YOUR WORD IS A LAMP TO MY FEET AND A LIGHT FOR MY PATH. PS 119:105

PRESENTED

TO

____

____

____

BY

____

____

ON

____

YOU KNIT ME TOGETHER IN MY
MOTHER'S WOMB. PS 139:13

BIRTHS

NAME

BORN TO DATE

NAME

BORN TO DATE

NAME

BORN TO DATE

NAME

BORN TO DATE

NAME

BORN TO DATE

NAME

BORN TO DATE

NAME

BORN TO DATE

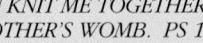

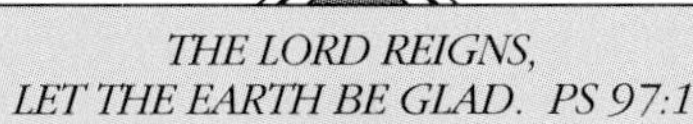

SPECIAL EVENTS

EVENT

PLACE DATE

EVENT

PLACE DATE

EVENT

PLACE DATE

EVENT

PLACE DATE

EVENT

PLACE DATE

EVENT

PLACE DATE

A MAN WILL... BE UNITED TO HIS WIFE, AND
THEY WILL BECOME ONE FLESH. GE 2:24

THIS CERTIFIES THAT

____

and

____

were united in

HOLY MATRIMONY

on ________________ *the* ________________

day of ________________ *A.D.* ________

at ________________________________

in accordance with the laws of ________________

Officiating ________________________________

Witness ________________________________

Witness ________________________________

LOVE IS PATIENT, LOVE IS KIND…
LOVE NEVER FAILS. 1 CO 13:4,8

MARRIAGES

HUSBAND

WIFE

PLACE DATE

HUSBAND

WIFE

PLACE DATE

HUSBAND

WIFE

PLACE DATE

HUSBAND

WIFE

PLACE DATE

HUSBAND

WIFE

PLACE DATE

HUSBAND

WIFE

PLACE DATE

BLESSED IS THE MAN
WHO FEARS THE LORD. PS 112:1

HUSBAND'S FAMILY TREE

NAME

BIRTHPLACE DATE

BROTHERS AND SISTERS

PARENTS

FATHER

NAME

BIRTHPLACE DATE

MOTHER

NAME

BIRTHPLACE DATE

GRANDPARENTS

PATERNAL

GRANDFATHER

BIRTHPLACE DATE

GRANDMOTHER

BIRTHPLACE DATE

MATERNAL

GRANDFATHER

BIRTHPLACE DATE

GRANDMOTHER

BIRTHPLACE DATE

GREAT-GRANDPARENTS

PATERNAL

GRANDFATHER'S FATHER

BIRTHPLACE DATE

GRANDFATHER'S MOTHER

BIRTHPLACE DATE

GRANDMOTHER'S FATHER

BIRTHPLACE DATE

GRANDMOTHER'S MOTHER

BIRTHPLACE DATE

MATERNAL

GRANDFATHER'S FATHER

BIRTHPLACE DATE

GRANDFATHER'S MOTHER

BIRTHPLACE DATE

GRANDMOTHER'S FATHER

BIRTHPLACE DATE

GRANDMOTHER'S MOTHER

BIRTHPLACE DATE

A WOMAN WHO FEARS THE LORD
IS TO BE PRAISED. PR 31:30

WIFE'S FAMILY TREE

NAME

BIRTHPLACE DATE

BROTHERS AND SISTERS

PARENTS

FATHER

NAME

BIRTHPLACE DATE

MOTHER

NAME

BIRTHPLACE DATE

GRANDPARENTS

PATERNAL

GRANDFATHER

BIRTHPLACE DATE

GRANDMOTHER

BIRTHPLACE DATE

MATERNAL

GRANDFATHER

BIRTHPLACE DATE

GRANDMOTHER

BIRTHPLACE DATE

GREAT-GRANDPARENTS

PATERNAL

GRANDFATHER'S FATHER

BIRTHPLACE DATE

GRANDFATHER'S MOTHER

BIRTHPLACE DATE

GRANDMOTHER'S FATHER

BIRTHPLACE DATE

GRANDMOTHER'S MOTHER

BIRTHPLACE DATE

MATERNAL

GRANDFATHER'S FATHER

BIRTHPLACE DATE

GRANDFATHER'S MOTHER

BIRTHPLACE DATE

GRANDMOTHER'S FATHER

BIRTHPLACE DATE

GRANDMOTHER'S MOTHER

BIRTHPLACE DATE

FOR TO ME, TO LIVE IS CHRIST AND TO DIE IS GAIN. PHP 1:21

DEATHS

NAME

DATE

NAME

DATE

NAME

DATE

NAME

DATE

NAME

DATE

NAME

DATE

NAME

DATE

KJV
PROPHECY
MARKED REFERENCE
STUDY BIBLE

GENERAL EDITOR
GRANT R. JEFFREY

Zondervan Publishing House
Grand Rapids, Michigan 49530, U.S.A.

KJV Prophecy Marked Reference Study Bible

Artwork:

Solomon's Temple, Zerubbabel's Temple, copyright © 1981 by Hugh Claycombe; Ezekiel's Temple, plan adapted from the design given in the Zondervan Pictorial Bible Dictionary. Copyright © 1975 by the Zondervan Corporation. Used by permission. "Harmony of the Gospels" adapted from "Analytical Outline for the NIV Harmony of the Gospels," pp. 15–23 from *The NIV Harmony of the Gospels,* by Robert L. Thomas and Stanley N. Gundry. Copyright © 1988 by Robert L. Thomas and Stanley N. Gundry. Reprinted by permission of HarperCollins Publishers, Inc..

Notes on the Subjects of Dispensations and Covenants:

Limited quotations and references from C.I. Scofield, taken from the *New Scofield Reference Bible* copyright © 1984 by Oxford University Press, Inc. Used by permission.

Library of Congress Catalog Card Number 98-61544
Published by Zondervan Publishing House
Grand Rapids, Michigan 49530, U.S.A.
http://www.zondervan.com

Printed in the United States of America

99 00 01 02 7 6 5 4 3 2 1

RRD

Table of Contents

Introduction

Prophecy Marked Reference Study Bible

ONE OF THE most amazing facts about the Bible is its endurance through the ages. Its persistent popularity into our present day is undiminished in the face of continuous, powerful, and relentless opposition. The Bible is one of the oldest books in the world; sections of it were written more than 25 centuries ago and no part of Scripture is less than 18 centuries old. Very few other ancient works are still circulated and read; those that are circulated and read lie nearly dormant on library shelves, referred to only by a few scholars or by college students as "required reading."

The Bible today is still a best seller, read frequently by millions. Its pages are thumbed and its covers are worn. Passages in the Bible such as the Psalms of David, the prophecies in Isaiah, the Sermon on the Mount in Matthew 5—7, the story of the prodigal son in Luke 15, and well-known chapters such as Romans 8 and John 14 have introduced salvation, encouraged discipleship, and provided hope and security for countless Christians.

It is evident, however, that many people who love to read the Bible have neither the time nor the specialized training for deep systematic study of the Scriptures. To gain a better understanding of the Bible, they must depend upon others who have made special studies of the Word of God. All Christians can be diligent readers of the Bible, but not all can be thorough students of the Scriptures.

The investigations of educated Bible scholars in colleges and seminaries are important, and their conclusions in commentaries, handbooks, and textbooks can be helpful. But for each Christian there is no substitute for reading the Biblical text itself in his or her own personal copy of the Bible. Better than the second-hand study of the Bible is the direct reading of the Word of God.

It is extremely important, however, that the reader learns to read the Bible meaningfully. To assist any follower of Christ who desires to read his own Bible with more purpose and meaning, the original *Marked Reference Bible* was conceived and developed to enable the student to master many of the key ideas and themes of God's Word. J. Gilchrist Lawson devoted many years to the preparation of the original four-theme edition.

The following statistics show the importance of four of the greatest themes of the Bible and over seventy subjects marked in this Bible:

1. On the theme of PROPHETIC SUBJECTS there are nearly 3,900 verses in the Old Testament and nearly 1,500 in the New Testament. One verse in six in the Bible has a more or less important bearing on prophetic subjects.

2. On the theme of THE HOLY SPIRIT there are over 500 verses, or one verse in forty-five, in the Old Testament; and over 660 verses, or one verse in twelve, in the New Testament. The Holy Spirit is mentioned over 400 times in the Bible, under 41 different names and titles. One verse in twenty-six in the Bible concerns the work of the Holy Spirit.

3. Out of a total of over 31,000 verses in the Bible, nearly 7,700 verses, or nearly one verse in four, concern the theme of SALVATION . This includes over 1,900 verses on the necessity of holy living, over 2,500 verses on the temporal punishment of unbelievers, over 400 verses on the future punishment of unbelievers, nearly 600 verses that show God's love for the sinner, and over 180 verses that show that God is no respecter of persons but saves all who are willing to meet the conditions of salvation.

Out of over 23,100 verses in the Old Testament, over 4,700 have some bearing on a person's need of salvation, or on the way of salvation; and nearly 3,000 verses out of a total of nearly 8,000 in the New Testament also concern the salvation of human beings.

4. On the theme of TEMPORAL BLESSINGS there are over 2,400 verses in the Old Testament and 1,091 in the New Testament. This includes nearly 330 verses on promises of examples of food or clothing

provided, and almost 90 verses recording promises and 760 verses recording examples of health and healing for the body, which makes one verse in thirty-six in the Bible on the subject of health or healing for the body. One verse in nine in the Bible concerns temporal blessings.

One-half of the Bible is devoted to these great themes. Thus, wherever there are readers and students of the Bible, there will be those who may receive help from this work. That it will increase interest in the Word of God, strengthen faith, build up true Christian character, and enlarge the kingdom of God is the hope of all who have taken part in its preparation.

Features of the KJV Prophecy Marked Reference Study Bible

Study Notes An outstanding feature of this Bible is the nearly 1200 notes it includes on the same pages as the verses and chapters they explain. Most of these notes illuminate various scriptural passages that have special prophetic significance.

Articles Another important feature of this study Bible is the inclusion of 30 articles on various topics related to Bible prophecy. These articles address significant prophetic topics such as Biblical dispensations, Biblical covenants, the rapture, the tribulation, the resurrection, signs of the Second Coming, the antichrist, Satan, the Millennium, heaven, hell, and many other important topics.

Introductions to Books Each book of the Bible has a unique introduction that includes a short description of the book's author, time of writing, and purpose; an outline of the Biblical book; and a section that gives additional historical, theological, and prophetic information pertaining to the book.

Chain of References The marked reference system color-highlights four key themes in Scripture. The color-highlighted verses along with the color marginal letters, which indicate the subjects, enable the reader to tell in an instant both the theme and the subject of any marked verse or passage. The Scripture references located at the bottom of a column indicate both the previous reference to a subject as well as the next reference to it. The "Complete Summary of Chain of References of Subjects" located on page xvi offers a resource showing a complete listing of all of the marked themes and subjects in the *KJV Prophecy Marked Reference Study Bible*. These references will enable the Bible student to make a careful, complete and objective study of any theme or subject marked in this Bible.

Maps In addition to the beautiful, four-color maps located in the back of this Bible, you will also find six in-text, two-color maps that graphically illustrate various subjects of prophetic significance.

Charts Fifteen in-text charts provide you with a quick pictorial view of various subjects and events, including the Biblical dispensations and covenants, the rapture, the Millennium, and a possible sequence of future events.

Illustrations This Bible also includes four finely detailed illustrations. Three of these depict the temples of Solomon, Ezekiel, and Zerubbabel, while another illustrates the four Gentile world empires described in the book of Daniel.

Concordance A concordance is included in the back of the *KJV Prophecy Marked Reference Study Bible* to help you find Bible verses quickly and easily. Key words in a Bible verse will help you find a verse for which you remember a word or two but not a location.

Subject, Article, and Color Map Indexes The subject index locates other references to persons, places, events and topics mentioned in the Study Bible notes, book introductions, and articles. The map index helps in locating place-names on a variety of full-color maps.

Harmony of the Gospels As an additional study tool for the Gospels and the life of Christ, this Bible contains a harmony of the Gospels.

Introduction to Prophecy

THE STUDY OF prophecy is known as eschatology, that is, "the study of last things." The *KJV Prophecy Marked Reference Study Bible* will focus primarily on the interpretation of the prophetic portions of the Scriptures. However, the role of the prophet and his message is much broader than simply the prediction of spiritually significant future events. In the Hebrew Bible three primary words describe a prophet. Together they reveal the role of the prophet both as seer as well as spokesperson of God's words. The message of the prophet is twofold: God's coming judgment of sin, and his declaration of immediate and ultimate triumph for truth and his sovereign purposes. Both the past and the future unite together in the message of the prophet. Ultimately, God is guiding human history toward the day when the kingdoms of this world will truly become the kingdom of God.

Principles of Prophetic Interpretation

The principles used to interpret Scripture are intimately related to the principles used to interpret the prophetic portions of Scripture. Several basic principles for the interpretation of prophecy include the following:

1. All Scripture should be understood according to its ordinary, usual, and common sense meaning, unless the context clearly indicates that the statement is symbolic.
2. The interpretation of symbolic language is usually clarified by reference to other Biblical passages.
3. God has consistently prophesied and set appointed times for Israel and the nations that have been fulfilled with accuracy and precision. The Lord has always dealt with Israel in terms of specifically appointed time periods and the promised land.
4. Scripture does not pinpoint the specific day or hour for the rapture.
5. The message of the prophet is for his own time and for all generations to follow. Its purpose is not simply to provide information but rather to challenge our behavior and our priorities in life.
6. God has never abandoned his eternal covenant with Israel.
7. Christ will return to usher in the long-awaited Messianic kingdom.

Historically, many in the church have forgotten Israel and the eternal promises that God made to her. They believe that God rejected and abandoned Israel forever because she rejected Jesus Christ, her Messiah. However, the apostle Paul warned the church against this mistake: "For I would not, brethren, that ye should be ignorant of this mystery, lest ye should be wise in your own conceits; that blindness in part is happened to Israel, until the fulness of the Gentiles be come in. And so all Israel shall be saved: as it is written, There shall come out of Zion the Deliverer, and shall turn away ungodliness from Jacob: For this is my covenant unto them, when I shall take away their sins" (Ro 11:25–27). God will still accomplish all of his promises.

The primary focus of this Bible is to present an interpretation of the prophecies concerning Israel, the nations, and the church. The notes and articles will explore the precise fulfillment of past prophecies and examine the prophecies that relate to the second coming of the Messiah. Those prophecies of the Bible, which have already been fulfilled, were fulfilled accurately. Therefore, we can have confidence that the prophecies about the "last days" will also be fulfilled as accurately as the specific predictions in regard to Christ's life, death, and resurrection.

The Bible declares that prophecy is clear evidence that God inspired the Word of God, distinguishing it from all other religious writings. The Lord declares that he is the only one who can prophesy the future and bring it to pass: "Remember the former things of old: for I am God, and there is none else; I am God, and there is none like me, Declaring the end from the beginning, and from ancient times the things that are not yet done, saying, My counsel shall stand, and I will do all my pleasure" (Isa 46:9–10).

Since one quarter of the verses in the Bible is prophetic, it is vital for us to properly understand God's revelation to his church. So how can we correctly interpret the prophecies of the Bible? Bible students have used two basic methods of interpretation to understand Biblical prophecy.

Understanding Biblical Prophecy: Two Approaches

The Allegorical Method Some scholars maintain that the prophecies of the Bible should be interpreted allegorically or symbolically rather than literally. This allegorical method of interpretation does not accept that certain prophecies point to second coming of Christ in our generation. For example, they interpret Christ's words in Matthew 24 in an allegorical manner. When they interpret Matthew 24, they understand that all of these prophetic signs were fulfilled when Rome destroyed Jerusalem in A.D. 70. They believe that the prophetic signs of worldwide earthquakes, famines, pestilence, the key prophetic role of Israel, the rebuilt temple, the abomination of desolation, the personal antichrist, and the Battle of Armageddon were totally fulfilled in the burning of the temple and the destruction of Jerusalem nearly 2,000 years ago.

The Literal Method Another method is the literal or common sense method. This approach assumes that the writer wrote his prophecy to be understood as any other type of writing. While the literal method acknowledges that prophecy contains symbols and figures of speech, it interprets these as pointing to a literal reality.

The literal method maintains that all fulfilled prophecies were fulfilled in a literal manner. To illustrate, nearly 50 distinct predictions from the Old Testament pertain to the life, death, and resurrection of Jesus Christ. Yet not one of those predictions was fulfilled in an allegorical or spiritual manner. Thus the conclusion reached by many respected Bible scholars over the centuries is that the Bible's prophecies should be interpreted literally.

This method maintains that the authors of the New Testament interpreted the Old Testament prophecies in a literal manner. For example, the apostle Peter declared, "We have also a more sure word of prophecy; whereunto ye do well that ye take heed, as unto a light that shineth in a dark place, until the day dawn, and the day star arise in your hearts: Knowing this first, that no prophecy of the scripture is of any private interpretation. For the prophecy came not in old time by the will of man: but holy men of God spake as they were moved by the Holy Ghost" (2Pe 1:19–21). This significant passage explains that prophecy helps Christians in several ways. First, it helps them understand their dark times. Second, it motivates them to holy living. Third, it encourages them to share the Gospel. It also tells us that prophecy does not come "by the will of man" or "of any private interpretation." The message of prophecy is an inspired message from the Holy Spirit to all generations of the church, encouraging the church to live expectantly for Jesus Christ's imminent return.

The Language of Prophecy

Prophecy is often written in a distinct form of religious literature called apocalyptic. While the Bible often uses symbolic language and figures, the Scriptures always interpret their own symbols; we need not guess their meaning. For example, in Revelation 12:7 we read that "Michael and his angels fought against the dragon." Instead of wondering what the dragon symbol represents, Revelation 12:9 reveals its identity: "And the great dragon was cast out, that old serpent, called the Devil, and Satan."

Why Prophecy Is Vital to the Church

There are four major reasons why prophecy is vital to the church.

1. Fulfilled prophecy authenticates the Bible as the inspired Word of God.
2. The message of the prophets calls the church to live in purity and holiness.
3. The prophetic message of the imminent return of Jesus Christ motivates us to witness to those around us.

4. The message of prophecy is a vital evangelistic tool for reaching the lost. God can use prophecy to help convince unbelievers that the Bible is the inspired Word of God, thereby bringing them to a place where they may consider the truth of the Gospel.

Reasons to Study Prophecy

While it is certainly true that many details in the unfolding plan of God will not be known until they come to pass, four factors encourage us to examine those prophecies that point to events leading up to Christ's return:

1. *The importance that God places on prophecy.* Over one quarter of the Bible is prophetic, and the Lord directs us to study prophecy (Rev 1:3).
2. *The literal fulfillment of past prophecies.* This leads us to believe that the prophecies that describe future events will be fulfilled in a similar literal manner. God will continue to fulfill his ancient prophecies as he has in the past, for the Lord himself says, "For I am the LORD, I change not" (Mal 3:6).
3. *Jesus Christ's criticism of the religious leaders of his day.* These leaders failed to pay attention to the prophecies and failed to "discern the signs of the times" (Mt 16:3).
4. *The apostle Paul's instructions.* Paul specifically reminded Christians that they knew that "the day of the Lord so cometh as a thief in the night" (1Th 5:2), yet he also reminded them, "But ye, brethren, are not in darkness, that that day should overtake you as a thief. Ye are all the children of light, and the children of the day: we are not of the night, nor of darkness. Therefore let us not sleep, as do others: but let us watch and be sober" (5:4–6).

These factors encourage us to carefully and prudently examine those prophecies that clearly relate to our generation. While the textual notes in the *KJV Prophecy Marked Reference Study Bible* will examine numerous prophecies that have already been fulfilled, we will also explore those prophecies that still await fulfillment.

Jesus Christ commanded his disciples to watch for the fulfillment of the prophetic signs that would indicate his coming. And he himself declared, "When these things begin to come to pass, then look up, and lift up your heads; for your redemption draweth nigh" (Lk 21:28).

Contents:
Articles

Contents:
Maps, Charts, Illustrations

Maps

Charts

Illustrations

Explanations:
Color Markings and Chain of References

Color Markings

All verses about **PROPHETIC SUBJECTS** are marked with **BLUE** ink.
All verses about the **HOLY SPIRIT** are marked with **DARK GREEN** ink.
All verses about **SALVATION** are marked with **RED** ink.
All verses about **TEMPORAL BLESSINGS** are marked with **LIGHT GREEN** ink.

Only the verses or words having a *very important* bearing on each subject are marked with colors in this Bible.

A summary of all the Bible verses on each subject marked is given at the front of the Bible (on pages xii–xv). In this summary the marked verses, or very important verses, are printed in colored type. Less important verses are not marked in color but are printed in lightface black type.

The letters on the margin of the verses marked in this Bible indicated the subjects of the verses marked.

The index on the following pages (pages xvi–xlviii) shows the letter that stands for each subject. This index also gives the first verse in the Old Testament and the first verse in the New Testament on each subject. These are given after each subject in the index. Under each subject in the index the most important verses in the Bible on the subject are given.

It will be noted that in the index all subjects are grouped under the four great themes of **PROPHETIC SUBJECTS,** the **HOLY SPIRIT, SALVATION,** and **TEMPORAL BLESSINGS,** and that the letter which stands for each subject is generally the first letter of the most important word in each subject. Thus, under the theme of **SALVATION** the letter **F** stands for FAITH, **H** for HELL, **R** for REPENTANCE, and so on. Under the theme of the **HOLY SPIRIT** the letter **F** stands for FRUITS of the Spirit, the letter **G** for GIFTS of the Spirit, the letter **B** for BAPTISM of the Spirit, and so on.

As *blue* ink is used for marking all verses on subjects under the theme of **PROPHETIC SUBJECTS,** so *blue* letters stand for all subjects under the theme of **PROPHETIC SUBJECTS.** In like manner *green* letters are used for all subjects under the theme of the **HOLY SPIRIT,** *red* letters for all subjects under the theme of **SALVATION,** and *light green* for all subjects under the theme of **TEMPORAL BLESSINGS.**

Chain of Reference System

After each verse or passage marked in this Bible there is a reference to the *next verse* or passage on the subject, thus forming a chain of reference that extends through the whole Bible. The letter in front of each reference corresponds to the same letter in the margin so as to enable the reader to select the proper reference for any subject marked.

The markings in this Bible will enable a person to give a Bible reading at a moment's notice on any subject marked, or a Bible reading may be given from either the Old or New Testament. The first verse on any subject is found by turning to the index on the following pages.

Other subjects may be marked by the Bible student personally, by arranging them under the heading "Miscellaneous Subjects," and using an appropriate letter or sign for each subject of special or personal interest.

Prophetic Subjects

	Subject	Key
A.	Dispensational **Ages** and Covenants Ge 2:16; 3:7, 15; 8:15; 9:8–16; 12:1; Ex 19:1; Dt 30:3; 2Sa 7:16; He 8:8–13; Rev 20:4	Ge 1:28 Ac 2:1
B.	Prophecies About Christ's **Birth** and First Coming Ge 3:15; Ps. 22:1–18; Isa 9:6–7; 52:13—53:12; Mic 5:1–4; Mt 1:21–23; Lk 1:30–35	Ge 3:15 Mt 1:21–23
C.	Prophecies About Christ's Second **Coming** Isa 64:1–2; Da 7:13; Mt 24:26–27, 31, 36–51; 25:1–13; Ac 1:11; 1Th 4:14; 5:4	Ps 97:2–7 Mt 16:27–28
D.	**Descent** of Christ and the Saints Job 19:25; Ps 96:13; Eze 43:1–2, 4–7; Zec 2:10; 14:4–5; 1Th 3:13; Rev 3:12	Job 19:25 Mt 25:31
E.	**Events** that Precede Christ's Second Coming Da 12:4; Lk 17:26–30; 1Th 5:1–4; 1Ti 4:1–3; 2Ti 3:1–4; 2Pe 3:3–4; Jude 17–18	Da 12:4 Mt 16:3
F.	The **First** Resurrection Job 19:26; Ps 17:15; Da 12:2; Lk 14:14; 1Co 15:23, 35–55; 1Th 4:16; Rev 20:6	Job 14:12–15 Mt 22:30–32
G.	Times of the **Gentile's** Ascendancy Dt 32:21; Da 2: 28–45; 7; 8; Mt 21:41, 43; Lk 21:24; Ro 11:17–22	Dt 32:21 Mt 21:41
H.	Marriage Supper and Church in **Heaven** Isa 26:20; Mt 22:1–14; 25:1–13; Eph 1:10; 5:27; Rev. 7:9–17; 14:1–5; 15:2–4; 19:7–9	Ps 45:14–15 Mt 22:2–3
I.	Prophecies About **Israel's** Restoration Isa 4; 49:13, 23; 54:1–14; 60; 62; Eze 37; Mt 19:28; Ro 11:25–26; Rev 7:1–8	Ge 13:15 Mt 2:2
J.	God's Prophetic **Judgments** Ecc 3:17; 12:14; Mt 10:15; 11:22, 24; 12:36, 42; 25:31–46; 2Co 5:10–11; Rev 20:11–15	Ge 6:2–4 Mt 10:15
K.	Triumph of God's **Kingdom** Isa 11:9; Hab 2:14; Zec 14:9; Mt 6:10; Ac 3:21; 1Co 15:24–28	Ps 10:16 Mt 6:10
M.	The **Millennial** Reign of Christ Isa 2:1–4; 11:4–10; 35; Jer 23:5–6; Da 2:44; Mic 4:3–4; Zec 9:10; Mt 19:28; Rev 20:1–6	Nu 14:21 Mt 2:2
N.	The **Never-ending** Life Ps 102:25–26; Isa 65:17; Heb 1:10–12; 12:26–28; 2Pe 3:10–14; Rev. 21:1–5; 22:3–5	Dt 4:40 Mt 5:5
P.	**Period** of Great Tribulation Ps 10:16; 11:6; 37:34; Pr 2:22; Isa 2:10–21; 13:6–13; Zep 1:14–18; Mal 4:1; Rev 6:12–17	Nu 24:17–19 Mt 3:12
Q.	**Question** of Recognizing Friends in Heaven Ge 15:15; 25:8; 35:29; 49:33; Dt 32:50; Jdg 2:10; Lk 16:23–25; 1Co 13:12	Ge 15:15 Lk 9:28–33
R.	**Rejection** and Scattering of Israel Dt. 29:22–28; Da 9:26–27; Hos 3:4; Mt 21:41, 43; 22:7; 23:37–39;24:14–22; Ro 11:17–28	Lev 26:18 Mt 10:6
S.	**Sorrow** and **Suffering** Cease Forever Ps 16:11; Isa 12:3; 25:8; 35:10; 51:11; 61:3; Rev. 7:17; 21:4	Ps 16:11 Rev 7:17
T.	**Translation** of the Saved Isa 26:20; Mt 13:30; 24:31; Lk 17:34–36; 1Co 15:50–55; 1Th 4:13–18	Ps 45:14–15 Mt 3:12
U.	Hope of **Universal** Peace Realized Isa 2:4; Hos 2:18; Mic 4:3–4; Mt 5:9; Lk 2:14; Heb 12:14	Ps 72:7 Mt 5:9
V.	Christ's Certain **Victory** Over All Enemies Isa 45:23; Da 2:44; 7:14; Mt 22:44; Php 2:9–10; Rev 11:15	Ps 45:6 Mt 22:44
W.	The Resurrection of the **Wicked** Da 12:2; Jn 5:25–29; Ac 24:15; 1Co 15:21–26; 1Ti 6:13; Rev 20:5–6	Da 12:2 Jn 5:25–29

The Holy Spirit

A.	**Asking For,** or Praying for the Spirit Isa 44:3; Hos 10:12; Lk 11:9–13; Jn 4:10; Ac 8:14–19; 9:17; 19:1–6	2Ki 2:9–10 Lk 11:9–13
B.	**Baptism** or Filling of the Spirit Ex 31:2–3; Dt 34:9; Lk 3:16; Jn 14:17; Ac 2:1–18; 8:14–19; 19:1–6; Eph 5:18	Ge 41:38 Mt 3:11
C.	The Holy Spirit **Convicts** of Sin Ge 6:3; Ps 51:12–13; Mic 3:8; Zec 12:10; Jn 16:8–11; Ac 2:37	Ge 6:3 Lk 1:17
D.	**Deity,** or Divinity, of the Holy Spirit Ps 68:18; Mt 28:19; Ac 5:3–4; 1Co 3:16; 2Co 3:17; 13:14; Eph 2:22; 1Jn 5:7	Ps 68:18 Mt 12:31–32
E.	**Examples** of the Holy Spirit's Work Ge 41:38–39; Nu 11:24–29; 1Ki 3:12; Da 1:17–20; Ac 2:1–18; 8:14–19; 19:1–6	Ge 1:2–3 Mt 1:18
F.	**Fruits** of the Holy Spirit Isa 63:14; Ac 2:46; 9:31; 13:52; Ro 5:5; 8:23; 14:17; 15:13; Gal 5:22–23	Ps 45:7 Ac 9:31
G.	**Gifts** of the Holy Spirit Ps 68:18; Isa 11:2; Joel 2:28; Mk 16:17–18; Ro 12:6–8; 1Co 12:14; Eph 4:7–16	Ge 41:38 Mt 10:19–20
H.	**Healing** and Resurrecting Power of the Spirit Eze 37:14; Mt 12:28; Ro 8:11; 1Co 12:9, 28, 30; 15:35–55; 1Pe 3:18; Rev 11:11	Job 33:4 Mt 12:28
J.	Comfort or **Joy** of the Holy Spirit Ps 45:7; Isa 61:3; Jn 14:16, 26; 15:26; 16:7; Ac 2:46; 9:31; 13:52; Ro 14:17	Ps 45:7 Mt 3:16
L.	**Leading** or Guiding of the Holy Spirit Ex 4:12, 15; Nu 22:38; 1Sa 10:7; 1Ki 22:14; Mt 10:19–20; Jn 16:13; Ac 2:4	Jdg 13:25 Mt 4:1
M.	Great **Might** or Power Given by the Spirit Jdg 14:6; 15:14–15; Mic 3:8; Zec 4:6; Lk 24:49; Ac 1:8; 2Co 10:4; Eph 3:16	Ge 1:2–3 Mt 3:11
N.	**Names** and Symbols of the Holy Spirit Job 32:19; Ps 23:5; 39:3; 45:7; Mt 3:16; Lk 3:16; Jn 7:38; Ac 2:2–3	Ge 1:2 Mt 3:11
P.	The Holy Spirit **Promised** Isa 44:3; Joel 2:28–29; Mal 3:10; Lk 3:16; 11:9–13; Jn 16:7–15; Ac 2:39	Ps 68:18 Mt 3:11
Q.	**Quenching,** Grieving, or Sinning Against the Spirit Ge 6:3; Isa 63:10; Mt 12:31–32; Eph 4:30; 1Th 5:19; Heb 10:29; 1Jn 5:16	Ge 6:3 Mt 12:31–32
R.	**Regeneration** as the Work of the Holy Spirit 1Sa 10:6; 9:26; Jer 31:33; Jn 3:5–8; Ro 8:15–16; 1Co 6:11; 12:13; Tit 3:5	1Sa 10:6 Lk 1:15–17
S.	**Sanctifying** Power of the Holy Spirit Ex 3:5; Ps 51:10; Eze 36:25–27; Ac 15:8–9; Ro 8:1–14; 15:16; 1Co 3:16–17	Ex 30:25 Lk 1:17
T.	**Teaching** or Enlightening of the Spirit Ge 41:39; 1Ki 3:12; 10:7; Da 1:20; Jn 16:13; Ac 4:13; 1Co 2; 2Co 12:4; 1Jn 2:27	Ge 41:38 Mt 10:19–20
W.	God **Wishes** Us to be Filled with the Spirit Nu 11:29; Isa 30:1; Lk 24:49; Jn 16:7; Ac 19:1–2; 1Co 12:1; Eph 5:18; 6:10–18	Nu 11:29 Lk 24:49

Salvation

A.	**ALL** Unsaved People are Sinners Ps 14:3; Ecc 7:20; Isa 53:6; Ro 3:12, 23; 5:12; Gal 3:22; 1Jn 1:8	1Ki 8:46 Mt 12:30
C.	**CONDITION** of Sinners Described Ps 1:4; 40:2; Isa 1:5–6; 64:6; Jer 17:9; Lk 12:16–21; Rev 3:17	Ge 2:17 Mt 3:7
D.	Christ **DIED** to Save Sinners Isa 53; Zec 13:1; Mt 26:28; Jn 1:29; 3:14–17; 1Pe 2:24; 1Jn 1:7; 2:2	Ge 3:15 Mt 1:21
E.	The Lord Knows **EVERY** Secret Thing Ps 139:1–12; Jer 2:22; Jn 4:29; Heb 4:12–13; 1Jn 3:20	Ge 6:5 Mt 9:4
F.	We are Saved Through **FAITH** 2Ch 20:20; Ps 34:22; Hab 2:4; Jn 3:14–16, 36; Ac 10:43; 16:31; Ro 1:18; 10:8–13	Ge 15:6 Mt. 11:12
G.	**GOOD WORKS** Alone Will Not Save Pr 16:2; Isa 64:6; Jer 17:5; Ro 3:20; 10:3; 1Co 13:3; Gal 2:16; Tit 3:5	Dt 32:31 Mt 5:20
H.	Punishment and **HELL** Await Sinners Da 12:2; Mt 25:46; Lk 16:19–31; Gal 6:7; Heb 6:2; Rev 20:10, 15	Ge 17:14 Mt 3:7
J.	All People will be **JUDGED** by the Lord Ecc 11:9; 12:14; Mt 25:31–46; 2Co 5:10–11; Heb 9:27; Rev 20:11–15	Ge 18:25 Mt 7:1–2
K.	Saving and **KEEPING** Power of God Dt 33:25, 27; Ps 121; Isa 26:4; 40:31; 41:10; 48:18; 59:1; Ro 8:33–39; 2Ti 1:12; Heb 7:25	Ge 15:1 Mt. 1:21
L.	The Lord **LOVES** and Saves Sinners Isa 1:18; 55:7; 65:2; Zec 13:1; Mt 18:11; Lk 15; Jn 6:37; 1Ti 1:15	Ex 20:6 Mt 1:21
M.	We Must be **MEEK** or Humble Before God Ps 34:18; 51:17; 147:3; 149:4; Isa 57:15; 66:2; Mt 18:3; Lk 18:9–14; 1Pe 5:5–6	Ex 32:9–10 Mt 5:3–5
N.	**NEGLECTING** or Rejecting Salvation Pr 1:24–32; 27:1; 29:1; Jer 8:20; Lk 12:16–21; 14:15–24; 2Co 6:2; Heb 2:3; Jas 4:13–14	Ge 6:3 Mt 10:14–15
O.	The Lord is the **ONLY** Way of Salvation Job 8:11–15; Isa 43:11; 45:22; Jer 17:13; Mt 22:37–38; Jn 3:3; 14:6; Ac 4:12; Rev 20:15	Ge 17:4 Mt 7:26–27
P.	The Lord Loves and **PARDONS** Backsliders 2Sa 12:13; 14:14; 2Ch 7:14; 30:9; Jer 3; Hos 14:4; Lk 15; 1Jn 2:1	Lev 26:40–42 Mt 10:6
R.	**REPENTANCE**, Confession, and Restitution Lev 6:1–6; Pr 28:13; Eze 18:27–28; Mt. 4:17; Ac 17:30; 20:21; 26:20; 1Jn 1:9	Ex 22:1–14 Mt 3:2
S.	Holy Living **SHOULD** Follow Conversion Lev 11:44; Ps 24:3–4; Ro 6; 1Th 4:3, 7; Heb 12:14; 1Jn 3:3–10; 5:18	Ge 2:17 Mt 1:21
T.	**TESTIFYING**, or Confessing the Lord Ps 40:10; 107:2; Isa 43:12; Mt 10:32–33; 12:34; Ro 10:8–10; 1Co 14:24–25	Dt 6:7 Mt 10:32–33
W.	"**WHOSOEVER WILL**" May Be Saved Isa 45:22; 55:1; Mt 11:28–30; Jn 3:16; 2Pe 3:9; 1Jn 2:2; Rev 3:20; 22:17	Nu 21:8–9 Mt 7:7–8

Temporal Blessings

A.	**All Things** Working for Good Ge 21:22; Ps 91:10; 121:7; Pr 12:21; Isa 58:11; Ro 8:28	Ge 21:22 Ro 8:28
B.	The Lord's **Blessing** on Fields and Flocks Lev 26:3–5; Dt 11:14–15; 28:3–5; Ps 65:9–13; Pr 3:9–10; 2Co 9:10	Ge 24:35 2Co 9:10
C.	**Clothing** Provided for God's Children Ge 28:20; Dt 10:8; 29:5; 33:25; Job 27:16–17; Mt 6:25–34	Ge 28:20 Mt 6:25–34
D.	Some Reasons Why **Diseases** are Allowed Lev 26:16; Dt 7:15; 28:21–22, 27, 35, 59–61; Jn 5:14; 1Co 11:29–32	Ge 12:17 Mt 13:58
E.	**Examples** of Healing for the Body Nu 21:9; Ps 105:37; Mt 8:16–17; 12:15; Mk 6:13, 54–56; Ac 5:14–16	Ge 17:15–17 Mt 4:23–24
F.	**Food** Provided for the Lord's Children Ex 16:35; Dt 10:18; Ps 37:3, 25; Isa 1:19; 33:16; Mt 6:11, 25–34; 2Co 9:10	Ge 21:19 Mt 4:11
H.	**Health** and Healing Promised Ex 15:26; 23:25; Dt 7:15; 33:25; Ps 91:10; 103:3; Isa 40:31; Mt 8:17; Jas 5:14–15	Ge 15:15 Mt 8:17
J.	**Joy** and Trust in Times of Trial Ne 8:10; Job 1:21; 13:15; Ps 23:4; 30:5; Isa 26:3; Hab 3:17–19; Jas 1:2; 1 Jn 4:18	Ne 8:10 Mt 5:11–12
L.	The Lord's **Love** and Care for His Children Dt 33:27; Ps 23; 91; Pr 18:24; Jer 31:3; Lk 12:6–7, 22–31; Heb 13:5; 1Jn 3:1	Ge 15:1 Mt 6:8
P.	**Prosperity** in Business and Finance Dt 8:18; 15:4–6; 1Sa 2:7–8; Pr 11:24–25; 19:17; Ecc 2:26; 2Co 9:6–11	Ge 15:14 Mt 6:31–33
R.	Blessing on Children, **Relatives**, and Friends Ge 26:24; 30:27; Job 42:15; Ps 37:26; 103:17–18; 112:2; 128:3; 144:12; Lk 1:13–15	Ge 26:24 Lk 1:13–15
S.	**Safety** From All Harm and Danger Ex 11:7; 1Ch 18:6; Ps 91:10–12; 121:5–8; Na 1:7; Lk 21:18; Ac 18:10	Ex 11:7 Mt 4:6
T.	Why **Temptations** and **Trials** are Allowed Dt 8:5–6; Job 5:17; Pr 3:11–12; Ro 5:3–4; 2Co 4:17; Heb 5:8; 12:5–13; Jas 1:2–4, 12	Dt 8:2 Ro 5:3–4
U.	The **Upright** are Blessed and Prospered Dt 28:1–13; 1Sa 2:30; Job 17:9; Ps 37:4–6; 84:11; Pr 4:18; Mk 10:28–30; 1Jn 3:22	Ge 12:1–3 Mt 5:5–12
V.	**Victory** Over Enemies and Troubles Jos 23:10; Ps 18:29; 34:17; Pr 16:7; Isa 54:17; Ac 5:39; Ro 8:37; 2Ti 4:18	Ex 23:22 Lk 21:18
W.	**Worry** and Anxiety Contrary to God's Will Dt 1:21; Jos 1:9; Ps 27:14; 55:22; Mt 6:25–34; Jn 14:1, 27; Php 4:4, 6–7; 1Pe 5:7	Ge 15:1 Mt 6:25–34

Complete Summary
of Chain of References on Subjects Marked in this Bible

The references printed in color type are the important ones, and are the only ones marked in the Bible. Those marked in black type are secondary references.

PROPHETIC SUBJECTS
(BLUE)

A
Dispensational AGES and Covenants

Ge 1:28;
2:16–17;
3:7, 15;
8:15;
9:1–3, 7–10,
11–17, 24–27;
12:1–3, 7;
13:14–16;
14:18–20;
15:4–5, 13–16,
18–21;
16:10–12;
17:2–21;
19:22–25;
21:18;
22:15–18;
24:60;
25:23;
26:2–5, 24;
27:28, 39–40;
28:3–4, 13–15;
32:27–28;
35:10–12;
37:6–7, 9;
41:1–7, 25–36,
47–48, 53–54;
46:2–4;
48:3–6, 15–16,
19–22;
49:1–28;
50:24–25
Ex 3:8–12, 17–21;
12:3–9;
23:16, 25–31;
32:13;
34:10–12
Lev 23:33–36;
25:8–17
Nu 23:24
Dt 33:6, 12–29

B
Prophecies About Christ's BIRTH and First Coming

Ge 3:15–21;
49:10
Nu 19:1–22
Dt 18:15–19
Ps 22:1–18
Isa 7:13–16;
9:6–7;
11:1–5;
50:6–9;
52:13—53:12;
61:1–3
Jer 22:29–30
Da 9:24–26
Mic 5:1–4
Hag 2:9
Zec 9:9;
11:12–13
Mt 1:21–23;
2:14–15, 23;
3:3;
4:13–15;
12:40–41;
27:9–10, 51
Mk 1:7;
8:31;
14:18–21, 27–28,
30, 42
Lk 1:30–35;
2:30–32, 34–35;
3:16;
9:22
Jn 1:29, 33;
2:19;
3:14;
7:42;
19:24, 36–37
Ac 7:37–38;
26:23

C
Prophecies About Christ's Second COMING

2Sa 22:10–13
Ps 77:15–18;
97:2–7;
109:8;
114:7
SS 1:2, 4;
2:7–8, 16, 17;
4:6;
5:6–7, 8;
6:11–12;
7:1–7, 8–9;
8:4, 14
Isa 64:1, 4
Da 7:13
Hag 2:6–7
Mt 16:27–28;
24:3, 4–25,
26–27, 28,
29–33, 34–35,
36–51;
25:1–13, 14–18,
19, 20–30;
26:64
Mk 4:26–28, 29;
8:38;
9:1–13;
13:26, 32–37;
14:62
Lk 9:26;
12:34, 35–47, 48;
17:23–24, 25,
26–30, 31–33,
34–37;
18:8;
19:15, 23;
21:27–31, 32–33,
34–36
Jn 14:2–3;
16:16;
21:22–23
Ac 1:9–10, 11, 20;
4:7, 13
Ro 13:11–12
1Co 1:7–8;
7:29–31;
10:11;
11:26
2Co 1:14
Php 1:6, 10;
2:16;
3:20–21;
4:5
Col 3:4
1Th 1:10;
2:19;
3:13;
4:14—5:4;
5:5–11, 23
2Th 1:7, 10;
2:1–3;
3:5
1Ti 6:14
2Ti 1:12;
4:8
Tit 2:13
Heb 9:26, 28;
10:25, 37
Jas 5:7–9
1Pe 1:5, 7, 13, 20;
4:7, 13
2Pe 1:16–19;
3:3–14
1Jn 2:28;
3:2–3
Rev 1:7, 13–17;
3:11;
22:7, 12, 20

D
DESCENT of Christ and the Saints

Job 19:25
Ps 96:12–13;
98:9;
102:16
SS 8:5
Eze 43:1–2, 4–7;
44:1–2
Zec 2:10;
14:4–7, 14–20

Mt 25:31
Mk 13:26
1Th 3:13
Rev 3:12

E

EVENTS that Precede Christ's Second Coming

SS 5:6–8;
6:1–2
Da 12:4, 8, 9–10
Mal 4:5
Mt 10:23;
16:2, 3;
24:3–6, 7–31, 32–33
Mk 13:5–13, 14–26, 22, 24, 27, 31–32
Lk 12:54–57;
17:26–30;
21:25–31
Ac 2:17, 19–20
1Th 5:1–4
2Th 2:1–9, 10–12
1Ti 4:1–3
2Ti 3:1–9;
4:3–4
Jas 5:1, 3, 4–6, 7
2Pe 3:3–10
1Jn 2:18
Jude 17–18
Rev 1:1, 3, 19;
4:1, 2;
5:1—6:11;
22:6–7, 10

F

The **FIRST** Resurrection

Job 14:12–15;
19:25–27
Ps 8:3–8;
16:9, 9–10;
17:15;
71:20;
88:10–12
Isa 25:8;
26:19
Eze 37:12–14
Da 12:2, 13
Hos 13:14
Mt 22:23–29, 30–32
Mk 12:18–23, 24–25, 26–27
Lk 14:13–14;
20:27–33, 34–38
Jn 5:21, 25–29;
6:39–40, 44, 54;
11:23–25
Ac 17:18;
23:6, 7, 8, 9;
24:15, 21;
26:6–8;
28:20
Ro 8:11, 17–25, 29
1Co 6:13, 14;
15:12–19, 20–26, 35–55
2Co 1:9;
4:14
Php 3:11–15, 21
1Th 4:13–18
1Ti 6:13
2Ti 2:17–18
Heb 6:2;
11:35
Rev 1:5, 18;
20:5–6

G

Times of the **GENTILE'S** Ascendancy

Dt 32:21
2Ch 36:23
Ezr 1:2
Est 1:1
SS 8:8–9
Isa 49:6;
65:1
Jer 16:19, 20–21
Da 2:1–27, 28–45;
7:1, 2–28;
8:1–26, 27;
9:26–27;
10:1, 2–13, 14, 15–19, 20—11:5;
11:6–30, 31, 32–45;
12:5, 6–7, 11–12
Zec 1:7–15, 18–21
Mal 1:11
Mt 21:41, 43;
22:9–10
Mk 12:9
Lk 14:21, 22–24;
20:16;
21:24
Jn 10:16
Ac 10:1–14, 15, 16–44, 45—11:1;
11:2–17, 18, 19–21;
13:44–45, 46–48;
14:27;
15:3, 6, 7–9, 10–11, 12, 13–19;
18:6;
21:19;
22:21;
28:28
Ro 9:30;
10:19–20;
11:11–12, 13–14, 15–29;
15:9–11, 12, 16, 27
Rev 11:2;
12:3–6;
13:1–18;
14:8;
17:1—18:3

H

Marriage Supper and Church in **HEAVEN**

Ps 45:14–15
SS 1:4;
2:4
Isa 26:20–21
Mt 22:1, 2–3, 4–7, 8–10, 11, 13, 14;
25:1–13
Lk 14:16;
22:16
Eph 1:10;
5:25–26, 27
Rev 7:9–17;
14:1–5;
15:2–4;
19:7–9

I

Prophecies About **ISRAEL'S** Restoration

Ge 12:7;
13:15;
15:18;
17:7–8, 19;
48:4
Ex 12:41;
32:13
Lev 26:40–42, 44–45
Nu 10:29;
24:7–9, 14–19;
34:1–12
Dt 1:35–39;
2:24–25;
3:2, 21–22;
4:22, 26–31, 32–38;
6:3;
7:4, 6–9, 14–15, 22;
11:12;
12:5;
17:14;
18:15–19;
26:19;
28:1–3;
30:1–10;
32:36, 43
Jos 1:2–9;
3:5, 7;
6:2–5, 16;
8:1–2, 7;
9:27;
10:8, 12, 19;
11:6;
17:18
Jdg 1:2;
2:1;
6:16;
7:13–14;
13:3, 5;
20:28
1Sa 7:3;
9:16;
12:22;
14:10;
17:36–37;
25:28
2Sa 3:18;
7:10–12, 23–24
1Ki 2:4;
5:5;
9:3;
18:1, 41
2Ki 7:1–2;
8:19;
13:15–19;
14:27;
19:30–31
1Ch 14:10, 15;
16:15–18, 35;
17:9, 22;
22:9, 13
2Ch 20:7
Ezr 3:11
Ne 1:9
Ps 14:7;
28:9;
29:11;
33:12;
47:3–4;
50:5;
53:6;
60:1–12;
68:13, 22–23;
69:35–36;
74:10, 11, 19–20;
77:7–10, 15;
79:5, 13;
80:1–2, 3–7, 14–15, 19;
85:1–13;
87:2, 3, 5;
90:13–17;
94:14;
97:8;
98:3;
99:4;
102:13–16, 21–22;
105:8–11, 12;
107:3–7;
111:5–6, 9;
112:3–9;
115:12;

125:1;
126:1–6;
129:1–8;
130:8;
132:13–15;
135:4, 14;
136:21–22;
147:2;
148:14
Isa 1:25–27;
2:1–5;
4:2–6;
9:1–4, 7;
10:20–21;
11:11–15, 14—16;
12:1–6, 4–5, 6;
14:1–3;
18:7;
22:20–24;
25:8–10;
26:1–2, 12, 19;
27:2–6, 7–11,
12–13;
28:5–6;
30:15, 18–26, 29;
31:4–5;
32:15–18;
33:20–22, 24;
37:31–32;
40:1–2, 3–7, 8–11,
27–28, 29–31;
41:2–7, 8–21;
42:16, 17–21;
43:1–4, 5–7,
8–18, 19–21,
22–24, 25, 26;
44:1–8, 21–23,
24–25, 26,
27–28;
45:17–19, 25;
46:3–4, 12–13;
49:5–6, 7, 8–23,
24–26;
50:2;
51:1–2, 3–4, 5–8,
9, 10, 11–12,
13–14, 15–17,
18–21, 22, 23;
52:1–3, 4–5, 6–9,
10;
54:1–14, 15–16,
17;
55:5, 8–11, 12–13;
56:1, 8;
57:16–19;
58:8–12, 14;
59:20, 21;
60:1–22;
61:3—62:12;
65:8–10, 16–25;
66:5–6, 7, 8, 9,
10–14, 15–17,
18–24

Jer 3:14–19;
4:1–2;
10:16;
12:14–17, 14,
16–17;
14:21;
16:14–16;
18:1–8;
23:1–2, 3–8;
25:12;
29:10–14;
30:1–3, 4–6,
7–10, 11–16,
14, 17–22,
23–24;
31:1, 2, 3–14,
15–27, 28–29,
30, 31–34,
35–37, 38–40;
32:36–42, 43, 44;
33:1, 2–3, 4–5,
6–11, 12–14,
15–16, 17–26;
35:18–19;
46:27–28;
50:4–5, 19–20;
51:5, 10, 19–23
La 3:31;
4:22;
5:20–21
Eze 4:4–6;
11:17–20;
16:53, 55, 60–63;
17:17, 22–24;
20:33, 34–38, 39,
40–42, 43–44;
28:25–26;
29:21;
34:11–16, 17–21,
22—31;
36:1–7, 8–12,
13–21;
37:1–28;
38:1–7, 8, 9–10,
11–12, 13, 14,
15, 16, 17–19,
20, 21—39:6;
39:7–10, 11–24,
25–29;
43:4, 5–7, 8, 9,
10–12;
45:1–2, 7, 8;
47:1—48:35
Da 8:19;
12:1
Hos 1:10–11;
2:7, 14–16, 17,
18–23;
3:5;
6:1–3;
11:8–12;
12:9;

13:9–10, 14;
14:4–8
Joel 2:21—3:2;
3:16–18, 19,
20–21
Am 9:11–15
Ob 17; 18–21
Mic 2:12, 13;
4:1–4, 5, 6–8,
9–11, 12–13;
5:1, 2, 3–15;
7:7–9, 10, 11–20
Na 1:12, 13–14, 15
Hab 3:13
Zep 2:6–7;
3:9–20
Hag 2:7
Zec 1:12—2:5;
2:1–5, 6–9,
10–13;
3:1, 2–5, 6–8,
9–10;
8:1–3, 4–6, 7–8,
9–19, 20–23;
9:9–10, 11—10:5;
10:6–8, 9–12;
12:6–7, 8—13:1;
13:2–6, 9;
14:8–11, 12–15,
16–21
Mal 3:2–4, 6–7, 9–12
Mt 2:1, 2, 3–5, 6,
7–20;
19:28;
21:5;
27:11, 28, 29,
30–31, 37, 42
Mk 11:10;
15:2, 9, 12, 16,
17–18, 19–20,
26, 32
Lk 1:32–33, 54–55,
68–79;
2:25–26, 38;
23:2–3, 36,
37–38;
24:13–20, 21
Jn 1:49;
12:12, 13–15, 16;
18:33–37, 38, 39;
19:2–3, 4–5,
12–15, 17–18,
19–22, 37
Ac 1:6–7;
2:29–31
Ro 3:1–2;
9:4, 8–24,
25–28;
10:21—11:5;
11:6–11, 12,
13–14, 15–29,

30–31, 32,
33–36;
15:8
2Co 3:16
Heb 8:7, 8–13;
10:16–17
Rev 1:7;
3:7;
7:1–8;
11:1–2;
12:14–17

J

God's Prophetic JUDGMENTS

Ge 6:2–4, 17;
11:6–8;
40:12–13, 18–19
Ex 14:4, 13;
16:23–30;
17:14, 16
Nu 14:22–30, 43;
24:14–24;
33:55–56
Jos 6:26;
23:13
Jdg 2:3, 21;
9:15, 20
1Sa 2:31;
12:25;
13:14
2Sa 12:14
1Ki 17:1;
21:19, 21–24, 29
2Ki 1:4;
2:3, 5, 9–10;
5:27;
7:19;
8:1, 10–13;
9:8–10, 26;
18:30;
19:7;
20:17–19
1Ch 21:9–13
2Ch 16:9;
21:14–16
Ps 1:5;
7:8;
9:7–8, 19;
69:25;
87:4–6
Ecc 3:17–18;
11:9;
12:14
Isa 10:33–34;
15:1–9;
20:1–6;
21:13–16;
23:1–17;
30:5–7;
48:14–15
Jer 1:13–16, 18–19;
9:26;

11:20;
27:22;
28:16;
29:21–22, 32;
44:30;
46:26;
47:5
Eze 12:13
21:28–31
24:21, 25–27;
25:15–17;
26:1–5, 12–21;
28:20–24;
29:1–6, 19–20;
35:1–15
Da 4:10–17, 20–26, 31–32;
5:5, 24–28;
7:10–11
Zep 2:4–15
Mt 10:15;
11:22, 24;
12:36, 42;
25:14–18, 19, 20–30, 31–46
Mk 6:11
Lk 10:12, 14;
11:31–32
Jn 12:48
Ac 17:31
Ro 2:5, 16;
14:10–13
1Co 4:5
2Co 5:9–11
2Ti 4:1
Heb 9:27;
10:30
1Pe 4:5
2Pe 2:4, 9;
3:7
1Jn 4:17
Jude 6
Rev 20:11–15

K

Triumph of God's KINGDOM

Ps 10:16;
92:9;
145:13
Isa 2:2–4;
11:9;
24:23
Jer 10:10;
31:34
Da 2:33, 35, 44–45;
4:3, 34;
6:26;
7:13–14, 27
Ob 21
Mic 4:7
Hab 2:14
Zec 14:9
Mt 6:10, 13;
13:33;
16:18–20
Mk 4:26–28;
9:1
Lk 11:2
Ac 3:21, 25
1Co 15:24–28
Rev 11:15

2Ki 4:16;
10:30;
20:5–10
2Ch 1:12;
9:8;
20:9;
34:28
Isa 38:18, 21–22;
45:1–5, 13
Jer 39:17–18
Da 2:28–32
Jnh 2:4
Mt 10:17–23;
26:13

M

The MILLENNIAL Reign of Christ

Ge 3:15;
49:10
Ex 15:17–18;
19:5
Nu 14:21;
24:17–19
1Sa 2:10
2Sa 7:12, 13–14, 14–15, 16, 17–29;
23:3–5
1Ki 2:45
1Ch 16:30–33, 34;
17:10–13, 13, 14, 15–27, 22;
28:4
2Ch 6:16;
13:5;
21:7
Ps 2:8–9;
9:8;
10:16;
14:7;
22:27–28;
24:1, 2–6, 7–10;
29:10;
45:1–5, 16;
46:4–11;
47:1–9;
48:2, 8;
49:14;
50:1–2, 4–6;
60:6–12;
66:4;
67:4;
68:16;
72:1–19;
76:1–12;
82:8;
85:9–13;
86:9;
89:2, 3–4, 26–32, 30–34, 35–37;
93:1–2;
96:1–3, 7–9, 10–13;
97:1;
98:3–9;
99:1–5, 9;
102:15–16, 22;
108:7–9;
110:1–7;
132:11–18
SS 1:11–17;
2:3–6, 11–13;
4:16—5:1;
7:10–13
Isa 2:1–5;
4:5–6;
9:6–7;
11:4–10, 12;
14:2;
16:5;
19:20–25;
22:20–24;
24:13–15, 23;
25:6–10;
26:1–2, 9;
29:17–24;
32:1–4;
33:6, 20–22;
35:1–10;
40:4–5;
41:18–20;
42:4;
44:3–5;
45:8, 23–24;
49:7–12;
52:13;
55:3, 12–13;
56:1;
57:13;
59:19, 21;
60:1–22;
65:16–25;
66:18–24
Jer 3:17;
23:5–6;
30:9;
33:15
Eze 21:26–27;
34:23–29
34:25–28
37:22–28;
43:5–7;
47:1–21;
48:1–7, 10–35
Da 2:34–35, 44–45;
7:13–14, 18, 22, 27
Hos 2:18, 21–22;
3:5
Joel 3:4, 18–20
Mic 4:3–4;
5:2
Hab 2:14, 20
Hag 2:23
Zec 2:5, 10–13;
6:9–11, 11–15;
8:3–8, 20–23;
9:1, 9–10;
14:9, 16–21
Mal 1:4–5;
3:1, 17–18;
4:2–3
Mt 2:1, 2, 3–5, 6;
5:35;
6:10, 13;
13:31–33, 43;
16:28—17:13;
19:28;
20:20–21, 22–24;
21:1–4, 5, 6–11, 33–37, 38;
22:43, 44;
25:21, 23;
27:11, 28, 29, 30–31, 37, 42
Mk 4:30–32;
10:35–36, 37, 38, 41–45, 39–40;
11:1–9, 10;
12:10–11, 36;
15:2, 9, 12, 16, 17–18, 19–20, 26, 32, 43
Lk 1:32–33;
2:26;
3:4, 5–6;
9:27–36;
11:2;
12:32, 44;
13:18, 19, 20, 21;
17:20–37;
19:11–26, 20–26, 27, 28–40;
20:9–13, 14, 17, 42–43;
22:29–30;
23:2–3, 36, 37–38, 42, 51
Jn 10:16;
12:12, 13–15, 16;
18:33–37, 38, 39, 40—19:5;
19:12–15, 17–18, 19–22
Ac 2:29–31, 34–35;
3:19–21;
17:7

Ro 4:13;
8:17–18;
14:11;
15:10, 12;
16:20
1Co 6:2–3;
10:26, 28;
15:24–28
Eph 1:10, 22
Php 2:9–11
Col 1:20
1Th 3:13
2Th 1:5
1Ti 6:15
2Ti 2:12;
4:1, 8, 18
Heb 1:2, 8, 13;
2:5–8;
5:6;
7:1, 2, 3–10, 11, 12–14, 15–17, 18, 19, 20–21, 22–24;
10:12, 13
1Pe 4:11, 13;
5:1, 4, 6
2Pe 1:19
Rev 1:5–6;
2:26–27;
3:7, 11–12, 21;
5:10;
11:15–19;
12:5;
19:16;
20:1–6

N

The **Never-Ending** Life

Dt 4:40
Job 26:10
Ps 37:9, 11, 22, 29, 34;
75:3;
78:69;
93:1;
96:10;
102:25–26;
104:5;
119:90
Pr 10:30
Ecc 1:4
Isa 51:16;
65:16–18
Mt 5:5
Eph 1:10;
6:3
Heb 1:10–12;
2:5;
6:5;
12:26–28
2Pe 3:13–14
1Jn 2:17
Rev 21:1–5, 6—22:2;
22:3–5, 14–15

P

Period of Great Tribulation

Nu 24:17–19
Dt 32:22, 41–43
1Sa 2:10
2Sa 22:14–18;
23:6–7
Job 38:13
Ps 2:1–6, 8–9, 12;
10:15–16;
11:6;
18:7–15;
37:34;
45:1–5;
46:6–9;
50:3;
59:5, 8;
66:3;
68:1–2;
72:9;
75:8, 10;
76:3–12;
82:5, 8;
83:13–17;
94:1–4;
98:1–2;
101:8;
104:35;
110:1, 5–6;
119:119;
132:18;
144:5–6
Pr 2:21–22
Isa 1:24, 28, 29, 30–31;
2:10–21;
9:18;
11:4;
13:1–22;
24:1, 2, 3, 4–5, 6, 7–12, 17–23;
25:10–12;
26:20–21;
27:1;
28:17–18, 19–20, 21–22;
29:20, 21;
30:27, 28, 30;
33:3–4, 10–11, 12;
34:1–4, 5, 5–17;
40:10, 24;
42:13–15;
45:23–24;
59:17–19;
61:2;
63:1–2, 3–6;
64:2–3;
66:5–6, 14–17, 24
Jer 9:25–26;
10:10, 15;
23:19–20;
25:29–33;
30:23–24;
45:5;
48:47;
49:2–6, 23–27, 39
Eze 38:1–23;
39:1–22
Da 12:1
Joel 1:15;
2:1–11, 19–32;
3:1–2, 9–17
Am 1:2–15;
5:18–20
Ob 1–10; 15–16
Mic 1:3–7, 9;
5:5, 15
Na 1:1, 2, 3–4, 5–12, 15
Hab 3:3–16
Zep 1:14–18;
3:8
Hag 2:20–21, 22
Zec 9:2, 5–8, 12–16;
11:8;
12:2–6, 9–14;
13:7–9;
14:12–21
Mal 3:2–5;
4:1, 2, 3, 5
Mt 3:12;
13:24–26, 27–30, 39–42, 47–50;
22:43–44;
24:50–51
Mk 13:19–20;
14:25
Lk 3:17;
12:45–47;
17:26–30;
18:1–6, 7–8;
19:27;
20:42–43;
21:5–7, 9–11, 25–26, 36
Ac 2:19–20
1Co 16:22
1Th 5:3, 4, 9
2Th 1:5–9, 6, 10;
2:8–9
2Pe 3:10–12
2Jn 7
Jude 14–15
Rev 1:7;
2:27;
3:10;
6:12—9:6;
9:7–11, 12–15, 16–17, 18, 19, 20, 21—10:4;
10:5–7, 8—11:13;
11:14, 15–17, 18–19;
12:9–17;
14:6–11, 13, 14—15:1;
15:2–4, 5—18:13;
18:14–18, 19—19:3;
19:4–10, 11—20:3;
21:9

Q

Question of Recognizing Friends in Heaven

Ge 15:15;
25:8, 17;
35:29;
49:29, 33
Nu 20:24, 26;
27:13;
31:2
Dt 32:50
Jdg 2:10
Mt 8:11;
17:4
Mk 9:4–5
Lk 9:28–33;
13:28;
16:23–25
1Co 13:12
Col 1:28
Phm 15
Heb 12:23
Rev 3:5

R

Rejection and Scattering of Israel

Lev 20:22;
26:5–10, 14–35, 15–17, 18, 19–23, 24, 25–27, 28, 29–30, 31–35, 36–39, 41–43, 43
Dt 4:27, 28, 30;
28:15–22, 23–25, 26–32, 33, 34–36, 37, 38–44, 45, 46–48, 49, 50–61, 62–65, 66–68;
29:22–28, 29;
30:1;
31:16, 17–18, 29;
32:9–19, 20, 21–25, 26, 36
Jos 23:15–16;
24:20

21:33–40, 41, 42, 43, 44–45;
22:3–6, 7–8;
23:34–36, 37–39;
24:1–3, 4–13, 15–22, 28;
27:25
Mk 12:1–8, 9, 10–12;
13:1–2, 3–13, 14–20
Lk 13:1–2, 3, 4, 5, 6–9, 34–35;
14:15–23, 24;
19:41–44;
20:9–16;
21:5–19, 20–24;
23:28, 29–31
Jn 7:35;
12:37–41
Ro 9:1–24, 25–29, 30;
11:1–5, 6, 7–12, 13–14, 15, 16, 17–28
2Co 3:14
1Th 2:14–15, 16
Rev 12:1–6, 7–9, 10–13

S

Sorrow and Suffering Cease Forever

Ps 16:11;
30:5;
98:4;
126:5
Isa 12:3;
25:8;
29:19;
35:2, 10;
49:13;
51:11;
52:9;
61:3;
65:14, 18–19
Jer 31:13
Lk 2:10
Jn 15:11;
16:22;
17:3
Ac 2:28
Gal 5:22
1Th 5:16
1Pe 1:8–9
1Jn 1:4
Rev 7:17;
21:4

T

Translation of the Saved

Ps 45:14–15
SS 1:4;
2:10;
6:10—12
Isa 26:20
Mt 3:12;
13:30;
24:31
Lk 3:17;
17:34–36
Jn 3:3–7, 8, 9–13;
14:2–3
Ro 8:17–18, 29
1Co 15:50–55
Php 3:21
1Th 4:15–18

U

Hope of Universal Peace Realized

Lev 26:6
Dt 33:28
1Ki 5:4
1Ch 22:9
Job 5:23
Ps 72:7
Isa 2:4;
9:6;
11:6–9;
32:17–18;
65:25
Jer 23:6;
31:40
Hos 2:18
Mic 4:3–4
Zec 9:10;
14:11
Mt 5:9
Lk 1:79;
2:14
Ro 16:20
Jas 3:18;
4:1–2

V

Christ's Certain Victory Over All Enemies

Ps 2:8–9;
45:6;
72:4, 8–9;
110:1;
132:11
Isa 9:6–7;
11:1–9;
16:5;
32:1;
42:1, 4;
45:23;
49:6;
55:4–5;
60:12
Jer 23:5–6;
30:9;
31:34
Eze 21:27;
34:23–24;
37:24
Da 2:34–35, 44, 45;
7:13, 14, 27;
9:25
Hos 3:5
Zec 9:10
Mt 21:5, 38, 44;
22:44;
28:18
Mk 12:36
Lk 1:32, 33;
2:32;
19:12, 15;
20:42–43;
22:29
Jn 3:35
Ac 2:34–35;
3:22–23
1Co 15:24–26
Eph 1:21–22
Php 2:9–10
2Th 2:8
1Ti 6:15
Heb 1:2, 8, 13
Rev 2:26–27;
5:13;
11:15;
12:5;
17:14;
19:15–16;
20:7–15

W

The Resurrection of the Wicked

Da 12:2
Jn 5:25–29
Ac 24:15
1Co 15:21–26
1Ti 6:13
Rev 20:5–6

THE HOLY SPIRIT
(DARK GREEN)

A

Asking for, or Praying for the Spirit

Ge 32:24–28
1Ki 3:5–12
2Ki 2:9–10
2Ch 1:7–12
Ps 51:10–13
Isa 44:3
Mt 5:6
Lk 11:9–13
Jn 4:10
Ac 1:4, 14;
4:29–31;
8:14–17;
10:31
Eph 1:16–17;
3:14–19
Col 1:9

B

Baptism or Filling of the Spirit

Ge 41:38
Ex 28:3;
29:7;
31:3;
35:31
Lev 8:12
Nu 27:18
Dt 34:9
2Ki 2:9–10
Job 32:18–19
Ps 45:7;
51:12–13;
68:18;
133:2
Isa 11:2;
42:1;
44:3;
61:1;
63:11
Eze 11:19;
36:26–27;
37:14
Da 4:8–9, 18;
5:11–12, 14;
6:3
Joel 2:28–29
Mic 3:8
Mal 3:10
Mt 3:11, 16;
12:18

12:6–7;
15:16, 18–19, 30
1Co 2:4–16;
3:1, 16;
6:11, 19;
7:40;
12:1–13, 28–31
2Co 1:21–22;
3:3, 6–18;
12:1–4
Gal 3:2–3, 5;
4:6;
5:5;
6:1
Eph 1:3, 13–14;
2:18, 22;
3:2–5;
4:3, 7–8, 30
Php 3:3
Col 1:8;
2:5
1Th 1:5–6;
4:8
2Th 2:13
1Ti 3:16;
4:1, 14
2Ti 1:6–7, 14
Tit 3:5–6
Heb 1:9;
2:4;
3:7;
9:8, 14;
10:15, 32;
11:11
1Pe 1:2, 11–12, 22;
2:5;
3:18–19;
4:10–11
2Pe 1:21
1Jn 2:20, 27;
3:24;
4:13;
5:6–8
Jude 19–20
Rev 1:4, 10;
2:7, 11, 17, 29;
3:1, 6, 13, 22;
4:2;
5:6;
9:17;
11:11;
14:13;
17:3;
21:10;
22:17

F

Fruits of the Holy Spirit

Ps 45:7;
51:12
Isa 61:3;
63:14
Mt 3:10;
7:16–20;
12:33;
13:8, 22–23
Mk 4:8, 20
Lk 3:9;
6:43–44;
8:8, 15;
13:9
Jn 4:10–15;
15:1–8
Ac 9:31;
13:52
Ro 5:5;
6:22;
8:6, 23;
14:17;
15:13, 30
2Co 13:14
Gal 5:22–23
Eph 1:3;
4:3;
5:9
Php 1:11;
2:1
Col 1:8
1Th 1:6
2Ti 1:7
Heb 1:9;
12:11
Jas 3:17–18
1Pe 1:22

G

Gifts of the Holy Spirit

Ge 41:38
Ex 4:10–15;
6:30—7:1;
25:31–40;
28:3;
31:3;
35:31, 34–35;
36:1;
37:17–24
Nu 11:25–29
Dt 34:9
1Sa 10:6–7, 10–12;
18:14–15, 30;
19:20–24
2Sa 14:17, 20;
16:23;
23:2
1Ki 3:5–14, 28;
4:29–34;
5:12;
10:1–9, 23–24;
11:41
2Ki 6:8–12
1Ch 22:12
2Ch 1:7–12;
2:12;
9:1–8, 22–23
Ezr 7:25
Ne 9:20
Job 32:8;
35:10–11;
38:36
Ps 51:6;
68:18
Pr 1:22–23;
2:3–8;
3:13–18
Ecc 2:26
Isa 11:2–3;
28:6, 9, 11;
42:1;
61:1
Jer 1:6–10;
5:14
Da 1:17, 20;
2:20–23;
4:8–9, 18;
5:11–12, 14
Joel 2:28–29
Mic 3:8
Zec 4:1–6
Mt 10:19–20;
12:42
Mk 13:11;
16:17–18
Lk 1:17, 67;
2:40;
11:31;
12:11–12;
21:14–15;
24:49
Jn 3:34;
14:26;
16:13–15
Ac 1:8;
2:3–18;
4:13;
6:3, 8–10;
10:38, 46;
11:27–28;
19:6;
20:28
Ro 1:11;
12:6–8;
15:19
1Co 1:4–7;
2:4–15;
3:1–2;
7:7;
12:1–31;
13:1–2, 8;
14:1–40
Eph 1:16–19;
3:2–5, 7, 14–19;
4:7–8, 11–14
Col 1:9
1Th 5:20
1Ti 4:14
2Ti 1:6–7, 14;
3:16
Heb 2:4
Jas 1:5
1Pe 4:10–11
2Pe 1:19, 21
1Jn 2:20, 27
Rev 1:4;
3:1;
4:5;
5:6;
19:10

H

Healing and Resurrecting Power of the Spirit

Job 33:4
Eze 37:1–12, 13–14
Mt 12:28
Jn 3:3–8;
6:63
Ro 1:4;
8:2, 11;
15:19
1Co 6:14;
12:9;
15:44–54
2Co 3:6
Eph 1:19–20
Heb 2:4
1Pe 3:18
Rev 11:11

J

Comfort or **Joy** of the Holy Spirit

Ps 45:7;
51:12
Isa 44:3;
61:3;
63:14
Mal 3:10
Mt 3:16;
5:6
Mk 1:10
Lk 3:22
Jn 1:32;
14:16–17, 26;
15:26;
16:7;
20:21–22
Ac 2:46;
9:31;
13:52
Ro 5:5;
8:1, 15;
14:17;
15:13
2Co 3:17
Gal 5:22
1Th 1:6
Heb 1:9

L

Leading or Guiding of the Holy Spirit

Ge 24:27
Nu 9:21
Jdg 13:25
1Sa 10:6–7
2Sa 5:24;
23:2
1Ki 18:12;
22:24
2Ki 2:16
1Ch 14:15
2Ch 18:23
Ne 2:12;
9:12, 20
Job 32:18–19
Ps 37:23;
39:3;
143:10
Pr 3:5–6;
6:22;
16:1, 9
Isa 30:21;
48:16;
58:1;
63:14
Jer 10:23;
20:9
Eze 1:12, 20;
2:2–3;
3:14, 22, 24;
11:1, 5;
13:3;
36:27
Mt 4:1;
10:19–20
Mk 1:12;
12:36;
13:11
Lk 2:27;
4:1, 14;
12:11–12;
21:14–15
Jn 4:23–24;
16:13
Ac 1:2;
2:4;
4:8;
6:10;
8:29, 39;
9:31;
10:19–20;
11:12;
13:2, 4, 9;
15:28;
16:6–7;
18:5;
20:22–23, 28;
21:4
Ro 7:6;
8:1–14, 26–27;
9:1;
12:6–8
1Co 7:40;
12:3;
14:15, 30, 32–33
2Co 12:18
Gal 5:5, 16–18, 22–25;
6:8
Eph 4:3–4;
5:18–19;
6:18
Php 3:3
1Th 5:19
Heb 9:14
1Pe 1:12, 22;
2:5;
3:18–19;
4:10–11
Jude 19–20
Rev 1:10;
4:2

M

Great **Might** or Power Given by the Spirit

Ge 1:2–3;
41:38
Ex 4:10–12;
40:34–35
Jdg 3:10;
6:34;
11:29;
14:6, 19;
15:14–15;
16:20
1Sa 10:10–12;
11:6;
19:20–23
1Ki 3:12;
4:29–34;
8:10–11;
10:1–9
2Ki 2:16
2Ch 5:14;
7:2
Job 26:13–14;
32:18–19;
33:4
Ps 51:12–13;
104:30;
139:7
Isa 9:5;
11:2;
28:6;
31:3;
32:15;
34:16;
40:7, 13;
44:3–4;
58:11;
59:19
Jer 1:6–10, 17–19;
5:14;
20:9
Eze 2:2–3;
3:12, 14, 24;
33:22;
36:27;
37:14
Da 4:8–9, 18;
5:11–12, 14;
6:3
Joel 2:28
Mic 2:7;
3:8
Zec 4:6;
6:8
Mal 3:10;
4:2–3
Mt 3:11;
12:28
Mk 13:11
Lk 1:15–17, 80;
2:40;
3:16;
4:14;
21:14–15;
24:32, 49
Jn 7:38–39;
14:26;
16:7–15
Ac 1:8;
2:1–18;
4:13, 29–31, 33;
6:8–10, 15;
10:38, 46;
11:24;
19:6
Ro 1:4, 11;
8:2, 26–27;
15:13, 19
1Co 2:4–10;
3:1;
4:20
2Co 3:5–18;
9:8
Gal 3:5
Eph 1:17–19;
3:2–5, 14–19;
6:10
Php 1:19
Col 1:9–11
1Th 1:5
2Ti 1:7
Heb 2:4
2Pe 1:21
1Jn 2:20, 27

N

Names and Symbols of the Holy Spirit

Ge 1:2
Ex 3:1–6;
13:21–22;
25:31–37;
29:7;
30:25;
34:29–35;
40:34–35
Lev 1:7;
6:13
1Ki 8:10–11;
18:46
2Ki 2:9;
3:15
2Ch 5:13–14;
7:1–22
Ne 9:12, 20
Job 26:13;
32:8, 18–19;
33:4
Ps 39:3;
45:2, 7;
51:12;
78:14;
84:11;
89:20;
104:30;
133:2;
139:7;
143:10
Ecc 11:5
Isa 4:4, 5;
6:6;
9:5;
11:2;
12:3;
30:1;
40:7;
44:3–4;
55:1;
61:3
Jer 2:13;
5:14;
17:13;
20:9
Eze 1:3–4, 13, 27–28;
3:12, 14, 22;
8:1, 3;
10:2–4;
34:26;
37:1;
40:1;
43:4–5
Da 5:12;
6:3
Hos 10:12
Joel 3:18
Zec 4:1–6;
6:8;
12:10
Mal 4:2
Mt 3:11, 16;
6:22;
25:4

Mk 1:10;
6:13
Lk 3:16, 22;
11:34–36;
24:32
Jn 1:32;
3:5, 8, 34;
4:10–14;
7:37–39;
14:16–17;
15:26
Ac 2:2–4, 13, 33;
4:31;
6:15;
8:39;
9:3;
10:45;
22:6;
26:13
Ro 1:4
1Co 2:11;
12:1–13
2Co 3:17;
4:6–7;
11:4
Gal 5:18
Eph 2:18;
3:16;
4:4;
5:18
Heb 9:14;
10:29
Jas 5:14
1Pe 4:14
1Jn 2:20, 27;
4:1–2, 6;
5:6, 7–8
Jude 19
Rev 1:4;
3:1, 18;
4:5;
5:6;
22:17

P

The Holy Spirit **Promised**

Nu 11:17;
12:6
1Sa 10:6
2Ki 2:9–10
Ps 68:18;
84:11
Pr 1:22–23
Isa 4:4;
9:5;
11:2;
12:3;
32:15;
41:17–18;
42:1;
44:3–4;
55:1;
59:21;
61:1
Eze 11:19;
36:26–27;
37:14;
39:29
Da 9:24
Hos 6:3;
10:12
Joel 2:28–29;
3:18
Zec 12:10
Mal 3:10;
4:2
Mt 3:11;
12:18
Mk 1:8
Lk 1:15, 35;
3:16;
4:17–18;
11:9–13;
24:29
Jn 1:33;
4:10;
7:37–39;
14:16–17, 26;
15:26;
16:7–15
Ac 1:4–5, 8;
2:15–18, 38–39;
11:16
Ro 15:29
Gal 3:14
2Pe 1:4
Rev 22:17

Q

Quenching, Grieving, or Sinning Against the Spirit

Ge 6:3
Jdg 16:20
1Sa 3:1;
16:14;
18:12
1Ki 22:24
2Ch 18:23
Ne 9:30
Ps 51:11
Isa 63:10
La 2:9
Mic 3:6
Zec 6:8
Mt 12:31–32
Mk 3:29
Lk 12:10
Ac 5:3–4, 9;
7:51
Eph 4:30
1Th 5:19
Heb 6:4–6;
10:29
1Jn 5:16, 17–18

R

Regeneration as the Work of the Holy Spirit

1Sa 10:6, 9
Ps 51:10, 12–13
Isa 4:4;
6:5–7;
61:1–3
Jer 31:33–34;
32:38–39
Eze 11:19;
36:25–27
Lk 1:17
Jn 3:3–8;
6:63
Ro 8:1–16
1Co 6:11;
12:13
2Co 3:3
Gal 3:2–3;
4:6, 29
Eph 1:13–14;
2:18
Tit 3:5
Heb 8:10–12;
10:16, 22

S

Sanctifying Power of the Holy Spirit

Ex 3:1–6;
28:41;
29:21;
30:25
Lev 8:12;
21:10–12
Dt 30:6
1Sa 24:6;
26:9
2Sa 1:14, 21
1Ch 16:22
Ps 51:10
Isa 4:3–4;
6:5–8;
9:5
Eze 11:19;
36:25–27
Mic 2:7
Lk 1:17
Ac 15:8–9
Ro 1:4;
8:1–16;
12:1–2;
15:16
1Co 3:1, 16–17;
6:11
2Co 3:18
Gal 5:16
Eph 4:22–24;
5:25–27
1Th 4:7–8;
5:23
2Th 2:13
Heb 10:14–15, 22, 29
1Pe 1:2, 22
Jude 19–20

T

Teaching or Enlightening of the Spirit

Ge 15:1;
41:38;
46:2
Ex 4:15;
28:3;
31:3;
35:31
Nu 11:25–29;
12:6;
22:38;
23:5, 12, 16;
24:2–3
Dt 34:9
1Sa 3:1;
10:6–7, 10–12
2Sa 16:23;
23:1–2
1Ki 3:5–14, 28;
4:29–34;
5:12;
10:1–9, 23–24;
22:14
2Ki 6:8–12, 17
1Ch 28:12, 19
2Ch 9:1–7, 23;
18:13;
20:14–15;
24:20;
26:5
Ezr 7:25
Ne 9:20
Job 4:13;
27:11;
32:8, 18–19;
33:14–15;
35:10–11;
38:36
Ps 143:10
Pr 1:22–23;
2:3–9;
28:5
Ecc 1:16;
2:26
Isa 11:2–3;
28:6, 9;
40:13;
42:1;
51:16;
61:1
Jer 1:6–10, 5–14;
31:33–34
La 2:9
Eze 1:1;
7:26;

8:3;
11:24;
13:3;
40:1–2
Da 1:17, 20;
2:19–23, 28;
4:8–9, 18;
5:11–12, 14;
7:1;
8:1–2, 16;
9:21;
10:1, 8, 16
Joel 2:28–29
Mic 3:8
Zec 7:12
Mt 6:22;
10:19–20;
12:42;
22:43–44
Mk 12:36;
13:11;
16:17
Lk 1:22, 41–42, 67;
2:40, 52;
4:18;
11:31;
12:11–12;
21:14–15
Jn 3:34;
14:26;
15:26;
16:7–15
Ac 1:2, 16;
2:1–18;
4:13;
6:3, 9–10;
7:55;
10:10–11, 17, 46;
11:28;
16:9;
19:6;
20:23;
21:4, 11;
22:17–18;
28:25
Ro 12:6–8
1Co 2:4–16;
7:40;
12:3, 8, 10;
14:30
2Co 12:1–4
Gal 1:11–12
Eph 1:17–19;
3:2–5, 16–19;
6:17
1Th 1:5
1Ti 4:1
2Ti 3:16
Heb 3:7;
6:4;
8:10–11;
10:16
1Pe 1:11, 22;
4:10–11
2Pe 1:21
1Jn 2:20, 27
Rev 1:10;
2:7, 11, 17, 29;
3:6, 13, 18, 22;
4:2;
14:13;
17:3

W

God **Wishes** Us to be Filled with the Spirit

Nu 11:29;
14:24;
27:18–20
Ps 68:18
Pr 1:22–23;
29:18
Isa 30:1
Jer 2:13
Hos 10:12
Mic 2:7
Zec 4:6
Lk 24:49
Jn 4:23–24;
6:63;
14:16–17;
16:7
Ac 1:4–5;
6:3;
7:51;
8:14–15;
9:17;
19:2
Ro 1:11;
7:6;
8:1–16;
12:1–2, 6–8;
14:17
1Co 1:4–7;
2:14;
3:1–2;
12:1–11, 31;
14:1, 5, 15
2Co 3:6–11, 17–18;
6:6;
13:14
Gal 3:3, 14;
5:16, 25
Eph 1:16–17;
2:22;
3:14–19;
4:3–4, 11–14;
5:9, 18
Php 3:3
Col 1:9
1Th 4:7–8
2Th 2:13
1Ti 4:12
1Pe 1:2;
2:5;
4:10–11
Jude 19–20
Rev 3:18

SALVATION
(RED)

A

All Unsaved People are Sinners

Ge 17:10, 14
Ex 12:43–49;
30:15
Dt 1:32;
11:26–28;
18:18–19;
32:20
1Sa 2:12;
8:7
1Ki 8:46
2Ch 6:36;
12:14
Job 9:2–3;
15:12–16;
25:4–6
Ps 14:1–4;
53:1–4;
58:1–2;
78:21–22;
130:3;
143:2
Pr 20:9;
30:12
Ecc 7:20
Isa 53:6
Mal 1:6;
3:18
Mt 4:8–9;
6:24;
7:13–14;
12:30;
13:38;
18:3;
22:11–14;
25:1–12
Mk 9:40;
10:15;
16:16
Lk 4:5–6;
11:23;
12:34;
13:1–5;
16:13, 15;
18:17
Jn 1:12;
3:3–7, 18, 19, 36;
5:38–42;
6:53;
7:7;
8:7–9, 23–24, 33–36, 42–44, 47;
10:1, 25–28;
12:48;
14:17, 30;
15:6, 18–19;
16:8–9;
17:14, 16, 25
Ac 3:22–23
Ro 1:20, 21;
3:9–12, 19, 22, 23;
5:12, 14–21;
6:16, 20–21;
7:5, 9, 14;
8:5–9, 13–14;
11:32
1Co 11:32
2Co 5:14;
13:5
Gal 1:4;
2:16, 21;
3:10–11, 22
Eph 2:1–3
Php 2:21
2Th 1:8
Heb 3:18
Jas 2:10;
4:4
1Jn 1:6, 8, 10;
2:15–16, 22;
3:1, 9, 10;
4:3;
5:10, 12, 19
2Jn 9–10
Rev 13:8;
20:15

C

Condition of Sinners Described

Ge 2:17;
3:3;

6:5, 11, 12;
8:21;
13:13;
18:20;
19:4–10
Ex 9:34;
32:7–9;
33:3, 5
Nu 16:38
Dt 9:6, 13, 18;
13:13;
29:4, 18–19;
31:27;
32:5, 20, 28–29
Jdg 2:19;
19:22
1Sa 2:12, 17, 25;
8:7;
24:13;
25:17
2Sa 23:6–7
1Ki 21:20, 25–26
2Ki 17:14–15, 17;
19:22;
21:22
2Ch 12:14;
24:20;
28:11, 22;
29:6
Ne 9:16–17
Job 5:13–14;
6:18;
15:16, 20–21, 23–26, 35;
20:4–13, 14–29;
21:14–15, 17–18;
22:10;
24:13, 17;
27:18
Ps 1:4;
5:9;
7:14;
10:4–6, 7–13;
11:2;
12:2;
14:1–4;
17:14;
28:5;
36:1–4;
37:12, 14;
38:4–5, 7;
40:2;
49:11–13, 20;
51:5;
52:1–3, 7;
53:1–4;
58:1–3, 4–5;
62:9–10;
64:3–6;
73:6, 8–9;
74:18, 22;
78:8, 10, 36–37;
82:5;
83:5;
94:11;
95:10;
107:10, 17;
119:53, 158
Pr 1:32;
2:13–14;
4:16–17, 19;
5:5, 22–23;
6:14;
8:36;
10:20, 23;
11:18;
12:5;
13:15, 19;
14:9, 13, 16, 34;
15:8–9, 26, 29;
16:27;
21:10, 16, 27;
30:12–13
Ecc 1:2;
5:1;
7:6, 29;
8:11;
9:3, 18;
10:2;
12:8
Isa 1:4–6;
3:9;
5:18, 20;
6:5, 9–10;
9:2;
26:10–11;
30:9–10;
33:11;
42:7;
43:8;
44:18, 20;
48:4, 22;
53:6;
55:2;
57:4, 20–21;
59:2–3, 4–7, 8, 12, 13;
61:1;
64:6;
65:2
Jer 2:19, 32;
4:22;
5:4, 21–25;
6:10, 15, 17, 28, 30;
7:24, 25, 26;
8:7, 9;
9:3, 26;
11:8;
13:10, 23;
16:12;
17:1, 9, 23;
23:12;
30:12;
44:10;
50:6
La 3:19–20
Eze 2:3, 4, 6;
3:7;
12:2;
20:16;
22:18;
33:30–32
Da 9:5
Hos 1:9;
4:2, 17;
6:4;
10:1–2, 13;
13:3
Am 5:7;
6:12, 13
Mic 7:2–4
Hab 2:4
Zep 1:12
Hag 1:5–7
Mal 3:13–14
Mt 3:7, 12;
4:16;
6:23;
7:16–20, 26–27;
8:22;
9:10–11, 12;
10:6;
12:30, 33;
13:14–15, 38;
15:14, 18–19;
18:11–14;
22:11–14;
23:17, 19, 25–28, 33;
25:2–3
Mk 2:16, 17;
4:12;
7:15, 20–23
Lk 1:79;
3:7;
5:30, 31;
6:39, 43–45, 49;
9:60;
11:23, 34–35, 39, 44;
12:15, 16–21;
15:6, 9, 16–17, 24, 32;
19:10
Jn 3:19–20;
6:44;
8:34, 44;
11:10;
12:40;
17:25
Ac 7:51;
8:23;
13:10;
26:18;
28:26–27
Ro 1:20–21, 22–23, 24, 25, 26, 27, 28–32;
3:9–12, 17–20;
6:16–17, 20;
7:5, 9–11, 14–25;
8:5–8;
11:8
1Co 2:14;
3:19–20;
6:9–10
2Co 4:3–4;
5:14;
10:12
Gal 5:19–21
Eph 2:1–3, 12, 19;
4:18;
5:5, 14
Php 2:21;
3:18–19
Col 1:13, 21;
2:13, 18;
3:5–7
1Th 4:13;
5:6
2Th 1:8;
2:10–12;
3:2
1Ti 1:9–10;
4:2;
5:6
2Ti 2:26;
3:1–5, 8, 13;
4:4
Tit 1:15, 16;
3:3
Heb 2:15;
3:10
Jas 1:14–15;
2:14–15;
4:5
1Pe 2:25;
4:3–5
2Pe 2:10–15, 17, 22;
3:3
1Jn 2:11, 15–17;
3:8, 14–15;
5:12, 19
Jude 12; 13; 16
Rev 3:17

D

Christ DIED to Save Sinners

Ge 3:15;
4:3–5;
8:20;
22:1–6, 7–8, 9–14;
31:54;
46:1
Ex 3:18;
5:3;
8:8, 25–29;

12:3–5,6–12, 13, 14–20, 21–23, 24–28;
20:24;
24:5–8;
28:38;
29:1, 10–13, 14, 15–18, 36–42;
30:10,15–16;
32:30
Lev 1:1–4, 10;
3:1–2, 6–8, 12–13;
4:1–3,4–11, 12, 13, 14,15–19, 20–21,22, 23, 24–27, 28, 29–31, 32, 33–35;
5:5–6,7–14, 15, 16–17, 18,19;
6:6–7,17, 25;
7:1–2,7, 37;
8:2, 14, 17–18, 22;
9:2–7, 11,15–18, 22;
10:16–19;
12:6–8;
14:4–7, 10–14, 19–25, 30–31;
15:14–15, 29–30;
16:3,5–11, 15, 21, 27;
17:3–10, 11–14;
19:21–22;
22:17–25;
23:4–5,8, 19, 26–32
Nu 5:8;
6:12–17;
7:10–88;
8:8, 10–13, 17–18, 21;
9:2–3, 13–14;
15:24–29;
16:46–47;
18:17;
19:1–9,17;
21:6–9;
23:1–3;
25:13;
28:3–4,9–10, 15–19, 22–23, 30–31;
29:1–40;
31:50
Dt 12:5–6, 13–14;
15:21;
16:1–6;
17:1
Jos 5:10;
8:30–31
Jdg 2:5;
20:26;
21:4
1Sa 1:3;
6:15;
7:9;
10:8;
11:15;
13:9–10;
15:15, 21;
20:6
2Sa 6:13, 17–18;
24:25
1Ki 3:4, 15;
8:5, 62-64;
9:25;
18:29, 36
2Ki 16:13–15;
23:21
1Ch 6:49;
16:1–2, 40;
21:26;
28:21
2Ch 2:4;
7:4–5;
8:12–13;
13:11;
15:11;
29:21–24, 27, 31–35;
30:1, 5,15, 22, 24;
31:2–3;
35:1,7–19
Ezr 3:2–6;
6:17, 19–20;
8:35
Ne 10:33;
12:43
Job 1:5;
42:8
Ps 22:13–18;
40:6–8;
69:22–21
Isa 52:14–15;
53:3–12;
56:7
Eze 40:39;
42:13;
43:18–27;
44:11, 27, 29;
45:15–25;
46:4–6, 11-12, 13, 14–15, 20
Da 9:24–26
Jnh 1:16
Zec 12:10;
13:1
Mal 1:8, 13–14
Mt 1:21;
20:28;
26:26–28
Mk 10:45;
14:22–24
Lk 9:56;
19:10;
22:17–20;
24:25–27, 44–47
Jn 1:29,36;
3:14–17;
6:51–56;
10:11, 15;
11:49–52;
12:32, 47;
15:13;
18:14
Ac 8:32–35;
20:28;
26:22–23
Ro 3:24–25;
5:1–2, 6–21;
8:3, 32,34;
14:9, 15
1Co 5:7;
6:20;
7:23;
8:11;
10:16;
11:23–25;
15:3
2Co 5:14–15, 18–21;
9:15
Gal 1:4;
2:20;
3:13,16;
4:4–5
Eph 1:4–5, 6–7, 10–11;
2:13–18;
4:32;
5:2, 25
Col 1:14, 20–22
1Th 5:9–10
1Ti 1:15;
2:5–6
Tit 2:14
Heb 1:3;
2:9, 14–17;
5:1–5;
7:27;
9:7, 11–28;
10:1–11, 12, 13–22;
12:24;
13:11–12,21
1Pe 1:2, 11, 18–19;
2:21, 24;
3:18;
4:1
2Pe 2:1
1Jn 1:7;
2:2,12;
3:5, 16;
4:9,10, 14;
5:8
Rev 1:5;
5:6, 9,12;
7:14;
12:11;
13:8

E

The Lord Knows **Every** Secret Thing

Ge 3:8–9;
6:5,11–12;
13:13;
18:20–21;
19:13;
20:6
Ex 32:9
Nu 32:23
Dt 9:13;
31:16, 21
Jos 22:22
1Sa 2:3,17;
16:7
1Ki 8:39;
19:18
2Ki 19:27
1Ch 28:9
2Ch 6:30;
16:9
Job 4:14;
10:4–7;
13:27;
14:16–17;
20:27;
22:12–17;
23:10;
26:6;
28:24–25;
31:4;
34:21–22,25;
42:2
Ps 7:9;
10:11–14;
11:4;
14:2;
17:3;
33:13–15;
44:21;
53:2;
56:8;
59:8–9;
64:5;
66:7;
69:5;
73:11;
87:6;
90:8;
94:7–11;
102:19;
139:1–16
Pr 5:21;
15:3, 11;
16:2;
17:3;
21:2;
24:12

Ecc 12:14
Isa 28:17; 29:15; 59:12
Jer 2:26; 11:20; 12:3; 13:27; 16:17; 17:1, 10; 18:23; 20:12; 23:23–24; 29:23; 32:19; 49:10
Eze 8:12; 9:9–10; 11:5
Da 2:22; 5:27
Hos 5:3; 7:2
Am 5:12; 8:7; 9:8
Jnh 1:2; 4:4
Zec 4:10
Mt 9:4; 10:26, 29–30; 12:25, 36
Mk 2:8; 4:22; 12:15
Lk 5:22; 6:8; 8:17; 9:47; 11:17; 12:2–3; 16:15
Jn 1:47–49; 2:24–25; 4:17–19, 29, 39; 5:42; 6:64; 10:14; 13:11, 21; 16:30; 21:17
Ac 1:24; 15:8, 18; 18:10
Ro 2:16; 8:27, 29; 11:4
1Co 3:13; 4:5; 8:3
2Co 11:31
1Th 2:4
2Ti 2:19
Heb 4:12–13
Jas 5:4
1Jn 3:20
Rev 2:23; 3:1

F

We are Saved Through **Faith**

Ge 15:6
2Sa 22:31
2Ch 20:20
Ps 2:12; 18:30; 32:10; 34:8, 22; 37:3, 40; 40:4; 84:12; 116:13; 125:1; 146:5; 147:11
Pr 16:20; 29:25
Isa 7:9; 26:3–4
Jer 17:7
Hab 2:4
Mt 9:2; 11:12; 21:31–32
Mk 1:15; 2:5; 16:16
Lk 5:20; 7:50; 8:12; 16:16; 18:42
Jn 1:12; 3:14–18, 36; 5:24; 6:28–29, 35, 40, 47; 7:38; 8:24; 9:35; 11:25–26; 12:36, 46; 14:12; 20:29, 31
Ac 8:37; 10:43; 13:38–39; 15:9; 16:30–31; 19:4; 20:21; 26:18
Ro 1:16, 17; 3:3, 21–30; 4:1–2, 3, 4–15, 16, 17–22, 23–24, 25; 5:1–2; 8:24; 9:30–33; 10:4, 6–11; 11:20, 23; 15:13
1Co 1:21; 15:2
Gal 2:16; 3:2, 6–9, 11, 14, 22, 24–26; 5:5–6
Eph 2:8; 3:12
Php 3:9
2Th 2:12–13
1Ti 1:16
2Ti 2:13; 3:15
Heb 3:18–19; 4:2–3, 6; 6:1, 12; 10:38–39; 11:1, 6, 7, 13
Jas 2:5, 23
1Pe 1:5, 8–9; 2:6
1Jn 3:23; 4:15; 5:1, 4–5, 9–10, 13

G

Good Works Alone Will Not Save

Ex 20:25
Dt 9:6; 10:17; 32:31, 37
Jdg 10:13–14
1Sa 2:9; 12:21; 16:7
1Ki 18:21
2Ch 19:7
Job 8:11–16; 9:2–3, 20, 29–31; 15:12, 16, 31; 27:18; 31:24; 34:19; 36:18–19; 40:3–4
Ps 16:4; 20:7; 33:16-17; 44:3, 6; 49:6–7; 52:7; 62:9–11; 75:6–7; 78:36–37; 118:8–9; 127:1; 143:2; 146:3
Pr 3:5–6, 7; 11:4, 28; 16:2; 18:11, 12; 19:21; 20:9; 21:2; 26:12; 28:26
Ecc 1:14–15; 7:13
Isa 1:11–14; 28:15–20; 29:8, 13–14; 30:1; 31:1; 36:6; 41:29; 45:20; 50:11; 52:3; 55:1–2; 59:6; 64:6
Jer 2:13, 22, 28, 35; 3:23; 4:14, 19–20; 8:9, 11; 9:23–24; 10:15; 13:23; 16:19; 17:5; 18:13–15; 23:17; 30:12; 34:17; 46:11; 48:7
La 3:37
Eze 7:19; 13:10–14; 29:6–7; 33:31
Hos 1:7; 5:13; 10:13; 14:3
Am 2:14–16
Jnh 2:8
Mic 6:7
Hab 2:13
Zep 1:18
Hag 1:5–7
Zec 4:6
Mt 3:9; 5:20;

7:26–27;
9:13;
15:8–9;
18:23–25;
19:16–26;
22:11–14;
25:1–2, 3, 4–13
Mk 7:6–7;
10:17–22, 23–27
Lk 6:49;
7:41–42;
11:39–40;
12:15;
16:15;
18:9–14, 16–22, 23–27
Jn 1:12–13;
3:3, 5;
6:28–29;
9:39;
10:1;
15:4
Ac 15:11
Ro 2:11, 28–29;
3:20, 27;
4:1–4, 13, 14;
8:9, 14;
9:11, 15–16, 31–32;
10:1–3;
11:5–6, 32
1Co 1:18–21, 26–31;
3:11, 19–20;
13:1–3;
15:10
2Co 10:18
Gal 1:8–9;
2:6, 16, 21;
3:2, 10–12, 17–18, 21;
4:21–31;
5:4, 6;
6:14–15
Eph 2:5, 8–9;
6:9
Php 3:3–10
1Ti 6:7, 17
2Ti 1:9
Tit 3:5
Heb 11:6
1Pe 1:18–19, 23–24
Rev 3:17–18

H

Punishment and **Hell** Await Sinners

Ge 2:17, 18;
3:3, 14–19;
4:7, 11–14;
6:7, 13, 17;
7:4, 21–23;
9:6;
11:7, 8;
12:17;
17:14;
19:11, 13, 24–26;
38:7, 10
Ex 4:24;
7:19–21;
8:1–6, 16, 18, 20–24;
9:1–6, 8–11, 13–15, 18–19, 22–25;
10:4–6, 12–15, 21–23;
11:4–6;
12:13, 15, 29–30;
14:23–28, 30;
15:4–5, 10;
19:13;
20:5, 7;
21:12, 14–17, 20, 22–25;
22:9, 20, 24;
23:7, 21, 27;
31:14–15;
32:10, 27–28, 33, 34;
33:2–3;
34:7;
35:2
Lev 10:1–2, 6–7, 10;
18:25, 28;
20:1–6, 9–21, 27;
22:9;
23:30;
25:13–21;
26:14–39, 41, 43
Nu 1:51;
3:4, 10, 38;
5:27;
8:17;
9:13;
11:1, 33–34;
14:11–12, 18, 22–23, 29–30, 32–37, 42–43;
15:30–36;
16:29–35, 39–40, 44–49;
17:12–13;
18:7, 22;
20:12, 24;
21:2–3, 6;
22:33;
23:20;
24:17, 20, 24;
25:3–9, 17;
26:10, 61, 64–65;
27:13–14;
31:16–17;
32:10–15, 23;
33:4, 52;
35:19, 21
Dt 1:34–37, 42–44;
2:14–15, 21, 34;
3:6;
4:3, 21, 24, 25, 27;
5:9, 11;
6:15;
7:1–5, 10, 23–24, 26;
8:19–20;
9:3–5, 13–14, 25;
10:10;
11:4–8, 16–17, 26–28;
13:4–11, 15;
17:2–7, 12–13;
18:12, 18–19;
19:11–13, 21;
20:16–17;
21:21–23;
24:7;
25:1;
27:14–26;
28:15–28, 29, 30–68;
29:19–28;
30:1, 15, 17–19;
31:16–17, 29;
32:22–23, 24–26, 35, 41, 42, 43, 49–52;
34:4–5
Jos 5:6;
6:17, 21;
7:1–26;
8:24, 26;
9:24;
10:11, 24–25, 28–41;
11:11–12, 14, 20–22;
13:22;
22:17–18, 20;
23:12–13, 15–16;
24:18, 19, 20
Jdg 1:6–7;
2:14–15, 20–21;
3:7–8;
4:1–2;
5:23, 31;
6:1;
10:6–9;
13:1;
20:13;
21:11
1Sa 2:9, 10, 24–25, 30–34;
3:11–12, 13–14;
4:7, 8, 10–11;
5:6–7, 9–12;
6:4, 19–20;
7:10, 13;
12:9, 15, 25;
15:1–23, 26, 33;
25:29, 38;
26:10;
28:18–19
2Sa 3:39;
6:7;
7:14;
12:1–15;
22:27–28;
24:10–15
1Ki 2:5–6, 33, 34, 44;
8:32–33, 35, 46;
9:6–9;
13:34;
14:10–11, 16;
16:1–4, 12–13;
17:1;
20:42;
21:20–24, 29
2Ki 1:10, 12, 14;
2:23–24;
9:8–10, 25;
10:18–25, 32;
13:3;
14:5–6;
17:6–7, 18–20, 22–23, 25;
18:11–12;
21:9–15;
22:13, 16–17;
23:26–27;
24:3;
25:21
1Ch 2:3;
5:25–26;
9:1;
10:13–14;
21:8–14;
27:24;
28:9
2Ch 6:23, 26, 36;
7:13, 19–22;
12:1, 2, 5;
15:2;
19:2;
22:7–8;
24:18, 20, 24;
25:3–4, 15–16, 20, 23;
26:16–21;
28:4–6, 10–11, 13, 19;
29:7–8;
30:7;
32:25;
33:10–11;
34:21, 24–25;
36:16, 17
Ezr 8:22

Ne 1:8;
4:5;
9:11, 26–28, 30
Est 7:10
Job 4:8–9;
8:11–15, 20, 22;
9:4;
10:14,15;
11:20;
15:20–22, 23–26,
30,31–33, 34;
18:18;
20:5–25, 26–27,
28–29;
21:17–20, 30;
22:15–16;
26:6;
27:7, 8, 19–23;
29:17;
31:3;
34:11–12, 25–26;
36:12–14;
38:15
Ps 1:4–6;
2:4–5, 8–9, 12;
3:7;
5:4–6,10;
7:11,12–15, 16;
9:3, 5,15–16,
17;
10:2, 14–16;
11:6;
12:3;
16:4;
18:13–14, 26;
21:8–9;
25:4–8, 26;
26:9;
27:14–15, 17;
28:1, 3–5;
31:23;
32:10;
34:16, 21;
36:12;
37:1–2, 9–10,
12–13, 20,22,
28, 33–36, 38;
39:11;
40:14;
50:3,21–22;
52:5–6;
53:5;
55:9, 15, 23;
57:6;
58:6–10;
59:5, 8, 12–13;
62:3, 12;
63:9–10;
64:7;
68:1–2, 21,23;
69:22, 23–24,25,
27–28;
70:2–3;
71:13;
72:9;
73:17–18,27;
74:1;
75:7–8, 10;
76:7;
78:21–22, 30–34,
43–51, 55–66;
79:5–6;
83:9–11, 13–16,
17;
86:13;
89:10, 23, 32;
91:8;
92:7,9;
94:1–2, 13, 23;
95:11;
97:3;
101:8;
103:4;
104:35;
105:27–36;
106:11, 14–15,
17–18, 23, 27,
29, 32, 34, 40,
42;
107:17, 33–34;
109:7–16, 17–19;
110:1,5–6;
112:10;
119:21, 32,118,
119;
120:3–4;
125:3;
129:4;
135:8–12;
136:10;
139:19;
140:9–11;
141:9–10;
143:7;
144:6;
145:20;
146:9;
147:6;
149:7
Pr 1:24–32;
2:18, 22;
3:25, 33–34;
5:4–5, 22,23;
6:15,27–28,
32–33;
7:27;
8:36;
9:18;
10:7, 14, 24–25,
27–31;
11:3, 5–7, 19, 21,
31;
12:2, 13, 21;
13:2–3, 6, 9,13,
15,20, 21,25;
14:11, 12,13–14,
27, 32;
15:10–11, 24,25;
16:4–5, 18, 25;
17:19;
18:7, 12;
19:5, 9, 19;
20:17, 20, 26;
21:7, 11–12,
15–16, 28;
22:3,8;
23:14,29–32;
24:12, 16, 20;
26:10,27;
27:12,20;
29:1;
30:17;
31:6
Ecc 7:6, 17;
8:11–13;
9:12;
10:8, 12
Isa 1:20, 24, 28,
30–31;
2:10–21;
3:8–10, 11,
14–15, 24;
5:5–6, 11–12,
16–18, 23;
8:15;
9:18;
11:4;
13:6–13,15–22;
14:4–6, 9, 11–12,
15, 19–25;
15:9;
16:6–11;
17:12–14;
23:1–11;
24:1–12, 17–23;
25:5, 10–12;
26:11, 20–21;
28:1–3, 15–18,
22;
29:1–8, 15;
30:1, 12–14, 17,
30,31, 33;
31:1–2;
33:11–12, 14;
34:1–17;
35:4;
40:2;
42:24–25;
43:17;
50:1;
51:17;
59:18;
60:12;
61:2;
63:3–4,6, 10;
65:6,7, 12,
13–14,15, 20;
66:14–16,17, 24
Jer 1:16;
2:16–17, 35;
3:3, 8;
4:4,6–9, 15,
18–20;
5:6, 9,14–19,
25, 29;
6:11–12, 15, 19,
21, 25–26;
7:12, 19–20, 29,
32–34;
8:12–18, 20;
9:9,11, 16, 19,
22, 25;
10:10,15, 18, 25;
11:8, 11, 20, 22;
12:5,9, 11–13, 17;
13:10, 14, 15–16,
17–23, 24,
25–27;
14:4, 10–12;
15:2–9;
16:4–5, 10–13,
18;
17:4,5–6, 10, 18;
18:9–11, 16–17,
23;
19:3, 6–15;
20:3–6, 11,12, 16;
21:4–7, 10, 12, 14;
22:5-13, 24–30;
23:1–2, 12,15,
17–19,20, 29,
34, 39, 40;
24:9–10;
25:8–38;
26:3–6;
27:8;
29:17–19, 22, 32;
30:6–7, 15, 20,
23–24;
31:28, 30;
32:18–19, 23–25,
28–29, 36;
33:5;
34:17, 20–22;
35:17;
36:3, 7,30–31;
42:16–18;
43:11–13;
44:2, 6–7, 11–14,
22–23, 27,
29–30;
46:5–6, 10,
14–16, 19–26;
47:4–7;
48:3–4, 7–10,
15–25, 36–46;
49:2–3, 8–10,
12–18, 20–29,
32–38;
50:3, 12–18,
21–32, 35–46;

51:3–4, 6, 11, 18, 20–64
La 1:5–8, 12–22; 2:1–12, 20; 3:20, 39,64–66; 4:5–6, 10–12, 22; 5:1–22
Eze 3:17–20; 5:1; 7:8,9–16, 17–18,19; 9:5–7, 10; 11:21; 12:13–15, 25; 13:8–9, 14,22; 14:8–10, 13–21; 15:7–8; 16:23,49–50; 17:16, 18–21; 18:4,13, 20, 23–24, 26, 30; 19:8–9; 20:8, 15, 21, 23; 22:20–22,31; 23:25–26, 32–34; 24:13–14, 23; 25:7, 13–16, 17; 26:4–8, 14–21; 28:7–10, 18–19; 29:8–10; 30:1–26; 31:11–18; 33:4–5, 8–10, 11, 12, 13,14–16, 18; 35:3–9, 14; 36:5–7; 38:20–23; 43:8; 44:12
Da 2:44; 5:1–6,20, 24–28; 6:24; 7:11, 26; 8:25; 9:11–14; 12:1,2
Hos 1:6; 2:2–3, 13; 4:2–3, 6–9, 14; 5:5, 9–14; 6:4–5; 7:12–13; 8:7,13–14; 9:9, 12; 10:7–10, 13–15; 12:2; 13:1, 3,16; 14:1, 9
Joel 1:15; 2:1–2,3–5, 6, 7–9, 10–11, 31; 3:13–14
Am 1:3; 2:6, 9, 14–16; 3:2, 14; 4:2, 6–11, 12; 5:6, 16–20,27; 6:1, 11; 8:3, 7,8–14; 9:1–4,8, 10
Ob 4, 8–10, 15
Jnh 1:2; 3:4
Mic 1:3–6; 2:1, 3, 10; 5:15; 6:13,14–15; 7:9–10, 17
Na 1:2–3, 5–6, 8–12; 2:10,13; 3:1, 10, 13–15
Hab 2:10; 3:12–13
Zep 1:2–3, 6–8, 12, 14–15, 17–18; 2:2–3; 3:8
Hag 2:17
Zec 3:2; 5:1–4; 7:17; 8:14; 9:4–5; 10:3, 5; 11:6; 14:3, 12, 18–19
Mal 1:4; 2:2,9; 3:2, 5; 4:1, 3
Mt 3:7, 10, 12; 5:13, 22, 29–30; 6:15; 7:13, 19,23, 26–27; 8:12; 10:14–15, 28,33; 11:20–24; 12:31–32, 36–37, 41–42; 13:30, 38–42, 46–50; 15:4, 13–14; 16:19, 26–27; 18:3, 6–9,18, 34–35; 19:24; 21:40–41, 44; 22:1–6, 7, 11–13, 44; 23:14–15,23, 25, 27, 29, 33,38; 24:21,40–41, 50–51; 25:11–12, 30–46; 26:24,52
Mk 3:28–29; 6:11; 7:10; 8:36–38; 9:42–49; 12:9, 36–40; 13:19; 14:21; 16:16
Lk 1:51; 2:34; 3:7, 9,17; 6:24, 25,26, 39, 49; 9:25–26; 10:12–15,18; 11:31–32, 42–44, 46–47, 50–52; 12:4–5,9–10, 16–19, 20–21, 46–48; 13:1–4, 5,6–8, 9, 24–28,35; 14:16–23, 24; 16:19–31; 17:1–2, 26–30, 32–36; 18:7; 19:27,41–46; 20:15–16, 18, 42–43, 47; 21:24, 25–26; 22:22; 23:30
Jn 3:3, 5, 16–19, 36; 5:14, 24, 29; 9:39; 12:48; 15:2, 6; 17:12
Ac 1:25; 2:34–35; 3:23; 5:1–11; 12:21–23; 13:6–11, 41; 18:6; 23:3
Ro 1:18,28–32; 2:2–13; 3:5–6, 8,16; 5:9, 12; 6:21, 23; 8:6, 13; 9:22; 11:9–10, 14, 20–22,25; 12:19; 13:2, 4; 14:15
1Co 1:18; 3:17; 6:9–10,13; 8:11; 9:22; 10:5–12; 11:32; 15:25,56; 16:22
2Co 2:15–16; 4:3; 5:10–11; 11:15
Gal 1:8–9; 5:19–21; 6:7–8
Eph 5:5–6
Php 1:28; 3:19
Col 3:5–6, 25
1Th 1:10; 2:16; 4:6; 5:3,9
2Th 1:5–9; 2:8, 11–12
1Ti 4:16; 5:12, 24; 6:9,10
2Ti 4:14
Heb 1:13; 2:2–3; 3:11, 17–19; 6:2, 7–8; 10:12–13, 26–31, 39; 11:28; 12:20–21, 25, 29; 13:4
Jas 1:15; 2:13; 3:1; 5:1–3
1Pe 3:12; 4:17–18
2Pe 2:1, 3–9, 12–13, 17,20, 21; 3:6–7,16
Jude 5–7;11; 13–15; 23
Rev 1:7; 2:5, 16, 21–23, 27; 3:3, 16; 6:15–17; 8:7–13; 9:1–21; 11:13–14, 18;

13:10;
14:10–11, 14–20;
15:1, 6–8;
17:8, 11;
18:4–8, 10, 15,
20–21;
19:3, 11–19, 20,
21;
20:2–3, 9–15;
21:8, 27;
22:12, 15

J

All People will be JUDGED by the Lord

Ge 18:25
Jdg 11:27
1Sa 2:10
1Ch 16:33
Ps 1:5;
7:8;
9:7–8;
37:32–3;
50:3–6;
58:11;
67:4;
75:7;
82:8;
94:2;
96:10, 13;
98:9;
109:7;
110:6
Ecc 3:17;
11:9;
12:14
Isa 2:4;
3:13–14;
33:22
Eze 7:27;
18:30;
33:20;
34:17, 20, 22
Da 7:9–10, 26
Joel 3:12
Am 4:12
Mal 3:5
Mt 7:1–2;
10:15;
11:22, 24;
12:36, 41–42;
25:31–46
Mk 6:11
Lk 10:12–14;
11:31–32
Jn 8:50;
12:48;
16:11
Ac 10:42;
17:31;
24:25
Ro 2:2–13, 16;
3:6;
14:10–12
1Co 4:4–5;
5:13
2Co 5:10
1Ti 5:24
2Ti 4:1, 8
Heb 9:27;
10:27, 30;
12:23;
13:4
Jas 2:12–13;
4:12;
5:9
1Pe 4:5
2Pe 2:4, 9;
3:7
1Jn 4:17
Jude 6; 14–15
Rev 11:18;
14:7;
19:11;
20:1–15

K

Saving and KEEPING Power of God

Ge 7:16;
14:19, 22;
15:1;
18:14;
22:18
Ex 12:13, 23;
15:2, 11, 13, 17;
19:5–6;
33:19
Nu 6:24–26;
11:23;
21:8–9;
23:19
Dt 30:6, 20;
32:15, 39;
33:25, 27, 29
Jos 1:5
Jdg 5:31
Ru 2:12
1Sa 2:2, 8–9;
25:29
2Sa 22:31, 36, 47
1Ki 8:57–58
2Ki 6:16–17
1Ch 4:10;
29:11–12
2Ch 2:5–6
Ne 8:10;
9:29
Job 1:10;
5:24;
17:9;
19:25;
36:7;
42:2
Ps 2:12;
3:8;
4:3;
12:7;
16:8;
17:8;
18:2, 16, 35–36,
46;
19:7;
20:5–6;
25:5;
26:1;
27:1;
31:5;
36:9;
37:27–28;
40:2;
51:7;
55:16, 22;
61:2;
62:1–2, 5–10,
11–12;
67:1–2;
68:13, 20;
69:32;
72:17;
73:26;
78:35;
80:3, 7, 19;
84:11;
89:8, 13, 15–16,
26;
91:3, 11;
94:18;
95:1;
103:3–4, 12;
106:8;
107:14;
118:14, 21;
119:130;
121:1–8;
125:1;
128:1–2;
130:7;
135:5–6;
144:15;
145:14;
146:5
Pr 14:17;
16:15;
19:21;
20:22;
23:11
Ecc 7:13
Isa 1:18, 25;
4:4, 6;
12:1–2;
25:4;
26:3–4;
28:16;
32:2;
40:8, 29, 30, 31;
41:10;
43:1–2;
47:4;
48:18;
50:2, 10;
51:6;
52:10;
53:5, 11;
55:7;
57:13;
59:1;
60:19–21;
63:1
Jer 8:22;
17:13–14;
18:14–15;
24:7;
31:33–34;
32:17–18, 27,
38–39;
33:8;
50:20, 34
Eze 11:19–20;
12:25;
20:13, 21;
36:25–26, 29, 33;
37:23
Joel 2:32
Am 5:4, 6, 8
Ob 17
Jnh 2:9
Mic 7:7
Zec 13:1
Mal 3:3
Mt 1:21, 25;
4:4;
6:13;
7:24–25;
9:2–5, 6, 7–8;
11:28–29;
19:26;
24:35;
27:42;
28:18
Mk 2:10;
10:27;
13:31;
14:36;
15:31
Lk 1:31, 37, 69,
77–79;
2:10–11, 21, 32,
38;
3:5–6;
5:24;
6:47–48;
11:4;
18:27;
21:33;
22:31–32;
23:35
Jn 1:4, 12, 29;
3:14–18;
4:10, 13–14, 42;
5:24;

6:27, 33–35,
39–40, 50–51,
54–58, 63, 68;
7:17, 38;
8:12, 36, 51, 52;
9:5;
10:7, 9–10,
28–29;
11:25–26;
12:46, 50;
14:6;
17:3, 11–12;
19:30;
20:23
Ac 2:25–26;
3:26;
5:31;
10:43;
13:23, 38–39, 47;
16:31;
20:32
Ro 1:16;
3:3–4, 24–25;
5:1–2, 9–11,
15–21;
7:24–25;
8:1–4, 33–39;
9:15, 18, 21, 23;
10:4, 11;
11:26;
15:29;
16:20, 25
1Co 1:9, 18, 23–24,
25, 30;
3:7;
6:9–11;
15:56–57
2Co 1:20;
2:14;
9:8
Eph 1:7;
2:18;
3:20;
5:14
Php 4:13, 19
Col 1:14
1Th 1:10;
5:9–10
2Th 3:3
1Ti 4:8
2Ti 1:12;
3:15
Tit 1:2;
2:11
Heb 2:18;
5:9;
6:16–17, 18–19;
7:25;
8:10–12;
9:13–14;
10:16–17;
12:24;
13:6, 8
Jas 1:21;
4:12
1Pe 1:4–5, 8, 9, 23,
25;
2:6, 24
2Pe 2:9
1Jn 1:7;
2:2;
3:5, 8;
4:4, 14;
5:4–5
Jude 24
Rev 1:18;
5:9;
7:9, 14;
12:11

L

The Lord **Loves** and Saves Sinners

Ge 15:16;
17:7;
18:23–32
Ex 20:6;
22:27;
25:17;
34:6–7
Lev 4:1–19, 20,
21–25, 26,
27–30, 31,
32–34, 35;
5:5–9, 10, 11–12,
13, 14–15, 16,
17, 18, 19;
6:4–6, 7;
19:22;
26:40–42
Nu 14:18–20;
15:25–28;
21:7–9;
30:5, 8, 12
Dt 4:7, 29, 30–31;
5:10;
7:7–8, 9;
11:26–27;
30:1–3, 11–15, 19
Jdg 3:8–9, 12–15;
4:1–7;
6:1–14;
13:1–5
1Sa 2:8;
7:9;
12:10–11, 20
2Sa 12:13;
22:28
1Ki 8:33–39, 47–50;
21:25–29
1Ch 16:34, 41;
28:9
2Ch 5:13;
6:26–30, 37–39;
7:3, 6, 14;
15:2, 3, 4, 15;
20:21;
30:9, 18–20;
33:11–13
Ezr 3:11;
8:22
Ne 1:9;
9:16, 17, 18–28,
31
Job 33:27–28
Ps 9:10;
22:5, 24, 26;
25:6–11;
30:5;
31:16;
32:5;
33:5, 18–19;
34:8, 18;
51:1–3, 17;
65:3;
68:13;
69:16, 32;
77:7–9;
78:34–37, 38–39;
79:9;
85:2–3, 9–10;
86:5, 13, 15;
89:34;
99:8;
100:5;
102:19–20;
103:1–4, 8–14, 17;
106:7–8, 45;
107:1, 9, 13, 19;
108:4;
109:26;
111:4;
112:4;
113:7;
116:5, 13;
118:1–5, 29;
119:64, 156;
130:3–4, 7–8;
136:1–26;
138:8;
145:8, 18;
147:3;
149:4
Pr 8:17;
21:21;
28:13
Isa 1:18–19, 25;
4:4, 6;
9:2;
12:1–3;
32:2, 3–4;
33:24;
38:17;
40:2;
42:6–7;
43:1, 25;
44:22;
45:22;
49:6;
52:3;
53:4–6, 11–12;
55:1–3, 6–7;
57:15–16, 18–19;
59:1;
61:1–3;
63:7, 9;
65:1, 2
Jer 3:1, 5, 12, 14, 22;
5:1;
9:24;
14:7;
18:8, 11–12;
21:8;
25:3–5;
26:3, 13, 19;
29:12, 13;
31:3, 20, 34;
32:18;
33:8, 11;
35:15;
36:3;
44:4–5;
50:20
La 3:22, 25, 32–33,
42
Eze 18:21–23, 27–28,
32;
33:11–12, 14–16,
19;
34:11–12;
36:25, 29, 33;
37:23
Da 9:9, 24
Hos 1:10;
2:19–20, 23;
5:15;
6:1, 3;
13:9, 14;
14:4
Joel 2:13
Am 5:4, 6–8;
7:3, 6
Jnh 3:10;
4:2, 11
Mic 6:6–8;
7:18–19
Hab 2:13
Zec 1:3;
3:1–5, 9;
13:1
Mal 3:7
Mt 1:21;
4:16;
5:5;
6:14;
7:7–8;
9:2, 10–11,
12–13;
10:6;
11:19, 28–29;
12:20, 31–32;
15:24;

18:11–14, 21–25, 26–27;
20:1–14;
21:27–30, 31–32;
22:1–8, 9–10;
23:37
Mk 2:5, 15–16, 17;
3:28;
6:34;
11:24–25;
16:9
Lk 1:50, 77–79;
2:10–11, 14, 32;
4:4, 18–19;
5:20, 29–30, 31–32;
6:35–36, 37;
7:34, 36–40, 41–42, 43–46, 47;
9:56;
11:9–10;
12:10;
13:34;
14:12–20, 21–23;
15:1–2, 3–24, 25–31, 32;
16:19–22;
17:3–4;
18:9–14;
19:1–9, 10, 41–42;
23:34, 39–41, 42–43;
24:46–47
Jn 1:7, 9, 12, 29;
3:14–17, 36;
4:6–9, 10, 11–41, 42;
5:24, 34;
6:35, 37, 40, 47;
7:17, 37;
8:3–10, 11–12, 51;
9:35–38, 39;
10:10;
11:25–26;
12:32, 46–47;
15:13;
20:31
Ac 3:14–18, 19, 25, 26;
5:31;
10:43;
11:18;
13:38–39, 47;
14:27;
15:7–10, 11, 14–17;
17:27, 28;
26:17–18, 23;
28:28
Ro 2:4;
3:21–30;
4:6, 12, 16, 22–24;
5:1, 6–21;
8:32;
9:23–26;
10:4–13, 20, 21;
11:23–24, 26–27, 32;
15:8–12, 21
1Co 1:26–31;
6:9–11, 20;
7:23;
15:3
2Co 1:3;
5:18–21;
6:2;
9:15
Gal 1:4;
2:21;
3:8, 22, 26;
4:4–5
Eph 1:6–7;
2:1–9, 11–18;
3:6–8;
4:32;
5:8, 14
Col 1:13–14, 19–22;
2:13;
3:13
1Th 1:10;
2:16;
5:9–10
1Ti 1:13, 15;
2:3–4;
4:10
2Ti 1:9;
2:13
Tit 1:2;
2:11;
3:3–5, 7
Heb 1:3;
2:14–17;
4:15;
5:2, 9;
7:25, 27;
8:12;
9:13–14, 28;
10:17;
13:8
Jas 2:5;
4:10;
5:7, 11
1Pe 1:10, 18–19;
2:6, 9–10, 24–25;
3:18
2Pe 3:9
1Jn 1:7, 9;
2:1–2, 12, 25;
3:5, 16;
4:8–10, 14;
5:1, 9–10, 16
Rev 1:5;
3:20;
21:6;
22:17

M

We Must be Meek or Humble Before God

Ex 10:3;
32:9–10;
33:3, 5;
34:8, 9
Lev 26:18–19, 40–42
Nu 12:3
Dt 9:13–14;
10:16–17;
31:27
Jos 7:6
Jdg 20:26
1Sa 1:10;
2:3
2Sa 22:28;
24:10
1Ki 8:33–34, 38–39, 47–50;
21:25–29
2Ki 17:14;
20:2–5;
22:19
1Ch 21:8
2Ch 6:24–27, 29–30, 37–39;
7:14;
12:6–7, 12;
30:8;
32:26;
33:12–13;
34:27;
36:12–13
Ezr 9:5–6, 7–15;
10:1, 2–12
Ne 1:4–6;
9:3, 29
Job 5:11;
22:29;
38:15;
40:3–5, 11–12;
41:34
Ps 6:1–4;
9:12;
10:4, 17;
12:3–4;
17:10;
18:27;
22:26;
25:9, 11, 16–18;
27:7–8;
30:5, 11;
31:9–10, 18;
34:18;
37:11, 35–36;
42:1–2;
51:1–17;
59:12;
61:1–2;
63:1–3;
72:12–13;
73:3–18;
76:9;
79:8–9;
84:2;
86:16;
94:2–4;
106:6;
113:7;
116:3–5;
119:21, 81;
123:1–3;
126:5;
138:6;
143:6–7;
145:14;
146:8;
147:3, 6;
149:4
Pr 3:7, 34;
4:24;
6:16–17;
8:13;
11:2;
14:3, 16;
15:25, 33;
16:5, 18;
17:19–20;
18:12;
26:12;
29:1, 20, 23;
30:12–13
Ecc 7:6
Isa 2:10–17;
5:14–16, 21;
10:15, 33;
13:11;
14:12–15;
16:6–11;
23:9;
25:11;
28:1–3;
29:4;
38:2–4;
46:12;
48:4;
57:15;
61:1–3;
66:2
Jer 2:35;
3:3;
4:3–4;
5:3;
6:10, 15;
7:24, 26;
8:12;
9:25–26;
13:9–10, 15–17;
14:7;

17:23;
19:15;
26:18–19;
29:12–13;
48:29–31;
49:16;
50:31–32
La 2:18–19;
3:19–21, 40–42
Eze 2:4;
3:7;
16:50;
31:10–14;
33:13;
34:16;
44:7
Da 4:30–33, 37;
5:20–24;
9:3–5, 6, 19, 20–21
Hos 5:5;
7:10;
10:12;
12:7–8
Joel 1:13;
2:13, 17
Am 7:2–3
Ob 3–4
Jnh 2:1–2;
3:5–10
Hab 2:4
Zep 2:2–3, 10
Mal 3:13;
4:1
Mt 5:3–5;
11:20–23, 25;
18:1–4, 26–27;
19:14, 23–24, 30;
20:16, 27;
23:12
Mk 10:14–15, 23–25, 31
Lk 1:51–52;
6:20–21;
10:13–15;
13:30;
14:11;
18:9–14, 24–25
Jn 7:48;
9:39
Ac 7:51;
8:22;
12:21–23
Ro 1:30;
12:16;
14:11
1Co 1:26–31;
10:12;
14:24–25
Col 2:18
1Ti 6:3–4
2Ti 3:2
Jas 1:10–11;
2:5;
4:6–10
1Pe 5:5–6
1Jn 2:16
Jude 15
Rev 3:17–18;
18:7–8

N

NEGLECTING or Rejecting Salvation

Ge 6:3;
7:16;
19:14, 17
Ex 16:28;
32:9–10;
33:5
Lev 26:14–26, 18, 21, 23–24, 27–28
Nu 14:11, 23, 27
Dt 9:13–14, 23–25;
10:16;
11:26–28;
18:18–19;
28:15;
29:19–20, 21;
30:15, 19;
31:27;
32:35
Jos 24:15
1Sa 12:15
2Sa 14:14
1Ki 18:4, 21;
19:10
2Ki 17:13–15;
18:11–12
1Ch 29:15
2Ch 12:14;
24:20–21;
25:16;
30:8;
33:10–11;
36:12, 13, 16
Ne 9:16, 26, 29–30
Job 4:19–20;
7:1, 6–10;
8:9, 11–15;
9:2–4;
11:20;
14:1–2, 5, 7–12;
15:12–13;
16:22;
20:5, 6–12;
21:13–14;
22:15–17;
24:13;
27:8–9;
34:15;
36:10–12
Ps 2:2–5;
27:8;
39:4–5;
49:10–14;
50:16–17, 21–22;
55:23;
58:4–5;
78:10, 22, 32–33, 39;
81:11–12;
89:48;
90:5–6, 9, 12;
95:8;
103:9, 15–16;
106:24–26;
112:10;
118:22;
144:4;
146:3–4
Pr 1:24–33;
8:17;
11:7;
14:16, 32;
22:3;
27:1, 12;
28:14;
29:1
Ecc 7:6;
8:8, 11–13;
9:4, 10–12;
12:1, 2–7
Isa 26:10–11;
28:12–13;
30:12–13;
40:6;
48:4;
55:6;
60:12;
63:10;
65:12, 13–14;
66:4
Jer 2:27;
3:5;
5:3–4, 12, 21–25;
6:15–17, 19;
7:13–15, 23–29;
8:9, 12, 20;
9:13–15;
11:7–8, 10–11;
13:10, 15–17;
17:23;
18:11–13;
19:15;
22:5;
25:4–5, 7–9;
26:3–6, 22–24;
29:17–19;
32:33;
35:14–15, 17;
37:15;
44:4–6
Eze 3:7;
12:2;
20:15–16;
33:1–3, 4–5, 6–8, 9, 31;
39:6
Da 5:1–6, 20;
8:25
Hos 4:17
Joel 3:14
Am 4:6–11, 12
Zec 1:4–5;
7:11–12
Mal 2:2
Mt 5:12;
10:14–15;
11:15–19, 20–24;
12:41–42;
13:3–9, 13–15, 18–23;
17:17;
21:33–43, 44;
22:1–7;
23:37–38;
24:36–41, 43–44, 50–51;
25:1–9, 10–11;
27:1
Mk 4:3–9, 14–20, 23;
6:11;
12:1–10;
16:15–16
Lk 4:28–29;
7:29–30;
8:4–15;
9:5;
10:10–16;
11:23, 31–32;
12:16–21, 39–40, 46–47;
13:24–25, 34–35;
14:16–24;
16:30–31;
17:26–30;
20:9–17, 18;
21:34–36
Jn 3:18–20, 36;
8:24, 47;
9:39–41;
10:1, 26–27;
12:35–36, 40, 48
Ac 2:23;
3:14–15, 22–23;
4:11–12, 27;
5:30;
7:51–53, 54–60;
12:1–4;
13:41, 46, 50–51;
14:19;
16:22–23;
18:6;
21:27;
24:25;
26:28–29;
28:26–27

Ro 1:20–22, 28;
2:5, 8;
13:12
1Co 1:18
2Co 2:15–16;
4:3–4;
6:2
1Th 2:15–16;
5:2–3
2Th 1:7–8;
2:10–12
1Ti 4:2
2Ti 3:8;
4:3–4
Heb 2:2–3;
3:7–9, 15, 18—
4:2;
4:6–7;
11:36–37;
12:25
Jas 4:13–14
1Pe 1:24;
2:7–8
2Pe 3:10–11
1Jn 5:10, 12
Jude 14; 15
Rev 2:21–22;
3:17–18;
6:15–16;
10:5–6;
13:9;
22:11–12

O

The Lord is the **Only** Way of Salvation

Ge 17:4
Ex 15:11
Dt 3:24;
4:35, 39;
6:4–5;
10:12;
18:15, 18–19;
30:15–16, 20;
32:31–32, 39
Jos 5:2–9
1Sa 2:2, 6–9
2Sa 7:22;
22:32
1Ki 8:60
2Ki 19:15, 19
1Ch 17:20
Job 8:11–15
Ps 3:8;
16:4;
18:31;
36:9;
62:1–2, 5–6,
11–12;
68:20;
73:25–27;
75:6–7;
86:10;
118:22;
127:1
Pr 19:21
Ecc 7:13;
12:13
Isa 37:16;
43:11;
44:6, 8;
45:5–9, 14, 18,
21–22;
46:9;
48:12;
50:10–11
Jer 2:13, 22;
3:23;
9:23–24;
13:23;
17:13–14
La 3:37
Hos 6:1;
13:4;
14:3
Jnh 2:9
Mic 6:7–8
Mt 7:26–27;
10:32–33;
12:21;
15:13;
16:16–18, 19;
18:3, 18;
19:16–22, 25–26;
21:42;
22:11–14, 35–40;
25:1–12
Mk 2:7;
8:38;
10:15, 17, 22,
26–27;
12:10, 28–34;
16:15–16
Lk 5:21;
6:47–49;
10:25–28;
12:8–9;
18:16–17, 18–27;
20:17;
24:46–47
Jn 1:4;
3:3, 5, 18–19,
36;
5:38–42;
6:53;
8:12, 24;
10:1, 7, 9;
12:48;
14:6;
15:1–5, 6;
20:23
Ac 3:22–23;
4:11–12;
13:38–39
Ro 8:9, 14;
9:15–16;
10:3–4;
11:36;
14:17
1Co 1:30–31;
2:2;
3:7, 11;
8:4, 6;
15:17
2Co 10:17–18;
13:5
Gal 1:8–9;
2:16;
3:11;
5:6;
6:14–15
Eph 1:6, 22;
4:15–16
Php 3:8–9
Col 1:16–18
1Ti 2:5
2Ti 2:11–12
Heb 9:22;
11:6
Jas 4:12
1Pe 1:18–19
1Jn 2:22–23;
5:12
Rev 1:8, 18;
3:17–18;
7:9–12, 14;
12:11;
19:1;
21:6;
22:13

P

The Lord Loves and **Pardons** Backsliders

Lev 26:40–42
Nu 14:19–20
Dt 4:29–31;
30:2–3
Jdg 10:15–16
1Sa 12:20
2Sa 12:13
1Ki 8:33–36, 38–39,
46–50
2Ch 6:24–27, 29–30,
36–39;
7:14;
15:3–4, 15;
30:9
Ne 1:9;
9:16–17
Ps 32:5;
51:1–10;
78:38;
106:43–45
Isa 49:14–16;
57:15–19
Jer 3:1, 5, 12–14,
20–22;
4:1;
25:3–5;
29:11–13;
30:17;
31:3, 20;
33:6–8;
35:15;
36:3, 7;
44:4, 5
La 3:40–42
Eze 2:3–5;
34:11–12
Da 9:9
Hos 6:1;
14:1–2, 4
Joel 2:12–13
Am 5:4, 6–8
Mic 7:18–19
Zec 1:3
Mal 3:7
Mt 10:6;
18:11–14
Lk 15:3–32
Ro 10:21;
11:23–24
Jas 5:19–20
1Jn 2:1–2;
5:16
Rev 2:5

R

Repentance, Confession, and Restitution

Ge 35:2–3
Ex 22:1–14;
34:13
Lev 5:5, 16;
16:21;
22:14;
26:40–41
Nu 5:6–8;
21:7;
22:34
Dt 4:29–30;
7:5;
12:3;
30:2, 8
Jos 7:19;
24:14, 23
Jdg 10:10, 15–16;
20:26
1Sa 1:14;
7:3–6;
12:3, 10–11;
15:24, 30–31;
26:21
2Sa 12:6, 13;
24:10
1Ki 8:33–36, 47–50;
21:25–29
2Ki 11:17–18;
17:13;
18:4–5;
23:3–8, 14–15

1Ch 21:8
2Ch 6:24–27, 37–39;
7:14;
14:3;
15:4, 8, 12, 15;
19:3;
23:16–19;
29:4–8;
30:8, 22;
31:1;
34:7, 31–33;
36:13
Ezr 9:5–10;
10:11, 12
Ne 1:6–7, 9;
5:11–13;
9:2–3, 33–35;
10:29;
13:3, 30
Job 7:20;
11:13–14;
13:23;
20:18;
22:23;
28:28;
31:33;
33:27–28;
34:31–32;
36:9–11;
40:3–4;
42:6
Ps 6:6;
7:11–12;
25:11;
32:5;
34:14, 18;
37:27;
38:1–10, 18;
39:8;
40:12–13;
41:4;
51:1–3, 17;
66:16–19;
78:34;
80:3, 7, 19;
106:6;
126:5;
147:3
Pr 1:23;
3:7;
6:30–31;
14:16;
28:13
Ecc 11:10
Isa 1:16–17;
9:13;
31:6;
55:7;
57:15;
58:5–10;
66:2
Jer 3:10, 12–13, 25;
4:1, 3–4, 14;
6:15;
7:3, 5–7;
8:5–6, 12;
14:7, 20;
18:7–8, 11;
23:22;
25:4–5;
26:3, 13;
29:12–13;
31:9, 18–19;
35:15;
36:3, 7;
44:5;
50:4
La 1:16, 18, 20;
2:11, 18–19;
3:40–41, 42;
5:21
Eze 3:19;
13:22;
14:6;
18:21–23, 27–28,
30–32;
20:43;
33:9, 11–12,
14–16, 19;
36:31;
43:9;
45:9–12
Da 4:27;
9:4–5, 15, 20
Hos 2:2, 7;
5:4, 15;
7:10;
10:12;
12:6;
14:1–2
Joel 1:13;
2:12–13
Am 5:14–15
Jnh 3:5–10
Hag 2:17
Zec 1:4–5;
12:10
Mal 3:7
Mt 3:2, 6, 8, 11;
4:17;
6:12, 14–15;
9:13;
11:20–22;
12:41;
18:35;
21:28–32;
26:75
Mk 1:4, 15;
2:17;
6:12;
11:25–26;
14:72
Lk 3:3, 8;
5:32;
6:37;
10:13–14;
11:4, 32;
13:3, 5;
15:7, 10, 18–22;
16:30;
17:3–4;
18:13–14;
19:8–9;
22:62;
24:47
Ac 2:37–38;
3:19, 26;
5:31;
8:22;
11:18;
13:24;
14:15;
17:30;
19:4, 18–20;
20:21;
26:18, 20
Ro 2:4
2Co 7:9–10;
12:21
1Th 1:9
2Ti 2:25
Heb 6:1, 6
Jas 1:21;
4:8;
5:16
2Pe 3:9
1Jn 1:9
Rev 2:5, 16, 21–22;
3:3, 19;
9:20–21;
16:9, 11

S

Holy Living Should Follow Conversion

Ge 2:17;
4:7;
7:1;
18:19;
19:26;
35:2
Ex 15:26;
16:28;
19:5–6;
20:6;
22:31;
23:2, 7, 18, 21;
32:33, 34;
34:11
Lev 11:4–8, 44–45;
18:4–5;
19:2, 12, 37;
20:7–8, 22–25,
26;
22:8, 31–32;
25:18;
26:2–4, 14–16,
23–24, 27–28
Nu 14:22–25, 30, 43;
15:30–31, 37, 40;
16:7, 23–26;
32:11, 23
Dt 4:1–2, 9, 40;
5:29, 32–33;
6:7, 12–18, 24,
25;
7:6, 9, 12, 26;
8:1, 3, 6, 11,
19–20;
10:12–13;
11:1, 8, 14,
16–22, 26–27,
32;
12:19, 25, 28, 32;
13:4–18;
14:2;
15:5;
16:12, 20;
17:7, 9–13, 20;
18:9–12, 13,
18–19;
19:9, 19–20;
21:9, 20–21;
22:21–24;
23:12–14;
24:7;
25:16;
26:16–19;
27:1, 9–10;
28:1–2, 9–10,
13–14, 15, 20,
45, 58–59, 62;
29:19–20;
30:2, 6, 8, 10–11,
15–20;
31:12–13;
32:5
Jos 1:7, 8;
5:6;
6:18;
7:1–18;
22:5, 16–20, 29;
23:6–8, 11, 16;
24:14, 15–16,
19–24, 27
Jdg 2:2, 11–15, 17,
19–22;
3:4, 7–8, 12;
4:1–2;
6:1, 10;
8:23;
10:6–7;
13:1;
20:13
1Sa 12:14, 15, 20–23,
24, 25;
15:1–21, 22–23,
24;
16:14;
24:13

2Sa 12:1–14;
22:21–27;
24:1–15
1Ki 2:3–4;
3:14;
6:12;
8:58, 61;
9:6–9;
11:4–11, 33, 38;
14:8, 16, 22;
15:3, 5, 14, 26, 30, 34;
16:13, 19, 25–26, 30–31, 33;
18:18, 21;
20:36;
22:52–53
2Ki 10:31;
13:2–3, 6, 11;
14:24;
15:9, 18, 28;
17:7–20, 33–41;
18:11–12;
20:3;
21:2, 6, 14–15, 20–22;
22:13, 17;
23:32, 37;
24:9, 19
1Ch 10:13–14;
16:29;
28:8, 9;
29:19
2Ch 6:14;
7:14;
8:17, 19–22;
12:1–2, 5;
15:2;
19:7–10;
20:21;
24:18, 20, 24;
27:2;
28:1, 6, 19, 22;
29:4–6;
30:7;
34:2, 21, 24–25, 31–33;
36:12
Ezr 8:28;
9:1–10, 12
Ne 1:5, 7–8;
9:16, 28–29;
10:29;
13:26–27
Job 4:8;
8:20;
11:14;
17:9;
22:23;
27:8;
28:7–8;
34:11, 26–27, 32;
36:10–11

Ps 1:1–2, 5;
4:2, 3–4;
5:4–6;
6:8;
7:10–11;
11:5;
15:1–2, 5;
18:20, 21–23, 24;
19:12–14;
24:3–5;
26:1, 5–6;
29:2;
34:12–16;
36:4;
37:3, 8–9, 27, 29–31, 34, 37–38;
50:16, 17–22, 23;
62:12;
66:18;
68:21;
69:28;
73:1, 27;
78:7–8, 10, 14, 56–66;
85:8–11;
89:30–32;
93:5;
96:9;
97:10;
101:2–3, 6–8;
105:45;
106:13, 21;
110:3;
119:1–3, 4, 8–9, 11, 15–16, 21, 30–31, 97, 101–106, 112, 115, 119, 126–129, 141, 153, 155, 159, 173;
125:3–4, 5;
128:1–2;
139:23–24;
140:13;
141:4
Pr 1:10, 15;
3:3, 6–7;
4:14–15, 23, 24–26, 27;
6:22, 27–28;
10:28, 29–30;
11:3–5, 6, 7–8;
14:9, 14, 16;
15:8, 9, 26, 29;
16:6, 7, 17;
17:15;
21:16, 21;
22:8;
24:12, 20, 24;
28:9

Ecc 5:6;
8:5;
11:13;
12:13–14
SS 6:10
Isa 1:4, 13–17, 19, 20, 27–28;
2:5;
3:10–11;
5:18, 23;
32:17;
33:14–17;
35:8–9;
48:18, 22;
52:1, 11;
57:20–21;
60:21;
62:12;
65:11–12;
66:4
Jer 1:16;
2:13, 17, 19, 20, 29, 32;
3:1, 6, 8;
4:14;
5:7;
6:28–30;
7:3, 5–7, 9–11, 12, 23, 24–29;
8:5;
9:13–15, 25;
11:3–4, 7–8;
12:17;
13:10, 25;
14:10, 11–14;
15:6;
16:10–12;
17:10, 13;
18:9–11;
19:3–4;
22:3, 8–9;
23:16–17, 21–22;
26:4–6, 13;
32:19, 23, 39–40;
40:3;
42:6, 21;
44:4–6, 23
Eze 3:20–21;
5:5–8;
6:9–11;
8:17–18;
9:4–6;
11:19–21;
13:22;
14:6–8, 11;
18:4, 20–27, 30–32;
20:11–13, 19, 21, 27, 39;
33:11–16, 18, 31;
36:25–27, 29;
37:23
Da 9:4, 11

Hos 4:6–7, 16;
6:4;
7:13;
8:1;
10:1, 2, 12–13;
11:7;
12:6;
13:1;
14:1
Joel 3:17
Am 2:4;
3:2, 3;
5:14–15;
6:12;
9:10
Ob 17
Jnh 2:8
Mic 2:10;
3:4;
6:7–8
Na 1:3
Zep 1:6–7;
2:3;
3:13
Zec 7:9–10;
8:16–17;
14:20–21
Mal 1:6;
2:11, 17;
3:7, 18
Mt 1:21;
3:10;
5:3–7, 8, 9, 13, 19–20, 29–30, 48;
6:21–24;
7:13–14, 16–24;
10:22, 37–38;
11:29;
12:33–37, 44–45, 50;
13:5–8, 20–22;
16:24, 27;
18:8–9, 15–16, 17, 23–35;
19:16–21;
21:28–31, 33, 34, 35–40, 41;
22:30, 35, 36–40;
23:23, 25–28;
24:13, 42–47, 48–51;
25:14–23, 24–30, 31–33, 34–36, 37–40, 41–43, 44–46;
28:20
Mk 3:35;
4:5–8, 16–20;
8:34;
9:43–50;

12:1, 2,3–9,
28–34;
13:13,34
Lk 1:74–75;
3:8, 9;
6:43–49;
8:6–8, 13–15,
21;
9:23, 62;
10:25–28;
11:28, 34;
12:1, 34–37,
45–47;
13:6–8, 9, 23–28;
14:26–27,28–31,
33–35;
16:10–12, 13;
17:32;
19:12–27;
20:9, 10,11–16,
19–21
Jn 4:23–24;
5:14, 29;
8:11–12, 31,
34–35,44, 51;
9:31;
12:26;
13:35;
14:15, 21;
15:1, 2,3–5, 6,
7–9, 10, 14,
16;
17:15–20
Ac 1:25;
3:26;
5:1–11, 32;
14:22
Ro 1:18;
2:6–13;
3:31;
6:1–2,3–5, 6,
7–10, 11–23;
7:4,5–6;
8:1–14;
11:16–19, 20–22;
12:1–2,9, 21;
13:8–13, 14;
14:10–12, 15–18
1Co 1:2, 30;
3:8, 12–13, 17;
5:7–8, 11, 13;
6:9–11,13, 15,
20;
8:11;
9:24–27;
10:5–10, 11–12,
13, 21, 31;
11:27–32;
13:1–7;
15:1, 2, 33–34
2Co 5:10, 15,17;
6:14;
7:1;
10:2;
12:21;
13:2, 11
Gal 1:10;
2:17–18,19, 20;
3:1;
5:6,13, 19–25;
6:7–9, 14–16
Eph 1:4;
2:10;
4:1,17–19,
20–24,26–32;
5:1–4, 5–6,
7–12, 25–27
Php 1:27;
2:12, 15;
3:17, 18,19–20;
4:8–9
Col 1:10, 21–23;
2:6, 11;
3:1–3, 5–10, 12,
17, 23–25;
4:6
1Th 2:11–12;
4:1–2, 3,4–5,
6–7;
5:22–23
2Th 1:8;
2:13;
3:6,14
1Ti 1:5, 19;
2:8–10, 15;
4:1–2, 12, 16;
5:8, 12;
6:8–11, 12,
13–14, 18–21
2Ti 2:10–12, 19,22;
3:1–5;
4:10
Tit 1:16;
2:11–14;
3:1, 8,14
Heb 2:1–3;
3:6,10–11,
12–14;
4:1, 11;
5:9;
6:1,4–7, 8,
11–12;
9:14;
10:26–31, 35–36,
38–39;
12:1, 14, 25;
13:4, 20–21
Jas 1:21–27;
2:8–26;
3:11–13,14–18;
4:4, 8, 17;
5:9, 19–20
1Pe 1:2,13–14,
15–17,22;
2:1, 11–17,
21–22, 24;
3:2–4, 8–9,
10–12,15;
4:1–7, 15,
17–18;
5:8–9
2Pe 1:4–8, 9–10;
2:9–10, 15,
19–21;
3:7, 11, 13–14
1Jn 1:5–7;
2:1, 3–6,11, 15,
16–17, 29;
3:3–10,14, 15,
20–21, 23, 24;
4:8, 20–21;
5:2–3,4, 16–17,
18
2Jn 8–9
3Jn 11
Jude 5–6;15,
19–21, 24
Rev 2:4–5,7, 10,11,
17, 23, 26;
3:1–5, 14–16,
21;
14:4–5, 13;
20:12–13;
21:7–8, 27;
22:12, 14–15

T

Testifying, or Confessing the Lord

Dt 6:7;
8:10;
26:1–3
Jos 4:1–9, 19–24
1Sa 7:12
2Sa 22:50
1Ch 16:8–10,23–24,
29, 34–36
Ps 9:11, 14;
20:5;
22:22–23, 25;
29:2, 9;
34:1–3,4–6;
35:18,27–28;
40:10,16;
44:8;
50:23;
51:15;
60:4;
63:3;
66:8, 16–17;
67:3;
68:26;
70:4;
71:8;
77:12;
78:4;
92:1;
96:2–4;
100:4;
105:1–2;
106:1–2;
107:1, 2,22, 31;
109:30;
111:1;
118:21, 28–29;
119:13, 27, 46, 108,
116–171;
128:2;
132:9;
134:1–3;
135:1–3, 19–20;
140:13;
145:1–7, 10–12,21;
146:1–2;
147:12;
148:1–14
Isa 12:1–3, 4,5–6;
38:19;
43:10, 12;
44:8
Jer 1:17
Da 4:37
Joel 2:26
Mal 3:16–17
Mt 10:32–33;
12:34, 37
Mk 5:19;
8:38
Lk 6:45;
9:25–26;
12:8–9
Jn 12:42–43
Ac 1:8
Ro 1:16;
10:8–10,11
1Co 14:3, 24–25
Php 1:28
2Ti 1:8;
2:12
Phm 6
Heb 2:11–12;
3:13;
13:6, 15–16
1Pe 2:9
1Jn 4:15
Rev 12:11;
19:5

W

"Whosoever Will" May Be Saved

Ge 12:3;
22:18;
26:4;
28:14
Nu 21:8–9
2Sa 22:31
1Ch 12:22
Ezr 8:22
Ps 2:12;
18:30;
22:27;

32:10;
34:8, 22;
49:1–2;
50:1;
84:12;
86:5;
145:9, 18
Pr 16:20;
29:25
Isa 1:18;
11:10;
42:3; 45:22;
49:6;
52:10;
53:6; 55:1, 6–7;
57:19;
59:1–2;
63:1
Jer 17:7
Eze 18:23, 32; 33:11
Zec 13:1
Mt 7:7–8, 24;
8:11;
9:12;
10:32;
11:15,28–29;
12:20, 31–32;
13:9;
20:1–16;
22:1–10;
26:28;
28:19
Mk 3:28;
4:9, 23;
10:45;
14:24;
16:15–16
Lk 1:79;
2:10–11, 30–32;
6:47–48;
11:9–10;
12:8;
13:29;
14:16–23;
15:7;
16:16;
19:10;
24:46–47
Jn 1:7, 9, 12, 29;
3:14–18, 36;
4:10,42;
5:24;
6:35, 37, 40, 47,
51, 54;
7:17,37;
9:5;
11:25,26;
12:32, 46, 47
Ac 2:21;
3:25;
10:34–35, 43;
11:18;
13:26, 38–39, 47;
15:7–11;
17:27;
26:13–18;
28:28
Ro 1:16;
3:21–24, 28–30;
4:6–13, 16;
5:6–17,18,
19–21;
9:33;
10:4, 6–13;
11:32;
15:10
2Co 5:14–15, 19–21
Gal 3:6–9, 14,22, 26
Eph 2:17–18;
3:6–8
Col 1:20–21
1Ti 1:15;
2:3–6;
4:10
Tit 2:11
Heb 2:9; 5:9;7:25;
9:13–14, 22, 28
2Pe 3:9
1Jn 1:7–9;
2:1–2;
4:14–15;
5:1, 9–10, 13
Rev 3:20;
5:9; 7:9; 14:6;
21:6;
22:17

TEMPORAL BLESSINGS
(LIGHT GREEN)

A

All Things Working for Good

Ge 21:22;
24:1;
45:5–8;
48:16
Dt 14:29;
15:10, 18;
29:9
1Ki 2:3
Ps 91:10;
121:7
Pr 12:21;
19:23
Isa 58:11
Ro 8:28
1Th 5:18

B

The Lord's **Blessing** on Fields and Flocks

Ge 15:7;
24:35;
26:12, 14;
27:28, 39;
30:43;
39:5
Ex 9:4–7, 26;
23:26;
33:3
Lev 20:24;
25:19, 20–22, 38;
26:3–5, 19–20
Dt 7:13, 14;
8:7–8, 13;
11:10, 11–12, 13,
14–15;
26:9;
28:3–5, 11–12,
23–24;
30:9
1Ki 8:35
2Ki 2:19–22
Job 42:12
Ps 65:9–13;
67:6;
85:12;
107:38;
144:13
Pr 3:9–10
Isa 4:2;
55:10
Eze 34:26–27;
36:30
Hos 2:8, 21–22
Joel 2:22, 24–26
Am 4:9;
9:13
Hag 1:10;
2:15–19
Zec 8:12
Mal 3:11–12
2Co 9:10

C

Clothing Provided for God's Children

Ge 28:20
Dt 2:7;
8:4;
10:18;
29:5;
33:25
Ne 9:21
Job 27:16–17
Eze 16:10
Mt 6:25–34;
10:10
Mk 6:8–9
Lk 9:3;
10:4;
12:22–31;
22:35

D

Some Reasons Why **Diseases** are Allowed

Ge 12:17;
19:11;
20:18
Ex 4:6;
5:3;
9:8–10, 11–14,
15;
15:26;
20:12;
23:25;
30:12;
32:35
Lev 14:19, 30–32, 34;
15:13–15;
18:30;
26:14–15, 16,
23–25, 36
Nu 5:20, 21, 27;
8:19;
11:33–34;
12:9–10;
14:12, 37;
16:46, 47–49;
21:6;
25:1–7, 8–9
Dt 7:15;
24:9;
28:21–22, 27, 35,
59–61;
29:22
Jos 22:17
1Sa 1:5–6;
5:6, 9, 11–12;
25:38
2Sa 3:29;
6:23;

12:15–18;
24:15
1Ki 13:4;
14:1–11, 12–13;
17:18
2Ki 1:2–4;
5:20–26, 27;
6:18;
15:5
1Ch 21:10, 13, 14–15
2Ch 7:13;
13:20;
21:14–15, 18–19;
26:16–18, 19–21
Job 2:3–6, 7, 8;
30:18–19;
33:17–22, 23–28, 29–30
Ps 78:30–31;
106:29
Pr 5:8–11
Jer 14:12;
21:6;
24:10;
29:17;
42:17;
44:13
Eze 5:12, 17;
6:12;
7:15;
14:19, 21;
28:23;
33:27;
38:22
Am 4:10
Mt 13:58
Mk 6:5–6
Lk 1:20;
4:23–27;
13:16
Jn 5:14;
9:1–3;
11:4
Ac 9:8–9;
10:38;
13:11
1Co 7:28;
10:8;
11:29–32
2Co 12:7–10
Php 2:30
Heb 12:5–13
Rev 16:3

E

EXAMPLES of Healing for the Body

Ge 5:5, 8, 11, 14, 17, 20, 23, 27, 31–32;
17:15–17;
18:12–14;
20:17;
25:7–8, 21;
29:31;
30:17, 22;
50:23
Ex 4:7
Lev 14:3
Nu 12:9–15;
16:46–50;
21:7–9;
25:8
Dt 8:4;
34:7
Jos 14:10–11
Jdg 13:2–3
1Sa 1:5–20;
2:5
2Sa 24:18–24, 25
1Ki 13:6;
17:17–21, 22–24
2Ki 4:12–31, 32–35, 39–41;
5:1–13, 14;
6:20;
8:4–5;
13:21;
20:1–11
1Ch 21:15–27;
29:28
2Ch 32:24
Ne 9:21
Job 42:16–17
Ps 30:2–3;
103:3;
105:37;
106:30;
107:20
Isa 38:1–22
Da 1:15
Hos 11:3
Mt 4:23–25;
7:22;
8:2–3, 4, 5–17, 28–32, 33–34;
9:2–8, 18–35;
10:1, 7–8;
11:4–5;
12:9–13, 15, 22–29;
13:58;
14:14, 34–36;
15:21–28, 30–31;
17:14–21;
19:1–2;
20:30–34;
21:14
Mk 1:23–34, 39–45;
2:3–12;
3:1–5, 7–9, 10–12, 14–15, 22–27;
5:1–20, 22–43;
6:5, 7, 13, 54–56;
7:25–37;
8:22–26;
9:14–29, 38–39;
10:46–52;
16:9
Lk 1:11–17, 18, 19–25, 36–37;
4:23–27, 33–41;
5:12–26;
6:6–11, 17–19;
7:1–22;
8:26–56;
9:1–2, 6, 11, 37–43, 49–50;
10:9, 17–20;
11:14–26;
13:11–17, 32–33;
14:1–6;
17:11–19;
18:35–43;
22:50–51
Jn 4:46–54;
5:1–16, 17–38;
6:2;
7:23;
9:1–7, 8–41;
11:1–38, 39–46, 47–54;
12:9–11, 17–19
Ac 2:22;
3:1–16;
4:8–10, 14–22;
5:14–16;
8:6–7;
9:12, 17, 18, 32–35;
10:38;
14:3, 8–10, 11–18, 19–20;
16:16–18, 19–24;
19:11–12, 13–17;
20:9–12;
22:11–13;
28:3–9
Ro 15:18–19
1Co 12:9, 28, 30
2Co 12:12
Php 2:25–26, 27
Heb 2:4;
11:11–12, 34–35

F

FOOD Provided for the Lord's Children

Ge 6:19–21;
21:19;
27:28;
28:20;
45:5–7;
48:15
Ex 15:23–25;
16:4–36;
17:5–6;
23:25
Lev 25:19, 20–22;
26:5
Nu 11:7–9, 18–23, 31–32;
20:7–11;
21:16, 17
Dt 2:7;
7:13;
8:3, 9–10, 15–16;
10:18;
11:14–15;
32:13–14
Jos 5:12
Jdg 15:18–19
Ru 1:6
1Sa 2:5
1Ki 17:1–16;
19:5–8
2Ki 3:9–20;
4:1–7, 42–44;
6:18, 19–20, 24—7:17
2Ch 20:9
Ne 9:15, 20–21
Job 5:20;
15:23
Ps 22:26;
23:1–2, 5;
33:18–19;
34:9–10;
37:3, 19, 25;
78:15–16, 19–29;
81:10, 16;
103:5;
104:27;
105:40–41;
107:9;
111:5;
114:8;
132:15;
136:25;
145:15;
146:7;
147:9, 14
Pr 10:3;
13:25;
30:8
Ecc 11:1
Isa 1:19;
33:16;
41:17, 18;
48:21;
49:9–10;
55:10;
58:11;
65:13
Hos 2:8;
11:4;
13:5–6
Joel 2:19, 24–26
Hab 3:17–18

Mt 4:11;
6:11, 25–34;
10:9–10;
14:15–21;
15:32–38;
16:5–10, 11–12
Mk 1:13;
6:8, 33–44;
8:1–9, 14–21
Lk 1:53;
4:25–26;
5:4–9;
9:3, 12–17;
10:4;
11:3;
12:22–31;
22:35
Jn 6:5–14, 31–32;
21:8–13
2Co 9:10
Rev 7:16

H

HEALTH and Healing Promised

Ge 15:15
Ex 9:4–5;
15:26;
20:12;
23:25;
30:12
Dt 4:40;
7:15;
11:21;
25:15;
32:39;
33:25
1Sa 2:6;
6:3
2Sa 12:22
1Ki 3:14;
8:37–39
2Ki 5:7
1Ch 29:12
2Ch 6:28–30;
7:13–14;
16:12;
20:9
Job 5:26;
33:23–30
Ps 34:12–13;
41:3;
67:2;
91:3, 5–7, 10, 16;
103:3, 5;
113:9;
128:6;
146:8
Pr 3:2, 8, 16;
4:10, 22;
9:11;
10:16, 27;
14:30;
17:22;
19:23
Isa 29:18;
32:3–4;
35:3–6;
38:16;
40:29–31;
42:6–7;
53:4
Jer 8:22;
17:14
Eze 34:4, 16;
47:12
Mt 8:17;
10:7–8
Mk 9:23;
16:17–18
Lk 4:18
Eph 6:2–3
Jas 5:13–18
1Pe 3:10
3Jn 2
Rev 22:2

J

JOY and Trust in Times of Trial

Ne 8:10
Job 1:21;
13:15
Ps 3:5–6;
18:29;
23:4;
27:1;
30:5;
31:13, 14;
42:5, 7–8, 11;
43:5;
46:1–3;
56:3–4, 11;
57:1;
61:2–4;
91:5–6;
112:7–8;
118:6;
119:83
Pr 1:33;
14:31
Isa 26:3;
51:12
Hab 3:17-19
Mt 5:11–12
Lk 6:22–23
Jn 16:33
Ac 5:41;
6:15;
16:25
Ro 5:3;
12:12
2Co 1:3–10;
2:14;
4:8–10, 15,
16–18;
7:4;
8:1–2;
11:23–33;
12:10
Eph 5:20
Php 1:28–29;
2:17;
3:8
Col 1:24
Heb 10:34;
13:6
Jas 1:2–4;
5:10, 11
1Pe 2:19–20;
3:14;
4:12–14, 16
1Jn 4:18

L

The Lord's LOVE and Care for His Children

Ge 6:7–8, 17–18;
7:1;
8:1;
12:3;
15:1;
16:13;
19:19–22, 29;
21:17–19, 22;
22:11–12;
24:27, 48;
26:3–4, 24, 28;
27:28–29;
28:15;
31:3, 24, 29;
35:3;
48:16
Ex 2:1–10, 24–25;
3:7–8, 15;
8:22;
9:4, 6, 26;
10:23;
11:7;
13:21–22;
14:19–20, 24–28;
15:13;
18:8–10;
19:4–6;
23:20;
29:45–46;
33:12, 22;
40:36–38
Nu 9:15–23;
14:14;
20:16;
22:12;
23:18–24;
24:9;
31:49
Dt 1:21, 29–33;
2:7;
4:7;
29:5;
31:6, 8, 23;
32:9–14;
33:12, 13–16, 27,
28–29
Jos 1:5, 9, 17;
3:7;
5:13–14;
6:27;
21:45;
23:14;
24:3–13
1Sa 2:9;
12:24;
17:37;
20:13;
25:29
2Sa 4:9;
6:11–12;
7:9–11, 23;
8:6, 14;
22:1, 2–4, 5–51
1Ki 1:29, 37, 47–48;
8:51–53, 56–59,
66;
9:4–5;
17:1–16;
19:5–8
2Ki 4:1–7;
6:16–17
1Ch 13:14;
16:21–22;
17:7–8, 21–22;
18:6;
28:20
2Ch 7:10;
32:22
Ne 9:11, 12, 13–15,
19
Est 4:14;
6:1—7:10;
8:16
Job 5:17–26;
23:6
Ps 3:3;
6:8–9;
13:6;
18:28;
20:1–2;
23:1–6;
27:4–5, 10;
28:7–9;
29:11;
30:5;
31:7, 19–20, 23;
32:8;
33:18, 20;
34:7–10, 15,
19–20, 22;
36:7–8;
37:39–40;
40:17;
41:12;
46:1;

P

Prosperity in Business and Finance

R

Blessing on Children, **Relatives**, and Friends

S

Safety From All Harm and Danger

22:12;
26:24
Ex 8:22;
9:4, 6, 26;
11:7;
12:13, 27;
33:22
Lev 25:18;
26:5, 6
Nu 14:9;
31:49
Dt 12:10;
33:28–29
2Sa 8:6, 14;
22:3
1Ch 18:6, 13
Job 5:21;
11:18–19;
34:29
Ps 3:3;
4:8;
9:9;
18:2;
27:5;
31:20, 23;
32:6–7;
34:9, 12–15;
37:4–6;
46:1;
59:16;
71:7;
84:11;
91:1–16;
97:10;
115:9–11;
118:6;
119:117;
121:1–8;
140:7;
142:5;
144:10
Pr 1:33;
3:23–26;
18:10;
29:25;
30:5
Isa 32:18;
43:2
Jer 16:19;
23:6;
32:37;
33:16;
42:11–12
Eze 34:25
Da 3:1–16, 17,
18–23, 24–25,
26, 27, 28–30;
6:4–21, 22–23,
27
Hos 2:18
Jnh 1:15–16, 17;
2:9, 10
Na 1:7
Mt 4:6
Mk 4:38–39, 40, 41
Lk 8:23–25;
21:18
Ac 18:10;
23:11;
27:22, 23–24,
25–44
Ro 8:31
Heb 11:33–34
2Pe 2:5, 7

T

Why TEMPTATIONS and TRIALS are Allowed

Dt 8:2, 5–6, 16
2Sa 7:14
Job 5:17;
23:10;
33:17–22;
34:31
Ps 17:3;
39:11;
66:10–12;
89:30–33;
94:12–13;
105:19;
119:67, 71, 75
Pr 3:11–12;
17:3;
25:4
Ecc 7:14
Isa 48:10
Jer 24:5;
31:18–19
Da 9:11–14;
11:35;
12:10
Hag 1:5–11;
2:15–19
Zec 13:9
Ro 5:3–4
1Co 11:32
2Co 1:6–9;
4:10–11, 17;
12:7–10
Heb 5:8;
12:5–13
Jas 1:2–4, 12
1Pe 1:6–7;
4:12–13;
5:10
Rev 3:10, 19

U

The UPRIGHT are Blessed and Prospered

Ge 9:1;
12:1–3, 3;
17:1–8;
21:22;
22:15–18;
24:1, 35;
25:11;
26:3, 24, 28–29;
28:3–4, 10–22;
31:3;
32:9–12;
35:9–12;
37:5–11;
39:2–3, 6, 21, 23;
41:51–52;
48:3–4;
49:22–24, 25–26;
50:24–25
Ex 1:21;
3:12, 21;
11:3;
15:26;
20:24
Lev 26:3–12
Nu 6:23, 24–27;
10:29, 32;
14:8;
23:8–9, 10;
24:5–9
Dt 4:40;
5:10, 29, 33;
6:3, 18;
7:12–13, 14–24;
11:26–27;
12:28;
14:29;
15:10, 18;
22:7;
23:20;
24:19;
26:15, 18–19;
28:1–14;
30:8–9, 15–16;
31:23;
33:13, 24, 28–29
Jos 1:9
Ru 2:12
1Sa 2:9, 30, 35;
3:19;
16:18;
18:12, 14, 28;
25:28–30
2Sa 7:3, 9;
22:20–21, 22–28
1Ki 2:3;
3:6, 13–14;
5:4;
6:11–13;
8:32;
9:4–5;
11:38
2Ki 18:7
1Ch 4:10;
11:9;
17:2, 7–8;
22:13;
28:7–8;
29:25, 28
2Ch 1:1, 12;
6:14;
15:2;
16:9;
19:11;
20:20;
26:5;
27:6;
31:5–9, 10, 20, 21;
32:26, 30
Ezr 8:22
Ne 1:5;
13:14, 22
Job 1:9–10;
4:7;
8:6–7;
11:13–19;
17:9;
22:21, 23, 28;
29:1–2, 3, 4–5, 6,
7–25;
36:7, 11, 16;
42:10, 11, 12,
13–17
Ps 1:1–3;
3:8;
4:7;
5:11–12;
7:10;
11:7;
15:1–2;
16:6, 11;
18:19–20, 21, 23,
24, 32, 33;
19:11;
21:1–7;
22:8;
24:3–4;
25:10, 14, 15;
28:25–31;
31:19–20, 23;
32:1–2, 10–11;
33:18;
34:7, 9, 12–15;
36:10;
37:4–6, 17–19,
23–28, 30, 31,
37;
41:1–3;
45:7;
55:22;
64:10;
65:4;
68:3;
73:1;
81:15–16;
84:4–5, 7, 10–12;
89:15–16;
91:1–16;
92:12–14;
97:10–12;
112:1–10;
115:12–15;

118:15;
119:1–2, 165;
125:4;
128:1–6;
132:9, 16;
140:13;
144:15;
145:18–19;
147:11
Pr 3:1–2, 5–6, 9, 10, 33;
4:18;
10:6, 22, 24;
11:8, 20, 24–25, 28, 31;
12:1–3, 13, 19, 21, 28;
13:21, 22;
14:9, 11, 19, 32;
15:8–9, 29;
16:3, 7, 20;
21:21;
23:17–18;
24:16, 25;
25:21–22;
28:10, 20, 25
Ecc 2:26;
7:18
Isa 1:19;
3:10;
32:17;
33:15–16;
55:2;
56:5, 7;
57:1–2;
58:7, 8, 10, 14;
62:4;
64:4–5;
65:13–14;
66:2
Jer 7:23;
17:7–8;
35:1–18, 19
Eze 34:26–27
Da 1:8–14, 15;
3:1–30;
6:4–23;
9:4;
10:12, 19;
12:3
Hos 13:1
Am 5:14–15
Hag 1:5–11;
2:15–19, 23
Zec 8:12
Mal 2:5;
3:10, 11–12, 16–17
Mt 5:5–12;
6:4, 6, 18, 33;
19:27–28, 29
Mk 10:28–30
Lk 12:31;
18:28, 29–30
Jn 9:31;
12:25–26;
14:21;
15:7, 11
Ac 7:9–10;
10:35
Ro 8:28
1Co 2:9
2Co 5:1, 2–9;
6:17—7:1
Gal 6:16
1Ti 4:8
Jas 5:16
1Pe 3:12
1Jn 1:4;
3:22

V

Victory Over Enemies and Troubles

Ge 14:20;
19:10–11;
22:17;
27:29;
31:5–9, 16, 42;
49:8
Ex 1:12;
3:7–10, 16–17, 19–22;
6:1, 6–8;
7:4–5;
11:1, 3;
12:33–36, 42;
13:14–15;
14:13–31;
15:1, 6, 9–10;
18:4, 8–11;
20:2;
23:22, 23, 27, 28;
33:2;
34:11, 24
Lev 26:6–8
Nu 10:9;
14:3, 9;
21:33–35;
22:12;
23:8–12, 19–24;
24:1–9;
33:52–53
Dt 1:29–31;
2:25, 33–36;
3:2–6, 21–24;
4:37–38;
5:6, 15;
6:18–23;
7:1–2, 15–24;
9:1–3;
11:4, 23–24, 25;
12:10;
20:1–3, 4;
23:5, 14;
25:19;
26:8;
28:7;
31:3–8;
32:30
Jos 1:5;
2:8–11, 24;
3:10;
5:1, 13;
6:21;
8:1, 18;
10:8–14, 24–25, 30, 32, 42;
11:1;
12:24;
13:6;
17:18;
21:44;
22:8;
23:3, 5, 9–10;
24:11–13, 17–18
Jdg 1:2–4;
3:10, 28–31;
4:9, 14–16, 23;
5:20;
6:8–9, 16;
7:1–25;
10:11–12;
11:21, 32–33, 36;
15:15;
16:28–30;
18:10
1Sa 2:1;
7:3, 9–13;
10:18–19;
11:13;
12:11;
14:6;
17:36–46, 47, 48–54;
20:15;
23:4–5;
25:29;
30:8
2Sa 3:18;
5:19–25;
7:9–11;
22:1–29, 30, 31–51;
23:10–12
1Ki 8:37–39, 44–45;
20:13, 27–30
2Ki 3:18–19;
6:13–23;
13:17–19;
17:39;
18:13–19, 37;
20:6
1Ch 5:20;
11:14;
14:10–11, 13–17;
17:10;
22:9, 18
2Ch 6:28–30, 34–35;
13:14–16, 18;
14:6, 7, 11, 12–14;
16:8, 9;
18:31;
20:5–14, 15, 16, 17, 27, 29;
32:7–8, 22
Ezr 8:31
Ne 4:4, 14–15, 20;
6:15–16;
9:11, 24–25, 27
Est 4:14;
5:14;
7:10;
8:4–11;
9:16–32
Job 5:15, 20–23, 24
Ps 3:5–6;
6:10;
9:3–4;
17:7;
18:3, 14, 17–18, 29, 34–50;
20:7–8;
22:4–5;
25:2–3;
27:1, 3, 5–6;
31:20;
34:6, 17, 19;
35:1–9, 10;
37:32, 33;
40:14–15;
41:2, 11;
44:1–3, 5–7;
45:5;
47:3;
50:15;
54:7;
55:18;
56:9;
59:1, 10;
60:12;
70:2;
78:42, 55;
81:13–14;
89:22–23;
91:1–16;
97:10;
106:10–11;
107:2;
108:13;
109:29, 31;
110:5;
112:8;
118:6–7, 10–14;
124:1–8;
132:18;
138:7
Pr 12:13;
16:7;
20:22

Isa 31:4; 36:1; 37:38; 38:6;
41:11–14;
49:25–26;
50:9;
54:15, 17
Jer 1:17–18, 19;
15:20–21;
20:11; 39:17–18;
42:11–12;
51:36
Da 3:6;
11:32
Hos 1:7
Joel 2:20
Zec 4:6;
12:8
Mt 8:23–27
Mk 4:36–39
Lk 8:22–25;
21:18
Ac 5:18, 19, 20–25, 38–39;
7:34;
12:5–6, 7–11, 12–19;
14:19–20;
16:25, 26, 27–28;
18:10;
27:9–44; 28:1–6
Ro 8:31, 35–39
1Co 15:57
2Co 2:14
2Ti 4:18
Heb 11:32–35
1Jn 5:4–5

W

Worry and Anxiety Contrary to God's Will

Ge 15:1;
21:17;
26:24
Dt 1:21;
20:8;
31:6–8, 23
Jos 1:6–7, 9;
8:1
Jdg 7:3
1Ch 22:13;
28:20
2Ch 19:11
Ne 8:10
Ps 23:4;
27:1, 14;
31:24;
37:1, 5;
42:5, 11;
43:5;
55:22;
91:5–6;
112:7–8;
119:165
Pr 1:33
Isa 12:2–3;
26:3–4; 32:17
Jer 10:2
Mt 6:25–34;
8:26
Mk 4:40
Lk 8:24–25;
12:22–32;
18:1
Jn 14:1, 27
2Co 13:11
Eph 5:20
Php 3:1;
4:4, 6–7, 11–13
Col 3:15
1Th 5:16, 18
1Ti 6:6, 8
Heb 13:5–6
1Pe 3:14;
5:7
1Jn 4:18

Epistle Dedicatory to the KJV

TO THE MOST HIGH AND MIGHTY PRINCE

JAMES

BY THE GRACE OF GOD

KING OF GREAT BRITAIN, FRANCE, AND IRELAND

DEFENDER OF THE FAITH, &C.

The Translators of the Bible wish Grace, Mercy, and Peace
through JESUS CHRIST our Lord

GREAT AND MANIFOLD were the blessings, most dread Sovereign, which Almighty God, the Father of all mercies, bestowed upon us the people of *England*, when first he sent Your Majesty's Royal Person to rule and reign over us. For whereas it was the expectation of many, who wished not well unto our *Sion*, that upon the setting of that bright *Occidental Star*, Queen *Elizabeth* of most happy memory, some thick and palpable clouds of darkness would so have overshadowed this Land, that men should have been in doubt which way they were to walk; and that it should hardly be known, who was to direct the unsettled State; the appearance of Your Majesty, as of the *Sun* in his strength, instantly dispelled those supposed and surmised mists, and gave unto all *what* were well affected exceeding cause of comfort; especially when we beheld the Government established in Your Highness, and Your hopeful Seed, by an undoubted Title, and this also accompanied with peace and tranquillity at home and abroad.

But among all our joys, there was no one that more filled our hearts, than the blessed continuance of the preaching of God's sacred Word among us; which is that inestimable treasure, which excelleth all the riches of the earth; because the fruit thereof extendeth itself, not only to the time spent in this transitory world, but directeth and disposeth men unto that eternal happiness which is above in heaven.

Then not to suffer this to fall to the ground, but rather to take it up, and to continue it in that state, wherein the famous Predecessor of Your Highness did leave it: nay, to go forward with the confidence and resolution of a Man in maintaining the truth of Christ, and propagating it far and near, is that which hath so bound and firmly knit the hearts of all Your Majesty's loyal and religious people unto You, that Your very name is precious among them: their eye doth behold You with comfort, and they bless You in their hearts, as that sanctified Person who, under God, is the immediate Author of their true happiness. And this their contentment doth not diminish or decay, but every day increaseth and taketh strength, when they observe, that the zeal of Your Majesty toward the house of God doth not slack or go backward, but is more and more kindled, manifesting itself abroad in the farthest parts of *Christendom*, by writing in defense of the Truth, (which hath given such a blow unto that man of sin, as will not be healed,) and every day at home, by religious and learned discourse, by frequenting the house of God, by hearing the Word preached, by cherishing the Teachers thereof, by caring for the Church, as a most tender and loving nursing Father.

There are infinite arguments of this right Christian and religious affection in Your Majesty; but none is more forcible to declare it to others than the vehement and perpetuated desire of accomplishing and publishing of this work, which now with all humility we present unto Your Majesty. For when Your Highness had once out of deep judgment apprehended how convenient it was, that out of the Original Sacred Tongues, together with comparing of the labours, both in our own, and other foreign Languages, of many worthy men who went before us, there should be one more exact Translation of the holy Scriptures into the *English Tongue*; Your majesty did never desist to urge and to excite those to whom it was commended, that the work might be hastened, and that the business might be expedited in so decent a manner, as a matter of such importance might justly require.

And now at last, by the mercy of God, and the continuance of our labours, it being brought unto such a conclusion, as that we have great hopes that the Church of *England* shall reap good fruit thereby; we hold it our duty to offer it to Your Majesty, not only as to our King and Sovereign, but as to the principal Mover and Author of the work: humbly craving of Your most Sacred Majesty, that since things of this quality have ever been subject to the censures of illmeaning and discontented persons, it may receive approbation and patronage from so learned and judicious a Prince as Your Highness is, whose allowance and acceptance of our labours shall more honour and encourage us, than all the calumniations and hard interpretations of other men shall dismay us. So that if, on the one side, we shall be traduced by Popish Persons at home or abroad, who therefore will malign us, because we are poor instruments to make God's holy Truth to be yet more and more known unto the people, whom they desire still to keep in ignorance and darkness, or if, on the other side, we shall be maligned by selfconceited Brethren, who run their own ways, and give liking unto nothing, but what is framed by themselves, and hammered on their anvil; we may rest secure, supported within by the truth and innocency of a good conscience, having walked the ways of simplicity and integrity, as before the Lord; and sustained without by the powerful protection of Your Majesty's grace and favor, which will ever give countenance to honest and Christian endeavors against bitter censures and uncharitable imputations.

The Lord of heaven and earth bless Your Majesty with many and happy days, that, as his heavenly hand hath enriched Your Highness with many singular and extraordinary graces, so You may be the wonder of the world in this latter age for happiness and true felicity, to the honour of that great GOD, and the good of his Church, through Jesus Christ our Lord and only Saviour.

How to Use
the Center Column Reference

CENTER COLUMN REFERENCES are a key to the connection between the text and the other passages in the Bible. They are an aid in clearing up for the reader obscure passages. This is their sole purpose. Great scholars have given readers of the Bible this chain of references to help them to understand the Holy Scriptures.

In the *KJV Prophecy Marked Reference Study Bible* you will find a small letter or a figure printed in the text to the left of certain words or phrases and above the level of the line of printing, such as [a]slain, or [1]for himself. These letters or figures refer the reader to the corresponding letters or figures in the center column references to the text.

For example, take a look at a familiar passage in the Bible, Psalm 23: "The Lord is [a]my shepherd; [b]I shall not want" (23:1) The letter superscript "a" is placed just before "my shepherd."

When we consult the references listed after "a" in the center reference section, we find that it refers to John 10:11, "I am the good shepherd." We also find another reference, Isaiah 40:11, "He shall feed his flock like a shepherd." These references present a picture of the Good Shepherd who made provision for our salvation.

Psalm 23:2 reads, "He maketh me to lie down in [1]green pastures: he leadeth me beside the [2]still waters." Here we find the a superscript italicized "1" before "green pastures." The corresponding number in the center gives the Hebrew rendering, "pastures of tender grass." Before the phrase "beside the still waters," you will find a superscript italicized "2." This number in the center column gives the Hebrew meaning, "waters of quietness." In Psalm 23:3 the superscript letter "a" before "he leadeth me" refers to Psalm 5:8, which reads, "Lead me, O LORD, in thy righteousness."

Through the study of these few references, we have a more vivid picture of the Good Shepherd. The more we go into the study of the center references, the greater will become our knowledge of the Bible. Thus we see the value and importance of the center references.

Now let's turn to the New Testament to examine a familiar passage. In Matthew 5:2–3 we read, "And he opened his mouth, and taught them, saying, [a]Blessed *are* the poor in spirit: for theirs is the kingdom of heaven." In the center column reference this "a" before "Blessed" refers to Psalm 51:17, which says, "The sacrifices of God *are* a broken spirit: a broken and contrite heart, O God, thou wilt not despise." Another central reference is to Proverbs 16:19, "Better *it is to be* of an humble spirit with the lowly, than to divide the spoil with the proud."

This simple study is adequate to convince us that the expression, "poor in spirit," means humility, a fundamental principle of Christianity.

Abbreviations
of the Books of the Bible

Genesis	Ge
Exodus	Ex
Leviticus	Lev
Numbers	Nu
Deuteronomy	Dt
Joshua	Jos
Judges	Jdg
Ruth	Ru
1 Samuel	1Sa
2 Samuel	2Sa
1 Kings	1Ki
2 Kings	2Ki
1 Chronicles	1Ch
2 Chronicles	2Ch
Ezra	Ezr
Nehemiah	Ne
Esther	Est
Job	Job
Psalm	Ps
Proverbs	Pr
Ecclesiastes	Ecc
Song of Solomon	SS
Isaiah	Isa
Jeremiah	Jer
Lamentations	La
Ezekiel	Eze
Daniel	Da
Hosea	Hos
Joel	Joel
Amos	Am
Obadiah	Ob
Jonah	Jnh
Micah	Mic
Nahum	Na
Habbakuk	Hab
Zephaniah	Zep
Haggai	Hag
Zechariah	Zec
Malachi	Mal
Matthew	Mt
Mark	Mk
Luke	Lk
John	Jn
Acts	Ac
Romans	Ro
1 Corinthians	1Co
2 Corinthians	2Co
Galatians	Gal
Ephesians	Eph
Philippians	Php
Colossians	Col
1 Thessalonians	1Th
2 Thessalonians	2Th
1 Timothy	1Ti
2 Timothy	2Ti
Titus	Tit
Philemon	Phm
Hebrews	Heb
James	Jas
1 Peter	1Pe
2 Peter	2Pe
1 John	1Jn
2 John	2Jn
3 John	3Jn
Jude	Jude
Revelation	Rev

OLD TESTAMENT

Genesis

Author: Moses

Theme: The beginning of all things

Date of Writing: c. 1446–1406 B.C.

Outline of Genesis

- I. God's Creation of the Universe (1:1—2:25)
- II. The First Sin and Promise of Redemption (3:1—5:32)
- III. The Flood and the History of Noah (6:1—9:29)
- IV. The Distribution of People (10:1—11:26)
- V. The Life of Abraham (Abram) (11:27—25:18)
- VI. The Life of Isaac (25:19—26:35)
- VII. The Life of Jacob and His Sons (27:1—37:1)
- VIII. The Life of Joseph (37:2—50:26)

GENESIS 1:1 OPENS with the Hebrew word *bereshith*, which means "by way of beginning" or "in [the] beginning." The book of Genesis is truly a book about beginnings, recording God's creation of the heavens, the earth, vegetation, animals and people. Genesis also chronicles the first sin—the disobedience of Adam and Eve to God's commands and their subsequent exile from Eden. The pages of Genesis reveal the breadth of humanity's sinful condition and broken relationship with God. Yet Genesis also introduces the progressive revelation of God's plan to redeem the earth and fallen humanity and defeat Satan through the sacrificial death on the cross of God's Son, Jesus Christ. Thus Genesis records the creation, fall and ultimate redemption of the human race.

The progressive revelation of God's divine nature and his plan of salvation through Jesus Christ are revealed in Scripture through eight major covenants. In each covenant God established specific conditions of relationship between himself and people. Genesis records the four initial covenants—the Edenic (2:15–17), Adamic (3:15–19), Noahic (9:8ff) and Abrahamic (15:4ff; 17:1–22). These four covenants set the stage for the four remaining covenants that are revealed in the balance of Scripture—the Mosaic (Sinaitic), Palestinian, Davidic and New covenants. Consequently a careful study of Genesis is essential to our understanding of the entire Bible.

The inspiration of Genesis is authenticated by the numerous quotations by the writers of the NT and by the word of Jesus Christ (see Mt 19:4–6; 24:37–39; Lk 17:26–29). Recent scientific discoveries also confirm the incredible accuracy of the scientific and medical statements found in this book. Though critics once doubted the existence of written language during Moses' day, modern-day archeologists have discovered many examples of ancient writing that predate the time of the exodus and further validate the historical reliability of Genesis.

The creation

1 IN THE [a]beginning [b]God created the heaven and the earth.

E M N 2 And the earth was [a]without form, and void; and darkness *was* upon the face of the deep. [b]And the spirit of God moved upon the face of the waters.

3 [a]And God said, [b]Let there be light: and there was light.

4 And God saw the light, that *it was* good: and God divided [1]the light from the darkness.

5 And God called the light [a]Day, and the darkness he called Night. [1]And the evening and the morning were the first day.

6 ¶ And God said, [a]Let there be a [1]firmament in the midst of the waters, and let it divide the waters from the waters.

7 And God made the firmament, [a]and divided the waters which *were* under the firmament from the waters which *were* [b]above the firmament: and it was so.

8 And God called the firmament Heaven. And the evening and the morning were the second day.

9 ¶ And God said, [a]Let the waters under the heaven be gathered together unto one place, and let the dry *land* appear: and it was so.

10 And God called the dry *land* Earth; and the gathering together of the waters called he Seas: and God saw that *it was* good.

11 And God said, Let the earth [a]bring forth [1]grass, the herb yielding seed, *and* the fruit tree yielding [b]fruit after his kind, whose seed *is* in itself, upon the earth: and it was so.

12 And the earth brought forth grass, *and* herb yielding seed after his kind, and the tree yielding fruit, whose seed *was* in itself, after his kind: and God saw that *it was* good.

13 And the evening and the morning were the third day.

14 ¶ And God said, Let there be lights in the firmament of the heaven to divide [1]the day from the night; and let them be for signs, and for seasons, and for days, and years:

15 And let them be for lights in the firmament of the heaven to give light upon the earth: and it was so.

16 And God made two great lights; the [a]greater light [1]to rule the day, and the [b]lesser light to rule the night: *he made* [c]the stars also.

17 And God set them in the firmament of the heaven to give light upon the earth,

18 And to [a]rule over the day and over the night, and to divide the light from the darkness: and God saw that *it was* good.

19 And the evening and the morning were the fourth day.

20 And God said, Let the waters bring forth abundantly the [1]moving creature that hath [2]life, and [3]fowl *that* may fly above the earth in the [4]open firmament of heaven.

21 And [a]God created great whales, and every living creature that moveth, which the waters brought forth abundantly, after their kind, and every winged fowl after his kind: and God saw that *it was* good.

22 And God blessed them, saying, [a]Be fruitful, and multiply, and fill the waters in the seas, and let fowl multiply in the earth.

23 And the evening and the morning were the fifth day.

24 ¶ And God said, Let the earth bring forth the living creature after his kind,

1:1 [a]John 1:1,2; Heb. 1:10 [b]Ps. 8:3; Is. 44:24; Acts 17:24; Rev. 4:11
2 [a]Jer. 4:23 [b]Ps. 33:6; Is. 40:13,14
3 [a]Ps. 33:9 [b]2 Cor. 4:6
4 [1]Heb. *between the light and between the darkness*
5 [a]Ps. 74:16 [1]Heb. *And the evening was, and the morning was*
6 [a]Job 37:18; Jer. 10:12 [1]Heb. *expansion*
7 [a]Prov. 8:28 [b]Ps. 148:4
9 [a]Job 26:10; Prov. 8:29; Jer. 5:22; 2 Pet. 3:5
11 [a]Heb. 6:7 [b]Luke 6:44 [1]Heb. *tender grass*
14 [1]Heb. *between the day and between the night*
16 [a]Ps. 136:8 [b]Ps. 8:3 [c]Job 38:7 [1]Heb. *for the rule of the day*
18 [a]Jer. 31:35
20 [1]Or, *creeping* [2]Heb. *soul* [3]Heb. *let fowl fly* [4]Heb. *face of the firmament of heaven*
21 [a]Ps. 104:26
22 [a]ch. 8:17

E ▶ *Ge 41:38* M ▶ *Ge 41:38* N ▶ *2Ki 2:9*

cattle, and creeping thing, and beast of the earth after his kind: and it was so.

25 And God made the beast of the earth after his kind, and cattle after their kind, and every thing that creepeth upon the earth after his kind: and God saw that *it was* good.

26 ¶ And God said, [a]Let us make man in our image, after our likeness: and [b]let them have dominion over the fish of the sea, and over the fowl of the air, and over the cattle, and over all the earth, and over every creeping thing that creepeth upon the earth.

27 So God created man in his *own* image, [a]in the image of God created he him; [b]male and female created he them.

A 28 And God blessed them, and God said unto them, [a]Be fruitful, and multiply, and replenish the earth, and subdue it: and have dominion over the fish of the sea, and over the fowl of the air, and over every living thing that ʹmoveth upon the earth.

29 ¶ And God said, Behold, I have given you every herb ʹbearing seed, which *is* upon the face of all the earth, and every tree, in the which *is* the fruit of a tree yielding seed; [a]to you it shall be for meat.

30 And to [a]every beast of the earth, and to every [b]fowl of the air, and to every thing that creepeth upon the earth, wherein *there is* ʹlife, *I have given* every green herb for meat: and it was so.

31 And [a]God saw every thing that he had made, and, behold, *it was* very good. And the evening and the morning were the sixth day.

2 THUS THE heavens and the earth were finished, and [a]all the host of them.

2 [a]And on the seventh day God ended his work which he had made; and he rested on the seventh day from all his work which he had made.

3 And God [a]blessed the seventh day, and sanctified it: because that in it he had rested from all his work which God ʹcreated and made.

Adam and Eve

4 ¶ [a]These *are* the generations of the heavens and of the earth when they were created, in the day that the LORD God made the earth and the heavens,

5 And every [a]plant of the field before it was in the earth, and every herb of the field before it grew: for the LORD God had not [b]caused it to rain upon the earth, and *there was* not a man [c]to till the ground.

6 But ʹthere went up a mist from the earth, and watered the whole face of the ground.

A ▶ *Ge 2:16–17*

26 [a]Ps. 100:3; Eccl. 7:29; Eph. 4:24; Jas. 3:9 [b]ch. 9:2; Ps. 8:6
27 [a]1 Cor. 11:7 [b]ch. 5:2; Mat. 19:4
28 [a]ch. 9:1,7; Lev. 26:9 ʹHeb. *creepeth*
29 [a]ch. 9:3; Ps. 104:14,15 ʹHeb. *seeding seed*
30 [a]Ps. 145:15 [b]Job 38:41 ʹHeb. *a living soul*
31 [a]Ps. 104:24
2:1 [a]Ps. 33:6
2 [a]Ex. 20:11; Heb. 4:4
3 [a]Is. 58:13 ʹHeb. *created to make*
4 [a]ch. 1:1
5 [a]ch. 1:12 [b]Job 38:26-28 [c]ch. 3:23
6 ʹOr, *a mist which went up from*

1:28 *Dispensation of Innocence.* Throughout Scripture, one can find seven distinct periods of time in which God commands obedience to a specific aspect or revelation of his will. These time periods may be referred to as dispensations. This verse introduces the first of those dispensations—the dispensation of innocence.

Adam and Eve were created as pure and innocent human beings, placed by God in a perfect world. God commanded Adam's adherence to one specific rule—not to eat of the tree of the knowledge of good and evil—and he warned Adam of the consequences of disobedience. But Adam and Eve failed this test of obedience. Eve yielded to Satan's temptation, and Adam chose to follow his wife's sinful rebellion. Their failure to obey God resulted in their eviction from the garden and their ultimate death.

The seven dispensations revealed in Scripture are the dispensations of innocence (Ge 1:28), conscience (3:7), human government (8:15), promise (12:1), law (Ex 19:1), the church (Ac 2:1) and the kingdom (Rev 20:4). For further information on the dispensations, see the article on p. 4.

The Seven Dispensations

1	2	3	4	5		6	7	
Innocence GE 1:28	**Conscience** GE 3:7	**Human Government** GE 8:15	**Promise** GE 12:1	**Law** EX 19:1		**Age of Grace Church Age** AC 2:1	**Kingdom Age** REV 20:4	
Creation	*Fall*	*Flood*	*Abraham*	*Moses*	*Crucifixion*	*Battle of Armageddon*		*Eternity*

The Seven Dispensations

A DISPENSATION IS a period of time in God's divine economy during which God gives a special revelation and commands people to obey that specific revelation. Scripture unveils seven distinct dispensations: innocence (Ge 1:28), conscience (3:7), human government (8:15), promise (12:1), law (Ex 19:1), the church (Ac 2:1) and the kingdom (Rev 20:4).

The Dispensation of Innocence (Ge 1:28)

God created Adam and Eve in total innocence and placed them in an environment of perfect harmony. God established one simple test of obedience: Adam and Eve were forbidden to eat from the tree of the knowledge of good and evil. Satan first tempted Eve, and Adam chose to follow his wife's rebellion. They both disobeyed God's test of obedience and instead yielded to sin. The consequence for their failure to obey God was their expulsion from Eden.

The Dispensation of Conscience (Ge 3:7)

As a result of Adam and Eve's sinful rebellion, people now possessed the knowledge of the difference between good and evil. God revealed a new test of obedience. People were to follow the dictates of conscience, rejecting evil and following good. Yet humanity failed this test of obedience too, resulting in worldwide corruption and violence. Consequently God sent a terrible flood to destroy the world, leaving only eight survivors from Noah's family.

The Dispensation of Human Government (Ge 8:15)

Noah's family was given the command to repopulate the world and to organize a society that would follow the principles of God's law. This new dispensation involved the creation of human government, under the command of God, to protect the sanctity of human life and to rule with righteousness on earth. Though God authorized human government, history tragically records humanity's failure to rule in righteousness. Human governments have been marked by cruelty, corruption and injustice. This dispensation of human government will be set aside when Jesus Christ returns at Armageddon to establish his kingdom in Jerusalem and to rule the earth in righteousness forever.

The Dispensation of Promise (Ge 12:1)

This dispensation revealed God's intent to use Abram and his descendants to provide a Savior for all people. Abram and his descendants were to be obedient to God and faithful to him. God unconditionally promised to bless them (see 15:15), make them a great nation (see 12:2) and give them the promised land as their eternal inheritance (see 15:18–21;

17:7–8). In addition, God promised to bless all who would bless Abram and his descendants (see 12:3), while those who cursed Abram and his offspring would reap judgment. The history of the rise and fall of many empires can be understood in light of this promise to bless or curse those who bless or curse Israel.

This dispensation of promise has not been eliminated even though Abram's descendants have not faithfully obeyed God. Though the dispensation of the law given to Moses at Mt. Sinai (see Ex 19:1–3) superseded this dispensation of promise, the Bible contains many promises about Israel's future blessing and restoration to the promised land (see Isa 44; 49: 51:3–9; 66:8–9; Jer 31:3–14).

The Dispensation of the Law (Ex 19:1)

This dispensation covered the time period from the giving of God's Law on Mt. Sinai until the death of Jesus Christ on the cross. Humanity had failed each of the previous tests of obedience, but Israel promised to obey this revelation of God's Law. The law provided Israel with a divinely sanctioned way of life that functioned as a tutor, or disciplinary schoolmaster, to test Israel's obedience to God's will (see Gal 3:24). Though God commanded the sacrifices, personal righteousness, rituals and worship ceremonies, these sacrifices and rituals could not, in themselves, ever eliminate sin. The law merely pointed to the need for a permanent salvation through Jesus Christ, the Lamb of God, slain for the sins of the world. Tragically, history records Israel's continual rebellion and violation of God's Law, proving that Israel failed this test of obedience. Therefore, it was necessary for God to send Jesus Christ to die as the perfect sacrifice for all sin.

The Dispensation of Grace (Ac 2:1)

This dispensation corresponds to the church age, beginning at the cross and continuing until the resurrection of the saints (see 1Th 4:13–17). During this time period, humanity faces the testing of their response to God's offer of salvation based on Jesus' sacrificial death. Many will deny Jesus' claims and introduce false doctrines into the church (see 1Ti 4:1–3). Others will scoff and refuse to accept God's gracious gift. Still others will verbally profess faith in Christ but never truly repent and will join in the apostasy of the false church during the last days. This dispensation of grace will conclude with the rapture of the saints, those who have truly repented and loved Jesus Christ, to their home in heaven.

The Dispensation of the Kingdom (Rev 20:4)

This last dispensation concludes God's plan of redemption for humanity, establishes his eternal kingdom on earth and ultimately fulfills God's unshakable promises to Israel, the Gentile nations, and the church. The Messiah, Jesus Christ, will rule the earth from the throne of David forever. Righteousness and justice will replace oppression and misrule. Israel will be restored and converted. And the final consummation of the dispensation of this coming kingdom will be the deliverance of creation from its bondage since the time of Eden.

For further information about the seven dispensations, see the chart on p. 3 or the study notes at Ge 1:28; 3:7; 8:15; 12:1; Ex 19:1; Ac 2:1 and Rev 20:4.

7 And the LORD God formed man ′of
the [a]dust of the ground, and [b]breathed
into his [c]nostrils the breath of life; and
[d]man became a living soul.
8 ¶ And the LORD God planted [a]a garden [b]eastward in [c]Eden; and there he put
the man whom he had formed.
9 And out of the ground made the LORD
God to grow [a]every tree that is pleasant
to the sight, and good for food; [b]the tree
of life also in the midst of the garden, and
the tree of knowledge of good and evil.
10 And a river went out of Eden to water the garden; and from thence it was
parted, and became into four heads.
11 The name of the first *is* Pison: that
is it which compasseth [a]the whole land
of Havilah, where *there is* gold;
12 And the gold of that land *is* good:
[a]there *is* bdellium and the onyx stone.
13 And the name of the second river *is*
Gihon: the same *is* it that compasseth the
whole land of ′Ethiopia.

7 [a]ch. 3:19,23; Ps. 103:14 [b]Job 33:4 [c]ch. 7:22 [d]1 Cor. 15:45 ′Heb. *dust of the ground*
8 [a]Is. 51:3 [b]ch. 3:24 [c]ch. 4:16
9 [a]Ezek. 31:8 [b]ch. 3:22; Rev. 2:7
11 [a]ch. 25:18
12 [a]Num. 11:7
13 ′Heb. *Cush*
14 [a]Dan. 10:4 ′Or, *eastward to Assyria*
15 ′Or, *Adam*
16 ′Heb. *eating thou shalt eat*
17 [a]ch. 3:1,3,11, 17 [b]ch. 3:3,19; Rom. 6:23 ′Heb. *dying thou shalt die*
18 [a]1 Cor. 11:9; 1 Tim. 2:13 ′Heb. *as before him*
19 [a]ch. 1:20,24 [b]Ps. 8:6

14 And the name of the third river *is*
[a]Hiddekel: that *is* it which goeth ′toward
the east of Assyria. And the fourth river *is*
Euphrates.
15 And the LORD God took ′the man,
and put him into the garden of Eden to
dress it and to keep it.
16 And the LORD God commanded the A
man, saying, Of every tree of the garden
′thou mayest freely eat:
17 But of the tree of the knowledge of C
good and evil, [a]thou shalt not eat of it: for S
in the day that thou eatest thereof [b]thou′
shalt surely die.
18 ¶ And the LORD God said, *It is* not
good that the man should be alone; [a]I
will make him an help ′meet for him.
19 [a]And out of the ground the LORD
God formed every beast of the field, and
every fowl of the air; and [b]brought *them*

A *Ge 1:28* ◀▶ *Ge 3:7* **C** ▶ *Ge 3:3*
S ▶ *Ge 7:1*

2:15–17 *Edenic Covenant.* This passage marks the Edenic covenant—the first of God's eight major covenants with humanity. In this solemn declaration of God's sovereignty the Lord established a relationship between himself and human beings involving the following elements:

1. People were to rule over the whole earth and "have dominion over the fish of the sea, and over the fowl of the air, and over every living thing that moveth upon the earth" (1:28).
2. People were to populate and fill the earth.
3. Adam was instructed to be a steward of the garden and allowed to partake of its fruits for food.
4. Adam was not allowed to eat of the fruit of the tree of the knowledge of good and evil on penalty of death.

NOTE: The seven additional covenants include the Adamic (3:15–17), Noahic (9:8ff), Abrahamic (15:4ff; 17:1–22), Mosaic (Ex 19:5), Palestinian (Dt 30:1–10), Davidic (2Sa 7:16) and New (Heb 8:8–12). See the chart below.

2:17 The description of the garden includes the mention of two specific trees. "The tree of the knowledge of good and evil" became the focus of Adam and Eve's temptation to disobey God, transcend themselves and "be as gods" (3:5). The other important tree in the middle of the garden was "the tree of life" (2:9). This tree yielded more than mere knowledge; its fruit conveyed immortality (see 3:22). The "tree of life" is referred to again in John's description of the new Jerusalem (see Rev 22:2). The righteous will apparently partake of this "tree of life" because sin's control over them will be destroyed and their eternity with God will be secure.

The Eight Covenants

Edenic GE 2:16	**Adamic** GE 3:15	**Noahic** GE 8:15	**Abrahamic** GE 12:2	**Mosaic** EX 19:5	**Palestinian** DT 30:3	**Davidic** 2 SA 7:16	**New Covenant** HEB 8:8
1	2	3	4	5	6	7	8
Creation	*The fall of Adam*	*After flood, government begins*	*Promise of land to Israel*	*The law given*	*God gives conditions to enter Promised Land*	*Promise David's throne forever*	*God Promised Final Redemption A new heart to be given to Israel*

Covenant: A declaration of God in which he establishes man's responsibility to obey a specific revelation from the Lord. Usually, these covenants are unconditional, as God declares "I will . . ." Man's obedience leads to blessing, while disobedience leads to discipline. However, man's sinful disobedience cannot interfere with God's ultimate fulfillment of his covenants.

unto [I]Adam to see what he would call them: and whatsoever Adam called every living creature, that *was* the name thereof.

20 And Adam [I]gave names to all cattle, and to the fowl of the air, and to every beast of the field; but for Adam there was not found an help meet for him.

21 And the LORD God caused a [a]deep sleep to fall upon Adam, and he slept: and he took one of his ribs, and closed up the flesh instead thereof;

22 And the rib, which the LORD God had taken from man, [I]made he a woman, and [a]brought her unto the man.

23 And Adam said, This *is* now [a]bone of my bones, and flesh of my flesh: she shall be called [I]Woman, because she was [b]taken out of [2]Man.

24 [a]Therefore shall a man leave his father and his mother, and shall cleave unto his wife: and they shall be one flesh.

25 [a]And they were both naked, the man and his wife, and were not [b]ashamed.

The fall of man

3 NOW [a]THE serpent was [b]more subtle than any beast of the field which the LORD God had made. And he said unto the woman, [I]Yea, hath God said, Ye shall not eat of every tree of the garden?

2 And the woman said unto the serpent, We may eat of the fruit of the trees of the garden:

C 3 But of the fruit of the tree which *is* in the midst of the garden, God hath said, Ye shall not eat of it, neither shall ye touch it, lest ye die.

4 [a]And the serpent said unto the woman, Ye shall not surely die:

5 For God doth know that in the day ye eat thereof, then your eyes shall be opened, and ye shall be as gods, knowing good and evil.

6 And when the woman saw that the tree *was* good for food, and that it *was* [I]pleasant to the eyes, and a tree to be desired to make *one* wise, she took of the fruit thereof, [a]and did eat, and gave also unto her husband with her; and he did eat.

7 And the eyes of them both were opened, [a]and they knew that they *were* naked; and they sewed fig leaves together, and made themselves [I]aprons. A

8 And they heard [a]the voice of the LORD God walking in the garden in the [I]cool of the day: and Adam and his wife [b]hid themselves from the presence of the LORD God amongst the trees of the garden.

9 And the LORD God called unto Adam, and said unto him, Where *art* thou?

10 And he said, I heard thy voice in the garden, [a]and I was afraid, because I *was* naked; and I hid myself.

11 And he said, Who told thee that thou *wast* naked? Hast thou eaten of the tree, whereof I commanded thee that thou shouldest not eat?

12 And the man said, [a]The woman whom thou gavest *to be* with me, she gave me of the tree, and I did eat.

13 And the LORD God said unto the woman, What *is* this *that* thou hast done? And the woman said, [a]The serpent beguiled me, and I did eat.

14 And the LORD God said unto the serpent, Because thou hast done this, thou *art* cursed above all cattle, and above every beast of the field; upon thy belly shalt thou go, and [a]dust shalt thou eat all the days of thy life:

19 [I]Or, *the man*
20 [I]Heb. *called*
21 [a]1 Sam. 26:12
22 [a]Heb. 13:4 [I]Heb. *builded*
23 [a]ch. 29:14; Eph. 5:30 [b]1 Cor. 11:8 [I]Heb. *Isha* [2]Heb. *Ish*
24 [a]Mat. 19:5; Eph. 5:31
25 [a]ch. 3:7,10 [b]Is. 47:3
3:1 [a]Rev. 12:9 [b]2 Cor. 11:3 [I]Heb. *Yea, because*
4 [a]2 Cor. 11:3
6 [a]1 Tim. 2:14 [I]Heb. *a desire*
7 [a]ch. 2:25 [I]Or, *things to gird about*
8 [a]Job 38:1 [b]Job 31:33; Jer. 23:24 [I]Heb. *wind*
10 [a]ch. 2:25; 1 John 3:20
12 [a]Prov. 28:13
13 [a]ver. 4; 2 Cor. 11:3; 1 Tim. 2:14
14 [a]Is. 65:25

C *Ge 2:17* ◀ ▶ *Ge 6:5*

A *Ge 2:16–17* ◀ ▶ *Ge 3:15*

3:7 *Dispensation of Conscience.* Adam and Eve disobeyed God's command and immediately felt a keen sense of guilt as they experienced what had heretofore been theoretical. They now knew the difference between good and evil, but had gained this knowledge by choosing disobedience rather than obedience to God's command. As a result of their sinful rebellion, humanity moved from innocence to a time of moral decision and faced God's test to follow the dictates of conscience, voluntarily choosing righteousness rather than wickedness. Tragically, humanity continued to reject obedience to God's revealed will and failed the test of obedience in this dispensation of conscience (see 6:5).

The seven dispensations revealed in Scripture are the dispensations of innocence (Ge 1:28), conscience (3:7), human government (8:15), promise (12:1), law (Ex 19:1), the church (Ac 2:1) and the kingdom (Rev 20:4). For further information on the dispensations, see the article on p. 4.

The Biblical Covenants

A COVENANT IS a formal, binding agreement between two parties to do or not to do something. Biblical covenants reflect God's sovereign declaration to establish a legal agreement between himself and human beings. Many Biblical covenants are unconditional—God commits himself to accomplish something regardless of whether or not humanity executes their part of the agreement. A Biblical covenant, however, usually contains promised blessings for adherence to the terms of the covenant and guarantees punishment for a refusal to comply. Though people may experience punishment in return for disobedience to a Biblical covenant, such disobedience does not negate the ultimate fulfillment of God's covenant promises.

Note that there are eight major covenants found in the Bible. These covenants help us understand God's unfolding plan to redeem humanity from the curse of sin and provide details about the establishment of his Messianic kingdom on earth. For additional details about each of the covenants listed below, refer to the study notes provided at each referenced location and review the chart provided on p. 6.

The Edenic Covenant (Ge 2:15)

The Edenic covenant is the first of God's great covenants with people. This covenant granted several rights and requirements for people: They were to rule the earth and its creatures, populate and fill the earth, take care of Eden and refrain from eating from the tree of the knowledge of good and evil. The blessings of this covenant were a beautiful environment, abundant fruits and food available in the garden and a close, personal relationship with God. The penalty for breaking this covenant was death.

The Adamic Covenant (Ge 3:15)

The Adamic covenant stipulated the conditions under which sinful people must live until the redemption of the earth in the millennial kingdom of Christ. These conditions included a curse upon the snake, a judgment on women because of Eve's fall and temptation of Adam, a curse upon the earth and a certainty of death for all people.

Yet hidden within each of these judgments was a seed of God's mercy. Though used as Satan's tool, the snake was not utterly destroyed but rather was given a lesser place of prominence in the animal kingdom. Though the earth was cursed because of sin, the ground would still yield enough food to allow the continuance of human beings and animals. Though the woman was cursed with sorrow in conception, pain in childbirth and a place of subjection in the marital relationship, God also showed mercy to the woman by granting her joy in the birth of her children (see Jn 16:21) and by establishing guidelines for a husband's leadership in marriage (see Eph 5:22–28).

Even the curse of death carried a promise from God. God had initially created Adam and Eve to live forever if they obeyed his commands. Because of their sin, Adam and Eve forfeited their immortality, received the curse of death and were evicted from the Garden. However, God extended his mercy to humanity in this covenant by promising that a future Redeemer would come through the woman's seed. This Messianic foreshadowing of the virgin birth is the first in a series of prophecies about Christ that occur throughout the Bible. This covenant also foreshadowed the rise of a seed of Satan—the antichrist—and his inevitable defeat. Though Satan would have a temporary victory, Christ would neutralize Satan's power through his triumphant resurrection and victory over death.

The Noahic Covenant *(Ge 9:8)*

God established the Noahic covenant to reconfirm the conditions of the Adamic covenant and to authorize human government as a control for violence and sin. The articles of this covenant included a confirmation of the seasons, the freedom for people to kill animals for food and a fear of humanity instilled in animals. God also required that people protect human life and control the actions of others through the creation of human government (see 9:5–6; Rom 13:1–7).

Specific instructions in this covenant were given to Noah's sons: Canaan's (Ham's) descendants would be the servants of their brothers; Japheth's line would be enlarged; Shem's descendants would serve the Lord in a unique way. Note that these specific instructions were also prophetic: Many of those gifted in art, science and government in ancient times were descendants of Japheth, while Jesus Christ was a descendant of Shem.

The promise of the Noahic covenant was sealed with a rainbow as God promised to never again destroy every living thing (see 8:21; 9:11–16) or increase the curse placed upon the ground.

The Abrahamic Covenant *(Ge 15:4)*

The Abrahamic covenant declared God's sovereign choice to bless Israel and the nations through Abraham and his descendant, the Messiah. The major aspects of this covenant included God's eternal promises to Abraham ensuring him innumerable descendants, considerable blessings and a great nation to come from his lineage. In this covenant God's promises of blessing also extended to all of humanity provided people blessed Abraham's descendants. If people chose to denounce Abraham's offspring, however, God would punish them. The reason for the rise and fall of many nations can be found in this solemn promise of God to Abraham and his descendants.

The Mosaic Covenant *(Ex 19:5)*

The Mosaic covenant did not change the covenant promise made to Abraham but instead expanded it. God promised to make the nation of Israel his chosen people. The people were required to obey God's commandments, judgments and ordinances to gain an understanding of God's righteousness and will for their lives. The law became Israel's schoolteacher, setting the limits for Israel's spiritual life and determining the rules that would govern Israel's daily life. This covenant would remain in effect until the Messiah comes.

The Palestinian Covenant (Dt 30:1–10)

The Palestinian covenant described the divinely appointed conditions that God established for Israel's occupation of the promised land. Blessings and punishments are offset in the terms of this covenant. If Israel rebelled against God, God said they would be removed from their land. Yet God promised that his people would eventually repent and be restored to the land of Canaan. When the Messiah comes Israel will be fully restored to the land, the nation will repent and God will judge Israel's enemies. Then Israel will enjoy eternal prosperity in the promised land.

Israel has never possessed Canaan under the terms of the unconditional Abrahamic covenant. The Palestinian covenant confirms those promises concerning the land and indicates that this covenant will not be totally fulfilled until the Millennium, under the rule of the Messiah.

The Davidic Covenant (2Sa 7:16)

God made additional promises to Israel through the Davidic covenant. This eternal agreement established David's throne and promised that David's descendants would rule his kingdom forever. This covenant was established upon God's promise that the future Messiah would come from David's line and someday rule Israel from David's throne. God guaranteed that despite the sins of David's sons, this covenant with David would be fulfilled eternally.

The New Covenant (Heb 8:8–12)

The New covenant is the last of the eight, major Biblical covenants and is unconditionally based on the promises of God to transform the hearts of his people. The promises of the New covenant affect all believers because this covenant asserts that all sin has been effectively forgiven forever through Christ's atoning work on the cross.

This final covenant also assures Israel that they will remain God's chosen people and that God will transform their sinful hearts so that they will love and obey him forever. God promises through his New covenant to ultimately redeem his chosen people and establish them in a new relationship with him forever in the promised land.

A 15 And I will put enmity between thee
B and the woman, and between [a]thy seed
D and [b]her seed; [c]it shall bruise thy head,
and thou shalt bruise his heel.
16 Unto the woman he said, I will
greatly multiply thy sorrow and thy conception; [a]in sorrow thou shalt bring forth
children; [b]and thy desire *shall be* [1]to thy
husband, and he shall [c]rule over thee.
17 And unto Adam he said, [a]Because
thou hast hearkened unto the voice of
thy wife, and hast eaten of the tree, [b]of
which I commanded thee, saying, Thou
shalt not eat of it: [c]cursed *is* the ground
for thy sake; [d]in sorrow shalt thou eat *of*
it all the days of thy life;
18 Thorns also and thistles shall it
[1]bring forth to thee; and [a]thou shalt eat
the herb of the field;
19 [a]In the sweat of thy face shalt thou
eat bread, till thou return unto the
ground; for out of it wast thou taken: [b]for

A *Ge 3:7* ◀ ▶ *Ge 8:15* **B** ▶ *Ge 49:10*
D ▶ *Ge 4:3–5*

15 [a]John 8:44; Acts 13:10; 1 John 3:8 [b]Is. 7:14; Luke 1:31,34,35 [c]Rom. 16:20; Rev. 12:7
16 [a]Is. 13:8; John 16:21 [b]ch. 4:7 [c]1 Cor. 11:3; Eph. 5:22 [1]Or, *subject to thy husband*
17 [a]1 Sam. 15:23 [b]ch. 2:17 [c]Rom. 8:20 [d]Eccl. 2:23
18 [a]Ps. 104:14 [1]Heb. *cause to bud*
19 [a]2 Thes. 3:10 [b]ch. 2:7

3:15 This verse has been called the *protevangelium*—the first proclamation of the gospel. It is the first in a chain of Messianic prophecies throughout the Scriptures that prefigure Christ's birth, life, death and resurrection. The first part of the verse infers the spiritual struggle that will arise between the woman's offspring and the offspring of the serpent—the continual battle between the children of the kingdom and the children of Satan. However, this prophecy also reveals that one ultimate victor will win this battle. Though Satan will "bruise his heel," inflicting temporary pain and suffering through his many skirmishes (see Rev 12:13–17), Christ will ultimately triumph over death and the grave, crushing the serpent's head and inflicting a mortal wound that will win the war. To the resounding, joyful cries of his children, Christ will one day destroy all of Satan's powers at the final defeat of the antichrist and in the last days deliver a wound to Satan's head that can never be healed.

3:15–17 *Adamic Covenant.* This verse introduces the agreement made between God and Adam and Eve after their sin but before their removal from the garden. This Adamic covenant specifies the elements of life for humanity on this earth until Christ's second coming (see Ro 8:21). The covenant consisted of curses and promises:

1. The curse upon the serpent (see 3:14; Isa 65:25; Ro 16:20; 2Co 11:3; Rev 12:9). Created to be under humanity's dominion and rule but abused as Satan's instrument, the serpent was reduced from a subtle "beast of the field" (3:1) to a slithering reptile, cursed more than any other beast and forced to eat dust. Although the words of the curse were directed toward a creature, the underlying thrust of the message was against "that old serpent, called the Devil" (Rev 12:9).
2. The curse upon Satan (3:15; see Eph 2:2; Col 2:13–15; Heb 2:14–15). The time will come when Satan will be completely crushed by the seed of the woman (see note on 3:15 above).
3. The curse upon women (see 3:16). As the one who yielded first to Satan and then tempted another to sin, the woman suffered a special punishment: (a) women would henceforth have multiplied pain, suffering and agony in childbirth as a perpetual reminder of the effects of sin; and (b) women were reduced to a position of subjection to their husbands. Within each of these pronouncements of judgment God also provided a promise. The experience of birth is an agony of the moment, but also a gift of joy: "A woman when she is in travail hath sorrow, because her hour is come: but as soon as she is delivered of the child, she remembereth no more the anguish, for joy that a man is born into the world" (Jn 16:21). The authority of a husband in a marriage can also be a blessing. When a husband exercises his leadership in the marriage under God's direction, he will cherish and love his wife "even as Christ also loved the church" (Eph 5:25; see Eph 5:23–28).
4. The curse upon the ground (see 3:17). The bountiful abundance of the garden would no longer be available to Adam and Eve. Weeds, thorns and thistles would now cover the ground and make harvesting food a toilsome process.
5. The curse upon humanity (see 3:17–19; Ro 5:12–21). From a life of ease to a life of toilsome labor, God's curse on Adam's sin also included the certainty of death for Adam, Eve and each of their descendants (see 3:19). Yet this judgment also contained a promise of grace—hard work would yield food to sustain life.
6. The promise of a future Redeemer (3:15). "That old serpent, called the Devil, and Satan, which deceiveth the whole world" (Rev 12:9) would be crushed by the seed of the woman, a descendant of Adam. The line of the Redeemer would eventually run from Adam through Seth, Noah, Shem and Abraham and on through the genealogy of the first chapter of Matthew concluding with Jesus (see 6:8–10; 11:10–32; 12:1–5; Mt 1:2–16).

NOTE: The seven additional covenants include the Edenic (Ge 2:15–17), Noahic (9:8ff), Abrahamic (15:4ff; 17:1–22), Mosaic (Ex 19:5), Palestinian (Dt 30:1–10), Davidic (2Sa 7:16) and New (Heb 8:8–12). See the article on p. 8.

dust thou *art,* and [c]unto dust shalt thou return.

20 And Adam called his wife's name [1]Eve; because she was the mother of all living.

21 Unto Adam also and to his wife did the LORD God make coats of skins, and clothed them.

22 ¶ And the LORD God said, Behold, the man is become as one of us, to know good and evil: and now, lest he put forth his hand, and take also of the tree of life, and eat, and live for ever:

23 Therefore the LORD God sent him forth from the garden of Eden, [a]to till the ground from whence he was taken.

24 So he drove out the man; and he placed [a]at the east of the garden of Eden [b]Cherubims, and a flaming sword which turned every way, to keep the way of the tree of life.

Cain and Abel

4 AND ADAM knew Eve his wife; and she conceived, and bare [1]Cain, and said, I have gotten a man from the LORD.

2 And she again bare his brother [1]Abel. And Abel was [2]a keeper of sheep, but Cain was a tiller of the ground.

D 3 And [1]in process of time it came to pass, that Cain brought [a]of the fruit of the ground an offering unto the LORD.

4 And Abel, he also brought of [a]the firstlings of his [1]flock and of [b]the fat thereof. And the LORD had [c]respect unto Abel and to his offering:

5 But unto Cain and to his offering he had not respect. And Cain was very wroth, [a]and his countenance fell.

6 And the LORD said unto Cain, Why art thou wroth? and why is thy countenance fallen?

7 If thou doest well, shalt thou not [1]be accepted? and if thou doest not well, sin lieth at the door. And [a]unto[2] thee *shall be* his desire, and thou shalt rule over him.

8 And Cain talked with Abel his brother: and it came to pass, when they were in the field, that Cain rose up against Abel his brother, and [a]slew him.

9 ¶ And the LORD said unto Cain, Where *is* Abel thy brother? And he said, [a]I know not: *Am* I my brother's keeper?

10 And he said, What hast thou done? the voice of thy brother's [1]blood [a]crieth unto me from the ground.

11 And now *art* thou cursed from the earth, which hath opened her mouth to receive thy brother's blood from thy hand;

12 When thou tillest the ground, it shall not henceforth yield unto thee her strength; a fugitive and a vagabond shalt thou be in the earth.

13 And Cain said unto the LORD, [1]My punishment *is* greater than I can bear.

14 Behold, thou hast driven me out this day from the face of the earth; and [a]from thy face shall I be hid; and I shall be a fugitive and a vagabond in the earth; and it shall come to pass, [b]*that* every one that findeth me shall slay me.

15 And the LORD said unto him, Therefore whosoever slayeth Cain, vengeance shall be taken on him [a]sevenfold. And the LORD set a mark upon Cain, lest any finding him should kill him.

16 ¶ And Cain [a]went out from the presence of the LORD, and dwelt in the land of Nod, on the east of Eden.

17 And Cain knew his wife; and she conceived, and bare [1]Enoch: and he builded a city, [a]and called the name of the city, after the name of his son, Enoch.

18 And unto Enoch was born Irad: and Irad begat Mehujael: and Mehujael begat Methusael: and Methusael begat [1]Lamech.

19 ¶ And Lamech took unto him two wives: the name of the one *was* Adah, and the name of the other Zillah.

20 And Adah bare Jabal: he was the father of such as dwell in tents, and *of such as have* cattle.

21 And his brother's name *was* Jubal: he was the father of all such as handle the harp and organ.

22 And Zillah, she also bare Tubal-

D *Ge 3:15* ◄ ► *Ge 22:7–8*

19 [c]Job 21:26; Eccl. 3:20
20 [1]Heb. *Chavah* i.e. *Living*
23 [a]ch. 4:2 & 9:20
24 [a]ch. 2:8 [b]Ps. 104:4; Heb. 1:7
4:1 [1]i.e.*Gotten*
2 [1]Heb. *Hebel* [2]Heb. *a feeder*
3 [a]Num. 18:12 [1]Heb. *at the end of days*
4 [a]Num. 18:17 [b]Lev. 3:16 [c]Heb. 11:4 [1]Heb. *sheep,* or, *goats*
5 [a]ch. 31:2
7 [a]ch. 3:16 [1]Or, *have the excellency?* [2]Or, *subject unto thee,*
8 [a]Mat. 23:35
9 [a]John 8:44
10 [a]Heb. 12:24; Rev. 6:10 [1]Heb. *bloods*
13 [1]Or, *Mine iniquity* is *greater than* that it may *be forgiven*
14 [a]Ps. 51:11 [b]ch. 9:6; Num. 35:19, 21,27
15 [a]Ps. 79:12
16 [a]2 Ki. 13:23 & 24:20; Jer. 23:39 & 52:3
17 [a]Ps. 49:11 [1]Heb. *Chanoch*
18 [1]Heb. *Lemech*

3:21 Because of Adam and Eve's awareness of their nakedness, God introduced death into the world by providing the "coats of skins" of animals to clothe them and cover their shame. God's sacrifice of an innocent animal to restore Adam and Eve's fellowship with him prefigures the ultimate sacrifice of Jesus Christ, who died on the cross to cover the shame of our sins and restore us to fellowship with God.

cain, an [1]instructor of every artificer in brass and iron: and the sister of Tubal-cain *was* Naamah.

23 And Lamech said unto his wives, Adah and Zillah, Hear my voice; ye wives of Lamech, hearken unto my speech: for [1]I have slain a man to my wounding, and a young man [2]to my hurt.

24 [a]If Cain shall be avenged sevenfold, truly Lamech seventy and sevenfold.

25 ¶ And Adam knew his wife again; and she bare a son, and [a]called his name [1]Seth[2]: For God, *said she,* hath appointed me another seed instead of Abel, whom Cain slew.

26 And to Seth, [a]to him also there was born a son; and he called his name [1]Enos: then began men [b]to[2] call upon the name of the LORD.

The descendants of Adam

5 THIS *IS* the book of the generations of Adam. In the day that God created man, in [a]the likeness of God made he him;

2 [a]Male and female created he them; and blessed them, and called their name Adam, in the day when they were created.

3 ¶ And Adam lived an hundred and thirty years, and begat *a son* in his own likeness, after his image; and [a]called his name Seth:

4 [a]And the days of Adam after he had begotten Seth were eight hundred years: [b]and he begat sons and daughters:

5 And all the days that Adam lived were nine hundred and thirty years: [a]and he died.

6 And Seth lived an hundred and five years, and [a]begat Enos:

7 And Seth lived after he begat Enos eight hundred and seven years, and begat sons and daughters:

8 And all the days of Seth were nine hundred and twelve years: and he died.

9 ¶ And Enos lived ninety years, and begat [1]Cainan:

10 And Enos lived after he begat Cainan eight hundred and fifteen years, and begat sons and daughters:

11 And all the days of Enos were nine hundred and five years: and he died.

12 ¶ And Cainan lived seventy years, and begat [1]Mahalaleel:

13 And Cainan lived after he begat Mahalaleel eight hundred and forty years, and begat sons and daughters:

14 And all the days of Cainan were nine hundred and ten years: and he died.

15 ¶ And Mahalaleel lived sixty and five years, and begat [1]Jared:

16 And Mahalaleel lived after he begat Jared eight hundred and thirty years, and begat sons and daughters:

17 And all the days of Mahalaleel were eight hundred ninety and five years: and he died.

18 ¶ And Jared lived an hundred sixty and two years, and he begat [a]Enoch:

19 And Jared lived after he begat Enoch eight hundred years, and begat sons and daughters:

20 And all the days of Jared were nine hundred sixty and two years: and he died.

21 ¶ And Enoch lived sixty and five years, and begat [1]Methuselah:

22 And Enoch [a]walked with God after he begat Methuselah three hundred years, and begat sons and daughters:

23 And all the days of Enoch were three hundred sixty and five years:

24 And [a]Enoch walked with God: and he *was* not; for God took him.

25 And Methuselah lived an hundred eighty and seven years, and begat [1]Lamech:

26 And Methuselah lived after he begat Lamech seven hundred eighty and two years, and begat sons and daughters:

27 And all the days of Methuselah were nine hundred sixty and nine years: and he died.

28 ¶ And Lamech lived an hundred eighty and two years, and begat a son:

29 And he called his name [1,2]Noah, saying, This *same* shall comfort us concerning our work and toil of our hands, because of the ground [a]which the LORD hath cursed.

30 And Lamech lived after he begat Noah five hundred ninety and five years, and begat sons and daughters:

31 And all the days of Lamech were seven hundred seventy and seven years: and he died.

32 And Noah was five hundred years old: and Noah begat [a]Shem, Ham, [b]and Japheth.

22 [1]Heb. *whetter*

23 [1]Or, *I would slay a man in my wound* [2]Or, *in my hurt*

24 [a]ver. 15

25 [a]ch. 5:3 [1]Heb. *Sheth* [2]i.e. *Appointed,* or, *Put*

26 [a]ch. 5:6 [b]1 Ki. 18:24; Ps. 116:17; 1 Cor. 1:2 [1]Heb. *Enosh* [2]Or, *to call themselves by the name of the LORD*

5:1 [a]ch. 1:26; Eph. 4:24; Col. 3:10

2 [a]ch. 1:27

3 [a]ch. 4:25

4 [a]1 Chr. 1:1 [b]ch. 1:28

5 [a]ch. 3:19; Heb. 9:27

6 [a]ch. 4:26

9 [1]Heb. *Kenan*

12 [1]Gk. *Maleleel*

15 [1]Heb. *Jered*

18 [a]Jude 14,15

21 [1]Gk. *Mathusala*

22 [a]ch. 6:9 & 17:1; 2 Ki. 20:3; Ps. 16:8; Mic. 6:8; Mal. 2:6

24 [a]2 Ki. 2:11; Heb. 11:5

25 [1]Heb. *Lemech*

29 [a]ch. 3:17 [1]Gk. *Noe;* see Luke 3:36; Heb. 11:7; 1 Pet. 3:20 [2]i.e. *Rest,* or, *Comfort*

32 [a]ch. 6:10 [b]ch. 10:21

The flood

6 AND IT came to pass, [a]when men began to multiply on the face of the earth, and daughters were born unto them,

J 2 That the sons of God saw the daughters of men that they *were* fair; and they [a]took them wives of all which they chose.

C Q N 3 And the LORD said, [a]My spirit shall not always strive with man, [b]for that he also *is* flesh: yet his days shall be an hundred and twenty years.

4 There were giants in the earth in those days; and also after that, when the sons of God came in unto the daughters of men, and they bare *children* to them, the same *became* mighty men which *were* of old, men of renown.

C E 5 ¶ And GOD saw that the wickedness of man *was* great in the earth, and *that* [1]every [a]imagination of the thoughts of his heart *was* only evil [2]continually.

6 And [a]it repented the LORD that he had made man on the earth, and it [b]grieved him at his heart.

7 And the LORD said, I will destroy man whom I have created from the face of the earth; [1]both man, and beast, and the creeping thing, and the fowls of the air; for it repenteth me that I have made them.

8 But Noah [a]found grace in the eyes of the LORD.

9 ¶ These *are* the generations of Noah: [a]Noah was a just man *and* [1]perfect in his generations, *and* Noah [b]walked with God.

10 And Noah begat three sons, [a]Shem, Ham, and Japheth.

11 The earth also was corrupt [a]before God, and the earth was [b]filled with violence.

12 And God [a]looked upon the earth, and, behold, it was corrupt; for all flesh had corrupted his way upon the earth. C

13 And God said unto Noah, [a]The end of all flesh is come before me; for the earth is filled with violence through them; [b]and, behold, I will destroy them [1]with the earth.

14 ¶ Make thee an ark of gopher wood; [1]rooms shalt thou make in the ark, and shalt pitch it within and without with pitch.

15 And this *is the fashion* which thou shalt make it *of:* The length of the ark *shall be* three hundred cubits, the

J ▶ *Ge 6:17* C ▶ *Ne 9:30* Q ▶ *Jdg 16:20*
N ▶ *Lev 26:21* C *Ge 3:3* ◀ ▶ *Ge 6:12*
E ▶ *Nu 32:23*

C *Ge 6:5* ◀ ▶ *Ge 8:21*

6:1 [a]ch. 1:28
2 [a]Deut. 7:3
3 [a]Gal. 5:16; 1 Pet. 3:19 [b]Ps. 78:39
5 [a]ch. 8:21 [1]Or, *the whole imagination:* the Hebrew word signifieth not only *the imagination,* but also *the purposes and desires* [2]Heb. *every day*
6 [a]1 Sam. 15:11, 29; 2 Sam. 24:16; Mal. 3:6; Jas. 1:17 [b]Is. 63:10
7 [1]Heb. *from man unto beast*
8 [a]ch. 19:19; Ex. 33:12; Luke 1:30; Acts 7:46
9 [a]ch. 7:1; Ezek. 14:14,20; Heb. 11:7; 2 Pet. 2:5 [b]ch. 5:22 [1]Or, *upright*
10 [a]ch. 5:32
11 [a]Rom. 2:13 [b]Ezek. 8:17
12 [a]Ps. 14:2 & 53:2,3
13 [a]Jer. 51:13; 1 Pet. 4:7 [b]ver. 17 [1]Or, *from the earth*
14 [1]Heb. *nests*

6:2 The phrase "sons of God" has been interpreted to mean either angels or human beings. Some use references in Job and Jude to apply this phrase to angels, suggesting that angels had sexual relations with human women (see Job 1:6; 2:1; 38:7; Jude 6). While ancient mythologies maintain that intermarriage between angels and human beings took place, Jesus' words refute the idea of angelic marriage (see Mt 22:30; Mk 12:25).

Other scholars believe that these "sons of God" were human beings. They may have been rulers who flaunted their power by having large harems. Others view this phrase figuratively and suggest that these "sons of God" were godly men descended from Seth who married sinful women descended from Cain, thus weakening the influence of the godly and allowing an increase in moral depravity.

6:3 As a result of this intermarriage God pronounced a judgment on humanity. Yet God offered a delay in his judgment for "an hundred and twenty years" giving people time to repent. During this delay, Noah preached repentance to his neighbors (see 1Pe 3:20; 2Pe 2:5), but to no avail.

6:4 The *Nephilim* or "giants" were probably people of great influence. In humanity's eyes they were "mighty men which were of old, men of renown" but in God's eyes they were sinners ripe for judgment. The term *Nephilim* also occurs in Nu 13:33.

6:9 Noah was "a just man, perfect in his generations." Since no one is sinless, this statement about Noah refers to his lifetime example of love and obedience to God in powerful contrast to the wicked lives of his contemporaries. Apparently Noah's was the last remaining family to follow the path of righteousness.

6:14 God commanded Noah to build a boat that measured 450 feet long, 75 feet wide and 45 feet high. Comparable in size to a modern ocean liner, the ark was 1.5 times the length of a football field with a height equal to a four-story building. Within this ark Noah was to stock sufficient food for a one-year journey for his family and for all of the animals God would send to him. Though most species require less food in a confined area than if they were living in the wild, this was still an enormous amount of cargo. Since there are approximately 18,000 known species of animals on earth today, it is quite possible that Noah and his family might have had to care for 40,000 animals on the ark.

breadth of it fifty cubits, and the height of
it thirty cubits.
16 A window shalt thou make to the
ark, and in a cubit shalt thou finish it
above; and the door of the ark shalt thou
set in the side thereof; *with* lower, second, and third *stories* shalt thou make it.
J 17 [a]And, behold, I, even I, do bring a
flood of waters upon the earth, to destroy
all flesh, wherein *is* the breath of life,
from under heaven; *and* every thing that
is in the earth shall die.
18 But with thee will I establish my
covenant; and [a]thou shalt come into the
ark, thou, and thy sons, and thy wife, and
thy sons' wives with thee.
19 And of every living thing of all
flesh, [a]two of every *sort* shalt thou bring
into the ark, to keep *them* alive with
thee; they shall be male and female.
20 Of fowls after their kind, and of
cattle after their kind, of every creeping
thing of the earth after his kind, two of
every *sort* [a]shall come unto thee, to keep
them alive.
21 And take thou unto thee of all food
that is eaten, and thou shalt gather *it* to
thee; and it shall be for food for thee, and
for them.
22 [a]Thus did Noah; [b]according to all
that God commanded him, so did he.
S 7 AND THE LORD said unto Noah,
[a]Come thou and all thy house into
the ark; for [b]thee have I seen righteous
before me in this generation.
2 Of every [a]clean beast thou shalt take
to thee by [l]sevens, the male and his female: [b]and of beasts that *are* not clean by
two, the male and his female.
3 Of fowls also of the air by sevens, the
male and the female; to keep seed alive
upon the face of all the earth.
4 For yet seven days, and I will cause it
to rain upon the earth [a]forty days and
forty nights; and every living substance
that I have made will I [l]destroy from off
the face of the earth.
5 [a]And Noah did according unto all
that the LORD commanded him.
6 And Noah *was* six hundred years old
when the flood of waters was upon the
earth.
7 ¶ [a]And Noah went in, and his sons,
and his wife, and his sons' wives with
him, into the ark, because of the waters
of the flood.
8 Of clean beasts, and of beasts that
are not clean, and of fowls, and of every
thing that creepeth upon the earth,
9 There went in two and two unto
Noah into the ark, the male and the female, as God had commanded Noah.
10 And it came to pass [l]after seven
days, that the waters of the flood were
upon the earth.
11 ¶ In the six hundredth year of
Noah's life, in the second month, the seventeenth day of the month, the same day
were all [a]the fountains of the great deep
broken up, and the [b]windows[l] of heaven
were opened.
12 [a]And the rain was upon the earth
forty days and forty nights.
13 In the selfsame day entered Noah,
and Shem, and Ham, and Japheth, the
sons of Noah, and Noah's wife, and the
three wives of his sons with them, into
the ark;
14 [a]They, and every beast after his
kind, and all the cattle after their kind,
and every creeping thing that creepeth
upon the earth after his kind, and every
fowl after his kind, every bird of every
[l]sort.
15 And they [a]went in unto Noah into
the ark, two and two of all flesh, wherein
is the breath of life.
16 And they that went in, went in
male and female of all flesh, [a]as God had
commanded him: and the LORD shut
him in.
17 [a]And the flood was forty days upon
the earth; and the waters increased, and

17 [a]ch. 7:4,21-23; 2 Pet. 2:5
18 [a]ch. 7:1,7,13; 1 Pet. 3:20; 2 Pet. 2:5
19 [a]ch. 7:8,9,15, 16
20 [a]ch. 7:9,15
22 [a]Heb. 11:7; See Ex. 40:16 [b]ch. 7:5, 9,16
7:1 [a]Mat. 24:38; Luke 17:26; Heb. 11:7; 1 Pet. 3:20; 2 Pet. 2:5 [b]ch. 6:9; Ps. 33:18; Prov. 10:9; 2 Pet. 2:9
2 [a]Lev. ch. 11 [b]Lev. 10:10; Ezek. 44:23 [l]Heb. *seven seven*
4 [a]ver. 12,17 [l]Heb. *blot out*
5 [a]ch. 6:22
7 [a]ver. 1
10 [l]Or, *on the seventh day*
11 [a]ch. 8:2; Prov. 8:28; Ezek. 26:19 [b]ch. 8:2; Ps. 78:23 [l]Or, *floodgates*
12 [a]ver. 4,17
14 [a]ch. 6:19 [l]Heb. *wing*
15 [a]ch. 6:20
16 [a]ver. 2,3
17 [a]ver. 4,12

J *Ge 6:2–4* ◀▶ *Ge 11:6–8*
S *Ge 2:17* ◀▶ *Ge 19:26*

6:17 God prophesied that the coming flood would destroy "all flesh, wherein is the breath of life, from under heaven; and every thing that is in the earth." Yet, in the very next verse, God promises a new covenant with Noah and his descendants. Out of universal death God would bring new life and rebuild the earth.

6:19 The Lord commanded that at least one pair of each species be preserved to restock the earth after the waters receded.

7:2 God further commanded Noah to gather seven of each of the ten species of clean animals (seventy clean animals) that were acceptable for sacrifice and for food (see 8:20; 9:3; Dt 14:1–8).

bare up the ark, and it was lift up above
the earth.
18 And the waters prevailed, and were
increased greatly upon the earth; [a]and
the ark went upon the face of the waters.
19 And the waters prevailed exceedingly upon the earth; and all the high
hills, that *were* under the whole heaven,
were covered.
20 Fifteen cubits upward did the waters prevail; and the mountains were
covered.
21 [a]And all flesh died that moved upon
the earth, both of fowl, and of cattle, and
of beast, and of every creeping thing that
creepeth upon the earth, and every man:
22 All in [a]whose nostrils *was* [l]the
breath of life, of all that *was* in the dry
land, died.
23 And every living substance was destroyed which was upon the face of the
ground, both man, and cattle, and the
creeping things, and the fowl of
the heaven; and they were destroyed
from the earth: and [a]Noah only remained
alive, and they that *were* with him in the
ark.
24 [a]And the waters prevailed upon the
earth an hundred and fifty days.

8 AND GOD [a]remembered Noah, and
every living thing, and all the cattle
that *was* with him in the ark: [b]and God
made a wind to pass over the earth, and
the waters assuaged;
2 [a]The fountains also of the deep and
the windows of heaven were stopped,
and [b]the rain from heaven was restrained;
3 And the waters returned from off the
earth [l]continually: and after the end [a]of
the hundred and fifty days the waters
were abated.
4 And the ark rested in the seventh
month, on the seventeenth day of the
month, upon the mountains of Ararat.
5 And the waters [l]decreased continually until the tenth month: in the tenth
month, on the first *day* of the month,
were the tops of the mountains seen.
6 ¶ And it came to pass at the end of
forty days, that Noah opened [a]the window of the ark which he had made:
7 And he sent forth a raven, which
went forth [l]to and fro, until the waters
were dried up from off the earth.
8 Also he sent forth a dove from him,
to see if the waters were abated from off
the face of the ground;
9 But the dove found no rest for the
sole of her foot, and she returned unto
him into the ark, for the waters *were* on
the face of the whole earth: then he put
forth his hand, and took her, and [l]pulled
her in unto him into the ark.
10 And he stayed yet other seven days;
and again he sent forth the dove out of
the ark;
11 And the dove came in to him in the
evening; and, lo, in her mouth *was* an
olive leaf plucked off: so Noah knew that
the waters were abated from off the
earth.
12 And he stayed yet other seven days;
and sent forth the dove; which returned
not again unto him any more.
13 ¶ And it came to pass in the six
hundredth and first year, in the first
month, the first *day* of the month, the
waters were dried up from off the earth:
and Noah removed the covering of the
ark, and looked, and, behold, the face of
the ground was dry.
14 And in the second month, on the
seven and twentieth day of the month,
was the earth dried.
15 ¶ And God spake unto Noah, A
saying,
16 Go forth of the ark, [a]thou, and thy

18 [a]Ps. 104:26
21 [a]ch. 6:13,17
22 [a]ch. 2:7 [l]Heb. *the breath of the spirit of life*
23 [a]1 Pet. 3:20; 2 Pet. 2:5
24 [a]ch. 8:3 & 8:4 compared with ver. 11 of this chapter
8:1 [a]ch. 19:29; Ex. 2:24; 1 Sam. 1:19; Ps. 106:4 [b]Ex. 14:21
2 [a]ch. 7:11 [b]Job 38:37
3 [a]ch. 7:24 [l]Heb. *in going and returning*
5 [l]Heb. *were in going and decreasing*
6 [a]ch. 6:16
7 [l]Heb. *in going forth and returning*
9 [l]Heb. *caused her to come*
16 [a]ch. 7:13

A *Ge 3:15* ◄► *Ge 9:1–3*

7:24 The 150 days mentioned in this verse are, in round numbers, equivalent to five months. This lengthy time period parallels the five months when the locusts will afflict sinners during the future tribulation (see Rev 9:5).

8:4 Due to its considerable size and weight, the ark rested on the mountain almost immediately after the water started to recede. Though the exact location of Ararat is uncertain, the mountain range is most probably in modern Armenia.

8:15 *Dispensation of Human Government.* After the destruction of the earth in the flood it was necessary for God to establish a new dispensation with the eight people who survived on the ark. This third dispensation instituted a new standard of conduct for Noah and his descendants that involved the creation of various laws to govern humanity and organize society. In addition to the internal workings of conscience, God established new external laws of civil government and rule, ways to punish wrongdoers and the means to worship God completely and correctly. By acting in submission to one another

wife, and thy sons, and thy sons' wives
with thee.
17 Bring forth with thee every living
thing that *is* with thee, of all flesh, *both*
of fowl, and of cattle, and of every creeping thing that creepeth upon the earth;
that they may breed abundantly in the
earth, and [a]be fruitful, and multiply upon
the earth.
18 And Noah went forth, and his sons,
and his wife, and his sons' wives with
him:
19 Every beast, every creeping thing,
and every fowl, *and* whatsoever creepeth
upon the earth, after their [1]kinds, went
forth out of the ark.
20 ¶ And Noah builded an altar unto
the LORD; and took of [a]every clean beast,
and of every clean fowl, and offered burnt
offerings on the altar.
C 21 And the LORD smelled [a]a [1] sweet savour; and the LORD said in his heart, I will
not again [b]curse the ground any more for
man's sake; [2]for the [c]imagination of
man's heart *is* evil from his youth; [d]nei-
ther will I again smite any more every
thing living, as I have done.
22 [a]While [1] the earth remaineth, seed-
time and harvest, and cold and heat, and
summer and winter, and [b]day and night
shall not cease.

C *Ge 6:12* ◀▶ *Dt 9:6*

17 [a]ch. 1:22
19 [1]Heb. *families*
20 [a]Lev. ch. 11
21 [a]Lev. 1:9; Ezek. 20:41; 2 Cor. 2:15; Eph. 5:2 [b]ch. 3:17 & 6:17 [c]ch. 6:5; Job 14:4; Jer. 17:9 [d]ch. 9:11,15 [1]Heb. *a saviour of rest* [2]Or, *though*
22 [a]Is. 54:9 [b]Jer. 33:20,25 [1]Heb. *As yet all the days of the earth*
9:1 [a]ver. 7,19; ch. 1:28 & 10:32
2 [a]ch. 1:28; Hos. 2:18
3 [a]Deut. 12:15 & 14:3,9,11; Acts 10:12,13 [b]ch. 1:29 [c]Rom. 14:14,20; 1 Cor. 10:23,26; Col. 2:16; 1 Tim. 4:3,4
4 [a]Lev. 17:10,11, 14; Deut. 12:23; 1 Sam. 14:33
5 [a]Ex. 21:28 [b]ch. 4:9,10; Ps. 9:12 [c]Acts 17:26
6 [a]Ex. 21:12,14; Lev. 24:17; Mat. 26:52 [b]ch. 1:27
7 [a]ver. 1,19
9 [a]ch. 6:18 [b]Is. 54:9

The covenant with Noah

9 AND GOD blessed Noah and his A
sons, and said unto them, [a]Be fruitful, and multiply, and replenish the earth.
2 [a]And the fear of you and the dread
of you shall be upon every beast of the
earth, and upon every fowl of the air,
upon all that moveth *upon* the earth, and
upon all the fishes of the sea; into your
hand are they delivered.
3 [a]Every moving thing that liveth shall
be meat for you; even as the [b]green herb
have I given you [c]all things.
4 [a]But flesh with the life thereof,
which is the blood thereof, shall ye not
eat.
5 And surely your blood of your lives
will I require; [a]at the hand of every beast
will I require it, and [b]at the hand of man;
at the hand of every [c]man's brother will I
require the life of man.
6 [a]Whoso sheddeth man's blood, by
man shall his blood be shed: [b]for in the
image of God made he man.
7 And you, [a]be ye fruitful, and multi- A
ply; bring forth abundantly in the earth,
and multiply therein.
8 ¶ And God spake unto Noah, and to
his sons with him, saying,
9 And I, [a]behold, I establish [b]my cov-

A *Ge 8:15* ◀▶ *Ge 9:7–10*
A *Ge 9:1–3* ◀▶ *Ge 9:11–17*

---

and to these laws, people would forge a corporate relationship with each other and live in obedience to God. Though people have failed in obedience to this dispensation, humanity's responsibility to obey government will continue until Christ sets up his heavenly kingdom.

The seven dispensations revealed in Scripture are the dispensations of innocence (Ge 1:28), conscience (3:7), human government (8:15), promise (12:1), law (Ex 19:1), the church (Ac 2:1) and the kingdom (Rev 20:4). For further information on the dispensations, see the article on p. 4.

9:8–16 *Noahic Covenant.* This covenant was made between God, Noah, Noah's descendants and all other living creatures on the earth (9:9–10). The Noahic covenant consisted of the following elements:

1. God promised that he would never destroy the earth and "every living thing" (8:21) with a flood again (9:11–16).
2. God reconfirmed the normal order of the earth and its seasons (see 8:22).
3. God reconfirmed his instructions to humanity to repopulate the earth (see 9:1).
4. God instilled a fear of humans in animals (see 9:2).
5. People were allowed to eat animals for food (see 9:3–4). Apparently humans were vegetarians in the garden and before the flood (see 1:29; 9:3). The only restriction to this allowance was the prohibition against eating "flesh with the life thereof, *which is* the blood thereof" (9:4).
6. God instituted basic civil government, including capital punishment for murder and people's accountability to protect human life (see 9:5–6). The NT also confirms God's role in the establishment of government and rulers (see Ro 13:1–5).
7. The covenant was unconditional and perpetual (9:12).
8. The covenant was sealed with the sign of the rainbow (9:13).

NOTE: The seven additional covenants include the Edenic (Ge 2:15–17), Adamic (3:15–19), Abrahamic (15:4ff; 17:1–22), Mosaic (Ex 19:5), Palestinian (Dt 30:1–10), Davidic (2Sa 7:16) and New (Heb 8:8–12). See the article on p. 8.

enant with you, and with your seed after you;

10 [a]And with every living creature that *is* with you, of the fowl, of the cattle, and of every beast of the earth with you; from all that go out of the ark, to every beast of the earth.

A 11 And [a]I will establish my covenant with you; neither shall all flesh be cut off any more by the waters of a flood; neither shall there any more be a flood to destroy the earth.

12 And God said, [a]This *is* the token of the covenant which I make between me and you and every living creature that *is* with you, for perpetual generations:

13 I do set [a]my bow in the cloud, and it shall be for a token of a covenant between me and the earth.

14 And it shall come to pass, when I bring a cloud over the earth, that the bow shall be seen in the cloud:

15 And [a]I will remember my covenant, which *is* between me and you and every living creature of all flesh; and the waters shall no more become a flood to destroy all flesh.

16 And the bow shall be in the cloud; and I will look upon it, that I may remember [a]the everlasting covenant between God and every living creature of all flesh that *is* upon the earth.

17 And God said unto Noah, This *is* the token of the covenant, which I have established between me and all flesh that *is* upon the earth.

18 ¶ And the sons of Noah, that went forth of the ark, were Shem, and Ham, and Japheth: [a]and Ham *is* the father of [l]Canaan.

19 [a]These *are* the three sons of Noah: [b]and of them was the whole earth overspread.

A *Ge 9:7–10* ◀ ▶ *Ge 9:24–27*

10 [a]Ps. 145:9
11 [a]Is. 54:9
12 [a]ch. 17:11
13 [a]Rev. 4:3
15 [a]Lev. 26:42,45
16 [a]ch. 17:13,19; Is. 55:3; Jer. 32:40; Heb. 13:20
18 [a]ch. 10:6 [l]Heb. *Chenaan*
19 [a]ch. 5:32 [b]ch. 10:32; 1 Chr. 1:4
20 [a]ch. 3:19,23 & 4:2; Prov. 12:11
21 [a]Prov. 20:1; 1 Cor. 10:12
23 [a]Ex. 20:12; Gal. 6:1
25 [a]Deut. 27:16; Josh. 9:23,27 [b]Josh. 9:23; 1 Ki. 9:20,21
26 [a]Ps. 144:15; Heb. 11:16 [l]Or, *servant to them*
27 [a]Eph. 2:13,14; & 3:6 [l]Or, *persuade*
10:1 [a]ch. 9:1,7,19
2 [a]1 Chr. 1:5
4 [l]Or, *Rodanim*

Canaan cursed; Shem blessed

20 And Noah began *to be* [a]an husbandman, and he planted a vineyard:

21 And he drank of the wine, [a]and was drunken; and he was uncovered within his tent.

22 And Ham, the father of Canaan, saw the nakedness of his father, and told his two brethren without.

23 [a]And Shem and Japheth took a garment, and laid *it* upon both their shoulders, and went backward, and covered the nakedness of their father; and their faces *were* backward, and they saw not their father's nakedness.

24 And Noah awoke from his wine, A
and knew what his younger son had done unto him.

25 And he said, [a]Cursed *be* Canaan; [b]a servant of servants shall he be unto his brethren.

26 And he said, [a]Blessed *be* the LORD God of Shem; and Canaan shall be [l]his servant.

27 God shall [l]enlarge Japheth, [a]and he shall dwell in the tents of Shem; and Canaan shall be his servant.

28 ¶ And Noah lived after the flood three hundred and fifty years.

29 And all the days of Noah were nine hundred and fifty years: and he died.

Descendants of Noah's sons

10 NOW THESE *are* the generations of the sons of Noah, Shem, Ham, and Japheth: [a]and unto them were sons born after the flood.

2 [a]The sons of Japheth; Gomer, and Magog, and Madai, and Javan, and Tubal, and Meshech, and Tiras.

3 And the sons of Gomer; Ashkenaz, and Riphath, and Togarmah.

4 And the sons of Javan; Elishah, and Tarshish, Kittim, and [l]Dodanim.

A *Ge 9:11–17* ◀ ▶ *Ge 12:1–3*

9:25–27 God made some direct promises to Noah's sons. Canaan and his descendants, who were Ham's offspring, would be servants of their brothers because of Ham's disrespectful actions toward his father (9:25–26). Historically, even before the Israelites occupied the promised land, the Canaanites were subject and inferior to the larger powers of Egypt and Assyria thus fulfilling this curse on Ham's (Canaan's) descendants.

On the other hand, Shem and Japheth's respect for their father would be rewarded. Blessings would be accorded to Shem. The Messianic line that began with Seth, Enoch and Noah before the flood would now run from Shem through Abraham and on to Jesus Christ (see 11:10–27; Mt 1:2–16). Japheth would also share in these blessings and would have his territories enlarged (9:27). It is noteworthy that the descendants of Japheth include the Medes and the Greeks, an obvious fulfillment of this prophecy as well.

5 By these were [a]the isles of the Gentiles divided in their lands; every one after his tongue, after their families, in
their nations.
6 ¶ [a]And the sons of Ham; Cush, and
Mizraim, and Phut, and Canaan.
7 And the sons of Cush; Seba, and Havilah, and Sabtah, and Raamah, and Sabtecha: and the sons of Raamah; Sheba, and
Dedan.
8 And Cush begat Nimrod: he began to
be a mighty one in the earth.
9 He was a mighty [a]hunter [b]before the
LORD: wherefore it is said, Even as Nimrod the mighty hunter before the LORD.
10 [a]And the beginning of his kingdom
was [1]Babel, and Erech, and Accad, and
Calneh, in the land of Shinar.
11 Out of that land [1]went forth Asshur, and builded Nineveh, and [2]the city
Rehoboth, and Calah,
12 And Resen between Nineveh and
Calah: the same *is* a great city.
13 And Mizraim begat Ludim, and
Anamim, and Lehabim, and Naphtuhim,
14 And Pathrusim, and Casluhim,
([a]out of whom came Philistim,) and
Caphtorim.
15 ¶ And Canaan begat [1]Sidon his
firstborn, and Heth,
16 And the Jebusite, and the Amorite,
and the Girgasite,
17 And the Hivite, and the Arkite, and
the Sinite,
18 And the Arvadite, and the Zemarite, and the Hamathite: and afterward
were the families of the Canaanites
spread abroad.
19 [a]And the border of the Canaanites
was from Sidon, as thou comest to Gerar,
unto [1]Gaza; as thou goest, unto Sodom,
and Gomorrah, and Admah, and Zeboim,
even unto Lasha.
20 These *are* the sons of Ham, after
their families, after their tongues, in their
countries, *and* in their nations.
21 ¶ Unto Shem also, the father of all
the children of Eber, the brother of Japheth the elder, even to him were *children* born.
22 The [a]children of Shem; Elam, and

5 [a] Ps. 72:10; Jer. 2:10 & 25:22
6 [a] 1 Chr. 1:8
9 [a] Jer. 16:16; Mic. 7:2 [b] ch. 6:11
10 [a] Mic. 5:6 [1] Gk. *Babylon*
11 [1] Or, *he went out into Assyria* [2] Or, *the streets of the city*
14 [a] 1 Chr. 1:12
15 [1] Heb. *Tzidon*
19 [a] ch. 13:12,14, 15,17 & 15:18-21 [1] Heb. *Azzah*
22 [a] 1 Chr. 1:17

Nations Descended from Noah's Sons

Ge 10:1

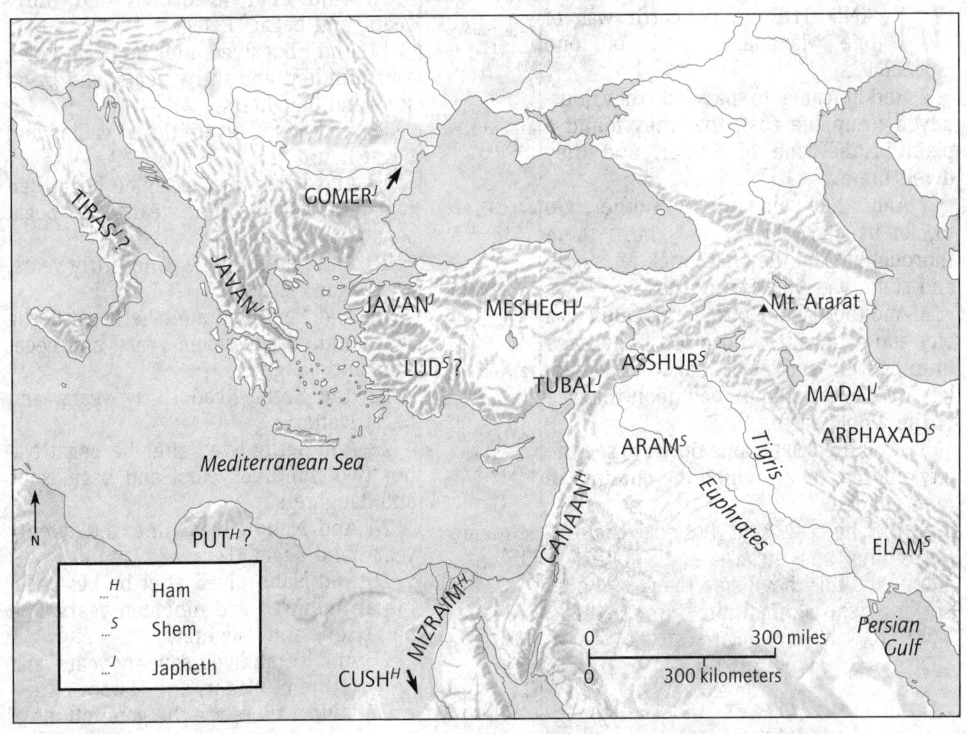

Asshur, and [1]Arphaxad, and Lud, and
Aram.
23 And the children of Aram; Uz, and
Hul, and Gether, and Mash.
24 And Arphaxad begat [a]Salah;[1] and
Salah begat Eber.
25 [a]And unto Eber were born two
sons: the name of one *was* [1]Peleg; for in
his days was the earth divided; and his
brother's name *was* Joktan.
26 And Joktan begat Almodad, and
Sheleph, and Hazarmaveth, and Jerah,
27 And Hadoram, and Uzal, and
Diklah,
28 And Obal, and Abimael, and Sheba,
29 And Ophir, and Havilah, and Jobab:
all these *were* the sons of Joktan.
30 And their dwelling was from Mesha, as thou goest unto Sephar a mount of
the east.
31 These *are* the sons of Shem, after
their families, after their tongues, in their
lands, after their nations.
32 [a]These *are* the families of the sons
of Noah, after their generations, in their
nations: [b]and by these were the nations
divided in the earth after the flood.

The tower of Babel

11 AND THE whole earth was of
one [1]language, and of one
[2]speech.
2 And it came to pass, as they journeyed [1]from the east, that they found a
plain in the land of Shinar; and they
dwelt there.
3 And [1]they said one to another, Go
to, let us make brick, and [2]burn them
thoroughly. And they had brick for stone,
and slime had they for mortar.
4 And they said, Go to, let us build us a
city and a tower, [a]whose top *may reach*
unto heaven; and let us make us a name,
lest we be scattered abroad upon the face
of the whole earth.
5 [a]And the LORD came down to see the
city and the tower, which the children of
men builded.
J 6 And the LORD said, Behold, [a]the people *is* one, and they have all [b]one language; and this they begin to do: and now
nothing will be restrained from them,
which they have [c]imagined to do.
7 Go to, [a]let us go down, and there
confound their language, that they may
[b]not understand one another's speech.
8 So [a]the LORD scattered them abroad
from thence [b]upon the face of all the
earth: and they left off to build the city.
9 Therefore is the name of it called
[1]Babel; [a]because the LORD did there confound the language of all the earth: and
from thence did the LORD scatter them
abroad upon the face of all the earth.

The descendants of Shem

10 ¶ [a]These *are* the generations of
Shem: Shem *was* an hundred years old,
and begat Arphaxad two years after the
flood:
11 And Shem lived after he begat Arphaxad five hundred years, and begat
sons and daughters.
12 And Arphaxad lived five and thirty
years, [a]and begat Salah:
13 And Arphaxad lived after he begat
Salah four hundred and three years, and
begat sons and daughters.
14 And Salah lived thirty years, and
begat Eber:
15 And Salah lived after he begat Eber
four hundred and three years, and begat
sons and daughters.
16 [a]And Eber lived four and thirty
years, and begat [b]Peleg:
17 And Eber lived after he begat Peleg
four hundred and thirty years, and begat
sons and daughters.
18 And Peleg lived thirty years, and
begat Reu:
19 And Peleg lived after he begat Reu
two hundred and nine years, and begat
sons and daughters.
20 And Reu lived two and thirty years,
and begat [a]Serug:
21 And Reu lived after he begat Serug
two hundred and seven years, and begat
sons and daughters.
22 And Serug lived thirty years, and
begat Nahor:
23 And Serug lived after he begat Nahor two hundred years, and begat sons
and daughters.
24 And Nahor lived nine and twenty
years, and begat [a]Terah:
25 And Nahor lived after he begat Terah an hundred and nineteen years, and
begat sons and daughters.
26 And Terah lived seventy years, and
[a]begat Abram, Nahor, and Haran.
27 ¶ Now these *are* the generations of

22 [1]Heb. *Arpachshad*
24 [a]ch. 11:12 [1]Heb. *Shelah*
25 [a]1 Chr. 1:19 [1]i.e. *Division*
32 [a]ver. 1 [b]ch. 9:19
11:1 [1]Heb. *lip* [2]Heb. *words*
2 [1]Or, *eastward*
3 [1]Heb. *a man said to his neighbour* [2]Heb. *burn them to a burning*
4 [a]Deut. 1:28
5 [a]ch. 18:21
6 [a]ch. 9:19; Acts 17:26 [b]ver. 1 [c]Ps. 2:1
7 [a]ch. 1:26 [b]ch. 42:23; 1 Cor. 14:2, 11
8 [a]Luke 1:51 [b]ch. 10:25,32
9 [a]1 Cor. 14:23 [1]i.e. *Confusion*
10 [a]ch. 10:22; 1 Chr. 1:17
12 [a]See Luke 3:36
16 [a]1 Chr. 1:19 [b]Called, Luke 3:35, *Phalec*
20 [a]Luke 3:35, *Saruch*
24 [a]Luke 3:34, *Thara*
26 [a]Josh. 24:2; 1 Chr. 1:26

J Ge 6:17 ◄► *Ge 40:12–13*

Terah: Terah begat Abram, Nahor, and Haran; and Haran begat Lot.

28 And Haran died before his father Terah in the land of his nativity, in Ur of the Chaldees.

29 And Abram and Nahor took them wives: the name of Abram's wife *was* [a]Sarai; and the name of Nahor's wife, [b]Milcah, the daughter of Haran, the father of Milcah, and the father of Iscah.

30 But [a]Sarai was barren; she *had* no child.

31 And Terah [a]took Abram his son, and Lot the son of Haran his son's son, and Sarai his daughter-in-law, his son Abram's wife; and they went forth with them from [b]Ur of the Chaldees, to go into [c]the land of Canaan; and they came unto Haran, and dwelt there.

32 And the days of Terah were two hundred and five years: and Terah died in Haran.

The call of Abram

A U 12 NOW THE [a]LORD had said unto Abram, Get thee out of thy country, and from thy kindred, and from thy father's house, unto a land that I will show thee:

2 [a]And I will make of thee a great nation, [b]and I will bless thee, and make thy name great; [c]and thou shalt be a blessing:

3 [a]And I will bless them that bless thee, and curse him that curseth thee: [b]and in thee shall all families of the earth be blessed.

4 So Abram departed, as the LORD had spoken unto him; and Lot went with him: and Abram *was* seventy and five years old when he departed out of Haran.

5 And Abram took Sarai his wife, and Lot his brother's son, and all their substance that they had gathered, and [a]the souls that they had gotten [b]in Haran; and they went forth to go into the land of Canaan; and into the land of Canaan they came.

6 ¶ And Abram [a]passed through the land unto the place of Sichem, [b]unto the plain of Moreh. [c]And the Canaanite *was* then in the land.

7 [a]And the LORD appeared unto Abram, and said, [b]Unto thy seed will I give this land: and there builded he an [c]altar unto the LORD, who appeared unto him. A

8 And he removed from thence unto a mountain on the east of Beth-el, and pitched his tent, *having* Beth-el on the west, and Hai on the east: and there he builded an altar unto the LORD, and [a]called upon the name of the LORD.

9 And Abram journeyed, [a]going[/] on still toward the south.

Abram goes to Egypt

10 ¶ And there was [a]a famine in the land: and Abram [b]went down into Egypt to sojourn there; for the famine *was* [c]grievous in the land.

11 And it came to pass, when he was come near to enter into Egypt, that he said unto Sarai his wife, Behold now, I know that thou *art* [a]a fair woman to look upon:

12 Therefore it shall come to pass, when the Egyptians shall see thee, that they shall say, This *is* his wife: and they

29 [a]ch. 17:15 & 20:12 [b]ch. 22:20
30 [a]ch. 16:1,2; Luke 1:36
31 [a]ch. 12:1 [b]Neh. 9:7; Acts 7:4 [c]ch. 10:19
12:1 [a]Acts 7:3; Heb. 11:8
2 [a]ch. 17:6 & 18:18; Deut. 26:5; 1 Ki. 3:8 [b]ch. 24:35 [c]ch. 28:4; Gal. 3:14
3 [a]ch. 27:29; Ex. 23:22; Num. 24:9 [b]ch. 18:18 & 22:18 & 26:4; Ps. 72:17; Acts 3:25; Gal. 3:8
5 [a]ch. 14:14 [b]ch. 11:31
6 [a]Heb. 11:9 [b]Deut. 11:30; Judg. 7:1 [c]ch. 10:18,19
7 [a]ch. 17:1 [b]ch. 13:15 & 17:8; Ps. 105:9,11 [c]ch. 13:4
8 [a]ch. 13:4
9 [a]ch. 13:3 [/]Heb. *in going and journeying*
10 [a]ch. 26:1 [b]Ps. 105:13 [c]ch. 43:1
11 [a]ver. 14; ch. 26:7

A *Ge 9:24–27* ◀ ▶ *Ge 12:7*
U ▶ *Ge 22:15–18*
A *Ge 12:1–3* ◀ ▶ *Ge 13:14–16*

12:1 *Dispensation of Promise.* In this time period God designated Abram and his descendants as the people who would be used in the fulfillment of God's plan of salvation. The dispensation of promise tested Abram and his descendants in their faithfulness and obedience to God. God unconditionally promised that individual obedience would be rewarded with individual blessing (see 12:2; 15:15; 22:18; 26:2–5); the promised land would be their eternal inheritance (see 17:7–8); they would be a great nation (see 12:2); and those nations and individuals who blessed Abram and his offspring would receive a blessing in return (see 12:3). This latter promise has seen fulfillment in the rise and fall of many empires. Anti-Semitism has brought many individuals and nations under God's curse.

The seven dispensations revealed in Scripture are the dispensations of innocence (Ge 1:28), conscience (3:7), human government (8:15), promise (12:1), law (Ex 19:1), the church (Ac 2:1) and the kingdom (Rev 20:4). For further information on the dispensations, see the article on p. 4.

12:7 This verse records a theophany—a visible manifestation of God's presence to someone. Whether in angelic or human form, the Lord frequently appeared to Abram and others, but not in all his glory (see Ex 33:18–20; Jn 1:18). We will not be given that opportunity until Christ's second coming (see 1Jn 3:2).

[a]will kill me, but they will save thee alive.

13 [a]Say, I pray thee, thou *art* my sister: that it may be well with me for thy sake; and my soul shall live because of thee.

14 ¶ And it came to pass, that, when Abram was come into Egypt, the Egyptians beheld the woman that she *was* very fair.

15 The princes also of Pharaoh saw her, and commended her before Pharaoh: and the woman was taken into Pharaoh's house.

16 And he [a]entreated Abram well for her sake: and he had sheep, and oxen, and he asses, and menservants, and maidservants, and she asses, and camels.

D 17 And the LORD [a]plagued Pharaoh and his house with great plagues because of Sarai Abram's wife.

18 And Pharaoh called Abram, and said, [a]What *is* this *that* thou hast done unto me? why didst thou not tell me that she *was* thy wife?

19 Why saidst thou, She *is* my sister?

D ► *Ge 19:11*

12 [a]ch. 20:11 & 26:7
13 [a]ch. 20:5,13
16 [a]ch. 20:14
17 [a]ch. 20:18; 1 Chr. 16:21; Ps. 105:14
18 [a]ch. 20:9 & 26:10
20 [a]Prov. 21:1
13:1 [a]ch. 12:9
2 [a]ch. 24:35; Ps. 112:3; Prov. 10:22
3 [a]ch. 12:8,9
4 [a]ch. 12:7,8 [b]Ps. 116:17
6 [a]ch. 36:7

so I might have taken her to me to wife: now therefore behold thy wife, take *her*, and go thy way.

20 [a]And Pharaoh commanded *his* men concerning him: and they sent him away, and his wife, and all that he had.

Abram and Lot part

13 AND ABRAM went up out of Egypt, he, and his wife, and all that he had, and Lot with him, [a]into the south.

2 [a]And Abram *was* very rich in cattle, in silver, and in gold.

3 And he went on his journeys [a]from the south even to Beth-el, unto the place where his tent had been at the beginning, between Beth-el and Hai;

4 Unto the [a]place of the altar, which he had made there at the first: and there Abram [b]called on the name of the LORD.

5 ¶ And Lot also, which went with Abram, had flocks, and herds, and tents.

6 And [a]the land was not able to bear them, that they might dwell together: for their substance was great, so that they could not dwell together.

Extent of Land Promised to Abraham

Ge 13:14–17; 15:18–21

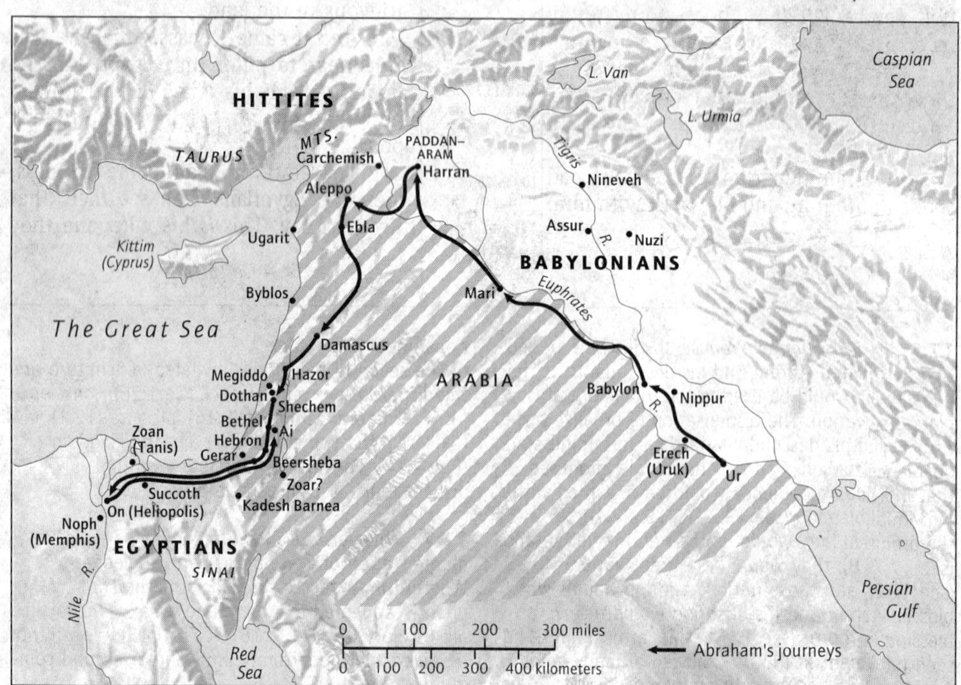

7 And there was [a]a strife between the herdmen of Abram's cattle and the herdmen of Lot's cattle: [b]and the Canaanite and the Perizzite dwelled then in the land.

8 And Abram said unto Lot, [a]Let there be no strife, I pray thee, between me and thee, and between my herdmen and thy herdmen; for we *be* [b]brethren.[1]

9 [a]*Is* not the whole land before thee? separate thyself, I pray thee, from me: [b]if *thou wilt take* the left hand, then I will go to the right; or if *thou depart* to the right hand, then I will go to the left.

10 And Lot lifted up his eyes, and beheld all [a]the plain of Jordan, that it *was* well watered every where, before the LORD [b]destroyed Sodom and Gomorrah, [c]*even* as the garden of the LORD, like the land of Egypt, as thou comest unto [d]Zoar.

11 Then Lot chose him all the plain of Jordan; and Lot journeyed east: and they separated themselves the one from the other.

12 Abram dwelled in the land of Canaan, and Lot [a]dwelled in the cities of the plain, and [b]pitched *his* tent toward Sodom.

13 But the men of Sodom [a]*were* wicked and [b]sinners before the LORD exceedingly.

A 14 ¶ And the LORD said unto Abram, after that Lot [a]was separated from him, Lift up now thine eyes, and look from the place where thou art [b]northward, and southward, and eastward, and westward:

I 15 For all the land which thou seest, [a]to thee will I give it, and [b]to thy seed for ever.

16 And [a]I will make thy seed as the dust of the earth: so that if a man can number the dust of the earth, *then* shall thy seed also be numbered.

17 Arise, walk through the land in the length of it and in the breadth of it; for I will give it unto thee.

18 Then Abram removed *his* tent, and came and [a]dwelt in the [1]plain of Mamre, [b]which *is* in Hebron, and built there an altar unto the LORD.

A *Ge 12:7* ◀ ▶ *Ge 14:18–20*
I ▶ *Ge 17:7–8*

7 [a]ch. 26:20 [b]ch. 12:6
8 [a]1 Cor. 6:7 [b]See ch. 11:27,31 [1]Heb. *men brethren*
9 [a]ch. 20:15 & 34:10 [b]Rom. 12:18
10 [a]ch. 19:17 [b]ch. 19:24 [c]ch. 2:10; Is. 51:3 [d]ch. 14:2,8 & 19:22
12 [a]ch. 19:29 [b]ch. 14:12 & 19:1
13 [a]ch. 18:20; 2 Pet. 2:7 [b]ch. 6:11
14 [a]ver. 11 [b]ch. 28:14
15 [a]ch. 12:7 & 15:18; Deut. 34:4; Acts 7:5 [b]2 Chr. 20:7; Ps. 37:22
16 [a]ch. 22:17; Ex. 32:13
18 [a]ch. 14:13 [b]ch. 35:27 [1]Heb. *plains*
14:1 [a]ch. 10:10 & 11:2 [b]Is. 11:11
2 [a]Deut. 29:23 [b]ch. 19:22
3 [a]Num. 34:12; Deut. 3:17; Josh. 3:16
4 [a]ch. 9:26
5 [a]ch. 15:20 [b]Deut. 2:20 [c]Deut. 2:10 [1]Or, *The plain of Kiriathaim*
6 [a]Deut. 2:12,22 [1]Or, *The plain of Paran*
7 [a]2 Chr. 20:2
10 [a]ch. 11:3 [b]ch. 19:17,30
11 [a]ver. 16,21

The wars of the kings

14 AND IT came to pass in the days of Amraphel king [a]of Shinar, Arioch king of Ellasar, Chedorlaomer king of [b]Elam, and Tidal king of nations;

2 *That these* made war with Bera king of Sodom, and with Birsha king of Gomorrah, Shinab king of [a]Admah, and Shemeber king of Zeboiim, and the king of Bela, which is [b]Zoar.

3 All these were joined together in the vale of Siddim, [a]which is the salt sea.

4 Twelve years [a]they served Chedorlaomer, and in the thirteenth year they rebelled.

5 And in the fourteenth year came Chedorlaomer, and the kings that *were* with him, and smote [a]the Rephaims in Ashteroth Karnaim, and [b]the Zuzims in Ham, [c]and the Emims in [1]Shaveh Kiriathaim,

6 [a]And the Horites in their mount Seir, unto [1]El-paran, which *is* by the wilderness.

7 And they returned, and came to En-mishpat, which *is* Kadesh, and smote all the country of the Amalekites, and also the Amorites, that dwelt [a]in Hazezon-tamar.

8 And there went out the king of Sodom, and the king of Gomorrah, and the king of Admah, and the king of Zeboiim, and the king of Bela (the same *is* Zoar;) and they joined battle with them in the vale of Siddim;

9 With Chedorlaomer the king of Elam, and with Tidal king of nations, and Amraphel king of Shinar, and Arioch king of Ellasar; four kings with five.

10 And the vale of Siddim *was full of* [a]slimepits; and the kings of Sodom and Gomorrah fled, and fell there; and they that remained fled [b]to the mountain.

11 And they took [a]all the goods of

13:14–16 In this passage God promised Abram that his descendants would possess Canaan forever. God's promise cannot be broken. Despite three major dispersions and exiles of the Jews from the promised land, God has always brought his people back to the land—and he always will (see 28:15; Ex 6:8; Jer 24:6; Eze 34:13; Am 9:14–15). In addition, the Lord promised that Abram would have "seed as the dust of the earth" (13:16) meaning Abram's descendants would be beyond numbering. This prophecy will not be completely fulfilled until the Messianic kingdom of Christ.

Sodom and Gomorrah, and all their victuals, and went their way.

12 And they took Lot, Abram's [a]brother's son, [b]who dwelt in Sodom, and his goods, and departed.

13 ¶ And there came one that had escaped, and told Abram the Hebrew; for [a]he dwelt in the plain of Mamre the Amorite, brother of Eshcol, and brother of Aner: [b]and these *were* confederate with Abram.

14 And when Abram heard that [a]his brother was taken captive, he [1]armed his [2]trained *servants,* [b]born in his own house, three hundred and eighteen, and pursued *them* [c]unto Dan.

15 And he divided himself against them, he and his servants, by night, and [a]smote them, and pursued them unto Hobah, which *is* on the left hand of Damascus.

16 And he brought back all the goods, and also brought again his brother Lot, and his goods, and the women also, and the people.

Melchizedek blesses Abram

17 ¶ And the king of Sodom [a]went out to meet him [b]after his return from the slaughter of Chedorlaomer, and of the kings that *were* with him, at the valley of Shaveh, which *is* the [c]king's dale.

A 18 And [a]Melchizedek king of Salem brought forth bread and wine: and he *was* [b]the priest of [c]the most high God.

19 And he blessed him, and said,

A *Ge 13:14–16* ◀ ▶ *Ge 15:4–5*

12 [a]ch. 12:5 [b]ch. 13:12
13 [a]ch. 13:18 [b]ver. 24
14 [a]ch. 13:8 [b]ch. 15:3 [c]Deut. 34:1 [1]Or, *led forth* [2]Or, *instructed*
15 [a]Is. 41:2,3
17 [a]1 Sam. 18:6 [b]Heb. 7:1 [c]2 Sam. 18:18
18 [a]Heb. 7:1 [b]Ps. 110:4; Heb. 5:6 [c]Acts 16:17
19 [a]Ruth 3:10 [b]ver. 22
20 [a]ch. 24:27 [b]Heb. 7:4
21 [1]Heb. *souls*
22 [a]Dan. 12:7 [b]ver. 19
23 [a]See Esth. 9:15, 16
15:1 [a]Dan. 10:1 [b]ch. 26:24; Dan. 10:12 [c]Ps. 3:3 & 84:11 & 91:4 [d]Prov. 11:18
2 [a]Acts 7:5
3 [a]ch. 14:14

[a]Blessed *be* Abram of the most high God, [b]possessor of heaven and earth:

20 And [a]blessed be the most high God, which hath delivered thine enemies into thy hand. And he gave him tithes [b]of all.

21 And the king of Sodom said unto Abram, Give me the [1]persons, and take the goods to thyself.

22 And Abram said to the king of Sodom, I [a]have lift up mine hand unto the LORD, the most high God, [b]the possessor of heaven and earth,

23 That [a]I will not *take* from a thread even to a shoelatchet, and that I will not take any thing that *is* thine, lest thou shouldest say, I have made Abram rich:

24 Save only that which the young men have eaten, and the portion of the men which went with me, Aner, Eshcol, and Mamre; let them take their portion.

The covenant with Abram

15 AFTER THESE things the word of the LORD came unto Abram [a]in a vision, saying, [b]Fear not, Abram: I *am* thy [c]shield, *and* thy exceeding [d]great reward. K L W

2 And Abram said, Lord GOD, what wilt thou give me, [a]seeing I go childless, and the steward of my house *is* this Eliezer of Damascus?

3 And Abram said, Behold, to me thou hast given no seed: and, lo, [a]one born in my house is mine heir.

4 And, behold, the word of the LORD A

K ▶ *Ge 18:14* L ▶ *Ge 26:28*
W ▶ *Dt 1:21*
A *Ge 14:18–20* ◀ ▶ *Ge 15:13–16*

14:18 This verse introduces us to Melchizedek, the king of Salem, a shortened form of "Jerusalem" (see Ps 76:2). Evidently the residents of this city worshiped "the most high God" under the leadership of this king-priest. Because of his double role in leadership, Melchizedek has been described as a type of Christ. (A "type" is an OT event, person, teaching or symbol that foreshadows something to come in the NT.) The psalmist referred to the Messiah as "a priest for ever after the order of Melchizedek" (Ps 110:4) while the writer of the book of Hebrews draws a parallel between Melchizedek's kingly priesthood and Christ's eternal high priesthood (see Heb 5:5–6; 6:20; 7:1ff).

15:4 *Abrahamic Covenant.* The Abrahamic covenant is closely allied to the dispensation of promise because of the similarity of their conditions. This covenant revealed God's sovereign plan to bless the world through the seed of Abraham:

1. God promised to make Abram a great nation with innumerable offspring (see 12:2; 13:16; 15:5; 17:6). Ultimately, all who belong to Christ are Abram's offspring too (see Gal 3:29).
2. God promised to personally bless Abram both spiritually and materially (see 15:6, 18; 24:34–35).
3. Abram would receive honor and be a blessing to others (see 12:2; Ro 4:1–22). This promise foreshadows the coming of Christ and the blessing of eternal life made available to all who believe on him.
4. This covenant was unconditional and its ultimate fulfillment rested on God's promise and power rather than on Israel's faithfulness.
5. The sign of this covenant was circumcision (see 17:1–21).

NOTE: The seven additional covenants include the Edenic (Ge 2:15–17), Adamic (3:15–19), Noahic

came unto him, saying, This shall not be
thine heir; but he that [a]shall come forth
out of thine own bowels shall be thine
heir.
5 And he brought him forth abroad,
and said, Look now toward heaven, and
[a]tell the [b]stars, if thou be able to number
them: and he said unto him, [c]So shall thy
seed be.
F 6 And he [a]believed in the LORD; and he
[b]counted it to him for righteousness.
7 And he said unto him, I *am* the LORD
that [a]brought thee out of [b]Ur of the Chaldees, [c]to give thee this land to inherit it.
8 And he said, Lord GOD, [a]whereby
shall I know that I shall inherit it?
9 And he said unto him, Take me an
heifer of three years old, and a she goat of
three years old, and a ram of three years
old, and a turtledove, and a young
pigeon.
10 And he took unto him all these, and
[a]divided them in the midst, and laid each
piece one against another: but [b]the birds
divided he not.
11 And when the fowls came down
upon the carcases, Abram drove them
away.
12 And when the sun was going down,
[a]a deep sleep fell upon Abram; and, lo, an
horror of great darkness fell upon him.
A 13 And he said unto Abram, Know of a
surety [a]that thy seed shall be a stranger
in a land *that is* not theirs, and shall serve
them; and [b]they shall afflict them four
hundred years;
P 14 And also that nation, whom they
shall serve, [a]will I judge: and afterward

F ▶ *2Ch 20:20*
A *Ge 15:4–5* ◀ ▶ *Ge 15:18–21*
P ▶ *Ge 24:1*

4 [a]2 Sam. 7:12
5 [a]Ps. 147:4 [b]Jer. 33:22 [c]Ex. 32:13; Heb. 11:12
6 [a]Rom. 4:3,9,22; Gal. 3:6 [b]Ps. 106:31
7 [a]ch. 12:1 [b]ch. 11:28,31 [c]Ps. 105:42,44
8 [a]See ch. 24:13, 14; 1 Sam. 14:9,10
10 [a]Jer. 34:18 [b]Lev. 1:17
12 [a]ch. 2:21
13 [a]Ex. 1:11; Acts 7:6 [b]Ex. 12:40
14 [a]Ex. 6:6 [b]Ex. 12:36
15 [a]Job 5:26 [b]Acts 13:36 [c]ch. 25:8
16 [a]Ex. 12:41 [b]1 Ki. 21:26 [c]Mat. 23:32
17 [1]Heb. *a lamp of fire*
18 [a]ch. 24:7 [b]ch. 12:7; Ex. 23:31; Num. 34:3; Deut. 11:24; Josh. 1:4
16:1 [a]ch. 15:2,3 [b]ch. 21:9 [c]Gal. 4:24
2 [a]ch. 30:3 [b]ch. 20:18 [c]ch. 30:3,9 [d]ch. 3:17 [1]Heb. *be builded by her*
3 [a]ch. 12:5

[b]shall they come out with great substance.
15 And [a]thou shalt go [b]to thy fathers Q
in peace; [c]thou shalt be buried in a good H
old age.
16 But [a]in the fourth generation they
shall come hither again: for the iniquity
[b]of the Amorites [c]*is* not yet full.
17 And it came to pass, that, when the
sun went down, and it was dark, behold a
smoking furnace, and [1]a burning lamp
that passed between those pieces.
18 In the same day the LORD [a]made a A
covenant with Abram, saying, [b]Unto thy
seed have I given this land, from the river
of Egypt unto the great river, the river
Euphrates:
19 The Kenites, and the Kenizzites,
and the Kadmonites,
20 And the Hittites, and the Perizzites,
and the Rephaims,
21 And the Amorites, and the Canaanites, and the Girgashites, and the Jebusites.

Hagar and Ishmael

16 NOW SARAI Abram's wife [a]bare
him no children: and she had an
handmaid, [b]an Egyptian, whose name
was [c]Hagar.
2 [a]And Sarai said unto Abram, Behold
now, the LORD [b]hath restrained me from
bearing: I pray thee, [c]go in unto my maid;
it may be that I may [1]obtain children by
her. And Abram [d]hearkened to the voice
of Sarai.
3 And Sarai Abram's wife took Hagar
her maid the Egyptian, after Abram [a]had
dwelt ten years in the land of Canaan,

Q ▶ *Ge 25:8* **H** ▶ *Ex 15:26*
A *Ge 15:13–16* ◀ ▶ *Ge 16:10–12*

(9:8ff), Mosaic (Ex 19:5), Palestinian (Dt 30:1–10), Davidic (2Sa 7:16) and New (Heb 8:8–12).

15:5 God declared to Abram that his descendants would be as numerous as the stars of the heavens. More than 8,000 stars are visible on a clear night in Israel, and we know that there are literally thousands of galaxies containing millions of stars each. Clearly this promise to Abram will not be completely fulfilled until Christ's kingdom comes, though it was initially fulfilled in Egypt (see Ex 1:7; Dt 1:10; Heb 11:13).

15:13–16 In this prophetic passage, the Lord predicts the slavery of the Israelites in Egypt while at the same time promising their deliverance and return to the promised land.

15:18–21 Ten Canaanite tribes occupied the land God promised to Abram in this passage. The Israelites only ruled all of this land briefly under the reigns of Solomon and Jeroboam II (see 1Ki 8:65; 2Ki 14:25). Even now, portions of the promised land remain outside Israeli control. Several prophecies in Scripture indicate that Israel will be exiled from the land but will ultimately regain possession of it (see Ge 15:13–16; Dt 28:62–65; 30:1–3). Twice before in history the Israelites have been exiled to foreign lands, but each time they have returned to the promised land as prophesied. The land will be completely theirs again when Christ returns (see Dt 30:3; Jer 23:5–8; Eze 37:21–25; Acts 15:14–17).

and gave her to her husband Abram to be his wife.

4 ¶ And he went in unto Hagar, and she conceived: and when she saw that she had conceived, her mistress was [a]despised in her eyes.

5 And Sarai said unto Abram, My wrong *be* upon thee: I have given my maid into thy bosom; and when she saw that she had conceived, I was despised in her eyes: [a]the LORD judge between me and thee.

6 [a]But Abram said unto Sarai, Behold, thy maid *is* in thy hand; do to her [1]as it pleaseth thee. And when Sarai [2]dealt hardly with her, [b]she fled from her face.

7 ¶ And the angel of the LORD found her by a fountain of water in the wilderness, [a]by the fountain in the way to [b]Shur.

8 And he said, Hagar, Sarai's maid, whence camest thou? and whither wilt thou go? And she said, I flee from the face of my mistress Sarai.

9 And the angel of the LORD said unto her, Return to thy mistress, and [a]submit thyself under her hands.

A 10 And the angel of the LORD said unto her, [a]I will multiply thy seed exceedingly, that it shall not be numbered for multitude.

11 And the angel of the LORD said unto her, Behold, thou *art* with child, and shalt bear a son, [a]and shalt call his name [1]Ishmael; because the LORD hath heard thy affliction.

12 [a]And he will be a wild man; his hand *will be* against every man, and every man's hand against him; [b]and he shall dwell in the presence of all his brethren.

13 And she called the name of the LORD that spake unto her, Thou God seest me: for she said, Have I also here looked after him [a]that seeth me?

14 Wherefore the well was called [a]Beer-lahai-roi;[1] behold, *it is* [b]between Kadesh and Bered.

15 ¶ And [a]Hagar bare Abram a son: and Abram called his son's name, which Hagar bare, Ishmael.

16 And Abram *was* fourscore and six years old, when Hagar bare Ishmael to Abram.

The covenant of circumcision

17 AND WHEN Abram was ninety years old and nine, the LORD appeared to Abram, and said unto him, [a]I *am* the Almighty God; [b]walk before me, and be thou [c]perfect.[1]

2 And I will make my covenant between me and thee, and [a]will multiply thee exceedingly. A

3 And Abram fell on his face: and God talked with him, saying,

4 As for me, behold, my covenant *is* with thee, and thou shalt be [a]a father of [1]many nations. O

5 Neither shall thy name any more be called Abram, but [a]thy name shall be [1]Abraham; [b]for a father of many nations have I made thee.

6 And I will make thee exceeding fruitful, and I will make [a]nations of thee, and [b]kings shall come out of thee.

7 And I will [a]establish my covenant be- I

A *Ge 15:18–21* ◀▶ *Ge 17:2–21*

A *Ge 16:10–12* ◀▶ *Ge 19:22–25*
O ▶ *Dt 4:35* I *Ge 13:15* ◀▶ *Ge 48:4*

4 [a]Prov. 30:21,23
5 [a]ch. 31:53
6 [a]1 Pet. 3:7 [b]Ex. 2:15 [1]Heb. that which is *good in thine eyes* [2]Heb. *afflicted her*
7 [a]ch. 25:18 [b]Ex. 15:22
9 [a]Tit. 2:9
10 [a]ch. 17:20
11 [a]Luke 1:13,31 [1]i.e. *God shall hear*
12 [a]ch. 21:20 [b]ch. 25:18
13 [a]ch. 31:42
14 [a]ch. 24:62 [b]Num. 13:26 [1]i.e. *The well of him that liveth* and *seeth me*
15 [a]Gal. 4:22
17:1 [a]ch. 28:3; Ex. 6:3 [b]2 Ki. 20:3 [c]Deut. 18:13 [1]Or, *upright*, or, *sincere*
2 [a]ch. 12:2
4 [a]Rom. 4:11,12, 16 [1]Heb. *multitude of nations*
5 [a]Neh. 9:7 [b]Rom. 4:17 [1]i.e. *Father of a great multitude*
6 [a]ch. 35:11 [b]Mat. 1:6
7 [a]Gal. 3:17

16:10 God promised Hagar that he would give her innumerable descendants. This promise was reaffirmed in 17:20, and initially fulfilled in 25:13–16. Today more than 200 million descendants of Ishmael live in the Arab countries surrounding Israel.

16:11 As a result of a lack of faith, Abram entered into a relationship with his wife's servant Hagar, attempting to produce a child to fulfill God's promise. Ishmael was the son born from this relationship. Because of hostility between Abram's wife and Hagar, Ishmael and his mother were forced to leave Abram's camp. Yet God took care of Hagar and Ishmael, as he had promised, and Ishmael fathered twelve sons—the ancestors of modern-day Arabs. The hostility between Ishmael's family and Abram's family continues today in both the political and spiritual arenas. Tragically, many Arabs refuse to follow the teachings of Jesus because he is a descendant of Abraham and choose instead to follow the teachings of Mohammed, a descendant of Ishmael and the founder of Islam.

16:12 The Lord described the future of Ishmael's race as being unceasingly in conflict with others and that Ishmael's enemies would be unable to drive them from the land. The history of Ishmael's descendants, the Arabs, clearly shows the fulfillment of this divine prediction. Even the British historian Edward Gibbon declared in *The Decline and Fall of the Roman Empire*: "The arms of Sesostris and Cyrus, of Pompey and Trajan could never achieve the conquest of Arabia."

tween me and thee and thy seed after
thee in their generations for an everlasting covenant, [b]to be a God unto thee, and
to [c]thy seed after thee.
8 And [a]I will give unto thee, and to thy
seed after thee, the land [b]wherein[/] thou
art a stranger, all the land of Canaan, for
an everlasting possession; and [c]I will be
their God.
9 ¶ And God said unto Abraham, Thou
shalt keep my covenant therefore, thou,
and thy seed after thee in their generations.
10 This *is* my covenant, which ye shall
keep, between me and you and thy seed
after thee; [a]Every man child among you
shall be circumcised.
11 And ye shall circumcise the flesh of
your foreskin; and it shall be [a]a token of
the covenant betwixt me and you.
12 And [/]he that is eight days old [a]shall
be circumcised among you, every man
child in your generations, he that is born
in the house, or bought with money of
any stranger, which *is* not of thy seed.
13 He that is born in thy house, and
he that is bought with thy money, must
needs be circumcised: and my covenant
shall be in your flesh for an everlasting
covenant.
H 14 And the uncircumcised man child
whose flesh of his foreskin is not circumcised, that soul [a]shall be cut off from his
people; he hath broken my covenant.
E 15 ¶ And God said unto Abraham, As
for Sarai thy wife, thou shalt not call her
name Sarai, but [/]Sarah *shall* her
name *be*.
16 And I will bless her, [a]and give thee
a son also of her: yea, I will bless her, and
[/]she shall be *a mother* [b]of nations; kings
of people shall be of her.
17 Then Abraham fell upon his face,
[a]and laughed, and said in his heart, Shall
a child be born unto him that is an hun-

H ▶ *Ex 12:13* **E** ▶ *Ge 18:12–14*

7 [b]ch. 26:24 & 28:13 [c]Rom. 9:8
8 [a]ch. 12:7 [b]ch. 23:4 & 28:4 [c]Ex. 6:7; Lev. 26:12 [/]Heb. *of thy sojournings*
10 [a]Acts 7:8
11 [a]Rom. 4:11
12 [a]Lev. 12:3; Luke 2:21 [/]Heb. *a son of eight days*
14 [a]Ex. 4:24
15 [/]i.e. *Princess*
16 [a]ch. 18:10 [b]ch. 35:11; Gal. 4:31; 1 Pet. 3:6 [/]Heb. *she shall become nations*
17 [a]ch. 18:12 & 21:6
19 [a]ch. 18:10 & 21:2; Gal. 4:28
20 [a]ch. 16:10 [b]ch. 25:12,16 [c]ch. 21:18
21 [a]ch. 21:2
27 [a]ch. 18:19
18:1 [a]ch. 13:18 & 14:13
2 [a]Heb. 13:2 [b]ch. 19:1; 1 Pet. 4:9

dred years old? and shall Sarah, that is
ninety years old, bear?
18 And Abraham said unto God,
O that Ishmael might live before thee!
19 And God said, [a]Sarah thy wife shall
bear thee a son indeed; and thou shalt
call his name Isaac: and I will establish
my covenant with him for an everlasting
covenant, *and* with his seed after him.
20 And as for Ishmael, I have heard
thee: Behold, I have blessed him, and will
make him fruitful, and [a]will multiply him
exceedingly; [b]twelve princes shall he beget, [c]and I will make him a great nation.
21 But my covenant will I establish
with Isaac, [a]which Sarah shall bear unto
thee at this set time in the next year.
22 And he left off talking with him,
and God went up from Abraham.
23 ¶ And Abraham took Ishmael his
son, and all that were born in his house,
and all that were bought with his money,
every male among the men of Abraham's
house; and circumcised the flesh of their
foreskin in the selfsame day, as God had
said unto him.
24 And Abraham *was* ninety years old
and nine, when he was circumcised in
the flesh of his foreskin.
25 And Ishmael his son *was* thirteen
years old, when he was circumcised in
the flesh of his foreskin.
26 In the selfsame day was Abraham
circumcised, and Ishmael his son.
27 And [a]all the men of his house, born
in the house, and bought with money of
the stranger, were circumcised with him.

The three visitors

18 AND THE LORD appeared unto
him in the [a]plains of Mamre: and
he sat in the tent door in the heat of the
day;
2 [a]And he lift up his eyes and looked,
and, lo, three men stood by him: [b]and
when he saw *them,* he ran to meet them
from the tent door, and bowed himself
toward the ground,

17:10 The Lord established circumcision as his appointed sign or token of his eternal covenant with Abraham (see 15:4). This act signified Abraham's commitment that the Lord alone would be his God; that he would trust in only God's Word (see Ro 4:11–12); and that he would consecrate, himself, his offspring and all he possessed to the Lord's service and mercy. Though other nations practiced circumcision (see Jer 9:25–26; Eze 32:18–19) only Israel observed this practice as a covenantal sign of consecration.

17:19–20 In this passage God reconfirmed his eternal covenant with Abraham's seed through Abraham's son Isaac and his descendants. God also reconfirmed his promise to bless Ishmael and make him a great nation too.

3 And said, My Lord, if now I have found favour in thy sight, pass not away, I pray thee, from thy servant:

4 Let [a]a little water, I pray you, be fetched, and wash your feet, and rest yourselves under the tree:

5 And [a]I will fetch a morsel of bread, and [b]comfort[1] ye your hearts; after that ye shall pass on: [c]for therefore [2]are ye come to your servant. And they said, So do, as thou hast said.

6 And Abraham hastened into the tent unto Sarah, and said, [1]Make ready quickly three measures of fine meal, knead *it,* and make cakes upon the hearth.

7 And Abraham ran unto the herd, and fetched a calf tender and good, and gave *it* unto a young man; and he hasted to dress it.

8 And [a]he took butter, and milk, and the calf which he had dressed, and set *it* before them; and he stood by them under the tree, and they did eat.

9 ¶ And they said unto him, Where *is* Sarah thy wife? And he said, Behold, [a]in the tent.

10 And he said, I [a]will certainly return unto thee [b]according to the time of life; and, lo, [c]Sarah thy wife shall have a son. And Sarah heard *it* in the tent door, which *was* behind him.

11 Now [a]Abraham and Sarah *were* old *and* well stricken in age; *and* it ceased to be with Sarah [b]after the manner of women.

12 Therefore Sarah [a]laughed within herself, saying, [b]After I am waxed old shall I have pleasure, my [c]lord being old also?

13 And the LORD said unto Abraham, Wherefore did Sarah laugh, saying, Shall I of a surety bear a child, which am old?

14 [a]Is any thing too hard for the LORD? [b]At the time appointed I will return unto thee, according to the time of life, and Sarah shall have a son.

15 Then Sarah denied, saying, I laughed not; for she was afraid. And he said, Nay; but thou didst laugh.

Abraham pleads for Sodom

16 ¶ And the men rose up from thence, and looked toward Sodom: and Abraham went with them [a]to bring them on the way.

17 And the LORD said, [a]Shall I hide from Abraham that thing which I do;

18 Seeing that Abraham shall surely become a great and mighty nation, and all the nations of the earth shall be [a]blessed in him?

19 For I know him, [a]that he will command his children and his household after him, and they shall keep the way of the LORD, to do justice and judgment; that the LORD may bring upon Abraham that which he hath spoken of him.

20 And the LORD said, Because [a]the cry of Sodom and Gomorrah is great, and because their sin is very grievous;

21 [a]I will go down now, and see whether they have done altogether according to the cry of it, which is come unto me; and if not, [b]I will know.

22 And the men turned their faces from thence, [a]and went toward Sodom: but Abraham [b]stood yet before the LORD.

23 ¶ And Abraham [a]drew near, and said, [b]Wilt thou also destroy the righteous with the wicked?

24 [a]Peradventure there be fifty righteous within the city: wilt thou also destroy and not spare the place for the fifty righteous that *are* therein?

25 That be far from thee to do after this manner, to slay the righteous with the wicked: and [a]that the righteous should be as the wicked, that be far from thee: [b]Shall not the Judge of all the earth do right?

26 And the LORD said, [a]If I find in Sodom fifty righteous within the city, then I will spare all the place for their sakes.

27 And Abraham answered and said, [a]Behold now, I have taken upon me to speak unto the Lord, which *am* [b]*but* dust and ashes:

28 Peradventure there shall lack five of the fifty righteous: wilt thou destroy all the city for *lack of* five? And he said, If I find there forty and five, I will not destroy *it.*

29 And he spake unto him yet again, and said, Peradventure there shall be forty found there. And he said, I will not do *it* for forty's sake.

30 And he said *unto him,* Oh let not

4 [a]ch. 19:2 & 43:24
5 [a]Judg. 6:18 & 13:15 [b]Judg. 19:5; Ps. 104:15 [c]ch. 19:8 & 33:10 [1]Heb. *stay* [2]Heb. *you have passed*
6 [1]Heb. *Hasten*
8 [a]ch. 19:3
9 [a]ch. 24:67
10 [a]ver. 14 [b]2 Ki. 4:16 [c]ch. 17:19,21 & 21:2; Rom. 9:9
11 [a]ch. 17:17; Rom. 4:19; Heb. 11:11,12,19 [b]ch. 31:35
12 [a]ch. 17:17 [b]Luke 1:18 [c]1 Pet. 3:6
14 [a]Num. 11:23; Jer. 32:17; Zech. 8:6; Mat. 3:9; Luke 1:37 [b]ver. 10; ch. 17:21; 2 Ki. 4:16
16 [a]Acts 15:3; Rom. 15:24; 3 John 6
17 [a]Ps. 25:14; Amos 3:7; John 15:15
18 [a]ch. 12:3 & 22:18; Acts 3:25; Gal. 3:8
19 [a]Deut. 4:9,10 & 6:7; Josh. 24:15; Eph. 6:4
20 [a]ch. 4:10
21 [a]ch. 11:5 [b]Deut. 8:2 & 13:3; Josh. 22:22; Luke 16:15; 2 Cor. 11:11
22 [a]ch. 19:1 [b]ver. 1
23 [a]Heb. 10:22 [b]Num. 16:22
24 [a]Jer. 5:1
25 [a]Job 8:20; Is. 3:10,11 [b]Job 8:3 & 34:17; Ps. 58:11 & 94:2; Rom. 3:6
26 [a]Jer. 5:1; Ezek. 22:30
27 [a]Luke 18:1 [b]ch. 3:19; Job 4:19; Eccl. 12:7; 1 Cor. 15:47, 48; 2 Cor. 5:1

E *Ge 17:15–17* ◀▶ *Ge 20:17*
K *Ge 15:1* ◀▶ *Ex 12:13*
J ▶ *1Sa 2:10*

the Lord be angry, and I will speak:
Peradventure there shall thirty be found
there. And he said, I will not do *it,* if I
find thirty there.
31 And he said, Behold now, I have
taken upon me to speak unto the Lord:
Peradventure there shall be twenty found
there. And he said, I will not destroy *it*
for twenty's sake.
32 And he said, [a]Oh let not the Lord
be angry, and I will speak yet but this
once: Peradventure ten shall be found
there. [b]And he said, I will not destroy *it*
for ten's sake.
33 And the LORD went his way, as soon
as he had left communing with Abraham:
and Abraham returned unto his place.

Sodom and Gomorrah destroyed

19 AND THERE [a]came two angels to
Sodom at even; and Lot sat in the
gate of Sodom: and [b]Lot seeing *them* rose
up to meet them; and he bowed himself
with his face toward the ground;
2 And he said, Behold now, my lords,
[a]turn in, I pray you, into your servant's
house, and tarry all night, and [b]wash
your feet, and ye shall rise up early, and
go on your ways. And they said, [c]Nay;
but we will abide in the street all night.
3 And he pressed upon them greatly;
and they turned in unto him, and entered
into his house; [a]and he made them a
feast, and did bake unleavened bread,
and they did eat.
4 ¶ But before they lay down, the men
of the city, *even* the men of Sodom, compassed the house round, both old and
young, all the people from every quarter:
5 [a]And they called unto Lot, and said
unto him, Where *are* the men which
came in to thee this night? [b]bring them
out unto us, that we [c]may know them.
6 And [a]Lot went out at the door unto
them, and shut the door after him,
7 And said, I pray you, brethren, do
not so wickedly.
8 [a]Behold now, I have two daughters
which have not known man; let me, I
pray you, bring them out unto you, and
do ye to them as *is* good in your eyes:
only unto these men do nothing; [b]for
therefore came they under the shadow of
my roof.
9 And they said, Stand back. And they
said *again,* This one *fellow* [a]came in to
sojourn, [b]and he will needs be a judge:
now will we deal worse with thee, than
with them. And they pressed sore upon
the man, *even* Lot, and came near to
break the door.
10 But the men put forth their hand,
and pulled Lot into the house to them,
and shut to the door.
11 And they smote the men that *were* D
at the door of the house with blindness,
both small and great: so that they wearied
themselves to find the door.
12 ¶ And the men said unto Lot, Hast
thou here any besides? son-in-law, and
thy sons, and thy daughters, and whatsoever thou hast in the city, [a]bring *them*
out of this place:
13 For we will destroy this place, because the [a]cry of them is waxen great
before the face of the LORD; and [b]the LORD
hath sent us to destroy it.
14 And Lot went out, and spake unto
his sons in law, [a]which married his
daughters, and said, [b]Up, get you out of
this place; for the LORD will destroy this
city. [c]But he seemed as one that mocked
unto his sons in law.
15 ¶ And when the morning arose,
then the angels hastened Lot, saying,
[a]Arise, take thy wife, and thy two daughters, which [1]are here; lest thou be consumed in the [2]iniquity of the city.
16 And while he lingered, the men
laid hold upon his hand, and upon the
hand of his wife, and upon the hand of
his two daughters; [a]the LORD being merciful unto him: [b]and they brought him
forth, and set him without the city.
17 ¶ And it came to pass, when they
had brought them forth abroad, that he
said, [a]Escape for thy life; [b]look not behind thee, neither stay thou in all the
plain; escape to the mountain, lest thou
be consumed.
18 And Lot said unto them, Oh, [a]not
so, my Lord:
19 Behold now, thy servant hath found
grace in thy sight, and thou hast magnified thy mercy, which thou hast shown
unto me in saving my life; and I cannot
escape to the mountain, lest some evil
take me, and I die:
20 Behold now, this city *is* near to flee
unto, and it *is* a little one: Oh, let me
escape thither, (*is* it not a little one?) and
my soul shall live.

32 [a]Judg. 6:39 [b]Jas. 5:16
19:1 [a]ch. 18:22 [b]ch. 18:1
2 [a]Heb. 13:2 [b]ch. 18:4 [c]See Luke 24:28
3 [a]ch. 18:8
5 [a]Is. 3:9 [b]Judg. 19:22 [c]ch. 4:1; Rom. 1:24,27; Jude 7
6 [a]Judg. 19:23
8 [a]See Judg. 19:24 [b]See ch. 18:5
9 [a]2 Pet. 2:7,8 [b]Ex. 2:14
12 [a]ch. 7:1; 2 Pet. 2:7,9
13 [a]ch. 18:20 [b]1 Chr. 21:15
14 [a]Mat. 1:18 [b]Num. 16:21,45 [c]Ex. 9:21; Luke 17:28 & 24:11
15 [a]Num. 16:24, 26; Rev. 18:4 [1]Heb. *are found* [2]Or, *punishment*
16 [a]Luke 18:13 [b]Ps. 34:22
17 [a]1 Ki. 19:3 [b]ver. 26; Mat. 24:16-18; Luke 9:62; Phil. 3:13,14
18 [a]Acts 10:14

D *Ge 12:17* ◄► *Ge 20:18*

21 And he said unto him, See, [a]I have accepted ʹthee concerning this thing also, that I will not overthrow this city, for the which thou hast spoken.

A 22 Haste thee, escape thither; for [a]I cannot do any thing till thou be come thither. Therefore [b]the name of the city was called ʹZoar.

23 ¶ The sun was ʹrisen upon the earth when Lot entered into Zoar.

24 Then [a]the LORD rained upon Sodom and upon Gomorrah brimstone and fire from the LORD out of heaven;

25 And he overthrew those cities, and all the plain, and all the inhabitants of the cities, and [a]that which grew upon the ground.

S 26 ¶ But his wife looked back from behind him, and she became [a]a pillar of salt.

27 ¶ And Abraham gat up early in the morning to the place where [a]he stood before the LORD:

28 And he looked toward Sodom and Gomorrah, and toward all the land of the plain, and beheld, and, lo, [a]the smoke of the country went up as the smoke of a furnace.

29 ¶ And it came to pass, when God destroyed the cities of the plain, that God [a]remembered Abraham, and sent Lot out of the midst of the overthrow, when he overthrew the cities in the which Lot dwelt.

The sin of Lot's daughters

30 ¶ And Lot went up out of Zoar, and [a]dwelt in the mountain, and his two daughters with him; for he feared to dwell in Zoar: and he dwelt in a cave, he and his two daughters.

31 And the firstborn said unto the younger, Our father *is* old, and *there is* not a man in the earth [a]to come in unto us after the manner of all the earth:

32 Come, let us make our father drink wine, and we will lie with him, that we [a]may preserve seed of our father.

33 And they made their father drink wine that night: and the firstborn went in, and lay with her father; and he perceived not when she lay down, nor when she arose.

34 And it came to pass on the morrow, that the firstborn said unto the younger, Behold, I lay yesternight with my father: let us make him drink wine this night also; and go thou in, *and* lie with him, that we may preserve seed of our father.

35 And they made their father drink wine that night also: and the younger arose, and lay with him; and he perceived not when she lay down, nor when she arose.

36 Thus were both the daughters of Lot with child by their father.

37 And the firstborn bare a son, and called his name Moab: [a]the same *is* the father of the Moabites unto this day.

38 And the younger, she also bare a son, and called his name Ben-ammi: [a]the same *is* the father of the children of Ammon unto this day.

Abraham and Abimelech

20 AND ABRAHAM journeyed from [a]thence toward the south country, and dwelled between [b]Kadesh and Shur, and [c]sojourned in Gerar.

2 And Abraham said of Sarah his wife, [a]She *is* my sister: and Abimelech king of Gerar sent, and [b]took Sarah.

3 But [a]God came to Abimelech [b]in a dream by night, and said to him, [c]Behold, thou *art but* a dead man, for the woman which thou hast taken; for she *is* ʹa man's wife.

4 But Abimelech had not come near her: and he said, Lord, [a]wilt thou slay also a righteous nation?

5 Said he not unto me, She *is* my sister? and she, even she herself said, He *is* my brother: [a]in the ʹintegrity of my heart and innocency of my hands have I done this.

21 [a]Job 42:8,9; Ps. 145:19 ʹHeb. *thy face*
22 [a]See ch. 32:25, 26; Ex. 32:10; Deut. 9:14; Mark 6:5 [b]ch. 13:10 & 14:2 ʹi.e. *Little*
23 ʹHeb. *gone forth*
24 [a]Deut. 29:23; Is. 13:19; Jer. 20:16; Ezek. 16:49, 50; Hos. 11:8; Luke 17:29; 2 Pet. 2:6; Jude 7
25 [a]ch. 14:3; Ps. 107:34
26 [a]Luke 17:32
27 [a]ch. 18:22
28 [a]Rev. 18:9
29 [a]ch. 8:1 & 18:23
30 [a]ver. 17,19
31 [a]ch. 16:2,4 & 38:8,9; Deut. 25:5
32 [a]Mark 12:19
37 [a]Deut. 2:9
38 [a]Deut. 2:19
20:1 [a]ch. 18:1 [b]ch. 16:7,14 [c]ch. 26:6
2 [a]ch. 12:13 & 26:7 [b]ch. 12:15
3 [a]Ps. 105:14 [b]Job 33:15 [c]ver. 7 ʹHeb. *married to an husband*
4 [a]ch. 18:23
5 [a]2 Ki. 20:3 ʹOr, *simplicity*, or, *sincerity*

A *Ge 17:2–21* ◀ ▶ *Ge 21:18*
S *Ge 7:1* ◀ ▶ *Ex 19:5–6*

19:22–25 The Lord's angels warned Abraham and Lot of the coming judgment on the cities of Sodom and Gomorrah. Lot and his family had to move quickly, choosing whether to obey God's command to flee to safety or disobey, stay and face judgment with the wicked. When Lot chose to obey God, note that God held off his judgment on Sodom and Gomorrah until Lot was safe (19:22). The very presence of godly people within these wicked cities would have prevented God's destruction of them (see 18:23–32). God cares about his people and watches over them to preserve them against indiscriminate judgment (see Eze 9:4; Rev 7:3).

6 And God said unto him in a dream, Yea, I know that thou didst this in the integrity of thy heart; for [a]I also withheld thee from sinning [b]against me: therefore suffered I thee not to touch her.

7 Now therefore restore the man *his* wife; [a]for he *is* a prophet, and he shall pray for thee, and thou shalt live: and if thou restore *her* not, [b]know thou that thou shalt surely die, thou, [c]and all that *are* thine.

8 Therefore Abimelech rose early in the morning, and called all his servants, and told all these things in their ears: and the men were sore afraid.

9 Then Abimelech called Abraham, and said unto him, What hast thou done unto us? and what have I offended thee, [a]that thou hast brought on me and on my kingdom a great sin? thou hast done deeds unto me [b]that ought not to be done.

10 And Abimelech said unto Abraham, What sawest thou, that thou hast done this thing?

11 And Abraham said, Because I thought, Surely [a]the fear of God *is* not in this place; and [b]they will slay me for my wife's sake.

12 And yet indeed [a]*she is* my sister; she *is* the daughter of my father, but not the daughter of my mother; and she became my wife.

13 And it came to pass, when [a]God caused me to wander from my father's house, that I said unto her, This *is* thy kindness which thou shalt show unto me; at every place whither we shall come, [b]say of me, He *is* my brother.

14 And Abimelech [a]took sheep, and oxen, and menservants, and womenservants, and gave *them* unto Abraham, and restored him Sarah his wife.

15 And Abimelech said, Behold, [a]my land *is* before thee: dwell [/]where it pleaseth thee.

16 And unto Sarah he said, Behold, I have given thy brother a thousand *pieces* of silver: [a]behold, he *is* to thee [b]a covering of the eyes, unto all that *are* with thee, and with all *other:* thus she was reproved.

E 17 ¶ So Abraham [a]prayed unto God: and God healed Abimelech, and his wife, and his maidservants; and they bare *children.*

18 For the LORD [a]had fast closed up all the wombs of the house of Abimelech, because of Sarah Abraham's wife. D

The birth of Isaac

21 AND THE LORD [a]visited Sarah as he had said, and the LORD did unto Sarah [b]as he had spoken.

2 For Sarah [a]conceived, and bare Abraham a son in his old age, [b]at the set time of which God had spoken to him.

3 And Abraham called the name of his son that was born unto him, whom Sarah bare to him, [a]Isaac.

4 And Abraham [a]circumcised his son Isaac being eight days old, [b]as God had commanded him.

5 And [a]Abraham was an hundred years old, when his son Isaac was born unto him.

6 ¶ And Sarah said, [a]God hath made me to laugh, *so that* all that hear [b]will laugh with me.

7 And she said, Who would have said unto Abraham, that Sarah should have given children suck? [a]for I have born *him* a son in his old age.

Hagar and Ishmael cast out

8 And the child grew, and was weaned: and Abraham made a great feast the *same* day that Isaac was weaned.

9 ¶ And Sarah saw the son of Hagar [a]the Egyptian, [b]which she had born unto Abraham, [c]mocking.

10 Wherefore she said unto Abraham, [a]Cast out this bondwoman and her son: for the son of this bondwoman shall not be heir with my son, *even* with Isaac.

11 And the thing was very grievous in Abraham's sight [a]because of his son.

12 ¶ And God said unto Abraham, Let it not be grievous in thy sight because of the lad, and because of thy bondwoman; in all that Sarah hath said unto thee, hearken unto her voice; for [a]in Isaac shall thy seed be called.

13 And also of the son of the bondwoman will I make [a]a nation, because he *is* thy seed.

14 And Abraham rose up early in the morning, and took bread, and a bottle of water, and gave *it* unto Hagar, putting *it*

6 [a]ch. 31:7 & 35:5; Ex. 34:24; 1 Sam. 25:26,34 [b]ch. 39:9; Lev. 6:2; Ps. 51:4
7 [a]1 Sam. 7:5; 2 Ki. 5:11; Job 42:8; Jas. 5:14,15 [b]ch. 2:17 [c]Num. 16:32,33
9 [a]ch. 26:10; Ex. 32:21; Josh. 7:25 [b]ch. 34:7
11 [a]ch. 42:18; Ps. 36:1; Prov. 16:6 [b]ch. 12:12 & 26:7
12 [a]See ch. 11:29
13 [a]ch. 12:1,9,11; Heb. 11:8 [b]ch. 12:13
14 [a]ch. 12:16
15 [a]ch. 13:9 [/]Heb. *as is good in thine eyes*
16 [a]ch. 26:11 [b]ch. 24:65
17 [a]Job 42:9
18 [a]ch. 12:17
21:1 [a]1 Sam. 2:21 [b]ch. 17:19; Gal. 4:23,28
2 [a]Acts 7:8; Gal. 4:22; Heb. 11:11 [b]ch. 17:21
3 [a]ch. 17:19
4 [a]Acts 7:8 [b]ch. 17:10,12
5 [a]ch. 17:1,17
6 [a]Ps. 126:2; Is. 54:1 [b]Luke 1:58
7 [a]ch. 18:11,12
9 [a]ch. 16:1 [b]ch. 16:15 [c]Gal. 4:29
10 [a]Gal. 4:30; See ch. 25:6 & 36:6,7
11 [a]ch. 17:18
12 [a]Rom. 9:7,8; Heb. 11:18
13 [a]ver. 18; ch. 16:10 & 17:20

on her shoulder, and the child, and [a]sent her away: and she departed, and wandered in the wilderness of Beer-sheba.

15 And the water was spent in the bottle, and she cast the child under one of the shrubs.

16 And she went, and sat her down over against *him* a good way off, as it were a bowshot: for she said, Let me not see the death of the child. And she sat over against *him,* and lift up her voice, and wept.

17 And [a]God heard the voice of the lad; and the angel of God called to Hagar out of heaven, and said unto her, What aileth thee, Hagar? fear not; for God hath heard the voice of the lad where he *is.*

A 18 Arise, lift up the lad, and hold him in thine hand; for [a]I will make him a great nation.

F 19 And [a]God opened her eyes, and she saw a well of water; and she went, and filled the bottle with water, and gave the lad drink.

20 And God [a]was with the lad; and he grew, and dwelt in the wilderness, [b]and became an archer.

21 And he dwelt in the wilderness of Paran: and his mother [a]took him a wife out of the land of Egypt.

Covenant with Abimelech

A 22 ¶ And it came to pass at that time, that [a]Abimelech and Phichol the chief captain of his host spake unto Abraham, saying, [b]God *is* with thee in all that thou doest:

23 Now therefore [a]swear unto me here by God [l]that thou wilt not deal falsely with me, nor with my son, nor with my son's son: *but* according to the kindness that I have done unto thee, thou shalt do unto me, and to the land wherein thou hast sojourned.

24 And Abraham said, I will swear.

25 And Abraham reproved Abimelech because of a well of water, which Abimelech's servants [a]had violently taken away.

26 And Abimelech said, I wot not who hath done this thing: neither didst thou tell me, neither yet heard I *of it,* but today.

27 And Abraham took sheep and oxen, and gave them unto Abimelech; and both of them [a]made a covenant.

28 And Abraham set seven ewe lambs of the flock by themselves.

29 And Abimelech said unto Abraham, [a]What *mean* these seven ewe lambs which thou hast set by themselves?

30 And he said, For *these* seven ewe lambs shalt thou take of my hand, that [a]they may be a witness unto me, that I have digged this well.

31 Wherefore he [a]called that place [l]Beer-sheba; because there they sware both of them.

32 Thus they made a covenant at Beer-sheba: then Abimelech rose up, and Phichol the chief captain of his host, and they returned into the land of the Philistines.

33 ¶ And *Abraham* planted a [l]grove in Beer-sheba, and [a]called there on the name of the LORD, [b]the everlasting God.

34 And Abraham sojourned in the Philistines' land many days.

God tests Abraham

22 AND IT came to pass after these things, that [a]God did tempt Abraham, and said unto him, Abraham: and he said, [l]Behold, *here* I *am.*

2 And he said, Take now thy son, [a]thine only *son* Isaac, whom thou lovest, and get thee [b]into the land of Moriah; and offer him there for a burnt offering upon one of the mountains which I will tell thee of.

3 ¶ And Abraham rose up early in the morning, and saddled his ass, and took two of his young men with him, and Isaac his son, and clave the wood for the burnt offering, and rose up, and went unto the place of which God had told him.

4 Then on the third day Abraham lifted up his eyes, and saw the place afar off.

5 And Abraham said unto his young men, Abide ye here with the ass; and I

14 [a]John 8:35
17 [a]Ex. 3:7
18 [a]ver. 13
19 [a]Num. 22:31
20 [a]ch. 28:15 & 39:2,3,21 [b]ch. 16:12
21 [a]ch. 24:4
22 [a]ch. 20:2 & 26:26 [b]ch. 26:28
23 [a]Josh. 2:12; 1 Sam. 24:21 [l]Heb. *if thou shalt lie unto me*
25 [a]See ch. 26:15, 18,20-22
27 [a]ch. 26:31 & 31:44; 1 Sam. 18:3
29 [a]ch. 33:8
30 [a]ch. 31:48,52
31 [a]ch. 26:33 [l]i.e. *The well of the oath*
33 [a]ch. 4:26 [b]Deut. 33:27 [l]Or, *tree*
22:1 [a]1 Cor. 10:13; Heb. 11:17; Jas. 1:12; 1 Pet. 1:7 [l]Heb. *Behold me*
2 [a]Heb. 11:17 [b]2 Chr. 3:1

A *Ge 19:22–25* ◀ ▶ *Ge 22:15–18*
F ▶ *Ge 27:28* **A** ▶ *Ge 24:1*

21:18 This prophecy assured Hagar that Ishmael would live and become the great nation that God had promised.

22:2–13 The record of Abraham's obedience to God in offering his son Isaac clearly prefigures the offering of God's own son Jesus to be the ultimate sacrifice for humanity.

and the lad will go yonder and worship, and come again to you.

6 And Abraham took the wood of the burnt offering, and [a]laid *it* upon Isaac his son; and he took the fire in his hand, and a knife; and they went both of them together.

D 7 And Isaac spake unto Abraham his father, and said, My father: and he said, [1]Here *am* I, my son. And he said, Behold the fire and the wood: but where *is* the [2]lamb for a burnt offering?

8 And Abraham said, My son, God will provide himself a lamb for a burnt offering: so they went both of them together.

9 And they came to the place which God had told him of; and Abraham built an altar there, and laid the wood in order, and bound Isaac his son, and [a]laid him on the altar upon the wood.

10 And Abraham stretched forth his hand, and took the knife to slay his son.

11 And the angel of the LORD called unto him out of heaven, and said, Abraham, Abraham: and he said, Here *am* I.

12 And he said, [a]Lay not thine hand upon the lad, neither do thou any thing unto him: for [b]now I know that thou fearest God, seeing thou hast not withheld thy son, thine only *son* from me.

13 And Abraham lifted up his eyes, and looked, and behold behind *him* a ram caught in a thicket by his horns: and Abraham went and took the ram, and offered him up for a burnt offering in the stead of his son.

14 And Abraham called the name of that place [1]Jehovah-jireh: as it is said *to* this day, In the mount of the LORD it shall be seen.

A U 15 ¶ And the angel of the LORD called unto Abraham out of heaven the second time,

16 And said, [a]By myself have I sworn, saith the LORD, for because thou hast done this thing, and hast not withheld thy son, thine only *son:*

17 That in blessing I will bless thee, and in multiplying I will multiply thy seed [a]as the stars of the heaven, [b]and as the sand which *is* upon the sea [1]shore; and [c]thy seed shall possess [d]the gate of his enemies;

18 [a]And in thy seed shall all the nations of the earth be blessed; [b]because thou hast obeyed my voice.

19 So Abraham returned unto his young men, and they rose up and went together to [a]Beer-sheba; and Abraham dwelt at Beer-sheba.

20 ¶ And it came to pass after these things, that it was told Abraham, saying, Behold, [a]Milcah, she hath also born children unto thy brother Nahor;

21 [a]Huz his firstborn, and Buz his brother, and Kemuel the father [b]of Aram,

22 And Chesed, and Hazo, and Pildash, and Jidlaph, and Bethuel.

23 And [a]Bethuel begat [b]Rebekah: these eight Milcah did bear to Nahor, Abraham's brother.

24 And his concubine, whose name *was* Reumah, she bare also Tebah, and Gaham, and Thahash, and Maachah.

The death of Sarah

23 AND SARAH was an hundred and seven and twenty years old: *these were* the years of the life of Sarah.

2 And Sarah died in [a]Kirjath-arba; the same *is* [b]Hebron in the land of Canaan: and Abraham came to mourn for Sarah, and to weep for her.

3 ¶ And Abraham stood up from before his dead, and spake unto the sons of Heth, saying,

4 [a]I *am* a stranger and a sojourner with you: [b]give me a possession of a buryingplace with you, that I may bury my dead out of my sight.

5 And the children of Heth answered Abraham, saying unto him,

6 Hear us, my lord: thou *art* [a]a [1] mighty prince among us: in the choice of our sepulchres bury thy dead; none of us shall withhold from thee his sepulchre, but that thou mayest bury thy dead.

7 And Abraham stood up, and bowed

6 [a]John 19:17
7 [1]Heb. *Behold me* [2]Or, *kid*
9 [a]Heb. 11:17; Jas. 2:21
12 [a]1 Sam. 15:22 [b]ch. 26:5; Jas. 2:22
14 [1]i.e. *The LORD will see,* or *provide*
16 [a]Ps. 105:9; Luke 1:73; Heb. 6:13,14
17 [a]ch. 15:5; Jer. 33:22 [b]ch. 13:16 [c]ch. 24:60 [d]Mic. 1:9 [1]Heb. *lip*
18 [a]ch. 12:3 & 18:18 & 26:4; Acts 3:25; Gal. 3:8,9,16, 18 [b]ver. 3,10; ch. 26:5
19 [a]ch. 21:31
20 [a]ch. 11:29
21 [a]Job 1:1 [b]Job 32:2
23 [a]ch. 24:15 [b]Called, Rom. 9:10, *Rebecca*
23:2 [a]Josh. 14:15 [b]ver. 19; ch. 13:18
4 [a]ch. 17:8; 1 Chr. 29:15; Ps. 105:12; Heb. 11:9,13 [b]Acts 7:5
6 [a]ch. 13:2 & 14:14 & 24:35 [1]Heb. *a prince of God*

D *Ge 4:3–5* ◄ ► *Ex 12:3–5*
A *Ge 21:18* ◄ ► *Ge 24:60*
U *Ge 12:1–3* ◄ ► *Ge 24:1*

22:15–18 The angel of the LORD reconfirmed God's covenant with Abraham regarding Abraham's innumerable descendants. Yet this passage adds an additional promise to the original covenant (see 15:4). The words "thy seed shall possess the gate of his enemies" (22:17) probably refer to the Israelites' victorious conquest of the promised land.

himself to the people of the land, *even* to the children of Heth.

8 And he communed with them, saying, If it be your mind that I should bury my dead out of my sight; hear me, and entreat for me to Ephron the son of Zohar,

9 That he may give me the cave of Machpelah, which he hath, which *is* in the end of his field; for [l]as much money as it is worth he shall give it me for a possession of a buryingplace amongst you.

10 And Ephron dwelt among the children of Heth: and Ephron the Hittite answered Abraham in the [l]audience of the children of Heth, *even* of all that [a]went in at the gate of his city, saying,

11 [a]Nay, my lord, hear me: the field give I thee, and the cave that *is* therein, I give it thee; in the presence of the sons of my people give I it thee: bury thy dead.

12 And Abraham bowed down himself before the people of the land.

13 And he spake unto Ephron in the audience of the people of the land, saying, But if thou *wilt give it,* I pray thee, hear me: I will give thee money for the field; take *it* of me, and I will bury my dead there.

14 And Ephron answered Abraham, saying unto him,

15 My lord, hearken unto me: the land *is worth* four hundred [a]shekels of silver; what *is* that betwixt me and thee? bury therefore thy dead.

16 And Abraham hearkened unto Ephron; and Abraham [a]weighed to Ephron the silver, which he had named in the audience of the sons of Heth, four hundred shekels of silver, current *money* with the merchant.

17 ¶ And [a]the field of Ephron, which *was* in Machpelah, which *was* before Mamre, the field, and the cave which *was* therein, and all the trees that *were* in the field, that *were* in all the borders round about, were made sure

18 Unto Abraham for a possession in the presence of the children of Heth, before all that went in at the gate of his city.

19 And after this, Abraham buried Sarah his wife in the cave of the field of Machpelah before Mamre: the same *is* Hebron in the land of Canaan.

20 And the field, and the cave that *is* therein, [a]were made sure unto Abraham for a possession of a buryingplace by the sons of Heth.

Isaac and Rebekah

24 AND ABRAHAM [a]was old, *and* [l]well stricken in age: and the LORD [b]had blessed Abraham in all things.

2 And Abraham said [a]unto his eldest servant of his house, that [b]ruled over all that he had, [c]Put, I pray thee, thy hand under my thigh:

3 And I will make thee [a]swear by the LORD, the God of heaven, and the God of the earth, that [b]thou shalt not take a wife unto my son of the daughters of the Canaanites, among whom I dwell:

4 [a]But thou shalt go [b]unto my country, and to my kindred, and take a wife unto my son Isaac.

5 And the servant said unto him, Peradventure the woman will not be willing to follow me unto this land: must I needs bring thy son again unto the land from whence thou camest?

6 And Abraham said unto him, Beware thou that thou bring not my son thither again.

7 ¶ The LORD God of heaven, which [a]took me from my father's house, and from the land of my kindred, and which spake unto me, and that sware unto me, saying, [b]Unto thy seed will I give this land; [c]he shall send his angel before thee, and thou shalt take a wife unto my son from thence.

8 And if the woman will not be willing to follow thee, then [a]thou shalt be clear from this my oath: only bring not my son thither again.

9 And the servant put his hand under the thigh of Abraham his master, and sware to him concerning that matter.

10 ¶ And the servant took ten camels of the camels of his master, and departed; [a]for[l] all the goods of his master *were* in his hand: and he arose, and went to Mesopotamia, unto [b]the city of Nahor.

11 And he made his camels to kneel down without the city by a well of water at the time of the evening, *even* the time [a]that[l] women go out to draw *water.*

12 And he said, [a]O LORD God of my master Abraham, I pray thee, [b]send me

A P U

9 [l]Heb. *full money*

10 [a]ch. 34:20,24; Ruth 4:4 [l]Heb. *ears*

11 [a]See 2 Sam. 24:21-24

15 [a]Ex. 30:13; Ezek. 45:12

16 [a]Jer. 32:9

17 [a]ch. 25:9 & 49:30-32 & 50:13; Acts 7:16

20 [a]Jer. 32:10,11

24:1 [a]ch. 21:5 [b]ver. 35; ch. 13:2; Ps. 112:3; Prov. 10:22 [l]Heb. *gone into days*

2 [a]ch. 15:2 [b]ver. 10; ch. 39:4-6 [c]ch. 47:29; 1 Chr. 29:24

3 [a]ch. 14:22; Deut. 6:13; Josh. 2:12 [b]ch. 26:35 & 28:2; Ex. 34:16; Deut. 7:3

4 [a]ch. 28:2 [b]ch. 12:1

7 [a]ch. 12:1 [b]ch. 12:7 & 13:15 & 17:8; Ex. 32:13; Deut. 1:8 & 34:4; Acts 7:5 [c]Ex. 23:20,23 & 33:2; Heb. 1:14

8 [a]Josh. 2:17,20

10 [a]ver. 2 [b]ch. 27:43 [l]Or, *and*

11 [a]Ex. 2:16; 1 Sam. 9:11 [l]Heb. *that women which draw* water *go forth*

12 [a]ver. 27; ch. 26:24 & 32:9; Ex. 3:6,15 [b]Neh. 1:11; Ps. 37:5

A Ge 21:22 ◀▶ Ge 48:16
P Ge 15:14 ◀▶ Ge 24:35
U Ge 22:15–18 ◀▶ Ge 24:35

good speed this day, and show kindness
unto my master Abraham.
13 Behold, [a]I stand *here* by the well of
water; and [b]the daughters of the men of
the city come out to draw water:
14 And let it come to pass, that the
damsel to whom I shall say, Let down thy
pitcher, I pray thee, that I may drink; and
she shall say, Drink, and I will give thy
camels drink also: *let the same be* she
that thou hast appointed for thy servant
Isaac; and [a]thereby shall I know that thou
hast shown kindness unto my master.
15 ¶ And it came to pass, before he
had done speaking, that, behold, Rebekah
came out, who was born to Bethuel, son
of [a]Milcah, the wife of Nahor, Abraham's
brother, with her pitcher upon her
shoulder.
16 And the damsel [a]*was* [/]very fair to
look upon, a virgin, neither had any man
known her: and she went down to the
well, and filled her pitcher, and came up.
17 And the servant ran to meet her,
and said, Let me, I pray thee, drink a little
water of thy pitcher.
18 [a]And she said, Drink, my lord: and
she hasted, and let down her pitcher
upon her hand, and gave him drink.
19 And when she had done giving him
drink, she said, I will draw *water* for thy
camels also, until they have done
drinking.
20 And she hasted, and emptied her
pitcher into the trough, and ran again
unto the well to draw *water,* and drew for
all his camels.
21 And the man wondering at her held
his peace, to wit whether [a]the LORD had
made his journey prosperous or not.
22 And it came to pass, as the camels
had done drinking, that the man took a
golden [a]earring[/] of half a shekel weight,
and two bracelets for her hands of ten
shekels weight of gold;
23 And said, Whose daughter *art* thou?
tell me, I pray thee: is there room *in* thy
father's house for us to lodge in?
24 And she said unto him, [a]I *am* the
daughter of Bethuel the son of Milcah,
which she bare unto Nahor.
25 She said moreover unto him, We
have both straw and provender enough,
and room to lodge in.
26 And the man [a]bowed down his
head, and worshipped the LORD.
27 And he said, [a]Blessed *be* the LORD
God of my master Abraham, who hath
not left destitute my master of [b]his mercy
and his truth: I *being* in the way, the LORD
[c]led me to the house of my master's
brethren.
28 And the damsel ran, and told *them*
of her mother's house these things.
29 ¶ And Rebekah had a brother, and
his name *was* [a]Laban: and Laban ran out
unto the man, unto the well.
30 And it came to pass, when he saw
the earring and bracelets upon his sister's
hands, and when he heard the words of
Rebekah his sister, saying, Thus spake
the man unto me; that he came unto the
man; and, behold, he stood by the camels
at the well.
31 And he said, Come in, [a]thou
blessed of the LORD; wherefore standest
thou without? for I have prepared the
house, and room for the camels.
32 ¶ And the man came into the
house: and he ungirded his camels, and
[a]gave straw and provender for the camels, and water to wash his feet, and the
men's feet that *were* with him.
33 And there was set *meat* before him
to eat: but he said, [a]I will not eat, until I
have told mine errand. And he said,
Speak on.
34 And he said, I *am* Abraham's
servant.
35 And the LORD [a]hath blessed my B
master greatly; and he is become great: P
and he hath given him flocks, and herds, U
and silver, and gold, and menservants,
and maidservants, and camels, and asses.
36 And Sarah my master's wife [a]bare a
son to my master when she was old: and
[b]unto him hath he given all that he hath.
37 And my master [a]made me swear,
saying, Thou shalt not take a wife to my
son of the daughters of the Canaanites, in
whose land I dwell:
38 [a]But thou shalt go unto my father's
house, and to my kindred, and take a wife
unto my son.
39 [a]And I said unto my master, Peradventure the woman will not follow me.
40 [a]And he said unto me, The LORD,
[b]before whom I walk, will send his angel
with thee, and prosper thy way; and thou
shalt take a wife for my son of my kindred, and of my father's house:

13 [a]ver. 43 [b]Ex. 2:16
14 [a]See Judg. 6:17, 37; 1 Sam. 6:7 & 14:10 & 20:7
15 [a]ch. 11:29 & 22:23
16 [a]ch. 26:7 [/]Heb. *good of countenance*
18 [a]1 Pet. 3:8
21 [a]ver. 12,56
22 [a]Ex. 32:2,3; Is. 3:19-21 [/]Or, *jewel for the forehead*
24 [a]ch. 22:23
26 [a]ver. 52; Ex. 4:31
27 [a]Ex. 18:10; Ruth 4:14; 1 Sam. 25:32,39 [b]ch. 32:10; Ps. 98:3 [c]ver. 48
29 [a]ch. 29:5
31 [a]ch. 26:29; Judg. 17:2; Ruth 3:10; Ps. 115:15
32 [a]ch. 43:24; Judg. 19:21
33 [a]Job 23:12; John 4:34; Eph. 6:5-7
35 [a]ver. 1; ch. 13:2
36 [a]ch. 21:2 [b]ch. 21:10 & 25:5
37 [a]ver. 3
38 [a]ver. 4
39 [a]ver. 5
40 [a]ver. 7 [b]ch. 17:1

B ▶ *Ge 26:12* **P** *Ge 24:1* ◀▶ *Dt 8:13*
U *Ge 24:1* ◀▶ *Ge 26:3*

41 [a]Then shalt thou be clear from *this*
my oath, when thou comest to my kindred; and if they give not thee *one,* thou
shalt be clear from my oath.
42 And I came this day unto the well,
and said, [a]O LORD God of my master Abraham, if now thou do prosper my way
which I go:
43 [a]Behold, I stand by the well of water; and it shall come to pass, that when
the virgin cometh forth to draw *water,*
and I say to her, Give me, I pray thee, a
little water of thy pitcher to drink;
44 And she say to me, Both drink
thou, and I will also draw for thy camels:
let the same *be* the woman whom the
LORD hath appointed out for my master's
son.
45 [a]And before I had done [b]speaking
in mine heart, behold, Rebekah came
forth with her pitcher on her shoulder;
and she went down unto the well, and
drew *water:* and I said unto her, Let me
drink, I pray thee.
46 And she made haste, and let down
her pitcher from her *shoulder,* and said,
Drink, and I will give thy camels drink
also: so I drank, and she made the camels
drink also.
47 And I asked her, and said, Whose
daughter *art* thou? And she said, The
daughter of Bethuel, Nahor's son, whom
Milcah bare unto him: and I [a]put the earring upon her face, and the bracelets
upon her hands.
48 [a]And I bowed down my head, and
worshipped the LORD, and blessed the
LORD God of my master Abraham, which
had led me in the right way to take [b]my
master's brother's daughter unto his son.
49 And now if ye will [a]deal kindly and
truly with my master, tell me: and if not,
tell me; that I may turn to the right hand,
or to the left.
50 Then Laban and Bethuel answered
and said, [a]The thing proceedeth from the
LORD: we cannot [b]speak unto thee bad or
good.
51 Behold, Rebekah [a]*is* before thee,
take *her,* and go, and let her be thy master's son's wife, as the LORD hath spoken.
52 And it came to pass, that, when
Abraham's servant heard their words, he
[a]worshipped the LORD, *bowing himself* to
the earth.
53 And the servant brought forth [a]jew-
els[1] of silver, and jewels of gold, and rai-

41 [a]ver. 8
42 [a]ver. 12
43 [a]ver. 13
45 [a]ver. 15 [b]1 Sam. 1:13
47 [a]Ezek. 16:11,12
48 [a]ver. 26 [b]ch. 22:23
49 [a]ch. 47:29; Josh. 2:14
50 [a]Ps. 118:23; Mat. 21:42 [b]ch. 31:24
51 [a]ch. 20:15
52 [a]ver. 26
53 [a]Ex. 3:22 & 11:2 & 12:35 [b]2 Chr. 21:3; Ezra 1:6 [1]Heb. *vessels*
54 [a]ver. 56,59
55 [1]Or, *a full year,* or, *ten* months
59 [a]ch. 35:8
60 [a]ch. 17:16 [b]ch. 22:17
62 [a]ch. 25:11
63 [a]Josh. 1:8; Ps. 1:2 & 77:12 & 119:15 & 143:5 [1]Or, *to pray*
64 [a]Josh. 15:18
67 [a]ch. 38:12

ment, and gave *them* to Rebekah: he gave
also to her brother and to her mother
[b]precious things.
54 And they did eat and drink, he and
the men that *were* with him, and tarried
all night; and they rose up in the morning, and he said, [a]Send me away unto my
master.
55 And her brother and her mother
said, Let the damsel abide with us [1]*a few*
days, at the least ten; after that she
shall go.
56 And he said unto them, Hinder me
not, seeing the LORD hath prospered my
way; send me away that I may go to my
master.
57 And they said, We will call the
damsel, and inquire at her mouth.
58 And they called Rebekah, and said
unto her, Wilt thou go with this man?
And she said, I will go.
59 And they sent away Rebekah their
sister, and [a]her nurse, and Abraham's
servant, and his men.
60 And they blessed Rebekah, and said A
unto her, Thou *art* our sister, be thou
[a]*the mother* of thousands of millions, and
[b]let thy seed possess the gate of those
which hate them.
61 ¶ And Rebekah arose, and her damsels, and they rode upon the camels, and
followed the man: and the servant took
Rebekah, and went his way.
62 And Isaac came from the way of the
[a]well Lahai-roi; for he dwelt in the south
country.
63 And Isaac went out [a]to[1] meditate in
the field at the eventide: and he lifted up
his eyes, and saw, and, behold, the camels *were* coming.
64 And Rebekah lifted up her eyes,
and when she saw Isaac, [a]she lighted off
the camel.
65 For she *had* said unto the servant,
What man *is* this that walketh in the field
to meet us? And the servant *had* said, It *is*
my master: therefore she took a veil, and
covered herself.
66 And the servant told Isaac all things
that he had done.
67 And Isaac brought her into his
mother Sarah's tent, and took Rebekah,
and she became his wife; and he loved
her: and Isaac [a]was comforted after his
mother's *death.*

A *Ge 22:15–18* ◀ ▶ *Ge 25:23*

The death of Abraham

25 THEN AGAIN Abraham took a wife, and her name *was* Keturah.

2 And [a]she bare him Zimran, and Jokshan, and Medan, and Midian, and Ishbak, and Shuah.

3 And Jokshan begat Sheba, and Dedan. And the sons of Dedan were Asshurim, and Letushim, and Leummim.

4 And the sons of Midian; Ephah, and Epher, and Hanoch, and Abidah, and Eldaah. All these *were* the children of Keturah.

5 ¶ And [a]Abraham gave all that he had unto Isaac.

6 But unto the sons of the concubines, which Abraham had, Abraham gave gifts, and [a]sent them away from Isaac his son, while he yet lived, eastward, unto [b]the east country.

7 And these *are* the days of the years of Abraham's life which he lived, an hundred threescore and fifteen years.

Q 8 Then Abraham gave up the ghost, and [a]died in a good old age, an old man, and full *of years;* and [b]was gathered to his people.

9 And [a]his sons Isaac and Ishmael buried him in the cave of Machpelah, in the field of Ephron the son of Zohar the Hittite, which *is* before Mamre;

10 [a]The field which Abraham purchased of the sons of Heth: [b]there was Abraham buried, and Sarah his wife.

11 ¶ And it came to pass after the death of Abraham, that God blessed his son Isaac; and Isaac dwelt by the [a]well Lahai-roi.

The descendants of Ishmael

12 ¶ Now these *are* the generations of Ishmael, Abraham's son, [a]whom Hagar the Egyptian, Sarah's handmaid, bare unto Abraham:

13 And [a]these *are* the names of the sons of Ishmael, by their names, according to their generations: the firstborn of Ishmael, Nebajoth; and Kedar, and Adbeel, and Mibsam,

Q *Ge 15:15* ◀ ▶ *Ge 35:29*

25:2 [a]1 Chr. 1:32
5 [a]ch. 24:36
6 [a]ch. 21:14 [b]Judg. 6:3
8 [a]ch. 15:15 [b]ch. 35:29 & 49:33
9 [a]ch. 35:29 & 50:13
10 [a]ch. 23:16 [b]ch. 49:31
11 [a]ch. 16:14
12 [a]ch. 16:15
13 [a]1 Chr. 1:29
15 [l]Or, *Hadad*
16 [a]ch. 17:20
17 [a]ver. 8
18 [a]1 Sam. 15:7 [b]ch. 16:12 [l]Heb. *fell*
19 [a]Mat. 1:2
20 [a]ch. 22:23 [b]ch. 24:29
21 [a]1 Chr. 5:20; 2 Chr. 33:13; Ezra 8:23 [b]Rom. 9:10
22 [a]1 Sam. 9:9 & 10:22
23 [a]ch. 17:16 & 24:60 [b]2 Sam. 8:14 [c]ch. 27:29; Mal. 1:3; Rom. 9:12
25 [a]ch. 27:11,16, 23
26 [a]Hos. 12:3 [b]ch. 27:36

14 And Mishma, and Dumah, and Massa,

15 [l]Hadar, and Tema, Jetur, Naphish, and Kedemah:

16 These *are* the sons of Ishmael, and these *are* their names, by their towns, and by their castles; [a]twelve princes according to their nations.

17 And these *are* the years of the life of Ishmael, an hundred and thirty and seven years: and [a]he gave up the ghost and died; and was gathered unto his people.

18 [a]And they dwelt from Havilah unto Shur, that *is* before Egypt, as thou goest toward Assyria: *and* he [l]died [b]in the presence of all his brethren.

Jacob and Esau

19 ¶ And these *are* the generations of Isaac, Abraham's son: [a]Abraham begat Isaac:

20 And Isaac was forty years old when he took Rebekah to wife, [a]the daughter of Bethuel the Syrian of Padan-aram, [b]the sister to Laban the Syrian.

21 And Isaac entreated the LORD for his wife, because she *was* barren: [a]and the LORD was entreated of him, and [b]Rebekah his wife conceived. E

22 And the children struggled together within her; and she said, If *it be* so, why *am* I thus? [a]And she went to inquire of the LORD.

23 And the LORD said unto her, [a]Two nations *are* in thy womb, and two manner of people shall be separated from thy bowels; and [b]*the one* people shall be stronger than *the other* people; and [c]the elder shall serve the younger. A

24 ¶ And when her days to be delivered were fulfilled, behold, *there were* twins in her womb.

25 And the first came out red, [a]all over like an hairy garment; and they called his name Esau.

26 And after that came his brother out, and [a]his hand took hold on Esau's heel; and [b]his name was called Jacob: and Isaac

E *Ge 20:17* ◀ ▶ *Ge 29:31*
A *Ge 24:60* ◀ ▶ *Ge 26:2–5*

25:23 God revealed that Rebekah would produce two sons in which "the elder shall serve the younger" indicating that Esau would be ruled by Jacob, despite Esau's position as the eldest son. God's designation of the younger son illustrates his sovereign right to do "whatsoever he hath pleased" (Ps 115:3) in accordance with his perfect will.

was threescore years old when she bare them.

27 And the boys grew: and Esau was [a]a cunning hunter, a man of the field; and Jacob *was* [b]a plain man, [c]dwelling in tents.

28 And Isaac loved Esau, because [1]he did [a]eat of *his* venison: [b]but Rebekah loved Jacob.

29 ¶ And Jacob sod pottage: and Esau came from the field, and he *was* faint:

30 And Esau said to Jacob, Feed me, I pray thee, [1]with that same red *pottage;* for I *am* faint: therefore was his name called [2]Edom.

31 And Jacob said, Sell me this day thy birthright.

32 And Esau said, Behold, I *am* [1]at the point to die: and what profit shall this birthright do to me?

33 And Jacob said, Swear to me this day; and he sware unto him: and [a]he sold his birthright unto Jacob.

34 Then Jacob gave Esau bread and pottage of lentiles; and [a]he did eat and drink, and rose up, and went his way: thus Esau despised *his* birthright.

Isaac and Abimelech

26 AND THERE was a famine in the land, beside the [a]first famine that was in the days of Abraham. And Isaac went unto [b]Abimelech king of the Philistines unto Gerar.

A 2 And the LORD appeared unto him, and said, Go not down into Egypt; dwell in [a]the land which I shall tell thee of:

U 3 [a]Sojourn in this land, and [b]I will be with thee, and [c]will bless thee; for unto thee, and unto thy seed, [d]I will give all these countries, and I will perform [e]the oath which I sware unto Abraham thy father;

4 And [a]I will make thy seed to multiply as the stars of heaven, and will give unto thy seed all these countries; [b]and in thy seed shall all the nations of the earth be blessed;

5 [a]Because that Abraham obeyed my voice, and kept my charge, my commandments, my statutes, and my laws.

6 ¶ And Isaac dwelt in Gerar:

7 And the men of the place asked *him* of his wife; and [a]he said, She *is* my sister: for [b]he feared to say, *She is* my wife; lest, *said he,* the men of the place should kill me for Rebekah; because she [c]*was* fair to look upon.

8 And it came to pass, when he had been there a long time, that Abimelech king of the Philistines looked out at a window, and saw, and, behold, Isaac *was* sporting with Rebekah his wife.

9 And Abimelech called Isaac, and said, Behold, of a surety she *is* thy wife: and how saidst thou, She *is* my sister? And Isaac said unto him, Because I said, Lest I die for her.

10 And Abimelech said, What *is* this thou hast done unto us? one of the people might lightly have lain with thy wife, and [a]thou shouldest have brought guiltiness upon us.

11 And Abimelech charged all *his* people, saying, He that [a]toucheth this man or his wife shall surely be put to death.

12 Then Isaac sowed in that land, and [1]received in the same year [a]an hundredfold: and the LORD [b]blessed him. B

13 And the man [a]waxed great, and [1]went forward, and grew until he became very great:

14 For he had possession of flocks, and possession of herds, and great store of [1]servants: and the Philistines [a]envied him.

15 For all the wells [a]which his father's servants had digged in the days of Abraham his father, the Philistines had stopped them, and filled them with earth.

16 And Abimelech said unto Isaac, Go from us; for [a]thou art much mightier than we.

17 ¶ And Isaac departed thence, and pitched his tent in the valley of Gerar, and dwelt there.

18 And Isaac digged again the wells of water, which they had digged in the days of Abraham his father; for the Philistines

27 [a]ch. 27:3,5 [b]Job 1:1,8 [c]Heb. 11:9
28 [a]ch. 27:19,25, 31 [b]ch. 27:6 [1]Heb. *venison* was *in his mouth*
30 [1]Heb. *with that red,* with that *red* pottage [2]i.e. *Red*
32 [1]Heb. *going to die*
33 [a]Heb. 12:16
34 [a]Eccl. 8:15; Is. 22:13; 1 Cor. 15:32
26:1 [a]ch. 12:10 [b]ch. 20:2
2 [a]ch. 12:1
3 [a]ch. 20:1; Ps. 39:12; Heb. 11:9 [b]ch. 28:15 [c]ch. 12:2 [d]ch. 13:15 [e]ch. 22:16; Ps. 105:9
4 [a]ch. 15:5 & 22:17 [b]ch. 12:3 & 22:18
5 [a]ch. 22:16,18
7 [a]ch. 12:13 & 20:2,13 [b]Prov. 29:25 [c]ch. 24:16
10 [a]ch. 20:9
11 [a]Ps. 105:15
12 [a]Mat. 13:8; Mark 4:8 [b]ver. 3; Job 42:12 [1]Heb. *found*
13 [a]ch. 24:35; Prov. 10:22 [1]Heb. *went going*
14 [a]ch. 37:11; Eccl. 4:4 [1]Or, *husbandry*
15 [a]ch. 21:30
16 [a]Ex. 1:9

A *Ge 25:23* ◄► *Ge 26:24*
U *Ge 24:35* ◄► *Ge 39:2–3*
B *Ge 24:35* ◄► *Ge 27:39*

26:3 In this verse the Lord reconfirmed with Isaac the Abrahamic covenant. God's promise to be a sustainer and protector of his people is repeated often throughout Scripture (see 28:13–15; 31:3; 35:11–12; Jos 1:5; Isa 41:10; Jer 1:19; Mt 28:20; Ac 18:10).

had stopped them after the death of Abraham: [a]and he called their names after the names by which his father had called them.

19 And Isaac's servants digged in the valley, and found there a well of [1]springing water.

20 And the herdmen of Gerar [a]did strive with Isaac's herdmen, saying, The water *is* ours: and he called the name of the well [1]Esek; because they strove with him.

21 And they digged another well, and strove for that also: and he called the name of it [1]Sitnah.

22 And he removed from thence, and digged another well; and for that they strove not: and he called the name of it [1]Rehoboth; and he said, For now the LORD hath made room for us, and we shall [a]be fruitful in the land.

23 And he went up from thence to Beer-sheba.

A R 24 And the LORD appeared unto him the same night, and said, [a]I *am* the God of Abraham thy father: [b]fear not, for [c]I *am* with thee, and will bless thee, and multiply thy seed for my servant Abraham's sake.

25 And he [a]builded an altar there, and [b]called upon the name of the LORD, and pitched his tent there: and there Isaac's servants digged a well.

26 ¶ Then Abimelech went to him from Gerar, and Ahuzzath one of his friends, [a]and Phichol the chief captain of his army.

27 And Isaac said unto them, Wherefore come ye to me, seeing [a]ye hate me, and have [b]sent me away from you?

L 28 And they said, [1]We saw certainly that the LORD [a]was with thee: and we said, Let there be now an oath betwixt us, *even* betwixt us and thee, and let us make a covenant with thee;

29 [1]That thou wilt do us no hurt, as we have not touched thee, and as we have done unto thee nothing but good, and have sent thee away in peace: [a]thou *art* now the blessed of the LORD.

30 [a]And he made them a feast, and they did eat and drink.

31 And they rose up betimes in the morning, and [a]sware one to another: and Isaac sent them away, and they departed from him in peace.

32 And it came to pass the same day, that Isaac's servants came, and told him concerning the well which they had digged, and said unto him, We have found water.

33 And he called it [1]Shebah: [a]therefore the name of the city *is* [2]Beer-sheba unto this day.

34 ¶ [a]And Esau was forty years old when he took to wife Judith the daughter of Beeri the Hittite, and Bashemath the daughter of Elon the Hittite:

35 Which [a]were [1]a grief of mind unto Isaac and to Rebekah.

Jacob's stolen blessing

27 AND IT came to pass, that when Isaac was old, and [a]his eyes were dim, so that he could not see, he called Esau his eldest son, and said unto him, My son: and he said unto him, Behold, *here am* I.

2 And he said, Behold now, I am old, I [a]know not the day of my death:

3 [a]Now therefore take, I pray thee, thy weapons, thy quiver and thy bow, and go out to the field, and [1]take me *some* venison;

4 And make me savoury meat, such as I love, and bring *it* to me, that I may eat; that my soul [a]may bless thee before I die.

5 And Rebekah heard when Isaac spake to Esau his son. And Esau went to the field to hunt *for* venison, *and* to bring *it*.

6 ¶ And Rebekah spake unto Jacob her son, saying, Behold, I heard thy father speak unto Esau thy brother, saying,

7 Bring me venison, and make me savoury meat, that I may eat, and bless thee before the LORD before my death.

8 Now therefore, my son, [a]obey my voice according to that which I command thee.

9 Go now to the flock, and fetch me from thence two good kids of the goats; and I will make them [a]savoury meat for thy father, such as he loveth:

10 And thou shalt bring *it* to thy father, that he may eat, and that he [a]may bless thee before his death.

11 And Jacob said to Rebekah his mother, Behold, [a]Esau my brother *is* a hairy man, and I *am* a smooth man:

12 My father peradventure will [a]feel

18 [a]ch. 21:31
19 [1]Heb. *living*
20 [a]ch. 21:25 [1]i.e. *Contention*
21 [1]i.e. *Hatred*
22 [a]ch. 17:6 & 28:3 & 41:52; Ex. 1:7 [1]i.e. *Room*
24 [a]ch. 17:7 & 24:12 [b]ch. 15:1 [c]ver. 3,4
25 [a]ch. 12:7 & 13:18 [b]Ps. 116:17
26 [a]ch. 21:22
27 [a]Judg. 11:7 [b]ver. 16
28 [a]ch. 21:22,23 [1]Heb. *Seeing we saw*
29 [a]ch. 24:31; Ps. 115:15 [1]Heb. *If thou shalt*
30 [a]ch. 19:3
31 [a]ch. 21:31
33 [a]ch. 21:31 [1]i.e. *An oath* [2]i.e. *The well of the oath*
34 [a]ch. 36:2
35 [a]ch. 27:46 & 28:1,8 [1]Heb. *bitterness of spirit*
27:1 [a]ch. 48:10; 1 Sam. 3:2
2 [a]Prov. 27:1; Jas. 4:14
3 [a]ch. 25:27,28 [1]Heb. *hunt*
4 [a]ver. 27; ch. 48:9,15 & 49:28; Deut. 33:1
8 [a]ver. 13
9 [a]ver. 4
10 [a]ver. 4
11 [a]ch. 25:25
12 [a]ver. 22

A *Ge 26:2–5* ◀ ▶ *Ge 27:28* **R** ▶ *Ge 30:27*
L *Ge 15:1* ◀ ▶ *Ge 28:15*

me, and I shall seem to him as a deceiver; and I shall bring [b]a curse upon me, and not a blessing.

13 And his mother said unto him, [a]Upon me *be* thy curse, my son: only obey my voice, and go fetch me *them.*

14 And he went, and fetched, and brought *them* to his mother: and his mother [a]made savoury meat, such as his father loved.

15 And Rebekah took [a]goodly[1] raiment of her eldest son Esau, which *were* with her in the house, and put them upon Jacob her younger son:

16 And she put the skins of the kids of the goats upon his hands, and upon the smooth of his neck:

17 And she gave the savoury meat and the bread, which she had prepared, into the hand of her son Jacob.

18 ¶ And he came unto his father, and said, My father: and he said, Here *am* I; who *art* thou, my son?

19 And Jacob said unto his father, I *am* Esau thy firstborn; I have done according as thou badest me: arise, I pray thee, sit and eat of my venison, [a]that thy soul may bless me.

20 And Isaac said unto his son, How *is it* that thou hast found *it* so quickly, my son? And he said, Because the LORD thy God brought *it* [1]to me.

21 And Isaac said unto Jacob, Come near, I pray thee, that I [a]may feel thee, my son, whether thou *be* my very son Esau or not.

22 And Jacob went near unto Isaac his father; and he felt him, and said, The voice *is* Jacob's voice, but the hands *are* the hands of Esau.

23 And he discerned him not, because [a]his hands were hairy, as his brother Esau's hands: so he blessed him.

24 And he said, *Art* thou my very son Esau? And he said, I *am.*

25 And he said, Bring *it* near to me, and I will eat of my son's venison, [a]that my soul may bless thee. And he brought *it* near to him, and he did eat: and he brought him wine, and he drank.

26 And his father Isaac said unto him, Come near now, and kiss me, my son.

27 And he came near, and kissed him: and he smelled the smell of his raiment, and blessed him, and said, See, [a]the smell of my son *is* as the smell of a field which the LORD hath blessed:

28 Therefore [a]God give thee of [b]the dew of heaven, and [c]the fatness of the earth, and [d]plenty of corn and wine: A F

29 [a]Let people serve thee, and nations bow down to thee: be lord over thy brethren, and [b]let thy mother's sons bow down to thee: [c]cursed *be* every one that curseth thee, and blessed *be* he that blesseth thee.

30 ¶ And it came to pass, as soon as Isaac had made an end of blessing Jacob, and Jacob was yet scarce gone out from the presence of Isaac his father, that Esau his brother came in from his hunting.

31 And he also had made savoury meat, and brought it unto his father, and said unto his father, Let my father arise, and [a]eat of his son's venison, that thy soul may bless me.

32 And Isaac his father said unto him, Who *art* thou? And he said, I *am* thy son, thy firstborn Esau.

33 And Isaac [1]trembled very exceedingly, and said, Who? where *is* he that hath [2]taken venison, and brought *it* me, and I have eaten of all before thou camest, and have blessed him? yea, [a]*and* he shall be blessed.

34 And when Esau heard the words of his father, [a]he cried with a great and exceeding bitter cry, and said unto his father, Bless me, *even* me also, O my father.

35 And he said, Thy brother came with subtlety, and hath taken away thy blessing.

36 And he said, [a]Is not he rightly named [1]Jacob? for he hath supplanted me these two times: [b]he took away my birthright; and, behold, now he hath taken away my blessing. And he said, Hast thou not reserved a blessing for me?

37 And Isaac answered and said unto Esau, [a]Behold, I have made him thy lord, and all his brethren have I given to him for servants; and [b]with corn and wine have I [1]sustained him: and what shall I do now unto thee, my son?

38 And Esau said unto his father, Hast thou but one blessing, my father? bless me, *even* me also, O my father. And Esau lifted up his voice, [a]and wept.

12 [b]ch. 9:25; Deut. 27:18
13 [a]ch. 43:9; 1 Sam. 25:24; 2 Sam. 14:9; Mat. 27:25
14 [a]Prov. 23:3; Luke 21:34
15 [a]ver. 27 [1]Heb. *desirable*
19 [a]ver. 4
20 [1]Heb. *before me*
21 [a]ver. 12
23 [a]ver. 16
25 [a]ver. 4,10,19, 31
27 [a]Sol. 4:11; Hos. 14:6
28 [a]Heb. 11:20 [b]Deut. 33:13,28; 2 Sam. 1:21; Ps. 133:3; Mic. 5:7 [c]ch. 45:18 [d]Deut. 33:28
29 [a]ch. 9:25 & 25:23 [b]ch. 49:8 [c]ch. 12:3; Num. 24:9; Zeph. 2:8
31 [a]ver. 4
33 [a]ch. 28:3,4; Rom. 11:29 [1]Heb. *trembled with a great trembling greatly* [2]Heb. *hunted*
34 [a]Heb. 12:17
36 [a]ch. 25:26 [b]ch. 25:33 [1]i.e. *A supplanter*
37 [a]Fulfilled 2 Sam. 8:14 [b]ver. 28 [1]Or, *supported*
38 [a]Heb. 12:17

A *Ge 26:24* ◀ ▶ *Ge 27:39–40*
F *Ge 21:19* ◀ ▶ *Ge 28:20*

39 And Isaac his father answered and said unto him, Behold, [a]thy dwelling shall be ʹthe fatness of the earth, and of the dew of heaven from above;

40 And by thy sword shalt thou live, and [a]shalt serve thy brother; and [b]it shall come to pass when thou shalt have the dominion, that thou shalt break his yoke from off thy neck.

Isaac sends Jacob to Laban

41 ¶ And Esau [a]hated Jacob because of the blessing wherewith his father blessed him: and Esau said in his heart, [b]The days of mourning for my father are at hand; [c]then will I slay my brother Jacob.

42 And these words of Esau her elder son were told to Rebekah: and she sent and called Jacob her younger son, and said unto him, Behold, thy brother Esau, as touching thee, doth [a]comfort himself, *purposing* to kill thee.

43 Now therefore, my son, obey my voice; and arise, flee thou to Laban my brother [a]to Haran;

44 And tarry with him a few days, until thy brother's fury turn away;

45 Until thy brother's anger turn away from thee, and he forget *that* which thou hast done to him: then I will send, and fetch thee from thence: why should I be deprived also of you both in one day?

46 And Rebekah said to Isaac, [a]I am weary of my life because of the daughters of Heth: [b]if Jacob take a wife of the daughters of Heth, such as these *which are* of the daughters of the land, what good shall my life do me?

28 AND ISAAC called Jacob, and [a]blessed him, and charged him, and said unto him, [b]Thou shalt not take a wife of the daughters of Canaan.

2 [a]Arise, go to [b]Padan-aram, to the house of [c]Bethuel thy mother's father; and take thee a wife from thence of the daughters of [d]Laban thy mother's brother.

3 [a]And God Almighty bless thee, and make thee fruitful, and multiply thee, that thou mayest be ʹa multitude of people;

4 And give thee [a]the blessing of Abraham, to thee, and to thy seed with thee; that thou mayest inherit the land [b]whereinʹ thou art a stranger, which God gave unto Abraham.

5 And Isaac sent away Jacob: and he went to Padan-aram unto Laban, son of Bethuel the Syrian, the brother of Rebekah, Jacob's and Esau's mother.

6 ¶ When Esau saw that Isaac had blessed Jacob, and sent him away to Padan-aram, to take him a wife from thence; and that as he blessed him he gave him a charge, saying, Thou shalt not take a wife of the daughters of Canaan;

7 And that Jacob obeyed his father and his mother, and was gone to Padan-aram;

8 And Esau seeing [a]that the daughters of Canaan ʹpleased not Isaac his father;

9 Then went Esau unto Ishmael, and took unto the wives which he had [a]Mahalath the daughter of Ishmael Abraham's son, [b]the sister of Nebajoth, to be his wife.

Jacob's dream at Beth-el

10 ¶ And Jacob [a]went out from Beer-sheba, and went toward [b]Haran.

11 And he lighted upon a certain place, and tarried there all night, because the sun was set; and he took of the stones of that place, and put *them for* his pillows, and lay down in that place to sleep.

12 And he [a]dreamed, and behold a ladder set up on the earth, and the top of it reached to heaven: and behold [b]the angels of God ascending and descending on it.

13 [a]And, behold, the LORD stood above it, and said, [b]I *am* the LORD God of Abraham thy father, and the God of Isaac: [c]the land whereon thou liest, to thee will I give it, and to thy seed;

14 And [a]thy seed shall be as the dust of the earth, and thou shalt ʹspread abroad [b]to the west, and to the east, and to the north, and to the south: and in thee and [c]in thy seed shall all the families of the earth be blessed.

15 And, behold, [a]I *am* with thee, and will [b]keep thee in all *places* whither thou goest, and will [c]bring thee again into this land; for [d]I will not leave thee, [e]until I have done *that* which I have spoken to thee of.

16 ¶ And Jacob awaked out of his

39 [a]ver. 28; Heb. 11:20 ʹOr, *of the fatness*
40 [a]ch. 25:23; 2 Sam. 8:14; Obad. 18-20 [b]2 Ki. 8:20
41 [a]ch. 37:4,8 [b]ch. 50:3,4,10 [c]Obad. 10
42 [a]Ps. 64:5
43 [a]ch. 11:31
46 [a]ch. 26:35 & 28:8 [b]ch. 24:3
28:1 [a]ch. 27:33 [b]ch. 24:3
2 [a]Hos. 12:12 [b]ch. 25:20 [c]ch. 22:23 [d]ch. 24:29
3 [a]ch. 17:1,6 ʹHeb. *an assembly of people*
4 [a]ch. 12:2 [b]ch. 17:8 ʹHeb. *of thy sojournings*
8 [a]ch. 24:3 & 26:35 ʹHeb. were *evil in the eyes*
9 [a]ch. 36:3, she is called *Bashemath* [b]ch. 25:13
10 [a]Hos. 12:12 [b]Called, Acts 7:2 *Charran*
12 [a]ch. 41:1 [b]John 1:51; Heb. 1:14
13 [a]ch. 35:1 & 48:3 [b]ch. 26:24 [c]ch. 13:15 & 35:12
14 [a]ch. 13:16 [b]ch. 13:14; Deut. 12:20 [c]ch. 12:3 & 18:18 & 22:18 & 26:4 ʹHeb. *break forth*
15 [a]See ver. 20,21 [b]ch. 48:16 [c]ch. 35:6 [d]Deut. 31:6,8; Josh. 1:5; 1 Ki. 8:57; Heb. 13:5 [e]Num. 23:19

A *Ge 27:28* ◄► *Ge 28:3–4*
B *Ge 26:12* ◄► *Ge 39:5*
A *Ge 27:39–40* ◄► *Ge 28:13–15*
A *Ge 28:3–4* ◄► *Ge 32:27–28*
L *Ge 26:28* ◄► *Ex 11:7*

sleep, and he said, Surely the LORD is in [a]this place; and I knew *it* not.

17 And he was afraid, and said, How dreadful *is* this place! this *is* none other but the house of God, and this *is* the gate of heaven.

18 And Jacob rose up early in the morning, and took the stone that he had put *for* his pillows, and [a]set it up *for* a pillar, [b]and poured oil upon the top of it.

19 And he called the name of [a]that place [1]Beth-el: but the name of that city *was called* Luz at the first.

C 20 [a]And Jacob vowed a vow, saying, If
F [b]God will be with me, and will keep me in this way that I go, and will give me [c]bread to eat, and raiment to put on,

21 So that [a]I come again to my father's house in peace; [b]then shall the LORD be my God:

22 And this stone, which I have set *for* a pillar, [a]shall be God's house: [b]and of all that thou shalt give me I will surely give the tenth unto thee.

Jacob meets Rachel

29 THEN JACOB [1]went on his journey, [a]and came into the land of the [2]people of the east.

2 And he looked, and behold a well in the field, and, lo, there *were* three flocks of sheep lying by it; for out of that well they watered the flocks: and a great stone *was* upon the well's mouth.

3 And thither were all the flocks gathered: and they rolled the stone from the well's mouth, and watered the sheep, and put the stone again upon the well's mouth in his place.

4 And Jacob said unto them, My brethren, whence *be* ye? And they said, Of Haran *are* we.

5 And he said unto them, Know ye Laban the son of Nahor? And they said, We know *him.*

6 And he said unto them, [a]*Is* [1] he well? And they said, *He is* well: and, behold, Rachel his daughter cometh with the sheep.

7 And he said, Lo, [1]*it is* yet high day, neither *is it* time that the cattle should be gathered together: water ye the sheep, and go *and* feed *them.*

8 And they said, We cannot, until all the flocks be gathered together, and *till* they roll the stone from the well's mouth; then we water the sheep.

9 ¶ And while he yet spake with them, [a]Rachel came with her father's sheep: for she kept them.

10 And it came to pass, when Jacob saw Rachel the daughter of Laban his mother's brother, and the sheep of Laban his mother's brother, that Jacob went near, and [a]rolled the stone from the well's mouth, and watered the flock of Laban his mother's brother.

11 And Jacob [a]kissed Rachel, and lifted up his voice, and wept.

12 And Jacob told Rachel that he *was* [a]her father's brother, and that he *was* Rebekah's son: [b]and she ran and told her father.

13 And it came to pass, when Laban heard the [1]tidings of Jacob his sister's son, that [a]he ran to meet him, and embraced him, and kissed him, and brought him to his house. And he told Laban all these things.

14 And Laban said to him, [a]Surely thou *art* my bone and my flesh. And he abode with him [1]the space of a month.

Jacob marries Leah and Rachel

15 ¶ And Laban said unto Jacob, Because thou *art* my brother, shouldest thou therefore serve me for nought? tell me, what *shall* thy wages *be?*

16 And Laban had two daughters: the name of the elder *was* Leah, and the name of the younger *was* Rachel.

17 Leah *was* tender eyed; but Rachel was beautiful and wellfavoured.

18 And Jacob loved Rachel; and said, [a]I will serve thee seven years for Rachel thy younger daughter.

19 And Laban said, *It is* better that I give her to thee, than that I should give her to another man: abide with me.

20 And Jacob [a]served seven years for Rachel; and they seemed unto him *but* a few days, for the love he had to her.

21 ¶ And Jacob said unto Laban, Give *me* my wife, for my days are fulfilled, that I may [a]go in unto her.

22 And Laban gathered together all the men of the place, and [a]made a feast.

23 And it came to pass in the evening, that he took Leah his daughter, and brought her to him; and he went in unto her.

16 [a]Ex. 3:5; Josh. 5:15
18 [a]ch. 31:13,45 [b]Lev. 8:10-12
19 [a]Judg. 1:23,26; Hos. 4:15 [1]i.e. *The house of God*
20 [a]ch. 31:13; Judg. 11:30; 2 Sam. 15:8 [b]ver. 15 [c]1 Tim. 6:8
21 [a]Judg. 11:31; 2 Sam. 19:24,30 [b]Deut. 26:17; 2 Sam. 15:8
22 [a]ch. 35:7,14 [b]Lev. 27:30
29:1 [a]Num. 23:7; Hos. 12:12 [1]Heb. *lift up his feet* [2]Heb. *children*
6 [a]ch. 43:27 [1]Heb. Is there *peace to him?*
7 [1]Heb. *yet the day* is *great*
9 [a]Ex. 2:16
10 [a]Ex. 2:17
11 [a]ch. 33:4 & 45:14,15
12 [a]ch. 13:8 & 14:14,16 [b]ch. 24:28
13 [a]ch. 24:29 [1]Heb. *hearing*
14 [a]ch. 2:23; Judg. 9:2; 2 Sam. 5:1 & 19:12,13 [1]Heb. *a month of days*
18 [a]ch. 31:41; 2 Sam. 3:14
20 [a]ch. 30:26; Hos. 12:12
21 [a]Judg. 15:1
22 [a]Judg. 14:10; John 2:1,2

24 And Laban gave unto his daughter Leah Zilpah his maid *for* an handmaid.

25 And it came to pass, that in the morning, behold, it *was* Leah: and he said to Laban, What *is* this thou hast done unto me? did not I serve with thee for Rachel? wherefore then hast thou beguiled me?

26 And Laban said, It must not be so done in our [1]country, to give the younger before the firstborn.

27 [a]Fulfil her week, and we will give thee this also for the service which thou shalt serve with me yet seven other years.

28 And Jacob did so, and fulfilled her week: and he gave him Rachel his daughter to wife also.

29 And Laban gave to Rachel his daughter Bilhah his handmaid to be her maid.

30 And he went in also unto Rachel, and he [a]loved also Rachel more than Leah, and served with him [b]yet seven other years.

The sons of Jacob

31 ¶ And when the LORD [a]saw that Leah *was* hated, he [b]opened her womb: but Rachel *was* barren.

32 And Leah conceived, and bare a son, and she called his name [1]Reuben: for she said, Surely the LORD hath [a]looked upon my affliction; now therefore my husband will love me.

33 And she conceived again, and bare a son; and said, Because the LORD hath heard that I *was* hated, he hath therefore given me this *son* also: and she called his name [1]Simeon.

34 And she conceived again, and bare a son; and said, Now this time will my husband be joined unto me, because I have born him three sons: therefore was his name called [1]Levi.

35 And she conceived again, and bare a son: and she said, Now will I praise the LORD: therefore she called his name [a]Judah;[1] and [2]left bearing.

30 AND WHEN Rachel saw that [a]she bare Jacob no children, Rachel [b]envied her sister; and said unto Jacob, Give me children, [c]or else I die.

2 And Jacob's anger was kindled against Rachel: and he said, [a]*Am* I in God's stead, who hath withheld from thee the fruit of the womb?

3 And she said, Behold [a]my maid Bilhah, go in unto her; [b]and she shall bear upon my knees, [a]that I may also [1]have children by her.

4 And she gave him Bilhah her handmaid [a]to wife: and Jacob went in unto her.

5 And Bilhah conceived, and bare Jacob a son.

6 And Rachel said, God hath [a]judged me, and hath also heard my voice, and hath given me a son: therefore called she his name [1]Dan.

7 And Bilhah Rachel's maid conceived again, and bare Jacob a second son.

8 And Rachel said, With [1]great wrestlings have I wrestled with my sister, and I have prevailed: and she called his name [a]Naphtali.[2]

9 When Leah saw that she had left bearing, she took Zilpah her maid, and [a]gave her Jacob to wife.

10 And Zilpah Leah's maid bare Jacob a son.

11 And Leah said, A troop cometh: and she called his name [1]Gad.

12 And Zilpah Leah's maid bare Jacob a second son.

13 And Leah said, [1]Happy am I, for the daughters [a]will call me blessed: and she called his name [2]Asher.

14 ¶ And Reuben went in the days of wheat harvest, and found mandrakes in the field, and brought them unto his mother Leah. Then Rachel said to Leah, [a]Give me, I pray thee, of thy son's mandrakes.

15 And she said unto her, [a]*Is it* a small matter that thou hast taken my husband? and wouldest thou take away my son's mandrakes also? And Rachel said, Therefore he shall lie with thee tonight for thy son's mandrakes.

16 And Jacob came out of the field in the evening, and Leah went out to meet him, and said, Thou must come in unto me; for surely I have hired thee with my son's mandrakes. And he lay with her that night.

17 And God hearkened unto Leah, and she conceived, and bare Jacob the fifth son.

18 And Leah said, God hath given me my hire, because I have given my maiden

26 [1]Heb. *place*
27 [a]Judg. 14:12
30 [a]Deut. 21:15 [b]ch. 30:26 & 31:41; Hos. 12:12
31 [a]Ps. 127:3 [b]ch. 30:1
32 [a]Ex. 4:31; Deut. 26:7; Ps. 25:18 [1]i.e. *See a son*
33 [1]i.e. *Hearing*
34 [1]i.e. *Joined*
35 [a]Mat. 1:2 [1]i.e. *Praise* [2]Heb. *stood from bearing*
30:1 [a]ch. 29:31 [b]ch. 37:11 [c]Job 5:2
2 [a]ch. 16:2; 1 Sam. 1:5
3 [a]ch. 16:2 [b]ch. 50:23; Job 3:12 [1]Heb. *be built by her*
4 [a]ch. 16:3
6 [a]Lam. 3:59 [1]i.e. *Judging*
8 [a]Called, Mat. 4:13, *Nephthalim* [1]Heb. *wrestlings of God* [2]i.e. *My wrestling*
9 [a]ver. 4
11 [1]i.e. *A troop, or, company*
13 [a]Prov. 31:28; Luke 1:48 [1]Heb. *In my happiness* [2]i.e. *Happy*
14 [a]ch. 25:30
15 [a]Num. 16:9,13

E Ge 25:21 ◀ ▶ Ge 30:22

to my husband: and she called his name
[1]Issachar.
19 And Leah conceived again, and
bare Jacob the sixth son.
20 And Leah said, God hath endued
me *with* a good dowry; now will my husband dwell with me, because I have born
him six sons: and she called his name
[a]Zebulun.[1]
21 And afterwards she bare a daughter, and called her name [1]Dinah.
E 22 ¶ And God [a]remembered Rachel,
and God hearkened to her, and [b]opened
her womb.
23 And she conceived, and bare a son;
and said, God hath taken away [a]my reproach:
24 And she called his name [1]Joseph;
and said, [a]The LORD shall add to me another son.

Jacob's bargain with Laban

25 ¶ And it came to pass, when Rachel
had born Joseph, that Jacob said unto Laban, [a]Send me away, that I may go unto
[b]mine own place, and to my country.
26 Give *me* my wives and my children,
[a]for whom I have served thee, and let me
go: for thou knowest my service which I
have done thee.
R 27 And Laban said unto him, I pray
thee, if I have found favour in thine eyes,
tarry: for [a]I have learned by experience
that the LORD hath blessed me [b]for thy
sake.
28 And he said, [a]Appoint me thy
wages, and I will give *it.*
29 And he said unto him, [a]Thou knowest how I have served thee, and how thy
cattle was with me.
30 For *it was* little which thou hadst
before I *came,* and it is *now* [1]increased
unto a multitude; and the LORD hath
blessed thee [2]since my coming: and now
when shall I [a]provide for mine own
house also?
31 And he said, What shall I give thee?
And Jacob said, Thou shalt not give me
any thing: if thou wilt do this thing for
me, I will again feed *and* keep thy
flock.
32 I will pass through all thy flock today, removing from thence all the speck-

18 [1]i.e. *An hire*

20 [a]Called, Mat. 4:13, *Zabulon* [1]i.e. Dwelling

21 [1]i.e. *Judgment*

22 [a]1 Sam. 1:19 [b]ch. 29:31

23 [a]1 Sam. 1:6; Is. 4:1; Luke 1:25

24 [a]ch. 35:17 [1]i.e. *Adding*

25 [a]ch. 24:54,56 [b]ch. 18:33

26 [a]ch. 29:20,30

27 [a]ch. 39:3,5 [b]See ch. 26:24

28 [a]ch. 29:15

29 [a]ch. 31:6, 38-40; Mat. 24:45; Tit. 2:10

30 [a]1 Tim. 5:8 [1]Heb. *broken forth* [2]Heb. *at my foot*

32 [a]ch. 31:8

33 [a]Ps. 37:6 [1]Heb. *tomorrow*

37 [a]See ch. 31:9-12

43 [a]ver. 30 [b]ch. 13:2 & 24:35 & 26:13,14

led and spotted cattle, and all the brown
cattle among the sheep, and the spotted
and speckled among the goats: and [a]*of
such* shall be my hire.
33 So shall my [a]righteousness answer
for me [1]in time to come, when it shall
come for my hire before thy face: every
one that *is* not speckled and spotted
among the goats, and brown among the
sheep, that shall be counted stolen
with me.
34 And Laban said, Behold, I would it
might be according to thy word.
35 And he removed that day the he
goats that were ringstraked and spotted,
and all the she goats that were speckled
and spotted, *and* every one that had *some*
white in it, and all the brown among the
sheep, and gave *them* into the hand of his
sons.
36 And he set three days' journey betwixt himself and Jacob: and Jacob fed the
rest of Laban's flocks.
37 ¶ And [a]Jacob took him rods of
green poplar, and of the hazel and chestnut tree; and pilled white strakes in
them, and made the white appear which
was in the rods.
38 And he set the rods which he had
pilled before the flocks in the gutters in
the watering troughs when the flocks
came to drink, that they should conceive
when they came to drink.
39 And the flocks conceived before the
rods, and brought forth cattle ringstraked,
speckled, and spotted.
40 And Jacob did separate the lambs,
and set the faces of the flocks toward the
ringstraked, and all the brown in the
flock of Laban; and he put his own flocks
by themselves, and put them not unto Laban's cattle.
41 And it came to pass, whensoever
the stronger cattle did conceive, that Jacob laid the rods before the eyes of the
cattle in the gutters, that they might conceive among the rods.
42 But when the cattle were feeble, he
put *them* not in: so the feebler were Laban's, and the stronger Jacob's.
43 And the man [a]increased exceedingly, and [b]had much cattle, and maidservants, and menservants, and camels, and
asses.

E Ge 29:31 ◀▶ Ex 4:7
R Ge 26:24 ◀▶ Ge 39:5

Jacob flees from Laban

31 AND HE heard the words of Laban's sons, saying, Jacob hath taken away all that *was* our father's; and of *that* which *was* our father's hath he gotten all this [a]glory.

2 And Jacob beheld [a]the countenance of Laban, and, behold, it *was* not [b]toward him [']as before.

3 And the LORD said unto Jacob, [a]Return unto the land of thy fathers, and to thy kindred; and I will be with thee.

4 And Jacob sent and called Rachel and Leah to the field unto his flock,

5 And said unto them, [a]I see your father's countenance, that it *is* not toward me as before; but the God of my father [b]hath been with me.

6 And [a]ye know that with all my power I have served your father.

7 And your father hath deceived me, and [a]changed my wages [b]ten times; but God [c]suffered him not to hurt me.

8 If he said thus, [a]The speckled shall be thy wages; then all the cattle bare speckled: and if he said thus, The ringstraked shall be thy hire; then bare all the cattle ringstraked.

9 Thus God hath [a]taken away the cattle of your father, and given *them* to me.

10 And it came to pass at the time that the cattle conceived, that I lifted up mine eyes, and saw in a dream, and, behold, the [']rams which leaped upon the cattle *were* ringstraked, speckled, and grisled.

11 And [a]the angel of God spake unto me in a dream, *saying,* Jacob: And I said, Here *am* I.

12 And he said, Lift up now thine eyes, and see, all the rams which leap upon the cattle *are* ringstraked, speckled, and grisled: for [a]I have seen all that Laban doeth unto thee.

13 I *am* the God of Beth-el, [a]where thou anointedst the pillar, *and* where thou vowedst a vow unto me: now [b]arise, get thee out from this land, and return unto the land of thy kindred.

14 And Rachel and Leah answered and said unto him, [a]*Is there* yet any portion or inheritance for us in our father's house?

15 Are we not counted of him strangers? for [a]he hath sold us, and hath quite devoured also our money.

16 For all the riches which God hath taken from our father, that *is* ours, and our children's: now then, whatsoever God hath said unto thee, do.

17 ¶ Then Jacob rose up, and set his sons and his wives upon camels;

18 And he carried away all his cattle, and all his goods which he had gotten, the cattle of his getting, which he had gotten in Padan-aram, for to go to Isaac his father in the land of Canaan.

19 And Laban went to shear his sheep: and Rachel had stolen the [a]images [b]that['] *were* her father's.

20 And Jacob stole away [']unawares to Laban the Syrian, in that he told him not that he fled.

21 So he fled with all that he had; and he rose up, and passed over the river, and [a]set his face *toward* the mount Gilead.

22 And it was told Laban on the third day that Jacob was fled.

23 And he took [a]his brethren with him, and pursued after him seven days' journey; and they overtook him in the mount Gilead.

24 And God [a]came to Laban the Syrian in a dream by night, and said unto him, Take heed that thou [b]speak not to Jacob [']either good or bad.

25 ¶ Then Laban overtook Jacob. Now Jacob had pitched his tent in the mount: and Laban with his brethren pitched in the mount of Gilead.

26 And Laban said to Jacob, What hast thou done, that thou hast stolen away unawares to me, and [a]carried away my daughters, as captives *taken* with the sword?

27 Wherefore didst thou flee away secretly, and [']steal away from me; and didst not tell me, that I might have sent thee away with mirth, and with songs, with tabret, and with harp?

28 And hast not suffered me [a]to kiss my sons and my daughters? [b]thou hast now done foolishly in *so* doing.

29 It is in the power of my hand to do you hurt: but the [a]God of your father spake unto me [b]yesternight, saying, Take thou heed that thou speak not to Jacob either good or bad.

30 And now, *though* thou wouldest needs be gone, because thou sore longedst after thy father's house, *yet* wherefore hast thou [a]stolen my gods?

31 And Jacob answered and said to Laban, Because I was afraid: for I said,

31:1 [a]Ps. 49:16
2 [a]ch. 4:5 [b]Deut. 28:54 [']Heb. *as yesterday and the day before*
3 [a]ch. 28:15,20, 21 & 32:9
5 [a]ver. 2 [b]ver. 3
6 [a]ver. 38-41; ch. 30:29
7 [a]ver. 41 [b]Num. 14:22; Neh. 4:12; Job 19:3; Zech. 8:23 [c]ch. 20:6; Job 1:10; Ps. 37:28 & 105:14
8 [a]ch. 30:32
9 [a]ver. 1,16
10 [']Or, *he goats*
11 [a]ch. 48:16
12 [a]Ex. 3:7; Ps. 139:3; Eccl. 5:8
13 [a]ch. 28:18-20 [b]ver. 3; ch. 32:9
14 [a]ch. 2:24
15 [a]ch. 29:15,27; Neh. 5:8
19 [a]ch. 35:2 [b]Judg. 17:5; 1 Sam. 19:13; Hos. 3:4 [']Heb. *teraphim*
20 [']Heb. *the heart of Laban*
21 [a]ch. 46:28; 2 Ki. 12:17; Luke 9:51,53
23 [a]ch. 13:8
24 [a]ch. 20:3; Job 33:15; Mat. 1:20 [b]ch. 24:50 [']Heb. *from good to bad*
26 [a]1 Sam. 30:2
27 [']Heb. *hast stolen me*
28 [a]ver. 55; Ruth 1:9,14; 1 Ki. 19:20; Acts 20:37 [b]1 Sam. 13:13; 2 Chr. 16:9
29 [a]ver. 53; ch. 28:13 [b]ver. 24
30 [a]ver. 19; Judg. 18:24

Peradventure thou wouldest take by force thy daughters from me.

32 With whomsoever thou findest thy gods, [a]let him not live: before our brethren discern thou what *is* thine with me, and take *it* to thee. For Jacob knew not that Rachel had stolen them.

33 And Laban went into Jacob's tent, and into Leah's tent, and into the two maidservants' tents; but he found *them* not. Then went he out of Leah's tent, and entered into Rachel's tent.

34 Now Rachel had taken the images, and put them in the camel's furniture, and sat upon them. And Laban [1]searched all the tent, but found *them* not.

35 And she said to her father, Let it not displease my lord that I cannot [a]rise up before thee; for the custom of women *is* upon me. And he searched, but found not the images.

36 ¶ And Jacob was wroth, and chode with Laban: and Jacob answered and said to Laban, What *is* my trespass? what *is* my sin, that thou hast so hotly pursued after me?

37 Whereas thou hast [1]searched all my stuff, what hast thou found of all thy household stuff? set *it* here before my brethren and thy brethren, that they may judge betwixt us both.

38 This twenty years *have* I *been* with thee; thy ewes and thy she goats have not cast their young, and the rams of thy flock have I not eaten.

39 [a]That which was torn *of beasts* I brought not unto thee; I bare the loss of it; of [b]my hand didst thou require it, *whether* stolen by day, or stolen by night.

40 *Thus* I was; in the day the drought consumed me, and the frost by night; and my sleep departed from mine eyes.

41 Thus have I been twenty years in thy house; I [a]served thee fourteen years for thy two daughters, and six years for thy cattle: and [b]thou hast changed my wages ten times.

42 [a]Except the God of my father, the God of Abraham, and [b]the fear of Isaac, had been with me, surely thou hadst sent me away now empty. [c]God hath seen mine affliction and the labour of my hands, and [d]rebuked *thee* yesternight.

43 ¶ And Laban answered and said unto Jacob, *These* daughters *are* my daughters, and *these* children *are* my children, and *these* cattle *are* my cattle, and all that thou seest *is* mine: and what can I do this day unto these my daughters, or unto their children which they have born?

44 Now therefore come thou, [a]let us make a covenant, I and thou; [b]and let it be for a witness between me and thee.

45 And Jacob [a]took a stone, and set it up *for* a pillar.

46 And Jacob said unto his brethren, Gather stones; and they took stones, and made an heap: and they did eat there upon the heap.

47 And Laban called it [1]Jegar-sahadutha: but Jacob called it [2]Galeed.

48 And Laban said, [a]This heap *is* a witness between me and thee this day. Therefore was the name of it called Galeed;

49 And [a]Mizpah;[1] for he said, The LORD watch between me and thee, when we are absent one from another.

50 If thou shalt afflict my daughters, or if thou shalt take *other* wives beside my daughters, no man *is* with us; see, God *is* witness betwixt me and thee.

51 And Laban said to Jacob, Behold this heap, and behold *this* pillar, which I have cast betwixt me and thee;

52 This heap *be* witness, and *this* pillar *be* witness, that I will not pass over this heap to thee, and that thou shalt not pass over this heap and this pillar unto me, for harm.

53 The God of Abraham, and the God of Nahor, the God of their father, [a]judge betwixt us. And Jacob [b]sware by [c]the fear of his father Isaac.

54 Then Jacob [1]offered sacrifice upon the mount, and called his brethren to eat bread: and they did eat bread, and tarried all night in the mount.

55 And early in the morning Laban rose up, and kissed his sons and his daughters, and [a]blessed them: and Laban departed, and [b]returned unto his place.

Jacob prepares to meet Esau

32 AND JACOB went on his way, and [a]the angels of God met him.

2 And when Jacob saw them, he said, This *is* God's [a]host: and he called the name of that place [1]Mahanaim.

3 And Jacob sent messengers before him to Esau his brother [a]unto the land of Seir, [b]the [1]country of Edom.

4 And he commanded them, saying,

32 [a]See ch. 44:9
34 [1]Heb. *felt*
35 [a]Ex. 20:12; Lev. 19:32
37 [1]Heb. *felt*
39 [a]Ex. 22:10 [b]Ex. 22:12
41 [a]ch. 29:27,28 [b]ver. 7
42 [a]Ps. 124:1,2 [b]ver. 53; Is. 8:13 [c]ch. 29:32; Ex. 3:7 [d]1 Chr. 12:17
44 [a]ch. 26:28 [b]Josh. 24:27
45 [a]ch. 28:18
47 [1]i.e. *The heap of witness* Chald. [2]i.e. *The heap of witness* Heb.
48 [a]Josh. 24:27
49 [a]Judg. 11:29; 1 Sam. 7:5 [1]i.e. *A beacon,* or, *watchtower*
53 [a]ch. 16:5 [b]ch. 21:23 [c]ver. 42
54 [1]Or, *killed beasts*
55 [a]ch. 28:1 [b]ch. 18:33 & 30:25; Num. 24:25
32:1 [a]Ps. 91:11; Heb. 1:14
2 [a]Josh. 5:14; Ps. 103:21 & 148:2; Luke 2:13 [1]i.e. *Two hosts,* or, *camps*
3 [a]ch. 33:14,16 [b]ch. 36:6-8; Deut. 2:5; Josh. 24:4 [1]Heb. *field*

[a]Thus shall ye speak unto my lord Esau;
Thy servant Jacob saith thus, I have sojourned with Laban, and stayed there until now:
5 And [a]I have oxen, and asses, flocks,
and menservants, and womenservants:
and I have sent to tell my lord, that [b]I
may find grace in thy sight.
6 ¶ And the messengers returned to
Jacob, saying, We came to thy brother
Esau, and also [a]he cometh to meet thee,
and four hundred men with him.
7 Then Jacob was greatly afraid and
[a]distressed: and he divided the people
that *was* with him, and the flocks, and
herds, and the camels, into two bands;
8 And said, If Esau come to the one
company, and smite it, then the other
company which is left shall escape.
9 ¶ [a]And Jacob said, [b]O God of my father Abraham, and God of my father
Isaac, the LORD [c]which saidst unto me,
Return unto thy country, and to thy kindred, and I will deal well with thee:
10 [l]I am not worthy of the least of all
the [a]mercies, and of all the truth, which
thou hast shown unto thy servant; for
with [b]my staff I passed over this Jordan;
and now I am become two bands.
11 [a]Deliver me, I pray thee, from the
hand of my brother, from the hand of
Esau: for I fear him, lest he will come and
smite me, *and* [b]the mother [l]with the
children.
12 And [a]thou saidst, I will surely do
thee good, and make thy seed as the sand
of the sea, which cannot be numbered for
multitude.
13 ¶ And he lodged there that same
night; and took of that which came to his
hand [a]a present for Esau his brother;
14 Two hundred she goats, and twenty
he goats, two hundred ewes, and twenty
rams,
15 Thirty milch camels with their
colts, forty kine, and ten bulls, twenty
she asses, and ten foals.
16 And he delivered *them* into the
hand of his servants, every drove by
themselves; and said unto his servants,
Pass over before me, and put a space betwixt drove and drove.
17 And he commanded the foremost,
saying, When Esau my brother meeteth
thee, and asketh thee, saying, Whose *art*
thou? and whither goest thou? and whose
are these before thee?

4 [a]Prov. 15:1
5 [a]ch. 30:43 [b]ch. 33:8,15
6 [a]ch. 33:1
7 [a]ch. 35:3
9 [a]Ps. 50:15 [b]ch. 28:13 [c]ch. 31:3,13
10 [a]ch. 24:27 [b]Job 8:7 [l]Heb. *I am less than all*
11 [a]Ps. 59:1,2 [b]Hos. 10:14 [l]Heb. *upon*
12 [a]ch. 28:13-15
13 [a]ch. 43:11; Prov. 18:16
20 [a]Prov. 21:14 [l]Heb. *my face*
22 [a]Deut. 3:16
23 [l]Heb. *caused to pass*
24 [a]Hos. 12:3,4 [l]Heb. *ascending of the morning*
25 [a]See Mat. 26:41; 2 Cor. 12:7
26 [a]See Luke 24:28 [b]Hos. 12:4
28 [a]ch. 35:10; 2 Ki. 17:34 [b]Hos. 12:3,4 [c]ch. 25:31 & 27:33 [l]i.e. *A prince of God*
29 [a]Judg. 13:18
30 [a]ch. 16:13; Ex. 24:11; Deut. 5:24; Judg. 6:22; Is. 6:5 [l]i.e. *The face of God*

18 Then thou shalt say, *They be* thy
servant Jacob's; it *is* a present sent unto
my lord Esau: and, behold, also he *is* behind us.
19 And so commanded he the second,
and the third, and all that followed the
droves, saying, On this manner shall ye
speak unto Esau, when ye find him.
20 And say ye moreover, Behold, thy
servant Jacob *is* behind us. For he said, I
will [a]appease him with the present that
goeth before me, and afterward I will see
his face; peradventure he will accept
[l]of me.
21 So went the present over before
him: and himself lodged that night in the
company.

Jacob's wrestling at Peniel

22 And he rose up that night, and took
his two wives, and his two womenservants, and his eleven sons, [a]and passed
over the ford Jabbok.
23 And he took them, and [l]sent them
over the brook, and sent over that he
had.
24 ¶ And Jacob was left alone; and
there [a]wrestled a man with him until the
[l]breaking of the day.
25 And when he saw that he prevailed
not against him, he touched the hollow
of his thigh; and [a]the hollow of Jacob's
thigh was out of joint, as he wrestled
with him.
26 And [a]he said, Let me go, for the day
breaketh. And he said, [b]I will not let thee
go, except thou bless me.
27 And he said unto him, What *is* thy A
name? And he said, Jacob.
28 And he said, [a]Thy name shall be
called no more Jacob, but [l]Israel: for as a
prince hast thou [b]power with God and
[c]with men, and hast prevailed.
29 And Jacob asked *him,* and said, Tell
me, I pray thee, thy name. And he said,
[a]Wherefore *is* it *that* thou dost ask after
my name? And he blessed him there.
30 And Jacob called the name of the
place [l]Peniel: for [a]I have seen God face
to face, and my life is preserved.
31 And as he passed over Penuel the
sun rose upon him, and he halted upon
his thigh.
32 Therefore the children of Israel eat
not *of* the sinew which shrank, which *is*

A *Ge 28:13–15* ◄► *Ge 35:10–12*

upon the hollow of the thigh, unto this
day: because he touched the hollow of
Jacob's thigh in the sinew that shrank.

Jacob and Esau meet

33 AND JACOB lifted up his eyes,
and looked, and, behold, [a]Esau
came, and with him four hundred men.
And he divided the children unto Leah,
and unto Rachel, and unto the two handmaids.
2 And he put the handmaids and their
children foremost, and Leah and her children after, and Rachel and Joseph hindermost.
3 And he passed over before them, and
[a]bowed himself to the ground seven
times, until he came near to his brother.
4 [a]And Esau ran to meet him, and embraced him, [b]and fell on his neck, and
kissed him: and they wept.
5 And he lifted up his eyes, and saw
the women and the children; and said,
Who *are* those [1]with thee? And he said,
The children [a]which God hath graciously
given thy servant.
6 Then the handmaidens came near,
they and their children, and they bowed
themselves.
7 And Leah also with her children
came near, and bowed themselves: and
after came Joseph near and Rachel, and
they bowed themselves.
8 And he said, [1]What *meanest* thou by
[a]all this drove which I met? And he said,
These are [b]to find grace in the sight of my
lord.
9 And Esau said, I have enough, my
brother; [1]keep that thou hast unto
thyself.
10 And Jacob said, Nay, I pray thee, if
now I have found grace in thy sight, then
receive my present at my hand: for therefore I [a]have seen thy face, as though I
had seen the face of God, and thou wast
pleased with me.
11 Take, I pray thee, [a]my blessing that
is brought to thee; because God hath
dealt graciously with me, and because I
have [1]enough. [b]And he urged him, and
he took *it*.
12 And he said, Let us take our journey, and let us go, and I will go before
thee.
13 And he said unto him, My lord
knoweth that the children *are* tender,
and the flocks and herds with young *are*
with me: and if men should overdrive
them one day, all the flock will die.
14 Let my lord, I pray thee, pass over
before his servant: and I will lead on
softly, [1]according as the cattle that goeth
before me and the children be able to endure, until I come unto my lord [a]unto
Seir.
15 And Esau said, Let me now [1]leave
with thee *some* of the folk that *are* with
me. And he said, [2]What needeth it? [a]let
me find grace in the sight of my lord.
16 ¶ So Esau returned that day on his
way unto Seir.
17 And Jacob journeyed to [a]Succoth,
and built him an house, and made booths
for his cattle: therefore the name of the
place is called [1]Succoth.
18 ¶ And Jacob came to [a]Shalem, a city
of [b]Shechem,[1] which *is* in the land of Canaan, when he came from Padan-aram;
and pitched his tent before the city.
19 And [a]he bought a parcel of a field,
where he had spread his tent, at the hand
of the children of [1]Hamor, Shechem's father, for an hundred [2]pieces of money.
20 And he erected there an altar, and
[a]called it [1]El-elohe-Israel.

The defiling of Dinah

34 AND [a]DINAH the daughter of
Leah, which she bare unto Jacob,
[b]went out to see the daughters of the
land.
2 And when Shechem the son of Hamor the Hivite, prince of the country,
[a]saw her, he [b]took her, and lay with her,
and [1]defiled her.
3 And his soul clave unto Dinah the
daughter of Jacob, and he loved the damsel, and spake kindly unto the damsel.
4 And Shechem [a]spake unto his father
Hamor, saying, Get me this damsel to
wife.
5 And Jacob heard that he had defiled
Dinah his daughter: now his sons were
with his cattle in the field: and Jacob
[a]held his peace until they were come.
6 ¶ And Hamor the father of Shechem
went out unto Jacob to commune with
him.
7 And the sons of Jacob came out of
the field when they heard *it:* and the
men were grieved, and they [a]were very
wroth, because he [b]had wrought folly in
Israel in lying with Jacob's daughter;
[c]which thing ought not to be done.

33:1 [a]ch. 32:6
3 [a]ch. 18:2 & 42:6
4 [a]ch. 32:28 [b]ch. 45:14,15
5 [a]ch. 48:9; Ps. 127:3; Is. 8:18 [1]Heb. *to thee?*
8 [a]ch. 32:16 [b]ch. 32:5 [1]Heb. *What is all this band to thee?*
9 [1]Heb. *be that to thee that* is *thine*
10 [a]ch. 43:3; 2 Sam. 3:13 & 14:24,28,32
11 [a]Judg. 1:15; 1 Sam. 25:27 & 30:26 [b]2 Ki. 5:23 [1]Heb. *all things*
14 [a]ch. 32:3 [1]Heb. *according to the foot of the work, &c. and according to the foot of the children*
15 [a]ch. 34:11 & 47:25; Ruth 2:13 [1]Heb. *set,* or, *place* [2]Heb. *Wherefore is this?*
17 [a]Josh. 13:27; Judg. 8:5; Ps. 60:6 [1]i.e. *Booths*
18 [a]John 3:23 [b]Josh. 24:1; Judg. 9:1 [1]Called *Sychem* in Acts 7:16
19 [a]Josh. 24:32; John 4:5 [1]Called *Emmor* in Acts 7:16 [2]Or, *lambs*
20 [a]ch. 35:7 [1]i.e. *God the God of Israel*
34:1 [a]ch. 30:21 [b]Tit. 2:5
2 [a]ch. 6:2; Judg. 14:1 [b]ch. 20:2 [1]Heb. *humbled her*
4 [a]Judg. 14:2
5 [a]1 Sam. 10:27; 2 Sam. 13:22
7 [a]ch. 49:7; 2 Sam. 13:21 [b]Josh. 7:15; Judg. 20:6 [c]Deut. 23:17; 2 Sam. 13:12

8 And Hamor communed with them, saying, The soul of my son Shechem longeth for your daughter: I pray you give her him to wife.

9 And make ye marriages with us, *and* give your daughters unto us, and take our daughters unto you.

10 And ye shall dwell with us: and [a]the land shall be before you; dwell and [b]trade ye therein, and [c]get you possessions therein.

11 And Shechem said unto her father and unto her brethren, Let me find grace in your eyes, and what ye shall say unto me I will give.

12 Ask me never so much [a]dowry and gift, and I will give according as ye shall say unto me: but give me the damsel to wife.

13 And the sons of Jacob answered Shechem and Hamor his father [a]deceitfully, and said, because he had defiled Dinah their sister:

14 And they said unto them, We cannot do this thing, to give our sister to one that is uncircumcised; for [a]that *were* a reproach unto us:

15 But in this will we consent unto you: If ye will be as we *be,* that every male of you be circumcised;

16 Then will we give our daughters unto you, and we will take your daughters to us, and we will dwell with you, and we will become one people.

17 But if ye will not hearken unto us, to be circumcised; then will we take our daughter, and we will be gone.

18 And their words pleased Hamor, and Shechem Hamor's son.

19 And the young man deferred not to do the thing, because he had delight in Jacob's daughter: and he *was* [a]more honourable than all the house of his father.

20 ¶ And Hamor and Shechem his son came unto the gate of their city, and communed with the men of their city, saying,

21 These men *are* peaceable with us; therefore let them dwell in the land, and trade therein; for the land, behold, *it is* large enough for them; let us take their daughters to us for wives, and let us give them our daughters.

22 Only herein will the men consent unto us for to dwell with us, to be one people, if every male among us be circumcised, as they *are* circumcised.

23 *Shall* not their cattle and their substance and every beast of theirs *be* ours? only let us consent unto them, and they will dwell with us.

24 And unto Hamor and unto Shechem his son hearkened all that [a]went out of the gate of his city; and every male was circumcised, all that went out of the gate of his city.

25 ¶ And it came to pass on the third day, when they were sore, that two of the sons of Jacob, [a]Simeon and Levi, Dinah's brethren, took each man his sword, and came upon the city boldly, and slew all the males.

26 And they slew Hamor and Shechem his son with the [1]edge of the sword, and took Dinah out of Shechem's house, and went out.

27 The sons of Jacob came upon the slain, and spoiled the city, because they had defiled their sister.

28 They took their sheep, and their oxen, and their asses, and that which *was* in the city, and that which *was* in the field,

29 And all their wealth, and all their little ones, and their wives took they captive, and spoiled even all that *was* in the house.

30 And Jacob said to Simeon and Levi, [a]Ye have [b]troubled me [c]to make me to stink among the inhabitants of the land, among the Canaanites and the Perizzites: [d]and I *being* few in number, they shall gather themselves together against me, and slay me; and I shall be destroyed, I and my house.

31 And they said, Should he deal with our sister as with an harlot?

Jacob returns to Beth-el

35 AND GOD said unto Jacob, Arise, go up to [a]Beth-el, and dwell there: and make there an altar unto God, [b]that appeared unto thee [c]when thou fleddest from the face of Esau thy brother.

2 Then Jacob said unto his [a]household, and to all that *were* with him, Put away [b]the strange gods that *are* among you, and [c]be clean, and change your garments:

3 And let us arise, and go up to Beth-el; and I will make there an altar unto God, [a]who answered me in the day of my distress, [b]and was with me in the way which I went.

10 [a]ch. 13:9 & 20:15 [b]ch. 42:34 [c]ch. 47:27
12 [a]Ex. 22:16,17; Deut. 22:29; 1 Sam. 18:25
13 [a]See 2 Sam. 13:24
14 [a]Josh. 5:9
19 [a]1 Chr. 4:9
24 [a]ch. 23:10,18
25 [a]ch. 49:5-7
26 [1]Heb. *mouth*
30 [a]ch. 49:6 [b]Josh. 7:25 [c]Ex. 5:21; 1 Sam. 13:4 [d]Deut. 4:27; Ps. 105:12
35:1 [a]ch. 28:19 [b]ch. 28:13 [c]ch. 27:43
2 [a]ch. 18:19; Josh. 24:15 [b]ch. 31:19, 34; Josh. 24:2,23; 1 Sam. 7:3 [c]Ex. 19:10
3 [a]ch. 32:7,24 [b]ch. 28:20 & 31:3,42

4 And they gave unto Jacob all the strange gods which *were* in their hand, and *all their* [a]earrings which *were* in their ears; and Jacob hid them under [b]the oak which *was* by Shechem.

5 And they journeyed: and [a]the terror of God was upon the cities that *were* round about them, and they did not pursue after the sons of Jacob.

6 ¶ So Jacob came to [a]Luz, which *is* in the land of Canaan, that *is,* Beth-el, he and all the people that *were* with him.

7 And he [a]built there an altar, and called the place [1]El-beth-el: because [b]there God appeared unto him, when he fled from the face of his brother.

8 But [a]Deborah Rebekah's nurse died, and she was buried beneath Beth-el under an oak: and the name of it was called [1]Allon-bachuth.

9 ¶ And [a]God appeared unto Jacob again, when he came out of Padan-aram, and blessed him.

A 10 And God said unto him, Thy name *is* Jacob: [a]thy name shall not be called any more Jacob, [b]but Israel shall be thy name: and he called his name Israel.

11 And God said unto him, [a]I *am* God Almighty: be fruitful and multiply; [b]a nation and a company of nations shall be of thee, and kings shall come out of thy loins;

12 And the land [a]which I gave Abraham and Isaac, to thee I will give it, and to thy seed after thee will I give the land.

13 And God [a]went up from him in the place where he talked with him.

14 And Jacob [a]set up a pillar in the place where he talked with him, *even* a pillar of stone: and he poured a drink offering thereon, and he poured oil thereon.

15 And Jacob called the name of the place where God spake with him, [a]Beth-el.

The deaths of Rachel and Isaac

16 ¶ And they journeyed from Beth-el; and there was but [1]a little way to come to Ephrath: and Rachel travailed, and she had hard labour.

17 And it came to pass, when she was in hard labour, that the midwife said unto her, Fear not; [a]thou shalt have this son also.

18 And it came to pass, as her soul was in departing, (for she died) that she called his name [1]Ben-oni: but his father called him [2]Benjamin.

19 And [a]Rachel died, and was buried in the way to [b]Ephrath, which *is* Beth-lehem.

20 And Jacob set a pillar upon her grave: that *is* the pillar of Rachel's grave [a]unto this day.

21 ¶ And Israel journeyed, and spread his tent beyond [a]the tower of Edar.

22 And it came to pass, when Israel dwelt in that land, that Reuben went and [a]lay with Bilhah his father's concubine: and Israel heard *it.* Now the sons of Jacob were twelve:

23 The sons of Leah; [a]Reuben, Jacob's firstborn, and Simeon, and Levi, and Judah, and Issachar, and Zebulun:

24 The sons of Rachel; Joseph, and Benjamin:

25 And the sons of Bilhah, Rachel's handmaid; Dan, and Naphtali:

26 And the sons of Zilpah, Leah's handmaid; Gad, and Asher: these *are* the sons of Jacob, which were born to him in Padan-aram.

27 ¶ And Jacob came unto Isaac his father unto [a]Mamre, unto the [b]city of Arbah, which *is* Hebron, where Abraham and Isaac sojourned.

28 And the days of Isaac were an hundred and fourscore years.

29 And Isaac gave up the ghost, and died, and [a]was gathered unto his people, *being* old and full of days: and [b]his sons Esau and Jacob buried him. Q

4 [a]Hos. 2:13 [b]Josh. 24:26; Judg. 9:6
5 [a]Ex. 15:16; Deut. 11:25; Josh. 2:9; 1 Sam. 14:15
6 [a]ch. 28:19,22
7 [a]Eccl. 5:4 [b]ch. 28:13 [1]i.e. *The God of Beth-el*
8 [a]ch. 24:59 [1]i.e. *The oak of weeping*
9 [a]Hos. 12:4
10 [a]ch. 17:5 [b]ch. 32:28
11 [a]ch. 17:1 & 48:3,4; Ex. 6:3 [b]ch. 17:5,6,16 & 28:3 & 48:4
12 [a]ch. 12:7 & 13:15 & 26:3,4 & 28:13
13 [a]ch. 17:22
14 [a]ch. 28:18
15 [a]ch. 28:19
16 [1]Heb. *a little piece of ground*
17 [a]ch. 30:24; 1 Sam. 4:20
18 [1]i.e. *The son of my sorrow* [2]i.e. *The son of the right hand*
19 [a]ch. 48:7 [b]Ruth 1:2; Mic. 5:2; Mat. 2:6
20 [a]1 Sam. 10:2
21 [a]Mic. 4:8
22 [a]ch. 49:4; 1 Chr. 5:1
23 [a]ch. 46:8; Ex. 1:2
27 [a]ch. 13:18 [b]Josh. 14:15
29 [a]ch. 15:15 & 25:8 [b]See ch. 25:9 & 49:31

A *Ge 32:27–28* ◀ ▶ *Ge 37:6–7*

Q *Ge 25:8* ◀ ▶ *Ge 49:29*

35:29 Isaac lived for 180 years, the longest living of the patriarchs. The phrase "gathered unto his people" occurs often in Scripture as part of a promise to a godly individual. It implies the Hebrew view of life after death that involved the reuniting of family members (see 2Sa 12:23). A thousand years later, Jesus referred to the gathered patriarchs (see Mt 22:32), confirming that ancient believers were indeed still alive and awaiting the resurrection from the dead at Christ's second coming.

The descendants of Esau

36 NOW THESE *are* the generations
of Esau, [a]who *is* Edom.
2 [a]Esau took his wives of the daughters of Canaan; Adah the daughter of Elon
the Hittite, and [b]Aholibamah the daughter of Anah the daughter of Zibeon the
Hivite;
3 And [a]Bashemath Ishmael's daughter,
sister of Nebajoth.
4 And [a]Adah bare to Esau Eliphaz; and
Bashemath bare Reuel;
5 And Aholibamah bare Jeush, and Jaalam, and Korah: these *are* the sons of
Esau, which were born unto him in the
land of Canaan.
6 And Esau took his wives, and his
sons, and his daughters, and all the [1]per-
sons of his house, and his cattle, and all
his beasts, and all his substance, which
he had got in the land of Canaan; and
went into the country from the face of his
brother Jacob.
7 [a]For their riches were more than
that they might dwell together; and [b]the
land wherein they were strangers could
not bear them because of their cattle.
8 Thus dwelt Esau in [a]mount Seir:
[b]Esau *is* Edom.
9 ¶ And these *are* the generations of
Esau the father of [1]the Edomites in
mount Seir:
10 These *are* the names of Esau's sons;
[a]Eliphaz the son of Adah the wife of
Esau, Reuel the son of Bashemath the
wife of Esau.
11 And the sons of Eliphaz were Teman, Omar, [1]Zepho, and Gatam, and
Kenaz.
12 And Timna was concubine to Eliphaz Esau's son; and she bare to Eliphaz
[a]Amalek: these *were* the sons of Adah
Esau's wife.
13 And these *are* the sons of Reuel;
Nahath, and Zerah, Shammah, and Mizzah: these were the sons of Bashemath
Esau's wife.
14 ¶ And these were the sons of
Aholibamah, the daughter of Anah the
daughter of Zibeon, Esau's wife: and she
bare to Esau Jeush, and Jaalam, and
Korah.
15 ¶ These *were* dukes of the sons of
Esau: the sons of Eliphaz the firstborn
son of Esau; duke Teman, duke Omar,
duke Zepho, duke Kenaz,
16 Duke Korah, duke Gatam, *and* duke
Amalek: these *are* the dukes *that came* of
Eliphaz in the land of Edom; these *were*
the sons of Adah.
17 ¶ And these *are* the sons of Reuel
Esau's son; duke Nahath, duke Zerah,
duke Shammah, duke Mizzah: these *are*
the dukes *that came* of Reuel in the land
of Edom; these *are* the sons of Bashemath
Esau's wife.
18 ¶ And these are the sons of
Aholibamah Esau's wife; duke Jeush,
duke Jaalam, duke Korah: these *were* the
dukes *that came* of Aholibamah the
daughter of Anah, Esau's wife.
19 These *are* the sons of Esau, who *is*
Edom, and these *are* their dukes.
20 ¶ [a]These *are* the sons of Seir [b]the
Horite, who inhabited the land; Lotan,
and Shobal, and Zibeon, and Anah,
21 And Dishon, and Ezer, and Dishan:
these *are* the dukes of the Horites, the
children of Seir in the land of Edom.
22 And the children of Lotan were
Hori and [1]Hemam; and Lotan's sister *was*
Timna.
23 And the children of Shobal *were*
these; [1]Alvan, and Manahath, and Ebal,
[2]Shepho, and Onam.
24 And these *are* the children of Zibeon; both Ajah, and Anah: this *was that*
Anah that found [a]the mules in the wilderness, as he fed the asses of Zibeon his
father.
25 And the children of Anah *were*
these; Dishon, and Aholibamah the
daughter of Anah.
26 And these *are* the children of Dishon; [1]Hemdan, and Eshban, and Ithran,
and Cheran.
27 The children of Ezer *are* these; Bilhan, and Zaavan, and [1]Akan.
28 The children of Dishan *are* these;
Uz, and Aran.
29 These *are* the dukes *that came* of
the Horites; duke Lotan, duke Shobal,
duke Zibeon, duke Anah,
30 Duke Dishon, duke Ezer, duke Dishan: these *are* the dukes *that came* of
Hori, among their dukes in the land of
Seir.

The kings of Edom

31 ¶ And [a]these *are* the kings that
reigned in the land of Edom, before there
reigned any king over the children of
Israel.

36:1 [a]ch. 25:30
2 [a]ch. 26:34 [b]ver. 25
3 [a]ch. 28:9
4 [a]1 Chr. 1:35
6 [1]Heb. *souls*
7 [a]ch. 13:6,11 [b]ch. 17:8 & 28:4
8 [a]ch. 32:3; Deut. 2:5; Josh. 24:4 [b]ver. 1
9 [1]Heb. *Edom*
10 [a]1 Chr. 1:35
11 [1]Or, *Zephi;* see 1 Chr. 1:36
12 [a]Ex. 17:8,14; Num. 24:20; 1 Sam. 15:2,3
20 [a]1 Chr. 1:38 [b]ch. 14:6; Deut. 2:12,22
22 [1]Or, *Homam;* see 1 Chr. 1:39
23 [1]Or, *Alian;* see 1 Chr. 1:40 [2]Or, *Shephi;* see 1 Chr. 1:40
24 [a]See Lev. 19:19
26 [1]Or, *Amram;* see 1 Chr. 1:41
27 [1]Or, *Jakan;* see 1 Chr. 1:42
31 [a]1 Chr. 1:43

32 And Bela the son of Beor reigned in Edom: and the name of his city *was* Dinhabah.

33 And Bela died, and Jobab the son of Zerah of Bozrah reigned in his stead.

34 And Jobab died, and Husham of the land of Temani reigned in his stead.

35 And Husham died, and Hadad the son of Bedad, who smote Midian in the field of Moab, reigned in his stead: and the name of his city *was* Avith.

36 And Hadad died, and Samlah of Masrekah reigned in his stead.

37 And Samlah died, and Saul of [a]Rehoboth *by* the river reigned in his stead.

38 And Saul died, and Baal-hanan the son of Achbor reigned in his stead.

39 And Baal-hanan the son of Achbor died, and [a]Hadar reigned in his stead: and the name of his city *was* Pau; and his wife's name *was* Mehetabel, the daughter of Matred, the daughter of Mezahab.

40 And these *are* the names of [a]the dukes *that came* of Esau, according to their families, after their places, by their names; duke Timnah, duke ʹAlvah, duke Jetheth,

41 Duke Aholibamah, duke Elah, duke Pinon,

42 Duke Kenaz, duke Teman, duke Mibzar,

43 Duke Magdiel, duke Iram: these *be* the dukes of Edom, according to their habitations in the land of their possession: he *is* Esau the father of ʹthe Edomites.

Joseph's dream

37 AND JACOB dwelt in the land [a]whereinʹ his father was a stranger, in the land of Canaan.

2 These *are* the generations of Jacob. Joseph, *being* seventeen years old, was feeding the flock with his brethren; and the lad *was* with the sons of Bilhah, and with the sons of Zilpah, his father's wives: and Joseph brought unto his father [a]their evil report.

3 Now Israel loved Joseph more than all his children, because he *was* [a]the son of his old age: and he made him a coat of *many* [b]colours.ʹ

4 And when his brethren saw that their father loved him more than all his brethren, they [a]hated him, and could not speak peaceably unto him.

5 ¶ And Joseph dreamed a dream, and he told *it* his brethren: and they hated him yet the more.

37 [a]ch. 10:11
39 [a]1 Chr. 1:50, *Hadad Pai*
40 [a]1 Chr. 1:51 ʹOr, *Aliah*
43 ʹHeb. *Edom*
37:1 [a]ch. 17:8 & 23:4 & 28:4 & 36:7; Heb. 11:9 ʹHeb. *of his father's sojournings*
2 [a]1 Sam. 2:22-24
3 [a]ch. 44:20 [b]Judg. 5:30; 2 Sam. 13:18 ʹOr, *pieces,*
4 [a]ch. 27:41 & 49:23
7 [a]ch. 42:6,9 & 43:26 & 44:14
9 [a]ch. 46:29
10 [a]ch. 27:29
11 [a]Acts 7:9 [b]Dan. 7:28; Luke 2:19,51
12 [a]ch. 33:18
14 [a]ch. 13:18 & 35:27 ʹHeb. *see the peace of thy brethren*
16 [a]Sol. 1:7
17 [a]2 Ki. 6:13

6 And he said unto them, Hear, I pray you, this dream which I have dreamed: **A**

7 For, [a]behold, we *were* binding sheaves in the field, and, lo, my sheaf arose, and also stood upright; and, behold, your sheaves stood round about, and made obeisance to my sheaf.

8 And his brethren said to him, Shalt thou indeed reign over us? or shalt thou indeed have dominion over us? And they hated him yet the more for his dreams, and for his words.

9 ¶ And he dreamed yet another dream, and told it his brethren, and said, Behold, I have dreamed a dream more; and, behold, [a]the sun and the moon and the eleven stars made obeisance to me. **A**

10 And he told *it* to his father, and to his brethren: and his father rebuked him, and said unto him, What *is* this dream that thou hast dreamed? Shall I and thy mother and [a]thy brethren indeed come to bow down ourselves to thee to the earth?

11 And [a]his brethren envied him; but his father [b]observed the saying.

Joseph sold to merchants

12 ¶ And his brethren went to feed their father's flock in [a]Shechem.

13 And Israel said unto Joseph, Do not thy brethren feed *the flock* in Shechem? come, and I will send thee unto them. And he said to him, Here *am I.*

14 And he said to him, Go, I pray thee, ʹsee whether it be well with thy brethren, and well with the flocks; and bring me word again. So he sent him out of the vale of [a]Hebron, and he came to Shechem.

15 ¶ And a certain man found him, and, behold, *he was* wandering in the field: and the man asked him, saying, What seekest thou?

16 And he said, I seek my brethren: [a]tell me, I pray thee, where they feed *their flocks.*

17 And the man said, They are departed hence; for I heard them say, Let us go to Dothan. And Joseph went after his brethren, and found them in [a]Dothan.

18 And when they saw him afar off,

A *Ge 35:10–12* ◄► *Ge 37:9*
A *Ge 37:6–7* ◄► *Ge 41:1–7*

even before he came near unto them, [a]they conspired against him to slay him.

19 And they said one to another, Behold, this [1]dreamer cometh.

20 [a]Come now therefore, and let us slay him, and cast him into some pit, and we will say, Some evil beast hath devoured him: and we shall see what will become of his dreams.

21 And [a]Reuben heard *it,* and he delivered him out of their hands; and said, Let us not kill him.

22 And Reuben said unto them, Shed no blood, *but* cast him into this pit that *is* in the wilderness, and lay no hand upon him; that he might rid him out of their hands, to deliver him to his father again.

23 ¶ And it came to pass, when Joseph was come unto his brethren, that they stripped Joseph out of his coat, *his* coat of *many* [1]colours that *was* on him;

24 And they took him, and cast him into a pit: and the pit *was* empty, *there was* no water in it.

25 [a]And they sat down to eat bread: and they lifted up their eyes and looked, and, behold, a company of [b]Ishmeelites came from Gilead with their camels bearing spicery and [c]balm and myrrh, going to carry *it* down to Egypt.

26 And Judah said unto his brethren, What profit *is it* if we slay our brother, and [a]conceal his blood?

27 Come, and let us sell him to the Ishmeelites, and [a]let not our hand be upon him; for he *is* [b]our brother *and* [c]our flesh. And his brethren [1]were content.

28 Then there passed by [a]Midianites merchantmen; and they drew and lifted up Joseph out of the pit, [b]and sold Joseph to the Ishmeelites for [c]twenty *pieces* of silver: and they brought Joseph into Egypt.

29 ¶ And Reuben returned unto the pit; and, behold, Joseph *was* not in the pit; and he [a]rent his clothes.

30 And he returned unto his brethren, and said, The child [a]*is* not; and I, whither shall I go?

31 And they took [a]Joseph's coat, and killed a kid of the goats, and dipped the coat in the blood;

32 And they sent the coat of *many* colours, and they brought *it* to their father; and said, This have we found: know now whether it *be* thy son's coat or no.

33 And he knew it, and said, *It is* my son's coat; an [a]evil beast hath devoured him; Joseph is without doubt rent in pieces.

34 And Jacob [a]rent his clothes, and put sackcloth upon his loins, and mourned for his son many days.

35 And all his sons and all his daughters [a]rose up to comfort him; but he refused to be comforted; and he said, For [b]I will go down into the grave unto my son mourning. Thus his father wept for him.

36 And [a]the Midianites sold him into Egypt unto Potiphar, an [1]officer of Pharaoh's, *and* [2,3]captain of the guard.

Judah and Tamar

38 AND IT came to pass at that time, that Judah went down from his brethren, and [a]turned in to a certain Adullamite, whose name *was* Hirah.

2 And Judah [a]saw there a daughter of a certain Canaanite, whose name *was* [b]Shuah; and he took her, and went in unto her.

3 And she conceived, and bare a son; and he called his name Er.

4 And she conceived again, and bare a son; and she called his name [a]Onan.

5 And she yet again conceived, and bare a son; and called his name [a]Shelah: and he was at Chezib, when she bare him.

6 And Judah [a]took a wife for Er his firstborn, whose name *was* Tamar.

7 And [a]Er, Judah's firstborn, was wicked in the sight of the LORD; [b]and the LORD slew him.

8 And Judah said unto Onan, Go in unto [a]thy brother's wife, and marry her, and raise up seed to thy brother.

9 And Onan knew that the seed should not be [a]his; and it came to pass, when he went in unto his brother's wife, that he spilled *it* on the ground, lest that he should give seed to his brother.

10 And the thing which he did [1]displeased the LORD: wherefore he slew [a]him also.

11 Then said Judah to Tamar his daughter-in-law, [a]Remain a widow at thy father's house, till Shelah my son be grown: for he said, Lest peradventure he die also, as his brethren *did.* And Tamar went and dwelt [b]in her father's house.

12 ¶ And [1]in process of time the daughter of Shuah Judah's wife died; and Judah [a]was comforted, and went up unto

18 [a]1 Sam. 19:1; Mat. 27:1; Mark 14:1; Acts 23:12
19 [1]Heb. *master of dreams*
20 [a]Prov. 1:11
21 [a]ch. 42:22
23 [1]Or, *pieces*
25 [a]Prov. 30:20 [b]See ver. 28,36 [c]Jer. 8:22
26 [a]ver. 20
27 [a]1 Sam. 18:17 [b]ch. 42:21 [c]ch. 29:14 [1]Heb. *hearkened*
28 [a]Judg. 6:3 [b]Ps. 105:17; Acts 7:9 [c]See Mat. 27:9
29 [a]Job 1:20
30 [a]ch. 42:13,36
31 [a]ver. 23
33 [a]ver. 20
34 [a]2 Sam. 3:31
35 [a]2 Sam. 12:17 [b]ch. 42:38
36 [a]ch. 39:1 [1]Heb. *eunuch:* But the word doth signify not only *eunuchs,* but also *chamberlains, courtiers,* and *officers* [2]Heb. *chief of the slaughtermen,* or, *executioners* [3]Or, *chief marshal*
38:1 [a]2 Ki. 4:8
2 [a]ch. 34:2 [b]1 Chr. 2:3
4 [a]Num. 26:19
5 [a]Num. 26:20
6 [a]ch. 21:21
7 [a]Num. 26:19 [b]1 Chr. 2:3
8 [a]Deut. 25:5
9 [a]Deut. 25:6
10 [a]ch. 46:12 [1]Heb. *was evil in the eyes of the LORD*
11 [a]Ruth 1:13 [b]Lev. 22:13
12 [a]2 Sam. 13:39 [1]Heb. *the days were multiplied*

his sheepshearers to Timnath, he and his friend Hirah the Adullamite.

13 And it was told Tamar, saying, Behold thy father-in-law goeth up [a]to Timnath to shear his sheep.

14 And she put her widow's garments off from her, and covered her with a veil, and wrapped herself, and [a]sat in [1]an open place, which *is* by the way to Timnath; for she saw [b]that Shelah was grown, and she was not given unto him to wife.

15 When Judah saw her, he thought her *to be* an harlot; because she had covered her face.

16 And he turned unto her by the way, and said, Go to, I pray thee, let me come in unto thee; (for he knew not that she *was* his daughter-in-law.) And she said, What wilt thou give me, that thou mayest come in unto me?

17 And he said, [a]I will send *thee* [1]a kid from the flock. And she said, [b]Wilt thou give *me* a pledge, till thou send *it?*

18 And he said, What pledge shall I give thee? And she said, [a]Thy signet, and thy bracelets, and thy staff that *is* in thine hand. And he gave *it* her, and came in unto her, and she conceived by him.

19 And she arose, and went away, and [a]laid by her veil from her, and put on the garments of her widowhood.

20 And Judah sent the kid by the hand of his friend the Adullamite, to receive *his* pledge from the woman's hand: but he found her not.

21 Then he asked the men of that place, saying, Where *is* the harlot, that *was* [1]openly by the way side? And they said, There was no harlot in this *place.*

22 And he returned to Judah, and said, I cannot find her; and also the men of the place said, *that* there was no harlot in this *place.*

23 And Judah said, Let her take *it* to her, lest we [1]be shamed: behold, I sent this kid, and thou hast not found her.

24 ¶ And it came to pass about three months after, that it was told Judah, saying, Tamar thy daughter-in-law hath [a]played the harlot; and also, behold, she *is* with child by whoredom. And Judah said, Bring her forth, [b]and let her be burnt.

25 When she *was* brought forth, she sent to her father-in-law, saying, By the man, whose these *are, am* I with child: and she said, [a]Discern, I pray thee, whose *are* these, [b]the signet, and bracelets, and staff.

26 And Judah [a]acknowledged *them,* and said, [b]She hath been more righteous than I; because that [c]I gave her not to Shelah my son. And he knew her again [d]no more.

27 ¶ And it came to pass in the time of her travail, that, behold, twins *were* in her womb.

28 And it came to pass, when she travailed, that *the one* put out *his* hand: and the midwife took and bound upon his hand a scarlet thread, saying, This came out first.

29 And it came to pass, as he drew back his hand, that, behold, his brother came out: and she said, [1]How hast thou broken forth? *this* breach *be* upon thee: therefore his name was called [a]Pharez.[2]

30 And afterward came out his brother, that had the scarlet thread upon his hand: and his name was called Zerah.

Joseph and Potiphar's wife

39 AND JOSEPH was brought down to Egypt; and [a]Potiphar, an officer of Pharaoh, captain of the guard, an Egyptian, [b]bought him of the hands of the Ishmeelites, which had brought him down thither.

2 And [a]the LORD was with Joseph, and he was a prosperous man; and he was in the house of his master the Egyptian. U

3 And his master saw that the LORD *was* with him, and that the LORD [a]made all that he did to prosper in his hand.

4 And Joseph [a]found grace in his sight, and he served him: and he made him [b]overseer over his house, and all *that* he had he put into his hand.

5 And it came to pass from the time *that* he had made him overseer in his house, and over all that he had, that [a]the LORD blessed the Egyptian's house for Joseph's sake; and the blessing of the LORD was upon all that he had in the house, and in the field. B R

6 And he left all that he had in Joseph's hand; and he knew not aught he had, save the bread which he did eat. And Jo-

13 [a]Josh. 15:10,57
14 [a]Prov. 7:12 [b]ver. 11,26 [1]Heb. *the door of eyes,* or, *of Enajim*
17 [a]Ezek. 16:33 [b]ver. 20 [1]Heb. *a kid of the goats*
18 [a]ver. 25
19 [a]ver. 14
21 [1]Or, *in Enajim*
23 [1]Heb. *become a contempt*
24 [a]Judg. 19:2 [b]Lev. 21:9; Deut. 22:21
25 [a]ch. 37:32 [b]ver. 18
26 [a]ch. 37:33 [b]1 Sam. 24:17 [c]ver. 14 [d]Job 34:31,32
29 [a]ch. 46:12; Num. 26:20; 1 Chr. 2:4; Mat. 1:3 [1]Or, *Wherefore hast thou made this breach against thee?* [2]i.e. *A breach*
39:1 [a]ch. 37:36; Ps. 105:17 [b]ch. 37:28
2 [a]ver. 21; ch. 21:22 & 26:24,28 & 28:15; 1 Sam. 16:18 & 18:14,28; Acts 7:9
3 [a]Ps. 1:3
4 [a]ver. 21 [b]ch. 24:2
5 [a]ch. 30:27

U *Ge 26:3* ◀ ▶ *Ge 39:23*
B *Ge 27:39* ◀ ▶ *Ex 23:26*
R *Ge 30:27* ◀ ▶ *Job 42:15*

seph [a]was *a* goodly *person,* and well-favoured.

7 ¶ And it came to pass after these things, that his master's wife cast her eyes upon Joseph; and she said, [a]Lie with me.

8 But he refused, and said unto his master's wife, Behold, my master wotteth not what *is* with me in the house, and he hath committed all that he hath to my hand;

9 *There is* none greater in this house than I; neither hath he kept back any thing from me but thee, because thou *art* his wife: [a]how then can I do this great wickedness, and [b]sin against God?

10 And it came to pass, as she spake to Joseph day by day, that he hearkened not unto her, to lie by her, *or* to be with her.

11 And it came to pass about this time, that *Joseph* went into the house to do his business; and *there was* none of the men of the house there within.

12 And [a]she caught him by his garment, saying, Lie with me: and he left his garment in her hand, and fled, and got him out.

13 And it came to pass, when she saw that he had left his garment in her hand, and was fled forth,

14 That she called unto the men of her house, and spake unto them, saying, See, he hath brought in an Hebrew unto us to mock us; he came in unto me to lie with me, and I cried with a [l]loud voice:

15 And it came to pass, when he heard that I lifted up my voice and cried, that he left his garment with me, and fled, and got him out.

16 And she laid up his garment by her, until his lord came home.

17 And she [a]spake unto him according to these words, saying, The Hebrew servant, which thou hast brought unto us, came in unto me to mock me:

18 And it came to pass, as I lifted up my voice and cried, that he left his garment with me, and fled out.

19 And it came to pass, when his master heard the words of his wife, which she spake unto him, saying, After this manner did thy servant to me; that his [a]wrath was kindled.

20 And Joseph's master took him, and [a]put him into the [b]prison, a place where the king's prisoners *were* bound: and he was there in the prison.

6 [a] 1 Sam. 16:12
7 [a] 2 Sam. 13:11
9 [a] Prov. 6:29,32 [b] ch. 20:6
12 [a] Prov. 7:13
14 [l] Heb. *great*
17 [a] Ex. 23:1; Ps. 120:3
19 [a] Prov. 6:34,35
20 [a] Ps. 105:18; 1 Pet. 2:19 [b] See ch. 40:3,15 & 41:14
21 [a] Ex. 3:21; Prov. 16:7; Dan. 1:9; Acts 7:9,10 [l] Heb. *extended kindness unto him*
22 [a] ch. 40:3,4
23 [a] ver. 2,3
40:1 [a] Neh. 1:11
2 [a] Prov. 16:14
3 [a] ch. 39:20,23
7 [l] Heb. are *your faces evil?*
8 [a] ch. 41:15 [b] See ch. 41:16; Dan. 2:11,28,47

21 ¶ But the LORD was with Joseph, and [l]showed him mercy, and [a]gave him favour in the sight of the keeper of the prison.

22 And the keeper of the prison [a]committed to Joseph's hand all the prisoners that *were* in the prison; and whatsoever they did there, he was the doer *of it.*

23 The keeper of the prison looked not to any thing *that was* under his hand; because [a]the LORD was with him, and *that* which he did, the LORD made *it* to prosper. U

Joseph interprets dreams

40 AND IT came to pass after these things, *that* the [a]butler of the king of Egypt and *his* baker had offended their lord the king of Egypt.

2 And Pharaoh was [a]wroth against two *of* his officers, against the chief of the butlers, and against the chief of the bakers.

3 [a]And he put them in ward in the house of the captain of the guard, into the prison, the place where Joseph *was* bound.

4 And the captain of the guard charged Joseph with them, and he served them: and they continued a season in ward.

5 ¶ And they dreamed a dream both of them, each man his dream in one night, each man according to the interpretation of his dream, the butler and the baker of the king of Egypt, which *were* bound in the prison.

6 And Joseph came in unto them in the morning, and looked upon them, and, behold, they *were* sad.

7 And he asked Pharaoh's officers that *were* with him in the ward of his lord's house, saying, Wherefore [l]look ye *so* sadly today?

8 And they said unto him, [a]We have dreamed a dream, and *there is* no interpreter of it. And Joseph said unto them, [b]*Do* not interpretations *belong* to God? tell me *them,* I pray you.

9 And the chief butler told his dream to Joseph, and said to him, In my dream, behold, a vine *was* before me;

10 And in the vine *were* three branches: and it *was* as though it budded, *and* her blossoms shot forth; and the

U Ge 39:2–3 ◀ ▶ Ge 49:25–26

clusters thereof brought forth ripe
grapes:
11 And Pharaoh's cup *was* in my hand:
and I took the grapes, and pressed them
into Pharaoh's cup, and I gave the cup
into Pharaoh's hand.
J 12 And Joseph said unto him, [a]This *is*
the interpretation of it: The three
branches [b]*are* three days:
13 Yet within three days shall Pharaoh
[a]lift′ up thine head, and restore thee
unto thy place: and thou shalt deliver
Pharaoh's cup into his hand, after the
former manner when thou wast his
butler.
14 But [a]think′ on me when it shall be
well with thee, and [b]show kindness, I
pray thee, unto me, and make mention of
me unto Pharaoh, and bring me out of
this house:
15 For indeed I was stolen away out of
the land of the Hebrews: [a]and here also
have I done nothing that they should put
me into the dungeon.
16 When the chief baker saw that the
interpretation was good, he said unto Joseph, I also *was* in my dream, and, behold, *I had* three [a]white baskets on my
head:
17 And in the uppermost basket *there
was* of all manner of ′bakemeats for Pharaoh; and the birds did eat them out of the
basket upon my head.
J 18 And Joseph answered and said,
[a]This *is* the interpretation thereof: The
three baskets *are* three days:
19 [a]Yet within three days shall Pharaoh ′lift up thy head from off thee, and
shall hang thee on a tree; and the birds
shall eat thy flesh from off thee.
20 ¶ And it came to pass the third day,
which was Pharaoh's [a]birthday, that he
[b]made a feast unto all his servants: and
he [c]lifted′ up the head of the chief butler
and of the chief baker among his servants.
21 And he [a]restored the chief butler
unto his butlership again; and [b]he gave
the cup into Pharaoh's hand:
22 But he [a]hanged the chief baker: as
Joseph had interpreted to them.
23 Yet did not the chief butler remember Joseph, but [a]forgat him.

J *Ge 11:6–8* ◀▶ *Ge 40:18–19*
J *Ge 40:12–13* ◀▶ *Ex 14:4*

12 [a]ver. 18; ch. 41:12,25; Judg. 7:14; Dan. 2:36 & 4:19 [b]ch. 41:26
13 [a]2 Ki. 25:27; Ps. 3:3; Jer. 52:31 ′Or, *reckon*
14 [a]Luke 23:42 [b]Josh. 2:12; 1 Sam. 20:14,15; 2 Sam. 9:1; 1 Ki. 2:7 ′Heb. *remember me with thee*
15 [a]ch. 39:20
16 [a]Or, *full of holes*
17 ′Heb. *meat of Pharaoh, the work of a baker,* or, *cook*
18 [a]ver. 12
19 [a]ver. 13 ′Or, *reckon thee,* and take thy office *from thee*
20 [a]Mat. 14:6 [b]Mark 6:21 [c]ver. 13,19; Mat. 25:19 ′Or, *reckoned*
21 [a]ver. 13 [b]Neh. 2:1
22 [a]ver. 19
23 [a]Job 19:14; Eccl. 9:15,16; Amos 6:6
41:5 ′Heb. *fat*
8 [a]Dan. 2:1 & 4:5, 19 [b]Ex. 7:11,22; Is. 29:14; Dan. 1:20 & 2:2 & 4:7 [c]Mat. 2:1
10 [a]ch. 40:2,3 [b]ch. 39:20
11 [a]ch. 40:5
12 [a]ch. 37:36 [b]ch. 40:12
13 [a]ch. 40:22
14 [a]Ps. 105:20 [b]Dan. 2:25 [c]1 Sam. 2:8; Ps. 113:7,8 ′Heb. *made him run*

Pharaoh's dreams

41 AND IT came to pass at the end A
of two full years, that Pharaoh
dreamed: and, behold, he stood by the
river.
2 And, behold, there came up out of
the river seven wellfavoured kine and fatfleshed; and they fed in a meadow.
3 And, behold, seven other kine came
up after them out of the river, ill favoured
and leanfleshed; and stood by the *other*
kine upon the brink of the river.
4 And the ill favoured and leanfleshed
kine did eat up the seven wellfavoured
and fat kine. So Pharaoh awoke.
5 And he slept and dreamed the second time: and, behold, seven ears of corn
came up upon one stalk, ′rank and good.
6 And, behold, seven thin ears and
blasted with the east wind sprung up after them.
7 And the seven thin ears devoured
the seven rank and full ears. And Pharaoh
awoke, and, behold, *it was* a dream.
8 And it came to pass in the morning
[a]that his spirit was troubled; and he sent
and called for all [b]the magicians of Egypt,
and all the [c]wise men thereof: and Pharaoh told them his dream; but *there was*
none that could interpret them unto
Pharaoh.
9 ¶ Then spake the chief butler unto
Pharaoh, saying, I do remember my faults
this day:
10 Pharaoh was [a]wroth with his servants, [b]and put me in ward in the captain
of the guard's house, *both* me and the
chief baker:
11 And [a]we dreamed a dream in one
night, I and he; we dreamed each man
according to the interpretation of his
dream.
12 And *there was* there with us a
young man, an Hebrew, [a]servant to the
captain of the guard; and we told him,
and he [b]interpreted to us our dreams; to
each man according to his dream he did
interpret.
13 And it came to pass, [a]as he interpreted to us, so it was; me he restored
unto mine office, and him he hanged.
14 ¶ [a]Then Pharaoh sent and called Joseph, and they [b]brought′ him hastily [c]out
of the dungeon: and he shaved *himself,*

A *Ge 37:9* ◀▶ *Ge 41:25–36*

and changed his raiment, and came in unto Pharaoh.

15 And Pharaoh said unto Joseph, I have dreamed a dream, and *there is* none that can interpret it: [a]and I have heard say of thee, *that* [l]thou canst understand a dream to interpret it.

16 And Joseph answered Pharaoh, saying, [a]*It is* not in me: [b]God shall give Pharaoh an answer of peace.

17 And Pharaoh said unto Joseph, [a]In my dream, behold, I stood upon the bank of the river:

18 And, behold, there came up out of the river seven kine, fatfleshed and wellfavoured; and they fed in a meadow:

19 And, behold, seven other kine came up after them, poor and very ill favoured and leanfleshed, such as I never saw in all the land of Egypt for badness:

20 And the lean and the ill favoured kine did eat up the first seven fat kine:

21 And when they had [l]eaten them up, it could not be known that they had eaten them; but they *were* still ill favoured, as at the beginning. So I awoke.

22 And I saw in my dream, and, behold, seven ears came up in one stalk, full and good:

23 And, behold, seven ears, [l]withered, thin, *and* blasted with the east wind, sprung up after them:

24 And the thin ears devoured the seven good ears: and [a]I told *this* unto the magicians; but *there was* none that could declare *it* to me.

A 25 ¶ And Joseph said unto Pharaoh, The dream of Pharaoh *is* one: [a]God hath shown Pharaoh what he *is* about to do.

26 The seven good kine *are* seven years; and the seven good ears *are* seven years: the dream *is* one.

27 And the seven thin and ill favoured kine that came up after them *are* seven years; and the seven empty ears blasted with the east wind shall be [a]seven years of famine.

28 [a]This *is* the thing which I have spoken unto Pharaoh: What God *is* about to do he showeth unto Pharaoh.

29 Behold, there come [a]seven years of great plenty throughout all the land of Egypt:

30 And there shall [a]arise after them seven years of famine; and all the plenty shall be forgotten in the land of Egypt; and the famine [b]shall consume the land;

31 And the plenty shall not be known in the land by reason of that famine following; for it *shall be* very [l]grievous.

32 And for that the dream was doubled unto Pharaoh twice; *it is* because the [a]thing *is* [l]established by God, and God will shortly bring it to pass.

33 Now therefore let Pharaoh look out a man discreet and wise, and set him over the land of Egypt.

34 Let Pharaoh do *this,* and let him appoint [l]officers over the land, and [a]take up the fifth part of the land of Egypt in the seven plenteous years.

35 And [a]let them gather all the food of those good years that come, and lay up corn under the hand of Pharaoh, and let them keep food in the cities.

36 And that food shall be for store to the land against the seven years of famine, which shall be in the land of Egypt; that the land [a]perish[l] not through the famine.

Pharaoh makes Joseph a ruler

37 ¶ And [a]the thing was good in the eyes of Pharaoh, and in the eyes of all his servants.

38 And Pharaoh said unto his servants, Can we find *such a one* as this *is,* a man [a]in whom the spirit of God *is?* B E G M T

39 And Pharaoh said unto Joseph, Forasmuch as God hath shown thee all this, *there is* none so discreet and wise as thou *art:*

40 [a]Thou shalt be over my house, and according unto thy word shall all my people [l]be ruled: only in the throne will I be greater than thou.

41 And Pharaoh said unto Joseph, See, I have [a]set thee over all the land of Egypt.

42 And Pharaoh [a]took off his ring from his hand, and put it upon Joseph's hand, and [b]arrayed him in vestures of [l]fine linen, [c]and put a gold chain about his neck;

43 And he made him to ride in the second chariot which he had; [a]and they cried before him, [1,2]Bow the knee: and he made him *ruler* [b]over all the land of Egypt.

15 [a]ver. 12; Dan. 5:16 [l]Or, *when thou hearest a dream thou canst interpret it*
16 [a]Dan. 2:30; Acts 3:12; 2 Cor. 3:5 [b]ch. 40:8; Dan. 2:22,28,47 & 4:2
17 [a]ver. 1
21 [l]Heb. *come to the inward parts of them*
23 [l]Or, *small*
24 [a]ver. 8; Dan. 4:7
25 [a]Dan. 2:28,29, 45; Rev. 4:1
27 [a]2 Ki. 8:1
28 [a]ver. 25
29 [a]ver. 47
30 [a]ver. 54 [b]ch. 47:13
31 [l]Heb. *heavy*
32 [a]Num. 23:19; Is. 46:10,11 [l]Or, *prepared of God*
34 [a]Prov. 6:6-8 [l]Or, *overseers*
35 [a]ver. 48
36 [a]ch. 47:15,19 [l]Heb. *be not cut off*
37 [a]Ps. 105:19; Acts 7:10
38 [a]Num. 27:18; Job 32:8; Prov. 2:6; Dan. 4:8,18 & 5:11,14 & 6:3
40 [a]Ps. 105:21; Acts 7:10 [l]Heb. *be armed,* or, *kiss*
41 [a]Dan. 6:3
42 [a]Esth. 3:10 [b]Esth. 8:15 [c]Dan. 5:7,29 [l]Or, *silk*
43 [a]Esth. 6:9 [b]ch. 42:6; Acts 7:10 [1]Or, *Tender father* [2]Heb. *Abrech*

A *Ge 41:1–7* ◀ ▶ *Ge 41:47–48*

B ▶ *Ex 28:3* **E** *Ge 1:2–3* ◀ ▶ *Ex 28:3*
G ▶ *Ex 28:3* **M** *Ge 1:2–3* ◀ ▶ *Jdg 3:10*
T ▶ *Ex 28:3*

44 And Pharaoh said unto Joseph, I *am* Pharaoh, and without thee shall no man lift up his hand or foot in all the land of Egypt.

45 And Pharaoh called Joseph's name [1]Zaphnath-paaneah; and he gave him to wife Asenath the daughter of Poti-pherah [2]priest of On. And Joseph went out over *all* the land of Egypt.

46 ¶ And Joseph *was* thirty years old when he [a]stood before Pharaoh king of Egypt. And Joseph went out from the presence of Pharaoh, and went throughout all the land of Egypt.

A 47 And in the seven plenteous years the earth brought forth by handfuls.

48 And he gathered up all the food of the seven years, which were in the land of Egypt, and laid up the food in the cities: the food of the field, which *was* round about every city, laid he up in the same.

49 And Joseph gathered corn [a]as the sand of the sea, very much, until he left numbering; for *it was* without number.

50 [a]And unto Joseph were born two sons before the years of famine came, which Asenath the daughter of Poti-pherah [1]priest of On bare unto him.

51 And Joseph called the name of the firstborn [1]Manasseh: For God, *said he,* hath made me forget all my toil, and all my father's house.

52 And the name of the second called he [1]Ephraim: For God hath caused me to be [a]fruitful in the land of my affliction.

A 53 ¶ And the seven years of plenteousness, that was in the land of Egypt, were ended.

54 [a]And the seven years of dearth began to come, [b]according as Joseph had said: and the dearth was in all lands; but in all the land of Egypt there was bread.

55 And when all the land of Egypt was famished, the people cried to Pharaoh for bread: and Pharaoh said unto all the Egyptians, Go unto Joseph; what he saith to you, do.

56 And the famine was over all the face of the earth: and Joseph opened [1]all the storehouses, and [a]sold unto the Egyptians; and the famine waxed sore in the land of Egypt.

57 [a]And all countries came into Egypt to Joseph for to buy *corn;* because that the famine was *so* sore in all lands.

Joseph's brethren visit Egypt

42 NOW WHEN [a]Jacob saw that there was corn in Egypt, Jacob said unto his sons, Why do ye look one upon another?

2 And he said, Behold, I have heard that there is corn in Egypt: get you down thither, and buy for us from thence; that we may [a]live, and not die.

3 ¶ And Joseph's ten brethren went down to buy corn in Egypt.

4 But Benjamin, Joseph's brother, Jacob sent not with his brethren; for he said, [a]Lest peradventure mischief befall him.

5 And the sons of Israel came to buy *corn* among those that came: for the famine was [a]in the land of Canaan.

6 And Joseph *was* the governor [a]over the land, *and* he *it was* that sold to all the people of the land: and Joseph's brethren came, and [b]bowed down themselves before him *with* their faces to the earth.

7 And Joseph saw his brethren, and he knew them, but made himself strange unto them, and spake [1]roughly unto them; and he said unto them, Whence come ye? And they said, From the land of Canaan to buy food.

8 And Joseph knew his brethren, but they knew not him.

9 And Joseph [a]remembered the dreams which he dreamed of them, and said unto them, Ye *are* spies; to see the nakedness of the land ye are come.

10 And they said unto him, Nay, my lord, but to buy food are thy servants come.

11 We *are* all one man's sons; we *are* true *men,* thy servants are no spies.

12 And he said unto them, Nay, but to see the nakedness of the land ye are come.

13 And they said, Thy servants *are* twelve brethren, the sons of one man in the land of Canaan; and, behold, the youngest *is* this day with our father, and one [a]*is* not.

14 And Joseph said unto them, That *is it* that I spake unto you, saying, Ye *are* spies:

15 Hereby ye shall be proved: [a]By the life of Pharaoh ye shall not go forth

45 [1]Which in the Coptic signifies, *A revealer of secrets,* or, *The man to whom secrets* are *revealed* [2]Or, *prince;* see Ex. 2:16; 2 Sam. 8:18 & 20:26

46 [a]1 Sam. 16:21; 1 Ki. 12:6,8; Dan. 1:19

49 [a]ch. 22:17; Judg. 7:12; 1 Sam. 13:5

50 [a]ch. 46:20 & 48:5 [1]Or, *prince*

51 [1]i.e. *Forgetting*

52 [a]ch. 49:22 [1]i.e. *Fruitful*

54 [a]Ps. 105:16; Acts 7:11 [b]ver. 30

56 [a]ch. 42:6 [1]Heb. *all wherein* was

57 [a]Deut. 9:28

42:1 [a]Acts 7:12

2 [a]ch. 43:8; Is. 38:1

4 [a]ver. 38

5 [a]Acts 7:11

6 [a]ch. 41:41 [b]ch. 37:7

7 [1]Heb. *hard things with them*

9 [a]ch. 37:5,9

13 [a]ch. 37:30; Lam. 5:7; See ch. 44:20

15 [a]See 1 Sam. 1:26 & 17:55

A *Ge 41:25–36* ◀ ▶ *Ge 41:53–54*
A *Ge 41:47–48* ◀ ▶ *Ge 46:2–4*

hence, except your youngest brother come hither.

16 Send one of you, and let him fetch your brother, and ye shall be [l]kept in prison, that your words may be proved, whether *there be any* truth in you: or else by the life of Pharaoh surely ye *are* spies.

17 And he [l]put them all together into ward three days.

18 And Joseph said unto them the third day, This do, and live; [a]*for* I fear God:

19 If ye *be* true *men,* let one of your brethren be bound in the house of your prison: go ye, carry corn for the famine of your houses:

20 But [a]bring your youngest brother unto me; so shall your words be verified, and ye shall not die. And they did so.

21 ¶ And they said one to another, [a]We *are* verily guilty concerning our brother, in that we saw the anguish of his soul, when he besought us, and we would not hear; [b]therefore is this distress come upon us.

22 And Reuben answered them, saying, [a]Spake I not unto you, saying, Do not sin against the child; and ye would not hear? therefore, behold, also his blood is [b]required.

23 And they knew not that Joseph understood *them;* for [l]he spake unto them by an interpreter.

24 And he turned himself about from them, and wept; and returned to them again, and communed with them, and took from them Simeon, and bound him before their eyes.

25 ¶ Then Joseph commanded to fill their sacks with corn, and to restore every man's money into his sack, and to give them provision for the way: and [a]thus did he unto them.

26 And they laded their asses with the corn, and departed thence.

27 And as [a]one of them opened his sack to give his ass provender in the inn, he espied his money; for, behold, it *was* in his sack's mouth.

28 And he said unto his brethren, My money is restored; and, lo, *it is* even in my sack: and their heart [l]failed *them,* and they were afraid, saying one to another, What *is* this *that* God hath done unto us?

29 ¶ And they came unto Jacob their father unto the land of Canaan, and told him all that befell unto them; saying,

30 The man, *who is* the lord of the land, [a]spake [l]roughly to us, and took us for spies of the country.

31 And we said unto him, We *are* true *men;* we are no spies:

32 We *be* twelve brethren, sons of our father; one *is* not, and the youngest *is* this day with our father in the land of Canaan.

33 And the man, the lord of the country, said unto us, [a]Hereby shall I know that ye *are* true *men;* leave one of your brethren *here* with me, and take *food for* the famine of your households, and be gone:

34 And bring your youngest brother unto me: then shall I know that ye *are* no spies, but *that* ye *are* true *men: so* will I deliver you your brother, and ye shall [a]traffic in the land.

35 ¶ And it came to pass as they emptied their sacks, that, behold, [a]every man's bundle of money *was* in his sack: and when *both* they and their father saw the bundles of money, they were afraid.

36 And Jacob their father said unto them, Me have ye [a]bereaved *of my children:* Joseph *is* not, and Simeon *is* not, and ye will take Benjamin *away:* all these things are against me.

37 And Reuben spake unto his father, saying, Slay my two sons, if I bring him not to thee: deliver him into my hand, and I will bring him to thee again.

38 And he said, My son shall not go down with you; for [a]his brother is dead, and he is left alone: [b]if mischief befall him by the way in the which ye go, then shall ye [c]bring down my gray hairs with sorrow to the grave.

The second trip to Egypt

43 AND THE famine *was* [a]sore in the land.

2 And it came to pass, when they had eaten up the corn which they had brought out of Egypt, their father said unto them, Go again, buy us a little food.

3 And Judah spake unto him, saying, The man [l]did solemnly protest unto us, saying, Ye shall not see my face, except your [a]brother *be* with you.

4 If thou wilt send our brother with us, we will go down and buy thee food:

5 But if thou wilt not send *him,* we

16 [l]Heb. *bound*
17 [l]Heb. *gathered*
18 [a]Lev. 25:43; Neh. 5:15
20 [a]ver. 34; ch. 43:5 & 44:23
21 [a]Job 36:8,9; Hos. 5:15 [b]Prov. 21:13; Mat. 7:2
22 [a]ch. 37:21 [b]ch. 9:5; 1 Ki. 2:32; 2 Chr. 24:22; Ps. 9:12; Luke 11:50, 51
23 [l]Heb. *an interpreter* was *between them*
25 [a]Mat. 5:44; Rom. 12:17,20,21
27 [a]See ch. 43:21
28 [l]Heb. *went forth*
30 [a]ver. 7 [l]Heb. *with us hard things*
33 [a]ver. 15,19,20
34 [a]ch. 34:10
35 [a]See ch. 43:21
36 [a]ch. 43:14
38 [a]ver. 13; ch. 37:33 & 44:28 [b]ver. 4; ch. 44:29 [c]ch. 37:35 & 44:31
43:1 [a]ch. 41:54,57
3 [a]ch. 42:20 & 44:23 [l]Heb. *protesting protested*

will not go down: for the man said unto us, Ye shall not see my face, except your brother *be* with you.

6 And Israel said, Wherefore dealt ye *so* ill with me, *as* to tell the man whether ye had yet a brother?

7 And they said, The man [1]asked us straitly of our state, and of our kindred, saying, *Is* your father yet alive? have ye *another* brother? and we told him according to the [2]tenor of these words: [3]could we certainly know that he would say, Bring your brother down?

8 And Judah said unto Israel his father, Send the lad with me, and we will arise and go; that we may live, and not die, both we, and thou, *and* also our little ones.

9 I will be surety for him; of my hand shalt thou require him: [a]if I bring him not unto thee, and set him before thee, then let me bear the blame for ever:

10 For except we had lingered, surely now we had returned [1]this second time.

11 And their father Israel said unto them, If *it must be* so now, do this; take of the best fruits in the land in your vessels, and [a]carry down the man a present, a little [b]balm, and a little honey, spices, and myrrh, nuts, and almonds:

12 And take double money in your hand; and the money [a]that was brought again in the mouth of your sacks, carry *it* again in your hand; peradventure it *was* an oversight:

13 Take also your brother, and arise, go again unto the man:

14 And God Almighty give you mercy before the man, that he may send away your other brother, and Benjamin. [a]If[1] I be bereaved *of my children,* I am bereaved.

15 ¶ And the men took that present, and they took double money in their hand, and Benjamin; and rose up, and went down to Egypt, and stood before Joseph.

16 And when Joseph saw Benjamin with them, he said to the [a]ruler of his house, Bring *these* men home, and [1]slay, and make ready; for *these* men shall [2]dine with me at noon.

17 And the man did as Joseph bade; and the man brought the men into Joseph's house.

18 And the men were afraid, because they were brought into Joseph's house; and they said, Because of the money that was returned in our sacks at the first time are we brought in; that he may [1]seek occasion against us, and fall upon us, and take us for bondmen, and our asses.

19 And they came near to the steward of Joseph's house, and they communed with him at the door of the house,

20 And said, O sir, [a]we[1] came indeed down at the first time to buy food:

21 And [a]it came to pass, when we came to the inn, that we opened our sacks, and, behold, *every* man's money *was* in the mouth of his sack, our money in full weight: and we have brought it again in our hand.

22 And other money have we brought down in our hands to buy food: we cannot tell who put our money in our sacks.

23 And he said, Peace *be* to you, fear not: your God, and the God of your father, hath given you treasure in your sacks: [1]I had your money. And he brought Simeon out unto them.

24 And the man brought the men into Joseph's house, and [a]gave *them* water, and they washed their feet; and he gave their asses provender.

25 And they made ready the present against Joseph came at noon: for they heard that they should eat bread there.

26 ¶ And when Joseph came home, they brought him the present which *was* in their hand into the house, and [a]bowed themselves to him to the earth.

27 And he asked them of *their* [a]welfare,[1] and said, [2]*Is* your father well, the old man [b]of whom ye spake? *Is* he yet alive?

28 And they answered, Thy servant our father *is* in good health, he *is* yet alive. [a]And they bowed down their heads, and made obeisance.

29 And he lifted up his eyes, and saw his brother Benjamin, [a]his mother's son, and said, *Is* this your younger brother, [b]of whom ye spake unto me? And he said, God be gracious unto thee, my son.

30 And Joseph made haste; for [a]his bowels did yearn upon his brother: and he sought *where* to weep; and he entered into *his* chamber, and [b]wept there.

31 And he washed his face, and went out, and refrained himself, and said, Set on [a]bread.

32 And they set on for him by himself, and for them by themselves, and for the

7 [1]Heb. *asking asked us* [2]Heb. *mouth* [3]Heb. *knowing could we know*

9 [a]ch. 44:32; Philem. 18,19

10 [1]Or, *twice by this*

11 [a]ch. 32:20; Prov. 18:16 [b]ch. 37:25; Jer. 8:22

12 [a]ch. 42:25,35

14 [a]Esth. 4:16 [1]Or, *And I, as I have been*

16 [a]ch. 24:2 & 39:4 & 44:1 [1]Heb. *kill a killing* [2]Heb. *eat*

18 [1]Heb. *roll himself upon us*

20 [a]ch. 42:3,10 [1]Heb. *coming down we came down*

21 [a]ch. 42:27,35

23 [1]Heb. *your money came to me*

24 [a]ch. 18:4 & 24:32

26 [a]ch. 37:7,10

27 [a]ch. 37:14 [b]ch. 42:11,13 [1]Heb. *peace,* [2]Heb. Is there *peace to your father?*

28 [a]ch. 37:7,10

29 [a]ch. 35:17,18 [b]ch. 42:13

30 [a]1 Ki. 3:26 [b]ch. 42:24

31 [a]ver. 25

Egyptians, which did eat with him, by themselves: because the Egyptians might not eat bread with the Hebrews; for that *is* [a]an abomination unto the Egyptians.

33 And they sat before him, the firstborn according to his birthright, and the youngest according to his youth: and the men marvelled one at another.

34 And he took *and sent* messes unto them from before him: but Benjamin's mess was [a]five times so much as any of theirs. And they drank, and [l]were merry with him.

The missing silver cup

44 AND HE commanded [l]the steward of his house, saying, Fill the men's sacks *with* food, as much as they can carry, and put every man's money in his sack's mouth.

2 And put my cup, the silver cup, in the sack's mouth of the youngest, and his corn money. And he did according to the word that Joseph had spoken.

3 As soon as the morning was light, the men were sent away, they and their asses.

4 *And* when they were gone out of the city, *and* not *yet* far off, Joseph said unto his steward, Up, follow after the men; and when thou dost overtake them, say unto them, Wherefore have ye rewarded evil for good?

5 *Is* not this *it* in which my lord drinketh, and whereby indeed he [l]divineth? ye have done evil in so doing.

6 ¶ And he overtook them, and he spake unto them these same words.

7 And they said unto him, Wherefore saith my lord these words? God forbid that thy servants should do according to this thing:

8 Behold, [a]the money, which we found in our sacks' mouths, we brought again unto thee out of the land of Canaan: how then should we steal out of thy lord's house silver or gold?

9 With whomsoever of thy servants it be found, [a]both let him die, and we also will be my lord's bondmen.

10 And he said, Now also *let* it *be* according unto your words: he with whom it is found shall be my servant; and ye shall be blameless.

11 Then they speedily took down every man his sack to the ground, and opened every man his sack.

32 [a]ch. 46:34; Ex. 8:26
34 [a]ch. 45:22 [l]Heb. *drank largely*
44:1 [l]Heb. him *that was over his house*
5 [l]Or, *maketh trial?*
8 [a]ch. 43:21
9 [a]ch. 31:32
13 [a]ch. 37:29,34; Num. 14:6; 2 Sam. 1:11
14 [a]ch. 37:7
15 [l]Or, *make trial?*; see ver. 5
16 [a]ver. 9
17 [a]Prov. 17:15
18 [a]ch. 18:30,32; Ex. 32:22
20 [a]ch. 37:3
21 [a]ch. 42:15,20
23 [a]ch. 43:3,5
25 [a]ch. 43:2

12 And he searched, *and* began at the eldest, and left at the youngest: and the cup was found in Benjamin's sack.

13 Then they [a]rent their clothes, and laded every man his ass, and returned to the city.

14 ¶ And Judah and his brethren came to Joseph's house; for he *was* yet there: and they [a]fell before him on the ground.

15 And Joseph said unto them, What deed *is* this that ye have done? wot ye not that such a man as I can certainly [l]divine?

16 And Judah said, What shall we say unto my lord? what shall we speak? or how shall we clear ourselves? God hath found out the iniquity of thy servants: behold, [a]we *are* my lord's servants, both we, and *he* also with whom the cup is found.

17 And he said, [a]God forbid that I should do so: *but* the man in whose hand the cup is found, he shall be my servant; and as for you, get you up in peace unto your father.

18 ¶ Then Judah came near unto him, and said, Oh my lord, let thy servant, I pray thee, speak a word in my lord's ears, and [a]let not thine anger burn against thy servant: for thou *art* even as Pharaoh.

19 My lord asked his servants, saying, Have ye a father, or a brother?

20 And we said unto my lord, We have a father, an old man, and [a]a child of his old age, a little one; and his brother is dead, and he alone is left of his mother, and his father loveth him.

21 And thou saidst unto thy servants, [a]Bring him down unto me, that I may set mine eyes upon him.

22 And we said unto my lord, The lad cannot leave his father: for *if* he should leave his father, *his father* would die.

23 And thou saidst unto thy servants, [a]Except your youngest brother come down with you, ye shall see my face no more.

24 And it came to pass when we came up unto thy servant my father, we told him the words of my lord.

25 And [a]our father said, Go again, *and* buy us a little food.

26 And we said, We cannot go down: if our youngest brother be with us, then will we go down: for we may not see the man's face, except our youngest brother *be* with us.

27 And thy servant my father said unto us, Ye know that [a]my wife bare me two *sons:*

28 And the one went out from me, and I said, [a]Surely he is torn in pieces; and I saw him not since:

29 And if ye [a]take this also from me, and mischief befall him, ye shall bring down my gray hairs with sorrow to the grave.

30 Now therefore when I come to thy servant my father, and the lad *be* not with us; seeing that [a]his life is bound up in the lad's life;

31 It shall come to pass, when he seeth that the lad *is* not *with us,* that he will die: and thy servants shall bring down the gray hairs of thy servant our father with sorrow to the grave.

32 For thy servant became surety for the lad unto my father, saying, [a]If I bring him not unto thee, then I shall bear the blame to my father for ever.

33 Now therefore, I pray thee, [a]let thy servant abide instead of the lad a bondman to my lord; and let the lad go up with his brethren.

34 For how shall I go up to my father, and the lad *be* not with me? lest peradventure I see the evil that shall ʹcome on my father.

Joseph reveals his identity

45 THEN JOSEPH could not refrain himself before all them that stood by him; and he cried, Cause every man to go out from me. And there stood no man with him, while Joseph made himself known unto his brethren.

2 And he wept aloud: and the Egyptians and the house of Pharaoh heard.

3 And Joseph said unto his brethren, [a]I *am* Joseph; doth my father yet live? And his brethren could not answer him; for they were [b]troubledʹ at his presence.

4 And Joseph said unto his brethren, Come near to me, I pray you. And they came near. And he said, I *am* Joseph your brother, [a]whom ye sold into Egypt.

5 Now therefore be not grieved, ʹnor angry with yourselves, that ye sold me hither: [a]for God did send me before you to preserve life.

6 For these two years *hath* the famine *been* in the land: and yet *there are* five years, in the which *there shall* neither *be* earing nor harvest.

27 [a]ch. 46:19
28 [a]ch. 37:33
29 [a]ch. 42:36,38
30 [a]1 Sam. 18:1
32 [a]ch. 43:9
33 [a]Ex. 32:32
34 ʹHeb. *find my father*
45:3 [a]Acts 7:13 [b]Job 4:5 & 23:15; Mat. 14:26; Mark 6:50 ʹOr, *terrified*
4 [a]ch. 37:28
5 [a]ch. 50:20; Ps. 105:16,17 ʹHeb. *neither let there be anger in your eyes*
7 ʹHeb. *to put for you a remnant*
8 [a]ch. 41:43; Judg. 17:10
10 [a]ch. 47:1
12 [a]ch. 42:23
13 [a]Acts 7:14
16 ʹHeb. *was good in the eyes of Pharaoh*
18 [a]ch. 27:28; Num. 18:12,29
20 ʹHeb. *let not your eye spare*
21 ʹHeb. *mouth*

7 And God sent me before you ʹto preserve you a posterity in the earth, and to save your lives by a great deliverance.

8 So now *it was* not you *that* sent me hither, but God: and he hath made me [a]a father to Pharaoh, and lord of all his house, and a ruler throughout all the land of Egypt.

9 Haste ye, and go up to my father, and say unto him, Thus saith thy son Joseph, God hath made me lord of all Egypt: come down unto me, tarry not:

10 And [a]thou shalt dwell in the land of Goshen, and thou shalt be near unto me, thou, and thy children, and thy children's children, and thy flocks, and thy herds, and all that thou hast:

11 And there will I nourish thee; for yet *there are* five years of famine; lest thou, and thy household, and all that thou hast, come to poverty.

12 And, behold, your eyes see, and the eyes of my brother Benjamin, that *it is* [a]my mouth that speaketh unto you.

13 And ye shall tell my father of all my glory in Egypt, and of all that ye have seen; and ye shall haste and [a]bring down my father hither.

14 And he fell upon his brother Benjamin's neck, and wept; and Benjamin wept upon his neck.

15 Moreover he kissed all his brethren, and wept upon them: and after that his brethren talked with him.

16 ¶ And the fame thereof was heard in Pharaoh's house, saying, Joseph's brethren are come: and it ʹpleased Pharaoh well, and his servants.

17 And Pharaoh said unto Joseph, Say unto thy brethren, This do ye; lade your beasts, and go, get you unto the land of Canaan;

18 And take your father and your households, and come unto me: and I will give you the good of the land of Egypt, and ye shall eat [a]the fat of the land.

19 Now thou art commanded, this do ye; take you wagons out of the land of Egypt for your little ones, and for your wives, and bring your father, and come.

20 Also ʹregard not your stuff; for the good of all the land of Egypt *is* yours.

21 And the children of Israel did so: and Joseph gave them wagons, according to the ʹcommandment of Pharaoh, and gave them provision for the way.

22 To all of them he gave each man

changes of raiment; but to Benjamin he gave three hundred *pieces* of silver, and [a]five changes of raiment.

23 And to his father he sent after this *manner;* ten asses [1]laden with the good things of Egypt, and ten she asses laden with corn and bread and meat for his father by the way.

24 So he sent his brethren away, and they departed: and he said unto them, See that ye fall not out by the way.

25 ¶ And they went up out of Egypt, and came into the land of Canaan unto Jacob their father,

26 And told him, saying, Joseph *is* yet alive, and he *is* governor over all the land of Egypt. [a]And [1]Jacob's heart fainted, for he believed them not.

27 And they told him all the words of Joseph, which he had said unto them: and when he saw the wagons which Joseph had sent to carry him, the spirit of Jacob their father revived:

28 And Israel said, *It is* enough; Joseph my son *is* yet alive: I will go and see him before I die.

Jacob goes to Egypt

46 AND ISRAEL took his journey with all that he had, and came to [a]Beer-sheba, and offered sacrifices [b]unto the God of his father Isaac.

A 2 And God spake unto Israel [a]in the visions of the night, and said, Jacob, Jacob. And he said, Here *am* I.

3 And he said, I *am* God, [a]the God of thy father: fear not to go down into Egypt; for I will there [b]make of thee a great nation:

4 [a]I will go down with thee into Egypt; and I will also surely [b]bring thee up *again:* and [c]Joseph shall put his hand upon thine eyes.

5 And [a]Jacob rose up from Beer-sheba: and the sons of Israel carried Jacob their father, and their little ones, and their wives, in the wagons [b]which Pharaoh had sent to carry him.

6 And they took their cattle, and their goods, which they had gotten in the land of Canaan, and came into Egypt, [a]Jacob, and all his seed with him:

7 His sons, and his sons' sons with him, his daughters, and his sons' daughters, and all his seed brought he with him into Egypt.

8 ¶ And [a]these *are* the names of the children of Israel, which came into Egypt, Jacob and his sons: [b]Reuben, Jacob's firstborn.

9 And the sons of Reuben; Hanoch, and Phallu, and Hezron, and Carmi.

10 ¶ And [a]the sons of Simeon; [1]Jemuel, and Jamin, and Ohad, and [2]Jachin, and [3]Zohar, and Shaul the son of a Canaanitish woman.

11 ¶ And the sons of [a]Levi; [1]Gershon, Kohath, and Merari.

12 ¶ And the sons of [a]Judah; Er, and Onan, and Shelah, and Pharez, and Zerah: but [b]Er and Onan died in the land of Canaan. And [c]the sons of Pharez were Hezron and Hamul.

13 ¶ [a]And the sons of Issachar; Tola, and [1]Phuvah, and Job, and Shimron.

14 ¶ And the sons of Zebulun; Sered, and Elon, and Jahleel.

15 These *be* the sons of Leah, which she bare unto Jacob in Padan-aram, with his daughter Dinah: all the souls of his sons and his daughters *were* thirty and three.

16 ¶ And the sons of Gad; [a]Ziphion, and Haggi, Shuni, and [1]Ezbon, Eri, and [2]Arodi, and Areli.

17 ¶ [a]And the sons of Asher; Jimnah, and Ishuah, and Isui, and Beriah, and Serah their sister: and the sons of Beriah; Heber, and Malchiel.

18 [a]These *are* the sons of Zilpah, [b]whom Laban gave to Leah his daughter, and these she bare unto Jacob, *even* sixteen souls.

19 The sons of Rachel [a]Jacob's wife; Joseph, and Benjamin.

20 ¶ [a]And unto Joseph in the land of Egypt were born Manasseh and Ephraim, which Asenath the daughter of Poti-pherah [1]priest of On bare unto him.

21 ¶ [a]And the sons of Benjamin *were* Belah, and Becher, and Ashbel, Gera, and Naaman, [b]Ehi, and Rosh, [c]Muppim, and [1]Huppim, and Ard.

22 These *are* the sons of Rachel, which were born to Jacob: all the souls *were* fourteen.

23 ¶ [a]And the sons of Dan; [1]Hushim.

24 ¶ [a]And the sons of Naphtali; Jahzeel, and Guni, and Jezer, and Shillem.

25 [a]These *are* the sons of Bilhah, [b]which Laban gave unto Rachel his

22 [a]ch. 43:34
23 [1]Heb. *carrying*
26 [a]Job 29:24; Ps. 126:1; Luke 24:11, 41 [1]Heb. *his*
46:1 [a]ch. 21:31, 33 & 28:10 [b]ch. 26:24,25 & 28:13 & 31:42
2 [a]ch. 15:1; Job 33:14,15
3 [a]ch. 28:13 [b]ch. 12:2; Deut. 26:5
4 [a]ch. 28:15 & 48:21 [b]ch. 15:16 & 50:13,24,25; Ex. 3:8 [c]ch. 50:1
5 [a]Acts 7:15 [b]ch. 45:19,21
6 [a]Deut. 26:5; Josh. 24:4; Ps. 105:23; Is. 52:4
8 [a]Ex. 1:1 [b]Num. 26:5
10 [a]Ex. 6:15 [1]Or, *Nemuel* [2]Or, *Jarib* [3]Or, *Zerah;* see 1 Chr. 4:24
11 [a]1 Chr. 6:1,16 [1]Or, *Gershom*
12 [a]1 Chr. 2:3 & 4:21 [b]ch. 38:3,7,10 [c]ch. 38:29
13 [a]1 Chr. 7:1 [1]Or, *Puah, and Jashub*
16 [a]Num. 26:15 *Zephon* [1]Or, *Ozni* [2]Or, *Arod*
17 [a]1 Chr. 7:30
18 [a]ch. 30:10 [b]ch. 29:24
19 [a]ch. 44:27
20 [a]ch. 41:50 [1]Or, *prince*
21 [a]1 Chr. 7:6 & 8:1 [b]Num. 26:38, *Ahiram* [c]Num. 26:39, Shupham; 1 Chr. 7:12, Shuppim [1]*Hupham;* see Num. 26:39
23 [a]1 Chr. 7:12 [1]Or, *Shuham;* see Num. 26:42
24 [a]1 Chr. 7:13
25 [a]ch. 30:5,7 [b]ch. 29:29

A *Ge 41:53–54* ◀▶ *Ge 48:3–6*

daughter, and she bare these unto Jacob: all the souls *were* seven.

26 [a]All the souls that came with Jacob into Egypt, which came out of his [l]loins, besides Jacob's sons' wives, all the souls *were* threescore and six;

27 And the sons of Joseph, which were born him in Egypt, *were* two souls: [a]all the souls of the house of Jacob, which came into Egypt, *were* threescore and ten.

28 ¶ And he sent Judah before him unto Joseph, [a]to direct his face unto Goshen; and they came [b]into the land of Goshen.

29 And Joseph made ready his chariot, and went up to meet Israel his father, to Goshen, and presented himself unto him; and he [a]fell on his neck, and wept on his neck a good while.

30 And Israel said unto Joseph, [a]Now let me die, since I have seen thy face, because thou *art* yet alive.

31 And Joseph said unto his brethren, and unto his father's house, [a]I will go up, and show Pharaoh, and say unto him, My brethren, and my father's house, which *were* in the land of Canaan, are come unto me;

32 And the men *are* shepherds, for [l]their trade hath been to feed cattle; and they have brought their flocks, and their herds, and all that they have.

33 And it shall come to pass, when Pharaoh shall call you, and shall say, [a]What *is* your occupation?

34 That ye shall say, Thy servants' [a]trade hath been about cattle [b]from our youth even until now, both we, *and* also our fathers: that ye may dwell in the land of Goshen; for every shepherd *is* [c]an abomination unto the Egyptians.

47 THEN JOSEPH [a]came and told Pharaoh, and said, My father and my brethren, and their flocks, and their herds, and all that they have, are come out of the land of Canaan; and, behold, they *are* in [b]the land of Goshen.

2 And he took some of his brethren, *even* five men, and [a]presented them unto Pharaoh.

3 And Pharaoh said unto his brethren, [a]What *is* your occupation? And they said unto Pharaoh, [b]Thy servants *are* shepherds, both we, *and* also our fathers.

4 They said moreover unto Pharaoh, [a]For to sojourn in the land are we come; for thy servants have no pasture for their flocks; [b]for the famine *is* sore in the land of Canaan: now therefore, we pray thee, let thy servants [c]dwell in the land of Goshen.

5 And Pharaoh spake unto Joseph, saying, Thy father and thy brethren are come unto thee:

6 [a]The land of Egypt *is* before thee; in the best of the land make thy father and brethren to dwell; [b]in the land of Goshen let them dwell: and if thou knowest *any* men of activity among them, then make them rulers over my cattle.

7 And Joseph brought in Jacob his father, and set him before Pharaoh: and Jacob blessed Pharaoh.

8 And Pharaoh said unto Jacob, [l]How old *art* thou?

9 And Jacob said unto Pharaoh, [a]The days of the years of my pilgrimage *are* an hundred and thirty years: [b]few and evil have the days of the years of my life been, and [c]have not attained unto the days of the years of the life of my fathers in the days of their pilgrimage.

10 And Jacob [a]blessed Pharaoh, and went out from before Pharaoh.

11 ¶ And Joseph placed his father and his brethren, and gave them a possession in the land of Egypt, in the best of the land, in the land of [a]Rameses, [b]as Pharaoh had commanded.

12 And Joseph nourished his father, and his brethren, and all his father's household, with bread, [1,2]according to *their* families.

Joseph and the famine

13 ¶ And *there was* no bread in all the land; for the famine *was* very sore, [a]so that the land of Egypt and *all* the land of Canaan fainted by reason of the famine.

14 [a]And Joseph gathered up all the money that was found in the land of Egypt, and in the land of Canaan, for the corn which they bought: and Joseph brought the money into Pharaoh's house.

15 And when money failed in the land of Egypt, and in the land of Canaan, all the Egyptians came unto Joseph, and said, Give us bread: for [a]why should we die in thy presence? for the money faileth.

16 And Joseph said, Give your cattle; and I will give you for your cattle, if money fail.

---

26 [a]Ex. 1:5 [l]Heb. *thigh;* see ch. 35:11
27 [a]Deut. 10:22; See Acts 7:14
28 [a]ch. 31:21 [b]ch. 47:1
29 [a]ch. 45:14
30 [a]Luke 2:29,30
31 [a]ch. 47:1
32 [l]Heb. *they are men of cattle*
33 [a]ch. 47:2,3
34 [a]ver. 32 [b]ch. 30:35 & 34:5 & 37:12 [c]ch. 43:32; Ex. 8:26
47:1 [a]ch. 46:31 [b]ch. 45:10 & 46:28
2 [a]Acts 7:13
3 [a]ch. 46:33 [b]ch. 46:34
4 [a]ch. 15:13; Deut. 26:5 [b]ch. 43:1; Acts 7:11 [c]ch. 46:34
6 [a]ch. 20:15 [b]ver. 4
8 [l]Heb. *How many are the days of the years of thy life?*
9 [a]Ps. 39:12; Heb. 11:9,13 [b]Job 14:1 [c]ch. 25:7 & 35:28
10 [a]ver. 7
11 [a]Ex. 1:11 & 12:37 [b]ver. 6
12 [1]Or, *as a little child is nourished* [2]Heb. *according to the little ones*
13 [a]ch. 41:30; Acts 7:11
14 [a]ch. 41:56
15 [a]ver. 19

17 And they brought their cattle unto Joseph: and Joseph gave them bread *in exchange* for horses, and for the flocks, and for the cattle of the herds, and for the asses: and he [l]fed them with bread for all their cattle for that year.

18 When that year was ended, they came unto him the second year, and said unto him, We will not hide *it* from my lord, how that our money is spent; my lord also hath our herds of cattle; there is not aught left in the sight of my lord, but our bodies, and our lands:

19 Wherefore shall we die before thine eyes, both we and our land? buy us and our land for bread, and we and our land will be servants unto Pharaoh: and give *us* seed, that we may live, and not die, that the land be not desolate.

20 And Joseph bought all the land of Egypt for Pharaoh; for the Egyptians sold every man his field, because the famine prevailed over them: so the land became Pharaoh's.

21 And as for the people, he removed them to cities from *one* end of the borders of Egypt even to the *other* end thereof.

22 [a]Only the land of the [l]priests bought he not; for the priests had a portion *assigned them* of Pharaoh, and did eat their portion which Pharaoh gave them: wherefore they sold not their lands.

23 Then Joseph said unto the people, Behold, I have bought you this day and your land for Pharaoh: lo, *here is* seed for you, and ye shall sow the land.

24 And it shall come to pass in the increase, that ye shall give the fifth *part* unto Pharaoh, and four parts shall be your own, for seed of the field, and for your food, and for them of your households, and for food for your little ones.

25 And they said, Thou hast saved our lives: [a]let us find grace in the sight of my lord, and we will be Pharaoh's servants.

26 And Joseph made it a law over the land of Egypt unto this day, *that* Pharaoh should have the fifth *part;* [a]except the land of the [l]priests only, *which* became not Pharaoh's.

27 ¶ And Israel [a]dwelt in the land of Egypt, in the country of Goshen; and they had possessions therein, and [b]grew, and multiplied exceedingly.

17 [l]Heb. *led them*
22 [a]Ezra 7:24 [l]Or, *princes;* see ch. 41:45
25 [a]ch. 33:15
26 [a]ver. 22 [l]Or, *princes;* see ver. 22
27 [a]ver. 11 [b]ch. 46:3
28 [l]Heb. *the days of the years of his life*
29 [a]See Deut. 31:14; 1 Ki. 2:1 [b]ch. 24:2 [c]ch. 24:49 [d]See ch. 50:25
30 [a]2 Sam. 19:37 [b]ch. 49:29 & 50:5, 13
31 [a]ch. 48:2; 1 Ki. 1:47; Heb. 11:21
48:3 [a]ch. 28:13, 19 & 35:6,9
4 [a]ch. 17:8
5 [a]ch. 41:50 & 46:20; Josh. 13:7 & 14:4

28 And Jacob lived in the land of Egypt seventeen years: so [l]the whole age of Jacob was an hundred forty and seven years.

29 And the time [a]drew nigh that Israel must die: and he called his son Joseph, and said unto him, If now I have found grace in thy sight, [b]put, I pray thee, thy hand under my thigh, and [c]deal kindly and truly with me; [d]bury me not, I pray thee, in Egypt:

30 But [a]I will lie with my fathers, and thou shalt carry me out of Egypt, and [b]bury me in their buryingplace. And he said, I will do as thou hast said.

31 And he said, Swear unto me. And he sware unto him. And [a]Israel bowed himself upon the bed's head.

Jacob blesses Joseph's sons

48 AND IT came to pass after these things, that *one* told Joseph, Behold, thy father *is* sick: and he took with him his two sons, Manasseh and Ephraim.

2 And *one* told Jacob, and said, Behold, thy son Joseph cometh unto thee: and Israel strengthened himself, and sat upon the bed.

3 And Jacob said unto Joseph, God Al- A
mighty appeared unto me at [a]Luz in the
land of Canaan, and blessed me,
4 And said unto me, Behold, I will I
make thee fruitful, and multiply thee, and
I will make of thee a multitude of people;
and will give this land to thy seed after
thee [a]*for* an everlasting possession.

5 ¶ And now thy [a]two sons, Ephraim and Manasseh, which were born unto thee in the land of Egypt before I came unto thee into Egypt, *are* mine; as Reuben and Simeon, they shall be mine.

6 And thy issue, which thou begettest after them, shall be thine, *and* shall be called after the name of their brethren in their inheritance.

7 And as for me, when I came from

A *Ge 46:2–4* ◀ ▶ *Ge 48:15–16*
I *Ge 17:7–8* ◀ ▶ *Ex 12:41*

48:4 In this verse Jacob briefly summarizes and reconfirms the divine covenant made with Abraham and his descendants.

Padan, [a]Rachel died by me in the land of Canaan in the way, when yet *there was* but a little way to come unto Ephrath: and I buried her there in the way of Ephrath; the same *is* Bethlehem.

8 And Israel beheld Joseph's sons, and said, Who *are* these?

9 And Joseph said unto his father, [a]They *are* my sons, whom God hath given me in this *place.* And he said, Bring them, I pray thee, unto me, and [b]I will bless them.

10 Now [a]the eyes of Israel were [′]dim for age, *so that* he could not see. And he brought them near unto him; and [b]he kissed them, and embraced them.

11 And Israel said unto Joseph, [a]I had not thought to see thy face: and, lo, God hath shown me also thy seed.

12 And Joseph brought them out from between his knees, and he bowed himself with his face to the earth.

13 And Joseph took them both, Ephraim in his right hand toward Israel's left hand, and Manasseh in his left hand toward Israel's right hand, and brought *them* near unto him.

14 And Israel stretched out his right hand, and laid *it* upon Ephraim's head, who *was* the younger, and his left hand upon Manasseh's head, [a]guiding his hands wittingly; for Manasseh *was* the firstborn.

15 ¶ And [a]he blessed Joseph, and said, God, [b]before whom my fathers Abraham and Isaac did walk, the God which fed me all my life long unto this day,

16 The Angel [a]which redeemed me from all evil, bless the lads; and let [b]my name be named on them, and the name of my fathers Abraham and Isaac; and let them [′]grow into a multitude in the midst of the earth.

17 And when Joseph saw that his father [a]laid his right hand upon the head of Ephraim, it [′]displeased him: and he held up his father's hand, to remove it from Ephraim's head unto Manasseh's head.

18 And Joseph said unto his father, Not so, my father: for this *is* the firstborn; put thy right hand upon his head.

19 And his father refused, and said, [a]I know *it,* my son, I know *it:* he also shall become a people, and he also shall be great: but truly [b]his younger brother shall be greater than he, and his seed shall become a [′]multitude of nations.

20 And he blessed them that day, saying, [a]In thee shall Israel bless, saying, God make thee as Ephraim and as Manasseh: and he set Ephraim before Manasseh.

21 And Israel said unto Joseph, Behold, I die: but [a]God shall be with you, and bring you again unto the land of your fathers.

22 Moreover [a]I have given to thee one portion above thy brethren, which I took out of the hand [b]of the Amorite with my sword and with my bow.

Jacob blesses his sons

49 AND JACOB called unto his sons, and said, Gather yourselves together, that I may [a]tell you *that* which shall befall you [b]in the last days.

2 Gather yourselves together, and hear, ye sons of Jacob; and hearken unto Israel your father.

3 ¶ Reuben, thou *art* [a]my firstborn, my might, and the beginning of my strength,

7 [a]ch. 35:9,16,19
9 [a]See ch. 33:5 [b]ch. 27:4
10 [a]ch. 27:1 [b]ch. 27:27 [′]Heb. *heavy*
11 [a]ch. 45:26
14 [a]ver. 19
15 [a]Heb. 11:21 [b]ch. 17:1
16 [a]ch. 28:15; Ps. 34:22 & 121:7 [b]Amos 9:12; Acts 15:17 [′]Heb. *as fishes do increase*
17 [a]ver. 14 [′]*was evil in his eyes*
19 [a]ver. 14 [b]Num. 1:33,35; Deut. 33:17 [′]Heb. *fulness*
20 [a]See Ruth 4:11, 12
21 [a]ch. 46:4
22 [a]Josh. 24:32; John 4:5 [b]ch. 34:28
49:1 [a]Deut. 33:1; Amos 3:7 [b]Deut. 4:30; Is. 39:6; Jer. 23:20; Heb. 1:2
3 [a]ch. 29:32

A *Ge 48:3–6* ◀▶ *Ge 48:19–22*
F *Ge 28:20* ◀▶ *Ex 15:23–25*
A *Ge 24:1* ◀▶ *Dt 14:29*

A *Ge 48:15–16* ◀▶ *Ge 49:1–28*
A *Ge 48:19–22* ◀▶ *Ge 50:24–25*

49:1 The phrase "last days" appears in this verse for the first time in the Scripture and is used repeatedly throughout the remainder of the Bible. Referring to a final point in history when God's purposes for a people or an individual will be completed, this expression is primarily used in the OT in conjunction with Israel's rebellion against God and return to him (see Dt 4:30; 31:29; Hos 3:5). The NT writers use this phrase in connection with the coming of Christ (see Heb 1:2; 1Pe 1:20); the end of the dispensation of the church (see 2Ti 3:1; 1Pe 1:5; 2Pe 3:3); and the final resurrection (see Jn 6:39–40, 44, 54; 11:24; 12:48).

49:1–27 It was common practice in the Middle East for a dying patriarch to announce his last blessings to his family (see 27:1–4). In this deathbed prophecy, Jacob covers the future destiny of his sons and their tribes from the occupation of the promised land to the return of Christ. Note that the way each son lived his life affected the final blessing they received.

49:3 Reuben, as the oldest son, was entitled to special privileges. Jacob acknowledged Reuben's position in the family line and noted his excellent qual-

the excellency of dignity, and the excellency of power:
4 Unstable as water, [1]thou shalt not
excel; because thou [a]wentest up to thy
father's bed; then defiledst thou *it:* [2]he
went up to my couch.
5 ¶ [a]Simeon and Levi *are* brethren;
[1]instruments of cruelty *are in* their habitations.
6 O my soul, [a]come not thou into their
secret; [b]unto their assembly, mine honour, be not thou united: for [c]in their anger they slew a man, and in their selfwill
they [1]digged down a wall.
7 Cursed *be* their anger, for *it was*
fierce; and their wrath, for it was cruel: I
will divide them in Jacob, and scatter
them in Israel.
8 ¶ [a]Judah, thou *art he* whom thy
brethren shall praise: [b]thy hand *shall be*
in the neck of thine enemies; [c]thy father's children shall bow down before
thee.

4 [a]ch. 35:22; Deut. 27:20 [1]Heb. *do not thou excel* [2]Or, *my couch is gone*
5 [a]ch. 29:33,34 [1]Or, *their swords are weapons of violence*
6 [a]Prov. 1:15,16 [b]Ps. 26:9; Eph. 5:11 [c]ch. 34:26 [1]Or, *houghed oxen*
8 [a]Deut. 33:7 [b]Ps. 18:40 [c]1 Chr. 5:2
9 [a]Rev. 5:5 [b]Num. 23:24 & 24:9
10 [a]Num. 24:17; Jer. 30:21 [b]Ps. 60:7 [c]Is. 11:1; Mat. 21:9 [d]Is. 60:1-5; Luke 2:30-32
13 [a]Deut. 33:18, 19; Josh. 19:10,11

9 Judah *is* [a]a lion's whelp: from the
prey, my son, thou art gone up: [b]he
stooped down, he couched as a lion, and
as an old lion; who shall rouse him up?
10 [a]The sceptre shall not depart from **B**
Judah, nor [b]a lawgiver from between his
feet, [c]until Shiloh come; [d]and unto him
shall the gathering of the people *be.*
11 Binding his foal unto the vine, and
his ass's colt unto the choice vine; he
washed his garments in wine, and his
clothes in the blood of grapes:
12 His eyes *shall be* red with wine,
and his teeth white with milk.
13 ¶ [a]Zebulun shall dwell at the haven
of the sea; and he *shall be* for an haven of
ships; and his border *shall be* unto Zidon.
14 ¶ Issachar *is* a strong ass couching
down between two burdens:
15 And he saw that rest *was* good, and
the land that *it was* pleasant; and bowed

B *Ge 3:15–21* ◄► *Nu 19:1–22*

---

ities, but Jacob also prophesied that Reuben would not achieve excellence in leadership because of his unstable character. In addition, due to Reuben's sexual encounter with Jacob's concubine Bilhah (see 35:22), Reuben's birthright, a double portion, would ultimately be divided between Joseph's sons Ephraim and Manasseh (see 48:4–22, 1Ch 5:1). In fulfillment of this prophecy, no leader, judge, prophet or national hero ever came from Reuben's line, and Reuben's tribe was the first tribe of Israel to be carried into captivity by Assyria (see Jdg 5:15–16; 1Ch 5:26).

49:5–7 In addition to their blood relationship as brothers, Simeon and Levi shared the traits of violence, anger and cruelty (see 34:25). When the time came for Jacob to bless these two sons, Jacob prophesied that their descendants would be divided and scattered throughout the promised land. As fulfillment of this prophecy, during Israel's desert wanderings the tribe of Simeon decreased in size. When Israel was ready to conquer the promised land, Simeon was the smallest of the twelve tribes and was therefore only allotted to settle a few cities within the boundaries of Judah (see Jos 19:1). The Levites were not assigned a specific territory in Canaan but were given cities throughout the promised land (see Jos 21:1–3). Because of their opposition to the idolatry of the golden calf God also allowed them to serve as the priestly tribe of Israel (see Ex 32:26).

49:8 Judah was the fourth son born to Jacob (see 29:35). Since Reuben, Simeon and Levi had forfeited their right to leadership, Jacob assigned the leadership position to Judah. Prefiguring the future royalty of Judah's offspring with "thy father's children shall bow down before thee" and likening Judah's increased military strength to a lion's, Jacob prophesied strength, success, and security for Judah's descendants. In fulfillment of this prophecy, the tribe of Judah grew in power and produced mighty leaders like Caleb, David and Solomon. Significantly, Jesus Christ is a descendant of Judah and called "the Lion of the tribe of Judah, the Root of David" (Rev 5:5).

49:10–12 This prophecy was initially fulfilled in Judah's superiority among the twelve tribes and in David's ascendancy to the kingly throne of Israel but will find its final fulfillment in the Messianic reign of Jesus Christ. All the nations will be subject to the Messiah when he returns to establish his eternal and just kingdom.

The phrases "his foal" and "his ass's colt" (49:11) echo Zechariah's reference to the donkey used as the Messiah's mount (see Zec 9:9) and Christ's fulfillment of this prophecy on his entry into Jerusalem on Palm Sunday (see Lk 19:33–38). The symbolism of washing clothes in wine gives a graphic picture of abundance and fruitfulness (see 27:28) as the Messiah ushers in spiritual blessings and restores what Adam had lost.

49:13 Though landlocked by the tribes of Asher and Manasseh, Zebulun would be within ten miles of the Mediterranean—close enough to "be for an haven of ships."

49:14–15 Issachar was prophetically compared to a strong, powerful donkey. In the ancient Middle East this was not a slanderous description but rather an indication that Issachar would be strong but docile, a people able to carry the burden of others but often satisfied with sitting on the sidelines. Issachar's location within the promised land placed it along

[a]his shoulder to bear, and became a servant unto tribute.
16 ¶ [a]Dan shall judge his people, as
one of the tribes of Israel.
17 [a]Dan shall be a serpent by the way,
ʹan adder in the path, that biteth the
horse heels, so that his rider shall fall
backward.
18 [a]I have waited for thy salvation,
O LORD.
19 ¶ [a]Gad, a troop shall overcome
him: but he shall overcome at the last.
20 ¶ [a]Out of Asher his bread *shall be*
fat, and he shall yield royal dainties.
21 ¶ [a]Naphtali *is* a hind let loose: he
giveth goodly words.
22 ¶ Joseph *is* a fruitful bough, *even* a
fruitful bough by a well; *whose* ʹbranches
run over the wall:
23 The archers have [a]sorely grieved
him, and shot *at him,* and hated him:
24 But his [a]bow abode in strength, and
the arms of his hands were made strong
by the hands of [b]the mighty *God* of Jacob;
([c]from thence [d]*is* the shepherd, [e]the
stone of Israel:)
U 25 [a]*Even* by the God of thy father, who
shall help thee; [b]and by the Almighty,
[c]who shall bless thee with blessings of

U *Ge 39:23* ◄► *Ge 50:24–25*

15 [a]1 Sam. 10:9
16 [a]Deut. 33:22
17 [a]Judg. 18:27 ʹHeb. *an arrow-snake*
18 [a]Ps. 25:5; Is. 25:9
19 [a]Deut. 33:20; 1 Chr. 5:18
20 [a]Deut. 33:24; Josh. 19:24
21 [a]Deut. 33:23
22 ʹHeb. *daughters*
23 [a]ch. 37:4,24; Ps. 118:13
24 [a]Job 29:20; Ps. 37:15 [b]Ps. 132:2,5 [c]ch. 45:11 & 47:12 [d]Ps. 80:1 [e]Is. 28:16
25 [a]ch. 28:13 & 35:3 & 43:23 [b]ch. 17:1 & 35:11 [c]Deut. 33:13
26 [a]Deut. 33:15; Hab. 3:6 [b]Deut. 33:16
27 [a]Judg. 20:21,25 [b]Num. 23:24; Esth. 8:11; Ezek. 39:10; Zech. 14:1
29 [a]ch. 15:15 & 25:8 [b]ch. 47:30; 2 Sam. 19:37 [c]ch. 50:13
30 [a]ch. 23:16

heaven above, blessings of the deep that
lieth under, blessings of the breasts, and
of the womb:
26 The blessings of thy father have
prevailed above the blessings of my
progenitors [a]unto the utmost bound of
the everlasting hills: [b]they shall be on the
head of Joseph, and on the crown of the
head of him that was separate from his
brethren.
27 ¶ Benjamin shall [a]ravin *as* a wolf: in
the morning he shall devour the prey,
[b]and at night he shall divide the spoil.

The death of Jacob

28 ¶ All these *are* the twelve tribes of
Israel: and this *is it* that their father spake
unto them, and blessed them; every one
according to his blessing he blessed
them.
29 And he charged them, and said Q
unto them, I [a]am to be gathered unto my
people: [b]bury me with my fathers [c]in the
cave that *is* in the field of Ephron the
Hittite,
30 In the cave that *is* in the field of
Machpelah, which *is* before Mamre, in
the land of Canaan, [a]which Abraham
bought with the field of Ephron the Hittite for a possession of a buryingplace.

Q *Ge 35:29* ◄► *Ge 49:33*

---

one of the major trade routes and allowed this tribe to flourish. Yet Issachar was slow to help fight Israel's battles and its name is missing from the description of the conquest of Canaan recorded in Judges (see Jdg 1).

49:16–17 Dan's assigned territory in the promised land was close to the Philistines. Though small in size, the tribe of Dan was warlike and withstood the threats of this powerful neighbor. One of the more famous Danites was a judge named Samson who celebrated several victories over the Philistines (see Jdg 16:30).

49:19 Jacob prophesied that enemies would attack Gad's descendants but the tribe would rally and be successful in driving them out of their territory (see Jdg 10:7ff; 11:1; 1Ch 5:18–22). The judge and deliverer Jephthah was from Gad.

49:20 Asher would be allotted territory in the fertile farmlands near the Mediterranean, ensuring Asher's prosperity and future blessing. Even today this area is one of the more fertile areas of Israel, producing large supplies of olive oil, wine and fragrances.

49:21 Naphtali's territory was a very fertile region in the hill country north of the Sea of Galilee. Somewhat isolated from the other tribes, Naphtali exhibited an independent spirit that manifested itself in swift, skilled warriors who were a strong defense for the nation against its enemies.

49:22 The blessing given to Joseph was eloquent and befitting Jacob's favorite son. Joseph's sons Ephraim and Manasseh would carry this blessing into Canaan and were allotted the most favored territories in the promised land, straddling both sides of the Jordan River. Jacob's flowery words also mentioned that Joseph's branches would "run over the wall," a prediction of the extra land Ephraim would need when settling in Canaan (see Jos 17:14–18).

49:27 Benjamin was known as a warlike tribe, filled with mighty, vigorous warriors who were skilled with the sling and bow (see Jdg 5:14; 1Ch 12:2). Ehud, Saul and Jonathan were some of Benjamin's more famous warriors who fulfilled this prophecy (see Jdg 3:12–30; 1Sa 11—15).

49:29 Jacob realized that the land of his fathers was his God-appointed homeland, so he requested that he be buried in the cave at Machpelah. Scripture records that Jacob "was gathered unto his people" (49:33) supporting Jacob's belief that his faithful ancestors, though dead, still existed and would one day be resurrected (see note at 35:29).

31 [a]There they buried Abraham and Sarah his wife; [b]there they buried Isaac and Rebekah his wife; and there I buried Leah.

32 The purchase of the field and of the cave that *is* therein *was* from the children of Heth.

Q 33 And when Jacob had made an end of commanding his sons, he gathered up his feet into the bed, and yielded up the ghost, and [a]was gathered unto his people.

50 AND JOSEPH [a]fell upon his father's face, and [b]wept upon him, and kissed him.

2 And Joseph commanded his servants the physicians to [a]embalm his father: and the physicians embalmed Israel.

3 And forty days were fulfilled for him; for so are fulfilled the days of those which are embalmed: and the Egyptians [a]mourned[ǀ] for him threescore and ten days.

4 And when the days of his mourning were past, Joseph spake unto [a]the house of Pharaoh, saying, If now I have found grace in your eyes, speak, I pray you, in the ears of Pharaoh, saying,

5 [a]My father made me swear, saying, Lo, I die: in my grave [b]which I have digged for me in the land of Canaan, there shalt thou bury me. Now therefore let me go up, I pray thee, and bury my father, and I will come again.

6 And Pharaoh said, Go up, and bury thy father, according as he made thee swear.

7 ¶ And Joseph went up to bury his father: and with him went up all the servants of Pharaoh, the elders of his house, and all the elders of the land of Egypt,

8 And all the house of Joseph, and his brethren, and his father's house: only their little ones, and their flocks, and their herds, they left in the land of Goshen.

9 And there went up with him both chariots and horsemen: and it was a very great company.

10 And they came to the threshingfloor of Atad, which *is* beyond Jordan, and there they [a]mourned with a great and very sore lamentation: [b]and he made a mourning for his father seven days.

11 And when the inhabitants of the land, the Canaanites, saw the mourning in the floor of Atad, they said, This *is* a grievous mourning to the Egyptians: wherefore the name of it was called [ǀ]Abel-mizraim, which *is* beyond Jordan.

12 And his sons did unto him according as he commanded them:

13 For [a]his sons carried him into the land of Canaan, and buried him in the cave of the field of Machpelah, which Abraham [b]bought with the field for a possession of a buryingplace of Ephron the Hittite, before Mamre.

14 ¶ And Joseph returned into Egypt, he, and his brethren, and all that went up with him to bury his father, after he had buried his father.

15 ¶ And when Joseph's brethren saw that their father was dead, [a]they said, Joseph will peradventure hate us, and will certainly requite us all the evil which we did unto him.

16 And they [ǀ]sent a messenger unto Joseph, saying, Thy father did command before he died, saying,

17 So shall ye say unto Joseph, Forgive, I pray thee now, the trespass of thy brethren, and their sin; [a]for they did unto thee evil: and now, we pray thee, forgive the trespass of the servants of [b]the God of thy father. And Joseph wept when they spake unto him.

18 And his brethren also went and [a]fell down before his face; and they said, Behold, we *be* thy servants.

19 And Joseph said unto them, [a]Fear not: [b]for *am* I in the place of God?

20 [a]But as for you, ye thought evil against me; *but* [b]God meant it unto good, to bring to pass, as *it is* this day, to save much people alive.

21 Now therefore fear ye not: [a]I will nourish you, and your little ones. And he comforted them, and spake [ǀ]kindly unto them.

The death of Joseph

22 ¶ And Joseph dwelt in Egypt, he, and his father's house: and Joseph lived an hundred and ten years.

23 And Joseph saw Ephraim's children [a]of the third *generation:* [b]the children also of Machir the son of Manasseh [c]were [ǀ]brought up upon Joseph's knees.

---

31 [a]ch. 23:19 & 25:9 [b]ch. 35:29
33 [a]ver. 29
50:1 [a]ch. 46:4 [b]2 Ki. 13:14
2 [a]ver. 26; 2 Chr. 16:14; Luke 24:1; John 19:39,40
3 [a]Num. 20:29; Deut. 34:8 [ǀ]Heb. *wept*
4 [a]Esth. 4:2
5 [a]ch. 47:29 [b]2 Chr. 16:14; Is. 22:16
10 [a]Acts 8:2 [b]1 Sam. 31:13; Job 2:13
11 [ǀ]i.e. *The mourning of the Egyptians*
13 [a]ch. 49:29; Acts 7:16 [b]ch. 23:16
15 [a]Job 15:21
16 [ǀ]Heb. *charged*
17 [a]Prov. 28:13 [b]ch. 49:25
18 [a]ch. 37:7,10
19 [a]ch. 45:5 [b]2 Ki. 5:7
20 [a]Ps. 56:5 [b]Acts 3:13-15
21 [a]Mat. 5:44 [ǀ]Heb. *to their hearts*
23 [a]Job 42:16 [b]Num. 32:39 [c]ch. 30:3 [ǀ]Heb. *borne*

Q *Ge 49:29* ◄► *Nu 20:24*

A 24 And Joseph said unto his brethren,
U I die: and [a]God will surely visit you, and
bring you out of this land unto the land
[b]which he sware to Abraham, to Isaac,
and to Jacob.

A *Ge 49:1–28* ◀▶ *Ex 3:8–12*
U *Ge 49:25–26* ◀▶ *Lev 26:3–12*

24 [a]ch. 15:14 & 46:4 & 48:21; Ex. 3:16,17; Heb. 11:22 [b]ch. 26:3 & 35:12 & 46:4

25 [a]Ex. 13:19; Josh. 24:32; Acts 7:16

25 And [a]Joseph took an oath of the
children of Israel, saying, God will surely
visit you, and ye shall carry up my bones
from hence.
26 So Joseph died, *being* an hundred
and ten years old: and they embalmed
him, and he was put in a coffin in
Egypt.

50:24–25 God had promised to make Abraham's family into a great nation and bring them into the promised land. Joseph's dying words clearly emphasized his belief that God would do what he had promised (see 15:16; 46:4; 48:21; Heb 11:25). In addition, Joseph expressed his confidence in his descendants' ability to transfer his bones from Egypt to his homeland in Canaan. Though several generations would pass before this prophecy was fulfilled, Moses brought Joseph's bones out of Egypt during the exodus. Joseph's bones were reburied at Shechem (see 33:19; Ex 13:19; Jos 24:32).

Exodus

Author: Moses

Theme: Israel's deliverance from bondage

Date of Writing: c. 1440–1406 B.C.

Outline of Exodus

I. Israel Under Bondage in Egypt (1:1—12:36)
   A. The slavery of Israel (1:1–22)
   B. The rise of a deliverer (2:1—4:31)
   C. Moses' struggle with Pharaoh (5:1—12:36)

II. The Exodus From Egypt (12:37—18:27)
   A. Leaving Egypt (12:37—13:16)
   B. Crossing the "Red Sea" (13:17—15:21)
   C. The journey to Sinai (15:22—18:27)

III. Israel's Experience in the Wilderness (19:1—40:38)
   A. God gives the law on Mt. Sinai (19:1—24:18)
   B. Building the tabernacle (25:1—40:38)

THE BOOK OF Exodus derives its name not from Hebrew but from the Greek word *exodos*, which means "exit" or "departure." The Septuagint, a Greek translation of the OT, uses this term in Ex 19:1 and titles this book *Exodos*—an apt title for a book that chronicles the escape of the Israelites from centuries of bondage as slaves in Egypt.

Exodus records God's deliverance of his chosen people from slavery in Egypt through a series of supernatural interventions. Observing the plagues that Pharaoh's hard heart brought on the land, the Israelites soon realized that their deliverance hinged on faithful obedience to God's revealed law. One such act of obedience was expressed through the sacrifice of an innocent lamb at the institution of the Passover (see Ex 12:1–13). Though the sacrificial system inaugurated in the book of Exodus could not fully eliminate a sinner's guilt, Israel's obedience to God's system of sacrifices foreshadowed the sacrifice of Jesus Christ, who paid the full price for the redemption of sins with his death on the cross.

After the deliverance from Egypt, Exodus documents the elements of a foundational theology in which God reveals his name, his attributes, his redemption, his law and how he is to be worshiped. God gave Moses the Ten Commandments on Mt. Sinai and commanded the Israelites to obey his law. Yet the Israelites' disobedience to God's commandments created the need for a system of priests and blood sacrifices. The book of Exodus details the rules for worship in the tabernacle and for Israel's forgiveness and cleansing from sin and restoration to fellowship, blessing and proper worship.

This second book of the Pentateuch also continues the progressive revelation of God's divine nature and his plan of salvation as revealed in the covenants. Genesis closed with the Abrahamic covenant (see Ge 15:4). The book of Exodus relates how the ancient covenant relationship between God and his people expands under the Mosaic covenant (see Ex 19:5) as God establishes his unbreakable covenant with the nation of Israel.

Note also a multitude of types presented throughout the book of Exodus. Moses, the Passover and the tabernacle all point to the future Messiah, Jesus Christ. See "The Language of the Prophets" section in the article entitled "Introduction to Prophecy," p. vi.

Israel's growth and bondage

1 NOW [a]THESE *are* the names of the
children of Israel, which came into
Egypt; every man and his household
came with Jacob.
2 Reuben, Simeon, Levi, and Judah,
3 Issachar, Zebulun, and Benjamin,
4 Dan, and Naphtali, Gad, and Asher.
5 And all the souls that came out of the
ʼloins of Jacob were [a]seventy souls: for
Joseph was in Egypt *already.*
6 And [a]Joseph died, and all his brethren, and all that generation.
7 ¶ [a]And the children of Israel were
fruitful, and increased abundantly, and
multiplied, and waxed exceeding mighty;
and the land was filled with them.
8 Now there arose up a new king over
Egypt, which knew not Joseph.
9 And he said unto his people, Behold,
[a]the people of the children of Israel *are*
more and mightier than we:
10 [a]Come on, let us [b]deal wisely with
them; lest they multiply, and it come to
pass, that, when there falleth out any
war, they join also unto our enemies, and
fight against us, and *so* get them up out of
the land.
11 Therefore they did set over them
taskmasters [a]to afflict them with their
[b]burdens. And they built for Pharaoh
treasure cities, Pithom [c]and Raamses.
12 ʼBut the more they afflicted them,
the more they multiplied and grew. And
they were grieved because of the children of Israel.
13 And the Egyptians made the children of Israel to serve with rigour:
14 And they [a]made their lives bitter
with hard bondage, [b]in mortar, and in
brick, and in all manner of service in the
field: all their service, wherein they made
them serve, *was* with rigour.
15 ¶ And the king of Egypt spake to
the Hebrew midwives, of which the
name of the one *was* Shiphrah, and the
name of the other Puah:
16 And he said, When ye do the office
of a midwife to the Hebrew women, and
see *them* upon the stools; if it *be* a son,
then ye shall kill him: but if it *be* a daughter, then she shall live.
17 But the midwives [a]feared God, and
did not [b]as the king of Egypt commanded
them, but saved the men children alive.
18 And the king of Egypt called for the
midwives, and said unto them, Why have
ye done this thing, and have saved the
men children alive?
19 And [a]the midwives said unto Pharaoh, Because the Hebrew women *are* not
as the Egyptian women; for they *are*
lively, and are delivered ere the midwives come in unto them.
20 [a]Therefore God dealt well with the

1:1 [a]Gen. 46:8
5 [a]Gen. 46:26,27 ʼHeb. *thigh*
6 [a]Gen. 50:26; Acts 7:15
7 [a]Gen. 46:3; Deut. 26:5; Ps. 105:24; Acts 7:17
9 [a]Ps. 105:24
10 [a]Ps. 83:3,4 [b]Prov. 16:25; Acts 7:19
11 [a]Gen. 15:13; ch. 3:7; Deut. 26:6 [b]ch. 5:4,5 [c]Gen. 47:11
12 ʼHeb. *And as they afflicted them, so they multiplied*
14 [a]ch. 2:23 & 6:9; Num. 20:15; Acts 7:19,34 [b]Ps. 81:6
17 [a]Prov. 16:6 [b]Dan. 3:16,18; Acts 5:29
19 [a]See Josh. 2:4; 2 Sam. 17:19,20
20 [a]Prov. 11:18; Eccl. 8:12; Is. 3:10; Heb. 6:10

midwives: and the people multiplied, and waxed very mighty.

21 And it came to pass, because the midwives feared God, [a]that he made them houses.

22 And Pharaoh charged all his people, saying, [a]Every son that is born ye shall cast into the river, and every daughter ye shall save alive.

Moses' birth

2 AND THERE went [a]a man of the house of Levi, and took *to wife* a daughter of Levi.

2 And the woman conceived, and bare a son: and [a]when she saw him that he *was a* goodly *child,* she hid him three months.

3 And when she could not longer hide him, she took for him an ark of bulrushes, and daubed it with slime and with pitch, and put the child therein; and she laid *it* in the flags by the river's brink.

4 [a]And his sister stood afar off, to wit what would be done to him.

5 ¶ And the [a]daughter of Pharaoh came down to wash *herself* at the river; and her maidens walked along by the river's side; and when she saw the ark among the flags, she sent her maid to fetch it.

6 And when she had opened *it,* she saw the child: and, behold, the babe wept. And she had compassion on him, and said, This *is one* of the Hebrews' children.

7 Then said his sister to Pharaoh's daughter, Shall I go and call to thee a nurse of the Hebrew women, that she may nurse the child for thee?

8 And Pharaoh's daughter said to her, Go. And the maid went and called the child's mother.

9 And Pharaoh's daughter said unto her, Take this child away, and nurse it for me, and I will give *thee* thy wages. And the woman took the child, and nursed it.

10 And the child grew, and she brought him unto Pharaoh's daughter, and he became [a]her son. And she called his name [1]Moses: and she said, Because I drew him out of the water.

Moses flees to Midian

11 ¶ And it came to pass in those days, [a]when Moses was grown, that he went out unto his brethren, and looked on their [b]burdens: and he spied an Egyptian smiting an Hebrew, one of his brethren.

12 And he looked this way and that way, and when he saw that *there was* no man, he [a]slew the Egyptian, and hid him in the sand.

13 And [a]when he went out the second day, behold, two men of the Hebrews strove together: and he said to him that did the wrong, Wherefore smitest thou thy fellow?

14 And he said, [a]Who made thee [1]a prince and a judge over us? intendest thou to kill me, as thou killedst the Egyptian? And Moses feared, and said, Surely this thing is known.

15 Now when Pharaoh heard this thing, he sought to slay Moses. But [a]Moses fled from the face of Pharaoh, and dwelt in the land of Midian: and he sat down by [b]a well.

16 [a]Now the [1]priest of Midian had seven daughters: [b]and they came and drew *water,* and filled the troughs to water their father's flock.

17 And the shepherds came and drove them away: but Moses stood up and helped them, and [a]watered their flock.

18 And when they came to [a]Reuel their father, he said, How *is it that* ye are come so soon today?

19 And they said, An Egyptian delivered us out of the hand of the shepherds, and also drew *water* enough for us, and watered the flock.

20 And he said unto his daughters, And where *is* he? why *is* it *that* ye have left the man? call him, that he may [a]eat bread.

21 And Moses was content to dwell with the man: and he gave Moses [a]Zipporah his daughter.

22 And she bare *him* a son, and he called his name [a]Gershom:[1] for he said, I have been [b]a stranger in a strange land.

23 ¶ And it came to pass [a]in process of time, that the king of Egypt died: and the children of Israel [b]sighed by reason of the bondage, and they cried, and [c]their cry came up unto God by reason of the bondage.

24 And God [a]heard their groaning, and God [b]remembered his [c]covenant with Abraham, with Isaac, and with Jacob.

25 And God [a]looked upon the children

21 [a]See 1 Sam. 2:35; 2 Sam. 7:11, 13,27,29; 1 Ki. 11:38; Ps. 127:1
22 [a]Acts 7:19
2:1 [a]ch. 6:20; Num. 26:59; 1 Chr. 23:14
2 [a]Acts 7:20; Heb. 11:23
4 [a]ch. 15:20; Num. 26:59
5 [a]Acts 7:21
10 [a]Acts 7:21 [1]i.e. *Drawn out*
11 [a]Acts 7:23,24; Heb. 11:24-26 [b]ch. 1:11
12 [a]Acts 7:24
13 [a]Acts 7:26
14 [a]Acts 7:27,28 [1]Heb. *a man, a prince;* see Gen. 13:8
15 [a]Acts 7:29; Heb. 11:27 [b]Gen. 24:11 & 29:2
16 [a]ch. 3:1 [b]Gen. 24:11; 1 Sam. 9:11 [1]Or, *prince;* see Gen. 41:45
17 [a]Gen. 29:10
18 [a]Num. 10:29; Called also *Jethro,* or, *Jether;* ch. 3:1 & 4:18
20 [a]Gen. 31:54
21 [a]ch. 18:2
22 [a]ch. 18:3 [b]Acts 7:29 [1]i.e. *A stranger here*
23 [a]Acts 7:30 [b]Deut. 26:7 [c]ch. 3:9; Jas. 5:4
24 [a]ch. 6:5 [b]ch. 6:5; Ps. 105:8,42 [c]Gen. 15:14
25 [a]ch. 4:31; Luke 1:25

of Israel, and God [b]had[l] respect unto *them.*

Moses and the burning bush

3 NOW MOSES kept the flock of Jethro his father-in-law, [a]the priest of Midian: and he led the flock to the backside of the desert, and came to [b]the mountain of God, *even* to Horeb.

2 And [a]the angel of the LORD appeared unto him in a flame of fire out of the midst of a bush: and he looked, and, behold, the bush burned with fire, and the bush *was* not consumed.

3 And Moses said, I will now turn aside, and see this [a]great sight, why the bush is not burnt.

4 And when the LORD saw that he turned aside to see, God called [a]unto him out of the midst of the bush, and said, Moses, Moses. And he said, Here *am* I.

5 And he said, Draw not nigh hither: [a]put off thy shoes from off thy feet, for the place whereon thou standest *is* holy ground.

6 Moreover he said, [a]I *am* the God of thy father, the God of Abraham, the God of Isaac, and the God of Jacob. And Moses hid his face; for [b]he was afraid to look upon God.

7 ¶ And the LORD said, [a]I have surely seen the affliction of my people which *are* in Egypt, and have heard their cry [b]by reason of their taskmasters; for [c]I know their sorrows;

A 8 And [a]I am come down to [b]deliver them out of the hand of the Egyptians, and to bring them up out of that land [c]unto a good land and a large, unto a land [d]flowing with milk and honey; unto the place of [e]the Canaanites, and the Hittites, and the Amorites, and the Perizzites, and the Hivites, and the Jebusites.

9 Now therefore, behold, [a]the cry of the children of Israel is come unto me: and I have also seen the [b]oppression wherewith the Egyptians oppress them.

10 [a]Come now therefore, and I will send thee unto Pharaoh, that thou mayest bring forth my people the children of Israel out of Egypt.

11 ¶ And Moses said unto God, [a]Who *am* I, that I should go unto Pharaoh, and that I should bring forth the children of Israel out of Egypt?

12 And he said, [a]Certainly I will be with thee; and this *shall be* a token unto thee, that I have sent thee: When thou hast brought forth the people out of Egypt, ye shall serve God upon this mountain.

13 And Moses said unto God, Behold, *when* I come unto the children of Israel, and shall say unto them, The God of your fathers hath sent me unto you; and they shall say to me, What *is* his name? what shall I say unto them?

14 And God said unto Moses, I AM THAT I AM: and he said, Thus shalt thou say unto the children of Israel, [a]I AM hath sent me unto you.

15 And God said moreover unto Moses, Thus shalt thou say unto the children of Israel, The LORD God of your fathers, the God of Abraham, the God of Isaac, and the God of Jacob, hath sent me unto you: this *is* [a]my name for ever, and this *is* my memorial unto all generations.

16 Go, and [a]gather the elders of Israel together, and say unto them, The LORD God of your fathers, the God of Abraham, of Isaac, and of Jacob, appeared unto me, saying, [b]I have surely visited you, and *seen* that which is done to you in Egypt:

17 And I have said, [a]I will bring you up out of the affliction of Egypt unto the land of the Canaanites, and the Hittites, and the Amorites, and the Perizzites, and the Hivites, and the Jebusites, unto a land flowing with milk and honey. A

18 And [a]they shall hearken to thy voice: and [b]thou shalt come, thou and the elders of Israel, unto the king of Egypt, and ye shall say unto him, The LORD God of the Hebrews hath [c]met with us: and now let us go, we beseech thee, three days' journey into the wilderness, that we may sacrifice to the LORD our God.

19 ¶ And I am sure that the king of Egypt [a]will not let you go, [l]no, not by a mighty hand.

20 And I will [a]stretch out my hand, and smite Egypt with [b]all my wonders which I will do in the midst thereof: and [c]after that he will let you go.

21 And [a]I will give this people favour in the sight of the Egyptians: and it shall come to pass, that, when ye go, ye shall not go empty:

22 [a]But every woman shall borrow of

25 [b]ch. 3:7 [l]Heb. *knew*
3:1 [a]ch. 2:16 [b]ch. 18:5; 1 Ki. 19:8
2 [a]Deut. 33:16; Acts 7:30
3 [a]Acts 7:31
4 [a]Deut. 33:16
5 [a]Josh. 5:15
6 [a]Gen. 28:13; ch. 4:5; Mat. 22:32; Acts 7:32 [b]See 1 Ki. 19:13
7 [a]ch. 2:23-25; Ps. 106:44 [b]ch. 1:11 [c]Gen. 18:21; ch. 2:25
8 [a]Gen. 50:24 [b]ch. 6:6,8 [c]Deut. 1:25 & 8:7-9 [d]ver. 17; ch. 13:5; Jer. 11:5; Ezek. 20:6 [e]Gen. 15:21
9 [a]ch. 2:23 [b]ch. 1:11,13,14
10 [a]Mic. 6:4
11 [a]See ch. 6:12; 1 Sam. 18:18
12 [a]Gen. 31:3; Josh. 1:5; Rom. 8:31
14 [a]ch. 6:3; John 8:58; Heb. 13:8
15 [a]Ps. 135:13
16 [a]ch. 4:29 [b]ch. 2:25; Luke 1:68
17 [a]Gen. 15:14,16
18 [a]ch. 4:31 [b]ch. 5:1,3 [c]Num. 23:3, 4,15,16
19 [a]ch. 5:2 [l]Or, *but by strong hand*
20 [a]ch. 6:6 & 9:15 [b]Deut. 6:22; Neh. 9:10; Acts 7:36 [c]ch. 12:31
21 [a]ch. 11:3 & 12:36; Prov. 16:7
22 [a]ch. 11:2

A *Ge 50:24–25* ◀▶ *Ex 3:17–21*

A *Ex 3:8–12* ◀▶ *Ex 12:3–9*

her neighbour, and of her that sojourneth in her house, jewels of silver, and jewels of gold, and raiment: and ye shall put *them* upon your sons, and upon your daughters; and [b]ye shall spoil [1]the Egyptians.

God equips Moses

4 AND MOSES answered and said, But, behold, they will not believe me, nor hearken unto my voice: for they will say, The LORD hath not appeared unto thee.

2 And the LORD said unto him, What *is* that in thine hand? And he said, [a]A rod.

3 And he said, Cast it on the ground. And he cast it on the ground, and it became a serpent; and Moses fled from before it.

4 And the LORD said unto Moses, Put forth thine hand, and take it by the tail. And he put forth his hand, and caught it, and it became a rod in his hand:

5 That they may [a]believe that [b]the LORD God of their fathers, the God of Abraham, the God of Isaac, and the God of Jacob, hath appeared unto thee.

D 6 ¶ And the LORD said furthermore unto him, Put now thine hand into thy bosom. And he put his hand into his bosom: and when he took it out, behold, his hand *was* leprous [a]as snow.

E 7 And he said, Put thine hand into thy bosom again. And he put his hand into his bosom again; and plucked it out of his bosom, and, behold, [a]it was turned again as his *other* flesh.

8 And it shall come to pass, if they will not believe thee, neither hearken to the voice of the first sign, that they will believe the voice of the latter sign.

9 And it shall come to pass, if they will not believe also these two signs, neither hearken unto thy voice, that thou shalt take of the water of the river, and pour *it* upon the dry *land:* and [a]the water which thou takest out of the river [1]shall become blood upon the dry *land.*

10 ¶ And Moses said unto the LORD, O my Lord, I *am* not [1]eloquent, neither [2]heretofore, nor since thou hast spoken unto thy servant: but [a]I *am* slow of speech, and of a slow tongue.

11 And the LORD said unto him, [a]Who hath made man's mouth? or who maketh the dumb, or deaf, or the seeing, or the blind? have not I the LORD?

12 Now therefore go, and I will be [a]with thy mouth, and teach thee what thou shalt say.

13 And he said, O my Lord, [a]send, I pray thee, by the hand *of him whom* thou [1]wilt send.

14 And the anger of the LORD was kindled against Moses, and he said, *Is* not Aaron the Levite thy brother? I know that he can speak well. And also, behold, [a]he cometh forth to meet thee: and when he seeth thee, he will be glad in his heart.

15 And [a]thou shalt speak unto him, and [b]put words in his mouth: and I will be with thy mouth, and with his mouth, and [c]will teach you what ye shall do.

16 And he shall be thy spokesman unto the people: and he shall be, *even* he shall be to thee instead of a mouth, and [a]thou shalt be to him instead of God.

17 And thou shalt take [a]this rod in thine hand, wherewith thou shalt do signs.

Moses returns to Egypt

18 ¶ And Moses went and returned to [1]Jethro his father-in-law, and said unto him, Let me go, I pray thee, and return unto my brethren which *are* in Egypt, and see whether they be yet alive. And Jethro said to Moses, Go in peace.

19 And the LORD said unto Moses in Midian, Go, return into Egypt: for [a]all the men are dead which sought thy life.

20 And Moses took his wife and his sons, and set them upon an ass, and he returned to the land of Egypt: and Moses took [a]the rod of God in his hand.

21 And the LORD said unto Moses, When thou goest to return into Egypt, see that thou do all those [a]wonders before Pharaoh, which I have put in thine hand: but [b]I will harden his heart, that he shall not let the people go.

22 And thou shalt say unto Pharaoh, Thus saith the LORD, [a]Israel *is* my son, [b]*even* my firstborn:

23 And I say unto thee, Let my son go, that he may serve me: and if thou refuse to let him go, behold, [a]I will slay thy son, *even* thy firstborn.

24 ¶ And it came to pass by the way in the inn, that the LORD [a]met him, and sought to [b]kill him.

22 [b]Job 27:17; Prov. 13:22; Ezek. 39:10 [1]Or, *Egypt*
4:2 [a]ver. 17,20
5 [a]ch. 19:9 [b]ch. 3:15
6 [a]Num. 12:10; 2 Ki. 5:27
7 [a]Num. 12:13,14; Deut. 32:39
9 [a]ch. 7:19 [1]Heb. *shall be and shall be*
10 [a]ch. 6:12; Jer. 1:6 [1]Heb. *a man of words* [2]Heb. *since yesterday, nor since the third day*
11 [a]Ps. 94:9
12 [a]Is. 50:4; Jer. 1:9; Mat. 10:19; Mark 13:11; Luke 12:11,12 & 21:14, 15
13 [a]See Jonah 1:3 [1]Or, *shouldest*
14 [a]ver. 27; 1 Sam. 10:2,3,5
15 [a]ch. 7:1,2 [b]Num. 23:5,12,16 [c]Deut. 5:31
16 [a]ch. 7:1
17 [a]ver. 2
18 [1]Heb. *Jether*
19 [a]ch. 2:15,23; Mat. 2:20
20 [a]Num. 20:8,9
21 [a]ch. 3:20 [b]ch. 7:3,13 & 9:12,35; Deut. 2:30; Josh. 11:20; Is. 63:17; John 12:40
22 [a]Hos. 11:1; Rom. 9:4; 2 Cor. 6:18 [b]Jer. 31:9; Jas. 1:18
23 [a]ch. 11:5 & 12:29
24 [a]Num. 22:22 [b]Gen. 17:14

D *Ge 20:18* ◀▶ *Ex 9:8–10*
E *Ge 30:22* ◀▶ *Nu 12:9–15*

25 Then Zipporah took [a]a sharp
[1]stone, and cut off the foreskin of her
son, and [2]cast *it* at his feet, and said,
Surely a bloody husband *art* thou to me.
26 So he let him go: then she said, A
bloody husband *thou art,* because of the
circumcision.
27 ¶ And the LORD said to Aaron, Go
into the wilderness [a]to meet Moses. And
he went, and met him in [b]the mount of
God, and kissed him.
28 And Moses told [a]Aaron all the
words of the LORD who had sent him, and
all the [b]signs which he had commanded
him.
29 ¶ And Moses and Aaron [a]went and
gathered together all the elders of the
children of Israel:
30 [a]And Aaron spake all the words
which the LORD had spoken unto Moses,
and did the signs in the sight of the
people.
31 And the people [a]believed: and
when they heard that the LORD had [b]vis-
ited the children of Israel, and that he
[c]had looked upon their affliction, then
[d]they bowed their heads and worshipped.

Pharaoh oppresses Israel

5 AND AFTERWARD Moses and
Aaron went in, and told Pharaoh,
Thus saith the LORD God of Israel, Let my
people go, that they may hold [a]a feast
unto me in the wilderness.
2 And Pharaoh said, [a]Who *is* the LORD,
that I should obey his voice to let Israel
go? I know not the LORD, [b]neither will I
let Israel go.
3 And they said, [a]The God of the Hebrews hath met with us: let us go, we
pray thee, three days' journey into the
desert, and sacrifice unto the LORD our
God; lest he fall upon us with pestilence,
or with the sword.
4 And the king of Egypt said unto
them, Wherefore do ye, Moses and
Aaron, let the people from their works?
get you unto your [a]burdens.
5 And Pharaoh said, Behold, the people of the land now *are* [a]many, and ye
make them rest from their burdens.
6 And Pharaoh commanded the same
day the [a]taskmasters of the people, and
their officers, saying,
7 Ye shall no more give the people
straw to make brick, as heretofore: let
them go and gather straw for themselves.
8 And the tale of the bricks, which
they did make heretofore, ye shall lay
upon them; ye shall not diminish *aught*
thereof: for they *be* idle; therefore they
cry, saying, Let us go *and* sacrifice to our
God.
9 [1]Let there more work be laid upon
the men, that they may labour therein;
and let them not regard vain words.
10 ¶ And the taskmasters of the people
went out, and their officers, and they
spake to the people, saying, Thus saith
Pharaoh, I will not give you straw.
11 Go ye, get you straw where ye can
find it: yet not aught of your work shall
be diminished.
12 So the people were scattered
abroad throughout all the land of Egypt to
gather stubble instead of straw.
13 And the taskmasters hasted *them,*
saying, Fulfil your works, [1]*your* daily
tasks, as when there was straw.
14 And the officers of the children of
Israel, which Pharaoh's taskmasters had
set over them, were beaten, *and* demanded, Wherefore have ye not fulfilled
your task in making brick both yesterday
and today, as heretofore?
15 ¶ Then the officers of the children
of Israel came and cried unto Pharaoh,
saying, Wherefore dealest thou thus with
thy servants?
16 There is no straw given unto thy
servants, and they say to us, Make brick:
and, behold, thy servants *are* beaten; but
the fault *is* in thine own people.
17 But he said, Ye *are* idle, *ye are* idle:
therefore ye say, Let us go *and* do sacrifice to the LORD.
18 Go therefore now, *and* work; for
there shall no straw be given you, yet
shall ye deliver the tale of bricks.
19 And the officers of the children of
Israel did see *that* they *were* in evil *case,*
after it was said, Ye shall not minish
aught from your bricks of your daily task.
20 ¶ And they met Moses and Aaron,
who stood in the way, as they came forth
from Pharaoh:
21 [a]And they said unto them, The
LORD look upon you, and judge; because
ye have made our savour [1]to be abhorred
in the eyes of Pharaoh, and in the eyes of
his servants, to put a sword in their hand
to slay us.

25 [a]Josh. 5:2,3 [1]Or, *knife* [2]Heb. *made* it *touch*
27 [a]ver. 14 [b]ch. 3:1
28 [a]ver. 15,16 [b]ver. 8,9
29 [a]ch. 3:16
30 [a]ver. 16
31 [a]ver. 8,9; ch. 3:18 [b]ch. 3:16 [c]ch. 2:25 & 3:7 [d]Gen. 24:26; 1 Chr. 29:20
5:1 [a]ch. 10:9
2 [a]2 Ki. 18:35; Job 21:15 [b]ch. 3:19
3 [a]ch. 3:18
4 [a]ch. 1:11
5 [a]ch. 1:7,9
6 [a]ch. 1:11
9 [1]Heb. *Let the work be heavy upon the men*
13 [1]Heb. *a matter of a day in his day*
21 [a]ch. 6:9 [1]Heb. *to stink;* see Gen. 34:30; 2 Sam. 10:6

God's promise of deliverance

22 And Moses returned unto the LORD, and said, Lord, wherefore hast thou *so* evil entreated this people? why *is* it *that* thou hast sent me?

23 For since I came to Pharaoh to speak in thy name, he hath done evil to this people; [l]neither hast thou delivered thy people at all.

6 THEN THE LORD said unto Moses, Now shalt thou see what I will do to Pharaoh: for [a]with a strong hand shall he let them go, and with a strong hand [b]shall he drive them out of his land.

2 And God spake unto Moses, and said unto him, I *am* [l]the LORD:

3 And I appeared unto Abraham, unto Isaac, and unto Jacob, by *the name of* [a]God Almighty, but by my name [b]JEHOVAH was I not known to them.

4 [a]And I have also established my covenant with them, [b]to give them the land of Canaan, the land of their pilgrimage, wherein they were strangers.

5 And [a]I have also heard the groaning of the children of Israel, whom the Egyptians keep in bondage; and I have remembered my covenant.

6 Wherefore say unto the children of Israel, I *am* the LORD, and [a]I will bring you out from under the burdens of the Egyptians, and I will rid you out of their bondage, and I will [b]redeem you with a stretched out arm, and with great judgments:

7 And I will [a]take you to me for a people, and [b]I will be to you a God: and ye shall know that I *am* the LORD your God, which bringeth you out [c]from under the burdens of the Egyptians.

8 And I will bring you in unto the land, concerning the which I did [a]swear[l] to give it to Abraham, to Isaac, and to Jacob; and I will give it you for an heritage: I *am* the LORD.

9 ¶ And Moses spake so unto the children of Israel: [a]but they hearkened not unto Moses for [l]anguish of spirit, and for cruel bondage.

10 And the LORD spake unto Moses, saying,

11 Go in, speak unto Pharaoh king of Egypt, that he let the children of Israel go out of his land.

12 And Moses spake before the LORD, saying, Behold, the children of Israel have not hearkened unto me; how then shall Pharaoh hear me, [a]who *am* of uncircumcised lips?

13 And the LORD spake unto Moses and unto Aaron, and gave them a charge unto the children of Israel, and unto Pharaoh king of Egypt, to bring the children of Israel out of the land of Egypt.

The descendants of Israel

14 ¶ These *be* the heads of their fathers' houses: [a]The sons of Reuben the firstborn of Israel; Hanoch, and Pallu, Hezron, and Carmi: these *be* the families of Reuben.

15 [a]And the sons of Simeon; Jemuel, and Jamin, and Ohad, and Jachin, and Zohar, and Shaul the son of a Canaanitish woman: these *are* the families of Simeon.

16 ¶ And these *are* the names of [a]the sons of Levi according to their generations; Gershon, and Kohath, and Merari: and the years of the life of Levi *were* an hundred thirty and seven years.

17 [a]The sons of Gershon; Libni, and Shimi, according to their families.

18 And [a]the sons of Kohath; Amram, and Izhar, and Hebron, and Uzziel: and the years of the life of Kohath *were* an hundred thirty and three years.

19 And [a]the sons of Merari; Mahali and Mushi: these *are* the families of Levi according to their generations.

20 And [a]Amram took him Jochebed his father's sister to wife; and she bare him Aaron and Moses: and the years of the life of Amram *were* an hundred and thirty and seven years.

21 ¶ And [a]the sons of Izhar; Korah, and Nepheg, and Zichri.

22 And [a]the sons of Uzziel; Mishael, and Elzaphan, and Zithri.

23 And Aaron took him Elisheba, daughter of [a]Amminadab, sister of Naashon, to wife; and she bare him [b]Nadab, and Abihu, Eleazar, and Ithamar.

24 And the [a]sons of Korah; Assir, and Elkanah, and Abiasaph: these *are* the families of the Korhites.

25 And Eleazar Aaron's son took him *one* of the daughters of Putiel to wife; and [a]she bare him Phinehas: these *are* the heads of the fathers of the Levites according to their families.

26 These *are* that Aaron and Moses, to whom the LORD said, Bring out the chil-

---

23 [l]Heb. *delivering thou hast not delivered*

6:1 [a]ch. 3:19 [b]ch. 12:31,33,39

2 [l]Or, *JEHOVAH*

3 [a]Gen. 17:1 & 35:11 & 48:3 [b]ch. 3:14; Ps. 83:18; John 8:58

4 [a]Gen. 15:18 [b]Gen. 28:4

5 [a]ch. 2:24

6 [a]ch. 3:17; Deut. 26:8 [b]Deut. 7:8; 1 Chr. 17:21

7 [a]Deut. 4:20; 2 Sam. 7:24 [b]ch. 29:45,46; Rev. 21:7 [c]ch. 5:4,5

8 [a]Gen. 15:18 & 26:3 [l]Heb. *lift up my hand;* see Gen. 14:22; Deut. 32:40

9 [a]ch. 5:21 [l]Heb. *shortness,* or, *straitness*

12 [a]ver. 30; ch. 4:10; Jer. 1:6

14 [a]Gen. 46:9; 1 Chr. 5:3

15 [a]Gen. 46:10; 1 Chr. 4:24

16 [a]Gen. 46:11; Num. 3:17

17 [a]1 Chr. 6:17

18 [a]1 Chr. 6:2,18

19 [a]1 Chr. 6:19 & 23:21

20 [a]ch. 2:1,2

21 [a]1 Chr. 6:37,38

22 [a]Lev. 10:4

23 [a]Ruth 4:19,20; Mat. 1:4 [b]Lev. 10:1; Num. 3:2 & 26:60

24 [a]Num. 26:11

25 [a]Num. 25:7,11; Josh. 24:33

dren of Israel from the land of Egypt according to their [a]armies.

27 These *are* they which spake to Pharaoh king of Egypt, [a]to bring out the children of Israel from Egypt: these *are* that Moses and Aaron.

Aaron to speak for Moses

28 ¶ And it came to pass on the day *when* the LORD spake unto Moses in the land of Egypt,

29 That the LORD spake unto Moses, saying, I *am* the LORD: [a]speak thou unto Pharaoh king of Egypt all that I say unto thee.

30 And Moses said before the LORD, Behold, [a]I *am* of uncircumcised lips, and how shall Pharaoh hearken unto me?

7 AND THE LORD said unto Moses, See, I have made thee [a]a god to Pharaoh: and Aaron thy brother shall be [b]thy prophet.

2 Thou [a]shalt speak all that I command thee: and Aaron thy brother shall speak unto Pharaoh, that he send the children of Israel out of his land.

3 And [a]I will harden Pharaoh's heart, and [b]multiply my [c]signs and my wonders in the land of Egypt.

4 But Pharaoh shall not hearken unto you, [a]that I may lay my hand upon Egypt, and bring forth mine armies, *and* my people the children of Israel, out of the land of Egypt [b]by great judgments.

5 And the Egyptians [a]shall know that I *am* the LORD, when I [b]stretch forth mine hand upon Egypt, and bring out the children of Israel from among them.

6 And Moses and Aaron [a]did as the LORD commanded them, so did they.

7 And Moses *was* [a]fourscore years old, and Aaron fourscore and three years old, when they spake unto Pharaoh.

The rod becomes a serpent

8 ¶ And the LORD spake unto Moses and unto Aaron, saying,

9 When Pharaoh shall speak unto you, saying, [a]Show a miracle for you: then thou shalt say unto Aaron, [b]Take thy rod, and cast *it* before Pharaoh, *and* it shall become a serpent.

10 ¶ And Moses and Aaron went in unto Pharaoh, and they did so [a]as the LORD had commanded: and Aaron cast down his rod before Pharaoh, and before his servants, and it [b]became a serpent.

11 Then Pharaoh also [a]called the wise men and [b]the sorcerers: now the magicians of Egypt, they also [c]did in like manner with their enchantments.

12 For they cast down every man his rod, and they became serpents: but Aaron's rod swallowed up their rods.

13 And he hardened Pharaoh's heart, that he hearkened not unto them; as the LORD had said.

The water becomes blood

14 ¶ And the LORD said unto Moses, [a]Pharaoh's heart *is* hardened, he refuseth to let the people go.

15 Get thee unto Pharaoh in the morning; lo, he goeth out unto the water; and thou shalt stand by the river's brink against he come; and [a]the rod which was turned to a serpent shalt thou take in thine hand.

16 And thou shalt say unto him, [a]The LORD God of the Hebrews hath sent me unto thee, saying, Let my people go, [b]that they may serve me in the wilderness: and, behold, hitherto thou wouldest not hear.

17 Thus saith the LORD, In this [a]thou shalt know that I *am* the LORD: behold, I will smite with the rod that *is* in mine hand upon the waters which *are* in the river, and [b]they shall be turned [c]to blood.

18 And the fish that *is* in the river shall die, and the river shall stink; and the Egyptians shall [a]loathe to drink of the water of the river.

19 ¶ And the LORD spake unto Moses, Say unto Aaron, Take thy rod, and [a]stretch out thine hand upon the waters of Egypt, upon their streams, upon their rivers, and upon their ponds, and upon all their [ƒ]pools of water, that they may become blood; and *that* there may be blood throughout all the land of Egypt, both in *vessels of* wood, and in *vessels of* stone.

20 And Moses and Aaron did so, as the LORD commanded; and he [a]lifted up the rod, and smote the waters that *were* in the river, in the sight of Pharaoh, and in the sight of his servants; and all the [b]waters that *were* in the river were turned to blood.

21 And the fish that *was* in the river died; and the river stank, and the Egyptians [a]could not drink of the water of the

26 [a]ch. 7:4 & 12:17,51; Num. 33:1
27 [a]ver. 13; ch. 32:7 & 33:1; Ps. 77:20
29 [a]ver. 11; ch. 7:2
30 [a]ver. 12; ch. 4:10
7:1 [a]ch. 4:16; Jer. 1:10 [b]ch. 4:16
2 [a]ch. 4:15
3 [a]ch. 4:21 [b]ch. 11:9 [c]ch. 4:7
4 [a]ch. 10:1 & 11:9 [b]ch. 6:6
5 [a]ver. 17; ch. 8:22 & 14:4,18; Ps. 9:16 [b]ch. 3:20
6 [a]ver. 2
7 [a]Deut. 29:5 & 31:2 & 34:7; Acts 7:23,30
9 [a]Is. 7:11; John 2:18 & 6:30 [b]ch. 4:2,17
10 [a]ver. 9 [b]ch. 4:3
11 [a]Gen. 41:8 [b]2 Tim. 3:8 [c]ver. 22; ch. 8:7,18
14 [a]ch. 8:15 & 10:1,20,27
15 [a]ver. 10; ch. 4:2,3
16 [a]ch. 3:18 [b]ch. 3:12,18 & 5:1,3
17 [a]ver. 5; ch. 5:2 [b]ch. 4:9 [c]Rev. 16:4,6
18 [a]ver. 24
19 [a]ch. 8:5,6,16 & 9:22 & 10:12,21 & 14:21,26 [ƒ]Heb. *gathering of their waters*
20 [a]ch. 17:5 [b]Ps. 78:44 & 105:29
21 [a]ver. 18

river; and there was blood throughout all the land of Egypt.

22 [a]And the magicians of Egypt did so with their enchantments: and Pharaoh's heart was hardened, neither did he hearken unto them; [b]as the LORD had said.

23 And Pharaoh turned and went into his house, neither did he set his heart to this also.

24 And all the Egyptians digged round about the river for water to drink; for they could not drink of the water of the river.

The plague of frogs

25 And seven days were fulfilled, after that the LORD had smitten the river.

8 AND THE LORD spake unto Moses, Go unto Pharaoh, and say unto him, Thus saith the LORD, Let my people go, [a]that they may serve me.

2 And if thou [a]refuse to let *them* go, behold, I will smite all thy borders with [b]frogs:

3 And the river shall bring forth frogs abundantly, which shall go up and come into thine house, and into [a]thy bedchamber, and upon thy bed, and into the house of thy servants, and upon thy people, and into thine ovens, and into thy [1]kneadingtroughs:

4 And the frogs shall come up both on thee, and upon thy people, and upon all thy servants.

5 ¶ And the LORD spake unto Moses, Say unto Aaron, [a]Stretch forth thine hand with thy rod over the streams, over the rivers, and over the ponds, and cause frogs to come up upon the land of Egypt.

6 And Aaron stretched out his hand over the waters of Egypt; and [a]the frogs came up, and covered the land of Egypt.

7 [a]And the magicians did so with their enchantments, and brought up frogs upon the land of Egypt.

8 ¶ Then Pharaoh called for Moses and Aaron, and said, [a]Entreat the LORD, that he may take away the frogs from me, and from my people; and I will let the people go, that they may do sacrifice unto the LORD.

9 And Moses said unto Pharaoh, [1]Glory over me: [2]when shall I entreat for thee, and for thy servants, and for thy people, [3]to destroy the frogs from thee and thy houses, *that* they may remain in the river only?

10 And he said, [1]Tomorrow. And he said, *Be it* according to thy word: that thou mayest know that [a]*there is* none like unto the LORD our God.

11 And the frogs shall depart from thee, and from thy houses, and from thy servants, and from thy people; they shall remain in the river only.

12 And Moses and Aaron went out from Pharaoh: and Moses [a]cried unto the LORD because of the frogs which he had brought against Pharaoh.

13 And the LORD did according to the word of Moses; and the frogs died out of the houses, out of the villages, and out of the fields.

14 And they gathered them together upon heaps: and the land stank.

15 But when Pharaoh saw that there was [a]respite, [b]he hardened his heart, and hearkened not unto them; as the LORD had said.

The plague of lice

16 ¶ And the LORD said unto Moses, Say unto Aaron, Stretch out thy rod, and smite the dust of the land, that it may become lice throughout all the land of Egypt.

17 And they did so; for Aaron stretched out his hand with his rod, and smote the dust of the earth, and [a]it became lice in man, and in beast; all the dust of the land became lice throughout all the land of Egypt.

18 And [a]the magicians did so with their enchantments to bring forth lice, but they [b]could not: so there were lice upon man, and upon beast.

19 Then the magicians said unto Pharaoh, This *is* [a]the finger of God: and Pharaoh's [b]heart was hardened, and he hearkened not unto them; as the LORD had said.

The swarms of flies

20 ¶ And the LORD said unto Moses, [a]Rise up early in the morning, and stand before Pharaoh; lo, he cometh forth to the water; and say unto him, Thus saith the LORD, [b]Let my people go, that they may serve me.

21 Else, if thou wilt not let my people go, behold, I will send [1]swarms *of flies* upon thee, and upon thy servants, and upon thy people, and into thy houses:

22 [a]ver. 11 [b]ver. 3
8:1 [a]ch. 3:12,18
2 [a]ch. 7:14 & 9:2 [b]Rev. 16:13
3 [a]Ps. 105:30 [1]Or, *dough*
5 [a]ch. 7:19
6 [a]Ps. 78:45 & 105:30
7 [a]ch. 7:11
8 [a]ch. 9:28 & 10:17
9 [1]Or, *Have this honour over me* [2]Or, *against when* [3]Heb. *to cut off*
10 [a]ch. 9:14; Deut. 33:26; 2 Sam. 7:22; 1 Chr. 17:20; Is. 46:9; Jer. 10:6,7 [1]Or, *Against tomorrow*
12 [a]ver. 30; ch. 9:33 & 10:18 & 32:11; Jas. 5:16-18
15 [a]Eccl. 8:11 [b]ch. 7:14
17 [a]Ps. 105:31
18 [a]ch. 7:11 [b]Dan. 5:8; 2 Tim. 3:8,9
19 [a]1 Sam. 6:3,9; Ps. 8:3; Mat. 12:28; Luke 11:20 [b]ver. 15
20 [a]ch. 7:15 [b]ver. 1
21 [1]Or, *a mixture of noisome beasts*

and the houses of the Egyptians shall be
full of swarms *of flies,* and also the
ground whereon they *are.*
22 And [a]I will sever in that day the
land of Goshen, in which my people
dwell, that no swarms *of flies* shall be
there; to the end thou mayest know that I
am the LORD in the midst of the earth.
23 And I will put [1]a division between
my people and thy people: [2]tomorrow
shall this sign be.
24 And the LORD did so; and [a]there
came a grievous swarm *of flies* into the
house of Pharaoh, and *into* his servants'
houses, and into all the land of Egypt:
the land was [1]corrupted by reason of the
swarm *of flies.*
25 ¶ And Pharaoh called for Moses and
for Aaron, and said, Go ye, sacrifice to
your God in the land.
26 And Moses said, It is not meet so to
do; for we shall sacrifice [a]the abomination of the Egyptians to the LORD our God:
lo, shall we sacrifice the abomination of
the Egyptians before their eyes, and will
they not stone us?
27 We will go [a]three days' journey
into the wilderness, and sacrifice to the
LORD our God, as [b]he shall command us.
28 And Pharaoh said, I will let you go,
that ye may sacrifice to the LORD your God
in the wilderness; only ye shall not go
very far away: [a]entreat for me.
29 And Moses said, Behold, I go out
from thee, and I will entreat the LORD that
the swarms *of flies* may depart from Pharaoh, from his servants, and from his people, tomorrow: but let not Pharaoh [a]deal
deceitfully any more in not letting the
people go to sacrifice to the LORD.
30 And Moses went out from Pharaoh,
and [a]entreated the LORD.
31 And the LORD did according to the
word of Moses; and he removed the
swarms *of flies* from Pharaoh, from his
servants, and from his people; there remained not one.
32 And Pharaoh [a]hardened his heart at
this time also, neither would he let the
people go.

The death of Egyptian cattle

9 THEN THE LORD said unto Moses,
[a]Go in unto Pharaoh, and tell him,
Thus saith the LORD God of the Hebrews,
Let my people go, that they may
serve me.
2 For if thou [a]refuse to let *them* go,
and wilt hold them still,
3 Behold, the [a]hand of the LORD is
upon thy cattle which *is* in the field,
upon the horses, upon the asses, upon
the camels, upon the oxen, and upon the
sheep: *there shall be* a very grievous
murrain.
4 And [a]the LORD shall sever between
the cattle of Israel and the cattle of Egypt:
and there shall nothing die of all *that is*
the children's of Israel.
5 And the LORD appointed a set time,
saying, Tomorrow the LORD shall do this
thing in the land.
6 And the LORD did that thing on the
morrow, and [a]all the cattle of Egypt died:
but of the cattle of the children of Israel
died not one.
7 And Pharaoh sent, and, behold,
there was not one of the cattle of the Israelites dead. And [a]the heart of Pharaoh
was hardened, and he did not let the people go.

The plague of boils and blains

8 ¶ And the LORD said unto Moses and D
unto Aaron, Take to you handfuls of ashes
of the furnace, and let Moses sprinkle it
toward the heaven in the sight of
Pharaoh.
9 And it shall become small dust in all
the land of Egypt, and shall be [a]a boil
breaking forth *with* blains upon man, and
upon beast, throughout all the land of
Egypt.
10 And they took ashes of the furnace,
and stood before Pharaoh; and Moses
sprinkled it up toward heaven; and it became [a]a boil breaking forth *with* blains
upon man, and upon beast.
11 And the [a]magicians could not stand
before Moses because of the boils; for the
boil was upon the magicians, and upon all
the Egyptians.
12 And the LORD hardened the heart of
Pharaoh, and he hearkened not unto
them; [a]as the LORD had spoken unto
Moses.

The plague of hail and fire

13 ¶ And the LORD said unto Moses,
[a]Rise up early in the morning, and stand
before Pharaoh, and say unto him, Thus

22 [a]ch. 9:4,6,26 & 10:23 & 11:6,7 & 12:13
23 [1]Heb. *a redemption* [2]Or, *by tomorrow*
24 [a]Ps. 78:45 & 105:31 [1]Or, *destroyed*
26 [a]Gen. 43:32 & 46:34; Deut. 7:25, 26 & 12:31
27 [a]ch. 3:18 [b]ch. 3:12
28 [a]ver. 8; ch. 9:28; 1 Ki. 13:6
29 [a]ver. 15
30 [a]ver. 12
32 [a]ver. 15; ch. 4:21
9:1 [a]ch. 8:1
2 [a]ch. 8:2
3 [a]ch. 7:4
4 [a]ch. 8:22
6 [a]Ps. 78:50
7 [a]ch. 7:14 & 8:32
9 [a]Rev. 16:2
10 [a]Deut. 28:27
11 [a]ch. 8:18,19; 2 Tim. 3:9
12 [a]ch. 4:21
13 [a]ch. 8:20

saith the LORD God of the Hebrews, Let my people go, that they may serve me.

14 For I will at this time send all my plagues upon thine heart, and upon thy servants, and upon thy people; [a]that thou mayest know that *there is* none like me in all the earth.

D 15 For now I will [a]stretch out my hand, that I may smite thee and thy people with pestilence; and thou shalt be cut off from the earth.

16 And in very deed for [a]this *cause* have I [l]raised thee up, for to show *in* thee my power; and that my name may be declared throughout all the earth.

17 As yet exaltest thou thyself against my people, that thou wilt not let them go?

18 Behold, tomorrow about this time I will cause it to rain a very grievous hail, such as hath not been in Egypt since the foundation thereof even until now.

19 Send therefore now, *and* gather thy cattle, and all that thou hast in the field; *for upon* every man and beast which shall be found in the field, and shall not be brought home, the hail shall come down upon them, and they shall die.

20 He that feared the word of the LORD among the servants of Pharaoh made his servants and his cattle flee into the houses:

21 And he that regarded not the word of the LORD left his servants and his cattle in the field.

22 ¶ And the LORD said unto Moses, Stretch forth thine hand toward heaven, that there may be [a]hail in all the land of Egypt, upon man, and upon beast, and upon every herb of the field, throughout the land of Egypt.

23 And Moses stretched forth his rod toward heaven: and [a]the LORD sent thunder and hail, and the fire ran along upon the ground; and the LORD rained hail upon the land of Egypt.

24 So there was hail, and fire mingled with the hail, very grievous, such as there was none like it in all the land of Egypt since it became a nation.

25 And the hail smote throughout all the land of Egypt all that *was* in the field, both man and beast; and the hail [a]smote every herb of the field, and brake every tree of the field.

26 [a]Only in the land of Goshen, where the children of Israel *were,* was there no hail.

27 ¶ And Pharaoh sent, and called for Moses and Aaron, and said unto them, [a]I have sinned this time: [b]the LORD *is* righteous, and I and my people *are* wicked.

28 [a]Entreat the LORD (for *it is* enough) that there be no *more* [l]mighty thunderings and hail; and I will let you go, and ye shall stay no longer.

29 And Moses said unto him, As soon as I am gone out of the city, I will [a]spread abroad my hands unto the LORD; *and* the thunder shall cease, neither shall there be any more hail; that thou mayest know how that the [b]earth *is* the LORD'S.

30 But as for thee and thy servants, [a]I know that ye will not yet fear the LORD God.

31 And the flax and the barley was smitten: [a]for the barley *was* in the ear, and the flax *was* bolled.

32 But the wheat and the rie were not smitten: for they *were* [l]not grown up.

33 And Moses went out of the city from Pharaoh, and [a]spread abroad his hands unto the LORD: and the thunders and hail ceased, and the rain was not poured upon the earth.

34 And when Pharaoh saw that the rain and the hail and the thunders were ceased, he sinned yet more, and hardened his heart, he and his servants.

35 And [a]the heart of Pharaoh was hardened, neither would he let the children of Israel go; as the LORD had spoken [l]by Moses.

The plague of locusts

10 AND THE LORD said unto Moses, Go in unto Pharaoh: [a]for I have hardened his heart, and the heart of his servants, [b]that I might show these my signs before him:

2 And that [a]thou mayest tell in the ears of thy son, and of thy son's son, what things I have wrought in Egypt, and my signs which I have done among them; that ye may know how that I *am* the LORD.

3 And Moses and Aaron came in unto Pharaoh, and said unto him, Thus saith the LORD God of the Hebrews, How long wilt thou refuse to [a]humble thyself before me? let my people go, that they may serve me.

---

14 [a]ch. 8:10
15 [a]ch. 3:20
16 [a]See ch. 14:17; Prov. 16:4; Rom. 9:17; 1 Pet. 2:9 [l]Heb. *made thee stand*
22 [a]Rev. 16:21
23 [a]Josh. 10:11; Ps. 18:13 & 78:47 & 105:32 & 148:8; Is. 30:30; Ezek. 38:22; Rev. 8:7
25 [a]Ps. 105:33
26 [a]ch. 8:22 & 9:4,6 & 10:23 & 11:7 & 12:13; Is. 32:18,19
27 [a]ch. 10:16 [b]2 Chr. 12:6; Lam. 1:18
28 [a]ch. 8:8,28 & 10:17; Acts 8:24 [l]Heb. *voices of God*
29 [a]1 Ki. 8:22,38; Ps. 143:6; Is. 1:15 [b]Ps. 24:1; 1 Cor. 10:26,28
30 [a]Is. 26:10
31 [a]Ruth 1:22 & 2:23
32 [l]Heb. *hidden, or, dark*
33 [a]ver. 29; ch. 8:12
35 [a]ch. 4:21 [l]Heb. *by the hand of Moses*
10:1 [a]ch. 4:21 & 7:14 [b]ch. 7:4
2 [a]Deut. 4:9; Ps. 44:1 & 71:18 & 78:5; Joel 1:3
3 [a]1 Ki. 21:29; Job 42:6; Jas. 4:10

4 Else, if thou refuse to let my people
go, behold, tomorrow will I bring the [a]lo-
custs into thy coast:
5 And they shall cover the [a]face['] of the
earth, that one cannot be able to see the
earth: and [b]they shall eat the residue of
that which is escaped, which remaineth
unto you from the hail, and shall eat every tree which groweth for you out of the
field:
6 And they shall fill thy houses, and
the houses of all thy servants, and the
houses of all the Egyptians; which neither
thy fathers, nor thy fathers' fathers have
seen, since the day that they were upon
the earth unto this day. And he turned
himself, and went out from Pharaoh.
7 And Pharaoh's servants said unto
him, How long shall this man be [a]a snare
unto us? let the men go, that they may
serve the LORD their God: knowest thou
not yet that Egypt is destroyed?
8 And Moses and Aaron were brought
again unto Pharaoh: and he said unto
them, Go, serve the LORD your God: *but*
[']who *are* they that shall go?
9 And Moses said, We will go with our
young and with our old, with our sons
and with our daughters, with our flocks
and with our herds will we go; for [a]we
must hold a feast unto the LORD.
10 And he said unto them, Let the
LORD be so with you, as I will let you go,
and your little ones: look *to it;* for evil *is*
before you.
11 Not so: go now ye *that are* men,
and serve the LORD; for that ye did desire.
And they were driven out from Pharaoh's
presence.
12 ¶ And the LORD said unto Moses,
[a]Stretch out thine hand over the land of
Egypt for the locusts, that they may come
up upon the land of Egypt, and [b]eat every
herb of the land, *even* all that the hail
hath left.
13 And Moses stretched forth his rod
over the land of Egypt, and the LORD
brought an east wind upon the land all
that day, and all *that* night; *and* when it
was morning, the east wind brought the
locusts.
14 And [a]the locusts went up over all
the land of Egypt, and rested in all the
coasts of Egypt: very grievous *were they;*
[b]before them there were no such locusts
as they, neither after them shall be such.
15 For they [a]covered the face of the
whole earth, so that the land was darkened; and they [b]did eat every herb of the
land, and all the fruit of the trees which
the hail had left: and there remained not
any green thing in the trees, or in the
herbs of the field, through all the land of
Egypt.
16 ¶ Then Pharaoh [']called for Moses
and Aaron in haste; and he said, [a]I have
sinned against the LORD your God, and
against you.
17 Now therefore forgive, I pray thee,
my sin only this once, and [a]entreat the
LORD your God, that he may take away
from me this death only.
18 And he [a]went out from Pharaoh,
and entreated the LORD.
19 And the LORD turned a mighty
strong west wind, which took away the
locusts, and [']cast them [a]into the Red sea;
there remained not one locust in all the
coasts of Egypt.
20 But the LORD [a]hardened Pharaoh's
heart, so that he would not let the children of Israel go.

The plague of darkness

21 ¶ And the LORD said unto Moses,
[a]Stretch out thine hand toward heaven,
that there may be darkness over the land
of Egypt, [']even darkness *which* may be
felt.
22 And Moses stretched forth his hand
toward heaven; and there was a [a]thick
darkness in all the land of Egypt three
days:
23 They saw not one another, neither
rose any from his place for three days:
[a]but all the children of Israel had light in
their dwellings.
24 ¶ And Pharaoh called unto Moses,
and [a]said, Go ye, serve the LORD; only let
your flocks and your herds be stayed: let
your [b]little ones also go with you.
25 And Moses said, Thou must give
[']us also sacrifices and burnt offerings,
that we may sacrifice unto the LORD our
God.
26 Our cattle also shall go with us;
there shall not an hoof be left behind; for
thereof must we take to serve the LORD
our God; and we know not with what
we must serve the LORD, until we come
thither.
27 ¶ But the LORD [a]hardened Pharaoh's
heart, and he would not let them go.
28 And Pharaoh said unto him, Get

4 [a]Prov. 30:27; Rev. 9:3
5 [a]ver. 15 [b]ch. 9:32; Joel 1:4 & 2:25 [']Heb. *eye*
7 [a]ch. 23:33; Josh. 23:13; 1 Sam. 18:21; Eccl. 7:26; 1 Cor. 7:35
8 [']Heb. *who, and who*
9 [a]ch. 5:1
12 [a]ch. 7:19 [b]ver. 4,5
14 [a]Ps. 78:46 & 105:34 [b]Joel 2:2
15 [a]ver. 5 [b]Ps. 105:35
16 [a]ch. 9:27 [']Heb. *hastened to call*
17 [a]ch. 9:28; 1 Ki. 13:6
18 [a]ch. 8:30
19 [a]Joel 2:20 [']Heb. *fastened*
20 [a]ch. 4:21 & 11:10
21 [a]ch. 9:22 [']Heb. *that one may feel darkness*
22 [a]Ps. 105:28
23 [a]ch. 8:22
24 [a]ver. 8 [b]ver. 10
25 [']Heb. *into our hands*
27 [a]ver. 20; ch. 4:21 & 14:4,8

thee from me, take heed to thyself, see my face no more; for in *that* day thou seest my face thou shalt die.

29 And Moses said, Thou hast spoken well, [a]I will see thy face again no more.

The last plague

11 AND THE LORD said unto Moses, Yet will I bring one plague *more* upon Pharaoh, and upon Egypt; afterwards he will let you go hence: [a]when he shall let *you* go, he shall surely thrust you out hence altogether.

2 Speak now in the ears of the people, and let every man borrow of his neighbour, and every woman of her neighbour, [a]jewels of silver, and jewels of gold.

3 [a]And the LORD gave the people favour in the sight of the Egyptians. Moreover the man [b]Moses *was* very great in the land of Egypt, in the sight of Pharaoh's servants, and in the sight of the people.

4 And Moses said, Thus saith the LORD, [a]About midnight will I go out into the midst of Egypt:

5 And [a]all the firstborn in the land of Egypt shall die, from the firstborn of Pharaoh that sitteth upon his throne, even unto the firstborn of the maidservant that *is* behind the mill; and all the firstborn of beasts.

6 [a]And there shall be a great cry throughout all the land of Egypt, such as there was none like it, nor shall be like it any more.

L
S 7 [a]But against any of the children of Israel [b]shall not a dog move his tongue, against man or beast: that ye may know how that the LORD doth put a difference between the Egyptians and Israel.

8 And [a]all these thy servants shall come down unto me, and bow down themselves unto me, saying, Get thee out, and all the people [1]that follow thee:

L *Ge 28:15* ◀▶ *Ex 15:13* **S** ▶ *Lev 25:18*

29 [a]Heb. 11:27
11:1 [a]ch. 12:31, 33,39
2 [a]ch. 3:22 & 12:35
3 [a]ch. 3:21 & 12:36; Ps. 106:46 [b]2 Sam. 7:9; Esth. 9:4
4 [a]ch. 12:12,23,29
5 [a]ch. 12:12,29; Amos 4:10
6 [a]ch. 12:30; Amos 5:17
7 [a]ch. 8:22 [b]Josh. 10:21
8 [a]ch. 12:33 [1]Heb. *that is at thy feet;* see Judg. 4:10 & 8:5 [2]Heb. *heat of anger*
9 [a]ch. 3:19 & 7:4; & 10:1 [b]ch. 7:3
10 [a]ch. 10:20,27; Rom. 2:5 & 9:22
12:2 [a]ch. 13:4; Deut. 16:1
3 [1]Or, *kid*
5 [a]Lev. 22:19-21; Mal. 1:8,14; Heb. 9:14 [1]Heb. *son of a year*
6 [a]Lev. 23:5; Num. 9:3; Deut. 16:1,6 [1]Heb. *between the two evenings*
8 [a]ch. 34:25; Deut. 16:3; 1 Cor. 5:8

and after that I will go out. And he went out from Pharaoh in [2]a great anger.

9 And the LORD said unto Moses, [a]Pharaoh shall not hearken unto you; that [b]my wonders may be multiplied in the land of Egypt.

10 And Moses and Aaron did all these wonders before Pharaoh: [a]and the LORD hardened Pharaoh's heart, so that he would not let the children of Israel go out of his land.

The Passover

12 AND THE LORD spake unto Moses and Aaron in the land of Egypt, saying,

2 [a]This month *shall be* unto you the beginning of months: it *shall be* the first month of the year to you.

3 ¶ Speak ye unto all the congregation A
of Israel, saying, In the tenth *day* of this D
month they shall take to them every man a [1]lamb, according to the house of *their* fathers, a lamb for an house:

4 And if the household be too little for the lamb, let him and his neighbour next unto his house take *it* according to the number of the souls; every man according to his eating shall make your count for the lamb.

5 Your lamb shall be [a]without blemish, a male [1]of the first year: ye shall take *it* out from the sheep, or from the goats:

6 And ye shall keep it up until the [a]fourteenth day of the same month: and the whole assembly of the congregation of Israel shall kill it [1]in the evening.

7 And they shall take of the blood, and strike *it* on the two side posts and on the upper door post of the houses, wherein they shall eat it.

8 And they shall eat the flesh in that night, roast with fire, and [a]unleavened

A *Ex 3:17–21* ◀▶ *Ex 23:16*
D *Ge 22:7–8* ◀▶ *Ex 12:13*

12:2 This verse marks the beginning of the religious calendar of the Israelites. The designation of this month as the start of Israel's religious year reminded the people of their deliverance and redemption from Egypt. Corresponding to our March-April, the Israelites called this month Abib after the Canaanite name. The name changed to Nisan, its Babylonian form, during the exile. Israel also maintained an agricultural calendar that began in the fall, with both calendars existing side by side until after the exile.

12:3–6 God commanded Israel to celebrate the Passover sacrifice each year on the fourteenth day of the month Nisan. This festival was to be a perpetual reminder of the first Passover in Egypt, signifying that for the people to be spared from death an innocent life had to be sacrificed in their place.

bread; *and* with bitter *herbs* they shall eat it.

9 Eat not of it raw, nor sodden at all with water, but [a]roast *with* fire; his head with his legs, and with the purtenance thereof.

10 [a]And ye shall let nothing of it remain until the morning; and that which remaineth of it until the morning ye shall burn with fire.

11 ¶ And thus shall ye eat it; *with* your loins girded, your shoes on your feet, and your staff in your hand; and ye shall eat it in haste: [a]it *is* the LORD's passover.

12 For I [a]will pass through the land of Egypt this night, and will smite all the firstborn in the land of Egypt, both man and beast; and [b]against all the [/]gods of Egypt I will execute judgment: [c]I *am* the LORD.

D H K 13 And the blood shall be to you for a token upon the houses where ye *are:* and when I see the blood, I will pass over you, and the plague shall not be upon you [/]to destroy *you,* when I smite the land of Egypt.

14 And this day shall be unto you [a]for a memorial; and ye shall keep it a [b]feast to the LORD throughout your generations; ye shall keep it a feast [c]by an ordinance for ever.

15 [a]Seven days shall ye eat unleavened bread; even the first day ye shall put away leaven out of your houses: for whosoever eateth leavened bread from the first day until the seventh day, [b]that soul shall be cut off from Israel.

16 And in the first day *there shall be* [a]an holy convocation, and in the seventh day there shall be an holy convocation to you; no manner of work shall be done in them, save *that* which every [/]man must eat, that only may be done of you.

17 And ye shall observe *the feast of* unleavened bread; for [a]in this selfsame day have I brought your armies out of the land of Egypt: therefore shall ye observe this day in your generations by an ordinance for ever.

18 ¶ [a]In the first *month,* on the fourteenth day of the month at even, ye shall eat unleavened bread, until the one and twentieth day of the month at even.

D *Ex 12:3–5* ◀▶ *Ex 12:21–23*
H *Ge 17:14* ◀▶ *Ex 23:7*
K *Ge 18:14* ◀▶ *Ex 15:13*

9 [a]Deut. 16:7
10 [a]ch. 23:18 & 34:25
11 [a]Deut. 16:5
12 [a]ch. 11:4,5; Amos 5:17 [b]Num. 33:4 [c]ch. 6:2 [/]Or, *princes*
13 [/]Heb. *for a destruction*
14 [a]ch. 13:9 [b]Lev. 23:4,5; 2 Ki. 23:21 [c]ver. 24,43; ch. 13:10
15 [a]ch. 13:6,7 & 23:15; Lev. 23:5,6; Deut. 16:3,8; 1 Cor. 5:7 [b]Gen. 17:14; Num. 9:13
16 [a]Lev. 23:7,8; Num. 28:18,25 [/]Heb. *soul*
17 [a]ch. 13:3
18 [a]Lev. 23:5; Num. 28:16
19 [a]ch. 23:15 & 34:18
21 [a]ver. 3; Num. 9:4; Josh. 5:10; 2 Ki. 23:21; Ezra 6:20; Mark 14:12-16 [/]Or, *kid*
22 [a]Heb. 11:28 [b]ver. 7
23 [a]ver. 12,13 [b]Ezek. 9:6; Rev. 7:3 [c]2 Sam. 24:16; 1 Cor. 10:10; Heb. 11:28
25 [a]ch. 3:8,17
26 [a]ch. 13:8,14; Deut. 32:7; Josh. 4:6
27 [a]ver. 11 [b]ch. 4:31
28 [a]Heb. 11:28
29 [a]ch. 11:4 [b]Num. 8:17 & 33:4; Ps. 78:51 & 105:36 [c]ch. 4:23 & 11:5 [/]Heb. *house of the pit*
30 [a]ch. 11:6; Prov. 21:13; Amos 5:17

19 [a]Seven days shall there be no leaven found in your houses: for whosoever eateth that which is leavened, even that soul shall be cut off from the congregation of Israel, whether he be a stranger, or born in the land.

20 Ye shall eat nothing leavened; in all your habitations shall ye eat unleavened bread.

21 ¶ Then Moses called for all the elders of Israel, and said unto them, [a]Draw out and take you a [/]lamb according to your families, and kill the passover. D

22 [a]And ye shall take a bunch of hyssop, and dip *it* in the blood that *is* in the basin, and [b]strike the lintel and the two side posts with the blood that *is* in the basin; and none of you shall go out at the door of his house until the morning.

23 [a]For the LORD will pass through to smite the Egyptians; and when he seeth the blood upon the lintel, and on the two side posts, the LORD will pass over the door, and [b]will not suffer [c]the destroyer to come in unto your houses to smite *you.*

24 And ye shall observe this thing for an ordinance to thee and to thy sons for ever.

25 And it shall come to pass, when ye be come to the land which the LORD will give you, [a]according as he hath promised, that ye shall keep this service.

26 [a]And it shall come to pass, when your children shall say unto you, What mean ye by this service?

27 That ye shall say, [a]It *is* the sacrifice of the LORD's passover, who passed over the houses of the children of Israel in Egypt, when he smote the Egyptians, and delivered our houses. And the people [b]bowed the head and worshipped.

28 And the children of Israel went away, and [a]did as the LORD had commanded Moses and Aaron, so did they.

29 ¶ [a]And it came to pass, that at midnight [b]the LORD smote all the firstborn in the land of Egypt, [c]from the firstborn of Pharaoh that sat on his throne unto the firstborn of the captive that *was* in the [/]dungeon; and all the firstborn of cattle.

30 And Pharaoh rose up in the night, he, and all his servants, and all the Egyptians; and there was a [a]great cry in Egypt;

D *Ex 12:13* ◀▶ *Ex 24:5–8*

Hebrew Calendar and Selected Events

NUMBER of MONTH		HEBREW NAME	MODERN EQUIVALENT	BIBLICAL REFERENCES	AGRICULTURE	FEASTS
1 Sacred sequence begins	7	**Abib; Nisan**	March–April	Ex 12:2; 13:4; 23:15; 34:18; Dt 16:1; Ne 2:1; Est 3:7	Spring (later) rains; barley and flax harvest begins	Passover; Unleavened Bread; Firstfruits
2	8	**Ziv (Iyyar)***	April–May	1Ki 6:1,37	Barley harvest; dry season begins	
3	9	**Sivan**	May–June	Est 8:9	Wheat harvest	Pentecost (Weeks)
4	10	**(Tammuz)***	June–July		Tending vines	
5	11	**(Ab)***	July–August		Ripening of grapes, figs and olives	
6	12	**Elul**	August–September	Ne 6:15	Processing grapes, figs and olives	
7	1 Civil sequence	**Ethanim (Tishri)***	September–October	1Ki 8:2	Autumn (early) rains begin; plowing	Trumpets; Atonement; Tabernacles (Booths)
8	2	**Bul (Marcheshvan)***	October–November	1Ki 6:38	Sowing of wheat and barley	
9	3	**Kislev**	November–December	Ne 1:1; Zec 7:1	Winter rains begin (snow in some areas)	Hanukkah ("Dedication")
10	4	**Tebeth**	December–January	Est 2:16		
11	5	**Shebat**	January–February	Zec 1:7		
12	6	**Adar**	February–March	Ezr 6:15; Est 3:7,13; 8:12; 9:1,15,17,19,21	Almond trees bloom; citrus fruit harvest	Purim
		(Adar Sheni)* Second Adar	— This intercalary month was added about every three years so the lunar calendar would correspond to the solar year.			

**Names in parentheses are not in the Bible*

for *there was* not a house where *there was* not one dead.

The exodus begins

31 ¶ And [a]he called for Moses and Aaron by night, and said, Rise up, *and* get you forth from among my people, [b]both ye and the children of Israel; and go, serve the LORD, as ye have said.

32 [a]Also take your flocks and your herds, as ye have said, and be gone; and [b]bless me also.

33 [a]And the Egyptians were urgent upon the people, that they might send them out of the land in haste; for they said, [b]We *be* all dead *men.*

34 And the people took their dough before it was leavened, their [/]kneadingtroughs being bound up in their clothes upon their shoulders.

35 And the children of Israel did according to the word of Moses; and they borrowed of the Egyptians [a]jewels of silver, and jewels of gold, and raiment:

36 [a]And the LORD gave the people favour in the sight of the Egyptians, so that they lent unto them *such things as they required.* And [b]they spoiled the Egyptians.

37 ¶ And [a]the children of Israel journeyed from [b]Rameses to Succoth, about [c]six hundred thousand on foot *that were* men, beside children.

38 And [/]a mixed multitude went up also with them; and flocks, and herds, *even* very much cattle.

39 And they baked unleavened cakes of the dough which they brought forth out of Egypt, for it was not leavened; because [a]they were thrust out of Egypt, and could not tarry, neither had they prepared for themselves any victual.

40 ¶ Now the sojourning of the children of Israel, who dwelt in Egypt, *was* [a]four hundred and thirty years.

41 And it came to pass at the end of the four hundred and thirty years, even the selfsame day it came to pass, that all [a]the hosts of the LORD went out from the land of Egypt.

42 It *is* [a]a night[/] to be much observed unto the LORD for bringing them out from the land of Egypt: this *is* that night of the LORD to be observed of all the children of Israel in their generations.

The law of the Passover

43 ¶ And the LORD said unto Moses and Aaron, This *is* [a]the ordinance of the passover: There shall no stranger eat thereof:

44 But every man's servant that is bought for money, when thou hast [a]circumcised him, then shall he eat thereof.

45 [a]A foreigner and an hired servant shall not eat thereof.

46 In one house shall it be eaten; thou shalt not carry forth aught of the flesh abroad out of the house; [a]neither shall ye break a bone thereof.

47 [a]All the congregation of Israel shall [/]keep it.

48 And [a]when a stranger shall sojourn with thee, and will keep the passover to the LORD, let all his males be circumcised, and then let him come near and keep it; and he shall be as one that is born in the land: for no uncircumcised person shall eat thereof.

49 [a]One law shall be to him that is homeborn, and unto the stranger that sojourneth among you.

50 Thus did all the children of Israel; as the LORD commanded Moses and Aaron, so did they.

51 [a]And it came to pass the selfsame day, *that* the LORD did bring the children of Israel out of the land of Egypt [b]by their armies.

The firstborn set apart

13 AND THE LORD spake unto Moses, saying,

2 [a]Sanctify unto me all the firstborn, whatsoever openeth the womb among the children of Israel, *both* of man and of beast: it *is* mine.

3 ¶ And Moses said unto the people, [a]Remember this day, in which ye came out from Egypt, out of the house of [/]bondage; for [b]by strength of hand the LORD brought you out from this *place:* [c]there shall no leavened bread be eaten.

4 [a]This day came ye out in the month Abib.

31 [a]ch. 11:1; Ps. 105:38 [b]ch. 10:9
32 [a]ch. 10:26 [b]Gen. 27:34
33 [a]ch. 11:8; Ps. 105:38 [b]Gen. 20:3
34 [/]Or, *dough*
35 [a]ch. 3:22
36 [a]ch. 3:21 [b]Gen. 15:14; ch. 3:22; Ps. 105:37
37 [a]Num. 33:3,5 [b]Gen. 47:11 [c]Gen. 12:2; Num. 11:21
38 [/]Heb. *a great mixture*
39 [a]ver. 33; ch. 6:1
40 [a]Gen. 15:13; Acts 7:6; Gal. 3:17
41 [a]ch. 7:4
42 [a]See Deut. 16:6 [/]Heb. *a night of observations*
43 [a]Num. 9:14
44 [a]Gen. 17:12,13
45 [a]Lev. 22:10
46 [a]Num. 9:12; John 19:33,36
47 [a]ver. 6; Num. 9:13 [/]Heb. *do it*
48 [a]Num. 9:14
49 [a]Num. 9:14 & 15:15,16; Gal. 3:28
51 [a]ver. 41 [b]ch. 6:26
13:2 [a]ver. 12,13, 15; ch. 22:29,30; Num. 3:13; Deut. 15:19; Luke 2:23
3 [a]ch. 12:42; Deut. 16:3 [b]ch. 6:1 [c]ch. 12:8 [/]Heb. *servants*
4 [a]ch. 23:15 & 34:18; Deut. 16:1

Ge 48:4 ◀ ▶ Ex 32:13

12:41 Moses records that the exodus occurred on the very day that God said it would when God initiated the Abrahamic covenant 430 years earlier (see Ge 15:13–16).

5 ¶ And it shall be when the LORD shall [a]bring thee into the land of the Canaanites, and the Hittites, and the Amorites, and the Hivites, and the Jebusites, which he [b]sware unto thy fathers to give thee, a land flowing with milk and honey, [c]that thou shalt keep this service in this month.

6 [a]Seven days thou shalt eat unleavened bread, and in the seventh day *shall be* a feast to the LORD.

7 Unleavened bread shall be eaten seven days; and there shall [a]no leavened bread be seen with thee, neither shall there be leaven seen with thee in all thy quarters.

8 ¶ And thou shalt [a]show thy son in that day, saying, *This is done* because of that *which* the LORD did unto me when I came forth out of Egypt.

9 And it shall be for [a]a sign unto thee upon thine hand, and for a memorial between thine eyes, that the LORD'S law may be in thy mouth: for with a strong hand hath the LORD brought thee out of Egypt.

10 [a]Thou shalt therefore keep this ordinance in his season from year to year.

11 ¶ And it shall be when the LORD shall bring thee into the land of the Canaanites, as he sware unto thee and to thy fathers, and shall give it thee,

12 [a]That thou shalt [l]set apart unto the LORD all that openeth the matrix, and every firstling that cometh of a beast which thou hast; the males *shall be* the LORD'S.

13 And [a]every firstling of an ass thou shalt redeem with a [l]lamb; and if thou wilt not redeem it, then thou shalt break his neck: and all the firstborn of man among thy children [b]shalt thou redeem.

14 ¶ [a]And it shall be when thy son asketh thee [l]in time to come, saying, What *is* this? that thou shalt say unto him, [b]By strength of hand the LORD brought us out from Egypt, from the house of bondage:

15 And it came to pass, when Pharaoh would hardly let us go, that [a]the LORD slew all the firstborn in the land of Egypt, both the firstborn of man, and the firstborn of beast: therefore I sacrifice to the LORD all that openeth the matrix, being males; but all the firstborn of my children I redeem.

16 And it shall be for [a]a token upon thine hand, and for frontlets between thine eyes: for by strength of hand the LORD brought us forth out of Egypt.

5 [a]ch. 3:8 [b]ch. 6:8 [c]ch. 12:25,26
6 [a]ch. 12:15,16
7 [a]ch. 12:19
8 [a]ver. 14; ch. 12:26
9 [a]See ver. 16; Deut. 6:8; Mat. 23:5
10 [a]ch. 12:14,24
12 [a]ver. 2; Lev. 27:26 [l]Heb. *cause to pass over*
13 [a]ch. 34:20; Num. 18:15 [b]Num. 3:46,47 & 18:15,16 [l]Or, *kid*
14 [a]ch. 12:26; Deut. 6:20; Josh. 4:6,21 [b]ver. 3 [l]Heb. *tomorrow*
15 [a]ch. 12:29
16 [a]ver. 9
17 [a]ch. 14:11; Num. 14:1-4 [b]Deut. 17:16
18 [a]ch. 14:2; Num. 33:6 [l]Or, *by five in a rank*
19 [a]Gen. 50:25; Josh. 24:32
20 [a]Num. 33:6
21 [a]ch. 14:19,24; Num. 9:15 & 14:14; Deut. 1:33; Neh. 9:12; Ps. 78:14 & 99:7; Is. 4:5; 1 Cor. 10:1
14:2 [a]ch. 13:18 [b]Num. 33:7 [c]Jer. 44:1
3 [a]Ps. 71:11
4 [a]ch. 4:21 & 7:3 [b]ver. 17,18; ch. 9:16; Rom. 9:17,22,23 [c]ch. 7:5

Crossing the Red sea

17 ¶ And it came to pass, when Pharaoh had let the people go, that God led them not *through* the way of the land of the Philistines, although that *was* near; for God said, Lest peradventure the people [a]repent when they see war, and [b]they return to Egypt:

18 But God [a]led the people about, *through* the way of the wilderness of the Red sea: and the children of Israel went up [l]harnessed out of the land of Egypt.

19 And Moses took the bones of Joseph with him: for he had straitly sworn the children of Israel, saying, [a]God will surely visit you; and ye shall carry up my bones away hence with you.

20 ¶ And [a]they took their journey from Succoth, and encamped in Etham, in the edge of the wilderness.

21 And [a]the LORD went before them by day in a pillar of a cloud, to lead them the way; and by night in a pillar of fire, to give them light; to go by day and night:

22 He took not away the pillar of the cloud by day, nor the pillar of fire by night, *from* before the people.

14

AND THE LORD spake unto Moses, saying,

2 Speak unto the children of Israel, [a]that they turn and encamp before [b]Pi-hahiroth, between [c]Migdol and the sea, over against Baal-zephon: before it shall ye encamp by the sea.

3 For Pharaoh will say of the children of Israel, [a]They *are* entangled in the land, the wilderness hath shut them in.

4 And [a]I will harden Pharaoh's heart, that he shall follow after them; and I [b]will be honoured upon Pharaoh, and upon all his host; [c]that the Egyptians may know that I *am* the LORD. And they did so. J

5 ¶ And it was told the king of Egypt

J *Ge 40:18–19* ◄► *Ex 14:13*

14:4 God prophesied that even though Pharaoh would again change his mind and pursue the Israelites, God would receive the ultimate honor. This prophecy was fulfilled in a miraculous way (see 14:13, 28).

that the people fled: and [a]the heart of Pharaoh and of his servants was turned against the people, and they said, Why have we done this, that we have let Israel go from serving us?

6 And he made ready his chariot, and took his people with him:

7 And he took [a]six hundred chosen chariots, and all the chariots of Egypt, and captains over every one of them.

8 And the LORD [a]hardened the heart of Pharaoh king of Egypt, and he pursued after the children of Israel: and [b]the children of Israel went out with an high hand.

9 But the [a]Egyptians pursued after them, all the horses *and* chariots of Pharaoh, and his horsemen, and his army, and overtook them encamping by the sea, beside Pi-hahiroth, before Baal-zephon.

10 ¶ And when Pharaoh drew nigh, the children of Israel lifted up their eyes, and, behold, the Egyptians marched after them; and they were sore afraid: and the children of Israel [a]cried out unto the LORD.

11 [a]And they said unto Moses, Because *there were* no graves in Egypt, hast thou taken us away to die in the wilderness? wherefore hast thou dealt thus with us, to carry us forth out of Egypt?

12 [a]*Is* not this the word that we did tell thee in Egypt, saying, Let us alone, that we may serve the Egyptians? For *it had been* better for us to serve the Egyptians, than that we should die in the wilderness.

J 13 ¶ And Moses said unto the people, [a]Fear ye not, stand still, and see the salvation of the LORD, which he will show to you today: [/]for the Egyptians whom ye have seen today, ye shall see them again no more for ever.

14 [a]The LORD shall fight for you, and ye shall [b]hold your peace.

15 ¶ And the LORD said unto Moses, Wherefore criest thou unto me? speak unto the children of Israel, that they go forward:

16 But [a]lift thou up thy rod, and stretch out thine hand over the sea, and divide it: and the children of Israel shall go on dry *ground* through the midst of the sea.

17 And I, behold, I will [a]harden the hearts of the Egyptians, and they shall follow them: and I will [b]get me honour upon Pharaoh, and upon all his host, upon his chariots, and upon his horsemen.

18 And the Egyptians [a]shall know that I *am* the LORD, when I have gotten me honour upon Pharaoh, upon his chariots, and upon his horsemen.

19 ¶ And the angel of God, [a]which went before the camp of Israel, removed and went behind them; and the pillar of the cloud went from before their face, and stood behind them:

20 And it came between the camp of the Egyptians and the camp of Israel; and [a]it was a cloud and darkness *to them,* but it gave light by night *to these:* so that the one came not near the other all the night.

21 And Moses stretched out his hand over the sea; and the LORD caused the sea to go *back* by a strong east wind all that night, and [a]made the sea dry *land,* and the waters were [b]divided.

22 And [a]the children of Israel went into the midst of the sea upon the dry *ground:* and the waters *were* [b]a wall unto them on their right hand, and on their left.

23 ¶ And the Egyptians pursued, and went in after them to the midst of the sea, *even* all Pharaoh's horses, his chariots, and his horsemen.

24 And it came to pass, that in the morning watch [a]the LORD looked unto the host of the Egyptians through the pillar of fire and of the cloud, and troubled the host of the Egyptians,

25 And took off their chariot wheels, [/]that they drave them heavily: so that the Egyptians said, Let us flee from the face of Israel; for the LORD [a]fighteth for them against the Egyptians.

26 ¶ And the LORD said unto Moses, Stretch out thine hand over the sea, that the waters may come again upon the

5 [a]Ps. 105:25
7 [a]ch. 15:4
8 [a]ver. 4 [b]ch. 6:1; & 13:9; Num. 33:3
9 [a]ch. 15:9; Josh. 24:6
10 [a]Josh. 24:7; Neh. 9:9; Ps. 34:17
11 [a]Ps. 106:7,8
12 [a]ch. 5:21
13 [a]2 Chr. 20:15, 17; Is. 41:10 [/]Or, *for whereas ye have seen the Egyptians today*
14 [a]ver. 25; Deut. 1:30; Josh. 10:14, 42; 2 Chr. 20:29; Is. 31:4 [b]Is. 30:15
16 [a]ver. 21,26
17 [a]ver. 8 [b]ver. 4
18 [a]ver. 4
19 [a]ch. 13:21; Is. 63:9
20 [a]See Is. 8:14; 2 Cor. 4:3
21 [a]Ps. 66:6 [b]ch. 15:8; Josh. 3:16; Neh. 9:11; Ps. 74:13; Is. 63:12
22 [a]ch. 15:19; Ps. 66:6; Is. 63:13; 1 Cor. 10:1; Heb. 11:29 [b]Hab. 3:10
24 [a]See Ps. 77:17
25 [a]ver. 14 [/]Or, *and made them to go heavily*

J *Ex 14:4* ◄► *Ex 16:23–30*

14:13 Moses told the Israelites at the moment they faced certain destruction that they would "see the salvation of the LORD." That very day God fulfilled this prophecy as he destroyed the Egyptian army in the Red Sea.

Egyptians, upon their chariots, and upon their horsemen.

27 And Moses stretched forth his hand over the sea, and the sea [a]returned to his strength when the morning appeared; and the Egyptians fled against it; and the LORD [b]overthrew [c]the[/] Egyptians in the midst of the sea.

28 And [a]the waters returned, and [b]covered the chariots, and the horsemen, *and* all the host of Pharaoh that came into the sea after them; there remained not so much as one of them.

29 But [a]the children of Israel walked upon dry *land* in the midst of the sea; and the waters *were* a wall unto them on their right hand, and on their left.

30 Thus the LORD [a]saved Israel that day out of the hand of the Egyptians; and Israel [b]saw the Egyptians dead upon the sea shore.

31 And Israel saw that great [/]work which the LORD did upon the Egyptians: and the people feared the LORD, and [a]believed the LORD, and his servant Moses.

The song of Moses

15 THEN SANG [a]Moses and the children of Israel this song unto the LORD, and spake, saying, I will sing unto the LORD, for he hath triumphed gloriously: the horse and his rider hath he thrown into the sea.

2 The LORD *is* my strength and [a]song, and he is become my salvation: he *is* my God, and I will prepare him [b]an habitation; my [c]father's God, and I [d]will exalt him.

3 The LORD *is* a man of [a]war: the LORD *is* his [b]name.

4 [a]Pharaoh's chariots and his host hath he cast into the sea: [b]his chosen captains also are drowned in the Red sea.

5 [a]The depths have covered them: [b]they sank into the bottom as a stone.

6 [a]Thy right hand, O LORD, is become glorious in power: thy right hand, O LORD, hath dashed in pieces the enemy.

7 And in the greatness of thine [a]excellency thou hast overthrown them that rose up against thee: thou sentest forth thy wrath, *which* [b]consumed them [c]as stubble.

8 And [a]with the blast of thy nostrils the waters were gathered together, [b]the floods stood upright as an heap, *and* the depths were congealed in the heart of the sea.

9 [a]The enemy said, I will pursue, I will overtake, I will [b]divide the spoil; my lust shall be satisfied upon them; I will draw my sword, my hand shall [/]destroy them.

10 Thou didst [a]blow with thy wind, [b]the sea covered them: they sank as lead in the mighty waters.

11 [a]Who *is* like unto thee, O LORD, among the [/]gods? who *is* like thee, [b]glorious in holiness, fearful *in* praises, [c]doing wonders?

12 Thou stretchedst out thy right hand, the earth swallowed them.

13 Thou in thy mercy hast [a]led forth the people *which* thou hast redeemed: thou hast guided *them* in thy strength unto [b]thy holy habitation. K L

14 [a]The people shall hear, *and* be afraid: [b]sorrow shall take hold on the inhabitants of Palestina.

15 [a]Then [b]the dukes of Edom shall be amazed; [c]the mighty men of Moab, trembling shall take hold upon them; [d]all the inhabitants of Canaan shall melt away.

16 [a]Fear and dread shall fall upon them; by the greatness of thine arm they shall be *as* still [b]as a stone; till thy people pass over, O LORD, till the people pass over, [c]*which* thou hast purchased.

17 Thou shalt bring them in, and [a]plant them in the mountain of thine inheritance, *in* the place, O LORD, *which* thou hast made for thee to dwell in, *in* the [b]Sanctuary, O LORD, *which* thy hands have established.

18 [a]The LORD shall reign for ever and ever.

19 For the [a]horse of Pharaoh went in with his chariots and with his horsemen into the sea, and [b]the LORD brought again the waters of the sea upon them; but the children of Israel went on dry *land* in the midst of the sea.

20 ¶ And Miriam [a]the prophetess, [b]the sister of Aaron, [c]took a timbrel in her hand; and all the women went out after her [d]with timbrels and with dances.

21 And Miriam [a]answered them, [b]Sing ye to the LORD, for he hath triumphed gloriously; the horse and his rider hath he thrown into the sea.

27 [a]Josh. 4:18 [b]ch. 15:1,7 [c]Neh. 9:11; Heb. 11:29 [/]Heb. *shook off*
28 [a]Hab. 3:8,13 [b]Ps. 106:11
29 [a]ver. 22; Ps. 78:52,53
30 [a]Ps. 106:8,10 [b]Ps. 59:10
31 [a]ch. 4:31; John 2:11 [/]Heb. *hand*
15:1 [a]Ps. 106:12
2 [a]Ps. 18:2; Is. 12:2; Hab. 3:18,19 [b]Gen. 28:21,22 [c]ch. 3:15,16 [d]Is. 25:1
3 [a]Rev. 19:11 [b]ch. 6:3; Ps. 83:18
4 [a]ch. 14:28 [b]ch. 14:7
5 [a]ch. 14:28 [b]Neh. 9:11
6 [a]Ps. 118:15
7 [a]Deut. 33:26 [b]Ps. 59:13 [c]Is. 5:24
8 [a]ch. 14:21 [b]Ps. 78:13
9 [a]Judg. 5:30 [b]Is. 53:12 [/]Or, *repossess*
10 [a]ch. 14:21 [b]ch. 14:28
11 [a]1 Ki. 8:23 [b]Is. 6:3 [c]Ps. 77:14 [/]Or, *mighty ones?*
13 [a]Ps. 77:15,20 [b]Ps. 78:54
14 [a]Josh. 2:9 [b]Ps. 48:6
15 [a]Gen. 36:40 [b]Deut. 2:4 [c]Num. 22:3 [d]Josh. 5:1
16 [a]Josh. 2:9 [b]1 Sam. 25:37 [c]Ps. 74:2; Jer. 31:11; 1 Pet. 2:9
17 [a]Ps. 44:2 [b]Ps. 78:54
18 [a]Is. 57:15
19 [a]ch. 14:23 [b]ch. 14:28
20 [a]Judg. 4:4 [b]Num. 26:59 [c]1 Sam. 18:6 [d]Judg. 11:34; 2 Sam. 6:16; Ps. 150:4
21 [a]1 Sam. 18:7 [b]ver. 1

K *Ex 12:13* ◀▶ *Ex 33:19*
L *Ex 11:7* ◀▶ *Ex 19:4–6*

Bitter waters made sweet

22 So Moses brought Israel from the Red sea, and they went out into the wilderness of [a]Shur; and they went three days in the wilderness, and found no water.

F 23 ¶ And when they came to [a]Marah, they could not drink of the waters of Marah, for they *were* bitter: therefore the name of it was called [I]Marah.

24 And the people [a]murmured against Moses, saying, What shall we drink?

25 And he cried unto the LORD; and the LORD showed him a tree, [a]*which* when he had cast into the waters, the waters were made sweet: there he [b]made for them a statute and an ordinance, and there [c]he proved them,

D 26 And said, [a]If thou wilt diligently
H hearken to the voice of the LORD thy God, and wilt do that which is right in his sight, and wilt give ear to his commandments, and keep all his statutes, I will put none of these [b]diseases upon thee, which I have brought upon the Egyptians: for I *am* the LORD [c]that healeth thee.

27 ¶ [a]And they came to Elim, where *were* twelve wells of water, and threescore and ten palm trees: and they encamped there by the waters.

Quails and manna provided

16 AND THEY [a]took their journey from Elim, and all the congregation of the children of Israel came unto the wilderness of [b]Sin, which *is* between Elim and Sinai, on the fifteenth day of the second month after their departing out of the land of Egypt.

2 And the whole congregation of the children of Israel [a]murmured against Moses and Aaron in the wilderness:

3 And the children of Israel said unto them, [a]Would to God we had died by the hand of the LORD in the land of Egypt, [b]when we sat by the flesh pots, *and* when we did eat bread to the full; for ye have brought us forth into this wilderness, to kill this whole assembly with hunger.

F 4 ¶ Then said the LORD unto Moses, Behold, I will rain [a]bread from heaven for you; and the people shall go out and gather [I]a certain rate every day, that I may [b]prove them, whether they will walk in my law, or no.

5 And it shall come to pass, that on the sixth day they shall prepare *that* which they bring in; and [a]it shall be twice as much as they gather daily.

6 And Moses and Aaron said unto all the children of Israel, [a]At even, then ye shall know that the LORD hath brought you out from the land of Egypt:

7 And in the morning, then ye shall see [a]the glory of the LORD; for that he heareth your murmurings against the LORD: and [b]what *are* we, that ye murmur against us?

8 And Moses said, *This shall be,* when the LORD shall give you in the evening flesh to eat, and in the morning bread to the full; for that the LORD heareth your murmurings which ye murmur against him: and what *are* we? your murmurings *are* not against us, but [a]against the LORD.

9 ¶ And Moses spake unto Aaron, Say unto all the congregation of the children of Israel, [a]Come near before the LORD: for he hath heard your murmurings.

10 And it came to pass, as Aaron spake unto the whole congregation of the children of Israel, that they looked toward the wilderness, and, behold, the glory of the LORD [a]appeared in the cloud.

11 ¶ And the LORD spake unto Moses, saying,

12 [a]I have heard the murmurings of the children of Israel: speak unto them, saying, [b]At even ye shall eat flesh, and [c]in the morning ye shall be filled with bread; and ye shall know that I *am* the LORD your God.

13 And it came to pass, that at even [a]the quails came up, and covered the camp: and in the morning [b]the dew lay round about the host.

14 And when the dew that lay was gone up, behold, upon the face of the wilderness *there lay* [a]a small round thing, *as* small as the hoar frost on the ground.

15 And when the children of Israel saw *it,* they said one to another, [I]It *is* manna: for they wist not what it *was.* And Moses said unto them, [a]This *is* the bread which the LORD hath given you to eat.

16 ¶ This *is* the thing which the LORD hath commanded, Gather of it every man

22 [a]Gen. 25:18
23 [a]Num. 33:8 [I]i.e. *Bitterness*
24 [a]ch. 16:2
25 [a]See 2 Ki. 2:21 [b]See Josh. 24:25 [c]Deut. 8:2,16; Judg. 3:1,4; Ps. 66:10
26 [a]Deut. 7:12,15 [b]Deut. 28:27,60 [c]ch. 23:25; Ps. 103:3
27 [a]Num. 33:9
16:1 [a]Num. 33:10, 11 [b]Ezek. 30:15
2 [a]1 Cor. 10:10
3 [a]Lam. 4:9 [b]Num. 11:4
4 [a]John 6:31 [b]Deut. 8:2,16 [I]Heb. *the portion of a day in his day*
5 [a]See ver. 22; Lev. 25:21
6 [a]See ver. 12,13; & ch. 6:7; Num. 16:28-30
7 [a]See ver. 10; Is. 35:2 & 40:5; John 11:4,40 [b]Num. 16:11
8 [a]See 1 Sam. 8:7; Luke 10:16; Rom. 13:2
9 [a]Num. 16:16
10 [a]ver. 7; ch. 13:21; Num. 16:19; 1 Ki. 8:10,11
12 [a]ver. 8 [b]ver. 6 [c]ver. 7
13 [a]Num. 11:31; Ps. 78:27,28 & 105:40 [b]Num. 11:9
14 [a]Num. 11:7; Deut. 8:3; Neh. 9:15; Ps. 78:24 & 105:40
15 [a]John 6:31,49, 58; 1 Cor. 10:3 [I]Or, *What is this?* or, *It is a portion*

F *Ge 48:15* ◀▶ *Ex 16:4–36*
D *Ex 9:15* ◀▶ *Ex 32:35*
H *Ge 15:15* ◀▶ *Ex 20:12*
F *Ex 15:23–25* ◀▶ *Ex 17:5–6*

according to his eating, [a]an omer [1]for every man, *according to* the number of your [2]persons; take ye every man for *them* which *are* in his tents.

17 And the children of Israel did so, and gathered, some more, some less.

18 And when they did mete *it* with an omer, [a]he that gathered much had nothing over, and he that gathered little had no lack; they gathered every man according to his eating.

19 And Moses said, Let no man leave of it till the morning.

20 Notwithstanding they hearkened not unto Moses; but some of them left of it until the morning, and it bred worms, and stank: and Moses was wroth with them.

21 And they gathered it every morning, every man according to his eating: and when the sun waxed hot, it melted.

22 ¶ And it came to pass, *that* on the sixth day they gathered twice as much bread, two omers for one *man:* and all the rulers of the congregation came and told Moses.

J 23 And he said unto them, This *is that* which the LORD hath said, Tomorrow *is* [a]the rest of the holy sabbath unto the LORD: bake *that* which ye will bake *today,* and seethe that ye will seethe; and that which remaineth over lay up for you to be kept until the morning.

24 And they laid it up till the morning, as Moses bade: and it did not [a]stink, neither was there any worm therein.

25 And Moses said, Eat that today; for today *is* a sabbath unto the LORD: today ye shall not find it in the field.

26 [a]Six days ye shall gather it; but on the seventh day, *which is* the sabbath, in it there shall be none.

27 ¶ And it came to pass, *that* there went out *some* of the people on the seventh day for to gather, and they found none.

28 And the LORD said unto Moses, How long [a]refuse ye to keep my commandments and my laws?

29 See, for that the LORD hath given you the sabbath, therefore he giveth you on the sixth day the bread of two days; abide ye every man in his place, let no man go out of his place on the seventh day.

16 [a]ver. 36 [1]Heb. *by the poll,* or, *head* [2]Heb. *souls*
18 [a]2 Cor. 8:15
23 [a]Gen. 2:3; ch. 20:8 & 31:15 & 35:3; Lev. 23:3
24 [a]ver. 20
26 [a]ch. 20:9,10
28 [a]2 Ki. 17:14; Ps. 78:10,22
31 [a]Num. 11:7,8
33 [a]Heb. 9:4
34 [a]ch. 25:16,21; & 40:20; Num. 17:10; Deut. 10:5
35 [a]Num. 33:38; John 6:31,49 [b]Josh. 5:12
17:1 [a]Num. 33:12, 14
2 [a]Num. 20:3 [b]Deut. 6:16; Ps. 78:18,41
3 [a]ch. 16:2
4 [a]ch. 14:15 [b]John 8:59 & 10:31
5 [a]Ezek. 2:6 [b]Num. 20:8
6 [a]Num. 20:10,11

30 So the people rested on the seventh day.

31 And the house of Israel called the name thereof Manna: and [a]it *was* like coriander seed, white; and the taste of it *was* like wafers *made* with honey.

32 ¶ And Moses said, This *is* the thing which the LORD commandeth, Fill an omer of it to be kept for your generations; that they may see the bread wherewith I have fed you in the wilderness, when I brought you forth from the land of Egypt.

33 And Moses said unto Aaron, [a]Take a pot, and put an omer full of manna therein, and lay it up before the LORD, to be kept for your generations.

34 As the LORD commanded Moses, so Aaron laid it up [a]before the Testimony, to be kept.

35 And the children of Israel did eat manna [a]forty years, [b]until they came to a land inhabited; they did eat manna, until they came unto the borders of the land of Canaan.

36 Now an omer *is* the tenth *part* of an ephah.

The water from the rock

17 AND [a]ALL the congregation of the children of Israel journeyed from the wilderness of Sin, after their journeys, according to the commandment of the LORD, and pitched in Rephidim: and *there was* no water for the people to drink.

2 [a]Wherefore the people did chide with Moses, and said, Give us water that we may drink. And Moses said unto them, Why chide ye with me? wherefore do ye [b]tempt the LORD?

3 And the people thirsted there for water; and the people [a]murmured against Moses, and said, Wherefore *is* this *that* thou hast brought us up out of Egypt, to kill us and our children and our cattle with thirst?

4 And Moses [a]cried unto the LORD, saying, What shall I do unto this people? they be almost ready to [b]stone me.

5 And the LORD said unto Moses, [a]Go on before the people, and take with thee of the elders of Israel; and thy rod, wherewith [b]thou smotest the river, take in thine hand, and go. F

6 [a]Behold, I will stand before thee

there upon the rock in Horeb; and thou shalt smite the rock, and there shall come water out of it, that the people may drink. And Moses did so in the sight of the elders of Israel.

7 And he called the name of the place [a]Massah,[1] and [2]Meribah, because of the chiding of the children of Israel, and because they tempted the LORD, saying, Is the LORD among us, or not?

The defeat of Amalek

8 ¶ [a]Then came Amalek, and fought with Israel in Rephidim.

9 And Moses said unto [a]Joshua, Choose us out men, and go out, fight with Amalek: tomorrow I will stand on the top of the hill with [b]the rod of God in mine hand.

10 So Joshua did as Moses had said to him, and fought with Amalek: and Moses, Aaron, and Hur went up to the top of the hill.

11 And it came to pass, when Moses [a]held up his hand, that Israel prevailed: and when he let down his hand, Amalek prevailed.

12 But Moses' hands *were* heavy; and they took a stone, and put *it* under him, and he sat thereon; and Aaron and Hur stayed up his hands, the one on the one side, and the other on the other side; and his hands were steady until the going down of the sun.

13 And Joshua discomfited Amalek and his people with the edge of the sword.

J 14 And the LORD said unto Moses, [a]Write this *for* a memorial in a book, and rehearse *it* in the ears of Joshua: for [b]I will utterly put out the remembrance of Amalek from under heaven.

15 And Moses built an altar, and called the name of it [1]Jehovah-nissi:

J 16 For he said, [1]Because [2]the LORD hath sworn *that* the LORD *will have* war with Amalek from generation to generation.

J *Ex 16:23–30* ◀▶ *Ex 17:16*
J *Ex 17:14* ◀▶ *Nu 14:22–30*

7 [a]Num. 20:13 [1]i.e. *Temptation* [2]i.e. *Chiding*, or, *Strife*
8 [a]Gen. 36:12; Deut. 25:17
9 [a]Called *Jesus* Acts 7:45 [b]ch. 4:20
11 [a]Jas. 5:16
14 [a]ch. 34:27 [b]1 Sam. 15:3,7 & 30:1,17
15 [1]i.e. *The LORD my banner*
16 [1]Or, *Because the hand* of Amalek is *against the throne of the LORD*, therefore [2]Heb. *the hand upon the throne of the LORD*
18:1 [a]ch. 2:16 [b]Ps. 106:2,8
2 [a]ch. 4:26
3 [a]Acts 7:29 [b]ch. 2:22 [1]i.e. *A stranger there*
4 [1]i.e. *My God is an help*
5 [a]ch. 3:1,12
7 [a]Gen. 18:2 [b]Gen. 29:13 [1]Heb. *peace*
8 [a]Ps. 81:7 [1]Heb. *found them*
10 [a]Gen. 14:20; 2 Sam. 18:28

The coming of Jethro

18 WHEN [a]JETHRO, the priest of Midian, Moses' father-in-law, heard of all that [b]God had done for Moses, and for Israel his people, *and* that the LORD had brought Israel out of Egypt;

2 Then Jethro, Moses' father-in-law, took Zipporah, Moses' wife, [a]after he had sent her back,

3 And her [a]two sons; of which the [b]name of the one *was* [1]Gershom; for he said, I have been an alien in a strange land:

4 And the name of the other *was* [1]Eliezer; for the God of my father, *said he, was* mine help, and delivered me from the sword of Pharaoh:

5 And Jethro, Moses' father-in-law, came with his sons and his wife unto Moses into the wilderness, where he encamped at [a]the mount of God:

6 And he said unto Moses, I thy father-in-law Jethro am come unto thee, and thy wife, and her two sons with her.

7 ¶ And Moses [a]went out to meet his father-in-law, and did obeisance, and [b]kissed him; and they asked each other of *their* [1]welfare; and they came into the tent.

8 And Moses told his father-in-law all that the LORD had done unto Pharaoh and to the Egyptians for Israel's sake, *and* all the travail that had [1]come upon them by the way, and *how* the LORD [a]delivered them.

9 And Jethro rejoiced for all the goodness which the LORD had done to Israel, whom he had delivered out of the hand of the Egyptians.

10 And Jethro said, [a]Blessed *be* the LORD, who hath delivered you out of the hand of the Egyptians, and out of the hand of Pharaoh, who hath delivered

17:14 Though some Biblical scholars challenge the Mosaic authorship of the first five books of the OT, many Jews and Christians alike have historically accepted the testimony of the Scriptures that Moses authored these books (see Dt 31:9, 24). Jesus Christ also affirmed the authorship and inspiration of these five books in numerous passages (see Mt 19:4–8; Mk 12:26; Jn 5:46; 7:19–23). In addition, recent analysis of the Hebrew text of these books by modern-day scholars and scientists strongly indicates the linguistic unity of the five books. Modern archeological discoveries have also confirmed the historicity of the culture and times reflected in the Pentateuch and strongly support Mosaic authorship and authority.

the people from under the hand of the Egyptians.

11 Now I know that the LORD *is* [a]greater than all gods: [b]for in the thing wherein they dealt [c]proudly *he was* above them.

12 And Jethro, Moses' father-in-law, took a burnt offering and sacrifices for God: and Aaron came, and all the elders of Israel, to eat bread with Moses' father-in-law [a]before God.

13 ¶ And it came to pass on the morrow, that Moses sat to judge the people: and the people stood by Moses from the morning unto the evening.

14 And when Moses' father-in-law saw all that he did to the people, he said, What *is* this thing that thou doest to the people? why sittest thou thyself alone, and all the people stand by thee from morning unto even?

15 And Moses said unto his father-in-law, Because [a]the people come unto me to inquire of God:

16 When they have [a]a matter, they come unto me; and I judge between [1]one and another, and I do [b]make *them* know the statutes of God, and his laws.

17 And Moses' father-in-law said unto him, The thing that thou doest *is* not good.

18 [1]Thou wilt surely wear away, both thou, and this people that *is* with thee: for this thing *is* too heavy for thee; [a]thou art not able to perform it thyself alone.

19 Hearken now unto my voice, I will give thee counsel, and [a]God shall be with thee: Be thou [b]for the people to God-ward, that thou mayest [c]bring the causes unto God:

20 And thou shalt [a]teach them ordinances and laws, and shalt show them [b]the way wherein they must walk, and [c]the work that they must do.

21 Moreover thou shalt provide out of all the people [a]able men, such as [b]fear God, [c]men of truth, [d]hating covetousness; and place *such* over them, *to be* rulers of thousands, *and* rulers of hundreds, rulers of fifties, and rulers of tens:

22 And let them judge the people [a]at all seasons: [b]and it shall be, *that* every great matter they shall bring unto thee, but every small matter they shall judge: so shall it be easier for thyself, and [c]they shall bear *the burden* with thee.

23 If thou shalt do this thing, and God command thee *so,* then thou shalt be [a]able to endure, and all this people shall also go to [b]their place in peace.

24 So Moses hearkened to the voice of his father-in-law, and did all that he had said.

25 And [a]Moses chose able men out of all Israel, and made them heads over the people, rulers of thousands, rulers of hundreds, rulers of fifties, and rulers of tens.

26 And they [a]judged the people at all seasons: the [b]hard causes they brought unto Moses, but every small matter they judged themselves.

27 ¶ And Moses let his father-in-law depart; and [a]he went his way into his own land.

At mount Sinai

19 IN THE third month, when the children of Israel were gone forth out of the land of Egypt, the same day [a]came they *into* the wilderness of Sinai.

2 For they were departed from [a]Rephidim, and were come *to* the desert of Sinai, and had pitched in the wilderness; and there Israel camped before [b]the mount.

3 And [a]Moses went up unto God, and the LORD [b]called unto him out of the mountain, saying, Thus shalt thou say to

11 [a]2 Chr. 2:5 [b]ch. 1:10,16,22 [c]Luke 1:51
12 [a]Deut. 12:7
15 [a]Lev. 24:12
16 [a]ch. 24:14 [b]Lev. 24:15 [1]Heb. *a man and his fellow*
18 [a]Num. 11:14, 17 [1]Heb. *Fading thou wilt fade*
19 [a]ch. 3:12 [b]ch. 4:16 [c]Num. 27:5
20 [a]Deut. 5:1 [b]Ps. 143:8 [c]Deut. 1:18
21 [a]ver. 25; 2 Chr. 19:5-10; Acts 6:3 [b]2 Sam. 23:3 [c]Ezek. 18:8 [d]Deut. 16:19
22 [a]ver. 26 [b]Lev. 24:11; Deut. 1:17 [c]Num. 11:17
23 [a]ver. 18 [b]ch. 16:29; 2 Sam. 19:39
25 [a]Deut. 1:15
26 [a]ver. 22 [b]Job 29:16
27 [a]Num. 10:29, 30
19:1 [a]Num. 33:15
2 [a]ch. 17:1,8 [b]ch. 3:1,12
3 [a]Acts 7:38 [b]ch. 3:4

19:1 *Dispensation of the Law.* The dispensation of promise was superseded, but not annulled, by this dispensation of the law given at Sinai. Covering the time period from the exodus to the preaching of John the Baptist (see Mt 11:13; Lk 16:16), this dispensation was given to test the Israelites' obedience to the Law of Moses in every detail. God gave the Law of Moses so that people would recognize their sinfulness in contrast with his righteousness. Though the Israelites witnessed the power of God through miracles in the wilderness, saw a visible manifestation of his presence day and night, received a special revelation from him containing a complete code of civil and religious laws and covenanted with God to be his consecrated people, their failure of the test of this dispensation is documented throughout the entire OT.

The seven dispensations revealed in Scripture are the dispensations of innocence (Ge 1:28), conscience (Ge 3:7), human government (Ge 8:15), promise (Ge 12:1), law (Ex 19:1), the church (Ac 2:1) and the kingdom (Rev 20:4). For further information on the dispensations, see the article on p. 4.

the house of Jacob, and tell the children of Israel;

L 4 [a]Ye have seen what I did unto the Egyptians, and *how* [b]I bare you on eagles' wings, and brought you unto myself.

S 5 Now [a]therefore, if ye will obey my voice indeed, and keep my covenant, then [b]ye shall be a peculiar treasure unto me above all people: for [c]all the earth *is* mine:

6 And ye shall be unto me a [a]kingdom of priests, and an [b]holy nation. These *are* the words which thou shalt speak unto the children of Israel.

7 ¶ And Moses came and called for the elders of the people, and laid before their faces all these words which the LORD commanded him.

8 And [a]all the people answered together, and said, All that the LORD hath spoken we will do. And Moses returned the words of the people unto the LORD.

9 And the LORD said unto Moses, Lo, I come unto thee [a]in a thick cloud, [b]that the people may hear when I speak with thee, and [c]believe thee for ever. And Moses told the words of the people unto the LORD.

10 ¶ And the LORD said unto Moses, Go unto the people, and [a]sanctify them today and tomorrow, and let them [b]wash their clothes,

11 And be ready against the third day: for the third day the LORD [a]will come down in the sight of all the people upon mount Sinai.

12 And thou shalt set bounds unto the people round about, saying, Take heed to yourselves, *that ye* go *not* up into the mount, or touch the border of it: [a]whosoever toucheth the mount shall be surely put to death:

13 There shall not an hand touch it, but he shall surely be stoned, or shot through; whether *it be* beast or man, it shall not live: when the [a]trumpet[1] soundeth long, they shall come up to the mount.

14 ¶ And Moses went down from the mount unto the people, and sanctified the people; and they washed their clothes.

15 And he said unto the people, Be ready against the third day: [a]come not at *your* wives.

16 ¶ And it came to pass on the third day in the morning, that there were [a]thunders and lightnings, and a [b]thick cloud upon the mount, and the [c]voice of the trumpet exceeding loud; so that all the people that *was* in the camp [d]trembled.

17 And [a]Moses brought forth the people out of the camp to meet with God; and they stood at the nether part of the mount.

18 And [a]mount Sinai was altogether on a smoke, because the LORD descended upon it [b]in fire: [c]and the smoke thereof ascended as the smoke of a furnace, and [d]the whole mount quaked greatly.

19 And when the voice of the trumpet sounded long, and waxed louder and louder, [a]Moses spake, and [b]God answered him by a voice.

20 And the LORD came down upon mount Sinai, on the top of the mount: and the LORD called Moses *up* to the top of the mount; and Moses went up.

21 And the LORD said unto Moses, Go down, [1]charge the people, lest they break through unto the LORD [a]to gaze, and many of them perish.

4 [a]Deut. 29:2 [b]Is. 63:9
5 [a]Deut. 5:2 [b]Deut. 7:6 & 14:2, 21; 1 Ki. 8:53; Ps. 135:4 [c]ch. 9:29; Deut. 10:14; Job 41:11; Ps. 24:1
6 [a]Deut. 33:2-4; 1 Pet. 2:5,9 [b]Deut. 7:6; Is. 62:12; 1 Cor. 3:17
8 [a]Deut. 5:27
9 [a]Mat. 17:5 [b]Deut. 4:12,36; John 12:29,30 [c]ch. 14:31
10 [a]Lev. 11:44,45; Heb. 10:22 [b]ver. 14
11 [a]ver. 16,18; ch. 34:5
12 [a]Heb. 12:20
13 [a]ver. 16,19 [1]Or, *cornet*
15 [a]1 Cor. 7:5
16 [a]Heb. 12:18,19; Rev. 8:5 [b]ch. 40:34; 2 Chr. 5:14 [c]Rev. 4:1 [d]Heb. 12:21
17 [a]Deut. 4:10
18 [a]Deut. 4:11 & 33:2; Judg. 5:5; Hab. 3:3 [b]ch. 3:2 & 24:17; 2 Chr. 7:1-3 [c]Gen. 15:17; Ps. 144:5; Rev. 15:8 [d]Ps. 68:8; Jer. 4:24; Heb. 12:26
19 [a]Heb. 12:21 [b]Neh. 9:13; Ps. 81:7
21 [a]See ch. 3:5; 1 Sam. 6:19 [1]Heb. *contest*

L *Ex 15:13* ◀ ▶ *Ex 33:12*
S *Ge 19:26* ◀ ▶ *Ex 20:6*

19:5–6 *Mosaic Covenant.* This conditional covenant between God and Israel at Mt. Sinai represented an enlargement of the covenant God made with Abraham 600 years earlier. In addition to God's promise to be Israel's God, protector and provider, God now called Israel his "peculiar treasure," a nation separated from all other nations, holy and devoted to God alone, whose citizens were all priests with access to God (see Dt 7:6; 14:2; 26:18; Ps 135:4; Mal 3:17). This feature of the Mosaic covenant foreshadows the divine blessing bestowed on Christians (see 1Pe 2:9; Rev 1:6; 5:10).

Chosen to represent God's way of life, teach his Word and serve as his channel of salvation for the world through the prophesied Messiah (see Ge 18:18; Isa 60:3), Israel's covenantal blessing was conditional upon her faith and obedience. At Mt. Sinai the Israelites promised to consecrate themselves to God, to live by his rule and to serve his purposes, yet history records their repeated failures in each of these areas.

NOTE: The seven additional covenants include the Edenic (Ge 2:15–17), Adamic (Ge 3:15–19), Noahic (Ge 9:8ff), Abrahamic (Ge 15:4ff; 17:1–22), Palestinian (Dt 30:1–10), Davidic (2Sa 7:16) and New (Heb 8:8–12). See article on p. 8.

22 And let the priests also, which come near to the LORD, [a]sanctify themselves, lest the LORD [b]break forth upon them.

23 And Moses said unto the LORD, The people cannot come up to mount Sinai: for thou chargedst us, saying, [a]Set bounds about the mount, and sanctify it.

24 And the LORD said unto him, Away, get thee down, and thou shalt come up, thou, and Aaron with thee: but let not the priests and the people break through to come up unto the LORD, lest he break forth upon them.

25 So Moses went down unto the people, and spake unto them.

The Ten Commandments

20 AND GOD spake [a]all these words, saying,

2 [a]I *am* the LORD thy God, which have brought thee out of the land of Egypt, [b]out of the house of [l]bondage.

3 [a]Thou shalt have no other gods before me.

4 [a]Thou shalt not make unto thee any graven image, or any likeness *of any thing* that *is* in heaven above, or that *is* in the earth beneath, or that *is* in the water under the earth:

5 [a]Thou shalt not bow down thyself to them, nor serve them: for I the LORD thy God *am* [b]a jealous God, [c]visiting the iniquity of the fathers upon the children unto the third and fourth *generation* of them that hate me;

L S 6 And [a]showing mercy unto thousands of them that love me, and keep my commandments.

7 [a]Thou shalt not take the name of the LORD thy God in vain; for the LORD [b]will not hold him guiltless that taketh his name in vain.

8 [a]Remember the sabbath day, to keep it holy.

9 [a]Six days shalt thou labour, and do all thy work:

10 But the [a]seventh day *is* the sabbath of the LORD thy God: *in it* thou shalt not do any work, thou, nor thy son, nor thy daughter, thy manservant, nor thy maidservant, nor thy cattle, [b]nor thy stranger that *is* within thy gates:

11 For [a]*in* six days the LORD made heaven and earth, the sea, and all that in them *is,* and rested the seventh day: wherefore the LORD blessed the sabbath day, and hallowed it.

12 ¶ [a]Honour thy father and thy mother: that thy days may be long upon the land which the LORD thy God giveth thee. H

13 [a]Thou shalt not kill.

14 [a]Thou shalt not commit adultery.

15 [a]Thou shalt not steal.

16 [a]Thou shalt not bear false witness against thy neighbour.

17 [a]Thou shalt not covet thy neighbour's house, [b]thou shalt not covet thy neighbour's wife, nor his manservant, nor his maidservant, nor his ox, nor his ass, nor any thing that *is* thy neighbour's.

18 ¶ And [a]all the people [b]saw the thunderings, and the lightnings, and the noise of the trumpet, and the mountain [c]smoking: and when the people saw *it,* they removed, and stood afar off.

19 And they said unto Moses, [a]Speak thou with us, and we will hear: but [b]let not God speak with us, lest we die.

20 And Moses said unto the people, [a]Fear not: [b]for God is come to prove you, and [c]that his fear may be before your faces, that ye sin not.

Making an altar of earth

21 And the people stood afar off, and Moses drew near unto [a]the thick darkness where God *was.*

22 ¶ And the LORD said unto Moses, Thus thou shalt say unto the children of Israel, Ye have seen that I have talked with you [a]from heaven.

23 Ye shall not make [a]with me gods of silver, neither shall ye make unto you gods of gold.

24 ¶ An altar of earth thou shalt make unto me, and shalt sacrifice thereon thy burnt offerings, and thy peace offerings, [a]thy sheep, and thine oxen: in all [b]places where I record my name I will come unto thee, and I will [c]bless thee.

25 And [a]if thou wilt make me an altar of stone, thou shalt not [l]build it of hewn stone: for if thou lift up thy tool upon it, thou hast polluted it.

26 Neither shalt thou go up by steps unto mine altar, that thy nakedness be not discovered thereon.

22 [a]Lev. 10:3 [b]2 Sam. 6:7,8
23 [a]ver. 12
20:1 [a]Deut. 5:22
2 [a]Hos. 13:4 [b]ch. 13:3 [l]Heb. *servants*
3 [a]Jer. 35:15
4 [a]Deut. 27:15
5 [a]Is. 44:15,19 [b]Deut. 4:24 [c]Num. 14:18,33; 1 Ki. 21:29; Ps. 79:8; Jer. 32:18
6 [a]Deut. 7:9; Rom. 11:28
7 [a]Mat. 5:33 [b]Mic. 6:11
8 [a]Lev. 26:2
9 [a]Ezek. 20:12; Luke 13:14
10 [a]Gen. 2:2,3 [b]Neh. 13:16-19
11 [a]Gen. 2:2
12 [a]Lev. 19:3; Deut. 5:16; Eph. 6:2
13 [a]Rom. 13:9
14 [a]Deut. 5:18
15 [a]Lev. 19:11
16 [a]ch. 23:1; Deut. 5:20
17 [a]Luke 12:15; Eph. 5:3,5; Heb. 13:5 [b]Mat. 5:28
18 [a]Heb. 12:18 [b]Rev. 1:10,12 [c]ch. 19:18
19 [a]Gal. 3:19 [b]Deut. 5:25
20 [a]Is. 41:10,13 [b]Deut. 13:3 [c]Prov. 16:6; Is. 8:13
21 [a]ch. 19:16
22 [a]Deut. 4:36
23 [a]ch. 32:1,2,4
24 [a]Lev. 1:2 [b]Deut. 16:6,11; 1 Ki. 9:3; 2 Chr. 6:6 [c]Gen. 12:2
25 [a]Deut. 27:5 [l]Heb. *build them with hewing*

Laws about servants

21 NOW THESE *are* the judgments
which thou shalt [a]set before
them.
2 [a]If thou buy an Hebrew servant, six
years he shall serve: and in the seventh
he shall go out free for nothing.
3 If he came in [l]by himself, he shall go
out by himself: if he were married, then
his wife shall go out with him.
4 If his master have given him a wife,
and she have born him sons or daughters;
the wife and her children shall be her
master's, and he shall go out by himself.
5 [a]And if the servant [l]shall plainly say,
I love my master, my wife, and my children; I will not go out free:
6 Then his master shall bring him unto
the [a]judges; he shall also bring him to the
door, or unto the door post; and his master shall [b]bore his ear through with an
awl; and he shall serve him for ever.
7 ¶ And if a man [a]sell his daughter to
be a maidservant, she shall not go out as
the menservants do.
8 If she [l]please not her master, who
hath betrothed her to himself, then shall
he let her be redeemed: to sell her unto a
strange nation he shall have no power,
seeing he hath dealt deceitfully with her.
9 And if he have betrothed her unto
his son, he shall deal with her after the
manner of daughters.
10 If he take him another *wife;* her
food, her raiment, [a]and her duty of marriage, shall he not diminish.
11 And if he do not these three unto
her, then shall she go out free without
money.

Laws about murder and strife

12 ¶ [a]He that smiteth a man, so that
he die, shall be surely put to death.
13 And [a]if a man lie not in wait, but
God [b]deliver *him* into his hand; then [c]I
will appoint thee a place whither he shall
flee.
14 But if a man come [a]presumptuously
upon his neighbour, to slay him with
guile; [b]thou shalt take him from mine altar, that he may die.
15 ¶ And he that smiteth his father, or
his mother, shall be surely put to death.
16 ¶ And [a]he that stealeth a man, and
[b]selleth him, or if he be [c]found in his
hand, he shall surely be put to death.
17 ¶ And [a]he that [l]curseth his father,
or his mother, shall surely be put to
death.
18 ¶ And if men strive together, and
one smite [l]another with a stone, or with
his fist, and he die not, but keepeth *his*
bed:
19 If he rise again, and walk abroad
[a]upon his staff, then shall he that smote
him be quit: only he shall pay *for* [l]the
loss of his time, and shall cause *him* to be
thoroughly healed.
20 ¶ And if a man smite his servant, or
his maid, with a rod, and he die under his
hand; he shall be surely [l]punished.
21 Notwithstanding, if he continue a
day or two, he shall not be punished: for
he *is* his money.
22 ¶ If men strive, and hurt a woman
with child, so that her fruit depart *from
her,* and yet no mischief follow: he shall
be surely punished, according as the
woman's husband will lay upon him; and
he shall [a]pay as the judges *determine.*
23 And if *any* mischief follow, then
thou shalt give life for life,
24 [a]Eye for eye, tooth for tooth, hand
for hand, foot for foot,
25 Burning for burning, wound for
wound, stripe for stripe.
26 ¶ And if a man smite the eye of his
servant, or the eye of his maid, that it
perish; he shall let him go free for his
eye's sake.
27 And if he smite out his manservant's tooth, or his maidservant's tooth;
he shall let him go free for his tooth's
sake.
28 ¶ If an ox gore a man or a woman,
that they die: then [a]the ox shall be surely
stoned, and his flesh shall not be eaten;
but the owner of the ox *shall be* quit.
29 But if the ox were wont to push
with his horn in time past, and it hath
been testified to his owner, and he hath
not kept him in, but that he hath killed a
man or a woman; the ox shall be stoned,
and his owner also shall be put to death.
30 If there be laid on him a sum of
money, then he shall give for [a]the ransom of his life whatsoever is laid upon
him.
31 Whether he have gored a son, or
have gored a daughter, according to this
judgment shall it be done unto him.
32 If the ox shall push a manservant or
a maidservant; he shall give unto their

21:1 [a]Deut. 4:14
2 [a]Jer. 34:14
3 [l]Heb. *with his body*
5 [a]Deut. 15:16,17 [l]Heb. *saying shall say*
6 [a]ch. 12:12 [b]Ps. 40:6
7 [a]Neh. 5:5
8 [l]Heb. *be evil in the eyes of*
10 [a]1 Cor. 7:5
12 [a]Gen. 9:6; Mat. 26:52
13 [a]Deut. 19:4,5 [b]1 Sam. 24:4,10,18 [c]Num. 35:11; Deut. 19:3; Josh. 20:2
14 [a]Deut. 19:11, 12; Heb. 10:26 [b]1 Ki. 2:28-34
16 [a]Deut. 24:7 [b]Gen. 37:28 [c]ch. 22:4
17 [a]Mark 7:10 [l]Or, *revileth*
18 [l]Or, *his neighbour*
19 [a]2 Sam. 3:29 [l]Heb. *his ceasing*
20 [l]Heb. *avenged*
22 [a]ver. 30; Deut. 22:18,19
24 [a]Lev. 24:20; Deut. 19:21; Mat. 5:38
28 [a]Gen. 9:5
30 [a]ver. 22; Num. 35:31

master [a]thirty shekels of silver, and the [b]ox shall be stoned.

33 ¶ And if a man shall open a pit, or if a man shall dig a pit, and not cover it, and an ox or an ass fall therein;

34 The owner of the pit shall make *it* good, *and* give money unto the owner of them; and the dead *beast* shall be his.

35 ¶ And if one man's ox hurt another's, that he die; then they shall sell the live ox, and divide the money of it; and the dead *ox* also they shall divide.

36 Or if it be known that the ox hath used to push in time past, and his owner hath not kept him in; he shall surely pay ox for ox; and the dead shall be his own.

Laws about property

R **22** IF A man shall steal an ox, or a [l]sheep, and kill it, or sell it; he shall restore five oxen for an ox, and [a]four sheep for a sheep.

2 ¶ If a thief be found [a]breaking up, and be smitten that he die, *there shall* [b]no blood *be shed* for him.

3 If the sun be risen upon him, *there shall be* blood *shed* for him; *for* he should make full restitution; if he have nothing, then he shall be [a]sold for his theft.

4 If the theft be certainly [a]found in his hand alive, whether it be ox, or ass, or sheep; he shall [b]restore double.

5 ¶ If a man shall cause a field or vineyard to be eaten, and shall put in his beast, and shall feed in another man's field; of the best of his own field, and of the best of his own vineyard, shall he make restitution.

6 ¶ If fire break out, and catch in thorns, so that the stacks of corn, or the standing corn, or the field, be consumed *therewith;* he that kindled the fire shall surely make restitution.

7 ¶ If a man shall deliver unto his neighbour money or stuff to keep, and it be stolen out of the man's house; [a]if the thief be found, let him pay double.

8 If the thief be not found, then the master of the house shall be brought unto the [a]judges, *to see* whether he have put his hand unto his neighbour's goods.

9 For all manner of trespass, *whether it be* for ox, for ass, for sheep, for raiment, *or* for any manner of lost thing, which *another* challengeth to be his, the [a]cause of both parties shall come before the judges; *and* whom the judges shall condemn, he shall pay double unto his neighbour.

10 If a man deliver unto his neighbour an ass, or an ox, or a sheep, or any beast, to keep; and it die, or be hurt, or driven away, no man seeing *it:*

11 *Then* shall an [a]oath of the LORD be between them both, that he hath not put his hand unto his neighbour's goods; and the owner of it shall accept *thereof,* and he shall not make *it* good.

12 And [a]if it be stolen from him, he shall make restitution unto the owner thereof.

13 If it be torn in pieces, *then* let him bring it *for* witness, *and* he shall not make good that which was torn.

14 ¶ And if a man borrow *aught* of his neighbour, and it be hurt, or die, the owner thereof *being* not with it, he shall surely make *it* good.

15 *But* if the owner thereof *be* with it, he shall not make *it* good: if it *be* an hired *thing,* it came for his hire.

Laws about personal actions

16 ¶ And [a]if a man entice a maid that is not betrothed, and lie with her, he shall surely endow her to be his wife.

17 If her father utterly refuse to give her unto him, he shall [l]pay money according to the [a]dowry of virgins.

18 ¶ [a]Thou shalt not suffer a witch to live.

19 ¶ [a]Whosoever lieth with a beast shall surely be put to death.

20 ¶ [a]He that sacrificeth unto *any* god, save unto the LORD only, he shall be utterly destroyed.

21 ¶ [a]Thou shalt neither vex a stranger, nor oppress him: for ye were strangers in the land of Egypt.

22 ¶ [a]Ye shall not afflict any widow, or fatherless child.

23 If thou afflict them in any wise, and they [a]cry at all unto me, I will surely [b]hear their cry;

24 And my [a]wrath shall wax hot, and I will kill you with the sword; and [b]your wives shall be widows, and your children fatherless.

25 ¶ [a]If thou lend money to *any of* my people *that is* poor by thee, thou shalt not be to him as an usurer, neither shalt thou lay upon him usury.

32 [a]See Zech. 11:12,13; Mat. 26:15 & 27:3,9 [b]ver. 28
22:1 [a]2 Sam. 12:6; See Prov. 6:31; Luke 19:8 [l]Or, *goat*
2 [a]Mat. 24:43 [b]Num. 35:27
3 [a]ch. 21:2
4 [a]ch. 21:16 [b]See ver. 1,7; Prov. 6:31
7 [a]ver. 4
8 [a]ch. 21:6; ver. 28
9 [a]Deut. 25:1; 2 Chr. 19:10
11 [a]Heb. 6:16
12 [a]Gen. 31:39
16 [a]Deut. 22:28, 29
17 [a]Gen. 34:12 [l]Heb. *weigh;* see Gen. 23:16
18 [a]1 Sam. 28:3
19 [a]Lev. 18:23
20 [a]Deut. 17:2,3,5
21 [a]Deut. 10:19
22 [a]Jas. 1:27
23 [a]Luke 18:7 [b]Ps. 18:6
24 [a]Ps. 69:24 [b]Ps. 109:9
25 [a]Ps. 15:5

R ▶ *Lev 5:5*

26 [a]If thou at all take thy neighbour's raiment to pledge, thou shalt deliver it unto him by that the sun goeth down:

27 For that *is* his covering only, it *is* his raiment for his skin: wherein shall he sleep? and it shall come to pass, when he crieth unto me, that I will hear; for I *am* [a]gracious.

28 ¶ [a]Thou shalt not revile the [b]gods,[1] nor curse the ruler of thy people.

29 ¶ Thou shalt not delay *to offer* [a]the[1] first of thy ripe fruits, and of thy [2]liquors: [b]the firstborn of thy sons shalt thou give unto me.

30 [a]Likewise shalt thou do with thine oxen, *and* with thy sheep: [b]seven days it shall be with his dam; on the eighth day thou shalt give it me.

S 31 ¶ And ye shall be [a]holy men unto me: [b]neither shall ye eat *any* flesh *that is* torn of beasts in the field; ye shall cast it to the dogs.

23 THOU [a]SHALT not [1]raise a false report: put not thine hand with the wicked to be an [b]unrighteous witness.

2 ¶ [a]Thou shalt not follow a multitude to *do* evil; [b]neither shalt thou [1]speak in a cause to decline after many to wrest *judgment:*

3 ¶ Neither shalt thou countenance a poor man in his cause.

4 ¶ [a]If thou meet thine enemy's ox or his ass going astray, thou shalt surely bring it back to him again.

5 [a]If thou see the ass of him that hateth thee lying under his burden, [1]and wouldest forbear to help him, thou shalt surely help with him.

6 [a]Thou shalt not wrest the judgment of thy poor in his cause.

H S 7 [a]Keep thee far from a false matter; [b]and the innocent and righteous slay thou not: for [c]I will not justify the wicked.

8 ¶ And [a]thou shalt take no gift: for the gift blindeth [1]the wise, and perverteth the words of the righteous.

9 ¶ Also [a]thou shalt not oppress a stranger: for ye know the [1]heart of a stranger, seeing ye were strangers in the land of Egypt.

S *Ex 20:6* ◀▶ *Ex 23:7*
H *Ex 12:13* ◀▶ *Ex 32:33*
S *Ex 22:31* ◀▶ *Ex 32:33*

26 [a]Deut. 24:6
27 [a]ch. 34:6
28 [a]Eccl. 10:20 [b]Ps. 82:6 [1]Or, *judges*
29 [a]ch. 23:16 [b]ch. 13:2,12 [1]Heb. *thy fulness* [2]Heb. *tear*
30 [a]Deut. 15:19 [b]Lev. 22:27
31 [a]Lev. 19:2 [b]Ezek. 4:14
23:1 [a]Ps. 101:5 [b]Acts 6:11 [1]Or, *receive*
2 [a]Gen. 7:1 [b]Lev. 19:15 [1]Heb. *answer*
4 [a]Rom. 12:20
5 [a]Deut. 22:4 [1]Or, *wilt thou cease to help him?* or, *and wouldest cease to leave* thy business *for him; thou shalt surely leave* it to join *with him*
6 [a]Eccl. 5:8
7 [a]Eph. 4:25 [b]Mat. 27:4 [c]Rom. 1:18
8 [a]Prov. 15:27 [1]Heb. *the seeing*
9 [a]ch. 22:21 [1]Heb. *soul*
10 [a]Lev. 25:3,4
11 [1]Or, *olive trees*
12 [a]Luke 13:14
13 [a]1 Tim. 4:16 [b]Num. 32:38
14 [a]ch. 34:23
15 [a]ch. 12:15 [b]ch. 34:20
16 [a]ch. 34:22 [b]Deut. 16:13
17 [a]Deut. 16:16
18 [a]Deut. 16:4 [1]Or, *feast*
19 [a]Deut. 26:10 [b]Deut. 14:21
20 [a]ch. 14:19
21 [a]Num. 14:11; Ps. 78:40,56 [b]Deut. 18:19; 1 John 5:16

The law about the Sabbath

10 And [a]six years thou shalt sow thy land, and shalt gather in the fruits thereof:

11 But the seventh *year* thou shalt let it rest and lie still; that the poor of thy people may eat: and what they leave the beasts of the field shall eat. In like manner thou shalt deal with thy vineyard, *and* with thy [1]oliveyard.

12 [a]Six days thou shalt do thy work, and on the seventh day thou shalt rest: that thine ox and thine ass may rest, and the son of thy handmaid, and the stranger, may be refreshed.

13 And in all *things* that I have said unto you [a]be circumspect: and [b]make no mention of the name of other gods, neither let it be heard out of thy mouth.

Laws about appointed feasts

14 ¶ [a]Three times thou shalt keep a feast unto me in the year.

15 [a]Thou shalt keep the feast of unleavened bread: (thou shalt eat unleavened bread seven days, as I commanded thee, in the time appointed of the month Abib; for in it thou camest out from Egypt: [b]and none shall appear before me empty:)

16 [a]And the feast of harvest, the first- A
fruits of thy labours, which thou hast sown in the field: and [b]the feast of ingathering, *which is* in the end of the year, when thou hast gathered in thy labours out of the field.

17 [a]Three times in the year all thy males shall appear before the Lord GOD.

18 [a]Thou shalt not offer the blood of my sacrifice with leavened bread; neither shall the fat of my [1]sacrifice remain until the morning.

19 [a]The first of the firstfruits of thy land thou shalt bring into the house of the LORD thy God. [b]Thou shalt not seethe a kid in his mother's milk.

Promise of God's protection

20 ¶ [a]Behold, I send an Angel before thee, to keep thee in the way, and to bring thee into the place which I have prepared.

21 Beware of him, and obey his voice, [a]provoke him not; for he will [b]not pardon

A *Ex 12:3–9* ◀▶ *Ex 23:25–31*

your transgressions: for [c]my name *is* in him.

V 22 But if thou shalt indeed obey his voice, and do all that I speak; then [a]I will be an enemy unto thine enemies, and [1]an adversary unto thine adversaries.

23 [a]For mine Angel shall go before thee, and [b]bring thee in unto the Amorites, and the Hittites, and the Perizzites, and the Canaanites, the Hivites, and the Jebusites: and I will cut them off.

24 Thou shalt not [a]bow down to their gods, nor serve them, [b]nor do after their works: [c]but thou shalt utterly overthrow them, and quite break down their images.

A F H 25 And ye shall [a]serve the LORD your God, and [b]he shall bless thy bread, and thy water; and [c]I will take sickness away from the midst of thee.

B 26 ¶ [a]There shall nothing cast their young, nor be barren, in thy land: the number of thy days I will [b]fulfil.

V 27 I will send [a]my fear before thee, and will [b]destroy all the people to whom thou shalt come, and I will make all thine enemies turn their [1]backs unto thee.

28 And [a]I will send hornets before thee, which shall drive out the Hivite, the Canaanite, and the Hittite, from before thee.

29 [a]I will not drive them out from before thee in one year; lest the land become desolate, and the beast of the field multiply against thee.

30 By little and little I will drive them out from before thee, until thou be increased, and inherit the land.

31 And [a]I will set thy bounds from the Red sea even unto the sea of the Philistines, and from the desert unto the river: for I will [b]deliver the inhabitants of the land into your hand; and thou shalt drive them out before thee.

32 [a]Thou shalt make no covenant with them, nor with their gods.

33 They shall not dwell in thy land, lest they make thee sin against me: for if thou serve their gods, [a]it will surely be a snare unto thee.

The covenant affirmed

24 AND HE said unto Moses, Come up unto the LORD, thou, and Aaron, [a]Nadab, and Abihu, [b]and seventy of the elders of Israel; and worship ye afar off.

2 And Moses alone shall come near the LORD: but they shall not come nigh; neither shall the people go up with him.

3 ¶ And Moses came and told the people all the words of the LORD, and all the judgments: and all the people answered with one voice, and said, [a]All the words which the LORD hath said will we do.

4 And Moses [a]wrote all the words of the LORD, and rose up early in the morning, and builded an altar under the hill, and twelve [b]pillars, according to the twelve tribes of Israel.

5 And he sent young men of the children of Israel, which offered burnt offerings, and sacrificed peace offerings of oxen unto the LORD. D

6 And Moses [a]took half of the blood, and put *it* in basins; and half of the blood he sprinkled on the altar.

7 And he [a]took the book of the covenant, and read in the audience of the people: and they said, All that the LORD hath said will we do, and be obedient.

8 And Moses took the blood, and sprinkled *it* on the people, and said, Behold [a]the blood of the covenant, which the LORD hath made with you concerning all these words.

9 ¶ Then went up Moses, and Aaron, Nadab, and Abihu, and seventy of the elders of Israel:

10 And they [a]saw the God of Israel: and *there was* under his feet as it were a paved work of a [b]sapphire stone, and as it were the [c]body of heaven in *his* clearness.

11 And upon the nobles of the children of Israel he [a]laid not his hand: also [b]they saw God, and did [c]eat and drink.

12 ¶ And the LORD said unto Moses, [a]Come up to me into the mount, and be there: and I will give thee [b]tables of stone, and a law, and commandments which I have written; that thou mayest teach them.

13 And Moses rose up, and [a]his minister Joshua: and Moses went up into the mount of God.

21 [c]Is. 9:6; Jer. 23:6
22 [a]Deut. 30:7; Jer. 30:20 [1]*Or, I will afflict them that afflict thee*
23 [a]ver. 20 [b]Josh. 24:8
24 [a]ch. 20:5 [b]Deut. 12:30,31 [c]Num. 33:52
25 [a]Deut. 6:13; Mat. 4:10 [b]Deut. 28:5 [c]ch. 15:26; Deut. 7:15
26 [a]Deut. 7:14 & 28:4; Mal. 3:11 [b]1 Chr. 23:1
27 [a]Deut. 2:25 [b]Deut. 7:23 [1]Heb. *neck*
28 [a]Josh. 24:12
29 [a]Deut. 7:22
31 [a]Gen. 15:18; Deut. 11:24; 1 Ki. 4:21,24 [b]Josh. 21:44
32 [a]ch. 34:12,15
33 [a]1 Sam. 18:21; Ps. 106:36
24:1 [a]Lev. 10:1,2 [b]ch. 1:5; Num. 11:16
3 [a]ver. 7; ch. 19:8; Deut. 5:27; Gal. 3:19
4 [a]Deut. 31:9 [b]Gen. 28:18
6 [a]Heb. 9:18
7 [a]Heb. 9:19
8 [a]1 Pet. 1:2
10 [a]John 1:18; 1 John 4:12 [b]Ezek. 1:26; Rev. 4:3 [c]Mat. 17:2
11 [a]ch. 19:21 [b]Gen. 32:30; Judg. 13:22 [c]1 Cor. 10:18
12 [a]ver. 2,15 [b]ch. 32:15
13 [a]ch. 32:17

V ▶ *Ex 23:27* **A** *Ex 23:16* ◀ ▶ *Ex 32:13*
F *Ex 17:5–6* ◀ ▶ *Lev 25:19*
H *Ex 20:12* ◀ ▶ *Dt 7:15*
B *Ge 39:5* ◀ ▶ *Lev 25:19*
V *Ex 23:22* ◀ ▶ *Lev 26:6–8*
D *Ex 12:21–23* ◀ ▶ *Ex 28:38*

14 And he said unto the elders, Tarry ye here for us, until we come again unto you: and, behold, Aaron and Hur *are* with you: if any man have any matters to do, let him come unto them.

15 And Moses went up into the mount, and [a]a cloud covered the mount.

16 And [a]the glory of the LORD abode upon mount Sinai, and the cloud covered it six days: and the seventh day he called unto Moses out of the midst of the cloud.

17 And the sight of the glory of the LORD *was* like [a]devouring fire on the top of the mount in the eyes of the children of Israel.

18 And Moses went into the midst of the cloud, and gat him up into the mount: and [a]Moses was in the mount forty days and forty nights.

Offerings for the tabernacle

25 AND THE LORD spake unto Moses, saying,

2 Speak unto the children of Israel, that they [1]bring me an [2]offering: [a]of every man that giveth it willingly with his heart ye shall take my offering.

3 And this *is* the offering which ye shall take of them; gold, and silver, and brass,

4 And blue, and purple, and scarlet, and [a]fine[1] linen, and goats' *hair,*

5 And rams' skins dyed red, and badgers' skins, and shittim wood,

6 [a]Oil for the light, [b]spices for anointing oil, and for [c]sweet incense,

7 Onyx stones, and stones to be set in the [a]ephod, and in the [b]breastplate.

8 And let them make me a [a]sanctuary; that [b]I may dwell among them.

9 [a]According to all that I show thee, *after* the pattern of the tabernacle, and the pattern of all the instruments thereof, even so shall ye make *it.*

The ark

10 ¶ [a]And they shall make an ark *of* shittim wood: two cubits and a half *shall be* the length thereof, and a cubit and a half the breadth thereof, and a cubit and a half the height thereof.

11 And thou shalt overlay it with pure gold, within and without shalt thou overlay it, and shalt make upon it a crown of gold round about.

12 And thou shalt cast four rings of gold for it, and put *them* in the four corners thereof; and two rings *shall be* in the one side of it, and two rings in the other side of it.

13 And thou shalt make staves *of* shittim wood, and overlay them with gold.

14 And thou shalt put the staves into the rings by the sides of the ark, that the ark may be borne with them.

15 [a]The staves shall be in the rings of the ark: they shall not be taken from it.

16 And thou shalt put into the ark [a]the testimony which I shall give thee.

17 And [a]thou shalt make a mercy seat *of* pure gold: two cubits and a half *shall be* the length thereof, and a cubit and a half the breadth thereof. L

18 And thou shalt make two cherubims *of* gold, *of* beaten work shalt thou make them, in the two ends of the mercy seat.

19 And make one cherub on the one end, and the other cherub on the other end: *even* [1]of the mercy seat shall ye make the cherubims on the two ends thereof.

20 And [a]the cherubims shall stretch forth *their* wings on high, covering the mercy seat with their wings, and their faces *shall look* one to another; toward the mercy seat shall the faces of the cherubims be.

21 [a]And thou shalt put the mercy seat above upon the ark; and [b]in the ark thou shalt put the testimony that I shall give thee.

22 And [a]there I will meet with thee, and I will commune with thee from above the mercy seat, from [b]between the two cherubims which *are* upon the ark of the testimony, of all *things* which I will

L *Ex 20:6* ◀ ▶ *Ex 34:6–7*

15 [a]ch. 19:9; Mat. 17:5
16 [a]ch. 16:10
17 [a]ch. 3:2; Deut. 4:36; Heb. 12:18, 29
18 [a]ch. 34:28; Deut. 9:9
25:2 [a]ch. 35:5,21; 1 Chr. 29:3,5,9,14; Ezra 2:68; Neh. 11:2; 2 Cor. 8:12 & 9:7 [1]Heb. *take for me* [2]Or, *heave offering*
4 [a]Gen. 41:42 [1]Or, *silk*
6 [a]ch. 27:20 [b]ch. 30:23 [c]ch. 30:34
7 [a]ch. 28:4,6 [b]ch. 28:15
8 [a]ch. 36:1,3,4; Lev. 4:6 & 10:4 & 21:12; Heb. 9:1,2 [b]ch. 29:45; 1 Ki. 6:13; 2 Cor. 6:16; Heb. 3:6; Rev. 21:3
9 [a]ver. 40
10 [a]ch. 37:1; Deut. 10:3; Heb. 9:4
15 [a]1 Ki. 8:8
16 [a]ch. 16:34 & 31:18; Deut. 31:26; 1 Ki. 8:9; 2 Ki. 11:12; Heb. 9:4
17 [a]ch. 37:6; Rom. 3:25; Heb. 9:5
19 [1]Or, *of the* matter *of the mercy seat*
20 [a]1 Ki. 8:7; 1 Chr. 28:18; Heb. 9:5
21 [a]ch. 26:34 [b]ver. 16
22 [a]ch. 29:42,43 [b]Num. 7:89; 1 Sam. 4:4; 2 Sam. 6:2; 2 Ki. 19:15; Ps. 80:1; Is. 37:16

25:8 God commanded Moses to have the Israelites make him "a sanctuary" or holy place where he would dwell among them. This sanctuary was to be a sign or token of his presence in their midst. In the wilderness the Israelites lived in tents, so God's sanctuary was also a tent. When the Israelites conquered Canaan and established permanent dwellings, the temple in Jerusalem provided a more permanent place of worship and sacrifice.

give thee in commandment unto the children of Israel.

The table

23 ¶ [a]Thou shalt also make a table *of* shittim wood: two cubits *shall be* the length thereof, and a cubit the breadth thereof, and a cubit and a half the height thereof.

24 And thou shalt overlay it with pure gold, and make thereto a crown of gold round about.

25 And thou shalt make unto it a border of an handbreadth round about, and thou shalt make a golden crown to the border thereof round about.

26 And thou shalt make for it four rings of gold, and put the rings in the four corners that *are* on the four feet thereof.

27 Over against the border shall the rings be for places of the staves to bear the table.

28 And thou shalt make the staves *of* shittim wood, and overlay them with gold, that the table may be borne with them.

29 And thou shalt make [a]the dishes thereof, and spoons thereof, and covers thereof, and bowls thereof, [1]to cover withal: *of* pure gold shalt thou make them.

30 And thou shalt set upon the table [a]showbread before me always.

The candlestick

31 ¶ [a]And thou shalt make a candlestick *of* pure gold: *of* beaten work shall the candlestick be made: his shaft, and his branches, his bowls, his knobs, and his flowers, shall be of the same.

32 And six branches shall come out of the sides of it; three branches of the candlestick out of the one side, and three branches of the candlestick out of the other side:

33 [a]Three bowls made like unto almonds, *with* a knob and a flower in one branch; and three bowls made like almonds in the other branch, *with* a knob and a flower: so in the six branches that come out of the candlestick.

34 And [a]in the candlestick *shall be* four bowls made like unto almonds, *with* their knobs and their flowers.

35 And *there shall be* a knob under two branches of the same, and a knob under two branches of the same, and a knob under two branches of the same, according to the six branches that proceed out of the candlestick.

36 Their knobs and their branches shall be of the same: all it *shall be* one beaten work *of* pure gold.

37 And thou shalt make the seven lamps thereof: and [a]they shall [1]light the lamps thereof, that they may [b]give light over against [2]it.

38 And the tongs thereof, and the snuffdishes thereof, *shall be of* pure gold.

39 *Of* a talent of pure gold shall he make it, with all these vessels.

40 And [a]look that thou make *them* after their pattern, [1]which was shown thee in the mount.

The tabernacle

26 MOREOVER [a]THOU shalt make the tabernacle *with* ten curtains *of* fine twined linen, and blue, and purple, and scarlet: *with* cherubims [1]of cunning work shalt thou make them.

2 The length of one curtain *shall be* eight and twenty cubits, and the breadth of one curtain four cubits: and every one of the curtains shall have one measure.

3 The five curtains shall be coupled together one to another; and *other* five curtains *shall be* coupled one to another.

4 And thou shalt make loops of blue upon the edge of the one curtain from the selvedge in the coupling; and likewise shalt thou make in the uttermost edge of *another* curtain, in the coupling of the second.

5 Fifty loops shalt thou make in the one curtain, and fifty loops shalt thou make in the edge of the curtain that *is* in the coupling of the second; that the loops may take hold one of another.

6 And thou shalt make fifty taches of gold, and couple the curtains together with the taches: and it shall be one tabernacle.

7 ¶ And [a]thou shalt make curtains *of* goats' *hair* to be a covering upon the tabernacle: eleven curtains shalt thou make.

8 The length of one curtain *shall be* thirty cubits, and the breadth of one curtain four cubits: and the eleven curtains *shall be all* of one measure.

9 And thou shalt couple five curtains by themselves, and six curtains by themselves, and shalt double the sixth curtain in the forefront of the tabernacle.

23 [a]ch. 37:10; 1 Ki. 7:48; 2 Chr. 4:8; Heb. 9:2
29 [a]ch. 37:16; Num. 4:7 [1]Or, *to pour out withal*
30 [a]Lev. 24:5,6
31 [a]ch. 37:17; 1 Ki. 7:49; Zech. 4:2; Heb. 9:2; Rev. 1:12
33 [a]ch. 37:19
34 [a]ch. 37:20-22
37 [a]ch. 27:21 & 30:8; Lev. 24:3,4; 2 Chr. 13:11 [b]Num. 8:2 [1]Or, *cause to ascend* [2]Heb. *the face of it*
40 [a]ch. 26:30; Num. 8:4; 1 Chr. 28:11,19; Acts 7:44; Heb. 8:5 [1]Heb. *which thou wast caused to see*
26:1 [a]ch. 36:8 [1]Heb. *the work of a cunning workman, or, embroiderer*
7 [a]ch. 36:14

10 And thou shalt make fifty loops on the edge of the one curtain *that is* outmost in the coupling, and fifty loops in the edge of the curtain which coupleth the second.

11 And thou shalt make fifty taches of brass, and put the taches into the loops, and couple the [l]tent together, that it may be one.

12 And the remnant that remaineth of the curtains of the tent, the half curtain that remaineth, shall hang over the backside of the tabernacle.

13 And a cubit on the one side, and a cubit on the other side [l]of that which remaineth in the length of the curtains of the tent, it shall hang over the sides of the tabernacle on this side and on that side, to cover it.

14 And [a]thou shalt make a covering for the tent *of* rams' skins dyed red, and a covering above *of* badgers' skins.

15 ¶ And thou shalt make boards for the tabernacle *of* shittim wood standing up.

16 Ten cubits *shall be* the length of a board, and a cubit and a half *shall be* the breadth of one board.

17 Two [l]tenons *shall there be* in one board, set in order one against another: thus shalt thou make for all the boards of the tabernacle.

18 And thou shalt make the boards for the tabernacle, twenty boards on the south side southward.

19 And thou shalt make forty sockets of silver under the twenty boards; two sockets under one board for his two tenons, and two sockets under another board for his two tenons.

20 And for the second side of the tabernacle on the north side *there shall be* twenty boards:

21 And their forty sockets *of* silver; two sockets under one board, and two sockets under another board.

22 And for the sides of the tabernacle westward thou shalt make six boards.

23 And two boards shalt thou make for the corners of the tabernacle in the two sides.

24 And they shall be [l]coupled together beneath, and they shall be coupled together above the head of it unto one ring: thus shall it be for them both; they shall be for the two corners.

25 And they shall be eight boards, and their sockets *of* silver, sixteen sockets; two sockets under one board, and two sockets under another board.

26 ¶ And thou shalt make bars *of* shittim wood; five for the boards of the one side of the tabernacle,

27 And five bars for the boards of the other side of the tabernacle, and five bars for the boards of the side of the tabernacle, for the two sides westward.

28 And the middle bar in the midst of the boards shall reach from end to end.

29 And thou shalt overlay the boards with gold, and make their rings *of* gold *for* places for the bars: and thou shalt overlay the bars with gold.

30 And thou shalt rear up the tabernacle [a]according to the fashion thereof which was shown thee in the mount.

31 ¶ And [a]thou shalt make a veil *of* blue, and purple, and scarlet, and fine twined linen of cunning work: with cherubims shall it be made:

32 And thou shalt hang it upon four pillars of shittim *wood* overlaid with gold: their hooks *shall be of* gold, upon the four sockets of silver.

33 ¶ And thou shalt hang up the veil under the taches, that thou mayest bring in thither within the veil [a]the ark of the testimony: and the veil shall divide unto you between [b]the holy *place* and the most holy.

34 And [a]thou shalt put the mercy seat upon the ark of the testimony in the most holy *place.*

35 And [a]thou shalt set the table without the veil, and [b]the candlestick over against the table on the side of the tabernacle toward the south: and thou shalt put the table on the north side.

36 And [a]thou shalt make an hanging for the door of the tent, *of* blue, and purple, and scarlet, and fine twined linen, wrought with needlework.

37 And thou shalt make for the hanging [a]five pillars *of* shittim *wood,* and overlay them with gold, *and* their hooks *shall be of* gold: and thou shalt cast five sockets of brass for them.

The altar

27 AND THOU shalt make [a]an altar *of* shittim wood, five cubits long, and five cubits broad; the altar shall be foursquare: and the height thereof *shall be* three cubits.

- 11 [l]Or, *covering*
- 13 [l]Heb. *in the remainder,* or, *surplusage*
- 14 [a]ch. 36:19
- 17 [l]Heb. *hands*
- 24 [l]Heb. *twinned*
- 30 [a]ch. 25:9,40 & 27:8; Acts 7:44; Heb. 8:5
- 31 [a]ch. 36:35; Lev. 16:2; 2 Chr. 3:14; Mat. 27:51; Heb. 9:3
- 33 [a]ch. 25:16 & 40:21 [b]Lev. 16:2; Heb. 9:2,3
- 34 [a]ch. 25:21 & 40:20; Heb. 9:5
- 35 [a]ch. 40:22; Heb. 9:2 [b]ch. 40:24
- 36 [a]ch. 36:37
- 37 [a]ch. 36:38
- 27:1 [a]ch. 38:1; Ezek. 43:13

2 And thou shalt make the horns of it upon the four corners thereof: his horns shall be of the same: and [a]thou shalt overlay it with brass.

3 And thou shalt make his pans to receive his ashes, and his shovels, and his basins, and his fleshhooks, and his firepans: all the vessels thereof thou shalt make *of* brass.

4 And thou shalt make for it a grate of network *of* brass; and upon the net shalt thou make four brasen rings in the four corners thereof.

5 And thou shalt put it under the compass of the altar beneath, that the net may be even to the midst of the altar.

6 And thou shalt make staves for the altar, staves *of* shittim wood, and overlay them with brass.

7 And the staves shall be put into the rings, and the staves shall be upon the two sides of the altar, to bear it.

8 Hollow with boards shalt thou make it: [a]as [/]it was shown thee in the mount, so shall they make *it.*

The court of the tabernacle

9 ¶ And [a]thou shalt make the court of the tabernacle: for the south side southward *there shall be* hangings for the court *of* fine twined linen of an hundred cubits long for one side:

10 And the twenty pillars thereof and their twenty sockets *shall be of* brass; the hooks of the pillars and their fillets *shall be of* silver.

11 And likewise for the north side in length *there shall be* hangings of an hundred *cubits* long, and his twenty pillars and their twenty sockets *of* brass; the hooks of the pillars and their fillets *of* silver.

12 ¶ And *for* the breadth of the court on the west side *shall be* hangings of fifty cubits: their pillars ten, and their sockets ten.

13 And the breadth of the court on the east side eastward *shall be* fifty cubits.

14 The hangings of one side *of the gate shall be* fifteen cubits: their pillars three, and their sockets three.

15 And on the other side *shall be* hangings fifteen *cubits:* their pillars three, and their sockets three.

16 ¶ And for the gate of the court *shall be* an hanging of twenty cubits, *of* blue, and purple, and scarlet, and fine twined linen, wrought with needlework: *and* their pillars *shall be* four, and their sockets four.

17 All the pillars round about the court *shall be* filleted with silver; their hooks *shall be of* silver, and their sockets *of* brass.

18 ¶ The length of the court *shall be* an hundred cubits, and the breadth [/]fifty every where, and the height five cubits *of* fine twined linen, and their sockets *of* brass.

19 All the vessels of the tabernacle in all the service thereof, and all the pins thereof, and all the pins of the court, *shall be of* brass.

Oil for the lamp

20 ¶ And [a]thou shalt command the children of Israel, that they bring thee pure oil olive beaten for the light, to cause the lamp [/]to burn always.

21 In the tabernacle of the congregation [a]without the veil, which *is* before the testimony, [b]Aaron and his sons shall order it from evening to morning before the LORD: [c]*it shall be* a statute for ever unto their generations on the behalf of the children of Israel.

The priest's garments

28 AND TAKE thou unto thee [a]Aaron thy brother, and his sons with him, from among the children of Israel, that he may minister unto me in the priest's office, *even* Aaron, Nadab and Abihu, Eleazar and Ithamar, Aaron's sons.

2 And [a]thou shalt make holy garments for Aaron thy brother for glory and for beauty.

3 And [a]thou shalt speak unto all *that are* wisehearted, [b]whom I have filled with the spirit of wisdom, that they may make Aaron's garments to consecrate him, that he may minister unto me in the priest's office. B E G T

4 And these *are* the garments which they shall make; [a]a breastplate, and [b]an ephod, and [c]a robe, and [d]a broidered coat, a mitre, and a girdle: and they shall make holy garments for Aaron thy

B *Ge 41:38* ◄► *Ex 31:3*
E *Ge 41:38* ◄► *Ex 31:3*
G *Ge 41:38* ◄► *Ex 31:3*
T *Ge 41:38* ◄► *Ex 31:3*

2 [a]See Num. 16:38
8 [a]ch. 25:40 & 26:30 [/]Heb. *he showed*
9 [a]ch. 38:9
18 [/]Heb. *fifty by fifty*
20 [a]Lev. 24:2 [/]Heb. *to ascend up*
21 [a]ch. 26:31,33 [b]ch. 30:8; 1 Sam. 3:3; 2 Chr. 13:11 [c]ch. 28:43 & 29:9, 28; Lev. 3:17 & 16:34; Num. 18:23 & 19:21
28:1 [a]Num. 18:7; Heb. 5:1,4
2 [a]ch. 29:5,29 & 31:10 & 39:1,2; Lev. 8:7,30; Num. 20:26,28
3 [a]ch. 31:6 & 36:1 [b]ch. 31:3 & 35:30, 31
4 [a]ver. 15 [b]ver. 6 [c]ver. 31 [d]ver. 39

brother, and his sons, that he may minister unto me in the priest's office.

5 And they shall take gold, and blue, and purple, and scarlet, and fine linen.

6 ¶ [a]And they shall make the ephod *of* gold, *of* blue, and *of* purple, *of* scarlet, and fine twined linen, with cunning work.

7 It shall have the two shoulderpieces thereof joined at the two edges thereof; and *so* it shall be joined together.

8 And the [1]curious girdle of the ephod, which *is* upon it, shall be of the same, according to the work thereof; *even of* gold, *of* blue, and purple, and scarlet, and fine twined linen.

9 And thou shalt take two onyx stones, and grave on them the names of the children of Israel:

10 Six of their names on one stone, and *the other* six names of the rest on the other stone, according to their birth.

11 With the work of an engraver in stone, *like* the engravings of a signet, shalt thou engrave the two stones with the names of the children of Israel: thou shalt make them to be set in ouches of gold.

12 And thou shalt put the two stones upon the shoulders of the ephod *for* stones of memorial unto the children of Israel: and [a]Aaron shall bear their names before the LORD upon his two shoulders [b]for a memorial.

13 ¶ And thou shalt make ouches *of* gold;

14 And two chains *of* pure gold at the ends; *of* wreathen work shalt thou make them, and fasten the wreathen chains to the ouches.

The priest's breastplate

15 ¶ And [a]thou shalt make the breastplate of judgment with cunning work; after the work of the ephod thou shalt make it; *of* gold, *of* blue, and *of* purple, and *of* scarlet, and *of* fine twined linen, shalt thou make it.

16 Foursquare it shall be *being* doubled; a span *shall be* the length thereof, and a span *shall be* the breadth thereof.

17 [a]And thou shalt [1]set in it settings of stones, *even* four rows of stones: *the first* row *shall be* a [2]sardius, a topaz, and a carbuncle: *this shall be* the first row.

18 And the second row *shall be* an emerald, a sapphire, and a diamond.

19 And the third row a ligure, an agate, and an amethyst.

20 And the fourth row a beryl, and an onyx, and a jasper: they shall be set in gold in their [1]inclosings.

21 And the stones shall be with the names of the children of Israel, twelve, according to their names, *like* the engravings of a signet; every one with his name shall they be according to the twelve tribes.

22 ¶ And thou shalt make upon the breastplate chains at the ends *of* wreathen work *of* pure gold.

23 And thou shalt make upon the breastplate two rings of gold, and shalt put the two rings on the two ends of the breastplate.

24 And thou shalt put the two wreathen *chains* of gold in the two rings *which are* on the ends of the breastplate.

25 And *the other* two ends of the two wreathen *chains* thou shalt fasten in the two ouches, and put *them* on the shoulderpieces of the ephod before it.

26 ¶ And thou shalt make two rings of gold, and thou shalt put them upon the two ends of the breastplate in the border thereof, which *is* in the side of the ephod inward.

27 And two *other* rings of gold thou shalt make, and shalt put them on the two sides of the ephod underneath, toward the forepart thereof, over against the *other* coupling thereof, above the curious girdle of the ephod.

28 And they shall bind the breastplate by the rings thereof unto the rings of the ephod with a lace of blue, that *it* may be above the curious girdle of the ephod, and that the breastplate be not loosed from the ephod.

29 And Aaron shall bear the names of the children of Israel in the breastplate of judgment upon his heart, when he goeth in unto the holy *place,* [a]for a memorial before the LORD continually.

30 ¶ And [a]thou shalt put in the breastplate of judgment the Urim and the Thummim; and they shall be upon Aaron's heart, when he goeth in before the LORD: and Aaron shall bear the judgment of the children of Israel upon his heart before the LORD continually.

---

6 [a]ch. 39:2
8 [1]Or, *embroidered*
12 [a]ver. 29; ch. 39:7 [b]See Josh. 4:7; Zech. 6:14
15 [a]ch. 39:8
17 [a]ch. 39:10 [1]Heb. *fill in it fillings of stone* [2]Or, *ruby*
20 [1]Heb. *fillings*
29 [a]ver. 12
30 [a]Lev. 8:8; Num. 27:21; Deut. 33:8; 1 Sam. 28:6; Ezra 2:63; Neh. 7:65

The priest's robe

31 ¶ And [a]thou shalt make the robe of the ephod all *of* blue.

32 And there shall be an hole in the top of it, in the midst thereof: it shall have a binding of woven work round about the hole of it, as it were the hole of an habergeon, that it be not rent.

33 ¶ And *beneath* upon the [1]hem of it thou shalt make pomegranates *of* blue, and *of* purple, and *of* scarlet, round about the hem thereof; and bells of gold between them round about:

34 A golden bell and a pomegranate, a golden bell and a pomegranate, upon the hem of the robe round about.

35 And it shall be upon Aaron to minister: and his sound shall be heard when he goeth in unto the holy *place* before the LORD, and when he cometh out, that he die not.

36 ¶ And [a]thou shalt make a plate *of* pure gold, and grave upon it, *like* the engravings of a signet, HOLINESS TO THE LORD.

37 And thou shalt put it on a blue lace, that it may be upon the mitre; upon the forefront of the mitre it shall be.

D 38 And it shall be upon Aaron's forehead, that Aaron may [a]bear the iniquity of the holy things, which the children of Israel shall hallow in all their holy gifts; and it shall be always upon his forehead, that they may be [b]accepted before the LORD.

39 ¶ And thou shalt embroider the coat of fine linen, and thou shalt make the mitre *of* fine linen, and thou shalt make the girdle *of* needlework.

40 ¶ [a]And for Aaron's sons thou shalt make coats, and thou shalt make for them girdles, and bonnets shalt thou make for them, for glory and for beauty.

41 And thou shalt put them upon Aaron thy brother, and his sons with him; and shalt [a]anoint them, and [b]consecrate[1] them, and sanctify them, that they may minister unto me in the priest's office.

42 And thou shalt make them [a]linen breeches to cover [1]their nakedness; from the loins even unto the thighs they shall [2]reach:

43 And they shall be upon Aaron, and upon his sons, when they come in unto the tabernacle of the congregation, or when they come near [a]unto the altar to minister in the holy *place;* that they [b]bear not iniquity, and die: [c]*it shall be* a statute for ever unto him and his seed after him.

Consecrating the priests

29 AND THIS *is* the thing that thou shalt do unto them to hallow them, to minister unto me in the priest's office: [a]Take one young bullock, and two rams without blemish,

2 And [a]unleavened bread, and cakes unleavened tempered with oil, and wafers unleavened anointed with oil: *of* wheaten flour shalt thou make them.

3 And thou shalt put them into one basket, and bring them in the basket, with the bullock and the two rams.

4 And Aaron and his sons thou shalt bring unto the door of the tabernacle of the congregation, [a]and shalt wash them with water.

5 [a]And thou shalt take the garments, and put upon Aaron the coat, and the robe of the ephod, and the ephod, and the breastplate, and gird him with [b]the curious girdle of the ephod:

6 [a]And thou shalt put the mitre upon his head, and put the holy crown upon the mitre.

7 Then shalt thou take the anointing [a]oil, and pour *it* upon his head, and anoint him.

8 And [a]thou shalt bring his sons, and put coats upon them.

9 And thou shalt gird them with girdles, Aaron and his sons, and [1]put the bonnets on them: and [a]the priest's office shall be theirs for a perpetual statute: and thou shalt [b]consecrate[2] Aaron and his sons.

10 And thou shalt cause a bullock to be brought before the tabernacle of the congregation: and [a]Aaron and his sons shall put their hands upon the head of the bullock.

11 And thou shalt kill the bullock before the LORD, *by* the door of the tabernacle of the congregation.

12 And thou [a]shalt take of the blood of the bullock, and put *it* upon [b]the horns of the altar with thy finger, and pour all the blood beside the bottom of the altar.

13 And [a]thou shalt take all the fat that covereth the inwards, and [1]the caul *that*

---

31 [a]ch. 39:22
33 [1]Or, *skirts*
36 [a]ch. 39:30; Zech. 14:20
38 [a]ver. 43; Lev. 10:17 & 22:9; Num. 18:1; Is. 53:11; Ezek. 4:4-6; John 1:29; Heb. 9:28; 1 Pet. 2:24 [b]Lev. 1:4 & 22:27; Is. 56:7
40 [a]ver. 4; ch. 39:27-29,41; Ezek. 44:17,18
41 [a]ch. 29:7 & 30:30 & 40:15; Lev. 10:7 [b]ch. 29:9; Lev. 8; Heb. 7:28 [1]Heb. *fill their hand*
42 [a]ch. 39:28; Lev. 6:10 & 16:4; Ezek. 44:18 [1]Heb. *flesh of their nakedness* [2]Heb. *be*
43 [a]ch. 20:26 [b]Lev. 5:1,17 & 20:19,20 & 22:9; Num. 9:13 & 18:22 [c]ch. 27:21; Lev. 17:7
29:1 [a]Lev. 8:2
2 [a]Lev. 2:4 & 6:20-22
4 [a]ch. 40:12; Lev. 8:6; Heb. 10:22
5 [a]ch. 28:2; Lev. 8:7 [b]ch. 28:8
6 [a]Lev. 8:9
7 [a]ch. 30:25; Lev. 8:12 & 10:7 & 21:10; Num. 35:25
8 [a]Lev. 8:13
9 [a]Num. 18:7 [b]ch. 28:41; Lev. 8:22; Heb. 7:28 [1]Heb. *bind* [2]Heb. *fill the hand of*
10 [a]Lev. 1:4 & 8:14
12 [a]Lev. 8:15 [b]ch. 27:2
13 [a]Lev. 3:3 [1]It seemeth by anatomy, and the Hebrew doctors, to be *the midriff*

D *Ex 24:5–8* ◀▶ *Ex 29:14*

is above the liver, and the two kidneys, and the fat that *is* upon them, and burn *them* upon the altar.

D 14 But [a]the flesh of the bullock, and his skin, and his dung, shalt thou burn with fire without the camp: it *is* a sin offering.

15 ¶ [a]Thou shalt also take one ram; and Aaron and his sons shall [b]put their hands upon the head of the ram.

16 And thou shalt slay the ram, and thou shalt take his blood, and sprinkle *it* round about upon the altar.

17 And thou shalt cut the ram in pieces, and wash the inwards of him, and his legs, and put *them* unto his pieces, and [l]unto his head.

18 And thou shalt burn the whole ram upon the altar: it *is* a burnt offering unto the LORD: it *is* a [a]sweet savour, an offering made by fire unto the LORD.

19 ¶ [a]And thou shalt take the other ram; and Aaron and his sons shall put their hands upon the head of the ram.

20 Then shalt thou kill the ram, and take of his blood, and put *it* upon the tip of the right ear of Aaron, and upon the tip of the right ear of his sons, and upon the thumb of their right hand, and upon the great toe of their right foot, and sprinkle the blood upon the altar round about.

21 And thou shalt take of the blood that *is* upon the altar, and of [a]the anointing oil, and sprinkle *it* upon Aaron, and upon his garments, and upon his sons, and upon the garments of his sons with him: and [b]he shall be hallowed, and his garments, and his sons, and his sons' garments with him.

22 Also thou shalt take of the ram the fat and the rump, and the fat that covereth the inwards, and the caul *above* the liver, and the two kidneys, and the fat that *is* upon them, and the right shoulder; for it *is* a ram of consecration:

23 [a]And one loaf of bread, and one cake of oiled bread, and one wafer out of the basket of the unleavened bread that *is* before the LORD:

24 And thou shalt put all in the hands of Aaron, and in the hands of his sons; and shalt [a]wave[l] them *for* a wave offering before the LORD.

25 [a]And thou shalt receive them of their hands, and burn *them* upon the altar for a burnt offering, for a sweet savour before the LORD: it *is* an offering made by fire unto the LORD.

26 And thou shalt take [a]the breast of the ram of Aaron's consecration, and wave it *for* a wave offering before the LORD: and [b]it shall be thy part.

27 And thou shalt sanctify [a]the breast of the wave offering, and the shoulder of the heave offering, which is waved, and which is heaved up, of the ram of the consecration, *even* of *that* which *is* for Aaron, and of *that* which is for his sons:

28 And it shall be Aaron's and his sons' [a]by a statute for ever from the children of Israel: for it *is* an heave offering: and [b]it shall be an heave offering from the children of Israel of the sacrifice of their peace offerings, *even* their heave offering unto the LORD.

29 ¶ And the holy garments of Aaron [a]shall be his sons' after him, [b]to be anointed therein, and to be consecrated in them.

30 *And* [a]that[l] son that is priest in his stead shall put them on [b]seven days, when he cometh into the tabernacle of the congregation to minister in the holy *place.*

31 ¶ And thou shalt take the ram of the consecration, and [a]seethe his flesh in the holy place.

32 And Aaron and his sons shall eat the flesh of the ram, and the [a]bread that *is* in the basket, *by* the door of the tabernacle of the congregation.

33 And [a]they shall eat those things wherewith the atonement was made, to consecrate *and* to sanctify them: [b]but a stranger shall not eat *thereof,* because they *are* holy.

34 And if aught of the flesh of the consecrations, or of the bread, remain unto the morning, then [a]thou shalt burn the remainder with fire: it shall not be eaten, because it *is* holy.

35 And thus shalt thou do unto Aaron, and to his sons, according to all *things* which I have commanded thee: [a]seven days shalt thou consecrate them.

36 And thou shalt [a]offer every day a bullock *for* a sin offering for atonement: and thou shalt cleanse the altar, when thou hast made an atonement for it, [b]and thou shalt anoint it, to sanctify it. D

14 [a]Lev. 4:11,12, 21; Heb. 13:11
15 [a]Lev. 8:18 [b]Lev. 1:4-9
17 [l]Or, *upon*
18 [a]Gen. 8:21
19 [a]ver. 3; Lev. 8:22
21 [a]ch. 30:25,31 [b]ver. 1; Heb. 9:22
23 [a]Lev. 8:26
24 [a]Lev. 7:30 [l]Or, *shake to and fro*
25 [a]Lev. 8:28
26 [a]Lev. 8:29 [b]Lev. 7:33
27 [a]Lev. 7:31,34; Num. 18:11,18; Deut. 18:3
28 [a]Lev. 10:15 [b]Lev. 7:34
29 [a]Num. 20:26, 28 [b]Num. 18:8
30 [a]Num. 20:28 [b]Lev. 8:35 & 9:1,8 [l]Heb. he *of his sons*
31 [a]Lev. 8:31
32 [a]Mat. 12:4
33 [a]Lev. 10:14,15, 17 [b]Lev. 22:10
34 [a]Lev. 7:18 & 8:32
35 [a]Lev. 8:33-35
36 [a]Heb. 10:11 [b]ch. 40:10

D *Ex 28:38* ◀▶ *Ex 29:36–42*

D *Ex 29:14* ◀▶ *Ex 30:10*

37 Seven days thou shalt make an atonement for the altar, and sanctify it; [a]and it shall be an altar most holy: [b]whatsoever toucheth the altar shall be holy.

38 ¶ Now this *is that* which thou shalt offer upon the altar; [a]two lambs of the first year [b]day by day continually.

39 The one lamb thou shalt offer [a]in the morning; and the other lamb thou shalt offer at even:

40 And with the one lamb a tenth deal of flour mingled with the fourth part of an hin of beaten oil; and the fourth part of an hin of wine *for* a drink offering.

41 And the other lamb thou shalt [a]offer at even, and shalt do thereto according to the meat offering of the morning, and according to the drink offering thereof, for a sweet savour, an offering made by fire unto the LORD.

42 *This shall be* [a]a continual burnt offering throughout your generations *at* the door of the tabernacle of the congregation before the LORD: [b]where I will meet you, to speak there unto thee.

43 And there I will meet with the children of Israel, and [1]*the tabernacle* [a]shall be sanctified by my glory.

44 And I will sanctify the tabernacle of the congregation, and the altar: I will [a]sanctify also both Aaron and his sons, to minister to me in the priest's office.

45 ¶ And [a]I will dwell among the children of Israel, and will be their God.

46 And they shall know that [a]I *am* the LORD their God, that brought them forth out of the land of Egypt, that I may dwell among them: I *am* the LORD their God.

The altar of incense

30 AND THOU shalt make [a]an altar [b]to burn incense upon: *of* shittim wood shalt thou make it.

2 A cubit *shall be* the length thereof, and a cubit the breadth thereof; foursquare shall it be: and two cubits *shall be* the height thereof: the horns thereof *shall be* of the same.

3 And thou shalt overlay it with pure gold, the [1]top thereof, and the [2]sides thereof round about, and the horns thereof; and thou shalt make unto it a crown of gold round about.

4 And two golden rings shalt thou make to it under the crown of it, by the two [1]corners thereof, upon the two sides of it shalt thou make *it;* and they shall be for places for the staves to bear it withal.

5 And thou shalt make the staves *of* shittim wood, and overlay them with gold.

6 And thou shalt put it before the veil that *is* by the ark of the testimony, before the [a]mercy seat that *is* over the testimony, where I will meet with thee.

7 And Aaron shall burn thereon [a]sweet[1] incense every morning: when [b]he dresseth the lamps, he shall burn incense upon it.

8 And when Aaron [1]lighteth the lamps [2]at even, he shall burn incense upon it, a perpetual incense before the LORD throughout your generations.

9 Ye shall offer no [a]strange incense thereon, nor burnt sacrifice, nor meat offering; neither shall ye pour drink offering thereon.

10 And [a]Aaron shall make an atonement upon the horns of it once in a year with the blood of the sin offering of atonements: once in the year shall he make atonement upon it throughout your generations: it *is* most holy unto the LORD. **D**

The offerings for the tabernacle

11 ¶ And the LORD spake unto Moses, saying,

12 [a]When thou takest the sum of the children of Israel after [1]their number, then shall they give every man [b]a ransom for his soul unto the LORD, when thou numberest them; that there be no [c]plague among them, when *thou* numberest them.

13 [a]This they shall give, every one that passeth among them that are numbered, half a shekel after the shekel of the sanctuary: ([b]a shekel *is* twenty gerahs:) [c]an half shekel *shall be* the offering of the LORD.

14 Every one that passeth among them that are numbered, from twenty years old and above, shall give an offering unto the LORD.

15 The [a]rich shall not [1]give more, and the poor shall not [2]give less than half a shekel, when *they* give an offering unto the LORD, to make an atonement for your souls.

16 And thou shalt take the atonement money of the children of Israel, and [a]shalt appoint it for the service of the tab-

37 [a]ch. 40:10 [b]Mat. 23:19
38 [a]Num. 28:3; 1 Chr. 16:40; Ezra 3:3 [b]See Dan. 12:11
39 [a]Ezek. 46:13-15
41 [a]1 Ki. 18:29,36; 2 Ki. 16:15; Ezra 9:4,5; Ps. 141:2
42 [a]ch. 30:8 [b]ch. 25:22
43 [a]1 Ki. 8:11; 2 Chr. 5:14; Ezek. 43:5; Hag. 2:7,9 [1]Or, Israel
44 [a]Lev. 21:15
45 [a]Ex. 25:8; Lev. 26:12; Zech. 2:10; John 14:17,23; Rev. 21:3
46 [a]ch. 20:2
30:1 [a]ch. 37:25 [b]See ver. 7,8,10; Rev. 8:3
3 [1]Heb. *roof* [2]Heb. *walls*
4 [1]Heb. *ribs*
6 [a]ch. 25:21,22
7 [a]ver. 34; 1 Sam. 2:28; 1 Chr. 23:13; Luke 1:9 [b]ch. 27:21 [1]Heb. *incense of spices*
8 [1]Or, *setteth up* Heb. *causeth to ascend* [2]Heb. *between the two evens*
9 [a]Lev. 10:1
10 [a]Lev. 16:18
12 [a]2 Sam. 24:2 [b]See Num. 31:50; Mat. 20:28; 1 Pet. 1:18,19 [c]2 Sam. 24:15 [1]Heb. *them that are to be numbered*
13 [a]Mat. 17:24 [b]Num. 3:47 [c]ch. 38:26
15 [a]Prov. 22:2; Eph. 6:9 [1]Heb. *multiply* [2]Heb. *diminish*
16 [a]ch. 38:25

D *Ex 29:36–42* ◄► *Lev 1:1–4*

ernacle of the congregation; that it may
be [b]a memorial unto the children of Israel
before the LORD, to make an atonement
for your souls.

The laver, oil and perfume

17 ¶ And the LORD spake unto Moses,
saying,
18 [a]Thou shalt also make a laver *of*
brass, and his foot *also of* brass, to wash
withal: and thou shalt [b]put it between the
tabernacle of the congregation and the altar, and thou shalt put water therein.
19 For Aaron and his sons [a]shall wash
their hands and their feet thereat:
20 When they go into the tabernacle of
the congregation, they shall wash with
water, that they die not; or when they
come near to the altar to minister, to
burn offering made by fire unto the LORD:
21 So they shall wash their hands and
their feet, that they die not: and [a]it shall
be a statute for ever to them, *even* to him
and to his seed throughout their generations.
22 ¶ Moreover the LORD spake unto
Moses, saying,
23 Take thou also unto thee [a]principal
spices, of pure [b]myrrh five hundred *shekels,* and of sweet cinnamon half so much,
even two hundred and fifty *shekels,* and
of sweet [c]calamus two hundred and fifty
shekels,
24 And of [a]cassia five hundred *shekels,* after the shekel of the sanctuary, and
of oil olive an [b]hin:
S 25 And thou shalt make it an oil of
holy ointment, an ointment compound after the art of the [1]apothecary: it shall be
[a]an holy anointing oil.
26 [a]And thou shalt anoint the tabernacle of the congregation therewith, and
the ark of the testimony,
27 And the table and all his vessels,
and the candlestick and his vessels, and
the altar of incense,
28 And the altar of burnt offering with
all his vessels, and the laver and his foot.
29 And thou shalt sanctify them, that

S ► *Lev 8:12*

16 [b]Num. 16:40
18 [a]ch. 38:8; 1 Ki. 7:38 [b]ch. 40:30
19 [a]ch. 40:31,32; Ps. 26:6; Is. 52:11; John 13:10; Heb. 10:22
21 [a]ch. 28:43
23 [a]Sol. 4:14; Ezek. 27:22 [b]Ps. 45:8; Prov. 7:17 [c]Sol. 4:14; Jer. 6:20
24 [a]Ps. 45:8 [b]ch. 29:40
25 [a]ch. 37:29; Num. 35:25; Ps. 89:20 & 133:2 [1]Or, *perfumer*
26 [a]ch. 40:9; Lev. 8:10; Num. 7:1
29 [a]ch. 29:37
30 [a]ch. 29:7; Lev. 8:12,30
32 [a]ver. 25,37
33 [a]ver. 38 [b]Gen. 17:14; ch. 12:15; Lev. 7:20,21
34 [a]ch. 25:6 & 37:29
35 [a]ver. 25 [1]Heb. *salted*
36 [a]ch. 29:42; Lev. 16:2 [b]ver. 32; ch. 29:37; Lev. 2:3
37 [a]ver. 32
38 [a]ver. 33
31:2 [a]ch. 35:30 & 36:1 [b]1 Chr. 2:20
3 [a]ch. 35:31; 1 Ki. 7:14

they may be most holy: [a]whatsoever
toucheth them shall be holy.
30 [a]And thou shalt anoint Aaron and
his sons, and consecrate them, that *they*
may minister unto me in the priest's
office.
31 And thou shalt speak unto the children of Israel, saying, This shall be an
holy anointing oil unto me throughout
your generations.
32 Upon man's flesh shall it not be
poured, neither shall ye make *any other*
like it, after the composition of it: [a]it *is*
holy, *and* it shall be holy unto you.
33 [a]Whosoever compoundeth *any* like
it, or whosoever putteth *any* of it upon a
stranger, [b]shall even be cut off from his
people.
34 ¶ And the LORD said unto Moses,
[a]Take unto thee sweet spices, stacte, and
onycha, and galbanum; *these* sweet
spices with pure frankincense: of each
shall there be a like *weight:*
35 And thou shalt make it a perfume, a
confection [a]after the art of the apothecary, [1]tempered together, pure *and* holy:
36 And thou shalt beat *some* of it very
small, and put of it before the testimony
in the tabernacle of the congregation,
[a]where I will meet with thee: [b]it shall be
unto you most holy.
37 And *as for* the perfume which thou
shalt make, [a]ye shall not make to yourselves according to the composition
thereof: it shall be unto thee holy for the
LORD.
38 [a]Whosoever shall make like unto
that, to smell thereto, shall even be cut
off from his people.

The appointment of the workmen

31 AND THE LORD spake unto Moses, saying,
2 [a]See, I have called by name Bezaleel
the [b]son of Uri, the son of Hur, of the
tribe of Judah:
3 And I have [a]filled him with the spirit B E G T

B *Ex 28:3* ◄ ► *Ex 35:31*
E *Ex 28:3* ◄ ► *Ex 35:31*
G *Ex 28:3* ◄ ► *Ex 35:31*
T *Ex 28:3* ◄ ► *Ex 35:31*

30:25 Moses recorded God's command to create the "holy anointing oil" to anoint the tabernacle, its furnishings, the ark of the covenant and the priests. Scripture also records that Solomon was anointed with this oil (see 1Ki 1:39). In addition, Daniel prophesied that this oil will be used "to anoint the most Holy" (Da 9:24) in the millennial temple at the conclusion of the seventy weeks.

of God, in wisdom, and in understanding,
and in knowledge, and in all manner of
workmanship,
4 To devise cunning works, to work in
gold, and in silver, and in brass,
5 And in cutting of stones, to set *them,*
and in carving of timber, to work in all
manner of workmanship.
6 And I, behold, I have given with him
[a]Aholiab, the son of Ahisamach, of the
tribe of Dan: and in the hearts of all that
are [b]wisehearted I have put wisdom, that
they may make all that I have commanded thee;
7 [a]The tabernacle of the congregation,
and [b]the ark of the testimony, and [c]the
mercy seat that *is* thereupon, and all the
[l]furniture of the tabernacle,
8 And [a]the table and his furniture, and
[b]the pure candlestick with all his furniture, and the altar of incense,
9 And [a]the altar of burnt offering with
all his furniture, and [b]the laver and his
foot,
10 And [a]the cloths of service, and the
holy garments for Aaron the priest, and
the garments of his sons, to minister in
the priest's office,
11 [a]And the anointing oil, and [b]sweet
incense for the holy *place:* according to
all that I have commanded thee shall
they do.

The Sabbath

12 ¶ And the LORD spake unto Moses,
saying,
13 Speak thou also unto the children
of Israel, saying, [a]Verily my sabbaths ye
shall keep: for it *is* a sign between me
and you throughout your generations;
that *ye* may know that I *am* the LORD that
doth sanctify you.
14 [a]Ye shall keep the sabbath therefore; for it *is* holy unto you: every one
that defileth it shall surely be put to
death: for [b]whosoever doeth *any* work
therein, that soul shall be cut off from
among his people.
15 [a]Six days may work be done; but in
the [b]seventh *is* the sabbath of rest, [l]holy

6 [a]ch. 35:34 [b]ch. 28:3 & 35:10,35 & 36:1
7 [a]ch. 36:8 [b]ch. 37:1 [c]ch. 37:6 [l]Heb. *vessels*
8 [a]ch. 37:10 [b]ch. 37:17
9 [a]ch. 38:1 [b]ch. 38:8
10 [a]ch. 39:1,41; Num. 4:5,6
11 [a]ch. 30:25,31 [b]ch. 30:34
13 [a]Lev. 19:3,30; & 26:2; Ezek. 20:12,20
14 [a]ch. 20:8; Deut. 5:12 [b]Num. 15:35
15 [a]ch. 20:9 [b]Gen. 2:2 [l]Heb. *holiness*
17 [a]ver. 13 [b]Gen. 2:2
18 [a]ch. 32:15; Deut. 4:13 & 5:22; 2 Cor. 3:3
32:1 [a]ch. 24:18; Deut. 9:9 [b]Acts 7:40 [c]ch. 13:21
2 [a]Judg. 8:24-27
4 [a]ch. 20:23; Deut. 9:16; Judg. 17:3,4; 1 Ki. 12:28; Neh. 9:18; Ps. 106:19; Acts 7:41
5 [a]Lev. 23:2,4,21, 37; 2 Ki. 10:20; 2 Chr. 30:5
6 [a]1 Cor. 10:7

to the LORD: whosoever doeth *any* work
in the sabbath day, he shall surely be put
to death.
16 Wherefore the children of Israel
shall keep the sabbath, to observe the
sabbath throughout their generations, *for*
a perpetual covenant.
17 It *is* [a]a sign between me and the
children of Israel for ever: for [b]*in* six days
the LORD made heaven and earth, and on
the seventh day he rested, and was refreshed.
18 ¶ And he gave unto Moses, when
he had made an end of communing with
him upon mount Sinai, [a]two tables of testimony, tables of stone, written with the
finger of God.

The golden calf

32 AND WHEN the people saw that
Moses [a]delayed to come down
out of the mount, the people gathered
themselves together unto Aaron, and said
unto him, [b]Up, make us gods, which shall
[c]go before us; for *as for* this Moses, the
man that brought us up out of the land of
Egypt, we wot not what is become of
him.
2 And Aaron said unto them, Break off
the [a]golden earrings, which *are* in the
ears of your wives, of your sons, and of
your daughters, and bring *them* unto me.
3 And all the people brake off the
golden earrings which *were* in their ears,
and brought *them* unto Aaron.
4 [a]And he received *them* at their hand,
and fashioned it with a graving tool, after
he had made it a molten calf: and they
said, These *be* thy gods, O Israel, which
brought thee up out of the land of Egypt.
5 And when Aaron saw *it,* he built an
altar before it; and Aaron made [a]procla-
mation, and said, Tomorrow *is* a feast to
the LORD.
6 And they rose up early on the morrow, and offered burnt offerings, and
brought peace offerings; and the [a]people
sat down to eat and to drink, and rose up
to play.
7 ¶ And the LORD said unto Moses,

31:13 The Lord established the perpetual observance of the Sabbath to signify God's relationship with Israel as his sanctified people. This was time set aside to rest and remember what God had done for them. Some scholars who subscribe to the view that a "day" in Scripture is actually equivalent to 1,000 years (see Ps 90:4; 2Pe 3:8) suggest that the Sabbath day of rest prefigures the final millennial rest mentioned in the NT (see Rev 20:6–7).

[a]Go, get thee down; for thy people,
which thou broughtest out of the land of
Egypt, [b]have corrupted *themselves:*
8 They have turned aside quickly out
of the way which [a]I commanded them:
they have made them a molten calf, and
have worshipped it, and have sacrificed
thereunto, and said, [b]These *be* thy gods,
O Israel, which have brought thee up out
of the land of Egypt.
M 9 And the LORD said unto Moses, [a]I
have seen this people, and, behold, it *is* a
stiffnecked people:
10 Now therefore [a]let me alone, that
[b]my wrath may wax hot against them,
and that I may consume them: and [c]I will
make of thee a great nation.
11 [a]And Moses besought [1]the LORD his
God, and said, LORD, why doth thy wrath
wax hot against thy people, which thou
hast brought forth out of the land of Egypt
with great power, and with a mighty
hand?
12 [a]Wherefore should the Egyptians
speak, and say, For mischief did he bring
them out, to slay them in the mountains,
and to consume them from the face of the
earth? Turn from thy fierce wrath, and
[b]repent of this evil against thy people.
A 13 Remember Abraham, Isaac, and Is-
I rael, thy servants, to whom thou [a]swarest
by thine own self, and saidst unto them,
[b]I will multiply your seed as the stars of
heaven, and all this land that I have spoken of will I give unto your seed, and
they shall inherit *it* for ever.
14 And the LORD [a]repented of the evil
which he thought to do unto his people.
15 ¶ And [a]Moses turned, and went
down from the mount, and the two tables
of the testimony *were* in his hand: the
tables *were* written on both their sides;
on the one side and on the other *were*
they written.
16 And the [a]tables *were* the work of
God, and the writing *was* the writing of
God, graven upon the tables.
17 And when Joshua heard the noise
of the people as they shouted, he said
unto Moses, *There is* a noise of war in the
camp.
18 And he said, *It is* not the voice of
them that shout for mastery, neither *is it*
the voice of *them that* cry for [1]being overcome: *but* the noise of *them that* sing do I
hear.
19 ¶ And it came to pass, as soon as he
came nigh unto the camp, that [a]he saw
the calf, and the dancing: and Moses' anger waxed hot, and he cast the tables out
of his hands, and brake them beneath the
mount.
20 [a]And he took the calf which they
had made, and burnt *it* in the fire, and
ground *it* to powder, and strawed *it* upon
the water, and made the children of Israel drink *of it.*
21 And Moses said unto Aaron, [a]What
did this people unto thee, that thou hast
brought so great a sin upon them?
22 And Aaron said, Let not the anger
of my lord wax hot: [a]thou knowest the
people, that they *are set* on mischief.
23 For they said unto me, Make us
gods, which shall go before us: for *as for*
this Moses, the man that brought us up
out of the land of Egypt, we wot not what
is become of him.
24 And I said unto them, Whosoever
hath any gold, let them break *it* off. So
they gave *it* me: then I cast it into the
fire, and there came out this calf.
25 ¶ And when Moses saw that the
people *were* [a]naked; (for Aaron [b]had
made them naked unto *their* shame
among [1]their enemies:)
26 Then Moses stood in the gate of the
camp, and said, Who *is* on the LORD'S
side? *let him come* unto me. And all the
sons of Levi gathered themselves together unto him.
27 And he said unto them, Thus saith
the LORD God of Israel, Put every man his
sword by his side, *and* go in and out from
gate to gate throughout the camp, and
[a]slay every man his brother, and every
man his companion, and every man his
neighbour.
28 And the children of Levi did according to the word of Moses: and there fell of
the people that day about three thousand
men.

7 [a]Deut. 9:12; Dan. 9:24 [b]Gen. 6:11,12
8 [a]ch. 20:3,4,23 [b]1 Ki. 12:28
9 [a]2 Chr. 30:8; Is. 48:4; Acts 7:51
10 [a]Deut. 9:14,19 [b]ch. 22:24 [c]Num. 14:12
11 [a]Deut. 9:18, 26-29 [1]Heb. *the face of the LORD*
12 [a]Num. 14:13 [b]ver. 14
13 [a]Gen. 22:16; Heb. 6:13 [b]Gen. 12:7 & 13:15 & 15:7,18 & 26:4 & 35:11,12
14 [a]2 Sam. 24:16
15 [a]Deut. 9:15
16 [a]ch. 31:18
18 [1]Heb. *weakness*
19 [a]Deut. 9:16,17
20 [a]Deut. 9:21
21 [a]Gen. 26:10
22 [a]ch. 14:11
25 [a]ch. 33:4,5 [b]2 Chr. 28:19 [1]Heb. *those that rose up against them*
27 [a]Num. 25:5

M ▶ *Lev 26:40–42*
A *Ex 23:25–31* ◀ ▶ *Ex 34:10–12*
I *Ex 12:41* ◀ ▶ *Lev 26:44–45*

32:13 In this verse Moses appeals to God's mercy reminding him of his promise to the patriarchs that he would increase their offspring "as the stars of heaven" and give them the promised land.

29 [a]For[1] Moses had said, [2]Consecrate yourselves today to the LORD, even every man upon his son, and upon his brother; that he may bestow upon you a blessing this day.

30 ¶ And it came to pass on the morrow, that Moses said unto the people, [a]Ye have sinned a great sin: and now I will go up unto the LORD; [b]peradventure I shall [c]make an atonement for your sin.

31 And Moses [a]returned unto the LORD, and said, Oh, this people have sinned a great sin, and have [b]made them gods of gold.

32 Yet now, if thou wilt forgive their sin—; and if not, [a]blot me, I pray thee, [b]out of thy book which thou hast written.

H S 33 And the LORD said unto Moses, [a]Whosoever hath sinned against me, him will I blot out of my book.

34 Therefore now go, lead the people unto *the place* of which I have spoken unto thee: [a]behold, mine Angel shall go before thee: nevertheless [b]in the day when I visit I will visit their sin upon them.

D 35 And the LORD plagued the people, because [a]they made the calf, which Aaron made.

The renewal of the covenant

33 AND THE LORD said unto Moses, Depart, *and* go up hence, thou [a]and the people which thou hast brought up out of the land of Egypt, unto the land which I sware unto Abraham, to Isaac, and to Jacob, saying, [b]Unto thy seed will I give it:

2 [a]And I will send an angel before thee; [b]and I will drive out the Canaanite, the Amorite, and the Hittite, and the Perizzite, the Hivite, and the Jebusite:

3 [a]Unto a land flowing with milk and honey: for I will not go up in the midst of thee; for thou *art* a [b]stiffnecked people: lest [c]I consume thee in the way.

4 ¶ And when the people heard these evil tidings, [a]they mourned: [b]and no man did put on him his ornaments.

5 For the LORD had said unto Moses, Say unto the children of Israel, Ye *are* a stiffnecked people: I will come up [a]into the midst of thee in a moment, and consume thee: therefore now put off thy ornaments from thee, that I may [b]know what to do unto thee.

6 And the children of Israel stripped themselves of their ornaments by the mount Horeb.

7 And Moses took the tabernacle, and pitched it without the camp, afar off from the camp, [a]and called it the Tabernacle of the congregation. And it came to pass, *that* every one which [b]sought the LORD went out unto the tabernacle of the congregation, which *was* without the camp.

8 And it came to pass, when Moses went out unto the tabernacle, *that* all the people rose up, and stood every man [a]*at* his tent door, and looked after Moses, until he was gone into the tabernacle.

9 And it came to pass, as Moses entered into the tabernacle, the cloudy pillar descended, and stood *at* the door of the tabernacle, and *the LORD* [a]*talked with Moses.*

10 And all the people saw the cloudy pillar stand *at* the tabernacle door: and all the people rose up and [a]worshipped, every man *in* his tent door.

11 And [a]the LORD spake unto Moses face to face, as a man speaketh unto his friend. And he turned again into the camp: but [b]his servant Joshua, the son of Nun, a young man, departed not out of the tabernacle.

12 ¶ And Moses said unto the LORD, See, [a]thou sayest unto me, Bring up this people: and thou hast not let me know whom thou wilt send with me. Yet thou hast said, [b]I know thee by name, and thou hast also found grace in my sight. L

13 Now therefore, I pray thee, [a]if I have found grace in thy sight, [b]show me now thy way, that I may know thee, that I may find grace in thy sight: and consider that this nation *is* [c]thy people.

14 And he said, [a]My presence shall go *with thee,* and I will give thee [b]rest.

29 [a]1 Sam. 15:18, 22; Prov. 21:3; Zech. 13:3 [1]*Or, And Moses said, Consecrate yourselves today to the LORD, because every man* hath been *against his son, and against his brother* [2]Heb. *Fill your hands*
30 [a]1 Sam. 12:20, 23 [b]2 Sam. 16:12 [c]Num. 25:13
31 [a]Deut. 9:18 [b]ch. 20:23
32 [a]Ps. 69:28; Rom. 9:3 [b]Dan. 12:1; Phil. 4:3; Rev. 3:5 & 21:27
33 [a]Lev. 23:30; Ezek. 18:4
34 [a]ch. 33:2,14 [b]Deut. 32:35; Rom. 2:5,6
35 [a]2 Sam. 12:9
33:1 [a]ch. 32:7 [b]Gen. 12:7
2 [a]ch. 32:34 [b]Josh. 24:11
3 [a]ch. 3:8 [b]ch. 32:9 [c]Num. 16:21, 45
4 [a]Num. 14:1,39 [b]Ezra 9:3; Esth. 4:1,4; Ezek. 24:17, 23
5 [a]See Num. 16:45,46 [b]Ps. 139:23
7 [a]ch. 29:42,43 [b]Deut. 4:29
8 [a]Num. 16:27
9 [a]ch. 25:22 & 31:18; Ps. 99:7
10 [a]ch. 4:31
11 [a]Num. 12:8; Deut. 34:10 [b]ch. 24:13
12 [a]ch. 32:34 [b]ver. 17; John 10:14,15; 2 Tim. 2:19
13 [a]ch. 34:9 [b]Ps. 25:4 & 27:11 & 86:11 & 119:33 [c]Deut. 9:26,29
14 [a]Is. 63:9 [b]Josh. 21:44

H *Ex 23:7* ◀▶ *Ex 34:7*
S *Ex 23:7* ◀▶ *Lev 11:44–45*
D *Ex 15:26* ◀▶ *Lev 26:16*

L *Ex 19:4–6* ◀▶ *Ex 40:36–38*

33:1–3 This prophecy includes God's promise to remove the original pagan inhabitants of Canaan and give his people "a land flowing with milk and honey," a phrase that indicated the land's abundance and fertility.

15 And he said unto him, [a]If thy presence go not *with me,* carry us not up hence.

16 For wherein shall it be known here that I and thy people have found grace in thy sight? [a]*is it* not in that thou goest with us? so [b]shall we be separated, I and thy people, from all the people that *are* upon the face of the earth.

Moses beholds God's glory

17 And the LORD said unto Moses, [a]I will do this thing also that thou hast spoken: for [b]thou hast found grace in my sight, and I know thee by name.

18 And he said, I beseech thee, show me [a]thy glory.

K 19 And he said, I will make all my goodness pass before thee, and I will proclaim the name of the LORD before thee; [a]and will be [b]gracious to whom I will be gracious, and will show mercy on whom I will show mercy.

20 And he said, Thou canst not see my face: for [a]there shall no man see me, and live.

21 And the LORD said, Behold, *there is* a place by me, and thou shalt stand upon a rock:

22 And it shall come to pass, while my glory passeth by, that I will put thee [a]in a cleft of the rock, and will [b]cover thee with my hand while I pass by:

23 And I will take away mine hand, and thou shalt see my back parts: but my face shall [a]not be seen.

The second tables of stone

34 AND THE LORD said unto Moses, [a]Hew thee two tables of stone like unto the first: [b]and I will write upon *these* tables the words that were in the first tables, which thou brakest.

2 And be ready in the morning, and come up in the morning unto mount Sinai, and present thyself there to me [a]in the top of the mount.

K *Ex 15:13* ◀▶ *Nu 6:24–26*

15 [a]ver. 3
16 [a]Num. 14:14 [b]ch. 34:10; Deut. 4:7,34
17 [a]Jas. 5:16 [b]ver. 12
18 [a]1 Tim. 6:16
19 [a]Rom. 9:15,16, 18 [b]Rom. 4:4,16
20 [a]Gen. 32:30
22 [a]Is. 2:21 [b]Ps. 91:1,4
23 [a]John 1:18
34:1 [a]ch. 32:16,19 [b]ver. 28; Deut. 10:2,4
2 [a]ch. 19:20
3 [a]ch. 19:12,13,21
5 [a]ch. 33:19
6 [a]Neh. 9:17; Joel 2:13 [b]Rom. 2:4 [c]Ps. 108:4
7 [a]ch. 20:6 [b]Ps. 103:3 & 130:4; Dan. 9:9; Eph. 4:32; 1 John 1:9 [c]Josh. 24:19; Job 10:14; Mic. 6:11; Nah. 1:3
8 [a]ch. 4:31
9 [a]ch. 33:15,16 [b]ch. 33:3 [c]Ps. 33:12 & 94:14
10 [a]Deut. 5:2 [b]Deut. 4:32; Ps. 77:14 [c]Ps. 145:6
11 [a]Deut. 6:25 [b]ch. 33:2

3 And no man shall [a]come up with thee, neither let any man be seen throughout all the mount; neither let the flocks nor herds feed before that mount.

4 ¶ And he hewed two tables of stone like unto the first; and Moses rose up early in the morning, and went up unto mount Sinai, as the LORD had commanded him, and took in his hand the two tables of stone.

5 And the LORD descended in the cloud, and stood with him there, and [a]proclaimed the name of the LORD.

6 And the LORD passed by before him, L and proclaimed, The LORD, The LORD [a]God, merciful and gracious, longsuffering, and abundant in [b]goodness and [c]truth,

7 [a]Keeping mercy for thousands, [b]for- H giving iniquity and transgression and sin, and [c]that will by no means clear *the guilty;* visiting the iniquity of the fathers upon the children, and upon the children's children, unto the third and to the fourth *generation.*

8 And Moses made haste, and [a]bowed his head toward the earth, and worshipped.

9 And he said, If now I have found grace in thy sight, O Lord, [a]let my Lord, I pray thee, go among us; for [b]it *is* a stiffnecked people; and pardon our iniquity and our sin, and take us for [c]thine inheritance.

10 ¶ And he said, Behold, [a]I make a A covenant: before all thy people I will [b]do marvels, such as have not been done in all the earth, nor in any nation: and all the people among which thou *art* shall see the work of the LORD: for it *is* [c]a terrible thing that I will do with thee.

11 [a]Observe thou that which I command thee this day: behold, [b]I drive out before thee the Amorite, and the Canaan-

L *Ex 25:17* ◀▶ *Lev 4:20*
H *Ex 32:33* ◀▶ *Nu 14:18*
A *Ex 32:13* ◀▶ *Lev 23:33–36*

34:10–12 Though Israel had broken their covenant with God by worshiping the golden calf, God willingly renewed it, promising miracles and a successful conquest of Canaan. Yet God reminded his people that they could not expect the benefit of his blessing unless they were obedient to his commands to abstain from idolatry and worship him alone. In order that the Israelites would not be tempted into idolatry again, God further instructed the people to abstain from friendship or alliances with the idolatrous people of Canaan. Tragically, the Israelites disobeyed God in this matter and suffered greatly because of it.

ite, and the Hittite, and the Perizzite, and
the Hivite, and the Jebusite.
12 [a]Take heed to thyself, lest thou
make a covenant with the inhabitants of
the land whither thou goest, lest it be for
[b]a snare in the midst of thee:
13 But ye shall [a]destroy their altars,
break their [/]images, and [b]cut down their
groves:
14 For thou shalt worship [a]no other
god: for the LORD, whose [b]name *is* Jealous, *is* a [c]jealous God:
15 [a]Lest thou make a covenant with
the inhabitants of the land, and they [b]go
a-whoring after their gods, and do sacrifice unto their gods, and *one* [c]call thee,
and thou [d]eat of his sacrifice;
16 And thou take of [a]their daughters
unto thy sons, and their daughters [b]go
a-whoring after their gods, and make thy
sons go a-whoring after their gods.
17 [a]Thou shalt make thee no molten
gods.
18 ¶ The feast of [a]unleavened bread
shalt thou keep. Seven days thou shalt eat
unleavened bread, as I commanded thee,
in the time of the month Abib: for in the
[b]month Abib thou camest out from
Egypt.
19 [a]All that openeth the matrix *is*
mine; and every firstling among thy cattle, *whether* ox or sheep, *that is male.*
20 But [a]the firstling of an ass thou
shalt redeem with a [/]lamb: and if thou
redeem *him* not, then shalt thou break
his neck. All the firstborn of thy sons
thou shalt redeem. And none shall appear
before me [b]empty.
21 ¶ [a]Six days thou shalt work, but on
the seventh day thou shalt rest: in earing
time and in harvest thou shalt rest.
22 ¶ [a]And thou shalt observe the feast
of weeks, of the firstfruits of wheat harvest, and the feast of ingathering at the
[/]year's end.
23 ¶ [a]Thrice in the year shall all your
menchildren appear before the Lord GOD,
the God of Israel.
24 For I will [a]cast out the nations before thee, and [b]enlarge thy borders: [c]nei-
ther shall any man desire thy land, when
thou shalt go up to appear before the LORD
thy God thrice in the year.
25 [a]Thou shalt not offer the blood of
my sacrifice with leaven; [b]neither shall
the sacrifice of the feast of the passover
be left unto the morning.
26 [a]The first of the firstfruits of thy
land thou shalt bring unto the house of
the LORD thy God. [a]Thou shalt not seethe
a kid in his mother's milk.
27 And the LORD said unto Moses,
Write thou [a]these words: for after the
tenor of these words I have made a covenant with thee and with Israel.
28 [a]And he was there with the LORD
forty days and forty nights; he did neither
eat bread, nor drink water. And [b]he
wrote upon the tables the words of the
covenant, the ten [/]commandments.

Moses' shining face

29 ¶ And it came to pass, when Moses
came down from mount Sinai with the
[a]two tables of testimony in Moses' hand,
when he came down from the mount,
that Moses wist not that [b]the skin of his
face shone while he talked with him.
30 And when Aaron and all the children of Israel saw Moses, behold, the
skin of his face shone; and they were
afraid to come nigh him.
31 And Moses called unto them; and
Aaron and all the rulers of the congregation returned unto him: and Moses talked
with them.
32 And afterward all the children of Israel came nigh: [a]and he gave them in
commandment all that the LORD had spoken with him in mount Sinai.
33 And *till* Moses had done speaking
with them, he put [a]a veil on his face.
34 But [a]when Moses went in before
the LORD to speak with him, he took the
veil off, until he came out. And he came
out, and spake unto the children of Israel
that which he was commanded.
35 And the children of Israel saw the
face of Moses, that the skin of Moses'
face shone: and Moses put the veil upon
his face again, until he went in to speak
with him.

Sabbath regulations

35 AND MOSES gathered all the
congregation of the children of Israel together, and said unto them, [a]These
are the words which the LORD hath commanded, that *ye* should do them.
2 [a]Six days shall work be done, but on
the seventh day there shall be to you [/]an
holy day, a sabbath of rest to the LORD:
whosoever doeth work therein shall be
put to death.

12 [a]ch. 23:32 [b]ch. 23:33
13 [a]Deut. 12:3 [b]2 Ki. 18:4; 2 Chr. 34:3,4 [/]Heb. *statues*
14 [a]ch. 20:3,5 [b]See Is. 9:6 & 57:15 [c]ch. 20:5
15 [a]ver. 12 [b]Judg. 2:17 [c]Num. 25:2 [d]1 Cor. 8:4,7,10
16 [a]Deut. 7:3; 1 Ki. 11:2; Ezra 9:2; Neh. 13:25 [b]Num. 25:1,2; 1 Ki. 11:4
17 [a]ch. 32:8
18 [a]ch. 12:15 [b]ch. 13:4
19 [a]ch. 22:29
20 [a]ch. 13:13 [b]ch. 23:15; Deut. 16:16; 1 Sam. 9:7,8; 2 Sam. 24:24 [/]Or, *kid*
21 [a]ch. 20:9; Luke 13:14
22 [a]ch. 23:16 [/]Heb. *revolution of the year*
23 [a]ch. 23:14,17
24 [a]ch. 33:2; Ps. 78:55 [b]Deut. 12:20 & 19:8 [c]See Gen. 35:5; Acts 18:10
25 [a]ch. 23:18 [b]ch. 12:10
26 [a]ch. 23:19
27 [a]Deut. 31:9
28 [a]ch. 24:18 [b]ver. 1; ch. 31:18; Deut. 4:13 & 10:2, 4 [/]Heb. *words*
29 [a]ch. 32:15 [b]Mat. 17:2; 2 Cor. 3:7,13
32 [a]ch. 24:3
33 [a]2 Cor. 3:13
34 [a]2 Cor. 3:16
35:1 [a]ch. 34:32
2 [a]ch. 20:9; Lev. 23:3 [/]Heb. *holiness*

3 [a]Ye shall kindle no fire throughout your habitations upon the sabbath day.

4 ¶ And Moses spake unto all the congregation of the children of Israel, saying, [a]This *is* the thing which the LORD commanded, saying,

5 Take ye from among you an offering unto the LORD: [a]whosoever *is* of a willing heart, let him bring it, an offering of the LORD; gold, and silver, and brass,

6 And blue, and purple, and scarlet, and fine linen, and goats' *hair,*

7 And rams' skins dyed red, and badgers' skins, and shittim wood,

8 And oil for the light, [a]and spices for anointing oil, and for the sweet incense,

9 And onyx stones, and stones to be set for the ephod, and for the breastplate.

10 And [a]every wisehearted among you shall come, and make all that the LORD hath commanded;

11 [a]The tabernacle, his tent, and his covering, his taches, and his boards, his bars, his pillars, and his sockets,

12 [a]The ark, and the staves thereof, *with* the mercy seat, and the veil of the covering,

13 The [a]table, and his staves, and all his vessels, [b]and the showbread,

14 [a]The candlestick also for the light, and his furniture, and his lamps, with the oil for the light,

15 [a]And the incense altar, and his staves, [b]and the anointing oil, and [c]the sweet incense, and the hanging for the door at the entering in of the tabernacle,

16 [a]The altar of burnt offering, with his brasen grate, his staves, and all his vessels, the laver and his foot,

17 [a]The hangings of the court, his pillars, and their sockets, and the hanging for the door of the court,

18 The pins of the tabernacle, and the pins of the court, and their cords,

19 [a]The cloths of service, to do service in the holy *place,* the holy garments for Aaron the priest, and the garments of his sons, to minister in the priest's office.

Offerings for the tabernacle

20 ¶ And all the congregation of the children of Israel departed from the presence of Moses.

21 And they came, every one [a]whose heart stirred him up, and every one whom his spirit made willing, *and* they brought the LORD'S offering to the work of the tabernacle of the congregation, and for all his service, and for the holy garments.

22 And they came, both men and women, as many as were willing-hearted, *and* brought bracelets, and earrings, and rings, and tablets, all jewels of gold: and every man that offered *offered* an offering of gold unto the LORD.

23 And [a]every man, with whom was found blue, and purple, and scarlet, and fine linen, and goats' *hair,* and red skins of rams, and badgers' skins, brought *them.*

24 Every one that did offer an offering of silver and brass brought the LORD'S offering: and every man, with whom was found shittim wood for any work of the service, brought *it.*

25 And all the women that were [a]wisehearted did spin with their hands, and brought that which they had spun, *both* of blue, and of purple, *and* of scarlet, and of fine linen.

26 And all the women whose heart stirred them up in wisdom spun goats' *hair.*

27 And [a]the rulers brought onyx stones, and stones to be set, for the ephod, and for the breastplate;

28 And [a]spice, and oil for the light, and for the anointing oil, and for the sweet incense.

29 The children of Israel brought a [a]willing offering unto the LORD, every man and woman, whose heart made them willing to bring for all manner of work, which the LORD had commanded to be made by the hand of Moses.

The workmen gathered

30 ¶ And Moses said unto the children of Israel, See, [a]the LORD hath called by name Bezaleel the son of Uri, the son of Hur, of the tribe of Judah;

31 And he hath filled him with the spirit of God, in wisdom, in understanding, and in knowledge, and in all manner of workmanship; B E G T

32 And to devise curious works, to work in gold, and in silver, and in brass,

33 And in the cutting of stones, to set

3 [a]ch. 16:23
4 [a]ch. 25:1,2
5 [a]ch. 25:2
8 [a]ch. 25:6
10 [a]ch. 31:6
11 [a]ch. 26:1,2
12 [a]ch. 25:10
13 [a]ch. 25:23 [b]ch. 25:30; Lev. 24:5,6
14 [a]ch. 25:31
15 [a]ch. 30:1 [b]ch. 30:25 [c]ch. 30:34
16 [a]ch. 27:1
17 [a]ch. 27:9
19 [a]ch. 31:10 & 39:1,41; Num. 4:5, 6
21 [a]ver. 5,22,26, 29; ch. 36:2
23 [a]1 Chr. 29:8
25 [a]ch. 28:3 & 31:6 & 36:1
27 [a]1 Chr. 29:6; Ezra 2:68
28 [a]ch. 30:23
29 [a]ver. 21; 1 Chr. 29:9
30 [a]ch. 31:2

B Ex 31:3 ◄► Nu 27:18
E Ex 31:3 ◄► Nu 11:17
G Ex 31:3 ◄► Nu 11:25–29
T Ex 31:3 ◄► Nu 11:25–29

them, and in carving of wood, to make
any manner of cunning work.
34 And he hath put in his heart that he
may teach, *both* he, and [a]Aholiab, the
son of Ahisamach, of the tribe of Dan.
35 Them hath he [a]filled with wisdom
of heart, to work all manner of work, of
the engraver, and of the cunning workman, and of the embroiderer, in blue,
and in purple, in scarlet, and in fine
linen, and of the weaver, *even* of them
that do any work, and of those that devise
cunning work.

36 THEN WROUGHT Bezaleel and
Aholiab, and every [a]wisehearted
man, in whom the LORD put wisdom and
understanding to know how to work all
manner of work for the service of the
[b]sanctuary, according to all that the LORD
had commanded.
2 And Moses called Bezaleel and Aholiab, and every wisehearted man, in
whose heart the LORD had put wisdom,
even every one [a]whose heart stirred him
up to come unto the work to do it:
3 And they received of Moses all the
offering, which the children of Israel
[a]had brought for the work of the service
of the sanctuary, to make it *withal.* And
they brought yet unto him free offerings
every morning.
4 And all the wise men, that wrought
all the work of the sanctuary, came every
man from his work which they made;
5 ¶ And they spake unto Moses, saying, [a]The people bring much more than
enough for the service of the work,
which the LORD commanded to make.
6 And Moses gave commandment, and
they caused it to be proclaimed throughout the camp, saying, Let neither man
nor woman make any more work for the
offering of the sanctuary. So the people
were restrained from bringing.
7 For the stuff they had was sufficient
for all the work to make it, and too much.

The work for the tabernacle

8 ¶ [a]And every wisehearted man
among them that wrought the work of
the tabernacle made ten curtains *of* fine
twined linen, and blue, and purple, and
scarlet: *with* cherubims of cunning work
made he them.
9 The length of one curtain *was*
twenty and eight cubits, and the breadth
of one curtain four cubits: the curtains
were all of one size.
10 And he coupled the five curtains
one unto another: and *the other* five curtains he coupled one unto another.
11 And he made loops of blue on the
edge of one curtain from the selvedge in
the coupling: likewise he made in the uttermost side of *another* curtain, in the
coupling of the second.
12 [a]Fifty loops made he in one curtain,
and fifty loops made he in the edge of the
curtain which *was* in the coupling of the
second: the loops held one *curtain* to another.
13 And he made fifty taches of gold,
and coupled the curtains one unto another with the taches: so it became one
tabernacle.
14 ¶ [a]And he made curtains *of* goats'
hair for the tent over the tabernacle:
eleven curtains he made them.
15 The length of one curtain *was* thirty
cubits, and four cubits *was* the breadth of
one curtain: the eleven curtains *were* of
one size.
16 And he coupled five curtains by
themselves, and six curtains by themselves.
17 And he made fifty loops upon the
uttermost edge of the curtain in the coupling, and fifty loops made he upon the
edge of the curtain which coupleth the
second.
18 And he made fifty taches *of* brass to
couple the tent together, that it might be
one.
19 [a]And he made a covering for the
tent *of* rams' skins dyed red, and a covering *of* badgers' skins above *that.*
20 ¶ [a]And he made boards for the tabernacle *of* [b]shittim wood, standing up.
21 The length of a board *was* ten cubits, and the breadth of a board one cubit
and a half.
22 One board had two tenons, equally
distant one from another: thus did he
make for all the boards of the tabernacle.
23 And he made boards for the tabernacle; twenty boards for the south side
southward:
24 And forty sockets of silver he made
under the twenty boards; two sockets under one board for his two tenons, and
two sockets under another board for his
two tenons.
25 And for the other side of the taber-

34 [a]ch. 31:6
35 [a]ver. 31; ch. 31:3,6; 1 Ki. 7:14; 2 Chr. 2:14; Is. 28:26
36:1 [a]ch. 28:3 & 31:6 & 35:10,35 [b]ch. 25:8
2 [a]ch. 35:21,26; 1 Chr. 29:5
3 [a]ch. 35:27
5 [a]2 Cor. 8:2,3
8 [a]ch. 26:1
12 [a]ch. 26:5
14 [a]ch. 26:7
19 [a]ch. 26:14
20 [a]ch. 26:15 [b]ch. 25:5,10; Num. 15:1; Deut. 10:3; Josh. 2:1

nacle, *which is* toward the north corner, he made twenty boards,

26 And their forty sockets of silver; two sockets under one board, and two sockets under another board.

27 And for the sides of the tabernacle westward he made six boards.

28 And two boards made he for the corners of the tabernacle in the two sides.

29 And they were [l]coupled beneath, and coupled together at the head thereof, to one ring: thus he did to both of them in both the corners.

30 And there were eight boards; and their sockets *were* sixteen sockets of silver, [l]under every board two sockets.

31 ¶ And he made [a]bars of shittim wood; five for the boards of the one side of the tabernacle,

32 And five bars for the boards of the other side of the tabernacle, and five bars for the boards of the tabernacle for the sides westward.

33 And he made the middle bar to shoot through the boards from the one end to the other.

34 And he overlaid the boards with gold, and made their rings *of* gold *to be* places for the bars, and overlaid the bars with gold.

35 ¶ And he made [a]a veil *of* blue, and purple, and scarlet, and fine twined linen: *with* cherubims made he it of cunning work.

36 And he made thereunto four pillars *of* shittim *wood,* and overlaid them with gold: their hooks *were of* gold; and he cast for them four sockets of silver.

37 ¶ And he made an [a]hanging for the tabernacle door *of* blue, and purple, and scarlet, and fine twined linen, [l]of needlework;

38 And the five pillars of it with their hooks: and he overlaid their chapiters and their fillets with gold: but their five sockets *were of* brass.

The construction of the ark

37 AND BEZALEEL made [a]the ark *of* shittim wood: two cubits and a half *was* the length of it, and a cubit and a half the breadth of it, and a cubit and a half the height of it:

2 And he overlaid it with pure gold within and without, and made a crown of gold to it round about.

3 And he cast for it four rings of gold, *to be set* by the four corners of it; even two rings upon the one side of it, and two rings upon the other side of it.

4 And he made staves *of* shittim wood, and overlaid them with gold.

5 And he put the staves into the rings by the sides of the ark, to bear the ark.

6 ¶ And he made the [a]mercy seat *of* pure gold: two cubits and a half *was* the length thereof, and one cubit and a half the breadth thereof.

7 And he made two cherubims *of* gold, beaten out of one piece made he them, on the two ends of the mercy seat;

8 One cherub [l]on the end on this side, and another cherub [l]on the *other* end on that side: out of the mercy seat made he the cherubims on the two ends thereof.

9 And the cherubims spread out *their* wings on high, *and* covered with their wings over the mercy seat, with their faces one to another; *even* to the mercy seatward were the faces of the cherubims.

The table and the candlestick

10 ¶ And he made [a]the table *of* shittim wood: two cubits *was* the length thereof, and a cubit the breadth thereof, and a cubit and a half the height thereof:

11 And he overlaid it with pure gold, and made thereunto a crown of gold round about.

12 Also he made thereunto a border of an handbreadth round about; and made a crown of gold for the border thereof round about.

13 And he cast for it four rings of gold, and put the rings upon the four corners that *were* in the four feet thereof.

14 Over against the border were the rings, the places for the staves to bear the table.

15 And he made the staves *of* shittim wood, and overlaid them with gold, to bear the table.

16 And he made the vessels which *were* upon the table, his [a]dishes, and his spoons, and his bowls, and his covers [l]to cover withal, *of* pure gold.

17 ¶ And he made the [a]candlestick *of* pure gold: *of* beaten work made he the candlestick; his shaft, and his branch, his bowls, his knobs, and his flowers, were of the same:

18 And six branches going out of the

29 [l]Heb. *twinned*

30 [l]Heb. *two sockets, two sockets under one board*

31 [a]ch. 26:26

35 [a]ch. 26:31

37 [a]ch. 26:36 [l]Heb. *the work of a needleworker,* or, *embroiderer*

37:1 [a]ch. 25:10

6 [a]ch. 25:17

8 [l]Or, *out of*

10 [a]ch. 25:23

16 [a]ch. 25:29 [l]Or, *to pour out withal*

17 [a]ch. 25:31

sides thereof; three branches of the
candlestick out of the one side thereof,
and three branches of the candlestick out
of the other side thereof:
19 Three bowls made after the fashion
of almonds in one branch, a knob and a
flower; and three bowls made like almonds in another branch, a knob and a
flower: so throughout the six branches
going out of the candlestick.
20 And in the candlestick *were* four
bowls made like almonds, his knobs, and
his flowers:
21 And a knob under two branches of
the same, and a knob under two branches
of the same, and a knob under two
branches of the same, according to the
six branches going out of it.
22 Their knobs and their branches
were of the same: all of it *was* one beaten
work *of* pure gold.
23 And he made his seven lamps, and
his snuffers, and his snuffdishes, *of* pure
gold.
24 *Of* a talent of pure gold made he it,
and all the vessels thereof.

The altar of incense

25 ¶ [a]And he made the incense altar *of*
shittim wood: the length of it *was* a cubit,
and the breadth of it a cubit; *it was* foursquare; and two cubits *was* the height of
it; the horns thereof were of the same.
26 And he overlaid it with pure gold,
both the top of it, and the sides thereof
round about, and the horns of it: also he
made unto it a crown of gold round
about.
27 And he made two rings of gold for it
under the crown thereof, by the two corners of it, upon the two sides thereof, to
be places for the staves to bear it withal.
28 And he made the staves *of* shittim
wood, and overlaid them with gold.
29 ¶ And he made [a]the holy anointing
oil, and the pure incense of sweet spices,
according to the work of the apothecary.

The altar of burnt offering

38 AND [a]HE made the altar of burnt
offering *of* shittim wood: five cubits *was* the length thereof, and five cubits the breadth thereof; *it was* foursquare; and three cubits the height
thereof.
2 And he made the horns thereof on
the four corners of it; the horns thereof

25 [a]ch. 30:1 & 40:26; 1 Ki. 9:25; 2 Chr. 29:6,7; Is. 60:6; Heb. 7:25

29 [a]ch. 30:23,34; Ps. 133:2; Is. 11:2 & 61:1; 1 John 2:20

38:1 [a]ch. 27:1

8 [a]ch. 30:18 [1]Or, *brasen glasses* [2]Heb. *assembling by troops* as 1 Sam. 2:22

9 [a]ch. 27:9

were of the same: and he overlaid it with
brass.
3 And he made all the vessels of the
altar, the pots, and the shovels, and the
basins, *and* the fleshhooks, and the firepans: all the vessels thereof made he *of*
brass.
4 And he made for the altar a brasen
grate of network under the compass
thereof beneath unto the midst of it.
5 And he cast four rings for the four
ends of the grate of brass, *to be* places for
the staves.
6 And he made the staves *of* shittim
wood, and overlaid them with brass.
7 And he put the staves into the rings
on the sides of the altar, to bear it withal;
he made the altar hollow with boards.
8 ¶ And he made [a]the laver *of* brass,
and the foot of it *of* brass, of the [1]looking
glasses of *the women* [2]assembling, which
assembled *at* the door of the tabernacle of
the congregation.

The court of the tabernacle

9 ¶ And he made [a]the court: on the
south side southward the hangings of the
court *were of* fine twined linen, an hundred cubits:
10 Their pillars *were* twenty, and their
brasen sockets twenty; the hooks of the
pillars and their fillets *were of* silver.
11 And for the north side *the hangings*
were an hundred cubits, their pillars
were twenty, and their sockets of brass
twenty; the hooks of the pillars and their
fillets *of* silver.
12 And for the west side *were* hangings of fifty cubits, their pillars ten, and
their sockets ten; the hooks of the pillars
and their fillets *of* silver.
13 And for the east side eastward fifty
cubits.
14 The hangings of the one side *of the*
gate were fifteen cubits; their pillars
three, and their sockets three.
15 And for the other side of the court
gate, on this hand and that hand, *were*
hangings of fifteen cubits; their pillars
three, and their sockets three.
16 All the hangings of the court round
about *were* of fine twined linen.
17 And the sockets for the pillars *were*
of brass; the hooks of the pillars and their
fillets *of* silver; and the overlaying of their
chapiters *of* silver; and all the pillars of
the court *were* filleted with silver.

18 And the hanging for the gate of the court *was* needlework, *of* blue, and purple, and scarlet, and fine twined linen: and twenty cubits *was* the length, and the height in the breadth *was* five cubits, answerable to the hangings of the court.

19 And their pillars *were* four, and their sockets *of* brass four; their hooks *of* silver, and the overlaying of their chapiters and their fillets *of* silver.

20 And all the [a]pins of the tabernacle, and of the court round about, *were of* brass.

21 ¶ This is the sum of the tabernacle, *even* of [a]the tabernacle of testimony, as it was counted, according to the commandment of Moses, *for* the service of the Levites, [b]by the hand of Ithamar, son to Aaron the priest.

22 And [a]Bezaleel the son of Uri, the son of Hur, of the tribe of Judah, made all that the LORD commanded Moses.

23 And with him *was* Aholiab, son of Ahisamach, of the tribe of Dan, an engraver, and a cunning workman, and an embroiderer in blue, and in purple, and in scarlet, and fine linen.

The valuable metals used

24 All the gold that was occupied for the work in all the work of the holy *place,* even the gold of the offering, was twenty and nine talents, and seven hundred and thirty shekels, after [a]the shekel of the sanctuary.

25 And the silver of them that were numbered of the congregation *was* an hundred talents, and a thousand seven hundred and threescore and fifteen shekels, after the shekel of the sanctuary:

26 [a]A bekah for [/]every man, *that is,* half a shekel, after the shekel of the sanctuary, for every one that went to be numbered, from twenty years old and upward, for [b]six hundred thousand and three thousand and five hundred and fifty *men.*

27 And of the hundred talents of silver were cast [a]the sockets of the sanctuary, and the sockets of the veil; an hundred sockets of the hundred talents, a talent for a socket.

28 And of the thousand seven hundred seventy and five *shekels* he made hooks for the pillars, and overlaid their chapiters, and [a]filleted them.

29 And the brass of the offering *was* seventy talents, and two thousand and four hundred shekels.

30 And therewith he made the sockets to the door of the tabernacle of the congregation, and the brasen altar, and the brasen grate for it, and all the vessels of the altar,

31 And the sockets of the court round about, and the sockets of the court gate, and all the pins of the tabernacle, and all the pins of the court round about.

The garments of the priesthood

39 AND OF [a]the blue, and purple, and scarlet, they made [b]cloths of service, to do service in the holy *place,* and made the holy garments for Aaron; [c]as the LORD commanded Moses.

2 [a]And he made the ephod *of* gold, blue, and purple, and scarlet, and fine twined linen.

3 And they did beat the gold into thin plates, and cut *it into* wires, to work *it* in the blue, and in the purple, and in the scarlet, and in the fine linen, *with* cunning work.

4 They made shoulderpieces for it, to couple *it* together: by the two edges was it coupled together.

5 And the curious girdle of his ephod, that *was* upon it, *was* of the same, according to the work thereof; *of* gold, blue, and purple, and scarlet, and fine twined linen; as the LORD commanded Moses.

6 ¶ [a]And they wrought onyx stones enclosed in ouches of gold, graven, as signets are graven, with the names of the children of Israel.

7 And he put them on the shoulders of the ephod, *that they should be* stones for a [a]memorial to the children of Israel; as the LORD commanded Moses.

The priest's breastplate

8 ¶ [a]And he made the breastplate *of* cunning work, like the work of the ephod; *of* gold, blue, and purple, and scarlet, and fine twined linen.

9 It was foursquare; they made the breastplate double: a span *was* the length thereof, and a span the breadth thereof, *being* doubled.

10 [a]And they set in it four rows of stones: *the first* row *was* a [/]sardius, a topaz, and a carbuncle: this *was* the first row.

20 [a]ch. 27:19
21 [a]Num. 1:50,53; & 9:15 & 10:11 & 17:7,8; 2 Chr. 24:6; Acts 7:44 [b]Num. 4:28,33
22 [a]ch. 31:2,6
24 [a]ch. 30:13,24; Lev. 5:15 & 27:3, 25; Num. 3:47 & 18:16
26 [a]ch. 30:13,15 [b]Num. 1:46 [/]Heb. *a poll*
27 [a]ch. 26:19,21, 25,32
28 [a]ch. 27:17
39:1 [a]ch. 35:23 [b]ch. 31:10 & 35:19 [c]ch. 28:4
2 [a]ch. 28:6
6 [a]ch. 28:9
7 [a]ch. 28:12
8 [a]ch. 28:15
10 [a]ch. 28:17 [/]Or, *ruby*

11 And the second row, an emerald, a sapphire, and a diamond.

12 And the third row, a ligure, an agate, and an amethyst.

13 And the fourth row, a beryl, an onyx, and a jasper: *they were* enclosed in ouches of gold in their enclosings.

14 And the stones *were* according to the names of the children of Israel, [a]twelve, according to their names, *like* the engravings of a signet, every one with his name, according to the twelve tribes.

15 And they made upon the breastplate chains at the ends, *of* wreathen work *of* pure gold.

16 And they made two ouches *of* gold, and two gold rings; and put the two rings in the two ends of the breastplate.

17 And they put the [a]two wreathen chains of gold in the two rings on the ends of the breastplate.

18 And the two ends of the two wreathen chains they fastened in the two ouches, and put them on the shoulderpieces of the ephod, before it.

19 And they made two rings of gold, and put *them* on the two ends of the breastplate, upon the border of it, which *was* on the side of the ephod inward.

20 And they made two *other* golden rings, and put them on the two sides of the ephod underneath, toward the forepart of it, over against the *other* coupling thereof, above the curious girdle of the ephod.

21 And they did bind the breastplate by his rings unto the rings of the ephod with a lace of blue, that it might be above the curious girdle of the ephod, and that the breastplate might not be loosed from the ephod; as the LORD commanded Moses.

The robe of the ephod

22 ¶ [a]And he made the robe of the ephod *of* woven work, all *of* blue.

23 And *there was* an hole in the midst of the robe, as the hole of an habergeon, *with* a band round about the hole, that it should not rend.

24 And they made upon the hems of the robe pomegranates *of* blue, and purple, and scarlet, *and* twined *linen.*

25 And they made [a]bells *of* pure gold, and put the bells between the pomegranates upon the hem of the robe, round about between the pomegranates;

14 [a]Rev. 21:12
17 [a]Ex. 28:40
22 [a]ch. 28:31
25 [a]ch. 28:33
27 [a]ch. 28:39,40
28 [a]ch. 28:4,39; Ezek. 44:18 [b]ch. 28:42
29 [a]ch. 28:39
30 [a]ch. 28:36,37
32 [a]ver. 42,43; ch. 25:40
38 [f]Heb. *the incense of sweet spices*

26 A bell and a pomegranate, a bell and a pomegranate, round about the hem of the robe to minister *in;* as the LORD commanded Moses.

27 ¶ [a]And they made coats *of* fine linen *of* woven work for Aaron, and for his sons,

28 [a]And a mitre *of* fine linen, and goodly bonnets *of* fine linen, and [b]linen breeches *of* fine twined linen,

29 [a]And a girdle *of* fine twined linen, and blue, and purple, and scarlet, *of* needlework; as the LORD commanded Moses.

30 ¶ [a]And they made the plate of the holy crown *of* pure gold, and wrote upon it a writing, *like to* the engravings of a signet, HOLINESS TO THE LORD.

31 And they tied unto it a lace of blue, to fasten *it* on high upon the mitre; as the LORD commanded Moses.

The tabernacle finished

32 ¶ Thus was all the work of the tabernacle of the tent of the congregation finished: and the children of Israel did [a]according to all that the LORD commanded Moses, so did they.

33 ¶ And they brought the tabernacle unto Moses, the tent, and all his furniture, his taches, his boards, his bars, and his pillars, and his sockets,

34 And the covering of rams' skins dyed red, and the covering of badgers' skins, and the veil of the covering,

35 The ark of the testimony, and the staves thereof, and the mercy seat,

36 The table, *and* all the vessels thereof, and the showbread,

37 The pure candlestick, *with* the lamps thereof, *even with* the lamps to be set in order, and all the vessels thereof, and the oil for light,

38 And the golden altar, and the anointing oil, and [f]the sweet incense, and the hanging for the tabernacle door,

39 The brasen altar, and his grate of brass, his staves, and all his vessels, the laver and his foot,

40 The hangings of the court, his pillars, and his sockets, and the hanging for the court gate, his cords, and his pins, and all the vessels of the service of the tabernacle, for the tent of the congregation,

41 The cloths of service to do service in the holy *place,* and the holy garments for Aaron the priest, and his sons' gar-

ments, to minister in the priest's office.

42 According to all that the LORD commanded Moses, so the children of Israel [a]made all the work.

43 And Moses did look upon all the work, and, behold, they had done it as the LORD had commanded, even so had they done it: and Moses [a]blessed them.

Assembling the tabernacle

40 AND THE LORD spake unto Moses, saying,

2 On the first day of the [a]first month shalt thou set up [b]the tabernacle of the tent of the congregation.

3 And [a]thou shalt put therein the ark of the testimony, and cover the ark with the veil.

4 And [a]thou shalt bring in the table, and [b]set in order [ǀ]the things that are to be set in order upon it; [c]and thou shalt bring in the candlestick, and light the lamps thereof.

5 [a]And thou shalt set the altar of gold for the incense before the ark of the testimony, and put the hanging of the door to the tabernacle.

6 And thou shalt set the altar of the burnt offering before the door of the tabernacle of the tent of the congregation.

7 And [a]thou shalt set the laver between the tent of the congregation and the altar, and shalt put water therein.

8 And thou shalt set up the court round about, and hang up the hanging at the court gate.

9 And thou shalt take the anointing oil, and [a]anoint the tabernacle, and all that *is* therein, and shalt hallow it, and all the vessels thereof: and it shall be holy.

10 And thou shalt anoint the altar of the burnt offering, and all his vessels, and sanctify the altar: and [a]it shall be an altar [ǀ]most holy.

11 And thou shalt anoint the laver and his foot, and sanctify it.

12 [a]And thou shalt bring Aaron and his sons unto the door of the tabernacle of the congregation, and wash them with water.

13 And thou shalt put upon Aaron the holy garments, [a]and anoint him, and sanctify him; that he may minister unto me in the priest's office.

14 And thou shalt bring his sons, and clothe them with coats:

15 And thou shalt anoint them, as thou didst anoint their father, that they may minister unto me in the priest's office: for their anointing shall surely be [a]an everlasting priesthood throughout their generations.

16 Thus did Moses: according to all that the LORD commanded him, so did he.

17 ¶ And it came to pass in the first month in the second year, on the first *day* of the month, *that* the [a]tabernacle was reared up.

18 And Moses reared up the tabernacle, and fastened his sockets, and set up the boards thereof, and put in the bars thereof, and reared up his pillars.

19 And he spread abroad the tent over the tabernacle, and put the covering of the tent above upon it; as the LORD commanded Moses.

20 ¶ And he took and put [a]the testimony into the ark, and set the staves on the ark, and put the mercy seat above upon the ark:

21 And he brought the ark into the tabernacle, and [a]set up the veil of the covering, and covered the ark of the testimony; as the LORD commanded Moses.

22 ¶ [a]And he put the table in the tent of the congregation, upon the side of the tabernacle northward, without the veil.

23 [a]And he set the bread in order upon it before the LORD; as the LORD had commanded Moses.

24 ¶ [a]And he put the candlestick in the tent of the congregation, over against the table, on the side of the tabernacle southward.

25 And [a]he lighted the lamps before the LORD; as the LORD commanded Moses.

26 ¶ [a]And he put the golden altar in the tent of the congregation before the veil:

27 [a]And he burnt sweet incense thereon; as the LORD commanded Moses.

28 ¶ [a]And he set up the hanging *at* the door of the tabernacle.

29 [a]And he put the altar of burnt offering *by* the door of the tabernacle of the tent of the congregation, and [b]offered upon it the burnt offering and the meat offering; as the LORD commanded Moses.

30 ¶ [a]And he set the laver between the tent of the congregation and the altar, and put water there, to wash *withal.*

31 And Moses and Aaron and his sons washed their hands and their feet thereat:

42 [a]ch. 35:10
43 [a]Lev. 9:22,23; Num. 6:23; Josh. 22:6; 2 Sam. 6:18; 1 Ki. 8:14; 2 Chr. 30:27
40:2 [a]ch. 12:2 & 13:4 [b]ver. 17; ch. 26:1,30
3 [a]ver. 21; ch. 26:33; Num. 4:5
4 [a]ver. 22; ch. 26:35 [b]ver. 23; ch. 25:30 [c]ver. 24,25 [ǀ]Heb. *the order thereof*
5 [a]ver. 26
7 [a]ver. 30; ch. 30:18
9 [a]ch. 30:26
10 [a]ch. 29:36,37 [ǀ]Heb. *holiness of holinesses*
12 [a]Lev. 8:1-13
13 [a]ch. 28:41
15 [a]Num. 25:13
17 [a]ver. 2; Num. 7:1
20 [a]ch. 25:16
21 [a]ch. 26:33
22 [a]ch. 26:35
23 [a]ver. 4
24 [a]ch. 26:35
25 [a]ver. 4; ch. 25:37
26 [a]ver. 5; ch. 30:6
27 [a]ch. 30:7
28 [a]ver. 5; ch. 26:36
29 [a]ver. 6 [b]ch. 29:38
30 [a]ver. 7; ch. 30:18

32 When they went into the tent of the congregation, and when they came near unto the altar, they washed; [a]as the LORD commanded Moses.

33 [a]And he reared up the court round about the tabernacle and the altar, and set up the hanging of the court gate. So Moses finished the work.

The glory of the LORD

34 ¶ [a]Then a cloud covered the tent of the congregation, and the glory of the LORD filled the tabernacle.

35 And Moses [a]was not able to enter into the tent of the congregation, because the cloud abode thereon, and the glory of the LORD filled the tabernacle.

36 [a]And when the cloud was taken up from over the tabernacle, the children of Israel [l]went onward in all their journeys: L

37 But [a]if the cloud were not taken up, then they journeyed not till the day that it was taken up.

38 For [a]the cloud of the LORD *was* upon the tabernacle by day, and fire was on it by night, in the sight of all the house of Israel, throughout all their journeys.

32 [a]ch. 30:19,20
33 [a]ver. 8; ch. 27:9,16
34 [a]ch. 29:43; Lev. 16:2; Num. 9:15; 1 Ki. 8:10,11; 2 Chr. 5:13 & 7:2; Is. 6:4; Hag. 2:7,9; Rev. 15:8
35 [a]Lev. 16:2; 1 Ki. 8:11; 2 Chr. 5:14
36 [a]Num. 9:17 & 10:11; Neh. 9:19 [l]Heb. *journeyed*
37 [a]Num. 9:19-22
38 [a]ch. 13:21; Num. 9:15

L *Ex 33:12* ◀ ▶ *Nu 9:15–23*

Leviticus

Author: Moses

Theme: Laws and regulations about holy living and worship

Date of Writing: c. 1440–1406 B.C.

Outline of Leviticus

I. Regulations Concerning Sacrifices (1:1—7:38)
II. The Priesthood (8:1—10:20)
III. Regulations for Purity (11:1—15:33)
IV. The Day of Atonement (16:1–34)
V. Regulations for Holy Living (17:1—22:33)
VI. The Festivals, Feasts and Seasons of Israel (23:1—25:55)
VII. Obedience Brings Blessing (26:1—27:34)

LEVITICUS DERIVES ITS name from the word *Levitikon*, the Septuagint's (the Greek translation of the OT) title for the book, which means "relating to the Levites." The Hebrew title *wayyiqra'* is the first word in the Hebrew text of the book and means "and he [i.e., the Lord] called." After the exodus, the Israelites needed instruction in the proper use of tabernacle, the ark of the covenant and the other elements of worship. This third book in the Pentateuch provides a detailed set of regulations regarding Israel's worship, including instructions for ceremonial cleanness, moral laws and holy days.

The key thought of Leviticus is the holiness of God and Israel's duties as a holy nation. The Hebrew word *qodesh*, which translates as "holy" or "holiness," occurs with frequency throughout Leviticus. God commanded the sanctification of the Israelites in all areas of body and spirit because "ye shall be holy; for I am holy" (11:44). Their sanctification also necessitated a clear knowledge of the difference "between holy and unholy, and between unclean and clean" (10:10) which Leviticus clearly provides.

Leviticus is also replete with the language of sacrifice. In Leviticus, God's system of sacrifice provided the sinful Israelites with a means for their atonement from sin, both individually and nationally. Repeatedly throughout Leviticus the Israelites were reminded that reconciliation was available only through their obedience to God's regulations. The addition of the system of festivals, feasts and Sabbaths further confirmed and reminded the Israelites of their covenant relationship with God.

One of the most powerful proofs for the divine inspiration and authority of the Bible is found within the book of Leviticus. Archeological findings have revealed the limited medical knowledge available to the ancient Egyptians at the time of Moses. Yet the book of Leviticus follows modern medical practice in its recognition of the dangers of improper food preparation, cleanliness and care for disease. God had promised the Israelites, "If thou wilt diligently hearken to the voice of the LORD thy God, and wilt do that which is right in his sight, and wilt give ear to his commandments, and keep all his statutes, I will put none of these diseases upon thee, which I have brought upon the Egyptians: for I am the LORD that healeth thee" (Ex 15:26). The advanced medical knowledge that appears in the chapters of Leviticus could come only from God's hand and further underscores the divine inspiration of this book. Several of the textual notes call attention to these medical practices.

The law of burnt offering

D 1 AND THE LORD [a]called unto Moses, and spake unto him [b]out of the tabernacle of the congregation, saying,

2 Speak unto the children of Israel, and say unto them, [a]If any man of you bring an offering unto the LORD, ye shall bring your offering of the cattle, *even* of the herd, and of the flock.

3 If his offering *be* a burnt sacrifice of the herd, let him offer a male [a]without blemish: he shall offer it of his own voluntary will at the door of the tabernacle of the congregation before the LORD.

4 [a]And he shall put his hand upon the head of the burnt offering; and it shall be [b]accepted for him [c]to make atonement for him.

5 And he shall kill the [a]bullock before the LORD: [b]and the priests, Aaron's sons, shall bring the blood, [c]and sprinkle the blood round about upon the altar that *is* by the door of the tabernacle of the congregation.

6 And he shall flay the burnt offering, and cut it into his pieces.

7 And the sons of Aaron the priest shall put fire upon the altar, and [a]lay the wood in order upon the fire:

8 And the priests, Aaron's sons, shall lay the parts, the head, and the fat, in order upon the wood that *is* on the fire which *is* upon the altar:

9 But his inwards and his legs shall he wash in water: and the priest shall burn all on the altar, *to be* a burnt sacrifice, an offering made by fire, of a [a]sweet savour unto the LORD.

10 ¶ And if his offering *be* of the flocks, *namely,* of the sheep, or of the goats, for a burnt sacrifice; he shall bring it a male [a]without blemish. D

11 [a]And he shall kill it on the side of the altar northward before the LORD: and the priests, Aaron's sons, shall sprinkle his blood round about upon the altar.

12 And he shall cut it into his pieces, with his head and his fat: and the priest shall lay them in order on the wood that *is* on the fire which *is* upon the altar:

13 But he shall wash the inwards and the legs with water: and the priest shall bring *it* all, and burn *it* upon the altar: it *is* a burnt sacrifice, an offering made by fire, of a sweet savour unto the LORD.

14 ¶ And if the burnt sacrifice for his offering to the LORD *be* of fowls, then he shall bring his offering of [a]turtledoves, or of young pigeons.

15 And the priest shall bring it unto the altar, and [I]wring off his head, and burn *it* on the altar; and the blood thereof shall be wrung out at the side of the altar:

16 And he shall pluck away his crop with [I]his feathers, and cast it [a]beside the altar on the east part, by the place of the ashes:

17 And he shall cleave it with the

1:1 [a]Ex. 19:3 [b]Ex. 40:34
2 [a]ch. 22:18,19
3 [a]Deut. 15:21; Eph. 5:27; Heb. 9:14; 1 Pet. 1:19
4 [a]ch. 3:2,8,13 & 4:15 [b]Rom. 12:1; Phil. 4:18 [c]2 Chr. 29:23,24
5 [a]Mic. 6:6 [b]2 Chr. 35:11 [c]Heb. 12:24
7 [a]Gen. 22:9
9 [a]Gen. 8:21; Ezek. 20:28,41; 2 Cor. 2:15
10 [a]ver. 3
11 [a]ver. 5; Ex. 40:22; Ezek. 8:5
14 [a]ch. 5:7
15 [I]Or, *pinch off the head with the nail*
16 [a]ch. 6:10 [I]Or, *the filth thereof*

wings thereof, *but* [a]shall not divide *it* asunder: and the priest shall burn it upon the altar, upon the wood that *is* upon the fire: [b]it *is* a burnt sacrifice, an offering made by fire, of a sweet savour unto the LORD.

The law of meat offerings

2 AND WHEN any will offer [a]a meat offering unto the LORD, his offering shall be *of* fine flour; and he shall pour oil upon it, and put frankincense thereon:

2 And he shall bring it to Aaron's sons the priests: and he shall take thereout his handful of the flour thereof, and of the oil thereof, with all the frankincense thereof; and the priest shall burn [a]the memorial of it upon the altar, *to be* an offering made by fire, of a sweet savour unto the LORD:

3 And [a]the remnant of the meat offering *shall be* Aaron's and his sons': [b]*it is* a thing most holy of the offerings of the LORD made by fire.

4 ¶ And if thou bring an oblation of a meat offering baked in the oven, *it shall be* unleavened cakes of fine flour mingled with oil, or unleavened wafers [a]anointed with oil.

5 ¶ And if thy oblation *be* a meat offering *baked* [l]in a pan, it shall be *of* fine flour unleavened, mingled with oil.

6 Thou shalt part it in pieces, and pour oil thereon: it *is* a meat offering.

7 ¶ And if thy oblation *be* a meat offering *baked* in the fryingpan, it shall be made *of* fine flour with oil.

8 And thou shalt bring the meat offering that is made of these things unto the LORD: and when it is presented unto the priest, he shall bring it unto the altar.

9 And the priest shall take from the meat offering [a]a memorial thereof, and shall burn *it* upon the altar: *it is* an [b]offering made by fire, of a sweet savour unto the LORD.

10 And [a]that which is left of the meat offering *shall be* Aaron's and his sons': *it is* a thing most holy of the offerings of the LORD made by fire.

11 No meat offering, which ye shall bring unto the LORD, shall be made with [a]leaven: for ye shall burn no leaven, nor any honey, in any offering of the LORD made by fire.

12 ¶ [a]As for the oblation of the firstfruits, ye shall offer them unto the LORD: but they shall not [l]be burnt on the altar for a sweet savour.

13 And every oblation of thy meat offering [a]shalt thou season with salt; neither shalt thou suffer [b]the salt of the covenant of thy God to be lacking from thy meat offering: [c]with all thine offerings thou shalt offer salt.

14 And if thou offer a meat offering of thy firstfruits unto the LORD, [a]thou shalt offer for the meat offering of thy firstfruits green ears of corn dried by the fire, *even* corn beaten out of [b]full ears.

15 And [a]thou shalt put oil upon it, and lay frankincense thereon: it *is* a meat offering.

16 And the priest shall burn [a]the memorial of it, *part* of the beaten corn thereof, and *part* of the oil thereof, with all the frankincense thereof: *it is* an offering made by fire unto the LORD.

The law of peace offerings

3 AND IF his oblation *be* a [a]sacrifice of D
peace offering, if he offer *it* of the herd; whether *it be* a male or female, he shall offer it [b]without blemish before the LORD.

2 And [a]he shall lay his hand upon the head of his offering, and kill it *at* the door of the tabernacle of the congregation: and Aaron's sons the priests shall sprinkle the blood upon the altar round about.

3 And he shall offer of the sacrifice of the peace offering an offering made by fire unto the LORD; [a]the [l]fat that covereth the inwards, and all the fat that *is* upon the inwards,

4 And the two kidneys, and the fat that *is* on them, which *is* by the flanks, and the [l]caul above the liver, with the kidneys, it shall he take away.

5 And Aaron's sons [a]shall burn it on the altar upon the burnt sacrifice, which *is* upon the wood that *is* on the fire: *it is* an offering made by fire, of a sweet savour unto the LORD.

6 ¶ And if his offering for a sacrifice of D
peace offering unto the LORD *be* of the flock; male or female, [a]he shall offer it without blemish.

7 If he offer a lamb for his offering, then shall he offer it before the LORD.

8 And he shall lay his hand upon the

D *Lev 1:10* ◄► *Lev 3:6–8*
D *Lev 3:1–2* ◄► *Lev 4:1–3*

17 [a]Gen. 15:10 [b]ver. 9,13
2:1 [a]ch. 6:14 & 9:17; Num. 15:4
2 [a]ver. 9; ch. 5:12; & 6:15 & 24:7; Is. 66:3; Acts 10:4
3 [a]ch. 7:9 & 10:12,13 [b]Ex. 29:37; Num. 18:9
4 [a]Ex. 29:2
5 [l]Or, *on a flat plate*, or, *slice*
9 [a]ver. 2; ch. 6:15 [b]Ex. 29:18
10 [a]ver. 3
11 [a]ch. 6:17; See Mat. 16:12; Mark 8:15; Luke 12:1; 1 Cor. 5:8; Gal. 5:9
12 [a]Ex. 22:29; ch. 23:10,11 [l]Heb. *ascend*
13 [a]Mark 9:49; Col. 4:6 [b]Num. 18:19 [c]Ezek. 43:24
14 [a]ch. 23:10,14 [b]2 Ki. 4:42
15 [a]ver. 1
16 [a]ver. 2
3:1 [a]ch. 7:11,29 & 22:21 [b]ch. 1:3
2 [a]Ex. 29:10; ch. 1:4,5
3 [a]Ex. 29:13,22; ch. 4:8,9 [l]Or, *suet*
4 [l]Or, *midriff over the liver,* and *over the kidneys*
5 [a]Ex. 29:13; ch. 6:12
6 [a]ver. 1

head of his offering, and kill it before the
tabernacle of the congregation: and
Aaron's sons shall sprinkle the blood
thereof round about upon the altar.
9 And he shall offer of the sacrifice of
the peace offering an offering made by
fire unto the LORD; the fat thereof, *and*
the whole rump, it shall he take off hard
by the backbone; and the fat that covereth the inwards, and all the fat that *is*
upon the inwards,
10 And the two kidneys, and the fat
that *is* upon them, which *is* by the flanks,
and the caul above the liver, with the kidneys, it shall he take away.
11 And the priest shall burn it upon
the altar: *it is* [a]the food of the offering
made by fire unto the LORD.
12 ¶ And if his offering *be* a goat, then
[a]he shall offer it before the LORD.
13 And he shall lay his hand upon the
head of it, and kill it before the tabernacle
of the congregation: and the sons of
Aaron shall sprinkle the blood thereof
upon the altar round about.
14 And he shall offer thereof his offering, *even* an offering made by fire unto
the LORD; the fat that covereth the inwards, and all the fat that *is* upon the
inwards,
15 And the two kidneys, and the fat
that *is* upon them, which *is* by the flanks,
and the caul above the liver, with the kidneys, it shall he take away.
16 And the priest shall burn them
upon the altar: *it is* the food of the offering made by fire for a sweet savour: [a]all
the fat *is* the LORD'S.
17 *It shall be* a [a]perpetual statute for
your generations throughout all your
dwellings, that ye eat neither [b]fat nor
[c]blood.

The sin offering

D 4 AND THE LORD spake unto Moses,
saying,
2 Speak unto the children of Israel,
saying, [a]If a soul shall sin through ignorance against any of the commandments
of the LORD *concerning things* which
ought not to be done, and shall do against
any of them:
3 [a]If the priest that is anointed do sin
according to the sin of the people; then
let him bring for his sin, which he hath
sinned, [b]a young bullock without blemish
unto the LORD for a sin offering.
4 And he shall bring the bullock [a]unto
the door of the tabernacle of the congregation before the LORD; and shall lay his
hand upon the bullock's head, and kill
the bullock before the LORD.
5 And the priest that is anointed [a]shall
take of the bullock's blood, and bring it to
the tabernacle of the congregation:
6 And the priest shall dip his finger in
the blood, and sprinkle of the blood
seven times before the LORD, before the
veil of the sanctuary.
7 And the priest shall [a]put *some* of the
blood upon the horns of the altar of sweet
incense before the LORD, which *is* in the
tabernacle of the congregation; and shall
pour [b]all the blood of the bullock at the
bottom of the altar of the burnt offering,
which *is at* the door of the tabernacle of
the congregation.
8 And he shall take off from it all the
fat of the bullock for the sin offering; the
fat that covereth the inwards, and all
the fat that *is* upon the inwards,
9 And the two kidneys, and the fat that
is upon them, which *is* by the flanks, and
the caul above the liver, with the kidneys, it shall he take away,
10 [a]As it was taken off from the bullock of the sacrifice of peace offerings: and
the priest shall burn them upon the altar
of the burnt offering.
11 [a]And the skin of the bullock, and all
his flesh, with his head, and with his
legs, and his inwards, and his dung,
12 Even the whole bullock shall he D
carry forth [1]without the camp unto a
clean place, [a]where the ashes are poured
out, and [b]burn him on the wood with
fire: [2]where the ashes are poured out
shall he be burnt.
13 ¶ And [a]if the whole congregation
of Israel sin through ignorance, [b]and the
thing be hid from the eyes of the assembly, and they have done *somewhat*
against any of the commandments of the
LORD *concerning things* which should not
be done, and are guilty;
14 When the sin, which they have D
sinned against it, is known, then the congregation shall offer a young bullock for

11 [a]See ch. 21:6,8, 17,21,22 & 22:25; Ezek. 44:7; Mal. 1:7,12
12 [a]ver. 1,7
16 [a]ch. 7:23,25; 1 Sam. 2:15; 2 Chr. 7:7
17 [a]ch. 6:18 & 7:36 & 17:7 & 23:14 [b]ver. 16 compare with Deut. 32:14; Neh. 8:10 [c]Gen. 9:4; ch. 7:23,26 & 17:10, 14; Deut. 12:16; 1 Sam. 14:33; Ezek. 44:7,15
4:2 [a]ch. 5:15,17; Num. 15:22; 1 Sam. 14:27; Ps. 19:12
3 [a]ch. 8:12 [b]ch. 9:2
4 [a]ch. 1:3,4
5 [a]ch. 16:14; Num. 19:4
7 [a]ch. 8:15 & 9:9 & 16:18 [b]ch. 5:9
10 [a]ch. 3:3-5
11 [a]Ex. 29:14; Num. 19:5
12 [a]ch. 6:11 [b]Heb. 13:11 [1]Heb. *to without the camp* [2]Heb. *at the pouring out of the ashes*
13 [a]Num. 15:24; Josh. 7:11 [b]ch. 5:2-4,17

D *Lev 3:6–8* ◄► *Lev 4:12*
D *Lev 4:1–3* ◄► *Lev 4:14*
D *Lev 4:12* ◄► *Lev 4:20–21*

the sin, and bring him before the tabernacle of the congregation.

15 And the elders of the congregation [a]shall lay their hands upon the head of the bullock before the LORD: and the bullock shall be killed before the LORD.

16 [a]And the priest that is anointed shall bring of the bullock's blood to the tabernacle of the congregation:

17 And the priest shall dip his finger *in some* of the blood, and sprinkle *it* seven times before the LORD, *even* before the veil.

18 And he shall put *some* of the blood upon the horns of the altar which *is* before the LORD, that *is* in the tabernacle of the congregation, and shall pour out all the blood at the bottom of the altar of the burnt offering, which *is at* the door of the tabernacle of the congregation.

19 And he shall take all his fat from him, and burn *it* upon the altar.

D L 20 And he shall do with the bullock as he did [a]with the bullock for a sin offering, so shall he do with this: [b]and the priest shall make an atonement for them, and it shall be forgiven them.

21 And he shall carry forth the bullock without the camp, and burn him as he burned the first bullock: it *is* a sin offering for the congregation.

22 ¶ When a ruler hath sinned, and [a]done *somewhat* through ignorance *against* any of the commandments of the LORD his God *concerning things* which should not be done, and is guilty;

D 23 Or [a]if his sin, wherein he hath sinned, come to his knowledge; he shall bring his offering, a kid of the goats, a male without blemish:

24 And [a]he shall lay his hand upon the head of the goat, and kill it in the place where they kill the burnt offering before the LORD: it *is* a sin offering.

25 [a]And the priest shall take of the blood of the sin offering with his finger, and put *it* upon the horns of the altar of burnt offering, and shall pour out his blood at the bottom of the altar of burnt offering.

L 26 And he shall burn all his fat upon the altar, as [a]the fat of the sacrifice of peace offerings: [b]and the priest shall make an atonement for him as concerning his sin, and it shall be forgiven him.

27 ¶ And [a]if [1]any one of the [2]common people sin through ignorance, while he doeth *somewhat against* any of the commandments of the LORD *concerning things* which ought not to be done, and be guilty;

28 Or [a]if his sin, which he hath sinned, come to his knowledge: then he shall bring his offering, a kid of the goats, a female without blemish, for his sin which he hath sinned. D

29 [a]And he shall lay his hand upon the head of the sin offering, and slay the sin offering in the place of the burnt offering.

30 And the priest shall take of the blood thereof with his finger, and put *it* upon the horns of the altar of burnt offering, and shall pour out all the blood thereof at the bottom of the altar.

31 And [a]he shall take away all the fat thereof, [b]as the fat is taken away from off the sacrifice of peace offerings; and the priest shall burn *it* upon the altar for a [c]sweet savour unto the LORD; [d]and the priest shall make an atonement for him, and it shall be forgiven him. L

32 And if he bring a lamb for a sin offering, [a]he shall bring it a female without blemish. D

33 And he shall lay his hand upon the head of the sin offering, and slay it for a sin offering in the place where they kill the burnt offering.

34 And the priest shall take of the blood of the sin offering with his finger, and put *it* upon the horns of the altar of burnt offering, and shall pour out all the blood thereof at the bottom of the altar:

35 And he shall take away all the fat thereof, as the fat of the lamb is taken away from the sacrifice of the peace offerings; and the priest shall burn them upon the altar, [a]according to the offerings made by fire unto the LORD: [b]and the priest shall make an atonement for his sin L

15 [a]ch. 1:4
16 [a]ver. 5; Heb. 9:12-14
20 [a]ver. 3 [b]Num. 15:25
22 [a]ver. 2,13
23 [a]ver. 14; ch. 5:4
24 [a]ver. 4; Is. 53:6
25 [a]ver. 30
26 [a]ch. 3:5 [b]ver. 20; Num. 15:28
27 [a]ver. 2; Num. 15:27 [1]Heb. *any soul* [2]Heb. *people of the land*
28 [a]ver. 23
29 [a]ver. 4,24
31 [a]ch. 3:14 [b]ch. 3:3 [c]Gen. 8:21; Ex. 29:18; ch. 1:9; Ezra 6:10 [d]ver. 26
32 [a]ver. 28
35 [a]ch. 3:5 [b]ver. 26,31

D *Lev 4:14* ◀▶ *Lev 4:23*
L *Ex 34:6–7* ◀▶ *Lev 4:26*
D *Lev 4:20–21* ◀▶ *Lev 4:28*
L *Lev 4:20* ◀▶ *Lev 4:31*
D *Lev 4:23* ◀▶ *Lev 4:32*
L *Lev 4:26* ◀▶ *Lev 4:35*
D *Lev 4:28* ◀▶ *Lev 5:5–6*
L *Lev 4:31* ◀▶ *Lev 5:10*

that he hath committed, and it shall be forgiven him.

5 AND IF a soul sin, [a]and hear the voice of swearing, and *is* a witness, whether he hath seen or known *of it;* if he do not utter *it,* then he shall [b]bear his iniquity.

2 Or [a]if a soul touch any unclean thing, whether *it be* a carcase of an unclean beast, or a carcase of unclean cattle, or the carcase of unclean creeping things, and *if* it be hidden from him; he also shall be unclean, and [b]guilty.

3 Or if he touch [a]the uncleanness of man, whatsoever uncleanness *it be* that a man shall be defiled withal, and it be hid from him; when he knoweth *of it,* then he shall be guilty.

4 Or if a soul swear, pronouncing with *his* lips [a]to do evil, or [b]to do good, whatsoever *it be* that a man shall pronounce with an oath, and it be hid from him; when he knoweth *of it,* then he shall be guilty in one of these.

D
R 5 And it shall be, when he shall be guilty in one of these *things,* that he shall [a]confess that he hath sinned in that *thing:*

6 And he shall bring his trespass offering unto the LORD for his sin which he hath sinned, a female from the flock, a lamb or a kid of the goats, for a sin offering; and the priest shall make an atonement for him concerning his sin.

7 And [a]if [1]he be not able to bring a lamb, then he shall bring for his trespass, which he hath committed, two [b]turtledoves, or two young pigeons, unto the LORD; one for a sin offering, and the other for a burnt offering.

8 And he shall bring them unto the priest, who shall offer *that* which *is* for the sin offering first, and [a]wring off his head from his neck, but shall not divide *it* asunder:

9 And he shall sprinkle of the blood of the sin offering upon the side of the altar; and [a]the rest of the blood shall be wrung out at the bottom of the altar: it *is* a sin offering.

L 10 And he shall offer the second *for* a burnt offering, according to the [a]manner:[1] [b]and the priest shall make an atonement for him for his sin which he hath sinned, and it shall be forgiven him.

11 ¶ But if he be not able to bring two turtledoves, or two young pigeons, then he that sinned shall bring for his offering the tenth part of an ephah of fine flour for a sin offering; [a]he shall put no oil upon it, neither shall he put *any* frankincense thereon: for it *is* a sin offering.

12 Then shall he bring it to the priest, and the priest shall take his handful of *it,* [a]*even* a memorial thereof, and burn *it* on the altar, [b]according to the offerings made by fire unto the LORD: it *is* a sin offering.

13 [a]And the priest shall make an atonement for him as touching his sin that he hath sinned in one of these, and it shall be forgiven him: and [b]*the remnant* shall be the priest's, as a meat offering. L

14 ¶ And the LORD spake unto Moses, saying,

15 [a]If a soul commit a trespass, and sin through ignorance, in the holy things of the LORD; then [b]he shall bring for his trespass unto the LORD a ram without blemish out of the flocks, with thy estimation by shekels of silver, after [c]the shekel of the sanctuary, for a trespass offering: D

16 And he shall make amends for the harm that he hath done in the holy thing, and [a]shall add the fifth part thereto, and give it unto the priest: [b]and the priest shall make an atonement for him with the ram of the trespass offering, and it shall be forgiven him. L R

17 ¶ And if a soul sin, and commit any of these things which are forbidden to be done by the commandments of the LORD; [a]though he wist *it* not, yet is he [b]guilty, and shall bear his iniquity.

18 [a]And he shall bring a ram without blemish out of the flock, with thy estimation, for a trespass offering, unto the priest: [b]and the priest shall make an atonement for him concerning his ignorance wherein he erred and wist *it* not, and it shall be forgiven him. D L

5:1 [a]1 Ki. 8:31; Prov. 29:24; Mat. 26:63 [b]ver. 17; ch. 7:18 & 17:16 & 19:8 & 20:17; Num. 9:13
2 [a]ch. 11:24,28, 31,39; Num. 19:11, 13,16 [b]ver. 17
3 [a]ch. 12 & 13 & 15
4 [a]See 1 Sam. 25:22; Acts 23:12 [b]See Mark 6:23
5 [a]ch. 16:21 & 26:40; Num. 5:7; Ezra 10:11,12
7 [a]ch. 12:8 & 14:21 [b]ch. 1:14 [1]Heb. *his hand cannot reach to the sufficiency of a lamb*
8 [a]ch. 1:15
9 [a]ch. 4:7,18,30, 34
10 [a]ch. 1:14 [b]ch. 4:26 [1]Or, *ordinance*
11 [a]Num. 5:15
12 [a]ch. 2:2 [b]ch. 4:35
13 [a]ch. 4:26 [b]ch. 2:3
15 [a]ch. 22:14 [b]Ezra 10:19 [c]Ex. 30:13; ch. 27:25
16 [a]ch. 6:5 & 22:14 & 27:13,15, 27,31; Num. 5:7 [b]ch. 4:26
17 [a]ver. 15; ch. 4:2,13,22,27 [b]ver. 1,2
18 [a]ver. 15 [b]ver. 16

D *Lev 4:32* ◀▶ *Lev 5:15*
R *Ex 22:1–14* ◀▶ *Lev 5:16*
L *Lev 4:35* ◀▶ *Lev 5:13*

L *Lev 5:10* ◀▶ *Lev 5:16*
D *Lev 5:5–6* ◀▶ *Lev 5:18*
L *Lev 5:13* ◀▶ *Lev 5:18*
R *Lev 5:5* ◀▶ *Lev 26:40–41*
D *Lev 5:15* ◀▶ *Lev 6:6–7*
L *Lev 5:16* ◀▶ *Lev 6:7*

19 It *is* a trespass offering: [a]he hath certainly trespassed against the LORD.

6 AND THE LORD spake unto Moses, saying,

2 If a soul sin, and [a]commit a trespass against the LORD, and [b]lie unto his neighbour in that [c]which was delivered him to keep, or in [1,2]fellowship, or in a thing taken away by violence, or hath [d]deceived his neighbour;

3 Or [a]have found that which was lost, and lieth concerning it, and [b]sweareth falsely; in any of all these that a man doeth, sinning therein:

4 Then it shall be, because he hath sinned, and is guilty, that he shall restore that which he took violently away, or the thing which he hath deceitfully gotten, or that which was delivered him to keep, or the lost thing which he found,

5 Or all that about which he hath sworn falsely; he shall even [a]restore it in the principal, and shall add the fifth part more thereto, *and* give it unto him to whom it appertaineth, [1,2]in the day of his trespass offering.

D 6 And he shall bring his trespass offering unto the LORD, [a]a ram without blemish out of the flock, with thy estimation, for a trespass offering, unto the priest:

L 7 [a]And the priest shall make an atonement for him before the LORD: and it shall be forgiven him for any thing of all that he hath done in trespassing therein.

The burnt offering

8 ¶ And the LORD spake unto Moses, saying,

9 Command Aaron and his sons, saying, This *is* the law of the burnt offering: It *is* the burnt offering, [1]because of the burning upon the altar all night unto the morning, and the fire of the altar shall be burning in it.

10 [a]And the priest shall put on his linen garment, and his linen breeches shall he put upon his flesh, and take up the ashes which the fire hath consumed with the burnt offering on the altar, and he shall put them [b]beside the altar.

11 And [a]he shall put off his garments, and put on other garments, and carry forth the ashes without the camp [b]unto a clean place.

12 And the fire upon the altar shall be burning in it; it shall not be put out: and the priest shall burn wood on it every morning, and lay the burnt offering in order upon it; and he shall burn thereon [a]the fat of the peace offerings.

13 The fire shall ever be burning upon the altar; it shall never go out.

The meat offering

14 ¶ [a]And this *is* the law of the meat offering: the sons of Aaron shall offer it before the LORD, before the altar.

15 And he shall take of it his handful, of the flour of the meat offering, and of the oil thereof, and all the frankincense which *is* upon the meat offering, and shall burn *it* upon the altar *for* a sweet savour, *even* the [a]memorial of it, unto the LORD.

16 And [a]the remainder thereof shall Aaron and his sons eat: [b]with unleavened bread shall it be eaten in the holy place; in the court of the tabernacle of the congregation they shall eat it.

17 [a]It shall not be baked with leaven. [b]I have given it *unto them for* their portion of my offerings made by fire; [c]it *is* most holy, as *is* the sin offering, and as the trespass offering.

18 [a]All the males among the children of Aaron shall eat of it. [b]*It shall be* a statute for ever in your generations concerning the offerings of the LORD made by fire: [c]every one that toucheth them shall be holy.

19 ¶ And the LORD spake unto Moses, saying,

20 [a]This *is* the offering of Aaron and of his sons, which they shall offer unto the LORD in the day when he is anointed; the tenth part of an [b]ephah of fine flour for a meat offering perpetual, half of it in the morning, and half thereof at night.

21 In a pan it shall be made with oil; *and when it is* baked, thou shalt bring it in: *and* the baked pieces of the meat offering shalt thou offer *for* a sweet savour unto the LORD.

22 And the priest of his sons [a]that is anointed in his stead shall offer it: *it is* a statute for ever unto the LORD; [b]it shall be wholly burnt.

23 For every meat offering for the priest shall be wholly burnt: it shall not be eaten.

19 [a]Ezra 10:2
6:2 [a]Num. 5:6 [b]ch. 19:11; Acts 5:4; Col. 3:9 [c]Ex. 22:7,10 [d]Prov. 24:28 & 26:19 [1]Or, *in dealing* [2]Heb. *putting of the hand*
3 [a]Deut. 22:1-3 [b]Ex. 22:11; ch. 19:12; Jer. 7:9; Zech. 5:4
5 [a]ch. 5:16; Num. 5:7; 2 Sam. 12:6 [1]Or, *in the day of his being found guilty* [2]Heb. *in the day of his trespass*
6 [a]ch. 5:15
7 [a]ch. 4:26
9 [1]Or, *for the burning*
10 [a]Ex. 28:39-41, 43; ch. 16:4; Ezek. 44:17,18 [b]ch. 1:16
11 [a]Ezek. 44:19 [b]ch. 4:12
12 [a]ch. 3:3,9,14
14 [a]ch. 2:1; Num. 15:4
15 [a]ch. 2:2,9
16 [a]ch. 2:3; Ezek. 44:29 [b]ver. 26; ch. 10:12,13; Num. 18:10
17 [a]ch. 2:11 [b]Num. 18:9,10 [c]ver. 25; Ex. 29:37; ch. 2:3 & 7:1
18 [a]ver. 29; Num. 18:10 [b]ch. 3:17 [c]Ex. 29:37; ch. 22:3-7
20 [a]Ex. 29:2 [b]Ex. 16:36
22 [a]ch. 4:3 [b]Ex. 29:25

D *Lev 5:18* ◀ ▶ *Lev 7:1–2*
L *Lev 5:18* ◀ ▶ *Lev 19:22*

Old Testament Sacrifices

SACRIFICE	OT REFERENCES	ELEMENTS	PURPOSE
Burnt Offering	Lev 1; 6:8-13; 8:18-21; 16:24	Bull, ram or male bird (dove or young pigeon for the poor); wholly consumed; no defect	Voluntary act of worship; atonement for unintentional sin in general; expression of devotion, commitment and complete surrender to God
Grain Offering	Lev 2; 6:14-23	Grain, fine flour, olive oil, incense, baked bread (cakes or wafers), salt; no yeast or honey; accompanied burnt offering and fellowship offering (along with drink offering)	Voluntary act of worship; recognition of God's goodness and provisions; devotion to God
Fellowship Offering	Lev 3; 7:11-34	Any animal without defect from herd or flock; variety of breads	Voluntary act of worship; thanksgiving and fellowship (it included a communal meal)
Sin Offering	Lev 4:1–5:13; 6:24-30; 8:14-17; 16:3-22	1. Young bull: for high priest and congregation 2. Male goat: for leader 3. Female goat or lamb: for common person 4. Dove or pigeon: for the poor 5. Tenth of an ephah of fine flour: for the very poor	Mandatory atonement for specific unintentional sin; confession of sin; forgiveness of sin; cleansing from defilement
Guilt Offering	Lev. 5:14–6:7; 7:1-6	Ram or lamb	Mandatory atonement for unintentional sin requiring restitution; cleansing from defilement; make restitution; pay 20% fine

When more than one kind of offering was presented (as in Nu 7:16,17), the procedure was usually as follows: (1) sin offering or guilt offering, (2) burnt offering, (3) fellowship offering and grain offering (along with a drink offering). This sequence furnishes part of the spiritual significance of the sacrificial system. First, sin had to be dealt with (sin offering or guilt offering). Second, the worshiper committed himself completely to God (burnt offering and grain offering). Third, fellowship or communion between the Lord, the priest and the worshiper (fellowship offering) was established. To state it another way, there were sacrifices of expiation (sin offerings and guilt offerings), consecration (burnt offerings and grain offerings) and communion (fellowship offerings—these included vow offerings, thank offerings and freewill offerings).

The sin offering

24 ¶ And the LORD spake unto Moses,
saying,
25 Speak unto Aaron and to his sons,
saying, [a]This *is* the law of the sin offering: [b]In the place where the burnt offering is killed shall the sin offering be killed
before the LORD: [c]it *is* most holy.
26 [a]The priest that offereth it for sin
shall eat it: [b]in the holy place shall it be
eaten, in the court of the tabernacle of
the congregation.
27 [a]Whatsoever shall touch the flesh
thereof shall be holy: and when there is
sprinkled of the blood thereof upon any
garment, thou shalt wash that whereon it
was sprinkled in the holy place.
28 But the earthen vessel wherein it is
sodden [a]shall be broken: and if it be sodden in a brasen pot, it shall be both
scoured, and rinsed in water.
29 [a]All the males among the priests
shall eat thereof: [b]it *is* most holy.
30 [a]And no sin offering, whereof *any*
of the blood is brought into the tabernacle of the congregation to reconcile
withal in the holy *place,* shall be eaten: it
shall be burnt in the fire.

The trespass offering

D 7 LIKEWISE [a]THIS *is* the law of the
trespass offering: [b]it *is* most holy.
2 [a]In the place where they kill the
burnt offering shall they kill the trespass
offering: and the blood thereof shall he
sprinkle round about upon the altar.
3 And he shall offer of it [a]all the fat
thereof; the rump, and the fat that covereth the inwards.
4 And the two kidneys, and the fat that
is on them, which *is* by the flanks, and
the caul *that is* above the liver, with the
kidneys, it shall he take away:
5 And the priest shall burn them upon
the altar *for* an offering made by fire unto
the LORD: it *is* a trespass offering.
6 [a]Every male among the priests shall
eat thereof: it shall be eaten in the holy
place: [b]it *is* most holy.
7 As the sin offering *is,* so *is* [a]the trespass offering: *there is* one law for them:
the priest that maketh atonement therewith shall have *it.*
8 And the priest that offereth any
man's burnt offering, *even* the priest shall
have to himself the skin of the burnt offering which he hath offered.
9 And [a]all the meat offering that is
baked in the oven, and all that is dressed
in the fryingpan, and [l]in the pan, shall be
the priest's that offereth it.
10 And every meat offering, mingled
with oil, and dry, shall all the sons of
Aaron have, one *as much* as another.

The peace offering

11 And [a]this *is* the law of the sacrifice
of peace offerings, which he shall offer
unto the LORD.
12 If he offer it for a thanksgiving,
then he shall offer with the sacrifice of
thanksgiving unleavened cakes mingled
with oil, and unleavened wafers
[a]anointed with oil, and cakes mingled
with oil, of fine flour, fried.
13 Besides the cakes, he shall offer *for*
his offering [a]leavened bread with the sacrifice of thanksgiving of his peace offerings.
14 And of it he shall offer one out of
the whole oblation *for* an heave offering
unto the LORD, [a]*and* it shall be the priest's
that sprinkleth the blood of the peace offerings.
15 [a]And the flesh of the sacrifice of his
peace offerings for thanksgiving shall be
eaten the same day that it is offered; he
shall not leave any of it until the
morning.
16 But [a]if the sacrifice of his offering
be a vow, or a voluntary offering, it shall

25 [a]ch. 4:2 [b]ch. 1:3,5,11 [c]ver. 17
26 [a]ch. 10:17,18; Num. 18:9,10; Ezek. 44:28,29 [b]ver. 16
27 [a]Ex. 29:37 & 30:29
28 [a]ch. 11:33 & 15:12
29 [a]ver. 18; Num. 18:10 [b]ver. 25
30 [a]ch. 4:7,11,12, 18,21 & 10:18 & 16:27; Heb. 13:11
7:1 [a]ch. 5 & 6:1-7 [b]ch. 6:17,25 & 21:22
2 [a]ch. 1:3,5,11 & 4:24,29,33
3 [a]Ex. 29:13; ch. 3:4,9,10,14-16 & 4:8,9
6 [a]ch. 6:16-18; Num. 18:9,10 [b]ch. 2:3
7 [a]ch. 6:25,26 & 14:13
9 [a]ch. 2:3,10; Num. 18:9; Ezek. 44:29 [l]Or, *on the flat plate,* or, *slice*
11 [a]ch. 3:1 & 22:18,21; Ezek. 45:15
12 [a]ch. 2:4; Num. 6:15
13 [a]Amos 4:5
14 [a]Num. 18:8,11, 19
15 [a]ch. 22:30
16 [a]ch. 19:6-8

D *Lev 6:6–7* ◀ ▶ *Lev 7:37*

6:28 Since clay was a porous material and absorbed some of the juices of the sacrifice during the cooking, the Lord's command to break the clay cooking pot served two purposes. For religious reasons the clay pot was broken to remove the remnants of the sacrifice that the pot absorbed, thereby ensuring that nothing of the offering was withheld from God. The porous clay pots also had to be destroyed for health reasons. Modern science realizes the peril of germ-laden cookware. Yet God's instructions protected his people centuries before the scientific discovery of germs. Since the Levites were required to eat the sacrifices cooked in these pots, destruction of a pot that harbored germs on its porous surface would prevent illness and contamination for the Levites. Bronze pots could be scoured and cleaned and therefore could be used again.

be eaten the same day that he offereth his
sacrifice: and on the morrow also the remainder of it shall be eaten:
17 But the remainder of the flesh of
the sacrifice on the third day shall be
burnt with fire.
18 And if *any* of the flesh of the sacrifice of his peace offerings be eaten at all
on the third day, it shall not be accepted,
neither shall it be [a]imputed unto him
that offereth it: it shall be an [b]abomina-
tion, and the soul that eateth of it shall
bear his iniquity.
19 And the flesh that toucheth any unclean *thing* shall not be eaten; it shall be
burnt with fire: and as for the flesh, all
that be clean shall eat thereof.
20 But the soul that eateth *of* the flesh
of the sacrifice of peace offerings, that
pertain unto the LORD, [a]having his uncleanness upon him, even that soul [b]shall
be cut off from his people.
21 Moreover the soul that shall touch
any unclean *thing, as* [a]the uncleanness
of man, or *any* [b]unclean beast, or any
[c]abominable unclean *thing*, and eat of
the flesh of the sacrifice of peace offerings, which *pertain* unto the LORD, even
that soul [d]shall be cut off from his people.

Forbidden portions

22 ¶ And the LORD spake unto Moses,
saying,
23 Speak unto the children of Israel,
saying, [a]Ye shall eat no manner of fat, of
ox, or of sheep, or of goat.
24 And the fat of the [a]beast[1] that dieth
of itself, and the fat of that which is torn
with beasts, may be used in any other
use: but ye shall in no wise eat of it.
25 For whosoever eateth the fat of the
beast, of which men offer an offering
made by fire unto the LORD, even the soul
that eateth *it* shall be cut off from his
people.
26 [a]Moreover ye shall eat no manner
of blood, *whether it be* of fowl or of beast,
in any of your dwellings.
27 Whatsoever soul *it be* that eateth
any manner of blood, even that soul shall
be cut off from his people.

18 [a]Num. 18:27 [b]ch. 11:10,11,41 & 19:7
20 [a]ch. 15:3; 1 Cor. 11:28 [b]Gen. 17:14
21 [a]ch. 12 & 13 & 15 [b]ch. 11:24,28 [c]Ezek. 4:14 [d]ver. 20
23 [a]ch. 3:17
24 [a]ch. 17:15; Deut. 14:21; Ezek. 4:14 & 44:31 [1]Heb. *carcase*
26 [a]Gen. 9:4; ch. 3:17 & 17:10-14; Ezek. 33:25; John 6:53; Acts 15:20,29
29 [a]ch. 3:1 & 22:21; Ezek. 45:15
30 [a]ch. 3:3,4,9,14 [b]Ex. 29:24,27; ch. 8:27 & 9:21; Num. 6:20
31 [a]ch. 3:5,11,16 [b]ver. 34
32 [a]ver. 34; ch. 9:21; Num. 6:20
34 [a]Ex. 29:28; ch. 10:14,15; Num. 18:18,19; Deut. 18:3
36 [a]Ex. 40:13,15; ch. 8:12,30
37 [a]ch. 6:9 [b]ch. 6:14 [c]ch. 6:25 [d]ver. 1 [e]Ex. 29:1; ch. 6:20 [f]ver. 11
38 [a]ch. 1:2

The portion for priests

28 ¶ And the LORD spake unto Moses,
saying,
29 Speak unto the children of Israel,
saying, [a]He that offereth the sacrifice of
his peace offerings unto the LORD shall
bring his oblation unto the LORD of the
sacrifice of his peace offerings.
30 [a]His own hands shall bring the offerings of the LORD made by fire, the fat
with the breast, it shall he bring, that
[b]the breast may be waved *for* a wave offering before the LORD.
31 [a]And the priest shall burn the fat
upon the altar: [b]but the breast shall be
Aaron's and his sons'.
32 And [a]the right shoulder shall ye
give unto the priest *for* an heave offering
of the sacrifices of your peace offerings.
33 He among the sons of Aaron, that
offereth the blood of the peace offerings,
and the fat, shall have the right shoulder
for *his* part.
34 For [a]the wave breast and the heave
shoulder have I taken of the children of
Israel from off the sacrifices of their peace
offerings, and have given them unto
Aaron the priest and unto his sons by a
statute for ever from among the children
of Israel.
35 ¶ This *is the portion* of the anointing of Aaron, and of the anointing of his
sons, out of the offerings of the LORD
made by fire, in the day *when* he presented them to minister unto the LORD in
the priest's office;
36 Which the LORD commanded to be
given them of the children of Israel, [a]in
the day that he anointed them, *by* a statute for ever throughout their generations.
37 This *is* the law [a]of the burnt offer- **D**
ing, [b]of the meat offering, [c]and of the sin
offering, [d]and of the trespass offering,
[e]and of the consecrations, and [f]of the
sacrifice of the peace offerings;
38 Which the LORD commanded Moses
in mount Sinai, in the day that he commanded the children of Israel [a]to offer
their oblations unto the LORD, in the wilderness of Sinai.

D *Lev 7:1–2* ◀▶ *Lev 8:14*

7:24 God commanded that the people were not allowed to eat the fat of any animal that died naturally or was violently killed by a predator. Doctors now know that such animals quickly produce harmful germs, especially in a warm climate like the Middle East.

The anointing of priests

8 AND THE LORD spake unto Moses,
saying,
2 [a]Take Aaron and his sons with him,
and [b]the garments, and [c]the anointing
oil, and a bullock for the sin offering, and
two rams, and a basket of unleavened
bread;
3 And gather thou all the congregation
together unto the door of the tabernacle
of the congregation.
4 And Moses did as the LORD commanded him; and the assembly was gathered together unto the door of the tabernacle of the congregation.
5 And Moses said unto the congregation, [a]This *is* the thing which the LORD
commanded to be done.
6 And Moses brought Aaron and his
sons, [a]and washed them with water.
7 [a]And he put upon him the [b]coat, and
girded him with the girdle, and clothed
him with the robe, and put the ephod
upon him, and he girded him with the
curious girdle of the ephod, and bound *it*
unto him therewith.
8 And he put the breastplate upon
him: also he [a]put in the breastplate the
Urim and the Thummim.
9 [a]And he put the mitre upon his
head; also upon the mitre, *even* upon his
forefront, did he put the golden plate,
the holy crown; as the LORD [b]commanded
Moses.
10 [a]And Moses took the anointing oil,
and anointed the tabernacle and all that
was therein, and sanctified them.
11 And he sprinkled thereof upon the
altar seven times, and anointed the altar
and all his vessels, both the laver and his
foot, to sanctify them.
S 12 And he [a]poured of the anointing oil
upon Aaron's head, and anointed him, to
sanctify him.
13 [a]And Moses brought Aaron's sons,
and put coats upon them, and girded
them with girdles, and [†]put bonnets
upon them; as the LORD commanded
Moses.
D 14 [a]And he brought the bullock for the
sin offering: and Aaron and his sons [b]laid
their hands upon the head of the bullock
for the sin offering.
15 And he slew *it;* [a]and Moses took
the blood, and put *it* upon the horns of
the altar round about with his finger, and
purified the altar, and poured the blood at
the bottom of the altar, and sanctified it,
to make reconciliation upon it.
16 [a]And he took all the fat that *was*
upon the inwards, and the caul *above* the
liver, and the two kidneys, and their fat,
and Moses burned *it* upon the altar.
17 But the bullock, and his hide, his D
flesh, and his dung, he burnt with fire
without the camp; as the LORD [a]com-
manded Moses.
18 ¶ [a]And he brought the ram for the
burnt offering: and Aaron and his sons
laid their hands upon the head of the
ram.
19 And he killed *it;* and Moses sprinkled the blood upon the altar round
about.
20 And he cut the ram into pieces; and
Moses burnt the head, and the pieces,
and the fat.
21 And he washed the inwards and
the legs in water; and Moses burnt the
whole ram upon the altar: it *was* a burnt
sacrifice for a sweet savour, *and* an offering made by fire unto the LORD; [a]as the
LORD commanded Moses.
22 ¶ And [a]he brought the other ram,
the ram of consecration: and Aaron and
his sons laid their hands upon the head of
the ram.
23 And he slew *it;* and Moses took of
the blood of it, and put *it* upon the tip of
Aaron's right ear, and upon the thumb of
his right hand, and upon the great toe
of his right foot.
24 And he brought Aaron's sons, and
Moses put of the blood upon the tip of
their right ear, and upon the thumbs of
their right hands, and upon the great toes
of their right feet: and Moses sprinkled
the blood upon the altar round about.
25 [a]And he took the fat, and the rump,
and all the fat that *was* upon the inwards,
and the caul *above* the liver, and the two

8:2 [a]Ex. 29:1-3 [b]Ex. 28:2,4 [c]Ex. 30:24,25
5 [a]Ex. 29:4
6 [a]Ex. 29:4
7 [a]Ex. 29:5 [b]Ex. 28:4
8 [a]Ex. 28:30
9 [a]Ex. 29:6 [b]Ex. 28:37
10 [a]Ex. 30:26-29
12 [a]Ex. 29:7 & 30:30; ch. 21:10, 12; Ps. 133:2
13 [a]Ex. 29:8,9 [†]Heb. *bound*
14 [a]Ex. 29:10; Ezek. 43:19 [b]ch. 4:4
15 [a]Ex. 29:12,36; ch. 4:7; Ezek. 43:20,26; Heb. 9:22
16 [a]Ex. 29:13; ch. 4:8
17 [a]Ex. 29:14; ch. 4:11,12
18 [a]Ex. 29:15
21 [a]Ex. 29:18
22 [a]Ex. 29:19,31
25 [a]Ex. 29:22

S *Ex 30:25* ◀ ▶ *Ps 51:10*
D *Lev 7:37* ◀ ▶ *Lev 8:17–18*
D *Lev 8:14* ◀ ▶ *Lev 9:2–7*

8:12 This passage mentions the anointing oil applied to the high priest, foreshadowing the anointing of "the most Holy" (see Da 9:24).

kidneys, and their fat, and the right shoulder:

26 [a]And out of the basket of unleavened bread, that *was* before the LORD, he took one unleavened cake, and a cake of oiled bread, and one wafer, and put *them* on the fat, and upon the right shoulder:

27 And he put all [a]upon Aaron's hands, and upon his sons' hands, and waved them *for* a wave offering before the LORD.

28 [a]And Moses took them from off their hands, and burnt *them* on the altar upon the burnt offering: they *were* consecrations for a sweet savour: it *is* an offering made by fire unto the LORD.

29 And Moses took the breast, and waved it *for* a wave offering before the LORD: *for* of the ram of consecration it was Moses' [a]part; as the LORD commanded Moses.

30 And [a]Moses took of the anointing oil, and of the blood which *was* upon the altar, and sprinkled *it* upon Aaron, *and* upon his garments, and upon his sons, and upon his sons' garments with him; and sanctified Aaron, *and* his garments, and his sons, and his sons' garments with him.

31 ¶ And Moses said unto Aaron and to his sons, [a]Boil the flesh *at* the door of the tabernacle of the congregation: and there eat it with the bread that *is* in the basket of consecrations, as I commanded, saying, Aaron and his sons shall eat it.

32 [a]And that which remaineth of the flesh and of the bread shall ye burn with fire.

33 And ye shall not go out of the door of the tabernacle of the congregation *in* seven days, until the days of your consecration be at an end: for [a]seven days shall he consecrate you.

34 [a]As he hath done this day, *so* the LORD hath commanded to do, to make an atonement for you.

35 Therefore shall ye abide *at* the door of the tabernacle of the congregation day and night seven days, and [a]keep the charge of the LORD, that ye die not: for so I am commanded.

36 So Aaron and his sons did all things which the LORD commanded by the hand of Moses.

26 [a]Ex. 29:23
27 [a]Ex. 29:24
28 [a]Ex. 29:25
29 [a]Ex. 29:26
30 [a]Ex. 29:21 & 30:30; Num. 3:3
31 [a]Ex. 29:31,32; 1 Sam. 2:13-17
32 [a]Ex. 29:34
33 [a]Ex. 29:30,35; Ezek. 43:25,26
34 [a]Heb. 7:16
35 [a]Num. 3:7 & 9:19; Deut. 11:1; 1 Ki. 2:3
9:1 [a]Ezek. 43:27
2 [a]Ex. 29:1; ch. 4:3 & 8:14 [b]ch. 8:18
3 [a]ch. 4:23; Ezra 6:17 & 10:19
4 [a]ch. 2:4 [b]ver. 6, 23; Ex. 29:43
6 [a]ver. 23; Ex. 24:16; 2 Chr. 5:13, 14
7 [a]ch. 4:3; 1 Sam. 3:14; Heb. 5:3 & 7:27 & 9:7 [b]ch. 4:16,20; Heb. 5:1
9 [a]ch. 8:15 [b]See ch. 4:7; Heb. 9:22, 23
10 [a]ch. 8:16 [b]ch. 4:8
11 [a]ch. 4:11 & 8:17
12 [a]ch. 1:5 & 8:19
13 [a]ch. 8:20

The offerings of Aaron

9 AND [a]IT came to pass on the eighth day, *that* Moses called Aaron and his sons, and the elders of Israel;

2 And he said unto Aaron, [a]Take thee a young calf for a sin offering, [b]and a ram for a burnt offering, without blemish, and offer *them* before the LORD. D

3 And unto the children of Israel thou shalt speak, saying, [a]Take ye a kid of the goats for a sin offering; and a calf and a lamb, *both* of the first year, without blemish, for a burnt offering;

4 Also a bullock and a ram for peace offerings, to sacrifice before the LORD; and [a]a meat offering mingled with oil: for [b]today the LORD will appear unto you.

5 ¶ And they brought *that* which Moses commanded before the tabernacle of the congregation: and all the congregation drew near and stood before the LORD.

6 And Moses said, This *is* the thing which the LORD commanded that ye should do: and [a]the glory of the LORD shall appear unto you.

7 And Moses said unto Aaron, Go unto the altar, and [a]offer thy sin offering, and thy burnt offering, and make an atonement for thyself, and for the people: and [b]offer the offering of the people, and make an atonement for them; as the LORD commanded.

8 ¶ Aaron therefore went unto the altar, and slew the calf of the sin offering, which *was* for himself.

9 [a]And the sons of Aaron brought the blood unto him: and he dipped his finger in the blood, and [b]put *it* upon the horns of the altar, and poured out the blood at the bottom of the altar:

10 [a]But the fat, and the kidneys, and the caul above the liver of the sin offering, he burnt upon the altar; [b]as the LORD commanded Moses.

11 [a]And the flesh and the hide he burnt with fire without the camp. D

12 And he slew the burnt offering; and Aaron's sons presented unto him the blood, [a]which he sprinkled round about upon the altar.

13 [a]And they presented the burnt offering unto him, with the pieces thereof, and the head: and he burnt *them* upon the altar.

D *Lev 8:17–18* ◄► *Lev 9:11*
D *Lev 9:2–7* ◄► *Lev 16:3*

14 [a]And he did wash the inwards and the legs, and burnt *them* upon the burnt offering on the altar.

15 ¶ [a]And he brought the people's offering, and took the goat, which *was* the sin offering for the people, and slew it, and offered it for sin, as the first.

16 And he brought the burnt offering, and offered it [a]according to the [/]manner.

17 And he brought [a]the meat offering, and [/]took an handful thereof, and burnt *it* upon the altar, [b]beside the burnt sacrifice of the morning.

18 He slew also the bullock and the ram *for* [a]a sacrifice of peace offerings, which *was* for the people: and Aaron's sons presented unto him the blood, which he sprinkled upon the altar round about,

19 And the fat of the bullock and of the ram, the rump, and that which covereth *the inwards,* and the kidneys, and the caul *above* the liver:

20 And they put the fat upon the breasts, [a]and he burnt the fat upon the altar:

21 And the breasts and the right shoulder Aaron waved [a]*for* a wave offering before the LORD; as Moses commanded.

22 And Aaron lifted up his hand toward the people, and [a]blessed them, and came down from offering of the sin offering, and the burnt offering, and peace offerings.

23 And Moses and Aaron went into the tabernacle of the congregation, and came out, and blessed the people: [a]and the glory of the LORD appeared unto all the people.

24 And [a]there came a fire out from before the LORD, and consumed upon the altar the burnt offering and the fat: *which* when all the people saw, [b]they shouted, and fell on their faces.

The death of Nadab and Abihu

10 AND [a]NADAB and Abihu, the sons of Aaron, [b]took either of them his censer, and put fire therein, and put incense thereon, and offered [c]strange fire before the LORD, which he commanded them not.

2 And there [a]went out fire from the LORD, and devoured them, and they died before the LORD.

3 Then Moses said unto Aaron, This *is it* that the LORD spake, saying, I will be sanctified in them [a]that come nigh me, and before all the people I will be [b]glorified. [c]And Aaron held his peace.

4 And Moses called Mishael and Elzaphan, the sons of [a]Uzziel the uncle of Aaron, and said unto them, Come near, carry your brethren from before the sanctuary out of the camp.

5 So they went near, and carried them in their coats out of the camp; as Moses had said.

6 And Moses said unto Aaron, and unto Eleazar and unto Ithamar, his sons, [a]Uncover not your heads, neither rend your clothes; lest ye die, and lest [b]wrath come upon all the people: but let your brethren, the whole house of Israel, bewail the burning which the LORD hath kindled.

7 [a]And ye shall not go out from the door of the tabernacle of the congregation, lest ye die: [b]for the anointing oil of the LORD *is* upon you. And they did according to the word of Moses.

8 ¶ And the LORD spake unto Aaron, saying,

9 [a]Do not drink wine nor strong drink, thou, nor thy sons with thee, when ye go into the tabernacle of the congregation, lest ye die: *it shall be* a statute for ever throughout your generations:

10 And that ye may [a]put difference between holy and unholy, and between unclean and clean;

11 [a]And that ye may teach the children of Israel all the statutes which the LORD hath spoken unto them by the hand of Moses.

12 ¶ And Moses spake unto Aaron, and unto Eleazar and unto Ithamar, his sons that were left, Take [a]the meat offering that remaineth of the offerings of the LORD made by fire, and eat it without leaven beside the altar: for [b]it *is* most holy:

13 And ye shall eat it in the holy place, because it *is* thy due, and thy sons' due,

14 [a]ch. 8:21
15 [a]ver. 3; Is. 53:10; Heb. 2:17 & 5:3
16 [a]ch. 1:3,10 [/]Or, *ordinance*
17 [a]ver. 4; ch. 2:1, 2 [b]Ex. 29:38 [/]Heb. *filled his hand out of it*
18 [a]ch. 3:1
20 [a]ch. 3:5,16
21 [a]Ex. 29:24; ch. 7:30-34
22 [a]Num. 6:23; Deut. 21:5; Luke 24:50
23 [a]ver. 6; Num. 14:10
24 [a]Gen. 4:4; Judg. 6:21; 1 Ki. 18:38; 2 Chr. 7:1; Ps. 20:3 [b]1 Ki. 18:39; 2 Chr. 7:3; Ezra 3:11
10:1 [a]Num. 3:3,4; 1 Chr. 24:2 [b]ch. 16:12 [c]Ex. 30:9
2 [a]Num. 16:35
3 [a]Ex. 19:22; Is. 52:11; Ezek. 20:41 [b]Ezek. 28:22 [c]Ps. 39:9
4 [a]Ex. 6:18,22; Num. 3:19,30
6 [a]ch. 21:10; Num. 6:6,7 [b]Num. 16:22, 46; Josh. 7:1; 2 Sam. 24:1
7 [a]ch. 21:12 [b]ch. 8:30
9 [a]Luke 1:15; 1 Tim. 3:3; Tit. 1:7
10 [a]Ezek. 44:23
11 [a]Deut. 24:8; Neh. 8:2,8; Jer. 18:18; Mal. 2:7
12 [a]Num. 18:9 [b]ch. 21:22

10:10 God's laws of sanctification clearly defined the difference between the sacred and the profane, the holy and the common, the right and the wrong. This verse marks the focus of the entire book of Leviticus.

of the sacrifices of the LORD made by fire: for [a]so I am commanded.

14 And [a]the wave breast and heave shoulder shall ye eat in a clean place; thou, and thy sons, and thy daughters with thee: for *they be* thy due, and thy sons' due, *which* are given out of the sacrifices of peace offerings of the children of Israel.

15 [a]The heave shoulder and the wave breast shall they bring with the offerings made by fire of the fat, to wave *it for* a wave offering before the LORD; and it shall be thine, and thy sons' with thee, by a statute for ever; as the LORD hath commanded.

16 ¶ And Moses diligently sought [a]the goat of the sin offering, and, behold, it was burnt: and he was angry with Eleazar and Ithamar, the sons of Aaron *which were* left *alive,* saying,

17 [a]Wherefore have ye not eaten the sin offering in the holy place, seeing it *is* most holy, and *God* hath given it you to bear the iniquity of the congregation, to make atonement for them before the LORD?

18 Behold, [a]the blood of it was not brought in within the holy *place:* ye should indeed have eaten it in the holy *place,* [b]as I commanded.

19 And Aaron said unto Moses, Behold, [a]this day have they offered their sin offering and their burnt offering before the LORD; and such things have befallen me: and *if* I had eaten the sin offering today, [b]should it have been accepted in the sight of the LORD?

20 And when Moses heard *that,* he was content.

Clean and unclean animals

11 AND THE LORD spake unto Moses and to Aaron, saying unto them,

2 Speak unto the children of Israel, saying, [a]These *are* the beasts which ye shall eat among all the beasts that *are* on the earth.

3 Whatsoever parteth the hoof, and is clovenfooted, *and* cheweth the cud, among the beasts, that shall ye eat.

4 Nevertheless these shall ye not eat of them that chew the cud, or of them that divide the hoof: *as* the camel, because he cheweth the cud, but divideth not the hoof; he *is* unclean unto you.

5 And the coney, because he cheweth the cud, but divideth not the hoof; he *is* unclean unto you.

6 And the hare, because he cheweth the cud, but divideth not the hoof; he *is* unclean unto you.

7 And the swine, though he divide the hoof, and be clovenfooted, yet he cheweth not the cud; [a]he *is* unclean to you.

8 Of their flesh shall ye not eat, and their carcase shall ye not touch; [a]they *are* unclean to you.

9 ¶ [a]These shall ye eat of all that *are* in the waters: whatsoever hath fins and scales in the waters, in the seas, and in the rivers, them shall ye eat.

10 And all that have not fins and scales in the seas, and in the rivers, of all that move in the waters, and of any living thing which *is* in the waters, they *shall be* an [a]abomination unto you:

11 They shall be even an abomination unto you; ye shall not eat of their flesh, but ye shall have their carcases in abomination.

12 Whatsoever hath no fins nor scales in the waters, that *shall be* an abomination unto you.

13 ¶ [a]And these *are they which* ye shall have in abomination among the fowls; they shall not be eaten, they *are* an abomination: the eagle, and the ossifrage, and the ospray,

14 And the vulture, and the kite after his kind;

15 Every raven after his kind;

16 And the owl, and the night hawk, and the cuckoo, and the hawk after his kind,

17 And the little owl, and the cormorant, and the great owl,

18 And the swan, and the pelican, and the gier eagle,

19 And the stork, the heron after her kind, and the lapwing, and the bat.

20 All fowls that creep, going upon *all*

13 [a]ch. 2:3 & 6:16
14 [a]Ex. 29:24,26, 27; ch. 7:31,34; Num. 18:11
15 [a]ch. 7:29,30
16 [a]ch. 9:3,15
17 [a]ch. 6:26,29
18 [a]ch. 6:30 [b]ch. 6:26,30
19 [a]ch. 9:8,12 [b]Is. 1:11-15
11:2 [a]Deut. 14:4; Ezek. 4:14; Dan. 1:8; Mat. 15:11; Acts 10:12,14; Rom. 14:14; Heb. 9:10 & 13:9
7 [a]Is. 65:4 & 66:3, 17
8 [a]Is. 52:11; Mark 7:2,15,18; Acts 10:14,15 & 15:29; 1 Cor. 8:8; Heb. 9:10
9 [a]Deut. 14:9
10 [a]ch. 7:18; Deut. 14:3
13 [a]Deut. 14:12

11:2–3 The animals acceptable for human consumption were those that chewed the cud and had a split hoof (11:3). The distinction between these "clean" animals and "unclean" ones had been made since God commanded Noah to take additional clean animals into the ark for use in future sacrifices (see Ge 7:2–3).

four, *shall be* an abomination unto you.
21 Yet these may ye eat of every flying
creeping thing that goeth upon *all* four,
which have legs above their feet, to leap
withal upon the earth;
22 *Even* these of them ye may eat; [a]the
locust after his kind, and the bald locust
after his kind, and the beetle after his
kind, and the grasshopper after his kind.
23 But all *other* flying creeping things,
which have four feet, *shall be* an abomination unto you.
24 And for these ye shall be unclean:
whosoever toucheth the carcase of them
shall be unclean until the even.
25 And whosoever beareth *aught* of
the carcase of them [a]shall wash his
clothes, and be unclean until the even.
26 *The carcases* of every beast which
divideth the hoof, and *is* not clovenfooted, nor cheweth the cud, *are* unclean
unto you: every one that toucheth them
shall be unclean.
27 And whatsoever goeth upon his
paws, among all manner of beasts that go
on *all* four, those *are* unclean unto you:
whoso toucheth their carcase shall be unclean until the even.
28 And he that beareth the carcase of
them shall wash his clothes, and be unclean until the even: they *are* unclean
unto you.
29 ¶ These also *shall be* unclean unto
you among the creeping things that creep
upon the earth; the weasel, and [a]the
mouse, and the tortoise after his kind,
30 And the ferret, and the chameleon,
and the lizard, and the snail, and the
mole.
31 These *are* unclean to you among all
that creep: whosoever doth touch them,
when they be dead, shall be unclean until
the even.
32 And upon whatsoever *any* of them,
when they are dead, doth fall, it shall be
unclean; whether *it be* any vessel of
wood, or raiment, or skin, or sack, whatsoever vessel *it be,* wherein *any* work is
done, [a]it must be put into water, and it
shall be unclean until the even; so it shall
be cleansed.
33 And every earthen vessel, where-

22 [a] Mat. 3:4; Mark 1:6
25 [a] ch. 14:8 & 15:5; Num. 19:10, 22 & 31:24; Rev. 7:14
29 [a] Is. 66:17
32 [a] ch. 15:12
33 [a] ch. 6:28 & 15:12; Ps. 2:9; Jer. 48:38; 2 Tim. 2:21; Rev. 2:27
36 [l] Heb. *a gathering together of waters*
40 [a] ch. 17:15 & 22:8; Deut. 14:21; Ezek. 4:14 & 44:31
42 [l] Heb. *doth multiply feet*
43 [a] ch. 20:25 [l] Heb. *souls*
44 [a] Ex. 19:6; ch. 19:2 & 20:7,26; Amos 3:3; Mat. 5:48; 1 Thes. 4:7; 1 Pet. 1:15,16; Rev. 22:11,14

into *any* of them falleth, whatsoever *is* in
it shall be unclean; and [a]ye shall break it.
34 Of all meat which may be eaten,
that on which *such* water cometh shall
be unclean: and all drink that may be
drunk in every *such* vessel shall be unclean.
35 And every *thing* whereupon *any*
part of their carcase falleth shall be unclean; *whether it be* oven, or ranges for
pots, they shall be broken down: *for* they
are unclean, and shall be unclean unto
you.
36 Nevertheless a fountain or pit,
[l]*wherein there is* plenty of water, shall
be clean: but that which toucheth their
carcase shall be unclean.
37 And if *any part* of their carcase fall
upon any sowing seed which is to be
sown, it *shall be* clean.
38 But if *any* water be put upon the
seed, and *any part* of their carcase fall
thereon, it *shall be* unclean unto you.
39 And if any beast, of which ye may
eat, die; he that toucheth the carcase
thereof shall be unclean until the even.
40 And [a]he that eateth of the carcase
of it shall wash his clothes, and be unclean until the even: he also that beareth
the carcase of it shall wash his clothes,
and be unclean until the even.
41 And every creeping thing that
creepeth upon the earth *shall be* an
abomination; it shall not be eaten.
42 Whatsoever goeth upon the belly,
and whatsoever goeth upon *all* four, or
whatsoever [l]hath more feet among all
creeping things that creep upon the
earth, them ye shall not eat; for they *are*
an abomination.
43 [a]Ye shall not make your [l]selves
abominable with any creeping thing that
creepeth, neither shall ye make yourselves unclean with them, that ye should
be defiled thereby.
44 For I *am* the LORD your God: ye shall S
therefore sanctify yourselves, and [a]ye
shall be holy; for I *am* holy: neither shall
ye defile yourselves with any manner of

S *Ex 32:33* ◀ ▶ *Lev 18:4–5*

11:32–35 God gave his people special instructions regarding the dead carcasses of unclean animals such as rats, weasels and lizards. These dead creatures could easily contaminate food, cooking pots or ovens.

creeping thing that creepeth upon the earth.

45 [a]For I *am* the LORD that bringeth you up out of the land of Egypt, to be your God: [b]ye shall therefore be holy, for I *am* holy.

46 This *is* the law of the beasts, and of the fowl, and of every living creature that moveth in the waters, and of every creature that creepeth upon the earth:

47 [a]To make a difference between the unclean and the clean, and between the beast that may be eaten and the beast that may not be eaten.

Purification after childbirth

12 AND THE LORD spake unto Moses, saying,

2 Speak unto the children of Israel, saying, If a [a]woman have conceived seed, and born a man child: then [b]she shall be unclean seven days; [c]according to the days of the separation for her infirmity shall she be unclean.

3 And in the [a]eighth day the flesh of his foreskin shall be circumcised.

4 And she shall then continue in the blood of her purifying three and thirty days; she shall touch no hallowed thing, nor come into the sanctuary, until the days of her purifying be fulfilled.

5 But if she bear a maid child, then she shall be unclean two weeks, as in her separation: and she shall continue in the blood of her purifying threescore and six days.

6 And [a]when the days of her purifying are fulfilled, for a son, or for a daughter, she shall bring a lamb [l]of the first year for a burnt offering, and a young pigeon, or a turtledove, for a sin offering, unto the door of the tabernacle of the congregation, unto the priest:

7 Who shall offer it before the LORD, and make an atonement for her; and she shall be cleansed from the issue of her blood. This *is* the law for her that hath born a male or a female.

8 [a]And if [l]she be not able to bring a lamb, then she shall bring two turtles, or two young pigeons; the one for the burnt offering, and the other for a sin offering: [b]and the priest shall make an atonement for her, and she shall be clean.

45 [a]Ex. 6:7 & 20:2; Ps. 105:43-45; Hos. 11:1 [b]ver. 44

47 [a]ch. 10:10; Ezek. 44:23; Mal. 3:18

12:2 [a]ch. 15:19; Job 14:4; Ps. 51:5 [b]Luke 2:22 [c]ch. 15:19

3 [a]Gen. 17:12; Luke 1:59 & 2:21; John 7:22,23; Rom. 3:19; Gal. 5:3

6 [a]Luke 2:22 [l]Heb. *a son of his year*

8 [a]ch. 5:7; Luke 2:24 [b]ch. 4:26 [l]Heb. *her hand find not sufficiency of*

13:2 [a]Deut. 28:27; Is. 3:17 [b]Deut. 17:8,9 & 24:8; Mal. 2:7; Luke 17:14 [l]Or, *swelling*

6 [a]ch. 11:25 & 14:8

10 [a]Num. 12:10, 12; 2 Ki. 5:27; 2 Chr. 26:20 [l]Heb. *the quickening of living flesh*

Laws about skin plagues

13 AND THE LORD spake unto Moses and Aaron, saying,

2 When a man shall have in the skin of his flesh a [l]rising, [a]a scab, or bright spot, and it be in the skin of his flesh *like* the plague of leprosy; [b]then he shall be brought unto Aaron the priest, or unto one of his sons the priests:

3 And the priest shall look on the plague in the skin of the flesh: and *when* the hair in the plague is turned white, and the plague in sight *be* deeper than the skin of his flesh, it *is* a plague of leprosy: and the priest shall look on him, and pronounce him unclean.

4 If the bright spot *be* white in the skin of his flesh, and in sight *be* not deeper than the skin, and the hair thereof be not turned white; then the priest shall shut up *him that hath* the plague seven days:

5 And the priest shall look on him the seventh day: and, behold, *if* the plague in his sight be at a stay, *and* the plague spread not in the skin; then the priest shall shut him up seven days more:

6 And the priest shall look on him again the seventh day: and, behold, *if* the plague *be* somewhat dark, *and* the plague spread not in the skin, the priest shall pronounce him clean: it *is but* a scab: and he [a]shall wash his clothes, and be clean.

7 But if the scab spread much abroad in the skin, after that he hath been seen of the priest for his cleansing, he shall be seen of the priest again:

8 And *if* the priest see that, behold, the scab spreadeth in the skin, then the priest shall pronounce him unclean: it *is* a leprosy.

9 ¶ When the plague of leprosy is in a man, then he shall be brought unto the priest;

10 [a]And the priest shall see *him:* and, behold, *if* the rising *be* white in the skin, and it have turned the hair white, and *there be* [l]quick raw flesh in the rising;

11 It *is* an old leprosy in the skin of his flesh, and the priest shall pronounce him unclean, and shall not shut him up: for he *is* unclean.

12 And if a leprosy break out abroad in the skin, and the leprosy cover all the skin of *him that hath* the plague from his head even to his foot, wheresoever the priest looketh;

13 Then the priest shall consider: and, behold, *if* the leprosy have covered all his flesh, he shall pronounce *him* clean *that hath* the plague: it is all turned white: he *is* clean.

14 But when raw flesh appeareth in him, he shall be unclean.

15 And the priest shall see the raw flesh, and pronounce him to be unclean: *for* the raw flesh *is* unclean: it *is* a leprosy.

16 Or if the raw flesh turn again, and be changed unto white, he shall come unto the priest;

17 And the priest shall see him: and, behold, *if* the plague be turned into white; then the priest shall pronounce *him* clean *that hath* the plague: he *is* clean.

18 ¶ The flesh also, in which, *even* in the skin thereof, was a [a]boil, and is healed,

19 And in the place of the boil there be a white rising, or a bright spot, white, and somewhat reddish, and it be shown to the priest;

20 And if, when the priest seeth it, behold, it *be* in sight lower than the skin, and the hair thereof be turned white; the priest shall pronounce him unclean: it *is* a plague of leprosy broken out of the boil.

21 But if the priest look on it, and, behold, *there be* no white hairs therein, and *if* it *be* not lower than the skin, but *be* somewhat dark; then the priest shall shut him up seven days:

22 And if it spread much abroad in the skin, then the priest shall pronounce him unclean: it *is* a plague.

23 But if the bright spot stay in his place, *and* spread not, it *is* a burning boil; and the priest shall pronounce him clean.

24 ¶ Or if there be *any* flesh, in the skin whereof *there is* [l]a hot burning, and the quick *flesh* that burneth have a white bright spot, somewhat reddish, or white;

25 Then the priest shall look upon it: and, behold, *if* the hair in the bright spot be turned white, and it *be in* sight deeper than the skin; it *is* a leprosy broken out of the burning: wherefore the priest shall pronounce him unclean: it *is* the [a]plague of leprosy.

26 But if the priest look on it, and, behold, *there be* no white hair in the bright spot, and it *be* no lower than the *other* skin, but *be* somewhat dark; then the priest shall shut him up seven days:

27 And the priest shall look upon him the seventh day: *and* if it be spread much abroad in the skin, then the priest shall pronounce him unclean: it *is* the plague of leprosy.

28 And if the bright spot stay in his place, *and* spread not in the skin, but it *be* somewhat dark; it *is* a rising of the burning, and the priest shall pronounce him clean: for it *is* an inflammation of the burning.

29 ¶ If a man or woman have a plague upon the head or the beard;

30 Then the [a]priest shall see the plague: and, behold, if it *be* in sight deeper than the skin; *and there be* in it a yellow thin hair; then the priest shall pronounce him unclean: it *is* a dry [b]scall, *even* a leprosy upon the head or beard.

31 And if the priest look on the plague of the scall, and, behold, it *be* not in sight deeper than the skin, and *that there is* no black hair in it; then the priest shall shut up *him that hath* the plague of the scall seven days:

32 And in the seventh day the priest shall look on the plague: and, behold, *if* the scall spread not, and there be in it no yellow hair, and the scall *be* not in sight deeper than the skin;

33 He shall be [a]shaven, but the scall shall he not shave; and the priest shall shut up *him that hath* the scall seven days more:

34 And in the seventh day the priest shall look on the scall: and, behold, *if* the scall be not spread in the skin, nor *be* in sight deeper than the skin; then the priest shall pronounce him clean: and he shall wash his clothes, and be clean.

35 But if the scall spread much in the skin after his cleansing;

36 Then the priest shall look on him: and, behold, if the scall be spread in the skin, the priest shall not seek for yellow hair; he *is* unclean.

37 But if the scall be in his sight at a stay, and *that* there is black hair grown up therein; the scall is healed, he *is* clean: and the [a]priest shall pronounce him clean.

38 ¶ If a man also or a woman have in the skin of their flesh bright spots, *even* white bright spots;

39 Then the priest shall look: and, be-

18 [a]Ex. 9:9 & 15:26

24 [l]Heb. *a burning of fire*

25 [a]Ex. 4:6,7; Num. 12:10; 2 Sam. 3:29; 2 Ki. 5:27; Luke 5:12-14

30 [a]Deut. 24:8; Mal. 2:7; 1 Cor. 12:9 [b]Deut. 28:27; Is. 3:17

33 [a]Job 1:20; Rom. 8:13

37 [a]ch. 10:10; Jer. 15:19; Ezek. 22:26 & 44:23

hold, *if* the bright spots in the skin of their flesh *be* darkish white; it *is* a freckled spot *that* groweth in the skin; he *is* clean.

40 And the man whose [l]hair is fallen off his head, he *is* [a]bald; *yet is* he clean.

41 And he that hath his hair fallen off from the part of his head toward his face, he *is* forehead bald: *yet is* he clean.

42 And if there be in the bald head, or bald forehead, a white reddish sore; it *is* a leprosy sprung up in his bald head, or his bald forehead.

43 Then the priest shall look upon it: and, behold, *if* the rising of the sore *be* white reddish in his bald head, or in his bald forehead, as the leprosy appeareth in the skin of the flesh;

44 He is a leprous man, he *is* unclean: the priest shall pronounce him utterly unclean; his plague *is* in his head.

45 And the leper in whom the plague *is,* his clothes shall be rent, and his head bare, and he shall [a]put a covering upon his upper lip, and shall cry, [b]Unclean, unclean.

46 All the days wherein the plague *shall be* in him he shall be defiled; he *is* unclean: he shall dwell alone; [a]without the camp *shall* his habitation *be.*

Leprosy in garments

47 ¶ The garment also that the plague of leprosy is in, *whether it be* a woollen garment, or a linen garment;

48 Whether *it be* in the warp, or woof; of linen, or of woollen; whether in a skin, or in any [l]thing made of skin;

49 And if the plague be greenish or reddish in the garment, or in the skin, either in the warp, or in the woof, or in any [l]thing of skin; it *is* a plague of leprosy, and shall be shown unto the priest:

50 And the priest shall look upon the plague, and shut up *it that hath* the plague seven days:

51 And he shall look on the plague on the seventh day: if the plague be spread in the garment, either in the warp, or in the woof, or in a skin, *or* in any work that is made of skin; the plague *is* [a]a fretting leprosy; it *is* unclean.

52 He shall therefore burn that garment, whether warp or woof, in woollen or in linen, or any thing of skin, wherein the plague is: for it *is* a fretting leprosy; it shall be burnt in the fire.

53 And if the priest shall look, and, behold, the plague be not spread in the garment, either in the warp, or in the woof, or in any thing of skin;

54 Then the priest shall command that they wash *the thing* wherein the plague *is,* and he shall shut it up seven days more:

55 And the priest shall look on the plague, after that it is washed: and, behold, *if* the plague have not changed his colour, and the plague be not spread; it *is* unclean; thou shalt burn it in the fire; it *is* fret inward, [l]*whether* it *be* bare within or without.

56 And if the priest look, and, behold, the plague *be* somewhat dark after the washing of it; then he shall rend it out of the garment, or out of the skin, or out of the warp, or out of the woof:

57 And if it appear still in the garment, either in the warp, or in the woof, or in any thing of skin; it *is* a spreading *plague:* thou shalt burn that wherein the plague *is* with fire.

58 And the garment, either warp, or woof, or whatsoever thing of skin *it be,* which thou shalt wash, if the plague be departed from them, then it shall be washed the second time, and shall be clean.

59 This *is* the law of the plague of leprosy in a garment of woollen or linen, either in the warp, or woof, or any thing of skins, to pronounce it clean, or to pronounce it unclean.

The cleansing of lepers

14 AND THE LORD spake unto Moses, saying,

2 This shall be the law of the leper in the day of his cleansing: He [a]shall be brought unto the priest:

3 And the priest shall go forth out of the camp; and the priest shall look, and, behold, *if* the plague of leprosy be healed in the leper;

4 Then shall the priest command to take for him that is to be cleansed two

40 [a]Is. 15:2; Amos 8:10 [l]Heb. *head is pilled*

45 [a]Ezek. 24:17, 22; Mic. 3:7 [b]Lam. 4:15

46 [a]Num. 5:2 & 12:14; 2 Ki. 7:3 & 15:5; 2 Chr. 26:21; Luke 17:12

48 [l]Heb. *work of*

49 [l]Heb. *vessel,* or, *instrument*

51 [a]ch. 14:44

55 [l]Heb. whether *it be bald in the head thereof,* or *in the forehead thereof*

14:2 [a]Mat. 8:2,4; Mark 1:40,44; Luke 5:12,14 & 17:14

13:46 In this passage Moses divinely demonstrates a knowledge of quarantine—a disease control method that was not formally recognized until the 1870s.

[1]birds alive *and* clean, and [a]cedar wood, and [b]scarlet, and [c]hyssop:

5 And the priest shall command that one of the birds be killed in an earthen vessel over running water:

6 As for the living bird, he shall take it, and the cedar wood, and the scarlet, and the hyssop, and shall dip them and the living bird in the blood of the bird *that was* killed over the running water:

7 And he shall [a]sprinkle upon him that is to be cleansed from the leprosy [b]seven times, and shall pronounce him clean, and shall let the living bird loose [1]into the open field.

8 And he that is to be cleansed [a]shall wash his clothes, and shave off all his hair, [b]and wash himself in water, that he may be clean: and after that he shall come into the camp, and [c]shall tarry abroad out of his tent seven days.

9 But it shall be on the seventh day, that he shall shave all his hair off his head and his beard and his eyebrows, even all his hair he shall shave off: and he shall wash his clothes, also he shall wash his flesh in water, and he shall be clean.

10 And on the eighth day [a]he shall take two he lambs without blemish, and one ewe lamb [1]of the first year without blemish, and three tenth deals of fine flour *for* [b]a meat offering, mingled with oil, and one log of oil.

11 And the priest that maketh *him* clean shall present the man that is to be made clean, and those things, before the LORD, *at* the door of the tabernacle of the congregation:

12 And the priest shall take one he lamb, and [a]offer him for a trespass offering, and the log of oil, and [b]wave them *for* a wave offering before the LORD:

13 And he shall slay the lamb [a]in the place where he shall kill the sin offering and the burnt offering, in the holy place: for [b]as the sin offering *is* the priest's, *so is* the trespass offering: [c]it *is* most holy:

14 And the priest shall take *some* of the blood of the trespass offering, and the priest shall put *it* [a]upon the tip of the right ear of him that is to be cleansed, and upon the thumb of his right hand, and upon the great toe of his right foot:

15 And the priest shall take *some* of the log of oil, and pour *it* into the palm of his own left hand:

16 And the priest shall dip his right finger in the oil that *is* in his left hand, and shall sprinkle of the oil with his finger seven times before the LORD:

17 And of the rest of the oil that *is* in his hand shall the priest put upon the tip of the right ear of him that is to be cleansed, and upon the thumb of his right hand, and upon the great toe of his right foot, upon the blood of the trespass offering:

18 And the remnant of the oil that *is* in the priest's hand he shall pour upon the head of him that is to be cleansed: [a]and the priest shall make an atonement for him before the LORD.

19 And the priest shall offer [a]the sin offering, and make an atonement for him that is to be cleansed from his uncleanness; and afterward he shall kill the burnt offering:

20 And the priest shall offer the burnt offering and the meat offering upon the altar: and the priest shall make an atonement for him, and he shall be clean.

21 And [a]if he *be* poor, and [1]cannot get so much; then he shall take one lamb *for* a trespass offering [2]to be waved, to make an atonement for him, and one tenth deal of fine flour mingled with oil for a meat offering, and a log of oil;

22 [a]And two turtledoves, or two young pigeons, such as he is able to get; and the one shall be a sin offering, and the other a burnt offering.

23 [a]And he shall bring them on the eighth day for his cleansing unto the priest, unto the door of the tabernacle of the congregation, before the LORD.

24 [a]And the priest shall take the lamb of the trespass offering, and the log of oil, and the priest shall wave them *for* a wave offering before the LORD:

25 And he shall kill the lamb of the trespass offering, [a]and the priest shall take *some* of the blood of the trespass offering, and put *it* upon the tip of the right ear of him that is to be cleansed, and upon the thumb of his right hand, and upon the great toe of his right foot:

26 And the priest shall pour of the oil into the palm of his own left hand:

27 And the priest shall sprinkle with his right finger *some* of the oil that *is* in his left hand seven times before the LORD:

28 And the priest shall put of the oil that *is* in his hand upon the tip of the right ear of him that is to be cleansed,

4 [a]Num. 19:6 [b]Heb. 9:19 [c]Ps. 51:7 [1]Or, *sparrows*

7 [a]Num. 19:18,19; Is. 52:15; Heb. 9:13,21 & 12:24 [b]2 Ki. 5:10,14; Ps. 51:2 [1]Heb. *upon the face of the field*

8 [a]ch. 13:6 [b]ch. 11:25; Eph. 5:26; Heb. 10:22; Rev. 1:5,6 [c]Num. 12:15

10 [a]Mat. 8:4; Mark 1:44; Luke 5:14 [b]ch. 2:1; Num. 15:4 [1]Heb. *the daughter of her year*

12 [a]ch. 5:2,18 & 6:6,7 [b]Ex. 29:24

13 [a]Ex. 29:11; ch. 1:5 & 4:4 [b]ch. 7:7 [c]ch. 2:3 & 7:6 & 21:22

14 [a]Ex. 29:20; ch. 8:23

18 [a]ch. 4:26 & 5:6

19 [a]ch. 5:1,6 & 12:7

21 [a]ch. 5:7 & 12:8 [1]Heb. *his hand reach not* [2]Heb. *for a waving*

22 [a]ch. 12:8 & 15:14,15

23 [a]ver. 10,11

24 [a]ver. 12

25 [a]ver. 14,17

and upon the thumb of his right hand, and upon the great toe of his right foot, upon the place of the blood of the trespass offering:

29 And the rest of the oil that *is* in the priest's hand he shall put upon the head of him that is to be cleansed, to make an atonement for him before the LORD.

30 And he shall offer the one of [a]the turtledoves, or of the young pigeons, such as he can get;

31 *Even* such as he is able to get, the one *for* a sin offering, and the other *for* a burnt offering, with the meat offering: and the priest shall make an atonement for him that is to be cleansed before the LORD.

32 This *is* the law *of him* in whom *is* the plague of leprosy, whose hand is not able to get [a]*that which pertaineth* to his cleansing.

Leprosy in houses

33 ¶ And the LORD spake unto Moses and unto Aaron, saying,

34 [a]When ye be come into the land of Canaan, which I give to you for a possession, and I put the plague of leprosy in a house of the land of your possession;

35 And he that owneth the house shall come and tell the priest, saying, It seemeth to me *there is* as it were [a]a plague in the house:

36 Then the priest shall command that they [1]empty the house, before the priest go *into it* to see the plague, that all that *is* in the house be not made unclean: and afterward the priest shall go in to see the house:

37 And he shall look on the plague, and, behold, *if* the plague *be* in the walls of the house with hollow strakes, greenish or reddish, which in sight *are* lower than the wall;

38 Then the priest shall go out of the house to the door of the house, and shut up the house seven days:

39 And the priest shall come again the seventh day, and shall look: and, behold, *if* the plague be spread in the walls of the house;

40 Then the priest shall command that they take away the stones in which the plague *is,* and they shall cast them into an unclean place without the city:

41 And he shall cause the house to be scraped within round about, and they shall pour out the dust that they scrape off without the city into an unclean place:

42 And they shall take other stones, and put *them* in the place of those stones; and he shall take other mortar, and shall plaster the house.

43 And if the plague come again, and break out in the house, after that he hath taken away the stones, and after he hath scraped the house, and after it is plastered;

44 Then the priest shall come and look, and, behold, *if* the plague be spread in the house, it *is* [a]a fretting leprosy in the house: it *is* unclean.

45 And he shall break down the house, the stones of it, and the timber thereof, and all the mortar of the house; and he shall carry *them* forth out of the city into an unclean place.

46 Moreover he that goeth into the house all the while that it is shut up shall be unclean until the even.

47 And he that lieth in the house shall wash his clothes; and he that eateth in the house shall wash his clothes.

48 And if the priest [1]shall come in, and look *upon it,* and, behold, the plague hath not spread in the house, after the house was plastered: then the priest shall pronounce the house clean, because the plague is healed.

49 And [a]he shall take to cleanse the house two birds, and cedar wood, and scarlet, and hyssop:

50 And he shall kill the one of the birds in an earthen vessel over running water:

51 And he shall take the cedar wood, and the hyssop, and the scarlet, and the living bird, and dip them in the blood of the slain bird, and in the running water, and sprinkle the house seven times:

52 And he shall cleanse the house with the blood of the bird, and with the running water, and with the living bird, and with the cedar wood, and with the hyssop, and with the scarlet:

53 But he shall let go the living bird out of the city into the open fields, and [a]make an atonement for the house: and it shall be clean.

54 This *is* the law for all manner of plague of leprosy, and [a]scall,

55 And for the [a]leprosy of a garment, [b]and of a house,

30 [a]ver. 22; ch. 15:14,15
32 [a]ver. 10
34 [a]Gen. 17:8; Num. 32:22; Deut. 7:1 & 32:49
35 [a]Ps. 91:10; Prov. 3:33; Zech. 5:4
36 [1]Or, *prepare*
44 [a]ch. 13:51; Zech. 5:4
48 [1]Heb. *in coming in shall come in*
49 [a]ver. 4
53 [a]ver. 20
54 [a]ch. 13:30
55 [a]ch. 13:47 [b]ver. 34

56 And [a]for a rising, and for a scab, and for a bright spot:

57 To [a]teach [l]when *it is* unclean, and when *it is* clean: this *is* the law of leprosy.

Laws about uncleanness

15 AND THE LORD spake unto Moses and to Aaron, saying,

2 Speak unto the children of Israel, and say unto them, [a]When any man hath a [l]running issue out of his flesh, *because of* his issue he *is* unclean.

3 And this shall be his uncleanness in his issue: whether his flesh run with his issue, or his flesh be stopped from his issue, it *is* his uncleanness.

4 Every bed, whereon he lieth that hath the issue, is unclean: and every [l]thing, whereon he sitteth, shall be unclean.

5 And whosoever toucheth his bed shall wash his clothes, [a]and bathe *himself* in water, and be unclean until the even.

6 And he that sitteth on *any* thing whereon he sat that hath the issue shall wash his clothes, and bathe *himself* in water, and be unclean until the even.

7 And he that toucheth the flesh of him that hath the issue shall wash his clothes, and bathe *himself* in water, and be unclean until the even.

8 And if he that hath the issue spit upon him that is clean; then he shall wash his clothes, and bathe *himself* in water, and be unclean until the even.

9 And what saddle soever he rideth upon that hath the issue shall be unclean.

10 And whosoever toucheth any thing that was under him shall be unclean until the even: and he that beareth *any of* those things shall wash his clothes, and bathe *himself* in water, and be unclean until the even.

11 And whomsoever he toucheth that hath the issue, and hath not rinsed his hands in water, he shall wash his clothes, and bathe *himself* in water, and be unclean until the even.

12 And the [a]vessel of earth, that he toucheth which hath the issue, shall be broken: and every vessel of wood shall be rinsed in water.

13 And when he that hath an issue is cleansed of his issue; then [a]he shall number to himself seven days for his cleansing, and wash his clothes, and bathe his flesh in running water, and shall be clean.

14 And on the eighth day he shall take to him [a]two turtledoves, or two young pigeons, and come before the LORD unto the door of the tabernacle of the congregation, and give them unto the priest:

15 And the priest shall offer them, [a]the one *for* a sin offering, and the other *for* a burnt offering; [b]and the priest shall make an atonement for him before the LORD for his issue.

16 And [a]if any man's seed of copulation go out from him, then he shall wash all his flesh in water, and be unclean until the even.

17 And every garment, and every skin, whereon is the seed of copulation, shall be washed with water, and be unclean until the even.

18 The woman also with whom man shall lie *with* seed of copulation, they shall *both* bathe *themselves* in water, and [a]be unclean until the even.

19 ¶ And [a]if a woman have an issue, *and* her issue in her flesh be blood, she shall be [l]put apart seven days: and whosoever toucheth her shall be unclean until the even.

20 And every thing that she lieth upon in her separation shall be unclean: every thing also that she sitteth upon shall be unclean.

21 And whosoever toucheth her bed shall wash his clothes, and bathe *himself* in water, and be unclean until the even.

22 And whosoever toucheth any thing that she sat upon shall wash his clothes, and bathe *himself* in water, and be unclean until the even.

23 And if it *be* on *her* bed, or on any thing whereon she sitteth, when he toucheth it, he shall be unclean until the even.

24 And [a]if any man lie with her at all, and her flowers be upon him, he shall be

56 [a]ch. 13:2
57 [a]Deut. 24:8; Ezek. 44:23 [l]Heb. *in the day of the unclean, and in the day of the clean*
15:2 [a]ch. 22:4; Num. 5:2; 2 Sam. 3:29 [l]Or, *running of the reins*
4 [l]Heb. *vessel*
5 [a]ch. 11:25 & 17:15
12 [a]ch. 6:28 & 11:32,33
13 [a]ver. 28; ch. 14:8; Num. 19:11, 12
14 [a]ch. 14:22,23
15 [a]ch. 14:30,31 [b]ch. 14:19,31
16 [a]ch. 22:4; Deut. 23:10
18 [a]Ex. 19:15; 1 Sam. 21:4; 1 Cor. 6:18
19 [a]ch. 12:2 [l]Heb. *in her separation*
24 [a]See ch. 20:18

15:13 The command in this verse for the man to "wash his clothes, and bathe his flesh in running water" is as modern as today's hospital manuals. Following God's command to wash in running water could have saved untold millions from disease and death throughout history.

unclean seven days; and all the bed whereon he lieth shall be unclean.

25 And if [a]a woman have an issue of her blood many days out of the time of her separation, or if it run beyond the time of her separation; all the days of the issue of her uncleanness shall be as the days of her separation: she *shall be* unclean.

26 Every bed whereon she lieth all the days of her issue shall be unto her as the bed of her separation: and whatsoever she sitteth upon shall be unclean, as the uncleanness of her separation.

27 And whosoever toucheth those things shall be unclean, and shall wash his clothes, and bathe *himself* in water, and be unclean until the even.

28 But [a]if she be cleansed of her issue, then she shall number to herself seven days, and after that she shall be clean.

29 And on the eighth day she shall take unto her two turtles, or two young pigeons, and bring them unto the priest, to the door of the tabernacle of the congregation.

30 And the priest shall offer the one *for* a sin offering, and the other *for* a burnt offering; and the priest shall make an atonement for her before the LORD for the issue of her uncleanness.

31 Thus shall ye [a]separate the children of Israel from their uncleanness; that they die not in their uncleanness, when they [b]defile my tabernacle that *is* among them.

32 [a]This *is* the law of him that hath an issue, [b]and *of him* whose seed goeth from him, and is defiled therewith;

33 [a]And of her that is sick of her flowers, and of him that hath an issue, of the man, [b]and of the woman, [c]and of him that lieth with her that is unclean.

The day of Atonement

16 AND THE LORD spake unto Moses after [a]the death of the two sons of Aaron, when they offered before the LORD, and died;

2 And the LORD said unto Moses, Speak unto Aaron thy brother, that he [a]come not at all times into the holy *place* within the veil before the mercy seat, which *is* upon the ark; that he die not: for [b]I will appear in the cloud upon the mercy seat.

25 [a]Mat. 9:20; Mark 5:25; Luke 8:43
28 [a]ver. 13-15
31 [a]ch. 11:47; Deut. 24:8; Ezek. 44:23; Heb. 12:15 [b]Num. 5:3 & 19:13,20; Ezek. 5:11 & 23:38
32 [a]ver. 2 [b]ver. 16
33 [a]ver. 19 [b]ver. 25 [c]ver. 24
16:1 [a]ch. 10:1,2
2 [a]Ex. 30:10; ch. 23:27; Heb. 9:7 & 10:19 [b]Ex. 25:22 & 40:34; 1 Ki. 8:10-12
3 [a]Ex. 25:21 [b]ch. 4:3
4 [a]Ex. 28:39,42, 43; ch. 6:10; Ezek. 44:17,18 [b]Ex. 30:20; ch. 8:6,7
5 [a]See ch. 4:14; Num. 29:11; 2 Chr. 29:21; Ezra 6:17; Ezek. 45:22,23
6 [a]ch. 9:7; Heb. 5:2 & 7:27,28 & 9:7
8 [1]Heb. *Azazel*
9 [1]Heb. *went up*
10 [a]1 John 2:2
12 [a]ch. 10:1; Num. 16:18,46; Rev. 8:5 [b]Ex. 30:34
13 [a]Ex. 30:7,8; Num. 16:7,18,46 [b]Ex. 25:21
14 [a]ch. 4:5; Heb. 9:25 & 10:4 [b]ch. 4:6
15 [a]Heb. 2:17 & 5:2 & 9:7,28

3 Thus shall Aaron [a]come into the holy *place:* [b]with a young bullock for a sin offering, and a ram for a burnt offering. **D**

4 He shall put on [a]the holy linen coat, and he shall have the linen breeches upon his flesh, and shall be girded with a linen girdle, and with the linen mitre shall he be attired: these *are* holy garments; therefore [b]shall he wash his flesh in water, and *so* put them on.

5 And he shall take of [a]the congregation of the children of Israel two kids of the goats for a sin offering, and one ram for a burnt offering.

6 And Aaron shall offer his bullock of the sin offering, which *is* for himself, and [a]make an atonement for himself, and for his house.

7 And he shall take the two goats, and present them before the LORD *at* the door of the tabernacle of the congregation.

8 And Aaron shall cast lots upon the two goats; one lot for the LORD, and the other lot for the [1]scapegoat.

9 And Aaron shall bring the goat upon which the LORD'S lot [1]fell, and offer him *for* a sin offering.

10 But the goat, on which the lot fell to be the scapegoat, shall be presented alive before the LORD, to make [a]an atonement with him, *and* to let him go for a scapegoat into the wilderness.

11 And Aaron shall bring the bullock of the sin offering, which *is* for himself, and shall make an atonement for himself, and for his house, and shall kill the bullock of the sin offering which *is* for himself:

12 And he shall take [a]a censer full of burning coals of fire from off the altar before the LORD, and his hands full of [b]sweet incense beaten small, and bring *it* within the veil:

13 [a]And he shall put the incense upon the fire before the LORD, that the cloud of the incense may cover the [b]mercy seat that *is* upon the testimony, that he die not:

14 And [a]he shall take of the blood of the bullock, and [b]sprinkle *it* with his finger upon the mercy seat eastward; and before the mercy seat shall he sprinkle of the blood with his finger seven times.

15 ¶ [a]Then shall he kill the goat of the sin offering, that *is* for the people, and

D *Lev 9:11* ◀▶ *Lev 16:21*

bring his blood [b]within the veil, and do with that blood as he did with the blood of the bullock, and sprinkle it upon the mercy seat, and before the mercy seat:

16 And he shall [a]make an atonement for the holy *place,* because of the uncleanness of the children of Israel, and because of their transgressions in all their sins: and so shall he do for the tabernacle of the congregation, that ʹremaineth among them in the midst of their uncleanness.

17 [a]And there shall be no man in the tabernacle of the congregation when he goeth in to make an atonement in the holy *place,* until he come out, and have made an atonement for himself, and for his household, and for all the congregation of Israel.

18 And he shall go out unto the altar that *is* before the LORD, and [a]make an atonement for it; and shall take of the blood of the bullock, and of the blood of the goat, and put *it* upon the horns of the altar round about.

19 And he shall sprinkle of the blood upon it with his finger seven times, and cleanse it, and [a]hallow it from the uncleanness of the children of Israel.

20 ¶ And when he hath made an end of [a]reconciling the holy *place,* and the tabernacle of the congregation, and the altar, he shall bring the live goat:

D 21 And Aaron shall lay both his hands upon the head of the live goat, and confess over him all the iniquities of the children of Israel, and all their transgressions in all their sins, [a]putting them upon the head of the goat, and shall send *him* away by the hand of ʹa fit man into the wilderness:

22 And the goat shall [a]bear upon him all their iniquities unto a land ʹnot inhabited: and he shall let go the goat in the wilderness.

23 And Aaron shall come into the tabernacle of the congregation, [a]and shall put off the linen garments, which he put on when he went into the holy *place,* and shall leave them there:

24 And he shall wash his flesh with water in the holy place, and put on his garments, and come forth, [a]and offer his burnt offering, and the burnt offering of

15 [b]ver. 2; Heb. 6:19 & 9:3,7,12
16 [a]See Ex. 29:36; Ezek. 45:18; Heb. 9:22,23 ʹHeb. *dwelleth*
17 [a]See Ex. 34:3; Luke 1:10
18 [a]Ex. 30:10; ch. 4:7,18; Heb. 9:22, 23
19 [a]Ezek. 43:20
20 [a]ver. 16; Ezek. 45:20
21 [a]Is. 53:6 ʹHeb. *a man of opportunity*
22 [a]Is. 53:11,12; John 1:29; Heb. 9:28; 1 Pet. 2:24 ʹHeb. *of separation*
23 [a]Ezek. 42:14 & 44:19
24 [a]ver. 3,5
25 [a]ch. 4:10
26 [a]ch. 15:5
27 [a]ch. 4:12,21 & 6:30; Heb. 13:11
29 [a]Ex. 30:10; ch. 23:27; Num. 29:7
30 [a]Jer. 33:8; Eph. 5:26; Heb. 9:13,14 & 10:1,2; 1 John 1:7,9
31 [a]ch. 23:32
32 [a]ch. 4:3,5,16 [b]Ex. 29:29,30; Num. 20:26,28 [c]ver. 4 ʹHeb. *fill his hand*
33 [a]ver. 6,16-18, 24
34 [a]ch. 23:31; Num. 29:7 [b]Ex. 30:10; Heb. 9:7,25

the people, and make an atonement for himself, and for the people.

25 And [a]the fat of the sin offering shall he burn upon the altar.

26 And he that let go the goat for the scapegoat shall wash his clothes, [a]and bathe his flesh in water, and afterward come into the camp.

27 [a]And the bullock *for* the sin offering, and the goat *for* the sin offering, whose blood was brought in to make atonement in the holy *place,* shall *one* carry forth without the camp; and they shall burn in the fire their skins, and their flesh, and their dung. D

28 And he that burneth them shall wash his clothes, and bathe his flesh in water, and afterward he shall come into the camp.

29 ¶ And *this* shall be a statute for ever unto you: *that* [a]in the seventh month, on the tenth *day* of the month, ye shall afflict your souls, and do no work at all, *whether it be* one of your own country, or a stranger that sojourneth among you:

30 For on that day shall *the priest* make an atonement for you, to [a]cleanse you, *that* ye may be clean from all your sins before the LORD.

31 [a]It *shall be* a sabbath of rest unto you, and ye shall afflict your souls, by a statute for ever.

32 [a]And the priest, whom he shall anoint, and whom he shall [b]consecrateʹ to minister in the priest's office in his father's stead, shall make the atonement, and [c]shall put on the linen clothes, *even* the holy garments:

33 And [a]he shall make an atonement for the holy sanctuary, and he shall make an atonement for the tabernacle of the congregation, and for the altar, and he shall make an atonement for the priests, and for all the people of the congregation.

34 [a]And this shall be an everlasting statute unto you, to make an atonement for the children of Israel for all their sins [b]once a year. And he did as the LORD commanded Moses.

Laws about special sacrifices

17 AND THE LORD spake unto Moses, saying,

2 Speak unto Aaron, and unto his sons, and unto all the children of Israel, and say

unto them; This *is* the thing which the LORD hath commanded, saying,

3 What man soever *there be* of the house of Israel, [a]that killeth an ox, or lamb, or goat, in the camp, or that killeth *it* out of the camp,

4 [a]And bringeth it not unto the door of the tabernacle of the congregation, to offer an offering unto the LORD before the tabernacle of the LORD; blood shall be [b]imputed unto that man; he hath shed blood; and that man [c]shall be cut off from among his people:

5 To the end that the children of Israel may bring their sacrifices, [a]which they offer in the open field, even that they may bring them unto the LORD, unto the door of the tabernacle of the congregation, unto the priest, and offer them *for* peace offerings unto the LORD.

6 And the priest [a]shall sprinkle the blood upon the altar of the LORD *at* the door of the tabernacle of the congregation, and [b]burn the fat for a sweet savour unto the LORD.

7 And they shall no more offer their sacrifices [a]unto devils, after whom they [b]have gone a-whoring. This shall be a statute for ever unto them throughout their generations.

8 ¶ And thou shalt say unto them, Whatsoever man *there be* of the house of Israel, or of the strangers which sojourn among you, [a]that offereth a burnt offering or sacrifice,

9 And bringeth it not unto the door of the tabernacle of the congregation, to offer it unto the LORD; even that man shall be cut off from among his people.

10 ¶ [a]And whatsoever man *there be* of the house of Israel, or of the strangers that sojourn among you, that eateth any manner of blood; [b]I will even set my face against that soul that eateth blood, and will cut him off from among his people.

D 11 For the life of the flesh *is* in the blood: and I have given it to you upon the altar [a]to make an atonement for your souls: for [b]it *is* the blood *that* maketh an atonement for the soul.

12 Therefore I said unto the children of Israel, No soul of you shall eat blood, neither shall any stranger that sojourneth among you eat blood.

13 And whatsoever man *there be* of the children of Israel, or of the strangers that sojourn among you, [1]which [a]hunteth and catcheth any beast or fowl that may be eaten; he shall even [b]pour out the blood thereof, and [c]cover it with dust.

14 [a]For *it is* the life of all flesh; the blood of it *is* for the life thereof: therefore I said unto the children of Israel, Ye shall eat the blood of no manner of flesh: for the life of all flesh *is* the blood thereof: whosoever eateth it shall be cut off.

15 [a]And every soul that eateth [1]that which died *of itself*, or that which was torn *with beasts, whether it be* one of your own country, or a stranger, [b]he shall both wash his clothes, [c]and bathe *himself* in water, and be unclean until the even: then shall he be clean.

16 But if he wash *them* not, nor bathe his flesh; then [a]he shall bear his iniquity.

Unlawful sexual relations

18 AND THE LORD spake unto Moses, saying,

2 Speak unto the children of Israel, and say unto them, [a]I am the LORD your God.

3 [a]After the doings of the land of Egypt, wherein ye dwelt, shall ye not do: and [b]after the doings of the land of Canaan, whither I bring you, shall ye not do: neither shall ye walk in their ordinances.

4 [a]Ye shall do my judgments, and keep mine ordinances, to walk therein: I *am* the LORD your God. S

5 Ye shall therefore keep my statutes, and my judgments: [a]which if a man do, he shall live in them: [b]I *am* the LORD.

6 ¶ None of you shall approach to any

D *Lev 16:27* ◀▶ *Lev 22:17–25*

S *Lev 11:44–45* ◀▶ *Lev 19:2*

17:3 [a]See Deut. 12:5,15,21
4 [a]Deut. 12:5,6,13,14 [b]Rom. 5:13 [c]Gen. 17:14
5 [a]Gen. 21:33 & 22:2 & 31:54; Deut. 12:2
6 [a]ch. 3:2 [b]Ex. 29:18; Num. 18:17
7 [a]Deut. 32:17; 2 Chr. 11:15; 1 Cor. 10:20 [b]Ex. 34:15; Deut. 31:16; Ezek. 23:8
8 [a]ch. 1:2,3
10 [a]Gen. 9:4; Deut. 12:16,23 & 15:23; 1 Sam. 14:33 [b]ch. 20:3,5,6
11 [a]Mat. 26:28; Rom. 3:25; Eph. 1:7; Col. 1:14,20; 1 Pet. 1:2; 1 John 1:7 [b]Heb. 9:22
13 [a]ch. 7:26 [b]Deut. 12:16,24 [c]Ezek. 24:7 [1]Heb. *that hunteth any hunting*
14 [a]ver. 11,12; Gen. 9:4; Deut. 12:23
15 [a]Ex. 22:31; Ezek. 4:14 & 44:31 [b]ch. 11:25 [c]ch. 15:5 [1]Heb. *a carcase*
16 [a]ch. 5:1
18:2 [a]Ex. 6:7; Ezek. 20:5,7,19,20
3 [a]Ezek. 20:7 [b]Ex. 23:24
4 [a]Ezek. 20:19
5 [a]Ezek. 20:11,13,21; Rom. 10:5; Gal. 3:12 [b]Ex. 6:2,6

17:11 Since life was sacred to God, the blood was also sacred as a symbol of life. The blood of a sacrificial animal took the place of the sinner's blood and symbolically redeemed the sinner. Thus the blood in the OT sacrifice foreshadowed the blood of "the Lamb of God, which taketh away the sin of the world" (Jn 1:29).

18:4–5 These two statements reminded the Israelites that the law was the way of life for the redeemed. Their faithful acts of obedience would result in blessing (see Eze 20:11, 13, 21; Ro 10:5).

that is [/]near of kin to him, to uncover *their* nakedness: I *am* the LORD.

7 [a]The nakedness of thy father, or the nakedness of thy mother, shalt thou not uncover: she *is* thy mother; thou shalt not uncover her nakedness.

8 [a]The nakedness of thy father's wife shalt thou not uncover: it *is* thy father's nakedness.

9 [a]The nakedness of thy sister, the daughter of thy father, or daughter of thy mother, *whether she be* born at home, or born abroad, *even* their nakedness thou shalt not uncover.

10 The nakedness of thy son's daughter, or of thy daughter's daughter, *even* their nakedness thou shalt not uncover: for theirs *is* thine own nakedness.

11 The nakedness of thy father's wife's daughter, begotten of thy father, she *is* thy sister, thou shalt not uncover her nakedness.

12 [a]Thou shalt not uncover the nakedness of thy father's sister: she *is* thy father's near kinswoman.

13 Thou shalt not uncover the nakedness of thy mother's sister: for she *is* thy mother's near kinswoman.

14 [a]Thou shalt not uncover the nakedness of thy father's brother, thou shalt not approach to his wife: she *is* thine aunt.

15 [a]Thou shalt not uncover the nakedness of thy daughter-in-law: she *is* thy son's wife; thou shalt not uncover her nakedness.

16 [a]Thou shalt not uncover the nakedness of thy brother's wife: it *is* thy brother's nakedness.

17 [a]Thou shalt not uncover the nakedness of a woman and her daughter, neither shalt thou take her son's daughter, or her daughter's daughter, to uncover her nakedness; *for* they *are* her near kinswomen: it *is* wickedness.

18 Neither shalt thou take [/]a wife to her sister, [a]to vex *her,* to uncover her nakedness, beside the other in her life *time.*

19 [a]Also thou shalt not approach unto a woman to uncover her nakedness, as long as she is put apart for her uncleanness.

20 Moreover [a]thou shalt not lie carnally with thy neighbour's wife, to defile thyself with her.

21 And thou shalt not let any of thy seed [a]pass through *the fire* to [b]Molech, neither shalt thou [c]profane the name of thy God: I *am* the LORD.

22 [a]Thou shalt not lie with mankind, as with womankind: it *is* abomination.

23 [a]Neither shalt thou lie with any beast to defile thyself therewith: neither shall any woman stand before a beast to lie down thereto: it *is* [b]confusion.

24 [a]Defile not ye yourselves in any of these things: [b]for in all these the nations are defiled which I cast out before you:

25 And [a]the land is defiled: therefore I do [b]visit the iniquity thereof upon it, and the land itself vomiteth out her inhabitants.

26 [a]Ye shall therefore keep my statutes and my judgments, and shall not commit *any* of these abominations; *neither* any of your own nation, nor any stranger that sojourneth among you:

27 (For all these abominations have the men of the land done, which *were* before you, and the land is defiled;)

28 That [a]the land spew not you out also, when ye defile it, as it spewed out the nations that *were* before you.

29 For whosoever shall commit any of these abominations, even the souls that commit *them* shall be cut off from among their people.

30 Therefore shall ye keep mine ordinance, [a]that *ye* commit not *any one* of these abominable customs, which were committed before you, and that ye defile not yourselves therein: I *am* the LORD your God.

Personal conduct

19 AND THE LORD spake unto Moses, saying,

2 Speak unto all the congregation of S
the children of Israel, and say unto them, [a]Ye shall be holy: for I the LORD your God *am* holy.

3 ¶ [a]Ye shall fear every man his mother, and his father, and [b]keep my sabbaths: I *am* the LORD your God.

4 ¶ [a]Turn ye not unto idols, [b]nor make to yourselves molten gods: I *am* the LORD your God.

5 ¶ And [a]if ye offer a sacrifice of peace offerings unto the LORD, ye shall offer it at your own will.

6 It shall be eaten the same day ye of-

6 [/]Heb. *remainder of his flesh*
7 [a]ch. 20:11
8 [a]Gen. 49:4; ch. 20:11; 1 Cor. 5:1
9 [a]ch. 20:17
12 [a]ch. 20:19
14 [a]ch. 20:20
15 [a]Gen. 38:18,26
16 [a]See Deut. 25:5
17 [a]ch. 20:14
18 [a]1 Sam. 1:6,8 [/]Or, one *wife to another*
19 [a]ch. 20:18; Ezek. 18:6 & 22:10
20 [a]Ex. 20:14; ch. 20:10; Deut. 5:18 & 22:22; Mat. 5:27; Rom. 2:22; 1 Cor. 6:9; Heb. 13:4
21 [a]ch. 20:2; 2 Ki. 16:3 [b]1 Ki. 11:7, 33; Called Acts 7:43, *Moloch* [c]ch. 19:12 & 20:3; Ezek. 36:20
22 [a]ch. 20:13; 1 Cor. 6:9; 1 Tim. 1:10
23 [a]Ex. 22:19 [b]ch. 20:12
24 [a]Mat. 15:18-20; 1 Cor. 3:17 [b]Deut. 18:12
25 [a]Num. 35:34; Ezek. 36:17 [b]Is. 26:21; Jer. 5:9
26 [a]ver. 5,30
28 [a]Jer. 9:19
30 [a]ver. 3
19:2 [a]ch. 11:44
3 [a]Ex. 20:12 [b]Ex. 20:8
4 [a]Ex. 20:4 [b]Ex. 34:17
5 [a]ch. 7:16

S *Lev 18:4–5* ◀▶ *Lev 20:7–8*

fer it, and on the morrow: and if aught remain until the third day, it shall be burnt in the fire.

7 And if it be eaten at all on the third day, it *is* abominable; it shall not be accepted.

8 Therefore *every one* that eateth it shall bear his iniquity, because he hath profaned the hallowed thing of the LORD: and that soul shall be cut off from among his people.

9 ¶ And [a]when ye reap the harvest of your land, thou shalt not wholly reap the corners of thy field, neither shalt thou gather the gleanings of thy harvest.

10 And thou shalt not glean thy vineyard, neither shalt thou gather *every* grape of thy vineyard; thou shalt leave them for the poor and stranger: I *am* the LORD your God.

11 ¶ [a]Ye shall not steal, neither deal falsely, [b]neither lie one to another.

12 ¶ And ye shall not [a]swear by my name falsely, [b]neither shalt thou profane the name of thy God: I *am* the LORD.

13 ¶ [a]Thou shalt not defraud thy neighbour, neither rob *him:* [b]the wages of him that is hired shall not abide with thee all night until the morning.

14 ¶ Thou shalt not curse the deaf, [a]nor put a stumblingblock before the blind, but shalt fear thy God: I *am* the LORD.

15 ¶ Ye shall do no unrighteousness in judgment: thou shalt not respect the person of the poor, nor honour the person of the mighty: *but* in righteousness shalt thou judge thy neighbour.

16 ¶ [a]Thou shalt not go up and down *as* a talebearer among thy people: neither shalt thou [b]stand against the blood of thy neighbour: I *am* the LORD.

17 ¶ [a]Thou shalt not hate thy brother in thine heart: [b]thou shalt in any wise rebuke thy neighbour, [1]and not suffer sin upon him.

18 ¶ [a]Thou shalt not avenge, nor bear any grudge against the children of thy people, [b]but thou shalt love thy neighbour as thyself: I *am* the LORD.

19 ¶ Ye shall keep my statutes. Thou shalt not let thy cattle gender with a diverse kind: [a]thou shalt not sow thy field with mingled seed: [b]neither shall a garment mingled of linen and woollen come upon thee.

20 ¶ And whosoever lieth carnally with a woman, that *is* a bondmaid, [1,2]betrothed to an husband, and not at all redeemed, nor freedom given her; [3,4]she shall be scourged; they shall not be put to death, because she was not free.

21 And [a]he shall bring his trespass offering unto the LORD, unto the door of the tabernacle of the congregation, *even* a ram for a trespass offering.

22 And the priest shall make an atonement for him with the ram of the trespass offering before the LORD for his sin which he hath done: and the sin which he hath done shall be forgiven him. **L**

23 ¶ And when ye shall come into the land, and shall have planted all manner of trees for food, then ye shall count the fruit thereof as uncircumcised: three years shall it be as uncircumcised unto you: it shall not be eaten of.

24 But in the fourth year all the fruit thereof shall be [1]holy [a]to praise the LORD *withal.*

25 And in the fifth year shall ye eat of the fruit thereof, that it may yield unto you the increase thereof: I *am* the LORD your God.

26 ¶ [a]Ye shall not eat *any thing* with the blood: [b]neither shall ye use enchantment, nor observe times.

27 [a]Ye shall not round the corners of your heads, neither shalt thou mar the corners of thy beard.

28 Ye shall not [a]make any cuttings in your flesh for the dead, nor print any marks upon you: I *am* the LORD.

29 ¶ [a]Do not [1]prostitute thy daughter, to cause her to be a whore; lest the land fall to whoredom, and the land become full of wickedness.

30 ¶ [a]Ye shall keep my sabbaths, and [b]reverence my sanctuary: I *am* the LORD.

31 ¶ [a]Regard not them that have familiar spirits, neither seek after wizards, to be defiled by them: I *am* the LORD your God.

32 ¶ [a]Thou shalt rise up before the hoary head, and honour the face of the old man, and [b]fear thy God: I *am* the LORD.

33 ¶ And [a]if a stranger sojourn with thee in your land, ye shall not [1]vex him.

34 [a]*But* the stranger that dwelleth with you shall be unto you as one born among you, and [b]thou shalt love him as

L *Lev 6:7* ◄ ► *Nu 14:18–20*

9 [a]Deut. 24:19
11 [a]Ex. 20:15 [b]Eph. 4:25
12 [a]Ex. 20:7; Deut. 5:11; Mat. 5:33; Jas. 5:12 [b]ch. 18:21
13 [a]Mark 10:19 [b]Mal. 3:5
14 [a]Deut 27:18
16 [a]Ex. 23:1 [b]Ex. 23:1,7; 1 Ki. 21:13
17 [a]1 John 2:9,11; & 3:15 [b]Mat. 18:15; Eph. 5:11; 1 Tim. 5:20 [1]Or, *that thou bear not sin for him*
18 [a]Rom. 12:17,19 [b]Mat. 5:43
19 [a]Deut. 22:9,10 [b]Deut. 22:11
20 [1]Or, *abused by any* [2]Heb. *reproached by,* or, *for man* [3]Or, *they* [4]Heb. *there shall be a scourging*
21 [a]ch. 5:15
24 [a]Deut. 12:17, 18; Prov. 3:9 [1]Heb. *holiness of praises to the LORD*
26 [a]ch. 17:10 [b]Deut. 18:10,11, 14; 1 Sam. 15:23; 2 Chr. 33:6; Mal. 3:5
27 [a]ch. 21:5; Is. 15:2; Jer. 9:26
28 [a]Jer. 16:6
29 [a]Deut. 23:17 [1]Heb. *profane*
30 [a]ver. 3; ch. 26:2 [b]Eccl. 5:1
31 [a]Ex. 22:18; Is. 8:19; Acts 16:16
32 [a]1 Tim. 5:1 [b]ver. 14
33 [a]Ex. 22:21 [1]Or, *oppress*
34 [a]Ex. 12:48 [b]Deut. 10:19

thyself; for ye were strangers in the land
of Egypt: I *am* the LORD your God.
35 ¶ [a]Ye shall do no unrighteousness
in judgment, in meteyard, in weight, or
in measure.
36 [a]Just balances, just [l]weights, a just
ephah, and a just hin, shall ye have: I *am*
the LORD your God, which brought you
out of the land of Egypt.
37 [a]Therefore shall ye observe all my
statutes, and all my judgments, and do
them: I *am* the LORD.

Punishments for sin

20 AND THE LORD spake unto Moses, saying,
2 [a]Again, thou shalt say to the children
of Israel, [b]Whosoever *he be* of the children of Israel, or of the strangers that sojourn in Israel, that giveth *any* of his seed
unto Molech; he shall surely be put to
death: the people of the land shall stone
him with stones.
3 And [a]I will set my face against that
man, and will cut him off from among his
people; because he hath given of his seed
unto Molech, to [b]defile my sanctuary,
and [c]to profane my holy name.
4 And if the people of the land do any
ways hide their eyes from the man, when
he giveth of his seed unto Molech, and
[a]kill him not:
5 Then [a]I will set my face against that
man, and [b]against his family, and will cut
him off, and all that [c]go a-whoring after
him, to commit whoredom with Molech,
from among their people.
6 ¶ And [a]the soul that turneth after
such as have familiar spirits, and after
wizards, to go a-whoring after them, I
will even set my face against that soul,
and will cut him off from among his
people.
S 7 ¶ [a]Sanctify yourselves therefore, and
be ye holy: for I *am* the LORD your God.
8 [a]And ye shall keep my statutes, and
do them: [b]I *am* the LORD which sanctify
you.
9 ¶ [a]For every one that curseth his father or his mother shall be surely put to
death: he hath cursed his father or his
mother; [b]his blood *shall be* upon him.
10 ¶ And [a]the man that committeth
adultery with *another* man's wife, *even*
he that committeth adultery with his
neighbour's wife, the adulterer and the
adulteress shall surely be put to death.
11 [a]And the man that lieth with his
father's wife hath uncovered his father's
nakedness: both of them shall surely be
put to death; their blood *shall be* upon
them.
12 [a]And if a man lie with his daughter-
in-law, both of them shall surely be put
to death: [b]they have wrought confusion;
their blood *shall be* upon them.
13 [a]If a man also lie with mankind, as
he lieth with a woman, both of them
have committed an abomination: they
shall surely be put to death; their blood
shall be upon them.
14 [a]And if a man take a wife and her
mother, it *is* wickedness: they shall be
burnt with fire, both he and they; that
there be no wickedness among you.
15 [a]And if a man lie with a beast, he
shall surely be put to death: and ye shall
slay the beast.
16 And if a woman approach unto any
beast, and lie down thereto, thou shalt
kill the woman, and the beast: they shall
surely be put to death; their blood *shall*
be upon them.
17 [a]And if a man shall take his sister,
his father's daughter, or his mother's
daughter, and see her nakedness, and she
see his nakedness; it *is* a wicked thing;
and they shall be cut off in the sight of
their people; he hath uncovered his sister's nakedness; he shall bear his iniquity.
18 [a]And if a man shall lie with a
woman having her sickness, and shall uncover her nakedness; he hath [l]discovered
her fountain, and she hath uncovered the
fountain of her blood: and both of them
shall be cut off from among their people.
19 [a]And thou shalt not uncover the nakedness of thy mother's sister, nor of thy
father's sister: [b]for he uncovereth his
near kin: they shall bear their iniquity.
20 [a]And if a man shall lie with his uncle's wife, he hath uncovered his uncle's
nakedness: they shall bear their sin; they
shall die childless.
21 [a]And if a man shall take his
brother's wife, it *is* [l]an unclean thing: he
hath uncovered his brother's nakedness;
they shall be childless.
22 ¶ Ye shall therefore keep all my
[a]statutes, and all my judgments, and do

35 [a]ver. 15
36 [a]Deut. 25:13, 15 [l]Heb. *stones*
37 [a]ch. 18:4,5; Deut. 4:5,6 & 5:1 & 6:25
20:2 [a]ch. 18:2 [b]ch. 18:21; 2 Ki. 23:10; 2 Chr. 33:6; Jer. 7:31
3 [a]ch. 17:10 [b]Ezek. 5:11 & 23:38,39 [c]ch. 18:21
4 [a]Deut. 17:2,3,5
5 [a]ch. 17:10 [b]Ex. 20:5 [c]ch. 17:7
6 [a]ch. 19:31
7 [a]ch. 19:2
8 [a]ch. 19:37 [b]Ex. 31:13
9 [a]Ex. 21:17; Deut. 27:16; Prov. 20:20; Mat. 15:4 [b]ver. 11, 12,13,16,27; 2 Sam. 1:16
10 [a]ch. 18:20; Deut. 22:22
11 [a]ch. 18:8; Deut. 27:23
12 [a]ch. 18:15 [b]ch. 18:23
13 [a]ch. 18:22; Deut. 23:17; Gen. 19:5; Judg. 19:22
14 [a]ch. 18:17; Deut. 27:23
15 [a]ch. 18:23; Deut. 27:21
17 [a]ch. 18:9; Deut. 27:22; Gen. 20:12
18 [a]ch. 15:24 [l]Heb. *made naked*
19 [a]ch. 18:12 [b]ch. 18:6
20 [a]ch. 18:14
21 [a]ch. 18:16 [l]Heb. *a separation*
22 [a]ch. 18:26 & 19:37

S *Lev 19:2* ◄► *Lev 20:26*

them: that the land, whither I bring you to dwell therein, [b]spew you not out.

23 [a]And ye shall not walk in the manners of the nation, which I cast out before you: for they committed all these things, and [b]therefore I abhorred them.

24 But [a]I have said unto you, Ye shall inherit their land, and I will give it unto you to possess it, a land that floweth with milk and honey: I *am* the LORD your God, [b]which have separated you from *other* people.

25 [a]Ye shall therefore put difference between clean beasts and unclean, and between unclean fowls and clean: [b]and ye shall not make your souls abominable by beast, or by fowl, or by any manner of living thing that [/]creepeth on the ground, which I have separated from you as unclean.

S 26 And ye shall be holy unto me: [a]for I the LORD *am* holy, and have severed you from *other* people, that ye should be mine.

27 ¶ [a]A man also or woman that hath a familiar spirit, or that is a wizard, shall surely be put to death: they shall stone them with stones: [b]their blood *shall be* upon them.

The sanctity of the priesthood

21 AND THE LORD said unto Moses, Speak unto the priests the sons of Aaron, and say unto them, [a]There shall none be defiled for the dead among his people:

2 But for his kin, that is near unto him, *that is,* for his mother, and for his father, and for his son, and for his daughter, and for his brother,

3 And for his sister a virgin, that is nigh unto him, which hath had no husband; for her may he be defiled.

4 *But* [/]he shall not defile himself, *being* a chief man among his people, to profane himself.

5 [a]They shall not make baldness upon their head, neither shall they shave off the corner of their beard, nor make any cuttings in their flesh.

6 They shall be holy unto their God, and [a]not profane the name of their God: for the offerings of the LORD made by fire, *and* the bread of their God, they do offer: therefore they shall be holy.

7 [a]They shall not take a wife *that is* a whore, or profane; neither shall they take a woman [b]put away from her husband: for he *is* holy unto his God.

8 Thou shalt sanctify him therefore; for he offereth the bread of thy God: he shall be holy unto thee: for I the LORD, which sanctify you, *am* holy.

9 ¶ [a]And the daughter of any priest, if she profane herself by playing the whore, she profaneth her father: she shall be burnt with fire.

10 [a]And *he that is* the high priest among his brethren, upon whose head the anointing oil was poured, and [b]that is consecrated to put on the garments, [c]shall not uncover his head, nor rend his clothes;

11 Neither shall he [a]go in to any dead body, nor defile himself for his father, or for his mother;

12 [a]Neither shall he go out of the sanctuary, nor profane the sanctuary of his God; for [b]the crown of the anointing oil of his God *is* upon him: I *am* the LORD.

13 And [a]he shall take a wife in her virginity.

14 A widow, or a divorced woman, or profane, *or* an harlot, these shall he not take: but he shall take a virgin of his own people to wife.

15 Neither shall he profane his seed among his people: for [a]I the LORD do sanctify him.

16 ¶ And the LORD spake unto Moses, saying,

17 Speak unto Aaron, saying, Whosoever *he be* of thy seed in their generations that hath *any* blemish, let him not [a]approach to offer the [/]bread of his God.

18 For whatsoever man *he be* that hath a blemish, he shall not approach: a blind man, or a lame, or he that hath a flat nose, or any thing [a]superfluous,

19 Or a man that is brokenfooted, or brokenhanded,

20 Or crookbacked, or [/]a dwarf, or that hath a blemish in his eye, or be scurvy, or scabbed, or [a]hath his stones broken;

21 No man that hath a blemish of the seed of Aaron the priest shall come nigh to [a]offer the offerings of the LORD made by fire: he hath a blemish; he shall not come nigh to offer the bread of his God.

22 He shall eat the bread of his God, *both* of the [a]most holy, and of the [b]holy.

22 [b]ch. 18:25
23 [a]ch. 18:3,24 [b]ch. 18:27; Deut. 9:5
24 [a]Ex. 3:17 & 6:8 [b]ver. 26; Ex. 19:5 & 33:16; Deut. 7:6 & 14:2; 1 Ki. 8:53
25 [a]ch. 11:47; Deut. 14:4 [b]ch. 11:43 [/]Or, *moveth*
26 [a]ver. 7; ch. 19:2; 1 Pet. 1:16
27 [a]ch. 19:31 [b]ver. 9
21:1 [a]Ezek. 44:25
4 [/]Or, *being an husband among his people, he shall not defile himself* for his wife; see Ezek. 24:16,17
5 [a]ch. 19:27
6 [a]ch. 18:21 & 19:12
7 [a]Ezek. 44:22 [b]See Deut. 24:1,2
9 [a]Gen. 38:24
10 [a]Ex. 29:29; ch. 8:12 [b]Ex. 28:2; ch. 16:32 [c]ch. 10:6
11 [a]Num. 19:14
12 [a]ch. 10:7 [b]Ex. 28:36; ch. 8:9,12, 30
13 [a]ver. 7; Ezek. 44:22
15 [a]ver. 8
17 [a]ch. 10:3; Num. 16:5 [/]Or, *food*
18 [a]ch. 22:23
20 [a]Deut. 23:1 [/]Or, *too slender*
21 [a]ver. 6
22 [a]ch. 2:3,10 & 6:17,29 & 7:1 & 24:9; Num. 18:9 [b]ch. 22:10-12; Num. 18:19

23 Only he shall not go in unto the veil, nor come nigh unto the altar, because he hath a blemish; that [a]he profane not my sanctuaries: for I the LORD do sanctify them.

24 And Moses told *it* unto Aaron, and to his sons, and unto all the children of Israel.

22 AND THE LORD spake unto Moses, saying,

2 Speak unto Aaron and to his sons, that they [a]separate themselves from the holy things of the children of Israel, and that they [b]profane not my holy name *in those things* which they [c]hallow unto me: I *am* the LORD.

3 Say unto them, Whosoever *he be* of all your seed among your generations, that goeth unto the holy things, which the children of Israel hallow unto the LORD, [a]having his uncleanness upon him, that soul shall be cut off from my presence: I *am* the LORD.

4 What man soever of the seed of Aaron *is* a leper, or hath [a]a [ʹ]running issue; he shall not eat of the holy things, [b]until he be clean. And [c]whoso toucheth any thing *that is* unclean *by* the dead, or [d]a man whose seed goeth from him;

5 Or [a]whosoever toucheth any creeping thing, whereby he may be made unclean, or [b]a man of whom he may take uncleanness, whatsoever uncleanness he hath;

6 The soul which hath touched any such shall be unclean until even, and shall not eat of the holy things, unless he [a]wash his flesh with water.

7 And when the sun is down, he shall be clean, and shall afterward eat of the holy things; because [a]it *is* his food.

8 [a]That which dieth of itself, or is torn *with beasts,* he shall not eat to defile himself therewith: I *am* the LORD.

9 They shall therefore keep mine ordinance, [a]lest they bear sin for it, and die therefore, if they profane it: I the LORD do sanctify them.

10 [a]There shall no stranger eat *of* the holy thing: a sojourner of the priest, or an hired servant, shall not eat *of* the holy thing.

11 But if the priest buy *any* soul [ʹ]with his money, he shall eat of it, and he that is born in his house: [a]they shall eat of his meat.

12 If the priest's daughter also be *married* unto [ʹ]a stranger, she may not eat of an offering of the holy things.

13 But if the priest's daughter be a widow, or divorced, and have no child, and is [a]returned unto her father's house, [b]as in her youth, she shall eat of her father's meat: but there shall no stranger eat thereof.

14 ¶ [a]And if a man eat *of* the holy thing unwittingly, then he shall put the fifth *part* thereof unto it, and shall give *it* unto the priest with the holy thing.

15 And [a]they shall not profane the holy things of the children of Israel, which they offer unto the LORD;

16 Or [ʹ]suffer them [a]to bear the iniquity of trespass, when they eat their holy things: for I the LORD do sanctify them.

Sacrifices of blemished animals

17 ¶ And the LORD spake unto Moses, saying, D

18 Speak unto Aaron, and to his sons, and unto all the children of Israel, and say unto them, [a]Whatsoever *he be* of the house of Israel, or of the strangers in Israel, that will offer his oblation for all his vows, and for all his freewill offerings, which they will offer unto the LORD for a burnt offering;

19 [a]*Ye shall offer* at your own will a male without blemish, of the beeves, of the sheep, or of the goats.

20 [a]*But* whatsoever hath a blemish, *that* shall ye not offer: for it shall not be acceptable for you.

21 And [a]whosoever offereth a sacrifice of peace offerings unto the LORD [b]to accomplish *his* vow, or a freewill offering in beeves or [ʹ]sheep, it shall be perfect to be accepted; there shall be no blemish therein.

22 [a]Blind, or broken, or maimed, or having a wen, or scurvy, or scabbed, ye shall not offer these unto the LORD, nor make [b]an offering by fire of them upon the altar unto the LORD.

23 Either a bullock or a [ʹ]lamb that hath any thing [a]superfluous or lacking in his parts, that mayest thou offer *for* a freewill offering; but for a vow it shall not be accepted.

24 Ye shall not offer unto the LORD that which is bruised, or crushed, or broken,

23 [a]ver. 12
22:2 [a]Num. 6:3 [b]ch. 18:21 [c]Ex. 28:38; Num. 18:32; Deut. 15:19
3 [a]ch. 7:20
4 [a]ch. 15:2 [b]ch. 14:2 & 15:13 [c]Num. 19:11 [d]ch. 15:16 [ʹ]Heb. *running of the reins*
5 [a]ch. 11:24 [b]ch. 15:7,19
6 [a]ch. 15:5
7 [a]ch. 21:22; Num. 18:11,13
8 [a]Ex. 22:31; ch. 17:15; Ezek. 44:31
9 [a]Ex. 28:43
10 [a]See 1 Sam. 21:6
11 [a]Num. 8:11,13 [ʹ]Heb. *with the purchase of his money*
12 [ʹ]Heb. *a man a stranger*
13 [a]Gen. 38:11 [b]ch. 10:14
14 [a]ch. 5:15,16; Num. 18:11,19
15 [a]Num. 18:32
16 [a]ver. 9 [ʹ]Or, *lade themselves with the iniquity of trespass in their eating*
18 [a]ch. 1:2,3,10
19 [a]ch. 1:3
20 [a]Deut. 15:21; Mal. 1:8,14; Eph. 5:27; Heb. 9:14; 1 Pet. 1:19
21 [a]ch. 3:1,6 [b]Num. 15:3,8; Ps. 61:8 & 65:1; Eccl. 5:4,5 [ʹ]Or, *goats*
22 [a]ver. 20; Mal. 1:8 [b]ch. 1:9,13 & 3:3,5
23 [a]ch. 21:18 [ʹ]Or, *kid*

D *Lev 17:11–14* ◀▶ *Lev 23:4–5*

or cut; neither shall ye make *any offering*
thereof in your land.
25 Neither [a]from a stranger's hand
shall ye offer [b]the bread of your God of
any of these; because their [c]corruption *is*
in them, *and* blemishes *be* in them: they
shall not be accepted for you.
26 ¶ And the LORD spake unto Moses,
saying,
27 [a]When a bullock, or a sheep, or a
goat, is brought forth, then it shall be
seven days under the dam; and from the
eighth day and thenceforth it shall be accepted for an offering made by fire unto
the LORD.
28 And *whether it be* cow or [1]ewe, ye
shall not kill it [a]and her young both in
one day.
29 And when ye will [a]offer a sacrifice
of thanksgiving unto the LORD, offer *it* at
your own will.
30 On the same day it shall be eaten
up; ye shall leave [a]none of it until the
morrow: I *am* the LORD.
S 31 [a]Therefore shall ye keep my commandments, and do them: I *am* the LORD.

S *Lev 20:26* ◄► *Nu 14:22–25*

25 [a]Num. 15:15, 16 [b]ch. 21:6,17 [c]Mal. 1:14
27 [a]Ex. 22:30
28 [a]Deut. 22:6 [1]Or, *she goat*
29 [a]ch. 7:12; Ps. 107:22 & 116:17; Amos 4:5
30 [a]ch. 7:15
31 [a]ch. 19:37; Num. 15:40; Deut. 4:40
32 [a]ch. 18:21 [b]ch. 10:3; Mat. 6:9; Luke 11:2 [c]ch. 20:8
33 [a]ch. 19:36; Num. 15:41
23:2 [a]ver. 4,37 [b]Ex. 32:5; 2 Ki. 10:20; Ps. 81:3
3 [a]Ex. 20:9 & 23:12 & 31:15; ch. 19:3; Deut. 5:13; Luke 13:14
4 [a]ver. 37; Ex. 23:14
5 [a]Ex. 12:6,14,18; & 13:3,10; Deut. 16:1-8

32 [a]Neither shall ye profane my holy
name; but [b]I will be hallowed among the
children of Israel: I *am* the LORD which
[c]hallow you,
33 [a]That brought you out of the land of
Egypt, to be your God: I *am* the LORD.

Feasts of the LORD

23 AND THE LORD spake unto Moses, saying,
2 Speak unto the children of Israel,
and say unto them, *Concerning* [a]the
feasts of the LORD, which ye shall [b]pro-
claim *to be* holy convocations, *even* these
are my feasts.
3 [a]Six days shall work be done: but the
seventh day *is* the sabbath of rest, an holy
convocation; ye shall do no work *therein:*
it *is* the sabbath of the LORD in all your
dwellings.
4 ¶ [a]These *are* the feasts of the LORD, D
even holy convocations, which ye shall
proclaim in their seasons.
5 [a]In the fourteenth *day* of the first
month at even *is* the LORD's passover.
6 And on the fifteenth day of the same

D *Lev 22:17–25* ◄► *Lev 23:26–32*

23:2–4 The "feasts of the LORD" (23:4) consisted of seven religious celebrations that the Israelites were to observe every year. The apostle Paul admonished young believers to beware of legalism when he spoke of these special days as "a shadow of things to come" (Col 2:17). Though these holy days were commanded, they were intended to be celebrations of God's faithfulness in the past and promised blessing in the future.

23:5 The Passover was the first of Israel's major feasts. It was celebrated on the fourteenth day of the first month (Nisan/Abib) of Israel's religious year. Significant anniversaries in the spiritual and national life of Israel have occurred on the Passover.

1. The first Passover supper in Egypt. On this night God sent the tenth plague on Egypt—the death of "all the firstborn in the land of Egypt" (Ex 12:29). Yet God passed over the homes of his people who had placed lamb's blood on the lintels of their doors. The next morning the Israelites were set free from Egypt (see Ex 12:41).
2. The first Passover in Canaan. None of the male children born during the forty years of the wilderness wandering had been circumcised. Yet God's law prohibited the uncircumcised from celebrating the Passover (see Ex 12:48). Joshua ordered the circumcision of all the males of Israel and then "kept the passover on the fourteenth day of the month" (Jos 5:10). The very next day the Israelites ate food from the promised land.
3. The return from captivity. After the Jews returned to Jerusalem under the decree of Cyrus the Great in 538 B.C., they rebuilt the temple, rededicated it, cleansed themselves and celebrated the Passover (see Ezr 6:19–22).
4. The Last Supper. Jesus and the disciples met in an upper room to celebrate the Passover. While there, Jesus invoked the words of the new covenant, saying, "This is my body which is given for you: this do in remembrance of me" (Lk 22:19).

For a full examination of the phenomenon of Biblical anniversaries, see the article "The Biblical Anniversaries of Israel," p. 184.

23:6–8 Although it begins at almost the same time, the Feast of Unleavened Bread is distinct from the Passover. Israel was required to eat bread made without yeast, hold several assemblies and make several designated offerings for this seven-day celebration. Three important anniversaries in the life of Israel have occurred during the Feast of Unleavened Bread:

1. The exodus from Egypt. The morning after God's destroying angel had passed over the Israelites' homes the Israelites left Egypt. In their haste "they baked unleavened cakes of the dough which they brought forth out of Egypt, for it was not leavened; because they were thrust out of Egypt, and could not tarry, neither

month *is* the feast of unleavened bread
unto the LORD: seven days ye must eat
unleavened bread.
7 [a]In the first day ye shall have an holy
convocation: ye shall do no servile work
therein.
8 But ye shall offer an offering made by
fire unto the LORD seven days: in the seventh day *is* an holy convocation: ye shall
do no servile work *therein.*
9 ¶ And the LORD spake unto Moses,
saying,
10 Speak unto the children of Israel,
and say unto them, [a]When ye be come
into the land which I give unto you, and
shall reap the harvest thereof, then ye
shall bring a [1,2]sheaf of [b]the firstfruits of
your harvest unto the priest:
11 And he shall [a]wave the sheaf before
the LORD, to be accepted for you: on the
morrow after the sabbath the priest shall
wave it.
12 And ye shall offer that day when ye
wave the sheaf an he lamb without blemish of the first year for a burnt offering
unto the LORD.
13 [a]And the meat offering thereof
shall be two tenth deals of fine flour mingled with oil, an offering made by fire
unto the LORD *for* a sweet savour: and the
drink offering thereof *shall be* of wine,
the fourth *part* of an hin.
14 And ye shall eat neither bread, nor
parched corn, nor green ears, until the
selfsame day that ye have brought an offering unto your God: *it shall be* a statute
for ever throughout your generations in
all your dwellings.
15 ¶ And [a]ye shall count unto you
from the morrow after the sabbath, from
the day that ye brought the sheaf of the
wave offering; seven sabbaths shall be
complete:
16 Even unto the morrow after the
seventh sabbath shall ye number [a]fifty
days; and ye shall offer [b]a new meat offering unto the LORD.
17 Ye shall bring out of your habitations two wave loaves of two tenth deals:
they shall be of fine flour; they shall be
baked with leaven; *they are* [a]the firstfruits unto the LORD.
18 And ye shall offer with the bread
seven lambs without blemish of the first
year, and one young bullock, and two
rams: they shall be *for* a burnt offering
unto the LORD, with their meat offering,
and their drink offerings, *even* an
offering made by fire, of sweet savour
unto the LORD.
19 Then ye shall sacrifice [a]one kid of
the goats for a sin offering, and two lambs
of the first year for a sacrifice of [b]peace
offerings.
20 And the priest shall wave them
with the bread of the firstfruits *for* a wave
offering before the LORD, with the two
lambs: [a]they shall be holy to the LORD for
the priest.
21 And ye shall proclaim on the self-

7 [a]Ex. 12:16; Num. 28:18,25
10 [a]Ex. 34:26; Deut. 16:9; Josh. 3:15 [b]Rom. 11:16; Jas. 1:18; Rev. 14:4 [1]Or, *handful* [2]Heb. *omer*
11 [a]Ex. 29:24
13 [a]ch. 2:14-16
15 [a]Ex. 34:22; ch. 25:8; Deut. 16:9
16 [a]Acts 2:1 [b]Num. 28:26
17 [a]Ex. 23:16,19; Num. 15:17-21
19 [a]ch. 4:23,28; Num. 28:30 [b]ch. 3:1
20 [a]Num. 18:12; Deut. 18:4

---

had they prepared for themselves any victual" (Ex 12:39).

2. The crucifixion of Christ. Jesus referred to himself as "the bread of life" (Jn 6:35). He was crucified, died and was buried during the Feast of Unleavened Bread.
3. The fall of Massada. A nearly impregnable fortress commanded by Jewish resistance fighters was located at Massada. Flavius Josephus, a Jewish historian, records that this fortress finally fell to Roman soldiers "on the fifteenth day of the month Nisan" in A.D. 72—the first day of the Feast of Unleavened Bread.

23:9–11 The Feast of Firstfruits was celebrated on the sixteenth day of the first month (Nisan/ Abib). This feast recognized the Lord's bounty in the land with a wave offering, burnt offering and grain offering. Manna also stopped falling on this feast day after the Israelites enjoyed some of the fruit of the promised land (see Jos 5:12). The NT writers also make reference to firstfruits (see Ro 8:23; 1Co 15:20).

23:15–16 The Feast of Weeks was one of the three annual feasts for which all males of Israel were required to gather together (see Ex 23:14–19). Celebrated fifty days after the Feast of Firstfruits, the Feast of Weeks was a festival of joy and thanksgiving to the Lord for the blessing of the harvest. Included in the celebration were mandatory and voluntary offerings, including the firstfruits of the wheat harvest. This annual feast also served in part as a remembrance of the giving of the law upon Mt. Sinai fifty days after the Israelites left Egypt.

In the NT, the Feast of Weeks corresponds to the day of Pentecost. Fifty days after Christ's death on the cross God poured out his Spirit upon the apostles (see Ac 2:1). On that day all Jewish males were gathered together in Jerusalem to celebrate the Feast of Weeks (see Ac 2:5). The disciples were given extraordinary spiritual power and ability to witness to those assembled in Jerusalem and "the same day there were added unto them about three thousand souls" (Ac 2:41).

same day, *that* it may be an holy convocation unto you: ye shall do no servile work *therein: it shall be* a statute for ever in all your dwellings throughout your generations.

22 ¶ And [a]when ye reap the harvest of your land, thou shalt not make clean riddance of the corners of thy field when thou reapest, neither shalt thou gather any gleaning of thy harvest: thou shalt leave them unto the poor, and to the stranger: I *am* the LORD your God.

23 ¶ And the LORD spake unto Moses, saying,

24 Speak unto the children of Israel, saying, In the [a]seventh month, in the first *day* of the month, shall ye have a sabbath, [b]a memorial of blowing of trumpets, an holy convocation.

25 Ye shall do no servile work *therein:* but ye shall offer an offering made by fire unto the LORD.

D 26 ¶ And the LORD spake unto Moses, saying,

27 [a]Also on the tenth *day* of this seventh month *there shall be* a day of atonement: it shall be an holy convocation unto you; and ye shall afflict your souls, and offer an offering made by fire unto the LORD.

28 And ye shall do no work in that same day: for it *is* a day of atonement, to make an atonement for you before the LORD your God.

29 For whatsoever soul *it be* that shall not be afflicted in that same day, [a]he shall be cut off from among his people.

30 And whatsoever soul *it be* that doeth any work in that same day, [a]the same soul will I destroy from among his people.

31 Ye shall do no manner of work: *it shall be* a statute for ever throughout your generations in all your dwellings.

32 It *shall be* unto you a sabbath of rest, and ye shall afflict your souls: in the ninth *day* of the month at even, from even unto even, shall ye [l]celebrate your sabbath.

33 ¶ And the LORD spake unto Moses, A
saying,

34 Speak unto the children of Israel, saying, [a]The fifteenth day of this seventh month *shall be* the feast of tabernacles *for* seven days unto the LORD.

35 On the first day *shall be* an holy convocation: ye shall do no servile work *therein.*

36 Seven days ye shall offer an offering made by fire unto the LORD: [a]on the eighth day shall be an holy convocation unto you; and ye shall offer an offering made by fire unto the LORD: it *is* a [b]solemn[l] assembly; *and* ye shall do no servile work *therein.*

37 [a]These *are* the feasts of the LORD, which ye shall proclaim *to be* holy convocations, to offer an offering made by fire unto the LORD, a burnt offering, and a meat offering, a sacrifice, and drink offerings, every thing upon his day:

38 [a]Beside the sabbaths of the LORD,

22 [a]ch. 19:9
24 [a]Num. 29:1 [b]ch. 25:9
27 [a]ch. 16:30; Num. 29:7
29 [a]Gen. 17:14
30 [a]ch. 20:3,5,6
32 [l]Heb. *rest*
34 [a]Ex. 23:16; Num. 29:12; Deut. 16:13; Ezra 3:4; Neh. 8:14; Zech. 14:16; John 7:2
36 [a]Num. 29:35; Neh. 8:18; John 7:37 [b]Deut. 16:8; 2 Chr. 7:9 [l]Heb. day of *restraint*
37 [a]ver. 2,4
38 [a]Num. 29:39

D *Lev 23:4–5* ◀ ▶ *Nu 8:17–18*

A *Ex 34:10–12* ◀ ▶ *Lev 25:8–17*

23:24–25 The Feast of Trumpets was celebrated on the first day of the seventh month (Tishri). Later called Rosh Hashanah, this celebration was Israel's New Year's Day, the first day of the civil year. This day was a time of rest commemorated with trumpet blasts and sacrifices intended to present Israel before the Lord. The Feast of Trumpets also figures in the historical anniversaries of the Jews. When the exiles returned from Babylon to Jerusalem, Ezra read the law to them on Rosh Hashanah, marking a reaffirmation of Israel's covenant with God.

23:27–32 Known also as Yom Kippur, the Day of Atonement was the holiest day of the Israelite year. On this day of rest, fasting and sacrifice the Israelites mourned and made atonement for their sins, cleansing the priests, the people and the tabernacle. The high priest would enter the holy place and sprinkle the blood of the sacrifice before the mercy seat. The blood sprinkled on the Day of Atonement prefigured the ultimate sacrifice of God's only begotten Son who "entered in once into the holy place, having obtained eternal redemption for us" (Heb 9:12).

23:34, 39 The Feast of Tabernacles was the last of the three annual celebrations. Lasting seven days, this celebration, also called the Feast of Booths, memorialized the journey from Egypt to Canaan and was characterized by offering sacrifices and by the building of small booths or tents made of branches. During this harvest feast people gave thanks for the productivity of Canaan. In postexilic times the Jews who returned from Babylon responded to Ezra's reading about the Feast of Tabernacles by celebrating it with great joy (see Ne 8:14–18). In fact, Scripture records that "since the days of Jeshua the son of Nun unto that day had not the children of Israel done so. And there was very great gladness" (Ne 8:17).

and beside your gifts, and beside all your
vows, and beside all your freewill offerings, which ye give unto the LORD.
39 Also in the fifteenth day of the seventh month, when ye have [a]gathered in
the fruit of the land, ye shall keep a feast
unto the LORD seven days: on the first day
shall be a sabbath, and on the eighth day
shall be a sabbath.
40 And [a]ye shall take you on the first
day the [/]boughs of goodly trees, branches
of palm trees, and the boughs of thick
trees, and willows of the brook; [b]and ye
shall rejoice before the LORD your God
seven days.
41 [a]And ye shall keep it a feast unto
the LORD seven days in the year. *It shall
be* a statute for ever in your generations:
ye shall celebrate it in the seventh
month.
42 [a]Ye shall dwell in booths seven
days; all that are Israelites born shall
dwell in booths:
43 [a]That your generations may know
that I made the children of Israel to dwell
in booths, when I brought them out of
the land of Egypt: I *am* the LORD your
God.
44 And Moses [a]declared unto the children of Israel the feasts of the LORD.

The oil and the showbread

24 AND THE LORD spake unto Mo-
ses, saying,
2 [a]Command the children of Israel,
that they bring unto thee pure oil olive
beaten for the light, [/]to cause the lamps
to burn continually.
3 Without the veil of the testimony, in
the tabernacle of the congregation, shall
Aaron order it from the evening unto the
morning before the LORD continually: *it
shall be* a statute for ever in your generations.
4 He shall order the lamps upon [a]the
pure candlestick before the LORD continually.
5 ¶ And thou shalt take fine flour, and
bake twelve [a]cakes thereof: two tenth
deals shall be in one cake.
6 And thou shalt set them in two rows,
six on a row, [a]upon the pure table before
the LORD.
7 And thou shalt put pure frankincense
upon *each* row, that it may be on the
bread for a memorial, *even* an offering
made by fire unto the LORD.
8 [a]Every sabbath he shall set it in order before the LORD continually, *being
taken* from the children of Israel by an
everlasting covenant.
9 And [a]it shall be Aaron's and his
sons'; [b]and they shall eat it in the holy
place: for it *is* most holy unto him of the
offerings of the LORD made by fire by a
perpetual statute.

Death for blasphemy

10 ¶ And the son of an Israelitish
woman, whose father *was* an Egyptian,
went out among the children of Israel:
and this son of the Israelitish *woman* and
a man of Israel strove together in the
camp;
11 And the Israelitish woman's son
blasphemed the name *of the LORD,* and
[a]cursed. And they [b]brought him unto
Moses: (and his mother's name *was* Shelomith, the daughter of Dibri, of the tribe
of Dan:)
12 And they [a]put him in ward, [b]that[/]
the mind of the LORD might be shown
them.
13 And the LORD spake unto Moses,
saying,
14 Bring forth him that hath cursed
without the camp; and let all that heard
him [a]lay their hands upon his head, and
let all the congregation stone him.
15 And thou shalt speak unto the children of Israel, saying, Whosoever curseth
his God [a]shall bear his sin.
16 And he that [a]blasphemeth the
name of the LORD, he shall surely be put
to death, *and* all the congregation shall
certainly stone him: as well the stranger,
as he that is born in the land, when he
blasphemeth the name *of the LORD,* shall
be put to death.
17 ¶ [a]And he that [/]killeth any man
shall surely be put to death.
18 [a]And he that killeth a beast shall
make it good; [/]beast for beast.
19 And if a man cause a blemish in his
neighbour; as [a]he hath done, so shall it
be done to him;
20 Breach for breach, eye for eye,
tooth for tooth: as he hath caused a blemish in a man, so shall it be done to him
again.
21 [a]And he that killeth a beast, he
shall restore it: [b]and he that killeth a
man, he shall be put to death.
22 Ye shall have [a]one manner of law,

39 [a]Ex. 23:16; Deut. 16:13
40 [a]Neh. 8:15 [b]Deut. 16:14,15 [/]Heb. *fruit*
41 [a]Num. 29:12; Neh. 8:18
42 [a]Neh. 8:14-16
43 [a]Deut. 31:13
44 [a]ver. 2
24:2 [a]Ex. 27:20 [/]Heb. *to cause to ascend*
4 [a]Ex. 31:8 & 39:37
5 [a]Ex. 25:30
6 [a]1 Ki. 7:48; 2 Chr. 4:19 & 13:11; Heb. 9:2
8 [a]Num. 4:7; 1 Chr. 9:32; 2 Chr. 2:4
9 [a]1 Sam. 21:6; Mat. 12:4; Mark 2:26; Luke 6:4 [b]Ex. 29:33; ch. 8:31
11 [a]Job 1:5,11,22; Is. 8:21 [b]Ex. 18:22, 26
12 [a]Num. 15:34 [b]Ex. 18:15; Num. 27:5 [/]Heb. *to expound unto them according to the mouth of the LORD*
14 [a]Deut. 13:9 & 17:7
15 [a]ch. 20:17; Num. 9:13
16 [a]1 Ki. 21:10,13; Mat. 12:31; Mark 3:28
17 [a]Ex. 21:12; Num. 35:31; Deut. 19:11,12 [/]Heb. *smiteth the life of a man*
18 [a]ver. 21 [/]Heb. *life for life*
19 [a]Ex. 21:24; Deut. 19:21; Mat. 5:38 & 7:2
21 [a]Ex. 21:33 [b]ver. 17
22 [a]Ex. 12:49; ch. 19:34; Num. 15:16

Old Testament Feasts and Other Sacred Days

NAME	OLD TESTAMENT REFERENCES	TIME	DESCRIPTION	NEW TESTAMENT REFERENCES
Sabbath	Exodus 20:8-11; 31:12-17; Leviticus 23:3; Deuteronomy 5:12-15	7th day	Day of rest; no work	Matthew 12:1-14; Mark 2:23–3:5; Luke 4:16-30; 6:1-10; 13:10-16; 14:1-5; John 5:1-15; 9:1-34; Acts 13:14-48; 17:2; 18:4; Hebrews 4:1-11
Sabbath Year	Exodus 23:10-11; Leviticus 25:1-7	7th year	Year of rest; fallow fields	
Year of Jubilee	Leviticus 25:8-55; 27:17-24; Numbers 36:4	50th year	Canceled debts; liberation of slaves and indentured servants; land returned to original family owners	
Passover	Exodus 12:1-14; Leviticus 23:5; Numbers 9:1-14; 28:16; Deuteronomy 16:1-7	1st month (Abib) 14	Slaying and eating a lamb, together with bitter herbs and bread made without yeast in every household	Matthew 26:1-2,17-29; Mark 14:12-26; Luke 22:7-38; John 2:13-25; 11:55-56; 13:1-30; 1 Corinthians 5:7
Unleavened Bread	Exodus 12:15-20; 13:3-10; 23:15; Leviticus 23:6-8; Numbers 28:17-25; Deuteronomy 16:3-4,8	1st month (Abib) 15-21	Eating bread made without yeast; holding several assemblies; making designated offerings	Matthew 26:17; Mark 14:1,12; Luke 22:1,7; Acts 12:3; 20:6; 1 Corinthians 5:6-8
Firstfruits	Leviticus 23:9-14	1st month (Abib) 16	Presenting a sheaf of the first of the barley harvest as a wave offering; making a burnt offering and a grain offering	Romans 8:23; 1 Corinthians 15:20-23
Weeks (Pentecost) (Harvest)	Exodus 23:16a; 34:22a; Leviticus 23:15-21; Numbers 28:26-31; Deuteronomy 16:9-12	3rd month (Sivan) 6	A festival of joy; mandatory and voluntary offerings, including the firstfruits of the wheat harvest	Acts 2:1-41; 20:16; 1 Corinthians 16:8
Trumpets (Later: Rosh Hashanah—New Year's Day)	Leviticus 23:23-25; Numbers 29:1-6	7th month (Tishri) 1	An assembly on a day of rest commemorated with trumpet blasts and sacrifices	
Day of Atonement (Yom Kippur)	Leviticus 16; 23:26-32; Numbers 29:7-11	7th month (Tishri) 10	A day of rest, fasting and sacrifices of atonement for priests and people and atonement for the tabernacle and altar	Acts 27:9; Romans 3:24-26; Hebrews 9:1-14,23-26; 10:19-22
Tabernacles (Booths) (Ingathering)	Exodus 23:16b; 34:22b; Leviticus 23:33-36,39-43; Numbers 29:12-34; Deuteronomy 16:13-15	7th month (Tishri) 15-21	A week of celebration for the harvest; living in booths and offering sacrifices	John 7:2-37
Sacred Assembly	Leviticus 23:36; Numbers 29:35-38	7th month (Tishri) 22	A day of convocation, rest and offering sacrifices	John 7:37-44
Dedication		9th month	A commemoration of the purification of the temple in the Maccabean era (166-160 b.c.)	John 10:22-39
Purim	Esther 9:18-32	12th month (Adar) 14,15	A day of joy and feasting and giving presents	

as well for the stranger, as for one of
your own country: for I *am* the LORD your
God.
23 ¶ And Moses spake to the children
of Israel, [a]that they should bring forth
him that had cursed out of the camp, and
stone him with stones. And the children
of Israel did as the LORD commanded
Moses.

Sabbath and jubilee years

25 AND THE LORD spake unto Moses
in mount Sinai, saying,
2 Speak unto the children of Israel,
and say unto them, When ye come into
the land which I give you, then shall
the land [/]keep [a]a sabbath unto the
LORD.
3 Six years thou shalt sow thy field,
and six years thou shalt prune thy vineyard, and gather in the fruit thereof;
4 But in the seventh year shall be a
sabbath of rest unto the land, a sabbath
for the LORD: thou shalt neither sow thy
field, nor prune thy vineyard.
5 [a]That which groweth of its own accord of thy harvest thou shalt not reap,
neither gather the grapes [/]of thy vine undressed: *for* it is a year of rest unto the
land.
6 And the sabbath of the land shall be
meat for you; for thee, and for thy servant, and for thy maid, and for thy hired
servant, and for thy stranger that sojourneth with thee,
7 And for thy cattle, and for the beast
that *are* in thy land, shall all the increase
thereof be meat.
8 ¶ And thou shalt number seven sab- A
baths of years unto thee, seven times
seven years; and the space of the seven
sabbaths of years shall be unto thee forty
and nine years.
9 Then shalt thou cause the trumpet
[/]of the jubilee to sound on the tenth *day*
of the seventh month, [a]in the day of
atonement shall ye make the trumpet
sound throughout all your land.
10 And ye shall hallow the fiftieth
year, and [a]proclaim liberty throughout *all*
the land unto all the inhabitants thereof:
it shall be a jubilee unto you; [b]and ye
shall return every man unto his possession, and ye shall return every man unto
his family.

A *Lev 23:33–36* ◄► *Nu 23:24*

23 [a]ver. 14
25:2 [a]Ex. 23:10; See ch. 26:34,35 [/]Heb. *rest*
5 [a]2 Ki. 19:29 [/]Heb. *of thy separation*
9 [a]ch. 23:24,27 [/]Heb. *loud of sound*
10 [a]Is. 61:2 & 63:4; Jer. 34:8,15, 17; Luke 4:19 [b]ver. 13; Num. 36:4

25:2–6 When Israel conquered the promised land, God commanded them to let the land stay unplowed every seventh year. This Sabbath for the land actually allowed the ground to rest and replenished some of the nutrients taken out of the soil during the planting and harvesting years. Some crops would self-seed and sprout on their own, providing enough food for the people during the Sabbath year (25:6).

25:8–10, 23 Every fifty years God commanded Israel to allow the land to stay unplowed, to return lands to their former owners and to free all Hebrew slaves. This Year of Jubilee was to be observed after seven Sabbath years. As in the regular Sabbath years, the unplowed ground would have a rest. God promised to provide enough extra food in the sixth year to carry people through the Year of Jubilee and through the succeeding years "until the ninth year; until her fruits come in" (25:22).

The return of lands and property was also an important part of the Year of Jubilee. Since God had divided the land among the twelve tribes as their inheritance, God opposed the permanent transfer of land from one person to another. The Year of Jubilee required that all land and property sold to a creditor be transferred back to the original family. By this arrangement, land and property were not sold permanently; the land was merely leased, and all leases expired in the jubilee year. This arrangement reinforced in the Israelites' mind God's control of the land (25:23). He was the owner; they were the tenants.

In addition, if any Israelites had sold themselves to a fellow Israelite because of crushing debt, they were to be treated as hired hands and not as slaves. Only people from pagan nations could be kept as slaves (see 25:44). In the Year of Jubilee any Israelite people sold into servitude were automatically freed and returned to their families (see 25:54).

Moses warned the people to follow these Sabbath laws. Blessing, safety and productivity were promised for obedience. Yet if the people did not obey and give the land its Sabbath, they would be removed from the land and then "as long as it lieth desolate it shall rest; because it did not rest in your sabbaths, when ye dwelt upon it" (26:35).

Apparently the Israelites did not follow these Sabbath regulations for the land (see 2Ch 36:21). Jeremiah's words ring with the Lord's anger: "Ye have not hearkened unto me, in proclaiming liberty, every one to his brother, and every man to his neighbor: behold, I proclaim a liberty for you, saith the LORD, to the sword, to the pestilence, and to the famine; and I will make you to be removed into all the kingdoms of the earth" (Jer 34:17). In return for their disobedience to the law of the Sabbaths of the land Israel endured seventy years of captivity in Babylon.

11 A jubilee shall that fiftieth year be unto you: [a]ye shall not sow, neither reap that which groweth of itself in it, nor gather *the grapes* in it of thy vine undressed.

12 For it *is* the jubilee; it shall be holy unto you: [a]ye shall eat the increase thereof out of the field.

13 [a]In the year of this jubilee ye shall return every man unto his possession.

14 And if thou sell aught unto thy neighbour, or buyest *aught* of thy neighbour's hand, ye shall not oppress one another:

15 [a]According to the number of years after the jubilee thou shalt buy of thy neighbour, *and* according unto the number of years of the fruits he shall sell unto thee:

16 According to the multitude of years thou shalt increase the price thereof, and according to the fewness of years thou shalt diminish the price of it: for *according* to the number *of the years* of the fruits doth he sell unto thee.

17 [a]Ye shall not therefore oppress one another; [b]but thou shalt fear thy God: for I *am* the LORD your God.

S 18 ¶ [a]Wherefore ye shall do my statutes, and keep my judgments, and do them; [b]and ye shall dwell in the land in safety.

B 19 And the land shall yield her fruit,
F and [a]ye shall eat your fill, and dwell therein in safety.

20 And if ye shall say, [a]What shall we eat the seventh year? behold, [b]we shall not sow, nor gather in our increase:

21 Then I will [a]command my blessing upon you in the sixth year, and it shall bring forth fruit for three years.

22 [a]And ye shall sow the eighth year, and eat *yet* of [b]old fruit until the ninth year; until her fruits come in ye shall eat *of* the old *store*.

23 ¶ The land shall not be sold [1,2]for ever: for [a]the land *is* mine; for ye *are* [b]strangers and sojourners with me.

24 And in all the land of your possession ye shall grant a redemption for the land.

25 ¶ [a]If thy brother be waxen poor, and hath sold away *some* of his possession, and if [b]any of his kin come to redeem it, then shall he redeem that which his brother sold.

26 And if the man have none to redeem it, and [1]himself be able to redeem it;

27 Then [a]let him count the years of the sale thereof, and restore the overplus unto the man to whom he sold it; that he may return unto his possession.

28 But if he be not able to restore *it* to him, then that which is sold shall remain in the hand of him that hath bought it until the year of jubilee: [a]and in the jubilee it shall go out, and he shall return unto his possession.

29 And if a man sell a dwelling house in a walled city, then he may redeem it within a whole year after it is sold; *within* a full year may he redeem it.

30 And if it be not redeemed within the space of a full year, then the house that *is* in the walled city shall be established for ever to him that bought it throughout his generations: it shall not go out in the jubilee.

31 But the houses of the villages which have no wall round about them shall be counted as the fields of the country: [1]they may be redeemed, and they shall go out in the jubilee.

32 Notwithstanding [a]the cities of the Levites, *and* the houses of the cities of their possession, may the Levites redeem at any time.

33 And if [1]a man purchase of the Levites, then the house that was sold, and the city of his possession, shall go out in *the year of* jubilee: for the houses of the cities of the Levites *are* their possession among the children of Israel.

34 But [a]the field of the suburbs of their cities may not be sold; for it *is* their perpetual possession.

35 ¶ And if thy brother be waxen poor, and [1]fallen in decay with thee; then thou shalt [a]relieve[2] him: *yea, though he be* a stranger, or a sojourner; that he may live with thee.

36 [a]Take thou no usury of him, or increase: but [b]fear thy God; that thy brother may live with thee.

37 Thou shalt not give him thy money upon usury, nor lend him thy victuals for increase.

38 [a]I *am* the LORD your God, which brought you forth out of the land of

11 [a]ver. 5
12 [a]ver. 6,7
13 [a]ver. 10; ch. 27:24; Num. 36:4
15 [a]ch. 27:18
17 [a]ver. 14 [b]ver. 43; ch. 19:14,32
18 [a]ch. 19:37 [b]ch. 26:5; Deut. 12:10; Ps. 4:8
19 [a]ch. 26:5; Ezek. 34:25
20 [a]Mat. 6:25 [b]ver. 4,5
21 [a]See Ex. 16:29
22 [a]2 Ki. 19:29 [b]Josh. 5:11
23 [a]Deut. 32:43 [b]Ps. 39:12 [1]Or, *to be quite cut off* [2]Heb. *for cutting off*
25 [a]Ruth 2:20 [b]See Ruth 3:2,9,12
26 [1]Heb. *his hand hath attained and found sufficiency*
27 [a]ver. 50-52
28 [a]ver. 13
31 [1]Heb. *redemption belongeth unto it*
32 [a]See Num. 35:2
33 [1]Or, one *of the Levites redeem them*
34 [a]See Acts 4:36, 37
35 [a]Deut. 15:7; Luke 6:35; 1 John 3:17 [1]Heb. *his hand faileth* [2]Heb. *strengthen*
36 [a]Ex. 22:25; Deut. 23:19 [b]Neh. 5:9
38 [a]ch. 22:32,33

S *Ex 11:7* ◀▶ *Lev 26:6*
B *Ex 23:26* ◀▶ *Lev 26:3–5*
F *Ex 23:25* ◀▶ *Lev 26:5*

Egypt, to give you the land of Canaan, *and* to be your God.

39 ¶ And [a]if thy brother *that dwelleth* by thee be waxen poor, and be sold unto thee; thou shalt not [l]compel him to serve as a bondservant:

40 *But* as an hired servant, *and* as a sojourner, he shall be with thee, *and* shall serve thee unto the year of jubilee:

41 And *then* shall he depart from thee, *both* he and his children [a]with him, and shall return unto his own family, and [b]unto the possession of his fathers shall he return.

42 For they *are* [a]my servants, which I brought forth out of the land of Egypt: they shall not be sold [l]as bondmen.

43 [a]Thou shalt not rule over him [b]with rigour; but [c]shalt fear thy God.

44 Both thy bondmen, and thy bondmaids, which thou shalt have, *shall be* of the heathen that are round about you; of them shall ye buy bondmen and bondmaids.

45 Moreover of [a]the children of the strangers that do sojourn among you, of them shall ye buy, and of their families that *are* with you, which they begat in your land: and they shall be your possession.

46 And [a]ye shall take them as an inheritance for your children after you, to inherit *them for* a possession; [l]they shall be your bondmen for ever: but over your brethren the children of Israel, ye shall not rule one over another with rigour.

47 ¶ And if a sojourner or stranger [l]wax rich by thee, and [a]thy brother *that dwelleth* by him wax poor, and sell himself unto the stranger *or* sojourner by thee, or to the stock of the stranger's family:

48 After that he is sold he may be redeemed again; one of his brethren may [a]redeem him:

49 Either his uncle, or his uncle's son, may redeem him, or *any* that is nigh of kin unto him of his family may redeem him; or if [a]he be able, he may redeem himself.

50 And he shall reckon with him that bought him from the year that he was sold to him unto the year of jubilee: and the price of his sale shall be according unto the number of years, [a]according to the time of an hired servant shall it be with him.

39 [a]Ex. 21:2; Deut. 15:12; 1 Ki. 9:22 [l]Heb. *serve thyself with him with the service;* see ver. 46

41 [a]Ex. 21:3 [b]ver. 28

42 [a]ver. 55; Rom. 6:22; 1 Cor. 7:23 [l]Heb. *with the sale of a bondman*

43 [a]Eph. 6:9 [b]Ex. 1:13 [c]Ex. 1:17; Deut. 25:18; Mal. 3:5

45 [a]Is. 56:3,6

46 [a]Is. 14:2 [l]Heb. *ye shall serve yourselves with them;* see ver. 39

47 [a]ver. 25,35 [l]Heb. *his hand obtain*

48 [a]Neh. 5:5

49 [a]ver. 26

50 [a]Job 7:1; Is. 16:14

54 [l]Or, *by these means*

26:1 [a]Ex. 20:4,5; Deut. 5:8 [l]Or, *pillar* [2]Or, *figured stone* [3]Heb. *a stone of picture*

2 [a]ch. 19:30

3 [a]Deut. 28:1-14

4 [a]Is. 30:23 [b]Ps. 67:6; Zech. 8:12

5 [a]Amos 9:13 [b]ch. 25:19 [c]ch. 25:18

6 [a]Is. 45:7 [b]Ps. 4:8; Hos. 2:18; Zeph. 3:13 [c]2 Ki. 17:25 [d]Ezek. 14:17 [l]Heb. *cause to cease*

8 [a]Deut. 32:30

51 If *there be* yet many years *behind,* according unto them he shall give again the price of his redemption out of the money that he was bought for.

52 And if there remain but few years unto the year of jubilee, then he shall count with him, *and* according unto his years shall he give him again the price of his redemption.

53 *And* as a yearly hired servant shall he be with him: *and the other* shall not rule with rigour over him in thy sight.

54 And if he be not redeemed [l]in these *years,* then he shall go out in the year of jubilee, *both* he, and his children with him.

55 For unto me the children of Israel *are* servants; they *are* my servants whom I brought forth out of the land of Egypt: I *am* the LORD your God.

The blessings for obedience

26 YE SHALL make you [a]no idols nor graven image, neither rear you up a [l]standing image, neither shall ye set up *any* [2,3]image of stone in your land, to bow down unto it: for I *am* the LORD your God.

2 ¶ [a]Ye shall keep my sabbaths, and reverence my sanctuary: I *am* the LORD.

3 ¶ [a]If ye walk in my statutes, and B
keep my commandments, and do them; U

4 [a]Then I will give you rain in due season, [b]and the land shall yield her increase, and the trees of the field shall yield their fruit.

5 And [a]your threshing shall reach unto R
the vintage, and the vintage shall reach F
unto the sowing time: and [b]ye shall eat your bread to the full, and [c]dwell in your land safely.

6 And [a]I will give peace in the land, S
and [b]ye shall lie down, and none shall V
make *you* afraid: and I will [l]rid [c]evil beasts out of the land, neither shall [d]the sword go through your land.

7 And ye shall chase your enemies, and they shall fall before you by the sword.

8 And [a]five of you shall chase an hundred, and an hundred of you shall put ten

B *Lev 25:19* ◀▶ *Dt 7:13*
U *Ge 50:24–25* ◀▶ *Nu 6:24–27*
R ▶ *Lev 26:14–35*
F *Lev 25:19* ◀▶ *Nu 11:7–9*
S *Lev 25:18* ◀▶ *Nu 31:49*
V *Ex 23:27* ◀▶ *Nu 10:9*

thousand to flight: and your enemies shall
fall before you by the sword.
9 For I will [a]have respect unto you,
and [b]make you fruitful, and multiply you,
and establish my covenant with you.
10 And ye shall eat [a]old store, and
bring forth the old because of the new.
11 [a]And I will set my tabernacle
among you: and my soul shall not abhor
you.
12 [a]And I will walk among you, and
will be your God, and ye shall be my
people.
13 I *am* the LORD your God, which
brought you forth out of the land of
Egypt, that ye should not be their bondmen; and I have broken the bands of your
yoke, and made you go upright.

The punishments for disobedience

R 14 ¶ [a]But if ye will not hearken unto
me, and will not do all these commandments;
15 And if ye shall despise my statutes,
or if your soul abhor my judgments, so
that ye will not do all my commandments, *but* that ye break my covenant:
D 16 I also will do this unto you; I will
even appoint [l]over you terror, [a]consump-
tion, and the burning ague, that shall
[b]consume the eyes, and cause sorrow of
heart: and [c]ye shall sow your seed in
vain, for your enemies shall eat it.
17 And [a]I will set my face against you,
and [b]ye shall be slain before your enemies: [c]they that hate you shall reign over

R *Lev 26:5–10* ◄► *Lev 26:18*
D *Ex 32:35* ◄► *Nu 5:21*

9 [a]Ex. 2:25 [b]Gen. 17:6,7; Ps. 107:38
10 [a]ch. 25:22
11 [a]Ex. 25:8; Josh. 22:19; Ps. 76:2; Rev. 21:3
12 [a]2 Cor. 6:16
14 [a]Deut. 28:15; Lam. 2:17; Mal. 2:2
16 [a]Deut. 28:22 [b]1 Sam. 2:33 [c]Deut. 28:33,51; Job 31:8; Mic. 6:15 [l]Heb. *upon you*
17 [a]ch. 17:10 [b]Deut. 28:25 [c]Ps. 106:41 [d]ver. 36; Ps. 53:5
18 [a]1 Sam. 2:5
19 [a]Is. 25:11 [b]Deut. 28:23
20 [a]Ps. 127:1 [b]Deut. 11:17
21 [l]Or, *at all adventures with me;* see ver. 24
22 [a]Deut. 32:24 [b]2 Chr. 15:5; Zech. 7:14
23 [a]Jer. 2:30; Amos 4:6-12
24 [a]Ps. 18:26
25 [a]Ezek. 5:17 [b]Deut. 28:21
26 [a]Ps. 105:16

you; and [d]ye shall flee when none pursueth you.
18 And if ye will not yet for all this R
hearken unto me, then I will punish you
[a]seven times more for your sins.
19 And I will [a]break the pride of your
power; and I [b]will make your heaven as
iron, and your earth as brass:
20 And your [a]strength shall be spent
in vain: for [b]your land shall not yield her
increase, neither shall the trees of the
land yield their fruits.
21 ¶ And if ye walk [l]contrary unto N
me, and will not hearken unto me; I will
bring seven times more plagues upon you
according to your sins.
22 [a]I will also send wild beasts among
you, which shall rob you of your children,
and destroy your cattle, and make you
few in number; and [b]your *high* ways shall
be desolate.
23 And if ye [a]will not be reformed by N
me by these things, but will walk contrary unto me;
24 [a]Then will I also walk contrary unto R
you, and will punish you yet seven times
for your sins.
25 And [a]I will bring a sword upon you,
that shall avenge the quarrel of *my* covenant: and when ye are gathered together within your cities, [b]I will send the
pestilence among you; and ye shall be delivered into the hand of the enemy.
26 [a]*And* when I have broken the staff

R *Lev 26:14–35* ◄► *Lev 26:24*
N *Ge 6:3* ◄► *Lev 26:23–24*
N *Lev 26:21* ◄► *Lev 26:27–28*
R *Lev 26:18* ◄► *Lev 26:28*

26:18 This verse highlights a critical principle for the people of Israel. The Lord declares four times in this chapter that, if Israel refuses to repent for its sinful rebellion, then God would make their punishment seven times worse.

26:22 Wild animals were a nuisance in underpopulated areas in the promised land (see Dt 7:22). This verse seems to indicate that one of the punishments for disobedience would be an increase in the number of wild animals and their attacks in all areas of the land (see 2Ki 2:24; 17:26). God will also use wild animals to carry out his punishments in the last days. One of the horrors of the tribulation will be the attack on humans by wild beasts (see Rev 6:8).

26:22–26 According to this prophecy, God's wrath against Israel would involve four key elements: wild beasts, the sword, pestilence and famine. It is significant that these four elements appear together several times in Scripture (see Jer 15:2–3; Eze 5:12, 17; 14:13–20; 33:27). The prophet Ezekiel refers to them most often and calls them the "four sore judgments upon Jerusalem" (Eze 14:21).

These four elements of the wrath of God are also poured out on sinful humanity during the opening days of the tribulation (see Rev 6:4–8). God's wrath will continue until the end of the Battle of Armageddon. Yet the righteous will be spared such wrath (see Ge 18:23–32; Eze 14:13–20). God chastens his children, but he will deliver them from his wrath. The apostle Paul comforted believers to this end when he urged them to "wait for his Son from heaven, whom he raised from the dead, even Jesus, which delivered us from the wrath to come" (1Th 1:10). For more information, see the article entitled "The Rapture," p. 1370.

of your bread, ten women shall bake your bread in one oven, and they shall deliver *you* your bread again by weight: and [b]ye shall eat, and not be satisfied.

N 27 And if ye will not for all this hearken unto me, but walk contrary unto me;

R 28 Then I will walk contrary unto you also [a]in fury; and I, even I, will chastise you seven times for your sins.

29 [a]And ye shall eat the flesh of your sons, and the flesh of your daughters shall ye eat.

30 And [a]I will destroy your high places, and cut down your images, and cast your carcases upon the carcases of your idols, and my soul shall abhor you.

R 31 And I will make your cities waste, and [a]bring your sanctuaries unto desolation, and I will not smell the savour of your sweet odours.

32 [a]And I will bring the land into desolation: and your enemies which dwell therein shall be astonished at it.

33 And [a]I will scatter you among the heathen, and will draw out a sword after you: and your land shall be desolate, and your cities waste.

34 [a]Then shall the land enjoy her sabbaths, as long as it lieth desolate, and ye *be* in your enemies' land; *even* then shall the land rest, and enjoy her sabbaths.

35 As long as it lieth desolate it shall rest; because it did not rest in your [a]sabbaths, when ye dwelt upon it.

36 And upon them that are left *alive* of you [a]I will send a faintness into their hearts in the lands of their enemies; and [b]the sound of a [/]shaken leaf shall chase them; and they shall flee, as fleeing from a sword; and they shall fall when none pursueth.

37 And [a]they shall fall one upon another, as it were before a sword, when none pursueth: and [b]ye shall have no power to stand before your enemies.

38 And ye shall perish among the heathen, and the land of your enemies shall eat you up.

39 And they that are left of you [a]shall pine away in their iniquity in your enemies' lands; and also in the iniquities of their fathers shall they pine away with them.

M P R 40 [a]If they shall confess their iniquity, and the iniquity of their fathers, with their trespass which they trespassed against me, and that also they have walked contrary unto me;

R 41 And *that* I also have walked contrary unto them, and have brought them into the land of their enemies; if then their [a]uncircumcised hearts be [b]humbled, and they then accept of the punishment of their iniquity:

42 Then will I [a]remember my covenant with Jacob, and also my covenant with Isaac, and also my covenant with Abraham will I remember; and I will [b]remember the land.

R 43 [a]The land also shall be left of them, and shall enjoy her sabbaths, while she lieth desolate without them: and they shall accept of the punishment of their iniquity: because, even because they [b]despised my judgments, and because their soul abhorred my statutes.

I 44 And yet for all that, when they be in the land of their enemies, [a]I will not cast them away, neither will I abhor them, to destroy them utterly, and to break my covenant with them: for I *am* the LORD their God.

45 But I will [a]for their sakes remember the covenant of their ancestors, [b]whom I brought forth out of the land of Egypt [c]in the sight of the heathen, that I might be their God: I *am* the LORD.

46 [a]These *are* the statutes and judgments and laws, which the LORD made between him and the children of Israel [b]in mount Sinai by the hand of Moses.

Vows and tithes to the LORD

27 AND THE LORD spake unto Moses, saying,

2 Speak unto the children of Israel, and say unto them, [a]When a man shall make a singular vow, the persons *shall be* for the LORD by thy estimation.

3 And thy estimation shall be of the male from twenty years old even unto sixty years old, even thy estimation shall

26 [b]Mic. 6:14
28 [a]Jer. 21:5; Ezek. 5:13,15 & 8:18
29 [a]Deut. 28:53
30 [a]2 Chr. 34:3; Ezek. 6:3-6,13
31 [a]Ps. 74:7
32 [a]Jer. 9:11
33 [a]Deut. 4:27; Ezek. 12:15 & 20:23 & 22:15; Zech. 7:14
34 [a]2 Chr. 36:21
35 [a]ch. 25:2
36 [a]Ezek. 21:7,12,15 [b]ver. 17; Prov. 28:1 [/]Heb. *driven*
37 [a]See Judg. 7:22; 1 Sam. 14:15,16; Is. 10:4 [b]Josh. 7:12,13; Judg. 2:14
39 [a]Deut. 28:65; Zech. 10:9
40 [a]Num. 5:7; Neh. 9:2; Luke 15:18; 1 John 1:9
41 [a]Acts 7:51; Rom. 2:29 [b]2 Chr. 12:6,7
42 [a]Ex. 2:24 & 6:5; Ezek. 16:60 [b]Ps. 136:23
43 [a]ver. 34,35 [b]ver. 15
44 [a]Deut. 4:31; 2 Ki. 13:23; Rom. 11:2
45 [a]Rom. 11:28 [b]ch. 22:33 & 25:38 [c]Ps. 98:2; Ezek. 20:9,14,22
46 [a]ch. 27:34; Deut. 6:1 & 12:1; John 1:17 [b]ch. 25:1
27:2 [a]Num. 6:2; See Judg. 11:30,31,39; 1 Sam. 1:11,28

N *Lev 26:23–24* ◀ ▶ *Nu 14:11*
R *Lev 26:24* ◀ ▶ *Lev 26:31–35*
R *Lev 26:28* ◀ ▶ *Lev 26:41–43*
M *Ex 32:9–10* ◀ ▶ *Dt 9:13–14*
P ▶ *Nu 14:19–20*
R *Lev 5:16* ◀ ▶ *Nu 5:6–8*
R *Lev 26:31–35* ◀ ▶ *Lev 26:43*
R *Lev 26:41–43* ◀ ▶ *Dt 4:27*
I *Ex 32:13* ◀ ▶ *Nu 10:29*

be fifty shekels of silver, [a]after the shekel of the sanctuary.

4 And if it *be* a female, then thy estimation shall be thirty shekels.

5 And if *it be* from five years old even unto twenty years old, then thy estimation shall be of the male twenty shekels, and for the female ten shekels.

6 And if *it be* from a month old even unto five years old, then thy estimation shall be of the male five shekels of silver, and for the female thy estimation *shall be* three shekels of silver.

7 And if *it be* from sixty years old and above; if *it be* a male, then thy estimation shall be fifteen shekels, and for the female ten shekels.

8 But if he be poorer than thy estimation, then he shall present himself before the priest, and the priest shall value him; according to his ability that vowed shall the priest value him.

9 And if *it be* a beast, whereof men bring an offering unto the LORD, all that *any man* giveth of such unto the LORD shall be holy.

10 He shall not alter it, nor change it, a good for a bad, or a bad for a good: and if he shall at all change beast for beast, then it and the exchange thereof shall be holy.

11 And if *it be* any unclean beast, of which they do not offer a sacrifice unto the LORD, then he shall present the beast before the priest:

12 And the priest shall value it, whether it be good or bad: [l]as thou valuest it, *who art* the priest, so shall it be.

13 [a]But if he will at all redeem it, then he shall add a fifth *part* thereof unto thy estimation.

14 ¶ And when a man shall sanctify his house *to be* holy unto the LORD, then the priest shall estimate it, whether it be good or bad: as the priest shall estimate it, so shall it stand.

15 [a]And if he that sanctified it will redeem his house, then he shall add the fifth *part* of the money of thy estimation unto it, and it shall be his.

16 And if a man shall sanctify unto the LORD *some part* of a field of his possession, then thy estimation shall be according to the seed thereof: [l]an homer of barley seed *shall be valued* at fifty shekels of silver.

17 If he sanctify his field from the year of jubilee, according to thy estimation it shall stand.

18 But if he sanctify his field after the jubilee, then the priest shall [a]reckon unto him the money according to the years that remain, even unto the year of the jubilee, and it shall be abated from thy estimation.

19 [a]And if he that sanctified the field will in any wise redeem it, then he shall add the fifth *part* of the money of thy estimation unto it, and it shall be assured to him.

20 And if he will not redeem the field, or if he have sold the field to another man, it shall not be redeemed any more.

21 But the field, [a]when it goeth out in the jubilee, shall be holy unto the LORD, as a field [b]devoted; [c]the possession thereof shall be the priest's.

22 And if *a man* sanctify unto the LORD a field which he hath bought, which *is* not of the fields of [a]his possession;

23 [a]Then the priest shall reckon unto him the worth of thy estimation, *even* unto the year of the jubilee: and he shall give thine estimation in that day, *as* a holy thing unto the LORD.

24 [a]In the year of the jubilee the field shall return unto him of whom it was bought, *even* to him to whom the possession of the land *did belong*.

25 And all thy estimations shall be according to the shekel of the sanctuary: [a]twenty gerahs shall be the shekel.

26 ¶ Only the [a]firstling[l] of the beasts, which should be the LORD'S firstling, no man shall sanctify it; whether *it be* ox, or sheep: it *is* the LORD'S.

27 And if *it be* of an unclean beast, then he shall redeem *it* according to thine estimation, [a]and shall add a fifth *part* of it thereto: or if it be not redeemed, then it shall be sold according to thy estimation.

28 [a]Notwithstanding no devoted thing, that a man shall devote unto the LORD of all that he hath, *both* of man and beast, and of the field of his possession, shall be sold or redeemed: every devoted thing *is* most holy unto the LORD.

29 [a]None devoted, which shall be devoted of men, shall be redeemed; *but* shall surely be put to death.

30 And [a]all the tithe of the land, *whether* of the seed of the land, *or* of the

3 [a]Ex. 30:13
12 [l]Heb. *according to thy estimation, O priest*
13 [a]ver. 15,19
15 [a]ver. 13
16 [l]Or, the land of *an homer*
18 [a]ch. 25:15,16
19 [a]ver. 13
21 [a]ch. 25:10,28, 31 [b]ver. 28 [c]Num. 18:14; Ezek. 44:29
22 [a]ch. 25:10,25
23 [a]ver. 18
24 [a]ch. 25:28
25 [a]Ex. 30:13; Num. 3:47 & 18:16; Ezek. 45:12
26 [a]Ex. 13:2,12 & 22:30 [l]Heb. *firstborn*
27 [a]ver. 11,12
28 [a]ver. 21; Josh. 6:17-19
29 [a]Num. 21:2
30 [a]Gen. 28:22; Num. 18:21,24; 2 Chr. 31:5,6,12; Neh. 13:12; Mal. 3:8

fruit of the tree, *is* the LORD'S: *it is* holy
unto the LORD.
31 [a]And if a man will at all redeem
aught of his tithes, he shall add thereto
the fifth *part* thereof.
32 And concerning the tithe of the
herd, or of the flock, *even* of whatsoever
[a]passeth under the rod, the tenth shall be
holy unto the LORD.

31 [a]ver. 13
32 [a]Jer. 33:13; Ezek. 20:37; Mic. 7:14
33 [a]ver. 10
34 [a]ch. 26:46

33 He shall not search whether it be
good or bad, [a]neither shall he change it:
and if he change it at all, then both it and
the change thereof shall be holy; it shall
not be redeemed.
34 [a]These *are* the commandments,
which the LORD commanded Moses for
the children of Israel in mount Sinai.

Numbers

Author: Moses

Theme: Israel's wilderness wanderings in Sinai

Date of Writing: c. 1440–1406 B.C.

Outline of Numbers

I. Preparing to Depart From Mount Sinai (1:1—9:23)
II. From Mount Sinai to Defiance and Judgment (10:1—14:45)
III. Discipline, Duties and Defeat Along the Journey (15:1—21:35)
IV. Balaam's Prophetic Words (22:1—25:18)
V. Practical Preparations for Entering Canaan (26:1—36:13)

THE TITLE OF the book of Numbers comes from Moses' counting (or numbering) of the Israelites (chs. 1; 26). This census taking occurred twice—once as the Israelites left Egypt and again, almost forty years later, as the Israelites prepared to enter the promised land.

Yet the Hebrew title of the book (*bemidbar*, which means "in the wilderness") more accurately describes Numbers' contents. Continuing the account begun in the book of Exodus, Numbers opens with the conclusion of God's instructions to Moses at Mt. Sinai. The opening chapters of the book (chs. 1—14) chronicle the beginning of Israel's wilderness experience. The majority of the book relates the story of Israel's journey from Mt. Sinai to the borders of Canaan on the eastern side of the Jordan River (chs. 15—20). The book closes by recording the events that transpired in the final few months in the wilderness (chs. 21—36).

The book of Numbers also tells of the murmuring and rebellion of God's people. Despite the miraculous deliverance from their enemies, the divine provision of daily food in the form of manna and the continued presence of God in their lives as evidenced by the pillar of cloud and fire, Numbers reveals the deep-seated unbelief of the Israelites. Rather than displaying attitudes of worship and obedience, the people whom God had redeemed from slavery in Egypt responded to his miracles with constant complaining, rebellion and mutiny. Loudly voicing a desire to return to their chains in Egypt and refusing to believe God's promise to help them overcome their enemies in Canaan, the community of the redeemed tragically lost not only their faith but their part in the promised land as well.

The census of the people

1 AND THE LORD spake unto Moses [a]in
the wilderness of Sinai, [b]in the tabernacle of the congregation, on the first *day*
of the second month, in the second year
after they were come out of the land of
Egypt, saying,
2 [a]Take ye the sum of all the congregation of the children of Israel, after their
families, by the house of their fathers,
with the number of *their* names, every
male by their polls;
3 From twenty years old and upward,
all that are able to go forth to war in Israel: thou and Aaron shall number them
by their armies.
4 And with you there shall be a man of
every tribe; every one head of the house
of his fathers.
5 ¶ And these *are* the names of the
men that shall stand with you: of *the tribe*
of Reuben; Elizur the son of Shedeur.
6 Of Simeon; Shelumiel the son of Zurishaddai.
7 Of Judah; [l]Nahshon the son of Amminadab.
8 Of Issachar; Nethaneel the son of
Zuar.
9 Of Zebulun; Eliab the son of Helon.
10 Of the children of Joseph: of
Ephraim; Elishama the son of Ammihud:
of Manasseh; Gamaliel the son of Pedahzur.
11 Of Benjamin; Abidan the son of
Gideoni.
12 Of Dan; Ahiezer the son of Ammishaddai.
13 Of Asher; Pagiel the son of Ocran.
14 Of Gad; Eliasaph the son of [l]Deuel.
15 Of Naphtali; Ahira the son of Enan.
16 [a]These *were* the renowned of the
congregation, princes of the tribes of
their fathers, [b]heads of thousands in
Israel.
17 ¶ And Moses and Aaron took these
men which are expressed [a]by *their*
names:
18 And they assembled all the congregation together on the first *day* of the
second month, and they declared their
[a]pedigrees after their families, by the
house of their fathers, according to the
number of the names, from twenty years
old and upward, by their polls.
19 As the LORD commanded Moses, so
he numbered them in the wilderness of
Sinai.
20 And the [a]children of Reuben, Israel's eldest son, by their generations, after their families, by the house of their
fathers, according to the number of the
names, by their polls, every male from
twenty years old and upward, all that
were able to go forth to war;
21 Those that were numbered of
them, *even* of the tribe of Reuben, *were*
forty and six thousand and five hundred.
22 ¶ Of the [a]children of Simeon, by
their generations, after their families, by
the house of their fathers, those that
were numbered of them, according to the
number of the names, by their polls, every male from twenty years old and upward, all that were able to go forth to
war;
23 Those that were numbered of
them, *even* of the tribe of Simeon, *were*
fifty and nine thousand and three
hundred.
24 ¶ Of the [a]children of Gad, by their
generations, after their families, by the
house of their fathers, according to the
number of the names, from twenty years
old and upward, all that were able to go
forth to war;
25 Those that were numbered of
them, *even* of the tribe of Gad, *were* forty
and five thousand six hundred and fifty.
26 ¶ Of the [a]children of Judah, by
their generations, after their families, by
the house of their fathers, according to
the number of the names, from twenty
years old and upward, all that were able
to go forth to war;
27 Those that were numbered of
them, *even* of the tribe of Judah, *were*
[a]threescore and fourteen thousand and
six hundred.
28 ¶ Of the [a]children of Issachar, by
their generations, after their families, by
the house of their fathers, according to
the number of the names, from twenty
years old and upward, all that were able
to go forth to war;
29 Those that were numbered of
them, *even* of the tribe of Issachar, *were*
fifty and four thousand and four hundred.
30 ¶ Of the [a]children of Zebulun, by
their generations, after their families, by
the house of their fathers, according to
the number of the names, from twenty

1:1 [a]Ex. 19:1; ch. 10:11,12 [b]Ex. 25:22
2 [a]Ex. 30:12 & 38:26; ch. 26:2,63, 64; 2 Sam. 24:2; 1 Chr. 21:2
7 [l]Called *Naasson* in Mat. 1:4
14 [l]ch. 2:14 he is called *Reuel*
16 [a]ch. 7:2; 1 Chr. 27:16 [b]Ex. 18:21, 25
17 [a]Is. 43:1
18 [a]Ezra 2:59
20 [a]ch. 2:10,11 & 32:6,15,21,29
22 [a]ch. 2:12,13 & 26:12-14
24 [a]ch. 2:14,15 & 26:15-18 & 32:2, 29 & 34:14
26 [a]ch. 2:3,4 & 26:19-22; 2 Sam. 24:9
27 [a]2 Chr. 17:14
28 [a]ch. 2:5,6
30 [a]ch. 2:7,8 & 26:26,27

years old and upward, all that were able
to go forth to war;
31 Those that were numbered of
them, *even* of the tribe of Zebulun, *were*
fifty and seven thousand and four
hundred.
32 ¶ Of the children of Joseph, *namely,*
of the [a]children of Ephraim, by their generations, after their families, by the house
of their fathers, according to the number
of the names, from twenty years old and
upward, all that were able to go forth to
war;
33 Those that were numbered of
them, *even* of the tribe of Ephraim, *were*
forty thousand and five hundred.
34 ¶ Of the [a]children of Manasseh, by
their generations, after their families, by
the house of their fathers, according to
the number of the names, from twenty
years old and upward, all that were able
to go forth to war;
35 Those that were numbered of
them, *even* of the tribe of Manasseh,
were thirty and two thousand and two
hundred.
36 ¶ Of the [a]children of Benjamin, by
their generations, after their families, by
the house of their fathers, according to
the number of the names, from twenty
years old and upward, all that were able
to go forth to war;
37 Those that were numbered of
them, *even* of the tribe of Benjamin, *were*
thirty and five thousand and four
hundred.
38 ¶ Of the [a]children of Dan, by their
generations, after their families, by the
house of their fathers, according to the
number of the names, from twenty years
old and upward, all that were able to go
forth to war;
39 Those that were numbered of
them, *even* of the tribe of Dan, *were*
threescore and two thousand and seven
hundred.

32 [a] ch. 2:18,19 & 26:35-37
34 [a] ch. 2:20,21 & 26:28-34
36 [a] ch. 2:22,23 & 26:38-41
38 [a] ch. 2:25,26 & 26:42,43
40 [a] ch. 2:27,28 & 26:44-47
44 [a] ch. 26:64
46 [a] Ex. 38:26; See Ex. 12:37; ch. 2:32 & 26:51
47 [a] ch. 2:33; See ch. 3 & 4 & 26:57; 1 Chr. 6 & 21:6
49 [a] ch. 2:33 & 26:62
50 [a] Ex. 38:21; ch. 3:7,8 & 4:15, 25-27,33

40 ¶ Of the [a]children of Asher, by
their generations, after their families, by
the house of their fathers, according to
the number of the names, from twenty
years old and upward, all that were able
to go forth to war;
41 Those that were numbered of
them, *even* of the tribe of Asher, *were*
forty and one thousand and five hundred.
42 ¶ Of the children of Naphtali,
throughout their generations, after their
families, by the house of their fathers, according to the number of the names,
from twenty years old and upward, all
that were able to go forth to war;
43 Those that were numbered of
them, *even* of the tribe of Naphtali, *were*
fifty and three thousand and four
hundred.
44 [a]These *are* those that were numbered, which Moses and Aaron numbered, and the princes of Israel, *being*
twelve men: each one was for the house
of his fathers.
45 So were all those that were numbered of the children of Israel, by the
house of their fathers, from twenty years
old and upward, all that were able to go
forth to war in Israel;
46 Even all they that were numbered
were [a]six hundred thousand and three
thousand and five hundred and fifty.
47 ¶ But [a]the Levites after the tribe of
their fathers were not numbered among
them.
48 For the LORD had spoken unto Moses, saying,
49 [a]Only thou shalt not number the
tribe of Levi, neither take the sum of
them among the children of Israel:
50 [a]But thou shalt appoint the Levites
over the tabernacle of testimony, and
over all the vessels thereof, and over all
things that *belong* to it: they shall bear
the tabernacle, and all the vessels
thereof; and they shall minister unto it,

1:45–46 This passage chronicles the first census of the Israelites, recording 603,550 as the number of those qualified to serve in the army. Except for Joshua and Caleb, all of these died in the desert. This large number of men suggests a population for the entire community of nearly 2.5 million.

Because Exodus records that "a mixed multitude went up also with them; and flocks, and herds, *even* very much cattle" (Ex 12:38) some scholars deny that the route of the exodus led through the Sinai desert, claiming the Sinai's inability to sustain a large population and their flocks. However, archeological discoveries indicate that the northern areas of the Sinai that are now desert were once cultivated, treed and well watered, suggesting that available pasture land existed at the time of the exodus. Since God provided manna for human consumption, it is likely that with a slight increase in rainfall the land could have easily supported abundant flocks and herds.

[b]and shall encamp round about the tabernacle.

51 [a]And when the tabernacle setteth forward, the Levites shall take it down: and when the tabernacle is to be pitched, the Levites shall set it up: [b]and the stranger that cometh nigh shall be put to death.

52 And the children of Israel shall pitch their tents, [a]every man by his own camp, and every man by his own standard, throughout their hosts.

53 [a]But the Levites shall pitch round about the tabernacle of testimony, that there be no [b]wrath upon the congregation of the children of Israel: and the Levites shall keep the charge of the tabernacle of testimony.

54 And the children of Israel did according to all that the LORD commanded Moses, so did they.

The camps and tribal captains

2 AND THE LORD spake unto Moses and unto Aaron, saying,

2 [a]Every man of the children of Israel shall pitch by his own standard, with the ensign of their father's house: [b]far[1] off about the tabernacle of the congregation shall they pitch.

3 And on the east side toward the rising of the sun shall they of the standard of the camp of Judah pitch throughout their armies: and [a]Nahshon the son of Amminadab *shall be* captain of the children of Judah.

4 And his host, and those that were numbered of them, *were* threescore and fourteen thousand and six hundred.

5 And those that do pitch next unto him *shall be* the tribe of Issachar: and Nethaneel the son of Zuar *shall be* captain of the children of Issachar.

6 And his host, and those that were numbered thereof, *were* fifty and four thousand and four hundred.

7 *Then* the tribe of Zebulun: and Eliab the son of Helon *shall be* captain of the children of Zebulun.

8 And his host, and those that were numbered thereof, *were* fifty and seven thousand and four hundred.

9 All that were numbered in the camp of Judah *were* an hundred thousand and fourscore thousand and six thousand and four hundred, throughout their armies. [a]These shall first set forth.

50 [b]ch. 3:23,29, 35,38
51 [a]ch. 10:17,21 [b]ch. 3:10,38 & 18:22
52 [a]ch. 2:2,34
53 [a]ver. 50 [b]Lev. 10:6; ch. 8:19 & 16:46 & 18:5; 1 Sam. 6:19
2:2 [a]ch. 1:52 [b]Josh. 3:4 [1]Heb. *over against*
3 [a]ch. 10:14; Ruth 4:20; 1 Chr. 2:10; Mat. 1:4
9 [a]ch. 10:14
14 [1]*Deuel;* see ch. 1:14 & 7:42,47 & 10:20
16 [a]ch. 10:18
17 [a]ch. 10:17,21

10 ¶ On the south side *shall be* the standard of the camp of Reuben according to their armies: and the captain of the children of Reuben *shall be* Elizur the son of Shedeur.

11 And his host, and those that were numbered thereof, *were* forty and six thousand and five hundred.

12 And those which pitch by him *shall be* the tribe of Simeon: and the captain of the children of Simeon *shall be* Shelumiel the son of Zurishaddai.

13 And his host, and those that were numbered of them, *were* fifty and nine thousand and three hundred.

14 Then the tribe of Gad: and the captain of the sons of Gad *shall be* Eliasaph the son of [1]Reuel.

15 And his host, and those that were numbered of them, *were* forty and five thousand and six hundred and fifty.

16 All that were numbered in the camp of Reuben *were* an hundred thousand and fifty and one thousand and four hundred and fifty, throughout their armies. [a]And they shall set forth in the second rank.

17 ¶ [a]Then the tabernacle of the congregation shall set forward with the camp of the Levites in the midst of the camp: as they encamp, so shall they set forward, every man in his place by their standards.

18 ¶ On the west side *shall be* the standard of the camp of Ephraim according to their armies: and the captain of the sons of Ephraim *shall be* Elishama the son of Ammihud.

19 And his host, and those that were numbered of them, *were* forty thousand and five hundred.

20 And by him *shall be* the tribe of Manasseh: and the captain of the children of Manasseh *shall be* Gamaliel the son of Pedahzur.

21 And his host, and those that were numbered of them, *were* thirty and two thousand and two hundred.

22 Then the tribe of Benjamin: and the captain of the sons of Benjamin *shall be* Abidan the son of Gideoni.

23 And his host, and those that were numbered of them, *were* thirty and five thousand and four hundred.

24 All that were numbered of the camp of Ephraim *were* an hundred thousand and eight thousand and an hundred,

throughout their armies. [a]And they shall go forward in the third rank.

25 ¶ The standard of the camp of Dan *shall be* on the north side by their armies: and the captain of the children of Dan *shall be* Ahiezer the son of Ammishaddai.

26 And his host, and those that were numbered of them, *were* threescore and two thousand and seven hundred.

27 And those that encamp by him *shall be* the tribe of Asher: and the captain of the children of Asher *shall be* Pagiel the son of Ocran.

28 And his host, and those that were numbered of them, *were* forty and one thousand and five hundred.

29 ¶ Then the tribe of [a]Naphtali: and the captain of the children of Naphtali *shall be* Ahira the son of Enan.

30 And his host, and those that were numbered of them, *were* fifty and three thousand and four hundred.

31 All they that were numbered in the camp of Dan *were* an hundred thousand and fifty and seven thousand and six hundred. [a]They shall go hindmost with their standards.

32 ¶ These *are* those which were numbered of the children of Israel by the house of their fathers: [a]all those that were numbered of the camps throughout their hosts *were* six hundred thousand and three thousand and five hundred and fifty.

33 But [a]the Levites were not numbered among the children of Israel; as the LORD commanded Moses.

34 And the children of Israel did according to all that the LORD commanded Moses: [a]so they pitched by their standards, and so they set forward, every one after their families, according to the house of their fathers.

The Levites

3 THESE ALSO *are* the generations of Aaron and Moses in the day *that* the LORD spake with Moses in mount Sinai.

2 And these *are* the names of the sons of Aaron; Nadab the [a]firstborn, and Abihu, Eleazar, and Ithamar.

3 These *are* the names of the sons of Aaron, [a]the priests which were anointed, [†]whom he consecrated to minister in the priest's office.

4 [a]And Nadab and Abihu died before the LORD, when they offered strange fire before the LORD, in the wilderness of Sinai, and they had no children: and Eleazar and Ithamar ministered in the priest's office in the sight of Aaron their father.

5 ¶ And the LORD spake unto Moses, saying,

6 [a]Bring the tribe of Levi near, and present them before Aaron the priest, that they may minister unto him.

7 And they shall keep his charge, and the charge of the whole congregation before the tabernacle of the congregation, to do [a]the service of the tabernacle.

8 And they shall keep all the instruments of the tabernacle of the congregation, and the charge of the children of Israel, to do the service of the tabernacle.

9 And [a]thou shalt give the Levites unto Aaron and to his sons: they *are* wholly given unto him out of the children of Israel.

10 And thou shalt appoint Aaron and his sons, [a]and they shall wait on their priest's office: [b]and the stranger that cometh nigh shall be put to death.

11 And the LORD spake unto Moses, saying,

12 And I, behold, [a]I have taken the Levites from among the children of Israel instead of all the firstborn that openeth the matrix among the children of Israel: therefore the Levites shall be mine;

13 Because [a]all the firstborn *are* mine; [b]*for* on the day that I smote all the firstborn in the land of Egypt I hallowed unto me all the firstborn in Israel, both man and beast: mine shall they be: I *am* the LORD.

14 ¶ And the LORD spake unto Moses in the wilderness of Sinai, saying,

15 Number the children of Levi after the house of their fathers, by their families: [a]every male from a month old and upward shalt thou number them.

16 And Moses numbered them according to the [†]word of the LORD, as he was commanded.

17 [a]And these were the sons of Levi by their names; Gershon, and Kohath, and Merari.

18 And these *are* the names of the sons of Gershon by their families; [a]Libni, and Shimei.

19 And the sons of Kohath by their families; [a]Amram, and Izehar, Hebron, and Uzziel.

20 [a]And the sons of Merari by their

---

24 [a]ch. 10:22
29 [a]Gen. 30:8 & 49:21; 2 Ki. 15:29; Rev. 7:6
31 [a]ch. 10:25
32 [a]Ex. 38:26; ch. 1:46 & 11:21
33 [a]ch. 1:47
34 [a]ch. 24:2,5,6
3:2 [a]Ex. 6:23
3 [a]Ex. 28:41; Lev. 8 [†]Heb. *whose hand he filled*
4 [a]Lev. 10:1; ch. 26:61; 1 Chr. 24:2
6 [a]ch. 8:6 & 18:2
7 [a]See ch. 1:50 & 8:11,15,24,26
9 [a]ch. 8:19 & 18:6
10 [a]ch. 18:7 [b]ver. 38; ch. 1:51 & 16:40
12 [a]ver. 41; ch. 8:16 & 18:6
13 [a]Ex. 13:2; Lev. 27:26; ch. 8:17; Luke 2:23 [b]Ex. 13:12,15; ch. 8:17
15 [a]ver. 39; ch. 26:62
16 [†]Heb. *mouth*
17 [a]Gen. 46:11; Ex. 6:16; ch. 26:57; 1 Chr. 6:1,16 & 23:6
18 [a]Ex. 6:17
19 [a]Ex. 6:18
20 [a]Ex. 6:19

families; Mahli, and Mushi. These *are* the families of the Levites according to the house of their fathers.

21 Of Gershon *was* the family of the Libnites, and the family of the Shimites: these *are* the families of the Gershonites.

22 Those that were numbered of them, according to the number of all the males, from a month old and upward, *even* those that were numbered of them *were* seven thousand and five hundred.

23 [a]The families of the Gershonites shall pitch behind the tabernacle westward.

24 And the chief of the house of the father of the Gershonites *shall be* Eliasaph the son of Lael.

25 And [a]the charge of the sons of Gershon in the tabernacle of the congregation *shall be* [b]the tabernacle, and [c]the tent, [d]the covering thereof, and [e]the hanging for the door of the tabernacle of the congregation,

26 And [a]the hangings of the court, and [b]the curtain for the door of the court, which *is* by the tabernacle, and by the altar round about, and [c]the cords of it for all the service thereof.

27 ¶ [a]And of Kohath *was* the family of the Amramites, and the family of the Izeharites, and the family of the Hebronites, and the family of the Uzzielites: these *are* the families of the Kohathites.

28 In the number of all the males, from a month old and upward, *were* eight thousand and six hundred, keeping the charge of the sanctuary.

29 [a]The families of the sons of Kohath shall pitch on the side of the tabernacle southward.

30 And the chief of the house of the father of the families of the Kohathites *shall be* Elizaphan the son of Uzziel.

31 And [a]their charge *shall be* [b]the ark, and [c]the table, and [d]the candlestick, and [e]the altars, and the vessels of the sanctuary wherewith they minister, and [f]the hanging, and all the service thereof.

32 And Eleazar the son of Aaron the priest *shall be* chief over the chief of the Levites, *and have* the oversight of them that keep the charge of the sanctuary.

33 ¶ Of Merari *was* the family of the Mahlites, and the family of the Mushites: these *are* the families of Merari.

34 And those that were numbered of them, according to the number of all the males, from a month old and upward, *were* six thousand and two hundred.

35 And the chief of the house of the father of the families of Merari *was* Zuriel the son of Abihail: [a]*these* shall pitch on the side of the tabernacle northward.

36 And [a]*under*[1] the custody and charge of the sons of Merari *shall be* the boards of the tabernacle, and the bars thereof, and the pillars thereof, and the sockets thereof, and all the vessels thereof, and all that serveth thereto,

37 And the pillars of the court round about, and their sockets, and their pins, and their cords.

38 ¶ [a]But those that encamp before the tabernacle toward the east, *even* before the tabernacle of the congregation eastward, *shall be* Moses, and Aaron and his sons, [b]keeping the charge of the sanctuary [c]for the charge of the children of Israel; and [d]the stranger that cometh nigh shall be put to death.

39 [a]All that were numbered of the Levites, which Moses and Aaron numbered at the commandment of the LORD, throughout their families, all the males from a month old and upward, *were* twenty and two thousand.

40 ¶ And the LORD said unto Moses, [a]Number all the firstborn of the males of the children of Israel from a month old and upward, and take the number of their names.

41 [a]And thou shalt take the Levites for me (I *am* the LORD) instead of all the firstborn among the children of Israel; and the cattle of the Levites instead of all the firstlings among the cattle of the children of Israel.

42 And Moses numbered, as the LORD commanded him, all the firstborn among the children of Israel.

43 And all the firstborn males by the number of names, from a month old and upward, of those that were numbered of them, were twenty and two thousand two hundred and threescore and thirteen.

44 ¶ And the LORD spake unto Moses, saying,

45 [a]Take the Levites instead of all the firstborn among the children of Israel, and the cattle of the Levites instead of their cattle; and the Levites shall be mine: I *am* the LORD.

46 And for those that are to be [a]re-

23 [a]ch. 1:53
25 [a]ch. 4:24-26 [b]Ex. 25:9 [c]Ex. 26:1 [d]Ex. 26:7,14 [e]Ex. 26:36
26 [a]Ex. 27:9 [b]Ex. 27:16 [c]Ex. 35:18
27 [a]1 Chr. 26:23
29 [a]ch. 1:53
31 [a]ch. 4:15 [b]Ex. 25:10 [c]Ex. 25:23 [d]Ex. 25:31 [e]Ex. 27:1 & 30:1 [f]Ex. 26:32
35 [a]ch. 1:53
36 [a]ch. 4:31,32 [1]Heb. *the office of the charge*
38 [a]ch. 1:53 [b]ch. 18:5 [c]ver. 7,8 [d]ver. 10
39 [a]See ch. 26:62
40 [a]ver. 15
41 [a]ver. 12,45
45 [a]ver. 12,41
46 [a]Ex. 13:13; ch. 18:15

deemed of the two hundred and threescore and thirteen of the firstborn of the children of Israel, [b]which are more than the Levites;

47 Thou shalt even take [a]five shekels apiece by the poll, after the shekel of the sanctuary shalt thou take *them:* ([b]the shekel *is* twenty gerahs:)

48 And thou shalt give the money, wherewith the odd number of them is to be redeemed, unto Aaron and to his sons.

49 And Moses took the redemption money of them that were over and above them that were redeemed by the Levites:

50 Of the firstborn of the children of Israel took he the money; [a]a thousand three hundred and threescore and five *shekels,* after the shekel of the sanctuary:

51 And Moses [a]gave the money of them that were redeemed unto Aaron and to his sons, according to the word of the LORD, as the LORD commanded Moses.

The descendants of Kohath

4 AND THE LORD spake unto Moses and unto Aaron, saying,

2 Take the sum of the sons of Kohath from among the sons of Levi, after their families, by the house of their fathers,

3 [a]From thirty years old and upward even until fifty years old, all that enter into the host, to do the work in the tabernacle of the congregation.

4 [a]This *shall be* the service of the sons of Kohath in the tabernacle of the congregation, *about* [b]the most holy things:

5 ¶ And when the camp setteth forward, Aaron shall come, and his sons, and they shall take down [a]the covering veil, and cover the [b]ark of testimony with it:

6 And shall put thereon the covering of badgers' skins, and shall spread over *it* a cloth wholly of blue, and shall put in [a]the staves thereof.

7 And upon the [a]table of showbread they shall spread a cloth of blue, and put thereon the dishes, and the spoons, and the bowls, and covers to [l]cover withal: and the continual bread shall be thereon:

8 And they shall spread upon them a cloth of scarlet, and cover the same with a covering of badgers' skins, and shall put in the staves thereof.

9 And they shall take a cloth of blue, and cover the [a]candlestick of the light, [b]and his lamps, and his tongs, and his snuffdishes, and all the oil vessels thereof, wherewith they minister unto it:

10 And they shall put it and all the vessels thereof within a covering of badgers' skins, and shall put *it* upon a bar.

11 And upon [a]the golden altar they shall spread a cloth of blue, and cover it with a covering of badgers' skins, and shall put to the staves thereof:

12 And they shall take all the instruments of ministry, wherewith they minister in the sanctuary, and put *them* in a cloth of blue, and cover them with a covering of badgers' skins, and shall put *them* on a bar:

13 And they shall take away the ashes from the altar, and spread a purple cloth thereon:

14 And they shall put upon it all the vessels thereof, wherewith they minister about it, *even* the censers, the fleshhooks, and the shovels, and the [l]basins, all the vessels of the altar; and they shall spread upon it a covering of badgers' skins, and put to the staves of it.

15 And when Aaron and his sons have made an end of covering the sanctuary, and all the vessels of the sanctuary, as the camp is to set forward; after that [a]the sons of Kohath shall come to bear *it:* [b]but they shall not touch *any* holy thing, lest they die. [c]These *things are* the burden of the sons of Kohath in the tabernacle of the congregation.

16 ¶ And to the office of Eleazar the son of Aaron the priest *pertaineth* [a]the oil for the light, and the [b]sweet incense, and [c]the daily meat offering, and the [d]anointing oil, *and* the oversight of all the tabernacle, and of all that therein *is,* in the sanctuary, and in the vessels thereof.

17 ¶ And the LORD spake unto Moses and unto Aaron, saying,

18 Cut ye not off the tribe of the families of the Kohathites from among the Levites:

19 But thus do unto them, that they may live, and not die, when they approach unto [a]the most holy things: Aaron and his sons shall go in, and appoint them every one to his service and to his burden:

20 [a]But they shall not go in to see when the holy things are covered, lest they die.

46 [b]ver. 39,43
47 [a]Lev. 27:6; ch. 18:16 [b]Ex. 30:13
50 [a]ver. 46,47
51 [a]ver. 48
4:3 [a]See ch. 8:24; 1 Chr. 23:3,24,27
4 [a]ver. 15 [b]ver. 19
5 [a]Ex. 26:31 [b]Ex. 25:10,16
6 [a]Ex. 25:13
7 [a]Ex. 25:23,29,30 [l]Or, *pour out withal*
9 [a]Ex. 25:31 [b]Ex. 25:37,38
11 [a]Ex. 30:1,3
14 [l]Or, *bowls*
15 [a]ch. 7:9 & 10:21; Deut. 31:9; 2 Sam. 6:13; 1 Chr. 15:2,15 [b]2 Sam. 6:6,7; 1 Chr. 13:9,10 [c]ch. 3:31
16 [a]Ex. 25:6; Lev. 24:2 [b]Ex. 30:34 [c]Ex. 29:38 [d]Ex. 30:25
19 [a]ver. 4
20 [a]See Ex. 19:21; 1 Sam. 6:19

The descendants of Gershon

21 ¶ And the LORD spake unto Moses, saying,

22 Take also the sum of the sons of Gershon, throughout the houses of their fathers, by their families;

23 [a]From thirty years old and upward until fifty years old shalt thou number them; all that enter in [l]to perform the service, to do the work in the tabernacle of the congregation.

24 This *is* the service of the families of the Gershonites, to serve, and for [l]burdens:

25 And [a]they shall bear the curtains of the tabernacle, and the tabernacle of the congregation, his covering, and the covering of the badgers' skins that *is* above upon it, and the hanging for the door of the tabernacle of the congregation,

26 And the hangings of the court, and the hanging for the door of the gate of the court, which *is* by the tabernacle and by the altar round about, and their cords, and all the instruments of their service, and all that is made for them: so shall they serve.

27 At the [l]appointment of Aaron and his sons shall be all the service of the sons of the Gershonites, in all their burdens, and in all their service: and ye shall appoint unto them in charge all their burdens.

28 This *is* the service of the families of the sons of Gershon in the tabernacle of the congregation: and their charge *shall be* [a]under the hand of Ithamar the son of Aaron the priest.

The descendants of Merari

29 ¶ As for the sons of Merari, thou shalt number them after their families, by the house of their fathers;

30 [a]From thirty years old and upward even unto fifty years old shalt thou number them, every one that entereth into the [l]service, to do the work of the tabernacle of the congregation.

31 And [a]this *is* the charge of their burden, according to all their service in the tabernacle of the congregation; [b]the boards of the tabernacle, and the bars thereof, and the pillars thereof, and sockets thereof,

32 And the pillars of the court round about, and their sockets, and their pins, and their cords, with all their instruments, and with all their service: and by name ye shall [a]reckon the instruments of the charge of their burden.

33 This *is* the service of the families of the sons of Merari, according to all their service, in the tabernacle of the congregation, under the hand of Ithamar the son of Aaron the priest.

The results of the census

34 ¶ [a]And Moses and Aaron and the chief of the congregation numbered the sons of the Kohathites after their families, and after the house of their fathers,

35 From thirty [a]years old and upward even unto fifty years old, every one that entereth into the service, for the work in the tabernacle of the congregation:

36 And those that were numbered of them by their families were two thousand seven hundred and fifty.

37 These *were* they that were numbered of the families of the Kohathites, all that might do service in the tabernacle of the congregation, which Moses and Aaron did number according to the commandment of the LORD by the hand of Moses.

38 And those that were numbered of the sons of Gershon, throughout their families, and by the house of their fathers,

39 From thirty years old and upward even unto fifty years old, every one that entereth into the service, for the work in the tabernacle of the congregation,

40 Even those that were numbered of them, throughout their families, by the house of their fathers, were two thousand and six hundred and thirty.

41 [a]These *are* they that were numbered of the families of the sons of Gershon, of all that might do service in the tabernacle of the congregation, whom Moses and Aaron did number according to the commandment of the LORD.

42 ¶ And those that were numbered of the families of the sons of Merari, throughout their families, by the house of their fathers,

43 From thirty years old and upward even unto fifty years old, every one that entereth into the service, for the work in the tabernacle of the congregation,

44 Even those that were numbered of them after their families, were three thousand and two hundred.

23 [a]ver. 3 [l]Heb. *to war the warfare*
24 [l]Or, *carriage*
25 [a]ch. 3:25,26
27 [l]Heb. *mouth*
28 [a]ver. 33
30 [a]ver. 3 [l]Heb. *warfare*
31 [a]ch. 3:36,37 [b]Ex. 26:15
32 [a]Ex. 38:21
34 [a]ver. 2
35 [a]ver. 47; ch. 8:24,26; 1 Chr. 23:24; Luke 3:23; 1 Tim. 3:6
41 [a]ver. 22

45 These *be* those that were numbered of the families of the sons of Merari, whom Moses and Aaron numbered [a]according to the word of the LORD by the hand of Moses.

46 All those that were numbered of the Levites, whom Moses and Aaron and the chief of Israel numbered, after their families, and after the house of their fathers,

47 [a]From thirty years old and upward even unto fifty years old, every one that came to do the service of the ministry, and the service of the burden in the tabernacle of the congregation,

48 Even those that were numbered of them, were eight thousand and five hundred and fourscore.

49 According to the commandment of the LORD they were numbered by the hand of Moses, [a]every one according to his service, and according to his burden: thus were they numbered of him, [b]as the LORD commanded Moses.

Concerning the unclean

5 AND THE LORD spake unto Moses, saying,

2 Command the children of Israel, that they put out of the camp every [a]leper, and every one that hath an [b]issue, and whosoever is defiled by the [c]dead:

3 Both male and female shall ye put out, without the camp shall ye put them; that they defile not their camps, [a]in the midst whereof I dwell.

4 And the children of Israel did so, and put them out without the camp: as the LORD spake unto Moses, so did the children of Israel.

Suspected adultery

5 ¶ And the LORD spake unto Moses, saying,

R 6 Speak unto the children of Israel, [a]When a man or woman shall commit any sin that men commit, to do a trespass against the LORD, and that person be guilty;

7 [a]Then they shall confess their sin which they have done: and he shall recompense his trespass [b]with the principal thereof, and add unto it the fifth *part* thereof, and give *it* unto *him* against whom he hath trespassed.

R *Lev 26:40–41* ◀ ▶ *Dt 4:29–30*

45 [a]ver. 29
47 [a]ver. 3,23,30
49 [a]ver. 15,24,31 [b]ver. 1,21
5:2 [a]Lev. 13:3,46 [b]Lev. 15:2 [c]Lev. 21:1; ch. 9:6,10 & 19:11,13 & 31:19
3 [a]Lev. 26:11,12; 2 Cor. 6:16
6 [a]Lev. 6:2,3
7 [a]Lev. 5:5 & 26:40; Josh. 7:19 [b]Lev. 6:5
8 [a]Lev. 6:6,7 & 7:7
9 [a]Ex. 29:28; Lev. 6:17,18,26 & 7:6, 7,9,10,14 [1]Or, *heave offering*
10 [a]Lev. 10:13
13 [a]Lev. 18:20
15 [a]Lev. 5:11 [b]1 Ki. 17:18; Ezek. 29:16
19 [1]Or, being *in the power of thy husband* [2]Heb. *under thy husband*

8 But if the man have no kinsman to recompense the trespass unto, let the trespass be recompensed unto the LORD, *even* to the priest; beside [a]the ram of the atonement, whereby an atonement shall be made for him.

9 And every [a]offering[1] of all the holy things of the children of Israel, which they bring unto the priest, shall be his.

10 And every man's hallowed things shall be his: whatsoever any man giveth the priest, it shall be [a]his.

11 ¶ And the LORD spake unto Moses, saying,

12 Speak unto the children of Israel, and say unto them, If any man's wife go aside, and commit a trespass against him,

13 And a man [a]lie with her carnally, and it be hid from the eyes of her husband, and be kept close, and she be defiled, and *there be* no witness against her, neither she be taken *with the manner;*

14 And the spirit of jealousy come upon him, and he be jealous of his wife, and she be defiled: or if the spirit of jealousy come upon him, and he be jealous of his wife, and she be not defiled:

15 Then shall the man bring his wife unto the priest, and he shall [a]bring her offering for her, the tenth *part* of an ephah of barley meal; he shall pour no oil upon it, nor put frankincense thereon; for it *is* an offering of jealousy, an offering of memorial, [b]bringing iniquity to remembrance.

16 And the priest shall bring her near, and set her before the LORD:

17 And the priest shall take holy water in an earthen vessel; and of the dust that is in the floor of the tabernacle the priest shall take, and put *it* into the water:

18 And the priest shall set the woman before the LORD, and uncover the woman's head, and put the offering of memorial in her hands, which *is* the jealousy offering: and the priest shall have in his hand the bitter water that causeth the curse:

19 And the priest shall charge her by an oath, and say unto the woman, If no man have lain with thee, and if thou hast not gone aside to uncleanness [1,2]*with another* instead of thy husband, be thou free from this bitter water that causeth the curse:

20 But if thou hast gone aside *to another* instead of thy husband, and if thou

be defiled, and some man have lain with thee beside thine husband:

D 21 Then the priest shall [a]charge the woman with an oath of cursing, and the priest shall say unto the woman, [b]The LORD make thee a curse and an oath among thy people, when the LORD doth make thy thigh to [1]rot, and thy belly to swell;

22 And this water that causeth the curse [a]shall go into thy bowels, to make *thy* belly to swell, and *thy* thigh to rot: [b]And the woman shall say, Amen, amen.

23 And the priest shall write these curses in a book, and he shall blot *them* out with the bitter water:

24 And he shall cause the woman to drink the bitter water that causeth the curse: and the water that causeth the curse shall enter into her, *and become* bitter.

25 Then the priest shall take the jealousy offering out of the woman's hand, and shall [a]wave the offering before the LORD, and offer it upon the altar:

26 [a]And the priest shall take an handful of the offering, *even* the memorial thereof, and burn *it* upon the altar, and afterward shall cause the woman to drink the water.

D 27 And when he hath made her to drink the water, then it shall come to pass, *that,* if she be defiled, and have done trespass against her husband, that the water that causeth the curse shall enter into her, *and become* bitter, and her belly shall swell, and her thigh shall rot: and the woman [a]shall be a curse among her people.

28 And if the woman be not defiled, but be clean; then she shall be free, and shall conceive seed.

29 This *is* the law of jealousies, when a wife goeth aside *to another* [a]instead of her husband, and is defiled;

30 Or when the spirit of jealousy cometh upon him, and he be jealous over his wife, and shall set the woman before the LORD, and the priest shall execute upon her all this law.

31 Then shall the man be guiltless from iniquity, and this woman [a]shall bear her iniquity.

The law of a Nazarite

6 AND THE LORD spake unto Moses, saying,

2 Speak unto the children of Israel, and say unto them, When either man or woman shall [a]separate[1] *themselves* to vow a vow of a Nazarite, to separate *themselves* unto the LORD:

3 [a]He shall separate *himself* from wine and strong drink, and shall drink no vinegar of wine, or vinegar of strong drink, neither shall he drink any liquor of grapes, nor eat moist grapes, or dried.

4 All the days of his [1]separation shall he eat nothing that is made of the [2]vine tree, from the kernels even to the husk.

5 All the days of the vow of his separation there shall no [a]razor come upon his head: until the days be fulfilled, in the which he separateth *himself* unto the LORD, he shall be holy, *and* shall let the locks of the hair of his head grow.

6 All the days that he separateth *himself* unto the LORD [a]he shall come at no dead body.

7 [a]He shall not make himself unclean for his father, or for his mother, for his brother, or for his sister, when they die: because the [1]consecration of his God *is* upon his head.

8 [a]All the days of his separation he *is* holy unto the LORD.

9 And if any man die very suddenly by him, and he hath defiled the head of his consecration; then he shall [a]shave his head in the day of his cleansing, on the seventh day shall he shave it.

10 And [a]on the eighth day he shall bring two turtles, or two young pigeons, to the priest, to the door of the tabernacle of the congregation:

11 And the priest shall offer the one for a sin offering, and the other for a burnt offering, and make an atonement

21 [a]Josh. 6:26; 1 Sam. 14:24; Neh. 10:29 [b]Jer. 29:22 [1]Heb. *fall*
22 [a]Ps. 109:18 [b]Deut. 27:15
25 [a]Lev. 8:27
26 [a]Lev. 2:2,9
27 [a]ver. 21
29 [a]ver. 19
31 [a]Lev. 20:17,19, 20
6:2 [a]Lev. 27:2; Judg. 13:5; Acts 21:23; Rom. 1:1 [1]Or, *make themselves Nazarites*
3 [a]Amos 2:12; Luke 1:15
4 [1]Or, *Nazariteship* [2]Heb. *vine of the wine*
5 [a]Judg. 13:5 & 16:17; 1 Sam. 1:11
6 [a]Lev. 21:11; ch. 19:11,16
7 [a]Lev. 21:1,2,11; ch. 9:6 [1]Heb. *separation*
8 [a]2 Cor. 6:17,18
9 [a]Acts 18:18 & 21:24
10 [a]Lev. 5:7 & 14:22 & 15:14,29

D *Lev 26:16* ◀▶ *Nu 5:27*
D *Nu 5:21* ◀▶ *Nu 11:33–34*

6:2–21 This section outlines God's laws concerning the vows of a Nazarite—an Israelite who was completely separated to God for a specified period of time or for some holy service. Though there were many restrictions on a Nazarite, this vow was a positive act of total devotion to the Lord. Samson, Samuel, John the Baptist and the apostle Paul were all Nazarites (see Jdg 13; 1Sa 1:9–11; Lk 1:15; Ac 18:18).

for him, for that he sinned by the dead,
and shall hallow his head that same day.
12 And he shall consecrate unto the
LORD the days of his separation, and shall
bring a lamb of the first year [a]for a trespass offering: but the days that were before shall ʹbe lost, because his separation
was defiled.
13 ¶ And this *is* the law of the Nazarite, [a]when the days of his separation are
fulfilled: he shall be brought unto the
door of the tabernacle of the congregation:
14 And he shall offer his offering unto
the LORD, one he lamb of the first year
without blemish for a burnt offering, and
one ewe lamb of the first year without
blemish [a]for a sin offering, and one ram
without blemish [b]for peace offerings,
15 And a basket of unleavened bread,
[a]cakes of fine flour mingled with oil, and
wafers of unleavened bread [b]anointed
with oil, and their meat offering, and
their [c]drink offerings.
16 And the priest shall bring *them* before the LORD, and shall offer his sin offering, and his burnt offering:
17 And he shall offer the ram *for* a sacrifice of peace offerings unto the LORD,
with the basket of unleavened bread: the
priest shall offer also his meat offering,
and his drink offering.
18 [a]And the Nazarite shall shave the
head of his separation *at* the door of the
tabernacle of the congregation, and shall
take the hair of the head of his separation, and put *it* in the fire which *is* under
the sacrifice of the peace offerings.
19 And the priest shall take the [a]sod-
den shoulder of the ram, and one unleavened cake out of the basket, and one unleavened wafer, and [b]shall put *them* upon
the hands of the Nazarite, after *the hair
of* his separation is shaven:
20 And the priest shall wave them *for*
a wave offering before the LORD: [a]this *is*
holy for the priest, with the wave breast
and heave shoulder: and after that the
Nazarite may drink wine.
21 This *is* the law of the Nazarite who
hath vowed, *and of* his offering unto the
LORD for his separation, beside *that* that
his hand shall get: according to the vow
which he vowed, so he must do after the
law of his separation.

The Aaronic benediction

22 ¶ And the LORD spake unto Moses,
saying,
23 Speak unto Aaron and unto his
sons, saying, On this wise [a]ye shall bless
the children of Israel, saying unto them,
24 The LORD bless thee, and [a]keep K
thee: U
25 The LORD [a]make his face shine upon
thee, and [b]be gracious unto thee:
26 [a]The LORD lift up his countenance
upon thee, and [b]give thee peace.
27 [a]And they shall put my name upon
the children of Israel; and [b]I will bless
them.

The dedication offerings

7 AND IT came to pass on the day that
Moses had fully [a]set up the tabernacle, and had anointed it, and sanctified it,
and all the instruments thereof, both the
altar and all the vessels thereof, and had
anointed them, and sanctified them;
2 That [a]the princes of Israel, heads of
the house of their fathers, who *were* the
princes of the tribes, ʹand were over
them that were numbered, offered:
3 And they brought their offering before the LORD, six covered wagons, and
twelve oxen; a wagon for two of the
princes, and for each one an ox: and they
brought them before the tabernacle.
4 And the LORD spake unto Moses,
saying,
5 Take *it* of them, that they may be to
do the service of the tabernacle of the
congregation; and thou shalt give them
unto the Levites, to every man according
to his service.
6 And Moses took the wagons and the
oxen, and gave them unto the Levites.
7 Two wagons and four oxen [a]he gave
unto the sons of Gershon, according to
their service:
8 [a]And four wagons and eight oxen he
gave unto the sons of Merari, according
unto their service, [b]under the hand of
Ithamar the son of Aaron the priest.
9 But unto the sons of Kohath he gave
none: because [a]the service of the sanctuary belonging unto them [b]*was that* they
should bear upon their shoulders.
10 ¶ And the princes offered for [a]dedi-
cating of the altar in the day that it was

12 [a]Lev. 5:6 ʹHeb. *fall*
13 [a]Acts 21:26
14 [a]Lev. 4:2,27,32 [b]Lev. 3:6
15 [a]Lev. 2:4 [b]Ex. 29:2 [c]ch. 15:5,7,10
18 [a]Acts 21:24
19 [a]1 Sam. 2:15 [b]Ex. 29:23,24
20 [a]Ex. 29:27,28
23 [a]Lev. 9:22; Deut. 10:8 & 21:5; Josh. 8:33; 1 Chr. 23:13
24 [a]Ps. 121:7; John 17:11
25 [a]Ps. 31:16 & 67:1 & 80:3,7,19 & 119:135; Dan. 9:17 [b]Gen. 43:29; Ex. 33:19; Mal. 1:9
26 [a]Ps. 4:6 [b]John 14:27; Phil. 4:7; 2 Thes. 3:16
27 [a]Deut. 28:10; 2 Chr. 7:14; Is. 43:7; Dan. 9:18,19 [b]ch. 23:20; Ps. 5:12 & 67:7 & 115:12,13; Eph. 1:3
7:1 [a]Ex. 40:18; Lev. 8:10,11
2 [a]ch. 1:4 ʹHeb. *who stood*
7 [a]ch. 4:23
8 [a]ch. 4:33 [b]ch. 4:28,33
9 [a]ch. 4:15 [b]ch. 4:6,8,10,12,14; 2 Sam. 6:13
10 [a]See Deut. 20:5; 1 Ki. 8:63; 2 Chr. 7:5,9; Ezra 6:16; Neh. 12:27

K *Ex 33:19* ◀▶ *Nu 11:23*
U *Lev 26:3–12* ◀▶ *Nu 10:29*

anointed, even the princes offered their offering before the altar.

11 And the LORD said unto Moses, They shall offer their offering, each prince on his day, for the dedicating of the altar.

12 ¶ And he that offered his offering the first day was [a]Nahshon the son of Amminadab, of the tribe of Judah:

13 And his offering *was* one silver charger, the weight thereof *was* an hundred and thirty *shekels,* one silver bowl of seventy shekels, after [a]the shekel of the sanctuary; both of them *were* full of fine flour mingled with oil for a [b]meat offering:

14 One spoon of ten *shekels* of gold, full of [a]incense:

15 [a]One young bullock, one ram, one lamb [b]of the first year, for a burnt offering:

16 One kid of the goats for a [a]sin offering:

17 And for [a]a sacrifice of peace offerings, two oxen, five rams, five he goats, five lambs of the first year: this *was* the offering of Nahshon the son of Amminadab.

18 ¶ On the second day Nethaneel the son of Zuar, prince of Issachar, did offer:

19 He offered *for* his offering one silver charger, the weight whereof *was* an hundred and thirty *shekels,* one silver bowl of seventy shekels, after the shekel of the sanctuary; both of them full of fine flour mingled with oil for a meat offering:

20 One spoon of gold of ten *shekels,* full of incense:

21 One young bullock, one ram, one lamb of the first year, for a burnt offering:

22 One kid of the goats for a sin offering:

23 And for a sacrifice of peace offerings, two oxen, five rams, five he goats, five lambs of the first year: this *was* the offering of Nethaneel the son of Zuar.

24 ¶ On the third day Eliab the son of Helon, prince of the children of Zebulun, *did offer:*

25 His offering *was* one silver charger, the weight whereof *was* an hundred and thirty *shekels,* one silver bowl of seventy shekels, after the shekel of the sanctuary; both of them full of fine flour mingled with oil for a meat offering:

26 One golden spoon of ten *shekels,* full of incense:

12 [a]ch. 2:3
13 [a]Ex. 30:13 [b]Lev. 2:1
14 [a]Ex. 30:34
15 [a]Lev. 1:2 [b]Ex. 12:5
16 [a]Lev. 4:23
17 [a]Lev. 3:1
30 [a]ch. 1:5 & 2:10
36 [a]ver. 41; ch. 1:6 & 2:12
42 [a]ch. 1:14 & 2:14 [I]Or, *Reuel*

27 One young bullock, one ram, one lamb of the first year, for a burnt offering:

28 One kid of the goats for a sin offering:

29 And for a sacrifice of peace offerings, two oxen, five rams, five he goats, five lambs of the first year: this *was* the offering of Eliab the son of Helon.

30 ¶ On the fourth day [a]Elizur the son of Shedeur, prince of the children of Reuben, *did offer:*

31 His offering *was* one silver charger of the weight of an hundred and thirty *shekels,* one silver bowl of seventy shekels, after the shekel of the sanctuary; both of them full of fine flour mingled with oil for a meat offering:

32 One golden spoon of ten *shekels,* full of incense:

33 One young bullock, one ram, one lamb of the first year, for a burnt offering:

34 One kid of the goats for a sin offering:

35 And for a sacrifice of peace offerings, two oxen, five rams, five he goats, five lambs of the first year: this *was* the offering of Elizur the son of Shedeur.

36 ¶ On the fifth day [a]Shelumiel the son of Zurishaddai, prince of the children of Simeon, *did offer:*

37 His offering *was* one silver charger, the weight whereof *was* an hundred and thirty *shekels,* one silver bowl of seventy shekels, after the shekel of the sanctuary; both of them full of fine flour mingled with oil for a meat offering:

38 One golden spoon of ten *shekels,* full of incense:

39 One young bullock, one ram, one lamb of the first year, for a burnt offering:

40 One kid of the goats for a sin offering:

41 And for a sacrifice of peace offerings, two oxen, five rams, five he goats, five lambs of the first year: this *was* the offering of Shelumiel the son of Zurishaddai.

42 ¶ On the sixth day [a]Eliasaph the son of [I]Deuel, prince of the children of Gad, *offered:*

43 His offering *was* one silver charger of the weight of an hundred and thirty *shekels,* a silver bowl of seventy shekels, after the shekel of the sanctuary; both of them full of fine flour mingled with oil for a meat offering:

44 One golden spoon of ten *shekels,* full of incense:

45 One young bullock, one ram, one lamb of the first year, for [a]a burnt offering:

46 One kid of the goats for a sin offering:

47 And for a sacrifice of peace offerings, two oxen, five rams, five he goats, five lambs of the first year: this *was* the offering of Eliasaph the son of Deuel.

48 ¶ On the seventh day [a]Elishama the son of Ammihud, prince of the children of Ephraim, *offered:*

49 His offering *was* one silver charger, the weight whereof *was* an hundred and thirty *shekels,* one silver bowl of seventy shekels, after the shekel of the sanctuary; both of them full of fine flour mingled with oil for a meat offering:

50 One golden spoon of ten *shekels,* full of [a]incense:

51 One young bullock, one ram, one lamb of the first year, for a burnt offering:

52 One kid of the goats for a sin offering:

53 And for a sacrifice of peace offerings, two oxen, five rams, five he goats, five lambs of the first year: this *was* the offering of Elishama the son of Ammihud.

54 ¶ On the eighth day *offered* [a]Gamaliel the son of Pedahzur, prince of the children of Manasseh:

55 His offering *was* one silver charger of the weight of an hundred and thirty *shekels,* one silver bowl of seventy shekels, after the shekel of the sanctuary; both of them full of fine flour mingled with oil for a meat offering:

56 One golden spoon of ten *shekels,* full of incense:

57 One young bullock, one ram, one lamb of the first year, for a burnt offering:

58 One kid of the goats for a sin offering:

59 And for a sacrifice of peace offerings, two oxen, five rams, five he goats, five lambs of the first year: this *was* the offering of Gamaliel the son of Pedahzur.

60 ¶ On the ninth day [a]Abidan the son of Gideoni, prince of the children of Benjamin, *offered:*

61 His offering *was* one silver charger, the weight whereof *was* an hundred and thirty *shekels,* one silver bowl of seventy shekels, after the shekel of the sanctuary;

45 [a]Ps. 40:6

48 [a]ch. 1:10 & 2:18

50 [a]Deut. 33:10; Ps. 66:15 & 141:2; Ezek. 8:11; Mal. 1:11; Luke 1:10; Rev. 5:8 & 8:3

54 [a]ch. 1:10 & 2:20

60 [a]ch. 1:11 & 2:22

66 [a]ch. 1:12 & 2:25

72 [a]ch. 1:13 & 2:27

78 [a]ch. 1:15 & 2:29

both of them full of fine flour mingled with oil for a meat offering:

62 One golden spoon of ten *shekels,* full of incense:

63 One young bullock, one ram, one lamb of the first year, for a burnt offering:

64 One kid of the goats for a sin offering:

65 And for a sacrifice of peace offerings, two oxen, five rams, five he goats, five lambs of the first year: this *was* the offering of Abidan the son of Gideoni.

66 ¶ On the tenth day [a]Ahiezer the son of Ammishaddai, prince of the children of Dan, *offered:*

67 His offering *was* one silver charger, the weight whereof *was* an hundred and thirty *shekels,* one silver bowl of seventy shekels, after the shekel of the sanctuary; both of them full of fine flour mingled with oil for a meat offering:

68 One golden spoon of ten *shekels,* full of incense:

69 One young bullock, one ram, one lamb of the first year, for a burnt offering:

70 One kid of the goats for a sin offering:

71 And for a sacrifice of peace offerings, two oxen, five rams, five he goats, five lambs of the first year: this *was* the offering of Ahiezer the son of Ammishaddai.

72 ¶ On the eleventh day [a]Pagiel the son of Ocran, prince of the children of Asher, *offered:*

73 His offering *was* one silver charger, the weight whereof *was* an hundred and thirty *shekels,* one silver bowl of seventy shekels, after the shekel of the sanctuary; both of them full of fine flour mingled with oil for a meat offering:

74 One golden spoon of ten *shekels,* full of incense:

75 One young bullock, one ram, one lamb of the first year, for a burnt offering:

76 One kid of the goats for a sin offering:

77 And for a sacrifice of peace offerings, two oxen, five rams, five he goats, five lambs of the first year: this *was* the offering of Pagiel the son of Ocran.

78 ¶ On the twelfth day [a]Ahira the son of Enan, prince of the children of Naphtali, *offered:*

79 His offering *was* one silver charger, the weight whereof *was* an hundred and thirty *shekels,* one silver bowl of seventy

shekels, after the shekel of the sanctuary; both of them full of fine flour mingled with oil for a meat offering:

80 One golden spoon of ten *shekels,* full of incense:

81 One young bullock, one ram, one lamb of the first year, for a burnt offering:

82 One kid of the goats for a sin offering:

83 And for a sacrifice of peace offerings, two oxen, five rams, five he goats, five lambs of the first year: this *was* the offering of Ahira the son of Enan.

84 This *was* [a]the dedication of the altar, in the day when it was anointed, by [b]the princes of Israel: twelve chargers of silver, twelve silver bowls, twelve spoons of gold:

85 Each charger of silver *weighing* an hundred and thirty *shekels,* each bowl seventy: all the silver vessels *weighed* two thousand and four hundred *shekels,* after the [a]shekel of the sanctuary:

86 The golden spoons *were* twelve, full of incense, *weighing* ten *shekels* apiece, after the shekel of the sanctuary: all the gold of the spoons *was* an hundred and twenty *shekels.*

87 All the oxen for the burnt offering *were* twelve bullocks, the rams twelve, the lambs of the first year twelve, with their meat offering: and the kids of the goats for sin offering twelve.

88 And all the oxen for the sacrifice of the peace offerings *were* twenty and four bullocks, the rams sixty, the he goats sixty, the lambs of the first year sixty. This *was* the dedication of the altar, after that it was [a]anointed.

89 And when Moses was gone into the tabernacle of the congregation [a]to speak with [1]him, then he heard [b]the voice of one speaking unto him from off the mercy seat that *was* upon the ark of testimony, from between the two cherubims: and he spake unto him.

The candlestick

8 AND THE LORD spake unto Moses, saying,

2 Speak unto Aaron, and say unto him, When thou [a]lightest the lamps, the seven lamps shall give light over against the candlestick.

3 And Aaron did so; he lighted the lamps thereof over against the candlestick, as the LORD commanded Moses.

4 [a]And this work of the candlestick *was of* beaten gold, unto the shaft thereof, unto the flowers thereof, *was* [b]beaten work: [c]according unto the pattern which the LORD had shown Moses, so he made the candlestick.

Purification of the Levites

5 ¶ And the LORD spake unto Moses, saying,

6 Take the Levites from among the children of Israel, and cleanse them.

7 And thus shalt thou do unto them, to cleanse them: Sprinkle [a]water of purifying upon them, and [b]let[1] them shave all their flesh, and let them wash their clothes, and *so* make themselves clean.

8 Then let them take a young bullock with [a]his meat offering, *even* fine flour mingled with oil, and another young bullock shalt thou take for a sin offering.

9 [a]And thou shalt bring the Levites before the tabernacle of the congregation: [b]and thou shalt gather the whole assembly of the children of Israel together:

10 And thou shalt bring the Levites before the LORD: and the children of Israel [a]shall put their hands upon the Levites:

11 And Aaron shall [1]offer the Levites before the LORD *for* an [2]offering of the children of Israel, that [3]they may execute the service of the LORD.

12 [a]And the Levites shall lay their hands upon the heads of the bullocks: and thou shalt offer the one *for* a sin offering, and the other *for* a burnt offering, unto the LORD, to make an atonement for the Levites.

13 And thou shalt set the Levites before Aaron, and before his sons, and offer them *for* an offering unto the LORD.

14 Thus shalt thou separate the Levites from among the children of Israel: and the Levites shall be [a]mine.

15 And after that shall the Levites go in to do the service of the tabernacle of the congregation: and thou shalt cleanse them, and [a]offer them *for* an offering.

16 For they *are* wholly given unto me from among the children of Israel; [a]instead of such as open every womb, *even instead of* the firstborn of all the children of Israel, have I taken them unto me.

17 [a]For all the firstborn of the children of Israel *are* mine, *both* man and beast: D

D *Lev 23:26–32* ◀ ▶ *Nu 8:21*

84 [a]2 Chr. 7:9 [b]Judg. 5:9
85 [a]Ex. 30:13,24; & 38:24-26; Lev. 5:15 & 27:3,25; ch. 3:47
88 [a]ver. 1
89 [a]Ex. 33:9,11 [b]Ex. 25:22 [1]i.e. *God*
8:2 [a]Ex. 25:37 & 40:25
4 [a]Ex. 25:31 [b]Ex. 25:18 [c]Ex. 25:40
7 [a]ch. 19:9,17,18 [b]Lev. 14:8,9 [1]Heb. *let them cause a razor to pass over*
8 [a]Lev. 2:1
9 [a]See Ex. 29:4 & 40:12 [b]Lev. 8:3
10 [a]Lev. 1:4
11 [1]Heb. *wave* [2]Heb. *wave offering* [3]Heb. *they may be to execute*
12 [a]Ex. 29:10
14 [a]ch. 3:45 & 16:9
15 [a]ver. 11,13
16 [a]ch. 3:12,45
17 [a]Ex. 13:2,12, 13,15; ch. 3:13; Luke 2:23

on the day that I smote every firstborn in the land of Egypt I sanctified them for myself.

18 And I have taken the Levites for all the firstborn of the children of Israel.

19 And [a]I have given the Levites *as* [/]a gift to Aaron and to his sons from among the children of Israel, to do the service of the children of Israel in the tabernacle of the congregation, and to make an atonement for the children of Israel: [b]that there be no plague among the children of Israel, when the children of Israel come nigh unto the sanctuary.

20 And Moses, and Aaron, and all the congregation of the children of Israel, did to the Levites according unto all that the LORD commanded Moses concerning the Levites, so did the children of Israel unto them.

D 21 [a]And the Levites were purified, and they washed their clothes; and Aaron offered them *as* an offering before the LORD; and Aaron made an atonement for them to cleanse them.

22 [a]And after that went the Levites in to do their service in the tabernacle of the congregation before Aaron, and before his sons: [b]as the LORD had commanded Moses concerning the Levites, so did they unto them.

23 ¶ And the LORD spake unto Moses, saying,

24 This *is it* that *belongeth* unto the Levites: [a]from twenty and five years old and upward they shall go in to wait upon the service of the tabernacle of the congregation:

25 And from the age of fifty years they shall [/]cease waiting upon the service *thereof,* and shall serve no more:

26 But shall minister with their brethren in the tabernacle of the congregation, [a]to keep the charge, and shall do no service. Thus shalt thou do unto the Levites touching their charge.

The Passover command

9 AND THE LORD spake unto Moses in the wilderness of Sinai, in the first month of the second year after they were come out of the land of Egypt, saying,

2 Let the children of Israel also keep [a]the passover at his appointed season.

3 In the fourteenth day of this month, [/]at even, ye shall keep it in his appointed season: according to all the rites of it, and according to all the ceremonies thereof, shall ye keep it.

4 And Moses spake unto the children of Israel, that they should keep the passover.

5 And [a]they kept the passover on the fourteenth day of the first month at even in the wilderness of Sinai: according to all that the LORD commanded Moses, so did the children of Israel.

6 ¶ And there were certain men, who were [a]defiled by the dead body of a man, that they could not keep the passover on that day: [b]and they came before Moses and before Aaron on that day:

7 And those men said unto him, We *are* defiled by the dead body of a man: wherefore are we kept back, that we may not offer an offering of the LORD in his appointed season among the children of Israel?

8 And Moses said unto them, Stand still, and [a]I will hear what the LORD will command concerning you.

9 ¶ And the LORD spake unto Moses, saying,

10 Speak unto the children of Israel, saying, If any man of you or of your posterity shall be unclean by reason of a dead body, or *be* in a journey afar off, yet he shall keep the passover unto the LORD.

11 [a]The fourteenth day of the second month at even they shall keep it, *and* [b]eat it with unleavened bread and bitter *herbs.*

12 [a]They shall leave none of it unto the morning, [b]nor break any bone of it: [c]according to all the ordinances of the passover they shall keep it.

13 But the man that *is* clean, and is not in a journey, and forbeareth to keep the passover, even the same soul [a]shall be cut off from among his people: because he [b]brought not the offering of the LORD in his appointed season, that man shall [c]bear his sin. D

14 And if a stranger shall sojourn among you, and will keep the passover unto the LORD; according to the ordinance of the passover, and according to the manner thereof, so shall he do: [a]ye shall have one ordinance, both for the

19 [a]ch. 3:9 [b]ch. 1:53 & 16:46 & 18:5; 2 Chr. 26:16 [/]Heb. *given*
21 [a]ver. 7
22 [a]ver. 15 [b]ver. 5
24 [a]See ch. 4:3; 1 Chr. 23:3,24,27
25 [/]Heb. *return from the warfare of the service*
26 [a]ch. 1:53
9:2 [a]Ex. 12:1; Lev. 23:5; ch. 28:16; Deut. 16:1,2
3 [/]Heb. *between the two evenings*
5 [a]Josh. 5:10
6 [a]ch. 5:2 & 19:11,16; See John 18:28 [b]Ex. 18:15, 19,26; ch. 27:2
8 [a]ch. 27:5
11 [a]2 Chr. 30:2,15 [b]Ex. 12:8
12 [a]Ex. 12:10 [b]Ex. 12:46; John 19:36 [c]Ex. 12:43
13 [a]Gen. 17:14; Ex. 12:15 [b]ver. 7 [c]ch. 5:31
14 [a]Ex. 12:49

D *Nu 8:17–18* ◀ ▶ *Nu 9:13–14*

D *Nu 8:21* ◀ ▶ *Nu 16:46–47*

stranger, and for him that was born in the
land.

The cloud of guidance

L 15 ¶ And [a]on the day that the tabernacle was reared up the cloud covered the
tabernacle, *namely,* the tent of the testimony: and [b]at even there was upon the
tabernacle as it were the appearance of
fire, until the morning.
16 So it was always: the cloud covered
it *by day,* and the appearance of fire by
night.
17 And when the cloud [a]was taken up
from the tabernacle, then after that the
children of Israel journeyed: and in the
place where the cloud abode, there
the children of Israel pitched their tents.
18 At the commandment of the LORD
the children of Israel journeyed, and at
the commandment of the LORD they
pitched: [a]as long as the cloud abode upon
the tabernacle they rested in their tents.
19 And when the cloud [I]tarried long
upon the tabernacle many days, then the
children of Israel [a]kept the charge of the
LORD, and journeyed not.
20 And *so* it was, when the cloud was
a few days upon the tabernacle; according to the commandment of the LORD they
abode in their tents, and according to the
commandment of the LORD they journeyed.
21 And *so* it was, when the cloud
[I]abode from even unto the morning, and
that the cloud was taken up in the morning, then they journeyed: whether *it was*
by day or by night that the cloud was
taken up, they journeyed.
22 Or *whether it were* two days, or a
month, or a year, that the cloud tarried
upon the tabernacle, remaining thereon,
the children of Israel [a]abode in their
tents, and journeyed not: but when it was
taken up, they journeyed.
23 At the commandment of the LORD

15 [a]Ex. 40:34; Neh. 9:12,19; Ps. 78:14 [b]Ex. 13:21 & 40:38
17 [a]Ex. 40:36; ch. 10:11,33,34; Ps. 80:1
18 [a]1 Cor. 10:1
19 [a]ch. 1:53 & 3:8 [I]Heb. *prolonged*
21 [I]Heb. *was*
22 [a]Ex. 40:36,37
23 [a]ver. 19
10:2 [a]Is. 1:13
3 [a]Jer. 4:5; Joel 2:15
4 [a]Ex. 18:21; ch. 1:16 & 7:2
5 [a]ch. 2:3
6 [a]ch. 2:10
7 [a]ver. 3 [b]Joel 2:1
8 [a]ch. 31:6; Josh. 6:4; 1 Chr. 15:24; 2 Chr. 13:12
9 [a]ch. 31:6; Josh. 6:5; 2 Chr. 13:14 [b]Judg. 2:18 & 4:3 & 6:9 & 10:8,12 [c]Gen. 8:1; Ps. 106:4
10 [a]ch. 29:1; Lev. 23:24; 1 Chr. 15:24

they rested in the tents, and at the commandment of the LORD they journeyed:
they [a]kept the charge of the LORD, at the
commandment of the LORD by the hand of
Moses.

The two silver trumpets

10 AND THE LORD spake unto Moses, saying,
2 Make thee two trumpets of silver; of
a whole piece shalt thou make them: that
thou mayest use them for the [a]calling of
the assembly, and for the journeying of
the camps.
3 And when [a]they shall blow with
them, all the assembly shall assemble
themselves to thee at the door of the tabernacle of the congregation.
4 And if they blow *but* with one *trumpet,* then the princes, *which are* [a]heads
of the thousands of Israel, shall gather
themselves unto thee.
5 When ye blow an alarm, then [a]the
camps that lie on the east parts shall go
forward.
6 When ye blow an alarm the second
time, then the camps that lie [a]on the
south side shall take their journey: they
shall blow an alarm for their journeys.
7 But when the congregation is to be
gathered together, [a]ye shall blow, but ye
shall not [b]sound an alarm.
8 [a]And the sons of Aaron, the priests,
shall blow with the trumpets; and they
shall be to you for an ordinance for ever
throughout your generations.
9 And [a]if ye go to war in your land V
against the enemy that [b]oppresseth you,
then ye shall blow an alarm with the
trumpets; and ye shall be [c]remembered
before the LORD your God, and ye shall be
saved from your enemies.
10 Also [a]in the day of your gladness,
and in your solemn days, and in the beginnings of your months, ye shall blow
with the trumpets over your burnt offer-

L Ex 40:36–38 ◀▶ Nu 14:14

V Lev 26:6–8 ◀▶ Nu 14:9

10:2–7 Israel was commanded to make two, silver trumpets—long, straight, slender metal tubes with flared ends. These trumpets were blown to call the whole assembly to the tabernacle or to announce Israel's special feasts. In addition, two blasts were blown from these trumpets when the Israelites were to break camp. The first blast alerted the camp to start to pack up their tents and the tabernacle furnishings. When the second blast was blown, the Israelites were to "take their journey" (Nu 10:6). This response to the trumpet call may be what Paul had in mind when he wrote, "We shall not all sleep, but we shall all be changed, In a moment, in the twinkling of an eye, at the last trump" (1Co 15:51–52). See the study notes accompanying 1Co 15:51.

ings, and over the sacrifices of your peace
offerings; that they may be to you [b]for a
memorial before your God: I *am* the LORD
your God.

The departure from Sinai

11 ¶ And it came to pass on the twentieth *day* of the second month, in the second year, that the cloud [a]was taken up
from off the tabernacle of the testimony.
12 And the children of Israel took
[a]their journeys out of the [b]wilderness of
Sinai; and the cloud rested in the [c]wilder-
ness of Paran.
13 And they first took their journey
[a]according to the commandment of the
LORD by the hand of Moses.
14 ¶ [a]In the first *place* went the standard of the camp of the children of Judah
according to their armies: and over his
host *was* [b]Nahshon the son of Amminadab.
15 And over the host of the tribe of the
children of Issachar *was* Nethaneel the
son of Zuar.
16 And over the host of the tribe of the
children of Zebulun *was* Eliab the son of
Helon.
17 And [a]the tabernacle was taken
down; and the sons of Gershon and the
sons of Merari set forward, [b]bearing the
tabernacle.
18 ¶ And [a]the standard of the camp of
Reuben set forward according to their armies: and over his host *was* Elizur the
son of Shedeur.
19 And over the host of the tribe of the
children of Simeon *was* Shelumiel the
son of Zurishaddai.
20 And over the host of the tribe of the
children of Gad *was* Eliasaph the son of
Deuel.
21 And the Kohathites set forward,
bearing the [a]sanctuary: and [†]*the other*
did set up the tabernacle against they
came.
22 ¶ And [a]the standard of the camp of
the children of Ephraim set forward according to their armies: and over his host
was Elishama the son of Ammihud.
23 And over the host of the tribe of the
children of Manasseh *was* Gamaliel the
son of Pedahzur.
24 And over the host of the tribe of the
children of Benjamin *was* Abidan the son
of Gideoni.
25 ¶ And [a]the standard of the camp of
the children of Dan set forward, *which*
was the rearward of all the camps
throughout their hosts: and over his host
was Ahiezer the son of Ammishaddai.
26 And over the host of the tribe of the
children of Asher *was* Pagiel the son of
Ocran.
27 And over the host of the tribe of the
children of Naphtali *was* Ahira the son of
Enan.
28 [a]Thus[†] *were* the journeyings of the
children of Israel according to their armies, when they set forward.
29 ¶ And Moses said unto Hobab, the I
son of [a]Raguel the Midianite, Moses' fa- U
ther-in-law, We are journeying unto the
place of which the LORD said, [b]I will give
it you: come thou with us, and [c]we will
do thee good: for [d]the LORD hath spoken
good concerning Israel.
30 And he said unto him, I will not go;
but I will depart to mine own land, and to
my kindred.
31 And he said, Leave us not, I pray
thee; forasmuch as thou knowest how
we are to encamp in the wilderness, and
thou mayest be to us [a]instead of eyes.
32 And it shall be, if thou go with us,
yea, it shall be, that [a]what goodness the
LORD shall do unto us, the same will we
do unto thee.
33 ¶ And they departed from [a]the
mount of the LORD three days' journey:
and the ark of the covenant of the LORD
[b]went before them in the three days'
journey, to search out a resting place for
them.
34 And [a]the cloud of the LORD *was*
upon them by day, when they went out
of the camp.
35 And it came to pass, when the ark
set forward, that Moses said, [a]Rise up,
LORD, and let thine enemies be scattered;

I *Lev 26:44–45* ◀▶ *Nu 24:7–9*
U *Nu 6:24–27* ◀▶ *Nu 23:10*

10 [b]ver. 9
11 [a]ch. 9:17
12 [a]Ex. 40:36; ch. 2:9,16 [b]Ex. 19:1; ch. 1:1 & 9:5 [c]Gen. 21:21; ch. 12:16 & 13:3,26
13 [a]ver. 5,6
14 [a]ch. 2:3,9 [b]ch. 1:7
17 [a]ch. 1:51 [b]ch. 4:24,31
18 [a]ch. 2:16
21 [a]ch. 4:4,15 & 7:9 [†]i.e. *the Gershonites and the Merarites;* see ver. 17; ch. 1:51
22 [a]ch. 2:24
25 [a]ch. 2:31; Josh. 6:9
28 [a]ch. 2:34 [†]Heb. *These*
29 [a]Ex. 2:18 [b]Gen. 12:7 [c]Judg. 1:16 [d]Gen. 32:12; Ex. 3:8
31 [a]Job 29:15
32 [a]Judg. 1:16
33 [a]See Ex. 3:1 [b]Deut. 1:33; Josh. 3:3,4,6; Ezek. 20:6
34 [a]Ex. 13:21; Neh. 9:12,19
35 [a]Ps. 68:1,2 & 132:8

10:29 Moses invited his brother-in-law, Hobab the Midianite, to join the Israelites. Hobab's skills in the desert would have undoubtedly been helpful to the Israelites. Moses recognized this and promised Hobab that he would be well treated and experience the blessings God promised to his chosen people.

and let them that hate thee flee before thee.

36 And when it rested, he said, Return, O LORD, unto the [1]many thousands of Israel.

The people complain

11 AND [a]*WHEN* the people [1]complained, [2]it displeased the LORD: and the LORD heard *it;* [b]and his anger was kindled; and the [c]fire of the LORD burnt among them, and consumed *them that were* in the uttermost parts of the camp.

2 And the people cried unto Moses; and when Moses [a]prayed unto the LORD, the fire [1]was quenched.

3 And he called the name of the place [1]Taberah: because the fire of the LORD burnt among them.

God sends quail

4 ¶ And the [a]mixed multitude that *was* among them [1]fell a-lusting: and the children of Israel also [2]wept again, and said, [b]Who shall give us flesh to eat?

5 [a]We remember the fish, which we did eat in Egypt freely; the cucumbers, and the melons, and the leeks, and the onions, and the garlic:

6 But now [a]our soul *is* dried away: *there is* nothing at all, beside this manna, *before* our eyes.

F 7 And [a]the manna *was* as coriander seed, and the [1]colour thereof as the colour of bdellium.

8 *And* the people went about, and gathered *it,* and ground *it* in mills, or beat *it* in a mortar, and baked *it* in pans, and made cakes of it: and [a]the taste of it was as the taste of fresh oil.

9 And [a]when the dew fell upon the camp in the night, the manna fell upon it.

10 ¶ Then Moses heard the people weep throughout their families, every man in the door of his tent: and [a]the anger of the LORD was kindled greatly; Moses also was displeased.

11 [a]And Moses said unto the LORD, Wherefore hast thou afflicted thy servant? and wherefore have I not found favour in thy sight, that thou layest the burden of all this people upon me?

12 Have I conceived all this people? have I begotten them, that thou shouldest say unto me, [a]Carry them in thy bosom, as a [b]nursing father beareth the sucking child, unto the land which thou [c]swarest unto their fathers?

13 [a]Whence should I have flesh to give unto all this people? for they weep unto me, saying, Give us flesh, that we may eat.

14 [a]I am not able to bear all this people alone, because *it is* too heavy for me.

15 And if thou deal thus with me, [a]kill me, I pray thee, out of hand, if I have found favour in thy sight; and let me not [b]see my wretchedness.

16 ¶ And the LORD said unto Moses, Gather unto me [a]seventy men of the elders of Israel, whom thou knowest to be the elders of the people, and [b]officers over them; and bring them unto the tabernacle of the congregation, that they may stand there with thee.

17 And I will [a]come down and talk with thee there: and [b]I will take of the spirit which *is* upon thee, and will put *it* upon them; and they shall bear the burden of the people with thee, that thou bear *it* not thyself alone. E

18 And say thou unto the people, [a]Sanctify yourselves against tomorrow, and ye shall eat flesh: for ye have wept [b]in the ears of the LORD, saying, Who shall give us flesh to eat? [c]for *it was* well with us in Egypt: therefore the LORD will give you flesh, and ye shall eat. F

19 Ye shall not eat one day, nor two days, nor five days, neither ten days, nor twenty days;

20 [a]*But* even a [1]whole month, until it come out at your nostrils, and it be loathsome unto you: because that ye have despised the LORD which *is* among you, and have wept before him, saying, [b]Why came we forth out of Egypt?

21 And Moses said, [a]The people, among whom I *am, are* six hundred thousand footmen; and thou hast said, I will give them flesh, that they may eat a whole month.

22 [a]Shall the flocks and the herds be slain for them, to suffice them? or shall all the fish of the sea be gathered together for them, to suffice them?

23 And the LORD said unto Moses, [a]Is the LORD's hand waxed short? thou shalt K

36 [1]Heb. *ten thousand thousands*
11:1 [a]Deut. 9:22 [b]Ps. 78:21 [c]Lev. 10:2; 2 Ki. 1:12 [1]Or, *were as it were complainers* [2]Heb. *it was evil in the ears of*
2 [a]Jas. 5:16 [1]Heb. *sunk*
3 [1]i.e. *A burning*
4 [a]As Ex. 12:38 [b]Ps. 78:18; 1 Cor. 10:6 [1]Heb. *lusted a lust* [2]Heb. *returned and wept*
5 [a]Ex. 16:3
6 [a]ch. 21:5
7 [a]Ex. 16:14,31 [1]Heb. *eye of it as the eye of*
8 [a]Ex. 16:31
9 [a]Ex. 16:13,14
10 [a]Ps. 78:21
11 [a]Deut. 1:12
12 [a]Is. 40:11 [b]Is. 49:23; 1 Thes. 2:7 [c]Gen. 26:3 & 50:24; Ex. 13:5
13 [a]Mat. 15:33; Mark 8:4
14 [a]Ex. 18:18
15 [a]See 1 Ki. 19:4; Jonah 4:3 [b]Rev. 3:17
16 [a]See Ex. 24:1,9 [b]Deut. 16:18
17 [a]ver. 25; Ex. 19:20 [b]1 Sam. 10:6; 2 Ki. 2:15
18 [a]Ex. 19:10 [b]Ex. 16:7 [c]ver. 5; Acts 7:39
20 [a]Ps. 78:29 & 106:15 [b]ch. 21:5 [1]Heb. *month of days*
21 [a]Gen. 12:2; Ex. 12:37; ch. 1:46
22 [a]See 2 Ki. 7:2
23 [a]Is. 50:2 & 59:1

F *Lev 26:5* ◀▶ *Nu 11:18–23*
E *Ex 35:31* ◀▶ *Nu 11:25–29*
F *Nu 11:7–9* ◀▶ *Nu 11:31–32*
K *Nu 6:24–26* ◀▶ *Nu 21:8–9*

see now whether [b]my word shall come to pass unto thee or not.

24 ¶ And Moses went out, and told the people the words of the LORD, and [a]gathered the seventy men of the elders of the people, and set them round about the tabernacle.

E G T 25 And the LORD [a]came down in a cloud, and spake unto him, and took of the spirit that *was* upon him, and gave *it* unto the seventy elders: and it came to pass, *that,* [b]when the spirit rested upon them, [c]they prophesied, and did not cease.

26 But there remained two *of the* men in the camp, the name of the one *was* Eldad, and the name of the other Medad: and the spirit rested upon them; and they *were* of them that were written, but [a]went not out unto the tabernacle: and they prophesied in the camp.

27 And there ran a young man, and told Moses, and said, Eldad and Medad do prophesy in the camp.

28 And Joshua the son of Nun, the servant of Moses, *one* of his young men, answered and said, My lord Moses, [a]forbid them.

W 29 And Moses said unto him, Enviest thou for my sake? [a]would God that all the LORD'S people were prophets, *and* that the LORD would put his spirit upon them!

30 And Moses gat him into the camp, he and the elders of Israel.

F 31 ¶ And there went forth a [a]wind from the LORD, and brought quails from the sea, and let *them* fall by the camp, [1]as it were a day's journey on this side, and as it were a day's journey on the other side, round about the camp, and as it were two cubits *high* upon the face of the earth.

32 And the people stood up all that day, and all *that* night, and all the next day, and they gathered the quails: he that gathered least gathered ten [a]homers: and they spread *them* all abroad for themselves round about the camp.

D 33 And while the [a]flesh *was* yet between their teeth, ere it was chewed, the wrath of the LORD was kindled against the people, and the LORD smote the people with a very great plague.

34 And he called the name of that place [1]Kibroth-hattaavah: because there they buried the people that lusted.

35 [a]*And* the people journeyed from Kibroth-hattaavah unto Hazeroth; and [1]abode at Hazeroth.

Miriam and Aaron

12 AND MIRIAM and Aaron spake against Moses because of the [1]Ethiopian woman whom he had married: for [a]he had [2]married an Ethiopian woman.

2 And they said, Hath the LORD indeed spoken only by Moses? [a]hath he not spoken also by us? And the LORD [b]heard *it.*

3 (Now the man Moses *was* very meek, above all the men which *were* upon the face of the earth.)

4 [a]And the LORD spake suddenly unto Moses, and unto Aaron, and unto Miriam, Come out ye three unto the tabernacle of the congregation. And they three came out.

5 [a]And the LORD came down in the pillar of the cloud, and stood *in* the door of the tabernacle, and called Aaron and Miriam: and they both came forth.

6 And he said, Hear now my words: If there be a prophet among you, *I* the LORD will make myself known unto him [a]in a vision, *and* will speak unto him [b]in a dream.

7 [a]My servant Moses *is* not so, [b]who *is* faithful in all [c]mine house.

8 With him will I speak [a]mouth to mouth, even [b]apparently, and not in dark speeches; and [c]the similitude of the LORD shall he behold: wherefore then [d]were ye not afraid to speak against my servant Moses?

9 And the anger of the LORD was kindled against them; and he departed. D E

10 And the cloud departed from off the tabernacle; and, [a]behold, Miriam *became* [b]leprous, *white* as snow: and Aaron looked upon Miriam, and, behold, *she was* leprous.

11 And Aaron said unto Moses, Alas, my lord, I beseech thee, [a]lay not the sin upon us, wherein we have done foolishly, and wherein we have sinned.

23 [b]ch. 23:19; Ezek. 12:25
24 [a]ver. 16
25 [a]ver. 17; ch. 12:5 [b]See 2 Ki. 2:15 [c]See 1 Sam. 10:5,6,10; Joel 2:28; Acts 2:17,18; 1 Cor. 14:1
26 [a]See 1 Sam. 20:26; Jer. 36:5
28 [a]See Mark 9:38; Luke 9:49
29 [a]1 Cor. 14:5
31 [a]Ex. 16:13; Ps. 78:26-28 [1]Heb. *as it were the way of a day*
32 [a]Ex. 16:36; Ezek. 45:11
33 [a]Ps. 78:30,31
34 [1]i.e. *The graves of lust*
35 [a]ch. 33:17 [1]Heb. *they were in*
12:1 [a]Ex. 2:21 [1]Or, *Cushite* [2]Heb. *taken*
2 [a]Ex. 15:20; Mic. 6:4 [b]Gen. 29:33; ch. 11:1; 2 Ki. 19:4; Is. 37:4; Ezek. 35:12,13
4 [a]Ps. 76:9
5 [a]ch. 11:25 & 16:19
6 [a]Gen. 46:2; Job 33:15; Ezek. 1:1; Dan. 8:2 & 10:8, 16; Luke 1:11; Acts 10:11,17 & 22:17, 18 [b]Gen. 31:10; 1 Ki. 3:5; Mat. 1:20
7 [a]Ps. 105:26 [b]Heb. 3:2,5 [c]1 Tim. 3:11
8 [a]Ex. 33:11; Deut. 34:10 [b]1 Cor. 13:12 [c]Ex. 33:19 [d]2 Pet. 2:10; Jude 8
10 [a]Deut. 24:9 [b]2 Ki. 5:27 & 15:5; 2 Chr. 26:19,20
11 [a]2 Sam. 24:10; Prov. 30:32

E *Nu 11:17* ◀ ▶ *Nu 14:24*
G *Ex 35:31* ◀ ▶ *Dt 34:9*
T *Ex 35:31* ◀ ▶ *Nu 24:2–3* **W** ▶ *Ps 68:18*
F *Nu 11:18–23* ◀ ▶ *Nu 20:7–11*
D *Nu 5:27* ◀ ▶ *Nu 12:9–10*
D *Nu 11:33–34* ◀ ▶ *Nu 14:12*
E *Ex 4:7* ◀ ▶ *Nu 16:46–50*

12 Let her not be [a]as one dead, of whom the flesh is half consumed when he cometh out of his mother's womb.

13 And Moses cried unto the LORD, saying, Heal her now, O God, I beseech thee.

14 ¶ And the LORD said unto Moses, If her father had but spit in her face, should she not be ashamed seven days? let her be [a]shut out from the camp seven days, and after that let her be received in *again.*

15 [a]And Miriam was shut out from the camp seven days: and the people journeyed not till Miriam was brought in *again.*

16 And afterward the people removed from [a]Hazeroth, and pitched in the wilderness of Paran.

Twelve spies sent to Canaan

13 AND THE LORD spake unto Moses, saying,

2 [a]Send thou men, that they may search the land of Canaan, which I give unto the children of Israel: of every tribe of their fathers shall ye send a man, every one a ruler among them.

3 And Moses by the commandment of the LORD sent them [a]from the wilderness of Paran: all those men *were* heads of the children of Israel.

4 And these *were* their names: of the tribe of Reuben, Shammua the son of Zaccur.

5 Of the tribe of Simeon, Shaphat the son of Hori.

6 [a]Of the tribe of Judah, [b]Caleb the son of Jephunneh.

7 Of the tribe of Issachar, Igal the son of Joseph.

8 Of the tribe of Ephraim, [a]Oshea the son of Nun.

9 Of the tribe of Benjamin, Palti the son of Raphu.

10 Of the tribe of Zebulun, Gaddiel the son of Sodi.

11 Of the tribe of Joseph, *namely,* of the tribe of Manasseh, Gaddi the son of Susi.

12 Of the tribe of Dan, Ammiel the son of Gemalli.

13 Of the tribe of Asher, Sethur the son of Michael.

14 Of the tribe of Naphtali, Nahbi the son of Vophsi.

15 Of the tribe of Gad, Geuel the son of Machi.

16 These *are* the names of the men which Moses sent to spy out the land. And Moses called [a]Oshea the son of Nun Jehoshua.

17 ¶ And Moses sent them to spy out the land of Canaan, and said unto them, Get you up this *way* [a]southward, and go up into [b]the mountain:

18 And see the land, what it *is;* and the people that dwelleth therein, whether they *be* strong or weak, few or many;

19 And what the land *is* that they dwell in, whether it *be* good or bad; and what cities *they be* that they dwell in, whether in tents, or in strong holds;

20 And what the land *is,* whether it *be* [a]fat or lean, whether there be wood therein, or not. And [b]be ye of good courage, and bring of the fruit of the land. Now the time *was* the time of the firstripe grapes.

21 ¶ So they went up, and searched the land [a]from the wilderness of Zin unto [b]Rehob, as men come to Hamath.

22 And they ascended by the south, and came unto Hebron; where [a]Ahiman, Sheshai, and Talmai, [b]the children of Anak, *were.* (Now [c]Hebron was built seven years before [d]Zoan in Egypt.)

23 [a]And they came unto the [1]brook of Eshcol, and cut down from thence a branch with one cluster of grapes, and they bare it between two upon a staff; and *they brought* of the pomegranates, and of the figs.

24 The place was called the [1]brook [2]Eshcol, because of the cluster of grapes which the children of Israel cut down from thence.

The spies return

25 And they returned from searching of the land after forty days.

26 ¶ And they went and came to Moses, and to Aaron, and to all the congregation of the children of Israel, [a]unto the wilderness of Paran, to [b]Kadesh; and brought back word unto them, and unto all the congregation, and showed them the fruit of the land.

12 [a]Ps. 88:4
14 [a]Lev. 13:46; ch. 5:2,3
15 [a]Deut. 24:9; 2 Chr. 26:20,21
16 [a]ch. 11:35 & 33:18
13:2 [a]ch. 32:8; Deut. 1:22
3 [a]ch. 12:16 & 32:8; Deut. 1:19 & 9:23
6 [a]ch. 34:19; 1 Chr. 4:15 [b]ver. 30; ch. 14:6,30; Josh. 14:6,7,13,14; Judg. 1:12
8 [a]ver. 16
16 [a]ver. 8; Ex. 17:9; ch. 14:6
17 [a]ver. 21 [b]Judg. 1:9
20 [a]Neh. 9:25,35; Ezek. 34:14 [b]Deut. 31:6,7,23
21 [a]ch. 34:3; Josh. 15:1 [b]Josh. 19:28
22 [a]Josh. 15:13,14 [b]ver. 33 [c]Josh. 21:11 [d]Ps. 78:12; Is. 19:11
23 [a]Deut. 1:24,25 [1]Or, *valley*
24 [1]Or, *valley* [2]i.e. *A cluster of grapes*
26 [a]ver. 3 [b]ch. 20:1; Deut. 1:19; Josh. 14:6

27 And they told him, and said, We came unto the land whither thou sentest us, and surely it floweth with [a]milk and honey; [b]and this *is* the fruit of it.

28 Nevertheless [a]the people *be* strong that dwell in the land, and the cities *are* walled, *and* very great: and moreover we saw [b]the children of Anak there.

29 [a]The Amalekites dwell in the land of the south: and the Hittites, and the Jebusites, and the Amorites, dwell in the mountains: and the Canaanites dwell by the sea, and by the coast of Jordan.

30 And [a]Caleb stilled the people before Moses, and said, Let us go up at once, and possess it; for we are well able to overcome it.

31 [a]But the men that went up with him said, We be not able to go up against the people; for they *are* stronger than we.

32 And they [a]brought up an evil report of the land which they had searched unto the children of Israel, saying, The land, through which we have gone to search it, *is* a land that eateth up the inhabitants thereof; and [b]all the people that we saw in it *are* [1]men of a great stature.

33 And there we saw the giants, [a]the sons of Anak, *which come* of the giants: and we were in our own sight [b]as grasshoppers, and so we were [c]in their sight.

The rebellion of Israel

14 AND ALL the congregation lifted up their voice, and cried; and [a]the people wept that night.

2 [a]And all the children of Israel murmured against Moses and against Aaron: and the whole congregation said unto them, Would God that we had died in the land of Egypt! or [b]would God we had died in this wilderness!

3 And wherefore hath the LORD brought us unto this land, to fall by the sword, that our wives and our children should be a prey? were it not better for us to return into Egypt?

4 And they said one to another, [a]Let us make a captain, and [b]let us return into Egypt.

5 Then [a]Moses and Aaron fell on their faces before all the assembly of the congregation of the children of Israel.

6 ¶ [a]And Joshua the son of Nun, and Caleb the son of Jephunneh, *which were* of them that searched the land, rent their clothes:

7 And they spake unto all the company of the children of Israel, saying, [a]The land, which we passed through to search it, *is* an exceeding good land.

8 If the LORD [a]delight in us, then he will bring us into this land, and give it us; [b]a land which floweth with milk and honey.

9 Only [a]rebel not ye against the LORD, [b]neither fear ye the people of the land; for [c]they *are* bread for us: their [1]defence is departed from them, [d]and the LORD *is* with us: fear them not. V

10 [a]But all the congregation bade stone them with stones. And [b]the glory of the LORD appeared in the tabernacle of the congregation before all the children of Israel.

11 ¶ And the LORD said unto Moses, How long will this people [a]provoke me? and how long will it be ere they [b]believe N

27 [a]Ex. 3:8 [b]Deut. 1:25
28 [a]Deut. 1:28 [b]ver. 33
29 [a]Ex. 17:8; Judg. 6:3
30 [a]See ch. 14:6, 24
31 [a]ch. 32:9; Deut. 1:28; Josh. 14:8
32 [a]ch. 14:36,37 [b]Amos 2:9 [1]Heb. *men of statures*
33 [a]Deut. 9:2 [b]Is. 40:22 [c]1 Sam. 17:42
14:1 [a]ch. 11:4
2 [a]Ex. 16:2 [b]See ver. 28,29
4 [a]Neh. 9:17 [b]See Deut. 17:16; Acts 7:39
5 [a]ch. 16:4,22
6 [a]ch. 13:6,8
7 [a]ch. 13:27
8 [a]Deut. 10:15; 2 Sam. 15:25,26; 1 Ki. 10:9; Ps. 147:11 [b]ch. 13:27
9 [a]Deut. 9:7,23,24 [b]Deut. 7:18 [c]ch. 24:8 [d]Gen. 48:21; Deut. 20:1,3,4 & 31:6,8 [1]Heb. *shadow*
10 [a]Ex. 17:4 [b]Ex. 16:10; Lev. 9:23
11 [a]ver. 23; Ps. 95:8; Heb. 3:8 [b]Deut. 9:23; Ps. 78:22,32,42; John 12:37

V *Nu 10:9* ◀ ▶ *Dt 11:25*
N *Lev 26:27–28* ◀ ▶ *Dt 11:26–28*

13:27–33 The report of the ten spies acknowledged that the promised land flowed "with milk and honey" (13:27). They also correctly reported that the cities were walled and well defended and that the people of the land were strong and very large. While Joshua and Caleb saw God's overcoming power through their eyes of faith, ten of the spies saw horrible obstacles through their eyes of fear as they told the terrified Israelites "we were in our own sight as grasshoppers" (Nu 13:33). See note on Ge 6:4.

14:1–2 The frightening words of the fearful spies caused the Israelites to lose faith in God's promises to help them possess the promised land. They preferred instead to return to slavery in Egypt. Focused on their problems instead of their provider, the Israelites had no hope. When Moses, Aaron and Caleb appealed to them to have faith in God's prophecies "all the congregation bade stone them with stones" (Nu 14:10).

14:11–12 This passage marks the second time since the exodus that God speaks of starting over with Moses to create a nation that would be faithful to God alone (see Ex 32:10). The Israelites were given the privilege to obey God and participate in his blessings, but many times they chose to disobey him. Yet God did not need their faithfulness to fulfill his purposes. He will always accomplish his perfect plan, with or without human obedience. But we will suffer the consequences of our disobedience, just as the Israelites did.

The Biblical Anniversaries of Israel

JUST AS WE attach special significance to certain happenings in our lives like birthdays or anniversaries, some of the significant happenings in the life of Israel occurred on some of the same days that had been important to their ancestors. In effect these days became Biblical anniversaries, visual reminders of God's sovereignty and plan for his people. Some of these visual reminders were tied to Israel's feasts. In giving the laws to his people, God set several appointed feasts for Israel to observe at specific times during the year (see Lev 23). Each feast commemorated a specific event in God's interaction with Israel. Some feasts were celebrated annually, such as Passover. Others were celebrated more often; the Sabbath was observed every week.

The apostle Paul understood that the feasts and celebrations were intended by the Lord as prophetic signs of future events and referred to them as "a shadow of things to come" (Col 2:17). Looking back from the vantage point of modern history we can observe specific prophecies that were fulfilled on or near several of these special celebrations. Just as we anticipate our next birthday, note that some of these "anniversaries" are still to come.

The First Day of Nisan

The first day of the month of Nisan was a time for ritual cleansing and new beginnings for the Jews. Nisan was the first month in the Jewish civil calendar. Three events symbolizing new beginnings have already transpired in Israel's history on this important anniversary. One event still remains to be fulfilled.

1. The dedication of the tabernacle (see Ex 40:17)
2. The cleansing of the temple by King Hezekiah (see 2Ch 29:2–3, 17)
3. Ezra and the exiles return to Jerusalem from Babylon (see Ezr 7:9)
4. The future cleansing of the millennial temple (see Eze 45:18)

The Tenth Day of Nisan

Sanctification is the theme associated with the tenth day of Nisan. It was the day connected with setting apart someone or something for a holy purpose. There are three major events associated with this special day.

1. The lamb is chosen for the Passover (see Ex 12:3–6)
2. Israel crosses the Jordan River and enters Canaan (see Jos 4:19)
3. Ezekiel's vision of the millennial temple (see Eze 40:1–2)

The Passover

"In the fourteenth day of the first month at even is the LORD's passover" (Lev 23:5). Passover was the first of three annual feasts that required mandatory attendance of all men at the temple. The Passover holds forth the promise of a final atonement when the Messiah will redeem all those who look to him for salvation. Six times in their history the Passover has marked a milestone in the spiritual and national life of Israel.

1. The Passover supper eaten in Egypt (see Ex 12:41)
2. The Passover supper eaten at Sinai (see Nu 9:5)
3. The first Passover in Canaan (see Jos 5:10)
4. King Josiah celebrates the Passover (see 2Ch 35:1)
5. Ezra and the exiles celebrate the Passover (see Ezr 6:16–19)
6. The Last Supper observed at Passover (see Lk 22:7–11)

The Feast of Pentecost

Celebrated fifty days after the Feast of Firstfruits, the Feast of Pentecost was the second of the three required celebrations at the temple in Jerusalem. Two special events took place on this feast, introducing a special time of spiritual stewardship to a specific new revelation of God.

1. The giving of the Law (see Ex 19:1–11)
2. The giving of the Holy Spirit (see Ac 2:1–4)

The Feast of Trumpets

This feast signaled the beginning of the agricultural calendar, a New Year's celebration marked by the blowing of trumpets, cessation of work and convening together to celebrate. At this time the people would be reminded of the long-awaited day when the Lord would be revealed as King and accepted as the ruler of the whole world. Two spiritually important events have already occurred on the anniversary of this feast.

1. God institutes the Feast of Trumpets (see Lev 23:23–24)
2. The high priest brings the first offering to the rebuilt altar (see Ezr 3:1–6)
3. Ezra reads the Law to the returned exiles (see Ne 8:2–3)

A Shadow of Things to Come

Of the seven appointed feasts mentioned in Leviticus 23, four of them have found prophetic fulfillment in the major events in the life of Jesus Christ. During the Passover Jesus instituted the Last Supper and the new covenant of his blood. The Feast of Unleavened Bread, the day after Passover, coincided with the crucifixion of Christ, the sinless Son of God who was untainted by the leaven of the Pharisees. The Feast of Firstfruits marked the day of resurrection when Christ became "the firstfruits of them that slept" (1Co 15:20). And the Feast of Pentecost heralded the giving of the Holy Spirit.

The three other major celebrations—the Feast of Trumpets, the Day of Atonement and the Feast of Tabernacles—are still only shadows of things to come and may be fulfilled at the climactic Battle of Armageddon as Christ ushers in his millennial kingdom. What better event could happen than the deliverance from persecution and the beginning of the prophesied kingdom of God on earth? That would be worth an anniversary forever in Jerusalem (see Zec 14:16).

me, for all the signs which I have shown among them?

D 12 I will smite them with the pestilence, and disinherit them, and [a]will make of thee a greater nation and mightier than they.

13 ¶ And [a]Moses said unto the LORD, Then the Egyptians shall hear *it,* (for thou broughtest up this people in thy might from among them;)

L 14 And they will tell *it* to the inhabitants of this land: [a]*for* they have heard that thou LORD *art* among this people, that thou LORD art seen face to face, and *that* [b]thy cloud standeth over them, and *that* thou goest before them, by day time in a pillar of a cloud, and in a pillar of fire by night.

15 ¶ Now *if* thou shalt kill *all* this people as one man, then the nations which have heard the fame of thee will speak, saying,

16 Because the LORD was not [a]able to bring this people into the land which he sware unto them, therefore he hath slain them in the wilderness.

17 And now, I beseech thee, let the power of my LORD be great, according as thou hast spoken, saying,

H L 18 The LORD *is* [a]longsuffering, and of great mercy, forgiving iniquity and transgression, and by no means clearing *the guilty,* [b]visiting the iniquity of the fathers upon the children unto the third and fourth *generation.*

P 19 [a]Pardon, I beseech thee, the iniquity of this people [b]according unto the greatness of thy mercy, and [c]as thou hast forgiven this people, from Egypt even [1]until now.

D Nu 12:9–10 ◀ ▶ Nu 14:37
L Nu 9:15–23 ◀ ▶ Nu 31:49
H Ex 34:7 ◀ ▶ Nu 32:23
L Lev 19:22 ◀ ▶ Dt 4:7
P Lev 26:40–42 ◀ ▶ Dt 4:29–31

12 [a]Ex. 32:10
13 [a]Ex. 32:12; Ezek. 20:9,14
14 [a]Ex. 15:14 [b]Ex. 13:21; Neh. 9:12
16 [a]Deut. 9:28
18 [a]Ex. 34:6,7 [b]Ex. 20:5
19 [a]Ex. 34:9 [b]Ps. 106:45 [c]Ps. 78:38 [1]Or, *hitherto*
20 [a]1 John 5:14-16
21 [a]Ps. 72:19
22 [a]Deut. 1:35; Heb. 3:17 [b]Gen. 31:7
23 [a]ch. 32:11; Ezek. 20:15 [1]Heb. *If they see the land*
24 [a]Josh. 14:6,8,9, 14 [b]ch. 32:12
25 [a]Deut. 1:40
27 [a]Ex. 16:28 [b]Ex. 16:12
28 [a]ver. 21; Deut. 1:35; Heb. 3:17 [b]See ver. 2
29 [a]ch. 1:45 & 26:64
30 [a]ver. 38; Deut. 1:36,38 [1]Heb. *lifted up my hand*

20 And the LORD said, I have pardoned [a]according to thy word:

21 But *as* truly *as* I live, [a]all the earth shall be filled with the glory of the LORD. M

22 [a]Because all those men which have seen my glory, and my miracles, which I did in Egypt and in the wilderness, and have tempted me now [b]these ten times, and have not hearkened to my voice; J S

23 [a]Surely[1] they shall not see the land which I sware unto their fathers, neither shall any of them that provoked me see it:

24 But my servant [a]Caleb, because he had another spirit with him, and [b]hath followed me fully, him will I bring into the land whereinto he went; and his seed shall possess it. E

25 (Now the Amalekites and the Canaanites dwelt in the valley.) Tomorrow turn you, [a]and get you into the wilderness by the way of the Red sea.

26 ¶ And the LORD spake unto Moses and unto Aaron, saying,

27 [a]How long *shall I bear with* this evil congregation, which murmur against me? [b]I have heard the murmurings of the children of Israel, which they murmur against me.

28 Say unto them, [a]*As truly as* I live, saith the LORD, [b]as ye have spoken in mine ears, so will I do to you:

29 Your carcases shall fall in this wilderness; and [a]all that were numbered of you, according to your whole number, from twenty years old and upward, which have murmured against me,

30 Doubtless ye shall not come into the land, *concerning* which I [1]sware to make you dwell therein, [a]save Caleb the

M ▶ Nu 24:17–19
J Ex 17:16 ◀ ▶ Nu 14:43
S Lev 22:31–32 ◀ ▶ Nu 15:30–31
E Nu 11:25–29 ◀ ▶ Nu 24:2

14:21 The phrase "all the earth shall be filled with the glory of the LORD" appears here for the first time. It occurs throughout Scripture in various forms (see Ps 72:19; 86:9; Isa 6:3; Hab 2:14; Mal 1:11). The coming kingdom of the Messiah will usher in the day when this phrase will be a reality (see Rev 4:11; 15:4).

14:22–23 Although God did not annihilate the Israelites because of their rebellion, justice required punishment. All throughout the exodus the Israelites had repeatedly disobeyed the Lord (see Ex 14:10–12; 15:22–24; 16:1–3, 19–20, 27–30; 17:1–4; 32:1–35; Nu 11:1–3, 4–34; 14:3). Consequently, God declared that every adult, above twenty years of age who had "not hearkened to my voice" (14:22) would die in the desert. In this way the nation would be purged of rebellion; only the children born on this arduous journey would see the promised land.

son of Jephunneh, and Joshua the son of
Nun.
31 [a]But your little ones, which ye said
should be a prey, them will I bring in,
and they shall know the land which [b]ye
have despised.
32 But *as for* you, [a]your carcases, they
shall fall in this wilderness.
33 And your children shall [a]wander[/]
in the wilderness [b]forty years, and [c]bear
your whoredoms, until your carcases be
wasted in the wilderness.
34 [a]After the number of the days in
which ye searched the land, *even* [b]forty
days, each day for a year, shall ye bear
your iniquities, *even* forty years, [c]and ye
shall know my [/]breach of promise.
35 [a]I the LORD have said, I will surely
do it unto all [b]this evil congregation, that
are gathered together against me: in this
wilderness they shall be consumed, and
there they shall die.
36 [a]And the men, which Moses sent
to search the land, who returned, and
made all the congregation to murmur
against him, by bringing up a slander
upon the land,
D 37 Even those men that did bring up
the evil report upon the land, [a]died by
the plague before the LORD.
38 [a]But Joshua the son of Nun, and Caleb the son of Jephunneh, *which were* of
the men that went to search the land,
lived *still.*
39 And Moses told these sayings unto
all the children of Israel: [a]and the people
mourned greatly.
40 ¶ And they rose up early in the
morning, and gat them up into the top of
the mountain, saying, Lo, [a]we *be here,*
and will go up unto the place which the

31 [a]Deut. 1:39 [b]Ps. 106:24
32 [a]1 Cor. 10:5
33 [a]ch. 32:13; Ps. 107:40 [b]See Deut. 2:14 [c]Ezek. 23:35 [/]Or, *feed*
34 [a]ch. 13:25 [b]Ps. 95:10; Ezek. 4:6 [c]See 1 Ki. 8:56; Heb. 4:1 [/]Or, *altering of my purpose*
35 [a]ch. 23:19 [b]ver. 27,29; 1 Cor. 10:5
36 [a]ch. 13:31,32
37 [a]1 Cor. 10:10
38 [a]Josh. 14:6,10
39 [a]Ex. 33:4
40 [a]Deut. 1:41
41 [a]ver. 25; 2 Chr. 24:20
42 [a]Deut. 1:42
43 [a]2 Chr. 15:2
44 [a]Deut. 1:43
45 [a]ver. 43; Deut. 1:44 [b]ch. 21:3; Judg. 1:17
15:2 [a]ver. 18; Lev. 23:10; Deut. 7:1
3 [a]Lev. 1:2,3 [b]Lev. 7:16 & 22:18,21 [c]Lev. 23:8,12,36; ch. 28:19,27; Deut. 16:10 [d]Gen. 8:21; Ex. 29:18 [/]Heb. *separating*
4 [a]Lev. 2:1 & 6:14 [b]Ex. 29:40; Lev. 23:13 [c]Lev. 14:10; ch. 28:5
5 [a]ch. 28:7,14

LORD hath promised: for we have sinned.
41 And Moses said, Wherefore now do
ye transgress [a]the commandment of the
LORD? but it shall not prosper.
42 [a]Go not up, for the LORD *is* not
among you; that ye be not smitten before
your enemies.
43 For the Amalekites and the Canaanites *are* there before you, and ye shall fall J
by the sword: [a]because ye are turned
away from the LORD, therefore the LORD
will not be with you.
44 [a]But they presumed to go up unto
the hill top: nevertheless the ark of the
covenant of the LORD, and Moses, departed not out of the camp.
45 [a]Then the Amalekites came down,
and the Canaanites which dwelt in that
hill, and smote them, and discomfited
them, *even* unto [b]Hormah.

Offerings required of Israel

15 AND THE LORD spake unto Moses, saying,
2 [a]Speak unto the children of Israel,
and say unto them, When ye be come
into the land of your habitations, which I
give unto you,
3 And [a]will make an offering by fire
unto the LORD, a burnt offering, or a sacrifice [b]in [/]performing a vow, or in a freewill offering, or [c]in your solemn feasts, to
make a [d]sweet savour unto the LORD, of
the herd, or of the flock:
4 Then [a]shall he that offereth his offering unto the LORD bring [b]a meat offering
of a tenth deal of flour mingled [c]with the
fourth *part* of an hin of oil.
5 [a]And the fourth *part* of an hin of
wine for a drink offering shalt thou pre-

D Nu 14:12 ◀ ▶ Nu 16:46
J Nu 14:22–30 ◀ ▶ Nu 24:14–24

14:32–34 The Lord punished the Israelites with one year in the desert for each day that the spies searched out the land—forty years for forty days. During that time the older generation of Israelites would die, leaving only the younger generation to enter the promised land.

14:36–37 The judgment on the ten spies who sinfully rebelled against the Lord's command to conquer Canaan was immediate—each one died of a plague. The two faithful spies, Joshua and Caleb, were the only adult Israelites who lived through the exodus from Egypt and crossed into Canaan forty years later.

14:39 After Moses' prophecy of judgment "the people mourned greatly," knowing they would all die in the wilderness. Yet Joshua and Caleb were spared this tragedy because of their faith in God. They were God's believing remnant in a nation of unbelievers. Believers, both Jew and Gentile, can faithfully hold on to God's promises and look expectantly to that great day when their Messiah will come to end their suffering. When the Messianic kingdom arrives, the mournful fasting and sorrow of Israel will be transformed and "shall be to the house of Judah joy and gladness, and cheerful feasts" (Zec 8:19).

pare with the burnt offering or sacrifice, for one lamb.

6 [a]Or for a ram, thou shalt prepare *for* a meat offering two tenth deals of flour mingled with the third *part* of an hin of oil.

7 And for a drink offering thou shalt offer the third *part* of an hin of wine, *for* a sweet savour unto the LORD.

8 And when thou preparest a bullock *for* a burnt offering, or *for* a sacrifice in performing a vow, or [a]peace offerings unto the LORD:

9 Then shall he bring [a]with a bullock a meat offering of three tenth deals of flour mingled with half an hin of oil.

10 And thou shalt bring for a drink offering half an hin of wine, *for* an offering made by fire, of a sweet savour unto the LORD.

11 [a]Thus shall it be done for one bullock, or for one ram, or for a lamb, or a kid.

12 According to the number that ye shall prepare, so shall ye do to every one according to their number.

13 All that are born of the country shall do these things after this manner, in offering an offering made by fire, of a sweet savour unto the LORD.

14 And if a stranger sojourn with you, or whosoever *be* among you in your generations, and will offer an offering made by fire, of a sweet savour unto the LORD; as ye do, so he shall do.

15 [a]One ordinance *shall be both* for you of the congregation, and also for the stranger that sojourneth *with you,* an ordinance for ever in your generations: as ye *are,* so shall the stranger be before the LORD.

16 One law and one manner shall be for you, and for the stranger that sojourneth with you.

17 ¶ And the LORD spake unto Moses, saying,

18 [a]Speak unto the children of Israel, and say unto them, When ye come into the land whither I bring you,

19 Then it shall be, that, when ye eat of [a]the bread of the land, ye shall offer up an heave offering unto the LORD.

20 [a]Ye shall offer up a cake of the first of your dough *for* an heave offering: as *ye do* [b]the heave offering of the threshingfloor, so shall ye heave it.

21 Of the first of your dough ye shall give unto the LORD an heave offering in your generations.

Offering for unintentional sins

22 ¶ And [a]if ye have erred, and not observed all these commandments, which the LORD hath spoken unto Moses,

23 *Even* all that the LORD hath commanded you by the hand of Moses, from the day that the LORD commanded *Moses,* and henceforward among your generations;

24 Then it shall be, [a]if *aught* be committed by ignorance [1]without the knowledge of the congregation, that all the congregation shall offer one young bullock for a burnt offering, for a sweet savour unto the LORD, [b]with his meat offering, and his drink offering, according to the [2]manner, and [c]one kid of the goats for a sin offering.

25 [a]And the priest shall make an atonement for all the congregation of the children of Israel, and it shall be forgiven them; for it *is* ignorance: and they shall bring their offering, a sacrifice made by fire unto the LORD, and their sin offering before the LORD, for their ignorance:

26 And it shall be forgiven all the congregation of the children of Israel, and the stranger that sojourneth among them; seeing all the people *were* in ignorance.

27 ¶ And [a]if any soul sin through ignorance, then he shall bring a she goat of the first year for a sin offering.

28 [a]And the priest shall make an atonement for the soul that sinneth ignorantly, when he sinneth by ignorance before the LORD, to make an atonement for him; and it shall be forgiven him.

29 [a]Ye shall have one law for him that [1]sinneth through ignorance, *both for* him that is born among the children of Israel, and for the stranger that sojourneth among them.

30 ¶ [a]But the soul that doeth *aught* [1]presumptuously, *whether he be* born in the land, or a stranger, the same reproacheth the LORD; and that soul shall be cut off from among his people. S

31 Because he hath [a]despised the word of the LORD, and hath broken his commandment, that soul shall utterly be cut off; [b]his iniquity *shall be* upon him.

S *Nu 14:22–25* ◄ ► *Nu 32:11*

6 [a]ch. 28:12,14
8 [a]Lev. 7:11
9 [a]ch. 28:12,14
11 [a]ch. 28
15 [a]ver. 29; Ex. 12:49; ch. 9:14
18 [a]ver. 2; Deut. 26:1
19 [a]Josh. 5:11,12
20 [a]Deut. 26:2,10; Prov. 3:9,10 [b]Lev. 2:14 & 23:10,16
22 [a]Lev. 4:2
24 [a]Lev. 4:13 [b]ver. 8-10 [c]See Lev. 4:23 [1]Heb. *from the eyes* [2]Or, *ordinance*
25 [a]Lev. 4:20
27 [a]Lev. 4:27,28
28 [a]Lev. 4:35
29 [a]ver. 15 [1]Heb. *doth*
30 [a]Deut. 17:12; Ps. 19:13; Heb. 10:26 [1]Heb. *with an high hand*
31 [a]2 Sam. 12:9; Prov. 13:13 [b]Lev. 5:1; Ezek. 18:20

Stoning the sabbath breaker

32 ¶ And while the children of Israel were in the wilderness, [a]they found a man that gathered sticks upon the sabbath day.

33 And they that found him gathering sticks brought him unto Moses and Aaron, and unto all the congregation.

34 And they put him [a]in ward, because it was not declared what should be done to him.

35 And the LORD said unto Moses, [a]The man shall be surely put to death: all the congregation shall [b]stone him with stones without the camp.

36 And all the congregation brought him without the camp, and stoned him with stones, and he died; as the LORD commanded Moses.

The fringes of remembrance

37 ¶ And the LORD spake unto Moses, saying,

38 Speak unto the children of Israel, and bid [a]them that they make them fringes in the borders of their garments throughout their generations, and that they put upon the fringe of the borders a ribband of blue:

39 And it shall be unto you for a fringe, that ye may look upon it, and remember all the commandments of the LORD, and do them; and that ye [a]seek not after your own heart and your own eyes, after which ye use [b]to go a-whoring:

40 That ye may remember, and do all my commandments, and be [a]holy unto your God.

41 I *am* the LORD your God, which brought you out of the land of Egypt, to be your God: I *am* the LORD your God.

The rebellion of Korah

16 NOW [a]KORAH, the son of Izhar, the son of Kohath, the son of Levi, and Dathan and Abiram, the sons of Eliab, and On, the son of Peleth, sons of Reuben, took *men:*

2 And they rose up before Moses, with certain of the children of Israel, two hundred and fifty princes of the assembly, [a]famous in the congregation, men of renown:

3 And [a]they gathered themselves together against Moses and against Aaron, and said unto them, [1]*Ye take* too much upon you, seeing [b]all the congregation *are* holy, every one of them, [c]and the LORD *is* among them: wherefore then lift ye up yourselves above the congregation of the LORD?

4 And when Moses heard *it,* [a]he fell upon his face:

5 And he spake unto Korah and unto all his company, saying, Even tomorrow the LORD will show who *are* his, and *who is* [a]holy; and will cause *him* to come near unto him: even *him* whom he hath [b]chosen will he cause to [c]come near unto him.

6 This do; Take you censers, Korah, and all his company;

7 And put fire therein, and put incense in them before the LORD tomorrow: and it shall be *that* the man whom the LORD doth choose, he *shall be* holy: *ye take* too much upon you, ye sons of Levi.

8 And Moses said unto Korah, Hear, I pray you, ye sons of Levi:

9 *Seemeth it but* [a]a small thing unto you, that the God of Israel hath [b]separated you from the congregation of Israel, to bring you near to himself to do the service of the tabernacle of the LORD, and to stand before the congregation to minister unto them?

10 And he hath brought thee near *to him,* and all thy brethren the sons of Levi with thee: and seek ye the priesthood also?

11 For which cause *both* thou and all thy company *are* gathered together against the LORD: [a]and what *is* Aaron, that ye murmur against him?

12 ¶ And Moses sent to call Dathan and Abiram, the sons of Eliab: which said, We will not come up:

13 *Is it* a small thing that thou hast brought us up out of a land that floweth with milk and honey, to kill us in the wilderness, except thou [a]make thyself altogether a prince over us?

14 Moreover thou hast not brought us into [a]a land that floweth with milk and honey, or given us inheritance of fields and vineyards: wilt thou [1]put out the eyes of these men? we will not come up.

15 And Moses was very wroth, and said unto the LORD, [a]Respect not thou their offering: [b]I have not taken one ass from them, neither have I hurt one of them.

16 And Moses said unto Korah, [a]Be thou and all thy company [b]before the

32 [a]Ex. 31:14,15 & 35:2,3
34 [a]Lev. 24:12
35 [a]Ex. 31:14,15 [b]Lev. 24:14; 1 Ki. 21:13; Acts 7:58
38 [a]Deut. 22:12; Mat. 23:5
39 [a]See Deut. 29:19 [b]Ps. 73:27 & 106:39; Jas. 4:4
40 [a]Lev. 11:44,45; Rom. 12:1; Col. 1:22; 1 Pet. 1:15,16
16:1 [a]Ex. 6:21; ch. 26:9 & 27:3; Jude 11
2 [a]ch. 26:9
3 [a]Ps. 106:16 [b]Ex. 19:6 [c]Ex. 29:45; ch. 14:14 & 35:34 [1]Heb. It is *much for you*
4 [a]ch. 14:5 & 20:6
5 [a]ver. 3; Lev. 21:6-8,12,15 [b]Ex. 28:1; ch. 17:5; 1 Sam. 2:28 [c]Ezek. 40:46 & 44:15,16
9 [a]1 Sam. 18:23; Is. 7:13 [b]ch. 3:41, 45 & 8:14; Deut. 10:8
11 [a]Ex. 16:8
13 [a]Ex. 2:14; Acts 7:27,35
14 [a]Ex. 3:8; Lev. 20:24 [1]Heb. *bore out*
15 [a]Gen. 4:4,5 [b]1 Sam. 12:3; Acts 20:33
16 [a]ver. 6,7 [b]1 Sam. 12:3,7

LORD, thou, and they, and Aaron, to-morrow:

17 And take every man his censer, and put incense in them, and bring ye before the LORD every man his censer, two hundred and fifty censers; thou also, and Aaron, each *of you* his censer.

18 And they took every man his censer, and put fire in them, and laid incense thereon, and stood in the door of the tabernacle of the congregation with Moses and Aaron.

19 And Korah gathered all the congregation against them unto the door of the tabernacle of the congregation: and [a]the glory of the LORD appeared unto all the congregation.

20 And the LORD spake unto Moses and unto Aaron, saying,

21 [a]Separate yourselves from among this congregation, that I may [b]consume them in a moment.

22 And they [a]fell upon their faces, and said, O God, [b]the God of the spirits of all flesh, shall one man sin, and wilt thou be wroth with all the congregation?

23 ¶ And the LORD spake unto Moses, saying,

24 Speak unto the congregation, saying, Get you up from about the tabernacle of Korah, Dathan, and Abiram.

25 And Moses rose up and went unto Dathan and Abiram; and the elders of Israel followed him.

26 And he spake unto the congregation, saying, [a]Depart, I pray you, from the tents of these wicked men, and touch nothing of theirs, lest ye be consumed in all their sins.

27 So they gat up from the tabernacle of Korah, Dathan, and Abiram, on every side: and Dathan and Abiram came out, and stood in the door of their tents, and their wives, and their sons, and their little children.

28 And Moses said, [a]Hereby ye shall know that the LORD hath sent me to do all these works; for *I have* not *done them* [b]of mine own mind.

29 If these men die [1]the common death of all men, or if they be [a]visited after the visitation of all men; *then* the LORD hath not sent me.

30 But if the LORD [1]make [a]a new thing, and the earth open her mouth, and swallow them up, with all that *appertain* unto them, and they [b]go down quick into the pit; then ye shall understand that these men have provoked the LORD.

31 ¶ [a]And it came to pass, as he had made an end of speaking all these words, that the ground clave asunder that *was* under them:

32 And the earth opened her mouth, and swallowed them up, and their houses, and [a]all the men that *appertained* unto Korah, and all *their* goods.

33 They, and all that *appertained* to them, went down alive into the pit, and the earth closed upon them: and they perished from among the congregation.

34 And all Israel that *were* round about them fled at the cry of them: for they said, Lest the earth swallow us up *also.*

35 And there [a]came out a fire from the LORD, and consumed [b]the two hundred and fifty men that offered incense.

36 ¶ And the LORD spake unto Moses, saying,

37 Speak unto Eleazar the son of Aaron the priest, that he take up the censers out of the burning, and scatter thou the fire yonder; for [a]they are hallowed.

38 The censers of these [a]sinners against their own souls, let them make them broad plates *for* a covering of the altar: for they offered them before the LORD, therefore they are hallowed: [b]and they shall be a sign unto the children of Israel.

39 And Eleazar the priest took the brasen censers, wherewith they that were burnt had offered; and they were made broad *plates for* a covering of the altar:

40 *To be* a memorial unto the children of Israel, [a]that no stranger, which *is* not of the seed of Aaron, come near to offer incense before the LORD; that he be not as Korah, and as his company: as the LORD said to him by the hand of Moses.

41 ¶ But on the morrow [a]all the congregation of the children of Israel murmured against Moses and against Aaron, saying, Ye have killed the people of the LORD.

42 And it came to pass, when the congregation was gathered against Moses and against Aaron, that they looked toward the tabernacle of the congregation: and, behold, [a]the cloud covered it, and [b]the glory of the LORD appeared.

43 And Moses and Aaron came before the tabernacle of the congregation.

19 [a]ver. 42; Ex. 16:7,10; Lev. 9:6, 23; ch. 14:10

21 [a]ver. 45; See Gen. 19:17,22; Jer. 51:6 [b]ver. 45; Ex. 32:10 & 33:5

22 [a]ver. 45; ch. 14:5 [b]ch. 27:16; Job 12:10; Eccl. 12:7; Heb. 12:9

26 [a]Gen. 19:12,14

28 [a]Ex. 3:12; John 5:36 [b]ch. 24:13; Ezek. 13:17; John 5:30 & 6:38

29 [a]Ex. 20:5 & 32:34; Job 35:15 [1]Heb. *as every man dieth*

30 [a]Job 31:3; Is. 28:21 [b]ver. 33; Ps. 55:15 [1]Heb. *create a creature*

31 [a]ch. 26:10 & 27:3; Deut. 11:6; Ps. 106:17

32 [a]See ver. 17 & ch. 26:11; 1 Chr. 6:22,37

35 [a]Lev. 10:2; ch. 11:1; Ps. 106:18 [b]ver. 17

37 [a]See Lev. 27:28

38 [a]Prov. 20:2; Hab. 2:10 [b]ch. 17:10 & 26:10; Ezek. 14:8

40 [a]ch. 3:10; 2 Chr. 26:18

41 [a]ch. 14:2; Ps. 106:25

42 [a]Ex. 40:34 [b]ver. 19; ch. 20:6

44 ¶ And the LORD spake unto Moses,
saying,
45 [a]Get you up from among this congregation, that I may consume them as
in a moment. And [b]they fell upon their
faces.
D 46 ¶ And Moses said unto Aaron, Take
D a censer, and put fire therein from off the
E altar, and put on incense, and go quickly
unto the congregation, and make an
atonement for them: [a]for there is wrath
gone out from the LORD; the plague is
begun.
47 And Aaron took as Moses commanded, and ran into the midst of the
congregation; and, behold, the plague
was begun among the people: and he put
on incense, and made an atonement for
the people.
48 And he stood between the dead and
the living; and [a]the plague was stayed.
49 Now they that died in the plague
were fourteen thousand and seven hundred, beside them that died about the
matter of Korah.
50 And Aaron returned unto Moses
unto the door of the tabernacle of the
congregation: and the plague was stayed.

The budding of Aaron's rod

17 AND THE LORD spake unto Moses, saying,
2 Speak unto the children of Israel,
and take of every one of them a rod according to the house of *their* fathers, of all
their princes according to the house of
their fathers twelve rods: write thou every man's name upon his rod.
3 And thou shalt write Aaron's name
upon the rod of Levi: for one rod *shall be*
for the head of the house of their fathers.
4 And thou shalt lay them up in the
tabernacle of the congregation before the
testimony, [a]where I will meet with you.
5 And it shall come to pass, *that* the
man's rod, [a]whom I shall choose, shall
blossom: and I will make to cease from
me the murmurings of the children of Israel, [b]whereby they murmur against you.
6 ¶ And Moses spake unto the children
of Israel, and every one of their princes
gave him [l]a rod apiece, for each prince
one, according to their fathers' houses,
even twelve rods: and the rod of Aaron
was among their rods.
7 And Moses laid up the rods before
the LORD in [a]the tabernacle of witness.
8 And it came to pass, that on the morrow Moses went into the tabernacle of
witness; and, behold, the rod of Aaron
for the house of Levi was budded, and
brought forth buds, and bloomed blossoms, and yielded almonds.
9 And Moses brought out all the rods
from before the LORD unto all the children
of Israel: and they looked, and took every
man his rod.
10 ¶ And the LORD said unto Moses,
Bring [a]Aaron's rod again before the testimony, to be kept [b]for a token against the
[l]rebels; [c]and thou shalt quite take away
their murmurings from me, that they die
not.
11 And Moses did *so:* as the LORD commanded him, so did he.
12 And the children of Israel spake
unto Moses, saying, Behold, we die, we
perish, we all perish.
13 [a]Whosoever cometh any thing near
unto the tabernacle of the LORD shall die:
shall we be consumed with dying?

Duties of priests and Levites

18 AND THE LORD said unto Aaron,
[a]Thou and thy sons and thy fa-
ther's house with thee shall [b]bear the iniquity of the sanctuary: and thou and thy
sons with thee shall bear the iniquity of
your priesthood.
2 And thy brethren also of the tribe of
Levi, the tribe of thy father, bring thou
with thee, that they may be [a]joined unto
thee, and [b]minister unto thee: but [c]thou
and thy sons with thee *shall minister* before the tabernacle of witness.

45 [a]ver. 21,24 [b]ver. 22; ch. 20:6
46 [a]Lev. 10:6; ch. 8:19 & 11:33; 1 Chr. 27:24
48 [a]ch. 25:8; Ps. 106:30
17:4 [a]Ex. 25:22 & 29:42,43 & 30:36
5 [a]ch. 16:5 [b]ch. 16:11
6 [l]Heb. *a rod for one prince, a rod for one prince*
7 [a]Ex. 38:21; ch. 18:2; Acts 7:44
10 [a]Heb. 9:4 [b]ch. 16:38 [c]ver. 5 [l]Heb. *children of rebellion*
13 [a]ch. 1:51,53 & 18:4,7
18:1 [a]ch. 17:13 [b]Ex. 28:38
2 [a]See Gen. 29:34 [b]ch. 3:6,7 [c]ch. 3:10

D *Nu 9:13–14* ◀▶ *Nu 18:17*
D *Nu 14:37* ◀▶ *Nu 21:6*
E *Nu 12:9–15* ◀▶ *Nu 21:7–9*

17:5–10 To prevent any further uprisings by the Israelites, God initiated a test to determine his choice for Israel's high priest. The head of each tribe brought Moses a dead, wooden walking stick. God said he would cause one of the rods to blossom and bring forth buds. The next day Aaron's rod was covered with buds, blossoms and fully developed almonds confirming God's choice and the exclusive legitimacy of Aaron as high priest. Aaron's rod joined the tablets of the law and the jar of manna within or near the ark of the covenant in the tabernacle (see Ex 16:33–34; Dt 10:1–3; Heb 9:4).

3 And they shall keep thy charge, and [a]the charge of all the tabernacle: [b]only they shall not come nigh the vessels of the sanctuary and the altar, [c]that neither they, nor ye also, die.

4 And they shall be joined unto thee, and keep the charge of the tabernacle of the congregation, for all the service of the tabernacle: [a]and a stranger shall not come nigh unto you.

5 And ye shall keep [a]the charge of the sanctuary, and the charge of the altar: [b]that there be no wrath any more upon the children of Israel.

6 And I, behold, I have [a]taken your brethren the Levites from among the children of Israel: [b]to you *they are* given *as* a gift for the LORD, to do the service of the tabernacle of the congregation.

7 Therefore [a]thou and thy sons with thee shall keep your priest's office for every thing of the altar, and [b]within the veil; and ye shall serve: I have given your priest's office *unto you as* a service of gift: and the stranger that cometh nigh shall be put to death.

Tithes and offerings

8 ¶ And the LORD spake unto Aaron, Behold, [a]I also have given thee the charge of mine heave offerings of all the hallowed things of the children of Israel; unto thee have I given them [b]by reason of the anointing, and to thy sons, by an ordinance for ever.

9 This shall be thine of the most holy things, *reserved* from the fire: every oblation of theirs, every [a]meat offering of theirs, and every [b]sin offering of theirs, and every [c]trespass offering of theirs, which they shall render unto me, *shall be* most holy for thee and for thy sons.

10 [a]In the most holy *place* shalt thou eat it; every male shall eat it: it shall be holy unto thee.

11 And this *is* thine; [a]the heave offering of their gift, with all the wave offerings of the children of Israel: I have given them unto thee, and to thy sons and to thy daughters with thee, by a statute for ever: [b]every one that is clean in thy house shall eat of it.

12 [a]All the [/]best of the oil, and all the best of the wine, and of the wheat, [b]the firstfruits of them which they shall offer unto the LORD, them have I given thee.

13 *And* whatsoever is first ripe in the land, [a]which they shall bring unto the LORD, shall be thine; every one that is clean in thine house shall eat *of* it.

14 [a]Every thing devoted in Israel shall be thine.

15 Every thing that openeth [a]the matrix in all flesh, which they bring unto the LORD, *whether it be* of men or beasts, shall be thine: nevertheless [b]the firstborn of man shalt thou surely redeem, and the firstling of unclean beasts shalt thou redeem.

16 And those that are to be redeemed from a month old shalt thou redeem, [a]according to thine estimation, for the money of five shekels, after the shekel of the sanctuary, [b]which *is* twenty gerahs.

17 [a]But the firstling of a cow, or the firstling of a sheep, or the firstling of a goat, thou shalt not redeem; they *are* holy: [b]thou shalt sprinkle their blood upon the altar, and shalt burn their fat *for* an offering made by fire, for a sweet savour unto the LORD. D

18 And the flesh of them shall be thine, as the [a]wave breast and as the right shoulder are thine.

19 All the heave offerings of the holy things, which the children of Israel offer unto the LORD, have I given thee, and thy sons and thy daughters with thee, by a statute for ever: [a]it *is* a covenant of salt for ever before the LORD unto thee and to thy seed with thee.

20 ¶ And the LORD spake unto Aaron, Thou shalt have no inheritance in their land, neither shalt thou have any part among them: [a]I *am* thy part and thine inheritance among the children of Israel.

21 And, behold, [a]I have given the children of Levi all the tenth in Israel for an inheritance, for their service which they serve, *even* [b]the service of the tabernacle of the congregation.

22 [a]Neither must the children of Israel henceforth come nigh the tabernacle of the congregation, [b]lest they bear sin, [/]and die.

23 [a]But the Levites shall do the service of the tabernacle of the congregation, and they shall bear their iniquity: *it shall be* a statute for ever throughout your genera-

3 [a]ch. 3:25,31,36 [b]ch. 16:40 [c]ch. 4:15
4 [a]ch. 3:10
5 [a]Ex. 27:21 & 30:7; Lev. 24:3; ch. 8:2 [b]ch. 16:46
6 [a]ch. 3:12,45 [b]ch. 3:9 & 8:19
7 [a]ver. 5; ch. 3:10 [b]Heb. 9:3,6
8 [a]Lev. 6:16,18 & 7:6,32; ch. 5:9 [b]Ex. 29:29 & 40:13,15
9 [a]Lev. 2:2,3 & 10:12,13 [b]Lev. 6:25,26 [c]Lev. 7:7
10 [a]Lev. 6:16,26
11 [a]Ex. 29:27,28 [b]Lev. 22:2,3
12 [a]Ex. 23:19; Neh. 10:35,36 [b]Ex. 22:29 [/]Heb. *fat*
13 [a]Ex. 23:19; Lev. 2:14; Deut. 26:2
14 [a]Lev. 27:28
15 [a]Ex. 13:2; Lev. 27:26; ch. 3:13 [b]Ex. 13:13
16 [a]Lev. 27:6 [b]Ex. 30:13
17 [a]Deut. 15:19 [b]Lev. 3:2,5
18 [a]Ex. 29:26,28
19 [a]Lev. 2:13; 2 Chr. 13:5
20 [a]Deut. 10:9 & 12:12 & 14:27,29 & 18:1,2; Josh. 13:14,33 & 14:3 & 18:7; Ezek. 44:28
21 [a]ver. 24,26; Lev. 27:30,32; Neh. 10:37 & 12:44; Heb. 7:5,8,9 [b]ch. 3:7,8
22 [a]ch. 1:51 [b]Lev. 22:9 [/]Heb. *to die*
23 [a]ch. 3:7

D *Nu 16:46–47* ◄► *Nu 19:1–9*

tions, that among the children of Israel
they have no inheritance.
24 But the tithes of the children of Israel, which they offer *as* an heave offering unto the LORD, I have given to the Levites to inherit: therefore I have said unto them, Among the children of Israel they shall have no inheritance.
25 ¶ And the LORD spake unto Moses, saying,
26 Thus speak unto the Levites, and say unto them, When ye take of the children of Israel the tithes which I have given you from them for your inheritance, then ye shall offer up an heave offering of it for the LORD, *even* [a]a tenth *part* of the tithe.
27 And *this* your heave offering shall be reckoned unto you, as though *it were* the corn of the threshingfloor, and as the fulness of the winepress.
28 Thus ye also shall offer an heave offering unto the LORD of all your tithes, which ye receive of the children of Israel; and ye shall give thereof the LORD'S heave offering to Aaron the priest.
29 Out of all your gifts ye shall offer every heave offering of the LORD, of all the [/]best thereof, *even* the hallowed part thereof out of it.
30 Therefore thou shalt say unto them, When ye have heaved the best thereof from it, [a]then it shall be counted unto the Levites as the increase of the threshing-floor, and as the increase of the winepress.
31 And ye shall eat it in every place, ye and your households: for it *is* [a]your reward for your service in the tabernacle of the congregation.
32 And ye shall [a]bear no sin by reason of it, when ye have heaved from it the best of it: neither shall ye [b]pollute the holy things of the children of Israel, lest ye die.

26 [a]Neh. 10:38
29 [/]Heb. *fat;* see ver. 12
30 [a]ver. 27
31 [a]Mat. 10:10; Luke 10:7; 1 Cor. 9:13; 1 Tim. 5:18
32 [a]Lev. 19:8 & 22:16 [b]Lev. 22:2, 15
19:2 [a]Deut. 21:3; 1 Sam. 6:7
3 [a]Lev. 4:12,21 & 16:27; Heb. 13:11
4 [a]Lev. 4:6 & 16:14,19; Heb. 9:13
5 [a]Ex. 29:14; Lev. 4:11,12

Purification of the unclean

19 AND THE LORD spake unto Moses and unto Aaron, saying, B D
2 This *is* the ordinance of the law which the LORD hath commanded, saying, Speak unto the children of Israel, that they bring thee a red heifer without spot, wherein *is* no blemish, [a]*and* upon which never came yoke:
3 And ye shall give her unto Eleazar the priest, that he may bring her [a]forth without the camp, and *one* shall slay her before his face:
4 And Eleazar the priest shall take of her blood with his finger, and [a]sprinkle of her blood directly before the tabernacle of the congregation seven times:
5 And *one* shall burn the heifer in his sight; [a]her skin, and her flesh, and her blood, with her dung, shall he burn:

B *Ge 49:10* ◀ ▶ *Dt 18:15–19*
D *Nu 18:17* ◀ ▶ *Nu 21:6–9*

19:2–12 In every respect the killing of the red heifer is distinct. It is a cow, not a bull or an ox, that is to be killed, not sacrificed. The animal was taken outside the camp, and though the priest was present, he did not identify himself with it. Except for a small amount of blood that the priest sprinkled toward the tabernacle seven times, the entire heifer, including its blood and feces, was burned to ash. When the ash was mixed with water, the solution could be used to purify anyone who had touched a dead body.

This unusual ritual is clearly symbolic. The red hide of the animal symbolized blood, God's requirement for cleansing. The use of a young female cow symbolized the giving of life back to one who had come in contact with death.

The killing of the red heifer is also a prophetic type of the ultimate sacrifice of Christ:

1. God instructed that the people bring a cow "without spot, wherein is no blemish" (19:2). This same description was applied to Christ, "a lamb without blemish and without spot" (1Pe 1:19), the only perfect "Lamb slain from the foundation of the world" (Rev 13:8). Jesus, who was perfectly sinless, became sin for us so that our sins could be judged and paid for by his completed work on the cross (see 2Co 5:21).
2. The red heifer was a female animal. Jesus was betrayed for thirty pieces of silver, the price of a female slave.
3. God commanded that this slaughter take place "without the camp" (19:3). Jesus also sanctified people with his blood and "suffered without the gate" (Heb 13:12).

Moses' words indicate that this ceremony was to be "a perpetual statute" (Nu 19:21). Though this ritual has not been performed for centuries, it is possible this ceremony will be reinstated in the last days. Ezekiel prophesied that the Lord would "sprinkle clean water upon you, and ye shall be clean" (Eze 36:25). The red cattle being bred in Israel may be used for reinstatement of this ceremony in the last days.

6 And the priest shall take [a]cedar wood, and hyssop, and scarlet, and cast *it* into the midst of the burning of the heifer.

7 [a]Then the priest shall wash his clothes, and he shall bathe his flesh in water, and afterward he shall come into the camp, and the priest shall be unclean until the even.

8 And he that burneth her shall wash his clothes in water, and bathe his flesh in water, and shall be unclean until the even.

9 And a man *that is* clean shall gather up [a]the ashes of the heifer, and lay *them* up without the camp in a clean place, and it shall be kept for the congregation of the children of Israel [b]for a water of separation: it *is* a purification for sin.

10 And he that gathereth the ashes of the heifer shall wash his clothes, and be unclean until the even: and it shall be unto the children of Israel, and unto the stranger that sojourneth among them, for a statute for ever.

11 ¶ [a]He that toucheth the dead body of any [1]man shall be unclean seven days.

12 [a]He shall purify himself with it on the third day, and on the seventh day he shall be clean: but if he purify not himself the third day, then the seventh day he shall not be clean.

13 Whosoever toucheth the dead body of any man that is dead, and purifieth not himself, [a]defileth the tabernacle of the LORD; and that soul shall be cut off from Israel: because [b]the water of separation was not sprinkled upon him, he shall be unclean; [c]his uncleanness *is* yet upon him.

14 This *is* the law, when a man dieth in a tent: all that come into the tent, and all that *is* in the tent, shall be unclean seven days.

15 And every [a]open vessel, which hath no covering bound upon it, *is* unclean.

16 And [a]whosoever toucheth one that is slain with a sword in the open fields, or a dead body, or a bone of a man, or a grave, shall be unclean seven days.

17 And for an unclean *person* they shall take of the [a]ashes[1] of the burnt heifer of purification for sin, and [2]running water shall be put thereto in a vessel:

18 And a clean person shall take [a]hyssop, and dip *it* in the water, and sprinkle *it* upon the tent, and upon all the vessels, and upon the persons that were there, and upon him that touched a bone, or one slain, or one dead, or a grave:

19 And the clean *person* shall sprinkle upon the unclean on the third day, and on the seventh day: [a]and on the seventh day he shall purify himself, and wash his clothes, and bathe himself in water, and shall be clean at even.

20 But the man that shall be unclean, and shall not purify himself, that soul shall be cut off from among the congregation, because he hath [a]defiled the sanctuary of the LORD: the water of separation hath not been sprinkled upon him; he *is* unclean.

21 And it shall be a perpetual statute unto them, that he that sprinkleth the water of separation shall wash his clothes; and he that toucheth the water of separation shall be unclean until even.

22 And [a]whatsoever the unclean *person* toucheth shall be unclean; and [b]the soul that toucheth *it* shall be unclean until even.

20 THEN [a]CAME the children of Israel, *even* the whole congregation, into the desert of Zin in the first month: and the people abode in Kadesh; and [b]Miriam died there, and was buried there.

Water from the rock

2 [a]And there was no water for the congregation: [b]and they gathered themselves together against Moses and against Aaron.

3 And the people [a]chode with Moses, and spake, saying, Would God that we had died [b]when our brethren died before the LORD!

4 And [a]why have ye brought up the congregation of the LORD into this wilderness, that we and our cattle should die there?

5 And wherefore have ye made us to come up out of Egypt, to bring us in unto this evil place? it *is* no place of seed, or of figs, or of vines, or of pomegranates; neither *is* there any water to drink.

6 And Moses and Aaron went from the presence of the assembly unto the door of the tabernacle of the congregation, and [a]they fell upon their faces: and [b]the glory of the LORD appeared unto them.

6 [a]Lev. 14:4,6,49
7 [a]Lev. 11:25 & 15:5
9 [a]Heb. 9:13 [b]ver. 13,20,21
11 [a]ver. 16; Lev. 21:1; ch. 5:2 & 9:6, 10 & 31:19; Lam. 4:14; Hag. 2:13 [1]Heb. *soul of man*
12 [a]ch. 31:19
13 [a]Lev. 15:31 [b]ver. 9; ch. 8:7 [c]Lev. 7:20 & 22:3
15 [a]Lev. 11:32; ch. 31:20
16 [a]ver. 11
17 [a]ver. 9 [1]Heb. *dust* [2]Heb. *living waters shall be given*
18 [a]Ps. 51:7
19 [a]Lev. 14:9
20 [a]ver. 13
22 [a]Hag. 2:13 [b]Lev. 15:5
20:1 [a]ch. 33:36 [b]Ex. 15:20; ch. 26:59
2 [a]Ex. 17:1 [b]ch. 16:19,42
3 [a]Ex. 17:2; ch. 14:2 [b]ch. 11:1,33 & 14:37 & 16:32, 35,49
4 [a]Ex. 17:3
6 [a]ch. 14:5 & 16:4,22,45 [b]ch. 14:10

F 7 ¶ And the LORD spake unto Moses, saying,

8 [a]Take the rod, and gather thou the assembly together, thou, and Aaron thy brother, and speak ye unto the rock before their eyes; and it shall give forth his water, and [b]thou shalt bring forth to them water out of the rock: so thou shalt give the congregation and their beasts drink.

9 And Moses took the rod [a]from before the LORD, as he commanded him.

10 And Moses and Aaron gathered the congregation together before the rock, and he said unto them, [a]Hear now, ye rebels; must we fetch you water out of this rock?

11 And Moses lifted up his hand, and with his rod he smote the rock twice: and [a]the water came out abundantly, and the congregation drank, and their beasts *also.*

12 ¶ And the LORD spake unto Moses and Aaron, Because [a]ye believed me not, to [b]sanctify me in the eyes of the children of Israel, therefore ye shall not bring this congregation into the land which I have given them.

13 [a]This *is* the water of [b]Meribah;[1] because the children of Israel strove with the LORD, and he was sanctified in them.

Edom refuses Israel passage

14 ¶ [a]And Moses sent messengers from Kadesh unto the king of Edom, [b]Thus saith thy brother Israel, Thou knowest all the travail that hath [1]befallen us:

15 [a]How our fathers went down into Egypt, [b]and we have dwelt in Egypt a long time; [c]and the Egyptians vexed us, and our fathers:

16 And [a]when we cried unto the LORD, he heard our voice, and [b]sent an angel, and hath brought us forth out of Egypt: and, behold, we *are* in Kadesh, a city in the uttermost of thy border:

F *Nu 11:31–32* ◄► *Nu 21:16*

8 [a]Ex. 17:5 [b]Neh. 9:15; Is. 43:20 & 48:21
9 [a]ch. 17:10
10 [a]Ps. 106:33
11 [a]Ex. 17:6; Deut. 8:15; 1 Cor. 10:4
12 [a]Deut. 1:37 [b]Lev. 10:3; Ezek. 20:41 & 36:23; 1 Pet. 3:15
13 [a]Deut. 33:8; Ps. 106:32 [b]Ex. 17:7 [1]i.e. *Strife*
14 [a]Judg. 11:16,17 [b]Deut. 2:4; Obad. 10,12 [1]Heb. *found us*
15 [a]Gen. 46:6; Acts 7:15 [b]Ex. 12:40 [c]Ex. 1:11; Deut. 26:6; Acts 7:19
16 [a]Ex. 2:23 & 3:7 [b]Ex. 3:2 & 14:19
17 [a]See ch. 21:22
19 [a]Deut. 2:6
20 [a]Judg. 11:17
21 [a]See Deut. 2:27,29 [b]Deut. 2:8; Judg. 11:18
22 [a]ch. 33:37 [b]ch. 21:4
24 [a]Gen. 25:8; Deut. 32:50 [b]ver. 12 [1]Heb. *mouth*
25 [a]ch. 33:38; Deut. 32:50

17 [a]Let us pass, I pray thee, through thy country: we will not pass through the fields, or through the vineyards, neither will we drink *of* the water of the wells: we will go by the king's *high* way, we will not turn to the right hand nor to the left, until we have passed thy borders.

18 And Edom said unto him, Thou shalt not pass by me, lest I come out against thee with the sword.

19 And the children of Israel said unto him, We will go by the high way: and if I and my cattle drink of thy water, [a]then I will pay for it: I will only, without *doing* any thing *else,* go through on my feet.

20 And he said, [a]Thou shalt not go through. And Edom came out against him with much people, and with a strong hand.

21 Thus Edom [a]refused to give Israel passage through his border: wherefore Israel [b]turned away from him.

The death of Aaron

22 ¶ And the children of Israel, *even* the whole congregation, journeyed from [a]Kadesh, [b]and came unto mount Hor.

23 And the LORD spake unto Moses and Aaron in mount Hor, by the coast of the land of Edom, saying,

24 Aaron shall be [a]gathered unto his people: for he shall not enter into the land which I have given unto the children of Israel, because [b]ye rebelled against my [1]word at the water of Meribah. Q

25 [a]Take Aaron and Eleazar his son, and bring them up unto mount Hor:

26 And strip Aaron of his garments, and put them upon Eleazar his son: and Aaron shall be gathered *unto his people,* and shall die there. Q

27 And Moses did as the LORD commanded: and they went up into mount Hor in the sight of all the congregation.

Q *Ge 49:33* ◄► *Nu 20:26*
Q *Nu 20:24* ◄► *Nu 27:13*

20:12 Despite almost forty years of faithful leadership, Moses reacted faithlessly to the Israelites' insistent demand for water. Displaying his lack of faith in God's ability to provide water with a mere word, Moses struck the rock. The end result of his failure to honor God was his exclusion from entering the promised land.

20:24–26 The Lord promised Moses that "Aaron shall be gathered unto his people" (20:24). This phrase occurs often in Scripture as a promise to a godly person, implying the reuniting of family members after death (see 2Sa 12:23). The promise is ours as well. Those who live godly lives can die secure in the knowledge that they will live eternally with God and their righteous ancestors in heaven. See note at Ge 35:29.

28 [a]And Moses stripped Aaron of his garments, and put them upon Eleazar his son; and [b]Aaron died there in the top of the mount: and Moses and Eleazar came down from the mount.

29 And when all the congregation saw that Aaron was dead, they mourned for Aaron [a]thirty days, *even* all the house of Israel.

21 AND *WHEN* [a]king Arad the Canaanite, which dwelt in the south, heard tell that Israel came [b]by the way of the spies; then he fought against Israel, and took *some* of them prisoners.

The serpent of brass

2 [a]And Israel vowed a vow unto the LORD, and said, If thou wilt indeed deliver this people into my hand, then [b]I will utterly destroy their cities.

3 And the LORD hearkened to the voice of Israel, and delivered up the Canaanites; and they utterly destroyed them and their cities: and he called the name of the place [1]Hormah.

4 ¶ And [a]they journeyed from mount Hor by the way of the Red sea, to [b]compass the land of Edom: and the soul of the people was much [1,2]discouraged because of the way.

5 And the people [a]spake against God, and against Moses, [b]Wherefore have ye brought us up out of Egypt to die in the wilderness? for *there is* no bread, neither *is there any* water; and [c]our soul loatheth this light bread.

6 And [a]the LORD sent [b]fiery serpents among the people, and they bit the people; and much people of Israel died.

7 ¶ [a]Therefore the people came to Moses, and said, We have sinned, for [b]we have spoken against the LORD, and against thee; [c]pray unto the LORD, that he take away the serpents from us. And Moses prayed for the people.

8 And the LORD said unto Moses, Make thee a fiery serpent, and set it upon a pole: and it shall come to pass, that every one that is bitten, when he looketh upon it, shall live.

9 And [a]Moses made a serpent of brass, and put it upon a pole, and it came to pass, that if a serpent had bitten any man, when he beheld the serpent of brass, he lived.

Israel moves on

10 ¶ And the children of Israel set forward, and [a]pitched in Oboth.

11 And they journeyed from Oboth, and [a]pitched at [1]Ije-abarim, in the wilderness which *is* before Moab, toward the sunrising.

12 ¶ [a]From thence they removed, and pitched in the valley of Zared.

13 From thence they removed, and pitched on the other side of Arnon, which *is* in the wilderness that cometh out of the coasts of the Amorites: for [a]Arnon *is* the border of Moab, between Moab and the Amorites.

14 Wherefore it is said in the book of the wars of the LORD, [1]What he did in the Red sea, and in the brooks of Arnon,

15 And at the stream of the brooks that goeth down to the dwelling of Ar, [a]and [1]lieth upon the border of Moab.

16 And from thence *they went* [a]to Beer: that *is* the well whereof the LORD spake unto Moses, Gather the people together, and I will give them water.

17 ¶ [a]Then Israel sang this song, [1]Spring up, O well; [2]sing ye unto it:

18 The princes digged the well, the nobles of the people digged it, by *the direction of* [a]the lawgiver, with their staves. And from the wilderness *they went* to Mattanah:

19 And from Mattanah to Nahaliel: and from Nahaliel to Bamoth:

20 And from Bamoth *in* the valley, that *is* in the [1]country of Moab, to the top of [2]Pisgah, which looketh [a]toward [3]Jeshimon.

Defeat of Sihon and Og

21 ¶ And [a]Israel sent messengers unto Sihon king of the Amorites, saying,

22 [a]Let me pass through thy land: we

D *Nu 19:1–9* ◀ ▶ *Nu 28:3–4*
D *Nu 16:46* ◀ ▶ *Nu 25:8–9*
E *Nu 16:46–50* ◀ ▶ *Nu 25:8*
K *Nu 11:23* ◀ ▶ *Nu 23:19* **W** ▶ *2Sa 22:31*
F *Nu 20:7–11* ◀ ▶ *Dt 2:7*

28 [a]Ex. 29:29,30 [b]ch. 33:38; Deut. 10:6
29 [a]Deut. 34:8
21:1 [a]ch. 33:40; Judg. 1:16 [b]ch. 13:21
2 [a]Gen. 28:20; Judg. 11:30 [b]Lev. 26:25
3 [1]i.e. *Utter destruction*
4 [a]ch. 20:22 & 33:41 [b]Judg. 11:18 [1]Or, *grieved* [2]Heb. *shortened*
5 [a]Ps. 78:19 [b]Ex. 17:3 [c]ch. 11:6
6 [a]1 Cor. 10:9 [b]Deut. 8:15
7 [a]Ps. 78:34 [b]ver. 5 [c]Ex. 8:8; 1 Sam. 12:19; 1 Ki. 13:6; Acts 8:24
9 [a]2 Ki. 18:4; John 3:14,15
10 [a]ch. 33:43
11 [a]ch. 33:44 [1]Or, *Heaps of Abarim*
12 [a]Deut. 2:13
13 [a]ch. 22:36; Judg. 11:18
14 [1]Or, *Vaheb in Suphah*
15 [a]Deut. 2:18,29 [1]Heb. *leaneth*
16 [a]Judg. 9:21
17 [a]Ex. 15:1; Ps. 105:2 & 106:12 [1]Heb. *Ascend* [2]Or, *answer*
18 [a]Is. 33:22
20 [a]ch. 23:28 [1]Heb. *field* [2]Or, *The hill* [3]Or, *The wilderness*
21 [a]Deut. 2:26,27; Judg. 11:19
22 [a]ch. 20:17

21:8 The bronze serpent on a pole points prophetically as a type of Jesus Christ. Just as the Israelites were saved when they faithfully gazed upon the bronze serpent, those who turn from their sins and gaze in faith upon the crucified and risen Christ will have everlasting life (see Jn 3:14–15).

will not turn into the fields, or into the
vineyards; we will not drink *of* the waters
of the well: *but* we will go along by the
king's *high* way, until we be past thy
borders.
23 [a]And Sihon would not suffer Israel
to pass through his border: but Sihon
gathered all his people together, and
went out against Israel into the wilderness: [b]and he came to Jahaz, and fought
against Israel.
24 And [a]Israel smote him with the
edge of the sword, and possessed his land
from Arnon unto Jabbok, even unto the
children of Ammon: for the border of the
children of Ammon *was* strong.
25 And Israel took all these cities: and
Israel dwelt in all the cities of the Amorites, in Heshbon, and in all the [/]villages
thereof.
26 For Heshbon *was* the city of Sihon
the king of the Amorites, who had fought
against the former king of Moab, and
taken all his land out of his hand, even
unto Arnon.
27 Wherefore they that speak in proverbs say, Come into Heshbon, let the city
of Sihon be built and prepared:
28 For there is [a]a fire gone out of
Heshbon, a flame from the city of Sihon:
it hath consumed [b]Ar of Moab, *and* the
lords of the high places of Arnon.
29 Woe to thee, Moab! thou art undone, O people of [a]Chemosh: he hath
given his sons that escaped, and his
daughters, into captivity unto Sihon king
of the Amorites.
30 We have shot at them; Heshbon is
perished even [a]unto Dibon, and we have
laid them waste even unto Nophah,
which *reacheth* unto [b]Medeba.
31 ¶ Thus Israel dwelt in the land of
the Amorites.
32 And Moses sent to spy out [a]Jaazer,
and they took the villages thereof, and
drove out the Amorites that *were* there.
33 ¶ [a]And they turned and went up by
the way of Bashan: and Og the king of
Bashan went out against them, he, and all
his people, to the battle [b]at Edrei.
34 And the LORD said unto Moses,
[a]Fear him not: for I have delivered him
into thy hand, and all his people, and his
land; and [b]thou shalt do to him as thou
didst unto Sihon king of the Amorites,
which dwelt at Heshbon.
35 [a]So they smote him, and his sons,
and all his people, until there was none
left him alive: and they possessed his
land.

Balak sends for Balaam

22 AND [a]THE children of Israel set
forward, and pitched in the
plains of Moab on this side Jordan *by*
Jericho.
2 ¶ And [a]Balak the son of Zippor saw
all that Israel had done to the Amorites.
3 And [a]Moab was sore afraid of the
people, because they *were* many: and
Moab was distressed because of the children of Israel.
4 And Moab said unto [a]the elders of
Midian, Now shall this company lick up
all *that are* round about us, as the ox lick-
eth up the grass of the field. And Balak
the son of Zippor *was* king of the Moabites at that time.
5 [a]He sent messengers therefore unto
Balaam the son of Beor to [b]Pethor, which
is by the river of the land of the children
of his people, to call him, saying, Behold,
there is a people come out from Egypt:
behold, they cover the [/]face of the earth,
and they abide over against me:
6 Come now therefore, I pray thee,
[a]curse me this people; for they *are* too
mighty for me: peradventure I shall prevail, *that* we may smite them, and *that* I
may drive them out of the land: for I wot
that he whom thou blessest *is* blessed,
and he whom thou cursest is cursed.
7 And the elders of Moab and the elders of Midian departed with [a]the rewards of divination in their hand; and
they came unto Balaam, and spake unto
him the words of Balak.
8 And he said unto them, [a]Lodge here
this night, and I will bring you word
again, as the LORD shall speak unto me:
and the princes of Moab abode with
Balaam.
9 [a]And God came unto Balaam, and
said, What men *are* these with thee?
10 And Balaam said unto God, Balak
the son of Zippor, king of Moab, hath
sent unto me, *saying,*
11 Behold, *there is* a people come out
of Egypt, which covereth the face of the
earth: come now, curse me them; peradventure [/]I shall be able to overcome
them, and drive them out.
12 And God said unto Balaam, Thou
shalt not go with them; thou shalt not

23 [a]Deut. 29:7 [b]Deut. 2:32; Judg. 11:20
24 [a]Deut. 2:33; Josh. 12:1; Neh. 9:22; Ps. 135:10 & 136:19; Amos 2:9
25 [/]Heb. *daughters*
28 [a]Jer. 48:45,46 [b]Deut. 2:9,18; Is. 15:1
29 [a]Judg. 11:24; 1 Ki. 11:7,33; 2 Ki. 23:13; Jer. 48:7,13
30 [a]Jer. 48:18,22 [b]Is. 15:2
32 [a]ch. 32:1; Jer. 48:32
33 [a]Deut. 3:1 & 29:7 [b]Josh. 13:12
34 [a]Deut. 3:2 [b]ver. 24; Ps. 135:10 & 136:20
35 [a]Deut. 3:3 & 29:7; Josh. 13:12; Ps. 135:10
22:1 [a]ch. 33:48
2 [a]Judg. 11:25
3 [a]Ex. 15:15
4 [a]ch. 31:8; Josh. 13:21
5 [a]Deut. 23:4; Josh. 13:22 & 24:9; Neh. 13:1,2; Mic. 6:5; 2 Pet. 2:15; Jude 11; Rev. 2:14 [b]See ch. 23:7; Deut. 23:4 [/]Heb. *eye*
6 [a]ch. 23:7
7 [a]1 Sam. 9:7,8
8 [a]ver. 19
9 [a]ver. 20; Gen. 20:3
11 [/]Heb. *I shall prevail in fighting against him*

curse the people: for [a]they *are* blessed.

13 And Balaam rose up in the morning, and said unto the princes of Balak, Get you into your land: for the LORD refuseth to give me leave to go with you.

14 And the princes of Moab rose up, and they went unto Balak, and said, Balaam refuseth to come with us.

15 ¶ And Balak sent yet again princes, more, and more honourable than they.

16 And they came to Balaam, and said to him, Thus saith Balak the son of Zippor, [1]Let nothing, I pray thee, hinder thee from coming unto me:

17 For I will promote thee unto very great honour, and I will do whatsoever thou sayest unto me: [a]come therefore, I pray thee, curse me this people.

18 And Balaam answered and said unto the servants of Balak, [a]If Balak would give me his house full of silver and gold, [b]I cannot go beyond the word of the LORD my God, to do less or more.

19 Now therefore, I pray you, [a]tarry ye also here this night, that I may know what the LORD will say unto me more.

20 [a]And God came unto Balaam at night, and said unto him, If the men come to call thee, rise up, *and* go with them; but [b]yet the word which I shall say unto thee, that shalt thou do.

Balaam's ass speaks

21 And Balaam rose up in the morning, and saddled his ass, and went with the princes of Moab.

22 ¶ And God's anger was kindled because he went: [a]and the angel of the LORD stood in the way for an adversary against him. Now he was riding upon his ass, and his two servants *were* with him.

23 And [a]the ass saw the angel of the LORD standing in the way, and his sword drawn in his hand: and the ass turned aside out of the way, and went into the field: and Balaam smote the ass, to turn her into the way.

24 But the angel of the LORD stood in a path of the vineyards, a wall *being* on this side, and a wall on that side.

25 And when the ass saw the angel of the LORD, she thrust herself unto the wall, and crushed Balaam's foot against the wall: and he smote her again.

26 And the angel of the LORD went further, and stood in a narrow place, where *was* no way to turn either to the right hand or to the left.

27 And when the ass saw the angel of the LORD, she fell down under Balaam: and Balaam's anger was kindled, and he smote the ass with a staff.

28 And the LORD [a]opened the mouth of the ass, and she said unto Balaam, What have I done unto thee, that thou hast smitten me these three times?

29 And Balaam said unto the ass, Because thou hast mocked me: I would there were a sword in mine hand, [a]for now would I kill thee.

30 [a]And the ass said unto Balaam, *Am* not I thine ass, [1]upon which thou hast ridden [2]ever since *I was* thine unto this day? was I ever wont to do so unto thee? And he said, Nay.

31 Then the LORD [a]opened the eyes of Balaam, and he saw the angel of the LORD standing in the way, and his sword drawn in his hand: and he [b]bowed down his head, and [1]fell flat on his face.

32 And the angel of the LORD said unto him, Wherefore hast thou smitten thine ass these three times? behold, I went out [1]to withstand thee, because *thy* way is [a]perverse before me:

33 And the ass saw me, and turned from me these three times: unless she had turned from me, surely now also I had slain thee, and saved her alive.

34 And Balaam said unto the angel of the LORD, [a]I have sinned; for I knew not that thou stoodest in the way against me: now therefore, if it [1]displease thee, I will get me back again.

35 And the angel of the LORD said unto Balaam, Go with the men: [a]but only the word that I shall speak unto thee, that thou shalt speak. So Balaam went with the princes of Balak.

36 ¶ And when Balak heard that Balaam was come, [a]he went out to meet him unto a city of Moab, [b]which *is* in the border of Arnon, which *is* in the utmost coast.

37 And Balak said unto Balaam, Did I not earnestly send unto thee to call thee? wherefore camest thou not unto me? am I not able indeed [a]to promote thee to honour?

38 And Balaam said unto Balak, Lo, I am come unto thee: have I now any power at all to say any thing? [a]the word

12 [a]ch. 23:20; Rom. 11:28
16 [1]Heb. *Be not thou letted from*
17 [a]ver. 6
18 [a]ch. 24:13 [b]1 Ki. 22:14; 2 Chr. 18:13
19 [a]ver. 8
20 [a]ver. 9 [b]ver. 35; ch. 23:12,26 & 24:13
22 [a]Ex. 4:24
23 [a]See 2 Ki. 6:17; Dan. 10:7; Acts 22:9; 2 Pet. 2:16; Jude 11
28 [a]2 Pet. 2:16
29 [a]Prov. 12:10
30 [a]2 Pet. 2:16 [1]Heb. *who hast ridden upon me* [2]Or, *ever since thou* wast
31 [a]See Gen. 21:19; 2 Ki. 6:17; Luke 24:16,31 [b]Ex. 34:8 [1]Or, *bowed himself*
32 [a]2 Pet. 2:14,15 [1]Heb. *to be an adversary unto thee*
34 [a]1 Sam. 15:24, 30 & 26:21; 2 Sam. 12:13; Job 34:31,32 [1]Heb. *be evil in thine eyes*
35 [a]ver. 20
36 [a]Gen. 14:17 [b]ch. 21:13
37 [a]ver. 17; ch. 24:11
38 [a]ch. 23:26 & 24:13; 1 Ki. 22:14; 2 Chr. 18:13

that God putteth in my mouth, that shall I
speak.
39 And Balaam went with Balak, and
they came unto [1]Kirjath-huzoth.
40 And Balak offered oxen and sheep,
and sent to Balaam, and to the princes
that *were* with him.
41 And it came to pass on the morrow,
that Balak took Balaam, and brought him
up into the [a]high places of Baal, that
thence he might see the utmost *part* of
the people.

Balaam's parables

23 AND BALAAM said unto Balak,
[a]Build me here seven altars, and
prepare me here seven oxen and seven
rams.
2 And Balak did as Balaam had spoken;
and Balak and Balaam [a]offered on *every*
altar a bullock and a ram.
3 And Balaam said unto Balak, [a]Stand
by thy burnt offering, and I will go: peradventure the LORD will come [b]to meet me:
and whatsoever he showeth me I will tell
thee. And [1]he went to an high place.
4 [a]And God met Balaam: and he said
unto him, I have prepared seven altars,
and I have offered upon *every* altar a bullock and a ram.
5 And the LORD [a]put a word in Balaam's mouth, and said, Return unto Balak, and thus thou shalt speak.
6 And he returned unto him, and, lo,
he stood by his burnt sacrifice, he, and all
the princes of Moab.
7 And he [a]took up his parable, and
said, Balak the king of Moab hath brought
me from Aram, out of the mountains of
the east, *saying,* [b]Come, curse me Jacob,
and come, [c]defy Israel.
8 [a]How shall I curse, whom God hath
not cursed? or how shall I defy, *whom*
the LORD hath not defied?
9 For from the top of the rocks I see
him, and from the hills I behold him: lo,
[a]the people shall dwell alone, and [b]shall
not be reckoned among the nations.

39 [1]Or, *A city of streets*
41 [a]Deut. 12:2
23:1 [a]ver. 29
2 [a]ver. 14,30
3 [a]ver. 15 [b]ch. 24:1 [1]Or, *he went solitary*
4 [a]ver. 16
5 [a]ver. 16; ch. 22:35; Deut. 18:18; Jer. 1:9
7 [a]ver. 18; ch. 24:3,15,23; Job 27:1 & 29:1; Ps. 78:2 [b]ch. 22:6,11, 17 [c]1 Sam. 17:10
8 [a]Is. 47:12
9 [a]Deut. 33:28 [b]Ex. 33:16; Ezra 9:2; Eph. 2:14
10 [a]Gen. 13:16 & 22:17 [b]Ps. 116:15 [1]Heb. *my soul,* or, *my life*
11 [a]ch. 22:11
12 [a]ch. 22:38
14 [a]ver. 1,2 [1]Or, *The hill*
16 [a]ver. 5; ch. 22:35
18 [a]Judg. 3:20
19 [a]1 Sam. 15:29; Mal. 3:6; Jas. 1:17
20 [a]Gen. 12:2 & 22:17; ch. 22:12
21 [a]Rom. 4:7,8 [b]Ps. 89:15
22 [a]ch. 24:8

10 [a]Who can count the dust of Jacob, U
and the number of the fourth *part* of Israel? Let [1]me die [b]the death of the righteous, and let my last end be like his!
11 And Balak said unto Balaam, What
hast thou done unto me? [a]I took thee to
curse mine enemies, and, behold, thou
hast blessed *them* altogether.
12 And he answered and said, [a]Must I
not take heed to speak that which the
LORD hath put in my mouth?
13 And Balak said unto him, Come, I
pray thee, with me unto another place,
from whence thou mayest see them: thou
shalt see but the utmost part of them, and
shalt not see them all: and curse me them
from thence.
14 ¶ And he brought him into the field
of Zophim, to the top of [1]Pisgah, [a]and
built seven altars, and offered a bullock
and a ram on *every* altar.
15 And he said unto Balak, Stand here
by thy burnt offering, while I meet *the*
LORD yonder.
16 And the LORD met Balaam, and [a]put
a word in his mouth, and said, Go again
unto Balak, and say thus.
17 And when he came to him, behold,
he stood by his burnt offering, and the
princes of Moab with him. And Balak said
unto him, What hath the LORD spoken?
18 And he took up his parable, and
said, [a]Rise up, Balak, and hear; hearken
unto me, thou son of Zippor:
19 [a]God *is* not a man, that he should K
lie; neither the son of man, that he
should repent: hath he said, and shall he
not do *it?* or hath he spoken, and shall
he not make it good?
20 Behold, I have received *command-*
ment to bless: and [a]he hath blessed: and I
cannot reverse it.
21 [a]He hath not beheld iniquity in Jacob, neither hath he seen perverseness in
Israel; the LORD his God *is* with him, [b]and
the shout of a king *is* among them.
22 [a]God brought them out of Egypt;

U *Nu 10:29* ◀▶ *Dt 5:10*
K *Nu 21:8–9* ◀▶ *Dt 30:6*

23:8–10 God led Balaam, the hired, pagan prophet, to prophesy and bless Israel despite the commands of the king of the Moabites. Balaam declared that he could not curse what God had blessed but rather prophesied that the Israelites would be innumerable, echoing God's direct prophecy to make Abram's "seed as the dust of the earth" (Ge 13:16). With Balaam's own words he fulfilled another of God's promises to Abram: " I will bless them that bless thee, and curse him that curseth thee" (Ge 12:3).

he hath as it were [b]the strength of an unicorn.

23 Surely *there is* no enchantment [l]against Jacob, neither *is there* any divination against Israel: according to this time it shall be said of Jacob and of Israel, [a]What hath God wrought!

A 24 Behold, the people shall rise up [a]as a great lion, and lift up himself as a young lion: [b]he shall not lie down until he eat *of* the prey, and drink the blood of the slain.

25 ¶ And Balak said unto Balaam, Neither curse them at all, nor bless them at all.

26 But Balaam answered and said unto Balak, Told not I thee, saying, [a]All that the LORD speaketh, that I must do?

27 ¶ And Balak said unto Balaam, [a]Come, I pray thee, I will bring thee unto another place; peradventure it will please God that thou mayest curse me them from thence.

28 And Balak brought Balaam unto the top of Peor, that looketh [a]toward Jeshimon.

29 And Balaam said unto Balak, [a]Build me here seven altars, and prepare me here seven bullocks and seven rams.

30 And Balak did as Balaam had said, and offered a bullock and a ram on *every* altar.

24 AND WHEN Balaam saw that it pleased the LORD to bless Israel, he went not, as at [a]other times, [l]to seek for enchantments, but he set his face toward the wilderness.

E T 2 And Balaam lifted up his eyes, and he saw Israel [a]abiding *in his tents* according to their tribes; and [b]the spirit of God came upon him.

3 [a]And he took up his parable, and said, Balaam the son of Beor hath said, and the man [l]whose eyes are open hath said:

4 He hath said, which heard the words of God, which saw the vision of the Almighty, [a]falling *into a trance,* but having his eyes open:

5 How goodly are thy tents, O Jacob, *and* thy tabernacles, O Israel!

6 As the valleys are they spread forth,

22 [b]Deut. 33:17; Job 39:10
23 [a]Ps. 31:19 & 44:1 [l]Or, *in*
24 [a]Gen. 49:9 [b]Gen. 49:27
26 [a]ver. 12; ch. 22:38
27 [a]ver. 13
28 [a]ch. 21:10
29 [a]ver. 1
24:1 [a]ch. 23:3,15 [l]Heb. *to the meeting of enchantments*
2 [a]ch. 2:2 [b]ch. 11:25; 1 Sam. 10:10 & 19:20,23; 2 Chr. 15:1
3 [a]ch. 23:7,18 [l]Heb. *who had his eyes shut,* but now opened
4 [a]See 1 Sam. 19:24; Ezek. 1:28
6 [a]Ps. 1:3; Jer. 17:8 [b]Ps. 104:16
7 [a]Jer. 51:13; Rev. 17:1,15 [b]1 Sam. 15:9 [c]2 Sam. 5:12; 1 Chr. 14:2
8 [a]ch. 23:22 [b]ch. 14:9 & 23:24 [c]Ps. 2:9; Jer. 50:17 [d]Ps. 45:5
9 [a]Gen. 49:9 [b]Gen. 12:3
10 [a]Ezek. 21:14,17 [b]ch. 23:11; Neh. 13:2
11 [a]ch. 22:17,37
13 [a]ch. 22:18
14 [a]Mic. 6:5; Rev. 2:14 [b]Gen. 49:1; Dan. 2:28

as gardens by the river's side, [a]as the trees of lign aloes [b]which the LORD hath planted, *and* as cedar trees beside the waters.

7 He shall pour the water out of his buckets, and his seed *shall be* [a]in many waters, and his king shall be higher than [b]Agag, and his [c]kingdom shall be exalted. I

8 [a]God brought him forth out of Egypt; he hath as it were the strength of an unicorn: he shall [b]eat up the nations his enemies, and shall [c]break their bones, and [d]pierce *them* through with his arrows.

9 [a]He couched, he lay down as a lion, and as a great lion: who shall stir him up? [b]Blessed *is* he that blesseth thee, and cursed *is* he that curseth thee.

10 ¶ And Balak's anger was kindled against Balaam, and he [a]smote his hands together: and Balak said unto Balaam, [b]I called thee to curse mine enemies, and, behold, thou hast altogether blessed *them* these three times.

11 Therefore now flee thou to thy place: [a]I thought to promote thee unto great honour; but, lo, the LORD hath kept thee back from honour.

12 And Balaam said unto Balak, Spake I not also to thy messengers which thou sentest unto me, saying,

13 [a]If Balak would give me his house full of silver and gold, I cannot go beyond the commandment of the LORD, to do *either* good or bad of mine own mind; *but* what the LORD saith, that will I speak?

14 And now, behold, I go unto my people: come *therefore, and* [a]I will advertise thee what this people shall do to thy people [b]in the latter days. I J

15 ¶ And he took up his parable, and said, Balaam the son of Beor hath said, and the man whose eyes are open hath said:

16 He hath said, which heard the words of God, and knew the knowledge of the most High, *which* saw the vision of the Almighty, falling *into a trance,* but having his eyes open:

A *Lev 25:8–17* ◀ ▶ *Dt 33:6*
E *Nu 14:24* ◀ ▶ *Nu 27:18*
T *Nu 11:25–29* ◀ ▶ *Dt 34:9*
I *Nu 10:29* ◀ ▶ *Nu 24:14–19*
I *Nu 24:7–9* ◀ ▶ *Nu 34:1–12*
J *Nu 14:43* ◀ ▶ *Nu 33:55–56*

M P 17 [a]I shall see him, but not now: I shall behold him, but not nigh: there shall come [b]a Star out of Jacob, and [c]a Sceptre shall rise out of Israel, and shall [d]smite[1] the corners of Moab, and destroy all the children of Sheth.

18 And [a]Edom shall be a possession, Seir also shall be a possession for his enemies; and Israel shall do valiantly.

19 [a]Out of Jacob shall come he that shall have dominion, and shall destroy him that remaineth of the city.

20 ¶ And when he looked on Amalek, he took up his parable, and said, Amalek *was* [a]the[1] first of the nations; but his latter end [b]*shall be*[2] that he perish for ever.

21 And he looked on the Kenites, and took up his parable, and said, Strong is thy dwellingplace, and thou puttest thy nest in a rock.

22 Nevertheless [1]the Kenite shall be wasted, [2]until Asshur shall carry thee away captive.

23 And he took up his parable, and said, Alas, who shall live when God doeth this!

24 And ships *shall come* from the coast of [a]Chittim, and shall afflict Asshur, and shall afflict [b]Eber, and he also shall perish for ever.

25 And Balaam rose up, and went and [a]returned to his place: and Balak also went his way.

Israel's idolatry in Shittim

25 AND ISRAEL abode in [a]Shittim, and [b]the people began to commit whoredom with the daughters of Moab.

2 And [a]they called the people unto [b]the sacrifices of their gods: and the people did eat, and [c]bowed down to their gods.

3 And Israel joined himself unto Baal-peor: and [a]the anger of the LORD was kindled against Israel.

4 And the LORD said unto Moses, [a]Take all the heads of the people, and hang them up before the LORD against the sun, [b]that the fierce anger of the LORD may be turned away from Israel.

5 And Moses said unto [a]the judges of Israel, [b]Slay ye every one his men that were joined unto Baal-peor.

6 ¶ And, behold, one of the children of Israel came and brought unto his brethren a Midianitish woman in the sight of Moses, and in the sight of all the congregation of the children of Israel, [a]who *were* weeping *before* the door of the tabernacle of the congregation.

7 And [a]when Phinehas, [b]the son of Eleazar, the son of Aaron the priest, saw *it,* he rose up from among the congregation, and took a javelin in his hand;

8 And he went after the man of Israel into the tent, and thrust both of them through, the man of Israel, and the woman through her belly. So [a]the plague was stayed from the children of Israel. D E

9 And [a]those that died in the plague were twenty and four thousand.

10 ¶ And the LORD spake unto Moses, saying,

11 [a]Phinehas, the son of Eleazar, the son of Aaron the priest, hath turned my wrath away from the children of Israel, while he was zealous [1]for my sake among them, that I consumed not the children of Israel in [b]my jealousy.

12 Wherefore say, [a]Behold, I give unto him my covenant of peace:

13 And he shall have it, and [a]his seed after him, *even* the covenant of [b]an everlasting priesthood; because he was [c]zealous for his God, and [d]made an atonement for the children of Israel.

17 [a]Rev. 1:7 [b]Mat. 2:2 [c]Gen. 49:10 [d]2 Sam. 8:2 [1]Or, *smite through the princes of Moab*
18 [a]2 Sam. 8:14
19 [a]Gen. 49:10
20 [a]Ex. 17:8 [b]Ex. 17:14 [1]Or, *the first of the nations that warred against Israel* [2]Or, shall be *even to destruction*
22 [1]Heb. *Kain* [2]Or, *how long* shall it be ere *Asshur carry thee away captive?*
24 [a]Gen. 10:4 [b]Gen. 10:21,25
25 [a]See ch. 31:8
25:1 [a]ch. 33:49; Josh. 2:1 [b]1 Cor. 10:8
2 [a]Josh. 22:17; Hos. 9:10 [b]Ex. 34:15 [c]Ex. 20:5
3 [a]Ps. 106:29
4 [a]Deut. 4:3 [b]ver. 11; Deut. 13:17
5 [a]Ex. 18:21 [b]Deut. 13:6,9
6 [a]Joel 2:17
7 [a]Ps. 106:30 [b]Ex. 6:25
8 [a]Ps. 106:30
9 [a]Deut. 4:3; 1 Cor. 10:8
11 [a]Ps. 106:30 [b]Ex. 20:5; Ps. 78:58; Ezek. 16:38 [1]Heb. *with my zeal*
12 [a]Mal. 2:4,5
13 [a]See 1 Chr. 6:4 [b]Ex. 40:15 [c]Acts 22:3; Rom. 10:2 [d]Heb. 2:17

M *Nu 14:21* ◀ ▶ *1Sa 2:10* **P** ▶ *Dt 32:22*
D *Nu 21:6* ◀ ▶ *Dt 7:15*
E *Nu 21:7–9* ◀ ▶ *Dt 8:4*

24:17 Though this prophecy was initially fulfilled in David's victory over the Moabites and Edomites (see 2Sa 8:2–14), this verse foreshadows the greater victory of Christ's second coming. This oracle describes the Messiah as "a Star out of Jacob, and a Sceptre . . . out of Israel." It is possible that Balaam's words gave direction to the wise men who saw an unusual star over the land of Judah and went to look for the one "born King of the Jews" (Mt 2:2).

24:19 This prophecy of the rise of the Messiah from the tribe of Jacob confirms the earlier prediction that the "sceptre shall not depart from Judah, nor a lawgiver from between his feet, until Shiloh come" (Ge 49:10).

24:20–24 Amalek was the first of the pagan nations to fight and oppose Israel in the wilderness (see Ex 17:8–16). At that time God promised to annihilate the Amalekites. Balaam's prophecy in these verses confirms God's intent toward Amalek.

14 Now the name of the Israelite that was slain, *even* that was slain with the Midianitish woman, *was* Zimri, the son of Salu, a prince of a [l]chief house among the Simeonites.

15 And the name of the Midianitish woman that was slain *was* Cozbi, the daughter of [a]Zur; he *was* head over a people, *and* of a chief house in Midian.

16 ¶ And the LORD spake unto Moses, saying,

17 [a]Vex the Midianites, and smite them:

18 For they vex you with their [a]wiles, wherewith they have beguiled you in the matter of Peor, and in the matter of Cozbi, the daughter of a prince of Midian, their sister, which was slain in the day of the plague for Peor's sake.

Israel's second census

26 AND IT came to pass after the plague, that the LORD spake unto Moses and unto Eleazar the son of Aaron the priest, saying,

2 [a]Take the sum of all the congregation of the children of Israel, [b]from twenty years old and upward, throughout their fathers' house, all that are able to go to war in Israel.

3 And Moses and Eleazar the priest spake with them [a]in the plains of Moab by Jordan *near* Jericho, saying,

4 *Take the sum of the people,* from twenty years old and upward; as the LORD [a]commanded Moses and the children of Israel, which went forth out of the land of Egypt.

5 ¶ [a]Reuben, the eldest son of Israel: the children of Reuben; Hanoch, *of whom cometh* the family of the Hanochites: of Pallu, the family of the Palluites:

6 Of Hezron, the family of the Hezronites: of Carmi, the family of the Carmites.

7 These *are* the families of the Reubenites: and they that were numbered of them were forty and three thousand and seven hundred and thirty.

8 And the sons of Pallu; Eliab.

9 And the sons of Eliab; Nemuel, and Dathan, and Abiram. This *is that* Dathan and Abiram, *which were* [a]famous in the congregation, who strove against Moses and against Aaron in the company of Korah, when they strove against the LORD:

10 [a]And the earth opened her mouth, and swallowed them up together with Korah, when that company died, what time the fire devoured two hundred and fifty men: [b]and they became a sign.

11 Notwithstanding [a]the children of Korah died not.

12 ¶ The sons of Simeon after their families: of [a]Nemuel, the family of the Nemuelites: of Jamin, the family of the Jaminites: of [b]Jachin, the family of the Jachinites:

13 Of [a]Zerah, the family of the Zarhites: of Shaul, the family of the Shaulites.

14 These *are* the families of the Simeonites, twenty and two thousand and two hundred.

15 ¶ The children of Gad after their families: of [a]Zephon, the family of the Zephonites: of Haggi, the family of the Haggites: of Shuni, the family of the Shunites:

16 Of [l]Ozni, the family of the Oznites: of Eri, the family of the Erites:

17 Of [a]Arod, the family of the Arodites: of Areli, the family of the Arelites.

18 These *are* the families of the children of Gad according to those that were numbered of them, forty thousand and five hundred.

19 ¶ [a]The sons of Judah *were* Er and Onan: and Er and Onan died in the land of Canaan.

20 And [a]the sons of Judah after their families were; of Shelah, the family of the Shelanites: of Pharez, the family of the Pharzites: of Zerah, the family of the Zarhites.

21 And the sons of Pharez were; of Hezron, the family of the Hezronites: of Hamul, the family of the Hamulites.

22 These *are* the families of Judah according to those that were numbered of them, threescore and sixteen thousand and five hundred.

23 ¶ [a]*Of* the sons of Issachar after their families: *of* Tola, the family of the Tolaites: of [l]Pua, the family of the Punites:

24 Of [l]Jashub, the family of the Jashubites: of Shimron, the family of the Shimronites.

25 These *are* the families of Issachar according to those that were numbered of them, threescore and four thousand and three hundred.

26 ¶ [a]*Of* the sons of Zebulun after their families: of Sered, the family of the

14 [l]Heb. *house of a father*
15 [a]ch. 31:8; Josh. 13:21
17 [a]ch. 31:2
18 [a]ch. 31:16; Rev. 2:14
26:2 [a]Ex. 30:12 & 38:25,26; ch. 1:2 [b]ch. 1:3
3 [a]ver. 63; ch. 22:1 & 31:12 & 33:48 & 35:1
4 [a]ch. 1:1
5 [a]Gen. 46:8; Ex. 6:14; 1 Chr. 5:1
9 [a]ch. 16:1,2
10 [a]ch. 16:32,35 [b]ch. 16:38; See 1 Cor. 10:6; 2 Pet. 2:6
11 [a]Ex. 6:24; 1 Chr. 6:22
12 [a]Gen. 46:10; Ex. 6:15 *Jemuel* [b]1 Chr. 4:24 *Jarib*
13 [a]Gen. 46:10 *Zohar*
15 [a]Gen. 46:16 *Ziphion*
16 [l]Or, *Ezbon* see Gen. 46:16
17 [a]Gen. 46:16 *Arodi*
19 [a]Gen. 38:2 & 46:12
20 [a]1 Chr. 2:3
23 [a]Gen. 46:13; 1 Chr. 7:1 [l]Or, *Phuvah*
24 [l]Or, *Job*
26 [a]Gen. 46:14

Sardites: of Elon, the family of the Elon-
ites: of Jahleel, the family of the Jahle-
elites.
27 These *are* the families of the Zebu-
lunites according to those that were numbered of them, threescore thousand and
five hundred.
28 ¶ [a]The sons of Joseph after their
families *were* Manasseh and Ephraim.
29 Of the sons of Manasseh: of [a]Ma-
chir, the family of the Machirites: and
Machir begat Gilead: of Gilead *come* the
family of the Gileadites.
30 These *are* the sons of Gilead: *of* [a]Je-
ezer, the family of the Jeezerites: of Helek, the family of the Helekites:
31 And *of* Asriel, the family of the As-
rielites: and *of* Shechem, the family of the
Shechemites:
32 And *of* Shemida, the family of the
Shemidaites: and *of* Hepher, the family of
the Hepherites.
33 ¶ And [a]Zelophehad the son of Hepher had no sons, but daughters: and the
names of the daughters of Zelophehad
were Mahlah, and Noah, Hoglah, Milcah,
and Tirzah.
34 These *are* the families of Manasseh,
and those that were numbered of them,
fifty and two thousand and seven
hundred.
35 ¶ These *are* the sons of Ephraim after their families: of Shuthelah, the family
of the Shuthalhites: of [a]Becher, the family of the Bachrites: of Tahan, the family
of the Tahanites.
36 And these *are* the sons of Shuthelah: of Eran, the family of the Eranites.
37 These *are* the families of the sons
of Ephraim according to those that were
numbered of them, thirty and two thousand and five hundred. These *are* the
sons of Joseph after their families.
38 ¶ [a]The sons of Benjamin after their
families: of Bela, the family of the Be-
laites: of Ashbel, the family of the Ashbel-
ites: of [b]Ahiram, the family of the Ahi-
ramites:
39 Of [a]Shupham, the family of the
Shuphamites: of Hupham, the family of
the Huphamites.
40 And the sons of Bela were [a]Ard and
Naaman: *of Ard,* the family of the Ar-
dites: *and* of Naaman, the family of the
Naamites.
41 These *are* the sons of Benjamin after their families: and they that were
numbered of them *were* forty and five
thousand and six hundred.
42 ¶ [a]These *are* the sons of Dan after
their families: of [1]Shuham, the family of
the Shuhamites. These *are* the families of
Dan after their families.
43 All the families of the Shuhamites,
according to those that were numbered
of them, *were* threescore and four thousand and four hundred.
44 ¶ [a]*Of* the children of Asher after
their families: of Jimna, the family of the
Jimnites: of Jesui, the family of the Je-
suites: of Beriah, the family of the Be-
riites.
45 Of the sons of Beriah: of Heber, the
family of the Heberites: of Malchiel, the
family of the Malchielites.
46 And the name of the daughter of
Asher *was* Sarah.
47 These *are* the families of the sons of
Asher according to those that were numbered of them; *who were* fifty and three
thousand and four hundred.
48 ¶ [a]*Of* the sons of Naphtali after
their families: of Jahzeel, the family of the
Jahzeelites: of Guni, the family of the Gu-
nites:
49 Of Jezer, the family of the Jezerites:
of [a]Shillem, the family of the Shillemites.
50 These *are* the families of Naphtali
according to their families: and they that
were numbered of them *were* forty and
five thousand and four hundred.
51 [a]These *were* the numbered of the
children of Israel, six hundred thousand
and a thousand seven hundred and thirty.
52 ¶ And the LORD spake unto Moses,
saying,
53 [a]Unto these the land shall be di-

28 [a]Gen. 46:20
29 [a]Josh. 17:1; 1 Chr. 7:14,15
30 [a]Called *Abiezer* Josh. 17:2; Judg. 6:11,24,34
33 [a]ch. 27:1 & 36:11
35 [a]1 Chr. 7:20 *Bered*
38 [a]Gen. 46:21; 1 Chr. 7:6 [b]Gen. 46:21 *Ehi;* 1 Chr. 8:1 *Aharah*
39 [a]Gen. 46:21 *Muppim and Huppim*
40 [a]1 Chr. 8:3 *Addar*
42 [a]Gen. 46:23 [1]Or, *Hushim*
44 [a]Gen. 46:17; 1 Chr. 7:30
48 [a]Gen. 46:24; 1 Chr. 7:13
49 [a]1 Chr. 7:13 *Shallum*
51 [a]See ch. 1:46
53 [a]Josh. 11:23 & 14:1

26:51–53 The second census of the Israelites yielded an astonishing result. Though the Israelites had spent forty years in the wilderness as a result of their sinful rebellion and an entire generation had died, the new census was nearly the same as the first. Of the 603,550 original adults, all but Joshua and Caleb died in the desert as decreed by the Lord (see 26:64–65). God replaced the rebellious generation of Israelite slaves with a new generation totaling 601,730 born in the freedom of the desert. This new generation eagerly awaited their land allotments following the conquest of the promised land.

vided for an inheritance according to the
number of names.
54 [a]To many thou shalt [1]give the more
inheritance, and to few thou shalt [2]give
the less inheritance: to every one shall
his inheritance be given according to
those that were numbered of him.
55 Notwithstanding the land shall be
[a]divided by lot: according to the names of
the tribes of their fathers they shall inherit.
56 According to the lot shall the possession thereof be divided between many
and few.
57 ¶ [a]And these *are* they that were
numbered of the Levites after their families: of Gershon, the family of the Gershonites: of Kohath, the family of the Kohathites: of Merari, the family of the
Merarites.
58 These *are* the families of the Levites: the family of the Libnites, the family of the Hebronites, the family of the
Mahlites, the family of the Mushites, the
family of the Korathites. And Kohath begat Amram.
59 And the name of Amram's wife *was*
[a]Jochebed, the daughter of Levi, whom
her mother bare to Levi in Egypt: and she
bare unto Amram Aaron and Moses, and
Miriam their sister.
60 [a]And unto Aaron was born Nadab,
and Abihu, Eleazar, and Ithamar.
61 And [a]Nadab and Abihu died, when
they offered strange fire before the LORD.
62 [a]And those that were numbered of
them were twenty and three thousand,
all males from a month old and upward:
[b]for they were not numbered among the
children of Israel, because there was [c]no
inheritance given them among the children of Israel.
63 ¶ These *are* they that were numbered by Moses and Eleazar the priest,
who numbered the children of Israel [a]in
the plains of Moab by Jordan *near*
Jericho.
64 [a]But among these there was not a
man of them whom Moses and Aaron the
priest numbered, when they numbered
the children of Israel in the wilderness of
Sinai.
65 For the LORD had said of them, They
[a]shall surely die in the wilderness. And
there was not left a man of them, [b]save
Caleb the son of Jephunneh, and Joshua
the son of Nun.

The daughters of Zelophehad

27 THEN CAME the daughters of
[a]Zelophehad, the son of Hepher,
the son of Gilead, the son of Machir, the
son of Manasseh, of the families of Manasseh the son of Joseph: and these *are*
the names of his daughters; Mahlah,
Noah, and Hoglah, and Milcah, and
Tirzah.
2 And they stood before Moses, and
before Eleazar the priest, and before the
princes and all the congregation, *by* the
door of the tabernacle of the congregation, saying,
3 Our father [a]died in the wilderness,
and he was not in the company of them
that gathered themselves together against
the LORD [b]in the company of Korah;
but died in his own sin, and had no
sons.
4 Why should the name of our father
be [1]done away from among his family,
because he hath no son? [a]Give unto us
therefore a possession among the brethren of our father.
5 And Moses [a]brought their cause before the LORD.
6 ¶ And the LORD spake unto Moses,
saying,
7 The daughters of Zelophehad speak
right: [a]thou shalt surely give them a possession of an inheritance among their father's brethren; and thou shalt cause the
inheritance of their father to pass unto
them.
8 And thou shalt speak unto the children of Israel, saying, If a man die, and
have no son, then ye shall cause his inheritance to pass unto his daughter.
9 And if he have no daughter, then ye
shall give his inheritance unto his
brethren.
10 And if he have no brethren, then ye
shall give his inheritance unto his father's
brethren.
11 And if his father have no brethren,
then ye shall give his inheritance unto his
kinsman that is next to him of his family,
and he shall possess it: and it shall be
unto the children of Israel [a]a statute of
judgment, as the LORD commanded
Moses.

Joshua to succeed Moses

12 ¶ And the LORD said unto Moses,
[a]Get thee up into this mount Abarim,

54 [a]ch. 33:54 [1]Heb. *multiply his inheritance* [2]Heb. *diminish his inheritance*
55 [a]ch. 33:54 & 34:13; Josh. 11:23 & 14:2
57 [a]Gen. 46:11; Ex. 6:16-19; 1 Chr. 6:1,16
59 [a]Ex. 2:1,2 & 6:20
60 [a]ch. 3:2
61 [a]Lev. 10:1,2; ch. 3:4; 1 Chr. 24:2
62 [a]See ch. 3:39 [b]ch. 1:49 [c]ch. 18:20,23,24; Deut. 10:9; Josh. 13:14, 33
63 [a]ver. 3
64 [a]ch. 1; Deut. 2:14,15
65 [a]ch. 14:28,29; 1 Cor. 10:5,6 [b]ch. 14:30
27:1 [a]ch. 26:33 & 36:1,11; Josh. 17:3
3 [a]ch. 14:35 & 26:64,65 [b]ch. 16:1,2
4 [a]Josh. 17:4 [1]Heb. *diminished*
5 [a]Ex. 18:15,19
7 [a]ch. 36:2
11 [a]ch. 35:29
12 [a]ch. 33:47; Deut. 3:27 & 32:49

and see the land which I have given unto the children of Israel.

Q 13 And when thou hast seen it, thou also [a]shalt be gathered unto thy people, as Aaron thy brother was gathered.

14 For ye [a]rebelled against my commandment in the desert of Zin, in the strife of the congregation, to sanctify me at the water before their eyes: that *is* the [b]water of Meribah in Kadesh in the wilderness of Zin.

15 ¶ And Moses spake unto the LORD, saying,

16 Let the LORD, [a]the God of the spirits of all flesh, set a man over the congregation,

17 [a]Which may go out before them, and which may go in before them, and which may lead them out, and which may bring them in; that the congregation of the LORD be not [b]as sheep which have no shepherd.

B 18 ¶ And the LORD said unto Moses,
E Take thee Joshua the son of Nun, a man
[a]in whom *is* the spirit, and [b]lay thine
hand upon him;

19 And set him before Eleazar the priest, and before all the congregation; and [a]give him a charge in their sight.

20 And [a]thou shalt put *some* of thine honour upon him, that all the congregation of the children of Israel [b]may be obedient.

21 [a]And he shall stand before Eleazar the priest, who shall ask *counsel* for him [b]after the judgment of Urim before the LORD: [c]at his word shall they go out, and at his word they shall come in, *both* he, and all the children of Israel with him, even all the congregation.

22 And Moses did as the LORD commanded him: and he took Joshua, and set him before Eleazar the priest, and before all the congregation:

23 And he laid his hands upon him, [a]and gave him a charge, as the LORD commanded by the hand of Moses.

Q *Nu 20:26* ◀▶ *Nu 31:2*
B *Ex 35:31* ◀▶ *Dt 34:9*
E *Nu 24:2* ◀▶ *Dt 34:9*

13 [a]ch. 20:24,28 & 31:2; Deut. 10:6
14 [a]ch. 20:12,24; Deut. 1:37 & 32:51; Ps. 106:32 [b]Ex. 17:7
16 [a]ch. 16:22; Heb. 12:9
17 [a]Deut. 31:2; 1 Sam. 8:20 & 18:13; 2 Chr. 1:10 [b]1 Ki. 22:17; Zech. 10:2; Mat. 9:36; Mark 6:34
18 [a]Gen. 41:38; Judg. 3:10; 1 Sam. 16:13,18 [b]Deut. 34:9
19 [a]Deut. 31:7
20 [a]See ch. 11:17, 28 [b]Josh. 1:16,17
21 [a]Judg. 20:18, 23,26; 1 Sam. 23:9 & 30:7 [b]Ex. 28:30 [c]Josh. 9:14; 1 Sam. 22:10,13,15
23 [a]Deut. 3:28 & 31:7
28:2 [a]Lev. 3:11 & 21:6,8; Mal. 1:7,12 [ʹ]Heb. *a savour of my rest*
3 [a]Ex. 29:38 [ʹ]Heb. *in a day*
4 [ʹ]Heb. *between the two evenings*
5 [a]Ex. 16:36; ch. 15:4 [b]Lev. 2:1 [c]Ex. 29:40
6 [a]Ex. 29:42; See Amos 5:25
7 [a]Ex. 29:42
10 [a]Ezek. 46:4
11 [a]ch. 10:10; 1 Sam. 20:5; 1 Chr. 23:31; 2 Chr. 2:4; Ezra 3:5; Neh. 10:33; Is. 1:13,14; Ezek. 45:17 & 46:6; Hos. 2:11; Col. 2:16

The daily burnt offering

28 AND THE LORD spake unto Moses, saying,

2 Command the children of Israel, and say unto them, My offering, *and* [a]my bread for my sacrifices made by fire, *for* [ʹ]a sweet savour unto me, shall ye observe to offer unto me in their due season.

3 And thou shalt say unto them, [a]This D
is the offering made by fire which ye shall offer unto the LORD; two lambs of the first year without spot [ʹ]day by day, *for* a continual burnt offering.

4 The one lamb shalt thou offer in the morning, and the other lamb shalt thou offer [ʹ]at even;

5 And [a]a tenth *part* of an ephah of flour for a [b]meat offering, mingled with the fourth *part* of an [c]hin of beaten oil.

6 *It is* [a]a continual burnt offering, which was ordained in mount Sinai for a sweet savour, a sacrifice made by fire unto the LORD.

7 And the drink offering thereof *shall be* the fourth *part* of an hin for the one lamb: [a]in the holy *place* shalt thou cause the strong wine to be poured unto the LORD *for* a drink offering.

8 And the other lamb shalt thou offer at even: as the meat offering of the morning, and as the drink offering thereof, thou shalt offer *it,* a sacrifice made by fire, of a sweet savour unto the LORD.

The offering on the Sabbath

9 ¶ And on the sabbath day two lambs of the first year without spot, and two tenth deals of flour *for* a meat offering, mingled with oil, and the drink offering thereof:

10 *This is* [a]the burnt offering of every sabbath, beside the continual burnt offering, and his drink offering.

The offering at the new moon

11 ¶ And [a]in the beginnings of your months ye shall offer a burnt offering unto the LORD; two young bullocks, and one ram, seven lambs of the first year without spot;

D *Nu 21:6–9* ◀▶ *Dt 15:21*

27:13–14 The Lord allowed Moses a glimpse of the promised land from the top of the mountain, but reconfirmed his judgment on Moses' unfaithfulness at Meribah. Moses' sin and failure to believe God and honor him cost Moses the blessing of entering Canaan. See note at 20:12.

12 And [a]three tenth deals of flour *for* a meat offering, mingled with oil, for one bullock; and two tenth deals of flour *for* a meat offering, mingled with oil, for one ram;

13 And a several tenth deal of flour mingled with oil *for* a meat offering unto one lamb; *for* a burnt offering of a sweet savour, a sacrifice made by fire unto the LORD.

14 And their drink offerings shall be half an hin of wine unto a bullock, and the third *part* of an hin unto a ram, and a fourth *part* of an hin unto a lamb: this *is* the burnt offering of every month throughout the months of the year.

15 And [a]one kid of the goats for a sin offering unto the LORD shall be offered, beside the continual burnt offering, and his drink offering.

The feast of unleavened bread

16 [a]And in the fourteenth day of the first month *is* the passover of the LORD.

17 [a]And in the fifteenth day of this month *is* the feast: seven days shall unleavened bread be eaten.

18 In the [a]first day *shall be* an holy convocation; ye shall do no manner of servile work *therein:*

19 But ye shall offer a sacrifice made by fire *for* a burnt offering unto the LORD; two young bullocks, and one ram, and seven lambs of the first year: [a]they shall be unto you without blemish:

20 And their meat offering *shall be of* flour mingled with oil: three tenth deals shall ye offer for a bullock, and two tenth deals for a ram;

21 A several tenth deal shalt thou offer for every lamb, throughout the seven lambs:

22 And [a]one goat *for* a sin offering, to make an atonement for you.

23 Ye shall offer these beside the burnt offering in the morning, which *is* for a continual burnt offering.

24 After this manner ye shall offer daily, throughout the seven days, the meat of the sacrifice made by fire, of a sweet savour unto the LORD: it shall be offered beside the continual burnt offering, and his drink offering.

25 And [a]on the seventh day ye shall have an holy convocation; ye shall do no servile work.

26 ¶ Also [a]in the day of the firstfruits, when ye bring a new meat offering unto the LORD, after your weeks *be out,* ye shall have an holy convocation; ye shall do no servile work:

27 But ye shall offer the burnt offering for a sweet savour unto the LORD; [a]two young bullocks, one ram, seven lambs of the first year;

28 And their meat offering of flour mingled with oil, three tenth deals unto one bullock, two tenth deals unto one ram,

29 A several tenth deal unto one lamb, throughout the seven lambs;

30 *And* one kid of the goats, to make an atonement for you.

31 Ye shall offer *them* beside the continual burnt offering, and his meat offering, ([a]they shall be unto you without blemish) and their drink offerings.

Feast of the trumpets offerings

29 AND IN the seventh month, on the first *day* of the month, ye shall have an holy convocation; ye shall do no servile work: [a]it is a day of blowing the trumpets unto you.

2 And ye shall offer a burnt offering for a sweet savour unto the LORD; one young bullock, one ram, *and* seven lambs of the first year without blemish:

3 And their meat offering *shall be of* flour mingled with oil, three tenth deals for a bullock, *and* two tenth deals for a ram,

4 And one tenth deal for one lamb, throughout the seven lambs:

5 And one kid of the goats *for* a sin offering, to make an atonement for you:

6 Beside [a]the burnt offering of the month, and his meat offering, and [b]the daily burnt offering, and his meat offering, and their drink offerings, [c]according unto their manner, for a sweet savour, a sacrifice made by fire unto the LORD.

Day of Atonement offerings

7 ¶ And [a]ye shall have on the tenth *day* of this seventh month an holy convocation; and ye shall [b]afflict your souls: ye shall not do any work *therein:*

8 But ye shall offer a burnt offering unto the LORD *for* a sweet savour; one young bullock, one ram, *and* seven lambs of the first year; [a]they shall be unto you without blemish:

9 And their meat offering *shall be of*

---

12 [a]ch. 15:4-12
15 [a]ver. 22; ch. 15:24
16 [a]Ex. 12:6,18; Lev. 23:5; ch. 9:3; Deut. 16:1; Ezek. 45:21
17 [a]Lev. 23:6
18 [a]Ex. 12:16; Lev. 23:7
19 [a]ver. 31; Lev. 22:20; ch. 29:8; Deut. 15:21
22 [a]ver. 15
25 [a]Ex. 13:6; Lev. 23:8
26 [a]Ex. 23:16 & 34:22; Lev. 23:10, 15; Deut. 16:10; Acts 2:1
27 [a]See Lev. 23:18,19
31 [a]ver. 19
29:1 [a]Lev. 23:24
6 [a]ch. 28:11 [b]ch. 28:3 [c]ch. 15:11,12
7 [a]Lev. 16:29 & 23:27 [b]Ps. 35:13; Is. 58:5
8 [a]ch. 28:19

flour mingled with oil, three tenth deals to a bullock, *and* two tenth deals to one ram,

10 A several tenth deal for one lamb, throughout the seven lambs:

11 One kid of the goats *for* a sin offering; beside [a]the sin offering of atonement, and the continual burnt offering, and the meat offering of it, and their drink offerings.

Feast of tabernacles offerings

12 ¶ And [a]on the fifteenth day of the seventh month ye shall have an holy convocation; ye shall do no servile work, and ye shall keep a feast unto the LORD seven days:

13 And [a]ye shall offer a burnt offering, a sacrifice made by fire, of a sweet savour unto the LORD; thirteen young bullocks, two rams, *and* fourteen lambs of the first year; they shall be without blemish:

14 And their meat offering *shall be of* flour mingled with oil, three tenth deals unto every bullock of the thirteen bullocks, two tenth deals to each ram of the two rams,

15 And a several tenth deal to each lamb of the fourteen lambs:

16 And one kid of the goats *for* a sin offering; beside the continual burnt offering, his meat offering, and his drink offering.

17 ¶ And on the second day *ye shall offer* twelve young bullocks, two rams, fourteen lambs of the first year without spot:

18 And their meat offering and their drink offerings for the bullocks, for the rams, and for the lambs, *shall be* according to their number, [a]after the manner:

19 And one kid of the goats *for* a sin offering; beside the continual burnt offering, and the meat offering thereof, and their drink offerings.

20 ¶ And on the third day eleven bullocks, two rams, fourteen lambs of the first year without blemish;

21 And their meat offering and their drink offerings for the bullocks, for the rams, and for the lambs, *shall be* according to their number, [a]after the manner:

22 And one goat *for* a sin offering; beside the continual burnt offering, and his meat offering, and his drink offering.

23 ¶ And on the fourth day ten bullocks, two rams, *and* fourteen lambs of the first year without blemish:

24 Their meat offering and their drink offerings for the bullocks, for the rams, and for the lambs, *shall be* according to their number, after the manner:

25 And one kid of the goats *for* a sin offering; beside the continual burnt offering, his meat offering, and his drink offering.

26 ¶ And on the fifth day nine bullocks, two rams, *and* fourteen lambs of the first year [a]without spot:

27 And their meat offering and their drink offerings for the bullocks, for the rams, and for the lambs, *shall be* according to their number, after the manner:

28 And one goat *for* a sin offering; beside the continual burnt offering, and his meat offering, and his drink offering.

29 ¶ And on the sixth day eight bullocks, two rams, *and* fourteen lambs of the first year without blemish:

30 And their meat offering and their drink offerings for the bullocks, for the rams, and for the lambs, *shall be* according to their number, after the manner:

31 And one goat *for* a sin offering; beside the continual burnt offering, his meat offering, and his drink offering.

32 ¶ And on the seventh day seven bullocks, two rams, *and* fourteen lambs of the first year without blemish:

33 And their meat offering and their drink offerings for the bullocks, for the rams, and for the lambs, *shall be* according to their number, after the manner:

34 And one goat *for* a sin offering; beside the continual burnt offering, his meat offering, and his drink offering.

35 ¶ On the eighth day ye shall have a [a]solemn assembly: ye shall do no servile work *therein:*

36 But ye shall offer a burnt offering, a sacrifice made by fire, of a sweet savour unto the LORD: one bullock, one ram, seven lambs of the first year without blemish:

37 Their meat offering and their drink offerings for the bullock, for the ram, and for the lambs, *shall be* according to their number, after the manner:

38 And one goat *for* a sin offering; beside the continual burnt offering, and his meat offering, and his drink offering.

39 These *things* ye shall [l]do unto the LORD in your [a]set feasts, beside your

11 [a]Lev. 16:3,5
12 [a]Lev. 23:34; Deut. 16:13; Ezek. 45:25
13 [a]Ezra 3:4; Dan. 9:24; Heb. 7:18,19 & 8:13 & 10:1-18
18 [a]ver. 3,4,9,10; ch. 15:12 & 28:7, 14
21 [a]ver. 18
26 [a]Heb. 7:26; 1 Pet. 1:19; Rev. 5:6-14
35 [a]Lev. 23:36
39 [a]Lev. 23:2; 1 Chr. 23:31; 2 Chr. 31:3; Ezra 3:5; Neh. 10:33; Is. 1:14 [l]Or, *offer*

[b]vows, and your freewill offerings, for your burnt offerings, and for your meat offerings, and for your drink offerings, and for your peace offerings.

40 And Moses told the children of Israel according to all that the LORD commanded Moses.

The laws about vows

30 AND MOSES spake unto [a]the heads of the tribes concerning the children of Israel, saying, This *is* the thing which the LORD hath commanded.

2 [a]If a man vow a vow unto the LORD, or [b]swear an oath to bind his soul with a bond; he shall not [/]break his word, he shall [c]do according to all that proceedeth out of his mouth.

3 If a woman also vow a vow unto the LORD, and bind *herself* by a bond, *being* in her father's house in her youth;

4 And her father hear her vow, and her bond wherewith she hath bound her soul, and her father shall hold his peace at her: then all her vows shall stand, and every bond wherewith she hath bound her soul shall stand.

5 But if her father disallow her in the day that he heareth; not any of her vows, or of her bonds wherewith she hath bound her soul, shall stand: and the LORD shall forgive her, because her father disallowed her.

6 And if she had at all an husband, when [a]she[/] vowed, or uttered aught out of her lips, wherewith she bound her soul;

7 And her husband heard *it,* and held his peace at her in the day that he heard *it:* then her vows shall stand, and her bonds wherewith she bound her soul shall stand.

8 But if her husband [a]disallowed her on the day that he heard *it;* then he shall make her vow which she vowed, and that which she uttered with her lips, wherewith she bound her soul, of none effect: and the LORD shall forgive her.

9 But every vow of a widow, and of her that is divorced, wherewith they have bound their souls, shall stand against her.

10 And if she vowed in her husband's house, or bound her soul by a bond with an oath;

11 And her husband heard *it,* and held his peace at her, *and* disallowed her not: then all her vows shall stand, and every bond wherewith she bound her soul shall stand.

12 But if her husband [/]hath utterly made them void on the day he heard *them; then* whatsoever proceeded out of her lips concerning her vows, or concerning the bond of her soul, shall not stand: her husband hath made them void; and the LORD shall forgive her.

13 Every vow, and every binding oath to afflict the soul, her husband may establish it, or her husband may make it void.

14 But if her husband altogether hold his peace at her from day to day; then he establisheth all her vows, or all her bonds, which *are* upon her: he confirmeth them, because he held his peace at her in the day that he heard *them.*

15 But if he shall any ways make them void after that he hath heard *them;* then he shall bear her iniquity.

16 These *are* the statutes, which the LORD commanded Moses, between a man and his wife, between the father and his daughter, *being yet* in her youth in her father's house.

The killing of the Midianites

31 AND THE LORD spake unto Moses, saying,

2 [a]Avenge the children of Israel of the Midianites: afterward shalt thou [b]be gathered unto thy people. Q

3 And Moses spake unto the people, saying, Arm some of yourselves unto the war, and let them go against the Midianites, and avenge the LORD of Midian.

4 [/]Of every tribe a thousand, throughout all the tribes of Israel, shall ye send to the war.

5 So there were delivered out of the thousands of Israel, a thousand of *every* tribe, twelve thousand armed for war.

6 And Moses sent them to the war, a

Q *Nu 27:13* ◀ ▶ *Dt 32:50*

39 [b]Lev. 7:11,16 & 22:21,23

30:1 [a]ch. 1:4,16 & 7:2

2 [a]Lev. 27:2; Deut. 23:21; Judg. 11:30, 35; Eccl. 5:4 [b]Lev. 5:4; Mat. 14:9; Acts 23:14 [c]Job 22:27; Ps. 22:25 & 50:14 & 66:13,14 & 116:14,18; Nah. 1:15 [/]Heb. *profane*

6 [a]Ps. 56:12 [/]Heb. *her vows were upon her*

8 [a]Gen. 3:16

12 [/]Heb. *making void hath made them void*

31:2 [a]ch. 25:17 [b]ch. 27:13

4 [/]Heb. *A thousand of a tribe, a thousand of a tribe*

31:2 God confirmed that Moses death was imminent but promised that Moses would "be gathered unto" his people. The repetition of this promise in Scripture reflects the Hebrew belief that godly individuals will be reunited with their godly ancestors in heaven and will one day be resurrected. See note at Ge 35:29.

thousand of *every* tribe, them and Phinehas the son of Eleazar the priest, to the
war, with the holy instruments, and [a]the
trumpets to blow in his hand.
7 And they warred against the Midianites, as the LORD commanded Moses; and
[a]they slew all the [b]males.
8 And they slew the kings of Midian,
beside the rest of them that were slain;
namely, [a]Evi, and Rekem, and Zur, and
Hur, and Reba, five kings of Midian: [b]Ba-
laam also the son of Beor they slew with
the sword.
9 And the children of Israel took *all* the
women of Midian captives, and their little ones, and took the spoil of all their
cattle, and all their flocks, and all their
goods.
10 And they burnt all their cities
wherein they dwelt, and all their goodly
castles, with fire.
11 And [a]they took all the spoil, and all
the prey, *both* of men and of beasts.
12 And they brought the captives, and
the prey, and the spoil, unto Moses, and
Eleazar the priest, and unto the congregation of the children of Israel, unto the
camp at the plains of Moab, which *are* by
Jordan *near* Jericho.

Purification of those who killed

13 ¶ And Moses, and Eleazar the
priest, and all the princes of the congregation, went forth to meet them without
the camp.
14 And Moses was wroth with the officers of the host, *with* the captains over
thousands, and captains over hundreds,
which came from the [l]battle.
15 And Moses said unto them, Have ye
saved [a]all the women alive?
16 Behold, [a]these caused the children
of Israel, through the [b]counsel of Balaam,
to commit trespass against the LORD in the
matter of Peor, and [c]there was a plague
among the congregation of the LORD.
17 Now therefore [a]kill every male
among the little ones, and kill every
woman that hath known man by lying
with [l]him.
18 But all the women children, that
have not known a man by lying with him,
keep alive for yourselves.
19 And [a]do ye abide without the camp
seven days: whosoever hath killed any
person, and [b]whosoever hath touched
any slain, purify *both* yourselves and your
captives on the third day, and on the seventh day.
20 And purify all *your* raiment, and all
[l]that is made of skins, and all work of
goats' *hair,* and all things made of wood.
21 ¶ And Eleazar the priest said unto
the men of war which went to the battle,
This *is* the ordinance of the law which
the LORD commanded Moses;
22 Only the gold, and the silver, the
brass, the iron, the tin, and the lead,
23 Every thing that may abide the fire,
ye shall make *it* go through the fire, and it
shall be clean: nevertheless it shall be purified [a]with the water of separation: and
all that abideth not the fire ye shall make
go through the water.
24 [a]And ye shall wash your clothes on
the seventh day, and ye shall be clean,
and afterward ye shall come into the
camp.

The division of the prey

25 ¶ And the LORD spake unto Moses,
saying,
26 Take the sum of the prey [l]that was
taken, *both* of man and of beast, thou,
and Eleazar the priest, and the chief fathers of the congregation:
27 And [a]divide the prey into two
parts; between them that took the war
upon them, who went out to battle, and
between all the congregation:
28 And levy a tribute unto the LORD of
the men of war which went out to battle:
[a]one soul of five hundred, *both* of the
persons, and of the beeves, and of the
asses, and of the sheep:
29 Take *it* of their half, and give *it* unto
Eleazar the priest, *for* an heave offering of
the LORD.
30 And of the children of Israel's half,
thou shalt take [a]one portion of fifty, of
the persons, of the beeves, of the asses,
and of the [l]flocks, of all manner of beasts,
and give them unto the Levites, [b]which
keep the charge of the tabernacle of the
LORD.
31 And Moses and Eleazar the priest
did as the LORD commanded Moses.
32 And the booty, *being* the rest of the
prey which the men of war had caught,
was six hundred thousand and seventy
thousand and five thousand sheep,
33 And threescore and twelve thousand beeves,

6 [a]ch. 10:9
7 [a]Deut. 20:13; Judg. 21:11; 1 Sam. 27:9; 1 Ki. 11:15, 16 [b]See Judg. 6:1, 2,33
8 [a]Josh. 13:21 [b]Josh. 13:22
11 [a]Deut. 20:14
14 [l]Heb. *host of war*
15 [a]See Deut. 20:14; 1 Sam. 15:3
16 [a]ch. 25:2 [b]ch. 24:14; 2 Pet. 2:15; Rev. 2:14 [c]ch. 25:9
17 [a]Judg. 21:11 [l]Heb. *a male*
19 [a]ch. 5:2 [b]ch. 19:11
20 [l]Heb. *instrument,* or, *vessel of skins*
23 [a]ch. 19:9,17
24 [a]Lev. 11:25
26 [l]Heb. *of the captivity*
27 [a]Josh. 22:8; 1 Sam. 30:24
28 [a]See ver. 30,47 & ch. 18:26
30 [a]See ver. 42-47 [b]ch. 3:7,8,25,31, 36 & 18:3,4 [l]Or, *goats*

34 And threescore and one thousand asses,

35 And thirty and two thousand persons in all, of women that had not known man by lying with him.

36 And the half, *which was* the portion of them that went out to war, was in number three hundred thousand and seven and thirty thousand and five hundred sheep:

37 And the LORD'S [a]tribute of the sheep was six hundred and threescore and fifteen.

38 And the beeves *were* thirty and six thousand; of which the LORD'S tribute *was* threescore and twelve.

39 And the asses *were* thirty thousand and five hundred; of which the LORD'S tribute *was* threescore and one.

40 And the persons *were* sixteen thousand; of which the LORD'S tribute *was* thirty and two persons.

41 And Moses gave the tribute, *which was* the LORD'S heave offering, unto Eleazar the priest, [a]as the LORD commanded Moses.

42 And of the children of Israel's half, which Moses divided from the men that warred,

43 (Now the half *that pertained unto* the congregation was three hundred thousand and thirty thousand *and* seven thousand and five hundred sheep,

44 And thirty and six thousand beeves,

45 And thirty thousand asses and five hundred,

46 And sixteen thousand persons;)

47 Even [a]of the children of Israel's half, Moses took one portion of fifty, *both* of man and of beast, and gave them unto the Levites, which kept the charge of the tabernacle of the LORD; as the LORD commanded Moses.

48 ¶ And the officers which *were* over thousands of the host, the captains of thousands, and captains of hundreds, came near unto Moses:

49 And they said unto Moses, Thy servants have taken the sum of the men of war which *are* under our ʹcharge, and there lacketh not one man of us.

50 We have therefore brought an oblation for the LORD, what every man hath ʹgotten, of jewels of gold, chains, and bracelets, rings, earrings, and tablets, [a]to make an atonement for our souls before the LORD.

51 And Moses and Eleazar the priest took the gold of them, *even* all wrought jewels.

52 And all the gold of the ʹoffering that they offered up to the LORD, of the captains of thousands, and of the captains of hundreds, was sixteen thousand seven hundred and fifty shekels.

53 (*For* [a]the men of war had taken spoil, every man for himself.)

54 And Moses and Eleazar the priest took the gold of the captains of thousands and of hundreds, and brought it into the tabernacle of the congregation, [a]*for* a memorial for the children of Israel before the LORD.

Tribes to possess Gilead

32 NOW THE children of Reuben and the children of Gad had a very great multitude of cattle: and when they saw the land of [a]Jazer, and the land of Gilead, that, behold, the place *was* a place for cattle;

2 The children of Gad and the children of Reuben came and spake unto Moses, and to Eleazar the priest, and unto the princes of the congregation, saying,

3 Ataroth, and Dibon, and Jazer, and [a]Nimrah, and Heshbon, and Elealeh, and [b]Shebam, and Nebo, and [c]Beon,

4 *Even* the country [a]which the LORD smote before the congregation of Israel, *is* a land for cattle, and thy servants have cattle:

5 Wherefore, said they, if we have found grace in thy sight, let this land be given unto thy servants for a possession, *and* bring us not over Jordan.

6 ¶ And Moses said unto the children of Gad and to the children of Reuben, Shall your brethren go to war, and shall ye sit here?

7 And wherefore ʹdiscourage ye the heart of the children of Israel from going over into the land which the LORD hath given them?

8 Thus did your fathers, [a]when I sent them from Kadesh-barnea [b]to see the land.

9 For [a]when they went up unto the valley of Eshcol, and saw the land, they discouraged the heart of the children of

37 [a]Lev. 25:23; Deut. 10:14; Job 41:11; Ps. 24:1 & 50:12; Prov. 3:9; Luke 20:25; 1 Cor. 10:26,28
41 [a]See ch. 18:8, 19
47 [a]ver. 30
49 ʹHeb. *hand*
50 [a]Ex. 30:12,16 ʹHeb. *found*
52 ʹHeb. *heave offering*
53 [a]Deut. 20:14
54 [a]Ex. 30:16
32:1 [a]ch. 21:32; Josh. 13:25; 2 Sam. 24:5
3 [a]ver. 36 *Beth-nimrah* [b]ver. 38 *Shibmah* [c]ver. 38 *Baal-meon*
4 [a]ch. 21:24,34
7 ʹHeb. *break*
8 [a]ch. 13:3,26 [b]Deut. 1:22
9 [a]ch. 13:24,31; Deut. 1:24,28

L *Nu 14:14* ◀▶ *Dt 1:29–33*
S *Lev 26:6* ◀▶ *2Sa 8:6*

Israel, that they should not go into the land which the LORD had given them.

10 [a]And the LORD'S anger was kindled the same time, and he sware, saying,

S 11 Surely none of the men that came up out of Egypt, [a]from twenty years old and upward, shall see the land which I sware unto Abraham, unto Isaac, and unto Jacob; because [b]they have not [/]wholly followed me:

12 Save Caleb the son of Jephunneh the Kenezite, and Joshua the son of Nun: [a]for they have wholly followed the LORD.

13 And the LORD'S anger was kindled against Israel, and he made them [a]wander in the wilderness forty years, until [b]all the generation, that had done evil in the sight of the LORD, was consumed.

14 And, behold, ye are risen up in your fathers' stead, an increase of sinful men, to augment yet the [a]fierce anger of the LORD toward Israel.

15 For if ye [a]turn away from after him, he will yet again leave them in the wilderness; and ye shall destroy all this people.

16 ¶ And they came near unto him, and said, We will build sheepfolds here for our cattle, and cities for our little ones:

17 But [a]we ourselves will go ready armed before the children of Israel, until we have brought them unto their place: and our little ones shall dwell in the fenced cities because of the inhabitants of the land.

18 [a]We will not return unto our houses, until the children of Israel have inherited every man his inheritance.

19 For we will not inherit with them on yonder side Jordan, or forward; [a]because our inheritance is fallen to us on this side Jordan eastward.

20 ¶ And [a]Moses said unto them, If ye will do this thing, if ye will go armed before the LORD to war,

21 And will go all of you armed over Jordan before the LORD, until he hath driven out his enemies from before him,

22 And [a]the land be subdued before the LORD: then afterward [b]ye shall return, and be guiltless before the LORD, and before Israel; and [c]this land shall be your possession before the LORD.

23 But if ye will not do so, behold, ye have sinned against the LORD: and be sure [a]your sin will find you out. E H S

24 [a]Build you cities for your little ones, and folds for your sheep; and do that which hath proceeded out of your mouth.

25 And the children of Gad and the children of Reuben spake unto Moses, saying, Thy servants will do as my lord commandeth.

26 [a]Our little ones, our wives, our flocks, and all our cattle, shall be there in the cities of Gilead:

27 [a]But thy servants will pass over, every man armed for war, before the LORD to battle, as my lord saith.

28 So [a]concerning them Moses commanded Eleazar the priest, and Joshua the son of Nun, and the chief fathers of the tribes of the children of Israel:

29 And Moses said unto them, If the children of Gad and the children of Reuben will pass with you over Jordan, every man armed to battle, before the LORD, and the land shall be subdued before you; then ye shall give them the land of Gilead for a possession:

30 But if they will not pass over with you armed, they shall have possessions among you in the land of Canaan.

31 And the children of Gad and the children of Reuben answered, saying, As the LORD hath said unto thy servants, so will we do.

32 We will pass over armed before the LORD into the land of Canaan, that the possession of our inheritance on this side Jordan *may be* ours.

33 And [a]Moses gave unto them, *even* to the children of Gad, and to the children of Reuben, and unto half the tribe of Manasseh the son of Joseph, [b]the kingdom of Sihon king of the Amorites, and the kingdom of Og king of Bashan, the

10 [a]ch. 14:11,21; Deut. 1:34
11 [a]ch. 14:28,29; Deut. 1:35 [b]ch. 14:24,30 [/]Heb. *fulfilled after me*
12 [a]ch. 14:24; Deut. 1:36; Josh. 14:8,9
13 [a]ch. 14:33-35 [b]ch. 26:64,65
14 [a]Deut. 1:34
15 [a]Deut. 30:17; Josh. 22:16,18; 2 Chr. 7:19
17 [a]Josh. 4:12,13
18 [a]Josh. 22:4
19 [a]ver. 33; Josh. 12:1 & 13:8
20 [a]Deut. 3:18; Josh. 1:14 & 4:12, 13
22 [a]Deut. 3:20; Josh. 11:23 & 18:1 [b]Josh. 22:4 [c]Deut. 3:12,15,16,18; Josh. 1:15 & 13:8, 32 & 22:4,9
23 [a]Gen. 4:7 & 44:16; Is. 59:12
24 [a]ver. 16,34
26 [a]Josh. 1:14
27 [a]Josh. 4:12
28 [a]Josh. 1:13
33 [a]Deut. 3:12-17 & 29:8; Josh. 12:6 & 13:8 & 22:4 [b]ch. 21:24,33,35

S *Nu 15:30–31* ◀▶ *Nu 32:23*

E *Ge 6:5* ◀▶ *1Sa 2:3*
H *Nu 14:18* ◀▶ *Dt 4:24*
S *Nu 32:11* ◀▶ *Dt 5:29*

32:11 Moses reminded the people that the disobedience and unfaithfulness of the ten spies resulted in judgment. Complete obedience to the Lord's commands was the only way for the Israelites to achieve blessing and military success.

land, with the cities thereof in the coasts,
even the cities of the country round
about.
34 ¶ And the children of Gad built [a]Di-
bon, and Ataroth, and [b]Aroer,
35 And Atroth, Shophan, and [a]Jaazer,
and Jogbehah,
36 And [a]Beth-nimrah, and Beth-haran,
[b]fenced cities: and folds for sheep.
37 And the children of Reuben [a]built
Heshbon, and Elealeh, and Kirjathaim,
38 And [a]Nebo and [b]Baal-meon, ([c]their
names being changed,) and Shibmah: and
[1]gave other names unto the cities which
they builded.
39 And the children of [a]Machir the
son of Manasseh went to Gilead, and took
it, and dispossessed the Amorite which
was in it.
40 And Moses [a]gave Gilead unto Machir the son of Manasseh; and he dwelt
therein.
41 And [a]Jair the son of Manasseh went
and took the small towns thereof, and
called them [b]Havoth-jair.
42 And Nobah went and took Kenath,
and the villages thereof, and called it Nobah, after his own name.

Journey from Egypt to Canaan

33 THESE *ARE* the journeys of the
children of Israel, which went
forth out of the land of Egypt with their
armies under the hand of Moses and
Aaron.
2 And Moses wrote their goings out
according to their journeys by the commandment of the LORD: and these *are*
their journeys according to their goings
out.
3 And they [a]departed from Rameses in
[b]the first month, on the fifteenth day of
the first month; on the morrow after the
passover the children of Israel went out
[c]with an high hand in the sight of all the
Egyptians.
4 For the Egyptians buried all *their*
firstborn, [a]which the LORD had smitten
among them: [b]upon their gods also the
LORD executed judgments.
5 [a]And the children of Israel removed
from Rameses, and pitched in Succoth.
6 And they departed from [a]Succoth,
and pitched in Etham, which *is* in the
edge of the wilderness.
7 And [a]they removed from Etham, and
turned again unto Pi-hahiroth, which *is*
before Baal-zephon: and they pitched before Migdol.
8 And they departed from before Pi-hahiroth, and [a]passed through the midst of
the sea into the wilderness, and went
three days' journey in the wilderness of
Etham, and pitched in Marah.
9 And they removed from Marah, and
[a]came unto Elim: and in Elim *were*
twelve fountains of water, and threescore
and ten palm trees; and they pitched
there.
10 And they removed from Elim, and
encamped by the Red sea.
11 And they removed from the Red
sea, and encamped in the [a]wilderness of
Sin.
12 And they took their journey out of
the wilderness of Sin, and encamped in
Dophkah.
13 And they departed from Dophkah,
and encamped in Alush.
14 And they removed from Alush, and
encamped at [a]Rephidim, where was no
water for the people to drink.
15 And they departed from Rephidim,
and pitched in the [a]wilderness of Sinai.
16 And they removed from the desert
of Sinai, and pitched [a]at [1]Kibroth-hat-
taavah.
17 And they departed from Kibroth-
hattaavah, and [a]encamped at Hazeroth.
18 And they departed from Hazeroth,
and pitched in [a]Rithmah.
19 And they departed from Rithmah,
and pitched at Rimmon-parez.
20 And they departed from Rimmon-
parez, and pitched in Libnah.
21 And they removed from Libnah,
and pitched at Rissah.
22 And they journeyed from Rissah,
and pitched in Kehelathah.
23 And they went from Kehelathah,
and pitched in mount Shapher.
24 And they removed from mount Shapher, and encamped in Haradah.
25 And they removed from Haradah,
and pitched in Makheloth.
26 And they removed from Makheloth, and encamped at Tahath.
27 And they departed from Tahath,
and pitched at Tarah.
28 And they removed from Tarah, and
pitched in Mithcah.
29 And they went from Mithcah, and
pitched in Hashmonah.

34 [a]ch. 33:45,46 [b]Deut. 2:36
35 [a]ver. 1,3 *Jazer*
36 [a]ver. 3 *Nimrah* [b]ver. 24
37 [a]ch. 21:27
38 [a]Is. 46:1 [b]ch. 22:41 [c]See ver. 3; Ex. 23:13; Josh. 23:7 [1]Heb. *they called by names the names of the cities*
39 [a]Gen. 50:23
40 [a]Deut. 3:12,13, 15; Josh. 13:31 & 17:1
41 [a]Deut. 3:14; Josh. 13:30; 1 Chr. 2:21 [b]Judg. 10:4; 1 Ki. 4:13
33:3 [a]Ex. 12:37 [b]Ex. 12:2 & 13:4 [c]Ex. 14:8
4 [a]Ex. 12:29 [b]Ex. 12:12 & 18:11; Is. 19:1; Rev. 12:8
5 [a]Ex. 12:37
6 [a]Ex. 13:20
7 [a]Ex. 14:2,9
8 [a]Ex. 14:22 & 15:22,23
9 [a]Ex. 15:27
11 [a]Ex. 16:1
14 [a]Ex. 17:1 & 19:2
15 [a]Ex. 16:1 & 19:1,2
16 [a]ch. 11:34 [1]i.e. *The graves of lust*
17 [a]ch. 11:35
18 [a]ch. 12:16

30 And they departed from Hashmonah, and [a]encamped at Moseroth.

31 And they departed from Moseroth, and pitched in Bene-jaakan.

32 And they removed from [a]Bene-jaakan, and [b]encamped at Hor-hagidgad.

33 And they went from Hor-hagidgad, and pitched in Jotbathah.

34 And they removed from Jotbathah, and encamped at Ebronah.

35 And they departed from Ebronah, [a]and encamped at Ezion-geber.

36 And they removed from Ezion-geber, and pitched in the [a]wilderness of Zin, which *is* Kadesh.

37 And they removed from [a]Kadesh, and pitched in mount Hor, in the edge of the land of Edom.

38 And [a]Aaron the priest went up into mount Hor at the commandment of the LORD, and died there, in the fortieth year after the children of Israel were come out of the land of Egypt, in the first *day* of the fifth month.

39 And Aaron *was* an hundred and twenty and three years old when he died in mount Hor.

40 And [a]king Arad the Canaanite, which dwelt in the south in the land of Canaan, heard of the coming of the children of Israel.

41 And they departed from mount [a]Hor, and pitched in Zalmonah.

42 And they departed from Zalmonah, and pitched in Punon.

43 And they departed from Punon, and [a]pitched in Oboth.

44 And [a]they departed from Oboth, and pitched in [a]Ije-abarim,[1] in the border of Moab.

45 And they departed from Iim, and pitched [a]in Dibon-gad.

46 And they removed from Dibon-gad, and encamped in Almon-[a]diblathaim.

47 And they removed from Almon-diblathaim, [a]and pitched in the mountains of Abarim, before Nebo.

48 And they departed from the mountains of Abarim, and [a]pitched in the plains of Moab by Jordan *near* Jericho.

49 And they pitched by Jordan, from Beth-jeshimoth *even* unto [a]Abel-shittim[1] in the plains of Moab.

50 ¶ And the LORD spake unto Moses in the plains of Moab by Jordan *near* Jericho, saying,

51 Speak unto the children of Israel, and say unto them, [a]When ye are passed over Jordan into the land of Canaan;

52 [a]Then ye shall drive out all the inhabitants of the land from before you, and destroy all their pictures, and destroy all their molten images, and quite pluck down all their high places:

53 And ye shall dispossess *the inhabitants of* the land, and dwell therein: for I have given you the land to possess it.

54 And [a]ye shall divide the land by lot for an inheritance among your families: *and* to the more ye shall [1]give the more inheritance, and to the fewer ye shall [2]give the less inheritance: every man's *inheritance* shall be in the place where his lot falleth; according to the tribes of your fathers ye shall inherit.

55 But if ye will not drive out the inhabitants of the land from before you; then it shall come to pass, that those which ye let remain of them *shall be* [a]pricks in your eyes, and thorns in your sides, and shall vex you in the land wherein ye dwell. J

56 Moreover it shall come to pass, *that* I shall do unto you, as I thought to do unto them.

The borders of Canaan

34 AND THE LORD spake unto Moses, saying, I

2 Command the children of Israel, and say unto them, When ye come into [a]the land of Canaan; (this *is* the land that shall fall unto you for an inheritance, *even* the land of Canaan with the coasts thereof:)

3 Then [a]your south quarter shall be from the wilderness of Zin along by the coast of Edom, and your south border shall be the outmost coast of [b]the salt sea eastward:

4 And your border shall turn from the south [a]to the ascent of Akrabbim, and

J *Nu 24:14–24* ◀▶ *Jos 6:26*
I *Nu 24:14–19* ◀▶ *Dt 1:35–39*

30 [a]Deut. 10:6
32 [a]See Gen. 36:27; Deut. 10:6; 1 Chr. 1:42 [b]Deut. 10:7
35 [a]Deut. 2:8; 1 Ki. 9:26 & 22:48
36 [a]ch. 20:1 & 27:14
37 [a]ch. 20:22,23; & 21:4
38 [a]ch. 20:25,28; Deut. 10:6 & 32:50
40 [a]ch. 21:1
41 [a]ch. 21:4
43 [a]ch. 21:10
44 [a]ch. 21:11 [1]Or, *Heaps of Abarim*
45 [a]ch. 32:34
46 [a]Jer. 48:22; Ezek. 6:14
47 [a]ch. 21:20; Deut. 32:49
48 [a]ch. 22:1
49 [a]ch. 25:1; Josh. 2:1 [1]Or, *The plains of Shittim*
51 [a]Deut. 7:1,2 & 9:1; Josh. 3:17
52 [a]Ex. 23:24,33; & 34:13; Deut. 7:2, 5 & 12:3; Josh. 11:12; Judg. 2:2
54 [a]ch. 26:53-55 [1]Heb. *multiply his inheritance* [2]Heb. *diminish his inheritance*
55 [a]Josh. 23:13; Judg. 2:3; Ps. 106:34,36
34:2 [a]Gen. 17:8; Deut. 1:7; Ps. 78:55; Ezek. 47:14
3 [a]Josh. 15:1; See Ezek. 47:13 [b]Gen. 14:3; Josh. 15:2
4 [a]Josh. 15:3

34:1–15 Moses records God's detailed outline of the future borders of the territory allotments in the promised land. This outline was not only for information, but to convey to the people again the greatness of God's gifts to his people.

pass on to Zin: and the going forth thereof shall be from the south [b]to Kadesh-barnea, and shall go on to [c]Hazar-addar, and pass on to Azmon:

5 And the border shall fetch a compass from Azmon [a]unto the river of Egypt, and the goings out of it shall be at the sea.

6 And *as for* the western border, ye shall even have the great sea for a border: this shall be your west border.

7 And this shall be your north border: from the great sea ye shall point out for you [a]mount Hor:

8 From mount Hor ye shall point out *your border* [a]unto the entrance of Hamath; and the goings forth of the border shall be to [b]Zedad:

9 ¶ And the border shall go on to Ziphron, and the goings out of it shall be at [a]Hazar-enan: this shall be your north border.

10 And ye shall point out your east border from Hazar-enan to Shepham:

11 And the coast shall go down from Shepham [a]to Riblah, on the east side of Ain; and the border shall descend, and shall reach unto the [1]side of the sea [b]of Chinnereth eastward:

12 And the border shall go down to Jordan, and the goings out of it shall be at [a]the salt sea: this shall be your land with the coasts thereof round about.

13 And Moses commanded the children of Israel, saying, [a]This *is* the land which ye shall inherit by lot, which the LORD commanded to give unto the nine tribes, and to the half tribe:

14 [a]For the tribe of the children of Reuben according to the house of their fathers, and the tribe of the children of Gad according to the house of their fathers, have received *their inheritance;* and half the tribe of Manasseh have received their inheritance:

15 The two tribes and the half tribe have received their inheritance on this side Jordan *near* Jericho eastward, toward the sunrising.

16 And the LORD spake unto Moses, saying,

17 These *are* the names of the men which shall divide the land unto you: [a]Eleazar the priest, and Joshua the son of Nun.

18 And ye shall take one [a]prince of every tribe, to divide the land by inheritance.

4 [b]ch. 13:26 & 32:8 [c]See Josh. 15:3,4
5 [a]Gen. 15:18; Josh. 15:4,47; 1 Ki. 8:65; Is. 27:12
7 [a]ch. 33:37
8 [a]ch. 13:21; 2 Ki. 14:25 [b]Ezek. 47:15
9 [a]Ezek. 47:17
11 [a]2 Ki. 23:33; Jer. 39:5,6 [b]Deut. 3:17; Josh. 11:2 & 19:35; Mat. 14:34; Luke 5:1 [1]Heb. *shoulder*
12 [a]ver. 3
13 [a]ver. 2; Josh. 14:1,2
14 [a]ch. 32:33; Josh. 14:2
17 [a]Josh. 14:1 & 19:51
18 [a]ch. 1:4,16
35:1 [a]See ch. 33:50
2 [a]Josh. 14:3,4 & 21:2; See Ezek. 45:1 & 48:8 [b]See Lev. 25:34

19 And the names of the men *are* these: Of the tribe of Judah, Caleb the son of Jephunneh.

20 And of the tribe of the children of Simeon, Shemuel the son of Ammihud.

21 Of the tribe of Benjamin, Elidad the son of Chislon.

22 And the prince of the tribe of the children of Dan, Bukki the son of Jogli.

23 The prince of the children of Joseph, for the tribe of the children of Manasseh, Hanniel the son of Ephod.

24 And the prince of the tribe of the children of Ephraim, Kemuel the son of Shiphtan.

25 And the prince of the tribe of the children of Zebulun, Elizaphan the son of Parnach.

26 And the prince of the tribe of the children of Issachar, Paltiel the son of Azzan.

27 And the prince of the tribe of the children of Asher, Ahihud the son of Shelomi.

28 And the prince of the tribe of the children of Naphtali, Pedahel the son of Ammihud.

29 These *are they* whom the LORD commanded to divide the inheritance unto the children of Israel in the land of Canaan.

Cities for the Levites

35 AND THE LORD spake unto Moses in [a]the plains of Moab by Jordan *near* Jericho, saying,

2 [a]Command the children of Israel, that they give unto the Levites of the inheritance of their possession cities to dwell in; and ye shall give *also* unto the Levites [b]suburbs for the cities round about them.

3 And the cities shall they have to dwell in; and the suburbs of them shall be for their cattle, and for their goods, and for all their beasts.

4 And the suburbs of the cities, which ye shall give unto the Levites, *shall reach* from the wall of the city and outward a thousand cubits round about.

5 And ye shall measure from without the city on the east side two thousand cubits, and on the south side two thousand cubits, and on the west side two thousand cubits, and on the north side two thousand cubits; and the city *shall be*

in the midst: this shall be to them the suburbs of the cities.

6 And among the cities which ye shall give unto the Levites *there shall be* [a]six cities for refuge, which ye shall appoint for the manslayer, that he may flee thither: and [ʹ]to them ye shall add forty and two cities.

7 *So* all the cities which ye shall give to the Levites *shall be* [a]forty and eight cities: them *shall ye give* with their suburbs.

8 And the cities which ye shall give *shall be* [a]of the possession of the children of Israel: [b]from *them that have* many ye shall give many; but from *them that have* few ye shall give few: every one shall give of his cities unto the Levites according to his inheritance which [ʹ]he inheriteth.

The cities of refuge

9 ¶ And the LORD spake unto Moses, saying,

10 Speak unto the children of Israel, and say unto them, [a]When ye be come over Jordan into the land of Canaan;

11 Then [a]ye shall appoint you cities to be cities of refuge for you; that the slayer may flee thither, which killeth any person [ʹ]at unawares.

12 [a]And they shall be unto you cities for refuge from the avenger; that the manslayer die not, until he stand before the congregation in judgment.

13 And of these cities which ye shall give [a]six cities shall ye have for refuge.

14 [a]Ye shall give three cities on this side Jordan, and three cities shall ye give in the land of Canaan, *which* shall be cities of refuge.

15 These six cities shall be a refuge, *both* for the children of Israel, and [a]for the stranger, and for the sojourner among them: that every one that killeth any person unawares may flee thither.

16 [a]And if he smite him with an instrument of iron, so that he die, he *is* a murderer: the murderer shall surely be put to death.

17 And if he smite him [ʹ]with throwing a stone, wherewith he may die, and he die, he *is* a murderer: the murderer shall surely be put to death.

18 Or *if* he smite him with an hand-weapon of wood, wherewith he may die, and he die, he *is* a murderer: the murderer shall surely be put to death.

19 [a]The revenger of blood himself shall slay the murderer: when he meeteth him, he shall slay him.

20 But [a]if he thrust him of hatred, or hurl at him [b]by laying of wait, that he die;

21 Or in enmity smite him with his hand, that he die: he that smote *him* shall surely be put to death; *for* he *is* a murderer: the revenger of blood shall slay the murderer, when he meeteth him.

22 But if he thrust him suddenly [a]without enmity, or have cast upon him any thing without laying of wait,

23 Or with any stone, wherewith a man may die, seeing *him* not, and cast *it* upon him, that he die, and *was* not his enemy, neither sought his harm:

24 Then [a]the congregation shall judge between the slayer and the revenger of blood according to these judgments:

25 And the congregation shall deliver the slayer out of the hand of the revenger of blood, and the congregation shall restore him to the city of his refuge, whither he was fled: and [a]he shall abide in it unto the death of the high priest, [b]which was anointed with the holy oil.

26 But if the slayer shall at any time come without the border of the city of his refuge, whither he was fled;

27 And the revenger of blood find him without the borders of the city of his refuge, and the revenger of blood kill the slayer; [a]he[ʹ] shall not be guilty of blood:

28 Because he should have remained in the city of his refuge until the death of the high priest: but after the death of the high priest the slayer shall return into the land of his possession.

29 So these *things* shall be for [a]a statute of judgment unto you throughout your generations in all your dwellings.

30 Whoso killeth any person, the murderer shall be put to death by the [a]mouth of witnesses: but one witness shall not testify against any person *to cause him* to die.

31 Moreover ye shall take no satisfaction for the life of a murderer, which *is* [ʹ]guilty of death: but he shall be surely put to death.

32 And ye shall take no satisfaction for him that is fled to the city of his refuge, that he should come again to dwell in the land, until the death of the priest.

33 So ye shall not pollute the land wherein ye *are:* for blood [a]it defileth the land: and [ʹ]the land cannot be cleansed of

---

6 [a]ver. 13; Deut. 4:41; Josh. 20:2,7, 8 & 21:3,13 [ʹ]Heb. *above them ye shall give*

7 [a]Josh. 21:41

8 [a]Josh. 21:3 [b]ch. 26:54 [ʹ]Heb. *they inherit*

10 [a]Deut. 19:2; Josh. 20:2

11 [a]Ex. 21:13 [ʹ]Heb. *by error*

12 [a]Deut. 19:6; Josh. 20:3,5,6

13 [a]ver. 6

14 [a]Deut. 4:41; Josh. 20:8

15 [a]ch. 15:16

16 [a]Ex. 21:12,14; Lev. 24:17; Deut. 19:11,12

17 [ʹ]Heb. *with a stone of the hand*

19 [a]ver. 21,24,27; Deut. 19:6,12; Josh. 20:3,5

20 [a]Gen. 4:8; 2 Sam. 3:27 & 20:10; 1 Ki. 2:31, 32 [b]Ex. 21:14; Deut. 19:11

22 [a]Ex. 21:13

24 [a]ver. 12; Josh. 20:6

25 [a]Josh. 20:6 [b]Ex. 29:7; Lev. 4:3 & 21:10

27 [a]Ex. 22:2 [ʹ]Heb. *no blood* shall be *to him*

29 [a]ch. 27:11

30 [a]Deut. 17:6 & 19:15; Mat. 18:16; 2 Cor. 13:1; Heb. 10:28

31 [ʹ]Heb. *faulty to die*

33 [a]Ps. 106:38; Mic. 4:11 [ʹ]Heb *there can be no expiation for the land*

the blood that is shed therein, but [b]by the blood of him that shed it.

34 [a]Defile not therefore the land which ye shall inhabit, wherein I dwell: for [b]I the LORD dwell among the children of Israel.

The marriage of heiresses

36 AND THE chief fathers of the families of the [a]children of Gilead, the son of Machir, the son of Manasseh, of the families of the sons of Joseph, came near, and spake before Moses, and before the princes, the chief fathers of the children of Israel:

2 And they said, [a]The LORD commanded my lord to give the land for an inheritance by lot to the children of Israel: and [b]my lord was commanded by the LORD to give the inheritance of Zelophehad our brother unto his daughters.

3 And if they be married to any of the sons of the *other* tribes of the children of Israel, then shall their inheritance be [a]taken from the inheritance of our fathers, and shall be put to the inheritance of the tribe [l]whereunto they are received: so shall it be taken from the lot of our inheritance.

4 And when [a]the jubilee of the children of Israel shall be, then shall their inheritance be put unto the inheritance of the tribe whereunto they are received: so shall their inheritance be taken away from the inheritance of the tribe of our fathers.

5 And Moses commanded the children of Israel according to the word of the LORD, saying, The tribe of the sons of Joseph [a]hath said well.

6 This *is* the thing which the LORD doth command concerning the daughters of Zelophehad, saying, Let them [l]marry to whom they think best; [a]only to the family of the tribe of their father shall they marry.

7 So shall not the inheritance of the children of Israel remove from tribe to tribe: for every one of the children of Israel shall [a]keep[l] himself to the inheritance of the tribe of his fathers.

8 And [a]every daughter, that possesseth an inheritance in any tribe of the children of Israel, shall be wife unto one of the family of the tribe of her father, that the children of Israel may enjoy every man the inheritance of his fathers.

9 Neither shall the inheritance remove from *one* tribe to another tribe; but every one of the tribes of the children of Israel shall keep himself to his own inheritance.

10 Even as the LORD commanded Moses, so did the daughters of Zelophehad:

11 [a]For Mahlah, Tirzah, and Hoglah, and Milcah, and Noah, the daughters of Zelophehad, were married unto their father's brothers' sons:

12 *And* they were married [l]into the families of the sons of Manasseh the son of Joseph, and their inheritance remained in the tribe of the family of their father.

13 These *are* the commandments and the judgments, [a]which the LORD commanded by the hand of Moses unto the children of Israel [b]in the plains of Moab by Jordan *near* Jericho.

33 [b]Gen. 9:6
34 [a]Lev. 18:25; Deut. 21:23 [b]Ex. 29:45,46
36:1 [a]ch. 26:29
2 [a]ch. 26:55 & 33:54; Josh. 17:4 [b]ch. 27:1,7; Josh. 17:3,4
3 [a]ch. 27:4 marg. [l]Heb. *unto whom they shall be*
4 [a]Lev. 25:10
5 [a]ch. 27:7
6 [a]ver. 11,12 [l]Heb. *be wives*
7 [a]1 Ki. 21:3 [l]Heb. *cleave to the*
8 [a]1 Chr. 23:22
11 [a]ch. 27:1
12 [l]Heb. *to some that were of the families*
13 [a]Deut. 33:4 [b]ch. 26:3 & 33:50

Deuteronomy

Author: Moses

Theme: Restatement of the laws in Exodus, Leviticus and Numbers

Date of Writing: c. 1406–1400 B.C.

Outline of Deuteronomy

I. A Historical Review of Israel's Wanderings (1:1—4:43)
II. A Restatement of God's Laws (4:44—11:32)
III. Practical Lessons in Righteous Living (12:1—26:19)
IV. Blessings and Curses (27:1—28:68)
V. The Palestinian Covenant (29:1—30:20)
VI. Final Words and Moses' Death (31:1—34:12)

DEUTERONOMY IS THE last book of the Pentateuch. Its name comes from a phrase in Dt 17:18 in the Greek Septuagint which means "second law-giving." The Hebrew title for this book, *debarim*, literally means "words" and is taken from the opening phrase in the first verse.

This was time of great anticipation for the Israelites. Encamped along the Jordan River, the countdown had begun. Everyone in the camp knew that the forty-year judgment promised by God was about to be completed. With the exception of Moses, Joshua and Caleb, a whole generation had died during the forty years in the wilderness. Moses' death loomed, but a new generation of Israelites stood poised on the riverbank, ready to conquer Canaan. The dream of the promised land was almost in their grasp.

Commencing with an overview of their experiences during the exodus and wilderness wandering, Moses admonishes Israel in this farewell address to obey the fundamental laws of God that were given at Sinai. This new generation of Israelites needed to understand their covenant relationship with God—his laws and their required obedience. Moses words came from his heart as he reminded the people to "take heed, and hearken, O Israel; this day thou art become the people of the LORD thy God. Thou shalt therefore obey the voice of the LORD thy God, and do his commandments and his statutes, which I command thee this day" (27:9–10). Moses also dictated a series of blessings and curses that were to be announced from Mt. Ebal and Mt. Gerizim after the Israelites had taken possession of the land. The great lawgiver of Israel concludes his remarks in Deuteronomy with a series of prophecies that span Israel's exile from the land and their ultimate return to Palestine. The book of Deuteronomy closes with God's appointment of Joshua as Moses' successor and the death of Moses on Mt. Nebo.

Deuteronomy's spiritual emphasis and its call to total commitment to the Lord in worship and obedience inspired references to its message throughout the rest of Scripture. The NT writers refer to it more than eighty times and Jesus quoted from Deuteronomy more than from any other OT book (see Mt 4:1–11; 22:37).

Moses tells of God's guidance

1 THESE *BE* the words which Moses spake unto all Israel [a]on this side Jordan in the wilderness, in the plain over against [l]the Red *sea,* between Paran, and Tophel, and Laban, and Hazeroth, and Dizahab.

2 (*There are* eleven days' *journey* from Horeb by the way of mount Seir [a]unto Kadesh-barnea.)

3 And it came to pass [a]in the fortieth year, in the eleventh month, on the first *day* of the month, *that* Moses spake unto the children of Israel, according unto all that the LORD had given him in commandment unto them;

4 [a]After he had slain Sihon the king of the Amorites, which dwelt in Heshbon, and Og the king of Bashan, which dwelt at Astaroth [b]in Edrei:

5 On this side Jordan, in the land of Moab, began Moses to declare this law, saying,

6 The LORD our God spake unto us [a]in Horeb, saying, Ye have dwelt long [b]enough in this mount:

7 Turn you, and take your journey, and go to the mount of the Amorites, and unto [l]all *the places* nigh thereunto, in the plain, in the hills, and in the vale, and in the south, and by the sea side, to the land of the Canaanites, and unto Lebanon, unto the great river, the river Euphrates.

8 Behold, I have [l]set the land before you: go in and possess the land which the LORD sware unto your fathers, [a]Abraham, Isaac, and Jacob, to give unto them and to their seed after them.

The choice of leaders

9 ¶ And [a]I spake unto you at that time, saying, I am not able to bear you myself alone:

10 The LORD your God hath multiplied you, and, behold, [a]ye *are* this day as the stars of heaven for multitude.

11 ([a]The LORD God of your fathers make you a thousand times so many more as ye *are,* and bless you, [b]as he hath promised you!)

12 [a]How can I myself alone bear your cumbrance, and your burden, and your strife?

13 [l]Take you wise men, and understanding, and known among your tribes, and I will make them rulers over you.

14 And ye answered me, and said, The thing which thou hast spoken *is* good *for us* to do.

15 So I took [a]the chief of your tribes, wise men, and known, [a]and [l]made them heads over you, captains over thousands, and captains over hundreds, and captains over fifties, and captains over tens, and officers among your tribes.

16 And I charged your judges at that time, saying, Hear *the causes* between your brethren, and [a]judge righteously be-

1:1 [a]Josh. 9:1,10 [l]Or, *Zuph*
2 [a]Num. 13:26; ch. 9:23
3 [a]Num. 33:38
4 [a]Num. 21:24,33 [b]Num. 21:33; Josh. 13:12
6 [a]Ex. 3:1 [b]See Ex. 19:1; Num. 10:11
7 [l]Heb. *all his neighbours*
8 [a]Gen. 12:7 & 15:18 & 17:7,8 & 26:4 & 28:13 [l]Heb. *given*
9 [a]Ex. 18:18; Num. 11:14
10 [a]Gen. 15:5; ch. 10:22 & 28:62
11 [a]2 Sam. 24:3 [b]Gen. 15:5 & 22:17 & 26:4; Ex. 32:13
12 [a]1 Ki. 3:8,9
13 [l]Heb. *Give*
15 [a]Ex. 18:25 [l]Heb. *gave*
16 [a]ch. 16:18; John 7:24

1:1–3 Moses' last great message confirmed Israel's eternal covenant with God. This discourse was delivered on the first day of the last month of the forty years spent in the wilderness. With the exception of Moses, Joshua and Caleb, the entire generation of Israelites who had escaped from Egypt during the exodus had died in the Sinai wilderness. Within the month Moses would die too, and the new generation would begin the conquest of the land.

tween *every* man and his [b]brother, and the stranger *that is* with him.

17 [a]Ye shall not ʹrespect persons in judgment; *but* ye shall hear the small as well as the great; ye shall not be afraid of the face of man; for [b]the judgment *is* God's: and the cause that is too hard for you, [c]bring *it* unto me, and I will hear it.

18 And I commanded you at that time all the things which ye should do.

The report of the spies

19 ¶ And when we departed from Horeb, [a]we went through all that great and terrible wilderness, which ye saw by the way of the mountain of the Amorites, as the LORD our God commanded us; and [b]we came to Kadesh-barnea.

20 And I said unto you, Ye are come unto the mountain of the Amorites, which the LORD our God doth give unto us.

W 21 Behold, the LORD thy God hath set the land before thee: go up *and* possess *it,* as the LORD God of thy fathers hath said unto thee; [a]fear not, neither be discouraged.

22 ¶ And ye came near unto me every one of you, and said, We will send men before us, and they shall search us out the land, and bring us word again by what way we must go up, and into what cities we shall come.

23 And the saying pleased me well: and [a]I took twelve men of you, one of a tribe:

24 And [a]they turned and went up into the mountain, and came unto the valley of Eshcol, and searched it out.

25 And they took of the fruit of the land in their hands, and brought *it* down unto us, and brought us word again, and said, [a]*It is* a good land which the LORD our God doth give us.

The murmuring of Israel

26 [a]Notwithstanding ye would not go up, but rebelled against the commandment of the LORD your God:

27 And ye murmured in your tents, and said, Because the LORD [a]hated us, he hath brought us forth out of the land of Egypt, to deliver us into the hand of the Amorites, to destroy us.

28 Whither shall we go up? our brethren have [a]discouragedʹ our heart, saying, [b]The people *is* greater and taller than we; the cities *are* great and walled up to heaven; and moreover we have seen the sons of the [c]Anakims there.

29 Then I said unto you, Dread not, neither be afraid of them. L

30 [a]The LORD your God which goeth before you, he shall fight for you, according to all that he did for you in Egypt before your eyes;

31 And in the wilderness, where thou hast seen how that the LORD thy God [a]bare thee, as a man doth bear his son, in all the way that ye went, until ye came into this place.

32 Yet in this thing [a]ye did not believe the LORD your God,

33 [a]Who went in the way before you, [b]to search you out a place to pitch your tents *in,* in fire by night, to show you by what way ye should go, and in a cloud by day.

34 And the LORD heard the voice of your words, and was wroth, [a]and sware, saying,

35 [a]Surely there shall not one of these men of this evil generation see that good land, which I sware to give unto your fathers, I

36 [a]Save Caleb the son of Jephunneh; he shall see it, and to him will I give the land that he hath trodden upon, and to his children, because [b]he hath ʹwholly followed the LORD.

37 [a]Also the LORD was angry with me for your sakes, saying, Thou also shalt not go in thither.

38 [a]*But* Joshua the son of Nun, [b]which standeth before thee, he shall go in thither: [c]encourage him: for he shall cause Israel to inherit it.

39 [a]Moreover your little ones, which [b]ye said should be a prey, and your children, which in that day [c]had no knowledge between good and evil, they shall go in thither, and unto them will I give it, and they shall possess it.

40 [a]But *as for* you, turn you, and take your journey into the wilderness by the way of the Red sea.

41 Then ye answered and said unto me, [a]We have sinned against the LORD, we will go up and fight, according to all

16 [b]Lev. 24:22
17 [a]Lev. 19:15; ch. 16:19; 1 Sam. 16:7; Prov. 24:23; Jas. 2:1 [b]2 Chr. 19:6 [c]Ex. 18:22,26 ʹHeb. *acknowledge faces*
19 [a]Num. 10:12; ch. 8:15; Jer. 2:6 [b]Num. 13:26
21 [a]Josh. 1:9
23 [a]Num. 13:3
24 [a]Num. 13:22-24
25 [a]Num. 13:27
26 [a]Num. 14:1-4; Ps. 106:24
27 [a]ch. 9:28
28 [a]Josh. 2:11 [b]Num. 13:28, 31-33; ch. 9:1,2 [c]Num. 13:28 ʹHeb. *melted*
30 [a]Ex. 14:14; Neh. 4:20
31 [a]Ex. 19:4; ch. 32:11,12; Is. 46:3, 4 & 63:9; Hos. 11:3; See Acts 13:18
32 [a]Ps. 106:24; Jude 5
33 [a]Ex. 13:21; Ps. 78:14 [b]Num. 10:33; Ezek. 20:6
34 [a]ch. 2:14,15
35 [a]Num. 14:22; Ps. 95:11
36 [a]Num. 14:24; Josh. 14:9 [b]Num. 14:24 ʹHeb. *fulfilled* to go *after*
37 [a]Num. 20:12 & 27:14; ch. 3:26 & 4:21 & 34:4; Ps. 106:32
38 [a]Num. 14:30 [b]Ex. 24:13 & 33:11; See 1 Sam. 16:22 [c]Num. 27:18,19; ch. 31:7, 23
39 [a]Num. 14:31 [b]Num. 14:3 [c]Is. 7:15,16; Rom. 9:11
40 [a]Num. 14:25
41 [a]Num. 14:40

W *Ge 15:1* ◀▶ *Dt 20:8*
L *Nu 31:49* ◀▶ *Dt 2:7*
I *Nu 34:1–12* ◀▶ *Dt 2:24–25*

that the LORD our God commanded us.
And when ye had girded on every man
his weapons of war, ye were ready to go
up into the hill.
42 And the LORD said unto me, Say
unto them, [a]Go not up, neither fight; for
I *am* not among you; lest ye be smitten
before your enemies.
43 So I spake unto you; and ye would
not hear, but rebelled against the commandment of the LORD, and [a]went[1] presumptuously up into the hill.
44 And the Amorites, which dwelt in
that mountain, came out against you, and
chased you, [a]as bees do, and destroyed
you in Seir, *even* unto Hormah.
45 And ye returned and wept before
the LORD; but the LORD would not hearken
to your voice, nor give ear unto you.
46 [a]So ye abode in Kadesh many days,
according unto the days that ye abode
there.

The years in the wilderness

2 THEN WE turned, and took our journey into the wilderness by the way
of the Red sea, [a]as the LORD spake unto
me: and we compassed mount Seir many
days.
2 And the LORD spake unto me, saying,
3 Ye have compassed this mountain
[a]long enough: turn you northward.
4 And command thou the people, saying, [a]Ye *are* to pass through the coast of
your brethren the children of Esau,
which dwell in Seir; and they shall be
afraid of you: take ye good heed unto
yourselves therefore:
5 Meddle not with them; for I will not
give you of their land, [1]no, not so much
as a footbreadth; [a]because I have given
mount Seir unto Esau *for* a possession.
6 Ye shall buy meat of them for money,
that ye may eat; and ye shall also buy
water of them for money, that ye may
drink.
C 7 For the LORD thy God hath blessed
F thee in all the works of thy hand: he
L knoweth thy walking through this great
wilderness: [a]these forty years the LORD
thy God *hath been* with thee; thou hast
lacked nothing.

C *Ge 28:20* ◀ ▶ *Dt 8:4*
F *Nu 21:16* ◀ ▶ *Dt 8:3*
L *Dt 1:29–33* ◀ ▶ *Dt 4:7*

8 [a]And when we passed by from our
brethren the children of Esau, which
dwelt in Seir, through the way of the
plain from [b]Elath, and from Ezion-geber,
we turned and passed by the way of the
wilderness of Moab.
9 And the LORD said unto me, [1]Distress
not the Moabites, neither contend with
them in battle: for I will not give thee of
their land *for* a possession; because I
have given [a]Ar unto [b]the children of Lot
for a possession.
10 [a]The Emims dwelt therein in times
past, a people great, and many, and tall,
as [b]the Anakims;
11 Which also were accounted giants,
as the Anakims; but the Moabites call
them Emims.
12 [a]The Horims also dwelt in Seir
beforetime; but the children of Esau [1]suc-
ceeded them, when they had destroyed
them from before them, and dwelt in
their [2]stead; as Israel did unto the land of
his possession, which the LORD gave unto
them.
13 Now rise up, *said I,* and get you
over [a]the [1]brook Zered. And we went
over the brook Zered.
14 And the space in which we came
[a]from Kadesh-barnea, until we were
come over the brook Zered, *was* thirty
and eight years; [b]until all the generation
of the men of war were wasted out from
among the host, [c]as the LORD sware unto
them.
15 For indeed the [a]hand of the LORD
was against them, to destroy them from
among the host, until they were consumed.
16 ¶ So it came to pass, when all the
men of war were consumed and dead
from among the people,
17 That the LORD spake unto me,
saying,
18 Thou art to pass over through Ar,
the coast of Moab, this day:
19 And *when* thou comest nigh over
against the children of Ammon, distress
them not, nor meddle with them: for I
will not give thee of the land of the children of Ammon *any* possession; because I
have given it unto [a]the children of Lot *for*
a possession.
20 (That also was accounted a land of
giants: giants dwelt therein in old time;

42 [a]Num. 14:42
43 [a]Num. 14:44 [1]Heb. *ye were presumptuous, and went up*
44 [a]Ps. 118:12
46 [a]Num. 13:25 & 20:1,22; Judg. 11:17
2:1 [a]Num. 14:25; ch. 1:40
3 [a]See ver. 7,14
4 [a]Num. 20:14
5 [a]Gen. 36:8; Josh. 24:4 [1]Heb. *even to the treading of the sole of the foot*
7 [a]ch. 8:2-4
8 [a]Judg. 11:18 [b]1 Ki. 9:26
9 [a]Num. 21:28 [b]Gen. 19:36,37 [1]Or, *Use no hostility against Moab*
10 [a]Gen. 14:5 [b]Num. 13:22,33; ch. 9:2
12 [a]ver. 22; Gen. 14:6 & 36:20 [1]Heb. *inherited them* [2]Or, *room*
13 [a]Num. 21:12 [1]Or, *valley*
14 [a]Num. 13:26 [b]Num. 14:33 & 26:64 [c]Num. 14:35; ch. 1:34,35; Ezek. 20:15
15 [a]Ps. 78:33 & 106:26
19 [a]Gen. 19:38

and the Ammonites call them [a]Zamzummims;

21 [a]A people great, and many, and tall, as the Anakims; but the LORD destroyed them before them; and they succeeded them, and dwelt in their stead:

22 As he did to the children of Esau, [a]which dwelt in Seir, when he destroyed [b]the Horims from before them; and they succeeded them, and dwelt in their stead even unto this day:

23 And [a]the Avims which dwelt in Hazerim, *even* unto Azzah, [b]the Caphtorims, which came forth out of Caphtor, destroyed them, and dwelt in their stead.)

24 ¶ Rise ye up, take your journey, and [a]pass over the river Arnon: behold, I have given into thine hand Sihon the Amorite, king of Heshbon, and his land: [†]begin to possess *it,* and contend with him in battle.

25 [a]This day will I begin to put the dread of thee and the fear of thee upon the nations *that are* under the whole heaven, who shall hear report of thee, and shall tremble, and be in anguish because of thee.

The victory over Sihon

26 ¶ And I sent messengers out of the wilderness of Kedemoth unto Sihon king of Heshbon [a]with words of peace, saying,

27 [a]Let me pass through thy land: I will go along by the high way, I will neither turn unto the right hand nor to the left.

28 Thou shalt sell me meat for money, that I may eat; and give me water for money, that I may drink: [a]only I will pass through on my feet;

29 ([a]As the children of Esau which dwell in Seir, and the Moabites which dwell in Ar, did unto me;) until I shall pass over Jordan into the land which the LORD our God giveth us.

30 [a]But Sihon king of Heshbon would not let us pass by him: for [b]the LORD thy God [c]hardened his spirit, and made his heart obstinate, that he might deliver him into thy hand, as *appeareth* this day.

31 And the LORD said unto me, Behold, I have begun to [a]give Sihon and his land before thee: begin to possess, that thou mayest inherit his land.

32 [a]Then Sihon came out against us, he and all his people, to fight at Jahaz.

33 And [a]the LORD our God delivered him before us; and [b]we smote him, and his sons, and all his people.

34 And we took all his cities at that time, and [a]utterly destroyed [†]the men, and the women, and the little ones, of every city, we left none to remain:

35 Only the cattle we took for a prey unto ourselves, and the spoil of the cities which we took.

36 [a]From Aroer, which *is* by the brink of the river of Arnon, and *from* the city that *is* by the river, even unto Gilead, there was not one city too strong for us: [b]the LORD our God delivered all unto us:

37 Only unto the land of the children of Ammon thou camest not, *nor* unto any place of the river [a]Jabbok, nor unto the cities in the mountains, nor unto [b]whatsoever the LORD our God forbad us.

The victory over Og

3 THEN WE turned, and went up the way to Bashan: and [a]Og the king of Bashan came out against us, he and all his people, to battle [b]at Edrei.

2 And the LORD said unto me, Fear him not: for I will deliver him, and all his people, and his land, into thy hand; and thou shalt do unto him as thou didst unto [a]Sihon king of the Amorites, which dwelt at Heshbon.

3 So the LORD our God delivered into

| Dt 1:35–39 ◄► Dt 3:2

| Dt 2:24–25 ◄► Dt 3:21–22

20 [a]Gen. 14:5 *Zuzims*
21 [a]See ver. 10
22 [a]Gen. 36:8 [b]Gen. 14:6 & 36:20-30
23 [a]Josh. 13:3 [b]Gen. 10:14; Amos 9:7
24 [a]Num. 21:13; Judg. 11:18 [†]Heb. *begin, possess*
25 [a]Ex. 15:14,15
26 [a]ch. 20:10
27 [a]Num. 21:21, 22; Judg. 11:19
28 [a]Num. 20:19
29 [a]See Num. 20:18; ch. 23:3,4; Judg. 11:17
30 [a]Num. 21:23 [b]Josh. 11:20 [c]Ex. 4:21
31 [a]ch. 1:8
32 [a]Num. 21:23
33 [a]ch. 7:2 & 20:16 [b]Num. 21:24; ch. 29:7
34 [a]Lev. 27:28; ch. 7:2,26 [†]Heb. *every city of men, and women, and little ones*
36 [a]ch. 3:12 & 4:48; Josh. 13:9 [b]Ps. 44:3
37 [a]Gen. 32:22; Num. 21:24; ch. 3:16 [b]ver. 5,9,19
3:1 [a]Num. 21:33; ch. 29:7 [b]ch. 1:4
2 [a]Num. 21:34

2:20–21 The giants that inhabited the territories around Canaan were probably descendants of the early inhabitants of Ashteroth Karnaim on the eastern slopes of the Jordan (see Ge 14:5). These Rephaites were probably descended from the same race, but were given different names by the different peoples who came in contact with them. The races identified with the Rephaites include the Zamzummin (2:20), who may be the same as the Zuzim mentioned in Ge 14:5; the Emim (see 2:10–11), a very tall race who lived in Moabite territory in the time of Abraham (see Ge 14:5); and the Anakim (see 1:28; 2:11), who lived in Hebron, the territory promised to Caleb (see Nu 13:22; Jos 15:13–14; 21:11; Jdg 1:20).

our hands Og also, the king of Bashan,
and all his people: [a]and we smote him
until none was left to him remaining.
4 And we took all his cities at that
time, there was not a city which we took
not from them, threescore cities, [a]all the
region of Argob, the kingdom of Og in
Bashan.
5 All these cities *were* fenced with
high walls, gates, and bars; beside unwalled towns a great many.
6 And we utterly destroyed them, as
we did unto Sihon king [a]of Heshbon, utterly destroying the men, women, and
children, of every city.
7 But all the cattle, and the spoil of the
cities, we took for a prey to ourselves.
8 And we took at that time out of the
hand of the two kings of the Amorites the
land that *was* on this side Jordan, from
the river of Arnon unto mount Hermon;
9 (*Which* [a]Hermon the Sidonians call
Sirion; and the Amorites call it [b]Shenir;)
10 [a]All the cities of the plain, and all
Gilead, and [b]all Bashan, unto Salchah and
Edrei, cities of the kingdom of Og in
Bashan.
11 [a]For only Og king of Bashan remained of the remnant of [b]giants; behold,
his bedstead *was* a bedstead of iron; *is* it
not in [c]Rabbath of the children of Ammon? nine cubits *was* the length thereof,
and four cubits the breadth of it, after the
cubit of a man.

The distribution of the land

12 And this land, *which* we possessed
at that time, [a]from Aroer, which *is* by the
river Arnon, and half mount Gilead, and
[b]the cities thereof, gave I unto the Reubenites and to the Gadites.
13 [a]And the rest of Gilead, and all Bashan, *being* the kingdom of Og, gave I
unto the half tribe of Manasseh; all the
region of Argob, with all Bashan, which
was called the land of giants.
14 [a]Jair the son of Manasseh took all
the country of Argob [b]unto the coasts of
Geshuri and Maachathi; and [c]called them
after his own name, Bashan-havoth-jair,
unto this day.
15 [a]And I gave Gilead unto Machir.
16 And unto the Reubenites [a]and unto
the Gadites I gave from Gilead even unto
the river Arnon half the valley, and the
border even unto the river Jabbok,
[b]*which is* the border of the children of
Ammon;
17 The plain also, and Jordan, and the
coast *thereof,* from [a]Chinnereth [b]even
unto the sea of the plain, [c]*even* the salt
sea, [†]under Ashdoth-pisgah eastward.
18 ¶ And I commanded you at that
time, saying, The LORD your God hath
given you this land to possess it: [a]ye shall
pass over armed before your brethren the
children of Israel, all *that are* [†]meet for
the war.
19 But your wives, and your little
ones, and your cattle, (*for* I know that ye
have much cattle,) shall abide in your cities which I have given you;
20 Until the LORD have given rest unto
your brethren, as well as unto you, and
until they also possess the land which the
LORD your God hath given them beyond
Jordan: and *then* shall ye [a]return every
man unto his possession, which I have
given you.
21 ¶ And [a]I commanded Joshua at that
time, saying, Thine eyes have seen all
that the LORD your God hath done unto
these two kings: so shall the LORD do unto
all the kingdoms whither thou passest.
22 Ye shall not fear them: for [a]the LORD
your God he shall fight for you.

Moses forbidden to cross Jordan

23 And [a]I besought the LORD at that
time, saying,
24 O Lord GOD, thou hast begun to
show thy servant [a]thy greatness, and thy
mighty hand: for [b]what God *is there* in
heaven or in earth, that can do according
to thy works, and according to thy might?
25 I pray thee, let me go over, and see

Dt 3:2 ◄ ► Dt 4:22

3 [a]Num. 21:35
4 [a]1 Ki. 4:13
6 [a]ch. 2:24; Ps. 135:10-12
9 [a]ch. 4:48 [b]1 Chr. 5:23
10 [a]ch. 4:49 [b]Josh. 12:5 & 13:11
11 [a]Amos 2:9 [b]Gen. 14:5 [c]2 Sam. 12:26; Jer. 49:2; Ezek. 21:20
12 [a]ch. 2:36; Josh. 12:2 [b]Num. 32:33; Josh. 12:6 & 13:8
13 [a]Josh. 13:29
14 [a]1 Chr. 2:22 [b]Josh. 13:13; 2 Sam. 3:3 & 10:6 [c]Num. 32:41
15 [a]Num. 32:39
16 [a]2 Sam. 24:5 [b]Num. 21:24; Josh. 12:2
17 [a]Num. 34:11 [b]Num. 34:12; ch. 4:49; Josh. 12:3 [c]Gen. 14:3 [†]Or, *under the springs of Pisgah,* or, *the hill*
18 [a]Num. 32:20 [†]Heb. *sons of power*
20 [a]Josh. 22:4
21 [a]Num. 27:23
22 [a]Ex. 14:14; ch. 1:30 & 20:4
23 [a]See 2 Cor. 12:8,9
24 [a]ch. 11:2 [b]Ex. 15:11; 2 Sam. 7:22; Ps. 71:19 & 86:8 & 89:6,8

3:11 Og was the king of Bashan, the last of the giant races of that part of Canaan. The Israelites conquered Og's kingdom immediately after the conquest of Sihon (see Nu 21:32–35; Dt 3:1–12), and Og and his people were "utterly destroyed" (3:6). Og's kingdom became part of the inheritance of Gad, Reuben and the half tribe of Manasseh (see Nu 32:33). The bed mentioned in this verse may refer to Og's sarcophagus (stone coffin) made of basalt, a stone as hard as iron. Yet the bed may have been Og's regular bed. In either case the dimensions of this bed—13.5 feet long by 6 feet wide—suggest that Og was a huge man and his defeat was a cause for rejoicing (see Ps 135:11; 136:20).

[a]the good land that *is* beyond Jordan, that goodly mountain, and Lebanon.

26 But the LORD [a]was wroth with me for your sakes, and would not hear me: and the LORD said unto me, Let it suffice thee; speak no more unto me of this matter.

27 [a]Get thee up into the top of [/]Pisgah, and lift up thine eyes westward, and northward, and southward, and eastward, and behold *it* with thine eyes: for thou shalt not go over this Jordan.

28 But [a]charge Joshua, and encourage him, and strengthen him: for he shall go over before this people, and he shall cause them to inherit the land which thou shalt see.

29 So we abode in [a]the valley over against Beth-peor.

Moses commands obedience

4 NOW THEREFORE hearken, O Israel, unto [a]the statutes and unto the judgments, which I teach you, for to do *them,* that ye may live, and go in and possess the land which the LORD God of your fathers giveth you.

2 [a]Ye shall not add unto the word which I command you, neither shall ye diminish *aught* from it, that ye may keep the commandments of the LORD your God which I command you.

3 Your eyes have seen what the LORD did because of [a]Baal-peor: for all the men that followed Baal-peor, the LORD thy God hath destroyed them from among you.

4 But ye that did cleave unto the LORD your God *are* alive every one of you this day.

5 Behold, I have taught you statutes and judgments, even as the LORD my God commanded me, that ye should do so in the land whither ye go to possess it.

6 Keep therefore and do *them;* for this *is* [a]your wisdom and your understanding in the sight of the nations, which shall hear all these statutes, and say, Surely this great nation *is* a wise and understanding people.

L 7 For [a]what nation *is there so* great,
L who *hath* [b]God *so* nigh unto them, as the LORD our God *is* in all *things that* we call upon him *for?*

8 And what nation *is there so* great, that hath statutes and judgments *so* righteous as all this law, which I set before you this day?

9 Only take heed to thyself, and [a]keep thy soul diligently, lest thou forget the things which thine eyes have seen, and lest they depart from thy heart all the days of thy life: but [b]teach them thy sons, and thy sons' sons;

10 *Specially* [a]the day that thou stoodest before the LORD thy God in Horeb, when the LORD said unto me, Gather me the people together, and I will make them hear my words, that they may learn to fear me all the days that they shall live upon the earth, and *that* they may teach their children.

11 And ye came near and stood under the mountain; and the [a]mountain burned with fire unto the [/]midst of heaven, with darkness, clouds, and thick darkness.

12 [a]And the LORD spake unto you out of the midst of the fire: ye heard the voice of the words, but saw no similitude; [b]only[/] *ye heard* a voice.

13 [a]And he declared unto you his covenant, which he commanded you to perform, *even* [b]ten commandments; and [c]he wrote them upon two tables of stone.

14 ¶ And [a]the LORD commanded me at that time to teach you statutes and judgments, that ye might do them in the land whither ye go over to possess it.

Idolatry forbidden

15 [a]Take ye therefore good heed unto yourselves; for ye saw no manner of [b]similitude on the day *that* the LORD spake unto you in Horeb out of the midst of the fire:

16 Lest ye [a]corrupt *yourselves,* and [b]make you a graven image, the similitude of any figure, [c]the likeness of male or female,

17 The likeness of any beast that *is* on the earth, the likeness of any winged fowl that flieth in the air,

18 The likeness of any thing that creepeth on the ground, the likeness of any fish that *is* in the waters beneath the earth:

19 And lest thou [a]lift up thine eyes unto heaven, and when thou seest the sun, and the moon, and the stars, *even* [b]all the host of heaven, shouldest be driven to [c]worship them, and serve them, which the LORD thy God hath [/]di-

25 [a]Ex. 3:8; ch. 4:22
26 [a]ch. 1:37 & 31:2
27 [a]Num. 27:12 [/]Or, *The hill*
28 [a]Num. 27:18, 23; ch. 31:3,7
29 [a]ch. 34:6
4:1 [a]Lev. 19:37; ch. 5:1; Ezek. 20:11; Rom. 10:5
2 [a]Josh. 1:7
3 [a]Josh. 22:17; Ps. 106:28
6 [a]Job 28:28; Ps. 19:7; Prov. 1:7
7 [a]2 Sam. 7:23 [b]Ps. 46:1; Is. 55:6
9 [a]Prov. 4:23 [b]Gen. 18:19; ch. 6:7 & 11:19; Ps. 78:5,6; Eph. 6:4
10 [a]Ex. 19:9,16
11 [a]Ex. 19:18 [/]Heb. *heart*
12 [a]ch. 5:4,22 [b]Ex. 20:22; 1 Ki. 19:12 [/]Heb. *save a voice*
13 [a]ch. 9:9,11 [b]Ex. 34:28 [c]Ex. 24:12 & 31:18
14 [a]Ex. 21:1 & ch. 22 & ch. 23
15 [a]Josh. 23:11 [b]Is. 40:18
16 [a]Ex. 32:7 [b]ver. 23; Ex. 20:4,5; ch. 5:8 [c]Rom. 1:23
19 [a]ch. 17:3; Job 31:26 [b]2 Ki. 21:3 [c]Rom. 1:25 [/]Or, *imparted*

L *Nu 14:18–20* ◀▶ *Dt 4:29*
L *Dt 2:7* ◀▶ *Dt 29:5*

vided unto all nations under the whole
heaven.
20 But the LORD hath taken you, and
[a]brought you forth out of the iron furnace, *even* out of Egypt, [b]to be unto him a
people of inheritance, as *ye are* this day.
21 Furthermore [a]the LORD was angry
with me for your sakes, and sware that I
should not go over Jordan, and that I
should not go in unto that good land,
which the LORD thy God giveth thee *for*
an inheritance:
I 22 But [a]I must die in this land, [b]I must
not go over Jordan: but ye shall go over,
and possess [c]that good land.
23 Take heed unto yourselves, [a]lest ye
forget the covenant of the LORD your God,
which he made with you, [b]and make you
a graven image, *or* the likeness of any
thing, which the LORD thy God hath forbidden thee.
H 24 For [a]the LORD thy God *is* a consuming fire, *even* [b]a jealous God.
25 ¶ When thou shalt beget children,
and children's children, and ye shall have
remained long in the land, and shall corrupt *yourselves,* and make a graven image, *or* the likeness of any *thing,* and
[a]shall do evil in the sight of the LORD thy
God, to provoke him to anger:
I 26 [a]I call heaven and earth to witness
against you this day, that ye shall soon
utterly perish from off the land whereunto ye go over Jordan to possess it; ye
shall not prolong *your* days upon it, but
shall utterly be destroyed.
R 27 And the LORD [a]shall scatter you
among the nations, and ye shall be left

20 [a]1 Ki. 8:51; Jer. 11:4 [b]Ex. 19:5; ch. 9:29
21 [a]Num. 20:12; ch. 1:37 & 3:26
22 [a]See 2 Pet. 1:13-15 [b]ch. 3:27 [c]ch. 3:25
23 [a]ver. 9 [b]ver. 16; Ex. 20:4,5
24 [a]Ex. 24:17; ch. 9:3; Is. 33:14; Heb. 12:29 [b]Ex. 20:5; ch. 6:15
25 [a]2 Ki. 17:17
26 [a]ch. 30:18,19; Is. 1:2; Mic. 6:2
27 [a]Lev. 26:33; Neh. 1:8
28 [a]ch. 28:64; 1 Sam. 26:19; Jer. 16:13 [b]Ps. 115:4,5 & 135:15,16; Is. 44:9 & 46:7
29 [a]Lev. 26:39; ch. 30:1-3; 2 Chr. 15:4; Neh. 1:9; Is. 55:6,7
30 [a]Gen. 49:1; ch. 31:29; Jer. 23:20; Hos. 3:5 [b]Joel 2:12 [1]Heb. *have found thee*
31 [a]2 Chr. 30:9; Neh. 9:31; Ps. 116:5; Jonah 4:2
32 [a]Job 8:8 [b]Mat. 24:31
33 [a]Ex. 24:11 & 33:20; ch. 5:24,26
34 [a]ch. 7:19 [b]Ex. 7:3 [c]Ex. 13:3 [d]Ex. 6:6 [e]ch. 26:8 & 34:12

few in number among the heathen,
whither the LORD shall lead you.
28 And [a]there ye shall serve gods, the
work of men's hands, wood and stone,
[b]which neither see, nor hear, nor eat,
nor smell.
29 [a]But if from thence thou shalt seek L
the LORD thy God, thou shalt find *him,* if P
thou seek him with all thy heart and with R
all thy soul.
30 When thou art in tribulation, and R
all these things [1]are come upon thee,
[a]*even* in the latter days, if thou [b]turn to
the LORD thy God, and shalt be obedient
unto his voice;
31 (For the LORD thy God *is* [a]a merciful
God;) he will not forsake thee, neither
destroy thee, nor forget the covenant of
thy fathers which he sware unto them.

Israel as a chosen nation

32 For [a]ask now of the days that are
past, which were before thee, since the
day that God created man upon the earth,
and *ask* [b]from the one side of heaven
unto the other, whether there hath been
any such thing as this great thing *is,* or
hath been heard like it?
33 [a]Did *ever* people hear the voice of
God speaking out of the midst of the fire,
as thou hast heard, and live?
34 Or hath God assayed to go *and* take
him a nation from the midst of *another*
nation, [a]by temptations, [b]by signs, and by
wonders, and by war, and [c]by a mighty
hand, and [d]by a stretched out arm, [e]and
by great terrors, according to all that the

I *Dt 3:21–22* ◀▶ *Dt 4:26–31*
H *Nu 32:23* ◀▶ *Dt 7:10*
I *Dt 4:22* ◀▶ *Dt 6:3*
R *Lev 26:43* ◀▶ *Dt 4:30*

L *Dt 4:7* ◀▶ *Dt 5:10*
P *Nu 14:19–20* ◀▶ *Jdg 10:15–16*
R *Nu 5:6–8* ◀▶ *Dt 30:2*
R *Dt 4:27* ◀▶ *Dt 28:23–25*

4:21–22 Moses was forbidden to enter the promised land because of his unbelief and failure to honor God at Meribah. (See note at Nu 20:12).
4:23 Because of their ancestors' sin with the golden calf in the desert of Sinai this new generation of Israelites was admonished to remember their covenant with God and his prohibition of idolatry (see Ex 20:4–5).
4:25–28 Moses acknowledged that the sin of idolatry could tempt Israel after their settlement in Canaan. He wanted this new generation to know that God would deal severely with this sin, causing them to "utterly perish from off the land" (4:26), be carried off to foreign nations and be forced to serve their gods (4:27–28). Tragically, the Israelites forgot Moses' words and worshiped the idols of Canaan. Moses' prophecy was fulfilled when the Israelites were exiled to Babylon and ordered to worship the golden image of Nebuchadnezzar (see Da 3:4–7).

4:29–31 God's judgment on the Israelites' idolatry was tempered with mercy. God promised that if the Israelites would repent and turn back to him, he would hear their prayers and forgive them. Nearly a thousand years later Nehemiah refers to these prophetic words of Moses when he appeals for God's forgiveness and mercy for the returning exiles (see Ne 1:1–11).

LORD your God did for you in Egypt before your eyes?

O 35 Unto thee it was shown, that thou mightest know that the LORD he *is* God; [a]*there is* none else beside him.

36 [a]Out of heaven he made thee to hear his voice, that he might instruct thee: and upon earth he showed thee his great fire; and thou heardest his words out of the midst of the fire.

37 And because [a]he loved thy fathers, therefore he chose their seed after them, and [b]brought thee out in his sight with his mighty power out of Egypt;

38 [a]To drive out nations from before thee greater and mightier than thou *art,* to bring thee in, to give thee their land *for* an inheritance, as *it is* this day.

O 39 Know therefore this day, and consider *it* in thine heart, that [a]the LORD he *is* God in heaven above, and upon the earth beneath: *there is* none else.

N 40 [a]Thou shalt keep therefore his statutes, and his commandments, which I command thee this day, [b]that it may go well with thee, and with thy children after thee, and that thou mayest prolong *thy* days upon the earth, which the LORD thy God giveth thee, for ever.

41 ¶ Then Moses [a]severed three cities on this side Jordan toward the sunrising;

42 [a]That the slayer might flee thither, which should kill his neighbour unawares, and hated him not in times past; and that fleeing unto one of these cities he might live:

43 *Namely,* [a]Bezer in the wilderness, in the plain country, of the Reubenites; and Ramoth in Gilead, of the Gadites; and Golan in Bashan, of the Manassites.

44 ¶ And this *is* the law which Moses set before the children of Israel:

45 These *are* the testimonies, and the statutes, and the judgments, which Moses spake unto the children of Israel, after they came forth out of Egypt,

46 On this side Jordan, [a]in the valley over against Beth-peor, in the land of Sihon king of the Amorites, who dwelt at Heshbon, whom Moses and the children of Israel [b]smote, after they were come forth out of Egypt:

47 And they possessed his land, and the land [a]of Og king of Bashan, two kings of the Amorites, which *were* on this side Jordan toward the sunrising;

48 [a]From Aroer, which *is* by the bank of the river Arnon, even unto mount Sion, which *is* [b]Hermon,

49 And all the plain on this side Jordan eastward, even unto the sea of the plain, under the [a]springs of Pisgah.

The Ten Commandments

5 AND MOSES called all Israel, and said unto them, Hear, O Israel, the statutes and judgments which I speak in your ears this day, that ye may learn them, and [l]keep, and do them.

2 [a]The LORD our God made a covenant with us in Horeb.

3 The LORD [a]made not this covenant with our fathers, but with us, *even* us, who *are* all of us here alive this day.

4 [a]The LORD talked with you face to face in the mount out of the midst of the fire,

5 ([a]I stood between the LORD and you at that time, to show you the word of the LORD: for [b]ye were afraid by reason of the fire, and went not up into the mount;) saying,

6 ¶ [a]I *am* the LORD thy God, which brought thee out of the land of Egypt, from the house of [l]bondage.

7 [a]Thou shalt have none other gods before me.

8 [a]Thou shalt not make thee *any* graven image, *or* any likeness *of any thing* that *is* in heaven above, or that *is* in the earth beneath, or that *is* in the waters beneath the earth:

9 Thou shalt not bow down thyself unto them, nor serve them: for I the LORD thy God *am* a jealous God, [a]visiting the iniquity of the fathers upon the children unto the third and fourth *generation* of them that hate me,

35 [a]ch. 32:39; 1 Sam. 2:2; Is. 45:5, 18; Mark 12:29
36 [a]Ex. 19:9,19 & 20:18,22 & 24:16; Heb. 12:18
37 [a]ch. 10:15 [b]Ex. 13:3,9,14
38 [a]ch. 7:1 & 9:1, 4,5
39 [a]Josh. 2:11
40 [a]Lev. 22:31 [b]ch. 5:16 & 6:3, 18 & 12:25,28 & 22:7; Eph. 6:3
41 [a]Num. 35:6
42 [a]ch. 19:4
43 [a]Josh. 20:8
46 [a]ch. 3:29 [b]Num. 21:24; ch. 1:4
47 [a]Num. 21:35; ch. 3:3,4
48 [a]ch. 2:36 & 3:12 [b]ch. 3:9; Ps. 133:3
49 [a]ch. 3:17
5:1 [l]Heb. *keep to do them*
2 [a]Ex. 19:5; ch. 4:23
3 [a]See Mat. 13:17; Heb. 8:9
4 [a]Ex. 19:9,19 & 20:22; ch. 4:33,36 & 34:10
5 [a]Ex. 20:21; Gal. 3:19 [b]Ex. 19:16 & 20:18 & 24:2
6 [a]Ex. 20:2 [l]Heb. *servants*
7 [a]Ex. 20:3
8 [a]Ex. 20:4
9 [a]Ex. 34:7

O *Ge 17:4* ◀▶ *Dt 4:39*
O *Dt 4:35* ◀▶ *Dt 18:18–19*　**N** ▶ *Job 26:10*

4:40 If the Israelites kept God's commandments, God made two promises to them in this verse: things would go well for them and they would "prolong [their] days upon the earth." Moses wanted the Israelites to understand that obedience to God's laws would bring blessings in all areas of their lives. Isaiah echoes this prophecy of long life with his description of the Messianic kingdom (see Isa 65:20). Earlier, God had also promised good health to the Israelites if they followed his statutes (see Ex 15:26).

L U 10 [a]And showing mercy unto thousands of them that love me and keep my commandments.

11 [a]Thou shalt not take the name of the LORD thy God in vain: for the LORD will not hold *him* guiltless that taketh his name in vain.

12 [a]Keep the sabbath day to sanctify it, as the LORD thy God hath commanded thee.

13 [a]Six days thou shalt labour, and do all thy work:

14 But the seventh day *is* the [a]sabbath of the LORD thy God: *in it* thou shalt not do any work, thou, nor thy son, nor thy daughter, nor thy manservant, nor thy maidservant, nor thine ox, nor thine ass, nor any of thy cattle, nor thy stranger that *is* within thy gates; that thy manservant and thy maidservant may rest as well as thou.

15 [a]And remember that thou wast a servant in the land of Egypt, and *that* the LORD thy God brought thee out thence [b]through a mighty hand and by a stretched out arm: therefore the LORD thy God commanded thee to keep the sabbath day.

16 ¶ [a]Honour thy father and thy mother, as the LORD thy God hath commanded thee; [b]that thy days may be prolonged, and that it may go well with thee, in the land which the LORD thy God giveth thee.

17 [a]Thou shalt not kill.

18 [a]Neither shalt thou commit adultery.

19 [a]Neither shalt thou steal.

20 [a]Neither shalt thou bear false witness against thy neighbour.

21 [a]Neither shalt thou desire thy neighbour's wife, neither shalt thou covet thy neighbour's house, his field, or his manservant, or his maidservant, his ox, or his ass, or any *thing* that *is* thy neighbour's.

22 ¶ These words the LORD spake unto all your assembly in the mount out of the midst of the fire, of the cloud, and of the thick darkness, with a great voice: and he added no more. And [a]he wrote them in two tables of stone, and delivered them unto me.

23 [a]And it came to pass, when ye heard the voice out of the midst of the darkness, (for the mountain did burn with fire,) that ye came near unto me, *even* all the heads of your tribes, and your elders;

24 And ye said, Behold, the LORD our God hath shown us his glory and his greatness, and [a]we have heard his voice out of the midst of the fire: we have seen this day that God doth talk with man, and he [b]liveth.

25 Now therefore why should we die? for this great fire will consume us: [a]if we [1]hear the voice of the LORD our God any more, then we shall die.

26 [a]For who *is there of* all flesh, that hath heard the voice of the living God speaking out of the midst of the fire, as we *have,* and lived?

27 Go thou near, and hear all that the LORD our God shall say: and [a]speak thou unto us all that the LORD our God shall speak unto thee; and we will hear *it,* and do *it.*

28 And the LORD heard the voice of your words, when ye spake unto me; and the LORD said unto me, I have heard the voice of the words of this people, which they have spoken unto thee: [a]they have well said all that they have spoken.

29 [a]O that there were such an heart in them, that they would fear me, and [b]keep all my commandments always, [c]that it might be well with them, and with their children for ever! S U

30 Go say to them, Get you into your tents again.

31 But as for thee, stand thou here by me, [a]and I will speak unto thee all the commandments, and the statutes, and the judgments, which thou shalt teach them, that they may do *them* in the land which I give them to possess it.

32 Ye shall observe to do therefore as the LORD your God hath commanded you: [a]ye shall not turn aside to the right hand or to the left.

33 Ye shall walk in [a]all the ways which the LORD your God hath commanded you, that ye may live, [b]and *that it may be* well with you, and *that* ye may prolong *your* days in the land which ye shall possess.

10 [a]Jer. 32:18; Dan. 9:4
11 [a]Ex. 20:7; Lev. 19:12; Mat. 5:33
12 [a]Ex. 20:8
13 [a]Ex. 23:12 & 35:2; Ezek. 20:12
14 [a]Gen. 2:2; Ex. 16:29; Heb. 4:4
15 [a]ch. 15:15 & 16:12 & 24:18,22 [b]ch. 4:34,37
16 [a]Ex. 20:12; Lev. 19:3; ch. 27:16; Eph. 6:2,3; Col. 3:20 [b]ch. 4:40
17 [a]Ex. 20:13; Mat. 5:21
18 [a]Ex. 20:14; Luke 18:20; Jas. 2:11
19 [a]Ex. 20:15; Rom. 13:9
20 [a]Ex. 20:16
21 [a]Ex. 20:17; Mic. 2:2; Hab. 2:9; Luke 12:15; Rom. 7:7
22 [a]Ex. 24:12 & 31:18; ch. 4:13
23 [a]Ex. 20:18,19
24 [a]Ex. 19:19 [b]ch. 4:33; Judg. 13:22
25 [a]ch. 18:16 [1]Heb. *add to hear*
26 [a]ch. 4:33
27 [a]Ex. 20:19; Heb. 12:19
28 [a]ch. 18:17
29 [a]ch. 32:29; Ps. 81:13; Is. 48:18; Mat. 23:37; Luke 19:42 [b]ch. 11:1 [c]ch. 4:40
31 [a]Gal. 3:19
32 [a]ch. 17:20 & 28:14; Josh. 1:7; Prov. 4:27
33 [a]ch. 10:12; Jer. 7:23 [b]ch. 4:40

Love the LORD *thy God*

6 NOW THESE *are* [a]the commandments, the statutes, and the judgments, which the LORD your God commanded to teach you, that ye might do
them in the land whither ye ʹgo to possess it:
2 [a]That thou mightest fear the LORD thy
God, to keep all his statutes and his commandments, which I command thee,
thou, and thy son, and thy son's son, all
the days of thy life; [b]and that thy days
may be prolonged.
I 3 ¶ Hear therefore, O Israel, and observe to do *it;* that it may be well with
thee, and that ye may increase mightily,
[a]as the LORD God of thy fathers hath
promised thee, in [b]the land that floweth
with milk and honey.
4 [a]Hear, O Israel: The LORD our God *is*
one LORD:
5 And [a]thou shalt love the LORD thy
God [b]with all thine heart, and with all
thy soul, and with all thy might.
6 And [a]these words, which I command
thee this day, shall be in thine heart:
S 7 And [a]thou shalt ʹteach them dili-
T gently unto thy children, and shalt talk of
them when thou sittest in thine house,
and when thou walkest by the way, and
when thou liest down, and when thou
risest up.
8 [a]And thou shalt bind them for a sign
upon thine hand, and they shall be as
frontlets between thine eyes.
9 [a]And thou shalt write them upon the
posts of thy house, and on thy gates.
10 And it shall be, when the LORD thy
God shall have brought thee into the land
which he sware unto thy fathers, to Abraham, to Isaac, and to Jacob, to give thee
great and goodly cities, [a]which thou
buildest not,
11 And houses full of all good *things,*
which thou filledst not, and wells digged,
which thou diggedst not, vineyards and
olive trees, which thou plantedst not;
[a]when thou shalt have eaten and be full;
12 *Then* beware lest thou forget the

I *Dt 4:26–31* ◀▶ *Dt 7:4*
S *Dt 5:29* ◀▶ *Dt 6:25* **T** ▶ *Dt 26:1–3*

6:1 [a]ch. 12:1 ʹHeb. *pass over*
2 [a]ch. 10:12,13; Eccl. 12:13 [b]ch. 4:40; Prov. 3:1,2
3 [a]Gen. 22:17 [b]Ex. 3:8
4 [a]John 17:3; 1 Cor. 8:4,6
5 [a]Mat. 22:37; Mark 12:30 [b]2 Ki. 23:25
6 [a]ch. 11:18; Ps. 119:11,98
7 [a]ch. 11:19; Ps. 78:4-6 ʹHeb. *whet,* or, *sharpen*
8 [a]Prov. 6:21 & 7:3
9 [a]ch. 11:20; Is. 57:8
10 [a]Josh. 24:13; Ps. 105:44
11 [a]ch. 8:10
12 ʹHeb. *bondmen,* or, *servants*
13 [a]Mat. 4:10; Luke 4:8 [b]Is. 45:23 & 65:16; Jer. 4:2
14 [a]ch. 13:7
15 [a]Ex. 20:5; ch. 4:24 [b]ch. 7:4 & 11:17
16 [a]Mat. 4:7; Luke 4:12 [b]1 Cor. 10:9
17 [a]Ps. 119:4
18 [a]Ex. 15:26; ch. 12:28 & 13:18
19 [a]Num. 33:52, 53
20 [a]Ex. 13:14 ʹHeb. *tomorrow*
21 [a]Ex. 13:3
22 [a]Ex. 7 & 8 & 9; & 10 ʹHeb. *evil*
24 [a]ver. 2 [b]Job 35:7,8; Jer. 32:39 [c]ch. 4:1; Ps. 41:2
25 [a]Lev. 18:5; Rom. 10:3,5

LORD, which brought thee forth out of the
land of Egypt, from the house of
ʹbondage.
13 Thou shalt [a]fear the LORD thy God,
and serve him, and [b]shalt swear by his
name.
14 Ye shall not go after other gods, [a]of
the gods of the people which *are* round
about you;
15 (For [a]the LORD thy God *is* a jealous
God among you) [b]lest the anger of the
LORD thy God be kindled against thee,
and destroy thee from off the face of the
earth.
16 ¶ [a]Ye shall not tempt the LORD your
God, [b]as ye tempted *him* in Massah.
17 Ye shall [a]diligently keep the commandments of the LORD your God, and his
testimonies, and his statutes, which he
hath commanded thee.
18 And thou [a]shalt do *that which is*
right and good in the sight of the LORD:
that it may be well with thee, and that
thou mayest go in and possess the good
land which the LORD sware unto thy fathers,
19 [a]To cast out all thine enemies from
before thee, as the LORD hath spoken.
20 *And* [a]when thy son asketh thee ʹin
time to come, saying, What *mean* the testimonies, and the statutes, and the judgments, which the LORD our God hath
commanded you?
21 Then thou shalt say unto thy son,
We were Pharaoh's bondmen in Egypt;
and the LORD brought us out of Egypt
[a]with a mighty hand:
22 [a]And the LORD showed signs and
wonders, great and ʹsore, upon Egypt,
upon Pharaoh, and upon all his household, before our eyes:
23 And he brought us out from thence,
that he might bring us in, to give us the
land which he sware unto our fathers.
24 And the LORD commanded us to do
all these statutes, [a]to fear the LORD our
God, [b]for our good always, that [c]he might
preserve us alive, as *it is* at this day.
25 And [a]it shall be our righteousness, S
if we observe to do all these command-

S *Dt 6:7* ◀▶ *Dt 7:6*

6:4–9 This passage is known as the *Shema,* a Hebrew word for "hear." These words affirm the Jews' loyalty to the one and only God and are recited daily by the pious (see Mt 22:37–38; Mk 12:29–30; Lk 10:27).

ments before the LORD our God, as he
hath commanded us.

God will defeat the nations

7 WHEN THE [a]LORD thy God shall
bring thee into the land whither
thou goest to possess it, and hath cast
out many nations before thee, [b]the Hittites, and the Girgashites, and the Amorites,
and the Canaanites, and the Perizzites,
and the Hivites, and the Jebusites, seven
nations [c]greater and mightier than thou;
2 And when the LORD thy God shall
[a]deliver them before thee; thou shalt
smite them, *and* [b]utterly destroy them;
[c]thou shalt make no covenant with them,
nor show mercy unto them:
3 [a]Neither shalt thou make marriages
with them; thy daughter thou shalt not
give unto his son, nor his daughter shalt
thou take unto thy son.
I 4 For they will turn away thy son from
following me, that they may serve other
gods: [a]so will the anger of the LORD be
kindled against you, and destroy thee
suddenly.
5 But thus shall ye deal with them; ye
shall [a]destroy their altars, and break
down their [/]images, and cut down their
groves, and burn their graven images
with fire.
I 6 [a]For thou *art* an holy people unto the
S LORD thy God: [b]the LORD thy God hath
chosen thee to be a special people unto
himself, above all people that *are* upon
the face of the earth.
L 7 The LORD did not set his love upon
you, nor choose you, because ye were
more in number than any people; for ye
were [a]the fewest of all people:
8 But [a]because the LORD loved you, and

I Dt 6:3 ◀▶ Dt 7:6–9
I Dt 7:4 ◀▶ Dt 7:14–15
S Dt 6:25 ◀▶ Dt 7:9
L Dt 5:10 ◀▶ Dt 11:26–27

7:1 [a]ch. 31:3 [b]Ex. 33:2 [c]ch. 4:38
2 [a]ch. 23:14 [b]Josh. 6:17 & 8:24 & 9:24 [c]Josh. 2:14; Judg. 1:24 & 2:2
3 [a]1 Ki. 11:2; Ezra 9:2
4 [a]ch. 6:15
5 [a]Ex. 23:24 & 34:13; ch. 12:2,3 [/]Heb. *statues,* or, *pillars*
6 [a]Ps. 50:5; Jer. 2:3 [b]Ex. 19:5; Amos 3:2; 1 Pet. 2:9
7 [a]ch. 10:22
8 [a]ch. 10:15 [b]Luke 1:55,72,73 [c]Ex. 13:3,14
9 [a]1 Cor. 1:9; 2 Cor. 1:18; 2 Thes. 3:3; 2 Tim. 2:13; Heb. 11:11 [b]Neh. 1:5; Dan. 9:4
10 [a]Is. 59:18 [b]ch. 32:35
12 [a]ch. 28:1 [b]Ps. 105:8,9 [/]Heb. *because*
13 [a]John 14:21 [b]ch. 28:4
14 [a]Ex. 23:26
15 [a]Ex. 15:26; ch. 28:27,60

because he would keep [b]the oath which
he had sworn unto your fathers, [c]hath
the LORD brought you out with a mighty
hand, and redeemed you out of the house
of bondmen, from the hand of Pharaoh
king of Egypt.
9 Know therefore that the LORD thy S
God, he *is* God, [a]the faithful God, [b]which
keepeth covenant and mercy with them
that love him and keep his commandments to a thousand generations;
10 And [a]repayeth them that hate him H
to their face, to destroy them: [b]he will
not be slack to him that hateth him, he
will repay him to his face.
11 Thou shalt therefore keep the commandments, and the statutes, and the
judgments, which I command thee this
day, to do them.
12 ¶ [a]Wherefore it shall come to pass, U
[/]if ye hearken to these judgments, and
keep, and do them, that the LORD thy God
shall keep unto thee [b]the covenant and
the mercy which he sware unto thy fathers:
13 And he will [a]love thee, and bless B
thee, and multiply thee: [b]he will also
bless the fruit of thy womb, and the fruit
of thy land, thy corn, and thy wine, and
thine oil, the increase of thy kine, and
the flocks of thy sheep, in the land which
he sware unto thy fathers to give thee.
14 Thou shalt be blessed above all peo- I
ple: [a]there shall not be male or female
barren among you, or among your cattle.
15 And the LORD will take away from D
thee all sickness, and will put none of the H
[a]evil diseases of Egypt, which thou know-

S Dt 7:6 ◀▶ Dt 8:3
H Dt 4:24 ◀▶ Dt 18:18–19
U Dt 5:29 ◀▶ Dt 11:26–27
B Lev 26:3–5 ◀▶ Dt 11:11–12
I Dt 7:6–9 ◀▶ Dt 7:22
D Nu 25:8–9 ◀▶ Dt 28:21–22
H Ex 23:25 ◀▶ Dt 33:25

7:6–10 These verses announced God's decision to make Israel a "special people unto himself, above all people that are upon the face of the earth" (7:6). This covenantal relationship was first articulated to Abram (see Ge 12:1–3) and reiterated to the Israelites throughout the OT. This covenant was not based on the numerical greatness of Israel or because of any virtue on their part. God chose Israel as his special people because of his love and mercy. Moses also declared that God would eternally keep his "covenant and mercy with them that love him and keep his commandments to a thousand generations" (7:9).

7:12–14 If Israel kept their part of the covenant, God promised to multiply their people, their livestock and their crops so that they would be "blessed above all people" (7:14). Obedience to God's commands would ensure fertility rather than sterility.

7:15 Obedience to God's commands would ensure good health for the Israelites (see Ex 15:26; Dt 28:27, 60), but God would bring disease and ill health "upon all them that hate thee."

est, upon thee; but will lay them upon all
them that hate thee.
16 And [a]thou shalt consume all the
people which the LORD thy God shall deliver thee; [b]thine eye shall have no pity
upon them: neither shalt thou serve their
gods; for that *will be* [c]a snare unto thee.
17 If thou shalt say in thine heart,
These nations *are* more than I; how can I
[a]dispossess them?
18 [a]Thou shalt not be afraid of them:
but shalt well [b]remember what the LORD
thy God did unto Pharaoh, and unto all
Egypt;
19 [a]The great temptations which thine
eyes saw, and the signs, and the wonders, and the mighty hand, and the
stretched out arm, whereby the LORD thy
God brought thee out: so shall the LORD
thy God do unto all the people of whom
thou art afraid.
20 [a]Moreover the LORD thy God will
send the hornet among them, until they
that are left, and hide themselves from
thee, be destroyed.
21 Thou shalt not be affrighted at
them: for the LORD thy God *is* [a]among
you, [b]a mighty God and terrible.
I 22 [a]And the LORD thy God will [/]put out
those nations before thee by little and little: thou mayest not consume them at
once, lest the beasts of the field increase
upon thee.
23 But the LORD thy God shall deliver
them [/]unto thee, and shall destroy them
with a mighty destruction, until they be
destroyed.
24 And [a]he shall deliver their kings
into thine hand, and thou shalt destroy

I *Dt 7:14–15* ◀▶ *Dt 12:5*

16 [a]ver. 2 [b]ch. 19:13,21 [c]Judg. 8:27
17 [a]Num. 33:53
18 [a]ch. 31:6 [b]Ps. 105:5
19 [a]ch. 4:34 & 29:3
20 [a]Josh. 24:12
21 [a]Num. 16:3; Josh. 3:10 [b]Neh. 9:32
22 [a]Ex. 23:29,30 [/]Heb. *pluck off*
23 [/]Heb. *before thy face*
24 [a]Josh. 10:24,25, 42 [b]Ex. 17:14 [c]Josh. 23:9
25 [a]Ex. 32:20; 1 Chr. 14:12 [b]Josh. 7:1,21 [c]Judg. 8:27; Zeph. 1:3 [d]ch. 17:1
26 [a]Lev. 27:28; Josh. 6:17 & 7:1
8:1 [a]ch. 4:1 & 5:32,33 & 6:1-3
2 [a]ch. 1:3 & 2:7; Amos 2:10 [b]Ex. 16:4; ch. 13:3 [c]John 2:25
3 [a]Ex. 16:2,3 [b]Ex. 16:12,14,35 [c]Mat. 4:4; Luke 4:4
4 [a]ch. 29:5; Neh. 9:21

their name [b]from under heaven: [c]there
shall no man be able to stand before thee,
until thou have destroyed them.
25 The graven images of their gods
[a]shall ye burn with fire: thou [b]shalt not
desire the silver or gold *that is* on them,
nor take *it* unto thee, lest thou be [c]snared
therein: for it *is* [d]an abomination to the
LORD thy God.
26 Neither shalt thou bring an abomination into thine house, lest thou be a
cursed thing like it: *but* thou shalt utterly
detest it, and thou shalt utterly abhor it;
[a]for it *is* a cursed thing.

God's mercies in the wilderness

8 ALL THE commandments which I
command thee this day [a]shall ye observe to do, that ye may live, and multiply, and go in and possess the land which
the LORD sware unto your fathers.
2 And thou shalt remember all the way T
which the LORD thy God [a]led thee these
forty years in the wilderness, to humble
thee, *and* [b]to prove thee, [c]to know what
was in thine heart, whether thou wouldest keep his commandments, or no.
3 And he humbled thee, and [a]suffered S
thee to hunger, and [b]fed thee with F
manna, which thou knewest not, neither
did thy fathers know; that he might make
thee know that man doth [c]not live by
bread only, but by every *word* that proceedeth out of the mouth of the LORD
doth man live.
4 [a]Thy raiment waxed not old upon C
E

T ▶ *Dt 8:5–6* S *Dt 7:9* ◀▶ *Dt 11:26–27*
F *Dt 2:7* ◀▶ *Dt 8:15–16*
C *Dt 2:7* ◀▶ *Dt 10:18*
E *Nu 25:8* ◀▶ *Dt 34:7*

7:16 Moses reaffirmed God's command to completely conquer all of the people in the land of Canaan and show them no pity.
7:20 This prophecy indicated that God would send hornets to drive out the remnant of Israel's enemies from the promised land (see Ex 23:28). The use of stinging insects was a metaphor used elsewhere in Scripture (see 1:44; Jos 24:12; Isa 7:18; Ps 118:12).
7:22–24 The Israelites' conquering of Canaan would be gradual so that large territories would not be left abandoned. Wild animals could quickly overtake these deserted areas and make reclamation more difficult for the Israelites. (See note on wild animals at Lev 26:22.) Yet eventually all the pagan kings and their armies would fall to the Israelites because God promised to fight for Israel.
8:2–3 These verses indicate an underlying reason for the forty-year wilderness wandering. In addition to the death of the rebellious generation of adults, the desert experience helped the Israelites see what was in their own hearts, whether they "wouldest keep his commandments, or no" (8:2). Forty years of experiencing God's miraculous daily provision of water and manna taught the Israelites that "man doth not live by bread only, but by every word that proceedeth out of the mouth of the LORD" (8:3).
8:4 One of the great miracles of the exodus was God's preservation of the Israelites' clothes and shoes throughout forty years of brutal, desert conditions. Resupply of clothing in the desert was virtually

thee, neither did thy foot swell, these forty years.

5 [a]Thou shalt also consider in thine heart, that, as a man chasteneth his son, *so* the LORD thy God chasteneth thee.

6 Therefore thou shalt keep the commandments of the LORD thy God, [a]to walk in his ways, and to fear him.

7 For the LORD thy God bringeth thee into a good land, [a]a land of brooks of water, of fountains and depths that spring out of valleys and hills;

8 A land of wheat, and barley, and vines, and fig trees, and pomegranates; a land [l]of oil olive, and honey;

9 A land wherein thou shalt eat bread without scarceness, thou shalt not lack any *thing* in it; a land [a]whose stones *are* iron, and out of whose hills thou mayest dig brass.

10 [a]When thou hast eaten and art full, then thou shalt bless the LORD thy God for the good land which he hath given thee.

Warning against pride

11 Beware that thou forget not the LORD thy God, in not keeping his commandments, and his judgments, and his statutes, which I command thee this day:

12 [a]Lest *when* thou hast eaten and art full, and hast built goodly houses, and dwelt *therein;*

13 And *when* thy herds and thy flocks multiply, and thy silver and thy gold is multiplied, and all that thou hast is multiplied;

14 [a]Then thine heart be lifted up, and thou [b]forget the LORD thy God, which brought thee forth out of the land of Egypt, from the house of bondage;

15 Who [a]led thee through that great and terrible wilderness, [b]*wherein were* fiery serpents, and scorpions, and drought, where *there was* no water; [c]who brought thee forth water out of the rock of flint;

16 Who fed thee in the wilderness with [a]manna, which thy fathers knew not, that he might humble thee, and that he might prove thee, [b]to do thee good at thy latter end;

17 [a]And thou say in thine heart, My power and the might of *mine* hand hath gotten me this wealth.

18 But thou shalt remember the LORD thy God: [a]for *it is* he that giveth thee power to get wealth, [b]that he may establish his covenant which he sware unto thy fathers, as *it is* this day.

19 And it shall be, if thou do at all forget the LORD thy God, and walk after other gods, and serve them, and worship them, [a]I testify against you this day that ye shall surely perish.

20 As the nations which the LORD destroyeth before your face, [a]so shall ye perish; because ye would not be obedient unto the voice of the LORD your God.

9 HEAR, O Israel: Thou *art* to [a]pass over Jordan this day, to go in to possess nations [b]greater and mightier than thyself, cities great and [c]fenced up to heaven,

2 A people great and tall, [a]the children of the Anakims, whom thou knowest, and *of whom* thou hast heard *say,* Who can stand before the children of Anak!

3 Understand therefore this day, that the LORD thy God *is* he which [a]goeth over before thee; *as* a [b]consuming fire [c]he shall destroy them, and he shall bring them down before thy face: [d]so shalt thou drive them out, and destroy them quickly, as the LORD hath said unto thee.

4 [a]Speak not thou in thine heart, after that the LORD thy God hath cast them out from before thee, saying, For my righteousness the LORD hath brought me in to

5 [a]2 Sam. 7:14; Ps. 89:32; Prov. 3:12; Heb. 12:5,6; Rev. 3:19
6 [a]ch. 5:33
7 [a]ch. 11:10-12
8 [l]Heb. *of olive tree of oil*
9 [a]ch. 33:25
10 [a]ch. 6:11,12
12 [a]ch. 28:47 & 32:15; Hos. 13:6
14 [a]1 Cor. 4:7 [b]Ps. 106:21
15 [a]Is. 63:12-14; Jer. 2:6 [b]Num. 21:6; Hos. 13:5 [c]Num. 20:11
16 [a]Ex. 16:15 [b]Jer. 24:5,6; Heb. 12:11
17 [a]ch. 9:4
18 [a]Prov. 10:22; Hos. 2:8 [b]ch. 7:8, 12
19 [a]ch. 4:26 & 30:18
20 [a]Dan. 9:11,12
9:1 [a]ch. 11:31; Josh. 3:16 & 4:19 [b]ch. 4:38 & 11:23 [c]ch. 1:28
2 [a]Num. 13:22,28, 32,33
3 [a]ch. 31:3; Josh. 3:11 [b]ch. 4:24; Heb. 12:29 [c]ch. 7:23 [d]Ex. 23:31; ch. 7:24
4 [a]ch. 8:17; Rom. 11:6,20; 1 Cor. 4:4,7

T *Dt 8:2* ◀▶ *Dt 8:16*
P *Ge 24:35* ◀▶ *Dt 8:18*
F *Dt 8:3* ◀▶ *Dt 10:18*
T *Dt 8:5–6* ◀▶ *2Sa 7:14*
P *Dt 8:13* ◀▶ *Dt 15:4–6*

---

impossible for that many people. Only God's divine intervention could have provided so abundantly (see 29:5)

8:11–20 Forgetfulness comes easily to all of us, so the Israelites were urged to remember the desert's bitter lessons of sin and its punishment. Forgetfulness could result in pride and the Israelites might ascribe their wealth to their own efforts. Therefore, when the Israelites became successful in the promised land, Moses instructed them to "remember the LORD thy God: for it is he that giveth thee power to get wealth" (8:18).

9:1 God commanded Israel to "pass over Jordan this day" to conquer nations that were larger and stronger than themselves. It is possible that this day coincided with the Feast of Firstfruits. See the article "The Biblical Anniversaries of Israel," p. 184.

possess this land: but [b]for the wickedness
of these nations the LORD doth drive them
out from before thee.
5 [a]Not for thy righteousness, or for the
uprightness of thine heart, dost thou go
to possess their land: but for the wickedness of these nations the LORD thy God
doth drive them out from before thee,
and that he may perform [b]the word
which the LORD sware unto thy fathers,
Abraham, Isaac, and Jacob.

The golden calf

C 6 Understand therefore, that the LORD
thy God giveth thee not this good land to
possess it for thy righteousness; for thou
art [a]a stiffnecked people.
7 ¶ Remember, *and* forget not, how
thou provokedst the LORD thy God to
wrath in the wilderness: [a]from the day
that thou didst depart out of the land of
Egypt, until ye came unto this place, ye
have been rebellious against the LORD.
8 Also [a]in Horeb ye provoked the LORD
to wrath, so that the LORD was angry with
you to have destroyed you.
9 [a]When I was gone up into the mount
to receive the tables of stone, *even* the
tables of the covenant which the LORD
made with you, then [b]I abode in the
mount forty days and forty nights, I neither did eat bread nor drink water:
10 [a]And the LORD delivered unto me
two tables of stone written with the finger of God; and on them *was written* according to all the words, which the LORD
spake with you in the mount out of the
midst of the fire [b]in the day of the assembly.
11 And it came to pass at the end of
forty days and forty nights, *that* the LORD
gave me the two tables of stone, *even* the
tables of the covenant.
12 And the LORD said unto me, [a]Arise,
get thee down quickly from hence; for
thy people which thou hast brought forth
out of Egypt have corrupted *themselves;*
they are [b]quickly turned aside out of the
way which I commanded them; they
have made them a molten image.
C 13 Furthermore [a]the LORD spake unto
M me, saying, I have seen this people, and,
behold, [b]it *is* a stiffnecked people:
14 [a]Let me alone, that I may destroy
them, and [b]blot out their name from under heaven: [c]and I will make of thee a
nation mightier and greater than they.
15 [a]So I turned and came down from
the mount, and [b]the mount burned with
fire: and the two tables of the covenant
were in my two hands.
16 And [a]I looked, and, behold, ye had
sinned against the LORD your God, *and*
had made you a molten calf: ye had
turned aside quickly out of the way
which the LORD had commanded you.
17 And I took the two tables, and cast
them out of my two hands, and brake
them before your eyes.
18 And I [a]fell down before the LORD, as
at the first, forty days and forty nights: I
did neither eat bread, nor drink water,
because of all your sins which ye sinned,
in doing wickedly in the sight of the LORD,
to provoke him to anger.
19 [a]For I was afraid of the anger and
hot displeasure, wherewith the LORD was
wroth against you to destroy you. [b]But
the LORD hearkened unto me at that time
also.
20 And the LORD was very angry with
Aaron to have destroyed him: and I
prayed for Aaron also the same time.
21 And [a]I took your sin, the calf which
ye had made, and burnt it with fire, and
stamped it, *and* ground *it* very small,
even until it was as small as dust: and I
cast the dust thereof into the brook that
descended out of the mount.
22 And at [a]Taberah, and at [b]Massah,
and at [c]Kibroth-hattaavah, ye provoked
the LORD to wrath.
23 Likewise [a]when the LORD sent you
from Kadesh-barnea, saying, Go up and
possess the land which I have given you;
then ye rebelled against the commandment of the LORD your God, and [b]ye believed him not, nor hearkened to his
voice.
24 [a]Ye have been rebellious against
the LORD from the day that I knew you.
25 [a]Thus I fell down before the LORD
forty days and forty nights, as I fell down
at the first; because the LORD had said he
would destroy you.
26 [a]I prayed therefore unto the LORD,
and said, O Lord GOD, destroy not thy
people and thine inheritance, which thou
hast redeemed through thy greatness,

C *Ge 8:21* ◀▶ *Dt 9:13*
C *Dt 9:6* ◀▶ *Dt 29:18–19*
M *Lev 26:40–42* ◀▶ *Dt 10:16–17*

4 [b]Gen. 15:16; Lev. 18:24; ch. 18:12
5 [a]Tit. 3:5 [b]Gen. 12:7 & 13:15 & 15:7 & 17:8 & 26:4
6 [a]ver. 13; Ex. 32:9 & 33:3 & 34:9
7 [a]Ex. 14:11 & 16:2 & 17:2; Num. 11:4 & 20:2 & 25:2; ch. 31:27
8 [a]Ex. 32:4; Ps. 106:19
9 [a]Ex. 24:12,15 [b]Ex. 24:18 & 34:28
10 [a]Ex. 31:18 [b]Ex. 19:17 & 20:1; ch. 4:10 & 10:4
12 [a]Ex. 32:7 [b]ch. 31:29; Judg. 2:17
13 [a]Ex. 32:9 [b]ver. 6; ch. 10:16 & 31:27; 2 Ki. 17:14
14 [a]Ex. 32:10 [b]ch. 29:20 [c]Num. 14:12
15 [a]Ex. 32:15 [b]Ex. 19:18; ch. 4:11 & 5:23
16 [a]Ex. 32:19
18 [a]Ex. 34:28
19 [a]Ex. 32:10,11 [b]Ex. 32:14 & 33:17; ch. 10:10; Ps. 106:23
21 [a]Ex. 32:20; Is. 31:7
22 [a]Num. 11:1,3,5 [b]Ex. 17:7 [c]Num. 11:4,34
23 [a]Num. 13:3 & 14:1 [b]Ps. 106:24, 25
24 [a]ch. 31:27
25 [a]ver. 18
26 [a]Ex. 32:11

which thou hast brought forth out of Egypt with a mighty hand.

27 Remember thy servants, Abraham, Isaac, and Jacob; look not unto the stubbornness of this people, nor to their wickedness, nor to their sin:

28 Lest [a]the land whence thou broughtest us out say, [b]Because the LORD was not able to bring them into the land which he promised them, and because he hated them, he hath brought them out to slay them in the wilderness.

29 [a]Yet they *are* thy people and thine inheritance, which thou broughtest out by thy mighty power and by thy stretched out arm.

The second tables of stone

10 AT THAT time the LORD said unto me, [a]Hew thee two tables of stone like unto the first, and come up unto me into the mount, and [b]make thee an ark of wood.

2 And I will write on the tables the words that were in the first tables which thou brakest, and [a]thou shalt put them in the ark.

3 And I made an ark of [a]shittim wood, and [b]hewed two tables of stone like unto the first, and went up into the mount, having the two tables in mine hand.

4 And he wrote on the tables, according to the first writing, the ten [†]commandments, [a]which the LORD spake unto you in the mount out of the midst of the fire in the day of the assembly: and the LORD gave them unto me.

5 And I turned myself and [a]came down from the mount, and [b]put the tables in the ark which I had made; [c]and there they be, as the LORD commanded me.

6 ¶ And the children of Israel took their journey from Beeroth [a]of the children of Jaakan to [b]Mosera: [c]there Aaron died, and there he was buried; and Eleazar his son ministered in the priest's office in his stead.

7 [a]From thence they journeyed unto Gudgodah; and from Gudgodah to Jotbath, a land of rivers of waters.

8 ¶ At that time [a]the LORD separated the tribe of Levi, [b]to bear the ark of the covenant of the LORD, [c]to stand before the LORD to minister unto him, and [d]to bless in his name, unto this day.

9 [a]Wherefore Levi hath no part nor inheritance with his brethren; the LORD *is* his inheritance, according as the LORD thy God promised him.

10 And [a]I stayed in the mount, according to the [†]first time, forty days and forty nights; and [b]the LORD hearkened unto me at that time also, *and* the LORD would not destroy thee.

11 [a]And the LORD said unto me, Arise, [†]take *thy* journey before the people, that they may go in and possess the land, which I sware unto their fathers to give unto them.

God's great requirement

12 ¶ And now, Israel, [a]what doth the LORD thy God require of thee, but [b]to fear the LORD thy God, [c]to walk in all his ways, and [d]to love him, and to serve the LORD thy God with all thy heart and with all thy soul,

13 To keep the commandments of the LORD, and his statutes, which I command thee this day [a]for thy good?

14 Behold, [a]the heaven and the heaven of heavens *is* the LORD'S thy God, [b]the earth *also,* with all that therein *is.*

15 [a]Only the LORD had a delight in thy fathers to love them, and he chose their seed after them, *even* you above all people, as *it is* this day.

16 Circumcise therefore [a]the foreskin M
of your heart, and be no more [b]stiffnecked.

17 For the LORD your God *is* [a]God of gods, and [b]Lord of lords, a great God, [c]a mighty, and a terrible, which [d]regardeth not persons, nor taketh reward:

18 [a]He doth execute the judgment of C
the fatherless and widow, and loveth the F
stranger, in giving him food and raiment.

19 [a]Love ye therefore the stranger: for ye were strangers in the land of Egypt.

20 [a]Thou shalt fear the LORD thy God; him shalt thou serve, and to him shalt thou [b]cleave, [c]and swear by his name.

21 [a]He *is* thy praise, and he *is* thy God, [b]that hath done for thee these great and terrible things, which thine eyes have seen.

22 Thy fathers went down into Egypt [a]with threescore and ten persons; and now the LORD thy God hath made thee [b]as the stars of heaven for multitude.

M *Dt 9:13–14* ◀▶ *1Sa 2:3*
C *Dt 8:4* ◀▶ *Dt 29:5*
F *Dt 8:15–16* ◀▶ *Dt 11:14–15*

28 [a]Ex. 6:6-8; 1 Sam. 14:25 [b]Ex. 32:12; Num. 14:16
29 [a]ch. 4:20; 1 Ki. 8:51; Neh. 1:10
10:1 [a]Ex. 34:1,2 [b]Ex. 25:10
2 [a]Ex. 25:16,21
3 [a]Ex. 25:5,10 [b]Ex. 34:4
4 [a]Ex. 20:1 [†]Heb. *words*
5 [a]Ex. 34:29 [b]Ex. 40:20 [c]1 Ki. 8:9
6 [a]Num. 33:31 [b]Num. 33:30 [c]Num. 20:28 & 33:38
7 [a]Num. 33:32,33
8 [a]Num. 3:6 [b]Num. 4:15 [c]ch. 18:5 [d]Num. 6:23; ch. 21:5
9 [a]ch. 18:1,2; Ezek. 44:28
10 [a]Ex. 34:28; ch. 9:18,25 [b]Ex. 32:14,33,34 & 33:17; ch. 9:19 [†]Or, *former days*
11 [a]Ex. 33:1 [†]Heb. *go in journey*
12 [a]Mic. 6:8 [b]ch. 6:13 [c]ch. 5:33 [d]ch. 6:5; Mat. 22:37
13 [a]ch. 6:24
14 [a]1 Ki. 8:27 [b]Ex. 19:5
15 [a]ch. 4:37
16 [a]ch. 30:6; Jer. 4:4; Rom. 2:28,29; Col. 2:11 [b]ch. 9:6, 13
17 [a]Dan. 2:47 [b]Rev. 19:16 [c]ch. 7:21 [d]Acts 10:34; Rom. 2:11; Eph. 6:9; 1 Pet. 1:17
18 [a]Ps. 68:5
19 [a]Lev. 19:33,34
20 [a]Mat. 4:10 [b]ch. 11:22 [c]Ps. 63:11
21 [a]Ex. 15:2; Jer. 17:14 [b]Ps. 106:21, 22
22 [a]Gen. 46:27; Acts 7:14 [b]Gen. 15:5

Love and obey God

11 THEREFORE THOU shalt [a]love
the LORD thy God, and [b]keep his
charge, and his statutes, and his judgments, and his commandments, always.
2 And know ye this day: for *I speak*
not with your children which have not
known, and which have not seen [a]the
chastisement of the LORD your God, [b]his
greatness, his mighty hand, and his
stretched out arm,
3 [a]And his miracles, and his acts,
which he did in the midst of Egypt unto
Pharaoh the king of Egypt, and unto all
his land;
4 And what he did unto the army of
Egypt, unto their horses, and to their
chariots; [a]how he made the water of the
Red sea to overflow them as they pursued
after you, and *how* the LORD hath destroyed them unto this day;
5 And what he did unto you in the wilderness, until ye came into this place;
6 And [a]what he did unto Dathan and
Abiram, the sons of Eliab, the son of Reuben: how the earth opened her mouth,
and swallowed them up, and their households, and their tents, and all the [1]sub-
stance that [2]*was* in their possession, in
the midst of all Israel:
7 But [a]your eyes have seen all the
great acts of the LORD which he did.
8 Therefore shall ye keep all the commandments which I command you this
day, that ye may [a]be strong, and go in
and possess the land, whither ye go to
possess it;
9 And [a]that ye may prolong *your* days
in the land, [b]which the LORD sware unto
your fathers to give unto them and to
their seed, [c]a land that floweth with milk
and honey.
10 ¶ For the land, whither thou goest
in to possess it, *is* not as the land of
Egypt, from whence ye came out, where
thou sowedst thy seed, and wateredst *it*
with thy foot, as a garden of herbs:
B 11 [a]But the land, whither ye go to possess it, *is* a land of hills and valleys, *and*
drinketh water of the rain of heaven:
12 A land which the LORD thy God
[1]careth for: [a]the eyes of the LORD thy God
are always upon it, from the beginning of
the year even unto the end of the year.
13 ¶ And it shall come to pass, if ye
shall hearken [a]diligently unto my commandments which I command you this
day, [b]to love the LORD your God, and to
serve him with all your heart and with all
your soul,
14 That [a]I will give *you* the rain of B
your land in his due season, [b]the first F
rain and the latter rain, that thou mayest
gather in thy corn, and thy wine, and
thine oil.
15 [a]And I will [1]send grass in thy fields
for thy cattle, that thou mayest [b]eat and
be full.
16 Take heed to yourselves, [a]that your
heart be not deceived, and ye turn aside,
and [b]serve other gods, and worship
them;
17 And *then* [a]the LORD'S wrath be kindled against you, and he [b]shut up the
heaven, that there be no rain, and that
the land yield not her fruit; and *lest* [c]ye
perish quickly from off the good land
which the LORD giveth you.
18 ¶ Therefore [a]shall ye lay up these
my words in your heart and in your soul,
and [b]bind them for a sign upon your
hand, that they may be as frontlets between your eyes.
19 [a]And ye shall teach them your children, speaking of them when thou sittest
in thine house, and when thou walkest
by the way, when thou liest down, and
when thou risest up.
20 [a]And thou shalt write them upon
the door posts of thine house, and upon
thy gates:
21 That [a]your days may be multiplied,
and the days of your children, in the land
which the LORD sware unto your fathers
to give them, [b]as the days of heaven upon
the earth.

B *Dt 7:13* ◀ ▶ *Dt 11:14–15*

B *Dt 11:11–12* ◀ ▶ *Dt 28:3–5*
F *Dt 10:18* ◀ ▶ *Dt 32:13–14*

11:1 [a]ch. 10:12 [b]Zech. 3:7
2 [a]ch. 8:5 [b]ch. 5:24
3 [a]Ps. 78:12 & 135:9
4 [a]Ps. 106:11
6 [a]Num. 16:1,31 [1]Or, *living substance which followed them* [2]Heb. *was at their feet*
7 [a]ch. 5:3 & 7:19
8 [a]Josh. 1:6,7
9 [a]ch. 4:40; Prov. 10:27 [b]ch. 9:5 [c]Ex. 3:8
11 [a]ch. 8:7
12 [a]1 Ki. 9:3 [1]Heb. *seeketh*
13 [a]ver. 22; ch. 6:17 [b]ch. 10:12
14 [a]Lev. 26:4; ch. 28:12 [b]Joel 2:23; Jas. 5:7
15 [a]Ps. 104:14 [b]ch. 6:11; Joel 2:19 [1]Heb. *give*
16 [a]ch. 29:18; Job 31:27 [b]ch. 8:19
17 [a]ch. 6:15 [b]1 Ki. 8:35; 2 Chr. 6:26 [c]ch. 4:26 & 8:19, 20; Josh. 23:13,15, 16
18 [a]ch. 6:6 & 32:46 [b]ch. 6:8
19 [a]ch. 4:9,10 & 6:7
20 [a]ch. 6:9
21 [a]ch. 4:40; Prov. 3:2 & 4:10 [b]Ps. 72:5 & 89:29

11:11–14 If the Israelites served God and rejected idolatry, God promised rain and abundant crops. Obedience would bring his blessing to them and their possessions. God's promises are still true. If we will love and serve him with all our heart and soul, he will provide for us too.

22 ¶ For if [a]ye shall diligently keep all these commandments which I command you, to do them, to love the LORD your God, to walk in all his ways, and [b]to cleave unto him;

23 Then will the LORD [a]drive out all these nations from before you, and ye shall [b]possess greater nations and mightier than yourselves.

24 [a]Every place whereon the soles of your feet shall tread shall be yours: [b]from the wilderness and Lebanon, from the river, the river Euphrates, even unto the uttermost sea shall your coast be.

V 25 [a]There shall no man be able to stand before you: *for* the LORD your God shall [b]lay the fear of you and the dread of you upon all the land that ye shall tread upon, [c]as he hath said unto you.

L 26 ¶ [a]Behold, I set before you this day
N a blessing and a curse;
S 27 [a]A blessing, if ye obey the com-
U mandments of the LORD your God, which
I command you this day:

28 And a [a]curse, if ye will not obey the commandments of the LORD your God, but turn aside out of the way which I command you this day, to go after other gods, which ye have not known.

29 And it shall come to pass, when the LORD thy God hath brought thee in unto the land whither thou goest to possess it, that thou shalt put [a]the blessing upon mount Gerizim, and the curse upon mount Ebal.

30 *Are* they not on the other side Jordan, by the way where the sun goeth down, in the land of the Canaanites, which dwell in the champaign over against Gilgal, [a]beside the plains of Moreh?

31 [a]For ye shall pass over Jordan to go in to possess the land which the LORD your God giveth you, and ye shall possess it, and dwell therein.

32 And ye shall observe [a]to do all the statutes and judgments which I set before you this day.

Sacrifice at one altar only

12 THESE [a]*ARE* the statutes and judgments, which ye shall observe to do in the land, which the LORD God of thy fathers giveth thee to possess it, [b]all the days that ye live upon the earth.

2 [a]Ye shall utterly destroy all the places, wherein the nations which ye shall [1]possess served their gods, [b]upon the high mountains, and upon the hills, and under every green tree:

3 And [a]ye shall [1]overthrow their altars, and break their pillars, and burn their groves with fire; and ye shall hew down the graven images of their gods, and destroy the names of them out of that place.

4 [a]Ye shall not do so unto the LORD your God.

5 But unto the place which the LORD I
your God shall [a]choose out of all your tribes to put his name there, *even* unto his habitation shall ye seek, and thither thou shalt come:

6 And [a]thither ye shall bring your burnt offerings, and your sacrifices, and your [b]tithes, and heave offerings of your hand, and your vows, and your freewill offerings, and the firstlings of your herds and of your flocks:

7 And [a]there ye shall eat before the LORD your God, and [b]ye shall rejoice in all that ye put your hand unto, ye and your households, wherein the LORD thy God hath blessed thee.

8 Ye shall not do after all *the things* that we do here this day, [a]every man whatsoever *is* right in his own eyes.

22 [a]ver. 13; ch. 6:17 [b]ch. 10:20 & 30:20
23 [a]ch. 4:38 [b]ch. 9:1
24 [a]Josh. 1:3 & 14:9 [b]Gen. 15:18; Ex. 23:31; Num. 34:3
25 [a]ch. 7:24 [b]ch. 2:25 [c]Ex. 23:27
26 [a]ch. 30:1,15,19
27 [a]ch. 28:2
28 [a]ch. 28:15
29 [a]ch. 27:12,13; Josh. 8:33
30 [a]Gen. 12:6; Judg. 7:1
31 [a]ch. 9:1; Josh. 1:11
32 [a]ch. 5:32 & 12:32
12:1 [a]ch. 6:1 [b]ch. 4:10; 1 Ki. 8:40
2 [a]Ex. 34:13; ch. 7:5 [b]2 Ki. 16:4 & 17:10,11; Jer. 3:6 [1]Or, *inherit*
3 [a]Num. 33:52; Judg. 2:2 [1]Heb. *break down*
4 [a]ver. 31
5 [a]ver. 11; ch. 26:2; Josh. 9:27; 1 Ki. 8:29; 2 Chr. 7:12
6 [a]Lev. 17:3,4 [b]ver. 17; ch. 14:22, 23 & 15:19,20
7 [a]ch. 14:26 [b]ver. 12,18; Lev. 23:40; ch. 16:11,14,15
8 [a]Judg. 17:6 & 21:25

V *Nu 14:9* ◀▶ *Dt 20:4*
L *Dt 7:7–8* ◀▶ *Dt 30:11–15*
N *Nu 14:11* ◀▶ *Dt 18:18–19*
S *Dt 8:3* ◀▶ *Dt 12:28*
U *Dt 7:12–13* ◀▶ *Dt 14:29*

I *Dt 7:22* ◀▶ *Dt 17:14*

11:22–28 This passage established the covenant rules that would govern God's agreement with Israel. If the Israelites diligently followed his commands, God promised to drive out their enemies regardless of size or strength. He also set the borders for the promised land, and guaranteed to "lay the fear of you and the dread of you upon all the land that ye shall tread upon" (11:25). Yet God also gave a spiritual ultimatum to his chosen people: a promise of blessing if they followed his commandments but a guarantee of judgment if they worshiped false gods.

12:5 God ultimately chose Jerusalem as the location for his sanctuary, but during the exodus and the conquest of Canaan the tabernacle was located in different places as God directed (see 12:10–11; 26:2; Jos 9:27).

9 For ye are not as yet come to the rest and to the inheritance, which the LORD your God giveth you.

10 But *when* [a]ye go over Jordan, and dwell in the land which the LORD your God giveth you to inherit, and *when* he giveth you rest from all your enemies round about, so that ye dwell in safety;

11 Then there shall be [a]a place which the LORD your God shall choose to cause his name to dwell there; thither shall ye bring all that I command you; your burnt offerings, and your sacrifices, your tithes, and the heave offering of your hand, and all [/]your choice vows which ye vow unto the LORD:

12 And [a]ye shall rejoice before the LORD your God, ye, and your sons, and your daughters, and your menservants, and your maidservants, and the Levite that *is* within your gates; forasmuch as [b]he hath no part nor inheritance with you.

13 [a]Take heed to thyself that thou offer not thy burnt offerings in every place that thou seest:

14 [a]But in the place which the LORD shall choose in one of thy tribes, there thou shalt offer thy burnt offerings, and there thou shalt do all that I command thee.

15 Notwithstanding [a]thou mayest kill and eat flesh in all thy gates, whatsoever thy soul lusteth after, according to the blessing of the LORD thy God which he hath given thee: [b]the unclean and the clean may eat thereof, [c]as of the roebuck, and as of the hart.

16 [a]Only ye shall not eat the blood; ye shall pour it upon the earth as water.

17 ¶ Thou mayest not eat within thy gates the tithe of thy corn, or of thy wine, or of thy oil, or the firstlings of thy herds or of thy flock, nor any of thy vows which thou vowest, nor thy freewill offerings, or heave offering of thine hand:

18 [a]But thou must eat them before the LORD thy God in the place which the LORD thy God shall choose, thou, and thy son, and thy daughter, and thy manservant, and thy maidservant, and the Levite that *is* within thy gates: and thou shalt rejoice before the LORD thy God in all that thou puttest thine hands unto.

19 [a]Take heed to thyself that thou forsake not the Levite [/]as long as thou livest upon the earth.

10 [a]ch. 11:31

11 [a]ver. 5,14,18, 21,26 & ch. 14:23 & 15:20 & 16:2; Josh. 18:1; 1 Ki. 8:29 [/]Heb. *the choice of your vows*

12 [a]ver. 7 [b]ch. 10:9 & 14:29

13 [a]Lev. 17:4

14 [a]ver. 11

15 [a]ver. 21 [b]ver. 22 [c]ch. 14:5 & 15:22

16 [a]Gen. 9:4; Lev. 7:26 & 17:10; ch. 15:23 & ver. 23

18 [a]ver. 11,12; ch. 14:23

19 [a]ch. 14:27 [/]Heb. *all thy days*

20 [a]Gen. 15:18 & 28:14; Ex. 34:24; ch. 11:24 & 19:8

22 [a]ver. 15

23 [a]ver. 16 [b]Gen. 9:4; Lev. 17:11,14 [/]Heb. *be strong*

25 [a]ch. 4:40; Is. 3:10 [b]Ex. 15:26; ch. 13:18; 1 Ki. 11:38

26 [a]Num. 5:9,10 [b]1 Sam. 1:21,22,24

27 [a]Lev. 1:5,9,13; & 17:11

28 [a]ver. 25

29 [a]Ex. 23:23; ch. 19:1; Josh. 23:4 [/]Heb. *inheritest,* or, *possessest them*

30 [/]Heb. *after them*

31 [a]Lev. 18:3,26, 30 [/]Heb. *abomination of the*

20 ¶ When the LORD thy God shall enlarge thy border, [a]as he hath promised thee, and thou shalt say, I will eat flesh, because thy soul longeth to eat flesh; thou mayest eat flesh, whatsoever thy soul lusteth after.

21 If the place which the LORD thy God hath chosen to put his name there be too far from thee, then thou shalt kill of thy herd and of thy flock, which the LORD hath given thee, as I have commanded thee, and thou shalt eat in thy gates whatsoever thy soul lusteth after.

22 [a]Even as the roebuck and the hart is eaten, so thou shalt eat them: the unclean and the clean shall eat *of* them alike.

23 [a]Only [/]be sure that thou eat not the blood: [b]for the blood *is* the life; and thou mayest not eat the life with the flesh.

24 Thou shalt not eat it; thou shalt pour it upon the earth as water.

25 Thou shalt not eat it; [a]that it may go well with thee, and with thy children after thee, [b]when thou shalt do *that which is* right in the sight of the LORD.

26 Only thy [a]holy things which thou hast, and [b]thy vows, thou shalt take, and go unto the place which the LORD shall choose:

27 And [a]thou shalt offer thy burnt offerings, the flesh and the blood, upon the altar of the LORD thy God: and the blood of thy sacrifices shall be poured out upon the altar of the LORD thy God, and thou shalt eat the flesh.

28 Observe and hear all these words which I command thee, [a]that it may go well with thee, and with thy children after thee for ever, when thou doest *that which is* good and right in the sight of the LORD thy God. **S**

29 ¶ When [a]the LORD thy God shall cut off the nations from before thee, whither thou goest to possess them, and thou [/]succeedest them, and dwellest in their land;

30 Take heed to thyself that thou be not snared [/]by following them, after that they be destroyed from before thee; and that thou inquire not after their gods, saying, How did these nations serve their gods? even so will I do likewise.

31 [a]Thou shalt not do so unto the LORD thy God: for every [/]abomination to the

S *Dt 11:26–27* ◀ ▶ *Dt 12:32*

LORD, which he hateth, have they done
unto their gods; for [b]even their sons and
their daughters they have burnt in the
fire to their gods.
S 32 What thing soever I command you,
observe to do it: [a]thou shalt not add
thereto, nor diminish from it.

Warning against idolatry

13 IF THERE arise among you a
prophet, or a [a]dreamer of
dreams, [b]and giveth thee a sign or a
wonder,
2 And [a]the sign or the wonder come to
pass, whereof he spake unto thee, saying,
Let us go after other gods, which thou
hast not known, and let us serve them;
3 Thou shalt not hearken unto the
words of that prophet, or that dreamer of
dreams: for the LORD your God [a]proveth
you, to know whether ye love the LORD
your God with all your heart and with all
your soul.
4 Ye shall [a]walk after the LORD your
God, and fear him, and keep his commandments, and obey his voice, and ye
shall serve him, and [b]cleave unto him.
5 And [a]that prophet, or that dreamer
of dreams, shall be put to death; because
he hath ʹspoken to turn *you* away from
the LORD your God, which brought you
out of the land of Egypt, and redeemed
you out of the house of bondage, to thrust
thee out of the way which the LORD thy
God commanded thee to walk in. [b]So
shalt thou put the evil away from the
midst of thee.
6 ¶ [a]If thy brother, the son of thy
mother, or thy son, or thy daughter, or
[b]the wife of thy bosom, or thy friend,
[c]which *is* as thine own soul, entice thee
secretly, saying, Let us go and serve other
gods, which thou hast not known, thou,
nor thy fathers;
7 *Namely,* of the gods of the people
which *are* round about you, nigh unto
thee, or far off from thee, from the *one*
end of the earth even unto the *other* end
of the earth;
8 Thou shalt [a]not consent unto him,
nor hearken unto him; neither shall thine
eye pity him, neither shalt thou spare,
neither shalt thou conceal him:
9 But [a]thou shalt surely kill him;
[b]thine hand shall be first upon him to put

31 [b]ch. 18:10; Jer. 32:35; Ezek. 23:37
32 [a]ch. 4:2; Josh. 1:7; Rev. 22:18
13:1 [a]Zech. 10:2 [b]Mat. 24:24; 2 Thes. 2:9
2 [a]See ch. 18:22; Mat. 7:22
3 [a]ch. 8:2; See Mat. 24:24; 2 Thes. 2:11
4 [a]2 Ki. 23:3; 2 Chr. 34:31 [b]ch. 30:20
5 [a]Jer. 14:15; Zech. 13:3 [b]ch. 17:7; 1 Cor. 5:13 ʹHeb. *spoken revolt against the LORD*
6 [a]ch. 17:2 [b]See Gen. 16:5; ch. 28:54; Prov. 5:20 [c]1 Sam. 18:1,3 & 20:17
8 [a]Prov. 1:10
9 [a]ch. 17:5 [b]ch. 17:7; Acts 7:58
10 ʹHeb. *bondmen*
11 [a]ch. 19:20
12 [a]Judg. 20:1,2
13 [a]1 John 2:19; Jude 19 [b]2 Ki. 17:21 [c]ver. 2,6 ʹOr, *naughty men*
15 [a]Lev. 27:28; Josh. 6:17,21
16 [a]Josh. 6:24 [b]Josh. 8:28; Jer. 49:2
17 [a]Josh. 6:18 [b]Josh. 7:26 [c]Gen. 22:17 & 26:4,24 & 28:14 ʹOr, *devoted*
18 [a]ch. 12:25,28, 32
14:1 [a]Rom. 8:16; & 9:8,26; Gal. 3:26 [b]Lev. 19:28 & 21:5; Jer. 16:6 & 41:5 & 47:5; 1 Thes. 4:13
2 [a]Lev. 20:26; ch. 7:6 & 26:18,19

him to death, and afterwards the hand of
all the people.
10 And thou shalt stone him with
stones, that he die; because he hath
sought to thrust thee away from the LORD
thy God, which brought thee out of the
land of Egypt, from the house of
ʹbondage.
11 And [a]all Israel shall hear, and fear,
and shall do no more any such wickedness as this is among you.
12 ¶ [a]If thou shalt hear *say* in one of
thy cities, which the LORD thy God hath
given thee to dwell there, saying,
13 *Certain* men, ʹthe children of Belial, [a]are gone out from among you, and
have [b]withdrawn the inhabitants of their
city, saying, [c]Let us go and serve other
gods, which ye have not known;
14 Then shalt thou inquire, and make
search, and ask diligently; and, behold, *if*
it be truth, *and* the thing certain, *that*
such abomination is wrought among you;
15 Thou shalt surely smite the inhabitants of that city with the edge of the
sword, [a]destroying it utterly, and all that
is therein, and the cattle thereof, with
the edge of the sword.
16 And thou shalt gather all the spoil
of it into the midst of the street thereof,
and shalt [a]burn with fire the city, and all
the spoil thereof every whit, for the LORD
thy God: and it shall be [b]an heap for ever;
it shall not be built again.
17 And [a]there shall cleave nought of
the ʹcursed thing to thine hand: that the
LORD may [b]turn from the fierceness of his
anger, and show thee mercy, and have
compassion upon thee, and multiply
thee, [c]as he hath sworn unto thy fathers;
18 When thou shalt hearken to the
voice of the LORD thy God, [a]to keep all his
commandments which I command thee
this day, to do *that which is* right in the
eyes of the LORD thy God.
14 YE *ARE* [a]the children of the LORD
your God: [b]ye shall not cut yourselves, nor make any baldness between
your eyes for the dead.
2 [a]For thou *art* an holy people unto the S
LORD thy God, and the LORD hath chosen
thee to be a peculiar people unto himself,
above all the nations that *are* upon the
earth.

Clean and unclean animals

3 ¶ [a]Thou shalt not eat any abominable thing.

4 [a]These *are* the beasts which ye shall eat: the ox, the sheep, and the goat,

5 The hart, and the roebuck, and the fallow deer, and the wild goat, and the [1,2]pygarg, and the wild ox, and the chamois.

6 And every beast that parteth the hoof, and cleaveth the cleft into two claws, *and* cheweth the cud among the beasts, that ye shall eat.

7 Nevertheless these ye shall not eat of them that chew the cud, or of them that divide the cloven hoof; *as* the camel, and the hare, and the coney: for they chew the cud, but divide not the hoof; *therefore* they *are* unclean unto you.

8 And the swine, because it divideth the hoof, yet cheweth not the cud, it *is* unclean unto you: ye shall not eat of their flesh, [a]nor touch their dead carcase.

9 ¶ [a]These ye shall eat of all that *are* in the waters: all that have fins and scales shall ye eat:

10 And whatsoever hath not fins and scales ye may not eat; it *is* unclean unto you.

11 ¶ *Of* all clean birds ye shall eat.

12 [a]But these *are they* of which ye shall not eat: the eagle, and the ossifrage, and the ospray,

13 And the glede, and the kite, and the vulture after his kind,

14 And every raven after his kind,

15 And the owl, and the night hawk, and the cuckoo, and the hawk after his kind,

16 The little owl, and the great owl, and the swan,

17 And the pelican, and the gier eagle, and the cormorant,

18 And the stork, and the heron after her kind, and the lapwing, and the bat.

19 And [a]every creeping thing that flieth *is* unclean unto you: [b]they shall not be eaten.

20 *But of* all clean fowls ye may eat.

21 ¶ [a]Ye shall not eat *of* any thing that dieth of itself: thou shalt give it unto the stranger that *is* in thy gates, that he may eat it; or thou mayest sell it unto an alien: [b]for thou *art* an holy people unto the LORD thy God. [c]Thou shalt not seethe a kid in his mother's milk.

3 [a]Ezek. 4:14; Acts 10:13,14
4 [a]Lev. 11:2
5 [1]Or, *bison* [2]Heb. *dishon*
8 [a]Lev. 11:26,27
9 [a]Lev. 11:9
12 [a]Lev. 11:13
19 [a]Lev. 11:20 [b]See Lev. 11:21
21 [a]Lev. 17:15 & 22:8; Ezek. 4:14 [b]ver. 2 [c]Ex. 23:19 & 34:26
22 [a]Lev. 27:30; ch. 12:6,17; Neh. 10:37
23 [a]ch. 12:5-7,17, 18 [b]ch. 15:19,20
24 [a]ch. 12:21
26 [a]ch. 12:7,18 & 26:11 [1]Heb. *asketh of thee*
27 [a]ch. 12:12,18, 19 [b]Num. 18:20; ch. 18:1,2
28 [a]ch. 26:12; Amos 4:4
29 [a]ch. 26:12 [b]ver. 27; ch. 12:12 [c]ch. 15:10; See Mal. 3:10
15:1 [a]Ex. 21:2 & 23:10,11; Lev. 25:2,4; ch. 31:10; Jer. 34:14
2 [1]Heb. *master of the lending of his hand*
3 [a]See ch. 23:20

Laws about tithes

22 [a]Thou shalt truly tithe all the increase of thy seed, that the field bringeth forth year by year.

23 [a]And thou shalt eat before the LORD thy God, in the place which he shall choose to place his name there, the tithe of thy corn, of thy wine, and of thine oil, and [b]the firstlings of thy herds and of thy flocks; that thou mayest learn to fear the LORD thy God always.

24 And if the way be too long for thee, so that thou art not able to carry it; *or* [a]if the place be too far from thee, which the LORD thy God shall choose to set his name there, when the LORD thy God hath blessed thee:

25 Then shalt thou turn *it* into money, and bind up the money in thine hand, and shalt go unto the place which the LORD thy God shall choose:

26 And thou shalt bestow that money for whatsoever thy soul lusteth after, for oxen, or for sheep, or for wine, or for strong drink, or for whatsoever thy soul [1]desireth: [a]and thou shalt eat there before the LORD thy God, and thou shalt rejoice, thou, and thine household,

27 And [a]the Levite that *is* within thy gates; thou shalt not forsake him; for [b]he hath no part nor inheritance with thee.

28 ¶ [a]At the end of three years thou shalt bring forth all the tithe of thine increase the same year, and shalt lay *it* up within thy gates:

29 [a]And the Levite, (because [b]he hath no part nor inheritance with thee,) and the stranger, and the fatherless, and the widow, which *are* within thy gates, shall come, and shall eat and be satisfied; that [c]the LORD thy God may bless thee in all the work of thine hand which thou doest. A U

The sabbath years of release

15 AT THE end of [a]*every* seven years thou shalt make a release.

2 And this *is* the manner of the release: Every [1]creditor that lendeth *aught* unto his neighbour shall release *it;* he shall not exact *it* of his neighbour, or of his brother; because it is called the LORD'S release.

3 [a]Of a foreigner thou mayest exact *it*

A Ge 48:16 ◄► Dt 15:10
U Dt 11:26–27 ◄► Dt 26:18–19

again: but *that* which is thine with thy brother thine hand shall release;

P 4 [1]Save when there shall be no poor among you; [a]for the LORD shall greatly bless thee in the land which the LORD thy God giveth thee *for* an inheritance to possess it:

5 Only [a]if thou carefully hearken unto the voice of the LORD thy God, to observe to do all these commandments which I command thee this day.

6 For the LORD thy God blesseth thee, as he promised thee: and [a]thou shalt lend unto many nations, but thou shalt not borrow; and [b]thou shalt reign over many nations, but they shall not reign over thee.

7 ¶ If there be among you a poor man of one of thy brethren within any of thy gates in thy land which the LORD thy God giveth thee, [a]thou shalt not harden thine heart, nor shut thine hand from thy poor brother:

8 [a]But thou shalt open thine hand wide unto him, and shalt surely lend him sufficient for his need, *in that* which he wanteth.

9 Beware that there be not a [1]thought in thy [2]wicked heart, saying, The seventh year, the year of release, is at hand; and thine [a]eye be evil against thy poor brother, and thou givest him nought; and [b]he cry unto the LORD against thee, and [c]it be sin unto thee.

A 10 Thou shalt surely give him, and
P [a]thine heart shall not be grieved when thou givest unto him: because that [b]for this thing the LORD thy God shall bless thee in all thy works, and in all that thou puttest thine hand unto.

11 For [a]the poor shall never cease out of the land: therefore I command thee, saying, Thou shalt open thine hand wide unto thy brother, to thy poor, and to thy needy, in thy land.

Hebrew slaves to be freed

12 ¶ *And* [a]if thy brother, an Hebrew man, or an Hebrew woman, be sold unto thee, and serve thee six years; then in the seventh year thou shalt let him go free from thee.

13 And when thou sendest him out free from thee, thou shalt not let him go away empty:

14 Thou shalt furnish him liberally out of thy flock, and out of thy floor, and out of thy winepress: *of that* wherewith the LORD thy God hath [a]blessed thee thou shalt give unto him.

15 And [a]thou shalt remember that thou wast a bondman in the land of Egypt, and the LORD thy God redeemed thee: therefore I command thee this thing today.

16 And it shall be, [a]if he say unto thee, I will not go away from thee; because he loveth thee and thine house, because he is well with thee;

17 Then thou shalt take an awl, and thrust *it* through his ear unto the door, and he shall be thy servant for ever. And also unto thy maidservant thou shalt do likewise.

18 It shall not seem hard unto thee, A
when thou sendest him away free from P
thee; for he hath been worth [a]a double hired servant *to thee,* in serving thee six years: and the LORD thy God shall bless thee in all that thou doest.

Offering the firstlings

19 ¶ [a]All the firstling males that come of thy herd and of thy flock thou shalt sanctify unto the LORD thy God: thou shalt do no work with the firstling of thy bullock, nor shear the firstling of thy sheep.

20 [a]Thou shalt eat *it* before the LORD thy God year by year in the place which the LORD shall choose, thou and thy household.

21 [a]And if there be *any* blemish D
therein, *as if it be* lame, or blind, *or have* any ill blemish, thou shalt not sacrifice it unto the LORD thy God.

22 Thou shalt eat it within thy gates: [a]the unclean and the clean *person shall eat it* alike, as the roebuck, and as the hart.

23 [a]Only thou shalt not eat the blood thereof; thou shalt pour it upon the ground as water.

4 [a]ch. 28:8 [1]Or, *To the end that there be no poor among you*
5 [a]ch. 28:1
6 [a]ch. 28:12,44 [b]ch. 28:13; Prov. 22:7
7 [a]1 John 3:17
8 [a]Lev. 25:35; Mat. 5:42; Luke 6:34,35
9 [a]ch. 28:54,56; Mat. 20:15 [b]ch. 24:15 [c]Mat. 25:41, 42 [1]Heb. *word* [2]Heb. *Belial*
10 [a]2 Cor. 9:5,7 [b]ch. 14:29 & 24:19
11 [a]Mat. 26:11; Mark 14:7; John 12:8
12 [a]Ex. 21:2; Lev. 25:39; Jer. 34:14
14 [a]Prov. 10:22
15 [a]ch. 5:15 & 16:12
16 [a]Ex. 21:5,6
18 [a]See Is. 16:14; & 21:16
19 [a]Ex. 13:2 & 34:19; Lev. 27:26; Num. 3:13
20 [a]ch. 12:5-7,17; & 14:23 & 16:11, 14
21 [a]Lev. 22:20
22 [a]ch. 12:15,22
23 [a]ch. 12:16,23

P *Dt 8:18* ◀ ▶ *Dt 15:10*
A *Dt 14:29* ◀ ▶ *Dt 15:18*
P *Dt 15:4–6* ◀ ▶ *Dt 15:18*
A *Dt 15:10* ◀ ▶ *1Ki 2:3*
P *Dt 15:10* ◀ ▶ *Dt 16:15*
D *Nu 28:3–4* ◀ ▶ *Dt 16:1–6*

The Passover

D **16** OBSERVE THE [a]month of Abib, and keep the passover unto the LORD thy God: for [b]in the month of Abib the LORD thy God brought thee forth out of Egypt [c]by night.

2 Thou shalt therefore sacrifice the passover unto the LORD thy God, of the flock and [a]the herd, in the [b]place which the LORD shall choose to place his name there.

3 [a]Thou shalt eat no leavened bread with it; seven days shalt thou eat unleavened bread therewith, *even* the bread of affliction; for thou camest forth out of the land of Egypt in haste: that thou mayest remember the day when thou camest forth out of the land of Egypt all the days of thy life.

4 [a]And there shall be no leavened bread seen with thee in all thy coast seven days; [b]neither shall there *any thing* of the flesh, which thou sacrificedst the first day at even, remain all night until the morning.

5 Thou mayest not [1]sacrifice the passover within any of thy gates, which the LORD thy God giveth thee:

6 But at the place which the LORD thy God shall choose to place his name in, there thou shalt sacrifice the passover [a]at even, at the going down of the sun, at the season that thou camest forth out of Egypt.

7 And thou shalt [a]roast and eat *it* [b]in the place which the LORD thy God shall choose: and thou shalt turn in the morning, and go unto thy tents.

8 Six days thou shalt eat unleavened bread: and [a]on the seventh day *shall be* a [1]solemn assembly to the LORD thy God: thou shalt do no work *therein.*

Feasts of weeks and tabernacles

9 ¶ [a]Seven weeks shalt thou number unto thee: begin to number the seven weeks from *such time as* thou beginnest *to put* the sickle to the corn.

10 And thou shalt keep the feast of weeks unto the LORD thy God with [1]a tribute of a freewill offering of thine hand, which thou shalt give *unto the LORD thy God,* [a]according as the LORD thy God hath blessed thee:

11 And [a]thou shalt rejoice before the LORD thy God, thou, and thy son, and thy daughter, and thy manservant, and thy maidservant, and the Levite that *is* within thy gates, and the stranger, and the fatherless, and the widow, that *are* among you, in the place which the LORD thy God hath chosen to place his name there.

12 [a]And thou shalt remember that thou wast a bondman in Egypt: and thou shalt observe and do these statutes.

13 ¶ [a]Thou shalt observe the feast of tabernacles seven days, after that thou hast gathered in thy [1]corn and thy wine:

14 And [a]thou shalt rejoice in thy feast, thou, and thy son, and thy daughter, and thy manservant, and thy maidservant, and the Levite, the stranger, and the fatherless, and the widow, that *are* within thy gates.

15 [a]Seven days shalt thou keep a solemn feast unto the LORD thy God in the place which the LORD shall choose: because the LORD thy God shall bless thee in all thine increase, and in all the works of thine hands, therefore thou shalt surely rejoice. P

16 ¶ [a]Three times in a year shall all thy males appear before the LORD thy God in the place which he shall choose; in the feast of unleavened bread, and in the feast of weeks, and in the feast of tabernacles: and [b]they shall not appear before the LORD empty:

17 Every man *shall give* [1]as he is able, [a]according to the blessing of the LORD thy God which he hath given thee.

Appointment of judges and officers

18 ¶ [a]Judges and officers shalt thou make thee in all thy gates, which the LORD thy God giveth thee, throughout thy tribes: and they shall judge the people with just judgment.

19 [a]Thou shalt not wrest judgment; [b]thou shalt not respect persons, [c]neither take a gift: for a gift doth blind the eyes of the wise, and pervert the [1]words of the righteous.

20 [1]That which is altogether just shalt thou follow, that thou mayest [a]live, and inherit the land which the LORD thy God giveth thee.

21 ¶ [a]Thou shalt not plant thee a grove of any trees near unto the altar of the

16:1 [a]Ex. 12:2 [b]Ex. 13:4 [c]Ex. 12:29,42
2 [a]Num. 28:19 [b]ch. 12:5,26
3 [a]Ex. 12:15,19, 39 & 13:3,6,7 & 34:18
4 [a]Ex. 13:7 [b]Ex. 12:10 & 34:25
5 [1]Or, *kill*
6 [a]Ex. 12:6
7 [a]Ex. 12:8,9; 2 Chr. 35:13 [b]2 Ki. 23:23; John 2:13 & 11:55
8 [a]Ex. 12:16 & 13:6; Lev. 23:8 [1]Heb. *restraint;* see Lev. 23:36
9 [a]Ex. 23:16 & 34:22; Lev. 23:15; Acts 2:1
10 [a]1 Cor. 16:2 [1]Or, *sufficiency*
11 [a]ver. 14; ch. 12:7,12
12 [a]ch. 15:15
13 [a]Ex. 23:16; Lev. 23:34; Num. 29:12 [1]Heb. *floor, and thy winepress*
14 [a]Neh. 8:9
15 [a]Lev. 23:39
16 [a]Ex. 23:14 & 34:23 [b]Ex. 23:15 & 34:20
17 [a]ver. 10 [1]Heb. *according to the gift of his hand*
18 [a]ch. 1:16; 1 Chr. 23:4; 2 Chr. 19:5
19 [a]Ex. 23:2,6; Lev. 19:15 [b]ch. 1:17 [c]Ex. 23:8; Eccl. 7:7 [1]Or, *matters*
20 [a]Ezek. 18:5 [1]Heb. *Justice, justice*
21 [a]Ex. 34:13; 1 Ki. 14:15 & 16:33; 2 Ki. 17:16 & 21:3; 2 Chr. 33:3

LORD thy God, which thou shalt make thee.

22 [a]Neither shalt thou set thee up *any* ʹimage; which the LORD thy God hateth.

D 17 THOU [a]SHALT not sacrifice unto the LORD thy God *any* bullock, or ʹsheep, wherein is blemish, *or* any evilfavouredness: for that *is* an abomination unto the LORD thy God.

The administration of justice

2 ¶ [a]If there be found among you, within any of thy gates which the LORD thy God giveth thee, man or woman, that hath wrought wickedness in the sight of the LORD thy God, [b]in transgressing his covenant,

3 And hath gone and served other gods, and worshipped them, either [a]the sun, or moon, or any of the host of heaven, [b]which I have not commanded;

4 [a]And it be told thee, and thou hast heard *of it,* and inquired diligently, and, behold, *it be* true, *and* the thing certain, *that* such abomination is wrought in Israel:

5 Then shalt thou bring forth that man or that woman, which have committed that wicked thing, unto thy gates, *even* that man or that woman, and [a]shalt stone them with stones, till they die.

6 [a]At the mouth of two witnesses, or three witnesses, shall he that is worthy of death be put to death; *but* at the mouth of one witness he shall not be put to death.

7 [a]The hands of the witnesses shall be first upon him to put him to death, and afterward the hands of all the people. So [b]thou shalt put the evil away from among you.

8 ¶ [a]If there arise a matter too hard for thee in judgment, [b]between blood and blood, between plea and plea, and between stroke and stroke, *being* matters of controversy within thy gates: then shalt thou arise, [c]and get thee up into the place which the LORD thy God shall choose;

9 And [a]thou shalt come unto the priests the Levites, and [b]unto the judge that shall be in those days, and inquire; [c]and they shall show thee the sentence of judgment:

10 And thou shalt do according to the sentence, which they of that place which the LORD shall choose shall show thee; and thou shalt observe to do according to all that they inform thee:

11 According to the sentence of the law which they shall teach thee, and according to the judgment which they shall tell thee, thou shalt do: thou shalt not decline from the sentence which they shall show thee, *to* the right hand, nor *to* the left.

12 And [a]the man that will do presumptuously, ʹand will not hearken unto the priest [b]that standeth to minister there before the LORD thy God, or unto the judge, even that man shall die: and [c]thou shalt put away the evil from Israel.

13 [a]And all the people shall hear, and fear, and do no more presumptuously.

The choice of a king

14 ¶ When thou art come unto the land which the LORD thy God giveth thee, and shalt possess it, and shalt dwell therein, and shalt say, [a]I will set a king over me, like as all the nations that *are* about me; I

15 Thou shalt in any wise set *him* king over thee, [a]whom the LORD thy God shall choose: *one* [b]from among thy brethren shalt thou set king over thee: thou mayest not set a stranger over thee, which *is* not thy brother.

16 But he shall not multiply [a]horses to himself, nor cause the people [b]to return to Egypt, to the end that he should multiply horses: forasmuch as [c]the LORD hath said unto you, [d]Ye shall henceforth return no more that way.

17 Neither shall he multiply wives to himself, that [a]his heart turn not away: neither shall he greatly multiply to himself silver and gold.

18 [a]And it shall be, when he sitteth upon the throne of his kingdom, that he shall write him a copy of this law in a book out of [b]*that which is* before the priests the Levites:

19 And [a]it shall be with him, and he shall read therein all the days of his life: that he may learn to fear the LORD his God, to keep all the words of this law and these statutes, to do them:

20 That his heart be not lifted up above his brethren, and that he [a]turn not aside from the commandment, *to* the

22 [a]Lev. 26:1 ʹOr, *statue,* or, *pillar*
17:1 [a]ch. 15:21; Mal. 1:8,13 ʹOr, *goat*
2 [a]ch. 13:6 [b]Josh. 7:11 & 23:16; Judg. 2:20; 2 Ki. 18:12; Hos. 8:1
3 [a]ch. 4:19; Job 31:26 [b]Jer. 7:22, 23 & 19:5 & 32:35
4 [a]ch. 13:12,14
5 [a]Lev. 24:14; ch. 13:10; Josh. 7:25
6 [a]Num. 35:30; ch. 19:15; Mat. 18:16; John 8:17; 2 Cor. 13:1; 1 Tim. 5:19; Heb. 10:28
7 [a]ch. 13:9; Acts 7:58 [b]ch. 13:5 & 19:19
8 [a]2 Chr. 19:10; Hag. 2:11; Mal. 2:7 [b]Ex. 21:13,20,22, 28 [c]ch. 12:5 & 19:17
9 [a]Jer. 18:18 [b]ch. 19:17 [c]Ezek. 44:24
12 [a]Num. 15:30 [b]ch. 18:5,7 [c]ch. 13:5 ʹHeb. *not to hearken*
13 [a]ch. 13:11 & 19:20
14 [a]1 Sam. 8:5,19, 20
15 [a]1 Sam. 10:24; 1 Chr. 22:10 [b]Jer. 30:21
16 [a]1 Ki. 4:26 & 10:26,28 [b]Is. 31:1; Ezek. 17:15 [c]Ex. 13:17; Num. 14:3 [d]ch. 28:68; Jer. 42:15; Hos. 11:5
17 [a]See 1 Ki. 11:3, 4
18 [a]2 Ki. 11:12 [b]ch. 31:9; 2 Ki. 22:8
19 [a]Ps. 119:97,98
20 [a]ch. 5:32; 1 Ki. 15:5

D *Dt 16:1–6* ◀▶ *2Ki 23:21*

I *Dt 12:5* ◀▶ *Dt 18:15–19*

right hand, or *to* the left: to the end that he may prolong *his* days in his kingdom, he, and his children, in the midst of Israel.

The portion for the priests

18 THE PRIESTS the Levites, *and* all the tribe of Levi, [a]shall have no part nor inheritance with Israel: they [b]shall eat the offerings of the LORD made by fire, and his inheritance.

2 Therefore shall they have no inheritance among their brethren: the LORD *is* their inheritance, as he hath said unto them.

3 ¶ And this shall be the priest's due from the people, from them that offer a sacrifice, whether *it be* ox or sheep; and [a]they shall give unto the priest the shoulder, and the two cheeks, and the maw.

4 [a]The firstfruit *also* of thy corn, of thy wine, and of thine oil, and the first of the fleece of thy sheep, shalt thou give him.

5 For [a]the LORD thy God hath chosen him out of all thy tribes, [b]to stand to minister in the name of the LORD, him and his sons for ever.

6 ¶ And if a Levite come from any of thy gates out of all Israel, where he [a]sojourned, and come with all the desire of his mind [b]unto the place which the LORD shall choose;

7 Then he shall minister in the name of the LORD his God, [a]as all his brethren the Levites *do,* which stand there before the LORD.

8 They shall have like [a]portions to eat, beside [/]that which cometh of the sale of his patrimony.

Forbidden pagan practices

9 ¶ When thou art come into the land which the LORD thy God giveth thee, [a]thou shalt not learn to do after the abominations of those nations.

10 There shall not be found among you *any one* that maketh his son or his daughter [a]to pass through the fire, [b]*or* that useth divination, *or* an observer of times, or an enchanter, or a witch,

11 [a]Or a charmer, or a consulter with familiar spirits, or a wizard, or a [b]necromancer.

12 For all that do these things *are* an abomination unto the LORD: and [a]because of these abominations the LORD thy God doth drive them out from before thee.

13 Thou shalt be [a]perfect[/] with the LORD thy God. S

14 For these nations, which thou shalt [/]possess, hearkened unto observers of times, and unto diviners: but as for thee, the LORD thy God hath not suffered thee so *to do.*

The promise of a prophet

15 ¶ [a]The LORD thy God will raise up unto thee a Prophet from the midst of thee, of thy brethren, like unto me; unto him ye shall hearken; B I

16 According to all that thou desiredst of the LORD thy God in Horeb [a]in the day of the assembly, saying, [b]Let me not hear again the voice of the LORD my God, neither let me see this great fire any more, that I die not.

17 And the LORD said unto me, [a]They have well *spoken that* which they have spoken.

18 [a]I will raise them up a Prophet from H N O

S *Dt 14:2* ◀▶ *Dt 25:16*
B *Nu 19:1–22* ◀▶ *Ps 22:1–18*
I *Dt 17:14* ◀▶ *Dt 26:19*
H *Dt 7:10* ◀▶ *Dt 28:29*
N *Dt 11:26–28* ◀▶ *Dt 29:19–20*
O *Dt 4:39* ◀▶ *Dt 32:39*

18:1 [a]Num. 18:20 & 26:62; ch. 10:9 [b]Num. 18:8; 1 Cor. 9:13
3 [a]Lev. 7:30-34
4 [a]Ex. 22:29; Num. 18:12
5 [a]Ex. 28:1; Num. 3:10 [b]ch. 10:8
6 [a]Num. 35:2 [b]ch. 12:5
7 [a]2 Chr. 31:2
8 [a]2 Chr. 31:4; Neh. 12:44 [/]Heb. *his sales by the fathers*
9 [a]Lev. 18:26,27, 30; ch. 12:29
10 [a]Lev. 18:21; ch. 12:31 [b]Lev. 20:27; Is. 8:19
11 [a]Lev. 20:27 [b]1 Sam. 28:7
12 [a]Lev. 18:24; ch. 9:4
13 [a]Gen. 17:1 [/]Or, *upright,* or, *sincere*
14 [/]Or, *inherit*
15 [a]John 1:45; Acts 3:22
16 [a]ch. 9:10 [b]Ex. 20:19; Heb. 12:19
17 [a]ch. 5:28
18 [a]John 1:45; Acts 3:22

18:9–12 This passage contains the most complete list of occult and spiritistic rites in the OT. One of the major Canaanite religions involved the worship of the god Molech and required child sacrifice. The Canaanites believed that such sacrifices would ensure material blessings. God referred to these practices as "abominations" (18:9). All forms of fortune telling, sorcery, witchcraft and occult practice were also forbidden in this passage. God's prohibition of these practices continues today; anyone involved with these activities needs to repent of their sin and seek God's forgiveness.

18:15–19 These verses contain one of the clearest, prophetic descriptions of Israel's Messiah. Moses indicated that God would raise up a prophet "like unto me" (18:15). Though this is a collective reference to all of the prophets that would follow Moses, it is also a reference to the Messiah and is uniquely fulfilled in Jesus (see Jn 1:21, 25, 45; 5:46; 6:14; 7:40; Ac 3:22–23; 7:37). Moses specifically warned Israel to listen to this prophet for God would hold everyone responsible if they rejected his words. For a more detailed discussion of the prophetic parallels between the life of Moses and the life of Jesus, see the article "A Prophet Like Unto Moses," p. 242.

A Prophet Like Unto Moses

Moses gave Israel one of the greatest Messianic prophecies. As a unique leader with abilities as prophet, priest, teacher and lawgiver, Moses prophesied that God would raise up the Messiah to be like Moses so that God's people would recognize him (see Dt 18:15–18; 34:10; Ac 3:22–23; 7:37).

This prophecy was fulfilled in many ways through the life, death and resurrection of Jesus (see Jn 1:21, 45; 6:14; Ac 7:37–38). In fact, an analysis of the life of Moses and the life of Jesus of Nazareth reveals at least fifty parallels in their lives. Both were prophets, priests, lawgivers, teachers and leaders of men. Both taught God's truth and confirmed their teaching with miracles. Both spent their early years in Egypt, miraculously protected from those who sought their lives. Moses' family initially did not accept his role of leadership, but later his brother Aaron and sister Miriam became his assistants. Similarly, Jesus' family initially failed to follow him, but later Jesus' brother James became the leader of the believers in Jerusalem.

The similarities are also evident in their leadership and authority. As Moses appointed seventy rulers over Israel, Jesus anointed seventy disciples to teach the nations. Moses stretched his hand over the Red Sea to command it, and Jesus rebuked the Sea of Galilee to quiet the waves. Moses sent twelve spies to explore Canaan; Jesus sent twelve apostles to reach the world. Moses and Jesus both cured lepers and proved their authority through miracles. The people were ungrateful and rebelled against the leadership of both men. The generations that rebelled against Moses died for their lack of faith in the wilderness. Those who rebelled against Jesus died in the Roman siege of Jerusalem in A.D. 70.

The parallelism is noticeable in the experiences of their personal lives too. The Bible never indicates that either one experienced sickness. Though Moses and Jesus both died on a hilltop, neither of their bodies remained in a tomb. Both fasted for forty days and faced spiritual crises on mountaintops. Both of their faces shone with the glory of heaven—Moses on Mt. Sinai, Jesus on the Mount of Transfiguration.

Yet the greatest resemblance between Moses and Jesus occurred in their ministries among people. During the Passover, both Moses and Jesus freed all people who would listen to them and trust God's Word. While Moses rescued Israel from the dead religion of pagan Egypt, Jesus rescued Israel from the dead letter of the law of tradition. As Moses conquered the great enemy of Israel, the Amalekites, with his upraised arms, Jesus conquered the great enemy of sin and death with his upraised arms on a cross. Moses lifted up the brazen serpent in the wilderness to heal his people; Jesus was lifted up on the cross to heal all people from sin. During the Feast of Firstfruits, God used Moses to bring about the resurrection of the children of Israel as they passed through the Red Sea; on the anniversary of that feast Jesus became the firstfruits of resurrection as he rose from the grave. Fifty days after the Red Sea, on Pentecost, God delivered the great gift to Israel of the Law; fifty days after Jesus' resurrection, God gave believers the great gift of the Holy Spirit.

God is a covenant-keeping God, and the promises made about the Messiah have all come true in Jesus Christ. That all of these similarities are beyond the ability of human control, compels one to believe that Jesus is the prophesied Messiah, a prophet like unto Moses.

among their brethren, like unto thee, and
[b]will put my words in his mouth; [c]and he
shall speak unto them all that I shall command him.
19 [a]And it shall come to pass, *that*
whosoever will not hearken unto my
words which he shall speak in my name,
I will require *it* of him.
20 But [a]the prophet, which shall presume to speak a word in my name, which
I have not commanded him to speak, or
[b]that shall speak in the name of other
gods, even that prophet shall die.
21 And if thou say in thine heart, How
shall we know the word which the LORD
hath not spoken?
22 [a]When a prophet speaketh in the
name of the LORD, [b]if the thing follow not,
nor come to pass, that *is* the thing which
the LORD hath not spoken, *but* the
prophet hath spoken it [c]presumptuously:
thou shalt not be afraid of him.

Cities of refuge for murderers

19 WHEN THE LORD thy God [a]hath
cut off the nations, whose land
the LORD thy God giveth thee, and thou
[1]succeedest them, and dwellest in their
cities, and in their houses;
2 [a]Thou shalt separate three cities for
thee in the midst of thy land, which the
LORD thy God giveth thee to possess it.
3 Thou shalt prepare thee a way, and
divide the coasts of thy land, which the
LORD thy God giveth thee to inherit, into
three parts, that every slayer may flee
thither.
4 ¶ And [a]this *is* the case of the slayer,
which shall flee thither, that he may live:
Whoso killeth his neighbour ignorantly,
whom he hated not [1]in time past;
5 As when a man goeth into the wood
with his neighbour to hew wood, and his
hand fetcheth a stroke with the axe to cut
down the tree, and the [1]head slippeth
from the [2]helve, and [3]lighteth upon his
neighbour, that he die; he shall flee unto
one of those cities, and live:
6 [a]Lest the avenger of the blood pursue the slayer, while his heart is hot, and
overtake him, because the way is long,
and [1]slay him; whereas he *was* not worthy of death, inasmuch as he hated him
not [2]in time past.
7 Wherefore I command thee, saying,
Thou shalt separate three cities for thee.
8 And if the LORD thy God [a]enlarge thy
coast, as he hath sworn unto thy fathers,
and give thee all the land which he promised to give unto thy fathers;
9 If thou shalt keep all these commandments to do them, which I command thee this day, to love the LORD thy
God, and to walk ever in his ways; [a]then
shalt thou add three cities more for thee,
beside these three:
10 That innocent blood be not shed in
thy land, which the LORD thy God giveth
thee *for* an inheritance, and *so* blood be
upon thee.
11 ¶ But [a]if any man hate his neighbour, and lie in wait for him, and rise up
against him, and smite him [1]mortally that
he die, and fleeth into one of these cities:
12 Then the elders of his city shall
send and fetch him thence, and deliver
him into the hand of the avenger of
blood, that he may die.
13 [a]Thine eye shall not pity him, [b]but
thou shalt put away *the guilt of* innocent
blood from Israel, that it may go well
with thee.
14 ¶ [a]Thou shalt not remove thy
neighbour's landmark, which they of old
time have set in thine inheritance, which
thou shalt inherit in the land that the
LORD thy God giveth thee to possess it.

Laws about witnesses

15 ¶ [a]One witness shall not rise up
against a man for any iniquity, or for any
sin, in any sin that he sinneth: at the
mouth of two witnesses, or at the mouth
of three witnesses, shall the matter be
established.
16 ¶ If a false witness [a]rise up against
any man to testify against him [1]*that
which is* wrong;
17 Then both the men, between
whom the controversy *is*, shall stand before the LORD, [a]before the priests and the
judges, which shall be in those days;
18 And the judges shall make diligent
inquisition: and, behold, *if* the witness *be*
a false witness, *and* hath testified falsely
against his brother;
19 [a]Then shall ye do unto him, as he
had thought to have done unto his
brother: so [b]shalt thou put the evil away
from among you.
20 [a]And those which remain shall
hear, and fear, and shall henceforth commit no more any such evil among you.
21 [a]And thine eye shall not pity; *but*

18 [b]Is. 51:16; John 17:8 [c]John 4:25 & 8:28 & 12:49,50
19 [a]Acts 3:23
20 [a]Jer. 14:14,15 [b]ch. 13:1,2; Jer. 2:8
22 [a]Jer. 28:9 [b]See ch. 13:2 [c]ver. 20
19:1 [a]ch. 12:29 [1]Heb. *inheritest*, or, *possessest*
2 [a]Ex. 21:13; Num. 35:10,14; Josh. 20:2
4 [a]Num. 35:15; ch. 4:42 [1]Heb. *from yesterday the third day*
5 [1]Heb. *iron* [2]Heb. *wood* [3]Heb. *findeth*
6 [a]Num. 35:12 [1]Heb. *smite him in life* [2]Heb. *from yesterday the third day*
8 [a]Gen. 15:18; ch. 12:20
9 [a]Josh. 20:7
11 [a]Num. 35:16, 24; ch. 27:24; Prov. 28:17 [1]Heb. *in life*
13 [a]ch. 13:8 [b]Num. 35:33,34; 1 Ki. 2:31
14 [a]ch. 27:17; Prov. 22:28; Hos. 5:10
15 [a]Num. 35:30; ch. 17:6; Mat. 18:16; John 8:17; 2 Cor. 13:1; 1 Tim. 5:19; Heb. 10:28
16 [a]Ps. 27:12 & 35:11 [1]Or, *falling away*
17 [a]ch. 17:9 & 21:5
19 [a]Prov. 19:5; Dan. 6:24 [b]ch. 13:5 & 17:7 & 21:21 & 22:21
20 [a]ch. 17:13 & 21:21
21 [a]ver. 13

[b]life *shall go* for life, eye for eye, tooth for tooth, hand for hand, foot for foot.

Laws about military service

20 WHEN THOU goest out to battle against thine enemies, and seest [a]horses, and chariots, *and* a people more than thou, be not afraid of them: for the LORD thy God *is* [b]with thee, which brought thee up out of the land of Egypt.

2 And it shall be, when ye are come nigh unto the battle, that the priest shall approach and speak unto the people,

3 And shall say unto them, Hear, O Israel, ye approach this day unto battle against your enemies: let not your hearts [1]faint, fear not, and do not [2]tremble, neither be ye terrified because of them;

V 4 For the LORD your God *is* he that goeth with you, [a]to fight for you against your enemies, to save you.

5 ¶ And the officers shall speak unto the people, saying, What man *is there* that hath built a new house, and hath not [a]dedicated it? let him go and return to his house, lest he die in the battle, and another man dedicate it.

6 And what man *is he* that hath planted a vineyard, and hath not *yet* [a]eaten of it? let him *also* go and return unto his house, lest he die in the battle, and another man eat of it.

7 [a]And what man *is there* that hath betrothed a wife, and hath not taken her? let him go and return unto his house, lest he die in the battle, and another man take her.

W 8 And the officers shall speak further unto the people, and they shall say, [a]What man *is there that is* fearful and fainthearted? let him go and return unto his house, lest his brethren's heart [1]faint as well as his heart.

9 And it shall be, when the officers have made an end of speaking unto the people, that they shall make captains of the armies [1]to lead the people.

10 ¶ When thou comest nigh unto a city to fight against it, [a]then proclaim peace unto it.

11 And it shall be, if it make thee answer of peace, and open unto thee, then it shall be, *that* all the people *that is* found therein shall be tributaries unto thee, and they shall serve thee.

12 And if it will make no peace with thee, but will make war against thee, then thou shalt besiege it:

13 And when the LORD thy God hath delivered it into thine hands, [a]thou shalt smite every male thereof with the edge of the sword:

14 But the women, and the little ones, and [a]the cattle, and all that is in the city, *even* all the spoil thereof, shalt thou [1]take unto thyself; and [b]thou shalt eat the spoil of thine enemies, which the LORD thy God hath given thee.

15 Thus shalt thou do unto all the cities *which are* very far off from thee, which *are* not of the cities of these nations.

16 But [a]of the cities of these people, which the LORD thy God doth give thee *for* an inheritance, thou shalt save alive nothing that breatheth:

17 But thou shalt utterly destroy them; *namely,* the Hittites, and the Amorites, the Canaanites, and the Perizzites, the Hivites, and the Jebusites; as the LORD thy God hath commanded thee:

18 That [a]they teach you not to do after all their abominations, which they have done unto their gods; so should ye [b]sin against the LORD your God.

19 ¶ When thou shalt besiege a city a long time, in making war against it to take it, thou shalt not destroy the trees thereof by forcing an axe against them: for thou mayest eat of them, and thou shalt not cut them down ([1]for the tree of the field *is* man's *life*) [2]to employ *them* in the siege:

20 Only the trees which thou knowest that they *be* not trees for meat, thou shalt destroy and cut them down; and thou shalt build bulwarks against the city that maketh war with thee, until [1]it be subdued.

Laws about unsolved murders

21 IF *ONE* be found slain in the land which the LORD thy God giveth thee to possess it, lying in the field, *and* it be not known who hath slain him:

2 Then thy elders and thy judges shall come forth, and they shall measure unto the cities which *are* round about him that is slain:

3 And it shall be, *that* the city *which is*

21 [b]Ex. 21:23,24; Lev. 24:20; Mat. 5:38
20:1 [a]See Ps. 20:7; Is. 31:1 [b]Num. 23:21; ch. 31:6,8; 2 Chr. 13:12 & 32:7,8
3 [1]Heb. *be tender* [2]Heb. *make haste*
4 [a]ch. 1:30 & 3:22; Josh. 23:10
5 [a]See Neh. 12:27
6 [a]See Lev. 19:23, 24; ch. 28:30
7 [a]ch. 24:5
8 [a]Judg. 7:3 [1]Heb. *melt*
9 [1]Heb. to be *in the head of the people*
10 [a]2 Sam. 20:18, 20
13 [a]Num. 31:7
14 [a]Josh. 8:2 [b]Josh. 22:8 [1]Heb. *spoil*
16 [a]Num. 21:2,3, 35 & 33:52; ch. 7:1,2; Josh. 11:14
18 [a]ch. 7:4 & 12:30,31 & 18:9 [b]Ex. 23:33
19 [1]Or, *for, O man, the tree of the field is to be employed in the siege* [2]Heb. *to go from before thee*
20 [1]Heb. *it come down*

V *Dt 11:25* ◀▶ *Dt 28:7*
W *Dt 1:21* ◀▶ *Dt 31:6–8*

next unto the slain man, even the elders of that city shall take an heifer, which hath not been wrought with, *and* which hath not drawn in the yoke;

4 And the elders of that city shall bring down the heifer unto a rough valley, which is neither eared nor sown, and shall strike off the heifer's neck there in the valley:

5 And the priests the sons of Levi shall come near; for [a]them the LORD thy God hath chosen to minister unto him, and to bless in the name of the LORD; and [b]by their [1]word shall every controversy and every stroke be *tried:*

6 And all the elders of that city, *that are* next unto the slain *man,* [a]shall wash their hands over the heifer that is beheaded in the valley:

7 And they shall answer and say, Our hands have not shed this blood, neither have our eyes seen *it.*

8 Be merciful, O LORD, unto thy people Israel, whom thou hast redeemed, [a]and lay not innocent blood [1]unto thy people of Israel's charge. And the blood shall be forgiven them.

9 So [a]shalt thou put away the *guilt of* innocent blood from among you, when thou shalt do *that which is* right in the sight of the LORD.

Laws about captive wives

10 ¶ When thou goest forth to war against thine enemies, and the LORD thy God hath delivered them into thine hands, and thou hast taken them captive,

11 And seest among the captives a beautiful woman, and hast a desire unto her, that thou wouldest have her to thy wife;

12 Then thou shalt bring her home to thine house; and she shall shave her head, and [1,2]pare her nails;

13 And she shall put the raiment of her captivity from off her, and shall remain in thine house, and [a]bewail her father and her mother a full month: and after that thou shalt go in unto her, and be her husband, and she shall be thy wife.

14 And it shall be, if thou have no delight in her, then thou shalt let her go whither she will; but thou shalt not sell her at all for money, thou shalt not make merchandise of her, because thou hast [a]humbled her.

Laws concerning sons

15 ¶ If a man have two wives, one beloved, [a]and another hated, and they have born him children, *both* the beloved and the hated; and *if* the firstborn son be hers that was hated:

16 Then it shall be, [a]when he maketh his sons to inherit *that* which he hath, *that* he may not make the son of the beloved firstborn before the son of the hated, *which is indeed* the firstborn:

17 But he shall acknowledge the son of the hated *for* the firstborn, [a]by giving him a double portion of all [1]that he hath: for he *is* [b]the beginning of his strength; [c]the right of the firstborn *is* his.

18 ¶ If a man have a stubborn and rebellious son, which will not obey the voice of his father, or the voice of his mother, and *that,* when they have chastened him, will not hearken unto them:

19 Then shall his father and his mother lay hold on him, and bring him out unto the elders of his city, and unto the gate of his place;

20 And they shall say unto the elders of his city, This our son *is* stubborn and rebellious, he will not obey our voice; *he is* a glutton, and a drunkard.

21 And all the men of his city shall stone him with stones, that he die: [a]so shalt thou put evil away from among you; [b]and all Israel shall hear, and fear.

Miscellaneous laws

22 ¶ And if a man have committed a sin [a]worthy of death, and he be to be put to death, and thou hang him on a tree:

23 [a]His body shall not remain all night upon the tree, but thou shalt in any wise bury him that day; (for [b]he that is hanged *is* [c]accursed[1] of God;) that [d]thy land be not defiled, which the LORD thy God giveth thee *for* an inheritance.

22 THOU [a]SHALT not see thy brother's ox or his sheep go astray, and hide thyself from them: thou shalt in any case bring them again unto thy brother.

2 And if thy brother *be* not nigh unto thee, or if thou know him not, then thou shalt bring it unto thine own house, and it shall be with thee until thy brother seek after it, and thou shalt restore it to him again.

3 In like manner shalt thou do with his ass; and so shalt thou do with his rai-

21:5 [a]ch. 10:8; 1 Chr. 23:13 [b]ch. 17:8,9 [1]Heb. *mouth*

6 [a]See Ps. 19:12 & 26:6; Mat. 27:24

8 [a]Jonah 1:14 [1]Heb. *in the midst*

9 [a]ch. 19:13

12 [1]Or, *suffer to grow* [2]Heb. *make,* or, *dress*

13 [a]See Ps. 45:10

14 [a]Gen. 34:2; ch. 22:29; Judg. 19:24

15 [a]Gen. 29:33

16 [a]1 Chr. 5:2 & 26:10; 2 Chr. 11:19,22

17 [a]See 1 Chr. 5:1 [b]Gen. 49:3 [c]Gen. 25:31,33 [1]Heb. *that is found with him*

21 [a]ch. 13:5 & 19:19,20 & 22:21, 24 [b]ch. 13:11

22 [a]ch. 19:6 & 22:26; Acts 23:29 & 25:11,25 & 26:31

23 [a]Josh. 8:29 & 10:26,27; John 19:31 [b]Gal. 3:13 [c]Num. 25:4; 2 Sam. 21:6 [d]Lev. 18:25; Num. 35:34 [1]Heb. *the curse of God*

22:1 [a]Ex. 23:4

ment; and with all lost thing of thy brother's, which he hath lost, and thou hast found, shalt thou do likewise: thou mayest not hide thyself.

4 ¶ [a]Thou shalt not see thy brother's ass or his ox fall down by the way, and hide thyself from them: thou shalt surely help him to lift *them* up again.

5 ¶ The woman shall not wear that which pertaineth unto a man, neither shall a man put on a woman's garment: for all that do so *are* abomination unto the LORD thy God.

6 ¶ If a bird's nest chance to be before thee in the way in any tree, or on the ground, *whether they be* young ones, or eggs, and the dam sitting upon the young, or upon the eggs, [a]thou shalt not take the dam with the young:

7 *But* thou shalt in any wise let the dam go, and take the young to thee; [a]that it may be well with thee, and *that* thou mayest prolong *thy* days.

8 ¶ When thou buildest a new house, then thou shalt make a battlement for thy roof, that thou bring not blood upon thine house, if any man fall from thence.

9 ¶ [a]Thou shalt not sow thy vineyard with divers seeds: lest the [l]fruit of thy seed which thou hast sown, and the fruit of thy vineyard, be defiled.

10 ¶ [a]Thou shalt not plow with an ox and an ass together.

11 ¶ [a]Thou shalt not wear a garment of divers sorts, *as* of woollen and linen together.

12 ¶ Thou shalt make thee [a]fringes upon the four [l]quarters of thy vesture, wherewith thou coverest *thyself.*

Laws about sexual conduct

13 ¶ If any man take a wife, and go in unto her, and hate her,

14 And give occasions of speech against her, and bring up an evil name upon her, and say, I took this woman, and when I came to her, I found her not a maid:

15 Then shall the father of the damsel, and her mother, take and bring forth *the tokens of* the damsel's virginity unto the elders of the city in the gate:

16 And the damsel's father shall say unto the elders, I gave my daughter unto this man to wife, and he hateth her;

17 And, lo, he hath given occasions of speech *against her,* saying, I found not thy daughter a maid; and yet these *are the tokens of* my daughter's virginity. And they shall spread the cloth before the elders of the city.

18 And the elders of that city shall take that man and chastise him;

19 And they shall amerce him in an hundred *shekels* of silver, and give *them* unto the father of the damsel, because he hath brought up an evil name upon a virgin of Israel: and she shall be his wife; he may not put her away all his days.

20 But if this thing be true, *and the tokens of* virginity be not found for the damsel:

21 Then they shall bring out the damsel to the door of her father's house, and the men of her city shall stone her with stones that she die: because she hath [a]wrought folly in Israel, to play the whore in her father's house: [b]so shalt thou put evil away from among you.

22 ¶ [a]If a man be found lying with a woman married to an husband, then they shall both of them die, *both* the man that lay with the woman, and the woman: so shalt thou put away evil from Israel.

23 ¶ If a damsel *that is* a virgin be [a]betrothed unto an husband, and a man find her in the city, and lie with her;

24 Then ye shall bring them both out unto the gate of that city, and ye shall stone them with stones that they die; the damsel, because she cried not, *being* in the city; and the man, because he hath [a]humbled his neighbour's wife: [b]so thou shalt put away evil from among you.

25 ¶ But if a man find a betrothed damsel in the field, and the man [a]force[l] her, and lie with her: then the man only that lay with her shall die:

26 But unto the damsel thou shalt do nothing; *there is* in the damsel no sin *worthy* of death: for as when a man riseth against his neighbour, and slayeth him, even so *is* this matter:

27 For he found her in the field, *and* the betrothed damsel cried, and *there was* none to save her.

28 ¶ [a]If a man find a damsel *that is* a virgin, which is not betrothed, and lay hold on her, and lie with her, and they be found;

29 Then the man that lay with her shall give unto the damsel's father fifty *shekels* of silver, and she shall be his

4 [a]Ex. 23:5
6 [a]Lev. 22:28
7 [a]ch. 4:40
9 [a]Lev. 19:19 [l]Heb. *fulness of thy seed*
10 [a]See 2 Cor. 6:14-16
11 [a]Lev. 19:19
12 [a]Num. 15:38 [l]Heb. *wings*
21 [a]Gen. 34:7; Judg. 20:6,10; 2 Sam. 13:12,13 [b]ch. 13:5
22 [a]Lev. 20:10; John 8:5; Num. 5:22-27
23 [a]Mat. 1:18,19
24 [a]ch. 21:14 [b]ver. 21,22; 1 Cor. 5:2,13
25 [a]2 Sam. 13:14 [l]Or, *take strong hold of her*
28 [a]Ex. 22:16,17

wife; [a]because he hath humbled her, he may not put her away all his days.

30 ¶ [a]A man shall not take his father's wife, nor [b]discover his father's skirt.

Persons to be excluded

23 HE THAT is wounded in the stones, or hath his privy member cut off, shall not enter into the congregation of the LORD.

2 A bastard shall not enter into the congregation of the LORD; even to his tenth generation shall he not enter into the congregation of the LORD.

3 [a]An Ammonite or Moabite shall not enter into the congregation of the LORD; even to their tenth generation shall they not enter into the congregation of the LORD for ever:

4 [a]Because they met you not with bread and with water in the way, when ye came forth out of Egypt; and [b]because they hired against thee Balaam the son of Beor of Pethor of Mesopotamia, to curse thee.

5 Nevertheless the LORD thy God would not hearken unto Balaam; but the LORD thy God turned the curse into a blessing unto thee, because the LORD thy God loved thee.

6 [a]Thou shalt not seek their peace nor their [ʹ]prosperity all thy days for ever.

7 ¶ Thou shalt not abhor an Edomite; [a]for he *is* thy brother: thou shalt not abhor an Egyptian; because [b]thou wast a stranger in his land.

8 The children that are begotten of them shall enter into the congregation of the LORD in their third generation.

Camp sanitation in wartime

9 ¶ When the host goeth forth against thine enemies, then keep thee from every wicked thing.

10 ¶ [a]If there be among you any man, that is not clean by reason of uncleanness that chanceth him by night, then shall he go abroad out of the camp, he shall not come within the camp:

11 But it shall be, when evening [ʹ]cometh on, [a]he shall wash *himself* with water: and when the sun is down, he shall come into the camp *again.*

12 ¶ Thou shalt have a place also without the camp, whither thou shalt go forth abroad:

13 And thou shalt have a paddle upon thy weapon; and it shall be, when thou [ʹ]wilt ease thyself abroad, thou shalt dig therewith, and shalt turn back and cover that which cometh from thee:

14 For the LORD thy God [a]walketh in the midst of thy camp, to deliver thee, and to give up thine enemies before thee; therefore shall thy camp be holy: that he see no [ʹ]unclean thing in thee, and turn away from thee.

Various laws

15 ¶ [a]Thou shalt not deliver unto his master the servant which is escaped from his master unto thee:

16 He shall dwell with thee, *even* among you, in that place which he shall choose in one of thy gates, where it [ʹ]liketh him best: [a]thou shalt not oppress him.

17 ¶ There shall be no [ʹ]whore [a]of the daughters of Israel, nor [b]a sodomite of the sons of Israel.

18 Thou shalt not bring the hire of a whore, or the price of a dog, into the house of the LORD thy God for any vow: for even both these *are* abomination unto the LORD thy God.

19 ¶ [a]Thou shalt not lend upon usury to thy brother; usury of money, usury of victuals, usury of any thing that is lent upon usury:

20 [a]Unto a stranger thou mayest lend upon usury; but unto thy brother thou shalt not lend upon usury: [b]that the LORD thy God may bless thee in all that thou settest thine hand to in the land whither thou goest to possess it.

21 ¶ [a]When thou shalt vow a vow unto the LORD thy God, thou shalt not slack to pay it: for the LORD thy God will surely require it of thee; and it would be sin in thee.

22 But if thou shalt forbear to vow, it shall be no sin in thee.

23 [a]That which is gone out of thy lips thou shalt keep and perform; *even* a freewill offering, according as thou hast vowed unto the LORD thy God, which thou hast promised with thy mouth.

24 ¶ When thou comest into thy neighbour's vineyard, then thou mayest eat grapes thy fill at thine own pleasure; but thou shalt not put *any* in thy vessel.

25 When thou comest into the standing corn of thy neighbour, [a]then thou mayest pluck the ears with thine hand;

---

29 [a]ver. 24
30 [a]Lev. 18:8 & 20:11; ch. 27:20; 1 Cor. 5:1 [b]See Ruth 3:9; Ezek. 16:8
23:3 [a]Neh. 13:1,2
4 [a]See ch. 2:29 [b]Num. 22:5,6
6 [a]Ezra 9:12 [ʹ]Heb. *good*
7 [a]Gen. 25:24-26; Obad. 10,12 [b]Ex. 22:21 & 23:9; Lev. 19:34; ch. 10:19
10 [a]Lev. 15:16
11 [a]Lev. 15:5 [ʹ]Heb. *turneth toward*
13 [ʹ]Heb. *sittest down*
14 [a]Lev. 26:12 [ʹ]Heb. *nakedness of anything*
15 [a]1 Sam. 30:15
16 [a]Ex. 22:21 [ʹ]Heb. *is good for him*
17 [a]Lev. 19:29; See Prov. 2:16 [b]Gen. 19:5; 2 Ki. 23:7 [ʹ]Or, *sodomitess*
19 [a]Ex. 22:25; Lev. 25:36,37
20 [a]See Lev. 19:34; ch. 15:3 [b]ch. 15:10
21 [a]Num. 30:2; Eccl. 5:4,5
23 [a]Num. 30:2; Ps. 66:13,14
25 [a]Mat. 12:1; Mark 2:23; Luke 6:1

but thou shalt not move a sickle unto thy neighbour's standing corn.

24 WHEN A [a]man hath taken a wife, and married her, and it come to pass that she find no favour in his eyes, because he hath found [1]some uncleanness in her: then let him write her a bill of [2]divorcement, and give *it* in her hand, and send her out of his house.

2 And when she is departed out of his house, she may go and be another man's *wife*.

3 And *if* the latter husband hate her, and write her a bill of divorcement, and giveth *it* in her hand, and sendeth her out of his house; or if the latter husband die, which took her *to be* his wife;

4 [a]Her former husband, which sent her away, may not take her again to be his wife, after that she is defiled; for that *is* abomination before the LORD: and thou shalt not cause the land to sin, which the LORD thy God giveth thee *for* an inheritance.

5 ¶ [a]When a man hath taken a new wife, he shall not go out to war, [1]neither shall he be charged with any business: *but* he shall be free at home one year, and shall [b]cheer up his wife which he hath taken.

6 ¶ No man shall take the nether or the upper millstone to pledge: for he taketh *a man's* life to pledge.

7 ¶ [a]If a man be found stealing any of his brethren of the children of Israel, and maketh merchandise of him, or selleth him; then that thief shall die; [b]and thou shalt put evil away from among you.

8 ¶ Take heed in [a]the plague of leprosy, that thou observe diligently, and do according to all that the priests the Levites shall teach you: as I commanded them, *so* ye shall observe to do.

9 [a]Remember what the LORD thy God did [b]unto Miriam by the way, after that ye were come forth out of Egypt.

10 ¶ When thou dost [1]lend thy brother any thing, thou shalt not go into his house to fetch his pledge.

11 Thou shalt stand abroad, and the man to whom thou dost lend shall bring out the pledge abroad unto thee.

12 And if the man *be* poor, thou shalt not sleep with his pledge:

13 [a]In any case thou shalt deliver him the pledge again when the sun goeth down, that he may sleep in his own raiment, and [b]bless thee: and [c]it shall be righteousness unto thee before the LORD thy God.

14 ¶ Thou shalt not [a]oppress an hired servant *that is* poor and needy, *whether he be* of thy brethren, or of thy strangers that *are* in thy land within thy gates:

15 At his day [a]thou shalt give *him* his hire, neither shall the sun go down upon it; for he *is* poor, and [1]setteth his heart upon it: [b]lest he cry against thee unto the LORD, and it be sin unto thee.

16 [a]The fathers shall not be put to death for the children, neither shall the children be put to death for the fathers: every man shall be put to death for his own sin.

17 ¶ [a]Thou shalt not pervert the judgment of the stranger, *nor* of the fatherless; [b]nor take a widow's raiment to pledge:

18 But [a]thou shalt remember that thou wast a bondman in Egypt, and the LORD thy God redeemed thee thence: therefore I command thee to do this thing.

19 ¶ [a]When thou cuttest down thine harvest in thy field, and hast forgot a sheaf in the field, thou shalt not go again to fetch it: it shall be for the stranger, for the fatherless, and for the widow: that the LORD thy God may [b]bless thee in all the work of thine hands. P

20 When thou beatest thine olive tree, [1]thou shalt not go over the boughs again: it shall be for the stranger, for the fatherless, and for the widow.

21 When thou gatherest the grapes of thy vineyard, thou shalt not glean *it* [1]afterward: it shall be for the stranger, for the fatherless, and for the widow.

22 And [a]thou shalt remember that thou wast a bondman in the land of Egypt: therefore I command thee to do this thing.

25 IF THERE be a [a]controversy between men, and they come unto judgment, that *the judges* may judge them; then they [b]shall justify the righteous, and condemn the wicked.

2 And it shall be, if the wicked man *be* [a]worthy to be beaten, that the judge shall cause him to lie down, [b]and to be beaten before his face, according to his fault, by a certain number.

3 [a]Forty stripes he may give him, *and*

24:1 [a]Mat. 5:31 & 19:7; Mark 10:4 [1]Heb. *matter of nakedness* [2]Heb. *cutting off*

4 [a]Jer. 3:1

5 [a]ch. 20:7 [b]Prov. 5:18 [1]Heb. *not any thing shall pass upon him*

7 [a]Ex. 21:16 [b]ch. 19:19

8 [a]Lev. 13:2 & 14:2

9 [a]See Luke 17:32; 1 Cor. 10:6 [b]Num. 12:10

10 [1]Heb. *lend the loan of any thing to*

13 [a]Ex. 22:26 [b]Job 29:11; 2 Cor. 9:13; 2 Tim. 1:18 [c]Dan. 4:27

14 [a]Mal. 3:5

15 [a]Lev. 19:13; Jer. 22:13; Jas. 5:4 [b]Jas. 5:4 [1]Heb. *lifteth his soul unto it*

16 [a]Jer. 31:29; Ezek. 18:20

17 [a]Prov. 22:22; Jer. 5:28; Ezek. 22:29; Zech. 7:10 [b]Ex. 22:26

18 [a]ver. 22; ch. 16:12

19 [a]Lev. 19:9 & 23:22 [b]Ps. 41:1; Prov. 19:17

20 [1]Heb. *thou shalt not bough it after thee*

21 [1]Heb. *after thee*

22 [a]ver. 18

25:1 [a]ch. 19:17; Ezek. 44:24 [b]See Prov. 17:15

2 [a]Luke 12:48 [b]Mat. 10:17

3 [a]2 Cor. 11:24

P Dt 16:15 ◄ ► Dt 28:8

not exceed: lest, *if* he should exceed, and
beat him above these with many stripes,
then thy brother should [b]seem vile unto
thee.
4 ¶ [a]Thou shalt not muzzle the ox
when he ʹtreadeth out *the corn.*
5 ¶ [a]If brethren dwell together, and
one of them die, and have no child, the
wife of the dead shall not marry without
unto a stranger: her [b]husband'sʹ brother
shall go in unto her, and take her to him
to wife, and perform the duty of an husband's brother unto her.
6 And it shall be, *that* the firstborn
which she beareth [a]shall succeed in the
name of his brother *which is* dead, that
[b]his name be not put out of Israel.
7 And if the man like not to take his
ʹbrother's wife, then let his brother's
wife go up to the [a]gate unto the elders,
and say, My husband's brother refuseth
to raise up unto his brother a name in
Israel, he will not perform the duty of my
husband's brother.
8 Then the elders of his city shall call
him, and speak unto him: and *if* he stand
to it, and say, [a]I like not to take her;
9 Then shall his brother's wife come
unto him in the presence of the elders,
and [a]loose his shoe from off his foot, and
spit in his face, and shall answer and say,
So shall it be done unto that man that will
not [b]build up his brother's house.
10 And his name shall be called in Israel, The house of him that hath his shoe
loosed.
11 ¶ When men strive together one
with another, and the wife of the one
draweth near for to deliver her husband
out of the hand of him that smiteth him,
and putteth forth her hand, and taketh
him by the secrets:
12 Then thou shalt cut off her hand,
[a]thine eye shall not pity *her.*
13 ¶ [a]Thou shalt not have in thy bag
ʹdivers weights, a great and a small.
14 Thou shalt not have in thine house
ʹdivers measures, a great and a small.
15 *But* thou shalt have a perfect and
just weight, a perfect and just measure
shalt thou have: [a]that thy days may be
lengthened in the land which the LORD
thy God giveth thee.
S 16 For [a]all that do such things, *and* all

3 [b]Job 18:3
4 [a]Prov. 12:10; 1 Tim. 5:18 ʹHeb. *thresheth*
5 [a]Mat. 22:24; Luke 20:28 [b]Gen. 38:8; Ruth 1:12,13 & 3:9 ʹOr, *next kinsman*
6 [a]Gen. 38:9 [b]Ruth 4:10
7 [a]Ruth 4:1,2 ʹOr, *next kinsman's wife*
8 [a]Ruth 4:6
9 [a]Ruth 4:7 [b]Ruth 4:11
12 [a]ch. 19:13
13 [a]Lev. 19:35,36; Prov. 11:1; Ezek. 45:10; Mic. 6:11 ʹHeb. *a stone and a stone*
14 ʹHeb. *an ephah and an ephah*
15 [a]Ex. 20:12
16 [a]Prov. 11:1; 1 Thes. 4:6
17 [a]Ex. 17:8
18 [a]Ps. 36:1; Prov. 16:6; Rom. 3:18
19 [a]1 Sam. 15:3 [b]Ex. 17:14
26:2 [a]Ex. 23:19 & 34:26; Num. 18:13; ch. 16:10; Prov. 3:9 [b]ch. 12:5
5 [a]Hos. 12:12 [b]Gen. 43:1,2 & 45:7,11 [c]Gen. 46:1,6; Acts 7:15 [d]Gen. 46:27; ch. 10:22
6 [a]Ex. 1:11,14
7 [a]Ex. 2:23-25 & 3:9 & 4:31
8 [a]Ex. 12:37,51 & 13:3,14,16; ch. 5:15

that do unrighteously, *are* an abomination unto the LORD thy God.
17 ¶ [a]Remember what Amalek did
unto thee by the way, when ye were
come forth out of Egypt;
18 How he met thee by the way, and
smote the hindmost of thee, *even* all *that*
were feeble behind thee, when thou *wast*
faint and weary; and he [a]feared not God.
19 Therefore it shall be, [a]when the
LORD thy God hath given thee rest from
all thine enemies round about, in the
land which the LORD thy God giveth thee
for an inheritance to possess it, *that* thou
shalt [b]blot out the remembrance of Amalek from under heaven; thou shalt not forget *it.*

Firstfruits and tithes

26 AND IT shall be, when thou *art* T
come in unto the land which the
LORD thy God giveth thee *for* an inheritance, and possessest it, and dwellest
therein;
2 [a]That thou shalt take of the first of all
the fruit of the earth, which thou shalt
bring of thy land that the LORD thy God
giveth thee, and shalt put *it* in a basket,
and shalt [b]go unto the place which the
LORD thy God shall choose to place his
name there.
3 And thou shalt go unto the priest
that shall be in those days, and say unto
him, I profess this day unto the LORD thy
God, that I am come unto the country
which the LORD sware unto our fathers for
to give us.
4 And the priest shall take the basket
out of thine hand, and set it down before
the altar of the LORD thy God.
5 And thou shalt speak and say before
the LORD thy God, [a]A Syrian [b]ready to
perish *was* my father, and [c]he went
down into Egypt, and sojourned there
with a [d]few, and became there a nation,
great, mighty, and populous:
6 And [a]the Egyptians evil entreated us,
and afflicted us, and laid upon us hard
bondage:
7 And [a]when we cried unto the LORD
God of our fathers, the LORD heard our
voice, and looked on our affliction, and
our labour, and our oppression:
8 And [a]the LORD brought us forth out of
Egypt with a mighty hand, and with an

outstretched arm, and [b]with great terribleness, and with signs, and with
wonders:
9 And he hath brought us into this
place, and hath given us this land, *even*
[a]a land that floweth with milk and honey.
10 And now, behold, I have brought
the firstfruits of the land, which thou,
O LORD, hast given me. And thou shalt set
it before the LORD thy God, and worship
before the LORD thy God:
11 And [a]thou shalt rejoice in every
good *thing* which the LORD thy God hath
given unto thee, and unto thine house,
thou, and the Levite, and the stranger
that *is* among you.
12 ¶ When thou hast made an end of
tithing all the [a]tithes of thine increase
the third year, *which is* [b]the year of tithing, and hast given *it* unto the Levite, the
stranger, the fatherless, and the widow,
that they may eat within thy gates, and
be filled;
13 Then thou shalt say before the LORD
thy God, I have brought away the hallowed things out of *mine* house, and also
have given them unto the Levite, and
unto the stranger, to the fatherless, and
to the widow, according to all thy commandments which thou hast commanded
me: I have not transgressed thy commandments, [a]neither have I forgotten
them:
14 [a]I have not eaten thereof in my
mourning, neither have I taken away
aught thereof for *any* unclean *use,* nor
given *aught* thereof for the dead: *but* I
have hearkened to the voice of the LORD
my God, *and* have done according to all
that thou hast commanded me.
15 [a]Look down from thy holy habitation, from heaven, and bless thy people
Israel, and the land which thou hast
given us, as thou swarest unto our fathers, a land that floweth with milk and
honey.
S 16 ¶ This day the LORD thy God hath
commanded thee to do these statutes and
judgments: thou shalt therefore keep and
do them with all thine heart, and with all
thy soul.
17 Thou hast [a]avouched the LORD this
day to be thy God, and to walk in his
ways, and to keep his statutes, and his
commandments, and his judgments, and
to hearken unto his voice:
18 And [a]the LORD hath avouched thee U
this day to be his peculiar people, as he
hath promised thee, and that *thou*
shouldest keep all his commandments;
19 And to make thee [a]high above all I
nations which he hath made, in praise,
and in name, and in honour; and that
thou mayest be [b]an holy people unto the
LORD thy God, as he hath spoken.

The altar at mount Ebal

27 AND MOSES with the elders of
Israel commanded the people,
saying, Keep all the commandments
which I command you this day.
2 And it shall be on the day [a]when ye
shall pass over Jordan unto the land
which the LORD thy God giveth thee, that
[b]thou shalt set thee up great stones, and
plaster them with plaster:
3 And thou shalt write upon them all
the words of this law, when thou art
passed over, that thou mayest go in unto
the land which the LORD thy God giveth
thee, a land that floweth with milk and
honey; as the LORD God of thy fathers
hath promised thee.
4 Therefore it shall be when ye be
gone over Jordan, *that* ye shall set up
these stones, which I command you this
day, [a]in mount Ebal, and thou shalt plaster them with plaster.
5 And there shalt thou build an altar
unto the LORD thy God, an altar of stones:
[a]thou shalt not lift up *any* iron *tool* upon
them.
6 Thou shalt build the altar of the LORD
thy God of whole stones: and thou shalt
offer burnt offerings thereon unto the
LORD thy God:
7 And thou shalt offer peace offerings,

8 [b]ch. 4:34
9 [a]Ex. 3:8
11 [a]ch. 12:7,12, 18 & 16:11
12 [a]Lev. 27:30; Num. 18:24 [b]ch. 14:28,29
13 [a]Ps. 119:141, 153,176
14 [a]Lev. 7:20 & 21:1,11; Hos. 9:4
15 [a]Is. 63:15; Zech. 2:13
17 [a]Ex. 20:19
18 [a]Ex. 6:7 & 19:5; ch. 7:6 & 14:2 & 28:9
19 [a]ch. 4:7,8 & 28:1 [b]Ex. 19:6; ch. 7:6 & 28:9; 1 Pet. 2:9
27:2 [a]Josh. 4:1 [b]Josh. 8:32
4 [a]ch. 11:29; Josh. 8:30,31
5 [a]Ex. 20:25; Josh. 8:31

S *Dt 25:16* ◀ ▶ *Dt 27:9–10*

U *Dt 14:29* ◀ ▶ *Dt 28:1–14*
I *Dt 18:15–19* ◀ ▶ *Dt 28:1–3*

27:4–10 Moses commanded Israel to gather stones, coat them with plaster, inscribe them with the words of the law and build them into a holy altar on the top of Mt. Ebal in the promised land. In this way the words written on them would stand out clearly, and the people would be reminded of their covenant relationship to obey God's laws and statutes every time they offered a sacrifice.

and shalt eat there, and rejoice before the
LORD thy God.
8 And thou shalt write upon the stones
all the words of this law very plainly.
S 9 ¶ And Moses and the priests the Levites spake unto all Israel, saying, Take
heed, and hearken, O Israel; [a]this day
thou art become the people of the LORD
thy God.
10 Thou shalt therefore obey the voice
of the LORD thy God, and do his commandments and his statutes, which I
command thee this day.
11 ¶ And Moses charged the people
the same day, saying,
12 These shall stand [a]upon mount Gerizim to bless the people, when ye are
come over Jordan; Simeon, and Levi, and
Judah, and Issachar, and Joseph, and Benjamin:
13 And [a]these shall stand upon mount
Ebal [†]to curse; Reuben, Gad, and Asher,
and Zebulun, Dan, and Naphtali.
14 ¶ And [a]the Levites shall speak, and
say unto all the men of Israel with a loud
voice,
15 [a]Cursed *be* the man that maketh
any graven or molten image, an abomination unto the LORD, the work of the hands
of the craftsman, and putteth *it* in *a* secret *place.* [b]And all the people shall answer and say, Amen.
16 [a]Cursed *be* he that setteth light by
his father or his mother. And all the people shall say, Amen.
17 [a]Cursed *be* he that removeth his
neighbour's landmark. And all the people
shall say, Amen.
18 [a]Cursed *be* he that maketh the
blind to wander out of the way. And all
the people shall say, Amen.
19 [a]Cursed *be* he that perverteth the
judgment of the stranger, fatherless, and
widow. And all the people shall say,
Amen.
20 [a]Cursed *be* he that lieth with his
father's wife; because he uncovereth his

S *Dt 26:16–19* ◄► *Dt 28:9–10*

9 [a]ch. 26:18
12 [a]ch. 11:29; Josh. 8:33; Judg. 9:7
13 [a]ch. 11:29; Josh. 8:33 [†]Heb. *for a cursing*
14 [a]ch. 33:10; Josh. 8:33; Dan. 9:11
15 [a]Ex. 20:4,23 & 34:17; Lev. 19:4 & 26:1; ch. 4:16,23 & 5:8; Is. 44:9; Hos. 13:2 [b]See Num. 5:22; Jer. 11:5; 1 Cor. 14:16
16 [a]Ex. 20:12 & 21:17; Lev. 19:3; ch. 21:18
17 [a]ch. 19:14; Prov. 22:28
18 [a]Lev. 19:14
19 [a]Ex. 22:21,22; ch. 10:18 & 24:17; Mal. 3:5
20 [a]Lev. 18:8; ch. 22:30
21 [a]Lev. 18:23
22 [a]Lev. 18:9
23 [a]Lev. 18:17
24 [a]Ex. 20:13; Lev. 24:17; Num. 35:31
25 [a]Ex. 23:7,8; ch. 10:17; Ezek. 22:12
26 [a]Jer. 11:3; Gal. 3:10
28:1 [a]Ex. 15:26; Lev. 26:3; Is. 55:2 [b]ch. 26:19
2 [a]Zech. 1:6
3 [a]Ps. 128:1,4 [b]Gen. 39:5
4 [a]Gen. 22:17 & 49:25; ch. 7:13; Prov. 10:22
5 [†]Or, *dough,* or, *kneading-trough*
6 [a]Ps. 121:8

father's skirt. And all the people shall say,
Amen.
21 [a]Cursed *be* he that lieth with any
manner of beast. And all the people shall
say, Amen.
22 [a]Cursed *be* he that lieth with his
sister, the daughter of his father, or the
daughter of his mother. And all the people shall say, Amen.
23 [a]Cursed *be* he that lieth with his
mother-in-law. And all the people shall
say, Amen.
24 [a]Cursed *be* he that smiteth his
neighbour secretly. And all the people
shall say, Amen.
25 [a]Cursed *be* he that taketh reward to
slay an innocent person. And all the people shall say, Amen.
26 [a]Cursed *be* he that confirmeth not
all the words of this law to do them. And
all the people shall say, Amen.

The blessings of obedience

28 AND IT shall come to pass, [a]if I
thou shalt hearken diligently U
unto the voice of the LORD thy God, to
observe *and* to do all his commandments
which I command thee this day, that the
LORD thy God [b]will set thee on high above
all nations of the earth:
2 And all these blessings shall come on
thee, and [a]overtake thee, if thou shalt
hearken unto the voice of the LORD thy
God.
3 [a]Blessed *shalt* thou *be* in the city, B
and blessed *shalt* thou *be* [b]in the field.
4 Blessed *shall be* [a]the fruit of thy
body, and the fruit of thy ground, and
the fruit of thy cattle, the increase of thy
kine, and the flocks of thy sheep.
5 Blessed *shall be* thy basket and thy
[†]store.
6 [a]Blessed *shalt* thou *be* when thou
comest in, and blessed *shalt* thou *be*
when thou goest out.

I *Dt 26:19* ◄► *Dt 30:1–10*
U *Dt 26:18–19* ◄► *Dt 30:8–9*
B *Dt 11:14–15* ◄► *Dt 28:11–12*

27:12–14 This curious passage recorded Moses' command to the tribes of Israel to separate into two groups after crossing into the promised land. Some of the tribes were to assemble on Mt. Gerizim and shout out the blessings of the law upon the people. The remaining tribes were to assemble on Mt. Ebal to shout out the curses of the law. Following this, the Levites would loudly shout a series of curses upon those who would violate God's laws. Chapters 28 and 29 contain these blessings and curses and form the basis for the Palestinian covenant established in 30:1–9.

V 7 The LORD [a]shall cause thine enemies that rise up against thee to be smitten before thy face: they shall come out against thee one way, and flee before thee seven ways.

P 8 The LORD shall [a]command the blessing upon thee in thy [1]storehouses, and in all that thou [b]settest thine hand unto; and he shall bless thee in the land which the LORD thy God giveth thee.

S 9 [a]The LORD shall establish thee an holy people unto himself, as he hath sworn unto thee, if thou shalt keep the commandments of the LORD thy God, and walk in his ways.

10 And all people of the earth shall see that thou art [a]called by the name of the LORD; and they shall be [b]afraid of thee.

B 11 And [a]the LORD shall make thee
P plenteous [1]in goods, in the fruit of thy [2]body, and in the fruit of thy cattle, and in the fruit of thy ground, in the land which the LORD sware unto thy fathers to give thee.

12 The LORD shall open unto thee his good treasure, the heaven [a]to give the rain unto thy land in his season, and [b]to bless all the work of thine hand: and [c]thou shalt lend unto many nations, and thou shalt not borrow.

13 And the LORD shall make thee [a]the head, and not the tail; and thou shalt be above only, and thou shalt not be beneath; if that thou hearken unto the commandments of the LORD thy God, which I command thee this day, to observe and to do *them:*

14 [a]And thou shalt not go aside from any of the words which I command thee this day, *to* the right hand, or *to* the left, to go after other gods to serve them.

The curses of disobedience

S 15 ¶ But it shall come to pass, [a]if thou wilt not hearken unto the voice of the LORD thy God, to observe to do all his commandments and his statutes which I command thee this day; that all these curses shall come upon thee, and overtake thee:

16 Cursed *shalt* thou *be* in the city, and cursed *shalt* thou *be* in the field.

17 Cursed *shall be* thy basket and thy store.

18 Cursed *shall be* the fruit of thy body, and the fruit of thy land, the increase of thy kine, and the flocks of thy sheep.

19 Cursed *shalt* thou *be* when thou comest in, and cursed *shalt* thou *be* when thou goest out.

20 The LORD shall send upon thee [a]cursing, [b]vexation, and [c]rebuke, in all that thou settest thine hand unto [1]for to do, until thou be destroyed, and until thou perish quickly; because of the wickedness of thy doings, whereby thou hast forsaken me.

21 The LORD shall make [a]the pestilence cleave unto thee, until he have consumed thee from off the land, whither thou goest to possess it. D

22 [a]The LORD shall smite thee with a consumption, and with a fever, and with an inflammation, and with an extreme burning, and with the [1]sword, and with [b]blasting, and with mildew; and they shall pursue thee until thou perish.

23 And [a]thy heaven that *is* over thy head shall be brass, and the earth that *is* under thee *shall be* iron. R

24 The LORD shall make the rain of thy land powder and dust: from heaven shall it come down upon thee, until thou be destroyed.

25 [a]The LORD shall cause thee to be smitten before thine enemies: thou shalt go out one way against them, and flee seven ways before them: and [b]shalt be [1]removed into all the kingdoms of the earth.

26 And [a]thy carcase shall be meat unto all fowls of the air, and unto the beasts of the earth, and no man shall fray *them* away.

7 [a]Lev. 26:7,8; 2 Sam. 22:38,39,41
8 [a]Lev. 25:21 [b]ch. 15:10 [1]Or, *barns*
9 [a]Ex. 19:5,6; ch. 7:6 & 26:18,19
10 [a]Num. 6:27; 2 Chr. 7:14; Is. 63:19; Dan. 9:18, 19 [b]ch. 11:25
11 [a]ch. 30:9; Prov. 10:22 [1]Or, *for good* [2]Heb. *belly*
12 [a]Lev. 26:4; ch. 11:14 [b]ch. 14:29 [c]ch. 15:6
13 [a]Is. 9:14,15
14 [a]ch. 5:32
15 [a]Lev. 26:14; Lam. 2:17; Dan. 9:11; Mal. 2:2
20 [a]Mal. 2:2 [b]1 Sam. 14:20; Zech. 14:13 [c]Is. 30:17 & 51:20 & 66:15 [1]Heb. *which thou wouldest do*
21 [a]Lev. 26:25
22 [a]Lev. 26:16 [b]Amos 4:9 [1]Or, *drought*
23 [a]Lev. 26:19
25 [a]ch. 32:30; Is. 30:17 [b]Jer. 15:4 & 24:9; Ezek. 23:46 [1]Heb. *for a removing*
26 [a]1 Sam. 17:44, 46; Jer. 7:33 & 16:4

V *Dt 20:4* ◀▶ *Dt 32:30*
P *Dt 24:19* ◀▶ *Dt 28:11–12*
S *Dt 27:9–10* ◀▶ *Dt 28:15*
B *Dt 28:3–5* ◀▶ *Dt 30:9*
P *Dt 28:8* ◀▶ *Dt 30:9*
S *Dt 28:9–10* ◀▶ *Dt 29:19–20*
D *Dt 7:15* ◀▶ *Dt 28:27*
R *Dt 4:30* ◀▶ *Dt 28:33*

28:23–25 Moses warned that a severe drought would turn the fertile land to dust if the Israelites broke their covenant with God. Furthermore, if the Israelites broke their covenant, their supernatural victories would become ruinous defeats and lead to their exile from the promised land.

D 27 The LORD will smite thee with [a]the botch of Egypt, and with [b]the emerods, and with the scab, and with the itch, whereof thou canst not be healed.

28 The LORD shall smite thee with madness, and blindness, and [a]astonishment of heart:

H 29 And thou shalt [a]grope at noonday, as the blind gropeth in darkness, and thou shalt not prosper in thy ways: and thou shalt be only oppressed and spoiled evermore, and no man shall save *thee.*

30 [a]Thou shalt betroth a wife, and another man shall lie with her: [b]thou shalt build an house, and thou shalt not dwell therein: [c]thou shalt plant a vineyard, and shalt not gather the grapes thereof.

31 Thine ox *shall be* slain before thine eyes, and thou shalt not eat thereof: thine ass *shall be* violently taken away from before thy face, and [l]shall not be restored to thee: thy sheep *shall be* given unto thine enemies, and thou shalt have none to rescue *them.*

32 Thy sons and thy daughters *shall be* given unto another people, and thine eyes shall look, and [a]fail *with longing* for them all the day long: and *there shall be* no might in thine hand.

R 33 [a]The fruit of thy land, and all thy labours, shall a nation which thou knowest not eat up; and thou shalt be only oppressed and crushed always:

34 So that thou shalt be mad for the sight of thine eyes which thou shalt see.

D 35 The LORD shall smite thee in the knees, and in the legs, with a sore botch that cannot be healed, from the sole of thy foot unto the top of thy head.

36 The LORD shall [a]bring thee, and thy king which thou shalt set over thee, unto a nation which neither thou nor thy fathers have known; and [b]there shalt thou serve other gods, wood and stone.

37 And thou shalt become [a]an astonishment, a proverb, [b]and a byword, among all nations whither the LORD shall lead thee. R

38 [a]Thou shalt carry much seed out into the field, and shalt gather *but* little in; for [b]the locust shall consume it.

39 Thou shalt plant vineyards, and dress *them,* but shalt neither drink *of* the wine, nor gather *the grapes;* for the worms shall eat them.

40 Thou shalt have olive trees throughout all thy coasts, but thou shalt not anoint *thyself* with the oil; for thine olive shall cast *his fruit.*

41 Thou shalt beget sons and daughters, but [l]thou shalt not enjoy them; for [a]they shall go into captivity.

42 All thy trees and fruit of thy land shall the locust [l]consume.

43 The stranger that *is* within thee shall get up above thee very high; and thou shalt come down very low.

44 [a]He shall lend to thee, and thou shalt not lend to him: [b]he shall be the head, and thou shalt be the tail.

45 Moreover [a]all these curses shall come upon thee, and shall pursue thee, and overtake thee, till thou be destroyed; because thou hearkenedst not unto the voice of the LORD thy God, to keep his commandments and his statutes which he commanded thee: R

46 And they shall be upon thee [a]for a sign and for a wonder, and upon thy seed for ever.

47 [a]Because thou servedst not the LORD thy God with joyfulness, and with gladness of heart, [b]for the abundance of all *things;*

48 Therefore shalt thou serve thine enemies which the LORD shall send against thee, in hunger, and in thirst, and in na-

27 [a]Ex. 15:26 [b]1 Sam. 5:6
28 [a]Jer. 4:9
29 [a]Job 5:14; Is. 59:10
30 [a]Job 31:10; Jer. 8:10 [b]Job 31:8; Jer. 12:13; Amos 5:11; Mic. 6:15; Zeph. 1:13 [c]ch. 20:6
31 [l]Heb. *shall not return to thee*
32 [a]Ps. 119:82
33 [a]Lev. 26:16; Jer. 5:17
36 [a]2 Ki. 17:4,6 & 24:12,14; 2 Chr. 33:11 [b]ch. 4:28; Jer. 16:13
37 [a]Jer. 24:9; Zech. 8:13 [b]Ps. 44:14
38 [a]Mic. 6:15; Hag. 1:6 [b]Joel 1:4
41 [a]Lam. 1:5 [l]Heb. *they shall not be thine*
42 [l]Or, *possess*
44 [a]ver. 12 [b]ver. 13
45 [a]ver. 15
46 [a]Is. 8:18; Ezek. 14:8
47 [a]Neh. 9:35-37 [b]ch. 32:15

D *Dt 28:21–22* ◀▶ *Dt 28:35*
H *Dt 18:18–19* ◀▶ *Dt 30:15*
R *Dt 28:23–25* ◀▶ *Dt 28:37*
D *Dt 28:27* ◀▶ *Dt 28:59–61*
R *Dt 28:33* ◀▶ *Dt 28:45*
R *Dt 28:37* ◀▶ *Dt 28:49*

28:33 More than 700 years before its fulfillment Moses prophesied about Israel's future destruction at the hands of the Babylonians and warned that this nation would someday oppress, crush and devour everything in the land of Israel.

28:37 Moses prophesied that the Israelites reputation would suffer irreparable damage. The nation that had once been a terror and a power among its neighbors would one day become "an astonishment, a proverb, and a byword, among all nations," thus proving the wisdom of Solomon's words that "sin is a reproach to any people" (Pr 14:34).

28:45 Over the last twenty-six centuries these curses fell upon the Israelites exactly as Moses had warned because the people refused to hear and obey God's commandments.

kedness, and in want of all *things:* and he [a]shall put a yoke of iron upon thy neck, until he have destroyed thee.

R 49 [a]The LORD shall bring a nation against thee from far, from the end of the earth, [b]*as swift* as the eagle flieth; a nation whose tongue thou shalt not [ʹ]understand;

50 A nation [a]of[ʹ] fierce countenance, [b]which shall not regard the person of the old, nor show favour to the young:

51 And he shall [a]eat the fruit of thy cattle, and the fruit of thy land, until thou be destroyed: which *also* shall not leave thee *either* corn, wine, or oil, *or* the increase of thy kine, or flocks of thy sheep, until he have destroyed thee.

52 And he shall [a]besiege thee in all thy gates, until thy high and fenced walls come down, wherein thou trustedst, throughout all thy land: and he shall besiege thee in all thy gates throughout all thy land, which the LORD thy God hath given thee.

53 And [a]thou shalt eat the fruit of thine own [ʹ]body, the flesh of thy sons and of thy daughters, which the LORD thy God hath given thee, in the siege, and in the straitness, wherewith thine enemies shall distress thee:

54 *So that* the man *that is* tender among you, and very delicate, [a]his eye shall be evil toward his brother, and toward [b]the wife of his bosom, and toward the remnant of his children which he shall leave:

55 So that he will not give to any of them of the flesh of his children whom he shall eat: because he hath nothing left him in the siege, and in the straitness, wherewith thine enemies shall distress thee in all thy gates.

56 The tender and delicate woman among you, which would not adventure to set the sole of her foot upon the ground for delicateness and tenderness, [a]her eye shall be evil toward the husband of her bosom, and toward her son, and toward her daughter,

57 And toward her [ʹ]young one that cometh out [a]from between her feet, and toward her children which she shall bear: for she shall eat them for want of all *things* secretly in the siege and straitness, wherewith thine enemy shall distress thee in thy gates.

58 If thou wilt not observe to do all the words of this law that are written in this book, that thou mayest fear [a]this glorious and fearful name, THE LORD THY GOD;

59 Then the LORD will make thy plagues [a]wonderful, and the plagues of thy seed, *even* great plagues, and of long continuance, and sore sicknesses, and of long continuance. D

60 Moreover he will bring upon thee all [a]the diseases of Egypt, which thou wast afraid of; and they shall cleave unto thee.

61 Also every sickness, and every plague, which *is* not written in the book of this law, them will the LORD [ʹ]bring upon thee, until thou be destroyed.

62 And ye [a]shall be left few in number, whereas ye were [b]as the stars of heaven for multitude; because thou wouldest not obey the voice of the LORD thy God. R

63 And it shall come to pass, *that* as the LORD [a]rejoiced over you to do you good, and to multiply you; so the LORD [b]will rejoice over you to destroy you, and to bring you to nought; and ye shall be plucked from off the land whither thou goest to possess it.

64 And the LORD [a]shall scatter thee among all people, from the one end of the

48 [a]Jer. 28:14
49 [a]Jer. 5:15 & 6:22,23; Luke 19:43 [b]Jer. 48:40 & 49:22; Lam. 4:19; Hos. 8:1 [ʹ]Heb. *hear*
50 [a]Prov. 7:13; Eccl. 8:1; Dan. 8:23 [b]2 Chr. 36:17; Is. 47:6 [ʹ]Heb. *strong of face*
51 [a]ver. 33; Is. 1:7
52 [a]2 Ki. 25:1,2,4
53 [a]Lev. 26:29; 2 Ki. 6:28,29; Jer. 19:9; Lam. 2:20 & 4:10 [ʹ]Heb. *belly*
54 [a]ch. 15:9 [b]ch. 13:6
56 [a]ver. 54
57 [a]Gen. 49:10 [ʹ]Heb. *afterbirth*
58 [a]Ex. 6:3
59 [a]Dan. 9:12
60 [a]ch. 7:15
61 [ʹ]Heb. *cause to ascend*
62 [a]ch. 4:27 [b]ch. 10:22; Neh. 9:23
63 [a]ch. 30:9; Jer. 32:41 [b]Prov. 1:26; Is. 1:24
64 [a]Lev. 26:33; ch. 4:27,28; Neh. 1:8; Jer. 16:13

R *Dt 28:45* ◀▶ *Dt 28:62–65*
D *Dt 28:35* ◀▶ *Dt 29:22*
R *Dt 28:49* ◀▶ *Dt 29:22–28*

28:49 God prophesied that an enemy nation "from the end of the earth" would conquer the Israelites. This enemy would speak a language that the people would not understand. This prophecy was fulfilled when Nebuchadnezzar of Babylon swiftly conquered Judah in 606 B.C.

28:62–65 Moses prophesied that God's judgment on Israel's sins would reduce the population of the Israelites until they were much fewer in number and dispersed throughout the world. Though God's promise to Abram included offspring as numerous as the stars (see Ge 15:5) the actual number of Jews has grown to only18 million worldwide today. Yet after almost two thousand years of oppression Jews have begun to return to their homeland and fulfill the words of Ezekiel: "Thus saith the Lord GOD; I will even gather you from the people, and assemble you out of the countries where ye have been scattered, and I will give you the land of Israel" (Eze 11:17).

earth even unto the other; and [b]there thou shalt serve other gods, which neither thou nor thy fathers have known, *even* wood and stone.

65 And [a]among these nations shalt thou find no ease, neither shall the sole of thy foot have rest: [b]but the LORD shall give thee there a trembling heart, and failing of eyes, and [c]sorrow of mind:

66 And thy life shall hang in doubt before thee; and thou shalt fear day and night, and shalt have none assurance of thy life:

67 [a]In the morning thou shalt say, Would God it were even! and at even thou shalt say, Would God it were morning! for the fear of thine heart wherewith thou shalt fear, and [b]for the sight of thine eyes which thou shalt see.

68 And the LORD [a]shall bring thee into Egypt again with ships, by the way whereof I spake unto thee, [b]Thou shalt see it no more again: and there ye shall be sold unto your enemies for bondmen and bondwomen, and no man shall buy *you.*

Keep the covenant

29 THESE *ARE* the words of the covenant, which the LORD commanded Moses to make with the children of Israel in the land of Moab, beside [a]the covenant which he made with them in Horeb.

2 ¶ And Moses called unto all Israel, and said unto them, [a]Ye have seen all that the LORD did before your eyes in the land of Egypt unto Pharaoh, and unto all his servants, and unto all his land;

3 [a]The great temptations which thine eyes have seen, the signs, and those great miracles:

4 Yet [a]the LORD hath not given you an heart to perceive, and eyes to see, and ears to hear, unto this day.

C L 5 [a]And I have led you forty years in the wilderness: [b]your clothes are not waxen old upon you, and thy shoe is not waxen old upon thy foot.

6 [a]Ye have not eaten bread, neither have ye drunk wine or strong drink: that ye might know that I *am* the LORD your God.

7 And when ye came unto this place, [a]Sihon the king of Heshbon, and Og the king of Bashan, came out against us unto battle, and we smote them:

8 And we took their land, and [a]gave it for an inheritance unto the Reubenites, and to the Gadites, and to the half tribe of Manasseh.

9 [a]Keep therefore the words of this covenant, and do them, that ye may [b]prosper in all that ye do.

10 ¶ Ye stand this day all of you before the LORD your God; your captains of your tribes, your elders, and your officers, *with* all the men of Israel,

11 Your little ones, your wives, and thy stranger that *is* in thy camp, from [a]the hewer of thy wood unto the drawer of thy water:

12 That thou shouldest [I]enter into covenant with the LORD thy God, and [a]into his oath, which the LORD thy God maketh with thee this day:

13 That he may [a]establish thee today for a people unto himself, and *that* he may be unto thee a God, [b]as he hath said unto thee, and [c]as he hath sworn unto thy fathers, to Abraham, to Isaac, and to Jacob.

14 Neither with you only [a]do I make this covenant and this oath;

15 But with *him* that standeth here with us this day before the LORD our God, [a]and also with *him* that *is* not here with us this day:

16 (For ye know how we have dwelt in the land of Egypt; and how we came through the nations which ye passed by;

17 And ye have seen their abominations, and their [I]idols, wood and stone, silver and gold, which *were* among them:)

18 Lest there should be among you man, or woman, or family, or tribe, [a]whose heart turneth away this day from the LORD our God, to go *and* serve the gods of these nations; [b]lest there should be among you a root that beareth [1,2]gall and wormwood; C

19 And it come to pass, when he heareth the words of this curse, that he bless himself in his heart, saying, I shall have peace, though I walk [a]in the [b]imagina- N S

64 [b]ver. 36
65 [a]Amos 9:4 [b]Lev. 26:36 [c]Lev. 26:16
67 [a]Job 7:4 [b]ver. 34
68 [a]Jer. 43:7; Hos. 8:13 & 9:3 [b]ch. 17:16
29:1 [a]ch. 5:2,3
2 [a]Ex. 19:4
3 [a]ch. 4:34 & 7:19
4 [a]See Is. 6:9,10 & 63:17; John 8:43; Acts 28:26,27; Eph. 4:18
5 [a]ch. 1:3 & 8:2 [b]ch. 8:4
6 [a]Ex. 16:12; ch. 8:3
7 [a]Num. 21:23,24, 33; ch. 2:32
8 [a]Num. 32:33; ch. 3:12,13
9 [a]ch. 4:6; 1 Ki. 2:3 [b]Josh. 1:7
11 [a]See Josh. 9:21, 23,27
12 [a]Neh. 10:29 [I]Heb. *pass*
13 [a]ch. 28:9 [b]Ex. 6:7 [c]Gen. 17:7
14 [a]Jer. 31:31
15 [a]Acts 2:39; 1 Cor. 7:14
17 [I]Heb. *dungy gods*
18 [a]ch. 11:16 [b]Acts 8:23; Heb. 12:15 [1]Or, *a poisonful herb* [2]Heb. *rosh*
19 [a]Num. 15:39; Eccl. 11:9 [b]Jer. 3:17 & 7:24

C *Dt 10:18* ◀▶ *Dt 33:25*
L *Dt 4:7* ◀▶ *Dt 31:6*
C *Dt 9:13* ◀▶ *Dt 32:5*
N *Dt 18:18–19* ◀▶ *Dt 30:15*
S *Dt 28:15* ◀▶ *Dt 30:6*

tion[1] of mine heart, [c]to add [2]drunkenness to thirst:

20 [a]The LORD will not spare him, but then [b]the anger of the LORD and [c]his jealousy shall smoke against that man, and all the curses that are written in this book shall lie upon him, and the LORD [d]shall blot out his name from under heaven.

21 And the LORD [a]shall separate him unto evil out of all the tribes of Israel, according to all the curses of the covenant that [1]are written in this book of the law:

R D 22 So that the generation to come of your children that shall rise up after you, and the stranger that shall come from a far land, shall say, when they see the plagues of that land, and the sicknesses [1]which the LORD hath laid upon it;

23 *And that* the whole land thereof *is* brimstone, [a]and salt, *and* burning, *that* it is not sown, nor beareth, nor any grass groweth therein, [b]like the overthrow of Sodom, and Gomorrah, Admah, and Zeboim, which the LORD overthrew in his anger, and in his wrath:

24 Even all nations shall say, [a]Wherefore hath the LORD done thus unto this land? what *meaneth* the heat of this great anger?

25 Then men shall say, Because they have forsaken the covenant of the LORD God of their fathers, which he made with them when he brought them forth out of the land of Egypt:

26 For they went and served other gods, and worshipped them, gods whom they knew not, and [1]*whom* he had not [2]given unto them:

27 And the anger of the LORD was kindled against this land, [a]to bring upon it all the curses that are written in this book:

28 And the LORD [a]rooted them out of their land in anger, and in wrath, and in great indignation, and cast them into another land, as *it is* this day.

29 The secret *things belong* unto the LORD our God: but those *things which are* revealed *belong* unto us and to our children for ever, that *we* may do all the words of this law.

The rewards of repentance

30 AND [a]IT shall come to pass, when [b]all these things are come upon thee, the blessing and the curse, which I have set before thee, and [c]thou I R

19 [c]Is. 30:1 [1]Or, *stubbornness* [2]Heb. *the drunken to the thirsty*
20 [a]Ezek. 14:7 [b]Ps. 74:1 [c]Ps. 79:5; Ezek. 23:25 [d]ch. 9:14
21 [a]Mat. 24:51 [1]Heb. *is written*
22 [1]Heb. *wherewith the LORD hath made it sick*
23 [a]Jer. 17:6; Zeph. 2:9 [b]Gen. 19:24; Jer. 20:16
24 [a]1 Ki. 9:8,9; Jer. 22:8,9
26 [1]Or, who *had not given to them* any portion [2]Heb. *divided*
27 [a]Dan. 9:11,13, 14
28 [a]1 Ki. 14:15; Ps. 52:5; Prov. 2:22
30:1 [a]Lev. 26:40 [b]ch. 28 [c]ch. 4:29, 30; 1 Ki. 8:47

R *Dt 28:62–65* ◀ ▶ *Dt 30:1*
D *Dt 28:59–61* ◀ ▶ *Jos 22:17*
I *Dt 28:1–3* ◀ ▶ *Dt 32:36*
R *Dt 29:22–28* ◀ ▶ *Dt 31:17–18*

29:22–28 This passage reveals that because of God's judgments, pagan nations would know that Israel had broken their covenant with him. Moses warned the Israelites that the desolation of the promised land would astonish all those who traveled through its ruins. Recent archeological discoveries have yielded proof that the land of Israel was once a fertile land that could have easily supported a flourishing population. Israel's sin brought judgment on the people and on the land too.

29:29 The "secret things" in this verse probably refer to Israel's unknown future. Only God knows these secret things. Yet God had revealed some of these secret things through his law, and the Israelites could determine the secret things of their future by their obedience or disobedience to God's revealed law (see Pr 3:32; Am 3:7).

30:1–20 *Palestinian Covenant.* This restatement of the Abrahamic covenant provides clear answers to Israel's' connection to the promised land. Though Israel had failed to keep their covenant with God, his promise still stood—the land was theirs. The Palestinian covenant contained seven elements:

1. Israel would be taken out of the land because of her disobedience to God's laws (30:1–3; see also 28:63–68; 29:22–28).
2. Israel will repent (30:2; see also 28:63–68).
3. Christ the Messiah will gather the exiles and bring them back to the land (30:3–6; Isa 11:11–12; Jer 23:3–8; Eze 37:21–25; Am 9:14).
4. The land will be restored to the Israelites (30:5). Thus far in history Israel has failed to possess the total area of land promised under God's unconditional covenant to Abram (Ge 12:2; 15:18).
5. Israel will be converted as a nation (30:6; see also Dt 28:9; Ro 11:26–27).
6. Those who oppressed Israel will be judged (30:7; Isa 14:1–2; Joel 3:1–8; Mt 25:31–46).
7. Israel will experience future prosperity (30:9; Am 9:11–15).

Other Biblical authors refer to these elements of the Palestinian covenant. Ezekiel uses it as the framework for his prophecy (see Eze 16:1–7, 35–52), Hosea alludes to the national repentance and conversion which is necessary for its fulfillment (see Hos 2:14–23) and Paul speaks about the salvation of Israel (see Ro 11:26–27). Since all of the elements of this covenant have not been

shalt call *them* to mind among all the nations, whither the LORD thy God hath
driven thee,
R 2 And shalt [a]return unto the LORD thy
God, and shalt obey his voice according
to all that I command thee this day, thou
and thy children, with all thine heart,
and with all thy soul;
3 [a]That then the LORD thy God will
turn thy captivity, and have compassion
upon thee, and will return and [b]gather
thee from all the nations, whither the
LORD thy God hath scattered thee.
4 [a]If *any* of thine be driven out unto
the outmost *parts* of heaven, from thence
will the LORD thy God gather thee, and
from thence will he fetch thee:
5 And the LORD thy God will bring thee
into the land which thy fathers possessed, and thou shalt possess it; and he
will do thee good, and multiply thee
above thy fathers.
K 6 And [a]the LORD thy God will circum-
S cise thine heart, and the heart of thy
seed, to love the LORD thy God with all
thine heart, and with all thy soul, that
thou mayest live.
7 And the LORD thy God will put all
these curses upon thine enemies, and on
them that hate thee, which persecuted
thee.
R 8 And thou shalt return and obey the
U voice of the LORD, and do all his commandments which I command thee this
day.
B 9 [a]And the LORD thy God will make
P thee plenteous in every work of thine
hand, in the fruit of thy body, and in the
fruit of thy cattle, and in the fruit of thy
land, for good: for the LORD will again [b]re-
joice over thee for good, as he rejoiced
over thy fathers:
10 If thou shalt hearken unto the voice
of the LORD thy God, to keep his commandments and his statutes which are
written in this book of the law, *and* if
thou turn unto the LORD thy God with all
thine heart, and with all thy soul.

Closing advice

11 ¶ For this commandment which I L
command thee this day, [a]it *is* not hidden
from thee, neither *is* it far off.
12 [a]It *is* not in heaven, that thou
shouldest say, Who shall go up for us to
heaven, and bring it unto us, that we may
hear it, and do it?
13 Neither *is* it beyond the sea, that
thou shouldest say, Who shall go over the
sea for us, and bring it unto us, that we
may hear it, and do it?
14 But the word *is* very nigh unto
thee, in thy mouth, and in thy heart, that
thou mayest do it.
15 ¶ See, [a]I have set before thee this H
day life and good, and death and evil; N
16 In that I command thee this day to
love the LORD thy God, to walk in his
ways, and to keep his commandments
and his statutes and his judgments, that
thou mayest live and multiply: and the
LORD thy God shall bless thee in the land
whither thou goest to possess it.
17 But if thine heart turn away, so that
thou wilt not hear, but shalt be drawn
away, and worship other gods, and serve
them;
18 [a]I denounce unto you this day, that
ye shall surely perish, *and that* ye shall
not prolong *your* days upon the land,

2 [a]Neh. 1:9; Is. 55:7; Lam. 3:40; Joel 2:12
3 [a]Ps. 106:45 & 126:1,4; Jer. 29:14; Lam. 3:22,32 [b]Ps. 147:2; Jer. 32:37; Ezek. 34:13 & 36:24
4 [a]ch. 28:64; Neh. 1:9
6 [a]ch. 10:16; Jer. 32:39; Ezek. 11:19 & 36:26
9 [a]ch. 28:11 [b]ch. 28:63; Jer. 32:41
11 [a]Is. 45:19
12 [a]Rom. 10:6
15 [a]ver. 1,19; ch. 11:26
18 [a]ch. 4:26 & 8:19

R *Dt 4:29–30* ◀▶ *Dt 30:8*
K *Nu 23:19* ◀▶ *Dt 30:20*
S *Dt 29:19–20* ◀▶ *Jos 1:8*
R *Dt 30:2* ◀▶ *Jos 7:19*
U *Dt 28:1–14* ◀▶ *1Sa 2:30*
B *Dt 28:11–12* ◀▶ *Job 42:12*
P *Dt 28:11–12* ◀▶ *1Sa 2:7–8*

L *Dt 11:26–27* ◀▶ *Dt 30:19*
H *Dt 28:29* ◀▶ *Dt 32:22–23*
N *Dt 29:19–20* ◀▶ *Dt 30:19*

---

fulfilled, the Palestinian covenant will play a major role in modern history until Christ's second coming.

NOTE: The seven additional covenants include the Edenic (Ge 2:15–17), Adamic (Ge 3:15–19), Noahic (Ge 9:8ff), Abrahamic (Ge 15:4ff; 17:1–22), Mosaic (Ex 19:5), Davidic (2Sa 7:16) and New (Heb 8:8–12). See the article on p. 8.

30:5–10 After many prophecies about the judgments on Israel's disobedience, God promised that he would bring the exiles back "into the land which thy fathers possessed" (30:5) if they repented of their sins and followed his commandments. This prophecy was initially fulfilled during the time of Nehemiah as a remnant returned from exile in Babylon. This century has also seen partial fulfillment of this prophecy as those Jews who have been scattered since NT times have begun to return to their homeland. The final fulfillment of this prophecy will not occur until the other elements of the Palestinian covenant are accomplished.

whither thou passest over Jordan to go to
possess it.
L 19 [a]I call heaven and earth to record
N this day against you, *that* [b]I have set before you life and death, blessing and cursing: therefore choose life, that both thou
and thy seed may live:
K 20 That thou mayest love the LORD thy
God, *and* that thou mayest obey his
voice, and that thou mayest cleave unto
him: for he *is* thy [a]life, and the length of
thy days: that thou mayest dwell in the
land which the LORD sware unto thy fathers, to Abraham, to Isaac, and to Jacob,
to give them.

The appointment of Joshua

31 AND MOSES went and spake
these words unto all Israel.
2 And he said unto them, I [a]*am* an
hundred and twenty years old this day; I
can no more [b]go out and come in: also
the LORD hath said unto me, [c]Thou shalt
not go over this Jordan.
3 The LORD thy God, [a]he will go over
before thee, *and* he will destroy these nations from before thee, and thou shalt
possess them: *and* Joshua, he shall go
over before thee, [b]as the LORD hath said.
4 [a]And the LORD shall do unto them [b]as
he did to Sihon and to Og, kings of the
Amorites, and unto the land of them,
whom he destroyed.
5 And [a]the LORD shall give them up before your face, that ye may do unto them
according unto all the commandments
which I have commanded you.
L 6 [a]Be strong and of a good courage,
W [b]fear not, nor be afraid of them: for the
LORD thy God, [c]he *it is* that doth go with
thee; [d]he will not fail thee, nor forsake
thee.
7 ¶ And Moses called unto Joshua, and
said unto him in the sight of all Israel,
[a]Be strong and of a good courage: for
thou must go with this people unto the
land which the LORD hath sworn unto
their fathers to give them; and thou shalt
cause them to inherit it.
L 8 And the LORD, [a]he *it is* that doth go
before thee; [b]he will be with thee, he
will not fail thee, neither forsake thee:
fear not, neither be dismayed.

Provision for teaching the law

9 ¶ And Moses wrote this law, [a]and
delivered it unto the priests the sons of
Levi, [b]which bare the ark of the covenant
of the LORD, and unto all the elders of
Israel.
10 And Moses commanded them, saying, At the end of *every* seven years, in
the solemnity of the [a]year of release, [b]in
the feast of tabernacles,
11 When all Israel is come to [a]appear
before the LORD thy God in the place
which he shall choose, [b]thou shalt read
this law before all Israel in their hearing.
12 [a]Gather the people together, men,
and women, and children, and thy
stranger that *is* within thy gates, that they
may hear, and that they may learn, and
fear the LORD your God, and observe to do
all the words of this law:
13 And *that* their children, [a]which
have not known *any thing,* [b]may hear,
and learn to fear the LORD your God, as
long as ye live in the land whither ye go
over Jordan to possess it.

The LORD appears to Moses

14 ¶ And the LORD said unto Moses,
[a]Behold, thy days approach that thou
must die: call Joshua, and present yourselves in the tabernacle of the congregation, that [b]I may give him a charge. And
Moses and Joshua went, and presented
themselves in the tabernacle of the congregation.
15 And [a]the LORD appeared in the tabernacle in a pillar of a cloud: and the pillar of the cloud stood over the door of the
tabernacle.
16 ¶ And the LORD said unto Moses,
Behold, thou shalt [l]sleep with thy fathers; and this people will [a]rise up, and
[b]go a-whoring after the gods of the
strangers of the land, whither they go *to
be* among them, and will [c]forsake me,
and [d]break my covenant which I have
made with them.

19 [a]ch. 4:26 & 31:28 [b]ver. 15
20 [a]Ps. 27:1 & 66:9; John 11:25
31:2 [a]Ex. 7:7; ch. 34:7 [b]Num. 27:17; 1 Ki. 3:7 [c]Num. 20:12 & 27:13; ch. 3:27
3 [a]ch. 9:3 [b]Num. 27:21; ch. 3:28
4 [a]ch. 3:21 [b]Num. 21:24,33
5 [a]ch. 7:2
6 [a]Josh. 10:25; 1 Chr. 22:13 [b]ch. 1:29 & 7:18 [c]ch. 20:4 [d]Josh. 1:5; Heb. 13:5
7 [a]ver. 23; ch. 1:38 & 3:28; Josh. 1:6
8 [a]Ex. 13:21 & 33:14; ch. 9:3 [b]Josh. 1:5,9; 1 Chr. 28:20
9 [a]ver. 25; ch. 17:18 [b]Num. 4:15; Josh. 3:3; 1 Chr. 15:12,15
10 [a]ch. 15:1 [b]Lev. 23:34
11 [a]ch. 16:16 [b]Josh. 8:34,35; 2 Ki. 23:2; Neh. 8:1-3
12 [a]ch. 4:10
13 [a]ch. 11:2 [b]Ps. 78:6,7
14 [a]Num. 27:13; ch. 34:5 [b]Num. 27:19
15 [a]Ex. 33:9
16 [a]Ex. 32:6 [b]Ex:34:15; Judg. 2:17 [c]ch. 32:15; Judg. 2:12 & 10:6, 13 [d]Judg. 2:20 [l]Heb. *lie down*

L *Dt 30:11–15* ◄► *1Sa 12:20*
N *Dt 30:15* ◄► *Dt 32:35*
K *Dt 30:6* ◄► *Dt 32:39*
L *Dt 29:5* ◄► *Dt 31:8*
W *Dt 20:8* ◄► *Jos 1:6–7*

L *Dt 31:6* ◄► *Dt 32:9–14*

R 17 Then my anger shall be kindled against them in that day, and [a]I will forsake them, and I will [b]hide my face from them, and they shall be devoured, and many evils and troubles shall [1]befall them; so that they will say in that day, [c]Are not these evils come upon us, because our God *is* [d]not among us?

18 And [a]I will surely hide my face in that day for all the evils which they shall have wrought, in that they are turned unto other gods.

19 Now therefore write ye this song for you, and teach it the children of Israel: put it in their mouths, that this song may be [a]a witness for me against the children of Israel.

20 For when I shall have brought them into the land which I sware unto their fathers, that floweth with milk and honey; and they shall have eaten and filled themselves, [a]and waxen fat; [b]then will they turn unto other gods, and serve them, and provoke me, and break my covenant.

21 And it shall come to pass, [a]when many evils and troubles are befallen them, that this song shall testify [1]against them as a witness; for it shall not be forgotten out of the mouths of their seed: for [b]I know their imagination [c]which they [2]go about, even now, before I have brought them into the land which I sware.

22 ¶ Moses therefore wrote this song the same day, and taught it the children of Israel.

23 [a]And he gave Joshua the son of Nun a charge, and said, [b]Be strong and of a good courage: for thou shalt bring the children of Israel into the land which I sware unto them: and I will be with thee.

24 ¶ And it came to pass, when Moses had made an end of writing the words of this law in a book, until they were finished,

25 That Moses commanded the Levites, which bare the ark of the covenant of the LORD, saying,

26 Take this book of the law, [a]and put it in the side of the ark of the covenant of the LORD your God, that it may be there [b]for a witness against thee.

27 [a]For I know thy rebellion, and thy [b]stiff neck: behold, while I am yet alive with you this day, ye have been rebellious against the LORD; and how much more after my death?

28 ¶ Gather unto me all the elders of your tribes, and your officers, that I may speak these words in their ears, [a]and call heaven and earth to record against them.

29 For I know that after my death ye will utterly [a]corrupt *yourselves,* and turn aside from the way which I have commanded you; and [b]evil will befall you [c]in the latter days; because ye will do evil in the sight of the LORD, to provoke him to anger through the work of your hands. R

The song of Moses

30 And Moses spake in the ears of all the congregation of Israel the words of this song, until they were ended.

32 GIVE [a]EAR, O ye heavens, and I will speak; and hear, O earth, the words of my mouth.

2 [a]My doctrine shall drop as the rain, my speech shall distil as the dew, [b]as the small rain upon the tender herb, and as the showers upon the grass:

3 Because I will publish the name of the LORD: [a]ascribe ye greatness unto our God.

4 *He is* [a]the Rock, [b]his work *is* perfect: for all his ways *are* judgment: [c]a God of truth and [d]without iniquity, just and right *is* he.

5 [a]They[1] have corrupted themselves, [2]their spot *is* not *the spot* of his children: *they are* a [b]perverse and crooked generation. C

6 Do ye thus [a]requite the LORD, O foolish people and unwise? *is* not he

17 [a]2 Chr. 15:2 [b]ch. 32:20; Is. 8:17 & 64:7; Ezek. 39:23 [c]Judg. 6:13 [d]Num. 14:42 [1]Heb. *find them*
18 [a]ver. 17
19 [a]ver. 26
20 [a]ch. 32:15; Neh. 9:25; Hos. 13:6 [b]ver. 16
21 [a]ver. 17 [b]Hos. 5:3 & 13:5,6 [c]Amos 5:25,26 [1]Heb. *before* [2]Heb. *do*
23 [a]ver. 14 [b]ver. 7; Josh. 1:6
26 [a]See 2 Ki. 22:8 [b]ver. 19
27 [a]ch. 9:24 & 32:20 [b]Ex. 32:9; ch. 9:6
28 [a]ch. 30:19 & 32:1
29 [a]ch. 32:5; Judg. 2:19; Hos. 9:9 [b]ch. 28:15 [c]Gen. 49:1; ch. 4:30
32:1 [a]Is. 1:2
2 [a]1 Cor. 3:6 [b]Ps. 72:6
3 [a]1 Chr. 29:11
4 [a]Ps. 18:2 [b]2 Sam. 22:31 [c]Jer. 10:10 [d]Job 34:10
5 [a]ch. 31:29 [b]Phil. 2:15 [1]Heb. *He hath corrupted to himself* [2]Or, that they are *not his children,* that is *their blot*
6 [a]Ps. 116:12

R *Dt 30:1* ◀ ▶ *Dt 31:29*
R *Dt 31:17–18* ◀ ▶ *Dt 32:20*
C *Dt 29:18–19* ◀ ▶ *Dt 32:28–29*

31:17–19 In ancient cultures, songs were used to teach and share information. To warn Israel away from the dangerous temptations to idolatry, God commanded Moses to teach the Israelites a song to remind them of their holy covenant, their history of deliverance from Egyptian slavery and their marvelous future when the Messiah returns.

31:29 Despite Moses' warnings, he knew that the Israelites would turn to idolatry after his death. Since he would no longer be able to direct their activities, his predictions were all the more grievous.

[b]thy father *that* hath [c]bought thee? hath he not [d]made thee, and established thee?

7 ¶ Remember the days of old, consider the years of [1]many generations: [a]ask thy father, and he will show thee; thy elders, and they will tell thee.

8 When the Most High [a]divided to the nations their inheritance, when he [b]separated the sons of Adam, he set the bounds of the people according to the number of the children of Israel.

L 9 For [a]the LORD'S portion *is* his people; Jacob *is* the [1]lot of his inheritance.

10 He found him [a]in a desert land, and in the waste howling wilderness; he [1]led him about, he instructed him, he [b]kept him as the apple of his eye.

11 [a]As an eagle stirreth up her nest, fluttereth over her young, spreadeth abroad her wings, taketh them, beareth them on her wings:

12 *So* the LORD alone did lead him, and *there was* no strange god with him.

F 13 [a]He made him ride on the high places of the earth, that he might eat the increase of the fields; and he made him to suck honey out of the rock, and oil out of the flinty rock;

14 Butter of kine, and milk of sheep, with fat of lambs, and rams of the breed of Bashan, and goats, [a]with the fat of kidneys of wheat; and thou didst drink the pure [b]blood of the grape.

15 ¶ But Jeshurun waxed fat, and kicked: [a]thou art waxen fat, thou art grown thick, thou art covered *with fatness;* then he [b]forsook God *which* [c]made him, and lightly esteemed the [d]Rock of his salvation.

16 [a]They provoked him to jealousy with strange *gods,* with abominations provoked they him to anger.

17 [a]They sacrificed unto devils, [1]not to God; to gods whom they knew not, to new *gods that* came newly up, whom your fathers feared not.

L Dt 31:8 ◀▶ Dt 33:12
F Dt 11:14–15 ◀▶ Jos 5:12

6 [b]Is. 63:16 [c]Ps. 74:2 [d]ver. 15
7 [a]Ex. 13:14 [1]Heb. *generation and generation*
8 [a]Zech. 9:2 [b]Gen. 11:8
9 [a]Ex. 19:5 [1]Heb. *cord*
10 [a]Jer. 2:6 [b]Ps. 17:8 [1]Or, *compassed him about*
11 [a]Is. 31:5
13 [a]Is. 58:14
14 [a]Ps. 81:16 [b]Gen. 49:11
15 [a]ch. 31:20 [b]Is. 1:4 [c]Is. 51:13 [d]Ps. 95:1
16 [a]1 Cor. 10:22
17 [a]Rev. 9:20 [1]Or, which were *not God;* see ver. 21
18 [a]Is. 17:10 [b]Jer. 2:32
19 [1]Or, *despised*
20 [a]Mat. 17:17
21 [a]Ps. 78:58 [b]Ps. 31:6 [c]Rom. 10:19
22 [a]Lam. 4:11 [1]Or, *hath burned* [2]Or, *hath consumed*
23 [a]Is. 26:15 [b]Ps. 7:12,13
24 [1]Heb. *burning coals*
25 [1]Heb. *from the chambers* [2]Heb. *bereave*
27 [1]Or, *Our high hand, and not the LORD, hath done all this*

18 [a]Of the Rock *that* begat thee thou art unmindful, and hast [b]forgotten God that formed thee.

19 And when the LORD saw *it,* he [1]abhorred *them,* because of the provoking of his sons, and of his daughters.

20 And he said, I will hide my face from them, I will see what their end *shall be:* for they *are* a very froward generation, [a]children in whom *is* no faith. R

21 [a]They have moved me to jealousy with *that which is* not God; they have provoked me to anger [b]with their vanities: and [c]I will move them to jealousy with *those which are* not a people; I will provoke them to anger with a foolish nation. G

22 For [a]a fire is kindled in mine anger, and [1]shall burn unto the lowest hell, and [2]shall consume the earth with her increase, and set on fire the foundations of the mountains. P H

23 I will [a]heap mischiefs upon them; [b]I will spend mine arrows upon them.

24 *They shall be* burnt with hunger, and devoured with [1]burning heat, and with bitter destruction: I will also send the teeth of beasts upon them, with the poison of serpents of the dust.

25 The sword without, and terror [1]within, shall [2]destroy both the young man and the virgin, the suckling *also* with the man of gray hairs.

26 I said, I would scatter them into corners, I would make the remembrance of them to cease from among men: R

27 Were it not that I feared the wrath of the enemy, lest their adversaries should behave themselves strangely, *and* lest they should say, [1]Our hand *is* high, and the LORD hath not done all this.

28 For they *are* a nation void of coun- C

R Dt 31:29 ◀▶ Dt 32:26 G ▶ SS 8:8–9
P Nu 24:17–19 ◀▶ Dt 32:41–43
H Dt 30:15 ◀▶ Dt 32:35
R Dt 32:20 ◀▶ Dt 32:36
C Dt 32:5 ◀▶ 1Sa 2:25

32:8–9 The exact translation of these verses is difficult to determine. If the Hebrew is best translated "children of Israel," then God may have set the boundaries of the nations during the exodus when Israel left Egypt. Yet if the Hebrew translates as "children of God," then the boundaries of the nations may have been set at an earlier time (see Ac 17:26).

32:20–26 In this passage Moses recorded God's rejection of those who turn from the true God to follow "that which is not God" (32:21) and prophesied that those who reject God's truth would "burn unto the lowest hell" (32:22). Even the memory about those who reject God's mercy and salvation will be lost forever.

sel, neither *is there any* understanding in
them.
29 [a]O that they were wise, *that* they
understood this, *that* they would consider
their latter end!
V 30 How should one chase a thousand,
and two put ten thousand to flight, except their Rock [a]had sold them, and the
LORD had shut them up?
G 31 For their rock *is* not as our Rock,
[a]even our enemies themselves *being*
judges.
32 For [a]their vine [1]*is* of the vine of
Sodom, and of the fields of Gomorrah:
their grapes *are* grapes of gall, their clusters *are* bitter:
33 Their wine *is* [a]the poison of dragons, and the cruel [b]venom of asps.
34 *Is* not this [a]laid up in store with
me, *and* sealed up among my treasures?
H 35 [a]To me *belongeth* vengeance, and
N recompence; their foot shall slide in *due*
time: for [b]the day of their calamity *is* at
hand, and the things that shall come
upon them make haste.
I 36 [a]For the LORD shall judge his peo-
R ple, [b]and repent himself for his servants,
when he seeth that *their* [1]power is gone,
and [c]*there is* none shut up, or left.
37 And he shall say, [a]Where *are* their
gods, *their* rock in whom they trusted,
38 Which did eat the fat of their sacrifices, *and* drank the wine of their drink
offerings? let them rise up and help you,
and be [1]your protection.
K 39 See now that [a]I, *even* I, *am* he, and
O [b]*there is* no god with me: [c]I kill, and I
make alive; I wound, and I heal: neither

V *Dt 28:7* ◀▶ *Jos 1:5* G ▶ *1Sa 16:7*
H *Dt 32:22–23* ◀▶ *Dt 32:41*
N *Dt 30:19* ◀▶ *Jos 24:15*
I *Dt 30:1–10* ◀▶ *Dt 32:43*
R *Dt 32:26* ◀▶ *Jos 23:15–16*
K *Dt 30:20* ◀▶ *Dt 33:25*
O *Dt 18:18–19* ◀▶ *1Sa 2:2*

29 [a]Luke 19:42
30 [a]Ps. 44:12
31 [a]1 Sam. 4:8; Jer. 40:3
32 [a]Is. 1:10 [1]Or, is worse *than the vine of Sodom*
33 [a]Ps. 58:4 [b]Rom. 3:13
34 [a]Jer. 2:22; Rom. 2:5
35 [a]Heb. 10:30 [b]2 Pet. 2:3
36 [a]Ps. 135:14 [b]Jer. 31:20; Joel 2:14 [c]2 Ki. 14:26 [1]Heb. *hand*
37 [a]Judg. 10:14; Jer. 2:28
38 [1]Heb. *an hiding for you*
39 [a]Ps. 102:27 [b]Is. 45:5,18,22 [c]1 Sam. 2:6; Hos. 6:1
41 [a]Is. 66:16
42 [a]Jer. 46:10 [b]Jer. 30:14; Lam. 2:5
43 [a]Rom. 15:10 [b]Rev. 19:2 [c]Ps. 85:1 [1]Or, *Praise his people, ye nations:* or, *Sing ye*
44 [1]Or, *Joshua*
46 [a]Ezek. 40:4
47 [a]Prov. 3:2; Rom. 10:5
48 [a]Num. 27:12, 13
49 [a]ch. 34:1

is there any that can deliver out of my
hand.
40 For I lift up my hand to heaven, and
say, I live for ever.
41 [a]If I whet my glittering sword, and P
mine hand take hold on judgment; I will H
render vengeance to mine enemies, and
will reward them that hate me.
42 I will make mine arrows [a]drunk
with blood, and my sword shall devour
flesh; *and that* with the blood of the slain
and of the captives, from the beginning of
[b]revengers upon the enemy.
43 [a]Rejoice,[1] O ye nations, *with* his I
people: for he will [b]avenge the blood of H
his servants, and will render vengeance
to his adversaries, and [c]will be merciful
unto his land, *and* to his people.
44 ¶ And Moses came and spake all
the words of this song in the ears of the
people, he, and [1]Hoshea the son of Nun.
45 And Moses made an end of speaking all these words to all Israel:
46 And he said unto them, [a]Set your
hearts unto all the words which I testify
among you this day, which ye shall command your children to observe to do, all
the words of this law.
47 For it *is* not a vain thing for you;
[a]because it *is* your life: and through this
thing ye shall prolong *your* days in the
land, whither ye go over Jordan to possess it.

Moses to die on mount Nebo

48 [a]And the LORD spake unto Moses
that selfsame day, saying,
49 Get thee up into this [a]mountain
Abarim, *unto* mount Nebo, which *is* in
the land of Moab, that *is* over against
Jericho; and behold the land of Canaan,

P *Dt 32:22* ◀▶ *1Sa 2:10*
H *Dt 32:35* ◀▶ *Dt 32:43*
I *Dt 32:36* ◀▶ *Jos 1:2–9*
H *Dt 32:41* ◀▶ *Jos 24:19*

32:36 Though the Lord would stand in judgment of his people, Israel had to realize that God was their only source of hope and help.

32:41–43 In his last words to the people, Moses declared that although God would execute final vengeance on his enemies, God promised to be merciful to the people as long as they repented of their sins. Echoing Moses' words, the prophet Isaiah reminded the people to "return unto the LORD, and he will have mercy upon him; and to our God, for he will abundantly pardon" (Isa 55:7).

32:48–52 This is one of the most poignant moments in Biblical history. Moses recorded God's announcement of his approaching death and the reason why he was forbidden from entering the promised land (see the note at Nu 20:12). This notation reminds all who read Moses' words that we serve a holy God who demands obedience from his children. Yet God let Moses view Canaan from the top of the mountain, confirming God's abundant grace and mercy to all who love him.

which I give unto the children of Israel for a possession:

Q 50 And die in the mount whither thou goest up, and be gathered unto thy people; as [a]Aaron thy brother died in mount Hor, and was gathered unto his people:

51 Because [a]ye trespassed against me among the children of Israel at the waters of [1]Meribah-Kadesh, in the wilderness of Zin; because ye [b]sanctified me not in the midst of the children of Israel.

52 [a]Yet thou shalt see the land before *thee;* but thou shalt not go thither unto the land which I give the children of Israel.

Moses blesses the tribes

33 AND THIS *is* [a]the blessing, wherewith Moses [b]the man of God blessed the children of Israel before his death.

2 And he said, [a]The LORD came from Sinai, and rose up from Seir unto them; he shined forth from mount Paran, and he came with [b]ten thousands of saints: from his right hand *went* [1]a fiery law for them.

3 Yea, [a]he loved the people; [b]all his saints *are* in thy hand: and they [c]sat down at thy feet; *every one* shall [d]receive of thy words.

4 [a]Moses commanded us a law, [b]*even* the inheritance of the congregation of Jacob.

5 And he was [a]king in [b]Jeshurun, when the heads of the people *and* the tribes of Israel were gathered together.

A 6 ¶ Let Reuben live, and not die; and let *not* his men be few.

7 ¶ And this *is the blessing* of Judah: and he said, Hear, LORD, the voice of Judah, and bring him unto his people: [a]let his hands be sufficient for him; and be thou [b]an help *to him* from his enemies.

8 ¶ And of Levi he said, [a]*Let* thy Thummim and thy Urim *be* with thy holy one, [b]whom thou didst prove at Massah, *and with* whom thou didst strive at the waters of Meribah;

9 Who said unto his father and to his mother, I have not [a]seen him; [b]neither did he acknowledge his brethren, nor knew his own children: for [c]they have observed thy word, and kept thy covenant.

10 [a]They[1] shall teach Jacob thy judgments, and Israel thy law: [2]they shall put incense [3]before thee, [b]and whole burnt sacrifice upon thine altar.

11 Bless, LORD, his substance, and [a]accept the work of his hands: smite through the loins of them that rise against him, and of them that hate him, that they rise not again.

12 ¶ *And* of Benjamin he said, The beloved of the LORD shall dwell in safety by him; *and the LORD* shall cover him all the day long, and he shall dwell between his shoulders. A L

13 ¶ And of Joseph he said, [a]Blessed of the LORD *be* his land, for the precious things of heaven, for [b]the dew, and for the deep that coucheth beneath,

14 And for the precious fruits *brought forth* by the sun, and for the precious things [1]put forth by the [2]moon,

15 And for the chief things of [a]the ancient mountains, and for the precious things [b]of the lasting hills,

16 And for the precious things of the earth and fulness thereof, and *for* the good will of [a]him that dwelt in the bush: let *the blessing* [b]come upon the head of Joseph, and upon the top of the head of him *that was* separated from his brethren.

17 His glory *is like* the [a]firstling of his bullock, and his horns *are like* [b]the horns of [1]unicorns: with them [c]he shall push the people together to the ends of the earth: and [d]they *are* the ten thousands of

Q *Nu 31:2* ◄► *Jdg 2:10*
A *Nu 23:24* ◄► *Dt 33:12–29*

A *Dt 33:6* ◄►
L *Dt 32:9–14* ◄► *Dt 33:27*

50 [a]Num. 20:25, 28
51 [a]Num. 20:11-13 [b]See Lev. 10:3 [1]Or, *Strife at Kadesh*
52 [a]Num. 27:12
33:1 [a]Gen. 49:28 [b]Ps. 90,title
2 [a]Hab. 3:3 [b]Dan. 7:10; Rev. 5:11 [1]Heb. *a fire of law*
3 [a]Ps. 47:4; Hos. 11:1 [b]1 Sam. 2:9 [c]Luke 10:39 [d]Prov. 2:1
4 [a]John 1:17 [b]Ps. 119:111
5 [a]See Gen. 36:31 [b]ch. 32:15
7 [a]Gen. 49:8 [b]Ps. 146:5
8 [a]Ex. 28:30 [b]ch. 8:2,3,16; Ps. 81:7
9 [a]Gen. 29:32 [b]Ex. 32:26,27,28 [c]Mal. 2:5,6
10 [a]Lev. 10:11; Mal. 2:7 [b]Lev. 1:9; Ps. 51:19 [1]Or, *Let them teach* [2]Or, *let them put incense* [3]Heb. *at thy nose*
11 [a]2 Sam. 24:23; Ezek. 20:40
13 [a]Gen. 49:25 [b]Gen. 27:28
14 [1]Heb. *thrust forth* [2]Heb. *moons*
15 [a]Gen. 49:26 [b]Hab. 3:6
16 [a]Ex. 3:2,4 [b]Gen. 49:26
17 [a]1 Chr. 5:1 [b]Num. 23:22 [c]Ps. 44:5 [d]Gen. 48:19 [1]Heb. *an unicorn*

33:2 Moses recounted the highlight of his ministry—his time with God on Mt. Sinai when he received the law—and traced God's movements with his people from Sinai through Seir (Edom) and on to the northern section of the Sinai peninsula (Paran). Moses also indicated that God's angels accompanied him when he gave the law to Moses. Several NT writers support this statement (see Ac 7:53; Gal 3:19; Heb 2:2).

33:5 *Jeshurun* is a Hebrew term of endearment that means "the upright one" (see Isa 44:2) and refers to Israel. This curious verse reinforces that the Lord, not a mere human, is to be the king over Israel (see 1Sa 12:12; Ps 10:16).

Ephraim, and they *are* the thousands of Manasseh.

18 ¶ And of Zebulun he said, [a]Rejoice, Zebulun, in thy going out; and, Issachar, in thy tents.

19 They shall [a]call the people unto the mountain; there [b]they shall offer sacrifices of righteousness: for they shall suck *of* the abundance of the seas, and *of* treasures hid in the sand.

20 ¶ And of Gad he said, Blessed *be* he that [a]enlargeth Gad: he dwelleth as a lion, and teareth the arm with the crown of the head.

21 And [a]he provided the first part for himself, because there, *in* a portion of the lawgiver, *was he* [1]seated; and [b]he came with the heads of the people, he executed the justice of the LORD, and his judgments with Israel.

22 ¶ And of Dan he said, Dan *is* a lion's whelp: [a]he shall leap from Bashan.

23 ¶ And of Naphtali he said, O Naphtali, [a]satisfied with favour, and full with the blessing of the LORD: [b]possess thou the west and the south.

24 ¶ And of Asher he said, [a]*Let* Asher *be* blessed with children; let him be acceptable to his brethren, and let him [b]dip his foot in oil.

K 25 [1]Thy shoes *shall be* [a]iron and brass;
C and as thy days, *so shall* thy strength *be*.
H 26 ¶ *There is* [a]none like unto the God of [b]Jeshurun, [c]*who* rideth upon the heaven in thy help, and in his excellency on the sky.

K 27 The eternal God *is thy* [a]refuge, and
L underneath *are* the everlasting arms: and [b]he shall thrust out the enemy from before thee; and shall say, Destroy *them*.

28 [a]Israel then shall dwell in safety alone: [b]the fountain of Jacob *shall be* upon a land of corn and wine; also his [c]heavens shall drop down dew.

K 29 [a]Happy *art* thou, O Israel: [b]who *is* like unto thee, O people saved by the LORD, [c]the shield of thy help, and who *is* the sword of thy excellency! and thine enemies [d]shall[1] be found liars unto thee; and [e]thou shalt tread upon their high places.

K *Dt 32:39* ◀▶ *Dt 33:27*
C *Dt 29:5* ◀▶ *Ne 9:21*
H *Dt 7:15* ◀▶ *1Ki 3:14*
K *Dt 33:25* ◀▶ *Dt 33:29*
L *Dt 33:12* ◀▶ *Jos 1:5*
K *Dt 33:27* ◀▶ *Jos 1:5*

18 [a]Gen. 49:13
19 [a]Is. 2:3 [b]Ps. 4:5
20 [a]1 Chr. 12:8
21 [a]Num. 32:16, 17 [b]Josh. 4:12 [1]Heb. *ceiled*
22 [a]Josh. 19:47
23 [a]Gen. 49:21 [b]See Josh. 19:32
24 [a]Gen. 49:20 [b]Job 29:6
25 [a]ch. 8:9 [1]Or, Under *thy shoes* shall be *iron*
26 [a]Ex. 15:11 [b]ch. 32:15 [c]Ps. 68:4
27 [a]Ps. 90:1 [b]ch. 9:3-5
28 [a]Jer. 23:6 [b]ch. 8:7,8 [c]Gen. 27:28
29 [a]Ps. 144:15 [b]2 Sam. 7:23 [c]Ps. 115:9 [d]Ps. 18:44 [e]ch. 32:13 [1]Or, *shall be subdued*
34:1 [a]Num. 27:12 [b]ch. 3:27 [c]Gen. 14:14 [1]Or, *The hill*
2 [a]ch. 11:24
3 [a]2 Chr. 28:15
4 [a]Gen. 12:7 [b]ch. 3:27
5 [a]ch. 32:50
6 [a]See Jude 9
7 [a]ch. 31:2 [b]Gen 27:1 [1]Heb. *moisture* [2]Heb. *fled*
8 [a]See Gen. 50:3, 10; Num. 20:29
9 [a]Is. 11:2; Dan. 6:3 [b]Num. 27:18, 23
10 [a]ch. 18:15 [b]Ex. 33:11; ch. 5:4
11 [a]ch. 7:19

The death of Moses

34 AND MOSES went up from the plains of Moab [a]unto the mountain of Nebo, to the top of [1]Pisgah, that *is* over against Jericho. And the LORD [b]showed him all the land of Gilead, [c]unto Dan,

2 And all Naphtali, and the land of Ephraim, and Manasseh, and all the land of Judah, [a]unto the utmost sea,

3 And the south, and the plain of the valley of Jericho, [a]the city of palm trees, unto Zoar.

4 And the LORD said unto him, [a]This *is* the land which I sware unto Abraham, unto Isaac, and unto Jacob, saying, I will give it unto thy seed: [b]I have caused thee to see *it* with thine eyes, but thou shalt not go over thither.

5 ¶ [a]So Moses the servant of the LORD died there in the land of Moab, according to the word of the LORD.

6 And he buried him in a valley in the land of Moab, over against Beth-peor: but [a]no man knoweth of his sepulchre unto this day.

7 ¶ [a]And Moses *was* an hundred and twenty years old when he died: [b]his eye was not dim, nor his [1]natural force [2]abated. E

8 ¶ And the children of Israel wept for Moses in the plains of Moab [a]thirty days: so the days of weeping *and* mourning for Moses were ended.

9 ¶ And Joshua the son of Nun was full B
of the [a]spirit of wisdom; for [b]Moses had E
laid his hands upon him: and the children G
of Israel hearkened unto him, and did as T
the LORD commanded Moses.

10 ¶ And there [a]arose not a prophet since in Israel like unto Moses, [b]whom the LORD knew face to face,

11 In all [a]the signs and the wonders, which the LORD sent him to do in the land of Egypt to Pharaoh, and to all his servants, and to all his land,

12 And in all that mighty hand, and in all the great terror which Moses showed in the sight of all Israel.

E *Dt 8:4* ◀▶ *Jos 14:10–11*
B *Nu 27:18* ◀▶ *Ps 45:7*
E *Nu 27:18* ◀▶ *Jdg 3:10*
G *Nu 11:25–29* ◀▶ *1Sa 10:6–7*
T *Nu 24:2–3* ◀▶ *1Sa 10:6–7*

Joshua

Author: Joshua

Theme: The conquest of Canaan

Date of Writing: c. 1390 B.C.

Outline of Joshua

I. Preparing to Enter Canaan (1:1—5:12)
II. Conquering the Land (5:13—12:24)
III. Dividing the Land by Tribes (13:1—21:45)
IV. Joshua's Farewell and Death (22:1—24:33)

THE BOOK OF Joshua is the first book in Scripture to bear the name of its author. Appointed by God to succeed Moses as Israel's leader, Joshua had been Moses' willing servant and pupil from the time of the giving of the law at Sinai through the forty years in the desert (see Ex 33:11). Joshua was also one of the twelve spies who originally explored the promised land, returning with a positive report (see Nu 14:6–9, 30). Described by Moses as "a man in whom is the spirit" (Nu 27:18), Joshua faithfully and "wholly followed the LORD" (Nu 32:12).

The book of Joshua records the military battles of the Israelites as they conquered the pagan cities of Canaan. As the Israelites entered the land, they confirmed their acceptance of God's covenant by circumcising all of the males that had been born during the forty years in the wilderness (see Jos 5:2–7). Then, following Joshua's bold leadership and trusting God's promises, the Israelites conquered Canaan, a process that took thirty years. The book concludes with God's detailed instructions for the division of the land among the twelve tribes, including the allotments to Reuben, Gad and the half tribe of Manasseh on the east bank of the Jordan.

Though God provided his presence and constant direction to the Israelites through his law and the visible pillar of cloud and fire, the Israelites rebelliously chose to ignore God's directions. The book of Joshua details the sins of Israel that brought about their numerous defeats. The example of the Israelites profoundly illustrates the opposition God's people will face when they attempt to possess the promises of God and underscores the peril of any disobedience (see Eph 1:3; 6:10–18).

The LORD *instructs Joshua*

1 NOW AFTER the death of Moses the servant of the LORD it came to pass, that the LORD spake unto Joshua the son of Nun, Moses' [a]minister, saying,

I 2 [a]Moses my servant is dead; now therefore arise, go over this Jordan, thou, and all this people, unto the land which I do give to them, *even* to the children of Israel.

3 [a]Every place that the sole of your foot shall tread upon, that have I given unto you, as I said unto Moses.

4 [a]From the wilderness and this Lebanon even unto the great river, the river Euphrates, all the land of the Hittites, and unto the great sea toward the going down of the sun, shall be your coast.

K 5 [a]There shall not any man be able to
L stand before thee all the days of thy life:
V [b]as I was with Moses, *so* [c]I will be with thee: [d]I will not fail thee, nor forsake thee.

W 6 [a]Be strong and of a good courage: for [/]unto this people shalt thou divide for an inheritance the land, which I sware unto their fathers to give them.

7 Only be thou strong and very courageous, that thou mayest observe to do according to all the law, [a]which Moses my servant commanded thee: [b]turn not from it *to* the right hand or *to* the left, that thou mayest [/]prosper whithersoever thou goest.

S 8 [a]This book of the law shall not depart out of thy mouth; but [b]thou shalt meditate therein day and night, that thou mayest observe to do according to all that is written therein: for then thou shalt make thy way prosperous, and then thou shalt [/]have good success.

L 9 [a]Have not I commanded thee? Be
W strong and of a good courage; [b]be not afraid, neither be thou dismayed: for the LORD thy God *is* with thee whithersoever thou goest.

10 ¶ Then Joshua commanded the officers of the people, saying,

11 Pass through the host, and command the people, saying, Prepare you victuals; for [a]within three days ye shall pass over this Jordan, to go in to possess the land, which the LORD your God giveth you to possess it.

12 ¶ And to the Reubenites, and to the Gadites, and to half the tribe of Manasseh, spake Joshua, saying,

13 Remember [a]the word which Moses the servant of the LORD commanded you, saying, The LORD your God hath given you rest, and hath given you this land.

14 Your wives, your little ones, and your cattle, shall remain in the land which Moses gave you on this side Jordan; but ye shall pass before your brethren [/]armed, all the mighty men of valour, and help them;

15 Until the LORD have given your brethren rest, as *he hath given* you, and they also have possessed the land which the LORD your God giveth them: [a]then ye shall return unto the land of your possession, and enjoy it, which Moses the LORD'S servant gave you on this side Jordan toward the sunrising.

16 ¶ And they answered Joshua, saying, All that thou commandest us we will do, and whithersoever thou sendest us, we will go.

17 According as we hearkened unto Moses in all things, so will we hearken unto thee: only the LORD thy God [a]be with thee, as he was with Moses.

18 Whosoever *he be* that doth rebel against thy commandment, and will not hearken unto thy words in all that thou commandest him, he shall be put to death: only be strong and of a good courage.

Two spies sent to Jericho

2 AND JOSHUA the son of Nun [/]sent [a]out of Shittim two men to spy secretly, saying, Go view the land, even Jericho. And they went, and [b]came into an

1:1 [a]Ex. 24:13; Deut. 1:38
2 [a]Deut. 34:5
3 [a]Deut. 11:24
4 [a]Gen. 15:18; Ex. 23:31; Num. 34:3-12
5 [a]Deut. 7:24 [b]Ex. 3:12 [c]Deut. 31:8, 23; ch. 3:7 & 6:27; Is. 43:2,5 [d]Deut. 31:6,8
6 [a]Deut. 31:7,23 [/]Or, *thou shalt cause this people to inherit the land*
7 [a]Num. 27:23; Deut. 31:7; ch. 11:15 [b]Deut. 5:32 & 28:14 [/]Or, *do wisely*
8 [a]Deut. 17:18,19 [b]Ps. 1:2 [/]Or, *do wisely*
9 [a]Deut. 31:7,8,23 [b]Ps. 27:1; Jer. 1:8
11 [a]Deut. 9:1 & 11:31
13 [a]Num. 32:20-28; ch. 22:2-4
14 [/]Heb. *marshalled by five* as Ex. 13:18
15 [a]ch. 22:4
17 [a]1 Sam. 20:13; 1 Ki. 1:37
2:1 [a]Num. 25:1 [b]Heb. 11:31; Jas. 2:25 [/]Or, *had sent*

I *Dt 32:43* ◀ ▶ *Jos 3:5*
K *Dt 33:29* ◀ ▶ *Jdg 5:31*
L *Dt 33:27* ◀ ▶ *Jos 1:9*
V *Dt 32:30* ◀ ▶ *Jos 21:44*
W *Dt 31:6–8* ◀ ▶ *Jos 1:9*
S *Dt 30:6* ◀ ▶ *Jos 5:6*
L *Jos 1:5* ◀ ▶ *Jos 21:45*
W *Jos 1:6–7* ◀ ▶ *Jos 8:1*

1:5–9 God's promised presence and strength would be Joshua's so that he could lead the Israelites to a successful conquest of the land promised to Abram and his descendants (see Ge 12:6; 13:14–15; 15:18–21).

harlot's house, named [c]Rahab, and [2]lodged there.

2 And [a]it was told the king of Jericho, saying, Behold, there came men in hither tonight of the children of Israel to search out the country.

3 And the king of Jericho sent unto Rahab, saying, Bring forth the men that are come to thee, which are entered into thine house: for they be come to search out all the country.

4 [a]And the woman took the two men, and hid them, and said thus, There came men unto me, but I wist not whence they *were:*

5 And it came to pass *about the time* of shutting of the gate, when it was dark, that the men went out: whither the men went I wot not: pursue after them quickly; for ye shall overtake them.

6 But [a]she had brought them up to the roof of the house, and hid them with the stalks of flax, which she had laid in order upon the roof.

7 And the men pursued after them the way to Jordan unto the fords: and as soon as they which pursued after them were gone out, they shut the gate.

8 ¶ And before they were laid down, she came up unto them upon the roof;

9 And she said unto the men, I know that the LORD hath given you the land, and that [a]your terror is fallen upon us, and that all the inhabitants of the land [1]faint because of you.

10 For we have heard how the LORD [a]dried up the water of the Red sea for you, when ye came out of Egypt; and [b]what ye did unto the two kings of the Amorites, that *were* on the other side Jordan, Sihon and Og, whom ye utterly destroyed.

11 And as soon as we had [a]heard *these things,* [b]our hearts did melt, neither [1]did there remain any more courage in any man, because of you: for [c]the LORD your God, he *is* God in heaven above, and in earth beneath.

12 Now therefore, I pray you, [a]swear unto me by the LORD, since I have shown you kindness, that ye will also show kindness unto [b]my father's house, and [c]give me a true token:

13 And *that* ye will save alive my father, and my mother, and my brethren, and my sisters, and all that they have, and deliver our lives from death.

14 And the men answered her, Our life [1]for yours, if ye utter not this our business. And it shall be, when the LORD hath given us the land, that [a]we will deal kindly and truly with thee.

15 Then she [a]let them down by a cord through the window: for her house *was* upon the town wall, and she dwelt upon the wall.

16 And she said unto them, Get you to the mountain, lest the pursuers meet you; and hide yourselves there three days, until the pursuers be returned: and afterward may ye go your way.

17 And the men said unto her, We *will be* [a]blameless of this thine oath which thou hast made us swear.

18 [a]Behold, *when* we come into the land, thou shalt bind this line of scarlet thread in the window which thou didst let us down by: [b]and thou shalt [1]bring thy father, and thy mother, and thy brethren, and all thy father's household, home unto thee.

19 And it shall be, *that* whosoever shall go out of the doors of thy house into the street, his blood *shall be* upon his head, and we *will be* guiltless: and whosoever shall be with thee in the house, [a]his blood *shall be* on our head, if *any* hand be upon him.

20 And if thou utter this our business, then we will be quit of thine oath which thou hast made us to swear.

21 And she said, According unto your words, so *be* it. And she sent them away, and they departed: and she bound the scarlet line in the window.

22 And they went, and came unto the mountain, and abode there three days, until the pursuers were returned: and the pursuers sought *them* throughout all the way, but found *them* not.

23 ¶ So the two men returned, and descended from the mountain, and passed over, and came to Joshua the son of Nun, and told him all *things* that befell them:

24 And they said unto Joshua, Truly [a]the LORD hath delivered into our hands all the land; for even all the inhabitants of the country do [1]faint because of us.

1 [c]Mat. 1:5 [2]Heb. *lay*
2 [a]ver. 22
4 [a]See 2 Sam. 17:19,20
6 [a]See Ex. 1:17; 2 Sam. 17:19
9 [a]Gen. 35:5; Ex. 23:27; Deut. 2:25 & 11:25 [1]Heb. *melt*
10 [a]Ex. 14:21; ch. 4:23 [b]Num. 21:24, 34,35
11 [a]Ex. 15:14,15 [b]ch. 5:1 & 7:5; Is. 13:7 [c]Deut. 4:39 [1]Heb. *rose up*
12 [a]See 1 Sam. 20:14,15,17 [b]See 1 Tim. 5:8 [c]ver. 18
14 [a]Judg. 1:24; Mat. 5:7 [1]Heb. *instead of you to die*
15 [a]Acts 9:25
17 [a]Ex. 20:7
18 [a]ver. 12 [b]ch. 6:23 [1]Heb. *gather*
19 [a]1 Ki. 2:32; Mat. 27:25
24 [a]Ex. 23:31; ch. 6:2 & 21:44 [1]Heb. *melt*

Israel crosses the Jordan

3 AND JOSHUA rose early in the morning; and they removed [a]from Shittim, and came to Jordan, he and all the children of Israel, and lodged there before they passed over.

2 And it came to pass [a]after three days, that the officers went through the host;

3 And they commanded the people, saying, [a]When ye see the ark of the covenant of the LORD your God, [b]and the priests the Levites bearing it, then ye shall remove from your place, and go after it.

4 [a]Yet there shall be a space between you and it, about two thousand cubits by measure: come not near unto it, that ye may know the way by which ye must go: for ye have not passed *this* way [†]heretofore.

I 5 And Joshua said unto the people, [a]Sanctify yourselves: for tomorrow the LORD will do wonders among you.

6 And Joshua spake unto the priests, saying, [a]Take up the ark of the covenant, and pass over before the people. And they took up the ark of the covenant, and went before the people.

I 7 ¶ And the LORD said unto Joshua, This day will I begin to [a]magnify thee in the sight of all Israel, that they may know that, [b]as I was with Moses, *so* I will be with thee.

8 And thou shalt command [a]the priests that bear the ark of the covenant, saying, When ye are come to the brink of the water of Jordan, [b]ye shall stand still in Jordan.

9 ¶ And Joshua said unto the children of Israel, Come hither, and hear the words of the LORD your God.

10 And Joshua said, Hereby ye shall know that [a]the living God *is* among you, and *that* he will without fail [b]drive out from before you the Canaanites, and the Hittites, and the Hivites, and the Perizzites, and the Girgashites, and the Amorites, and the Jebusites.

11 Behold, the ark of the covenant of [a]the Lord of all the earth passeth over before you into Jordan.

12 Now therefore [a]take you twelve men out of the tribes of Israel, out of every tribe a man.

I *Jos 1:2–9* ◄► *Jos 3:7*
I *Jos 3:5* ◄► *Jos 6:2–5*

3:1 [a]ch. 2:1
2 [a]ch. 1:10,11
3 [a]See Num. 10:33 [b]Deut. 31:9,25
4 [a]Ex. 19:12 [†]Heb. *since yesterday, and the third day*
5 [a]Ex. 19:10,14,15; Lev. 20:7; Num. 11:18; ch. 7:13; 1 Sam. 16:5; Joel 2:16
6 [a]Num. 4:15
7 [a]ch. 4:14; 1 Chr. 29:25; 2 Chr. 1:1 [b]ch. 1:5
8 [a]ver. 3 [b]ver. 17
10 [a]Deut. 5:26; 1 Sam. 17:26; 2 Ki. 19:4; Hos. 1:10; Mat. 16:16; 1 Thes. 1:9 [b]Ex. 33:2; Deut. 7:1; Ps. 44:2
11 [a]ver. 13; Mic. 4:13; Zech. 4:14 & 6:5
12 [a]ch. 4:2
13 [a]ver. 15,16 [b]ver. 11 [c]Ps. 78:13 & 114:3
14 [a]Acts 7:45
15 [a]ver. 13 [b]1 Chr. 12:15; Jer. 12:5 & 49:19 [c]ch. 4:18 & 5:10,12
16 [a]1 Ki. 4:12 & 7:46 [b]Deut. 3:17 [c]Gen. 14:3; Num. 34:3
17 [a]See Ex. 14:29
4:1 [a]Deut. 27:2; ch. 3:17
2 [a]ch. 3:12
3 [a]ch. 3:13 [b]ver. 19,20
6 [a]Ex. 12:26 & 13:14; Deut. 6:20

13 And it shall come to pass, [a]as soon as the soles of the feet of the priests that bear the ark of the LORD, [b]the Lord of all the earth, shall rest in the waters of Jordan, *that* the waters of Jordan shall be cut off *from* the waters that come down from above; and they [c]shall stand upon an heap.

14 ¶ And it came to pass, when the people removed from their tents, to pass over Jordan, and the priests bearing the [a]ark of the covenant before the people;

15 And as they that bare the ark were come unto Jordan, and [a]the feet of the priests that bare the ark were dipped in the brim of the water, (for [b]Jordan overfloweth all his banks [c]all the time of harvest,)

16 That the waters which came down from above stood *and* rose up upon an heap very far from the city Adam, that *is* beside [a]Zaretan: and those that came down [b]toward the sea of the plain, *even* [c]the salt sea, failed, *and* were cut off: and the people passed over right against Jericho.

17 And the priests that bare the ark of the covenant of the LORD stood firm on dry ground in the midst of Jordan, [a]and all the Israelites passed over on dry ground, until all the people were passed clean over Jordan.

4 AND IT came to pass, when all the people were clean passed [a]over Jordan, that the LORD spake unto Joshua, saying,

2 [a]Take you twelve men out of the people, out of every tribe a man,

3 And command ye them, saying, Take you hence out of the midst of Jordan, out of the place where [a]the priests' feet stood firm, twelve stones, and ye shall carry them over with you, and leave them in [b]the lodging place, where ye shall lodge this night.

4 Then Joshua called the twelve men, whom he had prepared of the children of Israel, out of every tribe a man:

5 And Joshua said unto them, Pass over before the ark of the LORD your God into the midst of Jordan, and take you up every man of you a stone upon his shoulder, according unto the number of the tribes of the children of Israel:

6 That this may be a sign among you, *that* [a]when your children ask *their* fa-

thers [1]in time to come, saying, What *mean* ye by these stones?

7 Then ye shall answer them, That [a]the waters of Jordan were cut off before the ark of the covenant of the LORD; when it passed over Jordan, the waters of Jordan were cut off: and these stones shall be for [b]a memorial unto the children of Israel for ever.

8 And the children of Israel did so as Joshua commanded, and took up twelve stones out of the midst of Jordan, as the LORD spake unto Joshua, according to the number of the tribes of the children of Israel, and carried them over with them unto the place where they lodged, and laid them down there.

9 And Joshua set up twelve stones in the midst of Jordan, in the place where the feet of the priests which bare the ark of the covenant stood: and they are there unto this day.

10 ¶ For the priests which bare the ark stood in the midst of Jordan, until every thing was finished that the LORD commanded Joshua to speak unto the people, according to all that Moses commanded Joshua: and the people hasted and passed over.

11 And it came to pass, when all the people were clean passed over, that the ark of the LORD passed over, and the priests, in the presence of the people.

12 And [a]the children of Reuben, and the children of Gad, and half the tribe of Manasseh, passed over armed before the children of Israel, as Moses spake unto them:

13 About forty thousand [1]prepared for war passed over before the LORD unto battle, to the plains of Jericho.

14 ¶ On that day the LORD [a]magnified Joshua in the sight of all Israel; and they feared him, as they feared Moses, all the days of his life.

15 And the LORD spake unto Joshua, saying,

16 Command the priests that bear [a]the ark of the testimony, that they come up out of Jordan.

17 Joshua therefore commanded the priests, saying, Come ye up out of Jordan.

18 And it came to pass, when the priests that bare the ark of the covenant of the LORD were come up out of the midst of Jordan, *and* the soles of the priests' feet were [1]lifted up unto the dry land, that the waters of Jordan returned unto their place, [a]and [2]flowed over all his banks, as *they did* before.

19 ¶ And the people came up out of Jordan on the tenth *day* of the first month, and encamped [a]in Gilgal, in the east border of Jericho.

20 And [a]those twelve stones, which they took out of Jordan, did Joshua pitch in Gilgal.

21 And he spake unto the children of Israel, saying, [a]When your children shall ask their fathers [1]in time to come, saying, What *mean* these stones?

22 Then ye shall let your children know, saying, [a]Israel came over this Jordan on dry land.

23 For the LORD your God dried up the waters of Jordan from before you, until ye were passed over, as the LORD your God did to the Red sea, [a]which he dried up from before us, until we were gone over:

24 [a]That all the people of the earth might know the hand of the LORD, that it *is* [b]mighty: that ye might [c]fear the LORD your God [1]for ever.

5 AND IT came to pass, when all the kings of the Amorites, which *were* on the side of Jordan westward, and all the kings of the Canaanites, [a]which *were* by the sea, [b]heard that the LORD had dried up the waters of the Jordan from before the children of Israel, until we were passed over, that their heart melted, [c]neither was there spirit in them any more, because of the children of Israel.

Circumcising of the nation

2 ¶ At that time the LORD said unto Joshua, Make thee [a]sharp[1] knives, and circumcise again the children of Israel the second time.

3 And Joshua made him sharp knives, and circumcised the children of Israel at [1]the hill of the foreskins.

4 And this *is* the cause why Joshua did circumcise: [a]All the people that came out of Egypt, *that were* males, *even* all the men of war, died in the wilderness by the way, after they came out of Egypt.

5 Now all the people that came out were circumcised: but all the people *that were* born in the wilderness by the way as they came forth out of Egypt, *them* they had not circumcised.

6 [1]Heb. *tomorrow*
7 [a]ch. 3:13,16 [b]Ex. 12:14; Num. 16:40
12 [a]Num. 32:20, 27,28
13 [1]Or, *ready armed*
14 [a]ch. 3:7
16 [a]Ex. 25:16,22
18 [a]ch. 3:15 [1]Heb. *plucked up* [2]Heb. *went*
19 [a]ch. 5:9
20 [a]ver. 3
21 [a]ver. 6 [1]Heb. *tomorrow*
22 [a]ch. 3:17
23 [a]Ex. 14:21
24 [a]1 Ki. 8:42,43; 2 Ki. 19:19 [b]Ex. 15:16; 1 Chr. 29:12 [c]Ex. 14:31; Deut. 6:2; Jer. 10:7 [1]Heb. *all days*
5:1 [a]Num. 13:29 [b]Ex. 15:14,15 [c]1 Ki. 10:5
2 [a]Ex. 4:25 [1]Or, *knives of flints*
3 [1]Or, *Gibeah-haaraloth*
4 [a]Num. 14:29 & 26:64,65; Deut. 2:16

S 6 For the children of Israel walked [a]forty years in the wilderness, till all the people *that were* men of war, which came out of Egypt, were consumed, because they obeyed not the voice of the LORD: unto whom the LORD sware that [b]he would not show them the land, which the LORD sware unto their fathers that he would give us, [c]a land that floweth with milk and honey.

7 And [a]their children, *whom* he raised up in their stead, them Joshua circumcised: for they were uncircumcised, because they had not circumcised them by the way.

8 And it came to pass, [1]when they had done circumcising all the people, that they abode in their places in the camp, [a]till they were whole.

9 And the LORD said unto Joshua, This day have I rolled away [a]the reproach of Egypt from off you. Wherefore the name of the place is called [b]Gilgal[1] unto this day.

10 ¶ And the children of Israel encamped in Gilgal, and kept the passover [a]on the fourteenth day of the month at even in the plains of Jericho.

11 And they did eat of the old corn of the land on the morrow after the passover, unleavened cakes, and parched *corn* in the selfsame day.

F 12 ¶ And [a]the manna ceased on the morrow after they had eaten of the old corn of the land; neither had the children of Israel manna any more; but they did eat of the fruit of the land of Canaan that year.

The fall of Jericho

13 ¶ And it came to pass, when Joshua was by Jericho, that he lifted up his eyes and looked, and, behold, there stood [a]a man over against him [b]with his sword drawn in his hand: and Joshua went unto him, and said unto him, *Art* thou for us, or for our adversaries?

14 And he said, Nay; but *as* [1]captain of the host of the LORD am I now come. And Joshua [a]fell on his face to the earth, and did worship, and said unto him, What saith my lord unto his servant?

15 And the captain of the LORD'S host said unto Joshua, [a]Loose thy shoe from off thy foot; for the place whereon thou standest *is* holy. And Joshua did so.

S *Jos 1:8* ◀▶ *Jos 24:14*
F *Dt 32:13–14* ◀▶ *Jdg 15:18–19*

6 NOW JERICHO [1]was straitly shut up because of the children of Israel: none went out, and none came in.

2 And the LORD said unto Joshua, See, [a]I have given into thine hand Jericho, and the [b]king thereof, *and* the mighty men of valour. I

3 And ye shall compass the city, all *ye* men of war, *and* go round about the city once. Thus shalt thou do six days.

4 And seven priests shall bear before the ark seven [a]trumpets of rams' horns: and the seventh day ye shall compass the city seven times, and [b]the priests shall blow with the trumpets.

5 And it shall come to pass, that when they make a long *blast* with the ram's horn, *and* when ye hear the sound of the trumpet, all the people shall shout with a great shout; and the wall of the city shall fall down [1]flat, and the people shall ascend up every man straight before him.

6 ¶ And Joshua the son of Nun called the priests, and said unto them, Take up the ark of the covenant, and let seven priests bear seven trumpets of rams' horns before the ark of the LORD.

7 And he said unto the people, Pass on, and compass the city, and let him that is armed pass on before the ark of the LORD.

8 ¶ And it came to pass, when Joshua had spoken unto the people, that the seven priests bearing the seven trumpets of rams' horns passed on before the LORD, and blew with the trumpets: and the ark of the covenant of the LORD followed them.

9 ¶ And the armed men went before the priests that blew with the trumpets, [a]and the [1]rearward came after the ark, *the priests* going on, and blowing with the trumpets.

10 And Joshua had commanded the

I *Jos 3:7* ◀▶ *Jos 6:16*

5:6 [a]Num. 14:33; Deut. 1:3 [b]Num. 14:23; Heb. 3:11 [c]Ex. 3:8
7 [a]Num. 14:31; Deut. 1:39
8 [a]See Gen. 34:25 [1]Heb. *when the people had made an end to be circumcised*
9 [a]Gen. 34:14 [b]ch. 4:19 [1]i.e. *Rolling*
10 [a]Ex. 12:6; Num. 9:5
12 [a]Ex. 16:35
13 [a]Gen. 18:2 & 32:24; Ex. 23:23; Zech. 1:8; Acts 1:10 [b]Num. 22:23
14 [a]Gen. 17:3 [1]Or, *prince; see* Dan. 10:13,21
15 [a]Ex. 3:5; Acts 7:33
6:1 [1]Heb. *did shut up, and was shut up*
2 [a]ch. 2:9,24 & 8:1 [b]Deut. 7:24
4 [a]See Judg. 7:16, 22 [b]Num. 10:8
5 [1]Heb. *under it*
9 [a]Num. 10:25 [1]Heb. *gathering host*

5:6 This piece of historical trivia records the fulfillment of the prophecy announced forty years earlier when God pronounced judgment on the Israelites for their lack of faith and rebellion against Moses' leadership (see Nu 14:32–34).

people, saying, Ye shall not shout, nor [1]make any noise with your voice, neither shall *any* word proceed out of your mouth, until the day I bid you shout; then shall ye shout.

11 So the ark of the LORD compassed the city, going about *it* once: and they came into the camp, and lodged in the camp.

12 ¶ And Joshua rose early in the morning, [a]and the priests took up the ark of the LORD.

13 And seven priests bearing seven trumpets of rams' horns before the ark of the LORD went on continually, and blew with the trumpets: and the armed men went before them; but the rearward came after the ark of the LORD, *the priests* going on, and blowing with the trumpets.

14 And the second day they compassed the city once, and returned into the camp: so they did six days.

15 And it came to pass on the seventh day, that they rose early about the dawning of the day, and compassed the city after the same manner seven times: only on that day they compassed the city seven times.

I 16 And it came to pass at the seventh time, when the priests blew with the trumpets, Joshua said unto the people, Shout; for the LORD hath given you the city.

17 ¶ And the city shall be [1]accursed, *even* it, and all that *are* therein, to the LORD: only Rahab the harlot shall live, she and all that *are* with her in the house, because [a]she hid the messengers that we sent.

18 And ye, [a]in any wise keep *yourselves* from the accursed thing, lest ye make *yourselves* accursed, when ye take of the accursed thing, and make the camp of Israel a curse, [b]and trouble it.

19 But all the silver, and gold, and vessels of brass and iron, *are* [1]consecrated unto the LORD: they shall come into the treasury of the LORD.

20 So the people shouted when *the priests* blew with the trumpets: and it came to pass, when the people heard the sound of the trumpet, and the people shouted with a great shout, that [a]the wall fell down [1]flat, so that the people went up into the city, every man straight before him, and they took the city.

21 And they [a]utterly destroyed all that *was* in the city, both man and woman, young and old, and ox, and sheep, and ass, with the edge of the sword.

22 But Joshua had said unto the two men that had spied out the country, Go into the harlot's house, and bring out thence the woman, and all that she hath, [a]as ye sware unto her.

23 And the young men that were spies went in, and brought out Rahab, [a]and her father, and her mother, and her brethren, and all that she had; and they brought out all her [1]kindred, and left them without the camp of Israel.

24 And they burnt the city with fire, and all that *was* therein: [a]only the silver, and the gold, and the vessels of brass and of iron, they put into the treasury of the house of the LORD.

25 And Joshua saved Rahab the harlot alive, and her father's household, and all that she had; and [a]she dwelleth in Israel *even* unto this day; because she hid the messengers, which Joshua sent to spy out Jericho.

26 ¶ And Joshua adjured *them* at that time, saying, [a]Cursed *be* the man before the LORD, that riseth up and buildeth this city Jericho: he shall lay the foundation thereof in his firstborn, and in his youngest *son* shall he set up the gates of it. J

27 [a]So the LORD was with Joshua; and [b]his fame was *noised* throughout all the country.

Achan's sin

7 BUT THE children of Israel committed a trespass in the accursed thing: for [a]Achan,[1] the son of Carmi, the son of [2]Zabdi, the son of Zerah, of the tribe of Judah, took of the accursed thing: and the anger of the LORD was kindled against the children of Israel.

2 And Joshua sent men from Jericho to Ai, which *is* beside Beth-aven, on the east side of Beth-el, and spake unto them, saying, Go up and view the country. And the men went up and viewed Ai.

3 And they returned to Joshua, and said unto him, Let not all the people go up; but let [1]about two or three thousand man go up and smite Ai; *and* make not all

10 [1]Heb. *make your voice to be heard*
12 [a]Deut. 31:25
17 [a]ch. 2:4 [1]Or, *devoted;* see Lev. 27:28
18 [a]Deut. 7:26 & 13:17; ch. 7:1,11, 12 [b]ch. 7:25; 1 Ki. 18:17,18; Jonah 1:12
19 [1]Heb. *holiness*
20 [a]ver. 5; Heb. 11:30 [1]Heb. *under it*
21 [a]Deut. 7:2
22 [a]ch. 2:14; Heb. 11:31
23 [a]ch. 2:13 [1]Heb. *families*
24 [a]ver. 19
25 [a]See Mat. 1:5
26 [a]1 Ki. 16:34
27 [a]ch. 1:5 [b]ch. 9:1,3
7:1 [a]ch. 22:20 [1]1 Chr. 2:7, *Achar* [2]Or, *Zimri;* see 1 Chr. 2:6
3 [1]Heb. *about 2000 men, or about 3000 men*

I *Jos 6:2–5* ◀▶ *Jos 8:1–2*
J *Nu 33:55–56* ◀▶ *Jos 23:13*

the people to labour thither; for they *are*
but few.
4 So there went up thither of the people about three thousand men: [a]and they
fled before the men of Ai.
5 And the men of Ai smote of them
about thirty and six men: for they chased
them *from* before the gate *even* unto
Shebarim, and smote them [l]in the going
down: wherefore [a]the hearts of the people melted, and became as water.
6 ¶ And Joshua [a]rent his clothes, and
fell to the earth upon his face before the
ark of the LORD until the eventide, he and
the elders of Israel, and [b]put dust upon
their heads.
7 And Joshua said, Alas, O Lord GOD,
[a]wherefore hast thou at all brought this
people over Jordan, to deliver us into
the hand of the Amorites, to destroy us?
would to God we had been content, and
dwelt on the other side Jordan!
8 O Lord, what shall I say, when Israel turneth their [l]backs before their enemies!
9 For the Canaanites and all the inhabitants of the land shall hear *of it,* and shall
environ us round, and [a]cut off our name
from the earth: and [b]what wilt thou do
unto thy great name?
10 ¶ And the LORD said unto Joshua,
Get thee up; wherefore [l]liest thou thus
upon thy face?
11 [a]Israel hath sinned, and they have
also transgressed my covenant which I
commanded them: [b]for they have even
taken of the accursed thing, and have also
stolen, and [c]dissembled also, and they
have put *it* even among their own stuff.
12 [a]Therefore the children of Israel
could not stand before their enemies, *but*
turned *their* backs before their enemies,
because [b]they were accursed: neither
will I be with you any more, except ye
destroy the accursed from among you.
13 Up, [a]sanctify the people, and say,
[b]Sanctify yourselves against tomorrow:
for thus saith the LORD God of Israel,
There is an accursed thing in the midst of
thee, O Israel: thou canst not stand before thine enemies, until ye take away
the accursed thing from among you.
14 In the morning therefore ye shall
be brought according to your tribes: and
it shall be, *that* the tribe which [a]the LORD
taketh shall come according to the families *thereof;* and the family which the
LORD shall take shall come by households;
and the household which the LORD shall
take shall come man by man.
15 [a]And it shall be, *that* he that is
taken with the accursed thing shall be
burnt with fire, he and all that he hath:
because he hath [b]transgressed the covenant of the LORD, and because he [c]hath
wrought [l]folly in Israel.
16 ¶ So Joshua rose up early in the
morning, and brought Israel by their
tribes; and the tribe of Judah was taken:
17 And he brought the family of Judah;
and he took the family of the Zarhites:
and he brought the family of the Zarhites
man by man; and Zabdi was taken:
18 And he brought his household man
by man; and Achan, the son of Carmi, the
son of Zabdi, the son of Zerah, of the
tribe of Judah, [a]was taken.
19 And Joshua said unto Achan, My R
son, [a]give, I pray thee, glory to the LORD
God of Israel, [b]and make confession unto
him; and [c]tell me now what thou hast
done; hide *it* not from me.
20 And Achan answered Joshua, and
said, Indeed I have sinned against the
LORD God of Israel, and thus and thus
have I done:
21 When I saw among the spoils a
goodly Babylonish garment, and two hundred shekels of silver, and a [l]wedge of
gold of fifty shekels weight, then I coveted them, and took them; and, behold,
they *are* hid in the earth in the midst of
my tent, and the silver under it.
22 ¶ So Joshua sent messengers, and
they ran unto the tent; and, behold, *it*
was hid in his tent, and the silver under it.
23 And they took them out of the
midst of the tent, and brought them unto
Joshua, and unto all the children of Israel,
and [l]laid them out before the LORD.
24 And Joshua, and all Israel with him,
took Achan the son of Zerah, and the silver, and the garment, and the wedge of
gold, and his sons, and his daughters, and
his oxen, and his asses, and his sheep,
and his tent, and all that he had: and they
brought them unto [a]the valley of Achor.
25 And Joshua said, [a]Why hast thou
troubled us? the LORD shall trouble thee
this day. [b]And all Israel stoned him with

4 [a]Lev. 26:17; Deut. 28:25
5 [a]ch. 2:9,11; Lev. 26:36 [l]Or, *in Morad*
6 [a]Gen. 37:29,34 [b]1 Sam. 4:12; 2 Sam. 1:2 & 13:19; Neh. 9:1; Job 2:12
7 [a]Ex. 17:3; Num. 21:5
8 [l]Heb. *necks*
9 [a]Deut. 32:26 [b]See Ex. 32:12; Num. 14:13
10 [l]Heb. *fallest*
11 [a]ver. 1 [b]ch. 6:17,18 [c]See Acts 5:1,2
12 [a]See Num. 14:45; Judg. 2:14 [b]Deut. 7:26; ch. 6:18; Hag. 2:13,14
13 [a]Ex. 19:10 [b]ch. 3:5
14 [a]Prov. 16:33
15 [a]See 1 Sam. 14:38,39 [b]ver. 11 [c]Gen. 34:7; Judg. 20:6 [l]Or, *wickedness*
18 [a]1 Sam. 14:42
19 [a]See 1 Sam. 6:5; Jer. 13:16; John 9:24 [b]Num. 5:6,7; 2 Chr. 30:22; Ezra 10:10,11; Dan. 9:4 [c]1 Sam. 14:43
21 [l]Heb. *tongue*
23 [l]Heb. *poured*
24 [a]ver. 26; ch. 15:7
25 [a]ch. 6:18; 1 Chr. 2:7; Gal. 5:12 [b]Deut. 17:5

R *Dt 30:8* ◀ ▶ *Jdg 10:15–16*

stones, and burned them with fire, after they had stoned them with stones.

26 And they [a]raised over him a great heap of stones unto this day. So [b]the LORD turned from the fierceness of his anger. Wherefore the name of that place was called, [c]The valley of [l]Achor, unto this day.

The destruction of Ai

I W **8** AND THE LORD said unto Joshua, [a]Fear not, neither be thou dismayed: take all the people of war with thee, and arise, go up to Ai: see, [b]I have given into thy hand the king of Ai, and his people, and his city, and his land:

2 And thou shalt do to Ai and her king as thou didst unto [a]Jericho and her king: only [b]the spoil thereof, and the cattle thereof, shall ye take for a prey unto yourselves: lay thee an ambush for the city behind it.

3 ¶ So Joshua arose, and all the people of war, to go up against Ai: and Joshua chose out thirty thousand mighty men of valour, and sent them away by night.

4 And he commanded them, saying, Behold, [a]ye shall lie in wait against the city, *even* behind the city: go not very far from the city, but be ye all ready:

5 And I, and all the people that *are* with me, will approach unto the city: and it shall come to pass, when they come out against us, as at the first, that [a]we will flee before them,

6 (For they will come out after us) till we have [l]drawn them from the city; for they will say, They flee before us, as at the first: therefore we will flee before them.

I 7 Then ye shall rise up from the ambush, and seize upon the city: for the LORD your God will deliver it into your hand.

8 And it shall be, when ye have taken the city, *that* ye shall set the city on fire: according to the commandment of the LORD shall ye do. [a]See, I have commanded you.

9 ¶ Joshua therefore sent them forth: and they went to lie in ambush, and abode between Beth-el and Ai, on the west side of Ai: but Joshua lodged that night among the people.

10 And Joshua rose up early in the morning, and numbered the people, and went up, he and the elders of Israel, before the people to Ai.

11 [a]And all the people, *even the people* of war that *were* with him, went up, and drew nigh, and came before the city, and pitched on the north side of Ai: now *there was* a valley between them and Ai.

12 And he took about five thousand men, and set them to lie in ambush between Beth-el and Ai, on the west side [l]of the city.

13 And when they had set the people, *even* all the host that *was* on the north of the city, and their liers in wait on the west of the city, Joshua went that night into the midst of the valley.

14 ¶ And it came to pass, when the king of Ai saw *it,* that they hasted and rose up early, and the men of the city went out against Israel to battle, he and all his people, at a time appointed, before the plain; but he [a]wist not that *there were* liers in ambush against him behind the city.

15 And Joshua and all Israel [a]made as if they were beaten before them, and fled by the way of the wilderness.

16 And all the people that *were* in Ai were called together to pursue after them: and they pursued after Joshua, and were drawn away from the city.

17 And there was not a man left in Ai or Beth-el, that went not out after Israel: and they left the city open, and pursued after Israel.

18 And the LORD said unto Joshua, Stretch out the spear that *is* in thy hand toward Ai; for I will give it into thine hand. And Joshua stretched out the spear that *he had* in his hand toward the city.

19 And the ambush arose quickly out of their place, and they ran as soon as he had stretched out his hand: and they entered into the city, and took it, and hasted and set the city on fire.

20 And when the men of Ai looked behind them, they saw, and, behold, the smoke of the city ascended up to heaven, and they had no [l]power to flee this way or that way: and the people that fled to the wilderness turned back upon the pursuers.

21 And when Joshua and all Israel saw

26 [a]ch. 8:29; 2 Sam. 18:17; Lam. 3:53 [b]Deut. 13:17; 2 Sam. 21:14 [c]ver. 24 [l]i.e. *Trouble*
8:1 [a]Deut. 1:21 & 7:18 & 31:8; ch. 1:9 [b]ch. 6:2
2 [a]ch. 6:21 [b]Deut. 20:14
4 [a]Judg. 20:29
5 [a]Judg. 20:32
6 [l]Heb. *pulled*
8 [a]2 Sam. 13:28
11 [a]ver. 5
12 [l]Or, *of Ai*
14 [a]Judg. 20:34; Eccl. 9:12
15 [a]Judg. 20:36
20 [l]Heb. *hand*

I *Jos 6:16* ◀ ▶ *Jos 8:7*
W *Jos 1:9* ◀ ▶ *1Ch 22:13*
I *Jos 8:1–2* ◀ ▶ *Jos 9:27*

that the ambush had taken the city, and
that the smoke of the city ascended, then
they turned again, and slew the men
of Ai.
22 And the other issued out of the city
against them; so they were in the midst
of Israel, some on this side, and some on
that side: and they smote them, so that
they [a]let none of them remain or escape.
23 And the king of Ai they took alive,
and brought him to Joshua.
24 And it came to pass, when Israel
had made an end of slaying all the inhabitants of Ai in the field, in the wilderness
wherein they chased them, and when
they were all fallen on the edge of the
sword, until they were consumed, that all
the Israelites returned unto Ai, and smote
it with the edge of the sword.
25 And *so* it was, *that* all that fell that
day, both of men and women, *were*
twelve thousand, *even* all the men of Ai.
26 For Joshua drew not his hand back,
wherewith he stretched out the spear,
until he had utterly destroyed all the inhabitants of Ai.
27 [a]Only the cattle and the spoil of
that city Israel took for a prey unto themselves, according unto the word of the
LORD which he [b]commanded Joshua.
28 And Joshua burnt Ai, and made it
[a]an heap for ever, *even* a desolation unto
this day.
29 [a]And the king of Ai he hanged on a
tree until eventide: [b]and as soon as the
sun was down, Joshua commanded that
they should take his carcase down from
the tree, and cast it at the entering of the
gate of the city, and [c]raise thereon a great
heap of stones, *that remaineth* unto this
day.

An altar built in mount Ebal

30 ¶ Then Joshua built an altar unto
the LORD God of Israel [a]in mount Ebal,
31 As Moses the servant of the LORD
commanded the children of Israel, as it is
written in the [a]book of the law of Moses,
an altar of whole stones, over which no
man hath lift up *any* iron: and [b]they offered thereon burnt offerings unto the
LORD, and sacrificed peace offerings.
32 ¶ And [a]he wrote there upon the
stones a copy of the law of Moses, which
he wrote in the presence of the children
of Israel.
33 And all Israel, and their elders, and
officers, and their judges, stood on this
side the ark and on that side before the
priests the Levites, [a]which bare the ark of
the covenant of the LORD, as well [b]the
stranger, as he that was born among
them; half of them over against mount
Gerizim, and half of them over against
mount Ebal; [c]as Moses the servant of the
LORD had commanded before, that they
should bless the people of Israel.
34 And afterward [a]he read all the
words of the law, [b]the blessings and curs-
ings, according to all that is written in the
book of the law.
35 There was not a word of all that
Moses commanded, which Joshua read
not before all the congregation of Israel,
[a]with the women, and the little ones,
and [b]the strangers that [l]were conversant
among them.

The trickery of the Gibeonites

9 AND IT came to pass, when all the
kings which *were* on this side Jordan, in the hills, and in the valleys, and
in all the coasts of [a]the great sea over
against Lebanon, [b]the Hittite, and the
Amorite, the Canaanite, the Perizzite,
the Hivite, and the Jebusite, heard
thereof;
2 That they [a]gathered themselves together, to fight with Joshua and with Israel, with one [l]accord.
3 ¶ And when the inhabitants of [a]Gib-
eon [b]heard what Joshua had done unto
Jericho and to Ai,
4 They did work wilily, and went and
made as if they had been ambassadors,
and took old sacks upon their asses, and
wine bottles, old, and rent, and
bound up;
5 And old shoes and clouted upon
their feet, and old garments upon them;
and all the bread of their provision was
dry *and* mouldy.
6 And they went to Joshua [a]unto the
camp at Gilgal, and said unto him, and to
the men of Israel, We be come from a far
country: now therefore make ye a league
with us.
7 And the men of Israel said unto the
[a]Hivites, Peradventure ye dwell among
us; and [b]how shall we make a league
with you?
8 And they said unto Joshua, [a]We *are*
thy servants. And Joshua said unto them,
Who *are* ye? and from whence come ye?

22 [a]Lev. 7:29; Deut. 7:2; Job 20:5; Luke 17:26-30; 1 Thes. 5:3
27 [a]Num. 31:22, 26 [b]ver. 2
28 [a]Deut. 13:16
29 [a]ch. 10:26 [b]Deut. 21:22,23; ch. 10:27 [c]ch. 7:26 & 10:27
30 [a]Deut. 27:4,5
31 [a]Ex. 20:25; Deut. 27:5,6 [b]Ex. 20:24
32 [a]Deut. 27:2,8
33 [a]Deut. 31:9,25 [b]Deut. 31:12 [c]Deut. 11:29 & 27:12
34 [a]Deut. 31:11; Neh. 8:3 [b]Deut. 28:2,15,45 & 29:20,21 & 30:19
35 [a]Deut. 31:12 [b]ver. 33 [l]Heb. *walked*
9:1 [a]Num. 34:6 [b]Ex. 3:17 & 23:23
2 [a]Ps. 83:3,5 [l]Heb. *mouth*
3 [a]ch. 10:2; 2 Sam. 21:1,2 [b]ch. 6:27
6 [a]ch. 5:10
7 [a]ch. 11:19 [b]Ex. 23:32; Deut. 7:2; Judg. 2:2
8 [a]Deut. 20:11

9 And they said unto him, [a]From a very far country thy servants are come because of the name of the LORD thy God: for we have [b]heard the fame of him, and all that he did in Egypt,

10 And [a]all that he did to the two kings of the Amorites, that *were* beyond Jordan, to Sihon king of Heshbon, and to Og king of Bashan, which *was* at Ashtaroth.

11 Wherefore our elders and all the inhabitants of our country spake to us, saying, Take victuals [ʹ]with you for the journey, and go to meet them, and say unto them, We *are* your servants: therefore now make ye a league with us.

12 This our bread we took hot *for* our provision out of our houses on the day we came forth to go unto you; but now, behold, it is dry, and it is mouldy:

13 And these bottles of wine, which we filled, *were* new; and, behold, they be rent: and these our garments and our shoes are become old by reason of the very long journey.

14 And [ʹ]the men took of their victuals, [a]and asked not *counsel* at the mouth of the LORD.

15 And Joshua [a]made peace with them, and made a league with them, to let them live: and the princes of the congregation sware unto them.

16 ¶ And it came to pass at the end of three days after they had made a league with them, that they heard that they *were* their neighbours, and *that* they dwelt among them.

17 And the children of Israel journeyed, and came unto their cities on the third day. Now their cities *were* [a]Gibeon, and Chephirah, and Beeroth, and Kirjath-jearim.

18 And the children of Israel smote them not, [a]because the princes of the congregation had sworn unto them by the LORD God of Israel. And all the congregation murmured against the princes.

19 But all the princes said unto all the congregation, We have sworn unto them by the LORD God of Israel: now therefore we may not touch them.

20 This we will do to them; we will even let them live, lest [a]wrath be upon us, because of the oath which we sware unto them.

21 And the princes said unto them, Let them live; but let them be [a]hewers of wood and drawers of water unto all the congregation; as the princes had [b]promised them.

22 ¶ And Joshua called for them, and he spake unto them, saying, Wherefore have ye beguiled us, saying, [a]We *are* very far from you; when [b]ye dwell among us?

23 Now therefore ye *are* [a]cursed, and there shall [ʹ]none of you be freed from being bondmen, and hewers of wood and drawers of water for the house of my God.

24 And they answered Joshua, and said, Because it was certainly told thy servants, how that the LORD thy God [a]commanded his servant Moses to give you all the land, and to destroy all the inhabitants of the land from before you, therefore [b]we were sore afraid of our lives because of you, and have done this thing.

25 And now, behold, we *are* [a]in thine hand: as it seemeth good and right unto thee to do unto us, do.

26 And so did he unto them, and delivered them out of the hand of the children of Israel, that they slew them not.

27 And Joshua [ʹ]made them that day [a]hewers of wood and drawers of water for the congregation, and for the altar of the LORD, even unto this day, [b]in the place which he should choose.

The sun stands still

10 NOW IT came to pass, when Adoni-zedec king of Jerusalem had heard how Joshua had taken Ai, and had utterly destroyed it; [a]as he had done to Jericho and her king, so he had done to [b]Ai and her king; and [c]how the inhabitants of Gibeon had made peace with Israel, and were among them;

2 That they [a]feared greatly, because Gibeon *was* a great city, as one of the [ʹ]royal cities, and because it *was* greater than Ai, and all the men thereof *were* mighty.

3 Wherefore Adoni-zedec king of Jerusalem sent unto Hoham king of Hebron, and unto Piram king of Jarmuth, and unto Japhia king of Lachish, and unto Debir king of Eglon, saying,

4 Come up unto me, and help me, that we may smite Gibeon: [a]for it hath made peace with Joshua and with the children of Israel.

9 [a]Deut. 20:15 [b]Ex. 15:14; Josh. 2:10
10 [a]Num. 21:24, 33
11 [ʹ]Heb. *in your hand*
14 [a]Num. 27:21 [ʹ]Or, *they received the men by reason of their victuals*
15 [a]ch. 11:19; 2 Sam. 21:2
17 [a]ch. 18:25,26, 28; Ezra 2:25
18 [a]Ps. 15:4; Eccl. 5:2
20 [a]See 2 Sam. 21:1,2,6; Ezek. 17:13,15,18,19; Zech. 5:3,4; Mal. 3:5
21 [a]Deut. 29:11 [b]ver. 15
22 [a]ver. 6,9 [b]ver. 16
23 [a]Gen. 9:25 [ʹ]Heb. *not be cut off from you*
24 [a]Ex. 23:32; Deut. 7:1,2 [b]Ex. 15:14
25 [a]Gen. 16:6
27 [a]ver. 21,23 [b]Deut. 12:5 [ʹ]Heb. *gave*, or, *delivered to be*
10:1 [a]ch. 6:21 [b]ch. 8:22,26,28 [c]ch. 9:15
2 [a]Ex. 15:14-16; Deut. 11:25 [ʹ]Heb. *cities of the kingdom*
4 [a]ver. 1; ch. 9:15

Jos 8:7 ◄ ► Jos 10:8

5 Therefore the five kings of the Amorites, the king of Jerusalem, the king of Hebron, the king of Jarmuth, the king of Lachish, the king of Eglon, [a]gathered themselves together, and went up, they and all their hosts, and encamped before Gibeon, and made war against it.

6 ¶ And the men of Gibeon sent unto Joshua [a]to the camp to Gilgal, saying, Slack not thy hand from thy servants; come up to us quickly, and save us, and help us: for all the kings of the Amorites that dwell in the mountains are gathered together against us.

7 So Joshua ascended from Gilgal, he, and [a]all the people of war with him, and all the mighty men of valour.

8 ¶ And the LORD said unto Joshua, [a]Fear them not: for I have delivered them into thine hand; [b]there shall not a man of them stand before thee.

9 Joshua therefore came unto them suddenly, *and* went up from Gilgal all night.

10 And the LORD [a]discomfited them before Israel, and slew them with a great slaughter at Gibeon, and chased them along the way that goeth up [b]to Beth-horon, and smote them to [c]Azekah, and unto Makkedah.

11 And it came to pass, as they fled from before Israel, *and* were in the going down to Beth-horon, [a]that the LORD cast down great stones from heaven upon them unto Azekah, and they died: *they were* more which died with hailstones than *they* whom the children of Israel slew with the sword.

12 ¶ Then spake Joshua to the LORD in the day when the LORD delivered up the Amorites before the children of Israel, and he said in the sight of Israel, [a]Sun, [ǀ]stand thou still upon Gibeon; and thou, Moon, in the valley of [b]Ajalon.

13 And the sun stood still, and the moon stayed, until the people had avenged themselves upon their enemies. [a]*Is* not this written in the book of [ǀ]Jasher? So the sun stood still in the midst of heaven, and hasted not to go down about a whole day.

14 And there was [a]no day like that before it or after it, that the LORD hearkened unto the voice of a man: for [b]the LORD fought for Israel.

15 ¶ [a]And Joshua returned, and all Israel with him, unto the camp to Gilgal.

16 But these five kings fled, and hid themselves in a cave at Makkedah.

17 And it was told Joshua, saying, The five kings are found hid in a cave at Makkedah.

18 And Joshua said, Roll great stones upon the mouth of the cave, and set men by it for to keep them:

19 And stay ye not, *but* pursue after your enemies, and [ǀ]smite the hindmost of them; suffer them not to enter into their cities: for the LORD your God hath delivered them into your hand.

20 And it came to pass, when Joshua and the children of Israel had made an end of slaying them with a very great slaughter, till they were consumed, that the rest *which* remained of them entered into fenced cities.

21 And all the people returned to the camp to Joshua at Makkedah in peace: [a]none moved his tongue against any of the children of Israel.

22 Then said Joshua, Open the mouth of the cave, and bring out those five kings unto me out of the cave.

23 And they did so, and brought forth those five kings unto him out of the cave, the king of Jerusalem, the king of Hebron, the king of Jarmuth, the king of Lachish, *and* the king of Eglon.

24 And it came to pass, when they brought out those kings unto Joshua, that Joshua called for all the men of Israel, and said unto the captains of the men of war which went with him, Come near, [a]put

5 [a]ch. 9:2
6 [a]ch. 5:10 & 9:6
7 [a]ch. 8:1
8 [a]ch. 11:6; Judg. 4:14 [b]ch. 1:5
10 [a]Judg. 4:15; 1 Sam. 7:10,12; Is. 28:21 [b]ch. 16:3,5 [c]ch. 15:35
11 [a]Is. 30:30; Rev. 16:21
12 [a]Is. 28:21; Hab. 3:11 [b]Judg. 12:12 [ǀ]Heb. *be silent*
13 [a]2 Sam. 1:18 [ǀ]Or, *The upright?*
14 [a]See Is. 38:8 [b]ver. 42; Deut. 1:30; ch. 23:3
15 [a]ver. 43
19 [ǀ]Heb. *cut off the tail*
21 [a]Ex. 11:7
24 [a]Ps. 107:40; Is. 26:5,6; Mal. 4:3

I *Jos 9:27* ◀ ▶ *Jos 10:12*
I *Jos 10:8* ◀ ▶ *Jos 10:19*
I *Jos 10:12* ◀ ▶ *Jos 11:6*

10:12–14 This passage records a miraculous answer to Joshua's prayer: "So the sun stood still in the midst of heaven, and hasted not to go down about a whole day" (10:13). Never before or never since has there been a day like that one. Whether God slowed the rotation of the earth on its axis to lengthen the hours of daylight or whether he cooled the sun's rays for an entire day so that the fighting could continue throughout the afternoon, we cannot say. Scripture does not record how God achieved this effect. It is enough to believe the Biblical record that it happened and trust that the God who created the universe could easily have created this phenomenon to save his chosen people.

your feet upon the necks of these kings. And they came near, and put their feet upon the necks of them.

25 And Joshua said unto them, [a]Fear not, nor be dismayed, be strong and of good courage: for [b]thus shall the LORD do to all your enemies against whom ye fight.

26 And afterward Joshua smote them, and slew them, and hanged them on five trees: and they [a]were hanging upon the trees until the evening.

27 And it came to pass at the time of the going down of the sun, *that* Joshua commanded, and they [a]took them down off the trees, and cast them into the cave wherein they had been hid, and laid great stones in the cave's mouth, *which remain* until this very day.

Conquest of the south

28 ¶ And that day Joshua took Makkedah, and smote it with the edge of the sword, and the king thereof he utterly destroyed, them, and all the souls that *were* therein; he let none remain: and he did to the king of Makkedah [a]as he did unto the king of Jericho.

29 Then Joshua passed from Makkedah, and all Israel with him, unto Libnah, and fought against Libnah:

30 And the LORD delivered it also, and the king thereof, into the hand of Israel; and he smote it with the edge of the sword, and all the souls that *were* therein; he let none remain in it; but did unto the king thereof as he did unto the king of Jericho.

31 ¶ And Joshua passed from Libnah, and all Israel with him, unto Lachish, and encamped against it, and fought against it:

32 And the LORD delivered Lachish into the hand of Israel, which took it on the second day, and smote it with the edge of the sword, and all the souls that *were* therein, according to all that he had done to Libnah.

33 ¶ Then Horam king of [a]Gezer came up to help Lachish; and Joshua smote him and his people, until he had left him none remaining.

34 ¶ And from Lachish Joshua passed unto Eglon, and all Israel with him; and they encamped against it, and fought against it:

35 And they took it on that day, and smote it with the edge of the sword, and all the souls that *were* therein he utterly destroyed that day, according to all that he had done to Lachish.

36 And Joshua went up from Eglon, and all Israel with him, unto [a]Hebron; and they fought against it:

37 And they took it, and smote it with the edge of the sword, and the king thereof, and all the cities thereof, and all the souls that *were* therein; he left none remaining, according to all that he had done to Eglon; but destroyed it utterly, and all the souls that *were* therein.

38 ¶ And Joshua returned, and all Israel with him, to [a]Debir; and fought against it:

39 And he took it, and the king thereof, and all the cities thereof; and they smote them with the edge of the sword, and utterly destroyed all the souls that *were* therein; he left none remaining: as he had done to Hebron, so he did to Debir, and to the king thereof; as he had done also to Libnah, and to her king.

40 ¶ So Joshua smote all the country of the hills, and of the south, and of the vale, and of the springs, and all their kings: he left none remaining, but utterly destroyed all that breathed, as the LORD God of Israel [a]commanded.

41 And Joshua smote them from Kadesh-barnea even unto [a]Gaza, [b]and all the country of Goshen, even unto Gibeon.

42 And all these kings and their land did Joshua take at one time, [a]because the LORD God of Israel fought for Israel.

43 And Joshua returned, and all Israel with him, unto the camp to Gilgal.

Conquest of the north

11 AND IT came to pass, when Jabin king of Hazor had heard *those things,* that he [a]sent to Jobab king of Madon, and to the king [b]of Shimron, and to the king of Achshaph,

2 And to the kings that *were* on the north of the mountains, and of the plains south of [a]Chinneroth, and in the valley, and in the borders [b]of Dor on the west,

3 *And to* the Canaanite on the east and on the west, and *to* the Amorite, and the Hittite, and the Perizzite, and the Jebusite in the mountains, [a]and *to* the Hivite under [b]Hermon [c]in the land of Mizpeh.

4 And they went out, they and all their

25 [a]Deut. 31:6,8; ch. 1:9 [b]Deut. 3:21 & 7:19
26 [a]ch. 8:29
27 [a]Deut. 21:23; ch. 8:29
28 [a]ch. 6:21
33 [a]ch. 16:3,10; 1 Ki. 9:16,17; 1 Chr. 20:4
36 [a]See ch. 14:13; & 15:13; Judg. 1:10
38 [a]See ch. 15:15; Judg. 1:11
40 [a]Deut. 20:16, 17
41 [a]Gen. 10:19 [b]ch. 11:16
42 [a]ver. 14
11:1 [a]ch. 10:3 [b]ch. 19:15
2 [a]Num. 34:11 [b]ch. 17:11; Judg. 1:27; 1 Ki. 4:11
3 [a]Judg. 3:3 [b]ch. 13:11 [c]Gen. 31:49

hosts with them, much people, [a]even as the sand that *is* upon the sea shore in multitude, with horses and chariots very many.

5 And when all these kings were [l]met together, they came and pitched together at the waters of Merom, to fight against Israel.

6 ¶ And the LORD said unto Joshua, [a]Be not afraid because of them: for tomorrow about this time will I deliver them up all slain before Israel: thou shalt [b]hough their horses, and burn their chariots with fire.

7 So Joshua came, and all the people of war with him, against them by the waters of Merom suddenly; and they fell upon them.

8 And the LORD delivered them into the hand of Israel, who smote them, and chased them unto [l]great Zidon, and unto [a]Misrephoth-maim,[2,3] and unto the valley of Mizpeh eastward; and they smote them, until they left them none remaining.

9 And Joshua did unto them as the LORD bade him: he houghed their horses, and burnt their chariots with fire.

10 ¶ And Joshua at that time turned back, and took Hazor, and smote the king thereof with the sword: for Hazor beforetime was the head of all those kingdoms.

11 And they smote all the souls that *were* therein with the edge of the sword, utterly destroying *them:* there was not [l]any left to breathe: and he burnt Hazor with fire.

12 And all the cities of those kings, and all the kings of them, did Joshua take, and smote them with the edge of the sword, *and* he utterly destroyed them, [a]as Moses the servant of the LORD commanded.

13 But *as for* the cities that stood still [l]in their strength, Israel burned none of them, save Hazor only; *that* did Joshua burn.

14 And all the spoil of these cities, and the cattle, the children of Israel took for a prey unto themselves; but every man they smote with the edge of the sword, until they had destroyed them, neither left they any to breathe.

15 ¶ [a]As the LORD commanded Moses his servant, so [b]did Moses command Joshua, and [c]so did Joshua; [l]he left nothing undone of all that the LORD commanded Moses.

16 So Joshua took all that land, [a]the hills, and all the south country, [b]and all the land of Goshen, and the valley, and the plain, and the mountain of Israel, and the valley of the same;

17 [a]*Even* from [l]the mount Halak, that goeth up to Seir, even unto Baal-gad in the valley of Lebanon under mount Hermon: and [b]all their kings he took, and smote them, and slew them.

18 Joshua made war a long time with all those kings.

19 There was not a city that made peace with the children of Israel, save [a]the Hivites the inhabitants of Gibeon: all *other* they took in battle.

20 For [a]it was of the LORD to harden their hearts, that they should come against Israel in battle, that he might destroy them utterly, *and* that they might have no favour, but that he might destroy them, [b]as the LORD commanded Moses.

21 ¶ And at that time came Joshua, and cut off [a]the Anakims from the mountains, from Hebron, from Debir, from Anab, and from all the mountains of Judah, and from all the mountains of Israel: Joshua destroyed them utterly with their cities.

22 There was none of the Anakims left in the land of the children of Israel: only in Gaza, in [a]Gath, [b]and in Ashdod, there remained.

23 So Joshua took the whole land, [a]according to all that the LORD said unto Moses; and Joshua gave it for an inheritance unto Israel [b]according to their divisions by their tribes. [c]And the land rested from war.

Defeated kings

12 NOW THESE *are* the kings of the land, which the children of Israel smote, and possessed their land on the other side Jordan toward the rising of the sun, [a]from the river Arnon [b]unto mount Hermon, and all the plain on the east:

2 [a]Sihon king of the Amorites, who dwelt in Heshbon, *and* ruled from Aroer, which *is* upon the bank of the river Arnon, and from the middle of the river, and from half Gilead, even unto the river Jabbok, *which is* the border of the children of Ammon;

4 [a]Gen. 22:17 & 32:12; Judg. 7:12; 1 Sam. 13:5
5 [l]Heb. *assembled by appointment*
6 [a]ch. 10:8 [b]2 Sam. 8:4
8 [a]ch. 13:6 [l]Or, *Zidon-rabbah* [2]Or, *Salt pits* [3]Heb. *Burnings*
11 [l]Heb. *any breath*
12 [a]Num. 33:52
13 [l]Heb. *on their heap*
15 [a]Ex. 34:11,12 [b]Deut. 31:7,8 [c]ch. 1:7 [l]Heb. *he removed nothing*
16 [a]ch. 12:8 [b]ch. 10:41
17 [a]ch. 12:7 [b]Deut. 7:24; ch. 12:7 [l]Or, *the smooth mountain*
19 [a]ch. 9:3,7
20 [a]Deut. 2:30; Judg. 14:4; 1 Sam. 2:25 [b]Deut. 20:16, 17
21 [a]Num. 13:22, 33; Deut. 1:28; ch. 15:13,14
22 [a]1 Sam. 17:4 [b]ch. 15:46
23 [a]Num. 34:2 [b]Num. 26:53; ch. 14 & 15 [c]ver. 18; ch. 14:15 & 21:44 & 22:4 & 23:1
12:1 [a]Num. 21:24 [b]Deut. 3:8,9
2 [a]Num. 21:24

3 And [a]from the plain to the sea of Chinneroth on the east, and unto the sea of the plain, *even* the salt sea on the east, [b]the way to Beth-jeshimoth; and from [1]the south, under [c]Ashdoth-pisgah:[2]

4 ¶ And [a]the coast of Og king of Bashan, *which was* of [b]the remnant of the giants, [c]that dwelt at Ashtaroth and at Edrei,

5 And reigned in [a]mount Hermon, [b]and in Salcah, and in all Bashan, [c]unto the border of the Geshurites and the Maachathites, and half Gilead, the border of Sihon king of Heshbon.

6 [a]Them did Moses the servant of the LORD and the children of Israel smite: and [b]Moses the servant of the LORD gave it *for* a possession unto the Reubenites, and the Gadites, and the half tribe of Manasseh.

7 ¶ And these *are* the kings of the country [a]which Joshua and the children of Israel smote on this side Jordan on the west, from Baal-gad in the valley of Lebanon even unto the mount Halak, that goeth up to [b]Seir; which Joshua [c]gave unto the tribes of Israel *for* a possession according to their divisions;

8 [a]In the mountains, and in the valleys, and in the plains, and in the springs, and in the wilderness, and in the south country; [b]the Hittites, the Amorites, and the Canaanites, the Perizzites, the Hivites, and the Jebusites:

9 ¶ [a]The king of Jericho, one; [b]the king of Ai, which *is* beside Beth-el, one;

10 [a]The king of Jerusalem, one; the king of Hebron, one;

11 The king of Jarmuth, one; the king of Lachish, one;

12 The king of Eglon, one; [a]the king of Gezer, one;

13 [a]The king of Debir, one; the king of Geder, one;

14 The king of Hormah, one; the king of Arad, one;

15 [a]The king of Libnah, one; the king of Adullam, one;

16 [a]The king of Makkedah, one; [b]the king of Beth-el, one;

17 The king of Tappuah, one; [a]the king of Hepher, one;

18 The king of Aphek, one; the king of Lasharon, one;

19 The king of Madon, one; [a]the king of Hazor, one;

3 [a] Deut. 3:17 [b] ch. 13:20 [c] Deut. 3:17 & 4:49 [1] Or, *Teman* [2] Or, *The springs of Pisgah,* or, *The hill*
4 [a] Num. 21:33; Deut. 3:4,10 [b] Deut. 3:11; ch. 13:12 [c] Deut. 1:4
5 [a] Deut. 3:8 [b] Deut. 3:10; ch. 13:11 [c] Deut. 3:14
6 [a] Num. 21:24,35 [b] Num. 32:29,33; ch. 13:8
7 [a] ch. 11:17 [b] Gen. 14:6 & 32:3; Deut. 2:1,4 [c] ch. 11:23
8 [a] ch. 10:40 & 11:16 [b] Ex. 3:8 & 23:23; ch. 9:1
9 [a] ch. 6:2 [b] ch. 8:29
10 [a] ch. 10:23
12 [a] ch. 10:33
13 [a] ch. 10:38,39
15 [a] ch. 10:29,30
16 [a] ch. 10:28 [b] ch. 8:17; Judg. 1:22
17 [a] 1 Ki. 4:10
19 [a] ch. 11:10
20 [a] ch. 11:1 & 19:15
22 [a] ch. 19:37
23 [a] ch. 11:2 [b] Gen. 14:1,2; Is. 9:1
13:1 [a] See ch. 14:10 [b] Deut. 31:3
2 [a] Judg. 3:1 [b] Joel 3:4 [c] ver. 13; 2 Sam. 3:3
3 [a] Jer. 2:18 [b] Judg. 3:3 [c] Deut. 2:23
4 [a] ch. 19:30 [b] See Judg. 1:34 [1] Or, *The cave*
5 [a] 1 Ki. 5:18; Ezek. 27:9 [b] ch. 12:7
6 [a] ch. 11:8 [b] ch. 23:13; Judg. 2:21, 23 [c] ch. 14:1,2
8 [a] Num. 32:33; Deut. 3:12,13; ch. 22:4
9 [a] ver. 16; Num. 21:30

20 The king of [a]Shimron-meron, one; the king of Achshaph, one;

21 The king of Taanach, one; the king of Megiddo, one;

22 [a]The king of Kedesh, one; the king of Jokneam of Carmel, one;

23 The king of Dor in the [a]coast of Dor, one; the king of [b]the nations of Gilgal, one;

24 The king of Tirzah, one: all the kings thirty and one.

Land yet to be conquered

13 NOW JOSHUA [a]was old *and* stricken in years; and the LORD said unto him, Thou art old *and* stricken in years, and there remaineth yet very much land [b]to be possessed.

2 [a]This *is* the land that yet remaineth: [b]all the borders of the Philistines, and all [c]Geshuri,

3 [a]From Sihor, which *is* before Egypt, even unto the borders of Ekron northward, *which* is counted to the Canaanite: [b]five lords of the Philistines; the Gazathites, and the Ashdothites, the Eshkalonites, the Gittites, and the Ekronites; also [c]the Avites:

4 From the south, all the land of the Canaanites, and [1]Mearah that *is* beside the Sidonians, [a]unto Aphek, to the borders of [b]the Amorites:

5 And the land of [a]the Giblites, and all Lebanon, toward the sunrising, [b]from Baal-gad under mount Hermon unto the entering into Hamath.

6 All the inhabitants of the hill country from Lebanon unto [a]Misrephoth-maim, *and* all the Sidonians, them [b]will I drive out from before the children of Israel: only [c]divide thou it by lot unto the Israelites for an inheritance, as I have commanded thee.

7 Now therefore divide this land for an inheritance unto the nine tribes, and the half tribe of Manasseh,

Land east of the Jordan

8 With whom the Reubenites and the Gadites have received their inheritance, [a]which Moses gave them, beyond Jordan eastward, *even* as Moses the servant of the LORD gave them;

9 From Aroer, that *is* upon the bank of the river Arnon, and the city that *is* in the midst of the river, [a]and all the plain of Medeba unto Dibon;

10 And [a]all the cities of Sihon king of
the Amorites, which reigned in Heshbon,
unto the border of the children of
Ammon;
11 [a]And Gilead, and the border of the
Geshurites and Maachathites, and all
mount Hermon, and all Bashan unto
Salcah;
12 All the kingdom of Og in Bashan,
which reigned in Ashtaroth and in Edrei,
who remained of [a]the remnant of the
giants: [b]for these did Moses smite, and
cast them out.
13 Nevertheless the children of Israel
expelled [a]not the Geshurites, nor the
Maachathites: but the Geshurites and the
Maachathites dwell among the Israelites
until this day.
14 [a]Only unto the tribe of Levi he gave
none inheritance; the sacrifices of the
LORD God of Israel made by fire *are* their
inheritance, [b]as he said unto them.
15 ¶ And Moses gave unto the tribe of
the children of Reuben *inheritance* according to their families.
16 And their coast was [a]from Aroer,
that *is* on the bank of the river Arnon,
[b]and the city that *is* in the midst of the
river, [c]and all the plain by Medeba;
17 Heshbon, and all her cities that *are*
in the plain; Dibon, and [a]Bamoth-baal,ʹ
and Beth-baal-meon,
18 [a]And Jahaza, and Kedemoth, and
Mephaath,
19 [a]And Kirjathaim, and [b]Sibmah, and
Zareth-shahar in the mount of the valley,
20 And Beth-peor, and [a]Ashdoth-pis-
gah,ʹ and Beth-jeshimoth,
21 [a]And all the cities of the plain, and
all the kingdom of Sihon king of the Amorites, which reigned in Heshbon, [b]whom
Moses smote [c]with the princes of Midian, Evi, and Rekem, and Zur, and Hur,
and Reba, *which were* dukes of Sihon,
dwelling in the country.
22 ¶ [a]Balaam also the son of Beor, the
ʹsoothsayer, did the children of Israel
slay with the sword among them that
were slain by them.
23 And the border of the children of
Reuben was Jordan, and the border
thereof. This *was* the inheritance of the
children of Reuben after their families,
the cities and the villages thereof.
24 And Moses gave *inheritance* unto
the tribe of Gad, *even* unto the children
of Gad according to their families.

25 [a]And their coast was Jazer, and all
the cities of Gilead, [b]and half the land of
the children of Ammon, unto Aroer that
is before [c]Rabbah;
26 And from Heshbon unto Ramath-
mizpeh, and Betonim; and from Mahanaim unto the border of Debir;
27 And in the valley, [a]Beth-aram, and
Beth-nimrah, [b]and Succoth, and Zaphon,
the rest of the kingdom of Sihon king of
Heshbon, Jordan and *his* border, *even*
unto the edge [c]of the sea of Chinnereth
on the other side Jordan eastward.
28 This *is* the inheritance of the children of Gad after their families, the cities,
and their villages.
29 ¶ And Moses gave *inheritance* unto
the half tribe of Manasseh: and *this* was
the possession of the half tribe of the
children of Manasseh by their families.
30 And their coast was from Mahanaim, all Bashan, all the kingdom of Og
king of Bashan, and [a]all the towns of Jair,
which *are* in Bashan, threescore cities:
31 And half Gilead, and [a]Ashtaroth,
and Edrei, cities of the kingdom of Og in
Bashan, *were pertaining* unto the children of Machir the son of Manasseh,
even to the one half of the [b]children of
Machir by their families.
32 These *are the countries* which Moses did distribute for inheritance in the
plains of Moab, on the other side Jordan,
by Jericho, eastward.
33 [a]But unto the tribe of Levi Moses
gave not *any* inheritance: the LORD God of
Israel *was* their inheritance, [b]as he said
unto them.

Land west of the Jordan

14 AND THESE *are the countries*
which the children of Israel inherited in the land of Canaan, [a]which Eleazar the priest, and Joshua the son of
Nun, and the heads of the fathers of the
tribes of the children of Israel, distributed
for inheritance to them.
2 [a]By lot *was* their inheritance, as the
LORD commanded by the hand of Moses,
for the nine tribes, and *for* the half tribe.
3 [a]For Moses had given the inheritance of two tribes and an half tribe on
the other side Jordan: but unto the Levites he gave none inheritance among
them.
4 For [a]the children of Joseph were two
tribes, Manasseh and Ephraim: therefore

10 [a]Num. 21:24, 25
11 [a]ch. 12:5
12 [a]Deut. 3:11; ch. 12:4 [b]Num. 21:24, 35
13 [a]ver. 11
14 [a]Num. 18:20, 23,24; ch. 14:3,4 [b]ver. 33
16 [a]ch. 12:2 [b]Num. 21:28 [c]ver. 9; Num. 21:30
17 [a]Num. 32:38 ʹOr, *The high places of Baal, and house of Baal-meon*
18 [a]Num. 21:23
19 [a]Num. 32:37 [b]Num. 32:38
20 [a]Deut. 3:17; ch. 12:3 ʹOr, *Springs of Pisgah,* or, *The hill*
21 [a]Deut. 3:10 [b]Num. 21:24 [c]Num. 31:8
22 [a]Num. 22:5 & 31:8 ʹOr, *diviner*
25 [a]Num. 32:35 [b]Compare Num. 21:26,28,29 with Deut. 2:19 & Judg. 11:13,15 [c]2 Sam. 11:1 & 12:26
27 [a]Num. 32:36 [b]Gen. 33:17; 1 Ki. 7:46 [c]Num. 34:11
30 [a]Num. 32:41; 1 Chr. 2:23
31 [a]ch. 12:4 [b]Num. 32:39,40
33 [a]ver. 14; ch. 18:7 [b]Num. 18:20; Deut. 10:9 & 18:1,2
14:1 [a]Num. 34:17, 18
2 [a]Num. 26:55 & 33:54 & 34:13
3 [a]ch. 13:8,32,33
4 [a]Gen. 48:5; 1 Chr. 5:1,2

they gave no part unto the Levites in the land, save cities to dwell *in,* with their suburbs for their cattle and for their substance.

5 [a]As the LORD commanded Moses, so the children of Israel did, and they divided the land.

6 ¶ Then the children of Judah came unto Joshua in Gilgal: and Caleb the son of Jephunneh the [a]Kenezite said unto him, Thou knowest [b]the thing that the LORD said unto Moses the man of God concerning me and thee [c]in Kadesh-barnea.

7 Forty years old *was* I when Moses the servant of the LORD [a]sent me from Kadesh-barnea to espy out the land; and I brought him word again as *it was* in mine heart.

8 Nevertheless [a]my brethren that went up with me made the heart of the people melt: but I wholly [b]followed the LORD my God.

9 And Moses sware on that day, saying, [a]Surely the land [b]whereon thy feet have trodden shall be thine inheritance, and thy children's for ever, because thou hast wholly followed the LORD my God.

E 10 And now, behold, the LORD hath kept me alive, [a]as he said, these forty and five years, even since the LORD spake this word unto Moses, while *the children of* Israel [/]wandered in the wilderness: and now, lo, I *am* this day fourscore and five years old.

11 [a]As yet I *am as* strong this day as *I was* in the day that Moses sent me: as my strength *was* then, even so *is* my strength now, for war, both [b]to go out, and to come in.

12 Now therefore give me this mountain, whereof the LORD spake in that day; for thou heardest in that day how [a]the Anakims *were* there, and *that* the cities *were* great *and* fenced: [b]if so be the LORD *will be* with me, then [c]I shall be able to drive them out, as the LORD said.

13 And Joshua [a]blessed him, [b]and gave unto Caleb the son of Jephunneh Hebron for an inheritance.

14 [a]Hebron therefore became the inheritance of Caleb the son of Jephunneh the Kenezite unto this day, because that he [b]wholly followed the LORD God of Israel.

15 And [a]the name of Hebron before *was* Kirjath-arba; *which Arba was* a great man among the Anakims. [b]And the land had rest from war.

The borders of Judah

15 *THIS* THEN was the lot of the tribe of the children of Judah by their families; [a]*even* to the border of Edom the [b]wilderness of Zin southward *was* the uttermost part of the south coast.

2 And their south border was from the shore of the salt sea, from the [/]bay that looketh southward:

3 And it went out to the south side [a]to [/]Maaleh-acrabbim, and passed along to Zin, and ascended up on the south side unto Kadesh-barnea, and passed along to Hezron, and went up to Adar, and fetched a compass to Karkaa:

4 *From thence* it passed [a]toward Azmon, and went out unto the river of Egypt; and the goings out of that coast were at the sea: this shall be your south coast.

5 And the east border *was* the salt sea, *even* unto the end of Jordan. And *their* border in the north quarter *was* from the bay of the sea at the uttermost part of Jordan:

6 And the border went up to [a]Beth-hoglah, and passed along by the north by Beth-arabah; and the border went up [b]to the stone of Bohan the son of Reuben:

7 And the border went up toward Debir from [a]the valley of Achor, and so northward, looking toward Gilgal, that *is* before the going up to Adummim, which *is* on the south side of the river: and the border passed toward the waters of En-shemesh, and the goings out thereof were at [b]En-rogel:

8 And the border went up [a]by the valley of the son of Hinnom unto the south side of the [b]Jebusite; the same *is* Jerusalem: and the border went up to the top of the mountain that *lieth* before the valley of Hinnom westward, which *is* at the end [c]of the valley of the giants northward:

9 And the border was drawn from the top of the hill unto [a]the fountain of the water of Nephtoah, and went out to the cities of mount Ephron; and the border was drawn [b]to Baalah, which *is* [c]Kirjath-jearim:

10 And the border compassed from Baalah westward unto mount Seir, and

5 [a]Num. 35:2; ch. 21:2
6 [a]Num. 32:12 & ch. 15:17 [b]Num. 14:24,30 [c]Num. 13:26
7 [a]Num. 13:6 & 14:6
8 [a]Num. 13:31,32 [b]Num. 14:24; Deut. 1:36
9 [a]Num. 14:23,24 [b]See Num. 13:22
10 [a]Num. 14:30 [/]Heb. *walked*
11 [a]See Deut. 34:7 [b]Deut. 31:2
12 [a]Num. 13:28, 33 [b]Rom. 8:31 [c]ch. 15:14; Judg. 1:20
13 [a]ch. 22:6 [b]ch. 10:37 & 15:13
14 [a]ch. 21:12 [b]ver. 8,9
15 [a]Gen. 23:2; ch. 15:13 [b]ch. 11:23
15:1 [a]Num. 34:3 [b]Num. 33:36
2 [/]Heb. *tongue*
3 [a]Num. 34:4 [/]Or, *The going up to Acrabbim*
4 [a]Num. 34:5
6 [a]ch. 18:19 [b]ch. 18:17
7 [a]ch. 7:26 [b]2 Sam. 17:17; 1 Ki. 1:9
8 [a]ch. 18:16; 2 Ki. 23:10; Jer. 19:2,6 [b]ch. 18:28; Judg. 1:21 & 19:10 [c]ch. 18:16
9 [a]ch. 18:15 [b]1 Chr. 13:6 [c]Judg. 18:12

passed along unto the side of mount Jearim, which *is* Chesalon, on the north side, and went down to Beth-shemesh, and passed on to [a]Timnah:

11 And the border went out unto the side of [a]Ekron northward: and the border was drawn to Shicron, and passed along to mount Baalah, and went out unto Jabneel; and the goings out of the border were at the sea.

12 And the west border *was* [a]to the great sea, and the coast *thereof.* This *is* the coast of the children of Judah round about according to their families.

13 ¶ [a]And unto Caleb the son of Jephunneh he gave a part among the children of Judah, according to the commandment of the LORD to Joshua, *even* [b]the['] city of Arba the father of Anak, which *city is* Hebron.

14 And Caleb drove thence [a]the three sons of Anak, [b]Sheshai, and Ahiman, and Talmai, the children of Anak.

15 And [a]he went up thence to the inhabitants of Debir: and the name of Debir before *was* Kirjath-sepher.

16 ¶ [a]And Caleb said, He that smiteth Kirjath-sepher, and taketh it, to him will I give Achsah my daughter to wife.

17 And [a]Othniel the [b]son of Kenaz, the brother of Caleb, took it: and he gave him Achsah his daughter to wife.

18 [a]And it came to pass, as she came *unto him,* that she moved him to ask of her father a field: and [b]she lighted off *her* ass; and Caleb said unto her, What wouldest thou?

19 Who answered, Give me a [a]blessing; for thou hast given me a south land; give me also springs of water. And he gave her the upper springs, and the nether springs.

20 This *is* the inheritance of the tribe of the children of Judah according to their families.

21 And the uttermost cities of the tribe of the children of Judah toward the coast of Edom southward were Kabzeel, and Eder, and Jagur,

22 And Kinah, and Dimonah, and Adadah,

23 And Kedesh, and Hazor, and Ithnan,

24 Ziph, and Telem, and Bealoth,

25 And Hazor, Hadattah, and Kerioth, *and* Hezron, which *is* Hazor,

26 Amam, and Shema, and Moladah,

10 [a]Gen. 38:13; Judg. 14:1

11 [a]ch. 19:43

12 [a]ver. 47; Num. 34:6,7

13 [a]ch. 14:13 [b]ch. 14:15 [']Or, *Kirjath-arba*

14 [a]Judg. 1:11,20 [b]Num. 13:22

15 [a]ch. 10:38; Judg. 1:11

16 [a]Judg. 1:12

17 [a]Judg. 1:13 & 3:9 [b]Num. 32:12; ch. 14:6

18 [a]Judg. 1:14 [b]See Gen. 24:64; 1 Sam. 25:23

19 [a]Gen. 33:11

31 [a]1 Sam. 27:6

33 [a]Num. 13:23

36 [']Or, *or*

38 [a]2 Ki. 14:7

46 [']Heb. *by the place of*

47 [a]ver. 4 [b]Num. 34:6

51 [a]ch. 10:41 & 11:16

53 [']Or, *Janus*

54 [a]ver. 13; ch. 14:15

27 And Hazar-gaddah, and Heshmon, and Beth-palet,

28 And Hazar-shual, and Beer-sheba, and Bizjothjah,

29 Baalah, and Iim, and Azem,

30 And Eltolad, and Chesil, and Hormah,

31 And [a]Ziklag, and Madmannah, and Sansannah,

32 And Lebaoth, and Shilhim, and Ain, and Rimmon: all the cities *are* twenty and nine, with their villages:

33 *And* in the valley, [a]Eshtaol, and Zoreah, and Ashnah,

34 And Zanoah, and En-gannim, Tappuah, and Enam,

35 Jarmuth, and Adullam, Socoh, and Azekah,

36 And Sharaim, and Adithaim, and Gederah, [']and Gederothaim; fourteen cities with their villages:

37 Zenan, and Hadashah, and Migdal-gad,

38 And Dilean, and Mizpeh, [a]and Joktheel,

39 Lachish, and Bozkath, and Eglon,

40 And Cabbon, and Lahmam, and Kithlish,

41 And Gederoth, Beth-dagon, and Naamah, and Makkedah; sixteen cities with their villages:

42 Libnah, and Ether, and Ashan,

43 And Jiphtah, and Ashnah, and Nezib,

44 And Keilah, and Achzib, and Mareshah; nine cities with their villages:

45 Ekron, with her towns and her villages:

46 From Ekron even unto the sea, all that *lay* [']near Ashdod, with their villages:

47 Ashdod with her towns and her villages, Gaza with her towns and her villages, unto [a]the river of Egypt, and [b]the great sea, and the border *thereof:*

48 ¶ And in the mountains, Shamir, and Jattir, and Socoh,

49 And Dannah, and Kirjath-sannah, which *is* Debir,

50 And Anab, and Eshtemoh, and Anim,

51 [a]And Goshen, and Holon, and Giloh; eleven cities with their villages:

52 Arab, and Dumah, and Eshean,

53 And [']Janum, and Beth-tappuah, and Aphekah,

54 And Humtah, and [a]Kirjath-arba,

which *is* Hebron, and Zior; nine cities with their villages:

55 Maon, Carmel, and Ziph, and Juttah,

56 And Jezreel, and Jokdeam, and Zanoah,

57 Cain, Gibeah, and Timnah; ten cities with their villages:

58 Halhul, Beth-zur, and Gedor,

59 And Maarath, and Beth-anoth, and Eltekon; six cities with their villages:

60 [a]Kirjath-baal, which *is* Kirjath-jearim, and Rabbah; two cities with their villages:

61 In the wilderness, Beth-arabah, Middin, and Secacah,

62 And Nibshan, and the city of Salt, and En-gedi; six cities with their villages.

63 ¶ As for the Jebusites the inhabitants of Jerusalem, [a]the children of Judah could not drive them out: [b]but the Jebusites dwell with the children of Judah at Jerusalem unto this day.

Ephraim and Manasseh

16 AND THE lot of the children of Joseph [1]fell from Jordan by Jericho, unto the water of Jericho on the east, to the wilderness that goeth up from Jericho throughout mount Beth-el,

2 And goeth out from Beth-el to [a]Luz, and passeth along unto the borders of Archi to Ataroth,

3 And goeth down westward to the coast of Japhleti, [a]unto the coast of Bethhoron the nether, and to [b]Gezer: and the goings out thereof are at the sea.

4 [a]So the children of Joseph, Manasseh and Ephraim, took their inheritance.

5 ¶ And the border of the children of Ephraim according to their families was *thus:* even the border of their inheritance on the east side was [a]Ataroth-addar, [b]unto Beth-horon the upper;

6 And the border went out toward the sea to [a]Michmethah on the north side; and the border went about eastward unto Taanath-shiloh, and passed by it on the east to Janohah;

7 And it went down from Janohah to Ataroth, [a]and to Naarath, and came to Jericho, and went out at Jordan.

8 The border went out from Tappuah westward unto the [a]river Kanah; and the goings out thereof were at the sea. This *is* the inheritance of the tribe of the children of Ephraim by their families.

9 And [a]the separate cities for the children of Ephraim *were* among the inheritance of the children of Manasseh, all the cities with their villages.

10 [a]And they drave not out the Canaanites that dwelt in Gezer: but the Canaanites dwell among the Ephraimites unto this day, and serve under tribute.

17 THERE WAS also a lot for the tribe of Manasseh; for he *was* the [a]firstborn of Joseph; *to wit,* for [b]Machir the firstborn of Manasseh, the father of Gilead: because he was a man of war, therefore he had [c]Gilead and Bashan.

2 There was also *a lot* for [a]the rest of the children of Manasseh by their families; [b]for the children of [1]Abiezer, and for the children of Helek, [c]and for the children of Asriel, and for the children of Shechem, [d]and for the children of Hepher, and for the children of Shemida: these *were* the male children of Manasseh the son of Joseph by their families.

3 ¶ But [a]Zelophehad, the son of Hepher, the son of Gilead, the son of Machir, the son of Manasseh, had no sons, but daughters: and these *are* the names of his daughters, Mahlah, and Noah, Hoglah, Milcah, and Tirzah.

4 And they came near before [a]Eleazar the priest, and before Joshua the son of Nun, and before the princes, saying, [b]The LORD commanded Moses to give us an inheritance among our brethren. Therefore according to the commandment of the LORD he gave them an inheritance among the brethren of their father.

5 And there fell ten portions to Manasseh, beside the land of Gilead and Bashan, which *were* on the other side Jordan;

6 Because the daughters of Manasseh had an inheritance among his sons: and the rest of Manasseh's sons had the land of Gilead.

7 ¶ And the coast of Manasseh was from Asher to [a]Michmethah, that *lieth* before Shechem; and the border went along on the right hand unto the inhabitants of En-tappuah.

8 *Now* Manasseh had the land of Tappuah: but [a]Tappuah on the border of Manasseh *belonged* to the children of Ephraim;

9 And the coast descended unto the [1]river Kanah, southward of the river: [a]these cities of Ephraim *are* among the

60 [a]ch. 18:14
63 [a]See Judg. 1:8, 21; 2 Sam. 5:6 [b]Judg. 1:21
16:1 [1]Heb. *went forth*
2 [a]ch. 18:13; Judg. 1:26
3 [a]ch. 18:13; 2 Chr. 8:5 [b]1 Ki. 9:15; 1 Chr. 7:28
4 [a]ch. 17:14
5 [a]ch. 18:13 [b]2 Chr. 8:5
6 [a]ch. 17:7
7 [a]1 Chr. 7:28
8 [a]ch. 17:9
9 [a]ch. 17:9
10 [a]Judg. 1:29; See 1 Ki. 9:16
17:1 [a]Gen. 41:51; & 46:20 & 48:18 [b]Gen. 50:23 [c]Deut. 3:15
2 [a]Num. 26:29-32 [b]1 Chr. 7:18 [c]Num. 26:31 [d]Num. 26:32 [1]Num. 26:30 in *Jeezer*
3 [a]Num. 26:33 & 27:1 & 36:2
4 [a]ch. 14:1 [b]Num. 27:6,7
7 [a]ch. 16:6
8 [a]ch. 16:8
9 [a]ch. 16:9 [1]Or, *brook of reeds*

cities of Manasseh: the coast of Manasseh also *was* on the north side of the river, and the outgoings of it were at the sea:

10 Southward *it was* Ephraim's, and northward *it was* Manasseh's, and the sea is his border; and they met together in Asher on the north, and in Issachar on the east.

11 [a]And Manasseh had in Issachar and in Asher [b]Beth-shean and her towns, and Ibleam and her towns, and the inhabitants of Dor and her towns, and the inhabitants of En-dor and her towns, and the inhabitants of Taanach and her towns, and the inhabitants of Megiddo and her towns, *even* three countries.

12 Yet [a]the children of Manasseh could not drive out *the inhabitants of* those cities; but the Canaanites would dwell in that land.

13 Yet it came to pass, when the children of Israel were waxen strong, that they put the Canaanites to [a]tribute; but did not utterly drive them out.

14 [a]And the children of Joseph spake unto Joshua, saying, Why hast thou given me *but* [b]one lot and one portion to inherit, seeing I *am* [c]a great people, forasmuch as the LORD hath blessed me hitherto?

15 And Joshua answered them, If thou *be* a great people, *then* get thee up to the wood *country,* and cut down for thyself there in the land of the Perizzites, and of the [/]giants, if mount Ephraim be too narrow for thee.

16 And the children of Joseph said, The hill is not enough for us: and all the Canaanites that dwell in the land of the valley have [a]chariots of iron, *both they* who *are* of Beth-shean and her towns, and *they* who *are* [b]of the valley of Jezreel.

17 And Joshua spake unto the house of Joseph, *even* to Ephraim and to Manasseh, saying, Thou *art* a great people, and hast great power: thou shalt not have one lot *only:*

I 18 But the mountain shall be thine; for it *is* a wood, and thou shalt cut it down: and the outgoings of it shall be thine: for thou shalt drive out the Canaanites, [a]though they have iron chariots, *and* though they *be* strong.

I *Jos 11:6* ◄► *Jdg 1:2*

11 [a]1 Chr. 7:29 [b]1 Sam. 31:10; 1 Ki. 4:12
12 [a]Judg. 1:27,28
13 [a]ch. 16:10
14 [a]ch. 16:4 [b]Gen. 48:22 [c]Gen. 48:19; Num. 26:34,37
15 [/]Or, *Rephaims;* see Gen. 14:5 & 15:20
16 [a]Judg. 1:19 & 4:3 [b]ch. 19:18; 1 Ki. 4:12
18 [a]Deut. 20:1
18:1 [a]ch. 19:51 & 21:2 & 22:9; Jer. 7:12 [b]Judg. 18:31; 1 Sam. 1:3,24 & 4:3,4
3 [a]Judg. 18:9
5 [a]ch. 15:1 [b]ch. 16:1,4
6 [a]ver. 10; ch. 14:2
7 [a]ch. 13:33 [b]ch. 13:8
12 [a]See ch. 16:1

Assigning the inherited land

18 AND THE whole congregation of the children of Israel assembled together [a]at Shiloh, and [b]set up the tabernacle of the congregation there. And the land was subdued before them.

2 And there remained among the children of Israel seven tribes, which had not yet received their inheritance.

3 And Joshua said unto the children of Israel, [a]How long *are* ye slack to go to possess the land, which the LORD God of your fathers hath given you?

4 Give out from among you three men for *each* tribe: and I will send them, and they shall rise, and go through the land, and describe it according to the inheritance of them; and they shall come *again* to me.

5 And they shall divide it into seven parts: [a]Judah shall abide in their coast on the south, and [b]the house of Joseph shall abide in their coasts on the north.

6 Ye shall therefore describe the land *into* seven parts, and bring *the description* hither to me, [a]that I may cast lots for you here before the LORD our God.

7 [a]But the Levites have no part among you; for the priesthood of the LORD *is* their inheritance: [b]and Gad, and Reuben, and half the tribe of Manasseh, have received their inheritance beyond Jordan on the east, which Moses the servant of the LORD gave them.

8 ¶ And the men arose, and went away: and Joshua charged them that went to describe the land, saying, Go and walk through the land, and describe it, and come again to me, that I may here cast lots for you before the LORD in Shiloh.

9 And the men went and passed through the land, and described it by cities into seven parts in a book, and came *again* to Joshua to the host at Shiloh.

10 ¶ And Joshua cast lots for them in Shiloh before the LORD: and there Joshua divided the land unto the children of Israel according to their divisions.

The land of Benjamin

11 ¶ And the lot of the tribe of the children of Benjamin came up according to their families: and the coast of their lot came forth between the children of Judah and the children of Joseph.

12 [a]And their border on the north side was from Jordan; and the border went up

to the side of Jericho on the north side, and went up through the mountains westward; and the goings out thereof were at the wilderness of Beth-aven.

13 And the border went over from thence toward Luz, to the side of Luz, [a]which *is* Beth-el, southward; and the border descended to Ataroth-adar, near the hill that *lieth* on the south side [b]of the nether Beth-horon.

14 And the border was drawn *thence,* and compassed the corner of the sea southward, from the hill that *lieth* before Beth-horon southward; and the goings out thereof were at [a]Kirjath-baal, which *is* Kirjath-jearim, a city of the children of Judah: this *was* the west quarter.

15 And the south quarter *was* from the end of Kirjath-jearim, and the border went out on the west, and went out to [a]the well of waters of Nephtoah:

16 And the border came down to the end of the mountain that *lieth* before [a]the valley of the son of Hinnom, *and* which *is* in the valley of the giants on the north, and descended to the valley of Hinnom, to the side of Jebusi on the south, and descended to [b]En-rogel,

17 And was drawn from the north, and went forth to En-shemesh, and went forth toward Geliloth, which *is* over against the going up of Adummim, and descended to [a]the stone of Bohan the son of Reuben,

18 And passed along toward the side over against [a]Arabah[f] northward, and went down unto Arabah:

19 And the border passed along to the side of Beth-hoglah northward: and the outgoings of the border were at the north [f]bay of the salt sea at the south end of Jordan: this *was* the south coast.

20 And Jordan was the border of it on the east side. This *was* the inheritance of the children of Benjamin, by the coasts thereof round about, according to their families.

21 Now the cities of the tribe of the children of Benjamin according to their families were Jericho, and Beth-hoglah, and the valley of Keziz,

22 And Beth-arabah, and Zemaraim, and Beth-el,

23 And Avim, and Parah, and Ophrah,

24 And Chephar-haammonai, and Ophni, and Gaba; twelve cities with their villages:

25 Gibeon, and Ramah, and Beeroth,

26 And Mizpeh, and Chephirah, and Mozah,

27 And Rekem, and Irpeel, and Taralah,

28 And Zelah, Eleph, and [a]Jebusi, which *is* Jerusalem, Gibeath, *and* Kirjath; fourteen cities with their villages. This *is* the inheritance of the children of Benjamin according to their families.

The land of Simeon

19 AND THE second lot came forth to Simeon, *even* for the tribe of the children of Simeon according to their families: [a]and their inheritance was within the inheritance of the children of Judah.

2 And [a]they had in their inheritance Beer-sheba, or Sheba, and Moladah,

3 And Hazar-shual, and Balah, and Azem,

4 And Eltolad, and Bethul, and Hormah,

5 And Ziklag, and Beth-marcaboth, and Hazar-susah,

6 And Beth-lebaoth, and Sharuhen; thirteen cities and their villages:

7 Ain, Remmon, and Ether, and Ashan; four cities and their villages:

8 And all the villages that *were* round about these cities to Baalath-beer, Ramath of the south. This *is* the inheritance of the tribe of the children of Simeon according to their families.

9 Out of the portion of the children of Judah *was* the inheritance of the children of Simeon: for the part of the children of Judah was too much for them: [a]therefore the children of Simeon had their inheritance within the inheritance of them.

The land of Zebulun

10 ¶ And the third lot came up for the children of Zebulun according to their families: and the border of their inheritance was unto Sarid:

11 [a]And their border went up toward the sea, and Maralah, and reached to Dabbasheth, and reached to the river that *is* [b]before Jokneam;

12 And turned from Sarid eastward toward the sunrising unto the border of Chisloth-tabor, and then goeth out to Daberath, and goeth up to Japhia,

13 And from thence passeth on along on the east to Gittah-hepher, to Ittah-ka-

13 [a]Gen. 28:19; Judg. 1:23 [b]ch. 16:3
14 [a]See ch. 15:9
15 [a]ch. 15:9
16 [a]ch. 15:8 [b]ch. 15:7
17 [a]ch. 15:6
18 [a]ch. 15:6 [f]Or, *The plain*
19 [f]Heb. *tongue*
28 [a]ch. 15:8
19:1 [a]ver. 9
2 [a]1 Chr. 4:28
9 [a]ver. 1
11 [a]Gen. 49:13 [b]ch. 12:22

zin, and goeth out to Remmon-[1]methoar
to Neah;
14 And the border compasseth it on
the north side to Hannathon: and the outgoings thereof are in the valley of
Jiphthah-el:
15 And Kattath, and Nahallal, and
Shimron, and Idalah, and Bethlehem:
twelve cities with their villages.
16 This *is* the inheritance of the children of Zebulun according to their families, these cities with their villages.

The land of Issachar

17 ¶ *And* the fourth lot came out to
Issachar, for the children of Issachar according to their families.
18 And their border was toward Jezreel, and Chesulloth, and Shunem,
19 And Haphraim, and Shion, and
Anaharath,
20 And Rabbith, and Kishion, and
Abez,
21 And Remeth, and En-gannim, and
En-haddah, and Beth-pazzez;
22 And the coast reacheth to Tabor,
and Shahazimah, and Beth-shemesh; and
the outgoings of their border were at Jordan: sixteen cities with their villages.
23 This *is* the inheritance of the tribe
of the children of Issachar according to
their families, the cities and their villages.

The land of Asher

24 ¶ And the fifth lot came out for the
tribe of the children of Asher according
to their families.
25 And their border was Helkath, and
Hali, and Beten, and Achshaph,
26 And Alammelech, and Amad, and
Misheal; and reacheth to Carmel westward, and to Shihor-libnath;
27 And turneth toward the sunrising
to Beth-dagon, and reacheth to Zebulun,
and to the valley of Jiphthah-el toward
the north side of Beth-emek, and Neiel,
and goeth out to Cabul on the left hand,
28 And Hebron, and Rehob, and Hammon, and Kanah, [a]*even* unto great Zidon;
29 And *then* the coast turneth to Ramah, and to the strong city [a]Tyre; and the
coast turneth to Hosah; and the outgoings
thereof are at the sea from the coast to
[b]Achzib:
30 Ummah also, and Aphek, and Rehob: twenty and two cities with their villages.
31 This *is* the inheritance of the tribe
of the children of Asher according to
their families, these cities with their villages.

The land of Naphtali

32 ¶ The sixth lot came out to the children of Naphtali, *even* for the children of
Naphtali according to their families.
33 And their coast was from Heleph,
from Allon to Zaanannim, and Adami,
Nekeb, and Jabneel, unto Lakum; and the
outgoings thereof were at Jordan:
34 And *then* [a]the coast turneth westward to Aznoth-tabor, and goeth out from
thence to Hukkok, and reacheth to Zebulun on the south side, and reacheth to
Asher on the west side, and to Judah
upon Jordan toward the sunrising.
35 And the fenced cities *are* Ziddim,
Zer, and Hammath, Rakkath, and [a]Chin-
nereth,
36 And Adamah, and Ramah, and
Hazor,
37 And Kedesh, and Edrei, and En-
hazor,
38 And Iron, and Migdal-el, Horem,
and Beth-anath, and Beth-shemesh; nineteen cities with their villages.
39 This *is* the inheritance of the tribe
of the children of Naphtali according to
their families, the cities and their villages.

The land of Dan

40 ¶ *And* the seventh lot came out for
the tribe of the children of Dan according
to their families.
41 And the coast of their inheritance
was Zorah, and Eshtaol, and Ir-shemesh,
42 And [a]Shaalabbin, and Ajalon, and
Jethlah,
43 And Elon, and Thimnathah, and
Ekron,
44 And Eltekeh, and Gibbethon, and
Baalath,
45 And Jehud, and Bene-berak, and
Gath-rimmon,
46 And Me-jarkon, and Rakkon, with
the border [1]before [2]Japho.
47 And [a]the coast of the children of
Dan went out *too little* for them: therefore the children of Dan went up to fight
against Leshem, and took it, and smote it
with the edge of the sword, and pos-

13 [1]Or, *which is drawn*
28 [a]ch. 11:8; Judg. 1:31
29 [a]2 Sam. 5:11 [b]Judg. 1:31
34 [a]Deut. 33:23
35 [a]Deut. 3:17; ch. 11:2 & 12:3; Mark 6:53; Luke 5:1
42 [a]Judg. 1:35
46 [1]Or, *over against* [2]Or, *Joppa;* see Acts 9:36
47 [a]See Judg. 18

sessed it, and dwelt therein, and called Leshem, [b]Dan, after the name of Dan their father.

48 This *is* the inheritance of the tribe of the children of Dan according to their families, these cities with their villages.

49 ¶ When they had made an end of dividing the land for inheritance by their coasts, the children of Israel gave an inheritance to Joshua the son of Nun among them:

50 According to the word of the LORD they gave him the city which he asked, *even* [a]Timnath-[b]serah in mount Ephraim: and he built the city, and dwelt therein.

51 [a]These *are* the inheritances, which Eleazar the priest, and Joshua the son of Nun, and the heads of the fathers of the tribes of the children of Israel, divided for an inheritance by lot [b]in Shiloh before the LORD, at the door of the tabernacle of the congregation. So they made an end of dividing the country.

The six cities of refuge

20 THE LORD also spake unto Joshua, saying,

2 Speak to the children of Israel, saying, [a]Appoint out for you cities of refuge, whereof I spake unto you by the hand of Moses:

3 That the slayer that killeth *any* person unawares *and* unwittingly may flee thither: and they shall be your refuge from the avenger of blood.

4 And when he that doth flee unto one of those cities shall stand at the entering of the gate of the city, and shall declare his cause in the ears of the elders of that city, they shall take him into the city unto them, and give him a place, that he may dwell among them.

5 [a]And if the avenger of blood pursue after him, then they shall not deliver the slayer up into his hand; because he smote his neighbour unwittingly, and hated him not beforetime.

6 And he shall dwell in that city, [a]until he stand before the congregation for judgment, *and* until the death of the high priest that shall be in those days: then shall the slayer return, and come unto his own city, and unto his own house, unto the city from whence he fled.

7 ¶ And they [/]appointed [a]Kedesh in Galilee in mount Naphtali, and [b]Shechem in mount Ephraim, and [c]Kirjath-arba, which *is* Hebron, in [d]the mountain of Judah.

8 And on the other side Jordan by Jericho eastward, they assigned [a]Bezer in the wilderness upon the plain out of the tribe of Reuben, and [b]Ramoth in Gilead out of the tribe of Gad, and [c]Golan in Bashan out of the tribe of Manasseh.

9 [a]These were the cities appointed for all the children of Israel, and for the stranger that sojourneth among them, that whosoever killeth *any* person at unawares might flee thither, and not die by the hand of the avenger of blood, [b]until he stood before the congregation.

Cities for the Levites

21 THEN CAME near the heads of the fathers of the Levites unto [a]Eleazar the priest, and unto Joshua the son of Nun, and unto the heads of the fathers of the tribes of the children of Israel;

2 And they spake unto them at [a]Shiloh in the land of Canaan, saying, [b]The LORD commanded by the hand of Moses to give us cities to dwell in, with the suburbs thereof for our cattle.

3 And the children of Israel gave unto the Levites out of their inheritance, at the commandment of the LORD, these cities and their suburbs.

4 And the lot came out for the families of the Kohathites: and [a]the children of Aaron the priest, *which were* of the Levites, [b]had by lot out of the tribe of Judah, and out of the tribe of Simeon, and out of the tribe of Benjamin, thirteen cities.

5 And [a]the rest of the children of Kohath *had* by lot out of the families of the tribe of Ephraim, and out of the tribe of Dan, and out of the half tribe of Manasseh, ten cities.

6 And [a]the children of Gershon *had* by lot out of the families of the tribe of Issachar, and out of the tribe of Asher, and out of the tribe of Naphtali, and out of the half tribe of Manasseh in Bashan, thirteen cities.

7 [a]The children of Merari by their families *had* out of the tribe of Reuben, and out of the tribe of Gad, and out of the tribe of Zebulun, twelve cities.

8 [a]And the children of Israel gave by lot unto the Levites these cities with their suburbs, [b]as the LORD commanded by the hand of Moses.

47 [b]Judg. 18:29
50 [a]ch. 24:30 [b]1 Chr. 7:24
51 [a]Num. 34:17; ch. 14:1 [b]ch. 18:1, 10
20:2 [a]Ex. 21:13; Num. 35:6,11,14; Deut. 19:2,9
5 [a]Num. 35:12
6 [a]Num. 35:12,25
7 [a]ch. 21:32; 1 Chr. 6:76 [b]ch. 21:21; 2 Chr. 10:1 [c]ch. 14:15 & 21:11,13 [d]Luke 1:39 [/]Heb. *sanctified*
8 [a]Deut. 4:43; ch. 21:36; 1 Chr. 6:78 [b]ch. 21:38; 1 Ki. 22:3 [c]ch. 21:27
9 [a]Num. 35:15 [b]ver. 6
21:1 [a]ch. 14:1 & 17:4
2 [a]ch. 18:1 [b]Num. 35:2
4 [a]ver. 8,19 [b]See ch. 24:33
5 [a]ver. 20
6 [a]ver. 27
7 [a]ver. 34
8 [a]ver. 3 [b]Num. 35:2

9 ¶ And they gave out of the tribe of the children of Judah, and out of the tribe of the children of Simeon, these cities which are *here* [I]mentioned by name,

10 Which the children of Aaron, *being* of the families of the Kohathites, *who were* of the children of Levi, had: for their's was the first lot.

11 [a]And they gave them [I]the city of Arba the father of [b]Anak, which *city is* Hebron, [c]in the hill *country* of Judah, with the suburbs thereof round about it.

12 But [a]the fields of the city, and the villages thereof, gave they to Caleb the son of Jephunneh for his possession.

13 ¶ Thus [a]they gave to the children of Aaron the priest [b]Hebron with her suburbs, *to be* a city of refuge for the slayer; [c]and Libnah with her suburbs,

14 And [a]Jattir with her suburbs, [b]and Eshtemoa with her suburbs,

15 And [a]Holon with her suburbs, [b]and Debir with her suburbs,

16 And [a]Ain with her suburbs, [b]and Juttah with her suburbs, *and* [c]Beth-shemesh with her suburbs; nine cities out of those two tribes.

17 And out of the tribe of Benjamin, [a]Gibeon with her suburbs, [b]Geba with her suburbs,

18 Anathoth with her suburbs, and [a]Almon with her suburbs; four cities.

19 All the cities of the children of Aaron, the priests, *were* thirteen cities with their suburbs.

20 ¶ [a]And the families of the children of Kohath, the Levites which remained of the children of Kohath, even they had the cities of their lot out of the tribe of Ephraim.

21 For they gave them [a]Shechem with her suburbs in mount Ephraim, *to be* a city of refuge for the slayer; and Gezer with her suburbs,

22 And Kibzaim with her suburbs, and Beth-horon with her suburbs; four cities.

23 And out of the tribe of Dan, Eltekeh with her suburbs, Gibbethon with her suburbs,

24 Aijalon with her suburbs, Gathrimmon with her suburbs; four cities.

25 And out of the half tribe of Manasseh, Tanach with her suburbs, and Gathrimmon with her suburbs; two cities.

26 All the cities *were* ten with their suburbs for the families of the children of Kohath that remained.

27 ¶ [a]And unto the children of Gershon, of the families of the Levites, out of the *other* half tribe of Manasseh *they gave* [b]Golan in Bashan with her suburbs, *to be* a city of refuge for the slayer; and Beeshterah with her suburbs; two cities.

28 And out of the tribe of Issachar, Kishon with her suburbs, Dabareh with her suburbs,

29 Jarmuth with her suburbs, En-gannim with her suburbs; four cities.

30 And out of the tribe of Asher, Mishal with her suburbs, Abdon with her suburbs,

31 Helkath with her suburbs, and Rehob with her suburbs; four cities.

32 And out of the tribe of Naphtali, [a]Kedesh in Galilee with her suburbs, *to be* a city of refuge for the slayer; and Hammoth-dor with her suburbs, and Kartan with her suburbs; three cities.

33 All the cities of the Gershonites according to their families *were* thirteen cities with their suburbs.

34 ¶ [a]And unto the families of the children of Merari, the rest of the Levites, out of the tribe of Zebulun, Jokneam with her suburbs, and Kartah with her suburbs,

35 Dimnah with her suburbs, Nahalal with her suburbs; four cities.

36 And out of the tribe of Reuben, [a]Bezer with her suburbs, and Jahazah with her suburbs,

37 Kedemoth with her suburbs, and Mephaath with her suburbs; four cities.

38 And out of the tribe of Gad, [a]Ramoth in Gilead with her suburbs, *to be* a city of refuge for the slayer; and Mahanaim with her suburbs,

39 Heshbon with her suburbs, Jazer with her suburbs; four cities in all.

40 So all the cities for the children of Merari by their families, which were remaining of the families of the Levites, were *by* their lot twelve cities.

41 [a]All the cities of the Levites within the possession of the children of Israel *were* forty and eight cities with their suburbs.

42 These cities were every one with their suburbs round about them: thus *were* all these cities.

43 ¶ And the LORD gave unto Israel [a]all the land which he sware to give unto their fathers; and they possessed it, and dwelt therein.

9 [I]Heb. *called*
11 [a]1 Chr. 6:55 [b]ch. 15:13,14 [c]ch. 20:7; Luke 1:39 [I]Or, *Kirjath-arba;* see Gen. 23:2
12 [a]ch. 14:14; 1 Chr. 6:56
13 [a]1 Chr. 6:57 [b]ch. 15:54 & 20:7 [c]ch. 15:42
14 [a]ch. 15:48 [b]ch. 15:50
15 [a]1 Chr. 6:58 *Hilen;* ch. 15:51 [b]ch. 15:49
16 [a]1 Chr. 6:59 *Ashan;* ch. 15:42 [b]ch. 15:55 [c]ch. 15:10
17 [a]ch. 18:25 [b]ch. 18:24 *Gaba*
18 [a]1 Chr. 6:60 *Alemeth*
20 [a]ver. 5; 1 Chr. 6:66
21 [a]ch. 20:7
27 [a]ver. 6; 1 Chr. 6:71 [b]ch. 20:8
32 [a]ch. 20:7
34 [a]ver. 7; See 1 Chr. 6:77
36 [a]ch. 20:8
38 [a]ch. 20:8
41 [a]Num. 35:7
43 [a]Gen. 13:15 & 15:18 & 26:3 & 28:4,13

V 44 [a]And the LORD gave them rest round about, according to all that he sware unto their fathers: and [b]there stood not a man of all their enemies before them; the LORD delivered all their enemies into their hand.

L 45 [a]There failed not aught of any good thing which the LORD had spoken unto the house of Israel; all came to pass.

Eastern tribes return home

22 THEN JOSHUA called the Reubenites, and the Gadites, and the half tribe of Manasseh,

2 And said unto them, Ye have kept [a]all that Moses the servant of the LORD commanded you, [b]and have obeyed my voice in all that I commanded you:

3 Ye have not left your brethren these many days unto this day, but have kept the charge of the commandment of the LORD your God.

4 And now the LORD your God hath given rest unto your brethren, as he promised them: therefore now return ye, and get you unto your tents, *and* unto the land of your possession, [a]which Moses the servant of the LORD gave you on the other side Jordan.

5 But [a]take diligent heed to do the commandment and the law, which Moses the servant of the LORD charged you, [b]to love the LORD your God, and to walk in all his ways, and to keep his commandments, and to cleave unto him, and to serve him with all your heart and with all your soul.

6 So Joshua [a]blessed them, and sent them away: and they went unto their tents.

7 ¶ Now to the *one* half of the tribe of Manasseh Moses had given *possession* in Bashan: [a]but unto the *other* half thereof gave Joshua among their brethren on this side Jordan westward. And when Joshua sent them away also unto their tents, then he blessed them,

8 And he spake unto them, saying, Return with much riches unto your tents, and with very much cattle, with silver, and with gold, and with brass, and with iron, and with very much raiment: [a]divide the spoil of your enemies with your brethren.

9 ¶ And the children of Reuben and the children of Gad and the half tribe of Manasseh returned, and departed from the children of Israel out of Shiloh, which *is* in the land of Canaan, to go unto [a]the country of Gilead, to the land of their possession, whereof they were possessed, according to the word of the LORD by the hand of Moses.

10 ¶ And when they came unto the borders of Jordan, that *are* in the land of Canaan, the children of Reuben and the children of Gad and the half tribe of Manasseh built there an altar by Jordan, a great altar to see to.

11 ¶ And the children of Israel [a]heard say, Behold, the children of Reuben and the children of Gad and the half tribe of Manasseh have built an altar over against the land of Canaan, in the borders of Jordan, at the passage of the children of Israel.

12 And when the children of Israel heard *of it,* [a]the whole congregation of the children of Israel gathered themselves together at Shiloh, to go up to war against them.

13 And the children of Israel [a]sent unto the children of Reuben, and to the children of Gad, and to the half tribe of Manasseh, into the land of Gilead, [b]Phinehas the son of Eleazar the priest,

14 And with him ten princes, of each [1]chief house a prince throughout all the tribes of Israel; and [a]each one *was* an head of the house of their fathers among the thousands of Israel.

15 ¶ And they came unto the children of Reuben, and to the children of Gad, and to the half tribe of Manasseh, unto the land of Gilead, and they spake with them, saying,

16 Thus saith the whole congregation of the LORD, What trespass *is* this that ye have committed against the God of Israel, to turn away this day from following the LORD, in that ye have builded you an altar, [a]that ye might rebel this day against the LORD?

17 *Is* the iniquity [a]of Peor too little for us, from which we are not cleansed until this day, although there was a plague in the congregation of the LORD, D

18 But that ye must turn away this day from following the LORD? and it will be,

44 [a]ch. 11:23 & 22:4 [b]Deut. 7:24
45 [a]ch. 23:14
22:2 [a]Num. 32:20; Deut. 3:18 [b]ch. 1:16,17
4 [a]Num. 32:33
5 [a]Deut. 6:6,17 & 11:22; Jer. 12:16 [b]Deut. 10:12
6 [a]Gen. 47:7; Ex. 39:43; ch. 14:13; 2 Sam. 6:18; Luke 24:50
7 [a]ch. 17:5
8 [a]Num. 31:27; 1 Sam. 30:24
9 [a]Num. 32:1,26, 29
11 [a]Deut. 13:12; Judg. 20:12
12 [a]Judg. 20:1
13 [a]Deut. 13:14; Judg. 20:12 [b]Ex. 6:25; Num. 25:7, 11-13
14 [a]Num. 1:4 [1]Heb. *house of the father*
16 [a]See Lev. 17:8, 9; Deut. 12:13,14
17 [a]Num. 25:3,4; Deut. 4:3

V *Jos 1:5* ◀▶ *Jos 23:9–10*
L *Jos 1:9* ◀▶ *1Sa 2:9*
D *Dt 29:22* ◀▶ *1Sa 5:6*

seeing ye rebel today against the LORD, that tomorrow [a]he will be wroth with the whole congregation of Israel.

19 Notwithstanding, if the land of your possession *be* unclean, *then* pass ye over unto the land of the possession of the LORD, [a]wherein the LORD'S tabernacle dwelleth, and take possession among us: but rebel not against the LORD, nor rebel against us, in building you an altar beside the altar of the LORD our God.

20 [a]Did not Achan the son of Zerah commit a trespass in the accursed thing, and wrath fell on all the congregation of Israel? and that man perished not alone in his iniquity.

21 ¶ Then the children of Reuben and the children of Gad and the half tribe of Manasseh answered, and said unto the heads of the thousands of Israel,

22 The LORD [a]God of gods, the LORD God of gods, he [b]knoweth, and Israel he shall know; if *it be* in rebellion, or if in transgression against the LORD, (save us not this day,)

23 That we have built us an altar to turn from following the LORD, or if to offer thereon burnt offering or meat offering, or if to offer peace offerings thereon, let the LORD himself [a]require *it;*

24 And if we have not *rather* done it for fear of *this* thing, saying, ['] In time to come your children might speak unto our children, saying, What have ye to do with the LORD God of Israel?

25 For the LORD hath made Jordan a border between us and you, ye children of Reuben and children of Gad; ye have no part in the LORD: so shall your children make our children cease from fearing the LORD.

26 Therefore we said, Let us now prepare to build us an altar, not for burnt offering, nor for sacrifice:

27 But *that* it *may be* [a]a witness between us, and you, and our generations after us, that we might [b]do the service of the LORD before him with our burnt offerings, and with our sacrifices, and with our peace offerings; that your children may not say to our children in time to come, Ye have no part in the LORD.

28 Therefore said we, that it shall be, when they should *so* say to us or to our generations in time to come, that we may say *again,* Behold the pattern of the altar of the LORD, which our fathers made, not for burnt offerings, nor for sacrifices; but it *is* a witness between us and you.

29 God forbid that we should rebel against the LORD, and turn this day from following the LORD, [a]to build an altar for burnt offerings, for meat offerings, or for sacrifices, beside the altar of the LORD our God that *is* before his tabernacle.

30 ¶ And when Phinehas the priest, and the princes of the congregation and heads of the thousands of Israel which *were* with him, heard the words that the children of Reuben and the children of Gad and the children of Manasseh spake, [']it pleased them.

31 And Phinehas the son of Eleazar the priest said unto the children of Reuben, and to the children of Gad, and to the children of Manasseh, This day we perceive that the LORD *is* [a]among us, because ye have not committed this trespass against the LORD: [']now ye have delivered the children of Israel out of the hand of the LORD.

32 ¶ And Phinehas the son of Eleazar the priest, and the princes, returned from the children of Reuben, and from the children of Gad, out of the land of Gilead, unto the land of Canaan, to the children of Israel, and brought them word again.

33 And the thing pleased the children of Israel; and the children of Israel [a]blessed God, and did not intend to go up against them in battle, to destroy the land wherein the children of Reuben and Gad dwelt.

34 And the children of Reuben and the children of Gad called the altar [a]*Ed:* ['] for it *shall be* a witness between us that the LORD *is* God.

Joshua's address to Israel

23 AND IT came to pass a long time after that the LORD [a]had given rest unto Israel from all their enemies round about, that Joshua [b]waxed old *and* [']stricken in age.

2 And Joshua [a]called for all Israel, *and* for their elders, and for their heads, and for their judges, and for their officers, and said unto them, I am old *and* stricken in age:

3 And ye have seen all that the LORD your God hath done unto all these nations because of you; for the [a]LORD your God *is* he that hath fought for you.

4 Behold, [a]I have divided unto you by

18 [a]Num. 16:22
19 [a]ch. 18:1
20 [a]ch. 7:1,5
22 [a]Deut. 10:17 [b]Job 10:7 & 23:10; Jer. 12:3; 2 Cor. 11:11,31
23 [a]Deut. 18:19; 1 Sam. 20:16
24 [']Heb. *Tomorrow*
27 [a]ver. 34; Gen. 31:48; ch. 24:27 [b]Deut. 12:5
29 [a]Deut. 12:13, 14
30 [']Heb. *it was good in their eyes*
31 [a]Lev. 26:11,12; 2 Chr. 15:2 [']Heb. *then*
33 [a]1 Chr. 29:20; Neh. 8:6; Dan. 2:19; Luke 2:28
34 [a]ch. 24:27 [']i.e. A witness
23:1 [a]ch. 21:44 & 22:4 [b]ch. 13:1 [']Heb. *come into days*
2 [a]Deut. 31:28; ch. 24:1; 1 Chr. 28:1
3 [a]Ex. 14:14; ch.10:14,42
4 [a]ch. 13:2,6 & 18:10

lot these nations that remain, to be an
inheritance for your tribes, from Jordan,
with all the nations that I have cut off,
even unto the great sea [l]westward.
5 And the LORD your God, [a]he shall expel them from before you, and drive
them from out of your sight; and ye shall
possess their land, [b]as the LORD your God
hath promised unto you.
6 [a]Be ye therefore very courageous to
keep and to do all that is written in the
book of the law of Moses, [b]that ye turn
not aside therefrom *to* the right hand or
to the left;
7 That ye [a]come not among these nations, these that remain among you; neither [b]make mention of the name of their
gods, nor cause to swear *by them,* neither
serve them, nor bow yourselves unto
them:
8 [l]But [a]cleave unto the LORD your God,
as ye have done unto this day.
V 9 [a]For[l] the LORD hath driven out from
before you great nations and strong: but
as for you, [b]no man hath been able to
stand before you unto this day.
10 [a]One man of you shall chase a thousand: for the LORD your God, he *it is* that
fighteth for you, [b]as he hath promised
you.
11 [a]Take good heed therefore unto
[l]yourselves, that ye love the LORD your
God.
12 Else if ye do in any wise [a]go back,
and cleave unto the remnant of these nations, *even* these that remain among you,
and shall [b]make marriages with them,
and go in unto them, and they to you:
J 13 Know for a certainty that [a]the LORD
your God will no more drive out *any of*
these nations from before you; [b]but they
shall be snares and traps unto you, and
scourges in your sides, and thorns in your
eyes, until ye perish from off this good
land which the LORD your God hath given
you.
14 And, behold, this day [a]I *am* going
the way of all the earth: and ye know in
all your hearts and in all your souls, that
[b]not one thing hath failed of all the good
things which the LORD your God spake
concerning you; all are come to pass unto
you, *and* not one thing hath failed
thereof.
15 [a]Therefore it shall come to pass, R
that as all good things are come upon
you, which the LORD your God promised
you; so shall the LORD bring upon you [b]all
evil things, until he have destroyed you
from off this good land which the LORD
your God hath given you.
16 When ye have transgressed the covenant of the LORD your God, which he
commanded you, and have gone and
served other gods, and bowed yourselves
to them; then shall the anger of the LORD
be kindled against you, and ye shall perish quickly from off the good land which
he hath given unto you.

Israel renews the covenant

24 AND JOSHUA gathered all the
tribes of Israel to [a]Shechem, and
[b]called for the elders of Israel, and for
their heads, and for their judges, and for
their officers; and they [c]presented themselves before God.
2 And Joshua said unto all the people,
Thus saith the LORD God of Israel, [a]Your
fathers dwelt on the other side of the
flood in old time, *even* Terah, the father
of Abraham, and the father of Nachor:
and [b]they served other gods.
3 And [a]I took your father Abraham
from the other side of the flood, and led
him throughout all the land of Canaan,
and multiplied his seed, and [b]gave him
Isaac.
4 And I gave unto Isaac [a]Jacob and
Esau: and I gave unto [b]Esau mount Seir,
to possess it; [c]but Jacob and his children
went down into Egypt.
5 [a]I sent Moses also and Aaron, and [b]I
plagued Egypt, according to that which I
did among them: and afterward I brought
you out.
6 And I [a]brought your fathers out of
Egypt: and [b]ye came unto the sea; [c]and
the Egyptians pursued after your fathers
with chariots and horsemen unto the Red
sea.

4 [l]Heb. *at the sunset*
5 [a]Ex. 23:30 & 33:2 & 34:11; Deut. 11:23; ch. 13:6 [b]Num. 33:53
6 [a]ch. 1:7 [b]Deut. 5:32 & 28:14
7 [a]Ex. 23:33; Deut. 7:2,3; Prov. 4:14; Eph. 5:11 [b]Ex. 23:13; Jer. 5:7; Zeph. 1:5; See Num. 32:38
8 [a]Deut. 10:20; ch. 22:5 [l]Or, *For if ye will cleave*
9 [a]Deut. 11:23 [b]ch. 1:5 [l]Or, *Then the* LORD *will drive*
10 [a]Lev. 26:8; Deut. 32:30 [b]Ex. 14:14; Deut. 3:22
11 [a]ch. 22:5 [l]Heb. *your souls*
12 [a]2 Pet. 2:20,21 [b]Deut. 7:3
13 [a]Judg. 2:3 [b]Ex. 23:33; 1 Ki. 11:4
14 [a]1 Ki. 2:2 [b]Luke 21:33
15 [a]Deut. 28:63 [b]Deut. 28:15,16
24:1 [a]Gen. 35:4 [b]ch. 23:2 [c]1 Sam. 10:19
2 [a]Gen. 11:26,31 [b]ver. 14
3 [a]Gen. 12:1; Acts 7:2,3 [b]Ps. 127:3
4 [a]Gen. 25:24-26 [b]Gen. 36:8; Deut. 2:5 [c]Gen. 46:1,6
5 [a]Ex. 3:10 [b]Ex. 7 & 8 & 9 & 10
6 [a]Ex. 12:37,51 [b]Ex. 14:2 [c]Ex. 14:9

V *Jos 21:44* ◀▶ *1Sa 14:6*
J *Jos 6:26* ◀▶ *Jdg 2:3*
R *Dt 32:36* ◀▶ *1Ki 9:6–9*

23:15–16 Joshua's last words to the people confirmed God's promise to bless Israel if they would obey his laws or to judge them if they rejected his laws and worshiped idols.

7 And when they cried unto the LORD, [a]he put darkness between you and the Egyptians, [b]and brought the sea upon them, and covered them; and [c]your eyes have seen what I have done in Egypt: and ye dwelt in the wilderness [d]a long season.

8 And I brought you into the land of the Amorites, which dwelt on the other side Jordan; [a]and they fought with you: and I gave them into your hand, that ye might possess their land; and I destroyed them from before you.

9 Then [a]Balak the son of Zippor, king of Moab, arose and warred against Israel, and [b]sent and called Balaam the son of Beor to curse you:

10 [a]But I would not hearken unto Balaam; [b]therefore he blessed you still: so I delivered you out of his hand.

11 And [a]ye went over Jordan, and came unto Jericho: and [b]the men of Jericho fought against you, the Amorites, and the Perizzites, and the Canaanites, and the Hittites, and the Girgashites, the Hivites, and the Jebusites; and I delivered them into your hand.

12 And [a]I sent the hornet before you, which drave them out from before you, *even* the two kings of the Amorites; *but* [b]not with thy sword, nor with thy bow.

13 And I have given you a land for which ye did not labour, and [a]cities which ye built not, and ye dwell in them; of the vineyards and oliveyards which ye planted not do ye eat.

S 14 ¶ [a]Now therefore fear the LORD, and serve him in [b]sincerity and in truth: and [c]put away the gods which your fathers served on the other side of the flood, and [d]in Egypt; and serve ye the LORD.

N 15 And if it seem evil unto you to serve the LORD, [a]choose you this day whom ye will serve; whether [b]the gods which your fathers served that *were* on the other side of the flood, or [c]the gods of the Amorites, in whose land ye dwell: [d]but as for me and my house, we will serve the LORD.

S *Jos 5:6* ◀ ▶ *1Sa 12:15*
N *Dt 32:35* ◀ ▶ *2Sa 14:14*

16 And the people answered and said, God forbid that we should forsake the LORD, to serve other gods;

17 For the LORD our God, he *it is* that brought us up and our fathers out of the land of Egypt, from the house of bondage, and which did those great signs in our sight, and preserved us in all the way wherein we went, and among all the people through whom we passed:

18 And the LORD drave out from before us all the people, even the Amorites which dwelt in the land: *therefore* will we also serve the LORD; for he *is* our God.

19 And Joshua said unto the people, H
[a]Ye cannot serve the LORD: for he *is* an [b]holy God; he *is* [c]a jealous God; [d]he will not forgive your transgressions nor your sins.

20 [a]If ye forsake the LORD, and serve strange gods, [b]then he will turn and do you hurt, and consume you, after that he hath done you good.

21 And the people said unto Joshua, Nay; but we will serve the LORD.

22 And Joshua said unto the people, Ye *are* witnesses against yourselves that [a]ye have chosen you the LORD, to serve him. And they said, *We are* witnesses.

23 Now therefore [a]put away, *said he,* the strange gods which *are* among you, and incline your heart unto the LORD God of Israel.

24 And the people said unto Joshua, The LORD our God will we serve, and his voice will we obey.

25 So Joshua [a]made a covenant with the people that day, and set them a statute and an ordinance [b]in Shechem.

26 ¶ And Joshua [a]wrote these words in the book of the law of God, and took [b]a great stone, and [c]set it up there [d]under an oak, that *was* by the sanctuary of the LORD.

27 And Joshua said unto all the people, Behold, this stone shall be [a]a witness unto us; for [b]it hath heard all the words of the LORD which he spake unto us: it shall be therefore a witness unto you, lest ye deny your God.

H *Dt 32:43* ◀ ▶ *Jdg 5:23*

7 [a]Ex. 14:20 [b]Ex. 14:27,28 [c]Deut. 4:34 [d]ch. 5:6
8 [a]Num. 21:21,33; Deut. 2:32
9 [a]Judg. 11:25 [b]Num. 22:5
10 [a]Deut. 23:5 [b]Num. 23:11,20
11 [a]ch. 3:14,17 [b]ch. 6:1 & 10:1
12 [a]Ex. 23:28; Deut. 7:20 [b]Ps. 44:3,6
13 [a]Deut. 6:10,11
14 [a]Deut. 10:12; 1 Sam. 12:24 [b]Gen. 17:1 & 20:5; Deut. 18:13; 2 Cor. 1:12 [c]ver. 2,23; Ezek. 20:18 [d]Ezek. 20:7, 8 & 23:3
15 [a]Ruth 1:15; 1 Ki. 18:21 [b]ver. 2 [c]Ex. 23:24,32,33 [d]Gen. 18:19
19 [a]Mat. 6:24 [b]1 Sam. 6:20 [c]Ex. 20:5 [d]Ex. 23:21
20 [a]1 Chr. 28:9; Ezra 8:22; Is. 1:28; Jer. 17:13 [b]ch. 23:15; Is. 63:10; Acts 7:42
22 [a]Ps. 119:173
23 [a]ver. 14; Gen. 35:2
25 [a]Ex. 15:25; 2 Ki. 11:17 [b]ver. 1
26 [a]Deut. 31:24 [b]Judg. 9:6 [c]Gen. 28:18; ch. 4:3 [d]Gen. 35:4
27 [a]See Gen. 31:48,52 [b]Deut. 32:1

24:15 The book of Joshua concludes with an ultimatum that required the Israelites to choose either to worship God or to follow pagan idols. The choices that the people made at this time became one of the most significant turning points in Israel's history.

28 So [a]Joshua let the people depart,
every man unto his inheritance.

The death of Joshua

29 ¶ [a]And it came to pass after these
things, that Joshua the son of Nun, the
servant of the LORD, died, *being* an hundred and ten years old.
30 And they buried him in the border
of his inheritance in [a]Timnath-serah,
which *is* in mount Ephraim, on the north
side of the hill of Gaash.
31 And [a]Israel served the LORD all the
days of Joshua, and all the days of the
elders that [I]overlived Joshua, and which
had [b]known all the works of the LORD,
that he had done for Israel.
32 ¶ And the [a]bones of Joseph, which
the children of Israel brought up out of
Egypt, buried they in Shechem, in a parcel of ground [b]which Jacob bought of the
sons of Hamor the father of Shechem for
an hundred [I]pieces of silver: and it became the inheritance of the children of
Joseph.
33 And Eleazar the son of Aaron died;
and they buried him in a hill *that pertained to* [a]Phinehas his son, which was
given him in mount Ephraim.

28 [a]Judg. 2:6
29 [a]Judg. 2:8
30 [a]ch. 19:50
31 [a]Judg. 2:7 [b]Deut. 11:2 [I]Heb. *prolonged* their *days after Joshua*
32 [a]Gen. 50:25; Ex. 13:19 [b]Gen. 33:19 [I]Or, *lambs*
33 [a]Ex. 6:25; Judg. 20:28

Judges

Author: Tradition suggests Samuel; authorship uncertain

Theme: Israel's disobedience, defeat and deliverance

Date of Writing: c. 1050–1000 B.C.

Outline of Judges

I. Failure to Purge the Land Leads to Apostasy (1:1—3:6)
II. The Cycle of Oppression and Deliverance (3:7—16:31)
III. Spiritual and Civil Disorder (17:1—21:25)

THIS BOOK TAKES its title from the leaders who governed Israel from the time of Joshua's death to the beginning of the monarchy. During this time, men and women from various tribes were chosen by God to provide direction and deliverance for the nation of Israel during times of spiritual disintegration and enemy oppression. These judges ruled over different parts of the promised land for several hundred years. While many of the judges ruled only a portion of the land, God granted some of the judges jurisdiction over the entire territory.

If the book of Joshua is a book of victory, then the book of Judges is a book of defeat. Joshua, who was Moses' second-in-command throughout the exodus, led the Israelites into Canaan and followed God's directions over the next thirty years to conquer the promised land. However, in the leadership vacuum that developed after Joshua's death, Israel did not consistently follow Joshua's example of submission to God. A careful analysis of the chronology of this book reveals that various periods of conquest by their pagan enemies interrupted Israel's peaceful years under the rule of a judge. Israel's spiritual history became a spiral of indifference, disobedience, defeat, domination, deliverance and restored divine approval that was tragically repeated for centuries. The book of Judges chronicles these cycles, noting the numerous defeats of the Israelites as well as their victories, highlighting the righteous judges that God raised up to conquer Israel's enemies and the restoring of his people to covenant fellowship with himself.

Fighting the Canaanites

1 NOW AFTER the death of Joshua it came to pass, that the children of Israel [a]asked the LORD, saying, Who shall go up for us against the Canaanites first, to fight against them?

2 And the LORD said, [a]Judah shall go up: behold, I have delivered the land into his hand.

3 And Judah said unto Simeon his brother, Come up with me into my lot, that we may fight against the Canaanites; and [a]I likewise will go with thee into thy lot. So Simeon went with him.

4 And Judah went up; and the LORD delivered the Canaanites and the Perizzites into their hand: and they slew of them in [a]Bezek ten thousand men.

5 And they found Adoni-bezek in Bezek: and they fought against him, and they slew the Canaanites and the Perizzites.

6 But Adoni-bezek fled; and they pursued after him, and caught him, and cut off his thumbs and his great toes.

7 And Adoni-bezek said, Threescore and ten kings, having [1]their thumbs and their great toes cut off, [2]gathered *their meat* under my table: [a]as I have done, so God hath requited me. And they brought him to Jerusalem, and there he died.

8 Now [a]the children of Judah had fought against Jerusalem, and had taken it, and smitten it with the edge of the sword, and set the city on fire.

9 ¶ [a]And afterward the children of Judah went down to fight against the Canaanites, that dwelt in the mountain, and in the south, and in the [1]valley.

10 And Judah went against the Canaanites that dwelt in Hebron: (now the name of Hebron before *was* [a]Kirjath-arba:) and they slew Sheshai, and Ahiman, and Talmai.

11 [a]And from thence he went against the inhabitants of Debir: and the name of Debir before *was* Kirjath-sepher:

12 [a]And Caleb said, He that smiteth Kirjath-sepher, and taketh it, to him will I give Achsah my daughter to wife.

13 And Othniel the son of Kenaz, [a]Caleb's younger brother, took it: and he gave him Achsah his daughter to wife.

14 [a]And it came to pass, when she came *to him,* that she moved him to ask of her father a field: and she lighted from off *her* ass; and Caleb said unto her, What wilt thou?

15 And she said unto him, [a]Give me a blessing: for thou hast given me a south land; give me also springs of water. And Caleb gave her the upper springs and the nether springs.

16 ¶ [a]And the children of the Kenite, Moses' father-in-law, went up out [b]of the city of palm trees with the children of Judah into the wilderness of Judah, which *lieth* in the south of [c]Arad; [d]and they went and dwelt among the people.

17 [a]And Judah went with Simeon his brother, and they slew the Canaanites that inhabited Zephath, and utterly destroyed it. And the name of the city was called [b]Hormah.

18 Also Judah took [a]Gaza with the coast thereof, and Askelon with the coast thereof, and Ekron with the coast thereof.

19 And [a]the LORD was with Judah; and [1]he drave out *the inhabitants of* the mountain; but could not drive out the inhabitants of the valley, because they had [b]chariots of iron.

20 [a]And they gave Hebron unto Caleb, as Moses said: and he expelled thence the three sons of Anak.

21 [a]And the children of Benjamin did not drive out the Jebusites that inhabited Jerusalem; but the Jebusites dwell with the children of Benjamin in Jerusalem unto this day.

22 ¶ And the house of Joseph, they also went up against Beth-el: [a]and the LORD *was* with them.

23 And the house of Joseph [a]sent to descry Beth-el. (Now the name of the city before *was* [b]Luz.)

24 And the spies saw a man come forth out of the city, and they said unto him, Show us, we pray thee, the entrance into the city, and [a]we will show thee mercy.

25 And when he showed them the entrance into the city, they smote the city with the edge of the sword; but they let go the man and all his family.

26 And the man went into the land of the Hittites, and built a city, and called the name thereof Luz: which *is* the name thereof unto this day.

27 ¶ [a]Neither did Manasseh drive out *the inhabitants of* Beth-shean and her

1:1 [a]Num. 27:21; ch. 20:18
2 [a]Gen. 49:8
3 [a]ver. 17
4 [a]1 Sam. 11:8
7 [a]Lev. 24:19; 1 Sam. 15:33; Jas. 2:13 [1]Heb. *the thumbs of their hands and of their feet* [2]Or, *gleaned*
8 [a]See Josh. 15:63
9 [a]Josh. 10:36 & 11:21 & 15:13 [1]Or, *low country*
10 [a]Josh. 14:15 & 15:13,14
11 [a]Josh. 15:15
12 [a]Josh. 15:16,17
13 [a]ch. 3:9
14 [a]Josh. 15:18,19
15 [a]Gen. 33:11
16 [a]ch. 4:11,17; 1 Sam. 15:6; 1 Chr. 2:55 [b]Deut. 34:3 [c]Num. 21:1 [d]1 Sam. 15:6
17 [a]ver. 3 [b]Num. 21:3; Josh. 19:4
18 [a]Josh. 11:22
19 [a]ver. 2; 2 Ki. 18:7 [b]Josh. 17:16, 18 [1]Or, *he possessed the mountain*
20 [a]Num. 14:24; Deut. 1:36; Josh. 14:9,13,14 & 15:13,14
21 [a]See Josh. 15:63 & 18:28
22 [a]ver. 19
23 [a]Josh. 2:1 & 7:2; ch. 18:2 [b]Gen. 28:19
24 [a]Josh. 2:12,14
27 [a]Josh. 17:11-13

towns, nor Taanach and her towns, nor the inhabitants of Dor and her towns, nor the inhabitants of Ibleam and her towns, nor the inhabitants of Megiddo and her towns: but the Canaanites would dwell in that land.

28 And it came to pass, when Israel was strong, that they put the Canaanites to tribute, and did not utterly drive them out.

29 ¶ [a]Neither did Ephraim drive out the Canaanites that dwelt in Gezer; but the Canaanites dwelt in Gezer among them.

30 ¶ Neither did Zebulun drive out the inhabitants of Kitron, nor the [a]inhabitants of Nahalol; but the Canaanites dwelt among them, and became tributaries.

31 ¶ [a]Neither did Asher drive out the inhabitants of Accho, nor the inhabitants of Zidon, nor of Ahlab, nor of Achzib, nor of Helbah, nor of Aphik, nor of Rehob:

32 But the Asherites [a]dwelt among the Canaanites, the inhabitants of the land: for they did not drive them out.

33 ¶ [a]Neither did Naphtali drive out the inhabitants of Beth-shemesh, nor the inhabitants of Beth-anath; but he [b]dwelt among the Canaanites, the inhabitants of the land: nevertheless the inhabitants of Beth-shemesh and of Beth-anath [c]became tributaries unto them.

34 And the Amorites forced the children of Dan into the mountain: for they would not suffer them to come down to the valley:

35 But the Amorites would dwell in mount Heres [a]in Aijalon, and in Shaalbim: yet the hand of the house of Joseph [1]prevailed, so that they became tributaries.

36 And the coast of the Amorites *was* [a]from [1]the going up to Akrabbim, from the rock, and upward.

29 [a]Josh. 16:10; 1 Ki. 9:16
30 [a]Josh. 19:15
31 [a]Josh. 19:24-30
32 [a]Ps. 106:34,35
33 [a]Josh. 19:38 [b]ver. 32 [c]ver. 30
35 [a]Josh. 19:42 [1]Heb. *was heavy*
36 [a]Num. 34:4; Josh. 15:3 [1]Or, *Maaleh-akrabbim*
2:1 [a]ver. 5 [b]Gen. 17:7 [1]Or, *messenger*
2 [a]Deut. 7:2 [b]Deut. 12:3 [c]Ps. 106:34
3 [a]Josh. 23:13 [b]ch. 3:6 [c]Ex. 23:33; Deut. 7:16; Ps. 106:36
5 [1]i.e. *Weepers*
6 [a]Josh. 22:6
7 [a]Josh. 24:31 [1]Heb. *prolonged days after Joshua*
8 [a]Josh. 24:29
9 [a]Josh. 24:30 [b]Josh. 19:50 & 24:30 *Timnath-serah*

Israel's disobedience

2 AND AN [1]angel of the LORD came up from Gilgal [a]to Bochim, and said, I made you to go up out of Egypt, and have brought you unto the land which I sware unto your fathers; and [b]I said, I will never break my covenant with you. I

2 And [a]ye shall make no league with the inhabitants of this land; [b]ye shall throw down their altars: [c]but ye have not obeyed my voice: why have ye done this?

3 Wherefore I also said, I will not drive them out from before you; but they shall be [a]*as thorns* in your sides, and [b]their gods shall be a [c]snare unto you. J

4 And it came to pass, when the angel of the LORD spake these words unto all the children of Israel, that the people lifted up their voice, and wept.

5 And they called the name of that place [1]Bochim: and they sacrificed there unto the LORD.

6 ¶ And when [a]Joshua had let the people go, the children of Israel went every man unto his inheritance to possess the land.

7 [a]And the people served the LORD all the days of Joshua, and all the days of the elders that [1]outlived Joshua, who had seen all the great works of the LORD, that he did for Israel.

8 And [a]Joshua the son of Nun, the servant of the LORD, died, *being* an hundred and ten years old.

9 [a]And they buried him in the border of his inheritance in [b]Timnath-heres, in the mount of Ephraim, on the north side of the hill Gaash.

10 And also all that generation were gathered unto their fathers: and there arose another generation after them, Q

I *Jdg 1:2* ◀ ▶ *Jdg 6:16*
J *Jos 23:13* ◀ ▶ *Jdg 2:21*
Q *Dt 32:50* ◀ ▶ *Lk 9:28–33*

2:1 The angel mentioned in this verse is actually the Lord himself. Whenever God appeared to individuals in the OT it was in this physical, angelic form. Such a visible manifestation of God to humanity is called a theophany. Scripture records other theophanies and other titles given to these visitors, including "the angel of God" (Ge 21:17), "the angel of his presence" (Isa 63:9) and the "messenger of the covenant" (Mal 3:1). Sometimes people recognized the angel's divinity (see Ge 16:13; 48:16) while at other times the angel clearly identified himself as God (see Ge 31:11–13; Ex 3:2–6). In each appearance the angel of the Lord carried out divine actions such as revelation, salvation and judgment, thus preparing God's people for the full expression of God in the form of Jesus Christ.

2:10 This verse refers to the Hebrew view of life after death and the resurrection of the Patriarchs to heaven (see note on Ge 35:29).

which [a]knew not the LORD, nor yet the works which he had done for Israel.

11 ¶ And the children of Israel did evil in the sight of the LORD, and served Baalim:

12 And they [a]forsook the LORD God of their fathers, which brought them out of the land of Egypt, and followed [b]other gods, of the gods of the people that *were* round about them, and [c]bowed themselves unto them, and provoked the LORD to anger.

13 And they forsook the LORD, [a]and served Baal and Ashtaroth.

14 ¶ [a]And the anger of the LORD was hot against Israel, and he [b]delivered them into the hands of spoilers that spoiled them, and [c]he sold them into the hands of their enemies round about, so that they [d]could not any longer stand before their enemies.

15 Whithersoever they went out, the hand of the LORD was against them for evil, as the LORD had said, and [a]as the LORD had sworn unto them: and they were greatly distressed.

The LORD raises up judges

16 ¶ Nevertheless [a]the LORD raised up judges, which [1]delivered them out of the hand of those that spoiled them.

17 And yet they would not hearken unto their judges, but they [a]went a-whoring after other gods, and bowed themselves unto them: they turned quickly out of the way which their fathers walked in, obeying the commandments of the LORD; *but* they did not so.

18 And when the LORD raised them up judges, then [a]the LORD was with the judge, and delivered them out of the hand of their enemies all the days of the judge: [b]for it repented the LORD because of their groanings by reason of them that oppressed them and vexed them.

19 And it came to pass, [a]when the judge was dead, *that* they returned, and [1]corrupted *themselves* more than their fathers, in following other gods to serve them, and to bow down unto them; [2]they ceased not from their own doings, nor from their stubborn way.

20 ¶ [a]And the anger of the LORD was hot against Israel; and he said, Because that this people hath [b]transgressed my covenant which I commanded their fathers, and have not hearkened unto my voice;

21 [a]I also will not henceforth drive out any from before them of the nations which Joshua left when he died: J

22 [a]That through them I may [b]prove Israel, whether they will keep the way of the LORD to walk therein, as their fathers did keep *it,* or not.

23 Therefore the LORD [1]left those nations, without driving them out hastily; neither delivered he them into the hand of Joshua.

3 NOW THESE *are* [a]the nations which the LORD left, to prove Israel by them, *even* as many *of Israel* as had not known all the wars of Canaan;

2 Only that the generations of the children of Israel might know, to teach them war, at the least such as before knew nothing thereof;

3 *Namely,* [a]five lords of the Philistines, and all the Canaanites, and the Sidonians, and the Hivites that dwelt in mount Lebanon, from mount Baal-hermon unto the entering in of Hamath.

4 [a]And they were to prove Israel by them, to know whether they would hearken unto the commandments of the LORD, which he commanded their fathers by the hand of Moses.

5 ¶ [a]And the children of Israel dwelt among the Canaanites, Hittites, and Amorites, and Perizzites, and Hivites, and Jebusites:

6 And [a]they took their daughters to be their wives, and gave their daughters to their sons, and served their gods.

Othniel

7 [a]And the children of Israel did evil in the sight of the LORD, and forgat the LORD their God, [b]and served Baalim and [c]the groves.

8 ¶ Therefore the anger of the LORD was hot against Israel, and he [a]sold them into the hand of [b]Chushan-rishathaim king of [1]Mesopotamia: and the children of Israel served Chushan-rishathaim eight years.

9 And when the children of Israel [a]cried unto the LORD, the LORD [b]raised up a [1]deliverer to the children of Israel, who delivered them, *even* [c]Othniel the son of Kenaz, Caleb's younger brother.

10 [a]Ex. 5:2; 1 Sam. 2:12; 1 Chr. 28:9; Gal. 4:8; Tit. 1:16
12 [a]Deut. 31:16 [b]Deut. 6:14 [c]Ex. 20:5
13 [a]ch. 10:6; Ps. 106:36
14 [a]ch. 3:8; Ps. 106:40-42 [b]2 Ki. 17:20 [c]ch. 3:8; Is. 50:1 [d]Lev. 26:37; Josh. 7:12,13
15 [a]Lev. 26; Deut. 28
16 [a]ch. 3:9,10,15 [1]Heb. *saved*
17 [a]Ex. 34:15; Lev. 17:7
18 [a]Josh. 1:5 [b]Gen. 6:6; Ps. 106:44
19 [a]ch. 3:12 [1]Or, *were corrupt* [2]Heb. *they let nothing fall of their*
20 [a]ver. 14 [b]Josh. 23:16
21 [a]Josh. 23:13
22 [a]ch. 3:1,4 [b]Deut. 8:2,16
23 [1]Or, *suffered*
3:1 [a]ch. 2:21,22
3 [a]Josh. 13:3
4 [a]ch. 2:22
5 [a]Ps. 106:35
6 [a]Ex. 34:16; Deut. 7:3
7 [a]ch. 2:11 [b]ch. 2:13 [c]Ex. 34:13; Deut. 16:21; ch. 6:25
8 [a]ch. 2:14 [b]Hab. 3:7 [1]Heb. *Aram-naharaim*
9 [a]ver. 15; ch. 4:3; & 6:7 & 10:10; Ps. 22:5 & 106:44 [b]ch. 2:16 [c]ch. 1:13 [1]Heb. *saviour*

J *Jdg 2:3* ◄► *Jdg 9:15*

E M 10 And [a]the spirit of the LORD [1]came upon him, and he judged Israel, and went out to war: and the LORD delivered Chushan-rishathaim king of [2]Mesopotamia into his hand; and his hand prevailed against Chushan-rishathaim.

11 And the land had rest forty years. And Othniel the son of Kenaz died.

Ehud

12 ¶ [a]And the children of Israel did evil again in the sight of the LORD: and the LORD strengthened [b]Eglon the king of Moab against Israel, because they had done evil in the sight of the LORD.

13 And he gathered unto him the children of Ammon and [a]Amalek, and went and smote Israel, and possessed [b]the city of palm trees.

14 So the children of Israel [a]served Eglon the king of Moab eighteen years.

15 But when the children of Israel [a]cried unto the LORD, the LORD raised them up a deliverer, Ehud the son of Gera, [1]a Benjamite, a man [b]lefthanded: and by him the children of Israel sent a present unto Eglon the king of Moab.

16 But Ehud made him a dagger which had two edges, of a cubit length; and he did gird it under his raiment upon his right thigh.

17 And he brought the present unto Eglon king of Moab: and Eglon *was* a very fat man.

18 And when he had made an end to offer the present, he sent away the people that bare the present.

19 But he himself turned again [a]from the [1]quarries that *were* by Gilgal, and said, I have a secret errand unto thee, O king: who said, Keep silence. And all that stood by him went out from him.

20 And Ehud came unto him; and he was sitting in [a]a summer parlour, which he had for himself alone. And Ehud said, I have a message from God unto thee. And he arose out of *his* seat.

21 And Ehud put forth his left hand, and took the dagger from his right thigh, and thrust it into his belly:

22 And the haft also went in after the blade; and the fat closed upon the blade, so that he could not draw the dagger out of his belly; and [1]the dirt came out.

23 Then Ehud went forth through the porch, and shut the doors of the parlour upon him, and locked them.

24 When he was gone out, his servants came; and when they saw that, behold, the doors of the parlour *were* locked, they said, Surely he [a]covereth[1] his feet in his summer chamber.

25 And they tarried till they were ashamed: and, behold, he opened not the doors of the parlour; therefore they took a key, and opened *them:* and, behold, their lord *was* fallen down dead on the earth.

26 And Ehud escaped while they tarried, and passed beyond the quarries, and escaped unto Seirath.

27 And it came to pass, when he was come, that [a]he blew a trumpet in the [b]mountain of Ephraim, and the children of Israel went down with him from the mount, and he before them.

28 And he said unto them, Follow after me: for [a]the LORD hath delivered your enemies the Moabites into your hand. And they went down after him, and took [b]the fords of Jordan toward Moab, and suffered not a man to pass over.

29 And they slew of Moab at that time about ten thousand men, all [1]lusty, and all men of valour; and there escaped not a man.

30 So Moab was subdued that day under the hand of Israel. And [a]the land had rest fourscore years.

31 ¶ And after him was [a]Shamgar the son of Anath, which slew of the Philistines six hundred men [b]with an ox goad: [c]and he also delivered [d]Israel.

Deborah

4 AND [a]THE children of Israel again did evil in the sight of the LORD, when Ehud was dead.

2 And the LORD [a]sold them into the hand of Jabin king of Canaan, that reigned in [b]Hazor; the captain of whose host *was* [c]Sisera, which dwelt in [d]Harosheth of the Gentiles.

3 And the children of Israel cried unto the LORD: for he had nine hundred [a]chariots of iron; and twenty years [b]he mightily oppressed the children of Israel.

4 ¶ And Deborah, a prophetess, the wife of Lapidoth, she judged Israel at that time.

5 [a]And she dwelt under the palm tree of Deborah between Ramah and Beth-el

10 [a]Num. 27:18; ch. 6:34 & 11:29 & 13:25 & 14:6,19; 1 Sam. 11:6; 2 Chr. 15:1 [1]Heb. *was* [2]Heb. *Aram*
12 [a]ch. 2:19 [b]1 Sam. 12:9
13 [a]ch. 5:14 [b]ch. 1:16
14 [a]Deut. 28:48
15 [a]ver. 9; Ps. 78:34 [b]ch. 20:16 [1]Or, *the son of Jemini*
19 [a]Josh. 4:20 [1]Or, *graven images*
20 [a]Amos 3:15
22 [1]Or, *it came out at the fundament*
24 [a]1 Sam. 24:3 [1]Or, *doeth his easement*
27 [a]ch. 5:14 & 6:34; 1 Sam. 13:3 [b]Josh. 17:15
28 [a]ch. 7:9,15; 1 Sam. 17:47 [b]Josh. 2:7; ch. 12:5
29 [1]Heb. *fat*
30 [a]ver. 11
31 [a]ch. 5:6,8; 1 Sam. 13:19,22; It seems to concern only the country next to the Philistines [b]1 Sam. 17:47,50 [c]ch. 2:16 [d]So part is called Israel, ch. 4:1,3 & 10:7,17 & 11:4; 1 Sam. 4:1
4:1 [a]ch. 2:19
2 [a]ch. 2:14 [b]Josh. 11:1,10 & 19:36 [c]1 Sam. 12:9; Ps. 83:9; It seems to concern only North Israel [d]ver. 13,16
3 [a]ch. 1:19 [b]ch. 5:8; Ps. 106:42
5 [a]Gen. 35:8

E *Dt 34:9* ◄► *Jdg 6:34*
M *Ge 41:38* ◄► *Jdg 6:34*

in mount Ephraim: and the children of Israel came up to her for judgment.

6 And she sent and called [a]Barak the son of Abinoam out [b]of Kedesh-naphtali, and said unto him, Hath not the LORD God of Israel commanded, *saying,* Go and draw toward mount Tabor, and take with thee ten thousand men of the children of Naphtali and of the children of Zebulun?

7 And [a]I will draw unto thee to the [b]river Kishon Sisera, the captain of Jabin's army, with his chariots and his multitude; and I will deliver him into thine hand.

8 And Barak said unto her, If thou wilt go with me, then I will go: but if thou wilt not go with me, *then* I will not go.

9 And she said, I will surely go with thee: notwithstanding the journey that thou takest shall not be for thine honour; for the LORD shall [a]sell Sisera into the hand of a woman. And Deborah arose, and went with Barak to Kedesh.

10 ¶ And Barak called [a]Zebulun and Naphtali to Kedesh; and he went up with ten thousand men [b]at his feet: and Deborah went up with him.

11 Now Heber [a]the Kenite, *which was* of the children of [b]Hobab the father-in-law of Moses, had severed himself from the Kenites, and pitched his tent unto the plain of Zaanaim, [c]which *is* by Kedesh.

12 And they showed Sisera that Barak the son of Abinoam was gone up to mount Tabor.

13 And Sisera [l]gathered together all his chariots, *even* nine hundred chariots of iron, and all the people that *were* with him, from Harosheth of the Gentiles unto the river of Kishon.

14 And Deborah said unto Barak, Up; for this *is* the day in which the LORD hath delivered Sisera into thine hand: [a]is not the LORD gone out before thee? So Barak went down from mount Tabor, and ten thousand men after him.

15 And [a]the LORD discomfited Sisera, and all *his* chariots, and all *his* host, with the edge of the sword before Barak; so that Sisera lighted down off *his* chariot, and fled away on his feet.

16 But Barak pursued after the chariots, and after the host, unto Harosheth of the Gentiles: and all the host of Sisera fell upon the edge of the sword; *and* there was not [l]a man left.

17 Howbeit Sisera fled away on his feet to the tent of Jael the wife of Heber the Kenite: for *there was* peace between Jabin the king of Hazor and the house of Heber the Kenite.

18 ¶ And Jael went out to meet Sisera, and said unto him, Turn in, my lord, turn in to me; fear not. And when he had turned in unto her into the tent, she covered him with a [l]mantle.

19 And he said unto her, Give me, I pray thee, a little water to drink; for I am thirsty. And she opened [a]a bottle of milk, and gave him drink, and covered him.

20 Again he said unto her, Stand in the door of the tent, and it shall be, when any man doth come and inquire of thee, and say, Is there any man here? that thou shalt say, No.

21 Then Jael Heber's wife [a]took a nail of the tent, and [l]took an hammer in her hand, and went softly unto him, and smote the nail into his temples, and fastened it into the ground: for he was fast asleep and weary. So he died.

22 And, behold, as Barak pursued Sisera, Jael came out to meet him, and said unto him, Come, and I will show thee the man whom thou seekest. And when he came into her *tent,* behold, Sisera lay dead, and the nail *was* in his temples.

23 So God subdued on that day Jabin the king of Canaan before the children of Israel.

24 And the hand of the children of Israel [l]prospered, and prevailed against Jabin the king of Canaan, until they had destroyed Jabin king of Canaan.

The song of Deborah

5 THEN [a]SANG Deborah and Barak the son of Abinoam on that day, saying,

2 Praise ye the LORD for the [a]avenging of Israel, [b]when the people willingly offered themselves.

3 [a]Hear, O ye kings; give ear, O ye princes; I, *even* I, will sing unto the LORD; I will sing *praise* to the LORD God of Israel.

4 LORD, [a]when thou wentest out of Seir, when thou marchedst out of the field of Edom, [b]the earth trembled, and the heavens dropped, the clouds also dropped water.

5 [a]The mountains [l]melted from before the LORD, *even* [b]that Sinai from before the LORD God of Israel.

6 [a]Heb. 11:32 [b]Josh. 19:37
7 [a]Ex. 14:4 [b]ch. 5:21; 1 Ki. 18:40; Ps. 83:9,10
9 [a]ch. 2:14
10 [a]ch. 5:18 [b]See Ex. 11:8; 1 Ki. 20:10
11 [a]ch. 1:16 [b]Num. 10:29 [c]ver. 6
13 [l]Heb. *gathered by cry,* or, *proclamation*
14 [a]Deut. 9:3; 2 Sam. 5:24; Ps. 68:7; Is. 52:12
15 [a]Ps. 83:9,10; See Josh. 10:10
16 [l]Heb. *unto one*
18 [l]Or, *rug,* or, *blanket*
19 [a]ch. 5:25
21 [a]ch. 5:26 [l]Heb. *put*
24 [l]Heb. *going went and was hard*
5:1 [a]See Ex. 15:1
2 [a]Ps. 18:47 [b]2 Chr. 17:16
3 [a]Deut. 32:1,3
4 [a]Deut. 33:2 [b]Ps. 68:8
5 [a]Ps. 97:5 [b]Ex. 19:18 [l]Heb. *flowed*

6 In the days of Shamgar the son of Anath, in the days of Jael, [a]the highways were unoccupied, and the [1]travellers walked through [2]byways.

7 *The inhabitants of* the villages ceased, they ceased in Israel, until that I Deborah arose, that I arose [a]a mother in Israel.

8 They [a]chose new gods; then *was* war in the gates: [b]was there a shield or spear seen among forty thousand in Israel?

9 My heart *is* toward the governors of Israel, that offered themselves willingly among the people. Bless ye the LORD.

10 [a]Speak,[1] ye [b]that ride on white asses, [c]ye that sit in judgment, and walk by the way.

11 *They that are delivered* from the noise of archers in the places of drawing water, there shall they rehearse the [a]righteous[1] acts of the LORD, *even* the righteous acts *toward the inhabitants* of his villages in Israel: then shall the people of the LORD go down to the gates.

12 [a]Awake, awake, Deborah: awake, awake, utter a song: arise, Barak, and [b]lead thy captivity captive, thou son of Abinoam.

13 Then he made him that remaineth [a]have dominion over the nobles among the people: the LORD made me have dominion over the mighty.

14 Out of Ephraim *was there* a root of them against Amalek; after thee, Benjamin, among thy people; out of Machir came down governors, and out of Zebulun they that [1]handle the pen of the writer.

15 And the princes of Issachar *were* with Deborah; even Issachar, and also Barak: he was sent on [1]foot into the valley. [2]For the divisions of Reuben *there were* great [3]thoughts of heart.

16 Why abodest thou among the sheepfolds, to hear the bleatings of the flocks? [1]For the divisions of Reuben *there were* great searchings of heart.

17 [a]Gilead abode beyond Jordan: and why did Dan remain in ships? [b]Asher continued on the sea [1]shore, and abode in his [2]breaches.

18 [a]Zebulun and Naphtali *were* a people *that* [1]jeoparded their lives unto the death in the high places of the field.

19 The kings came *and* fought, then fought the kings of Canaan in Taanach by the waters of Megiddo; [a]they took no gain of money.

20 [a]They fought from heaven; [b]the stars in their [1]courses fought against Sisera.

21 [a]The river of Kishon swept them away, that ancient river, the river Kishon. O my soul, thou hast trodden down strength.

22 Then were the horsehoofs broken by the means of the [1]pransings, the pransings of their mighty ones.

23 Curse ye Meroz, said the angel of the LORD, curse ye bitterly the inhabitants thereof; [a]because they came not to the help [b]of the LORD, to the help of the LORD against the mighty. H

24 Blessed above women shall [a]Jael the wife of Heber the Kenite be, [b]blessed shall she be above women in the tent.

25 [a]He asked water, *and* she gave *him* milk; she brought forth butter in a lordly dish.

26 She put her hand to the nail, and her right hand to the workmen's hammer; and [1]with the hammer she smote Sisera, she smote off his head, when she had pierced and stricken through his temples.

27 [1]At her feet he bowed, he fell, he lay down: at her feet he bowed, he fell: where he bowed, there he fell down [2]dead.

28 The mother of Sisera looked out at a window, and cried through the lattice, Why is his chariot *so* long in coming? why tarry the wheels of his chariot?

29 Her wise ladies answered her, yea, she returned [1]answer to herself,

30 [a]Have they not sped? have they *not* divided the prey; [1]to every man a damsel *or* two; to Sisera a prey of divers colours, a prey of divers colours of needlework, of divers colours of needlework on both sides, *meet* for the necks of *them that take* the spoil?

31 [a]So let all thine enemies perish, O LORD: but *let* them that love him *be* [b]as the sun [c]when he goeth forth in his might. And the land had rest forty years. K

H *Jos 24:19* ◄ ► *1Sa 2:9*
K *Jos 1:5* ◄ ► *Ru 2:12*

---

6 [a]Is. 33:8 [1]Heb. *walkers of paths* [2]Heb. *crooked ways*
7 [a]Is. 49:23
8 [a]Deut. 32:16 [b]1 Sam. 13:19,22
10 [a]Ps. 145:5 [b]ch. 10:4 [c]Ps. 107:32 [1]Or, *Meditate*
11 [a]Ps. 145:7 [1]Heb. *righteousnesses of the LORD*
12 [a]Ps. 57:8 [b]Ps. 68:18
13 [a]Ps. 49:14
14 [1]Heb. *draw with the pen*
15 [1]Heb. *his feet* [2]Or, *In the divisions* [3]Heb. *impressions*
16 [1]Or, *In*
17 [a]See Josh. 13:25,31 [b]Josh. 19:29 [1]Or, *port* [2]Or, *creeks*
18 [a]ch. 4:10 [1]Heb. *exposed to reproach*
19 [a]Ps. 44:12
20 [a]Ps. 77:17,18 [b]ch. 4:15 [1]Heb. *paths*
21 [a]ch. 4:7
22 [1]Or, *tramplings*, or, *plungings*
23 [a]Neh. 3:5 [b]1 Sam. 18:17
24 [a]ch. 4:17 [b]Luke 1:28
25 [a]ch. 4:19
26 [1]Heb. *she hammered*
27 [1]Heb. *Between* [2]Heb. *destroyed*
29 [1]Heb. *her words*
30 [a]Ex. 15:9 [1]Heb. *to the head of a man*
31 [a]Ps. 83:9,10 [b]2 Sam. 23:4 [c]Ps. 19:4,5

Gideon

6 AND [a]THE children of Israel did evil in the sight of the LORD: and the LORD delivered them into the hand [b]of Midian seven years.

2 And the hand of Midian [l]prevailed against Israel: *and* because of the Midianites the children of Israel made them [a]the dens which *are* in the mountains, and caves, and strong holds.

3 And *so* it was, when Israel had sown, that the Midianites came up, and [a]the Amalekites, [b]and the children of the east, even they came up against them;

4 And they encamped against them, and [a]destroyed the increase of the earth, till thou come unto Gaza, and left no sustenance for Israel, neither [l]sheep, nor ox, nor ass.

5 For they came up with their cattle and their tents, and they came [a]as grasshoppers for multitude; *for* both they and their camels were without number: and they entered into the land to destroy it.

6 And Israel was greatly impoverished because of the Midianites; and the children of Israel [a]cried unto the LORD.

7 ¶ And it came to pass, when the children of Israel cried unto the LORD because of the Midianites,

8 That the LORD sent [l]a prophet unto the children of Israel, which said unto them, Thus saith the LORD God of Israel, I brought you up from Egypt, and brought you forth out of the house of bondage;

9 And I delivered you out of the hand of the Egyptians, and out of the hand of all that oppressed you, and [a]drave them out from before you, and gave you their land;

10 And I said unto you, I *am* the LORD your God; [a]fear not the gods of the Amorites, in whose land ye dwell: but ye have not obeyed my voice.

11 ¶ And there came an angel of the LORD, and sat under an oak which *was* in Ophrah, that *pertained* unto Joash [a]the Abi-ezrite: and his son [b]Gideon threshed wheat by the winepress, [l]to hide *it* from the Midianites.

12 And the [a]angel of the LORD appeared unto him, and said unto him, The LORD *is* [b]with thee, thou mighty man of valour.

13 And Gideon said unto him, Oh my Lord, if the LORD be with us, why then is all this befallen us? and [a]where *be* all his miracles [b]which our fathers told us of, saying, Did not the LORD bring us up from Egypt? but now the LORD hath [c]forsaken us, and delivered us into the hands of the Midianites.

14 And the LORD looked upon him, and said, [a]Go in this thy might, and thou shalt save Israel from the hand of the Midianites: [b]have not I sent thee?

15 And he said unto him, Oh my Lord, wherewith shall I save Israel? behold, [a]my family *is* poor in Manasseh, and I *am* the least in my father's house.

16 And the LORD said unto him, [a]Surely I will be with thee, and thou shalt smite the Midianites as one man.

17 And he said unto him, If now I have found grace in thy sight, then [a]show me a sign that thou talkest with me.

18 [a]Depart not hence, I pray thee, until I come unto thee, and bring forth my [l]present, and set *it* before thee. And he said, I will tarry until thou come again.

19 ¶ [a]And Gideon went in, and made ready [l]a kid, and unleavened cakes of an ephah of flour: the flesh he put in a basket, and he put the broth in a pot, and brought *it* out unto him under the oak, and presented *it*.

20 And the angel of God said unto him, Take the flesh and the unleavened cakes, and [a]lay *them* upon this rock, and [b]pour out the broth. And he did so.

21 ¶ Then the angel of the LORD put forth the end of the staff that *was* in his hand, and touched the flesh and the unleavened cakes; and [a]there rose up fire out of the rock, and consumed the flesh and the unleavened cakes. Then the angel of the LORD departed out of his sight.

22 And when Gideon [a]perceived that he *was* an angel of the LORD, Gideon said, Alas, O Lord GOD! [b]for because I have seen an angel of the LORD face to face.

23 And the LORD said unto him, [a]Peace *be* unto thee; fear not: thou shalt not die.

24 Then Gideon built an altar there unto the LORD, and called it [l]Jehovah-shalom: unto this day it *is* yet [a]in Ophrah of the Abi-ezrites.

25 ¶ And it came to pass the same night, that the LORD said unto him, Take thy father's young bullock, [l]even the second bullock of seven years old, and throw

6:1 [a]ch. 2:19 [b]Hab. 3:7
2 [a]1 Sam. 13:6; Heb. 11:38 [l]Heb. *was strong*
3 [a]ch. 3:13 [b]Gen. 29:1; ch. 7:12; 1 Ki. 4:30; Job 1:3
4 [a]Lev. 26:16; Deut. 28:30; Mic. 6:15 [l]Or, *goat*
5 [a]ch. 7:12
6 [a]Hos. 5:15
8 [l]Heb. *a man a prophet*
9 [a]Ps. 44:2,3
10 [a]2 Ki. 17:35,37, 38; Jer. 10:2
11 [a]Josh. 17:2 [b]Heb. 11:32 called *Gideon* [l]Heb. *to cause* it *to flee*
12 [a]ch. 13:3; Luke 1:11,28 [b]Josh. 1:5
13 [a]Is. 59:1 [b]Ps. 44:1 [c]2 Chr. 15:2
14 [a]1 Sam. 12:11 [b]Josh. 1:9
15 [a]See 1 Sam. 9:21
16 [a]Ex. 3:12
17 [a]ver. 36,37; 2 Ki. 20:8; Ps. 86:17; Is. 7:11
18 [a]Gen. 18:3,5 [l]Or, *meat offering*
19 [a]Gen. 18:6-8 [l]Heb. *a kid of the goats*
20 [a]ch. 13:19 [b]See 1 Ki. 18:33,34
21 [a]Lev. 9:24
22 [a]ch. 13:21 [b]Gen. 16:13; Ex. 33:20; ch. 13:22
23 [a]Dan. 10:19
24 [a]ch. 8:32 [l]i.e. *The LORD send peace*
25 [l]Or, *and*

I *Jdg 2:1* ◄► *Jdg 7:13–14*

down the altar of Baal that thy father hath, and [a]cut down the grove that *is* by it:

26 And build an altar unto the LORD thy God upon the top of this [1]rock, [2]in the ordered place, and take the second bullock, and offer a burnt sacrifice with the wood of the grove which thou shalt cut down.

27 Then Gideon took ten men of his servants, and did as the LORD had said unto him: and *so* it was, because he feared his father's household, and the men of the city, that he could not do *it* by day, that he did *it* by night.

28 ¶ And when the men of the city arose early in the morning, behold, the altar of Baal was cast down, and the grove was cut down that *was* by it, and the second bullock was offered upon the altar *that was* built.

29 And they said one to another, Who hath done this thing? And when they inquired and asked, they said, Gideon the son of Joash hath done this thing.

30 Then the men of the city said unto Joash, Bring out thy son, that he may die: because he hath cast down the altar of Baal, and because he hath cut down the grove that *was* by it.

31 And Joash said unto all that stood against him, Will ye plead for Baal? will ye save him? he that will plead for him, let him be put to death whilst *it is yet* morning: if he *be* a god, let him plead for himself, because *one* hath cast down his altar.

32 Therefore on that day he called him [a]Jerubbaal,[1] saying, Let Baal plead against him, because he hath thrown down his altar.

33 ¶ Then all [a]the Midianites and the Amalekites and the children of the east were gathered together, and went over, and pitched in [b]the valley of Jezreel.

E 34 But [a]the spirit of the LORD [1]came
M upon Gideon, and he [b]blew a trumpet; and Abiezer [2]was gathered after him.

35 And he sent messengers throughout all Manasseh; who also was gathered after him: and he sent messengers unto Asher, and unto Zebulun, and unto Naphtali; and they came up to meet them.

36 ¶ And Gideon said unto God, If thou wilt save Israel by mine hand, as thou hast said,

37 [a]Behold, I will put a fleece of wool in the floor; *and* if the dew be on the fleece only, and *it be* dry upon all the earth *beside,* then shall I know that thou wilt save Israel by mine hand, as thou hast said.

38 And it was so: for he rose up early on the morrow, and thrust the fleece together, and wringed the dew out of the fleece, a bowl full of water.

39 And Gideon said unto God, [a]Let not thine anger be hot against me, and I will speak but this once: let me prove, I pray thee, but this once with the fleece; let it now be dry only upon the fleece, and upon all the ground let there be dew.

40 And God did so that night: for it was dry upon the fleece only, and there was dew on all the ground.

The defeat of the Midianites

7 THEN [a]JERUBBAAL, who *is* Gideon, and all the people that *were* with him, rose up early, and pitched beside the well of Harod: so that the host of the Midianites were on the north side of them, by the hill of Moreh, in the valley.

2 And the LORD said unto Gideon, The people that *are* with thee *are* too many for me to give the Midianites into their hands, lest Israel [a]vaunt themselves against me, saying, Mine own hand hath saved me.

3 Now therefore go to, proclaim in the ears of the people, saying, [a]Whosoever *is* fearful and afraid, let him return and depart early from mount Gilead. And there returned of the people twenty and two thousand; and there remained ten thousand.

4 And the LORD said unto Gideon, The people *are* yet *too* many; bring them down unto the water, and I will try them for thee there: and it shall be, *that* of whom I say unto thee, This shall go with thee, the same shall go with thee; and of whomsoever I say unto thee, This shall not go with thee, the same shall not go.

5 So he brought down the people unto the water: and the LORD said unto Gideon, Every one that lappeth of the water with his tongue, as a dog lappeth, him shalt thou set by himself; likewise every one that boweth down upon his knees to drink.

25 [a]Ex. 34:13; Deut. 7:5
26 [1]Heb. *strong place* [2]Or, *in an orderly manner*
32 [a]1 Sam. 12:11; 2 Sam. 11:21 *Jerubbesheth;* i.e. *Let the shameful thing plead:* See Jer. 11:13; Hos. 9:10 [1]i.e. *Let Baal plead*
33 [a]ver. 3 [b]Josh. 17:16
34 [a]ch. 3:10; 1 Chr. 12:18; 2 Chr. 24:20 [b]Num. 10:3; ch. 3:27 [1]Heb. *clothed* [2]Heb. *was called after him*
37 [a]See Ex. 4:3-7
39 [a]Gen. 18:32
7:1 [a]ch. 6:32
2 [a]Deut. 8:17; 1 Cor. 1:29
3 [a]Deut. 20:8

E *Jdg 3:10* ◄► *Jdg 11:29*
M *Jdg 3:10* ◄► *Jdg 11:29*

6 And the number of them that lapped, *putting* their hand to their mouth, were three hundred men: but all the rest of the people bowed down upon their knees to drink water.

7 And the LORD said unto Gideon, [a]By the three hundred men that lapped will I save you, and deliver the Midianites into thine hand: and let all the *other* people go every man unto his place.

8 So the people took victuals in their hand, and their trumpets: and he sent all *the rest of* Israel every man unto his tent, and retained those three hundred men: and the host of Midian was beneath him in the valley.

9 ¶ And it came to pass the same [a]night, that the LORD said unto him, Arise, get thee down unto the host; for I have delivered it into thine hand.

10 But if thou fear to go down, go thou with Phurah thy servant down to the host:

11 And thou shalt [a]hear what they say; and afterward shall thine hands be strengthened to go down unto the host. Then went he down with Phurah his servant unto the outside of the [1]armed men that *were* in the host.

12 And the Midianites and the Amalekites and [a]all the children of the east lay along in the valley like grasshoppers for multitude; and their camels *were* without number, as the sand by the sea side for multitude.

13 And when Gideon was come, behold, *there was* a man that told a dream unto his fellow, and said, Behold, I dreamed a dream, and, lo, a cake of barley bread tumbled into the host of Midian, and came unto a tent, and smote it that it fell, and overturned it, that the tent lay along.

14 And his fellow answered and said, This *is* nothing else save the sword of Gideon the son of Joash, a man of Israel: *for* into his hand hath God delivered Midian, and all the host.

15 ¶ And it was *so,* when Gideon heard the telling of the dream, and [1]the interpretation thereof, that he worshipped, and returned into the host of Israel, and said, Arise; for the LORD hath delivered into your hand the host of Midian.

7 [a]1 Sam. 14:6
9 [a]Gen. 46:2,3
11 [a]ver. 13-15; See Gen. 24:14; 1 Sam. 14:9,10 [1]Or, *ranks by five*
12 [a]ch. 6:5,33 & 8:10
15 [1]Heb. *the breaking thereof*
16 [1]Heb. *trumpets in the hand of all of them* [2]Or, *firebrands,* or, *torches*
21 [a]Ex. 14:13,14; 2 Chr. 20:17 [b]2 Ki. 7:7
22 [a]Josh. 6:4,16, 20; See 2 Cor. 4:7 [b]Ps. 83:9; Is. 9:4 [c]1 Sam. 14:20; 2 Chr. 20:23 [1]Or, *toward* [2]Heb. *lip*
24 [a]ch. 3:27 [b]ch. 3:28 [c]John 1:28
25 [a]ch. 8:3; Ps. 83:11 [b]Is. 10:26

16 And he divided the three hundred men *into* three companies, and he put [1]a trumpet in every man's hand, with empty pitchers, and [2]lamps within the pitchers.

17 And he said unto them, Look on me, and do likewise: and, behold, when I come to the outside of the camp, it shall be *that,* as I do, so shall ye do.

18 When I blow with a trumpet, I and all that *are* with me, then blow ye the trumpets also on every side of all the camp, and say, *The sword* of the LORD, and of Gideon.

19 ¶ So Gideon, and the hundred men that *were* with him, came unto the outside of the camp in the beginning of the middle watch; and they had but newly set the watch: and they blew the trumpets, and brake the pitchers that *were* in their hands.

20 And the three companies blew the trumpets, and brake the pitchers, and held the lamps in their left hands, and the trumpets in their right hands to blow *withal:* and they cried, The sword of the LORD, and of Gideon.

21 And they [a]stood every man in his place round about the camp: [b]and all the host ran, and cried, and fled.

22 And the three hundred [a]blew the trumpets, and [b]the LORD set [c]every man's sword against his fellow, even throughout all the host: and the host fled to Beth-shittah [1]in Zererath, *and* to the [2]border of Abel-meholah, unto Tabbath.

23 And the men of Israel gathered themselves together out of Naphtali, and out of Asher, and out of all Manasseh, and pursued after the Midianites.

24 ¶ And Gideon sent messengers throughout all [a]mount Ephraim, saying, Come down against the Midianites, and take before them the waters unto Beth-barah and Jordan. Then all the men of Ephraim gathered themselves together, and [b]took the waters unto [c]Beth-barah and Jordan.

25 And they took [a]two princes of the Midianites, Oreb and Zeeb; and they slew Oreb upon [b]the rock Oreb, and Zeeb they slew at the winepress of Zeeb, and pursued Midian, and brought the

Jdg 6:16 ◄► Jdg 13:3

heads of Oreb and Zeeb to Gideon on the [c]other side Jordan.

8 AND [a]THE men of Ephraim said unto him, [1]Why hast thou served us thus, that thou calledst us not, when thou wentest to fight with the Midianites? And they did chide with him [2]sharply.

2 And he said unto them, What have I done now in comparison of you? *Is* not the gleaning of the grapes of Ephraim better than the vintage of Abiezer?

3 [a]God hath delivered into your hands the princes of Midian, Oreb and Zeeb: and what was I able to do in comparison of you? Then their [b]anger[1] was abated toward him, when he had said that.

4 ¶ And Gideon came to Jordan, *and* passed over, he, and the three hundred men that *were* with him, faint, yet pursuing *them.*

5 And he said unto the men of [a]Succoth, Give, I pray you, loaves of bread unto the people that follow me; for they *be* faint, and I am pursuing after Zebah and Zalmunna, kings of Midian.

6 ¶ And the princes of Succoth said, [a]*Are* the hands of Zebah and Zalmunna now in thine hand, that [b]we should give bread unto thine army?

7 And Gideon said, Therefore when the LORD hath delivered Zebah and Zalmunna into mine hand, [a]then I will [1]tear your flesh with the thorns of the wilderness and with briers.

8 ¶ And he went up thence [a]to Penuel, and spake unto them likewise: and the men of Penuel answered him as the men of Succoth had answered *him.*

9 And he spake also unto the men of Penuel, saying, When I [a]come again in peace, [b]I will break down this tower.

10 ¶ Now Zebah and Zalmunna *were* in Karkor, and their hosts with them, about fifteen thousand *men,* all that were left of [a]all the hosts of the children of the east: for there fell [b]an hundred and twenty thousand men that drew sword.

11 ¶ And Gideon went up by the way of them that dwelt in tents on the east of [a]Nobah and Jogbehah, and smote the host: for the host was [b]secure.

12 And when Zebah and Zalmunna fled, he pursued after them, and [a]took the two kings of Midian, Zebah and Zalmunna, and [1]discomfited all the host.

13 ¶ And Gideon the son of Joash returned from battle before the sun *was up,*

14 And caught a young man of the men of Succoth, and inquired of him: and he [1]described unto him the princes of Succoth, and the elders thereof, *even* threescore and seventeen men.

15 And he came unto the men of Succoth, and said, Behold Zebah and Zalmunna, with whom ye did [a]upbraid me, saying, *Are* the hands of Zebah and Zalmunna now in thine hand, that we should give bread unto thy men *that are* weary?

16 [a]And he took the elders of the city, and thorns of the wilderness and briers, and with them he [1]taught the men of Succoth.

17 [a]And he beat down the tower of [b]Penuel, and slew the men of the city.

18 ¶ Then said he unto Zebah and Zalmunna, What manner of men *were they* whom ye slew at [a]Tabor? And they answered, As thou *art,* so *were* they; each one [1]resembled the children of a king.

19 And he said, they *were* my brethren, *even* the sons of my mother: *as* the LORD liveth, if ye had saved them alive, I would not slay you.

20 And he said unto Jether his firstborn, Up, *and* slay them. But the youth drew not his sword: for he feared, because he *was* yet a youth.

21 Then Zebah and Zalmunna said, Rise thou, and fall upon us: for as the man *is, so is* his strength. And Gideon arose, and [a]slew Zebah and Zalmunna, and took away the [1]ornaments that *were* on their camels' necks.

Gideon refuses the kingship

22 ¶ Then the men of Israel said unto Gideon, Rule thou over us, both thou, and thy son, and thy son's son also: for thou hast delivered us from the hand of Midian.

23 And Gideon said unto them, I will not rule over you, neither shall my son rule over you: [a]the LORD shall rule over you.

24 ¶ And Gideon said unto them, I would desire a request of you, that ye would give me every man the earrings of his prey. (For they had golden earrings, [a]because they *were* Ishmaelites.)

25 And they answered, We will willingly give *them.* And they spread a garment, and did cast therein every man the earrings of his prey.

25 [c]ch. 8:4
8:1 [a]See ch. 12:1; 2 Sam. 19:41 [1]Heb. *What thing is this thou hast done unto us* [2]Heb. *strongly*
3 [a]ch. 7:24,25; Phil. 2:3 [b]Prov. 15:1 [1]Heb. *spirit*
5 [a]Gen. 33:17; Ps. 60:6
6 [a]See 1 Ki. 20:11 [b]See 1 Sam. 25:11
7 [a]ver. 16 [1]Heb. *thresh*
8 [a]Gen. 32:30; 1 Ki. 12:25
9 [a]1 Ki. 22:27 [b]ver. 17
10 [a]ch. 7:12 [b]ch. 20:2,15,17,25; 2 Ki. 3:26
11 [a]Num. 32:35, 42 [b]ch. 18:27; 1 Thes. 5:3
12 [a]Ps. 83:11 [1]Heb. *terrified*
14 [1]Heb. *writ*
15 [a]ver. 6
16 [a]ver. 7 [1]Heb. *made to know*
17 [a]ver. 9 [b]1 Ki. 12:25
18 [a]ch. 4:6; Ps. 89:12 [1]Heb. *according to the form*
21 [a]Ps. 83:11 [1]Or, *ornaments like the moon*
23 [a]1 Sam. 8:7 & 10:19 & 12:12
24 [a]Gen. 25:13 & 37:25,28

26 And the weight of the golden earrings that he requested was a thousand and seven hundred *shekels* of gold; beside ornaments, and [l]collars, and purple raiment that *was* on the kings of Midian, and beside the chains that *were* about their camels' necks.

27 And Gideon [a]made an ephod thereof, and put it in his city, *even* [b]in Ophrah: and all Israel [c]went thither a-whoring after it: which thing became [d]a snare unto Gideon, and to his house.

28 ¶ Thus was Midian subdued before the children of Israel, so that they lifted up their heads no more. [a]And the country was in quietness forty years in the days of Gideon.

Gideon's death

29 ¶ And Jerubbaal the son of Joash went and dwelt in his own house.

30 And Gideon had [a]threescore and ten sons [l]of his body begotten: for he had many wives.

31 [a]And his concubine that *was* in Shechem, she also bare him a son, whose name he [l]called Abimelech.

32 ¶ And Gideon the son of Joash died [a]in a good old age, and was buried in the sepulchre of Joash his father, [b]in Ophrah of the Abi-ezrites.

33 And it came to pass, [a]as soon as Gideon was dead, that the children of Israel turned again, and [b]went a-whoring after Baalim, [c]and made Baal-berith their god.

34 And the children of Israel [a]remembered not the LORD their God, who had delivered them out of the hands of all their enemies on every side:

35 [a]Neither showed they kindness to the house of Jerubbaal, *namely,* Gideon, according to all the goodness which he had shown unto Israel.

Abimelech

9 AND ABIMELECH the son of Jerubbaal went to Shechem unto [a]his mother's brethren, and communed with them, and with all the family of the house of his mother's father, saying,

2 Speak, I pray you, in the ears of all the men of Shechem, [l]Whether *is* better for you, either that all the sons of Jerubbaal, *which are* [a]threescore and ten persons, reign over you, or that one reign over you? remember also that I *am* [b]your bone and your flesh.

3 And his mother's brethren spake of him in the ears of all the men of Shechem all these words: and their hearts inclined [l]to follow Abimelech; for they said, He *is* our [a]brother.

4 And they gave him threescore and ten *pieces* of silver out of the house of [a]Baal-berith, wherewith Abimelech hired [b]vain and light persons, which followed him.

5 And he went unto his father's house [a]at Ophrah, and [b]slew his brethren the sons of Jerubbaal, *being* threescore and ten persons, upon one stone: notwithstanding yet Jotham the youngest son of Jerubbaal was left; for he hid himself.

6 And all the men of Shechem gathered together, and all the house of Millo, and went, and made Abimelech king, [l]by the plain of the pillar that *was* in Shechem.

7 ¶ And when they told *it* to Jotham, he went and stood in the top of [a]mount Gerizim, and lifted up his voice, and cried, and said unto them, Hearken unto me, ye men of Shechem, that God may hearken unto you.

8 [a]The trees went forth *on a time* to anoint a king over them; and they said unto the olive tree, [b]Reign thou over us.

9 But the olive tree said unto them, Should I leave my fatness, [a]wherewith by me they honour God and man, and [l]go to be promoted over the trees?

10 And the trees said to the fig tree, Come thou, *and* reign over us.

11 But the fig tree said unto them, Should I forsake my sweetness, and my good fruit, and go to be promoted over the trees?

12 Then said the trees unto the vine, Come thou, *and* reign over us.

13 And the vine said unto them, Should I leave my wine, [a]which cheereth God and man, and go to be promoted over the trees?

14 Then said all the trees unto the [l]bramble, Come thou, *and* reign over us.

15 And the bramble said unto the trees, If in truth ye anoint me king over you, *then* come *and* put your trust in my [a]shadow: and if not, [b]let fire come out of J

26 [l]Or, *sweet jewels*
27 [a]ch. 17:5 [b]ch. 6:24 [c]Ps. 106:39 [d]Deut. 7:16
28 [a]ch. 5:31
30 [a]ch. 9:2,5 [l]Heb. *going out of his thigh*
31 [a]ch. 9:1 [l]Heb. *set*
32 [a]Gen. 25:8; Job 5:26 [b]ver. 27; ch. 6:24
33 [a]ch. 2:19 [b]ch. 2:17 [c]ch. 9:4,46
34 [a]Ps. 78:11,42; & 106:13,21
35 [a]ch. 9:16-18; Eccl. 9:14
9:1 [a]ch. 8:31
2 [a]ch. 8:30 [b]Gen. 29:14 [l]Heb. *What is good? whether*
3 [a]Gen. 29:15 [l]Heb. *after*
4 [a]ch. 8:33 [b]ch. 11:3; 2 Chr. 13:7; Acts 17:5
5 [a]ch. 6:24 [b]2 Ki. 11:1,2
6 [l]Or, *by the oak of the pillar;* see Josh. 24:26
7 [a]Deut. 11:29 & 27:12; Josh. 8:33; John 4:20
8 [a]See 2 Ki. 14:9 [b]ch. 8:22,23
9 [a]Ps. 104:15 [l]Heb. *go up and down for* other *trees*
13 [a]Ps. 104:15
14 [l]Or, *thistle*
15 [a]Is. 30:2; Dan. 4:12; Hos. 14:7 [b]ver. 20; Num. 21:28; Ezek. 19:14

J *Jdg 2:21* ◄► *Jdg 9:20*

the bramble, and devour the [c]cedars of
Lebanon.
16 Now therefore, if ye have done
truly and sincerely, in that ye have made
Abimelech king, and if ye have dealt well
with Jerubbaal and his house, and have
done unto him [a]according to the deserv-
ing of his hands;
17 (For my father fought for you, and
[ʹ]adventured his life far, and delivered
you out of the hand of Midian:
18 [a]And ye are risen up against my father's house this day, and have slain his
sons, threescore and ten persons, upon
one stone, and have made Abimelech,
the son of his maidservant, king over the
men of Shechem, because he *is* your
brother;)
19 If ye then have dealt truly and sincerely with Jerubbaal and with his house
this day, *then* [a]rejoice ye in Abimelech,
and let him also rejoice in you:
J 20 But if not, [a]let fire come out from
Abimelech, and devour the men of Shechem, and the house of Millo; and let fire
come out from the men of Shechem, and
from the house of Millo, and devour
Abimelech.
21 And Jotham ran away, and fled, and
went to [a]Beer, and dwelt there, for fear
of Abimelech his brother.
22 ¶ When Abimelech had reigned
three years over Israel,
23 Then [a]God sent an evil spirit between Abimelech and the men of Shechem; and the men of Shechem [b]dealt
treacherously with Abimelech:
24 [a]That the cruelty *done* to the threescore and ten sons of Jerubbaal might
come, and their blood be laid upon Abimelech their brother, which slew them;
and upon the men of Shechem, which
[ʹ]aided him in the killing of his brethren.
25 And the men of Shechem set liers
in wait for him in the top of the mountains, and they robbed all that came along
that way by them: and it was told Abimelech.
26 And Gaal the son of Ebed came
with his brethren, and went over to Shechem: and the men of Shechem put their
confidence in him.
27 And they went out into the fields,
and gathered their vineyards, and trode
the grapes, and made merry, and went

15 [c]2 Ki. 14:9; Is. 2:13 & 37:24; Ezek. 31:3
16 [a]ch. 8:35
17 [ʹ]Heb. *cast his life*
18 [a]ver. 5,6
19 [a]Is. 8:6; Phil. 3:3
20 [a]ver. 15,56,57
21 [a]2 Sam. 20:14
23 [a]1 Sam. 16:14; & 18:9,10; See 1 Ki. 22:22; 2 Chr. 18:22; Is. 19:14 [b]Is. 33:1
24 [a]1 Ki. 2:32; Esth. 9:25; Mat. 23:35,36 [ʹ]Heb. *strengthened his hands to kill*
27 [a]ver. 4
28 [a]1 Sam. 25:10; 1 Ki. 12:16 [b]Gen. 34:2,6
29 [a]2 Sam. 15:4
30 [ʹ]Or, *hot*
31 [ʹ]Heb. *craftily,* or, *to Tormah*
33 [ʹ]Heb. *as thine hand shall find*
37 [ʹ]Heb. *navel*
38 [a]ver. 28,29

into [a]the house of their god, and did eat
and drink, and cursed Abimelech.
28 And Gaal the son of Ebed said,
[a]Who *is* Abimelech, and who *is* Shechem, that we should serve him? *is* not
he the son of Jerubbaal? and Zebul his
officer? serve the men of [b]Hamor the father of Shechem: for why should we
serve him?
29 And [a]would to God this people
were under my hand! then would I remove Abimelech. And he said to Abimelech, Increase thine army, and come out.
30 ¶ And when Zebul the ruler of the
city heard the words of Gaal the son of
Ebed, his anger was [ʹ]kindled.
31 And he sent messengers unto
Abimelech [ʹ]privily, saying, Behold, Gaal
the son of Ebed and his brethren be come
to Shechem; and, behold, they fortify the
city against thee.
32 Now therefore up by night, thou
and the people that *is* with thee, and lie
in wait in the field:
33 And it shall be, *that* in the morning,
as soon as the sun is up, thou shalt rise
early, and set upon the city: and, behold,
when he and the people that *is* with him
come out against thee, then mayest thou
do to them [ʹ]as thou shalt find occasion.
34 ¶ And Abimelech rose up, and all
the people that *were* with him, by night,
and they laid wait against Shechem in
four companies.
35 And Gaal the son of Ebed went out,
and stood in the entering of the gate of
the city: and Abimelech rose up, and the
people that *were* with him, from lying in
wait.
36 And when Gaal saw the people, he
said to Zebul, Behold, there come people
down from the top of the mountains. And
Zebul said unto him, Thou seest the
shadow of the mountains as *if they were*
men.
37 And Gaal spake again and said, See
there come people down by the [ʹ]middle
of the land, and another company come
along by the plain of Meonenim.
38 Then said Zebul unto him, Where
is now thy mouth, wherewith thou
[a]saidst, Who *is* Abimelech, that we
should serve him? *is* not this the people
that thou hast despised? go out, I pray
now, and fight with them.
39 And Gaal went out before the men
of Shechem, and fought with Abimelech.

J *Jdg 9:15* ◄► *1Sa 2:31*

40 And Abimelech chased him, and he
fled before him, and many were overthrown *and* wounded, *even* unto the entering of the gate.
41 And Abimelech dwelt at Arumah:
and Zebul thrust out Gaal and his brethren, that they should not dwell in
Shechem.
42 And it came to pass on the morrow,
that the people went out into the field;
and they told Abimelech.
43 And he took the people, and divided them into three companies, and
laid wait in the field, and looked, and,
behold, the people *were* come forth out
of the city; and he rose up against them,
and smote them.
44 And Abimelech, and the company
that *was* with him, rushed forward, and
stood in the entering of the gate of the
city: and the two *other* companies ran
upon all *the people* that *were* in the
fields, and slew them.
45 And Abimelech fought against the
city all that day; and [a]he took the city,
and slew the people that *was* therein, and
[b]beat down the city, and sowed it with
salt.
46 ¶ And when all the men of the
tower of Shechem heard *that,* they entered into an hold of the house [a]of the
god Berith.
47 And it was told Abimelech, that all
the men of the tower of Shechem were
gathered together.
48 And Abimelech gat him up to
mount [a]Zalmon, he and all the people
that *were* with him; and Abimelech took
an axe in his hand, and cut down a bough
from the trees, and took it, and laid *it* on
his shoulder, and said unto the people
that *were* with him, What ye have seen
[1]me do, make haste, *and* do as I *have
done.*
49 And all the people likewise cut
down every man his bough, and followed
Abimelech, and put *them* to the hold, and
set the hold on fire upon them; so that all
the men of the tower of Shechem died
also, about a thousand men and women.
50 ¶ Then went Abimelech to Thebez,
and encamped against Thebez, and
took it.
51 But there was a strong tower
within the city, and thither fled all the
men and women, and all they of the city,
and shut *it* to them, and gat them up to
the top of the tower.
52 And Abimelech came unto the
tower, and fought against it, and went
hard unto the door of the tower to burn it
with fire.
53 And a certain woman [a]cast a piece
of a millstone upon Abimelech's head,
and all to brake his skull.
54 Then [a]he called hastily unto the
young man his armourbearer, and said
unto him, Draw thy sword, and slay me,
that men say not of me, A woman slew
him. And his young man thrust him
through, and he died.
55 And when the men of Israel saw
that Abimelech was dead, they departed
every man unto his place.
56 ¶ [a]Thus God rendered the wickedness of Abimelech, which he did unto his
father, in slaying his seventy brethren:
57 And all the evil of the men of Shechem did God render upon their heads:
and upon them came [a]the curse of Jotham the son of Jerubbaal.

Israel cries for deliverance

10 AND AFTER Abimelech there
[a]arose to [1,2]defend Israel Tola the
son of Puah, the son of Dodo, a man of
Issachar; and he dwelt in Shamir in
mount Ephraim.
2 And he judged Israel twenty and
three years, and died, and was buried in
Shamir.
3 ¶ And after him arose Jair, a Gileadite, and judged Israel twenty and two
years.
4 And he had thirty sons that [a]rode on
thirty ass colts, and they had thirty cities,
[b]which are called [c]Havoth-jair[1] unto this
day, which *are* in the land of Gilead.
5 And Jair died, and was buried in
Camon.
6 ¶ And [a]the children of Israel did evil
again in the sight of the LORD, and [b]served
Baalim, and Ashtaroth, and [c]the gods of
Syria, and the gods of [d]Zidon, and the
gods of Moab, and the gods of the children of Ammon, and the gods of the Philistines, and forsook the LORD, and served
not him.
7 And the anger of the LORD was hot
against Israel, and he [a]sold them into the
hands of the Philistines, and into the
hands of the children of Ammon.
8 And that year they vexed and [1]op-

45 [a]ver. 20 [b]Deut. 29:23; 1 Ki. 12:25; 2 Ki. 3:25
46 [a]ch. 8:33
48 [a]Ps. 68:14 [1]Heb. *I have done*
53 [a]2 Sam. 11:21
54 [a]1 Sam. 31:4
56 [a]ver. 24; Job 31:3; Prov. 5:22
57 [a]ver. 20
10:1 [a]ch. 2:16 [1]Or, *deliver* [2]Heb. *save*
4 [a]ch. 5:10 & 12:14 [b]Deut. 3:14 [c]Num. 32:41 [1]Or, *The villages of Jair*
6 [a]ch. 2:11 & 3:7; & 4:1 & 6:1 & 13:1 [b]ch. 2:13 [c]ch. 2:12 [d]1 Ki. 11:33; Ps. 106:36
7 [a]ch. 2:14; 1 Sam. 12:9
8 [1]Heb. *crushed*

pressed the children of Israel: eighteen years, all the children of Israel that *were* on the other side Jordan in the land of the Amorites, which *is* in Gilead.

9 Moreover the children of Ammon passed over Jordan to fight also against Judah, and against Benjamin, and against the house of Ephraim; so that Israel was sore distressed.

10 ¶ [a]And the children of Israel cried unto the LORD, saying, We have sinned against thee, both because we have forsaken our God, and also served Baalim.

11 And the LORD said unto the children of Israel, *Did* not *I deliver you* [a]from the Egyptians, and [b]from the Amorites, [c]from the children of Ammon, [d]and from the Philistines?

12 [a]The Zidonians also, [b]and the Amalekites, and the Maonites, [c]did oppress you; and ye cried to me, and I delivered you out of their hand.

13 [a]Yet ye have forsaken me, and served other gods: wherefore I will deliver you no more.

14 Go and [a]cry unto the gods which ye have chosen; let them deliver you in the time of your tribulation.

P 15 ¶ And the children of Israel said
R unto the LORD, We have sinned: [a]do thou unto us whatsoever [1]seemeth good unto thee; deliver us only, we pray thee, this day.

16 [a]And they put away the [1]strange gods from among them, and served the LORD: and [b]his soul [2]was grieved for the misery of Israel.

17 Then the children of Ammon were [1]gathered together, and encamped in Gilead. And the children of Israel assembled themselves together, and encamped in [a]Mizpeh.

18 And the people *and* princes of Gilead said one to another, What man *is he* that will begin to fight against the children of Ammon? he shall [a]be head over all the inhabitants of Gilead.

Jephthah

11 NOW [a]JEPHTHAH the Gileadite was [b]a mighty man of valour, and he *was* the son of [1]an harlot: and Gilead begat Jephthah.

2 And Gilead's wife bare him sons; and his wife's sons grew up, and they thrust out Jephthah, and said unto him, Thou shalt not inherit in our father's house; for thou *art* the son of a strange woman.

3 Then Jephthah fled [1]from his brethren, and dwelt in the land of Tob: and there were gathered [a]vain men to Jephthah, and went out with him.

4 ¶ And it came to pass [1]in process of time, that the children of Ammon made war against Israel.

5 And it was so, that when the children of Ammon made war against Israel, the elders of Gilead went to fetch Jephthah out of the land of Tob:

6 And they said unto Jephthah, Come, and be our captain, that we may fight with the children of Ammon.

7 And Jephthah said unto the elders of Gilead, [a]Did not ye hate me, and expel me out of my father's house? and why are ye come unto me now when ye are in distress?

8 [a]And the elders of Gilead said unto Jephthah, Therefore we [b]turn again to thee now, that thou mayest go with us, and fight against the children of Ammon, and be [a]our head over all the inhabitants of Gilead.

9 And Jephthah said unto the elders of Gilead, If ye bring me home again to fight against the children of Ammon, and the LORD deliver them before me, shall I be your head?

10 And the elders of Gilead said unto Jephthah, [a]The LORD [1]be witness between us, if we do not so according to thy words.

11 Then Jephthah went with the elders of Gilead, and the people made him [a]head and captain over them: and Jephthah uttered all his words [b]before the LORD in Mizpeh.

12 ¶ And Jephthah sent messengers unto the king of the children of Ammon, saying, What hast thou to do with me, that thou art come against me to fight in my land?

13 And the king of the children of Ammon answered unto the messengers of Jephthah, [a]Because Israel took away my land, when they came up out of Egypt, from Arnon even unto [b]Jabbok, and unto Jordan: now therefore restore those *lands* again peaceably.

14 And Jephthah sent messengers

10 [a]1 Sam. 12:10
11 [a]Ex. 14:30 [b]Num. 21:21,24,25 [c]ch. 3:12,13 [d]ch. 3:31
12 [a]ch. 5:19 [b]ch. 6:3 [c]Ps. 106:42,43
13 [a]Jer. 2:13
14 [a]Deut. 32:37, 38
15 [a]1 Sam. 3:18; 2 Sam. 15:26 [1]Heb. *is good in thine eyes*
16 [a]2 Chr. 7:14 & 15:8; Jer. 18:7,8 [b]Ps. 106:44,45; Is. 63:9 [1]Heb. *gods of strangers* [2]Heb. *was shortened*
17 [a]Gen. 31:49; ch. 11:11,29 [1]Heb. *cried together*
18 [a]ch. 11:8,11
11:1 [a]Heb. 11:32 called *Jephthae* [b]ch. 6:12; 2 Ki. 5:1 [1]Heb. *a woman an harlot*
3 [a]ch. 9:4; 1 Sam. 22:2 [1]Heb. *from the face*
4 [1]Heb. *after days*
7 [a]Gen. 26:27
8 [a]ch. 10:18 [b]Luke 17:4
10 [a]Jer. 42:5 [1]Heb. *be the hearer between us*
11 [a]ver. 8 [b]ch. 10:17 & 20:1; 1 Sam. 10:17 & 11:15
13 [a]Num. 21:24-26 [b]Gen. 32:22

P *Dt 4:29–31* ◀▶ *2Sa 12:13*
R *Jos 7:19* ◀▶ *1Sa 12:3*

again unto the king of the children of
Ammon:
15 And said unto him, Thus saith Jephthah, [a]Israel took not away the land of
Moab, nor the land of the children of
Ammon:
16 But when Israel came up from
Egypt, and walked through the wilderness unto the Red sea, and [a]came to
Kadesh;
17 Then [a]Israel sent messengers unto
the king of Edom, saying, Let me, I pray
thee, pass through thy land: [b]but the king
of Edom would not hearken *thereto.* And
in like manner they sent unto the king of
Moab: but he would not *consent:* and Israel [c]abode in Kadesh.
18 Then they went along through the
wilderness, and [a]compassed the land of
Edom, and the land of Moab, and [b]came
by the east side of the land of Moab, [c]and
pitched on the other side of Arnon, but
came not within the border of Moab: for
Arnon *was* the border of Moab.
19 And [a]Israel sent messengers unto
Sihon king of the Amorites, the king of
Heshbon; and Israel said unto him, [b]Let
us pass, we pray thee, through thy land
into my place.
20 [a]But Sihon trusted not Israel to pass
through his coast: but Sihon gathered all
his people together, and pitched in Jahaz,
and fought against Israel.
21 And the LORD God of Israel delivered Sihon and all his people into the
hand of Israel, and they [a]smote them: so
Israel possessed all the land of the Amorites, the inhabitants of that country.
22 And they possessed [a]all the coasts
of the Amorites, from Arnon even unto
Jabbok, and from the wilderness even
unto Jordan.
23 So now the LORD God of Israel hath
dispossessed the Amorites from before
his people Israel, and shouldest thou possess it?
24 Wilt not thou possess that which
[a]Chemosh thy god giveth thee to possess? So whomsoever [b]the LORD our God
shall drive out from before us, them will
we possess.
25 And now *art* thou any thing better
than [a]Balak the son of Zippor, king of
Moab? did he ever strive against Israel, or
did he ever fight against them,
26 While Israel dwelt in [a]Heshbon and
her towns, and in [b]Aroer and her towns,
and in all the cities that *be* along by the
coasts of Arnon, three hundred years?
why therefore did ye not recover *them*
within that time?
27 Wherefore I have not sinned
against thee, but thou doest me wrong to
war against me: the LORD [a]the Judge [b]be
judge this day between the children of
Israel and the children of Ammon.
28 Howbeit the king of the children of
Ammon hearkened not unto the words of
Jephthah which he sent him.
29 ¶ Then [a]the spirit of the LORD came E
upon [1]Jephthah, and he passed over Gil- M
ead, and Manasseh, and passed over Mizpeh of Gilead, and from Mizpeh of Gilead
he passed over *unto* the children of
Ammon.
30 And Jephthah [a]vowed a vow unto
the LORD, and said, If thou shalt without
fail deliver the children of Ammon into
mine hands,
31 Then it shall be, that [1]whatsoever
cometh forth of the doors of my house to
meet me, when I return in peace from
the children of Ammon, [a]shall surely be
the LORD'S, [b]and[2] I will offer it up for a
burnt offering.
32 ¶ So Jephthah passed over unto the
children of Ammon to fight against them;
and the LORD delivered them into his
hands.
33 And he smote them from Aroer,
even till thou come to [a]Minnith, *even*
twenty cities, and unto [1]the plain of the
vineyards, with a very great slaughter.
Thus the children of Ammon were subdued before the children of Israel.
34 ¶ And Jephthah came to [a]Mizpeh
unto his house, and, behold, [b]his daughter came out to meet him with timbrels
and with dances: and she *was his* only
child; [1,2]beside her he had neither son
nor daughter.
35 And it came to pass, when he saw
her, that he [a]rent his clothes, and said,
Alas, my daughter! thou hast brought me
very low, and thou art one of them that
trouble me: for I [b]have opened my mouth
unto the LORD, and [c]I cannot go back.
36 And she said unto him, My father,
if thou hast opened thy mouth unto the
LORD, [a]do to me according to that which
hath proceeded out of thy mouth; foras-

15 [a]Deut. 2:9,19
16 [a]Num. 13:26 & 20:1; Deut. 1:46
17 [a]Num. 20:14 [b]Num. 20:18,21 [c]Num. 20:1
18 [a]Num. 21:4; Deut. 2:1-8 [b]Num. 21:11 [c]Num. 21:13 & 22:36
19 [a]Num. 21:21; Deut. 2:26 [b]Num. 21:22; Deut. 2:27
20 [a]Num. 21:23; Deut. 2:32
21 [a]Num. 21:24, 25; Deut. 2:33,34
22 [a]Deut. 2:36
24 [a]Num. 21:29; 1 Ki. 11:7; Jer. 48:7 [b]Deut. 9:4,5 & 18:12; Josh. 3:10
25 [a]Num. 22:2; See Josh. 24:9
26 [a]Num. 21:25 [b]Deut. 2:36
27 [a]Gen. 18:25 [b]Gen. 16:5 & 31:53; 1 Sam. 24:12,15
29 [a]ch. 3:10 [1]Jephthah seems to have been Judge only of Northeast *Israel*
30 [a]Gen. 28:20
31 [a]See 1 Sam. 1:11,28 [b]Ps. 66:13 [1]Heb. *that which cometh forth, which shall come forth* [2]Or, *or I will offer it*
33 [a]Ezek. 27:17 [1]Or, *Abel*
34 [a]ver. 11; ch. 10:17 [b]Ex. 15:20; Ps. 68:25; Jer. 31:4 [1]Or, *he had not of his own either son or daughter* [2]Heb. *of himself*
35 [a]Gen. 37:29,34 [b]Eccl. 5:2 [c]Num. 30:2
36 [a]Num. 30:2

E *Jdg 6:34* ◀ ▶ *Jdg 13:25*
M *Jdg 6:34* ◀ ▶ *Jdg 14:6*

much as [b]the LORD hath taken vengeance
for thee of thine enemies, *even* of the
children of Ammon.
37 And she said unto her father, Let
this thing be done for me: let me alone
two months, that I may [1]go up and down
upon the mountains, and bewail my virginity, I and my fellows.
38 And he said, Go. And he sent her
away *for* two months: and she went with
her companions, and bewailed her virginity upon the mountains.
39 And it came to pass at the end of
two months, that she returned unto her
father, who [a]did with her *according* to
his vow which he had vowed: and she
knew no man. And it was a [1]custom in
Israel,
40 *That* the daughters of Israel went
[1]yearly [2]to lament the daughter of Jephthah the Gileadite four days in a year.

Jephthah and Ephraim

12 AND [a]THE men of Ephraim
[1]gathered themselves together,
and went northward, and said unto Jephthah, Wherefore passedst thou over to
fight against the children of Ammon, and
didst not call us to go with thee? we will
burn thine house upon thee with fire.
2 And Jephthah said unto them, I and
my people were at great strife with the
children of Ammon; and when I called
you, ye delivered me not out of their
hands.
3 And when I saw that ye delivered
me not, I [a]put my life in my hands, and
passed over against the children of Ammon, and the LORD delivered them into
my hand: wherefore then are ye come up
unto me this day, to fight against me?
4 Then Jephthah gathered together all
the men of Gilead, and fought with
Ephraim: and the men of Gilead smote
Ephraim, because they said, Ye Gileadites
[a]*are* fugitives of Ephraim among the
Ephraimites, *and* among the Manassites.
5 And the Gileadites took the [a]pas-
sages of Jordan before the Ephraimites:
and it was *so,* that when those Ephraimites which were escaped said, Let me go
over; that the men of Gilead said unto
him, *Art* thou an Ephraimite? If he said,
Nay;
6 Then said they unto him, Say now
[1]Shibboleth: and he said Sibboleth: for he
could not frame to pronounce *it* right.
Then they took him, and slew him at the
passages of Jordan: and there fell at that
time of the Ephraimites forty and two
thousand.
7 And Jephthah judged Israel six years.
Then died Jephthah the Gileadite, and
was buried in *one of* the cities of Gilead.

Ibzan, Elon and Abdon

8 ¶ And after him [1]Ibzan of Bethlehem
judged Israel.
9 And he had thirty sons, and thirty
daughters, *whom* he sent abroad, and
took in thirty daughters from abroad for
his sons. And he judged Israel seven
years.
10 Then died Ibzan, and was buried at
Bethlehem.
11 ¶ And after him [1]Elon, a Zebulonite, judged Israel; and he judged Israel
ten years.
12 And Elon the Zebulonite died, and
was buried in Aijalon in the country of
Zebulun.
13 ¶ And after him [1]Abdon the son of
Hillel, a Pirathonite, judged Israel.
14 And he had forty sons and thirty
[1]nephews, that [a]rode on threescore and
ten ass colts: and he judged Israel eight
years.
15 And Abdon the son of Hillel the Pirathonite died, and was buried in Pirathon
in the land of Ephraim, [a]in the mount of
the Amalekites.
13 AND THE children of Israel [a]did[1]
evil again in the sight of the LORD;
[2]and the LORD delivered them [b]into the
hand of the Philistines forty years.

The birth of Samson

2 ¶ And there was a certain man of E
[a]Zorah, of the family of the Danites,
whose name *was* Manoah; and his wife
was barren, and bare not.
3 And the [a]angel of the LORD appeared I
unto the woman, and said unto her, Behold now, thou *art* barren, and bearest
not: but thou shalt conceive, and bear a
son.
4 Now therefore beware, I pray thee,
and [a]drink not wine nor strong drink,
and eat not any unclean *thing:*
5 For, lo, thou shalt conceive, and bear I
a son; and no [a]razor shall come on his

36 [b]2 Sam. 18:19, 31
37 [1]Heb. *go and go down*
39 [a]ver. 31; 1 Sam. 1:22,24 [1]Or, *ordinance*
40 [1]Heb. *from year to year* [2]Or, *to talk with*
12:1 [a]See ch. 8:1 [1]Heb. *were called*
3 [a]1 Sam. 19:5; Ps. 119:109
4 [a]See 1 Sam. 25:10
5 [a]Josh. 22:11; ch. 3:28
6 [1]Which signifieth *a stream,* or, *flood*
8 [1]He seems to have been only a civil Judge to do justice in Northeast *Israel*
11 [1]A civil Judge in Northeast *Israel*
13 [1]A civil Judge also in Northeast *Israel*
14 [a]ch. 5:10 & 10:4 [1]Heb. *sons' sons*
15 [a]ch. 3:13,27 & 5:14
13:1 [a]ch. 2:11 & 3:7 & 4:1 & 6:1 & 10:6 [b]1 Sam. 12:9 [1]Heb. *added to commit* [2]This seems a partial captivity
2 [a]Josh. 19:41
3 [a]ch. 6:12; Luke 1:11,13,28,31
4 [a]ver. 14; Num. 6:2,3; Luke 1:15
5 [a]Num. 6:5; 1 Sam. 1:11

E *Jos 14:10–11* ◀ ▶ *1Sa 1:5–20*
I *Jdg 7:13–14* ◀ ▶ *Jdg 13:5*
I *Jdg 13:3* ◀ ▶ *Jdg 20:28*

head: for the child shall be [b]a Nazarite unto God from the womb: and he shall [c]begin to deliver Israel out of the hand of the Philistines.

6 ¶ Then the woman came and told her husband, saying, [a]A man of God came unto me, and his [b]countenance *was* like the countenance of an angel of God, very terrible: but I [c]asked him not whence he *was*, neither told he me his name:

7 But he said unto me, Behold, thou shalt conceive, and bear a son; and now drink no wine nor strong drink, neither eat any unclean *thing:* for the child shall be a Nazarite to God from the womb to the day of his death.

8 ¶ Then Manoah entreated the LORD, and said, O my Lord, let the man of God which thou didst send come again unto us, and teach us what we shall do unto the child that shall be born.

9 And God hearkened to the voice of Manoah; and the angel of God came again unto the woman as she sat in the field: but Manoah her husband *was* not with her.

10 And the woman made haste, and ran, and showed her husband, and said unto him, Behold, the man hath appeared unto me, that came unto me the *other* day.

11 And Manoah arose, and went after his wife, and came to the man, and said unto him, *Art* thou the man that spakest unto the woman? And he said, I *am.*

12 And Manoah said, Now let thy words come to pass. [1]How shall we order the child, and [2,3]*how* shall we do unto him?

13 And the angel of the LORD said unto Manoah, Of all that I said unto the woman let her beware.

14 She may not eat of any *thing* that cometh of the vine, [a]neither let her drink wine or strong drink, nor eat any unclean *thing:* all that I commanded her let her observe.

15 ¶ And Manoah said unto the angel of the LORD, I pray thee, [a]let us detain thee, until we shall have made ready a kid [1]for thee.

16 And the angel of the LORD said unto Manoah, Though thou detain me, I will not eat of thy bread: and if thou wilt offer a burnt offering, thou must offer it unto the LORD. For Manoah knew not that he *was* an angel of the LORD.

17 And Manoah said unto the angel of the LORD, What *is* thy name, that when thy sayings come to pass we may do thee honour?

18 And the angel of the LORD said unto him, [a]Why askest thou thus after my name, seeing it *is* secret?

19 So Manoah took a kid with a meat offering, [a]and offered *it* upon a rock unto the LORD: and *the angel* did wondrously; and Manoah and his wife looked on.

20 For it came to pass, when the flame went up toward heaven from off the altar, that the angel of the LORD ascended in the flame of the altar. And Manoah and his wife looked on *it,* and [a]fell on their faces to the ground.

21 But the angel of the LORD did no more appear to Manoah and to his wife. [a]Then Manoah knew that he *was* an angel of the LORD.

22 And Manoah said unto his wife, [a]We shall surely die, because we have seen God.

23 But his wife said unto him, If the LORD were pleased to kill us, he would not have received a burnt offering and a meat offering at our hands, neither would he have shown us all these *things,* nor would as at this time have told us *such things* as these.

24 ¶ And the woman bare a son, and called his name [a]Samson: and [b]the child grew, and the LORD blessed him.

25 [a]And the spirit of the LORD began to move him at times in [1]the camp of Dan [b]between Zorah and Eshtaol. E L

5 [b]Num. 6:2 [c]See 1 Sam. 7:13; 2 Sam. 8:1; 1 Chr. 18:1
6 [a]Deut. 33:1; 1 Sam. 2:27 & 9:6 [b]Mat. 28:3; Luke 9:29; Acts 6:15 [c]ver. 17,18
12 [1]Heb. *What shall be the manner of the* [2]Or, what *shall he do?* [3]Heb. what shall be *his work?*
14 [a]ver. 4
15 [a]Gen. 18:5; ch. 6:18 [1]Heb. *before thee*
18 [a]Gen. 32:29
19 [a]ch. 6:19,20
20 [a]Lev. 9:24; 1 Chr. 21:16; Ezek. 1:28; Mat. 17:6
21 [a]ch. 6:22
22 [a]Gen. 32:30; Ex. 33:20; Deut. 5:26; ch. 6:22
24 [a]Heb. 11:32 [b]1 Sam. 3:19; Luke 1:80 & 2:52
25 [a]ch. 3:10; 1 Sam. 11:6; Mat. 4:1 [b]Josh. 15:33; ch. 18:11 [1]Heb. *Mahaneh-dan* as ch. 18:12

E *Jdg 11:29* ◄ ► *Jdg 14:6* L ► *1Sa 10:6–7*

13:18 This angelic visitor is a theophany of Christ—a visible manifestation of God to humanity. The word translated "secret" is a Hebrew term for that which is "wonderful" or "beyond understanding." In Isa 9:6 a similar word occurs and is applied to the One who would come as "The mighty God." Since God is beyond our understanding, we will never be able to "name" him in adequate terms.

The marriage of Samson

14 AND SAMSON went down [a]to Timnath, and [b]saw a woman in Timnath of the daughters of the Philistines.

2 And he came up, and told his father and his mother, and said, I have seen a woman in Timnath of the daughters of the Philistines: now therefore [a]get her for me to wife.

3 Then his father and his mother said unto him, *Is there* never a woman among the daughters of [a]thy brethren, or among all my people, that thou goest to take a wife of the [b]uncircumcised Philistines? And Samson said unto his father, Get her for me; for [1]she pleaseth me well.

4 But his father and his mother knew not that it *was* [a]of the LORD, that he sought an occasion against the Philistines: for at that time [b]the Philistines had dominion over Israel.

5 ¶ Then went Samson down, and his father and his mother, to Timnath, and came to the vineyards of Timnath: and, behold, a young lion roared [1]against him.

E M 6 And [a]the spirit of the LORD came mightily upon him, and he rent him as he would have rent a kid, and *he had* nothing in his hand: but he told not his father or his mother what he had done.

7 And he went down, and talked with the woman; and she pleased Samson well.

8 ¶ And after a time he returned to take her, and he turned aside to see the carcase of the lion: and, behold, *there was* a swarm of bees and honey in the carcase of the lion.

9 And he took thereof in his hands, and went on eating, and came to his father and mother, and he gave them, and they did eat: but he told not them that he had taken the honey out of the carcase of the lion.

10 ¶ So his father went down unto the woman: and Samson made there a feast; for so used the young men to do.

11 And it came to pass, when they saw him, that they brought thirty companions to be with him.

12 ¶ And Samson said unto them, I will now [a]put forth a riddle unto you: if ye can certainly declare it me [b]within the seven days of the feast, and find *it* out, then I will give you thirty [1]sheets and thirty [c]change of garments:

13 But if ye cannot declare *it* me, then shall ye give me thirty sheets and thirty change of garments. And they said unto him, Put forth thy riddle, that we may hear it.

14 And he said unto them, Out of the eater came forth meat, and out of the strong came forth sweetness. And they could not in three days expound the riddle.

15 And it came to pass on the seventh day, that they said unto Samson's wife, [a]Entice thy husband, that he may declare unto us the riddle, [b]lest we burn thee and thy father's house with fire: have ye called us [1]to take that we have? *is it* not *so?*

16 And Samson's wife wept before him, and said, [a]Thou dost but hate me, and lovest me not: thou hast put forth a riddle unto the children of my people, and hast not told *it* me. And he said unto her, Behold, I have not told *it* my father nor my mother, and shall I tell *it* thee?

17 And she wept before him [1]the seven days, while their feast lasted: and it came to pass on the seventh day, that he told her, because she lay sore upon him: and she told the riddle to the children of her people.

18 And the men of the city said unto him on the seventh day before the sun went down, What *is* sweeter than honey? and what *is* stronger than a lion? And he said unto them, If ye had not plowed with my heifer, ye had not found out my riddle.

19 ¶ And [a]the spirit of the LORD came upon him, and he went down to Ashkelon, and slew thirty men of them, and took their [1]spoil, and gave change of garments unto them which expounded the riddle. And his anger was kindled, and he went up to his father's house. E M

20 But Samson's wife [a]was *given* to his companion, whom he had used as [b]his friend.

14:1 [a]Gen. 38:13; Josh. 15:10 [b]Gen. 34:2

2 [a]Gen. 21:21 & 34:4

3 [a]Gen. 24:3,4 [b]Gen. 34:14; Ex. 34:16; Deut. 7:3 [1]Heb. *she is right in mine eyes*

4 [a]Josh. 11:20; 1 Ki. 12:15; 2 Ki. 6:33; 2 Chr. 10:15 & 22:7 & 25:20 [b]ch. 13:1; Deut. 28:48

5 [1]Heb. *in meeting him*

6 [a]ch. 3:10 & 13:25; 1 Sam. 11:6

12 [a]1 Ki. 10:1; Ezek. 17:2; Luke 14:7 [b]Gen. 29:27 [c]Gen. 45:22; 2 Ki. 5:22 [1]Or, *shirts*

15 [a]ch. 16:5 [b]ch. 15:6 [1]Heb. *to possess us*, or, *to impoverish us?*

16 [a]ch. 16:15

17 [1]Or, the rest of *the seven days*

19 [a]ch. 3:10 & 13:25 [1]Or, *apparel*

20 [a]ch. 15:2 [b]John 3:29

E *Jdg 13:25* ◀▶ *Jdg 14:19*
M *Jdg 11:29* ◀▶ *Jdg 14:19*

E *Jdg 14:6* ◀▶ *Jdg 15:14–15*
M *Jdg 14:6* ◀▶ *Jdg 15:14–15*

The revenge of Samson

15 BUT IT came to pass within a while after, in the time of wheat harvest, that Samson visited his wife with a kid; and he said, I will go in to my wife into the chamber. But her father would not suffer him to go in.

2 And her father said, I verily thought that thou hadst utterly [a]hated her; therefore I gave her to thy companion: *is* not her younger sister fairer than she? [1]take her, I pray thee, instead of her.

3 ¶ And Samson said concerning them, [1]Now shall I be more blameless than the Philistines, though I do them a displeasure.

4 And Samson went and caught three hundred foxes, and took [1]firebrands, and turned tail to tail, and put a firebrand in the midst between two tails.

5 And when he had set the brands on fire, he let *them* go into the standing corn of the Philistines, and burnt up both the shocks, and also the standing corn, with the vineyards *and* olives.

6 ¶ Then the Philistines said, Who hath done this? And they answered, Samson, the son-in-law of the Timnite, because he had taken his wife, and given her to his companion. [a]And the Philistines came up, and burnt her and her father with fire.

7 ¶ And Samson said unto them, Though ye have done this, yet will I be avenged of you, and after that I will cease.

8 And he smote them hip and thigh with a great slaughter: and he went down and dwelt in the top of the rock Etam.

9 ¶ Then the Philistines went up, and pitched in Judah, and spread themselves [a]in Lehi.

10 And the men of Judah said, Why are ye come up against us? And they answered, To bind Samson are we come up, to do to him as he hath done to us.

11 Then three thousand men of Judah [1]went to the top of the rock Etam, and said to Samson, Knowest thou not that the Philistines *are* [a]rulers over us? what *is* this *that* thou hast done unto us? And he said unto them, As they did unto me, so have I done unto them.

12 And they said unto him, We are come down to bind thee, that we may deliver thee into the hand of the Philistines. And Samson said unto them, Swear unto me, that ye will not fall upon me yourselves.

13 And they spake unto him, saying, No; but we will bind thee fast, and deliver thee into their hand: but surely we will not kill thee. And they bound him with two new cords, and brought him up from the rock.

14 ¶ *And* when he came unto Lehi, the Philistines shouted against him: and [a]the spirit of the LORD came mightily upon him, and the cords that *were* upon his arms became as flax that was burnt with fire, and his bands [1]loosed from off his hands. E M

15 And he found a [1]new jawbone of an ass, and put forth his hand, and took it, and [a]slew a thousand men therewith.

16 And Samson said, With the jawbone of an ass, [1]heaps upon heaps, with the jaw of an ass have I slain a thousand men.

17 And it came to pass, when he had made an end of speaking, that he cast away the jawbone out of his hand, and called that place [1]Ramath-lehi.

18 ¶ And he was sore athirst, and called on the LORD, and said, [a]Thou hast given this great deliverance into the hand of thy servant: and now shall I die for thirst, and fall into the hand of the uncircumcised? F

19 But God clave an hollow place that *was* in [1]the jaw, and there came water thereout; and when he had drunk, [a]his spirit came again, and he revived: wherefore he called the name thereof [2]En-hakkore, which *is* in Lehi unto this day.

20 [1]And he judged Israel [a]in the days of the Philistines twenty years.

Samson and Delilah

16 THEN WENT Samson to Gaza, and saw there [1]an harlot, and went in unto her.

2 *And it was told* the Gazites, saying, Samson is come hither. And they [a]compassed *him* in, and laid wait for him all night in the gate of the city, and were [1]quiet all the night, saying, In the morning, when it is day, we shall kill him.

3 And Samson lay till midnight, and

15:2 [a]ch. 14:20 [1]Heb. *let her be thine*

3 [1]Or, *Now shall I be blameless from the Philistines, though*

4 [1]Or, *torches*

6 [a]ch. 14:15

9 [a]ver. 19

11 [a]ch. 14:4 [1]Heb. *went down*

14 [a]ch. 3:10 & 14:6 [1]Heb. *were melted*

15 [a]Lev. 26:8; Josh. 23:10; ch. 3:31 [1]Heb. *moist*

16 [1]Heb. *an heap, two heaps*

17 [1]i.e. *The lifting up of the jawbone,* or, *casting away of the jawbone*

18 [a]Ps. 3:7

19 [a]Gen. 45:27; Is. 40:29 [1]Or, *Lehi* [2]i.e. *The well of him that called,* or, *cried*

20 [a]ch. 13:1 [1]He seems to have judged Southwest Israel during twenty years of their servitude of the Philistines

16:1 [1]Heb. *a woman an harlot*

2 [a]1 Sam. 23:26; Acts 9:24 [1]Heb. *silent*

E *Jdg 14:19* ◄► *1Sa 10:6–7*
M *Jdg 14:19* ◄► *1Sa 10:10–12*
F *Jos 5:12* ◄► *Ru 1:6*

arose at midnight, and took the doors of the gate of the city, and the two posts, and went away with them, [1]bar and all, and put *them* upon his shoulders, and carried them up to the top of an hill that *is* before Hebron.

4 ¶ And it came to pass afterward, that he loved a woman [1]in the valley of Sorek, whose name *was* Delilah.

5 And the lords of the Philistines came up unto her, and said unto her, [a]Entice him, and see wherein his great strength *lieth,* and by what *means* we may prevail against him, that we may bind him to [1]afflict him: and we will give thee every one of us eleven hundred *pieces* of silver.

6 ¶ And Delilah said to Samson, Tell me, I pray thee, wherein thy great strength *lieth,* and wherewith thou mightest be bound to afflict thee.

7 And Samson said unto her, If they bind me with seven [1,2]green withs that were never dried, then shall I be weak, and be as [3]another man.

8 Then the lords of the Philistines brought up to her seven green withs which had not been dried, and she bound him with them.

9 Now *there were* men lying in wait, abiding with her in the chamber. And she said unto him, The Philistines *be* upon thee, Samson. And he brake the withs, as a thread of tow is broken when it [1]toucheth the fire. So his strength was not known.

10 And Delilah said unto Samson, Behold, thou hast mocked me, and told me lies: now tell me, I pray thee, wherewith thou mightest be bound.

11 And he said unto her, If they bind me fast with new ropes [1]that never were occupied, then shall I be weak, and be as another man.

12 Delilah therefore took new ropes, and bound him therewith, and said unto him, The Philistines *be* upon thee, Samson. And *there were* liers in wait abiding in the chamber. And he brake them from off his arms like a thread.

13 And Delilah said unto Samson, Hitherto thou hast mocked me, and told me lies: tell me wherewith thou mightest be bound. And he said unto her, If thou weavest the seven locks of my head with the web.

14 And she fastened *it* with the pin, and said unto him, The Philistines *be* upon thee, Samson. And he awaked out of his sleep, and went away with the pin of the beam, and with the web.

15 ¶ And she said unto him, [a]How canst thou say, I love thee, when thine heart *is* not with me? thou hast mocked me these three times, and hast not told me wherein thy great strength *lieth.*

16 And it came to pass, when she pressed him daily with her words, and urged him, *so* that his soul was [1]vexed unto death;

17 That he [a]told her all his heart, and said unto her, [b]There hath not come a razor upon mine head; for I *have been* a Nazarite unto God from my mother's womb: if I be shaven, then my strength will go from me, and I shall become weak, and be like any *other* man.

18 And when Delilah saw that he had told her all his heart, she sent and called for the lords of the Philistines, saying, Come up this once, for he hath shown me all his heart. Then the lords of the Philistines came up unto her, and brought money in their hand.

19 [a]And she made him sleep upon her knees; and she called for a man, and she caused him to shave off the seven locks of his head; and she began to afflict him, and his strength went from him.

20 And she said, The Philistines *be* upon thee, Samson. And he awoke out of his sleep, and said, I will go out as at other times before, and shake myself. And he wist not that the LORD [a]was departed from him. Q

21 ¶ But the Philistines took him, and [1]put out his eyes, and brought him down to Gaza, and bound him with fetters of brass; and he did grind in the prison house.

22 Howbeit the hair of his head began to grow again [1]after he was shaven.

Samson's revenge and death

23 Then the lords of the Philistines gathered them together for to offer a great sacrifice unto Dagon their god, and to rejoice: for they said, Our god hath delivered Samson our enemy into our hand.

24 And when the people saw him, they [a]praised their god: for they said, Our god hath delivered into our hands our en-

3 [1]Heb. *with the bar*
4 [1]Or, *by the brook*
5 [a]ch. 14:15 [1]Or, *humble*
7 [1]Or, *new cords* [2]Heb. *moist* [3]Heb. *one*
9 [1]Heb. *smelleth*
11 [1]Heb. *wherewith work hath not been done*
15 [a]ch. 14:16
16 [1]Heb. *shortened*
17 [a]Mic. 7:5 [b]Num. 6:5; ch. 13:5
19 [a]Prov. 7:26,27
20 [a]Num. 14:9,42, 43; Josh. 7:12; 1 Sam. 16:14 & 18:12 & 28:15,16; 2 Chr. 15:2
21 [1]Heb. *bored out*
22 [1]Or, *as when he was shaven*
24 [a]Dan. 5:4

Q Ge 6:3 ◄ ► 1Sa 16:14

emy, and the destroyer of our country,
[1]which slew many of us.
25 And it came to pass, when their
hearts were [a]merry, that they said, Call
for Samson, that he may make us sport.
And they called for Samson out of the
prison house; and he made [1]them sport:
and they set him between the pillars.
26 And Samson said unto the lad that
held him by the hand, Suffer me that I
may feel the pillars whereupon the house
standeth, that I may lean upon them.
27 Now the house was full of men and
women; and all the lords of the Philistines *were* there; and *there were* upon
the [a]roof about three thousand men and
women, that beheld while Samson made
sport.
28 And Samson called unto the LORD,
and said, O Lord GOD, [a]remember me, I
pray thee, and strengthen me, I pray
thee, only this once, O God, that I may
be at once avenged of the Philistines for
my two eyes.
29 And Samson took hold of the two
middle pillars upon which the house
stood, and [1]on which it was borne up, of
the one with his right hand, and of the
other with his left.
30 And Samson said, Let [1]me die with
the Philistines. And he bowed himself
with *all his* might; and the house fell
upon the lords, and upon all the people
that *were* therein. So the dead which he
slew at his death were more than *they*
which he slew in his life.
31 Then his brethren and all the house
of his father came down, and took him,
and brought *him* up, and [a]buried him between Zorah and Eshtaol in the buryingplace of Manoah his father. And he
judged Israel twenty years.

Micah's idols and priest

17 AND THERE was a man of mount
Ephraim, whose name *was*
Micah.
2 And he said unto his mother, The
eleven hundred *shekels* of silver that
were taken from thee, about which thou
cursedst, and spakest of also in mine ears,
behold, the silver *is* with me; I took it.
And his mother said, [a]Blessed *be thou* of
the LORD, my son.
3 And when he had restored the
eleven hundred *shekels* of silver to his
mother, his mother said, I had wholly

24 [1]Heb. *and who multiplied our slain*
25 [a]ch. 9:27 [1]Heb. *before them*
27 [a]Deut. 22:8
28 [a]Jer. 15:15
29 [1]Or, *he leaned on them*
30 [1]Heb. *my soul*
31 [a]ch. 13:25
17:2 [a]Gen. 14:19
3 [a]See Ex. 20:4,23; Lev. 19:4
4 [a]Is. 46:6
5 [a]ch. 8:27 [b]Gen. 31:19,30; Hos. 3:4 [c]Ex. 29:9 [1]Heb. *filled the hand*
6 [a]ch. 18:1 & 19:1 & 21:25 [b]Deut. 12:8
7 [a]See Josh. 19:15; ch. 19:1; Ruth 1:1, 2; Mic. 5:2; Mat. 2:1,5,6
8 [1]Heb. *in making his way*
10 [a]ch. 18:19 [b]Gen. 45:8; Job 29:16 [1]Or, *a double suit* [2]Heb. *an order of garments*
12 [a]ver. 5 [b]ch. 18:30
18:1 [a]ch. 17:6 & 21:25 [b]Josh. 19:47
2 [a]ch. 13:25 [b]Num. 13:17; Josh. 2:1 [1]Heb. *sons*

dedicated the silver unto the LORD from
my hand for my son, to [a]make a graven
image and a molten image: now therefore
I will restore it unto thee.
4 Yet he restored the money unto his
mother; and his mother [a]took two hundred *shekels* of silver, and gave them to
the founder, who made thereof a graven
image and a molten image: and they were
in the house of Micah.
5 And the man Micah had an house of
gods, and made an [a]ephod, and [b]tera-
phim, and [c]consecrated[1] one of his sons,
who became his priest.
6 [a]In those days *there was* no king in
Israel, [b]*but* every man did *that which was*
right in his own eyes.
7 ¶ And there was a young man out of
[a]Bethlehem-judah of the family of Judah,
who *was* a Levite, and he sojourned
there.
8 And the man departed out of the city
from Bethlehem-judah to sojourn where
he could find *a place:* and he came to
mount Ephraim to the house of Micah,
[1]as he journeyed.
9 And Micah said unto him, Whence
comest thou? And he said unto him, I *am*
a Levite of Bethlehem-judah, and I go to
sojourn where I may find *a place.*
10 And Micah said unto him, Dwell
with me, [a]and be unto me a [b]father and a
priest, and I will give thee ten *shekels* of
silver by the year, and [1,2]a suit of apparel,
and thy victuals. So the Levite went in.
11 And the Levite was content to
dwell with the man; and the young man
was unto him as one of his sons.
12 And Micah [a]consecrated the Levite;
and the young man [b]became his priest,
and was in the house of Micah.
13 Then said Micah, Now know I that
the LORD will do me good, seeing I have a
Levite to *my* priest.

Danites overtake Laish

18 IN [a]THOSE days *there was* no
king in Israel: and in those days
[b]the tribe of the Danites sought them an
inheritance to dwell in; for unto that day
all their inheritance had not fallen unto
them among the tribes of Israel.
2 And the children of Dan sent of their
family five men from their coasts, [1]men
of valour, from [a]Zorah, and from Eshtaol,
[b]to spy out the land, and to search it; and
they said unto them, Go, search the land:

who when they came to mount Ephraim, to the [c]house of Micah, they lodged there.

3 When they *were* by the house of Micah, they knew the voice of the young man the Levite: and they turned in thither, and said unto him, Who brought thee hither? and what makest thou in this *place?* and what hast thou here?

4 And he said unto them, Thus and thus dealeth Micah with me, and hath [a]hired me, and I am his priest.

5 And they said unto him, [a]Ask counsel, we pray thee, [b]of God, that we may know whether our way which we go shall be prosperous.

6 And the priest said unto them, [a]Go in peace: before the LORD *is* your way wherein ye go.

7 ¶ Then the five men departed, and came to [a]Laish, and saw the people that *were* therein, [b]how they dwelt careless, after the manner of the Zidonians, quiet and secure; and *there was* no [l]magistrate in the land, that might put *them* to shame in *any* thing; and they *were* far from the Zidonians, and had no business with *any* man.

8 And they came unto their brethren to [a]Zorah and Eshtaol: and their brethren said unto them, What *say* ye?

9 And they said, [a]Arise, that we may go up against them: for we have seen the land, and, behold, it *is* very good: and *are* ye [b]still? be not slothful to go, *and* to enter to possess the land.

10 When ye go, ye shall come unto a people [a]secure, and to a large land: for God hath given it into your hands; [b]a place where *there is* no want of any thing that *is* in the earth.

11 ¶ And there went from thence of the family of the Danites, out of Zorah and out of Eshtaol, six hundred men [l]appointed with weapons of war.

12 And they went up, and pitched in [a]Kirjath-jearim, in Judah: wherefore they called that place [b]Mahaneh-dan unto this day: behold, *it is* behind Kirjath-jearim.

13 And they passed thence unto mount Ephraim, and came unto [a]the house of Micah.

14 ¶ [a]Then answered the five men that went to spy out the country of Laish, and said unto their brethren, Do ye know that [b]there is in these houses an ephod, and teraphim, and a graven image, and a molten image? now therefore consider what ye have to do.

15 And they turned thitherward, and came to the house of the young man the Levite, *even* unto the house of Micah, and [l]saluted him.

16 And the [a]six hundred men appointed with their weapons of war, which *were* of the children of Dan, stood by the entering of the gate.

17 And [a]the five men that went to spy out the land went up, *and* came in thither, *and* took [b]the graven image, and the ephod, and the teraphim, and the molten image: and the priest stood in the entering of the gate with the six hundred men *that were* appointed with weapons of war.

18 And these went into Micah's house, and fetched the carved image, the ephod, and the teraphim, and the molten image. Then said the priest unto them, What do ye?

19 And they said unto him, Hold thy peace, [a]lay thine hand upon thy mouth, and go with us, [b]and be to us a father and a priest: *is it* better for thee to be a priest unto the house of one man, or that thou be a priest unto a tribe and a family in Israel?

20 And the priest's heart was glad, and he took the ephod, and the teraphim, and the graven image, and went in the midst of the people.

21 So they turned and departed, and put the little ones and the cattle and the carriage before them.

22 ¶ *And* when they were a good way from the house of Micah, the men that *were* in the houses near to Micah's house were gathered together, and overtook the children of Dan.

23 And they cried unto the children of Dan. And they turned their faces, and said unto Micah, What aileth thee, [l]that thou comest with such a company?

24 And he said, Ye have taken away my gods which I made, and the priest, and ye are gone away: and what have I more? and what *is* this *that* ye say unto me, What aileth thee?

25 And the children of Dan said unto him, Let not thy voice be heard among us, lest [l]angry fellows run upon thee, and thou lose thy life, with the lives of thy household.

26 And the children of Dan went their

2 [c] ch. 17:1
4 [a] ch. 17:10
5 [a] 1 Ki. 22:5; Is. 30:1; Hos. 4:12 [b] See ch. 17:5 & ver. 14
6 [a] 1 Ki. 22:6
7 [a] Josh. 19:47 called *Leshem* [b] ver. 27,28 [l] Heb. *possessor,* or, *heir of restraint*
8 [a] ver. 2
9 [a] Num. 13:30; Josh. 2:23,24 [b] 1 Ki. 22:3
10 [a] ver. 7,27 [b] Deut. 8:9
11 [l] Heb. *girded*
12 [a] Josh. 15:60 [b] ch. 13:25
13 [a] ver. 2
14 [a] 1 Sam. 14:28 [b] ch. 17:5
15 [l] Heb. *asked him of peace*
16 [a] ver. 11
17 [a] ver. 2,14 [b] ch. 17:4,5
19 [a] Job 21:5 & 29:9 & 40:4; Mic. 7:16 [b] ch. 17:10
23 [l] Heb. *that thou art gathered together?*
25 [l] Heb. *bitter of soul*

way: and when Micah saw that they *were* too strong for him, he turned and went back unto his house.

27 And they took *the things* which Micah had made, and the priest which he had, and came unto Laish, unto a people *that were* at quiet and secure: [a]and they smote them with the edge of the sword, and burnt the city with fire.

28 And *there was* no deliverer, because it *was* [a]far from Zidon, and they had no business with *any* man; and it was in the valley that *lieth* [b]by Beth-rehob. And they built a city, and dwelt therein.

29 And [a]they called the name of the city [b]Dan, after the name of Dan their father, who was born unto Israel: howbeit the name of the city *was* Laish at the first.

30 ¶ And the children of Dan set up the graven image: and Jonathan, the son of Gershom, the son of Manasseh, he and his sons were priests to the tribe of Dan [a]until the day of the captivity of the land.

31 And they set them up Micah's graven image, which he made, [a]all the time that the house of God was in Shiloh.

The Levite and his concubine

19

AND IT came to pass in those days, [a]when *there was* no king in Israel, that there was a certain Levite sojourning on the side of mount Ephraim, who took to him [1]a concubine out of [b]Bethlehem-judah.

2 And his concubine played the whore against him, and went away from him unto her father's house to Bethlehem-judah, and was there [1,2]four whole months.

3 And her husband arose, and went after her, to speak [1]friendly unto her, *and* to bring her again, having his servant with him, and a couple of asses: and she brought him into her father's house: and when the father of the damsel saw him, he rejoiced to meet him.

4 And his father-in-law, the damsel's father, retained him; and he abode with him three days: so they did eat and drink, and lodged there.

5 ¶ And it came to pass on the fourth day, when they arose early in the morning, that he rose up to depart: and the damsel's father said unto his son-in-law, [a]Comfort[1] thine heart with a morsel of bread, and afterward go your way.

6 And they sat down, and did eat and drink both of them together: for the damsel's father had said unto the man, Be content, I pray thee, and tarry all night, and let thine heart be merry.

7 And when the man rose up to depart, his father-in-law urged him: therefore he lodged there again.

8 And he arose early in the morning on the fifth day to depart: and the damsel's father said, Comfort thine heart, I pray thee. And they tarried [1]until afternoon, and they did eat both of them.

9 And when the man rose up to depart, he, and his concubine, and his servant, his father-in-law, the damsel's father, said unto him, Behold, now the day [1]draweth toward evening, I pray you tarry all night: behold, [2]the day groweth to an end, lodge here, that thine heart may be merry; and tomorrow get you early on your way, that thou mayest go [3]home.

10 But the man would not tarry that night, but he rose up and departed, and came [1]over against [a]Jebus, which *is* Jerusalem; and *there were* with him two asses saddled, his concubine also *was* with him.

11 *And* when they *were* by Jebus, the day was far spent; and the servant said unto his master, Come, I pray thee, and let us turn in into this city [a]of the Jebusites, and lodge in it.

12 And his master said unto him, We will not turn aside hither into the city of a stranger, that *is* not of the children of Israel; we will pass over [a]to Gibeah.

13 And he said unto his servant, Come, and let us draw near to one of these places to lodge all night, in Gibeah, or in [a]Ramah.

14 And they passed on and went their way; and the sun went down upon them *when they were* by Gibeah, which *belongeth* to Benjamin.

15 And they turned aside thither, to go in *and* to lodge in Gibeah: and when he went in, he sat him down in a street of the city: for *there was* no man that [a]took them into his house to lodging.

16 ¶ And, behold, there came an old man from [a]his work out of the field at even, which *was* also of mount Ephraim; and he sojourned in Gibeah: but the men of the place *were* Benjamites.

17 And when he had lifted up his eyes, he saw a wayfaring man in the street of

---

27 [a]Josh. 19:47
28 [a]ver. 7 [b]Num. 13:21; 2 Sam. 10:6
29 [a]Josh. 19:47 [b]Gen. 14:14; ch. 20:1; 1 Ki. 12:29, 30 & 15:20
30 [a]ch. 13:1; 1 Sam. 4:2,3,10,11
31 [a]Josh. 18:1; ch. 19:18 & 21:12
19:1 [a]ch. 17:6 & 18:1 & 21:25 [b]ch. 17:7 [1]Heb. *a woman a concubine*, or, *a wife a concubine*
2 [1]Or, *a year and four months* [2]Heb. *days four months*
3 [1]Heb. *to her heart*
5 [a]Gen. 18:5 [1]Heb. *Strengthen*
8 [1]Heb. *till the day declined*
9 [1]Heb. *is weak* [2]Heb. it is *the pitching* time *of the day* [3]Heb. *to thy tent*
10 [a]Josh. 18:28 [1]Heb. *to over against*
11 [a]Josh. 15:8,63
12 [a]Josh. 18:28
13 [a]Josh. 18:25
15 [a]Mat. 25:43
16 [a]Ps. 104:23

the city: and the old man said, Whither goest thou? and whence comest thou?

18 And he said unto him, We *are* passing from Bethlehem-judah toward the side of mount Ephraim; from thence *am* I: and I went to Bethlehem-judah, but I *am now* going to [a]the house of the LORD; and there *is* no man that receiveth me to house.

19 Yet there is both straw and provender for our asses; and there is bread and wine also for me, and for thy handmaid, and for the young man *which is* with thy servants: *there is* no want of any thing.

20 And the old man said, [a]Peace *be* with thee; howsoever *let* all thy wants *lie* upon me; [b]only lodge not in the street.

21 [a]So he brought him into his house, and gave provender unto the asses: [b]and they washed their feet, and did eat and drink.

22 ¶ *Now* as they were making their hearts merry, behold, [a]the men of the city, certain [b]sons of Belial, beset the house round about, *and* beat at the door, and spake to the master of the house, the old man, saying, [c]Bring forth the man that came into thine house, that we may know him.

23 And [a]the man, the master of the house, went out unto them, and said unto them, Nay, my brethren, *nay,* I pray you, do not *so* wickedly; seeing that this man is come into mine house, [b]do not this folly.

24 [a]Behold, *here is* my daughter a maiden, and his concubine; them I will bring out now, and [b]humble ye them, and do with them what seemeth good unto you: but unto this man do not [/]so vile a thing.

25 But the men would not hearken to him: so the man took his concubine, and brought her forth unto them; and they [a]knew her, and abused her all the night until the morning: and when the day began to spring, they let her go.

26 Then came the woman in the dawning of the day, and fell down at the door of the man's house where her lord *was,* till it was light.

27 And her lord rose up in the morning, and opened the doors of the house, and went out to go his way: and, behold, the woman his concubine was fallen down *at* the door of the house, and her hands *were* upon the threshold.

28 And he said unto her, Up, and let us be going. But [a]none answered. Then the man took her *up* upon an ass, and the man rose up, and gat him unto his place.

29 ¶ And when he was come into his house, he took a knife, and laid hold on his concubine, and [a]divided her, *together* with her bones, into twelve pieces, and sent her into all the coasts of Israel.

30 And it was so, that all that saw it said, There was no such deed done nor seen from the day that the children of Israel came up out of the land of Egypt unto this day: consider of it, [a]take advice, and speak *your minds.*

The rout of Benjamin

20 THEN [a]ALL the children of Israel went out, and the congregation was gathered together as one man, from [b]Dan even to Beer-sheba, with the land of Gilead, unto the LORD [c]in Mizpeh.

2 And the chief of all the people, *even* of all the tribes of Israel, presented themselves in the assembly of the people of God, four hundred thousand footmen [a]that drew sword.

3 (Now the children of Benjamin heard that the children of Israel were gone up to Mizpeh.) Then said the children of Israel, Tell *us,* how was this wickedness?

4 And [/]the Levite, the husband of the woman that was slain, answered and said, [a]I came into Gibeah that *belongeth* to Benjamin, I and my concubine, to lodge.

5 [a]And the men of Gibeah rose against me, and beset the house round about upon me by night, *and* thought to have slain me: [b]and my concubine have they [/]forced, that she is dead.

6 And [a]I took my concubine, and cut her in pieces, and sent her throughout all the country of the inheritance of Israel: for they [b]have committed lewdness and folly in Israel.

7 Behold, ye *are* all children of Israel; [a]give here your advice and counsel.

8 ¶ And all the people arose as one man, saying, We will not any *of us* go to his tent, neither will we any *of us* turn into his house.

9 But now this *shall be* the thing which we will do to Gibeah; *we will go up* by lot against it;

10 And we will take ten men of an hundred throughout all the tribes of Is-

18 [a]Josh. 18:1; ch. 18:31 & 20:18; 1 Sam. 1:3,7

20 [a]Gen 43:23; ch. 6:23 [b]Gen. 19:2

21 [a]Gen. 24:32 & 43:24 [b]Gen. 18:4; John 13:5

22 [a]Gen. 19:4; ch. 20:5; Hos. 9:9 & 10:9 [b]Deut. 13:13 [c]Gen 19:5; Rom. 1:26,27

23 [a]Gen. 19:6,7 [b]2 Sam. 13:12

24 [a]Gen. 19:8 [b]Gen. 34:2; Deut. 21:14 [/]Heb. *the matter of this folly*

25 [a]Gen. 4:1

28 [a]ch. 20:5

29 [a]ch. 20:6; See 1 Sam. 11:7

30 [a]ch. 20:7

20:1 [a]ver. 11; Josh. 22:12; ch. 21:5; 1 Sam. 11:7 [b]ch. 18:29; 1 Sam. 3:20; 2 Sam. 3:10 & 24:2 [c]Judg. 10:17 & 11:11; 1 Sam. 7:5 & 10:17

2 [a]ch. 8:10

4 [a]ch. 19:15 [/]Heb. *the man the Levite*

5 [a]ch. 19:22 [b]ch. 19:25,26 [/]Heb. *humbled*

6 [a]ch. 19:29 [b]Josh. 7:15

7 [a]ch. 19:30

rael, and an hundred of a thousand, and a thousand out of ten thousand, to fetch victual for the people, that they may do, when they come to Gibeah of Benjamin, according to all the folly that they have wrought in Israel.

11 So all the men of Israel were gathered against the city, [1]knit together as one man.

12 ¶ [a]And the tribes of Israel sent men through all the tribe of Benjamin, saying, What wickedness *is* this that is done among you?

13 Now therefore deliver *us* the men, [a]the children of Belial, which *are* in Gibeah, that we may put them to death, and [b]put away evil from Israel. But the children of Benjamin would not hearken to the voice of their brethren the children of Israel:

14 But the children of Benjamin gathered themselves together out of the cities unto Gibeah, to go out to battle against the children of Israel.

15 And the children of Benjamin were numbered at that time out of the cities twenty and six thousand men that drew sword, beside the inhabitants of Gibeah, which were numbered seven hundred chosen men.

16 Among all this people *there were* seven hundred chosen men [a]lefthanded; every one could sling stones at an hair *breadth,* and not miss.

17 And the men of Israel, beside Benjamin, were numbered four hundred thousand men that drew sword: all these *were* men of war.

18 ¶ And the children of Israel arose, and [a]went up to the house of God, and [b]asked counsel of God, and said, Which of us shall go up first to the battle against the children of Benjamin? And the LORD said, Judah *shall go up* first.

19 And the children of Israel rose up in the morning, and encamped against Gibeah.

20 And the men of Israel went out to battle against Benjamin; and the men of Israel put themselves in array to fight against them at Gibeah.

21 And [a]the children of Benjamin came forth out of Gibeah, and destroyed down to the ground of the Israelites that day twenty and two thousand men.

22 And the people the men of Israel encouraged themselves, and set their battle again in array in the place where they put themselves in array the first day.

23 ([a]And the children of Israel went up and wept before the LORD until even, and asked counsel of the LORD, saying, Shall I go up again to battle against the children of Benjamin my brother? And the LORD said, Go up against him.)

24 And the children of Israel came near against the children of Benjamin the second day.

25 And [a]Benjamin went forth against them out of Gibeah the second day, and destroyed down to the ground of the children of Israel again eighteen thousand men; all these drew the sword.

26 ¶ Then all the children of Israel, and all the people, [a]went up, and came unto the house of God, and wept, and sat there before the LORD, and fasted that day until even, and offered burnt offerings and peace offerings before the LORD.

27 And the children of Israel inquired of the LORD, (for [a]the ark of the covenant of God *was* there in those days,

28 [a]And Phinehas, the son of Eleazar, ❙
the son of Aaron, [b]stood before it in those days,) saying, Shall I yet again go out to battle against the children of Benjamin my brother, or shall I cease? And the LORD said, Go up; for tomorrow I will deliver them into thine hand.

29 And Israel [a]set liers in wait round about Gibeah.

30 And the children of Israel went up against the children of Benjamin on the third day, and put themselves in array against Gibeah, as at other times.

31 And the children of Benjamin went out against the people, *and* were drawn away from the city; and they began [1]to smite of the people, *and* kill, as at other times, in the highways, of which one goeth up to [2]the house of God, and the other to Gibeah in the field, about thirty men of Israel.

32 And the children of Benjamin said, They *are* smitten down before us, as at the first. But the children of Israel said, Let us flee, and draw them from the city unto the highways.

33 And all the men of Israel rose up out of their place, and put themselves in array at Baal-tamar: and the liers in wait

11 [1]Heb. *fellows*

12 [a]Deut. 13:14; Josh. 22:13,16

13 [a]Deut. 13:13; ch. 19:22 [b]Deut. 17:12

16 [a]ch. 3:15; 1 Chr. 12:2

18 [a]ver. 23,26 [b]Num. 27:21; ch. 1:1

21 [a]Gen. 49:27

23 [a]ver. 26,27

25 [a]ver. 21

26 [a]ver. 18

27 [a]Josh. 18:1; 1 Sam. 4:3,4

28 [a]Josh. 24:33 [b]Deut. 10:8 & 18:5

29 [a]See Josh. 8:4

31 [1]Heb. *to smite of the people wounded as at* [2]Or, *Beth-el*

of Israel came forth out of their places,
even out of the meadows of Gibeah.
34 And there came against Gibeah ten
thousand chosen men out of all Israel,
and the battle was sore: [a]but they knew
not that evil *was* near them.
35 And the LORD smote Benjamin before Israel: and the children of Israel destroyed of the Benjamites that day twenty
and five thousand and an hundred men:
all these drew the sword.
36 So the children of Benjamin saw
that they were smitten: [a]for the men of
Israel gave place to the Benjamites, because they trusted unto the liers in wait
which they had set beside Gibeah.
37 [a]And the liers in wait hasted, and
rushed upon Gibeah; and the liers in wait
[1]drew *themselves* along, and smote all
the city with the edge of the sword.
38 Now there was an appointed [1]sign
between the men of Israel [2]and the liers
in wait, that they should make a great
[3]flame with smoke rise up out of the city.
39 And when the men of Israel retired
in the battle, Benjamin began [1]to smite
and kill of the men of Israel about thirty
persons: for they said, Surely they are
smitten down before us, as *in* the first
battle.
40 But when the flame began to arise
up out of the city with a pillar of smoke,
the Benjamites [a]looked behind them,
and, behold, [1]the flame of the city ascended up to heaven.
41 And when the men of Israel turned
again, the men of Benjamin were
amazed: for they saw that evil [1]was come
upon them.
42 Therefore they turned *their backs*
before the men of Israel unto the way of
the wilderness; but the battle overtook
them; and them which *came* out of the
cities they destroyed in the midst of
them.
43 *Thus* they inclosed the Benjamites
round about, *and* chased them, *and* trode
them down [1]with ease [2]over against Gibeah toward the sunrising.
44 And there fell of Benjamin eighteen
thousand men; all these *were* men of
valour.
45 And they turned and fled toward
the wilderness unto the rock of [a]Rim-
mon: and they gleaned of them in the
highways five thousand men; and pursued hard after them unto Gidom, and
slew two thousand men of them.
46 So that all which fell that day of
Benjamin were twenty and five thousand
men that drew the sword; all these *were*
men of valour.
47 [a]But six hundred men turned and
fled to the wilderness unto the rock Rimmon, and abode in the rock Rimmon four
months.
48 And the men of Israel turned again
upon the children of Benjamin, and
smote them with the edge of the sword,
as well the men of *every* city, as the
beast, and all that [1]came to hand: also
they set on fire all the cities that [2]they
came to.

Wives for the Benjaminites

21 NOW [a]THE men of Israel had
sworn in Mizpeh, saying, There
shall not any of us give his daughter unto
Benjamin to wife.
2 And the people came [a]to the house
of God, and abode there till even before
God, and lifted up their voices, and wept
sore;
3 And said, O LORD God of Israel, why
is this come to pass in Israel, that there
should be today one tribe lacking in
Israel?
4 And it came to pass on the morrow,
that the people rose early, and [a]built
there an altar, and offered burnt offerings
and peace offerings.
5 And the children of Israel said, Who
is there among all the tribes of Israel that
came not up with the congregation unto
the LORD? [a]For they had made a great oath
concerning him that came not up to the
LORD to Mizpeh, saying, He shall surely be
put to death.
6 And the children of Israel repented
them for Benjamin their brother, and
said, There is one tribe cut off from Israel
this day.
7 How shall we do for wives for them
that remain, seeing we have sworn by
the LORD that we will not give them of our
daughters to wives?
8 ¶ And they said, What one *is there* of
the tribes of Israel that came not up to
Mizpeh to the LORD? And, behold, there
came none to the camp from [a]Jabesh-gil-
ead to the assembly.
9 For the people were numbered, and,

34 [a]Josh. 8:14; Is. 47:11
36 [a]Josh. 8:15
37 [a]Josh. 8:19 [1]Or, *made a long* sound with the trumpet
38 [1]Or, *time* [2]Heb. *with* [3]Heb. *elevation*
39 [1]Heb. *to smite the wounded*
40 [a]Josh. 8:20 [1]Heb. *the whole consumption*
41 [1]Heb. *touched them*
43 [1]Or, from Menuchah [2]Heb. *unto over against*
45 [a]Josh. 15:32
47 [a]ch. 21:13
48 [1]Heb. *was found* [2]Heb. *were found*
21:1 [a]ch. 20:1
2 [a]ch. 20:18,26
4 [a]2 Sam. 24:25
5 [a]ch. 5:23
8 [a]1 Sam 11:1 & 31:11

behold, *there were* none of the inhabitants of Jabesh-gilead there.
10 And the congregation sent thither
twelve thousand men of the valiantest,
and commanded them, saying, [a]Go and
smite the inhabitants of Jabesh-gilead
with the edge of the sword, with the
women and the children.
11 And this *is* the thing that ye shall
do, [a]Ye shall utterly destroy every male,
and every woman that [1]hath lain by man.
12 And they found among the inhabitants of Jabesh-gilead four hundred
[1]young virgins, that had known no man
by lying with any male: and they brought
them unto the camp to [a]Shiloh, which *is*
in the land of Canaan.
13 And the whole congregation sent
some [1]to speak to the children of Benjamin [a]that *were* in the rock Rimmon, and
to [b]call[2] peaceably unto them.
14 And Benjamin came again at that
time; and they gave them wives which
they had saved alive of the women of Jabesh-gilead: and yet so they sufficed them
not.
15 And the people [a]repented them for
Benjamin, because that the LORD had
made a breach in the tribes of Israel.
16 ¶ Then the elders of the congregation said, How shall we do for wives for
them that remain, seeing the women are
destroyed out of Benjamin?
17 And they said, *There must be* an
inheritance for them that be escaped of
Benjamin, that a tribe be not destroyed
out of Israel.
18 Howbeit we may not give them
wives of our daughters: [a]for the children
of Israel have sworn, saying, Cursed *be*
he that giveth a wife to Benjamin.
19 Then they said, Behold, *there is* a
feast of the LORD in Shiloh [1]yearly *in a*
place which *is* on the north side of Beth-
el, [2]on the east side [3]of the highway that
goeth up from Beth-el to Shechem, and
on the south of Lebonah.
20 Therefore they commanded the
children of Benjamin, saying, Go and lie
in wait in the vineyards;
21 And see, and, behold, if the daughters of Shiloh come out [a]to dance in
dances, then come ye out of the vineyards, and catch you every man his wife
of the daughters of Shiloh, and go to the
land of Benjamin.
22 And it shall be, when their fathers
or their brethren come unto us to complain, that we will say unto them, [1]Be
favourable unto them for our sakes: because we reserved not to each man his
wife in the war: for ye did not give unto
them at this time, *that* ye should be
guilty.
23 And the children of Benjamin did
so, and took *them* wives, according to
their number, of them that danced,
whom they caught: and they went and
returned unto their inheritance, and [a]re-
paired the cities, and dwelt in them.
24 And the children of Israel departed
thence at that time, every man to his
tribe and to his family, and they went
out from thence every man to his inheritance.
25 [a]In those days *there was* no king in
Israel: [b]every man did *that which was*
right in his own eyes.

10 [a]ver. 5; ch. 5:23; 1 Sam. 11:7
11 [a]Num. 31:17 [1]Heb. *knoweth the lying* with *man*
12 [a]Josh. 18:1 [1]Heb. *young women virgins*
13 [a]ch. 20:47 [b]Deut. 20:10 [1]Heb. *and spake and called* [2]Or, *proclaim peace*
15 [a]ver. 6
18 [a]ver. 1; ch. 11:35
19 [1]Heb. *from year to year* [2]Or, *toward the sunrising* [3]Or, *on*
21 [a]See Ex. 15:20; ch. 11:34; 1 Sam. 18:6
22 [1]Or, *Gratify us in them*
23 [a]See ch. 20:48
25 [a]ch. 17:6 & 18:1 & 19:1 [b]Deut. 12:8; ch. 17:6

Ruth

Author: Unknown

Theme: Devotion yields redemption and restoration

Date of Writing: c. 1000 B.C.

Outline of Ruth

I. Ruth's Selfless Decision (1:1–22)
II. Ruth's Favorable Reception (2:1—3:18)
III. Ruth's Compassionate Redemption (4:1–22)

THIS BOOK IS named after a young woman from Moab named Ruth, the great-grandmother of David and ancestress of Jesus (see 4: 22; Mt 1:1, 5). During a famine in Israel, Elimelech, Naomi and their two sons had abandoned their home in Bethlehem to find food in Moab. While they were there, Ruth met and married one of the sons. Years later, Naomi's and Ruth's husbands died, leaving both women widowed and stranded in Moab. Naomi chose to return to Bethlehem, and Ruth went with her. The book recounts this short story with charming simplicity and further chronicles Ruth's life in Bethlehem, her courtship and marriage, and the birth of her son Obed, the grandfather of King David.

Ancient Jewish manuscripts considered the book of Ruth and the book of Judges as one volume because the events in Ruth occurred during the period of the judges. Later Jewish manuscripts separated the two volumes and included Ruth, because of its literary beauty and subject matter, in a five-book grouping called the megilloth. According to Jewish custom certain books were to be read aloud in the synagogues (see Lk 4:16–17). The books of the megilloth were usually read at feast seasons, with the book of Ruth scheduled to be read at the Feast of Weeks (Pentecost).

The exact dating of this book is uncertain, but because the author explained customs that seemed unfamiliar to readers (see 4:6–8) many scholars believe this book was composed during the time of King David. Note also the reference to David's lineage in the last chapter (see 4:17–22)—a commonplace identifier used during the monarchical period.

Naomi and Ruth

1 NOW IT came to pass in the days when [a]the judges [1]ruled, that there was [b]a famine in the land. And a certain man of [c]Bethlehem-judah went to sojourn in the country of Moab, he, and his wife, and his two sons.

2 And the name of the man *was* Elimelech, and the name of his wife Naomi, and the name of his two sons Mahlon and Chilion, [a]Ephrathites of Bethlehem-judah. And they came [b]into the country of Moab, and [1]continued there.

3 And Elimelech Naomi's husband died; and she was left, and her two sons.

4 And they took them wives of the women of Moab; the name of the one *was* Orpah, and the name of the other Ruth: and they dwelled there about ten years.

5 And Mahlon and Chilion died also both of them; and the woman was left of her two sons and her husband.

F 6 ¶ Then she arose with her daughters-in-law, that she might return from the country of Moab: for she had heard in the country of Moab how that the LORD had [a]visited his people in [b]giving them bread.

7 Wherefore she went forth out of the place where she was, and her two daughters-in-law with her; and they went on the way to return unto the land of Judah.

8 And Naomi said unto her two daughters-in-law, [a]Go, return each to her mother's house: [b]the LORD deal kindly with you, as ye have dealt with [c]the dead, and with me.

9 The LORD grant you that ye may find [a]rest, each *of you* in the house of her husband. Then she kissed them; and they lifted up their voice, and wept.

10 And they said unto her, Surely we will return with thee unto thy people.

11 And Naomi said, Turn again, my daughters: why will ye go with me? *are* there yet *any more* sons in my womb, [a]that they may be your husbands?

12 Turn again, my daughters, go *your way;* for I am too old to have an husband. If I should say, I have hope, [1]*if* I should have an husband also tonight, and should also bear sons;

13 Would ye [1]tarry for them till they were grown? would ye stay for them from having husbands? nay, my daughters; for [2]it grieveth me much for your sakes that [a]the hand of the LORD is gone out against me.

14 And they lifted up their voice, and wept again: and Orpah kissed her mother-in-law; but Ruth [a]clave unto her.

15 And she said, Behold, thy sister-in-law is gone back unto her people, and unto [a]her gods: [b]return thou after thy sister-in-law.

16 And Ruth said, [a]Entreat[1] me not to leave thee, *or* to return from following after thee: for whither thou goest, I will go; and where thou lodgest, I will lodge: [b]thy people *shall be* my people, and thy God my God:

17 Where thou diest, will I die, and there will I be buried: [a]the LORD do so to me, and more also, *if aught* but death part thee and me.

18 [a]When she saw that she [1]was stedfastly minded to go with her, then she left speaking unto her.

19 ¶ So they two went until they came to Bethlehem. And it came to pass, when they were come to Bethlehem, that [a]all the city was moved about them, and they said, [b]*Is* this Naomi?

20 And she said unto them, Call me not [1]Naomi, call me [2]Mara: for the Almighty hath dealt very bitterly with me.

21 I went out full, [a]and the LORD hath brought me home again empty: why *then* call ye me Naomi, seeing the LORD hath testified against me, and the Almighty hath afflicted me?

22 So Naomi returned, and Ruth the Moabitess, her daughter-in-law, with her, which returned out of the country of Moab: and they came to Bethlehem [a]in the beginning of barley harvest.

Boaz speaks with Ruth

2 AND NAOMI had a [a]kinsman of her husband's, a mighty man of wealth, of the family of Elimelech; and his name *was* [b]Boaz.[1]

2 And Ruth the Moabitess said unto Naomi, Let me now go to the field, and [a]glean ears of corn after *him* in whose sight I shall find grace. And she said unto her, Go, my daughter.

3 And she went, and came, and gleaned in the field after the reapers: and her [1]hap was to light on a part of the field *belonging* unto Boaz, who *was* of the kindred of Elimelech.

1:1 [a]Judg. 2:16 [b]Gen. 12:10 & 26:1; 2 Ki. 8:1 [c]Judg. 17:8 [1]Heb. *judged*
2 [a]Gen. 35:19 [b]Judg. 3:30 [1]Heb. *were*
6 [a]Ex. 4:31; Luke 1:68 [b]Mat. 6:11
8 [a]See Josh. 24:15 [b]2 Tim. 1:16-18 [c]ver. 5; ch. 2:20
9 [a]ch. 3:1
11 [a]Gen. 38:11; Deut. 25:5
12 [1]Or, if *I were with an husband*
13 [a]Judg. 2:15; Job 19:21 [1]Heb. *hope* [2]Heb. *I have much bitterness*
14 [a]Prov. 17:17 & 18:24
15 [a]Judg. 11:24 [b]See Josh. 24:15, 19; 2 Ki. 2:2; Luke 24:28
16 [a]2 Ki. 2:2,4,6 [b]ch. 2:11,12 [1]Or, *Be not against me*
17 [a]1 Sam. 3:17 & 25:22; 2 Sam. 19:13; 2 Ki. 6:31
18 [a]Acts 21:14 [1]Heb. *strengthened herself*
19 [a]Mat. 21:10 [b]See Is. 23:7; Lam. 2:15
20 [1]i.e. *Pleasant* [2]i.e. *Bitter*
21 [a]Job 1:21
22 [a]Ex. 9:31,32; ch. 2:23; 2 Sam. 21:9
2:1 [a]ch. 3:2,12 [b]ch. 4:21 [1]Called *Booz* in Mat. 1:5
2 [a]Lev. 19:9; Deut. 24:19
3 [1]Heb. *hap happened*

4 ¶ And, behold, Boaz came from Bethlehem, and said unto the reapers, [a]The LORD *be* with you. And they answered him, The LORD bless thee.

5 Then said Boaz unto his servant that was set over the reapers, Whose damsel *is* this?

6 And the servant that was set over the reapers answered and said, It *is* the Moabitish damsel [a]that came back with Naomi out of the country of Moab:

7 And she said, I pray you, let me glean and gather after the reapers among the sheaves: so she came, and hath continued even from the morning until now, that she tarried a little in the house.

8 Then said Boaz unto Ruth, Hearest thou not, my daughter? Go not to glean in another field, neither go from hence, but abide here fast by my maidens:

9 *Let* thine eyes *be* on the field that they do reap, and go thou after them: have I not charged the young men that they shall not touch thee? and when thou art athirst, go unto the vessels, and drink of *that* which the young men have drawn.

10 Then she [a]fell on her face, and bowed herself to the ground, and said unto him, Why have I found grace in thine eyes, that thou shouldest take knowledge of me, seeing I *am* a stranger?

11 And Boaz answered and said unto her, It hath fully been shown me, [a]all that thou hast done unto thy mother-in-law since the death of thine husband: and *how* thou hast left thy father and thy mother, and the land of thy nativity, and art come unto a people which thou knewest not heretofore.

K 12 [a]The LORD recompense thy work, and a full reward be given thee of the LORD God of Israel, [b]under whose wings thou art come to trust.

13 Then she said, [a]Let[1] me find favour in thy sight, my lord; for that thou hast comforted me, and for that thou hast spoken [2]friendly unto thine handmaid, [b]though I be not like unto one of thine handmaidens.

14 And Boaz said unto her, At mealtime come thou hither, and eat of the bread, and dip thy morsel in the vinegar. And she sat beside the reapers: and he reached her parched *corn,* and she did eat, and [a]was sufficed, and left.

15 And when she was risen up to glean, Boaz commanded his young men, saying, Let her glean even among the sheaves, and [1]reproach her not:

16 And let fall also *some* of the handfuls of purpose for her, and leave *them,* that she may glean *them,* and rebuke her not.

17 So she gleaned in the field until even, and beat out that she had gleaned: and it was about an ephah of barley.

18 ¶ And she took *it* up, and went into the city: and her mother-in-law saw what she had gleaned: and she brought forth, and gave to her [a]that she had reserved after she was sufficed.

19 And her mother-in-law said unto her, Where hast thou gleaned today? and where wroughtest thou? blessed be he that did [a]take knowledge of thee. And she showed her mother-in-law with whom she had wrought, and said, The man's name with whom I wrought today *is* Boaz.

20 And Naomi said unto her daughter-in-law, [a]Blessed *be* he of the LORD, who [b]hath not left off his kindness to the living and to the dead. And Naomi said unto her, The man *is* near of kin unto us, [c]one[1] of our next kinsmen.

21 And Ruth the Moabitess said, He said unto me also, Thou shalt keep fast by my young men, until they have ended all my harvest.

22 And Naomi said unto Ruth her daughter-in-law, *It is* good, my daughter, that thou go out with his maidens, that they [1]meet thee not in any other field.

23 So she kept fast by the maidens of Boaz to glean unto the end of barley harvest and of wheat harvest; and dwelt with her mother-in-law.

Ruth visits Boaz

3 THEN NAOMI her mother-in-law said unto her, My daughter, [a]shall I not seek [b]rest for thee, that it may be well with thee?

2 And now *is* not Boaz of our kindred, [a]with whose maidens thou wast? Behold, he winnoweth barley tonight in the threshingfloor.

3 Wash thyself therefore, [a]and anoint thee, and put thy raiment upon thee, and get thee down to the floor: *but* make not

4 [a]Luke 1:28; 2 Thes. 3:16
6 [a]ch. 1:22
10 [a]1 Sam. 25:23
11 [a]ch. 1:14,16,17
12 [a]1 Sam. 24:19 [b]ch. 1:16; Ps. 17:8
13 [a]Gen. 33:15; 1 Sam. 1:18 [b]1 Sam. 25:41 [1]Or, *I find favour* [2]Heb. *to the heart*
14 [a]ver. 18
15 [1]Heb. *shame her not*
18 [a]ver. 14
19 [a]ver. 10; Ps. 41:1
20 [a]ch. 3:10; 2 Sam. 2:5; Job 29:13 [b]Prov. 17:17 [c]ch. 3:9 & 4:6 [1]Or, *one that hath right to redeem*
22 [1]Or, *fall upon thee*
3:1 [a]1 Cor. 7:36; 1 Tim. 5:8 [b]ch. 1:9
2 [a]ch. 2:8
3 [a]2 Sam. 14:2

thyself known unto the man, until he shall have done eating and drinking.

4 And it shall be, when he lieth down, that thou shalt mark the place where he shall lie, and thou shalt go in, and [l]uncover his feet, and lay thee down; and he will tell thee what thou shalt do.

5 And she said unto her, All that thou sayest unto me I will do.

6 ¶ And she went down unto the floor, and did according to all that her mother-in-law bade her.

7 And when Boaz had eaten and drunk, and [a]his heart was merry, he went to lie down at the end of the heap of corn: and she came softly, and uncovered his feet, and laid her down.

8 ¶ And it came to pass at midnight, that the man was afraid, and [l]turned himself: and, behold, a woman lay at his feet.

9 And he said, Who *art* thou? And she answered, I *am* Ruth thine handmaid: [a]spread therefore thy skirt over thine handmaid; for thou *art* [b]a [l] near kinsman.

10 And he said, [a]Blessed *be* thou of the LORD, my daughter: *for* thou hast shown more kindness in the latter end than [b]at the beginning, inasmuch as thou followedst not young men, whether poor or rich.

11 And now, my daughter, fear not; I will do to thee all that thou requirest: for all the [l]city of my people doth know that thou *art* [a]a virtuous woman.

12 And now it is true that I *am thy* [a]near kinsman: howbeit [b]there is a kinsman nearer than I.

13 Tarry this night, and it shall be in the morning, *that* if he will [a]perform unto thee the part of a kinsman, well; let him do the kinsman's part: but if he will not do the part of a kinsman to thee, then will I do the part of a kinsman to thee, [b]*as* the LORD liveth: lie down until the morning.

14 ¶ And she lay at his feet until the morning: and she rose up before one could know another. And he said, [a]Let it not be known that a woman came into the floor.

15 Also he said, Bring the [l]veil that *thou hast* upon thee, and hold it. And when she held it, he measured six *measures* of barley, and laid *it* on her: and she went into the city.

16 And when she came to her mother-in-law, she said, Who *art* thou, my daughter? And she told her all that the man had done to her.

17 And she said, These six *measures* of barley gave he me; for he said to me, Go not empty unto thy mother-in-law.

18 Then said she, [a]Sit still, my daughter, until thou know how the matter will fall: for the man will not be in rest, until he have finished the thing this day.

Boaz and Ruth marry

4 THEN WENT Boaz up to the gate, and sat him down there: and, behold, [a]the kinsman of whom Boaz spake came by; unto whom he said, Ho, such a one! turn aside, sit down here. And he turned aside, and sat down.

2 And he took ten men of [a]the elders of the city, and said, Sit ye down here. And they sat down.

3 And he said unto the kinsman, Naomi, that is come again out of the country of Moab, selleth a parcel of land, which *was* our brother Elimelech's:

4 And [l]I thought to advertise thee, saying, [a]Buy *it* [b]before the inhabitants, and before the elders of my people. If thou wilt redeem *it,* redeem *it:* but if thou wilt not redeem *it, then* tell me, that I may know: [c]for *there is* none to redeem *it* beside thee; and I *am* after thee. And he said, I will redeem *it.*

5 Then said Boaz, What day thou buyest the field of the hand of Naomi, thou must buy *it* also of Ruth the Moabitess, the wife of the dead, [a]to raise up the name of the dead upon his inheritance.

6 ¶ [a]And the kinsman said, I cannot redeem *it* for myself, lest I mar mine own inheritance: redeem thou my right to thyself; for I cannot redeem *it.*

7 [a]Now this *was the manner* in former time in Israel concerning redeeming and concerning changing, for to confirm all things; a man plucked off his shoe, and gave *it* to his neighbour: and this *was* a testimony in Israel.

8 Therefore the kinsman said unto Boaz, Buy *it* for thee. So he drew off his shoe.

9 ¶ And Boaz said unto the elders, and *unto* all the people, Ye *are* witnesses this day, that I have bought all that *was* Elimelech's, and all that *was* Chilion's and Mahlon's, of the hand of Naomi.

10 Moreover Ruth the Moabitess, the

4 [l]Or, *lift up the clothes that are on his feet*
7 [a]Judg. 19:6,9,22; 2 Sam. 13:28; Esth. 1:10
8 [l]Or, *took hold on*
9 [a]Ezek. 16:8 [b]ver. 12; ch. 2:20 [l]Or, *one that hath right to redeem*
10 [a]ch. 2:20 [b]ch. 1:8
11 [a]Prov. 12:4 [l]Heb. *gate*
12 [a]ver. 9 [b]ch. 4:1
13 [a]Deut. 25:5; ch. 4:5; Mat. 22:24 [b]Judg. 8:19; Jer. 4:2
14 [a]Rom. 12:17 & 14:16; 1 Cor. 10:32; 2 Cor. 8:21; 1 Thes. 5:22
15 [l]Or, *sheet,* or *apron*
18 [a]Ps. 37:3,5
4:1 [a]ch. 3:12
2 [a]1 Ki. 21:8; Prov. 31:23
4 [a]Jer. 32:7,8 [b]Gen. 23:18 [c]Lev. 25:25 [l]Heb. *I said I will reveal in thine ear*
5 [a]Gen. 38:8; Deut. 25:5,6; ch. 3:13; Mat. 22:24
6 [a]ch. 3:12,13
7 [a]Deut. 25:7,9

wife of Mahlon, have I purchased to be my wife, to raise up the name of the dead upon his inheritance, [a]that the name of the dead be not cut off from among his brethren, and from the gate of his place: ye *are* witnesses this day.

11 And all the people that *were* in the gate, and the elders, said, *We are* witnesses. [a]The LORD make the woman that is come into thine house like Rachel and like Leah, which two did [b]build the house of Israel: and [1]do thou worthily in [c]Ephratah, and [2]be famous in Bethlehem:

12 And let thy house be like the house of Pharez, [a]whom Tamar bare unto Judah, of [b]the seed which the LORD shall give thee of this young woman.

Obed is born: the Davidic line

13 ¶ So Boaz [a]took Ruth, and she was his wife: and when he went in unto her, [b]the LORD gave her conception, and she bare a son.

14 And [a]the women said unto Naomi, Blessed *be* the LORD, which hath not [1]left thee this day without a [2]kinsman, that his name may be famous in Israel.

15 And he shall be unto thee a restorer of *thy* life, and [1]a nourisher of [2]thine old age: for thy daughter-in-law, which loveth thee, which is [a]better to thee than seven sons, hath borne him.

16 And Naomi took the child, and laid it in her bosom, and became nurse unto it.

17 [a]And the women her neighbours gave it a name, saying, There is a son born to Naomi; and they called his name Obed: he *is* the father of Jesse, the father of David.

18 ¶ Now these *are* the generations of Pharez: [a]Pharez begat Hezron,

19 And Hezron begat Ram, and Ram begat Amminadab,

20 And Amminadab begat [a]Nahshon, and Nahshon begat [b]Salmon,[1]

21 And Salmon begat Boaz, and Boaz begat Obed,

22 And Obed begat Jesse, and Jesse begat [a]David.

10 [a]Deut. 25:6

11 [a]Ps. 127:3 & 128:3 [b]Deut. 25:9 [c]Gen. 35:16 [1]Or, *get thee riches,* or, *power* [2]Heb. *proclaim* thy name

12 [a]1 Chr. 2:4; Mat. 1:3 [b]1 Sam. 2:20

13 [a]ch. 3:11 [b]Gen. 29:31

14 [a]Luke 1:58 [1]Heb. *caused to cease unto thee* [2]Or, *redeemer*

15 [a]1 Sam. 1:8 [1]Heb. *to nourish* [2]Heb. *thy gray hairs*

17 [a]Luke 1:58

18 [a]1 Chr. 2:4

20 [a]Num. 1:7 [b]Mat. 1:4 [1]Or, *Salmah*

22 [a]1 Chr. 2:15; Mat. 1:6

1 Samuel

Author: Unknown

Theme: The careers of Samuel, Saul and David

Date of Writing: c. 925 B.C.

Outline of 1 Samuel

I. Samuel's Birth, Call and Training (1:1—4:22)
II. Samuel's Role as Judge and Deliverer (5:1—8:22)
III. A King Is Anointed and Ultimately Rejected (9:1—15:35)
IV. Saul's Descent and David's Rise (16:1—30:31)
V. Saul's Death (31:1–13)

ORIGINALLY THE BOOKS of 1 and 2 Samuel were contained on one scroll and considered one volume. Translators of the Greek version of the OT (Septuagint) divided this large book into two parts, referring to them as "The First and Second Books of Kingdoms." However, Hebrew tradition and most modern versions refer to these books as 1 and 2 Samuel since Samuel, more than any other individual during that time period, helped Israel maintain their covenantal relationship with God during the transition from the judges to the monarchy.

Together the books of 1 and 2 Samuel chronicle a seamless history of the establishment of the kingdom of Israel and the foundation of the Hebrew monarchy. The books open with the birth of Samuel during the time of Eli, the high priest, judge and governor of Israel at Shiloh. Several chapters record Samuel's influential career as prophet, priest and judge over Israel and detail the emergence of the monarchy as they describe the anointing of first Saul and then David as Israel's kings. The final chapters of 1 Samuel record Saul's disobedience and sins of presumption that bring about God's rejection of him as king and the anointing of God's replacement, David. Well-known stories in this book include the account of Hannah's infertility (ch. 1), David and Goliath (ch. 17), David and Jonathan (ch. 18) and Saul and the séance at Endor (ch. 28).

Samuel's birth

1 NOW THERE was a certain man of Ramathaim-zophim, of mount Ephraim, and his name *was* [a]Elkanah, the son of Jeroham, the son of Elihu, the son of Tohu, the son of Zuph, [b]an Ephrathite:

2 And he had two wives; the name of the one *was* Hannah, and the name of the other Peninnah: and Peninnah had children, but Hannah had no children.

3 And this man went up out of his city [a]yearly[1] [b]to worship and to sacrifice unto the LORD of hosts in [c]Shiloh. And the two sons of Eli, Hophni and Phinehas, the priests of the LORD, *were* there.

4 ¶ And when the time was that Elkanah [a]offered, he gave to Peninnah his wife, and to all her sons and her daughters, portions:

E 5 But unto Hannah he gave [1]a worthy portion; for he loved Hannah: [a]but the LORD had shut up her womb.

6 And her adversary also [a]provoked[1] her sore, for to make her fret, because the LORD had shut up her womb.

7 And *as* he did so year by year, [1,2]when she went up to the house of the LORD, so she provoked her; therefore she wept, and did not eat.

8 Then said Elkanah her husband to her, Hannah, why weepest thou? and why eatest thou not? and why is thy heart grieved? *am* not I [a]better to thee than ten sons?

9 ¶ So Hannah rose up after they had eaten in Shiloh, and after they had drunk. Now Eli the priest sat upon a seat by a post of [a]the temple of the LORD.

10 [a]And she *was* [1]in bitterness of soul, and prayed unto the LORD, and wept sore.

11 And she [a]vowed a vow, and said, O LORD of hosts, if thou wilt indeed [b]look on the affliction of thine handmaid, and [c]remember me, and not forget thine handmaid, but wilt give unto thine handmaid [1]a man child, then I will give him unto the LORD all the days of his life, and [d]there shall no razor come upon his head.

12 And it came to pass, as she [1]continued praying before the LORD, that Eli marked her mouth.

13 Now Hannah, she spake in her heart; only her lips moved, but her voice was not heard: therefore Eli thought she had been drunken.

14 And Eli said unto her, How long wilt thou be drunken? put away thy wine from thee.

15 And Hannah answered and said, No, my lord, I *am* a woman [1]of a sorrowful spirit: I have drunk neither wine nor strong drink, but have [a]poured out my soul before the LORD.

16 Count not thine handmaid for a daughter of [a]Belial: for out of the abundance of my [1]complaint and grief have I spoken hitherto.

17 Then Eli answered and said, [a]Go in peace: and [b]the God of Israel grant *thee* thy petition that thou hast asked of him.

18 And she said, [a]Let thine handmaid find grace in thy sight. So the woman [b]went her way, and did eat, and her countenance was no more *sad.*

19 ¶ And they rose up in the morning early, and worshipped before the LORD, and returned, and came to their house to Ramah: and Elkanah [a]knew Hannah his wife; and [b]the LORD remembered her.

20 Wherefore it came to pass, [1]when the time was come about after Hannah had conceived, that she bare a son, and called his name [2]Samuel, *saying,* Because I have asked him of the LORD.

Samuel dedicated

21 And the man Elkanah, and all his house, [a]went up to offer unto the LORD the yearly sacrifice, and his vow.

22 But Hannah went not up; for she said unto her husband, *I will not go up* until the child be weaned, and *then* I will [a]bring him, that he may appear before the LORD, and there [b]abide [c]for ever.

23 And [a]Elkanah her husband said unto her, Do what seemeth thee good; tarry until thou have weaned him; [b]only the LORD establish his word. So the woman abode, and gave her son suck until she weaned him.

24 ¶ And when she had weaned him, she [a]took him up with her, with three bullocks, and one ephah of flour, and a bottle of wine, and brought him unto [b]the house of the LORD in Shiloh: and the child *was* young.

25 And they slew a bullock, and [a]brought the child to Eli.

26 And she said, Oh my lord, [a]*as* thy soul liveth, my lord, I *am* the woman that stood by thee here, praying unto the LORD.

1:1 [a]1 Chr. 6:27, 34 [b]Ruth 1:2
3 [a]Ex. 23:14; Luke 2:41 [b]Deut. 12:5 [c]Josh. 18:1 [1]Heb. *from year to year*
4 [a]Deut. 12:17
5 [a]Gen. 30:2 [1]Or, *a double portion*
6 [a]Job 24:21 [1]Heb. *angered her*
7 [1]Or, *from the time that she* [2]Heb. *from her going up*
8 [a]Ruth 4:15
9 [a]ch. 3:3
10 [a]Job 7:11 [1]Heb. *bitter of soul*
11 [a]Gen. 28:20 [b]Ps. 25:18 [c]Gen. 8:1 [d]Num. 6:5 [1]Heb. *seed of men*
12 [1]Heb. *multiplied to pray*
15 [a]Ps. 62:8 [1]Heb. *hard of spirit*
16 [a]Deut. 13:13 [1]Or, *meditation*
17 [a]Judg. 18:6; Mark 5:34 [b]Ps. 20:4,5
18 [a]Ruth 2:13 [b]Eccl. 9:7
19 [a]Gen. 4:1 [b]Gen. 30:22
20 [1]Heb. *in revolution of days* [2]i.e. *Asked of God*
21 [a]ver. 3
22 [a]Luke 2:22 [b]ver. 11:28 [c]Ex. 21:6
23 [a]Num. 30:7 [b]2 Sam. 7:25
24 [a]Deut. 12:5,6, 11 [b]Josh. 18:1
25 [a]Luke 2:22
26 [a]2 Ki. 2:2,4,6

E *Jdg 13:2–3* ◄► *2Sa 24:25*

27 [a]For this child I prayed; and the LORD hath given me my petition which I asked of him:

28 Therefore also I have [1]lent him to the LORD; as long as he liveth [2]he shall be lent to the LORD. And he [a]worshipped the LORD there.

Hannah's song of praise

2 AND HANNAH [a]prayed, and said, [b]My heart rejoiceth in the LORD, [c]mine horn is exalted in the LORD: my mouth is enlarged over mine enemies; because I [d]rejoice in thy salvation.

K 2 [a]*There is* none holy as the LORD: for
O *there is* [b]none beside thee: neither *is*
there any rock like our God.
E 3 Talk no more so exceeding proudly;
M [a]let *not* [1]arrogancy come out of your
mouth: for the LORD *is* a God of knowledge, and by him actions are weighed.

4 [a]The bows of the mighty men *are* broken, and they that stumbled are girded with strength.

5 *They that were* full have hired out themselves for bread; and *they that were* hungry ceased: so that [a]the barren hath born seven; and [b]she that hath many children is waxed feeble.

6 [a]The LORD killeth, and maketh alive: he bringeth down to the grave, and bringeth up.

P 7 The LORD [a]maketh poor, and maketh rich: [b]he bringeth low, and lifteth up.
K 8 [a]He raiseth up the poor out of the dust, *and* lifteth up the beggar from the dunghill, [b]to set *them* among princes, and to make them inherit the throne of glory: for [c]the pillars of the earth *are* the LORD'S, and he hath set the world upon them.
H 9 [a]He will keep the feet of his saints,
L and the wicked shall be silent in darkness; for by strength shall no man prevail.

M 10 The adversaries of the LORD shall be
P [a]broken to pieces; [b]out of heaven shall he
J thunder upon them: [c]the LORD shall judge
the ends of the earth; and he shall give strength unto his king, and [d]exalt the horn of his anointed.

11 And Elkanah went to Ramah to his house. [a]And the child did minister unto the LORD before Eli the priest.

The sons of Eli

12 ¶ Now the sons of Eli *were* [1]sons of Belial; [a]they knew not the LORD.

13 And the priests' custom with the people *was, that,* when any man offered sacrifice, the priest's servant came, while the flesh was in seething, with a fleshhook of three teeth in his hand;

14 And he struck *it* into the pan, or kettle, or caldron, or pot; all that the fleshhook brought up the priest took for himself. So they did in Shiloh unto all the Israelites that came thither.

15 Also before they [a]burnt the fat, the priest's servant came, and said to the man that sacrificed, Give flesh to roast for the priest; for he will not have sodden flesh of thee, but raw.

16 And *if* any man said unto him, Let them not fail to burn the fat [1]presently, and *then* take *as much* as thy soul desireth; then he would answer him, *Nay;* but thou shalt give *it me* now: and if not, I will take *it* by force.

17 Wherefore the sin of the young men was very great [a]before the LORD: for men [b]abhorred the offering of the LORD.

18 ¶ [a]But Samuel ministered before the LORD, *being* a child, [b]girded with a linen ephod.

19 Moreover his mother made him a little coat, and brought *it* to him from year to year, when she [a]came up with her husband to offer the yearly sacrifice.

20 ¶ And Eli [a]blessed Elkanah and his wife, and said, The LORD give thee seed of this woman for the [1]loan which is [b]lent to the LORD. And they went unto their own home.

27 [a]Mat. 7:7
28 [a]Gen. 24:26,52 [1]Or, *returned him, whom I have obtained by petition, to the LORD* [2]Or, *he whom I have obtained by petition shall be returned*
2:1 [a]Phil. 4:6 [b]See Luke 1:46 [c]Ps. 92:10 [d]Ps. 9:14
2 [a]Ex. 15:11 [b]Deut. 4:35
3 [a]Ps. 94:4; Jude 15 [1]Heb. *hard*
4 [a]Ps. 37:15
5 [a]Ps. 113:9 [b]Is. 54:1
6 [a]Job 5:18; Hos. 6:1
7 [a]Job 1:21 [b]Ps. 75:7
8 [a]Luke 1:52 [b]Job 36:7 [c]Job 38:4-6
9 [a]Ps. 91:11
10 [a]Ps. 2:9 [b]Ps. 18:13 [c]Ps. 96:13 [d]Ps. 89:24
11 [a]ver. 18; ch. 3:1
12 [a]Judg. 2:10; Rom. 1:28 [1]Deut. 13:13
15 [a]Lev. 3:3,4,5, 16
16 [1]Heb. *as on the day*
17 [a]Gen. 6:11 [b]Mal. 2:8
18 [a]ver. 11 [b]Ex. 28:4
19 [a]ch. 1:3
20 [a]Gen. 14:19 [b]ch. 1:28 [1]Or, *petition which she asked*

K *Ru 2:12* ◀▶ *1Sa 2:8–9*
O *Dt 32:39* ◀▶ *2Sa 7:22*
E *Nu 32:23* ◀▶ *1Sa 16:7*
M *Dt 10:16–17* ◀▶ *2Sa 22:28*
P *Dt 30:9* ◀▶ *1Ki 3:13*
K *1Sa 2:2* ◀▶ *1Sa 25:29*
H *Jdg 5:23* ◀▶ *1Sa 3:13–14*
L *Jos 21:45* ◀▶ *1Sa 12:24*

M *Nu 24:17–19* ◀▶ *2Sa 7:13–14*
P *Dt 32:41–43* ◀▶ *2Sa 22:14–18*
J *Ge 18:25* ◀▶ *1Ch 16:33*

2:10 Samuel's mother, Hannah, spoke one of the first prophecies in Scripture anticipating the establishment of the monarchy in Israel as well as the future Messianic triumph over the enemies of God in the end times (see Lk 1:69) and the exaltation "of his anointed."

21 And the LORD [a]visited Hannah, so that she conceived, and bare three sons and two daughters. And the child Samuel [b]grew before the LORD.

22 ¶ Now Eli was very old, and heard all that his sons did unto all Israel; and how they lay with [a]the women that [1]assembled *at* the door of the tabernacle of the congregation.

23 And he said unto them, Why do ye such things? for [1]I hear of your evil dealings by all this people.

24 Nay, my sons; for *it is* no good report that I hear: ye make the LORD'S people [1]to transgress.

C 25 If one man sin against another, the judge shall judge him: but if a man [a]sin against the LORD, who shall entreat for him? Notwithstanding they hearkened not unto the voice of their father, [b]because the LORD would slay them.

26 And the child Samuel [a]grew on, and was [b]in favour both with the LORD, and also with men.

The prophecy of doom to Eli

27 ¶ [a]And there came a man of God unto Eli, and said unto him, Thus saith the LORD, [b]Did I plainly appear unto the house of thy father, when they were in Egypt in Pharaoh's house?

28 And did I [a]choose him out of all the tribes of Israel *to be* my priest, to offer upon mine altar, to burn incense, to wear an ephod before me? and [b]did I give unto the house of thy father all the offerings made by fire of the children of Israel?

29 Wherefore [a]kick ye at my sacrifice and at mine offering, which I have commanded *in my* [b]habitation; and honourest thy sons above me, to make yourselves fat with the chiefest of all the offerings of Israel my people?

U 30 Wherefore the LORD God of Israel saith, [a]I said indeed *that* thy house, and the house of thy father, should walk before me for ever: but now the LORD saith, [b]Be it far from me; for them that honour me [c]I will honour, and [d]they that despise me shall be lightly esteemed.

J 31 Behold, [a]the days come, that I will cut off thine arm, and the arm of thy father's house, that there shall not be an old man in thine house.

32 And thou shalt see [1]an enemy *in my* habitation, in all *the wealth* which *God* shall give Israel: and there shall not be [a]an old man in thine house for ever.

33 And the man of thine, *whom* I shall not cut off from mine altar, *shall be* to consume thine eyes, and to grieve thine heart: and all the increase of thine house shall die [1]in the flower of their age.

34 And this *shall be* [a]a sign unto thee, that shall come upon thy two sons, on Hophni and Phinehas; [b]in one day they shall die both of them.

35 And [a]I will raise me up a faithful priest, *that* shall do according to *that* which *is* in mine heart and in my mind: and [b]I will build him a sure house; and he shall walk before [c]mine anointed for ever.

36 [a]And it shall come to pass, *that* every one that is left in thine house shall come *and* crouch to him for a piece of silver and a morsel of bread, and shall say, [1]Put me, I pray thee, into [2]one of the priests' offices, that I may eat a piece of bread.

The LORD calls Samuel

3 AND [a]THE child Samuel ministered unto the LORD before Eli. And [b]the word of the LORD was precious in those days; *there was* no open vision.

2 And it came to pass at that time, when Eli *was* laid down in his place, and his eyes began to wax dim, *that* he could not see;

3 And ere [a]the lamp of God went out [b]in the temple of the LORD, where the ark of God *was,* and Samuel was laid down *to sleep;*

4 That the LORD called Samuel: and he answered, Here *am* I.

5 And he ran unto Eli, and said, Here *am* I; for thou calledst me. And he said, I called not; lie down again. And he went and lay down.

6 And the LORD called yet again, Samuel. And Samuel arose and went to Eli, and said, Here *am* I; for thou didst call me. And he answered, I called not, my son; lie down again.

7 [1]Now Samuel [a]did not yet know the LORD, neither was the word of the LORD yet revealed unto him.

8 And the LORD called Samuel again the

21 [a]Gen. 21:1 [b]ver. 26; Judg. 13:24
22 [a]Ex. 38:8 [1]Heb. *assembled by troops*
23 [1]Or, *I hear evil words of you*
24 [1]Or, *to cry out*
25 [a]Num. 15:30 [b]Josh. 11:20
26 [a]ver. 21 [b]Prov. 3:4
27 [a]1 Ki. 13:1 [b]Ex. 4:14,27
28 [a]Ex. 28:1,4; Num. 16:5 [b]Lev. 2:3,10 & 6:16 & 7:7,8,34,35; Num. 5:9
29 [a]Deut. 32:15 [b]Deut. 12:5
30 [a]Ex. 29:9 [b]Jer. 18:9,10 [c]Ps. 91:14 [d]Mal. 2:9
31 [a]1 Ki. 2:27; See ch. 4:11,18,20 & 14:3 & 22:18
32 [a]Zech. 8:4 [1]Or, *the affliction of the tabernacle, for all the wealth which God would have given Israel*
33 [1]Heb. *men*
34 [a]1 Ki. 13:3 [b]ch. 4:11
35 [a]1 Ki. 2:35; Ezek. 44:15 [b]2 Sam. 7:11,27; 1 Ki. 11:38 [c]Ps. 18:50
36 [a]1 Ki. 2:27 [1]Heb. *Join* [2]Or, *somewhat about the priesthood*
3:1 [a]ch. 2:11 [b]Ps. 74:9; Amos 8:11
3 [a]Ex. 27:20 [b]ch. 1:9
7 [a]See Acts 19:2 [1]Or, *Thus did Samuel before he knew the LORD, and before the word of the LORD was revealed unto him*

C *Dt 32:28–29* ◀ ▶ *1Sa 8:7*
U *Dt 30:8–9* ◀ ▶ *2Sa 22:20–21*
J *Jdg 9:20* ◀ ▶ *1Sa 12:25*

third time. And he arose and went to Eli,
and said, Here *am* I; for thou didst call
me. And Eli perceived that the LORD had
called the child.
9 Therefore Eli said unto Samuel, Go,
lie down: and it shall be, if he call thee,
that thou shalt say, Speak, LORD; for thy
servant heareth. So Samuel went and lay
down in his place.
10 And the LORD came, and stood, and
called as at other times, Samuel, Samuel.
Then Samuel answered, Speak; for thy
servant heareth.
11 ¶ And the LORD said to Samuel, Behold, I will do a thing in Israel, [a]at which
both the ears of every one that heareth it
shall tingle.
12 In that day I will perform against Eli
[a]all *things* which I have spoken concerning his house: [1]when I begin, I will also
make an end.
H 13 [a]For[1] I have told him that I will
[b]judge his house for ever for the iniquity
which he knoweth; because [c]his sons
made themselves [2]vile, and he [d]re-
strained[3] them not.
14 And therefore I have sworn unto
the house of Eli, that the iniquity of Eli's
house [a]shall not be purged with sacrifice
nor offering for ever.
15 ¶ And Samuel lay until the morning, and opened the doors of the house of
the LORD. And Samuel feared to show Eli
the vision.
16 Then Eli called Samuel, and said,
Samuel, my son. And he answered, Here
am I.
17 And he said, What *is* the thing that
the LORD hath said unto thee? I pray thee
hide *it* not from me: [a]God do so to thee,
and [1]more also, if thou hide *any* [2]thing
from me of all the things that he said unto
thee.
18 And Samuel told him [1]every whit,
and hid nothing from him. And he said,
[a]It *is* the LORD: let him do what seemeth
him good.
19 ¶ And Samuel [a]grew, and [b]the LORD
was with him, [c]and did let none of his
words fall to the ground.
20 And all Israel [a]from Dan even to
Beer-sheba knew that Samuel *was* [1]estab-
lished *to be* a prophet of the LORD.
21 And the LORD appeared again in Shiloh: for the LORD revealed himself to Samuel in Shiloh by [a]the word of the LORD.

Israel defeated by the Philistines

4 AND THE word of Samuel [1,2]came to
all Israel. Now Israel went out
against the Philistines to battle, and
pitched beside [a]Eben-ezer: and the Philistines pitched in Aphek.
2 And the Philistines put themselves
in array against Israel: and when [1]they
joined battle, Israel was smitten before
the Philistines: and they slew of [2]the
army in the field about four thousand
men.
3 ¶ And when the people were come
into the camp, the elders of Israel said,
Wherefore hath the LORD smitten us today before the Philistines? Let us [1]fetch
the ark of the covenant of the LORD out of
Shiloh unto us, that, when it cometh
among us, it may save us out of the hand
of our enemies.
4 So the people sent to Shiloh, that
they might bring from thence the ark of
the covenant of the LORD of hosts, [a]which
dwelleth *between* [b]the cherubims: and
the two sons of Eli, Hophni and Phinehas, *were* there with the ark of the covenant of God.
5 And when the ark of the covenant of
the LORD came into the camp, all Israel
shouted with a great shout, so that the
earth rang again.
6 And when the Philistines heard the
noise of the shout, they said, What *meaneth* the noise of this great shout in the
camp of the Hebrews? And they understood that the ark of the LORD was come
into the camp.
7 And the Philistines were afraid, for
they said, God is come into the camp.
And they said, Woe unto us! for there
hath not been such a thing [1]heretofore.
8 Woe unto us! who shall deliver us
out of the hand of these mighty Gods?
these *are* the Gods that smote the Egyptians with all the plagues in the wilderness.
9 [a]Be strong, and quit yourselves like
men, O ye Philistines, that ye be not servants unto the Hebrews, [b]as they have
been to you: [1]quit yourselves like men,
and fight.
10 ¶ And the Philistines fought, and
[a]Israel was smitten, and they fled every
man into his tent: and there was a very

11 [a]2 Ki. 21:12
12 [a]ch. 2:30-36 [1]Heb. *beginning and ending*
13 [a]ch. 2:29-31 [b]Ezek. 7:3 & 18:30 [c]ch. 2:12,17,22 [d]ch. 2:23,25 [1]Or, *And I will tell him* [2]Or, *accursed* [3]Heb. *frowned not upon them*
14 [a]Num. 15:30, 31
17 [a]Ruth 1:17 [1]Heb. *so add* [2]Or, *word*
18 [a]Job 1:21; Is. 39:8 [1]Heb. *all the things,* or, *words*
19 [a]ch. 2:21 [b]Gen. 39:2,21,23 [c]ch. 9:6
20 [a]Judg. 20:1 [1]Or, *faithful*
21 [a]ver. 1,4
4:1 [a]ch. 7:12 [1]Or, *came to pass* [2]Heb. *was*
2 [1]Heb. *the battle was spread* [2]Heb. *the array*
3 [1]Heb. *take unto us*
4 [a]2 Sam. 6:2 [b]Num. 7:89
7 [1]Heb. *yesterday, or, the third day*
9 [a]1 Cor. 16:13 [b]Judg. 13:1 [1]Heb. *be men*
10 [a]ver. 2; Lev. 26:17; Deut. 28:25

H *1Sa 2:9* ◄► *1Sa 25:29*

great slaughter; for there fell of Israel thirty thousand footmen.

11 And [a]the ark of God was taken; and [b]the two sons of Eli, Hophni and Phinehas, [/]were slain.

The death of Eli

12 ¶ And there ran a man of Benjamin out of the army, and [a]came to Shiloh the same day with his clothes rent, and [b]with earth upon his head.

13 And when he came, lo, Eli sat upon [a]a seat by the wayside watching: for his heart trembled for the ark of God. And when the man came into the city, and told *it,* all the city cried out.

14 And when Eli heard the noise of the crying, he said, What *meaneth* the noise of this tumult? And the man came in hastily, and told Eli.

15 Now Eli was ninety and eight years old; and [a]his eyes [/]were dim, that he could not see.

16 And the man said unto Eli, I *am* he that came out of the army, and I fled today out of the army. And he said, [a]What [/]is there done, my son?

17 And the messenger answered and said, Israel is fled before the Philistines, and there hath been also a great slaughter among the people, and thy two sons also, Hophni and Phinehas, are dead, and the ark of God is taken.

18 And it came to pass, when he made mention of the ark of God, that he fell from off the seat backward by the side of the gate, and his neck brake, and he died: for he was an old man, and heavy. [/]And he had judged Israel forty years.

19 ¶ And his daughter-in-law, Phinehas' wife, was with child, *near* [/]to be delivered: and when she heard the tidings that the ark of God was taken, and that her father-in-law and her husband were dead, she bowed herself and travailed; for her pains [2]came upon her.

20 And about the time of her death [a]the women that stood by her said unto her, Fear not; for thou hast borne a son. But she answered not, [/]neither did she regard *it.*

21 And she named the child [a]I-chabod,[/] saying, [b]The glory is departed from Israel: because the ark of God was taken, and because of her father-in-law and her husband.

22 And she said, The glory is departed from Israel: for the ark of God is taken.

The Philistines move the ark

5 AND THE Philistines took the ark of God, and brought it [a]from Eben-ezer unto Ashdod.

2 When the Philistines took the ark of God, they brought it into the house of [a]Dagon, and set it by Dagon.

3 ¶ And when they of Ashdod arose early on the morrow, behold, Dagon *was* [a]fallen upon his face to the earth before the ark of the LORD. And they took Dagon, and [b]set him in his place again.

4 And when they arose early on the morrow morning, behold, Dagon *was* fallen upon his face to the ground before the ark of the LORD; and [a]the head of Dagon and both the palms of his hands *were* cut off upon the threshold; only [/]*the stump of* Dagon was left to him.

5 Therefore neither the priests of Dagon, nor any that come into Dagon's house, [a]tread on the threshold of Dagon in Ashdod unto this day.

6 But [a]the hand of the LORD was heavy upon them of Ashdod, and he [b]destroyed them, and smote them with [c]emerods, *even* Ashdod and the coasts thereof. D

7 And when the men of Ashdod saw that *it was* so, they said, The ark of the God of Israel shall not abide with us: for his hand is sore upon us, and upon Dagon our god.

8 They sent therefore and gathered all the lords of the Philistines unto them, and said, What shall we do with the ark of the God of Israel? And they answered, Let the ark of the God of Israel be carried about unto Gath. And they carried the ark of the God of Israel about *thither.*

9 And it was *so,* that, after they had carried it about, [a]the hand of the LORD was against the city [b]with a very great destruction: and [c]he smote the men of the city, both small and great, and they had emerods in their secret parts. D

11 [a]ch. 2:32; Ps. 78:61 [b]ch. 2:34; Ps. 78:64 [/]Heb. *died*

12 [a]2 Sam. 1:2 [b]Josh. 7:6; 2 Sam. 13:19 & 15:32; Neh. 9:1; Job 2:12

13 [a]ch. 1:9

15 [a]ch. 3:2 [/]Heb. *stood*

16 [a]2 Sam. 1:4 [/]Heb. *is the thing*

18 [/]He seems to have been a Judge to do justice only, and that in Southwest *Israel*

19 [/]Or, *to cry out* [2]Heb. *were turned*

20 [a]Gen. 35:17 [/]Heb. *set not her heart*

21 [a]ch. 14:3 [b]Ps. 26:8 & 78:61 [/]i.e. *Where is the glory?* or, There is *no glory*

5:1 [a]ch. 4:1 & 7:12

2 [a]Judg. 16:23

3 [a]Is. 19:1 & 46:1, 2 [b]Is. 46:7

4 [a]Jer. 50:2; Ezek. 6:4,6; Mic. 1:7 [/]Or, *the fishy part*

5 [a]Zeph. 1:9

6 [a]ver. 7,11; Ex. 9:3; Ps. 32:4; Acts 13:11 [b]ch. 6:5 [c]Deut. 28:27; Ps. 78:66

9 [a]Deut. 2:15; ch. 7:13 & 12:15 [b]ver. 11 [c]ver. 6; Ps. 78:66

D *Jos 22:17* ◀▶ *1Sa 5:9*
D *1Sa 5:6* ◀▶ *1Sa 5:11–12*

10 ¶ Therefore they sent the ark of
God to Ekron. And it came to pass, as the
ark of God came to Ekron, that the Ekronites cried out, saying, They have
brought about the ark of the God of Israel
to [1]us, to slay us and our people.
D 11 So they sent and gathered together
all the lords of the Philistines, and said,
Send away the ark of the God of Israel,
and let it go again to his own place, that it
slay [1]us not, and our people: for there
was a deadly destruction throughout all
the city; [a]the hand of God was very heavy
there.
12 And the men that died not were
smitten with the emerods: and the cry of
the city went up to heaven.

The ark returned to Israel

6 AND THE ark of the LORD was in the
country of the Philistines seven
months.
2 And the Philistines [a]called for the
priests and the diviners, saying, What
shall we do to the ark of the LORD? tell us
wherewith we shall send it to his place.
3 And they said, If ye send away the
ark of the God of Israel, send it not
[a]empty; but in any wise return him [b]a
trespass offering: then ye shall be healed,
and it shall [c]be known to you why his
hand is not removed from you.
4 Then said they, What *shall be* the
trespass offering which we shall return to
him? They answered, Five golden emerods, and five golden mice, [a]*according to*
the number of the lords of the Philistines:
for one plague *was* on [1]you all, and on
your lords.
5 Wherefore ye shall make images of
your emerods, and images of your mice
that [a]mar the land; and ye shall [b]give
glory unto the God of Israel: peradventure he will [c]lighten his hand from off
you, and from off [d]your gods, and from off
your land.
6 Wherefore then do ye harden your
hearts, [a]as the Egyptians and Pharaoh
hardened their hearts? when he had
wrought [1]wonderfully among them, [b]did
they not let [2]the people go, and they departed?
7 Now therefore make [a]a new cart,
and take two milch kine, [b]on which there
hath come no yoke, and tie the kine to
the cart, and bring their calves home
from them:
8 And take the ark of the LORD, and lay
it upon the cart; and put [a]the jewels of
gold, which ye return him *for* a trespass
offering, in a coffer by the side thereof;
and send it away, that it may go.
9 And see, if it goeth up by the way of
his own coast to [a]Beth-shemesh, *then*
[1]he hath done us this great evil: but if
not, then [b]we shall know that *it is* not his
hand *that* smote us; it *was* a chance *that*
happened to us.
10 ¶ And the men did so; and took two
milch kine, and tied them to the cart, and
shut up their calves at home:
11 And they laid the ark of the LORD
upon the cart, and the coffer with the
mice of gold and the images of their
emerods.
12 And the kine took the straight way
to the way of Beth-shemesh, *and* went
along the highway, lowing as they went,
and turned not aside *to* the right hand or
to the left; and the lords of the Philistines
went after them unto the border of Beth-
shemesh.
13 And *they of* Beth-shemesh *were*
reaping their wheat harvest in the valley:
and they lifted up their eyes, and saw the
ark, and rejoiced to see *it*.
14 And the cart came into the field of
Joshua, a Beth-shemite, and stood there,
where *there was* a great stone: and they
clave the wood of the cart, and offered
the kine a burnt offering unto the LORD.
15 And the Levites took down the ark
of the LORD, and the coffer that *was* with
it, wherein the jewels of gold *were,* and
put *them* on the great stone: and the men
of Beth-shemesh offered burnt offerings

10 [1]Heb. *me, to slay me and my*
11 [a]ver. 6,9 [1]Heb. *me not, and my*
6:2 [a]Gen. 41:8; Ex. 7:11; Dan. 2:2 & 5:7; Mat. 2:4
3 [a]Ex. 23:15; Deut. 16:16 [b]Lev. 5:15, 16 [c]ver. 9
4 [a]See ver. 17,18; Josh. 13:3; Judg. 3:3 [1]Heb. *them*
5 [a]ch. 5:6 [b]Josh. 7:19; Is. 42:12; Mal. 2:2; John 9:24 [c]See ch. 5:6,11; Ps. 39:10 [d]ch. 5:3,4,7
6 [a]Ex. 7:13 & 8:15 & 14:17 [b]Ex. 12:31 [1]Or, *reproachfully* [2]Heb. *them*
7 [a]2 Sam. 6:3 [b]Num. 19:2
8 [a]ver. 4,5
9 [a]Josh. 15:10 [b]ver. 3 [1]Or, *it*

D 1Sa 5:9 ◀▶ 1Sa 25:38

5:10–11 Ekron was the most northerly of the five chief cities of the Philistines and was included in the territory of Dan (see Jos 19:43). After David killed Goliath, the Philistines fled to this fortified city (see 1Sa 17:52). In this story, the people of Ekron urged the other Philistines to return the captured ark of the covenant to Israel in order to avert destruction. The prophets called down God's judgment upon Ekron (see Am 1:8) and the city was destroyed. Recent archeological excavation has uncovered what appear to be the ruins of Ekron, including a stone inscription naming the city and five of its kings.

and sacrificed sacrifices the same day unto the LORD.

16 And when [a]the five lords of the Philistines had seen *it,* they returned to Ekron the same day.

17 [a]And these *are* the golden emerods which the Philistines returned *for* a trespass offering unto the LORD; for Ashdod one, for Gaza one, for Askelon one, for Gath one, for Ekron one;

18 And the golden mice, *according to* the number of all the cities of the Philistines *belonging* to the five lords, *both* of fenced cities, and of country villages, even unto the [/]great *stone of* Abel, whereon they set down the ark of the LORD: *which stone remaineth* unto this day in the field of Joshua, the Beth-shemite.

19 ¶ And [a]he smote the men of Beth-shemesh, because they had looked into the ark of the LORD, even he smote of the people fifty thousand and threescore and ten men: and the people lamented, because the LORD had smitten *many* of the people with a great slaughter.

20 And the men of Beth-shemesh said, [a]Who is able to stand before this holy LORD God? and to whom shall he go up from us?

21 ¶ And they sent messengers to the inhabitants of [a]Kirjath-jearim, saying, The Philistines have brought again the ark of the LORD; come ye down, *and* fetch it up to you.

7 AND THE men of [a]Kirjath-jearim came, and fetched up the ark of the LORD, and brought it into the house of [b]Abinadab in the hill, and sanctified Eleazar his son to keep the ark of the LORD.

2 And it came to pass, while the ark abode in Kirjath-jearim, that the time was long; for it was twenty years: and all the house of Israel lamented after the LORD.

Philistines defeated at Mizpah

I 3 ¶ And Samuel spake unto all the house of Israel, saying, If ye do [a]return unto the LORD with all your hearts, *then* [b]put away the strange gods and [c]Ashtaroth from among you, and [d]prepare your hearts unto the LORD, and [e]serve him only: and he will deliver you out of the hand of the Philistines.

4 Then the children of Israel did put away [a]Baalim and Ashtaroth, and served the LORD only.

5 And Samuel said, [a]Gather all Israel to Mizpeh, and I will pray for you unto the LORD.

6 And they gathered together to Mizpeh, [a]and drew water, and poured *it* out before the LORD, and [b]fasted on that day, and said there, [c]We have sinned against the LORD. And Samuel judged the children of Israel in Mizpeh.

7 And when the Philistines heard that the children of Israel were gathered together to Mizpeh, the lords of the Philistines went up against Israel. And when the children of Israel heard *it,* they were afraid of the Philistines.

8 And the children of Israel said to Samuel, [a]Cease[/] not to cry unto the LORD our God for us, that he will save us out of the hand of the Philistines.

9 ¶ And Samuel took a sucking lamb, and offered *it for* a burnt offering wholly unto the LORD: and [a]Samuel cried unto the LORD for Israel; and the LORD [/]heard him.

10 And as Samuel was offering up the burnt offering, the Philistines drew near to battle against Israel: [a]but the LORD thundered with a great thunder on that day upon the Philistines, and discomfited them; and they were smitten before Israel.

11 And the men of Israel went out of Mizpeh, and pursued the Philistines, and smote them, until *they came* under Beth-car.

12 Then Samuel [a]took a stone, and set *it* between Mizpeh and Shen, and called the name of it [b]Eben-ezer,[/] saying, Hitherto hath the LORD helped us. T

13 ¶ [a]So the Philistines were subdued, and they [b]came no more into the coast of Israel: and the hand of the LORD was against the Philistines all the days of Samuel.

14 And the cities which the Philistines

I *Jdg 20:28* ◀ ▶ *1Sa 9:16*

T *Dt 26:1–3* ◀ ▶ *1Ch 16:8–10*

16 [a]Josh. 13:3
17 [a]ver. 4
18 [/]Or, *great stone*
19 [a]See Ex. 19:21; 2 Sam. 6:7
20 [a]2 Sam. 6:9; Mal. 3:2
21 [a]Josh. 18:14; 1 Chr. 13:5,6
7:1 [a]ch. 6:21; Ps. 132:6 [b]2 Sam. 6:4
3 [a]Deut. 30:2-10; Is. 55:7; Hos. 6:1; Joel 2:12 [b]Gen. 35:2; Josh. 24:14 [c]Judg. 2:13 [d]2 Chr. 30:19; Job 11:13 [e]Deut. 6:13 & 10:20; Luke 4:8
4 [a]Judg. 2:11
5 [a]Judg. 20:1
6 [a]2 Sam. 14:14 [b]Neh. 9:1,2; Dan. 9:3-5; Joel 2:12 [c]Judg. 10:10; Ps. 106:6
8 [a]Is. 37:4 [/]Heb. *Be not silent from us from crying*
9 [a]Ps. 99:6; Jer. 15:1 [/]Or, *answered*
10 [a]Josh. 10:10; Judg. 4:15 & 5:20; ch. 2:10; 2 Sam. 22:14,15
12 [a]Gen. 28:18; Josh. 4:9 [b]ch. 4:1 [/]i.e. *The stone of help*
13 [a]Judg. 13:1 [b]ch. 13:5

7:3 Samuel prophesied Israel's divine deliverance from the Philistines if the Israelites would repent of their idolatry.

had taken from Israel were restored to
Israel, from Ekron even unto Gath; and
the coasts thereof did Israel deliver out of
the hands of the Philistines. And there
was peace between Israel and the Amorites.
15 And Samuel [a]judged Israel all the
days of his life.
16 And he went from year to year [1]in
circuit to Beth-el, and Gilgal, and Mizpeh, and judged Israel in all those places.
17 And [a]his return *was* to Ramah; for
there *was* his house; and there he judged
Israel; and there he [b]built an altar unto
the LORD.

Israel demands a king

8 AND IT came to pass, when Samuel
was old, that he [a]made his [b]sons
judges over Israel.
2 Now the name of his firstborn was
[1]Joel; and the name of his second, Abiah:
they were judges in Beer-sheba.
3 And his sons [a]walked not in his
ways, but turned aside [b]after lucre, and
[c]took bribes, and perverted judgment.
4 Then all the elders of Israel gathered
themselves together, and came to Samuel
unto Ramah,
5 And said unto him, Behold, thou art
old, and thy sons walk not in thy ways:
now [a]make us a king to judge us like all
the nations.
6 ¶ But the thing [1]displeased Samuel,
when they said, Give us a king to judge
us. And Samuel prayed unto the LORD.
C 7 And the LORD said unto Samuel,
Hearken unto the voice of the people in
all that they say unto thee: for [a]they have
not rejected thee, but [b]they have rejected
me, that I should not reign over them.
8 According to all the works which
they have done since the day that I
brought them up out of Egypt even unto
this day, wherewith they have forsaken
me, and served other gods, so do they
also unto thee.
9 Now therefore [1]hearken unto their
voice: [2]howbeit yet protest solemnly
unto them, and [a]show them the manner
of the king that shall reign over them.
10 ¶ And Samuel told all the words of
the LORD unto the people that asked of
him a king.
11 And he said, [a]This will be the man-

15 [a] ch. 12:11; Judg. 2:16

16 [1] Heb. *and he circuited*

17 [a] ch. 8:4 [b] Judg. 21:4

8:1 [a] Deut. 16:18; 2 Chr. 19:5 [b] Judg. 10:4 & 12:14 compared with Judg. 5:10

2 [1] *Vashni* in 1 Chr. 6:28

3 [a] Jer. 22:15-17 [b] Ex. 18:21; 1 Tim. 3:3 & 6:10 [c] Deut. 16:19; Ps. 15:5

5 [a] ver. 19,20; Deut. 17:14; Hos. 13:10; Acts 13:21

6 [1] Heb. *was evil in the eyes of Samuel*

7 [a] See Ex. 16:8 [b] ch. 10:19 & 12:17,19; Hos. 13:10,11

9 [a] ver. 11 [1] Or, *obey* [2] Or, *notwithstanding when thou hast solemnly protested against them, then thou shalt show*

11 [a] See Deut. 17:16; ch. 10:25 [b] ch. 14:52

14 [a] 1 Ki. 21:7; See Ezek. 46:18

15 [1] Heb. *eunuchs;* see Gen. 37:36

18 [a] Is. 1:15; Mic. 3:4

19 [a] Jer. 44:16

20 [a] ver. 5

22 [a] ver. 7; Hos. 13:11

9:1 [a] ch. 14:51; 1 Chr. 8:33 & 9:39 [1] Or, *the son of a man of Jemini* [2] Or, *substance*

ner of the king that shall reign over you:
[b]He will take your sons, and appoint
them for himself, for his chariots, and *to
be* his horsemen; and *some* shall run before his chariots.
12 And he will appoint him captains
over thousands, and captains over fifties;
and *will set them* to ear his ground, and
to reap his harvest, and to make his instruments of war, and instruments of his
chariots.
13 And he will take your daughters *to
be* confectionaries, and *to be* cooks, and
to be bakers.
14 And [a]he will take your fields, and
your vineyards, and your oliveyards, *even*
the best *of them,* and give *them* to his
servants.
15 And he will take the tenth of your
seed, and of your vineyards, and give to
his [1]officers, and to his servants.
16 And he will take your menservants,
and your maidservants, and your goodliest young men, and your asses, and put
them to his work.
17 He will take the tenth of your
sheep: and ye shall be his servants.
18 And ye shall cry out in that day because of your king which ye shall have
chosen you; and the LORD [a]will not hear
you in that day.
19 ¶ Nevertheless the people [a]refused
to obey the voice of Samuel; and they
said, Nay; but we will have a king
over us;
20 That we also may be [a]like all the
nations; and that our king may judge us,
and go out before us, and fight our
battles.
21 And Samuel heard all the words of
the people, and he rehearsed them in the
ears of the LORD.
22 And the LORD said to Samuel,
[a]Hearken unto their voice, and make
them a king. And Samuel said unto the
men of Israel, Go ye every man unto his
city.

Saul anointed by Samuel

9 NOW THERE was a man of Benjamin, whose name *was* [a]Kish, the son
of Abiel, the son of Zeror, the son of Be-
chorath, the son of Aphiah, [1]a Benjamite,
a mighty man of [2]power.
2 And he had a son, whose name *was*
Saul, a choice young man, and a goodly:
and *there was* not among the children of

C *1Sa 2:25* ◄► *1Sa 24:13*

Israel a goodlier person than he: [a]from
his shoulders and upward *he was* higher
than any of the people.
3 And the asses of Kish Saul's father
were lost. And Kish said to Saul his son,
Take now one of the servants with thee,
and arise, go seek the asses.
4 And he passed through mount
Ephraim, and passed through the land of
[a]Shalisha, but they found *them* not: then
they passed through the land of Shalim,
and *there they were* not: and he passed
through the land of the Benjamites, but
they found *them* not.
5 *And* when they were come to the
land of Zuph, Saul said to his servant that
was with him, Come, and let us return;
lest my father leave *caring* for the asses,
and take thought for us.
6 And he said unto him, Behold now,
there is in this city [a]a man of God, and *he*
is an honourable man; [b]all that he saith
cometh surely to pass: now let us go
thither; peradventure he can show us our
way that we should go.
7 Then said Saul to his servant, But,
behold, *if* we go, [a]what shall we bring
the man? for the bread [1]is spent in our
vessels, and *there is* not a present to
bring to the man of God: what [2]have we?
8 And the servant answered Saul
again, and said, Behold, [1]I have here at
hand the fourth part of a shekel of silver:
that will I give to the man of God, to tell
us our way.
9 (Beforetime in Israel, when a man
[a]went to inquire of God, thus he spake,
Come, and let us go to the seer: for *he*
that is now *called* a Prophet was beforetime called [b]a Seer.)
10 Then said Saul to his servant, [1]Well
said; come, let us go. So they went unto
the city where the man of God *was.*
11 ¶ *And* as they went up [1]the hill to
the city, [a]they found young maidens going out to draw water, and said unto
them, Is the seer here?
12 And they answered them, and said,
He is; behold, *he is* before you: make
haste now, for he came today to the city;
for [a]*there is* a [1]sacrifice of the people today [b]in the high place:
13 As soon as ye be come into the city,
ye shall straightway find him, before he
go up to the high place to eat: for the
people will not eat until he come, because he doth bless the sacrifice; *and* afterwards they eat that be bidden. Now
therefore get you up; for about [1]this time
ye shall find him.
14 And they went up into the city: *and*
when they were come into the city, behold, Samuel came out against them, for
to go up to the high place.
15 ¶ [a]Now the LORD had told Samuel in
his ear a day before Saul came, saying,
16 Tomorrow about this time I will ❙
send thee a man out of the land of Benjamin, [a]and thou shalt anoint him *to be*
captain over my people Israel, that he
may save my people out of the hand of
the Philistines: for I have [b]looked upon
my people, because their cry is come
unto me.
17 And when Samuel saw Saul, the
LORD said unto him, [a]Behold the man
whom I spake to thee of! this same shall
[1]reign over my people.
18 Then Saul drew near to Samuel in
the gate, and said, Tell me, I pray thee,
where the seer's house *is.*
19 And Samuel answered Saul, and
said, I *am* the seer: go up before me unto
the high place; for ye shall eat with me
today, and tomorrow I will let thee go,
and will tell thee all that *is* in thine heart.
20 And as for [a]thine asses that were
lost [1]three days ago, set not thy mind on
them; for they are found. And on whom
[b]*is* all the desire of Israel? *Is it* not on
thee, and on all thy father's house?
21 And Saul answered and said, [a]*Am*
not I a Benjamite, of the [b]smallest of the
tribes of Israel? and [c]my family the least
of all the families of the tribe of Benjamin? wherefore then speakest thou [1]so
to me?
22 And Samuel took Saul and his servant, and brought them into the parlour,
and made them sit in the chiefest place
among them that were bidden, which
were about thirty persons.
23 And Samuel said unto the cook,
Bring the portion which I gave thee, of
which I said unto thee, Set it by thee.
24 And the cook took up [a]the shoulder, and *that* which *was* upon it, and set
it before Saul. And *Samuel* said, Behold
that which is [1]left! set *it* before thee, *and*
eat: for unto this time hath it been kept
for thee since I said, I have invited the

2 [a]ch. 10:23
4 [a]2 Ki. 4:42
6 [a]Deut. 33:1; 1 Ki. 13:1 [b]ch. 3:19
7 [a]See Judg. 6:18; & 13:17; 1 Ki. 14:3; 2 Ki. 4:42 & 8:8 [1]Heb. *is gone out of* [2]Heb. *is with us*
8 [1]Heb. *there is found in my hand*
9 [a]Gen. 25:22 [b]2 Sam. 24:11; 2 Ki. 17:13; 1 Chr. 26:28 & 29:29; 2 Chr. 16:7,10; Is. 30:10; Amos 7:12
10 [1]Heb. *Thy word is good*
11 [a]Gen. 24:11 [1]Heb. *in the ascent of the city*
12 [a]Gen. 31:54; ch. 16:2 [b]1 Ki. 3:2 [1]Or, *feast*
13 [1]Heb. *today*
15 [a]ch. 15:1; Acts 13:21
16 [a]ch. 10:1 [b]Ex. 2:25 & 3:7,9
17 [a]ch. 16:12; Hos. 13:11 [1]Heb. *restrain in*
20 [a]ver. 3 [b]ch. 8:5,19 & 12:13 [1]Heb. *today three days*
21 [a]ch. 15:17 [b]Judg. 20:46-48 [c]See Judg. 6:15 [1]Heb. *according to this word?*
24 [a]Lev. 7:32,33; Ezek. 24:4 [1]Or, *reserved*

❙ *1Sa 7:3* ◄► *1Sa 12:22*

people. So Saul did eat with Samuel that day.

25 ¶ And when they were come down from the high place into the city, *Samuel* communed with Saul upon [a]the top of the house.

26 And they arose early: and it came to pass about the spring of the day, that Samuel called Saul to the top of the house, saying, Up, that I may send thee away. And Saul arose, and they went out both of them, he and Samuel, abroad.

27 *And* as they were going down to the end of the city, Samuel said to Saul, Bid the servant pass on before us, (and he passed on,) but stand thou still [1]a while, that I may show thee the word of God.

10 THEN [a]SAMUEL took a vial of oil, and poured *it* upon his head, [b]and kissed him, and said, *Is it* not because [c]the LORD hath anointed thee *to be* captain over [d]his inheritance?

2 When thou art departed from me today, then thou shalt find two men by [a]Rachel's sepulchre in the border of Benjamin [b]at Zelzah; and they will say unto thee, The asses which thou wentest to seek are found: and, lo, thy father hath left [1]the care of the asses, and sorroweth for you, saying, What shall I do for my son?

3 Then shalt thou go on forward from thence, and thou shalt come to the plain of Tabor, and there shall meet thee three men going up [a]to God to Beth-el, one carrying three kids, and another carrying three loaves of bread, and another carrying a bottle of wine:

4 And they will [1]salute thee, and give thee two *loaves* of bread; which thou shalt receive of their hands.

5 After that thou shalt come to the hill of God, [a]where *is* the garrison of the Philistines: and it shall come to pass, when thou art come thither to the city, that thou shalt meet a company of prophets coming down [b]from the high place with a psaltery, and a tabret, and a pipe, and a harp, before them; [c]and they shall prophesy:

E G L T 6 And [a]the spirit of the LORD will come upon thee, and [b]thou shalt prophesy with them, and shalt be turned into another man.

7 And [1]let it be, when these [a]signs are come unto thee, [b]*that*[2] thou do as occasion serve thee; for [c]God *is* with thee.

8 And thou shalt go down before me [a]to Gilgal; and, behold, I will come down unto thee, to offer burnt offerings, *and* to sacrifice sacrifices of peace offerings: [b]seven days shalt thou tarry, till I come to thee, and show thee what thou shalt do.

Saul becomes king of Israel

9 ¶ And it was *so,* that when he had turned his [1]back to go from Samuel, God [2]gave him another heart: and all those signs came to pass that day.

10 And [a]when they came thither to the hill, behold, [b]a company of prophets met him; and the spirit of God came upon him, and he prophesied among them. E G M T

11 And it came to pass, when all that knew him beforetime saw that, behold, he prophesied among the prophets, then the people said [1]one to another, What *is* this *that* is come unto the son of Kish? [a]*Is* Saul also among the prophets?

12 And one [1]of the same place answered and said, But [a]who *is* their father? Therefore it became a proverb, *Is* Saul also among the prophets?

13 And when he had made an end of prophesying, he came to the high place.

14 ¶ And Saul's uncle said unto him and to his servant, Whither went ye? And he said, To seek the asses: and when we saw that *they were* no where, we came to Samuel.

15 And Saul's uncle said, Tell me, I pray thee, what Samuel said unto you.

16 And Saul said unto his uncle, He told us plainly that the asses were found. But of the matter of the kingdom, whereof Samuel spake, he told him not.

17 ¶ And Samuel called the people together [a]unto the LORD [b]to Mizpeh;

18 And said unto the children of Israel, [a]Thus saith the LORD God of Israel, I brought up Israel out of Egypt, and delivered you out of the hand of the Egyptians, and out of the hand of all kingdoms, *and* of them that oppressed you:

25 [a]Deut. 22:8; 2 Sam. 11:2; Acts 10:9
27 [1]Heb. *today*
10:1 [a]ch. 9:16 & 16:13; 2 Ki. 9:3,6 [b]Ps. 2:12 [c]Acts 13:21 [d]Deut. 32:9
2 [a]Gen. 35:19,20 [b]Josh. 18:28 [1]Heb. *the business*
3 [a]Gen. 28:22 & 35:1,3,7
4 [1]Heb. *ask thee of peace* as Judg. 18:15
5 [a]ch. 13:3 [b]ch. 9:12 [c]Ex. 15:20,21; 2 Ki. 3:15; 1 Cor. 14:1
6 [a]Num. 11:25; ch. 16:13 [b]ver. 10; ch. 19:23,24
7 [a]Ex. 4:8; Luke 2:12 [b]Judg. 9:33 [c]Judg. 6:12 [1]Heb. *it shall come to pass, that when these signs* [2]Heb. *do for thee as thine hand shall find*
8 [a]ch. 11:14,15 [b]ch. 13:8
9 [1]Heb. *shoulder* [2]Heb. *turned*
10 [a]ver. 5 [b]ch. 19:20
11 [a]Mat. 13:54,55; John 7:15; Acts 4:13 [1]Heb. *a man to his neighbour*
12 [a]Is. 54:13; John 6:45 [1]Heb. *from thence*
17 [a]Judg. 11:11 & 20:1 [b]ch. 7:5,6
18 [a]Judg. 6:8,9

E *Jdg 15:14–15* ◄ ► *1Sa 10:10–12*
G *Dt 34:9* ◄ ► *1Sa 10:10–12*
L *Jdg 13:25* ◄ ► *2Sa 23:2*
T *Dt 34:9* ◄ ► *1Sa 10:10–12*

E *1Sa 10:6–7* ◄ ► *1Sa 19:20–23*
G *1Sa 10:6–7* ◄ ► *1Sa 19:20–24*
M *Jdg 15:14–15* ◄ ► *1Sa 11:6*
T *1Sa 10:6–7* ◄ ► *2Sa 23:1–2*

19 [a]And ye have this day rejected your God, who himself saved you out of all your adversities and your tribulations; and ye have said unto him, *Nay,* but set a king over us. Now therefore present yourselves before the LORD by your tribes, and by your thousands.

20 And when Samuel had [a]caused all the tribes of Israel to come near, the tribe of Benjamin was taken.

21 When he had caused the tribe of Benjamin to come near by their families, the family of Matri was taken, and Saul the son of Kish was taken: and when they sought him, he could not be found.

22 Therefore they [a]inquired of the LORD further, if the man should yet come thither. And the LORD answered, Behold, he hath hid himself among the stuff.

23 And they ran and fetched him thence: and when he stood among the people, [a]he was higher than any of the people from his shoulders and upward.

24 And Samuel said to all the people, See ye him [a]whom the LORD hath chosen, that *there is* none like him among all the people? And all the people shouted, and said, [b]God[l] save the king.

25 Then Samuel told the people [a]the manner of the kingdom, and wrote *it* in a book, and laid *it* up before the LORD. And Samuel sent all the people away, every man to his house.

26 ¶ And Saul also went home [a]to Gibeah; and there went with him a band of men, whose hearts God had touched.

27 [a]But the [b]children of Belial said, How shall this man save us? And they despised him, [c]and brought him no presents. But [l]he held his peace.

The Ammonites defeated

11 THEN [a]NAHASH the Ammonite came up, and encamped against [b]Jabesh-gilead: and all the men of Jabesh said unto Nahash, [c]Make a covenant with us, and we will serve thee.

2 And Nahash the Ammonite answered them, On this *condition* will I make *a covenant* with you, that I may thrust out all your right eyes, and lay it *for* [a]a reproach upon all Israel.

3 And the elders of Jabesh said unto him, [l]Give us seven days' respite, that we may send messengers unto all the coasts of Israel: and then, if *there be* no man to save us, we will come out to thee.

4 ¶ Then came the messengers [a]to Gibeah of Saul, and told the tidings in the ears of the people: and [b]all the people lifted up their voices, and wept.

5 And, behold, Saul came after the herd out of the field; and Saul said, What *aileth* the people that they weep? And they told him the tidings of the men of Jabesh.

6 [a]And the spirit of God came upon Saul when he heard those tidings, and his anger was kindled greatly. M

7 And he took a yoke of oxen, and [a]hewed them in pieces, and sent *them* throughout all the coasts of Israel by the hands of messengers, saying, [b]Whosoever cometh not forth after Saul and after Samuel, so shall it be done unto his oxen. And the fear of the LORD fell on the people, and they came out [l]with one consent.

8 And when he numbered them in [a]Bezek, the children [b]of Israel were three hundred thousand, and the men of Judah thirty thousand.

9 And they said unto the messengers that came, Thus shall ye say unto the men of Jabesh-gilead, Tomorrow, by *that time* the sun be hot, ye shall have [l]help. And the messengers came and showed *it* to the men of Jabesh; and they were glad.

10 Therefore the men of Jabesh said, Tomorrow [a]we will come out unto you, and ye shall do with us all that seemeth good unto you.

11 And it was *so* on the morrow, that [a]Saul put the people [b]in three companies; and they came into the midst of the host in the morning watch, and slew the Ammonites until the heat of the day: and it came to pass, that they which remained were scattered, so that two of them were not left together.

12 ¶ And the people said unto Samuel, [a]Who *is* he that said, Shall Saul reign over us? [b]bring the men, that we may put them to death.

13 And Saul said, [a]There shall not a man be put to death this day: for today [b]the LORD hath wrought salvation in Israel.

14 Then said Samuel to the people, Come, and let us go [a]to Gilgal, and renew the kingdom there.

15 And all the people went to Gilgal;

19 [a]ch. 8:7,19 & 12:12
20 [a]Acts 1:24,26
22 [a]ch. 23:2,4,10, 11
23 [a]ch. 9:2
24 [a]2 Sam. 21:6 [b]1 Ki. 1:25,39 [l]Heb. *Let the king live*
25 [a]ch. 8:11
26 [a]Judg. 20:14; ch. 11:4
27 [a]ch. 11:12 [b]Deut. 13:13 [c]2 Sam. 8:2; 1 Ki. 4:21; Mat. 2:11 [l]Or, *he was as though he had been deaf*
11:1 [a]ch. 12:12 [b]Judg. 21:8 [c]Gen. 26:28; 1 Ki. 20:34
2 [a]Gen. 34:14; ch. 17:26
3 [l]Heb. *Forbear us*
4 [a]ch. 10:26 & 15:34; 2 Sam. 21:6 [b]Judg. 2:4
6 [a]Judg. 3:10 & 6:34; ch. 10:10
7 [a]Judg. 19:29 [b]Judg. 21:5,8,10 [l]Heb. *as one man*
8 [a]Judg. 1:5 [b]2 Sam. 24:9
9 [l]Or, *deliverance*
10 [a]ver. 3
11 [a]See ch. 31:11 [b]Judg. 7:16
12 [a]ch. 10:27 [b]See Luke 19:27
13 [a]2 Sam. 19:22 [b]Ex. 14:13,30; ch. 19:5
14 [a]ch. 10:8

M *1Sa 10:10–12* ◄► *1Sa 19:20–23*

and there they made Saul king [a]before the LORD in Gilgal; and [b]there they sacrificed sacrifices of peace offerings before the LORD; and there Saul and all the men of Israel rejoiced greatly.

Samuel addresses the people

12 AND SAMUEL said unto all Israel, Behold, I have hearkened unto [a]your voice in all that ye said unto me, and [b]have made a king over you.

2 And now, behold, the king [a]walketh before you: [b]and I am old and grayheaded; and, behold, my sons *are* with you: and I have walked before you from my childhood unto this day.

R 3 Behold, here I *am:* witness against me before the LORD, and before [a]his anointed: [b]whose ox have I taken? or whose ass have I taken? or whom have I defrauded? whom have I oppressed? or of whose hand have I received *any* [1]bribe [2]to [c]blind mine eyes therewith? and I will restore it you.

4 And they said, Thou hast not defrauded us, nor oppressed us, neither hast thou taken aught of any man's hand.

5 And he said unto them, The LORD *is* witness against you, and his anointed *is* witness this day, [a]that ye have not found aught [b]in my hand. And they answered, *He is* witness.

6 ¶ And Samuel said unto the people, [a]*It is* the LORD that [1]advanced Moses and Aaron, and that brought your fathers up out of the land of Egypt.

7 Now therefore stand still, that I may [a]reason with you before the LORD of all the [b]righteous[1] acts of the LORD, which he did [2]to you and to your fathers.

8 [a]When Jacob was come into Egypt, and your fathers [b]cried unto the LORD, then the LORD [c]sent Moses and Aaron, which brought forth your fathers out of Egypt, and made them dwell in this place.

9 And when they [a]forgat the LORD their God, [b]he sold them into the hand of Sisera, captain of the host of Hazor, and into the hand of [c]the Philistines, and into the hand of the king [d]of Moab, and they fought against them.

10 And they cried unto the LORD, and said, [a]We have sinned, because we have forsaken the LORD, [b]and have served Baalim and Ashtaroth: but now [c]deliver us out of the hand of our enemies, and we will serve thee.

11 And the LORD sent [a]Jerubbaal, and Bedan, and [b]Jephthah, and [c]Samuel, and delivered you out of the hand of your enemies on every side, and ye dwelled safe.

12 And when ye saw that [a]Nahash the king of the children of Ammon came against you, [b]ye said unto me, Nay; but a king shall reign over us: when [c]the LORD your God *was* your king.

13 Now therefore [a]behold the king [b]whom ye have chosen, *and* whom ye have desired! and, behold, [c]the LORD hath set a king over you.

14 If ye will [a]fear the LORD, and serve him, and obey his voice, and not rebel against the [1]commandment of the LORD, then shall both ye and also the king that reigneth over you [2]continue following the LORD your God:

15 But if ye will [a]not obey the voice of the LORD, but rebel against the commandment of the LORD, then shall the hand of the LORD be against you, [b]as *it was* against your fathers. S

16 ¶ Now therefore [a]stand and see this great thing, which the LORD will do before your eyes.

17 *Is it* not [a]wheat harvest today? [b]I will call unto the LORD, and he shall send thunder and rain; that ye may perceive and see that [c]your wickedness *is* great, which ye have done in the sight of the LORD, in asking you a king.

18 So Samuel called unto the LORD; and the LORD sent thunder and rain that day: and [a]all the people greatly feared the LORD and Samuel.

19 And all the people said unto Samuel, [a]Pray for thy servants unto the LORD thy God, that we die not: for we have added unto all our sins *this* evil, to ask us a king.

20 ¶ And Samuel said unto the people, Fear not: ye have done all this wickedness: yet turn not aside from following the LORD, but serve the LORD with all your heart; L

21 And [a]turn ye not aside: [b]for *then should ye go* after vain *things,* which cannot profit nor deliver; for they *are* vain.

15 [a]ch. 10:17 [b]ch. 10:8
12:1 [a]ch. 8:5,19, 20 [b]ch. 10:24
2 [a]Num. 27:17; ch. 8:20 [b]ch. 8:1,5
3 [a]ch. 24:6; 2 Sam. 1:14,16 [b]Num. 16:15; Acts 20:33; 1 Thes. 2:5 [c]Deut. 16:19 [1]Heb. *ransom* [2]Or, *that I should hide mine eyes at him*
5 [a]John 18:38; Acts 23:9 [b]Ex. 22:4
6 [a]Mic. 6:4 [1]Or, *made*
7 [a]Is. 1:18; Mic. 6:2,3 [b]Judg. 5:11 [1]Heb. *righteousnesses,* or, *benefits* [2]Heb. *with*
8 [a]Gen. 46:5,6 [b]Ex. 2:23 [c]Ex. 3:10
9 [a]Judg. 3:7 [b]Judg. 4:2 [c]Judg. 10:7 [d]Judg. 3:12
10 [a]Judg. 10:10 [b]Judg. 2:13 [c]Judg. 10:15,16
11 [a]Judg. 6:14,32 [b]Judg. 11:1 [c]ch. 7:13
12 [a]ch. 11:1 [b]ch. 8:5,19 [c]Judg. 8:23; ch. 8:7
13 [a]ch. 10:24 [b]ch. 8:5 [c]Hos. 13:11
14 [a]Josh. 24:14 [1]Heb. *mouth* [2]Heb. *be after*
15 [a]Lev. 26:14; Deut. 28:15; Josh. 24:20 [b]ver. 9
16 [a]Ex. 14:13
17 [a]Prov. 26:1 [b]Josh. 10:12; ch. 7:9,10; Jas. 5:16-18 [c]ch. 8:7
18 [a]Ex. 14:31; Ezra 10:9
19 [a]Ex. 9:28 & 10:17; Jas. 5:15; 1 John 5:16
21 [a]Deut. 11:16 [b]Jer. 16:19; Hab. 2:18; 1 Cor. 8:4

R *Jdg 10:15–16* ◀▶ *2Sa 12:13*
S *Jos 24:14* ◀▶ *1Sa 12:24*
L *Dt 30:19* ◀▶ *2Sa 12:13*

I 22 For [a]the LORD will not forsake his people [b]for his great name's sake: because [c]it hath pleased the LORD to make you his people.

23 Moreover as for me, God forbid that I should sin against the LORD [a]in[l] ceasing to pray for you: but [b]I will teach you the [c]good and the right way:

S L 24 [a]Only fear the LORD, and serve him in truth with all your heart: for [b]consider [l]how [c]great *things* he hath done for you.

J 25 But if ye shall still do wickedly, [a]ye shall be consumed, [b]both ye and your king.

Samuel rebukes Saul

13 SAUL [l]REIGNED one year; and when he had reigned two years over Israel,

2 Saul chose him three thousand *men* of Israel; *whereof* two thousand were with Saul in Michmash and in mount Beth-el, and a thousand were with Jonathan in [a]Gibeah of Benjamin: and the rest of the people he sent every man to his tent.

3 And Jonathan smote [a]the garrison of the Philistines that *was* in [l]Geba, and the Philistines heard *of it.* And Saul blew the trumpet throughout all the land, saying, Let the Hebrews hear.

4 And all Israel heard say *that* Saul had smitten a garrison of the Philistines, and *that* Israel also [l]was had in abomination with the Philistines. And the people were called together after Saul to Gilgal.

5 ¶ And the Philistines gathered themselves together to fight with Israel, thirty thousand chariots, and six thousand horsemen, and people as the sand which *is* on the sea shore in multitude: and they came up, and pitched in Michmash, eastward from Beth-aven.

6 When the men of Israel saw that they were in a strait, (for the people were distressed,) then the people [a]did hide themselves in caves, and in thickets, and in rocks, and in high places, and in pits.

7 And *some of* the Hebrews went over Jordan to the land of Gad and Gilead. As for Saul, he *was* yet in Gilgal, and all the people [l]followed him trembling.

8 ¶ [a]And he tarried seven days, according to the set time that Samuel *had appointed:* but Samuel came not to Gilgal; and the people were scattered from him.

9 And Saul said, Bring hither a burnt offering to me, and peace offerings. And he offered the burnt offering.

10 And it came to pass, that as soon as he had made an end of offering the burnt offering, behold, Samuel came; and Saul went out to meet him, that he might [l]salute him.

11 ¶ And Samuel said, What hast thou done? And Saul said, Because I saw that the people were scattered from me, and *that* thou camest not within the days appointed, and *that* the Philistines gathered themselves together at Michmash;

12 Therefore said I, The Philistines will come down now upon me to Gilgal, and I have not [l]made supplication unto the LORD: I forced myself therefore, and offered a burnt offering.

13 And Samuel said to Saul, [a]Thou hast done foolishly: [b]thou hast not kept the commandment of the LORD thy God, which he commanded thee: for now would the LORD have established thy kingdom upon Israel for ever.

14 [a]But now thy kingdom shall not continue: [b]the LORD hath sought him a man after his own heart, and the LORD hath commanded him *to be* captain over his people, because thou hast not kept *that* which the LORD commanded thee. J

Saul's small army

15 And Samuel arose, and gat him up from Gilgal unto Gibeah of Benjamin. And Saul numbered the people *that were*

22 [a]1 Ki. 6:13 [b]Josh. 7:9; Jer. 14:21 [c]Deut. 7:7,8
23 [a]Acts 12:5; Rom. 1:9; Col. 1:9; 2 Tim. 1:3 [b]Ps. 34:11; Prov. 4:11 [c]1 Ki. 8:36; 2 Chr. 6:27; Jer. 6:16 [l]Heb. *from ceasing*
24 [a]Eccl. 12:13 [b]Is. 5:12 [c]Deut. 10:21 [l]Or, *what a great* thing
25 [a]Josh. 24:20 [b]Deut. 28:36
13:1 [l]Heb. *the son of one year in his reigning*
2 [a]ch. 10:26
3 [a]ch. 10:5 [l]Or, *The hill*
4 [l]Heb. *did stink;* see Gen. 34:30; Ex. 5:21
6 [a]Judg. 6:2
7 [l]Heb. *trembled after him*
8 [a]ch. 10:8
10 [l]Heb. *bless him*
12 [l]Heb. *entreated the face*
13 [a]2 Chr. 16:9 [b]ch. 15:11
14 [a]ch. 15:28 [b]Ps. 89:20; Acts 13:22

I *1Sa 9:16* ◀▶ *1Sa 14:10*
S *1Sa 12:15* ◀▶ *1Sa 15:22–23*
L *1Sa 2:9* ◀▶ *1Sa 25:29*
J *1Sa 2:31* ◀▶ *1Sa 13:14*

J *1Sa 12:25* ◀▶ *2Sa 12:14*

12:22 The Lord reconfirmed the unconditional nature of his eternal covenant with Israel and his intent to set them apart as his chosen nation (see Dt 7:6).

13:14 King Saul had overstepped his bounds and offered a sacrifice that should have only been offered by the high priest. By such a sinful presumption, Saul violated the divine position of trust he had been given as Israel's king and incurred God's judgment. Saul would be removed as king; God had already chosen "a man after his own heart" to be the next king of Israel—David.

[1]present with him, [a]about six hundred
men.
16 And Saul, and Jonathan his son, and
the people *that were* present with them,
abode in [1]Gibeah of Benjamin: but the
Philistines encamped in Michmash.
17 ¶ And the spoilers came out of the
camp of the Philistines in three companies: one company turned unto the way
that leadeth to [a]Ophrah, unto the land of
Shual:
18 And another company turned the
way *to* [a]Beth-horon: and another company turned *to* the way of the border that
looketh to the valley of [b]Zeboim toward
the wilderness.
19 ¶ Now [a]there was no smith found
throughout all the land of Israel: for the
Philistines said, Lest the Hebrews make
them swords or spears:
20 But all the Israelites went down to
the Philistines, to sharpen every man his
share, and his coulter, and his axe, and
his mattock.
21 Yet they had [1]a file for the mat-
tocks, and for the coulters, and for the
forks, and for the axes, and [2]to sharpen
the goads.
22 So it came to pass in the day of battle, that [a]there was neither sword nor
spear found in the hand of any of the people that *were* with Saul and Jonathan: but
with Saul and with Jonathan his son was
there found.
23 [a]And the [1]garrison of the Philistines went out to the passage of
Michmash.

Jonathan attacks the Philistines

14 NOW [1]IT came to pass upon a
day, that Jonathan the son of Saul
said unto the young man that bare his
armour, Come, and let us go over to the
Philistines' garrison, that *is* on the other
side. But he told not his father.
2 And Saul tarried in the uttermost
part of Gibeah under a pomegranate tree
which *is* in Migron: and the people that
were with him *were* [a]about six hundred
men;
3 And [a]Ahiah, the son of Ahitub, [b]Ich-
abod's brother, the son of Phinehas, the
son of Eli, the LORD's priest in Shiloh,
[c]wearing an ephod. And the people knew
not that Jonathan was gone.
4 ¶ And between the passages, by
which Jonathan sought to go over [a]unto
the Philistines' garrison, *there was* a
sharp rock on the one side, and a sharp
rock on the other side: and the name of
the one *was* Bozez, and the name of the
other Seneh.
5 The [1]forefront of the one *was* situate
northward over against Michmash, and
the other southward over against Gibeah.
6 And Jonathan said to the young man V
that bare his armour, Come, and let us go
over unto the garrison of these uncircumcised: it may be that the LORD will work
for us: for *there is* no restraint to the LORD
[a]to save by many or by few.
7 And his armourbearer said unto him,
Do all that *is* in thine heart: turn thee;
behold, I *am* with thee according to thy
heart.
8 Then said Jonathan, Behold, we will
pass over unto *these* men, and we will
discover ourselves unto them.
9 If they say thus unto us, [1]Tarry until
we come to you; then we will stand still
in our place, and will not go up unto
them.
10 But if they say thus, Come up unto I
us; then we will go up: for the LORD hath
delivered them into our hand: and [a]this
shall be a sign unto us.
11 And both of them discovered themselves unto the garrison of the Philistines:
and the Philistines said, Behold, the Hebrews come forth out of the holes where
they had hid themselves.
12 And the men of the garrison answered Jonathan and his armourbearer,
and said, Come up to us, and we will
show you a thing. And Jonathan said unto
his armourbearer, Come up after me: for
the LORD hath delivered them into the
hand of Israel.
13 And Jonathan climbed up upon his
hands and upon his feet, and his armourbearer after him: and they fell before Jonathan; and his armourbearer slew after
him.
14 And that first slaughter, which Jonathan and his armourbearer made, was
about twenty men, within as it were [1]an
half acre of land, *which* a yoke *of oxen*
might plow.
15 And [a]there was trembling in the
host, in the field, and among all the people: the garrison, and [b]the spoilers, they

15 [a]ch. 14:2 [1]Heb. *found*
16 [1]Heb. *Geba; see* ver. 3
17 [a]Josh. 18:23
18 [a]Josh. 16:3 & 18:13,14 [b]Neh. 11:34; Gen. 14:2
19 [a]See 2 Ki. 24:14; Jer. 24:1
21 [1]Heb. *a file with mouths* [2]Heb. *to set*
22 [a]See Judg. 5:8
23 [a]ch. 14:1,4 [1]Or, *standing camp*
14:1 [1]Or, *there was a day*
2 [a]ch. 13:15
3 [a]ch. 22:9,11,20 called *Ahimelech* [b]ch. 4:21 [c]ch. 2:28
4 [a]ch. 13:23
5 [1]Heb. *tooth*
6 [a]Judg. 7:4,7; 2 Chr. 14:11
9 [1]Heb. *Be still*
10 [a]See Gen. 24:14; Judg. 7:11
14 [1]Or, *half a furrow of an acre of land*
15 [a]2 Ki. 7:7; Job 18:11 [b]ch. 13:17

V *Jos 23:9–10* ◄► *1Sa 17:47*
I *1Sa 12:22* ◄► *1Sa 17:36–37*

also trembled, and the earth quaked: so it was [c]a[l] very great trembling.

The Philistines flee

16 And the watchmen of Saul in Gibeah of Benjamin looked; and, behold, the multitude melted away, and they [a]went on beating down *one another.*

17 Then said Saul unto the people that *were* with him, Number now, and see who is gone from us. And when they had numbered, behold, Jonathan and his armourbearer *were* not *there.*

18 And Saul said unto Ahiah, Bring hither the ark of God. For the ark of God was at that time with the children of Israel.

19 ¶ And it came to pass, while Saul [a]talked unto the priest, that the [l]noise that *was* in the host of the Philistines went on and increased: and Saul said unto the priest, Withdraw thine hand.

20 And Saul and all the people that *were* with him [l]assembled themselves, and they came to the battle: and, behold, [a]every man's sword was against his fellow, *and there was* a very great discomfiture.

21 Moreover the Hebrews *that* were with the Philistines before that time, which went up with them into the camp *from the country* round about, even they also *turned* to be with the Israelites that *were* with Saul and Jonathan.

22 Likewise all the men of Israel which [a]had hid themselves in mount Ephraim, *when* they heard that the Philistines fled, even they also followed hard after them in the battle.

23 [a]So the LORD saved Israel that day: and the battle passed over [b]unto Bethaven.

Jonathan breaks Saul's oath

24 ¶ And the men of Israel were distressed that day: for Saul had [a]adjured the people, saying, Cursed *be* the man that eateth *any* food until evening, that I may be avenged on mine enemies. So none of the people tasted *any* food.

25 [a]And all *they of* the land came to a wood; and there was [b]honey upon the ground.

26 And when the people were come into the wood, behold, the honey dropped; but no man put his hand to his mouth: for the people feared the oath.

27 But Jonathan heard not when his father charged the people with the oath: wherefore he put forth the end of the rod that *was* in his hand, and dipped it in an honeycomb, and put his hand to his mouth; and his eyes were enlightened.

28 Then answered one of the people, and said, Thy father straitly charged the people with an oath, saying, Cursed *be* the man that eateth *any* food this day. And the people were [l]faint.

29 Then said Jonathan, My father hath troubled the land: see, I pray you, how mine eyes have been enlightened, because I tasted a little of this honey.

30 How much more, if haply the people had eaten freely today of the spoil of their enemies which they found? for had there not been now a much greater slaughter among the Philistines?

31 And they smote the Philistines that day from Michmash to Aijalon: and the people were very faint.

32 And the people flew upon the spoil, and took sheep, and oxen, and calves, and slew *them* on the ground: and the people did eat *them* [a]with the blood.

33 ¶ Then they told Saul, saying, Behold, the people sin against the LORD, in that they eat with the blood. And he said, Ye have [l]transgressed: roll a great stone unto me this day.

34 And Saul said, Disperse yourselves among the people, and say unto them, Bring me hither every man his ox, and every man his sheep, and slay *them* here, and eat; and sin not against the LORD in eating with the blood. And all the people brought every man his ox [l]with him that night, and slew *them* there.

35 And Saul [a]built an altar unto the LORD: [l]the same was the first altar that he built unto the LORD.

36 ¶ And Saul said, Let us go down after the Philistines by night, and spoil them until the morning light, and let us not leave a man of them. And they said, Do whatsoever seemeth good unto thee. Then said the priest, Let us draw near hither unto God.

37 And Saul asked counsel of God, Shall I go down after the Philistines? wilt thou deliver them into the hand of Israel? But [a]he answered him not that day.

38 And Saul said, [a]Draw ye near hither, all the [b]chief of the people: and

15 [c]Gen. 35:5 [l]Heb. *a trembling of God*
16 [a]ver. 20
19 [a]Num. 27:21 [l]Or, *tumult*
20 [a]Judg. 7:22; 2 Chr. 20:23 [l]Heb. *were cried together*
22 [a]ch. 13:6
23 [a]Ex. 14:30; Hos. 1:7 [b]ch. 13:5
24 [a]Josh. 6:26
25 [a]Deut. 9:28; Mat. 3:5 [b]Ex. 3:8; Num. 13:27; Mat. 3:4
28 [l]Or, *weary*
32 [a]Lev. 3:17 & 7:26 & 17:10 & 19:26; Deut. 12:16, 23,24
33 [l]Or, *dealt treacherously*
34 [l]Heb. *in his hand*
35 [a]ch. 7:17 [l]Heb. *that altar he began to build unto the LORD*
37 [a]ch. 28:6
38 [a]Josh. 7:14; ch. 10:19 [b]Judg. 20:2

know and see wherein this sin hath been this day.

39 For, [a]*as* the LORD liveth, which saveth Israel, though it be in Jonathan my son, he shall surely die. But *there was* not a man among all the people *that* answered him.

40 Then said he unto all Israel, Be ye on one side, and I and Jonathan my son will be on the other side. And the people said unto Saul, Do what seemeth good unto thee.

41 Therefore Saul said unto the LORD God of Israel, [a]Give[1] a perfect *lot.* [b]And Saul and Jonathan were taken: but the people [2]escaped.

42 And Saul said, Cast *lots* between me and Jonathan my son. And Jonathan was taken.

43 Then Saul said to Jonathan, [a]Tell me what thou hast done. And Jonathan told him, and said, [b]I did but taste a little honey with the end of the rod that *was* in mine hand, *and,* lo, I must die.

44 And Saul answered, [a]God do so and more also: [b]for thou shalt surely die, Jonathan.

45 And the people said unto Saul, Shall Jonathan die, who hath wrought this great salvation in Israel? God forbid: [a]*as* the LORD liveth, there shall not one hair of his head fall to the ground; for he hath wrought with God this day. So the people rescued Jonathan, that he died not.

46 Then Saul went up from following the Philistines: and the Philistines went to their own place.

Saul wars against other nations

47 ¶ So Saul took the kingdom over Israel, and fought against all his enemies on every side, against Moab, and against the children of [a]Ammon, and against Edom, and against the kings of [b]Zobah, and against the Philistines: and whithersoever he turned himself, he vexed *them.*

48 And he [1]gathered an host, and [a]smote the Amalekites, and delivered Israel out of the hands of them that spoiled them.

49 Now [a]the sons of Saul were Jonathan, and Ishui, and Melch-ishua: and the names of his two daughters *were these;* the name of the firstborn Merab, and the name of the younger Michal:

50 And the name of Saul's wife *was* Ahinoam, the daughter of Ahimaaz: and the name of the captain of his host *was* [1]Abner, the son of Ner, Saul's uncle.

51 [a]And Kish *was* the father of Saul; and Ner the father of Abner *was* the son of Abiel.

52 And there was sore war against the Philistines all the days of Saul: and when Saul saw any strong man, or any valiant man, [a]he took him unto him.

Saul rejected as king

15 SAMUEL ALSO said unto Saul, [a]The LORD sent me to anoint thee *to be* king over his people, over Israel: now therefore hearken thou unto the voice of the words of the LORD.

2 Thus saith the LORD of hosts, I remember *that* which Amalek did to Israel, [a]how he laid *wait* for him in the way, when he came up from Egypt.

3 Now go and smite Amalek, and [a]utterly destroy all that they have, and spare them not; but slay both man and woman, infant and suckling, ox and sheep, camel and ass.

4 And Saul gathered the people together, and numbered them in Telaim, two hundred thousand footmen, and ten thousand men of Judah.

5 And Saul came to a city of Amalek, and [1]laid wait in the valley.

6 ¶ And Saul said unto [a]the Kenites, [b]Go, depart, get you down from among the Amalekites, lest I destroy you with them: for [c]ye showed kindness to all the children of Israel, when they came up out of Egypt. So the Kenites departed from among the Amalekites.

7 [a]And Saul smote the Amalekites from [b]Havilah *until* thou comest to [c]Shur, that *is* over against Egypt.

8 And [a]he took Agag the king of the Amalekites alive, and [b]utterly destroyed all the people with the edge of the sword.

9 But Saul and the people [a]spared Agag, and the best of the sheep, and of the oxen, and [1]of the fatlings, and the lambs, and all *that was* good, and would not utterly destroy them: but every thing *that was* vile and refuse, that they destroyed utterly.

10 ¶ Then came the word of the LORD unto Samuel, saying,

11 [a]It repenteth me that I have set up Saul *to be* king: for he is [b]turned back from following me, [c]and hath not performed my commandments. And it

39 [a]2 Sam. 12:5
41 [a]Prov. 16:33; Acts 1:24 [b]Josh. 7:16; ch. 10:20,21 [1]Or, *Show the innocent* [2]Heb. *went forth*
43 [a]Josh. 7:19 [b]ver. 27
44 [a]Ruth 1:17 [b]ver. 39
45 [a]2 Sam. 14:11; 1 Ki. 1:52; Luke 21:18
47 [a]ch. 11:11 [b]2 Sam. 10:6
48 [a]ch. 15:3,7 [1]Or, *wrought mightily*
49 [a]ch. 31:2; 1 Chr. 8:33
50 [1]Heb. *Abiner*
51 [a]ch. 9:1
52 [a]ch. 8:11
15:1 [a]ch. 9:16
2 [a]Ex. 17:8,14; Num. 24:20; Deut. 25:17-19
3 [a]Lev. 27:28,29; Josh. 6:17,21
5 [1]Or, *fought*
6 [a]Num. 24:21; Judg. 1:16 & 4:11 [b]Gen. 18:25 & 19:12,14; Rev. 18:4 [c]Ex. 18:10,19; Num. 10:29,32
7 [a]ch. 14:48 [b]Gen. 2:11 & 25:18 [c]Gen. 16:7
8 [a]See 1 Ki. 20:34, 35 [b]See ch. 30:1
9 [a]ver. 3,15 [1]Or, *of the second sort*
11 [a]ver. 35; Gen. 6:6,7; 2 Sam. 24:16 [b]Josh. 22:16; 1 Ki. 9:6 [c]ver. 3,9; ch. 13:13

[d]grieved Samuel; and he cried unto the LORD all night.

12 And when Samuel rose early to meet Saul in the morning, it was told Samuel, saying, Saul came to [a]Carmel, and, behold, he set him up a place, and is gone about, and passed on, and gone down to Gilgal.

13 And Samuel came to Saul: and Saul said unto him, [a]Blessed *be* thou of the LORD: I have performed the commandment of the LORD.

14 And Samuel said, What *meaneth* then this bleating of the sheep in mine ears, and the lowing of the oxen which I hear?

15 And Saul said, They have brought them from the Amalekites: [a]for the people spared the best of the sheep and of the oxen, to sacrifice unto the LORD thy God; and the rest we have utterly destroyed.

16 Then Samuel said unto Saul, Stay, and I will tell thee what the LORD hath said to me this night. And he said unto him, Say on.

17 And Samuel said, [a]When thou *wast* little in thine own sight, *wast* thou not *made* the head of the tribes of Israel, and the LORD anointed thee king over Israel?

18 And the LORD sent thee on a journey, and said, Go and utterly destroy the sinners the Amalekites, and fight against them until [/]they be consumed.

19 Wherefore then didst thou not obey the voice of the LORD, but didst fly upon the spoil, and didst evil in the sight of the LORD?

20 And Saul said unto Samuel, Yea, [a]I have obeyed the voice of the LORD, and have gone the way which the LORD sent me, and have brought Agag the king of Amalek, and have utterly destroyed the Amalekites.

21 [a]But the people took of the spoil, sheep and oxen, the chief of the things which should have been utterly destroyed, to sacrifice unto the LORD thy God in Gilgal.

S 22 And Samuel said, [a]Hath the LORD *as* *great* delight in burnt offerings and sacrifices, as in obeying the voice of the LORD? Behold, [b]to obey *is* better than sacrifice, *and* to hearken than the fat of rams.

23 For rebellion *is as* the sin of [/]witchcraft, and stubbornness *is as* iniquity and idolatry. Because thou hast rejected the word of the LORD, [a]he hath also rejected thee from *being* king.

24 ¶ [a]And Saul said unto Samuel, I have sinned: for I have transgressed the commandment of the LORD, and thy words: because I [b]feared the people, and obeyed their voice.

25 Now therefore, I pray thee, pardon my sin, and turn again with me, that I may worship the LORD.

26 And Samuel said unto Saul, I will not return with thee: [a]for thou hast rejected the word of the LORD, and the LORD hath rejected thee from being king over Israel.

27 And as Samuel turned about to go away, [a]he laid hold upon the skirt of his mantle, and it rent.

28 And Samuel said unto him, [a]The LORD hath rent the kingdom of Israel from thee this day, and hath given it to a neighbour of thine, *that is* better than thou.

29 And also the [/]Strength of Israel [a]will not lie nor repent: for he *is* not a man, that he should repent.

30 Then he said, I have sinned: *yet* [a]honour me now, I pray thee, before the elders of my people, and before Israel, and turn again with me, that I may worship the LORD thy God.

31 So Samuel turned again after Saul; and Saul worshipped the LORD.

32 ¶ Then said Samuel, Bring ye hither to me Agag the king of the Amalekites. And Agag came unto him delicately. And Agag said, Surely the bitterness of death is past.

33 And Samuel said, [a]As thy sword hath made women childless, so shall thy mother be childless among women. And Samuel hewed Agag in pieces before the LORD in Gilgal.

34 ¶ Then Samuel went to Ramah; and

11 [d]ver. 35; ch. 16:1
12 [a]Josh. 15:55
13 [a]Gen. 14:19; Judg. 17:2; Ruth 3:10
15 [a]ver. 9,21; Gen. 3:12; Prov. 28:13
17 [a]ch. 9:21
18 [/]Heb. *they consume them*
20 [a]ver. 13
21 [a]ver. 15
22 [a]Is. 1:11-13,16, 17; Jer. 7:22,23; Mic. 6:6-8; Heb. 10:6-9 [b]Eccl. 5:1; Hos. 6:6; Mat. 5:24 & 9:13 & 12:7; Mark 12:33
23 [a]ch. 13:14 [/]Heb. *divination*
24 [a]See 2 Sam. 12:13 [b]Ex. 23:2; Is. 51:12,13
26 [a]ch. 2:30
27 [a]See 1 Ki. 11:30
28 [a]ch. 28:17,18; 1 Ki. 11:31
29 [a]Num. 23:19; Ezek. 24:14; 2 Tim. 2:13; Tit. 1:2 [/]Or, *Eternity*, or, *Victory*
30 [a]John 5:44 & 12:43
33 [a]Ex. 17:11; Num. 14:45; See Judg. 1:7

S *1Sa 12:24* ◄ ► *1Sa 16:14*

15:22 Samuel revealed that God desired obedience more than the formal completion of the required sacrifices. Saul's rebellion and disobedience grew from the root of spiritual pride that in God's eyes was as abominable as witchcraft and idolatry (see 15:23)

Saul went up to his house to [a]Gibeah of
Saul.
35 And [a]Samuel came no more to see
Saul until the day of his death: nevertheless Samuel [b]mourned for Saul: and the
LORD [c]repented that he had made Saul
king over Israel.

David chosen to be king

16 AND THE LORD said unto Samuel,
[a]How long wilt thou mourn for
Saul, seeing [b]I have rejected him from
reigning over Israel? [c]fill thine horn with
oil, and go, I will send thee to Jesse the
Bethlehemite: for [d]I have provided me a
king among his sons.
2 And Samuel said, How can I go? if
Saul hear *it,* he will kill me. And the LORD
said, Take an heifer [1]with thee, and say,
[a]I am come to sacrifice to the LORD.
3 And call Jesse to the sacrifice, and [a]I
will show thee what thou shalt do: and
[b]thou shalt anoint unto me *him* whom I
name unto thee.
4 And Samuel did that which the LORD
spake, and came to Bethlehem. And the
elders of the town [a]trembled at his [1]com-
ing, and said, [b]Comest thou peaceably?
5 And he said, Peaceably: I am come to
sacrifice unto the LORD: [a]sanctify yourselves, and come with me to the sacrifice.
And he sanctified Jesse and his sons, and
called them to the sacrifice.
6 ¶ And it came to pass, when they
were come, that he looked on [a]Eliab, and
[b]said, Surely the LORD'S anointed *is* before
him.
E 7 But the LORD said unto Samuel, Look
G not on [a]his countenance, or on the
height of his stature; because I have refused him: [b]for *the LORD seeth* not as man
seeth; for man [c]looketh on the [1]outward
appearance, but the LORD looketh on the
[d]heart.
8 Then Jesse called [a]Abinadab, and
made him pass before Samuel. And he
said, Neither hath the LORD chosen this.
9 Then Jesse made [a]Shammah[1] to pass
by. And he said, Neither hath the LORD
chosen this.
10 Again, Jesse made seven of his sons
to pass before Samuel. And Samuel said
unto Jesse, The LORD hath not chosen
these.
11 And Samuel said unto Jesse, Are
here all *thy* children? And he said, [a]There
remaineth yet the youngest, and, behold,
he keepeth the sheep. And Samuel said
unto Jesse, [b]Send and fetch him: for we
will not sit [1]down till he come hither.
12 And he sent, and brought him in.
Now he *was* [a]ruddy, *and* withal [1]of a
beautiful countenance, and goodly to look
to. [b]And the LORD said, Arise, anoint him:
for this *is* he.
13 Then Samuel took the horn of oil,
and [a]anointed him in the midst of his
brethren: and [b]the spirit of the LORD came
upon David from that day forward. So
Samuel rose up, and went to Ramah.

David plays the harp

14 ¶ [a]But the spirit of the LORD de- Q
parted from Saul, and [b]an evil spirit from S
the LORD [1]troubled him.
15 And Saul's servants said unto him,
Behold now, an evil spirit from God troubleth thee.
16 Let our lord now command thy servants, *which are* [a]before thee, to seek out
a man, *who is* a cunning player on an
harp: and it shall come to pass, when the
evil spirit from God is upon thee, that he
shall [b]play with his hand, and thou shalt
be well.
17 And Saul said unto his servants,
Provide me now a man that can play well,
and bring *him* to me.
18 Then answered one of the servants,
and said, Behold, I have seen a son of

34 [a]ch. 11:4
35 [a]See ch. 19:24 [b]ver. 11; ch. 16:1 [c]ver. 11
16:1 [a]ch. 15:35 [b]ch. 15:23 [c]ch. 9:16; 2 Ki. 9:1 [d]Ps. 78:70; Acts 13:22
2 [a]ch. 9:12 & 20:29 [1]Heb. *in thine hand*
3 [a]Ex. 4:15 [b]ch. 9:16
4 [a]ch. 21:1 [b]1 Ki. 2:13; 2 Ki. 9:22 [1]Heb. *meeting*
5 [a]Ex. 19:10
6 [a]ch. 17:13; Called *Elihu* 1 Chr. 27:18 [b]1 Ki. 12:26
7 [a]Ps. 147:10 [b]Is. 55:8 [c]2 Cor. 10:7 [d]1 Ki. 8:39 [1]Heb. *eyes*
8 [a]ch. 17:13
9 [a]ch. 17:13 [1]*Shimeah* in 2 Sam. 13:3; *Shimma* in 1 Chr. 2:13
11 [a]ch. 17:12 [b]2 Sam. 7:8 [1]Heb. *round*
12 [a]ch. 17:42 [b]See ch. 9:17 [1]Heb. *fair of eyes*
13 [a]ch. 10:1 [b]Num. 27:18; Judg. 11:29 & 13:25; ch. 10:6,10
14 [a]Judg. 16:20 [b]Judg. 9:23 [1]Or, *terrified*
16 [a]ver. 21,22; Gen. 41:46 [b]ver. 23; 2 Ki. 3:15

E *1Sa 2:3* ◄► *1Ki 8:39*
G *Dt 32:31* ◄► *Job 8:11–16*

Q *Jdg 16:20* ◄► *1Ki 22:24*
S *1Sa 15:22–23* ◄► *1Sa 24:13*

16:7 God is more concerned with what is inside the heart than what is outwardly visible to others. Note that no one even considered the possibility that Samuel would anoint David (see 16:7–13). He was a young shepherd. He had no military experience or advantages by virtue of birth order. Yet God knew David's heart. Position, birth order, strength or beauty meant nothing. Though David was young and weak, God in his sovereign grace chose the man he wanted to use in his service regardless of natural advantage for God's "strength is made perfect in weakness" (2Co 12:9).

16:13 The anointing of David as the king of Israel prefigures the anointing of the true Messiah of Israel at the conclusion of the seventy weeks (see Da 9:24).

Jesse the Bethlehemite, *that is* cunning in playing, and [a]a mighty valiant man, and a man of war, and prudent in [1]matters, and a comely person, and [b]the LORD *is* with him.

19 ¶ Wherefore Saul sent messengers unto Jesse, and said, Send me David thy son, [a]which *is* with the sheep.

20 And Jesse [a]took an ass *laden* with bread, and a bottle of wine, and a kid, and sent *them* by David his son unto Saul.

21 And David came to Saul, and [a]stood before him: and he loved him greatly; and he became his armourbearer.

22 And Saul sent to Jesse, saying, Let David, I pray thee, stand before me; for he hath found favour in my sight.

23 And it came to pass, when [a]the *evil* spirit from God was upon Saul, that David took an harp, and played with his hand: so Saul was refreshed, and was well, and the evil spirit departed from him.

David and Goliath

17 NOW THE Philistines gathered together their armies to battle, and were gathered together at [a]Shochoh, which *belongeth* to Judah, and pitched between Shochoh and Azekah, in [1]Ephes-dammim.

2 And Saul and the men of Israel were gathered together, and pitched by the valley of Elah, and [1]set the battle in array against the Philistines.

3 And the Philistines stood on a mountain on the one side, and Israel stood on a mountain on the other side: and *there was* a valley between them.

4 ¶ And there went out a champion out of the camp of the Philistines, named [a]Goliath, of [b]Gath, whose height *was* six cubits and a span.

5 And *he had* an helmet of brass upon his head, and he *was* [1]armed with a coat of mail; and the weight of the coat *was* five thousand shekels of brass.

6 And *he had* greaves of brass upon his legs, and a [1]target of brass between his shoulders.

7 And the staff of his spear *was* like a weaver's beam; and his spear's head *weighed* six hundred shekels of iron: and one bearing a shield went before him.

8 And he stood and cried unto the armies of Israel, and said unto them, Why are ye come out to set *your* battle in array? *am* not I a Philistine, and ye [a]servants to Saul? choose you a man for you, and let him come down to me.

9 If he be able to fight with me, and to kill me, then will we be your servants: but if I prevail against him, and kill him, then shall ye be our servants, and [a]serve us.

10 And the Philistine said, I [a]defy the armies of Israel this day; give me a man, that we may fight together.

11 When Saul and all Israel heard those words of the Philistine, they were dismayed, and greatly afraid.

12 ¶ Now David *was* [a]the son of that [b]Ephrathite of Bethlehem-judah, whose name *was* Jesse; and he had [c]eight sons: and the man went among men *for* an old man in the days of Saul.

13 And the three eldest sons of Jesse went *and* followed Saul to the battle: and the [a]names of his three sons that went to the battle *were* Eliab the firstborn, and next unto him Abinadab, and the third Shammah.

14 And David *was* the youngest: and the three eldest followed Saul.

15 But David went and returned from Saul [a]to feed his father's sheep at Bethlehem.

16 And the Philistine drew near morning and evening, and presented himself forty days.

17 And Jesse said unto David his son, Take now for thy brethren an ephah of this parched *corn,* and these ten loaves, and run to the camp to thy brethren;

18 And carry these ten [1]cheeses unto the [2]captain of *their* thousand, and [a]look how thy brethren fare, and take their pledge.

19 Now Saul, and they, and all the men of Israel, *were* in the valley of Elah, fighting with the Philistines.

20 ¶ And David rose up early in the morning, and left the sheep with a keeper, and took, and went, as Jesse had commanded him; and he came to the [a]trench,[1] as the host was going forth to the [2]fight, and shouted for the battle.

21 For Israel and the Philistines had put the battle in array, army against army.

22 And David left [1]his carriage in the hand of the keeper of the carriage, and ran into the army, and came and saluted his brethren.

18 [a]ch. 17:32, 34-36 [b]ch. 3:19 & 18:12,14 [1]Or, *speech*
19 [a]ver. 11; ch. 17:15
20 [a]ch. 10:27 & 17:18
21 [a]Gen. 41:46
23 [a]ver. 14,16
17:1 [a]Josh. 15:35 [1]Or, *The coast of Dammim,* called *Pas-dammim* in 1 Chr. 11:13
2 [1]Heb. *ranged the battle*
4 [a]2 Sam. 21:19 [b]Josh. 11:22
5 [1]Heb. *clothed*
6 [1]Or, *gorget*
8 [a]ch. 8:17
9 [a]ch. 11:1
10 [a]ver. 26; 2 Sam. 21:21
12 [a]ver. 58; Ruth 4:22; ch. 16:1,18 [b]Gen. 35:19 [c]ch. 16:10,11; See 1 Chr. 2:13-15
13 [a]ch. 16:6,8,9
15 [a]ch. 16:19
18 [a]Gen. 37:14 [1]Heb. *cheeses of milk* [2]Heb. *captain of a thousand*
20 [a]ch. 26:5 [1]Or, *place of the carriage* [2]Or, *battle array,* or, *place of fight*
22 [1]Heb. *the vessels from upon him*

23 And as he talked with them, behold, there came up the champion, the Philistine of Gath, Goliath by name, out of the armies of the Philistines, and spake [a]according to the same words: and David heard *them.*

24 And all the men of Israel, when they saw the man, fled [1]from him, and were sore afraid.

25 And the men of Israel said, Have ye seen this man that is come up? surely to defy Israel is he come up: and it shall be, *that* the man who killeth him, the king will enrich him with great riches, and [a]will give him his daughter, and make his father's house free in Israel.

26 And David spake to the men that stood by him, saying, What shall be done to the man that killeth this Philistine, and taketh away [a]the reproach from Israel? for who *is* this [b]uncircumcised Philistine, that he should [c]defy the armies of [d]the living God?

27 And the people answered him after this manner, saying, [a]So shall it be done to the man that killeth him.

28 ¶ And Eliab his eldest brother heard when he spake unto the men; and Eliab's [a]anger was kindled against David, and he said, Why camest thou down hither? and with whom hast thou left those few sheep in the wilderness? I know thy pride, and the naughtiness of thine heart; for thou art come down that thou mightest see the battle.

29 And David said, What have I now done? [a]*Is there* not a cause?

30 ¶ And he turned from him toward another, and [a]spake after the same [1]manner: and the people answered him again after the former manner.

31 And when the words were heard which David spake, they rehearsed *them* before Saul: and he [1]sent for him.

32 ¶ And David said to Saul, [a]Let no man's heart fail because of him; [b]thy servant will go and fight with this Philistine.

33 And Saul said to David, [a]Thou art not able to go against this Philistine to fight with him: for thou *art but* a youth, and he a man of war from his youth.

34 And David said unto Saul, Thy servant kept his father's sheep, and there came a lion, and a bear, and took a [1]lamb out of the flock:

35 And I went out after him, and smote him, and delivered *it* out of his mouth: and when he arose against me, I caught *him* by his beard, and smote him, and slew him.

36 Thy servant slew both the lion and the bear: and this uncircumcised Philistine shall be as one of them, seeing he hath defied the armies of the living God.

37 David said moreover, [a]The LORD that delivered me out of the paw of the lion, and out of the paw of the bear, he will deliver me out of the hand of this Philistine. And Saul said unto David, Go, and [b]the LORD be with thee.

38 ¶ And Saul [1]armed David with his armour, and he put an helmet of brass upon his head; also he armed him with a coat of mail.

39 And David girded his sword upon his armour, and he assayed to go; for he had not proved *it.* And David said unto Saul, I cannot go with these; for I have not proved *them.* And David put them off him.

40 And he took his staff in his hand, and chose him five smooth stones out of the [1]brook, and put them in a shepherd's [2]bag which he had, even in a scrip; and his sling *was* in his hand: and he drew near to the Philistine.

41 And the Philistine came on and drew near unto David; and the man that bare the shield *went* before him.

42 And when the Philistine looked about, and saw David, he [a]disdained him: for he was *but* a youth, and [b]ruddy, and of a fair countenance.

43 And the Philistine said unto David, [a]*Am* I a dog, that thou comest to me with staves? And the Philistine cursed David by his gods.

44 And the Philistine [a]said to David, Come to me, and I will give thy flesh

❙ 1Sa 14:10 ◀ ▶ 1Sa 25:28

23 [a]ver. 8
24 [1]Heb. *from his face*
25 [a]Josh. 15:16
26 [a]ch. 11:2 [b]ch. 14:6 [c]ver. 10 [d]Deut. 5:26
27 [a]ver. 25
28 [a]Gen. 37:4,8, 11; Mat. 10:36
29 [a]ver. 17
30 [a]ver. 26,27 [1]Heb. *word*
31 [1]Heb. *took him*
32 [a]Deut. 20:1,3 [b]ch. 16:18
33 [a]See Num. 13:31; Deut. 9:2
34 [1]Or, *kid*
37 [a]2 Cor. 1:10; 2 Tim. 4:17,18 [b]ch. 20:13; 1 Chr. 22:11,16
38 [1]Heb. *clothed David with his clothes*
40 [1]Or, *valley* [2]Heb. *vessel*
42 [a]1 Cor. 1:27,28 [b]ch. 16:12
43 [a]ch. 24:14; 2 Sam. 3:8 & 9:8 & 16:9; 2 Ki. 8:13
44 [a]1 Ki. 20:10,11

17:40 Though David gathered five stones, this is not an indication of a lack of faith in God's power to help him defeat Goliath. Realizing that the death of their champion might anger the Philistines, David prudently gathered these extra stones for additional ammunition in case other Philistines decided to join the fight.

unto the fowls of the air, and to the beasts of the field.

45 Then said David to the Philistine, Thou comest to me with a sword, and with a spear, and with a shield: [a]but I come to thee in the name of the LORD of hosts, the God of the armies of Israel, whom thou hast [b]defied.

46 This day will the LORD [1]deliver thee into mine hand; and I will smite thee, and take thine head from thee; and I will give [a]the carcases of the host of the Philistines this day unto the fowls of the air, and to the wild beasts of the earth; [b]that all the earth may know that there is a God in Israel.

V 47 And all this assembly shall know that the LORD [a]saveth not with sword and spear: for [b]the battle *is* the LORD'S, and he will give you into our hands.

48 And it came to pass, when the Philistine arose, and came and drew nigh to meet David, that David hasted, and ran toward the army to meet the Philistine.

49 And David put his hand in his bag, and took thence a stone, and slang *it,* and smote the Philistine in his forehead, that the stone sunk into his forehead; and he fell upon his face to the earth.

50 So [a]David prevailed over the Philistine with a sling and with a stone, and smote the Philistine, and slew him; but *there was* no sword in the hand of David.

51 Therefore David ran, and stood upon the Philistine, and took his sword, and drew it out of the sheath thereof, and slew him, and cut off his head therewith. And when the Philistines saw their champion was dead, [a]they fled.

52 And the men of Israel and of Judah arose, and shouted, and pursued the Philistines, until thou come to the valley, and to the gates of Ekron. And the wounded of the Philistines fell down by the way to [a]Shaaraim, even unto Gath, and unto Ekron.

53 And the children of Israel returned from chasing after the Philistines, and they spoiled their tents.

54 And David took the head of the Philistine, and brought it to Jerusalem; but he put his armour in his tent.

55 ¶ And when Saul saw David go forth against the Philistine, he said unto Abner, the captain of the host, Abner, [a]whose son *is* this youth? And Abner said, *As* thy soul liveth, O king, I cannot tell.

56 And the king said, Inquire thou whose son the stripling *is.*

57 And as David returned from the slaughter of the Philistine, Abner took him, and brought him before Saul [a]with the head of the Philistine in his hand.

58 And Saul said to him, Whose son *art* thou, *thou* young man? And David answered, [a]*I am* the son of thy servant Jesse the Bethlehemite.

Saul's hatred of David

18 AND IT came to pass, when he had made an end of speaking unto Saul, that [a]the soul of Jonathan was knit with the soul of David, [b]and Jonathan loved him as his own soul.

2 And Saul took him that day, [a]and would let him go no more home to his father's house.

3 Then Jonathan and David made a covenant, because he loved him as his own soul.

4 And Jonathan stripped himself of the robe that *was* upon him, and gave it to David, and his garments, even to his sword, and to his bow, and to his girdle.

5 ¶ And David went out whithersoever Saul sent him, *and* [1]behaved himself wisely: and Saul set him over the men of war, and he was accepted in the sight of all the people, and also in the sight of Saul's servants.

6 And it came to pass as they came, when David was returned from the slaughter of the [1]Philistine, that [a]the women came out of all cities of Israel, singing and dancing, to meet king Saul, with tabrets, with joy, and with [2]instruments of music.

7 And the women [a]answered *one another* as they played, and said, [b]Saul hath slain his thousands, and David his ten thousands.

8 And Saul was very wroth, and the saying [a]displeased[1] him; and he said, They have ascribed unto David ten thousands, and to me they have ascribed *but* thousands: and *what* can he have more but [b]the kingdom?

9 And Saul eyed David from that day and forward.

10 ¶ And it came to pass on the morrow, that [a]the evil spirit from God came

---

45 [a]2 Sam. 22:33, 35; 2 Cor. 10:4; Heb. 11:33,34 [b]ver. 10
46 [a]Deut. 28:26 [b]Josh. 4:24; 1 Ki. 8:43 & 18:36; 2 Ki. 19:19; Is. 52:10 [1]Heb. *shut thee up*
47 [a]Hos. 1:7; Zech. 4:6 [b]2 Chr. 20:15
50 [a]ch. 21:9; See Judg. 3:31 & 15:15; 2 Sam. 23:21
51 [a]Heb. 11:34
52 [a]Josh. 15:36
55 [a]See ch. 16:21, 22
57 [a]ver. 54
58 [a]ver. 12
18:1 [a]Gen. 44:30 [b]ch. 19:2 & 20:17; 2 Sam. 1:26; Deut. 13:6
2 [a]ch. 17:15
5 [1]Or, *prospered;* see ver. 14,15,30
6 [a]Ex. 15:20; Judg. 11:34 [1]Or, *Philistines* [2]Heb. *three-stringed instruments*
7 [a]Ex. 15:21 [b]ch. 21:11 & 29:5
8 [a]Eccl. 4:4 [b]ch. 15:28 [1]Heb. *was evil in his eyes*
10 [a]ch. 16:14

upon Saul, [b]and he prophesied in the
midst of the house: and David played
with his hand, as at other times: [c]and
there was a javelin in Saul's hand.
11 And Saul [a]cast the javelin; for he
said, I will smite David even to the wall
with it. And David avoided out of his
presence twice.
12 ¶ And Saul was [a]afraid of David, because [b]the LORD was with him, and was
[c]departed from Saul.
13 Therefore Saul removed him from
him, and made him his captain over a
thousand; and [a]he went out and came in
before the people.
14 And David [/]behaved himself wisely
in all his ways; and [a]the LORD *was* with
him.
15 Wherefore when Saul saw that he
behaved himself very wisely, he was
afraid of him.
16 But [a]all Israel and Judah loved David, because he went out and came in
before them.
17 ¶ And Saul said to David, Behold
my elder daughter Merab, [a]her will I give
thee to wife: only be thou [/]valiant for
me, and fight [b]the LORD'S battles. For Saul
said, [c]Let not mine hand be upon him,
but let the hand of the Philistines be
upon him.
18 And David said unto Saul, [a]Who *am*
I? and what *is* my life, *or* my father's family in Israel, that I should be son-in-law to
the king?
19 But it came to pass at the time
when Merab Saul's daughter should have
been given to David, that she was given
unto [a]Adriel the [b]Meholathite to wife.
20 [a]And Michal Saul's daughter loved
David: and they told Saul, and the thing
[/]pleased him.
21 And Saul said, I will give him her,
that she may be a snare to him, and that
[a]the hand of the Philistines may be
against him. Wherefore Saul said to David, Thou shalt [b]this day be my son-in-
law in *the one of* the twain.
22 ¶ And Saul commanded his servants, *saying,* Commune with David secretly, and say, Behold, the king hath delight in thee, and all his servants love
thee: now therefore be the king's son-in-
law.
23 And Saul's servants spake those
words in the ears of David. And David
said, Seemeth it to you *a* light *thing* to be
a king's son-in-law, seeing that I *am* a
poor man, and lightly esteemed?
24 And the servants of Saul told him,
saying, [/]On this manner spake David.
25 And Saul said, Thus shall ye say to
David, The king desireth not any [a]dowry,
but an hundred foreskins of the Philistines, to be [b]avenged of the king's enemies. But Saul [c]thought to make David
fall by the hand of the Philistines.
26 And when his servants told David
these words, it pleased David well to be
the king's son-in-law: and [a]the days were
not [/]expired.
27 Wherefore David arose and went,
he and [a]his men, and slew of the Philistines two hundred men; and [b]David
brought their foreskins, and they gave
them in full tale to the king, that he
might be the king's son-in-law. And Saul
gave him Michal his daughter to wife.
28 ¶ And Saul saw and knew that the
LORD *was* with David, and *that* Michal
Saul's daughter loved him.
29 And Saul was yet the more afraid of
David; and Saul became David's enemy
continually.
30 Then the princes of the Philistines
[a]went forth: and it came to pass, after
they went forth, *that* David [b]behaved
himself more wisely than all the servants
of Saul; so that his name was much
[/]set by.

Saul tries to kill David

19 AND SAUL spake to Jonathan his
son, and to all his servants, that
they should kill David.
2 But Jonathan Saul's son [a]delighted
much in David: and Jonathan told David,
saying, Saul my father seeketh to kill
thee: now therefore, I pray thee, take
heed to thyself until the morning, and
abide in a secret *place,* and hide thyself:
3 And I will go out and stand beside
my father in the field where thou *art,* and
I will commune with my father of thee;
and what I see, that I will tell thee.
4 ¶ And Jonathan [a]spake good of David
unto Saul his father, and said unto him,
Let not the king [b]sin against his servant,
against David; because he hath not
sinned against thee, and because his
works *have been* to thee-ward very good:
5 For he did put his [a]life in his hand,
and [b]slew the Philistine, and [c]the LORD
wrought a great salvation for all Israel:

10 [b]ch. 19:24; 1 Ki. 18:29; Acts 16:16 [c]ch. 19:9
11 [a]ch. 19:10 & 20:33
12 [a]ver. 15,29 [b]ch. 16:13,18 [c]ch. 16:14 & 28:15
13 [a]ver. 16; Num. 27:17; 2 Sam. 5:2
14 [a]Gen. 39:2,3, 23; Josh. 6:27 [/]Or, *prospered;* see ver. 5
16 [a]ver. 5
17 [a]ch. 17:25 [b]Num. 32:20,27, 29; ch. 25:28 [c]ver. 21,25; 2 Sam. 12:9 [/]Heb. *a son of valour*
18 [a]See ver. 23; ch. 9:21; 2 Sam. 7:18
19 [a]2 Sam. 21:8 [b]Judg. 7:22
20 [a]ver. 28 [/]Heb. *was right in his eyes*
21 [a]ver. 17 [b]See ver. 26
24 [/]Heb. *According to these words*
25 [a]Gen. 34:12; Ex. 22:17 [b]ch. 14:24 [c]ver. 17
26 [a]See ver. 21 [/]Heb. *fulfilled*
27 [a]ver. 13 [b]2 Sam. 3:14
30 [a]2 Sam. 11:1 [b]ver. 5 [/]Heb. *precious*
19:2 [a]ch. 18:1
4 [a]Prov. 31:8,9 [b]Gen. 42:22; Prov. 17:13
5 [a]Judg. 9:17 [b]ch. 17:49,50 [c]1 Sam. 11:13; 1 Chr. 11:14

thou sawest *it,* and didst rejoice: [d]wherefore then wilt thou [e]sin against innocent blood, to slay David without a cause?

6 And Saul hearkened unto the voice of Jonathan: and Saul sware, *As* the LORD liveth, he shall not be slain.

7 And Jonathan called David, and Jonathan showed him all those things. And Jonathan brought David to Saul, and he was in his presence, [a]as [1]in times past.

8 ¶ And there was war again: and David went out, and fought with the Philistines, and slew them with a great slaughter; and they fled from [1]him.

9 And [a]the evil spirit from the LORD was upon Saul, as he sat in his house with his javelin in his hand: and David played with *his* hand.

10 And Saul sought to smite David even to the wall with the javelin; but he slipped away out of Saul's presence, and he smote the javelin into the wall: and David fled, and escaped that night.

11 [a]Saul also sent messengers unto David's house, to watch him, and to slay him in the morning: and Michal David's wife told him, saying, If thou save not thy life tonight, tomorrow thou shalt be slain.

12 ¶ So Michal [a]let David down through a window: and he went, and fled, and escaped.

13 And Michal took an [a]image,[1] and laid *it* in the bed, and put a pillow of goats' *hair* for his bolster, and covered *it* with a cloth.

14 And when Saul sent messengers to take David, she said, He *is* sick.

15 And Saul sent the messengers *again* to see David, saying, Bring him up to me in the bed, that I may slay him.

16 And when the messengers were come in, behold, *there was* an image in the bed, with a pillow of goats' *hair* for his bolster.

17 And Saul said unto Michal, Why hast thou deceived me so, and sent away mine enemy, that he is escaped? And Michal answered Saul, He said unto me, Let me go; [a]why should I kill thee?

18 ¶ So David fled, and escaped, and came to Samuel to Ramah, and told him all that Saul had done to him. And he and Samuel went and dwelt in Naioth.

19 And it was told Saul, saying, Behold, David *is* at Naioth in Ramah.

5 [d]ch. 20:32 [e]Mat. 27:4
7 [a]ch. 16:21 & 18:2,13 [1]Heb. *yesterday third day*
8 [1]Heb. *his face*
9 [a]ch. 16:14 & 18:10,11
11 [a]Ps. 59,title
12 [a]See Josh. 2:15; Acts 9:24,25
13 [a]Gen. 31:19 [1]Heb. *teraphim*
17 [a]2 Sam. 2:22
20 [a]See John 7:32, 45 [b]ch. 10:5,6; 1 Cor. 14:3,24,25 [c]Num. 11:25; Joel 2:28
23 [a]ch. 10:10
24 [a]Is. 20:2 [b]Mic. 1:8; See 2 Sam. 6:14,20 [c]ch. 10:11 [1]Heb. *fell;* see Num. 24:4
20:4 [1]Or, *Say what is thy mind, and I will do* [2]Heb. *speaketh,* or, *thinketh*
5 [a]Num. 10:10 & 28:11 [b]ch. 19:2

20 And [a]Saul sent messengers to take David: [b]and when they saw the company of the prophets prophesying, and Samuel standing *as* appointed over them, the spirit of God was upon the messengers of Saul, and they also [c]prophesied. E G M

21 And when it was told Saul, he sent other messengers, and they prophesied likewise. And Saul sent messengers again the third time, and they prophesied also.

22 Then went he also to Ramah, and came to a great well that *is* in Sechu: and he asked and said, Where *are* Samuel and David? And *one* said, Behold, *they be* at Naioth in Ramah.

23 And he went thither to Naioth in Ramah: and [a]the spirit of God was upon him also, and he went on, and prophesied, until he came to Naioth in Ramah.

24 [a]And he stripped off his clothes also, and prophesied before Samuel in like manner, and [1]lay down [b]naked all that day and all that night. Wherefore they say, [c]*Is* Saul also among the prophets?

David and Jonathan

20 AND DAVID fled from Naioth in Ramah, and came and said before Jonathan, What have I done? what *is* mine iniquity? and what *is* my sin before thy father, that he seeketh my life?

2 And he said unto him, God forbid; thou shalt not die: behold, my father will do nothing either great or small, but that he will show it me: and why should my father hide this thing from me? it *is* not *so.*

3 And David sware moreover, and said, Thy father certainly knoweth that I have found grace in thine eyes; and he saith, Let not Jonathan know this, lest he be grieved: but truly *as* the LORD liveth, and *as* thy soul liveth, *there is* but a step between me and death.

4 Then said Jonathan unto David, [1]Whatsoever thy soul [2]desireth, I will even do *it* for thee.

5 And David said unto Jonathan, Behold, tomorrow *is* the [a]new moon, and I should not fail to sit with the king at meat: but let me go, that I may [b]hide my-

E *1Sa 10:10–12* ◄► *2Sa 23:2*
G *1Sa 10:10–12* ◄► *2Sa 23:2*
M *1Sa 11:6* ◄► *2Ki 2:16*

self in the field unto the third *day* at even.

6 If thy father at all miss me, then say, David earnestly asked *leave* of me that he might run [a]to Bethlehem his city: for *there is* a yearly [b]sacrifice[1] there for all the family.

7 [a]If he say thus, *It is* well; thy servant shall have peace: but if he be very wroth, *then* be sure that [b]evil is determined by him.

8 Therefore thou shalt [a]deal kindly with thy servant; for [b]thou hast brought thy servant into a covenant of the LORD with thee: notwithstanding, [c]if there be in me iniquity, slay me thyself; for why shouldest thou bring me to thy father?

9 And Jonathan said, Far be it from thee: for if I knew certainly that evil were determined by my father to come upon thee, then would not I tell it thee?

10 Then said David to Jonathan, Who shall tell me? or what *if* thy father answer thee roughly?

11 ¶ And Jonathan said unto David, Come, and let us go out into the field. And they went out both of them into the field.

12 And Jonathan said unto David, O LORD God of Israel, when I have [1]sounded my father about tomorrow any time, *or* the third *day,* and, behold, *if there be* good toward David, and I then send not unto thee, and [2]show it thee;

13 [a]The LORD do so and much more to Jonathan: but if it please my father *to do* thee evil, then I will show it thee, and send thee away, that thou mayest go in peace: and [b]the LORD be with thee, as he hath been with my father.

14 And thou shalt not only while yet I live show me the kindness of the LORD, that I die not:

15 But *also* [a]thou shalt not cut off thy kindness from my house for ever: no, not when the LORD hath cut off the enemies of David every one from the face of the earth.

16 So Jonathan [1]made *a covenant* with the house of David, *saying,* [a]Let the LORD even require *it* at the hand of David's enemies.

17 And Jonathan caused David to swear again, [1]because he loved him: [a]for he loved him as he loved his own soul.

18 Then Jonathan said to David, [a]Tomorrow *is* the new moon: and thou shalt be missed, because thy seat will be [1]empty.

19 And *when* thou hast stayed three days, *then* thou shalt go down [1,2]quickly, and come to [a]the place where thou didst hide thyself [3]when the business was *in hand,* and shalt remain by the stone [4]Ezel.

20 And I will shoot three arrows on the side *thereof,* as though I shot at a mark.

21 And, behold, I will send a lad, *saying,* Go, find out the arrows. If I expressly say unto the lad, Behold, the arrows *are* on this side of thee, take them; then come thou: for *there is* peace to thee, and [1]no hurt; [a]*as* the LORD liveth.

22 But if I say thus unto the young man, Behold, the arrows *are* beyond thee; go thy way: for the LORD hath sent thee away.

23 And *as touching* [a]the matter which thou and I have spoken of, behold, the LORD *be* between thee and me for ever.

24 ¶ So David hid himself in the field: and when the new moon was come, the king sat him down to eat meat.

25 And the king sat upon his seat, as at other times, *even* upon a seat by the wall: and Jonathan arose, and Abner sat by Saul's side, and David's place was empty.

26 Nevertheless Saul spake not any thing that day: for he thought, Something hath befallen him, he *is* [a]not clean; surely he *is* not clean.

27 And it came to pass on the morrow, *which was* the second *day* of the month, that David's place was empty: and Saul said unto Jonathan his son, Wherefore cometh not the son of Jesse to meat, neither yesterday, nor today?

28 And Jonathan [a]answered Saul, David earnestly asked *leave* of me *to go* to Bethlehem:

29 And he said, Let me go, I pray thee; for our family hath a sacrifice in the city; and my brother, he hath commanded me *to be there:* and now, if I have found favour in thine eyes, let me get away, I pray thee, and see my brethren. Therefore he cometh not unto the king's table.

30 Then Saul's anger was kindled against Jonathan, and he said unto him, [1,2]Thou son of the perverse rebellious *woman,* do not I know that thou hast chosen the son of Jesse to thine own confu-

6 [a]ch:16:4 [b]ch. 9:12 [1]Or, *feast*

7 [a]See Deut. 1:23; 2 Sam. 17:4 [b]ch. 25:17; Esth. 7:7

8 [a]Josh. 2:14 [b]ver. 16; ch. 18:3 & 23:18 [c]2 Sam. 14:32

12 [1]Heb. *searched* [2]Heb. *uncover thine ear*

13 [a]Ruth 1:17 [b]Josh. 1:5; ch. 17:37; 1 Chr. 22:11,16

15 [a]2 Sam. 9:1,3,7; & 21:7

16 [a]ch. 25:22; See ch. 31:2; 2 Sam. 4:7 & 21:8 [1]Heb. *cut*

17 [a]ch. 18:1 [1]Or, *by his love toward him*

18 [a]ver. 5 [1]Heb. *missed*

19 [a]ch. 19:2 [1]Or, *diligently* [2]Heb. *greatly* [3]Heb. *in the day of the business* [4]Or, *that showeth the way*

21 [a]Jer. 4:2 [1]Heb. *not any thing*

23 [a]ver. 14,15; See ver. 42

26 [a]Lev. 7:21 & 15:5

28 [a]ver. 6

30 [1]Or, *Thou perverse rebel* [2]Heb. *Son of perverse rebellion*

sion, and unto the confusion of thy mother's nakedness?

31 For as long as the son of Jesse liveth upon the ground, thou shalt not be established, nor thy kingdom. Wherefore now send and fetch him unto me, for he [l]shall surely die.

32 And Jonathan answered Saul his father, and said unto him, [a]Wherefore shall he be slain? what hath he done?

33 And Saul [a]cast a javelin at him to smite him: [b]whereby Jonathan knew that it was determined of his father to slay David.

34 So Jonathan arose from the table in fierce anger, and did eat no meat the second day of the month: for he was grieved for David, because his father had done him shame.

35 ¶ And it came to pass in the morning, that Jonathan went out into the field at the time appointed with David, and a little lad with him.

36 And he said unto his lad, Run, find out now the arrows which I shoot. *And* as the lad ran, he shot an arrow [l]beyond him.

37 And when the lad was come to the place of the arrow which Jonathan had shot, Jonathan cried after the lad, and said, *Is* not the arrow beyond thee?

38 And Jonathan cried after the lad, Make speed, haste, stay not. And Jonathan's lad gathered up the arrows, and came to his master.

39 But the lad knew not any thing: only Jonathan and David knew the matter.

40 And Jonathan gave his [l]artillery unto [2]his lad, and said unto him, Go, carry *them* to the city.

41 ¶ *And* as soon as the lad was gone, David arose out of *a place* toward the south, and fell on his face to the ground, and bowed himself three times: and they kissed one another, and wept one with another, until David exceeded.

42 And Jonathan said to David, [a]Go in peace, [l]forasmuch as we have sworn both of us in the name of the LORD, saying, The LORD be between me and thee, and between my seed and thy seed for ever. And he arose and departed: and Jonathan went into the city.

David visits Ahimelech

21 THEN CAME David to Nob to [a]Ahimelech the priest: and Ahimelech was [b]afraid at the meeting of David, and said unto him, Why *art* thou alone, and no man with thee?

2 And David said unto Ahimelech the priest, The king hath commanded me a business, and hath said unto me, Let no man know any thing of the business whereabout I send thee, and what I have commanded thee: and I have appointed *my* servants to such and such a place.

3 Now therefore what is under thine hand? give *me* five *loaves of* bread in mine hand, or what there is [l]present.

4 And the priest answered David, and said, *There is* no common bread under mine hand, but there is [a]hallowed bread; [b]if the young men have kept themselves at least from women.

5 And David answered the priest, and said unto him, Of a truth women *have been* kept from us about these three days, since I came out, and the [a]vessels of the young men are holy, and *the bread is* in a manner common, [l]yea, though it were sanctified this day [b]in the vessel.

6 So the priest [a]gave him hallowed *bread:* for there was no bread there but the showbread, [b]that was taken from before the LORD, to put hot bread in the day when it was taken away.

7 Now a certain man of the servants of Saul *was* there that day, detained before the LORD; and his name *was* [a]Doeg, an Edomite, the chiefest of the herdmen that *belonged* to Saul.

David escapes to Gath

8 ¶ And David said unto Ahimelech, And is there not here under thine hand spear or sword? for I have neither brought my sword nor my weapons with me, because the king's business required haste.

9 And the priest said, The sword of Goliath the Philistine, whom thou slewest in [a]the valley of Elah, [b]behold, it *is here* wrapped in a cloth behind the ephod: if thou wilt take that, take *it:* for *there is* no other save that here. And David said, *There is* none like that; give it me.

10 ¶ And David arose, and fled that day for fear of Saul, and went to [l]Achish the king of Gath.

11 And [a]the servants of Achish said

31 [l]Heb. is *the son of death*

32 [a]ch. 19:5; Mat. 27:23; Luke 23:22

33 [a]ch. 18:11 [b]ver. 7

36 [l]Heb. *to pass over him*

40 [l]Heb. *instruments* [2]Heb. *that was his*

42 [a]ch. 1:17 [l]Or, the LORD be witness of that *which;* see ver. 23

21:1 [a]ch. 14:3 called *Ahiah;* Called also *Abiathar* Mark 2:26 [b]ch. 16:4

3 [l]Heb. *found*

4 [a]Ex. 25:30; Lev. 24:5; Mat. 12:4 [b]Ex. 19:15; Zech. 7:3

5 [a]1 Thes. 4:4 [b]Lev. 8:26 [l]Or, *especially when this day there is* other *sanctified in the vessel*

6 [a]Mat. 12:3,4; Mark 2:25,26; Luke 6:3,4 [b]Lev. 24:8,9

7 [a]ch. 22:9; Ps. 52, title

9 [a]ch. 17:2,50 [b]See ch. 31:10

10 [l]Or, *Abimelech;* see Ps. 34, title

11 [a]Ps. 56,title

unto him, *Is* not this David the king of the land? did they not sing one to another of him in dances, saying, [b]Saul hath slain his thousands, and David his ten thousands?

12 And David [a]laid up these words in his heart, and was sore afraid of Achish the king of Gath.

13 And [a]he changed his behaviour before them, and feigned himself mad in their hands, and [1]scrabbled on the doors of the gate, and let his spittle fall down upon his beard.

14 Then said Achish unto his servants, Lo, ye see the man [1]is mad: wherefore *then* have ye brought him to me?

15 Have I need of mad men, that ye have brought this *fellow* to play the mad man in my presence? shall this *fellow* come into my house?

David's flight continues

22 DAVID THEREFORE departed thence, and [a]escaped [b]to the cave Adullam: and when his brethren and all his father's house heard *it,* they went down thither to him.

2 [a]And every one *that was* in distress, and every one that [1]*was* in debt, and every one *that was* [2]discontented, gathered themselves unto him; and he became a captain over them: and there were with him about four hundred men.

3 ¶ And David went thence to Mizpeh of Moab: and he said unto the king of Moab, Let my father and my mother, I pray thee, come forth, *and be* with you, till I know what God will do for me.

4 And he brought them before the king of Moab: and they dwelt with him all the while that David was in the hold.

5 ¶ And the prophet [a]Gad said unto David, Abide not in the hold; depart, and get thee into the land of Judah. Then David departed, and came into the forest of Hareth.

6 ¶ When Saul heard that David was discovered, and the men that *were* with him, (now Saul abode in Gibeah under a [1]tree in Ramah, having his spear in his hand, and all his servants *were* standing about him;)

7 Then Saul said unto his servants that stood about him, Hear now, ye Benjamites; will the son of Jesse [a]give every one of you fields and vineyards, *and* make you all captains of thousands, and captains of hundreds;

8 That all of you have conspired against me, and *there is* none that showeth me that [a]my son hath made a league with the son of Jesse, and *there is* none of you that is sorry for me, or showeth unto me that my son hath stirred up my servant against me, to lie in wait, as at this day?

9 ¶ Then answered [a]Doeg the Edomite, which was set over the servants of Saul, and said, I saw the son of Jesse coming to Nob, to [b]Ahimelech the son of [c]Ahitub.

10 [a]And he inquired of the LORD for him, and [b]gave him victuals, and gave him the sword of Goliath the Philistine.

Saul has Ahimelech killed

11 Then the king sent to call Ahimelech the priest, the son of Ahitub, and all his father's house, the priests that *were* in Nob: and they came all of them to the king.

12 And Saul said, Hear now, thou son of Ahitub. And he answered, [1]Here I *am,* my lord.

13 And Saul said unto him, Why have ye conspired against me, thou and the son of Jesse, in that thou hast given him bread, and a sword, and hast inquired of God for him, that he should rise against me, to lie in wait, as at this day?

14 Then Ahimelech answered the king, and said, And who *is so* faithful among all thy servants as David, which is the king's son-in-law, and goeth at thy bidding, and is honourable in thine house?

15 Did I then begin to inquire of God for him? be it far from me: let not the king impute *any* thing unto his servant, *nor* to all the house of my father: for thy servant knew nothing of all this, [1]less or more.

16 And the king said, Thou shalt surely die, Ahimelech, thou, and all thy father's house.

17 ¶ And the king said unto the [1,2]footmen that stood about him, Turn, and slay the priests of the LORD; because their hand also *is* with David, and because they knew when he fled, and did not show it to me. But the servants of the king [a]would not put forth their hand to fall upon the priests of the LORD.

11 [b]ch. 18:7 & 29:5
12 [a]Luke 2:19
13 [a]Ps. 34,title [1]Or, *made marks*
14 [1]Or, *playeth the mad man*
22:1 [a]Ps. 57,title; & 142,title [b]2 Sam. 23:13
2 [a]Judg. 11:3 [1]Heb. *had a creditor* [2]Heb. *bitter of soul*
5 [a]2 Sam. 24:11; 1 Chr. 21:9; 2 Chr. 29:25
6 [1]Or, *grove in a high place*
7 [a]ch. 8:14
8 [a]ch. 18:3 & 20:30
9 [a]ch. 21:7; Ps. 52, title & ver. 1-3 [b]ch. 21:1 [c]ch. 14:3
10 [a]Num. 27:21 [b]ch. 21:6,9
12 [1]Heb. *Behold me*
15 [1]Heb. *little or great*
17 [a]See Ex. 1:17 [1]Or, *guard* [2]Heb. *runners*

18 And the king said to Doeg, Turn thou, and fall upon the priests. And Doeg the Edomite turned, and he fell upon the priests, and [a]slew on that day fourscore and five persons that did wear a linen ephod.

19 [a]And Nob, the city of the priests, smote he with the edge of the sword, both men and women, children and sucklings, and oxen, and asses, and sheep, with the edge of the sword.

20 ¶ [a]And one of the sons of Ahimelech the son of Ahitub, named Abiathar, [b]escaped, and fled after David.

21 And Abiathar showed David that Saul had slain the LORD'S priests.

22 And David said unto Abiathar, I knew *it* that day, when Doeg the Edomite *was* there, that he would surely tell Saul: I have occasioned *the death* of all the persons of thy father's house.

23 Abide thou with me, fear not: [a]for he that seeketh my life seeketh thy life: but with me thou *shalt be* in safeguard.

David at Keilah

23 THEN THEY told David, saying, Behold, the Philistines fight against [a]Keilah, and they rob the threshingfloors.

2 Therefore David [a]inquired of the LORD, saying, Shall I go and smite these Philistines? And the LORD said unto David, Go, and smite the Philistines, and save Keilah.

3 And David's men said unto him, Behold, we be afraid here in Judah: how much more then if we come to Keilah against the armies of the Philistines?

4 Then David inquired of the LORD yet again. And the LORD answered him and said, Arise, go down to Keilah; for I will deliver the Philistines into thine hand.

5 So David and his men went to Keilah, and fought with the Philistines, and brought away their cattle, and smote them with a great slaughter. So David saved the inhabitants of Keilah.

6 And it came to pass, when Abiathar the son of Ahimelech [a]fled to David to Keilah, *that* he came down *with* an ephod in his hand.

7 ¶ And it was told Saul that David was come to Keilah. And Saul said, God hath delivered him into mine hand; for he is shut in, by entering into a town that hath gates and bars.

8 And Saul called all the people together to war, to go down to Keilah, to besiege David and his men.

9 ¶ And David knew that Saul secretly practised mischief against him; and [a]he said to Abiathar the priest, Bring hither the ephod.

10 Then said David, O LORD God of Israel, thy servant hath certainly heard that Saul seeketh to come to Keilah, [a]to destroy the city for my sake.

11 Will the men of Keilah deliver me up into his hand? will Saul come down, as thy servant hath heard? O LORD God of Israel, I beseech thee, tell thy servant. And the LORD said, He will come down.

12 Then said David, Will the men of Keilah [1]deliver me and my men into the hand of Saul? And the LORD said, They will deliver *thee* up.

13 ¶ Then David and his men, [a]*which were* about six hundred, arose and departed out of Keilah, and went whithersoever they could go. And it was told Saul that David was escaped from Keilah; and he forbare to go forth.

14 And David abode in the wilderness in strong holds, and remained in [a]a mountain in the wilderness of [b]Ziph. And Saul [c]sought him every day, but God delivered him not into his hand.

Saul pursues David

15 And David saw that Saul was come out to seek his life: and David *was* in the wilderness of Ziph in a wood.

16 ¶ And Jonathan Saul's son arose, and went to David into the wood, and strengthened his hand in God.

17 And he said unto him, Fear not: for the hand of Saul my father shall not find thee; and thou shalt be king over Israel, and I shall be next unto thee; and [a]that also Saul my father knoweth.

18 And they two [a]made a covenant before the LORD: and David abode in the wood, and Jonathan went to his house.

19 ¶ Then [a]came up the Ziphites to Saul to Gibeah, saying, Doth not David hide himself with us in strong holds in the wood, in the hill of Hachilah, which *is* [1]on the south of [2]Jeshimon?

20 Now therefore, O king, come down according to all the desire of thy soul to come down; and [a]our part *shall be* to deliver him into the king's hand.

---

18 [a]See ch. 2:31
19 [a]ver. 9,11
20 [a]ch. 23:6 [b]ch. 2:33
23 [a]1 Ki. 2:26
23:1 [a]Josh. 15:44
2 [a]ver. 4,6,9; ch. 30:8; 2 Sam. 5:19, 23
6 [a]ch. 22:20
9 [a]Num. 27:21; ch. 30:7
10 [a]ch. 22:19
12 [1]Heb. *shut up*
13 [a]ch. 22:2 & 25:13
14 [a]Ps. 11:1 [b]Josh. 15:55 [c]Ps. 54:3,4
17 [a]ch. 24:20
18 [a]ch. 18:3 & 20:16,42; 2 Sam. 21:7
19 [a]See ch. 26:1; Ps. 54,title [1]Heb. *on the right hand* [2]Or, *The wilderness?*
20 [a]Ps. 54:3

21 And Saul said, Blessed *be* ye of the LORD; for ye have compassion on me.

22 Go, I pray you, prepare yet, and know and see his place where his ʹhaunt is, *and* who hath seen him there: for it is told me *that* he dealeth very subtly.

23 See therefore, and take knowledge of all the lurking places where he hideth himself, and come ye again to me with the certainty, and I will go with you: and it shall come to pass, if he be in the land, that I will search him out throughout all the thousands of Judah.

24 And they arose, and went to Ziph before Saul: but David and his men *were* in the wilderness [a]of Maon, in the plain on the south of Jeshimon.

25 Saul also and his men went to seek *him.* And they told David: wherefore he came down ʹinto a rock, and abode in the wilderness of Maon. And when Saul heard *that,* he pursued after David in the wilderness of Maon.

26 And Saul went on this side of the mountain, and David and his men on that side of the mountain: [a]and David made haste to get away for fear of Saul; for Saul and his men [b]compassed David and his men round about to take them.

27 ¶ [a]But there came a messenger unto Saul, saying, Haste thee, and come; for the Philistines have ʹinvaded the land.

28 Wherefore Saul returned from pursuing after David, and went against the Philistines: therefore they called that place ʹSela-hammahlekoth.

29 ¶ And David went up from thence, and dwelt in strong holds at [a]En-gedi.

David spares Saul

24 AND IT came to pass, [a]when Saul was returned from ʹfollowing the Philistines, that it was told him, saying, Behold, David *is* in the wilderness of En-gedi.

2 Then Saul took three thousand chosen men out of all Israel, and [a]went to seek David and his men upon the rocks of the wild goats.

3 And he came to the sheepcotes by the way, where *was* a cave; and [a]Saul went in to [b]cover his feet: and [c]David and his men remained in the sides of the cave.

4 [a]And the men of David said unto him, Behold the day of which the LORD said unto thee, Behold, I will deliver thine enemy into thine hand, that thou mayest do to him as it shall seem good unto thee. Then David arose, and cut off the skirt of ʹSaul's robe privily.

5 And it came to pass afterward, that [a]David's heart smote him, because he had cut off Saul's skirt.

6 And he said unto his men, [a]The LORD forbid that I should do this thing unto my master, the LORD'S anointed, to stretch forth mine hand against him, seeing he *is* the anointed of the LORD.

7 So David [a]stayedʹ his servants with these words, and suffered them not to rise against Saul. But Saul rose up out of the cave, and went on *his* way.

8 David also arose afterward, and went out of the cave, and cried after Saul, saying, My lord the king. And when Saul looked behind him, David stooped with his face to the earth, and bowed himself.

9 ¶ And David said to Saul, [a]Wherefore hearest thou men's words, saying, Behold, David seeketh thy hurt?

10 Behold, this day thine eyes have seen how that the LORD had delivered thee today into mine hand in the cave: and *some* bade *me* kill thee: but *mine eye* spared thee; and I said, I will not put forth mine hand against my lord; for he *is* the LORD'S anointed.

11 Moreover, my father, see, yea, see the skirt of thy robe in my hand: for in that I cut off the skirt of thy robe, and killed thee not, know thou and see that *there is* [a]neither evil nor transgression in mine hand, and I have not sinned against thee; yet thou [b]huntest my soul to take it.

12 [a]The LORD judge between me and thee, and the LORD avenge me of thee: but mine hand shall not be upon thee.

13 As saith the proverb of the an- **C**
cients, Wickedness proceedeth from the **S**
wicked: but mine hand shall not be upon thee.

14 After whom is the king of Israel come out? after whom dost thou pursue? [a]after a dead dog, after [b]a flea.

15 [a]The LORD therefore be judge, and judge between me and thee, and [b]see, and [c]plead my cause, and ʹdeliver me out of thine hand.

16 ¶ And it came to pass, when David

C *1Sa 8:7* ◀ ▶ *2Sa 23:6–7*
S *1Sa 16:14* ◀ ▶ *2Sa 22:21–27*

---

22 ʹHeb. *foot shall be*
24 [a]Josh. 15:55; ch. 25:2
25 ʹOr, *from the rock*
26 [a]Ps. 31:22 [b]Ps. 17:9
27 [a]See 2 Ki. 19:9 ʹHeb. *spread themselves upon*
28 ʹi.e. *The rock of divisions*
29 [a]2 Chr. 20:2
24:1 [a]ch. 23:28 ʹHeb. *after*
2 [a]Ps. 38:12
3 [a]ver. 10 [b]Judg. 3:24 [c]Ps. 57,title & 142,title
4 [a]ch. 26:8 ʹHeb. *the robe which was Saul's*
5 [a]2 Sam. 24:10
6 [a]ch. 26:11
7 [a]Ps. 7:4; Mat. 5:44; Rom. 12:17, 19 ʹHeb. *cut off*
9 [a]Ps. 141:6; Prov. 16:28 & 17:9
11 [a]Ps. 7:3 & 35:7 [b]ch. 26:20
12 [a]Gen. 16:5; Judg. 11:27; ch. 26:10; Job 5:8
14 [a]ch. 17:43; 2 Sam. 9:8 [b]ch. 26:20
15 [a]ver. 12 [b]2 Chr. 24:22 [c]Ps. 35:1 & 43:1; Mic. 7:9 ʹHeb. *judge*

had made an end of speaking these words
unto Saul, that Saul said, [a]*Is* this thy
voice, my son David? And Saul lifted up
his voice, and wept.
17 [a]And he said to David, Thou *art*
[b]more righteous than I: for [c]thou hast rewarded me good, whereas I have rewarded thee evil.
18 And thou hast shown this day how
that thou hast dealt well with me: forasmuch as when [a]the LORD had [b]delivered
me into thine hand, thou killedst me not.
19 For if a man find his enemy, will he
let him go well away? wherefore the LORD
reward thee good for that thou hast done
unto me this day.
20 And now, behold, [a]I know well that
thou shalt surely be king, and that the
kingdom of Israel shall be established in
thine hand.
21 [a]Swear now therefore unto me by
the LORD, [b]that thou wilt not cut off my
seed after me, and that thou wilt not destroy my name out of my father's house.
22 And David sware unto Saul. And
Saul went home; but David and his men
gat them up unto [a]the hold.

David, Nabal and Abigail

25 AND [a]SAMUEL died; and all the
Israelites were gathered together,
and [b]lamented him, and buried him in
his house at Ramah. And David arose,
and went down [c]to the wilderness of
Paran.
2 And *there was* a man [a]in Maon,
whose ʹpossessions *were* in [b]Carmel; and
the man *was* very great, and he had three
thousand sheep, and a thousand goats:
and he was shearing his sheep in Carmel.
3 Now the name of the man *was* Nabal; and the name of his wife Abigail: and
she was a woman of good understanding,
and of a beautiful countenance: but the
man *was* churlish and evil in his doings;
and he *was* of the house of Caleb.
4 ¶ And David heard in the wilderness
that Nabal did [a]shear his sheep.
5 And David sent out ten young men,
and David said unto the young men, Get
you up to Carmel, and go to Nabal, and
greet him in my name:
6 And thus shall ye say to him that liveth *in prosperity,* [a]Peace *be* both to thee,
and peace *be* to thine house, and peace
be unto all that thou hast.
7 And now I have heard that thou hast

16 [a]ch. 26:17
17 [a]ch. 26:21 [b]Gen. 38:26 [c]Mat. 5:44
18 [a]ch. 26:23 [b]ch. 23:12 & 26:8
20 [a]ch. 23:17
21 [a]Gen. 21:23 [b]2 Sam. 21:6,8
22 [a]ch. 23:29
25:1 [a]ch. 28:3 [b]Num. 20:29; Deut. 34:8 [c]Gen. 21:21; Ps. 120:5
2 [a]ch. 23:24 [b]Josh. 15:55 ʹOr, *business*
4 [a]Gen. 38:13; 2 Sam. 13:23
6 [a]1 Chr. 12:18; Luke 10:5
7 [a]ver. 15,21 ʹHeb. *shamed*
8 [a]Neh. 8:10; Esth. 9:19
9 ʹHeb. *rested*
10 [a]Judg. 9:28
11 [a]Judg. 8:6 ʹHeb. *slaughter*
13 [a]ch. 30:24
14 ʹHeb. *flew upon them*
15 [a]ver. 7 ʹHeb. *shamed*
16 [a]Ex. 14:22; Job 1:10
17 [a]ch. 20:7 [b]Deut. 13:13; Judg. 19:22
18 [a]Gen. 32:13; Prov. 18:16 & 21:14 ʹOr, *lumps*

shearers: now thy shepherds which were
with us, we ʹhurt them not, [a]neither was
there aught missing unto them, all the
while they were in Carmel.
8 Ask thy young men, and they will
show thee. Wherefore let the young men
find favour in thine eyes: for we come in
[a]a good day: give, I pray thee, whatsoever
cometh to thine hand unto thy servants,
and to thy son David.
9 And when David's young men came,
they spake to Nabal according to all those
words in the name of David, and ʹceased.
10 ¶ And Nabal answered David's servants, and said, [a]Who *is* David? and who
is the son of Jesse? there be many servants now a days that break away every
man from his master.
11 [a]Shall I then take my bread, and my
water, and my ʹflesh that I have killed for
my shearers, and give *it* unto men, whom
I know not whence they *be?*
12 So David's young men turned their
way, and went again, and came and told
him all those sayings.
13 And David said unto his men, Gird
ye on every man his sword. And they
girded on every man his sword; and David also girded on his sword: and there
went up after David about four hundred
men; and two hundred [a]abode by the
stuff.
14 ¶ But one of the young men told
Abigail, Nabal's wife, saying, Behold, David sent messengers out of the wilderness
to salute our master; and he ʹrailed on
them.
15 But the men *were* very good unto
us, and [a]we were not ʹhurt, neither
missed we any thing, as long as we were
conversant with them, when we were in
the fields:
16 They were [a]a wall unto us both by
night and day, all the while we were with
them keeping the sheep.
17 Now therefore know and consider
what thou wilt do; for [a]evil is determined
against our master, and against all his
household: for he *is such* a son of [b]Belial,
that *a man* cannot speak to him.
18 ¶ Then Abigail made haste, and
[a]took two hundred loaves, and two bottles of wine, and five sheep ready
dressed, and five measures of parched
corn, and an hundred ʹclusters of raisins,
and two hundred cakes of figs, and laid
them on asses.

19 And she said unto her servants, [a]Go on before me; behold, I come after you. But she told not her husband Nabal.

20 And it was *so, as* she rode on the ass, that she came down by the covert of the hill, and, behold, David and his men came down against her; and she met them.

21 Now David had said, Surely in vain have I kept all that this *fellow* hath in the wilderness, so that nothing was missed of all that *pertained* unto him: and he hath [a]requited me evil for good.

22 [a]So and more also do God unto the enemies of David, if I [b]leave of all that *pertain* to him by the morning light [c]any that pisseth against the wall.

23 And when Abigail saw David, she hasted, and [a]lighted off the ass, and fell before David on her face, and bowed herself to the ground,

24 And fell at his feet, and said, Upon me, my lord, *upon* me *let this* iniquity *be:* and let thine handmaid, I pray thee, speak in thine [1]audience, and hear the words of thine handmaid.

25 Let not my lord, I pray thee, [1]regard this man of Belial, *even* Nabal: for as his name *is,* so *is* he; [2]Nabal *is* his name, and folly *is* with him: but I thine handmaid saw not the young men of my lord, whom thou didst send.

26 Now therefore, my lord, [a]*as* the LORD liveth, and *as* thy soul liveth, seeing the LORD hath [b]withholden thee from coming to *shed* blood, and from [c]avenging[1] thyself with thine own hand, now [d]let thine enemies, and they that seek evil to my lord, be as Nabal.

27 And now [a]this [1]blessing which thine handmaid hath brought unto my lord, let it even be given unto the young men that follow my lord.

I 28 I pray thee, forgive the trespass of thine handmaid: for [a]the LORD will certainly make my lord a sure house; because my lord [b]fighteth the battles of the LORD, and [c]evil hath not been found in thee *all* thy days.

H 29 Yet a man is risen to pursue thee,
K and to seek thy soul: but the soul of my lord shall be bound in the bundle of life with the LORD thy God; and the souls of thine enemies, them shall he [a]sling out, [1]*as out* of the middle of a sling.

30 And it shall come to pass, when the LORD shall have done to my lord according to all the good that he hath spoken concerning thee, and shall have appointed thee ruler over Israel;

31 That this shall be [1]no grief unto thee, nor offence of heart unto my lord, either that thou hast shed blood causeless, or that my lord hath avenged himself: but when the LORD shall have dealt well with my lord, then remember thine handmaid.

32 ¶ And David said to Abigail, [a]Blessed *be* the LORD God of Israel, which sent thee this day to meet me:

33 And blessed *be* thy advice, and blessed *be* thou, which hast [a]kept me this day from coming to *shed* blood, and from avenging myself with mine own hand.

34 For in very deed, *as* the LORD God of Israel liveth, which hath [a]kept me back from hurting thee, except thou hadst hasted and come to meet me, surely there had [b]not been left unto Nabal by the morning light any that pisseth against the wall.

35 So David received of her hand *that* which she had brought him, and said unto her, [a]Go up in peace to thine house; see, I have hearkened to thy voice, and have [b]accepted thy person.

36 ¶ And Abigail came to Nabal; and, behold, [a]he held a feast in his house, like the feast of a king; and Nabal's heart *was* merry within him, for he *was* very drunken: wherefore she told him nothing, less or more, until the morning light.

37 But it came to pass in the morning, when the wine was gone out of Nabal, and his wife had told him these things, that his heart died within him, and he became *as* a stone.

38 And it came to pass about ten days *after,* that the LORD smote Nabal, that he died. D

39 ¶ And when David heard that Nabal was dead, he said, [a]Blessed *be* the LORD, that hath [b]pleaded the cause of my reproach from the hand of Nabal, and hath [c]kept his servant from evil: for the LORD hath [d]returned the wickedness of Nabal

19 [a]Gen. 32:16,20
21 [a]Ps. 109:5
22 [a]Ruth 1:17; ch. 3:17 & 20:13,16 [b]ver. 34 [c]1 Ki. 14:10 & 21:21; 2 Ki. 9:8
23 [a]Josh. 15:18; Judg. 1:14
24 [1]Heb. *ears*
25 [1]Heb. *lay it to his heart* [2]i.e. *Fool*
26 [a]2 Ki. 2:2 [b]ver. 33; Gen. 20:6 [c]Rom. 12:19 [d]2 Sam. 18:32 [1]Heb. *saving thyself*
27 [a]Gen. 33:11; ch. 30:26; 2 Ki. 5:15 [1]Or, *present*
28 [a]2 Sam. 7:11, 27; 1 Ki. 9:5; 1 Chr. 17:10,25 [b]ch. 18:17 [c]ch. 24:11
29 [a]Jer. 10:18 [1]Heb. *in the midst of the bought of a sling*
31 [1]Heb. *no staggering,* or, *stumbling*
32 [a]Gen. 24:27; Ex. 18:10; Luke 1:68
33 [a]ver. 26
34 [a]ver. 26 [b]ver. 22
35 [a]ch. 20:42; 2 Sam. 15:9; 2 Ki. 5:19; Luke 7:50 & 8:48 [b]Gen. 19:21
36 [a]2 Sam. 13:23
39 [a]ver. 32 [b]Prov. 22:23 [c]ver. 26,34 [d]1 Ki. 2:44

L
V
I *1Sa 17:36–37* ◀▶ *2Sa 3:18*
H *1Sa 3:13–14* ◀▶ *2Sa 3:39*
K *1Sa 2:8–9* ◀▶ *2Sa 22:31*
L *1Sa 12:24* ◀▶ *2Sa 22:2–4*
V *1Sa 17:47* ◀▶ *2Sa 22:30*

D *1Sa 5:11–12* ◀▶ *1Ki 13:4*

upon his own head. And David sent and communed with Abigail, to take her to him to wife.

40 And when the servants of David were come to Abigail to Carmel, they spake unto her, saying, David sent us unto thee, to take thee to him to wife.

41 And she arose, and bowed herself on *her* face to the earth, and said, Behold, *let* thine handmaid *be* a servant to wash the feet of the servants of my lord.

42 And Abigail hasted, and arose, and rode upon an ass, with five damsels of hers that went after her; and she went after the messengers of David, and became his wife.

43 David also took Ahinoam [a]of Jezreel; [b]and they were also both of them his wives.

44 ¶ But Saul had given [a]Michal his daughter, David's wife, to [l]Phalti the son of Laish, which *was* of [b]Gallim.

David spares Saul again

26 AND THE Ziphites came unto Saul to Gibeah, saying, [a]Doth not David hide himself in the hill of Hachilah, *which is* before Jeshimon?

2 Then Saul arose, and went down to the wilderness of Ziph, having three thousand chosen men of Israel with him, to seek David in the wilderness of Ziph.

3 And Saul pitched in the hill of Hachilah, which *is* before Jeshimon, by the way. But David abode in the wilderness, and he saw that Saul came after him into the wilderness.

4 David therefore sent out spies, and understood that Saul was come in very deed.

5 ¶ And David arose, and came to the place where Saul had pitched: and David beheld the place where Saul lay, and [a]Abner the son of Ner, the captain of his host: and Saul lay in the [b]trench,[l] and the people pitched round about him.

6 Then answered David and said to Ahimelech the Hittite, and to Abishai [a]the son of Zeruiah, brother to Joab, saying, Who will [b]go down with me to Saul to the camp? And Abishai said, I will go down with thee.

7 So David and Abishai came to the people by night: and, behold, Saul lay sleeping within the trench, and his spear stuck in the ground at his bolster: but Abner and the people lay round about him.

8 Then said Abishai to David, God hath [a]delivered thine enemy into thine hand this day: now therefore let me smite him, I pray thee, with the spear even to the earth at once, and I will not *smite* him the second time.

9 And David said to Abishai, Destroy him not: [a]for who can stretch forth his hand against the LORD'S anointed, and be guiltless?

10 David said furthermore, *As* the LORD liveth, [a]the LORD shall smite him; or [b]his day shall come to die; or he shall [c]descend into battle, and perish.

11 [a]The LORD forbid that I should stretch forth mine hand against the LORD'S anointed: but, I pray thee, take thou now the spear that *is* at his bolster, and the cruse of water, and let us go.

12 So David took the spear and the cruse of water from Saul's bolster; and they gat them away, and no man saw *it,* nor knew *it,* neither awaked: for they *were* all asleep; because [a]a deep sleep from the LORD was fallen upon them.

13 ¶ Then David went over to the other side, and stood on the top of an hill afar off; a great space *being* between them:

14 And David cried to the people, and to Abner the son of Ner, saying, Answerest thou not, Abner? Then Abner answered and said, Who *art* thou *that* criest to the king?

15 And David said to Abner, *Art* not thou a *valiant* man? and who *is* like to thee in Israel? wherefore then hast thou not kept thy lord the king? for there came one of the people in to destroy the king thy lord.

16 This thing *is* not good that thou hast done. *As* the LORD liveth, ye *are* [a]worthy to die, because ye have not kept your master, the LORD'S anointed. And now see where the king's spear *is,* and the cruse of water that *was* at his bolster.

17 And Saul knew David's voice, and said, [a]*Is* this thy voice, my son David? And David said, *It is* my voice, my lord, O king.

18 And he said, [a]Wherefore doth my lord thus pursue after his servant? for what have I done? or what evil *is* in mine hand?

19 Now therefore, I pray thee, let my lord the king hear the words of his servant. If the LORD have [a]stirred thee up

43 [a]Josh. 15:56 [b]ch. 27:3 & 30:5
44 [a]2 Sam. 3:14 [b]Is. 10:30 [l]*Phaltiel* in 2 Sam. 3:15
26:1 [a]ch. 23:19; Ps. 54,title
5 [a]ch. 14:50 & 17:55 [b]ch. 17:20 [l]Or, *midst of his carriages*
6 [a]1 Chr. 2:16 [b]Judg. 7:10,11
8 [a]ch. 24:18
9 [a]ch. 24:6,7; 2 Sam. 1:16
10 [a]ch. 25:38; Luke 18:7; Rom. 12:19 [b]See Gen. 47:29; Deut. 31:14; Job 7:1 & 14:5 [c]ch. 31:6
11 [a]ch. 24:6,12
12 [a]Gen. 2:21 & 15:12
16 [a]2 Sam. 12:5
17 [a]ch. 24:16
18 [a]ch. 24:9,11
19 [a]2 Sam. 16:11; & 24:1

against me, let him [1]accept an offering: but if *they be* the children of men, cursed *be* they before the LORD; [b]for they have driven me out this day from [2]abiding in the [c]inheritance of the LORD, saying, Go, serve other gods.

20 Now therefore, let not my blood fall to the earth before the face of the LORD: for the king of Israel is come out to seek [a]a flea, as when one doth hunt a partridge in the mountains.

21 ¶ Then said Saul, [a]I have sinned: return, my son David: for I will no more do thee harm, because my soul was [b]precious in thine eyes this day: behold, I have played the fool, and have erred exceedingly.

22 And David answered and said, Behold the king's spear! and let one of the young men come over and fetch it.

23 [a]The LORD render to every man his righteousness and his faithfulness: for the LORD delivered thee into *my* hand today, but I would not stretch forth mine hand against the LORD'S anointed.

24 And, behold, as thy life was much set by this day in mine eyes, so let my life be much set by in the eyes of the LORD, and let him deliver me out of all tribulation.

25 Then Saul said to David, Blessed *be* thou, my son David: thou shalt both do great *things,* and also shalt still [a]prevail. So David went on his way, and Saul returned to his place.

David lives with the Philistines

27 AND DAVID said in his heart, I shall now [1]perish one day by the hand of Saul: *there is* nothing better for me than that I should speedily escape into the land of the Philistines; and Saul shall despair of me, to seek me any more in any coast of Israel: so shall I escape out of his hand.

2 And David arose, [a]and he passed over with the six hundred men that *were* with him [b]unto Achish, the son of Maoch, king of Gath.

3 And David dwelt with Achish at Gath, he and his men, every man with his household, *even* David [a]with his two wives, Ahinoam the Jezreelitess, and Abigail the Carmelitess, Nabal's wife.

4 And it was told Saul that David was fled to Gath: and he sought no more again for him.

5 ¶ And David said unto Achish, If I have now found grace in thine eyes, let them give me a place in some town in the country, that I may dwell there: for why should thy servant dwell in the royal city with thee?

6 Then Achish gave him Ziklag that day: wherefore [a]Ziklag pertaineth unto the kings of Judah unto this day.

7 And [1]the time that David dwelt in the country of the Philistines was [a]a full year and four months.

8 ¶ And David and his men went up, and invaded [a]the Geshurites, [b]and the [1]Gezrites, and the [c]Amalekites: for those *nations were* of old the inhabitants of the land, [d]as thou goest to Shur, even unto the land of Egypt.

9 And David smote the land, and left neither man nor woman alive, and took away the sheep, and the oxen, and the asses, and the camels, and the apparel, and returned, and came to Achish.

10 And Achish said, [1]Whither have ye made a road today? And David said, Against the south of Judah, and against the south of [a]the Jerahmeelites, and against the south of [b]the Kenites.

11 And David saved neither man nor woman alive, to bring *tidings* to Gath, saying, Lest they should tell on us, saying, So did David, and so *will be* his manner all the while he dwelleth in the country of the Philistines.

12 And Achish believed David, saying, He hath made his people Israel [1]utterly to abhor him; therefore he shall be my servant for ever.

28 AND [a]IT came to pass in those days, that the Philistines gathered their armies together for warfare, to fight with Israel. And Achish said unto David, Know thou assuredly, that thou shalt go out with me to battle, thou and thy men.

2 And David said to Achish, Surely thou shalt know what thy servant can do. And Achish said to David, Therefore will I make thee keeper of mine head for ever.

Saul and the woman at Endor

3 ¶ Now [a]Samuel was dead, and all Israel had lamented him, and buried him in [b]Ramah, even in his own city. And Saul had put away [c]those that had familiar spirits, and the wizards, out of the land.

19 [b]Deut. 4:28 [c]2 Sam. 14:16 & 20:19 [1]Heb. *smell;* see Gen. 8:21; Lev. 26:31 [2]Heb. *cleaving*
20 [a]ch. 24:14
21 [a]ch. 15:24 & 24:17 [b]ch. 18:30
23 [a]Ps. 7:8 & 18:20
25 [a]Gen. 32:28
27:1 [1]Heb. *be consumed*
2 [a]ch. 25:13 [b]ch. 21:10
3 [a]ch. 25:43
6 [a]See Josh. 15:31; & 19:5
7 [a]ch. 29:3 [1]Heb. *the number of days*
8 [a]Josh. 13:2 [b]Josh. 16:10; Judg. 1:29 [c]Ex. 17:16; See ch. 15:7,8 [d]Gen. 25:18 [1]Or, *Gerzites*
10 [a]See 1 Chr. 2:9, 25 [b]Judg. 1:16 [1]Or, *Did you not make a road*
12 [1]Heb. *to stink*
28:1 [a]ch. 29:1
3 [a]ch. 5:1 [b]See ch 1:19 [c]ver. 9; Ex. 22:18; Lev. 19:31 & 20:2; Deut. 18:10,11

4 And the Philistines gathered themselves together, and came and pitched in [a]Shunem: and Saul gathered all Israel together, and they pitched in [b]Gilboa.

5 And when Saul saw the host of the Philistines, he was [a]afraid, and his heart greatly trembled.

6 And when Saul inquired of the LORD, [a]the LORD answered him not, neither by [b]dreams, nor [c]by Urim, nor by prophets.

7 ¶ Then said Saul unto his servants, Seek me a woman that hath a familiar spirit, that I may go to her, and inquire of her. And his servants said to him, Behold, *there is* a woman that hath a familiar spirit at En-dor.

8 And Saul disguised himself, and put on other raiment, and he went, and two men with him, and they came to the woman by night: and [a]he said, I pray thee, divine unto me by the familiar spirit, and bring me *him* up, whom I shall name unto thee.

9 And the woman said unto him, Behold, thou knowest what Saul hath done, how he hath [a]cut off those that have familiar spirits, and the wizards, out of the land: wherefore then layest thou a snare for my life, to cause me to die?

10 And Saul sware to her by the LORD, saying, *As* the LORD liveth, there shall no punishment happen to thee for this thing.

11 Then said the woman, Whom shall I bring up unto thee? And he said, Bring me up Samuel.

12 And when the woman saw Samuel, she cried with a loud voice: and the woman spake to Saul, saying, Why hast thou deceived me? for thou *art* Saul.

13 And the king said unto her, Be not afraid: for what sawest thou? And the woman said unto Saul, I saw [a]gods ascending out of the earth.

14 And he said unto her, [1]What form *is* he of? And she said, An old man cometh up; and he *is* covered with [a]a mantle. And Saul perceived that it *was* Samuel, and he stooped with *his* face to the ground, and bowed himself.

15 ¶ And Samuel said to Saul, Why hast thou disquieted me, to bring me up? And Saul answered, [a]I am sore distressed; for the Philistines make war against me, and [b]God is departed from me, and [c]answereth me no more, neither [1]by prophets, nor by dreams: therefore I have called thee, that thou mayest make known unto me what I shall do.

16 Then said Samuel, Wherefore then dost thou ask of me, seeing the LORD is departed from thee, and is become thine enemy?

17 And the LORD hath done [1]to him, [a]as he spake by [2]me: for the LORD hath rent the kingdom out of thine hand, and given it to thy neighbour, *even* to David:

18 [a]Because thou obeyedst not the voice of the LORD, nor executedst his fierce wrath upon Amalek, therefore hath the LORD done this thing unto thee this day.

19 Moreover the LORD will also deliver Israel with thee into the hand of the Philistines: and tomorrow *shalt* thou and thy sons *be* with me: the LORD also shall deliver the host of Israel into the hand of the Philistines.

20 Then Saul [1]fell straightway all along on the earth, and was sore afraid, because of the words of Samuel: and there was no strength in him; for he had eaten no bread all the day, nor all the night.

21 ¶ And the woman came unto Saul, and saw that he was sore troubled, and said unto him, Behold, thine handmaid hath obeyed thy voice, and I have [a]put my life in my hand, and have hearkened unto thy words which thou spakest unto me.

22 Now therefore, I pray thee, hearken thou also unto the voice of thine handmaid, and let me set a morsel of bread before thee; and eat, that thou mayest have strength, when thou goest on thy way.

23 But he refused, and said, I will not eat. But his servants, together with the woman, compelled him; and he hearkened unto their voice. So he arose from the earth, and sat upon the bed.

24 And the woman had a fat calf in the house; and she hasted, and killed it, and took flour, and kneaded *it*, and did bake unleavened bread thereof:

25 And she brought *it* before Saul, and before his servants; and they did eat. Then they rose up, and went away that night.

4 [a]Josh. 19:18; 2 Ki. 4:8 [b]ch. 31:1
5 [a]Job 18:11
6 [a]ch. 14:37; Prov. 1:28; Lam. 2:9 [b]Num. 12:6 [c]Ex. 28:30; Num. 27:21; Deut. 33:8
8 [a]Deut. 18:11; 1 Chr. 10:13; Is. 8:19
9 [a]ver. 3
13 [a]Ex. 22:28
14 [a]ch. 15:27; 2 Ki. 2:8,13 [1]Heb. *What is his form?*
15 [a]Prov. 5:11-13; & 14:14 [b]ch. 18:12 [c]ver. 6 [1]Heb. *by the hand of prophets*
17 [a]ch. 15:28 [1]Or, *for himself* [2]Heb. *mine hand*
18 [a]ch. 15:9; 1 Ki. 20:42; 1 Chr. 10:13; Jer. 48:10
20 [1]Heb. *made haste, and fell with the fulness of his stature*
21 [a]Judg. 12:3; ch. 19:5; Job 13:14

The Philistines dismiss David

29 NOW [a]THE Philistines gathered together all their armies [b]to Aphek: and the Israelites pitched by a fountain which *is* in Jezreel.

2 And the lords of the Philistines passed on by hundreds, and by thousands: but David and his men passed on in the rearward [a]with Achish.

3 Then said the princes of the Philistines, What *do* these Hebrews *here?* And Achish said unto the princes of the Philistines, *Is* not this David, the servant of Saul the king of Israel, which hath been with me [a]these days, or these years, and I have [b]found no fault in him since he fell *unto me* unto this day?

4 And the princes of the Philistines were wroth with him; and the princes of the Philistines said unto him, [a]Make this fellow return, that he may go again to his place which thou hast appointed him, and let him not go down with us to battle, lest [b]in the battle he be an adversary to us: for wherewith should he reconcile himself unto his master? *should it* not *be* with the heads of these men?

5 *Is* not this David, of whom they sang one to another in dances, saying, [a]Saul slew his thousands, and David his ten thousands?

6 ¶ Then Achish called David, and said unto him, Surely, *as* the LORD liveth, thou hast been upright, and [a]thy going out and thy coming in with me in the host *is* good in my sight: for [b]I have not found evil in thee since the day of thy coming unto me unto this day: nevertheless ʹthe lords favour thee not.

7 Wherefore now return, and go in peace, that thou ʹdisplease not the lords of the Philistines.

8 ¶ And David said unto Achish, But what have I done? and what hast thou found in thy servant so long as I have been ʹwith thee unto this day, that I may not go fight against the enemies of my lord the king?

9 And Achish answered and said to David, I know that thou *art* good in my sight, [a]as an angel of God: notwithstanding [b]the princes of the Philistines have said, He shall not go up with us to the battle.

10 Wherefore now rise up early in the morning with thy master's servants that are come with thee: and as soon as ye be up early in the morning, and have light, depart.

11 So David and his men rose up early to depart in the morning, to return into the land of the Philistines. [a]And the Philistines went up to Jezreel.

David smites the Amalekites

30 AND IT came to pass, when David and his men were come to Ziklag on the third day, that the [a]Amalekites had invaded the south, and Ziklag, and smitten Ziklag, and burned it with fire;

2 And had taken the women captives, that *were* therein: they slew not any, either great or small, but carried *them* away, and went on their way.

3 ¶ So David and his men came to the city, and, behold, *it was* burned with fire; and their wives, and their sons, and their daughters, were taken captives.

4 Then David and the people that *were* with him lifted up their voice and wept, until they had no more power to weep.

5 And David's [a]two wives were taken captives, Ahinoam the Jezreelitess, and Abigail the wife of Nabal the Carmelite.

6 And David was greatly distressed; [a]for the people spake of stoning him, because the soul of all the people was ʹgrieved, every man for his sons and for his daughters: but [b]David encouraged himself in the LORD his God.

7 [a]And David said to Abiathar the priest, Ahimelech's son, I pray thee, bring me hither the ephod. And Abiathar brought thither the ephod to David.

8 [a]And David inquired at the LORD, saying, Shall I pursue after this troop? shall I overtake them? And he answered him, Pursue: for thou shalt surely overtake *them,* and without fail recover *all.*

9 So David went, he and the six hundred men that *were* with him, and came to the brook Besor, where those that were left behind stayed.

10 But David pursued, he and four hundred men: [a]for two hundred abode behind, which were so faint that they could not go over the brook Besor.

11 ¶ And they found an Egyptian in the field, and brought him to David, and gave him bread, and he did eat; and they made him drink water;

12 And they gave him a piece of [a]a

29:1 [a]ch. 28:1 [b]ch. 4:1
2 [a]ch. 28:1,2
3 [a]See ch. 27:7 [b]Dan. 6:5
4 [a]1 Chr. 12:19 [b]As ch. 14:21
5 [a]ch. 18:7 & 21:11
6 [a]2 Sam. 3:25; 2 Ki. 19:27 [b]ver. 3 ʹHeb. *thou art not good in the eyes of the lords*
7 ʹHeb. *do not evil in the eyes of the lords*
8 ʹHeb. *before thee*
9 [a]2 Sam. 14:17, 20 & 19:27 [b]ver. 4
11 [a]2 Sam. 4:4
30:1 [a]See ch. 15:7; & 27:8
5 [a]ch. 25:42,43; 2 Sam. 2:2
6 [a]Ex. 17:4 [b]Ps. 42:5 & 56:3,4,11; Hab. 3:17,18 ʹHeb. *bitter*
7 [a]ch. 23:6,9
8 [a]ch. 23:2,4
10 [a]ver. 21
12 [a]ch. 25:18; 2 Ki. 20:7

cake of figs, and two clusters of raisins: and [b]when he had eaten, his spirit came again to him: for he had eaten no bread, nor drunk *any* water, three days and three nights.

13 And David said unto him, To whom *belongest* thou? and whence *art* thou? And he said, I *am* a young man of Egypt, servant to an Amalekite; and my master left me, because three days agone I fell sick.

14 We made an invasion *upon* the south of [a]the Cherethites, and upon *the coast* which *belongeth* to Judah, and upon the south of [b]Caleb; and we burned Ziklag with fire.

15 And David said to him, Canst thou bring me down to this company? And he said, Swear unto me by God, that thou wilt neither kill me, nor deliver me into the hands of my master, and I will bring thee down to this company.

16 ¶ And when he had brought him down, behold, *they were* spread abroad upon all the earth, [a]eating and drinking, and dancing, because of all the great spoil that they had taken out of the land of the Philistines, and out of the land of Judah.

17 And David smote them from the twilight even unto the evening of [1]the next day: and there escaped not a man of them, save four hundred young men, which rode upon camels, and fled.

18 And David recovered all that the Amalekites had carried away: and David rescued his two wives.

19 And there was nothing lacking to them, neither small nor great, neither sons nor daughters, neither spoil, nor any *thing* that they had taken to them: [a]David recovered all.

20 And David took all the flocks and the herds, *which* they drave before those *other* cattle, and said, This *is* David's spoil.

21 ¶ And David came to the [a]two hundred men, which were so faint that they could not follow David, whom they had made also to abide at the brook Besor: and they went forth to meet David, and to meet the people that *were* with him: and when David came near to the people, he [1]saluted them.

22 Then answered all the wicked men and *men* [a]of Belial, of [1]those that went with David, and said, Because they went not with us, we will not give them *aught* of the spoil that we have recovered, save to every man his wife and his children, that they may lead *them* away, and depart.

23 Then said David, Ye shall not do so, my brethren, with that which the LORD hath given us, who hath preserved us, and delivered the company that came against us into our hand.

24 For who will hearken unto you in this matter? but [a]as his part *is* that goeth down to the battle, so *shall* his part *be* that tarrieth by the stuff: they shall part alike.

25 And it was *so* from that day [1]forward, that he made it a statute and an ordinance for Israel unto this day.

26 ¶ And when David came to Ziklag, he sent of the spoil unto the elders of Judah, *even* to his friends, saying, Behold a [1]present for you of the spoil of the enemies of the LORD;

27 To *them* which *were* in Beth-el, and to *them* which *were* in [a]south Ramoth, and to *them* which *were* in [b]Jattir,

28 And to *them* which *were* in [a]Aroer, and to *them* which *were* in Siphmoth, and to *them* which *were* in [b]Eshtemoa,

29 And to *them* which *were* in Rachal, and to *them* which *were* in the cities of [a]the Jerahmeelites, and to *them* which *were* in the cities of the [b]Kenites,

30 And to *them* which *were* in [a]Hormah, and to *them* which *were* in Chorashan, and to *them* which *were* in Athach,

31 And to *them* which *were* in [a]Hebron, and to all the places where David himself and his men were wont to haunt.

The death of Saul

31 NOW [a]THE Philistines fought against Israel: and the men of Israel fled from before the Philistines, and fell down [1]slain in mount [b]Gilboa.

2 And the Philistines followed hard upon Saul and upon his sons; and the Philistines slew [a]Jonathan, and Abinadab, and Melchi-shua, Saul's sons.

3 And [a]the battle went sore against Saul, and the [1]archers [2]hit him; and he was sore wounded of the archers.

4 [a]Then said Saul unto his armourbearer, Draw thy sword, and thrust me through therewith; lest [b]these uncircumcised come and thrust me through, and [1]abuse me. But his armourbearer would

12 [b]Judg. 15:19; ch. 14:27
14 [a]ver. 16; 2 Sam. 8:18; 1 Ki. 1:38,44; Ezek. 25:16; Zeph. 2:5 [b]Josh. 14:13 & 15:13
16 [a]1 Thes. 5:3
17 [1]Heb. *their morrow*
19 [a]ver. 8
21 [a]ver. 10 [1]Or, *asked them how they did*
22 [a]Deut. 13:13; Judg. 19:22 [1]Heb. *men*
24 [a]See Num. 31:27; Josh. 22:8
25 [1]Heb. *and forward*
26 [1]Heb. *blessing*
27 [a]Josh. 19:8 [b]Josh. 15:48
28 [a]Josh. 13:16 [b]Josh. 15:50
29 [a]ch. 27:10 [b]Judg. 1:16
30 [a]Judg. 1:17
31 [a]Josh. 14:13; 2 Sam. 2:1
31:1 [a]1 Chr. 10:1-12 [b]ch. 28:4 [1]Or, *wounded*
2 [a]ch. 14:49
3 [a]See 2 Sam. 1:6 [1]Heb. *shooters, men with bows* [2]Heb. *found him*
4 [a]See Judg. 9:54 [b]ch. 14:6 [1]Or, *mock me*

not; [c]for he was sore afraid. Therefore
Saul took a sword, and [d]fell upon it.
5 And when his armourbearer saw that
Saul was dead, he fell likewise upon his
sword, and died with him.
6 So Saul died, and his three sons, and
his armourbearer, and all his men, that
same day together.
7 ¶ And when the men of Israel that
were on the other side of the valley, and
they that *were* on the other side Jordan,
saw that the men of Israel fled, and that
Saul and his sons were dead, they forsook
the cities, and fled; and the Philistines
came and dwelt in them.
8 And it came to pass on the morrow,
when the Philistines came to strip the
slain, that they found Saul and his three
sons fallen in mount Gilboa.
9 And they cut off his head, and
stripped off his armour, and sent into the
land of the Philistines round about, to
[a]publish *it in* the house of their idols, and
among the people.
10 [a]And they put his armour in the
house of [b]Ashtaroth: and [c]they fastened
his body to the wall of [d]Beth-shan.
11 ¶ [a]And when the inhabitants of Jabesh-gilead heard [I]of that which the Philistines had done to Saul;
12 [a]All the valiant men arose, and
went all night, and took the body of Saul
and the bodies of his sons from the wall
of Beth-shan, and came to Jabesh, and
[b]burnt them there.
13 And they took their bones, and
[a]buried *them* under a tree at Jabesh, [b]and
fasted seven days.

4 [c]2 Sam. 1:14 [d]ch. 14:6
9 [a]2 Sam. 1:20
10 [a]ch. 21:9 [b]Judg. 2:13 [c]2 Sam. 21:12 [d]Josh. 17:11; Judg. 1:27
11 [a]ch. 11:3,9,11 [I]Or, *concerning him*
12 [a]See ch. 11:1-11; 2 Sam. 2:4-7 [b]2 Chr. 16:14; Jer. 34:5; Amos 6:10
13 [a]2 Sam. 21:12-14 [b]Gen. 50:10

2 Samuel

Author: Unknown

Theme: The events of King David's reign

Date of writing: c. 925 B.C.

Outline of 2 Samuel

I. David's Rise to the Throne (1:1—4:12)
II. David's Accomplishments as King (5:1—9:13)
III. David's Weaknesses and Failures (10:1—20:26)
IV. Final Reflections About David's Reign (21:1—24:25)

IN THE ORIGINAL Hebrew manuscript the two books of 1 and 2 Samuel were combined into one scroll and identified by the title "Samuel." (For further information about the title, authorship and date of these books, see the introduction to 1 Samuel on p. 327.)

The book of 2 Samuel describes the events following the death of King Saul, detailing the establishment of the kingdom of Israel under King David. Spanning a period of forty years, the book of 2 Samuel records David's military victories over his enemies, his moral failure and adultery with Bathsheba, his flight from Absalom's rebellion and his unauthorized census of the people of Israel. This book also records the Davidic covenant (see 7:8–17), centering its focus on the throne of Jerusalem and the Messiah's promised descent from David's line.

The news of Saul's death

1 NOW IT came to pass after the death
of Saul, when David was returned
from [a]the slaughter of the Amalekites,
and David had abode two days in Ziklag;
2 It came even to pass on the third
day, that, behold, [a]a man came out of the
camp from Saul [b]with his clothes rent,
and earth upon his head: and *so* it was,
when he came to David, that he fell to
the earth, and did obeisance.
3 And David said unto him, From
whence comest thou? And he said unto
him, Out of the camp of Israel am I escaped.
4 And David said unto him, How went
the matter? I pray thee, tell me. And he
answered, That the people are fled from
the battle, and many of the people also
are fallen and dead; and Saul and Jonathan his son are dead also.
5 And David said unto the young man
that told him, How knowest thou that
Saul and Jonathan his son be dead?
6 And the young man that told him
said, As I happened by chance upon
[a]mount Gilboa, behold, [b]Saul leaned
upon his spear; and, lo, the chariots and
horsemen followed hard after him.
7 And when he looked behind him, he
saw me, and called unto me. And I answered, [I]Here *am* I.
8 And he said unto me, Who *art* thou?
And I answered him, I *am* an Amalekite.
9 He said unto me again, Stand, I pray
thee, upon me, and slay me: for [I]anguish
is come upon me, because my life *is* yet
whole in me.
10 So I stood upon him, and [a]slew
him, because I was sure that he could not
live after that he was fallen: and I took
the crown that *was* upon his head, and
the bracelet that *was* on his arm, and
have brought them hither unto my lord.
11 Then David took hold on his
clothes, and [a]rent them; and likewise all
the men that *were* with him:
12 And they mourned, and wept, and
fasted until even, for Saul, and for Jonathan his son, and for the people of the
LORD, and for the house of Israel; because
they were fallen by the sword.
13 ¶ And David said unto the young
man that told him, Whence *art* thou? And
he answered, I *am* the son of a stranger,
an Amalekite.
14 And David said unto him, [a]How
wast thou not [b]afraid to [c]stretch forth
thine hand to destroy the LORD'S
anointed?
15 And [a]David called one of the young
men, and said, Go near, *and* fall upon
him. And he smote him that he died.
16 And David said unto him, [a]Thy
blood *be* upon thy head; for [b]thy mouth
hath testified against thee, saying, I have
slain the LORD'S anointed.

David's lament

17 ¶ And David lamented with this
lamentation over Saul and over Jonathan
his son:
18 ([a]Also he bade them teach the children of Judah *the use of* the bow: behold,
it is written [b]in the book [I]of Jasher.)
19 The beauty of Israel is slain upon
thy high places: [a]how are the mighty
fallen!
20 [a]Tell *it* not in Gath, publish *it*
not in the streets of Askelon; lest [b]the
daughters of the Philistines rejoice,
lest the daughters of [c]the uncircumcised
triumph.
21 Ye [a]mountains of Gilboa, [b]*let there
be* no dew, neither *let there be* rain, upon
you, nor fields of offerings: for there the
shield of the mighty is vilely cast away,
the shield of Saul, *as though he had* not
been [c]anointed with oil.
22 From the blood of the slain, from
the fat of the mighty, [a]the bow of Jonathan turned not back, and the sword of
Saul returned not empty.
23 Saul and Jonathan *were* lovely and
[I]pleasant in their lives, and in their death
they were not divided: they were swifter
than eagles, they were [a]stronger than
lions.
24 Ye daughters of Israel, weep over
Saul, who clothed you in scarlet, with
other delights, who put on ornaments of
gold upon your apparel.
25 How are the mighty fallen in the
midst of the battle! O Jonathan, *thou
wast* slain in thine high places.
26 I am distressed for thee, my brother
Jonathan: very pleasant hast thou been
unto me: [a]thy love to me was wonderful,
passing the love of women.
27 [a]How are the mighty fallen, and the
weapons of war perished!

1:1 [a] 1 Sam. 30:17, 26
2 [a] ch. 4:10 [b] 1 Sam. 4:12
6 [a] 1 Sam. 31:1 [b] See 1 Sam. 31:2-4
7 [I] Heb. *Behold me*
9 [I] Or, *my coat of mail,* or, *my embroidered coat hindereth me, that my*
10 [a] Judg. 9:54
11 [a] ch. 3:31 & 13:31
14 [a] Num. 12:8 [b] 1 Sam. 31:4 [c] 1 Sam. 24:6 & 26:9; Ps. 105:15
15 [a] ch. 4:10,12
16 [a] 1 Sam. 26:9; 1 Ki. 2:32,33,37 [b] ver. 10; Luke 19:22
18 [a] 1 Sam. 31:3 [b] Josh. 10:13 [I] Or, *of the upright*
19 [a] ver. 27
20 [a] 1 Sam. 31:9; Mic. 1:10; See Judg. 16:23 [b] See Ex. 15:20; Judg. 11:34; 1 Sam. 18:6 [c] 1 Sam. 31:4
21 [a] 1 Sam. 31:1 [b] Judg. 5:23; Job 3:3,4; Jer. 20:14 [c] 1 Sam. 10:1
22 [a] 1 Sam. 18:4
23 [a] Judg. 14:18 [I] Or, *sweet*
26 [a] 1 Sam. 18:1,3; & 19:2 & 20:17,41 & 23:16
27 [a] ver. 19

David anointed king of Judah

2 AND IT came to pass after this, that David [a]inquired of the LORD, saying, Shall I go up into any of the cities of Judah? And the LORD said unto him, Go up. And David said, Whither shall I go up? And he said, Unto [b]Hebron.

2 So David went up thither, and his [a]two wives also, Ahinoam the Jezreelitess, and Abigail Nabal's wife the Carmelite.

3 And [a]his men that *were* with him did David bring up, every man with his household: and they dwelt in the cities of Hebron.

4 [a]And the men of Judah came, and there they anointed David king over the house of Judah. And they told David, saying, *That* [b]the men of Jabesh-gilead *were they* that buried Saul.

5 ¶ And David sent messengers unto the men of Jabesh-gilead, and said unto them, [a]Blessed *be* ye of the LORD, that ye have shown this kindness unto your lord, *even* unto Saul, and have buried him.

6 And now [a]the LORD show kindness and truth unto you: and I also will requite you this kindness, because ye have done this thing.

7 Therefore now let your hands be strengthened, and [1]be ye valiant: for your master Saul is dead, and also the house of Judah have anointed me king over them.

War between Israel and Judah

8 ¶ But [a]Abner the son of Ner, captain of [1]Saul's host, took [2]Ish-bosheth the son of Saul, and brought him over to Mahanaim;

9 And made him king over Gilead, and over the Ashurites, and over Jezreel, and over Ephraim, and over Benjamin, and over all Israel.

10 Ish-bosheth Saul's son *was* forty years old when he began to reign over Israel, and reigned two years. But the house of Judah followed David.

11 And [a]the [1]time that David was king in Hebron over the house of Judah was seven years and six months.

12 ¶ And Abner the son of Ner, and the servants of Ish-bosheth the son of Saul, went out from Mahanaim to [a]Gibeon.

13 And Joab the son of Zeruiah, and the servants of David, went out, and met [1]together by [a]the pool of Gibeon: and they sat down, the one on the one side of the pool, and the other on the other side of the pool.

14 And Abner said to Joab, Let the young men now arise, and play before us. And Joab said, Let them arise.

15 Then there arose and went over by number twelve of Benjamin, which *pertained* to Ish-bosheth the son of Saul, and twelve of the servants of David.

16 And they caught every one his fellow by the head, and *thrust* his sword in his fellow's side; so they fell down together: wherefore that place was called [1]Helkath-hazzurim, which *is* in Gibeon.

17 And there was a very sore battle that day; and Abner was beaten, and the men of Israel, before the servants of David.

18 ¶ And there were [a]three sons of Zeruiah there, Joab, and Abishai, and Asahel: and Asahel *was* [b]*as* light [1]of foot [c]as[2] a wild roe.

19 And Asahel pursued after Abner; and in going he turned not to the right hand nor to the left [1]from following Abner.

20 Then Abner looked behind him, and said, *Art* thou Asahel? And he answered, I *am*.

21 And Abner said to him, Turn thee aside to thy right hand or to thy left, and lay thee hold on one of the young men, and take thee his [a]armour.[1] But Asahel would not turn aside from following of him.

22 And Abner said again to Asahel, Turn thee aside from following me: wherefore should I smite thee to the ground? how then should I hold up my face to Joab thy brother?

23 Howbeit he refused to turn aside: wherefore Abner with the hinder end of the spear smote him [a]under the fifth *rib*, that the spear came out behind him; and he fell down there, and died in the same place: and it came to pass, *that* as many as came to the place where Asahel fell down and died stood still.

24 Joab also and Abishai pursued after Abner: and the sun went down when they were come to the hill of Ammah, that *lieth* before Giah by the way of the wilderness of Gibeon.

25 ¶ And the children of Benjamin gathered themselves together after Ab-

2:1 [a]Judg. 1:1; 1 Sam. 23:2,4,9 & 30:7,8 [b]ver. 11; 1 Sam. 30:31; ch. 5:1,3; 1 Ki. 2:11
2 [a]1 Sam. 30:5
3 [a]1 Sam. 27:2,3 & 30:1; 1 Chr. 12:1
4 [a]ver. 11; ch. 5:5 [b]1 Sam. 31:11,13
5 [a]Ruth 2:20 & 3:10
6 [a]2 Tim. 1:16,18
7 [1]Heb. *be ye the sons of valour*
8 [a]1 Sam. 14:50 [1]Heb. *the host which* was *Saul's* [2]Or, *Esh-baal;* see 1 Chr. 8:33 & 9:39
11 [a]ch. 5:5; 1 Ki. 2:11 [1]Heb. *number of days*
12 [a]Josh. 18:25
13 [a]Jer. 41:12 [1]Heb. *them together*
16 [1]i.e. *The field of strong men*
18 [a]1 Chr. 2:16 [b]1 Chr. 12:8 [c]Ps. 18:33 [1]Heb. *of his feet* [2]Heb. *as one of the roes that is in the field*
19 [1]Heb. *from after Abner*
21 [a]Judg. 14:19 [1]Or, *spoil*
23 [a]ch. 3:27 & 4:6 & 20:10

ner, and became one troop, and stood on the top of an hill.

26 Then Abner called to Joab, and said, Shall the sword devour for ever? knowest thou not that it will be bitterness in the latter end? how long shall it be then, ere thou bid the people return from following their brethren?

27 And Joab said, *As* God liveth, unless [a]thou hadst spoken, surely then [1]in the morning the people had [2]gone up every one from following his brother.

28 So Joab blew a trumpet, and all the people stood still, and pursued after Israel no more, neither fought they any more.

29 And Abner and his men walked all that night through the plain, and passed over Jordan, and went through all Bithron, and they came to Mahanaim.

30 And Joab returned from following Abner: and when he had gathered all the people together, there lacked of David's servants nineteen men and Asahel.

31 But the servants of David had smitten of Benjamin, and of Abner's men, *so that* three hundred and threescore men died.

32 ¶ And they took up Asahel, and buried him in the sepulchre of his father, which *was in* Bethlehem. And Joab and his men went all night, and they came to Hebron at break of day.

3 NOW THERE was long war between the house of Saul and the house of David: but David waxed stronger and stronger, and the house of Saul waxed weaker and weaker.

2 ¶ And [a]unto David were sons born in Hebron: and his firstborn was Amnon, [b]of Ahinoam the Jezreelitess;

3 And his second, [1]Chileab, of Abigail the wife of Nabal the Carmelite; and the third, Absalom the son of Maacah the daughter of Talmai king [a]of Geshur;

4 And the fourth, [a]Adonijah the son of Haggith; and the fifth, Shephatiah the son of Abital;

5 And the sixth, Ithream, by Eglah David's wife. These were born to David in Hebron.

6 ¶ And it came to pass, while there was war between the house of Saul and the house of David, that Abner made himself strong for the house of Saul.

7 And Saul had a concubine, whose name *was* [a]Rizpah, the daughter of Aiah: and *Ish-bosheth* said to Abner, Wherefore hast thou [b]gone in unto my father's concubine?

8 Then was Abner very wroth for the words of Ish-bosheth, and said, *Am* I [a]a dog's head, which against Judah do show kindness this day unto the house of Saul thy father, to his brethren, and to his friends, and have not delivered thee into the hand of David, that thou chargest me today with a fault concerning this woman?

9 [a]So do God to Abner, and more also, except, [b]as the LORD hath sworn to David, even so I do to him;

10 To translate the kingdom from the house of Saul, and to set up the throne of David over Israel and over Judah, [a]from Dan even to Beer-sheba.

11 And he could not answer Abner a word again, because he feared him.

12 ¶ And Abner sent messengers to David on his behalf, saying, Whose *is* the land? saying *also,* Make thy league with me, and, behold, my hand *shall be* with thee, to bring about all Israel unto thee.

13 ¶ And he said, Well; I will make a league with thee: but one thing I require of thee, [1]that is, [a]Thou shalt not see my face, except thou first bring [b]Michal Saul's daughter, when thou comest to see my face.

14 And David sent messengers to Ish-bosheth Saul's son, saying, Deliver *me* my wife Michal, which I espoused to me [a]for an hundred foreskins of the Philistines.

15 And Ish-bosheth sent, and took her from *her* husband, *even* from [a]Phaltiel the son of Laish.

16 And her husband went with her [1]along weeping behind her to [a]Bahurim. Then said Abner unto him, Go, return. And he returned.

Abner visits David

17 ¶ And Abner had communication with the elders of Israel, saying, Ye sought for David [1]in times past *to be* king over you:

18 Now then do *it:* [a]for the LORD hath spoken of David, saying, By the hand of my servant David I will save my people Israel out of the hand of the Philistines, and out of the hand of all their enemies. ▮

19 And Abner also spake in the ears of

27 [a]ver. 14; Prov. 17:14 [1]Heb. *from the morning* [2]Or, *gone away*
3:2 [a]1 Chr. 3:1-4 [b]1 Sam. 25:43
3 [a]1 Sam. 27:8; ch. 13:37 [1]Or, *Daniel* in 1 Chr. 3:1
4 [a]1 Ki. 1:5
7 [a]ch. 21:8,10 [b]ch. 16:21
8 [a]Deut. 23:18; 1 Sam. 24:14; ch. 9:8 & 16:9
9 [a]Ruth 1:17; 1 Ki. 19:2 [b]1 Sam. 15:28 & 16:1,12 & 28:17; 1 Chr. 12:23
10 [a]Judg. 20:1; ch. 17:11; 1 Ki. 4:25
13 [a]Gen. 43:3 [b]1 Sam. 18:20 [1]Heb. *saying*
14 [a]1 Sam. 18:25, 27
15 [a]1 Sam. 25:44, *Phalti*
16 [a]ch. 19:16 [1]Heb. *going and weeping*
17 [1]Heb. *both yesterday and the third day*
18 [a]ver. 9

▮ *1Sa 25:28* ◄► *2Sa 7:10–12*

[a]Benjamin: and Abner went also to speak in the ears of David in Hebron all that seemed good to Israel, and that seemed good to the whole house of Benjamin.

20 So Abner came to David to Hebron, and twenty men with him. And David made Abner and the men that *were* with him a feast.

21 And Abner said unto David, I will arise and go, and [a]will gather all Israel unto my lord the king, that they may make a league with thee, and that thou mayest [b]reign over all that thine heart desireth. And David sent Abner away; and he went in peace.

22 ¶ And, behold, the servants of David and Joab came from *pursuing* a troop, and brought in a great spoil with them: but Abner *was* not with David in Hebron; for he had sent him away, and he was gone in peace.

23 When Joab and all the host that *was* with him were come, they told Joab, saying, Abner the son of Ner came to the king, and he hath sent him away, and he is gone in peace.

24 Then Joab came to the king, and said, What hast thou done? behold, Abner came unto thee; why *is* it *that* thou hast sent him away, and he is quite gone?

25 Thou knowest Abner the son of Ner, that he came to deceive thee, and to know [a]thy going out and thy coming in, and to know all that thou doest.

Joab kills Abner

26 And when Joab was come out from David, he sent messengers after Abner, which brought him again from the well of Sirah: but David knew *it* not.

27 And when Abner was returned to Hebron, Joab [a]took him aside in the gate to speak with him [l]quietly, and smote him there [b]under the fifth *rib,* that he died, for the blood of [c]Asahel his brother.

28 ¶ And afterward when David heard *it,* he said, I and my kingdom *are* guiltless before the LORD for ever from the [l]blood of Abner the son of Ner:

29 [a]Let it rest on the head of Joab, and on all his father's house; and let there not [l]fail from the house of Joab one [b]that hath an issue, or that is a leper, or that leaneth on a staff, or that falleth on the sword, or that lacketh bread.

30 So Joab and Abishai his brother slew Abner, because he had slain their brother [a]Asahel at Gibeon in the battle.

31 ¶ And David said to Joab, and to all the people that *were* with him, [a]Rend your clothes, and [b]gird you with sackcloth, and mourn before Abner. And king David *himself* followed the [l]bier.

32 And they buried Abner in Hebron: and the king lifted up his voice, and wept at the grave of Abner; and all the people wept.

33 And the king lamented over Abner, and said, Died Abner as a [a]fool dieth?

34 Thy hands *were* not bound, nor thy feet put into fetters: as a man falleth before [l]wicked men, *so* fellest thou. And all the people wept again over him.

35 And when all the people came [a]to cause David to eat meat while it was yet day, David sware, saying, [b]So do God to me, and more also, if I taste bread, or aught else, [c]till the sun be down.

36 And all the people took notice *of it,* and it [l]pleased them: as whatsoever the king did pleased all the people.

37 For all the people and all Israel understood that day that it was not of the king to slay Abner the son of Ner.

38 And the king said unto his servants, Know ye not that there is a prince and a great man fallen this day in Israel?

39 And I *am* this day [l]weak, though anointed king; and these men the sons of Zeruiah [a]*be* too hard for me: [b]the LORD shall reward the doer of evil according to his wickedness. H

The murder of Ish-bosheth

4 AND WHEN Saul's son heard that Abner was dead in Hebron, [a]his hands were feeble, and all the Israelites were [b]troubled.

2 And Saul's son had two men *that were* captains of bands: the name of the one *was* Baanah, and the name of the [l]other Rechab, the sons of Rimmon a Beerothite, of the children of Benjamin: (for [a]Beeroth also was reckoned to Benjamin:

3 And the Beerothites fled to [a]Gittaim, and were sojourners there until this day.)

4 And [a]Jonathan, Saul's son, had a son *that was* lame of *his* feet. He was five years old when the tidings came of Saul and Jonathan [b]out of Jezreel, and his nurse took him up, and fled: and it came to pass, as she made haste to flee, that he

19 [a]1 Chr. 12:29
21 [a]ver. 10,12 [b]1 Ki. 11:37
25 [a]1 Sam. 29:6; Is. 37:28
27 [a]1 Ki. 2:5; ch. 20:9,10 [b]ch. 4:6 [c]ch. 2:23 [l]Or, *peaceably*
28 [l]Heb. *bloods*
29 [a]1 Ki. 2:32,33 [b]Lev. 15:2 [l]Heb. *be cut off*
30 [a]ch. 2:23
31 [a]Josh. 7:6; ch. 1:2,11 [b]Gen. 37:34 [l]Heb. *bed*
33 [a]ch. 13:12,13
34 [l]Heb. *children of iniquity*
35 [a]ch. 12:17; Jer. 16:7 [b]Ruth 1:17 [c]ch. 1:12
36 [l]Heb. *was good in their eyes*
39 [a]ch. 19:7 [b]See ch. 19:13; 1 Ki. 2:5, 6,33,34; 2 Tim. 4:14 [l]Heb. *tender*
4:1 [a]Ezra 4:4; Is. 13:7 [b]Mat. 2:3
2 [a]Josh. 18:25 [l]Heb. *second*
3 [a]Neh. 11:33
4 [a]ch. 9:3 [b]1 Sam. 29:1,11

H *1Sa 25:29* ◄► *1Ki 2:33*

fell, and became lame. And his name *was* [1]Mephibosheth.

5 And the sons of Rimmon the Beerothite, Rechab and Baanah, went, and came about the heat of the day to the house of Ish-bosheth, who lay on a bed at noon.

6 And they came thither into the midst of the house, *as though* they would have fetched wheat; and they smote him [a]under the fifth *rib:* and Rechab and Baanah his brother escaped.

7 For when they came into the house, he lay on his bed in his bedchamber, and they smote him, and slew him, and beheaded him, and took his head, and gat them away through the plain all night.

8 And they brought the head of Ish-bosheth unto David to Hebron, and said to the king, Behold the head of Ish-bosheth the son of Saul thine enemy, [a]which sought thy life; and the LORD hath avenged my lord the king this day of Saul, and of his seed.

9 ¶ And David answered Rechab and Baanah his brother, the sons of Rimmon the Beerothite, and said unto them, *As* the LORD liveth, [a]who hath redeemed my soul out of all adversity,

10 When [a]one told me, saying, Behold, Saul is dead, [1]thinking to have brought good tidings, I took hold of him, and slew him in Ziklag, [2]who *thought* that I would have given him a reward for his tidings:

11 How much more, when wicked men have slain a righteous person in his own house upon his bed? shall I not therefore now [a]require his blood of your hand, and take you away from the earth?

12 And David [a]commanded his young men, and they slew them, and cut off their hands and their feet, and hanged *them* up over the pool in Hebron. But they took the head of Ish-bosheth, and buried *it* in the [b]sepulchre of Abner in Hebron.

David made king of Israel

5 THEN [a]CAME all the tribes of Israel to David unto Hebron, and spake, saying, Behold, [b]we *are* thy bone and thy flesh.

2 Also in time past, when Saul was king over us, [a]thou wast he that leddest out and broughtest in Israel: and the LORD said to thee, [b]Thou shalt feed my people Israel, and thou shalt be a captain over Israel.

3 [a]So all the elders of Israel came to the king to Hebron; [b]and king David made a league with them in Hebron [c]before the LORD: and they anointed David king over Israel.

4 ¶ David *was* thirty years old when he began to reign, [a]*and* he reigned forty years.

5 In Hebron he reigned over Judah [a]seven years and six months: and in Jerusalem he reigned thirty and three years over all Israel and Judah.

The capture of Jerusalem

6 ¶ And the king and his men went [a]to Jerusalem unto [b]the Jebusites, the inhabitants of the land: which spake unto David, saying, Except thou take away the blind and the lame, thou shalt not come in hither: [1]thinking, David cannot come in hither.

7 Nevertheless David took the strong hold of Zion: [a]the same *is* the city of David.

8 And David said on that day, Whosoever getteth up to the gutter, and smiteth the Jebusites, and the lame and the blind, *that are* hated of David's soul, [a]*he shall be chief and captain.* [1]Wherefore they said, The blind and the lame shall not come into the house.

9 So David dwelt in the fort, and called it [a]the city of David. And David built round about from Millo and inward.

10 And David [1]went on, and grew great, and the LORD God of hosts *was* with him.

11 ¶ And [a]Hiram king of Tyre sent messengers to David, and cedar trees, and carpenters, and [1]masons: and they built David an house.

12 And David perceived that the LORD had established him king over Israel, and that he had exalted his kingdom for his people Israel's sake.

13 ¶ And [a]David took *him* more concubines and wives out of Jerusalem, after he was come from Hebron: and there were yet sons and daughters born to David.

14 And [a]these *be* the names of those that were born unto him in Jerusalem; [1]Shammuah, and Shobab, and Nathan, and Solomon,

4 [1]Or, *Merib-baal;* see 1 Chr. 8:34 & 9:40
6 [a]ch. 2:23
8 [a]1 Sam. 19:2,10, 11
9 [a]Gen. 48:16; 1 Ki. 1:29
10 [a]ch. 1:2,4,15 [1]Heb. *he was in his own eyes as a bringer* [2]Or, *which was the reward I gave him for his tidings*
11 [a]Gen. 9:5,6
12 [a]ch. 1:15 [b]ch. 3:32
5:1 [a]1 Chr. 11:1 [b]Gen. 29:14
2 [a]1 Sam. 18:13 [b]1 Sam. 16:1
3 [a]1 Chr. 11:3 [b]2 Ki. 11:17 [c]Judg. 11:11; 1 Sam. 23:18
4 [a]1 Chr. 26:31 & 29:27
5 [a]ch. 2:11; 1 Chr. 3:4
6 [a]Judg. 1:21 [b]Josh. 15:63; Judg. 1:8 & 19:11,12 [1]Or, *saying, David shall not*
7 [a]1 Ki. 2:10 & 8:1
8 [a]1 Chr. 11:6-9 [1]Or, *Because they had said, even the blind and the lame, He shall not come into the house*
9 [a]ver. 7
10 [1]Heb. *went going and growing*
11 [a]1 Ki. 5:2 [1]Heb. *hewers of the stone of the wall*
13 [a]Deut. 17:17; 1 Chr. 3:9
14 [a]1 Chr. 3:5 [1]Or, *Shimea;* see 1 Chr. 3:5

15 Ibhar also, and [1]Elishua, and Nepheg, and Japhia,

16 And Elishama, and [1]Eliada, and Eliphalet.

The Philistines defeated

17 ¶ [a]But when the Philistines heard that they had anointed David king over Israel, all the Philistines came up to seek David; and David heard *of it,* [b]and went down to the hold.

18 The Philistines also came and spread themselves in [a]the valley of Rephaim.

19 And David [a]inquired of the LORD, saying, Shall I go up to the Philistines? wilt thou deliver them into mine hand? And the LORD said unto David, Go up: for I will doubtless deliver the Philistines into thine hand.

20 And David came to [a]Baal-perazim, and David smote them there, and said, The LORD hath broken forth upon mine enemies before me, as the breach of waters. Therefore he called the name of that place [1]Baal-perazim.

21 And there they left their images, and David and his men [a]burned[1] them.

22 ¶ [a]And the Philistines came up yet again, and spread themselves in the valley of Rephaim.

23 And when [a]David inquired of the LORD, he said, Thou shalt not go up; *but* fetch a compass behind them, and come upon them over against the mulberry trees.

24 And let it be, when thou [a]hearest the sound of a going in the tops of the mulberry trees, that then thou shalt bestir thyself: for then [b]shall the LORD go out before thee, to smite the host of the Philistines.

25 And David did so, as the LORD had commanded him; and smote the Philistines from [a]Geba until thou come to [b]Gazer.

Bringing the ark to Jerusalem

6 AGAIN, DAVID gathered together all *the* chosen *men* of Israel, thirty thousand.

2 And [a]David arose, and went with all the people that *were* with him from [1]Baale of Judah, to bring up from thence the ark of God, [2]whose name is called by the name of the LORD of hosts [b]that dwelleth *between* the cherubims.

3 And they [1]set the ark of God upon a new cart, and brought it out of the house of Abinadab that *was* in [2]Gibeah: and Uzzah and Ahio, the sons of Abinadab, drave the new cart.

4 And they brought it out of [a]the house of Abinadab which *was* at Gibeah, [1]accompanying the ark of God: and Ahio went before the ark.

5 And David and all the house of Israel played before the LORD on all manner of *instruments made of* fir wood, even on harps, and on psalteries, and on timbrels, and on cornets, and on cymbals.

6 ¶ And when they came to [a]Nachon's threshingfloor, Uzzah put forth *his hand* to the ark of God, and took hold of it; for the oxen [1]shook *it.*

7 And the anger of the LORD was kindled against Uzzah; and [a]God smote him there for *his* [1]error; and there he died by the ark of God.

8 And David was displeased, because the LORD had [1]made a breach upon Uzzah: and he called the name of the place [2]Perez-uzzah to this day.

9 And [a]David was afraid of the LORD that day, and said, How shall the ark of the LORD come to me?

10 So David would not remove the ark of the LORD unto him into the city of David: but David carried it aside into the house of Obed-edom [a]the Gittite.

11 [a]And the ark of the LORD continued in the house of Obed-edom the Gittite three months: and the LORD [b]blessed Obed-edom, and all his household.

12 ¶ And it was told king David, saying, The LORD hath blessed the house of Obed-edom, and all that *pertaineth* unto him, because of the ark of God. [a]So David went and brought up the ark of God from the house of Obed-edom into the city of David with gladness.

13 And it was *so,* that when [a]they that bare the ark of the LORD had gone six paces, he sacrificed [b]oxen and fatlings.

14 And David [a]danced before the LORD with all *his* might; and David *was* girded [b]with a linen ephod.

15 [a]So David and all the house of Israel brought up the ark of the LORD with shouting, and with the sound of the trumpet.

16 And as the ark of the LORD came into the city of David, Michal Saul's daughter looked through a window, and

15 [1]Or, *Elishama;* see 1 Chr. 3:6
16 [1]Or, *Beeliada;* see 1 Chr. 14:7
17 [a]1 Chr. 11:16 [b]ch. 23:14
18 [a]Josh. 15:8; Is. 17:5
19 [a]1 Sam. 23:2,4
20 [a]Is. 28:21 [1]i.e. *The plain of breaches*
21 [a]Deut. 7:5,25 [1]Or, *took them away*
22 [a]1 Chr. 14:13
23 [a]ver. 19
24 [a]2 Ki. 7:6 [b]Judg. 4:14
25 [a]1 Chr. 14:16 *Gibeon* [b]Josh. 16:10
6:2 [a]1 Chr. 13:5,6 [b]1 Sam. 4:4; Ps. 80:1 [1]Or, *Baalah* i.e. *Kirjath-jearim;* see Josh. 15:9 [2]Or, *at which the name,* even *the name of the LORD of hosts, was called upon*
3 [1]Heb. *made to ride* [2]Or, *The hill*
4 [a]1 Sam. 7:1 [1]Heb. *with*
6 [a]1 Chr. 13:9; he is called *Chidon* [1]Or, *stumbled*
7 [a]1 Sam. 6:19 [1]Or, *rashness*
8 [1]Heb. *broken* [2]i.e. *The breach of Uzzah*
9 [a]Ps. 119:120
10 [a]1 Chr. 13:13
11 [a]1 Chr. 13:14 [b]Gen. 39:5
12 [a]1 Chr. 15:25
13 [a]Num. 4:15; Josh. 3:3; 1 Chr. 15:2,15 [b]See 1 Ki. 8:5
14 [a]Ps. 30:11 [b]1 Sam. 2:18
15 [a]1 Chr. 15:28

saw king David leaping and dancing before the LORD; and she despised him in
her heart.
17 ¶ And [a]they brought in the ark of
the LORD, and set it in [b]his place, in the
midst of the tabernacle that David had
'pitched for it: and David [c]offered burnt
offerings and peace offerings before the
LORD.
18 And as soon as David had made an
end of offering burnt offerings and peace
offerings, [a]he blessed the people in the
name of the LORD of hosts.
19 [a]And he dealt among all the people,
even among the whole multitude of Israel, as well to the women as men, to
every one a cake of bread, and a good
piece *of flesh,* and a flagon *of wine.* So
all the people departed every one to his
house.
20 ¶ [a]Then David returned to bless his
household. And Michal the daughter of
Saul came out to meet David, and said,
How glorious was the king of Israel today,
who [b]uncovered himself today in the
eyes of the handmaids of his servants, as
one of the [c]vain fellows 'shamelessly uncovereth himself!
21 And David said unto Michal, *It was*
before the LORD, [a]which chose me before
thy father, and before all his house, to
appoint me ruler over the people of the
LORD, over Israel: therefore will I play before the LORD.
22 And I will yet be more vile than
thus, and will be base in mine own sight:
and 'of the maidservants which thou hast
spoken of, of them shall I be had in
honour.
23 Therefore Michal the daughter of
Saul had no child [a]unto the day of her
death.

Nathan's prophecy

7 AND IT came to pass, [a]when the
king sat in his house, and the LORD
had given him rest round about from all
his enemies;
2 That the king said unto Nathan the
prophet, See now, I dwell in [a]an house
of cedar, [b]but the ark of God dwelleth
within [c]curtains.

17 [a]1 Chr. 16:1 [b]1 Chr. 15:1; Ps. 132:8 [c]1 Ki. 8:5, 62,63 'Heb. *stretched*
18 [a]1 Ki. 8:55
19 [a]1 Chr. 16:3
20 [a]Ps. 30,title [b]ver. 14,16 [c]Judg. 9:4 'Or, *openly*
21 [a]1 Sam. 13:14
22 'Or, *of the handmaids* of my servants
23 [a]See 1 Sam. 15:35; Is. 22:14
7:1 [a]1 Chr. 17:1
2 [a]ch. 5:11 [b]See Acts 7:46 [c]Ex. 26:1
5 [a]1 Ki. 5:3 & 8:19; 1 Chr. 22:8 'Heb. *to my servant, to David*
6 [a]1 Ki. 8:16 [b]Ex. 40:18,19,34
7 [a]Lev. 26:11; Deut. 23:14 [b]Mat. 2:6; Acts 20:28 'Or, *any of the judges;* see 1 Chr. 17:6
8 [a]1 Sam. 16:11,12 'Heb. *from after*
9 [a]1 Sam. 18:14; ch. 5:10 [b]1 Sam. 31:6 'Heb. *from thy face*
10 [a]Ps. 44:2 & 80:8; Jer. 24:6 [b]Ps. 89:22
11 [a]Judg. 2:14; 1 Sam. 12:9 [b]ver. 27; Ex. 1:21
12 [a]1 Ki. 2:1 [b]Deut. 31:16 [c]Ps. 132:11
13 [a]1 Ki. 5:5 & 8:19 [b]ver. 16

3 And Nathan said to the king, Go, do
all that *is* in thine heart; for the LORD *is*
with thee.
4 ¶ And it came to pass that night, that
the word of the LORD came unto Nathan,
saying,
5 Go and tell 'my servant David, Thus
saith the LORD, [a]Shalt thou build me an
house for me to dwell in?
6 Whereas I have not dwelt in *any*
house [a]since the time that I brought up
the children of Israel out of Egypt, even
to this day, but have walked in [b]a tent
and in a tabernacle.
7 In all *the places* wherein I have
[a]walked with all the children of Israel
spake I a word with 'any of the tribes of
Israel, whom I commanded [b]to feed my
people Israel, saying, Why build ye not
me an house of cedar?
8 Now therefore so shalt thou say unto
my servant David, Thus saith the LORD of
hosts, [a]I took thee from the sheepcote,
'from following the sheep, to be ruler
over my people, over Israel:
9 And [a]I was with thee whithersoever
thou wentest, [b]and have cut off all thine
enemies 'out of thy sight, and have made
thee a great name, like unto the name of
the great *men* that *are* in the earth.
10 Moreover I will appoint a place for **I**
my people Israel, and will [a]plant them,
that they may dwell in a place of their
own, and move no more; [b]neither shall
the children of wickedness afflict them
any more, as beforetime,
11 And as [a]since the time that I commanded judges *to be* over my people Israel, and have caused thee to rest from all
thine enemies. Also the LORD telleth thee
[b]that he will make thee an house.
12 ¶ And [a]when thy days be fulfilled,
and thou [b]shalt sleep with thy fathers, [c]I
will set up thy seed after thee, which
shall proceed out of thy bowels, and I will
establish his kingdom.
13 [a]He shall build an house for my **M**
name, and I will [b]stablish the throne of
his kingdom for ever.

I *2Sa 3:18* ◀ ▶ *2Sa 7:23–24*
M *1Sa 2:10* ◀ ▶ *2Sa 7:16*

7:10 The Lord promised to give Israel a secure place of their own. This prophecy will find complete fulfillment in the last days as Jewish exiles return to the promised land from all over the world.
7:13 God promised that David would have a son who would build a house for God. That son was Solo-

T 14 [a]I will be his father, and he shall be my son. [b]If he commit iniquity, I will chasten him with the rod of men, and with the stripes of the children of men:

15 But my mercy shall not depart away from him, [a]as I took *it* from Saul, whom I put away before thee.

M 16 And [a]thine house and thy kingdom shall be established for ever before thee: thy throne shall be established for ever.

17 According to all these words, and according to all this vision, so did Nathan speak unto David.

David's prayer

18 ¶ Then went king David in, and sat before the LORD, and he said, [a]Who *am* I, O Lord GOD? and what *is* my house, that thou hast brought me hitherto?

19 And this was yet a small thing in thy sight, O Lord GOD; but thou hast spoken also of thy servant's house for a great while to come. [a]And *is* this the [l]manner of man, O Lord GOD?

20 And what can David say more unto thee? for thou, Lord GOD, [a]knowest thy servant.

21 For thy word's sake, and according to thine own heart, hast thou done all these great things, to make thy servant know *them.*

O 22 Wherefore [a]thou art great, O LORD God: for [b]*there is* none like thee, neither *is there any* God beside thee, according to all that we have heard with our ears.

23 And [a]what one nation in the earth *is* like thy people, *even* like Israel, whom God went to redeem for a people to himself, and to make him a name, and to do for you great things and terrible, for thy land, before [b]thy people, which thou redeemedst to thee from Egypt, *from* the nations and their gods? I

24 For [a]thou hast confirmed to thyself thy people Israel *to be* a people unto thee for ever: [b]and thou, LORD, art become their God.

25 And now, O LORD God, the word that thou hast spoken concerning thy servant, and concerning his house, establish *it* for ever, and do as thou hast said.

26 And let thy name be magnified for ever, saying, The LORD of hosts *is* the God over Israel: and let the house of thy servant David be established before thee.

27 For thou, O LORD of hosts, God of Israel, hast revealed to thy servant, saying, I will build thee an house: therefore hath thy servant found in his heart to pray this prayer unto thee.

28 And now, O Lord GOD, thou *art* that God, and [a]thy words be true, and thou hast promised this goodness unto thy servant:

29 Therefore now [l]let it please thee to bless the house of thy servant, that it may continue for ever before thee: for thou, O Lord GOD, hast spoken *it:* and with thy blessing let the house of thy servant be blessed [a]for ever.

14 [a]Heb. 1:5 [b]Ps. 89:30
15 [a]1 Sam. 15:23, 28 & 16:14
16 [a]ver. 13; John 12:34
18 [a]Gen. 32:10
19 [a]Is. 55:8 [l]Heb. *law*
20 [a]Ps. 139:1
22 [a]1 Chr. 16:25; 2 Chr. 2:5; Jer. 10:6 [b]Deut. 3:24 & 4:35 & 32:39
23 [a]Ps. 147:20 [b]Deut. 9:26
24 [a]Deut. 26:18 [b]Ps. 48:14
28 [a]John 17:17
29 [a]ch. 22:51 [l]Heb. *be thou pleased and bless*

T *Dt 8:16* ◀ ▶ *Job 5:17*
M *2Sa 7:13–14* ◀ ▶ *2Sa 23:3–5*
O *1Sa 2:2* ◀ ▶ *2Sa 22:32*
I *2Sa 7:10–12* ◀ ▶ *1Ki 2:4*

mon (see 2Ch 6:7–10).

7:16 *Davidic Covenant.* The covenant promise made to Abram concerning the promised land was confirmed and expanded in the Palestinian covenant (see Dt 30:1–3). The Davidic covenant also expands the Abrahamic covenant, but concentrates its focus on the promise of offspring. This eternal covenant contains the following elements:

1. David will have a child who will succeed him and further establish the kingdom (see 7:12). This promise was initially fulfilled in the birth of Solomon.
2. This son (Solomon) will build the temple instead of David (see 7:13). This promise was fulfilled (see 2Ch 6:7–12).
3. Solomon's throne would be established forever (see 7:13). The exile to Babylon interrupted the kingdom, but did not set this promise aside.
4. If Solomon sinned he would be chastised but not removed from God's love (see 7:14–15).
5. David's house, kingdom and throne would be established forever (7:16). This promise will be ultimately fulfilled when David's son, the Christ, returns to earth to reign over David's covenanted kingdom. Each of the elements of this promise is eternal, indicating that there must be no end to the Messiah's reign from David's throne.

NOTE: The seven additional covenants include the Edenic (Ge 2:15–17), Adamic (Ge 3:15–19), Noahic (Ge 9:8ff), Abrahamic (Ge 15:4ff; 17:1–22), Mosaic (Ex 19:5), Palestinian (Dt 30:1–10) and New (Heb 8:8–12). See chart on p. 6.

7:23–24 Israel was unique among the nations because God had chosen them to be his special people (see Ex 19:5–6).

David's military victories

8 AND AFTER this it came to pass, that David smote the Philistines, and subdued them: and David took [1]Metheg-ammah out of the hand of the Philistines.

2 And [a]he smote Moab, and measured them with a line, casting them down to the ground; even with two lines measured he to put to death, and with one full line to keep alive. And *so* the Moabites became David's servants, *and* [b]brought gifts.

3 ¶ David smote also [1]Hadadezer, the son of Rehob, king of [a]Zobah, as he went to recover [b]his border at the river Euphrates.

4 And David took [1]from him a thousand [2]*chariots,* and seven hundred horsemen, and twenty thousand footmen: and David [a]houghed all the chariot *horses,* but reserved of them *for* an hundred chariots.

5 [a]And when the Syrians of Damascus came to succour Hadadezer king of Zobah, David slew of the Syrians two and twenty thousand men.

S 6 Then David put garrisons in Syria of Damascus: and the Syrians became servants to David, *and* brought gifts. [a]And the LORD preserved David whithersoever he went.

7 And David took [a]the shields of gold that were on the servants of Hadadezer, and brought them to Jerusalem.

8 And from [1]Betah, and from [2]Berothai, cities of Hadadezer, king David took exceeding much brass.

9 ¶ When [1]Toi king of Hamath heard that David had smitten all the host of Hadadezer,

10 Then Toi sent [a]Joram his son unto king David, to [1]salute him, and to bless him, because he had fought against Hadadezer, and smitten him: for Hadadezer [2]had wars with Toi. And *Joram* [3]brought with him vessels of silver, and vessels of gold, and vessels of brass:

11 Which also king David [a]did dedicate unto the LORD, with the silver and gold that he had dedicated of all nations which he subdued;

12 Of Syria, and of Moab, and of the children of Ammon, and of the Philistines, and of Amalek, and of the spoil of Hadadezer, son of Rehob, king of Zobah.

13 And David gat *him* a name when he returned from [1]smiting of the Syrians in [a]the valley of salt, [b]*being*[2] eighteen thousand *men.*

14 ¶ And he put garrisons in Edom; throughout all Edom put he garrisons, and [a]all they of Edom became David's servants. And the LORD preserved David whithersoever he went. S

15 And David reigned over all Israel; and David executed judgment and justice unto all his people.

16 [a]And Joab the son of Zeruiah *was* over the host; and [b]Jehoshaphat the son of Ahilud *was* [1]recorder;

17 And [a]Zadok the son of Ahitub, and Ahimelech the son of Abiathar, *were* the priests; and Seraiah *was* the [1]scribe;

18 [a]And Benaiah the son of Jehoiada *was over* both the [b]Cherethites and the Pelethites; and David's sons were [1]chief rulers.

David and Mephibosheth

9 AND DAVID said, Is there yet any that is left of the house of Saul, that I may [a]show him kindness for Jonathan's sake?

2 And *there was* of the house of Saul a servant whose name *was* [a]Ziba. And when they had called him unto David, the king said unto him, *Art* thou Ziba? And he said, Thy servant *is he.*

3 And the king said, *Is* there not yet any of the house of Saul, that I may show [a]the kindness of God unto him? And Ziba said unto the king, Jonathan hath yet a son, *which is* [b]lame on *his* feet.

4 And the king said unto him, Where *is* he? And Ziba said unto the king, Behold, he *is* in the house of [a]Machir, the son of Ammiel, in Lo-debar.

5 ¶ Then king David sent, and fetched him out of the house of Machir, the son of Ammiel, from Lo-debar.

6 Now when [1]Mephibosheth, the son of Jonathan, the son of Saul, was come unto David, he fell on his face, and did reverence. And David said, Mephibosheth. And he answered, Behold thy servant!

7 ¶ And David said unto him, Fear not: for I will surely show thee kindness for Jonathan thy father's sake, and will restore thee all the land of Saul thy father;

8:1 [1]Or, *The bridle of Ammah*
2 [a]Num. 24:17 [b]See 1 Sam. 10:27
3 [a]ch. 10:6; Ps. 60, title [b]See Gen. 15:18 [1]Or, *Hadarezer;* see 1 Chr. 18:3
4 [a]Josh. 11:6,9 [1]Or, *of his* [2]As 1 Chr. 18:4
5 [a]1 Ki. 11:23
6 [a]ver. 14; ch. 7:9
7 [a]See 1 Ki. 10:16
8 [1]Or, *Tibhath* [2]Or, *Chun;* see 1 Chr. 18:8
9 [1]*Tou;* see 1 Chr. 18:9
10 [a]1 Chr. 18:10, *Hadoram* [1]Heb. *ask him of peace* [2]Heb. *was a man of wars with* [3]Heb. *in his hand were*
11 [a]1 Ki. 7:51
13 [a]2 Ki. 14:7 [b]See 1 Chr. 18:12; Ps. 60,title [1]Heb. *his smiting* [2]Or, *slaying*
14 [a]Gen. 27:29,37, 40; Num. 24:18
16 [a]ch. 19:13 & 20:23; 1 Chr. 11:6 [b]1 Ki. 4:3 [1]Or, *remembrancer,* or, *writer of chronicles*
17 [a]1 Chr. 24:3 [1]Or, *secretary*
18 [a]1 Chr. 18:17 [b]1 Sam. 30:14 [1]Or, *princes*
9:1 [a]1 Sam. 18:3; Prov. 27:10
2 [a]ch. 16:1 & 19:17,29
3 [a]1 Sam. 20:14 [b]ch. 4:4
4 [a]ch. 17:27
6 [1]Called *Merib-baal* in 1 Chr. 8:34

S Nu 31:49 ◀▶ 2Sa 8:14 S 2Sa 8:6 ◀▶ 1Ch 18:6

and thou shalt eat bread at my table continually.
8 And he bowed himself, and said,
What *is* thy servant, that thou shouldest
look upon such [a]a dead dog as I *am?*
9 ¶ Then the king called to Ziba, Saul's
servant, and said unto him, [a]I have given
unto thy master's son all that pertained to
Saul and to all his house.
10 Thou therefore, and thy sons, and
thy servants, shall till the land for him,
and thou shalt bring in *the fruits,* that thy
master's son may have food to eat: but
Mephibosheth thy master's son [a]shall eat
bread always at my table. Now Ziba had
[b]fifteen sons and twenty servants.
11 Then said Ziba unto the king, According to all that my lord the king hath
commanded his servant, so shall thy servant do. As for Mephibosheth, *said the
king,* he shall eat at my table, as one of
the king's sons.
12 And Mephibosheth had a young
son, [a]whose name *was* Micha. And all
that dwelt in the house of Ziba *were* servants unto Mephibosheth.
13 So Mephibosheth dwelt in Jerusalem: [a]for he did eat continually at the
king's table; and [b]was lame on both his
feet.

Victory over the Ammonites

10 AND IT came to pass after this,
that the [a]king of the children of
Ammon died, and Hanun his son reigned
in his stead.
2 Then said David, I will show kindness unto Hanun the son of Nahash, as
his father showed kindness unto me. And
David sent to comfort him by the hand of
his servants for his father. And David's
servants came into the land of the children of Ammon.
3 And the princes of the children of
Ammon said unto Hanun their lord,
[1]Thinkest thou that David doth honour
thy father, that he hath sent comforters
unto thee? hath not David *rather* sent his
servants unto thee, to search the city, and
to spy it out, and to overthrow it?
4 Wherefore Hanun took David's servants, and shaved off the one half of their
beards, and cut off their garments in the
middle, [a]*even* to their buttocks, and sent
them away.
5 When they told *it* unto David, he
sent to meet them, because the men
were greatly ashamed: and the king said,
Tarry at Jericho until your beards be
grown, and *then* return.
6 ¶ And when the children of Ammon
saw that they [a]stank before David, the
children of Ammon sent and hired [b]the
Syrians of Beth-rehob, and the Syrians of
Zoba, twenty thousand footmen, and of
king Maacah a thousand men, and
of [c]Ish-tob[1] twelve thousand men.
7 And when David heard of *it,* he sent
Joab, and all the host of [a]the mighty men.
8 And the children of Ammon came
out, and put the battle in array at the entering in of the gate: and [a]the Syrians of
Zoba, and of Rehob, and Ish-tob, and Maacah, *were* by themselves in the field.
9 When Joab saw that the front of the
battle was against him before and behind,
he chose of all the choice *men* of Israel,
and put *them* in array against the Syrians:
10 And the rest of the people he delivered into the hand of Abishai his brother,
that he might put *them* in array against
the children of Ammon.
11 And he said, If the Syrians be too
strong for me, then thou shalt help me:
but if the children of Ammon be too
strong for thee, then I will come and help
thee.
12 [a]Be of good courage, and let us
[b]play the men for our people, and for the
cities of our God: and [c]the LORD do that
which seemeth him good.
13 And Joab drew nigh, and the people
that *were* with him, unto the battle
against the Syrians: and they fled before
him.
14 And when the children of Ammon
saw that the Syrians were fled, then fled
they also before Abishai, and entered into
the city. So Joab returned from the children of Ammon, and came to Jerusalem.
15 ¶ And when the Syrians saw that
they were smitten before Israel, they
gathered themselves together.
16 And Hadarezer sent, and brought
out the Syrians that *were* beyond [1]the
river: and they came to Helam; and [2]Sho-
bach the captain of the host of Hadarezer
went before them.
17 And when it was told David, he
gathered all Israel together, and passed
over Jordan, and came to Helam. And the
Syrians set themselves in array against
David, and fought with him.
18 And the Syrians fled before Israel;

8 [a]ch. 16:9
9 [a]ch. 16:4 & 19:29
10 [a]ver. 7,11,13; ch. 19:28 [b]ch. 19:17
12 [a]1 Chr. 8:34
13 [a]ver. 7,10; 2 Ki. 25:29 [b]ver. 3
10:1 [a]1 Chr. 19:1
3 [1]Heb. *In thine eyes doth David*
4 [a]Is. 20:4 & 47:2
6 [a]Gen. 34:30; Ex. 5:21; 1 Sam. 13:4 [b]ch. 8:3,5 [c]Judg. 11:3,5 [1]Or, *The men of Tob*
7 [a]ch. 23:8
8 [a]ver. 6
12 [a]Deut. 31:6 [b]1 Sam. 4:9; 1 Cor. 16:13 [c]1 Sam. 3:18
16 [1]i.e. *Euphrates* [2]Or, *Shophach;* see 1 Chr. 19:16

and David slew *the men of* seven hundred chariots of the Syrians, and forty
thousand [a]horsemen, and smote Shobach
the captain of their host, who died there.
19 And when all the kings *that were*
servants to Hadarezer saw that they were
smitten before Israel, they made peace
with Israel, and [a]served them. So the
Syrians feared to help the children of Ammon any more.

David's sin against Uriah

11 AND IT came to pass, [1]after the
year was expired, at the time
when kings go forth *to battle,* that [a]David
sent Joab, and his servants with him, and
all Israel; and they destroyed the children
of Ammon, and besieged Rabbah. But David tarried still at Jerusalem.
2 ¶ And it came to pass in an eveningtide, that David arose from off his bed,
[a]and walked upon the roof of the king's
house: and from the roof he [b]saw a
woman washing herself; and the woman
was very beautiful to look upon.
3 And David sent and inquired after
the woman. And *one* said, *Is* not this
[1]Bath-sheba, the daughter of [2]Eliam, the
wife [a]of Uriah the Hittite?
4 And David sent messengers, and
took her; and she came in unto him, and
[a]he lay with her; [1]for she was [b]purified
from her uncleanness: and she returned
unto her house.
5 And the woman conceived, and sent
and told David, and said, I *am* with child.
6 ¶ And David sent to Joab, *saying,*
Send me Uriah the Hittite. And Joab sent
Uriah to David.
7 And when Uriah was come unto
him, David demanded *of him* [1]how Joab
did, and how the people did, and how the
war prospered.
8 And David said to Uriah, Go down to
thy house, and [a]wash thy feet. And Uriah
departed out of the king's house, and
there [1]followed him a mess *of meat* from
the king.
9 But Uriah slept at the door of the
king's house with all the servants of his
lord, and went not down to his house.
10 And when they had told David, saying, Uriah went not down unto his house,
David said unto Uriah, Camest thou not
from *thy* journey? why *then* didst thou
not go down unto thine house?
11 And Uriah said unto David, [a]The

18 [a]1 Chr. 19:18 *footmen*
19 [a]ch. 8:6
11:1 [a]1 Chr. 20:1 [1]Heb. *at the return of the year*
2 [a]Deut. 22:8 [b]Gen. 34:2; Job 31:1; Mat. 5:28
3 [a]ch. 23:39 [1]Or, *Bath-shuah;* see 1 Chr. 3:5 [2]Or, *Ammiel*
4 [a]Ps. 51,title; Jas. 1:14 [b]Lev. 15:19, 28 & 18:19 [1]Or, *and when she had purified herself, &c., she returned*
7 [1]Heb. *of the peace of*
8 [a]Gen. 18:4 & 19:2 [1]Heb. *went out after him*
11 [a]ch. 7:2,6 [b]ch. 20:6
13 [a]Gen. 19:33,35 [b]ver. 9
14 [a]See 1 Ki. 21:8, 9
15 [a]ch. 12:9 [1]Heb. *strong* [2]Heb. *from after him*
21 [a]Judg. 9:53 [b]Judg. 6:32 *Jerubbaal*

ark, and Israel, and Judah, abide in tents;
and [b]my lord Joab, and the servants of my
lord, are encamped in the open fields;
shall I then go into mine house, to eat
and to drink, and to lie with my wife? *as*
thou livest, and *as* thy soul liveth, I will
not do this thing.
12 And David said to Uriah, Tarry here
today also, and tomorrow I will let thee
depart. So Uriah abode in Jerusalem that
day, and the morrow.
13 And when David had called him, he
did eat and drink before him; and he
made him [a]drunk: and at even he went
out to lie on his bed [b]with the servants of
his lord, but went not down to his house.
14 ¶ And it came to pass in the morning, that David [a]wrote a letter to Joab,
and sent *it* by the hand of Uriah.
15 And he wrote in the letter, saying,
Set ye Uriah in the forefront of the [1]hot-
test battle, and retire ye [2]from him, that
he may [a]be smitten, and die.
16 And it came to pass, when Joab observed the city, that he assigned Uriah
unto a place where he knew that valiant
men *were.*
17 And the men of the city went out,
and fought with Joab: and there fell *some*
of the people of the servants of David;
and Uriah the Hittite died also.
18 ¶ Then Joab sent and told David all
the things concerning the war;
19 And charged the messenger, saying, When thou hast made an end of telling the matters of the war unto the king,
20 And if so be that the king's wrath
arise, and he say unto thee, Wherefore
approached ye so nigh unto the city when
ye did fight? knew ye not that they would
shoot from the wall?
21 Who smote [a]Abimelech the son of
[b]Jerubbesheth? did not a woman cast a
piece of a millstone upon him from the
wall, that he died in Thebez? why went
ye nigh the wall? then say thou, Thy servant Uriah the Hittite is dead also.
22 ¶ So the messenger went, and came
and showed David all that Joab had sent
him for.
23 And the messenger said unto David, Surely the men prevailed against us,
and came out unto us into the field, and
we were upon them even unto the entering of the gate.
24 And the shooters shot from off the
wall upon thy servants; and *some* of the

king's servants be dead, and thy servant
Uriah the Hittite is dead also.
25 Then David said unto the messenger, Thus shalt thou say unto Joab, Let
not this thing [1]displease thee, for the
sword devoureth [2]one as well as another:
make thy battle more strong against the
city, and overthrow it: and encourage
thou him.
26 ¶ And when the wife of Uriah
heard that Uriah her husband was dead,
she mourned for her husband.
27 And when the mourning was past,
David sent and fetched her to his house,
and she [a]became his wife, and bare him a
son. But the thing that David had done
[1]displeased the LORD.

David repents

12 AND THE LORD sent Nathan unto
David. And [a]he came unto him,
and [b]said unto him, There were two men
in one city; the one rich, and the other
poor.
2 The rich *man* had exceeding many
flocks and herds:
3 But the poor *man* had nothing, save
one little ewe lamb, which he had bought
and nourished up: and it grew up together with him, and with his children; it
did eat of his own [1]meat, and drank of his
own cup, and lay in his bosom, and was
unto him as a daughter.
4 And there came a traveller unto the
rich man, and he spared to take of his
own flock and of his own herd, to dress
for the wayfaring man that was come
unto him; but took the poor man's lamb,
and dressed it for the man that was come
to him.
5 And David's anger was greatly kindled against the man; and he said to Nathan, *As* the LORD liveth, the man that
hath done this *thing* [a]shall[1] surely die:
6 And he shall restore the lamb [a]four-
fold, because he did this thing, and because he had no pity.
7 ¶ And Nathan said to David, Thou *art*
the man. Thus saith the LORD God of Israel, I [a]anointed thee king over Israel,
and I delivered thee out of the hand of
Saul;
8 And I gave thee thy master's house,
and thy master's wives into thy bosom,
and gave thee the house of Israel and of
Judah; and if *that had been* too little, I
would moreover have given unto thee
such and such things.
9 [a]Wherefore hast thou [b]despised the
commandment of the LORD, to do evil in
his sight? [c]thou hast killed Uriah the Hittite with the sword, and hast taken his
wife *to be* thy wife, and hast slain him
with the sword of the children of
Ammon.
10 Now therefore [a]the sword shall
never depart from thine house; because
thou hast despised me, and hast taken
the wife of Uriah the Hittite to be thy
wife.
11 Thus saith the LORD, Behold, I will
raise up evil against thee out of thine
own house, and I will [a]take thy wives
before thine eyes, and give *them* unto
thy neighbour, and he shall lie with thy
wives in the sight of this sun.
12 For thou didst *it* secretly: [a]but I will
do this thing before all Israel, and before
the sun.
13 [a]And David said unto Nathan, [b]I L
have sinned against the LORD. And Na- P
than said unto David, The LORD also hath R
[c]put away thy sin; thou shalt not die.
14 Howbeit, because by this deed thou J
hast given great occasion to the enemies
of the LORD [a]to blaspheme, the child also
that is born unto thee shall surely die.
15 ¶ And Nathan departed unto his
house. And the LORD struck the child that
Uriah's wife bare unto David, and it was
very sick.
16 David therefore besought God for
the child; and David [1]fasted, and went in,
and [a]lay all night upon the earth.
17 And the elders of his house arose,
and went to him, to raise him up from
the earth: but he would not, neither did
he eat bread with them.
18 And it came to pass on the seventh
day, that the child died. And the servants
of David feared to tell him that the child
was dead: for they said, Behold, while the
child was yet alive, we spake unto him,
and he would not hearken unto our
voice: how will he then [1]vex himself, if
we tell him that the child is dead?
19 But when David saw that his servants whispered, David perceived that

25 [1]Heb. *be evil in thine eyes* [2]Heb. *so and such*
27 [a]ch. 12:9 [1]Heb. *was evil in the eyes of*
12:1 [a]Ps. 51,title [b]See ch. 14:5; 1 Ki. 20:35-41; Is. 5:3
3 [1]Heb. *morsel*
5 [a]1 Sam. 26:16 [1]Or, *is worthy to die*, or, *is a son of death*
6 [a]Ex. 22:1; Luke 19:8
7 [a]1 Sam. 16:13
9 [a]See 1 Sam. 15:19 [b]Num. 15:31 [c]ch. 11:15-17,27
10 [a]Amos 7:9
11 [a]Deut. 28:30; ch. 16:22
12 [a]ch. 16:22
13 [a]See 1 Sam. 15:24 [b]ch. 24:10; Job 7:20; Prov. 28:13 [c]ch. 24:10; Job 7:21; Mic. 7:18; Zech. 3:4
14 [a]Is. 52:5; Ezek. 36:20,23; Rom. 2:24
16 [a]ch. 13:31 [1]Heb. *fasted a fast*
18 [1]Heb. *do hurt*

L *1Sa 12:20* ◀ ▶ *1Ch 28:9*
P *Jdg 10:15–16* ◀ ▶ *2Ch 7:14*
R *1Sa 12:3* ◀ ▶ *2Sa 24:10*
J *1Sa 13:14* ◀ ▶ *1Ki 17:1*

the child was dead: therefore David said unto his servants, Is the child dead? And they said, He is dead.

20 Then David arose from the earth, and washed, and anointed *himself,* and changed his apparel, and came into the house of the LORD, and [a]worshipped: then he came to his own house; and when he required, they set bread before him, and he did eat.

21 Then said his servants unto him, What thing *is* this that thou hast done? thou didst fast and weep for the child, *while it was* alive; but when the child was dead, thou didst rise and eat bread.

22 And he said, While the child was yet alive, I fasted and wept: [a]for I said, Who can tell *whether* GOD will be gracious to me, that the child may live?

23 But now he is dead, wherefore should I fast? can I bring him back again? I shall go to him, but [a]he shall not return to me.

24 ¶ And David comforted Bath-sheba his wife, and went in unto her, and lay with her: and [a]she bare a son, and [b]he called his name Solomon: and the LORD loved him.

25 And he sent by the hand of Nathan the prophet; and he called his name [1]Jedidiah, because of the LORD.

Victory over the Ammonites

26 ¶ And [a]Joab fought against [b]Rabbah of the children of Ammon, and took the royal city.

27 And Joab sent messengers to David, and said, I have fought against Rabbah, and have taken the city of waters.

28 Now therefore gather the rest of the people together, and encamp against the city, and take it: lest I take the city, and [1]it be called after my name.

29 And David gathered all the people together, and went to Rabbah, and fought against it, and took it.

30 [a]And he took their king's crown from off his head, the weight whereof *was* a talent of gold with the precious stones: and it was *set* on David's head. And he brought forth the spoil of the city [1]in great abundance.

31 And he brought forth the people that *were* therein, and put *them* under saws, and under harrows of iron, and under axes of iron, and made them pass through the brickkiln: and thus did he unto all the cities of the children of Ammon. So David and all the people returned unto Jerusalem.

Amnon defiles Tamar

13 AND IT came to pass after this, [a]that Absalom the son of David had a fair sister, whose name *was* [b]Tamar; and Amnon the son of David loved her.

2 And Amnon was so vexed, that he fell sick for his sister Tamar; for she *was* a virgin; and [1]Amnon thought it hard for him to do any thing to her.

3 But Amnon had a friend, whose name *was* Jonadab, [a]the son of Shimeah David's brother: and Jonadab *was* a very subtle man.

4 And he said unto him, Why *art* thou, *being* the king's son, [1]lean [2]from day to day? wilt thou not tell me? And Amnon said unto him, I love Tamar, my brother Absalom's sister.

5 And Jonadab said unto him, Lay thee down on thy bed, and make thyself sick: and when thy father cometh to see thee, say unto him, I pray thee, let my sister Tamar come, and give me meat, and dress the meat in my sight, that I may see *it,* and eat *it* at her hand.

6 ¶ So Amnon lay down, and made himself sick: and when the king was come to see him, Amnon said unto the king, I pray thee, let Tamar my sister come, and [a]make me a couple of cakes in my sight, that I may eat at her hand.

7 Then David sent home to Tamar, saying, Go now to thy brother Amnon's house, and dress him meat.

8 So Tamar went to her brother Amnon's house; and he was laid down. And she took [1]flour, and kneaded *it,* and made cakes in his sight, and did bake the cakes.

9 And she took a pan, and poured *them* out before him; but he refused to eat. And Amnon said, [a]Have out all men from me. And they went out every man from him.

10 And Amnon said unto Tamar, Bring the meat into the chamber, that I may eat of thine hand. And Tamar took the cakes which she had made, and brought *them* into the chamber to Amnon her brother.

11 And when she had brought *them* unto him to eat, he [a]took hold of her, and said unto her, Come lie with me, my sister.

---

20 [a]Job 1:20
22 [a]See Is. 38:1,5; Jonah 3:9
23 [a]Job 7:8-10
24 [a]Mat. 1:6 [b]1 Chr. 22:9
25 [1]i.e. *Beloved of the LORD*
26 [a]1 Chr. 20:1 [b]Deut. 3:11
28 [1]Heb. *my name be called upon it*
30 [a]1 Chr. 20:2 [1]Heb. *very great*
13:1 [a]ch. 3:2,3 [b]1 Chr. 3:9
2 [1]Heb. *it was marvellous,* or, *hidden in the eyes of Amnon*
3 [a]See 1 Sam. 16:9
4 [1]Heb. *thin* [2]Heb. *morning by morning*
6 [a]Gen. 18:6
8 [1]Or, *paste*
9 [a]Gen. 45:1
11 [a]Gen. 39:12

12 And she answered him, Nay, my brother, do not [a]force[1] me; for [b]no[2] such thing ought to be done in Israel: do not thou this [c]folly.

13 And I, whither shall I cause my shame to go? and as for thee, thou shalt be as one of the fools in Israel. Now therefore, I pray thee, speak unto the king; [a]for he will not withhold me from thee.

14 Howbeit he would not hearken unto her voice: but, being stronger than she, [a]forced her, and lay with her.

15 ¶ Then Amnon hated her [1]exceedingly; so that the hatred wherewith he hated her *was* greater than the love wherewith he had loved her. And Amnon said unto her, Arise, be gone.

16 And she said unto him, *There is* no cause: this evil in sending me away *is* greater than the other that thou didst unto me. But he would not hearken unto her.

17 Then he called his servant that ministered unto him, and said, Put now this *woman* out from me, and bolt the door after her.

18 And *she had* [a]a garment of divers colours upon her: for with such robes were the king's daughters *that were* virgins apparelled. Then his servant brought her out, and bolted the door after her.

19 ¶ And Tamar put [a]ashes on her head, and rent her garment of divers colours that *was* on her, and [b]laid her hand on her head, and went on crying.

20 And Absalom her brother said unto her, Hath [1]Amnon thy brother been with thee? but hold now thy peace, my sister: he *is* thy brother; [2]regard not this thing. So Tamar remained [3]desolate in her brother Absalom's house.

21 ¶ But when king David heard of all these things, he was very wroth.

22 And Absalom spake unto his brother Amnon [a]neither good nor bad: for Absalom [b]hated Amnon, because he had forced his sister Tamar.

Absalom kills Amnon

23 ¶ And it came to pass after two full years, that Absalom [a]had sheepshearers in Baal-hazor, which *is* beside Ephraim: and Absalom invited all the king's sons.

24 And Absalom came to the king, and said, Behold now, thy servant hath sheepshearers; let the king, I beseech thee, and his servants go with thy servant.

25 And the king said to Absalom, Nay, my son, let us not all now go, lest we be chargeable unto thee. And he pressed him: howbeit he would not go, but blessed him.

26 Then said Absalom, If not, I pray thee, let my brother Amnon go with us. And the king said unto him, Why should he go with thee?

27 But Absalom pressed him, that he let Amnon and all the king's sons go with him.

28 ¶ Now Absalom had commanded his servants, saying, Mark ye now when Amnon's [a]heart is merry with wine, and when I say unto you, Smite Amnon; then kill him, fear not: [1]have not I commanded you? be courageous, and be [2]valiant.

29 And the servants of Absalom did unto Amnon as Absalom had commanded. Then all the king's sons arose, and every man [1]gat him up upon his mule, and fled.

30 ¶ And it came to pass, while they were in the way, that tidings came to David, saying, Absalom hath slain all the king's sons, and there is not one of them left.

31 Then the king arose, and [a]tare his garments, and [b]lay on the earth; and all his servants stood by with their clothes rent.

32 And [a]Jonadab, the son of Shimeah David's brother, answered and said, Let not my lord suppose *that* they have slain all the young men the king's sons; for Amnon only is dead: for by the [1]appointment of Absalom this hath been [2]determined from the day that he forced his sister Tamar.

33 Now therefore [a]let not my lord the king take the thing to his heart, to think that all the king's sons are dead: for Amnon only is dead.

Absalom flees to Geshur

34 [a]But Absalom fled. And the young man that kept the watch lifted up his eyes, and looked, and, behold, there came much people by the way of the hill side behind him.

35 And Jonadab said unto the king, Behold, the king's sons come: [1]as thy servant said, so it is.

12 [a]Gen. 34:2 [b]Lev. 18:9,11 & 20:17 [c]Gen. 34:7; Judg. 19:23 & 20:6 [1]Heb. *humble me* [2]Heb. *it ought not so to be done*

13 [a]See Lev. 18:9, 11

14 [a]Deut. 22:25; See ch. 12:11

15 [1]Heb. *with great hatred greatly*

18 [a]Gen. 37:3; Judg. 5:30

19 [a]Josh. 7:6; ch. 1:2; Job 2:12 [b]Jer. 2:37

20 [1]Heb. *Aminon* [2]Heb. *set not thine heart* [3]Heb. *and desolate*

22 [a]Gen. 24:50 & 31:24 [b]Lev. 19:17, 18

23 [a]See Gen. 38:12,13; 1 Sam. 25:4,36

28 [a]Judg. 19:6,9, 22; Ruth 3:7; 1 Sam. 25:36; Esth. 1:10 [1]Or, *will you not, since I have commanded you?* [2]Heb. *sons of valour*

29 [1]Heb. *rode*

31 [a]ch. 1:11 [b]ch. 12:16

32 [a]ver. 3 [1]Heb. *mouth* [2]Or, *settled*

33 [a]ch. 19:19

34 [a]ver. 38

35 [1]Heb. *according to the word of thy servant*

36 And it came to pass, as soon as he had made an end of speaking, that, behold, the king's sons came, and lifted up their voice and wept: and the king also and all his servants wept [l]very sore.

37 ¶ But Absalom fled, and went to [a]Talmai, the son of [l]Ammihud, king of Geshur. And *David* mourned for his son every day.

38 So Absalom fled, and went to [a]Geshur, and was there three years.

39 And *the soul of* king David [l]longed to go forth unto Absalom: for he was [a]comforted concerning Amnon, seeing he was dead.

Absalom's return

14 NOW JOAB the son of Zeruiah perceived that the king's heart *was* [a]toward Absalom.

2 And Joab sent to [a]Tekoah, and fetched thence a wise woman, and said unto her, I pray thee, feign thyself to be a mourner, [b]and put on now mourning apparel, and anoint not thyself with oil, but be as a woman that had a long time mourned for the dead:

3 And come to the king, and speak on this manner unto him. So Joab [a]put the words in her mouth.

4 ¶ And when the woman of Tekoah spake to the king, she [a]fell on her face to the ground, and did obeisance, and said, [b]Help,[l] O king.

5 And the king said unto her, What aileth thee? And she answered, [a]I *am* indeed a widow woman, and mine husband is dead.

6 And thy handmaid had two sons, and they two strove together in the field, and *there was* [l]none to part them, but the one smote the other, and slew him.

7 And, behold, the whole family is risen against thine handmaid, and they said, Deliver him that smote his brother, that we may kill him, for the life of his brother whom he slew; and we will destroy the heir also: and so they shall quench my coal which is left, and shall not leave to my husband *neither* name nor remainder [l]upon the earth.

8 And the king said unto the woman, Go to thine house, and I will give charge concerning thee.

9 And the woman of Tekoah said unto the king, My lord, O king, [a]the iniquity *be* on me, and on my father's house: [b]and the king and his throne *be* guiltless.

10 And the king said, Whosoever saith *aught* unto thee, bring him to me, and he shall not touch thee any more.

11 Then said she, I pray thee, let the king remember the LORD thy God, [l]that thou wouldest not suffer [a]the revengers of blood to destroy any more, lest they destroy my son. And he said, [b]*As* the LORD liveth, there shall not one hair of thy son fall to the earth.

12 Then the woman said, Let thine handmaid, I pray thee, speak *one* word unto my lord the king. And he said, Say on.

13 And the woman said, Wherefore then hast thou thought such a thing against [a]the people of God? for the king doth speak this thing as one which is faulty, in that the king doth not fetch home again [b]his banished.

14 For we [a]must needs die, and *are* as water spilt on the ground, which cannot be gathered up again; [l]neither doth God respect *any* person: yet doth he [b]devise means, that his banished be not expelled from him. **N**

15 Now therefore that I am come to speak of this thing unto my lord the king, *it is* because the people have made me afraid: and thy handmaid said, I will now speak unto the king; it may be that the king will perform the request of his handmaid.

16 For the king will hear, to deliver his handmaid out of the hand of the man *that would* destroy me and my son together out of the inheritance of God.

17 Then thine handmaid said, The word of my lord the king shall now be [l]comfortable: for [a]as an angel of God, so *is* my lord the king [2]to discern good and bad: therefore the LORD thy God will be with thee.

18 Then the king answered and said unto the woman, Hide not from me, I pray thee, the thing that I shall ask thee. And the woman said, Let my lord the king now speak.

19 And the king said, *Is not* the hand of Joab with thee in all this? And the woman answered and said, *As* thy soul liveth, my lord the king, none can turn to the right hand or to the left from aught

36 [l]Heb. *with a great weeping greatly*
37 [a]ch. 3:3 [l]Or, *Ammihur*
38 [a]ch. 14:23,32; & 15:8
39 [a]Gen. 38:12 [l]Or, *was consumed*
14:1 [a]ch. 13:39
2 [a]2 Chr. 11:6 [b]See Ruth 3:3
3 [a]ver. 19; Ex. 4:15
4 [a]1 Sam. 20:41; ch. 1:2 [b]See 2 Ki. 6:26,28 [l]Heb. *Save*
5 [a]See ch. 12:1
6 [l]Heb. *no deliverer between them*
7 [l]Heb. *upon the face of the earth*
9 [a]Gen. 27:13; 1 Sam. 25:24; Mat. 27:25 [b]ch. 3:28,29; 1 Ki. 2:33
11 [a]Num. 35:19 [b]1 Sam. 14:45; Acts 27:34 [l]Heb. *that the revenger of blood do not multiply to destroy*
13 [a]Judg. 20:2 [b]ch. 13:37,38
14 [a]Job 34:15; Heb. 9:27 [b]Num. 35:15,25,28 [l]Or, *because God hath not taken away* his *life, he hath also devised means*
17 [a]ver. 20; ch. 19:27 [l]Heb. *for rest* [2]Heb. *to hear*

N *Jos 24:15* ◀ ▶ *1Ki 18:21*

that my lord the king hath spoken: for thy servant Joab, he bade me, and [a]he put all these words in the mouth of thine handmaid:

20 To fetch about this form of speech hath thy servant Joab done this thing: and my lord *is* wise, [a]according to the wisdom of an angel of God, to know all *things* that *are* in the earth.

21 ¶ And the king said unto Joab, Behold now, I have done this thing: go therefore, bring the young man Absalom again.

22 And Joab fell to the ground on his face, and bowed himself, and [1]thanked the king: and Joab said, Today thy servant knoweth that I have found grace in thy sight, my lord, O king, in that the king hath fulfilled the request of [2]his servant.

23 So Joab arose [a]and went to Geshur, and brought Absalom to Jerusalem.

24 And the king said, Let him turn to his own house, and let him [a]not see my face. So Absalom returned to his own house, and saw not the king's face.

25 ¶ [1]But in all Israel there was none to be so much praised as Absalom for his beauty: [a]from the sole of his foot even to the crown of his head there was no blemish in him.

26 And when he polled his head, (for it was at every year's end that he polled *it:* because *the hair* was heavy on him, therefore he polled it:) he weighed the hair of his head at two hundred shekels after the king's weight.

27 And [a]unto Absalom there were born three sons, and one daughter, whose name *was* Tamar: she was a woman of a fair countenance.

28 ¶ So Absalom dwelt two full years in Jerusalem, [a]and saw not the king's face.

29 Therefore Absalom sent for Joab, to have sent him to the king; but he would not come to him: and when he sent again the second time, he would not come.

30 Therefore he said unto his servants, See, Joab's field is [1]near mine, and he hath barley there; go and set it on fire. And Absalom's servants set the field on fire.

31 Then Joab arose, and came to Absalom unto *his* house, and said unto him, Wherefore have thy servants set my field on fire?

32 And Absalom answered Joab, Behold, I sent unto thee, saying, Come hither, that I may send thee to the king, to say, Wherefore am I come from Geshur? *it had been* good for me *to have been* there still: now therefore let me see the king's face; and if there be *any* iniquity in me, let him kill me.

33 So Joab came to the king, and told him: and when he had called for Absalom, he came to the king, and bowed himself on his face to the ground before the king: and the king [a]kissed Absalom.

Absalom's revolt against David

15 AND [a]IT came to pass after this, that Absalom [b]prepared him chariots and horses, and fifty men to run before him.

2 And Absalom rose up early, and stood beside the way of the gate: and it was *so,* that when any man that had a controversy [1]came to the king for judgment, then Absalom called unto him, and said, Of what city *art* thou? And he said, Thy servant *is* of one of the tribes of Israel.

3 And Absalom said unto him, See, thy matters *are* good and right; but [1]*there is* no man *deputed* of the king to hear thee.

4 Absalom said moreover, [a]Oh that I were made judge in the land, that every man which hath any suit or cause might come unto me, and I would do him justice!

5 And it was *so,* that when any man came nigh *to him* to do him obeisance, he put forth his hand, and took him, and kissed him.

6 And on this manner did Absalom to all Israel that came to the king for judgment: [a]so Absalom stole the hearts of the men of Israel.

7 ¶ And it came to pass [a]after forty years, that Absalom said unto the king, I pray thee, let me go and pay my vow, which I have vowed unto the LORD, in Hebron.

8 [a]For thy servant [b]vowed a vow [c]while I abode at Geshur in Syria, saying, If the LORD shall bring me again indeed to Jerusalem, then I will serve the LORD.

9 And the king said unto him, Go in peace. So he arose, and went to Hebron.

10 ¶ But Absalom sent spies throughout all the tribes of Israel, saying, As soon as ye hear the sound of the trumpet, then ye shall say, Absalom reigneth in Hebron.

---

19 [a]ver. 3
20 [a]ver. 17; ch. 19:27
22 [1]Heb. *blessed* [2]Or, *thy*
23 [a]ch. 13:37
24 [a]Gen. 43:3; ch. 3:13
25 [a]Is. 1:6 [1]Heb. *And as Absalom there was not a beautiful man in all Israel to praise greatly*
27 [a]See ch. 18:18
28 [a]ver. 24
30 [1]Heb. *near my place*
33 [a]Gen. 33:4 & 45:15; Luke 15:20
15:1 [a]ch. 12:11 [b]1 Ki. 1:5
2 [1]Heb. *to come*
3 [1]Or, *none will hear thee from the king* downward
4 [a]Judg. 9:29
6 [a]Rom. 16:18
7 [a]1 Sam. 16:1
8 [a]1 Sam. 16:2 [b]Gen. 28:20,21 [c]ch. 13:38

11 And with Absalom went two hundred men out of Jerusalem, *that were* [a]called; and they went [b]in their simplicity, and they knew not any thing.

12 And Absalom sent for Ahithophel the Gilonite, [a]David's counsellor, from his city, *even* from [b]Giloh, while he offered sacrifices. And the conspiracy was strong; for the people [c]increased continually with Absalom.

David and his household flee

13 ¶ And there came a messenger to David, saying, [a]The hearts of the men of Israel are after Absalom.

14 And David said unto all his servants that *were* with him at Jerusalem, Arise, and let us [a]flee; for we shall not *else* escape from Absalom: make speed to depart, lest he overtake us suddenly, and [ℓ]bring evil upon us, and smite the city with the edge of the sword.

15 And the king's servants said unto the king, Behold, thy servants *are ready to do* whatsoever my lord the king shall [ℓ]appoint.

16 And [a]the king went forth, and all his household [ℓ]after him. And the king left [b]ten women, *which were* concubines, to keep the house.

17 And the king went forth, and all the people after him, and tarried in a place that was far off.

18 And all his servants passed on beside him; [a]and all the Cherethites, and all the Pelethites, and all the Gittites, six hundred men which came after him from Gath, passed on before the king.

19 ¶ Then said the king to [a]Ittai the Gittite, Wherefore goest thou also with us? return to thy place, and abide with the king: for thou *art* a stranger, and also an exile.

20 Whereas thou camest *but* yesterday, should I this day [ℓ]make thee go up and down with us? seeing I go [a]whither I may, return thou, and take back thy brethren: mercy and truth *be* with thee.

21 And Ittai answered the king, and said, [a]*As* the LORD liveth, and *as* my lord the king liveth, surely in what place my lord the king shall be, whether in death or life, even there also will thy servant be.

22 And David said to Ittai, Go and pass over. And Ittai the Gittite passed over, and all his men, and all the little ones that *were* with him.

23 And all the country wept with a loud voice, and all the people passed over: the king also himself passed over the brook [ℓ]Kidron, and all the people passed over, toward the way of the [a]wilderness.

24 ¶ And lo Zadok also, and all the Levites *were* with him, bearing the ark of the covenant of God: and they set down the ark of God; and Abiathar went up, until all the people had done passing out of the city.

25 And the king said unto Zadok, Carry back the ark of God into the city: if I shall find favour in the eyes of the LORD, he [a]will bring me again, and show me *both* it, and his habitation:

26 But if he thus say, I have no [a]delight in thee; behold, *here am* I, [b]let him do to me as seemeth good unto him.

27 The king said also unto Zadok the priest, *Art not* thou a [a]seer? return into the city in peace, and [b]your two sons with you, Ahimaaz thy son, and Jonathan the son of Abiathar.

28 See, [a]I will tarry in the plain of the wilderness, until there come word from you to certify me.

29 Zadok therefore and Abiathar carried the ark of God again to Jerusalem: and they tarried there.

30 ¶ And David went up by the ascent of *mount* Olivet, [ℓ]and wept as he went up, and [a]had his head covered, and he went [b]barefoot: and all the people that *was* with him [c]covered every man his head, and they went up, [d]weeping as they went up.

31 ¶ And *one* told David, saying, [a]Ahithophel *is* among the conspirators with Absalom. And David said, O LORD, I pray thee, [b]turn the counsel of Ahithophel into foolishness.

32 ¶ And it came to pass, that *when* David was come to the top *of the mount,* where he worshipped God, behold, Hushai the [a]Archite came to meet him [b]with his coat rent, and earth upon his head:

33 Unto whom David said, If thou passest on with me, then thou shalt be [a]a burden unto me:

34 But if thou return to the city, and say unto Absalom, [a]I will be thy servant, O king; *as* I *have been* thy father's ser-

11 [a]1 Sam. 9:13 & 16:3,5 [b]Gen. 20:5
12 [a]Ps. 41:9 & 55:12-14 [b]Josh. 15:51 [c]Ps. 3:1
13 [a]ver. 6; Judg. 9:3
14 [a]ch. 19:9; Ps. 3, title [ℓ]Heb. *thrust*
15 [ℓ]Heb. *choose*
16 [a]Ps. 3, title [b]ch. 16:21,22 [ℓ]Heb. *at his feet*
18 [a]ch. 8:18
19 [a]ch. 18:2
20 [a]1 Sam. 23:13 [ℓ]Heb. *make thee wander in going*
21 [a]Ruth 1:16,17
23 [a]ch. 16:2 [ℓ]Called *Cedron* in John 18:1
25 [a]Ps. 43:3
26 [a]Num. 14:8; ch. 22:20; 1 Ki. 10:9; 2 Chr. 9:8; Is. 62:4 [b]1 Sam. 3:18
27 [a]1 Sam. 9:9 [b]See ch. 17:17
28 [a]ch. 17:16
30 [a]ch. 19:4; Esth. 6:12 [b]Is. 20:2,4 [c]Jer. 14:3,4 [d]Ps. 126:6 [ℓ]Heb. *going up, and weeping*
31 [a]Ps. 3:1,2 & 55:12 [b]ch. 16:23 & 17:14,23
32 [a]Josh. 16:2 [b]ch. 1:2
33 [a]ch. 19:35
34 [a]ch. 16:19

vant hitherto, so *will* I now also *be* thy servant: then mayest thou for me defeat the counsel of Ahithophel.

35 And *hast thou* not there with thee Zadok and Abiathar the priests? therefore it shall be, *that* what thing soever thou shalt hear out of the king's house, [a]thou shalt tell *it* to Zadok and Abiathar the priests.

36 Behold, *they have* there [a]with them their two sons, Ahimaaz Zadok's *son,* and Jonathan Abiathar's *son;* and by them ye shall send unto me every thing that ye can hear.

37 So Hushai [a]David's friend came into the city, [b]and Absalom came into Jerusalem.

Ziba's lie

16 AND [a]WHEN David was a little past the top *of the hill,* behold, [b]Ziba the servant of Mephibosheth met him, with a couple of asses saddled, and upon them two hundred *loaves* of bread, and an hundred bunches of raisins, and an hundred of summer fruits, and a bottle of wine.

2 And the king said unto Ziba, What meanest thou by these? And Ziba said, The asses *be* for the king's household to ride on; and the bread and summer fruit for the young men to eat; and the wine, [a]that such as be faint in the wilderness may drink.

3 And the king said, And where *is* thy master's son? [a]And Ziba said unto the king, Behold, he abideth at Jerusalem: for he said, Today shall the house of Israel restore me the kingdom of my father.

4 Then said the king to Ziba, Behold, thine *are* all that *pertained* unto Mephibosheth. And Ziba said, [l]I humbly beseech thee *that* I may find grace in thy sight, my lord, O king.

Shimei curses David

5 ¶ And when king David came to Bahurim, behold, thence came out a man of the family of the house of Saul, whose name *was* [a]Shimei, the son of Gera: [l]he came forth, and cursed still as he came.

6 And he cast stones at David, and at all the servants of king David: and all the people and all the mighty men *were* on his right hand and on his left.

7 And thus said Shimei when he cursed, Come out, come out, thou [l]bloody man, and thou [a]man of Belial:

8 The LORD hath [a]returned upon thee all [b]the blood of the house of Saul, in whose stead thou hast reigned; and the LORD hath delivered the kingdom into the hand of Absalom thy son: and, [l]behold, thou *art taken* in thy mischief, because thou *art* a bloody man.

9 ¶ Then said Abishai the son of Zeruiah unto the king, Why should this [a]dead dog [b]curse my lord the king? let me go over, I pray thee, and take off his head.

10 And the king said, [a]What have I to do with you, ye sons of Zeruiah? so let him curse, because [b]the LORD hath said unto him, Curse David. [c]Who shall then say, Wherefore hast thou done so?

11 And David said to Abishai, and to all his servants, Behold, [a]my son, which [b]came forth of my bowels, seeketh my life: how much more now *may this* Benjamite *do it?* let him alone, and let him curse; for the LORD hath bidden him.

12 It may be that the LORD will look on mine [l]affliction, and that the LORD will [a]requite me good for his cursing this day.

13 And as David and his men went by the way, Shimei went along on the hill's side over against him, and cursed as he went, and threw stones at him, and [l]cast dust.

14 And the king, and all the people that *were* with him, came weary, and refreshed themselves there.

The advice of Ahithophel

15 ¶ And [a]Absalom, and all the people the men of Israel, came to Jerusalem, and Ahithophel with him.

16 And it came to pass, when Hushai the Archite, [a]David's friend, was come unto Absalom, that Hushai said unto Absalom, [l]God save the king, God save the king.

17 And Absalom said to Hushai, *Is* this thy kindness to thy friend? [a]why wentest thou not with thy friend?

18 And Hushai said unto Absalom, Nay; but whom the LORD, and this people, and all the men of Israel, choose, his will I be, and with him will I abide.

19 And again, [a]whom should I serve? *should I* not *serve* in the presence of his son? as I have served in thy father's presence, so will I be in thy presence.

20 ¶ Then said Absalom to Ahithophel,

35 [a]ch. 17:15,16
36 [a]ver. 27
37 [a]ch. 16:16; 1 Chr. 27:33 [b]ch. 16:15
16:1 [a]ch. 15:30,32 [b]ch. 9:2
2 [a]ch. 15:23 & 17:29
3 [a]ch. 19:27
4 [l]Heb. *I do obeisance*
5 [a]ch. 19:16; 1 Ki. 2:8,44 [l]Or, *he still came forth and cursed*
7 [a]Deut. 13:13 [l]Heb. *man of blood*
8 [a]Judg. 9:24,56,57; 1 Ki. 2:32,33 [b]See ch. 1:16 & 3:28,29 & 4:11,12 [l]Heb. *behold thee in thy evil*
9 [a]1 Sam. 24:14; ch. 9:8 [b]Ex. 22:28
10 [a]ch. 19:22; 1 Pet. 2:23 [b]See 2 Ki. 18:25; Lam. 3:38 [c]Rom. 9:20
11 [a]ch. 12:11 [b]Gen. 15:4
12 [a]Rom. 8:28 [l]Or, *tears*
13 [l]Heb. *dusted* him *with dust*
15 [a]ch. 15:37
16 [a]ch. 15:37 [l]Heb. *Let the king live*
17 [a]ch. 19:25; Prov. 17:17
19 [a]ch. 15:34

Give counsel among you what we
shall do.
21 And Ahithophel said unto Absalom,
Go in unto thy father's [a]concubines,
which he hath left to keep the house;
and all Israel shall hear that thou [b]art abhorred of thy father: then shall [c]the
hands of all that *are* with thee be strong.
22 So they spread Absalom a tent upon
the top of the house; and Absalom went
in unto his father's concubines [a]in the
sight of all Israel.
23 And the counsel of Ahithophel,
which he counselled in those days, *was*
as if a man had inquired at the [l]oracle of
God: so *was* all the counsel of Ahithophel
[a]both with David and with Absalom.
17 MOREOVER AHITHOPHEL said
unto Absalom, Let me now
choose out twelve thousand men, and I
will arise and pursue after David this
night:
2 And I will come upon him while he
is [a]weary and weak handed, and will
make him afraid: and all the people that
are with him shall flee; and I will [b]smite
the king only:
3 And I will bring back all the people
unto thee: the man whom thou seekest *is*
as if all returned: *so* all the people shall
be in peace.
4 And the saying [a]pleased[l] Absalom
well, and all the elders of Israel.

The advice of Hushai

5 Then said Absalom, Call now Hushai
the Archite also, and let us hear likewise
[l]what he saith.
6 And when Hushai was come to Absalom, Absalom spake unto him, saying,
Ahithophel hath spoken after this manner: shall we do *after* his [l]saying? if not;
speak thou.
7 And Hushai said unto Absalom, The
counsel that Ahithophel hath [l]given *is*
not good at this time.
8 For, said Hushai, thou knowest thy
father and his men, that they *be* mighty
men, and they *be* [l]chafed in their minds,
as [a]a bear robbed of her whelps in the
field: and thy father *is* a man of war, and
will not lodge with the people.
9 Behold, he is hid now in some pit, or
in some *other* place: and it will come to
pass, when some of them be [l]overthrown
at the first, that whosoever heareth it will

21 [a]ch. 15:16 & 20:3 [b]Gen. 34:30; 1 Sam. 13:4 [c]ch. 2:7; Zech. 8:13
22 [a]ch. 12:11,12
23 [a]ch. 15:12 [l]Heb. *word*
17:2 [a]See Deut. 25:18; ch:16:14 [b]Zech. 13:7
4 [a]1 Sam. 18:20 [l]Heb. *was right in the eyes of*
5 [l]Heb. *what is in his mouth*
6 [l]Heb. *word?*
7 [l]Heb. *counselled*
8 [a]Hos. 13:8 [l]Heb. *bitter of soul*
9 [l]Heb. *fallen*
10 [a]Josh. 2:11
11 [a]Judg. 20:1 [b]Gen. 22:17 [l]Heb. *that thy face*, or, *presence go*
14 [a]ch. 15:31,34 [l]Heb. *commanded*
15 [a]ch. 15:35
16 [a]ch. 15:28
17 [a]ch. 15:27,36 [b]Josh. 2:4 [c]Josh. 15:7 & 18:16
18 [a]ch. 16:5
19 [a]See Josh. 2:6

say, There is a slaughter among the people that follow Absalom.
10 And he also *that is* valiant, whose
heart *is* as the heart of a lion, shall utterly
[a]melt: for all Israel knoweth that thy father *is* a mighty man, and *they* which *be*
with him *are* valiant men.
11 Therefore I counsel that all Israel
be generally gathered unto thee, [a]from
Dan even to Beer-sheba, [b]as the sand that
is by the sea for multitude; and [l]that thou
go to battle in thine own person.
12 So shall we come upon him in some
place where he shall be found, and we
will light upon him as the dew falleth on
the ground: and of him and of all the men
that *are* with him there shall not be left
so much as one.
13 Moreover, if he be gotten into a
city, then shall all Israel bring ropes to
that city, and we will draw it into the
river, until there be not one small stone
found there.
14 And Absalom and all the men of Israel said, The counsel of Hushai the Archite *is* better than the counsel of Ahithophel. For [a]the LORD had [l]appointed to
defeat the good counsel of Ahithophel, to
the intent that the LORD might bring evil
upon Absalom.
15 ¶ [a]Then said Hushai unto Zadok
and to Abiathar the priests, Thus and
thus did Ahithophel counsel Absalom and
the elders of Israel; and thus and thus
have I counselled.
16 Now therefore send quickly, and
tell David, saying, Lodge not this night
[a]in the plains of the wilderness, but
speedily pass over; lest the king be swallowed up, and all the people that *are* with
him.
17 [a]Now Jonathan and Ahimaaz
[b]stayed by [c]En-rogel; for they might not
be seen to come into the city: and a
wench went and told them; and they
went and told king David.
18 Nevertheless a lad saw them, and
told Absalom: but they went both of them
away quickly, and came to a man's house
[a]in Bahurim, which had a well in his
court; whither they went down.
19 And [a]the woman took and spread a
covering over the well's mouth, and
spread ground corn thereon; and the
thing was not known.
20 And when Absalom's servants
came to the woman to the house, they

said, Where *is* Ahimaaz and Jonathan? And [a]the woman said unto them, They be gone over the brook of water. And when they had sought and could not find *them,* they returned to Jerusalem.

21 And it came to pass, after they were departed, that they came up out of the well, and went and told king David, and said unto David, [a]Arise, and pass quickly over the water: for thus hath Ahithophel counselled against you.

22 Then David arose, and all the people that *were* with him, and they passed over Jordan: by the morning light there lacked not one of them that was not gone over Jordan.

23 ¶ And when Ahithophel saw that his counsel was not [1]followed, he saddled *his* ass, and arose, and gat him home to his house, to [a]his city, and [b]put[2] his household in order, and [c]hanged himself, and died, and was buried in the sepulchre of his father.

24 Then David came to [a]Mahanaim. And Absalom passed over Jordan, he and all the men of Israel with him.

25 ¶ And Absalom made Amasa captain of the host instead of Joab: which Amasa *was* a man's son, whose name *was* [1]Ithra an Israelite, that went in to [a]Abigail[2] the daughter of [3]Nahash, sister to Zeruiah Joab's mother.

26 So Israel and Absalom pitched in the land of Gilead.

27 ¶ And it came to pass, when David was come to Mahanaim, that [a]Shobi the son of Nahash of Rabbah of the children of Ammon, and [b]Machir the son of Ammiel of Lo-debar, and [c]Barzillai the Gileadite of Rogelim,

28 Brought beds, and [1]basins, and earthen vessels, and wheat, and barley, and flour, and parched *corn,* and beans, and lentiles, and parched *pulse,*

29 And honey, and butter, and sheep, and cheese of kine, for David, and for the people that *were* with him, to eat: for they said, The people *is* hungry, and weary, and thirsty, [a]in the wilderness.

Absalom killed by Joab

18 AND DAVID numbered the people that *were* with him, and set captains of thousands and captains of hundreds over them.

2 And David sent forth a third part of the people under the hand of Joab, and a third part under the hand of Abishai the son of Zeruiah, Joab's brother, [a]and a third part under the hand of Ittai the Gittite. And the king said unto the people, I will surely go forth with you myself also.

3 [a]But the people answered, Thou shalt not go forth: for if we flee away, they will not [1]care for us; neither if half of us die, will they care for us: but now *thou art* [2]worth ten thousand of us: therefore now *it is* better that thou [3]succour us out of the city.

4 And the king said unto them, What seemeth you best I will do. And the king stood by the gate side, and all the people came out by hundreds and by thousands.

5 And the king commanded Joab and Abishai and Ittai, saying, *Deal* gently for my sake with the young man, *even* with Absalom. [a]And all the people heard when the king gave all the captains charge concerning Absalom.

6 ¶ So the people went out into the field against Israel: and the battle was in the [a]wood of Ephraim;

7 Where the people of Israel were slain before the servants of David, and there was there a great slaughter that day of twenty thousand *men.*

8 For the battle was there scattered over the face of all the country: and the wood [1]devoured more people that day than the sword devoured.

9 ¶ And Absalom met the servants of David. And Absalom rode upon a mule, and the mule went under the thick boughs of a great oak, and his head caught hold of the oak, and he was taken up between the heaven and the earth; and the mule that *was* under him went away.

10 And a certain man saw *it,* and told Joab, and said, Behold, I saw Absalom hanged in an oak.

11 And Joab said unto the man that told him, And, behold, thou sawest *him,* and why didst thou not smite him there to the ground? and I would have given thee ten *shekels* of silver, and a girdle.

12 And the man said unto Joab, Though I should [1]receive a thousand *shekels* of silver in mine hand, *yet* would I not put forth mine hand against the king's son: [a]for in our hearing the king charged thee and Abishai and Ittai, saying, [2]Beware that none *touch* the young man Absalom.

20 [a]See Ex. 1:19; Josh. 2:4,5
21 [a]ver. 15,16
23 [a]ch. 15:12 [b]2 Ki. 20:1 [c]Mat. 27:5 [1]Heb. *done* [2]Heb. *gave charge concerning his house*
24 [a]Gen. 32:2; Josh. 13:26; ch. 2:8
25 [a]1 Chr. 2:16,17 [1]Or, *Jether an Ishmaelite* [2]Heb. *Abigal* [3]Or, *Jesse;* see 1 Chr. 2:13,16
27 [a]See ch. 10:1 & 12:29 [b]ch. 9:4 [c]ch. 19:31,32; 1 Ki. 2:7
28 [1]Or, *cups*
29 [a]ch. 16:2
18:2 [a]ch. 15:19
3 [a]ch. 21:17 [1]Heb. *set their heart on us* [2]Heb. *as ten thousand of us* [3]Heb. *be to succour*
5 [a]ver. 12
6 [a]Josh. 17:15,18
8 [1]Heb. *multiplied to devour*
12 [a]ver. 5 [1]Heb. *weigh upon mine hand* [2]Heb. *Beware whosoever ye be of*

13 Otherwise I should have wrought falsehood against mine own life: for there is no matter hid from the king, and thou thyself wouldest have set thyself against *me.*

14 Then said Joab, I may not tarry thus [1]with thee. And he took three darts in his hand, and thrust them through the heart of Absalom, while he *was* yet alive in the [2]midst of the oak.

15 And ten young men that bare Joab's armour compassed about and smote Absalom, and slew him.

16 And Joab blew the trumpet, and the people returned from pursuing after Israel: for Joab held back the people.

17 And they took Absalom, and cast him into a great pit in the wood, and [a]laid a very great heap of stones upon him: and all Israel fled every one to his tent.

18 ¶ Now Absalom in his lifetime had taken and reared up for himself a pillar, which *is* in [a]the king's dale: for he said, [b]I have no son to keep my name in remembrance: and he called the pillar after his own name: and it is called unto this day, Absalom's place.

David told of Absalom's death

19 ¶ Then said Ahimaaz the son of Zadok, Let me now run, and bear the king tidings, how that the LORD hath [1]avenged him of his enemies.

20 And Joab said unto him, Thou shalt not [1]bear tidings this day, but thou shalt bear tidings another day: but this day thou shalt bear no tidings, because the king's son is dead.

21 Then said Joab to Cushi, Go tell the king what thou hast seen. And Cushi bowed himself unto Joab, and ran.

22 Then said Ahimaaz the son of Zadok yet again to Joab, But [1]howsoever, let me, I pray thee, also run after Cushi. And Joab said, Wherefore wilt thou run, my son, seeing that thou hast no tidings [2]ready?

23 But howsoever, *said he,* let me run. And he said unto him, Run. Then Ahimaaz ran by the way of the plain, and overran Cushi.

24 And David sat between the two gates: and [a]the watchman went up to the roof over the gate unto the wall, and lifted up his eyes, and looked, and behold a man running alone.

25 And the watchman cried, and told the king. And the king said, If he *be* alone, *there is* tidings in his mouth. And he came apace, and drew near.

26 And the watchman saw another man running: and the watchman called unto the porter, and said, Behold *another* man running alone. And the king said, He also bringeth tidings.

27 And the watchman said, [1]Me thinketh the running of the foremost is like the running of Ahimaaz the son of Zadok. And the king said, He *is* a good man, and cometh with good tidings.

28 And Ahimaaz called, and said unto the king, [1,2]All is well. And he fell down to the earth upon his face before the king, and said, Blessed *be* the LORD thy God, which hath [3]delivered up the men that lifted up their hand against my lord the king.

29 And the king said, [1]Is the young man Absalom safe? And Ahimaaz answered, When Joab sent the king's servant, and *me* thy servant, I saw a great tumult, but I knew not what *it was.*

30 And the king said *unto him,* Turn aside, *and* stand here. And he turned aside, and stood still.

31 And, behold, Cushi came; and Cushi said, [1]Tidings, my lord the king: for the LORD hath avenged thee this day of all them that rose up against thee.

32 And the king said unto Cushi, *Is* the young man Absalom safe? And Cushi answered, The enemies of my lord the king, and all that rise against thee to do *thee* hurt, be as *that* young man *is.*

33 ¶ And the king was much moved, and went up to the chamber over the gate, and wept: and as he went, thus he said, [a]O my son Absalom, my son, my son Absalom! would God I had died for thee, O Absalom, my son, my son!

19

AND IT was told Joab, Behold, the king weepeth and mourneth for Absalom.

2 And the [1]victory that day was *turned* into mourning unto all the people: for the people heard say that day how the king was grieved for his son.

3 And the people gat them by stealth that day [a]into the city, as people being ashamed steal away when they flee in battle.

4 But the king [a]covered his face, and the king cried with a loud voice, [b]O my

14 [1]Heb. *before thee* [2]Heb. *heart*
17 [a]Josh. 7:26
18 [a]Gen. 14:17 [b]See ch. 14:27
19 [1]Heb. *judged him from the hand*
20 [1]Heb. *be a man of tidings*
22 [1]Heb. *be what may* [2]Or, *convenient*
24 [a]2 Ki. 9:17
27 [1]Heb. *I see the running*
28 [1]Or, *Peace be to thee* [2]Heb. *Peace* [3]Heb. *shut up*
29 [1]Heb. Is there *peace?*
31 [1]Heb. *Tidings is brought*
33 [a]ch. 19:4
19:2 [1]Heb. *salvation, or, deliverance*
3 [a]ver. 32
4 [a]ch. 15:30 [b]ch. 18:33

son Absalom, O Absalom, my son, my son!

5 And Joab came into the house to the king, and said, Thou hast shamed this day the faces of all thy servants, which this day have saved thy life, and the lives of thy sons and of thy daughters, and the lives of thy wives, and the lives of thy concubines;

6 [1]In that thou lovest thine enemies, and hatest thy friends. For thou hast declared this day, [2]that thou regardest neither princes nor servants: for this day I perceive, that if Absalom had lived, and all we had died this day, then it had pleased thee well.

7 Now therefore arise, go forth, and speak [1]comfortably unto thy servants: for I swear by the LORD, if thou go not forth, there will not tarry one with thee this night: and that will be worse unto thee than all the evil that befell thee from thy youth until now.

8 Then the king arose, and sat in the gate. And they told unto all the people, saying, Behold, the king doth sit in the gate. And all the people came before the king: for Israel had fled every man to his tent.

David's return to Jerusalem

9 ¶ And all the people were at strife throughout all the tribes of Israel, saying, The king saved us out of the hand of our enemies, and he delivered us out of the hand of the Philistines; and now he is [a]fled out of the land for Absalom.

10 And Absalom, whom we anointed over us, is dead in battle. Now therefore why [1]speak ye not a word of bringing the king back?

11 ¶ And king David sent to Zadok and to Abiathar the priests, saying, Speak unto the elders of Judah, saying, Why are ye the last to bring the king back to his house? seeing the speech of all Israel is come to the king, *even* to his house.

12 Ye *are* my brethren, ye *are* [a]my bones and my flesh: wherefore then are ye the last to bring back the king?

13 [a]And say ye to Amasa, *Art* thou not of my bone, and of my flesh? [b]God do so to me, and more also, if thou be not captain of the host before me continually in the room of Joab.

14 And he bowed the heart of all the men of Judah, [a]even as *the heart of* one man; so that they sent *this word* unto the king, Return thou, and all thy servants.

15 So the king returned, and came to Jordan. And Judah came to [a]Gilgal, to go to meet the king, to conduct the king over Jordan.

16 ¶ And [a]Shimei the son of Gera, a Benjamite, which *was* of Bahurim, hasted and came down with the men of Judah to meet king David.

17 And *there were* a thousand men of Benjamin with him, and [a]Ziba the servant of the house of Saul, and his fifteen sons and his twenty servants with him; and they went over Jordan before the king.

18 And there went over a ferry boat to carry over the king's household, and to do [1]what he thought good. And Shimei the son of Gera fell down before the king, as he was come over Jordan;

19 And said unto the king, [a]Let not my lord impute iniquity unto me, neither do thou remember [b]that which thy servant did perversely the day that my lord the king went out of Jerusalem, that the king should [c]take it to his heart.

20 For thy servant doth know that I have sinned: therefore, behold, I am come the first this day of all [a]the house of Joseph to go down to meet my lord the king.

21 But Abishai the son of Zeruiah answered and said, Shall not Shimei be put to death for this, because he [a]cursed the LORD'S anointed?

22 And David said, [a]What have I to do with you, ye sons of Zeruiah, that ye should this day be adversaries unto me? [b]shall there any man be put to death this day in Israel? for do not I know that I *am* this day king over Israel?

23 Therefore [a]the king said unto Shimei, Thou shalt not die. And the king sware unto him.

24 ¶ And [a]Mephibosheth the son of Saul came down to meet the king, and had neither dressed his feet, nor trimmed his beard, nor washed his clothes, from the day the king departed until the day he came *again* in peace.

25 And it came to pass, when he was come to Jerusalem to meet the king, that the king said unto him, [a]Wherefore wentest not thou with me, Mephibosheth?

26 And he answered, My lord, O king,

6 [1]Heb. *By loving* [2]Heb. *that princes* or, *servants are not to thee*
7 [1]Heb. *to the heart of thy servants*
9 [a]ch. 15:14
10 [1]Heb. are *ye silent?*
12 [a]ch. 5:1
13 [a]ch. 17:25 [b]Ruth 1:17
14 [a]Judg. 20:1
15 [a]Josh. 5:9
16 [a]ch. 16:5; 1 Ki. 2:8
17 [a]ch. 9:2,10 & 16:1,2
18 [1]Heb. *the good in his eyes*
19 [a]1 Sam. 22:15 [b]ch. 16:5,6 [c]ch. 13:33
20 [a]See ch. 16:5
21 [a]Ex. 22:28; 1 Sam. 26:9
22 [a]ch. 16:10 [b]1 Sam. 11:13
23 [a]1 Ki. 2:8,9,37, 46
24 [a]ch. 9:6
25 [a]ch. 16:17

my servant deceived me: for thy servant said, I will saddle me an ass, that I may ride thereon, and go to the king; because thy servant *is* lame.

27 And [a]he hath slandered thy servant unto my lord the king; [b]but my lord the king *is* as an angel of God: do therefore *what is* good in thine eyes.

28 For all *of* my father's house were but [1]dead men before my lord the king: [a]yet didst thou set thy servant among them that did eat at thine own table. What right therefore have I yet to cry any more unto the king?

29 And the king said unto him, Why speakest thou any more of thy matters? I have said, Thou and Ziba divide the land.

30 And Mephibosheth said unto the king, Yea, let him take all, forasmuch as my lord the king is come again in peace unto his own house.

31 ¶ And [a]Barzillai the Gileadite came down from Rogelim, and went over Jordan with the king, to conduct him over Jordan.

32 Now Barzillai was a very aged man, *even* fourscore years old: and [a]he had provided the king of sustenance while he lay at Mahanaim; for he *was* a very great man.

33 And the king said unto Barzillai, Come thou over with me, and I will feed thee with me in Jerusalem.

34 And Barzillai said unto the king, [1]How long have I to live, that I should go up with the king unto Jerusalem?

35 I *am* this day [a]fourscore years old: *and* can I discern between good and evil? can thy servant taste what I eat or what I drink? can I hear any more the voice of singing men and singing women? wherefore then should thy servant be yet a burden unto my lord the king?

36 Thy servant will go a little way over Jordan with the king: and why should the king recompense it me with such a reward?

37 Let thy servant, I pray thee, turn back again, that I may die in mine own city, *and be buried* by the grave of my father and of my mother. But behold thy servant [a]Chimham; let him go over with my lord the king; and do to him what shall seem good unto thee.

38 And the king answered, Chimham shall go over with me, and I will do to him that which shall seem good unto thee: and whatsoever thou shalt [1]require of me, *that* will I do for thee.

39 And all the people went over Jordan. And when the king was come over, the king [a]kissed Barzillai, and blessed him; and he returned unto his own place.

40 Then the king went on to Gilgal, and [1]Chimham went on with him: and all the people of Judah conducted the king, and also half the people of Israel.

41 ¶ And, behold, all the men of Israel came to the king, and said unto the king, Why have our brethren the men of Judah stolen thee away, and [a]have brought the king, and his household, and all David's men with him, over Jordan?

42 And all the men of Judah answered the men of Israel, Because the king *is* [a]near of kin to us: wherefore then be ye angry for this matter? have we eaten at all of the king's *cost?* or hath he given us any gift?

43 And the men of Israel answered the men of Judah, and said, We have ten parts in the king, and we have also more *right* in David than ye: why then did ye [1]despise us, that our advice should not be first had in bringing back our king? And [a]the words of the men of Judah were fiercer than the words of the men of Israel.

Sheba leads Israel to revolt

20 AND THERE happened to be there a man of Belial, whose name *was* Sheba, the son of Bichri, a Benjamite: and he blew a trumpet, and said, [a]We have no part in David, neither have we inheritance in the son of Jesse: [b]every man to his tents, O Israel.

2 So every man of Israel went up from after David, *and* followed Sheba the son of Bichri: but the men of Judah clave unto their king, from Jordan even to Jerusalem.

3 ¶ And David came to his house at Jerusalem; and the king took the ten women *his* [a]concubines, whom he had left to keep the house, and put them in [1]ward, and fed them, but went not in unto them. So they were [2]shut up unto the day of their death, [3]living in widowhood.

4 ¶ Then said the king to Amasa, [a]Assemble[1] me the men of Judah within three days, and be thou here present.

5 So Amasa went to assemble *the men*

27 [a]ch. 16:3 [b]ch. 14:17,20
28 [a]ch. 9:7,10,13 [1]Heb. *men of death*
31 [a]1 Ki. 2:7
32 [a]ch. 17:27
34 [1]Heb. *How many days are the years of my life?*
35 [a]Ps. 90:10
37 [a]1 Ki. 2:7; Jer. 41:17
38 [1]Heb. *choose*
39 [a]Gen. 31:55
40 [1]Heb. *Chimhan*
41 [a]ver. 15
42 [a]ver. 12
43 [a]See Judg. 8:1; & 12:1 [1]Heb. *set us at light*
20:1 [a]ch. 19:43 [b]1 Ki. 12:16; 2 Chr. 10:16
3 [a]ch. 15:16 & 16:21,22 [1]Heb. *an house of ward* [2]Heb. *bound* [3]Heb. *in widowhood of life*
4 [a]ch. 19:13 [1]Heb. *Call*

of Judah: but he tarried longer than the
set time which he had appointed him.
6 And David said to Abishai, Now shall
Sheba the son of Bichri do us more harm
than *did* Absalom: take thou [a]thy lord's
servants, and pursue after him, lest he
get him fenced cities, and [l]escape us.
7 And there went out after him Joab's
men, and the [a]Cherethites, and the Pelethites, and all the mighty men: and they
went out of Jerusalem, to pursue after
Sheba the son of Bichri.
8 When they *were* at the great stone
which *is* in Gibeon, Amasa went before
them. And Joab's garment that he had put
on was girded unto him, and upon it a
girdle *with* a sword fastened upon his
loins in the sheath thereof; and as he
went forth it fell out.
9 And Joab said to Amasa, *Art* thou in
health, my brother? [a]And Joab took Amasa by the beard with the right hand to
kiss him.
10 But Amasa took no heed to the
sword that *was* in Joab's hand: so [a]he
smote him therewith [b]in the fifth *rib,* and
shed out his bowels to the ground, and
[l]struck him not again; and he died. So
Joab and Abishai his brother pursued after Sheba the son of Bichri.
11 And one of Joab's men stood by
him, and said, He that favoureth Joab,
and he that *is* for David, *let him go* after
Joab.
12 And Amasa wallowed in blood in
the midst of the highway. And when the
man saw that all the people stood still, he
removed Amasa out of the highway into
the field, and cast a cloth upon him,
when he saw that every one that came by
him stood still.
13 When he was removed out of the
highway, all the people went on after
Joab, to pursue after Sheba the son of
Bichri.
14 ¶ And he went through all the
tribes of Israel unto [a]Abel, and to Beth-
maachah, and all the Berites: and they
were gathered together, and went also after him.
15 And they came and besieged him in
Abel of Beth-maachah, and they [a]cast up
a bank against the city, and [l]it stood in
the trench: and all the people that *were*
with Joab [2]battered the wall, to throw it
down.
16 ¶ Then cried a wise woman out of
the city, Hear, hear; say, I pray you, unto
Joab, Come near hither, that I may speak
with thee.
17 And when he was come near unto
her, the woman said, *Art* thou Joab? And
he answered, I *am he.* Then she said unto
him, Hear the words of thine handmaid.
And he answered, I do hear.
18 Then she spake, saying, [l]They
were wont to speak in old time, saying,
They shall surely ask *counsel* at Abel: and
so they ended *the matter.*
19 I *am one of them that are* peaceable
and faithful in Israel: thou seekest to destroy a city and a mother in Israel: why
wilt thou swallow up [a]the inheritance of
the LORD?
20 And Joab answered and said, Far be
it, far be it from me, that I should swallow up or destroy.
21 The matter *is* not so: but a man of
mount Ephraim, Sheba the son of Bichri
[l]by name, hath lifted up his hand against
the king, *even* against David: deliver him
only, and I will depart from the city. And
the woman said unto Joab, Behold, his
head shall be thrown to thee over the
wall.
22 Then the woman went unto all the
people [a]in her wisdom. And they cut off
the head of Sheba the son of Bichri, and
cast *it* out to Joab. And he blew a trumpet, and they [l]retired from the city, every
man to his tent. And Joab returned to Jerusalem unto the king.
23 ¶ Now [a]Joab *was* over all the host
of Israel: and Benaiah the son of Jehoiada
was over the Cherethites and over the
Pelethites:
24 And Adoram *was* [a]over the tribute:
and [b]Jehoshaphat the son of Ahilud *was*
[l]recorder:
25 And Sheva *was* scribe: and [a]Zadok
and Abiathar *were* the priests:
26 [a]And Ira also the Jairite was [b]a[l]
chief ruler about David.

David repays the Gibeonites

21 THEN THERE was a famine in
the days of David three years,
year after year; and David [l]inquired of
the LORD. And the LORD answered, *It is* for
Saul, and for *his* bloody house, because
he slew the Gibeonites.
2 And the king called the Gibeonites,
and said unto them; (now the Gibeonites
were not of the children of Israel, but [a]of

6 [a]ch. 11:11; 1 Ki. 1:33 [l]Heb. *deliver himself from our eyes*
7 [a]ch. 8:18; 1 Ki. 1:38
9 [a]Mat. 26:49; Luke 22:47
10 [a]1 Ki. 2:5 [b]ch. 2:23 [l]Heb. *doubled not his stroke*
14 [a]2 Ki. 15:29; 2 Chr. 16:4
15 [a]2 Ki. 19:32 [l]Or, *it stood against the outmost wall* [2]Heb. *marred to throw down*
18 [l]Or, *They plainly spake in the beginning, saying, Surely they will ask of Abel, and so make an end*
19 [a]1 Sam. 26:19; ch. 21:3
21 [l]Heb. *by his name*
22 [a]Eccl. 9:14,15 [l]Heb. *were scattered*
23 [a]ch. 8:16,18
24 [a]1 Ki. 4:6 [b]ch. 8:16; 1 Ki. 4:3 [l]Or, *remembrancer*
25 [a]ch. 8:17; 1 Ki. 4:4
26 [a]ch. 23:38 [b]Gen. 41:45; Ex. 2:16; ch. 8:18 [l]Or, *a prince*
21:1 [l]Heb. *sought the face*
2 [a]Josh. 9:3,15-17

the remnant of the Amorites; and the
children of Israel had sworn unto them:
and Saul sought to slay them in his zeal to
the children of Israel and Judah.)
3 Wherefore David said unto the Gibeonites, What shall I do for you? and
wherewith shall I make the atonement,
that ye may bless [a]the inheritance of the
LORD?
4 And the Gibeonites said unto him,
[1]We will have no silver nor gold of Saul,
nor of his house; neither for us shalt thou
kill any man in Israel. And he said, What
ye shall say, *that* will I do for you.
5 And they answered the king, The
man that consumed us, and that [1]devised
against us *that* we should be destroyed
from remaining in any of the coasts of
Israel,
6 Let seven men of his sons be delivered unto us, and we will hang them up
unto the LORD [a]in Gibeah of Saul, [b]*whom*[1]
the LORD did choose. And the king said, I
will give *them.*
7 But the king spared Mephibosheth,
the son of Jonathan the son of Saul, because of [a]the LORD'S oath that *was* between them, between David and Jonathan the son of Saul.
8 But the king took the two sons of
[a]Rizpah the daughter of Aiah, whom she
bare unto Saul, Armoni and Mephibosheth; and the five sons of [1]Michal the
daughter of Saul, whom she [2]brought up
for Adriel the son of Barzillai the Mehola-
thite:
9 And he delivered them into the
hands of the Gibeonites, and they hanged
them in the hill [a]before the LORD: and
they fell *all* seven together, and were put
to death in the days of harvest, in the first
days, in the beginning of barley harvest.
10 ¶ And [a]Rizpah the daughter of Aiah
took sackcloth, and spread it for her upon
the rock, [b]from the beginning of harvest
until water dropped upon them out of
heaven, and suffered neither the birds of
the air to rest on them by day, nor the
beasts of the field by night.
11 And it was told David what Rizpah
the daughter of Aiah, the concubine of
Saul, had done.
12 ¶ And David went and took the
bones of Saul and the bones of Jonathan
his son from the men of [a]Jabesh-gilead,
which had stolen them from the street of
Beth-shan, where the Philistines had
hanged them, when the Philistines had
slain Saul in Gilboa:
13 And he brought up from thence the
bones of Saul and the bones of Jonathan
his son; and they gathered the bones of
them that were hanged.
14 And the bones of Saul and Jonathan
his son buried they in the country of Benjamin in [a]Zelah, in the sepulchre of Kish
his father: and they performed all that the
king commanded. And after that [b]God
was entreated for the land.

Victories over the Philistines

15 ¶ Moreover the Philistines had yet
war again with Israel; and David went
down, and his servants with him, and
fought against the Philistines: and David
waxed faint.
16 And Ishbi-benob, which *was* of the
sons of [1]the giant, the weight of whose
[2]spear *weighed* three hundred *shekels* of
brass in weight, he being girded with
a new *sword,* thought to have slain
David.
17 But Abishai the son of Zeruiah succoured him, and smote the Philistine,
and killed him. Then the men of David
sware unto him, saying, [a]Thou shalt go
no more out with us to battle, that thou
quench not the [b]light[1] of Israel.
18 [a]And it came to pass after this, that
there was again a battle with the Philistines at Gob: then [b]Sibbechai the Hushathite slew [1]Saph, which *was* of the
sons of [2]the giant.
19 And there was again a battle in Gob
with the Philistines, where Elhanan the
son of [1]Jaare-oregim, a Bethlehemite,
slew [a]*the brother of* Goliath the Gittite,
the staff of whose spear *was* like a
weaver's beam.
20 And [a]there was yet a battle in Gath,
where was a man of *great* stature, that
had on every hand six fingers, and on
every foot six toes, four and twenty in
number; and he also was born to [1]the
giant.
21 And when he [1]defied Israel, Jonathan the son of [a]Shimeah the brother of
David slew him.
22 [a]These four were born to the giant
in Gath, and fell by the hand of David,
and by the hand of his servants.

3 [a]ch. 20:19
4 [1]Or, It is *not silver nor gold that we have to do with Saul or his house, neither* pertains it *to us to kill*
5 [1]Or, *cut us off*
6 [a]1 Sam. 10:26 [b]1 Sam. 10:24 [1]Or, *chosen of the LORD*
7 [a]1 Sam. 18:3 & 20:8,15
8 [a]ch. 3:7 [1]Or, *Michal's sister* [2]Heb. *bare to Adriel;* see 1 Sam. 18:19
9 [a]ch. 6:17
10 [a]ver. 8; ch. 3:7 [b]See Deut. 21:23
12 [a]1 Sam. 31:11-13
14 [a]Josh. 18:28 [b]See Josh. 7:26; ch. 24:25
16 [1]Or, *Rapha* [2]Heb. *the staff,* or, *the head*
17 [a]ch. 18:3 [b]1 Ki. 11:36 [1]Heb. *candle,* or, *lamp*
18 [a]1 Chr. 20:4 [b]1 Chr. 11:29 [1]Or, *Sippai* [2]Or, *Rapha*
19 [a]See 1 Chr. 20:5 [1]Or, *Jair*
20 [a]1 Chr. 20:6 [1]Or, *Rapha*
21 [a]1 Sam. 16:9, *Shammah* [1]Or, *reproached*
22 [a]1 Chr. 20:8

David's psalm of praise

22 AND DAVID [a]spake unto the LORD the words of this song in the day *that* the LORD had [b]delivered him out of the hand of all his enemies, and out of the hand of Saul:

L 2 And he said, [a]The LORD *is* my rock, and my fortress, and my deliverer;

3 The God of my rock; [a]in him will I trust: *he is* my [b]shield, and the [c]horn of my salvation, my high [d]tower, and my [e]refuge, my saviour; thou savest me from violence.

4 I will call on the LORD, *who is* worthy to be praised: so shall I be saved from mine enemies.

5 When the [1]waves of death compassed me, the floods of [2]ungodly men made me afraid;

6 The [a]sorrows[1] of hell compassed me about; the snares of death prevented me;

7 In my distress [a]I called upon the LORD, and cried to my God: and he did [b]hear my voice out of his temple, and my cry *did enter* into his ears.

8 Then [a]the earth shook and trembled; [b]the foundations of heaven moved and shook, because he was wroth.

9 There went up a smoke [1]out of his nostrils, and [a]fire out of his mouth devoured: coals were kindled by it.

10 He [a]bowed the heavens also, and came down; and [b]darkness *was* under his feet.

11 And he rode upon a cherub, and did fly: and he was seen [a]upon the wings of the wind.

12 And he made [a]darkness pavilions round about him, [1]dark waters, *and* thick clouds of the skies.

13 Through the brightness before him were [a]coals of fire kindled.

P 14 The LORD [a]thundered from heaven, and the most High uttered his voice.

15 And he sent out [a]arrows, and scattered them; lightning, and discomfited them.

16 And the channels of the sea appeared, the foundations of the world were discovered, at the [a]rebuking of the LORD, at the blast of the breath of his nostrils.

17 [a]He sent from above, he took me; he drew me out of [1]many waters;

18 [a]He delivered me from my strong enemy, *and* from them that hated me: for they were too strong for me.

19 They prevented me in the day of my calamity: but the LORD was my stay.

20 [a]He brought me forth also into a U
large place: he delivered me, because he [b]delighted in me.

21 [a]The LORD rewarded me according S
to my righteousness: according to the [b]cleanness of my hands hath he recompensed me.

22 For I have [a]kept the ways of the LORD, and have not wickedly departed from my God.

23 For all his [a]judgments *were* before me: and *as for* his statutes, I did not depart from them.

24 I was also [a]upright [1]before him, and have kept myself from mine iniquity.

25 Therefore [a]the LORD hath recompensed me according to my righteousness; according to my cleanness [1]in his eyesight.

26 With [a]the merciful thou wilt show thyself merciful, *and* with the upright man thou wilt show thyself upright.

27 With the pure thou wilt show thyself pure; and [a]with the froward thou wilt [1]show thyself unsavoury.

28 And the [a]afflicted people thou wilt M
save: but thine eyes *are* upon [b]the haughty, *that* thou mayest bring *them* down.

29 For thou *art* my [1]lamp, O LORD: and the LORD will lighten my darkness.

30 For by thee I have [1]run through a V
troop: by my God have I leaped over a wall.

31 *As for* God, [a]his way *is* perfect; [b]the K
word of the LORD *is* [1]tried: he *is* a buckler W
to all them that trust in him.

22:1 [a]Ex. 15:1; Judg. 5:1 [b]Ps. 18, title, & 34:19
2 [a]Deut. 32:4
3 [a]Heb. 2:13 [b]Gen. 15:1 [c]Luke 1:69 [d]Prov. 18:10 [e]Ps. 9:9; Jer. 16:19
5 [1]Or, *pangs* [2]Heb. *Belial*
6 [a]Ps. 116:3 [1]Or, *cords*
7 [a]Ps. 116:4 [b]Ex. 3:7
8 [a]Ps. 77:18 [b]Job 26:11
9 [a]Ps. 97:3 [1]Heb. *by*
10 [a]Is. 64:1 [b]Ex. 20:21
11 [a]Ps. 104:3
12 [a]Ps. 97:2 [1]Heb. *binding of waters*
13 [a]ver. 9
14 [a]1 Sam. 2:10
15 [a]Ps. 7:13
16 [a]Ex. 15:8
17 [a]Ps. 144:7 [1]Or, *great*
18 [a]ver. 1
20 [a]Ps. 31:8 [b]ch. 15:26
21 [a]Ps. 7:8 [b]Ps. 24:4
22 [a]Ps. 119:3
23 [a]Deut. 7:12
24 [a]Job 1:1 [1]Heb. *to him*
25 [a]ver. 21 [1]Heb. *before his eyes*
26 [a]Mat. 5:7
27 [a]Lev. 26:23 [1]Or, *wrestle*
28 [a]Ps. 72:12 [b]Job 40:11
29 [1]Or, *candle*
30 [1]Or, *broken a troop*
31 [a]Dan. 4:37 [b]Ps. 12:6 [1]Or, *refined*

L *1Sa 25:29* ◀▶ *2Ki 6:16–17*
P *1Sa 2:10* ◀▶ *2Sa 23:6–7*

U *1Sa 2:30* ◀▶ *1Ki 3:6*
S *1Sa 24:13* ◀▶ *1Ki 8:61*
M *1Sa 2:3* ◀▶ *2Sa 24:10*
V *1Sa 25:29* ◀▶ *2Ch 14:7*
K *1Sa 25:29* ◀▶ *2Sa 22:36*
W *Nu 21:8–9* ◀▶ *Ezr 8:22*

22:14–18 David's song of praise is also given in Ps 18:1–50. In this song David declares his total dependence upon God's direction and his trust in God's ability to deliver Israel from all their enemies.

O 32 For [a]who *is* God, save the LORD? and who *is* a rock, save our God?

33 God *is* my [a]strength *and* power: and he [b]maketh[1] my way [c]perfect.

34 He [1]maketh my feet [a]like hinds' *feet:* and [b]setteth me upon my high places.

35 [a]He teacheth my hands [1]to war; so that a bow of steel is broken by mine arms.

K 36 Thou hast also given me the shield of thy salvation: and thy gentleness hath [1]made me great.

37 Thou hast [a]enlarged my steps under me; so that my [1]feet did not slip.

38 I have pursued mine enemies, and destroyed them; and turned not again until I had consumed them.

39 And I have consumed them, and wounded them, that they could not arise: yea, they are fallen [a]under my feet.

40 For thou hast [a]girded me with strength to battle: [b]them that rose up against me hast thou [1]subdued under me.

41 Thou hast also given me the [a]necks of mine enemies, that I might destroy them that hate me.

42 They looked, but *there was* none to save; *even* [a]unto the LORD, but he answered them not.

43 Then did I beat them as small [a]as the dust of the earth, I did stamp them [b]as the mire of the street, *and* did spread them abroad.

44 [a]Thou also hast delivered me from the strivings of my people, thou hast kept me *to be* [b]head of the heathen: [c]a people *which* I knew not shall serve me.

45 [1]Strangers shall [2]submit themselves unto me: as soon as they hear, they shall be obedient unto me.

46 Strangers shall fade away, and they shall be afraid [a]out of their close places.

47 The LORD liveth; and blessed *be* my rock; and exalted be the God of the [a]rock of my salvation.

48 It *is* God that [a]avengeth[1] me, and that [b]bringeth down the people under me,

49 And that bringeth me forth from mine enemies: thou also hast lifted me up on high above them that rose up against me: thou hast delivered me from the [a]violent man.

50 Therefore I will give thanks unto thee, O LORD, among [a]the heathen, and I will sing praises unto thy name.

51 [a]*He is* the tower of salvation for his king: and showeth mercy to his [b]anointed, unto David, and [c]to his seed for evermore.

David's last words

23 NOW THESE *be* the last words of David. David the son of Jesse said, [a]and the man *who was* raised up on high, [b]the anointed of the God of Jacob, and the sweet psalmist of Israel, said, T

2 [a]The spirit of the LORD spake by me, and his word *was* in my tongue. E G

3 The God of Israel said, [a]the Rock of Israel spake to me, [1]He that ruleth over men *must be* just, ruling [b]in the fear of God. L M

4 And *he shall be* as the light of the morning, *when* the sun riseth, *even* a morning without clouds; *as* the tender grass *springing* out of the earth by clear shining after rain.

5 Although my house *be* not so with God; [a]yet he hath made with me an everlasting covenant, ordered in all *things,* and sure: for *this is* all my salvation, and all *my* desire, although he make *it* not to grow.

6 ¶ But *the sons* of Belial *shall be* all of them as thorns thrust away, because they cannot be taken with hands: P C

7 But the man *that* shall touch them must be [1]fenced with iron and the staff of a spear; and they shall be utterly burned with fire in the *same* place.

32 [a]Is. 45:5,6
33 [a]Ps. 27:1; Is. 12:2 [b]Heb. 13:21 [c]Ps. 101:2,6 [1]Heb. *riddeth,* or, *looseth*
34 [a]ch. 2:18 [b]Is. 33:16 [1]Heb. *equalleth*
35 [a]Ps. 144:1 [1]Heb. *for the war*
36 [1]Heb. *multiplied me*
37 [a]Prov. 4:12 [1]Heb. *ankles*
39 [a]Mal. 4:3
40 [a]Ps. 18:32 [b]Ps. 44:5 [1]Heb. *caused to bow*
41 [a]Gen. 49:8
42 [a]Prov. 1:28
43 [a]Ps. 18:42 [b]Is. 10:6
44 [a]ch. 3:1 [b]Deut. 28:13 [c]Is. 55:5
45 [1]Heb. *Sons of the stranger* [2]Or, *yield feigned obedience*
46 [a]Mic. 7:17
47 [a]Ps. 89:26
48 [a]1 Sam. 25:39 [b]Ps. 144:2 [1]Heb. *giveth avengement for me*
49 [a]Ps. 140:1
50 [a]Rom. 15:9
51 [a]Ps. 144:10 [b]Ps. 89:20 [c]Ps. 89:29
23:1 [a]Ps. 78:70 [b]1 Sam. 16:12,13; Ps. 89:20
2 [a]2 Pet. 1:21
3 [a]Deut. 32:4 [b]Ex. 18:21 [1]Or, *Be thou ruler*
5 [a]Ps. 89:29
7 [1]Heb. *filled*

O *2Sa 7:22* ◀▶ *1Ki 8:60*
K *2Sa 22:31* ◀▶ *2Ki 6:16–17*

T *1Sa 10:10–12* ◀▶ *1Ch 28:12*
E *1Sa 19:20–23* ◀▶ *1Ki 18:12*
G *1Sa 19:20–24* ◀▶ *Ne 9:20*
L *1Sa 10:6–7* ◀▶ *1Ki 18:12*
M *2Sa 7:16* ◀▶ *1Ki 2:45*
P *2Sa 22:14–18* ◀▶ *Job 38:13*
C *1Sa 24:13* ◀▶ *1Ki 21:20*

23:3–5 These verses clearly declared that God alone sets the standards for righteous government. Humanity must rule one another in conformity to God's justice. See the discussion concerning the dispensation of human government at Ge 8:15.

David's mighty men

8 ¶ These *be* the names of the mighty men whom David had: [1]The Tachmonite that sat in the seat, chief among the captains; the same *was* Adino the Eznite: [2]*he lift up his spear* against eight hundred, [3]whom he slew at one time.

9 And after him *was* [a]Eleazar the son of Dodo the Ahohite, *one* of the three mighty men with David, when they defied the Philistines *that* were there gathered together to battle, and the men of Israel were gone away:

10 He arose, and smote the Philistines until his hand was weary, and his hand clave unto the sword: and the LORD wrought a great victory that day; and the people returned after him only to spoil.

11 And after him *was* [a]Shammah the son of Agee the Hararite. [b]And the Philistines were gathered together [1]into a troop, where was a piece of ground full of lentiles: and the people fled from the Philistines.

12 But he stood in the midst of the ground, and defended it, and slew the Philistines: and the LORD wrought a great victory.

13 And [a]three[1] of the thirty chief went down, and came to David in the harvest time unto [b]the cave of Adullam: and the troop of the Philistines pitched in [c]the valley of Rephaim.

14 And David *was* then in [a]an hold, and the garrison of the Philistines *was* then *in* Bethlehem.

15 And David longed, and said, Oh that one would give me drink of the water of the well of Bethlehem, which *is* by the gate!

16 And the three mighty men brake through the host of the Philistines, and drew water out of the well of Bethlehem, that *was* by the gate, and took *it,* and brought *it* to David: nevertheless he would not drink thereof, but poured it out unto the LORD.

17 And he said, Be it far from me, O LORD, that I should do this: *is not this* [a]the blood of the men that went in jeopardy of their lives? therefore he would not drink it. These things did these three mighty men.

18 And [a]Abishai, the brother of Joab, the son of Zeruiah, was chief among three. And he lifted up his spear against three hundred, [1]*and* slew *them,* and had the name among three.

19 Was he not most honourable of three? therefore he was their captain: howbeit he attained not unto the *first* three.

20 And Benaiah the son of Jehoiada, the son of a valiant man, of [a]Kabzeel, [1]who had done many acts, [b]he slew two [2]lionlike men of Moab: he went down also and slew a lion in the midst of a pit in time of snow:

21 And he slew an Egyptian, [a]a[1] goodly man: and the Egyptian had a spear in his hand; but he went down to him with a staff, and plucked the spear out of the Egyptian's hand, and slew him with his own spear.

22 These *things* did Benaiah the son of Jehoiada, and had the name among three mighty men.

23 He was [1]more honourable than the thirty, but he attained not to the *first* three. And David set him [a]over his [2]guard.

24 [a]Asahel the brother of Joab *was* one of the thirty; Elhanan the son of Dodo of Bethlehem,

25 [a]Shammah the Harodite, Elika the Harodite,

26 Helez the Paltite, Ira the son of Ikkesh the Tekoite,

27 Abiezer the Anethothite, Mebunnai the Hushathite,

28 Zalmon the Ahohite, Maharai the Netophathite,

29 Heleb the son of Baanah, a Netophathite, Ittai the son of Ribai out of Gibeah of the children of Benjamin,

30 Benaiah the Pirathonite, Hiddai of the [1]brooks of [a]Gaash,

31 Abi-albon the Arbathite, Azmaveth the Barhumite,

32 Eliahba the Shaalbonite, of the sons of Jashen, Jonathan,

33 Shammah the Hararite, Ahiam the son of Sharar the Hararite,

34 Eliphelet the son of Ahasbai, the son of the Maachathite, Eliam the son of Ahithophel the Gilonite,

35 Hezrai the Carmelite, Paarai the Arbite,

36 Igal the son of Nathan of Zobah, Bani the Gadite,

37 Zelek the Ammonite, Nahari the Beerothite, armourbearer to Joab the son of Zeruiah,

8 [1]Or, *Josheb-bassebet the Tachmonite, head of the three* [2]See 1 Chr. 11:11 [3]Heb. *slain*

9 [a]1 Chr. 11:12

11 [a]1 Chr. 11:27 [b]See 1 Chr. 11:13, 14 [1]Or, *for foraging*

13 [a]1 Chr. 11:15 [b]1 Sam. 22:1 [c]ch. 5:18 [1]Or, *the three captains over the thirty*

14 [a]1 Sam. 22:4,5

17 [a]Lev. 17:10

18 [a]1 Chr. 11:20 [1]Heb. *slain*

20 [a]Josh. 15:21 [b]Ex. 15:15 [1]Heb. *great of acts* [2]Heb. *lions of God*

21 [a]1 Chr. 11:23 [1]Heb. *a man of countenance,* or, *sight:* called

23 [a]ch. 8:18 & 20:23 [1]Or, *honourable among the thirty* [2]Or, *council*

24 [a]ch. 2:18

25 [a]See 1 Chr. 11:27

30 [a]Judg. 2:9 [1]Or, *valleys*

38 [a]Ira an Ithrite, Gareb an Ithrite,

39 [a]Uriah the Hittite: thirty and seven in all.

The census of Israel and Judah

24 AND [a]AGAIN the anger of the LORD was kindled against Israel, and he moved David against them to say, [b]Go, number Israel and Judah.

2 For the king said to Joab the captain of the host, which *was* with him, [l]Go now through all the tribes of Israel, [a]from Dan even to Beer-sheba, and number ye the people, that [b]I may know the number of the people.

3 And Joab said unto the king, Now the LORD thy God add unto the people, how many soever they be, an hundredfold, and that the eyes of my lord the king may see *it:* but why doth my lord the king delight in this thing?

4 Notwithstanding the king's word prevailed against Joab, and against the captains of the host. And Joab and the captains of the host went out from the presence of the king, to number the people of Israel.

5 ¶ And they passed over Jordan, and pitched in [a]Aroer, on the right side of the city that *lieth* in the midst of the [l]river of Gad, and toward [b]Jazer:

6 Then they came to Gilead, and to the [l]land of Tahtim-hodshi; and they came to [a]Dan-jaan, and about to [b]Zidon,

7 And came to the strong hold of Tyre, and to all the cities of the Hivites, and of the Canaanites: and they went out to the south of Judah, *even* to Beer-sheba.

8 So when they had gone through all the land, they came to Jerusalem at the end of nine months and twenty days.

9 And Joab gave up the sum of the number of the people unto the king: [a]and there were in Israel eight hundred thousand valiant men that drew the sword; and the men of Judah *were* five hundred thousand men.

M R 10 ¶ And [a]David's heart smote him after that he had numbered the people. And David said unto the LORD, [b]I have sinned greatly in that I have done: and now, I beseech thee, O LORD, take away the iniquity of thy servant; for I have [c]done very foolishly.

M *2Sa 22:28* ◀▶ *1Ki 21:25–29*
R *2Sa 12:13* ◀▶ *2Ki 17:13*

38 [a]ch. 20:26
39 [a]ch. 11:3,6
24:1 [a]ch. 20:1 [b]1 Chr. 27:23,24
2 [a]Judg. 20:1 [b]Jer. 17:5 [l]Or, *Compass*
5 [a]Deut. 2:36; Josh. 13:9,16 [b]Num. 32:1,3 [l]Or, *valley*
6 [a]Josh. 19:47; Judg. 18:29 [b]Josh. 19:28; Judg. 18:28 [l]Or, *nether land newly inhabited*
9 [a]See 1 Chr. 21:5
10 [a]1 Sam. 24:5 [b]ch. 12:13 [c]1 Sam. 13:13
11 [a]1 Sam. 22:5 [b]1 Sam. 9:9; 1 Chr. 29:29
13 [a]See 1 Chr. 21:12
14 [a]Ps. 103:8,13, 14 & 119:156 [b]See Is. 47:6; Zech. 1:15 [l]Or, *many*
15 [a]1 Chr. 21:14; & 27:24
16 [a]Ex. 12:23 [b]Gen. 6:6; 1 Sam. 15:11; Joel 2:13,14 [c]1 Chr. 21:15, *Ornan:* See ver. 18; 2 Chr. 3:1
17 [a]1 Chr. 21:17
18 [a]1 Chr. 21:18 [l]Heb. *Araniah*
21 [a]See Gen. 23:8-16

11 For when David was up in the morning, the word of the LORD came unto the prophet [a]Gad, David's [b]seer, saying,

12 Go and say unto David, Thus saith the LORD, I offer thee three *things;* choose thee one of them, that I may *do it* unto thee.

13 So Gad came to David, and told him, and said unto him, Shall [a]seven years of famine come unto thee in thy land? or wilt thou flee three months before thine enemies, while they pursue thee? or that there be three days' pestilence in thy land? now advise, and see what answer I shall return to him that sent me.

14 And David said unto Gad, I am in a great strait: let us fall now into the hand of the LORD; [a]for his mercies *are* [l]great: and [b]let me not fall into the hand of man.

15 ¶ So [a]the LORD sent a pestilence upon Israel from the morning even to the time appointed: and there died of the people from Dan even to Beer-sheba seventy thousand men.

16 [a]And when the angel stretched out his hand upon Jerusalem to destroy it, [b]the LORD repented him of the evil, and said to the angel that destroyed the people, It is enough: stay now thine hand. And the angel of the LORD was by the threshingplace of [c]Araunah the Jebusite.

17 And David spake unto the LORD when he saw the angel that smote the people, and said, Lo, [a]I have sinned, and I have done wickedly: but these sheep, what have they done? let thine hand, I pray thee, be against me, and against my father's house.

David builds an altar

18 ¶ And Gad came that day to David, and said unto him, [a]Go up, rear an altar unto the LORD in the threshingfloor of [l]Araunah the Jebusite.

19 And David, according to the saying of Gad, went up as the LORD commanded.

20 And Araunah looked, and saw the king and his servants coming on toward him: and Araunah went out, and bowed himself before the king on his face upon the ground.

21 And Araunah said, Wherefore is my lord the king come to his servant? [a]And David said, To buy the threshingfloor of thee, to build an altar unto the LORD, that

[b]the plague may be stayed from the
people.
22 And Araunah said unto David, Let
my lord the king take and offer up what
seemeth good unto him: [a]behold, *here be*
oxen for burnt sacrifice, and threshing instruments and *other* instruments of the
oxen for wood.
23 All these *things* did Araunah, *as* a
king, give unto the king. And Araunah
said unto the king, The LORD thy God [a]ac-
cept thee.
24 And the king said unto Araunah,

21 [b]Num. 16:48, 50
22 [a]1 Ki. 19:21
23 [a]Ezek. 20:40,41
24 [a]See 1 Chr. 21:24,25
25 [a]ch. 21:14 [b]ver. 21

Nay; but I will surely buy *it* of thee at a
price: neither will I offer burnt offerings
unto the LORD my God of that which doth
cost me nothing. So [a]David bought the
threshingfloor and the oxen for fifty shekels of silver.
25 And David built there an altar unto
the LORD, and offered burnt offerings and
peace offerings. [a]So the LORD was entreated for the land, and [b]the plague was
stayed from Israel.

E 1Sa 1:5–20 ◄ ► 1Ki 13:6

24:24 Though Araunah had freely offered this land to David, David insisted on paying for it. David declared that an offering must cost the giver something. By purchasing this threshing floor, this land became David's property and ultimately the future site of the temple (see 1Ch 22:1; 2Ch 3:1). The principle of sacrificial giving applies to us as well. While God's gift of grace is free, it was bought with the high price of Jesus' death. We should take our worship of God seriously and offer him only our best, regardless of personal cost (see Lk 21:1–4).

1 Kings

Author: Unknown

Theme: The united and divided kingdom of Israel

Date of Writing: c. 560–550 B.C.

Outline of 1 Kings

I. King David's Reign Ends (1:1—2:11)
II. The Reign of Solomon (2:12—11:43)
III. The Kingdom Is Divided (12:1—14:31)
IV. Kings of Judah and Israel (15:1—16:28)
V. The Reign of Ahab (16:29—22:40)
VI. Jehoshaphat and Ahaziah (22:41–53)

THE BOOKS OF 1 and 2 Kings (like 1 and 2 Samuel) were originally treated as one book and called simply "Kings" in the ancient Hebrew manuscripts. Translators of the Septuagint (the Greek version of the OT) divided the larger Hebrew manuscript into the two books modern translations refer to as 1 and 2 Kings. The books of 1 and 2 Kings combined with 1 and 2 Samuel cover the history of Israel through the monarchies of the united and divided kingdoms until its ultimate destruction and exile under the Babylonians. Though authorship of 1 and 2 Kings is uncertain, these books were probably written after King Jehoiachin's release from prison (562 B.C.) but before the end of the Babylonian exile (538 B.C.).

The book of 1 Kings begins with the account of King Solomon's reign, describing the building of the temple and recording Solomon's journey from wisdom to folly. Following Solomon's reign, rebellion among the people broke the nation apart. The northern ten tribes re-formed as the kingdom of Israel and the remaining two southern tribes re-formed as the kingdom of Judah. The remainder of 1 Kings traces the reigns of the kings of these new kingdoms, highlighting the success of the kings who followed God's law while pointing out the destruction that followed those who disobeyed. Note that the majority of the northern kings were evil, but many southern kings initiated revivals and returned their people to the worship of God. The book of 1 Kings closes with the reign of King Ahaziah of Israel and King Jehoshaphat of Judah. Some important stories in 1 Kings include Solomon's prayer for wisdom (ch. 3), the Queen of Sheba's visit (ch. 10), Elijah and the prophets of Baal (ch. 18) and Ahab and Jezebel (chs. 21—22).

Adonijah seeks to be king

1 NOW KING David was old *and* [1]stricken in years; and they covered him with clothes, but he gat no heat.

2 Wherefore his servants said unto him, [1]Let there be sought for my lord the king [2]a young virgin: and let her stand before the king, and let her [3]cherish him, and let her lie in thy bosom, that my lord the king may get heat.

3 So they sought for a fair damsel throughout all the coasts of Israel, and found Abishag a [a]Shunammite, and brought her to the king.

4 And the damsel *was* very fair, and cherished the king, and ministered to him: but the king knew her not.

5 ¶ Then [a]Adonijah the son of Haggith exalted himself, saying, I will [1]be king: and he prepared him chariots and horsemen, and fifty men to run before him.

6 And his father had not displeased him [1]at any time in saying, Why hast thou done so? and he also *was a* very goodly *man;* [a]and *his mother* bare him after Absalom.

7 And [1]he conferred with Joab the son of Zeruiah, and with [a]Abiathar the priest: and [b]they [2]following Adonijah helped *him.*

8 But Zadok the priest, and Benaiah the son of Jehoiada, and Nathan the prophet, and [a]Shimei, and Rei, and [b]the mighty men which *belonged* to David, were not with Adonijah.

9 And Adonijah slew sheep and oxen and fat cattle by the stone of Zoheleth, which *is* by [1]En-rogel, and called all his brethren the king's sons, and all the men of Judah the king's servants:

10 But Nathan the prophet, and Benaiah, and the mighty men, and Solomon his brother, he called not.

11 ¶ Wherefore Nathan spake unto Bath-sheba the mother of Solomon, saying, Hast thou not heard that Adonijah the son of [a]Haggith doth reign, and David our lord knoweth *it* not?

12 Now therefore come, let me, I pray thee, give thee counsel, that thou mayest save thine own life, and the life of thy son Solomon.

13 Go and get thee in unto king David, and say unto him, Didst not thou, my lord, O king, swear unto thine handmaid, saying, [a]Assuredly Solomon thy son shall reign after me, and he shall sit upon my throne? why then doth Adonijah reign?

14 Behold, while thou yet talkest there with the king, I also will come in after thee, and [1]confirm thy words.

15 ¶ And Bath-sheba went in unto the king into the chamber: and the king was very old; and Abishag the Shunammite ministered unto the king.

16 And Bath-sheba bowed, and did obeisance unto the king. And the king said, [1]What wouldest thou?

17 And she said unto him, My lord, [a]thou swarest by the LORD thy God unto thine handmaid, *saying,* Assuredly Solomon thy son shall reign after me, and he shall sit upon my throne.

18 And now, behold, Adonijah reigneth; and now, my lord the king, thou knowest *it* not:

19 [a]And he hath slain oxen and fat cattle and sheep in abundance, and hath called all the sons of the king, and Abiathar the priest, and Joab the captain of the host: but Solomon thy servant hath he not called.

20 And thou, my lord, O king, the eyes of all Israel *are* upon thee, that thou shouldest tell them who shall sit on the throne of my lord the king after him.

21 Otherwise it shall come to pass, when my lord the king shall [a]sleep with his fathers, that I and my son Solomon shall be counted [1]offenders.

22 ¶ And, lo, while she yet talked with the king, Nathan the prophet also came in.

23 And they told the king, saying, Behold Nathan the prophet. And when he was come in before the king, he bowed himself before the king with his face to the ground.

24 And Nathan said, My lord, O king, hast thou said, Adonijah shall reign after me, and he shall sit upon my throne?

25 [a]For he is gone down this day, and hath slain oxen and fat cattle and sheep in abundance, and hath called all the king's sons, and the captains of the host, and Abiathar the priest; and, behold, they eat and drink before him, and say, [b]God [1] save king Adonijah.

26 But me, *even* me thy servant, and Zadok the priest, and Benaiah the son of Jehoiada, and thy servant Solomon, hath he not called.

27 Is this thing done by my lord the

1:1 [1]Heb. *entered into days*
2 [1]Heb. *Let them seek* [2]Heb. *a damsel, a virgin* [3]Heb. *be a cherisher unto him*
3 [a]Josh. 19:18
5 [a]2 Sam. 3:4 [1]Heb. *reign*
6 [a]2 Sam. 3:3; 1 Chr. 3:2 [1]Heb. *from his days*
7 [a]2 Sam. 20:25 [b]ch. 2:22,28 [1]Heb. *his words were with Joab* [2]Heb. *helped after Adonijah*
8 [a]ch. 4:18 [b]2 Sam. 23:8
9 [1]Or, *The well Rogel*
11 [a]2 Sam. 3:4
13 [a]1 Chr. 22:9
14 [1]Heb. *fill up*
16 [1]Heb. *What to thee?*
17 [a]ver. 13,30
19 [a]ver. 7-9,25
21 [a]Deut. 31:16; ch. 2:10 [1]Heb. *sinners*
25 [a]ver. 19 [b]1 Sam. 10:24 [1]Heb. *Let king Adonijah live*

king, and thou hast not showed *it* unto
thy servant, who should sit on the throne
of my lord the king after him?

Solomon anointed king

28 ¶ Then king David answered and
said, Call me Bath-sheba. And she came
[1]into the king's presence, and stood before the king.
29 And the king sware, and said, [a]*As*
the LORD liveth, that hath redeemed my
soul out of all distress,
30 [a]Even as I sware unto thee by the
LORD God of Israel, saying, Assuredly Solomon thy son shall reign after me, and he
shall sit upon my throne in my stead;
even so will I certainly do this day.
31 Then Bath-sheba bowed with *her*
face to the earth, and did reverence to
the king, and said, [a]Let my lord king David live for ever.
32 ¶ And king David said, Call me Zadok the priest, and Nathan the prophet,
and Benaiah the son of Jehoiada. And
they came before the king.
33 The king also said unto them, [a]Take
with you the servants of your lord, and
cause Solomon my son to ride upon
[1]mine own mule, and bring him down to
[b]Gihon:
34 And let Zadok the priest and Nathan the prophet [a]anoint him there king
over Israel: and [b]blow ye with the trumpet, and say, God save king Solomon.
35 Then ye shall come up after him,
that he may come and sit upon my
throne; for he shall be king in my stead:
and I have appointed him to be ruler over
Israel and over Judah.
36 And Benaiah the son of Jehoiada answered the king, and said, Amen: the
LORD God of my lord the king say so *too.*
37 [a]As the LORD hath been with my
lord the king, even so be he with Solomon, and [b]make his throne greater than
the throne of my lord king David.
38 So Zadok the priest, and Nathan the
prophet, [a]and Benaiah the son of Jehoiada, and the Cherethites, and the Pelethites, went down, and caused Solomon
to ride upon king David's mule, and
brought him to Gihon.
39 And Zadok the priest took an horn
of [a]oil out of the tabernacle, and
[b]anointed Solomon. And they blew the
trumpet; [c]and all the people said, God
save king Solomon.

28 [1]Heb. *before the king*
29 [a]2 Sam. 4:9
30 [a]ver. 17
31 [a]Neh. 2:3; Dan 2:4
33 [a]2 Sam. 20:6 [b]2 Chr. 32:30 [1]Heb. *which* belongeth *to me*
34 [a]1 Sam. 10:1 & 16:3,12; 2 Sam. 2:4 & 5:3; ch. 19:16; 2 Ki. 9:3 & 11:12 [b]2 Sam. 15:10; 2 Ki 9:13 & 11:14
37 [a]Josh. 1:5,17; 1 Sam. 20:13 [b]ver. 47
38 [a]2 Sam. 8:18 & 23:20-23
39 [a]Ex. 30:23,25, 32; Ps. 89:20 [b]1 Chr. 29:22 [c]1 Sam. 10:24
40 [1]Or, *flutes*
42 [a]2 Sam. 18:27
46 [a]1 Chr. 29:23
47 [a]ver. 37 [b]Gen. 47:31
48 [a]ch. 3:6; Ps. 132:11,12
50 [a]ch. 2:28
52 [a]1 Sam. 14:45; 2 Sam. 14:11

40 And all the people came up after
him, and the people piped with [1]pipes,
and rejoiced with great joy, so that the
earth rent with the sound of them.
41 ¶ And Adonijah and all the guests
that *were* with him heard *it* as they had
made an end of eating. And when Joab
heard the sound of the trumpet, he said,
Wherefore *is this* noise of the city being
in an uproar?
42 And while he yet spake, behold,
Jonathan the son of Abiathar the priest
came: and Adonijah said unto him, Come
in; for [a]thou *art* a valiant man, and bringest good tidings.
43 And Jonathan answered and said to
Adonijah, Verily our lord king David hath
made Solomon king.
44 And the king hath sent with him
Zadok the priest, and Nathan the
prophet, and Benaiah the son of Jehoiada,
and the Cherethites, and the Pelethites,
and they have caused him to ride upon
the king's mule:
45 And Zadok the priest and Nathan
the prophet have anointed him king in
Gihon: and they are come up from thence
rejoicing, so that the city rang again. This
is the noise that ye have heard.
46 And also Solomon [a]sitteth on the
throne of the kingdom.
47 And moreover the king's servants
came to bless our lord king David, saying,
[a]God make the name of Solomon better
than thy name, and make his throne
greater than thy throne. [b]And the king
bowed himself upon the bed.
48 And also thus said the king, Blessed
be the LORD God of Israel, which hath
[a]given *one* to sit on my throne this day,
mine eyes even seeing *it.*
49 And all the guests that *were* with
Adonijah were afraid, and rose up, and
went every man his way.
50 ¶ And Adonijah feared because of
Solomon, and arose, and went, and
[a]caught hold on the horns of the altar.
51 And it was told Solomon, saying,
Behold, Adonijah feareth king Solomon:
for, lo, he hath caught hold on the horns
of the altar, saying, Let king Solomon
swear unto me today that he will not slay
his servant with the sword.
52 And Solomon said, If he will show
himself a worthy man, [a]there shall not an
hair of him fall to the earth: but if wickedness shall be found in him, he shall die.

53 So king Solomon sent, and they brought him down from the altar. And he came and bowed himself to king Solomon: and Solomon said unto him, Go to thine house.

David's last words and death

2 NOW [a]THE days of David drew nigh that he should die; and he charged Solomon his son, saying,

2 [a]I go the way of all the earth: [b]be thou strong therefore, and show thyself a man;

A 3 And keep the charge of the LORD thy God, to walk in his ways, to keep his statutes, and his commandments, and his judgments, and his testimonies, as it is written in the law of Moses, that thou mayest [a]prosper[1] in all that thou doest, and whithersoever thou turnest thyself:

I 4 That the LORD may [a]continue his word which he spake concerning me, saying, [b]If thy children take heed to their way, to [c]walk before me in truth with all their heart and with all their soul, [d]there shall not [1]fail thee (said he) a man on the throne of Israel.

5 Moreover thou knowest also what Joab the son of Zeruiah [a]did to me, *and* what he did to the two captains of the hosts of Israel, unto [b]Abner the son of Ner, and unto [c]Amasa the son of Jether, whom he slew, and [1]shed the blood of war in peace, and put the blood of war upon his girdle that *was* about his loins, and in his shoes that *were* on his feet.

6 Do therefore [a]according to thy wisdom, and let not his hoar head go down to the grave in peace.

7 But show kindness unto the sons of [a]Barzillai the Gileadite, and let them be of those that [b]eat at thy table: for so [c]they came to me when I fled because of Absalom thy brother.

8 And, behold, *thou hast* with thee [a]Shimei the son of Gera, a Benjamite of Bahurim, which cursed me with a [1]grievous curse in the day when I went to Mahanaim: but [b]he came down to meet me at Jordan, and [c]I sware to him by the LORD, saying, I will not put thee to death with the sword.

9 Now therefore [a]hold him not guiltless: for thou *art* a wise man, and knowest what thou oughtest to do unto him; but his hoar head [b]bring thou down to the grave with blood.

10 So [a]David slept with his fathers, and was buried in [b]the city of David.

11 And the days that David [a]reigned over Israel *were* forty years: seven years reigned he in Hebron, and thirty and three years reigned he in Jerusalem.

12 ¶ [a]Then sat Solomon upon the throne of David his father; and his kingdom was established greatly.

13 ¶ And Adonijah the son of Haggith came to Bath-sheba the mother of Solomon. And she said, [a]Comest thou peaceably? And he said, Peaceably.

14 He said moreover, I have somewhat to say unto thee. And she said, Say on.

15 And he said, Thou knowest that the kingdom was mine, and *that* all Israel set their faces on me, that I should reign: howbeit the kingdom is turned about, and is become my brother's: for [a]it was his from the LORD.

16 And now I ask one petition of thee, [1]deny me not. And she said unto him, Say on.

17 And he said, Speak, I pray thee, unto Solomon the king, (for he will not say thee nay,) that he give me [a]Abishag the Shunammite to wife.

18 And Bath-sheba said, Well; I will speak for thee unto the king.

19 ¶ Bath-sheba therefore went unto king Solomon, to speak unto him for Adonijah. And the king rose up to meet her, and [a]bowed himself unto her, and sat down on his throne, and caused a seat to be set for the king's mother; [b]and she sat on his right hand.

20 Then she said, I desire one small petition of thee; *I pray thee,* say me not nay. And the king said unto her, Ask on, my mother: for I will not say thee nay.

21 And she said, Let Abishag the Shunammite be given to Adonijah thy brother to wife.

22 And king Solomon answered and

2:1 [a]Gen. 47:29; Deut. 31:14
2 [a]Josh. 23:14 [b]Deut. 17:19,20
3 [a]Deut. 29:9; Josh. 1:7; 1 Chr. 22:12, 13 [1]Or, *do wisely*
4 [a]2 Sam. 7:25 [b]Ps. 132:12 [c]2 Ki. 20:3 [d]2 Sam. 7:12, 13; ch. 8:25 [1]Heb. *be cut off from thee from the throne*
5 [a]2 Sam. 3:39 & 18:5,12,14 [b]2 Sam. 3:27 [c]2 Sam. 20:10 [1]Heb. *put*
6 [a]ver. 9; Prov. 20:26
7 [a]2 Sam. 19:31,38 [b]2 Sam. 9:7,10 & 19:28 [c]2 Sam. 17:27
8 [a]2 Sam. 16:5 [b]2 Sam. 19:18 [c]2 Sam. 19:23 [1]Heb. *strong*
9 [a]Ex. 20:7; Job 9:28 [b]Gen. 42:38 & 44:31
10 [a]ch. 1:21; Acts 2:29 & 13:36 [b]2 Sam. 5:7
11 [a]2 Sam. 5:4; 1 Chr. 29:26,27
12 [a]1 Chr. 29:23; 2 Chr. 1:1
13 [a]1 Sam. 16:4,5
15 [a]1 Chr. 22:9, 10 & 28:5-7; Dan. 2:21
16 [1]Heb. *turn not away my face*
17 [a]ch. 1:3,4
19 [a]Ex. 20:12 [b]See Ps. 45:9

A *Dt 15:18* ◀▶ *Ps 91:10*
I *2Sa 7:23–24* ◀▶ *1Ki 5:5*

2:2–4 As King David lay on his deathbed he prophesied that God would prosper the reign of Solomon if he would "keep his statutes, and his commandments" (2:3). David then prophesied that his descendants would continue to rule Israel forever if they obeyed God.

said unto his mother, And why dost thou ask Abishag the Shunammite for Adonijah? ask for him the kingdom also; for he *is* mine elder brother; even for him, and for [a]Abiathar the priest, and for Joab the son of Zeruiah.

23 Then king Solomon sware by the LORD, saying, [a]God do so to me, and more also, if Adonijah have not spoken this word against his own life.

24 Now therefore, *as* the LORD liveth, which hath established me, and set me on the throne of David my father, and who hath made me an house, as he [a]promised, Adonijah shall be put to death this day.

25 And king Solomon sent by the hand of Benaiah the son of Jehoiada; and he fell upon him that he died.

26 ¶ And unto Abiathar the priest said the king, Get thee to [a]Anathoth, unto thine own fields; for thou *art* [l]worthy of death: but I will not at this time put thee to death, [b]because thou barest the ark of the Lord GOD before David my father, and because [c]thou hast been afflicted in all wherein my father was afflicted.

27 So Solomon thrust out Abiathar from being priest unto the LORD; that he might [a]fulfil the word of the LORD, which he spake concerning the house of Eli in Shiloh.

28 ¶ Then tidings came to Joab: for Joab [a]had turned after Adonijah, though he turned not after Absalom. And Joab fled unto the tabernacle of the LORD, and [b]caught hold on the horns of the altar.

29 And it was told king Solomon that Joab was fled unto the tabernacle of the LORD; and, behold, *he is* by the altar. Then Solomon sent Benaiah the son of Jehoiada, saying, Go, fall upon him.

30 And Benaiah came to the tabernacle of the LORD, and said unto him, Thus saith the king, Come forth. And he said, Nay; but I will die here. And Benaiah brought the king word again, saying, Thus said Joab, and thus he answered me.

31 And the king said unto him, [a]Do as he hath said, and fall upon him, and bury him; [b]that thou mayest take away the innocent blood, which Joab shed, from me, and from the house of my father.

32 And the LORD [a]shall return his blood upon his own head, who fell upon two men more righteous [b]and better than he, and slew them with the sword, my father David not knowing *thereof, to wit,* [c]Abner the son of Ner, captain of the host of Israel, and [d]Amasa the son of Jether, captain of the host of Judah.

33 Their blood shall therefore return upon the head of Joab, and [a]upon the head of his seed for ever: [b]but upon David, and upon his seed, and upon his house, and upon his throne, shall there be peace for ever from the LORD. **H**

34 So Benaiah the son of Jehoiada went up, and fell upon him, and slew him: and he was buried in his own house in the wilderness.

35 ¶ And the king put Benaiah the son of Jehoiada in his room over the host: and [a]Zadok the priest did the king put in the room of [b]Abiathar.

36 ¶ And the king sent and called for [a]Shimei, and said unto him, Build thee an house in Jerusalem, and dwell there, and go not forth thence any whither.

37 For it shall be, *that* on the day thou goest out, and passest over [a]the brook Kidron, thou shalt know for certain that thou shalt surely die: [b]thy blood shall be upon thine own head.

38 And Shimei said unto the king, The saying *is* good: as my lord the king hath said, so will thy servant do. And Shimei dwelt in Jerusalem many days.

39 And it came to pass at the end of three years, that two of the servants of Shimei ran away unto [a]Achish son of Maachah king of Gath. And they told Shimei, saying, Behold, thy servants *be* in Gath.

40 And Shimei arose, and saddled his ass, and went to Gath to Achish to seek his servants: and Shimei went, and brought his servants from Gath.

41 And it was told Solomon that Shimei had gone from Jerusalem to Gath, and was come again.

42 And the king sent and called for Shimei, and said unto him, Did I not make thee to swear by the LORD, and protested unto thee, saying, Know for a certain, on the day thou goest out, and walkest abroad any whither, that thou shalt surely die? and thou saidst unto me, The word *that* I have heard *is* good.

43 Why then hast thou not kept the

22 [a]ch. 1:7
23 [a]Ruth 1:17
24 [a]2 Sam. 7:11, 13; 1 Chr. 22:10
26 [a]Josh. 21:18 [b]1 Sam. 23:6; 2 Sam. 15:24,29 [c]1 Sam. 22:20,23; 2 Sam. 15:24 [l]Heb. *a man of death*
27 [a]1 Sam. 2:31-35
28 [a]ch. 1:7 [b]ch. 1:50
31 [a]Ex. 21:14 [b]Num. 35:33; Deut. 19:13 & 21:8,9
32 [a]Judg. 9:24,57 [b]2 Chr. 21:13 [c]2 Sam. 3:27 [d]2 Sam. 20:10
33 [a]2 Sam. 3:29 [b]Prov. 25:5
35 [a]Num. 25:11-13; 1 Sam. 2:35; See 1 Chr. 6:53 & 24:3 [b]ver. 27
36 [a]ver. 8; 2 Sam. 16:5
37 [a]2 Sam. 15:23 [b]Lev. 20:9; Josh. 2:19; 2 Sam. 1:16
39 [a]1 Sam. 27:2

oath of the LORD, and the commandment
that I have charged thee with?
44 The king said moreover to Shimei,
Thou knowest [a]all the wickedness which
thine heart is privy to, that thou didst to
David my father: therefore the LORD shall
[b]return thy wickedness upon thine own
head;
45 And king Solomon *shall be* blessed,
and [a]the throne of David shall be established before the LORD for ever.
46 So the king commanded Benaiah
the son of Jehoiada; which went out, and
fell upon him, that he died. And the
[a]kingdom was established in the hand of
Solomon.

Prayer for wisdom granted

3 AND [a]SOLOMON made affinity with
Pharaoh king of Egypt, and took
Pharaoh's daughter, and brought her into
the [b]city of David, until he had made an
end of building his [c]own house, and [d]the
house of the LORD, and [e]the wall of Jerusalem round about.
2 [a]Only the people sacrificed in high
places, because there was no house built
unto the name of the LORD, until those
days.
3 And Solomon [a]loved the LORD, [b]walk-
ing in the statutes of David his father:
only he sacrificed and burnt incense in
high places.
4 And [a]the king went to Gibeon to sacrifice there; [b]for that *was* the great high
place: a thousand burnt offerings did Solomon offer upon that altar.
5 ¶ [a]In Gibeon the LORD appeared to
Solomon [b]in a dream by night: and God
said, Ask what I shall give thee.
6 [a]And Solomon said, Thou hast
shown unto thy servant David my father
great [1]mercy, according as he [b]walked
before thee in truth, and in righteousness, and in uprightness of heart with
thee; and thou hast kept for him this
great kindness, that thou [c]hast given him
a son to sit on his throne, as *it is* this day.
7 And now, O LORD my God, thou hast
made thy servant king instead of David
my father: and I *am but* a little child: I
know not *how* [a]to go out or come in.
8 And thy servant *is* in the midst of thy
people which thou [a]hast chosen, a great
people, [b]that cannot be numbered nor
counted for multitude.
9 [a]Give therefore thy servant an [1]un-
derstanding heart [b]to judge thy people,
that I may [c]discern between good and
bad: for who is able to judge this thy so
great a people?
10 And the speech pleased the Lord,
that Solomon had asked this thing.
11 And God said unto him, Because
thou hast asked this thing, and hast [a]not
asked for thyself [1]long life; neither hast
asked riches for thyself, nor hast asked
the life of thine enemies; but hast asked
for thyself understanding [2]to discern
judgment;
12 [a]Behold, I have done according to
thy words: [b]lo, I have given thee a wise
and an understanding heart; so that there
was none like thee before thee, neither
after thee shall any arise like unto thee.
13 And I have also [a]given thee that
which thou hast not asked, both [b]riches,
and honour: so that there [1]shall not be
any among the kings like unto thee all thy
days.
14 And if thou wilt walk in my ways,
to keep my statutes and my commandments, [a]as thy father David did walk,
then I will [b]lengthen thy days.
15 And Solomon [a]awoke; and, behold,
it was a dream. And he came to Jerusalem, and stood before the ark of the covenant of the LORD, and offered up burnt
offerings, and offered peace offerings, and
[b]made a feast to all his servants.

Solomon's wise decision

16 ¶ Then came there two women,
that were harlots, unto the king, and
[a]stood before him.
17 And the one woman said, O my
lord, I and this woman dwell in one
house; and I was delivered of a child with
her in the house.
18 And it came to pass the third day
after that I was delivered, that this

44 [a]2 Sam. 16:5 [b]Ezek. 17:19
45 [a]Prov. 25:5
46 [a]ver. 12; 2 Chr. 1:1
3:1 [a]ch. 7:8 & 9:24 [b]2 Sam. 5:7 [c]ch. 7:1 [d]ch. 6 [e]ch. 9:15,19
2 [a]Lev. 17:3-5; Deut. 12:2,4,5; ch. 22:43
3 [a]Deut. 6:5 & 30:16,20; Rom. 8:28; 1 Cor. 8:3 [b]ver. 6,14
4 [a]2 Chr. 1:3 [b]1 Chr. 16:39; 2 Chr. 1:3
5 [a]ch. 9:2; 2 Chr. 1:7 [b]Num. 12:6; Mat. 1:20
6 [a]2 Chr. 1:8 [b]ch. 2:4 & 9:4; 2 Ki. 20:3 [c]ch. 1:48 [1]Or, *bounty*
7 [a]Num. 27:17
8 [a]Deut. 7:6 [b]Gen. 13:16 & 15:5
9 [a]2 Chr. 1:10; Prov. 2:3-9; Jas. 1:5 [b]Ps. 72:1,2 [c]Heb. 5:14 [1]Heb. *hearing*
11 [a]Jas. 4:3 [1]Heb. *many days* [2]Heb. *to hear*
12 [a]1 John 5:14,15 [b]ch. 4:29-31; Eccl. 1:16
13 [a]Mat. 6:33; Eph. 3:20 [b]ch. 4:21,24 [1]Or, *hath not been*
14 [a]ch. 15:5 [b]Ps. 91:16; Prov. 3:2
15 [a]Gen. 41:7 [b]Gen. 40:20; ch. 8:65; Esth. 1:3; Dan. 5:1; Mark 6:21
16 [a]Num. 27:2

M *2Sa 23:3–5* ◀ ▶ *1Ch 16:30–33*
U *2Sa 22:20–21* ◀ ▶ *1Ki 3:13–14*

P *1Sa 2:7–8* ◀ ▶ *1Ch 29:12*
U *1Ki 3:6* ◀ ▶ *1Ch 4:10*
H *Dt 33:25* ◀ ▶ *1Ki 8:37–39*

2:45 Solomon reiterates the promise that the "throne of David" would continue forever.

woman was delivered also: and we *were*
together; *there was* no stranger with us
in the house, save we two in the house.
19 And this woman's child died in the
night; because she overlaid it.
20 And she arose at midnight, and
took my son from beside me, while thine
handmaid slept, and laid it in her bosom,
and laid her dead child in my bosom.
21 And when I rose in the morning to
give my child suck, behold, it was dead:
but when I had considered it in the
morning, behold, it was not my son,
which I did bear.
22 And the other woman said, Nay;
but the living *is* my son, and the dead *is*
thy son. And this said, No; but the dead *is*
thy son, and the living *is* my son. Thus
they spake before the king.
23 Then said the king, The one saith,
This *is* my son that liveth, and thy son *is*
the dead: and the other saith, Nay; but
thy son *is* the dead, and my son *is* the
living.
24 And the king said, Bring me a
sword. And they brought a sword before
the king.
25 And the king said, Divide the living
child in two, and give half to the one, and
half to the other.
26 Then spake the woman whose the
living child *was* unto the king, for [a]her
bowels [1]yearned upon her son, and she
said, O my lord, give her the living child,
and in no wise slay it. But the other said,
Let it be neither mine nor thine, *but* divide *it.*
27 Then the king answered and said,
Give her the living child, and in no wise
slay it: she *is* the mother thereof.
28 And all Israel heard of the judgment
which the king had judged; and they
feared the king: for they saw that the
[a]wisdom of God *was* [1]in him, to do
judgment.

Appointment of court officials

4 SO KING Solomon was king over all
Israel.
2 And these *were* the princes which
he had; Azariah the son of Zadok [1]the
priest,
3 Elihoreph and Ahiah, the sons of Shisha, [1]scribes; [a]Jehoshaphat the son of
Ahilud, the [2]recorder.
4 And [a]Benaiah the son of Jehoiada
was over the host: and Zadok and [b]Abia-
thar *were* the priests:
5 And Azariah the son of Nathan *was*
over [a]the officers: and Zabud the son of
Nathan *was* [b]principal officer, *and* [c]the
king's friend:
6 And Ahishar *was* over the household: and [a]Adoniram the son of Abda *was*
over the [1]tribute.
7 ¶ And Solomon had twelve officers
over all Israel, which provided victuals
for the king and his household: each man
his month in a year made provision.
8 And these *are* their names: [1]The son
of Hur, in mount Ephraim:
9 [1]The son of Dekar, in Makaz, and in
Shaalbim, and Beth-shemesh, and Elon-
beth-hanan:
10 [1]The son of Hesed, in Aruboth; to
him *pertained* Sochoh, and all the land of
Hepher:
11 [1]The son of Abinadab, in all the region of Dor; which had Taphath the
daughter of Solomon to wife:
12 Baana the son of Ahilud; *to him
pertained* Taanach and Megiddo, and all
Beth-shean, which *is* by Zartanah beneath Jezreel, from Beth-shean to Abel-
meholah, *even* unto *the place that is* beyond Jokneam:
13 [1]The son of Geber, in Ramoth-gilead; to him *pertained* [a]the towns of Jair
the son of Manasseh, which *are* in Gilead; to him *also pertained* [b]the region of
Argob, which *is* in Bashan, threescore
great cities with walls and brasen bars:
14 Ahinadab the son of Iddo *had* [1]Ma-
hanaim:
15 Ahimaaz *was* in Naphtali; he also
took Basmath the daughter of Solomon to
wife:
16 Baanah the son of Hushai *was* in
Asher and in Aloth:
17 Jehoshaphat the son of Paruah, in
Issachar:
18 Shimei the son of Elah, in Benjamin:
19 Geber the son of Uri *was* in the
country of Gilead, *in* [a]the country of Sihon king of the Amorites, and of Og king
of Bashan; and *he was* the only officer
which *was* in the land.
20 ¶ Judah and Israel *were* many, [a]as
the sand which *is* by the sea in multitude,
[b]eating and drinking, and making merry.
21 And [a]Solomon reigned over all
kingdoms from [b]the river unto the land of

26 [a]Gen. 43:30; Is. 49:15; Jer. 31:20; Hos. 11:8 [1]Heb. *were hot*
28 [a]ver. 9,11,12 [1]Heb. *in the midst of him*
4:2 [1]Or, *the chief officer*
3 [a]2 Sam. 8:16 & 20:24 [1]Or, *secretaries* [2]Or, *remembrancer*
4 [a]ch. 2:35 [b]See ch. 2:27
5 [a]ver. 7 [b]2 Sam. 8:18 & 20:26 [c]2 Sam. 15:37 & 16:16; 1 Chr. 27:33
6 [a]ch. 5:14 [1]Or, *levy*
8 [1]Or, *Ben-hur*
9 [1]Or, *Ben-dekar*
10 [1]Or, *Ben-hesed*
11 [1]Or, *Ben-abinadab*
13 [a]Num. 32:41 [b]Deut. 3:4 [1]Or, *Ben-geber*
14 [1]Or, *to Mahanaim*
19 [a]Deut. 3:8
20 [a]Gen. 22:17; ch. 3:8; Prov. 14:28 [b]Ps. 72:3,7; Mic. 4:4
21 [a]2 Chr. 9:26; Ps. 72:8 [b]Gen. 15:18; Josh. 1:4

the Philistines, and unto the border of Egypt: [c]they brought presents, and served Solomon all the days of his life.

The household provisions

22 ¶ And Solomon's [1]provision for one day was thirty [2]measures of fine flour, and threescore measures of meal,

23 Ten fat oxen, and twenty oxen out of the pastures, and an hundred sheep, beside harts, and roebucks, and fallowdeer, and fatted fowl.

24 For he had dominion over all *the region* on this side the river, from Tiphsah even to Azzah, over [a]all the kings on this side the river: and [b]he had peace on all sides round about him.

25 And Judah and Israel [a]dwelt [1]safely, [b]every man under his vine and under his fig tree, [c]from Dan even to Beer-sheba, all the days of Solomon.

26 ¶ And [a]Solomon had forty thousand stalls of [b]horses for his chariots, and twelve thousand horsemen.

27 And [a]those officers provided victual for king Solomon, and for all that came unto king Solomon's table, every man in his month: they lacked nothing.

28 Barley also and straw for the horses and [1]dromedaries brought they unto the place where *the officers* were, every man according to his charge.

Solomon's great wisdom

29 ¶ And [a]God gave Solomon wisdom and understanding exceeding much, and largeness of heart, even as the sand that *is* on the sea shore.

30 And Solomon's wisdom excelled the wisdom of all the children [a]of the east country, and all [b]the wisdom of Egypt.

31 For he was [a]wiser than all men; [b]than Ethan the Ezrahite, [c]and Heman, and Chalcol, and Darda, the sons of Mahol: and his fame was in all nations round about.

32 And [a]he spake three thousand proverbs: and his [b]songs were a thousand and five.

33 And he spake of trees, from the cedar tree that *is* in Lebanon even unto the hyssop that springeth out of the wall: he spake also of beasts, and of fowl, and of creeping things, and of fishes.

34 And [a]there came of all people to hear the wisdom of Solomon, from all kings of the earth, which had heard of his wisdom.

Preparing to build the temple

5 AND [a]HIRAM king of Tyre sent his servants unto Solomon; for he had heard that they had anointed him king in the room of his father: [b]for Hiram was ever a lover of David.

2 And [a]Solomon sent to Hiram, saying,

3 Thou knowest how that David my father could not build an house unto the name of the LORD his God [a]for the wars which were about him on every side, until the LORD put them under the soles of his feet.

4 But now the LORD my God hath given me [a]rest on every side, *so that there is* neither adversary nor evil occurrent.

5 [a]And, behold, I [1]purpose to build an house unto the name of the LORD my God, [b]as the LORD spake unto David my father, saying, Thy son, whom I will set upon thy throne in thy room, he shall build an house unto my name.

6 Now therefore command thou that they hew me [a]cedar trees out of Lebanon; and my servants shall be with thy servants: and unto thee will I give hire for thy servants according to all that thou shalt [1]appoint: for thou knowest that *there is* not among us any that can skill to hew timber like unto the Sidonians.

7 ¶ And it came to pass, when Hiram heard the words of Solomon, that he rejoiced greatly, and said, Blessed *be* the LORD this day, which hath given unto David a wise son over this great people.

8 And Hiram sent to Solomon, saying, I have [1]considered the things which thou sentest to me for: *and* I will do all thy desire concerning timber of cedar, and concerning timber of fir.

9 My servants shall bring *them* down from Lebanon unto the sea: and I will convey them by sea in floats unto the place that thou shalt [1]appoint me, and

1Ki 2:4 ◀▶ 1Ki 9:3

21 [c]Ps. 68:29 & 72:10,11
22 [1]Heb. *bread* [2]Heb. *cors*
24 [a]Ps. 72:11 [b]1 Chr. 22:9
25 [a]See Jer. 23:6 [b]Mic. 4:4; Zech. 3:10 [c]Judg. 20:1 [1]Heb. *confidently*
26 [a]ch. 10:26; 2 Chr. 1:14 [b]See Deut. 17:16
27 [a]ver. 7
28 [1]Or, *mules*, or, *swift beasts*
29 [a]ch. 3:12
30 [a]Gen. 25:6 [b]See Acts 7:22
31 [a]ch. 3:12 [b]1 Chr. 15:19; Ps. 89,title [c]See 1 Chr. 2:6 & 6:33 & 15:19; Ps. 88,title
32 [a]Prov. 1:1; Eccl. 12:9 [b]Sol. 1:1
34 [a]ch. 10:1; 2 Chr. 9:1,23
5:1 [a]ver. 10,18; 2 Chr. 2:3 *Huram* [b]2 Sam. 5:11; 1 Chr. 14:1; Amos 1:9
2 [a]2 Chr. 2:3
3 [a]1 Chr. 22:8 & 28:3
4 [a]ch. 4:24; 1 Chr. 22:9
5 [a]2 Chr. 2:4 [b]2 Sam. 7:13; 1 Chr. 17:12 [1]Heb. *say*
6 [a]2 Chr. 2:8,10 [1]Heb. *say*
8 [1]Heb. *heard*
9 [1]Heb. *send*

5:5 Solomon confirms the promise God made to David, that his son would build God's temple (see 2Sa 7:13; 1Ch 17:12).

will cause them to be discharged there, and thou shalt receive *them:* and thou shalt accomplish my desire, [a]in giving food for my household.

10 So Hiram gave Solomon cedar trees and fir trees *according to* all his desire.

11 [a]And Solomon gave Hiram twenty thousand [1]measures of wheat *for* food to his household, and twenty measures of pure oil: thus gave Solomon to Hiram year by year.

12 And the LORD gave Solomon wisdom, [a]as he promised him: and there was peace between Hiram and Solomon; and they two made a league together.

13 ¶ And king Solomon raised a [1]levy out of all Israel; and the levy was thirty thousand men.

14 And he sent them to Lebanon, ten thousand a month by courses: a month they were in Lebanon, *and* two months at home: and [a]Adoniram *was* over the levy.

15 [a]And Solomon had threescore and ten thousand that bare burdens, and fourscore thousand hewers in the mountains;

16 Beside the chief of Solomon's officers which *were* over the work, three thousand and three hundred, which ruled over the people that wrought in the work.

17 And the king commanded, and they brought great stones, costly stones, *and* [a]hewed stones, to lay the foundation of the house.

18 And Solomon's builders and Hiram's builders did hew *them,* and the [1]stonesquarers: so they prepared timber and stones to build the house.

The description of the temple

6 AND [a]IT came to pass in the four hundred and eightieth year after the children of Israel were come out of the land of Egypt, in the fourth year of Solomon's reign over Israel, in the month Zif, which *is* the second month, that [b]he [1]began to build the house of the LORD.

2 And [a]the house which king Solomon built for the LORD, the length thereof *was* threescore cubits, and the breadth thereof twenty *cubits,* and the height thereof thirty cubits.

3 And the porch before the temple of the house, twenty cubits *was* the length thereof, according to the breadth of the house; *and* ten cubits *was* the breadth thereof before the house.

4 And for the house he made [a]windows[1] of narrow lights.

5 ¶ And [1]against the wall of the house he built [a]chambers[2] round about, *against* the walls of the house round about, *both* of the temple [b]and of the oracle: and he made [3]chambers round about:

6 The nethermost chamber *was* five cubits broad, and the middle *was* six cubits broad, and the third *was* seven cubits broad: for without *in the wall* of the house he made [1]narrowed rests round about, that *the beams* should not be fastened in the walls of the house.

7 And [a]the house, when it was in building, was built of stone made ready before it was brought thither: so that there was neither hammer nor axe *nor* any tool of iron heard in the house, while it was in building.

8 The door for the middle chamber *was* in the right [1]side of the house: and they went up with winding stairs into the middle *chamber,* and out of the middle into the third.

9 [a]So he built the house, and finished it; and covered the house [1]with beams and boards of cedar.

10 And *then* he built chambers against all the house, five cubits high: and they rested on the house with timber of cedar.

11 ¶ And the word of the LORD came to Solomon, saying,

12 *Concerning* this house which thou art in building, [a]if thou wilt walk in my statutes, and execute my judgments, and keep all my commandments to walk in them; then will I perform my word with thee, [b]which I spake unto David thy father:

13 And I [a]will dwell among the children of Israel, and will not [b]forsake my people Israel.

14 So Solomon built the house, and finished it.

15 And he built the walls of the house within with boards of cedar, [1]both the floor of the house, and the walls of the ceiling: *and* he covered *them* on the inside with wood, and covered the floor of the house with planks of fir.

16 And he built twenty cubits on the sides of the house, both the floor and the

9 [a]See Ezra 3:7; Ezek. 27:17; Acts 12:20
11 [a]See 2 Chr. 2:10 [1]Heb. *cors*
12 [a]ch. 3:12
13 [1]Heb. *tribute of men*
14 [a]ch. 4:6
15 [a]ch. 9:21; 2 Chr. 2:18
17 [a]1 Chr. 22:2
18 [1]Or, *Giblites* as Ezek. 27:9
6:1 [a]2 Chr. 3:1,2 [b]Acts 7:47 [1]Heb. *built*
2 [a]See Ezek. 41:1
4 [a]See Ezek. 40:16 [1]Or, *windows broad* within, and *narrow* without: or, *skewed* and *closed*
5 [a]See Ezek. 41:6 [b]ver. 16,19-21,31 [1]Or, *upon,* or, *joining to* [2]Heb. *floors* [3]Heb. *ribs*
6 [1]Heb. *narrowings,* or, *rebatements*
7 [a]See Deut. 27:5,6
8 [1]Heb. *shoulder*
9 [a]ver. 14,38 [1]Or, *the vault-beams and the ceilings with cedar*
12 [a]ch. 2:4 & 9:4 [b]2 Sam. 7:13; 1 Chr. 22:10
13 [a]Ex. 25:8; 2 Cor. 6:16; Rev. 21:3 [b]Deut. 31:6
15 [1]Or, *from the floor of the house unto the walls*

walls with boards of cedar: he even built
them for it within, *even* for the oracle,
even for the [a]most holy *place.*
17 And the house, that *is,* the temple
before it, was forty cubits *long.*
18 And the cedar of the house within
was carved with [1]knobs and [2]open flowers: all *was* cedar; there was no stone
seen.
19 And the oracle he prepared in the
house within, to set there the ark of the
covenant of the LORD.
20 And the oracle in the forepart *was*
twenty cubits in length, and twenty cubits in breadth, and twenty cubits in the
height thereof: and he overlaid it with
[1]pure gold; and *so* covered the altar
which was of cedar.
21 So Solomon overlaid the house
within with pure gold: and he made a
partition by the chains of gold before the
oracle; and he overlaid it with gold.
22 And the whole house he overlaid
with gold, until he had finished all the
house: also [a]the whole altar that *was* by
the oracle he overlaid with gold.
23 ¶ And within the oracle [a]he made
two cherubims *of* [1,2]olive tree, *each* ten
cubits high.
24 And five cubits *was* the one wing
of the cherub, and five cubits the other
wing of the cherub: from the uttermost
part of the one wing unto the uttermost
part of the other *were* ten cubits.
25 And the other cherub *was* ten cubits: both the cherubims *were* of one
measure and one size.
26 The height of the one cherub *was*
ten cubits, and so *was it* of the other
cherub.

16 [a]Ex. 26:33; Lev. 16:2; ch. 8:6; 2 Chr. 3:8; Ezek. 45:3

18 [1]Or, *goards* [2]Heb. *openings of flowers*

20 [1]Heb. *shut up*

22 [a]Ex. 30:1,3,6

23 [a]Ex. 37:7-9; 2 Chr. 3:10-12 [1]Or, *oily* [2]Heb. *trees of oil*

Solomon's Temple

960–586 B.C.

Temple source materials are subject to academic interpretation, and subsequent art reconstructions vary.

This reconstruction recognizes influence from the desert tabernacle, accepts general Near Eastern cultural diffusion, and rejects overt pagan Canaanite symbols. It uses known archaeological parallels to supplement the text, and assumes interior dimensions from 1 Ki 6:17-20.

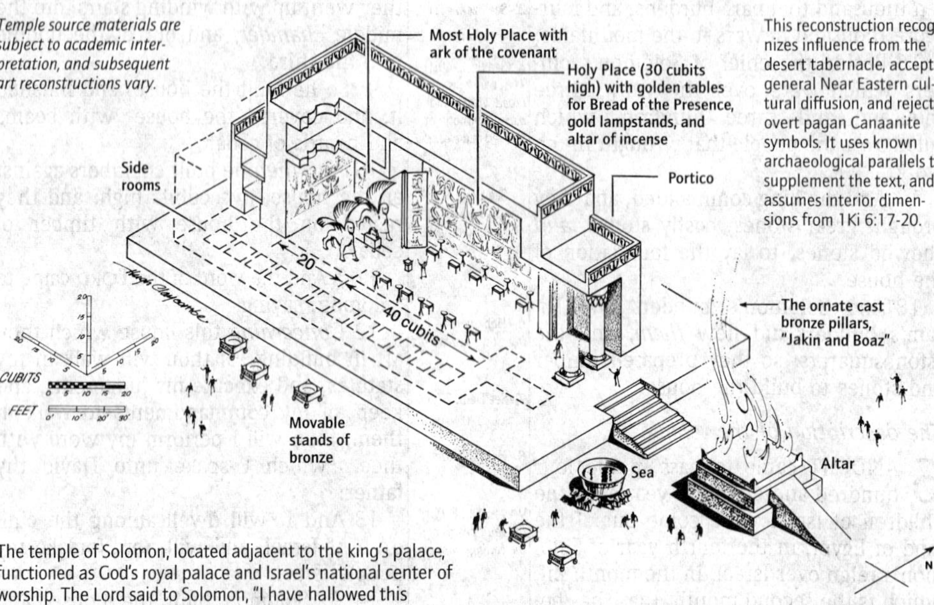

©1986 Hugh Claycombe

The temple of Solomon, located adjacent to the king's palace, functioned as God's royal palace and Israel's national center of worship. The Lord said to Solomon, "I have hallowed this house… to put my name there for ever; and mine eyes and mine heart shall be there perpetually" (1 Ki 9:3). By its cosmological and royal symbolism, the sanctuary taught the absolute sovereignty of the Lord over the whole creation and his special headship over Israel.

The floor plan is a type that has a long history in Semitic religion, particularly among the West Semites. An early example of the tripartite division into *'ulam*, *hekal*, and *debir* (portico, main hall, and inner sanctuary) has been found at Syrian Ebla (c. 2300 B.C.) and, much later but more contemporaneous with Solomon, at Tell Tainat in the Orontes basin (c. 900 B.C.). Like Solomon's, the later temple has three divisions, contains two columns supporting the entrance, and is located adjacent to the royal palace.

Many archaeological parallels can be drawn to the methods of construction used in the temple, e.g., the "stone and cedar beam" technique described in 1 Ki 6:36. Interestingly, evidence for the largest bronze-casting industry ever found in Palestine comes from the same locale and period as that indicated in Scripture: Zarethan in the Jordan Valley c. 1000 B.C.

27 And he set the cherubims within
the inner house: and [a]they[1] stretched
forth the wings of the cherubims, so that
the wing of the one touched the *one* wall,
and the wing of the other cherub touched
the other wall; and their wings touched
one another in the midst of the house.
28 And he overlaid the cherubims
with gold.
29 And he carved all the walls of the
house round about with carved figures of
cherubims and palm trees and [1]open
flowers, within and without.
30 And the floor of the house he overlaid with gold, within and without.
31 ¶ And for the entering of the oracle
he made doors *of* olive tree: the lintel
and side posts *were* [1]a fifth part *of the
wall.*
32 The [1]two doors also *were of* olive
tree; and he carved upon them carvings
of cherubims and palm trees and [2]open
flowers, and overlaid *them* with gold, and
spread gold upon the cherubims, and
upon the palm trees.
33 So also made he for the door of the
temple posts *of* olive tree, [1]a fourth part
of the wall.
34 And the two doors *were of* fir tree:
the [a]two leaves of the one door *were* folding, and the two leaves of the other door
were folding.
35 And he carved *thereon* cherubims
and palm trees and open flowers: and
covered *them* with gold fitted upon the
carved work.
36 ¶ And he built the inner court with
three rows of hewed stone, and a row of
cedar beams.
37 ¶ [a]In the fourth year was the foundation of the house of the LORD laid, in
the month Zif:
38 And in the eleventh year, in the
month Bul, which *is* the eighth month,
was the house finished [1]throughout all
the parts thereof, and according to all the
fashion of it. So was he [a]seven years in
building it.

The palace buildings

7 BUT SOLOMON was building his
own house [a]thirteen years, and he
finished all his house.
2 ¶ He built also the house of the forest
of Lebanon; the length thereof *was* an
hundred cubits, and the breadth thereof
fifty cubits, and the height thereof thirty
cubits, upon four rows of cedar pillars,
with cedar beams upon the pillars.
3 And *it was* covered with cedar above
upon the [1]beams, that *lay* on forty-five
pillars, fifteen *in* a row.
4 And *there were* windows *in* three
rows, and [1]light *was* against light *in* three
ranks.
5 And all the [1]doors and posts *were*
square, with the windows: and light *was*
against light *in* three ranks.
6 ¶ And he made a porch of pillars;
the length thereof *was* fifty cubits, and the
breadth thereof thirty cubits: and the
porch *was* [1]before them: and the *other*
pillars and the thick beam *were* [1]before
them.
7 ¶ Then he made a porch for the
throne where he might judge, *even* the
porch of judgment: and *it was* covered
with cedar [1]from one side of the floor to
the other.
8 ¶ And his house where he dwelt *had*
another court within the porch, *which*
was of the like work. Solomon made also
an house for Pharaoh's daughter, [a]whom
he had taken *to wife,* like unto this
porch.
9 All these *were of* costly stones, according to the measures of hewed stones,
sawed with saws, within and without,
even from the foundation unto the cop-
ing, and *so* on the outside toward the
great court.
10 And the foundation *was of* costly
stones, even great stones, stones of ten
cubits, and stones of eight cubits.
11 And above *were* costly stones, after
the measures of hewed stones, and
cedars.
12 And the great court round about
was with three rows of hewed stones,
and a row of cedar beams, both for the
inner court of the house of the LORD, [a]and
for the porch of the house.

The temple furnishings

13 ¶ And king Solomon sent and
fetched [a]Hiram out of Tyre.
14 [a]He *was* [1]a widow's son of the tribe
of Naphtali, and [b]his father *was* a man of
Tyre, a worker in brass: and [c]he was
filled with wisdom, and understanding,
and cunning to work all works in brass.
And he came to king Solomon, and
wrought all his work.
15 For he [1]cast [a]two pillars of brass, of

27 [a]Ex. 25:20 & 37:9; 2 Chr. 5:8 [1]Or, *the cherubims stretched forth their wings*
29 [1]Heb. *openings of flowers*
31 [1]Or, *fivesquare*
32 [1]Or, *leaves of the doors* [2]Heb. *openings of flowers*
33 [1]Or, *foursquare*
34 [a]Ezek. 41:23-25
37 [a]ver. 1
38 [a]Compare ver. 1 [1]Or, *with all the appurtenances thereof, and with all the ordinances thereof*
7:1 [a]ch. 9:10; 2 Chr. 8:1
3 [1]Heb. *ribs*
4 [1]Heb. *sight against sight*
5 [1]Or, *spaces and pillars were square in prospect*
6 [1]Or, *according to them*
7 [1]Heb. *from floor to floor*
8 [a]ch. 3:1; 2 Chr. 8:11
12 [a]John 10:23; Acts 3:11
13 [a]2 Chr. 4:11; *Huram:* See ver. 40
14 [a]2 Chr. 2:14 [b]2 Chr. 4:16 [c]Ex. 31:3 & 36:1 [1]Heb. *the son of a widow woman*
15 [a]2 Ki. 25:17; 2 Chr. 3:15 & 4:12; Jer. 52:21 [1]Heb. *fashioned*

eighteen cubits high apiece: and a line of
twelve cubits did compass either of them
about.
16 And he made two chapiters *of* molten brass, to set upon the tops of the pillars: the height of the one chapiter *was*
five cubits, and the height of the other
chapiter *was* five cubits:
17 *And* nets of checker work, and
wreaths of chain work, for the chapiters
which *were* upon the top of the pillars;
seven for the one chapiter, and seven for
the other chapiter.
18 And he made the pillars, and two
rows round about upon the one network,
to cover the chapiters that *were* upon the
top, with pomegranates: and so did he for
the other chapiter.
19 And the chapiters that *were* upon
the top of the pillars *were* of lily work in
the porch, four cubits.
20 And the chapiters upon the two pillars *had pomegranates* also above, over
against the belly which *was* by the network: and the pomegranates *were* [a]two
hundred in rows round about upon the
other chapiter.
21 [a]And he set up the pillars in the
porch of the temple: and he set up the
right pillar, and called the name thereof
[1]Jachin: and he set up the left pillar, and
called the name thereof [2]Boaz.
22 And upon the top of the pillars *was*
lily work: so was the work of the pillars
finished.
23 ¶ And he made [a]a molten sea, ten
cubits [1]from the one brim to the other: *it*
was round all about, and his height *was*
five cubits: and a line of thirty cubits did
compass it round about.
24 And under the brim of it round
about *there were* knobs compassing it,
ten in a cubit, [a]compassing the sea round
about: the knobs *were* cast in two rows,
when it was cast.
25 It stood upon [a]twelve oxen, three
looking toward the north, and three looking toward the west, and three looking
toward the south, and three looking toward the east: and the sea *was set* above
upon them, and all their hinder parts
were inward.
26 And it *was* an handbreadth thick,
and the brim thereof was wrought like
the brim of a cup, with flowers of lilies: it
contained [a]two thousand baths.
27 ¶ And he made ten bases of brass;

20 [a]See 2 Chr. 3:16 & 4:13; Jer. 52:23
21 [a]2 Chr. 3:17 [1]i.e. *He shall establish* [2]i.e. *In it is strength*
23 [a]2 Ki. 25:13; 2 Chr. 4:2; Jer. 52:17 [1]Heb. *from his brim to his brim*
24 [a]2 Chr. 4:3
25 [a]2 Chr. 4:4,5; Jer. 52:20
26 [a]See 2 Chr. 4:5
29 [a]Gen. 3:24; ch. 6:27; Ps. 18:10; Ezek. 1:10 & 41:18,19; Rev. 4:6-8
32 [1]Heb. *in the base*
36 [1]Heb. *nakedness*
38 [a]2 Chr. 4:6
39 [1]Heb. *shoulder*
40 [1]Heb. *Hirom;* see ver. 13

four cubits *was* the length of one base,
and four cubits the breadth thereof, and
three cubits the height of it.
28 And the work of the bases *was* on
this *manner:* they had borders, and the
borders *were* between the ledges:
29 And on the borders that *were* between the ledges *were* [a]lions, oxen, and
cherubims: and upon the ledges *there*
was a base above: and beneath the lions
and oxen *were* certain additions made of
thin work.
30 And every base had four brasen
wheels, and plates of brass: and the four
corners thereof had undersetters: under
the laver *were* undersetters molten, at
the side of every addition.
31 And the mouth of it within the
chapiter and above *was* a cubit: but the
mouth thereof *was* round *after* the work
of the base, a cubit and an half: and also
upon the mouth of it *were* gravings with
their borders, foursquare, not round.
32 And under the borders *were* four
wheels; and the axletrees of the wheels
were [1]*joined* to the base: and the height
of a wheel *was* a cubit and half a cubit.
33 And the work of the wheels *was*
like the work of a chariot wheel: their
axletrees, and their naves, and their
felloes, and their spokes, *were* all molten.
34 And *there were* four undersetters to
the four corners of one base: *and* the undersetters *were* of the very base itself.
35 And in the top of the base *was*
there a round compass of half a cubit
high: and on the top of the base the
ledges thereof and the borders thereof
were of the same.
36 For on the plates of the ledges
thereof, and on the borders thereof, he
graved cherubims, lions, and palm trees,
according to the [1]proportion of every
one, and additions round about.
37 After this *manner* he made the ten
bases: all of them had one casting, one
measure, *and* one size.
38 ¶ Then [a]made he ten lavers of
brass: one laver contained forty baths:
and every laver was four cubits: *and* upon
every one of the ten bases one laver.
39 And he put five bases on the right
[1]side of the house, and five on the left
side of the house: and he set the sea on
the right side of the house eastward over
against the south.
40 ¶ And [1]Hiram made the lavers, and

the shovels, and the basins. So Hiram made an end of doing all the work that he made king Solomon for the house of the LORD:

41 The two pillars, and the *two* bowls of the chapiters that *were* on the top of the two pillars; and the two [a]networks, to cover the two bowls of the chapiters which *were* upon the top of the pillars;

42 And four hundred pomegranates for the two networks, *even* two rows of pomegranates for one network, to cover the two bowls of the chapiters that *were* [l]upon the pillars;

43 And the ten bases, and ten lavers on the bases;

44 And one sea, and twelve oxen under the sea;

45 [a]And the pots, and the shovels, and the basins: and all these vessels, which Hiram made to king Solomon for the house of the LORD, *were of* [l]bright brass.

46 [a]In the plain of Jordan did the king cast them, [l]in the clay ground between [b]Succoth and [c]Zarthan.

47 And Solomon left all the vessels *unweighed,* [l]because they were exceeding many: neither was the weight of the brass [a]found[2] out.

48 And Solomon made all the vessels that *pertained* unto the house of the LORD: [a]the altar of gold, and [b]the table of gold, whereupon [c]the showbread *was,*

49 And the candlesticks of pure gold, five on the right *side,* and five on the left, before the oracle, with the flowers, and the lamps, and the tongs *of* gold,

50 And the bowls, and the snuffers, and the basins, and the spoons, and the [l]censers *of* pure gold; and the hinges *of* gold, *both* for the doors of the inner house, the most holy *place, and* for the doors of the house, *to wit,* of the temple.

51 So was ended all the work that king Solomon made for the house of the LORD. And Solomon brought in the [l]things [a]which David his father had dedicated; *even* the silver, and the gold, and the vessels, did he put among the treasures of the house of the LORD.

The ark brought to the temple

8 THEN [a]SOLOMON assembled the elders of Israel, and all the heads of the tribes, the [l]chief of the fathers of the children of Israel, unto king Solomon in Jerusalem, [b]that they might bring up the ark of the covenant of the LORD [c]out of the city of David, which *is* Zion.

2 And all the men of Israel assembled themselves unto king Solomon at the [a]feast in the month Ethanim, which *is* the seventh month.

3 And all the elders of Israel came, [a]and the priests took up the ark.

4 And they brought up the ark of the LORD, [a]and the tabernacle of the congregation, and all the holy vessels that *were* in the tabernacle, even those did the priests and the Levites bring up.

5 And king Solomon, and all the congregation of Israel, that were assembled unto him, *were* with him before the ark, [a]sacrificing sheep and oxen, that could not be told nor numbered for multitude.

6 And the priests [a]brought in the ark of the covenant of the LORD unto [b]his place, into the oracle of the house, to the most holy *place, even* [c]under the wings of the cherubims.

7 For the cherubims spread forth *their* two wings over the place of the ark, and the cherubims covered the ark and the staves thereof above.

8 And they [a]drew out the staves, that the [l]ends of the staves were seen out in the [2]holy *place* before the oracle, and they were not seen without: and there they are unto this day.

9 [a]*There was* nothing in the ark [b]save the two tables of stone, which Moses [c]put there at Horeb, [d]when[l] the LORD made *a covenant* with the children of Israel, when they came out of the land of Egypt.

10 And it came to pass, when the priests were come out of the holy *place,* that the cloud [a]filled the house of the LORD,

11 So that the priests could not stand to minister because of the cloud: for the glory of the LORD had filled the house of the LORD.

12 ¶ [a]Then spake Solomon, The LORD said that he would dwell [b]in the thick darkness.

13 [a]I have surely built thee an house to dwell in, [b]a settled place for thee to abide in for ever.

14 And the king turned his face about, and [a]blessed all the congregation of Israel: (and all the congregation of Israel stood;)

15 And he said, [a]Blessed *be* the LORD

41 [a]ver. 17,18
42 [l]Heb. *upon the face of the pillars*
45 [a]Ex. 27:3; 2 Chr. 4:16 [l]Heb. *made bright,* or, *scoured*
46 [a]2 Chr. 4:17 [b]Gen. 33:17 [c]Josh. 3:16 [l]Heb. *in the thickness of the ground*
47 [a]1 Chr. 22:14 [l]Heb. *for the exceeding multitude* [2]Heb. *searched*
48 [a]Ex. 37:25 [b]Ex. 37:10 [c]Lev. 24:5-8
50 [l]Heb. *ash pans*
51 [a]2 Sam. 8:11 [l]Heb. *holy things of David*
8:1 [a]2 Chr. 5:2 [b]2 Sam. 6:17 [c]2 Sam. 5:7 & 6:12,16 [l]Heb. *princes*
2 [a]Lev. 23:34; 2 Chr. 7:8
3 [a]Num. 4:15
4 [a]2 Chr. 1:3
5 [a]2 Sam. 6:13
6 [a]2 Sam. 6:17 [b]Ex. 26:33,34; ch. 6:19 [c]ch. 6:27
8 [a]Ex. 25:14 [l]Heb. *heads* [2]Or, *ark as* 2 Chr. 5:9
9 [a]Ex. 25:21; Deut. 10:2 [b]Deut. 10:5; Heb. 9:4 [c]Ex. 40:20 [d]Ex. 34:27, 28 [l]Or, *where*
10 [a]Ex. 40:34
12 [a]2 Chr. 6:1 [b]Ps. 18:11
13 [a]2 Sam. 7:13 [b]Ps. 132:14
14 [a]2 Sam. 6:18
15 [a]Luke 1:68

God of Israel, which [b]spake with his
mouth unto David my father, and hath
with his hand fulfilled *it,* saying,
16 Since the day that I brought forth
my people Israel out of Egypt, I chose no
city out of all the tribes of Israel to build
an house, that [a]my name might be
therein; but I chose [b]David to be over my
people Israel.
17 And [a]it was in the heart of David
my father to build an house for the name
of the LORD God of Israel.
18 [a]And the LORD said unto David my
father, Whereas it was in thine heart to
build an house unto my name, thou didst
well that it was in thine heart.
19 Nevertheless [a]thou shalt not build
the house; but thy son that shall come
forth out of thy loins, he shall build the
house unto my name.
20 And the LORD hath performed his
word that he spake, and I am risen up in
the room of David my father, and sit on
the throne of Israel, [a]as the LORD promised, and have built an house for the
name of the LORD God of Israel.
21 And I have set there a place for the
ark, wherein *is* [a]the covenant of the LORD,
which he made with our fathers, when
he brought them out of the land of Egypt.

Solomon's prayer of dedication

22 ¶ And Solomon stood before [a]the
altar of the LORD in the presence of all the
congregation of Israel, and [b]spread forth
his hands toward heaven:
23 And he said, LORD God of Israel,
[a]*there is* no God like thee, in heaven
above, or on earth beneath, [b]who keepest
covenant and mercy with thy servants
that [c]walk before thee with all their
heart:
24 Who hast kept with thy servant David my father that thou promisedst him:
thou spakest also with thy mouth, and
hast fulfilled *it* with thine hand, as *it is*
this day.
25 Therefore now, LORD God of Israel,
keep with thy servant David my father
that thou promisedst him, saying,
[a]There[1] shall not fail thee a man in my
sight to sit on the throne of Israel; [2]so
that thy children take heed to their way,
that they walk before me as thou hast
walked before me.
26 [a]And now, O God of Israel, let thy
word, I pray thee, be verified, which thou
spakest unto thy servant David my father.
27 But [a]will God indeed dwell on the
earth? behold, the heaven and [b]heaven of
heavens cannot contain thee; how much
less this house that I have builded?
28 Yet have thou respect unto the
prayer of thy servant, and to his supplication, O LORD my God, to hearken unto the
cry and to the prayer, which thy servant
prayeth before thee today:
29 That thine eyes may be open toward this house night and day, *even* toward the place of which thou hast said,
[a]My name shall be there: that thou mayest hearken unto the prayer which thy
servant shall make [b]toward[1] this place.
30 [a]And hearken thou to the supplication of thy servant, and of thy people Israel, when they shall pray [1]toward this
place: and hear thou in heaven thy dwellingplace: and when thou hearest, forgive.
31 ¶ If any man trespass against his
neighbour, [a]and[1] [b]an oath be laid upon
him to cause him to swear, and the oath
come before thine altar in this house:
32 Then hear thou in heaven, and do,
and judge thy servants, [a]condemning the
wicked, to bring his way upon his head;
and justifying the righteous, to give him
according to his righteousness.
33 ¶ [a]When thy people Israel be smitten down before the enemy, because
they have sinned against thee, and [b]shall
turn again to thee, and confess thy name,
and pray, and make supplication unto
thee [1]in this house:
34 Then hear thou in heaven, and forgive the sin of thy people Israel, and
bring them again unto the land which
thou gavest unto their fathers.
35 ¶ [a]When heaven is shut up, and
there is no rain, because they have
sinned against thee; if they pray toward
this place, and confess thy name, and

15 [b]2 Sam. 7:5,25
16 [a]ver. 29 [b]1 Sam. 16:1; 2 Sam. 7:8; 1 Chr. 28:4
17 [a]2 Sam. 7:2
18 [a]2 Chr. 6:8,9
19 [a]2 Sam. 7:5,12, 13
20 [a]1 Chr. 28:5,6
21 [a]ver. 9; Deut. 31:26
22 [a]2 Chr. 6:12 [b]Ex. 9:33; Ezra 9:5
23 [a]Ex. 15:11; 2 Sam. 7:22 [b]Deut. 7:9; Neh. 1:5; Dan. 9:4 [c]Gen. 17:1; ch. 3:6; 2 Ki. 20:3
25 [a]2 Sam. 7:12, 16; ch. 2:4 [1]Heb. *There shall not be cut off unto thee a man from my sight* [2]Heb. *only if*
26 [a]2 Sam. 7:25
27 [a]2 Chr. 2:6; Is. 66:1; Jer. 23:24; Acts 7:49 & 17:24 [b]2 Cor. 12:2
29 [a]Deut. 12:11 [b]Dan. 6:10 [1]Or, *in this place*
30 [a]Neh. 1:6 [1]Or, *in this place*
31 [a]Lev. 5:1 [b]Ex. 22:11 [1]Heb. *and he require an oath of him*
32 [a]Deut. 25:1
33 [a]Lev. 26:17; Deut. 28:25 [b]Lev. 26:39 [1]Or, *toward*
35 [a]Lev. 26:19; Deut. 28:23

8:29 Solomon asked God to graciously listen to the prayers of those who prayed to him when they were at the temple. Even today religious Jews worship and pray at the "wailing wall" in Jerusalem—the only surviving remnant of Solomon's temple—and insert written prayers in the cracks of the stones in this sacred, western wall.

turn from their sin, when thou afflictest them:

36 Then hear thou in heaven, and forgive the sin of thy servants, and of thy people Israel, that thou [a]teach them [b]the good way wherein they should walk, and give rain upon thy land, which thou hast given to thy people for an inheritance.

H 37 ¶ [a]If there be in the land famine, if there be pestilence, blasting, mildew, locust, *or* if there be caterpillar; if their enemy besiege them in the land of their [l]cities; whatsoever plague, whatsoever sickness *there be;*

38 What prayer and supplication soever be *made* by any man, *or* by all thy people Israel, which shall know every man the plague of his own heart, and spread forth his hands toward this house:

E 39 Then hear thou in heaven thy dwellingplace, and forgive, and do, and give to every man according to his ways, whose heart thou knowest; (for thou, *even* thou only, [a]knowest the hearts of all the children of men;)

40 [a]That they may fear thee all the days that they live in the land which thou gavest unto our fathers.

41 Moreover concerning a stranger, that *is* not of thy people Israel, but cometh out of a far country for thy name's sake;

42 (For they shall hear of thy great name, and of thy [a]strong hand, and of thy stretched out arm;) when he shall come and pray toward this house;

43 Hear thou in heaven thy dwellingplace, and do according to all that the stranger calleth to thee for: [a]that all people of the earth may know thy name, to [b]fear thee, as *do* thy people Israel; and that they may know that [l]this house, which I have builded, is called by thy name.

44 ¶ If thy people go out to battle against their enemy, whithersoever thou shalt send them, and shall pray unto the LORD [l]toward the city which thou hast chosen, and *toward* the house that I have built for thy name:

45 Then hear thou in heaven their prayer and their supplication, and maintain their [l]cause.

A 46 If they sin against thee, ([a]for *there* *is* no man that sinneth not,) and thou be angry with them, and deliver them to the enemy, so that they carry them away captives [b]unto the land of the enemy, far or near;

47 [a]*Yet* if they shall [l]bethink themselves in the land whither they were carried captives, and repent, and make supplication unto thee in the land of them that carried them captives, [b]saying, We have sinned, and have done perversely, we have committed wickedness;

48 And *so* [a]return unto thee with all their heart, and with all their soul, in the land of their enemies, which led them away captive, and [b]pray unto thee toward their land, which thou gavest unto their fathers, the city which thou hast chosen, and the house which I have built for thy name:

49 Then hear thou their prayer and their supplication in heaven thy dwellingplace, and maintain their [l]cause,

50 And forgive thy people that have sinned against thee, and all their transgressions wherein they have transgressed against thee, and [a]give them compassion before them who carried them captive, that they may have compassion on them:

51 For [a]they *be* thy people, and thine inheritance, which thou broughtest forth out of Egypt, [b]from the midst of the furnace of iron:

52 That thine eyes may be open unto the supplication of thy servant, and unto the supplication of thy people Israel, to hearken unto them in all that they call for unto thee.

53 For thou didst separate them from among all the people of the earth, *to be* thine inheritance, [a]as thou spakest by the hand of Moses thy servant, when thou broughtest our fathers out of Egypt, O Lord GOD.

54 And it was *so,* that when Solomon had made an end of praying all this prayer and supplication unto the LORD, he arose from before the altar of the LORD, from kneeling on his knees with his hands spread up to heaven.

55 And he stood, [a]and blessed all the congregation of Israel with a loud voice, saying,

56 Blessed *be* the LORD, that hath given rest unto his people Israel, according to all that he promised: [a]there hath not [l]failed one word of all his good promise,

36 [a]Ps. 25:4 & 27:11 & 94:12 [b]1 Sam. 12:23
37 [a]Lev. 26:16,25,26 [l]Or, *jurisdiction*
39 [a]1 Sam. 16:7; 1 Chr. 28:9; Ps. 11:4; Jer. 17:10; Acts 1:24
40 [a]Ps. 130:4
42 [a]Deut. 3:24
43 [a]1 Sam. 17:46; 2 Ki. 19:19 [b]Ps. 102:15 [l]Heb. *thy name is called upon this house*
44 [l]Heb. *the way of the city*
45 [l]Or, *right*
46 [a]2 Chr. 6:36; Eccl. 7:20; Jas. 3:2; 1 John 1:8,10 [b]Lev. 26:34,44; Deut. 28:36,64
47 [a]Lev. 26:40 [b]Neh. 1:6; Ps. 106:6; Dan. 9:5 [l]Heb. *bring back to their heart*
48 [a]Jer. 29:12-14 [b]Dan. 6:10
49 [l]Or, *right*
50 [a]Ezra 7:6; Ps. 106:46
51 [a]Deut. 9:29; Neh. 1:10 [b]Deut. 4:20; Jer. 11:4
53 [a]Ex. 19:5; Deut. 9:26,29
55 [a]2 Sam. 6:18
56 [a]Deut. 12:10; Josh. 21:45 & 23:14 [l]Heb. *fallen*

H *1Ki 3:14* ◄ ► *2Ch 6:28–30*
E *1Sa 16:7* ◄ ► *2Ki 19:27* A ► *2Ch 6:36*

which he promised by the hand of Moses his servant.

57 The LORD our God be with us, as he was with our fathers: [a]let him not leave us, nor forsake us:

58 That he may [a]incline our hearts unto him, to walk in all his ways, and to keep his commandments, and his statutes, and his judgments, which he commanded our fathers.

59 And let these my words, wherewith I have made supplication before the LORD, be nigh unto the LORD our God day and night, that he maintain the cause of his servant, and the cause of his people Israel [l]at all times, as the matter shall require:

O 60 [a]That all the people of the earth may know that [b]the LORD *is* God, *and that there is* none else.

S 61 Let your [a]heart therefore be perfect with the LORD our God, to walk in his statutes, and to keep his commandments, as at this day.

The offering and feast

62 ¶ And [a]the king, and all Israel with him, offered sacrifice before the LORD.

63 And Solomon offered a sacrifice of peace offerings, which he offered unto the LORD, two and twenty thousand oxen, and an hundred and twenty thousand sheep. So the king and all the children of Israel dedicated the house of the LORD.

64 [a]The same day did the king hallow the middle of the court that *was* before the house of the LORD: for there he offered burnt offerings, and meat offerings, and the fat of the peace offerings: because [b]the brasen altar that *was* before the LORD *was* too little to receive the burnt offerings, and meat offerings, and the fat of the peace offerings.

65 And at that time Solomon held [a]a feast, and all Israel with him, a great congregation, from [b]the entering in of Hamath unto [c]the river of Egypt, before the LORD our God, [d]seven days and seven days, *even* fourteen days.

O *2Sa 22:32* ◀▶ *1Ch 17:20*
S *2Sa 22:21–27* ◀▶ *1Ki 18:21*

57 [a]Deut. 31:6; Josh. 1:5
58 [a]Ps. 119:36
59 [l]Heb. *the thing of a day in his day*
60 [a]Josh. 4:24; 1 Sam. 17:46 [b]Deut. 4:35,39
61 [a]ch. 11:4 & 15:3,14; 2 Ki. 20:3
62 [a]2 Chr. 7:4
64 [a]2 Chr. 7:7 [b]2 Chr. 4:1
65 [a]ver. 2; Lev. 23:34 [b]Num. 34:8; Josh. 13:5; Judg. 3:3; 2 Ki. 14:25 [c]Gen. 15:18; Num. 34:5 [d]2 Chr. 7:8
66 [a]2 Chr. 7:9 [l]Or, *thanked*
9:1 [a]2 Chr. 7:11 [b]ch. 7:1 [c]2 Chr. 8:6
2 [a]ch. 3:5
3 [a]2 Ki. 20:5; Ps. 10:17 [b]ch. 8:29 [c]Deut. 11:12
4 [a]Gen. 17:1 [b]ch. 15:5
5 [a]2 Sam. 7:12,16; ch. 2:4; 1 Chr. 22:10
6 [a]2 Sam. 7:14; 2 Chr. 7:19,20
7 [a]2 Ki. 17:23 & 25:21 [b]Jer. 7:14 [c]Deut. 28:37
8 [a]2 Chr. 7:21

66 [a]On the eighth day he sent the people away: and they [l]blessed the king, and went unto their tents joyful and glad of heart for all the goodness that the LORD had done for David his servant, and for Israel his people.

The covenant with Solomon

9 AND [a]IT came to pass, when Solomon had finished the building of the house of the LORD, [b]and the king's house, and [c]all Solomon's desire which he was pleased to do,

2 That the LORD appeared to Solomon the second time, [a]as he had appeared unto him at Gibeon.

3 And the LORD said unto him, [a]I have heard thy prayer and thy supplication, that thou hast made before me: I have hallowed this house, which thou hast built, [b]to put my name there for ever; [c]and mine eyes and mine heart shall be there perpetually. I

4 And if thou wilt [a]walk before me, [b]as David thy father walked, in integrity of heart, and in uprightness, to do according to all that I have commanded thee, *and* wilt keep my statutes and my judgments:

5 Then I will establish the throne of thy kingdom upon Israel for ever, [a]as I promised to David thy father, saying, There shall not fail thee a man upon the throne of Israel.

6 [a]*But* if ye shall at all turn from following me, ye or your children, and will not keep my commandments *and* my statutes which I have set before you, but go and serve other gods, and worship them: R

7 [a]Then will I cut off Israel out of the land which I have given them; and this house, which I have hallowed [b]for my name, will I cast out of my sight; [c]and Israel shall be a proverb and a byword among all people: R

8 And [a]at this house, *which* is high, every one that passeth by it shall be astonished, and shall hiss; and they shall

I *1Ki 5:5* ◀▶ *1Ki 18:1*
R *Jos 23:15–16* ◀▶ *1Ki 9:7–8*
R *1Ki 9:6–9* ◀▶ *1Ki 11:11*

9:3 God proclaimed his intent toward the temple "to put my name there for ever." This is why orthodox Jews believe they must rebuild the temple on the same site as Solomon's temple.

9:6–9 This prophecy of the future desolation of the temple would come to pass if Israel turned from worshiping the true God to "go and serve other gods" (9:6). Such destruction would stand as a witness to other nations of Israel's rebellion and God's punishment for their sins.

say, [b]Why hath the LORD done thus unto this land, and to this house?

9 And they shall answer, Because they forsook the LORD their God, who brought forth their fathers out of the land of Egypt, and have taken hold upon other gods, and have worshipped them, and served them: therefore hath the LORD brought upon them all this evil.

Solomon's accomplishments

10 ¶ And [a]it came to pass at the end of twenty years, when Solomon had built the two houses, the house of the LORD, and the king's house,

11 [a](*Now* Hiram the king of Tyre had furnished Solomon with cedar trees and fir trees, and with gold, according to all his desire,) that then king Solomon gave Hiram twenty cities in the land of Galilee.

12 And Hiram came out from Tyre to see the cities which Solomon had given him; and they [I]pleased him not.

13 And he said, What cities *are* these which thou hast given me, my brother? [a]And he called them the land of [I]Cabul unto this day.

14 And Hiram sent to the king sixscore talents of gold.

15 ¶ And this *is* the reason of [a]the levy which king Solomon raised; for to build the house of the LORD, and his own house, and [b]Millo, and the wall of Jerusalem, and [c]Hazor, and [d]Megiddo, and [e]Gezer.

16 *For* Pharaoh king of Egypt had gone up, and taken Gezer, and burnt it with fire, [a]and slain the Canaanites that dwelt in the city, and given it *for* a present unto his daughter, Solomon's wife.

17 And Solomon built Gezer, and [a]Beth-horon the nether,

18 And [a]Baalath, and Tadmor in the wilderness, in the land,

19 And all the cities of store that Solomon had, and cities for [a]his chariots, and cities for his horsemen, and [I]that which Solomon [b]desired to build in Jerusalem, and in Lebanon, and in all the land of his dominion.

20 [a]*And* all the people *that were* left of the Amorites, Hittites, Perizzites, Hivites, and Jebusites, which *were* not of the children of Israel,

21 Their children [a]that were left after them in the land, [b]whom the children of Israel also were not able utterly to destroy, [c]upon those did Solomon levy a tribute of [d]bondservice unto this day.

22 But of the children of Israel did Solomon [a]make no bondmen: but they *were* men of war, and his servants, and his princes, and his captains, and rulers of his chariots, and his horsemen.

23 These *were* the chief of the officers that *were* over Solomon's work, [a]five hundred and fifty, which bare rule over the people that wrought in the work.

24 ¶ But [a]Pharaoh's daughter came up out of the city of David unto [b]her house which *Solomon* had built for her: [c]then did he build Millo.

25 ¶ [a]And three times in a year did Solomon offer burnt offerings and peace offerings upon the altar which he built unto the LORD, and he burnt incense [I]upon the altar that *was* before the LORD. So he finished the house.

26 ¶ And [a]king Solomon made a navy of ships in [b]Ezion-geber, which *is* beside Eloth, on the [I]shore of the Red sea, in the land of Edom.

27 [a]And Hiram sent in the navy his servants, shipmen that had knowledge of the sea, with the servants of Solomon.

28 And they came to [a]Ophir, and fetched from thence gold, four hundred and twenty talents, and brought *it* to king Solomon.

The visit of the Queen of Sheba

10 AND WHEN the [a]queen of Sheba heard of the fame of Solomon concerning the name of the LORD, she came [b]to prove him with hard questions.

2 And she came to Jerusalem with a very great train, with camels that bare spices, and very much gold, and precious stones: and when she was come to Solomon, she communed with him of all that was in her heart.

3 And Solomon told her all her [I]questions: there was not *any* thing hid from the king, which he told her not.

4 And when the queen of Sheba had seen all Solomon's wisdom, and the house that he had built,

5 And the meat of his table, and the sitting of his servants, and the [I]attendance of his ministers, and their apparel, and his [2]cupbearers, [a]and his ascent by which he went up unto the house of the LORD; there was no more spirit in her.

---

8 [b]Deut. 29:24-26; Jer. 22:8,9
10 [a]ch. 6:37,38 & 7:1; 2 Chr. 8:1
11 [a]2 Chr. 8:2
12 [I]Heb. *were not right in his eyes*
13 [a]Josh. 19:27 [I]i.e. *Displeasing*, or, *Dirty*
15 [a]ch. 5:13 [b]ver. 24; 2 Sam. 5:9 [c]Josh. 19:36 [d]Josh. 17:11 [e]Josh. 16:10
16 [a]Josh. 16:10
17 [a]Josh. 16:3; 2 Chr. 8:5
18 [a]Josh. 19:44; 2 Chr. 8:4,6
19 [a]ch. 4:26 [b]ver. 1 [I]Heb. *the desire of Solomon which he desired*
20 [a]2 Chr. 8:7
21 [a]Judg. 3:1 [b]Josh. 15:63 & 17:12 [c]Judg. 1:28 [d]Ezra 2:55,58; Neh. 7:57
22 [a]Lev. 25:39
23 [a]See 2 Chr. 8:10
24 [a]ch. 3:1; 2 Chr. 8:11 [b]ch. 7:8 [c]2 Sam. 5:9; ch. 11:27; 2 Chr. 32:5
25 [a]2 Chr. 8:12, 13,16 [I]Heb. *upon it*
26 [a]2 Chr. 8:17,18 [b]Num. 33:35; Deut. 2:8; ch. 22:48 [I]Heb. *lip*
27 [a]ch. 10:11
28 [a]Job 22:24
10:1 [a]2 Chr. 9:1; Mat. 12:42; Luke 11:31 [b]See Judg. 14:12; Prov. 1:6
3 [I]Heb. *words*
5 [a]1 Chr. 26:16 [I]Heb. *standing* [2]Or, *butlers*

6 And she said to the king, It was a true [a]report that I heard in mine own land of thy [b]acts and of thy wisdom.

7 Howbeit I believed not the words, until I came, and mine eyes had seen *it:* and, behold, the half was not told me: [1]thy wisdom and prosperity exceedeth the fame which I heard.

8 [a]Happy *are* thy men, happy *are* these thy servants, which stand continually before thee, *and* that near thy wisdom.

9 [a]Blessed be the LORD thy God, which delighted in thee, to set thee on the throne of Israel: because the LORD loved Israel for ever, therefore made he thee king, [b]to do judgment and justice.

10 And she [a]gave the king an hundred and twenty talents of gold, and of spices very great store, and precious stones: there came no more such abundance of spices as these which the queen of Sheba gave to king Solomon.

11 [a]And the navy also of Hiram, that brought gold from Ophir, brought in from Ophir great plenty of [b]almug[1] trees, and precious stones.

12 [a]And the king made of the almug trees [1,2]pillars for the house of the LORD, and for the king's house, harps also and psalteries for singers: there came no such [b]almug trees, nor were seen unto this day.

13 And king Solomon gave unto the queen of Sheba all her desire, whatsoever she asked, beside *that* which Solomon gave her [1]of his royal bounty. So she turned and went to her own country, she and her servants.

The splendor of Solomon

14 ¶ Now the weight of gold that came to Solomon in one year was six hundred threescore and six talents of gold,

15 Beside *that he had* of the merchantmen, and of the traffic of the spice merchants, and [a]of all the kings of Arabia, and of the [1]governors of the country.

16 ¶ And king Solomon made two hundred targets *of* beaten gold: six hundred *shekels* of gold went to one target.

17 And *he made* [a]three hundred shields *of* beaten gold; three pound of gold went to one shield: and the king put them in the [b]house of the forest of Lebanon.

18 ¶ [a]Moreover the king made a great throne of ivory, and overlaid it with the best gold.

19 The throne had six steps, and the top of the throne *was* round [1]behind: and *there were* [2]stays on either side on the place of the seat, and two lions stood beside the stays.

20 And twelve lions stood there on the one side and on the other upon the six steps: there was not [1]the like made in any kingdom.

21 ¶ [a]And all king Solomon's drinking vessels *were of* gold, and all the vessels of the house of the forest of Lebanon *were of* pure gold; [1]none *were of* silver: it was nothing accounted of in the days of Solomon.

22 For the king had at sea a navy of [a]Tharshish with the navy of Hiram: once in three years came the navy of Tharshish, bringing gold, and silver, [1]ivory, and apes, and peacocks.

23 So [a]king Solomon exceeded all the kings of the earth for riches and for wisdom.

24 ¶ And all the earth [1]sought to Solomon, to hear his wisdom, which God had put in his heart.

25 And they brought every man his present, vessels of silver, and vessels of gold, and garments, and armour, and spices, horses, and mules, a rate year by year.

26 ¶ [a]And Solomon [b]gathered together chariots and horsemen: and he had a thousand and four hundred chariots, and twelve thousand horsemen, whom he bestowed in the cities for chariots, and with the king at Jerusalem.

27 [a]And the king [1]made silver *to be* in Jerusalem as stones, and cedars made he *to be* as the sycamore trees that *are* in the vale, for abundance.

28 ¶ [a]And[1] Solomon had horses brought out of Egypt, and linen yarn: the king's merchants received the linen yarn at a price.

29 And a chariot came up and went out of Egypt for six hundred *shekels* of silver, and an horse for an hundred and fifty: [a]and so for all the kings of the Hittites, and for the kings of Syria, did they bring *them* out [1]by their means.

6 [a]Heb. *word* [b]Or, *sayings*
7 [1]Heb. *thou hast added wisdom and goodness to the fame*
8 [a]Prov. 8:34
9 [a]ch. 5:7 [b]2 Sam. 8:15; Ps. 72:2; Prov. 8:15
10 [a]Ps. 72:10,15
11 [a]ch. 9:27 [b]2 Chr. 2:8 & 9:10,11 [1]Or, *algum trees*
12 [a]2 Chr. 9:11 [b]2 Chr. 9:10 [1]Or, *rails* [2]Heb. *a prop*
13 [1]Heb. *according to the hand of king Solomon*
15 [a]2 Chr. 9:24; Ps. 72:10 [1]Or, *captains*
17 [a]ch. 14:26 [b]ch. 7:2
18 [a]2 Chr. 9:17
19 [1]Heb. *on the hinder part thereof* [2]Heb. *hands*
20 [1]Heb. *so*
21 [a]2 Chr. 9:20 [1]Or, there was *no silver* in them
22 [a]Gen. 10:4; 2 Chr. 20:36 [1]Or, *elephants' teeth*
23 [a]ch. 3:12,13 & 4:30
24 [1]Heb. *sought the face of*
26 [a]ch. 4:26; 2 Chr. 1:14 & 9:25 [b]Deut. 17:16
27 [a]2 Chr. 1:15-17 [1]Heb. *gave*
28 [a]Deut. 17:16; 2 Chr. 1:16 & 9:28 [1]Heb. *And the going forth of the horses which* was *Solomon's*
29 [a]Josh. 1:4; 2 Ki. 7:6 [1]Heb. *by their hand*

Solomon takes foreign wives

11 BUT [a]KING Solomon loved
[b]many strange women, [l]together
with the daughter of Pharaoh, women of
the Moabites, Ammonites, Edomites,
Zidonians, *and* Hittites;
2 Of the nations *concerning* which the
LORD said unto the children of Israel, [a]Ye
shall not go in to them, neither shall they
come in unto you: *for* surely they will
turn away your heart after their gods: Solomon clave unto these in love.
3 And he had seven hundred wives,
princesses, and three hundred concubines: and his wives turned away his
heart.
4 For it came to pass, when Solomon
was old, [a]*that* his wives turned away his
heart after other gods: and his [b]heart was
not perfect with the LORD his God, [c]as
was the heart of David his father.
5 For Solomon went after [a]Ashtoreth
the goddess of the Zidonians, and after
[l]Milcom the abomination of the Ammonites.
6 And Solomon did evil in the sight of
the LORD, and [l]went not fully after the
LORD, as *did* David his father.
7 [a]Then did Solomon build an high
place for [b]Chemosh, the abomination of
Moab, in [c]the hill that *is* before Jerusalem, and for Molech, the abomination of
the children of Ammon.
8 And likewise did he for all his
strange wives, which burnt incense and
sacrificed unto their gods.
9 ¶ And the LORD was angry with Solomon, because his heart was turned from
the LORD God of Israel, [a]which had appeared unto him twice,
10 And [a]had commanded him concerning this thing, that he should not go
after other gods: but he kept not that
which the LORD commanded.
R 11 Wherefore the LORD said unto Solomon, Forasmuch as this [l]is done of thee,
and thou hast not kept my covenant and
my statutes, which I have commanded
thee, [a]I will surely rend the kingdom

R *1Ki 9:7–8* ◀ ▶ *1Ki 11:30–31*

11:1 [a]Neh. 13:26 [b]Deut. 17:17 [l]Or, *beside*
2 [a]Ex. 34:16; Deut. 7:3,4
4 [a]Deut. 17:17; Neh. 13:26 [b]ch. 8:61 [c]ch. 9:4
5 [a]ver. 33; Judg. 2:13; 2 Ki. 23:13 [l]Called *Molech* in ver. 7
6 [l]Heb. *fulfilled not after*
7 [a]Num. 33:52 [b]Num. 21:29; Judg. 11:24 [c]2 Ki. 23:13
9 [a]ch. 3:5 & 9:2
10 [a]ch. 6:12 & 9:6
11 [a]ver. 31; ch. 12:15,16 [l]Heb. *is with thee*
13 [a]2 Sam. 7:15 [b]ch. 12:20 [c]Deut. 12:11
14 [a]1 Chr. 5:26
15 [a]2 Sam. 8:14; 1 Chr. 18:12 [b]Num. 24:19; Deut. 20:13
21 [a]ch. 2:10,34 [l]Heb. *Send me away*
22 [l]Heb. *Not*

from thee, and will give it to thy servant.
12 Notwithstanding in thy days I will
not do it for David thy father's sake: *but* I
will rend it out of the hand of thy son.
13 [a]Howbeit I will not rend away all
the kingdom; *but* will give [b]one tribe to
thy son for David my servant's sake, and
for Jerusalem's sake [c]which I have
chosen.

Solomon's adversaries

14 ¶ And the LORD [a]stirred up an adversary unto Solomon, Hadad the Edomite: he *was* of the king's seed in Edom.
15 [a]For it came to pass, when David
was in Edom, and Joab the captain of the
host was gone up to bury the slain, [b]after
he had smitten every male in Edom;
16 (For six months did Joab remain
there with all Israel, until he had cut off
every male in Edom:)
17 That Hadad fled, he and certain
Edomites of his father's servants with
him, to go into Egypt; Hadad *being* yet a
little child.
18 And they arose out of Midian, and
came to Paran: and they took men with
them out of Paran, and they came to
Egypt, unto Pharaoh king of Egypt; which
gave him an house, and appointed him
victuals, and gave him land.
19 And Hadad found great favour in
the sight of Pharaoh, so that he gave him
to wife the sister of his own wife, the
sister of Tahpenes the queen.
20 And the sister of Tahpenes bare
him Genubath his son, whom Tahpenes
weaned in Pharaoh's house: and Genubath was in Pharaoh's household among
the sons of Pharaoh.
21 [a]And when Hadad heard in Egypt
that David slept with his fathers, and that
Joab the captain of the host was dead,
Hadad said to Pharaoh, [l]Let me depart,
that I may go to mine own country.
22 Then Pharaoh said unto him, But
what hast thou lacked with me, that, behold, thou seekest to go to thine own
country? And he answered, [l]Nothing:
howbeit let me go in any wise.
23 ¶ And God stirred him up *another*

11:11–13 King Solomon's apostasy in the final years of his reign caused God to declare that he would "surely rend the kingdom from thee" (11:11). Yet God's profound love for Solomon's father, David, delayed this judgment until after Solomon's death and allowed Solomon's son Rehoboam to retain rule over Jerusalem and the tribes of Judah.

adversary, Rezon the son of Eliadah,
which fled from his lord [a]Hadadezer king
of Zobah:
24 And he gathered men unto him,
and became captain over a band, [a]when
David slew them *of Zobah:* and they went
to Damascus, and dwelt therein, and
reigned in Damascus.
25 And he was an adversary to Israel
all the days of Solomon, beside the mischief that Hadad *did:* and he abhorred Israel, and reigned over Syria.

Jeroboam's rebellion

26 ¶ And [a]Jeroboam the son of Nebat,
an Ephrathite of Zereda, Solomon's servant, whose mother's name *was* Zeruah,
a widow woman, even he [b]lifted up *his*
hand against the king.
27 And this *was* the cause that he
lifted up *his* hand against the king: [a]Solo-
mon built Millo, *and* [1]repaired the
breaches of the city of David his father.
28 And the man Jeroboam *was* a
mighty man of valour: and Solomon seeing the young man that he [1]was industri-
ous, he made him ruler over all the
[2]charge of the house of Joseph.
29 And it came to pass at that time
when Jeroboam went out of Jerusalem,
that the prophet [a]Ahijah the Shilonite
found him in the way; and he had clad
himself with a new garment; and they
two *were* alone in the field:
R 30 And Ahijah caught the new garment that *was* on him, and [a]rent it *in*
twelve pieces:
31 And he said to Jeroboam, Take thee
ten pieces: for [a]thus saith the LORD, the
God of Israel, Behold, I will rend the
kingdom out of the hand of Solomon, and
will give ten tribes to thee:
32 (But he shall have one tribe for my
servant David's sake, and for Jerusalem's
sake, the city which I have chosen out of
all the tribes of Israel:)
33 [a]Because that they have forsaken
me, and have worshipped Ashtoreth the
goddess of the Zidonians, Chemosh the
god of the Moabites, and Milcom the god
of the children of Ammon, and have not
walked in my ways, to do *that which is*
right in mine eyes, and *to keep* my statutes and my judgments, as *did* David his
father.
34 Howbeit I will not take the whole
kingdom out of his hand: but I will make
him prince all the days of his life for David my servant's sake, whom I chose, because he kept my commandments and
my statutes:
35 But [a]I will take the kingdom out of
his son's hand, and will give it unto thee,
even ten tribes.
36 And unto his son will I give one
tribe, that [a]David my servant may have a
[1]light always before me in Jerusalem, the
city which I have chosen me to put my
name there.
37 And I will take thee, and thou shalt
reign according to all that thy soul desireth, and shalt be king over Israel.
38 And it shall be, if thou wilt hearken
unto all that I command thee, and wilt
walk in my ways, and do *that is* right in
my sight, to keep my statutes and my
commandments, as David my servant
did; that [a]I will be with thee, and [b]build
thee a sure house, as I built for David,
and will give Israel unto thee.
39 And I will for this afflict the seed of
David, but not for ever.
40 Solomon sought therefore to kill
Jeroboam. And Jeroboam arose, and fled
into Egypt, unto Shishak king of Egypt,
and was in Egypt until the death of
Solomon.

The death of Solomon

41 ¶ And [a]the rest of the [1]acts of Solomon, and all that he did, and his wisdom,
are they not written in the book of the
acts of Solomon?
42 [a]And the [1]time that Solomon
reigned in Jerusalem over all Israel *was*
forty years.
43 [a]And Solomon slept with his fathers, and was buried in the city of David

23 [a]2 Sam. 8:3
24 [a]2 Sam. 8:3 & 10:8,18
26 [a]ch. 12:2; 2 Chr. 13:6 [b]2 Sam. 20:21
27 [a]ch. 9:24 [1]Heb. *closed*
28 [1]Heb. *did work* [2]Heb. *burden*
29 [a]ch. 14:2
30 [a]See 1 Sam. 15:27 & 24:5
31 [a]ver. 11,13
33 [a]ver. 5-7
35 [a]ch. 12:16,17
36 [a]ch. 15:4; 2 Ki. 8:19 [1]Heb. *lamp,* or, *candle*
38 [a]Josh. 1:5 [b]2 Sam. 7:11,27
41 [a]2 Chr. 9:29 [1]Or, *words,* or, *things*
42 [a]2 Chr. 9:30 [1]Heb. *days*
43 [a]2 Chr. 9:31

R *1Ki 11:11* ◀ ▶ *1Ki 13:2–3*

11:28–32 God arranged the meeting of the prophet Ahijah and Jeroboam, governor over the territory of the tribe of Joseph. Ahijah acted out a symbolic prophecy by ripping his garment into twelve pieces. After giving Jeroboam ten pieces, the prophet Ahijah prophesied that God would "rend the kingdom out of the hand of Solomon"(11:31) and give the leadership of the ten tribes to Jeroboam. Ahijah reaffirmed that two tribes would remain loyal to the house of David.

his father: and [b]Rehoboam his son reigned in his stead.

Rehoboam, king of Israel

12 AND [a]REHOBOAM went to Shechem: for all Israel were come to Shechem to make him king.

2 And it came to pass, when [a]Jeroboam the son of Nebat, who was yet in [b]Egypt, heard *of it,* (for he was fled from the presence of king Solomon, and Jeroboam dwelt in Egypt;)

3 That they sent and called him. And Jeroboam and all the congregation of Israel came, and spake unto Rehoboam, saying,

4 Thy father made our [a]yoke grievous: now therefore make thou the grievous service of thy father, and his heavy yoke which he put upon us, lighter, and we will serve thee.

5 And he said unto them, Depart yet *for* three days, then come again to me. And the people departed.

6 ¶ And king Rehoboam consulted with the old men, that stood before Solomon his father while he yet lived, and said, How do ye advise that I may answer this people?

7 And they spake unto him, saying, [a]If thou wilt be a servant unto this people this day, and wilt serve them, and answer them, and speak good words to them, then they will be thy servants for ever.

8 But he forsook the counsel of the old men, which they had given him, and consulted with the young men that were grown up with him, *and* which stood before him:

9 And he said unto them, What counsel give ye that we may answer this people, who have spoken to me, saying, Make the yoke which thy father did put upon us lighter?

10 And the young men that were grown up with him spake unto him, saying, Thus shalt thou speak unto this people that spake unto thee, saying, Thy father made our yoke heavy, but make thou *it* lighter unto us; thus shalt thou say unto them, My little *finger* shall be thicker than my father's loins.

11 And now whereas my father did lade you with a heavy yoke, I will add to your yoke: my father hath chastised you with whips, but I will chastise you with scorpions.

12 ¶ So Jeroboam and all the people came to Rehoboam the third day, as the king had appointed, saying, Come to me again the third day.

13 And the king answered the people [ʹ]roughly, and forsook the old men's counsel that they gave him;

14 And spake to them after the counsel of the young men, saying, My father made your yoke heavy, and I will add to your yoke: my father *also* chastised you with whips, but I will chastise you with scorpions.

15 Wherefore the king hearkened not unto the people; for [a]the cause was from the LORD, that he might perform his saying, which the LORD [b]spake by Ahijah the Shilonite unto Jeroboam the son of Nebat.

16 ¶ So when all Israel saw that the king hearkened not unto them, the people answered the king, saying, [a]What portion have we in David? neither *have we* inheritance in the son of Jesse: to your tents, O Israel: now see to thine own house, David. So Israel departed unto their tents.

17 But [a]*as for* the children of Israel which dwelt in the cities of Judah, Rehoboam reigned over them.

18 Then king Rehoboam [a]sent Adoram, who *was* over the tribute; and all Israel stoned him with stones, that he died. Therefore king Rehoboam [ʹ]made speed to get him up to his chariot, to flee to Jerusalem.

19 So [a]Israel [ʹ]rebelled against the house of David unto this day.

20 And it came to pass, when all Israel heard that Jeroboam was come again, that they sent and called him unto the congregation, and made him king over all Israel: there was none that followed the house of David, but the tribe of Judah [a]only.

21 ¶ And when [a]Rehoboam was come to Jerusalem, he assembled all the house of Judah, with the tribe of Benjamin, an hundred and fourscore thousand chosen men, which were warriors, to fight against the house of Israel, to bring the kingdom again to Rehoboam the son of Solomon.

22 But [a]the word of God came unto Shemaiah the man of God, saying,

23 Speak unto Rehoboam, the son of Solomon, king of Judah, and unto all the

43 [b]Mat. 1:7 called *Roboam*
12:1 [a]2 Chr. 10:1
2 [a]ch. 11:26 [b]ch. 11:40
4 [a]1 Sam. 8:11-18; ch. 4:7
7 [a]2 Chr. 10:7; Prov. 15:1
13 [ʹ]Heb. *hardly*
15 [a]ver. 24; Judg. 14:4; 2 Chr. 10:15 & 22:7 & 25:20 [b]ch. 11:11,31
16 [a]2 Sam. 20:1
17 [a]ch. 11:13,36
18 [a]ch. 4:6 & 5:14 [ʹ]Heb. *strengthened himself*
19 [a]2 Ki. 17:21 [ʹ]Or, *fell away*
20 [a]ch. 11:13,32
21 [a]2 Chr. 11:1
22 [a]2 Chr. 11:2

house of Judah and Benjamin, and to the remnant of the people, saying,

24 Thus saith the LORD, Ye shall not go up, nor fight against your brethren the children of Israel: return every man to his house; [a]for this thing is from me. They hearkened therefore to the word of the LORD, and returned to depart, according to the word of the LORD.

Two golden calves

25 ¶ Then Jeroboam [a]built Shechem in mount Ephraim, and dwelt therein; and went out from thence, and built [b]Penuel.

26 And Jeroboam said in his heart, Now shall the kingdom return to the house of David:

27 If this people [a]go up to do sacrifice in the house of the LORD at Jerusalem, then shall the heart of this people turn again unto their lord, *even* unto Rehoboam king of Judah, and they shall kill me, and go again to Rehoboam king of Judah.

28 Whereupon the king took counsel, and [a]made two calves *of* gold, and said unto them, It is too much for you to go up to Jerusalem: [b]behold thy gods, O Israel, which brought thee up out of the land of Egypt.

29 And he set the one in [a]Beth-el, and the other put he in [b]Dan.

30 And this thing became [a]a sin: for the people went *to worship* before the one, *even* unto Dan.

31 And he made an [a]house of high places, [b]and made priests of the lowest of the people, which were not of the sons of Levi.

32 And Jeroboam ordained a feast in the eighth month, on the fifteenth day of the month, like unto [a]the feast that *is* in Judah, and he [1]offered upon the altar. So did he in Beth-el, [2]sacrificing unto the calves that he had made: [b]and he placed in Beth-el the priests of the high places which he had made.

33 So he [1]offered upon the altar which he had made in Beth-el the fifteenth day of the eighth month, *even* in the month

24 [a]ver. 15
25 [a]See Judg. 9:45 [b]Judg. 8:17
27 [a]Deut. 12:5,6
28 [a]2 Ki. 10:29 & 17:16 [b]Ex. 32:4,8
29 [a]Gen. 28:19; Hos. 4:15 [b]Judg. 18:29
30 [a]ch. 13:34; 2 Ki. 17:21
31 [a]ch. 13:32 [b]Num. 3:10; ch. 13:33; 2 Ki. 17:32; 2 Chr. 11:14,15
32 [a]Lev. 23:33,34; Num. 29:12; ch. 8:2,5 [b]Amos 7:13 [1]Or, *went up to the altar* [2]Or, *to sacrifice*
33 [a]Num. 15:39 [b]ch. 13:1 [1]Or, *went up to the altar* [2]Heb. *to burn incense*
13:1 [a]2 Ki. 23:17 [b]ch. 12:32,33 [1]Or, *to offer*
2 [a]2 Ki. 23:15,16
3 [a]Is. 7:14; John 2:18; 1 Cor. 1:22
6 [a]Ex. 8:8 & 9:28; & 10:17; Num. 21:7; Acts 8:24; Jas. 5:16 [1]Heb. *the face of the LORD*
7 [a]1 Sam. 9:7; 2 Ki. 5:15
8 [a]Num. 22:18 & 24:13

which he had [a]devised of his own heart; and ordained a feast unto the children of Israel: and he offered upon the altar, [2]and [b]burnt incense.

The man of God from Judah

13 AND, BEHOLD, there [a]came a man of God out of Judah by the word of the LORD unto Beth-el: [b]and Jeroboam stood by the altar [1]to burn incense.

2 And he cried against the altar in the word of the LORD, and said, O altar, altar, thus saith the LORD; Behold, a child shall be born unto the house of David, [a]Josiah by name; and upon thee shall he offer the priests of the high places that burn incense upon thee, and men's bones shall be burnt upon thee. R

3 And he gave [a]a sign the same day, saying, This *is* the sign which the LORD hath spoken; Behold, the altar shall be rent, and the ashes that *are* upon it shall be poured out.

4 And it came to pass, when king Jeroboam heard the saying of the man of God, which had cried against the altar in Beth-el, that he put forth his hand from the altar, saying, Lay hold on him. And his hand, which he put forth against him, dried up, so that he could not pull it in again to him. D

5 The altar also was rent, and the ashes poured out from the altar, according to the sign which the man of God had given by the word of the LORD.

6 And the king answered and said unto the man of God, [a]Entreat now the face of the LORD thy God, and pray for me, that my hand may be restored me again. And the man of God besought [1]the LORD, and the king's hand was restored him again, and became as *it was* before. E

7 And the king said unto the man of God, Come home with me, and refresh thyself, and [a]I will give thee a reward.

8 And the man of God said unto the king, [a]If thou wilt give me half thine

R *1Ki 11:30–31* ◀ ▶ *1Ki 13:22*
D *1Sa 25:38* ◀ ▶ *1Ki 14:12–13*
E *2Sa 24:25* ◀ ▶ *1Ki 17:22–24*

13:1–3 An unnamed prophet of God from Judah came to Bethel to confront King Jeroboam. Jeroboam had sinfully created two golden calves for the Israelites to worship rather than have them travel south to Jerusalem to worship God (see 12:28). The man of God prophesied that a descendant of David named Josiah would destroy this idol worship by sacrificing the bodies of the idolatrous priests on their idolatrous altar. Three centuries later King Josiah fulfilled this prophecy (see 2Ki 23:1–15).

house, I will not go in with thee, neither
will I eat bread nor drink water in this
place:
9 For so was it charged me by the word
of the LORD, saying, [a]Eat no bread, nor
drink water, nor turn again by the same
way that thou camest.
10 So he went another way, and returned not by the way that he came to
Beth-el.
11 ¶ Now there dwelt an old prophet
in Beth-el; and his [l]sons came and told
him all the works that the man of God
had done that day in Beth-el: the words
which he had spoken unto the king, them
they told also to their father.
12 And their father said unto them,
What way went he? For his sons had seen
what way the man of God went, which
came from Judah.
13 And he said unto his sons, Saddle
me the ass. So they saddled him the ass;
and he rode thereon,
14 And went after the man of God,
and found him sitting under an oak: and
he said unto him, *Art* thou the man of
God that camest from Judah? And he
said, I *am*.
15 Then he said unto him, Come
home with me, and eat bread.
16 And he said, [a]I may not return with
thee, nor go in with thee: neither will I
eat bread nor drink water with thee in
this place:
17 For [l]it was said to me [a]by the word
of the LORD, Thou shalt eat no bread nor
drink water there, nor turn again to go by
the way that thou camest.
18 He said unto him, I *am* a prophet
also as thou *art;* and an angel spake unto
me by the word of the LORD, saying, Bring
him back with thee into thine house, that
he may eat bread and drink water. *But* he
lied unto him.
19 So he went back with him, and did
eat bread in his house, and drank water.
20 ¶ And it came to pass, as they sat at
the table, that the word of the LORD came
unto the prophet that brought him back:
21 And he cried unto the man of God
that came from Judah, saying, Thus saith
the LORD, Forasmuch as thou hast disobeyed the mouth of the LORD, and hast
not kept the commandment which the
LORD thy God commanded thee,

9 [a] 1 Cor. 5:11
11 [l] Heb. *son*
16 [a] ver. 8:9
17 [a] ch. 20:35; 1 Thes. 4:15 [l] Heb. *a word* was
24 [a] ch. 20:36
26 [l] Heb. *broken*
28 [l] Heb. *broken*
30 [a] Jer. 22:18
31 [a] 2 Ki. 23:17,18
32 [a] ver. 2; 2 Ki. 23:16,19 [b] See ch. 16:24
33 [a] ch. 12:31,32; 2 Chr. 11:15 & 13:9 [l] Heb. *returned and made*

22 But camest back, and hast eaten R
bread and drunk water in the place, of
the which *the* LORD did say to thee, Eat no
bread, and drink no water; thy carcase
shall not come unto the sepulchre of thy
fathers.
23 ¶ And it came to pass, after he had
eaten bread, and after he had drunk, that
he saddled for him the ass, *to wit,* for the
prophet whom he had brought back.
24 And when he was gone, [a]a lion met
him by the way, and slew him: and his
carcase was cast in the way, and the ass
stood by it, the lion also stood by the
carcase.
25 And, behold, men passed by, and
saw the carcase cast in the way, and the
lion standing by the carcase: and they
came and told *it* in the city where the old
prophet dwelt.
26 And when the prophet that brought
him back from the way heard *thereof,* he
said, It *is* the man of God, who was disobedient unto the word of the LORD:
therefore the LORD hath delivered him
unto the lion, which hath [l]torn him, and
slain him, according to the word of the
LORD, which he spake unto him.
27 And he spake to his sons, saying,
Saddle me the ass. And they saddled *him.*
28 And he went and found his carcase
cast in the way, and the ass and the lion
standing by the carcase: the lion had not
eaten the carcase, nor [l]torn the ass.
29 And the prophet took up the carcase of the man of God, and laid it upon
the ass, and brought it back: and the old
prophet came to the city, to mourn and to
bury him.
30 And he laid his carcase in his own
grave; and they mourned over him, *saying,* [a]Alas, my brother!
31 And it came to pass, after he had
buried him, that he spake to his sons, saying, When I am dead, then bury me in
the sepulchre wherein the man of God *is*
buried; [a]lay my bones beside his bones:
32 [a]For the saying which he cried by R
the word of the LORD against the altar in
Beth-el, and against all the houses of the
high places which *are* in the cities of [b]Sa-
maria, shall surely come to pass.
33 ¶ [a]After this thing Jeroboam returned not from his evil way, but [l]made

R *1Ki 13:2–3* ◄► *1Ki 13:32*
R *1Ki 13:22* ◄► *1Ki 14:10–16*

again of the lowest of the people priests of the high places: whosoever would, he [b]consecrated[2] him, and he became *one* of the priests of the high places.

34 [a]And this thing became sin unto the house of Jeroboam, even [b]to cut *it* off, and to destroy *it* from off the face of the earth.

The prophecy against Jeroboam

14 AT THAT time Abijah the son of Jeroboam fell sick.

2 And Jeroboam said to his wife, Arise, I pray thee, and disguise thyself, that thou be not known to be the wife of Jeroboam; and get thee to Shiloh: behold, there *is* Ahijah the prophet, which told me that [a]*I should be* king over this people.

3 [a]And take [1]with thee ten loaves, and [2]cracknels, and a [3]cruse of honey, and go to him: he shall tell thee what shall become of the child.

4 And Jeroboam's wife did so, and arose, [a]and went to Shiloh, and came to the house of Ahijah. But Ahijah could not see; for his eyes [1]were set by reason of his age.

5 ¶ And the LORD said unto Ahijah, Behold, the wife of Jeroboam cometh to ask a thing of thee for her son; for he *is* sick: thus and thus shalt thou say unto her: for it shall be, when she cometh in, that she shall feign herself *to be* another *woman.*

6 And it was *so,* when Ahijah heard the sound of her feet, as she came in at the door, that he said, Come in, thou wife of Jeroboam; why feignest thou thyself *to be* another? for I *am* sent to thee *with* [1]heavy *tidings.*

7 Go, tell Jeroboam, Thus saith the LORD God of Israel, [a]Forasmuch as I exalted thee from among the people, and made thee prince over my people Israel,

8 And [a]rent the kingdom away from the house of David, and gave it thee: and *yet* thou hast not been as my servant David, [b]who kept my commandments, and who followed me with all his heart, to do *that* only *which was* right in mine eyes;

9 But hast done evil above all that were before thee: [a]for thou hast gone and made thee other gods, and molten images, to provoke me to anger, and [b]hast cast me behind thy back:

10 Therefore, behold, [a]I will bring evil upon the house of Jeroboam, and [b]will cut off from Jeroboam him that pisseth against the wall, [c]*and* him that is shut up and left in Israel, and will take away the remnant of the house of Jeroboam, as a man taketh away dung, till it be all gone. R

11 [a]Him that dieth of Jeroboam in the city shall the dogs eat; and him that dieth in the field shall the fowls of the air eat: for the LORD hath spoken *it.*

12 Arise thou therefore, get thee to thine own house: *and* [a]when thy feet enter into the city, the child shall die. D

13 And all Israel shall mourn for him, and bury him: for he only of Jeroboam shall come to the grave, because in him [a]there is found *some* good thing toward the LORD God of Israel in the house of Jeroboam.

14 [a]Moreover the LORD shall raise him up a king over Israel, who shall cut off the house of Jeroboam that day: but what? even now.

15 For the LORD shall smite Israel, as a reed is shaken in the water, and he shall [a]root up Israel out of this [b]good land, which he gave to their fathers, and shall scatter them [c]beyond the river, [d]because they have made their groves, provoking the LORD to anger.

16 And he shall give Israel up because of the sins of Jeroboam, [a]who did sin, and who made Israel to sin.

17 ¶ And Jeroboam's wife arose, and departed, and came to [a]Tirzah: *and* [b]when she came to the threshold of the door, the child died;

18 And they buried him; and all Israel mourned for him, [a]according to the word

R *1Ki 13:32* ◄► *2Ki 13:23*
D *1Ki 13:4* ◄► *2Ki 1:2–4*

33 [b]Judg. 17:12 [2]Heb. *filled his hand*
34 [a]ch. 12:30 [b]ch. 14:10
14:2 [a]ch. 11:31
3 [a]See 1 Sam. 9:7,8 [1]Heb. *in thine hand* [2]Or, *cakes* [3]Or, *bottle*
4 [a]ch. 11:29 [1]Heb. *stood for his hoariness*
6 [1]Heb. *hard*
7 [a]See 2 Sam. 12:7, 8
8 [a]ch. 11:31 [b]ch. 11:33,38 & 15:5
9 [a]ch. 12:28; 2 Chr. 11:15 [b]Neh. 9:26; Ps. 50:17
10 [a]ch. 15:29 [b]ch. 21:21; 2 Ki. 9:8 [c]Deut. 32:36; 2 Ki. 14:26
11 [a]ch. 16:4 & 21:24
12 [a]ver. 17
13 [a]2 Chr. 12:12; & 19:3
14 [a]ch. 15:27-29
15 [a]2 Ki. 17:6; Ps. 52:5 [b]Josh. 23:15, 16 [c]2 Ki. 15:29 [d]Ex. 34:13; Deut. 12:3
16 [a]ch. 12:30 & 13:34 & 15:30,34 & 16:2
17 [a]ch. 16:6,8 [b]ver. 12
18 [a]ver. 13

14:10–16 The prophet Ahijah, who earlier prophesied to Jeroboam that he would become king of Israel, now came to the king and announced that all his descendants would die without honor because of Jeroboam's idolatry. Ahijah further prophesied that God would raise up another king who would kill King Jeroboam's son and end his dynasty (see 15:28). Because of Jeroboam's evil influence God would also "root up Israel out of this good land, which he gave to their fathers, and shall scatter them beyond the river" (14:15), a prophecy of exile that was fulfilled in 722 B.C.

of the LORD, which he spake by the hand of his servant Ahijah the prophet.

19 And the rest of the acts of Jeroboam, how he [a]warred, and how he reigned, behold, they *are* written in the book of the chronicles of the kings of Israel.

20 And the days which Jeroboam reigned *were* two and twenty years: and he [l]slept with his fathers, and Nadab his son reigned in his stead.

Rehoboam, king of Judah

21 ¶ And Rehoboam the son of Solomon reigned in Judah. [a]Rehoboam *was* forty and one years old when he began to reign, and he reigned seventeen years in Jerusalem, the city [b]which the LORD did choose out of all the tribes of Israel, to put his name there. [c]And his mother's name *was* Naamah an Ammonitess.

22 [a]And Judah did evil in the sight of the LORD, and they [b]provoked him to jealousy with their sins which they had committed, above all that their fathers had done.

23 For they also built them [a]high places, and [l]images, [b]and groves, on every high hill, and [c]under every green tree.

24 [a]And there were also sodomites in the land: *and* they did according to all the abominations of the nations which the LORD cast out before the children of Israel.

25 ¶ [a]And it came to pass in the fifth year of king Rehoboam, *that* Shishak king of Egypt came up against Jerusalem:

26 [a]And he took away the treasures of the house of the LORD, and the treasures of the king's house; he even took away all: and he took away all the shields of gold [b]which Solomon had made.

27 And king Rehoboam made in their stead brasen shields, and committed *them* unto the hands of the chief of the [l]guard, which kept the door of the king's house.

28 And it was *so,* when the king went into the house of the LORD, that the guard bare them, and brought them back into the guard chamber.

29 ¶ [a]Now the rest of the acts of Rehoboam, and all that he did, *are* they not written in the book of the chronicles of the kings of Judah?

30 And there was [a]war between Rehoboam and Jeroboam all *their* days.

19 [a]2 Chr. 13:2

20 [l]Heb. *lay down*

21 [a]2 Chr. 12:13 [b]ch. 11:36 [c]ver. 31

22 [a]2 Chr. 12:1 [b]Deut. 32:21

23 [a]Deut. 12:2; Ezek. 16:24,25 [b]2 Ki. 17:9,10 [c]Is. 57:5 [l]Or, *standing images,* or, *statues*

24 [a]Deut. 23:17; ch. 15:12; 2 Ki. 23:7

25 [a]ch. 11:40; 2 Chr. 12:2

26 [a]2 Chr. 12:9-11 [b]ch. 10:17

27 [l]Heb. *runners*

29 [a]2 Chr. 12:15

30 [a]ch. 12:24 & 15:6; 2 Chr. 12:15

31 [a]2 Chr. 12:16 [b]ver. 21 [c]2 Chr. 12:16 *Abijah;* Mat. 1:7 *Abia*

15:1 [a]2 Chr. 13:1

2 [a]2 Chr. 11:20-22 [b]2 Chr. 13:2 *Michaiah the daughter of Uriel* [c]2 Chr. 11:21 *Absalom*

3 [a]ch. 11:4; Ps. 119:80

4 [a]ch. 11:32,36; 2 Chr. 21:7 [b]ch. 11:36 [l]Or, *candle*

5 [a]ch. 14:8 [b]2 Sam. 11:4,15 & 12:9

6 [a]ch. 14:30

7 [a]2 Chr. 13:2,3, 22

8 [a]2 Chr. 14:1

10 [l]i.e. *grandmother's;* see ver. 2

11 [a]2 Chr. 14:2

12 [a]ch. 14:24 & 22:46

13 [a]2 Chr. 15:16

31 [a]And Rehoboam slept with his fathers, and was buried with his fathers in the city of David. [b]And his mother's name *was* Naamah an Ammonitess. And [c]Abijam his son reigned in his stead.

Abijam, king of Judah

15 NOW [a]IN the eighteenth year of king Jeroboam the son of Nebat reigned Abijam over Judah.

2 Three years reigned he in Jerusalem. [a]And his mother's name *was* [b]Maachah, the daughter of [c]Abishalom.

3 And he walked in all the sins of his father, which he had done before him: and [a]his heart was not perfect with the LORD his God, as the heart of David his father.

4 Nevertheless [a]for David's sake did the LORD his God give him a [b]lamp[l] in Jerusalem, to set up his son after him, and to establish Jerusalem:

5 Because David [a]did *that which was* right in the eyes of the LORD, and turned not aside from any *thing* that he commanded him all the days of his life, [b]save only in the matter of Uriah the Hittite.

6 [a]And there was war between Rehoboam and Jeroboam all the days of his life.

7 [a]Now the rest of the acts of Abijam, and all that he did, *are* they not written in the book of the chronicles of the kings of Judah? And there was war between Abijam and Jeroboam.

8 [a]And Abijam slept with his fathers; and they buried him in the city of David: and Asa his son reigned in his stead.

Asa, king of Judah

9 ¶ And in the twentieth year of Jeroboam king of Israel reigned Asa over Judah.

10 And forty and one years reigned he in Jerusalem. And his [l]mother's name *was* Maachah, the daughter of Abishalom.

11 [a]And Asa did *that which was* right in the eyes of the LORD, as *did* David his father.

12 [a]And he took away the sodomites out of the land, and removed all the idols that his fathers had made.

13 And also [a]Maachah his mother, even her he removed from *being* queen, because she had made an idol in a grove;

and Asa [l]destroyed her idol, and [b]burnt *it* by the brook Kidron.

14 [a]But the high places were not removed: nevertheless Asa's [b]heart was perfect with the LORD all his days.

15 And he brought in the [l]things which his father had dedicated, and the things which himself had dedicated, into the house of the LORD, silver, and gold, and vessels.

16 ¶ And there was war between Asa and Baasha king of Israel all their days.

17 And [a]Baasha king of Israel went up against Judah, and built [b]Ramah, [c]that he might not suffer any to go out or come in to Asa king of Judah.

18 Then Asa took all the silver and the gold *that were* left in the treasures of the house of the LORD, and the treasures of the king's house, and delivered them into the hand of his servants: and king Asa sent them to [a]Ben-hadad, the son of Tabrimon, the son of Hezion, king of Syria, that dwelt at [b]Damascus, saying,

19 *There is* a league between me and thee, *and* between my father and thy father: behold, I have sent unto thee a present of silver and gold; come and break thy league with Baasha king of Israel, that he may [l]depart from me.

20 So Ben-hadad hearkened unto king Asa, and sent the captains of the hosts which he had against the cities of Israel, and smote [a]Ijon, and [b]Dan, and [c]Abel-beth-maachah, and all Cinneroth, with all the land of Naphtali.

21 And it came to pass, when Baasha heard *thereof,* that he left off building of Ramah, and dwelt in Tirzah.

22 [a]Then king Asa made a proclamation throughout all Judah; none *was* [l]exempted: and they took away the stones of Ramah, and the timber thereof, wherewith Baasha had builded; and king Asa built with them [b]Geba of Benjamin, and [c]Mizpah.

23 The rest of all the acts of Asa, and all his might, and all that he did, and the cities which he built, *are* they not written in the book of the chronicles of the kings of Judah? Nevertheless [a]in the time of his old age he was diseased in his feet.

24 And Asa slept with his fathers, and was buried with his fathers in the city of David his father: [a]and [b]Jehoshaphat his son reigned in his stead.

Nadab, king of Israel

25 ¶ And Nadab the son of Jeroboam [l]began to reign over Israel in the second year of Asa king of Judah, and reigned over Israel two years.

26 And he did evil in the sight of the LORD, and walked in the way of his father, and in [a]his sin wherewith he made Israel to sin.

27 ¶ [a]And Baasha the son of Ahijah, of the house of Issachar, conspired against him; and Baasha smote him at [b]Gibbethon, which *belonged* to the Philistines; for Nadab and all Israel laid siege to Gibbethon.

28 Even in the third year of Asa king of Judah did Baasha slay him, and reigned in his stead.

29 And it came to pass, when he reigned, *that* he smote all the house of Jeroboam; he left not to Jeroboam any that breathed, until he had destroyed him, according unto [a]the saying of the LORD, which he spake by his servant Ahijah the Shilonite:

30 [a]Because of the sins of Jeroboam which he sinned, and which he made Israel sin, by his provocation wherewith he provoked the LORD God of Israel to anger.

31 ¶ Now the rest of the acts of Nadab, and all that he did, *are* they not written in the book of the chronicles of the kings of Israel?

32 [a]And there was war between Asa and Baasha king of Israel all their days.

Baasha, king of Israel

33 In the third year of Asa king of Judah began Baasha the son of Ahijah to reign over all Israel in Tirzah, twenty and four years.

34 And he did evil in the sight of the LORD, and walked in [a]the way of Jeroboam, and in his sin wherewith he made Israel to sin.

16 THEN THE word of the LORD came to [a]Jehu the son of Hanani against Baasha, saying,

2 [a]Forasmuch as I exalted thee out of

13 [b]Ex. 32:20 [l]Heb. *cut off*
14 [a]ch. 22:43; 2 Chr. 15:17,18 [b]See ver. 3
15 [l]Heb. *holy*
17 [a]2 Chr. 16:1 [b]Josh. 18:25 [c]See ch. 12:27
18 [a]2 Chr. 16:2 [b]ch. 11:23,24
19 [l]Heb. *go up*
20 [a]2 Ki. 15:29 [b]Judg. 18:29 [c]2 Sam. 20:14
22 [a]2 Chr. 16:6 [b]Josh. 21:17 [c]Josh. 18:26 [l]Heb. *free*
23 [a]2 Chr. 16:12
24 [a]2 Chr. 17:1 [b]Mat. 1:8 called *Josaphat*
25 [l]Heb. *reigned*
26 [a]ch. 12:30 & 14:16
27 [a]ch. 14:14 [b]Josh. 19:44
29 [a]ch. 14:10,14
30 [a]ch. 14:9,16
32 [a]ver. 16
34 [a]ch. 12:28,29; & 13:33 & 14:16
16:1 [a]ver. 7; 2 Chr. 19:2 & 20:34
2 [a]ch. 14:7

15:27–28 Baasha, from the tribe of Issachar, conspired and killed King Nadab, the son of King Jeroboam, as prophesied by Ahijah years earlier (see 14:14).

the dust, and made thee prince over my people Israel; and [b]thou hast walked in the way of Jeroboam, and hast made my people Israel to sin, to provoke me to anger with their sins;

3 Behold, I will [a]take away the posterity of Baasha, and the posterity of his house; and will make thy house like [b]the house of Jeroboam the son of Nebat.

4 [a]Him that dieth of Baasha in the city shall the dogs eat; and him that dieth of his in the fields shall the fowls of the air eat.

5 Now the rest of the acts of Baasha, and what he did, and his might, [a]*are* they not written in the book of the chronicles of the kings of Israel?

6 So Baasha slept with his fathers, and was buried in [a]Tirzah: and Elah his son reigned in his stead.

7 And also by the hand of the prophet [a]Jehu the son of Hanani came the word of the LORD against Baasha, and against his house, even for all the evil that he did in the sight of the LORD, in provoking him to anger with the work of his hands, in being like the house of Jeroboam; and because [b]he killed him.

Elah, king of Israel

8 ¶ In the twenty and sixth year of Asa king of Judah began Elah the son of Baasha to reign over Israel in Tirzah, two years.

9 [a]And his servant Zimri, captain of half *his* chariots, conspired against him, as he was in Tirzah, drinking himself drunk in the house of Arza [/]steward of *his* house in Tirzah.

10 And Zimri went in and smote him, and killed him, in the twenty and seventh year of Asa king of Judah, and reigned in his stead.

11 ¶ And it came to pass, when he began to reign, as soon as he sat on his throne, *that* he slew all the house of Baasha: he left him [a]not one that pisseth against a wall, [/]neither of his kinsfolks, nor of his friends.

12 Thus did Zimri destroy all the house of Baasha, [a]according to the word of the LORD, which he spake against Baasha [b]by[/] Jehu the prophet,

13 For all the sins of Baasha, and the sins of Elah his son, by which they sinned, and by which they made Israel to sin, in provoking the LORD God of Israel to anger [a]with their vanities.

14 Now the rest of the acts of Elah, and all that he did, *are* they not written in the book of the chronicles of the kings of Israel?

Zimri, king of Israel

15 ¶ In the twenty and seventh year of Asa king of Judah did Zimri reign seven days in Tirzah. And the people *were* encamped [a]against Gibbethon, which *belonged* to the Philistines.

16 And the people *that were* encamped heard say, Zimri hath conspired, and hath also slain the king: wherefore all Israel made Omri, the captain of the host, king over Israel that day in the camp.

17 And Omri went up from Gibbethon, and all Israel with him, and they besieged Tirzah.

18 And it came to pass, when Zimri saw that the city was taken, that he went into the palace of the king's house, and burnt the king's house over him with fire, and died,

19 For his sins which he sinned in doing evil in the sight of the LORD, [a]in walking in the way of Jeroboam, and in his sin which he did, to make Israel to sin.

20 Now the rest of the acts of Zimri, and his treason that he wrought, *are* they not written in the book of the chronicles of the kings of Israel?

Omri, king of Israel

21 ¶ Then were the people of Israel divided into two parts: half of the people followed Tibni the son of Ginath, to make him king; and half followed Omri.

22 But the people that followed Omri prevailed against the people that followed Tibni the son of Ginath: so Tibni died, and Omri reigned.

23 ¶ In the thirty and first year of Asa king of Judah began Omri to reign over Israel, twelve years: six years reigned he in Tirzah.

24 And he bought the hill Samaria of Shemer for two talents of silver, and built on the hill, and called the name of the city which he built, after the name of Shemer, owner of the hill, [a]Samaria.[/]

2 [b]ch. 15:34
3 [a]ver. 11 [b]ch. 14:10 & 15:29
4 [a]ch. 14:11
5 [a]2 Chr. 16:1
6 [a]ch. 14:17 & 15:21
7 [a]ver. 1 [b]ch. 15:27,29; See Hos. 1:4
9 [a]2 Ki. 9:31 [/]Heb. *which was over*
11 [a]1 Sam. 25:22 [/]Or, *both his kinsmen and his friends*
12 [a]ver. 3 [b]ver. 1 [/]Heb. *by the hand of*
13 [a]Deut. 32:21; 1 Sam. 12:21; Is. 41:29; Jonah 2:8; 1 Cor. 8:4 & 10:19
15 [a]ch. 15:27
19 [a]ch. 12:28 & 15:26,34
24 [a]See ch. 13:32; 2 Ki. 17:24; John 4:4 [/]Heb. *Shomeron*

25 ¶ But [a]Omri wrought evil in the
eyes of the LORD, and did worse than all
that *were* before him.
26 For he [a]walked in all the way of
Jeroboam the son of Nebat, and in his sin
wherewith he made Israel to sin, to provoke the LORD God of Israel to anger with
their [b]vanities.
27 Now the rest of the acts of Omri
which he did, and his might that he
showed, *are* they not written in the
book of the chronicles of the kings of
Israel?
28 So Omri slept with his fathers, and
was buried in Samaria: and Ahab his son
reigned in his stead.

Ahab, king of Israel

29 ¶ And in the thirty and eighth year
of Asa king of Judah began Ahab the son
of Omri to reign over Israel: and Ahab the
son of Omri reigned over Israel in Samaria twenty and two years.
30 And Ahab the son of Omri did evil
in the sight of the LORD above all that
were before him.
31 And it came to pass, [†]as if it had
been a light thing for him to walk in the
sins of Jeroboam the son of Nebat, [a]that
he took to wife Jezebel the daughter of
Ethbaal king of the [b]Zidonians, [c]and
went and served Baal, and worshipped
him.
32 And he reared up an altar for Baal
in [a]the house of Baal, which he had built
in Samaria.
33 [a]And Ahab made a grove; and Ahab
[b]did more to provoke the LORD God of
Israel to anger than all the kings of Israel
that were before him.
34 ¶ In his days did Hiel the Beth-elite
build Jericho: he laid the foundation
thereof in Abiram his firstborn, and set
up the gates thereof in his youngest *son*
Segub, [a]according to the word of the
LORD, which he spake by Joshua the son
of Nun.

25 [a]Mic. 6:16
26 [a]ver. 19 [b]ver. 13
31 [a]Deut. 7:3 [b]Judg. 18:7 [c]ch. 21:25,26; 2 Ki. 10:18 & 17:16 [†]Heb. *was it a light thing*
32 [a]2 Ki. 10:21,26, 27
33 [a]2 Ki. 13:6 & 17:10 & 21:3; Jer. 17:2 [b]ver. 30; ch. 21:25
34 [a]Josh. 6:26
17:1 [a]2 Ki. 3:14 [b]Deut. 10:8 [c]Jas. 5:17 [d]Luke 4:25 [†]Heb. *Elijahu;* in Luke 1:17 & 4:25, he is called *Elias*
7 [†]Heb. *at the end of days*
9 [a]Obad. 20; Luke 4:26 called *Sarepta*

Elijah fed by ravens

17 AND [†]ELIJAH the Tishbite, *who* J
was of the inhabitants of Gilead, F
said unto Ahab, [a]*As* the LORD God of Israel liveth, [b]before whom I stand, [c]there
shall not be dew nor rain [d]these years,
but according to my word.
2 And the word of the LORD came unto
him, saying,
3 Get thee hence, and turn thee eastward, and hide thyself by the brook
Cherith, that *is* before Jordan.
4 And it shall be, *that* thou shalt drink
of the brook; and I have commanded the
ravens to feed thee there.
5 So he went and did according unto
the word of the LORD: for he went and
dwelt by the brook Cherith, that *is* before
Jordan.
6 And the ravens brought him bread
and flesh in the morning, and bread and
flesh in the evening; and he drank of the
brook.
7 And it came to pass [†]after a while,
that the brook dried up, because there
had been no rain in the land.

Elijah raises the widow's son

8 ¶ And the word of the LORD came
unto him, saying,
9 Arise, get thee to [a]Zarephath, which
belongeth to Zidon, and dwell there: behold, I have commanded a widow woman
there to sustain thee.
10 So he arose and went to Zarephath.
And when he came to the gate of the city,
behold, the widow woman *was* there
gathering of sticks: and he called to her,
and said, Fetch me, I pray thee, a little
water in a vessel, that I may drink.
11 And as she was going to fetch *it,* he
called to her, and said, Bring me, I pray
thee, a morsel of bread in thine hand.
12 And she said, *As* the LORD thy God
liveth, I have not a cake, but an handful
of meal in a barrel, and a little oil in a

J *2Sa 12:14* ◀ ▶ *1Ki 21:19*
F *Ru 1:6* ◀ ▶ *1Ki 19:5–8*

16:34 This verse records the deaths of Abiram and Segub, the youngest and oldest sons of Hiel, the builder who ignored Joshua's curse uttered six centuries earlier: "Cursed be the man before the LORD, that riseth up and buildeth this city Jericho: he shall lay the foundation thereof in his firstborn, and in his youngest son shall he set up the gates of it" (Jos 6:26).

17:1 Elijah prophesied to King Ahab that there would be a drought. In fulfillment of Elijah's words, it did not rain for over three years (see Jas 5:17). This period of judgment corresponds to the same length of time of the ministry of God's two witnesses during the tribulation period (see Rev 11:3).

cruse: and, behold, I *am* gathering two sticks, that I may go in and dress it for me and my son, that we may eat it, and die.

13 And Elijah said unto her, Fear not; go *and* do as thou hast said: but make me thereof a little cake first, and bring *it* unto me, and after make for thee and for thy son.

14 For thus saith the LORD God of Israel, The barrel of meal shall not waste, neither shall the cruse of oil fail, until the day *that* the LORD [1]sendeth rain upon the earth.

15 And she went and did according to the saying of Elijah: and she, and he, and her house, did eat [1]*many* days.

16 *And* the barrel of meal wasted not, neither did the cruse of oil fail, according to the word of the LORD, which he spake [1]by Elijah.

17 ¶ And it came to pass after these things, *that* the son of the woman, the mistress of the house, fell sick; and his sickness was so sore, that there was no breath left in him.

18 And she said unto Elijah, [a]What have I to do with thee, O thou man of God? art thou come unto me to call my sin to remembrance, and to slay my son?

19 And he said unto her, Give me thy son. And he took him out of her bosom, and carried him up into a loft, where he abode, and laid him upon his own bed.

20 And he cried unto the LORD, and said, O LORD my God, hast thou also brought evil upon the widow with whom I sojourn, by slaying her son?

21 [a]And he [1]stretched himself upon the child three times, and cried unto the LORD, and said, O LORD my God, I pray thee, let this child's soul come [2]into him again.

E 22 And the LORD heard the voice of Elijah; and the soul of the child came into him again, and he [a]revived.

23 And Elijah took the child, and brought him down out of the chamber into the house, and delivered him unto

E *1Ki 13:6* ◄► *2Ki 4:32–35*

14 [1]Heb. *giveth*
15 [1]Or, *a full year*
16 [1]Heb. *by the hand of*
18 [a]See Luke 5:8
21 [a]2 Ki. 4:34,35 [1]Heb. *measured* [2]Heb. *into his inward parts*
22 [a]Heb. 11:35
24 [a]John 3:2 & 16:30
18:1 [a]Luke 4:25; Jas. 5:17 [b]Deut. 28:12
3 [1]Heb. *Obadiahu* [2]Heb. *over his house*
4 [1]Heb. *Izebel*
5 [1]Heb. *that we cut not off* ourselves *from the beasts*

his mother: and Elijah said, See, thy son liveth.

24 ¶ And the woman said to Elijah, Now by this [a]I know that thou *art* a man of God, *and* that the word of the LORD in thy mouth *is* truth.

Elijah and Obadiah meet

18 AND IT came to pass *after* [a]many days, that the word of the LORD came to Elijah in the third year, saying, Go, show thyself unto Ahab; and [b]I will send rain upon the earth. I

2 And Elijah went to show himself unto Ahab. And *there was* a sore famine in Samaria.

3 And Ahab called [1]Obadiah, which *was* [2]the governor of *his* house. (Now Obadiah feared the LORD greatly:

4 For it was *so,* when [1]Jezebel cut off the prophets of the LORD, that Obadiah took an hundred prophets, and hid them by fifty in a cave, and fed them with bread and water.)

5 And Ahab said unto Obadiah, Go into the land, unto all fountains of water, and unto all brooks: peradventure we may find grass to save the horses and mules alive, [1]that we lose not all the beasts.

6 So they divided the land between them to pass throughout it: Ahab went one way by himself, and Obadiah went another way by himself.

7 ¶ And as Obadiah was in the way, behold, Elijah met him: and he knew him, and fell on his face, and said, *Art* thou that my lord Elijah?

8 And he answered him, I *am:* go, tell thy lord, Behold, Elijah *is here.*

9 And he said, What have I sinned, that thou wouldest deliver thy servant into the hand of Ahab, to slay me?

10 *As* the LORD thy God liveth, there is no nation or kingdom, whither my lord hath not sent to seek thee: and when they said, *He is* not *there;* he took an oath of the kingdom and nation, that they found thee not.

I *1Ki 9:3* ◄► *1Ki 18:41*

17:24 This widow declared that the true test of a prophet's message was in its fulfillment. The words of a man of God would come true.

18:3–4 This verse indicates that there were many godly prophets in Israel who banded together for safety. That Obadiah was able to hide one hundred of these godly prophets from the evil Queen Jezebel during a famine is a miracle of God.

11 And now thou sayest, Go, tell thy lord, Behold, Elijah *is here.*

E L 12 And it shall come to pass, *as soon as* I am gone from thee, that [a]the spirit of the LORD shall carry thee whither I know not; and *so* when I come and tell Ahab, and he cannot find thee, he shall slay me: but I thy servant fear the LORD from my youth.

13 Was it not told my lord what I did when Jezebel slew the prophets of the LORD, how I hid an hundred men of the LORD'S prophets by fifty in a cave, and fed them with bread and water?

14 And now thou sayest, Go, tell thy lord, Behold, Elijah *is here:* and he shall slay me.

15 And Elijah said, *As* the LORD of hosts liveth, before whom I stand, I will surely show myself unto him today.

16 So Obadiah went to meet Ahab, and told him: and Ahab went to meet Elijah.

Elijah on mount Carmel

17 ¶ And it came to pass, when Ahab saw Elijah, that Ahab said unto him, [a]*Art* thou he that [b]troubleth Israel?

18 And he answered, I have not troubled Israel; but thou, and thy father's house, [a]in that ye have forsaken the commandments of the LORD, and thou hast followed Baalim.

19 Now therefore send, *and* gather to me all Israel unto mount [a]Carmel, and the prophets of Baal four hundred and fifty, [b]and the prophets of the groves four hundred, which eat at Jezebel's table.

20 So Ahab sent unto all the children of Israel, and [a]gathered the prophets together unto mount Carmel.

N S 21 And Elijah came unto all the people, and said, [a]How long halt ye between two [1]opinions? if the LORD *be* God, follow him: but if Baal, [b]*then* follow him. And the people answered him not a word.

22 Then said Elijah unto the people, [a]I, *even* I only, remain a prophet of the LORD; [b]but Baal's prophets *are* four hundred and fifty men.

23 Let them therefore give us two bullocks; and let them choose one bullock for themselves, and cut it in pieces, and lay *it* on wood, and put no fire *under:* and I will dress the other bullock, and lay *it* on wood, and put no fire *under:*

24 And call ye on the name of your gods, and I will call on the name of the LORD: and the God that [a]answereth by fire, let him be God. And all the people answered and said, [1]It is well spoken.

25 And Elijah said unto the prophets of Baal, Choose you one bullock for yourselves, and dress *it* first; for ye *are* many; and call on the name of your gods, but put no fire *under.*

26 And they took the bullock which was given them, and they dressed *it,* and called on the name of Baal from morning even until noon, saying, O Baal, [1]hear us. But *there was* [a]no voice, nor any that [2]answered. And they [3]leaped upon the altar which was made.

27 And it came to pass at noon, that Elijah mocked them, and said, Cry [1]aloud: for he *is* a god; either [2]he is talking, or he [3]is pursuing, or he is in a journey, *or* peradventure he sleepeth, and must be awaked.

28 And they cried aloud, and [a]cut themselves after their manner with knives and lancets, till [1]the blood gushed out upon them.

29 And it came to pass, when midday was past, [a]and they prophesied until the *time* of the [1]offering of the *evening* sacrifice, that *there was* [b]neither voice, nor any to answer, nor any [2]that regarded.

30 And Elijah said unto all the people, Come near unto me. And all the people came near unto him. [a]And he repaired the altar of the LORD *that was* broken down.

31 And Elijah took twelve stones, according to the number of the tribes of the sons of Jacob, unto whom the word of the LORD came, saying, [a]Israel shall be thy name:

32 And with the stones he built an altar [a]in the name of the LORD: and he made a trench about the altar, as great as would contain two measures of seed.

33 And he [a]put the wood in order, and cut the bullock in pieces, and laid *him* on the wood, and said, Fill four barrels with water, and [b]pour *it* on the burnt sacrifice, and on the wood.

34 And he said, Do *it* the second time. And they did *it* the second time. And he

12 [a]2 Ki. 2:16; Ezek. 3:12,14; Mat. 4:1; Acts 8:39
17 [a]ch. 21:20 [b]Josh. 7:25; Acts 16:20
18 [a]2 Chr. 15:2
19 [a]Josh. 19:26 [b]ch. 16:33
20 [a]ch. 22:6
21 [a]2 Ki. 17:41; Mat. 6:24 [b]See Josh. 24:15 [1]Or, *thoughts?*
22 [a]ch. 19:10,14 [b]ver. 19
24 [a]ver. 38; 1 Chr. 21:26 [1]Heb. *The word* is *good*
26 [a]Ps. 115:5; Jer. 10:5; 1 Cor. 8:4 [1]Or, *answer* [2]Or, *heard* [3]Or, *leaped up and down at the altar*
27 [1]Heb. *with a great voice* [2]Or, *he meditateth* [3]Heb. *hath a pursuit*
28 [a]Lev. 19:28; Deut. 14:1 [1]Heb. *poured out blood upon them*
29 [a]1 Cor. 11:4,5 [b]ver. 26 [1]Heb. *ascending* [2]Heb. *attention*
30 [a]ch. 19:10
31 [a]Gen. 32:28; 2 Ki. 17:34
32 [a]Col. 3:17
33 [a]Lev. 1:6-8 [b]See Judg. 6:20

E *2Sa 23:2* ◄► *1Ki 22:24*
L *2Sa 23:2* ◄► *1Ki 22:24*
N *2Sa 14:14* ◄► *2Ki 17:13–15*
S *1Ki 8:61* ◄► *1Ch 16:29*

said, Do *it* the third time. And they did *it*
the third time.
35 And the water [/]ran round about the
altar; and he filled [a]the trench also with
water.
36 And it came to pass at *the time of*
the offering of the *evening* sacrifice, that
Elijah the prophet came near, and said,
LORD [a]God of Abraham, Isaac, and of Israel, [b]let it be known this day that thou
art God in Israel, and *that* I *am* thy servant, and *that* [c]I have done all these
things at thy word.
37 Hear me, O LORD, hear me, that this
people may know that thou *art* the LORD
God, and *that* thou hast turned their
heart back again.
38 Then [a]the fire of the LORD fell, and
consumed the burnt sacrifice, and the
wood, and the stones, and the dust, and
licked up the water that *was* in the
trench.
39 And when all the people saw *it,*
they fell on their faces: and they said,
[a]The LORD, he *is* the God; the LORD, he *is*
the God.
40 And Elijah said unto them, [a]Take[/]
the prophets of Baal; let not one of them
escape. And they took them: and Elijah
brought them down to the brook Kishon,
and [b]slew them there.
I 41 ¶ And Elijah said unto Ahab, Get
thee up, eat and drink; for *there is* [/]a
sound of abundance of rain.
42 So Ahab went up to eat and to
drink. And Elijah went up to the top of
Carmel; [a]and he cast himself down upon
the earth, and put his face between his
knees,
43 And said to his servant, Go up now,
look toward the sea. And he went up, and
looked, and said, *There is* nothing. And
he said, Go again seven times.
44 And it came to pass at the seventh
time, that he said, Behold, there ariseth a
little cloud out of the sea, like a man's
hand. And he said, Go up, say unto Ahab,
[/]Prepare *thy chariot,* and get thee down,
that the rain stop thee not.
45 And it came to pass in the mean
while, that the heaven was black with
clouds and wind, and there was a great
rain. And Ahab rode, and went to Jezreel.
46 And the hand of the LORD was on
Elijah; and he [a]girded up his loins, and
ran before Ahab [/]to the entrance of
Jezreel.

Elijah flees from Jezebel

19 AND AHAB told Jezebel all that
Elijah had done, and withal how
he had [a]slain all the prophets with the
sword.
2 Then Jezebel sent a messenger unto
Elijah, saying, [a]So let the gods do *to me,*
and more also, if I make not thy life as the
life of one of them by tomorrow about
this time.
3 And when he saw *that,* he arose, and
went for his life, and came to Beer-sheba,
which *belongeth* to Judah, and left his
servant there.
4 ¶ But he himself went a day's journey into the wilderness, and came and
sat down under a juniper tree: and he
[a]requested [/]for himself that he might die;
and said, It is enough; now, O LORD, take
away my life; for I *am* not better than my
fathers.
5 And as he lay and slept under a juni- F
per tree, behold, then an angel touched
him, and said unto him, Arise *and* eat.
6 And he looked, and, behold, *there
was* a cake baked on the coals, and a
cruse of water at his [/]head. And he did
eat and drink, and laid him down again.
7 And the angel of the LORD came again
the second time, and touched him, and
said, Arise *and* eat; because the journey
is too great for thee.
8 And he arose, and did eat and drink,
and went in the strength of that meat
[a]forty days and forty nights unto [b]Horeb
the mount of God.

Elijah in the mountain cave

9 ¶ And he came thither unto a cave,
and lodged there; and, behold, the word
of the LORD *came* to him, and he said unto
him, What doest thou here, Elijah?
10 And he said, [a]I have been very

35 [a]ver. 32,38 [/]Heb. *went*
36 [a]Ex. 3:6 [b]ch. 8:43; 2 Ki. 19:19 [c]Num. 16:28
38 [a]Lev. 9:24; Judg. 6:21; 1 Chr. 21:26; 2 Chr. 7:1
39 [a]ver. 24
40 [a]2 Ki. 10:25 [b]Deut. 13:5 & 18:20 [/]Or, *Apprehend*
41 [/]Or, *a sound of a noise of rain*
42 [a]Jas. 5:17,18
44 [/]Heb. *Tie,* or, *Bind*
46 [a]2 Ki. 4:29 & 9:1 [/]Heb. *till thou come to Jezreel*
19:1 [a]ch. 18:40
2 [a]Ruth 1:17; ch. 20:10; 2 Ki. 6:31
4 [a]Num. 11:15; Jonah 4:3,8 [/]Heb. *for his life*
6 [/]Heb. *bolster*
8 [a]Ex. 34:28; Deut. 9:9,18; Mat. 4:2 [b]Ex. 3:1
10 [a]Rom. 11:3

I *1Ki 18:1* ◄► *2Ki 7:1–2*

F *1Ki 17:1–16* ◄► *2Ki 3:9–20*

18:41–46 Elijah bravely approached the king who hated him and announced that the rains would begin again and end God's judgment of drought and famine throughout Israel. The rains began as promised, and Elijah was miraculously empowered to run from Mt. Carmel to Jezreel (about 17 miles).

[b]jealous for the LORD God of hosts: for the children of Israel have forsaken thy covenant, thrown down thine altars, and [c]slain thy prophets with the sword; and [d]I, *even* I only, am left; and they seek my life, to take it away.

11 And he said, Go forth, and stand [a]upon the mount before the LORD. And, behold, the LORD passed by, and [b]a great and strong wind rent the mountains, and brake in pieces the rocks before the LORD; *but* the LORD *was* not in the wind: and after the wind an earthquake; *but* the LORD *was* not in the earthquake:

12 And after the earthquake a fire; *but* the LORD *was* not in the fire: and after the fire a still small voice.

13 And it was *so,* when Elijah heard *it,* that [a]he wrapped his face in his mantle, and went out, and stood in the entering in of the cave. [b]And, behold, *there came* a voice unto him, and said, What doest thou here, Elijah?

14 [a]And he said, I have been very jealous for the LORD God of hosts: because the children of Israel have forsaken thy covenant, thrown down thine altars, and slain thy prophets with the sword; and I, *even* I only, am left; and they seek my life, to take it away.

15 And the LORD said unto him, Go, return on thy way to the wilderness of Damascus: [a]and when thou comest, anoint Hazael *to be* king over Syria:

16 And [a]Jehu the son of Nimshi shalt thou anoint *to be* king over Israel: and [b]Elisha the son of Shaphat of Abel-meholah shalt thou anoint *to be* prophet in thy room.

17 And [a]it shall come to pass, *that* him that escapeth the sword of Hazael shall Jehu slay: and him that escapeth from the sword of Jehu [b]shall Elisha slay.

18 [a]Yet [I]I have left *me* seven thousand in Israel, all the knees which have not bowed unto Baal, [b]and every mouth which hath not kissed him.

10 [b]Num. 25:11, 13; Ps. 69:9 [c]ch. 18:4 [d]ch. 18:22; Rom. 11:3
11 [a]Ex. 24:12 [b]Ezek. 1:4 & 37:7
13 [a]Ex. 3:6; Is. 6:2 [b]ver. 9
14 [a]ver. 10
15 [a]2 Ki. 8:12,13
16 [a]2 Ki. 9:1-3 [b]Luke 4:27 called *Eliseus*
17 [a]2 Ki. 8:12 & 9:14 & 10:6 & 13:3 [b]See Hos. 6:5
18 [a]Rom. 11:4 [b]See Hos. 13:2 [I]Or, *I will leave*
20 [a]Mat. 8:21,22; Luke 9:61,62 [I]Heb. *Go return*
21 [a]2 Sam. 24:22

Elijah and Elisha

19 ¶ So he departed thence, and found Elisha the son of Shaphat, who *was* plowing *with* twelve yoke *of oxen* before him, and he with the twelfth: and Elijah passed by him, and cast his mantle upon him.

20 And he left the oxen, and ran after Elijah, and said, [a]Let me, I pray thee, kiss my father and my mother, and *then* I will follow thee. And he said unto him, [I]Go back again: for what have I done to thee?

21 And he returned back from him, and took a yoke of oxen, and slew them, and [a]boiled their flesh with the instruments of the oxen, and gave unto the people, and they did eat. Then he arose, and went after Elijah, and ministered unto him.

Ahab defeats Ben-hadad

20 AND BEN-HADAD the king of Syria gathered all his host together: and *there were* thirty and two kings with him, and horses, and chariots: and he went up and besieged Samaria, and warred against it.

2 And he sent messengers to Ahab king of Israel into the city, and said unto him, Thus saith Ben-hadad,

3 Thy silver and thy gold *is* mine; thy wives also and thy children, *even* the goodliest, *are* mine.

4 And the king of Israel answered and said, My lord, O king, according to thy saying, I *am* thine, and all that I have.

5 And the messengers came again, and said, Thus speaketh Ben-hadad, saying, Although I have sent unto thee, saying, Thou shalt deliver me thy silver, and thy gold, and thy wives, and thy children;

6 Yet I will send my servants unto thee tomorrow about this time, and they shall search thine house, and the houses of thy servants; and it shall be, *that* whatsoever

---

19:15–18 God commanded Elijah to anoint Hazael as king of Syria, Jehu as king of Israel and Elisha as his successor as the chief prophet of Israel. God promised that none of his evil enemies would escape Hazael, Jehu or Elisha. While Elijah complained bitterly that he was the only faithful man of God left in Israel (see 19:10), God responded that he had "seven thousand in Israel, all the knees which have not bowed unto Baal, and every mouth which hath not kissed him" (19:18). God's message is the same today. Despite widespread apostasy, God is still in control and has under his care many men and women who truly love him and his Word.

19:19 Elijah obeyed God's command and found his successor plowing a field. By placing his cloak on the shoulders of this younger man of God, Elijah symbolically passed his prophetic office to Elisha.

is [1]pleasant in thine eyes, they shall put *it*
in their hand, and take *it* away.
7 Then the king of Israel called all the
elders of the land, and said, Mark, I pray
you, and see how this *man* seeketh mischief: for he sent unto me for my wives,
and for my children, and for my silver,
and for my gold; and [1]I denied him not.
8 And all the elders and all the people
said unto him, Hearken not *unto him,*
nor consent.
9 Wherefore he said unto the messengers of Ben-hadad, Tell my lord the king,
All that thou didst send for to thy servant
at the first I will do: but this thing I may
not do. And the messengers departed,
and brought him word again.
10 And Ben-hadad sent unto him, and
said, [a]The gods do so unto me, and more
also, if the dust of Samaria shall suffice
for handfuls for all the people that [1]fol-
low me.
11 And the king of Israel answered
and said, Tell *him,* Let not him that girdeth on *his harness* boast himself as he
that putteth it off.
12 And it came to pass, when *Ben-hadad* heard this [1]message, as he *was*
[a]drinking, he and the kings in the [2]pavil-
ions, that he said unto his servants, [3]Set
yourselves in array. And they set *themselves in array* against the city.
13 ¶ And, behold, there [1]came a
prophet unto Ahab king of Israel, saying,
Thus saith the LORD, Hast thou seen all
this great multitude? behold, [a]I will deliver it into thine hand this day; and thou
shalt know that I *am* the LORD.
14 And Ahab said, By whom? And he
said, Thus saith the LORD, *Even* by the
[1]young men of the princes of the provinces. Then he said, Who shall [2]order the
battle? And he answered, Thou.
15 Then he numbered the young men
of the princes of the provinces, and they
were two hundred and thirty two: and
after them he numbered all the people,
even all the children of Israel, *being*
seven thousand.
16 And they went out at noon. But
Ben-hadad *was* [a]drinking himself drunk
in the pavilions, he and the kings, the
thirty and two kings that helped him.
17 And the young men of the princes
of the provinces went out first; and Ben-
hadad sent out, and they told him, saying,
There are men come out of Samaria.
18 And he said, Whether they be come
out for peace, take them alive; or
whether they be come out for war, take
them alive.
19 So these young men of the princes
of the provinces came out of the city, and
the army which followed them.
20 And they slew every one his man:
and the Syrians fled; and Israel pursued
them: and Ben-hadad the king of Syria
escaped on an horse with the horsemen.
21 And the king of Israel went out, and
smote the horses and chariots, and slew
the Syrians with a great slaughter.
22 ¶ And the prophet came to the king
of Israel, and said unto him, Go,
strengthen thyself, and mark, and see
what thou doest: [a]for at the return of the
year the king of Syria will come up
against thee.
23 And the servants of the king of
Syria said unto him, Their gods *are* gods
of the hills; therefore they were stronger
than we; but let us fight against them in
the plain, and surely we shall be stronger
than they.
24 And do this thing, Take the kings
away, every man out of his place, and put
captains in their rooms:
25 And number thee an army, like the
army [1]that thou hast lost, horse for horse,
and chariot for chariot: and we will fight
against them in the plain, *and* surely we
shall be stronger than they. And he
hearkened unto their voice, and did so.
26 And it came to pass at the return of
the year, that Ben-hadad numbered the
Syrians, and went up to [a]Aphek, [1]to fight
against Israel.
27 And the children of Israel were
numbered, and [1]were all present, and
went against them: and the children of
Israel pitched before them like two little
flocks of kids; but the Syrians filled the
country.
28 ¶ And there came a man of God,
and spake unto the king of Israel, and
said, Thus saith the LORD, Because the
Syrians have said, The LORD *is* God of the
hills, but he *is* not God of the valleys,
therefore [a]will I deliver all this great multitude into thine hand, and ye shall know
that I *am* the LORD.
29 And they pitched one over against
the other seven days. And *so* it was, that
in the seventh day the battle was joined:
and the children of Israel slew of the Syri-

20:6 [1]Heb. *desirable*
7 [1]Heb. *I kept not back from him*
10 [a]ch. 19:2 [1]Heb. are *at my feet*
12 [a]ver. 16 [1]Heb. *word* [2]Or, *tents* [3]Or, *Place* the engines *And they placed* engines
13 [a]ver. 28 [1]Heb. *approached*
14 [1]Or, *servants* [2]Heb. *bind,* or, *tie*
16 [a]ver. 12; ch. 16:9
22 [a]2 Sam. 11:1
25 [1]Heb. *that was fallen*
26 [a]Josh. 13:4 [1]Heb. *to the war with Israel*
27 [1]Or, *were victualled*
28 [a]ver. 13

ans an hundred thousand footmen in one
day.
30 But the rest fled to Aphek, into the
city; and *there* a wall fell upon twenty
and seven thousand of the men *that were*
left. And Ben-hadad fled, and came into
the city, [1,2]into an inner chamber.
31 ¶ And his servants said unto him,
Behold now, we have heard that the
kings of the house of Israel *are* merciful
kings: let us, I pray thee, [a]put sackcloth
on our loins, and ropes upon our heads,
and go out to the king of Israel: peradventure he will save thy life.
32 So they girded sackcloth on their
loins, and *put* ropes on their heads, and
came to the king of Israel, and said, Thy
servant Ben-hadad saith, I pray thee, let
me live. And he said, *Is* he yet alive? he *is*
my brother.
33 Now the men did diligently observe
whether *any thing would come* from
him, and did hastily catch *it:* and they
said, Thy brother Ben-hadad. Then he
said, Go ye, bring him. Then Ben-hadad
came forth to him; and he caused him to
come up into the chariot.
34 And *Ben-hadad* said unto him, [a]The
cities, which my father took from thy father, I will restore; and thou shalt make
streets for thee in Damascus, as my father
made in Samaria. Then *said Ahab,* I will
send thee away with this covenant. So he
made a covenant with him, and sent him
away.

Ahab judged

35 ¶ And a certain man of [a]the sons of
the prophets said unto his neighbour [b]in
the word of the LORD, Smite me, I pray
thee. And the man refused to smite him.
36 Then said he unto him, Because
thou hast not obeyed the voice of the
LORD, behold, as soon as thou art departed
from me, a lion shall slay thee. And as
soon as he was departed from him, [a]a
lion found him, and slew him.
37 Then he found another man, and
said, Smite me, I pray thee. And the man
smote him, [1]so that in smiting he
wounded *him.*
38 So the prophet departed, and
waited for the king by the way, and disguised himself with ashes upon his face.
39 And [a]as the king passed by, he
cried unto the king: and he said, Thy servant went out into the midst of the battle;
and, behold, a man turned aside, and
brought a man unto me, and said, Keep
this man: if by any means he be missing,
then [b]shall thy life be for his life, or else
thou shalt [1]pay a talent of silver.
40 And as thy servant was busy here
and there, [1]he was gone. And the king of
Israel said unto him, So *shall* thy judgment *be;* thyself hast decided *it.*
41 And he hasted, and took the ashes
away from his face; and the king of Israel
discerned him that he *was* of the
prophets.
42 And he said unto him, Thus saith
the LORD, [a]Because thou hast let go out of
thy hand a man whom I appointed to utter destruction, therefore thy life shall go
for his life, and thy people for his people.
43 And the king of Israel [a]went to his
house heavy and displeased, and came to
Samaria.

Naboth's vineyard

21 AND IT came to pass after these
things, *that* Naboth the Jezreelite
had a vineyard, which *was* in Jezreel,
hard by the palace of Ahab king of Samaria.
2 And Ahab spake unto Naboth, saying, Give me thy [a]vineyard, that I may
have it for a garden of herbs, because it *is*
near unto my house: and I will give thee
for it a better vineyard than it; *or,* if it
[1]seem good to thee, I will give thee the
worth of it in money.
3 And Naboth said to Ahab, The LORD
forbid it me, [a]that I should give the inheritance of my fathers unto thee.
4 And Ahab came into his house heavy
and displeased because of the word
which Naboth the Jezreelite had spoken
to him: for he had said, I will not give
thee the inheritance of my fathers. And
he laid him down upon his bed, and
turned away his face, and would eat no
bread.
5 ¶ But Jezebel his wife came to him,
and said unto him, Why is thy spirit so
sad, that thou eatest no bread?
6 And he said unto her, Because I
spake unto Naboth the Jezreelite, and
said unto him, Give me thy vineyard for
money; or else, if it please thee, I will
give thee *another* vineyard for it: and he
answered, I will not give thee my
vineyard.
7 And Jezebel his wife said unto him,

30 [1]Or, *from chamber to chamber* [2]Heb. *into a chamber within a chamber*
31 [a]Gen. 37:34
34 [a]ch. 15:20
35 [a]2 Ki. 2:3,5,7, 15 [b]ch. 13:17,18
36 [a]ch. 13:24
37 [1]Heb. *smiting and wounding*
39 [a]See 2 Sam. 12:1 [b]2 Ki. 10:24 [1]Heb. *weigh*
40 [1]Heb. *he was not*
42 [a]ch. 22:31-37
43 [a]ch. 21:4
21:2 [a]1 Sam. 8:14 [1]Heb. *be good in thine eyes*
3 [a]Lev. 25:23; Num. 36:7; Ezek. 46:18

Dost thou now govern the kingdom of Israel? arise, *and* eat bread, and let thine heart be merry: I will give thee the vineyard of Naboth the Jezreelite.

8 So she wrote letters in Ahab's name, and sealed *them* with his seal, and sent the letters unto the elders and to the nobles that *were* in his city, dwelling with Naboth.

9 And she wrote in the letters, saying, Proclaim a fast, and set Naboth [l]on high among the people:

10 And set two men, sons of Belial, before him, to bear witness against him, saying, Thou didst [a]blaspheme God and the king. And *then* carry him out, and [b]stone him, that he may die.

11 And the men of his city, *even* the elders and the nobles who were the inhabitants in his city, did as Jezebel had sent unto them, *and* as it *was* written in the letters which she had sent unto them.

12 [a]They proclaimed a fast, and set Naboth on high among the people.

13 And there came in two men, children of Belial, and sat before him: and the men of Belial witnessed against him, *even* against Naboth, in the presence of the people, saying, Naboth did blaspheme God and the king. [a]Then they carried him forth out of the city, and stoned him with stones, that he died.

14 Then they sent to Jezebel, saying, Naboth is stoned, and is dead.

15 ¶ And it came to pass, when Jezebel heard that Naboth was stoned, and was dead, that Jezebel said to Ahab, Arise, take possession of the vineyard of Naboth the Jezreelite, which he refused to give thee for money: for Naboth is not alive, but dead.

16 And it came to pass, when Ahab heard that Naboth was dead, that Ahab rose up to go down to the vineyard of Naboth the Jezreelite, to take possession of it.

17 ¶ [a]And the word of the LORD came to Elijah the Tishbite, saying,

18 Arise, go down to meet Ahab king of Israel, [a]which *is* in Samaria: behold, *he* *is* in the vineyard of Naboth, whither he is gone down to possess it.

19 And thou shalt speak unto him, saying, Thus saith the LORD, Hast thou killed, and also taken possession? And thou shalt speak unto him, saying, Thus saith the LORD, [a]In the place where dogs licked the blood of Naboth shall dogs lick thy blood, even thine. J

20 And Ahab said to Elijah, [a]Hast thou found me, O mine enemy? And he answered, I have found *thee:* because [b]thou hast sold thyself to work evil in the sight of the LORD. C

21 Behold, [a]I will bring evil upon thee, and will take away thy posterity, and will cut off from Ahab [b]him that pisseth against the wall, and [c]him that is shut up and left in Israel, J

22 And will make thine house like the house of [a]Jeroboam the son of Nebat, and like the house of [b]Baasha the son of Ahijah, for the provocation wherewith thou hast provoked *me* to anger, and made Israel to sin.

23 And [a]of Jezebel also spake the LORD, saying, The dogs shall eat Jezebel by the [l]wall of Jezreel.

24 [a]Him that dieth of Ahab in the city the dogs shall eat; and him that dieth in the field shall the fowls of the air eat.

25 ¶ But [a]there was none like unto Ahab, which did sell himself to work wickedness in the sight of the LORD, [b]whom Jezebel his wife [l]stirred up. M

26 And he did very abominably in following idols, according to all *things* [a]as did the Amorites, whom the LORD cast out before the children of Israel.

27 And it came to pass, when Ahab heard those words, that he rent his clothes, and [a]put sackcloth upon his flesh, and fasted, and lay in sackcloth, and went softly.

28 And the word of the LORD came to Elijah the Tishbite, saying,

9 [l]Heb. *in the top of the people*
10 [a]Ex. 22:28; Lev. 24:15,16; Acts 6:11 [b]Lev. 24:14
12 [a]Is. 58:4
13 [a]See 2 Ki. 9:26
17 [a]Ps. 9:12
18 [a]ch. 13:32; 2 Chr. 22:9
19 [a]ch. 22:38
20 [a]ch. 18:17 [b]2 Ki. 17:17; Rom. 7:14
21 [a]ch. 14:10; 2 Ki. 9:8 [b]1 Sam. 25:22 [c]ch. 14:10
22 [a]ch. 15:29 [b]ch. 16:3,11
23 [a]2 Ki. 9:36 [l]Or, *ditch*
24 [a]ch. 14:11 & 16:4
25 [a]ch. 16:30 [b]ch. 16:31 [l]Or, *incited*
26 [a]Gen. 15:16; 2 Ki. 21:11
27 [a]Gen. 37:34

J *1Ki 17:1* ◀ ▶ *1Ki 21:21–24*
C *2Sa 23:6–7* ◀ ▶ *2Ki 17:14–15*
J *1Ki 21:19* ◀ ▶ *1Ki 21:29*
M *2Sa 24:10* ◀ ▶ *2Ki 22:19*

21:21–29 Elijah announced God's verdict upon King Ahab's dynasty because of Ahab's idolatry: all of Ahab's descendants would die dishonorably, his dynasty would be destroyed and dogs would eat his wife's dead body. In response to this terrible judgment, Ahab repented, and God graciously delayed this punishment until after Ahab's death, allowing the judgment to fall on Ahab's evil son instead.

J 29 Seest thou how Ahab humbleth himself before me? because he humbleth himself before me, I will not bring the evil in his days: *but* [a]in his son's days will I bring the evil upon his house.

Micaiah's prophecy

22 AND THEY continued three years without war between Syria and Israel.

2 And it came to pass in the third year, that [a]Jehoshaphat the king of Judah came down to the king of Israel.

3 And the king of Israel said unto his servants, Know ye that [a]Ramoth in Gilead *is* ours, and we *be* [l]still, *and* take it not out of the hand of the king of Syria?

4 And he said unto Jehoshaphat, Wilt thou go with me to battle to Ramoth-gilead? And Jehoshaphat said to the king of Israel, [a]I *am* as thou *art,* my people as thy people, my horses as thy horses.

5 And Jehoshaphat said unto the king of Israel, Inquire, I pray thee, at the word of the LORD today.

6 Then the king of Israel [a]gathered the prophets together, about four hundred men, and said unto them, Shall I go against Ramoth-gilead to battle, or shall I forbear? And they said, Go up; for the Lord shall deliver *it* into the hand of the king.

7 And [a]Jehoshaphat said, *Is there* not here a prophet of the LORD besides, that we might inquire of him?

8 And the king of Israel said unto Jehoshaphat, *There is* yet one man, Micaiah the son of Imlah, by whom we may inquire of the LORD: but I hate him; for he doth not prophesy good concerning me, but evil. And Jehoshaphat said, Let not the king say so.

9 Then the king of Israel called an [l]officer, and said, Hasten *hither* Micaiah the son of Imlah.

10 And the king of Israel and Jehoshaphat the king of Judah sat each on his throne, having put on their robes, in a [l]void place in the entrance of the gate of Samaria; and all the prophets prophesied before them.

11 And Zedekiah the son of Chenaanah made him horns of iron: and he said, Thus saith the LORD, With these shalt thou push the Syrians, until thou have consumed them.

12 And all the prophets prophesied so, saying, Go up to Ramoth-gilead, and prosper: for the LORD shall deliver *it* into the king's hand.

13 And the messenger that was gone to call Micaiah spake unto him, saying, Behold now, the words of the prophets *declare* good unto the king with one mouth: let thy word, I pray thee, be like the word of one of them, and speak *that which is* good.

14 And Micaiah said, *As* the LORD liveth, [a]what the LORD saith unto me, that will I speak.

15 ¶ So he came to the king. And the king said unto him, Micaiah, shall we go against Ramoth-gilead to battle, or shall we forbear? And he answered him, Go, and prosper: for the LORD shall deliver *it* into the hand of the king.

16 And the king said unto him, How many times shall I adjure thee that thou tell me nothing but *that which is* true in the name of the LORD?

17 And he said, I saw all Israel [a]scattered upon the hills, as sheep that have not a shepherd: and the LORD said, These have no master: let them return every man to his house in peace.

18 And the king of Israel said unto Jehoshaphat, Did I not tell thee that he would prophesy no good concerning me, but evil?

19 And he said, Hear thou therefore the word of the LORD: [a]I saw the LORD sitting on his throne, [b]and all the host of heaven standing by him on his right hand and on his left.

20 And the LORD said, Who shall [l]persuade Ahab, that he may go up and fall at Ramoth-gilead? And one said on this manner, and another said on that manner.

21 And there came forth a spirit, and stood before the LORD, and said, I will persuade him.

22 And the LORD said unto him, Wherewith? And he said, I will go forth, and I will be a lying spirit in the mouth of all his prophets. And he said, [a]Thou shalt persuade *him,* and prevail also: go forth, and do so.

23 [a]Now therefore, behold, the LORD hath put a lying spirit in the mouth of all

29 [a]2 Ki. 9:25
22:2 [a]2 Chr. 18:2
3 [a]Deut. 4:43 [l]Heb. *silent from taking it*
4 [a]2 Ki. 3:7
6 [a]ch. 18:19
7 [a]2 Ki. 3:11
9 [l]Or, *eunuch*
10 [l]Heb. *floor*
14 [a]Num. 22:38
17 [a]Mat. 9:36
19 [a]Is. 6:1; Dan. 7:9 [b]Job 1:6 & 2:1; Dan. 7:10; Zech. 1:10; Mat. 18:10; Heb. 1:7,14
20 [l]Or, *deceive*
22 [a]Judg. 9:23; Job 12:16; Ezek. 14:9; 2 Thes. 2:11
23 [a]Ezek. 14:9

J *1Ki 21:21–24* ◄► *2Ki 1:4*

these thy prophets, and the LORD hath spoken evil concerning thee.

E L Q 24 But Zedekiah the son of Chenaanah went near, and smote Micaiah on the cheek, and said, [a]Which way went the spirit of the LORD from me to speak unto thee?

25 And Micaiah said, Behold, thou shalt see in that day, when thou shalt go [1]into [2]an inner chamber to hide thyself.

26 And the king of Israel said, Take Micaiah, and carry him back unto Amon the governor of the city, and to Joash the king's son;

27 And say, Thus saith the king, Put this *fellow* in the prison, and feed him with bread of affliction and with water of affliction, until I come in peace.

28 And Micaiah said, If thou return at all in peace, [a]the LORD hath not spoken by me. And he said, Hearken, O people, every one of you.

Ahab's defeat and death

29 So the king of Israel and Jehoshaphat the king of Judah went up to Ramoth-gilead.

30 And the king of Israel said unto Jehoshaphat, [1]I will disguise myself, and enter into the battle; but put thou on thy robes. And the king of Israel [a]disguised himself, and went into the battle.

31 But the king of Syria commanded his thirty and two captains that had rule over his chariots, saying, Fight neither with small nor great, save only with the king of Israel.

32 And it came to pass, when the captains of the chariots saw Jehoshaphat, that they said, Surely it *is* the king of Israel. And they turned aside to fight against him: and Jehoshaphat [a]cried out.

33 And it came to pass, when the captains of the chariots perceived that it *was* not the king of Israel, that they turned back from pursuing him.

34 And a *certain* man drew a bow at a venture, and smote the king of Israel between the [1]joints of the harness: wherefore he said unto the driver of his chariot, Turn thine hand, and carry me out of the host; for I am [2]wounded.

35 And the battle [1]increased that day: and the king was stayed up in his chariot against the Syrians, and died at even: and the blood ran out of the wound into the [2]midst of the chariot.

36 And there went a proclamation throughout the host about the going down of the sun, saying, Every man to his city, and every man to his own country.

37 ¶ So the king died, and [1]was brought to Samaria; and they buried the king in Samaria.

38 And *one* washed the chariot in the pool of Samaria; and the dogs licked up his blood; and they washed his armour; according [a]unto the word of the LORD which he spake.

39 Now the rest of the acts of Ahab, and all that he did, and [a]the ivory house which he made, and all the cities that he built, *are* they not written in the book of the chronicles of the kings of Israel?

40 So Ahab slept with his fathers; and Ahaziah his son reigned in his stead.

Jehoshaphat, king of Judah

41 ¶ And [a]Jehoshaphat the son of Asa began to reign over Judah in the fourth year of Ahab king of Israel.

42 Jehoshaphat *was* thirty and five years old when he began to reign; and he reigned twenty and five years in Jerusalem. And his mother's name *was* Azubah the daughter of Shilhi.

43 And [a]he walked in all the ways of Asa his father; he turned not aside from it, doing *that which was* right in the eyes of the LORD: nevertheless [b]the high places were not taken away; *for* the people offered and burnt incense yet in the high places.

44 And [a]Jehoshaphat made peace with the king of Israel.

45 Now the rest of the acts of Jehoshaphat, and his might that he showed, and how he warred, *are* they not written in the book of the chronicles of the kings of Judah?

46 [a]And the remnant of the sodomites, which remained in the days of his father Asa, he took out of the land.

47 [a]*There was* then no king in Edom: a deputy *was* king.

48 [a]Jehoshaphat [b]made[1] ships of Tharshish to go to Ophir for gold: [c]but they went not; for the ships were broken at [d]Ezion-geber.

49 Then said Ahaziah the son of Ahab

24 [a]2 Chr. 18:23
25 [1]Or, *from chamber to chamber* [2]Heb. *a chamber in a chamber*
28 [a]Num. 16:29; Deut. 18:20-22
30 [a]2 Chr. 35:22 [1]Or, *when he was to disguise himself, and enter into the battle*
32 [a]2 Chr. 18:31; Prov. 13:20
34 [1]Heb. *joints and the breastplate* [2]Heb. *made sick*
35 [1]Heb. *ascended* [2]Heb. *bosom*
37 [1]Heb. *came*
38 [a]ch. 21:19
39 [a]Amos 3:15
41 [a]2 Chr. 20:31
43 [a]2 Chr. 17:3 [b]ch. 14:23 & 15:14; 2 Ki. 12:3
44 [a]2 Chr. 19:2; 2 Cor. 6:14
46 [a]ch. 14:24 & 15:12
47 [a]Gen. 25:23; 2 Sam. 8:14; 2 Ki. 3:9 & 8:20
48 [a]2 Chr. 20:35 [b]ch. 10:22 [c]2 Chr. 20:37 [d]ch. 9:26 [1]Or, had *ten ships*

E 1Ki 18:12 ◀ ▶ 2Ki 2:9–10
L 1Ki 18:12 ◀ ▶ 2Ki 2:16
Q 1Sa 16:14 ◀ ▶ 2Ch 18:23

unto Jehoshaphat, Let my servants go
with thy servants in the ships. But Jehoshaphat would not.
50 ¶ And [a]Jehoshaphat slept with his
fathers, and was buried with his fathers
in the city of David his father: and Jehoram his son reigned in his stead.

Ahaziah, king of Israel

51 ¶ [a]Ahaziah the son of Ahab began
to reign over Israel in Samaria the seventeenth year of Jehoshaphat king of Judah,
and reigned two years over Israel.
52 And he did evil in the sight of the
LORD, and [a]walked in the way of his father, and in the way of his mother, and in
the way of Jeroboam the son of Nebat,
who made Israel to sin:
53 For [a]he served Baal, and worshipped him, and provoked to anger the
LORD God of Israel, according to all that
his father had done.

50 [a] 2 Chr. 21:1
51 [a] ver. 40
52 [a] ch. 15:26
53 [a] Judg. 2:11; ch. 16:31

2 Kings

Author: Unknown

Theme: The history of the divided kingdom

Date of Writing: c. 560–550 B.C.

Outline of 2 Kings

I. The Ministries of Elijah and Elisha (1:1—8:15)
II. Israel's Decline and Exile (8:16—17:41)
III. Judah's Descent Into Sin (18:1—23:30)
IV. The Babylonian Exile (23:31—25:30)

THE BOOKS OF 1 and 2 Kings were originally part of one large manuscript that the Hebrews simply called "Kings." (For further information about the title, authorship and date of these books, see the introduction to 1 Kings on p. 395.)

The book of 2 Kings begins with the rebellion of Moab following the death of King Ahab. The narrative describes a short-lived alliance between Israel and Judah and then follows the events in Israel's spiritual apostasy and final fall to the Assyrians. The account of 2 Kings then follows the reigns of Judah's kings until that kingdom's final destruction by the armies of Babylon.

Quoting from various historical records and royal accounts that have not survived the centuries, the author of 2 Kings consistently records God's blessing for obedience and promised judgment for idolatry. Also included in this narrative are the miracles of Elisha, including the healing of a Syrian leper named Naaman (ch. 5).

Elijah's prophecy to Ahaziah

1 THEN MOAB [a]rebelled against Israel
[b]after the death of Ahab.
D 2 And Ahaziah fell down through a lattice in his upper chamber that *was* in Samaria, and was sick: and he sent messengers, and said unto them, Go, inquire of
Baal-zebub the god of [a]Ekron whether I
shall recover of this disease.
3 But the angel of the LORD said to Elijah the Tishbite, Arise, go up to meet the
messengers of the king of Samaria, and
say unto them, *Is it* not because *there is*
not a God in Israel, *that* ye go to inquire
of Baal-zebub the god of Ekron?
J 4 Now therefore thus saith the LORD,
[†]Thou shalt not come down from that
bed on which thou art gone up, but shalt
surely die. And Elijah departed.
5 ¶ And when the messengers turned
back unto him, he said unto them, Why
are ye now turned back?
6 And they said unto him, There came
a man up to meet us, and said unto us,
Go, turn again unto the king that sent
you, and say unto him, Thus saith the
LORD, *Is it* not because *there is* not a God
in Israel, *that* thou sendest to inquire of
Baal-zebub the god of Ekron? therefore
thou shalt not come down from that bed
on which thou art gone up, but shalt
surely die.
7 And he said unto them, [†]What manner of man *was he* which came up to
meet you, and told you these words?
8 And they answered him, *He was* [a]an
hairy man, and girt with a girdle of
leather about his loins. And he said, It *is*
Elijah the Tishbite.
9 Then the king sent unto him a captain of fifty with his fifty. And he went up
to him: and, behold, he sat on the top of
an hill. And he spake unto him, Thou
man of God, the king hath said, Come
down.
10 And Elijah answered and said to the
captain of fifty, If I *be* a man of God, then
[a]let fire come down from heaven, and
consume thee and thy fifty. And there
came down fire from heaven, and consumed him and his fifty.
11 Again also he sent unto him another captain of fifty with his fifty. And
he answered and said unto him, O man
of God, thus hath the king said, Come
down quickly.
12 And Elijah answered and said unto
them, If I *be* a man of God, let fire come
down from heaven, and consume thee
and thy fifty. And the fire of God came
down from heaven, and consumed him
and his fifty.
13 ¶ And he sent again a captain of the
third fifty with his fifty. And the third
captain of fifty went up, and came and
[†]fell on his knees before Elijah, and besought him, and said unto him, O man of
God, I pray thee, let my life, and the life
of these fifty thy servants, [a]be precious in
thy sight.
14 Behold, there came fire down from
heaven, and burnt up the two captains of
the former fifties with their fifties: therefore let my life now be precious in thy
sight.
15 And the angel of the LORD said unto
Elijah, Go down with him: be not afraid
of him. And he arose, and went down
with him unto the king.
16 And he said unto him, Thus saith
the LORD, Forasmuch as thou hast sent
messengers to inquire of Baal-zebub the
god of Ekron, *is it* not because *there is*
no God in Israel to inquire of his word?
therefore thou shalt not come down off
that bed on which thou art gone up, but
shalt surely die.
17 ¶ So he died according to the word
of the LORD which Elijah had spoken. And
[†]Jehoram reigned in his stead in the second year of Jehoram the son of Jehoshaphat king of Judah; because he had no
son.
18 Now the rest of the acts of Ahaziah
which he did, *are* they not written in the
book of the chronicles of the kings of Israel?

Elijah taken up to heaven

2 AND IT came to pass, when the LORD
would [a]take up Elijah into heaven by
a whirlwind, that Elijah went with [b]Eli-
sha from Gilgal.
2 And Elijah said unto Elisha, [a]Tarry
here, I pray thee; for the LORD hath sent
me to Beth-el. And Elisha said *unto him,*
As the LORD liveth, and [b]*as* thy soul liveth, I will not leave thee. So they went
down to Beth-el.

1:1 [a]2 Sam. 8:2 [b]ch. 3:5
2 [a]1 Sam. 5:10
4 [†]Heb. *The bed whither thou art gone up, thou shall not come down from it*
7 [†]Heb. *What* was *the manner of the man?*
8 [a]See Zech. 13:4; Mat. 3:4
10 [a]Luke 9:54
13 [a]1 Sam. 26:21; Ps. 72:14 [†]Heb. *bowed*
17 [†]The second year that *Jehoram* was *Prorex,* and the eighteenth of *Jehoshaphat;* see ch. 3:1
2:1 [a]Gen. 5:24 [b]1 Ki. 19:21
2 [a]See Ruth 1:15, 16 [b]ver. 4,6; 1 Sam. 1:26; ch. 4:30

D *1Ki 14:12–13* ◄► *2Ki 5:27*
J *1Ki 21:29* ◄► *2Ki 2:3*

J 3 And [a]the sons of the prophets that *were* at Beth-el came forth to Elisha, and said unto him, Knowest thou that the LORD will take away thy master from thy head today? And he said, Yea, I know *it;* hold ye your peace.
4 And Elijah said unto him, Elisha, tarry here, I pray thee; for the LORD hath sent me to Jericho. And he said, *As* the LORD liveth, and *as* thy soul liveth, I will not leave thee. So they came to Jericho.
J 5 And the sons of the prophets that *were* at Jericho came to Elisha, and said unto him, Knowest thou that the LORD will take away thy master from thy head today? And he answered, Yea, I know *it;* hold ye your peace.
6 And Elijah said unto him, Tarry, I pray thee, here; for the LORD hath sent me to Jordan. And he said, *As* the LORD liveth, and *as* thy soul liveth, I will not leave thee. And they two went on.
7 And fifty men of the sons of the prophets went, and stood [1]to view afar off: and they two stood by Jordan.
8 And Elijah took his mantle, and wrapped *it* together, and smote the waters, and [a]they were divided hither and thither, so that they two went over on dry ground.
J E N 9 ¶ And it came to pass, when they were gone over, that Elijah said unto Elisha, Ask what I shall do for thee, before I be taken away from thee. And Elisha said, I pray thee, let a double portion of thy spirit be upon me.
10 And he said, [1]Thou hast asked a hard thing: *nevertheless,* if thou see me *when I am* taken from thee, it shall be so unto thee; but if not, it shall not be *so.*
11 And it came to pass, as they still went on, and talked, that, behold, *there appeared* [a]a chariot of fire, and horses of fire, and parted them both asunder; and Elijah went up by a whirlwind into heaven.
12 ¶ And Elisha saw *it,* and he cried, [a]My father, my father, the chariot of Israel, and the horsemen thereof. And he saw him no more: and he took hold of his own clothes, and rent them in two pieces.

Beginning of Elisha's ministry

13 He took up also the mantle of Elijah that fell from him, and went back, and stood by the [1]bank of Jordan;
14 And he took the mantle of Elijah that fell from him, and smote the waters, and said, Where *is* the LORD God of Elijah? and when he also had smitten the waters, [a]they parted hither and thither: and Elisha went over.
15 And when the sons of the prophets which *were* [a]to view at Jericho saw him, they said, The spirit of Elijah doth rest on Elisha. And they came to meet him, and bowed themselves to the ground before him. E
16 ¶ And they said unto him, Behold now, there be with thy servants fifty [1]strong men; let them go, we pray thee, and seek thy master: [a]lest peradventure the spirit of the LORD hath taken him up, and cast him upon [2]some mountain, or into some valley. And he said, Ye shall not send. L M
17 And when they urged him till he was ashamed, he said, Send. They sent therefore fifty men; and they sought three days, but found him not.
18 And when they came again to him, (for he tarried at Jericho,) he said unto them, Did I not say unto you, Go not?
19 ¶ And the men of the city said unto Elisha, Behold, I pray thee, the situation of this city *is* pleasant, as my lord seeth: but the water *is* naught, and the ground [1]barren.
20 And he said, Bring me a new cruse,

3 [a]ver. 5,7,15; 1 Ki. 20:35; ch. 4:1, 38 & 9:1
7 [1]Heb. *in sight,* or, *over against*
8 [a]ver. 14; Ex. 14:21; Josh. 3:16
10 [1]Heb. *Thou hast done hard in asking*
11 [a]ch. 6:17; Ps. 104:4
12 [a]ch. 13:14
13 [1]Heb. *lip*
14 [a]ver. 8
15 [a]ver. 7
16 [a]See 1 Ki. 18:12; Ezek. 8:3; Acts 8:39; ch. 1:17 [1]Heb. *sons of strength* [2]Heb. *one of the mountains*
19 [1]Heb. *causing to miscarry*

J *2Ki 1:4* ◀ ▶ *2Ki 2:5*
J *2Ki 2:3* ◀ ▶ *2Ki 2:9–10*
J *2Ki 2:5* ◀ ▶ *2Ki 5:27*
E *1Ki 22:24* ◀ ▶ *2Ki 2:15–16*
N *Ge 1:2* ◀ ▶ *Ne 9:20*
E *2Ki 2:9–10* ◀ ▶ *2Ki 3:15*
L *1Ki 22:24* ◀ ▶ *2Ch 18:23*
M *1Sa 19:20–23* ◀ ▶ *Job 26:13–14*

2:11–12 These verses mention the second time that God supernaturally took someone to heaven without a death experience. The first such rapture happened to Enoch (see Ge 5:24). These OT raptures foreshadow the final rapture of believers (see 1Co 15:51; 1Th 4:16–17) when Jesus Christ comes again to take his church to the marriage supper of the Lamb (see Rev 19:17–19). Notice that Elisha's description of this miraculous event includes chariots and horsemen, symbols that are used throughout Scripture to indicate strength and might (see Ps 104:3).

and put salt therein. And they brought *it* to him.

21 And he went forth unto the spring of the waters, and [a]cast the salt in there, and said, Thus saith the LORD, I have healed these waters; there shall not be from thence any more death or barren *land.*

22 So the waters were healed unto this day, according to the saying of Elisha which he spake.

23 ¶ And he went up from thence unto Beth-el: and as he was going up by the way, there came forth little children out of the city, and mocked him, and said unto him, Go up, thou bald head; go up, thou bald head.

24 And he turned back, and looked on them, and cursed them in the name of the LORD. And there came forth two she bears out of the wood, and tare forty and two children of them.

25 And he went from thence to mount Carmel, and from thence he returned to Samaria.

Jehoram's siege against Moab

3 NOW JEHORAM the son of Ahab began to reign over Israel in Samaria the eighteenth year of Jehoshaphat king of Judah, and reigned twelve years.

2 And he wrought evil in the sight of the LORD; but not like his father, and like his mother: for he put away the [/]image of Baal [a]that his father had made.

3 Nevertheless he cleaved unto [a]the sins of Jeroboam the son of Nebat, which made Israel to sin; he departed not therefrom.

4 ¶ And Mesha king of Moab was a sheepmaster, and rendered unto the king of Israel an hundred thousand [a]lambs, and an hundred thousand rams, with the wool.

5 But it came to pass, when [a]Ahab was dead, that the king of Moab rebelled against the king of Israel.

6 ¶ And king Jehoram went out of Samaria the same time, and numbered all Israel.

7 And he went and sent to Jehoshaphat the king of Judah, saying, The king of Moab hath rebelled against me: wilt thou go with me against Moab to battle? And he said, I will go up: [a]I *am* as thou *art,* my people as thy people, *and* my horses as thy horses.

8 And he said, Which way shall we go up? And he answered, The way through the wilderness of Edom.

9 So the king of Israel went, and the king of Judah, and the king of Edom: and they fetched a compass of seven days' journey: and there was no water for the host, and for the cattle [/]that followed them. F

10 And the king of Israel said, Alas! that the LORD hath called these three kings together, to deliver them into the hand of Moab!

11 But [a]Jehoshaphat said, *Is there* not here a prophet of the LORD, that we may inquire of the LORD by him? And one of the king of Israel's servants answered and said, Here *is* Elisha the son of Shaphat, which poured water on the hands of Elijah.

12 And Jehoshaphat said, The word of the LORD is with him. So the king of Israel and Jehoshaphat and the king of Edom [a]went down to him.

13 And Elisha said unto the king of Israel, [a]What have I to do with thee? [b]get thee to [c]the prophets of thy father, and to the prophets of thy mother. And the king of Israel said unto him, Nay: for the LORD hath called these three kings together, to deliver them into the hand of Moab.

14 And Elisha said, [a]*As* the LORD of hosts liveth, before whom I stand, surely, were it not that I regard the presence of Jehoshaphat the king of Judah, I would not look toward thee, nor see thee.

15 But now bring me [a]a minstrel. And it came to pass, when the minstrel played, that [b]the hand of the LORD came upon him. E

16 And he said, Thus saith the LORD, [a]Make this valley full of ditches.

F *1Ki 19:5–8* ◄► *2Ki 4:1–7*
E *2Ki 2:15–16* ◄► *1Ch 12:18*

21 [a]See Ex. 15:25; ch. 4:41 & 6:6; John 9:6
3:2 [a]1 Ki. 16:31, 32 [/]Heb. *statue*
3 [a]1 Ki. 12:28,31, 32
4 [a]See Is. 16:1
5 [a]ch. 1:1
7 [a]1 Ki. 22:4
9 [/]Heb. *at their feet*
11 [a]1 Ki. 22:7
12 [a]ch. 2:25
13 [a]Ezek. 14:3 [b]Judg. 10:14; Ruth 1:15 [c]1 Ki. 18:19
14 [a]1 Ki. 17:1; ch. 5:16
15 [a]See 1 Sam. 10:5 [b]Ezek. 1:3 & 3:14,22 & 8:1
16 [a]ch. 4:3

3:15–20 Elisha prophesied to the three kings of Judah, Israel and Edom that God would supernaturally fill these man-made ditches in the desolate valley with water. In addition, Elisha prophesied that the three kings would defeat the Moabites and conquer their land because of the Moabite's rebellion from Israel's rule after the death of King Ahab.

17 For thus saith the LORD, Ye shall not
see wind, neither shall ye see rain; yet
that valley shall be filled with water, that
ye may drink, both ye, and your cattle,
and your beasts.
18 And this is *but* a light thing in the
sight of the LORD: he will deliver the Moabites also into your hand.
19 And ye shall smite every fenced
city, and every choice city, and shall fell
every good tree, and stop all wells of water, and [1]mar every good piece of land
with stones.
20 And it came to pass in the morning,
when [a]the meat offering was offered,
that, behold, there came water by the
way of Edom, and the country was filled
with water.
21 ¶ And when all the Moabites heard
that the kings were come up to fight
against them, they [1]gathered all that
were able to [2]put on armour, and upward, and stood in the border.
22 And they rose up early in the morning, and the sun shone upon the water,
and the Moabites saw the water on the
other side *as* red as blood:
23 And they said, This *is* blood: the
kings are surely [1]slain, and they have
smitten one another: now therefore,
Moab, to the spoil.
24 And when they came to the camp
of Israel, the Israelites rose up and smote
the Moabites, so that they fled before
them: but [1]they went forward smiting
the Moabites, even in *their* country.
25 And they beat down the cities, and
on every good piece of land cast every
man his stone, and filled it; and they
stopped all the wells of water, and felled
all the good trees: [1]only in [a]Kir-hara-
seth left they the stones thereof; howbeit the slingers went about *it*, and
smote it.
26 ¶ And when the king of Moab saw
that the battle was too sore for him, he
took with him seven hundred men that
drew swords, to break through *even* unto
the king of Edom: but they could not.
27 Then [a]he took his eldest son that
should have reigned in his stead, and
offered him *for* a burnt offering upon
the wall. And there was great indignation against Israel: [b]and they departed
from him, and returned to *their own*
land.

19 [1]Heb. *grieve*
20 [a]Ex. 29:39,40
21 [1]Heb. *were cried together* [2]Heb. *gird himself with a girdle*
23 [1]Heb. *destroyed*
24 [1]Or, *they smote in it even smiting*
25 [a]Is. 16:7,11 [1]Heb. *until he left the stones thereof in Kir-haraseth*
27 [a]Amos 2:1 [b]ch. 8:20
4:1 [a]1 Ki. 20:35 [b]See Lev. 25:39; Mat. 18:25
3 [a]See ch. 3:16 [1]Or, *scant not*
7 [1]Or, *creditor*
8 [a]Josh. 19:18 [1]Heb. *there was a day* [2]Heb. *laid hold on him*

The widow's pot of oil

4 NOW THERE cried a certain woman
of the wives of [a]the sons of the
prophets unto Elisha, saying, Thy servant
my husband is dead; and thou knowest
that thy servant did fear the LORD: and the
creditor is come [b]to take unto him my
two sons to be bondmen.
2 And Elisha said unto her, What shall
I do for thee? tell me, what hast thou in
the house? And she said, Thine handmaid hath not any thing in the house,
save a pot of oil.
3 Then he said, Go, borrow thee vessels abroad of all thy neighbours, *even*
empty vessels; [a]borrow[1] not a few.
4 And when thou art come in, thou
shalt shut the door upon thee and upon
thy sons, and shalt pour out into all those
vessels, and thou shalt set aside that
which is full.
5 So she went from him, and shut the
door upon her and upon her sons, who
brought *the vessels* to her; and she
poured out.
6 And it came to pass, when the vessels were full, that she said unto her son,
Bring me yet a vessel. And he said unto
her, *There is* not a vessel more. And the
oil stayed.
7 Then she came and told the man of
God. And he said, Go, sell the oil, and
pay thy [1]debt, and live thou and thy children of the rest.

The Shunammite's son

8 ¶ And [1]it fell on a day, that Elisha
passed to [a]Shunem, where *was* a great
woman; and she [2]constrained him to eat
bread. And *so* it was, *that* as oft as he
passed by, he turned in thither to eat
bread.
9 And she said unto her husband, Behold now, I perceive that this *is* an holy
man of God, which passeth by us continually.
10 Let us make a little chamber, I pray
thee, on the wall; and let us set for him
there a bed, and a table, and a stool, and
a candlestick: and it shall be, when he
cometh to us, that he shall turn in
thither.
11 And it fell on a day, that he came
thither, and he turned into the chamber,
and lay there.

F
F 2Ki 3:9–20 ◀▶ 2Ki 4:42–44

12 And he said to Gehazi his servant, Call this Shunammite. And when he had called her, she stood before him.

13 And he said unto him, Say now unto her, Behold, thou hast been careful for us with all this care; what *is* to be done for thee? wouldest thou be spoken for to the king, or to the captain of the host? And she answered, I dwell among mine own people.

14 And he said, What then *is* to be done for her? And Gehazi answered, Verily she hath no child, and her husband is old.

15 And he said, Call her. And when he had called her, she stood in the door.

L 16 And he said, [a]About this [1]season, according to the time of life, thou shalt embrace a son. And she said, Nay, my lord, *thou* man of God, [b]do not lie unto thine handmaid.

17 And the woman conceived, and bare a son at that season that Elisha had said unto her, according to the time of life.

18 ¶ And when the child was grown, it fell on a day, that he went out to his father to the reapers.

19 And he said unto his father, My head, my head. And he said to a lad, Carry him to his mother.

20 And when he had taken him, and brought him to his mother, he sat on her knees till noon, and *then* died.

21 And she went up, and laid him on the bed of the man of God, and shut *the door* upon him, and went out.

22 And she called unto her husband, and said, Send me, I pray thee, one of the young men, and one of the asses, that I may run to the man of God, and come again.

23 And he said, Wherefore wilt thou go to him today? *it is* neither new moon, nor sabbath. And she said, *It shall be* [1]well.

24 Then she saddled an ass, and said to her servant, Drive, and go forward; [1]slack not *thy* riding for me, except I bid thee.

25 So she went and came unto the man of God [a]to mount Carmel. And it came to pass, when the man of God saw her afar off, that he said to Gehazi his servant, Behold, *yonder is* that Shunammite:

26 Run now, I pray thee, to meet her, and say unto her, *Is it* well with thee? *is it* well with thy husband? *is it* well with the child? And she answered, *It is* well.

27 And when she came to the man of God to the hill, she caught [a]him[1] by the feet: but Gehazi came near to thrust her away. And the man of God said, Let her alone; for her soul *is* [b]vexed[2] within her: and the LORD hath hid *it* from me, and hath not told me.

28 Then she said, Did I desire a son of my lord? [a]did I not say, Do not deceive me?

29 Then he said to Gehazi, [a]Gird up thy loins, and take my staff in thine hand, and go thy way: if thou meet any man, [b]salute him not; and if any salute thee, answer him not again: and [c]lay my staff upon the face of the child.

30 And the mother of the child said, [a]*As* the LORD liveth, and *as* thy soul liveth, I will not leave thee. And he arose, and followed her.

31 And Gehazi passed on before them, and laid the staff upon the face of the child; but *there was* neither voice, nor [1]hearing. Wherefore he went again to meet him, and told him, saying, The child is [a]not awaked.

32 And when Elisha was come into the house, behold, the child was dead, *and* laid upon his bed. E

33 He [a]went in therefore, and shut the door upon them twain, [b]and prayed unto the LORD.

34 And he went up, and lay upon the child, and put his mouth upon his mouth, and his eyes upon his eyes, and his hands upon his hands: and [a]he stretched himself upon the child; and the flesh of the child waxed warm.

35 Then he returned, and walked in the house [1]to and fro; and went up, and [a]stretched himself upon him: and [b]the child sneezed seven times, and the child opened his eyes.

36 And he called Gehazi, and said, Call this Shunammite. So he called her. And when she was come in unto him, he said, Take up thy son.

37 Then she went in, and fell at his

16 [a]Gen. 18:10,14 [b]ver. 28 [1]Heb. *set time*

23 [1]Heb. *peace*

24 [1]Heb. *restrain not for me to ride*

25 [a]ch. 2:25

27 [a]Mat. 28:9 [b]1 Sam. 1:10 [1]Heb. *by his feet* [2]Heb. *bitter*

28 [a]ver. 16

29 [a]1 Ki. 18:46; ch. 9:1 [b]Luke 10:4 [c]See Ex. 7:19 & 14:16; ch. 2:8,14; Acts 19:12

30 [a]ch. 2:2

31 [a]John 11:11 [1]Heb. *attention*

33 [a]ver. 4; Mat. 6:6 [b]1 Ki. 17:20

34 [a]1 Ki. 17:21; Acts 20:10

35 [a]1 Ki. 17:21 [b]ch. 8:1,5 [1]Heb. *once hither, and once thither*

feet, and bowed herself to the ground,
and [a]took up her son, and went out.

Poisonous food made harmless

38 ¶ And Elisha came again to [a]Gilgal:
and *there was* a [b]dearth in the land; and
the sons of the prophets *were* [c]sitting before him: and he said unto his servant,
Set on the great pot, and seethe pottage
for the sons of the prophets.
E 39 And one went out into the field to
gather herbs, and found a wild vine, and
gathered thereof wild gourds his lap full,
and came and shred *them* into the pot of
pottage: for they knew *them* not.
40 So they poured out for the men to
eat. And it came to pass, as they were
eating of the pottage, that they cried out,
and said, O *thou* man of God, *there is*
[a]death in the pot. And they could not eat
thereof.
41 But he said, Then bring meal. And
[a]he cast *it* into the pot; and he said, Pour
out for the people, that they may eat. And
there was no [1]harm in the pot.

The feeding of the hundred men

F 42 ¶ And there came a man from
[a]Baal-shalisha, [b]and brought the man of
God bread of the firstfruits, twenty loaves
of barley, and full ears of corn [1]in the
husk thereof. And he said, Give unto the
people, that they may eat.
43 And his servitor said, [a]What,
should I set this before an hundred men?
He said again, Give the people, that they
may eat: for thus saith the LORD, [b]They
shall eat, and shall leave *thereof.*
44 So he set *it* before them, and they
did eat, [a]and left *thereof,* according to the
word of the LORD.

The cure of Naaman the leper

5 NOW [a]NAAMAN, captain of the
host of the king of Syria, was [b]a great
man [1]with his master, and [2,3]honourable,
because by him the LORD had given [4]de-
liverance unto Syria: he was also a mighty
man in valour, *but he was* a leper.
2 And the Syrians had gone out by
companies, and had brought away captive
out of the land of Israel a little maid; and
she [1]waited on Naaman's wife.
3 And she said unto her mistress,
Would God my lord *were* [1]with the
prophet that *is* in Samaria! for he would
[2]recover him of his leprosy.
4 And *one* went in, and told his lord,
saying, Thus and thus said the maid that
is of the land of Israel.
5 And the king of Syria said, Go to, go,
and I will send a letter unto the king of
Israel. And he departed, and [a]took [1]with
him ten talents of silver, and six thousand
pieces of gold, and ten changes of
raiment.
6 And he brought the letter to the king
of Israel, saying, Now when this letter is
come unto thee, behold, I have *therewith*
sent Naaman my servant to thee, that
thou mayest recover him of his leprosy.
7 And it came to pass, when the king
of Israel had read the letter, that he rent
his clothes, and said, *Am* I [a]God, to kill
and to make alive, that this man doth
send unto me to recover a man of his
leprosy? wherefore consider, I pray you,
and see how he seeketh a quarrel
against me.
8 ¶ And it was *so,* when Elisha the
man of God had heard that the king of
Israel had rent his clothes, that he sent
to the king, saying, Wherefore hast thou
rent thy clothes? let him come now to
me, and he shall know that there is a
prophet in Israel.
9 So Naaman came with his horses and
with his chariot, and stood at the door of
the house of Elisha.
10 And Elisha sent a messenger unto
him, saying, Go and [a]wash in Jordan
seven times, and thy flesh shall come
again to thee, and thou shalt be clean.
11 But Naaman was wroth, and went
away, and said, Behold, [1,2]I thought, He
will surely come out to me, and stand,
and call on the name of the LORD his God,
and [3]strike his hand over the place, and
recover the leper.
12 *Are* not [1]Abana and Pharpar, rivers
of Damascus, better than all the waters of
Israel? may I not wash in them, and be
clean? So he turned and went away in a
rage.
13 And his servants came near, and
spake unto him, and said, My father, *if*
the prophet had bid thee *do some* great
thing, wouldest thou not have done *it?*
how much rather then, when he saith to
thee, Wash, and be clean?

37 [a]1 Ki. 17:23; Heb. 11:35
38 [a]ch. 2:1 [b]ch. 8:1 [c]ch. 2:3; Luke 10:39; Acts 22:3
40 [a]Ex. 10:17
41 [a]See Ex. 15:25; ch. 2:21 & 5:10; John 9:6 [1]Heb. *evil thing*
42 [a]1 Sam. 9:4 [b]1 Sam. 9:7; 1 Cor. 9:11; Gal. 6:6 [1]Or, *in his scrip,* or, *garment*
43 [a]Luke 9:13; John 6:9 [b]Luke 9:17; John 6:11
44 [a]Mat. 14:20 & 15:37; John 6:13
5:1 [a]Luke 4:27 [b]Ex. 11:3 [1]Heb. *before* [2]Or, *gracious* [3]Heb. *lifted up,* or, *accepted in countenance* [4]Or, *victory*
2 [1]Heb. *was before*
3 [1]Heb. *before* [2]Heb. *gather in*
5 [a]1 Sam. 9:8; ch. 8:8,9 [1]Heb. *in his hand*
7 [a]Gen. 30:2; Deut. 32:39; 1 Sam. 2:6
10 [a]See ch. 4:41; John 9:7
11 [1]Heb. *I said* [2]Or, *I said with myself, He will surely come out* [3]Heb. *move up and down*
12 [1]Or, *Amana*

E 2Ki 4:32–35 ◀ ▶ 2Ki 5:14
F 2Ki 4:1–7 ◀ ▶ 2Ki 6:18

E 14 Then went he down, and dipped himself seven times in Jordan, according to the saying of the man of God: and [a]his flesh came again like unto the flesh of a little child, and [b]he was clean.

15 ¶ And he returned to the man of God, he and all his company, and came, and stood before him: and he said, Behold, now I know that *there is* [a]no God in all the earth, but in Israel: now therefore, I pray thee, take [b]a blessing of thy servant.

16 But he said, [a]*As* the LORD liveth, before whom I stand, [b]I will receive none. And he urged him to take *it;* but he refused.

17 And Naaman said, Shall there not then, I pray thee, be given to thy servant two mules' burden of earth? for thy servant will henceforth offer neither burnt offering nor sacrifice unto other gods, but unto the LORD.

18 In this thing the LORD pardon thy servant, *that* when my master goeth into the house of Rimmon to worship there, and [a]he leaneth on my hand, and I bow myself in the house of Rimmon: when I bow down myself in the house of Rimmon, the LORD pardon thy servant in this thing.

19 And he said unto him, Go in peace. So he departed from him a little way.

20 ¶ But Gehazi, the servant of Elisha the man of God, said, Behold, my master hath spared Naaman this Syrian, in not receiving at his hands that which he brought: but, *as* the LORD liveth, I will run after him, and take somewhat of him.

21 So Gehazi followed after Naaman. And when Naaman saw *him* running after him, he lighted down from the chariot to meet him, and said, [l]*Is* all well?

22 And he said, All *is* well. My master hath sent me, saying, Behold, even now there be come to me from mount Ephraim two young men of the sons of the prophets: give them, I pray thee, a talent of silver, and two changes of garments.

23 And Naaman said, Be content, take two talents. And he urged him, and bound two talents of silver in two bags, with two changes of garments, and laid *them* upon two of his servants; and they bare *them* before him.

14 [a]Job 33:25 [b]Luke 4:27

15 [a]Dan 2:47 & 3:29 & 6:26,27 [b]Gen. 33:11

16 [a]ch. 3:14 [b]Gen. 14:23; See Mat. 10:8; Acts 8:18,20

18 [a]ch. 7:2,17

21 [l]Heb. Is there *peace?*

24 [l]Or, *secret place*

25 [l]Heb. *not hither or thither*

27 [a]1 Tim. 6:10 [b]Ex. 4:6; Num. 12:10; ch. 15:5

6:1 [a]ch. 4:38

5 [l]Heb. *iron*

6 [a]ch. 2:21

8 [l]Or, *encamping*

24 And when he came to the [l]tower, he took *them* from their hand, and bestowed *them* in the house: and he let the men go, and they departed.

25 But he went in, and stood before his master. And Elisha said unto him, Whence *comest thou,* Gehazi? And he said, Thy servant went [l]no whither.

26 And he said unto him, Went not mine heart *with thee,* when the man turned again from his chariot to meet thee? *Is it* a time to receive money, and to receive garments, and oliveyards, and vineyards, and sheep, and oxen, and menservants, and maidservants?

27 The leprosy therefore of Naaman [a]shall cleave unto thee, and unto thy seed for ever. And he went out from his presence [b]a leper *as white* as snow. J D

Recovery of the lost axe head

6 AND [a]THE sons of the prophets said unto Elisha, Behold now, the place where we dwell with thee is too strait for us.

2 Let us go, we pray thee, unto Jordan, and take thence every man a beam, and let us make us a place there, where we may dwell. And he answered, Go ye.

3 And one said, Be content, I pray thee, and go with thy servants. And he answered, I will go.

4 So he went with them. And when they came to Jordan, they cut down wood.

5 But as one was felling a beam, the [l]axe head fell into the water: and he cried, and said, Alas, master! for it was borrowed.

6 And the man of God said, Where fell it? And he showed him the place. And [a]he cut down a stick, and cast *it* in thither; and the iron did swim.

7 Therefore said he, Take *it* up to thee. And he put out his hand, and took it.

Elisha strikes the Syrians blind

8 ¶ Then the king of Syria warred against Israel, and took counsel with his servants, saying, In such and such a place *shall be* my [l]camp.

9 And the man of God sent unto the king of Israel, saying, Beware that thou

E *2Ki 4:39–41* ◀ ▶ *2Ki 6:20*

J *2Ki 2:9–10* ◀ ▶ *2Ki 7:19*
D *2Ki 1:2–4* ◀ ▶ *2Ki 6:18*

pass not such a place; for thither the Syrians are come down.

10 And the king of Israel sent to the place which the man of God told him and warned him of, and saved himself there, not once nor twice.

11 Therefore the heart of the king of Syria was sore troubled for this thing; and he called his servants, and said unto them, Will ye not show me which of us *is* for the king of Israel?

12 And one of his servants said, [l]None, my lord, O king: but Elisha, the prophet that *is* in Israel, telleth the king of Israel the words that thou speakest in thy bedchamber.

13 ¶ And he said, Go and spy where he *is,* that I may send and fetch him. And it was told him, saying, Behold, *he is* in [a]Dothan.

14 Therefore sent he thither horses, and chariots, and a [l]great host: and they came by night, and compassed the city about.

15 And when the [l]servant of the man of God was risen early, and gone forth, behold, an host compassed the city both with horses and chariots. And his servant said unto him, Alas, my master! how shall we do?

K 16 And he answered, Fear not: for
L [a]they that *be* with us *are* more than they that *be* with them.

17 And Elisha prayed, and said, LORD, I pray thee, open his eyes, that he may see. And the LORD opened the eyes of the young man; and he saw: and, behold, the mountain *was* full of [a]horses and chariots of fire round about Elisha.

D 18 And when they came down to him,
F Elisha prayed unto the LORD, and said, Smite this people, I pray thee, with blindness. And [a]he smote them with blindness according to the word of Elisha.

19 ¶ And Elisha said unto them, This *is* not the way, neither *is* this the city: [l]follow me, and I will bring you to the man whom ye seek. But he led them to Samaria.

20 And it came to pass, when they were come into Samaria, that Elisha said, LORD, open the eyes of these *men,* that they may see. And the LORD opened their eyes, and they saw; and, behold, *they were* in the midst of Samaria. E

21 And the king of Israel said unto Elisha, when he saw them, My father, shall I smite *them?* shall I smite *them?*

22 And he answered, Thou shalt not smite *them:* wouldest thou smite those whom thou hast taken captive with thy sword and with thy bow? [a]set bread and water before them, that they may eat and drink, and go to their master.

23 And he prepared great provision for them: and when they had eaten and drunk, he sent them away, and they went to their master. So [a]the bands of Syria came no more into the land of Israel.

Famine in Samaria

24 ¶ And it came to pass after this, that Ben-hadad king of Syria gathered all his host, and went up, and besieged Samaria.

25 And there was a great famine in Samaria: and, behold, they besieged it, until an ass's head was *sold* for fourscore *pieces* of silver, and the fourth part of a cab of dove's dung for five *pieces* of silver.

26 And as the king of Israel was passing by upon the wall, there cried a woman unto him, saying, Help, my lord, O king.

27 And he said, [l]If the LORD do not help thee, whence shall I help thee? out of the barnfloor, or out of the winepress?

28 And the king said unto her, What aileth thee? And she answered, This woman said unto me, Give thy son, that we may eat him today, and we will eat my son tomorrow.

29 So [a]we boiled my son, and did eat him: and I said unto her on the [l]next day, Give thy son, that we may eat him: and she hath hid her son.

30 ¶ And it came to pass, when the

12 [l]Heb. *No*
13 [a]Gen. 37:17
14 [l]Heb. *heavy*
15 [l]Or, *minister*
16 [a]2 Chr. 32:7; Ps. 55:18; Rom. 8:31
17 [a]ch. 2:11; Ps. 34:7 & 68:17; Zech. 1:8 & 6:1-7
18 [a]Gen. 19:11
19 [l]Heb. *come ye after me*
22 [a]Rom. 12:20
23 [a]ver. 8,9; ch. 5:2
27 [l]Or, *Let not the LORD save thee*
29 [a]Lev. 26:29; Deut. 28:53,57 [l]Heb. *other*

K *2Sa 22:36* ◄► *1Ch 4:10*
L *2Sa 22:2–4* ◄► *1Ch 16:21–22*
D *2Ki 5:27* ◄► *2Ki 15:5*
F *2Ki 4:42–44* ◄► *2Ch 20:9*
E *2Ki 5:14* ◄► *2Ki 8:4–5*

6:15–17 These verses reveal the difference between natural vision and spiritual vision. Though natural vision viewed a difficult situation as overwhelming, spiritual vision recognized God's powerful hosts of heaven outnumbering the enemy. As believers, we are surrounded by angels who do God's bidding and help care for us (see Heb 1:14).

king heard the words of the woman, that he [a]rent his clothes; and he passed by upon the wall, and the people looked, and, behold, *he had* sackcloth within upon his flesh.

31 Then he said, [a]God do so and more also to me, if the head of Elisha the son of Shaphat shall stand on him this day.

The prophecy of Elisha

32 But Elisha sat in his house, and [a]the elders sat with him; and *the king* sent a man from before him: but ere the messenger came to him, he said to the elders, [b]See ye how this son of [c]a murderer hath sent to take away mine head? look, when the messenger cometh, shut the door, and hold him fast at the door: *is* not the sound of his master's feet behind him?

33 And while he yet talked with them, behold, the messenger came down unto him: and he said, Behold, this evil *is* of the LORD; [a]what should I wait for the LORD any longer?

I 7 THEN ELISHA said, Hear ye the word of the LORD; Thus saith the LORD, [a]Tomorrow about this time *shall* a measure of fine flour *be sold* for a shekel, and two measures of barley for a shekel, in the gate of Samaria.

2 [a]Then [b]a[*l*] lord on whose hand the king leaned answered the man of God, and said, Behold, [c]*if* the LORD would make windows in heaven, might this thing be? And he said, Behold, thou shalt see *it* with thine eyes, but shalt not eat thereof.

3 ¶ And there were four leprous men [a]at the entering in of the gate: and they said one to another, Why sit we here until we die?

4 If we say, We will enter into the city, then the famine *is* in the city, and we shall die there: and if we sit still here, we die also. Now therefore come, and let us fall unto the host of the Syrians: if they save us alive, we shall live; and if they kill us, we shall but die.

5 And they rose up in the twilight, to go unto the camp of the Syrians: and when they were come to the uttermost part of the camp of Syria, behold, *there was* no man there.

6 For the Lord had made the host of the Syrians [a]to hear a noise of chariots, and a noise of horses, *even* the noise of a great host: and they said one to another, Lo, the king of Israel hath hired against us [b]the kings of the Hittites, and the kings of the Egyptians, to come upon us.

7 Wherefore they [a]arose and fled in the twilight, and left their tents, and their horses, and their asses, even the camp as it *was,* and fled for their life.

8 And when these lepers came to the uttermost part of the camp, they went into one tent, and did eat and drink, and carried thence silver, and gold, and raiment, and went and hid *it;* and came again, and entered into another tent, and carried thence *also,* and went and hid *it.*

9 Then they said one to another, We do not well: this day *is* a day of good tidings, and we hold our peace: if we tarry till the morning light, [*l*]some mischief will come upon us: now therefore come, that we may go and tell the king's household.

10 So they came and called unto the porter of the city: and they told them, saying, We came to the camp of the Syrians, and, behold, *there was* no man there, neither voice of man, but horses tied, and asses tied, and the tents as they *were.*

11 And he called the porters; and they told *it* to the king's house within.

12 ¶ And the king arose in the night, and said unto his servants, I will now show you what the Syrians have done to us. They know that we *be* hungry; therefore are they gone out of the camp to hide themselves in the field, saying, When

I *1Ki 18:41* ◄► *2Ki 8:19*

30 [a]1 Ki. 21:27
31 [a]Ruth 1:17; 1 Ki. 19:2
32 [a]Ezek. 8:1 & 20:1 [b]Luke 13:32 [c]1 Ki. 18:4
33 [a]Job 2:9
7:1 [a]ver. 18,19
2 [a]ver. 17,19,20 [b]ch. 5:18 [c]Mal. 3:10 [*l*]Heb. *a lord which* belonged *to the king leaning upon his hand*
3 [a]Lev. 13:46
6 [a]2 Sam. 5:24; ch. 19:7; Job 15:21 [b]1 Ki. 10:29
7 [a]Ps. 48:4-6; Prov. 28:1
9 [*l*]Heb. *we shall find punishment*

7:1–2 Elisha prophesied that the siege of the Syrian army would miraculously end overnight. Furthermore, Elisha said that the ensuing surplus of food would cause food prices to drop overnight too. One of the nobles of Israel mocked this seemingly impossible prophecy. As a result, Elisha predicted that this doubter would live to see the miracle but he would not live to eat the food. In fulfillment of this prophecy, God supernaturally frightened the Syrian army causing them to flee their camp and leave their enormous stores of food behind. Every detail of Elisha's prediction was fulfilled, including the death of the unbelieving noble (see 7:18–20).

they come out of the city, we shall catch
them alive, and get into the city.
13 And one of his servants answered
and said, Let *some* take, I pray thee, five
of the horses that remain, which are left
[l]in the city, (behold, they *are* as all the
multitude of Israel that are left in it: behold, *I say,* they *are* even as all the multitude of the Israelites that are consumed:)
and let us send and see.
14 They took therefore two chariot
horses; and the king sent after the host of
the Syrians, saying, Go and see.
15 And they went after them unto Jordan: and, lo, all the way *was* full of garments and vessels, which the Syrians had
cast away in their haste. And the messengers returned, and told the king.
16 And the people went out, and
spoiled the tents of the Syrians. So a measure of fine flour was *sold* for a shekel,
and two measures of barley for a shekel,
[a]according to the word of the LORD.
17 ¶ And the king appointed the lord
on whose hand he leaned to have the
charge of the gate: and the people trode
upon him in the gate, and he died, [a]as
the man of God had said, who spake
when the king came down to him.
18 And it came to pass as the man of
God had spoken to the king, saying, [a]Two
measures of barley for a shekel, and a
measure of fine flour for a shekel, shall be
tomorrow about this time in the gate of
Samaria:
J 19 And that lord answered the man of
God, and said, Now, behold, *if* the LORD
should make windows in heaven, might
such a thing be? And he said, Behold,
thou shalt see it with thine eyes, but shalt
not eat thereof.
20 And so it fell out unto him: for the
people trode upon him in the gate, and
he died.

The Shunammite comes home

J 8 THEN SPAKE Elisha unto the
woman, [a]whose son he had restored
to life, saying, Arise, and go thou and
thine household, and sojourn wheresoever thou canst sojourn: for the LORD
[b]hath called for a famine; and it shall also
come upon the land seven years.
2 And the woman arose, and did after
the saying of the man of God: and she
went with her household, and sojourned
in the land of the Philistines seven years.
3 And it came to pass at the seven
years' end, that the woman returned out
of the land of the Philistines: and she
went forth to cry unto the king for her
house and for her land.
4 And the king talked with [a]Gehazi E
the servant of the man of God, saying,
Tell me, I pray thee, all the great things
that Elisha hath done.
5 And it came to pass, as he was telling
the king how he had [a]restored a dead
body to life, that, behold, the woman,
whose son he had restored to life, cried
to the king for her house and for her land.
And Gehazi said, My lord, O king, this *is*
the woman, and this *is* her son, whom
Elisha restored to life.
6 And when the king asked the
woman, she told him. So the king appointed unto her a certain [l]officer, saying, Restore all that *was* hers, and all the
fruits of the field since the day that she
left the land, even until now.

Hazael anointed king of Syria

7 ¶ And Elisha came to Damascus; and
Ben-hadad the king of Syria was sick; and
it was told him, saying, The man of God
is come hither.
8 And the king said unto [a]Hazael,
[b]Take a present in thine hand, and go,
meet the man of God, and [c]inquire of the
LORD by him, saying, Shall I recover of
this disease?
9 So Hazael went to meet him, and
took a present [l]with him, even of every
good thing of Damascus, forty camels'
burden, and came and stood before him,
and said, Thy son Ben-hadad king of Syria
hath sent me to thee, saying, Shall I recover of this disease?
10 And Elisha said unto him, Go, say J
unto him, Thou mayest certainly recover:
howbeit the LORD hath shown me that
[a]he shall surely die.
11 And he settled his countenance
[l]stedfastly, until he was ashamed: and
the man of God [a]wept.
12 And Hazael said, Why weepeth my
lord? And he answered, Because I know
[a]the evil that thou wilt do unto the chil-

13 [l]Heb. *in it*
16 [a]ver. 1
17 [a]ver. 2
18 [a]ver. 1
8:1 [a]ch. 4:35 [b]Ps. 105:16; Hag. 1:11
4 [a]ch. 5:27
5 [a]ch. 4:35
6 [l]Or, *eunuch*
8 [a]1 Ki. 19:15 [b]1 Sam. 9:7; 1 Ki. 14:3; ch. 5:5 [c]ch. 1:2
9 [l]Heb. *in his hand*
10 [a]ver. 15
11 [a]Luke 19:41 [l]Heb. *and set* it
12 [a]ch. 10:32 & 12:17 & 13:3,7; Amos 1:3

J *2Ki 5:27* ◀ ▶ *2Ki 8:1*
J *2Ki 7:19* ◀ ▶ *2Ki 8:10–13*
E *2Ki 6:20* ◀ ▶ *2Ki 13:21*
J *2Ki 8:1* ◀ ▶ *2Ki 9:8–10*

dren of Israel: their strong holds wilt thou
set on fire, and their young men wilt thou
slay with the sword, and [b]wilt dash their
children, and rip up their women with
child.
13 And Hazael said, But what, [a]*is* thy
servant a dog, that he should do this great
thing? And Elisha answered, [b]The LORD
hath shown me that thou *shalt be* king
over Syria.
14 So he departed from Elisha, and
came to his master; who said to him,
What said Elisha to thee? And he answered, He told me *that* thou shouldest
surely recover.
15 And it came to pass on the morrow,
that he took a thick cloth, and dipped *it*
in water, and spread *it* on his face, so that
he died: and Hazael reigned in his stead.

Jehoram, king of Judah

16 ¶ And in the fifth year of Joram the
son of Ahab king of Israel, Jehoshaphat
being then king of Judah, [a]Jehoram the
son of Jehoshaphat king of Judah [1]began
to reign.
17 [a]Thirty and two years old was he
when he began to reign; and he reigned
eight years in Jerusalem.
18 And he walked in the way of the
kings of Israel, as did the house of Ahab:
for [a]the daughter of Ahab was his wife:
and he did evil in the sight of the LORD.
19 Yet the LORD would not destroy Judah for David his servant's sake, [a]as he
promised him to give him always a [1]light,
and to his children.
20 ¶ In his days [a]Edom revolted from
under the hand of Judah, [b]and made a
king over themselves.
21 So Joram went over to Zair, and all
the chariots with him: and he rose by
night, and smote the Edomites which
compassed him about, and the captains
of the chariots: and the people fled into
their tents.
22 [1]Yet Edom revolted from under the
hand of Judah unto this day. [a]Then Libnah revolted at the same time.
23 And the rest of the acts of Joram,
and all that he did, *are* they not written
in the book of the chronicles of the kings
of Judah?
24 And Joram slept with his fathers,
and was buried with his fathers in the
city of David: and [a]Ahaziah[1] his son
reigned in his stead.

Ahaziah, king of Judah

25 ¶ In the twelfth year of Joram the
son of Ahab king of Israel did Ahaziah the
son of Jehoram king of Judah begin to
reign.
26 [a]Two and twenty years old *was*
Ahaziah when he began to reign; and he
reigned one year in Jerusalem. And his
mother's name *was* Athaliah, the [1]daugh-
ter of Omri king of Israel.
27 [a]And he walked in the way of the
house of Ahab, and did evil in the sight of
the LORD, as *did* the house of Ahab: for he
was the son-in-law of the house of Ahab.
28 ¶ And he went [a]with Joram the son
of Ahab to the war against Hazael king of
Syria in Ramoth-gilead; and the Syrians
wounded Joram.
29 And [a]king Joram went back to be
healed in Jezreel of the wounds [1]which
the Syrians had given him at [2]Ramah,
when he fought against Hazael king of
Syria. [b]And Ahaziah the son of Jehoram
king of Judah went down to see Joram the
son of Ahab in Jezreel, because he was
[3]sick.

Jehu anointed king of Israel

9 AND ELISHA the prophet called one
of the [a]children of the prophets, and
said unto him, [b]Gird up thy loins, and
take this box of oil in thine hand, [c]and go
to Ramoth-gilead:
2 And when thou comest thither, look
out there Jehu the son of Jehoshaphat the
son of Nimshi, and go in, and make him
arise up from among [a]his brethren, and
carry him to an [1]inner chamber;
3 Then [a]take the box of oil, and pour *it*
on his head, and say, Thus saith the LORD,
I have anointed thee king over Israel.
Then open the door, and flee, and tarry
not.
4 ¶ So the young man, *even* the young
man the prophet, went to Ramoth-gilead.
5 And when he came, behold, the cap-

12 [b]ch. 15:16; Hos. 13:16; Amos 1:13
13 [a]1 Sam. 17:43 [b]1 Ki. 19:15
16 [a]2 Chr. 21:3 [1]Heb. *reigned.* Began to reign in consort with his father
17 [a]2 Chr. 21:5
18 [a]ver. 26
19 [a]2 Sam. 7:13; 1 Ki. 11:36 & 15:4; 2 Chr. 21:7 [1]Heb. *candle,* or, *lamp*
20 [a]Gen. 27:40; ch. 3:27; 2 Chr. 21:8-10 [b]1 Ki. 22:47
22 [a]2 Chr. 21:10 [1]And see fulfilled in Gen. 27:40
24 [a]2 Chr. 22:1 [1]Called *Azariah* in 2 Chr. 22:6 and *Jehoahaz* in 2 Chr. 21:17 & 25:23
26 [a]See 2 Chr. 22:2 [1]Or, *granddaughter;* see ver. 18
27 [a]2 Chr. 22:3,4
28 [a]2 Chr. 22:5
29 [a]ch. 9:15 [b]ch. 9:16; 2 Chr. 22:6,7 [1]Heb. *wherewith the Syrians had wounded* [2]Called *Ramoth* in ver. 28 [3]Heb. *wounded*
9:1 [a]1 Ki. 20:35 [b]ch. 4:29; Jer. 1:17 [c]ch. 8:28,29
2 [a]ver. 5,11 [1]Heb. *chamber in a chamber*
3 [a]1 Ki. 19:16

I *2Ki 7:1–2* ◄► *2Ki 13:15–19*

9:4 Some scholars suggest that this young prophet, who was "one of the children of the prophets" (9:1), was the prophet Jonah, son of Amittai, who was later sent by God to Nineveh.

tains of the host *were* sitting; and he said, I have an errand to thee, O captain. And Jehu said, Unto which of all us? And he said, To thee, O captain.

6 And he arose, and went into the house; and he poured the oil on his head, and said unto him, [a]Thus saith the LORD God of Israel, I have anointed thee king over the people of the LORD, *even* over Israel.

7 And thou shalt smite the house of Ahab thy master, that I may avenge the blood of my servants the prophets, and the blood of all the servants of the LORD, [a]at the hand of Jezebel.

J 8 For the whole house of Ahab shall perish: and [a]I will cut off from Ahab [b]him that pisseth against the wall, and [c]him that is shut up and left in Israel:

9 And I will make the house of Ahab like the house of [a]Jeroboam the son of Nebat, and like the house of [b]Baasha the son of Ahijah:

10 [a]And the dogs shall eat Jezebel in the portion of Jezreel, and *there shall be* none to bury *her.* And he opened the door, and fled.

11 ¶ Then Jehu came forth to the servants of his lord: and *one* said unto him, *Is* all well? wherefore came [a]this mad *fellow* to thee? And he said unto them, Ye know the man, and his communication.

12 And they said, *It is* false; tell us now. And he said, Thus and thus spake he to me, saying, Thus saith the LORD, I have anointed thee king over Israel.

13 Then they hasted, and [a]took every man his garment, and put *it* under him on the top of the stairs, and blew with trumpets, saying, Jehu [1]is king.

Jehu kills Joram and Ahaziah

14 So Jehu the son of Jehoshaphat the son of Nimshi conspired against Joram. (Now Joram had kept Ramoth-gilead, he and all Israel, because of Hazael king of Syria.

15 But [a]king [1]Joram was returned to be healed in Jezreel of the wounds which the Syrians [2]had given him, when he fought with Hazael king of Syria.) And Jehu said, If it be your minds, *then* [3]let none go forth *nor* escape out of the city to go to tell *it* in Jezreel.

16 So Jehu rode in a chariot, and went to Jezreel; for Joram lay there. [a]And Ahaziah king of Judah was come down to see Joram.

17 And there stood a watchman on the tower in Jezreel, and he spied the company of Jehu as he came, and said, I see a company. And Joram said, Take an horseman, and send to meet them, and let him say, *Is it* peace?

18 So there went one on horseback to meet him, and said, Thus saith the king, *Is it* peace? And Jehu said, What hast thou to do with peace? turn thee behind me. And the watchman told, saying, The messenger came to them, but he cometh not again.

19 Then he sent out a second on horseback, which came to them, and said, Thus saith the king, *Is it* peace? And Jehu answered, What hast thou to do with peace? turn thee behind me.

20 And the watchman told, saying, He came even unto them, and cometh not again: and the [1]driving *is* like the driving of Jehu the son of Nimshi; for he driveth [2]furiously.

21 And Joram said, [1]Make ready. And his chariot was made ready. And [a]Joram king of Israel and Ahaziah king of Judah went out, each in his chariot, and they went out against Jehu, and [2]met him in the portion of Naboth the Jezreelite.

22 And it came to pass, when Joram saw Jehu, that he said, *Is it* peace, Jehu? And he answered, What peace, so long as the whoredoms of thy mother Jezebel and her witchcrafts *are so* many?

23 And Joram turned his hands, and fled, and said to Ahaziah, *There is* treachery, O Ahaziah.

24 And Jehu [1]drew a bow with his full strength, and smote Jehoram between his arms, and the arrow went out at his heart, and he [2]sunk down in his chariot.

25 Then said *Jehu* to Bidkar his captain, Take up, *and* cast him in the portion of the field of Naboth the Jezreelite: for remember how that, when I and thou rode together after Ahab his father, [a]the LORD laid this burden upon him;

26 Surely I have seen yesterday the [1]blood of Naboth, and the blood of his sons, saith the LORD; and I will requite thee in this [2]plat, saith the LORD. Now therefore take *and* cast him into the plat J

6 [a]1 Ki. 19:16; 2 Chr. 22:7
7 [a]1 Ki. 18:4 & 21:15
8 [a]1 Ki. 14:10 & 21:21 [b]1 Sam. 25:22 [c]Deut. 32:36
9 [a]1 Ki. 14:10 & 15:29 & 21:22 [b]1 Ki. 16:3,11
10 [a]ver. 35,36; 1 Ki. 21:23
11 [a]Jer. 29:26; John 10:20; Acts 26:24; 1 Cor. 4:10
13 [a]Mat. 21:7 [1]Heb. *reigneth*
15 [a]ch. 8:29 [1]Heb. *Jehoram* [2]Heb. *smote* [3]Heb. *let no escaper go*
16 [a]ch. 8:29
20 [1]Or, *marching* [2]Heb. *in madness*
21 [a]2 Chr. 22:7 [1]Heb. *Bind* [2]Heb. *found*
24 [1]Heb. *filled his hand with a bow* [2]Heb. *bowed*
25 [a]1 Ki. 21:29
26 [1]Heb. *bloods* [2]Or, *portion*

of ground, according to the word of the LORD.

27 ¶ But when Ahaziah the king of Judah saw *this,* he fled by the way of the garden house. And Jehu followed after him, and said, Smite him also in the chariot. *And they did so* at the going up to Gur, which *is* by Ibleam. And he fled to [a]Megiddo, and died there.

28 And his servants carried him in a chariot to Jerusalem, and buried him in his sepulchre with his fathers in the city of David.

29 And in the eleventh year of Joram the son of Ahab began Ahaziah to reign over Judah.

The death of Jezebel

30 ¶ And when Jehu was come to Jezreel, Jezebel heard *of it;* [a]and she [l]painted her face, and tired her head, and looked out at a window.

31 And as Jehu entered in at the gate, she said, [a]*Had* Zimri peace, who slew his master?

32 And he lifted up his face to the window, and said, Who *is* on my side? who? And there looked out to him two *or* three [l]eunuchs.

33 And he said, Throw her down. So they threw her down: and *some* of her blood was sprinkled on the wall, and on the horses: and he trode her under foot.

34 And when he was come in, he did eat and drink, and said, Go, see now this cursed *woman,* and bury her: for [a]she *is* a king's daughter.

35 And they went to bury her: but they found no more of her than the skull, and the feet, and the palms of *her* hands.

36 Wherefore they came again, and told him. And he said, This *is* the word of the LORD, which he spake [l]by his servant Elijah the Tishbite, saying, [a]In the portion of Jezreel shall dogs eat the flesh of Jezebel:

37 And the carcase of Jezebel shall be [a]as dung upon the face of the field in the portion of Jezreel; *so* that they shall not say, This *is* Jezebel.

Ahab's kin destroyed

10 AND AHAB had seventy sons in Samaria. And Jehu wrote letters, and sent to Samaria, unto the rulers of Jezreel, to the elders, and to [l]them that brought up Ahab's *children,* saying,

2 Now as soon as this letter cometh to you, seeing your master's sons *are* with you, and *there are* with you chariots and horses, a fenced city also, and armour;

3 Look even out the best and meetest of your master's sons, and set *him* on his father's throne, and fight for your master's house.

4 But they were exceedingly afraid, and said, Behold, two kings stood not before him: how then shall we stand?

5 And he that *was* over the house, and he that *was* over the city, the elders also, and the bringers up *of the children,* sent to Jehu, saying, *We are* thy servants, and will do all that thou shalt bid us; we will not make any king: do thou *that which is* good in thine eyes.

6 Then he wrote a letter the second time to them, saying, If ye *be* [l]mine, and *if* ye will hearken unto my voice, take ye the heads of the men your master's sons, and come to me to Jezreel by tomorrow this time. Now the king's sons, *being* seventy persons, *were* with the great men of the city, which brought them up.

7 And it came to pass, when the letter came to them, that they took the king's sons, and [a]slew seventy persons, and put their heads in baskets, and sent him *them* to Jezreel.

8 ¶ And there came a messenger, and told him, saying, They have brought the heads of the king's sons. And he said, Lay ye them in two heaps at the entering in of the gate until the morning.

9 And it came to pass in the morning, that he went out, and stood, and said to all the people, Ye *be* righteous: behold, [a]I conspired against my master, and slew him: but who slew all these?

10 Know now that there shall [a]fall unto the earth nothing of the word of the LORD, which the LORD spake concerning the house of Ahab: for the LORD hath done *that* which he spake [b]by[l] his servant Elijah.

11 So Jehu slew all that remained of the house of Ahab in Jezreel, and all his great men, and his [l]kinsfolks, and his priests, until he left him none remaining.

12 ¶ And he arose and departed, and came to Samaria. *And* as he *was* at the [l]shearing house in the way,

13 [a]Jehu [l]met with the brethren of Ahaziah king of Judah, and said, Who *are* ye? And they answered, We *are* the

27 [a]In the kingdom of *Samaria;* 2 Chr. 22:9
30 [a]Ezek. 23:40 [l]Heb. *put her eyes in painting*
31 [a]1 Ki. 16:9-20
32 [l]Or, *chamberlains*
34 [a]1 Ki. 16:31
36 [a]1 Ki. 21:23 [l]Heb. *by the hand of*
37 [a]Ps. 83:10
10:1 [l]Heb. *nourishers*
6 [l]Heb. *for me*
7 [a]1 Ki. 21:21
9 [a]ch. 9:14,24
10 [a]1 Sam. 3:19; Jer. 44:28 [b]1 Ki. 21:19,21,29 [l]Heb. *by the hand of*
11 [l]Or, *acquaintance*
12 [l]Heb. *house of shepherds binding sheep*
13 [a]ch. 8:29; 2 Chr. 22:8 [l]Heb. *found*

brethren of Ahaziah; and we go down [2]to salute the children of the king and the children of the queen.

14 And he said, Take them alive. And they took them alive, and slew them at the pit of the shearing house, *even* two and forty men: neither left he any of them.

15 ¶ And when he was departed thence, He [1]lighted on [a]Jehonadab the son of [b]Rechab *coming* to meet him: and he [2]saluted him, and said to him, Is thine heart right, as my heart *is* with thy heart? And Jehonadab answered, It is. If it be, [c]give *me* thine hand. And he gave *him* his hand; and he took him up to him into the chariot.

16 And he said, Come with me, and see my [a]zeal for the LORD. So they made him ride in his chariot.

17 And when he came to Samaria, [a]he slew all that remained unto Ahab in Samaria, till he had destroyed him, according to the saying of the LORD, [b]which he spake to Elijah.

Massacre of Baal worshippers

18 ¶ And Jehu gathered all the people together, and said unto them, [a]Ahab served Baal a little; *but* Jehu shall serve him much.

19 Now therefore call unto me all the [a]prophets of Baal, all his servants, and all his priests; let none be wanting: for I have a great sacrifice *to do* to Baal; whosoever shall be wanting, he shall not live. But Jehu did *it* in subtlety, to the intent that he might destroy the worshippers of Baal.

20 And Jehu said, [1]Proclaim a solemn assembly for Baal. And they proclaimed *it*.

21 And Jehu sent through all Israel: and all the worshippers of Baal came, so that there was not a man left that came not. And they came into the [a]house of Baal; and the house of Baal was [1]full from one end to another.

22 And he said unto him that *was* over the vestry, Bring forth vestments for all the worshippers of Baal. And he brought them forth vestments.

23 And Jehu went, and Jehonadab the son of Rechab, into the house of Baal, and said unto the worshippers of Baal, Search, and look that there be here with you none of the servants of the LORD, but the worshippers of Baal only.

24 And when they went in to offer sacrifices and burnt offerings, Jehu appointed fourscore men without, and said, *If* any of the men whom I have brought into your hands escape, *he that letteth him go,* [a]his life *shall be* for the life of him.

25 And it came to pass, as soon as he had made an end of offering the burnt offering, that Jehu said to the guard and to the captains, Go in, *and* slay them; let none come forth. And they smote them with [1]the edge of the sword; and the guard and the captains cast *them* out, and went to the city of the house of Baal.

26 And they brought forth the [a]images[1] out of the house of Baal, and burned them.

27 And they brake down the image of Baal, and brake down the house of Baal, [a]and made it a draught house unto this day.

28 Thus Jehu destroyed Baal out of Israel.

29 ¶ Howbeit *from* the sins of Jeroboam the son of Nebat, who made Israel to sin, Jehu departed not from after them, *to wit,* [a]the golden calves that *were* in Beth-el, and that *were* in Dan.

30 And the LORD said unto Jehu, Because thou hast done well in executing *that which is* right in mine eyes, *and* hast done unto the house of Ahab according to all that *was* in mine heart, [a]thy children of the fourth *generation* shall sit on the throne of Israel. L

31 But Jehu [1]took no heed to walk in the law of the LORD God of Israel with all his heart: for he departed not from [a]the sins of Jeroboam, which made Israel to sin.

32 ¶ In those days the LORD began [1]to cut Israel short: and [a]Hazael smote them in all the coasts of Israel;

33 From Jordan [1]eastward, all the land of Gilead, the Gadites, and the Reubenites, and the Manassites, from Aroer, which *is* by the river Arnon, [2]even [a]Gilead and Bashan.

34 Now the rest of the acts of Jehu, and all that he did, and all his might, *are* they not written in the book of the chronicles of the kings of Israel?

13 [2]Heb. *to the peace of*
15 [a]Jer. 35:6 [b]1 Chr. 2:55 [c]Ezra 10:19 [1]Heb. *found* [2]Heb. *blessed*
16 [a]1 Ki. 19:10
17 [a]ch. 9:8; 2 Chr. 22:8 [b]1 Ki. 21:21
18 [a]1 Ki. 16:31,32
19 [a]1 Ki. 22:6
20 [1]Heb. *Sanctify*
21 [a]1 Ki. 16:32 [1]Or, so *full,* that they stood *mouth to mouth*
24 [a]1 Ki. 20:39
25 [1]Heb. *the mouth*
26 [a]1 Ki. 14:23 [1]Heb. *statues*
27 [a]Ezra 6:11; Dan. 2:5 & 3:29
29 [a]1 Ki. 12:28,29
30 [a]See ver. 35; ch. 13:1,10 & 14:23 & 15:8,12
31 [a]1 Ki. 14:16 [1]Heb. *observed not*
32 [a]ch. 8:12 [1]Heb. *to cut off the ends*
33 [a]Amos 1:3 [1]Heb. *toward the rising of the sun* [2]Or, *even to Gilead and Bashan*

L *2Ki 4:16* ◄► *2Ki 20:5–10*

35 And Jehu slept with his fathers: and they buried him in Samaria. And Jehoahaz his son reigned in his stead.

36 And [l]the time that Jehu reigned over Israel in Samaria *was* twenty and eight years.

Jehoash, king of Judah

11 AND WHEN [a]Athaliah [b]the mother of Ahaziah saw that her son was dead, she arose and destroyed all the [l]seed royal.

2 But [l]Jehosheba, the daughter of king Joram, sister of Ahaziah, took [2]Joash the son of Ahaziah, and stole him from among the king's sons *which were* slain; and they hid him, *even* him and his nurse, in the bedchamber from Athaliah, so that he was not slain.

3 And he was with her hid in the house of the LORD six years. And Athaliah did reign over the land.

4 ¶ And [a]the seventh year Jehoiada sent and fetched the rulers over hundreds, with the captains and the guard, and brought them to him into the house of the LORD, and made a covenant with them, and took an oath of them in the house of the LORD, and showed them the king's son.

5 And he commanded them, saying, This *is* the thing that ye shall do; A third part of you that enter in [a]on the sabbath shall even be keepers of the watch of the king's house;

6 And a third part *shall be* at the gate of Sur; and a third part at the gate behind the guard: so shall ye keep the watch of the house, [l]that it be not broken down.

7 And two [1,2]parts of all you that go forth on the sabbath, even they shall keep the watch of the house of the LORD about the king.

8 And ye shall compass the king round about, every man with his weapons in his hand: and he that cometh within the ranges, let him be slain: and be ye with the king as he goeth out and as he cometh in.

9 [a]And the captains over the hundreds did according to all *things* that Jehoiada the priest commanded: and they took every man his men that were to come in on the sabbath, with them that should go out on the sabbath, and came to Jehoiada the priest.

10 And to the captains over hundreds did the priest give king David's spears and shields, [a]that *were* in the temple of the LORD.

11 And the guard stood, every man with his weapons in his hand, round about the king, from the right [l]corner of the temple to the left corner of the temple, *along* by the altar and the temple.

12 And he brought forth the king's son, and put the crown upon him, and *gave him* the testimony; and they made him king, and anointed him; and they clapped their hands, and said, [a]God [l]save the king.

13 ¶ [a]And when Athaliah heard the noise of the guard *and* of the people, she came to the people into the temple of the LORD.

14 And when she looked, behold, the king stood by [a]a pillar, as the manner *was,* and the princes and the trumpeters by the king, and all the people of the land rejoiced, and blew with trumpets: and Athaliah rent her clothes, and cried, Treason, Treason.

15 But Jehoiada the priest commanded the captains of the hundreds, the officers of the host, and said unto them, Have her forth without the ranges: and him that followeth her kill with the sword. For the priest had said, Let her not be slain in the house of the LORD.

16 And they laid hands on her; and she went by the way by the which the horses came into the king's house: and there was she slain.

17 ¶ [a]And Jehoiada made a covenant between the LORD and the king and the people, that they should be the LORD'S people; [b]between the king also and the people.

18 And all the people of the land went into the [a]house of Baal, and brake it down; his altars and his images [b]brake they in pieces thoroughly, and slew Mattan the priest of Baal before the altars. And [c]the priest appointed [l]officers over the house of the LORD.

19 And he took the rulers over hundreds, and the captains, and the guard, and all the people of the land; and they brought down the king from the house of the LORD, and came by the way of the gate of the guard to the king's house. And he sat on the throne of the kings.

20 And all the people of the land rejoiced, and the city was in quiet: and they

---

36 [l]Heb. *the days were*
11:1 [a]2 Chr. 22:10 [b]ch. 8:26 [l]Heb. *seed of the kingdom*
2 [l]*Jehoshabeath* in 2 Chr. 22:11 [2]Or, *Jehoash*
4 [a]2 Chr. 23:1
5 [a]1 Chr. 9:25
6 [l]Or, *from breaking up*
7 [l]Or, *companies* [2]Heb. *hands*
9 [a]2 Chr. 23:8
10 [a]2 Sam. 8:7
11 [l]Heb. *shoulder*
12 [a]1 Sam. 10:24 [l]Heb. *Let the king live*
13 [a]2 Chr. 23:12
14 [a]ch. 23:3; 2 Chr. 34:31
17 [a]2 Chr. 23:16 [b]2 Sam. 5:3
18 [a]ch. 10:26 [b]Deut. 12:3; 2 Chr. 23:17 [c]2 Chr. 23:18 [l]Heb. *offices*

slew Athaliah with the sword *beside* the
king's house.
21 [a]Seven years old *was* Jehoash when
he began to reign.
12 IN THE seventh year of Jehu [a]Je-
hoash began to reign; and forty
years reigned he in Jerusalem. And his
mother's name *was* Zibiah of Beer-sheba.
2 And Jehoash did *that which was*
right in the sight of the LORD all his days
wherein Jehoiada the priest instructed
him.
3 But [a]the high places were not taken
away: the people still sacrificed and burnt
incense in the high places.

Jehoash repairs the temple

4 ¶ And Jehoash said to the priests,
[a]All the money of the [1,2]dedicated things
that is brought into the house of the LORD,
even [b]the money of every one that passeth *the account,* [3]the money that every
man is set at, *and* all the money that
[c]cometh[4] into any man's heart to bring
into the house of the LORD,
5 Let the priests take *it* to them, every
man of his acquaintance: and let them
repair the breaches of the house,
wheresoever any breach shall be found.
6 But it was *so, that* [1]in the three and
twentieth year of king Jehoash [a]the
priests had not repaired the breaches of
the house.
7 [a]Then king Jehoash called for Jehoiada the priest, and the *other* priests, and
said unto them, Why repair ye not the
breaches of the house? now therefore receive no *more* money of your acquaintance, but deliver it for the breaches of
the house.
8 And the priests consented to receive
no *more* money of the people, neither to
repair the breaches of the house.
9 But Jehoiada the priest took [a]a chest,
and bored a hole in the lid of it, and set it
beside the altar, on the right side as one
cometh into the house of the LORD: and
the priests that kept the [1]door put
therein all the money *that was* brought
into the house of the LORD.
10 And it was *so,* when they saw that
there was much money in the chest, that
the king's [1]scribe and the high priest
came up, and they [2]put up in bags, and
told the money that was found in the
house of the LORD.
11 And they gave the money, being
told, into the hands of them that did the
work, that had the oversight of the house
of the LORD: and they [1]laid it out to the
carpenters and builders, that wrought
upon the house of the LORD,
12 And to masons, and hewers of
stone, and to buy timber and hewed
stone to repair the breaches of the house
of the LORD, and for all that [1]was laid out
for the house to repair *it.*
13 Howbeit [a]there were not made for
the house of the LORD bowls of silver,
snuffers, basins, trumpets, any vessels of
gold, or vessels of silver, of the money
that was brought into the house of the
LORD:
14 But they gave that to the workmen,
and repaired therewith the house of the
LORD.
15 Moreover [a]they reckoned not with
the men, into whose hand they delivered
the money to be bestowed on workmen:
for they dealt faithfully.
16 [a]The trespass money and sin
money was not brought into the house of
the LORD: [b]it was the priests'.
17 ¶ Then [a]Hazael king of Syria went
up, and fought against Gath, and took it:
and [b]Hazael set his face to go up to Jerusalem.
18 And Jehoash king of Judah [a]took all
the hallowed things that Jehoshaphat,
and Jehoram, and Ahaziah, his fathers,
kings of Judah, had dedicated, and his
own hallowed things, and all the gold
that was found in the treasures of the
house of the LORD, and in the king's
house, and sent *it* to Hazael king of Syria:
and he [1]went away from Jerusalem.
19 ¶ And the rest of the acts of Joash,
and all that he did, *are* they not written
in the book of the chronicles of the kings
of Judah?
20 And [a]his servants arose, and made
a conspiracy, and slew Joash in the
[1]house of Millo, which goeth down to
Silla.
21 For [a]Jozachar the son of Shimeath,
and Jehozabad the son of [1]Shomer, his
servants, smote him, and he died; and
they buried him with his fathers in the
city of David: and [b]Amaziah his son
reigned in his stead.

---

21 [a]2 Chr. 24:1
12:1 [a]2 Chr. 24:1
3 [a]1 Ki. 15:14 & 22:43; ch. 14:4
4 [a]ch. 22:4 [b]Ex. 30:13 [c]Ex. 35:5; 1 Chr. 29:9 [1]Or, *holy things* [2]Heb. *holinesses* [3]Heb. *the money of the souls of his estimation* [4]Heb. *ascendeth upon the heart of a man*
6 [a]2 Chr. 24:5 [1]Heb. *in the twentieth year and third year*
7 [a]2 Chr. 24:6
9 [a]2 Chr. 24:8 [1]Heb. *threshold*
10 [1]Or, *secretary* [2]Heb. *bound up*
11 [1]Heb. *brought it forth*
12 [1]Heb. *went forth*
13 [a]See 2 Chr. 24:14
15 [a]ch. 22:7
16 [a]Lev. 5:15,18 [b]Lev. 7:7; Num. 18:9
17 [a]ch. 8:12 [b]See 2 Chr. 24:23
18 [a]1 Ki. 15:18; ch. 18:15,16 [1]Heb. *went up*
20 [a]ch. 14:5; 2 Chr. 24:25 [1]Or, *Beth-millo*
21 [a]2 Chr. 24:26 *Zabad* [b]2 Chr. 24:27 [1]Or, *Shimrith*

Jehoahaz, king of Israel

13 IN [1]THE three and twentieth year of Joash the son of Ahaziah king of Judah Jehoahaz the son of Jehu began to reign over Israel in Samaria, *and reigned* seventeen years.

2 And he did *that which was* evil in the sight of the LORD, and [1]followed the sins of Jeroboam the son of Nebat, which made Israel to sin; he departed not therefrom.

3 ¶ And [a]the anger of the LORD was kindled against Israel, and he delivered them into the hand of [b]Hazael king of Syria, and into the hand of Ben-hadad the son of Hazael, all *their* days.

4 And Jehoahaz [a]besought the LORD, and the LORD hearkened unto him: for [b]he saw the oppression of Israel, because the king of Syria oppressed them.

5 ([a]And the LORD gave Israel a saviour, so that they went out from under the hand of the Syrians: and the children of Israel dwelt in their tents, [1]as beforetime.

6 Nevertheless they departed not from the sins of the house of Jeroboam, who made Israel sin, *but* [1]walked therein: [a]and there [2]remained the grove also in Samaria.)

7 Neither did he leave of the people to Jehoahaz but fifty horsemen, and ten chariots, and ten thousand footmen; for the king of Syria had destroyed them, [a]and had made them like the dust by threshing.

8 ¶ Now the rest of the acts of Jehoahaz, and all that he did, and his might, *are* they not written in the book of the chronicles of the kings of Israel?

9 And Jehoahaz slept with his fathers; and they buried him in Samaria: and [1]Joash his son reigned [2]in his stead.

Jehoash, king of Israel

10 ¶ In the thirty and seventh year of Joash king of Judah began [1]Jehoash the son of Jehoahaz to reign over Israel in Samaria, *and reigned* sixteen years.

11 And he did *that which was* evil in the sight of the LORD; he departed not from all the sins of Jeroboam the son of Nebat, who made Israel sin: *but* he walked therein.

12 [a]And the rest of the acts of Joash, and [b]all that he did, and [c]his might wherewith he fought against Amaziah king of Judah, *are* they not written in the book of the chronicles of the kings of Israel?

13 And Joash slept with his fathers; and Jeroboam sat upon his throne: and Joash was buried in Samaria with the kings of Israel.

The death of Elisha

14 ¶ Now Elisha was fallen sick of his sickness whereof he died. And Joash the king of Israel came down unto him, and wept over his face, and said, O my father, my father, [a]the chariot of Israel, and the horsemen thereof.

15 And Elisha said unto him, Take bow and arrows. And he took unto him bow and arrows. I

16 And he said to the king of Israel, [1]Put thine hand upon the bow. And he put his hand *upon it:* and Elisha put his hands upon the king's hands.

17 And he said, Open the window eastward. And he opened *it.* Then Elisha said, Shoot. And he shot. And he said, The arrow of the LORD's deliverance, and the arrow of deliverance from Syria: for thou shalt smite the Syrians in [a]Aphek, till thou have consumed *them.*

18 And he said, Take the arrows. And he took *them.* And he said unto the king of Israel, Smite upon the ground. And he smote thrice, and stayed.

19 And the man of God was wroth with him, and said, Thou shouldest have smitten five or six times; then hadst thou smitten Syria till thou hadst consumed *it:* [a]whereas now thou shalt smite Syria *but* thrice.

20 ¶ And Elisha died, and they buried him. And the bands of the Moabites invaded the land at the coming in of the year.

21 And it came to pass, as they were burying a man, that, behold, they spied a band *of men;* and they cast the man into the sepulchre of Elisha: and when the man [1]was let down, and touched the bones of Elisha, he revived, and stood up on his feet. E

22 ¶ But [a]Hazael king of Syria oppressed Israel all the days of Jehoahaz.

23 And the LORD was gracious unto them, and had compassion on them, and R

13:1 [1]Heb. *the twentieth year and third year*
2 [1]Heb. *walked after*
3 [a]Judg. 2:14 [b]ch. 8:12
4 [a]Ps. 78:34 [b]Ex. 3:7; ch. 14:26
5 [a]See ver. 25; ch. 14:25,27 [1]Heb. *as yesterday,* and *third day*
6 [a]1 Ki. 16:33 [1]Heb. *he walked* [2]Heb. *stood*
7 [a]Amos 1:3
9 [1]*Jehoash* in ver. 10 [2]Alone
10 [1]In consort with his father; see ch. 14:1
12 [a]ch. 14:15 [b]See ver. 14 & 25 [c]ch. 14:9; 2 Chr. 25:17
14 [a]ch. 2:12
16 [1]Heb. *Make thine hand to ride*
17 [a]1 Ki. 20:26
19 [a]ver. 25
21 [1]Heb. *went down*
22 [a]ch. 8:12

I *2Ki 8:19* ◀ ▶ *2Ki 14:27*
E *2Ki 8:4–5* ◀ ▶ *2Ki 20:1–11*
R *1Ki 14:10–16* ◀ ▶ *2Ki 17:6*

[a]had respect unto them, [b]because of his
covenant with Abraham, Isaac, and Jacob,
and would not destroy them, neither cast
he them from his ʹpresence as yet.
24 So Hazael king of Syria died; and
Ben-hadad his son reigned in his stead.
25 And Jehoash the son of Jehoahaz
ʹtook again out of the hand of Ben-hadad
the son of Hazael the cities, which he had
taken out of the hand of Jehoahaz his father by war. [a]Three times did Joash beat
him, and recovered the cities of Israel.

Amaziah, king of Judah

14 IN [a]THE second year of Joash son
of Jehoahaz king of Israel reigned
[b]Amaziah the son of Joash king of Judah.
2 He was twenty and five years old
when he began to reign, and reigned
twenty and nine years in Jerusalem. And
his mother's name *was* Jehoaddan of Jerusalem.
3 And he did *that which was* right in
the sight of the LORD, yet not like David
his father: he did according to all things
as Joash his father did.
4 [a]Howbeit the high places were not
taken away: as yet the people did sacrifice and burnt incense on the high places.
5 ¶ And it came to pass, as soon as the
kingdom was confirmed in his hand, that
he slew his servants [a]which had slain the
king his father.
6 But the children of the murderers he
slew not: according unto that which is
written in the book of the law of Moses,
wherein the LORD commanded, saying,
[a]The fathers shall not be put to death for
the children, nor the children be put to
death for the fathers; but every man shall
be put to death for his own sin.
7 [a]He slew of Edom in [b]the valley of
salt ten thousand, and took ʹSelah by
war, [c]and called the name of it Joktheel
unto this day.
8 ¶ [a]Then Amaziah sent messengers to
Jehoash, the son of Jehoahaz son of Jehu,
king of Israel, saying, Come, let us look
one another in the face.
9 And Jehoash the king of Israel sent to
Amaziah king of Judah, saying, [a]The thistle that *was* in Lebanon sent to the [b]cedar
that *was* in Lebanon, saying, Give thy
daughter to my son to wife: and there
passed by a wild beast that *was* in Lebanon, and trode down the thistle.
10 Thou hast indeed smitten Edom,
and [a]thine heart hath lifted thee up: glory
of this, and tarry ʹat home: for why
shouldest thou meddle to *thy* hurt, that
thou shouldest fall, *even* thou, and Judah
with thee?
11 But Amaziah would not hear.
Therefore Jehoash king of Israel went up;
and he and Amaziah king of Judah looked
one another in the face at [a]Beth-shemesh, which *belongeth* to Judah.
12 And Judah ʹwas put to the worse
before Israel; and they fled every man to
their tents.
13 And Jehoash king of Israel took Amaziah king of Judah, the son of Jehoash
the son of Ahaziah, at Beth-shemesh, and
came to Jerusalem, and brake down the
wall of Jerusalem from [a]the gate of
Ephraim unto [b]the corner gate, four hundred cubits.
14 And he took all [a]the gold and silver,
and all the vessels that were found in the
house of the LORD, and in the treasures of
the king's house, and hostages, and returned to Samaria.
15 ¶ [a]Now the rest of the acts of Jehoash which he did, and his might, and
how he fought with Amaziah king of Judah, *are* they not written in the book of
the chronicles of the kings of Israel?
16 And Jehoash slept with his fathers,
and was buried in Samaria with the kings
of Israel; and Jeroboam his son reigned in
his stead.
17 ¶ [a]And Amaziah the son of Joash
king of Judah lived after the death of Jehoash son of Jehoahaz king of Israel fifteen years.
18 And the rest of the acts of Amaziah,
are they not written in the book of the
chronicles of the kings of Judah?
19 Now [a]they made a conspiracy
against him in Jerusalem: and he fled to
[b]Lachish; but they sent after him to Lachish, and slew him there.
20 And they brought him on horses:
and he was buried at Jerusalem with his
fathers in the city of David.
21 ¶ And all the people of Judah took
[a]Azariah, which *was* sixteen years old,
and made him king instead of his father
Amaziah.
22 He built [a]Elath, and restored it to
Judah, after that the king slept with his
fathers.

23 [a]Ex. 2:24,25 [b]Ex. 32:13 ʹHeb. *face*
25 [a]ver. 18,19 ʹHeb. *returned and took*
14:1 [a]ch. 13:10 [b]2 Chr. 25:1
4 [a]ch. 12:3
5 [a]ch. 12:20
6 [a]Deut. 24:16; Ezek. 18:4,20
7 [a]2 Chr. 25:11 [b]2 Sam. 8:13; Ps. 60,title [c]Josh. 15:38 ʹOr, *The rock*
8 [a]2 Chr. 25:17,18
9 [a]See Judg. 9:8 [b]1 Ki. 4:33
10 [a]Deut. 8:14; 2 Chr. 32:25; Ezek. 28:2,5,17; Hab. 2:4 ʹHeb. *at thy house*
11 [a]Josh. 19:38 & 21:16
12 ʹHeb. *was smitten*
13 [a]Neh. 8:16 & 12:39 [b]Jer. 31:38; Zech. 14:10
14 [a]1 Ki. 7:51
15 [a]ch. 13:12
17 [a]2 Chr. 25:25
19 [a]2 Chr. 25:27 [b]Josh. 10:31
21 [a]ch. 15:13 & 2 Chr. 26:1, he is called *Uzziah*
22 [a]ch. 16:6; 2 Chr. 26:2

Jeroboam II, king of Israel

23 ¶ In the fifteenth year of Amaziah the son of Joash king of Judah Jeroboam the son of Joash king of Israel began to reign in Samaria, *and reigned* forty and one years.

24 And he did *that which was* evil in the sight of the LORD: he departed not from all the sins of Jeroboam the son of Nebat, who made Israel to sin.

25 He restored the coast of Israel [a]from the entering of Hamath unto [b]the sea of the plain, according to the word of the LORD God of Israel, which he spake by the hand of his servant [c]Jonah, the son of Amittai, the prophet, which *was* of [d]Gath-hepher.

26 For the LORD [a]saw the affliction of Israel, *that it was* very bitter: for [b]*there was* not any shut up, nor any left, nor any helper for Israel.

I 27 [a]And the LORD said not that he would blot out the name of Israel from under heaven: but he saved them by the hand of Jeroboam the son of Joash.

28 ¶ Now the rest of the acts of Jeroboam, and all that he did, and his might, how he warred, and how he recovered Damascus, and Hamath, [a]*which belonged* to Judah, for Israel, *are* they not written in the book of the chronicles of the kings of Israel?

29 And Jeroboam slept with his fathers, *even* with the kings of Israel; and [a]Zachariah his son reigned in his stead.

Azariah, king of Judah

15 IN THE twenty and seventh year of Jeroboam king of Israel [a]began [b]Azariah son of Amaziah king of Judah to reign.

2 Sixteen years old was he when he began to reign, and he reigned two and fifty years in Jerusalem. And his mother's name *was* Jecholiah of Jerusalem.

3 And he did *that which was* right in the sight of the LORD, according to all that his father Amaziah had done;

4 [a]Save that the high places were not removed: the people sacrificed and burnt incense still on the high places.

5 ¶ And the LORD [a]smote the king, so that he was a leper unto the day of his death, and [b]dwelt in a several house. And Jotham the king's son *was* over the house, judging the people of the land. D

6 And the rest of the acts of Azariah, and all that he did, *are* they not written in the book of the chronicles of the kings of Judah?

7 So Azariah slept with his fathers; and [a]they buried him with his fathers in the city of David: and Jotham his son reigned in his stead.

Zechariah, king of Israel

8 ¶ In the thirty and eighth year of Azariah king of Judah did Zachariah the son of Jeroboam reign over Israel in Samaria six months.

9 And he did *that which was* evil in the sight of the LORD, as his fathers had done: he departed not from the sins of Jeroboam the son of Nebat, who made Israel to sin.

10 And Shallum the son of Jabesh conspired against him, and [a]smote him before the people, and slew him, and reigned in his stead.

11 And the rest of the acts of Zachariah, behold, they *are* written in the book of the chronicles of the kings of Israel.

12 This *was* [a]the word of the LORD which he spake unto Jehu, saying, Thy sons shall sit on the throne of Israel unto the fourth *generation.* And so it came to pass.

Shallum, king of Israel

13 ¶ Shallum the son of Jabesh began to reign in the nine and thirtieth year of [a]Uzziah king of Judah; and he reigned [l]a full month in Samaria.

14 For Menahem the son of Gadi went up from [a]Tirzah, and came to Samaria, and smote Shallum the son of Jabesh in Samaria, and slew him, and reigned in his stead.

15 And the rest of the acts of Shallum, and his conspiracy which he made, behold, they *are* written in the book of the chronicles of the kings of Israel.

16 ¶ Then Menahem smote [a]Tiphsah,

25 [a]Num. 13:21 & 34:8 [b]Deut. 3:17 [c]Jonah 1:1; Mat. 12:39,40, called *Jonas* [d]Josh. 19:13
26 [a]ch. 13:4 [b]Deut. 32:36
27 [a]ch. 13:5
28 [a]2 Sam. 8:6; 1 Ki. 11:24; 2 Chr. 8:3
29 [a]After an interregnum of 11 years; ch. 15:8
15:1 [a]ch. 14:21; 2 Chr. 26:1,3,4 [b]Called *Uzziah* ver. 13,30; 2 Chr. 26:1
4 [a]ver. 35; ch. 12:3 & 14:4
5 [a]2 Chr. 26:19-21 [b]Lev. 13:46
7 [a]2 Chr. 26:23
10 [a]As prophesied, Amos 7:9
12 [a]ch. 10:30
13 [a]Mat. 1:8,9 called *Ozias* and ver. 1 *Azariah* [l]Heb. *a month of days*
14 [a]1 Ki. 14:17
16 [a]1 Ki. 4:24

I *2Ki 13:15–19* ◀▶ *2Ki 19:30–31*

D *2Ki 6:18* ◀▶ *1Ch 21:14–15*

14:27 Though God would judge Israel for its idolatry and rebellion, he would never "blot out the name of Israel from under heaven."

and all that *were* therein, and the coasts thereof from Tirzah: because they opened not *to him,* therefore he smote *it; and* all [b]the women therein that were with child he ripped up.

Menahem, king of Israel

17 In the nine and thirtieth year of Azariah king of Judah began Menahem the son of Gadi to reign over Israel, *and reigned* ten years in Samaria.

18 And he did *that which was* evil in the sight of the LORD: he departed not all his days from the sins of Jeroboam the son of Nebat, who made Israel to sin.

19 *And* [a]Pul the king of Assyria came against the land: and Menahem gave Pul a thousand talents of silver, that his hand might be with him to [b]confirm the kingdom in his hand.

20 And Menahem [l]exacted the money of Israel, *even* of all the mighty men of wealth, of each man fifty shekels of silver, to give to the king of Assyria. So the king of Assyria turned back, and stayed not there in the land.

21 ¶ And the rest of the acts of Menahem, and all that he did, *are* they not written in the book of the chronicles of the kings of Israel?

22 And Menahem slept with his fathers; and Pekahiah his son reigned in his stead.

Pekahiah, king of Israel

23 ¶ In the fiftieth year of Azariah king of Judah Pekahiah the son of Menahem began to reign over Israel in Samaria, *and reigned* two years.

24 And he did *that which was* evil in the sight of the LORD: he departed not from the sins of Jeroboam the son of Nebat, who made Israel to sin.

25 But Pekah the son of Remaliah, a captain of his, conspired against him, and smote him in Samaria, in the palace of the king's house, with Argob and Arieh, and with him fifty men of the Gileadites: and he killed him, and reigned in his room.

26 And the rest of the acts of Pekahiah, and all that he did, behold, they *are* written in the book of the chronicles of the kings of Israel.

Pekah, king of Israel

27 ¶ In the two and fiftieth year of Azariah king of Judah [a]Pekah the son of Remaliah began to reign over Israel in Samaria, *and reigned* twenty years.

28 And he did *that which was* evil in the sight of the LORD: he departed not from the sins of Jeroboam the son of Nebat, who made Israel to sin.

29 In the days of Pekah king of Israel [a]came Tiglath-pileser king of Assyria, and took [b]Ijon, and Abel-beth-maachah, and Janoah, and Kedesh, and Hazor, and Gilead, and Galilee, all the land of Naphtali, and carried them captive to Assyria.

30 And Hoshea the son of Elah made a conspiracy against Pekah the son of Remaliah, and smote him, and slew him, and [a]reigned in his stead, [b]in the twentieth year of Jotham the son of Uzziah.

31 And the rest of the acts of Pekah, and all that he did, behold, they *are* written in the book of the chronicles of the kings of Israel.

Jotham, king of Judah

32 ¶ In the second year of Pekah the son of Remaliah king of Israel began [a]Jotham the son of Uzziah king of Judah to reign.

33 Five and twenty years old was he when he began to reign, and he reigned sixteen years in Jerusalem. And his mother's name *was* Jerusha, the daughter of Zadok.

34 And he did *that which was* right in the sight of the LORD: he did [a]according to all that his father Uzziah had done.

35 ¶ [a]Howbeit the high places were not removed: the people sacrificed and burned incense still in the high places. [b]He built the higher gate of the house of the LORD.

36 ¶ Now the rest of the acts of Jotham, and all that he did, *are* they not written in the book of the chronicles of the kings of Judah?

37 In those days the LORD began to send against Judah [a]Rezin the king of Syria, and [b]Pekah the son of Remaliah.

38 And Jotham slept with his fathers, and was buried with his fathers in the city of David his father: and Ahaz his son reigned in his stead.

16 [b]ch. 8:12
19 [a]1 Chr. 5:26; Is. 66:19; Hos. 8:9 [b]ch. 14:5
20 [l]Heb. *caused to come forth*
27 [a]Is. 7:1
29 [a]1 Chr. 5:26; Is. 9:1 [b]1 Ki. 15:20
30 [a]After an anarchy for some years ch. 17:1; Hos. 10:3,7,15 [b]in the fourth year of Ahaz,in the twentieth year after Jotham had begun to reign: *Ush*
32 [a]2 Chr. 27:1
34 [a]ver. 3
35 [a]ver. 4 [b]2 Chr. 27:3
37 [a]ch. 16:5; Is. 7:1 [b]ver. 27

Ahaz, king of Judah

16 IN THE seventeenth year of Pekah the son of Remaliah [a]Ahaz the son of Jotham king of Judah began to reign.

2 Twenty years old *was* Ahaz when he began to reign, and reigned sixteen years in Jerusalem, and did not *that which was* right in the sight of the LORD his God, like David his father.

3 But he walked in the way of the kings of Israel, yea, [a]and made his son to pass through the fire, according to the [b]abominations of the heathen, whom the LORD cast out from before the children of Israel.

4 And he sacrificed and burnt incense in the high places, and [a]on the hills, and under every green tree.

5 ¶ [a]Then Rezin king of Syria and Pekah son of Remaliah king of Israel came up to Jerusalem to war: and they besieged Ahaz, but could not overcome *him.*

6 At that time Rezin king of Syria [a]recovered Elath to Syria, and drave the Jews from [/]Elath: and the Syrians came to Elath, and dwelt there unto this day.

7 So Ahaz sent messengers [a]to [/]Tiglath-pileser king of Assyria, saying, I *am* thy servant and thy son: come up, and save me out of the hand of the king of Syria, and out of the hand of the king of Israel, which rise up against me.

8 And Ahaz [a]took the silver and gold that was found in the house of the LORD, and in the treasures of the king's house, and sent *it for* a present to the king of Assyria.

9 And the king of Assyria hearkened unto him: for the king of Assyria went up against [/]Damascus, and [a]took it, and carried *the people of* it captive to Kir, and slew Rezin.

10 ¶ And king Ahaz went to Damascus to meet Tiglath-pileser king of Assyria, and saw an altar that *was* at Damascus: and king Ahaz sent to Urijah the priest the fashion of the altar, and the pattern of it, according to all the workmanship thereof.

11 And Urijah the priest built an altar according to all that king Ahaz had sent from Damascus: so Urijah the priest made *it* against king Ahaz came from Damascus.

12 And when the king was come from Damascus, the king saw the altar: and [a]the king approached to the altar, and offered thereon.

13 And he burnt his burnt offering and his meat offering, and poured his drink offering, and sprinkled the blood of [/]his peace offerings, upon the altar.

14 And he brought also [a]the brasen altar, which *was* before the LORD, from the forefront of the house, from between the altar and the house of the LORD, and put it on the north side of the altar.

15 And king Ahaz commanded Urijah the priest, saying, Upon the great altar burn [a]the morning burnt offering, and the evening meat offering, and the king's burnt sacrifice, and his meat offering, with the burnt offering of all the people of the land, and their meat offering, and their drink offerings; and sprinkle upon it all the blood of the burnt offering, and all the blood of the sacrifice: and the brasen altar shall be for me to inquire *by.*

16 Thus did Urijah the priest, according to all that king Ahaz commanded.

17 ¶ [a]And king Ahaz cut off [b]the borders of the bases, and removed the laver from off them; and took down [c]the sea from off the brasen oxen that *were* under it, and put it upon a pavement of stones.

18 And the covert for the sabbath that they had built in the house, and the king's entry without, turned he from the house of the LORD for the king of Assyria.

19 ¶ Now the rest of the acts of Ahaz which he did, *are* they not written in the book of the chronicles of the kings of Judah?

20 And Ahaz slept with his fathers, and [a]was buried with his fathers in the city of David: and Hezekiah his son reigned in his stead.

Samaria captured by Assyria

17 IN THE twelfth year of Ahaz king of Judah began [a]Hoshea the son of Elah to reign in Samaria over Israel nine years.

2 And he did *that which was* evil in the sight of the LORD, but not as the kings of Israel that were before him.

3 ¶ Against him came up [a]Shalmaneser king of Assyria; and Hoshea became his servant, and gave him [/]presents.

4 And the king of Assyria found conspiracy in Hoshea: for he had sent messengers to So king of Egypt, and brought

---

16:1 [a]2 Chr. 28:1
3 [a]Lev. 18:21; 2 Chr. 28:3; Ps. 106:37,38 [b]Deut. 12:31
4 [a]Deut. 12:2; 1 Ki. 14:23
5 [a]Is. 7:1,4
6 [a]ch. 14:22 [/]Heb. *Eloth*
7 [a]ch. 15:29 [/]Heb. *Tilgath-pileser;* 1 Chr. 5:26 & 2 Chr. 28:20 have *Tilgath-pilneser*
8 [a]ch. 12:18; See 2 Chr. 28:21
9 [a]Foretold Amos 1:5 [/]Heb. *Dammesek*
12 [a]2 Chr. 26:16, 19
13 [/]Heb. *which were his*
14 [a]2 Chr. 4:1
15 [a]Ex. 29:39-41
17 [a]2 Chr. 28:24 [b]1 Ki. 7:27,28 [c]1 Ki. 7:23,25
20 [a]2 Chr. 28:27
17:1 [a]After an interregnum; ch. 15:30
3 [a]ch. 18:9 [/]Or, *tribute*

no present to the king of Assyria, as *he*
had done year by year: therefore the king
of Assyria shut him up, and bound him in
prison.
5 ¶ Then [a]the king of Assyria came up
throughout all the land, and went up to
Samaria, and besieged it three years.
R 6 ¶ [a]In the ninth year of Hoshea the
king of Assyria took Samaria, and [b]carried
Israel away into Assyria, [c]and placed
them in Halah and in Habor *by* the river
of Gozan, and in the cities of the Medes.

The sins of Israel and Judah

7 For *so* it was, that the children of
Israel had sinned against the LORD their
God, which had brought them up out of
the land of Egypt, from under the hand of
Pharaoh king of Egypt, and had feared
other gods,
8 And [a]walked in the statutes of the
heathen, whom the LORD cast out from
before the children of Israel, and of the
kings of Israel, which they had made.
9 And the children of Israel did secretly *those* things that *were* not right
against the LORD their God, and they built
them high places in all their cities, [a]from
the tower of the watchmen to the fenced
city.
10 [a]And they set them up [l]images and
[b]groves [c]in every high hill, and under every green tree:
11 And there they burnt incense in all
the high places, as *did* the heathen whom
the LORD carried away before them; and
wrought wicked things to provoke the
LORD to anger:
12 For they served idols, [a]whereof the
LORD had said unto them, [b]Ye shall not do
this thing.
N 13 Yet the LORD testified against Israel,
R and against Judah, [l]by all the prophets,
and by all [a]the seers, saying, [b]Turn ye
from your evil ways, and keep my commandments *and* my statutes, according to
all the law which I commanded your fathers, and which I sent to you by my servants the prophets.
14 Notwithstanding they would not C
hear, but [a]hardened their necks, like to
the neck of their fathers, that did not believe in the LORD their God.
15 And they rejected his statutes, [a]and
his covenant that he made with their fathers, and his testimonies which he testified against them; and they followed
[b]vanity, and [c]became vain, and went after the heathen that *were* round about
them, *concerning* whom the LORD had
charged them, that they should [d]not do
like them.
16 And they left all the commandments of the LORD their God, and [a]made
them molten images, *even* two calves,
[b]and made a grove, and worshipped all
the host of heaven, [c]and served Baal.
17 [a]And they caused their sons and
their daughters to pass through the fire,
and [b]used divination and enchantments,
and [c]sold themselves to do evil in the
sight of the LORD, to provoke him to
anger.
18 Therefore the LORD was very angry R
with Israel, and removed them out of his
sight: there was none left [a]but the tribe
of Judah only.
19 Also [a]Judah kept not the commandments of the LORD their God, but walked
in the statutes of Israel which they made.
20 And the LORD rejected all the seed R
of Israel, and afflicted them, and [a]deliv-
ered them into the hand of spoilers, until
he had cast them out of his sight.
21 For [a]he rent Israel from the house
of David; and [b]they made Jeroboam the
son of Nebat king: and Jeroboam drave
Israel from following the LORD, and made
them sin a great sin.
22 For the children of Israel walked in
all the sins of Jeroboam which he did;
they departed not from them;

5 [a]ch. 18:9
6 [a]ch. 18:10,11; Hos. 13:16 Foretold [b]Lev. 26:32,33; Deut. 28:36,64 & 29:27, 28 [c]1 Chr. 5:26
8 [a]Lev. 18:3; Deut. 18:9; ch. 16:3
9 [a]ch. 18:8
10 [a]1 Ki. 14:23; Is. 57:5 [b]Ex. 34:13; Deut. 16:21; Mic. 5:14 [c]Deut. 12:2; ch. 16:4 [l]Heb. *statues*
12 [a]Ex. 20:3,4; Lev. 26:1; Deut. 5:7,8 [b]Deut. 4:19
13 [a]1 Sam. 9:9 [b]Jer. 18:11 & 25:5 & 35:15 [l]Heb. *by the hand of all*
14 [a]Deut. 31:27; Prov. 29:1
15 [a]Deut. 29:25 [b]Deut. 32:21; 1 Ki. 16:13; 1 Cor. 8:4 [c]Ps. 115:8; Rom. 1:21 [d]Deut. 12:30, 31
16 [a]Ex. 32:8; 1 Ki. 12:28 [b]1 Ki. 14:15 [c]1 Ki. 16:31 & 22:53; ch. 11:18
17 [a]Lev. 18:21; ch. 16:3; Ezek. 23:37 [b]Deut. 18:10 [c]1 Ki. 21:20
18 [a]1 Ki. 11:13,32
19 [a]Jer. 3:8
20 [a]ch. 13:3 & 15:29
21 [a]1 Ki. 11:11,31 [b]1 Ki. 12:20,28

R *2Ki 13:23* ◀▶ *2Ki 17:18*
N *1Ki 18:21* ◀▶ *1Ch 29:15*
R *2Sa 24:10* ◀▶ *1Ch 21:8*

C *1Ki 21:20* ◀▶ *2Ki 19:22*
R *2Ki 17:6* ◀▶ *2Ki 17:20*
R *2Ki 17:18* ◀▶ *2Ki 17:23*

17:6 The rebellion of Israel had to be punished, so God let the Assyrians conquer Israel and carry into exile the ten tribes of Israel. This was the first example in history of an enemy transporting an entire conquered population to another location in order to prevent rebellion and assure future loyalty.

17:18–20 God had allowed Israel's defeat and exile due to their idol worship. Only the southern kingdom of Judah (the tribes of Judah and Benjamin) escaped the Assyrian conquest.

R 23 Until the LORD removed Israel out of his sight, [a]as he had said by all his servants the prophets. [b]So was Israel carried away out of their own land to Assyria unto this day.

Israel resettled with Assyrians

24 ¶ [a]And the king of Assyria brought *men* from Babylon, and from Cuthah, and from [b]Ava, and from Hamath, and from Sepharvaim, and placed *them* in the cities of Samaria instead of the children of Israel: and they possessed Samaria, and dwelt in the cities thereof.

25 And *so* it was at the beginning of their dwelling there, *that* they feared not the LORD: therefore the LORD sent lions among them, which slew *some* of them.

26 Wherefore they spake to the king of Assyria, saying, The nations which thou hast removed, and placed in the cities of Samaria, know not the manner of the God of the land: therefore he hath sent lions among them, and, behold, they slay them, because they know not the manner of the God of the land.

27 Then the king of Assyria commanded, saying, Carry thither one of the priests whom ye brought from thence; and let them go and dwell there, and let him teach them the manner of the God of the land.

28 Then one of the priests whom they had carried away from Samaria came and dwelt in Beth-el, and taught them how they should fear the LORD.

29 Howbeit every nation made gods of their own, and put *them* in the houses of the high places which the Samaritans had made, every nation in their cities wherein they dwelt.

30 And the men of [a]Babylon made Succoth-benoth, and the men of Cuth made Nergal, and the men of Hamath made Ashima,

31 [a]And the Avites made Nibhaz and Tartak, and the Sepharvites [b]burnt their children in fire to Adrammelech and Anammelech, the gods of Sepharvaim.

32 So they feared the LORD, [a]and made unto themselves of the lowest of them priests of the high places, which sacrificed for them in the houses of the high places.

33 [a]They feared the LORD, and served their own gods, after the manner of the nations [/]whom they carried away from thence.

34 Unto this day they do after the former manners: they fear not the LORD, neither do they after their statutes, or after their ordinances, or after the law and commandment which the LORD commanded the children of Jacob, [a]whom he named Israel;

35 With whom the LORD had made a covenant, and charged them, saying, [a]Ye shall not fear other gods, nor [b]bow yourselves to them, nor serve them, nor sacrifice to them:

36 But the LORD, who brought you up out of the land of Egypt with great power and [a]a stretched out arm, [b]him shall ye fear, and him shall ye worship, and to him shall ye do sacrifice.

37 And the statutes, and the ordinances, and the law, and the commandment, which he wrote for you, [a]ye shall observe to do for evermore; and ye shall not fear other gods.

38 And the covenant that I have made with you [a]ye shall not forget; neither shall ye fear other gods.

39 But the LORD your God ye shall fear; and he shall deliver you out of the hand of all your enemies.

40 Howbeit they did not hearken, but they did after their former manner.

41 [a]So these nations feared the LORD, and served their graven images, both their children, and their children's children: as did their fathers, so do they unto this day.

Hezekiah, king of Judah

18 NOW IT came to pass in the third year of Hoshea son of Elah king of Israel, *that* [a]Hezekiah the son of Ahaz king of Judah began to reign.

2 Twenty and five years old was he when he began to reign; and he reigned twenty and nine years in Jerusalem. His mother's name also *was* [a]Abi, the daughter of Zachariah.

23 [a]1 Ki. 14:16 [b]ver. 6
24 [a]Ezra 4:2,10 [b]ch. 18:34 *Ivah*
30 [a]ver. 24
31 [a]Ezra 4:9 [b]Lev. 18:21; Deut. 12:31
32 [a]1 Ki. 12:31
33 [a]Zeph. 1:5 [/]Or, *who carried them away from thence*
34 [a]Gen. 32:28 & 35:10; 1 Ki. 18:31
35 [a]Judg. 6:10 [b]Ex. 20:5
36 [a]Ex. 6:6 [b]Deut. 10:20
37 [a]Deut. 5:32
38 [a]Deut. 4:23
41 [a]ver. 32,33
18:1 [a]2 Chr. 28:27 & 29:1; He is called *Ezekias* Mat. 1:9
2 [a]2 Chr. 29:1 *Abijah*

R *2Ki 17:20* ◀ ▶ *2Ki 18:9–12*

17:23 Scripture repeatedly affirms that God will ultimately restore all twelve tribes to the promised land in the last days (see Eze 37:15–28).

3 And he did *that which was* right in the sight of the LORD, according to all that David his father did.

4 ¶ [a]He removed the high places, and brake the [1]images, and cut down the groves, and brake in pieces the [b]brasen serpent that Moses had made: for unto those days the children of Israel did burn incense to it: and he called it [2]Nehushtan.

5 He [a]trusted in the LORD God of Israel; [b]so that after him was none like him among all the kings of Judah, nor *any* that were before him.

6 For he [a]clave to the LORD, *and* departed not [1]from following him, but kept his commandments, which the LORD commanded Moses.

7 And the LORD [a]was with him; *and* he [b]prospered whithersoever he went forth: and he [c]rebelled against the king of Assyria, and served him not.

8 [a]He smote the Philistines, *even* unto [1]Gaza, and the borders thereof, [b]from the tower of the watchmen to the fenced city.

R 9 ¶ And [a]it came to pass in the fourth year of king Hezekiah, which *was* the seventh year of Hoshea son of Elah king of Israel, *that* Shalmaneser king of Assyria came up against Samaria, and besieged it.

10 And at the end of three years they took it: *even* in the sixth year of Hezekiah, that *is* [a]the ninth year of Hoshea king of Israel, Samaria was taken.

11 [a]And the king of Assyria did carry away Israel unto Assyria, and put them [b]in Halah and in Habor *by* the river of Gozan, and in the cities of the Medes:

12 Because they obeyed not the voice of the LORD their God, but transgressed his covenant, *and* all that Moses the servant of the LORD commanded, and would not hear *them,* nor do *them.*

13 ¶ Now [a]in the fourteenth year of king Hezekiah did [1]Sennacherib king of Assyria come up against all the fenced cities of Judah, and took them.

14 And Hezekiah king of Judah sent to the king of Assyria to Lachish, saying, I have offended; return from me: that which thou puttest on me will I bear. And the king of Assyria appointed unto Hezekiah king of Judah three hundred talents of silver and thirty talents of gold.

15 And Hezekiah [a]gave *him* all the silver that was found in the house of the LORD, and in the treasures of the king's house.

16 At that time did Hezekiah cut off *the gold from* the doors of the temple of the LORD, and *from* the pillars which Hezekiah king of Judah had overlaid, and gave [1]it to the king of Assyria.

The Assyrian threats

17 ¶ And the king of Assyria sent Tartan and Rabsaris and Rab-shakeh from Lachish to king Hezekiah with a [1]great host against Jerusalem. And they went up and came to Jerusalem. And when they were come up, they came and stood by the conduit of the upper pool, [a]which *is* in the highway of the fuller's field.

18 And when they had called to the king, there came out to them Eliakim the son of Hilkiah, which *was* over the household, and Shebna the [1]scribe, and Joah the son of Asaph the recorder.

19 And Rab-shakeh said unto them, Speak ye now to Hezekiah, Thus saith the great king, the king of Assyria, [a]What confidence *is* this wherein thou trustest?

20 Thou [1]sayest, (but *they are but* [2]vain words,) [3]*I have* counsel and strength for the war. Now on whom dost thou trust, that thou rebellest against me?

21 [a]Now, behold, thou [1]trustest upon the staff of this bruised reed, *even* upon Egypt, on which if a man lean, it will go into his hand, and pierce it: so *is* Pharaoh king of Egypt unto all that trust on him.

22 But if ye say unto me, We trust in the LORD our God: *is* not that he, [a]whose high places and whose altars Hezekiah hath taken away, and hath said to Judah and Jerusalem, Ye shall worship before this altar in Jerusalem?

23 Now therefore, I pray thee, give [1]pledges to my lord the king of Assyria, and I will deliver thee two thousand

4 [a]2 Chr. 31:1 [b]Num. 21:9 [1]Heb. *statues* [2]i.e. *A piece of brass*
5 [a]ch. 19:10; Job 13:15; Ps. 13:5 [b]ch. 23:25
6 [a]Deut. 10:20; Josh. 23:8 [1]Heb. *from after him*
7 [a]2 Chr. 15:2 [b]1 Sam. 18:5,14; Ps. 60:12 [c]ch. 16:7
8 [a]1 Chr. 4:41; Is. 14:29 [b]ch. 17:9 [1]Heb. *Azzah*
9 [a]ch. 17:3
10 [a]ch. 17:6
11 [a]ch. 17:6 [b]1 Chr. 5:26
13 [a]2 Chr. 32:1; Is. 36:1 [1]Heb. *Sanherib*
15 [a]ch. 16:8
16 [1]Heb. *them*
17 [a]Is. 7:3 [1]Heb. *heavy*
18 [1]Or, *secretary*
19 [a]2 Chr. 32:10
20 [1]Or, *talkest* [2]Heb. *word of the lips* [3]Or, *But counsel and strength* are *for the war*
21 [a]Ezek. 29:6,7 [1]Heb. *trustest thee*
22 [a]ver. 4; 2 Chr. 31:1 & 32:12
23 [1]Or, *hostages*

R *2Ki 17:23* ◀▶ *2Ki 21:7–9*

18:9–12 This passage confirms the fulfillment of prophecies that warned of Israel's exile from the promised land if the Israelites persisted in their idolatry and "transgressed his covenant" (18:9; see Dt 28:62–65).

horses, if thou be able on thy part to set
riders upon them.
24 How then wilt thou turn away the
face of one captain of the least of my master's servants, and put thy trust on Egypt
for chariots and for horsemen?
25 Am I now come up without the
LORD against this place to destroy it? The
LORD said to me, Go up against this land,
and destroy it.
26 Then said Eliakim the son of Hilkiah, and Shebna, and Joah, unto Rab-
shakeh, Speak, I pray thee, to thy servants in the Syrian language; for we
understand *it:* and talk not with us in the
Jews' language in the ears of the people
that *are* on the wall.
27 But Rab-shakeh said unto them,
Hath my master sent me to thy master,
and to thee, to speak these words? *hath
he* not *sent me* to the men which sit on
the wall, that they may eat their own
dung, and drink [1]their own piss with
you?
28 Then Rab-shakeh stood and cried
with a loud voice in the Jews' language,
and spake, saying, Hear the word of the
great king, the king of Assyria:
29 Thus saith the king, [a]Let not Hezekiah deceive you: for he shall not be able
to deliver you out of his hand:
J 30 Neither let Hezekiah make you
trust in the LORD, saying, The LORD will
surely deliver us, and this city shall not
be delivered into the hand of the king of
Assyria.
31 Hearken not to Hezekiah: for thus
saith the king of Assyria, [1,2]Make *an
agreement* with me by a present, and
come out to me, and *then* eat ye every
man of his own vine, and every one of his
fig tree, and drink ye every one the waters of his [3]cistern:
32 Until I come and take you away to a
land like your own land, [a]a land of corn
and wine, a land of bread and vineyards,
a land of oil olive and of honey, that ye
may live, and not die: and hearken not
unto Hezekiah, when he [1]persuadeth
you, saying, The LORD will deliver us.
33 [a]Hath any of the gods of the nations
delivered at all his land out of the hand of
the king of Assyria?
34 [a]Where *are* the gods of Hamath,
and of Arpad? where *are* the gods of

J 2Ki 9:26 ◄► 2Ki 19:7

27 [1]Heb. *the water of their feet*
29 [a]2 Chr. 32:15
31 [1]Or, *Seek my favour* [2]Heb. *Make with me a blessing* [3]Or, *pit*
32 [a]Deut. 8:7,8 [1]Or, *deceiveth*
33 [a]ch. 19:12; 2 Chr. 32:14; Is. 10:10,11
34 [a]ch. 19:13 [b]ch. 17:24 *Ava*
35 [a]Dan. 3:15
37 [a]Is. 33:7
19:1 [a]Is. 37:1
2 [a]Luke 3:4 called *Esaias*
3 [1]Or, *provocation*
4 [a]2 Sam. 16:12 [b]ch. 18:35 [c]Ps. 50:21 [1]Heb. *found*
6 [a]Is. 37:6 [b]ch. 18:17
7 [a]ver. 35-37; Jer. 51:1

Sepharvaim, Hena, and [b]Ivah? have they
delivered Samaria out of mine hand?
35 Who *are* they among all the gods of
the countries, that have delivered their
country out of mine hand, [a]that the LORD
should deliver Jerusalem out of mine
hand?
36 But the people held their peace,
and answered him not a word: for the
king's commandment was, saying, Answer him not.
37 Then came Eliakim the son of Hilkiah, which *was* over the household, and
Shebna the scribe, and Joah the son of
Asaph the recorder, to Hezekiah [a]with
their clothes rent, and told him the words
of Rab-shakeh.

Hezekiah sends to Isaiah

19 AND [a]IT came to pass, when
king Hezekiah heard *it,* that he
rent his clothes, and covered himself
with sackcloth, and went into the house
of the LORD.
2 And he sent Eliakim, which *was* over
the household, and Shebna the scribe,
and the elders of the priests, covered
with sackcloth, to [a]Isaiah the prophet the
son of Amoz.
3 And they said unto him, Thus saith
Hezekiah, This day *is* a day of trouble,
and of rebuke, and [1]blasphemy: for the
children are come to the birth, and *there
is* not strength to bring forth.
4 [a]It may be the LORD thy God will hear
all the words of Rab-shakeh, [b]whom the
king of Assyria his master hath sent to
reproach the living God; and will [c]re-
prove the words which the LORD thy God
hath heard: wherefore lift up *thy* prayer
for the remnant that are [1]left.
5 So the servants of king Hezekiah
came to Isaiah.
6 ¶ [a]And Isaiah said unto them, Thus
shall ye say to your master, Thus saith the
LORD, Be not afraid of the words which
thou hast heard, with which the [b]ser-
vants of the king of Assyria have blasphemed me.
7 Behold, I will send [a]a blast upon J
him, and he shall hear a rumour, and
shall return to his own land; and I will
cause him to fall by the sword in his own
land.
8 ¶ So Rab-shakeh returned, and found

J 2Ki 18:30 ◄► 2Ki 20:17–19

the king of Assyria warring against Libnah: for he had heard that he was departed [a]from Lachish.

9 And [a]when he heard say of Tirhakah king of Ethiopia, Behold, he is come out to fight against thee: he sent messengers again unto Hezekiah, saying,

10 Thus shall ye speak to Hezekiah king of Judah, saying, Let not thy God [a]in whom thou trustest deceive thee, saying, Jerusalem shall not be delivered into the hand of the king of Assyria.

11 Behold, thou hast heard what the kings of Assyria have done to all lands, by destroying them utterly: and shalt thou be delivered?

12 [a]Have the gods of the nations delivered them which my fathers have destroyed; *as* Gozan, and Haran, and Rezeph, and the children of [b]Eden which *were* in Thelasar?

13 [a]Where *is* the king of Hamath, and the king of Arpad, and the king of the city of Sepharvaim, of Hena, and Ivah?

Hezekiah's prayer

14 ¶ [a]And Hezekiah received the letter of the hand of the messengers, and read it: and Hezekiah went up into the house of the LORD, and spread it before the LORD.

15 And Hezekiah prayed before the LORD, and said, O LORD God of Israel, [a]which dwellest *between* the cherubims, [b]thou art the God, *even* thou alone, of all the kingdoms of the earth; thou hast made heaven and earth.

16 LORD, [a]bow down thine ear, and hear: [b]open, LORD, thine eyes, and see: and hear the words of Sennacherib, [c]which hath sent him to reproach the living God.

17 Of a truth, LORD, the kings of Assyria have destroyed the nations and their lands,

18 And have [1]cast their gods into the fire: for they *were* no gods, but [a]the work of men's hands, wood and stone: therefore they have destroyed them.

19 Now therefore, O LORD our God, I beseech thee, save thou us out of his hand, [a]that all the kingdoms of the earth may know that thou *art* the LORD God, *even* thou only.

The divine deliverance

20 ¶ Then Isaiah the son of Amoz sent to Hezekiah, saying, Thus saith the LORD God of Israel, [a]*That* which thou hast prayed to me against Sennacherib king of Assyria [b]I have heard.

21 This *is* the word that the LORD hath spoken concerning him; The virgin [a]the daughter of Zion hath despised thee, *and* laughed thee to scorn; the daughter of Jerusalem [b]hath shaken her head at thee.

22 Whom hast thou reproached and blasphemed? and against whom hast thou exalted *thy* voice, and lifted up thine eyes on high? *even* against [a]the Holy *One* of Israel. C

23 [a]By[1] thy messengers thou hast reproached the Lord, and hast said, [b]With the multitude of my chariots I am come up to the height of the mountains, to the sides of Lebanon, and will cut down [2]the tall cedar trees thereof, *and* the choice fir trees thereof: and I will enter into the lodgings of his borders, *and into* [3]the forest of his Carmel.

24 I have digged and drunk strange waters, and with the sole of my feet have I dried up all the rivers of [1]besieged places.

25 [1]Hast thou not heard long ago *how* [a]I have done it, *and* of ancient times that I have formed it? now have I brought it to pass, that [b]thou shouldest be to lay waste fenced cities *into* ruinous heaps.

26 Therefore their inhabitants were [1]of small power, they were dismayed and confounded; they were *as* the grass of the field, and *as* the green herb, *as* [a]the grass on the housetops, and *as corn* blasted before it be grown up.

27 But [a]I know thy [1]abode, and thy going out, and thy coming in, and thy rage against me. E

28 Because thy rage against me and thy tumult is come up into mine ears, therefore [a]I will put my hook in thy nose, and my bridle in thy lips, and I will turn thee back [b]by the way by which thou camest.

29 And this *shall be* a sign unto thee, Ye shall eat this year such things as grow of themselves, and in the second year that which springeth of the same; and in the third year sow ye, and reap, and plant vineyards, and eat the fruits thereof.

C *2Ki 17:14–15* ◀ ▶ *2Ki 21:22*
E *1Ki 8:39* ◀ ▶ *1Ch 28:9*

8 [a]ch. 18:14
9 [a]See 1 Sam. 23:27
10 [a]ch. 18:5
12 [a]ch. 18:33,34 [b]Ezek. 27:23
13 [a]ch. 18:34
14 [a]Is. 37:14
15 [a]Ps. 80:1 [b]Is. 44:6
16 [a]Ps. 31:2 [b]2 Chr. 6:40 [c]ver. 4
18 [a]Jer. 10:3 [1]Heb. *given*
19 [a]Ps. 83:18
20 [a]Is. 37:21 [b]Ps. 65:2
21 [a]Lam. 2:13 [b]Ps. 22:7,8
22 [a]Jer. 51:5
23 [a]ch. 18:17 [b]Ps. 20:7 [1]Heb. *By the hand of* [2]Heb. *the tallness* [3]Or, *the forest* and *his fruitful field;* see Is. 10:18
24 [1]Or, *fenced*
25 [a]Is. 45:7 [b]Is. 10:5 [1]Or, *Hast thou not heard* how *I have made it long ago, and formed it of ancient times? should I now bring it to be laid waste,* and *fenced cities* to be *ruinous heaps?*
26 [a]Ps. 129:6 [1]Heb. *short of hand*
27 [a]Ps. 139:1 [1]Or, *sitting*
28 [a]Ezek. 29:4 [b]ver. 33,36

I 30 [a]And [l]the remnant that is escaped of the house of Judah shall yet again take root downward, and bear fruit upward.

31 For out of Jerusalem shall go forth a remnant, and [l]they that escape out of mount Zion: [a]the zeal of the LORD *of hosts* shall do this.

32 Therefore thus saith the LORD concerning the king of Assyria, He shall not come into this city, nor shoot an arrow there, nor come before it with shield, nor cast a bank against it.

33 By the way that he came, by the same shall he return, and shall not come into this city, saith the LORD.

34 For [a]I will defend this city, to save it, for mine own sake, and [b]for my servant David's sake.

35 ¶ And [a]it came to pass that night, that the angel of the LORD went out, and smote in the camp of the Assyrians an hundred fourscore and five thousand: and when they arose early in the morning, behold, they *were* all dead corpses.

36 So Sennacherib king of Assyria departed, and went and returned, and dwelt at [a]Nineveh.

37 And it came to pass, as he was worshipping in the house of Nisroch his god, that [a]Adrammelech and Sharezer his sons [b]smote him with the sword: and they escaped into the land of [l]Armenia. And [c]Esar-haddon his son reigned in his stead.

The sickness of Hezekiah

E 20 IN [a]THOSE days was Hezekiah sick unto death. And the prophet Isaiah the son of Amoz came to him, and said unto him, Thus saith the LORD, [l]Set thine house in order; for thou shalt die, and not live.

2 Then he turned his face to the wall, and prayed unto the LORD, saying,

3 I beseech thee, O LORD, [a]remember now how I have walked before thee in truth and with a perfect heart, and have done *that which is* good in thy sight. And Hezekiah wept [l]sore.

4 And it came to pass, afore Isaiah was gone out into the middle [l]court, that the word of the LORD came to him, saying,

5 Turn again, and tell Hezekiah [a]the captain of my people, Thus saith the LORD, the God of David thy father, [b]I have heard thy prayer, I have seen [c]thy tears: behold, I will heal thee: on the third day thou shalt go up unto the house of the LORD. L

6 And I will add unto thy days fifteen years; and I will deliver thee and this city out of the hand of the king of Assyria; and [a]I will defend this city for mine own sake, and for my servant David's sake.

7 And [a]Isaiah said, Take a lump of figs. And they took and laid *it* on the boil, and he recovered.

8 ¶ And Hezekiah said unto Isaiah, [a]What *shall be* the sign that the LORD will heal me, and that I shall go up into the house of the LORD the third day?

9 And Isaiah said, [a]This sign shalt thou have of the LORD, that the LORD will do the thing that he hath spoken: shall the shadow go forward ten degrees, or go back ten degrees?

10 And Hezekiah answered, It is a light thing for the shadow to go down ten degrees: nay, but let the shadow return backward ten degrees.

11 And Isaiah the prophet cried unto the LORD: and [a]he brought the shadow ten degrees backward, by which it had gone down in the [l]dial of Ahaz.

Hezekiah's foolishness

12 ¶ [a]At that time [l]Berodach-baladan, the son of Baladan, king of Babylon, sent letters and a present unto Hezekiah: for he had heard that Hezekiah had been sick.

13 And [a]Hezekiah hearkened unto them, and showed them all the house of his [l]precious things, the silver, and the gold, and the spices, and the precious ointment, and *all* the house of his [2,3]armour, and all that was found in his treasures: there was nothing in his house, nor in all his dominion, that Hezekiah showed them not.

14 ¶ Then came Isaiah the prophet

30 [a]2 Chr. 32:22 [l]Heb. *the escaping of the house of Judah that remaineth*
31 [a]Is. 9:7 [l]Heb. *the escaping*
34 [a]ch. 20:6 [b]1 Ki. 11:12
35 [a]Is. 37:36
36 [a]Gen. 10:11
37 [a]2 Chr. 32:21 [b]ver. 7 [c]Ezra 4:2 [l]Heb. *Ararat*
20:1 [a]Is. 38:1 [l]Heb. *Give charge concerning thine house*
3 [a]Neh. 13:22 [l]Heb. *with a great weeping*
4 [l]Or, *city*
5 [a]1 Sam. 9:16 & 10:1 [b]ch. 19:20; Ps. 65:2 [c]Ps. 39:12 & 56:8
6 [a]ch. 19:34
7 [a]Is. 38:21
8 [a]See Judg. 6:17, 37,39; Is. 7:11,14 & 38:22
9 [a]See Is. 38:7,8
11 [a]See Is. 38:8 [l]Heb. *degrees*
12 [a]Is. 39:1 [l]Or, *Merodach-baladan*
13 [a]2 Chr. 32:27, 31 [l]Or, *spicery* [2]Or, *jewels* [3]Heb. *vessels*

I *2Ki 14:27* ◀ ▶ *1Ch 14:10*
E *2Ki 13:21* ◀ ▶ *2Ch 32:24*
L *2Ki 10:30* ◀ ▶ *2Ch 1:12*

19:30–31 The Lord promised that some from Judah would escape captivity because they had not yet fallen into idolatry and because of Judah's godly King Hezekiah (see 2Ch 32:22).

unto king Hezekiah, and said unto him, What said these men? and from whence came they unto thee? And Hezekiah said, They are come from a far country, *even* from Babylon.

15 And he said, What have they seen in thine house? And Hezekiah answered, [a]All *the things* that *are* in mine house have they seen: there is nothing among my treasures that I have not showed them.

16 And Isaiah said unto Hezekiah, Hear the word of the LORD.

J 17 Behold, the days come, that all that *is* in thine house, and that which thy fathers have laid up in store unto this day, [a]shall be carried into Babylon: nothing shall be left, saith the LORD.

18 And of thy sons that shall issue from thee, which thou shalt beget, [a]shall they take away; and they shall be eunuchs in the palace of the king of Babylon.

19 Then said Hezekiah unto Isaiah, [a]Good *is* the word of the LORD which thou hast spoken. And he said, [1]*Is it* not *good,* if peace and truth be in my days?

20 ¶ [a]And the rest of the acts of Hezekiah, and all his might, and how he [b]made a pool, and a conduit, and [c]brought water into the city, *are* they not written in the book of the chronicles of the kings of Judah?

21 And [a]Hezekiah slept with his fathers: and Manasseh his son reigned in his stead.

Manasseh, king of Judah

21 MANASSEH [a]*WAS* twelve years old when he began to reign, and reigned fifty and five years in Jerusalem. And his mother's name *was* Hephzibah.

2 And he did *that which was* evil in the sight of the LORD, [a]after the abominations of the heathen, whom the LORD cast out before the children of Israel.

3 For he built up again the high places [a]which Hezekiah his father had destroyed; and he reared up altars for Baal, and made a grove, [b]as did Ahab king of Israel; and [c]worshipped all the host of heaven, and served them.

4 And [a]he built altars in the house of the LORD, of which the LORD said, [b]In Jerusalem will I put my name.

5 And he built altars for all the host of heaven in the two courts of the house of the LORD.

6 [a]And he made his son pass through the fire, and observed [b]times, and used enchantments, and dealt with familiar spirits and wizards: he wrought much wickedness in the sight of the LORD, to provoke *him* to anger.

7 And he set a graven image of the grove that he had made in the house, of which the LORD said to David, and to Solomon his son, [a]In this house, and in Jerusalem, which I have chosen out of all tribes of Israel, will I put my name for ever: R

8 [a]Neither will I make the feet of Israel move any more out of the land which I gave their fathers; only if they will observe to do according to all that I have commanded them, and according to all the law that my servant Moses commanded them.

9 But they hearkened not: and Manasseh [a]seduced them to do more evil than did the nations whom the LORD destroyed before the children of Israel.

10 ¶ And the LORD spake by his servants the prophets, saying,

11 [a]Because Manasseh king of Judah hath done these abominations, [b]*and* hath done wickedly above all that the Amorites did, which *were* before him, and [c]hath made Judah also to sin with his idols:

12 Therefore thus saith the LORD God of Israel, Behold, I *am* bringing *such* evil upon Jerusalem and Judah, that whosoever heareth of it, both [a]his ears shall tingle. R

13 And I will stretch over Jerusalem [a]the line of Samaria, and the plummet of

15 [a]ver. 13
17 [a]ch. 24:13 & 25:13; Jer. 27:21 & 52:17
18 [a]ch. 24:12; 2 Chr. 33:11
19 [a]1 Sam. 3:18; Job 1:21; Ps. 39:9 [1]*Or, Shall there not be peace and truth*
20 [a]2 Chr. 32:32 [b]Neh. 3:16 [c]2 Chr. 32:30
21 [a]2 Chr. 32:33
21:1 [a]2 Chr. 33:1
2 [a]ch. 16:3
3 [a]ch. 18:4 [b]1 Ki. 16:32 [c]Deut. 4:19 & 17:3; ch. 17:16
4 [a]Jer. 32:34 [b]2 Sam. 7:13; 1 Ki. 8:29 & 9:3
6 [a]Lev. 18:21 & 20:2; ch. 16:3 & 17:17 [b]Lev. 19:26, 31; Deut. 18:10,11; ch. 17:17
7 [a]2 Sam. 7:13; 1 Ki. 8:29 & 9:3; ch. 23:27; Jer. 32:34
8 [a]2 Sam. 7:10
9 [a]Prov. 29:12
11 [a]ch. 23:26,27 & 24:3,4; Jer. 15:4 [b]1 Ki. 21:26 [c]ver. 9
12 [a]1 Sam. 3:11; Jer. 19:3
13 [a]See Is. 34:11; Lam. 2:8; Amos 7:7,8

J *2Ki 19:7* ◀▶ *1Ch 21:9–13*

R *2Ki 18:9–12* ◀▶ *2Ki 21:12–15*
R *2Ki 21:7–9* ◀▶ *2Ki 22:15–20*

21:7–8 Evil King Manasseh of Judah sacrificed his son to pagan god Molech and established widespread idolatry and wickedness during his long reign. God had warned David and Solomon centuries earlier that he would protect Israel from exile only if Israel obeyed their covenant with God.

21:12–15 God announced the destruction of Judah and Jerusalem and the exile of the people as punishment for their continuing sins.

the house of Ahab: and I will wipe Jerusalem as *a man* wipeth a dish, [|]wiping *it,* and turning *it* upside down.

14 And I will forsake the remnant of mine inheritance, and deliver them into the hand of their enemies; and they shall become a prey and a spoil to all their enemies;

15 Because they have done *that which was* evil in my sight, and have provoked me to anger, since the day their fathers came forth out of Egypt, even unto this day.

16 [a]Moreover Manasseh shed innocent blood very much, till he had filled Jerusalem [|]from one end to another; beside his sin wherewith he made Judah to sin, in doing *that which was* evil in the sight of the LORD.

17 ¶ Now [a]the rest of the acts of Manasseh, and all that he did, and his sin that he sinned, *are* they not written in the book of the chronicles of the kings of Judah?

18 And [a]Manasseh slept with his fathers, and was buried in the garden of his own house, in the garden of Uzza: and Amon his son reigned in his stead.

Amon, king of Judah

19 ¶ [a]Amon *was* twenty and two years old when he began to reign, and he reigned two years in Jerusalem. And his mother's name *was* Meshullemeth, the daughter of Haruz of Jotbah.

20 And he did *that which was* evil in the sight of the LORD, [a]as his father Manasseh did.

21 And he walked in all the way that his father walked in, and served the idols that his father served, and worshipped them:

C 22 And he [a]forsook the LORD God of his fathers, and walked not in the way of the LORD.

23 ¶ [a]And the servants of Amon conspired against him, and slew the king in his own house.

24 And the people of the land slew all them that had conspired against king Amon; and the people of the land made Josiah his son king in his stead.

25 Now the rest of the acts of Amon which he did, *are* they not written in the book of the chronicles of the kings of Judah?

26 And he was buried in his sepulchre in the garden of Uzza: and [a]Josiah his son reigned in his stead.

The book of the law found

22 JOSIAH [a]*WAS* eight years old when he began to reign, and he reigned thirty and one years in Jerusalem. And his mother's name *was* Jedidah, the daughter of Adaiah of [b]Boscath.

2 And he did *that which was* right in the sight of the LORD, and walked in all the way of David his father, and [a]turned not aside to the right hand or to the left.

3 ¶ [a]And it came to pass in the eighteenth year of king Josiah, *that* the king sent Shaphan the son of Azaliah, the son of Meshullam, the scribe, to the house of the LORD, saying,

4 Go up to Hilkiah the high priest, that he may sum the silver which is [a]brought into the house of the LORD, which [b]the keepers of the [|]door have gathered of the people:

5 And let them [a]deliver it into the hand of the doers of the work, that have the oversight of the house of the LORD: and let them give it to the doers of the work which *is* in the house of the LORD, to repair the breaches of the house,

6 Unto carpenters, and builders, and masons, and to buy timber and hewn stone to repair the house.

7 Howbeit [a]there was no reckoning made with them of the money that was delivered into their hand, because they dealt faithfully.

8 ¶ And Hilkiah the high priest said unto Shaphan the scribe, [a]I have found the book of the law in the house of the LORD. And Hilkiah gave the book to Shaphan, and he read it.

9 And Shaphan the scribe came to the king, and brought the king word again, and said, Thy servants have [|]gathered the money that was found in the house, and have delivered it into the hand of them that do the work, that have the oversight of the house of the LORD.

10 And Shaphan the scribe showed the king, saying, Hilkiah the priest hath delivered me a book. And Shaphan read it before the king.

11 And it came to pass, when the king

13 [|]Heb. *he wipeth and turneth* it *upon the face thereof*
16 [a]ch. 24:4 [|]Heb. *from mouth to mouth*
17 [a]2 Chr. 33:11-19
18 [a]2 Chr. 33:20
19 [a]2 Chr. 33:21-23
20 [a]ver. 2
22 [a]1 Ki. 11:33
23 [a]2 Chr. 33:24, 25
26 [a]Mat. 1:10 called *Josias*
22:1 [a]2 Chr. 34:1 [b]Josh. 15:39
2 [a]Deut. 5:32
3 [a]2 Chr. 34:8
4 [a]ch. 12:4 [b]ch. 12:9 [|]Heb. *threshold*
5 [a]ch. 12:11,12,14
7 [a]ch. 12:15
8 [a]Deut. 31:24; 2 Chr. 34:14
9 [|]Heb. *melted*

had heard the words of the book of the law, that he rent his clothes.

12 And the king commanded Hilkiah the priest, and Ahikam the son of Shaphan, and [a]Achbor the son of [1]Michaiah, and Shaphan the scribe, and Asahiah a servant of the king's, saying,

13 Go ye, inquire of the LORD for me, and for the people, and for all Judah, concerning the words of this book that is found: for great *is* [a]the wrath of the LORD that is kindled against us, because our fathers have not hearkened unto the words of this book, to do according unto all that which is written concerning us.

14 So Hilkiah the priest, and Ahikam, and Achbor, and Shaphan, and Asahiah, went unto Huldah the prophetess, the wife of Shallum the son of [a]Tikvah, the son of [1]Harhas, keeper of the [2]wardrobe; (now she dwelt in Jerusalem [3]in the college;) and they communed with her.

R 15 ¶ And she said unto them, Thus saith the LORD God of Israel, Tell the man that sent you to me,

16 Thus saith the LORD, Behold, [a]I will bring evil upon this place, and upon the inhabitants thereof, *even* all the words of the book which the king of Judah hath read:

17 [a]Because they have forsaken me, and have burned incense unto other gods, that they might provoke me to anger with all the works of their hands; therefore my wrath shall be kindled against this place, and shall not be quenched.

18 But to [a]the king of Judah which sent you to inquire of the LORD, thus shall ye say to him, Thus saith the LORD God of Israel, *As touching* the words which thou hast heard;

M 19 Because thine [a]heart was tender, and thou hast [b]humbled thyself before the LORD, when thou heardest what I spake against this place, and against the inhabitants thereof, that they should become [c]a desolation and [d]a curse, and hast rent thy clothes, and wept before me; I also have heard *thee,* saith the LORD.

20 Behold therefore, I will gather thee unto thy fathers, and thou [a]shalt be gathered into thy grave in peace; and thine eyes shall not see all the evil which I will bring upon this place. And they brought the king word again.

The renewal of the covenant

23 AND [a]THE king sent, and they gathered unto him all the elders of Judah and of Jerusalem.

2 And the king went up into the house of the LORD, and all the men of Judah and all the inhabitants of Jerusalem with him, and the priests, and the prophets, and all the people, [1]both small and great: and he read in their ears all the words of the book of the covenant [a]which was found in the house of the LORD.

3 ¶ And the king [a]stood by a pillar, and made a covenant before the LORD, to walk after the LORD, and to keep his commandments and his testimonies and his statutes with all *their* heart and all *their* soul, to perform the words of this covenant that were written in this book. And all the people stood to the covenant.

4 And the king commanded Hilkiah the high priest, and the priests of the second order, and the keepers of the door, to bring forth out of the temple of the LORD all the vessels that were made for Baal, and for [a]the grove, and for all the host of heaven: and he burned them without Jerusalem in the fields of Kidron, and carried the ashes of them unto Beth-el.

5 And he [1]put down the [2]idolatrous priests, whom the kings of Judah had ordained to burn incense in the high places in the cities of Judah, and in the places round about Jerusalem; them also that burned incense unto Baal, to the sun, and to the moon, and to the [3]planets, and to [a]all the hosts of heaven.

6 And he brought out the [a]grove from the house of the LORD, without Jerusalem, unto the brook Kidron, and burned it at the brook Kidron, and stamped *it* small

12 [a]*Abdon* 2 Chr. 34:20 [1]Or, *Micah*
13 [a]Deut. 29:27
14 [a]*Tikvath* 2 Chr. 34:22 [1]Or, *Hasrah* [2]Heb. *garments* [3]Or, *in the second part*
16 [a]Deut. 29:27; Dan. 9:11-14
17 [a]Deut. 29:25-27
18 [a]2 Chr. 34:26
19 [a]Ps. 51:17; Is. 57:15 [b]1 Ki. 21:29 [c]Lev. 26:31,32 [d]Jer. 26:6 & 44:22
20 [a]Ps. 37:37; Is. 57:1,2
23:1 [a]2 Chr. 34:29,30
2 [a]ch. 22:8 [1]Heb. *from small even unto great*
3 [a]ch. 11:14,17
4 [a]ch. 21:3,7
5 [a]ch. 21:3 [1]Heb. *caused to cease* [2]Heb. *Chemarim* [3]Or, *twelve signs, or, constellations*
6 [a]ch. 21:7

R *2Ki 21:12–15* ◀ ▶ *2Ki 23:26–27*
M *1Ki 21:25–29* ◀ ▶ *1Ch 21:8*

22:15–20 When Josiah became the king of Judah, he ordered repairs be made to the temple. During these repairs someone found the book of the law (Deuteronomy) that had been misplaced during the years of evil rulers and priests. The prophetess Huldah predicted that God would fulfill the prophecies of judgment because of Judah's sin. However, God promised to delay this judgment until after Josiah's death because of Josiah's genuine repentance.

to powder, and cast the powder thereof upon [b]the graves of the children of the people.

7 And he brake down the houses [a]of the sodomites, that *were* by the house of the LORD, [b]where the women wove [l]hangings for the grove.

8 And he brought all the priests out of the cities of Judah, and defiled the high places where the priests had burned incense, from [a]Geba to Beer-sheba, and brake down the high places of the gates that *were* in the entering in of the gate of Joshua the governor of the city, which *were* on a man's left hand at the gate of the city.

9 [a]Nevertheless the priests of the high places came not up to the altar of the LORD in Jerusalem, [b]but they did eat of the unleavened bread among their brethren.

10 And he defiled [a]Topheth, which *is* in [b]the valley of the children of Hinnom, [c]that no man might make his son or his daughter to pass through the fire to Molech.

11 And he took away the horses that the kings of Judah had given to the sun, at the entering in of the house of the LORD, by the chamber of Nathan-melech the [l]chamberlain, which *was* in the suburbs, and burned the chariots of the sun with fire.

12 And the altars that *were* [a]on the top of the upper chamber of Ahaz, which the kings of Judah had made, and the altars which [b]Manasseh had made in the two courts of the house of the LORD, did the king beat down, and [l]brake *them* down from thence, and cast the dust of them into the brook Kidron.

13 And the high places that *were* before Jerusalem, which *were* on the right hand of [l]the mount of corruption, which [a]Solomon the king of Israel had builded for Ashtoreth the abomination of the Zidonians, and for Chemosh the abomination of the Moabites, and for Milcom the abomination of the children of Ammon, did the king defile.

14 And he [a]brake in pieces the [l]images, and cut down the groves, and filled their places with the bones of men.

15 ¶ Moreover the altar that *was* at Beth-el, *and* the high place [a]which Jeroboam the son of Nebat, who made Israel to sin, had made, both that altar and the high place he brake down, and burned the high place, *and* stamped *it* small to powder, and burned the grove.

16 And as Josiah turned himself, he spied the sepulchres that *were* there in the mount, and sent, and took the bones out of the sepulchres, and burned *them* upon the altar, and polluted it, according to the [a]word of the LORD which the man of God proclaimed, who proclaimed these words.

17 Then he said, What title *is* that that I see? And the men of the city told him, *It is* [a]the sepulchre of the man of God, which came from Judah, and proclaimed these things that thou hast done against the altar of Beth-el.

18 And he said, Let him alone; let no man move his bones. So they let his bones [l]alone, with the bones of [a]the prophet that came out of Samaria.

19 And all the houses also of the high places that *were* [a]in the cities of Samaria, which the kings of Israel had made to provoke *the* LORD to anger, Josiah took away, and did to them according to all the acts that he had done in Beth-el.

20 And [a]he [b]slew[l] all the priests of the high places that *were* there upon the altars, and [c]burned men's bones upon them, and returned to Jerusalem.

21 ¶ And the king commanded all the people, saying, [a]Keep the passover unto the LORD your God, [b]as *it is* written in the book of this covenant. D

22 Surely [a]there was not holden such a passover from the days of the judges that judged Israel, nor in all the days of the kings of Israel, nor of the kings of Judah;

23 But in the eighteenth year of king Josiah, *wherein* this passover was holden to the LORD in Jerusalem.

24 ¶ Moreover the *workers with* familiar spirits, and the wizards, and the [a]images,[l] and the idols, and all the abominations that were spied in the land of Judah and in Jerusalem, did Josiah put away, that he might perform the words of [b]the law which were written in the book that Hilkiah the priest found in the house of the LORD.

25 [a]And like unto him was there no king before him, that turned to the LORD with all his heart, and with all his soul, and with all his might, according to all

6 [b]2 Chr. 34:4
7 [a]1 Ki. 14:24 & 15:12 [b]Ezek. 16:16 [l]Heb. *houses*
8 [a]1 Ki. 15:22
9 [a]See Ezek. 44:10-14 [b]1 Sam. 2:36
10 [a]Is. 30:33; Jer. 7:31 & 19:6,11-13 [b]Josh. 15:8 [c]Lev. 18:21; Deut. 18:10; Ezek. 23:37,39
11 [l]Or, *eunuch,* or, *officer*
12 [a]See Jer. 19:13; Zeph. 1:5 [b]ch. 21:5 [l]Or, *ran from thence*
13 [a]1 Ki. 11:7 [l]i.e. the mount of Olives
14 [a]Ex. 23:24; Deut. 7:5,25 [l]Heb. *statues*
15 [a]1 Ki. 12:28,33
16 [a]1 Ki. 13:2
17 [a]1 Ki. 13:1,30
18 [a]1 Ki. 13:31 [l]Heb. *to escape*
19 [a]See 2 Chr. 34:6,7
20 [a]1 Ki. 13:2 [b]Ex. 22:20; 1 Ki. 18:40; ch. 11:18 [c]2 Chr. 34:5 [l]Or, *sacrificed*
21 [a]2 Chr. 35:1 [b]Ex. 12:3; Lev. 23:5; Num. 9:2; Deut. 16:2
22 [a]2 Chr. 35:18, 19
24 [a]Gen. 31:19 [b]Lev. 19:31 & 20:27; Deut. 18:11 [l]Or, *teraphim*
25 [a]ch. 18:5

D *Dt 17:1* ◄► *2Ch 30:1*

the law of Moses; neither after him arose there *any* like him.

R 26 ¶ Notwithstanding the LORD turned not from the fierceness of his great wrath, wherewith his anger was kindled against Judah, [a]because of all the [1]provocations that Manasseh had provoked him withal.

27 And the LORD said, I will remove Judah also out of my sight, as [a]I have removed Israel, and will cast off this city Jerusalem which I have chosen, and the house of which I said, [b]My name shall be there.

28 Now the rest of the acts of Josiah, and all that he did, *are* they not written in the book of the chronicles of the kings of Judah?

29 ¶ [a]In his days Pharaoh-nechoh king of Egypt went up against the king of Assyria to the river Euphrates: and king Josiah went against him; and he slew him at [b]Megiddo, when he [c]had seen him.

30 [a]And his servants carried him in a chariot dead from Megiddo, and brought him to Jerusalem, and buried him in his own sepulchre. And [b]the people of the land took Jehoahaz the son of Josiah, and anointed him, and made him king in his father's stead.

Jehoahaz, king of Judah

31 ¶ [1]Jehoahaz *was* twenty and three years old when he began to reign; and he reigned three months in Jerusalem. And his mother's name *was* [a]Hamutal, the daughter of Jeremiah of Libnah.

32 And he did *that which was* evil in the sight of the LORD, according to all that his fathers had done.

33 And Pharaoh-nechoh put him in bands [a]at Riblah in the land of Hamath, [1]that he might not reign in Jerusalem; and [b]put[2] the land to a tribute of an hundred talents of silver, and a talent of gold.

34 And [a]Pharaoh-nechoh made Eliakim the son of Josiah king in the room of Josiah his father, and [b]turned his name to [c]Johoiakim, and took Jehoahaz away: [d]and he came to Egypt, and died there.

35 And Jehoiakim gave [a]the silver and the gold to Pharaoh; but he taxed the land to give the money according to the commandment of Pharaoh: he exacted the silver and the gold of the people of the land, of every one according to his taxation, to give *it* unto Pharaoh-nechoh.

Jehoiakim, king of Judah

36 ¶ [a]Jehoiakim *was* twenty and five years old when he began to reign; and he reigned eleven years in Jerusalem. And his mother's name was Zebudah, the daughter of Pedaiah of Rumah.

37 And he did *that which was* evil in the sight of the LORD, according to all that his fathers had done.

24

IN [a]HIS days Nebuchadnezzar king of Babylon came up, and Jehoiakim became his servant three years: then he turned and rebelled against him.

2 [a]And the LORD sent against him bands of the Chaldees, and bands of the Syrians, and bands of the Moabites, and bands of the children of Ammon, and sent them against Judah to destroy it, [b]according to the word of the LORD, which he spake [1]by his servants the prophets. R

3 Surely at the commandment of the LORD came *this* upon Judah, to remove *them* out of his sight, [a]for the sins of Manasseh, according to all that he did;

4 [a]And also for the innocent blood that he shed: for he filled Jerusalem with innocent blood; which the LORD would not pardon.

5 ¶ Now the rest of the acts of Jehoiakim, and all that he did, *are* they not written in the book of the chronicles of the kings of Judah?

6 [a]So Jehoiakim slept with his fathers: and Jehoiachin his son reigned in his stead.

7 And [a]the king of Egypt came not again any more out of his land: for [b]the king of Babylon had taken from the river of Egypt unto the river Euphrates all that pertained to the king of Egypt.

Jehoiachin, king of Judah

8 ¶ [a]Jehoiachin[1] *was* eighteen years

26 [a] ch. 21:11,12 & 24:3,4; Jer. 15:4 [1] Heb. *angers*
27 [a] ch. 17:18,20; & 18:11 & 21:13 [b] 1 Ki. 8:29 & 9:3; ch. 21:4,7
29 [a] 2 Chr. 35:20 [b] Zech. 12:11 [c] ch. 14:8
30 [a] 2 Chr. 35:24 [b] 2 Chr. 36:1
31 [a] ch. 24:18 [1] Called *Shallum* in 1 Chr. 3:15; Jer. 22:11
33 [a] ch. 25:6; Jer. 52:27 [b] 2 Chr. 36:3 [1] Or, *because he reigned* [2] Heb. *set a mulct upon the land*
34 [a] 2 Chr. 36:4 [b] ch. 24:17; Dan. 1:7 [c] Mat. 1:11 called *Jakim* [d] Jer. 22:11; Ezek. 19:3
35 [a] ver. 33
36 [a] 2 Chr. 36:5
24:1 [a] 2 Chr. 36:6; Jer. 25:1,9; Dan. 1:1
2 [a] Jer. 25:9 & 32:28; Ezek. 19:8 [b] ch. 20:17 & 21:12-14 & 23:27 [1] Heb. *by the hand of*
3 [a] ch. 21:2,11 & 23:26
4 [a] ch. 21:16
6 [a] See 2 Chr. 36:6, 8; Jer. 22:18 & 36:30
7 [a] Jer. 37:5,7 [b] Jer. 46:2
8 [a] 2 Chr. 36:9 [1] Called *Jeconiah* in 1 Chr. 3:16; Jer. 24:1 and *Coniah* in Jer. 22:24

R *2Ki 22:15–20* ◀ ▶ *2Ki 24:2–3*

R *2Ki 23:26–27* ◀ ▶ *2Ki 24:14*

23:26–27 Despite King Josiah's righteousness, God declared that the sins of Judah would receive full judgment in the future generation.

24:2–3 In fulfillment of God's words to his prophets, the Lord sent the combined armies of Babylon, Moab, Ammon and Aramea against Judah.

old when he began to reign, and he reigned in Jerusalem three months. And his mother's name *was* Nehushta, the daughter of Elnathan of Jerusalem.

9 And he did *that which was* evil in the sight of the LORD, according to all that his father had done.

10 ¶ [a]At that time the servants of Nebuchadnezzar king of Babylon came up against Jerusalem, and the city [/]was besieged.

11 And Nebuchadnezzar king of Babylon came against the city, and his servants did besiege it.

12 [a]And Jehoiachin the king of Judah went out to the king of Babylon, he, and his mother, and his servants, and his princes, and his [/]officers: [b]and the king of Babylon [c]took him [d]in the eighth year of his reign.

13 [a]And he carried out thence all the treasures of the house of the LORD, and the treasures of the king's house, and [b]cut in pieces all the vessels of gold which Solomon king of Israel had made in the temple of the LORD, [c]as the LORD had said.

R 14 And [a]he carried away all Jerusalem, and all the princes, and all the mighty men of valour, [b]*even* ten thousand captives, and [c]all the craftsmen and smiths: none remained, save [d]the poorest sort of the people of the land.

15 And [a]he carried away Jehoiachin to Babylon, and the king's mother, and the king's wives, and his [/]officers, and the mighty of the land, *those* carried he into captivity from Jerusalem to Babylon.

16 And [a]all the men of might, *even* seven thousand, and craftsmen and smiths a thousand, all *that were* strong *and* apt for war, even them the king of Babylon brought captive to Babylon.

17 ¶ And [a]the king of Babylon made Mattaniah [b]his father's brother king in his stead, and [c]changed his name to Zedekiah.

R 2Ki 24:2–3 ◀▶ 2Ki 25:7–12

10 [a]Dan. 1:1 [/]Heb. *came into siege*
12 [a]Jer. 24:1 & 29:1,2; Ezek. 17:12 [b]*Nebuchadnezzar's* eighth year; Jer. 25:1 [c]ch. 25:27 [d]Jer. 52:28 [/]Or, *eunuchs*
13 [a]ch. 20:17; Is. 39:6 [b]Dan. 5:2,3 [c]Jer. 20:5
14 [a]Jer. 24:1 [b]Jer. 52:28 [c]1 Sam. 13:19,22 [d]ch. 25:12
15 [a]2 Chr. 36:10; Esth. 2:6; Jer. 22:24 [/]Or, *eunuchs*
16 [a]Jer. 52:28
17 [a]Jer. 37:1 [b]1 Chr. 3:15; 2 Chr. 36:10 [c]2 Chr. 36:4
18 [a]2 Chr. 36:11; Jer. 52:1 [b]ch. 23:31
19 [a]2 Chr. 36:12
20 [a]2 Chr. 36:13; Ezek. 17:15
25:1 [a]2 Chr. 36:17; Jer. 34:2; Ezek. 24:1
3 [a]Jer. 39:2
4 [a]Jer. 39:2 [b]Jer. 39:4-7; Ezek. 12:12
6 [a]ch. 23:33; Jer. 52:9 [/]Heb. *spake judgment with him*
7 [a]Jer. 39:7 [/]Heb. *made blind*

Zedekiah, king of Judah

18 [a]Zedekiah *was* twenty and one years old when he began to reign, and he reigned eleven years in Jerusalem. And his mother's name *was* [b]Hamutal, the daughter of Jeremiah of Libnah.

19 [a]And he did *that which was* evil in the sight of the LORD, according to all that Jehoiakim had done.

20 For through the anger of the LORD it came to pass in Jerusalem and Judah, until he had cast them out from his presence, [a]that Zedekiah rebelled against the king of Babylon.

Jerusalem destroyed

25 AND IT came to pass [a]in the ninth year of his reign, in the tenth month, in the tenth *day* of the month, *that* Nebuchadnezzar king of Babylon came, he, and all his host, against Jerusalem, and pitched against it; and they built forts against it round about.

2 And the city was besieged unto the eleventh year of king Zedekiah.

3 And on the ninth *day* of the [a]*fourth* month the famine prevailed in the city, and there was no bread for the people of the land.

4 ¶ And [a]the city was broken up, and all the men of war *fled* by night by the way of the gate between two walls, which *is* by the king's garden: (now the Chaldees *were* against the city round about:) and [b]*the king* went the way toward the plain.

5 And the army of the Chaldees pursued after the king, and overtook him in the plains of Jericho: and all his army were scattered from him.

6 So they took the king, and brought him up to the king of Babylon [a]to Riblah; and they [/]gave judgment upon him.

7 And they slew the sons of Zedekiah before his eyes, and [a]put[/] out the eyes of Zedekiah, and bound him with fetters of brass, and carried him to Babylon. R

R 2Ki 24:14 ◀▶ 2Ki 25:21

24:14 Nebuchadnezzar of Babylon conquered Jerusalem in 586 B.C., plundering the precious treasures of the temple and taking ten thousand skilled craftsmen, nobles (including Daniel) and fighting men back to Babylon.

25:7–12 The Babylonians killed the sons of King Zedekiah before his eyes and then blinded him in fulfillment of Ezekiel's prophecy (see Eze 12:13). Nebuchadnezzar ordered his troops to burn the city of Jerusalem, destroy the temple and carry off most of the remaining population to slavery in Babylon. Only the poorest people of Judah were left to tend the land under the rule of Babylon.

8 ¶ And in the fifth month, [a]on the
seventh *day* of the month, which *is* [b]the
nineteenth year of king Nebuchadnezzar
king of Babylon, [c]came Nebuzar-adan,
[1]captain of the guard, a servant of the
king of Babylon, unto Jerusalem:
9 [a]And he burnt the house of the LORD,
[b]and the king's house, and all the houses
of Jerusalem, and every great *man's*
house burnt he with fire.
10 And all the army of the Chaldees,
that *were with* the captain of the guard,
[a]brake down the walls of Jerusalem
round about.
11 [a]Now the rest of the people *that*
were left in the city, and the [1]fugitives
that fell away to the king of Babylon, with
the remnant of the multitude, did Nebuzar-adan the captain of the guard carry
away.
12 But the captain of the guard [a]left of
the poor of the land *to be* vinedressers
and husbandmen.
13 And [a]the [b]pillars of brass that *were*
in the house of the LORD, and [c]the bases,
and [d]the brasen sea that *was* in the house
of the LORD, did the Chaldees break in
pieces, and carried the brass of them to
Babylon.
14 And [a]the pots, and the shovels, and
the snuffers, and the spoons, and all the
vessels of brass wherewith they ministered, took they away.
15 And the firepans, and the bowls,
and such things as *were* of gold, *in* gold,
and of silver, *in* silver, the captain of the
guard took away.
16 The two pillars, [1]one sea, and the
bases which Solomon had made for the
house of the LORD; [a]the brass of all these
vessels was without weight.
17 [a]The height of the one pillar *was*
eighteen cubits, and the chapiter upon it
was brass: and the height of the chapiter
three cubits; and the wreathen work, and
pomegranates upon the chapiter round
about, all of brass: and like unto these
had the second pillar with wreathen
work.
18 ¶ [a]And the captain of the guard
took [b]Seraiah the chief priest, and [c]Zeph-
aniah the second priest, and the three
keepers of the [1]door:

8 [a]Jer. 52:12 [b]ch. 24:12 [c]Jer. 39:9 [1]Or, *chief marshal*
9 [a]2 Chr. 36:19 [b]Jer. 39:8; Amos 2:5
10 [a]Neh. 1:3; Jer. 52:14
11 [a]Jer. 39:9 [1]Heb. *fallen away*
12 [a]ch. 24:14
13 [a]Jer. 27:19 & 52:17 [b]1 Ki. 7:15 [c]1 Ki. 7:27 [d]1 Ki. 7:23
14 [a]Ex. 27:3; 1 Ki. 7:45
16 [a]1 Ki. 7:47 [1]Heb. *the one sea*
17 [a]1 Ki. 7:15; Jer. 52:21
18 [a]Jer. 52:24 [b]1 Chr. 6:14; Ezra 7:1 [c]Jer. 21:1 [1]Heb. *threshold*
19 [a]Jer. 52:25 [1]Or, *eunuch* [2]Heb. *saw the king's face* [3]Or, *scribe of the captain of the host*
21 [a]Lev. 26:33; Deut. 28:36,64; ch. 23:27
22 [a]Jer. 40:5
23 [a]Jer. 40:7-9
25 [a]Jer. 41:1,2 [1]Heb. *of the kingdom*
26 [a]Jer. 43:4,7
27 [a]Jer. 52:31

19 And out of the city he took an [1]offi-
cer that was set over the men of war,
and [a]five men of them that [2]were in the
king's presence, which were found in the
city, and the [3]principal scribe of the host,
which mustered the people of the land,
and threescore men of the people of the
land *that were* found in the city:
20 And Nebuzar-adan captain of the
guard took these, and brought them to
the king of Babylon to Riblah:
21 And the king of Babylon smote **R**
them, and slew them at Riblah in the
land of Hamath. [a]So Judah was carried
away out of their land.
22 ¶ [a]And *as for* the people that remained in the land of Judah, whom Nebuchadnezzar king of Babylon had left,
even over them he made Gedaliah the
son of Ahikam, the son of Shaphan, ruler.
23 And when all the [a]captains of the
armies, they and their men, heard that
the king of Babylon had made Gedaliah
governor, there came to Gedaliah to Mizpah, even Ishmael the son of Nethaniah,
and Johanan the son of Careah, and Seraiah the son of Tanhumeth the Netophathite, and Jaazaniah the son of a Maachathite, they and their men.
24 And Gedaliah sware to them, and
to their men, and said unto them, Fear
not to be the servants of the Chaldees:
dwell in the land, and serve the king of
Babylon; and it shall be well with you.
25 But [a]it came to pass in the seventh
month, that Ishmael the son of Nethaniah, the son of Elishama, of the seed
[1]royal, came, and ten men with him, and
smote Gedaliah, that he died, and the
Jews and the Chaldees that were with
him at Mizpah.
26 And all the people, both small and
great, and the captains of the armies,
arose, [a]and came to Egypt: for they were
afraid of the Chaldees.

Jehoiachin in captivity

27 ¶ [a]And it came to pass in the seven
and thirtieth year of the captivity of Jehoiachin king of Judah, in the twelfth
month, on the seven and twentieth *day* of

R *2Ki 25:7–12* ◀ ▶ *1Ch 5:26*

25:21 The king of Babylon killed the leaders of Judah for their continual rebellion against Babylonian rule. Significantly, rebellion was the same reason for God's judgment against the leaders of Judah.

the month, *that* Evil-merodach king of
Babylon in the year that he began to reign
[b]did lift up the head of Jehoiachin king of
Judah out of prison;
28 And he spake [l]kindly to him, and
set his throne above the throne of the
kings that *were* with him in Babylon;

27 [b]See Gen. 40:13,20

28 [l]Heb. *good things with him*

29 [a]2 Sam. 9:7

29 And changed his prison garments:
and he did [a]eat bread continually before
him all the days of his life.
30 And his allowance *was* a continual
allowance given him of the king, a
daily rate for every day, all the days of
his life.

1 Chronicles

Author: Authorship uncertain; possibly Ezra

Theme: The life and lineage of King David

Date of Writing: c. 450–400 B.C.

Outline of 1 Chronicles

I. Genealogies From Adam to David (1:1—9:44)
II. The Death of Saul (10:1—10:14)
III. The Reign of David (11:1—29:21)
IV. David's Death and Solomon's Accession (29:22–30)

ORIGINAL HEBREW MANUSCRIPTS combined 1 and 2 Chronicles as one book and titled it "the events (or annals) of the days (or years)," deriving this title from the opening words of the narrative. Septuagint (the Greek translation of the OT) translators called the book "the things omitted" since they regarded its information as supplemental to the narratives of Samuel and Kings. The title "Chronicles" found acceptance after a Latin translation was made of the text by a scholar named Jerome.

The first nine chapters of 1 Chronicles trace the genealogy of King David. This unbroken lineage from the time of the patriarchs to the rise of the monarchy established a rich heritage for the Jewish exiles who returned from Babylon to rebuild their temple and nation. The Chronicles' accounts reflect a priestly view of the events in Israel's life by firmly establishing the basis of God's eternal covenant with his chosen people. The central chapters of 1 Chronicles indicate that this covenantal relationship reached its peak under King David and provide additional details about David's reign that are not recorded in 1 and 2 Kings (see 1Ch 22:1–5; 23—29).

Descendants of the patriarchs

1 ADAM, [a]SHETH, Enosh,

2 Kenan, Mahalaleel, Jered,

3 Henoch, Methuselah, Lamech,

4 Noah, Shem, Ham, and Japheth.

5 ¶ [a]The sons of Japheth; Gomer, and Magog, and Madai, and Javan, and Tubal, and Meshech, and Tiras.

6 And the sons of Gomer; Ashchenaz, and [1]Riphath, and Togarmah.

7 And the sons of Javan; Elishah, and Tarshish, Kittim, and [1]Dodanim.

8 ¶ [a]The sons of Ham; Cush, and Mizraim, Put, and Canaan.

9 And the sons of Cush; Seba, and Havilah, and Sabta, and Raamah, and Sabtecha. And the sons of Raamah; Sheba, and Dedan.

10 And Cush [a]begat Nimrod: he began to be mighty upon the earth.

11 And Mizraim begat Ludim, and Anamim, and Lehabim, and Naphtuhim,

12 And Pathrusim, and Casluhim, (of whom came the Philistines,) and [a]Caphthorim.

13 And [a]Canaan begat Zidon his firstborn, and Heth,

14 The Jebusite also, and the Amorite, and the Girgashite,

15 And the Hivite, and the Arkite, and the Sinite,

16 And the Arvadite, and the Zemarite, and the Hamathite.

17 ¶ The sons of [a]Shem; Elam, and Asshur, and Arphaxad, and Lud, and Aram, and Uz, and Hul, and Gether, and [1]Meshech.

18 And Arphaxad begat Shelah, and Shelah begat Eber.

19 And unto Eber were born two sons: the name of the one *was* [a]Peleg;[1] because in his days the earth was divided: and his brother's name *was* Joktan.

20 And [a]Joktan begat Almodad, and Sheleph, and Hazarmaveth, and Jerah,

21 Hadoram also, and Uzal, and Diklah,

22 And Ebal, and Abimael, and Sheba,

23 And Ophir, and Havilah, and Jobab. All these *were* the sons of Joktan.

24 ¶ [a]Shem, Arphaxad, Shelah,

25 [a]Eber, Peleg, Reu,

26 Serug, Nahor, Terah,

27 [a]Abram; the same *is* Abraham.

28 The sons of Abraham; [a]Isaac, and [b]Ishmael.

29 ¶ These *are* their generations: The [a]firstborn of Ishmael, Nebaioth; then Kedar, and Adbeel, and Mibsam,

30 Mishma, and Dumah, Massa, [1]Hadad, and Tema,

31 Jetur, Naphish, and Kedemah. These are the sons of Ishmael.

32 ¶ Now [a]the sons of Keturah, Abraham's concubine: she bare Zimran, and Jokshan, and Medan, and Midian, and Ishbak, and Shuah. And the sons of Jokshan; Sheba, and Dedan.

33 And the sons of Midian; Ephah, and Epher, and Henoch, and Abida, and Eldaah. All these *are* the sons of Keturah.

34 And [a]Abraham begat Isaac. [b]The sons of Isaac; Esau and Israel.

35 ¶ The sons of [a]Esau; Eliphaz, Reuel, and Jeush, and Jaalam, and Korah.

36 The sons of Eliphaz; Teman, and Omar, [1]Zephi, and Gatam, Kenaz, and Timna, and Amalek.

37 The sons of Reuel; Nahath, Zerah, Shammah, and Mizzah.

38 And [a]the sons of Seir; Lotan, and Shobal, and Zibeon, and Anah, and Dishon, and Ezar, and Dishan.

39 And the sons of Lotan; Hori, and [1]Homam: and Timna *was* Lotan's sister.

40 The sons of Shobal; [1]Alian, and Manahath, and Ebal, [2]Shephi, and Onam. And the sons of Zibeon; Aiah, and Anah.

41 The sons of Anah; [a]Dishon. And the sons of Dishon; [1]Amram, and Eshban, and Ithran, and Cheran.

42 The sons of Ezer; Bilhan, and Zavan, *and* [1]Jakan. The sons of Dishan; Uz, and Aran.

The kings of Edom

43 ¶ Now these *are* the [a]kings that reigned in the land of Edom before *any* king reigned over the children of Israel; Bela the son of Beor: and the name of his city *was* Dinhabah.

44 And when Bela was dead, Jobab the son of Zerah of Bozrah reigned in his stead.

45 And when Jobab was dead, Husham of the land of the Temanites reigned in his stead.

46 And when Husham was dead, Hadad the son of Bedad, which smote Midian in the field of Moab, reigned in his stead: and the name of his city *was* Avith.

47 And when Hadad was dead, Samlah of Masrekah reigned in his stead.

1:1 [a]Gen. 4:25,26 & 5:3,9
5 [a]Gen. 10:2
6 [1]Or, *Diphath,* as it is in some copies
7 [1]Or, *Rodanim,* according to some copies
8 [a]Gen. 10:6
10 [a]Gen. 10:8,13
12 [a]Deut. 2:23
13 [a]Gen. 10:15
17 [a]Gen. 10:22 & 11:10 [1]Or, *Mash;* see Gen. 10:23
19 [a]Gen. 10:25 [1]i.e. *Division*
20 [a]Gen. 10:26
24 [a]Gen. 11:10; Luke 3:36
25 [a]Gen. 11:15
27 [a]Gen. 17:5
28 [a]Gen. 21:2 [b]Gen. 16:11,15
29 [a]Gen. 25:13-16
30 [1]Or, *Hadar;* see Gen. 25:15
32 [a]Gen. 25:1
34 [a]Gen. 21:2 [b]Gen. 25:25,26
35 [a]Gen. 36:9,10
36 [1]Or, *Zepho;* see Gen. 36:11
38 [a]Gen. 36:20
39 [1]Or, *Heman;* see Gen. 36:22
40 [1]Or, *Alvan;* see Gen. 36:23 [2]Or, *Shepho;* see Gen. 36:23
41 [a]Gen. 36:25 [1]Or, *Hemdan;* see Gen. 36:26
42 [1]Or, *Akan;* see Gen. 36:27
43 [a]Gen. 36:31

48 [a]And when Samlah was dead, Shaul
of Rehoboth by the river reigned in his
stead.
49 And when Shaul was dead, Baal-hanan the son of Achbor reigned in his
stead.
50 And when Baal-hanan was dead,
[1]Hadad reigned in his stead: and the
name of his city *was* [2]Pai; and his wife's
name *was* Mehetabel, the daughter of
Matred, the daughter of Mezahab.
51 ¶ Hadad died also. And the [a]dukes
of Edom were; duke Timnah, duke
[1]Aliah, duke Jetheth,
52 Duke Aholibamah, duke Elah, duke
Pinon,
53 Duke Kenaz, duke Teman, duke
Mibzar,
54 Duke Magdiel, duke Iram. These
are the dukes of Edom.

From Israel to David

2 THESE *ARE* the sons of [1]Israel; [a]Reu-
ben, Simeon, Levi, and Judah, Issachar, and Zebulun,
2 Dan, Joseph, and Benjamin, Naphtali, Gad, and Asher.
3 ¶ The sons of [a]Judah; Er, and Onan,
and Shelah: *which* three were born unto
him of the daughter of [b]Shua the Canaan-
itess. And [c]Er, the firstborn of Judah,
was evil in the sight of the LORD; and he
slew him.
4 And [a]Tamar his daughter-in-law bare
him Pharez and Zerah. All the sons of
Judah *were* five.
5 The sons of [a]Pharez; Hezron, and
Hamul.
6 And the sons of Zerah; [1]Zimri, [a]and
Ethan, and Heman, and Calcol, and
[2]Dara: five of them in all.
7 And the sons of [a]Carmi; [1]Achar, the
troubler of Israel, who transgressed in the
thing [b]accursed.
8 And the sons of Ethan; Azariah.
9 The sons also of Hezron, that were
born unto him; Jerahmeel, and [1]Ram, and
[2]Chelubai.
10 And Ram [a]begat Amminadab; and
Amminadab begat Nahshon, [b]prince of
the children of Judah;
11 And Nahshon begat [1]Salma, and
Salma begat Boaz,
12 And Boaz begat Obed, and Obed
begat Jesse.
13 ¶ [a]And Jesse begat his firstborn
Eliab, and Abinadab the second, and
[1]Shimma the third,
14 Nethaneel the fourth, Raddai the
fifth,
15 Ozem the sixth, David the seventh:
16 Whose sisters *were* Zeruiah, and
Abigail. [a]And the sons of Zeruiah;
Abishai, and Joab, and Asahel, three.
17 And [a]Abigail bare Amasa: and the
father of Amasa *was* [1]Jether the Ishmaelite.
18 ¶ And Caleb the son of Hezron begat *children* of Azubah *his* wife, and of
Jerioth: her sons *are* these; Jesher, and
Shobab, and Ardon.
19 And when Azubah was dead, Caleb
took unto him [a]Ephrath, which bare him
Hur.
20 And Hur begat Uri, and Uri begat
[a]Bezaleel.
21 ¶ And afterward Hezron went in to
the daughter of [a]Machir the father of Gilead, whom he [1]married when he *was*
threescore years old; and she bare him
Segub.
22 And Segub begat Jair, who had
three and twenty cities in the land of
Gilead.
23 [a]And he took Geshur, and Aram,
with the towns of Jair, from them, with
Kenath, and the towns thereof, *even*
threescore cities. All these *belonged to*
the sons of Machir the father of Gilead.
24 And after that Hezron was dead in
Caleb-ephratah, then Abiah Hezron's
wife bare him [a]Ashur the father of Tekoa.
25 ¶ And the sons of Jerahmeel the
firstborn of Hezron were, Ram the firstborn, and Bunah, and Oren, and Ozem,
and Ahijah.
26 Jerahmeel had also another wife,
whose name *was* Atarah; she *was* the
mother of Onam.

48 [a]Gen. 36:37
50 [1]Or, *Hadar;* see Gen. 36:39 [2]Or, *Pau;* see Gen. 36:39
51 [a]Gen. 36:40 [1]Or, *Alvah*
2:1 [a]Gen. 29:32 & 30:5 & 35:18,22 & 46:8 [1]Or, *Jacob*
3 [a]Gen. 38:3 & 46:12; Num. 26:19 [b]Gen. 38:2 [c]Gen. 38:7
4 [a]Gen. 38:29,30
5 [a]Gen. 46:12; Ruth 4:18
6 [a]1 Ki. 4:31 [1]Or, *Zabdi;* see Josh. 7:1 [2]Or, *Darda*
7 [a]See ch. 4:1 [b]Josh. 6:18 & 7:1 [1]Or, *Achan*
9 [1]Or, *Aram;* see Mat. 1:3,4 [2]Or, *Caleb;* see ver. 18,42
10 [a]Ruth 4:19,20; Mat. 1:4 [b]Num. 1:7 & 2:3
11 [1]Or, *Salmon;* see Ruth 4:21; Mat. 1:4
13 [a]1 Sam. 16:6 [1]Or, *Shammah;* see 1 Sam. 16:9
16 [a]2 Sam. 2:18
17 [a]2 Sam. 17:25 [1]Or, *Ithra an Israelite;* see 2 Sam. 17:25
19 [a]ver. 50
20 [a]Ex. 31:2
21 [a]Num. 27:1 [1]Heb. *took*
23 [a]Num. 32:41; Deut. 3:14; Josh. 13:30
24 [a]ch. 4:5

2:15 David was not Jesse's firstborn son but rather the seventh in line. No one even considered the possibility of David being the son that Samuel would anoint as Israel's future king (see 1Sa 16:7–13). The customs of ancient Israel provided added benefits to the firstborn son in terms of inheritance and birthright blessings. Yet God in his sovereign grace chose to make Jesse's seventh son the forefather of the Messiah, regardless of his position, birth order or natural advantage.

27 And the sons of Ram the firstborn of Jerahmeel were, Maaz, and Jamin, and Eker.

28 And the sons of Onam were, Shammai, and Jada. And the sons of Shammai; Nadab, and Abishur.

29 And the name of the wife of Abishur *was* Abihail, and she bare him Ahban, and Molid.

30 And the sons of Nadab; Seled, and Appaim: but Seled died without children.

31 And the sons of Appaim; Ishi. And the sons of Ishi; Sheshan. And [a]the children of Sheshan; Ahlai.

32 And the sons of Jada the brother of Shammai; Jether, and Jonathan: and Jether died without children.

33 And the sons of Jonathan; Peleth, and Zaza. These were the sons of Jerahmeel.

34 ¶ Now Sheshan had no sons, but daughters. And Sheshan had a servant, an Egyptian, whose name *was* Jarha.

35 And Sheshan gave his daughter to Jarha his servant to wife; and she bare him Attai.

36 And Attai begat Nathan, and Nathan begat [a]Zabad,

37 And Zabad begat Ephlal, and Ephlal begat Obed,

38 And Obed begat Jehu, and Jehu begat Azariah,

39 And Azariah begat Helez, and Helez begat Eleasah,

40 And Eleasah begat Sisamai, and Sisamai begat Shallum,

41 And Shallum begat Jekamiah, and Jekamiah begat Elishama.

42 ¶ Now the sons of Caleb the brother of Jerahmeel *were,* Mesha his firstborn, which *was* the father of Ziph; and the sons of Mareshah the father of Hebron.

43 And the sons of Hebron; Korah, and Tappuah, and Rekem, and Shema.

44 And Shema begat Raham, the father of Jorkoam: and Rekem begat Shammai.

45 And the son of Shammai *was* Maon: and Maon *was* the father of Beth-zur.

46 And Ephah, Caleb's concubine, bare Haran, and Moza, and Gazez: and Haran begat Gazez.

47 And the sons of Jahdai; Regem, and Jotham, and Gesham, and Pelet, and Ephah, and Shaaph.

48 Maachah, Caleb's concubine, bare Sheber, and Tirhanah.

31 [a]See ver. 34,35
36 [a]ch. 11:41
49 [a]Josh. 15:17
50 [1]Or, *Ephrath;* see ver. 19
52 [1]Or, *Reaiah;* see ch. 4:2 [2]Or, *half of the Menuchites,* or, *Hatsiham-menuchoth*
54 [1]Or, *Atarites,* or, *crowns of the house of Joab*
55 [a]Judg. 1:16 [b]Jer. 35:2
3:1 [a]2 Sam. 3:2 [b]Josh. 15:56 [1]Or, *Chileab;* see 2 Sam. 3:3
3 [a]2 Sam. 3:5
4 [a]2 Sam. 2:11 [b]2 Sam. 5:5
5 [a]ch. 14:4 [b]2 Sam. 12:24 [1]Or, *Shammua;* see 2 Sam. 5:14 [2]Or, *Bath-sheba;* see 2 Sam. 11:3 [3]Or, *Eliam;* see 2 Sam. 11:3
6 [1]Or, *Elishua;* see 2 Sam. 5:15
8 [a]See 2 Sam. 5:14-16 [1]Or, *Beeliada;* see ch. 14:7
9 [a]2 Sam. 13:1

49 She bare also Shaaph the father of Madmannah, Sheva the father of Machbenah, and the father of Gibea: and the daughter of Caleb *was* [a]Achsah.

50 ¶ These were the sons of Caleb the son of Hur, the firstborn of [1]Ephratah; Shobal the father of Kirjath-jearim,

51 Salma the father of Bethlehem, Hareph the father of Beth-gader.

52 And Shobal the father of Kirjath-jearim had sons; [1]Haroeh, *and* [2]half of the Manahethites.

53 And the families of Kirjath-jearim; the Ithrites, and the Puhites, and the Shumathites, and the Mishraites; of them came the Zareathites, and the Eshtaulites.

54 The sons of Salma; Bethlehem, and the Netophathites, [1]Ataroth, the house of Joab, and half of the Manahethites, the Zorites.

55 And the families of the scribes which dwelt at Jabez; the Tirathites, the Shimeathites, *and* Suchathites. These *are* the [a]Kenites that came of Hemath, the father of the house of [b]Rechab.

The family of David

3 NOW THESE were the sons of David, which were born unto him in Hebron; the firstborn [a]Amnon, of Ahinoam the [b]Jezreelitess; the second [1]Daniel, of Abigail the Carmelitess:

2 The third, Absalom the son of Maachah the daughter of Talmai king of Geshur: the fourth, Adonijah the son of Haggith:

3 The fifth, Shephatiah of Abital: the sixth, Ithream by [a]Eglah his wife.

4 *These* six were born unto him in Hebron; and [a]there he reigned seven years and six months: and [b]in Jerusalem he reigned thirty and three years.

5 [a]And these were born unto him in Jerusalem; [1]Shimea, and Shobab, and Nathan, and [b]Solomon, four, of [2]Bath-shua the daughter of [3]Ammiel:

6 Ibhar also, and [1]Elishama, and Eliphelet,

7 And Nogah, and Nepheg, and Japhia,

8 And Elishama, and [1]Eliada, and Eliphelet, [a]nine.

9 *These were* all the sons of David, beside the sons of the concubines, and [a]Tamar their sister.

The family of Solomon

10 ¶ And Solomon's son *was* [a]Reho-
boam, [1]Abia his son, Asa his son, Jehoshaphat his son,
11 Joram his son, [1]Ahaziah his son, Joash his son,
12 Amaziah his son, [1]Azariah his son,
Jotham his son,
13 Ahaz his son, Hezekiah his son,
Manasseh his son,
14 Amon his son, Josiah his son.
15 And the sons of Josiah *were,* the
firstborn [1]Johanan, the second [2]Jehoia-
kim, the third [3]Zedekiah, the fourth
Shallum.
16 And the sons of [a]Jehoiakim: [1]Jeco-
niah his son, Zedekiah [b]his son.
17 ¶ And the sons of Jeconiah; Assir,
[1]Salathiel [a]his son,
18 Malchiram also, and Pedaiah, and
Shenazar, Jecamiah, Hoshama, and Ned-
abiah.
19 And the sons of Pedaiah *were,* Zerubbabel, and Shimei: and the sons of Zerubbabel; Meshullam, and Hananiah, and
Shelomith their sister:
20 And Hashubah, and Ohel, and
Berechiah, and Hasadiah, Jushab-hesed,
five.
21 And the sons of Hananiah; Pelatiah,
and Jesaiah: the sons of Rephaiah, the
sons of Arnan, the sons of Obadiah, the
sons of Shechaniah.
22 And the sons of Shechaniah; Shemaiah: and the sons of Shemaiah; [a]Hat-
tush, and Igeal, and Bariah, and Neariah,
and Shaphat, six.
23 And the sons of Neariah; Elioenai,
and [1]Hezekiah, and Azrikam, three.
24 And the sons of Elioenai *were,* Ho-
daiah, and Eliashib, and Pelaiah, and Akkub, and Johanan, and Dalaiah, and
Anani, seven.

The family of Judah

4 THE SONS of Judah; [a]Pharez, Hezron, and [1]Carmi, and Hur, and
Shobal.
2 And [1]Reaiah the son of Shobal begat
Jahath; and Jahath begat Ahumai, and La-
had. These *are* the families of the Zo-
rathites.
3 And these *were of* the father of
Etam; Jezreel, and Ishma, and Idbash:
and the name of their sister *was* Haze-
lelponi:
4 And Penuel the father of Gedor, and
Ezer the father of Hushah. These *are* the
sons of [a]Hur, the firstborn of Ephratah,
the father of Bethlehem.
5 ¶ And [a]Ashur the father of Tekoa
had two wives, Helah and Naarah.
6 And Naarah bare him Ahuzam, and
Hepher, and Temeni, and Haahashtari.
These *were* the sons of Naarah.
7 And the sons of Helah *were,* Zereth,
and Jezoar, and Ethnan.
8 And Coz begat Anub, and Zobebah,
and the families of Aharhel the son of
Harum.
9 ¶ And Jabez was [a]more honourable
than his brethren: and his mother called
his name [1]Jabez, saying, Because I bare
him with sorrow.
10 And Jabez called on the God of Is- K
rael, saying, [1]Oh that thou wouldest bless U
me indeed, and enlarge my coast, and
that thine hand might be with me, and
that thou wouldest [2]keep *me* from evil,
that it may not grieve me! And God
granted him that which he requested.
11 ¶ And Chelub the brother of Shuah
begat Mehir, which *was* the father of
Eshton.
12 And Eshton begat Beth-rapha, and
Paseah, and Tehinnah the father of [1]Ir-
nahash. These *are* the men of Rechah.
13 And the sons of Kenaz; [a]Othniel,
and Seraiah: and the sons of Othniel;
[1]Hathath.
14 And Meonothai begat Ophrah: and
Seraiah begat Joab, the father of [a]the [1]val-
ley of [2]Charashim; for they were
craftsmen.
15 And the sons of Caleb the son of
Jephunneh; Iru, Elah, and Naam: and the
sons of Elah, [1]even Kenaz.
16 And the sons of Jehaleleel; Ziph,
and Ziphah, Tiria, and Asareel.
17 And the sons of Ezra *were,* Jether,
and Mered, and Epher, and Jalon: and
she bare Miriam, and Shammai, and Ish-
bah the father of Eshtemoa.
18 And his wife [1]Jehudijah bare Jered
the father of Gedor, and Heber the father
of Socho, and Jekuthiel the father of Zanoah. And these *are* the sons of Bithiah
the daughter of Pharaoh, which Mered
took.
19 And the sons of *his* wife [1]Hodiah
the sister of Naham, the father of Keilah

3:10 [a]1 Ki. 11:43 [1]Called *Abijam* in 1 Ki. 15:1
11 [1]Called *Azariah* in 2 Chr. 22:6; *Jehoahaz* in 2 Chr. 21:17
12 [1]Called *Uzziah* in 2 Ki. 15:30
15 [1]Called *Jehoahaz* in 2 Ki. 23:30 [2]Called *Eliakim* in 2 Ki. 23:34 [3]Called *Mattaniah* in 2 Ki. 24:17
16 [a]Mat. 1:11 [b]2 Ki. 24:17 being his uncle [1]Called *Jehoiachin* in 2 Ki. 24:6; *Coniah* in Jer. 22:24
17 [a]Mat. 1:12 [1]Heb. *Shealtiel*
22 [a]Ezra 8:2
23 [1]Heb. *Hiskijahu*
4:1 [a]Gen. 46:12 [1]Called *Chelubai* in ch. 2:9; *Caleb* in ch. 2:18
2 [1]Or, *Haroeh;* see ch. 2:52
4 [a]ch. 2:50
5 [a]ch. 2:24
9 [a]Gen. 34:19 [1]i.e. *sorrowful*
10 [1]Heb. *If thou wilt* [2]Heb. *do* me
12 [1]Or, *the city of Nahash*
13 [a]Josh. 15:17 [1]Or, *Hathath* and *Meonothai, who begat*
14 [a]Neh. 11:35 [1]Or, inhabitants *of the valley* [2]i.e. *Craftsmen*
15 [1]Or, *Uknaz*
18 [1]Or, *the Jewess*
19 [1]Or, *Jehudijah,* mentioned before

K *2Ki 6:16–17* ◀ ▶ *1Ch 29:11–12*
U *1Ki 3:13–14* ◀ ▶ *1Ch 11:9*

the Garmite, and Eshtemoa the Maachathite.

20 And the sons of Shimon *were,* Amnon, and Rinnah, Ben-hanan, and Tilon. And the sons of Ishi *were,* Zoheth, and Ben-zoheth.

21 ¶ The sons of Shelah [a]the son of Judah *were,* Er the father of Lecah, and Laadah the father of Mareshah, and the families of the house of them that wrought fine linen, of the house of Ashbea,

22 And Jokim, and the men of Chozeba, and Joash, and Saraph, who had the dominion in Moab, and Jashubi-lehem. And *these are* ancient things.

23 These *were* the potters, and those that dwelt among plants and hedges: there they dwelt with the king for his work.

The family of Simeon

24 ¶ The sons of Simeon *were,* [1]Nemuel, and Jamin, [2]Jarib, Zerah, *and* Shaul:

25 Shallum his son, Mibsam his son, Mishma his son.

26 And the sons of Mishma; Hamuel his son, Zacchur his son, Shimei his son.

27 And Shimei had sixteen sons and six daughters; but his brethren had not many children, neither did all their family multiply, [1]like to the children of Judah.

28 And they dwelt at [a]Beer-sheba, and Moladah, and Hazar-shual,

29 And at [1]Bilhah, and at Ezem, and at [2]Tolad,

30 And at Bethuel, and at Hormah, and at Ziklag,

31 And at Beth-marcaboth, and [1]Hazar-susim, and at Beth-birei, and at Shaaraim. These *were* their cities unto the reign of David.

32 And their villages *were,* [1]Etam, and Ain, Rimmon, and Tochen, and Ashan, five cities:

33 And all their villages that *were* round about the same cities, unto [1]Baal. These *were* their habitations, and [2]their genealogy.

34 And Meshobab, and Jamlech, and Joshah the son of Amaziah,

35 And Joel, and Jehu the son of Josibiah, the son of Seraiah, the son of Asiel,

36 And Elioenai, and Jaakobah, and Jeshohaiah, and Asaiah, and Adiel, and Jesimiel, and Benaiah,

37 And Ziza the son of Shiphi, the son of Allon, the son of Jedaiah, the son of Shimri, the son of Shemaiah;

38 These [1]mentioned by *their* names *were* princes in their families: and the house of their fathers increased greatly.

39 ¶ And they went to the entrance of Gedor, *even* unto the east side of the valley, to seek pasture for their flocks.

40 And they found fat pasture and good, and the land *was* wide, and quiet, and peaceable; for *they* of Ham had dwelt there of old.

41 And these written by name came in the days of Hezekiah king of Judah, and [a]smote their tents, and the habitations that were found there, and destroyed them utterly unto this day, and dwelt in their rooms: because *there was* pasture there for their flocks.

42 And *some* of them, *even* of the sons of Simeon, five hundred men, went to mount Seir, having for their captains Pelatiah, and Neariah, and Rephaiah, and Uzziel, the sons of Ishi.

43 And they smote [a]the rest of the Amalekites that were escaped, and dwelt there unto this day.

The family of Reuben

5 NOW THE sons of Reuben the firstborn of Israel, (for [a]he *was* the firstborn; but, forasmuch as he [b]defiled his father's bed, [c]his birthright was given unto the sons of Joseph the son of Israel: and the genealogy is not to be reckoned after the birthright.

2 For [a]Judah prevailed above his brethren, and of him *came* the [b]chief [1]ruler; but the birthright *was* Joseph's:)

3 The sons, *I say,* of [a]Reuben the firstborn of Israel *were,* Hanoch, and Pallu, Hezron, and Carmi.

4 The sons of Joel; Shemaiah his son, Gog his son, Shimei his son,

5 Micah his son, Reaia his son, Baal his son,

6 Beerah his son, whom [1]Tilgath-pilneser king of Assyria carried away *captive:* he *was* prince of the Reubenites.

7 And his brethren by their families, [a]when the genealogy of their generations was reckoned, *were* the chief, Jeiel, and Zechariah,

8 And Bela the son of Azaz, the son of [1]Shema, the son of Joel, who dwelt in [a]Aroer, even unto Nebo and Baal-meon:

21 [a]Gen. 38:1,5

24 [1]Or, *Jemeul;* see Gen. 46:10; Ex. 6:15; Num. 26:12 [2]Or, *Jachin, Zohar*

27 [1]Heb. *unto*

28 [a]Josh. 19:2

29 [1]Or, *Balah;* see Josh. 19:3 [2]Or, *Eltolad;* see Josh. 19:4

31 [1]Or, *Hazarsusah;* see Josh. 19:5

32 [1]Or, *Ether;* see Josh. 19:7

33 [1]Or, *Baalathbeer;* see Josh. 19:8 [2]Or, *as they divided themselves by nations among them*

38 [1]Heb. *coming*

41 [a]2 Ki. 18:8

43 [a]See 1 Sam. 15:8 & 30:17 & 2 Sam. 8:12

5:1 [a]Gen. 29:32 & 49:3 [b]Gen. 35:22 & 49:4 [c]Gen. 48:15,22

2 [a]Gen. 49:8,10; Ps. 60:7 & 108:8 [b]Mic. 5:2; Mat. 2:6 [1]Or, *prince*

3 [a]Gen. 46:9; Ex. 6:14; Num. 26:5

6 [1]Or, *Tiglathpileser;* see 2 Ki. 15:29 & 16:7

7 [a]See ver. 17

8 [a]Josh. 13:15,16 [1]Or, *Shemaiah;* see ver. 4

9 And eastward he inhabited unto the
entering in of the wilderness from the
river Euphrates: because their cattle were
multiplied [a]in the land of Gilead.
10 And in the days of Saul they made
war [a]with the Hagarites, who fell by their
hand: and they dwelt in their tents
[1]throughout all the east *land* of Gilead.

The family of Gad

11 ¶ And the children of Gad dwelt
over against them, in the land of [a]Bashan
unto Salcah:
12 Joel the chief, and Shapham the
next, and Jaanai, and Shaphat in Bashan.
13 And their brethren of the house of
their fathers *were,* Michael, and Meshullam, and Sheba, and Jorai, and Jachan,
and Zia, and Heber, seven.
14 These *are* the children of Abihail
the son of Huri, the son of Jaroah, the son
of Gilead, the son of Michael, the son of
Jeshishai, the son of Jahdo, the son of
Buz;
15 Ahi the son of Abdiel, the son of
Guni, chief of the house of their fathers.
16 And they dwelt in Gilead in Bashan, and in her towns, and in all the
suburbs of [a]Sharon, upon [1]their borders.
17 All these were reckoned by genealogies in the days of [a]Jotham king of Judah, and in the days of [b]Jeroboam king of
Israel.
18 ¶ The sons of Reuben, and the Gadites, and half the tribe of Manasseh, [1]of
valiant men, men able to bear buckler
and sword, and to shoot with bow, and
skilful in war, *were* four and forty thousand seven hundred and threescore, that
went out to the war.
19 And they made war with the Hagarites, with [a]Jetur, and Nephish, and
Nodab.
20 And [a]they were helped against
them, and the Hagarites were delivered
into their hand, and all that *were* with
them: for they cried to God in the battle,
and he was entreated of them; because
they [b]put their trust in him.
21 And they [1]took away their cattle; of
their camels fifty thousand, and of sheep
two hundred and fifty thousand, and of
asses two thousand, and of [2]men an hundred thousand.
22 For there fell down many slain, because the war *was* of God. And they
dwelt in their steads until [a]the captivity.

The half tribe of Manasseh

23 ¶ And the children of the half tribe
of Manasseh dwelt in the land: they increased from Bashan unto Baal-hermon
and Senir, and unto mount Hermon.
24 And these *were* the heads of the
house of their fathers, even Epher, and
Ishi, and Eliel, and Azriel, and Jeremiah,
and Hodaviah, and Jahdiel, mighty men
of valour, [1]famous men, *and* heads of the
house of their fathers.
25 ¶ And they transgressed against the
God of their fathers, and went [a]a-whor-
ing after the gods of the people of the
land, whom God destroyed before them.
26 And the God of Israel stirred up the **R**
spirit of [a]Pul king of Assyria, and the
spirit of [b]Tilgath-pilneser king of Assyria,
and he carried them away, even the Reubenites, and the Gadites, and the half
tribe of Manasseh, and brought them
unto [c]Halah, and Habor, and Hara, and to
the river Gozan, unto this day.

The family of Levi

6 THE SONS of Levi; [a]Gershon,[1] Kohath, and Merari.
2 And the sons of Kohath; Amram, [a]Iz-
har, and Hebron, and Uzziel.
3 And the children of Amram; Aaron,
and Moses, and Miriam. The sons also of
Aaron; [a]Nadab, and Abihu, Eleazar, and
Ithamar.
4 ¶ Eleazar begat Phinehas, Phinehas
begat Abishua,
5 And Abishua begat Bukki, and Bukki
begat Uzzi,
6 And Uzzi begat Zerahiah, and Zerahiah begat Meraioth,
7 Meraioth begat Amariah, and Amariah begat Ahitub,
8 And [a]Ahitub begat Zadok, and [b]Za-
dok begat Ahimaaz,
9 And Ahimaaz begat Azariah, and Azariah begat Johanan,

R *2Ki 25:21* ◀▶ *1Ch 6:15*

9 [a]Josh. 22:9
10 [a]Gen. 25:12 [1]Heb. *upon all the face of the east*
11 [a]Josh. 13:11,24
16 [a]ch. 27:29 [1]Heb. *their goings forth*
17 [a]2 Ki. 15:5,32 [b]2 Ki. 14:16,28
18 [1]Heb. *sons of valour*
19 [a]Gen. 25:15; ch. 1:31
20 [a]See ver. 22 [b]Ps. 22:4,5
21 [1]Heb. *led captive* [2]Heb. *souls of men*
22 [a]2 Ki. 15:29 & 17:6
24 [1]Heb. *men of names*
25 [a]2 Ki. 17:7
26 [a]2 Ki. 15:19 [b]2 Ki. 15:29 [c]2 Ki. 17:6 & 18:11
6:1 [a]Gen. 46:11; Ex. 6:16; Num. 26:57; ch. 23:6 [1]Or, *Gershom;* see ver. 16
2 [a]See ver. 22
3 [a]Lev. 10:1
8 [a]2 Sam. 8:17 [b]2 Sam. 15:27

5:26 God used the king of Assyria to accomplish his judgment of sinful Israel. The Assyrians captured the tribes that settled on the eastern side of the Jordan River (Reuben, Gad and the half-tribe of Manasseh) and exiled them to Assyria (modern-day Iraq, Iran and Afghanistan).

10 And Johanan begat Azariah, (he *it is* [a]that executed the priest's office [1]in the [b]temple that Solomon built in Jerusalem:)

11 And [a]Azariah begat Amariah, and Amariah begat Ahitub,

12 And Ahitub begat Zadok, and Zadok begat [1]Shallum,

13 And Shallum begat Hilkiah, and Hilkiah begat Azariah,

14 And Azariah begat [a]Seraiah, and Seraiah begat Jehozadak,

R 15 And Jehozadak went *into captivity,* [a]when the LORD carried away Judah and Jerusalem by the hand of Nebuchadnezzar.

16 ¶ The sons of Levi; [a]Gershom,[1] Kohath, and Merari.

17 And these *be* the names of the sons of Gershom; Libni, and Shimei.

18 And the sons of Kohath *were,* Amram, and Izhar, and Hebron, and Uzziel.

19 The sons of Merari; Mahli, and Mushi. And these *are* the families of the Levites according to their fathers.

20 Of Gershom; Libni his son, Jahath his son, [a]Zimmah his son,

21 [1]Joah his son, [2]Iddo his son, Zerah his son, [3]Jeaterai his son.

22 The sons of Kohath; [1]Amminadab his son, Korah his son, Assir his son,

23 Elkanah his son, and Ebiasaph his son, and Assir his son,

24 Tahath his son, [1]Uriel his son, Uzziah his son, and Shaul his son.

25 And the sons of Elkanah; [a]Amasai, and Ahimoth.

26 *As for* Elkanah: the sons of Elkanah; [1]Zophai his son, and [a]Nahath his son,

27 [a]Eliab his son, Jeroham his son, Elkanah his son.

28 And the sons of Samuel; the firstborn [1]Vashni, and Abiah.

29 The sons of Merari; Mahli, Libni his son, Shimei his son, Uzza his son,

30 Shimea his son, Haggiah his son, Asaiah his son.

31 And these *are they* whom David set over the service of song in the house of the LORD, after that the [a]ark had rest.

32 And they ministered before the dwellingplace of the tabernacle of the congregation with singing, until Solomon had built the house of the LORD in Jerusalem: and *then* they waited on their office according to their order.

33 And these *are* they that [1]waited with their children. Of the sons of the Kohathites: Heman a singer, the son of Joel, the son of Shemuel,

34 The son of Elkanah, the son of Jeroham, the son of Eliel, the son of [1]Toah,

35 The son of [1]Zuph, the son of Elkanah, the son of Mahath, the son of Amasai,

36 The son of Elkanah, the son of Joel, the son of Azariah, the son of Zephaniah,

37 The son of Tahath, the son of Assir, the son of [a]Ebiasaph, the son of Korah,

38 The son of Izhar, the son of Kohath, the son of Levi, the son of Israel.

39 And his brother Asaph, who stood on his right hand, *even* Asaph the son of Berachiah, the son of Shimea,

40 The son of Michael, the son of Baaseiah, the son of Malchiah,

41 The son of [a]Ethni, the son of Zerah, the son of Adaiah,

42 The son of Ethan, the son of Zimmah, the son of Shimei,

43 The son of Jahath, the son of Gershom, the son of Levi.

44 And their brethren the sons of Merari *stood* on the left hand: [1]Ethan the son of [2]Kishi, the son of Abdi, the son of Malluch,

45 The son of Hashabiah, the son of Amaziah, the son of Hilkiah,

46 The son of Amzi, the son of Bani, the son of Shamer,

47 The son of Mahli, the son of Mushi, the son of Merari, the son of Levi.

48 Their brethren also the Levites *were* appointed unto all manner of service of the tabernacle of the house of God.

The family of Aaron

49 ¶ But Aaron and his sons offered [a]upon the altar of the burnt offering, and [b]on the altar of incense, *and were appointed* for all the work of the *place* most holy, and to make an atonement for Is-

10 [a]See 2 Chr. 26:17,18 [b]1 Ki. 6; 2 Chr. 3 [1]Heb. *in the house*
11 [a]See Ezra 7:3
12 [1]Or, *Meshullam;* see ch. 9:11
14 [a]Neh. 11:11
15 [a]2 Ki. 25:18
16 [a]Ex. 6:16 [1]Or, *Gershon;* see ver. 1
20 [a]ver. 42
21 [1]Or, *Ethan;* see ver. 42 [2]Or, *Adaiah;* see ver. 41 [3]Or, *Ethni;* see ver. 41
22 [1]Or, *Izhar;* see ver. 2,18
24 [1]Or, *Zephaniah, Azariah, Joel;* see ver. 36
25 [a]See ver. 35,36
26 [a]ver. 34 *Toah* [1]Or, *Zuph;* see ver. 35; 1 Sam. 1:1
27 [a]ver. 34 *Eliel*
28 [1]Called also *Joel* in ver. 33; 1 Sam. 8:2
31 [a]ch. 16:1
33 [1]Heb. *stood*
34 [1]Or, *Nahath;* see ver. 26
35 [1]Or, *Zophai*
37 [a]Ex. 6:24
41 [a]See ver. 21
44 [1]Called *Jeduthun* in ch. 9:16 & 25:1,3,6 [2]Or, *Kushaiah;* see ch. 15:17
49 [a]Lev. 1:9 [b]Ex. 30:7

R *1Ch 5:26* ◄► *1Ch 9:1*

6:15 Jehozadak, son of the high priest of the temple, was taken captive to Babylon. Apparently he is the same man as Josedech (see Hag 1:1). His son Joshua returned with Zerubbabel, governor of Judah, at the end of the Babylonian captivity to rebuild the temple.

rael, according to all that Moses the servant of God had commanded.

50 And these *are* the sons of Aaron; Eleazar his son, Phinehas his son, Abishua his son,

51 Bukki his son, Uzzi his son, Zerahiah his son,

52 Meraioth his son, Amariah his son, Ahitub his son,

53 Zadok his son, Ahimaaz his son.

54 ¶ [a]Now these *are* their dwelling places throughout their castles in their coasts, of the sons of Aaron, of the families of the Kohathites: for theirs was the lot.

55 [a]And they gave them Hebron in the land of Judah, and the suburbs thereof round about it.

56 [a]But the fields of the city, and the villages thereof, they gave to Caleb the son of Jephunneh.

57 And [a]to the sons of Aaron they gave the cities of Judah, *namely*, Hebron, *the city* of refuge, and Libnah with her suburbs, and Jattir, and Eshtemoa, with their suburbs,

58 And [1]Hilen with her suburbs, Debir with her suburbs,

59 And [1]Ashan with her suburbs, and Beth-shemesh with her suburbs:

60 And out of the tribe of Benjamin; Geba with her suburbs, and [1]Alemeth with her suburbs, and Anathoth with her suburbs. All their cities throughout their families *were* thirteen cities.

61 And unto the sons of Kohath, [a]*which were* left of the family of that tribe, *were cities given* out of the half tribe, *namely, out of* the half *tribe* of Manasseh, [b]by lot, ten cities.

62 And to the sons of Gershom throughout their families out of the tribe of Issachar, and out of the tribe of Asher, and out of the tribe of Naphtali, and out of the tribe of Manasseh in Bashan, thirteen cities.

63 Unto the sons of Merari *were given* by lot, throughout their families, out of the tribe of Reuben, and out of the tribe of Gad, and out of the tribe of Zebulun, [a]twelve cities.

64 And the children of Israel gave to the Levites *these* cities with their suburbs.

65 And they gave by lot out of the tribe of the children of Judah, and out of the tribe of the children of Simeon, and out of the tribe of the children of Benjamin, these cities, which are called by *their* names.

66 And [a]*the residue* of the families of the sons of Kohath had cities of their coasts out of the tribe of Ephraim.

67 [a]And they gave unto them, *of* the cities of refuge, Shechem in mount Ephraim with her suburbs; *they gave* also Gezer with her suburbs,

68 And [a]Jokmeam with her suburbs, and Beth-horon with her suburbs,

69 And Aijalon with her suburbs, and Gath-rimmon with her suburbs:

70 And out of the half tribe of Manasseh; Aner with her suburbs, and Bileam with her suburbs, for the family of the remnant of the sons of Kohath.

71 Unto the sons of Gershom *were given* out of the family of the half tribe of Manasseh, Golan in Bashan with her suburbs, and [a]Ashtaroth with her suburbs:

72 And out of the tribe of Issachar; [a]Kedesh with her suburbs, Daberath with her suburbs,

73 And Ramoth with her suburbs, and Anem with her suburbs:

74 And out of the tribe of Asher; Mashal with her suburbs, and Abdon with her suburbs,

75 And Hukok with her suburbs, and Rehob with her suburbs:

76 And out of the tribe of Naphtali; Kedesh in Galilee with her suburbs, and Hammon with her suburbs, and Kirjathaim with her suburbs.

77 Unto the rest of the children of Merari *were given* out of the tribe of Zebulun, Rimmon with her suburbs, Tabor with her suburbs:

78 And on the other side Jordan by Jericho, on the east side of Jordan, *were given them* out of the tribe of Reuben, Bezer in the wilderness with her suburbs, and Jahzah with her suburbs,

79 Kedemoth also with her suburbs, and Mephaath with her suburbs:

80 And out of the tribe of Gad; Ramoth in Gilead with her suburbs, and Mahanaim with her suburbs,

81 And Heshbon with her suburbs, and Jazer with her suburbs.

54 [a]Josh. 21
55 [a]Josh. 21:11,12
56 [a]Josh. 14:13 & 15:13
57 [a]Josh. 21:13
58 [1]Or, *Holon;* see Josh. 21:15
59 [1]Or, *Ain;* see Josh. 21:16
60 [1]Or, *Almon;* see Josh. 21:18
61 [a]ver. 66 [b]Josh. 21:5
63 [a]Josh. 21:7,34
66 [a]ver. 61
67 [a]Josh. 21:21
68 [a]See Josh. 21:22-35 where many of these cities have other names
71 [a]Josh. 21:27 *Beeshterah*
72 [a]Josh. 21:28 *Kishon*

The family of Issachar

7 NOW THE sons of Issachar *were,* [a]Tola, and [1]Puah, Jashub, and Shimrom, four.

2 And the sons of Tola; Uzzi, and Rephaiah, and Jeriel, and Jahmai, and Jibsam, and Shemuel, heads of their father's house, *to wit,* of Tola: *they were* valiant men of might in their generations; [a]whose number *was* in the days of David two and twenty thousand and six hundred.

3 And the sons of Uzzi; Izrahiah: and the sons of Izrahiah; Michael and Obadiah, and Joel, Ishiah, five: all of them chief men.

4 And with them, by their generations, after the house of their fathers, *were* bands of soldiers for war, six and thirty thousand *men:* for they had many wives and sons.

5 And their brethren among all the families of Issachar *were* valiant men of might, reckoned in all by their genealogies fourscore and seven thousand.

The family of Benjamin

6 ¶ *The sons* of [a]Benjamin: Bela, and Becher, and Jediael, three.

7 And the sons of Bela; Ezbon, and Uzzi, and Uzziel, and Jerimoth, and Iri, five; heads of the house of *their* fathers, mighty men of valour; and were reckoned by their genealogies twenty and two thousand and thirty and four.

8 And the sons of Becher; Zemira, and Joash, and Eliezer, and Elioenai, and Omri, and Jerimoth, and Abiah, and Anathoth, and Alameth. All these *are* the sons of Becher.

9 And the number of them, after their genealogy by their generations, heads of the house of their fathers, mighty men of valour, *was* twenty thousand and two hundred.

10 The sons also of Jediael; Bilhan: and the sons of Bilhan; Jeush, and Benjamin, and Ehud, and Chenaanah, and Zethan, and Tharshish, and Ahishahar.

11 All these the sons of Jediael, by the heads of their fathers, mighty men of valour, *were* seventeen thousand and two hundred *soldiers,* fit to go out for war *and* battle.

12 [a]Shuppim also, and Huppim, the children of [1]Ir, *and* Hushim, the sons of [2]Aher.

The family of Naphtali

13 ¶ The sons of Naphtali; Jahziel, and Guni, and Jezer, and [a]Shallum, the sons of Bilhah.

14 ¶ The sons of Manasseh; Ashriel, whom she bare: (*but* his concubine the Aramitess bare Machir the father of Gilead:

15 And Machir took to wife *the sister* of Huppim and Shuppim, whose sister's name *was* Maachah;) and the name of the second *was* Zelophehad: and Zelophehad had daughters.

16 And Maachah the wife of Machir bare a son, and she called his name Peresh; and the name of his brother *was* Sheresh; and his sons *were* Ulam and Rakem.

17 And the sons of Ulam; [a]Bedan. These *were* the sons of Gilead, the son of Machir, the son of Manasseh.

18 And his sister Hammoleketh bare Ishod, and [a]Abiezer, and Mahalah.

19 And the sons of Shemidah were, Ahian, and Shechem, and Likhi, and Aniam.

The family of Ephraim

20 ¶ And [a]the sons of Ephraim; Shuthelah, and Bered his son, and Tahath his son, and Eladah his son, and Tahath his son,

21 ¶ And Zabad his son, and Shuthelah his son, and Ezer, and Elead, whom the men of Gath *that were* born in *that* land slew, because they came down to take away their cattle.

22 And Ephraim their father mourned many days, and his brethren came to comfort him.

23 ¶ And when he went in to his wife, she conceived, and bare a son, and he called his name Beriah, because it went evil with his house.

24 (And his daughter *was* Sherah, who built Beth-horon the nether, and the upper, and Uzzen-sherah.)

25 And Rephah *was* his son, also Resheph, and Telah his son, and Tahan his son,

26 Laadan his son, Ammihud his son, Elishama his son,

27 [1]Non his son, Jehoshuah his son.

28 ¶ And their possessions and habitations *were,* Beth-el and the towns thereof, and eastward [a]Naaran, and westward Gezer, with the [1]towns thereof;

7:1 [a]Gen. 46:13; Num. 26:23 [1]*Phuvah, Job*
2 [a]2 Sam. 24:1,2; ch. 27:1
6 [a]Gen. 46:21; Num. 26:38; ch. 8:1
12 [a]Num. 26:39 *Shupham* and *Hupham* [1]Or, *Iri;* see ver. 7 [2]Or, *Ahiram;* see Num. 26:38
13 [a]Gen. 46:24 *Shillem*
17 [a]1 Sam. 12:11
18 [a]Num. 26:30 *Jeezer*
20 [a]Num. 26:35
27 [1]Or, *Nun;* see Num. 13:8,16
28 [a]Josh. 16:7 *Naarath* [1]Heb. *daughters*

Shechem also and the towns thereof,
unto Gaza and the towns thereof:
29 And by the borders of the children
of [a]Manasseh, Beth-shean and her towns,
Taanach and her towns, [b]Megiddo and
her towns, Dor and her towns. In these
dwelt the children of Joseph the son of
Israel.

The family of Asher

30 ¶ [a]The sons of Asher; Imnah, and
Isuah, and Ishuai, and Beriah, and Serah
their sister.
31 And the sons of Beriah; Heber, and
Malchiel, who *is* the father of Birzavith.
32 And Heber begat Japhlet, and [a]Sho-
mer, and Hotham, and Shua their sister.
33 And the sons of Japhlet; Pasach,
and Bimhal, and Ashvath. These *are* the
children of Japhlet.
34 And the sons of [a]Shamer; Ahi, and
Rohgah, Jehubbah, and Aram.
35 And the sons of his brother Helem;
Zophah, and Imna, and Shelesh, and
Amal.
36 The sons of Zophah; Suah, and Har-
nepher, and Shual, and Beri, and Imrah,
37 Bezer, and Hod, and Shamma, and
Shilshah, and Ithran, and Beera.
38 And the sons of Jether; Jephunneh,
and Pispah, and Ara.
39 And the sons of Ulla; Arah, and
Haniel, and Rezia.
40 All these *were* the children of
Asher, heads of *their* father's house,
choice *and* mighty men of valour, chief of
the princes. And the number throughout
the genealogy of them that were apt
to the war *and* to battle *was* twenty and
six thousand men.

The family of Benjamin

8 NOW BENJAMIN begat [a]Bela his
firstborn, Ashbel the second, and
Aharah the third,
2 Nohah the fourth, and Rapha the
fifth.
3 And the sons of Bela were, [I]Addar,
and Gera, and Abihud,
4 And Abishua, and Naaman, and
Ahoah,
5 And Gera, and [I]Shephuphan, and
Huram.
6 And these *are* the sons of Ehud:
these are the heads of the fathers of the
inhabitants of Geba, and they removed
them to [a]Manahath:
7 And Naaman, and Ahiah, and Gera,
he removed them, and begat Uzza, and
Ahihud.
8 And Shaharaim begat *children* in the
country of Moab, after he had sent them
away; Hushim and Baara *were* his wives.
9 And he begat of Hodesh his wife, Jobab, and Zibia, and Mesha, and Malcham,
10 And Jeuz, and Shachia, and Mirma.
These *were* his sons, heads of the fathers.
11 And of Hushim he begat Abitub,
and Elpaal.
12 The sons of Elpaal; Eber, and Mi-
sham, and Shamed, who built Ono, and
Lod, with the towns thereof:
13 Beriah also, and [a]Shema, who *were*
heads of the fathers of the inhabitants of
Aijalon, who drove away the inhabitants
of Gath:
14 And Ahio, Shashak, and Jeremoth,
15 And Zebadiah, and Arad, and Ader,
16 And Michael, and Ispah, and Joha,
the sons of Beriah;
17 And Zebadiah, and Meshullam, and
Hezeki, and Heber,
18 Ishmerai also, and Jezliah, and Jobab, the sons of Elpaal;
19 And Jakim, and Zichri, and Zabdi,
20 And Elienai, and Zilthai, and Eliel,
21 And Adaiah, and Beraiah, and
Shimrath, the sons of [I]Shimhi;
22 And Ishpan, and Heber, and Eliel,
23 And Abdon, and Zichri, and Hanan,
24 And Hananiah, and Elam, and Anto-
thijah,
25 And Iphedeiah, and Penuel, the
sons of Shashak;
26 And Shamsherai, and Shehariah,
and Athaliah,
27 And Jaresiah, and Eliah, and Zichri,
the sons of Jeroham.
28 These *were* heads of the fathers, by
their generations, chief *men.* These dwelt
in Jerusalem.
29 And at Gibeon dwelt the [I]father of
Gibeon; whose [a]wife's name *was*
Maachah:
30 And his firstborn son Abdon, and
Zur, and Kish, and Baal, and Nadab,
31 And Gedor, and Ahio, and [I]Zacher.
32 And Mikloth begat [I]Shimeah. And
these also dwelt with their brethren in
Jerusalem, over against them.
33 ¶ And [a]Ner begat Kish, and Kish
begat Saul, and Saul begat Jonathan, and
Malchi-shua, and [b]Abinadab, and [I]Esh-
baal.

29 [a]Josh. 17:7 [b]Josh. 17:11
30 [a]Gen. 46:17; Num. 26:44
32 [a]ver. 34 *Shamer*
34 [a]ver. 32 *Shomer*
8:1 [a]Gen. 46:21; Num. 26:38; ch. 7:6
3 [I]Or, *Ard;* see Gen. 46:21
5 [I]Or, *Shupham;* see Num. 26:39; see ch. 7:12
6 [a]ch. 2:52
13 [a]ver. 21
21 [I]Or, *Shema;* see ver. 13
29 [a]ch. 9:35 [I]Called *Jehiel* in ch. 9:35
31 [I]Or, *Zechariah;* see ch. 9:37
32 [I]Or, *Shimeam;* see ch. 9:38
33 [a]1 Sam. 14:51 [b]1 Sam. 14:49 *Ishui* [I]Or, *Ish-bosheth;* see 2 Sam. 2:8

34 And the son of Jonathan *was* [l]Merib-baal; and Merib-baal begat [a]Micah.

35 And the sons of Micah *were,* Pithon, and Melech, and [l]Tarea, and Ahaz.

36 And Ahaz begat [a]Jehoadah; and Jehoadah begat Alemeth, and Azmaveth, and Zimri; and Zimri begat Moza,

37 And Moza begat Binea: [a]Rapha *was* his son, Eleasah his son, Azel his son:

38 And Azel had six sons, whose names *are* these, Azrikam, Bocheru, and Ishmael, and Sheariah, and Obadiah, and Hanan. All these *were* the sons of Azel.

39 And the sons of Eshek his brother *were,* Ulam his firstborn, Jehush the second, and Eliphelet the third.

40 And the sons of Ulam were mighty men of valour, archers, and had many sons, and sons' sons, an hundred and fifty. All these *are* of the sons of Benjamin.

Inhabitants in Jerusalem

R 9 SO [a]ALL Israel were reckoned by genealogies; and, behold, they *were* written in the book of the kings of Israel and Judah, *who* were carried away to Babylon for their transgression.

2 ¶ [a]Now the first inhabitants that *dwelt* in their possessions in their cities *were,* the Israelites, the priests, Levites, and [b]the Nethinims.

3 And in [a]Jerusalem dwelt of the children of Judah, and of the children of Benjamin, and of the children of Ephraim, and Manasseh;

4 Uthai the son of Ammihud, the son of Omri, the son of Imri, the son of Bani, of the children of Pharez the son of Judah.

5 And of the Shilonites; Asaiah the firstborn, and his sons.

6 And of the sons of Zerah; Jeuel, and their brethren, six hundred and ninety.

7 And of the sons of Benjamin; Sallu the son of Meshullam, the son of Hodaviah, the son of Hasenuah,

8 And Ibneiah the son of Jeroham, and Elah the son of Uzzi, the son of Michri, and Meshullam the son of Shephathiah, the son of Reuel, the son of Ibnijah;

9 And their brethren, according to their generations, nine hundred and fifty and six. All these men *were* chief of the fathers in the house of their fathers.

10 ¶ [a]And of the priests; Jedaiah, and Jehoiarib, and Jachin,

11 And [l]Azariah the son of Hilkiah, the son of Meshullam, the son of Zadok, the son of Meraioth, the son of Ahitub, the ruler of the house of God;

12 And Adaiah the son of Jeroham, the son of Pashur, the son of Malchijah, and Maasiai the son of Adiel, the son of Jahzerah, the son of Meshullam, the son of Meshillemith, the son of Immer;

13 And their brethren, heads of the house of their fathers, a thousand and seven hundred and threescore; [l]very able men for the work of the service of the house of God.

14 And of the Levites; Shemaiah the son of Hasshub, the son of Azrikam, the son of Hashabiah, of the sons of Merari;

15 And Bakbakkar, Heresh, and Galal, and Mattaniah the son of Micah, the son of Zichri, the son of Asaph;

16 And Obadiah the son of Shemaiah, the son of Galal, the son of Jeduthun, and Berechiah the son of Asa, the son of Elkanah, that dwelt in the villages of the Netophathites.

17 And the porters *were,* Shallum, and Akkub, and Talmon, and Ahiman, and their brethren: Shallum *was* the chief;

18 Who hitherto *waited* in the king's gate eastward: they *were* porters in the companies of the children of Levi.

19 And Shallum the son of Kore, the son of Ebiasaph, the son of Korah, and his brethren, of the house of his father, the Korahites, *were* over the work of the service, keepers of the [l]gates of the tabernacle: and their fathers, *being* over the host of the LORD, *were* keepers of the entry.

20 And [a]Phinehas the son of Eleazar was the ruler over them in time past, *and* the LORD *was* with him.

21 *And* Zechariah the son of Meshelemiah *was* porter of the door of the tabernacle of the congregation.

22 All these *which were* chosen to be

R *1Ch 6:15* ◀ ▶ *2Ch 7:20*

34 [a]2 Sam. 9:12 [l]Or, *Mephibosheth;* see 2 Sam. 4:4 & 9:6,10
35 [l]Or, *Tahrea;* see ch. 9:41
36 [a]*Jarah;* ch. 9:42
37 [a]ch. 9:43 *Rephaiah*
9:1 [a]Ezra 2:59
2 [a]Ezra 2:70; Neh. 7:73 [b]Josh. 9:27; Ezra 2:43 & 8:20
3 [a]Neh. 11:1
10 [a]Neh. 11:10
11 [l]Or, *Seraiah;* see Neh. 11:11
13 [l]Heb. *mighty men of valour*
19 [l]Heb. *thresholds*
20 [a]Num. 31:6

9:1 This "book of the kings of Israel and Judah" was an official court record that has been lost and should not be confused with our books of 1 and 2 Kings.

porters in the gates *were* two hundred and twelve. These were reckoned by their genealogy in their villages, whom [a]David and Samuel [b]the seer [1]did ordain in their [2]set office.

23 So they and their children *had* the oversight of the gates of the house of the LORD, *namely,* the house of the tabernacle, by wards.

24 In four quarters were the porters, toward the east, west, north, and south.

25 And their brethren, *which were* in their villages, *were* to come [a]after seven days from time to time with them.

26 For these Levites, the four chief porters, were in *their* [1]set office, and were over the [2]chambers and treasuries of the house of God.

27 ¶ And they lodged round about the house of God, because the charge *was* upon them, and the opening thereof every morning *pertained* to them.

28 And *certain* of them had the charge of the ministering vessels, that they should [1]bring them in and out by tale.

29 *Some* of them also *were* appointed to oversee the vessels, and all the [1]instruments of the sanctuary, and the fine flour, and the wine, and the oil, and the frankincense, and the spices.

30 And *some* of the sons of the priests made [a]the ointment of the spices.

31 And Mattithiah, *one* of the Levites, who *was* the firstborn of Shallum the Korahite, had the [1]set office [a]over the things that were made [2]in the pans.

32 And *other* of their brethren, of the sons of the Kohathites, [a]*were* over the [1]showbread, to prepare *it* every sabbath.

33 And these *are* [a]the singers, chief of the fathers of the Levites, *who remaining* in the chambers *were* free: for [1]they were employed in *that* work day and night.

34 These chief fathers of the Levites *were* chief throughout their generations; these dwelt at Jerusalem.

The family of Saul

35 ¶ And in Gibeon dwelt the father of Gibeon, Jehiel, whose wife's name *was* [a]Maachah:

36 And his firstborn son Abdon, then Zur, and Kish, and Baal, and Ner, and Nadab,

37 And Gedor, and Ahio, and Zechariah, and Mikloth.

38 And Mikloth begat Shimeam. And they also dwelt with their brethren at Jerusalem, over against their brethren.

39 [a]And Ner begat Kish; and Kish begat Saul; and Saul begat Jonathan, and Malchi-shua, and Abinadab, and Eshbaal.

40 And the son of Jonathan *was* Merib-baal: and Merib-baal begat Micah.

41 And the sons of Micah *were,* Pithon, and Melech, and Tahrea, [a]*and Ahaz.*

42 And Ahaz begat Jarah; and Jarah begat Alemeth, and Azmaveth, and Zimri; and Zimri begat Moza;

43 And Moza begat Binea; and Rephaiah his son, Eleasah his son, Azel his son.

44 And Azel had six sons, whose names *are* these, Azrikam, Bocheru, and Ishmael, and Sheariah, and Obadiah, and Hanan: these *were* the sons of Azel.

Saul killed on mount Gilboa

10 NOW [a]THE Philistines fought against Israel; and the men of Israel fled from before the Philistines, and fell down [1]slain in mount Gilboa.

2 And the Philistines followed hard after Saul, and after his sons; and the Philistines slew Jonathan, and [1]Abinadab, and Malchi-shua, the sons of Saul.

3 And the battle went sore against Saul, and the [1]archers [2]hit him, and he was wounded of the archers.

4 Then said Saul to his armourbearer, Draw thy sword, and thrust me through therewith; lest these uncircumcised come and [1]abuse me. But his armourbearer would not; for he was sore afraid. So Saul took a sword, and fell upon it.

5 And when his armourbearer saw that Saul was dead, he fell likewise on the sword, and died.

6 So Saul died, and his three sons, and all his house died together.

7 And when all the men of Israel that *were* in the valley saw that they fled, and that Saul and his sons were dead, then they forsook their cities, and fled: and the Philistines came and dwelt in them.

8 ¶ And it came to pass on the morrow, when the Philistines came to strip the slain, that they found Saul and his sons fallen in mount Gilboa.

9 And when they had stripped him, they took his head, and his armour, and sent into the land of the Philistines round

22 [a]ch. 26:1,2 [b]1 Sam. 9:9 [1]Heb. *founded* [2]Or, *trust*

25 [a]2 Ki. 11:5

26 [1]Or, *trust* [2]Or, *storehouses*

28 [1]Heb. *bring them in by tale, and carry them out by tale*

29 [1]Or, *vessels*

30 [a]Ex. 30:23

31 [a]Lev. 2:5 & 6:21 [1]Or, *trust* [2]Or, *on flat plates,* or, *slices*

32 [a]Lev. 24:8 [1]Heb. *bread of ordering*

33 [a]ch. 6:31 & 25:1 [1]Heb. *upon them*

35 [a]ch. 8:29

39 [a]ch. 8:33

41 [a]ch. 8:35

10:1 [a]1 Sam. 31:1, 2 [1]Or, *wounded*

2 [1]Or, *Ishui;* see 1 Sam. 14:49

3 [1]Heb. *shooters with bows* [2]Heb. *found him*

4 [1]Or, *mock me*

about, to carry tidings unto their idols, and to the people.

10 [a]And they put his armour in the house of their gods, and fastened his head in the temple of Dagon.

11 ¶ And when all Jabesh-gilead heard all that the Philistines had done to Saul,

12 They arose, all the valiant men, and took away the body of Saul, and the bodies of his sons, and brought them to Jabesh, and buried their bones under the oak in Jabesh, and fasted seven days.

13 ¶ So Saul died for his transgression which he [1]committed against the LORD, [a]*even* against the word of the LORD, which he kept not, and also for asking *counsel* of *one that had* a familiar spirit, [b]to inquire *of it;*

14 And inquired not of the LORD: therefore he slew him, and [a]turned the kingdom unto David the son of [1]Jesse.

David, king of all Israel

11 THEN [a]ALL Israel gathered themselves to David unto Hebron, saying, Behold, we *are* thy bone and thy flesh.

2 And moreover [1]in time past, even when Saul was king, thou *wast* he that leddest out and broughtest in Israel: and the LORD thy God said unto thee, Thou shalt [a]feed[2] my people Israel, and thou shalt be ruler over my people Israel.

3 Therefore came all the elders of Israel to the king to Hebron; and David made a covenant with them in Hebron before the LORD; and [a]they anointed David king over Israel, according to the word of the LORD [1]by [b]Samuel.

4 ¶ And David and all Israel [a]went to Jerusalem, which *is* Jebus; [b]where the Jebusites *were,* the inhabitants of the land.

5 And the inhabitants of Jebus said to David, Thou shalt not come hither. Nevertheless David took the castle of Zion, which *is* the city of David.

6 And David said, Whosoever smiteth the Jebusites first shall be [1]chief and captain. So Joab the son of Zeruiah went first up, and was chief.

7 And David dwelt in the castle; therefore they called [1]it the city of David.

8 And he built the city round about, even from Millo round about: and Joab [1]repaired the rest of the city.

9 So David [1]waxed greater and greater: for the LORD of hosts *was* with him. U

David's mighty men

10 ¶ [a]These also *are* the chief of the mighty men whom David had, who [1]strengthened themselves with him in his kingdom, *and* with all Israel, to make him king, according to [b]the word of the LORD concerning Israel.

11 And this *is* the number of the mighty men whom David had; Jashobeam, [1]an Hachmonite, the chief of the captains: he lifted up his spear against three hundred slain *by him* at one time.

12 And after him *was* Eleazar the son of Dodo, the Ahohite, who *was one* of the three mighties.

13 He was with David at [1]Pas-dammim, and there the Philistines were gathered together to battle, where was a parcel of ground full of barley; and the people fled from before the Philistines.

14 And they [1]set themselves in the midst of *that* parcel, and delivered it, and slew the Philistines; and the LORD saved *them* by a great [a]deliverance.

15 ¶ Now [1]three of the thirty captains [a]went down to the rock to David, into the cave of Adullam; and the host of the Philistines encamped [b]in the valley of Rephaim.

16 And David *was* then in the hold, and the Philistines' garrison *was* then at Bethlehem.

17 And David longed, and said, Oh that one would give me drink of the water of the well of Bethlehem, that *is* at the gate!

18 And the three brake through the host of the Philistines, and drew water out of the well of Bethlehem, that *was* by the gate, and took *it,* and brought *it* to David: but David would not drink *of* it, but poured it out to the LORD,

19 And said, My God forbid it me, that I should do this thing: shall I drink the blood of these men [1]that have put their lives in jeopardy? for with *the jeopardy of* their lives they brought it. Therefore he would not drink it. These things did these three mightiest.

20 ¶ [a]And Abishai the brother of Joab, he was chief of the three: for lifting up his spear against three hundred, he slew

10 [a]1 Sam. 31:10
13 [a]1 Sam. 13:13; & 15:23 [b]1 Sam. 28:7 [1]Heb. *transgressed*
14 [a]1 Sam. 15:28; 2 Sam. 3:9,10 & 5:3 [1]Heb. *Isai*
11:1 [a]2 Sam. 5:1
2 [a]Ps. 78:71 [1]Heb. *both yesterday and the third day* [2]Or, *rule*
3 [a]2 Sam. 5:3 [b]1 Sam. 16:1,12,13 [1]Heb. *by the hand of*
4 [a]2 Sam. 5:6 [b]Judg. 1:21 & 19:10
6 [1]Heb. *head*
7 [1]i.e. *Zion;* see 2 Sam. 5:7
8 [1]Heb. *revived*
9 [1]Heb. *went in going and increasing*
10 [a]2 Sam. 23:8 [b]1 Sam. 16:1,12 [1]Or, *held strongly with him*
11 [1]Or, *son of Hachmoni*
13 [1]Or, *Ephes-dammim;* see 1 Sam. 17:1
14 [a]Judg. 1:21 & 19:10 [1]Or, *stood*
15 [a]2 Sam. 23:13 [b]ch. 14:9 [1]Or, *three captains over the thirty*
19 [1]Heb. *with their lives?*
20 [a]2 Sam. 23:18

U 1Ch 4:10 ◄► 2Ch 1:12

them, and had a name among the three.
21 [a]Of the three, he was more honourable than the two; for he was their captain: howbeit he attained not to the *first*
three.
22 Benaiah the son of Jehoiada, the
son of a valiant man of Kabzeel, [1]who had
done many acts; [a]he slew two lionlike
men of Moab: also he went down and
slew a lion in a pit in a snowy day.
23 And he slew an Egyptian, [1]a man of
great stature, five cubits high; and in the
Egyptian's hand *was* a spear like a
weaver's beam; and he went down to
him with a staff, and plucked the spear
out of the Egyptian's hand, and slew him
with his own spear.
24 These *things* did Benaiah the son of
Jehoiada, and had the name among the
three mighties.
25 Behold, he was honourable among
the thirty, but attained not to the *first*
three: and David set him over his guard.
26 ¶ Also the valiant men of the armies *were,* [a]Asahel the brother of Joab,
Elhanan the son of Dodo of Bethlehem,
27 [1]Shammoth the [2]Harorite, Helez
the [3]Pelonite,
28 Ira the son of Ikkesh the Tekoite,
Abiezer the Antothite,
29 [1]Sibbecai the Hushathite, [2]Ilai the
Ahohite,
30 Maharai the Netophathite, [1]Heled
the son of Baanah the Netophathite,
31 Ithai the son of Ribai of Gibeah,
that pertained to the children of Benjamin, Benaiah the Pirathonite,
32 [1]Hurai of the brooks of Gaash,
[2]Abiel the Arbathite,
33 Azmaveth the Baharumite, Eliahba
the Shaalbonite,
34 The sons of [1]Hashem the Gizonite,
Jonathan the son of Shage the Hararite,
35 Ahiam the son of [1]Sacar the Hararite, [2]Eliphal the son of [3]Ur,
36 Hepher the Mecherathite, Ahijah
the Pelonite,
37 [1]Hezro the Carmelite, [2]Naarai the
son of Ezbai,
38 Joel the brother of Nathan, Mibhar
[1]the son of Haggeri,
39 Zelek the Ammonite, Naharai the
Berothite, the armourbearer of Joab the
son of Zeruiah,
40 Ira the Ithrite, Gareb the Ithrite,
41 Uriah the Hittite, Zabad the son of
Ahlai,
42 Adina the son of Shiza the Reuben-
ite, a captain of the Reubenites, and
thirty with him,
43 Hanan the son of Maachah, and
Joshaphat the Mithnite,
44 Uzzia the Ashterathite, Shama and
Jehiel the sons of Hothan the Aroerite,
45 Jediael the [1]son of Shimri, and Joha
his brother, the Tizite,
46 Eliel the Mahavite, and Jeribai, and
Joshaviah, the sons of Elnaam, and Ith-
mah the Moabite,
47 Eliel, and Obed, and Jasiel the
Mesobaite.

David's supporters

12 NOW [a]THESE *are* they that came
to David to [b]Ziklag, [1]while he yet
kept himself close because of Saul the son
of Kish: and they *were* among the mighty
men, helpers of the war.
2 *They were* armed with bows, and
could use both the right hand and [a]the
left in *hurling* stones and *shooting* arrows
out of a bow, *even* of Saul's brethren of
Benjamin.
3 The chief *was* Ahiezer, then Joash,
the sons of [1]Shemaah the Gibeathite; and
Jeziel, and Pelet, the sons of Azmaveth;
and Berachah, and Jehu the Antothite,
4 And Ismaiah the Gibeonite, a mighty
man among the thirty, and over the
thirty; and Jeremiah, and Jahaziel, and Johanan, and Josabad the Gederathite,
5 Eluzai, and Jerimoth, and Bealiah,
and Shemariah, and Shephatiah the Haru-
phite,
6 Elkanah, and Jesiah, and Azareel,
and Joezer, and Jashobeam, the Korhites,
7 And Joelah, and Zebadiah, the sons
of Jeroham of Gedor.
8 And of the Gadites there separated
themselves unto David into the hold to
the wilderness men of might, *and* men
[1]of war *fit* for the battle, that could handle shield and buckler, whose faces *were*
like the faces of lions, and *were* [a]as[2] swift
as the roes upon the mountains;
9 Ezer the first, Obadiah the second,
Eliab the third,
10 Mishmannah the fourth, Jeremiah
the fifth,
11 Attai the sixth, Eliel the seventh,
12 Johanan the eighth, Elzabad the
ninth,
13 Jeremiah the tenth, Machbanai the
eleventh.

21 [a]2 Sam. 23:19
22 [a]2 Sam. 23:20 [1]Heb. *great of deeds*
23 [1]Heb. *a man of measure*
26 [a]2 Sam. 23:24
27 [1]Or, *Shammah* [2]Or, *Harodite;* see 2 Sam. 23:25 [3]Or, *Paltite;* see 2 Sam. 23:26
29 [1]Or, *Mebunnai* [2]Or, *Zalmon*
30 [1]Or, *Heleb*
32 [1]Or, *Hiddai* [2]Or, *Abi-albon*
34 [1]Or, *Jashen;* see 2 Sam. 23:32,33
35 [1]Or, *Sharar* [2]Or, *Eliphelet* [3]Or, *Ahasbai*
37 [1]Or, *Hezrai* [2]Or, *Paarai the Arbite*
38 [1]Or, *the Haggerite*
45 [1]Or, *Shimrite*
12:1 [a]1 Sam. 27:2 [b]1 Sam. 27:6 [1]Heb. being *yet shut up*
2 [a]Judg. 20:16
3 [1]Or, *Hasmaah*
8 [a]2 Sam. 2:18 [1]Heb. *of the host* [2]Heb. *as the roes upon the mountains to make haste*

14 These *were* of the sons of Gad, captains of the host: [1]one of the least *was* over an hundred, and the greatest over a thousand.

15 These *are* they that went over Jordan in the first month, when it had [1]overflown all his [a]banks; and they put to flight all *them* of the valleys, *both* toward the east, and toward the west.

16 And there came of the children of Benjamin and Judah to the hold unto David.

17 And David went out [1]to meet them, and answered and said unto them, If ye be come peaceably unto me to help me, mine heart shall [2]be knit unto you: but if *ye be come* to betray me to mine enemies, seeing *there is* no [3]wrong in mine hands, the God of our fathers look *thereon,* and rebuke *it.*

E 18 Then [a]the[1] spirit came upon [b]Amasai, *who was* chief of the captains, *and he said,* Thine *are we,* David, and on thy side, thou son of Jesse: peace, peace *be* unto thee, and peace *be* to thine helpers; for thy God helpeth thee. Then David received them, and made them captains of the band.

19 And there fell *some* of Manasseh to David, [a]when he came with the Philistines against Saul to battle: but they helped them not: for the lords of the Philistines upon advisement sent him away, saying, [b]He will fall to his master Saul [1]to *the jeopardy of* our heads.

20 As he went to Ziklag, there fell to him of Manasseh, Adnah, and Jozabad, and Jediael, and Michael, and Jozabad, and Elihu, and Zilthai, captains of the thousands that *were* of Manasseh.

21 And they helped David [1]against [a]the band *of the rovers:* for they *were* all mighty men of valour, and were captains in the host.

22 For at *that* time day by day there came to David to help him, until *it was* a great host, like the host of God.

The number of David's men

23 ¶ And these *are* the numbers of the [1,2]bands *that were* ready armed to the war, *and* [a]came to David to Hebron, to [b]turn the kingdom of Saul to him, [c]according to the word of the LORD.

24 The children of Judah that bare shield and spear *were* six thousand and eight hundred, ready [1]armed to the war.

25 Of the children of Simeon, mighty men of valour for the war, seven thousand and one hundred.

26 Of the children of Levi four thousand and six hundred.

27 And Jehoiada *was* the leader of the Aaronites, and with him *were* three thousand and seven hundred;

28 And [a]Zadok, a young man mighty of valour, and of his father's house twenty and two captains.

29 And of the children of Benjamin, the [1]kindred of Saul, three thousand: for hitherto [a]the[2] greatest part of them had kept the ward of the house of Saul.

30 And of the children of Ephraim twenty thousand and eight hundred, mighty men of valour, [1]famous throughout the house of their fathers.

31 And of the half tribe of Manasseh eighteen thousand, which were expressed by name, to come and make David king.

32 And of the children of Issachar, [a]*which were men* that had understanding of the times, to know what Israel ought to do; the heads of them *were* two hundred; and all their brethren *were* at their commandment.

33 Of Zebulun, such as went forth to battle, [1]expert in war, with all instruments of war, fifty thousand, which could [2]keep rank: *they were* [a]not[3] of double heart.

34 And of Naphtali a thousand captains, and with them with shield and spear thirty and seven thousand.

35 And of the Danites expert in war twenty and eight thousand and six hundred.

36 And of Asher, such as went forth to battle, [1]expert in war, forty thousand.

37 And on the other side of Jordan, of the Reubenites, and the Gadites, and of

14 [1]Or, *one that was least could resist an hundred, and the greatest a thousand*
15 [a]Josh. 3:15 [1]Heb. *filled over*
17 [1]Heb. *before them* [2]Heb. *be one* [3]Or, *violence*
18 [a]Judg. 6:34 [b]2 Sam. 17:25 [1]Heb. *the spirit clothed Amasai*
19 [a]1 Sam. 29:2 [b]1 Sam. 29:4 [1]Heb. *on our heads*
21 [a]1 Sam. 30:1,9, 10 [1]Or, *with a band*
23 [a]2 Sam. 2:3 [b]ch. 10:14 [c]1 Sam. 16:1 [1]Or, *captains,* or, *men* [2]Heb. *heads*
24 [1]Or, *prepared*
28 [a]2 Sam. 8:17
29 [a]2 Sam. 2:8,9 [1]Heb. *brethren* [2]Heb. *a multitude of them*
30 [1]Heb. *men of names*
32 [a]Esth. 1:13
33 [a]Ps. 12:2 [1]Or, *rangers of battle,* or, *ranged in battle* [2]Or, *set the battle in array* [3]Heb. *without a heart and a heart*
36 [1]Or, *keeping their rank*

E *2Ki 3:15* ◀▶ *1Ch 28:12*

12:32 The tribe of Issachar was made up of "men that had understanding of the times, to know what Israel ought to do." A proper understanding of God's plan is a benefit to any generation. We, too, should be aware of God's plan, live holy lives, long for Christ's return and look for the fulfillment of God's prophecies in our time.

the half tribe of Manasseh, with all manner of instruments of war for the battle, an hundred and twenty thousand.

38 All these men of war, that could keep rank, came with a perfect heart to Hebron, to make David king over all Israel: and all the rest also of Israel *were* of one heart to make David king.

39 And there they were with David three days, eating and drinking: for their brethren had prepared for them.

40 Moreover they that were nigh them, *even* unto Issachar and Zebulun and Naphtali, brought bread on asses, and on camels, and on mules, and on oxen, *and* [1]meat, meal, cakes of figs, and bunches of raisins, and wine, and oil, and oxen, and sheep abundantly: for *there was* joy in Israel.

The ark taken to Obed-edom

13 AND DAVID consulted with the captains of thousands and hundreds, *and* with every leader.

2 And David said unto all the congregation of Israel, If *it seem* good unto you, and *that it be* of the LORD our God, [1]let us send abroad unto our brethren every where, *that are* [a]left in all the land of Israel, and with them *also* to the priests and Levites *which are* [2]in their cities *and* suburbs, that they may gather themselves unto us:

3 And let us [1]bring again the ark of our God to us: [a]for we inquired not at it in the days of Saul.

4 And all the congregation said that they would do so: for the thing was right in the eyes of all the people.

5 So [a]David gathered all Israel together, from [b]Shihor of Egypt even unto the entering of Hemath, to bring the ark of God [c]from Kirjath-jearim.

6 And David went up, and all Israel, to [a]Baalah, *that is,* to Kirjath-jearim, which *belonged* to Judah, to bring up thence the ark of God the LORD, [b]that dwelleth *between* the cherubims, whose name is called *on it.*

7 And they [1]carried the ark of God [a]in a new cart [b]out of the house of Abinadab: and Uzza and Ahio drave the cart.

8 [a]And David and all Israel played before God with all *their* might, and with [1]singing, and with harps, and with psalteries, and with timbrels, and with cymbals, and with trumpets.

40 [1]Or, *victual of meal*

13:2 [a]1 Sam. 31:1; Is. 37:4 [1]Heb. *let us break forth* and *send* [2]Heb. *in the cities of their suburbs*

3 [a]1 Sam. 7:1,2 [1]Heb. *bring about*

5 [a]1 Sam. 7:5 [b]Josh. 13:3 [c]1 Sam. 6:21 & 7:1

6 [a]Josh. 15:9,60 [b]1 Sam. 4:4; 2 Sam. 6:2

7 [a]See Num. 4:15 [b]1 Sam. 7:1 [1]Heb. *made the ark to ride*

8 [a]2 Sam. 6:5 [1]Heb. *songs*

9 [1]Called *Nachon* in 2 Sam. 6:6 [2]Heb. *shook* it

10 [a]Num. 4:15; ch. 15:13,15 [b]Lev. 10:2

11 [1]i.e. *The breach of Uzza*

13 [1]Heb. *removed*

14 [a]2 Sam. 6:11 [b]As Gen. 30:27; ch. 26:5

14:1 [a]2 Sam. 5:11

3 [1]Heb. *yet*

4 [a]ch. 3:5

7 [1]Or, *Eliada;* see 2 Sam. 5:16

8 [a]2 Sam. 5:17

9 [a]ch. 11:15

9 ¶ And when they came unto the threshingfloor of [1]Chidon, Uzza put forth his hand to hold the ark; for the oxen [2]stumbled.

10 And the anger of the LORD was kindled against Uzza, and he smote him, [a]because he put his hand to the ark: and there he [b]died before God.

11 And David was displeased, because the LORD had made a breach upon Uzza: wherefore that place is called [1]Perez-uzza to this day.

12 And David was afraid of God that day, saying, How shall I bring the ark of God *home* to me?

13 So David [1]brought not the ark *home* to himself to the city of David, but carried it aside into the house of Obed-edom the Gittite.

14 [a]And the ark of God remained with the family of Obed-edom in his house three months. And the LORD blessed [b]the house of Obed-edom, and all that he had.

David defeats the Philistines

14 NOW [a]HIRAM king of Tyre sent messengers to David, and timber of cedars, with masons and carpenters, to build him an house.

2 And David perceived that the LORD had confirmed him king over Israel, for his kingdom was lifted up on high, because of his people Israel.

3 ¶ And David took [1]more wives at Jerusalem: and David begat more sons and daughters.

4 Now [a]these *are* the names of *his* children which he had in Jerusalem; Shammua, and Shobab, Nathan, and Solomon,

5 And Ibhar, and Elishua, and Elpalet,

6 And Nogah, and Nepheg, and Japhia,

7 And Elishama, and [1]Beeliada, and Eliphalet.

8 ¶ And when the Philistines heard that [a]David was anointed king over all Israel, all the Philistines went up to seek David. And David heard *of it,* and went out against them.

9 And the Philistines came and spread themselves [a]in the valley of Rephaim.

10 And David inquired of God, saying, Shall I go up against the Philistines? and wilt thou deliver them into mine hand? I

I *2Ki 19:30–31* ◀▶ *1Ch 14:15*

And the LORD said unto him, Go up; for I
will deliver them into thine hand.
11 So they came up to Baal-perazim;
and David smote them there. Then David
said, God hath broken in upon mine enemies by mine hand like the breaking
forth of waters: therefore they called the
name of that place [l]Baal-perazim.
12 And when they had left their gods
there, David gave a commandment, and
they were burned with fire.
13 [a]And the Philistines yet again
spread themselves abroad in the valley.
14 Therefore David inquired again of
God; and God said unto him, Go not up
after them; turn away from them, [a]and
come upon them over against the mulberry trees.
15 And it shall be, when thou shalt
hear a sound of going in the tops of the
mulberry trees, *that* then thou shalt go
out to battle: for God is gone forth before
thee to smite the host of the Philistines.
16 David therefore did as God commanded him: and they smote the host of
the Philistines from [a]Gibeon even to
Gazer.
17 And [a]the fame of David went out
into all lands; and the LORD [b]brought the
fear of him upon all nations.

The ark brought to Jerusalem

15 AND *DAVID* made him houses in
the city of David, and prepared a
place for the ark of God, [a]and pitched for
it a tent.
2 Then David said, [l]None ought to
carry the [a]ark of God but the Levites: for
them hath the LORD chosen to carry the
ark of God, and to minister unto him for
ever.
3 And David [a]gathered all Israel together to Jerusalem, to bring up the ark of
the LORD unto his place, which he had
prepared for it.
4 And David assembled the children of
Aaron, and the Levites:
5 Of the sons of Kohath; Uriel the
chief, and his [l]brethren an hundred and
twenty:
6 Of the sons of Merari; Asaiah the
chief, and his brethren two hundred and
twenty:
7 Of the sons of Gershom; Joel the
chief, and his brethren an hundred and
thirty:
8 Of the sons of [a]Elizaphan; Shemaiah
the chief, and his brethren two hundred:
9 Of the sons of [a]Hebron; Eliel the
chief, and his brethren fourscore:
10 Of the sons of Uzziel; Amminadab
the chief, and his brethren an hundred
and twelve.
11 And David called for Zadok and
Abiathar the priests, and for the Levites,
for Uriel, Asaiah, and Joel, Shemaiah, and
Eliel, and Amminadab,
12 And said unto them, Ye *are* the
chief of the fathers of the Levites: Sanctify yourselves, *both* ye and your brethren, that ye may bring up the ark of the
LORD God of Israel unto *the place that* I
have prepared for it.
13 For [a]because ye *did it* not at the
first, [b]the LORD our God made a breach
upon us, for that we sought him not after
the due order.
14 So the priests and the Levites sanctified themselves to bring up the ark of
the LORD God of Israel.
15 And the children of the Levites
bare the ark of God upon their shoulders
with the staves thereon, as [a]Moses commanded according to the word of the
LORD.
16 And David spake to the chief of the
Levites to appoint their brethren *to be*
the singers with instruments of music,
psalteries and harps and cymbals, sounding, by lifting up the voice with joy.
17 So the Levites appointed [a]Heman
the son of Joel; and of his brethren,
[b]Asaph the son of Berechiah; and of the
sons of Merari their brethren, [c]Ethan the
son of Kushaiah;
18 And with them their brethren of
the second *degree,* Zechariah, Ben, and
Jaaziel, and Shemiramoth, and Jehiel, and
Unni, Eliab, and Benaiah, and Maaseiah,
and Mattithiah, and Elipheleh, and Mikneiah, and Obed-edom, and Jeiel, the
porters.
19 So the singers, Heman, Asaph, and
Ethan, *were appointed* to sound with
cymbals of brass;
20 And Zechariah, and [l]Aziel, and
Shemiramoth, and Jehiel, and Unni, and
Eliab, and Maaseiah, and Benaiah, with
psalteries [a]on Alamoth;
21 And Mattithiah, and Elipheleh, and
Mikneiah, and Obed-edom, and Jeiel, and

11 [l]i.e. *A place of breaches*
13 [a]2 Sam. 5:22
14 [a]2 Sam. 5:23
16 [a]2 Sam. 5:25 *Geba*
17 [a]Josh. 6:27; 2 Chr. 26:8 [b]Deut. 2:25 & 11:25
15:1 [a]ch. 16:1
2 [a]Num. 4:2,15; Deut. 10:8 & 31:9 [l]Heb. It is *not to carry the ark of God, but for the Levites*
3 [a]1 Ki. 8:1; ch. 13:5
5 [l]Or, *kinsmen*
8 [a]Ex. 6:22
9 [a]Ex. 6:18
13 [a]2 Sam. 6:3; ch. 13:7 [b]ch. 13:10,11
15 [a]Ex. 25:14; Num. 4:15 & 7:9
17 [a]ch. 6:33 [b]ch. 6:39 [c]ch. 6:44
20 [a]Ps. 46,title [l]Or, *Jaaziel;* see ver. 18

1Ch 14:10 ◀ ▶ 1Ch 16:15–18

Azaziah, with harps [a]on the Sheminith to excel.

22 And Chenaniah, chief of the Levites, [1]*was* for [2]song: he instructed about the song, because he *was* skilful.

23 And Berechiah and Elkanah *were* doorkeepers for the ark.

24 And Shebaniah, and Jehoshaphat, and Nethaneel, and Amasai, and Zechariah, and Benaiah, and Eliezer, the priests, [a]did blow with the trumpets before the ark of God: and Obed-edom and Jehiah *were* doorkeepers for the ark.

25 ¶ So [a]David, and the elders of Israel, and the captains over thousands, went to bring up the ark of the covenant of the LORD out of the house of Obed-edom with joy.

26 And it came to pass, when God helped the Levites that bare the ark of the covenant of the LORD, that they offered seven bullocks and seven rams.

27 And David *was* clothed with a robe of fine linen, and all the Levites that bare the ark, and the singers, and Chenaniah the master of the [1]song with the singers: David also *had* upon him an ephod of linen.

28 [a]Thus all Israel brought up the ark of the covenant of the LORD with shouting, and with sound of the cornet, and with trumpets, and with cymbals, making a noise with psalteries and harps.

29 ¶ And it came to pass, [a]*as* the ark of the covenant of the LORD came to the city of David, that Michal the daughter of Saul looking out at a window saw king David dancing and playing: and she despised him in her heart.

16 SO [a]THEY brought the ark of God, and set it in the midst of the tent that David had pitched for it: and they offered burnt sacrifices and peace offerings before God.

2 And when David had made an end of offering the burnt offerings and the peace offerings, he blessed the people in the name of the LORD.

3 And he dealt to every one of Israel, both man and woman, to every one a loaf of bread, and a good piece of flesh, and a flagon *of wine.*

21 [a]Ps. 6,title
22 [1]Or, was *for the carriage: he instructed about the carriage* [2]Heb. *lifting up*
24 [a]Num. 10:8; Ps. 81:3
25 [a]2 Sam. 6:12,13; 1 Ki. 8:1
27 [1]Or, *carriage*
28 [a]ch. 13:8
29 [a]2 Sam. 6:16
16:1 [a]2 Sam. 6:17-19
4 [a]Ps. 38 & 70,title
5 [1]Heb. *with instruments of psalteries and harps*
7 [a]See 2 Sam. 23:1
8 [a]Ps. 105:1-15
16 [a]Gen. 17:2 & 26:3 & 28:13 & 35:11
18 [1]Heb. *the cord*
19 [a]Gen. 34:30 [1]Heb. *men of number*

4 ¶ And he appointed *certain* of the Levites to minister before the ark of the LORD, and to [a]record, and to thank and praise the LORD God of Israel:

5 Asaph the chief, and next to him Zechariah, Jeiel, and Shemiramoth, and Jehiel, and Mattithiah, and Eliab, and Benaiah, and Obed-edom: and Jeiel [1]with psalteries and with harps; but Asaph made a sound with cymbals;

6 Benaiah also and Jahaziel the priests with trumpets continually before the ark of the covenant of God.

David's psalm of gratitude

7 ¶ Then on that day David delivered [a]first *this psalm* to thank the LORD into the hand of Asaph and his brethren.

8 [a]Give thanks unto the LORD, call upon his name, make known his deeds among the people. T

9 Sing unto him, sing psalms unto him, talk ye of all his wondrous works.

10 Glory ye in his holy name: let the heart of them rejoice that seek the LORD.

11 Seek the LORD and his strength, seek his face continually.

12 Remember his marvellous works that he hath done, his wonders, and the judgments of his mouth;

13 O ye seed of Israel his servant, ye children of Jacob, his chosen ones.

14 He *is* the LORD our God; his judgments *are* in all the earth.

15 Be ye mindful always of his covenant; the word *which* he commanded to a thousand generations; I

16 *Even of the* [a]*covenant* which he made with Abraham, and of his oath unto Isaac;

17 And hath confirmed the same to Jacob for a law, *and* to Israel *for* an everlasting covenant,

18 Saying, Unto thee will I give the land of Canaan, [1]the lot of your inheritance;

19 When ye were but [1]few, [a]even a few, and strangers in it.

20 And *when* they went from nation to

T *1Sa 7:12* ◀ ▶ *Ps 22:22–23*
I *1Ch 14:15* ◀ ▶ *1Ch 16:35*

16:15 King David reminded Israel of the eternal covenant that God had made with Abraham regarding their possession of the land of Canaan and their position as God's chosen nation (see note on Abrahamic covenant at Ge15:4).

nation, and from *one* kingdom to another people;

L 21 He suffered no man to do them wrong: yea, he [a]reproved kings for their sakes,

22 *Saying,* [a]Touch not mine anointed, and do my prophets no harm.

23 [a]Sing unto the LORD, all the earth; show forth from day to day his salvation.

24 Declare his glory among the heathen; his marvellous works among all nations.

25 For great *is* the LORD, and greatly to be praised: he also *is* to be feared above all gods.

26 For all the gods [a]of the people *are* idols: but the LORD made the heavens.

27 Glory and honour *are* in his presence; strength and gladness *are* in his place.

28 Give unto the LORD, ye kindreds of the people, give unto the LORD glory and strength.

S 29 Give unto the LORD the glory *due* unto his name: bring an offering, and come before him: worship the LORD in the beauty of holiness.

M 30 Fear before him, all the earth: the world also shall be stable, that it be not moved.

31 Let the heavens be glad, and let the earth rejoice: and let *men* say among the nations, The LORD reigneth.

32 Let the sea roar, and the fulness thereof: let the fields rejoice, and all that *is* therein.

J 33 Then shall the trees of the wood sing out at the presence of the LORD, because he cometh to judge the earth.

34 [a]O give thanks unto the LORD; for *he is* good; for his mercy *endureth* for ever.

I 35 [a]And say ye, Save us, O God of our salvation, and gather us together, and deliver us from the heathen, that we may give thanks to thy holy name, *and* glory in thy praise.

36 [a]Blessed *be* the LORD God of Israel for ever and ever. And all [b]the people said, Amen, and praised the LORD.

37 ¶ So he left there before the ark of the covenant of the LORD Asaph and his brethren, to minister before the ark continually, as every day's work required:

38 And Obed-edom with their brethren, threescore and eight; Obed-edom also the son of Jeduthun and Hosah *to be* porters:

39 And Zadok the priest, and his brethren the priests, [a]before the tabernacle of the LORD [b]in the high place that *was* at Gibeon,

40 To offer burnt offerings unto the LORD upon the altar of the burnt offering continually [a]morningʹ and evening, and *to do* according to all that is written in the law of the LORD, which he commanded Israel;

41 And with them Heman and Jeduthun, and the rest that were chosen, who were expressed by name, to give thanks to the LORD, [a]because his mercy *endureth* for ever;

42 And with them Heman and Jeduthun with trumpets and cymbals for those that should make a sound, and with musical instruments of God. And the sons of Jeduthun *were* ʹporters.

43 [a]And all the people departed every man to his house: and David returned to bless his house.

Nathan's warning to David

17 NOW [a]IT came to pass, as David sat in his house, that David said to Nathan the prophet, Lo, I dwell in an house of cedars, but the ark of the covenant of the LORD *remaineth* under curtains.

2 Then Nathan said unto David, Do all that *is* in thine heart; for God *is* with thee.

3 ¶ And it came to pass the same night, that the word of God came to Nathan, saying,

4 Go and tell David my servant, Thus saith the LORD, Thou shalt not build me an house to dwell in:

5 For I have not dwelt in an house since the day that I brought up Israel unto this day; but ʹhave gone from tent to tent, and from *one* tabernacle *to another.*

6 Wheresoever I have walked with all Israel, spake I a word to any of the judges of Israel, whom I commanded to feed my people, saying, Why have ye not built me an house of cedars?

7 Now therefore thus shalt thou say

16:21 [a]Gen. 12:17 & 20:3; Ex. 7:15-18
22 [a]Ps. 105:15
23 [a]Ps. 96:1
26 [a]Lev. 19:4
34 [a]Ps. 106:1 & 107:1 & 118:1 & 136:1
35 [a]Ps. 106:47,48
36 [a]1 Ki. 8:15 [b]Deut. 27:15
39 [a]ch. 21:29; 2 Chr. 1:3 [b]1 Ki. 3:4
40 [a]Ex. 29:38; Num. 28:3 ʹHeb. *in the morning, and in the evening*
41 [a]ver. 34; 2 Chr. 5:13 & 7:3; Ezra 3:11; Jer. 33:11
42 ʹHeb. *for the gate*
43 [a]2 Sam. 6:19,20
17:1 [a]2 Sam. 7:1
5 ʹHeb. *have been*

L *2Ki 6:16–17* ◀ ▶ *1Ch 28:20*
S *1Ki 18:21* ◀ ▶ *1Ch 28:9*
M *1Ki 2:45* ◀ ▶ *1Ch 17:10–13*
J *1Sa 2:10* ◀ ▶ *Ps 1:5*
I *1Ch 16:15–18* ◀ ▶ *1Ch 17:9*

unto my servant David, Thus saith the LORD of hosts, I took thee from the sheepcote, *even* [l]from following the sheep, that thou shouldest be ruler over my people Israel:

8 And I have been with thee whithersoever thou hast walked, and have cut off all thine enemies from before thee, and have made thee a name like the name of the great men that *are* in the earth.

I 9 Also I will ordain a place for my people Israel, and will plant them, and they shall dwell in their place, and shall be moved no more; neither shall the children of wickedness waste them any more, as at the beginning,

M 10 And since the time that I commanded judges *to be* over my people Israel. Moreover I will subdue all thine enemies. Furthermore I tell thee that the LORD will build thee an house.

11 ¶ And it shall come to pass, when thy days be expired that thou must go *to be* with thy fathers, that I will raise up thy seed after thee, which shall be of thy sons; and I will establish his kingdom.

12 He shall build me an house, and I will establish his throne for ever.

13 [a]I will be his father, and he shall be my son: and I will not take my mercy away from him, as I took *it* from *him* that was before thee:

M 14 But [a]I will settle him in mine house and in my kingdom for ever: and his throne shall be established for evermore.

15 According to all these words, and according to all this vision, so did Nathan speak unto David.

David's prayer

16 ¶ [a]And David the king came and sat before the LORD, and said, Who *am* I, O LORD God, and what *is* mine house, that thou hast brought me hitherto?

17 And *yet* this was a small thing in thine eyes, O God; for thou hast *also* spoken of thy servant's house for a great while to come, and hast regarded me according to the estate of a man of high degree, O LORD God.

18 What can David *speak* more to thee for the honour of thy servant? for thou knowest thy servant.

19 O LORD, for thy servant's sake, and according to thine own heart, hast thou done all this greatness, in making known all *these* [l]great things.

20 O LORD, *there is* none like thee, neither *is there any* God beside thee, according to all that we have heard with our ears. O

21 And what one nation in the earth *is* like thy people Israel, whom God went to redeem *to be* his own people, to make thee a name of greatness and terribleness, by driving out nations from before thy people, whom thou hast redeemed out of Egypt?

22 For thy people Israel didst thou make thine own people for ever; and thou, LORD, becamest their God. I M

23 Therefore now, LORD, let the thing that thou hast spoken concerning thy servant and concerning his house be established for ever, and do as thou hast said.

24 Let it even be established, that thy name may be magnified for ever, saying, The LORD of hosts *is* the God of Israel, *even* a God to Israel: and *let* the house of David thy servant *be* established before thee.

25 For thou, O my God, [l]hast told thy servant that thou wilt build him an house: therefore thy servant hath found *in his heart* to pray before thee.

26 And now, LORD, thou art God, and hast promised this goodness unto thy servant:

27 Now therefore [l]let it please thee to bless the house of thy servant, that it may be before thee for ever: for thou blessest, O LORD, and *it shall be* blessed for ever.

7 [l]Heb. *from after*
13 [a]2 Sam. 7:14,15
14 [a]Luke 1:33
16 [a]2 Sam. 7:18
19 [l]Heb. *greatnesses*
25 [l]Heb. *hast revealed the ear of thy servant*
27 [l]Or, *it hath pleased thee*

I *1Ch 16:35* ◀▶ *1Ch 17:22*
M *1Ch 16:30–33* ◀▶ *1Ch 17:14*
M *1Ch 17:10–13* ◀▶ *1Ch 17:22*

O *1Ki 8:60* ◀▶ *Job 8:11–15*
I *1Ch 17:9* ◀▶ *1Ch 22:9*
M *1Ch 17:14* ◀▶ *1Ch 28:4*

17:9 God promised to settle Israel in the land, and they would never be removed from it. This prophecy will not be completely fulfilled until the return of Christ.

17:14 Though this prophecy was initially fulfilled in David's son Solomon, this prophecy also extends into the future to David's descendant Jesus Christ, God's Messiah, who will rule Israel forever (see note on Davidic covenant at 2Sa 7:16).

David's victories

18 NOW AFTER this [a]it came to pass, that David smote the Philistines, and subdued them, and took Gath and her towns out of the hand of the Philistines.

2 And he smote Moab; and the Moabites became David's servants, *and* brought gifts.

3 ¶ And David smote [1]Hadarezer king of Zobah unto Hamath, as he went to stablish his dominion by the river Euphrates.

4 And David took from him a thousand chariots, and [a]seven thousand horsemen, and twenty thousand footmen: David also houghed all the chariot *horses,* but reserved of them an hundred chariots.

5 And when the Syrians of [1]Damascus came to help Hadarezer king of Zobah, David slew of the Syrians two and twenty thousand men.

S 6 Then David put *garrisons* in Syria-damascus; and the Syrians became David's servants, *and* brought gifts. Thus the LORD preserved David whithersoever he went.

7 And David took the shields of gold that were on the servants of Hadarezer, and brought them to Jerusalem.

8 Likewise from [1]Tibhath, and from Chun, cities of Hadarezer, brought David very much brass, wherewith [a]Solomon made the brasen sea, and the pillars, and the vessels of brass.

9 ¶ Now when [1]Tou king of Hamath heard how David had smitten all the host of Hadarezer king of Zobah;

10 He sent [1]Hadoram his son to king David, [2]to inquire of his welfare, and [3]to congratulate him, because he had fought against Hadarezer, and smitten him; (for Hadarezer [4]had war with Tou;) and *with him* all manner of vessels of gold and silver and brass.

11 ¶ Them also king David dedicated unto the LORD, with the silver and the gold that he brought from all *these* nations; from Edom, and from Moab, and from the children of Ammon, and from the Philistines, and from Amalek.

12 Moreover [1]Abishai the son of Zeruiah slew of the Edomites in the valley of salt [a]eighteen thousand.

S 13 ¶ [a]And he put garrisons in Edom; and all the Edomites became David's servants. Thus the LORD preserved David whithersoever he went.

14 ¶ So David reigned over all Israel, and executed judgment and justice among all his people.

15 And Joab the son of Zeruiah *was* over the host; and Jehoshaphat the son of Ahilud, [1]recorder.

16 And Zadok the son of Ahitub, and [1]Abimelech the son of Abiathar, *were* the priests; and [2]Shavsha was scribe;

17 [a]And Benaiah the son of Jehoiada *was* over the Cherethites and the Pelethites; and the sons of David *were* chief [1]about the king.

David and the Ammonites

19 NOW [a]IT came to pass after this, that Nahash the king of the children of Ammon died, and his son reigned in his stead.

2 And David said, I will show kindness unto Hanun the son of Nahash, because his father showed kindness to me. And David sent messengers to comfort him concerning his father. So the servants of David came into the land of the children of Ammon to Hanun, to comfort him.

3 But the princes of the children of Ammon said to Hanun, [1]Thinkest thou that David doth honour thy father, that he hath sent comforters unto thee? are not his servants come unto thee for to search, and to overthrow, and to spy out the land?

4 Wherefore Hanun took David's servants, and shaved them, and cut off their garments in the midst hard by their buttocks, and sent them away.

5 Then there went *certain,* and told David how the men were served. And he sent to meet them: for the men were greatly ashamed. And the king said, Tarry at Jericho until your beards be grown, and *then* return.

6 ¶ And when the children of Ammon saw that they had made themselves [1]odious to David, Hanun and the children of Ammon sent a thousand talents of silver to hire them chariots and horsemen out of Mesopotamia, and out of Syria-maachah, [a]and out of Zobah.

7 So they hired thirty and two thousand chariots, and the king of Maachah and his people; who came and pitched before Medeba. And the children of Am-

S 2Sa 8:14 ◄► 1Ch 18:13
S 1Ch 18:6 ◄► Job 34:29

18:1 [a]2 Sam. 8:1
3 [1]Or, *Hadadezer;* see 2 Sam. 8:3
4 [a]2 Sam. 8:4 *seven hundred*
5 [1]Heb. *Darmesek*
8 [a]1 Ki. 7:15,23; 2 Chr. 4:12,15,16 [1]Called *Betah* and *Berothai* in 2 Sam. 8:8
9 [1]Or, *Toi;* see 2 Sam. 8:9
10 [1]Or, *Joram;* see 2 Sam. 8:10 [2]Or, *to salute* [3]Heb. *to bless* [4]Heb. *was the man of wars*
12 [a]2 Sam. 8:13 [1]Heb. *Abshai*
13 [a]2 Sam. 8:14
15 [1]Or, *remembrancer*
16 [1]Called *Ahimelech* in 2 Sam. 8:17 [2]Called *Seraiah* in 2 Sam. 8:17 and *Shisha* in 1 Ki. 4:3
17 [a]2 Sam. 8:18 [1]Heb. *at the hand of the king*
19:1 [a]2 Sam. 10:1
3 [1]Heb. *In thine eyes doth David*
6 [a]ch. 18:5,9 [1]Heb. *to stink*

mon gathered themselves together from their cities, and came to battle.

8 And when David heard *of it,* he sent Joab, and all the host of the mighty men.

9 And the children of Ammon came out, and put the battle in array before the gate of the city: and the kings that were come *were* by themselves in the field.

10 Now when Joab saw that [1]the battle was set against him before and behind, he chose out of all the [2]choice of Israel, and put *them* in array against the Syrians.

11 And the rest of the people he delivered unto the hand of [1]Abishai his brother, and they set *themselves* in array against the children of Ammon.

12 And he said, If the Syrians be too strong for me, then thou shalt help me: but if the children of Ammon be too strong for thee, then I will help thee.

13 Be of good courage, and let us behave ourselves valiantly for our people, and for the cities of our God: and let the LORD do *that which is* good in his sight.

14 So Joab and the people that *were* with him drew nigh before the Syrians unto the battle; and they fled before him.

15 And when the children of Ammon saw that the Syrians were fled, they likewise fled before Abishai his brother, and entered into the city. Then Joab came to Jerusalem.

16 ¶ And when the Syrians saw that they were put to the worse before Israel, they sent messengers, and drew forth the Syrians that *were* beyond the [1]river: and [2]Shophach the captain of the host of Hadarezer *went* before them.

17 And it was told David; and he gathered all Israel, and passed over Jordan, and came upon them, and set *the battle* in array against them. So when David had put the battle in array against the Syrians, they fought with him.

18 But the Syrians fled before Israel; and David slew of the Syrians seven thousand *men which fought in* chariots, and forty thousand footmen, and killed Shophach the captain of the host.

19 And when the servants of Hadarezer saw that they were put to the worse before Israel, they made peace with David, and became his servants: neither would the Syrians help the children of Ammon any more.

10 [1]Heb. *the face of the battle was* [2]Or, *young men*
11 [1]Heb. *Abshai*
16 [1]i.e. *Euphrates* [2]Or, *Shobach;* see 2 Sam. 10:16
20:1 [a]2 Sam. 11:1 [b]2 Sam. 12:26 [1]Heb. *at the return of the year*
2 [a]2 Sam. 12:30,31 [1]Heb. *the weight of*
4 [a]2 Sam. 21:18 [b]ch. 11:29 [1]Or, *continued* [2]Heb. *stood* [3]Or, *Gob* [4]Or, *Saph;* see 2 Sam. 21:18 [5]Or, *Rapha*
5 [1]Called *Jaareoregim* in 2 Sam. 21:19
6 [a]2 Sam. 21:20 [1]Heb. *a man of measure* [2]Heb. *born to the giant,* or, *Rapha*
7 [1]Or, *reproached* [2]Called *Shammah* in 1 Sam. 16:9
21:1 [a]2 Sam. 24:1
2 [a]ch. 27:23

War with the Philistines

20 AND [a]IT came to pass, that [1]after the year was expired, at the time that kings go out *to battle,* Joab led forth the power of the army, and wasted the country of the children of Ammon, and came and besieged Rabbah. But David tarried at Jerusalem. And [b]Joab smote Rabbah, and destroyed it.

2 And David [a]took the crown of their king from off his head, and found it [1]to weigh a talent of gold, and *there were* precious stones in it; and it was set upon David's head: and he brought also exceeding much spoil out of the city.

3 And he brought out the people that *were* in it, and cut *them* with saws, and with harrows of iron, and with axes. Even so dealt David with all the cities of the children of Ammon. And David and all the people returned to Jerusalem.

4 ¶ And it came to pass after this, [a]that there [1,2]arose war at [3]Gezer with the Philistines; at which time [b]Sibbechai the Hushathite slew [4]Sippai, *that was* of the children of [5]the giant: and they were subdued.

5 And there was war again with the Philistines; and Elhanan the son of [1]Jair slew Lahmi the brother of Goliath the Gittite, whose spear staff *was* like a weaver's beam.

6 And yet again [a]there was war at Gath, where was [1]a man of *great* stature, whose fingers and toes *were* four and twenty, six *on each hand,* and six *on each foot:* and he also was [2]the son of the giant.

7 But when he [1]defied Israel, Jonathan the son of [2]Shimea David's brother slew him.

8 These were born unto the giant in Gath; and they fell by the hand of David, and by the hand of his servants.

David's census

21 AND [a]SATAN stood up against Israel, and provoked David to number Israel.

2 And David said to Joab and to the rulers of the people, Go, number Israel from Beer-sheba even to Dan; [a]and bring the number of them to me, that I may know *it.*

3 And Joab answered, The LORD make his people an hundred times so many more as they *be:* but, my lord the king,

are they not all my lord's servants? why then doth my lord require this thing? why will he be a cause of trespass to Israel?

4 Nevertheless the king's word prevailed against Joab. Wherefore Joab departed, and went throughout all Israel, and came to Jerusalem.

5 ¶ And Joab gave the sum of the number of the people unto David. And all *they of* Israel were a thousand thousand and an hundred thousand men that drew sword: and Judah *was* four hundred threescore and ten thousand men that drew sword.

6 [a]But Levi and Benjamin counted he not among them: for the king's word was abominable to Joab.

7 [′]And God was displeased with this thing; therefore he smote Israel.

M R 8 And David said unto God, [a]I have sinned greatly, because I have done this thing: [b]but now, I beseech thee, do away the iniquity of thy servant; for I have done very foolishly.

J 9 ¶ And the LORD spake unto Gad, David's [a]seer, saying,

10 Go and tell David, saying, Thus saith the LORD, I [′]offer thee three *things:* choose thee one of them, that I may do *it* unto thee.

11 So Gad came to David, and said unto him, Thus saith the LORD, [′]Choose thee

12 [a]Either three years' famine; or three months to be destroyed before thy foes, while that the sword of thine enemies overtaketh *thee;* or else three days the sword of the LORD, even the pestilence, in the land, and the angel of the LORD destroying throughout all the coasts of Israel. Now therefore advise thyself what word I shall bring again to him that sent me.

13 And David said unto Gad, I am in a great strait: let me fall now into the hand of the LORD; for very [′]great *are* his mercies: but let me not fall into the hand of man.

D 14 ¶ So the LORD sent pestilence upon Israel: and there fell of Israel seventy thousand men.

15 And God sent an [a]angel unto Jerusalem to destroy it: and as he was destroying, the LORD beheld, and [b]he repented him of the evil, and said to the angel that destroyed, It is enough, stay now thine hand. And the angel of the LORD stood by the threshingfloor of [′]Ornan the Jebusite.

16 And David lifted up his eyes, and [a]saw the angel of the LORD stand between the earth and the heaven, having a drawn sword in his hand stretched out over Jerusalem. Then David and the elders *of Israel, who were* clothed in sackcloth, fell upon their faces.

17 And David said unto God, *Is it* not I *that* commanded the people to be numbered? even I it is that have sinned and done evil indeed; but *as for* these sheep, what have they done? let thine hand, I pray thee, O LORD my God, be on me, and on my father's house; but not on thy people, that they should be plagued.

18 ¶ Then the [a]angel of the LORD commanded Gad to say to David, that David should go up, and set up an altar unto the LORD in the threshingfloor of Ornan the Jebusite.

19 And David went up at the saying of Gad, which he spake in the name of the LORD.

20 [′]And Ornan turned back, and saw the angel; and his four sons with him hid themselves. Now Ornan was threshing wheat.

21 And as David came to Ornan, Ornan looked and saw David, and went out of the threshingfloor, and bowed himself to David with *his* face to the ground.

22 Then David said to Ornan, [′]Grant me the place of *this* threshingfloor, that I may build an altar therein unto the LORD: thou shalt grant it me for the full price: that the plague may be stayed from the people.

23 And Ornan said unto David, Take *it* to thee, and let my lord the king do *that which is* good in his eyes: lo, I give *thee* the oxen *also* for burnt offerings, and the threshing instruments for wood, and the wheat for the meat offering; I give it all.

24 And king David said to Ornan, Nay; but I will verily buy it for the full price: for I will not take *that* which *is* thine for the LORD, nor offer burnt offerings without cost.

25 So [a]David gave to Ornan for the

6 [a]ch. 27:24
7 [′]Heb. *And it was evil in the eyes of the LORD concerning this thing*
8 [a]2 Sam. 24:10 [b]2 Sam. 12:13
9 [a]See 1 Sam. 9:9
10 [′]Heb. *stretch out*
11 [′]Heb. *Take to thee*
12 [a]2 Sam. 24:13
13 [′]Or, *many*
15 [a]2 Sam. 24:16 [b]See Gen. 6:6 [′]Or, *Araunah;* see 2 Sam. 24:18
16 [a]2 Chr. 3:1
18 [a]2 Chr. 3:1
20 [′]Or, *When Ornan turned back and saw the angel,* then he *and his four sons with him hid themselves*
22 [′]Heb. *Give*
25 [a]2 Sam. 24:24

M *2Ki 22:19* ◄► *2Ch 7:14*
R *2Ki 17:13* ◄► *2Ch 7:14*
J *2Ki 20:17–19* ◄► *2Ch 16:9*
D *2Ki 15:5* ◄► *2Ch 26:19–21*

place six hundred shekels of gold by weight.

26 And David built there an altar unto the LORD, and offered burnt offerings and peace offerings, and called upon the LORD; and [a]he answered him from heaven by fire upon the altar of burnt offering.

27 And the LORD commanded the angel; and he put up his sword again into the sheath thereof.

28 ¶ At that time when David saw that the LORD had answered him in the threshingfloor of Ornan the Jebusite, then he sacrificed there.

29 [a]For the tabernacle of the LORD, which Moses made in the wilderness, and the altar of the burnt offering, *were* at that season in the high place at [b]Gibeon.

30 But David could not go before it to inquire of God: for he was afraid because of the sword of the angel of the LORD.

22 THEN DAVID said, [a]This *is* the house of the LORD God, and this *is* the altar of the burnt offering for Israel.

Preparing to build the temple

2 And David commanded to gather together [a]the strangers that *were* in the land of Israel; and he set masons to hew wrought stones to build the house of God.

3 And David prepared iron in abundance for the nails for the doors of the gates, and for the joinings; and brass in abundance [a]without weight;

4 Also cedar trees in abundance: for the [a]Zidonians and they of Tyre brought much cedar wood to David.

5 And David said, [a]Solomon my son *is* young and tender, and the house *that is* to be builded for the LORD *must be* exceeding magnifical, of fame and of glory throughout all countries: I will *therefore* now make preparation for it. So David prepared abundantly before his death.

6 ¶ Then he called for Solomon his son, and charged him to build an house for the LORD God of Israel.

7 And David said to Solomon, My son, as for me, [a]it was in my mind to build an house [b]unto the name of the LORD my God:

26 [a]Lev. 9:24; 2 Chr. 3:1 & 7:1
29 [a]ch. 16:39 [b]1 Ki. 3:4; ch. 16:39; 2 Chr. 1:3
22:1 [a]Deut. 12:5; 2 Sam. 24:18; ch. 21:18,19,26,28; 2 Chr. 3:1
2 [a]1 Ki. 9:21
3 [a]ver. 14; 1 Ki. 7:47
4 [a]1 Ki. 5:6
5 [a]ch. 29:1
7 [a]2 Sam. 7:2; 1 Ki. 8:17; ch. 17:1 & 28:2 [b]Deut. 12:5, 11
8 [a]1 Ki. 5:3
9 [a]ch. 28:5 [b]1 Ki. 4:25 & 5:4 [f]i.e. *Peaceable*
10 [a]2 Sam. 7:13; 1 Ki. 5:5; ch. 17:12, 13 & 28:6 [b]Heb. 1:5
11 [a]ver. 16
12 [a]1 Ki. 3:9,12
13 [a]Josh. 1:7,8; ch. 28:7 [b]Deut. 31:7,8; Josh. 1:6,7,9; ch. 28:20
14 [a]As ver. 3 [f]Or, *in my poverty*
15 [f]i.e. *masons and carpenters*
16 [a]ver. 11

8 But the word of the LORD came to me, saying, [a]Thou hast shed blood abundantly, and hast made great wars: thou shalt not build an house unto my name, because thou hast shed much blood upon the earth in my sight.

9 [a]Behold, a son shall be born to thee, who shall be a man of rest; and I will give him [b]rest from all his enemies round about: for his name shall be [f]Solomon, and I will give peace and quietness unto Israel in his days. I

10 [a]He shall build an house for my name; and [b]he shall be my son, and I *will be* his father; and I will establish the throne of his kingdom over Israel for ever.

11 Now, my son, [a]the LORD be with thee; and prosper thou, and build the house of the LORD thy God, as he hath said of thee.

12 Only the LORD [a]give thee wisdom and understanding, and give thee charge concerning Israel, that thou mayest keep the law of the LORD thy God.

13 [a]Then shalt thou prosper, if thou takest heed to fulfil the statutes and judgments which the LORD charged Moses with concerning Israel: [b]be strong, and of good courage; dread not, nor be dismayed. I W

14 Now, behold, [f]in my trouble I have prepared for the house of the LORD an hundred thousand talents of gold, and a thousand thousand talents of silver; and of brass and iron [a]without weight; for it is in abundance: timber also and stone have I prepared; and thou mayest add thereto.

15 Moreover *there are* workmen with thee in abundance, hewers and [f]workers of stone and timber, and all manner of cunning men for every manner of work.

16 Of the gold, the silver, and the brass, and the iron, *there is* no number. Arise *therefore,* and be doing, and [a]the LORD be with thee.

17 ¶ David also commanded all the princes of Israel to help Solomon his son, *saying,*

I *1Ch 17:22* ◀▶ *1Ch 22:13*
I *1Ch 22:9* ◀▶ *2Ch 20:7*
W *Jos 8:1* ◀▶ *1Ch 28:20*

22:8–10 God had refused to allow David to build the temple. Rather, his son Solomon would rule in peace and would build the temple in Jerusalem. God would also establish his throne forever.

18 *Is* not the LORD your God with you?
[a]and hath he *not* given you rest on every
side? for he hath given the inhabitants of
the land into mine hand; and the land is
subdued before the LORD, and before his
people.
19 Now set your heart and your soul to
seek the LORD your God; arise therefore,
and build ye the sanctuary of the LORD
God, to [a]bring the ark of the covenant of
the LORD, and the holy vessels of God,
into the house that is to be built [b]to the
name of the LORD.

Priests and Levites assembled

23 SO WHEN David was old and full
of days, he made [a]Solomon his
son king over Israel.
2 ¶ And he gathered together all the
princes of Israel, with the priests and the
Levites.
3 Now the Levites were numbered
from the age of [a]thirty years and upward:
and their number by their polls, man by
man, was thirty and eight thousand.
4 Of which, twenty and four thousand
were [1]to set forward the work of the
house of the LORD; and six thousand *were*
[a]officers and judges:
5 Moreover four thousand *were* porters; and four thousand praised the LORD
with the instruments [a]which I made, *said
David,* to praise *therewith.*
6 And [a]David divided them into
[1]courses among the sons of Levi, *namely,*
Gershon, Kohath, and Merari.
7 ¶ Of the [a]Gershonites *were,* [1]Laa-
dan, and Shimei.
8 The sons of Laadan; the chief *was* Jehiel, and Zetham, and Joel, three.
9 The sons of Shimei; Shelomith, and
Haziel, and Haran, three. These *were* the
chief of the fathers of Laadan.
10 And the sons of Shimei *were,* Jahath, [1]Zina, and Jeush, and Beriah. These
four *were* the sons of Shimei.
11 And Jahath was the chief, and Zizah
the second: but Jeush and Beriah [1]had
not many sons; therefore they were in
one reckoning, according to *their* father's
house.
12 ¶ [a]The sons of Kohath; Amram, Izhar, Hebron, and Uzziel, four.
13 The sons of [a]Amram; Aaron and
Moses: and [b]Aaron was separated, that
he should sanctify the most holy things,
he and his sons for ever, [c]to burn incense
before the LORD, [d]to minister unto him,
and [e]to bless in his name for ever.
14 Now *concerning* Moses the man of
God, [a]his sons were named of the tribe of
Levi.
15 [a]The sons of Moses *were,* Gershom, and Eliezer.
16 Of the sons of Gershom, [a]Shebuel[1]
was the chief.
17 And the sons of Eliezer *were,* [a]Re-
habiah [1]the chief. And Eliezer had none
other sons; but the sons of Rehabiah
[2]were very many.
18 Of the sons of Izhar; [1]Shelomith the
chief.
19 [a]Of the sons of Hebron; Jeriah the
first, Amariah the second, Jahaziel the
third, and Jekameam the fourth.
20 Of the sons of Uzziel; Michah the
first, and Jesiah the second.
21 ¶ [a]The sons of Merari; Mahli, and
Mushi. The sons of Mahli; Eleazar, and
[b]Kish.
22 And Eleazar died, and [a]had no
sons, but daughters: and their [1]brethren
the sons of Kish [b]took them.
23 [a]The sons of Mushi; Mahli, and
Eder, and Jeremoth, three.

The duties of the Levites

24 ¶ These *were* the sons of [a]Levi after
the house of their fathers; *even* the chief
of the fathers, as they were counted by
number of names by their polls, that did
the work for the service of the house of
the LORD, from the age of [b]twenty years
and upward.
25 For David said, The LORD God of Israel [a]hath given rest unto his people,
[1]that they may dwell in Jerusalem for
ever:
26 And also unto the Levites; they
shall no *more* [a]carry the tabernacle, nor
any vessels of it for the service thereof.
27 For by the last words of David the
Levites *were* [1]numbered from twenty
years old and above:
28 Because [a]their[1] office *was* to wait
on the sons of Aaron for the service of the
house of the LORD, in the courts, and in
the chambers, and in the purifying of all
holy things, and the work of the service
of the house of God;
29 Both for [a]the showbread, and for
[b]the fine flour for meat offering, and for
[c]the unleavened cakes, and for [d]*that
which is baked in* the [1]pan, and for that

18 [a]Deut. 12:10; Josh. 22:4; 2 Sam. 7:1; ch. 23:25
19 [a]2 Chr. 5:7 [b]1 Ki. 5:3
23:1 [a]1 Ki. 1:33
3 [a]Num. 4:3
4 [a]Deut. 16:18; 2 Chr. 19:8 [1]Or, *to oversee*
5 [a]2 Chr. 29:25,26
6 [a]Ex. 6:16; Num. 26:57; 2 Chr. 8:14 [1]Heb. *divisions*
7 [a]ch. 26:21 [1]Or, *Libni;* see ch. 6:17
10 [1]Or, *Zizah*
11 [1]Heb. *did not multiply sons*
12 [a]Ex. 6:18
13 [a]Ex. 6:20 [b]Ex. 28:1; Heb. 5:4 [c]Ex. 30:7; 1 Sam. 2:28 [d]Deut. 21:5 [e]Num. 6:23
14 [a]ch. 26:23
15 [a]Ex. 18:3,4
16 [a]ch. 26:24 [1]Or, *Shubael;* see ch. 24:20
17 [a]ch. 26:25 [1]Or, *the first* [2]Heb. *were highly multiplied*
18 [1]Or, *Shelomoth;* see ch. 24:22
19 [a]ch. 24:23
21 [a]ch. 24:26 [b]ch. 24:29
22 [a]ch. 24:28 [b]Num. 36:6 [1]Or, *kinsmen*
23 [a]ch. 24:30
24 [a]Num. 10:17, 21 [b]Num. 1:3; Ezra 3:8
25 [a]ch. 22:18 [1]Or, *and he dwelleth in Jerusalem*
26 [a]Num. 4:5
27 [1]Heb. *number*
28 [a]Neh. 11:24 [1]Heb. *their station was at the hand of the sons of Aaron*
29 [a]Ex. 25:30 [b]Lev. 6:20 [c]Lev. 2:4 [d]Lev. 2:5,7 [1]Or, *flat plate*

which is fried, and for all manner of [e]measure and size;

30 And to stand every morning to thank and praise the LORD, and likewise at even;

31 And to offer all burnt sacrifices unto the LORD [a]in the sabbaths, in the new moons, and on the [b]set feasts, by number, according to the order commanded unto them, continually before the LORD:

32 And that they should [a]keep the charge of the tabernacle of the congregation, and the charge of the holy *place,* and [b]the charge of the sons of Aaron their brethren, in the service of the house of the LORD.

The division of the priests

24 NOW *THESE are* the divisions of the sons of Aaron. [a]The sons of Aaron; Nadab, and Abihu, Eleazar, and Ithamar.

2 But [a]Nadab and Abihu died before their father, and had no children: therefore Eleazar and Ithamar executed the priest's office.

3 And David distributed them, both Zadok of the sons of Eleazar, and Ahimelech of the sons of Ithamar, according to their offices in their service.

4 And there were more chief men found of the sons of Eleazar than of the sons of Ithamar; and *thus* were they divided. Among the sons of Eleazar *there were* sixteen chief men of the house of *their* fathers, and eight among the sons of Ithamar according to the house of their fathers.

5 Thus were they divided by lot, one sort with another; for the governors of the sanctuary, and governors *of the house* of God, were of the sons of Eleazar, and of the sons of Ithamar.

6 And Shemaiah the son of Nethaneel the scribe, *one* of the Levites, wrote them before the king, and the princes, and Zadok the priest, and Ahimelech the son of Abiathar, and *before* the chief of the fathers of the priests and Levites: one [f]principal household being taken for Eleazar, and *one* taken for Ithamar.

7 Now the first lot came forth to Jehoiarib, the second to Jedaiah,

8 The third to Harim, the fourth to Seorim,

9 The fifth to Malchijah, the sixth to Mijamin,

10 The seventh to Hakkoz, the eighth to [a]Abijah,

11 The ninth to Jeshuah, the tenth to Shecaniah,

12 The eleventh to Eliashib, the twelfth to Jakim,

13 The thirteenth to Huppah, the fourteenth to Jeshebeab,

14 The fifteenth to Bilgah, the sixteenth to Immer,

15 The seventeenth to Hezir, the eighteenth to Aphses,

16 The nineteenth to Pethahiah, the twentieth to Jehezekel,

17 The one and twentieth to Jachin, the two and twentieth to Gamul,

18 The three and twentieth to Delaiah, the four and twentieth to Maaziah.

19 These *were* the orderings of them in their service [a]to come into the house of the LORD, according to their manner, under Aaron their father, as the LORD God of Israel had commanded him.

20 ¶ And the rest of the sons of Levi *were these:* Of the sons of Amram; [a]Shubael: of the sons of Shubael; Jehdeiah.

21 Concerning [a]Rehabiah: of the sons of Rehabiah, the first *was* Isshiah.

22 Of the Izharites; [a]Shelomoth: of the sons of Shelomoth; Jahath.

23 And the sons *of* [a]*Hebron;* Jeriah *the first,* Amariah the second, Jahaziel the third, Jekameam the fourth.

24 *Of* the sons of Uzziel; Michah: of the sons of Michah; Shamir.

25 The brother of Michah *was* Isshiah: of the sons of Isshiah; Zechariah.

26 [a]The sons of Merari *were* Mahli and Mushi: the sons of Jaaziah; Beno.

27 ¶ The sons of Merari by Jaaziah; Beno, and Shoham, and Zaccur, and Ibri.

28 Of Mahli *came* Eleazar, [a]who had no sons.

29 Concerning Kish: the son of Kish *was* Jerahmeel.

30 [a]The sons also of Mushi; Mahli, and Eder, and Jerimoth. These *were* the sons of the Levites after the house of their fathers.

31 These likewise cast lots over against their brethren the sons of Aaron in the presence of David the king, and Zadok, and Ahimelech, and the chief of the fathers of the priests and Levites, even the principal fathers over against their younger brethren.

29 [e]Lev. 19:35
31 [a]Num. 10:10 [b]Lev. 23:4
32 [a]Num. 1:53 [b]Num. 3:6-9
24:1 [a]Lev. 10:1,6; Num. 26:60
2 [a]Num. 3:4 & 26:61
6 [f]Heb. *house of the father*
10 [a]Neh. 12:4,17; Luke 1:5
19 [a]ch. 9:25
20 [a]ch. 23:16 *Shebuel*
21 [a]ch. 23:17
22 [a]ch. 23:18 *Shelomith*
23 [a]ch. 23:19 & 26:31
26 [a]Ex. 6:19; ch. 23:21
28 [a]ch. 23:22
30 [a]ch. 23:23

The arrangements for music

25 MOREOVER DAVID and the captains of the host separated to the service of the sons of [a]Asaph, and of Heman, and of Jeduthun, who should prophesy with harps, with psalteries, and with cymbals: and the number of the workmen according to their service was:

2 Of the sons of Asaph; Zaccur, and Joseph, and Nethaniah, and [1]Asarelah, the sons of Asaph under the hands of Asaph, which prophesied [a]according[2] to the order of the king.

3 Of Jeduthun: the sons of Jeduthun; Gedaliah, and [1]Zeri, and Jeshaiah, Hashabiah, and Mattithiah, [2]six, under the hands of their father Jeduthun, who prophesied with a harp, to give thanks and to praise the LORD.

4 Of Heman: the sons of Heman; Bukkiah, Mattaniah, [1]Uzziel, [2]Shebuel, and Jerimoth, Hananiah, Hanani, Eliathah, Giddalti, and Romamti-ezer, Joshbekashah, Mallothi, Hothir, *and* Mahazioth:

5 All these *were* the sons of Heman the king's seer in the [1]words of God, to lift up the horn. And God gave to Heman fourteen sons and three daughters.

6 All these *were* under the hands of their father for song *in* the house of the LORD, with cymbals, psalteries, and harps, for the service of the house of God, [a]according[1] to the king's order to Asaph, Jeduthun, and Heman.

7 So the number of them, with their brethren that were instructed in the songs of the LORD, *even* all that were cunning, was two hundred fourscore and eight.

8 ¶ And they cast lots, ward against *ward,* as well the small as the great, [a]the teacher as the scholar.

9 Now the first lot came forth for Asaph to Joseph: the second to Gedaliah, who with his brethren and sons *were* twelve:

10 The third to Zaccur, *he,* his sons, and his brethren, *were* twelve:

11 The fourth to Izri, *he,* his sons, and his brethren, *were* twelve:

12 The fifth to Nethaniah, *he,* his sons, and his brethren, *were* twelve:

13 The sixth to Bukkiah, *he,* his sons, and his brethren, *were* twelve:

14 The seventh to Jesharelah, *he,* his sons, and his brethren, *were* twelve:

15 The eighth to Jeshaiah, *he,* his sons, and his brethren, *were* twelve:

16 The ninth to Mattaniah, *he,* his sons, and his brethren, *were* twelve:

17 The tenth to Shimei, *he,* his sons, and his brethren, *were* twelve:

18 The eleventh to Azareel, *he,* his sons, and his brethren, *were* twelve:

19 The twelfth to Hashabiah, *he,* his sons, and his brethren, *were* twelve:

20 The thirteenth to Shubael, *he,* his sons, and his brethren, *were* twelve:

21 The fourteenth to Mattithiah, *he,* his sons, and his brethren, *were* twelve:

22 The fifteenth to Jeremoth, *he,* his sons, and his brethren, *were* twelve:

23 The sixteenth to Hananiah, *he,* his sons, and his brethren, *were* twelve:

24 The seventeenth to Joshbekashah, *he,* his sons, and his brethren, *were* twelve:

25 The eighteenth to Hanani, *he,* his sons, and his brethren, *were* twelve:

26 The nineteenth to Mallothi, *he,* his sons, and his brethren, *were* twelve:

27 The twentieth to Eliathah, *he,* his sons, and his brethren, *were* twelve:

28 The one and twentieth to Hothir, *he,* his sons, and his brethren, *were* twelve:

29 The two and twentieth to Giddalti, *he,* his sons, and his brethren, *were* twelve:

30 The three and twentieth to Mahazioth, *he,* his sons, and his brethren, *were* twelve:

31 The four and twentieth to Romamti-ezer, *he,* his sons, and his brethren, *were* twelve.

The arrangements for porters

26 CONCERNING THE divisions of the porters: Of the Korhites *was* [1]Meshelemiah the son of Kore, of the sons of [2]Asaph.

2 And the sons of Meshelemiah *were,* Zechariah the firstborn, Jediael the second, Zebadiah the third, Jathniel the fourth,

3 Elam the fifth, Jehohanan the sixth, Elioenai the seventh.

4 Moreover the sons of Obed-edom *were,* Shemaiah the firstborn, Jehozabad the second, Joah the third, and Sacar the fourth, and Nethaneel the fifth,

5 Ammiel the sixth, Issachar the sev-

25:1 [a]ch. 6:33,39, 44

2 [a]ver. 6 [1]Otherwise called *Jesharelah;* see ver. 14 [2]Heb. *by the hands of the king*

3 [1]Or, *Izri;* see ver. 11 [2]With Shimei mentioned; see ver. 17

4 [1]Or, *Azareel;* see ver. 18 [2]Or, *Shubael;* see ver. 20

5 [1]Or, *matters*

6 [a]ver. 2 [1]Heb. *by the hands of the king*

8 [a]2 Chr. 23:13

26:1 [1]Or, *Shelemiah;* see ver. 14 [2]Or, *Ebiasaph;* see ch. 6:37 & 9:19

enth, Peulthai the eighth: for God blessed
[1]him.
6 Also unto Shemaiah his son were
sons born, that ruled throughout the
house of their father: for they *were*
mighty men of valour.
7 The sons of Shemaiah; Othni, and
Rephael, and Obed, Elzabad, whose
brethren *were* strong men, Elihu, and
Semachiah.
8 All these of the sons of Obed-edom:
they and their sons and their brethren,
able men for strength for the service,
were threescore and two of Obed-edom.
9 And Meshelemiah had sons and
brethren, strong men, eighteen.
10 Also [a]Hosah, of the children of Merari, had sons; Simri the chief, (for
though he was not the firstborn, yet his
father made him the chief;)
11 Hilkiah the second, Tebaliah the
third, Zechariah the fourth: all the sons
and brethren of Hosah *were* thirteen.
12 Among these *were* the divisions of
the porters, *even* among the chief men,
having wards one against another, to
minister in the house of the LORD.
13 ¶ And they cast lots, [1]as well the
small as the great, according to the house
of their fathers, for every gate.
14 And the lot eastward fell to [1]Shele-
miah. Then for Zechariah his son, a wise
counsellor, they cast lots; and his lot
came out northward.
15 To Obed-edom southward; and to
his sons the house of [1]Asuppim.
16 To Shuppim and Hosah *the lot*
came forth westward, with the gate Shal-
lecheth, by the causeway of the going
[a]up, ward against ward.
17 Eastward *were* six Levites, northward four a day, southward four a day,
and toward Asuppim two *and* two.
18 At Parbar westward, four at the
causeway, *and* two at Parbar.
19 These *are* the divisions of the porters among the sons of Kore, and among
the sons of Merari.

The arrangements for treasures

20 ¶ And of the Levites, Ahijah *was*
[a]over the treasures of the house of God,
and over the treasures of the [1]dedicated
things.
21 *As concerning* the sons of [1]Laadan;
the sons of the Gershonite Laadan, chief
fathers, *even* of Laadan the Gershonite,
were [2]Jehieli.
22 The sons of Jehieli; Zetham, and
Joel his brother, *which were* over the
treasures of the house of the LORD.
23 Of the Amramites, *and* the Izharites, the Hebronites, *and* the Uzzielites:
24 And [a]Shebuel the son of Gershom,
the son of Moses, *was* ruler of the treasures.
25 And his brethren by Eliezer; Rehabiah his son, and Jeshaiah his son, and
Joram his son, and Zichri his son, and
[a]Shelomith his son.
26 Which Shelomith and his brethren
were over all the treasures of the dedicated things, which David the king, and
the chief fathers, the captains over thousands and hundreds, and the captains of
the host, had dedicated.
27 [1]Out of the spoils won in battles did
they dedicate to maintain the house of
the LORD.
28 And all that Samuel [a]the seer, and
Saul the son of Kish, and Abner the son of
Ner, and Joab the son of Zeruiah, had
dedicated; *and* whosoever had dedicated
any thing, it was under the hand of Shelomith, and of his brethren.

The officers and judges

29 ¶ Of the Izharites, Chenaniah and
his sons *were* for the outward business
over Israel, for [a]officers and judges.
30 *And* of the Hebronites, Hashabiah
and his brethren, men of valour, a thousand and seven hundred, *were* [1]officers
among them of Israel on this side Jordan
westward in all the business of the LORD,
and in the service of the king.
31 Among the Hebronites *was* [a]Jerijah
the chief, *even* among the Hebronites, according to the generations of his fathers.
In the fortieth year of the reign of David
they were sought for, and there were
found among them mighty men of valour
[b]at Jazer of Gilead.
32 And his brethren, men of valour,
were two thousand and seven hundred
chief fathers, whom king David made rulers over the Reubenites, the Gadites, and
the half tribe of Manasseh, for every matter pertaining to God, and [a]affairs[1] of the
king.

5 [1]i.e. Obed-edom as ch. 13:14
10 [a]ch. 16:38
13 [1]Or, *as well for the small as for the great*
14 [1]Called *Meshelemiah* in ver. 1
15 [1]Heb. *Gatherings*
16 [a]1 Ki. 10:5; 2 Chr. 9:4
20 [a]ch. 28:12; Mal. 3:10 [1]Heb. *holy things*
21 [1]Or, *Libni;* see ch. 6:17 [2]Or, *Jehiel;* see ch. 23:8 & 29:8
24 [a]ch. 23:16
25 [a]ch. 23:18
27 [1]Heb. *Out of the battles and spoils*
28 [a]1 Sam. 9:9
29 [a]ch. 23:4
30 [1]Heb. *over the charge*
31 [a]ch. 23:19 [b]See Josh. 21:39
32 [a]2 Chr. 19:11 [1]Heb. *thing*

Military and civil officials

27 NOW THE children of Israel after
their number, *to wit,* the chief fathers and captains of thousands and hundreds, and their officers that served the
king in any matter of the courses, which
came in and went out month by month
throughout all the months of the year, of
every course *were* twenty and four
thousand.
2 Over the first course for the first
month *was* [a]Jashobeam the son of Zabdiel: and in his course *were* twenty and
four thousand.
3 Of the children of Perez *was* the
chief of all the captains of the host for the
first month.
4 And over the course of the second
month *was* [l]Dodai an Ahohite, and of his
course *was* Mikloth also the ruler: in his
course likewise *were* twenty and four
thousand.
5 The third captain of the host for the
third month *was* Benaiah the son of Jehoiada, a [l]chief priest: and in his course
were twenty and four thousand.
6 This *is that* Benaiah, *who was*
[a]mighty *among* the thirty, and above the
thirty: and in his course *was* Ammizabad
his son.
7 The fourth *captain* for the fourth
month *was* [a]Asahel the brother of Joab,
and Zebadiah his son after him: and in his
course *were* twenty and four thousand.
8 The fifth captain for the fifth month
was Shamhuth the Izrahite: and in his
course *were* twenty and four thousand.
9 The sixth *captain* for the sixth
month *was* [a]Ira the son of Ikkesh the Tekoite: and in his course *were* twenty and
four thousand.
10 The seventh *captain* for the seventh month *was* [a]Helez the Pelonite, of
the children of Ephraim: and in his
course *were* twenty and four thousand.
11 The eighth *captain* for the eighth
month *was* [a]Sibbecai the Hushathite, of
the Zarhites: and in his course *were*
twenty and four thousand.
12 The ninth *captain* for the ninth
month *was* [a]Abiezer the Anetothite, of
the Benjamites: and in his course *were*
twenty and four thousand.
13 The tenth *captain* for the tenth
month *was* [a]Maharai the Netophathite,
of the Zarhites: and in his course *were*
twenty and four thousand.
14 The eleventh *captain* for the eleventh month *was* [a]Benaiah the Pirathonite, of the children of Ephraim: and in his
course *were* twenty and four thousand.
15 The twelfth *captain* for the twelfth
month *was* [l]Heldai the Netophathite, of
Othniel: and in his course *were* twenty
and four thousand.
16 ¶ Furthermore over the tribes of Israel: the ruler of the Reubenites *was* Eliezer the son of Zichri: of the Simeonites,
Shephatiah the son of Maachah:
17 Of the Levites, [a]Hashabiah the son
of Kemuel: of the Aaronites, Zadok:
18 Of Judah, [a]Elihu, *one* of the brethren of David: of Issachar, Omri the son of
Michael:
19 Of Zebulun, Ishmaiah the son of
Obadiah: of Naphtali, Jerimoth the son of
Azriel:
20 Of the children of Ephraim, Hoshea
the son of Azaziah: of the half tribe of
Manasseh, Joel the son of Pedaiah:
21 Of the half *tribe* of Manasseh in Gilead, Iddo the son of Zechariah: of Benjamin, Jaasiel the son of Abner:
22 Of Dan, Azareel the son of Jeroham. These *were* the princes of the tribes
of Israel.
23 ¶ But David took not the number of
them from twenty years old and under:
because [a]the LORD had said he would increase Israel like to the stars of the
heavens.
24 Joab the son of Zeruiah began to
number, but he finished not, because
[a]there fell wrath for it against Israel; neither [l]was the number put in the account
of the chronicles of king David.
25 ¶ And over the king's treasures *was*
Azmaveth the son of Adiel: and over the
storehouses in the fields, in the cities,
and in the villages, and in the castles, *was*
Jehonathan the son of Uzziah:
26 And over them that did the work of
the field for tillage of the ground *was* Ezri
the son of Chelub:
27 And over the vineyards *was* Shimei
the Ramathite: [l]over the increase of the
vineyards for the wine cellars *was* Zabdi
the Shiphmite:
28 And over the olive trees and the
sycamore trees that *were* in the low
plains *was* Baal-hanan the Gederite: and
over the cellars of oil *was* Joash:

27:2 [a]2 Sam. 23:8; ch. 11:11
4 [l]Or, *Dodo; see* 2 Sam. 23:9
5 [l]Or, *principal officer;* see 1 Ki. 4:5
6 [a]2 Sam. 23:20, 22,23; ch. 11:22
7 [a]2 Sam. 23:24; ch. 11:26
9 [a]ch. 11:28
10 [a]ch. 11:27
11 [a]2 Sam. 21:18
12 [a]ch. 11:28
13 [a]2 Sam. 23:28; ch. 11:30
14 [a]ch. 11:31
15 [l]Or, *Heled;* see ch. 11:30
17 [a]ch. 26:30
18 [a]1 Sam. 16:6 *Eliab*
23 [a]Gen. 15:5
24 [a]2 Sam. 24:15; ch 21:7 [l]Heb. *ascended*
27 [l]Heb. *over that which was of the vineyards*

29 And over the herds that fed in Sharon *was* Shitrai the Sharonite: and over the herds *that were* in the valleys *was* Shaphat the son of Adlai:

30 Over the camels also *was* Obil the Ishmaelite: and over the asses *was* Jehdeiah the Meronothite:

31 And over the flocks *was* Jaziz the Hagerite. All these *were* the rulers of the substance which *was* king David's.

32 Also Jonathan David's uncle was a counsellor, a wise man, and a [1]scribe: and Jehiel the [2]son of Hachmoni *was* with the king's sons:

33 And [a]Ahithophel *was* the king's counsellor: and [b]Hushai the Archite *was* the king's companion:

34 And after Ahithophel *was* Jehoiada the son of Benaiah, and [a]Abiathar: and the general of the king's army *was* [b]Joab.

David's instructions to Solomon

28 AND DAVID assembled all the princes of Israel, [a]the princes of the tribes, and [b]the captains of the companies that ministered to the king by course, and the captains over the thousands, and captains over the hundreds, and [c]the stewards over all the substance and [1]possession of the king, [2]and of his sons, with the [3]officers, and with [d]the mighty men, and with all the valiant men, unto Jerusalem.

2 Then David the king stood up upon his feet, and said, Hear me, my brethren, and my people: *As for me,* [a]I *had* in mine heart to build an house of rest for the ark of the covenant of the LORD, and for [b]the footstool of our God, and had made ready for the building:

3 But God said unto me, [a]Thou shalt not build an house for my name, because thou *hast been* a man of war, and hast shed [1]blood.

M 4 Howbeit the LORD God of Israel [a]chose me before all the house of my father to be king over Israel for ever: for he hath chosen [b]Judah *to be* the ruler; and of the house of Judah, [c]the house of my father; and [d]among the sons of my father he liked me to make *me* king over all Israel:

5 [a]And of all my sons, (for the LORD hath given me many sons,) [b]he hath chosen Solomon my son to sit upon the throne of the kingdom of the LORD over Israel.

6 And he said unto me, [a]Solomon thy son, he shall build my house and my courts: for I have chosen him *to be* my son, and I will be his father.

7 Moreover I will establish his kingdom for ever, [a]if he be [1]constant to do my commandments and my judgments, as at this day.

8 Now therefore in the sight of all Israel the congregation of the LORD, and in the audience of our God, keep and seek for all the commandments of the LORD your God: that ye may possess this good land, and leave *it* for an inheritance for your children after you for ever.

9 ¶ And thou, Solomon my son, [a]know thou the God of thy father, and serve him [b]with a perfect heart and with a willing mind: for [c]the LORD searcheth all hearts, and understandeth all the imaginations of the thoughts: [d]if thou seek him, he will be found of thee; but if thou forsake him, he will cast thee off for ever. E H L S

10 Take heed now; [a]for the LORD hath chosen thee to build an house for the sanctuary: be strong, and do *it.*

11 ¶ Then David gave to Solomon his son [a]the pattern of the porch, and of the houses thereof, and of the treasuries thereof, and of the upper chambers thereof, and of the inner parlours thereof, and of the place of the mercy seat,

12 And the pattern [1]of all that he had by the spirit, of the courts of the house of the LORD, and of all the chambers round about, [a]of the treasuries of the house of God, and of the treasuries of the dedicated things: E T

32 [1]Or, *secretary* [2]Or, *Hachmonite*
33 [a]2 Sam. 15:12 [b]2 Sam. 15:37 & 16:16
34 [a]1 Ki. 1:7 [b]ch. 11:6
28:1 [a]ch. 27:16 [b]ch. 27:1,2 [c]ch. 27:25 [d]ch. 11:10 [1]Or, *cattle* [2]Or, *and his sons* [3]Or, *eunuchs*
2 [a]2 Sam. 7:2 [b]Ps. 99:5 & 132:7
3 [a]2 Sam. 7:5,13; 1 Ki. 5:3; ch. 17:4 & 22:8 [1]Heb. *bloods*
4 [a]1 Sam. 16:7-13 [b]Gen. 49:8; ch. 5:2 [c]1 Sam. 16:1 [d]1 Sam. 16:12,13
5 [a]ch. 3:1 & 23:1 [b]ch. 22:9
6 [a]2 Sam. 7:13,14; ch. 22:9,10; 2 Chr. 1:9
7 [a]ch. 22:13 [1]Heb. *strong*
9 [a]Jer. 9:24; Hos. 4:1; John 17:3 [b]2 Ki. 20:3 [c]1 Sam. 16:7; 1 Ki. 8:39; ch. 29:17; Jer. 11:20 & 17:10 & 20:12; Rev. 2:23 [d]2 Chr. 15:2
10 [a]ver. 6
11 [a]ver. 19; See Ex. 25:40
12 [a]ch. 26:20 [1]Heb. *of all that was with him*

M *1Ch 17:22* ◀▶ *2Ch 6:16*

E *2Ki 19:27* ◀▶ *2Ch 6:30*
H *1Ki 2:33* ◀▶ *2Ch 36:16*
L *2Sa 12:13* ◀▶ *2Ch 7:14*
S *1Ch 16:29* ◀▶ *2Ch 7:14*
E *1Ch 12:18* ◀▶ *2Ch 15:1*
T *2Sa 23:1–2* ◀▶ *2Ch 20:14–15*

28:4 David declared that God had chosen him "to be king over Israel for ever" indicating that one of David's descendants would rule forever from David's throne as the Messiah. This prophecy will be fulfilled when Christ assumes the throne in his Messianic kingdom.

13 Also for the courses of the priests and the Levites, and for all the work of the service of the house of the LORD, and for all the vessels of service in the house of the LORD.

14 *He gave* of gold by weight for *things* of gold, for all instruments of all manner of service; *silver also* for all instruments of silver by weight, for all instruments of every kind of service:

15 Even the weight for the candlesticks of gold, and for their lamps of gold, by weight for every candlestick, and for the lamps thereof: and for the candlesticks of silver by weight, *both* for the candlestick, and *also* for the lamps thereof, according to the use of every candlestick.

16 And by weight *he gave* gold for the tables of showbread, for every *table; and likewise* silver for the tables of silver:

17 Also pure gold for the fleshhooks, and the bowls, and the cups: and for the golden basins *he gave gold* by weight for every basin; and *likewise silver* by weight for every basin of silver:

18 And for the altar of incense refined gold by weight; and gold for the pattern of the chariot of the [a]cherubims, that spread out *their wings,* and covered the ark of the covenant of the LORD.

19 All *this, said David,* [a]the LORD made me understand in writing by *his* hand upon me, *even* all the works of this pattern.

L W 20 And David said to Solomon his son, [a]Be strong and of good courage, and do *it:* fear not, nor be dismayed: for the LORD God, *even* my God, *will be* with thee; [b]he will not fail thee, nor forsake thee, until thou hast finished all the work for the service of the house of the LORD.

21 And, behold, [a]the courses of the priests and the Levites, *even they shall be with thee* for all the service of the house of God: and *there shall be* with thee for all manner of workmanship [b]every willing skilful man, for any manner of service: also the princes and all the people *will be* wholly at thy commandment.

L *1Ch 16:21–22* ◄► *2Ch 32:22*
W *1Ch 22:13* ◄► *2Ch 19:11*

18 [a]Ex. 25:18-22; 1 Sam. 4:4; 1 Ki. 6:23
19 [a]ver. 11,12; See Ex. 25,40
20 [a]Deut. 31:7,8; Josh. 1:6,7,9; ch. 22:13 [b]Josh. 1:5
21 [a]ch. 24 & 25 & 26 [b]Ex. 35:25,26
29:1 [a]1 Ki. 3:7; ch. 22:5; Prov. 4:3
2 [a]See Is. 54:11, 12; Rev. 21:18
4 [a]1 Ki. 9:28
5 [1]Heb. *to fill his hand*
6 [a]ch. 27:1 [b]ch. 27:25
8 [a]ch. 26:21
9 [a]2 Cor. 9:7

David invites the people to give

29 FURTHERMORE DAVID the king said unto all the congregation, Solomon my son, whom alone God hath chosen, *is yet* [a]young and tender, and the work *is* great: for the palace *is* not for man, but for the LORD God.

2 Now I have prepared with all my might for the house of my God the gold for *things to be made* of gold, and the silver for *things* of silver, and the brass for *things* of brass, the iron for *things* of iron, and wood for *things* of wood; [a]onyx stones, and *stones* to be set, glistering stones, and of divers colours, and all manner of precious stones, and marble stones in abundance.

3 Moreover, because I have set my affection to the house of my God, I have of mine own proper good, of gold and silver, *which* I have given to the house of my God, over and above all that I have prepared for the holy house,

4 *Even* three thousand talents of gold, of the gold of [a]Ophir, and seven thousand talents of refined silver, to overlay the walls of the houses *withal:*

5 The gold for *things* of gold, and the silver for *things* of silver, and for all manner of work *to be made* by the hands of artificers. And who *then* is willing [1]to consecrate his service this day unto the LORD?

6 ¶ Then [a]the chief of the fathers and princes of the tribes of Israel, and the captains of thousands and of hundreds, with [b]the rulers of the king's work, offered willingly,

7 And gave for the service of the house of God of gold five thousand talents and ten thousand drams, and of silver ten thousand talents, and of brass eighteen thousand talents, and one hundred thousand talents of iron.

8 And they with whom *precious* stones were found gave *them* to the treasure of the house of the LORD, by the hand of [a]Jehiel the Gershonite.

9 Then the people rejoiced, for that they offered willingly, because with perfect heart they [a]offered willingly to the LORD: and David the king also rejoiced with great joy.

David's prayer

10 ¶ Wherefore David blessed the LORD before all the congregation: and David

said, Blessed *be* thou, LORD God of Israel
our father, for ever and ever.
K 11 [a]Thine, O LORD, *is* the greatness,
and the power, and the glory, and the
victory, and the majesty: for all *that is* in
the heaven and in the earth *is thine;*
thine *is* the kingdom, O LORD, and thou
art exalted as head above all.
P 12 [a]Both riches and honour *come* of
thee, and thou reignest over all; and in
thine hand *is* power and might; and in
thine hand *it is* to make great, and to give
strength unto all.
13 Now therefore, our God, we thank
thee, and praise thy glorious name.
14 But who *am* I, and what *is* my people, that we should [1]be able to offer so
willingly after this sort? for all things
come of thee, and [2]of thine own have we
given thee.
N 15 For [a]we *are* strangers before thee,
and sojourners, as *were* all our fathers:
[b]our days on the earth *are* as a shadow,
and *there is* none [1]abiding.
16 O LORD our God, all this store that
we have prepared to build thee an house
for thine holy name *cometh* of thine
hand, and *is* all thine own.
17 I know also, my God, that thou [a]tri-
est the heart, and [b]hast pleasure in uprightness. As for me, in the uprightness
of mine heart I have willingly offered all
these things: and now have I seen with
joy thy people, which are [1]present here,
to offer willingly unto thee.
18 O LORD God of Abraham, Isaac, and
of Israel, our fathers, keep this for ever in
the imagination of the thoughts of the
heart of thy people, and [1]prepare their
heart unto thee:
19 And [a]give unto Solomon my son a
perfect heart, to keep thy commandments, thy testimonies, and thy statutes,
and to do all *these things,* and to build
the palace, *for* the which [b]I have made
provision.
20 ¶ And David said to all the congregation, Now bless the LORD your God.
And all the congregation blessed the LORD
God of their fathers, and bowed down
their heads, and worshipped the LORD,
and the king.
21 And they sacrificed sacrifices unto
the LORD, and offered burnt offerings unto
the LORD, on the morrow after that day,
even a thousand bullocks, a thousand
rams, *and* a thousand lambs, with their
drink offerings, and sacrifices in abundance for all Israel:

Solomon made king

22 And did eat and drink before the
LORD on that day with great gladness. And
they made Solomon the son of David king
the second time, and [a]anointed *him* unto
the LORD *to be* the chief governor, and
Zadok *to be* priest.
23 Then Solomon sat on the throne of
the LORD as king instead of David his father, and prospered; and all Israel obeyed
him.
24 And all the princes, and the mighty
men, and all the sons likewise of king
David, [a]submitted themselves unto Solomon the king.
25 And the LORD magnified Solomon
exceedingly in the sight of all Israel, and
[a]bestowed upon him *such* royal majesty
as had not been on any king before him
in Israel.

The death of David

26 ¶ Thus David the son of Jesse
reigned over all Israel.
27 [a]And the time that he reigned over
Israel *was* forty years; [b]seven years
reigned he in Hebron, and thirty and
three *years* reigned he in Jerusalem.
28 And he [a]died in a good old age,
[b]full of days, riches, and honour: and Solomon his son reigned in his stead.
29 Now the acts of David the king,
first and last, behold, they *are* written in
the [1]book[2] of Samuel the seer, and in the
book of Nathan the prophet, and in the
book of Gad the seer,
30 With all his reign and his might,
[a]and the times that went over him, and
over Israel, and over all the kingdoms of
the countries.

11 [a]Mat. 6:13; 1 Tim. 1:17; Rev. 5:13
12 [a]Rom. 11:36
14 [1]Heb. *retain,* or, *obtain strength* [2]Heb. *of thine hand*
15 [a]Ps. 39:12; Heb. 11:13; 1 Pet. 2:11 [b]Job 14:2; Ps. 90:9 [1]Heb. *expectation*
17 [a]1 Sam. 16:7; ch. 28:9 [b]Prov. 11:20 [1]Or, *found*
18 [1]Or, *stablish*
19 [a]Ps. 72:1 [b]ver. 2; ch. 22:14
22 [a]1 Ki. 1:35,39
24 [a]2 Chr. 30:8; Eccl. 8:2; Ezek. 17:18
25 [a]1 Ki. 3:13; 2 Chr. 1:12; Eccl. 2:9
27 [a]2 Sam. 5:4; 1 Ki. 2:11 [b]2 Sam. 5:5
28 [a]Gen. 25:8 [b]ch. 23:1
29 [1]Or, *history* [2]Heb. *words*
30 [a]Dan. 2:21

K *1Ch 4:10* ◀ ▶ *Job 1:10*
P *1Ki 3:13* ◀ ▶ *2Ch 1:12*
N *2Ki 17:13–15* ◀ ▶ *2Ch 12:14*

2 Chronicles

Author: Authorship uncertain; possibly Ezra

Theme: The kingdom from Solomon to the Babylonian exile

Date of Writing: c. 450–400 B.C.

Outline of 2 Chronicles

I. Solomon's Reign (1:1—9:31)
II. The Kings of Judah (10:1—36:14)
III. Jerusalem's Destruction (36:15–23)

In the original Hebrew canon 1 and 2 Chronicles formed one book. (For further information about the title and character of these books, see the introduction to 1 Chronicles on p. 469.)

The book of 2 Chronicles continues the history of King David's family, covering the same period of time as 1 and 2 Kings but omitting all references to the kings of the northern kingdom since David's line ran through the southern kings of Judah. The first nine chapters deal with King Solomon's reign, the building of the temple and Solomon's fall into idolatry. The bulk of 2 Chronicles covers the steady decline of the land of Judah and its continual struggle with idolatry. Though the book highlights several spiritual reformations, including a detailed account of the revival under King Hezekiah (chs. 29—31), the continued apostasy of Judah ultimately brought about its destruction and exile to Babylon. The writer concludes this book with a decree from King Cyrus of Persia that allowed the exiles to leave Babylon and end their seventy years of captivity.

Solomon asks for wisdom

1 AND [a]SOLOMON the son of David was strengthened in his kingdom, and [b]the LORD his God *was* with him, and [c]magnified him exceedingly.

2 Then Solomon spake unto all Israel, to [a]the captains of thousands and of hundreds, and to the judges, and to every governor in all Israel, the chief of the fathers.

3 So Solomon, and all the congregation with him, went to the high place that *was* at [a]Gibeon; for there was the tabernacle of the congregation of God, which Moses the servant of the LORD had made in the wilderness.

4 [a]But the ark of God had David brought up from Kirjath-jearim to *the place which* David had prepared for it: for he had pitched a tent for it at Jerusalem.

5 Moreover [a]the brasen altar, that [b]Bezaleel the son of Uri, the son of Hur, had made, ʹhe put before the tabernacle of the LORD: and Solomon and the congregation sought unto it.

6 And Solomon went up thither to the brasen altar before the LORD, which *was* at the tabernacle of the congregation, and [a]offered a thousand burnt offerings upon it.

7 ¶ [a]In that night did God appear unto Solomon, and said unto him, Ask what I shall give thee.

8 And Solomon said unto God, Thou hast shown great mercy unto David my father, and hast made me [a]to reign in his stead.

9 Now, O LORD God, let thy promise unto David my father be established: [a]for thou hast made me king over a people ʹlike the dust of the earth in multitude.

10 [a]Give me now wisdom and knowledge, that I may [b]go out and come in before this people: for who can judge this thy people, *that is so* great?

11 [a]And God said to Solomon, Because this was in thine heart, and thou hast not asked riches, wealth, or honour, nor the life of thine enemies, neither yet hast asked long life; but hast asked wisdom and knowledge for thyself, that thou mayest judge my people, over whom I have made thee king:

12 Wisdom and knowledge *is* granted unto thee; and I will give thee riches, and wealth, and honour, such as [a]none of the kings have had that *have been* before thee, neither shall there any after thee have the like. L P U

13 ¶ Then Solomon came *from his journey* to the high place that *was* at Gibeon to Jerusalem, from before the tabernacle of the congregation, and reigned over Israel.

14 [a]And Solomon gathered chariots and horsemen: and he had a thousand and four hundred chariots, and twelve thousand horsemen, which he placed in the chariot cities, and with the king at Jerusalem.

15 [a]And the king ʹmade silver and gold at Jerusalem *as plenteous* as stones, and cedar trees made he as the sycamore trees that *are* in the vale for abundance.

16 [a]And ʹSolomon had horses brought out of Egypt, and linen yarn: the king's merchants received the linen yarn at a price.

17 And they fetched up, and brought forth out of Egypt a chariot for six hundred *shekels* of silver, and an horse for an hundred and fifty: and so brought they out *horses* for all the kings of the Hittites, and for the kings of Syria, ʹby their means.

Preparing to build the temple

2 AND SOLOMON [a]determined to build an house for the name of the LORD, and an house for his kingdom.

2 And [a]Solomon told out threescore and ten thousand men to bear burdens, and fourscore thousand to hew in the mountain, and three thousand and six hundred to oversee them.

3 ¶ And Solomon sent to ʹHuram the king of Tyre, saying, [a]As thou didst deal with David my father, and didst send him cedars to build him an house to dwell therein, *even so deal with me.*

4 Behold, [a]I build an house to the name of the LORD my God, to dedicate *it* to him, *and* [b]to burn before him ʹsweet incense, and for [c]the continual showbread, and for [d]the burnt offerings morning and evening, on the sabbaths, and on

1:1 [a]1 Ki. 2:46 [b]Gen. 39:2 [c]1 Chr. 29:25
2 [a]1 Chr. 27:1
3 [a]1 Ki. 3:4; 1 Chr. 16:39 & 21:29
4 [a]2 Sam. 6:2,17; 1 Chr. 15:1
5 [a]Ex. 27:1,2 & 38:1,2 [b]Ex. 31:2 ʹOr, was *there*
6 [a]1 Ki. 3:4
7 [a]1 Ki. 3:5
8 [a]1 Chr. 28:5
9 [a]1 Ki. 3:7,8 ʹHeb. *much as the dust of the earth*
10 [a]1 Ki. 3:9 [b]Num. 27:17; Deut. 31:2
11 [a]1 Ki. 3:11-13
12 [a]1 Chr. 29:25; ch. 9:22; Eccl. 2:9
14 [a]1 Ki. 4:26 & 10:26; ch. 9:25
15 [a]1 Ki. 10:27; ch. 9:27; Job 22:24 ʹHeb. *gave*
16 [a]1 Ki. 10:28; ch. 9:28 ʹHeb. *the going forth of the horses which was Solomon's*
17 ʹHeb. *by their hand*
2:1 [a]1 Ki. 5:5
2 [a]ver. 18; 1 Ki. 5:15
3 [a]1 Chr. 14:1 ʹOr, *Hiram*
4 [a]ver. 1 [b]Ex. 30:7 [c]Ex. 25:30; Lev. 24:8 [d]Num. 28:3,9, 11 ʹHeb. *incense of spices*

L *2Ki 20:5–10* ◄► *2Ch 9:8*
P *1Ch 29:12* ◄► *2Ch 25:9*
U *1Ch 11:9* ◄► *2Ch 6:14*

the new moons, and on the solemn feasts of the LORD our God. This *is an ordinance* for ever to Israel.

5 And the house which I build *is* great: for [a]great *is* our God above all gods.

6 [a]But who [1]is able to build him an house, seeing the heaven and heaven of heavens cannot contain him? who *am* I then, that I should build him an house, save only to burn sacrifice before him?

7 Send me now therefore a man cunning to work in gold, and in silver, and in brass, and in iron, and in purple, and crimson, and blue, and that can skill [1]to grave with the cunning men that *are* with me in Judah and in Jerusalem, [a]whom David my father did provide.

8 [a]Send me also cedar trees, fir trees, and [1]algum trees, out of Lebanon: for I know that thy servants can skill to cut timber in Lebanon; and, behold, my servants *shall be* with thy servants,

9 Even to prepare me timber in abundance: for the house which I am about to build *shall be* [1]wonderful great.

10 [a]And, behold, I will give to thy servants, the hewers that cut timber, twenty thousand measures of beaten wheat, and twenty thousand measures of barley, and twenty thousand baths of wine, and twenty thousand baths of oil.

11 ¶ Then Huram the king of Tyre answered in writing, which he sent to Solomon, [a]Because the LORD hath loved his people, he hath made thee king over them.

12 Huram said moreover, [a]Blessed *be* the LORD God of Israel, [b]that made heaven and earth, who hath given to David the king a wise son, [1]endued with prudence and understanding, that might build an house for the LORD, and an house for his kingdom.

13 And now I have sent a cunning man, endued with understanding, of Huram my father's,

14 [a]The son of a woman of the daughters of Dan, and his father *was* a man of Tyre, skilful to work in gold, and in silver, in brass, in iron, in stone, and in timber, in purple, in blue, and in fine linen, and in crimson; also to grave any manner of graving, and to find out every device which shall be put to him, with thy cunning men, and with the cunning men of my lord David thy father.

15 Now therefore the wheat, and the barley, the oil, and the wine, which [a]my lord hath spoken of, let him send unto his servants:

16 [a]And we will cut wood out of Lebanon, [1]as much as thou shalt need: and we will bring it to thee in floats by sea to [2]Joppa; and thou shalt carry it up to Jerusalem.

17 ¶ [a]And Solomon numbered all [1]the strangers that *were* in the land of Israel, after the numbering wherewith [b]David his father had numbered them; and they were found an hundred and fifty thousand and three thousand and six hundred.

18 And he set [a]threescore and ten thousand of them *to be* bearers of burdens, and fourscore thousand *to be* hewers in the mountain, and three thousand and six hundred overseers to set the people awork.

Building the temple

3 THEN [a]SOLOMON began to build the house of the LORD at [b]Jerusalem in mount Moriah, [1]where *the* LORD appeared unto David his father, in the place that David had prepared in the threshingfloor of [c]Ornan[2] the Jebusite.

2 And he began to build in the second *day* of the second month, in the fourth year of his reign.

3 ¶ Now these *are the things* [a]*wherein* Solomon was [1]instructed for the building of the house of God. The length by cubits after the first measure *was* threescore cubits, and the breadth twenty cubits.

4 And the [a]porch that *was* in the front *of the house,* the length *of it was* according to the breadth of the house, twenty cubits, and the height *was* an hundred and twenty: and he overlaid it within with pure gold.

5 And [a]the greater house he ceiled with fir tree, which he overlaid with fine gold, and set thereon palm trees and chains.

6 And he [1]garnished the house with precious stones for beauty: and the gold *was* gold of Parvaim.

7 He overlaid also the house, the beams, the posts, and the walls thereof, and the doors thereof, with gold; and graved cherubims on the walls.

8 And he made the most holy house, the length whereof *was* according to the breadth of the house, twenty cubits, and

5 [a]Ps. 135:5
6 [a]1 Ki. 8:27; Is. 66:1 [1]Heb. *hath retained,* or, *obtained strength*
7 [a]1 Chr. 22:15 [1]Heb. *to grave gravings*
8 [a]1 Ki. 5:6 [1]Or, *almuggim;* see 1 Ki. 10:11
9 [1]Heb. *great and wonderful*
10 [a]1 Ki. 5:11
11 [a]1 Ki. 10:9; ch. 9:8
12 [a]1 Ki. 5:7 [b]Gen. 1 & 2; Acts 4:24 & 14:15; Rev. 10:6 [1]Heb. *knowing prudence and understanding*
14 [a]1 Ki. 7:13
15 [a]ver. 10
16 [a]1 Ki. 5:8,9 [1]Heb. *according to all thy need* [2]Heb. *Japho;* see Josh. 19:46; Acts 9:36
17 [a]As ver. 2; 1 Ki. 5:13; ch. 8:7,8 [b]1 Chr. 22:2 [1]Heb. *the men the strangers*
18 [a]As it is ver. 2
3:1 [a]1 Ki. 6:1 [b]Gen. 22:2 [c]1 Chr. 21:18 & 22:1 [1]Or, *which was seen of David his father* [2]Or, *Araunah;* see 2 Sam. 24:18
3 [a]1 Ki. 6:2 [1]Heb. *founded*
4 [a]1 Ki. 6:3
5 [a]1 Ki. 6:15
6 [1]Heb. *covered*

the breadth thereof twenty cubits: and he overlaid it with fine gold, *amounting* to six hundred talents.

9 And the weight of the nails *was* fifty shekels of gold. And he overlaid the upper chambers with gold.

10 [a]And in the most holy house he made two cherubims [1]of image work, and overlaid them with gold.

11 ¶ And the wings of the cherubims *were* twenty cubits long: one wing *of the one cherub was* five cubits, reaching to the wall of the house: and the other wing *was likewise* five cubits, reaching to the wing of the other cherub.

12 And *one* wing of the other cherub *was* five cubits, reaching to the wall of the house: and the other wing *was* five cubits *also,* joining to the wing of the other cherub.

13 The wings of these cherubims spread themselves forth twenty cubits: and they stood on their feet, and their faces *were* [1]inward.

14 ¶ And he made the [a]veil *of* blue, and purple, and crimson, and fine linen, and [1]wrought cherubims thereon.

15 Also he made before the house [a]two pillars of thirty and five cubits [1]high, and the chapiter that *was* on the top of each of them *was* five cubits.

16 And he made chains, *as* in the oracle, and put *them* on the heads of the pillars; and made [a]an hundred pomegranates, and put *them* on the chains.

17 And he [a]reared up the pillars before the temple, one on the right hand, and the other on the left; and called the name of that on the right hand [1]Jachin, and the name of that on the left [2]Boaz.

The furnishings of the temple

4 MOREOVER HE made [a]an altar of brass, twenty cubits the length thereof, and twenty cubits the breadth thereof, and ten cubits the height thereof.

2 ¶ [a]Also he made a molten sea of ten cubits [1]from brim to brim, round in compass, and five cubits the height thereof; and a line of thirty cubits did compass it round about.

3 [a]And under it *was* the similitude of oxen, which did compass it round about: ten in a cubit, compassing the sea round about. Two rows of oxen *were* cast, when it was cast.

4 It stood upon twelve oxen, three looking toward the north, and three looking toward the west, and three looking toward the south, and three looking toward the east: and the sea *was set* above upon them, and all their hinder parts *were* inward.

5 And the thickness of it *was* an handbreadth, and the brim of it like the work of the brim of a cup, [1]with flowers of lilies; *and* it received and held [a]three thousand baths.

6 ¶ He made also [a]ten lavers, and put five on the right hand, and five on the left, to wash in them: [1]such things as they offered for the burnt offering they washed in them; but the sea *was* for the priests to wash in.

7 [a]And he made ten candlesticks of gold [b]according to their form, and set *them* in the temple, five on the right hand, and five on the left.

8 [a]He made also ten tables, and placed *them* in the temple, five on the right side, and five on the left. And he made an hundred [1]basins of gold.

9 ¶ Furthermore [a]he made the court of the priests, and the great court, and doors for the court, and overlaid the doors of them with brass.

10 And [a]he set the sea on the right side of the east end, over against the south.

11 And [a]Huram made the pots, and the shovels, and the [1]basins. And Huram [2]finished the work that he was to make for king Solomon for the house of God;

12 *To wit,* the two pillars, and [a]the pommels, and the chapiters *which were* on the top of the two pillars, and the two wreaths to cover the two pommels of the chapiters which *were* on the top of the pillars;

13 And [a]four hundred pomegranates on the two wreaths; two rows of pomegranates on each wreath, to cover the two pommels of the chapiters which *were* [1]upon the pillars.

14 He made also [a]bases, and [1]lavers made he upon the bases;

15 One sea, and twelve oxen under it.

16 The pots also, and the shovels, and the fleshhooks, and all their instruments, did [a]Huram his father make to king Solomon for the house of the LORD of [1]bright brass.

17 [a]In the plain of Jordan did the king

10 [a] 1 Ki. 6:23 [1] Or, (as some think) *of moveable work*

13 [1] Or, *toward the house*

14 [a] Ex. 26:31; Mat. 27:51; Heb. 9:3 [1] Heb. *caused to ascend*

15 [a] 1 Ki. 7:15; Jer. 52:21 [1] Heb. *long*

16 [a] 1 Ki. 7:20

17 [a] 1 Ki. 7:21 [1] i.e. *He shall establish* [2] i.e. *In it is strength*

4:1 [a] Ex. 27:1,2; 2 Ki. 16:14; Ezek. 43:13,16

2 [a] 1 Ki. 7:23 [1] Heb. *from his brim to his brim*

3 [a] 1 Ki. 7:24-26

5 [a] See 1 Ki. 7:26 [1] Or, *like a lilyflower*

6 [a] 1 Ki. 7:38 [1] Heb. *the work of burnt offering*

7 [a] 1 Ki. 7:49 [b] Ex. 25:31; 1 Chr. 28:12,19

8 [a] 1 Ki. 7:48 [1] Or, *bowls*

9 [a] 1 Ki. 6:36

10 [a] 1 Ki. 7:39

11 [a] See 1 Ki. 7:40 [1] Or, *bowls* [2] Heb. *finished to make*

12 [a] 1 Ki. 7:41

13 [a] See 1 Ki. 7:20 [1] Heb. *upon the face*

14 [a] 1 Ki. 7:27,43 [1] Or, *caldrons*

16 [a] 1 Ki. 7:14,45 [1] Heb. *made bright,* or, *scoured*

17 [a] 1 Ki. 7:46

cast them, in the [l]clay ground between Succoth and Zeredathah.

18 [a]Thus Solomon made all these vessels in great abundance: for the weight of the brass could not be found out.

19 ¶ And [a]Solomon made all the vessels that *were for* the house of God, the golden altar also, and the tables whereon [b]the showbread *was set;*

20 Moreover the candlesticks with their lamps, that they should burn [a]after the manner before the oracle, of pure gold;

21 And [a]the flowers, and the lamps, and the tongs, *made he of* gold, *and* that [l]perfect gold;

22 And the snuffers, and the [l]basins, and the spoons, and the censers, *of* pure gold: and the entry of the house, the inner doors thereof for the most holy *place,* and the doors of the house of the temple, *were of* gold.

5 THUS [a]ALL the work that Solomon made for the house of the LORD was finished: and Solomon brought in *all* the things that David his father had dedicated; and the silver, and the gold, and all the instruments, put he among the treasures of the house of God.

Bringing the ark to the temple

2 ¶ [a]Then Solomon assembled the elders of Israel, and all the heads of the tribes, the chief of the fathers of the children of Israel, unto Jerusalem, to bring up the ark of the covenant of the LORD [b]out of the city of David, which *is* Zion.

3 [a]Wherefore all the men of Israel assembled themselves unto the king [b]in the feast which *was* in the seventh month.

4 And all the elders of Israel came; and the Levites took up the ark.

5 And they brought up the ark, and the tabernacle of the congregation, and all the holy vessels that *were* in the tabernacle, these did the priests *and* the Levites bring up.

6 Also king Solomon, and all the congregation of Israel that were assembled unto him before the ark, sacrificed sheep and oxen, which could not be told nor numbered for multitude.

7 And the priests brought in the ark of the covenant of the LORD unto his place, to the oracle of the house, into the most holy *place, even* under the wings of the cherubims:

17 [l]Heb. *thicknesses of the ground*
18 [a]1 Ki. 7:47
19 [a]1 Ki. 7:48-50 [b]Ex. 25:30
20 [a]Ex. 27:20,21
21 [a]Ex. 25:31 [l]Heb. *perfections of gold*
22 [l]Or, *bowls*
5:1 [a]1 Ki. 7:51
2 [a]1 Ki. 8:1 [b]2 Sam. 6:12
3 [a]1 Ki. 8:2 [b]See ch. 7:8-10
10 [a]Deut. 10:2,5; ch. 6:11 [l]Or, *where*
11 [l]Heb. *found*
12 [a]1 Chr. 25:1 [b]1 Chr. 15:24
13 [a]Ps. 136; See 1 Chr. 16:34,41
14 [a]Ex. 40:35; ch. 7:2
6:1 [a]1 Ki. 8:12 [b]Lev. 16:2

8 For the cherubims spread forth *their* wings over the place of the ark, and the cherubims covered the ark and the staves thereof above.

9 And they drew out the staves *of the ark,* that the ends of the staves were seen from the ark before the oracle; but they were not seen without. And there it is unto this day.

10 *There was* nothing in the ark save the two tables which Moses [a]put *therein* at Horeb, [l]when the LORD made *a covenant* with the children of Israel, when they came out of Egypt.

11 ¶ And it came to pass, when the priests were come out of the holy *place:* (for all the priests *that were* [l]present were sanctified, *and* did not *then* wait by course:

12 [a]Also the Levites *which were* the singers, all of them of Asaph, of Heman, of Jeduthun, with their sons and their brethren, *being* arrayed in white linen, having cymbals and psalteries and harps, stood at the east end of the altar, [b]and with them an hundred and twenty priests sounding with trumpets:)

13 It came even to pass, as the trumpeters and singers *were* as one, to make one sound to be heard in praising and thanking the LORD; and when they lifted up *their* voice with the trumpets and cymbals and instruments of music, and praised the LORD, *saying,* [a]For *he is* good; for his mercy *endureth* for ever: that *then* the house was filled with a cloud, *even* the house of the LORD;

14 So that the priests could not stand to minister by reason of the cloud: [a]for the glory of the LORD had filled the house of God.

6 THEN [a]SAID Solomon, The LORD hath said that he would dwell in the [b]thick darkness.

2 But I have built an house of habitation for thee, and a place for thy dwelling for ever.

3 And the king turned his face, and blessed the whole congregation of Israel: and all the congregation of Israel stood.

4 And he said, Blessed *be* the LORD God of Israel, who hath with his hands fulfilled *that* which he spake with his mouth to my father David, saying,

5 Since the day that I brought forth my people out of the land of Egypt I chose no city among all the tribes of Israel to build

an house in, that my name might be
there; neither chose I any man to be a
ruler over my people Israel:
6 [a]But I have chosen Jerusalem, that
my name might be there; and [b]have chosen David to be over my people Israel.
7 Now [a]it was in the heart of David my
father to build an house for the name of
the LORD God of Israel.
8 But the LORD said to David my father,
Forasmuch as it was in thine heart to
build an house for my name, thou didst
well in that it was in thine heart:
9 Notwithstanding thou shalt not build
the house; but thy son which shall come
forth out of thy loins, he shall build the
house for my name.
10 The LORD therefore hath performed
his word that he hath spoken: for I am
risen up in the room of David my father,
and am set on the throne of Israel, as the
LORD promised, and have built the house
for the name of the LORD God of Israel.
11 And in it have I put the ark,
[a]wherein *is* the covenant of the LORD,
that he made with the children of Israel.

Solomon's prayer of dedication

12 ¶ [a]And he stood before the altar of
the LORD in the presence of all the congregation of Israel, and spread forth his
hands:
13 For Solomon had made a brasen
scaffold, of five cubits [1]long, and five cubits broad, and three cubits high, and had
set it in the midst of the court: and upon
it he stood, and kneeled down upon his
knees before all the congregation of Israel, and spread forth his hands toward
heaven,
U 14 And said, O LORD God of Israel,
[a]*there is* no God like thee in the heaven,
nor in the earth; which keepest covenant, and *showest* mercy unto thy servants, that walk before thee with all their
hearts:
15 [a]Thou which hast kept with thy
servant David my father that which thou
hast promised him; and spakest with thy
mouth, and hast fulfilled *it* with thine
hand, as *it is* this day.
M 16 Now therefore, O LORD God of Israel, keep with thy servant David my father that which thou hast promised him,
saying, [a]There[1] shall not fail thee a man
in my sight to sit upon the throne of Israel; [b]yet so that thy children take heed
to their way to walk in my law, as thou
hast walked before me.
17 Now then, O LORD God of Israel, let
thy word be verified, which thou hast
spoken unto thy servant David.
18 But will God in very deed dwell
with men on the earth? [a]behold, heaven
and the heaven of heavens cannot contain thee; how much less this house
which I have built!
19 Have respect therefore to the
prayer of thy servant, and to his supplication, O LORD my God, to hearken unto
the cry and the prayer which thy servant
prayeth before thee:
20 That thine eyes may be open upon
this house day and night, upon the place
whereof thou hast said that thou wouldest put thy name there; to hearken unto
the prayer which thy servant prayeth [1]to-
ward this place.
21 Hearken therefore unto the supplications of thy servant, and of thy people
Israel, which they shall [1]make toward
this place: hear thou from thy dwelling
place, *even* from heaven; and when thou
hearest, forgive.
22 ¶ If a man sin against his neighbour, [1]and an oath be laid upon him to
make him swear, and the oath come before thine altar in this house;
23 Then hear thou from heaven, and
do, and judge thy servants, by requiting
the wicked, by recompensing his way
upon his own head; and by justifying the
righteous, by giving him according to his
righteousness.
24 ¶ And if thy people Israel [1]be put
to the worse before the enemy, because
they have sinned against thee; and shall
return and confess thy name, and pray
and make supplication before thee [2]in
this house;
25 Then hear thou from the heavens,
and forgive the sin of thy people Israel,
and bring them again unto the land
which thou gavest to them and to their
fathers.
26 ¶ When the [a]heaven is shut up,
and there is no rain, because they have
sinned against thee; yet if they pray toward this place, and confess thy name,
and turn from their sin, when thou dost
afflict them;

6 [a]ch. 12:13 [b]1 Chr. 28:4
7 [a]2 Sam. 7:2; 1 Chr. 17:1 & 28:2
11 [a]ch. 5:10
12 [a]1 Ki. 8:22
13 [1]Heb. *the length thereof*
14 [a]Ex. 15:11; Deut. 4:39 & 7:9
15 [a]1 Chr. 22:9
16 [a]2 Sam. 7:12, 16; 1 Ki. 2:4 & 6:12; ch. 7:18 [b]Ps. 132:12 [1]Heb. *There shall not a man be cut off*
18 [a]ch. 2:6; Is. 66:1; Acts 7:49
20 [1]Or, *in this place*
21 [1]Heb. *pray*
22 [1]Heb. *and he require an oath of him*
24 [1]Or, *be smitten* [2]Or, *toward*
26 [a]1 Ki. 17:1

U *2Ch 1:12* ◀ ▶ *2Ch 15:2*
M *1Ch 28:4* ◀ ▶ *2Ch 13:5*

27 Then hear thou from heaven, and
forgive the sin of thy servants, and of thy
people Israel, when thou hast taught
them the good way, wherein they should
walk; and send rain upon thy land, which
thou hast given unto thy people for an
inheritance.
H 28 ¶ If there [a]be dearth in the land, if
there be pestilence, if there be blasting,
or mildew, locusts, or caterpillars; if their
enemies besiege them [1]in the cities of
their land; whatsoever sore or whatsoever sickness *there be:*
29 *Then* what prayer *or* what supplication soever shall be made of any man, or
of all thy people Israel, when every one
shall know his own sore and his own
grief, and shall spread forth his hands [1]in
this house:
E 30 Then hear thou from heaven thy
dwellingplace, and forgive, and render
unto every man according unto all his
ways, whose heart thou knowest; (for
thou only [a]knowest the hearts of the children of men:)
31 That they may fear thee, to walk in
thy ways, [1]so long as they live [2]in the
land which thou gavest unto our fathers.
32 ¶ Moreover concerning the
stranger, [a]which is not of thy people Israel, but is come from a far country for
thy great name's sake, and thy mighty
hand, and thy stretched out arm; if they
come and pray in this house;
33 Then hear thou from the heavens,
even from thy dwellingplace, and do according to all that the stranger calleth to
thee for; that all people of the earth may
know thy name, and fear thee, as *doth*
thy people Israel, and may know that
[1]this house which I have built is called by
thy name.
34 If thy people go out to war against
their enemies by the way that thou shalt
send them, and they pray unto thee toward this city which thou hast chosen,
and the house which I have built for thy
name;
35 Then hear thou from the heavens
their prayer and their supplication, and
maintain their [1]cause.
A 36 If they sin against thee, (for *there is*
[a]no man which sinneth not,) and thou be
angry with them, and deliver them over
before *their* enemies, and [1]they carry
them away captives unto a land far off or
near;
37 Yet *if* they [1]bethink themselves in
the land whither they are carried captive,
and turn and pray unto thee in the land of
their captivity, saying, We have sinned,
we have done amiss, and have dealt
wickedly;
38 If they return to thee with all their
heart and with all their soul in the land of
their captivity, whither they have carried
them captives, and pray toward their
land, which thou gavest unto their fathers, and *toward* the city which thou
hast chosen, and toward the house which
I have built for thy name:
39 Then hear thou from the heavens,
even from thy dwellingplace, their prayer
and their supplications, and maintain
their [1]cause, and forgive thy people
which have sinned against thee.
40 Now, my God, let, I beseech thee,
thine eyes be open, and *let* thine ears *be*
attent [1]unto the prayer *that is made* in
this place.
41 Now [a]therefore arise, O LORD God,
into thy [b]resting place, thou, and the ark
of thy strength: let thy priests, O LORD
God, be clothed with salvation, and let
thy saints [c]rejoice in goodness.
42 O LORD God, turn not away the face
of thine anointed: [a]remember the mercies of David thy servant.

Dedicating the house of God

7 NOW [a]WHEN Solomon had made an
end of praying, the [b]fire came down
from heaven, and consumed the burnt offering and the sacrifices; and [c]the glory of
the LORD filled the house.
2 [a]And the priests could not enter into
the house of the LORD, because the glory
of the LORD had filled the LORD'S house.
3 And when all the children of Israel
saw how the fire came down, and the
glory of the LORD upon the house, they
bowed themselves with their faces to the
ground upon the pavement, and worshipped, and praised the LORD, [a]*saying,*
For *he is* good; [b]for his mercy *endureth*
for ever.
4 ¶ [a]Then the king and all the people
offered sacrifices before the LORD.
5 And king Solomon offered a sacrifice
of twenty and two thousand oxen, and an

28 [a]ch. 20:9 [1]Heb. *in the land of their gates*
29 [1]Or, *toward this house*
30 [a]1 Chr. 28:9
31 [1]Heb. *all the days which* [2]Heb. *upon the face of the land*
32 [a]John 12:20; Acts 8:27
33 [1]Heb. *thy name is called upon this house*
35 [1]Or, *right*
36 [a]Prov. 20:9; Eccl. 7:20; Jas. 3:2; 1 John 1:8 [1]Heb. *they that take them captives carry them away*
37 [1]Heb. *bring back to their heart*
39 [1]Or, *right*
40 [1]Heb. *to the prayer of this place*
41 [a]Ps. 132:8-10, 16 [b]1 Chr. 28:2 [c]Neh. 9:25
42 [a]Ps. 132:1; Is. 55:3
7:1 [a]1 Ki. 8:54 [b]Lev. 9:24; Judg. 6:21; 1 Ki. 18:38; 1 Chr. 21:26 [c]1 Ki. 8:10,11
2 [a]ch. 5:14
3 [a]ch. 5:13; Ps. 136:1 [b]1 Chr. 16:41; ch. 20:21
4 [a]1 Ki. 8:62,63

H *1Ki 8:37–39* ◀▶ *2Ch 7:13–14*
E *1Ch 28:9* ◀▶ *2Ch 16:9*
A *1Ki 8:46* ◀▶ *Ps 14:1–4*

hundred and twenty thousand sheep: so the king and all the people dedicated the house of God.

6 [a]And the priests waited on their offices: the Levites also with instruments of music of the LORD, which David the king had made to praise the LORD, because his mercy *endureth* for ever, when David praised [l]by their ministry; and [b]the priests sounded trumpets before them, and all Israel stood.

7 Moreover [a]Solomon hallowed the middle of the court that *was* before the house of the LORD: for there he offered burnt offerings, and the fat of the peace offerings, because the brasen altar which Solomon had made was not able to receive the burnt offerings, and the meat offerings, and the fat.

8 ¶ [a]Also at the same time Solomon kept the feast seven days, and all Israel with him, a very great congregation, from the entering in of Hamath unto [b]the river of Egypt.

9 And in the eighth day they made [l]a solemn assembly: for they kept the dedication of the altar seven days, and the feast seven days.

10 And [a]on the three and twentieth day of the seventh month he sent the people away into their tents, glad and merry in heart for the goodness that the LORD had shown unto David, and to Solomon, and to Israel his people.

The LORD's promise to Solomon

11 Thus [a]Solomon finished the house of the LORD, and the king's house: and all that came into Solomon's heart to make in the house of the LORD, and in his own house, he prosperously effected.

12 ¶ And the LORD appeared to Solomon by night, and said unto him, I have heard thy prayer, [a]and have chosen this place to myself for an house of sacrifice.

13 [a]If I shut up heaven that there be no rain, or if I command the locusts to devour the land, or if I send pestilence among my people;

H 2Ch 6:28–30 ◀▶ 2Ch 16:12

6 [a]1 Chr. 15:16 [b]ch. 5:12 [l]Heb. *by their hand*
7 [a]1 Ki. 8:64
8 [a]1 Ki. 8:65 [b]Josh. 13:3
9 [l]Heb. *a restraint*
10 [a]1 Ki. 8:66
11 [a]1 Ki. 9:1
12 [a]Deut. 12:5
13 [a]ch. 6:26,28
14 [a]Jas. 4:10 [b]ch. 6:27,30 [l]Heb. *upon whom my name is called*
15 [a]ch. 6:40 [l]Heb. *to the prayer of this place*
16 [a]1 Ki. 9:3; ch. 6:6
17 [a]1 Ki. 9:4
18 [a]ch. 6:16 [l]Heb. *There shall not be cut off to thee*
19 [a]Lev. 26:14,33; Deut. 28:15,36,37
21 [a]Deut. 29:24

14 If my people, [l]which are called by my name, shall [a]humble themselves, and pray, and seek my face, and turn from their wicked ways; [b]then will I hear from heaven, and will forgive their sin, and will heal their land.

15 Now [a]mine eyes shall be open, and mine ears attent [l]unto the prayer *that is made* in this place.

16 For now have [a]I chosen and sanctified this house, that my name may be there for ever: and mine eyes and mine heart shall be there perpetually.

17 [a]And as for thee, if thou wilt walk before me, as David thy father walked, and do according to all that I have commanded thee, and shalt observe my statutes and my judgments;

18 Then will I stablish the throne of thy kingdom, according as I have covenanted with David thy father, saying, [a]There[l] shall not fail thee a man *to be* ruler in Israel.

19 [a]But if ye turn away, and forsake my statutes and my commandments, which I have set before you, and shall go and serve other gods, and worship them;

20 Then will I pluck them up by the roots out of my land which I have given them; and this house, which I have sanctified for my name, will I cast out of my sight, and will make it *to be* a proverb and a byword among all nations.

21 And this house, which is high, shall be an astonishment to every one that passeth by it; so that he shall say, [a]Why hath the LORD done thus unto this land, and unto this house?

22 And it shall be answered, Because they forsook the LORD God of their fathers, which brought them forth out of the land of Egypt, and laid hold on other gods, and worshipped them, and served them: therefore hath he brought all this evil upon them.

L *1Ch 28:9* ◀▶ *2Ch 15:2*
M *1Ch 21:8* ◀▶ *2Ch 12:6–7*
P *2Sa 12:13* ◀▶ *2Ch 15:3–4*
R *1Ch 21:8* ◀▶ *2Ch 15:4*
S *1Ch 28:9* ◀▶ *2Ch 15:2*
R *1Ch 9:1* ◀▶ *2Ch 7:20–22*
R *2Ch 7:20* ◀▶ *2Ch 28:23*

7:20 God spoke to Solomon and reminded him of his promise to exile Israel and "pluck them up by the roots" out of the land if they turned away from God's law.

Solomon's other achievements

8 AND [a]IT came to pass at the end of
twenty years, wherein Solomon had
built the house of the LORD, and his own
house,
2 That the cities which Huram had restored to Solomon, Solomon built them,
and caused the children of Israel to dwell
there.
3 And Solomon went to Hamath-zo-
bah, and prevailed against it.
4 [a]And he built Tadmor in the wilderness, and all the store cities, which he
built in Hamath.
5 Also he built Beth-horon the upper,
and Beth-horon the nether, fenced cities,
with walls, gates, and bars;
6 And Baalath, and all the store cities
that Solomon had, and all the chariot cities, and the cities of the horsemen, and
[l]all that Solomon desired to build in Jerusalem, and in Lebanon, and throughout
all the land of his dominion.
7 ¶ [a]*As for* all the people *that were* left
of the Hittites, and the Amorites, and the
Perizzites, and the Hivites, and the Jebusites, which *were* not of Israel,
8 *But* of their children, who were left
after them in the land, whom the children of Israel consumed not, them did
Solomon make to pay tribute until this
day.
9 But of the children of Israel did Solomon make no servants for his work; but
they *were* men of war, and chief of his
captains, and captains of his chariots and
horsemen.
10 And these *were* the chief of king
Solomon's officers, *even* [a]two hundred
and fifty, that bare rule over the people.
11 ¶ And Solomon [a]brought up the
daughter of Pharaoh out of the city of David unto the house that he had built for
her: for he said, My wife shall not dwell
in the house of David king of Israel, because *the places are* [l]holy, whereunto
the ark of the LORD hath come.
12 ¶ Then Solomon offered burnt offerings unto the LORD on the altar of the
LORD, which he had built before the
porch,
13 Even after a certain rate [a]every day,
offering according to the commandment
of Moses, on the sabbaths, and on the
new moons, and on the solemn feasts,
[b]three times in the year, *even* in the feast
of unleavened bread, and in the feast of
weeks, and in the feast of tabernacles.
14 ¶ And he appointed, according to
the order of David his father, the
[a]courses of the priests to their service,
and [b]the Levites to their charges, to
praise and minister before the priests, as
the duty of every day required: the [c]por-
ters also by their courses at every gate:
for [l]so had David the man of God commanded.
15 And they departed not from the
commandment of the king unto the
priests and Levites concerning any matter, or concerning the treasures.
16 Now all the work of Solomon was
prepared unto the day of the foundation
of the house of the LORD, and until it was
finished. *So* the house of the LORD was
perfected.
17 ¶ Then went Solomon to [a]Ezion-ge-
ber, and to [l]Eloth, at the sea side in the
land of Edom.
18 [a]And Huram sent him by the hands
of his servants ships, and servants that
had knowledge of the sea; and they went
with the servants of Solomon to Ophir,
and took thence four hundred and fifty
talents of gold, and brought *them* to king
Solomon.

The visit of the queen of Sheba

9 AND [a]WHEN the queen of Sheba
heard of the fame of Solomon, she
came to prove Solomon with hard questions at Jerusalem, with a very great company, and camels that bare spices, and
gold in abundance, and precious stones:
and when she was come to Solomon, she
communed with him of all that was in
her heart.
2 And Solomon told her all her questions: and there was nothing hid from
Solomon which he told her not.
3 And when the queen of Sheba had
seen the wisdom of Solomon, and the
house that he had built,
4 And the meat of his table, and the
sitting of his servants, and the attendance
of his ministers, and their apparel; his
[l]cupbearers also, and their apparel; and
his ascent by which he went up into the
house of the LORD; there was no more
spirit in her.
5 And she said to the king, *It was* a
true [l]report which I heard in mine own
land of thine [2]acts, and of thy wisdom:

8:1 [a] 1 Ki. 9:10
4 [a] 1 Ki. 9:17
6 [l] Heb. *all the desire of Solomon which he desired to build*
7 [a] 1 Ki. 9:20
10 [a] See 1 Ki. 9:23
11 [a] 1 Ki. 3:1 & 7:8 & 9:24 [l] Heb. *holiness*
13 [a] Ex. 29:38; Num. 28:3,9,11,26 & 29:1 [b] Ex. 23:14; Deut. 16:16
14 [a] 1 Chr. 24:3 [b] 1 Chr. 25:1 [c] 1 Chr. 9:17 & 26:1 [l] Heb. *so* was *the commandment of David the man of God*
17 [a] 1 Ki. 9:26 [l] Or, *Elath;* see Deut. 2:8; 2 Ki. 14:22
18 [a] 1 Ki. 9:27; ch. 9:10,13
9:1 [a] 1 Ki. 10:1; Mat. 12:42; Luke 11:31
4 [l] Or, *butlers*
5 [l] Heb. *word* [2] Or, *sayings*

6 Howbeit I believed not their words, until I came, and mine eyes had seen *it:* and, behold, the one half of the greatness of thy wisdom was not told me: *for* thou exceedest the fame that I heard.

7 Happy *are* thy men, and happy *are* these thy servants, which stand continually before thee, and hear thy wisdom.

L 8 Blessed be the LORD thy God, which delighted in thee to set thee on his throne, *to be* king for the LORD thy God: because thy God loved Israel, to establish them for ever, therefore made he thee king over them, to do judgment and justice.

9 And she gave the king an hundred and twenty talents of gold, and of spices great abundance, and precious stones: neither was there any such spice as the queen of Sheba gave king Solomon.

10 And the servants also of Huram, and the servants of Solomon, [a]which brought gold from Ophir, brought [b]algum trees and precious stones.

11 And the king made *of* the algum trees [1,2]terraces to the house of the LORD, and to the king's palace, and harps and psalteries for singers: and there were none such seen before in the land of Judah.

12 And king Solomon gave to the queen of Sheba all her desire, whatsoever she asked, beside *that* which she had brought unto the king. So she turned, and went away to her own land, she and her servants.

Solomon's wealth and wisdom

13 ¶ Now the weight of gold that came to Solomon in one year was six hundred and threescore and six talents of gold;

14 Beside *that which* chapmen and merchants brought. And all the kings of Arabia and [1]governors of the country brought gold and silver to Solomon.

15 ¶ And king Solomon made two hundred targets *of* beaten gold: six hundred *shekels* of beaten gold went to one target.

16 And three hundred shields *made he of* beaten gold: three hundred *shekels* of gold went to one shield. And the king put them in the house of the forest of Lebanon.

17 Moreover the king made a great throne of ivory, and overlaid it with pure gold.

18 And *there were* six steps to the throne, with a footstool of gold, *which were* fastened to the throne, and [1]stays on each side of the sitting place, and two lions standing by the stays:

19 And twelve lions stood there on the one side and on the other upon the six steps. There was not the like made in any kingdom.

20 ¶ And all the drinking vessels of king Solomon *were of* gold, and all the vessels of the house of the forest of Lebanon *were of* [1]pure gold: [2]none *were of* silver; it was *not* any thing accounted of in the days of Solomon.

21 For the king's ships went to Tarshish with the servants of Huram: every three years once came the ships of Tarshish bringing gold, and silver, [1]ivory, and apes, and peacocks.

22 And king Solomon passed all the kings of the earth in riches and wisdom.

23 ¶ And all the kings of the earth sought the presence of Solomon, to hear his wisdom, that God had put in his heart.

24 And they brought every man his present, vessels of silver, and vessels of gold, and raiment, harness, and spices, horses, and mules, a rate year by year.

25 ¶ And Solomon [a]had four thousand stalls for horses and chariots, and twelve thousand horsemen; whom he bestowed in the chariot cities, and with the king at Jerusalem.

26 ¶ [a]And he reigned over all the kings [b]from the [1]river even unto the land of the Philistines, and to the border of Egypt.

27 [a]And the king [1]made silver in Jerusalem as stones, and cedar trees made he as the sycamore trees that *are* in the low plains in abundance.

28 [a]And they brought unto Solomon horses out of Egypt, and out of all lands.

Solomon's death and successor

29 ¶ [a]Now the rest of the acts of Solomon, first and last, *are* they not written in the [1]book of Nathan the prophet, and in the prophecy of [b]Ahijah the Shilonite, and in the visions of [c]Iddo the seer against Jeroboam the son of Nebat?

30 [a]And Solomon reigned in Jerusalem over all Israel forty years.

10 [a]ch. 8:18 [b]1 Ki. 10:11 *almug trees*
11 [1]Or, *stairs* [2]Heb. *highways*
14 [1]Or, *captains*
18 [1]Heb. *hands*
20 [1]Heb. *shut up* [2]Or, there was *no silver* in them
21 [1]Or, *elephants' teeth*
25 [a]1 Ki. 4:26 & 10:26; ch. 1:14
26 [a]1 Ki. 4:21 [b]Gen. 15:18; Ps. 72:8 [1]i.e. *Euphrates*
27 [a]1 Ki. 10:27; ch. 1:15 [1]Heb. *gave*
28 [a]1 Ki. 10:28; ch. 1:16
29 [a]1 Ki. 11:41 [b]1 Ki. 11:29 [c]ch. 12:15 & 13:22 [1]Heb. *words*
30 [a]1 Ki. 11:42,43

L *2Ch 1:12* ◄► *2Ch 20:9*

31 And Solomon slept with his fathers, and he was buried in the city of David his father: and Rehoboam his son reigned in his stead.

Rehoboam's harsh rule

10 AND [a]REHOBOAM went to Shechem: for to Shechem were all Israel come to make him king.

2 And it came to pass, when Jeroboam the son of Nebat, who *was* in Egypt, [a]whither he had fled from the presence of Solomon the king, heard *it,* that Jeroboam returned out of Egypt.

3 And they sent and called him. So Jeroboam and all Israel came and spake to Rehoboam, saying,

4 Thy father made our yoke grievous: now therefore ease thou somewhat the grievous servitude of thy father, and his heavy yoke that he put upon us, and we will serve thee.

5 And he said unto them, Come again unto me after three days. And the people departed.

6 ¶ And king Rehoboam took counsel with the old men that had stood before Solomon his father while he yet lived, saying, What counsel give ye *me* to return answer to this people?

7 And they spake unto him, saying, If thou be kind to this people, and please them, and speak good words to them, they will be thy servants for ever.

8 But he forsook the counsel which the old men gave him, and took counsel with the young men that were brought up with him, that stood before him.

9 And he said unto them, What advice give ye that we may return answer to this people, which have spoken to me, saying, Ease somewhat the yoke that thy father did put upon us?

10 And the young men that were brought up with him spake unto him, saying, Thus shalt thou answer the people that spake unto thee, saying, Thy father made our yoke heavy, but make thou *it* somewhat lighter for us; thus shalt thou say unto them, My little *finger* shall be thicker than my father's loins.

11 For whereas my father [l]put a heavy yoke upon you, I will put more to your yoke: my father chastised you with whips, but I *will chastise you* with scorpions.

12 So Jeroboam and all the people came to Rehoboam on the third day, as the king bade, saying, Come again to me on the third day.

13 And the king answered them roughly; and king Rehoboam forsook the counsel of the old men,

14 And answered them after the advice of the young men, saying, My father made your yoke heavy, but I will add thereto: my father chastised you with whips, but I *will chastise you* with scorpions.

15 So the king hearkened not unto the people: [a]for the cause was of God, that the LORD might perform his word, which he spake by the [b]hand of Ahijah the Shilonite to Jeroboam the son of Nebat.

16 ¶ And when all Israel *saw* that the king would not hearken unto them, the people answered the king, saying, What portion have we in David? and *we have* none inheritance in the son of Jesse: every man to your tents, O Israel: *and* now, David, see to thine own house. So all Israel went to their tents.

17 But *as for* the children of Israel that dwelt in the cities of Judah, Rehoboam reigned over them.

18 Then king Rehoboam sent Hadoram that *was* over the tribute; and the children of Israel stoned him with stones, that he died. But king Rehoboam [l]made speed to get him up to *his* chariot, to flee to Jerusalem.

19 [a]And Israel rebelled against the house of David unto this day.

Rehoboam builds strongholds

11 AND [a]WHEN Rehoboam was come to Jerusalem, he gathered of the house of Judah and Benjamin an hundred and fourscore thousand chosen *men,* which were warriors, to fight against Israel, that he might bring the kingdom again to Rehoboam.

2 But the word of the LORD came [a]to Shemaiah the man of God, saying,

3 Speak unto Rehoboam the son of Solomon, king of Judah, and to all Israel in Judah and Benjamin, saying,

4 Thus saith the LORD, Ye shall not go up, nor fight against your brethren: return every man to his house: for this thing is done of me. And they obeyed the words of the LORD, and returned from going against Jeroboam.

10:1 [a]1 Ki. 12:1
2 [a]1 Ki. 11:40
11 [l]Heb. *laded*
15 [a]1 Sam. 2:25; 1 Ki. 12:15,24 [b]1 Ki. 11:29
18 [l]Heb. *strengthened himself*
19 [a]1 Ki. 12:19
11:1 [a]1 Ki. 12:21
2 [a]ch. 12:15

5 ¶ And Rehoboam dwelt in Jerusalem, and built cities for defence in Judah.

6 He built even Bethlehem, and Etam, and Tekoa,

7 And Beth-zur, and Shoco, and Adullam,

8 And Gath, and Mareshah, and Ziph,

9 And Adoraim, and Lachish, and Azekah,

10 And Zorah, and Aijalon, and Hebron, which *are* in Judah and in Benjamin fenced cities.

11 And he fortified the strong holds, and put captains in them, and store of victual, and of oil and wine.

12 And in every several city *he put* shields and spears, and made them exceeding strong, having Judah and Benjamin on his side.

13 ¶ And the priests and the Levites that *were* in all Israel [l]resorted to him out of all their coasts.

14 For the Levites left [a]their suburbs and their possession, and came to Judah and Jerusalem: for [b]Jeroboam and his sons had cast them off from executing the priest's office unto the LORD:

15 [a]And he ordained him priests for the high places, and for [b]the devils, and for [c]the calves which he had made.

16 [a]And after them out of all the tribes of Israel such as set their hearts to seek the LORD God of Israel came to Jerusalem, to sacrifice unto the LORD God of their fathers.

17 So they [a]strengthened the kingdom of Judah, and made Rehoboam the son of Solomon strong, three years: for three years they walked in the way of David and Solomon.

Rehoboam's many wives

18 ¶ And Rehoboam took him Mahalath the daughter of Jerimoth the son of David to wife, *and* Abihail the daughter of Eliab the son of Jesse;

19 Which bare him children; Jeush, and Shamariah, and Zaham.

20 And after her he took [a]Maachah the daughter of Absalom; which bare him Abijah, and Attai, and Ziza, and Shelomith.

21 And Rehoboam loved Maachah the daughter of Absalom above all his wives and his concubines: (for he took eighteen wives, and threescore concubines; and begat twenty and eight sons, and threescore daughters.)

22 And Rehoboam [a]made Abijah the son of Maachah the chief, *to be* ruler among his brethren: for *he thought* to make him king.

23 And he dealt wisely, and dispersed of all his children throughout all the countries of Judah and Benjamin, unto every fenced city: and he gave them victual in abundance. And he desired [l]many wives.

Egyptians raid Jerusalem

12 AND [a]IT came to pass, when Rehoboam had established the kingdom, and had strengthened himself, [b]he forsook the law of the LORD, and all Israel with him.

2 [a]And it came to pass, *that* in the fifth year of king Rehoboam Shishak king of Egypt came up against Jerusalem, because they had transgressed against the LORD,

3 With twelve hundred chariots, and threescore thousand horsemen: and the people *were* without number that came with him out of Egypt; [a]the Lubims, the Sukkiims, and the Ethiopians.

4 And he took the fenced cities which *pertained* to Judah, and came to Jerusalem.

5 ¶ Then came [a]Shemaiah the prophet to Rehoboam, and *to* the princes of Judah, that were gathered together to Jerusalem because of Shishak, and said unto them, Thus saith the LORD, Ye have forsaken me, and therefore have I also left you in the hand of Shishak.

6 Whereupon the princes of Israel and the king [a]humbled themselves; and they said, [b]The LORD *is* righteous. M

7 And when the LORD saw that they humbled themselves, [a]the word of the LORD came to Shemaiah, saying, They have humbled themselves; *therefore* I will not destroy them, but I will grant them [l]some deliverance; and my wrath shall not be poured out upon Jerusalem by the hand of Shishak.

8 Nevertheless [a]they shall be his servants; that they may know [b]my service, and the service of the kingdoms of the countries.

9 [a]So Shishak king of Egypt came up

13 [l]Heb. *presented themselves to him*
14 [a]Num. 35:2 [b]ch. 13:9
15 [a]1 Ki. 12:31 & 13:33 & 14:9; Hos. 13:2 [b]Lev. 17:7; 1 Cor. 10:20 [c]1 Ki. 12:28
16 [a]See ch. 15:9 & 30:11,18
17 [a]ch. 12:1
20 [a]1 Ki. 15:2; She is called Michaiah the daughter of Uriel ch. 13:2
22 [a]See Deut. 21:15-17
23 [l]Heb. *a multitude of wives*
12:1 [a]ch. 11:17 [b]1 Ki. 14:22-24
2 [a]1 Ki. 14:24,25
3 [a]ch. 16:8
5 [a]ch. 11:2
6 [a]Jas. 4:10 [b]Ex. 9:27
7 [a]1 Ki. 21:28,29 [l]Or, *a little while*
8 [a]See Is. 26:13 [b]Deut. 28:47,48
9 [a]1 Ki. 14:25,26

M *2Ch 7:14* ◄► *2Ch 12:12*

against Jerusalem, and took away the treasures of the house of the LORD, and the treasures of the king's house; he took all: he carried away also the shields of gold which Solomon had [b]made.

10 Instead of which king Rehoboam made shields of brass, and committed *them* [a]to the hands of the chief of the guard, that kept the entrance of the king's house.

11 And when the king entered into the house of the LORD, the guard came and fetched them, and brought them again into the guard chamber.

M 12 And when he humbled himself, the wrath of the LORD turned from him, that he would not destroy *him* altogether: [a]andʹ also in Judah things went well.

13 ¶ So king Rehoboam strengthened himself in Jerusalem, and reigned: for [a]Rehoboam *was* one and forty years old when he began to reign, and he reigned seventeen years in Jerusalem, [b]the city which the LORD had chosen out of all the tribes of Israel, to put his name there. And his mother's name *was* Naamah an Ammonitess.

C N 14 And he did evil, because he ʹprepared not his heart to seek the LORD.

15 Now the acts of Rehoboam, first and last, *are* they not written in the ʹbook of Shemaiah the prophet, [a]and of Iddo the seer concerning genealogies? [b]And *there were* wars between Rehoboam and Jeroboam continually.

16 And Rehoboam slept with his fathers, and was buried in the city of David: and [a]Abijah his son reigned in his stead.

Abijah, king of Judah

13 NOW [a]IN the eighteenth year of king Jeroboam began Abijah to reign over Judah.

2 He reigned three years in Jerusalem. His mother's name also *was* [a]Michaiah the daughter of Uriel of Gibeah. And there was war between Abijah and Jeroboam.

3 And Abijah ʹset the battle in array with an army of valiant men of war, *even* four hundred thousand chosen men: Jeroboam also set the battle in array against him with eight hundred thousand chosen men, *being* mighty men of valour.

4 ¶ And Abijah stood up upon mount [a]Zemaraim, which *is* in mount Ephraim, and said, Hear me, thou Jeroboam, and all Israel;

5 Ought ye not to know that the LORD God of Israel [a]gave the kingdom over Israel to David for ever, *even* to him and to his sons [b]by a covenant of salt? M

6 Yet Jeroboam the son of Nebat, the servant of Solomon the son of David, is risen up, and hath [a]rebelled against his lord.

7 And there are gathered unto him [a]vain men, the children of Belial, and have strengthened themselves against Rehoboam the son of Solomon, when Rehoboam was young and tender-hearted, and could not withstand them.

8 And now ye think to withstand the kingdom of the LORD in the hand of the sons of David; and ye *be* a great multitude, and *there are* with you golden calves, which Jeroboam [a]made you for gods.

9 [a]Have ye not cast out the priests of the LORD, the sons of Aaron, and the Levites, and have made you priests after the manner of the nations of *other* lands? [b]so that whosoever cometh [c]toʹ consecrate himself with a young bullock and seven rams, *the same* may be a priest of *them that are* no gods.

10 But as for us, the LORD *is* our God, and we have not forsaken him; and the priests, which minister unto the LORD, *are* the sons of Aaron, and the Levites *wait* upon *their* business:

11 [a]And they burn unto the LORD every morning and every evening burnt sacrifices and sweet incense: the [b]showbread also *set they in order* upon the pure table; and the candlestick of gold with the lamps thereof, [c]to burn every evening: for we keep the charge of the LORD our God; but ye have forsaken him.

12 And, behold, God himself *is* with us for *our* captain, [a]and his priests with sounding trumpets to cry alarm against you. O children of Israel, fight ye not against the LORD God of your fathers; for ye shall not prosper.

13 ¶ But Jeroboam caused an ambushment to come about behind them: so they

9 [b]1 Ki. 10:16,17; ch. 9:15,16
10 [a]1 Ki. 14:27
12 [a]Gen. 18:24 & 1 Ki. 14:13; ch. 19:3 ʹOr, *and yet in Judah there were good things*
13 [a]1 Ki. 14:21 [b]ch. 6:6
14 ʹOr, *fixed*
15 [a]ch. 9:29 & 13:22 [b]1 Ki. 14:30 ʹHeb. *words*
16 [a]1 Ki. 14:31 *Abijam*
13:1 [a]1 Ki. 15:1
2 [a]See ch. 11:20
3 ʹHeb. *bound together*
4 [a]Josh. 18:22
5 [a]2 Sam. 7:12,13, 16 [b]Num. 18:19
6 [a]1 Ki. 11:26 & 12:20
7 [a]Judg. 9:4
8 [a]1 Ki. 12:28 & 14:9; Hos. 8:6
9 [a]ch. 11:14,15 [b]Ex. 29:35 [c]Ex. 29:1; Lev. 8:2 ʹHeb. *to fill his hand*
11 [a]ch. 2:4 [b]Lev. 24:6 [c]Ex. 27:20,21; Lev. 24:2,3
12 [a]Num. 10:8

M *2Ch 12:6–7* ◀ ▶ *2Ch 30:8*
C *2Ki 21:22* ◀ ▶ *2Ch 24:20*
N *1Ch 29:15* ◀ ▶ *2Ch 36:13*
M *2Ch 6:16* ◀ ▶ *2Ch 21:7*

were before Judah, and the ambushment *was* behind them.

14 And when Judah looked back, behold, the battle *was* before and behind: and they cried unto the LORD, and the priests sounded with the trumpets.

15 Then the men of Judah gave a shout: and as the men of Judah shouted, it came to pass, that God [a]smote Jeroboam and all Israel before Abijah and Judah.

16 And the children of Israel fled before Judah: and God delivered them into their hand.

17 And Abijah and his people slew them with a great slaughter: so there fell down slain of Israel five hundred thousand chosen men.

18 Thus the children of Israel were brought under at that time, and the children of Judah prevailed, [a]because they relied upon the LORD God of their fathers.

19 And Abijah pursued after Jeroboam, and took cities from him, Beth-el with the towns thereof, and Jeshanah with the towns thereof, and [a]Ephrain with the towns thereof.

20 Neither did Jeroboam recover strength again in the days of Abijah: and the LORD [a]struck him, and [b]he died.

21 ¶ But Abijah waxed mighty, and married fourteen wives, and begat twenty and two sons, and sixteen daughters.

22 And the rest of the acts of Abijah, and his ways, and his sayings, *are* written in the [/]story of the prophet [a]Iddo.

Asa, king of Judah

14 SO ABIJAH slept with his fathers, and they buried him in the city of David: and [a]Asa his son reigned in his stead. In his days the land was quiet ten years.

2 And Asa did *that which was* good and right in the eyes of the LORD his God:

3 For he took away the altars of the strange *gods,* and [a]the high places, and [b]brake down the [/]images, [c]and cut down the groves:

4 And commanded Judah to seek the LORD God of their fathers, and to do the law and the commandment.

5 Also he took away out of all the cities of Judah the high places and the [/]images: and the kingdom was quiet before him.

6 ¶ And he built fenced cities in Judah: for the land had rest, and he had no war in those years; because the LORD had given him rest.

7 Therefore he said unto Judah, Let us build these cities, and make about *them* walls, and towers, gates, and bars, *while* the land *is* yet before us; because we have sought the LORD our God, we have sought *him,* and he hath given us rest on every side. So they built and prospered. V

8 And Asa had an army *of men* that bare targets and spears, out of Judah three hundred thousand; and out of Benjamin, that bare shields and drew bows, two hundred and fourscore thousand: all these *were* mighty men of valour.

9 ¶ [a]And there came out against them Zerah the Ethiopian with an host of a thousand thousand, and three hundred chariots; and came unto [b]Mareshah.

10 Then Asa went out against him, and they set the battle in array in the valley of Zephathah at Mareshah.

11 And Asa [a]cried unto the LORD his God, and said, LORD, *it is* [b]nothing with thee to help, whether with many, or with them that have no power: help us, O LORD our God; for we rest on thee, and [c]in thy name we go against this multitude. O LORD, thou *art* our God; let not [/]man prevail against thee. V

12 So the LORD [a]smote the Ethiopians before Asa, and before Judah; and the Ethiopians fled.

13 And Asa and the people that *were* with him pursued them unto [a]Gerar: and the Ethiopians were overthrown, that they could not recover themselves; for they were [/]destroyed before the LORD, and before his host; and they carried away very much spoil.

14 And they smote all the cities round about Gerar; for [a]the fear of the LORD came upon them: and they spoiled all the cities; for there was exceeding much spoil in them.

15 They smote also the tents of cattle, and carried away sheep and camels in abundance, and returned to Jerusalem.

15 [a]ch. 14:12
18 [a]1 Chr. 5:20; Ps. 22:5
19 [a]Josh. 15:9
20 [a]1 Sam. 25:38 [b]1 Ki. 14:20
22 [a]ch. 12:15 [/]Or, *commentary*
14:1 [a]1 Ki. 15:8
3 [a]See 1 Ki. 15:14; ch. 15:17 [b]Ex. 34:13 [c]1 Ki. 11:7 [/]Heb. *statues*
5 [/]Heb. *sun images*
9 [a]ch. 16:8 [b]Josh. 15:44
11 [a]Ex. 14:10; ch. 13:14; Ps. 22:5 [b]1 Sam. 14:6 [c]1 Sam. 17:45; Prov. 18:10 [/]Or, *mortal man*
12 [a]ch. 13:15
13 [a]Gen. 10:19 & 20:1 [/]Heb. *broken*
14 [a]Gen. 35:5; ch. 17:10

V *2Sa 22:30* ◄► *2Ch 14:11*
V *2Ch 14:7* ◄► *2Ch 16:9*

Asa's reform movement

E 15 AND [a]THE spirit of God came
upon Azariah the son of Oded:
L 2 And he went out [1]to meet Asa, and
S said unto him, Hear ye me, Asa, and all
U Judah and Benjamin; [a]The LORD *is* with
you, while ye be with him; and [b]if ye
seek him, he will be found of you; but [c]if
ye forsake him, he will forsake you.
P 3 Now [a]for a long season Israel *hath
been* without the true God, and without
[b]a teaching priest, and without law.
L 4 But [a]when they in their trouble did
R turn unto the LORD God of Israel, and
sought him, he was found of them.

5 And in those times *there was* no peace to him that went out, nor to him that came in, but great vexations *were* upon all the inhabitants of the countries.

6 [a]And nation was [1]destroyed of nation, and city of city: for God did vex them with all adversity.

7 Be ye strong therefore, and let not your hands be weak: for your work shall be rewarded.

8 And when Asa heard these words, and the prophecy of Oded the prophet, he took courage, and put away the [1]abominable idols out of all the land of Judah and Benjamin, and out of the cities [a]which he had taken from mount Ephraim, and renewed the altar of the LORD, that *was* before the porch of the LORD.

9 And he gathered all Judah and Benjamin, and [a]the strangers with them out of Ephraim and Manasseh, and out of Simeon: for they fell to him out of Israel in abundance, when they saw that the LORD his God *was* with him.

10 So they gathered themselves together at Jerusalem in the third month, in the fifteenth year of the reign of Asa.

11 [a]And they offered unto the LORD [1]the same time, of [b]the spoil *which* they had brought, seven hundred oxen and seven thousand sheep.

12 And they [a]entered into a covenant to seek the LORD God of their fathers with all their heart and with all their soul;

13 [a]That whosoever would not seek the LORD God of Israel [b]should be put to death, whether small or great, whether man or woman.

14 And they sware unto the LORD with a loud voice, and with shouting, and with trumpets, and with cornets.

15 And all Judah rejoiced at the oath: L
for they had sworn with all their heart, and [a]sought him with their whole desire; and he was found of them: and the LORD gave them rest round about.

16 ¶ And also *concerning* [a]Maachah the [1]mother of Asa the king, he removed her from *being* queen, because she had made an [2]idol in a grove: and Asa cut down her idol, and stamped *it,* and burnt *it* at the brook Kidron.

17 But [a]the high places were not taken away out of Israel: nevertheless the heart of Asa was perfect all his days.

18 ¶ And he brought into the house of God the things that his father had dedicated, and that he himself had dedicated, silver, and gold, and vessels.

19 And there was no *more* war unto the five and thirtieth year of the reign of Asa.

The end of Asa's reign

16 IN THE six and thirtieth year of the reign of Asa [a]Baasha king of Israel came up against Judah, and built Ramah, [b]to the intent that he might let none go out or come in to Asa king of Judah.

2 Then Asa brought out silver and gold out of the treasures of the house of the LORD and of the king's house, and sent to Ben-hadad king of Syria, that dwelt at [1]Damascus, saying,

3 *There is* a league between me and thee, as *there was* between my father and thy father: behold, I have sent thee silver and gold; go, break thy league with Baasha king of Israel, that he may depart from me.

4 And Ben-hadad hearkened unto king Asa, and sent the captains of [1]his armies against the cities of Israel; and they smote Ijon, and Dan, and Abel-maim, and all the store cities of Naphtali.

15:1 [a]Num. 24:2; Judg. 3:10; ch. 20:14
2 [a]Jas. 4:8 [b]ver. 4, 15; 1 Chr. 28:9; ch. 33:12,13; Jer. 29:13; Mat. 7:7 [c]ch. 24:20 [1]Heb. *before Asa*
3 [a]Hos. 3:4 [b]Lev. 10:11
4 [a]Deut. 4:29
6 [a]Mat. 24:7 [1]Heb. *beaten in pieces*
8 [a]ch. 13:19 [1]Heb. *abominations*
9 [a]ch. 11:16
11 [a]ch. 14:15 [b]ch. 14:13 [1]Heb. *in that day*
12 [a]2 Ki. 23:3; ch. 34:31; Neh. 10:29
13 [a]Ex. 22:20 [b]Deut. 13:5,9,15
15 [a]ver. 2
16 [a]1 Ki. 15:13 [1]i.e. *grandmother;* see 1 Ki. 15:2,10 [2]Heb. *horror*
17 [a]ch. 14:3,5; 1 Ki. 15:14
16:1 [a]1 Ki. 15:17 [b]ch. 15:9
2 [1]Heb. *Darmesek*
4 [1]Heb. *which were his*

E *1Ch 28:12* ◀▶ *2Ch 20:14*
L *2Ch 7:14* ◀▶ *2Ch 15:4*
S *2Ch 7:14* ◀▶ *2Ch 20:21*
U *2Ch 6:14* ◀▶ *2Ch 16:9*
P *2Ch 7:14* ◀▶ *2Ch 30:9*
L *2Ch 15:2* ◀▶ *2Ch 15:15*
R *2Ch 7:14* ◀▶ *Ezr 10:11*
L *2Ch 15:4* ◀▶ *2Ch 30:9*

5 And it came to pass, when Baasha heard *it,* that he left off building of Ramah, and let his work cease.

6 Then Asa the king took all Judah; and they carried away the stones of Ramah, and the timber thereof, wherewith Baasha was building; and he built therewith Geba and Mizpah.

7 ¶ And at that time [a]Hanani the seer came to Asa king of Judah, and said unto him, [b]Because thou hast relied on the king of Syria, and not relied on the LORD thy God, therefore is the host of the king of Syria escaped out of thine hand.

8 Were not [a]the Ethiopians and [b]the Lubims [1]a huge host, with very many chariots and horsemen? yet, because thou didst rely on the LORD, he delivered them into thine hand.

J E U V 9 [a]For the eyes of the LORD run to and fro throughout the whole earth, [1]to show himself strong in the behalf of *them* whose heart *is* perfect toward him. Herein [b]thou hast done foolishly: therefore from henceforth [c]thou shalt have wars.

10 Then Asa was wroth with the seer, and [a]put him in a prison house; for *he was* in a rage with him because of this *thing.* And Asa [1]oppressed *some* of the people the same time.

11 ¶ [a]And, behold, the acts of Asa, first and last, lo, they *are* written in the book of the kings of Judah and Israel.

H 12 And Asa in the thirty and ninth year of his reign was diseased in his feet, until his disease *was* exceeding *great:* yet in his disease he [a]sought not to the LORD, but to the physicians.

13 ¶ [a]And Asa slept with his fathers, and died in the one and fortieth year of his reign.

14 And they buried him in his own sepulchres, which he had [1]made for himself in the city of David, and laid him in the bed which was filled [a]with sweet odours and divers kinds *of spices* prepared by the apothecaries' art: and they made [b]a very great burning for him.

J *1Ch 21:9–13 ◀ ▶ 2Ch 21:14–16*
E *2Ch 6:30 ◀ ▶ Job 4:14*
U *2Ch 15:2 ◀ ▶ 2Ch 19:11*
V *2Ch 14:11 ◀ ▶ 2Ch 20:15*
H *2Ch 7:13–14 ◀ ▶ 2Ch 20:9*

Jehoshaphat, king of Judah

17 AND [a]JEHOSHAPHAT his son reigned in his stead, and strengthened himself against Israel.

2 And he placed forces in all the fenced cities of Judah, and set garrisons in the land of Judah, and in the cities of Ephraim, [a]which Asa his father had taken.

3 And the LORD was with Jehoshaphat, because he walked in the first ways [1]of his father David, and sought not unto Baalim;

4 But sought to the *LORD* God of his father, and walked in his commandments, and not after [a]the doings of Israel.

5 Therefore the LORD stablished the kingdom in his hand; and all Judah [a]brought[1] to Jehoshaphat presents; [b]and he had riches and honour in abundance.

6 And his heart [1]was lifted up in the ways of the LORD: moreover [a]he took away the high places and groves out of Judah.

7 ¶ Also in the third year of his reign he sent to his princes, *even* to Ben-hail, and to Obadiah, and to Zechariah, and to Nethaneel, and to Michaiah, [a]to teach in the cities of Judah.

8 And with them *he sent* Levites, *even* Shemaiah, and Nethaniah, and Zebadiah, and Asahel, and Shemiramoth, and Jehonathan, and Adonijah, and Tobijah, and Tob-adonijah, Levites; and with them Elishama and Jehoram, priests.

9 [a]And they taught in Judah, and *had* the book of the law of the LORD with them, and went about throughout all the cities of Judah, and taught the people.

10 ¶ And [a]the fear of the LORD [1]fell upon all the kingdoms of the lands that *were* round about Judah, so that they made no war against Jehoshaphat.

11 Also *some* of the Philistines [a]brought Jehoshaphat presents, and tribute silver; and the Arabians brought him flocks, seven thousand and seven hundred rams, and seven thousand and seven hundred he goats.

12 ¶ And Jehoshaphat waxed great exceedingly; and he built in Judah [1]castles, and cities of store.

13 And he had much business in the cities of Judah: and the men of war, mighty men of valour, *were* in Jerusalem.

14 And these *are* the numbers of them

7 [a]1 Ki. 16:1; ch. 19:2 [b]Is. 31:1; Jer. 17:5
8 [a]ch. 14:9 [b]ch. 12:3 [1]Heb. *in abundance*
9 [a]Job 34:21; Prov. 5:21 & 15:3; Jer. 16:17 & 32:19; Zech. 4:10 [b]1 Sam. 13:13 [c]1 Ki. 15:32 [1]Or, *strongly to hold with* them
10 [a]ch. 18:26; Jer. 20:2; Mat. 14:3 [1]Heb. *crushed*
11 [a]1 Ki. 15:23
12 [a]Jer. 17:5
13 [a]1 Ki. 15:24
14 [a]Gen. 50:2; Mark 16:1; John 19:39,40 [b]ch. 21:19; Jer. 34:5 [1]Heb. *digged*
17:1 [a]1 Ki. 15:24
2 [a]ch. 15:8
3 [1]Or, *of his father,* and *of David*
4 [a]1 Ki. 12:28
5 [a]1 Sam. 10:27; 1 Ki. 10:25 [b]1 Ki. 10:27; ch. 18:1 [1]Heb. *gave*
6 [a]1 Ki. 22:43; ch. 15:17 & 19:3 & 20:33 [1]i.e. *was encouraged*
7 [a]ch. 15:3
9 [a]ch. 35:3; Neh. 8:7
10 [a]Gen. 35:5 [1]Heb. *was*
11 [a]2 Sam. 8:2
12 [1]Or, *palaces*

according to the house of their fathers: Of Judah, the captains of thousands; Adnah the chief, and with him mighty men of valour three hundred thousand.

15 And [1]next to him *was* Jehohanan the captain, and with him two hundred and fourscore thousand.

16 And next him *was* Amasiah the son of Zichri, [a]who willingly offered himself unto the LORD; and with him two hundred thousand mighty men of valour.

17 And of Benjamin; Eliada a mighty man of valour, and with him armed men with bow and shield two hundred thousand.

18 And next him *was* Jehozabad, and with him an hundred and fourscore thousand ready prepared for the war.

19 These waited on the king, beside [a]*those* whom the king put in the fenced cities throughout all Judah.

The prophecy against Ahab

18 NOW JEHOSHAPHAT [a]had riches and honour in abundance, and [b]joined affinity with Ahab.

2 [a]And [1]after *certain* years he went down to Ahab to Samaria. And Ahab killed sheep and oxen for him in abundance, and for the people that *he had* with him, and persuaded him to go up *with him* to Ramoth-gilead.

3 And Ahab king of Israel said unto Jehoshaphat king of Judah, Wilt thou go with me to Ramoth-gilead? And he answered him, I *am* as thou *art,* and my people as thy people; and *we will be* with thee in the war.

4 ¶ And Jehoshaphat said unto the king of Israel, [a]Inquire, I pray thee, at the word of the LORD today.

5 Therefore the king of Israel gathered together of prophets four hundred men, and said unto them, Shall we go to Ramoth-gilead to battle, or shall I forbear? And they said, Go up; for God will deliver *it* into the king's hand.

6 But Jehoshaphat said, *Is there* not here a prophet of the LORD [1]besides, that we might inquire of him?

7 And the king of Israel said unto Jehoshaphat, *There is* yet one man, by whom we may inquire of the LORD: but I hate him; for he never prophesied good unto me, but always evil: the same *is* Micaiah the son of Imla. And Jehoshaphat said, Let not the king say so.

15 [1]Heb. *at his hand*

16 [a]Judg. 5:2,9

19 [a]ver. 2

18:1 [a]ch. 17:5 [b]2 Ki. 8:18

2 [a]1 Ki. 22:2 [1]Heb. *at the end of years*

4 [a]1 Sam. 23:2,4,9; 2 Sam. 2:1

6 [1]Heb. *yet,* or, *more*

8 [1]Or, *eunuchs* [2]Heb. *Hasten*

9 [1]Or, *floor*

10 [1]Heb. thou *consume them*

12 [1]Heb. *with one mouth*

13 [a]Num. 22:18, 20,35 & 23:12,26 & 24:13; 1 Ki. 22:14

17 [1]Or, *but for evil?*

8 And the king of Israel called for one *of his* [1]officers, and said, [2]Fetch quickly Micaiah the son of Imla.

9 And the king of Israel and Jehoshaphat king of Judah sat either of them on his throne, clothed in *their* robes, and they sat in a [1]void place at the entering in of the gate of Samaria; and all the prophets prophesied before them.

10 And Zedekiah the son of Chenaanah had made him horns of iron, and said, Thus saith the LORD, With these thou shalt push Syria until [1]they be consumed.

11 And all the prophets prophesied so, saying, Go up to Ramoth-gilead, and prosper: for the LORD shall deliver *it* into the hand of the king.

12 And the messenger that went to call Micaiah spake to him, saying, Behold, the words of the prophets *declare* good to the king [1]with one assent; let thy word therefore, I pray thee, be like one of theirs, and speak thou good.

13 And Micaiah said, *As* the LORD liveth, [a]even what my God saith, that will I speak.

14 And when he was come to the king, the king said unto him, Micaiah, shall we go to Ramoth-gilead to battle, or shall I forbear? And he said, Go ye up, and prosper, and they shall be delivered into your hand.

15 And the king said to him, How many times shall I adjure thee that thou say nothing but the truth to me in the name of the LORD?

16 Then he said, I did see all Israel scattered upon the mountains, as sheep that have no shepherd: and the LORD said, These have no master; let them return *therefore* every man to his house in peace.

17 And the king of Israel said to Jehoshaphat, Did I not tell thee *that* he would not prophesy good unto me, [1]but evil?

18 Again he said, Therefore hear the word of the LORD; I saw the LORD sitting upon his throne, and all the host of heaven standing on his right hand and *on* his left.

19 And the LORD said, Who shall entice Ahab king of Israel, that he may go up and fall at Ramoth-gilead? And one spake saying after this manner, and another saying after that manner.

20 Then there came out a [a]spirit, and stood before the LORD, and said, I will entice him. And the LORD said unto him, Wherewith?

21 And he said, I will go out, and be a lying spirit in the mouth of all his prophets. And *the LORD* said, Thou shalt entice *him,* and thou shalt also prevail: go out, and do *even* so.

22 Now therefore, behold, [a]the LORD hath put a lying spirit in the mouth of these thy prophets, and the LORD hath spoken evil against thee.

L 23 Then Zedekiah the son of Chenaanah came near, and [a]smote Micaiah upon the cheek, and said, Which way went the spirit of the LORD from me to speak unto thee?

Q

24 And Micaiah said, Behold, thou shalt see on that day when thou shalt go [1]into [2]an inner chamber to hide thyself.

25 Then the king of Israel said, Take ye Micaiah, and carry him back to Amon the governor of the city, and to Joash the king's son;

26 And say, Thus saith the king, [a]Put this *fellow* in the prison, and feed him with bread of affliction and with water of affliction, until I return in peace.

27 And Micaiah said, If thou certainly return in peace, *then* hath not the LORD spoken by me. And he said, Hearken, all ye people.

The defeat and death of Ahab

28 So the king of Israel and Jehoshaphat the king of Judah went up to Ramoth-gilead.

29 And the king of Israel said unto Jehoshaphat, I will disguise myself, and will go to the battle; but put thou on thy robes. So the king of Israel disguised himself; and they went to the battle.

30 Now the king of Syria had commanded the captains of the chariots that *were* with him, saying, Fight ye not with small or great, save only with the king of Israel.

31 And it came to pass, when the captains of the chariots saw Jehoshaphat, that they said, It *is* the king of Israel. Therefore they compassed about him to fight: but Jehoshaphat cried out, and the LORD helped him; and God moved them *to depart* from him.

32 For it came to pass, that, when the captains of the chariots perceived that it was not the king of Israel, they turned back again [1]from pursuing him.

33 And a *certain* man drew a bow [1]at a venture, and smote the king of Israel [2]between the joints of the harness: therefore he said to his chariot man, Turn thine hand, that thou mayest carry me out of the host; for I am [3]wounded.

34 And the battle increased that day: howbeit the king of Israel stayed *himself* up in *his* chariot against the Syrians until the even: and about the time of the sun going down he died.

Reforms by Jehoshaphat

19 AND JEHOSHAPHAT the king of Judah returned to his house in peace to Jerusalem.

2 And Jehu the son of Hanani [a]the seer went out to meet him, and said to king Jehoshaphat, Shouldest thou help the ungodly, and [b]love them that hate the LORD? therefore *is* [c]wrath upon thee from before the LORD.

3 Nevertheless there are [a]good things found in thee, in that thou hast taken away the groves out of the land, and hast [b]prepared thine heart to seek God.

4 And Jehoshaphat dwelt at Jerusalem: and [1]he went out again through the people from Beer-sheba to mount Ephraim, and brought them back unto the LORD God of their fathers.

5 ¶ And he set judges in the land throughout all the fenced cities of Judah, city by city,

6 And said to the judges, Take heed what ye do: for [a]ye judge not for man, but for the LORD, [b]who *is* with you [1]in the judgment.

7 Wherefore now let the fear of the LORD be upon you; take heed and do *it:* for [a]*there is* no iniquity with the LORD our God, nor [b]respect of persons, nor taking of gifts.

8 ¶ Moreover in Jerusalem did Jehoshaphat [a]set of the Levites, and *of* the priests, and of the chief of the fathers of Israel, for the judgment of the LORD, and for controversies, when they returned to Jerusalem.

9 And he charged them, saying, Thus

---

20 [a]Job 1:6
22 [a]Job 12:16; Is. 19:14; Ezek. 14:9
23 [a]Jer. 20:2; Mark 14:65; Acts 23:2
24 [1]Or, *from chamber to chamber* [2]Heb. *a chamber in a chamber*
26 [a]ch. 16:10
32 [1]Heb. *from after him*
33 [1]Heb. *in his simplicity* [2]Heb. *between the joints and between the breastplate* [3]Heb. *made sick*
19:2 [a]1 Sam. 9:9 [b]Ps. 139:21 [c]ch. 32:25
3 [a]ch. 17:4,6 [b]ch. 30:19; Ezra 7:10
4 [1]Heb. *he returned and went out*
6 [a]Deut. 1:17 [b]Ps. 82:1; Eccl. 5:8 [1]Heb. *in the matter of judgment*
7 [a]Deut. 32:4; Rom. 9:14 [b]Deut. 10:17; Job 34:19; Acts 10:34; Rom. 2:11; Gal. 2:6; Eph. 6:9; Col. 3:25
8 [a]Deut. 16:18; ch. 17:8

L 2Ki 2:16 ◄► Job 32:18–19
Q 1Ki 22:24 ◄► Ne 9:30

shall ye do [a]in the fear of the LORD, faithfully, and with a perfect heart.

10 [a]And what cause soever shall come to you of your brethren that dwell in their cities, between blood and blood, between law and commandment, statutes and judgments, ye shall even warn them that they trespass not against the LORD, and *so* [b]wrath come upon [c]you, and upon your brethren: this do, and ye shall not trespass.

U W 11 And, behold, Amariah the chief priest *is* over you [a]in all matters of the LORD; and Zebadiah the son of Ishmael, the ruler of the house of Judah, for all the king's matters: also the Levites *shall be* officers before you. [1]Deal courageously, and the LORD shall be [b]with the good.

Moab and Ammon defeated

20 IT CAME to pass after this also, *that* the children of Moab, and the children of Ammon, and with them *other* beside the Ammonites, came against Jehoshaphat to battle.

2 Then there came some that told Jehoshaphat, saying, There cometh a great multitude against thee from beyond the sea on this side Syria; and, behold, they *be* [a]in Hazazon-tamar, which *is* [b]En-gedi.

3 And Jehoshaphat feared, and set [1]himself to [a]seek the LORD, and [b]proclaimed a fast throughout all Judah.

4 And Judah gathered themselves together, to ask *help* of the LORD: even out of all the cities of Judah they came to seek the LORD.

5 ¶ And Jehoshaphat stood in the congregation of Judah and Jerusalem, in the house of the LORD, before the new court,

6 And said, O LORD God of our fathers, *art* not thou [a]God in heaven? and [b]rulest *not* thou over all the kingdoms of the heathen? and [c]in thine hand *is there not* power and might, so that none is able to withstand thee?

I 7 *Art* not thou [a]our God, [1]*who* [b]didst drive out the inhabitants of this land before thy people Israel, and gavest it to the seed of Abraham [c]thy friend for ever?

U 2Ch 16:9 ◄► 2Ch 20:20
W 1Ch 28:20 ◄► Ne 8:10
I 1Ch 22:13 ◄► Ezr 3:11

9 [a]2 Sam. 23:3
10 [a]Deut. 17:8 [b]Num. 16:46 [c]Ezek. 3:18
11 [a]1 Chr. 26:30 [b]ch. 15:2 [1]Heb. *Take courage and do*
20:2 [a]Gen. 14:7 [b]Josh. 15:62
3 [a]ch. 19:3 [b]Ezra 8:21; Jer. 36:9; Jonah 3:5 [1]Heb. *his face*
6 [a]Deut. 4:39; Josh. 2:11; 1 Ki. 8:23; Mat. 6:9 [b]Ps. 47:2, 8; Dan. 4:17 [c]1 Chr. 29:12; Ps. 62:11; Mat. 6:13
7 [a]Gen. 17:7; Ex. 6:7 [b]Ps. 44:2 [c]Is. 41:8; Jas. 2:23 [1]Heb. *thou*
9 [a]1 Ki. 8:33,37; ch. 6:28-30 [b]ch. 6:20
10 [a]Deut. 2:4,9,19 [b]Num. 20:21
11 [a]Ps. 83:12
12 [a]1 Sam. 3:13 [b]Ps. 25:15 & 121:1,2 & 123:1,2 & 141:8
14 [a]Num. 11:25, 26 & 24:2; ch. 15:1
15 [a]Ex. 14:13,14; Deut. 1:29,30 & 31:6,8; ch. 32:7
16 [1]Heb. *ascent* [2]Or, *valley*
17 [a]Ex. 14:13,14

8 And they dwelt therein, and have built thee a sanctuary therein for thy name, saying,

9 [a]If, *when* evil cometh upon us, *as* the sword, judgment, or pestilence, or famine, we stand before this house, and in thy presence, (for thy [b]name *is* in this house,) and cry unto thee in our affliction, then thou wilt hear and help. L F H

10 And now, behold, the children of Ammon and Moab and mount Seir, whom thou [a]wouldest not let Israel invade, when they came out of the land of Egypt, but [b]they turned from them, and destroyed them not;

11 Behold, *I say, how* they reward us, [a]to come to cast us out of thy possession, which thou hast given us to inherit.

12 O our God, wilt thou not [a]judge them? for we have no might against this great company that cometh against us; neither know we what to do: but [b]our eyes *are* upon thee.

13 And all Judah stood before the LORD, with their little ones, their wives, and their children.

14 ¶ Then upon Jahaziel the son of Zechariah, the son of Benaiah, the son of Jeiel, the son of Mattaniah, a Levite of the sons of Asaph, [a]came the spirit of the LORD in the midst of the congregation; E T

15 And he said, Hearken ye, all Judah, and ye inhabitants of Jerusalem, and thou king Jehoshaphat, Thus saith the LORD unto you, [a]Be not afraid nor dismayed by reason of this great multitude; for the battle *is* not yours, but God's. V

16 Tomorrow go ye down against them: behold, they come up by the [1]cliff of Ziz; and ye shall find them at the end of the [2]brook, before the wilderness of Jeruel.

17 [a]Ye shall not *need* to fight in this *battle:* set yourselves, stand ye *still,* and see the salvation of the LORD with you, O Judah and Jerusalem: fear not, nor be V

L 2Ch 9:8 ◄► 2Ch 34:28
F 2Ki 6:18 ◄► Ne 9:15
H 2Ch 16:12 ◄► Job 5:26
E 2Ch 15:1 ◄► 2Ch 24:20
T 1Ch 28:12 ◄► 2Ch 24:20
V 2Ch 16:9 ◄► 2Ch 20:17
V 2Ch 20:15 ◄► 2Ch 32:7–8

20:7 King Jehoshaphat reminded God of his eternal covenant with Abraham to give Israel the land of Canaan (see note on the Abrahamic covenant at Ge 15:4).

dismayed; tomorrow go out against them: [b]for the LORD *will be* with you.

18 And Jehoshaphat [a]bowed his head with *his* face to the ground: and all Judah and the inhabitants of Jerusalem fell before the LORD, worshipping the LORD.

19 And the Levites, of the children of the Kohathites, and of the children of the Korhites, stood up to praise the LORD God of Israel with a loud voice on high.

F U 20 ¶ And they rose early in the morning, and went forth into the wilderness of Tekoa: and as they went forth, Jehoshaphat stood and said, Hear me, O Judah, and ye inhabitants of Jerusalem; [a]Believe in the LORD your God, so shall ye be established; believe his prophets, so shall ye prosper.

S 21 And when he had consulted with the people, he appointed singers unto the LORD, [a]and [1]that should praise the beauty of holiness, as they went out before the army, and to say, [b]Praise the LORD; [c]for his mercy *endureth* for ever.

22 ¶ [1]And when they began [2]to sing and to praise, [a]the LORD set ambushments against the children of Ammon, Moab, and mount Seir, which were come against Judah; and [3]they were smitten.

23 For the children of Ammon and Moab stood up against the inhabitants of mount Seir, utterly to slay and destroy *them:* and when they had made an end of the inhabitants of Seir, every one helped [1]to destroy another.

24 And when Judah came toward the watchtower in the wilderness, they looked unto the multitude, and, behold, they *were* dead bodies fallen to the earth, and [1]none escaped.

25 And when Jehoshaphat and his people came to take away the spoil of them, they found among them in abundance both riches with the dead bodies, and precious jewels, which they stripped off for themselves, more than they could carry away: and they were three days in gathering of the spoil, it was so much.

26 ¶ And on the fourth day they assembled themselves in the valley of [1]Berachah; for there they blessed the LORD: therefore the name of the same place was called, The valley of Berachah, unto this day.

27 Then they returned, every man of Judah and Jerusalem, and Jehoshaphat in the [1]forefront of them, to go again to Jerusalem with joy; for the LORD had [a]made them to rejoice over their enemies.

28 And they came to Jerusalem with psalteries and harps and trumpets unto the house of the LORD.

29 And [a]the fear of God was on all the kingdoms of *those* countries, when they had heard that the LORD fought against the enemies of Israel.

30 So the realm of Jehoshaphat was quiet: for his [a]God gave him rest round about.

The death of Jehoshaphat

31 ¶ [a]And Jehoshaphat reigned over Judah: *he was* thirty and five years old when he began to reign, and he reigned twenty and five years in Jerusalem. And his mother's name *was* Azubah the daughter of Shilhi.

32 And he walked in the way of Asa his father, and departed not from it, doing *that which was* right in the sight of the LORD.

33 Howbeit [a]the high places were not taken away: for as yet the people had not [b]prepared their hearts unto the God of their fathers.

34 Now the rest of the acts of Jehoshaphat, first and last, behold, they *are* written in the [1]book of Jehu the son of Hanani, [a]who [2]*is* mentioned in the book of the kings of Israel.

35 ¶ And after this [a]did Jehoshaphat king of Judah join himself with Ahaziah king of Israel, who did very wickedly:

36 [1]And he joined himself with him to make ships to go to Tarshish: and they made the ships in Ezion-geber.

37 Then Eliezer the son of Dodavah of Mareshah prophesied against Jehoshaphat, saying, Because thou hast joined thyself with Ahaziah, the LORD hath broken thy works. [a]And the ships were broken, that they were not able to go [b]to Tarshish.

Jehoram, king of Judah

21 NOW [a]JEHOSHAPHAT slept with his fathers, and was buried with his fathers in the city of David. And Jehoram his son [1]reigned in his stead.

17 [b]Num. 14:9; ch. 15:2 & 32:8
18 [a]Ex. 4:31
20 [a]Is. 7:9
21 [a]1 Chr. 16:29 [b]1 Chr. 16:34; Ps 136:1 [c]1 Chr. 16:41; ch. 5:13 [1]Heb. *praisers*
22 [a]Judg. 7:22; 1 Sam. 14:20 [1]Heb. *And in the time that they* [2]Heb. *in singing and praise* [3]Or, *they smote one another*
23 [1]Heb. *for the destruction*
24 [1]Heb. there was *not an escaping*
26 [1]i.e. *Blessing*
27 [a]Neh. 12:43 [1]Heb. *head*
29 [a]ch. 17:10
30 [a]ch. 15:15; Job 34:29
31 [a]1 Ki. 22:41
33 [a]See ch. 17:6 [b]ch. 12:14 & 19:3
34 [a]1 Ki. 16:1,7 [1]Heb. *words* [2]Heb. *was made to ascend*
35 [a]1 Ki. 22:48,49
36 [1]At first Jehoshaphat was unwilling; see 1 Ki. 22:49
37 [a]1 Ki. 22:48 [b]ch. 9:21
21:1 [a]1 Ki. 22:50 [1]Alone

F *Ge 15:6* ◀▶ *Ps 2:12*
U *2Ch 19:11* ◀▶ *2Ch 26:5*
S *2Ch 15:2* ◀▶ *2Ch 24:20*

2 And he had brethren the sons of Jehoshaphat, Azariah, and Jehiel, and Zechariah, and Azariah, and Michael, and Shephatiah: all these *were* the sons of Jehoshaphat king of Israel.

3 And their father gave them great gifts of silver, and of gold, and of precious things, with fenced cities in Judah: but the kingdom gave he to [1]Jehoram; because he *was* the firstborn.

4 Now when Jehoram was risen up to the kingdom of his father, he strengthened himself, and slew all his brethren with the sword, and *divers* also of the princes of Israel.

5 ¶ [a]Jehoram *was* thirty and two years old when he began to reign, and he reigned eight years in Jerusalem.

6 And he walked in the way of the kings of Israel, like as did the house of Ahab: for he had the daughter of [a]Ahab to wife: and he wrought *that which was* evil in the eyes of the LORD.

M 7 Howbeit the LORD would not destroy the house of David, because of the covenant that he had made with David, and as he promised to give a [1]light to him and to his [a]sons for ever.

8 ¶ [a]In his days the Edomites revolted from under the [1]dominion of Judah, and made themselves a king.

9 Then Jehoram went forth with his princes, and all his chariots with him: and he rose up by night, and smote the Edomites which compassed him in, and the captains of the chariots.

10 So the Edomites revolted from under the hand of Judah unto this day. The same time *also* did Libnah revolt from under his hand; because he had forsaken the LORD God of his fathers.

11 Moreover he made high places in the mountains of Judah, and caused the inhabitants of Jerusalem to [a]commit fornication, and compelled Judah *thereto.*

12 ¶ And there came a writing to him from Elijah the prophet, saying, Thus saith the LORD God of David thy father, Because thou hast not walked in the ways of Jehoshaphat thy father, nor in the ways of Asa king of Judah,

13 But hast walked in the way of the kings of Israel, and hast [a]made Judah and the inhabitants of Jerusalem to [b]go a-whoring, like to the [c]whoredoms of the house of Ahab, and also hast [d]slain thy brethren of thy father's house, *which were* better than thyself:

14 Behold, with [1]a great plague will the LORD smite thy people, and thy children, and thy wives, and all thy goods: J

15 And thou *shalt have* great sickness by [a]disease of thy bowels, until thy bowels fall out by reason of the sickness day by day.

16 ¶ Moreover the LORD stirred up against Jehoram the spirit of the Philistines, and of the Arabians, that *were* near the Ethiopians:

17 And they came up into Judah, and brake into it, and [1]carried away all the substance that was found in the king's house, and [a]his sons also, and his wives; so that there was never a son left him, save [2]Jehoahaz, the youngest of his sons.

18 ¶ And after all this the LORD smote him [a]in his bowels with an incurable disease.

19 And it came to pass, that in process of time, after the end of two years, his bowels fell out by reason of his sickness: so he died of sore diseases. And his people made no burning for him, like [a]the burning of his fathers.

20 Thirty and two years old was he when he began to reign, and he reigned in Jerusalem eight years, and departed without being desired. Howbeit they buried him in the city of David, but not in the sepulchres of the kings.

Ahaziah, king of Judah

22 AND THE inhabitants of Jerusalem made [a]Ahaziah his youngest son king in his stead: for the band of men that came with the Arabians to the camp had slain all the [b]eldest. So Ahaziah the son of Jehoram king of Judah reigned.

2 [a]Forty and two years old *was* Aha-

3 [1]Jehoram made partner of the kingdom with his father; see 2 Ki. 8:16
5 [a]In consort 2 Ki. 8:17
6 [a]ch. 22:2
7 [a]2 Sam. 7:12,13; 1 Ki. 11:36; 2 Ki. 8:19; Ps. 132:11 [1]Heb. *lamp,* or, *candle*
8 [a]2 Ki. 8:20 [1]Heb. *hand*
11 [a]Lev. 20:5
13 [a]ver. 11 [b]Ex. 34:15; Deut. 31:16 [c]1 Ki. 16:31-33; 2 Ki. 9:22 [d]ver. 4
14 [1]Heb. *a great stroke*
15 [a]ver. 18,19
17 [a]ch. 24:7 [1]Heb. *carried captive;* see ch. 22:1 [2]Or, *Ahaziah* in ch. 22:1, or, *Azariah* in ch. 22:6
18 [a]ver. 15
19 [a]ch. 16:14
22:1 [a]ver. 6; ch. 21:17 [b]ch. 21:17
2 [a]2 Ki. 8:26

M *2Ch 13:5* ◀ ▶ *Ps 2:8–9*

J *2Ch 16:9* ◀ ▶ *Ps 1:5*

21:7 Though King Jehoram was an evil king, God showed mercy to David's descendants in faithfulness to his covenant with David to establish David's house forever (see note on the Davidic covenant at 2Sa 7:16).

ziah when he began to reign, and he
reigned one year in Jerusalem. His
mother's name also *was* [b]Athaliah the
daughter of Omri.
3 He also walked in the ways of the
house of Ahab: for his mother was his
counsellor to do wickedly.
4 Wherefore he did evil in the sight of
the LORD like the house of Ahab: for they
were his counsellors after the death of his
father to his destruction.
5 ¶ He walked also after their counsel,
and [a]went with Jehoram the son of Ahab
king of Israel to war against Hazael king
of Syria at Ramoth-gilead: and the Syrians
smote Joram.
6 [a]And he returned to be healed in Jezreel because of the wounds [1]which were
given him at Ramah, when he fought
with Hazael king of Syria. And [2]Azariah
the son of Jehoram king of Judah went
down to see Jehoram the son of Ahab at
Jezreel, because he was sick.
7 And the [1]destruction of Ahaziah
[a]was of God by coming to Joram: for
when he was come, he [b]went out with
Jehoram against Jehu the son of Nimshi,
[c]whom the LORD had anointed to cut off
the house of Ahab.
8 And it came to pass, that, when Jehu
was [a]executing judgment upon the house
of Ahab, and [b]found the princes of Judah,
and the sons of the brethren of Ahaziah,
that ministered to Ahaziah, he slew
them.
9 [a]And he sought Ahaziah: and they
caught him, (for he was hid in Samaria,)
and brought him to Jehu: and when they
had slain him, they buried him: Because,
said they, he *is* the son of Jehoshaphat,
who [b]sought the LORD with all his heart.
So the house of Ahaziah had no power to
keep still the kingdom.

The murder of the royal family

10 ¶ [a]But when Athaliah the mother of
Ahaziah saw that her son was dead, she
arose and destroyed all the seed royal of
the house of Judah.
11 But [a]Jehoshabeath, the daughter of
the king, took Joash the son of Ahaziah,
and stole him from among the king's sons
that were slain, and put him and his
nurse in a bedchamber. So Jehoshabeath,
the daughter of king Jehoram, the wife of
Jehoiada the priest, (for she was the sister
of Ahaziah,) hid him from Athaliah, so
that she slew him not.
12 And he was with them hid in the
house of God six years: and Athaliah
reigned over the land.

23 AND [a]IN the seventh year Jehoiada strengthened himself, and
took the captains of hundreds, Azariah
the son of Jeroham, and Ishmael the son
of Jehohanan, and Azariah the son of
Obed, and Maaseiah the son of Adaiah,
and Elishaphat the son of Zichri, into covenant with him.
2 And they went about in Judah, and
gathered the Levites out of all the cities of
Judah, and the chief of the fathers of Israel, and they came to Jerusalem.
3 And all the congregation made a covenant with the king in the house of God.
And he said unto them, Behold, the
king's son shall reign, as the LORD hath
[a]said of the sons of David.
4 This *is* the thing that ye shall do; A
third part of you [a]entering on the sabbath, of the priests and of the Levites,
shall be porters of the [1]doors;
5 And a third part *shall be* at the king's
house; and a third part at the gate of the
foundation: and all the people *shall be* in
the courts of the house of the LORD.
6 But let none come into the house of
the LORD, save the priests, and [a]they that
minister of the Levites; they shall go in,
for they *are* holy: but all the people shall
keep the watch of the LORD.
7 And the Levites shall compass the
king round about, every man with his
weapons in his hand; and whosoever *else*
cometh into the house, he shall be put to
death: but be ye with the king when he
cometh in, and when he goeth out.
8 So the Levites and all Judah did according to all things that Jehoiada the
priest had commanded, and took every
man his men that were to come in on the
sabbath, with them that were to go *out*
on the sabbath: for Jehoiada the priest
dismissed not [a]the courses.
9 Moreover Jehoiada the priest delivered to the captains of hundreds spears,
and bucklers, and shields, that *had been*
king David's, which *were* in the house of
God.
10 And he set all the people, every
man having his weapon in his hand, from
the right [1]side of the [2]temple to the left

2 [b]ch. 21:6
5 [a]2 Ki. 8:28
6 [a]2 Ki. 9:15 [1]Heb. *wherewith they wounded him* [2]Otherwise called *Ahaziah* in ver. 1 and *Jehoahaz* in ch. 21:17
7 [a]Judg. 14:4; 1 Ki. 12:15; ch. 10:15 [b]2 Ki. 9:21 [c]2 Ki. 9:6,7 [1]Heb. *treading down*
8 [a]2 Ki. 10:10,11 [b]2 Ki. 10:13,14
9 [a]2 Ki. 9:27; at *Megiddo* in the kingdom of *Samaria* [b]ch. 17:4
10 [a]2 Ki. 11:1
11 [a]2 Ki. 11:2 *Jehosheba*
23:1 [a]2 Ki. 11:4
3 [a]2 Sam. 7:12; 1 Ki. 2:4 & 9:5; ch. 6:16 & 7:18 & 21:7
4 [a]1 Chr. 9:25 [1]Heb. *thresholds*
6 [a]1 Chr. 23:28,29
8 [a]See 1 Chr. 24 & 25
10 [1]Heb. *shoulder* [2]Heb. *house*

side of the temple, along by the altar and
the temple, by the king round about.
11 Then they brought out the king's
son, and put upon him the crown, and
[a]*gave him* the testimony, and made him
king. And Jehoiada and his sons anointed
him, and said, ′God save the king.
12 ¶ Now when Athaliah heard the
noise of the people running and praising
the king, she came to the people into the
house of the LORD:
13 And she looked, and, behold, the
king stood at his pillar at the entering in,
and the princes and the trumpets by the
king: and all the people of the land rejoiced, and sounded with trumpets, also
the singers with instruments of music,
and [a]such as taught to sing praise. Then
Athaliah rent her clothes, and said,
′Treason, Treason.
14 Then Jehoiada the priest brought
out the captains of hundreds that were
set over the host, and said unto them,
Have her forth of the ranges: and whoso
followeth her, let him be slain with the
sword. For the priest said, Slay her not in
the house of the LORD.
15 So they laid hands on her; and
when she was come to the entering [a]of
the horse gate by the king's house, they
slew her there.
16 ¶ And Jehoiada made a covenant
between him, and between all the people, and between the king, that they
should be the LORD'S people.
17 Then all the people went to the
house of Baal, and brake it down, and
brake his altars and his images in pieces,
and [a]slew Mattan the priest of Baal before the altars.
18 Also Jehoiada appointed the offices
of the house of the LORD by the hand of
the priests the Levites, whom David had
[a]distributed in the house of the LORD, to
offer the burnt offerings of the LORD, as *it*
is written in the [b]law of Moses, with rejoicing and with singing, *as it was or-*
dained [c]by′ David.
19 And he set the [a]porters at the gates
of the house of the LORD, that none *which*
was unclean in any thing should enter in.
20 [a]And he took the captains of hundreds, and the nobles, and the governors
of the people, and all the people of the
land, and brought down the king from
the house of the LORD: and they came
through the high gate into the king's
house, and set the king upon the throne
of the kingdom.
21 And all the people of the land rejoiced: and the city was quiet, after that
they had slain Athaliah with the sword.

Joash restores the temple

24 JOASH [a]*WAS* seven years old
when he began to reign, and he
reigned forty years in Jerusalem. His
mother's name also *was* Zibiah of Beer-
sheba.
2 And Joash [a]did *that which was* right
in the sight of the LORD all the days of
Jehoiada the priest.
3 And Jehoiada took for him two
wives; and he begat sons and daughters.
4 ¶ And it came to pass after this, *that*
Joash was minded ′to repair the house of
the LORD.
5 And he gathered together the priest
and the Levites, and said to them, Go out
unto the cities of Judah, and [a]gather of all
Israel money to repair the house of your
God from year to year, and see that ye
hasten the matter. Howbeit the Levites
hastened *it* not.
6 [a]And the king called for Jehoiada the
chief, and said unto him, Why hast thou
not required of the Levites to bring in out
of Judah and out of Jerusalem the collection, *according to the commandment* of
[b]Moses the servant of the LORD, and of
the congregation of Israel, for the [c]taber-
nacle of witness?
7 For [a]the sons of Athaliah, that
wicked woman, had broken up the house
of God; and also all the [b]dedicated things
of the house of the LORD did they bestow
upon Baalim.
8 And at the king's commandment
[a]they made a chest, and set it without at
the gate of the house of the LORD.
9 And they made ′a proclamation
through Judah and Jerusalem, to bring in
to the LORD [a]the collection *that* Moses the
servant of God *laid* upon Israel in the wilderness.
10 And all the princes and all the people rejoiced, and brought in, and cast into
the chest, until they had made an end.
11 Now it came to pass, that at what
time the chest was brought unto the
king's office by the hand of the Levites,
and [a]when they saw that *there was* much
money, the king's scribe and the high
priest's officer came and emptied the

11 [a]Deut. 17:18 ′Heb. *Let the king live*
13 [a]1 Chr. 25:8 ′Heb. *Conspiracy*
15 [a]Neh. 3:28
17 [a]Deut. 13:9
18 [a]1 Chr. 23:6, 30,31 & 24:1 [b]Num. 28:2 [c]1 Chr. 25:2,6 ′Heb. *by the hands of David*
19 [a]1 Chr. 26:1
20 [a]2 Ki. 11:19
24:1 [a]2 Ki. 11:21 & 12:1
2 [a]See ch. 26:5
4 ′Heb. *to renew*
5 [a]2 Ki. 12:4
6 [a]2 Ki. 12:7 [b]Ex. 30:12-14,16 [c]Num. 1:50; Acts 7:44
7 [a]ch. 21:17 [b]2 Ki. 12:4
8 [a]2 Ki. 12:9
9 [a]ver. 6 ′Heb. *a voice*
11 [a]2 Ki. 12:10

chest, and took it, and carried it to his place again. Thus they did day by day, and gathered money in abundance.

12 And the king and Jehoiada gave it to such as did the work of the service of the house of the LORD, and hired masons and carpenters to repair the house of the LORD, and also such as wrought iron and brass to mend the house of the LORD.

13 So the workmen wrought, and [1]the work was perfected by them, and they set the house of God in his state, and strengthened it.

14 And when they had finished *it,* they brought the rest of the money before the king and Jehoiada, [a]whereof were made vessels for the house of the LORD, *even* vessels to minister, and [1]to offer *withal,* and spoons, and vessels of gold and silver. And they offered burnt offerings in the house of the LORD continually all the days of Jehoiada.

15 ¶ But Jehoiada waxed old, and was full of days when he died; an hundred and thirty years old *was he* when he died.

16 And they buried him in the city of David among the kings, because he had done good in Israel, both toward God, and toward his house.

17 Now after the death of Jehoiada came the princes of Judah, and made obeisance to the king. Then the king hearkened unto them.

18 And they left the house of the LORD God of their fathers, and served [a]groves and idols: and [b]wrath came upon Judah and Jerusalem for this their trespass.

19 Yet he [a]sent prophets to them, to bring them again unto the LORD; and they testified against them: but they would not give ear.

E T C S 20 And the spirit of God [a]came[1] upon Zechariah the son of Jehoiada the priest, which stood above the people, and said unto them, Thus saith God, [b]Why transgress ye the commandments of the LORD, that ye cannot prosper? [c]because ye have forsaken the LORD, he hath also forsaken you.

21 And they conspired against him, and [a]stoned him with stones at the commandment of the king in the court of the house of the LORD.

22 Thus Joash the king remembered not the kindness which Jehoiada his father had done to him, but slew his son. And when he died, he said, The LORD look upon *it,* and require *it.*

The defeat and death of Joash

23 ¶ And it came to pass [1]at the end of the year, *that* [a]the host of Syria came up against him: and they came to Judah and Jerusalem, and destroyed all the princes of the people from among the people, and sent all the spoil of them unto the king of [2]Damascus.

24 For the army of the Syrians [a]came with a small company of men, and the LORD [b]delivered a very great host into their hand, because they had forsaken the LORD God of their fathers. So they [c]executed judgment against Joash.

25 And when they were departed from him, (for they left him in great diseases,) [a]his own servants conspired against him for the blood of the [b]sons of Jehoiada the priest, and slew him on his bed, and he died: and they buried him in the city of David, but they buried him not in the sepulchres of the kings.

26 And these are they that conspired against him; [1]Zabad the son of Shimeath an Ammonitess, and Jehozabad the son of [2]Shimrith a Moabitess.

27 ¶ Now *concerning* his sons, and the greatness of [a]the burdens *laid* upon him, and the [1]repairing of the house of God, behold, they *are* written in the [2]story of the book of the kings. [b]And Amaziah his son reigned in his stead.

Amaziah, king of Judah

25 AMAZIAH [a]*WAS* twenty and five years old *when* he began to reign, and he reigned twenty and nine years in Jerusalem. And his mother's name *was* Jehoaddan of Jerusalem.

2 And he did *that which was* right in the sight of the LORD, [a]but not with a perfect heart.

3 ¶ [a]Now it came to pass, when the kingdom was [1]established to him, that he slew his servants that had killed the king his father.

4 But he slew not their children, but *did* as *it is* written in the law in the book of Moses, where the LORD commanded,

13 [1]Heb. *the healing went up upon the work*

14 [a]See 2 Ki. 12:13 [1]Or, *pestils*

18 [a]1 Ki. 14:23 [b]Judg. 5:8; ch. 19:2 & 28:13 & 29:8 & 32:25

19 [a]ch. 36:15; Jer. 7:25,26 & 25:4

20 [a]Judg. 6:34 [b]Num. 14:41 [c]ch. 15:2 [1]Heb. *clothed*

21 [a]Mat. 23:35; Acts 7:58,59

23 [a]2 Ki. 12:17 [1]Heb. *in the revolution of the year* [2]Heb. *Darmesek*

24 [a]Lev. 26:8; Deut. 32:30; Is. 30:17 [b]Lev. 26:25; Deut. 28:25 [c]ch. 22:8; Is. 10:5

25 [a]2 Ki. 12:20 [b]ver. 21

26 [1]Or, *Jozachar;* see 2 Ki. 12:21 [2]Or, *Shomer*

27 [a]2 Ki. 12:18 [b]2 Ki. 12:21 [1]Heb. *founding* [2]Or, *commentary*

25:1 [a]2 Ki. 14:1

2 [a]ver. 14; See 2 Ki. 14:4

3 [a]2 Ki. 14:5 [1]Heb. *confirmed upon him*

E *2Ch 20:14 ◄► Ne 9:20*
T *2Ch 20:14–15 ◄► Ne 9:20*
C *2Ch 12:14 ◄► 2Ch 28:11*
S *2Ch 20:21 ◄► Ezr 8:28*

saying, [a]The fathers shall not die for the children, neither shall the children die for the fathers, but every man shall die for his own sin.

5 ¶ Moreover Amaziah gathered Judah together, and made them captains over thousands, and captains over hundreds, according to the houses of *their* fathers, throughout all Judah and Benjamin: and he numbered them [a]from twenty years old and above, and found them three hundred thousand choice *men, able* to go forth to war, that could handle spear and shield.

6 He hired also an hundred thousand mighty men of valour out of Israel for an hundred talents of silver.

7 But there came a man of God to him, saying, O king, let not the army of Israel go with thee; for the LORD *is* not with Israel, *to wit, with* all the children of Ephraim.

8 But if thou wilt go, do *it,* be strong for the battle: God shall make thee fall before the enemy: for God hath [a]power to help, and to cast down.

P 9 And Amaziah said to the man of God, But what shall we do for the hundred talents which I have given to the [1]army of Israel? And the man of God answered, [a]The LORD is able to give thee much more than this.

10 Then Amaziah separated them, *to wit,* the army that was come to him out of Ephraim, to go [1]home again: wherefore their anger was greatly kindled against Judah, and they returned home [2]in great anger.

11 ¶ And Amaziah strengthened himself, and led forth his people, and went to [a]the valley of salt, and smote of the children of Seir ten thousand.

12 And *other* ten thousand *left* alive did the children of Judah carry away captive, and brought them unto the top of the rock, and cast them down from the top of the rock, that they all were broken in pieces.

13 ¶ But [1]the soldiers of the army which Amaziah sent back, that they should not go with him to battle, fell upon the cities of Judah, from Samaria even unto Beth-horon, and smote three thousand of them, and took much spoil.

14 ¶ Now it came to pass, after that Amaziah was come from the slaughter of the Edomites, that [a]he brought the gods of the children of Seir, and set them up *to be* [b]his gods, and bowed down himself before them, and burned incense unto them.

15 Wherefore the anger of the LORD was kindled against Amaziah, and he sent unto him a prophet, which said unto him, Why hast thou sought after [a]the gods of the people, which [b]could not deliver their own people out of thine hand?

16 And it came to pass, as he talked with him, that *the king* said unto him, Art thou made of the king's counsel? forbear; why shouldest thou be smitten? Then the prophet forbare, and said, I know that God hath [a]determined[1] to destroy thee, because thou hast done this, and hast not hearkened unto my counsel.

17 ¶ Then [a]Amaziah king of Judah took advice, and sent to Joash, the son of Jehoahaz, the son of Jehu, king of Israel, saying, Come, let us see one another in the face.

18 And Joash king of Israel sent to Amaziah king of Judah, saying, The [1]thistle that *was* in Lebanon sent to the cedar that *was* in Lebanon, saying, Give thy daughter to my son to wife: and there passed by [2]a wild beast that *was* in Lebanon, and trode down the thistle.

19 Thou sayest, Lo, thou hast smitten the Edomites; and thine heart lifteth thee up to boast: abide now at home; why shouldest thou meddle to *thine* hurt, that thou shouldest fall, *even* thou, and Judah with thee?

20 But Amaziah would not hear; for [a]it *came* of God, that he might deliver them into the hand *of their enemies,* because they [b]sought after the gods of Edom.

21 So Joash the king of Israel went up; and they saw one another in the face, *both* he and Amaziah king of Judah, at Beth-shemesh, which *belongeth* to Judah.

22 And Judah was [1]put to the worse before Israel, and they fled every man to his tent.

23 And Joash the king of Israel took Amaziah king of Judah, the son of Joash, the son of [a]Jehoahaz, at Beth-shemesh, and brought him to Jerusalem, and brake down the wall of Jerusalem from the gate of Ephraim to [1]the corner gate, four hundred cubits.

24 And *he took* all the gold and the

4 [a]Deut. 24:16; 2 Ki. 14:6; Jer. 31:30; Ezek. 18:20
5 [a]Num. 1:3
8 [a]ch. 20:6
9 [a]Prov. 10:22 [1]Heb. *band*
10 [1]Heb. *to their place* [2]Heb. *in heat of anger*
11 [a]2 Ki. 14:7
13 [1]Heb. *the sons of the band*
14 [a]See ch. 28:23 [b]Ex. 20:3,5
15 [a]Ps. 96:5 [b]ver. 11
16 [a]1 Sam. 2:25 [1]Heb. *counselled*
17 [a]2 Ki. 14:8,9
18 [1]Or, *furze bush,* or, *thorn* [2]Heb. *a beast of the field*
20 [a]1 Ki. 12:15; ch. 22:7 [b]ver. 14
22 [1]Heb. *smitten*
23 [a]See ch. 21:17; & 22:1,6 [1]Heb. *the gate of it that looketh*

silver, and all the vessels that were found in the house of God with Obed-edom, and the treasures of the king's house, the hostages also, and returned to Samaria.

25 ¶ [a]And Amaziah the son of Joash king of Judah lived after the death of Joash son of Jehoahaz king of Israel fifteen years.

26 Now the rest of the acts of Amaziah, first and last, behold, *are* they not written in the book of the kings of Judah and Israel?

27 ¶ Now after the time that Amaziah did turn away [1]from following the LORD they [2]made a conspiracy against him in Jerusalem; and he fled to Lachish: but they sent to Lachish after him, and slew him there.

28 And they brought him upon horses, and buried him with his fathers in the city of [1]Judah.

Uzziah, king of Judah

26 THEN ALL the people of Judah took [a]Uzziah,[1] who *was* sixteen years old, and made him king in the room of his father Amaziah.

2 He built Eloth, and restored it to Judah, after that the king slept with his fathers.

3 Sixteen years old *was* Uzziah when he began to reign, and he reigned fifty and two years in Jerusalem. His mother's name also *was* Jecoliah of Jerusalem.

4 And he did *that which was* right in the sight of the LORD, according to all that his father Amaziah did.

U 5 And [a]he sought God in the days of Zechariah, who [b]had understanding [1]in the visions of God: and as long as he sought the LORD, God made him to prosper.

6 And he went forth and [a]warred against the Philistines, and brake down the wall of Gath, and the wall of Jabneh, and the wall of Ashdod, and built cities [1]about Ashdod, and among the Philistines.

7 And God helped him against [a]the Philistines, and against the Arabians that dwelt in Gur-baal, and the Mehunims.

8 And the Ammonites [a]gave gifts to Uzziah: and his name [1]spread abroad *even* to the entering in of Egypt; for he strengthened *himself* exceedingly.

9 Moreover Uzziah built towers in Jerusalem at the [a]corner gate, and at the valley gate, and at the turning *of the wall,* and [1]fortified them.

10 Also he built towers in the desert, and [1]digged many wells: for he had much cattle, both in the low country, and in the plains: husbandmen *also,* and vine dressers in the mountains, and in [2]Carmel: for he loved [3]husbandry.

11 Moreover Uzziah had an host of fighting men, that went out to war by bands, according to the number of their account by the hand of Jeiel the scribe and Maaseiah the ruler, under the hand of Hananiah, *one* of the king's captains.

12 The whole number of the chief of the fathers of the mighty men of valour *were* two thousand and six hundred.

13 And under their hand *was* [1]an army, three hundred thousand and seven thousand and five hundred, that made war with mighty power, to help the king against the enemy.

14 And Uzziah prepared for them throughout all the host shields, and spears, and helmets, and habergeons, and bows, and [1]slings *to cast* stones.

15 And he made in Jerusalem engines, invented by cunning men, to be on the towers and upon the bulwarks, to shoot arrows and great stones withal. And his name [1]spread far abroad; for he was marvellously helped, till he was strong.

16 ¶ But [a]when he was strong, his heart was [b]lifted up to *his* destruction: for he transgressed against the LORD his God, and [c]went into the temple of the LORD to burn incense upon the altar of incense.

17 And [a]Azariah the priest went in after him, and with him fourscore priests of the LORD, *that were* valiant men:

18 And they withstood Uzziah the king, and said unto him, *It* [a]*appertaineth* not unto thee, Uzziah, to burn incense unto the LORD, but to the [b]priests the sons of Aaron, that are consecrated to burn incense: go out of the sanctuary; for thou hast trespassed; neither *shall it be* for thine honour from the LORD God.

19 Then Uzziah was wroth, and *had* a censer in his hand to burn incense: and while he was wroth with the priests, [a]the leprosy even rose up in his forehead be- D

25 [a]2 Ki. 14:17
27 [1]Heb. *from after* [2]Heb. *conspired a conspiracy*
28 [1]i.e. *The city of David*
26:1 [a]2 Ki. 14:21, 22 & 15:1 [1]Or, *Azariah*
5 [a]See ch. 24:2 [b]Gen. 41:15; Dan. 1:17 & 10:1 [1]Heb. *in the seeing of God*
6 [a]Is. 14:29 [1]Or, *in the country of Ashdod*
7 [a]ch. 21:16
8 [a]2 Sam. 8:2; ch. 17:11 [1]Heb. *went*
9 [a]2 Ki. 14:13; Neh. 3:13,19,32; Zech. 14:10 [1]Or, *repaired*
10 [1]Or, *cut out many cisterns* [2]Or, *Fruitful fields* [3]Heb. *ground*
13 [1]Heb. *the power of an army*
14 [1]Heb. *stones of slings*
15 [1]Heb. *went forth*
16 [a]Deut. 32:15 [b]Deut. 8:14; ch. 25:19 [c]2 Ki. 16:12, 13
17 [a]1 Chr. 6:10
18 [a]Num. 16:40 & 18:7 [b]Ex. 30:7,8
19 [a]Num. 12:10; 2 Ki. 5:27

fore the priests in the house of the LORD, from beside the incense altar.

20 And Azariah the chief priest, and all the priests, looked upon him, and, behold, he *was* leprous in his forehead, and they thrust him out from thence; yea, himself [a]hasted also to go out, because the LORD had smitten him.

21 [a]And Uzziah the king was a leper unto the day of his death, and dwelt in a [b]several[ǀ] house, *being* a leper; for he was cut off from the house of the LORD: and Jotham his son *was* over the king's house, judging the people of the land.

22 ¶ Now the rest of the acts of Uzziah, first and last, did [a]Isaiah the prophet, the son of Amoz, write.

23 [a]So Uzziah slept with his fathers, and they buried him with his fathers in the field of the burial which *belonged* to the kings; for they said, He *is* a leper: and Jotham his son reigned in his stead.

Jotham, king of Judah

27 JOTHAM [a]*WAS* twenty and five years old when he began to reign, and he reigned sixteen years in Jerusalem. His mother's name also *was* Jerushah, the daughter of Zadok.

2 And he did *that which was* right in the sight of the LORD, according to all that his father Uzziah did: howbeit he entered not into the temple of the LORD. And [a]the people did yet corruptly.

3 He built the high gate of the house of the LORD, and on the wall of [ǀ]Ophel he built much.

4 Moreover he built cities in the mountains of Judah, and in the forests he built castles and towers.

5 ¶ He fought also with the king of the Ammonites, and prevailed against them. And the children of Ammon gave him the same year an hundred talents of silver, and ten thousand measures of wheat, and ten thousand of barley. [ǀ]So much did the children of Ammon pay unto him, both the second year, and the third.

U 6 So Jotham became mighty, because he [ǀ]prepared his ways before the LORD his God.

7 ¶ Now the rest of the acts of Jotham, and all his wars, and his ways, lo, they *are* written in the book of the kings of Israel and Judah.

8 He was five and twenty years old when he began to reign, and reigned sixteen years in Jerusalem.

9 ¶ [a]And Jotham slept with his fathers, and they buried him in the city of David: and Ahaz his son reigned in his stead.

Ahaz, king of Judah

28 AHAZ [a]*WAS* twenty years old when he began to reign, and he reigned sixteen years in Jerusalem: but he did not *that which was* right in the sight of the LORD, like David his father:

2 For he walked in the ways of the kings of Israel, and made also [a]molten images for [b]Baalim.

3 Moreover he [ǀ]burnt incense in [a]the valley of the son of Hinnom, and burnt [b]his children in the fire, after the abominations of the heathen whom the LORD had cast out before the children of Israel.

4 He sacrificed also and burnt incense in the high places, and on the hills, and under every green tree.

5 Wherefore [a]the LORD his God delivered him into the hand of the king of Syria; and they [b]smote him, and carried away a great multitude of them captives, and brought *them* to [ǀ]Damascus. And he was also delivered into the hand of the king of Israel, who smote him with a great slaughter.

6 ¶ For [a]Pekah the son of Remaliah slew in Judah an hundred and twenty thousand in one day, *which were* all [ǀ]valiant men; because they had forsaken the LORD God of their fathers.

7 And Zichri, a mighty man of Ephraim, slew Maaseiah the king's son, and Azrikam the governor of the house, and Elkanah *that was* [ǀ]next to the king.

8 And the children of Israel carried away captive of their [a]brethren two hundred thousand, women, sons, and daughters, and took also away much spoil from them, and brought the spoil to Samaria.

9 But a prophet of the LORD was there, whose name *was* Oded: and he went out before the host that came to Samaria, and said unto them, Behold, [a]because the LORD God of your fathers was wroth with Judah, he hath delivered them into your hand, and ye have slain them in a rage *that* [b]reacheth up unto heaven.

10 And now ye purpose to keep under the children of Judah and Jerusalem for [a]bondmen and bondwomen unto you:

20 [a]As Esth. 6:12
21 [a]2 Ki. 15:5 [b]Lev. 13:46; Num. 5:2 [ǀ]Heb. *free*
22 [a]Is. 1:1
23 [a]2 Ki. 15:7; Is. 6:1
27:1 [a]2 Ki. 15:32
2 [a]2 Ki. 15:35
3 [ǀ]Or, *The tower;* see ch. 33:14; Neh. 3:26
5 [ǀ]Heb. *This*
6 [ǀ]Or, *established*
9 [a]2 Ki. 15:38
28:1 [a]2 Ki. 16:2
2 [a]Ex. 34:17; Lev. 19:4 [b]Judg. 2:11
3 [a]2 Ki. 23:10 [b]Lev. 18:21; 2 Ki. 16:3; ch. 33:6 [ǀ]Or, *offered sacrifice*
5 [a]Is. 7:1 [b]2 Ki. 16:5,6 [ǀ]Heb. *Darmesek*
6 [a]2 Ki. 15:27 [ǀ]Heb. *sons of valour*
7 [ǀ]Heb. *the second to the king*
8 [a]ch. 11:4
9 [a]Is. 10:5 & 47:6; Ezek. 25:12,15 & 26:2; Obad. 10; Zech. 1:15 [b]Ezra 9:6; Rev. 18:5
10 [a]Lev. 25:39,42, 43,46

U *2Ch 26:5* ◄ ► *2Ch 31:10*

but are there not with you, even with you, sins against the LORD your God?

C 11 Now hear me therefore, and deliver the captives again, which ye have taken captive of your brethren: [a]for the fierce wrath of the LORD *is* upon you.

12 Then certain of the heads of the children of Ephraim, Azariah the son of Johanan, Berechiah the son of Meshillemoth, and Jehizkiah the son of Shallum, and Amasa the son of Hadlai, stood up against them that came from the war,

13 And said unto them, Ye shall not bring in the captives hither: for whereas we have offended against the LORD *already,* ye intend to add *more* to our sins and to our trespass: for our trespass is great, and *there is* fierce wrath against Israel.

14 So the armed men left the captives and the spoil before the princes and all the congregation.

15 And the men [a]which were expressed by name rose up, and took the captives, and with the spoil clothed all that were naked among them, and arrayed them, and shod them, and [b]gave them to eat and to drink, and anointed them, and carried all the feeble of them upon asses, and brought them to Jericho, [c]the city of palm trees, to their brethren: then they returned to Samaria.

16 ¶ [a]At that time did king Ahaz send unto the kings of Assyria to help him.

17 For again the Edomites had come and smitten Judah, and carried away [1]captives.

18 [a]The Philistines also had invaded the cities of the low country, and of the south of Judah, and had taken Beth-shemesh, and Ajalon, and Gederoth, and Shocho with the villages thereof, and Timnah with the villages thereof, Gimzo also and the villages thereof: and they dwelt there.

19 For the LORD brought Judah low because of Ahaz king of [a]Israel; for he [b]made Judah naked, and transgressed sore against the LORD.

20 And [a]Tilgath-pilneser king of Assyria came unto him, and distressed him, but strengthened him not.

21 For Ahaz took away a portion *out* of the house of the LORD, and *out* of the house of the king, and of the princes, and gave *it* unto the king of Assyria: but he helped him not.

22 ¶ And in the time of his distress did he trespass yet more against the LORD: this *is that* king Ahaz.

23 For [a]he sacrificed unto the gods of [1]Damascus, which smote him: and he said, Because the gods of the kings of Syria help them, *therefore* will I sacrifice to them, that [b]they may help me. But they were the ruin of him, and of all Israel. R

24 And Ahaz gathered together the vessels of the house of God, and cut in pieces the vessels of the house of God, [a]and shut up the doors of the house of the LORD, and he made him altars in every corner of Jerusalem.

25 And in every several city of Judah he made high places [1]to burn incense unto other gods, and provoked to anger the LORD God of his fathers.

26 ¶ [a]Now the rest of his acts and of all his ways, first and last, behold, they *are* written in the book of the kings of Judah and Israel.

27 And Ahaz slept with his fathers, and they buried him in the city, *even* in Jerusalem: but they brought him not into the sepulchres of the kings of Israel: and Hezekiah his son reigned in his stead.

Hezekiah cleanses the temple

29 HEZEKIAH [a]BEGAN to reign *when he was* five and twenty years old, and he reigned nine and twenty years in Jerusalem. And his mother's name *was* Abijah, the daughter [b]of Zechariah.

2 And he did *that which was* right in the sight of the LORD, according to all that David his father had done.

3 ¶ He in the first year of his reign, in the first month, [a]opened the doors of the house of the LORD, and repaired them.

4 And he brought in the priests and

11 [a]Jas. 2:13
15 [a]ver. 12 [b]2 Ki. 6:22; Luke 6:27; Rom. 12:20 [c]Deut. 34:3; Judg. 1:16
16 [a]2 Ki. 16:7
17 [1]Heb. *a captivity*
18 [a]Ezek. 16:27,57
19 [a]ch. 21:2 [b]Ex. 32:25
20 [a]2 Ki. 15:29 & 16:7-9
23 [a]See ch. 25:14 [b]Jer. 44:17,18 [1]Heb. *Darmesek*
24 [a]See ch. 29:3,7
25 [1]Or, *to offer*
26 [a]2 Ki. 16:19,20
29:1 [a]2 Ki. 18:1 [b]ch. 26:5
3 [a]ver. 7; See ch. 28:24

C *2Ch 24:20* ◀▶ *Ne 9:16–17*

R *2Ch 7:20–22* ◀▶ *2Ch 29:8*

28:23 King Ahaz worshiped the idol Molech, which required child sacrifices to ensure prosperity. Such apostasy led to Ahaz's downfall and Israel's destruction.

the Levites, and gathered them together
into the east street,
5 And said unto them, Hear me, ye Levites, [a]sanctify now yourselves, and sanctify the house of the LORD God of your
fathers, and carry forth the filthiness out
of the holy *place.*
6 For our fathers have trespassed, and
done *that which was* evil in the eyes of
the LORD our God, and have forsaken him,
and have [a]turned away their faces from
the habitation of the LORD, and [1]turned
their backs.
7 [a]Also they have shut up the doors of
the porch, and put out the lamps, and
have not burned incense nor offered
burnt offerings in the holy *place* unto the
God of Israel.
R 8 Wherefore the [a]wrath of the LORD
was upon Judah and Jerusalem, and he
hath delivered them to [b]trouble,[1] to astonishment, and to [c]hissing, as ye see
with your eyes.
9 For, lo, [a]our fathers have fallen by
the sword, and our sons and our daughters and our wives *are* in captivity for
this.
10 Now *it is* in mine heart to make [a]a
covenant with the LORD God of Israel, that
his fierce wrath may turn away from us.
11 My sons, [1]be not now negligent: for
the LORD hath [a]chosen you to stand before him, to serve him, and that ye should
minister unto him, and [2]burn incense.
12 ¶ Then the Levites arose, Mahath
the son of Amasai, and Joel the son of
Azariah, of the sons of the Kohathites:
and of the sons of Merari, Kish the son of
Abdi, and Azariah the son of Jehalelel:
and of the Gershonites; Joah the son of
Zimmah, and Eden the son of Joah:
13 And of the sons of Elizaphan;
Shimri, and Jeiel: and of the sons of
Asaph; Zechariah, and Mattaniah:
14 And of the sons of Heman; Jehiel,
and Shimei: and of the sons of Jeduthun;
Shemaiah, and Uzziel.
15 And they gathered their brethren,
and [a]sanctified themselves, and came, according to the commandment of the king,
[b]by[1] the words of the LORD, [c]to cleanse
the house of the LORD.
16 And the priests went into the inner
part of the house of the LORD, to cleanse
it, and brought out all the uncleanness
that they found in the temple of the LORD
into the court of the house of the LORD.
And the Levites took *it,* to carry *it* out
abroad into the brook Kidron.
17 Now they began on the first *day* of
the first month to sanctify, and on the
eighth day of the month came they to the
porch of the LORD: so they sanctified
the house of the LORD in eight days; and
in the sixteenth day of the first month
they made an end.
18 Then they went in to Hezekiah the
king, and said, We have cleansed all the
house of the LORD, and the altar of burnt
offering, with all the vessels thereof, and
the showbread table, with all the vessels
thereof.
19 Moreover all the vessels, which
king Ahaz in his reign did [a]cast away in
his transgression, have we prepared and
sanctified, and, behold, they *are* before
the altar of the LORD.
20 ¶ Then Hezekiah the king rose
early, and gathered the rulers of the city,
and went up to the house of the LORD.
21 And they brought seven bullocks,
and seven rams, and seven lambs, and
seven he goats, for a [a]sin offering for the
kingdom, and for the sanctuary, and for
Judah. And he commanded the priests
the sons of Aaron to offer *them* on the
altar of the LORD.
22 So they killed the bullocks, and the
priests received the blood, and [a]sprinkled
it on the altar: likewise, when they had
killed the rams, they sprinkled the blood
upon the altar: they killed also the lambs,
and they sprinkled the blood upon the
altar.
23 And they brought [1]forth the he
goats *for* the sin offering before the king
and the congregation; and they laid their
[a]hands upon them:
24 And the priests killed them, and
they made reconciliation with their blood
upon the altar, [a]to make an atonement
for all Israel: for the king commanded

5 [a]1 Chr. 15:12; ch. 35:6
6 [a]Jer. 2:27; Ezek. 8:16 [1]Heb. *given the neck*
7 [a]ch. 28:24
8 [a]ch. 24:18 [b]Deut. 28:25 [c]1 Ki. 9:8; Jer. 18:16 & 19:8 & 25:9,18 & 29:18 [1]Heb. *commotion*
9 [a]ch. 28:5,6,8,17
10 [a]ch. 15:12
11 [a]Num. 3:6 & 8:14 & 18:2,6 [1]Or, *be not now deceived* [2]Or, *offer sacrifice*
15 [a]ver. 5 [b]ch. 30:12 [c]1 Chr. 23:28 [1]Or, *in the business of the LORD*
19 [a]ch. 28:24
21 [a]Lev. 4:3,14
22 [a]Lev. 8:14,15, 19,24; Heb. 9:21
23 [a]Lev. 4:15,24 [1]Heb. *near*
24 [a]Lev. 14:20

R *2Ch 28:23* ◄► *2Ch 30:6–7*

29:8 King Hezekiah repented of the sins of his fathers, recognizing that because of his forefathers' sins of idolatry Judah and Jerusalem were suffering God's judgment.

that the burnt offering and the sin offering *should be made* for all Israel.

25 [a]And he set the Levites in the house of the LORD with cymbals, with psalteries, and with harps, [b]according to the commandment of David, and of [c]Gad the king's seer, and Nathan the prophet: [d]for *so was* the commandment [1]of the LORD [2]by his prophets.

26 And the Levites stood with the instruments [a]of David, and the priests with [b]the trumpets.

27 And Hezekiah commanded to offer the burnt offering upon the altar. And [1]when the burnt offering began, [a]the song of the LORD began *also* with the trumpets, and with the [2]instruments *ordained* by David king of Israel.

28 And all the congregation worshipped, and the [1]singers sang, and the trumpeters sounded: *and* all *this continued* until the burnt offering was finished.

29 And when they had made an end of offering, [a]the king and all that were [1]present with him bowed themselves, and worshipped.

30 Moreover Hezekiah the king and the princes commanded the Levites to sing praise unto the LORD with the words of David, and of Asaph the seer. And they sang praises with gladness, and they bowed their heads and worshipped.

31 Then Hezekiah answered and said, Now ye have [a]consecrated[1] yourselves unto the LORD, come near and bring sacrifices and [b]thank offerings into the house of the LORD. And the congregation brought in sacrifices and thank offerings; and as many as were of a free heart burnt offerings.

32 And the number of the burnt offerings, which the congregation brought, was threescore and ten bullocks, an hundred rams, *and* two hundred lambs: all these *were* for a burnt offering to the LORD.

33 And the consecrated things *were* six hundred oxen and three thousand sheep.

34 But the priests were too few, so that they could not flay all the burnt offerings: wherefore [a]their brethren the Levites [1]did help them, till the work was ended, and until the *other* priests had sanctified themselves: [b]for the Levites *were* more [c]upright in heart to sanctify themselves than the priests.

35 And also the burnt offerings *were* in abundance, with [a]the fat of the peace offerings, and [b]the drink offerings for *every* burnt offering. So the service of the house of the LORD was set in order.

36 And Hezekiah rejoiced, and all the people, that God had prepared the people: for the thing was *done* suddenly.

The observance of the Passover

30 AND HEZEKIAH sent to all Israel D
and Judah, and wrote letters also to Ephraim and Manasseh, that they should come to the house of the LORD at Jerusalem, to keep the passover unto the LORD God of Israel.

2 For the king had taken counsel, and his princes, and all the congregation in Jerusalem, to keep the passover in the second [a]month.

3 For they could not keep it [a]at that time, [b]because the priests had not sanctified themselves sufficiently, neither had the people gathered themselves together to Jerusalem.

4 And the thing [1]pleased the king and all the congregation.

5 So they established a decree to make D
proclamation throughout all Israel, from Beer-sheba even to Dan, that they should come to keep the passover unto the LORD God of Israel at Jerusalem: for they had not done *it* of a long *time in such sort* as it was written.

6 So the posts went with the letters R
[1]from the king and his princes throughout all Israel and Judah, and according to the commandment of the king, saying, Ye children of Israel, [a]turn again unto the LORD God of Abraham, Isaac, and Israel, and he will return to the remnant of you, that are escaped out of the hand of [b]the kings of Assyria.

7 And be not ye [a]like your fathers, and

D *2Ki 23:21* ◀▶ *2Ch 30:5*
D *2Ch 30:1* ◀▶ *2Ch 35:1*
R *2Ch 29:8* ◀▶ *2Ch 34:24–25*

25 [a]1 Chr. 16:4 & 25:6 [b]1 Chr. 23:5 & 25:1; ch. 8:14 [c]2 Sam. 24:11 [d]ch. 30:12 [1]Heb. *by the hand of the LORD* [2]Heb. *by the hand of*
26 [a]1 Chr. 23:5; Amos 6:5 [b]Num. 10:8,10; 1 Chr. 15:24 & 16:6
27 [a]ch. 23:18 [1]Heb. *in the time* [2]Heb. *hands of instruments*
28 [1]Heb. *song*
29 [a]ch. 20:18 [1]Heb. *found*
31 [a]ch. 13:9 [b]Lev. 7:12 [1]Or, *filled your hand*
34 [a]ch. 35:11 [b]ch. 30:3 [c]Ps. 7:10 [1]Heb. *strengthened them*
35 [a]Lev. 3:16 [b]Num. 15:5,7,10
30:2 [a]Num. 9:10, 11
3 [a]Ex. 12:6,18 [b]ch. 29:34
4 [1]Heb. *was right in the eyes of the king*
6 [a]Jer. 4:1; Joel 2:13 [b]2 Ki. 15:19 [1]Heb. *from the hand*
7 [a]Ezek. 20:18

30:6–7 King Hezekiah wrote letters to all of Israel and Judah encouraging them to return to the true worship of God and reject idol worship so that God might reestablish his blessings and protection for his people.

like your brethren, which trespassed against the LORD God of their fathers, *who* therefore [b]gave them up to desolation, as ye see.

M 8 Now [1]be ye not [a]stiffnecked, as your fathers *were, but* [b]yield[2] yourselves unto the LORD, and enter into his sanctuary, which he hath sanctified for ever: and serve the LORD your God, [c]that the fierceness of his wrath may turn away from you.

L 9 For if ye turn again unto the LORD, **P** your brethren and your children *shall find* [a]compassion before them that lead them captive, so that they shall come again into this land: for the LORD your God *is* [b]gracious and merciful, and will not turn away *his* face from you, if ye [c]return unto him.

10 So the posts passed from city to city through the country of Ephraim and Manasseh even unto Zebulun: but [a]they laughed them to scorn, and mocked them.

11 Nevertheless [a]divers of Asher and Manasseh and of Zebulun humbled themselves, and came to Jerusalem.

12 Also in Judah [a]the hand of God was to give them one heart to do the commandment of the king and of the princes, [b]by the word of the LORD.

13 ¶ And there assembled at Jerusalem much people to keep the feast of unleavened bread in the second month, a very great congregation.

14 And they arose and took away the [a]altars that *were* in Jerusalem, and all the altars for incense took they away, and cast *them* into the brook Kidron.

15 Then they killed the passover on the fourteenth *day* of the second month: and the priests and the Levites were [a]ashamed, and sanctified themselves, and brought in the burnt offerings into the house of the LORD.

16 And they stood in [1]their place after their manner, according to the law of Moses the man of God: the priests sprinkled the blood, *which they received* of the hand of the Levites.

17 For *there were* many in the congregation that were not sanctified: [a]therefore the Levites had the charge of the killing of the passovers for every one *that was* not clean, to sanctify *them* unto the LORD.

18 For a multitude of the people, *even* [a]many of Ephraim, and Manasseh, Issachar, and Zebulun, had not cleansed themselves, [b]yet did they eat the passover otherwise than it was written. But Hezekiah prayed for them, saying, The good LORD pardon every one

19 *That* [a]prepareth his heart to seek God, the LORD God of his fathers, though *he be* not *cleansed* according to the purification of the sanctuary.

20 And the LORD hearkened to Hezekiah, and healed the people.

21 And the children of Israel that were [1]present at Jerusalem kept [a]the feast of unleavened bread seven days with great gladness: and the Levites and the priests praised the LORD day by day, *singing* with [2]loud instruments unto the LORD.

22 And Hezekiah spake [a]comfortably[1] unto all the Levites [b]that taught the good knowledge of the LORD: and they did eat throughout the feast seven days, offering peace offerings, and [c]making confession to the LORD God of their fathers.

23 And the whole assembly took counsel to keep [a]other seven days: and they kept *other* seven days with gladness.

24 For Hezekiah king of Judah [a]did[1] give to the congregation a thousand bullocks and seven thousand sheep; and the princes gave to the congregation a thousand bullocks and ten thousand sheep: and a great number of priests [b]sanctified themselves.

25 And all the congregation of Judah, with the priests and the Levites, and all the congregation [a]that came out of Israel, and the strangers that came out of the land of Israel, and that dwelt in Judah, rejoiced.

26 So there was great joy in Jerusalem: for since the time of Solomon the son of David king of Israel *there was* not the like in Jerusalem.

27 ¶ Then the priests the Levites arose and [a]blessed the people: and their voice was heard, and their prayer came *up* to [b]his[1] holy dwellingplace, *even* unto heaven.

31

NOW WHEN all this was finished, all Israel that were [1]present went out to the cities of Judah, and [a]brake the [b]images[2] in pieces, and

7 [b]ch. 29:8
8 [a]Deut. 10:16 [b]1 Chr. 29:24; Ezra 10:19 [c]ch. 29:10 [1]Heb. *harden not your necks* [2]Heb. *give the hand*
9 [a]Ps. 106:46 [b]Ex. 34:6 [c]Is. 55:7
10 [a]ch. 36:16
11 [a]ver. 18,21; ch. 11:16
12 [a]Phil. 2:13 [b]ch. 29:25
14 [a]ch. 28:24
15 [a]ch. 29:34
16 [1]Heb. *their standing*
17 [a]ch. 29:34
18 [a]ver. 1,11 [b]Ex. 12:43
19 [a]ch. 19:3
21 [a]Ex. 12:15 & 13:6 [1]Heb. *found* [2]Heb. *instruments of strength*
22 [a]Is. 40:2 [b]Deut. 33:10; ch. 17:9 & 35:3 [c]Ezra 10:11 [1]Heb. *to the heart of all*
23 [a]See 1 Ki. 8:65
24 [a]ch. 35:7,8 [b]ch. 29:34 [1]Heb. *lifted up,* or, *offered*
25 [a]ver. 11,18
27 [a]Num. 6:23 [b]Ps. 68:5 [1]Heb. *the habitation of his holiness*
31:1 [a]2 Ki. 18:4 [b]ch. 30:14 [1]Heb. *found* [2]Heb. *statues*

M *2Ch 12:12* ◄► *2Ch 32:26*
L *2Ch 15:15* ◄► *Ezr 8:22*
P *2Ch 15:3–4* ◄► *Ps 32:5*

cut down the groves, and threw down the high places and the altars out of all Judah and Benjamin, in Ephraim also and Manasseh, [3]until they had utterly destroyed them all. Then all the children of Israel returned, every man to his possession, into their own cities.

Hezekiah's reforms

2 ¶ And Hezekiah appointed [a]the courses of the priests and the Levites after their courses, every man according to his service, the priests and Levites [b]for burnt offerings and for peace offerings, to minister, and to give thanks, and to praise in the gates of the tents of the LORD.

3 *He appointed* also the king's portion of his substance for the burnt offerings, *to wit,* for the morning and evening burnt offerings, and the burnt offerings for the sabbaths, and for the new moons, and for the set feasts, as *it is* written in [a]the law of the LORD.

4 Moreover he commanded the people that dwelt in Jerusalem to give the [a]portion of the priests and the Levites, that they might be encouraged in [b]the law of the LORD.

5 ¶ And as soon as the commandment [1]came abroad, the children of Israel brought in abundance [a]the firstfruits of corn, wine, and oil, and [2]honey, and of all the increase of the field; and the tithe of all *things* brought they in abundantly.

6 And *concerning* the children of Israel and Judah, that dwelt in the cities of Judah, they also brought in the tithe of oxen and sheep, and the [a]tithe of holy things which were consecrated unto the LORD their God, and laid *them* [1]by heaps.

7 In the third month they began to lay the foundation of the heaps, and finished *them* in the seventh month.

8 And when Hezekiah and the princes came and saw the heaps, they blessed the LORD, and his people Israel.

9 Then Hezekiah questioned with the priests and the Levites concerning the heaps.

P U 10 And Azariah the chief priest of the house of Zadok answered him, and said, [a]Since *the people* began to bring the offerings into the house of the LORD, we have had enough to eat, and have left plenty: for the LORD hath blessed his people; and that which is left *is* this great store.

11 ¶ Then Hezekiah commanded to prepare [1]chambers in the house of the LORD; and they prepared *them,*

12 And brought in the offerings and the tithes and the dedicated *things* faithfully: [a]over which Cononiah the Levite *was* ruler, and Shimei his brother *was* the next.

13 And Jehiel, and Azaziah, and Nahath, and Asahel, and Jerimoth, and Jozabad, and Eliel, and Ismachiah, and Mahath, and Benaiah, *were* overseers [1]under the hand of Cononiah and Shimei his brother, at the commandment of Hezekiah the king, and Azariah the ruler of the house of God.

14 And Kore the son of Imnah the Levite, the porter toward the east, *was* over the freewill offerings of God, to distribute the oblations of the LORD, and the most holy things.

15 And [1]next him *were* Eden, and Miniamin, and Jeshua, and Shemaiah, Amariah, and Shecaniah, in [a]the cities of the priests, in *their* set office, to give to their brethren by courses, as well to the great as to the small:

16 Beside their genealogy of males, from three years old and upward, *even* unto every one that entereth into the house of the LORD, his daily portion for their service in their charges according to their courses;

17 Both to the genealogy of the priests by the house of their fathers, and the Levites [a]from twenty years old and upward, in their charges by their courses;

18 And to the genealogy of all their little ones, their wives, and their sons, and their daughters, through all the congregation: for in their [1]set office they sanctified themselves in holiness:

19 Also of the sons of Aaron the priests, *which were* in [a]the fields of the suburbs of their cities, in every several city, the men that were [b]expressed by name, to give portions to all the males among the priests, and to all that were reckoned by genealogies among the Levites.

20 ¶ And thus did Hezekiah throughout all Judah, and [a]wrought *that which*

1 [3]Heb. *until to make an end*
2 [a]1 Chr. 23:6 & 24:1 [b]1 Chr. 23:30,31
3 [a]Num. 28 & 29
4 [a]Num. 18:8; Neh. 13:10 [b]Mal. 2:7
5 [a]Ex. 22:29; Neh. 13:12 [1]Heb. *brake forth* [2]Or, *dates*
6 [a]Lev. 27:30; Deut. 14:28 [1]Heb. *heaps, heaps*
10 [a]Mal. 3:10
11 [1]Or, *storehouses*
12 [a]Neh. 13:13
13 [1]Heb. *at the hand*
15 [a]Josh. 21:9 [1]Heb. *at his hand*
17 [a]1 Chr. 23:24, 27
18 [1]Or, *trust*
19 [a]Lev. 25:34; Num. 35:2 [b]ver. 12-15
20 [a]2 Ki. 20:3

P 2Ch 25:9 ◄► 2Ch 32:29
U 2Ch 27:6 ◄► 2Ch 31:21

was good and right and truth before the LORD his God.

U 21 And in every work that he began in the service of the house of God, and in the law, and in the commandments, to seek his God, he did *it* with all his heart, and prospered.

The defeat of Sennacherib

32 AFTER [a]THESE things, and the establishment thereof, Sennacherib king of Assyria came, and entered into Judah, and encamped against the fenced cities, and thought ʹto win them for himself.

2 And when Hezekiah saw that Sennacherib was come, and that ʹhe was purposed to fight against Jerusalem,

3 He took counsel with his princes and his mighty men to stop the waters of the fountains which *were* without the city: and they did help him.

4 So there was gathered much people together, who stopped all the fountains, and the brook that ʹran through the midst of the land, saying, Why should the kings of Assyria come, and find much water?

5 Also [a]he strengthened himself, [b]and built up all the wall that was broken, and raised *it* up to the towers, and another wall without, and repaired [c]Millo *in* the city of David, and made ʹdarts and shields in abundance.

6 And he set captains of war over the people, and gathered them together to him in the street of the gate of the city, and [a]spakeʹ comfortably to them, saying,

V 7 [a]Be strong and courageous, [b]be not afraid nor dismayed for the king of Assyria, nor for all the multitude that *is* with him: for [c]*there be* more with us than with him:

8 With him *is* an [a]arm of flesh; but [b]with us *is* the LORD our God to help us, and to fight our battles. And the people ʹrested themselves upon the words of Hezekiah king of Judah.

9 ¶ [a]After this did Sennacherib king of Assyria send his servants to Jerusalem, (but he *himself laid siege* against Lachish, and all his ʹpower with him,) unto Hezekiah king of Judah, and unto all Judah that *were* at Jerusalem, saying,

10 [a]Thus saith Sennacherib king of Assyria, Whereon do ye trust, that ye abide ʹin the siege in Jerusalem?

11 Doth not Hezekiah persuade you to give over yourselves to die by famine and by thirst, saying, [a]The LORD our God shall deliver us out of the hand of the king of Assyria?

12 [a]Hath not the same Hezekiah taken away his high places and his altars, and commanded Judah and Jerusalem, saying, Ye shall worship before one altar, and burn incense upon it?

13 Know ye not what I and my fathers have done unto all the people of *other* lands? [a]were the gods of the nations of those lands any ways able to deliver their lands out of mine hand?

14 Who *was there* among all the gods of those nations that my fathers utterly destroyed, that could deliver his people out of mine hand, that your God should be able to deliver you out of mine hand?

15 Now therefore [a]let not Hezekiah deceive you, nor persuade you on this manner, neither yet believe him: for no god of any nation or kingdom was able to deliver his people out of mine hand, and out of the hand of my fathers: how much less shall your God deliver you out of mine hand?

16 And his servants spake yet *more* against the LORD God, and against his servant Hezekiah.

17 [a]He wrote also letters to rail on the LORD God of Israel, and to speak against him, saying, [b]As the gods of the nations of *other* lands have not delivered their people out of mine hand, so shall not the God of Hezekiah deliver his people out of mine hand.

18 [a]Then they cried with a loud voice in the Jews' speech unto the people of Jerusalem that *were* on the wall, to affright them, and to trouble them; that they might take the city.

19 And they spake against the God of Jerusalem, as against the gods of the people of the earth, *which were* [a]the work of the hands of man.

20 [a]And for this *cause* Hezekiah the king, and [b]the prophet Isaiah the son of Amoz, prayed and cried to heaven.

21 ¶ [a]And the LORD sent an angel, which cut off all the mighty men of valour, and the leaders and captains in the camp of the king of Assyria. So he re-

32:1 [a]2 Ki. 18:13; Is. 36:1 ʹHeb. *to break them up*
2 ʹHeb. *his face was to war*
4 ʹHeb. *overflowed*
5 [a]Is. 22:9,10 [b]ch. 25:23 [c]2 Sam. 5:9; 1 Ki. 9:24 ʹOr, *swords, or, weapons*
6 [a]ch. 30:22; Is. 40:2 ʹHeb. *spake to their heart*
7 [a]Deut. 31:6 [b]ch. 20:15 [c]2 Ki. 6:16
8 [a]Jer. 17:5; 1 John 4:4 [b]ch. 13:12; Rom. 8:31 ʹHeb. *leaned*
9 [a]2 Ki. 18:17 ʹHeb. *dominion*
10 [a]2 Ki. 18:19 ʹOr, *in the strong hold*
11 [a]2 Ki. 18:30
12 [a]2 Ki. 18:22
13 [a]2 Ki. 18:33-35
15 [a]2 Ki. 18:29
17 [a]2 Ki. 19:9 [b]2 Ki. 19:12
18 [a]2 Ki. 18:28
19 [a]2 Ki. 19:18
20 [a]2 Ki. 19:15 [b]2 Ki. 19:2,4
21 [a]2 Ki. 19:35

U 2Ch 31:10 ◄► 2Ch 32:30
V 2Ch 20:17 ◄► Ne 4:20

turned with shame of face to his own land. And when he was come into the house of his god, they that came forth of his own bowels 'slew him there with the sword.

L 22 Thus the LORD saved Hezekiah and the inhabitants of Jerusalem from the hand of Sennacherib the king of Assyria, and from the hand of all *other,* and guided them on every side.

23 And many brought gifts unto the LORD to Jerusalem, and [a]presents' to Hezekiah king of Judah: so that he was [b]magnified in the sight of all nations from thenceforth.

Hezekiah's sickness and death

E 24 ¶ [a]In those days Hezekiah was sick to the death, and prayed unto the LORD: and he spake unto him, and he 'gave him a sign.

25 But Hezekiah [a]rendered not again according to the benefit *done* unto him; for [b]his heart was lifted up: [c]therefore there was wrath upon him, and upon Judah and Jerusalem.

M 26 [a]Notwithstanding Hezekiah humbled himself for 'the pride of his heart, *both* he and the inhabitants of Jerusalem, so that the wrath of the LORD came not upon them [b]in the days of Hezekiah.

27 ¶ And Hezekiah had exceeding much riches and honour: and he made himself treasuries for silver, and for gold, and for precious stones, and for spices, and for shields, and for all manner of 'pleasant jewels;

28 Storehouses also for the increase of corn, and wine, and oil; and stalls for all manner of beasts, and cotes for flocks.

P 29 Moreover he provided him cities, and possessions of flocks and herds in abundance: for [a]God had given him substance very much.

U 30 [a]This same Hezekiah also stopped the upper watercourse of Gihon, and brought it straight down to the west side of the city of David. And Hezekiah prospered in all his works.

31 ¶ Howbeit in *the business of* the 'ambassadors of the princes of Babylon, who [a]sent unto him to inquire of the wonder that was *done* in the land, God left him, to [b]try him, that he might know all *that was* in his heart.

32 ¶ Now the rest of the acts of Hezekiah, and his 'goodness, behold, they *are* written in [a]the vision of Isaiah the prophet, the son of Amoz, *and* in the [b]book of the kings of Judah and Israel.

33 [a]And Hezekiah slept with his fathers, and they buried him in the 'chiefest of the sepulchres of the sons of David: and all Judah and the inhabitants of Jerusalem did him [b]honour at his death. And Manasseh his son reigned in his stead.

Manasseh, king of Judah

33 MANASSEH [a]*WAS* twelve years old when he began to reign, and he reigned fifty and five years in Jerusalem:

2 But did *that which was* evil in the sight of the LORD, like unto the [a]abominations of the heathen, whom the LORD had cast out before the children of Israel.

3 ¶ For 'he built again the high places which Hezekiah his father had [a]broken down, and he reared up altars for Baalim, and [b]made groves, and worshipped [c]all the host of heaven, and served them.

4 Also he built altars in the house of the LORD, whereof the LORD had said, [a]In Jerusalem shall my name be for ever.

5 And he built altars for all the host of heaven [a]in the two courts of the house of the LORD.

6 [a]And he caused his children to pass through the fire in the valley of the son of Hinnom: also he observed times, and used enchantments, and used witchcraft, and [b]dealt with a familiar spirit, and with wizards: he wrought much evil in the sight of the LORD, to provoke him to anger.

7 And [a]he set a carved image, the idol which he had made, in the house of God, of which God had said to David and to Solomon his son, In this house, and in Jerusalem, which I have chosen before all the tribes of Israel, will I put my name for ever:

8 [a]Neither will I any more remove the foot of Israel from out of the land which I have appointed for your fathers; so that they will take heed to do all that I have commanded them, according to the whole law and the statutes and the ordinances by the hand of Moses.

21 'Heb. *made him fall*

23 [a]ch. 17:5 [b]ch. 1:1 'Heb. *precious things*

24 [a]2 Ki. 20:1; Is. 38:1 'Or, *wrought a miracle for him*

25 [a]Ps. 116:12 [b]ch. 26:16; Hab. 2:4 [c]ch. 24:18

26 [a]Jer. 26:18 [b]2 Ki. 20:19 'Heb. *the lifting up*

27 'Heb. *instruments of desire*

29 [a]1 Chr. 29:12

30 [a]Is. 22:9,11

31 [a]2 Ki. 20:12; Is. 39:1 [b]Deut. 8:2 'Heb. *interpreters*

32 [a]Is. 36 & 37 & 38 & 39 [b]2 Ki. 18 & 19 & 20 'Heb. *kindnesses*

33 [a]2 Ki. 20:21 [b]Prov. 10:7 'Or, *highest*

33:1 [a]2 Ki. 21:1

2 [a]Deut. 18:9; 2 Chr. 28:3

3 [a]2 Ki. 18:4; ch. 30:14 & 31:1 [b]Deut. 16:21 [c]Deut. 17:3 'Heb. *he returned and built*

4 [a]Deut. 12:11; 1 Ki. 8:29 & 9:3; ch. 6:6 & 7:16

5 [a]ch. 4:9

6 [a]Lev. 18:21; Deut. 18:10; 2 Ki. 23:10; ch. 28:3; Ezek. 23:37,39 [b]2 Ki. 21:6

7 [a]2 Ki. 21:7

8 [a]2 Sam. 7:10

L *1Ch 28:20 ◀▶ Ne 9:12*
E *2Ki 20:1–11 ◀▶ Ne 9:21*
M *2Ch 30:8 ◀▶ 2Ch 33:12–13*
P *2Ch 31:10 ◀▶ Job 1:10*
U *2Ch 31:21 ◀▶ Ezr 8:22*

9 So Manasseh made Judah and the inhabitants of Jerusalem to err, *and* to do worse than the heathen, whom the LORD had destroyed before the children of Israel.

10 And the LORD spake to Manasseh, and to his people: but they would not hearken.

11 ¶ [a]Wherefore the LORD brought upon them the captains of the host [1]of the king of Assyria, which took Manasseh among the thorns, and [b]bound him with [2]fetters, and carried him to Babylon.

M 12 And when he was in affliction, he besought the LORD his God, and [a]humbled himself greatly before the God of his fathers,

13 And prayed unto him: and he was [a]entreated of him, and heard his supplication, and brought him again to Jerusalem into his kingdom. Then Manasseh [b]knew that the LORD he *was* God.

14 Now after this he built a wall without the city of David, on the west side of [a]Gihon, in the valley, even to the entering in at the fish gate, and compassed [b]about [1]Ophel, and raised it up a very great height, and put captains of war in all the fenced cities of Judah.

15 And he took away [a]the strange gods, and the idol out of the house of the LORD, and all the altars that he had built in the mount of the house of the LORD, and in Jerusalem, and cast *them* out of the city.

16 And he repaired the altar of the LORD, and sacrificed thereon peace offerings and [a]thank offerings, and commanded Judah to serve the LORD God of Israel.

17 [a]Nevertheless the people did sacrifice still in the high places, *yet* unto the LORD their God only.

18 ¶ Now the rest of the acts of Manasseh, and his prayer unto his God, and the words of [a]the seers that spake to him in the name of the LORD God of Israel, behold, they *are written* in the book of the kings of Israel.

19 His prayer also, and *how God* was entreated of him, and all his sins, and his trespass, and the places wherein he built high places, and set up groves and graven images, before he was humbled: behold, they *are* written among the sayings of [1]the seers.

20 ¶ [a]So Manasseh slept with his fathers, and they buried him in his own house: and Amon his son reigned in his stead.

Amon, king of Judah

21 ¶ [a]Amon *was* two and twenty years old when he began to reign, and reigned two years in Jerusalem.

22 But he did *that which was* evil in the sight of the LORD, as did Manasseh his father: for Amon sacrificed unto all the carved images which Manasseh his father had made, and served them;

23 And humbled not himself before the LORD, [a]as Manasseh his father had humbled himself; but Amon [1]trespassed more and more.

24 [a]And his servants conspired against him, and slew him in his own house.

25 ¶ But the people of the land slew all them that had conspired against king Amon; and the people of the land made Josiah his son king in his stead.

Josiah repairs the temple

34 JOSIAH [a]*WAS* eight years old when he began to reign, and he reigned in Jerusalem one and thirty years.

2 And he did *that which was* right in the sight of the LORD, and walked in the ways of David his father, and declined *neither* to the right hand, nor to the left.

3 ¶ For in the eighth year of his reign, while he was yet young, he began to [a]seek after the God of David his father: and in the twelfth year he began [b]to purge Judah and Jerusalem [c]from the high places, and the groves, and the carved images, and the molten images.

4 [a]And they brake down the altars of Baalim in his presence; and the [1]images, that *were* on high above them, he cut down; and the groves, and the carved images, and the molten images, he brake in pieces, and made dust *of them,* [b]and strewed *it* upon the [2]graves of them that had sacrificed unto them.

5 And he [a]burnt the bones of the priests upon their altars, and cleansed Judah and Jerusalem.

6 And *so did he* in the cities of Manasseh, and Ephraim, and Simeon, even unto Naphtali, with their [1]mattocks round about.

11 [a]Deut. 28:36 [b]Job 36:8; Ps. 107:10,11 [1]Heb. *which* were *the king's* [2]Or, *chains*
12 [a]1 Pet. 5:6
13 [a]1 Chr. 5:20; Ezra 8:23 [b]Ps. 9:16; Dan. 4:25
14 [a]1 Ki. 1:33 [b]ch. 27:3 [1]Or, *The tower*
15 [a]ver. 3,5,7
16 [a]Lev. 7:12
17 [a]ch. 32:12
18 [a]1 Sam. 9:9
19 [1]Or, *Hosai*
20 [a]2 Ki. 21:18
21 [a]2 Ki. 21:19
23 [a]ver. 12 [1]Heb. *multiplied trespass*
24 [a]2 Ki. 21:23,24
34:1 [a]2 Ki. 22:1
3 [a]ch. 15:2 [b]1 Ki. 13:2 [c]ch. 33:17,22
4 [a]Lev. 26:30; 2 Ki. 23:4 [b]2 Ki. 23:6 [1]Or, *sun images* [2]Heb. *face of the graves*
5 [a]1 Ki. 13:2
6 [1]Or, *mauls*

M *2Ch 32:26* ◄► *2Ch 34:27*

7 And when he had broken down the altars and the groves, and had [a]beaten the graven images [1]into powder, and cut down all the idols throughout all the land of Israel, he returned to Jerusalem.

8 ¶ Now [a]in the eighteenth year of his reign, when he had purged the land, and the house, he sent Shaphan the son of Azaliah, and Maaseiah the governor of the city, and Joah the son of Joahaz the recorder, to repair the house of the LORD his God.

9 And when they came to Hilkiah the high priest, they delivered [a]the money that was brought into the house of God, which the Levites that kept the doors had gathered of the hand of Manasseh and Ephraim, and of all the remnant of Israel, and of all Judah and Benjamin; and they returned to Jerusalem.

10 And they put *it* in the hand of the workmen that had the oversight of the house of the LORD, and they gave it to the workmen that wrought in the house of the LORD, to repair and amend the house:

11 Even to the artificers and builders gave they *it,* to buy hewn stone, and timber for couplings, and [1]to floor the houses which the kings of Judah had destroyed.

12 And the men did the work faithfully: and the overseers of them *were* Jahath and Obadiah, the Levites, of the sons of Merari; and Zechariah and Meshullam, of the sons of the Kohathites, to set *it* forward; and *other of* the Levites, all that could skill of instruments of music.

13 Also *they were* over the bearers of burdens, and *were* overseers of all that wrought the work in any manner of service: [a]and of the Levites *there were* scribes, and officers, and porters.

Discovery of the book of the law

14 ¶ And when they brought out the money that was brought into the house of the LORD, Hilkiah the priest [a]found a book of the law of the LORD *given* [1]by Moses.

15 And Hilkiah answered and said to Shaphan the scribe, I have found the book of the law in the house of the LORD. And Hilkiah delivered the book to Shaphan.

16 And Shaphan carried the book to the king, and brought the king word back again, saying, All that was committed [1]to thy servants, they do *it.*

17 And they have [1]gathered together the money that was found in the house of the LORD, and have delivered it into the hand of the overseers, and to the hand of the workmen.

18 Then Shaphan the scribe told the king, saying, Hilkiah the priest hath given me a book. And Shaphan read [1]it before the king.

19 And it came to pass, when the king had heard the words of the law, that he rent his clothes.

20 And the king commanded Hilkiah, and Ahikam the son of Shaphan, and [1]Abdon the son of Micah, and Shaphan the scribe, and Asaiah a servant of the king's, saying,

21 Go, inquire of the LORD for me, and for them that are left in Israel and in Judah, concerning the words of the book that is found: for great *is* the wrath of the LORD that is poured out upon us, because our fathers have not kept the word of the LORD, to do after all that is written in this book.

22 And Hilkiah, and *they* that the king *had appointed,* went to Huldah the prophetess, the wife of Shallum the son of [a]Tikvath, the son of [1]Hasrah, keeper of the [2]wardrobe; (now she dwelt in Jerusalem [3]in the college:) and they spake to her to that *effect.*

23 ¶ And she answered them, Thus saith the LORD God of Israel, Tell ye the man that sent you to me,

24 Thus saith the LORD, Behold, I will bring evil upon this place, and upon the inhabitants thereof, *even* all the curses that are written in the book which they have read before the king of Judah: R

25 Because they have forsaken me, and have burned incense unto other gods, that they might provoke me to anger with all the works of their hands;

R *2Ch 30:6–7 ◄ ► 2Ch 36:17–21*

7 [a]Deut. 9:21 [1]Heb. *to make powder*
8 [a]2 Ki. 22:3
9 [a]See 2 Ki. 12:4
11 [1]Or, *to rafter*
13 [a]1 Chr. 23:4,5
14 [a]2 Ki. 22:8 [1]Heb. *by the hand of*
16 [1]Heb. *to the hand of*
17 [1]Heb. *poured out,* or, *melted*
18 [1]Heb. *in it*
20 [1]Or, *Achbor;* see 2 Ki. 22:12
22 [a]2 Ki. 22:14 [1]Or, *Harhas* [2]Heb. *garments* [3]Or, *in the school,* or, *in the second part*

34:24–25 After the discovery of the book of the law in the temple, Huldah prophesied that God would still deliver his judgment and punishment upon the people because of their idolatry, but God would delay this judgment until after the death of King Josiah.

therefore my wrath shall be poured out upon this place, and shall not be quenched.

26 And as for the king of Judah, who sent you to inquire of the LORD, so shall ye say unto him, Thus saith the LORD God of Israel *concerning* the words which thou hast heard;

M 27 Because thine heart was tender, and thou didst humble thyself before God, when thou heardest his words against this place, and against the inhabitants thereof, and humbledst thyself before me, and didst rend thy clothes, and weep before me; I have even heard *thee* also, saith the LORD.

L 28 Behold, I will gather thee to thy fathers, and thou shalt be gathered to thy grave in peace, neither shall thine eyes see all the evil that I will bring upon this place, and upon the inhabitants of the same. So they brought the king word again.

29 ¶ [a]Then the king sent and gathered together all the elders of Judah and Jerusalem.

30 And the king went up into the house of the LORD, and all the men of Judah, and the inhabitants of Jerusalem, and the priests, and the Levites, and all the people, [/]great and small: and he read in their ears all the words of the book of the covenant that was found in the house of the LORD.

31 And the king stood in [a]his place, and made a covenant before the LORD, to walk after the LORD, and to keep his commandments, and his testimonies, and his statutes, with all his heart, and with all his soul, to perform the words of the covenant which are written in this book.

32 And he caused all that were [/]present in Jerusalem and Benjamin to stand *to it.* And the inhabitants of Jerusalem did according to the covenant of God, the God of their fathers.

33 And Josiah took away all the [a]abominations out of all the countries that *pertained* to the children of Israel, and made all that were present in Israel to serve, *even* to serve the LORD their God. [b]*And* all his days they departed not [/]from following the LORD, the God of their fathers.

M *2Ch 33:12–13* ◀ ▶ *Ezr 9:5–6*
L *2Ch 20:9* ◀ ▶ *Isa 38:18*

29 [a]2 Ki. 23:1
30 [/]Heb. *from great even to small*
31 [a]2 Ki. 11:14 & 23:3; ch. 6:13
32 [/]Heb. *found*
33 [a]1 Ki. 11:5 [b]Jer. 3:10 [/]Heb. *from after*
35:1 [a]2 Ki. 23:21, 22 [b]Ex. 12:6; Ezra 6:19
2 [a]ch. 23:18; Ezra 6:18 [b]ch. 29:5,11
3 [a]Deut. 33:10 [b]See ch. 34:14 [c]ch. 5:7 [/]1 Chr. 23:26
4 [a]1 Chr. 9:10 [b]1 Chr. 23 & 24 & 25 & 26 [c]ch. 8:14
5 [a]Ps. 134:1 [/]Heb. *the house of the fathers* [2]Heb. *the sons of the people*
6 [a]ch. 29:5,15
7 [a]ch. 30:24 [/]Heb. *offered*
8 [/]Heb. *offered*
9 [/]Heb. *offered*
10 [a]Ezra 6:18
11 [a]ch. 29:22

Observance of the Passover

35 MOREOVER [a]JOSIAH kept a passover unto the LORD in Jerusalem: and they killed the passover on the [b]fourteenth *day* of the first month. D

2 And he set the priests in their [a]charges, and [b]encouraged them to the service of the house of the LORD,

3 And said unto the Levites [a]that taught all Israel, which were holy unto the LORD, [b]Put the holy ark [c]in the house which Solomon the son of David king of Israel did build; [/]*it shall* not *be* a burden upon *your* shoulders: serve now the LORD your God, and his people Israel,

4 And prepare *yourselves* [a]by the houses of your fathers, after your courses, according to the [b]writing of David king of Israel, and according to the [c]writing of Solomon his son.

5 And [a]stand in the holy *place* according to the divisions of [/]the families of the fathers of your brethren [2]the people, and *after* the division of the families of the Levites.

6 So kill the passover, and [a]sanctify yourselves, and prepare your brethren, that *they* may do according to the word of the LORD by the hand of Moses.

7 And Josiah [a]gave[/] to the people, of the flock, lambs and kids, all for the passover offerings, for all that were present, to the number of thirty thousand, and three thousand bullocks: these *were* of the king's substance.

8 And his princes [/]gave willingly unto the people, to the priests, and to the Levites: Hilkiah and Zechariah and Jehiel, rulers of the house of God, gave unto the priests for the passover offerings two thousand and six hundred *small cattle,* and three hundred oxen.

9 Conaniah also, and Shemaiah and Nethaneel, his brethren, and Hashabiah and Jeiel and Jozabad, chief of the Levites, [/]gave unto the Levites for passover offerings five thousand *small cattle,* and five hundred oxen.

10 So the service was prepared, and the priests [a]stood in their place, and the Levites in their courses, according to the king's commandment.

11 And they killed the passover, and the priests [a]sprinkled *the blood* from

D *2Ch 30:5* ◀ ▶ *Ezr 6:19–20*

their hands, and the Levites [b]flayed *them.*

12 And they removed the burnt offerings, that they might give according to the divisions of the families of the people, to offer unto the LORD, as *it is* written [a]in the book of Moses. And so *did they* with the oxen.

13 And they [a]roasted the passover with fire according to the ordinance: but the *other* holy *offerings* [b]sod they in pots, and in caldrons, and in pans, and [1]divided *them* speedily among all the people.

14 And afterward they made ready for themselves, and for the priests: because the priests the sons of Aaron *were busied* in offering of burnt offerings and the fat until night; therefore the Levites prepared for themselves, and for the priests the sons of Aaron.

15 And the singers the sons of Asaph *were* in their [1]place, according to the [a]commandment of David, and Asaph, and Heman, and Jeduthun the king's seer; and the porters [b]*waited* at every gate; they might not depart from their service; for their brethren the Levites prepared for them.

16 So all the service of the LORD was prepared the same day, to keep the passover, and to offer burnt offerings upon the altar of the LORD, according to the commandment of king Josiah.

17 And the children of Israel that were [1]present kept the passover at that time, and the feast of [a]unleavened bread seven days.

18 And [a]there was no passover like to that kept in Israel from the days of Samuel the prophet; neither did all the kings of Israel keep such a passover as Josiah kept, and the priests, and the Levites, and all Judah and Israel that were present, and the inhabitants of Jerusalem.

19 In the eighteenth year of the reign of Josiah was this passover kept.

The death of Josiah

20 ¶ [a]After all this, when Josiah had prepared the [1]temple, Necho king of Egypt came up to fight against Carchemish by Euphrates: and Josiah went out against him.

21 But he sent ambassadors to him, saying, What have I to do with thee, thou king of Judah? *I come* not against thee this day, but against [1]the house wherewith I have war: for God commanded me to make haste: forbear thee from *meddling with* God, who *is* with me, that he destroy thee not.

22 Nevertheless Josiah would not turn his face from him, but disguised himself, that he might fight with him, and hearkened not unto the words of Necho from the mouth of God, and came to fight in the valley of Megiddo.

23 And the archers shot at king Josiah; and the king said to his servants, Have me away; for I am sore [a]wounded.[1]

24 [a]His servants therefore took him out of that chariot, and put him in the second chariot that he had; and they brought him to Jerusalem, and he died, and was buried [1]in *one of* the sepulchres of his fathers. And [b]all Judah and Jerusalem mourned for Josiah.

25 ¶ And Jeremiah [a]lamented for Josiah: and [b]all the singing men and the singing women spake of Josiah in their lamentations to this day, [c]and made them an ordinance in Israel: and, behold, they *are* written in the lamentations.

26 Now the rest of the acts of Josiah, and his [1]goodness, according to *that which was* written in the law of the LORD,

27 And his deeds, first and last, behold, they *are* written in the book of the kings of Israel and Judah.

From Josiah to the captivity

36 THEN [a]THE people of the land took Jehoahaz the son of Josiah, and made him king in his father's stead in Jerusalem.

2 Jehoahaz *was* twenty and three years old when he began to reign, and he reigned three months in Jerusalem.

3 And the king of Egypt [1]put him down at Jerusalem, and [2]condemned the land in an hundred talents of silver and a talent of gold.

4 And the king of Egypt made Eliakim his brother king over Judah and Jerusalem, and turned his name to Jehoiakim. And Necho took Jehoahaz his brother, and carried him to Egypt.

5 ¶ [a]Jehoiakim *was* twenty and five years old when he began to reign, and he reigned eleven years in Jerusalem: and he did *that which was* evil in the sight of the LORD his God.

---

11 [b]See ch. 29:34
12 [a]Lev. 3:3
13 [a]Ex. 12:8,9; Deut. 16:7 [b]1 Sam. 2:13-15 [1]Heb. *made them run*
15 [a]1 Chr. 25:1 [b]1 Chr. 9:17,18 & 26:14 [1]Heb. *station*
17 [a]Ex. 12:15 & 13:6; ch. 30:21 [1]Heb. *found*
18 [a]2 Ki. 23:22,23
20 [a]2 Ki. 23:29 [1]Heb. *house*
21 [1]Heb. *the house of my war*
23 [a]1 Ki. 22:34 [1]Heb. *made sick*
24 [a]2 Ki. 23:30 [b]Zech. 12:11 [1]Or, *among the sepulchres*
25 [a]Lam. 4:20 [b]See Mat. 9:23 [c]Jer. 22:20
26 [1]Heb. *kindnesses*
36:1 [a]2 Ki. 23:30
3 [1]Heb. *removed him* [2]Heb. *mulcted*
5 [a]2 Ki. 23:36,37

6 [a]Against him came up Nebuchadnezzar king of Babylon, and bound him in [1]fetters, to [b]carry him to Babylon.

7 [a]Nebuchadnezzar also carried of the vessels of the house of the LORD to Babylon, and put them in his temple at Babylon.

8 Now the rest of the acts of Jehoiakim, and his abominations which he did, and that which was found in him, behold, they *are* written in the book of the kings of Israel and Judah: and [1]Jehoiachin his son reigned in his stead.

9 ¶ [a]Jehoiachin *was* eight years old when he began to reign, and he reigned three months and ten days in Jerusalem: and he did *that which was* evil in the sight of the LORD.

10 And [1]when the year was expired, [a]king Nebuchadnezzar sent, and brought him to Babylon, [b]with the [2]goodly vessels of the house of the LORD, and made [c]Zedekiah [d]his[3] brother king over Judah and Jerusalem.

11 ¶ [a]Zedekiah *was* one and twenty years old when he began to reign, and reigned eleven years in Jerusalem.

12 And he did *that which was* evil in the sight of the LORD his God, *and* humbled not himself before Jeremiah the prophet *speaking* from the mouth of the LORD.

N 13 And he also rebelled against king Nebuchadnezzar, who had made him swear by God: but he [a]stiffened his neck, and hardened his heart from turning unto the LORD God of Israel.

14 ¶ Moreover all the chief of the priests, and the people, transgressed very much after all the abominations of the heathen; and polluted the house of the LORD which he had hallowed in Jerusalem.

N *2Ch 12:14* ◀▶ *2Ch 36:16*

6 [a]2 Ki. 24:1; Foretold, Hab. 1:6 [b]Jer. 36:30 [1]*Or, chains*

7 [a]2 Ki. 24:13; Dan. 1:1,2

8 [1]*Called Jeconiah* in 1 Chr. 3:16, or, *Coniah* in Jer. 22:24

9 [a]2 Ki. 24:8

10 [a]2 Ki. 24:10-17 [b]Dan. 1:1,2 [c]Jer. 37:1 [d]2 Ki. 24:17 [1]*Heb. at the return of the year* [2]*Heb. vessels of desire* [3]*Or, Mattaniah, his father's brother*

11 [a]2 Ki. 24:18; Jer. 52:1

13 [a]2 Ki. 17:14

15 [a]Jer. 25:3,4 [1]*Heb. by the hand of his messengers* [2]*i.e. continually and carefully*

16 [a]Jer. 5:12 [b]Prov. 1:25 [c]Jer. 38:6; Mat. 23:34 [d]Ps. 79:5 [1]*Heb. healing*

17 [a]Deut. 28:49; 2 Ki. 25:1; Ezra 9:7 [b]Ps. 74:20

18 [a]2 Ki. 25:13

19 [a]2 Ki. 25:9; Ps. 79:1,7

20 [a]2 Ki. 25:11 [b]Jer. 27:7 [1]*Heb. the remainder from the sword*

21 [a]Jer. 26:6,7 [b]Lev. 26:34; Dan. 9:2 [c]Lev. 25:4,5

22 [a]Ezra 1:1

15 [a]And the LORD God of their fathers sent to them [1]by his messengers, rising up [2]betimes, and sending; because he had compassion on his people, and on his dwelling place:

16 But [a]they mocked the messengers of God, and [b]despised his words, and [c]misused his prophets, until the [d]wrath of the LORD arose against his people, till *there was* no [1]remedy. H N

Defeat and exile to Babylon

17 [a]Therefore he brought upon them the king of the Chaldees, who [b]slew their young men with the sword in the house of their sanctuary, and had no compassion upon young man or maiden, old man, or him that stooped for age: he gave *them* all into his hand. R

18 [a]And all the vessels of the house of God, great and small, and the treasures of the house of the LORD, and the treasures of the king, and of his princes; all *these* he brought to Babylon.

19 [a]And they burnt the house of God, and brake down the wall of Jerusalem, and burnt all the palaces thereof with fire, and destroyed all the goodly vessels thereof.

20 And [a]them[1] that had escaped from the sword carried he away to Babylon; [b]where they were servants to him and his sons until the reign of the kingdom of Persia:

21 To fulfil the word of the LORD by the mouth of [a]Jeremiah, until the land [b]had enjoyed her sabbaths: *for* as long as she lay desolate [c]she kept sabbath, to fulfil threescore and ten years.

Cyrus promises end of captivity

22 ¶ [a]Now in the first year of Cyrus

H *1Ch 28:9* ◀▶ *Ezr 8:22*
N *2Ch 36:13* ◀▶ *Ne 9:29–30*
R *2Ch 34:24–25* ◀▶ *Ne 1:8*

36:17–21 In fulfillment of Jeremiah's prophecy, God allowed the Babylonians to overrun Judah, capture Jerusalem, burn the temple and take the population captive to Babylon. This tragedy occurred in part because Israel had refused to follow God's law of the Sabbath of the land (allowing the land lie unplowed every seven years). Because Israel had willingly refused to obey God's Sabbath laws, God would forcibly give the land its Sabbaths by removing Israel from the land for seventy years.

king of Persia, that the word of the LORD
spoken by the mouth of [b]Jeremiah might
be accomplished, the LORD stirred up the
spirit of [c]Cyrus king of Persia, that he
made a proclamation throughout all his
kingdom, and *put it* also in writing,
saying,

22 [b]Jer. 29:10
[c]Is. 44:28

23 [a]Ezra 1:2,3

23 [a]Thus saith Cyrus king of Persia, All
the kingdoms of the earth hath the LORD
God of heaven given me; and he hath
charged me to build him an house in Jerusalem, which *is* in Judah. Who *is there*
among you of all his people? The LORD his
God *be* with him, and let him go up.

Ezra

Author: Ezra

Theme: Return of the faithful remnant

Date of Writing: c. 440 B.C.

Outline of Ezra

I. The First Exiles Return to the Land (1:1—2:70)
II. The Temple Is Rebuilt (3:1—6:22)
III. Ezra's Return and Ministry (7:1—10:44)

THIS BOOK IS named after Ezra, a scribe in Israel and main character in this story. Though some ancient texts combined Ezra and Nehemiah into one book, later translators divided them. As a historical narrative, Ezra continues Israel's story following the period of Samuel, Kings and Chronicles.

Using genealogies (2:1–70), official documents (4:7–16) and personal letters (7:27—9:15), Ezra relates the exiles' return to their homeland, commencing with King Cyrus's edict that released the exiles from their seventy-year captivity in Babylon. A remnant of Jews returned to Israel at this time under the supervision of Zerubbabel to begin the reconstruction of the temple. Though enemies opposed this rebuilding project for years, an appeal to Cyrus's successor, Darius, re-authorized the project. Encouraged by Haggai and Zechariah the people redoubled their efforts and completed the temple in 516 B.C.

In 458 B.C. Ezra led another group of Jews back to Jerusalem. Nehemiah returned with a third group in 445 B.C. to rebuild the city's walls. Though Nehemiah was the civil leader of these exiles, Ezra quickly became their teacher, initiating reforms and guiding the people in rebuilding their spiritual foundations as God's chosen nation. Ezra's concern for the people and his personal devotion to God provided effective leadership and spiritual guidance for the people in a very unsettled time.

The proclamation of Cyrus

1 NOW IN the first year of Cyrus king of Persia, that the word of the LORD [a]by the mouth of Jeremiah might be fulfilled, the LORD stirred up the spirit of Cyrus king of Persia, [b]that he [1]made a proclamation throughout all his kingdom, and *put it* also in writing, saying,

2 Thus saith Cyrus king of Persia, The LORD God of heaven hath given me all the kingdoms of the earth; and he hath [a]charged me to build him an house at Jerusalem, which *is* in Judah.

3 Who *is there* among you of all his people? his God be with him, and let him go up to Jerusalem, which *is* in Judah, and build the house of the LORD God of Israel, ([a]he *is* the God,) which *is* in Jerusalem.

4 And whosoever remaineth in any place where he sojourneth, let the men of his place [1]help him with silver, and with gold, and with goods, and with beasts, beside the freewill offering for the house of God that *is* in Jerusalem.

5 ¶ Then rose up the chief of the fathers of Judah and Benjamin, and the priests, and the Levites, with all *them* whose spirit [a]God had raised, to go up to build the house of the LORD which *is* in Jerusalem.

6 And all they that *were* about them [1]strengthened their hands with vessels of silver, with gold, with goods, and with beasts, and with precious things, beside all *that* was willingly offered.

7 ¶ [a]Also Cyrus the king brought forth the vessels of the house of the LORD, [b]which Nebuchadnezzar had brought forth out of Jerusalem, and had put them in the house of his gods;

8 Even those did Cyrus king of Persia bring forth by the hand of Mithredath the treasurer, and numbered them unto [a]Sheshbazzar, the prince of Judah.

9 And this *is* the number of them: thirty chargers of gold, a thousand chargers of silver, nine and twenty knives,

10 Thirty basins of gold, silver basins of a second *sort* four hundred and ten, *and* other vessels a thousand.

11 All the vessels of gold and of silver *were* five thousand and four hundred. All *these* did Sheshbazzar bring up with *them of* [1]the captivity that were brought up from Babylon unto Jerusalem.

1:1 [a]2 Chr. 36:22, 23 [b]ch. 5:13,14 [1]Heb. *(caused a voice to pass)*
2 [a]Is. 44:28 & 45:1,13
3 [a]Dan. 6:26
4 [1]Heb. *lift him up*
5 [a]Phil. 2:13
6 [1]i.e. *helped them*
7 [a]ch. 5:14 & 6:5 [b]2 Ki. 24:13; 2 Chr. 36:7
8 [a]See ch. 5:14
11 [1]Heb. *the transportation*
2:1 [a]Neh. 7:6 [b]2 Ki. 24:14-16 & 25:11; 2 Chr. 36:20
2 [1]Or, *Azariah;* see Neh. 7:7 [2]Or, *Raamiah* [3]Or, *Mispereth* [4]Or, *Nehum*
5 [a]See Neh. 7:10
6 [a]Neh. 7:11
10 [1]Or, *Binnui;* see Neh. 7:15
18 [1]Or, *Hariph;* see Neh. 7:24
20 [1]Or, *Gibeon;* see Neh. 7:25

The people who returned

2 NOW [a]THESE *are* the children of the province that went up out of the captivity, of those which had been carried away, [b]whom Nebuchadnezzar the king of Babylon had carried away unto Babylon, and came again unto Jerusalem and Judah, every one unto his city;

2 Which came with Zerubbabel: Jeshua, Nehemiah, [1]Seraiah, [2]Reelaiah, Mordecai, Bilshan, [3]Mizpar, Bigvai, [4]Rehum, Baanah. The number of the men of the people of Israel:

3 The children of Parosh, two thousand an hundred seventy and two.

4 The children of Shephatiah, three hundred seventy and two.

5 The children of Arah, [a]seven hundred seventy and five.

6 The children of [a]Pahath-moab, of the children of Jeshua *and* Joab, two thousand eight hundred and twelve.

7 The children of Elam, a thousand two hundred fifty and four.

8 The children of Zattu, nine hundred forty and five.

9 The children of Zaccai, seven hundred and threescore.

10 The children of [1]Bani, six hundred forty and two.

11 The children of Bebai, six hundred twenty and three.

12 The children of Azgad, a thousand two hundred twenty and two.

13 The children of Adonikam, six hundred sixty and six.

14 The children of Bigvai, two thousand fifty and six.

15 The children of Adin, four hundred fifty and four.

16 The children of Ater of Hezekiah, ninety and eight.

17 The children of Bezai, three hundred twenty and three.

18 The children of [1]Jorah, an hundred and twelve.

19 The children of Hashum, two hundred twenty and three.

20 The children of [1]Gibbar, ninety and five.

21 The children of Bethlehem, an hundred twenty and three.

22 The men of Netophah, fifty and six.

23 The men of Anathoth, an hundred twenty and eight.

24 The children of [1]Azmaveth, forty
and two.
25 The children of Kirjath-arim, Chephirah, and Beeroth, seven hundred and
forty and three.
26 The children of Ramah and Gaba,
six hundred twenty and one.
27 The men of Michmas, an hundred
twenty and two.
28 The men of Beth-el and Ai, two
hundred twenty and three.
29 The children of Nebo, fifty and two.
30 The children of Magbish, an hundred fifty and six.
31 The children of the other [a]Elam, a
thousand two hundred fifty and four.
32 The children of Harim, three hundred and twenty.
33 The children of Lod, [1]Hadid, and
Ono, seven hundred twenty and five.
34 The children of Jericho, three hundred forty and five.
35 The children of Senaah, three thousand and six hundred and thirty.
36 ¶ The priests: the children of [a]Jeda-
iah, of the house of Jeshua, nine hundred
seventy and three.
37 The children of [a]Immer, a thousand
fifty and two.
38 The children of [a]Pashur, a thousand
two hundred forty and seven.
39 The children of [a]Harim, a thousand
and seventeen.
40 ¶ The Levites: the children of
Jeshua and Kadmiel, of the children of
[1]Hodaviah, seventy and four.
41 ¶ The singers: the children of
Asaph, an hundred twenty and eight.
42 ¶ The children of the porters: the
children of Shallum, the children of Ater,
the children of Talmon, the children of
Akkub, the children of Hatita, the children of Shobai, *in* all an hundred thirty
and nine.
43 ¶ [a]The Nethinims: the children of
Ziha, the children of Hasupha, the children of Tabbaoth,
44 The children of Keros, the children
of [1]Siaha, the children of Padon,
45 The children of Lebanah, the children of Hagabah, the children of Akkub,
46 The children of Hagab, the children
of [1]Shalmai, the children of Hanan,
47 The children of Giddel, the children of Gahar, the children of Reaiah,
48 The children of Rezin, the children
of Nekoda, the children of Gazzam,

24 [1]Or, *Beth-azmaveth;* see Neh. 7:28

31 [a]See ver. 7

33 [1]Or, *Harid,* as it is in some copies

36 [a]1 Chr. 24:7

37 [a]1 Chr. 24:14

38 [a]1 Chr. 9:12

39 [a]1 Chr. 24:8

40 [1]Or, *Judah;* see ch. 3:9; called also *Hodevah* in Neh. 7:43

43 [a]1 Chr. 9:2

44 [1]Or, *Sia*

46 [1]Or, *Shamlai*

50 [1]Or, *Nephishesim*

52 [1]Or, *Bazlith;* see Neh. 7:54

55 [a]1 Ki. 9:21 [1]Or, *Perida;* see Neh. 7:57

57 [1]Or, *Amon;* see Neh. 7:59

58 [a]Josh. 9:21,27; 1 Chr. 9:2 [b]1 Ki. 9:21

59 [1]Or, *Addon;* see Neh. 7:61 [2]Or, *pedigree*

61 [a]2 Sam. 17:27

62 [a]Num. 3:10 [1]Heb. *they were polluted from the priesthood*

63 [a]Lev. 22:2,10, 15,16 [b]Ex. 28:30; Num. 27:21 [1]Or, *governor;* see Neh. 8:9

64 [a]Neh. 7:66

49 The children of Uzza, the children
of Paseah, the children of Besai,
50 the children of Asnah, the children
of Mehunim, the children of [1]Nephusim,
51 The children of Bakbuk, the children of Hakupha, the children of Harhur,
52 The children of [1]Bazluth, the children of Mehida, the children of Harsha,
53 The children of Barkos, the children of Sisera, the children of Thamah,
54 The children of Neziah, the children of Hatipha.
55 ¶ The children of [a]Solomon's servants: the children of Sotai, the children
of Sophereth, the children of [1]Peruda,
56 The children of Jaalah, the children
of Darkon, the children of Giddel,
57 The children of Shephatiah, the
children of Hattil, the children of Poche-
reth of Zebaim, the children of [1]Ami.
58 All the [a]Nethinims, and the children of [b]Solomon's servants, *were* three
hundred ninety and two.
59 And these *were* they which went
up from Tel-melah, Tel-harsa, Cherub,
[1]Addan, *and* Immer: but they could not
show their father's house, and their
[2]seed, whether they *were* of Israel:
60 The children of Delaiah, the children of Tobiah, the children of Nekoda,
six hundred fifty and two.
61 ¶ And of the children of the priests:
the children of Habaiah, the children of
Koz, the children of Barzillai; which took
a wife of the daughters of [a]Barzillai the
Gileadite, and was called after their
name:
62 These sought their register *among*
those that were reckoned by genealogy,
but they were not found: [a]therefore
[1]were they, as polluted, put from the
priesthood.
63 And the [1]Tirshatha said unto them,
that they [a]should not eat of the most holy
things, till there stood up a priest with
[b]Urim and with Thummim.
64 ¶ [a]The whole congregation together *was* forty and two thousand three
hundred *and* threescore,
65 Beside their servants and their
maids, of whom *there were* seven thousand three hundred thirty and seven: and
there were among them two hundred
singing men and singing women.
66 Their horses *were* seven hundred
thirty and six; their mules, two hundred
forty and five;

67 Their camels, four hundred thirty and five; *their* asses, six thousand seven hundred and twenty.

68 ¶ [a]And *some* of the chief of the fathers, when they came to the house of the LORD which *is* at Jerusalem, offered freely for the house of God to set it up in his place:

69 They gave after their ability unto the [a]treasure of the work threescore and one thousand drams of gold, and five thousand pound of silver, and one hundred priests' garments.

70 [a]So the priests, and the Levites, and *some* of the people, and the singers, and the porters, and the Nethinims, dwelt in their cities, and all Israel in their cities.

The altar rebuilt

3 AND WHEN the seventh month was come, and the children of Israel *were* in the cities, the people gathered themselves together as one man to Jerusalem.

2 Then stood up [1]Jeshua the son of Jozadak, and his brethren the priests, and [2]Zerubbabel the son of [a]Shealtiel, and his brethren, and builded the altar of the God of Israel, to offer burnt offerings thereon, as *it is* [b]written in the law of Moses the man of God.

3 And they set the altar upon his bases; for fear *was* upon them because of the people of those countries: and they offered burnt offerings thereon unto the LORD, *even* [a]burnt offerings morning and evening.

4 [a]They kept also the feast of tabernacles, [b]as *it is* written, and [c]*offered* the daily burnt offerings by number, according to the custom, [1]as the duty of every day required;

5 And afterward *offered* the [a]continual burnt offering, both of the new moons, and of all the set feasts of the LORD that were consecrated, and of every one that willingly offered a freewill offering unto the LORD.

6 From the first day of the seventh month began they to offer burnt offerings unto the LORD. But [1]the foundation of the temple of the LORD was not *yet* laid.

7 They gave money also unto the masons, and to the [1]carpenters; and [a]meat, and drink, and oil, unto them of Zidon, and to them of Tyre, to bring cedar trees from Lebanon to the sea of [b]Joppa, [c]according to the grant that they had of Cyrus king of Persia.

68 [a]Neh. 7:70
69 [a]1 Chr. 26:20
70 [a]ch. 6:16,17; Neh. 7:73
3:2 [a]Mat. 1:12 & Luke 3:27 called *Salathiel* [b]Deut. 12:5 [1]Or, *Joshua;* see Hag. 1:1 & 2:2; Zech. 3:1 [2]Called *Zorobabel* in Mat. 1:12; Luke 3:27
3 [a]Num. 28:3
4 [a]Neh. 8:14; Zech. 14:16 [b]Ex. 23:16 [c]Num. 29:12 [1]Heb. *the matter of the day in his day*
5 [a]Ex. 29:38; Num. 28:3,11,19,26
6 [1]Heb. *the temple of the LORD was not yet founded*
7 [a]1 Ki. 5:6,9; 2 Chr. 2:10; Acts 12:20 [b]2 Chr. 2:16; Acts 9:36 [c]ch. 6:3 [1]Or, *workmen*
8 [a]1 Chr. 23:24,27
9 [a]ch. 2:40 [1]Or, *Hodaviah;* see ch. 2:40 [2]Heb. *as one*
10 [a]1 Chr. 16:5 [b]1 Chr. 6:31 & 16:4 & 25:1
11 [a]Ex. 15:21; 2 Chr. 7:3; Neh. 12:24 [b]1 Chr. 16:34; Ps. 136:1 [c]1 Chr. 16:41; Jer. 33:11

Rebuilding of the temple begun

8 ¶ Now in the second year of their coming unto the house of God at Jerusalem, in the second month, began Zerubbabel the son of Shealtiel, and Jeshua the son of Jozadak, and the remnant of their brethren the priests and the Levites, and all they that were come out of the captivity unto Jerusalem; [a]and appointed the Levites, from twenty years old and upward, to set forward the work of the house of the LORD.

9 Then stood [a]Jeshua *with* his sons and his brethren, Kadmiel and his sons, the sons of [1]Judah, [2]together, to set forward the workmen in the house of God: the sons of Henadad, *with* their sons and their brethren the Levites.

10 And when the builders laid the foundation of the temple of the LORD, [a]they set the priests in their apparel with trumpets, and the Levites the sons of Asaph with cymbals, to praise the LORD, after the [b]ordinance of David king of Israel.

11 [a]And they sang together by course in praising and giving thanks unto the LORD; [b]because *he is* good, [c]for his mercy *endureth* for ever toward Israel. And all the people shouted with a great shout, when they praised the LORD, because the foundation of the house of the LORD was laid.

12 But many of the priests and Levites and chief of the fathers, *who were* ancient men, that had seen the first house, when the foundation of this house was laid before their eyes, wept with a loud voice; and many shouted aloud for joy:

13 So that the people could not discern the noise of the shout of joy from the noise of the weeping of the people: for the people shouted with a loud shout, and the noise was heard afar off.

2Ch 20:7 ◀ ▶ *Ne 1:9*

3:11 During this victory celebration, Ezra recorded that the people's praise and thanks were directed toward the Lord "because he is good, for his mercy endureth for ever toward Israel."

Adversaries of Judah

4 NOW WHEN [a]the adversaries of Judah and Benjamin heard that [1]the children of the captivity builded the temple unto the LORD God of Israel;

2 Then they came to Zerubbabel, and to the chief of the fathers, and said unto them, Let us build with you: for we seek your God, as ye *do;* and we do sacrifice unto him since [a]the days of Esar-haddon king of Assur, which brought us up hither.

3 But Zerubbabel, and Jeshua, and the rest of the chief of the fathers of Israel, said unto them, [a]Ye have nothing to do with us to build an house unto our God; but we ourselves together will build unto the LORD God of Israel, as [b]king Cyrus the king of Persia hath commanded us.

4 Then [a]the people of the land weakened the hands of the people of Judah, and troubled them in building,

5 And hired counsellors against them, to frustrate their purpose, all the days of Cyrus king of Persia, even until the reign of Darius king of Persia.

6 And in the reign of [1]Ahasuerus, in the beginning of his reign, wrote they *unto him* an accusation against the inhabitants of Judah and Jerusalem.

The letter to Artaxerxes

7 ¶ And in the days of Artaxerxes wrote [1]Bishlam, Mithredath, Tabeel, and the rest of their [2]companions, unto Artaxerxes king of Persia; and the writing of the letter *was* written in the Syrian tongue, and interpreted in the Syrian tongue.

8 Rehum the chancellor and Shimshai the [1]scribe wrote a letter against Jerusalem to Artaxerxes the king in this sort:

9 Then *wrote* Rehum the chancellor, and Shimshai the scribe, and the rest of their [1]companions; [a]the Dinaites, the Apharsathchites, the Tarpelites, the Apharsites, the Archevites, the Babylonians, the Susanchites, the Dehavites, *and* the Elamites,

10 [a]And the rest of the nations whom the great and noble Asnapper brought over, and set in the cities of Samaria, and the rest *that are* on this side the river, [b]and [1]at such a time.

11 ¶ This *is* the copy of the letter that they sent unto him, *even* unto Artaxerxes the king; Thy servants the men on this side the river, and at such a time.

12 Be it known unto the king, that the Jews which came up from thee to us are come unto Jerusalem, building the rebellious and the bad city, and have [1]set up the walls *thereof,* and [2]joined the foundations.

13 Be it known now unto the king, that, if this city be builded, and the walls set up *again, then* will they not [1]pay [a]toll, tribute, and custom, and *so* thou shalt endamage the [2]revenue of the kings.

14 Now because [1]we have maintenance from *the king's* palace, and it was not meet for us to see the king's dishonour, therefore have we sent and certified the king;

15 That search may be made in the book of the records of thy fathers: so shalt thou find in the book of the records, and know that this city *is* a rebellious city, and hurtful unto kings and provinces, and that they have [1]moved sedition [2]within the same of old time: for which cause was this city destroyed.

16 We certify the king that, if this city be builded *again,* and the walls thereof set up, by this means thou shalt have no portion on this side the river.

17 ¶ *Then* sent the king an answer unto Rehum the chancellor, and *to* Shimshai the scribe, and *to* the rest of their [1]companions that dwell in Samaria, and *unto* the rest beyond the river, Peace, and at such a time.

18 The letter which ye sent unto us hath been plainly read before me.

19 And [1]I commanded, and search hath been made, and it is found that this city of old time hath [2]made insurrection against kings, and *that* rebellion and sedition have been made therein.

20 There have been mighty kings also over Jerusalem, which have [a]ruled over all *countries* [b]beyond the river; and toll, tribute, and custom, was paid unto them.

21 [1]Give ye now commandment to cause these men to cease, and that this city be not builded, until *another* commandment shall be given from me.

22 Take heed now that ye fail not to do this: why should damage grow to the hurt of the kings?

23 ¶ Now when the copy of king Artaxerxes' letter *was* read before Rehum, and Shimshai the scribe, and their com-

4:1 [a]See ver. 7-9 [1]Heb. *the sons of the transportation*
2 [a]ver. 10; 2 Ki. 17:24,32,33 & 19:37
3 [a]Neh. 2:20 [b]ch. 1:1-3
4 [a]ch. 3:3
6 [1]Heb. *Ahashverosh*
7 [1]Or, *in peace* [2]Heb. *societies*
8 [1]Or, *secretary*
9 [a]2 Ki. 17:30,31 [1]Chald. *societies*
10 [a]ver. 1 [b]ver. 11,17 & ch 7:12 [1]Chald. *Cheeneth*
12 [1]Or, *finished* [2]Chald. *sewed together*
13 [a]ch. 7:24 [1]Chald. *give* [2]Or, *strength*
14 [1]Chald. *we are salted with the salt of the palace*
15 [1]Chald. *made* [2]Chald. *in the midst thereof*
17 [1]Chald. *societies*
19 [1]Chald. *by me a decree is set* [2]Chald. *lifted up itself*
20 [a]1 Ki. 4:21; Ps. 72:8 [b]Gen. 15:18; Josh. 1:4
21 [1]Chald. *Make a decree*

panions, they went up in haste to Jerusalem unto the Jews, and made them to
cease [1]by force and power.
24 Then ceased the work of the house
of God which *is* at Jerusalem. So it ceased
unto the second year of the reign of Darius king of Persia.

Zerubbabel begins to build again

5 THEN THE prophets, [a]Haggai the
prophet, and [b]Zechariah the son of
Iddo, prophesied unto the Jews that *were*
in Judah and Jerusalem in the name of
the God of Israel, *even* unto them.
2 Then rose up [a]Zerubbabel the son of
Shealtiel, and Jeshua the son of Jozadak,
and began to build the house of God
which *is* at Jerusalem: and with them
were the prophets of God helping them.
3 ¶ At the same time came to them
[a]Tatnai, governor on this side the river,
and Shethar-boznai, and their companions, and said thus unto them, [b]Who hath
commanded you to build this house, and
to make up this wall?
4 [a]Then said we unto them after this
manner, What are the names of the men
[1]that make this building?
5 But [a]the eye of their God was upon
the elders of the Jews, that they could not
cause them to cease, till the matter came
to Darius: and then they returned [b]an-
swer by letter concerning this *matter.*
6 ¶ The copy of the letter that Tatnai,
governor on this side the river, and Shethar-boznai, [a]and his companions the
Apharsachites, which *were* on this side
the river, sent unto Darius the king:
7 They sent a letter unto him,
[1]wherein was written thus; Unto Darius
the king, all peace.
8 Be it known unto the king, that we
went into the province of Judea, to the
house of the great God, which is builded
with [1]great stones, and timber is laid in
the walls, and this work goeth fast on,
and prospereth in their hands.
9 Then asked we those elders, *and* said
unto them thus, [a]Who commanded you
to build this house, and to make up these
walls?
10 We asked their names also, to certify thee, that we might write the names
of the men that *were* the chief of them.
11 And thus they returned us answer,
saying, We are the servants of the God of
heaven and earth, and build the house

23 [1]Chald. *by arm and power*
5:1 [a]Hag. 1:1 [b]Zech. 1:1
2 [a]ch. 3:2
3 [a]ver. 6; ch. 6:6 [b]ver. 9
4 [a]ver. 10 [1]Chald. *that build this building?*
5 [a]See ch. 7:6,28; Ps. 33:18 [b]ch. 6:6
6 [a]ch. 4:9
7 [1]Chald. *in the midst whereof*
8 [1]Chald. *stones of rolling*
9 [a]ver. 3,4
11 [a]1 Ki. 6:1
12 [a]2 Chr. 36:16, 17 [b]2 Ki. 24:2 & 25:8,9,11
13 [a]ch. 1:1
14 [a]ch. 1:7,8 & 6:5 [b]Hag. 1:14 & 2:2,21 [1]Or, *deputy*
16 [a]ch. 3:8,10 [b]ch. 6:15
17 [a]ch. 6:1,2
6:1 [a]ch. 5:17 [1]Chald. *books* [2]Chald. *made to descend*
2 [1]Or, *Ecbatana, or, in a coffer*
4 [a]1 Ki. 6:36

that was builded these many years ago,
which a great king of Israel builded [a]and
set up.
12 But [a]after that our fathers had provoked the God of heaven unto wrath, he
gave them into the hand of [b]Nebuchad-
nezzar the king of Babylon, the Chaldean,
who destroyed this house, and carried
the people away into Babylon.
13 But in the first year of [a]Cyrus the
king of Babylon *the same* king Cyrus
made a decree to build this house of God.
14 And [a]the vessels also of gold and
silver of the house of God, which Nebuchadnezzar took out of the temple that
was in Jerusalem, and brought them into
the temple of Babylon, those did Cyrus
the king take out of the temple of Babylon, and they were delivered unto *one,*
[b]whose name *was* Sheshbazzar, whom he
had made [1]governor;
15 And said unto him, Take these vessels, go, carry them into the temple that
is in Jerusalem, and let the house of God
be builded in his place.
16 Then came the same Sheshbazzar,
and [a]laid the foundation of the house of
God which *is* in Jerusalem: and since that
time even until now hath it been in building, and [b]*yet* it is not finished.
17 Now therefore, if *it seem* good to
the king, [a]let there be search made in the
king's treasure house, which *is* there at
Babylon, whether it be *so,* that a decree
was made of Cyrus the king to build this
house of God at Jerusalem, and let the
king send his pleasure to us concerning
this matter.

Darius' search and reply

6 THEN DARIUS the king made a decree, [a]and search was made in the
house of the [1]rolls, where the treasures
were [2]laid up in Babylon.
2 And there was found at [1]Achmetha,
in the palace that *is* in the province of the
Medes, a roll, and therein *was* a record
thus written:
3 In the first year of Cyrus the king *the*
same Cyrus the king made a decree *con-*
cerning the house of God at Jerusalem,
Let the house be builded, the place
where they offered sacrifices, and let the
foundations thereof be strongly laid; the
height thereof threescore cubits, *and*
the breadth thereof threescore cubits;
4 [a]*With* three rows of great stones, and

a row of new timber: and let the expenses be given out of the king's house:
5 And also let [a]the golden and silver
vessels of the house of God, which Nebuchadnezzar took forth out of the temple
which *is* at Jerusalem, and brought unto
Babylon, be restored, and [l]brought again
unto the temple which *is* at Jerusalem,
every one to his place, and place *them* in
the house of God.
6 [a]Now *therefore,* Tatnai, governor beyond the river, Shethar-boznai, and [l]your
companions the Apharsachites, which
are beyond the river, be ye far from
thence:
7 Let the work of this house of God
alone; let the governor of the Jews and
the elders of the Jews build this house of
God in his place.
8 Moreover [l]I make a decree what ye
shall do to the elders of these Jews for the
building of this house of God: that of the
king's goods, *even* of the tribute beyond
the river, forthwith expenses be given
unto these men, that they be not [2]hin-
dered.
9 And that which they have need of,
both young bullocks, and rams, and
lambs, for the burnt offerings of the God
of heaven, wheat, salt, wine, and oil, according to the appointment of the priests
which *are* at Jerusalem, let it be given
them day by day without fail:
10 [a]That they may offer sacrifices [l]of
sweet savours unto the God of heaven,
and pray for the life of the king, and of his
sons.
11 Also I have made a decree, that
whosoever shall alter this word, let timber be pulled down from his house, and
being set up, [l]let him be hanged thereon;
[a]and let his house be made a dunghill for
this.
12 And the God that hath caused his
[a]name to dwell there destroy all kings
and people, that shall put to their hand to
alter *and* to destroy this house of God
which *is* at Jerusalem. I Darius have
made a decree; let it be done with speed.

The temple rebuilt and dedicated

13 ¶ Then Tatnai, governor on this
side the river, Shethar-boznai, and their
companions, according to that which Darius the king had sent, so they did
speedily.
14 [a]And the elders of the Jews
builded, and they prospered through the
prophesying of Haggai the prophet and
Zechariah the son of Iddo. And they
builded, and finished *it,* according to the
commandment of the God of Israel, and
according to the [l]commandment of [b]Cy-
rus, and [c]Darius, and [d]Artaxerxes king of
Persia.
15 And this house was finished on the
third day of the month Adar, which was
in the sixth year of the reign of Darius
the king.
16 ¶ And the children of Israel, the
priests, and the Levites, and the rest of
[l]the children of the captivity, kept [a]the
dedication of this house of God with joy,
17 And [a]offered at the dedication of
this house of God an hundred bullocks,
two hundred rams, four hundred lambs;
and for a sin offering for all Israel, twelve
he goats, according to the number of the
tribes of Israel.
18 And they set the priests in their [a]di-
visions, and the Levites in their [b]courses,
for the service of God, which *is* at Jerusalem; [c]as[l] it is written in the book of
Moses.
19 And the children of the captivity D
kept the passover [a]upon the fourteenth
day of the first month.
20 For the priests and the Levites were
[a]purified together, all of them *were* pure,
and [b]killed the passover for all the children of the captivity, and for their brethren the priests, and for themselves.
21 And the children of Israel, which
were come again out of captivity, and all
such as had separated themselves unto
them from the [a]filthiness of the heathen
of the land, to seek the LORD God of Israel,
did eat,
22 And kept the [a]feast of unleavened
bread seven days with joy: for the LORD
had made them joyful, and [b]turned the
heart [c]of the king of Assyria unto them,
to strengthen their hands in the work of
the house of God, the God of Israel.

Ezra's genealogy and career

7 NOW AFTER these things, in the
reign of [a]Artaxerxes king of Persia,
Ezra [b]the son of Seraiah, the son of Azariah, the son of Hilkiah,
2 The son of Shallum, the son of Zadok, the son of Ahitub,

D *2Ch 35:1* ◀▶ *Ps 22:13–18*

5 [a]ch. 1:7,8 & 5:14 [l]Chald. *go*
6 [a]ch. 5:3 [l]Chald. *their societies*
8 [l]Chald. *by me a decree is made* [2]Chald. *made to cease*
10 [a]ch. 7:23 [l]Chald. *of rest*
11 [a]Dan. 2:5 & 3:29 [l]Chald. *let him be destroyed*
12 [a]1 Ki. 9:3
14 [a]ch. 5:1,2 [b]ver. 3; ch. 1:1 & 5:13 [c]ch. 4:24 [d]ch. 7:1 [l]Chald. *decree*
16 [a]1 Ki. 8:63; 2 Chr. 7:5 [l]Chald. *the sons of the transportation*
17 [a]ch. 8:35
18 [a]1 Chr. 24:1 [b]1 Chr. 23:6 [c]Num. 3:6 & 8:9 [l]Chald. *according to the writing*
19 [a]Ex. 12:6
20 [a]2 Chr. 30:15 [b]2 Chr. 35:11
21 [a]ch. 9:11
22 [a]Ex. 12:15 & 13:6; 2 Chr. 30:21 & 35:17 [b]Prov. 21:1 [c]2 Ki. 23:29; 2 Chr. 33:11; ch. 1:1
7:1 [a]Neh. 2:1 [b]1 Chr. 6:14

3 The son of Amariah, the son of Azariah, the son of Meraioth,
4 The son of Zerahiah, the son of Uzzi,
the son of Bukki,
5 The son of Abishua, the son of Phinehas, the son of Eleazar, the son of Aaron
the chief priest:
6 This Ezra went up from Babylon; and
he *was* [a]a ready scribe in the law of Moses, which the LORD God of Israel had
given: and the king granted him all his
request, [b]according to the hand of the
LORD his God upon him.
7 [a]And there went up *some* of the children of Israel, and of the priests, and [b]the
Levites, and the singers, and the porters,
and [c]the Nethinims, unto Jerusalem, in
the seventh year of Artaxerxes the king.
8 And he came to Jerusalem in the fifth
month, which *was* in the seventh year of
the king.
9 For upon the first *day* of the first
month ʹbegan he to go up from Babylon,
and on the first *day* of the fifth month
came he to Jerusalem, [a]according to the
good hand of his God upon him.
10 For Ezra had prepared his heart to
[a]seek the law of the LORD, and to do *it,*
and to [b]teach in Israel statutes and judgments.

Ezra's letter from Artaxerxes

11 ¶ Now this *is* the copy of the letter
that the king Artaxerxes gave unto Ezra
the priest, the scribe, *even* a scribe of the
words of the commandments of the LORD,
and of his statutes to Israel.
12 Artaxerxes, [a]king of kings, ʹunto
Ezra the priest, a scribe of the law of the
God of heaven, perfect *peace,* [b]and at
such a time.
13 I make a decree, that all they of the
people of Israel, and *of* his priests and
Levites, in my realm, which are minded
of their own freewill to go up to Jerusalem, go with thee.
14 Forasmuch as thou art sent ʹof the
king, and of his [a]seven counsellors, to inquire concerning Judah and Jerusalem,
according to the law of thy God which *is*
in thine hand;
15 And to carry the silver and gold,
which the king and his counsellors have
freely offered unto the God of Israel,
[a]whose habitation *is* in Jerusalem,
16 [a]And all the silver and gold that
thou canst find in all the province of Babylon, with the freewill offering of the people, and of the priests, [b]offering willingly
for the house of their God which *is* in
Jerusalem:
17 That thou mayest buy speedily with
this money bullocks, rams, lambs, with
their [a]meat offerings and their drink offerings, and [b]offer them upon the altar of
the house of your God which *is* in Jerusalem.
18 And whatsoever shall seem good to
thee, and to thy brethren, to do with the
rest of the silver and the gold, that do
after the will of your God.
19 The vessels also that are given thee
for the service of the house of thy God,
those deliver thou before the God of Jerusalem.
20 And whatsoever more shall be
needful for the house of thy God, which
thou shalt have occasion to bestow, bestow *it* out of the king's treasure house.
21 And I, *even* I Artaxerxes the king,
do make a decree to all the treasurers
which *are* beyond the river, that whatsoever Ezra the priest, the scribe of the law
of the God of heaven, shall require of
you, it be done speedily,
22 Unto an hundred talents of silver,
and to an hundred ʹmeasures of wheat,
and to an hundred baths of wine, and to
an hundred baths of oil, and salt without
prescribing *how much.*
23 ʹWhatsoever is commanded by the
God of heaven, let it be diligently done
for the house of the God of heaven: for
why should there be wrath against the
realm of the king and his sons?
24 Also we certify you, that touching
any of the priests and Levites, singers,
porters, Nethinims, or ministers of this
house of God, it shall not be lawful to
impose toll, tribute, or custom, upon
them.
25 And thou, Ezra, after the wisdom of
thy God, that *is* in thine hand, [a]set magistrates and judges, which may judge all
the people that *are* beyond the river, all
such as know the laws of thy God; and
[b]teach ye them that know *them* not.
26 And whosoever will not do the law
of thy God, and the law of the king, let
judgment be executed speedily upon
him, whether *it be* unto death, or ʹto
banishment, or to confiscation of goods,
or to imprisonment.
27 ¶ [a]Blessed *be* the LORD God of our

6 [a]ver. 11,12 [b]ch. 8:22
7 [a]ch. 8:1 [b]See ch. 8:15 [c]ch. 2:43 & 8:20
9 [a]Neh. 2:8,18 ʹHeb. was *the foundation of the going up*
10 [a]Ps. 119:45 [b]ver. 6,25; Deut. 33:10; Neh. 8:1-8; Mal. 2:7
12 [a]Ezek. 26:7; Dan. 2:37 [b]ch. 4:10 ʹOr, *to Ezra the priest, a perfect scribe of the law of the God of heaven,* peace,
14 [a]Esth. 1:14 ʹChald. *from before the king*
15 [a]2 Chr. 6:2; Ps. 135:21
16 [a]ch. 8:25 [b]1 Chr. 29:6,9
17 [a]Num. 15:4-13 [b]Deut. 12:5,11
22 ʹChald. *cors*
23 ʹHeb. *Whatsoever is of the decree*
25 [a]Ex. 18:21,22; Deut. 16:18 [b]ver. 10; 2 Chr. 17:7; Mal. 2:7; Mat. 23:2,3
26 ʹChald. *to rooting out*
27 [a]1 Chr. 29:10

fathers, [b]which hath put *such a thing* as this in the king's heart, to beautify the house of the LORD which *is* in Jerusalem:

28 And [a]hath extended mercy unto me before the king, and his counsellors, and before all the king's mighty princes. And I was strengthened as [b]the hand of the LORD my God *was* upon me, and I gathered together out of Israel chief men to go up with me.

People returning with Ezra

8 THESE *ARE* now the chief of their fathers, and *this is* the genealogy of them that went up with me from Babylon, in the reign of Artaxerxes the king.

2 Of the sons of Phinehas; Gershom: of the sons of Ithamar; Daniel: of the sons of David; [a]Hattush.

3 Of the sons of Shechaniah, of the sons of [a]Pharosh; Zechariah: and with him were reckoned by genealogy of the males an hundred and fifty.

4 Of the sons of Pahath-moab; Elihoenai the son of Zerahiah, and with him two hundred males.

5 Of the sons of Shechaniah; the son of Jahaziel, and with him three hundred males.

6 Of the sons also of Adin; Ebed the son of Jonathan, and with him fifty males.

7 And of the sons of Elam; Jeshaiah the son of Athaliah, and with him seventy males.

8 And of the sons of Shephatiah; Zebadiah the son of Michael, and with him fourscore males.

9 Of the sons of Joab; Obadiah the son of Jehiel, and with him two hundred and eighteen males.

10 And of the sons of Shelomith; the son of Josiphiah, and with him an hundred and threescore males.

11 And of the sons of Bebai; Zechariah the son of Bebai, and with him twenty and eight males.

12 And of the sons of Azgad; Johanan [1]the son of Hakkatan, and with him an hundred and ten males.

13 And of the last sons of Adonikam, whose names *are* these, Eliphelet, Jeiel, and Shemaiah, and with them threescore males.

14 Of the sons also of Bigvai; Uthai, and [1]Zabbud, and with them seventy males.

27 [b] ch. 6:22

28 [a] ch. 9:9 [b] ver. 6,9; See ch. 5:5 & 8:18

8:2 [a] 1 Chr. 3:22

3 [a] ch. 2:3

12 [1] Or, *the youngest son*

14 [1] Or, *Zaccur,* as some read

15 [a] See ch. 7:7 [1] Or, *pitched*

17 [1] Heb. *I put words in their mouth*

18 [a] Neh. 8:7 & 9:4,5

20 [a] See ch. 2:43

21 [a] 2 Chr. 20:3 [b] Lev. 16:29 & 23:29; Is. 58:3,5 [c] Ps. 5:8

22 [a] 1 Cor. 9:15 [b] ch. 7:6,9,28 [c] Ps. 33:18,19 & 34:15, 22; Rom. 8:28 [d] Ps. 34:16 [e] 2 Chr. 15:2

23 [a] 1 Chr. 5:20; 2 Chr. 33:13; Is. 19:22

The return to Jerusalem

15 ¶ And I gathered them together to the river that runneth to Ahava; and there [1]abode we in tents three days: and I viewed the people, and the priests, and found there none of the [a]sons of Levi.

16 Then sent I for Eliezer, for Ariel, for Shemaiah, and for Elnathan, and for Jarib, and for Elnathan, and for Nathan, and for Zechariah, and for Meshullam, chief men; also for Joiarib, and for Elnathan, men of understanding.

17 And I sent them with commandment unto Iddo the chief at the place Casiphia, and [1]I told them what they should say unto Iddo, *and* to his brethren the Nethinims, at the place Casiphia, that they should bring unto us ministers for the house of our God.

18 And by the good hand of our God upon us they [a]brought us a man of understanding, of the sons of Mahli, the son of Levi, the son of Israel; and Sherebiah, with his sons and his brethren, eighteen;

19 And Hashabiah, and with him Jeshaiah of the sons of Merari, his brethren and their sons, twenty;

20 [a]Also of the Nethinims, whom David and the princes had appointed for the service of the Levites, two hundred and twenty Nethinims: all of them were expressed by name.

21 ¶ Then I [a]proclaimed a fast there, at the river of Ahava, that we might [b]afflict ourselves before our God, to seek of him a [c]right way for us, and for our little ones, and for all our substance.

22 For [a]I was ashamed to require of H
the king a band of soldiers and horsemen L
to help us against the enemy in the way: W
because we had spoken unto the king, U
saying, [b]The hand of our God *is* upon all
them for [c]good that seek him; but his
power and his wrath *is* [d]against all them
that [e]forsake him.

23 So we fasted and besought our God for this: and he was [a]entreated of us.

24 ¶ Then I separated twelve of the chief of the priests, Sherebiah, Hashabiah, and ten of their brethren with them,

H *2Ch 36:16* ◀ ▶ *Job 4:8–9*
L *2Ch 30:9* ◀ ▶ *Ne 9:17*
W *2Sa 22:31* ◀ ▶ *Ps 2:12*
U *2Ch 32:30* ◀ ▶ *Ne 1:5*

25 And weighed unto them [a]the silver, and the gold, and the vessels, *even* the offering of the house of our God, which the king, and his counsellors, and his lords, and all Israel *there* present, had offered:

26 I even weighed unto their hand six hundred and fifty talents of silver, and silver vessels an hundred talents, *and* of gold an hundred talents;

27 Also twenty basins of gold, of a thousand drams; and two vessels of [1]fine copper, [2]precious as gold.

S 28 And I said unto them, Ye *are* [a]holy unto the LORD; the vessels *are* [b]holy also; and the silver and the gold *are* a freewill offering unto the LORD God of your fathers.

29 Watch ye, and keep *them,* until ye weigh *them* before the chief of the priests and the Levites, and chief of the fathers of Israel, at Jerusalem, in the chambers of the house of the LORD.

30 So took the priests and the Levites the weight of the silver, and the gold, and the vessels, to bring *them* to Jerusalem unto the house of our God.

31 ¶ Then we departed from the river of Ahava on the twelfth *day* of the first month, to go unto Jerusalem: and [a]the hand of our God was upon us, and he delivered us from the hand of the enemy, and of such as lay in wait by the way.

32 And we [a]came to Jerusalem, and abode there three days.

33 ¶ Now on the fourth day was the silver and the gold and the vessels [a]weighed in the house of our God by the hand of Meremoth the son of Uriah the priest; and with him *was* Eleazar the son of Phinehas; and with them *was* Jozabad the son of Jeshua, and Noadiah the son of Binnui, Levites;

34 By number *and* by weight of every one: and all the weight was written at that time.

35 *Also* the children of those that had been carried away, which were come out of the captivity, [a]offered burnt offerings unto the God of Israel, twelve bullocks for all Israel, ninety and six rams, seventy and seven lambs, twelve he goats *for* a sin offering: all *this was* a burnt offering unto the LORD.

36 ¶ And they delivered the king's [a]commissions unto the king's lieutenants, and to the governors on this side the river: and they furthered the people, and the house of God.

25 [a]ch. 7:15,16
27 [1]Heb. *yellow,* or, *shining brass* [2]Heb. *desirable*
28 [a]Lev. 21:6-8; Deut. 33:8 [b]Lev. 22:2,3; Num. 4:4, 15,19,20
31 [a]ch. 7:6,9,28
32 [a]Neh. 2:11
33 [a]ver. 26,30
35 [a]ch. 6:17
36 [a]ch. 7:21

Ezra's prayer

9 NOW WHEN these things were done, the princes came to me, saying, The people of Israel, and the priests, and the Levites, have not [a]separated themselves from the people of the lands, [b]*doing* according to their abominations, *even* of the Canaanites, the Hittites, the Perizzites, the Jebusites, the Ammonites, the Moabites, the Egyptians, and the Amorites.

2 For they have [a]taken of their daughters for themselves, and for their sons: so that the [b]holy seed have [c]mingled themselves with the people of *those* lands: yea, the hand of the princes and rulers hath been chief in this trespass.

3 And when I heard this thing, [a]I rent my garment and my mantle, and plucked off the hair of my head and of my beard, and sat down [b]astonied.

4 Then were assembled unto me every one that [a]trembled at the words of the God of Israel, because of the transgression of those that had been carried away; and I sat astonied until the [b]evening sacrifice.

5 ¶ And at the evening sacrifice I arose up from my [1]heaviness; and having rent my garment and my mantle, I fell upon my knees, and [a]spread out my hands unto the LORD my God, M

6 And said, O my God, I am [a]ashamed and blush to lift up my face to thee, my God: for [b]our iniquities are increased over *our* head, and our [1]trespass is [c]grown up unto the heavens.

7 Since the days of our fathers *have* [a]we *been* in a great trespass unto this day; and for our iniquities [b]have we, our kings, *and* our priests, been delivered into the hand of the kings of the lands, to the sword, to captivity, and to a spoil, and to [c]confusion of face, as *it is* this day.

8 And now for a [1]little space grace hath been *shown* from the LORD our God, to leave us a remnant to escape, and to give us [a]a [2] nail in his holy place, that our God may [b]lighten our eyes, and give us a little reviving in our bondage.

9:1 [a]ch. 6:21; Neh. 9:2 [b]Deut. 12:30, 31
2 [a]Ex. 34:16; Deut. 7:3 [b]Ex. 22:31; Deut. 7:6 [c]2 Cor. 6:14
3 [a]Job 1:20 [b]Ps. 143:4
4 [a]ch. 10:3 [b]Ex. 29:39
5 [a]Ex. 9:29 [1]Or, *affliction*
6 [a]Dan. 9:7,8 [b]Ps. 38:4 [c]2 Chr. 28:9; Rev. 18:5 [1]Or, *guiltiness*
7 [a]Ps. 106:6; Dan. 9:5,6 [b]Deut. 28:36; Neh. 9:30 [c]Dan. 9:7,8
8 [a]Is. 22:23 [b]Ps. 34:5 [1]Heb. *moment* [2]Or, *a pin:* i.e. *a constant and sure abode*

9 [a]For we *were* bondmen; [b]yet our God hath not forsaken us in our bondage, but [c]hath extended mercy unto us in the sight of the kings of Persia, to give us a reviving, to set up the house of our God, and [1]to repair the desolations thereof, and to give us [d]a wall in Judah and in Jerusalem.

10 And now, O our God, what shall we say after this? for we have forsaken thy commandments,

11 Which thou hast commanded [1]by thy servants the prophets, saying, The land, unto which ye go to possess it, is an unclean land with the filthiness of the people of the lands, with their abominations, which have filled it [a]from[2] one end to another with their uncleanness.

12 Now therefore [a]give not your daughters unto their sons, neither take their daughters unto your sons, [b]nor seek their peace or their wealth for ever: that ye may be strong, and eat the good of the land, and [c]leave *it* for an inheritance to your children for ever.

13 And after all that is come upon us for our evil deeds, and for our great trespass, seeing that thou our God [a]hast[1] punished us less than our iniquities *deserve,* and hast given us *such* deliverance as this;

14 Should we [a]again break thy commandments, and [b]join in affinity with the people of these abominations? wouldest not thou be [c]angry with us till thou hadst consumed *us,* so that *there should be* no remnant nor escaping?

15 O LORD God of Israel, [a]thou *art* righteous: for we remain yet escaped, as *it is* this day: behold, we *are* [b]before thee [c]in our trespasses: for we cannot stand before thee because of this.

The people's confession

M 10 NOW [a]WHEN Ezra had prayed, and when he had confessed, weeping and casting himself down [b]before the house of God, there assembled unto him out of Israel a very great congregation of men and women and children: for the people [1]wept very sore.

2 And Shechaniah the son of Jehiel, *one* of the sons of Elam, answered and said unto Ezra, We have [a]trespassed against our God, and have taken strange wives of the people of the land: yet now there is hope in Israel concerning this thing.

3 Now therefore let us make [a]a covenant with our God [1]to put away all the wives, and such as are born of them, according to the counsel of my lord, and of those that [b]tremble at [c]the commandment of our God; and let it be done according to the law.

4 Arise; for *this* matter *belongeth* unto thee: we also *will be* with thee: [a]be of good courage, and do *it.*

5 Then arose Ezra, and made the chief priests, the Levites, and all Israel, [a]to swear that they should do according to this word. And they sware.

6 ¶ Then Ezra rose up from before the house of God, and went into the chamber of Johanan the son of Eliashib: and *when* he came thither, he [a]did eat no bread, nor drink water: for he mourned because of the transgression of them that had been carried away.

7 And they made proclamation throughout Judah and Jerusalem unto all the children of the captivity, that they should gather themselves together unto Jerusalem;

8 And that whosoever would not come within three days, according to the counsel of the princes and the elders, all his substance should be [1]forfeited, and himself separated from the congregation of those that had been carried away.

9 ¶ Then all the men of Judah and Benjamin gathered themselves together unto Jerusalem within three days. It *was* the ninth month, on the twentieth *day* of the month; and [a]all the people sat in the street of the house of God, trembling because of *this* matter, and for [1]the great rain.

10 And Ezra the priest stood up, and said unto them, Ye have transgressed, and [1]have taken strange wives, to increase the trespass of Israel.

11 Now therefore [a]make confession unto the LORD God of your fathers, and do his pleasure: and [b]separate yourselves from the people of the land, and from the strange wives. R

12 Then all the congregation answered and said with a loud voice, As thou hast said, so must we do.

9 [a]Neh. 9:36 [b]Ps. 136:23 [c]ch. 7:28 [d]Is. 5:2 [1]Heb. *to set up*
11 [a]2 Ki. 21:16 [1]Heb. *by the hand of thy servants* [2]Heb. *from mouth to mouth*
12 [a]Ex. 23:32; Deut. 7:3 [b]Deut. 23:6 [c]Prov. 20:7
13 [a]Ps. 103:10 [1]Heb. *hast withheld beneath our iniquities*
14 [a]John 5:14; 2 Pet. 2:20 [b]Neh. 13:23 [c]Deut. 9:8
15 [a]Neh. 9:33; Dan. 9:14 [b]Rom. 3:19 [c]1 Cor. 15:17
10:1 [a]Dan. 9:20 [b]2 Chr. 20:9 [1]Heb. *wept a great weeping*
2 [a]Neh. 13:27
3 [a]2 Chr. 34:31 [b]ch. 9:4 [c]Deut. 7:2,3 [1]Heb. *to bring forth*
4 [a]1 Chr. 28:10
5 [a]Neh. 5:12
6 [a]Deut. 9:18
8 [1]Heb. *devoted*
9 [a]See 1 Sam. 12:18 [1]Heb. *the showers*
10 [1]Heb. *have caused to dwell,* or, *have brought back*
11 [a]Josh. 7:19; Prov. 28:13 [b]ver. 3

M *Ezr 9:5–6* ◀ ▶ *Ne 1:4–6*

R *2Ch 15:4* ◀ ▶ *Job 11:13–14*

13 But the people *are* many, and *it is* a time of much rain, and we are not able to stand without, neither *is this* a work of one day or two: for [l]we are many that have transgressed in this thing.

14 Let now our rulers of all the congregation stand, and let all them which have taken strange wives in our cities come at appointed times, and with them the elders of every city, and the judges thereof, until [a]the fierce wrath of our God [l]for this matter be turned from us.

15 ¶ Only Jonathan the son of Asahel and Jahaziah the son of Tikvah [l]were employed about this *matter:* and Meshullam and Shabbethai the Levite helped them.

16 And the children of the captivity did so. And Ezra the priest, *with* certain chief of the fathers, after the house of their fathers, and all of them by *their* names, were separated, and sat down in the first day of the tenth month to examine the matter.

17 And they made an end with all the men that had taken strange wives by the first day of the first month.

Priests with foreign wives

18 ¶ And among the sons of the priests there were found that had taken strange wives: *namely,* of the sons of Jeshua the son of Jozadak, and his brethren; Maaseiah, and Eliezer, and Jarib, and Gedaliah.

19 And they [a]gave their hands that they would put away their wives; and *being* [b]guilty, *they offered* a ram of the flock for their trespass.

20 And of the sons of Immer; Hanani, and Zebadiah.

21 And of the sons of Harim; Maaseiah, and Elijah, and Shemaiah, and Jehiel, and Uzziah.

22 And of the sons of Pashur; Elioenai, Maaseiah, Ishmael, Nethaneel, Jozabad, and Elasah.

23 Also of the Levites; Jozabad, and Shimei, and Kelaiah, (the same *is* Kelita,) Pethahiah, Judah, and Eliezer.

13 [l]Or, *we have greatly offended in this thing*

14 [a]2 Chr. 30:8 [l]Or, *till this matter be* dispatched

15 [l]Heb. *stood*

19 [a]2 Ki. 10:15; 1 Chr. 29:24; 2 Chr. 30:8 [b]Lev. 6:4,6

40 [l]Or, *Mabnadebai,* according to some copies

24 Of the singers also; Eliashib: and of the porters; Shallum, and Telem, and Uri.

25 Moreover of Israel: of the sons of Parosh; Ramiah, and Jeziah, and Malchiah, and Miamin, and Eleazar, and Malchijah, and Benaiah.

26 And of the sons of Elam; Mattaniah, Zechariah, and Jehiel, and Abdi, and Jeremoth, and Eliah.

27 And of the sons of Zattu; Elioenai, Eliashib, Mattaniah, and Jeremoth, and Zabad, and Aziza.

28 Of the sons also of Bebai; Jehohanan, Hananiah, Zabbai, *and* Athlai.

29 And of the sons of Bani; Meshullam, Malluch, and Adaiah, Jashub, and Sheal, and Ramoth.

30 And of the sons of Pahath-moab; Adna, and Chelal, Benaiah, Maaseiah, Mattaniah, Bezaleel, and Binnui, and Manasseh.

31 And *of* the sons of Harim; Eliezer, Ishijah, Malchiah, Shemaiah, Shimeon,

32 Benjamin, Malluch, *and* Shemariah.

33 Of the sons of Hashum; Mattenai, Mattathah, Zabad, Eliphelet, Jeremai, Manasseh, *and* Shimei.

34 Of the sons of Bani; Maadai, Amram, and Uel,

35 Benaiah, Bedeiah, Chelluh,

36 Vaniah, Meremoth, Eliashib,

37 Mattaniah, Mattenai, and Jaasau,

38 And Bani, and Binnui, Shimei,

39 And Shelemiah, and Nathan, and Adaiah,

40 [l]Machnadebai, Shashai, Sharai,

41 Azareel, and Shelemiah, Shemariah,

42 Shallum, Amariah, *and* Joseph.

43 Of the sons of Nebo; Jeiel, Mattithiah, Zabad, Zebina, Jadau, and Joel, Benaiah.

44 All these had taken strange wives: and *some* of them had wives by whom they had children.

Nehemiah

Author: Nehemiah

Theme: Rebuilding Jerusalem's walls

Date of Writing: c. 430 B.C.

Outline of Nehemiah

I. Nehemiah Returns to Rebuild the Walls (1:1—2:8)
II. Rebuilding the Walls of Jerusalem (2:9—7:73)
III. The Great Revival Under Ezra (8:1—10:39)
IV. Nehemiah's Policies and Programs (11:1—13:31)

THIS BOOK IS named for Nehemiah, a governor of Judah and one of the main characters in this narrative. Containing vivid details, Nehemiah's book completes the history of the restoration of Jerusalem that was begun under Ezra's leadership.

Formerly a cupbearer to King Artaxerxes, Nehemiah was sent to Jerusalem to act as governor and to help rebuild Jerusalem's city walls. The temple had already been rebuilt, as recorded in Ezra, yet the city walls remained in ruins. With energy, piety and honesty, Nehemiah faced the obstacles that had stalled the project and brought the reconstruction to completion in a record fifty-two days. Nehemiah tackled this project with a deep dependence on God, praying for God's help more than ten times in this short book.

The book of Nehemiah is important prophetically because it marks the beginning of Daniel's prophecy "that from the going forth of the commandment to restore and to build Jerusalem unto the Messiah the Prince shall be seven weeks" (Da 9:25). Though other decrees had been issued to other exiles to rebuild the temple, Artaxerxes' decree recorded for the first time that permission had been granted to rebuild the city of Jerusalem (2:1–8). Thus Nehemiah's book inaugurates the divine time period of Daniel's prophecy.

Nehemiah's prayer for Israel

1 THE WORDS of [a]Nehemiah the son of Hachaliah. And it came to pass in the month Chisleu, in the twentieth year, as I was in Shushan the palace,

2 That Hanani, one of my brethren, came, he and *certain* men of Judah; and I asked them concerning the Jews that had escaped, which were left of the captivity, and concerning Jerusalem.

3 And they said unto me, The remnant that are left of the captivity there in the province *are* in great affliction and reproach: [a]the wall of Jerusalem also [b]*is* broken down, and the gates thereof are burned with fire.

M 4 ¶ And it came to pass, when I heard these words, that I sat down and wept, and mourned *certain* days, and fasted, and prayed before the God of heaven,

U 5 And said, I beseech thee, [a]O LORD God of heaven, the great and terrible God, [b]that keepeth covenant and mercy for them that love him and observe his commandments:

6 Let thine ear now be attentive, and [a]thine eyes open, that thou mayest hear the prayer of thy servant, which I pray before thee now, day and night, for the children of Israel thy servants, and [b]confess the sins of the children of Israel, which we have sinned against thee: both I and my father's house have sinned.

7 [a]We have dealt very corruptly against thee, and have [b]not kept the commandments, nor the statutes, nor the judgments, which thou commandest thy servant Moses.

R 8 Remember, I beseech thee, the word that thou commandedst thy servant Moses, saying, [a]*If* ye transgress, I will scatter you abroad among the nations:

I 9 [a]But *if* ye turn unto me, and keep my commandments, and do them; [b]though there were of you cast out unto the uttermost part of the heaven, *yet* will I gather them from thence, and will bring them unto the place that I have chosen to set my name there.

10 [a]Now these *are* thy servants and thy people, whom thou hast redeemed by thy great power, and by thy strong hand.

11 O Lord, I beseech thee, [a]let now thine ear be attentive to the prayer of thy servant, and to the prayer of thy servants, who [b]desire to fear thy name: and prosper, I pray thee, thy servant this day, and grant him mercy in the sight of this man. For I was the king's [c]cupbearer.

Nehemiah's request

2 AND IT came to pass in the month Nisan, in the twentieth year of [a]Artaxerxes the king, *that* wine *was* before him: and [b]I took up the wine, and gave *it* unto the king. Now I had not been *beforetime* sad in his presence.

2 Wherefore the king said unto me, Why *is* thy countenance sad, seeing thou *art* not sick? this *is* nothing *else* but [a]sorrow of heart. Then I was very sore afraid,

3 And said unto the king, [a]Let the king live for ever: why should not my countenance be sad, when [b]the city, the place of my fathers' sepulchres, *lieth* waste, and the gates thereof are consumed with fire?

4 Then the king said unto me, For what dost thou make request? So I prayed to the God of heaven.

5 And I said unto the king, If it please the king, and if thy servant have found favour in thy sight, that thou wouldest send me unto Judah, unto the city of my fathers' sepulchres, that I may build it.

6 And the king said unto me, (the [l]queen also sitting by him,) For how long shall thy journey be? and when wilt thou return? So it pleased the king to send me; and I set him [a]a time.

7 Moreover I said unto the king, If it please the king, let letters be given me to the governors beyond the river, that they may convey me over till I come into Judah;

8 And a letter unto Asaph the keeper of the king's forest, that he may give me timber to make beams for the gates of the palace which *appertained* [a]to the house, and for the wall of the city, and for the

1:1 [a]ch. 10:1
3 [a]ch. 2:17 [b]2 Ki. 25:10
5 [a]Dan. 9:4 [b]Ex. 20:6
6 [a]1 Ki. 8:28,29; 2 Chr. 6:40; Dan. 9:17,18 [b]Dan. 9:20
7 [a]Ps. 106:6; Dan. 9:5 [b]Deut. 28:15
8 [a]Lev. 26:33; Deut. 4:25-27 & 28:64
9 [a]Lev. 26:39; Deut. 4:29-31 & 30:2 [b]Deut. 30:4
10 [a]Deut. 9:29; Dan. 9:15
11 [a]ver. 6 [b]Is. 26:8; Heb. 13:18 [c]ch. 2:1
2:1 [a]Ezra 7:1 [b]ch. 1:11
2 [a]Prov. 15:13
3 [a]1 Ki. 1:31; Dan. 2:4 & 5:10 & 6:6, 21 [b]ch. 1:3
6 [a]ch. 5:14 & 13:6 [l]Heb. *wife*
8 [a]ch. 3:7

M *Ezr 10:1* ◀▶ *Ne 9:3*
U *Ezr 8:22* ◀▶ *Job 1:9–10*
R *2Ch 36:17–21* ◀▶ *Ps 74:1–2*
I *Ezr 3:11* ◀▶ *Ps 14:7*

1:8–9 Once again the promise is given, if Israel sins "I will scatter you abroad among the nations" (1:8), but repentance would result in their return to "the place that I have chosen to set my name" (1:9). See note on the Palestinian covenant at Dt 30:1–20.

house that I shall enter into. And the king granted me, [b]according to the good hand of my God upon me.

Nehemiah's inspection of the walls

9 ¶ Then I came to the governors beyond the river, and gave them the king's letters. Now the king had sent captains of the army and horsemen with me.

10 When Sanballat the Horonite, and Tobiah the servant, the Ammonite, heard *of it,* it grieved them exceedingly that there was come a man to seek the welfare of the children of Israel.

11 So I [a]came to Jerusalem, and was there three days.

12 ¶ And I arose in the night, I and some few men with me; neither told I *any* man what my God had put in my heart to do at Jerusalem: neither *was there any* beast with me, save the beast that I rode upon.

13 And I went out by night [a]by the gate of the valley, even before the dragon well, and to the dung port, and viewed the walls of Jerusalem, which were [b]broken down, and the gates thereof were consumed with fire.

14 Then I went on to the [a]gate of the fountain, and to the king's pool: but *there was* no place for the beast *that was* under me to pass.

15 Then went I up in the night by the [a]brook, and viewed the wall, and turned back, and entered by the gate of the valley, and *so* returned.

16 And the rulers knew not whither I went, or what I did; neither had I as yet told *it* to the Jews, nor to the priests, nor to the nobles, nor to the rulers, nor to the rest that did the work.

17 ¶ Then said I unto them, Ye see the distress that we *are* in, how Jerusalem *lieth* waste, and the gates thereof are burned with fire: come, and let us build up the wall of Jerusalem, that we be no more [a]a reproach.

18 Then I told them of [a]the hand of my God which was good upon me; as also the king's words that he had spoken unto me. And they said, Let us rise up and build. So they [b]strengthened their hands for *this* good *work.*

19 But when Sanballat the Horonite, and Tobiah the servant, the Ammonite, and Geshem the Arabian, heard *it,* they laughed us to scorn, and despised us, and

8 [b]ver. 18; Ezra 5:5 & 7:6,9,28
11 [a]Ezra 8:32
13 [a]2 Chr. 26:9; ch. 3:13 [b]ver. 17 & ch. 1:3
14 [a]ch. 3:15
15 [a]2 Sam. 15:23; Jer. 31:40
17 [a]ch. 1:3; Ps. 44:13 & 79:4; Jer. 24:9; Ezek. 5:14, 15 & 22:4
18 [a]ver. 8 [b]2 Sam. 2:7
19 [a]ch. 6:6
20 [a]Ezra 4:3
3:1 [a]ch. 12:10 [b]John 5:2 [c]ch. 12:39 [d]Jer. 31:38; Zech. 14:10
2 [a]Ezra 2:34 [1]Heb. *at his hand*
3 [a]2 Chr. 33:14; ch. 12:39; Zeph. 1:10 [b]See ch. 6:1 & 7:1
5 [a]Judg. 5:23
6 [a]ch. 12:39
7 [a]ch. 2:8
8 [a]ch. 12:38 [1]Or, *left Jerusalem unto the broad wall*
11 [a]ch. 12:38 [1]Heb. *second measure*

said, What *is* this thing that ye do? [a]will ye rebel against the king?

20 Then answered I them, and said unto them, The God of heaven, he will prosper us; therefore we his servants will arise and build: [a]but ye have no portion, nor right, nor memorial, in Jerusalem.

The rebuilding begun

3 THEN [a]ELIASHIB the high priest rose up with his brethren the priests, [b]and they builded the sheep gate; they sanctified it, and set up the doors of it; [c]even unto the tower of Meah they sanctified it, unto the tower of [d]Hananeel.

2 And [1]next unto him builded [a]the men of Jericho. And next to them builded Zaccur the son of Imri.

3 [a]But the fish gate did the sons of Hassenaah build, who *also* laid the beams thereof, and [b]set up the doors thereof, the locks thereof, and the bars thereof.

4 And next unto them repaired Meremoth the son of Urijah, the son of Koz. And next unto them repaired Meshullam the son of Berechiah, the son of Meshezabeel. And next unto them repaired Zadok the son of Baana.

5 And next unto them the Tekoites repaired; but their nobles put not their necks to [a]the work of their Lord.

6 Moreover [a]the old gate repaired Jehoiada the son of Paseah, and Meshullam the son of Besodeiah; they laid the beams thereof, and set up the doors thereof, and the locks thereof, and the bars thereof.

7 And next unto them repaired Melatiah the Gibeonite, and Jadon the Meronothite, the men of Gibeon, and of Mizpah, unto the [a]throne of the governor on this side the river.

8 Next unto him repaired Uzziel the son of Harhaiah, of the goldsmiths. Next unto him also repaired Hananiah the son of *one of* the apothecaries, and they [1]fortified Jerusalem unto the [a]broad wall.

9 And next unto them repaired Rephaiah the son of Hur, the ruler of the half part of Jerusalem.

10 And next unto them repaired Jedaiah the son of Harumaph, even over against his house. And next unto him repaired Hattush the son of Hashabniah.

11 Malchijah the son of Harim, and Hashub the son of Pahath-moab, repaired the [1]other piece, [a]and the tower of the furnaces.

12 And next unto him repaired Shallum the son of Halohesh, the ruler of the
half part of Jerusalem, he and his
daughters.
13 [a]The valley gate repaired Hanun,
and the inhabitants of Zanoah; they built
it, and set up the doors thereof, the locks
thereof, and the bars thereof, and a thousand cubits on the wall unto [b]the dung
gate.
14 But the dung gate repaired Malchiah the son of Rechab, the ruler of part
of Beth-haccerem; he built it, and set up
the doors thereof, the locks thereof, and
the bars thereof.
15 But [a]the gate of the fountain repaired Shallun the son of Col-hozeh, the
ruler of part of Mizpah; he built it, and
covered it, and set up the doors thereof,
the locks thereof, and the bars thereof,
and the wall of the pool of [b]Siloah by the
king's garden, and unto the stairs that go
down from the city of David.
16 After him repaired Nehemiah the
son of Azbuk, the ruler of the half part of
Beth-zur, unto *the place* over against the
sepulchres of David, and to the [a]pool that
was made, and unto the house of the
mighty.
17 After him repaired the Levites, Rehum the son of Bani. Next unto him repaired Hashabiah, the ruler of the half
part of Keilah, in his part.
18 After him repaired their brethren,
Bavai the son of Henadad, the ruler of the
half part of Keilah.
19 And next to him repaired Ezer the
son of Jeshua, the ruler of Mizpah, another piece over against the going up to
the armoury at the [a]turning *of the wall.*
20 After him Baruch the son of [1]Zabbai
earnestly repaired the other piece, from
the turning *of the wall* unto the door of
the house of Eliashib the high priest.
21 After him repaired Meremoth the
son of Urijah the son of Koz another
piece, from the door of the house of Eliashib even to the end of the house of Eliashib.
22 And after him repaired the priests,
the men of the plain.
23 After him repaired Benjamin and
Hashub over against their house. After
him repaired Azariah the son of Maaseiah
the son of Ananiah by his house.
24 After him repaired Binnui the son
of Henadad another piece, from the
house of Azariah unto [a]the turning *of the*
wall, even unto the corner.
25 Palal the son of Uzai, over against
the turning *of the wall,* and the tower
which lieth out from the king's high
house, that *was* by the [a]court of the
prison. After him Pedaiah the son of
Parosh.
26 Moreover [a]the Nethinims [1]dwelt in
[b]Ophel,[2] unto *the place* over against [c]the
water gate toward the east, and the tower
that lieth out.
27 After them the Tekoites repaired
another piece, over against the great
tower that lieth out, even unto the wall of
Ophel.
28 From above the [a]horse gate repaired the priests, every one over against
his house.
29 After them repaired Zadok the son
of Immer over against his house. After
him repaired also Shemaiah the son of
Shechaniah, the keeper of the east gate.
30 After him repaired Hananiah the
son of Shelemiah, and Hanun the sixth
son of Zalaph, another piece. After him
repaired Meshullam the son of Berechiah
over against his chamber.
31 After him repaired Malchiah the
goldsmith's son unto the place of the
Nethinims, and of the merchants, over
against the gate Miphkad, and to the [1]go-
ing up of the corner.
32 And between the going up of the
corner unto the sheep gate repaired the
goldsmiths and the merchants.

Defence against a conspiracy

4 BUT IT came to pass, [a]that when
Sanballat heard that we builded the
wall, he was wroth, and took great indignation, and mocked the Jews.
2 And he spake before his brethren
and the army of Samaria, and said, What
do these feeble Jews? will they [1]fortify
themselves? will they sacrifice? will they
make an end in a day? will they revive
the stones out of the heaps of the rubbish
which are burned?
3 Now [a]Tobiah the Ammonite *was* by
him, and he said, Even that which they
build, if a fox go up, he shall even break
down their stone wall.
4 [a]Hear, O our God; for we are [1]de-
spised: and [b]turn their reproach upon
their own head, and give them for a prey
in the land of captivity:

13 [a]ch. 2:13 [b]ch:2:13
15 [a]ch. 2:14 [b]John 9:7
16 [a]2 Ki. 20:20; Is. 22:11
19 [a]2 Chr. 26:9
20 [1]Or, *Zaccai*
24 [a]ver. 19
25 [a]Jer. 32:2 & 33:1 & 37:21
26 [a]Ezra 2:43; ch. 11:21 [b]2 Chr. 27:3 [c]ch. 8:1,3 & 12:37 [1]Or, which *dwelt in Ophel,* repaired *unto* [2]Or, *The tower*
28 [a]2 Ki. 11:16; 2 Chr. 23:15; Jer. 31:40
31 [1]Or, *corner chambers*
4:1 [a]ch. 2:10,19
2 [1]Heb. *leave to themselves*
3 [a]ch. 2:10,19
4 [a]Ps. 123:3,4 [b]Ps. 79:12; Prov. 3:34 [1]Heb. *despite*

5 And [a]cover not their iniquity, and let not their sin be blotted out from before thee: for they have provoked *thee* to anger before the builders.

6 So built we the wall; and all the wall was joined together unto the half thereof: for the people had a mind to work.

7 ¶ But it came to pass, *that* [a]when Sanballat, and Tobiah, and the Arabians, and the Ammonites, and the Ashdodites, heard that the walls of Jerusalem [ʹ]were made up, *and* that the breaches began to be stopped, then they were very wroth,

8 And [a]conspired all of them together to come *and* to fight against Jerusalem, and [ʹ]to hinder it.

9 Nevertheless [a]we made our prayer unto our God, and set a watch against them day and night, because of them.

10 And Judah said, The strength of the bearers of burdens is decayed, and *there is* much rubbish; so that we are not able to build the wall.

11 And our adversaries said, They shall not know, neither see, till we come in the midst among them, and slay them, and cause the work to cease.

12 And it came to pass, that when the Jews which dwelt by them came, they said unto us ten times, [ʹ]From all places whence ye shall return unto us *they will be upon you.*

13 ¶ Therefore set I [ʹ]in the lower places behind the wall, *and* on the higher places, I even set the people after their families with their swords, their spears, and their bows.

14 And I looked, and rose up, and said unto the nobles, and to the rulers, and to the rest of the people, [a]Be not ye afraid of them: remember the Lord, *which is* [b]great and terrible, and [c]fight for your brethren, your sons, and your daughters, your wives, and your houses.

15 And it came to pass, when our enemies heard that it was known unto us, [a]and God had brought their counsel to nought, that we returned all of us to the wall, every one unto his work.

16 And it came to pass from that time forth, *that* the half of my servants wrought in the work, and the other half of them held both the spears, the shields, and the bows, and the habergeons; and the rulers *were* behind all the house of Judah.

17 They which builded on the wall, and they that bare burdens, with those that laded, *every one* with one of his hands wrought in the work, and with the other *hand* held a weapon.

18 For the builders, every one had his sword girded [ʹ]by his side, and *so* builded. And he that sounded the trumpet *was* by me.

19 ¶ And I said unto the nobles, and to the rulers, and to the rest of the people, The work *is* great and large, and we are separated upon the wall, one far from another.

20 In what place *therefore* ye hear the sound of the trumpet, resort ye thither unto us: [a]our God shall fight for us. V

21 So we laboured in the work: and half of them held the spears from the rising of the morning till the stars appeared.

22 Likewise at the same time said I unto the people, Let every one with his servant lodge within Jerusalem, that in the night they may be a guard to us, and labour on the day.

23 So neither I, nor my brethren, nor my servants, nor the men of the guard which followed me, none of us put off our clothes, [ʹ]*saving that* every one put them off for washing.

Poverty and famine

5 AND THERE was a great [a]cry of the people and of their wives against their [b]brethren the Jews.

2 For there were that said, We, our sons, and our daughters, *are* many: therefore we take up corn *for them,* that we may eat, and live.

3 *Some* also there were that said, We have mortgaged our lands, vineyards, and houses, that we might buy corn, because of the dearth.

4 There were also that said, We have borrowed money for the king's tribute, *and that upon* our lands and vineyards.

5 Yet now [a]our flesh *is* as the flesh of our brethren, our children as their children: and, lo, we [b]bring into bondage our sons and our daughters to be servants, and *some* of our daughters are brought unto bondage *already:* neither *is it* in our power *to redeem them;* for other men have our lands and vineyards.

6 ¶ And I was very angry when I heard their cry and these words.

5 [a]Ps. 69:27,28 & 109:14,15; Jer. 18:23
7 [a]ver. 1 [ʹ]Heb. *ascended*
8 [a]Ps. 83:3-5 [ʹ]Heb. *to make an error to it*
9 [a]Ps. 50:15
12 [ʹ]Or, *That from all places ye must return to us*
13 [ʹ]Heb. *from the lower parts of the place*
14 [a]Num. 14:9; Deut. 1:29 [b]Deut. 10:17 [c]2 Sam. 10:12
15 [a]Job 5:12
18 [ʹ]Heb. *on his loins*
20 [a]Ex. 14:14,25; Deut. 1:30 & 3:22 & 20:4; Josh. 23:10
23 [ʹ]Or, *every one went with his weapon for water*
5:1 [a]Is. 5:7 [b]Lev. 25:35-37; Deut. 15:7
5 [a]Is. 58:7 [b]Ex. 21:7; Lev. 25:39

7 Then [I]I consulted with myself, and I rebuked the nobles, and the rulers, and said unto them, [a]Ye exact usury, every one of his brother. And I set a great assembly against them.

8 And I said unto them, We after our ability have [a]redeemed our brethren the Jews, which were sold unto the heathen; and will ye even sell your brethren? or shall they be sold unto us? Then held they their peace, and found nothing *to answer.*

9 Also I said, It *is* not good that ye do: ought ye not to walk [a]in the fear of our God [b]because of the reproach of the heathen our enemies?

10 I likewise, *and* my brethren, and my servants, might exact of them money and corn: I pray you, let us leave off this usury.

11 Restore, I pray you, to them, even this day, their lands, their vineyards, their oliveyards, and their houses, also the hundredth *part* of the money, and of the corn, the wine, and the oil, that ye exact of them.

12 Then said they, We will restore *them,* and will require nothing of them; so will we do as thou sayest. Then I called the priests, [a]and took an oath of them, that they should do according to this promise.

13 Also [a]I shook my lap, and said, So God shake out every man from his house, and from his labour, that performeth not this promise, even thus be he shaken out, and [I]emptied. And all the congregation said, Amen, and praised the LORD. [b]And the people did according to this promise.

14 ¶ Moreover from the time that I was appointed to be their governor in the land of Judah, from the twentieth year [a]even unto the two and thirtieth year of Artaxerxes the king, *that is,* twelve years, I and my brethren have not [b]eaten the bread of the governor.

15 But the former governors that *had been* before me were chargeable unto the people, and had taken of them bread and wine, beside forty shekels of silver; yea, even their servants bare rule over the people: but [a]so did not I, because of the [b]fear of God.

16 Yea, also I continued in the work of this wall, neither bought we any land: and all my servants *were* gathered thither unto the work.

7 [a]Ex. 22:25; Lev. 25:36; Ezek. 22:12 [I]Heb. *my heart consulted in me*

8 [a]Lev. 25:48

9 [a]Lev. 25:36 [b]2 Sam. 12:14; Rom. 2:24; 1 Pet. 2:12

12 [a]Ezra 10:5; Jer. 34:8,9

13 [a]Mat. 10:14; Acts 13:51 & 18:6 [b]2 Ki. 23:3 [I]Heb. *empty,* or, *void*

14 [a]ch. 13:6 [b]1 Cor. 9:4,15

15 [a]2 Cor. 11:9 & 12:13 [b]ver. 9

17 [a]2 Sam. 9:7; 1 Ki. 18:19

18 [a]1 Ki. 4:22 [b]ver. 14,15

19 [a]ch. 13:22

6:1 [a]ch. 2:10,19 [b]ch. 3:1,3 [I]Or, *Gashmu;* see ver. 6

2 [a]Prov. 26:24,25 [b]1 Chr. 8:12; ch. 11:35 [c]Ps. 37:12, 32

6 [a]ch. 2:19 [I]Or, *Geshem;* see ver. 1

17 Moreover *there were* [a]at my table an hundred and fifty of the Jews and rulers, beside those that came unto us from among the heathen that *are* about us.

18 Now *that* [a]which was prepared *for me* daily *was* one ox *and* six choice sheep; also fowls were prepared for me, and once in ten days store of all sorts of wine: yet for all this [b]required not I the bread of the governor, because the bondage was heavy upon this people.

19 [a]Think upon me, my God, for good, *according* to all that I have done for this people.

False rumours about Nehemiah

6 NOW IT came to pass, [a]when Sanballat, and Tobiah, and [I]Geshem the Arabian, and the rest of our enemies, heard that I had builded the wall, and *that* there was no breach left therein; ([b]though at that time I had not set up the doors upon the gates;)

2 That Sanballat and Geshem [a]sent unto me, saying, Come, let us meet together in *some one of* the villages in the plain of [b]Ono. But they [c]thought to do me mischief.

3 And I sent messengers unto them, saying, I *am* doing a great work, so that I cannot come down: why should the work cease, whilst I leave it, and come down to you?

4 Yet they sent unto me four times after this sort; and I answered them after the same manner.

5 Then sent Sanballat his servant unto me in like manner the fifth time with an open letter in his hand;

6 Wherein *was* written, It is reported among the heathen, and [I]Gashmu saith *it,* [a]*that* thou and the Jews think to rebel: for which cause thou buildest the wall, that thou mayest be their king, according to these words.

7 And thou hast also appointed prophets to preach of thee at Jerusalem, saying, *There is* a king in Judah: and now shall it be reported to the king according to these words. Come now therefore, and let us take counsel together.

8 Then I sent unto him, saying, There are no such things done as thou sayest, but thou feignest them out of thine own heart.

9 For they all made us afraid, saying, Their hands shall be weakened from the

work, that it be not done. Now therefore, *O God,* strengthen my hands.

10 Afterward I came unto the house of Shemaiah the son of Delaiah the son of Mehetabeel, who *was* shut up; and he said, Let us meet together in the house of God, within the temple, and let us shut the doors of the temple: for they will come to slay thee; yea, in the night will they come to slay thee.

11 And I said, Should such a man as I flee? and who *is there,* that, *being* as I *am,* would go into the temple to save his life? I will not go in.

12 And, lo, I perceived that God had not sent him; but that [a]he pronounced this prophecy against me: for Tobiah and Sanballat had hired him.

13 Therefore *was* he hired, that I should be afraid, and do so, and sin, and *that* they might have *matter* for an evil report, that they might reproach me.

14 [a]My God, think thou upon Tobiah and Sanballat according to these their works, and on the [b]prophetess Noadiah, and the rest of the prophets, that would have put me in fear.

Building of the walls finished

15 ¶ So the wall was finished in the twenty and fifth *day* of *the month* Elul, in fifty and two days.

16 And it came to pass, that [a]when all our enemies heard *thereof,* and all the heathen that *were* about us saw *these things,* they were much cast down in their own eyes: for [b]they perceived that this work was wrought of our God.

17 ¶ Moreover in those days the nobles of Judah [l]sent many letters unto Tobiah, and *the letters* of Tobiah came unto them.

18 For *there were* many in Judah sworn unto him, because he *was* the son-in-law of Shechaniah the son of Arah; and his son Johanan had taken the daughter of Meshullam the son of Berechiah.

19 Also they reported his good deeds before me, and uttered my [l]words to him. *And* Tobiah sent letters to put me in fear.

7 NOW IT came to pass, when the wall was built, and I had [a]set up the doors, and the porters and the singers and the Levites were appointed,

2 That I gave my brother Hanani, and Hananiah the ruler [a]of the palace, charge over Jerusalem: for he *was* a faithful man, and [b]feared God above many.

3 And I said unto them, Let not the gates of Jerusalem be opened until the sun be hot; and while they stand by, let them shut the doors, and bar *them:* and appoint watches of the inhabitants of Jerusalem, every one in his watch, and every one *to be* over against his house.

4 Now the city *was* [l]large and great: but the people *were* few therein, and the houses *were* not builded.

List of those who returned

5 ¶ And my God put into mine heart to gather together the nobles, and the rulers, and the people, that they might be reckoned by genealogy. And I found a register of the genealogy of them which came up at the first, and found written therein,

6 [a]These *are* the children of the province, that went up out of the captivity, of those that had been carried away, whom Nebuchadnezzar the king of Babylon had carried away, and came again to Jerusalem and to Judah, every one unto his city;

7 Who came with Zerubbabel, Jeshua, Nehemiah, [l]Azariah, Raamiah, Nahamani, Mordecai, Bilshan, Mispereth, Bigvai, Nehum, Baanah. The number, *I say,* of the men of the people of Israel *was this;*

8 The children of Parosh, two thousand an hundred seventy and two.

9 The children of Shephatiah, three hundred seventy and two.

10 The children of Arah, six hundred fifty and two.

11 The children of Pahath-moab, of the children of Jeshua and Joab, two thousand and eight hundred *and* eighteen.

12 The children of Elam, a thousand two hundred fifty and four.

13 The children of Zattu, eight hundred forty and five.

14 The children of Zaccai, seven hundred and threescore.

15 The children of [l]Binnui, six hundred forty and eight.

16 The children of Bebai, six hundred twenty and eight.

17 The children of Azgad, two thousand three hundred twenty and two.

18 The children of Adonikam, six hundred threescore and seven.

12 [a]Ezek. 13:22
14 [a]ch. 13:29 [b]Ezek. 13:17
16 [a]ch. 2:10 & 4:1,7 & 6:1 [b]Ps. 126:2
17 [l]Heb. *multiplied their letters passing to Tobiah*
19 [l]Or, *matters*
7:1 [a]ch. 6:1
2 [a]ch. 2:8 [b]Ex. 18:21
4 [l]Heb. *broad in spaces*
6 [a]Ezra 2:1
7 [l]Or, *Seraiah;* see Ezra 2:2
15 [l]Or, *Bani*

19 The children of Bigvai, two thousand threescore and seven.
20 The children of Adin, six hundred
fifty and five.
21 The children of Ater of Hezekiah,
ninety and eight.
22 The children of Hashum, three
hundred twenty and eight.
23 The children of Bezai, three hundred twenty and four.
24 The children of [1]Hariph, an hundred and twelve.
25 The children of [1]Gibeon, ninety
and five.
26 The men of Bethlehem and Netophah, an hundred fourscore and eight.
27 The men of Anathoth, an hundred
twenty and eight.
28 The men of [1]Beth-azmaveth, forty
and two.
29 The men of [1]Kirjath-jearim, Chephirah, and Beeroth, seven hundred forty
and three.
30 The men of Ramah and Gaba, six
hundred twenty and one.
31 The men of Michmas, an hundred
and twenty and two.
32 The men of Beth-el and Ai, an hundred twenty and three.
33 The men of the other Nebo, fifty
and two.
34 The children of the other [a]Elam, a
thousand two hundred fifty and four.
35 The children of Harim, three hundred and twenty.
36 The children of Jericho, three hundred forty and five.
37 The children of Lod, Hadid, and
Ono, seven hundred twenty and one.
38 The children of Senaah, three thousand nine hundred and thirty.
39 ¶ The priests: the children of [a]Jeda-
iah, of the house of Jeshua, nine hundred
seventy and three.
40 The children of [a]Immer, a thousand
fifty and two.
41 The children of [a]Pashur, a thousand
two hundred forty and seven.
42 The children of [a]Harim, a thousand
and seventeen.
43 ¶ The Levites: the children of
Jeshua, of Kadmiel, *and* of the children of
[1]Hodevah, seventy and four.
44 ¶ The singers: the children of
Asaph, an hundred forty and eight.
45 ¶ The porters: the children of Shallum, the children of Ater, the children of
Talmon, the children of Akkub, the children of Hatita, the children of Shobai, an
hundred thirty and eight.
46 ¶ The Nethinims: the children of
Ziha, the children of Hashupha, the children of Tabbaoth,
47 The children of Keros, the children
of [1]Sia, the children of Padon,
48 The children of Lebana, the children of Hagaba, the children of [1]Shalmai,
49 The children of Hanan, the children
of Giddel, the children of Gahar,
50 The children of Reaiah, the children of Rezin, the children of Nekoda,
51 The children of Gazzam, the children of Uzza, the children of Phaseah,
52 The children of Besai, the children
of Meunim, the children of [1]Nephi-
shesim,
53 The children of Bakbuk, the children of Hakupha, the children of Harhur,
54 The children of [1]Bazlith, the children of Mehida, the children of Harsha,
55 The children of Barkos, the children of Sisera, the children of Tamah,
56 The children of Neziah, the children of Hatipha.
57 ¶ The children of Solomon's servants: the children of Sotai, the children
of Sophereth, the children of [1]Perida,
58 The children of Jaala, the children
of Darkon, the children of Giddel,
59 The children of Shephatiah, the
children of Hattil, the children of Poche-
reth of Zebaim, the children of [1]Amon.
60 All the Nethinims, and the children
of Solomon's servants, *were* three hundred ninety and two.
61 [a]And these *were* they which went
up *also* from Tel-melah, Tel-haresha,
Cherub, [1]Addon, and Immer: but they
could not show their father's house, nor
their [2]seed, whether they *were* of Israel.
62 The children of Delaiah, the children of Tobiah, the children of Nekoda,
six hundred forty and two.
63 ¶ And of the priests: the children of
Habaiah, the children of Koz, the children of Barzillai, which took *one* of the
daughters of Barzillai the Gileadite to
wife, and was called after their name.
64 These sought their register *among*
those that were reckoned by genealogy,
but it was not found: therefore were
they, as polluted, put from the
priesthood.
65 And [1]the Tirshatha said unto them,

24 [1]Or, *Jora*
25 [1]Or, *Gibbar*
28 [1]Or, *Azmaveth*
29 [1]Or, *Kirjath-arim*
34 [a]See ver. 12
39 [a]1 Chr. 24:7
40 [a]1 Chr. 24:14
41 [a]See 1 Chr. 9:12 & 24:9
42 [a]1 Chr. 24:8
43 [1]Or, *Hodaviah;* see Ezra 2:40; or, *Judah;* see Ezra 3:9
47 [1]Or, *Siaha*
48 [1]Or, *Shamlai*
52 [1]Or, *Nephusim*
54 [1]Or, *Bazluth*
57 [1]Or, *Peruda*
59 [1]Or, *Ami*
61 [a]Ezra 2:59 [1]Or, *Addan* [2]Or, *pedigree*
65 [1]Or, *the governor;* see ch. 8:9

that they should not eat of the most holy
things, till there stood *up* a priest with
Urim and Thummim.
66 ¶ The whole congregation together
was forty and two thousand three hundred and threescore,
67 Beside their manservants and their
maidservants, of whom *there were* seven
thousand three hundred thirty and seven:
and they had two hundred forty and five
singing men and singing women.
68 Their horses, seven hundred thirty
and six: their mules, two hundred forty
and five:
69 *Their* camels, four hundred thirty
and five: six thousand seven hundred and
twenty asses.
70 ¶ And 'some of the chief of the fathers gave unto the work. [a]The Tirshatha
gave to the treasure a thousand drams of
gold, fifty basins, five hundred and thirty
priests' garments.
71 And *some* of the chief of the fathers
gave to the treasure of the work [a]twenty
thousand drams of gold, and two thousand and two hundred pound of silver.
72 And *that* which the rest of the people gave *was* twenty thousand drams of
gold, and two thousand pound of silver,
and threescore and seven priests' garments.
73 So the priests, and the Levites, and
the porters, and the singers, and *some* of
the people, and the Nethinims, and all
Israel, dwelt in their cities; [a]and when
the seventh month came, the children of
Israel *were* in their cities.

The law read and explained

8 AND ALL [a]the people gathered
themselves together as one man into
the street that *was* [b]before the water
gate; and they spake unto Ezra the
[c]scribe to bring the book of the law of
Moses, which the LORD had commanded
to Israel.
2 And Ezra the priest brought [a]the law
before the congregation both of men and
women, and all 'that could hear with understanding, [b]upon the first day of the
seventh month.
3 And he read therein before the street
that *was* before the water gate 'from the
morning until midday, before the men
and the women, and those that could understand; and the ears of all the people
were attentive unto the book of the law.
4 And Ezra the scribe stood upon a
'pulpit of wood, which they had made for
the purpose; and beside him stood Mattithiah, and Shema, and Anaiah, and Urijah, and Hilkiah, and Maaseiah, on his
right hand; and on his left hand, Pedaiah,
and Mishael, and Malchiah, and Hashum,
and Hashbadana, Zechariah, *and* Meshullam.
5 And Ezra opened the book in the
'sight of all the people; (for he was above
all the people;) and when he opened it,
all the people [a]stood up:
6 And Ezra blessed the LORD, the great
God. And all the people [a]answered,
Amen, Amen, with [b]lifting up their
hands: and they [c]bowed their heads, and
worshipped the LORD with *their* faces to
the ground.
7 Also Jeshua, and Bani, and Sherebiah, Jamin, Akkub, Shabbethai, Hodijah,
Maaseiah, Kelita, Azariah, Jozabad, Hanan, Pelaiah, and the Levites, [a]caused the
people to understand the law: and the
people *stood* in their place.
8 So they read in the book in the law of
God distinctly, and gave the sense, and
caused *them* to understand the reading.
9 ¶ [a]And Nehemiah, which *is* 'the Tirshatha, and Ezra the priest the scribe,
and the Levites that taught the people,
said unto all the people, [b]This day *is* holy
unto the LORD your God; [c]mourn not, nor
weep. For all the people wept, when they
heard the words of the law.
10 Then he said unto them, Go your J
way, eat the fat, and drink the sweet, W
[a]and send portions unto them for whom
nothing is prepared: for *this* day *is* holy
unto our Lord: neither be ye sorry; for the
joy of the LORD is your strength.
11 So the Levites stilled all the people,
saying, Hold your peace, for the day *is*
holy; neither be ye grieved.
12 And all the people went their way
to eat, and to drink, and to [a]send portions, and to make great mirth, because
they had [b]understood the words that
were declared unto them.
13 ¶ And on the second day were gathered together the chief of the fathers of
all the people, the priests, and the Levites, unto Ezra the scribe, even 'to understand the words of the law.
14 And they found written in the law

70 [a]ch. 8:9 'Heb. *part*
71 [a]Ezra 2:69
73 [a]Ezra 3:1
8:1 [a]Ezra 3:1 [b]ch. 3:26 [c]Ezra 7:6
2 [a]Deut. 31:11,12 [b]Lev. 23:24 'Heb. *that understood in hearing*
3 'Heb. *from the light*
4 'Heb. *tower of wood*
5 [a]Judg. 3:20 'Heb. *eyes*
6 [a]1 Cor. 14:16 [b]Lam. 3:41; 1 Tim. 2:8 [c]Ex. 4:31 & 12:27; 2 Chr. 20:18
7 [a]Lev. 10:11; Deut. 33:10; 2 Chr. 17:7; Mal. 2:7
9 [a]Ezra 2:63; ch. 7:65 & 10:1 [b]Lev. 23:24; Num. 29:1 [c]Deut. 16:14; Eccl. 3:4 'Or, *the governor*
10 [a]Esth. 9:19; Rev. 11:10
12 [a]ver. 10 [b]ver. 7,8
13 'Or, *that they might instruct in the words of the law*

which the LORD had commanded [ǀ]by Moses, that the children of Israel should dwell in [a]booths in the feast of the seventh month:

15 And [a]that they should publish and proclaim in all their cities, and [b]in Jerusalem, saying, Go forth unto the mount, and [c]fetch olive branches, and pine branches, and myrtle branches, and palm branches, and branches of thick trees, to make booths, as *it is* written.

16 ¶ So the people went forth, and brought *them,* and made themselves booths, every one upon the [a]roof of his house, and in their courts, and in the courts of the house of God, and in the street of the [b]water gate, [c]and in the street of the gate of Ephraim.

17 And all the congregation of them that were come again out of the captivity made booths, and sat under the booths: for since the days of Jeshua the son of Nun unto that day had not the children of Israel done so. And there was very [a]great gladness.

18 Also [a]day by day, from the first day unto the last day, he read in the book of the law of God. And they kept the feast seven days; and on the eighth day *was* [ǀ]a solemn assembly, [b]according unto the manner.

Ezra's prayer

9 NOW IN the twenty and fourth day of [a]this month the children of Israel were assembled with fasting, and with sackclothes, [b]and earth upon them.

2 And [a]the seed of Israel separated themselves from all [ǀ]strangers, and stood and confessed their sins, and the iniquities of their fathers.

M 3 And they stood up in their place, and [a]read in the book of the law of the LORD their God *one* fourth part of the day; and *another* fourth part they confessed, and worshipped the LORD their God.

4 ¶ Then stood up upon the [ǀ]stairs, of the Levites, Jeshua, and Bani, Kadmiel, Shebaniah, Bunni, Sherebiah, Bani, *and* Chenani, and cried with a loud voice unto the LORD their God.

5 Then the Levites, Jeshua, and Kadmiel, Bani, Hashabniah, Sherebiah, Hodijah, Shebaniah, *and* Pethahiah, said, Stand up *and* bless the LORD your God for ever and ever: and blessed be [a]thy glorious name, which is exalted above all blessing and praise.

6 [a]Thou, *even* thou, *art* LORD alone; [b]thou hast made heaven, [c]the heaven of heavens, with [d]all their host, the earth, and all *things* that *are* therein, the seas, and all that *is* therein, and thou [e]preservest them all; and the host of heaven worshippeth thee.

7 Thou *art* the LORD the God, who didst choose [a]Abram, and broughtest him forth out of Ur of the Chaldees, and gavest him the name of [b]Abraham;

8 And foundest his heart [a]faithful before thee, and madest a [b]covenant with him to give the land of the Canaanites, the Hittites, the Amorites, and the Perizzites, and the Jebusites, and the Girgashites, to give *it, I say,* to his seed, and [c]hast performed thy words; for thou *art* righteous:

9 [a]And didst see the affliction of our fathers in Egypt, and [b]heardest their cry by the Red sea;

10 And [a]showedst signs and wonders upon Pharaoh, and on all his servants, and on all the people of his land: for thou knewest that they [b]dealt proudly against them. So didst thou [c]get thee a name, as *it is* this day.

11 [a]And thou didst divide the sea before them, so that they went through the midst of the sea on the dry land; and their persecutors thou threwest into the deeps, [b]as a stone into the mighty waters.

12 Moreover thou [a]leddest them in the day by a cloudy pillar; and in the night by a pillar of fire, to give them light in the way wherein they should go. L

13 [a]Thou camest down also upon mount Sinai, and spakest with them from heaven, and gavest them [b]right judgments, and [ǀ]true laws, good statutes and commandments:

14 And madest known unto them thy [a]holy sabbath, and commandedst them precepts, statutes, and laws, by the hand of Moses thy servant:

15 And [a]gavest them bread from heaven for their hunger, and [b]broughtest forth water for them out of the rock for their thirst, and promisedst them that they should [c]go in to possess the land F

14 [a]Lev. 23:34,42; Deut. 16:13 [ǀ]Heb. *by the hand of*
15 [a]Lev. 23:4 [b]Deut. 16:16 [c]Lev. 23:40
16 [a]Deut. 22:8 [b]ch. 12:37 [c]2 Ki. 14:13; ch. 12:39
17 [a]2 Chr. 30:21
18 [a]Deut. 31:10 [b]Lev. 23:36; Num. 29:35 [ǀ]Heb. *a restraint*
9:1 [a]ch. 8:2 [b]Josh. 7:6; 1 Sam. 4:12; 2 Sam. 1:2; Job 2:12
2 [a]Ezra 10:11; ch. 13:3,30 [ǀ]Heb. *strange children*
3 [a]ch. 8:7,8
4 [ǀ]Or, *scaffold*
5 [a]1 Chr. 29:13
6 [a]2 Ki. 19:15,19; Ps. 86:10; Is. 37:16, 20 [b]Gen. 1:1; Ex. 20:11; Rev. 14:7 [c]Deut. 10:14; 1 Ki. 8:27 [d]Gen. 2:1 [e]Ps. 36:6
7 [a]Gen. 11:31 [b]Gen. 17:5
8 [a]Gen. 15:6 [b]Gen. 15:18 [c]Josh. 23:14
9 [a]Ex. 2:25 [b]Ex. 14:10
10 [a]Ex. 7-10,12,14 [b]Ex. 18:11 [c]Jer. 32:20
11 [a]Ex. 14:21; Ps. 78:13 [b]Ex. 15:5
12 [a]Ex. 13:21
13 [a]Ex. 20:1 [b]Rom. 7:12 [ǀ]Heb. *laws of truth*
14 [a]Gen. 2:3; Ex. 20:8
15 [a]Ex. 16:14; John 6:31 [b]Ex. 17:6 [c]Deut. 1:8

M *Ne 1:4–6* ◄► *Job 22:29*

L *2Ch 32:22* ◄► *Est 8:16*
F *2Ch 20:9* ◄► *Ne 9:20–21*

[d]which[1] thou hadst sworn to give them.

C 16 [a]But they and our fathers dealt proudly, and [b]hardened their necks, and hearkened not to thy commandments,

L 17 And refused to obey, [a]neither were mindful of thy wonders that thou didst among them; but hardened their necks, and in their rebellion appointed [b]a captain to return to their bondage: but thou *art* [1]a God ready to pardon, [c]gracious and merciful, slow to anger, and of great kindness, and forsookest them not.

18 Yea, [a]when they had made them a molten calf, and said, This *is* thy God that brought thee up out of Egypt, and had wrought great provocations;

19 Yet thou in thy [a]manifold mercies forsookest them not in the wilderness: the [b]pillar of the cloud departed not from them by day, to lead them in the way; neither the pillar of fire by night, to show them light, and the way wherein they should go.

E 20 Thou gavest also thy [a]good spirit to
G instruct them, and withheldest not thy
N [b]manna from their mouth, and gavest
T them [c]water for their thirst.
F 21 Yea, [a]forty years didst thou sustain
C them in the wilderness, *so that* they
E lacked nothing; their [b]clothes waxed not
old, and their feet swelled not.

22 Moreover thou gavest them kingdoms and nations, and didst divide them into corners: so they possessed the land of [a]Sihon, and the land of the king of Heshbon, and the land of Og king of Bashan.

23 [a]Their children also multipliedst thou as the stars of heaven, and broughtest them into the land, concerning which thou hadst promised to their fathers, that they should go in to possess *it*.

24 So [a]the children went in and possessed the land, and [b]thou subduedst before them the inhabitants of the land, the Canaanites, and gavest them into their hands, with their kings, and the people of the land, that they might do with them [1]as they would.

25 And they took strong cities, and a [a]fat land, and possessed [b]houses full of all goods, [1]wells digged, vineyards, and oliveyards, and [2]fruit trees in abundance: so they did eat, and were filled, and [c]became fat, and delighted themselves in thy great [d]goodness.

26 Nevertheless they [a]were disobedient, and rebelled against thee, and [b]cast thy law behind their backs, and slew thy [c]prophets which testified against them to turn them to thee, and they wrought great provocations.

27 [a]Therefore thou deliveredst them into the hand of their enemies, who vexed them: and in the time of their trouble, when they cried unto thee, thou [b]heardest *them* from heaven; and according to thy manifold mercies [c]thou gavest them saviours, who saved them out of the hand of their enemies.

28 But after they had rest, [a]they[1] did evil again before thee: therefore leftest thou them in the hand of their enemies, so that they had the dominion over them: yet when they returned, and cried unto thee, thou heardest *them* from heaven; and [b]many times didst thou deliver them according to thy mercies;

29 And testifiedst against them, that N
thou mightest bring them again unto thy law: yet they dealt proudly, and hearkened not unto thy commandments, but sinned against thy judgments, ([a]which if a man do, he shall live in them;) and [b]withdrew[1] the shoulder, and hardened their neck, and would not hear.

30 Yet many years didst thou [1]forbear C
them, and testifiedst [a]against them by thy E
spirit [b]in[2] thy prophets: yet would they Q
not give ear: [c]therefore gavest thou them into the hand of the people of the lands.

31 Nevertheless for thy great mercies' L
sake [a]thou didst not utterly consume them, nor forsake them; for thou *art* a gracious and merciful God.

32 Now therefore, our God, the great, the [a]mighty, and the terrible God, who keepest covenant and mercy, let not all

15 [d]Num. 14:30 [1]Heb. *which thou hadst lift up thine hand to give them*
16 [a]Ps. 106:6 [b]Deut. 31:27
17 [a]Ps. 78:11 [b]Num. 14:4 [c]Joel 2:13 [1]Heb. *a God of pardons*
18 [a]Ex. 32:4
19 [a]Ps. 106:45 [b]1 Cor. 10:1
20 [a]Num. 11:17; Is. 63:11 [b]Ex. 16:15; Josh. 5:12 [c]Ex. 17:6
21 [a]Deut. 2:7 [b]Deut. 8:4 & 29:5
22 [a]Num. 21:21
23 [a]Gen. 22:17
24 [a]Josh. 1:2 [b]Ps. 44:2,3 [1]Heb. *according to their will*
25 [a]Num. 13:27 [b]Deut. 6:11 [c]Deut. 32:15 [d]Hos. 3:5 [1]Or, *cisterns* [2]Heb. *tree of food*
26 [a]Judg. 2:11 [b]1 Ki. 14:9; Ps. 50:17 [c]1 Ki. 18:4
27 [a]Judg. 2:14; Ps. 106:41 [b]Ps. 106:44 [c]Judg. 2:18
28 [a]Judg. 3:11 [b]Ps. 106:43 [1]Heb. *they returned to do evil*
29 [a]Lev. 18:5; Rom. 10:5; Gal. 3:12 [b]Zech. 7:11 [1]Heb. *they gave a withdrawing shoulder*
30 [a]2 Ki. 17:13; 2 Chr. 36:15; Jer. 7:25 [b]Acts 7:51; 1 Pet. 1:11; 2 Pet. 1:21 [c]Is. 5:5 [1]Heb. *protract over them* [2]Heb. *in the hand of thy prophets*
31 [a]Jer. 4:27
32 [a]Ex. 34:6,7

C *2Ch 28:11* ◀▶ *Job 5:13–14*
L *Ezr 8:22* ◀▶ *Ne 9:31*
E *2Ch 24:20* ◀▶ *Ne 9:30*
G *2Sa 23:2* ◀▶ *Job 32:8*
N *2Ki 2:9* ◀▶ *Job 26:13*
T *2Ch 24:20* ◀▶ *Job 32:8*
F *Ne 9:15* ◀▶ *Job 5:20*
C *Dt 33:25* ◀▶ *Job 27:16–17*
E *2Ch 32:24* ◀▶ *Job 42:16–17*

N *2Ch 36:16* ◀▶ *Job 4:19–20*
C *Ge 6:3* ◀▶ *Ps 51:12–13*
E *Ne 9:20* ◀▶ *Job 26:13*
Q *2Ch 18:23* ◀▶ *Ps 51:11*
L *Ne 9:17* ◀▶ *Job 33:27–28*

the [1]trouble seem little before thee, [2]that
hath come upon us, on our kings, on our
princes, and on our priests, and on our
prophets, and on our fathers, and on all
thy people, [b]since the time of the kings of
Assyria unto this day.
33 Howbeit [a]thou *art* just in all that is
brought upon us; for thou hast done
right, but [b]we have done wickedly:
34 Neither have our kings, our
princes, our priests, nor our fathers, kept
thy law, nor hearkened unto thy commandments and thy testimonies, wherewith thou didst testify against them.
35 For they have [a]not served thee in
their kingdom, and in thy great goodness
that thou gavest them, and in the large
and fat land which thou gavest before
them, neither turned they from their
wicked works.
36 Behold, [a]we *are* servants this day,
and *for* the land that thou gavest unto our
fathers to eat the fruit thereof and the
good thereof, behold, we *are* servants
in it:
37 And [a]it yieldeth much increase
unto the kings whom thou hast set over
us because of our sins: also they have
[b]dominion over our bodies, and over our
cattle, at their pleasure, and we *are* in
great distress.

The covenant signed

38 And because of all this we [a]make a
sure *covenant,* and write *it;* and our
princes, Levites, *and* priests, [1]seal
unto it.

10 NOW [1]THOSE that sealed *were,*
Nehemiah, [2]the Tirshatha, [a]the
son of Hachaliah, and Zidkijah,
2 [a]Seraiah, Azariah, Jeremiah,
3 Pashur, Amariah, Malchijah,
4 Hattush, Shebaniah, Malluch,
5 Harim, Meremoth, Obadiah,
6 Daniel, Ginnethon, Baruch,
7 Meshullam, Abijah, Mijamin,
8 Maaziah, Bilgai, Shemaiah: these
were the priests.
9 And the Levites: both Jeshua the son
of Azaniah, Binnui of the sons of Henadad, Kadmiel;
10 And their brethren, Shebaniah,
Hodijah, Kelita, Pelaiah, Hanan,
11 Micha, Rehob, Hashabiah,
12 Zaccur, Sherebiah, Shebaniah,
13 Hodijah, Bani, Beninu.

32 [b]2 Ki. 17:3 [1]Heb. *weariness* [2]Heb. *that hath found us*
33 [a]Ps. 119:137; Dan. 9:14 [b]Ps. 106:6; Dan. 9:5,6,8
35 [a]Deut. 28:47
36 [a]Deut. 28:48; Ezra 9:9
37 [a]Deut. 28:33, 51 [b]Deut. 28:48
38 [a]2 Ki. 23:3; 2 Chr. 29:10; Ezra 10:3 [1]Heb. are *at the sealing,* or, *sealed*
10:1 [a]ch. 1:1 [1]Heb. *at the sealings* [2]Or, *the governor*
2 [a]ch. 12:1-21
14 [a]Ezra 2:3; ch. 7:8
28 [a]Ezra 2:36-43 [b]Ezra 9:1; ch. 13:3
29 [a]Deut. 29:12; Ps. 119:106 [b]2 Ki. 23:3; 2 Chr. 34:31 [1]Heb. *by the hand of*
30 [a]Ex. 34:16; Deut. 7:3; Ezra 9:12
31 [a]Ex. 20:10; Lev. 23:3; Deut. 5:12 [b]Ex. 23:10; Lev. 25:4 [c]Deut. 15:1; ch. 5:12 [1]Heb. *every hand*
33 [a]Lev. 24:5; 2 Chr. 2:4 [b]See Num. 28 & 29
34 [a]ch. 13:31; Is. 40:16 [b]Lev. 6:12

14 The chief of the people; [a]Parosh,
Pahath-moab, Elam, Zatthu, Bani,
15 Bunni, Azgad, Bebai,
16 Adonijah, Bigvai, Adin,
17 Ater, Hizkijah, Azzur,
18 Hodijah, Hashum, Bezai,
19 Hariph, Anathoth, Nebai,
20 Magpiash, Meshullam, Hezir,
21 Meshezabeel, Zadok, Jaddua,
22 Pelatiah, Hanan, Anaiah,
23 Hoshea, Hananiah, Hashub,
24 Hallohesh, Pileha, Shobek,
25 Rehum, Hashabnah, Maaseiah,
26 And Ahijah, Hanan, Anan,
27 Malluch, Harim, Baanah.
28 ¶ [a]And the rest of the people, the
priests, the Levites, the porters, the singers, the Nethinims, [b]and all they that had
separated themselves from the people of
the lands unto the law of God, their
wives, their sons, and their daughters,
every one having knowledge, and having
understanding;
29 They clave to their brethren, their
nobles, [a]and entered into a curse, and
into an oath, [b]to walk in God's law,
which was given [1]by Moses the servant
of God, and to observe and do all the
commandments of the LORD our Lord, and
his judgments and his statutes;
30 And that we would not give [a]our
daughters unto the people of the land,
nor take their daughters for our sons:
31 [a]And *if* the people of the land bring
ware or any victuals on the sabbath day
to sell, *that* we would not buy it of them
on the sabbath, or on the holy day: and
that we would leave the [b]seventh year,
and the [c]exaction of [1]every debt.
32 Also we made ordinances for us, to
charge ourselves yearly with the third
part of a shekel for the service of the
house of our God;
33 For [a]the showbread, and for the
[b]continual meat offering, and for the continual burnt offering, of the sabbaths, of
the new moons, for the set feasts, and for
the holy *things,* and for the sin offerings
to make an atonement for Israel, and *for*
all the work of the house of our God.
34 And we cast the lots among the
priests, the Levites, and the people, [a]for
the wood offering, to bring *it* into the
house of our God, after the houses of our
fathers, at times appointed year by year,
to burn upon the altar of the LORD our
God, [b]as *it is* written in the law:

35 And [a]to bring the firstfruits of our ground, and the firstfruits of all fruit of all trees, year by year, unto the house of the LORD:

36 Also the firstborn of our sons, and of our cattle, as *it is* written [a]in the law, and the firstlings of our herds and of our flocks, to bring to the house of our God, unto the priests that minister in the house of our God:

37 [a]And *that* we should bring the firstfruits of our dough, and our offerings, and the fruit of all manner of trees, of wine and of oil, unto the priests, to the chambers of the house of our God; and [b]the tithes of our ground unto the Levites, that the same Levites might have the tithes in all the cities of our tillage.

38 And the priest the son of Aaron shall be with the Levites, [a]when the Levites take tithes: and the Levites shall bring up the tithe of the tithes unto the house of our God, to [b]the chambers, into the treasure house.

39 For the children of Israel and the children of Levi [a]shall bring the offering of the corn, of the new wine, and the oil, unto the chambers, where *are* the vessels of the sanctuary, and the priests that minister, and the porters, and the singers: [b]and we will not forsake the house of our God.

The repeopling of Jerusalem

11 AND THE rulers of the people dwelt at Jerusalem: the rest of the people also cast lots, to bring one of ten to dwell in Jerusalem [a]the holy city, and nine parts *to dwell* in *other* cities.

2 And the people blessed all the men, that [a]willingly offered themselves to dwell at Jerusalem.

3 ¶ [a]Now these *are* the chief of the province that dwelt in Jerusalem: but in the cities of Judah dwelt every one in his possession in their cities, *to wit,* Israel, the priests, and the Levites, and [b]the Nethinims, and [c]the children of Solomon's servants.

4 And [a]at Jerusalem dwelt *certain* of the children of Judah, and of the children of Benjamin. Of the children of Judah; Athaiah the son of Uzziah, the son of Zechariah, the son of Amariah, the son of Shephatiah, the son of Mahalaleel, of the children of [b]Perez;

5 And Maaseiah the son of Baruch, the son of Col-hozeh, the son of Hazaiah, the son of Adaiah, the son of Joiarib, the son of Zechariah, the son of Shiloni.

6 All the sons of Perez that dwelt at Jerusalem *were* four hundred threescore and eight valiant men.

7 And these *are* the sons of Benjamin; Sallu the son of Meshullam, the son of Joed, the son of Pedaiah, the son of Kolaiah, the son of Maaseiah, the son of Ithiel, the son of Jesaiah.

8 And after him Gabbai, Sallai, nine hundred twenty and eight.

9 And Joel the son of Zichri *was* their overseer: and Judah the son of Senuah *was* second over the city.

10 [a]Of the priests: Jedaiah the son of Joiarib, Jachin.

11 Seraiah the son of Hilkiah, the son of Meshullam, the son of Zadok, the son of Meraioth, the son of Ahitub, *was* the ruler of the house of God.

12 And their brethren that did the work of the house *were* eight hundred twenty and two: and Adaiah the son of Jeroham, the son of Pelaliah, the son of Amzi, the son of Zechariah, the son of Pashur, the son of Malchiah,

13 And his brethren, chief of the fathers, two hundred forty and two: and Amashai the son of Azareel, the son of Ahasai, the son of Meshillemoth, the son of Immer.

14 And their brethren, mighty men of valour, an hundred twenty and eight: and their overseer *was* Zabdiel, [ǀ]the son of *one of* the great men.

15 Also of the Levites: Shemaiah the son of Hashub, the son of Azrikam, the son of Hashabiah, the son of Bunni;

16 And Shabbethai and Jozabad, of the chief of the Levites, [ǀ]*had* the oversight of [a]the outward business of the house of God.

17 And Mattaniah the son of Micha, the son of Zabdi, the son of Asaph, *was* the principal to begin the thanksgiving in prayer: and Bakbukiah the second among his brethren, and Abda the son of Shammua, the son of Galal, the son of Jeduthun.

18 All the Levites in [a]the holy city *were* two hundred fourscore and four.

19 Moreover the porters, Akkub, Talmon, and their brethren that kept [ǀ]the gates, *were* an hundred seventy and two.

20 ¶ And the residue of Israel, of the

10:35 [a] Ex. 23:19; Lev. 19:23; Num. 18:12
36 [a] Ex. 13:2,12, 13; Lev. 27:26,27; Num. 18:15,16
37 [a] Lev. 23:17; Num. 15:19 & 18:12; Deut. 18:4 & 26:2 [b] Lev. 27:30; Num. 18:21
38 [a] Num. 18:26 [b] 1 Chr. 9:26; 2 Chr. 31:11
39 [a] Deut. 12:6,11; 2 Chr. 31:12; ch. 13:12 [b] ch. 13:10, 11
11:1 [a] ver. 18; Mat. 4:5 & 27:53
2 [a] Judg. 5:9
3 [a] 1 Chr. 9:2,3 [b] Ezra 2:43 [c] Ezra 2:55
4 [a] 1 Chr. 9:3 [b] Gen. 38:29 *Pharez*
10 [a] 1 Chr. 9:10
14 [ǀ] Or, *the son of Haggedolim*
16 [a] 1 Chr. 26:29 [ǀ] Heb. *were over*
18 [a] ver. 1
19 [ǀ] Heb. *at the gates*

priests, *and* the Levites, *were* in all the cities of Judah, every one in his inheritance.

21 [a]But the Nethinims dwelt in [1]Ophel: and Ziha and Gispa *were* over the Nethinims.

22 The overseer also of the Levites at Jerusalem *was* Uzzi the son of Bani, the son of Hashabiah, the son of Mattaniah, the son of Micha. Of the sons of Asaph, the singers *were* over the business of the house of God.

23 For [a]*it was* the king's commandment concerning them, that [1]a certain portion should be for the singers, due for every day.

24 And Pethahiah the son of Meshezabeel, of the children of [a]Zerah the son of Judah, *was* [b]at the king's hand in all matters concerning the people.

The villages outside Jerusalem

25 And for the villages, with their fields, *some* of the children of Judah dwelt at [a]Kirjath-arba, and *in* the villages thereof, and at Dibon, and *in* the villages thereof, and at Jekabzeel, and *in* the villages thereof,

26 And at Jeshua, and at Moladah, and at Beth-phelet,

27 And at Hazar-shual, and at Beer-sheba, and *in* the villages thereof,

28 And at Ziklag, and at Mekonah, and in the villages thereof,

29 And at En-rimmon, and at Zareah, and at Jarmuth,

30 Zanoah, Adullam, and *in* their villages, at Lachish, and the fields thereof, at Azekah, and *in* the villages thereof. And they dwelt from Beer-sheba unto the valley of Hinnom.

31 The children also of Benjamin [1]from Geba *dwelt* [2]at Michmash, and Aija, and Beth-el, and *in* their villages,

32 *And* at Anathoth, Nob, Ananiah,

33 Hazor, Ramah, Gittaim,

34 Hadid, Zeboim, Neballat,

35 Lod, and Ono, [a]the valley of craftsmen.

36 And of the Levites *were* divisions *in* Judah, *and* in Benjamin.

Priests and Levites

12 NOW THESE *are* the [a]priests and the Levites that went up with Zerubbabel the son of Shealtiel, and Jeshua: [b]Seraiah, Jeremiah, Ezra,

2 Amariah, [1]Malluch, Hattush,

3 [1]Shechaniah, [2]Rehum, [3]Meremoth,

4 Iddo, [1]Ginnetho, [a]Abijah,

5 [1]Miamin, [2]Maadiah, Bilgah,

6 Shemaiah, and Joiarib, Jedaiah,

7 [1]Sallu, Amok, Hilkiah, Jedaiah. These *were* the chief of the priests and of their brethren in the days of [a]Jeshua.

8 Moreover the Levites: Jeshua, Binnui, Kadmiel, Sherebiah, Judah, *and* Mattaniah, [a]*which was* over [1]the thanksgiving, he and his brethren.

9 Also Bakbukiah and Unni, their brethren, *were* over against them in the watches.

10 ¶ And Jeshua begat Joiakim, Joiakim also begat Eliashib, and Eliashib begat Joiada,

11 And Joiada begat Jonathan, and Jonathan begat Jaddua.

12 And in the days of Joiakim were priests, the chief of the fathers: of Seraiah, Meraiah; of Jeremiah, Hananiah;

13 Of Ezra, Meshullam; of Amariah, Jehohanan;

14 Of Melicu, Jonathan; of Shebaniah, Joseph;

15 Of Harim, Adna; of Meraioth, Helkai;

16 Of Iddo, Zechariah; of Ginnethon, Meshullam;

17 Of Abijah, Zichri; of Miniamin, of Moadiah, Piltai;

18 Of Bilgah, Shammua; of Shemaiah, Jehonathan;

19 And of Joiarib, Mattenai; of Jedaiah, Uzzi;

20 Of Sallai, Kallai; of Amok, Eber;

21 Of Hilkiah, Hashabiah; of Jedaiah, Nethaneel.

22 ¶ The Levites in the days of Eliashib, Joiada, and Johanan, and Jaddua, *were* recorded chief of the fathers: also the priests, to the reign of Darius the Persian.

23 The sons of Levi, the chief of the fathers, *were* written in the book of the [a]chronicles, even until the days of Johanan the son of Eliashib.

24 And the chief of the Levites: Hashabiah, Sherebiah, and Jeshua the son of Kadmiel, with their brethren over against them, to praise *and* to give thanks, [a]according to the commandment of David the man of God, [b]ward over against ward.

25 Mattaniah, and Bakbukiah, Obadiah, Meshullam, Talmon, Akkub, *were*

21 [a]See ch. 3:26 [1]Or, *The tower*

23 [a]See Ezra 6:8,9; & 7:20 [1]Or, *a sure ordinance*

24 [a]Gen. 38:30 *Zarah* [b]1 Chr. 18:17 & 23:28

25 [a]Josh. 14:15

31 [1]Or, *of Geba* [2]Or, *to Michmash*

35 [a]1 Chr. 4:14

12:1 [a]Ezra 2:1,2 [b]See ch. 10:2-8

2 [1]Or, *Melicu;* see ver. 14

3 [1]Or, *Shebaniah;* see ver. 14 [2]Or, *Harim;* see ver. 15 [3]Or, *Meraioth;* see ver. 15

4 [a]Luke 1:5 [1]Or, *Ginnethon;* see ver. 16

5 [1]Or, *Miniamin;* see ver. 17 [2]Or, *Moadiah;* see ver. 17

7 [a]Ezra 3:2; Hag. 1:1; Zech. 3:1 [1]Or, *Sallai;* see ver. 20

8 [a]ch. 11:17 [1]i.e. *the psalms of thanksgiving*

23 [a]1 Chr. 9:14

24 [a]1 Chr. 23 & 25 & 26 [b]Ezra 3:11

porters keeping the ward at the [1]thresholds of the gates.

26 These *were* in the days of Joiakim the son of Jeshua, the son of Jozadak, and in the days of Nehemiah [a]the governor, and of Ezra the priest, [b]the scribe.

Dedication of the city walls

27 ¶ And at [a]the dedication of the wall of Jerusalem they sought the Levites out of all their places, to bring them to Jerusalem, to keep the dedication with gladness, [b]both with thanksgivings, and with singing, *with* cymbals, psalteries, and with harps.

28 And the sons of the singers gathered themselves together, both out of the plain country round about Jerusalem, and from the villages of Netophathi;

29 Also from the house of Gilgal, and out of the fields of Geba and Azmaveth: for the singers had builded them villages round about Jerusalem.

30 And the priests and the Levites purified themselves, and purified the people, and the gates, and the wall.

31 Then I brought up the princes of Judah upon the wall, and appointed two great *companies of them that gave* thanks, *whereof* [a]*one* went on the right hand upon the wall [b]toward the dung gate:

32 And after them went Hoshaiah, and half of the princes of Judah,

33 And Azariah, Ezra, and Meshullam,

34 Judah, and Benjamin, and Shemaiah, and Jeremiah,

35 And *certain* of the priests' sons [a]with trumpets; *namely,* Zechariah the son of Jonathan, the son of Shemaiah, the son of Mattaniah, the son of Michaiah, the son of Zaccur, the son of Asaph:

36 And his brethren, Shemaiah, and Azarael, Milalai, Gilalai, Maai, Nethaneel, and Judah, Hanani, with [a]the musical instruments of David the man of God, and Ezra the scribe before them.

37 [a]And at the fountain gate, which was over against them, they went up by [b]the stairs of the city of David, at the going up of the wall, above the house of David, even unto [c]the water gate eastward.

38 [a]And the other *company of them that gave* thanks went over against *them,* and I after them, and the half of the people upon the wall, from beyond [b]the tower of the furnaces even unto [c]the broad wall;

39 [a]And from above the gate of Ephraim, and above [b]the old gate, and above [c]the fish gate, [d]and the tower of Hananeel, and the tower of Meah, even unto [e]the sheep gate: and they stood still in [f]the prison gate.

40 So stood the two *companies of them that gave* thanks in the house of God, and I, and the half of the rulers with me:

41 And the priests; Eliakim, Maaseiah, Miniamin, Michaiah, Elioenai, Zechariah, *and* Hananiah, with trumpets;

42 And Maaseiah, and Shemaiah, and Eleazar, and Uzzi, and Jehohanan, and Malchijah, and Elam, and Ezer. And the singers [1]sang loud, with Jezrahiah *their* overseer.

43 Also that day they offered great sacrifices, and rejoiced: for God had made them rejoice with great joy: the wives also and the children rejoiced: so that the joy of Jerusalem was heard even afar off.

44 ¶ [a]And at that time were some appointed over the chambers for the treasures, for the offerings, for the firstfruits, and for the tithes, to gather into them out of the fields of the cities the portions [1]of the law for the priests and Levites: [2]for Judah rejoiced for the priests and for the Levites [3]that waited.

45 And both the singers and the porters kept the ward of their God, and the ward of the purification, [a]according to the commandment of David, *and* of Solomon his son.

46 For in the days of David [a]and Asaph of old *there were* chief of the singers, and songs of praise and thanksgiving unto God.

47 And all Israel in the days of Zerubbabel, and in the days of Nehemiah, gave the portions of the singers and the porters, every day his portion: [a]and they [1]sanctified *holy things* unto the Levites; [b]and the Levites sanctified *them* unto the children of Aaron.

Nehemiah's reforms

13 ON THAT day [a]they[1] read in the book of Moses in the [2]audience of the people; and therein was found written, [b]that the Ammonite and the Moabite should not come into the congregation of God for ever;

25 [1]Or, *treasuries,* or, *assemblies*

26 [a]ch. 8:9 [b]Ezra 7:6,11

27 [a]Deut. 20:5; Ps. 30,title [b]1 Chr. 25:6; 2 Chr. 5:13 & 7:6

31 [a]See ver. 38 [b]ch. 2:13 & 3:13

35 [a]Num. 10:2,8

36 [a]1 Chr. 23:5

37 [a]ch. 2:14 & 3:15 [b]ch. 3:15 [c]ch. 3:26 & 8:1,3,16

38 [a]See ver. 31 [b]ch. 3:11 [c]ch. 3:8

39 [a]2 Ki. 14:13; ch. 8:16 [b]ch. 3:6 [c]ch. 3:3 [d]ch. 3:1 [e]ch. 3:32 [f]Jer. 32:2

42 [1]Heb. *made* their voice *to be heard*

44 [a]2 Chr. 31:11, 12; ch. 13:5,12,13 [1]i.e. *appointed by the law* [2]Heb. *for the joy of Judah* [3]Heb. *that stood*

45 [a]1 Chr. 25 & 26

46 [a]1 Chr. 25:1

47 [a]Num. 18:21, 24 [b]Num. 18:26 [1]i.e. *set apart*

13:1 [a]Deut. 31:11, 12; 2 Ki. 23:2; ch. 8:3,8 & 9:3; Is. 34:16 [b]Deut. 23:3, 4 [1]Heb. *there was read* [2]Heb. *ears*

2 Because they met not the children of
Israel with bread and with water, but
[a]hired Balaam against them, that he
should curse them: [b]howbeit our God
turned the curse into a blessing.
3 Now it came to pass, when they had
heard the law, [a]that they separated from
Israel all the mixed multitude.
4 ¶ And before this, Eliashib the priest,
[a]having[1] the oversight of the chamber of
the house of our God, *was* allied unto
Tobiah:
5 And he had prepared for him a great
chamber, [a]where aforetime they laid the
meat offerings, the frankincense, and the
vessels, and the tithes of the corn,
the new wine, and the oil, [b]which[1] was
commanded *to be given* to the Levites,
and the singers, and the porters; and the
offerings of the priests.
6 But in all this *time* was not I at Jerusalem: [a]for in the two and thirtieth year
of Artaxerxes king of Babylon came I
unto the king, and [1]after certain days [2]ob-
tained I leave of the king:
7 And I came to Jerusalem, and understood of the evil that Eliashib did for Tobiah, in [a]preparing him a chamber in the
courts of the house of God.
8 And it grieved me sore: therefore I
cast forth all the household stuff of Tobiah out of the chamber.
9 Then I commanded, and they
[a]cleansed the chambers: and thither
brought I again the vessels of the house
of God, with the meat offering and the
frankincense.
10 ¶ And I perceived that the portions
of the Levites had [a]not been given *them:*
for the Levites and the singers, that did
the work, were fled every one to [b]his
field.
11 Then [a]contended I with the rulers,
and said, [b]Why is the house of God forsaken? And I gathered them together,
and set them in their [1]place.
12 [a]Then brought all Judah the tithe of
the corn and the new wine and the oil
unto the [1]treasuries.
13 [a]And I made treasurers over the
treasuries, Shelemiah the priest, and Zadok the scribe, and of the Levites, Pedaiah: and [1]next to them *was* Hanan the
son of Zaccur, the son of Mattaniah: for
they were counted [b]faithful, and [2]their
office *was* to distribute unto their
brethren.

14 [a]Remember me, O my God, concerning this, and wipe not out my [1]good
deeds that I have done for the house of
my God, and for the [2]offices thereof.
15 ¶ In those days saw I in Judah *some*
treading wine presses [a]on the sabbath,
and bringing in sheaves, and lading asses;
as also wine, grapes, and figs, and all
manner of burdens, [b]which they brought
into Jerusalem on the sabbath day: and I
testified *against them* in the day wherein
they sold victuals.
16 There dwelt men of Tyre also
therein, which brought fish, and all manner of ware, and sold on the sabbath unto
the children of Judah, and in Jerusalem.
17 Then I contended with the nobles
of Judah, and said unto them, What evil
thing *is* this that ye do, and profane the
sabbath day?
18 [a]Did not your fathers thus, and did
not our God bring all this evil upon us,
and upon this city? yet ye bring more
wrath upon Israel by profaning the
sabbath.
19 And it came to pass, that when the
gates of Jerusalem [a]began to be dark before the sabbath, I commanded that the
gates should be shut, and charged that
they should not be opened till after the
sabbath: [b]and *some* of my servants set I at
the gates, *that* there should no burden be
brought in on the sabbath day.
20 So the merchants and sellers of all
kind of ware lodged without Jerusalem
once or twice.
21 Then I testified against them, and
said unto them, Why lodge ye [1]about the
wall? if ye do *so* again, I will lay hands on
you. From that time forth came they no
more on the sabbath.
22 And I commanded the Levites that
[a]they should cleanse themselves, and
that they should come *and* keep the
gates, to sanctify the sabbath day. Remember me, O my God, *concerning* this
also, and spare me according to the
[1]greatness of thy mercy.
23 ¶ In those days also saw I Jews *that*
[a]had[1] married wives of Ashdod, of Ammon, *and* of Moab:
24 And their children spake half in the
speech of Ashdod, and [1]could not speak
in the Jews' language, but according to
the language [2]of each people.
25 And I [a]contended with them, and
[1]cursed them, and smote certain of them,

2 [a]Num. 22:5; Josh. 24:9,10 [b]Num. 23:11 & 24:10; Deut. 23:5
3 [a]ch. 9:2 & 10:28
4 [a]ch. 12:44 [1]Heb. *being set over*
5 [a]ch. 12:44 [b]Num. 18:21,24 [1]Heb. *the commandment of the Levites*
6 [a]ch. 5:14 [1]Heb. *at the end of days* [2]Or, *I earnestly requested*
7 [a]ver. 1,5
9 [a]2 Chr. 29:5
10 [a]Mal. 3:8 [b]Num. 35:2
11 [a]ver. 17,25 [b]ch. 10:39 [1]Heb. *standing*
12 [a]ch. 10:38 [1]Or, *storehouses*
13 [a]2 Chr. 31:12; ch. 12:44 [b]1 Cor. 4:2 [1]Heb. *at their hand* [2]Heb. it was *upon them*
14 [a]ch. 5:19 [1]Heb. *kindnesses* [2]Or, *observations*
15 [a]Ex. 20:10 [b]ch. 10:31; Jer. 17:21
18 [a]Jer. 17:21
19 [a]Lev. 23:32 [b]Jer. 17:21
21 [1]Heb. *before the wall?*
22 [a]ch. 12:30 [1]Or, *multitude*
23 [a]Ezra 9:2 [1]Heb. *had made to dwell* with them
24 [1]Heb. *they discerned not to speak* [2]Heb. *of people and people*
25 [a]Prov. 28:4 [1]Or, *reviled them*

and plucked off their hair, and made
them [b]swear by God, *saying,* Ye shall not
give your daughters unto their sons, nor
take their daughters unto your sons, or
for yourselves.
26 [a]Did not Solomon king of Israel sin
by these things? yet among many nations
was there no king like him, [b]who was
beloved of his God, and God made him
king over all Israel: [c]nevertheless even
him did outlandish women cause to sin.
27 Shall we then hearken unto you to
do all this great evil, to [a]transgress
against our God in marrying strange
wives?

28 And *one* of the sons [a]of Joiada, the
son of Eliashib the high priest, *was* son-
in-law to Sanballat the Horonite: therefore I chased him from me.
29 [a]Remember them, O my God, [/]be-
cause they have defiled the priesthood,
and [b]the covenant of the priesthood, and
of the Levites.
30 [a]Thus cleansed I them from all
strangers, and [b]appointed the wards of
the priests and the Levites, every one in
his business;
31 And for [a]the wood offering, at
times appointed, and for the firstfruits.
[b]Remember me, O my God, for good.

25 [b]Ezra 10:5; ch. 10:29
26 [a]1 Ki. 11:1 [b]2 Sam. 12:24 [c]1 Ki. 11:4
27 [a]Ezra 10:2
28 [a]ch. 12:10,22
29 [a]ch. 6:14 [b]Mal. 2:4,11,12 [/]Heb. *for the defilings*
30 [a]ch. 10:30 [b]ch. 12:1
31 [a]ch. 10:34 [b]ver. 14,22

Esther

Author: Unknown

Theme: God provides for those who trust him

Date of Writing: c. 460–350 B.C.

Outline of Esther

I. King Ahasuerus and His Court (1:1—2:23)
II. Esther's People Are Threatened (3:1—5:14)
III. The Jews Triumph Over Haman (6:1—10:3)

THIS BOOK BEARS the name of its leading lady, Esther, whom the Persian king Ahasuerus (Xerxes) chose to be his queen. The book of Esther is one book in a five-book grouping in the Hebrew canon known as the megilloth. According to Jewish custom, certain books were to be read aloud in the synagogues (see Lk 4:16–17). The books of the megilloth were read aloud at feast seasons, with the book of Esther scheduled to be read at the Feast of Purim. The four other books in the megilloth are Ruth, Lamentations, Song of Solomon and Ecclesiastes.

The events in Esther took place in the Persian capital of Shushan during the reign of King Ahasuerus and may correspond to a time just after the dedication of the rebuilt temple but prior to Nehemiah's arrival in Judah. Although the name of God does not appear in the text of this book, Esther's story clearly demonstrates God's control over his covenant people as it portrays the plight of the Jews in Persian exile.

Although the author of Esther is unknown, contemporary customs, the royal palace and Persian history are accurately described. Note also the inauguration of the Feast of Purim. While not one of the feasts given to Moses by God in the desert (see Lev 23:1–39), the Feast of Purim is commemorated annually by the Jews worldwide, confirming the historicity of Esther's account.

The removal of queen Vashti

1 NOW IT came to pass in the days of [a]Ahasuerus, (this *is* Ahasuerus which reigned, [b]from India even unto Ethiopia, [c]*over* an hundred and seven and twenty provinces:)

2 *That* in those days, when the king Ahasuerus [a]sat on the throne of his kingdom, which *was* in [b]Shushan the palace,

3 In the third year of his reign, he [a]made a feast unto all his princes and his servants; the power of Persia and Media, the nobles and princes of the provinces, *being* before him:

4 When he showed the riches of his glorious kingdom and the honour of his excellent majesty many days, *even* an hundred and fourscore days.

5 And when these days were expired, the king made a feast unto all the people that were [1]present in Shushan the palace, both unto great and small, seven days, in the court of the garden of the king's palace;

6 *Where were* white, green, and [1]blue, *hangings,* fastened with cords of fine linen and purple to silver rings and pillars of marble: [a]the beds *were of* gold and silver, upon a pavement [2]of red, and blue, and white, and black, marble.

7 And they gave *them* drink in vessels of gold, (the vessels being diverse one from another,) and [1]royal wine in abundance, [2]according to the state of the king.

8 And the drinking *was* according to the law; none did compel: for so the king had appointed to all the officers of his house, that they should do according to every man's pleasure.

9 Also Vashti the queen made a feast for the women *in* the royal house which *belonged* to king Ahasuerus.

10 ¶ On the seventh day, when the heart of the king was merry with wine, he commanded Mehuman, Biztha, [a]Harbona, Bigtha, and Abagtha, Zethar, and Carcas, the seven [1]chamberlains that served in the presence of Ahasuerus the king,

11 To bring Vashti the queen before the king with the crown royal, to show the people and the princes her beauty: for she *was* [1]fair to look on.

1:1 [a]Ezra 4:6; Dan. 9:1 [b]ch. 8:9 [c]Dan. 6:1
2 [a]1 Ki. 1:46 [b]Neh. 1:1
3 [a]Gen. 40:20; ch. 2:18
5 [1]Heb. *found*
6 [a]ch. 7:8; Amos 2:8 & 6:4 [1]Or, *violet* [2]Or, *of porphyre, and marble, and alabaster, and stone of blue colour*
7 [1]Heb. *wine of the kingdom* [2]Heb. *according to the hand of the king*
10 [a]ch. 7:9 [1]Or, *eunuchs*
11 [1]Heb. *good of countenance*
12 [1]Heb. *which was by the hand of his eunuchs*
13 [a]Jer. 10:7; Dan. 2:12; Mat. 2:1 [b]1 Chr. 12:32
14 [a]Ezra 7:14 [b]2 Ki. 25:19
15 [1]Heb. *What to do*
17 [a]Eph. 5:33
19 [a]ch. 8:8; Dan. 6:8 [1]Heb. *If it be good with the king* [2]Heb. *from before him* [3]Heb. *that it pass not away* [4]Heb. *unto her companion*
20 [a]Eph. 5:33; Col. 3:18; 1 Pet. 3:1
21 [1]Heb. *was good in the eyes of the king*

12 But the queen Vashti refused to come at the king's commandment [1]by *his* chamberlains: therefore was the king very wroth, and his anger burned in him.

13 ¶ Then the king said to the [a]wise men, [b]which knew the times, (for so *was* the king's manner toward all that knew law and judgment:

14 And the next unto him *was* Carshena, Shethar, Admatha, Tarshish, Meres, Marsena, *and* Memucan, the [a]seven princes of Persia and Media, [b]which saw the king's face, *and* which sat the first in the kingdom;)

15 [1]What shall we do unto the queen Vashti according to law, because she hath not performed the commandment of the king Ahasuerus by the chamberlains?

16 And Memucan answered before the king and the princes, Vashti the queen hath not done wrong to the king only, but also to all the princes, and to all the people that *are* in all the provinces of the king Ahasuerus.

17 For *this* deed of the queen shall come abroad unto all women, so that they shall [a]despise their husbands in their eyes, when it shall be reported, The king Ahasuerus commanded Vashti the queen to be brought in before him, but she came not.

18 *Likewise* shall the ladies of Persia and Media say this day unto all the king's princes, which have heard of the deed of the queen. Thus *shall there arise* too much contempt and wrath.

19 [1]If it please the king, let there go a royal commandment [2]from him, and let it be written among the laws of the Persians and the Medes, [a]that[3] it be not altered, That Vashti come no more before king Ahasuerus; and let the king give her royal estate [4]unto another that is better than she.

20 And when the king's decree which he shall make shall be published throughout all his empire, (for it is great,) all the wives shall [a]give to their husbands honour, both to great and small.

21 And the saying [1]pleased the king and the princes; and the king did according to the word of Memucan:

22 For he sent letters into all the

1:13 The wise men were probably astrologers that advised the royal court of Persia. They were also conversant with the law of Moses (see Ezr 7:14).

king's provinces, [a]into every province according to the writing thereof, and to every people after their language, that every man should [b]bear rule in his own house, and [1]that *it* should be published according to the language of every people.

Esther chosen to be queen

2 AFTER THESE things, when the wrath of king Ahasuerus was appeased, he remembered Vashti, and what she had done, and [a]what was decreed against her.

2 Then said the king's servants that ministered unto him, Let there be fair young virgins sought for the king:

3 And let the king appoint officers in all the provinces of his kingdom, that they may gather together all the fair young virgins unto Shushan the palace, to the house of the women, [1]unto the custody of [2]Hege the king's chamberlain, keeper of the women; and let their things for purification be given *them:*

4 And let the maiden which pleaseth the king be queen instead of Vashti. And the thing pleased the king; and he did so.

5 ¶ *Now* in Shushan the palace there was a certain Jew, whose name *was* Mordecai, the son of Jair, the son of Shimei, the son of Kish, a Benjamite;

6 [a]Who had been carried away from Jerusalem with the captivity which had been carried away with [1]Jeconiah king of Judah, whom Nebuchadnezzar the king of Babylon had carried away.

7 And he [1]brought up Hadassah, that *is,* Esther, [a]his uncle's daughter: for she had neither father nor mother, and the maid *was* [2]fair and beautiful; whom Mordecai, when her father and mother were dead, took for his own daughter.

8 ¶ So it came to pass, when the king's commandment and his decree was heard, and when many maidens were [a]gathered together unto Shushan the palace, to the custody of Hegai, that Esther was brought also unto the king's house, to the custody of Hegai, keeper of the women.

9 And the maiden pleased him, and she obtained kindness of him; and he speedily gave her her [a]things for purification, with [1]such things as belonged to her, and seven maidens, *which were* meet to be given her, out of the king's house: and [2]he preferred her and her maids unto the best *place* of the house of the women.

10 [a]Esther had not shown her people nor her kindred: for Mordecai had charged her that she should not show *it.*

11 And Mordecai walked every day before the court of the women's house, [1]to know how Esther did, and what should become of her.

12 ¶ Now when every maid's turn was come to go in to king Ahasuerus, after that she had been twelve months, according to the manner of the women, (for so were the days of their purifications accomplished, *to wit,* six months with oil of myrrh, and six months with sweet odours, and with *other* things for the purifying of the women;)

13 Then thus came *every* maiden unto the king; whatsoever she desired was given her to go with her out of the house of the women unto the king's house.

14 In the evening she went, and on the morrow she returned into the second house of the women, to the custody of Shaashgaz, the king's chamberlain, which kept the concubines: she came in unto the king no more, except the king delighted in her, and that she were called by name.

15 ¶ Now when the turn of Esther, [a]the daughter of Abihail the uncle of Mordecai, who had taken her for his daughter, was come to go in unto the king, she required nothing but what Hegai the king's chamberlain, the keeper of the women, appointed. And Esther obtained favour in the sight of all them that looked upon her.

16 So Esther was taken unto king Ahasuerus into his house royal in the tenth month, which *is* the month Tebeth, in the seventh year of his reign.

17 And the king loved Esther above all the women, and she obtained grace and [1]favour [2]in his sight more than all the virgins; so that he set the royal crown upon her head, and made her queen instead of Vashti.

18 Then the king [a]made a great feast unto all his princes and his servants, *even* Esther's feast; and he made a [1]release to the provinces, and gave gifts, according to the state of the king.

The plot to kill Ahasuerus fails

19 And when the virgins were gath-

22 [a] ch. 8:9 [b] Eph. 5:22-24; 1 Tim. 2:12 [1] Heb. *that one should publish* it *according to the language of his people*

2:1 [a] ch. 1:19,20

3 [1] Heb. *unto the hand* [2] Or, *Hegai;* see ver. 8

6 [a] 2 Ki. 24:14,15; 2 Chr. 36:10,20; Jer. 24:1 [1] Or, *Jehoiachin;* see 2 Ki. 24:6

7 [a] ver. 15 [1] Heb. *nourished* [2] Heb. *fair of form, and good of countenance*

8 [a] ver. 3

9 [a] ver. 3,12 [1] Heb. *her portions* [2] Heb. *he changed her*

10 [a] ver. 20

11 [1] Heb. *to know the peace*

15 [a] ver. 7

17 [1] Or, *kindness* [2] Heb. *before him*

18 [a] ch. 1:3 [1] Heb. *rest*

ered together the second time, then Mordecai sat [a]in the king's gate.

20 [a]Esther had not *yet* shown her kindred nor her people; as Mordecai had charged her: for Esther did the commandment of Mordecai, like as when she was brought up with him.

21 ¶ In those days, while Mordecai sat in the king's gate, two of the king's chamberlains, [1]Bigthan and Teresh, of those which kept [2]the door, were wroth, and sought to lay hand on the king Ahasuerus.

22 And the thing was known to Mordecai, [a]who told *it* unto Esther the queen; and Esther certified the king *thereof* in Mordecai's name.

23 And when inquisition was made of the matter, it was found out; therefore they were both hanged on a tree: and it was written in [a]the book of the chronicles before the king.

Haman's plot against the Jews

3 AFTER THESE things did king Ahasuerus promote Haman the son of Hammedatha the [a]Agagite, and advanced him, and set his seat above all the princes that *were* with him.

2 And all the king's servants, that *were* [a]in the king's gate, bowed, and reverenced Haman: for the king had so commanded concerning him. But Mordecai [b]bowed not, nor did *him* reverence.

3 Then the king's servants, which *were* in the king's gate, said unto Mordecai, Why transgressest thou the [a]king's commandment?

4 Now it came to pass, when they spake daily unto him, and he hearkened not unto them, that they told Haman, to see whether Mordecai's matters would stand: for he had told them that he *was* a Jew.

5 And when Haman saw that Mordecai [a]bowed not, nor did him reverence, then was Haman [b]full of wrath.

6 And he thought scorn to lay hands on Mordecai alone; for they had shown him the people of Mordecai: wherefore Haman [a]sought to destroy all the Jews that *were* throughout the whole kingdom of Ahasuerus, *even* the people of Mordecai.

7 ¶ In the first month, that *is,* the month Nisan, in the twelfth year of king Ahasuerus, [a]they cast Pur, that *is,* the lot, before Haman from day to day, and from month to month, *to* the twelfth *month,* that *is,* the month Adar.

8 ¶ And Haman said unto king Ahasuerus, There is a certain people scattered abroad and dispersed among the people in all the provinces of thy kingdom; and [a]their laws *are* diverse from all people; neither keep they the king's laws: therefore it *is* not [1]for the king's profit to suffer them.

9 If it please the king, let it be written [1]that they may be destroyed: and I will [2]pay ten thousand talents of silver to the hands of those that have the charge of the business, to bring *it* into the king's treasuries.

10 And the king [a]took [b]his ring from his hand, and gave it unto Haman the son of Hammedatha the Agagite, the Jews' [1]enemy.

11 And the king said unto Haman, The silver *is* given to thee, the people also, to do with them as it seemeth good to thee.

12 [a]Then were the king's [1]scribes called on the thirteenth day of the first month, and there was written according to all that Haman had commanded unto the king's lieutenants, and to the governors that *were* over every province, and to the rulers of every people of every province [b]according to the writing thereof, and *to* every people after their language; [c]in the name of king Ahasuerus was it written, and sealed with the king's ring.

13 And the letters were [a]sent by posts into all the king's provinces, to destroy, to kill, and to cause to perish, all Jews, both young and old, little children and women, [b]in one day, *even* upon the thirteenth *day* of the twelfth month, which *is* the month Adar, and [c]*to take* the spoil of them for a prey.

14 [a]The copy of the writing for a commandment to be given in every province was published unto all people, that they should be ready against that day.

15 The posts went out, being hastened by the king's commandment, and the decree was given in Shushan the palace. And the king and Haman sat down to

19 [a]ver. 21; ch. 3:2
20 [a]ver. 10
21 [1]Or, *Bigthana;* see ch. 6:2 [2]Heb. *the threshold*
22 [a]ch. 6:2
23 [a]ch. 6:1
3:1 [a]Num. 24:7; 1 Sam. 15:8
2 [a]ch. 2:19 [b]ver. 5; Ps. 15:4
3 [a]ver. 2
5 [a]ver. 2; ch. 5:9 [b]Dan. 3:19
6 [a]Ps. 83:4
7 [a]ch. 9:24
8 [a]Ezra 4:13; Acts 16:20 [1]Heb. *meet,* or, *equal*
9 [1]Heb. *to destroy them* [2]Heb. *weigh*
10 [a]Gen. 41:42 [b]ch. 8:2,8 [1]Or, *oppressor;* see ch. 7:6
12 [a]ch. 8:9 [b]ch. 1:22 [c]1 Ki. 21:8; ch. 8:8,10 [1]Or, *secretaries*
13 [a]ch. 8:10 [b]ch. 8:12 [c]ch. 8:11
14 [a]ch. 8:13,14

drink; but [a]the city Shushan was perplexed.

4 WHEN MORDECAI perceived all that was done, Mordecai [a]rent his clothes, and put on sackcloth [b]with ashes, and went out into the midst of the city, and [c]cried with a loud and a bitter cry;

2 And came even before the king's gate: for none *might* enter into the king's gate clothed with sackcloth.

3 And in every province, whithersoever the king's commandment and his decree came, *there was* great mourning among the Jews, and fasting, and weeping, and wailing; and [l]many lay in sackcloth and ashes.

Mordecai asks Esther for help

4 ¶ So Esther's maids and her [l]chamberlains came and told *it* her. Then was the queen exceedingly grieved; and she sent raiment to clothe Mordecai, and to take away his sackcloth from him: but he received *it* not.

5 Then called Esther for Hatach, *one* of the king's chamberlains, [l]whom he had appointed to attend upon her, and gave him a commandment to Mordecai, to know what it *was,* and why it *was.*

6 So Hatach went forth to Mordecai unto the street of the city, which *was* before the king's gate.

7 And Mordecai told him of all that had happened unto him, and of [a]the sum of the money that Haman had promised to pay to the king's treasuries for the Jews, to destroy them.

8 Also he gave him [a]the copy of the writing of the decree that was given at Shushan to destroy them, to show *it* unto Esther, and to declare *it* unto her, and to charge her that she should go in unto the king, to make supplication unto him, and to make request before him for her people.

9 And Hatach came and told Esther the words of Mordecai.

10 ¶ Again Esther spake unto Hatach, and gave him commandment unto Mordecai;

11 All the king's servants, and the people of the king's provinces, do know, that whosoever, whether man or woman, shall come unto the king into [a]the inner court, who is not called, [b]*there is* one law of his to put *him* to death, except such [c]to whom the king shall hold out the golden sceptre, that he may live: but I have not been called to come in unto the king these thirty days.

12 And they told to Mordecai Esther's words.

13 Then Mordecai commanded to answer Esther, Think not with thyself that thou shalt escape in the king's house, more than all the Jews.

14 For if thou altogether holdest thy peace at this time, *then* shall there enlargement and deliverance arise to the Jews from another place; but thou and thy father's house shall be destroyed: and who knoweth whether thou art come to the kingdom for *such* a time as this?

15 ¶ Then Esther bade *them* return Mordecai *this answer,*

16 Go, gather together all the Jews that are [l]present in Shushan, and fast ye for me, and neither eat nor drink [a]three days, night or day: I also and my maidens will fast likewise; and so will I go in unto the king, which *is* not according to the law: [b]and if I perish, I perish.

17 So Mordecai [l]went his way, and did according to all that Esther had commanded him.

15 [a]See ch. 8:15; Prov. 29:2
4:1 [a]2 Sam. 1:11 [b]Josh. 7:6; Ezek. 27:30 [c]Gen. 27:34
3 [l]Heb. *sackcloth and ashes were laid under many*
4 [l]Heb. *eunuchs*
5 [l]Heb. *whom he had set before her*
7 [a]ch. 3:9
8 [a]ch. 3:14,15
11 [a]ch. 5:1 [b]Dan. 2:9 [c]ch. 5:2 & 8:4
16 [a]See ch. 5:1 [b]See Gen. 43:14 [l]Heb. *found*
17 [l]Heb. *passed*

4:16 Our method of marking time differs from the ancient Jews' method of calculating time. While we follow a full measure of time to calculate the passage of days and years (one day means 24 hours; one year means 365 days; half a day means 12 hours, etc.), in ancient societies any part of one day counted as a whole day when calculating time. When Esther asked Mordecai to fast for three days, she was not referring to a full measure of seventy-two hours, but rather regarded the three days to have begun on the day she spoke with Mordecai, continuing through the next full day and ending sometime during the day after that—the third day. Note that 5:1 bears out this inclusive mode of time calculation.

Understanding this ancient mode of time calculation is important for us in understanding the precise chronology of some key Biblical events such as Jonah's incarceration in the whale (see Jnh 1:17) and Christ's crucifixion and resurrection (see Mt 12:40).

Esther's intervention

5 NOW IT came to pass [a]on the third day, that Esther put on *her* royal *apparel,* and stood in [b]the inner court of the king's house, over against the king's house: and the king sat upon his royal throne in the royal house, over against the gate of the house.

2 And it was so, when the king saw Esther the queen standing in the court, *that* [a]she obtained favour in his sight: and [b]the king held out to Esther the golden sceptre that *was* in his hand. So Esther drew near, and touched the top of the sceptre.

3 Then said the king unto her, What wilt thou, queen Esther? and what *is* thy request? [a]it shall be even given thee to the half of the kingdom.

4 And Esther answered, If *it seem* good unto the king, let the king and Haman come this day unto the banquet that I have prepared for him.

5 Then the king said, Cause Haman to make haste, that he may do as Esther hath said. So the king and Haman came to the banquet that Esther had prepared.

6 ¶ [a]And the king said unto Esther at the banquet of wine, [b]What *is* thy petition? and it shall be granted thee: and what *is* thy request? even to the half of the kingdom it shall be performed.

7 Then answered Esther, and said, My petition and my request *is:*

8 If I have found favour in the sight of the king, and if it please the king to grant my petition, and [1]to perform my request, let the king and Haman come to the banquet that I shall prepare for them, and I will do tomorrow as the king hath said.

Haman has gallows made

9 ¶ Then went Haman forth that day joyful and with a glad heart: but when Haman saw Mordecai in the king's gate, [a]that he stood not up, nor moved for him, he was full of indignation against Mordecai.

10 Nevertheless Haman [a]refrained himself: and when he came home, he sent and [1]called for his friends, and Zeresh his wife.

11 And Haman told them of the glory of his riches, and [a]the multitude of his children, and all *the things* wherein the king had promoted him, and how he had advanced him above the princes and servants of the king.

12 Haman said moreover, Yea, Esther the queen did let no man come in with the king unto the banquet that she had prepared but myself; and tomorrow am I invited unto her also with the king.

13 Yet all this availeth me nothing, so long as I see Mordecai the Jew sitting at the king's gate.

14 ¶ Then said Zeresh his wife and all his friends unto him, Let a [a]gallows[1] be made of fifty cubits high, and tomorrow [b]speak thou unto the king that Mordecai may be hanged thereon: then go thou in merrily with the king unto the banquet. And the thing pleased Haman; and he caused [c]the gallows to be made.

Mordecai honoured

6 ON THAT night [1]could not the king sleep, and he commanded to bring [a]the book of records of the chronicles; and they were read before the king.

2 And it was found written, that Mordecai had told of [1]Bigthana and Teresh, two of the king's chamberlains, the keepers of the [2]door, who sought to lay hand on the king Ahasuerus.

3 And the king said, What honour and dignity hath been done to Mordecai for this? Then said the king's servants that ministered unto him, There is nothing done for him.

4 ¶ And the king said, Who *is* in the court? Now Haman was come into [a]the outward court of the king's house, [b]to speak unto the king to hang Mordecai on the gallows that he had prepared for him.

5 And the king's servants said unto him, Behold, Haman standeth in the court. And the king said, Let him come in.

6 So Haman came in. And the king said unto him, What shall be done unto the man [1]whom the king delighteth to honour? Now Haman thought in his heart, To whom would the king delight to do honour more than to myself?

7 And Haman answered the king, For the man [1]whom the king delighteth to honour,

8 [1]Let the royal apparel be brought [2]which the king *useth* to wear, and [a]the horse that the king rideth upon, and the crown royal which is set upon his head:

9 And let this apparel and horse be de-

5:1 [a]See ch. 4:16 [b]See ch. 4:11 & 6:4
2 [a]Prov. 21:1 [b]ch. 4:11 & 8:4
3 [a]Mark 6:23
6 [a]ch. 7:2 [b]ch. 9:12
8 [1]Heb *to do*
9 [a]ch. 3:5
10 [a]2 Sam. 13:22 [1]Heb. *caused to come*
11 [a]ch. 9:7
14 [a]ch. 7:9 [b]ch. 6:4 [c]ch. 7:10 [1]Heb. *tree*
6:1 [a]ch. 2:23 [1]Heb. *the king's sleep fled away*
2 [1]Or, *Bigthan;* see ch. 2:21 [2]Heb. *threshold*
4 [a]See ch. 5:1 [b]ch. 5:14
6 [1]Heb. *in whose honour the king delighteth*
7 [1]Heb. *in whose honour the king delighteth*
8 [a]1 Ki. 1:33 [1]Heb. *Let them bring the royal apparel* [2]Heb. *wherewith the king clotheth* himself

livered to the hand of one of the king's
most noble princes, that they may array
the man *withal* whom the king delighteth
to honour, and [1]bring him on horseback
through the street of the city, [a]and proclaim before him, Thus shall it be done to
the man whom the king delighteth to
honour.
10 Then the king said to Haman, Make
haste, *and* take the apparel and the horse,
as thou hast said, and do even so to Mordecai the Jew, that sitteth at the king's
gate: [1]let nothing fail of all that thou hast
spoken.
11 Then took Haman the apparel and
the horse, and arrayed Mordecai, and
brought him on horseback through the
street of the city, and proclaimed before
him, Thus shall it be done unto the man
whom the king delighteth to honour.
12 ¶ And Mordecai came again to the
king's gate. But Haman [a]hasted to his
house mourning, [b]and having his head
covered.
13 And Haman told Zeresh his wife
and all his friends every *thing* that had
befallen him. Then said his wise men and
Zeresh his wife unto him, If Mordecai *be*
of the seed of the Jews, before whom
thou hast begun to fall, thou shalt not
prevail against him, but shalt surely fall
before him.
14 And while they *were* yet talking
with him, came the king's chamberlains,
and hasted to bring Haman unto [a]the
banquet that Esther had prepared.

The downfall of Haman

7 SO THE king and Haman came [1]to
banquet with Esther the queen.
2 And the king said again unto Esther
on the second day [a]at the banquet of
wine, What *is* thy petition, queen Esther?
and it shall be granted thee: and what *is*
thy request? and it shall be performed,
even to the half of the kingdom.
3 Then Esther the queen answered
and said, If I have found favour in thy
sight, O king, and if it please the king, let
my life be given me at my petition, and
my people at my request:
4 For we are [a]sold, I and my people,
[1]to be destroyed, to be slain, and to perish. But if we had been sold for bondmen
and bondwomen, I had held my tongue,
although the enemy could not countervail
the king's damage.
5 ¶ Then the king Ahasuerus answered
and said unto Esther the queen, Who is
he, and where is he, [1]that durst presume
in his heart to do so?
6 And Esther said, [1]The adversary and
enemy *is* this wicked Haman. Then Haman was afraid [2]before the king and the
queen.
7 ¶ And the king arising from the banquet of wine in his wrath *went* into the
palace garden: and Haman stood up to
make request for his life to Esther the
queen; for he saw that there was evil determined against him by the king.
8 Then the king returned out of the
palace garden into the place of the banquet of wine; and Haman was fallen upon
[a]the bed whereon Esther *was.* Then said
the king, Will he force the queen also
[1]before me in the house? As the word
went out of the king's mouth, they [b]cov-
ered Haman's face.
9 And [a]Harbonah, one of the chamberlains, said before the king, Behold also,
[b]the [1]gallows fifty cubits high, which Haman had made for Mordecai, who had
spoken good for the king, standeth in the
house of Haman. Then the king said,
Hang him thereon.
10 So [a]they hanged Haman on the gallows that he had prepared for Mordecai.
Then was the king's wrath pacified.

The decree is revoked

8 ON THAT day did the king Ahasuerus give the house of Haman the
Jew's enemy unto Esther the queen. And
Mordecai came before the king; for Esther had told [a]what he *was* unto her.
2 And the king took off [a]his ring,
which he had taken from Haman, and
gave it unto Mordecai. And Esther set
Mordecai over the house of Haman.
3 ¶ And Esther spake yet again before
the king, and fell down at his feet, [1]and
besought him with tears to put away the
mischief of Haman the Agagite, and his
device that he had devised against the
Jews.
4 Then [a]the king held out the golden
sceptre toward Esther. So Esther arose,
and stood before the king,
5 And said, If it please the king, and if I
have found favour in his sight, and the
thing *seem* right before the king, and I *be*
pleasing in his eyes, let it be written to
reverse [1]the letters devised by Haman

9 [a]Gen. 41:43 [1]Heb. *cause him to ride*
10 [1]Heb. *suffer not a whit to fall*
12 [a]2 Chr. 26:20 [b]2 Sam. 15:30; Jer. 14:3,4
14 [a]ch. 5:8
7:1 [1]Heb. *to drink*
2 [a]ch. 5:6
4 [a]ch. 3:9 [1]Heb. *that they should destroy, and kill, and cause to perish*
5 [1]Heb. *whose heart hath filled him*
6 [1]Heb. *The man adversary* [2]Or, *at the presence of*
8 [a]ch. 1:6 [b]Job 9:24 [1]Heb. *with me*
9 [a]ch. 1:10 [b]ch. 5:14; Ps. 7:16; Prov. 11:5,6 [1]Heb. *tree*
10 [a]Ps. 37:35,36; Dan. 6:24
8:1 [a]ch. 2:7
2 [a]ch. 3:10
3 [1]Heb. *and she wept, and besought him*
4 [a]ch. 4:11 & 5:2
5 [1]Heb. *the device*

the son of Hammedatha the Agagite,
[2]which he wrote to destroy the Jews
which *are* in all the king's provinces:
6 For how can I [1]endure to see [a]the
evil that shall come unto my people? or
how can I endure to see the destruction
of my kindred?
7 ¶ Then the king Ahasuerus said unto
Esther the queen and to Mordecai the
Jew, Behold, [a]I have given Esther the
house of Haman, and him they have
hanged upon the gallows, because he laid
his hand upon the Jews.
8 Write ye also for the Jews, as it liketh
you, in the king's name, and seal *it* with
the king's ring: for the writing which is
written in the king's name, and sealed
with the king's ring, [a]may no man reverse.
9 [a]Then were the king's scribes called
at that time in the third month, that *is,*
the month Sivan, on the three and twentieth *day* thereof; and it was written according to all that Mordecai commanded
unto the Jews, and to the lieutenants, and
the deputies and rulers of the provinces
which *are* [b]from India unto Ethiopia, an
hundred twenty and seven provinces,
unto every province [c]according to the
writing thereof, and unto every people after their language, and to the Jews according to their writing, and according to
their language.
10 [a]And he wrote in the king Ahasuerus' name, and sealed *it* with the king's
ring, and sent letters by posts on horseback, *and* riders on mules, camels, *and*
young dromedaries:
11 Wherein the king granted the Jews
which *were* in every city to gather themselves together, and to stand for their life,
to destroy, to slay, and to cause to perish,
all the power of the people and province
that would assault them, *both* little ones
and women, and [a]*to take* the spoil of
them for a prey,
12 [a]Upon one day in all the provinces
of king Ahasuerus, *namely,* upon the thirteenth *day* of the twelfth month, which *is*
the month Adar.
13 [a]The copy of the writing for a commandment to be given in every province
was [1]published unto all people, and that
the Jews should be ready against that day
to avenge themselves on their enemies.
14 *So* the posts that rode upon mules
and camels went out, being hastened and
pressed on by the king's commandment.
And the decree was given at Shushan the
palace.
15 ¶ And Mordecai went out from the
presence of the king in royal apparel of
[1]blue and white, and with a great crown
of gold, and with a garment of fine linen
and purple: and [a]the city of Shushan rejoiced and was glad.
16 The Jews had [a]light, and gladness, L
and joy, and honour.
17 And in every province, and in every
city, whithersoever the king's commandment and his decree came, the Jews had
joy and gladness, a feast [a]and a good day.
And many of the people of the land [b]be-
came Jews; for [c]the fear of the Jews fell
upon them.

The victory of the Jews

9 NOW [a]IN the twelfth month, that *is,*
the month Adar, on the thirteenth
day of the same, [b]when the king's commandment and his decree drew near to
be put in execution, in the day that the
enemies of the Jews hoped to have power
over them, (though it was turned to the
contrary, that the Jews [c]had rule over
them that hated them;)
2 The Jews [a]gathered themselves together in their cities throughout all the
provinces of the king Ahasuerus, to lay
hand on such as [b]sought their hurt: and
no man could withstand them; for [c]the
fear of them fell upon all people.
3 And all the rulers of the provinces,
and the lieutenants, and the deputies,
and [1]officers of the king, helped the Jews;
because the fear of Mordecai fell upon
them.
4 For Mordecai *was* great in the king's
house, and his fame went out throughout
all the provinces: for this man Mordecai
[a]waxed greater and greater.
5 Thus the Jews smote all their enemies with the stroke of the sword, and
slaughter, and destruction, and did [1]what
they would unto those that hated them.
6 And in Shushan the palace the Jews
slew and destroyed five hundred men.
7 And Parshandatha, and Dalphon, and
Aspatha,

5 [2]Or, *who wrote*
6 [a]Neh. 2:3; ch. 7:4 [1]Heb. *be able that I may see*
7 [a]ver. 1; Prov. 13:22
8 [a]See ch. 1:19; Dan. 6:8,12,15
9 [a]ch. 3:12 [b]ch. 1:1 [c]ch. 1:22 & 3:12
10 [a]1 Ki. 21:8; ch. 3:12,13
11 [a]See ch. 9:10, 15,16
12 [a]ch. 3:13 & 9:1
13 [a]ch. 3:14,15 [1]Heb. *revealed*
15 [a]See ch. 3:15; Prov. 29:2 [1]Or, *violet*
16 [a]Ps. 97:11
17 [a]1 Sam. 25:8 [b]Ps. 18:43 [c]Gen. 35:5; Ex. 15:16; Deut. 2:25 & 11:25; ch. 9:2
9:1 [a]ch. 8:12 [b]ch. 3:13 [c]2 Sam. 22:41
2 [a]ver. 16 & ch. 8:11 [b]Ps. 71:13,24 [c]ch. 8:17
3 [1]Heb. *those which did the business that belonged to the king*
4 [a]2 Sam. 3:1; 1 Chr. 11:9; Prov. 4:18
5 [1]Heb. *according to their will*

L Ne 9:12 ◄► Job 5:17–26

8 And Poratha, and Adalia, and
Aridatha,
9 And Parmashta, and Arisai, and
Aridai, and Vajezatha,
10 [a]The ten sons of Haman the sons
of Hammedatha, the enemy of the Jews,
slew they; [b]but on the spoil laid they not
their hand.
11 On that day the number of those
that were slain in Shushan the palace
ʹwas brought before the king.
12 ¶ And the king said unto Esther the
queen, The Jews have slain and destroyed
five hundred men in Shushan the palace,
and the ten sons of Haman; what have
they done in the rest of the king's provinces? now [a]what *is* thy petition? and it
shall be granted thee: or what *is* thy request further? and it shall be done.
13 Then said Esther, If it please the
king, let it be granted to the Jews which
are in Shushan to do tomorrow also [a]ac-
cording unto this day's decree, and ʹlet
Haman's ten sons [b]be hanged upon the
gallows.
14 And the king commanded it so to
be done: and the decree was given at
Shushan; and they hanged Haman's ten
sons.
15 For the Jews that *were* in Shushan
[a]gathered themselves together on the
fourteenth day also of the month Adar,
and slew three hundred men at Shushan;
[b]but on the prey they laid not their
hand.
16 But the other Jews that *were* in the
king's provinces [a]gathered themselves together, and stood for their lives, and had
rest from their enemies, and slew of their
foes seventy and five thousand, [b]but they
laid not their hands on the prey,
17 On the thirteenth day of the month
Adar; and on the fourteenth day ʹof the
same rested they, and made it a day of
feasting and gladness.

The feast of Purim instituted

18 But the Jews that *were* at Shushan
assembled together [a]on the thirteenth
day thereof, and on the fourteenth
thereof; and on the fifteenth *day* of the
same they rested, and made it a day of
feasting and gladness.
19 Therefore the Jews of the villages,
that dwelt in the unwalled towns, made

10 [a]ch. 5:11; Job 18:19 & 27:13-15; Ps. 21:10 [b]See ch. 8:11
11 ʹHeb. *came*
12 [a]ch. 5:6 & 7:2
13 [a]ch. 8:11 [b]2 Sam. 21:6,9 ʹHeb. *let men hang*
15 [a]ver. 2 & ch. 8:11 [b]ver. 10
16 [a]ver. 2 & ch. 8:11 [b]See ch. 8:11
17 ʹHeb. *in it*
18 [a]ver. 11,15
19 [a]Deut. 16:11, 14 [b]ch. 8:17 [c]ver. 22; Neh. 8:10,12
22 [a]ver. 19 & Neh. 8:10
24 [a]ch. 3:6,7 ʹHeb. *crush*
25 [a]ver. 13,14; ch. 7:5 & 8:3 [b]ch. 7:10; Ps. 7:16 ʹHeb. *when she came*
26 [a]ver. 20 ʹi.e. *Lot*
27 [a]ch. 8:17; Is. 56:3,6; Zech. 2:11 ʹHeb. *pass*
28 ʹHeb. *pass* [2]Heb. *be ended*
29 [a]ch. 2:15

the fourteenth day of the month Adar [a]*a
day of* gladness and feasting, [b]and a good
day, and of [c]sending portions one to another.
20 ¶ And Mordecai wrote these things,
and sent letters unto all the Jews that
were in all the provinces of the king
Ahasuerus, *both* nigh and far,
21 To stablish *this* among them, that
they should keep the fourteenth day of
the month Adar, and the fifteenth day of
the same, yearly,
22 As the days wherein the Jews
rested from their enemies, and the
month which was turned unto them from
sorrow to joy, and from mourning into a
good day: that they should make them
days of feasting and joy, and of [a]sending
portions one to another, and gifts to the
poor.
23 And the Jews undertook to do as
they had begun, and as Mordecai had
written unto them;
24 Because Haman the son of Hammedatha, the Agagite, the enemy of all the
Jews, [a]had devised against the Jews to
destroy them, and had cast Pur, that *is,*
the lot, to ʹconsume them, and to destroy
them;
25 But [a]whenʹ *Esther* came before the
king, he commanded by letters that his
wicked device, which he devised against
the Jews, should [b]return upon his own
head, and that he and his sons should be
hanged on the gallows.
26 Wherefore they called these days
Purim after the name of ʹPur. Therefore
for all the words of [a]this letter, and *of
that* which they had seen concerning
this matter, and which had come unto
them,
27 The Jews ordained, and took upon
them, and upon their seed, and upon all
such as [a]joined themselves unto them, so
as it should not ʹfail, that they would
keep these two days according to their
writing, and according to their *appointed*
time every year;
28 And *that* these days *should be* remembered and kept throughout every
generation, every family, every province,
and every city; and *that* these days of Purim should not ʹfail from among the Jews,
nor the memorial of them [2]perish from
their seed.
29 Then Esther the queen, [a]the daugh-

ter of Abihail, and Mordecai the Jew,
wrote with [/]all authority, to confirm this
[b]second letter of Purim.
30 And he sent the letters unto all the
Jews, to [a]the hundred twenty and seven
provinces of the kingdom of Ahasuerus,
with words of peace and truth,
31 To confirm these days of Purim in
their times *appointed,* according as Mordecai the Jew and Esther the queen had
enjoined them, and as they had decreed
[/]for themselves and for their seed, the
matters of [a]the fastings and their cry.
32 And the decree of Esther confirmed
these matters of Purim; and it was written in the book.

29 [b]See ch. 8:10 & ver. 20 [/]Heb. *all strength*

30 [a]ch. 1:1

31 [a]ch. 4:3,16 [/]Heb. *for their souls*

10:1 [a]Gen. 10:5; Ps. 72:10; Is. 24:15

2 [a]ch. 8:15 & 9:4 [/]Heb. *made him great*

3 [a]Gen. 41:40; 2 Chr. 28:7 [b]Neh. 2:10; Ps. 122:8,9

The greatness of Mordecai

10 AND THE king Ahasuerus laid a
tribute upon the land, and *upon*
[a]the isles of the sea.
2 And all the acts of his power and of
his might, and the declaration of the
greatness of Mordecai, [a]whereunto the
king [/]advanced him, *are* they not written
in the book of the chronicles of the kings
of Media and Persia?
3 For Mordecai the Jew *was* [a]next
unto king Ahasuerus, and great among
the Jews, and accepted of the multitude
of his brethren, [b]seeking the wealth of
his people, and speaking peace to all his
seed.

Job

Author: Unknown

Theme: The problem of human suffering

Date of Writing: Unknown

Outline of Job

I. Behind the Scenes of Job's Life (1:1—2:13)
II. Job's Dialogue With His Three Friends (3:1—27:23)
III. What Is Wisdom? (28:1–28)
IV. Job, Elihu and God Speak (29:1—42:6)
V. Job's Fortunes Restored (42:7–17)

ALTHOUGH THIS BOOK consists of the words of Job and his friends, Job himself was not the author. Jewish tradition suggests that Job was written before the time of Moses, but it may have been written as late as the time of Esther. Authorship is uncertain, but we can ascertain from the way the text is grammatically constructed that the writer was an Israelite sharing the story of a non-Israelite from Uz. Using unusual words and literary styles, this book is difficult to translate, but the overarching message of God's justice despite human suffering cannot be missed.

The dialogue between Job and his three friends forms the major part of the book. Job and his friends did not know about Satan's contest with God to test Job's reasons for his righteous lifestyle. Missing this vital piece of the puzzle, Job's friends proceeded to dissect Job's life, attitudes and actions to explain away Job's suffering. Despite his overwhelming losses, calamities and betrayal by his friends and family, Job continued in his complete devotion to God (see 1:6–22; 2:1—3:26). Though Job did eventually succumb to self-pity, he never attacked God or questioned his sovereignty but expressed his unshakable confidence in God's redemption (see 19:25).

The book also presents several clear Messianic passages (see 9:33; 16:19; 19:25; 33:23–24; 36:18) pointing the reader to an eternal hope of deliverance. Job acknowledges that though the righteous may suffer, God has a purpose in suffering that may be beyond human comprehension. It is the response of the righteous to merely trust and obey.

Job and his background

1 THERE WAS a man [a]in the land of Uz, whose name *was* [b]Job; and that man was [c]perfect and upright, and one that [d]feared God, and eschewed evil.

2 And there were born unto him seven sons and three daughters.

3 His [1]substance also was seven thousand sheep, and three thousand camels, and five hundred yoke of oxen, and five hundred she asses, and a very great [2]household; so that this man was the greatest of all the [3]men of the east.

4 And his sons went and feasted *in their* houses, every one his day; and sent and called for their three sisters to eat and to drink with them.

5 And it was so, when the days of *their* feasting were gone about, that Job sent and sanctified them, and rose up early in the morning, [a]and offered burnt offerings *according* to the number of them all: for Job said, It may be that my sons have sinned, and [b]cursed God in their hearts. Thus did Job [1]continually.

Satan permitted to tempt Job

6 ¶ Now [a]there was a day when the sons of God came to present themselves before the LORD, and [1]Satan came also [2]among them.

7 And the LORD said unto Satan, Whence comest thou? Then Satan answered the LORD, and said, From [a]going to and fro in the earth, and from walking up and down in it.

8 And the LORD said unto Satan, [1]Hast thou considered my servant Job, that *there is* none like him in the earth, a perfect and an upright man, one that feareth God, and escheweth evil?

U 9 Then Satan answered the LORD, and said, Doth Job fear God for nought?

K 10 [a]Hast not thou made an hedge
P about him, and about his house, and
about all that he hath on every side?
[b]thou hast blessed the work of his hands, and his [1]substance is increased in the land.

11 [a]But put forth thine hand now, and touch all that he hath, [1]and he will [b]curse thee to thy face.

12 And the LORD said unto Satan, Behold, all that he hath *is* in thy [a]power;[1] only upon himself put not forth thine hand. So Satan went forth from the presence of the LORD.

13 ¶ And there was a day [a]when his sons and his daughters *were* eating and drinking wine in their eldest brother's house:

14 And there came a messenger unto Job, and said, The oxen were plowing, and the asses feeding beside them:

15 And the Sabeans fell *upon them,* and took them away; yea, they have slain the servants with the edge of the sword; and I only am escaped alone to tell thee.

16 While he *was* yet speaking, there came also another, and said, [1]The fire of God is fallen from heaven, and hath burned up the sheep, and the servants, and consumed them; and I only am escaped alone to tell thee.

17 While he *was* yet speaking, there came also another, and said, The Chaldeans made out three bands, and [1]fell upon the camels, and have carried them away, yea, and slain the servants with the edge of the sword; and I only am escaped alone to tell thee.

18 While he *was* yet speaking, there came also another, and said, [a]Thy sons and thy daughters *were* eating and drinking wine in their eldest brother's house:

19 And, behold, there came a great wind [1]from the wilderness, and smote the four corners of the house, and it fell upon the young men, and they are dead; and I only am escaped alone to tell thee.

20 Then Job arose, [a]and rent his [1]mantle, and shaved his head, and [b]fell down upon the ground, and worshipped,

21 And said, [a]Naked came I out of my mother's womb, and naked shall I return thither: the LORD [b]gave, and the LORD hath J

1:1 [a] 1 Chr. 1:17 [b] Ezek. 14:14; Jas. 5:11 [c] Gen. 17:1 [d] Prov. 16:6
3 [1] Or, *cattle* [2] Or, *husbandry* [3] Heb. *sons of the east*
5 [a] ch. 42:8 [b] 1 Ki. 21:10 [1] Heb. *all the days*
6 [a] ch. 2:1 [1] Heb. *the Adversary* [2] Heb. *in the midst of them*
7 [a] 1 Pet. 5:8
8 [1] Heb. *Hast thou set thy heart on*
10 [a] Ps. 34:7; Is. 5:2 [b] Ps. 128:1,2; Prov. 10:22 [1] Or, *cattle*
11 [a] ch. 2:5 & 19:21 [b] Is. 8:21; Mal. 3:13,14 [1] Heb. *if he curse thee not to thy face*
12 [a] Gen. 16:6 [1] Heb. *hand*
13 [a] Eccl. 9:12
16 [1] Or, *A great fire*
17 [1] Heb. *rushed*
18 [a] ver. 4,13
19 [1] Heb. *from aside*
20 [a] Gen. 37:29; Ezra 9:3 [b] 1 Pet. 5:6 [1] Or, *robe*
21 [a] Ps. 49:17; Eccl. 5:15; 1 Tim. 6:7 [b] Eccl. 5:19; Jas. 1:17

U *Ne 1:5* ◀ ▶ *Job 8:6–7*
K *1Ch 29:11–12* ◀ ▶ *Job 17:9*
P *2Ch 32:29* ◀ ▶ *Job 22:24–25*
J *Ne 8:10* ◀ ▶ *Job 13:15*

1:6–7 Satan, the chief of the fallen angels, "walketh about, seeking whom he may devour" (1Pe 5:8). Satan's freedom will end when Christ casts him into the bottomless pit for a thousand years following the defeat of the antichrist at the end of the Battle of Armageddon (see Rev 20:1–3).

[c]taken away; [d]blessed be the name of the
LORD.
22 [a]In all this Job sinned not, nor
[l]charged God foolishly.

Satan's second request of God

2 AGAIN [a]THERE was a day when the
sons of God came to present themselves before the LORD, and Satan came
also among them to present himself before the LORD.
2 And the LORD said unto Satan, From
whence comest thou? And [a]Satan answered the LORD, and said, From going to
and fro in the earth, and from walking up
and down in it.
3 And the LORD said unto Satan, Hast
thou considered my servant Job, that
there is none like him in the earth, [a]a
perfect and an upright man, one that feareth God, and escheweth evil? and still he
[b]holdeth fast his integrity, although thou
movedst me against him, [c]to[l] destroy
him without cause.
4 And Satan answered the LORD, and
said, Skin for skin, yea, all that a man
hath will he give for his life.
5 [a]But put forth thine hand now, and
touch his [b]bone and his flesh, and he will
curse thee to thy face.
6 [a]And the LORD said unto Satan, Behold, he *is* in thine hand; [l]but save his
life.
D 7 ¶ So went Satan forth from the presence of the LORD, and smote Job with sore
boils [a]from the sole of his foot unto his
crown.
8 And he took him a potsherd to
scrape himself withal; [a]and he sat down
among the ashes.
9 ¶ Then said his wife unto him, Dost
thou still retain thine integrity? curse
God, and die.
10 But he said unto her, Thou speakest
as one of the foolish women speaketh.
What? [a]shall we receive good at the hand
of God, and shall we not receive evil? [b]In
all this did not Job [c]sin with his lips.

The friends of Job

11 ¶ Now when Job's three friends
heard of all this evil that was come upon
him, they came every one from his own
place; Eliphaz the [a]Temanite, and Bildad
the [b]Shuhite, and Zophar the Naama-

D 2Ch 26:19–21 ◀ ▶ Job 33:17–22

21 [c]Gen. 31:16 [d]Eph. 5:20; 1 Thes. 5:18
22 [a]ch. 2:10 [l]Or, *attributed folly to God*
2:1 [a]ch. 1:6
2 [a]ch. 1:7
3 [a]ch. 1:1,8 [b]ch. 27:5,6 [c]ch. 9:17 [l]Heb. *to swallow him up*
5 [a]ch. 1:11 [b]ch. 19:20
6 [a]ch. 1:12 [l]Or, *only*
7 [a]Is. 1:6
8 [a]2 Sam. 13:19; ch. 42:6; Ezek. 27:30; Mat. 11:21
10 [a]ch. 1:21; Heb. 12:6; Jas. 5:10,11 [b]ch. 1:22 [c]Ps. 39:1
11 [a]Gen. 36:11; Jer. 49:7 [b]Gen. 25:2 [c]ch. 42:11; Rom. 12:15
12 [a]Neh. 9:1; Lam. 2:10; Ezek. 27:30
13 [a]Gen. 50:10
3:2 [l]Heb. *answered*
3 [a]Jer. 20:14
5 [a]ch. 10:21; Jer. 13:16; Amos 5:8 [l]Or, *challenge it*
6 [l]Or, *let it not rejoice among the days*
8 [a]Jer. 9:17 [l]Or, *a leviathan*
9 [l]Heb. *the eyelids of the morning;* see ch. 41:18
11 [a]ch. 10:18
12 [a]Gen. 30:3
14 [a]ch. 15:28
16 [a]Ps. 58:8

thite: for they had made an appointment
together to come [c]to mourn with him
and to comfort him.
12 And when they lifted up their eyes
afar off, and knew him not, they lifted up
their voice, and wept; and they rent every one his mantle, and [a]sprinkled dust
upon their heads toward heaven.
13 So they sat down with him upon
the ground [a]seven days and seven nights,
and none spake a word unto him: for they
saw that *his* grief was very great.

The speech of Job

3 AFTER THIS opened Job his mouth,
and cursed his day.
2 And Job [l]spake, and said,
3 [a]Let the day perish wherein I was
born, and the night *in which* it was said,
There is a man child conceived.
4 Let that day be darkness; let not God
regard it from above, neither let the light
shine upon it.
5 Let darkness and [a]the shadow of
death [l]stain it; let a cloud dwell upon it;
let the blackness of the day terrify it.
6 *As for* that night, let darkness seize
upon it; [l]let it not be joined unto the days
of the year, let it not come into the number of the months.
7 Lo, let that night be solitary, let no
joyful voice come therein.
8 Let them curse it that curse the day,
[a]who are ready to raise up [l]their
mourning.
9 Let the stars of the twilight thereof
be dark; let it look for light, but *have*
none; neither let it see [l]the dawning of
the day:
10 Because it shut not up the doors of
my *mother's* womb, nor hid sorrow from
mine eyes.
11 [a]Why died I not from the womb?
why did I *not* give up the ghost when I
came out of the belly?
12 [a]Why did the knees prevent me? or
why the breasts that I should suck?
13 For now should I have lain still and
been quiet, I should have slept: then had
I been at rest,
14 With kings and counsellors of the
earth, which [a]built desolate places for
themselves;
15 Or with princes that had gold, who
filled their houses with silver:
16 Or [a]as an hidden untimely birth I

had not been; as infants *which* never saw light.

17 There the wicked cease *from* troubling; and there the [1]weary be at rest.

18 *There* the prisoners rest together; [a]they hear not the voice of the oppressor.

19 The small and great are there; and the servant *is* free from his master.

20 [a]Wherefore is light given to him that is in misery, and life unto the [b]bitter *in* soul;

21 Which [a]long[1] for death, but it *cometh* not; and dig for it more than [b]for hid treasures;

22 Which rejoice exceedingly, *and* are glad, when they can find the grave?

23 *Why is light given* to a man whose way is hid, [a]and whom God hath hedged in?

24 For my sighing cometh [1]before I eat, and my roarings are poured out like the waters.

25 For [1]the thing which I greatly feared is come upon me, and that which I was afraid of is come unto me.

26 I was not in safety, neither had I rest, neither was I quiet; yet trouble came.

The speech of Eliphaz

4 THEN ELIPHAZ the Temanite answered and said,

2 *If* we assay [1]to commune with thee, wilt thou be grieved? but [2]who can withhold himself from speaking?

3 Behold, thou hast instructed many, and thou [a]hast strengthened the weak hands.

4 Thy words have upholden him that was falling, and thou [a]hast strengthened [b]the[1] feeble knees.

5 But now it is come upon thee, and thou faintest; it toucheth thee, and thou art troubled.

6 *Is* not *this* [a]thy fear, [b]thy confidence, thy hope, and the uprightness of thy ways?

7 Remember, I pray thee, [a]who *ever* perished, being innocent? or where were the righteous cut off ?

H 8 Even as I have seen, [a]they that plow
S iniquity, and sow wickedness, reap the same.

9 By the blast of God they perish, and [1]by the breath of his nostrils are they consumed.

10 The roaring of the lion, and the voice of the fierce lion, and [a]the teeth of the young lions, are broken.

11 [a]The old lion perisheth for lack of prey, and the stout lion's whelps are scattered abroad.

12 Now a thing was [1]secretly brought to me, and mine ear received a little thereof.

13 [a]In thoughts from the visions of the night, when deep sleep falleth on men,

14 Fear [1]came upon me, and [a]trembling, which made [2]all my bones to shake. E

15 Then a spirit passed before my face; the hair of my flesh stood up:

16 It stood still, but I could not discern the form thereof: an image *was* before mine eyes, [1]*there was* silence, and I heard a voice, *saying,*

17 Shall mortal man be more just than God? shall a man be more pure than his maker?

18 Behold, he [a]put no trust in his servants; [1]and his angels he charged with folly:

19 How much less *in* them that dwell in houses of clay, whose foundation *is* in the dust, *which* are crushed before the moth? N

20 [a]They are [1]destroyed from morning to evening: they perish for ever without any regarding *it.*

21 Doth not their excellency *which is* in them go away? they die, even without wisdom.

5 CALL NOW, if there be any that will answer thee; and to which of the saints wilt thou [1]turn?

2 For wrath killeth the foolish man, and [1]envy slayeth the silly one.

3 [a]I have seen the foolish taking root: but suddenly I cursed his habitation.

4 His children are far from safety, and they are crushed in the gate, neither *is there* any to deliver *them.*

5 Whose harvest the hungry eateth up, and taketh it even out of the thorns, and the robber swalloweth up their substance.

6 Although [1]affliction cometh not forth

17 [1]Heb. *wearied in strength*
18 [a]ch. 39:7
20 [a]Jer. 20:18 [b]2 Ki. 4:27
21 [a]Rev. 9:6 [b]Prov. 2:4 [1]Heb. *wait*
23 [a]Lam. 3:7
24 [1]Heb. *before my meat*
25 [1]Heb. *I feared a fear, and it came upon me*
4:2 [1]Heb. *a word* [2]Heb. *who can refrain from words?*
3 [a]Is. 35:3
4 [a]Is. 35:3 [b]Heb. 12:12 [1]Heb. *the bowing knees*
6 [a]ch. 1:1 [b]Prov. 3:26
7 [a]Ps. 37:25
8 [a]Prov. 22:8
9 [1]i.e. *by his anger* as Is. 30:33
10 [a]Ps. 58:6
11 [a]Ps. 34:10
12 [1]Heb. *by stealth*
13 [a]ch. 33:15
14 [a]Hab. 3:16 [1]Heb. *met me* [2]Heb. *the multitude of my bones*
16 [1]Or, *I heard a still voice*
18 [a]ch. 15:15 [1]Or, *nor in his angels,* in whom *he put light*
20 [a]Ps. 90:5,6 [1]Heb. *beaten in pieces*
5:1 [1]Or, *look?*
2 [1]Or, *indignation*
3 [a]Jer. 12:2,3
6 [1]Or, *iniquity*

H *Ezr 8:22* ◀▶ *Job 8:22*
S *Ezr 8:28* ◀▶ *Job 8:20*
E *2Ch 16:9* ◀▶ *Job 14:16–17*
N *Ne 9:29–30* ◀▶ *Job 7:1*

of the dust, neither doth trouble spring out of the ground;

7 Yet man is born unto [1]trouble, as [2]the sparks fly upward.

8 I would seek unto God, and unto God would I commit my cause:

9 Which doeth great things [1]and unsearchable; marvellous things [2]without number:

10 Who giveth rain upon the earth, and sendeth waters upon the [1]fields:

11 [a]To set up on high those that be low; that those which mourn may be exalted to safety.

12 [a]He disappointeth the devices of the crafty, so that their hands [1]cannot perform *their* enterprise.

C 13 He taketh the wise in their own craftiness: and the counsel of the froward is carried headlong.

14 They [1]meet with darkness in the daytime, and grope in the noonday as in the night.

15 But [a]he saveth the poor from the sword, from their mouth, and from the hand of the mighty.

16 [a]So the poor hath hope, and iniquity stoppeth her mouth.

L 17 [a]Behold, happy *is* the man whom
T God correcteth: therefore despise not thou the chastening of the Almighty:

18 [a]For he maketh sore, and bindeth up: he woundeth, and his hands make whole.

19 [a]He shall deliver thee in six troubles: yea, in seven [b]there shall no evil touch thee.

F 20 [a]In famine he shall redeem thee
V from death: and in war [1]from the power of the sword.

21 [a]Thou shalt be hid [1]from the scourge of the tongue: neither shalt thou be afraid of destruction when it cometh.

22 At destruction and famine thou shalt laugh: [a]neither shalt thou be afraid of the beasts of the earth.

23 [a]For thou shalt be in league with the stones of the field: and the beasts of the field shall be at peace with thee.

24 And thou shalt know [1]that thy tabernacle *shall be* in peace; and thou shalt visit thy habitation, and shalt not [2]sin.

25 Thou shalt know also that [a]thy seed *shall be* [1]great, and thine offspring [b]as the grass of the earth.

26 [a]Thou shalt come to *thy* grave in a full age, like as a shock of corn [1]cometh in in his season. H

27 Lo this, we have [a]searched it, so it *is;* hear it, and know thou *it* [1]for thy good.

Job's reply

6 BUT JOB answered and said,

2 Oh that my grief were thoroughly weighed, and my calamity [1]laid in the balances together!

3 For now it would be heavier than the sand of the sea: therefore [1]my words are swallowed up.

4 [a]For the arrows of the Almighty *are* within me, the poison whereof drinketh up my spirit: [b]the terrors of God do set themselves in array against me.

5 Doth the wild ass bray [1]when he hath grass? or loweth the ox over his fodder?

6 Can that which is unsavoury be eaten without salt? or is there *any* taste in the white of an egg?

7 The things *that* my soul refused to touch *are* as my sorrowful meat.

8 Oh that I might have my request; and that God would grant *me* [1]the thing that I long for!

9 Even that it would please God to destroy me; that he would let loose his hand, and cut me off!

10 Then should I yet have comfort; yea, I would harden myself in sorrow: let him not spare; for [a]I have not concealed the words of [b]the Holy One.

11 What *is* my strength, that I should hope? and what *is* mine end, that I should prolong my life?

12 *Is* my strength the strength of stones? or *is* my flesh [1]of brass?

13 *Is* not my help in me? and is wisdom driven quite from me?

14 [a]To[1] him that is afflicted pity *should be shown* from his friend; but he forsaketh the fear of the Almighty.

15 [a]My brethren have dealt deceitfully as a brook, *and* [b]as the stream of brooks they pass away;

7 [1]Or, *labour* [2]Heb. *the sons of the burning coal lift up to fly*
9 [1]Heb. *and there is no search* [2]Heb. *till there be no number*
10 [1]Heb. *outplaces*
11 [a]Ps. 113:7
12 [a]Neh. 4:15 [1]Or, *cannot perform any thing*
14 [1]Or, *run into*
15 [a]Ps. 35:10
16 [a]1 Sam. 2:8
17 [a]Ps. 94:12
18 [a]1 Sam. 2:6
19 [a]Ps. 34:19 [b]Ps. 91:10
20 [a]Ps. 33:19 [1]Heb. *from the hands*
21 [a]Ps. 31:20 [1]Or, *when the tongue scourgeth*
22 [a]Is. 11:9
23 [a]Ps. 91:12
24 [1]Or, *that peace is thy tabernacle* [2]Or, *err*
25 [a]Ps. 112:2 [b]Ps. 72:16 [1]Or, *much*
26 [a]Prov. 10:27 [1]Heb. *ascendeth*
27 [a]Ps. 111:2 [1]Heb. *for thyself*
6:2 [1]Heb. *lifted up*
3 [1]i.e. *I want words to express my grief*
4 [a]Ps. 38:2 [b]Ps. 88:15
5 [1]Heb. *at grass*
8 [1]Heb. *my expectation*
10 [a]Acts 20:20 [b]Lev. 19:2; Is. 57:15
12 [1]Heb. *brasen?*
14 [a]Prov. 17:17 [1]Heb. *To him that melteth*
15 [a]Ps. 38:11 [b]Jer. 15:18

C *Ne 9:16–17* ◀▶ *Job 6:18*
L *Est 8:16* ◀▶ *Ps 13:6*
T *2Sa 7:14* ◀▶ *Job 23:10*
F *Ne 9:20–21* ◀▶ *Ps 22:26*
V *Ne 4:20* ◀▶ *Ps 3:5–6*
H *2Ch 20:9* ◀▶ *Job 33:23–30*

16 Which are blackish by reason of the ice, *and* wherein the snow is hid:

17 What time they wax warm, [1]they vanish: [2]when it is hot, they are [3]consumed out of their place.

C 18 The paths of their way are turned aside; they go to nothing, and perish.

19 The troops of [a]Tema looked, the companies of [b]Sheba waited for them.

20 They were [a]confounded because they had hoped; they came thither, and were ashamed.

21 [1]For now [a]ye are [2]nothing; ye see *my* casting down, and [b]are afraid.

22 Did I say, Bring unto me? or, Give a reward for me of your substance?

23 Or, Deliver me from the enemy's hand? or, Redeem me from the hand of the mighty?

24 Teach me, and I will hold my tongue: and cause me to understand wherein I have erred.

25 How forcible are right words! but what doth your arguing reprove?

26 Do ye imagine to reprove words, and the speeches of one that is desperate, *which are* as wind?

27 Yea, [1]ye overwhelm the fatherless, and ye [a]dig *a pit* for your friend.

28 Now therefore be content, look upon me; for *it is* [1]evident unto you if I lie.

29 [a]Return, I pray you, let it not be iniquity; yea, return again, my righteousness *is* [1]in it.

30 Is there iniquity in my tongue? cannot [1]my taste discern perverse things?

N **7** *IS THERE* not [a]an[1] appointed time to man upon earth? *are not* his days also like the days of an hireling?

2 As a servant [1]earnestly desireth the shadow, and as an hireling looketh for *the reward of* his work:

3 So am I made to possess [a]months of vanity, and wearisome nights are appointed to me.

4 [a]When I lie down, I say, When shall I arise, and [1]the night be gone? and I am full of tossings to and fro unto the dawning of the day.

5 My flesh is [a]clothed with worms and clods of dust; my skin is broken, and become loathsome.

6 [a]My days are swifter than a weaver's shuttle, and are spent without hope.

7 O remember that [a]my life *is* wind: mine eye [1]shall no more [2]see good.

8 [a]The eye of him that hath seen me shall see me no *more:* thine eyes *are* upon me, and [1]I *am* not.

9 *As* the cloud is consumed and vanisheth away: so [a]he that goeth down to the grave shall come up no *more.*

10 He shall return no more to his house, [a]neither shall his place know him any more.

11 Therefore I will [a]not refrain my mouth; I will speak in the anguish of my spirit; I will [b]complain in the bitterness of my soul.

12 *Am* I a sea, or a whale, that thou settest a watch over me?

13 [a]When I say, My bed shall comfort me, my couch shall ease my complaint;

14 Then thou scarest me with dreams, and terrifiest me through visions:

15 So that my soul chooseth strangling, *and* death rather [1]than my life.

16 [a]I loathe *it;* I would not live always: [b]let me alone; for [c]my days *are* vanity.

17 [a]What *is* man, that thou shouldest magnify him? and that thou shouldest set thine heart upon him?

18 And *that* thou shouldest visit him every morning, *and* try him every moment?

19 How long wilt thou not depart from me, nor let me alone till I swallow down my spittle?

20 I have sinned; what shall I do unto thee, [a]O thou preserver of men? why [b]hast thou set me as a mark against thee, so that I am a burden to myself?

21 And why dost thou not pardon my transgression, and take away mine iniquity? for now shall I sleep in the dust; and thou shalt seek me in the morning, but I *shall* not *be.*

17 [1]Heb. *they are cut off* [2]Heb. *in the heat thereof* [3]Heb. *extinguished*
19 [a]Gen. 25:15 [b]Ps. 72:10
20 [a]Jer. 14:3
21 [a]ch. 13:4 [b]Ps. 38:11 [1]Or, *For now ye are like to them* Heb. *to it* [2]Heb. *not*
27 [a]Ps. 57:6 [1]Heb. *ye cause to fall upon*
28 [1]Heb. *before your face*
29 [a]ch. 17:10 [1]i.e. *in this matter*
30 [1]Heb. *my palate*
7:1 [a]ch. 14:5 [1]Or, *a warfare*
2 [1]Heb. *gapeth after*
3 [a]ch. 29:2
4 [a]Deut. 28:67 [1]Heb. *the evening be measured?*
5 [a]Is. 14:11
6 [a]ch. 9:25
7 [a]Ps. 78:39 [1]Heb. *shall not return* [2]*to see,* i.e. *to enjoy*
8 [a]ch. 20:9 [1]i.e. *I can live no longer*
9 [a]2 Sam. 12:23
10 [a]ch. 8:18
11 [a]Ps. 39:1,9 [b]1 Sam. 1:10
13 [a]ch. 9:27
15 [1]Heb. *than my bones*
16 [a]ch. 10:1 [b]ch. 14:6 [c]Ps. 62:9
17 [a]Ps. 8:4
20 [a]Ps. 36:6 [b]Ps. 21:12; Lam. 3:12

C *Job 5:13–14* ◀ ▶ *Job 15:16*
N *Job 4:19–20* ◀ ▶ *Job 8:9*

7:1–3 These verses indicate that God is in charge of the destiny of every one of us (see Ps 31:15; Ac 17:26).

The speech of Bildad

8 THEN ANSWERED Bildad the Shuhite, and said,

2 How long wilt thou speak these *things?* and *how long shall* the words of thy mouth *be like* a strong wind?

3 [a]Doth God pervert judgment? or doth the Almighty pervert justice?

4 If [a]thy children have sinned against him, and he have cast them away [l]for their transgression;

5 [a]If thou wouldest seek unto God betimes, and make thy supplication to the Almighty;

U 6 If thou *wert* pure and upright; surely now he would awake for thee, and make the habitation of thy righteousness prosperous.

7 Though thy beginning was small, yet thy latter end should greatly increase.

8 [a]For inquire, I pray thee, of the former age, and prepare thyself to the search of their fathers:

N 9 (For [a]we *are but of* yesterday, and know [l]nothing, because our days upon earth *are* a shadow:)

10 Shall not they teach thee, *and* tell thee, and utter words out of their heart?

G 11 Can the rush grow up without
O mire? can the flag grow without water?

12 [a]Whilst it *is* yet in his greenness, *and* not cut down, it withereth before any *other* herb.

13 So *are* the paths of all that forget God; and the [a]hypocrite's hope shall perish:

14 Whose hope shall be cut off, and whose trust *shall be* [a]a[l] spider's web.

15 [a]He shall lean upon his house, but it shall not stand: he shall hold it fast, but it shall not endure.

16 He *is* green before the sun, and his branch shooteth forth in his garden.

17 His roots are wrapped about the heap, *and* seeth the place of stones.

18 [a]If he destroy him from his place, then *it* shall deny him, *saying,* I have not seen thee.

19 Behold, this *is* the joy of his way, and [a]out of the earth shall others grow.

S 20 Behold, God will not cast away a perfect *man,* neither will he [l]help the evil doers:

21 Till he fill thy mouth with laughing, and thy lips with [l]rejoicing.

22 They that hate thee shall be [a]clothed with shame; and the dwelling-place of the wicked [l]shall come to nought. H

Job's reply

9 THEN JOB answered and said,

2 I know *it is* so of a truth: but how should [a]man be just [l]with God? N

3 If he will contend with him, he cannot answer him one of a thousand.

4 [a]*He is* wise in heart, and mighty in strength: who hath hardened *himself* against him, and hath prospered? H

5 Which removeth the mountains, and they know not: which overturneth them in his anger.

6 Which [a]shaketh the earth out of her place, and [b]the pillars thereof tremble.

7 Which commandeth the sun, and it riseth not; and sealeth up the stars.

8 [a]Which alone spreadeth out the heavens, and treadeth upon the [l]waves of the sea.

9 [a]Which maketh [l]Arcturus, Orion, and Pleiades, and the chambers of the south.

10 [a]Which doeth great things past finding out; yea, and wonders without number.

11 [a]Lo, he goeth by me, and I see *him* not: he passeth on also, but I perceive him not.

12 [a]Behold, he taketh away, [b]who[l] can hinder him? who will say unto him, What doest thou?

13 *If* God will not withdraw his anger, [a]the [l]proud helpers do stoop under him.

14 How much less shall I answer him, *and* choose out my words *to reason* with him?

15 [a]Whom, though I were righteous, *yet* would I not answer, *but* I would make supplication to my judge.

16 If I had called, and he had answered me; *yet* would I not believe that he had hearkened unto my voice.

17 For he breaketh me with a tempest,

8:3 [a]Gen. 18:25
4 [a]ch. 1:5,18 [l]Heb. *in the hand of their transgression*
5 [a]ch. 11:13
8 [a]Deut. 4:32
9 [a]Gen. 47:9; 1 Chr. 29:15; ch. 7:6 [l]Heb. *not*
12 [a]Ps. 129:6; Jer. 17:6
13 [a]ch. 11:20; Prov. 10:28
14 [a]Is. 59:5,6 [l]Heb. *a spider's house*
15 [a]ch. 27:18
18 [a]ch. 7:10; Ps. 37:36
19 [a]Ps. 113:7
20 [l]Heb. *take the ungodly by the hand*
21 [l]Heb. *shouting for joy*
22 [a]Ps. 35:26 & 109:29 [l]Heb. *shall not be*
9:2 [a]Ps. 143:2; Rom. 3:20 [l]Or, *before God?*
4 [a]ch. 36:5
6 [a]Is. 2:19,21; Hag. 2:6; Heb. 12:26 [b]ch. 26:11
8 [a]Gen. 1:6; Ps. 104:2,3 [l]Heb. *heights*
9 [a]Gen. 1:16; Amos 5:8 [l]Heb. *Ash, Cesil, and Cimah*
10 [a]Ps. 71:15
11 [a]ch. 23:8,9
12 [a]Is. 45:9; Jer. 18:6; Rom. 9:20 [b]ch. 11:10 [l]Heb. *who can turn him away?*
13 [a]ch. 26:12 [l]Heb. *helpers of pride,* or, *strength*
15 [a]ch. 10:15

U *Job 1:9–10* ◀ ▶ *Job 17:9*
N *Job 7:1* ◀ ▶ *Job 9:2–4*
G *1Sa 16:7* ◀ ▶ *Job 9:20*
O *1Ch 17:20* ◀ ▶ *Ps 3:8*
S *Job 4:8* ◀ ▶ *Job 11:14*
H *Job 4:8–9* ◀ ▶ *Job 9:4*
N *Job 8:9* ◀ ▶ *Job 11:20*
H *Job 8:22* ◀ ▶ *Job 10:14*

and multiplieth my wounds [a]without cause.

18 He will not suffer me to take my breath, but filleth me with bitterness.

19 If *I speak* of strength, lo, *he is* strong: and if of judgment, who shall set me a time *to plead?*

G 20 If I justify myself, mine own mouth shall condemn me: *if I say,* I *am* perfect, it shall also prove me perverse.

21 *Though* I *were* perfect, *yet* would I not know my soul: I would despise my life.

22 This *is* one *thing,* therefore I said *it,* [a]He destroyeth the perfect and the wicked.

23 If the scourge slay suddenly, he will laugh at the trial of the innocent.

24 The earth is given into the hand of the wicked: he covereth the faces of the judges thereof; if not, where, *and* who *is* he?

25 Now [a]my days are swifter than a post: they flee away, they see no good.

26 They are passed away as the [1,2]swift ships: [a]as the eagle *that* hasteth to the prey.

27 [a]If I say, I will forget my complaint, I will leave off my heaviness, and comfort *myself:*

28 [a]I am afraid of all my sorrows, I know that thou [b]wilt not hold me innocent.

G 29 *If* I be wicked, why then labour I in vain?

30 [a]If I wash myself with snow water, and make my hands never so clean;

31 Yet shalt thou plunge me in the ditch, and mine own clothes shall [1]abhor me.

32 For [a]*he is* not a man, as I *am, that* I should answer him, *and* we should come together in judgment.

33 [a]Neither is there [1]any [2]daysman betwixt us, *that* might lay his hand upon us both.

34 [a]Let him take his rod away from me, and let not his fear terrify me:

35 *Then* would I speak, and not fear him; [1]but *it is* not so with me.

10 MY [a]SOUL is [1]weary of my life; I will leave my complaint upon myself; [b]I will speak in the bitterness of my soul.

2 I will say unto God, Do not condemn me; show me wherefore thou contendest with me.

3 *Is it* good unto thee that thou shouldest oppress, that thou shouldest despise [1]the work of thine hands, and shine upon the counsel of the wicked?

4 Hast thou eyes of flesh? or [a]seest thou as man seeth?

5 *Are* thy days as the days of man? *are* thy years as man's days,

6 That thou inquirest after mine iniquity, and searchest after my sin?

7 [1]Thou knowest that I am not wicked; and *there is* none that can deliver out of thine hand.

8 [a]Thine hands [1]have made me and fashioned me together round about; yet thou dost destroy me.

9 Remember, I beseech thee, that [a]thou hast made me as the clay; and wilt thou bring me into dust again?

10 [a]Hast thou not poured me out as milk, and curdled me like cheese?

11 Thou hast clothed me with skin and flesh, and hast [1]fenced me with bones and sinews.

12 Thou hast granted me life and favour, and thy visitation hath preserved my spirit.

13 And these *things* hast thou hid in thine heart: I know that this *is* with thee.

14 If I sin, then [a]thou markest me, and thou wilt not acquit me from mine iniquity. H

15 If I be wicked, [a]woe unto me; [b]and *if* I be righteous, *yet* will I not lift up my head. *I am* full of confusion; therefore [c]see thou mine affliction;

16 For it increaseth. [a]Thou huntest me as a fierce lion: and again thou showest thyself marvellous upon me.

17 Thou renewest [a]thy[1] witnesses against me, and increasest thine indignation upon me; changes and war *are* against me.

18 [a]Wherefore then hast thou brought me forth out of the womb? Oh that I had given up the ghost, and no eye had seen me!

19 I should have been as though I had not been; I should have been carried from the womb to the grave.

20 [a]*Are* not my days few? cease *then,*

G *Job 8:11–16* ◀ ▶ *Job 9:29–31*
G *Job 9:20* ◀ ▶ *Job 15:12*
H *Job 9:4* ◀ ▶ *Job 11:20*

17 [a]ch. 2:3
22 [a]Eccl. 9:2,3; Ezek. 21:3
25 [a]ch. 7:6,7
26 [a]Hab. 1:8 [1]Heb. *ships of desire* [2]Or, *ships of Ebeh*
27 [a]ch. 7:13
28 [a]Ps. 119:120 [b]Ex. 20:7
30 [a]Jer. 2:22
31 [1]Or, *make me to be abhorred*
32 [a]Eccl. 6:10; Is. 45:9; Rom. 9:20
33 [a]1 Sam. 2:25 [1]Heb. *one that should argue* [2]Or, *umpire*
34 [a]ch. 13:20; Ps. 39:10
35 [1]Heb. *but I am not so with myself*
10:1 [a]1 Ki. 19:4; Jonah 4:3 [b]ch. 7:11 [1]Or, *cut off while I live*
3 [1]Heb. *the labour of thine hands*
4 [a]1 Sam. 16:7
7 [1]Heb. *It is upon thy knowledge*
8 [a]Ps. 119:73 [1]Heb. *took pains about me*
9 [a]Gen. 2:7; Is. 64:8
10 [a]Ps. 139:14-16
11 [1]Heb. *hedged*
14 [a]Ps. 139:1
15 [a]Is. 3:11 [b]ch. 9:12,15 [c]Ps. 25:18
16 [a]Is. 38:13; Lam. 3:10
17 [a]Ruth 1:21 [1]i.e. *thy plagues*
18 [a]ch. 3:11
20 [a]Ps. 39:5

and [b]let me alone, that I may take comfort a little,
21 Before I go *whence* I shall not return, [a]*even* to the land of darkness [b]and
the shadow of death;
22 A land of darkness, as darkness *itself; and* of the shadow of death, without
any order, and *where* the light *is* as darkness.

The speech of Zophar

11 THEN ANSWERED Zophar the
Naamathite, and said,
2 Should not the multitude of words be
answered? and should [1]a man full of talk
be justified?
3 Should thy [1]lies make men hold their
peace? and when thou mockest, shall no
man make thee ashamed?
4 For [a]thou hast said, My doctrine *is*
pure, and I am clean in thine eyes.
5 But oh that God would speak, and
open his lips against thee;
6 And that he would show thee the secrets of wisdom, that *they are* double to
that which is! Know therefore that [a]God
exacteth of thee *less* than thine iniquity
deserveth.
7 [a]Canst thou by searching find out
God? canst thou find out the Almighty
unto perfection?
8 *It is* [1]as high as heaven; what canst
thou do? deeper than hell; what canst
thou know?
9 The measure thereof *is* longer than
the earth, and broader than the sea.
10 [a]If he [1]cut off, and shut up, or
gather together, then [2]who can hinder
him?
11 For [a]he knoweth vain men: he
seeth wickedness also; will he not then
consider *it?*
12 For [a]vain[1] man would be wise,
though man be born *like* a wild ass's colt.
R 13 If thou [a]prepare thine heart, and
[b]stretch out thine hands toward him;
S 14 If iniquity *be* in thine hand, put it
far away, and [a]let not wickedness dwell
in thy tabernacles.
15 [a]For then shalt thou lift up thy face
without spot; yea, thou shalt be stedfast,
and shalt not fear:
16 Because thou shalt [a]forget *thy* misery, *and* remember *it* as waters *that* pass
away:
17 And *thine* age [a]shall[1] be clearer
than the noonday; thou shalt shine forth,
thou shalt be as the morning.
18 And thou shalt be secure, because
there is hope; yea, thou shalt dig *about
thee, and* [a]thou shalt take thy rest in
safety.
19 Also thou shalt lie down, and none
shall make *thee* afraid; yea, many shall
[1]make suit unto thee.
20 But [a]the eyes of the wicked shall H
fail, and [1]they shall not escape, and [b]their N
hope *shall be as* [2]the giving up of the
ghost.

Job's reply

12 AND JOB answered and said,
2 No doubt but ye *are* the people,
and wisdom shall die with you.
3 But I have [1]understanding as well as
you; [2]I *am* not inferior to you: yea, [3]who
knoweth not such things as these?
4 [a]I am *as* one mocked of his neighbour, who [b]calleth upon God, and he answereth him: the just upright *man is*
laughed to scorn.
5 [a]He that is ready to slip with *his* feet
is as a lamp despised in the thought of
him that is at ease.
6 [a]The tabernacles of robbers prosper,
and they that provoke God are secure;
into whose hand God bringeth *abundantly.*
7 But ask now the beasts, and they
shall teach thee; and the fowls of the air,
and they shall tell thee:
8 Or speak to the earth, and it shall
teach thee: and the fishes of the sea shall
declare unto thee.
9 Who knoweth not in all these that
the hand of the LORD hath wrought this?
10 In whose hand *is* the [1]soul of every
living thing, and the breath of [2]all
mankind.
11 Doth not the ear try words? and the
[a]mouth[1] taste his meat?
12 With the ancient *is* wisdom; and in
length of days understanding.
13 [1]With him *is* wisdom and strength,
he hath counsel and understanding.
14 Behold, he breaketh down, and it

20 [b]ch. 7:16,19
21 [a]Ps. 88:12 [b]Ps. 23:4
11:2 [1]Heb. *a man of lips*
3 [1]Or, *devices*
4 [a]ch. 6:30
6 [a]Ezra 9:13
7 [a]Eccl. 3:11
8 [1]Heb. *the heights of heaven*
10 [a]ch. 9:12; Rev. 3:7 [1]Or, *make a change* [2]Heb. *who can turn him away?*
11 [a]Ps. 10:14
12 [a]Rom. 1:22 [1]Heb. *empty*
13 [a]1 Sam. 7:3 [b]Ps. 88:9
14 [a]Ps. 101:3
15 [a]ch. 22:26; Ps. 119:6; 1 John 3:21
16 [a]Is. 65:16
17 [a]Ps. 37:6; Prov. 4:18; Is. 58:8,10 [1]Heb. *shall arise above the noonday*
18 [a]Lev. 26:5,6; Ps. 3:5; Prov. 3:24
19 [1]Heb. *entreat thy face*
20 [a]Lev. 26:16; Deut. 28:65 [b]ch. 18:14; Prov. 11:7 [1]Heb. *flight shall perish from them* [2]Or, *a puff of breath*
12:3 [1]Heb. *an heart* [2]Heb. *I fall not lower than you* [3]Heb. *with whom are not such as these?*
4 [a]ch. 21:3 [b]Ps. 91:15
5 [a]Prov. 14:2
6 [a]Jer. 12:1; Mal. 3:15
10 [1]Or, *life* [2]Heb. *all flesh of man*
11 [a]ch. 6:30 [1]Heb. *palate*
13 [1]i.e. *With God*

R *Ezr 10:11* ◄► *Job 31:33*
S *Job 8:20* ◄► *Job 17:9*
H *Job 10:14* ◄► *Job 15:23–26*
N *Job 9:2–4* ◄► *Job 15:12–13*

cannot be built again: he shutteth [1]up a
man, and there can be no opening.
15 Behold, he [a]withholdeth the waters, and they dry up: also he [b]sendeth
them out, and they overturn the earth.
16 With him *is* strength and wisdom:
the deceived and the deceiver *are* his.
17 He leadeth counsellors away
spoiled, and maketh the judges fools.
18 He looseth the bond of kings, and
girdeth their loins with a girdle.
19 He leadeth princes away spoiled,
and overthroweth the mighty.
20 [a]He removeth away [1]the speech of
the trusty, and taketh away the understanding of the aged.
21 [a]He poureth contempt upon
princes, and [1]weakeneth the strength of
the mighty.
22 He discovereth deep things out of
darkness, and bringeth out to light the
shadow of death.
23 [a]He increaseth the nations, and destroyeth them: he enlargeth the nations,
and [1]straiteneth them *again.*
24 He taketh away the heart of the
chief of the people of the earth, and
[a]causeth them to wander in a wilderness
where there is no way.
25 [a]They grope in the dark without
light, and he maketh them to [b]stagger[1]
like *a* drunken *man.*

13 LO, MINE eye hath seen all *this,*
mine ear hath heard and understood it.
2 [a]What ye know, *the same* do I know
also: I *am* not inferior unto you.
3 [a]Surely I would speak to the Almighty, and I desire to reason with God.
4 But ye *are* forgers of lies, [a]ye *are* all
physicians of no value.
5 O that ye would altogether hold your
peace! and [a]it should be your wisdom.
6 Hear now my reasoning, and
hearken to the pleadings of my lips.
7 [a]Will ye speak wickedly for God? and
talk deceitfully for him?
8 Will ye accept his person? will ye
contend for God?
9 Is it good that he should search you
out? or as one man mocketh another, do
ye *so* mock him?
10 He will surely reprove you, if ye do
secretly accept persons.
11 Shall not his excellency make you
afraid? and his dread fall upon you?
12 Your remembrances *are* like unto
ashes, your bodies to bodies of clay.
13 [1]Hold your peace, let me alone,
that I may speak, and let come on me
what *will.*
14 Wherefore [a]do I take my flesh in
my teeth, and put my life in mine hand?
15 [a]Though he slay me, yet will I trust
in him: [b]but I will [1]maintain mine own
ways before him.
16 He also *shall be* my salvation: for an
hypocrite shall not come before him.
17 Hear diligently my speech, and my
declaration with your ears.
18 Behold now, I have ordered *my*
cause; I know that I shall be justified.
19 [a]Who *is* he *that* will plead with me?
for now, if I hold my tongue, I shall give
up the ghost.
20 [a]Only do not two *things* unto me:
then will I not hide myself from thee.
21 [a]Withdraw thine hand far from me:
and let not thy dread make me afraid.
22 Then call thou, and I will answer:
or let me speak, and answer thou me.
23 How many *are* mine iniquities and
sins? make me to know my transgression
and my sin.
24 [a]Wherefore hidest thou thy face,
and [b]holdest me for thine enemy?
25 [a]Wilt thou break a leaf driven to
and fro? and wilt thou pursue the dry
stubble?
26 For thou writest bitter things
against me, and [a]makest me to possess
the iniquities of my youth.
27 [a]Thou puttest my feet also in the
stocks, and [1]lookest narrowly unto all my
paths; thou settest a print upon the
[2]heels of my feet.
28 And he, as a rotten thing, consumeth, as a garment that is motheaten.

J Job 1:21 ◄► Ps 3:5–6

14 [1]Heb. *upon*
15 [a]1 Ki. 8:35 [b]Gen. 7:11
20 [a]ch. 32:9 [1]Heb. *the lip of the faithful*
21 [a]Ps. 107:40; Dan. 2:21 [1]Or, *looseth the girdle of the strong*
23 [a]Ps. 107:38; Is. 9:3 [1]Heb. *leadeth in*
24 [a]Ps. 107:4
25 [a]ch. 5:14 [b]Ps. 107:27 [1]Heb. *wander*
13:2 [a]ch. 12:3
3 [a]ch. 23:3
4 [a]ch. 6:21
5 [a]Prov. 17:28
7 [a]ch. 36:4
13 [1]Heb. *Be silent from me*
14 [a]ch. 18:4
15 [a]Ps. 23:4; Prov. 14:32 [b]ch. 27:5 [1]Heb. *prove,* or, *argue*
19 [a]Is. 50:8
20 [a]ch. 9:34
21 [a]Ps. 39:10
24 [a]Deut. 32:20; Is. 8:17 [b]Deut. 32:42; ch. 16:9; Lam. 2:5
25 [a]Is. 42:3
26 [a]ch. 20:11; Ps. 25:7
27 [a]ch. 33:11 [1]Heb. *observest* [2]Heb. *roots*

13:15 Job expressed his unshakable confidence in God when he surrendered his own life to God's will despite his circumstances. Satan had intimated that Job's obedience hinged only on God's hand of blessing. When God allowed Satan to remove all that Job possessed, it was clear that Job's righteousness was motivated by his love of God, not by his blessings. Job's struggles illustrate that though circumstances change, our relationship with God is eternal.

14 MAN *THAT is* born of a woman *is* [1]of few days, and [a]full of trouble.

2 [a]He cometh forth like a flower, and is cut down: he fleeth also as a shadow, and continueth not.

3 And [a]dost thou open thine eyes upon such an one, and [b]bringest me into judgment with thee?

4 [1]Who [a]can bring a clean *thing* out of an unclean? not one.

5 [a]Seeing his days *are* determined, the number of his months *are* with thee, thou hast appointed his bounds that he cannot pass;

6 [a]Turn from him, that he may [1]rest, till he shall accomplish, [b]as an hireling, his day.

7 For there is hope of a tree, if it be cut down, that it will sprout again, and that the tender branch thereof will not cease.

8 Though the root thereof wax old in the earth, and the stock thereof die in the ground;

9 *Yet* through the scent of water it will bud, and bring forth boughs like a plant.

10 But man dieth, and [1]wasteth away: yea, man giveth up the ghost, and where *is* he?

11 *As* the waters fail from the sea, and the flood decayeth and drieth up:

F 12 So man lieth down, and riseth not: [a]till the heavens *be* no more, they shall not awake, nor be raised out of their sleep.

13 O that thou wouldest hide me in the grave, that thou wouldest keep me secret, until thy wrath be past, that thou wouldest appoint me a set time, and remember me!

14 If a man die, shall he live *again?* all the days of my appointed time [a]will I wait, till my change come.

15 [a]Thou shalt call, and I will answer thee: thou wilt have a desire to the work of thine hands.

F ▶ *Job 19:25–27*

14:1 [a]Eccl. 2:23 [1]Heb. *short of days*
2 [a]ch. 8:9; Ps. 90:5,6
3 [a]Ps. 144:3 [b]Ps. 143:2
4 [a]Ps. 51:2,5,10; John 3:6; Rom. 5:12; Eph. 2:3 [1]Heb. *Who will give*
5 [a]ch. 7:1
6 [a]ch. 7:16,19; Ps. 39:13 [b]ch. 7:1 [1]Heb. *cease*
10 [1]Heb. *is weakened,* or, *cut off*
12 [a]Is. 51:6; Acts 3:21; Rom. 8:20; 2 Pet. 3:7; Rev. 20:11 & 21:1
14 [a]ch. 13:15
15 [a]ch. 13:22
16 [a]ch. 10:6,14; Prov. 5:21; Jer. 32:19
17 [a]Deut. 32:34; Hos. 13:12
18 [1]Heb. *fadeth*
19 [1]Heb. *overflowest*
21 [a]Eccl. 9:5; Is. 63:16
15:2 [1]Heb. *knowledge of wind*
4 [1]Heb. *thou makest void* [2]Or, *speech*
5 [1]Heb. *teacheth*
6 [a]Luke 19:22
7 [a]Ps. 90:2; Prov. 8:25
8 [a]Rom. 11:34; 1 Cor. 2:11
9 [a]ch. 13:2
10 [a]ch. 32:6,7

16 [a]For now thou numberest my steps: dost thou not watch over my sin? E

17 [a]My transgression *is* sealed up in a bag, and thou sewest up mine iniquity.

18 And surely the mountain falling [1]cometh to nought, and the rock is removed out of his place.

19 The waters wear the stones: thou [1]washest away the things which grow *out* of the dust of the earth; and thou destroyest the hope of man.

20 Thou prevailest for ever against him, and he passeth: thou changest his countenance, and sendest him away.

21 His sons come to honour, and [a]he knoweth *it* not; and they are brought low, but he perceiveth *it* not of them.

22 But his flesh upon him shall have pain, and his soul within him shall mourn.

Eliphaz responds

15 THEN ANSWERED Eliphaz the Temanite, and said,

2 Should a wise man utter [1]vain knowledge, and fill his belly with the east wind?

3 Should he reason with unprofitable talk? or with speeches wherewith he can do no good?

4 Yea, [1]thou castest off fear, and restrainest [2]prayer before God.

5 For thy mouth [1]uttereth thine iniquity, and thou choosest the tongue of the crafty.

6 [a]Thine own mouth condemneth thee, and not I: yea, thine own lips testify against thee.

7 *Art* thou the first man *that* was born? [a]or wast thou made before the hills?

8 [a]Hast thou heard the secret of God? and dost thou restrain wisdom to thyself ?

9 [a]What knowest thou, that we know not? *what* understandest thou, which *is* not in us?

10 [a]With us *are* both the grayheaded

E *Job 4:14* ◀ ▶ *Job 22:12–17*

14:12 The phrase "till the heavens be no more" foreshadows the new heaven that will be created after the white throne judgment (see Rev 21:1).
14:14 The book of Job asks three questions that have puzzled humanity for centuries: (1) Where can we find God? (2) How can one be righteous before God? and the question posed in this verse (3) "If a man die, shall he live again?" The answer to each of these questions can only be found in Jesus Christ: He is God incarnate; his atoning death purchased our salvation; and we can only find immortality through his resurrection.

and very aged men, much elder than thy father.

11 *Are* the consolations of God small with thee? is there any secret thing with thee?

G 12 Why doth thine heart carry thee
N away? and what do thy eyes wink at,

13 That thou turnest thy spirit against God, and lettest *such* words go out of thy mouth?

14 [a]What *is* man, that he should be clean? and *he which is* born of a woman, that he should be righteous?

15 [a]Behold, he putteth no trust in his saints; yea, the heavens are not clean in his sight.

C 16 [a]How much more abominable and
G filthy *is* man, [b]which drinketh iniquity like water?

17 I will show thee, hear me; and that *which* I have seen I will declare;

18 Which wise men have told [a]from their fathers, and have not hid *it:*

19 Unto whom alone the earth was given, and [a]no stranger passed among them.

C 20 The wicked man travaileth with pain all *his* days, [a]and the number of years is hidden to the oppressor.

21 'A dreadful sound *is* in his ears: [a]in prosperity the destroyer shall come upon him.

22 He believeth not that he shall return out of darkness, and he is waited for of the sword.

C 23 He [a]wandereth abroad for bread,
H *saying,* Where *is it?* he knoweth that [b]the day of darkness is ready at his hand.

24 Trouble and anguish shall make him afraid; they shall prevail against him, as a king ready to the battle.

25 For he stretcheth out his hand against God, and strengtheneth himself against the Almighty.

26 He runneth upon him, *even* on *his* neck, upon the thick bosses of his bucklers:

27 [a]Because he covereth his face with his fatness, and maketh collops of fat on *his* flanks.

28 And he dwelleth in desolate cities, *and* in houses which no man inhabiteth, which are ready to become heaps.

29 He shall not be rich, neither shall his substance continue, neither shall he prolong the perfection thereof upon the earth.

30 He shall not depart out of darkness; H
the flame shall dry up his branches, and by the breath of his mouth shall he go away.

31 Let not him that is deceived [a]trust G
in vanity: for vanity shall be his recompence.

32 It shall be 'accomplished [a]before his time, and his branch shall not be green.

33 He shall shake off his unripe grape as the vine, and shall cast off his flower as the olive.

34 For the congregation of hypocrites H
shall be desolate, and fire shall consume the tabernacles of bribery.

35 [a]They conceive mischief, and bring forth 'vanity, and their belly prepareth deceit.

Job answers

16 THEN JOB answered and said,
2 I have heard many such things: [a]miserable' comforters *are* ye all.

3 Shall 'vain words have an end? or what emboldeneth thee that thou answerest?

4 I also could speak as ye *do:* if your soul were in my soul's stead, I could heap up words against you, and [a]shake mine head at you.

5 *But* I would strengthen you with my mouth, and the moving of my lips should assuage *your grief.*

6 Though I speak, my grief is not assuaged: and *though* I forbear, 'what am I eased?

7 But now he hath made me weary: thou hast made desolate all my company.

8 And thou hast filled me with wrinkles, *which* is a witness *against me:* and my leanness rising up in me beareth witness to my face.

9 [a]He teareth *me* in his wrath, who hateth me: he gnasheth upon me with his

14 [a]ch. 14:4; Prov. 20:9; Eccl. 7:20; 1 John 1:8,10
15 [a]ch. 4:18 & 25:5
16 [a]ch. 4:19; Ps. 14:3 & 53:3 [b]ch. 34:7; Prov. 19:28
18 [a]ch. 8:8
19 [a]Joel 3:17
20 [a]Ps. 90:12
21 [a]1 Thes. 5:3 'Heb. *A sound of fears*
23 [a]Ps. 59:15 & 109:10 [b]ch. 18:12
27 [a]Ps. 17:10
31 [a]Is. 59:4
32 [a]ch. 22:16; Ps. 55:23 'Or, *cut off*
35 [a]Ps. 7:14; Is. 59:4; Hos. 10:13 'Or, *iniquity*
16:2 [a]ch. 13:4 'Or, *troublesome*
3 'Heb. *words of wind*
4 [a]Ps. 22:7 & 109:25; Lam. 2:15
6 'Heb. *what goeth from me?*
9 [a]ch. 10:16,17

G *Job 9:29–31* ◀▶ *Job 15:16*
N *Job 11:20* ◀▶ *Job 16:22*
C *Job 6:18* ◀▶ *Job 15:20–21*
G *Job 15:12* ◀▶ *Job 15:31*
C *Job 15:16* ◀▶ *Job 15:23–26*
C *Job 15:20–21* ◀▶ *Job 20:4–13*
H *Job 11:20* ◀▶ *Job 15:30*

H *Job 15:23–26* ◀▶ *Job 15:34*
G *Job 15:16* ◀▶ *Ps 52:7*
H *Job 15:30* ◀▶ *Job 18:18*

teeth; [b]mine enemy sharpeneth his eyes
upon me.
10 They have [a]gaped upon me with
their mouth; [b]they have smitten me upon
the cheek reproachfully; they have gathered themselves together against me.
11 God [a]hath[l] delivered me to the ungodly, and turned me over into the hands
of the wicked.
12 I was at ease, but he hath broken
me asunder: he hath also taken *me* by my
neck, and shaken me to pieces, and [a]set
me up for his mark.
13 His archers compass me round
about, he cleaveth my reins asunder, and
doth not spare; he poureth out my gall
upon the ground.
14 He breaketh me with breach upon
breach, he runneth upon me like a giant.
15 I have sewed sackcloth upon my
skin, and [a]defiled my horn in the dust.
16 My face is foul with weeping, and
on my eyelids *is* the shadow of death;
17 Not for *any* injustice in mine hands:
also my prayer *is* pure.
18 O earth, cover not thou my blood,
and [a]let my cry have no place.
19 Also now, behold, [a]my witness *is* in
heaven, and my record *is* [l]on high.
20 My friends [l]scorn me: *but* mine eye
poureth out *tears* unto God.
21 [a]O that one might plead for a man
with God, as a man *pleadeth* for his
[l]neighbour!
N 22 When [l]a few years are come, then
I shall [a]go the way *whence* I shall not
return.

17 MY [l]BREATH is corrupt, my days
are extinct, [a]the graves *are ready*
for me.
2 *Are there* not mockers with me? and
doth not mine eye [l]continue in their
[a]provocation?
3 Lay down now, put me in a surety
with thee; who *is* he *that* [a]will strike
hands with me?
4 For thou hast hid their heart from
understanding: therefore shalt thou not
exalt *them.*
5 He that speaketh flattery to *his*
friends, even the eyes of his children
shall fail.
6 He hath made me also [a]a byword of
the people; and [l]aforetime I was as a
tabret.
7 [a]Mine eye also is dim by reason of
sorrow, and all [l]my members *are* as a
shadow.
8 Upright *men* shall be astonied at
this, and the innocent shall stir up himself against the hypocrite.
9 The righteous also shall hold on his K
way, and he that hath [a]clean hands [l]shall S
be stronger and stronger. U
10 But as for you all, [a]do ye return,
and come now: for I cannot find *one* wise
man among you.
11 [a]My days are past, my purposes are
broken off, *even* [l]the thoughts of my
heart.
12 They change the night into day: the
light *is* [l]short because of darkness.
13 If I wait, the grave *is* mine house: I
have made my bed in the darkness.
14 I have [l]said to corruption, Thou *art*
my father: to the worm, *Thou art* my
mother, and my sister.
15 And where *is* now my hope? as for
my hope, who shall see it?
16 They shall go down [a]to the bars of
the pit, when *our* [b]rest together *is* in the
dust.

Bildad reproves Job

18 THEN ANSWERED Bildad the
Shuhite, and said,
2 How long *will it be ere* ye make an
end of words? mark, and afterwards we
will speak.
3 Wherefore are we counted [a]as
beasts, *and* reputed vile in your sight?
4 [a]He teareth [l]himself in his anger:
shall the earth be forsaken for thee? and
shall the rock be removed out of his
place?
5 Yea, [a]the light of the wicked shall be
put out, and the spark of his fire shall not
shine.
6 The light shall be dark in his tabernacle, [a]and his [l]candle shall be put out with
him.
7 The steps of his strength shall be
straitened, and [a]his own counsel shall
cast him down.
8 For [a]he is cast into a net by his own
feet, and he walketh upon a snare.
9 The gin shall take *him* by the heel,
and [a]the robber shall prevail against him.

9 [b]ch. 13:24
10 [a]Ps. 22:13 [b]Lam. 3:30; Mic. 5:1
11 [a]ch. 1:15,17 [l]Heb. *hath shut me up*
12 [a]ch. 7:20
15 [a]ch. 30:19; Ps. 7:5
18 [a]ch. 27:9; Ps. 66:18
19 [a]Rom. 1:9 [l]Heb. *in the high places*
20 [l]Heb. *are my scorners*
21 [a]ch. 31:35; Eccl. 6:10; Is. 45:9; Rom. 9:20 [l]Or, *friend*
22 [a]Eccl. 12:5 [l]Heb. *years of number*
17:1 [a]Ps. 88:3,4 [l]Or, *spirit is spent*
2 [a]1 Sam. 1:6 [l]Heb. *lodge*
3 [a]Prov. 17:18
6 [a]ch. 30:9 [l]Or, *before them*
7 [a]Ps. 6:7 & 31:9 [l]Or, *my thoughts*
9 [a]Ps. 24:4 [l]Heb. *shall add strength*
10 [a]ch. 6:29
11 [a]ch. 7:6 [l]Heb. *the possessions*
12 [l]Heb. *near*
14 [l]Heb. *cried, or, called*
16 [a]Jonah 2:6 [b]ch. 3:17-19
18:3 [a]Ps. 73:22
4 [a]ch. 13:14 [l]Heb. *his soul*
5 [a]Prov. 13:9
6 [a]ch. 21:17; Ps. 18:28 [l]Or, *lamp*
7 [a]ch. 5:13
8 [a]ch. 22:10; Ps. 9:15 & 35:8
9 [a]ch. 5:5

N *Job 15:12–13* ◀▶ *Job 20:5*
K *Job 1:10* ◀▶ *Job 19:25*
S *Job 11:14* ◀▶ *Job 27:8*
U *Job 8:6–7* ◀▶ *Job 22:21*

10 The snare *is* [l]laid for him in the
ground, and a trap for him in the way.
11 [a]Terrors shall make him afraid on
every side, and shall [l]drive him to his
feet.
12 His strength shall be hungerbitten,
and [a]destruction *shall be* ready at his
side.
13 It shall devour the [l]strength of his
skin: *even* the firstborn of death shall devour his strength.
14 [a]His confidence shall be rooted out
of his tabernacle, and it shall bring him to
the king of terrors.
15 It shall dwell in his tabernacle, because *it is* none of his: brimstone shall be
scattered upon his habitation.
16 [a]His roots shall be dried up beneath, and above shall his branch be cut
off.
17 [a]His remembrance shall perish
from the earth, and he shall have no
name in the street.
H 18 [l]He shall be driven from light into
darkness, and chased out of the world.
19 [a]He shall neither have son nor
nephew among his people, nor any remaining in his dwellings.
20 They that come after *him* shall be
astonied at his day, as they that [l]went
before [2]were affrighted.
21 Surely such *are* the dwellings of the
wicked, and this *is* the place *of him that*
[a]knoweth not God.

Job's response

19 THEN JOB answered and said,
2 How long will ye vex my soul,
and break me in pieces with words?
3 These ten times have ye reproached
me: ye are not ashamed *that* ye [l]make
yourselves strange to me.
4 And be it indeed *that* I have erred,
mine error remaineth with myself.
5 If indeed ye will [a]magnify *yourselves*
against me, and plead against me my reproach:
6 Know now that God hath overthrown me, and hath compassed me with
his net.
7 Behold, I cry out of [l]wrong, but I am
not heard: I cry aloud, but *there is* no
judgment.
8 He hath fenced up my way that I cannot pass, and he hath set darkness in my
paths.
9 He hath stripped me of my glory, and
taken the crown *from* my head.
10 He hath destroyed me on every
side, and I am gone: and mine hope hath
he removed like a tree.
11 He hath also kindled his wrath
against me, and [a]he counteth me unto
him as *one of* his enemies.
12 His troops come together, and raise
up their way against me, and encamp
round about my tabernacle.
13 He hath put my brethren far from
me, and mine acquaintance are verily estranged from me.
14 My kinsfolk have failed, and my familiar friends have forgotten me.
15 They that dwell in mine house, and
my maids, count me for a stranger: I am
an alien in their sight.
16 I called my servant, and he gave
me no answer; I entreated him with my
mouth.
17 My breath is strange to my wife,
though I entreated for the children's *sake*
of [l]mine own body.
18 Yea, [a]young[l] children despised me;
I arose, and they spake against me.
19 [a]All [l]my inward friends abhorred
me: and they whom I loved are turned
against me.
20 [a]My bone cleaveth to my skin [l]and
to my flesh, and I am escaped with the
skin of my teeth.
21 Have pity upon me, have pity upon
me, O ye my friends; for the hand of God
hath touched me.
22 Why do ye [a]persecute me as God,
and are not satisfied with my flesh?
23 [l]Oh that my words were now written! oh that they were printed in a book!
24 That they were graven with an iron
pen and lead in the rock for ever!
25 For I know *that* my redeemer liv- D F K

10 [l]Heb. *hidden*
11 [a]ch. 20:25; Jer. 6:25 & 20:3,4 [l]Heb. *scatter him*
12 [a]ch. 15:23
13 [l]Heb. *bars*
14 [a]ch. 11:20; Ps. 112:10; Prov. 10:28
16 [a]ch. 29:19; Is. 5:24; Amos 2:9; Mal. 4:1
17 [a]Ps. 34:16 & 109:13; Prov. 2:22 & 10:7
18 [l]Heb. *They shall drive him*
19 [a]Is. 14:22; Jer. 22:30
20 [l]Or, *lived with him* [2]Heb. *laid hold on horror*
21 [a]Jer. 9:3; 1 Thes. 4:5
19:3 [l]Or, *harden yourselves against me*
5 [a]Ps. 38:16
7 [l]Or, *violence*
11 [a]ch. 13:24
17 [l]Heb. *my belly*
18 [a]2 Ki. 2:23 [l]Or, *the wicked*
19 [a]Ps. 55:13 [l]Heb. *the men of my secret*
20 [a]Ps. 102:5 [l]Or, *as*
22 [a]Ps. 69:26
23 [l]Heb. *Who will give*

H *Job 15:34* ◀ ▶ *Job 20:26–27*

D ▶ *Ps 96:12–13*
F *Job 14:12–15* ◀ ▶ *Ps 8:3–8*
K *Job 17:9* ◀ ▶ *Job 36:7*

19:25–27 Job affirmed his confidence in his redemption and in his physical resurrection noting that "in my flesh shall I see God: Whom I shall see for myself, and mine eyes shall behold, and not another"

eth, and *that* he shall stand at the latter *day* upon the earth:

26 [1]And *though* after my skin *worms* destroy this *body,* yet [a]in my flesh shall I see God:

27 Whom I shall see for myself, and mine eyes shall behold, and not [1]another; [2]*though* my reins be consumed [3]within me.

28 But ye should say, Why persecute we him, [1]seeing the root of the matter is found in me?

29 Be ye afraid of the sword: for wrath *bringeth* the punishments of the sword, that ye may know *there is* a judgment.

Zophar's speech

20 THEN ANSWERED Zophar the Naamathite, and said,

2 Therefore do my thoughts cause me to answer, and for *this* [1]I make haste.

3 I have heard the check of my reproach, and the spirit of my understanding causeth me to answer.

C 4 Knowest thou *not* this of old, since man was placed upon earth,

N 5 [a]That the triumphing of the wicked *is* [1]short, and the joy of the hypocrite *but* for a moment?

6 [a]Though his excellency mount up to the heavens, and his head reach unto the [1]clouds;

7 *Yet* he shall perish for ever like his own dung: they which have seen him shall say, Where *is* he?

8 He shall fly away [a]as a dream, and shall not be found: yea, he shall be chased away as a vision of the night.

9 The eye also *which* saw him shall *see him* no more; neither shall his place any more behold him.

10 [1]His children shall seek to please the poor, and his hands shall restore their goods.

11 His bones are full *of* [a]*the sin* of his youth, [b]which shall lie down with him in the dust.

12 Though wickedness be sweet in his mouth, *though* he hide it under his tongue;

13 *Though* he spare it, and forsake it not; but keep it still [1]within his mouth:

14 *Yet* his meat in his bowels is turned, *it is* the gall of asps within him.

15 He hath swallowed down riches, and he shall vomit them up again: God shall cast them out of his belly.

16 He shall suck the poison of asps: the viper's tongue shall slay him.

17 He shall not see [a]the rivers, [1]the floods, the brooks of honey and butter.

18 That which he laboured for shall he restore, and shall not swallow *it* down: [1]according to *his* substance *shall* the restitution *be,* and he shall not rejoice *therein.*

19 Because he hath [1]oppressed *and* hath forsaken the poor; *because* he hath violently taken away an house which he builded not;

20 [a]Surely he shall not [1]feel quietness in his belly, he shall not save of that which he desired.

21 [1]There shall none of his meat be left; therefore shall no man look for his goods.

22 In the fulness of his sufficiency he shall be in straits: every hand of the [1]wicked shall come upon him.

23 *When* he is about to fill his belly, *God* shall cast the fury of his wrath upon him, and shall rain *it* upon him while he is eating.

24 [a]He shall flee from the iron weapon, *and* the bow of steel shall strike him through.

25 It is drawn, and cometh out of the body; yea, [a]the glittering sword cometh out of his gall: [b]terrors *are* upon him.

26 All darkness *shall be* hid in his secret places: [a]a fire not blown shall consume him; it shall go ill with him that is left in his tabernacle. H

27 The heaven shall reveal his iniquity; and the earth shall rise up against him.

28 The increase of his house shall depart, *and his goods* shall flow away in the day of his wrath.

29 [a]This *is* the portion of a wicked

26 [a]Ps. 17:15; 1 Cor. 13:12 [1]Or, *After I shall awake, though this body be destroyed, yet out of my flesh shall I see God*
27 [1]Heb. *a stranger* [2]Or, *my reins within me are consumed with earnest desire* [for that day] [3]Heb. *in my bosom*
28 [1]Or, *and what root of matter is found in me?*
20:2 [1]Heb. *my haste is in me*
5 [a]Ps. 37:35 [1]Heb. *from near*
6 [a]Is. 14:13,14; Obad. 3,4 [1]Heb. *cloud*
8 [a]Ps. 73:20
10 [1]Or, *The poor shall oppress his children*
11 [a]ch. 13:26 [b]ch. 21:26
13 [1]Heb. *in the midst of his palate*
17 [a]Ps. 36:8; Jer. 17:8 [1]Or, *streaming brooks*
18 [1]Heb. *according to the substance of his exchange*
19 [1]Heb. *crushed*
20 [a]Eccl. 5:13 [1]Heb. *know*
21 [1]Or, *There shall be none left for his meat*
22 [1]Or, *troublesome*
24 [a]Is. 24:18; Amos 5:19
25 [a]ch. 16:13 [b]ch. 18:11
26 [a]Ps. 21:9
29 [a]ch. 27:13

C *Job 15:23–26* ◀ ▶ *Job 21:14–15*
N *Job 16:22* ◀ ▶ *Job 21:13–14*
H *Job 18:18* ◀ ▶ *Job 21:17–20*

(19:26–27). Job's words contradict those who teach that spiritual individuality is lost at the resurrection (see also 14:13–14).

man from God, and the heritage [1]appointed unto him by God.

Job disagrees with his friends

21 BUT JOB answered and said,
2 Hear diligently my speech, and let this be your consolations.

3 Suffer me that I may speak; and after that I have spoken, [a]mock on.

4 As for me, *is* my complaint to man? and if *it were so,* why should not my spirit be [1]troubled?

5 [1]Mark me, and be astonished, [a]and lay *your* hand upon *your* mouth.

6 Even when I remember I am afraid, and trembling taketh hold on my flesh.

7 [a]Wherefore do the wicked live, become old, yea, are mighty in power?

8 Their seed is established in their sight with them, and their offspring before their eyes.

9 Their houses [1]*are* safe from fear, [a]neither *is* the rod of God upon them.

10 Their bull gendereth, and faileth not; their cow calveth, and [a]casteth not her calf.

11 They send forth their little ones like a flock, and their children dance.

12 They take the timbrel and harp, and rejoice at the sound of the organ.

N 13 They [a]spend their days [1]in wealth, and in a moment go down to the grave.

C 14 [a]Therefore they say unto God, Depart from us; for we desire not the knowledge of thy ways.

15 [a]What *is* the Almighty, that we should serve him? and [b]what profit should we have, if we pray unto him?

16 Lo, their good *is* not in their hand: [a]the counsel of the wicked is far from me.

C 17 How oft is the [1]candle of the
H wicked put out! and *how oft* cometh their destruction upon them! *God* [a]distributeth sorrows in his anger.

18 [a]They are as stubble before the wind, and as chaff that the storm [1]carrieth away.

19 God layeth up [1]his iniquity [a]for his children: he rewardeth him, and he shall know *it.*

20 His eyes shall see his destruction, and [a]he shall drink of the wrath of the Almighty.

21 For what pleasure *hath* he in his house after him, when the number of his months is cut off in the midst?

22 [a]Shall *any* teach God knowledge? seeing he judgeth those that are high.

23 One dieth [1]in his full strength, being wholly at ease and quiet.

24 His [1]breasts are full of milk, and his bones are moistened with marrow.

25 And another dieth in the bitterness of his soul, and never eateth with pleasure.

26 They shall [a]lie down alike in the dust, and the worms shall cover them.

27 Behold, I know your thoughts, and the devices *which* ye wrongfully imagine against me.

28 For ye say, Where *is* the house of the prince? and where *are* [1]the dwelling places of the wicked?

29 Have ye not asked them that go by the way? and do ye not know their tokens,

30 [a]That the wicked is reserved to the H
day of destruction? they shall be brought forth to [1]the day of wrath.

31 Who shall declare his way to his face? and who shall repay him *what* he hath done?

32 Yet shall he be brought to the [1]grave, and shall [2]remain in the tomb.

33 The clods of the valley shall be sweet unto him, and [a]every man shall draw after him, as *there are* innumerable before him.

34 How then comfort ye me in vain, seeing in your answers there remaineth [1]falsehood?

29 [1]Heb. *of his decree from God*
21:3 [a]ch. 16:10
4 [1]Heb. *shortened?*
5 [a]Judg. 18:19; ch. 40:4 [1]Heb. *Look unto me.*
7 [a]ch. 12:6; Ps. 73:3,12; Jer. 12:1
9 [a]Ps. 73:5 [1]Heb. *are peace from fear*
10 [a]Ex. 23:26
13 [a]ch. 36:11 [1]Or, *in mirth*
14 [a]ch. 22:17
15 [a]Ex. 5:2 [b]Mal. 3:14
16 [a]Ps. 1:1; Prov. 1:10
17 [a]Luke 12:46 [1]Or, *lamp*
18 [a]Ps. 1:4 [1]Heb. *stealeth away*
19 [a]Ex. 20:5 [1]i.e. *the punishment of his iniquity*
20 [a]Ps. 75:8; Is. 51:17
22 [a]Is. 40:13
23 [1]Heb. *in his very perfection,* or, *in the strength of his perfection*
24 [1]Or, *milk pails*
26 [a]Eccl. 9:2
28 [1]Heb. *the tent of the tabernacles of the wicked*
30 [a]Prov. 16:4 [1]Heb. *the day of wraths*
32 [1]Heb. *graves* [2]Heb. *watch in the heap*
33 [a]Heb. 9:27
34 [1]Heb. *transgression?*

N *Job 20:5* ◀▶ *Job 22:15–17*
C *Job 20:4–13* ◀▶ *Job 21:17–18*
C *Job 21:14–15* ◀▶ *Job 24:13*
H *Job 20:26–27* ◀▶ *Job 21:30*
H *Job 21:17–20* ◀▶ *Job 27:8*

21:30 Job declared that the wicked would be judged and delivered to "the day of wrath" with the same certainty that he affirmed the promise of a heavenly resurrection to those who repented of their sins.

Eliphaz accuses Job again

22 THEN ELIPHAZ the Temanite answered and said,

2 [a]Can a man be profitable unto God, [1]as he that is wise may be profitable unto himself?

3 *Is it* any pleasure to the Almighty, that thou art righteous? or *is it* gain *to him,* that thou makest thy ways perfect?

4 Will he reprove thee for fear of thee? will he enter with thee into judgment?

5 *Is* not thy wickedness great? and thine iniquities infinite?

6 For thou hast [a]taken a pledge from thy brother for nought, and [1]stripped the naked of their clothing.

7 Thou hast not given water to the weary to drink, and thou [a]hast withholden bread from the hungry.

8 But *as for* [1]the mighty man, he had the earth; and the [2]honourable man dwelt in it.

9 Thou hast sent widows away empty, and the arms of the fatherless have been broken.

10 Therefore snares *are* round about thee, and sudden fear troubleth thee;

11 Or darkness, *that* thou canst not see; and abundance of [a]waters cover thee.

E 12 *Is* not God in the height of heaven? and behold [1]the height of the stars, how high they are!

13 And thou sayest, [a]How[1] doth God know? can he judge through the dark cloud?

14 Thick clouds *are* a covering to him, that he seeth not; and he walketh in the circuit of heaven.

N 15 Hast thou marked the old way which wicked men have trodden?

16 Which [a]were cut down out of time, [1]whose foundation was overflown with a flood:

17 [a]Which said unto God, Depart from us: and what can the Almighty do [1]for them?

18 Yet he filled their houses with good *things:* but the counsel of the wicked is far from me.

19 [a]The righteous see *it,* and are glad: and the innocent laugh them to scorn.

20 Whereas our [1]substance is not cut down, but [2]the remnant of them the fire consumeth.

21 Acquaint now thyself [1]with him, and [a]be at peace: thereby good shall come unto thee. U

22 Receive, I pray thee, the law from his mouth, and [a]lay up his words in thine heart.

23 If thou return to the Almighty, thou shalt be built up, thou shalt put away iniquity far from thy tabernacles. U

24 Then shalt thou [a]lay up gold [1]as dust, and the *gold* of Ophir as the stones of the brooks. P

25 Yea, the Almighty shall be thy [1]defence, and thou shalt have [2]plenty of silver.

26 For then shalt thou have thy [a]delight in the Almighty, and shalt lift up thy face unto God.

27 [a]Thou shalt make thy prayer unto him, and he shall hear thee, and thou shalt pay thy vows.

28 Thou shalt also decree a thing, and it shall be established unto thee: and the light shall shine upon thy ways. U

29 When *men* are cast down, then thou shalt say, *There is* lifting up; and [a]he shall save [1]the humble person. M

30 [1]He shall deliver the island of the innocent: and it is delivered by the pureness of thine hands.

Job's response to Eliphaz

23 THEN JOB answered and said,

2 Even today *is* my complaint bitter: [1]my stroke is heavier than my groaning.

3 Oh that I knew where I might find him! *that* I might come *even* to his seat!

4 I would order *my* cause before him, and fill my mouth with arguments.

5 I would know the words *which* he would answer me, and understand what he would say unto me.

6 [a]Will he plead against me with *his* great power? No; but he would put *strength* in me.

7 There the righteous might dispute with him; so should I be delivered for ever from my judge.

8 [a]Behold, I go forward, but he *is* not

22:2 [a]Ps. 16:2 [1]Or, *if he may be profitable,* doth his good success depend *thereon?*
6 [a]Ex. 22:26 [1]Heb. *stripped the clothes of the naked*
7 [a]Deut. 15:7
8 [1]Heb. *the man of arm* [2]Heb. *eminent,* or, *accepted for countenance*
11 [a]Ps. 69:1,2
12 [1]Heb. *the head of the stars*
13 [a]Ps. 73:11 [1]Or, *What*
16 [a]ch. 15:32 [1]Heb. *a flood was poured upon their foundation*
17 [a]ch. 21:14 [1]Or, *to them?*
19 [a]Ps. 58:10
20 [1]Or, *estate* [2]Or, *their excellency*
21 [a]Is. 27:5 [1]i.e. *with God*
22 [a]Ps. 119:11
24 [a]2 Chr. 1:15 [1]Or, *on the dust*
25 [1]Or, *gold* [2]Heb. *silver of strength*
26 [a]ch. 27:10
27 [a]Is. 58:9
29 [a]1 Pet. 5:5 [1]Heb. *him that hath low eyes*
30 [1]Or, *The innocent shall deliver the island*
23:2 [1]Heb. *my hand*
6 [a]Is. 57:16
8 [a]ch. 9:11

E *Job 14:16–17* ◀ ▶ *Job 26:6*
N *Job 21:13–14* ◀ ▶ *Job 27:8–9*
U *Job 17:9* ◀ ▶ *Job 22:23*
U *Job 22:21* ◀ ▶ *Job 22:28*
P *Job 1:10* ◀ ▶ *Job 27:16–17*
U *Job 22:23* ◀ ▶ *Job 29:3*
M *Ne 9:3* ◀ ▶ *Ps 10:4*

there; and backward, but I cannot perceive him:

9 On the left hand, where he doth work, but I cannot behold *him:* he hideth himself on the right hand, that I cannot see *him:*

T 10 But he [a]knoweth [1]the way that I take: *when* [b]he hath tried me, I shall come forth as gold.

11 [a]My foot hath held his steps, his way have I kept, and not declined.

12 Neither have I gone back from the commandment of his lips; [a]I[1] have esteemed the words of his mouth more than [2]my necessary *food.*

13 But he *is* in one *mind,* and who can turn him? and *what* [a]his soul desireth, even *that* he doeth.

14 For he performeth *the thing that is* [a]appointed for me: and many such *things are* with him.

15 Therefore am I troubled at his presence: when I consider, I am afraid of him.

16 For God [a]maketh my heart soft, and the Almighty troubleth me:

17 Because I was not cut off before the darkness, *neither* hath he covered the darkness from my face.

24

WHY, SEEING [a]times are not hidden from the Almighty, do they that know him not see his days?

2 *Some* remove the [a]landmarks; they violently take away flocks, and [1]feed *thereof.*

3 They drive away the ass of the fatherless, they [a]take the widow's ox for a pledge.

4 They turn the needy out of the way: [a]the poor of the earth hide themselves together.

5 Behold, *as* wild asses in the desert, go they forth to their work; rising betimes for a prey: the wilderness *yieldeth* food for them *and* for *their* children.

6 They reap *every one* his [1]corn in the field: and [2]they gather the vintage of the wicked.

7 They [a]cause the naked to lodge without clothing, that *they have* no covering in the cold.

8 They are wet with the showers of the mountains, and [a]embrace the rock for want of a shelter.

9 They pluck the fatherless from the breast, and take a pledge of the poor.

10 They cause *him* to go naked without clothing, and they take away the sheaf *from* the hungry;

11 *Which* make oil within their walls, *and* tread *their* winepresses, and suffer thirst.

12 Men groan from out of the city, and the soul of the wounded crieth out: yet God layeth not folly *to them.*

13 They are of those that rebel against the light; they know not the ways thereof, nor abide in the paths thereof. C

14 [a]The murderer rising with the light killeth the poor and needy, and in the night is as a thief.

15 [a]The eye also of the adulterer waiteth for the twilight, [b]saying, No eye shall see me: and [1]disguiseth *his* face.

16 In the dark they dig through houses, *which* they had marked for themselves in the daytime: [a]they know not the light.

17 For the morning *is* to them even as the shadow of death: if *one* know *them, they are in* the terrors of the shadow of death. C

18 He *is* swift as the waters; their portion is cursed in the earth: he beholdeth not the way of the vineyards.

19 Drought and heat [1]consume the snow waters: *so doth* the grave *those which* have sinned.

20 The womb shall forget him; the worm shall feed sweetly on him; [a]he shall be no more remembered; and wickedness shall be broken as a tree.

21 He evil entreateth the barren *that* beareth not: and doeth not good to the widow.

22 He draweth also the mighty with

10 [a]Ps. 139:1-3 [b]Ps. 17:3 & 66:10; Jas. 1:12 [1]Heb. *the way that is with me*
11 [a]Ps. 44:18
12 [a]John 4:32,34 [1]Heb. *I have hid,* or, *laid up* [2]Or, *my appointed portion*
13 [a]Ps. 115:3
14 [a]1 Thes. 3:3
16 [a]Ps. 22:14
24:1 [a]Acts 1:7
2 [a]Deut. 19:14 & 27:17; Prov. 22:28 & 23:10; Hos. 5:10 [1]Or, *feed* them
3 [a]Deut. 24:6,10, 12,17; ch. 22:6
4 [a]Prov. 28:28
6 [1]Heb. *mingled corn,* or, *dredge* [2]Heb. *the wicked gather the vintage*
7 [a]Ex. 22:26; Deut. 24:12,13; ch. 22:6
8 [a]Lam. 4:5
14 [a]Ps. 10:8
15 [a]Prov. 7:9 [b]Ps. 10:11 [1]Heb. *setteth his face in secret*
16 [a]John 3:20
19 [1]Heb. *violently take*
20 [a]Prov. 10:7

T *Job 5:17* ◀ ▶ *Job 33:17–22*
C *Job 21:17–18* ◀ ▶ *Job 24:17*
C *Job 24:13* ◀ ▶ *Job 27:18*

23:10 Job declared that God knew in advance what Job's conduct would be when he was subjected to various tests and temptations. These trials were designed to test Job's character and his devotion to God despite his circumstances. Just as an assay test examines the mineral content of an ore sample to determine its purity, Job's tests of character revealed what was in the core of Job's heart—his complete trust in God.

his power: he riseth up, [1]and no *man* is
sure of life.
23 *Though* it be given him *to be* in
safety, whereon he resteth; yet [a]his eyes
are upon their ways.
24 They are exalted for a little while,
but [1]are gone and brought low; they are
[2]taken out of the way as all *other,* and cut
off as the tops of the ears of corn.
25 And if *it be* not *so* now, who will
make me a liar, and make my speech
nothing worth?

Bildad answers

25 THEN ANSWERED Bildad the
Shuhite, and said,
2 Dominion and fear *are* with him, he
maketh peace in his high places.
3 Is there any number of his armies?
and upon whom doth not [a]his light arise?
4 [a]How then can man be justified with
God? or how can he be clean *that is* born
of a woman?
5 Behold even to the moon, and it
shineth not; yea, the stars are not pure in
his sight.
6 How much less man, *that is* [a]a
worm? and the son of man, *which is* a
worm?

Job's final speech

26 BUT JOB answered and said,
2 How hast thou helped *him that*
is without power? *how* savest thou the
arm *that hath* no strength?
3 How hast thou counselled *him that*
hath no wisdom? and *how* hast thou plentifully declared the thing as it is?
4 To whom hast thou uttered words?
and whose spirit came from thee?
5 Dead *things* are formed from under

22 [1]Or, *he trusteth not* his own *life*
23 [a]Ps. 11:4; Prov. 15:3
24 [1]Heb. *are not* [2]Heb. *closed up*
25:3 [a]Jas. 1:17
4 [a]ch. 4:17 & 15:14
6 [a]Ps. 22:6
26:5 [1]Or, *with the inhabitants*
6 [a]Ps. 139:8; Prov. 15:11; Heb. 4:13
7 [a]ch. 9:8; Ps. 24:2 & 104:2
8 [a]Prov. 30:4
10 [a]ch. 38:8; Ps. 33:7 & 104:9 [1]Heb. *until the end of light with darkness*
12 [a]Ex. 14:21; Is. 51:15; Jer. 31:35 [1]Heb. *pride*
13 [a]Ps. 33:6 [b]Is. 27:1
27:1 [1]Heb. *added to take up*
2 [a]ch. 34:5 [b]Ruth 1:20; 2 Ki. 4:27 [1]Heb. *made my soul bitter*
3 [1]i.e. *the breath which God gave him;* see Gen. 2:7

the waters, [1]and the inhabitants thereof.
6 [a]Hell *is* naked before him, and de- **E**
struction hath no covering.
7 [a]He stretcheth out the north over
the empty place, *and* hangeth the earth
upon nothing.
8 [a]He bindeth up the waters in his
thick clouds; and the cloud is not rent
under them.
9 He holdeth back the face of his
throne, *and* spreadeth his cloud upon it.
10 [a]He hath compassed the waters **N**
with bounds, [1]until the day and night
come to an end.
11 The pillars of heaven tremble and
are astonished at his reproof.
12 [a]He divideth the sea with his
power, and by his understanding he smiteth through [1]the proud.
13 [a]By his spirit he hath garnished the **E**
heavens; his hand hath formed [b]the **M**
crooked serpent. **N**
14 Lo, these *are* parts of his ways: but
how little a portion is heard of him? but
the thunder of his power who can understand?
27 MOREOVER JOB [1]continued his
parable, and said,
2 *As* God liveth, [a]*who* hath taken away
my judgment; and the Almighty, *who*
hath [b]vexed[1] my soul;
3 All the while my breath *is* in me, and
[1]the spirit of God *is* in my nostrils;
4 My lips shall not speak wickedness,
nor my tongue utter deceit.

E *Job 22:12–17* ◀ ▶ *Job 28:24–25*
N *Dt 4:40* ◀ ▶ *Ps 37:9*
E *Ne 9:30* ◀ ▶ *Job 32:8*
M *2Ki 2:16* ◀ ▶ *Job 32:18–19*
N *Ne 9:20* ◀ ▶ *Job 32:8*

25:4 Job's question of justification mirrors the discussion Jesus had with Nicodemus (see Jn 3:1–16) and provides the framework for the book of Romans. God is holy and he cannot ignore our sinfulness. However, we are incapable of living a sinless life and are in need of justification to satisfy God's entrance requirements to heaven (see Ro 3:23). The only way we can obtain this justification is through repentance and acceptance of Christ's sacrificial atonement for our sins. When a person repents of their sins, asks God for forgiveness and accepts Christ's death on the cross as payment for their sin, God wipes away the sin in their life and views that repentant sinner through the righteousness of Christ. Christ's perfect obedience and righteousness, applied to the heart of each repentant sinner, qualifies each one for acceptance into the holiness of heaven.

26:7 The Hebrew for this verse indicates that God created a zone of emptiness in space to the north of the earth. To the naked eye, the northern area of the night sky seems just as full of stars as other parts of the heavens. Yet scientists have recently discovered an area just north of the axis of the earth (near the north polar star) that seems to be almost empty of stars for millions of light-years, as if there were a hole in space, confirming the accuracy of Job's words.

26:10 Note the similarity between this verse and 38:8. God is in control of the boundaries of the water and the land as he promised Noah he would be (see Ge 9:15).

5 God forbid that I should justify you: till I die [a]I will not remove mine integrity from me.

6 My righteousness I [a]hold fast, and will not let it go: [b]my heart shall not reproach *me* [/]so long as I live.

7 Let mine enemy be as the wicked, and he that riseth up against me as the unrighteous.

H N S 8 [a]For what *is* the hope of the hypocrite, though he hath gained, when God taketh away his soul?

9 [a]Will God hear his cry when trouble cometh upon him?

10 [a]Will he delight himself in the Almighty? will he always call upon God?

11 I will teach you [/]by the hand of God: *that* which *is* with the Almighty will I not conceal.

12 Behold, all ye yourselves have seen *it;* why then are ye thus altogether vain?

13 [a]This *is* the portion of a wicked man with God, and the heritage of oppressors, *which* they shall receive of the Almighty.

14 [a]If his children be multiplied, *it is* for the sword: and his offspring shall not be satisfied with bread.

15 Those that remain of him shall be buried in death: and [a]his widows shall not weep.

C P 16 Though he heap up silver as the dust, and prepare raiment as the clay;

17 He may prepare *it,* but [a]the just shall put *it* on, and the innocent shall divide the silver.

C H 18 He buildeth his house as a moth, and [a]as a booth *that* the keeper maketh.

19 The rich man shall lie down, but he shall not be gathered: he openeth his eyes, and he *is* not.

20 [a]Terrors take hold on him as waters, a tempest stealeth him away in the night.

21 The east wind carrieth him away, and he departeth: and as a storm hurleth him out of his place.

22 For *God* shall cast upon him, and not spare: [/]he would fain flee out of his hand.

H *Job 21:30* ◄► *Job 27:19–23*
N *Job 22:15–17* ◄► *Ps 27:8*
S *Job 17:9* ◄► *Job 28:7–8*
C *Ne 9:21* ◄► *Eze 16:10*
P *Job 22:24–25* ◄► *Job 42:10*
C *Job 24:17* ◄► *Ps 1:4*
H *Job 27:8* ◄► *Job 31:3*

5 [a]ch. 2:9 & 13:15
6 [a]ch. 2:3 [b]Acts 24:16 [/]Heb. *from my days*
8 [a]Mat. 16:26; Luke 12:20
9 [a]ch. 35:12; Prov. 1:28 & 28:9; Is. 1:15; Jer. 14:12; Ezek. 8:18; Mic. 3:4; John 9:31; Jas. 4:3
10 [a]See ch. 22:26, 27
11 [/]Or, being *in the hand*
13 [a]ch. 20:29
14 [a]Deut. 28:41; Esth. 9:10; Hos. 9:13
15 [a]Ps. 78:64
17 [a]Prov. 28:8; Eccl. 2:26
18 [a]Is. 1:8; Lam. 2:6
20 [a]ch. 18:11
22 [/]Heb. *in fleeing he would flee*
28:1 [/]Or, *a mine*
2 [/]Or, *dust*
6 [/]Or, *gold ore*
9 [/]Or, *flint*
11 [/]Heb. *from weeping*
12 [a]Eccl. 7:24
13 [a]Prov. 3:15
14 [a]ver. 22; Rom. 11:33
15 [a]Prov. 3:13-15; & 8:10,11,19 [/]Heb. *Fine gold shall not be given for it*
17 [/]Or, *vessels of fine gold*
18 [/]Or, *Ramoth*

23 *Men* shall clap their hands at him, and shall hiss him out of his place.

28 SURELY THERE is [/]a vein for the silver, and a place for gold *where* they refine *it.*

2 Iron is taken out of the [/]earth, and brass *is* molten *out of* the stone.

3 He setteth an end to darkness, and searcheth out all perfection: the stones of darkness, and the shadow of death.

4 The flood breaketh out from the inhabitant; *even the waters* forgotten of the foot: they are dried up, they are gone away from men.

5 *As for* the earth, out of it cometh bread: and under it is turned up as it were fire.

6 The stones of it *are* the place of sapphires: and it hath [/]dust of gold.

7 *There is* a path which no fowl knoweth, and which the vulture's eye hath not seen: S

8 The lion's whelps have not trodden it, nor the fierce lion passed by it.

9 He putteth forth his hand upon the [/]rock; he overturneth the mountains by the roots.

10 He cutteth out rivers among the rocks; and his eye seeth every precious thing.

11 He bindeth the floods [/]from overflowing; and *the thing that is* hid bringeth he forth to light.

12 [a]But where shall wisdom be found? and where *is* the place of understanding?

13 Man knoweth not the [a]price thereof; neither is it found in the land of the living.

14 [a]The depth saith, It *is* not in me: and the sea saith, *It is* not with me.

15 [/]It [a]cannot be gotten for gold, neither shall silver be weighed *for* the price thereof.

16 It cannot be valued with the gold of Ophir, with the precious onyx, or the sapphire.

17 The gold and the crystal cannot equal it: and the exchange of it *shall not be for* [/]jewels of fine gold.

18 No mention shall be made of [/]coral, or of pearls: for the price of wisdom *is* above rubies.

19 The topaz of Ethiopia shall not equal it, neither shall it be valued with pure gold.

S *Job 27:8* ◄► *Job 34:11*

20 [a]Whence then cometh wisdom?
and where *is* the place of understanding?
21 Seeing it is hid from the eyes of all
living, and kept close from the fowls of
the [1]air.
22 [a]Destruction and death say, We
have heard the fame thereof with our
ears.
23 God understandeth the way
thereof, and he knoweth the place
thereof.
E 24 For he looketh to the ends of the
earth, *and* [a]seeth under the whole
heaven;
25 [a]To make the weight for the winds;
and he weigheth the waters by measure.
26 When he [a]made a decree for the
rain, and a way for the lightning of the
thunder:
27 Then did he see it, and [1]declare it;
he prepared it, yea, and searched it out.
28 And unto man he said, Behold, [a]the
fear of the Lord, that *is* wisdom; and to
depart from evil *is* understanding.

29 MOREOVER JOB [1]continued his
parable, and said,
2 Oh that I were as *in* months past, as
in the days *when* God preserved me;
U 3 [a]When his [1]candle shined upon my
head, *and when* by his light I walked
through darkness;
4 As I was in the days of my youth,
when [a]the secret of God *was* upon my
tabernacle;
5 When the Almighty *was* yet with
me, *when* my children *were* about me;
U 6 When [a]I washed my steps with butter, and [b]the rock poured [1]me out rivers
of oil;
7 When I went out to the gate through
the city, *when* I prepared my seat in the
street!
8 The young men saw me, and hid
themselves: and the aged arose, *and*
stood up.
9 The princes refrained talking, and
[a]laid *their* hand on their mouth.
10 [1]The nobles held their peace, and
their [a]tongue cleaved to the roof of their
mouth.
11 When the ear heard *me,* then it
blessed me; and when the eye saw *me,* it
gave witness to me:
12 Because [a]I delivered the poor that
cried, and the fatherless, and *him that*
had none to help him.
13 The blessing of him that was ready
to perish came upon me: and I caused the
widow's heart to sing for joy.
14 [a]I put on righteousness, and it
clothed me: my judgment *was* as a robe
and a diadem.
15 I was [a]eyes to the blind, and feet
was I to the lame.
16 I *was* a father to the poor: and [a]the
cause *which* I knew not I searched out.
17 And I brake [a]the[1] jaws of the
wicked, and [2]plucked the spoil out of his
teeth.
18 Then I said, [a]I shall die in my nest,
and I shall multiply *my* days as the sand.
19 [a]My root *was* [1]spread out [b]by the
waters, and the dew lay all night upon my
branch.
20 My glory *was* [1]fresh in me, and my
[a]bow was [2]renewed in my hand.
21 Unto me *men* gave ear, and waited,
and kept silence at my counsel.
22 After my words they spake not
again; and my speech dropped upon
them.
23 And they waited for me as for the
rain; and they opened their mouth wide
as for [a]the latter rain.
24 *If* I laughed on them, they believed
it not; and the light of my countenance
they cast not down.
25 I chose out their way, and sat chief,
and dwelt as a king in the army, as one
that comforteth the mourners.

30 BUT NOW *they that are* [1]younger
than I have me in derision,
whose fathers I would have disdained to
have set with the dogs of my flock.
2 Yea, whereto *might* the strength of
their hands *profit* me, in whom old age
was perished?
3 For want and famine *they were* [1]soli-
tary; fleeing into the wilderness [2]in former time desolate and waste.
4 Who cut up mallows by the bushes,
and juniper roots *for* their meat.
5 They were driven forth from among
men, (they cried after them as *after* a
thief;)
6 To dwell in the cliffs of the valleys, *in*
[1]caves of the earth, and *in* the rocks.
7 Among the bushes they brayed; under the nettles they were gathered together.

20 [a]ver. 12
21 [1]Or, *heaven*
22 [a]ver. 14
24 [a]Prov. 15:3
25 [a]Ps. 135:7
26 [a]ch. 38:25
27 [1]Or, *number it*
28 [a]Deut. 4:6; Prov. 1:7
29:1 [1]Heb. *added to take up*
3 [a]ch. 18:6 [1]Or, *lamp*
4 [a]Ps. 25:14
6 [a]Gen. 49:11; Deut. 32:13; ch. 20:17 [b]Ps. 81:16 [1]Heb. *with me*
9 [a]ch. 21:5
10 [a]Ps. 137:6 [1]Heb. *The voice of the nobles was hid*
12 [a]Ps. 72:12; Prov. 21:13 & 24:11
14 [a]Deut. 24:13; Is. 59:17 & 61:10; Eph. 6:14; 1 Thes. 5:8
15 [a]Num. 10:31
16 [a]Prov. 29:7
17 [a]Ps. 58:6; Prov. 30:14 [1]Heb. *the jawteeth,* or, *the grinders* [2]Heb. *cast*
18 [a]Ps. 30:6
19 [a]ch. 18:16 [b]Ps. 1:3; Jer. 17:8 [1]Heb. *opened*
20 [a]Gen. 49:24 [1]Heb. *new* [2]Heb. *changed*
23 [a]Zech. 10:1
30:1 [1]Heb. *of fewer days than I*
3 [1]Or, *dark as the night* [2]Heb. *yesternight*
6 [1]Heb. *holes*

E *Job 26:6* ◀▶ *Job 31:4*
U *Job 22:28* ◀▶ *Job 29:6*
U *Job 29:3* ◀▶ *Job 36:7*

8 *They were* children of fools, yea, children of [l]base men: they were viler than the earth.

9 [a]And now am I their song, yea, I am their byword.

10 They abhor me, they flee far from me, [l]and spare not [a]to spit in my face.

11 Because he [a]hath loosed my cord, and afflicted me, they have also let loose the bridle before me.

12 Upon *my* right *hand* rise the youth; they push away my feet, and [a]they raise up against me the ways of their destruction.

13 They mar my path, they set forward my calamity, they have no helper.

14 They came *upon me* as a wide breaking in *of waters:* in the desolation they rolled themselves *upon me.*

15 Terrors are turned upon me: they pursue [l]my soul as the wind: and my welfare passeth away as a cloud.

16 [a]And now my soul is poured out upon me; the days of affliction have taken hold upon me.

17 My bones are pierced in me in the night season: and my sinews take no rest.

18 By the great force *of my disease* is my garment changed: it bindeth me about as the collar of my coat.

19 He hath cast me into the mire, and I am become like dust and ashes.

20 I cry unto thee, and thou dost not hear me: I stand up, and thou regardest me *not.*

21 Thou art [l]become cruel to me: with [2]thy strong hand thou opposest thyself against me.

22 Thou liftest me up to the wind; thou causest me to ride *upon it,* and dissolvest my [l]substance.

23 For I know *that* thou wilt bring me *to* death, and *to* the house [a]appointed for all living.

24 Howbeit he will not stretch out *his* hand to the [l]grave, though they cry in his destruction.

25 [a]Did not I weep [l]for him that was in trouble? was *not* my soul grieved for the poor?

26 [a]When I looked for good, then evil came *unto me:* and when I waited for light, there came darkness.

27 My bowels boiled, and rested not: the days of affliction prevented me.

28 [a]I went mourning without the sun: I stood up, *and* I cried in the congregation.

29 [a]I am a brother to dragons, and a companion to [l]owls.

30 [a]My skin is black upon me, and [b]my bones are burned with heat.

31 My harp also is *turned* to mourning, and my organ into the voice of them that weep.

31

I MADE a covenant with mine [a]eyes; why then should I think upon a maid?

2 For what [a]portion of God *is there* from above? and *what* inheritance of the Almighty from on high?

3 *Is* not destruction to the wicked? and a strange *punishment* to the workers of iniquity? H

4 [a]Doth not he see my ways, and count all my steps? E

5 If I have walked with vanity, or if my foot hath hasted to deceit;

6 [l]Let me be weighed in an even balance, that God may know mine integrity.

7 If my step hath turned out of the way, and [a]mine heart walked after mine eyes, and if any blot hath cleaved to mine hands;

8 *Then* [a]let me sow, and let another eat; yea, let my offspring be rooted out.

9 If mine heart have been deceived by a woman, or *if* I have laid wait at my neighbour's door;

10 *Then* let my wife grind unto [a]another, and let others bow down upon her.

11 For this *is* an heinous crime; yea, [a]it *is* an iniquity *to be punished by* the judges.

12 For it *is* a fire *that* consumeth to destruction, and would root out all mine increase.

13 If I did despise the cause of my manservant or of my maidservant, when they contended with me;

14 What then shall I do when [a]God riseth up? and when he visiteth, what shall I answer him?

15 [a]Did not he that made me in the womb make him? and [l]did not one fashion us in the womb?

16 If I have withheld the poor from *their* desire, or have caused the eyes of the widow to fail;

17 Or have eaten my morsel myself

8 [l]Heb. *men of no name*
9 [a]ch. 17:6; Ps. 35:15 & 69:12; Lam. 3:14
10 [a]Num. 12:14; Deut. 25:9; Is. 50:6; Mat. 26:67 & 27:30 [l]Heb. *and withhold not spittle from my face*
11 [a]See ch. 12:18
12 [a]ch. 19:12
15 [l]Heb. *my principal one*
16 [a]Ps. 42:4
21 [l]Heb. *turned to be cruel* [2]Heb. *the strength of thy hand*
22 [l]Or, *wisdom*
23 [a]Heb. 9:27
24 [l]Heb. *heap*
25 [a]Ps. 35:13; Rom. 12:15 [l]Heb. *for him that was hard of day?*
26 [a]Jer. 8:15
28 [a]Ps. 42:9
29 [a]Ps. 102:6; Mic. 1:8 [l]Or, *ostriches*
30 [a]Ps. 119:83; Lam. 4:8 [b]Ps. 102:3
31:1 [a]Mat. 5:28
2 [a]ch. 20:29
4 [a]2 Chr. 16:9; Prov. 5:21; Jer. 32:19
6 [l]Heb. *Let him weigh me in balances of justice*
7 [a]See Num. 15:39; Eccl. 11:9; Ezek. 6:9; Mat. 5:29
8 [a]Lev. 26:16; Deut. 28:30,38
10 [a]2 Sam. 12:11; Jer. 8:10
11 [a]Gen. 38:24; Lev. 20:10; See ver. 28
14 [a]Ps. 44:21
15 [a]ch. 34:19 [l]Or, *did he not fashion us in one womb?*

H *Job 27:19–23* ◀▶ *Ps 2:8–9*
E *Job 28:24–25* ◀▶ *Job 34:21–22*

alone, and the fatherless hath not eaten thereof;

18 (For from my youth he was brought up with me, as *with* a father, and I have guided [1]her from my mother's womb;)

19 If I have seen any perish for want of clothing, or any poor without covering;

20 If his loins have not [a]blessed me, and *if* he were *not* warmed with the fleece of my sheep;

21 If I have lifted up my hand [a]against the fatherless, when I saw my help in the gate:

22 *Then* let mine arm fall from my shoulder blade, and mine arm be broken from [1]the bone.

23 For [a]destruction *from* God *was* a terror to me, and by reason of his highness I could not endure.

24 [a]If I have made gold my hope, or have said to the fine gold, *Thou art* my confidence;

25 [a]If I rejoiced because my wealth *was* great, and because mine hand had [1]gotten much;

26 [a]If I beheld [1]the sun when it shined, or the moon walking [2]*in* brightness;

27 And my heart hath been secretly enticed, or [1]my mouth hath kissed my hand:

28 This also *were* an iniquity *to be punished by* the judge: for I should have denied the God *that is* above.

29 [a]If I rejoiced at the destruction of him that hated me, or lifted up myself when evil found him:

30 [a]Neither have I suffered [1]my mouth to sin by wishing a curse to his soul.

31 If the men of my tabernacle said not, Oh that we had of his flesh! we cannot be satisfied.

32 [a]The stranger did not lodge in the street: *but* I opened my doors [1]to the traveller.

R 33 If I covered my transgressions [a]as[1] Adam, by hiding mine iniquity in my bosom:

34 Did I fear a great [a]multitude, or did the contempt of families terrify me, that I kept silence, *and* went not out of the door?

35 Oh that one would hear me! [1]behold, my desire *is,* [a]*that* the Almighty would answer me, and *that* mine adversary had written a book.

36 Surely I would take it upon my shoulder, *and* bind it *as* a crown to me.

37 I would declare unto him the number of my steps; as a prince would I go near unto him.

38 If my land cry against me, or that the furrows likewise thereof [1]complain;

39 If [a]I have eaten [1]the fruits thereof without money, or [b]have [2]caused the owners thereof to lose their life:

40 Let [a]thistles grow instead of wheat, and [1]cockle instead of barley. The words of Job are ended.

Elihu declares his opinion

32 SO THESE three men ceased [1]to answer Job, because he *was* [a]righteous in his own eyes.

2 Then was kindled the wrath of Elihu the son of Barachel the Buzite, of the kindred of Ram: against Job was his wrath kindled, because he justified [1]himself rather than God.

3 Also against his three friends was his wrath kindled, because they had found no answer, and *yet* had condemned Job.

4 Now Elihu had [1]waited till Job had spoken, because they *were* [2]elder than he.

5 When Elihu saw that *there was* no answer in the mouth of *these* three men, then his wrath was kindled.

6 And Elihu the son of Barachel the Buzite answered and said, I *am* [1]young, and ye *are* very old; wherefore I was afraid, and [2]durst not show you mine opinion.

7 I said, Days should speak, and multitude of years should teach wisdom.

8 But *there is* a spirit in man: and [a]the inspiration of the Almighty giveth them understanding. E G N T

9 [a]Great men are not *always* wise: neither do the aged understand judgment.

10 Therefore I said, Hearken to me; I also will show mine opinion.

11 Behold, I waited for your words; I gave ear to your [1]reasons, whilst ye searched out [2]what to say.

12 Yea, I attended unto you, and, be-

18 [1]i.e. *the widow*
20 [a]Deut. 24:13
21 [a]ch. 22:9
22 [1]Or, *the chanel-bone*
23 [a]Is. 13:6
24 [a]Mark 10:24
25 [a]Ps. 62:10 [1]Heb. *found much*
26 [a]Ezek. 8:16 [1]Heb. *the light* [2]Heb. *bright*
27 [1]Heb. *my hand hath kissed my mouth*
29 [a]Prov. 17:5
30 [a]Mat. 5:44 [1]Heb. *my palate*
32 [a]Gen. 19:2,3 [1]Or, *to the way*
33 [a]Prov. 28:13 [1]Or, *after the manner of men*
34 [a]Ex. 23:2
35 [a]ch. 13:22 [1]Or, *behold, my sign is that the Almighty will answer me*
38 [1]Heb. *weep*
39 [a]Jas. 5:4 [b]1 Ki. 21:19 [1]Heb. *the strength thereof* [2]Heb. *caused the soul of the owners thereof to expire,* or, *breathe out*
40 [a]Gen. 3:18 [1]Or, *noisome weeds*
32:1 [a]ch. 33:9 [1]Heb. *from answering*
2 [1]Heb. *his soul*
4 [1]Heb. *expected Job in words* [2]Heb. *elder for days*
6 [1]Heb. *few of days* [2]Heb. *feared*
8 [a]Prov. 2:6
9 [a]1 Cor. 1:26
11 [1]Heb. *understandings* [2]Heb. *words*

R *Job 11:13–14* ◀ ▶ *Job 33:27–28*

E *Job 26:13* ◀ ▶ *Job 32:18–19*
G *Ne 9:20* ◀ ▶ *Ps 68:18*
N *Job 26:13* ◀ ▶ *Job 33:4*
T *Ne 9:20* ◀ ▶ *Job 32:18–19*

hold, *there was* none of you that convinced Job, *or* that answered his words:
13 [a]Lest ye should say, We have found
out wisdom: God thrusteth him down,
not man.
14 Now he hath not [1]directed *his*
words against me: neither will I answer
him with your speeches.
15 They were amazed, they answered
no more: [1]they left off speaking.
16 When I had waited, (for they spake
not, but stood still, *and* answered no
more;)
17 *I said,* I will answer also my part, I
also will show mine opinion.
E 18 For I am full of [1]matter, [2]the spirit
L within me constraineth me.
M 19 Behold, my belly *is* as wine *which*
T [1]hath no vent; it is ready to burst like
new bottles.
20 I will speak, [1]that I may be refreshed: I will open my lips and answer.
21 Let me not, I pray you, accept any
man's person, neither let me give flattering titles unto man.
22 For I know not to give flattering titles; *in so doing* my maker would soon
take me away.

33 WHEREFORE, JOB, I pray thee,
hear my speeches, and hearken
to all my words.
2 Behold, now I have opened my
mouth, my tongue hath spoken [1]in my
mouth.
3 My words *shall be of* the uprightness
of my heart: and my lips shall utter
knowledge clearly.
E 4 [a]The spirit of God hath made me,
H and the breath of the Almighty hath
M given me life.
N 5 If thou canst answer me, set *thy*
words in order before me, stand up.
6 [a]Behold, I *am* [1]according to thy wish
in God's stead: I also am [2]formed out of
the clay.
7 [a]Behold, my terror shall not make
thee afraid, neither shall my hand be
heavy upon thee.
8 Surely thou hast spoken [1]in mine
hearing, and I have heard the voice of *thy*
words, *saying,*
9 [a]I am clean without transgression, I
am innocent; neither *is there* iniquity
in me.
10 Behold, he findeth occasions
against me, [a]he counteth me for his
enemy,
11 [a]He putteth my feet in the stocks,
he marketh all my paths.
12 Behold, *in* this thou art not just: I
will answer thee, that God is greater than
man.
13 Why dost thou [a]strive against him?
for [1]he giveth not account of any of his
matters.
14 [a]For God speaketh once, yea twice,
yet man perceiveth it not.
15 [a]In a dream, in a vision of the
night, when deep sleep falleth upon men,
in slumberings upon the bed;
16 [a]Then [1]he openeth the ears of men,
and sealeth their instruction,
17 That he may withdraw man *from* D
his [1]purpose, and hide pride from man. T
18 He keepeth back his soul from the
pit, and his life [1]from perishing by the
sword.
19 He is chastened also with pain
upon his bed, and the multitude of his
bones with strong *pain:*
20 [a]So that his life abhorreth bread,
and his soul [1]dainty meat.
21 His flesh is consumed away, that it
cannot be seen; and his bones *that* were
not seen stick out.
22 Yea, his soul draweth near unto the
grave, and his life to the destroyers.
23 If there be a messenger with him, H
an interpreter, one among a thousand, to
show unto man his uprightness:
24 Then he is gracious unto him, and
saith, Deliver him from going down to
the pit: I have found [1]a ransom.
25 His flesh shall be fresher [1]than a
child's: he shall return to the days of his
youth:
26 He shall pray unto God, and he will
be favourable unto him: and he shall see
his face with joy: for he will render unto
man his righteousness.

13 [a]Jer. 9:23
14 [1]Or, *ordered his words*
15 [1]Heb. *they removed speeches from themselves*
18 [1]Heb. *words* [2]Heb. *the spirit of my belly*
19 [1]Heb. *is not opened*
20 [1]Heb. *that I may breathe*
33:2 [1]Heb. *in my palate*
4 [a]Gen. 2:7
6 [a]ch. 9:32,33 [1]Heb. *according to thy mouth* [2]Heb. *cut out of the clay*
7 [a]ch. 9:34
8 [1]Heb. *in mine ears*
9 [a]ch. 10:7
10 [a]ch. 16:9
11 [a]ch. 13:27
13 [a]Is. 45:9 [1]Heb. *he answereth not*
14 [a]Ps. 62:11
15 [a]Num. 12:6
16 [a]ch. 36:10,15 [1]Heb. *he revealeth,* or, *uncovereth*
17 [1]Heb. *work*
18 [1]Heb. *from passing by the sword*
20 [a]Ps. 107:18 [1]Heb. *meat of desire*
24 [1]Or, *an atonement*
25 [1]Heb. *than childhood*

E *Job 32:8* ◄ ► *Job 33:4*
L *2Ch 18:23* ◄ ► *Ps 39:3*
M *Job 26:13–14* ◄ ► *Job 33:4*
T *Job 32:8* ◄ ► *Ps 143:10*
E *Job 32:18–19* ◄ ► *Ps 104:30*
H ► *Eze 37:13–14*
M *Job 32:18–19* ◄ ► *Ps 51:12–13*
N *Job 32:8* ◄ ► *Ps 51:12*
D *Job 2:7* ◄ ► *Job 33:29–30*
T *Job 23:10* ◄ ► *Job 34:31*
H *Job 5:26* ◄ ► *Ps 34:12–13*

L 27 ʹHe looketh upon men, and *if any*
R [a]say, I have sinned, and perverted *that which was* right, and it [b]profited me not;

28 ʹHe will [a]deliver his soul from going into the pit, and his life shall see the light.

D 29 Lo, all these *things* worketh God ʹoftentimes with man,

30 [a]To bring back his soul from the pit, to be enlightened with the light of the living.

31 Mark well, O Job, hearken unto me: hold thy peace, and I will speak.

32 If thou hast any thing to say, answer me: speak, for I desire to justify thee.

33 If not, [a]hearken unto me: hold thy peace, and I shall teach thee wisdom.

34

FURTHERMORE ELIHU answered and said,

2 Hear my words, O ye wise *men;* and give ear unto me, ye that have knowledge.

3 [a]For the ear trieth words, as the ʹmouth tasteth meat.

4 Let us choose to us judgment: let us know among ourselves what *is* good.

5 For Job hath said, [a]I am righteous: and [b]God hath taken away my judgment.

6 [a]Should I lie against my right? ʹmy wound *is* incurable without transgression.

7 What man *is* like Job, [a]*who* drinketh up scorning like water?

8 Which goeth in company with the workers of iniquity, and walketh with wicked men.

9 For [a]he hath said, It profiteth a man nothing that he should delight himself with God.

10 Therefore hearken unto me, ye ʹmen of understanding: [a]far be it from God, *that he should do* wickedness; and *from* the Almighty, *that he should commit* iniquity.

S 11 [a]For the work of a man shall he render unto him, and cause every man to find according to *his* ways.

12 Yea, surely God will not do wickedly, neither will the Almighty [a]pervert judgment.

13 Who hath given him a charge over the earth? or who hath disposed ʹthe whole world?

14 If he set his heart ʹupon man, *if* he [a]gather unto himself his spirit and his breath;

15 [a]All flesh shall perish together, and man shall turn again unto dust.

16 If now *thou hast* understanding, hear this: hearken to the voice of my words.

17 [a]Shall even he that hateth right ʹgovern? and wilt thou condemn him that is most just?

18 [a]*Is it fit* to say to a king, *Thou art* wicked? *and* to princes, *Ye are* ungodly?

19 *How much less to him* that [a]accepteth not the persons of princes, nor regardeth the rich more than the poor? for [b]they all *are* the work of his hands.

20 In a moment shall they die, and the people shall be troubled [a]at midnight, and pass away: and ʹthe mighty shall be taken away without hand.

21 [a]For his eyes *are* upon the ways of E
man, and he seeth all his goings.

22 [a]*There is* no darkness, nor shadow of death, where the workers of iniquity may hide themselves.

23 For he will not lay upon man more *than right;* that he should ʹenter into judgment with God.

24 [a]He shall break in pieces mighty men ʹwithout number, and set others in their stead.

25 Therefore he knoweth their works, and he overturneth *them* in the night, so that they are ʹdestroyed.

26 He striketh them as wicked men ʹin the open sight of others;

27 Because they [a]turned back ʹfrom him, and [b]would not consider any of his ways:

28 So that they [a]cause the cry of the poor to come unto him, and he [b]heareth the cry of the afflicted.

29 When he giveth quietness, who S
then can make trouble? and when he hideth *his* face, who then can behold him? whether *it be done* against a nation, or against a man only:

30 That the hypocrite reign not, lest [a]the people be ensnared.

27 [a]2 Sam. 12:13; Prov. 28:13; Luke 15:21; 1 John 1:9 [b]Rom. 6:21 ʹOr, *He shall look upon men, and say, I have sinned*
28 [a]Is. 38:17 ʹOr, *He hath delivered my soul, &c., and my life*
29 ʹHeb. *twice* and *thrice*
30 [a]Ps. 56:13
33 [a]Ps. 34:11
34:3 [a]ch. 6:30 & 12:11 ʹHeb. *palate*
5 [a]ch. 33:9 [b]ch. 27:2
6 [a]ch. 9:17 ʹHeb. *mine arrow*
7 [a]ch. 15:16
9 [a]Mal. 3:14
10 [a]ch. 8:3 ʹHeb. *men of heart*
11 [a]Ps. 62:12; Prov. 24:12; Mat. 16:27
12 [a]ch. 8:3
13 ʹHeb. *all of it?*
14 [a]Ps. 104:29 ʹHeb. *upon him*
15 [a]Gen. 3:19
17 [a]2 Sam. 23:3 ʹHeb. *bind?*
18 [a]Ex. 22:28
19 [a]Deut. 10:17 [b]ch. 31:15
20 [a]Ex. 12:29 ʹHeb. *they shall take away the mighty*
21 [a]ch. 31:4
22 [a]Ps. 139:12; Amos 9:2,3
23 ʹHeb. *go*
24 [a]Dan. 2:21 ʹHeb. *without searching out*
25 ʹHeb. *crushed*
26 ʹHeb. *in the place of beholders*
27 [a]1 Sam. 15:11 [b]Ps. 28:5; Is. 5:12 ʹHeb. *from after him*
28 [a]Jas. 5:4 [b]Ex. 22:23
30 [a]1 Ki. 12:28,30

L *Ne 9:31* ◀ ▶ *Ps 9:10*
R *Job 31:33* ◀ ▶ *Job 34:31–32*
D *Job 33:17–22* ◀ ▶ *Ps 106:29*
S *Job 28:7–8* ◀ ▶ *Job 34:32*
E *Job 31:4* ◀ ▶ *Job 42:2*
S *1Ch 18:13* ◀ ▶ *Ps 4:8*

R 31 Surely it is meet to be said unto
T God, I have borne *chastisement,* I will
not offend *any more:*
S 32 *That which* I see not teach thou me:
if I have done iniquity, I will do no more.

33 [1]*Should it be* according to thy mind? he will recompense it, whether thou refuse, or whether thou choose; and not I: therefore speak what thou knowest.

34 Let men [1]of understanding tell me, and let a wise man hearken unto me.

35 [a]Job hath spoken without knowledge, and his words *were* without wisdom.

36 [1]My desire *is that* Job may be tried unto the end because of *his* answers for wicked men.

37 For he addeth rebellion unto his sin, he clappeth *his hands* among us, and multiplieth his words against God.

35

ELIHU SPAKE moreover, and said,

2 Thinkest thou this to be right, *that* thou saidst, My righteousness *is* more than God's?

3 For [a]thou saidst, What advantage will it be unto thee? *and,* What profit shall I have, [1]*if I be cleansed* from my sin?

4 [1]I will answer thee, and [a]thy companions with thee.

5 [a]Look unto the heavens, and see; and behold the clouds *which* are higher than thou.

6 If thou sinnest, what doest thou [a]against him? or *if* thy transgressions be multiplied, what doest thou unto him?

7 [a]If thou be righteous, what givest thou him? or what receiveth he of thine hand?

8 Thy wickedness *may hurt* a man as thou *art;* and thy righteousness *may profit* the son of man.

9 [a]By reason of the multitude of oppressions they make *the oppressed* to cry: they cry out by reason of the arm of the mighty.

10 But none saith, [a]Where *is* God my maker, [b]who giveth songs in the night;

11 Who [a]teacheth us more than the beasts of the earth, and maketh us wiser than the fowls of heaven?

12 [a]There they cry, but none giveth answer, because of the pride of evil men.

13 [a]Surely God will not hear vanity, neither will the Almighty regard it.

14 [a]Although thou sayest thou shalt not see him, *yet* judgment *is* before him; therefore [b]trust thou in him.

15 But now, because *it is* not *so,* [1]he hath [a]visited in his anger; yet [2]he knoweth *it* not in great extremity:

16 [a]Therefore doth Job open his mouth in vain; he multiplieth words without knowledge.

36

ELIHU ALSO proceeded, and said,

2 Suffer me a little, and I will show thee [1]that *I have* yet to speak on God's behalf.

3 I will fetch my knowledge from afar, and will ascribe righteousness to my Maker.

4 For truly my words *shall* not *be* false: he that is perfect in knowledge *is* with thee.

5 Behold, God *is* mighty, and despiseth not *any:* [a]*he is* mighty in strength *and* [1]wisdom.

6 He preserveth not the life of the wicked: but giveth right to the [1]poor.

7 [a]He withdraweth not his eyes from K
the righteous: but [b]with kings *are they* on U
the throne; yea, he doth establish them
for ever, and they are exalted.

8 And [a]if *they be* bound in fetters, *and* be holden in cords of affliction;

9 Then he showeth them their work, R
and their transgressions that they have
exceeded.

10 [a]He openeth also their ear to disci- S
pline, and commandeth that they return
from iniquity.

11 If they obey and serve *him,* they U
shall [a]spend their days in prosperity, and
their years in pleasures.

12 But if they obey not, [1]they shall perish by the sword, and they shall die without knowledge.

13 But the hypocrites in heart [a]heap up wrath: they cry not when he bindeth them.

33 [1]Heb. Should it be *from with thee?*
34 [1]Heb. *of heart*
35 [a]ch. 35:16
36 [1]Or, *My father, let Job be tried*
35:3 [a]ch. 21:15 [1]Or, by it *more than by my sin?*
4 [a]ch. 34:8 [1]Heb. *I will return to thee words*
5 [a]ch. 22:12
6 [a]Prov. 8:36; Jer. 7:19
7 [a]Ps. 16:2; Prov. 9:12
9 [a]ch. 34:28
10 [a]Is. 51:13 [b]Ps. 42:8; Acts 16:25
11 [a]Ps. 94:12
12 [a]Prov. 1:28
13 [a]Is. 1:15; Jer. 11:11
14 [a]ch. 9:11 [b]Ps. 37:5,6
15 [a]Ps. 89:32 [1]i.e. *God* [2]i.e. *Job*
16 [a]ch. 34:35
36:2 [1]Heb. *that there are yet words for God*
5 [a]ch. 9:4 [1]Heb. *heart*
6 [1]Or, *afflicted*
7 [a]Ps. 33:18 [b]Ps. 113:8
8 [a]Ps. 107:10
10 [a]ch. 33:16
11 [a]ch. 21:13; Is. 1:19,20
12 [1]Heb. *they shall pass away by the sword*
13 [a]Rom. 2:5

R *Job 33:27–28* ◀ ▶ *Job 36:9–11*
T *Job 33:17–22* ◀ ▶ *Ps 39:11*
S *Job 34:11* ◀ ▶ *Job 36:10–11*

K *Job 19:25* ◀ ▶ *Job 42:2*
U *Job 29:6* ◀ ▶ *Job 36:11*
R *Job 34:31–32* ◀ ▶ *Job 42:6*
S *Job 34:32* ◀ ▶ *Ps 1:5*
U *Job 36:7* ◀ ▶ *Job 36:16*

14 [a]They[1] die in youth, and their life
is among the unclean.
15 He delivereth the [1]poor in his affliction, and openeth their ears in oppression.
16 Even so would he have removed
thee out of the strait [a]*into* a broad place,
where *there is* no straitness; and [b]that[1]
which should be set on thy table *should*
be full of [c]fatness.
17 But thou hast fulfilled the judgment
of the wicked: [1]judgment and justice take
hold *on thee.*
18 Because *there is* wrath, *beware* lest
he take thee away with *his* stroke: then
[a]a great ransom cannot [1]deliver thee.
19 [a]Will he esteem thy riches? *no,* not
gold, nor all the forces of strength.
20 Desire not the night, when people
are cut off in their place.
21 Take heed, [a]regard not iniquity: for
[b]this hast thou chosen rather than affliction.
22 Behold, God exalteth by his power:
[a]who teacheth like him?
23 [a]Who hath enjoined him his way?
or [b]who can say, Thou hast wrought iniquity?
24 Remember that thou [a]magnify his
work, which men behold.
25 Every man may see it; man may behold *it* afar off.
26 Behold, God *is* great, and we
[a]know *him* not, [b]neither can the number
of his years be searched out.
27 For he [a]maketh small the drops of
water: they pour down rain according to
the vapour thereof:
28 [a]Which the clouds do drop *and* distil upon man abundantly.
29 Also can *any* understand the
spreadings of the clouds, *or* the noise of
his tabernacle?
30 Behold, he [a]spreadeth his light
upon it, and covereth [1]the bottom of the
sea.
31 For [a]by them judgeth he the people; he [b]giveth meat in abundance.
32 [a]With clouds he covereth the light;
and commandeth it *not to shine* by *the*
cloud that cometh betwixt.
33 [a]The noise thereof showeth concerning it, the cattle also concerning [1]the
vapour.

37 AT THIS also my heart trembleth,
and is moved out of his place.
2 [1]Hear attentively the noise of his
voice, and the sound *that* goeth out of his
mouth.
3 He directeth it under the whole
heaven, and his [1]lightning unto the [2]ends
of the earth.
4 After it [a]a voice roareth: he thundereth with the voice of his excellency; and
he will not stay them when his voice is
heard.
5 God thundereth marvellously with
his voice; [a]great things doeth he, which
we cannot comprehend.
6 For [a]he saith to the snow, Be thou
on the earth; [1]likewise to the small rain,
and to the great rain of his strength.
7 He sealeth up the hand of every man;
[a]that all men may know his work.
8 Then the beasts [a]go into dens, and
remain in their places.
9 [1]Out of the south cometh the whirlwind: and cold out of the [2]north.
10 [a]By the breath of God frost is given:
and the breadth of the waters is
straitened.
11 Also by watering he wearieth the
thick cloud: he scattereth [1]his bright
cloud:
12 And it is turned round about by his
counsels: that they may [a]do whatsoever
he commandeth them upon the face of
the world in the earth.
13 [a]He causeth it to come, whether
for [1]correction, or [b]for his land, or [c]for
mercy.

Consider his wondrous works

14 Hearken unto this, O Job: stand
still, and [a]consider the wondrous works
of God.
15 Dost thou know when God disposed them, and caused the light of his
cloud to shine?
16 [a]Dost thou know the balancings of

14 [a]Ps. 55:23 [1]Heb. *Their soul dieth*
15 [1]Or, *afflicted*
16 [a]Ps. 18:19 & 31:8 [b]Ps. 23:5 [c]Ps. 36:8 [1]Heb. *the rest of thy table*
17 [1]Or, *judgment and justice should uphold* thee
18 [a]Ps. 49:7 [1]Heb. *turn thee aside*
19 [a]Prov. 11:4
21 [a]Ps. 66:18 [b]Heb. 11:25
22 [a]Is. 40:13; 1 Cor. 2:16
23 [a]ch. 34:13 [b]ch. 34:10
24 [a]Ps. 92:5; Rev. 15:3
26 [a]1 Cor. 13:12 [b]Ps. 90:2; Heb. 1:12
27 [a]Ps. 147:8
28 [a]Prov. 3:20
30 [a]ch. 37:3 [1]Heb. *the roots*
31 [a]ch. 37:13 [b]Acts 14:17
32 [a]Ps. 147:8
33 [a]1 Ki. 18:41 [1]Heb. *that which goeth up*
37:2 [1]Heb. *Hear in hearing*
3 [1]Heb. *light* [2]Heb. *wings of the earth*
4 [a]Ps. 29:3
5 [a]ch. 5:9
6 [a]Ps. 147:16 [1]Heb. *and to the shower of rain, and to the showers of rain of his strength*
7 [a]Ps. 109:27
8 [a]Ps. 104:22
9 [1]Heb. *Out of the chamber* [2]Heb. *scattering* winds
10 [a]Ps. 147:17
11 [1]Heb. *the cloud of his light*
12 [a]Ps. 148:8
13 [a]Ex. 9:18 [b]ch. 38:26 [c]2 Sam. 21:10; 1 Ki. 18:45 [1]Heb. *a rod*
14 [a]Ps. 111:2
16 [a]ch. 36:29

U Job 36:11 ◀▶ Job 42:10

37:16 Elihu mentioned God's marvelously complex influence on the world's climate as "the balancings of the clouds." Scientists now recognize that the amount of water vapor within the clouds influences the amount of rain, evaporation and global weather patterns. Once again, science upholds the Word of God written more than 3,000 years ago.

the clouds, the wondrous works of [b]him
which is perfect in knowledge?
17 How thy garments *are* warm, when
he quieteth the earth by the south *wind?*
18 Hast thou with him [a]spread out the
sky, *which is* strong, *and* as a molten
lookingglass?
19 Teach us what we shall say unto
him; *for* we cannot order *our speech* by
reason of darkness.
20 Shall it be told him that I speak? if
a man speak, surely he shall be swallowed up.
21 And now *men* see not the bright
light which *is* in the clouds: but the wind
passeth, and cleanseth them.
22 [1]Fair weather cometh out of the
north: with God *is* terrible majesty.
23 *Touching* the Almighty, [a]we cannot
find him out: [b]*he is* excellent in power,
and in judgment, and in plenty of justice:
he will not afflict.
24 Men do therefore [a]fear him: he respecteth not any *that are* [b]wise of heart.

The LORD *speaks*

38 THEN THE LORD answered Job
[a]out of the whirlwind, and said,
2 [a]Who *is* this that darkeneth counsel
by [b]words without knowledge?
3 [a]Gird up now thy loins like a man;
for I will demand of thee, and [1]answer
thou me.
4 [a]Where wast thou when I laid the
foundations of the earth? declare, [1]if thou
hast understanding.
5 Who hath laid the measures thereof,
if thou knowest? or who hath stretched
the line upon it?
6 Whereupon are the [1]foundations
thereof [2]fastened? or who laid the corner
stone thereof;
7 When the morning stars sang together, and all [a]the sons of God shouted
for joy?
8 [a]Or *who* shut up the sea with doors,
when it brake forth, *as if* it had issued out
of the womb?
9 When I made the cloud the garment
thereof, and thick darkness a swaddling-
band for it,
10 And [a]brake[1] up for it my decreed
place, and set bars and doors,
11 And said, Hitherto shalt thou come,
but no further: and here shall [1]thy proud
waves [a]be stayed?
12 Hast thou [a]commanded the morning since thy days; *and* caused the day-
spring to know his place;
13 That it might take hold of the [1]ends P
of the earth, that [a]the wicked might be
shaken out of it?
14 It is turned as clay *to* the seal; and
they stand as a garment.
15 And from the wicked their [a]light is
withholden, and [b]the high arm shall be
broken.
16 Hast thou [a]entered into the springs
of the sea? or hast thou walked in the
search of the depth?
17 Have [a]the gates of death been
opened unto thee? or hast thou seen the
doors of the shadow of death?
18 Hast thou perceived the breadth of
the earth? declare if thou knowest it all.
19 Where *is* the way *where* light
dwelleth? and *as for* darkness, where *is*
the place thereof,
20 That thou shouldest take it [1]to the
bound thereof, and that thou shouldest
know the paths *to* the house thereof ?
21 Knowest thou *it,* because thou wast
then born? or *because* the number of thy
days *is* great?
22 Hast thou entered into [a]the treasures of the snow? or hast thou seen the
treasures of the hail,
23 [a]Which I have reserved against the
time of trouble, against the day of battle
and war?
24 By what way is the light parted,
which scattereth the east wind upon the
earth?
25 Who [a]hath divided a watercourse
for the overflowing of waters, or a way
for the lightning of thunder;
26 To cause it to rain on the earth,
where no man *is; on* the wilderness,
wherein *there is* no man;
27 [a]To satisfy the desolate and waste

16 [b]ch. 36:4
18 [a]Gen. 1:6; Is. 44:24
22 [1]Heb. *Gold*
23 [a]1 Tim. 6:16 [b]ch. 36:5
24 [a]Mat. 10:28 [b]Mat. 11:25
38:1 [a]Ex. 19:16
2 [a]ch. 34:35 [b]1 Tim. 1:7
3 [a]ch. 40:7 [1]Heb. *make me know*
4 [a]Ps. 104:5; Prov. 8:29 [1]Heb. *if thou knowest understanding*
6 [1]Heb. *sockets* [2]Heb. *made to sink?*
7 [a]ch. 1:6
8 [a]Gen. 1:9
10 [a]ch. 26:10 [1]Or, *established my decree upon it*
11 [a]Ps. 89:9 [1]Heb. *the pride of thy waves*
12 [a]Ps. 148:5
13 [a]Ps. 104:35 [1]Heb. *wings*
15 [a]ch. 18:5 [b]Ps. 10:15
16 [a]Ps. 77:19
17 [a]Ps. 9:13
20 [1]Or, *at*
22 [a]Ps. 135:7
23 [a]Ex. 9:18; Josh. 10:11; Is. 30:30; Ezek. 13:11,13; Rev. 16:21
25 [a]ch. 28:26
27 [a]Ps. 107:35

P *2Sa 23:6–7* ◀ ▶ *Ps 2:1–6*

38:13 This verse metaphorically says that dawn will shake the wicked out of the earth. These words may allude prophetically to the final battle of this age (Armageddon) when the wicked leaders and armies of this world will be destroyed and "shaken out of it" by God.

ground; and to cause the bud of the tender herb to spring forth?

28 [a]Hath the rain a father? or who hath begotten the drops of dew?

29 Out of whose womb came the ice? and the [a]hoary frost of heaven, who hath gendered it?

30 The waters are hid as *with* a stone, and the face of the deep [1]is [a]frozen.

31 Canst thou bind the sweet influences of [a]Pleiades,[1,2] or loose the bands of [3]Orion?

32 Canst thou bring forth [1]Mazzaroth in his season? or canst thou [2]guide Arcturus with his sons?

33 Knowest thou [a]the ordinances of heaven? canst thou set the dominion thereof in the earth?

34 Canst thou lift up thy voice to the clouds, that abundance of waters may cover thee?

35 Canst thou send lightnings, that they may go, and say unto thee, [1]Here we *are?*

36 [a]Who hath put wisdom in the inward parts? or who hath given understanding to the heart?

37 Who can number the clouds in wisdom? or [1]who can stay the bottles of heaven,

38 [1]When the dust [2]groweth into hardness, and the clods cleave fast together?

39 [a]Wilt thou hunt the prey for the lion? or fill [1]the appetite of the young lions,

40 When they couch in *their* dens, *and* abide in the covert to lie in wait?

41 [a]Who provideth for the raven his food? when his young ones cry unto God, they wander for lack of meat.

39

KNOWEST THOU the time when the wild goats of the rock bring forth? *or* canst thou mark when [a]the hinds do calve?

2 Canst thou number the months *that* they fulfil? or knowest thou the time when they bring forth?

3 They bow themselves, they bring forth their young ones, they cast out their sorrows.

4 Their young ones are in good liking, they grow up with corn; they go forth, and return not unto them.

5 Who hath sent out the wild ass free? or who hath loosed the bands of the wild ass?

6 [a]Whose house I have made the wilderness, and the [1]barren land his dwellings.

7 He scorneth the multitude of the city, neither regardeth he the crying [a]of[1] the driver.

8 The range of the mountains *is* his pasture, and he searcheth after every green thing.

9 Will the [a]unicorn be willing to serve thee, or abide by thy crib?

10 Canst thou bind the unicorn with his band in the furrow? or will he harrow the valleys after thee?

11 Wilt thou trust him, because his strength *is* great? or wilt thou leave thy labour to him?

12 Wilt thou believe him, that he will bring home thy seed, and gather *it into* thy barn?

13 *Gavest thou* the goodly wings unto the peacocks? or [1]wings and feathers unto the ostrich?

14 Which leaveth her eggs in the earth, and warmeth them in dust,

15 And forgetteth that the foot may crush them, or that the wild beast may break them.

16 She is [a]hardened against her young ones, as though *they were* not hers: her labour is in vain without fear;

17 Because God hath deprived her of wisdom, neither hath he [a]imparted to her understanding.

18 What time she lifteth up herself on high, she scorneth the horse and his rider.

19 Hast thou given the horse strength? hast thou clothed his neck with thunder?

20 Canst thou make him afraid as a grasshopper? the glory of his nostrils *is* [1]terrible.

21 [1]He paweth in the valley, and rejoiceth in *his* strength: [a]he goeth on to meet [2]the armed men.

22 He mocketh at fear, and is not af-

28 [a]Ps. 147:8; Jer. 14:22
29 [a]Ps. 147:16
30 [a]ch. 37:10 [1]Heb. *is taken*
31 [a]ch. 9:9; Amos 5:8 [1]Or, *The seven stars* [2]Heb. *Cimah* [3]Heb. *Cesil?*
32 [1]Or, *The twelve signs* [2]Heb. *guide them*
33 [a]Jer. 31:35
35 [1]Heb. *Behold us?*
36 [a]ch. 32:8; Ps. 51:6; Eccl. 2:26
37 [1]Heb. *who can cause to lie down*
38 [1]Or, *When the dust is turned into mire* [2]Heb. *is poured*
39 [a]Ps. 104:21 & 145:15 [1]Heb. *the life*
41 [a]Ps. 147:9; Mat. 6:26
39:1 [a]Ps. 29:9
6 [a]ch. 24:5; Jer. 2:24; Hos. 8:9 [1]Heb. *salt places*
7 [a]ch. 3:18 [1]Heb. *of the exactor*
9 [a]Num. 23:22; Deut. 33:17
13 [1]Or, *the feathers of the stork and ostrich*
16 [a]Lam. 4:3
17 [a]ch. 35:11
20 [1]Heb. *terror*
21 [a]Jer. 8:6 [1]Or, His feet *dig* [2]Heb. *the armour*

38:30 Job's words confirm the divine inspiration of this book in this reference to frozen waters that are as hard as stone. Since Job lived in the Middle East it is unlikely that he had ever seen a frozen body of water or a polar ice cap, yet his description of both is profoundly accurate.

frighted; neither turneth he back from the sword.

23 The quiver rattleth against him, the glittering spear and the shield.

24 He swalloweth the ground with fierceness and rage: neither believeth he that *it is* the sound of the trumpet.

25 He saith among the trumpets, Ha, ha; and he smelleth the battle afar off, the thunder of the captains, and the shouting.

26 Doth the hawk fly by thy wisdom, *and* stretch her wings toward the south?

27 Doth the eagle mount up [1]at thy command, and [a]make her nest on high?

28 She dwelleth and abideth on the rock, upon the crag of the rock, and the strong place.

29 From thence she seeketh the prey, *and* her eyes behold afar off.

30 Her young ones also suck up blood: and [a]where the slain *are,* there *is* she.

40 MOREOVER THE LORD answered Job, and said,

2 Shall he that [a]contendeth with the Almighty instruct *him?* he that reproveth God, let him answer it.

3 ¶ Then Job answered the LORD, and said,

4 [a]Behold, I am vile; what shall I answer thee? [b]I will lay mine hand upon my mouth.

5 Once have I spoken; but I will not answer: yea, twice; but I will proceed no further.

6 ¶ [a]Then answered the LORD unto Job out of the whirlwind, and said,

7 [a]Gird up thy loins now like a man: [b]I will demand of thee, and declare thou unto me.

8 [a]Wilt thou also disannul my judgment? wilt thou condemn me, that thou mayest be righteous?

9 Hast thou an arm like God? or canst thou thunder with [a]a voice like him?

10 [a]Deck thyself now *with* majesty and excellency; and array thyself with glory and beauty.

11 Cast abroad the rage of thy wrath: and behold every one *that is* proud, and abase him.

12 Look on every one *that is* [a]proud, *and* bring him low; and tread down the wicked in their place.

13 Hide them in the dust together; *and* bind their faces in secret.

14 Then will I also confess unto thee that thine own right hand can save thee.

15 ¶ Behold now [1]behemoth, which I made with thee; he eateth grass as an ox.

16 Lo now, his strength *is* in his loins, and his force *is* in the navel of his belly.

17 [1]He moveth his tail like a cedar: the sinews of his stones are wrapped together.

18 His bones *are as* strong pieces of brass; his bones *are* like bars of iron.

19 He *is* the chief of the ways of God: he that made him can make his sword to approach *unto him.*

20 Surely the mountains [a]bring him forth food, where all the beasts of the field play.

21 He lieth under the shady trees, in the covert of the reed, and fens.

22 The shady trees cover him *with* their shadow; the willows of the brook compass him about.

23 Behold, [1]he drinketh up a river, *and* hasteth not: he trusteth that he can draw up Jordan into his mouth.

24 He taketh it with his eyes: *his* nose pierceth through snares.

41 CANST THOU draw out [a]leviathan[1] with an hook? or his tongue with a cord [2]*which* thou lettest down?

2 Canst thou [a]put an hook into his nose? or bore his jaw through with a thorn?

3 Will he make many supplications unto thee? will he speak soft *words* unto thee?

4 Will he make a covenant with thee? wilt thou take him for a servant for ever?

5 Wilt thou play with him as *with* a bird? or wilt thou bind him for thy maidens?

6 Shall the companions make a banquet of him? shall they part him among the merchants?

7 Canst thou fill his skin with barbed irons? or his head with fish spears?

8 Lay thine hand upon him, remember the battle, do no more.

9 Behold, the hope of him is in vain: shall not *one* be cast down even at the sight of him?

10 None *is so* fierce that dare stir him up: who then is able to stand before me?

11 [a]Who hath prevented me, that I should repay *him?* [b]*whatsoever* is under the whole heaven is mine.

27 [a]Jer. 49:16; Obad. 4 [1]Heb. *by thy mouth*
30 [a]Mat. 24:28; Luke 17:37
40:2 [a]ch. 33:13
4 [a]Ezra 9:6; ch. 42:6; Ps. 51:4 [b]ch. 29:9; Ps. 39:9
6 [a]ch. 38:1
7 [a]ch. 38:3 [b]ch. 42:4
8 [a]Ps. 51:4; Rom. 3:4
9 [a]ch. 37:4; Ps. 29:3,4
10 [a]Ps. 93:1 & 104:1
12 [a]Is. 2:12; Dan. 4:37
15 [1]Or, *the elephant,* as some think
17 [1]Or, *He setteth up*
20 [a]Ps. 104:14
23 [1]Heb. *he oppresseth*
41:1 [a]Ps. 104:26; Is. 27:1 [1]i.e. *a whale,* or, *a whirlpool* [2]Heb. which *thou drownest?*
2 [a]Is. 37:29
11 [a]Rom. 11:35 [b]Ex. 19:5; Deut. 10:14; Ps. 24:1 & 50:12; 1 Cor. 10:26,28

12 I will not conceal his parts, nor his power, nor his comely proportion.

13 Who can discover the face of his garment? *or* who can come *to him* [I]with his double bridle?

14 Who can open the doors of his face? his teeth *are* terrible round about.

15 *His* [I]scales *are his* pride, shut up together *as with* a close seal.

16 One is so near to another, that no air can come between them.

17 They are joined one to another, they stick together, that they cannot be sundered.

18 By his sneezings a light doth shine, and his eyes *are* like the eyelids of the morning.

19 Out of his mouth go burning lamps, *and* sparks of fire leap out.

20 Out of his nostrils goeth smoke, as *out* of a seething pot or caldron.

21 His breath kindleth coals, and a flame goeth out of his mouth.

22 In his neck remaineth strength, and [I]sorrow is turned into joy before him.

23 [I]The flakes of his flesh are joined together: they are firm in themselves; they cannot be moved.

24 His heart is as firm as a stone; yea, as hard as a piece of the nether *millstone.*

25 When he raiseth up himself, the mighty are afraid: by reason of breakings they purify themselves.

26 The sword of him that layeth at him cannot hold: the spear, the dart, nor the [I]habergeon.

27 He esteemeth iron as straw, *and* brass as rotten wood.

28 The arrow cannot make him flee: slingstones are turned with him into stubble.

29 Darts are counted as stubble: he laugheth at the shaking of a spear.

30 [I]Sharp stones *are* under him: he spreadeth sharp pointed things upon the mire.

31 He maketh the deep to boil like a pot: he maketh the sea like a pot of ointment.

32 He maketh a path to shine after him; *one* would think the deep *to be* hoary.

33 Upon earth there is not his like, [I]who is made without fear.

34 He beholdeth all high *things:* he *is* a king over all the children of pride.

Job repents in dust and ashes

42 THEN JOB answered the LORD, and said,

2 I know that thou [a]canst do every E
thing, and *that* [I]no thought can be with- K
holden from thee.

3 [a]Who *is* he that hideth counsel without knowledge? therefore have I uttered that I understood not; [b]things too wonderful for me, which I knew not.

4 Hear, I beseech thee, and I will speak: [a]I will demand of thee, and declare thou unto me.

5 I have heard of thee by the hearing of the ear: but now mine eye seeth thee.

6 Wherefore I [a]abhor *myself,* and re- R
pent in dust and ashes.

7 ¶ And it was *so,* that after the LORD had spoken these words unto Job, the LORD said to Eliphaz the Temanite, My wrath is kindled against thee, and against thy two friends: for ye have not spoken of me *the thing that is* right, as my servant Job *hath.*

8 Therefore take unto you now [a]seven bullocks and seven rams, and [b]go to my servant Job, and offer up for yourselves a burnt offering; and my servant Job shall [c]pray for you: for [I]him will I accept: lest I deal with you *after your* folly, in that ye have not spoken of me *the thing which is* right, like my servant Job.

9 So Eliphaz the Temanite and Bildad the Shuhite *and* Zophar the Naamathite went, and did according as the LORD commanded them: the LORD also accepted [I]Job.

Job's fortunes restored

10 [a]And the LORD turned the captivity P
of Job, when he prayed for his friends: U

E *Job 34:21–22* ◀ ▶ *Ps 7:9*
K *Job 36:7* ◀ ▶ *Ps 2:12*
R *Job 36:9–11* ◀ ▶ *Ps 32:5*
P *Job 27:16–17* ◀ ▶ *Job 42:12*
U *Job 36:16* ◀ ▶ *Job 42:12*

13 [I]Or, *within*
15 [I]Heb. *strong pieces of shields*
22 [I]Heb. *sorrow rejoiceth*
23 [I]Heb. *The fallings*
26 [I]Or, *breastplate*
30 [I]Heb. *Sharp pieces of potsherd*
33 [I]Or, *who behave themselves without fear*
42:2 [a]Gen. 18:14; Mat. 19:26; Mark 10:27 & 14:36; Luke 18:27 [I]Or, *no thought of thine can be hindered*
3 [a]ch. 38:2 [b]Ps. 40:5 & 131:1 & 139:6
4 [a]ch. 38:3 & 40:7
6 [a]Ezra 9:6; ch. 40:4
8 [a]Num. 23:1 [b]Mat. 5:24 [c]Gen. 20:17; Jas. 5:15,16; 1 John 5:16 [I]Heb. *his face,* or, *person*
9 [I]Heb. *the face of Job*
10 [a]Ps. 14:7 & 126:1

42:10 God reversed the fortunes of Job and prospered him "when he prayed for his friends." When Job looked beyond his own pain and prayed for God to bless his friends despite their accusations and useless advice, the Lord answered his prayer, reconciling him to his friends and restoring to Job more than he

also the LORD [l]gave Job [b]twice as much as he had before.

11 Then came there unto him [a]all his brethren, and all his sisters, and all they that had been of his acquaintance before, and did eat bread with him in his house: and they bemoaned him, and comforted him over all the evil that the LORD had brought upon him: every man also gave him a piece of money, and every one an earring of gold.

B 12 So the LORD blessed [a]the latter end
P of Job more than his beginning: for he
U had [b]fourteen thousand sheep, and six thousand camels, and a thousand yoke of oxen, and a thousand she asses.

13 [a]He had also seven sons and three daughters.

14 And he called the name of the first, Jemima; and the name of the second, Kezia; and the name of the third, Keren-happuch.

15 And in all the land were no women R
found *so* fair as the daughters of Job: and their father gave them inheritance among their brethren.

16 After this [a]lived Job an hundred E
and forty years, and saw his sons, and his sons' sons, *even* four generations.

17 So Job died, *being* old and [a]full of days.

10 [b]Is. 40:2 [l]Heb. *added all that had been to Job unto the double*
11 [a]See ch. 19:13
12 [a]ch. 8:7; Jas. 5:11 [b]See ch. 1:3
13 [a]ch. 1:2
16 [a]ch. 5:26; Prov. 3:16
17 [a]Gen. 25:8

B *Dt 30:9* ◀ ▶ *Ps 65:9–13*
P *Job 42:10* ◀ ▶ *Ps 105:37*
U *Job 42:10* ◀ ▶ *Ps 1:1–3*

R *Ge 39:5* ◀ ▶ *Ps 37:26*
E *Ne 9:21* ◀ ▶ *Ps 30:2–3*

had lost to Satan's attacks.

42:12 Despite Job's terrible trials, God's love for Job remained unchanged and "the LORD blessed the latter end of Job more than his beginning."

Psalms

Author: King David and others

Theme: A book of prayer and praise

Date of Writing: c. 1400–400 B.C.

Outline of Psalms

Book I. (1—41)
Book II. (42—72)
Book III. (73—89)
Book IV. (90—106)
Book V. (107—150)

THE COMBINATION OF poems, songs and laments included in the book of Psalms was originally called in Hebrew *tehillim*, meaning "praises." The name "Psalms" or "Psalter" came from the Septuagint (the Greek translation of the OT) title for this collection of poetry and is the title commonly used today. Characterized throughout by heartfelt praise to God, the 150 poems in the book of Psalms reflect a wide variety of feelings, attitudes and circumstances from its various authors. King David authored the majority of the psalms (73). Other authors include Solomon, Moses, Asaph, the sons of Korah, Heman and Ethan. Still other psalms are anonymous. Superscriptions preceding each psalm indicate its authorship, its use in worship and the circumstance for the writing of the psalm, if known.

Because it contains more verses than any other book of the Bible, the book of Psalms is usually divided into five sections. Each psalm within the section is separate and complete, with the last psalm in the section serving as a doxology. Significantly, the final psalm ends with its own doxology: "Let every thing that hath breath praise the LORD. Praise ye the LORD" (Ps 150:6).

The psalms may also be classified into categories. Psalms 104—106 are historical, Psalms 120—130 are liturgical and Psalms 95—100 and 146—150 are psalms of praise. In addition, several of the psalms are Messianic in content (2; 21; 22; 45; 50; 69; 72; 97; 98; 110) with Psalm 110 being the most frequently quoted psalm in the entire NT. Though Psalms is not a prophetical book, the NT quotes these passages as testimonies to Christ, for in him they are truly fulfilled (see Lk 24:44).

Book I

The way of the righteous

U **1** BLESSED [a]*IS* the man that walketh not in the counsel of the [1]ungodly, nor standeth in the way of sinners, [b]nor sitteth in the seat of the scornful.

2 But [a]his delight *is* in the law of the LORD; [b]and in his law doth he meditate day and night.

3 And he shall be like a tree [a]planted by the rivers of water, that bringeth forth his fruit in his season; his leaf also shall not [1]wither; and whatsoever he doeth shall [b]prosper.

C 4 The ungodly *are* not so: but *are* [a]like the chaff which the wind driveth away.

J 5 Therefore the ungodly shall not
J stand in the judgment, nor sinners in the
S congregation of the righteous.

6 For [a]the LORD knoweth the way of the righteous: but the way of the ungodly shall perish.

The triumph of the king

P **2** WHY[a] DO the heathen [1]rage, and the people [2]imagine a vain thing?

2 The kings of the earth set themselves, and the rulers take counsel together, against the LORD, and against his [a]anointed, *saying,*

3 [a]Let us break their bands asunder, and cast away their cords from us.

4 He that sitteth in the heavens [a]shall laugh: the Lord shall have them in derision.

5 Then shall he speak unto them in his wrath, and [1]vex them in his sore displeasure.

6 Yet have I [1]set my king [a]upon[2] my holy hill of Zion.

7 I will declare [1]the decree: the LORD hath said unto me, [a]Thou *art* my Son; this day have I begotten thee.

8 [a]Ask of me, and I shall give *thee* the M
heathen *for* thine inheritance, and the ut- P
termost parts of the earth *for* thy pos- H
session.

9 [a]Thou shalt break them with a rod of iron; thou shalt dash them in pieces like a potter's vessel.

10 Be wise now therefore, O ye kings: be instructed, ye judges of the earth.

11 [a]Serve the LORD with fear, and rejoice [b]with trembling.

12 [a]Kiss the Son, lest he be angry, and P
ye perish *from* the way, when [b]his wrath F
is kindled but a little. [c]Blessed *are* all H
they that put their trust in him. K
W

Confidence facing the enemy

A Psalm of David, [a]when he fled from Absalom his son.

3 LORD, [b]HOW are they increased that trouble me! many *are* they that rise up against me.

2 Many *there be* which say of my [a]*soul, There is* no help for him in God. Selah.

3 But thou, O LORD, *art* [a]a shield [1]for me; my glory, and [b]the lifter up of mine head.

1:1 [a]Prov. 4:14 [b]Ps. 26:4; Jer. 15:17 [1]Or, *wicked*
2 [a]Ps. 119:35 [b]Josh. 1:8; Ps. 119:1
3 [a]Jer. 17:8; Ezek. 47:12 [b]Gen. 39:3; Is. 3:10 [1]Heb. *fade*
4 [a]Job 21:18; Is. 17:13
6 [a]Ps. 37:18; 2 Tim. 2:19
2:1 [a]Acts 4:25 [1]Or, *tumultuously assemble* [2]Heb. *meditate*
2 [a]John 1:41
3 [a]Luke 19:14
4 [a]Ps. 37:13; Prov. 1:26
5 [1]Or, *trouble*
6 [a]2 Sam. 5:7 [1]Heb. *anointed* [2]Heb. *upon Zion, the hill of my holiness*
7 [a]Acts 13:33 [1]Or, *for a decree*
8 [a]Ps. 22:27
9 [a]Ps. 89:23; Rev. 2:27
11 [a]Heb. 12:28 [b]Phil. 2:12
12 [a]John 5:23 [b]Rev. 6:16 [c]Ps. 34:8; Is. 30:18; Rom. 9:33
3:1 [a]2 Sam. 15-18 [b]2 Sam. 15:12
2 [a]Ps. 71:11
3 [a]Ps. 28:7 [b]Ps. 27:6 [1]Or, *about*

U *Job 42:12* ◀▶ *Ps 3:8*
C *Job 27:18* ◀▶ *Ps 7:14*
J *2Ch 21:14–16* ◀▶ *Ps 7:8*
J *1Ch 16:33* ◀▶ *Ps 7:8*
S *Job 36:10–11* ◀▶ *Ps 4:3–4*
P *Job 38:13* ◀▶ *Ps 2:8–9*

M *2Ch 21:7* ◀▶ *Ps 10:16*
P *Ps 2:1–6* ◀▶ *Ps 2:12*
H *Job 31:3* ◀▶ *Ps 2:12*
P *Ps 2:8–9* ◀▶ *Ps 10:15–16*
F *2Ch 20:20* ◀▶ *Ps 34:8*
H *Ps 2:8–9* ◀▶ *Ps 5:4–6*
K *Job 42:2* ◀▶ *Ps 3:8*
W *Ezr 8:22* ◀▶ *Ps 18:30*

1:5 This verse affirms the principle that the ungodly will be unable to withstand God's wrath in the day of judgment. Furthermore, sinners will not be allowed to assemble in God's sanctuary because God will separate them out to judgment in hell.

2:1–3 This is the first of the major Messianic psalms. It foreshadows Christ's victory in the final battle of Armageddon. David used the phrase "his anointed" (2:2) referring to Jesus as the Messiah (see Ac 4:25–28). Other psalms also speak of the role of the Messiah (see 21; 22; 45; 50; 69; 72; 97; 98; 110).

2:8–9 These verses confirm God's plan to make the nations the Messiah's eternal possession when he establishes his kingdom. Ultimately the Messiah's rule will encompass all that God himself rules.

2:12 The "Son" clearly refers to the Messiah; and the NT defines the Messiah as Jesus Christ (see Heb 5:5). A kiss was a sign of submission (see 1Sa 10:1; 1Ki 19:18).

4 I cried unto the LORD with my voice,
and [a]he heard me out of his [b]holy hill.
Selah.
J 5 [a]I laid me down and slept; I awaked;
V for the LORD sustained me.
6 [a]I will not be afraid of ten thousands
of people, that have set *themselves*
against me round about.
7 Arise, O LORD; save me, O my God:
[a]for thou hast smitten all mine enemies
upon the cheek bone; thou hast broken
the teeth of the ungodly.
K 8 [a]Salvation *belongeth* unto the
O LORD: thy blessing *is* upon thy people.
U Selah.

Thoughts in the night

To the [1]chief Musician on Neginoth, A
Psalm of David.

4 HEAR ME when I call, O God of my
righteousness: thou hast enlarged
me *when I was* in distress; [2]have mercy
upon me, and hear my prayer.
2 O ye sons of men, how long *will ye*
turn my glory into shame? *how long* will
ye love vanity, *and* seek after leasing?
Selah.
S 3 But know that [a]the LORD hath set
apart him that is godly for himself:
the LORD will hear when I call unto
him.
4 [a]Stand in awe, and sin not: [b]com-
mune with your own heart upon your
bed, and be still. Selah.
5 Offer [a]the sacrifices of righteousness, and [b]put your trust in the LORD.
6 *There be* many that say, Who will
show us *any* good? [a]LORD, lift thou up the
light of thy countenance upon us.
U 7 Thou hast put [a]gladness in my heart,
more than in the time *that* their corn and
their wine increased.
S 8 [a]I will both lay me down in peace,
and sleep: [b]for thou, LORD, only makest
me dwell in safety.

J *Job 13:15 ◀ ▶ Ps 18:29*
V *Job 5:20–23 ◀ ▶ Ps 9:3–4*
K *Ps 2:12 ◀ ▶ Ps 12:7*
O *Job 8:11–15 ◀ ▶ Ps 18:31*
U *Ps 1:1–3 ◀ ▶ Ps 4:7*
S *Ps 1:5 ◀ ▶ Ps 5:4–6*
U *Ps 3:8 ◀ ▶ Ps 5:11–12*
S *Job 34:29 ◀ ▶ Ps 27:5*

4 [a]Ps. 34:4 [b]Ps. 2:6
5 [a]Lev. 26:6; Prov. 3:24
6 [a]Ps. 27:3
7 [a]Job 16:10; Lam. 3:30
8 [a]Is. 43:11
4:1 [1]Or, *overseer* [2]Or, *be gracious unto me*
3 [a]2 Tim. 2:19; 2 Pet. 2:9
4 [a]Eph. 4:26 [b]Ps. 77:6
5 [a]Deut. 33:19; Ps. 50:14 [b]Ps. 37:3
6 [a]Num. 6:26
7 [a]Is. 9:3
8 [a]Ps. 3:5 [b]Lev. 25:18
5:2 [a]Ps. 3:4
3 [a]Ps. 30:5
5 [1]Heb. *before thine eyes*
6 [a]Rev. 21:8 [b]Ps. 55:23 [1]Heb. *the man of bloods and deceit*
7 [1]Heb. *the temple of thy holiness*
8 [a]Ps. 25:5 [1]Heb. *those which observe me*
9 [a]Luke 11:44; Rom. 3:13 [b]Ps. 62:4 [1]Or, *stedfastness* [2]Heb. *in his mouth,* i.e. *in the mouth of any of them* [3]Heb. *wickednesses*
10 [1]Or, *Make them guilty* [2]Or, *from their counsels*
11 [a]Is. 65:13 [1]Heb. *thou coverest over,* or, *protectest them*
12 [1]Heb. *crown him*
6:1 [a]1 Chr. 15:21; Ps. 12, title [1]Or, *upon the eighth*

A morning prayer

To the chief Musician upon Nehiloth, A
Psalm of David.

5 GIVE EAR to my words, O LORD, consider my meditation.
2 Hearken unto the [a]voice of my cry,
my King, and my God: for unto thee will I
pray.
3 [a]My voice shalt thou hear in the
morning, O LORD; in the morning will I
direct *my prayer* unto thee, and will
look up.
4 For thou *art* not a God that hath plea- H
sure in wickedness: neither shall evil S
dwell with thee.
5 The foolish shall not stand [1]in thy
sight: thou hatest all workers of iniquity.
6 [a]Thou shalt destroy them that speak
leasing: [b]the LORD will abhor [1]the bloody
and deceitful man.
7 But as for me, I will come *into* thy
house in the multitude of thy mercy: *and*
in thy fear will I worship toward [1]thy
holy temple.
8 [a]Lead me, O LORD, in thy righteousness because of [1]mine enemies; make thy
way straight before my face.
9 For *there is* no [1]faithfulness [2]in their
mouth; their inward part *is* [3]very wickedness; [a]their throat *is* an open sepulchre;
[b]they flatter with their tongue.
10 [1]Destroy thou them, O God; let
them fall [2]by their own counsels; cast
them out in the multitude of their transgressions; for they have rebelled against
thee.
11 But let all those that put their trust U
in thee [a]rejoice: let them ever shout for
joy, because [1]thou defendest them: let
them also that love thy name be joyful in
thee.
12 For thou, LORD, wilt bless the righteous; with favour wilt thou [1]compass
him as *with* a shield.

Prayer for mercy during trouble

To the chief Musician on Neginoth [a]upon[1]
Sheminith, A Psalm of David.

6 O LORD, rebuke me not in thine anger, neither chasten me in thy hot
displeasure.
2 Have mercy upon me, O LORD; for I

H *Ps 2:12 ◀ ▶ Ps 7:11*
S *Ps 4:3–4 ◀ ▶ Ps 7:10–11*
U *Ps 4:7 ◀ ▶ Ps 7:10*

am weak: O LORD, [a]heal me; for my bones
are vexed.
3 My soul is also sore vexed: but thou,
O LORD, how long?
4 Return, O LORD, deliver my soul: oh
save me for thy mercies' sake.
5 [a]For in death *there is* no remembrance of thee: in the grave who shall
give thee thanks?
6 I am weary with my groaning; [/]all
the night make I my bed to swim; I water
my couch with my tears.
7 [a]Mine eye is consumed because of
grief; it waxeth old because of all mine
enemies.
8 [a]Depart from me, all ye workers of
iniquity; for the LORD hath [b]heard the
voice of my weeping.
9 The LORD hath heard my supplication; the LORD will receive my prayer.
10 Let all mine enemies be ashamed
and sore vexed: let them return *and* be
ashamed suddenly.

The prayer of a wronged man

[a]Shiggaion of David, which he sang unto
the LORD, [b]concerning the [/]words of Cush
the Benjamite.

7 O LORD my God, in thee do I put my
trust: [c]save me from all them that
persecute me, and deliver me:
2 [a]Lest he tear my soul like a lion,
[b]rending *it* in pieces, while *there is*
[/]none to deliver.
3 O LORD my God, [a]if I have done this;
if there be [b]iniquity in my hands;
4 If I have rewarded evil unto him that
was at peace with me; (yea, [a]I have delivered him that without cause is mine
enemy:)
5 Let the enemy persecute my soul,
and take *it;* yea, let him tread down my
life upon the earth, and lay mine honour
in the dust. Selah.
6 Arise, O LORD, in thine anger, [a]lift up
thyself because of the rage of mine enemies: and [b]awake for me *to* the judgment
that thou hast commanded.
7 So shall the congregation of the people compass thee about: for their sakes
therefore return thou on high.

2 [a]Hos. 6:1
5 [a]Ps. 30:9
6 [/]Or, *every night*
7 [a]Job 17:7
8 [a]Mat. 25:41 [b]Ps. 3:4
7:1 [a]Hab. 3:1 [b]2 Sam. 16 [c]Ps. 31:15 [/]Or, *business*
2 [a]Is. 38:13 [b]Ps. 50:22 [/]Heb. *not a deliverer*
3 [a]2 Sam. 16:7 [b]1 Sam. 24:11
4 [a]1 Sam. 24:7
6 [a]Ps. 94:2 [b]Ps. 44:23
8 [a]Ps. 18:20
9 [a]1 Sam. 16:7
10 [a]Ps. 125:4 [/]Heb. *My buckler is upon God*
11 [/]Or, *God is a righteous judge*
12 [a]Deut. 32:41
14 [a]Job 15:35
15 [a]Job 4:8 [/]Heb. *He hath digged a pit*
16 [a]Esth. 9:25
8:1 [a]Ps. 81, title & 84, title [b]Ps. 148:13 [c]Ps. 113:4
2 [a]1 Cor. 1:27 [b]Ps. 44:16 [/]Heb. *founded*
3 [a]Ps. 111:2
4 [a]Job 7:17

8 The LORD shall judge the people: J
judge me, O LORD, [a]according to my righ- J
teousness, and according to mine integrity *that is* in me.
9 Oh let the wickedness of the wicked E
come to an end; but establish the just:
[a]for the righteous God trieth the hearts
and reins.
10 [/]My defence *is* of God, which sav- S
eth the [a]upright in heart. U
11 [/]God judgeth the righteous, and H
God is angry *with the wicked* every day.
12 If he turn not, he will [a]whet his
sword; he hath bent his bow, and made it
ready.
13 He hath also prepared for him the
instruments of death; he ordaineth his arrows against the persecutors.
14 [a]Behold, he travaileth with iniq- C
uity, and hath conceived mischief, and
brought forth falsehood.
15 [/]He made a pit, and digged it, [a]and
is fallen into the ditch *which* he made.
16 [a]His mischief shall return upon his H
own head, and his violent dealing shall
come down upon his own pate.
17 I will praise the LORD according to
his righteousness: and will sing praise to
the name of the LORD most high.

God's glory and man's honour

To the chief Musician [a]upon Gittith, A
Psalm of David.

8 O LORD our Lord, how [b]excellent *is*
thy name in all the earth! who [c]hast
set thy glory above the heavens.
2 [a]Out of the mouth of babes and sucklings hast thou [/]ordained strength because of thine enemies, that thou mightest still [b]the enemy and the avenger.
3 When I [a]consider thy heavens, the F
work of thy fingers, the moon and the
stars, which thou hast ordained;
4 [a]What is man, that thou art mindful

J *Ps 1:5* ◀ ▶ *Ps 9:7–8*
J *Ps 1:5* ◀ ▶ *Ps 9:7–8*
E *Job 42:2* ◀ ▶ *Ps 10:11–14*
S *Ps 5:4–6* ◀ ▶ *Ps 11:5*
U *Ps 5:11–12* ◀ ▶ *Ps 11:7*
H *Ps 5:4–6* ◀ ▶ *Ps 7:16*
C *Ps 1:4* ◀ ▶ *Ps 10:4–6*
H *Ps 7:11* ◀ ▶ *Ps 9:5*
F *Job 19:25–27* ◀ ▶ *Ps 16:9*

7:8 The psalmist appeals to God to judge all the people of the earth according to God's standards of righteousness and integrity.

8:4 Though this psalm is not eschatological in

of him? and the son of man, that thou visitest him?

5 For thou hast made him a little lower than the angels, and hast crowned him with glory and honour.

6 [a]Thou madest him to have dominion over the works of thy hands; [b]thou hast put all *things* under his feet:

7 [1]All sheep and oxen, yea, and the beasts of the field;

8 The fowl of the air, and the fish of the sea, *and whatsoever* passeth through the paths of the seas.

9 [a]O LORD our Lord, how excellent *is* thy name in all the earth!

Praise to God for deliverance

To the chief Musician upon Muth-labben, A Psalm of David.

9 I WILL praise *thee,* O LORD, with my whole heart; I will show forth all thy marvellous works.

2 I will be glad and [a]rejoice in thee: I will sing praise to thy name, O [b]thou most High.

V 3 When mine enemies are turned back, they shall fall and perish at thy presence.

4 For [1]thou hast maintained my right and my cause; thou satest in the throne judging [2]right.

H 5 Thou hast rebuked the heathen, thou hast destroyed the wicked, thou hast [a]put out their name for ever and ever.

6 [1]O thou enemy, destructions are come to a perpetual end: and thou hast destroyed cities; their memorial is perished with them.

J 7 [a]But the LORD shall endure for ever:
J he hath prepared his throne for judgment.

8 And [a]he shall judge the world in righteousness, he shall minister judgment to the people in uprightness.

9 [a]The LORD also will be [1]a refuge for the oppressed, a refuge in times of trouble.

10 And they that [a]know thy name will put their trust in thee: for thou, LORD, hast not forsaken them that seek thee. L

11 Sing praises to the LORD, which dwelleth in Zion: [a]declare among the people his doings.

12 [a]When he maketh inquisition for blood, he remembereth them: he forgetteth not the cry of the [1]humble.

13 Have mercy upon me, O LORD; consider my trouble *which I suffer* of them that hate me, thou that liftest me up from the gates of death:

14 That I may show forth all thy praise in the gates of the daughter of Zion: I will [a]rejoice in thy salvation.

15 [a]The heathen are sunk down in the pit *that* they made: in the net which they hid is their own foot taken.

16 The LORD is [a]known *by* the judgment *which* he executeth: the wicked is snared in the work of his own hands. [b]Higgaion. [1] Selah.

17 The wicked shall be turned into hell, *and* all the nations [a]that forget God. H

18 [a]For the needy shall not always be forgotten: [b]the expectation of the poor shall *not* perish for ever.

19 Arise, O LORD; let not man prevail: let the heathen be judged in thy sight.

20 Put them in fear, O LORD: *that* the nations may know themselves *to be but* men. Selah.

God hears and acts

10 WHY STANDEST thou afar off, O LORD? *why* hidest thou *thyself* in times of trouble?

2 [1]The wicked in *his* pride doth persecute the poor: [a]let them be taken in the devices that they have imagined.

3 For the wicked [a]boasteth of his

V *Ps 3:5–6* ◀▶ *Ps 17:7*
H *Ps 7:16* ◀▶ *Ps 9:17*
J *Ps 7:8* ◀▶ *Ps 69:25*
J *Ps 7:8* ◀▶ *Ps 50:3–6*
L *Job 33:27–28* ◀▶ *Ps 22:26*
H *Ps 9:5* ◀▶ *Ps 11:6*

6 [a]Gen. 1:26 [b]Heb. 2:8
7 [1]Heb. *Flocks and oxen all of them*
9 [a]ver. 1
9:2 [a]Ps. 5:11 [b]Ps. 83:18
4 [1]Heb. *thou hast made my judgment* [2]Heb. *in righteousness*
5 [a]Prov. 10:7
6 [1]Or, *The destructions of the enemy are come to a perpetual end: and* their *cities hast thou destroyed*
7 [a]Heb. 1:11
8 [a]Ps. 96:13
9 [a]Ps. 32:7 [1]Heb. *an high place*
10 [a]Ps. 91:14
11 [a]Ps. 107:22
12 [a]Gen. 9:5 [1]Or, *afflicted*
14 [a]Ps. 13:5
15 [a]Ps. 7:15,16
16 [a]Ex. 7:5 [b]Ps. 92:3 [1]i.e. *Meditation*
17 [a]Job 8:13
18 [a]Ps. 12:5 [b]Prov. 23:18
10:2 [a]Ps. 7:16 [1]Heb. *In the pride of the wicked he doth persecute*
3 [a]Ps. 94:4

---

character, Heb 2:6–9 applies these verses to Jesus. Adam, representing the human race, fell from perfect obedience. Jesus, who is both the perfect man and the one in whom humanity's destiny is fully realized, provided redemption for humanity with his atoning death on the cross.

8:8 The phrase "the paths of the seas" refers to the huge currents of water that flow beneath the ocean's surface, such as the Gulf Stream, the Japan Current and the Humboldt Current.

9:7–8 David confirmed that God will ultimately judge the nations according to God's standards of righteousness.

[1]heart's desire, and [b]blesseth[2] the covetous, *whom* the LORD abhorreth.
C 4 The wicked, through the pride of his
M countenance, will not seek *after God:*
[1]God *is* not in all his [a]thoughts.
5 His ways are always grievous; thy
judgments *are* far above out of his sight:
as for all his enemies, he puffeth at them.
6 [a]He hath said in his heart, I shall not
be moved: [b]for *I shall* [1]never *be* in adversity.
7 [a]His mouth is full of cursing and [1]de-
ceit and fraud: under his tongue *is* mischief and [2]vanity.
8 He sitteth in the lurking places of the
villages: in the secret places doth he murder the innocent: his eyes [1]are privily set
against the poor.
9 He lieth in wait [1]secretly as a lion in
his den: he lieth in wait to catch the
poor: he doth catch the poor, when he
draweth him into his net.
10 [1]He croucheth, *and* humbleth himself, that the poor may fall [2]by his strong
ones.
E 11 He hath said in his heart, God hath
forgotten: [a]he hideth his face; he will
never see *it*.
12 Arise, O LORD; O God, [a]lift up thine
hand: forget not the [1]humble.
13 Wherefore doth the wicked contemn God? he hath said in his heart,
Thou wilt not require *it*.
14 Thou hast seen *it;* for thou beholdest mischief and spite, to requite *it* with
thy hand: the poor [a]committeth[1] himself
unto thee; [b]thou art the helper of the fatherless.
P 15 Break thou the arm of the wicked
and the evil *man:* seek out his wickedness *till* thou find none.
K 16 [a]The LORD *is* King for ever and ever:
M the heathen are perished out of his land.
17 LORD, thou hast heard the desire of
the humble: thou wilt [1]prepare their
heart, thou wilt cause thine ear to hear:
18 To [a]judge the fatherless and the oppressed, that the man of the earth may no
more [1]oppress.

The LORD our refuge

To the chief Musician, *A Psalm* of David.

11 IN[a] THE LORD put I my trust: how
say ye to my soul, Flee *as* a bird
to your mountain?
2 For, lo, [a]the wicked bend *their* bow,
they make ready their arrow upon the
string, that they may [1]privily shoot at the
upright in heart.
3 [a]If the foundations be destroyed,
what can the righteous do?
4 The LORD *is* in his holy temple, the E
LORD'S throne *is* in heaven: [a]his eyes behold, his eyelids try, the children of men.
5 The LORD [a]trieth the righteous: but S
the wicked and him that loveth violence
his soul hateth.
6 Upon the wicked he shall rain P
[1]snares, fire and brimstone, and [2]an hor- H
rible tempest: [a]*this shall be* the portion of
their cup.
7 For the righteous LORD [a]loveth righ- U
teousness; his countenance doth behold
the upright.

Good thoughts for bad times

To the chief Musician [a]upon[1] Sheminith, A
Psalm of David.

12 HELP,[2] LORD; for the godly man
ceaseth; for the faithful fail from
among the children of men.
2 [a]They speak vanity every one with
his neighbour: *with* flattering lips *and*
with [1]a double heart do they speak.
3 The LORD shall cut off all flattering M
lips, *and* the tongue that speaketh [1]proud
things:
4 Who have said, With our tongue will
we prevail; our lips [1]*are* our own: who *is*
lord over us?
5 For the oppression of the poor, for
the sighing of the needy, now will I arise,

3 [b]Prov. 28:4 [1]Heb. soul's [2]Or, *the covetous blesseth* himself, *he abhorreth the LORD*
4 [a]Ps. 14:1 [1]Or, *all his thoughts* are, There is *no God*
6 [a]Eccl. 8:11; Is. 56:12 [b]Rev. 18:7 [1]Heb. *unto generation and generation*
7 [a]Rom. 3:14 [1]Heb. *deceits* [2]Or, *iniquity*
8 [1]Heb. *hide themselves*
9 [1]Heb. *in the secret places*
10 [1]Heb. *He breaketh himself* [2]Or, *into his strong parts*
11 [a]Job 22:13
12 [a]Mic. 5:9 [1]Or, *afflicted*
14 [a]2 Tim. 1:12 [b]Ps. 68:5 [1]Heb. *leaveth*
16 [a]Ps. 29:10
17 [1]Or, *establish*
18 [a]Ps. 82:3 [1]Or, *terrify*
11:1 [a]Ps. 56:11
2 [a]Ps. 64:3,4 [1]Heb. *in darkness*
3 [a]Ps. 82:5
4 [a]Ps. 33:13 & 34:15,16
5 [a]Gen. 22:1
6 [a]Gen. 43:34; 1 Sam. 1:4; Ps. 75:8 [1]Or, *quick burning coal* [2]Or, *a burning tempest*
7 [a]Ps. 45:7
12:1 [a]Ps. 6, title [1]Or, *upon the eighth* [2]Or, *Save*
2 [a]Ps. 10:7 [1]Heb. *an heart and an heart*
3 [1]Heb. *great things*
4 [1]Heb. are *with us*

C *Ps 7:14* ◀▶ *Ps 14:1–4*
M *Job 22:29* ◀▶ *Ps 12:3–4*
E *Ps 7:9* ◀▶ *Ps 11:4* **P Ps 2:12** ◀▶ *Ps 11:6*
K ▶ *Ps 92:9* **M** *Ps 2:8–9* ◀▶ *Ps 14:7*

E *Ps 10:11–14* ◀▶ *Ps 33:13–15*
S *Ps 7:10–11* ◀▶ *Ps 15:1–2*
P *Ps 10:15–16* ◀▶ *Ps 18:7–15*
H *Ps 9:17* ◀▶ *Ps 21:8–9*
U *Ps 7:10* ◀▶ *Ps 15:1–2*
M *Ps 10:4* ◀▶ *Ps 25:11*

10:15–16 The wicked will be destroyed by God who is the "King for ever and ever" (10:16).
11:6 This verse may be recalling God's judgment on Sodom and Gomorrah as it predicts the ultimate destruction of the wicked (see Rev. 14:10; 20:10; 21:8).

saith the LORD; I will set *him* in safety
from him that [l]puffeth at him.
6 The words of the LORD *are* [a]pure
words: *as* silver tried in a furnace of
earth, purified seven times.
K 7 Thou shalt keep them, O LORD, thou
shalt preserve [l]them from this generation
for ever.
8 The wicked walk on every side,
when [l]the vilest men are exalted.

The deserted soul

To the [l]chief Musician, A Psalm of David.

13 HOW LONG wilt thou forget me,
O LORD? for ever? [a]how long wilt
thou hide thy face from me?
2 How long shall I take counsel in my
soul, *having* sorrow in my heart daily?
how long shall mine enemy be exalted
over me?
3 Consider *and* hear me, O LORD my
God: [a]lighten mine eyes, [b]lest I sleep the
sleep of death;
4 Lest mine enemy say, I have prevailed against him; *and* those that trouble
me rejoice when I am moved.
5 But I have trusted in thy mercy; my
heart shall rejoice in thy salvation.
L 6 I will sing unto the LORD, because he
hath dealt bountifully with me.

The fate of the fool

To the chief Musician, *A Psalm* of David.

A 14 THE [a]FOOL hath said in his
C heart, *There is* no God. They are
corrupt, they have done abominable
works, *there is* none that doeth good.
2 [a]The LORD looked down from heaven
upon the children of men, to see if there
were any that did understand, *and* seek
God.
3 They are all gone aside, they are *all*
together become [l]filthy: *there is* none
that doeth good, no, not one.
4 Have all the workers of iniquity no
knowledge? who eat up my people *as*
they eat bread, and [a]call not upon the
LORD.
5 There [l]were they in great fear: for
God *is* in the generation of the righteous.
6 Ye have shamed the counsel of the
poor, because the LORD *is* his [a]refuge.
7 [a]Oh [l] that the salvation of Israel *were* I
come out of Zion! [b]when the LORD bring- M
eth back the captivity of his people, Jacob
shall rejoice, *and* Israel shall be glad.

The happiness of the holy

A Psalm of David.

15 LORD, [a]WHO shall [l]abide in thy S
tabernacle? who shall dwell in U
thy holy hill?
2 He that walketh uprightly, and worketh righteousness, and speaketh the truth
in his heart.
3 *He that* backbiteth not with his
tongue, nor doeth evil to his neighbour,
[a]nor [l]taketh up a reproach against his
neighbour.
4 [a]In whose eyes a vile person is contemned; but he honoureth them that fear
the LORD. *He that* sweareth to *his own*
hurt, and changeth not.
5 *He that* putteth not out his money to S
usury, nor taketh reward against the innocent. He that doeth these *things* [a]shall
never be moved.

Joy in God's presence

[a]Michtam [l] of David.

16 PRESERVE ME, O God: for in
thee do I put my trust.
2 *O my soul,* thou hast said unto the
LORD, Thou *art* my Lord: [a]my goodness
extendeth not to thee;
3 *But* to the saints that *are* in the
earth, and *to* the excellent, in whom *is* all
my delight.
4 Their sorrows shall be multiplied
that [l]hasten *after* another *god:* their
drink offerings of blood will I not offer,
[a]nor take up their names into my lips.
5 The LORD *is* the portion [l]of mine inheritance and of my cup: thou maintain-
est my lot.

5 [l]Or, *would ensnare him*
6 [a]2 Sam. 22:31; Ps. 18:30; Prov. 30:5
7 [l]Heb. *him:* i.e. *every one of them*
8 [l]Heb. *the vilest of the sons of men are exalted*
13:1 [a]Job 13:24 [l]Or, *overseer*
3 [a]Ezra 9:8 [b]Jer. 51:39
14:1 [a]Ps. 10:4
2 [a]Ps. 33:13
3 [l]Heb. *stinking*
4 [a]Is. 64:7
5 [l]Heb. *they feared a fear*
6 [a]Ps. 9:9
7 [a]Ps. 53:6 [b]Job 42:10 [l]Heb. *Who will give*
15:1 [a]Ps. 24:3 [l]Heb. *sojourn*
3 [a]Ex. 23:1 [l]Or, *receiveth,* or, *endureth*
4 [a]Esth. 3:2
5 [a]2 Pet. 1:10
16:1 [a]Ps. 56-60 [l]Or, *A golden Psalm of David*
2 [a]Job 35:7
4 [a]Ex. 23:13 [l]Or, *give gifts to another*
5 [l]Heb. *of my part*

K *Ps 3:8* ◀▶ *Ps 16:8*
L *Job 5:17–26* ◀▶ *Ps 18:28*
A *2Ch 6:36* ◀▶ *Ps 53:1–4*
C *Ps 10:4–6* ◀▶ *Ps 17:14*
I *Ne 1:9* ◀▶ *Ps 28:9*
M *Ps 10:16* ◀▶ *Ps 22:27–28*
S *Ps 11:5* ◀▶ *Ps 15:5*
U *Ps 11:7* ◀▶ *Ps 16:6*
S *Ps 15:1–2* ◀▶ *Ps 18:21–23*

14:7 The psalmist looks forward to Israel's ultimate deliverance from her enemies through the victory of the Messiah.

U 6 The lines are fallen unto me in pleasant *places;* yea, I have a goodly heritage.

7 I will bless the LORD, who hath given me counsel: my reins also instruct me in the night seasons.

K 8 I have set the LORD always before me: because *he is* at my right hand, I shall not be moved.

F F 9 Therefore my heart is glad, and my glory rejoiceth: my flesh also shall [1]rest in hope.

10 [a]For thou wilt not leave my soul in hell; neither wilt thou suffer thine Holy One to see corruption.

S U 11 Thou wilt show me the [a]path of life: in thy presence *is* fulness of joy; at thy right hand *there are* pleasures for evermore.

Deliverance from the wicked

A Prayer of David.

17 HEAR [1]THE right, O LORD, attend unto my cry, give ear unto my prayer, *that goeth* [2]not out of feigned lips.

2 Let my sentence come forth from thy presence; let thine eyes behold the things that are equal.

3 Thou hast proved mine heart; thou hast visited *me* in the night; [a]thou hast tried me, *and* shalt find nothing; I am purposed *that* my mouth shall not transgress.

4 Concerning the works of men, by the word of thy lips I have kept *me from* the paths of the destroyer.

5 [a]Hold up my goings in thy paths, *that* my footsteps [1]slip not.

6 [a]I have called upon thee, for thou wilt hear me, O God: incline thine ear unto me, *and hear* my speech.

V 7 Show thy marvellous lovingkindness, O thou [1]that savest by thy right hand them which put their trust *in thee* from those that rise up *against them.*

8 Keep me as the apple of the eye, hide me under the shadow of thy wings, K

9 From the wicked [1]that oppress me, *from* [2]my deadly enemies, *who* compass me about.

10 They are inclosed in their own fat: with their mouth they [a]speak proudly.

11 They have now compassed us in our steps: they have set their eyes bowing down to the earth;

12 [1]Like as a lion *that* is greedy of his prey, and as it were a young lion [2]lurking in secret places.

13 Arise, O LORD, [1]disappoint him, cast him down: deliver my soul from the wicked, [2]*which is* thy sword:

14 From men [1]*which are* thy hand, O LORD, from men of the world, *which have* their portion in *this* life, and whose belly thou fillest with thy hid *treasure:* [2]they are full of children, and leave the rest of their *substance* to their babes. C

15 As for me, [a]I will behold thy face in righteousness: [b]I shall be satisfied, when I awake, with thy likeness. F

Calling upon God in distress

To the chief Musician, *A Psalm* of David, [a]the servant of the LORD, who spake unto the LORD the words of [b]this song in the day *that* the LORD delivered him from the hand of all his enemies, and from the hand of Saul: And he said,

18 I [c]WILL love thee, O LORD, my strength.

2 The LORD *is* my rock, and my fortress, and my deliverer; my God, [1]my strength, [a]in whom I will trust; my buckler, and the horn of my salvation, *and* my high tower. K

3 I will call upon the LORD, [a]*who is worthy* to be praised: so shall I be saved from mine enemies. V

4 [a]The sorrows of death compassed me, and the floods of [1]ungodly men made me afraid.

5 The [1]sorrows of hell compassed me about: the snares of death prevented me.

U *Ps 15:1–2* ◀▶ *Ps 16:11*
K *Ps 12:7* ◀▶ *Ps 17:8*
F *Ps 8:3–8* ◀▶ *Ps 16:9–10*
F *Ps 16:9* ◀▶ *Ps 17:15* S ▶ *Isa 12:3*
U *Ps 16:6* ◀▶ *Ps 18:19–20*
V *Ps 9:3–4* ◀▶ *Ps 18:3*

K *Ps 16:8* ◀▶ *Ps 18:2*
C *Ps 14:1–4* ◀▶ *Ps 36:1–4*
F *Ps 16:9–10* ◀▶ *Ps 71:20*
K *Ps 17:8* ◀▶ *Ps 18:16*
V *Ps 17:7* ◀▶ *Ps 18:29*

9 [1]Heb. *dwell confidently*
10 [a]Ps. 49:15
11 [a]Mat. 7:14
17:1 [1]Heb. *justice* [2]Heb. *without lips of deceit*
3 [a]Job 23:10
5 [a]Ps. 119:133 [1]Heb. *be not moved*
6 [a]Ps. 116:2
7 [1]Or, *that savest them which trust in thee from those that rise up against thy right hand*
9 [1]Heb. *that waste me* [2]Heb. *my enemies against the soul*
10 [a]1 Sam. 2:3
12 [1]Heb. *The likeness of him* (i.e. *of every one of them*) *is as a lion that desireth to ravin* [2]Heb. *sitting*
13 [1]Heb. *prevent his face* [2]Or, *by thy sword*
14 [1]Or, *by thine hand* [2]Or, *their children are full*
15 [a]1 John 3:2 [b]Ps. 4:6,7 & 16:11
18:1 [a]Ps. 36, title [b]2 Sam. 22 [c]Ps. 144:1
2 [a]Heb. 2:13 [1]Heb. *my rock*
3 [a]Ps. 76:4
4 [a]Ps. 116:3 [1]Heb. *Belial*
5 [1]Or, *cords*

16:9–11 Hidden in these words of assurance is David's confidence in a personal resurrection (see 17:15; 73:24). Peter declares that David's words also foretold Christ's resurrection and his victory over death and the grave (see Ac 2:25–31).

6 In my distress I called upon the LORD, and cried unto my God: he heard my voice out of his temple, and my cry came before him, *even* into his ears.

P 7 [a]Then the earth shook and trembled; the foundations also of the hills moved and were shaken, because he was wroth.

8 There went up a smoke ʹout of his nostrils, and fire out of his mouth devoured: coals were kindled by it.

9 [a]He bowed the heavens also, and came down: and darkness *was* under his feet.

10 [a]And he rode upon a cherub, and did fly: yea, [b]he did fly upon the wings of the wind.

11 He made darkness his secret place; [a]his pavilion round about him *were* dark waters *and* thick clouds of the skies.

12 [a]At the brightness *that was* before him his thick clouds passed, hail *stones* and coals of fire.

13 The LORD also thundered in the heavens, and the Highest gave [a]his voice; hail *stones* and coals of fire.

14 [a]Yea, he sent out his arrows, and scattered them; and he shot out lightnings, and discomfited them.

15 Then the channels of waters were seen, and the foundations of the world were discovered at thy rebuke, O LORD, at the blast of the breath of thy nostrils.

K 16 [a]He sent from above, he took me, he drew me out of ʹmany waters.

17 He delivered me from my strong enemy, and from them which hated me: for they were too strong for me.

18 They prevented me in the day of my calamity: but the LORD was my stay.

U 19 [a]He brought me forth also into a large place; he delivered me, because he delighted in me.

20 [a]The LORD rewarded me according to my righteousness; according to the cleanness of my hands hath he recompensed me.

S 21 For I have kept the ways of the LORD, and have not wickedly departed from my God.

22 For all his judgments *were* before me, and I did not put away his statutes from me.

23 I was also upright ʹbefore him, and I kept myself from mine iniquity.

24 [a]Therefore hath the LORD recompensed me according to my righteousness, according to the cleanness of my hands ʹin his eyesight. U

25 [a]With the merciful thou wilt show thyself merciful; with an upright man thou wilt show thyself upright;

26 With the pure thou wilt show thyself pure; and [a]with the froward thou wilt ʹshow thyself froward.

27 For thou wilt save the afflicted people; but wilt bring down [a]high looks.

28 [a]For thou wilt light my ʹcandle: the LORD my God will enlighten my darkness. L

29 For by thee I have ʹrun through a troop; and by my God have I leaped over a wall. J V

30 *As for* God, [a]his way *is* perfect: [b]the word of the LORD is ʹtried: he *is* a buckler [c]to all those that trust in him. W

31 [a]For who *is* God save the LORD? or who *is* a rock save our God? O

32 *It is* God that [a]girdeth me with strength, and maketh my way perfect. U

33 [a]He maketh my feet like hinds' *feet,* and [b]setteth me upon my high places.

34 [a]He teacheth my hands to war, so that a bow of steel is broken by mine arms.

35 Thou hast also given me the shield of thy salvation: and thy right hand hath holden me up, and ʹthy gentleness hath made me great. K

36 Thou hast enlarged my steps under me, [a]that ʹmy feet did not slip.

37 I have pursued mine enemies, and

7 [a]Acts 4:31
8 ʹHeb. *by his*
9 [a]Ps. 144:5
10 [a]Ps. 99:1 [b]Ps. 104:3
11 [a]Ps. 97:2
12 [a]Ps. 97:3
13 [a]Ps. 29:3
14 [a]Josh. 10:10; Ps. 144:6; Is. 30:30
16 [a]Ps. 144:7 ʹOr, *great waters*
19 [a]Ps. 31:8 & 118:5
20 [a]1 Sam. 24:19
23 ʹHeb. *with*
24 [a]1 Sam. 26:23 ʹHeb. *before his eyes*
25 [a]1 Ki. 8:32
26 [a]Lev. 26:23,24, 27,28; Prov. 3:34 ʹOr, *wrestle*
27 [a]Ps. 101:5; Prov. 6:17
28 [a]Job 18:6 ʹOr, *lamp*
29 ʹOr, *broken*
30 [a]Deut. 32:4; Dan. 4:37; Rev. 15:3 [b]Ps. 12:6 & 119:140; Prov. 30:5 [c]Ps. 17:7 ʹOr, *refined*
31 [a]Deut. 32:31, 39; 1 Sam. 2:2; Ps. 86:8; Is. 45:5
32 [a]Ps. 91:2
33 [a]2 Sam. 2:18; Hab. 3:19 [b]Deut. 32:13 & 33:29
34 [a]Ps. 144:1
35 ʹOr, *with thy meekness thou hast multiplied me*
36 [a]Prov. 4:12 ʹHeb. *mine ankles*

P *Ps 11:6* ◀ ▶ *Ps 37:34*
K *Ps 18:2* ◀ ▶ *Ps 18:35–36*
U *Ps 16:11* ◀ ▶ *Ps 18:24*
S *Ps 15:5* ◀ ▶ *Ps 19:12–14*
U *Ps 18:19–20* ◀ ▶ *Ps 18:32*
L *Ps 13:6* ◀ ▶ *Ps 23:1–6*
J *Ps 3:5–6* ◀ ▶ *Ps 23:4*
V *Ps 18:3* ◀ ▶ *Ps 20:7–8*
W *Ps 2:12* ◀ ▶ *Ps 34:8*
O *Ps 3:8* ◀ ▶ *Ps 36:9*
U *Ps 18:24* ◀ ▶ *Ps 19:11*
K *Ps 18:16* ◀ ▶ *Ps 19:7*

18:7–15 This psalm is a restatement of 2Sa 22 and celebrates David's deliverance from his mortal enemies.

overtaken them: neither did I turn again till they were consumed.

38 I have wounded them that they were not able to rise: they are fallen under my feet.

39 For thou hast girded me with strength unto the battle: thou hast [1]subdued under me those that rose up against me.

40 Thou hast also given me the necks of mine enemies; that I might destroy them that hate me.

41 They cried, but *there was* none to save *them:* [a]*even* unto the LORD, but he answered them not.

42 Then did I beat them small as the dust before the wind: I did [a]cast them out as the dirt in the streets.

43 Thou hast delivered me from the strivings of the people; *and* [a]thou hast made me the head of the heathen: [b]a people *whom* I have not known shall serve me.

44 [1]As soon as they hear of me, they shall obey me: [2]the strangers shall [3,4]submit themselves unto me.

45 [a]The strangers shall fade away, and be afraid out of their close places.

46 The LORD liveth; and blessed *be* my rock; and let the God of my salvation be exalted.

47 *It is* God that [1]avengeth me, [a]and [2]subdueth the people under me.

48 He delivereth me from mine enemies: yea, [a]thou liftest me up above those that rise up against me: thou hast delivered me from the [1]violent man.

49 [a]Therefore will I [1]give thanks unto thee, O LORD, among the heathen, and sing praises unto thy name.

50 [a]Great deliverance giveth he to his king; and showeth mercy to his anointed, to David, and to his seed for evermore.

The works and word of God

To the chief Musician, A Psalm of David.

19 THE [a]HEAVENS declare the glory of God; and the firmament showeth his handiwork.

2 Day unto day uttereth speech, and night unto night showeth knowledge.

3 *There is* no speech nor language, [1,2]*where* their voice is not heard.

4 [a]Their[1] line is gone out through all the earth, and their words to the end of the world. In them hath he set a tabernacle for the sun,

5 Which *is* as a bridegroom coming out of his chamber, [a]*and* rejoiceth as a strong man to run a race.

6 His going forth *is* from the end of the heaven, and his circuit unto the ends of it: and there is nothing hid from the heat thereof.

7 [a]The [1]law of the LORD *is* perfect, [2]converting the soul: the testimony of the LORD *is* sure, making wise the simple. K

8 The statutes of the LORD *are* right, rejoicing the heart: the commandment of the LORD *is* pure, enlightening the eyes.

9 The fear of the LORD *is* clean, enduring for ever: the judgments of the LORD *are* [1]true *and* righteous altogether.

10 More to be desired *are they* than gold, yea, than much fine gold: sweeter also than honey and [1]the honeycomb.

11 Moreover by them is thy servant warned: *and* in keeping of them *there is* great reward. U

12 Who can understand *his* errors? cleanse thou me from secret *faults.* S

13 Keep back thy servant also from presumptuous *sins;* let them not have dominion over me: then shall I be upright, and I shall be innocent from [1]the great transgression.

14 Let the words of my mouth, and the meditation of my heart, be acceptable in thy sight, O LORD, [1]my strength, and my [a]redeemer.

A prayer for the king

To the chief Musician, A Psalm of David.

20 THE LORD hear thee in the day of trouble; the name of the God of Jacob [1]defend thee;

2 Send [1]thee help from the sanctuary, and [2]strengthen thee out of Zion;

K *Ps 18:35–36* ◄ ► *Ps 20:5–6*
U *Ps 18:32* ◄ ► *Ps 21:1–7*
S *Ps 18:21–23* ◄ ► *Ps 24:3–5*

39 [1]Heb. *caused to bow*
41 [a]Job 27:9; Prov. 1:28; Jer. 11:11
42 [a]Zech. 10:5
43 [a]2 Sam. 8 [b]Is. 52:15
44 [1]Heb. *At the hearing of the ear* [2]Heb. *the sons of the stranger* [3]Or, *yield feigned obedience* [4]Heb. *lie*
45 [a]Mic. 7:17
47 [a]Ps. 47:3 [1]Heb. *giveth avengements for me* [2]Or, *destroyeth*
48 [a]Ps. 59:1 [1]Heb. *man of violence*
49 [a]Rom. 15:9 [1]Or, *confess*
50 [a]Ps. 144:10
19:1 [a]Is. 40:22
3 [1]Or, *without these their voice is heard* [2]Heb. *without their voice heard*
4 [a]Rom. 10:18 [1]Or, *Their rule,* or, *direction*
5 [a]Eccl. 1:5
7 [a]Ps. 111:7 [1]Or, *doctrine* [2]Or, *restoring*
9 [1]Heb. *truth*
10 [1]Heb. *the dropping of honeycombs*
13 [1]Or, *much*
14 [a]Is. 47:4 [1]Heb. *my rock*
20:1 [1]Heb. *set thee on an high place*
2 [1]Heb. *thy help* [2]Heb. *support thee*

19:6 While the sun is easily observed in its path from east to west during daylight hours, recent scientific discoveries have found that the sun also makes a "circuit" or orbit through the galaxy, confirming this divinely inspired record.

3 Remember all thy offerings, and [1]accept thy burnt sacrifice; Selah.
4 Grant thee according to thine own heart, and fulfil all thy counsel.
K 5 We will rejoice in thy salvation, and in the name of our God we will set up *our* banners: the LORD fulfil all thy petitions.
6 Now know I that the LORD saveth his anointed; he will hear him [1]from his holy heaven [2]with the saving strength of his right hand.
V 7 Some *trust* in chariots, and some in horses: but we will remember the name of the LORD our God.
8 They are brought down and fallen: but we are risen, and stand upright.
9 Save, LORD: let the king hear us when we call.

Splendor and success of the king

To the chief Musician, A Psalm of David.

U 21 THE KING shall joy in thy strength, O LORD; and in thy salvation how greatly shall he rejoice!
2 Thou hast given him his heart's desire, and hast not withholden the request of his lips. Selah.
3 For thou preventest him with the blessings of goodness: thou settest a crown of pure gold on his head.
4 [a]He asked life of thee, *and* thou gavest *it* him, *even* length of days for ever and ever.
5 His glory *is* great in thy salvation: honour and majesty hast thou laid upon him.
6 For thou hast [a]made[1] him most blessed for ever: thou hast [2]made him exceeding glad with thy countenance.
7 For the king trusteth in the LORD, and through the mercy of the most High he shall not be moved.
H 8 Thine hand shall find out all thine enemies: thy right hand shall find out those that hate thee.

3 [1]Heb. *turn to ashes:* or, *make fat*
6 [1]Heb. *from the heaven of his holiness* [2]Heb. *by the strength of the salvation of his right hand*
21:4 [a]Ps. 61:5,6
6 [a]Ps. 72:17 [1]Heb. *set him to be blessings* [2]Heb. *gladded him with joy*
12 [1]Heb. *shoulder*
22:1 [a]Mark 15:34 [1]Or, *the hind of the morning* [2]Heb. *from my salvation*
2 [1]Heb. there is *no silence to me*
3 [a]Deut. 10:21
5 [a]Is. 49:23
6 [a]Job 25:6 [b]Is. 53:3
7 [a]Mat. 27:39 [b]Job 16:4 [1]Heb. *open*
8 [a]Mat. 27:43 [b]Ps. 91:14 [1]Heb. *He rolled* himself *on the* LORD [2]Or, *if he delight in him*
9 [a]Ps. 71:6 [1]Or, *keptest me in safety*

9 Thou shalt make them as a fiery oven in the time of thine anger: the LORD shall swallow them up in his wrath, and the fire shall devour them.
10 Their fruit shalt thou destroy from the earth, and their seed from among the children of men.
11 For they intended evil against thee: they imagined a mischievous device, *which* they are not able *to perform.*
12 Therefore shalt thou make them turn their [1]back, *when* thou shalt make ready *thine arrows* upon thy strings against the face of them.
13 Be thou exalted, LORD, in thine own strength: *so* will we sing and praise thy power.

A cry of anguish

To the chief Musician upon [1]Aijeleth Shahar, A Psalm of David.

22 MY [a]GOD, my God, why hast thou forsaken me? *why art thou so* far [2]from helping me, *and from* the words of my roaring? B
2 O my God, I cry in the daytime, but thou hearest not; and in the night season, and [1]am not silent.
3 But thou *art* holy, *O thou* that inhabitest the [a]praises of Israel.
4 Our fathers trusted in thee: they trusted, and thou didst deliver them. V
5 They cried unto thee, and were delivered: [a]they trusted in thee, and were not confounded.
6 But I *am* [a]a worm, and no man; [b]a reproach of men, and despised of the people.
7 [a]All they that see me laugh me to scorn: they [1]shoot out the lip, [b]they shake the head, *saying,*
8 [a]He[1] trusted on the LORD *that* he would deliver him: [b]let him deliver him, [2]seeing he delighted in him.
9 [a]But thou *art* he that took me out of the womb: thou [1]didst make me hope *when I was* upon my mother's breasts.

K *Ps 19:7* ◀▶ *Ps 26:1*
V *Ps 18:29* ◀▶ *Ps 22:4–5*
U *Ps 19:11* ◀▶ *Ps 24:3–4*
H *Ps 11:6* ◀▶ *Ps 26:9*

B *Dt 18:15–19* ◀▶ *Isa 7:13–16*
V *Ps 20:7–8* ◀▶ *Ps 25:2–3*

22:1–2 The prophetic words of the psalmist "My God, my God, why hast thou forsaken me?" (22:1) were reiterated in Jesus' cry from the cross (see Mt 27:46). When Jesus took the sins of the world upon himself so that those sins could be judged and justified through his sacrifice, God in his holiness had to turn away (see 2Co 5:21).
22:6–8 David's prophecy described the rejection and the mockery that Jesus took upon himself on the cross. Matthew records the fulfillment of this psalm in his record of the crucifixion (see Mt 27:39–43).
22:9–10 In contrast to other OT references that

10 I was cast upon thee from the
womb: [a]thou *art* my God from my
mother's belly.
11 Be not far from me; for trouble *is*
near; for *there is* [1]none to help.
12 [a]Many bulls have compassed me:
strong *bulls* of Bashan have beset me
round.
D 13 [a]They [1]gaped upon me *with* their
mouths, *as* a ravening and a roaring lion.
14 I am poured out like water, [a]and all
my bones are [1]out of joint: my heart is
like wax; it is melted in the midst of my
bowels.
15 [a]My strength is dried up like a potsherd; and [b]my tongue cleaveth to my
jaws; and thou hast brought me into the
dust of death.
16 For dogs have compassed me: the
assembly of the wicked have inclosed me:
[a]they pierced my hands and my feet.
17 I may tell all my bones: [a]they look
and stare upon me.
18 [a]They part my garments among
them, and cast lots upon my vesture.
19 But be not thou far from me,
O LORD: O my strength, haste thee to
help me.
20 Deliver my soul from the sword;
[a]my[1] darling [2]from the power of the dog.
21 [a]Save me from the lion's mouth:
[b]for thou hast heard me from the horns of
the unicorns.

A song of praise

T 22 [a]I will declare thy name unto [b]my
brethren: in the midst of the congregation will I praise thee.
23 [a]Ye that fear the LORD, praise him;
all ye the seed of Jacob, glorify him; and
fear him, all ye the seed of Israel.
24 For he hath not despised nor abhorred the affliction of the afflicted;
neither hath he hid his face from
[a]him; but when he cried unto him, he
heard.
25 [a]My praise *shall be* of thee in the T
great congregation: [b]I will pay my vows
before them that fear him.
26 The meek shall eat and be satisfied: L
they shall praise the LORD that seek him: F
your heart shall live for ever.
27 All the ends of the world shall re- M
member and turn unto the LORD: and all
the kindreds of the nations shall worship
before thee.
28 [a]For the kingdom *is* the LORD'S: and
he *is* the governor among the nations.
29 [a]All *they that be* fat upon earth
shall eat and worship: [b]all they that
go down to the dust shall bow before
him: and none can keep alive his own
soul.
30 A seed shall serve him; [a]it shall
be accounted to the Lord for a generation.
31 [a]They shall come, and shall declare
his righteousness unto a people that shall
be born, that he hath done *this.*

10 [a]Is. 46:3
11 [1]Heb. *not a helper*
12 [a]Ps. 68:30
13 [a]Lam. 2:16 [1]Heb. *opened their mouths against me*
14 [a]Dan. 5:6 [1]Or, *sundered*
15 [a]Prov. 17:22 [b]John 19:28
16 [a]Mat. 27:35
17 [a]Luke 23:27,35
18 [a]Luke 23:34
20 [a]Ps. 35:17 [1]Heb. *my only one* [2]Heb. *from the hand*
21 [a]2 Tim. 4:17 [b]Is. 34:7
22 [a]Heb. 2:12 [b]Rom. 8:29
23 [a]Ps. 135:19
24 [a]Heb. 5:7
25 [a]Ps. 35:18 [b]Eccl. 5:4
28 [a]Mat. 6:13
29 [a]Ps. 45:12 [b]Is. 26:19
30 [a]Ps. 87:6
31 [a]Ps. 78:6

D *Ezr 6:19–20* ◀▶ *Ps 69:22–21*
T *1Ch 16:8–10* ◀▶ *Ps 22:25*
T *Ps 22:22–23* ◀▶ *Ps 34:1–3*
L *Ps 9:10* ◀▶ *Ps 30:5*
F *Job 5:20* ◀▶ *Ps 23:1–2*
M *Ps 14:7* ◀▶ *Ps 24:1*

---

identify a person through their father's lineage, this prophecy of the Messiah mentioned only the mother of the Messiah, foreshadowing the virgin birth.

22:11–18 This psalm predicted the horrible aspects of the crucifixion including thirst (see Jn 19:28) and the mocking of the priests and soldiers (see Jn 19:1–3). The startling prophetic words "they pierced my hands and my feet" (22:16) describe a method of execution that was not known until the Roman occupation several centuries later. The reference to gambling for the clothes of the victim was also fulfilled as the Roman soldiers gambled for the robe of Jesus (see Jn 19:24). Though some suggest that Jesus' familiarity with the Scriptures allowed him to arrange his life so that he could conveniently fulfill the Messianic prophecies, this argument does not bear itself out in Scripture.

Overwhelming historical evidence proves that Jesus of Nazareth is God's Messiah, the one who fulfilled the prophecies recorded in Scripture centuries before he was born.

22:27–31 David predicted that "all the ends of the world shall remember and turn unto the LORD" (22:27). The world already remembers the Lord when they record a date in history using the notation B.C. (Before Christ) or A.D. (*Anno Domini*, meaning "in the year of our Lord"). However, the final fulfillment of this prophecy will occur in the millennial kingdom of Christ. Note that vv. 30 and 31 may refer to those who witness about Christ to the survivors of Armageddon and those that are born during the millenium. These people must decide whether they will repent and follow Jesus or not. Some will still reject faith in Christ and join Satan's final rebellion at the end of the Millennium (see Rev 20:3). See the article on "The Millennium," p. 1480.

The shepherd psalm

A Psalm of David.

23 THE LORD *is* [a]my shepherd; [b]I shall not want.

2 [a]He maketh me to lie down in [1]green pastures: [b]he leadeth me beside the [2]still waters.

3 He restoreth my soul: [a]he leadeth me in the paths of righteousness for his name's sake.

4 Yea, though I walk through the valley of [a]the shadow of death, [b]I will fear no evil: [c]for thou *art* with me; thy rod and thy staff they comfort me.

5 Thou preparest a table before me in the presence of mine enemies: thou [a]anointest[1] my head with oil; my cup runneth over.

6 Surely goodness and mercy shall follow me all the days of my life: and I will dwell in the house of the LORD [1]for ever.

Song to the King of glory

A Psalm of David.

24 THE [a]EARTH *is* the LORD'S, and the fulness thereof; the world, and they that dwell therein.

2 For he hath founded it upon the seas, and established it upon the floods.

3 [a]Who shall ascend into the hill of the LORD? or who shall stand in his holy place?

4 [1]He that hath [a]clean hands, and [b]a pure heart; who hath not lifted up his soul unto vanity, nor [c]sworn deceitfully.

5 He shall receive the blessing from the LORD, and righteousness from the God of his salvation.

6 This *is* the generation of them that seek him, that [a]seek thy face, [1]O Jacob. Selah.

7 [a]Lift up your heads, O ye gates; and be ye lift up, ye everlasting doors; [b]and the King of glory shall come in.

8 Who *is* this King of glory? The LORD strong and mighty, the LORD mighty in battle.

9 Lift up your heads, O ye gates; even lift *them* up, ye everlasting doors; and the King of glory shall come in.

10 Who is this King of glory? The LORD of hosts, he *is* the King of glory. Selah.

Prayer for guidance and protection

A Psalm of David.

25 UNTO [a]THEE, O LORD, do I lift up my soul.

2 O my God, I [a]trust in thee: let me not be ashamed, [b]let not mine enemies triumph over me.

3 Yea, let none that wait on thee be ashamed: let them be ashamed which transgress without cause.

4 [a]Show me thy ways, O LORD; teach me thy paths.

5 Lead me in thy truth, and teach me: for thou *art* the God of my salvation; on thee do I wait all the day.

6 Remember, O LORD, [a]thy[1] tender mercies and thy lovingkindnesses; for they *have been* ever of old.

7 Remember not [a]the sins of my youth, nor my transgressions: [b]according to thy mercy remember thou me for thy goodness' sake, O LORD.

8 Good and upright *is* the LORD: therefore will he teach sinners in the way.

9 The meek will he guide in judgment: and the meek will he teach his way.

10 All the paths of the LORD *are* mercy and truth unto such as keep his covenant and his testimonies.

11 [a]For thy name's sake, O LORD, pardon mine iniquity; [b]for it *is* great.

12 What man *is* he that feareth the LORD? [a]him shall he teach in the way *that* he shall choose.

13 [a]His soul [1]shall dwell at ease; and [b]his seed shall inherit the earth.

14 [a]The secret of the LORD *is* with

23:1 [a]Is. 40:11; John 10:11 [b]Phil. 4:19
2 [a]Ezek. 34:14 [b]Rev. 7:17 [1]Heb. *pastures of tender grass* [2]Heb. *waters of quietness*
3 [a]Ps. 5:8
4 [a]Job 10:21,22; Ps. 44:19 [b]Ps. 3:6 [c]Is. 43:2
5 [a]Ps. 92:10 [1]Heb. *makest fat*
6 [1]Heb. *to length of days*
24:1 [a]Ex. 9:29; Job 41:11
3 [a]Ps. 15:1
4 [a]Job 17:9; 1 Tim. 2:8 [b]Mat. 5:8 [c]Ps. 15:4 [1]Heb. *The clean of hands*
6 [a]Ps. 27:8 [1]Or, O God of *Jacob*
7 [a]Is. 26:2 [b]Ps. 97:6; Hag. 2:7; Mal. 3:1
25:1 [a]Ps. 86:4
2 [a]Ps. 34:8; Is. 28:16 [b]Ps. 13:4
4 [a]Ex. 33:13; Ps. 5:8
6 [a]Ps. 103:17; Is. 63:15 [1]Heb. *thy bowels*
7 [a]Job 13:26; Jer. 3:25 [b]Ps. 51:1
11 [a]Ps. 31:3 & 79:9 [b]Rom. 5:20
12 [a]Ps. 37:23
13 [a]Prov. 19:23 [b]Ps. 37:11 [1]Heb. *shall lodge in goodness*
14 [a]Prov. 3:32; John 7:17

F *Ps 22:26* ◀ ▶ *Ps 23:5*
L *Ps 18:28* ◀ ▶ *Ps 27:4–5*
J *Ps 18:29* ◀ ▶ *Ps 27:1*
W *Ne 8:10* ◀ ▶ *Ps 27:1*
F *Ps 23:1–2* ◀ ▶ *Ps 33:18–19*
M *Ps 22:27–28* ◀ ▶ *Ps 24:7–10*
S *Ps 19:12–14* ◀ ▶ *Ps 26:1*
U *Ps 21:1–7* ◀ ▶ *Ps 25:10*
M *Ps 24:1* ◀ ▶ *Ps 45:16*

V *Ps 22:4–5* ◀ ▶ *Ps 27:3*
U *Ps 24:3–4* ◀ ▶ *Ps 25:14*
M *Ps 12:3–4* ◀ ▶ *Ps 30:5*
U *Ps 25:10* ◀ ▶ *Ps 31:19–20*

24:1, 7–10 This psalm foreshadows the establishment of the Messianic kingdom when the whole world will acknowledge Jesus as the "King of glory" (24:7).

them that fear him; [l]and he will show them his covenant.

15 [a]Mine eyes *are* ever toward the LORD; for he shall [l]pluck my feet out of the net.

16 [a]Turn thee unto me, and have mercy upon me; for I *am* desolate and afflicted.

17 The troubles of my heart are enlarged: *O* bring thou me out of my distresses.

18 [a]Look upon mine affliction and my pain; and forgive all my sins.

19 Consider mine enemies; for they are many; and they hate me with [l]cruel hatred.

20 O keep my soul, and deliver me: let me not be ashamed; for I put my trust in thee.

21 Let integrity and uprightness preserve me; for I wait on thee.

22 [a]Redeem Israel, O God, out of all his troubles.

The basis of judgment

A Psalm of David.

K S 26 JUDGE [a]ME, O LORD; for I have [b]walked in mine integrity: [c]I have trusted also in the LORD; *therefore* I shall not slide.

2 [a]Examine me, O LORD, and prove me; try my reins and my heart.

3 For thy lovingkindness *is* before mine eyes: and [a]I have walked in thy truth.

4 [a]I have not sat with vain persons, neither will I go in with dissemblers.

S 5 I have [a]hated the congregation of evildoers; [b]and will not sit with the wicked.

6 [a]I will wash mine hands in innocency: so will I compass thine altar, O LORD:

7 That I may publish with the voice of thanksgiving, and tell of all thy wondrous works.

8 LORD, [a]I have loved the habitation of thy house, and the place [l]where thine honour dwelleth.

H 9 [a]Gather[l] not my soul with sinners, nor my life with [2]bloody men:

K *Ps 20:5–6 ◀ ▶ Ps 27:1*
S *Ps 24:3–5 ◀ ▶ Ps 26:5–6*
S *Ps 26:1 ◀ ▶ Ps 29:2*
H *Ps 21:8–9 ◀ ▶ Ps 36:12*

10 In whose hands *is* mischief, and their right hand is [l]full of [a]bribes.

11 But as for me, I will walk in mine integrity: redeem me, and be merciful unto me.

12 [a]My foot standeth in an [b]even place: [c]in the congregations will I bless the LORD.

David's song of confidence

A Psalm of David.

27 THE LORD *is* [a]my light and [b]my salvation; whom shall I fear? [c]the LORD *is* the strength of my life; of whom shall I be afraid? K J W

2 When the wicked, *even* mine enemies and my foes, [l]came upon me to [a]eat up my flesh, they stumbled and fell.

3 [a]Though an host should encamp against me, my heart shall not fear: though war should rise against me, in this *will* I *be* confident. V

4 [a]One *thing* have I desired of the LORD, that will I seek after; that I may [b]dwell in the house of the LORD all the days of my life, to behold [c]the[l] beauty of the LORD, and to inquire in his temple. L

5 For [a]in the time of trouble he shall hide me in his pavilion: in the secret of his tabernacle shall he hide me; he shall [b]set me up upon a rock. S

6 And now shall [a]mine head be lifted up above mine enemies round about me: therefore will I offer in his tabernacle sacrifices [l]of joy; I will sing, yea, I will sing praises unto the LORD.

7 Hear, O LORD, *when* I cry with my voice: have mercy also upon me, and answer me.

8 [l]*When thou saidst,* Seek ye my face; my heart said unto thee, Thy face, LORD, will I seek. N

9 [a]Hide not thy face *far* from me; put not thy servant away in anger: thou hast been my help; leave me not, neither forsake me, O God of my salvation.

10 [a]When my father and my mother L

K *Ps 26:1 ◀ ▶ Ps 36:9*
J *Ps 23:4 ◀ ▶ Ps 30:5*
W *Ps 23:4 ◀ ▶ Ps 27:14*
V *Ps 25:2–3 ◀ ▶ Ps 34:6*
L *Ps 23:1–6 ◀ ▶ Ps 27:10*
S *Ps 4:8 ◀ ▶ Ps 31:20*
N *Job 27:8–9 ◀ ▶ Ps 49:10–14*
L *Ps 27:4–5 ◀ ▶ Ps 31:19–20*

---

14 [l]Or, *and his covenant to make them know* it
15 [a]Ps. 141:8 [l]Heb. *bring forth*
16 [a]Ps. 69:16
18 [a]2 Sam. 16:12
19 [l]Heb. *hatred of violence*
22 [a]Ps. 130:8
26:1 [a]Ps. 7:8 [b]2 Ki. 20:3 [c]Ps. 28:7; Prov. 29:25
2 [a]Ps. 17:3
3 [a]2 Ki. 20:3
4 [a]Ps. 1:1
5 [a]Ps. 31:6 [b]Ps. 1:1
6 [a]Ps. 73:13
8 [a]Ps. 27:4 [l]Heb. *of the tabernacle of thy honour*
9 [a]Ps. 28:3 [l]Or, *Take not away* [2]Heb. *men of blood*
10 [a]1 Sam. 8:3 [l]Heb. *filled with*
12 [a]Ps. 40:2 [b]Ps. 27:11 [c]Ps. 111:1
27:1 [a]Is. 60:19 [b]Ex. 15:2 [c]Ps. 62:2
2 [a]Ps. 14:4 [l]Heb. *approached against me*
3 [a]Ps. 3:6
4 [a]Ps. 26:8 [b]Luke 2:37 [c]Ps. 90:17 [l]Or, *the delight*
5 [a]Ps. 91:1 [b]Ps. 40:2
6 [a]Ps. 3:3 [l]Heb. *of shouting*
8 [l]Or, *My heart said unto thee, Let my face seek thy face*
9 [a]Ps. 69:17
10 [a]Is. 49:15

forsake me, then the LORD [1]will take
me up.
11 [a]Teach me thy way, O LORD, and
lead me in [1]a plain path, because of
[2]mine enemies.
12 Deliver me not over unto the will
of mine enemies: for false witnesses are
risen up against me, and such as breathe
out cruelty.
13 *I had fainted,* unless I had believed
to see the goodness of the LORD [a]in the
land of the living.
14 Wait on the LORD: be of good courage, and he shall strengthen thine heart:
wait, I say, on the LORD.

A prayer for help

A Psalm of David.

28 UNTO THEE will I cry, O LORD
my rock; [a]be not silent [1]to me:
[b]lest, *if* thou be silent to me, I become
like them that go down into the pit.
2 Hear the voice of my supplications,
when I cry unto thee, [a]when I lift up my
hands [b]toward[1] thy holy oracle.
3 Draw me not away with the wicked,
and with the workers of iniquity, [a]which
speak peace to their neighbours, but mischief *is* in their hearts.
4 [a]Give them according to their deeds,
and according to the wickedness of their
endeavours: give them after the work of
their hands; render to them their desert.
5 Because [a]they regard not the works
of the LORD, nor the operation of his
hands, he shall destroy them, and not
build them up.
6 Blessed *be* the LORD, because he hath
heard the voice of my supplications.
7 The LORD *is* [a]my strength and my
shield; my heart [b]trusted in him, and I
am helped: therefore my heart greatly rejoiceth; and with my song will I praise
him.
8 The LORD *is* [1]their strength, and he *is*
the [a]saving[2] strength of his anointed.
9 Save thy people, and bless [a]thine inheritance: [1]feed them also, [b]and lift them
up for ever.

W *Ps 27:1* ◀▶ *Ps 31:24*
I *Ps 14:7* ◀▶ *Ps 47:3–4*

10 [1]Heb. *will gather me*
11 [a]Ps. 25:4 [1]Heb. *a way of plainness* [2]Heb. *those which observe me*
13 [a]Ezek. 26:20
28:1 [a]Ps. 83:1 [b]Ps. 88:4 [1]Heb. *from me*
2 [a]Ps. 5:7 [b]Ps. 138:2 [1]Or, *toward the oracle of thy sanctuary*
3 [a]Ps. 12:2
4 [a]Rev. 18:6
5 [a]Is. 5:12
7 [a]Ps. 18:2 [b]Ps. 13:5
8 [a]Ps. 20:6 [1]Or, *his strength* [2]Heb. *strength of salvations*
9 [a]Deut. 9:29 [b]Ezra 1:4 [1]Or, *rule*
29:1 [a]1 Chr. 16:28 [1]Heb. *ye sons of the mighty*
2 [a]2 Chr. 20:21 [1]Heb. *the honour of his name* [2]Or, *in his glorious sanctuary*
3 [a]Job 37:4,5 [1]Or, *great waters*
4 [1]Heb. *in power* [2]Heb. *in majesty*
5 [a]Is. 2:13
6 [a]Ps. 114:4 [b]Deut. 3:9
7 [1]Heb. *cutteth out*
8 [a]Num. 13:26
9 [1]Or, *to be in pain* [2]Or, *every whit of it uttereth*
10 [a]Ps. 10:16
11 [a]Ps. 28:8
30:1 [a]Deut. 20:5 [b]Ps. 28:9 [c]Ps. 25:2
3 [a]Ps. 86:13
4 [1]Or, *to the memorial*

The LORD of the thunderstorm

A Psalm of David.

29 GIVE[a] UNTO the LORD, O [1]ye
mighty, give unto the LORD glory
and strength.
2 Give unto the LORD [1]the glory due
unto his name; worship the LORD [2]in [a]the
beauty of holiness.
3 The voice of the LORD *is* upon the
waters: [a]the God of glory thundereth: the
LORD *is* upon [1]many waters.
4 The voice of the LORD *is* [1]powerful;
the voice of the LORD *is* [2]full of majesty.
5 The voice of the LORD breaketh the
cedars; yea, the LORD breaketh [a]the cedars of Lebanon.
6 [a]He maketh them also to skip like a
calf; Lebanon and [b]Sirion like a young
unicorn.
7 The voice of the LORD [1]divideth the
flames of fire.
8 The voice of the LORD shaketh the
wilderness; the LORD shaketh the wilderness of [a]Kadesh.
9 The voice of the LORD maketh the
hinds [1]to calve, and discovereth the forests: and in his temple [2]doth every one
speak of *his* glory.
10 The LORD sitteth upon the flood;
yea, [a]the LORD sitteth King for ever.
11 [a]The LORD will give strength unto
his people; the LORD will bless his people
with peace.

The LORD my helper

A Psalm *and* Song [a]*at* the dedication of the
house of David.

30 I WILL extol thee, O LORD; for
thou hast [b]lifted me up, and hast
not made my foes to [c]rejoice over me.
2 O LORD my God, I cried unto thee,
and thou hast healed me.
3 O LORD, [a]thou hast brought up my
soul from the grave: thou hast kept me
alive, that I should not go down to the
pit.
4 Sing unto the LORD, O ye saints of
his, and give thanks [1]at the remembrance
of his holiness.

S *Ps 26:5–6* ◀▶ *Ps 34:12–16*
E *Job 42:16–17* ◀▶ *Ps 103:3*

28:9 David appealed to the Lord to save and bless his people. Note the eternal nature of this appeal that forms a restatement of God's covenant with his people to care for them forever.

5 For [a]his[1] anger *endureth but* a moment; [b]in his favour *is* life: weeping may endure [2]for a night, but [3]joy *cometh* in the morning.

6 And in my prosperity I said, I shall never be moved.

7 LORD, by thy favour thou hast [1]made my mountain to stand strong: [a]thou didst hide thy face, *and* I was troubled.

8 I cried to thee, O LORD; and unto the LORD I made supplication.

9 What profit *is there* in my blood, when I go down to the pit? [a]Shall the dust praise thee? shall it declare thy truth?

10 Hear, O LORD, and have mercy upon me: LORD, be thou my helper.

11 Thou hast turned for me my mourning into dancing: thou hast put off my sackcloth, and girded me with gladness;

12 To the end that [a]*my*[1] glory may sing praise to thee, and not be silent. O LORD my God, I will give thanks unto thee for ever.

My times are in thy hand

To the chief Musician, A Psalm of David.

31 IN[a] THEE, O LORD, do I put my trust; let me never be ashamed: deliver me in thy righteousness.

2 [a]Bow down thine ear to me; deliver me speedily: be thou [1]my strong rock, for an house of defence to save me.

3 [a]For thou *art* my rock and my fortress; therefore [b]for thy name's sake lead me, and guide me.

4 Pull me out of the net that they have laid privily for me: for thou *art* my strength.

5 [a]Into thine hand I commit my spirit: thou hast redeemed me, O LORD God of truth.

6 I have hated them [a]that regard lying vanities: but I trust in the LORD.

7 I will be glad and rejoice in thy mercy: for thou hast considered my trouble; thou hast [a]known my soul in adversities;

8 And hast not [a]shut me up into the hand of the enemy: thou hast set my feet in a large room.

9 Have mercy upon me, O LORD, for I am in trouble: [a]mine eye is consumed with grief, *yea,* my soul and my belly.

10 For my life is spent with grief, and my years with sighing: my strength faileth because of mine iniquity, and my bones are consumed.

11 [a]I was a reproach among all mine enemies, but [b]especially among my neighbours, and a fear to mine acquaintance: [c]they that did see me without fled from me.

12 [a]I am forgotten as a dead man out of mind: I am like [1]a broken vessel.

13 [a]For I have heard the slander of many: [b]fear *was* on every side: while they [c]took counsel together against me, they devised to take away my life.

14 But I trusted in thee, O LORD: I said, Thou *art* my God.

15 My times *are* in thy hand: deliver me from the hand of mine enemies, and from them that persecute me.

16 [a]Make thy face to shine upon thy servant: save me for thy mercies' sake.

17 [a]Let me not be ashamed, O LORD; for I have called upon thee: let the wicked be ashamed, *and* [b]let[1] them be silent in the grave.

18 [a]Let the lying lips be put to silence; which [b]speak [1]grievous things proudly and contemptuously against the righteous.

19 [a]*Oh* how great *is* thy goodness, which thou hast laid up for them that fear thee; *which* thou hast wrought for them that trust in thee before the sons of men!

20 [a]Thou shalt hide them in the secret of thy presence from the pride of man: [b]thou shalt keep them secretly in a pavilion from the strife of tongues.

21 Blessed *be* the LORD: for [a]he hath shown me his marvellous kindness [b]in a [1]strong city.

22 For [a]I said in my haste, [b]I am cut off from before thine eyes: nevertheless thou heardest the voice of my supplications when I cried unto thee.

23 [a]O love the LORD, all ye his saints: *for* the LORD preserveth the faithful, and plentifully rewardeth the proud doer.

5 [a]Ps. 103:9 [b]Ps. 63:3 [1]Heb. there is but *a moment in his anger* [2]Heb. *in the evening* [3]Heb. *singing*
7 [a]Ps. 104:29 [1]Heb. *settled strength for my mountain*
9 [a]Ps. 6:5
12 [a]Ps. 57:8 [1]i.e. my *tongue*, or, my *soul*
31:1 [a]Ps. 22:5
2 [a]Ps. 71:2 [1]Heb. *to me for a rock of strength*
3 [a]Ps. 18:2 [b]Ps. 23:3
5 [a]Luke 23:46
6 [a]Jonah 2:8
7 [a]John 10:27
8 [a]Deut. 32:30
9 [a]Ps. 6:7
11 [a]Is. 53:4 [b]Job 19:13 [c]Ps. 64:8
12 [a]Ps. 88:4,5 [1]Heb. *a vessel that perisheth*
13 [a]Jer. 20:10 [b]Lam. 2:22 [c]Mat. 27:1
16 [a]Ps. 4:6
17 [a]Ps. 25:2 [b]Ps. 115:17 [1]Or, *let them be cut off for the grave*
18 [a]Ps. 120:2 [b]Ps. 94:4 [1]Heb. *a hard thing*
19 [a]Is. 64:4
20 [a]Ps. 27:5 [b]Job 5:21
21 [a]Ps. 17:7 [b]1 Sam. 23:7 [1]Or, *fenced city*
22 [a]Ps. 116:11 [b]Lam. 3:54
23 [a]Ps. 34:9

L *Ps 22:26 ◀ ▶ Ps 32:5*
M *Ps 25:11 ◀ ▶ Ps 34:18*
J *Ps 27:1 ◀ ▶ Ps 31:14*
J *Ps 30:5 ◀ ▶ Ps 42:5*
L *Ps 27:10 ◀ ▶ Ps 31:23*
U *Ps 25:14 ◀ ▶ Ps 31:23*
S *Ps 27:5 ◀ ▶ Ps 31:23*
L *Ps 31:19–20 ◀ ▶ Ps 32:8*
S *Ps 31:20 ◀ ▶ Ps 32:6–7*
U *Ps 31:19–20 ◀ ▶ Ps 32:1–2*

W 24 [a]Be of good courage, and he shall strengthen your heart, all ye that hope in the LORD.

A prayer during distress

[l]*A Psalm* of David, Maschil.

U **32** BLESSED *IS he whose* [a]transgression *is* forgiven, *whose* sin *is* covered.

2 Blessed *is* the man unto whom the LORD [a]imputeth not iniquity, and [b]in whose spirit *there is* no guile.

3 When I kept silence, my bones waxed old through my roaring all the day long.

4 For day and night thy [a]hand was heavy upon me: my moisture is turned into the drought of summer. Selah.

L P R 5 I acknowledged my sin unto thee, and mine iniquity have I not hid. [a]I said, I will confess my transgressions unto the LORD; and thou forgavest the iniquity of my sin. Selah.

S 6 [a]For this shall every one that is godly [b]pray unto thee [l]in a time when thou mayest be found: surely in the floods of great waters they shall not come nigh unto him.

7 [a]Thou *art* my hiding place; thou shalt preserve me from trouble; thou shalt compass me about with [b]songs of deliverance. Selah.

L 8 I will instruct thee and teach thee in the way which thou shalt go: [l]I will guide thee with mine eye.

9 [a]Be ye not as the horse, *or* as the mule, *which* have [b]no understanding: whose mouth must be held in with bit and bridle, lest they come near unto thee.

U 10 [a]Many sorrows *shall be* to the wicked: but [b]he that trusteth in the LORD, mercy shall compass him about.

11 [a]Be glad in the LORD, and rejoice, ye righteous: and shout for joy, all *ye that are* upright in heart.

W *Ps 27:14* ◀ ▶ *Ps 37:1*
U *Ps 31:23* ◀ ▶ *Ps 32:10–11*
L *Ps 30:5* ◀ ▶ *Ps 34:8*
P *2Ch 30:9* ◀ ▶ *Ps 78:38*
R *Job 42:6* ◀ ▶ *Ps 34:14*
S *Ps 31:23* ◀ ▶ *Ps 34:9*
L *Ps 31:23* ◀ ▶ *Ps 34:7–10*
U *Ps 32:1–2* ◀ ▶ *Ps 34:9*

The LORD provides and delivers

33 REJOICE [a]IN the LORD, O ye righteous: *for* [b]praise is comely for the upright.

2 Praise the LORD with harp: sing unto him with the psaltery [a]*and* an instrument of ten strings.

3 [a]Sing unto him a new song; play skilfully with a loud noise.

4 For the word of the LORD *is* right; and all his works *are done* in truth.

5 [a]He loveth righteousness and judgment: [b]the earth is full of the [l]goodness of the LORD.

6 [a]By the word of the LORD were the heavens made; and all the host of them [b]by the breath of his mouth.

7 [a]He gathereth the waters of the sea together as an heap: he layeth up the depth in storehouses.

8 Let all the earth fear the LORD: let all the inhabitants of the world stand in awe of him.

9 For [a]he spake, and it was *done;* he commanded, and it stood fast.

10 [a]The LORD [l]bringeth the counsel of the heathen to nought: he maketh the devices of the people of none effect.

11 [a]The counsel of the LORD standeth for ever, the thoughts of his heart [l]to all generations.

12 Blessed *is* the nation whose God *is* the LORD; *and* the people *whom* he hath [a]chosen for his own inheritance.

13 [a]The LORD looketh from heaven; he beholdeth all the sons of men. E

14 From the place of his habitation he looketh upon all the inhabitants of the earth.

15 He fashioneth their hearts alike; [a]he considereth all their works.

16 [a]There is no king saved by the multitude of an host: a mighty man is not delivered by much strength.

17 [a]An horse *is* a vain thing for safety: neither shall he deliver *any* by his great strength.

18 [a]Behold, the eye of the LORD *is* [b]upon them that fear him, upon them that hope in his mercy; F

19 To deliver their soul from death, and [a]to keep them alive in famine.

20 [a]Our soul waiteth for the LORD: he *is* our help and our shield.

E *Ps 11:4* ◀ ▶ *Ps 44:21*
F *Ps 23:5* ◀ ▶ *Ps 34:9–10*

24 [a]Ps. 27:14
32:1 [a]Ps. 85:2 [l]Or, A Psalm *of David giving instruction*
2 [a]2 Cor. 5:19 [b]John 1:47
4 [a]Job 33:7
5 [a]Prov. 28:13
6 [a]1 Tim. 1:16 [b]Is. 55:6 [l]Heb. *in a time of finding*
7 [a]Ps. 9:9 [b]Ex. 15:1
8 [l]Heb. *I will counsel* thee, *mine eye* shall be *upon thee*
9 [a]Prov. 26:3 [b]Job 35:11
10 [a]Rom. 2:9 [b]Prov. 16:20
11 [a]Ps. 64:10
33:1 [a]Ps. 32:11 [b]Ps. 147:1
2 [a]Ps. 92:3
3 [a]Ps. 96:1
5 [a]Ps. 11:7 [b]Ps. 119:64 [l]Or, *mercy*
6 [a]Heb. 11:3 [b]Job 26:13
7 [a]Job 26:10
9 [a]Gen. 1:3
10 [a]Is. 8:10 [l]Heb. *maketh frustrate*
11 [a]Job 23:13 [l]Heb. *to generation and generation*
12 [a]Ex. 19:5; Deut. 7:6
13 [a]Job 28:24; Ps. 11:4
15 [a]Jer. 32:19
16 [a]Ps. 44:6
17 [a]Ps. 20:7; Prov. 21:31
18 [a]Job 36:7; Ps. 34:15 [b]Ps. 147:11
19 [a]Job 5:20
20 [a]Ps. 130:6

21 For our [a]heart shall rejoice in him, because we have trusted in his holy name.

22 Let thy mercy, O LORD, be upon us, according as we hope in thee.

A psalm of praise and trust

A Psalm of David, when he changed his behaviour before [1]Abimelech; who drove him away, and he departed.

T 34 I WILL [a]bless the LORD at all times: his praise *shall* continually *be* in my mouth.

2 My soul shall make her [a]boast in the LORD: [b]the humble shall hear *thereof,* and be glad.

3 O [a]magnify the LORD with me, and let us exalt his name together.

4 I [a]sought the LORD, and he heard me, and delivered me from all my fears.

5 [1]They looked unto him, and were lightened: and their faces were not ashamed.

V 6 [a]This poor man cried, and the LORD heard *him,* and [b]saved him out of all his troubles.

L 7 [a]The angel of the LORD [b]encampeth round about them that fear him, and delivereth them.

F L W 8 O [a]taste and see that the LORD *is* good: [b]blessed *is* the man *that* trusteth in him.

F S 9 O fear the LORD, ye his saints: for *there is* no want to them that fear him.

U 10 The young lions do lack, and suffer hunger: [a]but they that seek the LORD shall not want any good *thing.*

11 Come, ye children, hearken unto me: [a]I will teach you the fear of the LORD.

S H S 12 [a]What man *is he that* desireth life, *and* loveth *many* days, that he may see good?

U 13 Keep thy tongue from evil, and thy lips from speaking guile.

14 [a]Depart from evil, and do good; [b]seek peace, and pursue it. R

15 [a]The eyes of the LORD *are* upon the righteous, and his ears *are open* unto their cry. L

16 [a]The face of the LORD *is* against them that do evil, [b]to cut off the remembrance of them from the earth.

17 *The righteous* cry, and [a]the LORD heareth, and delivereth them out of all their troubles. V

18 [a]The LORD *is* nigh [b]unto[1] them that are of a broken heart; and saveth such as be [2]of a contrite spirit. L M R

19 [a]Many *are* the afflictions of the righteous: [b]but the LORD delivereth him out of them all. L V

20 He keepeth all his bones: [a]not one of them is broken.

21 [a]Evil shall slay the wicked: and they that hate the righteous [1]shall be desolate.

22 The LORD [a]redeemeth the soul of his servants: and none of them that trust in him shall be desolate. F W L

A plea for judgment

A Psalm of David.

35 PLEAD [a]*MY cause,* O LORD, with them that strive with me: [b]fight against them that fight against me.

2 [a]Take hold of shield and buckler, and stand up for mine help.

3 Draw out also the spear, and stop *the way* against them that persecute me: say unto my soul, I *am* thy salvation.

4 [a]Let them be confounded and put to shame that seek after my soul: let them be turned back and brought to confusion that devise my hurt.

5 [a]Let them be as chaff before the wind: and let the angel of the LORD chase *them.*

6 Let their way be [a]dark[1] and slippery: and let the angel of the LORD persecute them.

7 For without cause have they [a]hid for

---

21 [a]John 16:22
34:1 [a]Eph. 5:20 [1]Or, *Achish;* see 1 Sam. 21:13
2 [a]Jer. 9:24 [b]Ps. 119:74
3 [a]Luke 1:46
4 [a]Mat. 7:7
5 [1]Or, *They flowed unto him*
6 [a]Ps. 3:4 [b]ver. 17, 19
7 [a]Dan. 6:22 [b]2 Ki. 6:17
8 [a]1 Pet. 2:3 [b]Ps. 2:12
10 [a]Ps. 84:11
11 [a]Ps. 32:8
12 [a]1 Pet. 3:10
14 [a]Ps. 37:27 [b]Heb. 12:14
15 [a]Job 36:7
16 [a]Lev. 17:10 [b]Prov. 10:7
17 [a]Ps. 145:19
18 [a]Ps. 145:18 [b]Is. 57:15 [1]Heb. *to the broken of heart* [2]Heb. *contrite of spirit*
19 [a]Prov. 24:16 [b]ver. 6,17
20 [a]John 19:36
21 [a]Ps. 94:23 [1]Or, *shall be guilty*
22 [a]1 Ki. 1:29; Ps. 71:23
35:1 [a]Ps. 43:1 [b]Ex. 14:25
2 [a]Is. 42:13
4 [a]Ps. 70:2,3
5 [a]Job 21:18; Ps. 1:4
6 [a]Ps. 73:18 [1]Heb. *darkness and slipperiness*
7 [a]Ps. 9:15

T *Ps 22:25* ◀ ▶ *Ps 35:18*
V *Ps 27:3* ◀ ▶ *Ps 34:17*
L *Ps 32:8* ◀ ▶ *Ps 34:15*
F *Ps 2:12* ◀ ▶ *Ps 34:22*
L *Ps 32:5* ◀ ▶ *Ps 34:18*
W *Ps 18:30* ◀ ▶ *Ps 34:22*
F *Ps 33:18–19* ◀ ▶ *Ps 37:3*
S *Ps 32:6–7* ◀ ▶ *Ps 34:12–15*
U *Ps 32:10–11* ◀ ▶ *Ps 34:12–15*
S *Ps 29:2* ◀ ▶ *Ps 37:3*
H *Job 33:23–30* ◀ ▶ *Ps 41:3*
S *Ps 34:9* ◀ ▶ *Ps 37:4–6*
U *Ps 34:9* ◀ ▶ *Ps 37:4–6*

R *Ps 32:5* ◀ ▶ *Ps 34:18*
L *Ps 34:7–10* ◀ ▶ *Ps 34:19–20*
V *Ps 34:6* ◀ ▶ *Ps 34:19*
L *Ps 34:8* ◀ ▶ *Ps 51:1–3*
M *Ps 30:5* ◀ ▶ *Ps 51:1–17*
R *Ps 34:14* ◀ ▶ *Ps 37:27*
L *Ps 34:15* ◀ ▶ *Ps 34:22*
V *Ps 34:17* ◀ ▶ *Ps 35:10*
F *Ps 34:8* ◀ ▶ *Ps 37:3*
W *Ps 34:8* ◀ ▶ *Ps 50:1*
L *Ps 34:19–20* ◀ ▶ *Ps 36:7–8*

me their net *in* a pit, *which* without
cause they have digged for my soul.
8 Let [a]destruction come upon him [1]at
unawares; and let his net that he hath hid
catch himself: into that very destruction
let him fall.
9 And my soul shall be joyful in the
LORD: it shall rejoice in his salvation.
V 10 All my bones shall say, LORD, [a]who
is like unto thee, which deliverest the
poor from him that is too strong for him,
yea, the poor and the needy from him
that spoileth him?
11 [1]False witnesses did rise up; [2]they
laid to my charge *things* that I knew not.
12 [a]They rewarded me evil for good *to*
the [1]spoiling of my soul.
13 But as for me, [a]when they were
sick, my clothing *was* sackcloth: I [1]hum-
bled my soul with fasting; and my prayer
returned into mine own bosom.
14 I [1]behaved myself [2]as though *he*
had been my friend *or* brother: I bowed
down heavily, as one that mourneth *for*
his mother.
15 But in mine [1]adversity they rejoiced, and gathered themselves together:
yea, [a]the abjects gathered themselves together against me, and I knew *it* not; they
did [b]tear *me,* and ceased not:
16 With hypocritical mockers in feasts,
[a]they gnashed upon me with their teeth.
17 Lord, how long wilt thou [a]look on?
rescue my soul from their destructions,
[b]my[1] darling from the lions.
T 18 I will give thee thanks in the great
congregation: I will praise thee among
[1]much people.
19 [a]Let not them that are mine enemies [b]wrongfully[1] rejoice over me: *nei-*
ther [c]let them wink with the eye [d]that
hate me without a cause.
20 For they speak not peace: but they
devise deceitful matters against *them that*
are quiet in the land.
21 Yea, they [a]opened their mouth
wide against me, *and* said, [b]Aha, aha, our
eye hath seen *it.*
22 *This* thou hast [a]seen, O LORD: [b]keep
not silence: O Lord, be not [c]far from me.
23 [a]Stir up thyself, and awake to my
judgment, *even* unto my cause, my God
and my Lord.
24 Judge me, O LORD my God, [a]accord-
ing to thy righteousness; and let them not
rejoice over me.
25 Let them not say in their hearts,
[1]Ah, so would we have it: let them not
say, [a]We have swallowed him up.
26 Let them be ashamed and brought
to confusion together that rejoice at mine
hurt: let them be [a]clothed with shame
and dishonour that magnify *themselves*
against me.
27 [a]Let them shout for joy, and be
glad, that favour [1]my righteous cause:
yea, let them say continually, Let the
LORD be magnified, which hath pleasure
in the prosperity of his servant.
28 And my tongue shall speak of thy
righteousness *and* of thy praise all the day
long.

Wickedness confronts God's love

To the chief Musician, *A Psalm* of David the servant of the LORD.

36 THE TRANSGRESSION of the C
wicked saith within my heart,
that [a]*there is* no fear of God before his
eyes.
2 For he flattereth himself in his own
eyes, [1]until his iniquity be found to be
hateful.
3 The words of his mouth *are* iniquity
and deceit: [a]he hath left off to be wise,
and to do good.
4 [a]He deviseth [1]mischief upon his bed;
he setteth himself [b]in a way *that is* not
good; he abhorreth not evil.
5 Thy mercy, O LORD, *is* in the heavens; *and* thy faithfulness *reacheth* unto
the clouds.
6 Thy righteousness *is* like [1]the great
mountains; [a]thy judgments *are* a great
deep: O LORD, thou preservest man and
beast.
7 How [1]excellent *is* thy lovingkind- L
ness, O God! therefore the children of
men [a]put their trust under the shadow of
thy wings.
8 [a]They shall be [1]abundantly satisfied
with the fatness of thy house; and thou
shalt make them drink of [b]the river of thy
pleasures.
9 [a]For with thee *is* the fountain of life: K
[b]in thy light shall we see light. O

8 [a]1 Thes. 5:3 [1]Heb. which *he knoweth not of*
10 [a]Ex. 15:11
11 [1]Heb. *Witnesses of wrong* [2]Heb. *they asked me*
12 [a]John 10:32 [1]Heb. *depriving*
13 [a]Job 30:25 [1]Or, *afflicted*
14 [1]Heb. *walked* [2]Heb. *as a friend, as a brother to me*
15 [a]Job 30:1,8 [b]Job 16:9 [1]Heb. *halting*
16 [a]Job 16:9; Lam. 2:16
17 [a]Hab. 1:13 [b]Ps. 22:20 [1]Heb. *my only one*
18 [1]Heb. *strong*
19 [a]Ps. 13:4 [b]Ps. 38:19 [c]Job 15:12 [d]Ps. 69:4 [1]Heb. *falsely*
21 [a]Ps. 22:13 [b]Ps. 40:15
22 [a]Ex. 3:7 [b]Ps. 28:1 [c]Ps. 10:1
23 [a]Ps. 44:23
24 [a]2 Thes. 1:6
25 [a]Lam. 2:16 [1]Heb. *Ah, ah, our soul*
26 [a]Ps. 109:29
27 [a]Rom. 12:15 [1]Heb. *my righteousness*
36:1 [a]Rom. 3:18
2 [1]Heb. *to find his iniquity to hate*
3 [a]Jer. 4:22
4 [a]Prov. 4:16 [b]Is. 65:2 [1]Or, *vanity*
6 [a]Rom. 11:33 [1]Heb. *the mountains of God*
7 [a]Ps. 17:8 [1]Heb. *precious*
8 [a]Ps. 65:4 [b]Job 20:17; Rev. 22:1 [1]Heb. *watered*
9 [a]Jer. 2:13 [b]1 Pet. 2:9

V *Ps 34:19* ◀ ▶ *Ps 37:33*
T *Ps 34:1–3* ◀ ▶ *Ps 40:10*

C *Ps 17:14* ◀ ▶ *Ps 38:4–5*
L *Ps 34:22* ◀ ▶ *Ps 37:39–40*
K *Ps 27:1* ◀ ▶ *Ps 37:27–28*
O *Ps 18:31* ◀ ▶ *Ps 62:11–12*

10 O ′continue thy lovingkindness unto them that know thee; and thy righteousness to the upright in heart.

11 Let not the foot of pride come against me, and let not the hand of the wicked remove me.

H 12 There are the workers of iniquity fallen: they are cast down, and shall not be able to rise.

Blessings to the righteous

A Psalm of David.

W **37** FRET [a]NOT thyself because of evildoers, neither be thou envious against the workers of iniquity.

2 For they shall soon be cut down [a]like the grass, and wither as the green herb.

F
S 3 Trust in the LORD, and do good; *so* shalt thou dwell in the land, and ′verily
F thou shalt be fed.

S 4 [a]Delight thyself also in the LORD; and
U he shall give thee the desires of thine heart.

W 5 [a]Commit′ thy way unto the LORD; trust also in him; and he shall bring *it* to pass.

6 [a]And he shall bring forth thy righteousness as the light, and thy judgment as the noonday.

7 ′Rest in the LORD, [a]and wait patiently for him: fret not thyself because of him who prospereth in his way, because of the man who bringeth wicked devices to pass.

S 8 Cease from anger, and forsake wrath: [a]fret not thyself in any wise to do evil.

N 9 For evildoers shall be cut off: but those that wait upon the LORD, they shall [a]inherit the earth.

10 For [a]yet for a little while, and the wicked *shall* not *be:* yea, [b]thou shalt diligently consider his place, and it *shall* not *be.*

11 [a]But the meek shall inherit the N
earth; and shall delight themselves in the abundance of peace.

12 The wicked ′plotteth against the H
just, [a]and gnasheth upon him with his teeth.

13 [a]The Lord shall laugh at him: for he seeth that [b]his day is coming.

14 The wicked have drawn out the sword, and have bent their bow, to cast down the poor and needy, *and* to slay ′such as be of upright conversation.

15 [a]Their sword shall enter into their own heart, and their bows shall be broken.

16 [a]A little that a righteous man hath *is* better than the riches of many wicked.

17 For [a]the arms of the wicked shall U
be broken: but the LORD upholdeth the righteous.

18 The LORD [a]knoweth the days of the upright: and their inheritance shall be [b]for ever.

19 They shall not be ashamed in the F
evil time: and [a]in the days of famine they shall be satisfied.

20 But the wicked shall perish, and the H
enemies of the LORD *shall be* as ′the fat of lambs: they shall consume; [a]into smoke shall they consume away.

21 The wicked borroweth, and payeth not again: but [a]the righteous showeth mercy, and giveth.

22 [a]For *such as be* blessed of him shall N
inherit the earth; and *they that be* cursed of him shall be cut off.

23 [a]The steps of a *good* man are ′or- U
dered by the LORD: and he delighteth in his way.

24 [a]Though he fall, he shall not be utterly cast down: for the LORD upholdeth *him with* his hand.

10 ′Heb. *draw out at length*
37:1 [a]Ps. 73:3; Prov. 23:17
2 [a]Ps. 90:5,6
3 ′Heb. *in truth,* or, *stableness*
4 [a]Is. 58:14
5 [a]Ps. 55:22; Mat. 6:25 ′Heb. *Roll thy way upon the LORD*
6 [a]Job 11:17
7 [a]Lam. 3:26 ′Heb. *Be silent to the LORD*
8 [a]Ps. 73:3; Eph. 4:26
9 [a]Is. 57:13
10 [a]Heb. 10:36 [b]Job 7:10
11 [a]Mat. 5:5
12 [a]Ps. 35:16 ′Or, *practiseth*
13 [a]Ps. 2:4 [b]1 Sam. 26:10
14 ′Heb. *the upright of way*
15 [a]Ps. 9:16
16 [a]Prov. 15:16
17 [a]Ps. 10:15
18 [a]Ps. 1:6 [b]Is. 60:21
19 [a]Ps. 33:19
20 [a]Ps. 102:3 ′Heb. *the preciousness of lambs*
21 [a]Ps. 112:5,9
22 [a]Prov. 3:33
23 [a]1 Sam. 2:9 ′Or, *established*
24 [a]Prov. 24:16

H *Ps 26:9* ◀▶ *Ps 37:12–13*
W *Ps 31:24* ◀▶ *Ps 37:5*
F *Ps 34:22* ◀▶ *Ps 84:12*
S *Ps 34:12–16* ◀▶ *Ps 37:8–9*
F *Ps 34:9–10* ◀▶ *Ps 37:19*
S *Ps 34:12–15* ◀▶ *Ps 46:1*
U *Ps 34:12–15* ◀▶ *Ps 37:17–19*
W *Ps 37:1* ◀▶ *Ps 42:5*
S *Ps 37:3* ◀▶ *Ps 37:27*
N *Job 26:10* ◀▶ *Ps 37:11*
N *Ps 37:9* ◀▶ *Ps 37:22*
H *Ps 36:12* ◀▶ *Ps 37:20*
U *Ps 37:4–6* ◀▶ *Ps 37:23–28*
F *Ps 37:3* ◀▶ *Ps 37:25*
H *Ps 37:12–13* ◀▶ *Ps 37:38*
N *Ps 37:11* ◀▶ *Ps 37:29*
U *Ps 37:17–19* ◀▶ *Ps 37:31*

37:9–34 Several times throughout this passage the psalmist says that God will ultimately punish and "cut off" those who choose to reject his mercy and forgiveness. However, those "that wait upon the LORD" (37:9) will ultimately be blessed forever in Christ's Messianic kingdom when they "inherit the earth" (37:22) and witness with their own eyes God's final judgment of the wicked (37:34).

F 25 I have been young, and *now* am
old; yet have I not seen the righteous forsaken, nor his seed [a]begging bread.

R 26 [a]*He is* [/]ever merciful, and lendeth;
and his seed *is* blessed.

K 27 [a]Depart from evil, and do good; and
R dwell for evermore.

S 28 For the LORD [a]loveth judgment, and
forsaketh not his saints; they are preserved for ever: [b]but the seed of the
wicked shall be cut off.

N 29 [a]The righteous shall inherit the
S land, and dwell therein for ever.

30 [a]The mouth of the righteous speaketh wisdom, and his tongue talketh of
judgment.

U 31 [a]The law of his God *is* in his heart;
none of his [/]steps shall slide.

32 The wicked [a]watcheth the righteous, and seeketh to slay him.

V 33 The LORD [a]will not leave him in his
hand, nor [b]condemn him when he is
judged.

N 34 [a]Wait on the LORD, and keep his
P way, and he shall exalt thee to inherit the
S land: [b]when the wicked are cut off, thou
shalt see *it.*

35 [a]I have seen the wicked in great
power, and spreading himself like [/]a
green bay tree.

36 Yet he [a]passed away, and, lo, he
was not: yea, I sought him, but he could
not be found.

S 37 Mark the perfect *man,* and behold
U the upright: for [a]the end of *that* man *is*
peace.

H 38 [a]But the transgressors shall be destroyed together: the end of the wicked
shall be cut off.

L 39 But [a]the salvation of the righteous
is of the LORD: *he is* their strength [b]in the
time of trouble.

40 And [a]the LORD shall help them, and
deliver them: he shall deliver them from
the wicked, and save them, [b]because
they trust in him.

The burden of suffering

A Psalm of David, [a]to bring to
remembrance.

38 O [b]LORD, rebuke me not in thy
wrath: neither chasten me in thy
hot displeasure.

2 For [a]thine arrows stick fast in me,
and [b]thy hand presseth me sore.

3 *There is* no soundness in my flesh
because of thine anger; [a]neither *is there*
any [/]rest in my bones because of my sin.

4 For [a]mine iniquities are gone over C
mine head: as an heavy burden they are
too [b]heavy for me.

5 My wounds stink *and* are corrupt because of my foolishness.

6 I am [/]troubled; [a]I am bowed down
greatly; [b]I go mourning all the day long.

7 For my loins are filled with a [a]loath- C
some *disease:* and *there is* no soundness
in my flesh.

8 I am feeble and sore broken: [a]I have
roared by reason of the disquietness of
my heart.

9 Lord, all my desire *is* before thee;
and my groaning is not hid from thee.

10 My heart panteth, my strength faileth me: as for [a]the light of mine eyes, it
also [/]is gone from me.

11 [a]My lovers and my friends [b]stand
aloof from my [/]sore; and [2]my kinsmen
[c]stand afar off.

12 They also that seek after my life
[a]lay snares *for me:* and they that seek my
hurt [b]speak mischievous things, and
imagine deceits all the day long.

13 But [a]I, as a deaf *man,* heard not;
[b]and *I was* as a dumb man *that* openeth
not his mouth.

14 Thus I was as a man that heareth
not, and in whose mouth *are* no reproofs.

15 For [/]in thee, O LORD, [a]do I hope:
thou wilt [2]hear, O Lord my God.

16 For I said, *Hear me,* [a]lest *otherwise*
they should rejoice over me: when my
foot slippeth, they [b]magnify *themselves*
against me.

25 [a]Job 15:23
26 [a]Deut. 15:8 [/]Heb. *all the day*
27 [a]Ps. 34:14
28 [a]Is. 30:18 [b]Ps. 21:10
29 [a]Prov. 2:21
30 [a]Mat. 12:35
31 [a]Deut. 6:6 [/]Or, *goings*
32 [a]Ps. 10:8
33 [a]2 Pet. 2:9 [b]Ps. 109:31
34 [a]Ps. 27:14 [b]Ps. 52:5,6
35 [a]Job 5:3 [/]Or, *a green tree that groweth in his own soil*
36 [a]Job 20:5
37 [a]Is. 32:17
38 [a]Ps. 1:4
39 [a]Ps. 3:8 [b]Ps. 9:9
40 [a]Is. 31:5 [b]1 Chr. 5:20
38:1 [a]Ps. 70, title [b]Ps. 6:1
2 [a]Job 6:4 [b]Ps. 32:4
3 [a]Ps. 6:2 [/]Heb. *peace, or, health*
4 [a]Ezra 9:6 [b]Mat. 11:28
6 [a]Ps. 35:14 [b]Job 30:28 [/]Heb. *wried*
7 [a]Job 7:5
8 [a]Job 3:24
10 [a]Ps. 6:7 [/]Heb. *is not with me*
11 [a]Ps. 31:11 [b]Luke 10:31 [c]Luke 23:49 [/]Heb. *stroke* [2]Or, *my neighbours*
12 [a]2 Sam. 17:1 [b]2 Sam. 16:7
13 [a]2 Sam. 16:10 [b]Ps. 39:2,9
15 [a]Ps. 39:7 [/]Or, *thee do I wait for* [2]Or, *answer*
16 [a]Ps. 13:4 [b]Ps. 35:26

F *Ps 37:19* ◀ ▶ *Ps 78:15–16*
R *Job 42:15* ◀ ▶ *Ps 102:28*
K *Ps 36:9* ◀ ▶ *Ps 40:2*
R *Ps 34:18* ◀ ▶ *Ps 38:18*
S *Ps 37:8–9* ◀ ▶ *Ps 37:29–31*
N *Ps 37:22* ◀ ▶ *Ps 37:34*
S *Ps 37:27* ◀ ▶ *Ps 37:34*
U *Ps 37:23–28* ◀ ▶ *Ps 37:37*
V *Ps 35:10* ◀ ▶ *Ps 41:2*
N *Ps 37:29* ◀ ▶ *Ps 75:3*
P *Ps 18:7–15* ◀ ▶ *Ps 45:1–5*
S *Ps 37:29–31* ◀ ▶ *Ps 37:37–38*
S *Ps 37:34* ◀ ▶ *Ps 50:16*
U *Ps 37:31* ◀ ▶ *Ps 41:1–3*
H *Ps 37:20* ◀ ▶ *Ps 50:3*
L *Ps 36:7–8* ◀ ▶ *Ps 46:1*

C *Ps 36:1–4* ◀ ▶ *Ps 38:7*
C *Ps 38:4–5* ◀ ▶ *Ps 40:2*

17 For I *am* ready ʹto halt, and my sorrow *is* continually before me.

R 18 For I will [a]declare mine iniquity; I will be [b]sorry for my sin.

19 But mine enemies ʹ*are* lively, *and* they are strong: and they that hate me wrongfully are multiplied.

20 They also [a]that render evil for good are mine adversaries; because I follow *the thing that* good *is.*

21 Forsake me not, O LORD: O my God, [a]be not far from me.

22 Make haste ʹto help me, O Lord my salvation.

In time of trouble

To the chief Musician, *even to* [a]Jeduthun, A Psalm of David.

39 I SAID, I will [b]take heed to my ways, that I sin not with my tongue: I will keep ʹmy mouth with a bridle, while the wicked is before me.

2 [a]I was dumb with silence, I held my peace, *even* from good; and my sorrow was ʹstirred.

L 3 My heart was hot within me, while I was musing the fire burned: *then* spake I with my tongue,

4 LORD, make me to know mine end, and the measure of my days, what it *is;* *that* I may know ʹhow frail I *am.*

5 Behold, thou hast made my days *as* an handbreadth; and mine age *is* as nothing before thee: verily every man ʹat his best state *is* altogether vanity. Selah.

6 Surely every man walketh in ʹa vain show: surely they are disquieted in vain: [a]he heapeth up *riches,* and knoweth not who shall gather them.

7 And now, Lord, what wait I for? my hope *is* in thee.

8 Deliver me from all my transgressions: make me not [a]the reproach of the foolish.

9 [a]I was dumb, I opened not my mouth; because [b]thou didst *it.*

10 Remove thy stroke away from me: I am consumed by the ʹblow of thine hand.

T 11 When thou with rebukes dost correct man for iniquity, thou makest ʹhis beauty [a]to consume away like a moth: surely every man *is* vanity. Selah.

12 Hear my prayer, O LORD, and give ear unto my cry; hold not thy peace at my tears: for I *am* a stranger with thee, *and* a sojourner, [a]as all my fathers *were.*

13 [a]O spare me, that I may recover strength, before I go hence, and [b]be no more.

Delight in the will of the LORD

To the chief Musician, A Psalm of David.

40 I [a]WAITEDʹ patiently for the LORD; and he inclined unto me, and heard my cry.

2 He brought me up also out of ʹan C
horrible pit, out of [a]the miry clay, and K
[b]set my feet upon a rock, *and* established my goings.

3 [a]And he hath put a new song in my mouth, *even* praise unto our God: many shall see *it,* and fear, and shall trust in the LORD.

4 [a]Blessed *is* that man that maketh the LORD his trust, and respecteth not the proud, nor such as turn aside to lies.

5 [a]Many, O LORD my God, *are* thy wonderful works *which* thou hast done, [b]and thy thoughts *which are* to us-ward: ʹthey cannot be reckoned up in order unto thee: *if* I would declare and speak *of them,* they are more than can be numbered.

6 Sacrifice and offering thou didst not desire; mine ears hast thou ʹopened: burnt offering and sin offering hast thou not required.

7 Then said I, Lo, I come: in the volume of the book *it is* written of me,

8 [a]I delight to do thy will, O my God: yea, thy law *is* [b]withinʹ my heart.

9 [a]I have preached righteousness in the great congregation: lo, [b]I have not refrained my lips, O LORD, thou knowest.

10 [a]I have not hid thy righteousness T
within my heart; I have declared thy faithfulness and thy salvation: I have not concealed thy lovingkindness and thy truth from the great congregation.

11 Withhold not thou thy tender mercies from me, O LORD: [a]let thy lovingkindness and thy truth continually preserve me.

12 For innumerable evils have compassed me about: [a]mine iniquities have

17 ʹHeb. *for halting*
18 [a]Prov. 28:13 [b]2 Cor. 7:9
19 ʹHeb. being *living, are strong*
20 [a]Ps. 35:12
21 [a]Ps. 35:22
22 ʹHeb. *for my help*
39:1 [a]1 Chr. 16:41; Ps. 62, title & 77, title [b]1 Ki. 2:4 ʹHeb. *a bridle,* or, *muzzle for my mouth*
2 [a]Ps. 38:13 ʹHeb. *troubled*
4 ʹOr, *what time I have here*
5 ʹHeb. *settled*
6 [a]Luke 12:20 ʹHeb. *an image*
8 [a]Ps. 44:13
9 [a]Lev. 10:3 [b]Job 2:10
10 ʹHeb. *conflict*
11 [a]Job 13:28 ʹHeb. *that which is to be desired in him to melt away*
12 [a]Gen. 47:9
13 [a]Job 10:20 [b]Job 14:10
40:1 [a]Ps. 27:14 ʹHeb. *In waiting I waited*
2 [a]Ps. 69:2,14 [b]Ps. 27:5 ʹHeb. *a pit of noise*
3 [a]Ps. 33:3
4 [a]Ps. 34:8
5 [a]Job 9:10 [b]Is. 55:8 ʹOr, *none can order them unto thee*
6 ʹHeb. *digged*
8 [a]John 4:34 [b]Ps. 37:31; Jer. 31:33 ʹHeb. *in the midst of my bowels*
9 [a]Ps. 22:22 [b]Ps. 119:13
10 [a]Acts 20:20
11 [a]Ps. 43:3
12 [a]Ps. 38:4

R *Ps 37:27* ◀ ▶ *Ps 51:1–3*
L *Job 32:18–19* ◀ ▶ *Ps 143:10*
T *Job 34:31* ◀ ▶ *Ps 66:10–12*

C *Ps 38:7* ◀ ▶ *Ps 51:5*
K *Ps 37:27–28* ◀ ▶ *Ps 51:7*
T *Ps 35:18* ◀ ▶ *Ps 50:23*

taken hold upon me, so that I am not able to look up; they are more than the hairs of mine head: therefore my heart [1]faileth me.

13 [a]Be pleased, O LORD, to deliver me: O LORD, make haste to help me.

14 [a]Let them be ashamed and confounded together that seek after my soul to destroy it; let them be driven backward and put to shame that wish me evil.

15 Let them be [a]desolate for a reward of their shame that say unto me, Aha, aha.

16 [a]Let all those that seek thee rejoice and be glad in thee: let such as love thy salvation [b]say continually, The LORD be magnified.

17 [a]But I *am* poor and needy; *yet* the Lord thinketh upon me: thou *art* my help and my deliverer; make no tarrying, O my God.

Psalm of the compassionate

To the chief Musician, A Psalm of David.

U 41 BLESSED *IS* he that considereth [1]the poor: the LORD will deliver him [2]in time of trouble.

V 2 The LORD will preserve him, and keep him alive; *and* he shall be blessed upon the earth: [a]and [1]thou wilt not deliver him unto the will of his enemies.

H 3 The LORD will strengthen him upon the bed of languishing: thou wilt [1]make all his bed in his sickness.

4 I said, LORD, be merciful unto me: heal my soul; for I have sinned against thee.

5 Mine enemies speak evil of me, When shall he die, and his name perish?

6 And if he come to see *me,* he speaketh vanity: his heart gathereth iniquity to itself; *when* he goeth abroad, he telleth *it.*

7 All that hate me whisper together against me: against me do they devise [1]my hurt.

U *Ps 37:37* ◀ ▶ *Ps 45:7*
V *Ps 37:33* ◀ ▶ *Ps 41:11*
H *Ps 34:12–13* ◀ ▶ *Ps 67:2*

8 [1]An evil disease, *say they,* cleaveth fast unto him: and *now* that he lieth he shall rise up no more.

9 [a]Yea, [1]mine own familiar friend, in whom I trusted, [b]which did eat of my bread, hath [2]lifted up *his* heel against me.

10 But thou, O LORD, be merciful unto me, and raise me up, that I may requite them.

11 By this I know that thou favourest me, because mine enemy doth not triumph over me. V

12 And as for me, thou upholdest me in mine integrity, and [a]settest me before thy face for ever.

13 [a]Blessed *be* the LORD God of Israel from everlasting, and to everlasting. Amen, and Amen.

Book II

Yearning for God

To the chief Musician, [1]Maschil, for the sons of Korah.

42 AS THE hart [2]panteth after the water brooks, so panteth my soul after thee, O God.

2 [a]My soul thirsteth for God, for the living God: when shall I come and appear before God?

3 [a]My tears have been my meat day and night, while they continually say unto me, Where *is* thy God?

4 When I remember these *things,* [a]I pour out my soul in me: for I had gone with the multitude, [b]I went with them to the house of God, with the voice of joy and praise, with a multitude that kept holyday.

5 [a]Why art thou [1]cast down, O my soul? and *why* art thou disquieted in me? [b]hope thou in God: for I shall yet [2]praise him [3]*for* the help of his countenance. J W

6 O my God, my soul is cast down within me: therefore will I remember

V *Ps 41:2* ◀ ▶ *Ps 44:5–7*
J *Ps 31:14* ◀ ▶ *Ps 42:7–8*
W *Ps 37:5* ◀ ▶ *Ps 42:11*

12 [1]Heb. *forsaketh*
13 [a]Ps. 70:1
14 [a]Ps. 35:4
15 [a]Ps. 73:19
16 [a]Ps. 70:4 [b]Ps. 35:27
17 [a]Ps. 70:5
41:1 [1]Or, *the weak,* or, *sick* [2]Heb. *in the day of evil*
2 [a]Ps. 27:12 [1]Or, *do not thou deliver*
3 [1]Heb. *turn*
7 [1]Heb. *evil to me*
8 [1]Heb. *A thing of Belial*
9 [a]2 Sam. 15:12; Job 19:19; Ps. 55:12 [b]Obad. 7; John 13:18 [1]Heb. *the man of my peace* [2]Heb. *magnified*
12 [a]Job 36:7; Ps. 34:15
13 [a]Ps. 106:48
42:1 [1]Or, A Psalm *giving instruction of the sons* [2]Heb. *brayeth*
2 [a]Ps. 63:1
3 [a]Ps. 80:5
4 [a]Job 30:16 [b]Is. 30:29
5 [a]ver. 11 [b]Lam. 3:24 [1]Heb. *bowed down* [2]Or, *give thanks* [3]Or, *his presence is salvation*

41:9 David's prophecy of betrayal by a close friend prefigures two future events: the betrayal of King David and the betrayal of Jesus. David's trusted counselor Ahithophel betrayed him by joining Absalom's rebellion and advising David's son how to defeat his father and steal his throne. The words of this psalm also portend the betrayal of Jesus Christ by Judas Iscariot for thirty pieces of silver (see Jn 13:18–19).

thee from the land of Jordan, and of the Hermonites, from [1]the hill Mizar.

7 Deep calleth unto deep at the noise of thy waterspouts: [a]all thy waves and thy billows are gone over me.

8 *Yet* the LORD will command his lovingkindness in the daytime, and [a]in the night his song *shall be* with me, *and* my prayer unto the God of my life.

9 I will say unto God my rock, Why hast thou forgotten me? [a]why go I mourning because of the oppression of the enemy?

10 *As* with a [1]sword in my bones, mine enemies reproach me; [a]while they say daily unto me, Where *is* thy God?

11 [a]Why art thou cast down, O my soul? and why art thou disquieted within me? hope thou in God: for I shall yet praise him, *who is* the health of my countenance, and my God.

A plea for judgment

43 JUDGE[a] ME, O God, and [b]plead my cause against an [1]ungodly nation: O deliver me [2]from the deceitful and unjust man.

2 For thou *art* the God of my strength: why dost thou cast me off? [a]why go I mourning because of the oppression of the enemy?

3 [a]O send out thy light and thy truth: let them lead me; let them bring me unto [b]thy holy hill, and to thy tabernacles.

4 Then will I go unto the altar of God, unto God [1]my exceeding joy: yea, upon the harp will I praise thee, O God my God.

5 [a]Why art thou cast down, O my soul? and why art thou disquieted within me? hope in God: for I shall yet praise him, *who is* the health of my countenance, and my God.

Appeal to God for deliverance

To the chief Musician for the sons of Korah, Maschil.

44 WE HAVE heard with our ears, O God, [a]our fathers have told us, *what* work thou didst in their days, in the times of old.

2 *How* [a]thou didst drive out the heathen with thy hand, and plantedst them; *how* thou didst afflict the people, and cast them out.

3 For [a]they got not the land in possession by their own sword, neither did their own arm save them: but thy right hand, and thine arm, and the light of thy countenance, [b]because thou hadst a favour unto them.

4 [a]Thou art my King, O God: command deliverances for Jacob.

5 Through thee [a]will we push down our enemies: through thy name will we tread them under that rise up against us.

6 For [a]I will not trust in my bow, neither shall my sword save me.

7 But thou hast saved us from our enemies, and hast [a]put them to shame that hated us.

8 [a]In God we boast all the day long, and praise thy name for ever. Selah.

9 But [a]thou hast cast off, and put us to shame; and goest not forth with our armies.

10 Thou makest us to [a]turn back from the enemy: and they which hate us spoil for themselves.

11 [a]Thou hast given us [1]like sheep *appointed* for meat; and hast [b]scattered us among the heathen.

12 [a]Thou sellest thy people [1]for nought, and dost not increase *thy wealth* by their price.

13 [a]Thou makest us a reproach to our neighbours, a scorn and a derision to them that are round about us.

14 [a]Thou makest us a byword among the heathen, a [b]shaking of the head among the people.

15 My confusion *is* continually before me, and the shame of my face hath covered me,

16 For the voice of him that reproacheth and blasphemeth; [a]by reason of the enemy and avenger.

17 [a]All this is come upon us; yet have we not forgotten thee, neither have we dealt falsely in thy covenant.

18 Our heart is not turned back, [a]neither have our [1]steps declined from thy way;

19 Though thou hast sore broken us in [a]the place of dragons, and covered us [b]with the shadow of death.

---

6 [1]Or, *the little hill*
7 [a]Ps. 88:7
8 [a]Job 35:10
9 [a]Ps. 38:6
10 [a]Joel 2:17; Mic. 7:10 [1]Or, *killing*
11 [a]Ps. 43:5
43:1 [a]Ps. 26:1 [b]Ps. 35:1 [1]Or, *unmerciful* [2]Heb. *from a man of deceit and iniquity*
2 [a]Ps. 42:9
3 [a]Ps. 40:11 & 57:3 [b]Ps. 3:4
4 [1]Heb. *the gladness of my joy*
5 [a]Ps. 42:5,11
44:1 [a]Ex. 12:26; Ps. 78:3
2 [a]Ex. 15:17; Deut. 7:1; Ps. 80:8
3 [a]Deut. 8:17; Josh. 24:12 [b]Deut. 7:7,8
4 [a]Ps. 74:12
5 [a]Dan. 8:4
6 [a]Ps. 33:16
7 [a]Ps. 40:14
8 [a]Ps. 34:2; Jer. 9:24
9 [a]Ps. 60:1
10 [a]Lev. 26:17; Deut. 28:25
11 [a]Rom. 8:36 [b]Deut. 28:64; Ps. 60:1 [1]Heb. *as sheep of meat*
12 [a]Is. 52:3,4; Jer. 15:13 [1]Heb. *without riches*
13 [a]Deut. 28:37
14 [a]Jer. 24:9 [b]Job 16:4; Ps. 22:7
16 [a]Ps. 8:2
17 [a]Dan. 9:13
18 [a]Job 23:11 [1]Or, *goings*
19 [a]Is. 34:13 [b]Ps. 23:4

J Ps 42:5 ◄► Ps 42:11
J Ps 42:7–8 ◄► Ps 43:5
W Ps 42:5 ◄► Ps 43:5
J Ps 42:11 ◄► Ps 46:1–3
W Ps 42:11 ◄► Ps 55:22

V Ps 41:11 ◄► Ps 50:15

20 If we have forgotten the name of our God, or [a]stretched out our hands to a strange god;

E 21 [a]Shall not God search this out? for he knoweth the secrets of the heart.

22 [a]Yea, for thy sake are we killed all the day long; we are counted as sheep for the slaughter.

23 [a]Awake, why sleepest thou, O Lord? arise, cast *us* not off for ever.

24 [a]Wherefore hidest thou thy face, *and* forgettest our affliction and our oppression?

25 For [a]our soul is bowed down to the dust: our belly cleaveth unto the earth.

26 Arise [1]for our help, and redeem us for thy mercies' sake.

The king's marriage

To the chief Musician [a]upon Shoshannim, for the sons of Korah, [1]Maschil, A Song of loves.

P **45** MY HEART [2]is inditing a good matter: I speak of the things which I have made touching the king: my tongue *is* the pen of a ready writer.

2 Thou art fairer than the children of men: [a]grace is poured into thy lips: therefore God hath blessed thee for ever.

3 Gird thy [a]sword upon *thy* thigh, [b]O *most* mighty, with thy glory and thy majesty.

4 [a]And in thy majesty [1]ride prosperously because of truth and meekness *and* righteousness; and thy right hand shall teach thee terrible things.

5 Thine arrows *are* sharp in the heart of the king's enemies; *whereby* the people fall under thee.

V 6 [a]Thy throne, O God, *is* for ever and ever: the sceptre of thy kingdom *is* a right sceptre.

B F J U 7 [a]Thou lovest righteousness, and hatest wickedness: therefore [b]God,[1] thy God, [c]hath anointed thee with the oil [d]of gladness above thy fellows.

8 [a]All thy garments *smell* of myrrh, and aloes, *and* cassia, out of the ivory palaces, whereby they have made thee glad.

9 Kings' daughters *were* among thy honourable women: [a]upon thy right hand did stand the queen in gold of Ophir.

10 Hearken, O daughter, and consider, and incline thine ear; [a]forget also thine own people, and thy father's house;

11 So shall the king greatly desire thy beauty: [a]for he *is* thy Lord; and worship thou him.

12 And the daughter of Tyre *shall be there* with a gift; *even* [a]the rich among the people shall entreat [1]thy favour.

13 [a]The king's daughter *is* all glorious within: her clothing *is* of wrought gold.

14 [a]She shall be brought unto the king in raiment of needlework: the virgins her companions that follow her shall be brought unto thee. H T

15 With gladness and rejoicing shall they be brought: they shall enter into the king's palace.

16 Instead of thy fathers shall be thy children, [a]whom thou mayest make princes in all the earth. M

17 I will make thy name to be remembered in all generations: therefore shall the people praise thee for ever and ever.

The presence of God in calamity

To the chief Musician [1]for the sons of Korah, [a]A Song upon [b]Alamoth.

46 GOD *IS* our refuge and strength, [c]a very present help in trouble. J L

2 Therefore will not we fear, though the earth be removed, and though the mountains be carried into [1]the midst of the sea; S

3 [a]*Though* the waters thereof roar *and* be troubled, *though* the mountains shake with the swelling thereof. Selah.

4 *There is* [a]a river, the streams M

20 [a]Deut. 6:14; Ps. 88:9
21 [a]Job 31:14; Ps. 139:1
22 [a]Rom. 8:36
23 [a]Ps. 7:6
24 [a]Job 13:24; Ps. 13:1
25 [a]Ps. 119:25
26 [1]Heb. *a help for us*
45:1 [a]Ps. 69, title; & 80, title [1]Or, *of instruction* [2]Heb. *boileth,* or, *bubbleth up*
2 [a]Luke 4:22
3 [a]Is. 49:2; Heb. 4:12; Rev. 1:16 [b]Is. 9:6
4 [a]Rev. 6:2 [1]Heb. *prosper thou, ride thou*
6 [a]Ps. 93:2; Heb. 1:8
7 [a]Ps. 33:5 [b]Is. 61:1 [c]1 Ki. 1:39; Ps. 79:4 [d]Ps. 21:6 [1]Or, *O God*
8 [a]Sol. 1:3
9 [a]1 Ki. 2:19
10 [a]See Deut. 21:13
11 [a]Ps. 95:6; Is. 54:5
12 [a]Is. 49:23 [1]Heb. *thy face*
13 [a]Is. 61:10
14 [a]Sol. 1:4
16 [a]1 Pet. 2:9; Rev. 1:6 & 20:6
46:1 [a]Ps. 48 & 66 [b]1 Chr. 15:20 [c]Deut. 4:7 [1]Or, *of*
2 [1]Heb. *the heart of the seas*
3 [a]Ps. 93:3,4
4 [a]See Is. 8:7

E *Ps 33:13–15* ◀▶ *Ps 56:8*
P *Ps 37:34* ◀▶ *Ps 46:6–9* **V** ▶ *Ps 72:8–9*
B *Dt 34:9* ◀▶ *Ps 51:12–13* **F** ▶ *Ps 51:12*
J ▶ *Ps 51:12* **U** *Ps 41:1–3* ◀▶ *Ps 55:22*

H ▶ *SS 1:4* **T** ▶ *SS 1:4*
M *Ps 24:7–10* ◀▶ *Ps 46:4–11*
J *Ps 43:5* ◀▶ *Ps 56:3–4*
L *Ps 37:39–40* ◀▶ *Ps 48:14*
S *Ps 37:4–6* ◀▶ *Ps 91:1–16*
M *Ps 45:16* ◀▶ *Ps 47:1–9*

45:1–6 This psalm describes the certainty of Messiah's victory over his enemies at the end of the tribulation period and the establishment of his eternal throne and sceptre (see Ge 49:10).

45:14–16 David prophetically described the resurrected saints and the glorious marriage supper of the Lamb (see Mt 22:2–14; 25:10–13; Rev 19:7–9).

46:4–5 David foresaw the joy and peace that would accompany Christ's presence in Jerusalem

whereof shall make glad [b]the city of God, the holy *place* of the tabernacles of the most High.

5 God *is* [a]in the midst of her; she shall not be moved: God shall help her, '*and that* right early.

P 6 [a]The heathen raged, the kingdoms were moved: he uttered his voice, [b]the earth melted.

7 The LORD of hosts *is* with us; the God of Jacob *is* [a]our' refuge. Selah.

8 [a]Come, behold the works of the LORD, what desolations he hath made in the earth.

9 [a]He maketh wars to cease unto the end of the earth; [b]he breaketh the bow, and cutteth the spear in sunder; [c]he burneth the chariot in the fire.

10 Be still, and know that I *am* God: [a]I will be exalted among the heathen, I will be exalted in the earth.

11 The LORD of hosts *is* with us; the God of Jacob *is* our refuge. Selah.

God the King of the earth

To the chief Musician, A Psalm 'for the sons of Korah.

M **47** O [a]CLAP your hands, all ye people; shout unto God with the voice of triumph.

2 For the LORD most high *is* [a]terrible; [b]*he is* a great King over all the earth.

I 3 [a]He shall subdue the people under us, and the nations under our feet.

4 He shall choose our [a]inheritance for us, the excellency of Jacob whom he loved. Selah.

5 [a]God is gone up with a shout, the LORD with the sound of a trumpet.

6 Sing praises to God, sing praises: sing praises unto our King, sing praises.

P *Ps 45:1–5* ◀ ▶ *Ps 50:3*
M *Ps 46:4–11* ◀ ▶ *Ps 48:2*
I *Ps 28:9* ◀ ▶ *Ps 50:5*

4 [b]Ps. 48:1,8; Is. 60:14
5 [a]Is. 12:6; Ezek. 43:7 'Heb. *when the morning appeareth*
6 [a]Ps. 2:1 [b]Josh. 2:9
7 [a]Ps. 9:9 'Heb. *an high place for us*
8 [a]Ps. 66:5
9 [a]Is. 2:4 [b]Ps. 76:3 [c]Ezek. 39:9
10 [a]Is. 2:11,17
47:1 [a]Is. 55:12 'Or, *of*
2 [a]Deut. 7:21; Ps. 76:12 [b]Mal. 1:14
3 [a]Ps. 18:47
4 [a]1 Pet. 1:4
5 [a]Ps. 68:33
7 [a]Zech. 14:9 [b]1 Cor. 14:15 'Or, every one *that hath understanding*
8 [a]1 Chr. 16:31; Ps. 93:1; Rev. 19:6
9 [a]Ps. 89:18 'Or, *The voluntary of the people are gathered* unto *the people of the God of Abraham*
48:1 [a]Ps. 46:4 [b]Is. 2:2,3; Mic. 4:1; Zech. 8:3 'Or, *of*
2 [a]Ps. 50:2; Jer. 3:19 [b]Is. 14:13 [c]Mat. 5:35
4 [a]2 Sam. 10:6,14, 16,18,19
6 [a]Ex. 15:15
7 [a]Ezek. 27:26 [b]Jer. 18:17
9 [a]Ps. 26:3
10 [a]Deut. 28:58

7 [a]For God *is* the King of all the earth: [b]sing ye praises 'with understanding.

8 [a]God reigneth over the heathen: God sitteth upon the throne of his holiness.

9 'The princes of the people are gathered together, *even* the people of the God of Abraham: [a]for the shields of the earth *belong* unto God: he is greatly exalted.

A song to mount Zion

A Song *and* Psalm 'for the sons of Korah.

48 GREAT *IS* the LORD, and greatly to be praised [a]in the city of our God, *in* the [b]mountain of his holiness.

2 [a]Beautiful for situation, the joy of the whole earth, *is* mount Zion, [b]*on* the sides of the north, [c]the city of the great King. M

3 God is known in her palaces for a refuge.

4 For, lo, [a]the kings were assembled, they passed by together.

5 They saw *it, and* so they marvelled; they were troubled, *and* hasted away.

6 Fear [a]took hold upon them there, *and* pain, as of a woman in travail.

7 Thou [a]breakest the ships of Tarshish [b]with an east wind.

8 As we have heard, so have we seen in the city of the LORD of hosts, in the city of our God: God will establish it for ever. Selah. M

9 We have thought of [a]thy lovingkindness, O God, in the midst of thy temple.

10 According to [a]thy name, O God, so *is* thy praise unto the ends of the earth: thy right hand is full of righteousness.

11 Let mount Zion rejoice, let the daughters of Judah be glad, because of thy judgments.

12 Walk about Zion, and go round about her: tell the towers thereof.

M *Ps 47:1–9* ◀ ▶ *Ps 48:8*
M *Ps 48:2* ◀ ▶ *Ps 50:1–2*

---

during the millennial kingdom of God on earth.

46:6–11 This psalm celebrates the security of Jerusalem as God's great city as it declares the effects of God's triumph over the nations. These words also prophetically envision God's climactic salvation in the birth, life, death, resurrection and second coming of Christ. Only when the Messiah rules in his kingdom will Israel experience this glorious peace.

47:1–9 This psalm exalts the glorious and powerful victory of God over the heathen enemies of Israel and foreshadows God's rule through Jesus Christ in the millennial kingdom. God will vindicate those who have faith in him and will defeat the armies of the ungodly nations.

48:2 David likened Jerusalem to Mt. Zaphon, the residence of the Phoenicians' chief god El, thus signifying that Mt. Zion is "the joy of the whole earth" and abode of the only true God.

48:12–13 This curious command to walk around the city and take note of its construction would ultimately serve two purposes. Not only would it give the current residents of Jerusalem a sense of God's

13 [1]Mark ye well her bulwarks, [2]consider her palaces; that ye may tell *it* to the generation following.

L 14 For this God *is* our God for ever and ever: he will be our guide *even* unto death.

The folly of trusting riches

To the chief Musician, A Psalm [1]for the sons of Korah.

49 HEAR THIS, all *ye* people; give ear, all *ye* inhabitants of the world:

2 Both low and high, rich and poor, together.

3 My mouth shall speak of wisdom; and the meditation of my heart *shall be* of understanding.

4 [a]I will incline mine ear to a parable: I will open my dark saying upon the harp.

5 Wherefore should I fear in the days of evil, *when* the iniquity of my heels shall compass me about?

6 They that [a]trust in their wealth, and boast themselves in the multitude of their riches;

7 None *of them* can by any means redeem his brother, nor [a]give to God a ransom for him:

8 (For [a]the redemption of their soul *is* precious, and it ceaseth for ever:)

9 That he should still live for ever, *and* [a]not see corruption.

N 10 For he seeth *that* [a]wise men die, likewise the fool and the brutish person perish, [b]and leave their wealth to others.

11 Their inward thought *is, that* their houses *shall continue* for ever, *and* their dwelling places [1]to all generations; they [a]call *their* lands after their own names.

12 Nevertheless man *being* in honour abideth not: he is like the beasts *that* perish.

13 This their way *is* their [a]folly: yet their posterity [1]approve their sayings. Selah.

14 Like sheep they are laid in the grave; death shall feed on them; and [a]the upright shall have dominion over them in the morning; [b]and their [1]beauty shall consume [2]in the grave from their dwelling.

15 But God [a]will redeem my soul [1]from the power of [2]the grave: for he shall receive me. Selah.

16 Be not thou afraid when one is made rich, when the glory of his house is increased;

17 For when he dieth he shall carry nothing away: his glory shall not descend after him.

18 Though [1]while he lived [a]he blessed his soul: and *men* will praise thee, when thou doest well to thyself.

19 [1]He shall go to the generation of his fathers; they shall never see [a]light.

20 Man *that is* in honour, and understandeth not, [a]is like the beasts *that* perish.

True and false religion

A Psalm [a]of[1] Asaph.

50 THE [b]MIGHTY God, *even* the LORD, hath spoken, and called the earth from the rising of the sun unto the going down thereof. M W

2 Out of Zion, the perfection of beauty, [a]God hath shined.

3 Our God shall come, and shall not keep silence: [a]a fire shall devour before him, and it shall be very tempestuous round about him. P H J

4 [a]He shall call to the heavens from above, and to the earth, that he may judge his people. M

5 Gather [a]my saints together unto me; [b]those that have made a covenant with me by sacrifice. I

6 And the heavens shall declare his righteousness: for [a]God *is* judge himself. Selah.

13 [1]Heb. *Set your heart to her bulwarks* [2]Or, *raise up*
49:1 [1]Or, *of*
4 [a]Ps. 78:2; Mat. 13:35
6 [a]Mark 10:24
7 [a]Job 36:18
8 [a]Mat. 16:26
9 [a]Ps. 89:48
10 [a]Eccl. 2:16 [b]Eccl. 2:18
11 [a]Gen. 4:17 [1]Heb. *to generation and generation*
13 [a]Luke 12:20 [1]Heb. *delight in their mouth*
14 [a]Ps. 47:3; Dan. 7:22; Mal. 4:3 [b]Job 4:21 [1]Or, *strength* [2]Or, *the grave being an habitation to every one of them*
15 [a]Hos. 13:14 [1]Heb. *from the hand of the grave* [2]Or, *hell*
18 [a]Deut. 29:19 [1]Heb. *in his life*
19 [a]Job 33:30 [1]Heb. The soul *shall go*
20 [a]Eccl. 3:19
50:1 [a]1 Chr. 15:17; 2 Chr. 29:30 [b]Is. 9:6 [1]Or, *for Asaph*
2 [a]Ps. 80:1
3 [a]Ps. 97:3; Dan. 7:10
4 [a]Deut. 4:26
5 [a]Deut. 33:3 [b]Ex. 24:7
6 [a]Ps. 75:7

L *Ps 46:1 ◀▶ Ps 50:15*
N *Ps 27:8 ◀▶ Ps 78:39*

M *Ps 48:8 ◀▶ Ps 50:4–6*
W *Ps 34:22 ◀▶ Ps 86:5*
P *Ps 46:6–9 ◀▶ Ps 59:5*
H *Ps 37:38 ◀▶ Ps 55:23*
J *Ps 9:7–8 ◀▶ Ps 67:4*
M *Ps 50:1–2 ◀▶ Ps 66:4*
I *Ps 47:3–4 ◀▶ Ps 53:6*

---

blessing in providing such a beautiful city for his habitation, but by remembering the city and sharing its wonders with future generations, those who ultimately returned from Babylonian exile would have verbal reminders to help them rebuild the city and its temple.

50:1–6 This psalm of Asaph warns the Israelites that the God of Zion is the God of the covenant (see Ex 19:16–20), and he is coming to correct and rebuke his people for their sins.

7 Hear, O my people, and I will speak; O Israel, and I will testify against thee: [a]I *am* God, *even* thy God.

8 [a]I will not reprove thee [b]for thy sacrifices or thy burnt offerings, *to have been* continually before me.

9 [a]I will take no bullock out of thy house, *nor* he goats out of thy folds.

10 For every beast of the forest *is* mine, *and* the cattle upon a thousand hills.

11 I know all the fowls of the mountains: and the wild beasts of the field *are* [l]mine.

12 If I were hungry, I would not tell thee: [a]for the world *is* mine, and the fulness thereof.

13 Will I eat the flesh of bulls, or drink the blood of goats?

14 [a]Offer unto God thanksgiving; and [b]pay thy vows unto the most High:

L V 15 And [a]call upon me in the day of trouble: I will deliver thee, and thou shalt [b]glorify me.

S 16 But unto the wicked God saith, What hast thou to do to declare my statutes, or *that* thou shouldest take my covenant in thy mouth?

17 [a]Seeing thou hatest instruction, and [b]castest my words behind thee.

18 When thou sawest a thief, then thou [a]consentedst with him, and [l]hast been [b]partaker with adulterers.

19 [l]Thou givest thy mouth to evil, and [a]thy tongue frameth deceit.

20 Thou sittest *and* speakest against thy brother; thou slanderest thine own mother's son.

21 These *things* hast thou done, [a]and I kept silence; [b]thou thoughtest that I was altogether *such an one* as thyself: *but* [c]I will reprove thee, and set *them* in order before thine eyes.

22 Now consider this, ye that [a]forget God, lest I tear *you* in pieces, and *there be* none to deliver.

S T 23 [a]Whoso offereth praise glorifieth me: and [b]to him [l]that ordereth *his* conversation *aright* will I show the salvation of God.

L *Ps 48:14* ◀ ▶ *Ps 54:4*
V *Ps 44:5–7* ◀ ▶ *Ps 54:7*
S *Ps 37:37–38* ◀ ▶ *Ps 50:23*
S *Ps 50:16* ◀ ▶ *Ps 62:12*
T *Ps 40:10* ◀ ▶ *Ps 60:4*

7 [a]Ex. 20:2
8 [a]Jer. 7:22 [b]Hos. 6:6
9 [a]Acts 17:25
11 [l]Heb. *with me*
12 [a]Job 41:11
14 [a]Heb. 13:15 [b]Deut. 23:21
15 [a]Job 22:27 [b]Ps. 22:23
17 [a]Rom. 2:21 [b]Neh. 9:26
18 [a]Rom. 1:32 [b]1 Tim. 5:22 [l]Heb. *thy portion was with adulterers*
19 [a]Ps. 52:2 [l]Heb. *Thou sendest*
21 [a]Eccl. 8:11 [b]Ps. 10:11 [c]Ps. 90:8
22 [a]Job 8:13; Ps. 9:17; Is. 51:13
23 [a]Ps. 27:6 [b]Gal. 6:16 [l]Heb. *that disposeth* his way
51:1 [a]2 Sam. 12:1; & 11:2,4 [b]Is. 43:25; Col. 2:14
2 [a]Heb. 9:14; 1 John 1:7
4 [a]2 Sam. 12:13 [b]Luke 15:21 [c]Rom. 3:4
5 [a]Job 14:4 [l]Heb. *warm me*
7 [a]Lev. 14:4; Heb. 9:19 [b]Is. 1:18
8 [a]Mat. 5:4
9 [a]Jer. 16:17
10 [a]Ezek. 18:31; Acts 15:19 [l]Or, *a constant spirit*
11 [a]Gen 4:14 [b]Luke 11:13; Eph. 4:30
12 [a]2 Cor. 3:17
14 [a]2 Sam. 12:9 [l]Heb. *bloods*

The penitent's psalm

To the chief Musician, A Psalm of David, [a]when Nathan the prophet came unto him, after he had gone in to Bath-sheba.

51 HAVE MERCY upon me, O God, according to thy lovingkindness: according unto the multitude of thy tender mercies [b]blot out my transgressions. **L M R**

2 [a]Wash me thoroughly from mine iniquity, and cleanse me from my sin.

3 For I acknowledge my transgressions: and my sin *is* ever before me.

4 [a]Against thee, thee only, have I sinned, and done *this* evil [b]in thy sight: [c]that thou mightest be justified when thou speakest, *and* be clear when thou judgest.

5 [a]Behold, I was shapen in iniquity; [a]and in sin did my mother [l]conceive me. **C**

6 Behold, thou desirest truth in the inward parts: and in the hidden *part* thou shalt make me to know wisdom.

7 [a]Purge me with hyssop, and I shall be clean: wash me, and I shall be [b]whiter than snow. **K**

8 Make me to hear joy and gladness; *that* the bones *which* thou hast broken [a]may rejoice.

9 [a]Hide thy face from my sins, and blot out all mine iniquities.

10 [a]Create in me a clean heart, O God; and renew [l]a right spirit within me. **A R**

11 Cast me not away [a]from thy presence; and take not thy [b]holy spirit from me. **S Q**

12 Restore unto me the joy of thy salvation; and uphold me *with thy* [a]free spirit. **B C F**

13 *Then* will I teach transgressors thy ways; and sinners shall be converted unto thee. **J M N**

14 Deliver me from [a]bloodguiltiness,[l] O God, thou God of my salvation: *and* **R**

L *Ps 34:18* ◀ ▶ *Ps 51:17*
M *Ps 34:18* ◀ ▶ *Ps 116:3–5*
R *Ps 38:18* ◀ ▶ *Ps 51:17*
C *Ps 40:2* ◀ ▶ *Ps 53:1–4*
K *Ps 40:2* ◀ ▶ *Ps 55:16* **A** ▶ *Lk 11:9–13*
R ▶ *Ps 51:12–13* **S** *Lev 8:12* ◀ ▶ *Isa 4:3–4*
Q *Ne 9:30* ◀ ▶ *Isa 63:10*
B *Ps 45:7* ◀ ▶ *Isa 11:2*
C *Ne 9:30* ◀ ▶ *Ps 139:7*
F *Ps 45:7* ◀ ▶ *Isa 63:14*
J *Ps 45:7* ◀ ▶ *Isa 44:3*
M *Job 33:4* ◀ ▶ *Ps 104:30*
N *Job 33:4* ◀ ▶ *Ps 104:30*
R *Ps 51:10* ◀ ▶ *Isa 4:4*

[b]my tongue shall sing aloud of thy righteousness.

15 O Lord, open thou my lips: and my mouth shall show forth thy praise.

16 For [a]thou desirest not sacrifice; 'else would I give *it:* thou delightest not in burnt offering.

L 17 [a]The sacrifices of God *are* a broken
R spirit: a broken and a contrite heart, O God, thou wilt not despise.

18 Do good in thy good pleasure unto Zion: build thou the walls of Jerusalem.

19 Then shalt thou be pleased with [a]the sacrifices of righteousness, with burnt offering and whole burnt offering: then shall they offer bullocks upon thine altar.

The fate of the wicked

To the chief Musician, Maschil, *A Psalm* of David, [a]when Doeg the Edomite came and [b]told Saul, and said unto him, David is come to the house of Ahimelech.

52 WHY BOASTEST thou thyself in mischief, O [c]mighty man? the goodness of God *endureth* continually.

2 [a]Thy tongue deviseth mischiefs; [b]like a sharp razor, working deceitfully.

3 Thou lovest evil more than good; *and* [a]lying rather than to speak righteousness. Selah.

4 Thou lovest all devouring words, 'O *thou* deceitful tongue.

5 God shall likewise 'destroy thee for ever, he shall take thee away, and pluck thee out of *thy* dwellingplace, and [a]root thee out of the land of the living. Selah.

6 [a]The righteous also shall see, and fear, [b]and shall laugh at him:

G 7 Lo, *this is* the man *that* made not God his strength; but [a]trusted in the abundance of his riches, *and* strengthened himself in his 'wickedness.

8 But I *am* [a]like a green olive tree in the house of God: I trust in the mercy of God for ever and ever.

9 I will praise thee for ever, because thou hast done *it:* and I will wait on thy name; [a]for *it is* good before thy saints.

L *Ps 51:1–3* ◀▶ *Ps 65:3*
R *Ps 51:1–3* ◀▶ *Ps 126:5*
G *Job 15:31* ◀▶ *Ps 62:9–11*

14 [b]Ps. 35:28
16 [a]1 Sam. 15:22; Ps. 40:6; Is. 1:11; Jer. 7:22 '*Or, that I should give* it
17 [a]Ps. 34:18; Is. 57:15
19 [a]Ps. 4:5; Mal. 3:3
52:1 [a]1 Sam. 22:9 [b]Ezek. 22:9 [c]1 Sam. 21:7
2 [a]Ps. 50:19 [b]Ps. 57:4
3 [a]Jer. 9:4,5
4 'Or, and *the deceitful tongue*
5 [a]Prov. 2:22 'Heb. *beat thee down*
6 [a]Job 22:19; Ps. 37:34; Mal. 1:5 [b]Ps. 58:10
7 [a]Ps. 49:6 'Or, *substance*
8 [a]Jer. 11:16; Hos. 14:6
9 [a]Ps. 54:6
53:1 [a]Rom. 3:10 'Ps. 10:4
2 [a]Ps. 33:13 [b]2 Chr. 15:2
4 [a]Jer. 4:22
5 [a]Lev. 26:17 [b]Ezek. 6:5 'Heb. *they feared a fear*
6 [a]Ps. 14:7 'Heb. *Who will give salvations*
54:1 [a]1 Sam. 23:19
3 [a]Ps. 86:14
4 [a]Ps. 118:7
5 [a]Ps. 89:49 'Heb. *those that observe me*
6 [a]Ps. 52:9

The fate of the fool

To the chief Musician upon Mahalath, Maschil, *A Psalm* of David.

53 THE 'FOOL hath said in his heart, *There is* no God. Corrupt are they, and have done abominable iniquity: [a]*there is* none that doeth good. A C

2 God [a]looked down from heaven upon the children of men, to see if there were *any* that did understand, that did [b]seek God.

3 Every one of them is gone back: they are altogether become filthy; *there is* none that doeth good, no, not one.

4 Have the workers of iniquity [a]no knowledge? who eat up my people *as* they eat bread: they have not called upon God.

5 [a]There 'were they in great fear, *where* no fear was: for God hath [b]scattered the bones of him that encampeth *against* thee: thou hast put *them* to shame, because God hath despised them.

6 [a]Oh' that the salvation of Israel *were come* out of Zion! When God bringeth back the captivity of his people, Jacob shall rejoice, *and* Israel shall be glad. I

A prayer for deliverance

To the chief Musician on Neginoth, Maschil, *A Psalm* of David, [a]when the Ziphims came and said to Saul, Doth not David hide himself with us?

54 SAVE ME, O God, by thy name, and judge me by thy strength.

2 Hear my prayer, O God; give ear to the words of my mouth.

3 For [a]strangers are risen up against me, and oppressors seek after my soul: they have not set God before them. Selah.

4 Behold, God *is* mine helper: [a]the Lord *is* with them that uphold my soul. L

5 He shall reward evil unto 'mine enemies: cut them off [a]in thy truth.

6 I will freely sacrifice unto thee: I will praise thy name, O LORD; [a]for *it is* good.

A *Ps 14:1–4* ◀▶ *Ps 130:3*
C *Ps 51:5* ◀▶ *Ps 58:1–3*
I *Ps 50:5* ◀▶ *Ps 68:13*
L *Ps 50:15* ◀▶ *Ps 56:8*

53:6 This psalm contains material similar to Ps 14. David longed for the ultimate deliverance of his people from their enemies and that God's kingdom on earth would be established. Then his people could rejoice and be glad.

V 7 For he hath delivered me out of all trouble: [a]and mine eye hath seen *his desire* upon mine enemies.

The LORD *will sustain*

To the chief Musician on Neginoth,
Maschil, *A Psalm* of David.

55 GIVE EAR to my prayer, O God; and hide not thyself from my supplication.

2 Attend unto me, and hear me: I [a]mourn in my complaint, and make a noise;

3 Because of the voice of the enemy, because of the oppression of the wicked: [a]for they cast iniquity upon me, and in wrath they hate me.

4 [a]My heart is sore pained within me: and the terrors of death are fallen upon me.

5 Fearfulness and trembling are come upon me, and horror hath [1]overwhelmed me.

6 And I said, Oh that I had wings like a dove! *for then* would I fly away, and be at rest.

7 Lo, *then* would I wander far off, *and* remain in the wilderness. Selah.

8 I would hasten my escape from the windy storm *and* tempest.

9 Destroy, O Lord, *and* divide their tongues: for I have seen [a]violence and strife in the city.

10 Day and night they go about it upon the walls thereof: mischief also and sorrow *are* in the midst of it.

11 Wickedness *is* in the midst thereof: deceit and guile depart not from her streets.

12 [a]For *it was* not an enemy *that* reproached me; then I could have borne *it:* neither *was it* he that hated me *that* did [b]magnify *himself* against me; then I would have hid myself from him:

13 But *it was* thou, [1]a man mine equal, [a]my guide, and mine acquaintance.

14 [1]We took sweet counsel together, *and* [a]walked unto the house of God in company.

15 Let death seize upon them, *and* let them [a]go down quick into [1]hell: for wickedness *is* in their dwellings, *and* among them.

16 As for me, I will call upon God; and the LORD shall save me. K

17 [a]Evening, and morning, and at noon, will I pray, and cry aloud: and he shall hear my voice.

18 He hath delivered my soul in peace from the battle *that was* against me: for [a]there were many with me.

19 God shall hear, and afflict them, [a]even he that abideth of old. Selah. [1]Because they have no changes, therefore they fear not God.

20 He hath [a]put forth his hands against such as [b]be at peace with him: [1]he hath broken his covenant.

21 [a]*The words* of his mouth were smoother than butter, but war *was* in his heart: his words were softer than oil, yet *were* they drawn swords.

22 [a]Cast thy [1]burden upon the LORD, K
and he shall sustain thee: [b]he shall never U
suffer the righteous to be moved. W

23 But thou, O God, shalt bring them H
down into the pit of destruction: [a]bloody[1] and deceitful men [b]shall[2] not live out half their days; but I will trust in thee.

A song for the distressed

To the chief Musician upon
Jonath-elem-rechokim, [1]Michtam of David,
when the [a]Philistines took him in Gath.

56 BE [b]MERCIFUL unto me, O God: for man would swallow me up; he fighting daily oppresseth me.

2 [1]Mine enemies would daily [a]swallow *me* up: for *they be* many that fight against me, O thou most High.

3 What time I am afraid, I will trust in J
thee.

4 In God I will praise his word, in God I have put my trust; [a]I will not fear what flesh can do unto me.

5 Every day they wrest my words: all their thoughts *are* against me for evil.

6 [a]They gather themselves together, they hide themselves, they mark my steps, [b]when they wait for my soul.

7 Shall they escape by iniquity? in *thine* anger cast down the people, O God.

7 [a]Ps. 59:10
55:2 [a]Is. 38:14
3 [a]2 Sam. 16:7,8
4 [a]Ps. 116:3
5 [1]Heb. *covered me*
9 [a]Jer. 6:7
12 [a]Ps. 41:9 [b]Ps. 35:26
13 [a]2 Sam. 15:12; Ps. 41:9; Jer. 9:4 [1]Heb. *a man according to my rank*
14 [a]Ps. 42:4 [1]Heb. *Who sweetened counsel*
15 [a]Num. 16:30 [1]Or, *the grave*
17 [a]Luke 18:1
18 [a]2 Chr. 32:7,8
19 [a]Deut. 33:27 [1]Or, *With whom* also there be *no changes, yet they fear not God*
20 [a]Acts 12:1 [b]Ps. 7:4 [1]Heb. *he hath profaned*
21 [a]Ps. 28:3
22 [a]Ps. 37:5; Mat. 6:25 [b]Ps. 37:24 [1]Or, *gift*
23 [a]Ps. 5:6 [b]Job 15:32; Prov. 10:27; Eccl. 7:17 [1]Heb. *men of bloods and deceit* [2]Heb. *shall not half their days*
56:1 [a]1 Sam. 21:11 [b]Ps. 57:1 [1]Or, *A golden* Psalm *of David*
2 [a]Ps. 57:3 [1]Heb. *Mine observers*
4 [a]Ps. 118:6; Is. 31:3
6 [a]Ps. 59:3 [b]Ps. 71:10

V *Ps 50:15* ◀▶ *Ps 56:9*

K *Ps 51:7* ◀▶ *Ps 55:22*
K *Ps 55:16* ◀▶ *Ps 62:1–2*
U *Ps 45:7* ◀▶ *Ps 64:10*
W *Ps 43:5* ◀▶ *Ps 91:5–6*
H *Ps 50:3* ◀▶ *Ps 68:1–2*
J *Ps 46:1–3* ◀▶ *Ps 56:11*

8 Thou tellest my wanderings: put
thou my tears into thy bottle: *are they* not
in thy book?
9 When I cry *unto thee,* then shall
mine enemies turn back: this I know; for
[a]God *is* for me.
10 In God will I praise *his* word: in the
LORD will I praise *his* word.
11 In God have I put my trust: I
will not be afraid what man can do
unto me.
12 Thy vows *are* upon me, O God: I
will render praises unto thee.
13 For [a]thou hast delivered my soul
from death: *wilt* not *thou deliver* my feet
from falling, that I may walk before God
in [b]the light of the living?

The mercy and truth of God

To the chief Musician, [1]Al-taschith,
Michtam of David, [a]when he fled from Saul
in the cave.

57 BE MERCIFUL unto me, O God,
be merciful unto me: for my soul
trusteth in thee: [b]yea, in the shadow of
thy wings will I make my refuge, [c]until
these calamities be overpast.
2 I will cry unto God most high;
unto God [a]that performeth *all things*
for me.
3 He shall send from heaven, and save
me [1]*from* the reproach of him that would
swallow me up. Selah. God [a]shall send
forth his mercy and his truth.
4 My soul *is* among lions: *and* I lie
even among them that are set on fire,
even the sons of men, [a]whose teeth *are*
spears and arrows, and their tongue a
sharp sword.
5 [a]Be thou exalted, O God, above the
heavens; *let* thy glory *be* above all the
earth.
6 [a]They have prepared a net for my
steps; my soul is bowed down: they have
digged a pit before me, into the midst
whereof they are fallen *themselves.*
Selah.
7 [a]My heart is [1]fixed, O God, my
heart is fixed: I will sing and give praise.
8 Awake up, [a]my glory; awake, psaltery and harp: I *myself* will awake
early.
9 [a]I will praise thee, O Lord, among
the people: I will sing unto thee among
the nations.
10 [a]For thy mercy *is* great unto
the heavens, and thy truth unto the
clouds.
11 [a]Be thou exalted, O God, above the
heavens: *let* thy glory *be* above all the
earth.

The punishment of the wicked

To the chief Musician, [a]Al-taschith,[1]
Michtam of David.

58 DO YE indeed speak righteousness, O congregation? do ye
judge uprightly, O ye sons of men?
2 Yea, in heart ye work wickedness; ye
weigh the violence of your hands in the
earth.
3 [a]The wicked are estranged from the
womb: they go astray [1]as soon as they be
born, speaking lies.
4 [a]Their poison *is* [1]like the poison of a
serpent: *they are* like the deaf [2]adder *that*
stoppeth her ear;
5 Which will not hearken to the voice
of charmers, [1]charming never so wisely.
6 [a]Break their teeth, O God, in their
mouth: break out the great teeth of the
young lions, O LORD.
7 Let them melt away as waters *which*
run continually: *when* he bendeth *his*
bow to shoot his arrows, let them be as
cut in pieces.
8 As a snail *which* melteth, let *every*
one of them pass away: [a]*like* the untimely birth of a woman, *that* they may
not see the sun.
9 Before your pots can feel the thorns,
he shall take them away [a]as with a whirlwind, [1]both living, and in *his* wrath.
10 The righteous shall rejoice when he
seeth the vengeance: [a]he shall wash his
feet in the blood of the wicked.
11 [a]So that a man shall say, Verily
there is [1]a reward for the righteous:
verily he is a God that judgeth in the
earth.

9 [a]Rom. 8:31
13 [a]Ps. 116:8 [b]Job 33:30
57:1 [a]1 Sam. 22:1; Ps. 142, title [b]Ps. 17:8 [c]Is. 26:20 [1]Or, *Destroy not, A golden* Psalm
2 [a]Ps. 138:8
3 [a]Ps. 43:3 [1]Or, *he reproacheth him that would swallow me up*
4 [a]Prov. 30:14
5 [a]Ps. 108:5
6 [a]Ps. 9:15
7 [a]Ps. 108:1 [1]Or, *prepared*
8 [a]Ps. 16:9
9 [a]Ps. 108:3
10 [a]Ps. 103:11
11 [a]ver. 5
58:1 [a]Ps. 57, title [1]Or, *Destroy not, A golden* Psalm *of David*
3 [a]Is. 48:8 [1]Heb. *from the belly*
4 [a]Eccl. 10:11 [1]Heb. *according to the likeness* [2]Or, *asp*
5 [1]Or, be *the charmer never so cunning*
6 [a]Job 4:10
8 [a]Job 3:16
9 [a]Prov. 10:25 [1]Heb. *as living as wrath*
10 [a]Ps. 68:23
11 [a]Ps. 92:15 [1]Heb. *fruit of the*

E *Ps 44:21* ◀▶ *Ps 66:7*
L *Ps 54:4* ◀▶ *Ps 63:3–7*
V *Ps 54:7* ◀▶ *Ps 60:12*
J *Ps 56:3–4* ◀▶ *Ps 57:1*
J *Ps 56:11* ◀▶ *Ps 61:2–4*
C *Ps 53:1–4* ◀▶ *Ps 74:18*

Triumph over enemies

To the chief Musician, [a]Al-taschith,[1] Michtam of David; [b]when Saul sent, and they watched the house to kill him.

59 DELIVER ME from mine enemies, O my God: [2]defend me from them that rise up against me.
2 Deliver me from the workers of iniquity, and save me from bloody men.
3 For, lo, they lie in wait for my soul: [a]the mighty are gathered against me; not *for* my transgression, nor *for* my sin, O LORD.
4 They run and prepare themselves without *my* fault: [a]awake [1]to help me, and behold.
P 5 Thou therefore, O LORD God of hosts, the God of Israel, awake to visit all the heathen: be not merciful to any wicked transgressors. Selah.
6 [a]They return at evening: they make a noise like a dog, and go round about the city.
7 Behold, they belch out with their mouth: [a]swords *are* in their lips: for [b]who, *say they,* doth hear?
P 8 But [a]thou, O LORD, shalt laugh at them; thou shalt have all the heathen in derision.
9 *Because of* his strength will I wait upon thee: [a]for God *is* [1]my defence.
10 The God of my mercy shall [a]prevent me: God shall let [b]me see *my desire* upon [1]mine enemies.
11 Slay them not, lest my people forget: scatter them by thy power; and bring them down, O Lord our shield.
12 [a]*For* the sin of their mouth *and* the words of their lips let them even be taken in their pride: and for cursing and lying *which* they speak.
13 Consume *them* in wrath, consume *them,* that they *may* not *be:* and let them know that God ruleth in Jacob unto the ends of the earth. Selah.
14 And [a]at evening let them return; *and* let them make a noise like a dog, and go round about the city.
15 Let them [a]wander up and down [1]for meat, [2]and grudge if they be not satisfied.
16 But I will sing of thy power; yea, I will sing aloud of thy mercy in the morning: for thou hast been my defence and refuge in the day of my trouble.
17 Unto thee, [a]O my strength, will I sing: for God *is* my defence, *and* the God of my mercy.

Prayer for national deliverance

To the chief Musician [a]upon Shushan-eduth, [1]Michtam of David, to teach; [b]when he strove with Aram-naharaim and with Aram-zobah, when Joab returned, and smote of Edom in the valley of salt twelve thousand.

60 O GOD, [c]thou hast cast us off, thou hast [2]scattered us, thou hast been displeased; O turn thyself to us again.
2 Thou hast made the earth to tremble; thou hast broken it: [a]heal the breaches thereof; for it shaketh.
3 [a]Thou hast shown thy people hard things: [b]thou hast made us to drink the wine of astonishment.
4 [a]Thou hast given a banner to them that fear thee, that it may be displayed because of the truth. Selah. T
5 [a]That thy beloved may be delivered; save *with* thy right hand, and hear me.
6 God hath [a]spoken in his holiness; I will rejoice, I will [b]divide [c]Shechem, and mete out [d]the valley of Succoth.
7 Gilead *is* mine, and Manasseh *is* mine; [a]Ephraim also *is* the strength of mine head; [b]Judah *is* my lawgiver;
8 Moab *is* my washpot; over Edom will I cast out my shoe: [a]Philistia, [1]triumph thou because of me.
9 Who will bring me *into* the [1]strong city? who will lead me into Edom?
10 *Wilt* not thou, O God, *which* [a]hadst cast us off ? and *thou,* O God, *which* didst [b]not go out with our armies?
11 Give us help from trouble: for vain *is* the [1]help of man.
12 Through God [a]we shall do valiantly: V

59:1 [a]Ps. 57, title [b]1 Sam. 19:11 [1]Or, *Destroy not, A golden Psalm of David* [2]Heb. *set me on high*
3 [a]Ps. 56:6
4 [a]Ps. 35:23 [1]Heb. *to meet me*
6 [a]ver. 14
7 [a]Ps. 57:4; Prov. 12:18 [b]Ps. 10:11
8 [a]Prov. 1:26
9 [a]Ps. 62:2 [1]Heb. *my high place*
10 [a]Ps. 21:3 [b]Ps. 54:7 [1]Heb. *mine observers*
12 [a]Prov. 12,13
14 [a]ver. 6
15 [a]Job 15:23 [1]Heb. *to eat* [2]Or, *if they be not satisfied, then they will stay all night*
17 [a]Ps. 18:1
60:1 [a]Ps. 80 [b]2 Sam. 8:3; 1 Chr. 18:3 [c]Ps. 44:9 [1]Or, *A golden Psalm* [2]Heb. *broken*
2 [a]2 Chr. 7:14
3 [a]Ps. 71:20 [b]Jer. 25:15
4 [a]Ps. 20:5
5 [a]Ps. 108:6
6 [a]Ps. 89:35 [b]Josh. 1:6 [c]Gen. 12:6 [d]Josh. 13:27
7 [a]Deut. 33:17 [b]Gen. 49:10
8 [a]2 Sam. 8:1 [1]Or, *triumph thou over me* (by an irony)
9 [1]Heb. *city of strength?*
10 [a]Ps. 108:11 [b]Josh. 7:12
11 [1]Heb. *salvation*
12 [a]Num. 24:18

P *Ps 50:3* ◀▶ *Ps 59:8*
P *Ps 59:5* ◀▶ *Ps 66:3*
T *Ps 50:23* ◀▶ *Ps 66:8*
V *Ps 56:9* ◀▶ *Ps 81:13–14*

59:5, 8 The psalmist asked God not to show mercy to the heathen in the day of judgment because they were "wicked transgressors" (59:5). Rather God should openly show contempt for those who have derided him and his people.

for he *it is that* shall tread down our enemies.

The prayer of a troubled heart

To the chief Musician upon Neginah, *A Psalm* of David.

61 HEAR MY cry, O God; attend unto my prayer.

J 2 From the end of the earth will I cry unto thee, when my heart is overwhelmed: lead me to the rock *that* is higher than I.

3 For thou hast been a shelter for me, *and* [a]a strong tower from the enemy.

4 I will abide in thy tabernacle for ever: [a]I will [1]trust in the covert of thy wings. Selah.

5 For thou, O God, hast heard my vows: thou hast given *me* the heritage of those that fear thy name.

6 [1]Thou wilt prolong the king's life: *and* his years [2]as many generations.

7 He shall abide before God for ever: O prepare mercy [a]and truth, *which* may preserve him.

8 So will I sing praise unto thy name for ever, that I may daily perform my vows.

Confidence in God

To the chief Musician, to [a]Jeduthun, A Psalm of David.

K 62 TRULY[1] [b]MY soul [2]waiteth upon God: from him *cometh* my salvation.

2 He only *is* my rock and my salvation; *he is* my [a]defence;[1] I shall not be greatly moved.

3 How long will ye imagine mischief against a man? ye shall be slain all of you: [a]as a bowing wall *shall ye be, and as* a tottering fence.

4 They only consult to cast *him* down from his excellency: they delight in lies: [a]they bless with their mouth, but they curse [1]inwardly. Selah.

5 My soul, wait thou only upon God; for my expectation *is* from him.

6 He only *is* my rock and my salvation: *he is* my defence; I shall not be moved.

7 [a]In God *is* my salvation and my glory: the rock of my strength, *and* my refuge, *is* in God.

8 Trust in him at all times; ye people, [a]pour out your heart before him: God *is* a refuge for us. Selah.

9 [a]Surely men of low degree *are* vanity, *and* men of high degree *are* a lie: to be laid in the balance, they *are* [1]altogether *lighter* than vanity. G

10 Trust not in oppression, and become not vain in robbery: [a]if riches increase, set not your heart *upon them.*

11 God hath spoken [a]once; twice have I heard this; that [1]power *belongeth* unto God. K O

12 Also unto thee, O Lord, *belongeth* mercy: for [a]thou renderest to every man according to his work. S

The thirsty soul

A Psalm of David, [a]when he was in the wilderness of Judah.

63 O GOD, thou *art* my God; early will I seek thee: [b]my soul thirsteth for thee, my flesh longeth for thee in a dry and [1]thirsty land, [2]where no water is;

2 To see [a]thy power and thy glory, so *as* I have seen thee in the sanctuary.

3 Because thy lovingkindness *is* better than life, my lips shall praise thee. L

4 Thus will I bless thee while I live: I will lift up my hands in thy name.

5 My soul shall be satisfied as *with* [1]marrow and fatness; and my mouth shall praise *thee* with joyful lips:

6 When [a]I remember thee upon my bed, *and* meditate on thee in the *night* watches.

7 Because thou hast been my help, therefore in the shadow of thy wings will I rejoice.

8 My soul followeth hard after thee: thy right hand upholdeth me.

9 But those *that* seek my soul, to destroy *it,* shall go into the lower parts of the earth.

10 [1]They shall fall by the sword: they shall be a portion for foxes.

11 But the king shall rejoice in God; [a]every one that sweareth by him shall glory: but the mouth of them that speak lies shall be stopped.

61:3 [a]Prov. 18:10
4 [a]Ps. 91:4 [1]Or, *make my refuge*
6 [1]Heb. *Thou shalt add days to the days of the king* [2]Heb. *as generation and generation*
7 [a]Ps. 40:11
62:1 [a]1 Chr. 25:1 [b]Ps. 33:20 [1]Or, *Only* [2]Heb. *is silent*
2 [a]Ps. 59:9,17 [1]Heb. *high place*
3 [a]Is. 30:13
4 [a]Ps. 28:3 [1]Heb. *in their inward parts*
7 [a]Jer. 3:23
8 [a]1 Sam. 1:15; Lam. 2:19
9 [a]Ps. 39:5; Is. 40:17 [1]Or, *alike*
10 [a]Luke 12:15
11 [a]Job 33:14 [1]Or, *strength*
12 [a]Mat. 16:27
63:1 [a]1 Sam. 22:5 [b]Ps. 42:2 [1]Heb. *weary* [2]Heb. *without water*
2 [a]Ps. 27:4
5 [1]Heb. *fatness*
6 [a]Ps. 42:8
10 [1]Heb. *They shall make him run out like water by the hands of the sword*
11 [a]Deut. 6:13

J *Ps 57:1 ◀▶ Ps 91:5–6*
K *Ps 55:22 ◀▶ Ps 62:11–12*

G *Ps 52:7 ◀▶ Ps 75:6–7*
K *Ps 62:1–2 ◀▶ Ps 67:1–2*
O *Ps 36:9 ◀▶ Ps 68:20*
S *Ps 50:23 ◀▶ Ps 68:21*
L *Ps 56:8 ◀▶ Ps 68:5*

Appeal for aid against enemies

To the chief Musician, A Psalm of David.

64 HEAR MY voice, O God, in my prayer: preserve my life from fear of the enemy.

2 Hide me from the secret counsel of the wicked; from the insurrection of the workers of iniquity:

3 Who whet their tongue like a sword, [a]*and* bend *their bows to shoot* their arrows, *even* bitter words:

4 That they may shoot in secret at the perfect: suddenly do they shoot at him, and fear not.

5 They encourage themselves *in* an evil [1]matter: they commune [2]of laying snares privily; [a]they say, Who shall see them?

6 They search out iniquities; [1]they accomplish [2]a diligent search: both the inward *thought* of every one *of them,* and the heart, *is* deep.

7 But God shall shoot at them *with* an arrow; suddenly [1]shall they be wounded.

8 So they shall make their own tongue to fall upon themselves: [a]all that see them shall flee away.

9 And all men shall fear, and shall [a]declare the work of God; for they shall wisely consider of his doing.

U 10 The righteous shall be glad in the LORD, and shall trust in him; and all the upright in heart shall glory.

God's provisions for the earth

To the chief Musician, A Psalm *and* Song of David.

65 PRAISE [a]WAITETH[1] for thee, O God, in Zion: and unto thee shall the vow be performed.

2 O thou that hearest prayer, [a]unto thee shall all flesh come.

L 3 [1]Iniquities prevail against me: *as for* our transgressions, thou shalt [a]purge them away.

U 4 [a]Blessed *is the man whom* thou [b]choosest, and causest to approach *unto thee, that* he may dwell in thy courts: [c]we shall be satisfied with the goodness of thy house, *even* of thy holy temple.

5 *By* terrible things in righteousness wilt thou answer us, O God of our salvation; *who art* the confidence of all the ends of the earth, and of them that are afar off *upon* the sea:

6 Which by his strength setteth fast the mountains; [a]*being* girded with power:

7 [a]Which stilleth the noise of the seas, the noise of their waves, [b]and the tumult of the people.

8 They also that dwell in the uttermost parts are afraid at thy tokens: thou makest the outgoings of the morning and evening [1]to rejoice.

9 Thou visitest the earth, and [a]waterest[1] it: thou greatly enrichest it [b]with the river of God, *which* is full of water: thou preparest them corn, when thou hast so provided for it. B

10 Thou waterest the ridges thereof abundantly: [1]thou settlest the furrows thereof: [2]thou makest it soft with showers: thou blessest the springing thereof.

11 Thou crownest [1]the year with thy goodness; and thy paths drop fatness.

12 They drop *upon* the pastures of the wilderness: and the little hills [1]rejoice on every side.

13 The pastures are clothed with flocks; [a]the valleys also are covered over with corn; they shout for joy, they also sing.

God's power and works

To the chief Musician, A Song *or* Psalm.

66 MAKE[a] A joyful noise unto God, [1]all ye lands:

2 Sing forth the honour of his name: make his praise glorious.

3 Say unto God, How [a]terrible *art thou in* thy works! through the greatness of thy power shall thine enemies [b]submit[1] themselves unto thee. P

4 [a]All the earth shall worship thee, M

64:3 [a]Ps. 58:7
5 [a]Ps. 10:11 [1]Or, *speech* [2]Heb. *to hide snares*
6 [1]Or, *we are consumed by that which they have* thoroughly searched [2]Heb. *a search searched*
7 [1]Heb. *their wound shall be*
8 [a]Ps. 31:11
9 [a]Jer. 50:28 & 51:10
65:1 [a]Ps. 62:1 [1]Heb. *is silent*
2 [a]Is. 66:23
3 [a]Heb. 9:14 [1]Heb. *Words,* or, *Matters of iniquities*
4 [a]Ps. 33:12 [b]Ps. 4:3 [c]Ps. 36:8
6 [a]Ps. 93:1
7 [a]Mat. 8:26 [b]Is. 17:13
8 [1]Or, *to sing*
9 [a]Jer. 5:24 [b]Ps. 46:4 [1]Or, *after thou hadst made it to desire* rain
10 [1]Or, *thou causest rain to descend* into *the furrows thereof* [2]Heb. *thou dissolvest it*
11 [1]Heb. *the year of thy goodness*
12 [1]Heb. *are girded with joy*
13 [a]Is. 55:12
66:1 [a]Ps. 100:1 [1]Heb. *all the earth*
3 [a]Ps. 65:5 [b]Ps. 18:44 [1]Heb. *lie*
4 [a]Ps. 117:1

U *Ps 55:22* ◄► *Ps 65:4*
L *Ps 51:17* ◄► *Ps 68:13*
U *Ps 64:10* ◄► *Ps 68:3*
B *Job 42:12* ◄► *Ps 67:6*
P *Ps 59:8* ◄► *Ps 68:1–2*
M *Ps 50:4–6* ◄► *Ps 67:4*

66:3–4 The psalmist indicates that in the millennial kingdom God's enemies will "submit themselves unto thee" (66:3) and that all nations and peoples throughout the earth will join in glorious worship of God forever.

and shall sing unto thee; they shall sing *to* thy name. Selah.

5 Come and see the works of God: *he is* terrible *in his* doing toward the children of men.

6 [a]He turned the sea into dry *land:* they went through the flood on foot: there did we rejoice in him.

E 7 He ruleth by his power for ever; his eyes behold the nations: let not the rebellious exalt themselves. Selah.

T 8 O bless our God, ye people, and make the voice of his praise to be heard:

9 Which [l]holdeth our soul in life, and suffereth not our feet to be moved.

T 10 For [a]thou, O God, hast proved us: [b]thou hast tried us, as silver is tried.

11 [a]Thou broughtest us into the net; thou laidst affliction upon our loins.

12 [a]Thou hast caused men to ride over our heads; [b]we went through fire and through water: but thou broughtest us out into a [l]wealthy *place.*

13 I will go into thy house with burnt offerings: [a]I will pay thee my vows,

14 Which my lips have [l]uttered, and my mouth hath spoken, when I was in trouble.

15 I will offer unto thee burnt sacrifices of [l]fatlings, with the incense of rams; I will offer bullocks with goats. Selah.

T 16 Come *and* hear, all ye that fear God, and I will declare what he hath done for my soul.

17 I cried unto him with my mouth, and he was extolled with my tongue.

18 [a]If I regard iniquity in my heart, the Lord will not hear *me:*

19 *But* verily God [a]hath heard *me;* he hath attended to the voice of my prayer.

20 Blessed *be* God, which hath not turned away my prayer, nor his mercy from me.

E *Ps 56:8 ◀▶ Ps 69:5*
T *Ps 60:4 ◀▶ Ps 66:16–17*
T *Ps 39:11 ◀▶ Ps 89:30–33*
T *Ps 66:8 ◀▶ Ps 78:4*

6 [a]Ex. 14:21
9 [l]Heb. *putteth*
10 [a]Ps. 17:3; Is. 48:10 [b]Zech. 13:9; 1 Pet. 1:7
11 [a]Lam. 1:13
12 [a]Is. 51:23 [b]Is. 43:2 [l]Heb. *moist*
13 [a]Eccl. 5:4
14 [l]Heb. *opened*
15 [l]Heb. *marrow*
18 [a]Is. 1:15; John 9:31; Jas. 4:3
19 [a]Ps. 116:1,2
67:1 [a]Num. 6:25; Ps. 4:6 [l]Heb. *with us*
2 [a]Acts 18:25 [b]Is. 52:10; Tit. 2:11
4 [a]Ps. 96:10 [l]Heb. *lead*
6 [a]Lev. 26:4; Ps:85:12; Ezek. 34:27
68:1 [a]Num. 10:35; Is. 33:3 [l]Heb. *from his face*
2 [a]Is. 9:18; Hos. 13:3 [b]Mic. 1:4
3 [a]Ps. 32:11 [l]Heb. *rejoice with gladness*
4 [a]Deut. 33:26 [b]Ex. 6:3
5 [a]Ps. 10:14

God governs the nations

To the chief Musician on Neginoth, A Psalm *or* Song.

67 GOD BE merciful unto us, and bless us; *and* [a]cause his face to shine [l]upon us; Selah. K

2 That [a]thy way may be known upon earth, [b]thy saving health among all nations. H

3 Let the people praise thee, O God; let all the people praise thee.

4 O let the nations be glad and sing for joy: for [a]thou shalt judge the people righteously, and [l]govern the nations upon earth. Selah. M J

5 Let the people praise thee, O God; let all the people praise thee.

6 [a]*Then* shall the earth yield her increase; *and* God, *even* our own God, shall bless us. B

7 God shall bless us; and all the ends of the earth shall fear him.

The God of Israel

To the chief Musician, A Psalm *or* Song of David.

68 LET [a]GOD arise, let his enemies be scattered: let them also that hate him flee [l]before him. P H

2 [a]As smoke is driven away, *so* drive *them* away: [b]as wax melteth before the fire, *so* let the wicked perish at the presence of God.

3 But [a]let the righteous be glad; let them rejoice before God: yea, let them [l]exceedingly rejoice. U

4 Sing unto God, sing praises to his name: [a]extol him that rideth upon the heavens [b]by his name JAH, and rejoice before him.

5 [a]A father of the fatherless, and a L

K *Ps 62:11–12 ◀▶ Ps 68:13*
H *Ps 41:3 ◀▶ Ps 91:3*
M *Ps 66:4 ◀▶ Ps 68:16*
J *Ps 50:3–6 ◀▶ Ps 96:10*
B *Ps 65:9–13 ◀▶ Ps 85:12*
P *Ps 66:3 ◀▶ Ps 72:9*
H *Ps 55:23 ◀▶ Ps 68:21*
U *Ps 65:4 ◀▶ Ps 73:1*
L *Ps 63:3–7 ◀▶ Ps 68:19*

67:4 One of the great blessings of the Millennium will be that Jesus Christ will "judge the people righteously, and govern the nations." The oppressed of our world cry out for justice, but only Christ's millennial kingdom will bring true justice and peace.

68:1–2 David exults in the certain knowledge that God will "let his enemies be scattered" (68:1) and that the wicked will "perish at the presence of God" (68:2) during the coming tribulation period.

judge of the widows, *is* God in his holy habitation.

6 [a]God setteth the solitary [1]in families: [b]he bringeth out those which are bound with chains: but [c]the rebellious dwell in a dry *land.*

7 O God, [a]when thou wentest forth before thy people, when thou didst march through the wilderness; Selah:

8 The earth shook, the heavens also dropped at the presence of God: *even* Sinai itself *was moved* at the presence of God, the God of Israel.

9 [a]Thou, O God, didst [1]send a plentiful rain, whereby thou didst [2]confirm thine inheritance, when it was weary.

10 Thy congregation hath dwelt therein: [a]thou, O God, hast prepared of thy goodness for the poor.

11 The Lord gave the word: great *was* the [1]company of those that published *it.*

12 [a]Kings of armies [1]did flee apace: and she that tarried at home divided the spoil.

I K L 13 [a]Though ye have lain among the pots, [b]*yet shall ye be as* the wings of a dove covered with silver, and her feathers with yellow gold.

14 [a]When the Almighty scattered kings [1]in it, it was *white* as snow in Salmon.

15 The hill of God *is as* the hill of Bashan; an high hill *as* the hill of Bashan.

M 16 Why leap ye, ye high hills? [a]*this is* the hill *which* God desireth to dwell in; yea, the LORD will dwell *in it* for ever.

17 [a]The chariots of God *are* twenty thousand, [1]*even* thousands of angels: the Lord *is* among them, *as in* Sinai, in the holy *place.*

I *Ps 53:6* ◀▶ *Ps 68:22–23*
K *Ps 67:1–2* ◀▶ *Ps 68:20*
L *Ps 65:3* ◀▶ *Ps 69:32*
M *Ps 67:4* ◀▶ *Ps 72:1–19*

6 [a]1 Sam. 2:5; Ps. 107:4-7 [b]Acts 12:6 [c]Ps. 107:34 [1]Heb. *in a house*
7 [a]Ex. 13:21; Judg. 4:14
9 [a]Deut. 11:11 [1]Heb. *shake out* [2]Heb. *confirm it*
10 [a]Deut. 26:5; Ps. 74:19
11 [1]Heb. *army*
12 [a]Num. 31:8; Josh. 10:16 [1]Heb. *did flee, did flee*
13 [a]Ps. 81:6 [b]Ps. 105:37
14 [a]Josh. 10:10 [1]Or, *for her, she was*
16 [a]Deut. 12:5; 1 Ki. 9:3
17 [a]Deut. 33:2 [1]Or, even *many thousands*
18 [a]Eph. 4:8 [b]Judg. 5:12 [c]Acts 2:4,33 [d]1 Tim. 1:13 [e]Ps. 78:60 [1]Heb. *in the man*
20 [a]Deut. 32:39
21 [a]Hab. 3:13 [b]Ps. 55:23
22 [a]Num. 21:33 [b]Ex. 14:22
23 [a]Ps. 58:10 [b]1 Ki. 21:19 [1]Or, *red*
25 [a]1 Chr. 13:8
26 [a]Deut. 33:28; Is. 48:1 [1]Or, ye that are *of the fountain of Israel*
27 [a]1 Sam. 9:21 [1]Or, with *their company*
28 [a]Ps. 42:8

18 [a]Thou hast ascended on high, [b]thou hast led captivity captive: [c]thou hast received gifts [1]for men; yea, *for* [d]the rebellious also, [e]that the LORD God might dwell *among them.* D G P W

19 Blessed *be* the Lord, *who* daily loadeth us *with benefits, even* the God of our salvation. Selah. L

20 *He that is* our God *is* the God of salvation; and [a]unto GOD the Lord *belong* the issues from death. K O

21 But [a]God shall wound the head of his enemies, [b]*and* the hairy scalp of such an one as goeth on still in his trespasses. H S

22 The Lord said, I will bring [a]again from Bashan, I will bring *my people* again [b]from the depths of the sea: I

23 [a]That thy foot may be [1]dipped in the blood of *thine* enemies, [b]*and* the tongue of thy dogs in the same.

24 They have seen thy goings, O God; *even* the goings of my God, my King, in the sanctuary.

25 [a]The singers went before, the players on instruments *followed* after; among *them were* the damsels playing with timbrels.

26 Bless ye God in the congregations, *even* the Lord, [1]from [a]the fountain of Israel.

27 There *is* [a]little Benjamin *with* their ruler, the princes of Judah [1]*and* their council, the princes of Zebulun, *and* the princes of Naphtali.

28 Thy God hath [a]commanded thy strength: strengthen, O God, that which thou hast wrought for us.

D ▶ *Ps 139:7* **G** *Job 32:8* ◀▶ *Pr 1:22–23*
P ▶ *Pr 1:22–23*
W *Nu 11:29* ◀▶ *Pr 1:22–23*
L *Ps 68:5* ◀▶ *Ps 71:3*
K *Ps 68:13* ◀▶ *Ps 69:32*
O *Ps 62:11–12* ◀▶ *Ps 73:25–27*
H *Ps 68:1–2* ◀▶ *Ps 69:23–24*
S *Ps 62:12* ◀▶ *Ps 69:28*
I *Ps 68:13* ◀▶ *Ps 69:35–36*

68:13 Despite the apparent difficulties facing Israel, David prophesied that God would restore the nation. He likened Israel unto a dove that is covered with silver and gold—symbols of glory and victory.
68:16 Though the mountains of Bashan, including Mt. Hermon, were taller than Mt. Zion (also called Mt. Moriah), God had chosen it as the place for his eternal temple (see 2Ch 3:1). Note that this hill is probably the same location where God commanded Abraham to sacrifice a ram as a divinely-provided substitute for his son, Isaac (see Ge 22:2). This hill was also the site of Araunah's threshing floor and the place where David offered a sacrifice to halt the plague of the avenging angel (see note at 2Sa 24:24).
68:22–23 David foresaw the restoration of Israel from the highest plateaus of Bashan to the deepest depths of the sea. This return of God's people to the promised land is still under way and will find its ultimate fulfillment when Christ returns.

29 Because of thy temple at Jerusalem [a]shall kings bring presents unto thee.

30 Rebuke the company of spearmen, [a]the multitude of the bulls, with the calves of the people, *till every one* [b]submit himself with pieces of silver: [1]scatter thou the people *that* delight in war.

31 [a]Princes shall come out of Egypt; [b]Ethiopia shall soon [c]stretch out her hands unto God.

32 Sing unto God, ye kingdoms of the earth; O sing praises unto the Lord; Selah:

33 To him [a]that rideth upon the heavens of heavens, *which were* of old; lo, he doth [1]send out his voice, *and that* a mighty voice.

34 [a]Ascribe ye strength unto God: his excellency *is* over Israel, and his strength *is* in the [1]clouds.

35 O God, [a]*thou art* terrible out of thy holy places: the God of Israel *is* he that giveth strength and power unto *his* people. Blessed *be* God.

The prayer for deliverance

To the chief Musician [a]upon Shoshannim, *A Psalm* of David.

69 SAVE ME, O God; for [b]the waters are come in unto *my* soul.

2 [a]I sink in [1]deep mire, where *there is* no standing: I am come into [2]deep waters, where the floods overflow me.

3 [a]I am weary of my crying: my throat is dried: [b]mine eyes fail while I wait for my God.

4 They that [a]hate me without a cause are more than the hairs of mine head: they that would destroy me, *being* mine enemies wrongfully, are mighty: then I restored *that* which I took not away.

E 5 O God, thou knowest my foolishness; and my [1]sins are not hid from thee.

6 Let not them that wait on thee, O Lord GOD of hosts, be ashamed for my sake: let not those that seek thee be confounded for my sake, O God of Israel.

7 Because for thy sake I have borne reproach; shame hath covered my face.

8 [a]I am become a stranger unto my brethren, and an alien unto my mother's children.

9 [a]For the zeal of thine house hath eaten me up; [b]and the reproaches of them that reproached thee are fallen upon me.

10 [a]When I wept, *and chastened* my soul with fasting, that was to my reproach.

11 I made sackcloth also my garment; [a]and I became a proverb to them.

12 They that sit in the gate speak against me; and [a]I *was* the song of the [1]drunkards.

13 But as for me, my prayer *is* unto thee, O LORD, [a]*in* an acceptable time: O God, in the multitude of thy mercy hear me, in the truth of thy salvation.

14 Deliver me out of the mire, and let me not sink: [a]let me be delivered from them that hate me, and out of [b]the deep waters.

15 Let not the waterflood overflow me, neither let the deep swallow me up, and let not the pit [a]shut her mouth upon me.

16 Hear me, O LORD; for thy lovingkindness *is* good: [a]turn unto me according to the multitude of thy tender mercies.

17 And [a]hide not thy face from thy servant; for I am in trouble: [1]hear me speedily.

18 Draw nigh unto my soul, *and* redeem it: deliver me because of mine enemies.

19 Thou hast known [a]my reproach, and my shame, and my dishonour: mine adversaries *are* all before thee.

20 Reproach hath broken my heart; and I am full of heaviness: and [a]I looked *for some* [1]to take pity, but *there was* none; and for [b]comforters, but I found none.

21 They gave me also gall for my meat; [a]and in my thirst they gave me vinegar to drink.

22 [a]Let their table become a snare before them: and *that which should have been* for *their* welfare, *let it become* a trap. D

23 [a]Let their eyes be darkened, that they see not; and make their loins continually to shake. H

24 [a]Pour out thine indignation upon them, and let thy wrathful anger take hold of them.

29 [a]Ps. 72:10
30 [a]Ps. 22:12 [b]2 Sam. 8:2 [1]Or, *he scattereth*
31 [a]Is. 19:21 [b]Is. 45:14 [c]Ps. 44:20
33 [a]Ps. 18:10 [1]Heb. *give*
34 [a]Ps. 29:1 [1]Or, *heavens*
35 [a]Ps. 76:12
69:1 [a]Ps. 45, title [b]Jonah 2:5
2 [a]Ps. 40:2 [1]Heb. *the mire of depth* [2]Heb. *depth of waters*
3 [a]Ps. 6:6 [b]Ps. 119:82; Is. 38:14
4 [a]Ps. 35:19; John 15:25
5 [1]Heb. *guiltiness*
8 [a]Is. 53:3
9 [a]John 2:17 [b]Rom. 15:3
10 [a]Ps. 35:13
11 [a]Jer. 24:9
12 [a]Job 30:9 [1]Heb. *drinkers of strong drink*
13 [a]Is. 49:8
14 [a]Ps. 144:7 [b]ver. 1,2,15
15 [a]Num. 16:33
16 [a]Ps. 25:16
17 [a]Ps. 27:9 [1]Heb. *make haste to hear me*
19 [a]Ps. 22:6,7; Is. 53:3
20 [a]Is. 63:5 [b]Job 16:2 [1]Heb. *to lament* with me
21 [a]Mat. 27:34; Mark 15:23; John 19:29
22 [a]Rom. 11:9
23 [a]Is. 6:9,10; Rom. 11:10
24 [a]1 Thes. 2:16

E *Ps 66:7 ◀▶ Ps 87:6*

D *Ps 22:13–18 ◀▶ Isa 52:14–15*
H *Ps 68:21 ◀▶ Ps 69:27–28*

J 25 [a]Let ′their habitation be desolate; *and* [2]let none dwell in their tents.

26 For they persecute [a]*him* whom thou hast smitten; and they talk to the grief of ′those whom thou hast wounded.

H 27 [a]Add ′iniquity unto their iniquity: [b]and let them not come into thy righteousness.

S 28 Let them [a]be blotted out of the book of the living, [b]and not be written with the righteous.

29 But I *am* poor and sorrowful: let thy salvation, O God, set me up on high.

30 [a]I will praise the name of God with a song, and will magnify him with thanksgiving.

31 [a]*This* also shall please the LORD better than an ox *or* bullock that hath horns and hoofs.

K 32 [a]The ′humble shall see *this, and* be
L glad: and [b]your heart shall live that seek God.

33 For the LORD heareth the poor, and despiseth not [a]his prisoners.

34 [a]Let the heaven and earth praise him, the seas, [b]and every thing that ′moveth therein.

I 35 [a]For God will save Zion, and will build the cities of Judah: that they may dwell there, and have it in possession.

36 [a]The seed also of his servants shall inherit it: and they that love his name shall dwell therein.

Deliverance from persecutors

To the chief Musician, *A Psalm* of David, [a]to bring to remembrance.

70 *MAKE HASTE,* [b]O God, to deliver me; make haste ′to help me, O LORD.

2 [a]Let them be ashamed and confounded that seek after my soul: let them be turned backward, and put to confusion, that desire my hurt.

3 [a]Let them be turned back for a reward of their shame that say, Aha, aha.

4 Let all those that seek thee rejoice and be glad in thee: and let such as love thy salvation say continually, Let God be magnified.

5 [a]But I *am* poor and needy: [b]make haste unto me, O God: thou *art* my help and my deliverer; O LORD, make no tarrying.

The prayer of an aged man

71 IN [a]THEE, O LORD, do I put my trust: let me never be put to confusion.

2 [a]Deliver me in thy righteousness, and cause me to escape: [b]incline thine ear unto me, and save me.

3 [a]Be′ thou my strong habitation, whereunto I may continually resort: thou hast given [b]commandment to save me; for thou *art* my rock and my fortress. L

4 [a]Deliver me, O my God, out of the hand of the wicked, out of the hand of the unrighteous and cruel man.

5 For thou *art* [a]my hope, O Lord GOD: *thou art* my trust from my youth.

6 [a]By thee have I been holden up from the womb: thou art he that took me out of my mother's bowels: my praise *shall be* continually of thee. L

7 [a]I am as a wonder unto many; but thou *art* my strong refuge.

8 Let [a]my mouth be filled *with* thy praise *and with* thy honour all the day.

9 [a]Cast me not off in the time of old age; forsake me not when my strength faileth.

10 For mine enemies speak against me; and they that ′lay wait for my soul [a]take counsel together,

11 Saying, God hath forsaken him: per-

25 [a]Mat. 23:38 ′Heb. *their palace* [2]Heb. *let there not be a dweller*
26 [a]Is. 53:4 ′Heb. *thy wounded*
27 [a]Rom. 1:28 [b]Is. 26:10 ′Or, *punishment of iniquity*
28 [a]Ex. 32:32; Phil. 4:3 [b]Ezek. 13:9
30 [a]Ps. 28:7
31 [a]Ps. 50:13
32 [a]Ps. 34:2 [b]Ps. 22:26 ′Or, *meek*
33 [a]Eph. 3:1
34 [a]Ps. 96:11 & 148:1; Is. 44:23 [b]Is. 55:12 ′Heb. *creepeth*
35 [a]Ps. 51:18; Is. 44:26
36 [a]Ps. 102:28
70:1 [a]Ps. 38, title [b]Ps. 40:13 ′Heb. *to my help*
2 [a]Ps. 35:4,26
3 [a]Ps. 40:15
5 [a]Ps. 40:17 [b]Ps. 141:1
71:1 [a]Ps. 25:2,3
2 [a]Ps. 31:1 [b]Ps. 17:6
3 [a]Ps. 31:2,3 [b]Ps. 44:4 ′Heb. *Be thou to me for a rock of habitation*
4 [a]Ps. 140:1,4
5 [a]Jer. 17:7
6 [a]Ps. 22:9,10; Is 46:3
7 [a]Is. 8:18
8 [a]Ps. 35:28
9 [a]ver. 18
10 [a]2 Sam. 17:1; Mat. 27:1 ′Heb. *watch,* or, *observe*

J *Ps 9:7–8* ◀▶ *Ps 87:4–6*
H *Ps 69:23–24* ◀▶ *Ps 73:17–18*
S *Ps 68:21* ◀▶ *Ps 73:27*
K *Ps 68:20* ◀▶ *Ps 73:26*
L *Ps 68:13* ◀▶ *Ps 77:7–9*
I *Ps 68:22–23* ◀▶ *Ps 74:10*

L *Ps 68:19* ◀▶ *Ps 71:6*
L *Ps 71:3* ◀▶ *Ps 73:23–24*

69:25 The apostle Peter applied this verse to Judas after his betrayal of Jesus and subsequent suicide. Since Judas sought to remove Jesus from his place as Messiah, Peter said that Judas was removed from his place among the twelve disciples and another leader had to be found to take his place (see Acts 1:20).

69:35–36 These predictive verses were initially fulfilled when the exiles returned from their Babylonian captivity. The ultimate fulfillment will occur in the coming Millennium when Jesus Christ, God's Messiah, will obtain victory over his enemies. Then Jerusalem will be rebuilt and "they that love his name shall dwell therein" (69:36).

Old Testament Prophecies Fulfilled in Christ

OT TEXT	NT TEXT	SUBJECT
Ge 3:15	Lk 22:53	Satan against Jesus
Ge 3:15	Heb 2:14; 1Jn 3:8	Jesus' victory over Satan
Ge 12:3	Ac 3:25; Gal 3:8	Gentiles blessed through Christ as the seed of Abraham
Ge 13:15	Gal 3:15–16, 19	Messiah as the seed of Abraham
Ge 14:18–20	Heb 7	Jesus' priesthood according to the likeness of Melchizedek
Ge 18:18	Ac 3:25; Gal 3:8	Gentiles blessed through Christ as the seed of Abraham
Ge 22:18	Ac 3:25; Gal 3:8	Gentiles blessed through Christ as the seed of Abraham
Ge 26:4	Ac 3:25; Gal 3:8	Gentiles blessed through Christ as the seed of Abraham
Ge 49:10	Lk 1:32–33	Coming ruler from Judah
Ex 12:1—14:46	Jn 19:31–36; 1Co 5:7; 1Pe 1:19	The Messiah as the Passover Lamb
Ex 16:4	Jn 6:31–33	Messiah to give true bread from heaven
Ex 24:8	Heb 9:11–28	The Messiah's blood to be shed as sacrifice
Lev 16:15–17	Ro 3:25; Heb 9:1–14, 24; 1Jn 2:2	Atoning sacrifice of blood
Nu 21:8–9	Jn 3:14–15	Life through looking at one on a cross
Nu 24:17	Lk 1:32–33	Coming ruler from Jacob
Nu 24:17	Rev 22:16	Coming Star out of Jacob
Dt 18:17	Jn 6:14; 12:49–50; Ac 3:22–23	Coming prophet sent from God
Dt 21:23	Gal 3:13	Messiah cursed for hanging on a tree
Dt 30:12–14	Ro 10:6–8	Jesus is God's word near to us
2Sa 7:14	Heb 1:5	Messiah to be God's Son
2Sa 7:16	Lk 1:32–33; Rev 19:11–16	David's Son as eternal king
1Ch 17:13	Heb 1:5	Messiah to be God's Son
1Ch 17:14	Lk 1:32–33; Rev 19:11–16	David's Son as eternal king
Ps 2:7	Mt 3:17; 17:5; Mk 1:11; 9:7; Lk 3:22; 9:35; Ac 13:33; Heb 1:5	God's address to His Son
Ps 2:9	Rev 2:27	Messiah to rule the nations with power
Ps 8:2	Mt 21:16	Children to praise God's Son

Old Testament Prophecies Fulfilled in Christ

OT TEXT	NT TEXT	SUBJECT
Ps 8:4–5	Heb 2:6–9	Jesus lower than the angels
Ps 8:6	1Co 15:27–28; Eph 1:22	Everything subject to God's Son
Ps 16:8–11	Ac 2:25–32; 13:35–37	David's Son to be raised from the dead
Ps 22:1	Mt 27:46; Mk 15:34	God-forsaken cry by the Messiah
Ps 22:7–8	Mt 27:29, 41–44; Mk 15:18, 29–32; Lk 23:35–39	Messiah mocked by a crowd
Ps 22:18	Mt 27:35; Mk 15:24; Lk 23:34; Jn 19:24	Casting lots for Jesus' clothes
Ps 22:22	Heb 2:12	Jesus to declare his name in the church
Ps 31:5	Lk 23:46	Messiah to commit his spirit to God
Ps 34:20	Jn 19:31–36	Messiah to have no broken bones
Ps 35:19	Jn 15:25	Messiah experiencing hatred for no reason
Ps 40:6–8	Jn 6:48; Heb 10:5–9	Messiah to do God's perfect will
Ps 41:9	Jn 13:18	The Messiah's betrayal by a friend
Ps 45:6–7	Heb 1:8–9	Characteristics of the coming King
Ps 68:18	Eph 4:7–11	Ascension and giving gifts to humans
Ps 69:4	Jn 15:25	Messiah experiencing hatred for no reason
Ps 69:9	Jn 2:14–22	The Messiah's zeal for God's house
Ps 69:21	Jn 19:29	The thirst of the suffering Messiah
Ps 69:25	Ac 1:20	Judgment on the Messiah's persecutor
Ps 78:2	Mt 13:34–35	Messiah to speak in parables
Ps 102:25–27	Heb 1:10–12	Characteristics of the coming King
Ps 110:1	Ac 2:34–35; 1Co 15:25; Eph 1:20–22; Heb 1:13; 10:12–13	Jesus exalted in power at God's right hand
Ps 110:1	Mt 22:41–45; Mk 12:35–37; Lk 20:41–44	Jesus as Son and Lord of David
Ps 110:4	Heb 5:6; 7:11–22	Jesus' priesthood after Melchizedek
Ps 118:22–23	Mt 21:42–44; Mk 12:10–12; Lk 20:17–19; Ac 4:10–11; 1Pe 2:7–8	Rejected stone to become head of the corner
Ps 118:26	Mt 21:9; Mk 11:9; Lk 19:38; Jn 12:13	Messiah to come in the name of the Lord
Isa 6:9–10	Mt 13:14–15; Mk 4:12; Lk 8:10; Jn 12:37–41	Hearts to be closed to the gospel
Isa 7:14	Mt 1:18–23; Lk 1:26–35	Virgin birth of the Messiah
Isa 8:14	Ro 9:32–33; 1Pe 2:7–8	A stone on which people stumble
Isa 9:1–2	Mt 4:13–16; Mk 1:14–15; Lk 4:14–15	Ministry to begin in Galilee

Old Testament Prophecies Fulfilled in Christ

OT TEXT	NT TEXT	SUBJECT
Isa 9:6–7	Lk 1:32–33	David's Son as eternal king
Isa 9:7	Jn 1:1, 18	The Messiah to be God
Isa 9:7	Eph 2:14–17	The Messiah to be a man of peace
Isa 11:1–2	Mt 3:16; Mk 1:16; Lk 3:21–22	Rod of Jesse (David) to receive the Spirit
Isa 11:10	Lk 1:32–33	Rod of Jesse (David) as coming ruler
Isa 11:10	Ro 15:12	Salvation to be available for Gentiles
Isa 22:22	Rev 3:7	Jesus to receive the key of David
Isa 25:8	1Co 15:54	Death to be swallowed up in victory
Isa 28:16	Ro 9:32–33; 1Pe 2:6	Messiah to be the chief corner stone
Isa 35:5–6	Mt 11:4–6; Lk 7:22	Messiah to be a mighty worker of miracles
Isa 40:3–5	Mt 3:3; Mk 1:3; Lk 3:4–6; Jn 1:23	Jesus' forerunner, a voice in the wilderness
Isa 42:1–4	Mt 12:15–21	Messiah as the chosen servant of the Lord
Isa 45:23	Ro 14:11; Php 2:10	Every knee to bow before the Messiah
Isa 49:6	Ac 13:46–47	Messiah as a light to the Gentiles
Isa 50:6	Mt 27:26–30; Mk 14:65; 15:15, 19; Lk 22:63; Jn 19:1, 3	Beating God's servant
Isa 50:6	Mt 26:67; Mk 14:65	Spitting on God's servant
Isa 53:1	Jn 12:38; Ro 10:16	Israel not to believe in the Messiah
Isa 53:3	Jn 1:11	Messiah to be rejected by His own people
Isa 53:4–5	Mt 8:16–17; Mk 1:32–34; Lk. 4:40–41; 1Pe 2:24	Healing ministry of God's servant
Isa 53:7–8	Jn 1:29, 36; Ac 8:30–35; 1Pe 1:19; Rev 5:6, 12	Suffering Lamb of God
Isa 53:9	Heb 4:15; 1Pe 2:22	The sinless servant of God
Isa 53:9	Mt 27:57–60	Messiah to be buried in a rich man's grave
Isa 53:12	Mt 27:38; Mk 15:27–28; Lk 22:37; 23:33; Jn 19:18	God's servant numbered with transgressors
Isa 55:3	Lk 22:20; 1Co 11:25	Everlasting covenant through the Messiah
Isa 55:3	Ac 13:33	Blessings of David given to the Messiah
Isa 59:20–21	Ro 11:26–27	Israel's Deliverer to come from Zion
Isa 60:1–3	Mt 2:11; Ro 15:8–12	Gentiles coming to worship the Messiah
Isa 61:1–2	Mt 3:16; Mk 1:10; Lk 4:18–21	The Messiah anointed by the Holy Spirit
Isa 65:1	Ro 10:20	Gentiles would believe in the Messiah
Isa 65:2	Ro 10:21	Israel would reject the Messiah
Jer 23:5	Lk 1:32–33	David's Son to be a great King
Jer 23:6	Mt 1:21	David's Son to be Savior

Old Testament Prophecies Fulfilled in Christ

OT TEXT	NT TEXT	SUBJECT
Jer 23:6	1Co 1:30	Messiah to be named "Our Righteousness"
Jer 31:5	Mt 2:16–18	Rachel weeping when God's Son is born
Jer 31:31–34	Lk 22:20; 1Co 11:25; Heb 8:8–12; 10:15–18	Jesus and the new covenant
Jer 32:40	Lk 22:20; 1Co 11:25	Everlasting covenant through the Messiah
Jer 33:15	Lk 1:32–33	David's Son to be a great King
Jer 33:16	Mt 1:21	David's Son to be Savior
Jer 33:16	1Co 1:30	Messiah to be named "Our Righteousness"
Eze 21:26–27	Lk 1:32–33	A rightful crown for the Messiah
Eze 34:23–24	Jn 10:11, 14, 16; Heb 13:20; 1Pe 5:4	The coming good shepherd
Eze 37:24–25	Lk 1:32–33	Messiah to be David's Son and a king
Eze 37:24–25	Jn 10:11, 14, 16; Heb 13:20; 1Pe 5:4	The coming good shepherd
Eze 37:26	Lk 22:20; 1Co 11:25	Messiah's everlasting covenant of peace
Da 7:13–14	Mt 24:30; 26:64; Mk 13:26; 14:62; Lk 21:27; Rev 1:13; 14:14	The coming of the Son of Man
Da 7:27	Rev 11:15	The coming everlasting kingdom of the Messiah
Da 9:24–26	Gal 4:4	Timetable for the Messiah's coming
Hos 11:1	Mt 2:14–15	Jesus to return from Egypt
Joel 2:28–32	Ac 2:14–21	God's Spirit to be poured out
Am 9:11–12	Ac 15:13–18	Gentiles would believe in the Messiah
Jnh 1:17	Mt 12:39–40	Messiah to be three days and nights in grave
Mic 5:2	Mt 2:1–6	The Messiah to be born in Bethlehem
Mic 5:2	Lk 1:32–33	The Messiah as an eternal king
Mic 5:4	Jn 10:11, 14	The coming shepherd of God's flock
Mic 5:5	Eph 2:14–17	The Messiah to be a man of peace
Zec 9:9	Mt 21:1–9; Mk 11:1–10; Lk 19:28–38; Jn 12:12–16	The coming ruler on a donkey
Zec 11:12–13	Mt 27:1–10	Thirty pieces of silver for a potter's field
Zec 12:10	Jn 19:37; Rev 1:7	Looking on the pierced Messiah
Zec 13:7	Mt 26:31; 26:55–56; Mk 14:27; 14:48–50	Striking the coming shepherd; the sheep flee
Mal 3:1	Mt 11:7–10; Mk 1:2–4; Lk 7:24–27	The forerunner to the Messiah
Mal 4:5–6	Mt 11:14; 17:11–13; Mk 9:11–13; Lk 1:16–17	The forerunner as Elijah returned

secute and take him; for *there is* none to deliver *him.*

12 [a]O God, be not far from me: O my God, [b]make haste for my help.

13 [a]Let them be confounded *and* consumed that are adversaries to my soul; let them be covered *with* reproach and dishonour that seek my hurt.

14 But I will hope continually, and will yet praise thee more and more.

15 [a]My mouth shall show forth thy righteousness *and* thy salvation all the day; for [b]I know not the numbers *thereof.*

16 I will go in the strength of the Lord GOD: I will make mention of thy righteousness, *even* of thine only.

17 O God, thou hast taught me from my youth: and hitherto have I declared thy wondrous works.

18 [a]Now also [1]when I am old and grayheaded, O God, forsake me not; until I have shown [2]thy strength unto *this* generation, *and* thy power to every one *that* is to come.

19 [a]Thy righteousness also, O God, *is* very high, who hast done great things: [b]O God, who *is* like unto thee!

F 20 [a]*Thou,* which hast shown me great and sore troubles, [b]shalt quicken me again, and shalt bring me up again from the depths of the earth.

21 Thou shalt increase my greatness, and comfort me on every side.

22 I will also praise thee [a]with[1] the psaltery, *even* thy truth, O my God: unto thee will I sing with the harp, O thou [b]Holy One of Israel.

23 My lips shall greatly rejoice when I sing unto thee; and [a]my soul, which thou hast redeemed.

24 My tongue also shall talk of thy righteousness all the day long: for they are confounded, for they are brought unto shame, that seek my hurt.

F *Ps 17:15* ◀▶ *Ps 88:10–12*

12 [a]Ps. 35:22 [b]Ps. 70:1
13 [a]ver. 24
15 [a]Ps. 35:28 [b]Ps. 40:5
18 [a]ver. 9 [1]Heb. *unto old age and gray hairs* [2]Heb. *thine arm*
19 [a]Ps. 57:10 [b]Ps. 35:10
20 [a]Ps. 60:3 [b]Hos. 6:1,2
22 [a]Ps. 92:1-3 [b]2 Ki. 19:22; Is. 60:9 [1]Heb. *with the instrument of psaltery*
23 [a]Ps. 103:4
72:1 [a]Ps. 127, title [1]Or, *of*
2 [a]Is. 32:1
3 [a]Ps. 85:10; Is. 32:17
4 [a]Is. 11:4
5 [a]ver. 7:17
6 [a]Hos. 6:3
7 [a]Is. 2:4; Jer. 33:6; Luke 1:33 [1]Heb. *till* there be *no moon*
8 [a]Ex. 23:31; Zech. 9:10
9 [a]Ps. 74:14 [b]Is. 49:23
10 [a]2 Chr. 9:21
11 [a]Is. 49:23
12 [a]Job 29:12
14 [a]Ps. 116:15
15 [1]Heb. one *shall give*

A prayer for the king

A Psalm [a]for[1] Solomon.

72 GIVE THE king thy judgments, O God, and thy righteousness unto the king's son. M

2 [a]He shall judge thy people with righteousness, and thy poor with judgment.

3 [a]The mountains shall bring peace to the people, and the little hills, by righteousness.

4 [a]He shall judge the poor of the people, he shall save the children of the needy, and shall break in pieces the oppressor.

5 They shall fear thee [a]as long as the sun and moon endure, throughout all generations.

6 [a]He shall come down like rain upon the mown grass: as showers *that* water the earth.

7 In his days shall the righteous flourish; [a]and abundance of peace [1]so long as the moon endureth. U

8 [a]He shall have dominion also from sea to sea, and from the river unto the ends of the earth. V

9 [a]They that dwell in the wilderness shall bow before him; [b]and his enemies shall lick the dust. P

10 [a]The kings of Tarshish and of the isles shall bring presents: the kings of Sheba and Seba shall offer gifts.

11 [a]Yea, all kings shall fall down before him: all nations shall serve him.

12 For he [a]shall deliver the needy when he crieth; the poor also, and *him* that hath no helper.

13 He shall spare the poor and needy, and shall save the souls of the needy.

14 He shall redeem their soul from deceit and violence: and [a]precious shall their blood be in his sight.

15 And he shall live, and to him [1]shall

M *Ps 68:16* ◀▶ *Ps 82:8* **U** ▶ *Isa 2:4*
V *Ps 45:6* ◀▶ *Ps 110:1*
P *Ps 68:1–2* ◀▶ *Ps 75:8*

71:20 This is a clear OT prophecy of physical resurrection from "the depths of the earth" for God's righteous saints.

72:1–19 This prophetic psalm is a prayer for the king, a son of David, expressing the desire that the king's reign will be a just and righteous reign. Note that this description for the king can also apply to the Messiah, who will rule righteously in glory and power in his eternal kingdom on earth.

72:5–7 This psalm of Solomon prophesied the eternal reverence and fear of God that the nations will express during the coming Millennium.

72:8 This prophecy looks forward to the ultimate dominion of Jesus Christ as the Messiah who will rule the earth forever because of his righteousness.

be given of the gold of Sheba: prayer also
shall be made for him continually; *and*
daily shall he be praised.
16 There shall be an handful of corn in
the earth upon the top of the mountains;
the fruit thereof shall shake like Lebanon:
[a]and *they* of the city shall flourish like
grass of the earth.
17 [a]His name [1]shall endure for ever:
[2]his name shall be continued as long as
the sun: and [b]*men* shall be blessed in
him: [c]all nations shall call him blessed.
18 [a]Blessed *be* the LORD God, the God
of Israel, [b]who only doeth wondrous
things.
19 And [a]blessed *be* his glorious name
for ever: [b]and let the whole earth be
filled *with* his glory; Amen, and Amen.
20 The prayers of David the son of
Jesse are ended.

Book III

God delivers the righteous

[1]A Psalm of [a]Asaph.

U 73 TRULY[2] GOD *is* good to Israel,
even to such as are [3]of a clean
heart.
2 But as for me, my feet were almost
gone; my steps had well nigh slipped.
3 [a]For I was envious at the foolish,
when I saw the prosperity of the wicked.
4 For *there are* no bands in their death:
but their strength *is* [1]firm.
5 [a]They *are* not [1]in trouble *as other*
men; neither are they plagued [2]like *other*
men.
6 Therefore pride compasseth them
about as a chain; violence covereth them
[a]*as* a garment.
7 [a]Their eyes stand out with fatness:
[1]they have more than heart could wish.
8 [a]They are corrupt, and speak wickedly *concerning* oppression: they [b]speak
loftily.
9 They set their mouth [a]against the
heavens, and their tongue walketh
through the earth.
10 Therefore his people return hither:
[a]and waters of a full *cup* are wrung out to
them.

11 And they say, [a]How doth God
know? and is there knowledge in the
most High?
12 Behold, these *are* the ungodly, who
prosper in the world; they increase *in*
riches.
13 [a]Verily I have cleansed my heart *in*
vain, and [b]washed my hands in innocency.
14 For all the day long have I been
plagued, and [1]chastened every morning.
15 If I say, I will speak thus; behold, I
should offend *against* the generation of
thy children.
16 [a]When I thought to know this, [1]it
was too painful for me;
17 Until [a]I went into the sanctuary of H
God; *then* understood I [b]their end.
18 Surely [a]thou didst set them in slippery places: thou castedst them down
into destruction.
19 How are they *brought* into desolation, as in a moment! they are utterly
consumed with terrors.
20 [a]As a dream when *one* awaketh;
so, O Lord, when thou awakest, thou
shalt despise their image.
21 Thus my heart was grieved, and I
was pricked in my reins.
22 [a]So foolish *was* I, and [1]ignorant: I
was *as* a beast [2]before thee.
23 Nevertheless I *am* continually with L
thee: thou hast holden *me* by my right
hand.
24 [a]Thou shalt guide me with thy
counsel, and afterward receive me *to*
glory.
25 [a]Whom have I in heaven *but thee?* O
and *there is* none upon earth *that* I desire
beside thee.
26 [a]My flesh and my heart faileth: *but* K
God *is* the [1]strength of my heart, and my
portion for ever.
27 For, lo, [a]they that are far from thee S
shall perish: thou hast destroyed all them
that go a-whoring from thee.
28 But *it is* good for me to [a]draw near

16 [a] 1 Ki. 4:20
17 [a] Ps. 89:36 [b] Gen. 12:3; Jer. 4:2 [c] Luke 1:48 [1] Heb. *shall be* [2] Heb. *shall be as a son to continue his father's name for ever*
18 [a] 1 Chr. 29:10 [b] Ex. 15:11
19 [a] Neh. 9:5 [b] Num. 14:21; Hab. 2:14
73:1 [a] Ps. 50, title [1] Or, *A Psalm for Asaph* [2] Or, *Yet* [3] Heb. *clean of heart*
3 [a] Job 21:7; Ps. 37:1
4 [1] Heb. *fat*
5 [a] Job 21:9 [1] Heb. *in the trouble of* other *men* [2] Heb. *with*
6 [a] Ps. 109:18
7 [a] Jer. 5:28 [1] Heb. *they pass the thoughts of the heart*
8 [a] Ps. 53:1 [b] Jude 16
9 [a] Rev. 13:6
10 [a] Ps. 75:8
11 [a] Job 22:13
13 [a] Job 34:9; Mal. 3:14 [b] Ps:26:6
14 [1] Heb. *my chastisement* was
16 [a] Eccl. 8:17 [1] Heb. *it* was *labour in mine eyes*
17 [a] Ps. 77:13 [b] Ps. 37:38
18 [a] Ps. 35:6
20 [a] Job 20:8; Ps. 90:5
22 [a] Ps. 92:6; Prov. 30:2 [1] Heb. *I knew not* [2] Heb. *with thee*
24 [a] Ps. 32:8 & 48:14
25 [a] Phil. 3:8
26 [a] Ps. 84:2 & 119:81 [1] Heb. *rock*
27 [a] Ps. 119:155
28 [a] Heb. 10:22

U *Ps 68:3* ◀ ▶ *Ps 81:15–16*

H *Ps 69:27–28* ◀ ▶ *Ps 75:7–8*
L *Ps 71:6* ◀ ▶ *Ps 78:52–53*
O *Ps 68:20* ◀ ▶ *Ps 75:6–7*
K *Ps 69:32* ◀ ▶ *Ps 80:3*
S *Ps 69:28* ◀ ▶ *Ps 93:5*

72:17 Solomon's words conclude with a benediction that the Messiah's eternal and prosperous reign will bless the entire world.

to God: I have put my trust in the Lord GOD, that I may declare all thy works.

A plea for relief

[l]Maschil of Asaph.

R **74** O GOD, why hast thou [a]cast *us* off for ever? *why* doth thine anger [b]smoke against [c]the sheep of thy pasture?

2 Remember thy congregation, *which* thou hast purchased of old; the [l]rod of thine inheritance, *which* thou hast redeemed; this mount Zion, wherein thou hast dwelt.

3 Lift up thy feet unto the perpetual desolations; *even* all *that* the enemy hath done wickedly in the sanctuary.

4 Thine enemies roar in the midst of thy congregations; [a]they set up their ensigns *for* signs.

5 *A man* was famous according as he had lifted up axes upon the thick trees.

6 But now they break down the carved work thereof at once with axes and hammers.

R 7 [l]They have cast fire into thy sanctuary, they have defiled *by casting down* the dwellingplace of thy name to the ground.

8 [a]They said in their hearts, Let us [l]destroy them together: they have burned up all the synagogues of God in the land.

9 We see not our signs: [a]*there is* no more any prophet: neither *is there* among us any that knoweth how long.

I 10 O God, how long shall the adversary reproach? shall the enemy blaspheme thy name for ever?

11 [a]Why withdrawest thou thy hand, even thy right hand? pluck *it* out of thy bosom.

12 For [a]God *is* my King of old, working salvation in the midst of the earth.

13 [a]Thou didst [l]divide the sea by thy strength; [b]thou brakest the heads of the [2]dragons in the waters.

14 Thou brakest the heads of leviathan in pieces, *and* gavest him [a]*to be* meat to the people inhabiting the wilderness.

15 [a]Thou didst cleave the fountain and the flood: [b]thou driedst up [l]mighty rivers.

16 The day *is* thine, the night also *is* thine: thou hast prepared the light and the sun.

17 Thou hast set all the borders of the earth: [a]thou hast [l]made summer and winter.

18 [a]Remember this, *that* the enemy hath reproached, O LORD, and *that* [b]the foolish people have blasphemed thy name. C

19 O deliver not the soul [a]of thy turtledove unto the multitude *of the wicked:* [b]forget not the congregation of thy poor for ever.

20 [a]Have respect unto the covenant: for the dark places of the earth are full of the habitations of cruelty.

21 O let not the oppressed return ashamed: let the poor and needy praise thy name.

22 Arise, O God, plead thine own cause: [a]remember how the foolish man reproacheth thee daily. C

23 Forget not the voice of thine enemies: the tumult of those that rise up against thee [a]increaseth[l] continually.

The justice of God

To the chief Musician, [a]Al-taschith,[l] A Psalm *or* Song [2]of Asaph.

75 UNTO THEE, O God, do we give thanks, *unto thee* do we give thanks: for *that* thy name is near thy wondrous works declare.

2 [l]When I shall receive the congregation I will judge uprightly.

3 The earth and all the inhabitants thereof are dissolved: I bear up the pillars of it. Selah. N

74:1 [a]Ps. 44:9,23; Jer. 31:37 [b]Deut. 29:20 [c]Ps. 95:7 [l]Or, A Psalm *for Asaph to give instruction*
2 [l]Or, *tribe*
4 [a]Dan. 6:27
7 [l]Heb. *They have sent thy sanctuary into the fire*
8 [a]Ps. 83:4 [l]Heb. *break*
9 [a]Amos 8:11
11 [a]Lam. 2:3
12 [a]Ps. 44:4
13 [a]Ex. 14:21 [b]Is. 51:9,10; Ezek. 29:3 [l]Heb. *break* [2]Or, *whales*
14 [a]Num. 14:9
15 [a]Ex. 17:5,6; Num. 20:11 [b]Josh. 3:13 [l]Heb. *rivers of strength*
17 [a]Gen. 8:22 [l]Heb. *made them*
18 [a]ver. 22 [b]Ps. 39:8
19 [a]Sol. 2:14 [b]Ps. 68:10
20 [a]Gen. 17:7,8; Ps. 106:45
22 [a]Ps. 89:51
23 [a]Jonah 1:2 [l]Heb. *ascendeth*
75:1 [a]Ps. 57, title [l]Or, *Destroy not* [2]Or, *for Asaph*
2 [l]Or, *When I shall take a set time*

R *Ne 1:8 ◀▶ Ps 74:7–11*
R *Ps 74:1–2 ◀▶ Ps 78:67*
I *Ps 69:35–36 ◀▶ Ps 79:5*
C *Ps 58:1–3 ◀▶ Ps 74:22*
C *Ps 74:18 ◀▶ Ps 94:11*
N *Ps 37:34 ◀▶ Ps 78:69*

74:1–2 Asaph prophesied the rejection and scattering of Israel. This prophecy was fulfilled when the Assyrians and Babylonians carried Israel and Judah into exile.

74:7–11 Asaph declared that God's people would cry in despair that "there is no more any prophet" (74:9). Both of the prophets Ezekiel and Jeremiah had been carried into exile, leaving no one behind to tell the people how long their suffering would last.

75:3 This prophecy anticipates the ultimate redemption of the earth when the Messiah returns. Though the whole moral order of the world seems to have crumbled, God is still in control and will uphold "the pillars of it."

4 I said unto the fools, Deal not foolishly: and to the wicked, [a]Lift not up the horn:

5 Lift not up your horn on high: speak *not with* a stiff neck.

G 6 For promotion *cometh* neither from
O the east, nor from the west, nor from the *l*south.

H 7 But [a]God *is* the judge: [b]he putteth down one, and setteth up another.

P 8 For [a]in the hand of the LORD *there is* a cup, and the wine is red; it is [b]full of mixture; and he poureth out of the same: [c]but the dregs thereof, all the wicked of the earth shall wring *them* out, *and* drink *them.*

9 But I will declare for ever; I will sing praises to the God of Jacob.

P 10 [a]All the horns of the wicked also
H will I cut off; *but* [b]the horns of the righteous shall be exalted.

The victorious power of God

To the chief Musician on Neginoth, A Psalm *or* Song *l*of Asaph.

76 IN [a]JUDAH *is* God known: his name *is* great in Israel.

2 In Salem also is his tabernacle, and his dwellingplace in Zion.

3 [a]There brake he the arrows of the bow, the shield, and the sword, and the battle. Selah.

4 Thou *art* more glorious *and* excellent [a]than the mountains of prey.

5 [a]The stout-hearted are spoiled, [b]they have slept their sleep: and none of the men of might have found their hands.

6 [a]At thy rebuke, O God of Jacob, both the chariot and horse are cast into a dead sleep.

H 7 Thou, *even* thou, *art* to be feared: and [a]who may stand in thy sight when once thou art angry?

8 [a]Thou didst cause judgment to be heard from heaven; [b]the earth feared, and was still,

9 When God [a]arose to judgment, to save all the meek of the earth. Selah.

10 [a]Surely the wrath of man shall praise thee: the remainder of wrath shalt thou restrain.

11 [a]Vow, and pay unto the LORD your God: [b]let all that be round about him bring presents *l*unto him that ought to be feared.

12 He shall cut off the spirit of princes: [a]*he is* terrible to the kings of the earth.

The call to God for help

To the chief Musician, [a]to Jeduthun, A Psalm *l*of Asaph.

77 I [b]CRIED unto God with my voice, *even* unto God with my voice; and he gave ear unto me.

2 [a]In the day of my trouble I [b]sought the Lord: *l*my sore ran in the night, and ceased not: my soul refused to be comforted.

3 I remembered God, and was troubled: I complained, and [a]my spirit was overwhelmed. Selah.

4 Thou holdest mine eyes waking: I am so troubled that I cannot speak.

5 [a]I have considered the days of old, the years of ancient times.

6 I call to remembrance [a]my song in the night: [b]I commune with mine own heart: and my spirit made diligent search.

7 [a]Will the Lord cast off for ever? and L
will he [b]be favourable no more?

8 Is his mercy clean gone for ever? doth [a]*his* promise fail *l*for evermore?

9 Hath God [a]forgotten to be gracious? hath he in anger shut up his tender mercies? Selah.

10 And I said, This *is* [a]my infirmity: *but I will remember* the years of the right hand of the most High.

11 [a]I will remember the works of the LORD: surely I will remember thy wonders of old.

12 I will meditate also of all thy work, and talk of thy doings.

13 [a]Thy way, O God, *is* in the sanctu-

G *Ps 62:9–11* ◀▶ *Ps 143:2*
O *Ps 73:25–27* ◀▶ *Ps 127:1*
H *Ps 73:17–18* ◀▶ *Ps 75:10*
P *Ps 72:9* ◀▶ *Ps 75:10*
P *Ps 75:8* ◀▶ *Ps 83:13–17*
H *Ps 75:7–8* ◀▶ *Ps 76:7*
H *Ps 75:10* ◀▶ *Ps 83:17*

L *Ps 69:32* ◀▶ *Ps 78:38–39*

4 [a]Zech. 1:21
6 *l*Heb. *desert*
7 [a]Ps. 50:6 [b]1 Sam. 2:7; Dan. 2:21
8 [a]Job 21:20; Jer. 25:15; Rev. 14:10 & 16:19 [b]Prov. 23:30 [c]Ps. 73:10
10 [a]Ps. 101:8; Jer. 48:25 [b]Ps. 89:17 & 148:14
76:1 [a]Ps. 48:1 *l*Or, *for Asaph*
3 [a]Ps. 46:9; Ezek. 39:9
4 [a]Ezek. 38:12
5 [a]Is. 46:12 [b]Ps. 13:3; Jer. 51:39
6 [a]Ex. 15:1,21; Ezek. 39:20; Nah. 2:13; Zech. 12:4
7 [a]Nah. 1:6
8 [a]Ex. 19:10 [b]2 Chr. 20:29,30
9 [a]Ps. 9:7-9 & 72:4
10 [a]Ps. 65:7; Dan. 3:28
11 [a]Eccl. 5:4-6 [b]2 Chr. 32:22,23; Ps. 68:29 *l*Heb. *to fear*
12 [a]Ps. 68:35
77:1 [a]Ps. 39, title; & 62, title [b]Ps. 3:4 *l*Or, *for Asaph*
2 [a]Ps. 50:15 [b]Is. 26:9,16 *l*Heb. *my hand*
3 [a]Ps. 143:4
5 [a]Deut. 32:7; Ps. 143:5; Is. 51:9
6 [a]Ps. 42:8 [b]Ps. 4:4
7 [a]Ps. 74:1 [b]Ps. 85:1
8 [a]Rom. 9:6 *l*Heb. *to generation and generation?*
9 [a]Is. 49:15
10 [a]Ps. 31:22
11 [a]Ps. 143:5
13 [a]Ps. 73:17

75:8–10 This prophecy looks forward to the final victory of Jesus Christ over the wicked during the terrors of the great tribulation when God will defeat the wicked, "but the horns of the righteous shall be exalted" (75:10).

ary: [b]who *is so* great a God as *our* God?
14 Thou *art* the God that doest wonders: thou hast declared thy strength
among the people.
15 [a]Thou hast with *thine* arm redeemed thy people, the sons of Jacob and
Joseph. Selah.
16 [a]The waters saw thee, O God, the
waters saw thee; they were afraid: the
depths also were troubled.
17 [l]The clouds poured out water: the
skies sent out a sound: [a]thine arrows also
went abroad.
18 The voice of thy thunder *was* in
the heaven: the lightnings lightened the
world: [a]the earth trembled and shook.
19 [a]Thy way *is* in the sea, and thy path
in the great waters, [b]and thy footsteps are
not known.
20 [a]Thou leddest thy people like a
flock by the hand of Moses and Aaron.

God's guidance of his people

[a]Maschil[l] of Asaph.

78 GIVE[b] EAR, O my people, *to* my
law: incline your ears to the
words of my mouth.
2 [a]I will open my mouth in a parable: I
will utter dark sayings of old:
3 [a]Which we have heard and known,
and our fathers have told us.
T 4 [a]We will not hide *them* from their
children, [b]showing to the generation to
come the praises of the LORD, and his
strength, and his wonderful works that
he hath done.
5 For [a]he established a testimony in Jacob, and appointed a law in Israel, which
he commanded our fathers, [b]that they
should make them known to their
children:
6 [a]That the generation to come might
know *them, even* the children *which*
should be born; *who* should arise and declare *them* to their children:
7 That they might set their hope in
God, and not forget the works of God, but
keep his commandments:
8 And [a]might not be as their fathers,
[b]a stubborn and rebellious generation; a
generation [c]*that*[l] set not their heart
aright, and whose spirit was not stedfast
with God.
9 The children of Ephraim, *being*
armed, *and* [l]carrying bows, turned back
in the day of battle.
10 [a]They kept not the covenant of
God, and refused to walk in his law;
11 And [a]forgat his works, and his wonders that he had shown them.
12 [a]Marvellous things did he in the
sight of their fathers, in the land of Egypt,
[b]*in* the field of Zoan.
13 [a]He divided the sea, and caused
them to pass through; and [b]he made the
waters to stand as an heap.
14 [a]In the daytime also he led them
with a cloud, and all the night with a light
of fire.
15 [a]He clave the rocks in the wilder- F
ness, and gave *them* drink as *out of* the
great depths.
16 He brought [a]streams also out of the
rock, and caused waters to run down like
rivers.
17 And they sinned yet more against
him by [a]provoking the most High in the
wilderness.
18 And [a]they tempted God in their
heart by asking meat for their lust.
19 [a]Yea, they spake against God; they F
said, Can God [l]furnish a table in the wilderness?
20 [a]Behold, he smote the rock, that
the waters gushed out, and the streams
overflowed; can he give bread also? can
he provide flesh for his people?
21 Therefore the LORD heard *this,* and
[a]was wroth: so a fire was kindled against
Jacob, and anger also came up against
Israel;
22 Because they [a]believed not in God,
and trusted not in his salvation:
23 Though he had commanded the
clouds from above, [a]and opened the
doors of heaven,
24 [a]And had rained down manna upon
them to eat, and had given them of the
corn of heaven.

T *Ps 66:16–17* ◀▶ *Ps 105:1–2*

F *Ps 37:25* ◀▶ *Ps 78:19–29*
F *Ps 78:15–16* ◀▶ *Ps 81:10*

13 [b]Ex. 15:11
15 [a]Ex. 6:6; Deut. 9:29
16 [a]Ex. 14:21
17 [a]2 Sam. 22:15 [l]Heb. *The clouds were poured forth with water*
18 [a]2 Sam. 22:8
19 [a]Hab. 3:15 [b]Ex. 14:28
20 [a]Ex. 13:21; Is. 63:11,12
78:1 [a]Ps. 74, title [b]Is. 51:4 [l]Or, A Psalm *for Asaph to give instruction*
2 [a]Mat. 13:35
3 [a]Ps. 44:1
4 [a]Deut. 6:7; Joel 1:3 [b]Ex. 13:8,14
5 [a]Ps. 147:19 [b]Deut. 4:9
6 [a]Ps. 102:18
8 [a]2 Ki. 17:14 [b]Ex. 32:9 [c]ver. 37 [l]Heb. that *prepared not their heart*
9 [l]Heb. *throwing forth*
10 [a]2 Ki. 17:15
11 [a]Ps. 106:13
12 [a]Ex. 7-12 [b]Num. 13:22
13 [a]Ex. 14:21 [b]Ex. 15:8
14 [a]Ex. 13:21
15 [a]Num. 20:11
16 [a]Deut. 9:21
17 [a]Heb. 3:16
18 [a]Ex. 16:2
19 [a]Num. 11:4 [l]Heb. *order*
20 [a]Num. 20:11
21 [a]Num. 11:1
22 [a]Heb. 3:18
23 [a]Mal. 3:10
24 [a]John 6:31

78:24–25 The psalmist calls this heavenly manna "angels' food" (78:25), indicating that the angels have the capacity to eat (see Ge 18:1–8). The NT also suggests that resurrected bodies will still eat (see Lk 24:36–43; Rev 19:7–9).

25 [1]Man did eat angels' food: he sent them meat to the full.

26 [a]He caused an east wind [1]to blow in the heaven: and by his power he brought in the south wind.

27 He rained flesh also upon them as dust, and [1]feathered fowls like as the sand of the sea:

28 And he let *it* fall in the midst of their camp, round about their habitations.

29 [a]So they did eat, and were well filled: for he gave them their own desire;

30 They were not estranged from their lust. But [a]while their meat *was* yet in their mouths,

31 The wrath of God came upon them, and slew the fattest of them, and [1]smote down the [2]chosen *men* of Israel.

32 For all this [a]they sinned still, and [b]believed not for his wondrous works.

33 [a]Therefore their days did he consume in vanity, and their years in trouble.

34 [a]When he slew them, then they sought him: and they returned and inquired early after God.

35 And they remembered that [a]God *was* their rock, and the high God [b]their redeemer.

36 Nevertheless they did [a]flatter him with their mouth, and they lied unto him with their tongues.

37 For their heart was not right with him, neither were they stedfast in his covenant.

L 38 [a]But he, *being* full of compassion,
P forgave *their* iniquity, and destroyed *them* not: yea, many a time [b]turned he his anger away, [c]and did not stir up all his wrath.

N 39 For [a]he remembered [b]that they *were but* flesh; [c]a wind that passeth away, and cometh not again.

40 How oft did they [a]provoke[1] him in the wilderness, *and* grieve him in the desert!

41 Yea, [a]they turned back and tempted God, and limited the Holy One of Israel.

42 They remembered not his hand, *nor* the day when he delivered them [1]from the enemy.

43 How he had [1]wrought his signs in Egypt, and his wonders in the field of Zoan:

44 [a]And had turned their rivers into blood; and their floods, that they could not drink.

45 [a]He sent divers sorts of flies among them, which devoured them; and [b]frogs, which destroyed them.

46 He gave also their increase unto the caterpillar, and their labour unto the locust.

47 [a]He [1]destroyed their vines with hail, and their sycamore trees with [2]frost.

48 [a]He[1] gave up their cattle also to the hail, and their flocks to [2]hot thunderbolts.

49 He cast upon them the fierceness of his anger, wrath, and indignation, and trouble, by sending evil angels *among them.*

50 [1]He made a way to his anger; he spared not their soul from death, but gave [2]their life over to the pestilence;

51 [a]And smote all the firstborn in Egypt; the chief of *their* strength in [b]the tabernacles of Ham:

52 But [a]made his own people to go forth like sheep, and guided them in the wilderness like a flock. L

53 And he [a]led them on safely, so that they feared not: but the sea [b]overwhelmed[1] their enemies.

54 And he brought them to the border of his [a]sanctuary, *even to* this mountain, [b]*which* his right hand had purchased.

55 [a]He cast out the heathen also before them, and [b]divided them an inheritance by line, and made the tribes of Israel to dwell in their tents.

56 [a]Yet they tempted and provoked the most high God, and kept not his testimonies:

57 But [a]turned back, and dealt unfaithfully like their fathers: they were turned aside [b]like a deceitful bow.

58 [a]For they provoked him to anger with their [b]high places, and moved him to jealousy with their graven images.

59 When God heard *this,* he was wroth, and greatly abhorred Israel:

60 So that he forsook the tabernacle of Shiloh, the tent *which* he placed among men;

61 [a]And delivered his strength into

25 [1]Or, *Every one did eat the bread of the mighty*
26 [a]Num. 11:31 [1]Heb. *to go*
27 [1]Heb. *fowl of wing*
29 [a]Num. 11:20
30 [a]Num. 11:33
31 [1]Heb. *made to bow* [2]Or, *young men*
32 [a]Num. 14 & 16 & 17 [b]ver. 22
33 [a]Num. 14:29
34 [a]Hos. 5:15
35 [a]Deut. 32:4,15, 31 [b]Is. 41:14 & 63:9
36 [a]Ezek. 33:31
38 [a]Num. 14:18, 20 [b]Is. 48:9 [c]1 Ki. 21:29
39 [a]Ps. 103:14 [b]John 3:6 [c]Job 7:7, 16
40 [a]Ps. 95:8-10; Heb. 3:16 [1]Or, *rebel against him*
41 [a]Num. 14:22; Deut. 6:16
42 [1]Or, *from affliction*
43 [1]Heb. *set*
44 [a]Ex. 7:20; Ps. 105:29
45 [a]Ex. 8:24; Ps. 105:31 [b]Ex. 8:6
47 [a]Ex. 9:23,25; Ps. 105:33 [1]Heb. *killed* [2]Or, *great hailstones*
48 [a]Ex. 9:23-25 [1]Heb. *He shut up* [2]Or, *lightnings*
50 [1]Heb. *He weighed a path* [2]Or, *their beasts to the murrain*
51 [a]Ex. 12:29 [b]Ps. 106:22
52 [a]Ps. 77:20
53 [a]Ex. 14:19 [b]Ex. 14:27 [1]Heb. *covered*
54 [a]Ex. 15:17 [b]Ps. 44:3
55 [a]Ps. 44:2 [b]Josh. 13:7
56 [a]Judg. 2:11
57 [a]Ezek. 20:27 [b]Hos. 7:16
58 [a]Deut. 32:16, 21; Judg. 2:12 [b]Deut. 12:2
61 [a]Judg. 18:30

L *Ps 77:7–9* ◀▶ *Ps 85:2–3*
P *Ps 32:5* ◀▶ *Isa 57:15–19*
N *Ps 49:10–14* ◀▶ *Ps 89:48*

L *Ps 73:23–24* ◀▶ *Ps 81:10*

captivity, and his glory into the enemy's hand.

62 [a]He gave his people over also unto the sword; and was wroth with his inheritance.

63 The fire consumed their young men; and [a]their maidens were not [/]given to marriage.

64 [a]Their priests fell by the sword; and [b]their widows made no lamentation.

65 Then the Lord awaked as one out of sleep, *and* [a]like a mighty man that shouteth by reason of wine.

66 And [a]he smote his enemies in the hinder parts: he put them to a perpetual reproach.

R 67 Moreover he refused the tabernacle of Joseph, and chose not the tribe of Ephraim:

68 But chose the tribe of Judah, the mount Zion [a]which he loved.

N 69 And he built his sanctuary like high *palaces,* like the earth which he hath [/]established for ever.

70 [a]He chose David also his servant, and took him from the sheepfolds:

71 [/]From following [a]the ewes great with young he brought him [b]to feed Jacob his people, and Israel his inheritance.

72 So he fed them according to the [a]integrity of his heart; and guided them by the skilfulness of his hands.

A lament for Jerusalem

A Psalm [/]of Asaph.

R **79** O GOD, the heathen are come into [a]thine inheritance; thy holy temple have they defiled; [b]they have laid Jerusalem on heaps.

2 [a]The dead bodies of thy servants have they given *to be* meat unto the fowls of the heaven, the flesh of thy saints unto the beasts of the earth.

3 Their blood have they shed like water round about Jerusalem; and *there was* none to bury *them.*

4 We are become a reproach to our neighbours, a scorn and derision to them that are round about us. R

5 [a]How long, LORD? wilt thou be angry for ever? shall thy [b]jealousy burn like fire? I

6 [a]Pour out thy wrath upon the heathen that have [b]not known thee, and upon the kingdoms that have [c]not called upon thy name.

7 For they have devoured Jacob, and laid waste his dwellingplace.

8 [a]O remember not against us [/]former iniquities: let thy tender mercies speedily prevent us: for we are brought very low.

9 Help us, O God of our salvation, for the glory of thy name: and deliver us, and purge away our sins, [a]for thy name's sake.

10 [a]Wherefore should the heathen say, Where *is* their God? let him be known among the heathen in our sight *by* the [/]revenging of the blood of thy servants *which is* shed.

11 Let [a]the sighing of the prisoner come before thee; according to the greatness of [/]thy power [2]preserve thou those that are appointed to die;

12 And render unto our neighbours [a]sevenfold into their bosom [b]their reproach, wherewith they have reproached thee, O Lord.

13 So [a]we thy people and sheep of thy pasture will give thee thanks for ever: [b]we will show forth thy praise [/]to all generations. I

62 [a]1 Sam. 4:10
63 [a]Jer. 7:34 [/]Heb. *praised*
64 [a]1 Sam. 22:18 [b]Job 27:15
65 [a]Is. 42:13
66 [a]1 Sam. 5:6
68 [a]Ps. 87:2
69 [/]Heb. *founded*
70 [a]1 Sam. 16:11, 12
71 [a]Is. 40:11 [b]2 Sam. 5:2 [/]Heb. *From after*
72 [a]1 Ki. 9:4
79:1 [a]Ps. 74:2 [b]Mic. 3:12 [/]Or, *for Asaph*
2 [a]Jer:7:33
5 [a]Ps. 74:1,9 [b]Zeph. 3:8
6 [a]Jer. 10:25; Rev. 16:1 [b]Is. 45:4,5; 2 Thes. 1:8 [c]Ps. 53:4
8 [a]Is. 64:9 [/]Or, *the iniquities of them that were before us*
9 [a]Jer. 14:7
10 [a]Ps. 42:10 [/]Heb. *vengeance*
11 [a]Ps. 102:20 [/]Heb. *thine arm* [2]Heb. *reserve the children of death*
12 [a]Gen. 4:15; Is. 65:6,7; Jer. 32:18; Luke 6:38 [b]Ps. 74:18
13 [a]Ps. 74:1 & 95:7 [b]Is. 43:21 [/]Heb. *to generation and generation*

R *Ps 74:7–11* ◀▶ *Ps 79:1*
N *Ps 75:3* ◀▶ *Ps 93:1*
R *Ps 78:67* ◀▶ *Ps 79:4–7*
R *Ps 79:1* ◀▶ *Ps 80:4–6*
I *Ps 74:10* ◀▶ *Ps 79:13*
I *Ps 79:5* ◀▶ *Ps 80:3–7*

78:67–70 God had chosen Mt. Zion, in the territory allocated to the tribe of Judah, as the location for his temple. This sanctuary was as secure and enduring as the earth. A new earth will be revealed at the end of the Millennium (see Rev 21:1) and will be the home of the people who survive the Millennium. The new Jerusalem will descend to this perfected earth, and the resurrected believers will continue to rule there forever. For further information, see the article entitled "A New Heaven and a New Earth," p. 1488.

79:1 In this psalm Asaph complained to God that the enemies of Israel had defiled God's temple and destroyed Jerusalem, referring to the conquest of Jerusalem by the Babylonian army of Nebuchadnezzar in 586 B.C.

79:4–7 Note the similarity between vv. 6–7 and Jer 10:25. Perhaps Asaph is quoting the prophet here in his prayer for justice.

79:13 The psalmist rejoiced in his prophetic vision of the final victory over the heathen.

A call to God for help

To the chief Musician [a]upon Shoshannim-Eduth, A Psalm [/]of Asaph.

80 GIVE EAR, O Shepherd of Israel, thou that leadest Joseph [b]like a flock; thou that dwellest *between* the cherubims, [c]shine forth.

2 Before Ephraim and Benjamin and Manasseh stir up thy strength, and [/]come *and* save us.

3 [a]Turn us again, O God, [b]and cause thy face to shine; and we shall be saved.

4 O LORD God of hosts, how long [/]wilt thou be angry against the prayer of thy people?

5 [a]Thou feedest them with the bread of tears; and givest them tears to drink in great measure.

6 Thou makest us a strife unto our neighbours: and our enemies laugh among themselves.

7 Turn us again, O God of hosts, and cause thy face to shine; and we shall be saved.

8 Thou hast brought [a]a vine out of Egypt: [b]thou hast cast out the heathen, and planted it.

9 Thou preparedst *room* before it, and didst cause it to take deep root, and it filled the land.

10 The hills were covered with the shadow of it, and the boughs thereof *were like* [/]the goodly cedars.

11 She sent out her boughs unto the sea, and her branches unto the river.

12 Why hast thou *then* [a]broken down her hedges, so that all they which pass by the way do pluck her?

13 The boar out of the wood doth waste it, and the wild beast of the field doth devour it.

14 Return, we beseech thee, O God of hosts: [a]look down from heaven, and behold, and visit this vine;

15 And the vineyard which thy right hand hath planted, and the branch *that* thou madest strong for thyself.

16 *It is* burned with fire, *it is* cut down: [a]they perish at the rebuke of thy countenance.

17 [a]Let thy hand be upon the man of thy right hand, upon the son of man *whom* thou madest strong for thyself.

18 So will not we go back from thee: quicken us, and we will call upon thy name.

19 Turn us again, O LORD God of hosts, cause thy face to shine; and we shall be saved.

God's goodness to Israel

To the chief Musician [a]upon Gittith, *A Psalm* [/]of Asaph.

81 SING ALOUD unto God our strength: make a joyful noise unto the God of Jacob.

2 Take a psalm, and bring hither the timbrel, the pleasant harp with the psaltery.

3 Blow up the trumpet in the new moon, in the time appointed, on our solemn feast day.

4 For this *was* a statute for Israel, *and* a law of the God of Jacob.

5 This he ordained in Joseph *for* a testimony, when he went out [/]through the land of Egypt: [a]*where* I heard a language *that* I understood not.

6 I removed his shoulder from the burden: his hands [/]were delivered from the pots.

7 [a]Thou calledst in trouble, and I delivered thee; [b]I answered thee in the secret place of thunder: I [c]proved thee at the waters of [/]Meribah. Selah.

8 [a]Hear, O my people, and I will testify unto thee: O Israel, if thou wilt hearken unto me;

9 There shall no [a]strange god be in thee; neither shalt thou worship any strange god.

10 [a]I *am* the LORD thy God, which brought thee out of the land of Egypt:

80:1 [a]Ps. 45, title & 69, title [b]Ps. 77:20 [c]Deut. 33:2; Ps. 50:2 [/]Or, *for Asaph*
2 [/]Heb. *come for salvation to us*
3 [a]Lam. 5:21 [b]Num. 6:25; Ps. 4:6
4 [/]Heb. *wilt thou smoke*
5 [a]Ps. 42:3; Is. 30:20
8 [a]Is. 5:1,7; Jer. 2:21; Ezek. 15:6 [b]Ps. 44:2
10 [/]Heb. *the cedars of God*
12 [a]Is. 5:5; Nah. 2:2
14 [a]Is. 63:15
16 [a]Ps. 39:11 & 76:7
17 [a]Ps. 89:21
81:1 [a]Ps. 8, title [/]Or, *for Asaph*
5 [a]Ps. 114:1 [/]Or, *against*
6 [/]Heb. *passed away*
7 [a]Ex. 2:23; Ps. 50:15 [b]Ex. 19:19 [c]Ex. 17:6,7 [/]Or, *Strife*
8 [a]Ps. 50:7
9 [a]Deut. 32:12; Is. 43:12
10 [a]Ex. 20:2

I *Ps 79:13* ◀▶ *Ps 80:14–15*
K *Ps 73:26* ◀▶ *Ps 80:7*
R *Ps 79:4–7* ◀▶ *Ps 80:12–16*
K *Ps 80:3* ◀▶ *Ps 80:19*
R *Ps 80:4–6* ◀▶ *Isa 1:7–9*
I *Ps 80:3–7* ◀▶ *Ps 80:19*
I *Ps 80:14–15* ◀▶ *Ps 85:1–13*
K *Ps 80:7* ◀▶ *Ps 84:11*
F *Ps 78:19–29* ◀▶ *Ps 81:16*
L *Ps 78:52–53* ◀▶ *Ps 86:7*

80:3 The psalmist calls upon God for restoration and revival with words that echo the priestly benediction of Nu 6:25.

80:3–16, 19 Asaph expressed his confidence in God's ultimate sovereignty and deliverance despite a time of great destruction.

[b]open thy mouth wide, and I will fill it.

11 But my people would not hearken to my voice; and Israel would [a]none of me.

12 [a]So I gave them up [l]unto their own hearts' lust: *and* they walked in their own counsels.

V 13 [a]Oh that my people had hearkened unto me, *and* Israel had walked in my ways!

14 I should soon have subdued their enemies, and turned my hand against their adversaries.

U 15 [a]The haters of the LORD should have [b][l]submitted themselves unto him: but their time should have endured for ever.

F 16 He should [a]have fed them also [l]with the finest of the wheat: and with honey [b]out of the rock should I have satisfied thee.

Unjust judgments rebuked

A Psalm [l]of Asaph.

82 GOD [a]STANDETH in the congregation of the mighty; he judgeth among [b]the gods.

2 How long will ye judge unjustly, and [a]accept the persons of the wicked? Selah.

3 [l]Defend the poor and fatherless: [a]do justice to the afflicted and needy.

4 [a]Deliver the poor and needy: rid *them* out of the hand of the wicked.

5 They [a]know not, neither will they understand; they walk on in darkness: [b]all the foundations of the earth are [l]out of course.

6 [a]I have said, Ye *are* gods; and all of you *are* children of the most High.

7 But [a]ye shall die like men, and fall like one of the princes.

M 8 [a]Arise, O God, judge the earth: [b]for thou shalt inherit all nations.

V *Ps 60:12 ◀ ▶ Ps 89:22–23*
U *Ps 73:1 ◀ ▶ Ps 84:4–5*
F *Ps 81:10 ◀ ▶ Ps 103:5*
M *Ps 72:1–19 ◀ ▶ Ps 85:9–13*

10 [b]Ps. 103:5
11 [a]Ex. 32:1; Deut. 32:15
12 [a]Acts 7:42 [l]Or, *to the hardness of their hearts,* or, *imaginations*
13 [a]Deut. 5:29 & 32:29; Is. 48:18
15 [a]Rom. 1:30 [b]Ps. 18:44 [l]Or, *yielded feigned obedience*
16 [a]Deut. 32:14 [b]Job 29:6 [l]Heb. *with the fat of wheat*
82:1 [a]2 Chr. 19:6 [b]ver. 6 [l]Or, *for Asaph*
2 [a]Deut. 1:17
3 [a]Jer. 22:3 [l]Heb. *Judge*
4 [a]Job 29:12; Prov. 24:11
5 [a]Mic. 3:1 [b]Ps. 11:3 [l]Heb. *moved*
6 [a]Ex. 22:28; John 10:34
7 [a]Ps. 49:12
8 [a]Mic. 7:2,7 [b]Ps. 2:8; Rev. 11:15
83:1 [a]Ps. 28:1 [l]Or, *for Asaph*
2 [a]Ps. 2:1 [b]Ps. 81:15
3 [a]Ps. 27:5
4 [a]Jer. 11:19
5 [l]Heb. *heart*
6 [a]See 2 Chr. 20:1, 10,11
8 [l]Heb. *they have been an arm to the children of Lot*
9 [a]Judg. 4:15
10 [a]Zeph. 1:17
11 [a]Judg. 8:12
13 [a]Is. 17:13 [b]Ps. 35:5
14 [a]Deut. 32:22

Prayer for Israel's defence

A Song *or* Psalm [l]of Asaph.

83 KEEP [a]NOT thou silence, O God: hold not thy peace, and be not still, O God.

2 For, lo, [a]thine enemies make a tumult: and they that [b]hate thee have lifted up the head.

3 They have taken crafty counsel against thy people, and consulted [a]against thy hidden ones.

4 They have said, Come, and [a]let us cut them off from *being* a nation; that the name of Israel may be no more in remembrance.

5 For they have consulted together with one [l]consent: they are confederate against thee:

6 [a]The tabernacles of Edom, and the Ishmaelites; of Moab, and the Hagarenes;

7 Gebal, and Ammon, and Amalek; the Philistines with the inhabitants of Tyre;

8 Assur also is joined with them: [l]they have helped the children of Lot. Selah.

9 Do unto them as *unto* the Midianites; as *to* [a]Sisera, as *to* Jabin, at the brook of Kison:

10 *Which* perished at En-dor: [a]they became *as* dung for the earth.

11 Make their nobles like Oreb, and like Zeeb: yea, all their princes as [a]Zebah, and as Zalmunna:

12 Who said, Let us take to ourselves the houses of God in possession.

13 [a]O my God, make them like a wheel; [b]as the stubble before the wind. P

14 As the fire burneth a wood, and as the flame [a]setteth the mountains on fire;

15 So persecute them with thy tempest, and make them afraid with thy storm.

16 Fill their faces with shame; that they may seek thy name, O LORD.

17 Let them be confounded and troubled for ever; yea, let them be put to shame, and perish: H

P *Ps 75:10 ◀ ▶ Ps 94:1–4*
H *Ps 76:7 ◀ ▶ Ps 86:13*

82:8 Asaph confirmed the great truth that God will ultimately judge all of his inheritance.

83:13–17 These verses plead for God to destroy his enemies so that God's kingdom of righteousness and peace will come. Though this was the plea of most of the kings of Israel and Judah, these words also foreshadow the time when Jesus Christ will defeat his enemies during the seven years of the great tribulation.

18 [a]That *men* may know that thou, whose [b]name alone *is* JEHOVAH, *art* [c]the most high over all the earth.

Longing for the sanctuary

To the chief Musician [a]upon Gittith, A Psalm [1]for the sons of Korah.

84 HOW [b]AMIABLE *are* thy tabernacles, O LORD of hosts!

2 [a]My soul longeth, yea, even fainteth for the courts of the LORD: my heart and my flesh crieth out for the living God.

3 Yea, the sparrow hath found an house, and the swallow a nest for herself, where she may lay her young, *even* thine altars, O LORD of hosts, my King, and my God.

U 4 Blessed *are* they that dwell in thy house: they will be still praising thee. Selah.

5 Blessed *is* the man whose strength *is* in thee; in whose heart *are* the ways *of them.*

6 *Who* passing through the valley [a]of [1] Baca make it a well; the rain also [2]filleth the pools.

U 7 They go [a]from[1] strength to strength, *every one of them* in Zion [b]appeareth before God.

8 O LORD God of hosts, hear my prayer: give ear, O God of Jacob. Selah.

9 Behold, [a]O God our shield, and look upon the face of thine anointed.

U 10 For a day in thy courts *is* better than a thousand. [1]I had rather be a doorkeeper in the house of my God, than to dwell in the tents of wickedness.

K 11 For the LORD God *is* [a]a sun and [b]shield: the LORD will give grace and glory: [c]no good *thing* will he withhold from them that walk uprightly.

F 12 O LORD of hosts, [a]blessed *is* the man that trusteth in thee.

U *Ps 81:15–16* ◀▶ *Ps 84:7*
U *Ps 84:4–5* ◀▶ *Ps 84:10–12*
U *Ps 84:7* ◀▶ *Ps 89:15–16*
K *Ps 80:19* ◀▶ *Ps 89:15–16*
F *Ps 37:3* ◀▶ *Ps 125:1*

18 [a]Ps. 59:13
18 [b]Ex. 6:3 [c]Ps. 92:8
84:1 [a]Ps. 8, title [b]Ps. 27:4 [1]*Or, of*
2 [a]Ps. 42:1,2
6 [a]2 Sam. 5:23 [1]*Or, of mulberry trees make him a well* [2]Heb. *covereth*
7 [a]Prov. 4:18 [b]Deut. 16:16 [1]*Or, from company to company*
9 [a]ver. 11
10 [1]Heb. *I would choose rather to sit at the threshold*
11 [a]Is. 60:19 [b]Gen. 15:1; Ps. 115:9; Prov. 2:7 [c]Ps. 34:9
12 [a]Ps. 2:12
85:1 [a]Ps. 42, title [b]Ps. 77:7 [c]Ezra 1:11; Jer. 30:18; Ezek. 39:25; Joel 3:1 [1]*Or, of* [2]*Or, well pleased*
3 [1]*Or, thou hast turned thine anger from waxing hot*
4 [a]Ps. 80:7
5 [a]Ps. 79:5
6 [a]Hab. 3:2
8 [a]Hab. 2:1 [b]Zech. 9:10 [c]2 Pet. 2:20
9 [a]Is. 46:13 [b]Zech. 2:5
10 [a]Ps. 72:3; Is. 32:17; Luke 2:14
12 [a]Ps. 84:11; Jas. 1:17
13 [a]Ps. 89:14

Prayer for mercy to Israel

To the chief Musician, A Psalm [a]for[1] the sons of Korah.

85 LORD, THOU hast been [b]favourable[2] unto thy land: thou hast [c]brought back the captivity of Jacob. I

2 Thou hast forgiven the iniquity of thy people, thou hast covered all their sin. Selah. L

3 Thou hast taken away all thy wrath: [1]thou hast turned *thyself* from the fierceness of thine anger.

4 [a]Turn us, O God of our salvation, and cause thine anger toward us to cease

5 [a]Wilt thou be angry with us for ever? wilt thou draw out thine anger to all generations?

6 Wilt thou not [a]revive us again: that thy people may rejoice in thee?

7 Show us thy mercy, O LORD, and grant us thy salvation.

8 [a]I will hear what God the LORD will speak: for [b]he will speak peace unto his people, and to his saints: but let them not [c]turn again to folly.

9 Surely [a]his salvation *is* nigh them that fear him; [b]that glory may dwell in our land. M L

10 Mercy and truth are met together; [a]righteousness and peace have kissed *each other.*

11 Truth shall spring out of the earth; and righteousness shall look down from heaven.

12 [a]Yea, the LORD shall give *that which is* good; and our land shall yield her increase. B

13 [a]Righteousness shall go before him; and shall set *us* in the way of his steps.

I *Ps 80:19* ◀▶ *Ps 87:3*
L *Ps 78:38–39* ◀▶ *Ps 85:9–10*
M *Ps 82:8* ◀▶ *Ps 86:9*
L *Ps 85:2–3* ◀▶ *Ps 86:5*
B *Ps 67:6* ◀▶ *Ps 107:38*

85:1–13 This psalm recalls God's powerful deeds and his past faithfulness to help bring hope in a difficult time. In the Millennium, people will enjoy the blessings of God's victory again as the Messiah overcomes the nations that have resisted God's commands. This victory will allow for the proclamation of his righteousness among the captive nations.

Prayer for deliverance

[1]A Prayer of David.

86 BOW DOWN thine ear, O LORD, hear me: for I *am* poor and needy.
2 Preserve my soul; for I *am* [1]holy: O thou my God, save thy servant that trusteth in thee.
3 [a]Be merciful unto me, O Lord: for I cry unto thee [1]daily.
4 Rejoice the soul of thy servant: [a]for unto thee, O Lord, do I lift up my soul.
L 5 [a]For thou, Lord, *art* good, and ready
W to forgive; and plenteous in mercy unto all them that call upon thee.
6 Give ear, O LORD, unto my prayer; and attend to the voice of my supplications.
L 7 In the day of my trouble I will call upon thee: for thou wilt answer me.
8 [a]Among the gods *there is* none like unto thee, O Lord; [b]neither *are there any works* like unto thy works.
M 9 [a]All nations whom thou hast made shall come and worship before thee, O Lord; and shall glorify thy name.
10 For thou *art* great, and [a]doest wondrous things: [b]thou *art* God alone.
11 [a]Teach me thy way, O LORD; I will walk in thy truth: unite my heart to fear thy name.
12 I will praise thee, O Lord my God, with all my heart: and I will glorify thy name for evermore.
H 13 For great *is* thy mercy toward me: and thou hast delivered my soul from the lowest [1]hell.
14 O God, the proud are risen against me, and the assemblies of [1]violent *men* have sought after my soul; and have not set thee before them.
L 15 [a]But thou, O Lord, *art* a God full of compassion, and gracious, longsuffering, and plenteous in mercy and truth.

86:1 [1]Or, *A Prayer,* being a Psalm *of David*
2 [1]Or, *one whom thou favourest*
3 [a]Ps. 56:1 & 57:1 [1]Or, *all the day*
4 [a]Ps. 25:1 & 143:8
5 [a]Ps. 130:7 & 145:9; Joel 2:13
8 [a]Ex. 15:11; Ps. 89:6 [b]Deut. 3:24
9 [a]Ps. 22:31; Is. 43:7; Rev. 15:4
10 [a]Ex. 15:11; Ps. 72:18 [b]Deut. 6:4; Mark 12:29
11 [a]Ps. 25:4
13 [1]Or, *grave*
14 [1]Heb. *terrible*
15 [a]Ex. 34:6; Neh. 9:17; Ps. 103:8; Joel 2:13
87:1 [1]Or, *of*
2 [a]Ps. 78:68
3 [a]See Is. 60
6 [a]Ezek. 13:9
88:1 [a]1 Ki. 4:31; 1 Chr. 2:6 [b]Ps. 27:9 [1]Or, *of* [2]Or, *A Psalm of Heman the Ezrahite, giving instruction*
3 [a]Ps. 107:18
4 [a]Ps. 28:1

16 O turn unto me, and have mercy upon me; give thy strength unto thy servant, and save the son of thine handmaid.
17 Show me a token for good; that they which hate me may see *it,* and be ashamed: because thou, LORD, hast helped me, and comforted me.

Privileges of living in Zion

A Psalm *or* Song [1]for the sons of Korah.

87 HIS FOUNDATION *is* in the holy mountains.
2 [a]The LORD loveth the gates of Zion more than all the dwellings of Jacob.
3 [a]Glorious things are spoken of thee, I
O city of God. Selah.
4 I will make mention of Rahab and J
Babylon to them that know me: behold Philistia, and Tyre, with Ethiopia; this *man* was born there.
5 And of Zion it shall be said, This and I
that man was born in her: and the highest himself shall establish her.
6 The LORD shall count, when he [a]writ- E
eth up the people, *that* this *man* was born there. Selah.
7 As well the singers as the players on instruments *shall be there:* all my springs *are* in thee.

Prayer in the face of death

A Song *or* Psalm [1]for the sons of Korah, to the chief Musician upon Mahalath Leannoth, [2]Maschil of [a]Heman the Ezrahite.

88 O LORD [b]God of my salvation, I have cried day *and* night before thee:
2 Let my prayer come before thee: incline thine ear unto my cry;
3 For my soul is full of troubles: and my life [a]draweth nigh unto the grave.
4 [a]I am counted with them that go down into the pit: I am as a man *that hath* no strength:
5 Free among the dead, like the slain

L *Ps 85:9–10* ◀▶ *Ps 86:15*
W *Ps 50:1* ◀▶ *Ps 145:9*
L *Ps 81:10* ◀▶ *Ps 90:1*
M *Ps 85:9–13* ◀▶ *Ps 89:3–4*
H *Ps 83:17* ◀▶ *Ps 92:7*
L *Ps 86:5* ◀▶ *Ps 99:8*

I *Ps 85:1–13* ◀▶ *Ps 87:5*
J *Ps 69:25* ◀▶ *Ecc 3:17–18*
I *Ps 87:3* ◀▶ *Ps 94:14*
E *Ps 69:5* ◀▶ *Ps 90:8*

86:9 David prophetically announced that humanity would finally repent of its sin and glorify God. This prophecy will not be fulfilled until the Millennium.

87:3–5 One day, in the Millennium, humanity will speak glorious things of Jerusalem. Note that at that time native-born citizens will have special honor and privileges.

that lie in the grave, whom thou rememberest no more: and they are [a]cut off [1]from thy hand.

6 Thou hast laid me in the lowest pit, in darkness, in the deeps.

7 Thy wrath lieth hard upon me, and [a]thou hast afflicted *me* with all thy waves. Selah.

8 [a]Thou hast put away mine acquaintance far from me; thou hast made me an abomination unto them: [b]*I am* shut up, and I cannot come forth.

9 [a]Mine eye mourneth by reason of affliction: LORD, [b]I have called daily upon thee, [c]I have stretched out my hands unto thee.

F 10 [a]Wilt thou show wonders to the dead? shall the dead arise *and* praise thee? Selah.

11 Shall thy lovingkindness be declared in the grave? *or* thy faithfulness in destruction?

12 [a]Shall thy wonders be known in the dark? and thy righteousness in the land of forgetfulness?

13 But unto thee have I cried, O LORD; and [a]in the morning shall my prayer prevent thee.

14 LORD, why castest thou off my soul? *why* [a]hidest thou thy face from me?

15 I *am* afflicted and ready to die from *my* youth up: *while* [a]I suffer thy terrors I am distracted.

16 Thy fierce wrath goeth over me; thy terrors have cut me off.

17 They came round about me [1]daily like water; they [a]compassed me about together.

18 [a]Lover and friend hast thou put far from me, *and* mine acquaintance into darkness.

F *Ps 71:20* ◀ ▶ *Isa 25:8*

5 [a]Is. 53:8 [1]*Or, by thy hand*
7 [a]Ps. 42:7
8 [a]Job 19:13 [b]Lam. 3:7
9 [a]Ps. 38:10 [b]Ps. 86:3 [c]Ps. 143:6
10 [a]Ps. 6:5; Is. 38:18
12 [a]Job 10:21
13 [a]Ps. 5:3
14 [a]Job 13:24; Ps. 13:1
15 [a]Job 6:4
17 [a]Ps. 22:16 [1]*Or, all the day*
18 [a]Job 19:13
89:1 [a]1 Ki. 4:31; 1 Chr. 2:6 [b]Ps. 101:1 [c]ver. 4; Ps. 119:90 [1]Or, A Psalm *for Ethan the Ezrahite, to give instruction* [2]Heb. *to generation and generation*
2 [a]Ps. 119:89
3 [a]1 Ki. 8:16; 1 Chr. 28:4 [b]2 Sam. 7:13
4 [a]Luke 1:33
5 [a]Ps. 19:1
7 [a]Ps. 76:7,11
9 [a]Ps. 65:7
10 [a]Ps. 87:4 [1]*Or, Egypt* [2]Heb. *with the arm of thy strength*
11 [a]Gen. 1:1
12 [a]Josh. 19:22 [b]Josh. 12:1

God's covenant with David

[1]Maschil of [a]Ethan the Ezrahite.

89 I [b]WILL sing of the mercies of the LORD for ever: with my mouth will I make known thy faithfulness [c]to[2] all generations.

2 For I have said, Mercy shall be built up for ever: [a]thy faithfulness shalt thou establish in the very heavens.

3 [a]I have made a covenant with my chosen, I have [b]sworn unto David my servant, M

4 Thy seed will I establish for ever, and build up thy throne [a]to all generations. Selah.

5 And [a]the heavens shall praise thy wonders, O LORD: thy faithfulness also in the congregation of the saints.

6 For who in the heaven can be compared unto the LORD? *who* among the sons of the mighty can be likened unto the LORD?

7 [a]God is greatly to be feared in the assembly of the saints, and to be had in reverence of all *them that are* about him.

8 O LORD God of hosts, who *is* a strong LORD like unto thee? or to thy faithfulness round about thee?

9 [a]Thou rulest the raging of the sea: when the waves thereof arise, thou stillest them.

10 [a]Thou hast broken [1]Rahab in pieces, as one that is slain; thou hast scattered thine enemies [2]with thy strong arm.

11 [a]The heavens *are* thine, the earth also *is* thine: *as for* the world and the fulness thereof, thou hast founded them.

12 The north and the south thou hast created them: [a]Tabor and [b]Hermon shall rejoice in thy name.

M *Ps 86:9* ◀ ▶ *Ps 89:26–32*

88:10–12 This psalm expressed a cry of abandonment from one who felt the heavy hand of God's judgment on Israel. The Scriptures often record the deep emotions of the godly as they face struggles. Yet other passages provide God's answer to those questions of the heart: In everything God reigns supreme, "For the LORD of hosts hath purposed, and who shall disannul it?" (Isa 14:27).

89:3–4 Though it appeared that God had violated his covenant with David in allowing his downfall, the Lord reconfirmed the unbreakable covenant that he had made centuries earlier with David (see note at 2Sa 7:16). In the NT, the apostle Peter reminded his listeners that God had promised by an oath to King David that "of the fruit of his loins, according to the flesh, he would raise up Christ to sit on his throne" (Ac 2:30). The genealogical records trace Jesus' line back to the throne of David (see Mt 1:1–16; Lk 3:23–38) giving him the legal status as David's descendant to rule from David's throne as the Messiah.

13 Thou hast [1]a mighty arm: strong is thy hand, *and* high is thy right hand.

14 Justice and judgment *are* the [1]habitation of thy throne: mercy and truth shall go before thy face.

K 15 Blessed *is* the people that know the
U [a]joyful sound: they shall walk, O LORD, in the light of thy countenance.

16 In thy name shall they rejoice all the day: and in thy righteousness shall they be exalted.

17 For thou *art* the glory of their strength: and in thy favour our horn shall be exalted.

18 For [a]the[1] LORD *is* our defence; and the Holy One of Israel *is* our king.

19 Then thou spakest in vision to thy holy one, and saidst, I have laid help upon *one that is* mighty; I have exalted *one* [a]chosen out of the people.

20 [a]I have found David my servant; with my holy oil have I anointed him:

21 [a]With whom my hand shall be established: mine arm also shall strengthen him.

V 22 [a]The enemy shall not exact upon him; nor the son of wickedness afflict him.

23 [a]And I will beat down his foes before his face, and plague them that hate him.

24 But [a]my faithfulness and my mercy *shall be* with him: and in my name shall his horn be exalted.

25 I will set his hand also in the sea, and his right hand in the rivers.

M 26 He shall cry unto me, Thou *art* [a]my father, my God, and [b]the rock of my salvation.

27 Also I will make him [a]*my* firstborn, [b]higher than the kings of the earth.

28 [a]My mercy will I keep for him for evermore, and my covenant shall stand fast with him.

K *Ps 84:11* ◀▶ *Ps 91:3*
U *Ps 84:10–12* ◀▶ *Ps 91:1–16*
V *Ps 81:13–14* ◀▶ *Ps 91:1–16*
M *Ps 89:3–4* ◀▶ *Ps 89:35–37*

13 [1]Heb. *an arm with might*
14 [1]Or, *establishment*
15 [a]Ps. 98:6
18 [a]Ps. 47:9 [1]Or, *our shield is of the LORD, and our king is of the Holy One of Israel*
19 [a]1 Ki. 11:34
20 [a]1 Sam. 16:1
21 [a]Ps. 80:17
22 [a]2 Sam. 7:10
23 [a]2 Sam. 7:9
24 [a]2 Sam. 7:15
26 [a]1 Chr. 22:10 [b]2 Sam. 22:47
27 [a]Col. 1:15 [b]Num. 24:7
28 [a]Is. 55:3
29 [a]Jer. 33:17 [b]Deut. 11:21
30 [a]2 Sam. 7:14 [b]Ps. 119:53; Jer. 9:13
31 [1]Heb. *profane my statutes*
32 [a]2 Sam. 7:14
33 [a]2 Sam. 7:15 [1]Heb. *I will not make void from him* [2]Heb. *to lie*
35 [a]Amos 4:2 [1]Heb. *if I lie*
36 [a]Luke 1:33 [b]Ps. 72:17
38 [a]1 Chr. 28:9 [b]Deut. 32:19
39 [a]Lam. 5:16
41 [a]Ps. 44:13
44 [1]Heb. *brightness*
46 [a]Ps. 79:5

29 His seed also will I make *to endure* for ever, [a]and his throne [b]as the days of heaven.

30 [a]If his children [b]forsake my law, T
and walk not in my judgments;

31 If they [1]break my statutes, and keep not my commandments;

32 Then [a]will I visit their transgression with the rod, and their iniquity with stripes.

33 [a]Nevertheless my lovingkindness [1]will I not utterly take from him, nor suffer my faithfulness [2]to fail.

34 My covenant will I not break, nor alter the thing that is gone out of my lips.

35 Once have I sworn [a]by my holiness M
[1]that I will not lie unto David.

36 [a]His seed shall endure for ever, and his throne [b]as the sun before me.

37 It shall be established for ever as the moon, and *as* a faithful witness in heaven. Selah.

38 But thou hast [a]cast off and [b]abhorred, thou hast been wroth with thine anointed.

39 Thou hast made void the covenant of thy servant: [a]thou hast profaned his crown *by casting it* to the ground.

40 Thou hast broken down all his hedges; thou hast brought his strong holds to ruin.

41 All that pass by the way spoil him: he is [a]a reproach to his neighbours.

42 Thou hast set up the right hand of his adversaries; thou hast made all his enemies to rejoice.

43 Thou hast also turned the edge of his sword, and hast not made him to stand in the battle.

44 Thou hast made his [1]glory to cease, and cast his throne down to the ground.

45 The days of his youth hast thou shortened: thou hast covered him with shame. Selah.

46 [a]How long, LORD? wilt thou hide

T *Ps 66:10–12* ◀▶ *Ps 94:12–13*
M *Ps 89:26–32* ◀▶ *Ps 93:1–2*

89:27–29 Note the similarity between this prophecy about the Messiah as God's "firstborn, higher than the kings of the earth" (89:27) and the description of Jesus Christ as "the image of the invisible God, the firstborn of every creature" (Col 1:15) and "his only begotten Son" (Jn 3:16).

89:34–37 The Lord reconfirmed his unbreakable covenant with David and his descendants. However, he warned David's descendants that disobedience to God's laws would be punished severely. The downward spiral of Israel's refusal to repent and return to worship God resulted in the division of David's kingdom (see 1Ki 11:26–40) and the Assyrian and Babylonian captivities.

thyself for ever? shall thy wrath burn like
fire?
47 [a]Remember how short my time is:
wherefore hast thou made all men in
vain?
N 48 [a]What man *is he that* liveth, and
shall not [b]see death? shall he deliver his
soul from the hand of the grave? Selah.
49 Lord, where *are* thy former lovingkindnesses, *which* thou [a]swarest unto
David [b]in thy truth?
50 Remember, Lord, the reproach of
thy servants; [a]*how* I do bear in my bosom
the reproach of all the mighty people;
51 [a]Wherewith thine enemies have
reproached, O LORD; wherewith they
have reproached the footsteps of thine
anointed.
52 [a]Blessed *be* the LORD for evermore.
Amen, and Amen.

Book IV

Eternal God and mortal man

[1]A Prayer [a]of Moses the man of God.

L **90** LORD, [b]THOU hast been our
dwellingplace [2]in all generations.
2 [a]Before the mountains were brought
forth, or ever thou hadst formed the earth
and the world, even from everlasting to
everlasting, thou *art* God.
3 Thou turnest man to destruction;
and sayest, [a]Return, ye children of men.
4 [a]For a thousand years in thy sight *are*
but as yesterday [1]when it is past, and *as* a
watch in the night.
N 5 Thou carriest them away as with a
flood; [a]they are *as* a sleep: in the morning
[b]*they are* like grass *which* [1]groweth up.

N *Ps 78:39* ◀▶ *Ps 90:5–6*
L *Ps 86:7* ◀▶ *Ps 91:1–16*
N *Ps 89:48* ◀▶ *Ps 90:9*

47 [a]Job 7:7
48 [a]Ps. 49:9 [b]Heb. 11:5
49 [a]2 Sam. 7:15 [b]Ps. 54:5
50 [a]Ps. 69:9,19
51 [a]Ps. 74:22
52 [a]Ps. 41:13
90:1 [a]Deut. 33:1 [b]Ezek. 11:16 [1]Or, *A Prayer,* being a Psalm *of Moses* [2]Heb. *in generation and generation*
2 [a]Prov. 8:25
3 [a]Gen. 3:19
4 [a]2 Pet. 3:8 [1]Or, *when he hath passed* them
5 [a]Ps. 73:20 [b]Is. 40:6 [1]Or, *is changed*
8 [a]Ps. 50:21 [b]Ps. 19:12
9 [1]Heb. *turned away* [2]Or, *as a meditation*
10 [1]Heb. As for *the days of our years, in them* are *seventy years*
12 [a]Ps. 39:4 [1]Heb. *cause to come*
13 [a]Deut. 32:36; Ps. 135:14
14 [a]Ps. 85:6
16 [a]Hab. 3:2
17 [a]Ps. 27:4 [b]Is. 26:12

6 In the morning it flourisheth, and
groweth up; in the evening it is cut
down, and withereth.
7 For we are consumed by thine anger,
and by thy wrath are we troubled.
8 [a]Thou hast set our iniquities before E
thee, our [b]secret *sins* in the light of thy
countenance.
9 For all our days are [1]passed away in N
thy wrath: we spend our years [2]as a tale
that is told.
10 [1]The days of our years *are* threescore years and ten; and if by reason of
strength *they be* fourscore years, yet *is*
their strength labour and sorrow; for it is
soon cut off, and we fly away.
11 Who knoweth the power of thine
anger? even according to thy fear, *so is*
thy wrath.
12 [a]So teach *us* to number our days, N
that we may [1]apply *our* hearts unto
wisdom.
13 Return, O LORD, how long? and
let it [a]repent thee concerning thy
servants.
14 O satisfy us early with thy mercy;
[a]that we may rejoice and be glad all our
days.
15 Make us glad according to the days
wherein thou hast afflicted us, *and* the
years *wherein* we have seen evil.
16 Let [a]thy work appear unto thy
servants, and thy glory unto their
children.
17 [a]And let the beauty of the LORD our
God be upon us: and [b]establish thou the
work of our hands upon us; yea, the work
of our hands establish thou it.

E *Ps 87:6* ◀▶ *Ps 94:7–11*
N *Ps 90:5–6* ◀▶ *Ps 90:12*
N *Ps 90:9* ◀▶ *Ps 95:8*

90:4 The eternal God is not bound by our sense of time; one thousand years to him is but one day. In the NT the apostle Peter also reminded believers of this view of time (see 2Pe 3:8). These verses have prompted various interpretations. Some early church scholars taught that the relationship of one day to a thousand years could be used to determine a Biblical timeline. They believed that the six days of creation symbolized six thousand years of humanity's dominion on earth and concluded that the Sabbath day of rest was a symbol for the peaceful Millennium.

While this theory was widely taught in the early church, Scripture warns against any dogmatic declarations of when certain Biblical events will occur because "of that day and that hour knoweth no man, no, not the angels which are in heaven, neither the Son, but the Father" (Mk 13:32). Instead, we should be watchful and aware of the prophecies in Scripture, looking for their fulfillment, so that "when these things begin to come to pass" we can then "look up, and lift up your heads; for your redemption draweth nigh" (Lk 21:28). Until our Lord returns and the trumpet calls us to meet him in the air, we should be actively going about his business so that he will number us among his faithful servants (see Mt 25:21; Col 3:17; 2Ti 4:8).

The security of the godly

L S U V **91** HE [a]THAT dwelleth in the secret place of the most High shall [1]abide [b]under the shadow of the Almighty.

2 [a]I will say of the LORD, *He is* my refuge and my fortress: my God; in him will I trust.

K H 3 Surely [a]he shall deliver thee from the snare of the fowler, *and* from the noisome pestilence.

4 [a]He shall cover thee with his feathers, and under his wings shalt thou trust: his truth *shall be thy* shield and buckler.

H J W 5 [a]Thou shalt not be afraid for the terror by night; *nor* for the arrow *that* flieth by day;

6 *Nor* for the pestilence *that* walketh in darkness; *nor* for the destruction *that* wasteth at noonday.

7 A thousand shall fall at thy side, and ten thousand at thy right hand; *but* it shall not come nigh thee.

8 Only [a]with thine eyes shalt thou behold and see the reward of the wicked.

9 Because thou hast made the LORD, *which is* [a]my refuge, *even* the most High, [b]thy habitation;

A H 10 [a]There shall no evil befall thee, neither shall any plague come nigh thy dwelling.

K 11 [a]For he shall give his angels charge over thee, to keep thee in all thy ways.

12 They shall bear thee up in *their* hands, [a]lest thou dash thy foot against a stone.

13 Thou shalt tread upon the lion and [1]adder: the young lion and the dragon shalt thou trample under feet.

14 Because he hath set his love upon me, therefore will I deliver him: I will set him on high, because he hath [a]known my name.

15 [a]He shall call upon me, and I will answer him: [b]I *will be* with him in trouble; I will deliver him, and [c]honour him.

16 With [a]long[1] life will I satisfy him, and show him my salvation. H

Praise for the LORD's goodness

A Psalm *or* Song for the sabbath day.

92 *IT IS a* [a]good *thing* to give thanks unto the LORD, and to sing praises unto thy name, O most High:

2 To [a]show forth thy lovingkindness in the morning, and thy faithfulness [1]every night,

3 [a]Upon an instrument of ten strings, and upon the psaltery; [1]upon the harp with [2]a solemn sound.

4 For thou, LORD, hast made me glad through thy work: I will triumph in the works of thy hands.

5 [a]O LORD, how great are thy works! *and* [b]thy thoughts are very deep.

6 [a]A brutish man knoweth not; neither doth a fool understand this.

7 When [a]the wicked spring as the grass, and when all the workers of iniquity do flourish; *it is* that they shall be destroyed for ever: H

8 [a]But thou, LORD, *art most* high for evermore.

9 For, lo, thine enemies, O LORD, for, lo, thine enemies shall perish; all the workers of iniquity shall [a]be scattered. K

10 But [a]my horn shalt thou exalt like *the horn of* an unicorn: I shall be [b]anointed with fresh oil.

11 [a]Mine eye also shall see *my desire* on mine enemies, *and* mine ears shall hear *my desire* of the wicked that rise up against me.

12 [a]The righteous shall flourish like the palm tree: he shall grow like a cedar in Lebanon.

13 Those that be planted in the house of the LORD shall flourish [a]in the courts of our God.

14 They shall still bring forth fruit in

91:1 [a]Ps. 31:20 [b]Ps. 17:8 [1]Heb. *lodge*
2 [a]Ps. 142:5
3 [a]Ps. 124:7
4 [a]Ps. 17:8
5 [a]Job 5:19; Ps. 112:7; Prov. 3:23; Is. 43:2
8 [a]Mal. 1:5
9 [a]ver. 2 [b]Ps. 90:1
10 [a]Prov. 12:21
11 [a]Ps. 34:7 & 71:3; Mat. 4:6; Luke 4:10; Heb. 1:14
12 [a]Job 5:23; Ps. 37:24
13 [1]Or, *asp*
14 [a]Ps. 9:10
15 [a]Ps. 50:15 [b]Is. 43:2 [c]1 Sam. 2:30
16 [a]Prov. 3:2 [1]Heb. *length of days*
92:1 [a]Ps. 147:1
2 [a]Ps. 89:1 [1]Heb. *in the nights*
3 [a]1 Chr. 23:5; Ps. 33:2 [1]Or, *upon the solemn sound with the harp* [2]Heb. *Higgaion;* see Ps. 9:16
5 [a]Ps. 40:5 [b]Is. 28:29; Rom. 11:33
6 [a]Ps. 73:22
7 [a]Job 12:6 & 21:7; Ps. 37:1,2; Jer. 12:1,2; Mal. 3:15
8 [a]Ps. 83:18
9 [a]Ps. 68:1
10 [a]Ps. 89:17 [b]Ps. 23:5
11 [a]Ps. 54:7 & 59:10
12 [a]Ps. 52:8; Is. 65:22; Hos. 14:5,6
13 [a]Ps. 100:4

L *Ps 90:1* ◀▶ *Ps 94:18*
S *Ps 46:1* ◀▶ *Ps 118:6*
U *Ps 89:15–16* ◀▶ *Ps 97:10–12*
V *Ps 89:22–23* ◀▶ *Ps 97:10*
K *Ps 89:15–16* ◀▶ *Ps 91:11*
H *Ps 67:2* ◀▶ *Ps 91:5–7*
H *Ps 91:3* ◀▶ *Ps 91:10*
J *Ps 61:2–4* ◀▶ *Ps 112:7–8*
W *Ps 55:22* ◀▶ *Ps 112:7–8*
A *1Ki 2:3* ◀▶ *Ps 121:7*
H *Ps 91:5–7* ◀▶ *Ps 91:16*
K *Ps 91:3* ◀▶ *Ps 94:18*
H *Ps 91:10* ◀▶ *Ps 103:3*
H *Ps 86:13* ◀▶ *Ps 109:17–19*
K *Ps 10:16* ◀▶ *Ps 145:13*

92:9 This psalm was a song for the Sabbath that prophetically declared the certainty of God's judgment on "all the workers of iniquity."

old age; they shall be fat and [1]flourishing;
15 To show that the LORD *is* upright: [a]*he is* my rock, and [b]*there is* no unrighteousness in him.

The majesty of the LORD

M N 93 THE [a]LORD reigneth, [b]he is clothed with majesty; the LORD is clothed with strength, [c]*wherewith* he hath girded himself: the world also is stablished, that it cannot be moved.
2 [a]Thy throne *is* established [1]of old: thou *art* from everlasting.
3 The floods have lifted up, O LORD, the floods have lifted up their voice; the floods lift up their waves.
4 [a]The LORD on high *is* mightier than the noise of many waters, *yea, than* the mighty waves of the sea.
S 5 Thy testimonies are very sure: holiness becometh thine house, O LORD, [1]for ever.

An appeal for God to avenge

P 94 O LORD [1]God, [a]to whom vengeance belongeth; O God, to whom vengeance belongeth, [2]shew thyself.
2 [a]Lift up thyself, thou [b]judge of the earth: render a reward to the proud.
3 LORD, [a]how long shall the wicked, how long shall the wicked triumph?
4 *How long* shall they [a]utter *and* speak hard things? *and* all the workers of iniquity boast themselves?
5 They break in pieces thy people, O LORD, and afflict thine heritage.
6 They slay the widow and the stranger, and murder the fatherless.
E 7 [a]Yet they say, The LORD shall not see, neither shall the God of Jacob regard *it.*
8 [a]Understand, ye brutish among the people: and *ye* fools, when will ye be wise?
9 [a]He that planted the ear, shall he not hear? he that formed the eye, shall he not see?
10 He that chastiseth the heathen, shall not he correct? he that [a]teacheth man knowledge, *shall not he know?*
11 [a]The LORD knoweth the thoughts of man, that they *are* vanity. C
12 [a]Blessed *is* the man whom thou chastenest, O LORD, and teachest him out of thy law; T
13 That thou mayest give him rest from the days of adversity, until the pit be digged for the wicked.
14 [a]For the LORD will not cast off his people, neither will he forsake his inheritance. I
15 But judgment shall return unto righteousness: and all the upright in heart [1]shall follow it.
16 Who will rise up for me against the evildoers? *or* who will stand up for me against the workers of iniquity?
17 [a]Unless the LORD *had been* my help, my soul had [1]almost dwelt in silence.
18 When I said, [a]My foot slippeth; thy mercy, O LORD, held me up. K L
19 In the multitude of my thoughts within me thy comforts delight my soul.
20 Shall [a]the throne of iniquity have fellowship with thee, which [b]frameth mischief by a law?
21 [a]They gather themselves together against the soul of the righteous, and [b]condemn the innocent blood.
22 But the LORD is [a]my defence; and my God *is* the rock of my refuge.
23 And [a]he shall bring upon them their own iniquity, and shall cut them off in their own wickedness; *yea,* the LORD our God shall cut them off.

14 [1]Heb. *green*
15 [a]Deut. 32:4 [b]Rom. 9:14
93:1 [a]Ps. 96:10 & 97:1; Is. 52:7; Rev. 19:6 [b]Ps. 104:1 [c]Ps. 65:6
2 [a]Ps. 45:6; Prov. 8:22 [1]Heb. *from then*
4 [a]Ps. 65:7 & 89:9
5 [1]Heb. *to length of days*
94:1 [a]Nah. 1:2 [1]Heb. *God of revenges* [2]Heb. *shine forth;* see Ps. 80:1
2 [a]Ps. 7:6 [b]Gen. 18:25
3 [a]Job 20:5
4 [a]Ps. 31:18; Jude 15
7 [a]Ps. 10:11
8 [a]Ps. 73:22 & 92:6
9 [a]Ex. 4:11
10 [a]Job 35:11; Is. 28:26
11 [a]1 Cor. 3:20
12 [a]Job 5:17; Heb. 12:5
14 [a]1 Sam. 12:22; Rom. 11:1
15 [1]Heb. shall be *after it*
17 [a]Ps. 124:1,2 [1]Or, *quickly*
18 [a]Ps. 38:16
20 [a]Amos 6:3 [b]Is. 10:1
21 [a]Mat. 27:1 [b]Prov. 17:15
22 [a]Ps. 59:9
23 [a]Ps. 7:16; Prov. 2:22

M *Ps 89:35–37* ◀ ▶ *Ps 96:10–13*
N *Ps 78:69* ◀ ▶ *Ps 96:10*
S *Ps 73:27* ◀ ▶ *Ps 96:9*
P *Ps 83:13–17* ◀ ▶ *Ps 98:1–2*
E *Ps 90:8* ◀ ▶ *Ps 102:19*

C *Ps 74:22* ◀ ▶ *Ps 95:10*
T *Ps 89:30–33* ◀ ▶ *Ps 105:19*
I *Ps 87:5* ◀ ▶ *Ps 97:8*
K *Ps 91:11* ◀ ▶ *Ps 103:3–4*
L *Ps 91:1–16* ◀ ▶ *Ps 97:10*

93:1–2 This hymn of prophecy anticipated the glorious appearance of Jesus Christ as the reigning Messiah in the coming millennial kingdom.
94:1–4 This lament voiced the complaint of the writer as he witnessed the apparent victory of the wicked and prophetically called upon God to fulfill his promise of judgment.
94:14 The psalmist reconfirmed God's faithfulness to Israel and his guarantee that he will never forget his inheritance.

A call to praise the LORD

95 O COME, let us sing unto the LORD: [a]let us make a joyful noise to [b]the rock of our salvation.

2 Let us [1]come before his presence with thanksgiving, and make a joyful noise unto him with psalms.

3 For [a]the LORD *is* a great God, and a great King above all gods.

4 [1]In his hand *are* the deep places of the earth: [2]the strength of the hills *is* his also.

5 [a]The[1] sea *is* his, and he made it: and his hands formed the dry *land.*

6 O come, let us worship and bow down: let [a]us kneel before the LORD our maker.

7 For he *is* our God; and [a]we *are* the people of his pasture, and the sheep of his hand. [b]Today if ye will hear his voice,

N 8 Harden not your heart, [a]as in the [1]provocation, *and* as *in* the day of temptation in the wilderness:

9 When [a]your fathers tempted me, proved me, and [b]saw my work.

C 10 [a]Forty years long was I grieved with *this* generation, and said, It *is* a people that do err in their heart, and they have not known my ways:

11 Unto whom [a]I sware in my wrath [1]that they should not enter into my rest.

A call to worship the LORD

96 O [a]SING unto the LORD a new song: sing unto the LORD, all the earth.

2 Sing unto the LORD, bless his name; show forth his salvation from day to day.

3 Declare his glory among the heathen, his wonders among all people.

4 For [a]the LORD *is* great, and [b]greatly to be praised: [c]he *is* to be feared above all gods.

5 For [a]all the gods of the nations *are* idols: [b]but the LORD made the heavens.

6 Honour and majesty *are* before him: strength and [a]beauty *are* in his sanctuary.

7 [a]Give unto the LORD, O ye kindreds of the people, give unto the LORD glory and strength.

8 Give unto the LORD the glory [1]*due unto* his name: bring an offering, and come into his courts.

9 O worship the LORD [a]in[1] the beauty S
of holiness: fear before him, all the earth.

10 Say among the heathen *that* [a]the M
LORD reigneth: the world also shall be es- N
tablished that it shall not be moved: [b]he J
shall judge the people righteously.

11 [a]Let the heavens rejoice, and let the earth be glad; [b]let the sea roar, and the fulness thereof.

12 Let the field be joyful, and all that *is* D
therein: then shall all the trees of the wood rejoice

13 Before the LORD: for he cometh, for J
he cometh to judge the earth: [a]he shall judge the world with righteousness, and the people with his truth.

The LORD*'s power and dominion*

97 THE [a]LORD reigneth; let the M
earth rejoice; let the [1]multitude of [b]isles be glad *thereof.*

2 [a]Clouds and darkness *are* round C
about him: [b]righteousness and judgment *are* the [1]habitation of his throne.

3 [a]A fire goeth before him, and burneth up his enemies round about.

4 [a]His lightnings enlightened the world: the earth saw, and trembled.

5 [a]The hills melted like wax at the presence of the LORD, at the presence of the Lord of the whole earth.

6 [a]The heavens declare his righteousness, and all the people see his glory.

7 [a]Confounded be all they that serve graven images, that boast themselves of idols: [b]worship him, all *ye* gods.

95:1 [a]Ps. 100:1 [b]Deut. 32:15; 2 Sam. 22:47
2 [1]Heb. *prevent his face*
3 [a]Ps. 96:4
4 [1]Heb. *In whose* [2]Or, *the heights of the hills* are his
5 [a]Gen. 1:9,10 [1]Heb. *Whose the sea* is
6 [a]Phil. 2:10
7 [a]Ps. 79:13 & 100:3 [b]Heb. 3:7
8 [a]Ex. 17:2,7 [1]Heb. *contention*
9 [a]Ps. 78:18; 1 Cor. 10:9 [b]Num. 14:22
10 [a]Heb. 3:10
11 [a]Heb. 4:3,5 [1]Heb. *if they enter into my rest*
96:1 [a]1 Chr. 16:23-33
4 [a]Ps. 145:3 [b]Ps. 18:3 [c]Ps. 95:3
5 [a]Jer. 10:11 [b]Ps. 115:15; Is. 42:5
6 [a]Ps. 29:2
7 [a]Ps. 29:1,2
8 [1]Heb. *of his name*
9 [a]Ps. 29:2 [1]Or, *in the glorious sanctuary*
10 [a]Ps. 97:1 [b]Ps. 67:4
11 [a]Ps. 69:34 [b]Ps. 98:7
13 [a]Rev. 19:11
97:1 [a]Ps. 96:10 [b]Is. 60:9 [1]Heb. *many,* or, *great isles*
2 [a]Ps. 18:11 [b]Ps. 89:14 [1]Or, *establishment*
3 [a]Ps. 18:8
4 [a]Ex. 19:18
5 [a]Mic. 1:4
6 [a]Ps. 19:1
7 [a]Ex. 20:4; Lev. 26:1 [b]Heb. 1:6

N *Ps 90:12* ◀▶ *Ps 103:15–16*
C *Ps 94:11* ◀▶ *Ps 107:10*
S *Ps 93:5* ◀▶ *Ps 97:10*
M *Ps 93:1–2* ◀▶ *Ps 97:1*
N *Ps 93:1* ◀▶ *Ps 102:25–26*
J *Ps 67:4* ◀▶ *Ps 96:13*
D *Job 19:25* ◀▶ *Ps 98:9*
J *Ps 96:10* ◀▶ *Ps 98:9*
M *Ps 96:10–13* ◀▶ *Ps 98:3–9*
C ▶ *Ps 109:8*

96:10–13 This psalm reflects the universal joy that all nations will express when the Messiah "shall judge the people righteously" (96:10) and rule the earth from the throne of David with truth and justice.

97:1–8 This prophetic psalm describes the victory of the Messiah and prophesies about the battles that will defeat the armies of the antichrist, ushering in the millennial reign of Christ.

I 8 Zion heard, and was glad; and the daughters of Judah rejoiced because of thy judgments, O LORD.

9 For thou, LORD, *art* [a]high above all the earth: [b]thou art exalted far above all gods.

S 10 Ye that love the LORD, [a]hate evil:
L [b]he preserveth the souls of his saints; [c]he
U delivereth them out of the hand of the
V wicked.

11 [a]Light is sown for the righteous, and gladness for the upright in heart.

12 [a]Rejoice in the LORD, ye righteous; [b]and give thanks ʹat the remembrance of his holiness.

Praise to a righteous LORD

A Psalm.

P **98** O [a]SING unto the LORD a new song; for [b]he hath done marvellous things: [c]his right hand, and his holy arm, hath gotten him the victory.

2 [a]The LORD hath made known his salvation: [b]his righteousness hath he ʹopenly shown in the sight of the heathen.

I 3 He hath [a]remembered his mercy and
M his truth toward the house of Israel: [b]all the ends of the earth have seen the salvation of our God.

4 [a]Make a joyful noise unto the LORD, all the earth: make a loud noise, and rejoice, and sing praise.

5 Sing unto the LORD with the harp; with the harp, and the voice of a psalm.

6 [a]With trumpets and sound of cornet make a joyful noise before the LORD, the King.

7 Let the sea roar, and the fulness thereof; the world, and they that dwell therein.

8 Let the floods [a]clap *their* hands: let the hills be joyful together

I *Ps 94:14* ◀ ▶ *Ps 98:3*
S *Ps 96:9* ◀ ▶ *Ps 101:6–8*
L *Ps 94:18* ◀ ▶ *Ps 103:13*
U *Ps 91:1–16* ◀ ▶ *Ps 112:1–10*
V *Ps 91:1–16* ◀ ▶ *Ps 108:13*
P *Ps 94:1–4* ◀ ▶ *Ps 104:35*
I *Ps 97:8* ◀ ▶ *Ps 102:13–16*
M *Ps 97:1* ◀ ▶ *Ps 102:15–16*

9 [a]Ps. 83:18 [b]Ex. 18:11; Ps. 95:3
10 [a]Ps. 34:14; Amos 5:15 [b]Prov. 2:8 [c]Ps. 37:39; Dan. 3:28
11 [a]Job 22:28; Prov. 4:18
12 [a]Ps. 33:1 [b]Ps. 30:4 ʹOr, *to the memorial*
98:1 [a]Ps. 96:1; Is. 42:10 [b]Ex. 15:11; Ps. 77:14 [c]Ex. 15:6; Is. 63:5
2 [a]Is. 52:10; Luke 2:30 [b]Is. 62:2 ʹOr, *revealed*
3 [a]Luke 1:54 [b]Is. 49:6
4 [a]Ps. 95:1
6 [a]Num. 10:10
8 [a]Is. 55:12
9 [a]Ps. 96:10
99:1 [a]Ex. 25:22 ʹHeb. *stagger*
2 [a]Ps. 97:9
4 [a]Job 36:5-7
5 [a]Ps. 132:7 [b]Lev. 19:2 ʹOr, *it is holy*
6 [a]Jer. 15:1 [b]Ex. 14:15; 1 Sam. 7:9
7 [a]Ex. 33:9
8 [a]Num. 14:20 [b]Deut. 9:20
9 [a]Ps. 34:3
100:1 [a]Ps. 145, title [b]Ps. 95:1 ʹOr, *thanksgiving* ²Heb. *all the earth*
3 [a]Eph. 2:10 [b]Ezek. 34:31 ʹOr, *and his we are*
4 [a]Ps. 116:17
5 [a]Ps. 136:1

9 Before the LORD; [a]for he cometh to D
judge the earth: with righteousness shall J
he judge the world, and the people with equity.

Praise to a holy God

99 THE LORD reigneth; let the people tremble: [a]he sitteth *between* the cherubims; let the earth ʹbe moved.

2 The LORD *is* great in Zion; and he *is* [a]high above all the people.

3 Let them praise thy great and terrible name; *for* it *is* holy.

4 [a]The king's strength also loveth judgment; thou dost establish equity, thou executest judgment and righteousness in Jacob.

5 Exalt ye the LORD our God, and worship at [a]his footstool; *for* [b]heʹ *is* holy.

6 [a]Moses and Aaron among his priests, and Samuel among them that call upon his name; they [b]called upon the LORD, and he answered them.

7 [a]He spake unto them in the cloudy pillar: they kept his testimonies, and the ordinance *that* he gave them.

8 Thou answeredst them, O LORD our L
God: [a]thou wast a God that forgavest them, though [b]thou tookest vengeance of their inventions.

9 [a]Exalt the LORD our God, and worship at his holy hill; for the LORD our God *is* holy.

A song of praise and joy

[a]A Psalm of ʹpraise.

100 MAKE [b]A joyful noise unto the LORD, ²all ye lands.

2 Serve the LORD with gladness: come before his presence with singing.

3 Know ye that the LORD he *is* God: [a]*it is* he *that* hath made us, ʹand not we ourselves; [b]*we are* his people, and the sheep of his pasture.

4 [a]Enter into his gates with thanksgiving, *and* into his courts with praise: be thankful unto him, *and* bless his name.

5 For the LORD *is* good; [a]his mercy *is*

D *Ps 96:12–13* ◀ ▶ *SS 8:5*
J *Ps 96:13* ◀ ▶ *Ecc 3:17*
L *Ps 86:15* ◀ ▶ *Ps 102:19–20*

98:1–9 The beginning and ending of this psalm echoes Ps 96 in its description of humanity's joy at the establishment of Christ's righteous government in the millennial kingdom.

everlasting; and his truth *endureth* [b]to [l]
all generations.

A perfect heart

A Psalm of David.

101 I WILL sing of mercy and
judgment: unto thee, O LORD,
will I sing.
2 I will [a]behave myself wisely in a perfect way. O when wilt thou come unto
me? I will [b]walk within my house with a
perfect heart.
3 I will set no [l]wicked thing before
mine eyes: [a]I hate the work of them [b]that
turn aside; *it* shall not cleave to me.
4 A froward heart shall depart from
me: I will not [a]know a wicked *person.*
5 Whoso privily slandereth his neighbour, him will I cut off: [a]him that hath an
high look and a proud heart will not I
suffer.
S 6 Mine eyes *shall be* upon the faithful
of the land, that they may dwell with me:
he that walketh [l]in a perfect way, he
shall serve me.
7 He that worketh deceit shall not
dwell within my house: he that telleth
lies [l]shall not tarry in my sight.
8 I will [a]early destroy all the wicked of
the land; that I may cut off all wicked
doers [b]from the city of the LORD.

God's years and man's days

A Prayer [l]of the afflicted, [a]when he is overwhelmed, and poureth out his complaint before the LORD.

102 HEAR MY prayer, O LORD, and
let my cry [b]come unto thee.
2 [a]Hide not thy face from me in the
day *when* I am in trouble; [b]incline thine
ear unto me: in the day *when* I call answer me speedily.
3 [a]For my days are consumed [l]like
smoke, and [b]my bones are burned as an
hearth.
4 My heart is smitten, and [a]withered
like grass; so that I forget to eat my bread.
5 By reason of the voice of my groaning [a]my bones cleave to my [l]skin.
6 [a]I am like [b]a pelican of the wilderness: I am like an owl of the desert.
7 I [a]watch, and am as a sparrow [b]alone
upon the house top.
8 Mine enemies reproach me all the
day; *and* they that are [a]mad against me
are [b]sworn against me.
9 For I have eaten ashes like bread,
and [a]mingled my drink with weeping,
10 Because of thine indignation and
thy wrath: for [a]thou hast lifted me up,
and cast me down.
11 [a]My days *are* like a shadow that declineth; and [b]I am withered like grass.
12 But [a]thou, O LORD, shalt endure for
ever; and [b]thy remembrance unto all generations.
13 Thou shalt arise, *and* [a]have mercy I
upon Zion: for the time to favour her,
yea, the [b]set time, is come.
14 For thy servants take pleasure in
[a]her stones, and favour the dust thereof.
15 So the heathen shall [a]fear the name M
of the LORD, and all the kings of the earth
thy glory.
16 When the LORD shall build up Zion,
[a]he shall appear in his glory.
17 [a]He will regard the prayer of the
destitute, and not despise their prayer.
18 This shall be [a]written for the generation to come: and [b]the people which
shall be created shall praise the LORD.
19 For he hath [a]looked down from the E
L

5 [b]Ps. 89:1 [l]Heb. *to generation and generation*
101:2 [a]1 Sam. 18:14 [b]1 Ki. 11:4
3 [a]Ps. 97:10 [b]Josh. 23:6 [l]Heb. *thing of Belial*
4 [a]Ps. 119:115
5 [a]Prov. 6:17
6 [l]Or, *perfect in the way*
7 [l]Heb. *shall not be established*
8 [a]Ps. 75:10; Jer. 21:12 [b]Ps. 48:2,8
102:1 [a]Ps. 61:2 [b]Ps. 18:6 [l]Or, *for*
2 [a]Ps. 69:17 [b]Ps. 71:2
3 [a]Jas. 4:14 [b]Job 30:30; Ps. 31:10 [l]Or, (as some read) *into smoke*
4 [a]Ps. 37:2
5 [a]Job 19:20 [l]Or, *flesh*
6 [a]Job 30:29 [b]Is. 34:11
7 [a]Ps. 77:4 [b]Ps. 38:11
8 [a]Acts 26:11 [b]Acts 23:12
9 [a]Ps. 42:3
10 [a]Ps. 30:7
11 [a]Eccl. 6:12 [b]Is. 40:6-8; Jas. 1:10
12 [a]Ps. 9:7 [b]Ps. 135:13
13 [a]Is. 60:10 [b]Is. 40:2
14 [a]Ps. 79:1
15 [a]1 Ki. 8:43
16 [a]Is. 60:1,2
17 [a]Neh. 1:6
18 [a]Rom. 15:4 [b]Ps. 22:31
19 [a]Deut. 26:15

S *Ps 97:10* ◀ ▶ *Ps 119:1–3*

I *Ps 98:3* ◀ ▶ *Ps 102:21–22*
M *Ps 98:3–9* ◀ ▶ *Ps 102:22*
E *Ps 94:7–11* ◀ ▶ *Ps 139:1–16*
L *Ps 99:8* ◀ ▶ *Ps 103:1–4*

102:13–18 Several different interpretations have been given for this passage. Some scholars suggest that these verses pertain to our time. They suggest that Christ will return in our generation, basing their belief on the phrase "the set time, is come" (102:13) and citing the increase of modern-day Israel's interest in archeology as a prophetic fulfillment of "thy servants take pleasure in her stones, and favour the dust thereof" (102:14). Other scholars view these verses as prophecies from the time of the exile, noting that after seventy years of Babylonian captivity God's "set time" had transpired and the exiles could now return to the city that meant so much to them.

Still others view this psalm as a prophecy about the millennial kingdom and the eternal King who will hear the prayer of the destitute and restore Zion. These scholars note that though the promised land has experienced an influx of returning Jews in our century and that Jerusalem is being restored to her former strength and beauty, these verses will find their full expression in the new Jerusalem of Christ's millennial kingdom (see Rev 21).

height of his sanctuary; from heaven did
the LORD behold the earth;
20 [a]To hear the groaning of the prisoner; to loose ʹthose that are appointed
to death;
I 21 To [a]declare the name of the LORD in
Zion, and his praise in Jerusalem;
M 22 When the people are gathered together, and the kingdoms, to serve the
LORD.
23 He ʹweakened my strength in the
way; he [a]shortened my days.
24 [a]I said, O my God, take me not
away in the midst of my days: [b]thy years
are throughout all generations.
N 25 [a]Of old hast thou laid the foundation of the earth: and the heavens *are* the
work of thy hands.
26 [a]They shall perish, but thou shalt
ʹendure: yea, all of them shall wax old
like a garment; as a vesture shalt thou
change them, and they shall be changed:
27 But [a]thou *art* the same, and thy
years shall have no end.
R 28 [a]The children of thy servants shall
continue, and their seed shall be established before thee.

The benefits of the LORD

A Psalm of David.

L 103 BLESS [a]THE LORD, O my soul:
and all that is within me,
bless his holy name.
2 Bless the LORD, O my soul, and forget
not all his benefits:
K 3 [a]Who forgiveth all thine iniquities;
E who [b]healeth all thy diseases;
H 4 Who redeemeth thy life from destruction; [a]who crowneth thee with lovingkindness and tender mercies;
F 5 Who satisfieth thy mouth with good
H

I Ps 102:13–16 ◀▶ Ps 105:8–11
M Ps 102:15–16 ◀▶ Ps 110:1–7
N Ps 96:10 ◀▶ Ps 104:5
R Ps 37:26 ◀▶ Ps 103:17–18
L Ps 102:19–20 ◀▶ Ps 103:8–14
K Ps 94:18 ◀▶ Ps 103:12
E Ps 30:2–3 ◀▶ Ps 105:37
H Ps 91:16 ◀▶ Ps 103:5
F Ps 81:16 ◀▶ Ps 105:40–41
H Ps 103:3 ◀▶ Ps 113:9

things; so that [a]thy youth is renewed like
the eagle's.
6 The LORD executeth righteousness
and judgment for all that are oppressed.
7 [a]He made known his ways unto Moses, his acts unto the children of Israel.
8 [a]The LORD *is* merciful and gracious, L
slow to anger, and ʹplenteous in mercy.
9 [a]He will not always chide: neither
will he keep *his anger* for ever.
10 [a]He hath not dealt with us after our
sins; nor rewarded us according to our
iniquities.
11 For ʹas the heaven is high above
the earth, *so* great is his mercy toward
them that fear him.
12 As far as the east is from the west, K
so far hath he [a]removed our transgressions from us.
13 [a]Like as a father pitieth *his* chil- L
dren, *so* the LORD pitieth them that fear
him.
14 For he knoweth our frame; he remembereth that we *are* [a]dust.
15 *As for* man, [a]his days *are* as grass: N
[b]as a flower of the field, so he flourisheth.
16 For the wind passeth over it, and ʹit
is gone; and [a]the place thereof shall
know it no more.
17 But the mercy of the LORD *is* from L
everlasting to everlasting upon them that L
fear him, and his righteousness unto chil- R
dren's children;
18 [a]To such as keep his covenant, and
to those that remember his commandments to do them.
19 The LORD hath prepared his throne
in the heavens; and [a]his kingdom ruleth
over all.
20 [a]Bless the LORD, ye his angels, ʹthat
excel in strength, that [b]do his commandments, hearkening unto the voice of his
word.
21 Bless ye the LORD, all *ye* [a]his hosts;

L Ps 103:1–4 ◀▶ Ps 103:17
K Ps 103:3–4 ◀▶ Ps 107:14
L Ps 97:10 ◀▶ Ps 103:17–18
N Ps 95:8 ◀▶ Ps 144:4
L Ps 103:8–14 ◀▶ Ps 107:9
L Ps 103:13 ◀▶ Ps 105:14–15
R Ps 102:28 ◀▶ Ps 112:1–2

20 [a]Ps. 79:11 ʹHeb. *the children of death*
21 [a]Ps. 22:22
23 [a]Job 21:21 ʹHeb. *afflicted*
24 [a]Is. 38:10 [b]Ps. 90:2
25 [a]Heb. 1:10
26 [a]Is. 34:4 ʹHeb. *stand*
27 [a]Mal. 3:6; Heb. 13:8
28 [a]Ps. 69:36
103:1 [a]Ps. 104:1
3 [a]Ps. 130:8; Is. 33:24 [b]Ex. 15:26
4 [a]Ps. 5:12
5 [a]Is. 40:31
7 [a]Ps. 147:19
8 [a]Ex. 34:6,7 ʹHeb. *great of mercy*
9 [a]Ps. 30:5
10 [a]Ezra 9:13
11 ʹHeb. *according to the height of the heaven*
12 [a]Is. 43:25
13 [a]Mal. 3:17
14 [a]Eccl. 12:7
15 [a]1 Pet. 1:24 [b]Job 14:1,2
16 [a]Job 7:10 ʹHeb. *it is not*
18 [a]Deut. 7:9
19 [a]Ps. 47:2; Dan. 4:25
20 [a]Ps. 148:2 [b]Mat. 6:10 ʹHeb. *mighty in strength*
21 [a]Gen. 32:2

102:21–22 The psalmist announced in this millennial prophecy that the name of the LORD will be declared in Zion and Jerusalem "when the people are gathered together, and the kingdoms, to serve the LORD" (102:22). This prophecy will be fulfilled after the victory at Armageddon.

102:25–26 This prophecy deals with "a new heaven and a new earth" (Rev 21:1).

[b]ye ministers of his, that do his pleasure.
22 Bless the LORD, all his works in all
places of his dominion: bless the LORD,
O my soul.

God the creator of the earth

104 BLESS [a]THE LORD, O my soul.
O LORD my God, thou art very
great; thou art clothed with honour and
majesty.
2 [a]Who coverest *thyself* with light as
with a garment: [b]who stretchest out the
heavens like a curtain:
3 [a]Who layeth the beams of his chambers in the waters: [b]who maketh the
clouds his chariot: [c]who walketh upon
the wings of the wind:
4 [a]Who maketh his angels spirits; his
ministers a flaming fire:
N 5 [a]*Who*[l] laid the foundations of the
earth, *that* it should not be removed for
ever.
6 [a]Thou coveredst it with the deep as
with a garment: the waters stood above
the mountains.
7 At thy rebuke they fled; at the voice
of thy thunder they hasted away.
8 [a]They[l] go up by the mountains; they
go down by the valleys unto the place
which thou hast founded for them.
9 [a]Thou hast set a bound that they may
not pass over; [b]that they turn not again to
cover the earth.
10 [l]He sendeth the springs into the
valleys, *which* [2]run among the hills.
11 They give drink to every beast of
the field: the wild asses [l]quench their
thirst.
12 By them shall the fowls of the
heaven have their habitation, *which*
[l]sing among the branches.
13 [a]He watereth the hills from his
chambers: the earth is satisfied with [b]the
fruit of thy works.
14 [a]He causeth the grass to grow for
the cattle, and herb for the service of
man: that he may bring forth [b]food out of
the earth;
15 And [a]wine *that* maketh glad the
heart of man, *and* [l]oil to make *his* face
to shine, and bread *which* strengtheneth
man's heart.
16 The trees of the LORD are full *of sap;*
the cedars of Lebanon, which he hath
planted;
17 Where the birds make their nests:
as for the stork, the fir trees *are* her
house.
18 The high hills *are* a refuge for the
wild goats; *and* the rocks for the conies.
19 [a]He appointed the moon for sea
sons: the sun knoweth his going down.
20 [a]Thou makest darkness, and it is
night: wherein [l]all the beasts of the forest do creep *forth.*
21 [a]The young lions roar after their
prey, and seek their meat from God.
22 The sun ariseth, they gather themselves together, and lay them down in
their dens.
23 Man goeth forth unto [a]his work
and to his labour until the evening.
24 [a]O LORD, how manifold are thy
works! in wisdom hast thou made them
all: the earth is full of thy riches.
25 *So is* this great and wide sea,
wherein *are* things creeping innumerable, both small and great beasts.
26 There go the ships: *there is* that [a]le-
viathan, *whom* thou hast [l]made to play
therein.
27 [a]These wait all upon thee; that
thou mayest give *them* their meat in due
season.
28 *That* thou givest them they gather:
thou openest thine hand, they are filled
with good.
29 Thou hidest thy face, they are troubled: [a]thou takest away their breath, they
die, and return to their dust.
30 [a]Thou sendest forth thy spirit, they E
are created: and thou renewest the face M
of the earth. N
31 The glory of the LORD [l]shall endure
for ever: the LORD [a]shall rejoice in his
works.
32 He looketh on the earth, and it

21 [b]Heb. 1:14
104:1 [a]Ps. 103:1
2 [a]Dan. 7:9 [b]Is. 40:22
3 [a]Amos 9:6 [b]Is. 19:1 [c]Ps. 18:10
4 [a]Heb. 1:7
5 [a]Job 26:7 [l]Heb. *He hath founded the earth upon her bases*
6 [a]Gen. 7:19
8 [a]Gen. 8:5 [l]Or, *The mountains ascend, the valleys descend*
9 [a]Job 26:10 [b]Gen. 9:11
10 [l]Heb. *Who sendeth* [2]Heb. *walk*
11 [l]Heb. *break*
12 [l]Heb. *give a voice*
13 [a]Ps. 147:8 [b]Jer. 10:13
14 [a]Gen. 1:29 [b]Job 28:5; Ps. 136:25
15 [a]Judg. 9:13 [l]Heb. *to make his face shine with oil, or, more than oil*
19 [a]Gen. 1:14
20 [a]Is. 45:7 [l]Heb. *all the beasts thereof do trample on the forest*
21 [a]Job 38:39
23 [a]Gen. 3:19
24 [a]Prov. 3:19
26 [a]Job 41:1 [l]Heb. *formed*
27 [a]Ps. 136:25
29 [a]Job 34:15; Eccl. 12:7
30 [a]Is. 32:15; Ezek. 37:9
31 [a]Gen. 1:31 [l]Heb. *shall be*

N *Ps 102:25–26* ◀ ▶ *Pr 10:30*

E *Job 33:4* ◀ ▶ *Ps 139:7*
M *Ps 51:12–13* ◀ ▶ *Ps 139:7*
N *Ps 51:12* ◀ ▶ *Ps 139:7*

104:5 In this hymn to the Creator the psalmist echoes God's question to Job: "Where wast thou when I laid the foundations of the earth?" (Job 38:4). The NT clearly answers the question of Creator's identity—he is Jesus Christ (see Jn 1:3; Eph 3:9).

[a]trembleth: [b]he toucheth the hills, and they smoke.

33 [a]I will sing unto the LORD as long as I live: I will sing praise to my God while I have my being.

34 My meditation of him shall be sweet: I will be glad in the LORD.

P 35 Let [a]the sinners be consumed out of the earth, and let the wicked be no more. Bless thou the LORD, O my soul. Praise ye the LORD.

The LORD remembers his covenant

T **105** O [a]GIVE thanks unto the LORD; call upon his name: [b]make known his deeds among the people.

2 Sing unto him, sing psalms unto him: [a]talk ye of all his wondrous works.

3 Glory ye in his holy name: let the heart of them rejoice that seek the LORD.

4 Seek the LORD, and his strength: [a]seek his face evermore.

5 [a]Remember his marvellous works that he hath done; his wonders, and the judgments of his mouth;

6 O ye seed of Abraham his servant, ye children of Jacob his chosen.

7 He *is* the LORD our God: [a]his judgments *are* in all the earth.

I 8 He hath [a]remembered his covenant for ever, the word *which* he commanded to a thousand generations.

9 [a]Which *covenant* he made with Abraham, and his oath unto Isaac;

10 And confirmed the same unto Jacob for a law, *and* to Israel *for* an everlasting covenant:

11 Saying, [a]Unto thee will I give the land of Canaan, [/]the lot of your inheritance:

12 [a]When they were *but* a few men in number; yea, very few, [b]and strangers in it.

13 When they went from one nation to another, from *one* kingdom to another people;

14 [a]He suffered no man to do them wrong: yea, [b]he reproved kings for their sakes; L

15 *Saying,* Touch not mine anointed, and do my prophets no harm.

16 Moreover [a]he called for a famine upon the land: he brake the whole [b]staff of bread.

17 [a]He sent a man before them, *even* Joseph, *who* [b]was sold for a servant:

18 [a]Whose feet they hurt with fetters: [/]he was laid in iron:

19 Until the time that his word came: [a]the word of the LORD tried him. T

20 [a]The king sent and loosed him; *even* the ruler of the people, and let him go free.

21 [a]He made him lord of his house, and ruler of all his [/]substance:

22 To bind his princes at his pleasure; and teach his senators wisdom.

23 [a]Israel also came into Egypt; and Jacob sojourned [b]in the land of Ham.

24 And [a]he increased his people greatly; and made them stronger than their enemies.

25 [a]He turned their heart to hate his people, to deal subtly with his servants.

26 [a]He sent Moses his servant; *and* Aaron whom he had chosen.

27 [a]They showed [/]his signs among them, [b]and wonders in the land of Ham.

28 [a]He sent darkness, and made it dark; and [b]they rebelled not against his word.

29 [a]He turned their waters into blood, and slew their fish.

30 [a]Their land brought forth frogs in

32 [a]Hab. 3:10 [b]Ps. 144:5
33 [a]Ps. 63:4
35 [a]Ps. 37:38; Prov. 2:22
105:1 [a]1 Chr. 16:8; Is. 12:4 [b]Ps. 145:5
2 [a]Ps. 119:27
4 [a]Ps. 27:8
5 [a]Ps. 77:11
7 [a]Is. 26:9
8 [a]Luke 1:72
9 [a]Gen. 17:2 & 22:16
11 [a]Gen. 13:15 & 15:18 [/]Heb. *the cord*
12 [a]Gen. 34:30; Deut. 7:7 [b]Heb. 11:9
14 [a]Gen. 35:5 [b]Gen. 12:17
16 [a]Gen. 41:54 [b]Lev. 26:26; Is. 3:1
17 [a]Gen. 45:5 [b]Gen. 37:28
18 [a]Gen. 40:15 [/]Heb. *his soul came into iron*
19 [a]Gen. 41:25
20 [a]Gen. 41:14
21 [a]Gen. 41:40 [/]Heb. *possession*
23 [a]Gen. 46:6 [b]Ps. 78:51
24 [a]Ex. 1:7
25 [a]Ex. 1:8
26 [a]Ex. 3:10
27 [a]Ex. 7-12 [b]Ps. 106:22 [/]Heb. *words of his signs*
28 [a]Ex. 10:22 [b]Ps. 99:7
29 [a]Ex. 7:20; Ps. 78:44
30 [a]Ex. 8:6; Ps. 78:45

P *Ps 98:1–2 ◀ ▶ Ps 110:1*
T *Ps 78:4 ◀ ▶ Ps 107:2*
I *Ps 102:21–22 ◀ ▶ Ps 111:5–6*
L *Ps 103:17–18 ◀ ▶ Ps 107:6*
T *Ps 94:12–13 ◀ ▶ Ps 119:67*

104:35 The psalmist calls for God's judgment on the wicked. This judgment will occur during the seven-year tribulation period when the wicked will be overthrown and refused entrance into God's kingdom (see Rev 21:27). The Scriptures are very clear that the wicked who reject God's forgiveness will continue in hell forever (see Mt 18:8; Mk 3:29; 2Th 1:9).

105:8–11 The psalmist reconfirmed the Abrahamic covenant and the disposition of the land of Canaan (see note at Ge 15:4). Some have attempted to use this passage to determine the exact time of the Lord's second coming, basing their calculations on the length of "a thousand generations" (105:8). However, relating the Lord's second coming to this phrase is inaccurate because the phrase refers specifically to God's "word which he commanded" (105:8)—his eternal promise to Abraham and his descendants.

abundance, in the chambers of their kings.

31 [a]He spake, and there came divers sorts of flies, *and* lice in all their coasts.

32 [a]He[l] gave them hail for rain, *and* flaming fire in their land.

33 [a]He smote their vines also and their fig trees; and brake the trees of their coasts.

34 [a]He spake, and the locusts came, and caterpillars, and that without number,

35 And did eat up all the herbs in their land, and devoured the fruit of their ground.

36 [a]He smote also all the firstborn in their land, [b]the chief of all their strength.

E P 37 [a]He brought them forth also with silver and gold: and *there was* not one feeble *person* among their tribes.

38 [a]Egypt was glad when they departed: for the fear of them fell upon them.

39 [a]He spread a cloud for a covering; and fire to give light in the night.

F 40 [a]*The people* asked, and he brought quails, and [b]satisfied them with the bread of heaven.

41 [a]He opened the rock, and the waters gushed out; they ran in the dry places *like* a river.

42 For he remembered [a]his holy promise, *and* Abraham his servant.

43 And he brought forth his people with joy, *and* his chosen with [l]gladness:

44 [a]And gave them the lands of the heathen: and they inherited the labour of the people;

45 [a]That they might observe his statutes, and keep his laws. [l]Praise ye the LORD.

God's mercy to Israel

106 PRAISE[l] YE the LORD. [a]O give thanks unto the LORD; for *he is* good: for his mercy *endureth* for ever.

2 Who can utter the mighty acts of the LORD? *who* can show forth all his praise?

3 Blessed *are* they that keep judgment, *and* he that [a]doeth righteousness at [b]all times.

4 [a]Remember me, O LORD, with the favour *that thou bearest unto* thy people: O visit me with thy salvation;

5 That I may see the good of thy chosen, that I may rejoice in the gladness of thy nation, that I may glory with thine inheritance.

6 [a]We have sinned with our fathers, we have committed iniquity, we have done wickedly.

7 Our fathers understood not thy wonders in Egypt; they remembered not the multitude of thy mercies; [a]but provoked *him* at the sea, *even* at the Red sea.

8 Nevertheless he saved them for his name's sake, [a]that he might make his mighty power to be known.

9 [a]He rebuked the Red sea also, and it was dried up: so [b]he led them through the depths, as through the wilderness.

10 And he [a]saved them from the hand of him that hated *them,* and redeemed them from the hand of the enemy.

11 [a]And the waters covered their enemies: there was not one of them left.

12 [a]Then believed they his words; they sang his praise.

13 [a]They[l] soon forgat his works; they waited not for his counsel:

14 [a]But [l]lusted exceedingly in the wilderness, and tempted God in the desert.

15 [a]And he gave them their request; but [b]sent leanness into their soul.

16 [a]They envied Moses also in the camp, *and* Aaron the saint of the LORD.

17 [a]The earth opened and swallowed up Dathan, and covered the company of Abiram.

18 [a]And a fire was kindled in their company; the flame burned up the wicked.

19 [a]They made a calf in Horeb, and worshipped the molten image.

20 Thus [a]they changed their glory into the similitude of an ox that eateth grass.

21 They [a]forgat God their saviour, which had done great things in Egypt;

22 Wondrous works in [a]the land of Ham, *and* terrible things by the Red sea.

23 [a]Therefore he said that he would destroy them, had not Moses his chosen [b]stood before him in the breach, to turn away his wrath, lest he should destroy *them.*

24 Yea, they despised [a]the[l] pleasant land, they [b]believed not his word:

25 [a]But murmured in their tents, *and* hearkened not unto the voice of the LORD.

31 [a]Ex. 8:17; Ps. 78:45
32 [a]Ex. 9:23; Ps. 78:48 [l]Heb. *He gave their rain hail*
33 [a]Ps. 78:47
34 [a]Ex. 10:4; Ps. 78:46
36 [a]Ex. 12:29; Ps. 78:51 [b]Gen. 49:3
37 [a]Ex. 12:35
38 [a]Ex. 12:33
39 [a]Ex. 13:21; Neh. 9:12
40 [a]Ex. 16:12; Ps. 78:18 [b]Ps. 78:24
41 [a]Ex. 17:6; Ps. 78:15; 1 Cor. 10:4
42 [a]Gen. 15:14
43 [l]Heb. *singing*
44 [a]Josh. 13:7
45 [a]Deut. 4:1 & 6:21-25 [l]Heb. *Hallelujah*
106:1 [a]1 Chr. 16:34 [l]Heb. *Hallelujah*
3 [a]Ps. 15:2 [b]Gal. 6:9
4 [a]Ps. 119:132
6 [a]Dan. 9:5
7 [a]Ex. 14:11
8 [a]Ex. 9:16
9 [a]Ex. 14:21; Ps. 18:15; Nah. 1:4 [b]Is. 63:11
10 [a]Ex. 14:30
11 [a]Ex. 14:27
12 [a]Ex. 15:1
13 [a]Ex. 15:24 [l]Heb. *They made haste, they forgat*
14 [a]1 Cor. 10:6 [l]Heb. *lusted a lust*
15 [a]Num. 11:31 [b]Is. 10:16
16 [a]Num. 16:1
17 [a]Deut. 11:6
18 [a]Num. 16:35, 46
19 [a]Ex. 32:4
20 [a]Jer. 2:11; Rom. 1:23
21 [a]Ps. 78:11
22 [a]Ps. 78:51
23 [a]Ex. 32:10; Deut. 9:19 [b]Ezek. 22:30
24 [a]Deut. 8:7; Ezek. 20:6 [b]Heb. 3:18 [l]Heb. *a land of desire*
25 [a]Num. 14:2

E *Ps 103:3* ◀ ▶ *Ps 107:20*
P *Job 42:12* ◀ ▶ *Ps 112:3*
F *Ps 103:5* ◀ ▶ *Ps 111:5*

26 [a]Therefore he lifted up his hand against them, [b]to overthrow them in the wilderness:

27 [a]To[1] overthrow their seed also among the nations, and to scatter them in the lands.

28 [a]They joined themselves also unto Baal-peor, and ate the sacrifices of the dead.

D 29 Thus they provoked *him* to anger with their inventions: and the plague brake in upon them.

30 [a]Then stood up Phinehas, and executed judgment: and *so* the plague was stayed.

31 And that was counted unto him [a]for righteousness unto all generations for evermore.

32 [a]They angered *him* also at the waters of strife, so that it went ill with Moses for their sakes:

33 [a]Because they provoked his spirit, so that he spake unadvisedly with his lips.

34 [a]They did not destroy the nations, [b]concerning whom the LORD commanded them:

35 [a]But were mingled among the heathen, and learned their works.

36 And [a]they served their idols: [b]which were a snare unto them.

37 Yea, [a]they sacrificed their sons and their daughters unto [b]devils,

38 And shed innocent blood, *even* the blood of their sons and of their daughters, whom they sacrificed unto the idols of Canaan: and [a]the land was polluted with blood.

39 Thus were they [a]defiled with their own works, and [b]went a-whoring with their own inventions.

40 Therefore [a]was the wrath of the LORD kindled against his people, insomuch that he abhorred [b]his own inheritance.

41 And [a]he gave them into the hand of the heathen; and they that hated them ruled over them.

42 Their enemies also oppressed them, and they were brought into subjection under their hand.

43 [a]Many times did he deliver them; but they provoked *him* with their counsel, and were [1]brought low for their iniquity.

44 Nevertheless he regarded their affliction, when [a]he heard their cry:

45 [a]And he remembered for them his covenant, and [b]repented [c]according to the multitude of his mercies.

46 [a]He made them also to be pitied of all those that carried them captives.

47 [a]Save us, O LORD our God, and gather us from among the heathen, to give thanks unto thy holy name, *and* to triumph in thy praise.

48 [a]Blessed *be* the LORD God of Israel from everlasting to everlasting: and let all the people say, Amen. [1]Praise ye the LORD.

Book V

The LORD's goodness to men

107 O [a]GIVE thanks unto the LORD, for [b]*he is* good: for his mercy *endureth* for ever.

2 Let the redeemed of the LORD say *so*, [a]whom he hath redeemed from the hand of the enemy; T

3 And [a]gathered them out of the lands, from the east, and from the west, from the north, and [1]from the south.

4 They wandered in [a]the wilderness in a solitary way; they found no city to dwell in.

5 Hungry and thirsty, their soul fainted in them.

6 [a]Then they cried unto the LORD in their trouble, *and* he delivered them out of their distresses. L

7 And he led them forth by the [a]right way, that they might go to a city of habitation.

8 [a]Oh that *men* would praise the LORD *for* his goodness, and *for* his wonderful works to the children of men!

9 For [a]he satisfieth the longing soul, and filleth the hungry soul with goodness. L

10 Such as [a]sit in darkness and in the shadow of death, *being* [b]bound in affliction and iron; C

11 Because they [a]rebelled against the words of God, and contemned [b]the counsel of the most High:

12 Therefore he brought down their

26 [a]Ezek. 20:15 [b]Num. 14:29
27 [a]Lev. 26:33 [1]Heb. *To make them fall*
28 [a]Hos. 9:10
30 [a]Num. 25:7
31 [a]Num. 25:11
32 [a]Num. 20:3; Ps. 81:7
33 [a]Num. 20:10
34 [a]Judg. 1:21 [b]Deut. 7:2; Judg. 2:2
35 [a]Judg. 3:5,6; Is. 2:6
36 [a]Judg. 2:12 [b]Deut. 7:16
37 [a]2 Ki. 16:3 [b]Lev. 17:7
38 [a]Num. 35:33
39 [a]Ezek. 20:18 [b]Lev. 17:7; Num. 15:39; Ezek. 20:30
40 [a]Judg. 2:14 [b]Deut. 9:29
41 [a]Judg. 2:14; Neh. 9:27
43 [a]Judg. 2:16; Neh. 9:27 [1]Or, *impoverished*, or, *weakened*
44 [a]Judg. 10:10
45 [a]Lev. 26:41 [b]Judg. 2:18 [c]Ps. 69:16
46 [a]Ezra 9:9; Jer. 42:12
47 [a]1 Chr. 16:35
48 [a]Ps. 41:13 [1]Heb. *Hallelujah*
107:1 [a]Ps. 106:1 [b]Ps. 119:68
2 [a]Ps. 106:10
3 [a]Ps. 106:47 [1]Heb. *from the sea*
4 [a]Deut. 32:10
6 [a]Ps. 50:15; Hos. 5:15
7 [a]Ezra 8:21
8 [a]ver. 15,21
9 [a]Ps. 34:10; Luke 1:53
10 [a]Luke 1:79 [b]Job 36:8
11 [a]Lam. 3:42 [b]Ps. 73:24; Luke 7:30; Acts 20:27

D *Job 33:29–30* ◀ ▶ *Jer 21:6*

T *Ps 105:1–2* ◀ ▶ *Ps 119:46*
L *Ps 105:14–15* ◀ ▶ *Ps 107:13*
L *Ps 103:17* ◀ ▶ *Ps 108:4*
C *Ps 95:10* ◀ ▶ *Pr 4:19*

heart with labour; they fell down, and *there was* [a]none to help.

L 13 Then they cried unto the LORD in their trouble, *and* he saved them out of their distresses.

K 14 [a]He brought them out of darkness and the shadow of death, and brake their bands in sunder.

15 [a]Oh that *men* would praise the LORD *for* his goodness, and *for* his wonderful works to the children of men!

16 For he hath [a]broken the gates of brass, and cut the bars of iron in sunder.

17 Fools [a]because of their transgression, and because of their iniquities, are afflicted.

18 [a]Their soul abhorreth all manner of meat; and they [b]draw near unto the gates of death.

L 19 Then they cry unto the LORD in their trouble, *and* he saveth them out of their distresses.

E 20 [a]He sent his word, and [b]healed them, and [c]delivered *them* from their destructions.

21 Oh that *men* would praise the LORD *for* his goodness, and *for* his wonderful works to the children of men!

22 [a]And let them sacrifice the sacrifices of thanksgiving, and [b]declare his works with [1]rejoicing.

23 They that go down to the sea in ships, that do business in great waters;

24 These see the works of the LORD, and his wonders in the deep.

25 For he commandeth, and [a]raiseth[1] the stormy wind, which lifteth up the waves thereof.

26 They mount up to the heaven, they go down again to the depths: [a]their soul is melted because of trouble.

27 They reel to and fro, and stagger like a drunken man, and [1]are at their wit's end.

L 28 [a]Then they cry unto the LORD in their trouble, and he bringeth them out of their distresses.

29 [a]He maketh the storm a calm, so that the waves thereof are still.

30 Then are they glad because they be quiet; so he bringeth them unto their desired haven.

31 [a]Oh that *men* would praise the LORD *for* his goodness, and *for* his wonderful works to the children of men!

32 Let them exalt him also [a]in the congregation of the people, and praise him in the assembly of the elders.

33 He [a]turneth rivers into a wilderness, and the watersprings into dry ground;

34 A [a]fruitful land into [1]barrenness, for the wickedness of them that dwell therein.

35 [a]He turneth the wilderness into a standing water, and dry ground into watersprings.

36 And there he maketh the hungry to dwell, that they may prepare a city for habitation;

37 And sow the fields, and plant vineyards, which may yield fruits of increase.

38 [a]He blesseth them also, so that they [b]are multiplied greatly; and suffereth not their cattle to decrease. B

39 Again, they are [a]minished and brought low through oppression, affliction, and sorrow.

40 [a]He poureth contempt upon princes, and causeth them to wander in the [1]wilderness, *where there is* no way.

41 [a]Yet setteth he the poor on high [1]from affliction, and [b]maketh *him* families like a flock.

42 [a]The righteous shall see *it,* and rejoice: and all [b]iniquity shall stop her mouth.

43 [a]Whoso *is* wise, and will observe these *things,* even they shall understand the lovingkindness of the LORD.

A song of confidence in God

A Song *or* Psalm of David.

108 O [a]GOD, my heart is fixed; I will sing and give praise, even with my glory.

2 [a]Awake, psaltery and harp: I *myself* will awake early.

3 I will praise thee, O LORD, among the people: and I will sing praises unto thee among the nations.

4 For thy mercy *is* great above the heavens: and thy truth *reacheth* unto the [1]clouds. L

12 [a]Ps. 22:11; Is. 63:5
14 [a]Ps. 68:6; Acts 12:7
15 [a]ver. 8,21,31
16 [a]Is. 45:2
17 [a]Lam. 3:39
18 [a]Job 33:20 [b]Job 33:22; Ps. 9:13
20 [a]Mat. 8:8 [b]Ps. 30:2 & 103:3 [c]Job 33:28; Ps. 30:3 & 49:15
22 [a]Lev. 7:12; Ps. 116:17; Heb. 13:15 [b]Ps. 9:11 & 73:28 & 118:17 [1]Heb. *singing*
25 [a]Jonah 1:4 [1]Heb. *maketh to stand*
26 [a]Ps. 22:14
27 [1]Heb. *all their wisdom is swallowed up*
28 [a]ver. 6,13,19
29 [a]Ps. 89:9; Mat. 8:26
31 [a]ver. 8,15,21
32 [a]Ps. 22:22,25
33 [a]1 Ki. 17:1,7
34 [a]Gen. 13:10 & 14:3 & 19:25 [1]Heb. *saltness*
35 [a]Ps. 114:8; Is. 41:18
38 [a]Gen. 12:2 & 17:16,20 [b]Ex. 1:7
39 [a]2 Ki. 10:32
40 [a]Job 12:21,24 [1]Or, *void place*
41 [a]1 Sam. 2:8; Ps. 113:7,8 [b]Ps. 78:52 [1]Or, *after*
42 [a]Job 5:15,16 [b]Job 5:16; Ps. 63:11; Prov. 10:11; Rom. 3:19
43 [a]Ps. 64:9; Jer. 9:12; Hos. 14:9
108:1 [a]Ps. 57:7
2 [a]Ps. 57:8-11
4 [1]Or, *skies*

L *Ps 107:6* ◀▶ *Ps 107:19*
K *Ps 103:12* ◀▶ *Ps 121:1-8*
L *Ps 107:13* ◀▶ *Ps 107:28*
E *Ps 105:37* ◀▶ *Isa 38:1-22*
L *Ps 107:19* ◀▶ *Ps 116:15*
B *Ps 85:12* ◀▶ *Pr 3:9-10*
L *Ps 107:9* ◀▶ *Ps 111:4*

5 [a]Be thou exalted, O God, above the heavens: and thy glory above all the earth;

6 [a]That thy beloved may be delivered: save *with* thy right hand, and answer me.

7 God hath spoken in his holiness; I will rejoice, I will divide Shechem, and mete out the valley of Succoth.

8 Gilead *is* mine; Manasseh *is* mine; Ephraim also *is* the strength of mine head; [a]Judah *is* my lawgiver;

9 Moab *is* my washpot; over Edom will I cast out my shoe; over Philistia will I triumph.

10 [a]Who will bring me into the strong city? who will lead me into Edom?

11 *Wilt* not *thou,* O God, *who* hast cast us off ? and wilt not thou, O God, go forth with our hosts?

12 Give us help from trouble: for vain *is* the help of man.

V 13 [a]Through God we shall do valiantly: for he *it is that* shall tread down our enemies.

A cry to God for help

To the chief Musician, A Psalm of David.

109 HOLD [a]NOT thy peace, O God of my praise;

2 For the mouth of the wicked and the [1]mouth of the deceitful [2]are opened against me: they have spoken against me with a lying tongue.

3 They compassed me about also with words of hatred; and fought against me [a]without a cause.

4 For my love they are my adversaries: but I *give myself unto* prayer.

5 And [a]they have rewarded me evil for good, and hatred for my love.

6 Set thou a wicked man over him: and let [a]Satan[1] stand at his right hand.

7 When he shall be judged, let him [1]be condemned: and [a]let his prayer become sin.

C 8 Let his days be few; *and* [a]let another take his [1]office.

V *Ps 97:10* ◀▶ *Ps 112:8*
C *Ps 97:2–7* ◀▶ *SS 2:7–8*

5 [a]Ps. 57:5,11
6 [a]Ps. 60:5
8 [a]Gen. 49:10
10 [a]Ps. 60:9
13 [a]Ps. 60:12
109:1 [a]Ps. 83:1
2 [1]Heb. *mouth of deceit* [2]Heb. *have opened* themselves
3 [a]Ps. 35:7 & 69:4; John 15:25
5 [a]Ps. 35:7,12 & 38:20
6 [a]Zech. 3:1 [1]Or, *an adversary*
7 [a]Prov. 28:9 [1]Heb. *go out guilty,* or, *wicked*
8 [a]Acts 1:20 [1]Or, *charge*
9 [a]Ex. 22:24
11 [a]Job 5:5 & 18:9
13 [a]Job 18:19; Ps. 37:28 [b]Prov. 10:7
14 [a]Ex. 20:5 [b]Neh. 4:5; Jer. 18:23
15 [a]Job 18:17; Ps. 34:16
16 [a]Ps. 34:18
17 [a]Prov. 14:14; Ezek. 35:6
18 [a]Num. 5:22 [1]Heb. *within him*
23 [a]Ps. 102:11
24 [a]Heb. 12:12
25 [a]Ps. 22:6,7

9 [a]Let his children be fatherless, and his wife a widow.

10 Let his children be continually vagabonds, and beg: let them seek *their bread* also out of their desolate places.

11 [a]Let the extortioner catch all that he hath; and let the strangers spoil his labour.

12 Let there be none to extend mercy unto him: neither let there be any to favour his fatherless children.

13 [a]Let his posterity be cut off; *and* in the generation following let their [b]name be blotted out.

14 [a]Let the iniquity of his fathers be remembered with the LORD; and let not the sin of his mother [b]be blotted out.

15 Let them be before the LORD continually, that he may [a]cut off the memory of them from the earth.

16 Because that he remembered not to show mercy, but persecuted the poor and needy man, that he might even slay the [a]broken in heart.

17 [a]As he loved cursing, so let it come unto him: as he delighted not in blessing, so let it be far from him. H

18 As he clothed himself with cursing like as with his garment, so let it [a]come [1]into his bowels like water, and like oil into his bones.

19 Let it be unto him as the garment *which* covereth him, and for a girdle wherewith he is girded continually.

20 *Let* this *be* the reward of mine adversaries from the LORD, and of them that speak evil against my soul.

21 But do thou for me, O GOD the Lord, for thy name's sake: because thy mercy *is* good, deliver thou me.

22 For I *am* poor and needy, and my heart is wounded within me.

23 I am gone [a]like the shadow when it declineth: I am tossed up and down as the locust.

24 My [a]knees are weak through fasting; and my flesh faileth of fatness.

25 I became also [a]a reproach unto

H *Ps 92:7* ◀▶ *Ps 110:1*

109:8 The apostle Peter combined this verse with Ps 69:25 in reference to Judas after his betrayal of Jesus (see Ac 1:20). Judas's suicide removed him from his place among the twelve disciples and another leader had to be found to take his place. The early church chose Matthias, one who had been with Jesus and could testify to his words and deeds based on eyewitness accounts of his ministry, as Judas' successor (see Ac 1:12–26).

them: *when* they looked upon me [b]they
shaked their heads.
26 Help me, O LORD my God: O save
me according to thy mercy:
27 [a]That they may know that this *is*
thy hand; *that* thou, LORD, hast done it.
28 [a]Let them curse, but bless thou:
when they arise, let them be ashamed;
but let [b]thy servant rejoice.
29 [a]Let mine adversaries be clothed
with shame, and let them cover themselves with their own confusion, as with
a mantle.
30 I will greatly praise the LORD with
my mouth; yea, [a]I will praise him among
the multitude.
31 For [a]he shall stand at the right hand
of the poor, to save *him* [1]from those that
condemn his soul.

The king as priest and victor

A Psalm of David.

M 110 THE [a]LORD said unto my
P Lord, Sit thou at my right
V hand, until I make thine enemies thy
H footstool.
2 The LORD shall send the rod of thy
strength out of Zion: rule thou in the
midst of thine enemies.
3 [a]Thy people *shall be* willing in the
day of thy power, [b]in the beauties of holiness [1]from the womb of the morning:
thou hast the dew of thy youth.
4 The LORD hath sworn, and [a]will not
repent, Thou *art* a priest for ever after the
order of Melchizedek.
P 5 The Lord [a]at thy right hand shall
strike through kings [b]in the day of his
wrath.
6 He shall judge among the heathen,
he shall fill *the places* with the dead bodies; [a]he shall wound the heads over
[1]many countries.

M *Ps 102:22 ◀▶ Ps 132:11–18*
P *Ps 104:35 ◀▶ Ps 110:5–6*
V *Ps 72:8–9 ◀▶ Isa 9:6–7*
H *Ps 109:17–19 ◀▶ Ps 119:32*
P *Ps 110:1 ◀▶ Ps 144:5–6*

25 [b]Mat. 27:39
27 [a]Job 37:7
28 [a]2 Sam. 16:11 [b]Is. 65:14
29 [a]Ps. 35:26 & 132:18
30 [a]Ps. 35:18 & 111:1
31 [a]Ps. 16:8 & 73:23 [1]Heb. *from the judges of his soul*
110:1 [a]Mat. 22:44; Mark 12:36; Luke 20:42; Acts 2:34; 1 Cor. 15:25
3 [a]Judg. 5:2 [b]Ps. 96:9 [1]Or, *more than the womb of the morning: thou shalt have*
4 [a]Num. 23:19
5 [a]Ps. 16:8 [b]Ps. 2:5,12; Rom. 2:5
6 [a]Ps. 68:21; Hab. 3:13 [1]Or, *great*
7 [a]Is. 53:12
111:1 [a]Ps. 35:18; & 89:5 & 107:32 [1]Heb. *Hallelujah*
2 [a]Job 38-41; Ps. 92:5 [b]Ps. 143:5
3 [a]Ps. 145:4
4 [a]Ps. 86:5 & 103:8
5 [a]Mat. 6:26 [1]Heb. *prey*
7 [a]Rev. 15:3 [b]Ps. 19:7
8 [a]Is. 40:8 [b]Rev:15:3 [1]Heb. *are established*
9 [a]Luke 1:68 [b]Luke 1:49
10 [a]Eccl. 12:13 [b]Prov. 3:4 [1]Or, *good success* [2]Heb. *that do them*
112:1 [a]Ps. 119:16 [1]Heb. *Hallelujah*
2 [a]Ps. 102:28

7 He shall drink of the brook in the
way: [a]therefore shall he lift up the head.

The LORD's wonderful works

111 PRAISE[1] YE the LORD. [a]I will
praise the LORD with *my*
whole heart, in the assembly of the upright, and *in* the congregation.
2 [a]The works of the LORD *are* great,
[b]sought out of all them that have pleasure
therein.
3 His work *is* [a]honourable and glorious: and his righteousness endureth for
ever.
4 He hath made his wonderful works L
to be remembered: [a]the LORD *is* gracious
and full of compassion.
5 He hath given [a]meat[1] unto them that I
fear him: he will ever be mindful of his F
covenant.
6 He hath shown his people the power
of his works, that he may give them the
heritage of the heathen.
7 The works of his hands *are* [a]verity
and judgment; [b]all his commandments
are sure.
8 [a]They [1]stand fast for ever and ever,
and are [b]done in truth and uprightness.
9 [a]He sent redemption unto his peo- I
ple: he hath commanded his covenant for
ever: [b]holy and reverend *is* his name.
10 [a]The fear of the LORD *is* the beginning of wisdom: [b]a[1] good understanding
have all they [2]that do *his commandments:* his praise endureth for ever.

The prosperity of the righteous

112 PRAISE[1] YE the LORD. Blessed R
is the man *that* feareth the U
LORD, *that* [a]delighteth greatly in his commandments.
2 [a]His seed shall be mighty upon

L *Ps 108:4 ◀▶ Ps 112:4*
I *Ps 105:8–11 ◀▶ Ps 111:9*
F *Ps 105:40–41 ◀▶ Ps 114:8*
I *Ps 111:5–6 ◀▶ Ps 126:1–6*
R *Ps 103:17–18 ◀▶ Ps 128:3*
U *Ps 97:10–12 ◀▶ Ps 115:12–15*

110:1–7 This psalm is frequently referred to in the NT because of its vivid description of the Messiah. Beginning with the coronation of the King, David affirms the kingly and priestly roles of the Messiah (see Ge 14:18; Jn 14:6; 1Ti 2:5–6; Heb 5:6; 7:1–28; Rev 3:21). David also alludes to the conversion of Israel (see Dt 30:1–9; Joel 2:27; Zec 13:9) and the tribulation period when Jesus, as "the rod of thy strength out of Zion" (110:2), will defeat the antichrist and "judge among the heathen" (110:6).

111:5–9 The psalmist praised God for fulfilling his covenant with Israel by delivering them from the heathen and sending them redemption.

earth: the generation of the upright shall be blessed.

3 [a]Wealth and riches *shall be* in his house: and his righteousness endureth for ever.

4 [a]Unto the upright there ariseth light in the darkness: *he is* gracious, and full of compassion, and righteous.

5 [a]A good man showeth favour, and lendeth: he will guide his affairs [b]with [l]discretion.

6 Surely he shall not be moved for ever: [a]the righteous shall be in everlasting remembrance.

7 [a]He shall not be afraid of evil tidings: his [b]heart is fixed, [c]trusting in the LORD.

8 His heart *is* established, [a]he shall not be afraid, until he [b]see *his desire* upon his enemies.

9 [a]He hath dispersed, he hath given to the poor; his righteousness endureth for ever; [b]his horn shall be exalted with honour.

10 [a]The wicked shall see *it,* and be grieved; [b]he shall gnash with his teeth, and [c]melt away: [d]the desire of the wicked shall perish.

A hymn of praise to God

113 PRAISE[l] YE the LORD. [a]Praise, O ye servants of the LORD, praise the name of the LORD.

2 [a]Blessed be the name of the LORD from this time forth and for evermore.

3 [a]From the rising of the sun unto the going down of the same the LORD'S name *is* to be praised.

4 The LORD *is* [a]high above all nations, *and* [b]his glory above the heavens.

5 [a]Who *is* like unto the LORD our God, who [l]dwelleth on high,

6 [a]Who humbleth *himself* to behold *the things that are* in heaven, and in the earth!

7 [a]He raiseth up the poor out of the dust, *and* lifteth the needy out of the dunghill;

8 That he may [a]set *him* with princes, *even* with the princes of his people.

9 [a]He maketh the barren woman [l]to keep house, *and to be* a joyful mother of children. Praise ye the LORD.

The God of the exodus

114 WHEN [a]ISRAEL went out of Egypt, the house of Jacob [b]from a people of strange language;

2 [a]Judah was his sanctuary, *and* Israel his dominion.

3 [a]The sea saw *it,* and fled: [b]Jordan was driven back.

4 [a]The mountains skipped like rams, *and* the little hills like lambs.

5 [a]What *ailed* thee, O thou sea, that thou fleddest? thou Jordan, *that* thou wast driven back?

6 Ye mountains, *that* ye skipped like rams; *and* ye little hills, like lambs?

7 Tremble, thou earth, at the presence of the Lord, at the presence of the God of Jacob;

8 [a]Which turned the rock *into* a standing water, the flint into a fountain of waters.

To God alone belongs glory

115 NOT [a]UNTO us, O LORD, not unto us, but unto thy name give glory, for thy mercy, *and* for thy truth's sake.

2 Wherefore should the heathen say, [a]Where *is* now their God?

3 [a]But our God *is* in the heavens: he hath done whatsoever he hath pleased.

4 [a]Their idols *are* silver and gold, the work of men's hands.

5 They have mouths, but they speak not: eyes have they, but they see not:

6 They have ears, but they hear not: noses have they, but they smell not:

7 They have hands, but they handle not: feet have they, but they walk not: neither speak they through their throat.

8 [a]They that make them are like unto them; *so is* every one that trusteth in them.

9 [a]O Israel, trust thou in the LORD: [b]he *is* their help and their shield.

10 O house of Aaron, trust in the LORD: he *is* their help and their shield.

11 Ye that fear the LORD, trust in the LORD: he *is* their help and their shield.

12 The LORD hath been mindful of us: he will bless *us;* he will bless the house of

---

3 [a]Mat. 6:33
4 [a]Job 11:17; Ps. 97:11
5 [a]Ps. 37:26 [b]Eph. 5:15; Col. 4:5 [l]Heb. *judgment*
6 [a]Prov. 10:7
7 [a]Prov. 1:33 [b]Ps. 57:7 [c]Ps. 64:10
8 [a]Prov. 1:33 [b]Ps. 59:10 & 118:7
9 [a]2 Cor. 9:9 [b]Ps. 75:10
10 [a]Luke 13:28 [b]Ps. 37:12 [c]Ps. 58:7,8 [d]Prov. 11:7
113:1 [a]Ps. 135:1 [l]Heb. *Hallelujah*
2 [a]Dan. 2:20
3 [a]Is. 59:19; Mal. 1:11
4 [a]Ps. 97:9 & 99:2 [b]Ps. 8:1
5 [a]Ps. 89:6 [l]Heb. *exalteth* himself *to dwell*
6 [a]Ps. 11:4 & 138:6; Is. 57:15
7 [a]1 Sam. 2:8; Ps. 107:41
8 [a]Job 36:7
9 [a]1 Sam. 2:5; Ps. 68:6; Is. 54:1; Gal. 4:27 [l]Heb. *to dwell in an house*
114:1 [a]Ex. 13:3 [b]Ps. 81:5
2 [a]Ex. 6:7; Deut. 27:9
3 [a]Ex. 14:21; Ps. 77:16 [b]Josh. 3:13
4 [a]Ps. 29:6 & 68:16
5 [a]Hab. 3:8
8 [a]Ex. 17:6; Num. 20:11; Ps. 107:35
115:1 [a]Is. 48:11; Ezek. 36:32
2 [a]Ps. 42:3,10 & 79:10; Joel 2:17
3 [a]1 Chr. 16:26; Ps. 135:6; Dan. 4:35
4 [a]Deut. 4:28; Ps. 135:15; Jer. 10:3
8 [a]Ps. 135:18; Is. 44:9-11
9 [a]Ps. 118:2,3 [b]Ps. 33:20

P *Ps 105:37* ◀ ▶ *Pr 3:9–10*
L *Ps 111:4* ◀ ▶ *Ps 116:5*
J *Ps 91:5–6* ◀ ▶ *Ps 118:6*
W *Ps 91:5–6* ◀ ▶ *Ps 119:165*
V *Ps 108:13* ◀ ▶ *Ps 138:7*
H *Ps 103:5* ◀ ▶ *Ps 128:6*
F *Ps 111:5* ◀ ▶ *Ps 132:15*
U *Ps 112:1–10* ◀ ▶ *Ps 118:15*

Israel; he will bless the house of Aaron.
13 [a]He will bless them that fear the
LORD, *both* small ['] and great.
14 The LORD shall increase you more
and more, you and your children.
15 Ye *are* [a]blessed of the LORD [b]which
made heaven and earth.
16 The heaven, *even* the heavens, *are*
the LORD'S: but the earth hath he given to
the children of men.
17 [a]The dead praise not the LORD, neither any that go down into silence.
18 [a]But we will bless the LORD from
this time forth and for evermore. Praise
the LORD.

Deliverance from death

116 I [a]LOVE the LORD, because he
hath heard my voice *and* my
supplications.
2 Because he hath inclined his ear
unto me, therefore will I call upon *him*
[']as long as I live.
M 3 [a]The sorrows of death compassed
me, and the pains of hell [']gat hold upon
me: I found trouble and sorrow.
4 Then called I upon the name of the
LORD; O LORD, I beseech thee, deliver my
soul.
L 5 [a]Gracious *is* the LORD, and [b]righ-
teous; yea, our God *is* merciful.
6 The LORD preserveth the simple: I
was brought low, and he helped me.
7 Return unto thy [a]rest, O my soul; for
[b]the LORD hath dealt bountifully with
thee.
8 [a]For thou hast delivered my soul
from death, mine eyes from tears, *and* my
feet from falling.
9 I will walk before the LORD [a]in the
land of the living.
10 [a]I believed, therefore have I spoken: I was greatly afflicted:
11 [a]I said in my haste, [b]All men *are*
liars.
12 What shall I render unto the LORD
for all his benefits toward me?
13 I will take the cup of salvation, and
call upon the name of the LORD.
14 [a]I will pay my vows unto the LORD
now in the presence of all his people.
L 15 [a]Precious in the sight of the LORD *is*
the death of his saints.
16 O LORD, truly [a]I *am* thy servant; I
am thy servant, *and* [b]the son of thine
handmaid: thou hast loosed my bonds.
17 I will offer to thee [a]the sacrifice of
thanksgiving, and will call upon the name
of the LORD.
18 I will pay my vows unto the LORD
now in the presence of all his people,
19 In the [a]courts of the LORD'S house,
in the midst of thee, O Jerusalem. Praise
ye the LORD.

Praise for God's steadfast love

117 O [a]PRAISE the LORD, all ye
nations: praise him, all ye
people.
2 For his merciful kindness is great toward us: and [a]the truth of the LORD *endureth* for ever. Praise ye the LORD.

The LORD's mercy

118 O [a]GIVE thanks unto the
LORD; for *he is* good: because
his mercy *endureth* for ever.
2 [a]Let Israel now say, that his mercy
endureth for ever.
3 Let the house of Aaron now say, that
his mercy *endureth* for ever.
4 Let them now that fear the LORD say,
that his mercy *endureth* for ever.
5 [a]I called upon the LORD [']in distress:
the LORD answered me, *and* [b]*set me* in a
large place.
6 [a]The LORD *is* [']on my side; I will not J
fear: what can man do unto me? S
7 [a]The LORD taketh my part with them
that help me: therefore shall [b]I see *my
desire* upon them that hate me.
8 [a]*It is* better to trust in the LORD than L
to put confidence in man.
9 [a]*It is* better to trust in the LORD than
to put confidence in princes.
10 All nations compassed me about:
but in the name of the LORD will I [']de-
stroy them.
11 They [a]compassed me about; yea,
they compassed me about: but in the
name of the LORD I will destroy them.
12 They compassed me about [a]like
bees; they are quenched [b]as the fire of
thorns: for in the name of the LORD I will
[']destroy them.
13 Thou hast thrust sore at me that I
might fall: but the LORD helped me.

115:13 [a]Ps. 128:1 [']Heb. *with*
15 [a]Gen. 14:19 [b]Gen. 1:1; Ps. 96:5
17 [a]Ps. 6:5 & 88:10-12; Is. 38:18
18 [a]Ps. 113:2; Dan. 2:20
116:1 [a]Ps. 18:1
2 [']Heb. *in my days*
3 [a]Ps. 18:4-6 [']Heb. *found me*
5 [a]Ps. 103:8 [b]Ezra 9:15; Neh. 9:8; Ps. 119:137 & 145:17
7 [a]Jer. 6:16; Mat. 11:29 [b]Ps. 13:6 & 119:17
8 [a]Ps. 56:13
9 [a]Ps. 27:13
10 [a]2 Cor. 4:13
11 [a]Ps. 31:22 [b]Rom. 3:4
14 [a]ver. 18; Ps. 22:25; Jonah 2:9
15 [a]Ps. 72:14
16 [a]Ps. 119:125 & 143:12 [b]Ps. 86:16
17 [a]Lev. 7:12; Ps. 50:14 & 107:22
19 [a]Ps. 96:8 & 100:4
117:1 [a]Rom. 15:11
2 [a]Ps. 100:5
118:1 [a]1 Chr. 16:8; Ps. 106:1 & 107:1
2 [a]Ps. 115:9
5 [a]Ps. 120:1 [b]Ps. 18:19 [']Heb. *out of distress*
6 [a]Ps. 27:1; Heb. 13:6 [']Heb. *for me*
7 [a]Ps. 54:4 [b]Ps. 59:10
8 [a]Ps. 40:4 & 62:8,9
9 [a]Ps. 146:3
10 [']Heb. *cut them off*
11 [a]Ps. 88:17
12 [a]Deut. 1:44 [b]Eccl. 7:6; Nah. 1:10 [']Heb. *cut down*

M *Ps 51:1–17* ◀▶ *Ps 126:5*
L *Ps 112:4* ◀▶ *Ps 130:3–4*
L *Ps 107:28* ◀▶ *Ps 118:8*
J *Ps 112:7–8* ◀▶ *Pr 1:33*
S *Ps 91:1–16* ◀▶ *Ps 119:117*
L *Ps 116:15* ◀▶ *Ps 121:1–8*

14 [a]The LORD *is* my strength and song, and is become my salvation.

U 15 The voice of rejoicing and salvation *is* in the tabernacles of the righteous: the right hand of the LORD doeth valiantly.

16 [a]The right hand of the LORD is exalted: the right hand of the LORD doeth valiantly.

17 [a]I shall not die, but live, and [b]declare the works of the LORD.

18 The LORD hath [a]chastened me sore: but he hath not given me over unto death.

19 [a]Open to me the gates of righteousness: I will go into them, *and* I will praise the LORD:

20 [a]This gate of the LORD, [b]into which the righteous shall enter.

21 I will praise thee: for thou hast [a]heard me, and [b]art become my salvation.

22 [a]The stone *which* the builders refused is become the head *stone* of the corner.

23 ʹThis is the LORD'S doing; it *is* marvellous in our eyes.

24 This *is* the day *which* the LORD hath made; we will rejoice and be glad in it.

25 Save now, I beseech thee, O LORD: O LORD, I beseech thee, send now prosperity.

26 [a]Blessed *be* he that cometh in the name of the LORD: we have blessed you out of the house of the LORD.

27 God *is* the LORD, which hath shown us [a]light: bind the sacrifice with cords, *even* unto the horns of the altar.

28 Thou *art* my God, and I will praise thee: [a]*thou art* my God, I will exalt thee.

29 [a]O give thanks unto the LORD; for *he is* good: for his mercy *endureth* for ever.

Keepers of God's law

ALEPH.

S U 119 BLESSED *ARE* the ʹundefiled in the way, [a]who walk in the law of the LORD.

2 Blessed *are* they that keep his testimonies, *and that* seek him with the whole heart.

3 [a]They also do no iniquity: they walk in his ways.

U *Ps 115:12–15* ◀ ▶ *Ps 119:1–2*
S *Ps 101:6–8* ◀ ▶ *Ps 119:119*
U *Ps 118:15* ◀ ▶ *Ps 119:165*

14 [a]Ex. 15:2; Is. 12:2
16 [a]Ex. 15:6
17 [a]Ps. 6:5; Hab. 1:12 [b]Ps. 73:28
18 [a]2 Cor. 6:9
19 [a]Is. 26:2
20 [a]Ps. 24:7 [b]Is. 35:8; Rev. 22:14
21 [a]Ps. 116:1 [b]ver. 14
22 [a]Mat. 21:42; Mark 12:10; Luke 20:17; Acts 4:11
23 ʹHeb. *This is from the LORD*
26 [a]Mat. 21:9; Mark 11:9; Luke 19:38; See Zech. 4:7
27 [a]Esth. 8:16; 1 Pet. 2:9
28 [a]Ex. 15:2; Is. 25:1
29 [a]ver. 1
119:1 [a]Ps. 128:1 ʹOr, *perfect*, or, *sincere*
3 [a]1 John 3:9 & 5:18
6 [a]Job 22:26; 1 John 2:28
7 [a]ver. 171 ʹHeb. *judgments of thy righteousness*
10 [a]2 Chr. 15:15 [b]ver. 21,118
11 [a]Ps. 37:31; Luke 2:19
12 [a]ver. 26,33; Ps. 25:4
13 [a]Ps. 34:11
15 [a]ver. 23,48; Ps. 1:2
16 [a]Ps. 1:2
17 [a]Ps. 116:7
18 ʹHeb. *Reveal*
19 [a]Gen. 47:9; 1 Chr. 29:15; Ps. 39:12; 2 Cor. 5:6; Heb. 11:13
20 [a]Ps. 42:1,2 & 63:1 & 84:2
21 [a]ver. 10,110
22 [a]Ps. 39:8
23 [a]ver. 15
24 [a]ver. 77,92 ʹHeb. *men of my counsel*

4 Thou hast commanded *us* to keep thy precepts diligently.

5 O that my ways were directed to keep thy statutes!

6 [a]Then shall I not be ashamed, when I have respect unto all thy commandments.

7 [a]I will praise thee with uprightness of heart, when I shall have learned ʹthy righteous judgments.

8 I will keep thy statutes: O forsake me not utterly.

Purity, the fruit of the law

BETH.

9 Wherewithal shall a young man cleanse his way? by taking heed *thereto* according to thy word.

10 With my whole heart have I [a]sought thee: O let me not [b]wander from thy commandments.

11 [a]Thy word have I hid in mine heart, that I might not sin against thee.

12 Blessed *art* thou, O LORD: [a]teach me thy statutes.

13 With my lips have I [a]declared all the judgments of thy mouth.

14 I have rejoiced in the way of thy testimonies, as *much as* in all riches.

15 I will [a]meditate in thy precepts, and have respect unto thy ways.

16 I will [a]delight myself in thy statutes: I will not forget thy word.

Eyes to see God's law

GIMEL.

17 [a]Deal bountifully with thy servant, *that* I may live, and keep thy word.

18 ʹOpen thou mine eyes, that I may behold wondrous things out of thy law.

19 [a]I *am* a stranger in the earth: hide not thy commandments from me.

20 [a]My soul breaketh for the longing *that it hath* unto thy judgments at all times.

21 Thou hast rebuked the proud *that are* cursed, which do [a]err from thy commandments.

22 [a]Remove from me reproach and contempt; for I have kept thy testimonies.

23 Princes also did sit *and* speak against me: *but* thy servant did [a]meditate in thy statutes.

24 [a]Thy testimonies also *are* my delight *and* ʹmy counsellors.

Prayer for understanding the law

DALETH.

25 [a]My soul cleaveth unto the dust: [b]quicken thou me according to thy word.

26 I have declared my ways, and thou heardest me: [a]teach me thy statutes.

27 Make me to understand the way of thy precepts: so [a]shall I talk of thy wondrous works.

28 [a]My soul [/]melteth for heaviness: strengthen thou me according unto thy word.

29 Remove from me the way of lying: and grant me thy law graciously.

30 I have chosen the way of truth: thy judgments have I laid *before me.*

31 I have stuck unto thy testimonies: O LORD, put me not to shame.

H 32 I will run the way of thy commandments, when thou shalt [a]enlarge my heart.

Living the LORD's way

HE.

33 [a]Teach me, O LORD, the way of thy statutes; and I shall keep it [b]*unto* the end.

34 Give me understanding, and I shall keep thy law; yea, I shall observe it with *my* whole heart.

35 Make me to go in the path of thy commandments; for therein do I [a]delight.

36 Incline my heart unto thy testimonies, and not to [a]covetousness.

37 [a]Turn[/] away mine eyes from [b]beholding vanity; *and* quicken thou me in thy way.

38 [a]Stablish thy word unto thy servant, who *is devoted* to thy fear.

39 Turn away my reproach which I fear: for thy judgments *are* good.

40 Behold, I have [a]longed after thy precepts: [b]quicken me in thy righteousness.

Salvation through God's law

VAU.

41 [a]Let thy mercies come also unto me, O LORD, *even* thy salvation, according to thy word.

42 [/]So shall I have wherewith to answer him that reproacheth me: for I trust in thy word.

43 And take not the word of truth utterly out of my mouth; for I have hoped in thy judgments.

44 So shall I keep thy law continually for ever and ever.

45 And I will walk [/]at liberty: for I seek thy precepts.

46 [a]I will speak of thy testimonies also before kings, and will not be ashamed. T

47 And I will [a]delight myself in thy commandments, which I have loved.

48 My hands also will I lift up unto thy commandments, which I have loved; and I will [a]meditate in thy statutes.

Comfort in God's law

ZAIN.

49 Remember the word unto thy servant, upon which thou hast caused me to [a]hope.

50 This *is* my [a]comfort in my affliction: for thy word hath quickened me.

51 The proud have had me greatly [a]in derision: *yet* have I not [b]declined from thy law.

52 I remembered thy judgments of old, O LORD; and have comforted myself.

53 [a]Horror hath taken hold upon me because of the wicked that forsake thy law.

54 Thy statutes have been my songs in the house of my pilgrimage.

55 [a]I have remembered thy name, O LORD, in the night, and have kept thy law.

56 This I had, because I kept thy precepts.

The LORD our portion

CHETH.

57 [a]*Thou art* my portion, O LORD: I have said that I would keep thy words.

58 I entreated thy favour with *my* whole heart: be merciful unto me [a]according to thy word.

59 I [a]thought on my ways, and turned my feet unto thy testimonies.

60 I made haste, and delayed not to keep thy commandments.

61 The [/]bands of the wicked have robbed me: *but* I have not forgotten thy law.

62 [a]At midnight I will rise to give thanks unto thee because of thy righteous judgments.

25 [a]Ps. 44:25 [b]Ps. 143:11
26 [a]Ps. 25:4 & 27:11 & 86:11
27 [a]Ps. 145:5,6
28 [a]Ps. 107:26 [/]Heb. *droppeth*
32 [a]1 Ki. 4:29; Is. 60:5; 2 Cor. 6:11
33 [a]ver. 12 [b]Mat. 10:22; Rev. 2:26
35 [a]ver. 16
36 [a]Ezek. 33:31; Mark 7:21; Luke 12:15; Heb. 13:5
37 [a]Is. 33:15 [b]Prov. 23:5 [/]Heb. *Make to pass*
38 [a]2 Sam. 7:25
40 [a]ver. 20 [b]ver. 25,37
41 [a]ver. 77; Ps. 106:4
42 [/]Or, *So shall I answer him that reproacheth me in a thing*
45 [/]Heb. *at large*
46 [a]Ps. 138:1; Mat. 10:18; Acts 26
47 [a]ver. 16
48 [a]ver. 15
49 [a]ver. 74,81
50 [a]Rom. 15:4
51 [a]Jer. 20:7 [b]ver. 157; Job 23:11; Ps. 44:18
53 [a]Ezra 9:3
55 [a]Ps. 63:6
57 [a]Ps. 16:5; Jer. 10:16; Lam. 3:24
58 [a]ver. 41
59 [a]Luke 15:17
61 [/]Or, *companies*
62 [a]Acts 16:25

H *Ps 110:1 ◄► Ps 119:119*

T *Ps 107:2 ◄► Ps 119:108*

63 I *am* a companion of all *them* that fear thee, and of them that keep thy precepts.
64 [a]The earth, O LORD, is full of thy mercy: [b]teach me thy statutes.

God's law taught by affliction

TETH.

65 Thou hast dealt well with thy servant, O LORD, according unto thy word.
66 Teach me good judgment and knowledge: for I have believed thy commandments.
T 67 [a]Before I was afflicted I went astray: but now have I kept thy word.
68 Thou *art* [a]good, and doest good; [b]teach me thy statutes.
69 The proud have [a]forged a lie against me: *but* I will keep thy precepts with *my* whole heart.
70 [a]Their heart is as fat as grease; *but* I [b]delight in thy law.
T 71 [a]*It is* good for me that I have been afflicted; that I might learn thy statutes.
72 [a]The law of thy mouth *is* better unto me than thousands of gold and silver.

Confidence in the law

JOD.

73 [a]Thy hands have made me and fashioned me: [b]give me understanding, that I may learn thy commandments.
74 [a]They that fear thee will be glad when they see me; because [b]I have hoped in thy word.
T 75 I know, O LORD, that thy judgments *are* [1]right, and [a]*that* thou in faithfulness hast afflicted me.
76 Let, I pray thee, thy merciful kindness be [1]for my comfort, according to thy word unto thy servant.
77 [a]Let thy tender mercies come unto me, that I may live: for [b]thy law *is* my delight.
78 Let the proud [a]be ashamed; [b]for they dealt perversely with me without a cause: *but* I will [c]meditate in thy precepts.
79 Let those that fear thee turn unto me, and those that have known thy testimonies.

T *Ps 105:19* ◀▶ *Ps 119:71*
T *Ps 119:67* ◀▶ *Ps 119:75*
T *Ps 119:71* ◀▶ *Pr 3:11–12*

64 [a]Ps. 33:5 [b]ver. 12,26
67 [a]ver. 71; Jer. 31:18; Heb. 12:11
68 [a]Ps. 106:1 & 107:1; Mat. 19:17 [b]ver. 12,26
69 [a]Job 13:4; Ps. 109:2
70 [a]Ps. 17:10; Is. 6:10; Acts 28:27 [b]ver. 35
71 [a]ver. 67; Heb. 12:10
72 [a]Ps. 19:10; Prov. 8:10,11,19
73 [a]Job 10:8; Ps. 100:3 & 138:8 & 139:14 [b]ver. 34, 144
74 [a]Ps. 34:2 [b]ver. 49,147
75 [a]Heb. 12:10 [1]Heb. *righteousness*
76 [1]Heb. *to comfort me*
77 [a]ver. 41 [b]ver. 24,47
78 [a]Ps. 25:3 [b]ver. 86 [c]ver. 23
81 [a]Ps. 73:26 & 84:2 [b]ver. 74,114
82 [a]ver. 123; Ps. 69:3
83 [a]Job 30:30
84 [a]Ps. 39:4 [b]Rev. 6:10
85 [a]Ps. 35:7; Prov. 16:27
86 [a]ver. 78 [b]Ps. 35:19 [1]Heb. *faithfulness*
88 [a]ver. 40
89 [a]Ps. 89:2; Mat. 24:34; 1 Pet. 1:25
90 [1]Heb. *to generation and generation* [2]Heb. *standeth*
91 [a]Jer. 33:25
92 [a]ver. 24
96 [a]Mat. 5:18
97 [a]Ps. 1:2

80 Let my heart be sound in thy statutes; that I be not ashamed.

A longing for comfort

CAPH.

81 [a]My soul fainteth for thy salvation: *but* [b]I hope in thy word.
82 [a]Mine eyes fail for thy word, saying, When wilt thou comfort me?
83 For [a]I am become like a bottle in the smoke; *yet* do I not forget thy statutes.
84 [a]How many *are* the days of thy servant? [b]when wilt thou execute judgment on them that persecute me?
85 [a]The proud have digged pits for me, which *are* not after thy law.
86 All thy commandments *are* [1]faithful: [a]they persecute me [b]wrongfully; help thou me.
87 They had almost consumed me upon earth; but I forsook not thy precepts.
88 [a]Quicken me after thy lovingkindness; so shall I keep the testimony of thy mouth.

God's unchangeable law

LAMED.

89 [a]For ever, O LORD, thy word is settled in heaven.
90 Thy faithfulness *is* [1]unto all generations: thou hast established the earth, and it [2]abideth.
91 They continue this day according to [a]thine ordinances: for all *are* thy servants.
92 Unless [a]thy law *had been* my delights, I should then have perished in mine affliction.
93 I will never forget thy precepts: for with them thou hast quickened me.
94 I *am* thine, save me; for I have sought thy precepts.
95 The wicked have waited for me to destroy me: *but* I will consider thy testimonies.
96 [a]I have seen an end of all perfection: *but* thy commandment *is* exceeding broad.

The love of God's law

MEM.

97 O how love I thy law! [a]it *is* my meditation all the day.
98 Thou through thy commandments

hast made me [a]wiser than mine enemies: for [/]they *are* ever with me.

99 I have more understanding than all my teachers: [a]for thy testimonies *are* my meditation.

100 [a]I understand more than the ancients, because I keep thy precepts.

101 I have [a]refrained my feet from every evil way, that I might keep thy word.

102 I have not departed from thy judgments: for thou hast taught me.

103 [a]How sweet are thy words unto my [/]taste! *yea, sweeter* than honey to my mouth!

104 Through thy precepts I get understanding: therefore [a]I hate every false way.

God's law a lamp to the feet

NUN.

105 [a]Thy word *is* a [/]lamp unto my feet, and a light unto my path.

106 [a]I have sworn, and I will perform *it*, that I will keep thy righteous judgments.

107 I am afflicted very much: [a]quicken me, O LORD, according unto thy word.

T 108 Accept, I beseech thee, [a]the freewill offerings of my mouth, O LORD, and [b]teach me thy judgments.

109 [a]My soul *is* continually in my hand: yet do I not forget thy law.

110 [a]The wicked have laid a snare for me: yet I [b]erred not from thy precepts.

111 [a]Thy testimonies have I taken as an heritage for ever: for [b]they *are* the rejoicing of my heart.

112 I have inclined mine heart [/]to perform thy statutes always, [a]*even unto* the end.

God's law a hiding place

SAMECH.

113 I hate *vain* thoughts: but thy law do I love.

114 [a]Thou *art* my hiding place and my shield: [b]I hope in thy word.

115 [a]Depart from me, ye evildoers: for I will keep the commandments of my God.

116 Uphold me according unto thy word, that I may live: and let me not [a]be ashamed of my hope.

S 117 Hold thou me up, and I shall be safe: and I will have respect unto thy statutes continually.

118 Thou hast trodden down all them that [a]err from thy statutes: for their deceit *is* falsehood.

119 Thou [/]puttest away all the wicked of the earth [a]*like* dross: therefore I love thy testimonies. H S

120 [a]My flesh trembleth for fear of thee; and I am afraid of thy judgments.

The psalmist loves God's law

AIN.

121 I have done judgment and justice: leave me not to mine oppressors.

122 Be [a]surety for thy servant for good: let not the proud oppress me.

123 [a]Mine eyes fail for thy salvation, and for the word of thy righteousness.

124 Deal with thy servant according unto thy mercy, and [a]teach me thy statutes.

125 [a]I *am* thy servant; give me understanding, that I may know thy testimonies.

126 *It is* time for *thee*, LORD, to work: *for* they have made void thy law.

127 [a]Therefore I love thy commandments above gold; yea, above fine gold.

128 Therefore I esteem all *thy* precepts *concerning* all *things to be* right; *and* I [a]hate every false way.

The psalmist keeps God's law

PE.

129 Thy testimonies *are* wonderful: therefore doth my soul keep them.

130 The entrance of thy words giveth light; [a]it giveth understanding unto the simple.

131 I opened my mouth, and panted: for I [a]longed for thy commandments.

132 [a]Look thou upon me, and be merciful unto me, [b]as[/] thou usest to do unto those that love thy name.

133 [a]Order my steps in thy word: and [b]let not any iniquity have dominion over me.

134 [a]Deliver me from the oppression of man: so will I keep thy precepts.

135 [a]Make thy face to shine upon thy servant; and [b]teach me thy statutes.

136 [a]Rivers of waters run down mine eyes, because they keep not thy law.

98 [a]Deut. 4:6 [/]Heb. *it is ever with me*
99 [a]2 Tim. 3:15
100 [a]Job 32:7-9
101 [a]Prov. 1:15
103 [a]Ps. 19:10; Prov. 8:11 [/]Heb. *palate*
104 [a]ver. 128
105 [a]Prov. 6:23 [/]Or, *candle*
106 [a]Neh. 10:29
107 [a]ver. 88
108 [a]Hos. 14:2; Heb. 13:15 [b]ver. 12,26
109 [a]Job 13:14
110 [a]Ps. 140:5 [b]ver. 10,21
111 [a]Deut. 33:4 [b]ver. 77,92
112 [a]ver. 33 [/]Heb. *to do*
114 [a]Ps. 32:7 [b]ver. 81
115 [a]Ps. 6:8; Mat. 7:23
116 [a]Ps. 25:2; Rom. 5:5
118 [a]ver. 21
119 [a]Ezek. 22:18 [/]Heb. *causest to cease*
120 [a]Hab. 3:16
122 [a]Heb. 7:22
123 [a]ver. 81,82
124 [a]ver. 12
125 [a]Ps. 116:16
127 [a]Ps. 19:10
128 [a]ver. 104
130 [a]Ps. 19:7
131 [a]ver. 20
132 [a]Ps. 106:4 [b]2 Thes. 1:6 [/]Heb. *according to the custom towards those*
133 [a]Ps. 17:5 [b]Ps. 19:13; Rom. 6:12
134 [a]Luke 1:74
135 [a]Ps. 4:6 [b]ver. 12,26
136 [a]Jer. 9:1; Ezek. 9:4

T *Ps 119:46* ◀▶ *Ps 132:9*
S *Ps 118:6* ◀▶ *Ps 121:1–8*
H *Ps 119:32* ◀▶ *Pr 1:24–32*
S *Ps 119:1–3* ◀▶ *Ps 119:155*

God's law is true

TZADDI.

137 [a]Righteous *art* thou, O LORD, and upright *are* thy judgments.

138 [a]Thy testimonies *that* thou hast commanded *are* [1]righteous and very [2]faithful.

139 [a]My zeal hath [1]consumed me, because mine enemies have forgotten thy words.

140 [a]Thy word *is* very [1]pure: therefore thy servant loveth it.

141 I *am* small and despised: *yet* do not I forget thy precepts.

142 Thy righteousness *is* an everlasting righteousness, and thy law *is* [a]the truth.

143 Trouble and anguish have [1]taken hold on me: *yet* thy commandments *are* [a]my delights.

144 The righteousness of thy testimonies *is* everlasting: [a]give me understanding, and I shall live.

A cry for salvation

KOPH.

145 I cried with *my* whole heart; hear me, O LORD: I will keep thy statutes.

146 I cried unto thee; save me, [1]and I shall keep thy testimonies.

147 [a]I prevented the dawning of the morning, and cried: [b]I hoped in thy word.

148 [a]Mine eyes prevent the *night* watches, that I might meditate in thy word.

149 Hear my voice according unto thy lovingkindness: O LORD, [a]quicken me according to thy judgment.

150 They draw nigh that follow after mischief: they are far from thy law.

151 Thou *art* [a]near, O LORD; [b]and all thy commandments *are* truth.

152 Concerning thy testimonies, I have known of old that thou hast founded them [a]for ever.

Keeping God's law in adversity

RESH.

153 [a]Consider mine affliction, and deliver me: for I do not forget thy law.

154 [a]Plead my cause, and deliver me: [b]quicken me according to thy word.

155 [a]Salvation *is* far from the wicked: for they seek not thy statutes. **S**

156 [1]Great *are* thy tender mercies, O LORD: [a]quicken me according to thy judgments.

157 Many *are* my persecutors and mine enemies; *yet* do I not [a]decline from thy testimonies.

158 I beheld the transgressors, and [a]was grieved; because they kept not thy word.

159 Consider how I love thy precepts: [a]quicken me, O LORD, according to thy lovingkindness.

160 [1]Thy word *is* true *from* the beginning: and every one of thy righteous judgments *endureth* for ever.

SCHIN.

Peace in keeping God's law

161 [a]Princes have persecuted me without a cause: but my heart standeth in awe of thy word.

162 I rejoice at thy word, as one that findeth great spoil.

163 I hate and abhor lying: *but* thy law do I love.

164 Seven times a day do I praise thee because of thy righteous judgments.

165 [a]Great peace have they which love thy law: and [1]nothing shall offend them. **U** **W**

166 [a]LORD, I have hoped for thy salvation, and done thy commandments.

167 My soul hath kept thy testimonies; and I love them exceedingly.

168 I have kept thy precepts and thy testimonies: [a]for all my ways *are* before thee.

A prayer for understanding

TAU

169 Let my cry come near before thee, O LORD: [a]give me understanding according to thy word.

170 Let my supplication come before thee: deliver me according to thy word.

171 [a]My lips shall utter praise, when thou hast taught me thy statutes.

172 My tongue shall speak of thy word: for all thy commandments *are* righteousness.

S *Ps 119:119* ◀ ▶ *Ps 125:5*
U *Ps 119:1–2* ◀ ▶ *Ps 128:1–6*
W *Ps 112:7–8* ◀ ▶ *Pr 1:33*

137 [a]Neh. 9:33
138 [a]Ps. 19:7-9 [1]Heb. *righteousness* [2]Heb. *faithfulness*
139 [a]Ps. 69:9; John 2:17 [1]Heb. *cut me off*
140 [a]Ps. 12:6 [1]Heb. *tried, or, refined*
142 [a]Ps. 19:9
143 [a]ver. 77 [1]Heb. *found me*
144 [a]ver. 34,73
146 [1]Or, *that I may keep*
147 [a]Ps. 5:3 [b]ver. 74
148 [a]Ps. 63:1,6
149 [a]ver. 40
151 [a]Ps. 145:18 [b]ver. 142
152 [a]Luke 21:33
153 [a]Lam. 5:1
154 [a]1 Sam. 24:15 [b]ver. 40
155 [a]Job 5:4
156 [a]ver. 149 [1]Or, *Many*
157 [a]Ps. 44:18
158 [a]Ezek. 9:4
159 [a]ver. 88
160 [1]Heb. *The beginning of thy word is true*
161 [a]1 Sam. 24:11
165 [a]Prov. 3:2; Is. 32:17 [1]Heb. *they shall have no stumblingblock*
166 [a]Gen. 49:18
168 [a]Prov. 5:21
169 [a]ver. 144
171 [a]ver. 7

173 Let thine hand help me; for [a]I have chosen thy precepts.

174 [a]I have longed for thy salvation, O LORD; and [b]thy law *is* my delight.

175 Let my soul live, and it shall praise thee; and let thy judgments help me.

176 [a]I have gone astray like a lost sheep; seek thy servant; for I do not forget thy commandments.

A prayer for deliverance

A Song of degrees.

120 IN [a]MY distress I cried unto the LORD, and he heard me.

2 Deliver my soul, O LORD, from lying lips, *and* from a deceitful tongue.

3 [1]What shall be given unto thee? or what shall be [2]done unto thee, thou false tongue?

4 [1]Sharp arrows of the mighty, with coals of juniper.

5 Woe is me, that I sojourn in [a]Mesech, [b]*that* I dwell in the tents of Kedar!

6 My soul hath long dwelt with him that hateth peace.

7 I *am* [1]*for* peace: but when I speak, they *are* for war.

Help from the LORD

A Song of degrees.

K **121** I[a] WILL[1] lift up mine eyes unto the hills, from whence
L
S cometh my help.

2 [a]My help *cometh* from the LORD, which made heaven and earth.

3 [a]He will not suffer thy foot to be moved: [b]he that keepeth thee will not slumber.

4 Behold, he that keepeth Israel shall neither slumber nor sleep.

5 The LORD *is* thy keeper: the LORD *is* [a]thy shade [b]upon thy right hand.

6 [a]The sun shall not smite thee by day, nor the moon by night.

A 7 The LORD shall preserve thee from all evil: he shall [a]preserve thy soul.

8 The LORD shall [a]preserve thy going out and thy coming in from this time forth, and even for evermore.

K *Ps 107:14* ◄► *Ps 125:1*
L *Ps 118:8* ◄► *Ps 125:1–2*
S *Ps 119:117* ◄► *Ps 140:7*
A *Ps 91:10* ◄► *Pr 12:21*

The peace of Jerusalem

A Song of degrees of David.

122 I WAS glad when they said unto me, [a]Let us go into the house of the LORD.

2 Our feet shall stand within thy gates, O Jerusalem.

3 Jerusalem is builded as a city that is [a]compact together:

4 [a]Whither the tribes go up, the tribes of the LORD, unto [b]the testimony of Israel, to give thanks unto the name of the LORD.

5 [a]For there [1]are set thrones of judgment, the thrones of the house of David.

6 [a]Pray for the peace of Jerusalem: they shall prosper that love thee.

7 Peace be within thy walls, *and* prosperity within thy palaces.

8 For my brethren and companions' sakes, I will now say, Peace *be* within thee.

9 Because of the house of the LORD our God I will [a]seek thy good.

A song of confidence in God

A Song of degrees.

123 UNTO THEE [a]lift I up mine eyes, O thou [b]that dwellest in the heavens.

2 Behold, as the eyes of servants *look* unto the hand of their masters, *and* as the eyes of a maiden unto the hand of her mistress; so our eyes *wait* upon the LORD our God, until that he have mercy upon us.

3 Have mercy upon us, O LORD, have mercy upon us: for we are exceedingly filled with contempt.

4 Our soul is exceedingly filled with the scorning of those that are at ease, *and* with the contempt of the proud.

God's deliverance

A Song of degrees of David.

124 IF *IT had not been* the LORD who was on our side, [a]now may Israel say;

2 If *it had not been* the LORD who was on our side, when men rose up against us:

3 Then they had [a]swallowed us up quick, when their wrath was kindled against us:

4 Then the waters had overwhelmed us, the stream had gone over our soul:

---

173 [a]Josh. 24:22
174 [a]ver. 166 [b]ver. 16,24
176 [a]Is. 53:6
120:1 [a]Jonah 2:2
3 [1]Or, *What shall* the deceitful tongue *give unto thee?* or, *What shall it profit thee?* [2]Heb. *added*
4 [1]Or, It is as *the sharp arrows of the mighty* man, *with coals of juniper*
5 [a]Gen. 10:2; Ezek. 27:13 [b]Gen. 25:13; 1 Sam. 25:1; Jer. 49:28
7 [1]Or, a man *of peace*
121:1 [a]Jer. 3:23 [1]Or, *Shall I lift up mine eyes to the hills? whence should my help come?*
2 [a]Ps. 124:8
3 [a]1 Sam. 2:9 [b]Ps. 127:1; Is. 27:3
5 [a]Is. 25:4 [b]Ps. 16:8
6 [a]Ps. 91:5; Is. 49:10
7 [a]Ps. 41:2
8 [a]Deut. 28:6
122:1 [a]Is. 2:3; Zech. 8:21
3 [a]See 2 Sam. 5:9
4 [a]Ex. 23:17; Deut. 16:16 [b]Ex. 16:34
5 [a]Deut. 17:8; 2 Chr. 19:8 [1]Heb. *do sit*
6 [a]Ps. 51:18
9 [a]Neh. 2:10
123:1 [a]Ps. 121:1; & 141:8 [b]Ps. 2:4 & 11:4 & 115:3
124:1 [a]Ps. 129:1
3 [a]Ps. 56:1,2 & 57:3; Prov. 1:12

5 Then the proud waters had gone over our soul.

6 Blessed *be* the LORD, who hath not given us *as* a prey to their teeth.

7 Our soul is escaped [a]as a bird out of the snare of the fowlers: the snare is broken, and we are escaped.

8 [a]Our help *is* in the name of the LORD, [b]who made heaven and earth.

The LORD the protector

A Song of degrees.

F K L

125 THEY THAT trust in the LORD *shall be* as mount Zion, *which* cannot be removed, *but* abideth for ever.

2 *As* the mountains *are* round about Jerusalem, so the LORD *is* round about his people from henceforth even for ever.

3 For [a]the rod of [1]the wicked shall not rest upon the lot of the righteous; lest the righteous put forth their hands unto iniquity.

4 Do good, O LORD, unto *those that be* good, and to *them that are* upright in their hearts.

S

5 As for such as turn aside unto their [a]crooked ways, the LORD shall lead them forth with the workers of iniquity: *but* [b]peace *shall be* upon Israel.

Zion's captivity

A Song of degrees.

I

126 WHEN THE LORD [a]turned[1] again the captivity of Zion, [b]we were like them that dream.

2 Then [a]was our mouth filled with laughter, and our tongue with singing: then said they among the heathen, The LORD [1]hath done great things for them.

3 The LORD hath done great things for us; *whereof* we are glad.

4 Turn again our captivity, O LORD, as the streams in the south.

M R

5 [a]They that sow in tears shall reap in [1]joy.

6 He that goeth forth and weepeth, bearing [1]precious seed, shall doubtless come again with rejoicing, bringing his sheaves *with him.*

The vanity of work without God

A Song of degrees [1]for Solomon.

O

127 EXCEPT THE LORD build the house, they labour in vain [2]that build it: except [a]the LORD keep the city, the watchman waketh *but* in vain.

2 *It is* vain for you to rise up early, to sit up late, to [a]eat the bread of sorrows: *for* so he giveth his beloved sleep.

3 Lo, [a]children *are* an heritage of the LORD *and* [b]the fruit of the womb *is his* reward.

4 As arrows *are* in the hand of a mighty man; so *are* children of the youth.

5 Happy *is* the man that [1]hath his quiver full of them: [a]they shall not be ashamed, but they [2]shall speak with the enemies in the gate.

The God-fearing family

A Song of degrees.

K U

128 BLESSED [a]*IS* every one that feareth the LORD; that walketh in his ways.

2 [a]For thou shalt eat the labour of thine hands: happy *shalt* thou *be*, and *it shall be* well with thee.

R

3 Thy wife *shall be* [a]as a fruitful vine by the sides of thine house: thy children [b]like olive plants round about thy table.

4 Behold, that thus shall the man be blessed that feareth the LORD.

5 [a]The LORD shall bless thee out of Zion: and thou shalt see the good of Jerusalem all the days of thy life.

H

6 Yea, thou shalt [a]see thy children's children, *and* [b]peace upon Israel.

7 [a]Ps. 91:3; Prov. 6:5
8 [a]Ps. 121:2 [b]Gen. 1:1; Ps. 134:3
125:3 [a]Prov. 22:8; Is. 14:5 [1]Heb. *wickedness*
5 [a]Prov. 2:15 [b]Ps. 128:6
126:1 [a]Ps. 53:6 & 85:1; Hos. 6:11; Joel 3:1 [b]Acts 12:9 [1]Heb. *returned the returning of Zion*
2 [a]Job 8:21 [1]Heb. *hath magnified to do with them*
5 [a]See Jer. 31:9 [1]Or, *singing*
6 [1]Or, *seed basket*
127:1 [a]Ps. 121:3-5 [1]Or, *of Solomon;* see Ps. 72, title [2]Heb. that are *builders of it in it*
2 [a]Gen. 3:17,19
3 [a]Gen. 33:5 & 48:4; Josh. 24:3,4 [b]Deut. 28:4
5 [a]Job 5:4; Prov. 27:11 [1]Heb. *hath filled his quiver with them* [2]Or, *shall subdue,* or, *destroy*
128:1 [a]Ps. 119:1
2 [a]Is. 3:10
3 [a]Ezek. 19:10 [b]Ps. 52:8 & 144:12
5 [a]Ps. 134:3
6 [a]Gen. 50:23; Job 42:16 [b]Ps. 125:5

F *Ps 84:12* ◀▶ *Pr 29:25*
K *Ps 121:1–8* ◀▶ *Ps 128:1–2*
L *Ps 121:1–8* ◀▶ *Ps 142:3*
S *Ps 119:155* ◀▶ *Ps 139:23–24*
I *Ps 111:9* ◀▶ *Ps 130:8*

M *Ps 116:3–5* ◀▶ *Ps 138:6*
R *Ps 51:17* ◀▶ *Ps 147:3*
O *Ps 75:6–7* ◀▶ *Pr 19:21*
K *Ps 125:1* ◀▶ *Ps 130:7*
U *Ps 119:165* ◀▶ *Ps 132:9*
R *Ps 112:1–2* ◀▶ *Ps 144:12*
H *Ps 113:9* ◀▶ *Ps 146:8*

126:1–6 This psalm of praise rejoices in the exiles' restoration to Zion and prefigures the rejoicing that will accompany the Messiah's victory in the millennial kingdom. The psalmist also reminds his readers that we must remain faithful despite adversity for "they that sow in tears shall reap in joy" (126:5).

Israel's enemies

A Song of degrees.

129 MANY[1] A time have they afflicted me from [a]my youth,
[b]may Israel now say:
2 Many a time have they afflicted me
from my youth: yet they have not prevailed against me.
3 The plowers plowed upon my back:
they made long their furrows.
4 The LORD *is* righteous: he hath cut
asunder the cords of the wicked.
5 Let them all be confounded and
turned back that hate Zion.
6 Let them be as [a]the grass *upon* the
housetops, which withereth afore it
groweth up:
7 Wherewith the mower filleth not his
hand; nor he that bindeth sheaves his
bosom.
8 Neither do they which go by say,
[a]The blessing of the LORD *be* upon you:
we bless you in the name of the LORD.

Waiting on the LORD

A Song of degrees.

130 OUT [a]OF the depths have I
cried unto thee, O LORD.
2 Lord, hear my voice: let thine ears be
attentive to the voice of my supplications.
A 3 [a]If thou, LORD, shouldest mark iniqui-
L ties, O Lord, who shall stand?
4 But *there is* [a]forgiveness with thee,
that [b]thou mayest be feared.
5 [a]I wait for the LORD, my soul doth
wait, and [b]in his word do I hope.
6 [a]My soul *waiteth* for the Lord more
than they that watch for the morning: [1]*I
say, more than* they that watch for the
morning.
K 7 [a]Let Israel hope in the LORD: for
L [b]with the LORD *there is* mercy, and with
him *is* plenteous redemption.
8 And [a]he shall redeem Israel from all I
his iniquities.

A song of the humble

A Song of degrees of David.

131 LORD, MY heart is not
haughty, nor mine eyes lofty:
[a]neither do I [1]exercise myself in great
matters, or in things too [b]high[2] for me.
2 Surely I have behaved and quieted
[1]myself, [a]as a child that is weaned of his
mother: my soul *is* even as a weaned
child.
3 [a]Let Israel hope in the LORD [1]from
henceforth and for ever.

The promise to David and Zion

A Song of degrees.

132 LORD, REMEMBER David,
and all his afflictions:
2 How he sware unto the LORD, [a]*and*
vowed unto [b]the mighty *God* of Jacob;
3 Surely I will not come into the tabernacle of my house, nor go up into my
bed;
4 I will [a]not give sleep to mine eyes, *or*
slumber to mine eyelids,
5 Until I [a]find out a place for the LORD,
[1]an habitation for the mighty *God* of
Jacob.
6 Lo, we heard of it [a]at Ephratah: [b]we
found it [c]in the fields of the wood.
7 We will go into his tabernacles: [a]we
will worship at his footstool.
8 [a]Arise, O LORD, into thy rest; thou,
and [b]the ark of thy strength.
9 Let thy priests [a]be clothed with righ- T
teousness; and let thy saints shout for joy. U
10 For thy servant David's sake turn
not away the face of thine anointed.
11 [a]The LORD hath sworn *in* truth unto M
David; he will not turn from it; [b]Of the
fruit of [1]thy body will I set upon thy
throne.

129:1 [a]Ezek. 23:3; Hos. 2:15 [b]Ps. 124:1 [1]Or, *Much*
6 [a]Ps. 37:2
8 [a]Ruth 2:4; Ps. 118:26
130:1 [a]Lam. 3:55; Jonah 2:2
3 [a]Ps. 143:2; Rom. 3:20
4 [a]Ex. 34:7 [b]1 Ki. 8:40; Ps. 2:11; Jer. 33:8
5 [a]Ps. 27:14; Is. 8:17 [b]Ps. 119:81
6 [a]Ps:119:147 [1]Or, *which watch unto the morning*
7 [a]Ps. 131:3 [b]Ps. 86:5; Is. 55:7
8 [a]Ps. 103:3,4; Mat. 1:21
131:1 [a]Rom. 12:16 [b]Job 42:3; Ps. 139:6 [1]Heb. *walk* [2]Heb. *wonderful*
2 [a]Mat. 18:3; 1 Cor. 14:20 [1]Heb. *my soul*
3 [a]Ps. 130:7 [1]Heb. *from now*
132:2 [a]Ps. 65:1 [b]Gen. 49:24
4 [a]Prov. 6:4
5 [a]Acts 7:46 [1]Heb. *habitations*
6 [a]1 Sam. 17:12 [b]1 Sam. 7:1 [c]1 Chr. 13:5
7 [a]Ps. 5:7 & 99:5
8 [a]Num. 10:35; 2 Chr. 6:41 [b]Ps. 78:61
9 [a]Job 29:14; Is. 61:10
11 [a]Ps. 89:3,4 [b]2 Sam. 7:12; 1 Ki. 8:25 [1]Heb. *thy belly*

A *Ps 53:1–4* ◀ ▶ *Ps 143:2*
L *Ps 116:5* ◀ ▶ *Ps 130:7–8*
K *Ps 128:1–2* ◀ ▶ *Pr 23:11*
L *Ps 130:3–4* ◀ ▶ *Ps 145:8*
I *Ps 126:1–6* ◀ ▶ *Ps 132:13–15*
T *Ps 119:108* ◀ ▶ *Ps 134:1–3*
U *Ps 128:1–6* ◀ ▶ *Ps 132:16*
M *Ps 110:1–7* ◀ ▶ *SS 2:3–6*

130:8 This prophecy confirmed God's promise to redeem Israel from their sins if they would turn from iniquity and repent of their sins.
132:11–18 This psalm prophetically confirmed God's unbreakable promise to David to establish David's seed upon the throne of Israel forever. The final fulfillment of this prophecy will be realized during the millennial kingdom. When the Messiah returns, the temple will be reestablished, sacred worship reinstated and righteous priests will worship God in true holiness.

12 If thy children will keep my covenant and my testimony that I shall teach them, their children shall also sit upon thy throne for evermore.

I 13 [a]For the LORD hath chosen Zion; he hath desired *it* for his habitation.

14 [a]This *is* my rest for ever: here will I dwell; for I have desired it.

F 15 [a]I will /abundantly bless her provision: I will satisfy her poor with bread.

U 16 [a]I will also clothe her priests with salvation: [b]and her saints shall shout aloud for joy.

17 [a]There will I make the horn of David to bud: [b]I have ordained a /lamp for mine anointed.

18 His enemies will I [a]clothe with shame: but upon himself shall his crown flourish.

Brotherly unity

A Song of degrees of David.

133 BEHOLD, HOW good and how pleasant *it is* for [a]brethren to dwell /together in unity!

2 *It is* like [a]the precious ointment upon the head, that ran down upon the beard, *even* Aaron's beard: that went down to the skirts of his garments;

3 As the dew of [a]Hermon, *and as the dew* that descended upon the mountains of Zion: for [b]there the LORD commanded the blessing, *even* life for evermore.

Blessing for the night watch

A Song of degrees.

T **134** BEHOLD, BLESS ye the LORD, [a]all *ye* servants of the LORD, [b]which by night stand in the house of the LORD.

2 [a]Lift up your hands /*in* the sanctuary, and bless the LORD.

3 [a]The LORD that made heaven and earth [b]bless thee out of Zion.

Praise to the LORD

135 PRAISE YE the LORD. Praise ye the name of the LORD; [a]praise *him,* O ye servants of the LORD.

2 [a]Ye that stand in the house of the LORD, in [b]the courts of the house of our God,

3 Praise the LORD; for [a]the LORD *is* good: sing praises unto his name; [b]for *it is* pleasant.

4 For [a]the LORD hath chosen Jacob unto himself, *and* Israel for his peculiar treasure.

5 For I know that [a]the LORD *is* great, and *that* our Lord *is* above all gods.

6 [a]Whatsoever the LORD pleased, *that* did he in heaven, and in earth, in the seas, and all deep places.

7 [a]He causeth the vapours to ascend from the ends of the earth; [b]he maketh lightnings for the rain; he bringeth the wind out of his [c]treasuries.

8 [a]Who smote the firstborn of Egypt, /both of man and beast.

9 [a]*Who* sent tokens and wonders into the midst of thee, O Egypt, [b]upon Pharaoh, and upon all his servants.

10 [a]Who smote great nations, and slew mighty kings;

11 Sihon king of the Amorites, and Og king of Bashan, and [a]all the kingdoms of Canaan:

12 [a]And gave their land *for* an heritage, an heritage unto Israel his people.

13 [a]Thy name, O LORD, *endureth* for ever; *and* thy memorial, O LORD, /throughout all generations.

14 [a]For the LORD will judge his people, and he will repent himself concerning his servants. I

15 [a]The idols of the heathen *are* silver and gold, the work of men's hands.

16 They have mouths, but they speak not; eyes have they, but they see not;

17 They have ears, but they hear not; neither is there *any* breath in their mouths.

18 They that make them are like unto them: *so is* every one that trusteth in them.

19 [a]Bless the LORD, O house of Israel: bless the LORD, O house of Aaron:

20 Bless the LORD, O house of Levi: ye that fear the LORD, bless the LORD.

21 Blessed be the LORD [a]out of Zion, which dwelleth at Jerusalem. Praise ye the LORD.

13 [a]Ps. 48:1,2
14 [a]Ps. 68:16
15 [a]Ps. 147:14 /Or, *surely*
16 [a]2 Chr. 6:41 [b]Hos. 11:12
17 [a]Ezek. 29:21; Luke 1:69 [b]1 Ki. 11:36 /Or, *candle*
18 [a]Ps. 35:26 & 109:29
133:1 [a]Gen. 13:8; Heb. 13:1 /Heb. *even together*
2 [a]Ex. 30:25
3 [a]Deut. 4:48 [b]Lev. 25:21; Deut. 28:8; Ps. 42:8
134:1 [a]Ps. 135:1,2 [b]1 Chr. 9:33
2 [a]1 Tim. 2:8 /Or, in *holiness*
3 [a]Ps. 124:8 [b]Ps. 128:5 & 135:21
135:1 [a]Ps. 113:1; & 134:1
2 [a]Luke 2:37 [b]Ps. 116:19
3 [a]Ps. 119:68 [b]Ps. 147:1
4 [a]Ex. 19:5; Deut. 7:6,7
5 [a]Ps. 95:3 & 97:9
6 [a]Ps. 115:3
7 [a]Jer. 10:13 [b]Job 28:25; Zech. 10:1 [c]Job 38:22
8 [a]Ex. 12:12; Ps. 78:51 /Heb. *from man unto beast*
9 [a]Ex. 7-10 [b]Ps. 136:15
10 [a]Num. 21:24; Ps. 136:17
11 [a]Josh. 12:7
12 [a]Ps. 78:55 & 136:21,22
13 [a]Ex. 3:15; Ps. 102:12 /Heb. *to generation and generation*
14 [a]Deut. 32:36
15 [a]Ps. 115:4-8
19 [a]Ps. 115:9
21 [a]Ps. 134:3

I *Ps 130:8* ◀▶ *Ps 135:14*
F *Ps 114:8* ◀▶ *Ps 146:7*
U *Ps 132:9* ◀▶ *Ps 140:13*
T *Ps 132:9* ◀▶ *Ps 145:1–7*

I *Ps 132:13–15* ◀▶ *Ps 147:2*

A litany of God's wonders

136 O [a]GIVE thanks unto the
LORD; for *he is* good: [b]for his
mercy *endureth* for ever.
2 O give thanks unto [a]the God of gods:
for his mercy *endureth* for ever.
3 O give thanks to the Lord of lords:
for his mercy *endureth* for ever.
4 To him [a]who alone doeth great wonders: for his mercy *endureth* for ever.
5 [a]To him that by wisdom made the
heavens: for his mercy *endureth* for ever.
6 [a]To him that stretched out the earth
above the waters: for his mercy *endureth*
for ever.
7 [a]To him that made great lights: for
his mercy *endureth* for ever:
8 [a]The sun [1]to rule by day: for his
mercy *endureth* for ever:
9 The moon and stars to rule by night:
for his mercy *endureth* for ever.
10 [a]To him that smote Egypt in their
firstborn: for his mercy *endureth* for ever:
11 [a]And brought out Israel from
among them: for his mercy *endureth* for
ever:
12 [a]With a strong hand, and with a
stretched out arm: for his mercy *endureth* for ever.
13 [a]To him which divided the Red sea
into parts: for his mercy *endureth* for
ever:
14 And made Israel to pass through
the midst of it: for his mercy *endureth* for
ever:
15 [a]But [1]overthrew Pharaoh and his
host in the Red sea: for his mercy *endureth* for ever.
16 [a]To him which led his people
through the wilderness: for his mercy *endureth* for ever.
17 [a]To him which smote great kings:
for his mercy *endureth* for ever:
18 [a]And slew famous kings: for his
mercy *endureth* for ever:
19 [a]Sihon king of the Amorites: for his
mercy *endureth* for ever:
20 [a]And Og the king of Bashan: for his
mercy *endureth* for ever:
21 [a]And gave their land for an heritage: for his mercy *endureth* for ever:
22 *Even* an heritage unto Israel his servant: for his mercy *endureth* for ever.
23 Who [a]remembered us in our low
estate: for his mercy *endureth* for ever:
24 And hath redeemed us from our enemies: for his mercy *endureth* for ever.
25 [a]Who giveth food to all flesh: for his
mercy *endureth* for ever.
26 O give thanks unto the God of
heaven: for his mercy *endureth* for ever.

Captives in Babylon

137 BY THE rivers of Babylon,
there we sat down, yea, we
wept, when we remembered Zion.
2 We hanged our harps upon the willows in the midst thereof.
3 For there they that carried us away
captive required of us [1]a song; and they
that [a]wasted[2] us *required of us* mirth,
saying, Sing us *one* of the songs of Zion.
4 How shall we sing the LORD's song in
a [1]strange land?
5 If I forget thee, O Jerusalem, let my
right hand forget *her cunning.*
6 If I do not remember thee, let my
[a]tongue cleave to the roof of my mouth; if
I prefer not Jerusalem above [1]my chief
joy.
7 Remember, O LORD, [a]the children of
Edom in the day of Jerusalem; who said,
[1]Rase *it,* rase *it, even* to the foundation
thereof.
8 O daughter of Babylon, [a]who art to
be [1]destroyed; happy *shall he be,* [b]that[2]
rewardeth thee as thou hast served us.
9 Happy *shall he be,* that taketh and
[a]dasheth thy little ones against [1]the
stones.

The LORD a faithful God

A *Psalm* of David.

138 I WILL praise thee with my
whole heart: [a]before the gods
will I sing praise unto thee.
2 [a]I will worship [b]toward thy holy
temple, and praise thy name for thy lovingkindness and for thy truth: for thou
hast [c]magnified thy word above all thy
name.
3 In the day when I cried thou answeredst me, *and* strengthenedst me
with strength in my soul.
4 [a]All the kings of the earth shall
praise thee, O LORD, when they hear the
words of thy mouth.
5 Yea, they shall sing in the ways of
the LORD: for great *is* the glory of the LORD.
6 [a]Though the LORD *be* high, yet [b]hath M

M *Ps 126:5* ◄ ► *Ps 149:4*

136:1 [a]Ps. 106:1 [b]1 Chr. 16:34
2 [a]Deut. 10:17
4 [a]Ps. 72:18
5 [a]Gen. 1:1; Prov. 3:19; Jer. 51:15
6 [a]Gen. 1:9; Ps. 24:2; Jer. 10:12
7 [a]Gen. 1:14
8 [a]Gen. 1:16 [1]Heb. *for the rulings by day*
10 [a]Ex. 12:29; Ps. 135:8
11 [a]Ex. 12:51
12 [a]Ex. 6:6
13 [a]Ex. 14:21; Ps. 78:13
15 [a]Ex. 14:27; Ps. 135:9 [1]Heb. *shaked off*
16 [a]Ex. 13:18
17 [a]Ps. 135:10
18 [a]Deut. 29:7
19 [a]Num. 21:21
20 [a]Num. 21:33
21 [a]Josh. 12:1; Ps. 135:12
23 [a]Gen. 8:1; Deut. 32:36; Ps. 113:7
25 [a]Ps. 104:27 & 145:15
137:3 [a]Ps. 79:1 [1]Heb. *the words of song* [2]Heb. *laid us on heaps*
4 [1]Heb. *land of a stranger?*
6 [a]Ezek. 3:26 [1]Heb. *the head of my joy*
7 [a]Jer. 49:7; Lam. 4:22; Ezek. 25:12; Obad. 10 [1]Heb. *Make bare*
8 [a]Is. 13:1,6; Jer. 25:12 [b]Jer. 50:15; Rev. 18:6 [1]Heb. *wasted* [2]Heb. *that recompenseth unto thee thy deed which thou didst to us*
9 [a]Is. 13:16 [1]Heb. *the rock*
138:1 [a]Ps. 119:46
2 [a]Ps. 28:2 [b]1 Ki. 8:29; Ps. 5:7 [c]Is. 42:21
4 [a]Ps. 102:15
6 [a]Ps. 113:5,6; Is. 57:15 [b]Prov. 3:34; Jas. 4:6; 1 Pet. 5:5

he respect unto the lowly: but the proud he knoweth afar off.

V 7 [a]Though I walk in the midst of trouble, thou wilt revive me: thou shalt stretch forth thine hand against the wrath of mine enemies, and thy right hand shall save me.

8 [a]The LORD will perfect *that which* concerneth me: thy mercy, O LORD, *endureth* for ever: [b]forsake not the works of thine own hands.

The prayer of a believing heart

To the chief Musician, A Psalm of David.

E 139 O LORD, [a]thou hast searched me, and known *me.*

2 [a]Thou knowest my downsitting and mine uprising, thou [b]understandest my thought afar off.

3 [a]Thou [1]compassest my path and my lying down, and art acquainted *with* all my ways.

4 For *there is* not a word in my tongue, *but,* lo, O LORD, [a]thou knowest it altogether.

5 Thou hast beset me behind and before, and laid thine hand upon me.

6 [a]*Such* knowledge *is* too wonderful for me; it is high, I cannot *attain* unto it.
C 7 [a]Whither shall I go from thy spirit?
D or whither shall I flee from thy presence?
E 8 [a]If I ascend up into heaven, thou *art*
M there: [b]if I make my bed in hell, behold,
N thou *art there.*

9 *If* I take the wings of the morning, *and* dwell in the uttermost parts of the sea;

10 Even there shall thy hand lead me, and thy right hand shall hold me.

11 If I say, Surely the darkness shall cover me; even the night shall be light about me.

12 Yea, [a]the darkness [1]hideth not from thee; but the night shineth as the day: [2]the darkness and the light *are* both alike *to thee.*

13 For thou hast possessed my reins: thou hast covered me in my mother's womb.

14 I will praise thee; for I am fearfully *and* wonderfully made: marvellous *are* thy works; and *that* my soul knoweth [1]right well.

15 [a]My [1]substance was not hid from thee, when I was made in secret, *and* curiously wrought in the lowest parts of the earth.

16 Thine eyes did see my substance, yet being unperfect; and in thy book [1]all *my members* were written, [2]*which* in continuance were fashioned, when *as yet there was* none of them.

17 [a]How precious also are thy thoughts unto me, O God! how great is the sum of them!

18 *If* I should count them, they are more in number than the sand: when I awake, I am still with thee.

19 Surely thou wilt [a]slay the wicked, O God: [b]depart from me therefore, ye bloody men.

20 For they [a]speak against thee wickedly, *and* thine enemies take *thy name* in vain.

21 [a]Do not I hate them, O LORD, that hate thee? and am not I grieved with those that rise up against thee?

22 I hate them with perfect hatred: I count them mine enemies.

23 [a]Search me, O God, and know my S
heart: try me, and know my thoughts:

24 And see if *there be any* [1]wicked way in me, and [a]lead me in the way everlasting.

For protection against enemies

To the chief Musician, A Psalm of David.

140 DELIVER ME, O LORD, from the evil man: preserve me from the [1]violent man;

2 Which imagine mischiefs in *their* heart; [a]continually are they gathered together *for* war.

3 They have sharpened their tongues like a serpent; [a]adders' poison *is* under their lips. Selah.

4 [a]Keep me, O LORD, from the hands of the wicked; preserve me from the violent man; who have purposed to overthrow my goings.

5 [a]The proud have hid a snare for me, and cords; they have spread a net by the wayside; they have set gins for me. Selah.

6 I said unto the LORD, Thou *art* my

7 [a]Ps. 23:3,4
8 [a]Ps. 57:2; Phil. 1:6 [b]Job 10:3,8
139:1 [a]Ps. 17:3; Jer. 12:3
2 [a]2 Ki. 19:27 [b]Mat. 9:4; John 2:24
3 [a]Job 31:4 [1]Or, *winnowest*
4 [a]Heb. 4:13
6 [a]Job 42:3; Ps. 40:5
7 [a]Jer. 23:24; Jonah 1:3
8 [a]Amos 9:2 [b]Prov. 15:11
12 [a]Job 34:22 [1]Heb. *darkeneth not* [2]Heb. *as is the darkness, so is the light*
14 [1]Heb. *greatly*
15 [a]Job 10:8,9 [1]Or, *strength,* or, *body*
16 [1]Heb. *all of them* [2]Or, *what days they should be fashioned*
17 [a]Ps. 40:5
19 [a]Is. 11:4 [b]Ps. 119:115
20 [a]Jude 15
21 [a]2 Chr. 19:2
23 [a]Job 31:6
24 [a]Ps. 5:8 [1]Heb. *way of pain*
140:1 [1]Heb. *man of violences*
2 [a]Ps. 56:6
3 [a]Ps. 58:4
4 [a]Ps. 71:4
5 [a]Jer. 18:22

V *Ps 112:8* ◀▶ *Pr 12:13*
E *Ps 102:19* ◀▶ *Pr 5:21*
C *Ps 51:12–13* ◀▶ *Mic 3:8*
D *Ps 68:18* ◀▶ *Isa 40:13*
E *Ps 104:30* ◀▶ *Ps 143:10*
M *Ps 104:30* ◀▶ *Isa 11:2*
N *Ps 104:30* ◀▶ *Ps 143:10*

S *Ps 125:5* ◀▶ *Pr 3:6–7*

God: hear the voice of my supplications, O LORD.

S 7 O GOD the Lord, the strength of my salvation, thou hast covered my head in the day of battle.

8 Grant not, O LORD, the desires of the wicked: further not his wicked device; [a]*lest*[1] they exalt themselves. Selah.

9 *As for* the head of those that compass me about, [a]let the mischief of their own lips cover them.

10 [a]Let burning coals fall upon them: let them be cast into the fire; into deep pits, that they rise not up again.

11 Let not [1,2]an evil speaker be established in the earth: evil shall hunt the violent man to overthrow *him.*

12 I know that the LORD will [a]maintain the cause of the afflicted, *and* the right of the poor.

U 13 Surely the righteous shall give thanks unto thy name: the upright shall dwell in thy presence.

Conduct amidst trial

A Psalm of David.

141 LORD, I cry unto thee: [a]make haste unto me; give ear unto my voice, when I cry unto thee.

2 Let [a]my prayer be [1]set forth before thee [b]*as* incense; *and* [c]the lifting up of my hands *as* [d]the evening sacrifice.

3 Set a watch, O LORD, before my mouth; keep the door of my lips.

4 Incline not my heart to *any* evil thing, to practise wicked works with men that work iniquity: [a]and let me not eat of their dainties.

5 [a]Let[1] the righteous smite me; *it shall be* a kindness: and let him reprove me; *it shall be* an excellent oil, *which* shall not break my head: for yet my prayer also *shall be* in their calamities.

6 When their judges are overthrown in stony places, they shall hear my words; for they are sweet.

7 Our bones are scattered at the grave's mouth, as when one cutteth and cleaveth *wood* upon the earth.

8 But [a]mine eyes *are* unto thee, O GOD the Lord: in thee is my trust; [1]leave not my soul destitute.

9 Keep me from [a]the snares *which* they have laid for me, and the gins of the workers of iniquity.

10 [a]Let the wicked fall into their own nets, whilst that I withal [1]escape.

The prisoner's prayer

[a]Maschil[1] of David; A Prayer [b]when he was in the cave.

142 I CRIED unto the LORD with my voice; with my voice unto the LORD did I make my supplication.

2 [a]I poured out my complaint before him; I showed before him my trouble.

3 [a]When my spirit was overwhelmed within me, then thou knewest my path. [b]In the way wherein I walked have they privily laid a snare for me. L

4 [a]I[1] looked on *my* right hand, and beheld, but [b]*there was* no man that would know me: refuge [2]failed me; [3]no man cared for my soul.

5 I cried unto thee, O LORD: I said, [a]Thou *art* my refuge *and* [b]my portion [c]in the land of the living.

6 Attend unto my cry; for I am [a]brought very low: deliver me from my persecutors; for they are stronger than I.

7 Bring my soul out of prison, that I may praise thy name: [a]the righteous shall compass me about; [b]for thou shalt deal bountifully with me.

The prayer of a soul in distress

A Psalm of David.

143 HEAR MY prayer, O LORD, give ear to my supplications: [a]in thy faithfulness answer me, *and* in thy righteousness.

2 And [a]enter not into judgment with thy servant: for [b]in thy sight shall no man living be justified. A G

3 For the enemy hath persecuted my soul; he hath smitten my life down to the ground; he hath made me to dwell in darkness, as those that have been long dead.

4 [a]Therefore is my spirit overwhelmed within me; my heart within me is desolate.

5 [a]I remember the days of old; I meditate on all thy works; I muse on the work of thy hands.

6 [a]I stretch forth my hands unto thee:

8 [a]Deut. 32:27 [1]Or, *let them not be exalted*
9 [a]Ps. 7:16
10 [a]Ps. 11:6
11 [1]Heb. *a man of tongue* [2]Or, *an evil speaker, a wicked man of violence, be established in the earth: let him be hunted to his overthrow*
12 [a]Ps. 9:4
141:1 [a]Ps. 70:5
2 [a]Rev. 5:8 [b]Rev. 8:3 [c]1 Tim. 2:8 [d]Ex. 29:39 [1]Heb. *directed*
4 [a]Prov. 23:6
5 [a]Prov. 9:8 [1]Or, *Let the righteous smite me kindly, and reprove me; let not their precious oil break my head*
8 [a]Ps. 25:15 [1]Heb. *make not my soul bare*
9 [a]Ps. 119:110
10 [a]Ps. 35:8 [1]Heb. *pass over*
142:1 [a]Ps. 57, title [b]1 Sam. 22:1 [1]Or, A Psalm *of David, giving instruction*
2 [a]Is. 26:16
3 [a]Ps. 143:4 [b]Ps. 140:5
4 [a]Ps. 69:20 [b]Ps. 31:11 [1]Or, *Look on the right hand, and see* [2]Heb. *perished from me* [3]Heb. *no man sought after my soul*
5 [a]Ps. 46:1 [b]Lam. 3:24 [c]Ps. 27:13
6 [a]Ps. 116:6
7 [a]Ps. 34:2 [b]Ps. 13:6
143:1 [a]Ps. 31:1
2 [a]Job 14:3 [b]Ex. 34:7
4 [a]Ps. 77:3
5 [a]Ps. 77:5
6 [a]Ps. 88:9

S *Ps 121:1–8* ◀▶ *Pr 1:33*
U *Ps 132:16* ◀▶ *Ps 144:15*
L *Ps 125:1–2* ◀▶ *Ps 144:2*
A *Ps 130:3* ◀▶ *Pr 20:9*
G *Ps 75:6–7* ◀▶ *Pr 3:5–6*

[b]my soul *thirsteth* after thee, as a thirsty land. Selah.

7 Hear me speedily, O LORD: my spirit faileth: hide not thy face from me, [a]lest[1] I be like unto them that go down into the pit.

8 Cause me to hear thy lovingkindness [a]in the morning; for in thee do I trust: cause me to know the way wherein I should walk; for [b]I lift up my soul unto thee.

9 Deliver me, O LORD, from mine enemies: I [1]flee unto thee to hide me.

10 [a]Teach me to do thy will; for thou *art* my God: [b]thy spirit *is* good; lead me into [c]the land of uprightness.

11 [a]Quicken me, O LORD, for thy name's sake: for thy righteousness' sake bring my soul out of trouble.

12 And of thy mercy [a]cut off mine enemies, and destroy all them that afflict my soul: for I *am* thy servant.

The warrior's psalm

A Psalm of David.

144 BLESSED *BE* the LORD [a]my[1] strength, [b]which teacheth my hands [2]to war, *and* my fingers to fight:

2 [1]My goodness, and my fortress; my high tower, and my deliverer; my shield, and *he* in whom I trust; who subdueth my people under me.

3 [a]LORD, what *is* man, that thou takest knowledge of him! *or* the son of man, that thou makest account of him!

4 [a]Man is like to vanity: [b]his days *are* as a shadow that passeth away.

5 [a]Bow thy heavens, O LORD, and come down: [b]touch the mountains, and they shall smoke.

6 [a]Cast forth lightning, and scatter them: shoot out thine arrows, and destroy them.

7 Send thine [1]hand from above; rid me, and deliver me out of great waters, from the hand of strange children;

8 Whose mouth [a]speaketh vanity, and their right hand *is* a right hand of falsehood.

9 I will [a]sing a new song unto thee, O God: upon a psaltery *and* an instrument of ten strings will I sing praises unto thee.

10 [a]*It is he* that giveth [1]salvation unto kings: who delivereth David his servant from the hurtful sword.

11 Rid me, and deliver me from the hand of strange children, whose mouth speaketh vanity, and their right hand *is* a right hand of falsehood:

12 That our sons *may be* [a]as plants grown up in their youth; *that* our daughters *may be* as corner stones, [1]polished *after* the similitude of a palace:

13 *That* our garners *may be* full, affording [1]all manner of store: *that* our sheep may bring forth thousands and ten thousands in our streets:

14 *That* our oxen *may be* [1]strong to labour; *that there be* no breaking in, nor going out; that *there be* no complaining in our streets.

15 [a]Happy *is that* people, that is in such a case: *yea,* happy *is that* people, whose God *is* the LORD.

The goodness of the LORD

David's [a]*Psalm* of praise.

145 I WILL extol thee, my God, O king; and I will bless thy name for ever and ever.

2 Every day will I bless thee; and I will praise thy name for ever and ever.

3 [a]Great *is* the LORD, and greatly to be praised; [1]and [b]his greatness *is* unsearchable.

4 [a]One generation shall praise thy works to another, and shall declare thy mighty acts.

5 I will speak of the glorious honour of thy majesty, and of thy wondrous [1]works.

6 And *men* shall speak of the might of thy terrible acts: and I will [1]declare thy greatness.

143:6 [b]Ps. 63:1
7 [a]Ps. 28:1 [1]Or, *for I am become like*
8 [a]Ps. 46:5 [b]Ps. 25:1
9 [1]Heb. *hide me with thee*
10 [a]Ps. 25:4,5 [b]Neh. 9:20 [c]Is. 26:10
11 [a]Ps. 119:25
12 [a]Ps. 54:5
144:1 [a]Ps. 18:2,31 [b]2 Sam. 22:35; Ps. 18:34 [1]Heb. my *rock* [2]Heb. *to the war*
2 [1]Or, *My mercy*
3 [a]Job 7:17; Ps. 8:4; Heb. 2:6
4 [a]Job 4:19 [b]Ps. 102:11
5 [a]Ps. 18:9 [b]Ps. 104:32
6 [a]Ps. 18:13
7 [1]Heb. *hands*
8 [a]Ps. 12:2
9 [a]Ps. 33:2,3
10 [a]Ps. 18:50 [1]Or, *victory*
12 [a]Ps. 128:3 [1]Heb. *cut*
13 [1]Heb *from kind to kind*
14 [1]Heb. *able to bear burdens,* or, *loaden* with flesh
15 [a]Ps. 33:12
145:1 [a]Ps. 100, title
3 [a]Ps. 147:5 [b]Rom. 11:33 [1]Heb. *and of his greatness* there is *no search*
4 [a]Is. 38:9
5 [1]Heb. *things,* or, *words*
6 [1]Heb. *declare it*

E *Ps 139:7 ◀▶ Isa 30:1*
L *Ps 39:3 ◀▶ Isa 48:16*
N *Ps 139:7 ◀▶ Isa 4:4*
T *Job 32:18–19 ◀▶ Pr 1:22–23*
L *Ps 142:3 ◀▶ Ps 145:18*
N *Ps 103:15–16 ◀▶ Pr 1:24–33*
P *Ps 110:5–6 ◀▶ Pr 2:21–22*
R *Ps 128:3 ◀▶ Lk 1:13–15*
U *Ps 140:13 ◀▶ Ps 147:11*
T *Ps 134:1–3 ◀▶ Ps 145:10–12*

144:5–6 This prayer for deliverance over treacherous enemies bears some resemblance to Ps 18:9, 14.

7 They shall abundantly utter the memory of thy great goodness, and shall sing of thy righteousness.

L 8 [a]The LORD *is* gracious, and full of compassion; slow to anger, and [i]of great mercy.

W 9 [a]The LORD *is* good to all: and his tender mercies *are* over all his works.

T 10 [a]All thy works shall praise thee, O LORD; and thy saints shall bless thee.

11 They shall speak of the glory of thy kingdom, and talk of thy power;

12 To make known to the sons of men his mighty acts, and the glorious majesty of his kingdom.

K 13 [a]Thy kingdom *is* [i]an everlasting kingdom, and thy dominion *endureth* throughout all generations.

14 The LORD upholdeth all that fall, and [a]raiseth up all *those that be* bowed down.

15 [a]The eyes of all [i]wait upon thee; and [b]thou givest them their meat in due season.

16 Thou openest thine hand, [a]and satisfiest the desire of every living thing.

17 The LORD *is* righteous in all his ways, and [i]holy in all his works.

L W L 18 [a]The LORD *is* nigh unto all them that call upon him, to all that call upon him [b]in truth.

19 He will fulfil the desire of them that fear him: he also will hear their cry, and will save them.

L 20 [a]The LORD preserveth all them that love him: but all the wicked will he destroy.

21 My mouth shall speak the praise of the LORD: and let all flesh bless his holy name for ever and ever.

L *Ps 130:7–8* ◀▶ *Ps 145:18*
W *Ps 86:5* ◀▶ *Ps 145:18*
T *Ps 145:1–7* ◀▶ *Isa 12:4*
K *Ps 92:9* ◀▶ *Isa 11:9*
L *Ps 145:8* ◀▶ *Ps 147:3*
W *Ps 145:9* ◀▶ *Pr 29:25*
L *Ps 144:2* ◀▶ *Ps 145:20*
L *Ps 145:18* ◀▶ *Ps 146:5*

8 [a]Num. 14:18 [i]Heb. *great in mercy*
9 [a]Nah. 1:7
10 [a]Ps. 19:1
13 [a]1 Tim. 1:17 [i]Heb. *a kingdom of all ages*
14 [a]Ps. 146:8
15 [a]Ps. 104:27 [b]Ps. 136:25 [i]Or, *look unto thee*
16 [a]Ps. 104:21
17 [i]Or, *merciful,* or, *bountiful*
18 [a]Deut. 4:7 [b]John 4:24
20 [a]Ps. 31:23
146:1 [a]Ps. 103:1 [i]Heb. *Hallelujah*
2 [a]Ps. 104:33
3 [a]Is. 2:22 [i]Or, *salvation*
4 [a]Eccl. 12:7 [b]1 Cor. 2:6
5 [a]Jer. 17:7
6 [a]Rev. 14:7
7 [a]Ps. 103:6 [b]Ps. 107:9 [c]Ps. 107:10
8 [a]Mat. 9:30 [b]Luke 13:13
9 [a]Deut. 10:18; Ps. 68:5 [b]Ps. 147:6
10 [a]Ex. 15:18; Ps. 10:16
147:1 [a]Ps. 92:1 [b]Ps. 135:3 [c]Ps. 33:1
2 [a]Ps. 102:16 [b]Deut. 30:3
3 [a]Ps. 51:17 [i]Heb. *griefs*
4 [a]Is. 40:26

An exhortation to trust God

146 PRAISE[i] YE the LORD. [a]Praise the LORD, O my soul.

2 [a]While I live will I praise the LORD: I will sing praises unto my God while I have any being.

3 [a]Put not your trust in princes, *nor* in the son of man, in whom *there is* no [i]help.

4 [a]His breath goeth forth, he returneth to his earth; in that very day [b]his thoughts perish.

5 [a]Happy *is he* that *hath* the God of Jacob for his help, whose hope *is* in the LORD his God: L

6 [a]Which made heaven, and earth, the sea, and all that therein *is:* which keepeth truth for ever:

7 [a]Which executeth judgment for the oppressed: [b]which giveth food to the hungry. [c]The LORD looseth the prisoners: F

8 [a]The LORD openeth *the eyes of* the blind: [b]the LORD raiseth them that are bowed down: the LORD loveth the righteous: H

9 [a]The LORD preserveth the strangers; he relieveth the fatherless and widow: [b]but the way of the wicked he turneth upside down.

10 [a]The LORD shall reign for ever, *even* thy God, O Zion, unto all generations. Praise ye the LORD.

The might and grace of the LORD

147 PRAISE YE the LORD: for [a]*it is* good to sing praises unto our God; [b]for *it is* pleasant; *and* [c]praise is comely.

2 The LORD doth [a]build up Jerusalem: [b]he gathereth together the outcasts of Israel. I

3 [a]He healeth the broken in heart, and bindeth up their [i]wounds. L R

4 [a]He telleth the number of the stars; he calleth them all by *their* names.

L *Ps 145:20* ◀▶ *Pr 2:8*
F *Ps 132:15* ◀▶ *Ps 147:9*
H *Ps 128:6* ◀▶ *Pr 3:2*
I *Ps 135:14* ◀▶ *Isa 1:25–27*
L *Ps 145:18* ◀▶ *Ps 149:4*
R *Ps 126:5* ◀▶ *Pr 3:7*

145:13 Unlike earthly kingdoms that flourish for a few centuries and then fade away, the kingdom of the Messiah "is an everlasting kingdom."

147:2 This verse refers to the postexilic return of the Jews to Palestine that began in Nehemiah's day and has gained momentum in this generation, initially fulfilling this ancient prophecy.

5 [a]Great *is* our Lord, and of [b]great power: [c]his[/] understanding *is* infinite.

6 [a]The LORD lifteth up the meek: he casteth the wicked down to the ground.

7 Sing unto the LORD with thanksgiving; sing praise upon the harp unto our God:

8 [a]Who covereth the heaven with clouds, who prepareth rain for the earth, who maketh grass to grow upon the mountains.

F 9 [a]He giveth to the beast his food, *and* [b]to the young ravens which cry.

10 [a]He delighteth not in the strength of the horse: he taketh not pleasure in the legs of a man.

U 11 The LORD taketh pleasure in them that fear him, in those that hope in his mercy.

12 Praise the LORD, O Jerusalem; praise thy God, O Zion.

13 For he hath strengthened the bars of thy gates; he hath blessed thy children within thee.

F 14 [a]He[/] maketh peace *in* thy borders, *and* [b]filleth thee with the [2]finest of the wheat.

15 [a]He sendeth forth his commandment *upon* earth: his word runneth very swiftly.

16 [a]He giveth snow like wool: he scattereth the hoarfrost like ashes.

17 He casteth forth his ice like morsels: who can stand before his cold?

18 [a]He sendeth out his word, and melteth them: he causeth his wind to blow, *and* the waters flow.

19 [a]He showeth [/]his word unto Jacob, [b]his statutes and his judgments unto Israel.

20 [a]He hath not dealt so with any nation: and *as for his* judgments, they have not known them. Praise ye the LORD.

Nature's praise of the LORD

148 PRAISE[/] YE the LORD. Praise ye the LORD from the heavens: praise him in the heights.

2 Praise ye him, all his angels: praise ye him, all his hosts.

3 Praise ye him, sun and moon: praise him, all ye stars of light.

4 Praise him, [a]ye heavens of heavens, and [b]ye waters that *be* above the heavens.

5 Let them praise the name of the LORD: for [a]he commanded, and they were created.

6 [a]He hath also stablished them for ever and ever; he hath made a decree which shall not pass.

7 Praise the LORD from the earth, [a]ye dragons, and all deeps:

8 Fire, and hail; snow, and vapour; stormy wind [a]fulfilling his word:

9 [a]Mountains, and all hills; fruitful trees, and all cedars:

10 Beasts, and all cattle; creeping things, and [/]flying fowl:

11 Kings of the earth, and all people; princes, and all judges of the earth:

12 Both young men, and maidens; old men, and children:

13 Let them praise the name of the LORD: for [a]his name alone is [/]excellent; [b]his glory *is* above the earth and heaven.

14 [a]He also exalteth the horn of his people, [b]the praise of all his saints; *even* of the children of Israel, [c]a people near unto him. Praise ye the LORD.

The LORD's love of Israel

149 PRAISE[/] YE the LORD. [a]Sing unto the LORD a new song, *and* his praise in the congregation of saints.

2 Let Israel rejoice in [a]him that made him: let the children of Zion be joyful in their [b]King.

3 [a]Let them praise his name [/]in the dance: let them sing praises unto him with the timbrel and harp.

4 For [a]the LORD taketh pleasure in his people: [b]he will beautify the meek with salvation. L M

5 Let the saints be joyful in glory: let them [a]sing aloud upon their beds.

6 *Let* the high *praises* of God *be* [/]in their mouth, and [a]a twoedged sword in their hand;

7 To execute vengeance upon the heathen, *and* punishments upon the people;

8 To bind their kings with chains, and their nobles with fetters of iron;

9 [a]To execute upon them the judgment written: [b]this honour have all his saints. Praise ye the LORD.

---

5 [a]Ps. 48:1 [b]Nah. 1:3 [c]Is. 40:28 [/]Heb. *of his understanding* there is *no number*

6 [a]Ps. 146:8

8 [a]Job 38:26; Ps. 104:13

9 [a]Job 38:41; Ps. 104:27 [b]Mat. 6:26

10 [a]Ps. 33:16; Hos. 1:7

14 [a]Is. 60:17,18 [b]Ps. 132:15 [/]Heb. *Who maketh thy border peace* [2]Heb. *fat of wheat*

15 [a]Ps. 107:20

16 [a]Job 37:6

18 [a]Job 37:10

19 [a]Deut. 33:4; Ps. 76:1 [b]Mal. 4:4 [/]Heb. *his words*

20 [a]Rom. 3:1,2

148:1 [/]Heb. *Hallelujah*

4 [a]1 Ki. 8:27; 2 Cor. 12:2 [b]Gen. 1:7

5 [a]Gen. 1:1,6; Ps. 33:6,9

6 [a]Ps. 89:37; Jer. 33:25

7 [a]Is. 43:20

8 [a]Ps. 147:15-18

9 [a]Is. 44:23

10 [/]Heb. *birds of wing*

13 [a]Is. 12:4 [b]Ps. 113:4 [/]Heb. *exalted*

14 [a]Ps. 75:10 [b]Ps. 149:9 [c]Eph. 2:17

149:1 [a]Ps. 33:3; Is. 42:10 [/]Heb. *Hallelujah*

2 [a]Job 35:10; Ps. 100:3; Is. 54:5 [b]Zech. 9:9; Mat. 21:5

3 [a]Ps. 81:2 [/]Or, *with the pipe*

4 [a]Ps. 35:27 [b]Ps. 132:16

5 [a]Job 35:10

6 [a]Heb. 4:12; Rev. 1:16 [/]Heb. *in their throat*

9 [a]Deut. 7:1,2 [b]Ps. 148:14

F *Ps 146:7* ◀ ▶ *Ps 147:14*
U *Ps 144:15* ◀ ▶ *Pr 3:5–6*
F *Ps 147:9* ◀ ▶ *Pr 10:3*
L *Ps 147:3* ◀ ▶ *Pr 8:17*
M *Ps 138:6* ◀ ▶ *Pr 3:7*

Let every thing praise the LORD

150 PRAISE[I] YE the LORD. Praise
God in his sanctuary: praise
him in the firmament of his power.
2 [a]Praise him for his mighty acts;
praise him according to his excellent
[b]greatness.
3 Praise him with the sound of the
[a]trumpet:[I] [b]praise him with the psaltery
and harp.
4 Praise him [a]with the timbrel and
[b]dance:[I] praise him with [c]stringed instruments and organs.
5 Praise him upon the loud [a]cymbals:
praise him upon the high sounding
cymbals.
6 Let every thing that hath breath
praise the LORD. Praise ye the LORD.

150:1 [I]Heb. *Hallelujah*
2 [a]Ps. 145:5 [b]Deut. 3:24
3 [a]Ps. 98:6 [b]Ps. 81:2 [I]Or, *cornet*
4 [a]Ex. 15:20 [b]Ps. 149:3 [c]Ps. 33:2; Is. 38:20 [I]Or, *pipe*
5 [a]1 Chr. 15:16,19,28

150:6 This psalm follows the pattern of the rest of the book by ending this section of Psalms with a doxology. In fact, this particular psalm may have been composed specifically to close this book with a final call to "Praise ye the LORD."

Proverbs

Author: King Solomon and others

Theme: God's wisdom gives guidance for right living

Date of Writing: C. 970–700 B.C.

Outline of Proverbs

I. Purpose and Theme Are Introduced (1:1–7)
II. Following the Way of Wisdom (1:8—9:18)
III. Proverbs of Solomon (10:1—22:16)
IV. Words From the Wise (22:17—24:34)
V. More Proverbs of Solomon (25:1—29:27)
VI. Proverbs of Agur and Lemuel (30:1—31:9)
VII. An Excellent Wife (31:10–31)

COMPLETED ABOUT 700 B.C., the book of Proverbs consists of wise sayings, comparisons and moral assertions that illustrate truths about human behavior. The use of proverbs as a teaching tool was widely accepted in ancient societies. Since a proverb usually describes a self-evident or axiomatic truth, the 900 maxims in this book helped provide practical knowledge in discerning between good and evil, truth and error, uprightness and foolishness.

The proverbs used in this book came from a variety of sources. Many of the maxims in the opening chapters of this book probably came from Solomon's personal experience. In fact, Proverbs credits these wise sayings to King Solomon (see 1:1; 10:1). Additional proverbs may have been well known in the literature of that period and recorded by other authors. Later, King Solomon's reputation for wisdom prompted scholars in Hezekiah's day to copy down more of Solomon's proverbs (see 25:1; 1Ki 4:29–32), adding chapters 25—29 to the original collection. Additional entries by Agur and Lemuel complete the book as it appears today.

The purpose of Proverbs

1 THE [a]PROVERBS of Solomon the son of David, king of Israel;

2 To know wisdom and instruction; to perceive the words of understanding;

3 To receive the instruction of wisdom, justice, and judgment, and [l]equity;

4 To give subtlety to the simple, to the young man knowledge and [l]discretion.

5 [a]A wise *man* will hear, and will increase learning; and a man of understanding shall attain unto wise counsels:

6 To understand a proverb, and [l]the interpretation; the words of the wise, and their [a]dark sayings.

7 ¶ [a]The fear of the LORD *is* [l]the beginning of knowledge: *but* fools despise wisdom and instruction.

8 [a]My son, hear the instruction of thy father, and forsake not the law of thy mother:

9 For they *shall be* [l]an ornament of grace unto thy head, and chains about thy neck.

Warnings against violence

10 ¶ My son, if sinners entice thee, [a]consent thou not.

11 If they say, Come with us, let us [a]lay wait for blood, let us lurk privily for the innocent without cause:

12 Let us swallow them up alive as the grave; and whole, [a]as those that go down into the pit:

13 We shall find all precious substance, we shall fill our houses with spoil:

14 Cast in thy lot among us; let us all have one purse:

15 My son, [a]walk not thou in the way with them; [b]refrain thy foot from their path:

16 [a]For their feet run to evil, and make haste to shed blood.

17 Surely in vain the net is spread [l]in the sight of any bird.

18 And they lay wait for their *own* blood; they lurk privily for their *own* lives.

19 [a]So *are* the ways of every one that is greedy of gain; *which* taketh away the life of the owners thereof.

Result of rejecting wisdom

20 ¶ [a]Wisdom[l] crieth without; she uttereth her voice in the streets:

21 She crieth in the chief place of concourse, in the openings of the gates: in the city she uttereth her words, *saying,*

22 How long, ye simple ones, will ye love simplicity? and the scorners delight in their scorning, and fools hate knowledge? G P T W

23 Turn you at my reproof: behold, [a]I will pour out my spirit unto you, I will make known my words unto you.

24 ¶ [a]Because I have called, and ye refused; I have stretched out my hand, and no man regarded; H N

25 But ye [a]have set at nought all my counsel, and would none of my reproof:

26 [a]I also will laugh at your calamity; I will mock when your fear cometh;

27 When [a]your fear cometh as desolation, and your destruction cometh as a whirlwind; when distress and anguish cometh upon you.

28 [a]Then shall they call upon me, but I will not answer; they shall seek me early, but they shall not find me:

29 For that they [a]hated knowledge, and did not [b]choose the fear of the LORD:

30 [a]They would none of my counsel: they despised all my reproof.

31 Therefore [a]shall they eat of the fruit of their own way, and be filled with their own devices.

32 For the [l]turning away of the simple shall slay them, and the prosperity of fools shall destroy them.

33 But [a]whoso hearkeneth unto me shall dwell safely, and [b]shall be quiet from fear of evil. J S W

The reward of wisdom

2 MY SON, if thou wilt receive my words, and [a]hide my commandments with thee;

2 So that thou incline thine ear unto wisdom, *and* apply thine heart to understanding;

3 Yea, if thou criest after knowledge, *and* [l]liftest up thy voice for understanding;

4 [a]If thou seekest her as silver, and searchest for her as *for* hid treasures;

1:1 [a]1 Ki. 4:32; Eccl. 12:9
3 [l]Heb. *equities*
4 [l]Or, *advisement*
5 [a]ch. 9:9
6 [a]Ps. 78:2 [l]Or, *an eloquent speech*
7 [a]Job 28:28; Ps. 111:10; Eccl. 12:13 [l]Or, *the principal part*
8 [a]ch. 4:1
9 [l]Heb. *an adding*
10 [a]Gen. 39:7
11 [a]Jer. 5:26
12 [a]Ps. 28:1
15 [a]Ps. 1:1 [b]Ps. 119:101
16 [a]Is. 59:7
17 [l]Heb. *in the eyes of every thing that hath a wing*
19 [a]1 Tim. 6:10
20 [a]John 7:37 [l]Heb. *Wisdoms,* i.e. *Excellent wisdom*
23 [a]Joel 2:28
24 [a]Is. 66:4; Jer. 7:13; Zech. 7:11
25 [a]Ps. 107:11; Luke 7:30
26 [a]Ps. 2:4
27 [a]ch. 10:24
28 [a]Job 27:9; Is. 1:15; Jer. 14:12; Ezek. 8:18; Mic. 3:4; Zech. 7:13; Jas. 4:3
29 [a]Job 21:14 [b]Ps:119:173
30 [a]Ps. 81:11
31 [a]Job 4:8; Is. 3:11; Jer. 6:19
32 [l]Or, *ease of the simple*
33 [a]Ps. 25:12 [b]Ps. 112:7
2:1 [a]ch. 4:21
3 [l]Heb. *givest thy voice*
4 [a]ch. 3:14; Mat. 13:44

G *Ps 68:18 ◄► Isa 11:2–3*
P *Ps 68:18 ◄► Isa 4:4*
T *Ps 143:10 ◄► Isa 11:2–3*
W *Ps 68:18 ◄► Isa 30:1*
H *Ps 119:119 ◄► Pr 5:4–5*
N *Ps 144:4 ◄► Pr 8:17*
J *Ps 118:6 ◄► Isa 26:3*
S *Ps 140:7 ◄► Pr 3:23–26*
W *Ps 119:165 ◄► Isa 12:2–3*

5 Then shalt thou understand the fear of the LORD, and find the knowledge of God.

6 [a]For the LORD giveth wisdom: out of his mouth *cometh* knowledge and understanding.

7 He layeth up sound wisdom for the righteous: [a]*he is* a buckler to them that walk uprightly.

L 8 He keepeth the paths of judgment, and [a]preserveth the way of his saints.

9 Then shalt thou understand righteousness, and judgment, and equity; *yea,* every good path.

10 ¶ When wisdom entereth into thine heart, and knowledge is pleasant unto thy soul;

11 Discretion shall preserve thee, [a]understanding shall keep thee:

12 To deliver thee from the way of the evil *man,* from the man that speaketh froward things;

13 Who leave the paths of uprightness, to [a]walk in the ways of darkness;

14 Who [a]rejoice to do evil, *and* [b]delight in the frowardness of the wicked;

15 [a]Whose ways *are* crooked, and *they* froward in their paths:

16 To deliver thee from [a]the strange woman, [b]*even* from the stranger *which* flattereth with her words;

17 [a]Which forsaketh the guide of her youth, and forgetteth the covenant of her God.

18 For [a]her house inclineth unto death, and her paths unto the dead.

19 None that go unto her return again, neither take they hold of the paths of life.

20 That thou mayest walk in the way of good *men,* and keep the paths of the righteous.

P 21 [a]For the upright shall dwell in the land, and the perfect shall remain in it,

22 [a]But the wicked shall be cut off from the earth, and the transgressors shall be [1]rooted out of it.

L *Ps 146:5* ◀▶ *Pr 18:24*
P *Ps 144:5–6* ◀▶ *Isa 1:24*

The blessing of wisdom

3 MY SON, forget not my law; [a]but let thine heart keep my commandments:

2 For length of days, and [1]long life, and [a]peace, shall they add to thee. H

3 Let not mercy and truth forsake thee: [a]bind them about thy neck; [b]write them upon the table of thine heart:

4 [a]So shalt thou find favour and [1]good understanding in the sight of God and man.

5 ¶ [a]Trust in the LORD with all thine heart; [b]and lean not unto thine own understanding. G U

6 [a]In all thy ways acknowledge him, and he shall [b]direct thy paths. S

7 ¶ [a]Be not wise in thine own eyes: [b]fear the LORD, and depart from evil. M R

8 It shall be [1]health to thy navel, and [a]marrow[2] to thy bones. H

9 [a]Honour the LORD with thy substance, and with the firstfruits of all thine increase: B P U

10 [a]So shall thy barns be filled with plenty, and thy presses shall burst out with new wine.

11 ¶ [a]My son, despise not the chastening of the LORD; neither be weary of his correction: T

12 For whom the LORD loveth he correcteth; [a]even as a father the son *in whom* he delighteth.

13 ¶ [a]Happy *is* the man *that* findeth wisdom, and [1]the man *that* getteth understanding.

14 [a]For the merchandise of it *is* better than the merchandise of silver, and the gain thereof than fine gold.

15 She *is* more precious than rubies:

H *Ps 146:8* ◀▶ *Pr 3:8*
G *Ps 143:2* ◀▶ *Pr 16:2*
U *Ps 147:11* ◀▶ *Pr 3:9*
S *Ps 139:23–24* ◀▶ *Pr 4:23*
M *Ps 149:4* ◀▶ *Pr 3:34*
R *Ps 147:3* ◀▶ *Pr 14:16*
H *Pr 3:2* ◀▶ *Pr 3:16*
B *Ps 107:38* ◀▶ *Eze 34:26–27*
P *Ps 112:3* ◀▶ *Pr 3:16*
U *Pr 3:5–6* ◀▶ *Pr 3:33*
T *Ps 119:75* ◀▶ *Pr 17:3*

6 [a]1 Ki. 3:9; Jas. 1:5
7 [a]Ps. 84:11
8 [a]1 Sam. 2:9; Ps. 66:9
11 [a]ch. 6:22
13 [a]John 3:19
14 [a]Jer. 11:15 [b]Rom. 1:32
15 [a]Ps. 125:5
16 [a]ch. 5:20 [b]ch. 5:3
17 [a]See Mal. 2:14, 15
18 [a]ch. 7:27
21 [a]Ps. 37:29
22 [a]Job 18:17; Ps. 37:28 [1]Or, *plucked up*
3:1 [a]Deut. 8:1
2 [a]Ps. 119:165 [1]Heb. *years of life*
3 [a]Ex. 13:9; Deut. 6:8 [b]2 Cor. 3:3
4 [a]Rom. 14:18 [1]Or, *good success*
5 [a]Ps. 37:3,5 [b]Jer. 9:23
6 [a]1 Chr. 28:9 [b]Jer. 10:23
7 [a]Rom. 12:16 [b]ch. 16:6
8 [a]Job 21:24 [1]Heb. *medicine* [2]Heb. *watering,* or, *moistening*
9 [a]Ex. 22:29
10 [a]Deut. 28:8
11 [a]Job 5:17; Ps. 94:12
12 [a]Deut. 8:5
13 [a]ch. 8:34,35 [1]Heb. *the man* that *draweth out understanding*
14 [a]Job 28:13; Ps. 19:10

2:21–22 Solomon announced prophetically the final victory of the righteous and the defeat of the wicked who will be "cut off from the earth" (2:22). This prophecy will be fulfilled at the Battle of Armageddon and will usher in the Millennium.

and [a]all the things thou canst desire are not to be compared unto her.

H P 16 [a]Length of days *is* in her right hand; *and* in her left hand riches and honour.

17 [a]Her ways *are* ways of pleasantness, and all her paths *are* peace.

18 She *is* [a]a tree of life to them that lay hold upon her: and happy *is every one* that retaineth her.

19 [a]The LORD by wisdom hath founded the earth; by understanding hath he [l]established the heavens.

20 [a]By his knowledge the depths are broken up, and [b]the clouds drop down the dew.

21 ¶ My son, let not them depart from thine eyes: keep sound wisdom and discretion:

22 So shall they be life unto thy soul, and [a]grace to thy neck.

S 23 [a]Then shalt thou walk in thy way safely, and thy foot shall not stumble.

24 [a]When thou liest down, thou shalt not be afraid: yea, thou shalt lie down, and thy sleep shall be sweet.

25 [a]Be not afraid of sudden fear, neither of the desolation of the wicked, when it cometh.

26 For the LORD shall be thy confidence, and shall keep thy foot from being taken.

27 ¶ [a]Withhold not good from [l]them to whom it is due, when it is in the power of thine hand to do *it.*

28 [a]Say not unto thy neighbour, Go, and come again, and tomorrow I will give; when thou hast it by thee.

29 [l]Devise not evil against thy neighbour, seeing he dwelleth securely by thee.

30 ¶ [a]Strive not with a man without cause, if he have done thee no harm.

31 ¶ [a]Envy thou not [l]the oppressor, and choose none of his ways.

32 For the froward *is* abomination to the LORD: [a]but his secret *is* with the righteous.

U 33 ¶ [a]The curse of the LORD *is* in the house of the wicked: but [b]he blesseth the habitation of the just.

H *Pr 3:8* ◀▶ *Pr 4:10*
P *Pr 3:9–10* ◀▶ *Pr 8:18*
S *Pr 1:33* ◀▶ *Pr 18:10*
U *Pr 3:9* ◀▶ *Pr 4:18*

15 [a]Mat. 13:44
16 [a]1 Tim. 4:8
17 [a]Mat. 11:29
18 [a]Gen. 2:9
19 [a]Ps. 104:24 [l]Or, *prepared*
20 [a]Gen. 1:9 [b]Deut. 33:28; Job 36:28
22 [a]ch. 1:9
23 [a]Ps. 37:24
24 [a]Lev. 26:6; Ps. 3:5
25 [a]Ps. 91:5
27 [a]Rom. 13:7; Gal. 6:10 [l]Heb. *the owners thereof*
28 [a]Lev. 19:13
29 [l]Or, *Practise no evil*
30 [a]Rom. 12:18
31 [a]Ps. 37:1 [l]Heb. *a man of violence*
32 [a]Ps. 25:14
33 [a]Zech. 5:3,4; Mal. 2:2 [b]Ps. 1:3
34 [a]Jas. 4:6; 1 Pet. 5:5
35 [l]Heb. *exalteth the fools*
4:1 [a]Ps. 34:11; ch. 1:8
3 [a]1 Chr. 29:1
4 [a]1 Chr. 28:9; Eph. 6:4 [b]ch. 7:2
5 [a]ch. 2:2,3
6 [a]2 Thes. 2:10
7 [a]Mat. 13:44; Luke 10:42
8 [a]1 Sam. 2:30
9 [a]ch. 1:9 & 3:22 [l]Or, *she shall compass thee with a crown of glory*
10 [a]ch. 3:2
12 [a]Ps. 18:36 [b]Ps. 91:11,12
14 [a]Ps. 1:1; ch. 1:10,15
16 [a]Ps. 36:4; Is. 57:20

34 [a]Surely he scorneth the scorners: but he giveth grace unto the lowly. M

35 The wise shall inherit glory: but shame [l]shall be the promotion of fools.

The command to obtain wisdom

4 HEAR, [a]YE children, the instruction of a father, and attend to know understanding.

2 For I give you good doctrine, forsake ye not my law.

3 For I was my father's son, [a]tender and only *beloved* in the sight of my mother.

4 [a]He taught me also, and said unto me, Let thine heart retain my words: [b]keep my commandments, and live.

5 [a]Get wisdom, get understanding: forget *it* not; neither decline from the words of my mouth.

6 Forsake her not, and she shall preserve thee: [a]love her, and she shall keep thee.

7 [a]Wisdom *is* the principal thing; *therefore* get wisdom: and with all thy getting get understanding.

8 [a]Exalt her, and she shall promote thee: she shall bring thee to honour, when thou dost embrace her.

9 She shall give to thine head [a]an ornament of grace: [l]a crown of glory shall she deliver to thee.

10 Hear, O my son, and receive my sayings; [a]and the years of thy life shall be many. H

11 I have taught thee in the way of wisdom; I have led thee in right paths.

12 When thou goest, [a]thy steps shall not be straitened; [b]and when thou runnest, thou shalt not stumble.

13 Take fast hold of instruction; let *her* not go: keep her; for she *is* thy life.

14 ¶ [a]Enter not into the path of the wicked, and go not in the way of evil *men.*

15 Avoid it, pass not by it, turn from it, and pass away.

16 [a]For they sleep not, except they have done mischief; and their sleep is taken away, unless they cause *some* to fall.

17 For they eat the bread of wickedness, and drink the wine of violence.

M *Pr 3:7* ◀▶ *Pr 6:16–17*
H *Pr 3:16* ◀▶ *Pr 4:22*

U 18 [a]But the path of the just [b]*is* as the shining light, that shineth more and more unto the perfect day.

C 19 [a]The way of the wicked *is* as darkness: they know not at what they stumble.

20 ¶ My son, attend to my words; incline thine ear unto my sayings.

21 [a]Let them not depart from thine eyes; [b]keep them in the midst of thine heart.

H 22 For they *are* life unto those that find them, and [a]health[1] to all their flesh.

S 23 ¶ Keep thy heart [1]with all diligence; for out of it *are* the issues of life.

24 Put away from thee [1]a froward mouth, and perverse lips put far from thee.

25 Let thine eyes look right on, and let thine eyelids look straight before thee.

26 Ponder the path of thy feet, and [1]let all thy ways be established.

S 27 [a]Turn not to the right hand nor to the left: [b]remove thy foot from evil.

Warning against unchastity

5 MY SON, attend unto my wisdom, *and* bow thine ear to my understanding:

2 That thou mayest regard discretion, and *that* thy lips may [a]keep knowledge.

3 ¶ [a]For the lips of a strange woman drop *as* an honeycomb, and her [1]mouth *is* [b]smoother than oil:

H 4 But her end is [a]bitter as wormwood, [b]sharp as a twoedged sword.

5 [a]Her feet go down to death; her steps take hold on hell.

6 Lest thou shouldest ponder the path of life, her ways are moveable, *that* thou canst not know *them.*

7 Hear me now therefore, O ye children, and depart not from the words of my mouth.

8 Remove thy way far from her, and come not nigh the door of her house:

9 Lest thou give thine honour unto others, and thy years unto the cruel:

10 Lest strangers be filled with [1]thy wealth; and thy labours *be* in the house of a stranger;

11 And thou mourn at the last, when thy flesh and thy body are consumed,

12 And say, How have I [a]hated instruction, and my heart [b]despised reproof;

13 And have not obeyed the voice of my teachers, nor inclined mine ear to them that instructed me!

14 I was almost in all evil in the midst of the congregation and assembly.

15 ¶ Drink waters out of thine own cistern, and running waters out of thine own well.

16 Let thy fountains be dispersed abroad, *and* rivers of waters in the streets.

17 Let them be only thine own, and not strangers' with thee.

18 Let thy fountain be blessed: and rejoice with [a]the wife of thy youth.

19 [a]*Let her be as* the loving hind and pleasant roe; let her breasts [1]satisfy thee at all times; and [2]be thou ravished always with her love.

20 And why wilt thou, my son, be ravished with [a]a strange woman, and embrace the bosom of a stranger?

21 [a]For the ways of man *are* before the E eyes of the LORD, and he pondereth all his goings.

22 ¶ [a]His own iniquities shall take the C wicked himself, and he shall be holden H with the cords of his [1]sins.

23 [a]He shall die without instruction; and in the greatness of his folly he shall go astray.

Warnings against idleness

6 MY SON, [a]if thou be surety for thy friend, *if* thou hast stricken thy hand with a stranger,

2 Thou art snared with the words of thy mouth, thou art taken with the words of thy mouth.

3 Do this now, my son, and deliver thyself, when thou art come into the hand of thy friend; go, humble thyself, [1]and make sure thy friend.

4 [a]Give not sleep to thine eyes, nor slumber to thine eyelids.

5 Deliver thyself as a roe from the hand *of the hunter,* and as a bird from the hand of the fowler.

18 [a]Mat. 5:14,45; Phil. 2:15 [b]2 Sam. 23:4
19 [a]1 Sam. 2:9; Job 18:5,6; Is. 59:9,10; Jer. 23:12; John 12:35
21 [a]ch. 3:3,21 [b]ch. 2:1
22 [a]ch. 3:8 & 12:18 [1]Heb. *medicine*
23 [1]Heb. *above all keeping*
24 [1]Heb. *frowardness of mouth, and perverseness of lips*
26 [1]Or, *all thy ways shall be ordered aright*
27 [a]Deut. 5:32 & 28:14; Josh. 1:7 [b]Is. 1:16; Rom. 12:9
5:2 [a]Mal. 2:7
3 [a]ch. 2:16 & 6:24 [b]Ps. 55:21 [1]Heb. *palate*
4 [a]Eccl. 7:26 [b]Heb. 4:12
5 [a]ch. 7:27
10 [1]Heb. *thy strength*
12 [a]ch. 1:29 [b]ch. 1:25 & 12:1
18 [a]Mal. 2:14
19 [a]Sol. 2:9 & 4:5 [1]Heb. *water thee* [2]Heb. *err thou always in her love*
20 [a]ch. 2:16
21 [a]2 Chr. 16:9; Job 31:4; ch. 15:3; Jer. 16:17; Hos. 7:2; Heb. 4:13
22 [a]Ps. 9:15 [1]Heb. *sin*
23 [a]Job 4:21 & 36:12
6:1 [a]ch. 11:15
3 [1]Or, *so shalt thou prevail with thy friend*
4 [a]Ps. 132:4

U *Pr 3:33* ◀ ▶ *Pr 10:6*
C *Ps 107:10* ◀ ▶ *Pr 5:22–23*
H *Pr 4:10* ◀ ▶ *Pr 9:11*
S *Pr 3:6–7* ◀ ▶ *Pr 4:27*
S *Pr 4:23* ◀ ▶ *Pr 10:29–30*
H *Pr 1:24–32* ◀ ▶ *Pr 5:22*

E *Ps 139:1–16* ◀ ▶ *Pr 15:3*
C *Pr 4:19* ◀ ▶ *Pr 8:36*
H *Pr 5:4–5* ◀ ▶ *Pr 6:15*

6 ¶ [a]Go to the ant, thou sluggard; consider her ways, and be wise:

7 Which having no guide, overseer, or ruler,

8 Provideth her meat in the summer, *and* gathereth her food in the harvest.

9 [a]How long wilt thou sleep, O sluggard? when wilt thou arise out of thy sleep?

10 *Yet* a little sleep, a little slumber, a little folding of the hands to sleep:

11 [a]So shall thy poverty come as one that travelleth, and thy want as an armed man.

Warning against sowing discord

12 ¶ A naughty person, a wicked man, walketh with a froward mouth.

13 [a]He winketh with his eyes, he speaketh with his feet, he teacheth with his fingers;

14 Frowardness *is* in his heart, [a]he deviseth mischief continually; [b]he ′soweth discord.

H 15 Therefore shall his calamity come suddenly; suddenly shall he [a]be broken [b]without remedy.

M 16 ¶ These six *things* doth the LORD hate: yea, seven *are* an abomination ′unto him:

17 [a]A′ proud look, [b]a lying tongue, and [c]hands that shed innocent blood,

18 [a]An heart that deviseth wicked imaginations, [b]feet that be swift in running to mischief,

19 [a]A false witness *that* speaketh lies, and he [b]that soweth discord among brethren.

Warning against adultery

20 ¶ [a]My son, keep thy father's commandment, and forsake not the law of thy mother:

21 [a]Bind them continually upon thine heart, *and* tie them about thy neck.

22 [a]When thou goest, it shall lead thee; when thou sleepest, [b]it shall keep thee; and *when* thou awakest, it shall talk with thee.

23 [a]For the commandment *is* a ′lamp; and the law *is* light; and reproofs of instruction *are* the way of life:

24 [a]To keep thee from the evil woman, from the flattery ′of the tongue of a strange woman.

25 [a]Lust not after her beauty in thine heart; neither let her take thee with her eyelids.

26 For [a]by means of a whorish woman *a man is brought* to a piece of bread: [b]and ′the adulteress will [c]hunt for the precious life.

27 Can a man take fire in his bosom, and his clothes not be burned?

28 Can one go upon hot coals, and his feet not be burned?

29 So he that goeth in to his neighbour's wife; whosoever toucheth her shall not be innocent.

30 *Men* do not despise a thief, if he steal to satisfy his soul when he is hungry;

31 But *if* he be found, [a]he shall restore sevenfold; he shall give all the substance of his house.

32 *But* whoso committeth adultery with a woman [a]lacketh ′understanding: he *that* doeth it destroyeth his own soul.

33 A wound and dishonour shall he get; and his reproach shall not be wiped away.

34 For jealousy *is* the rage of a man: therefore he will not spare in the day of vengeance.

35 ′He will not regard any ransom; neither will he rest content, though thou givest many gifts.

7 MY SON, keep my words, and [a]lay up my commandments with thee.

2 [a]Keep my commandments, and live; [b]and my law as the apple of thine eye.

3 [a]Bind them upon thy fingers, write them upon the table of thine heart.

4 Say unto wisdom, Thou *art* my sister; and call understanding *thy* kinswoman:

5 [a]That they may keep thee from the strange woman, from the stranger *which* flattereth with her words.

6 ¶ For at the window of my house I looked through my casement,

7 And beheld among the simple ones, I discerned among ′the youths, a young man [a]void of understanding,

8 Passing through the street near her corner; and he went the way to her house,

9 [a]In the twilight, ′in the evening, in the black and dark night:

10 And, behold, there met him a

6 [a]Job 12:7
9 [a]ch. 24:33
11 [a]ch. 10:4
13 [a]Job 15:12; ch. 10:10
14 [a]Mic. 2:1 [b]ver. 19 ′Heb. *casteth forth*
15 [a]Jer. 19:11 [b]2 Chr. 36:16
16 ′Heb. *of his soul*
17 [a]Ps. 101:5 [b]Ps. 120:2,3 [c]Is. 1:15 ′Heb. *Haughty eyes*
18 [a]Gen. 6:5 [b]Is. 59:7
19 [a]Ps. 27:12 [b]ver. 14
20 [a]Eph. 6:1
21 [a]ch. 3:3
22 [a]ch. 3:23 [b]ch. 2:11
23 [a]Ps. 19:8 ′Or, *candle*
24 [a]ch. 2:16 ′Or, *of the strange tongue*
25 [a]Mat. 5:28
26 [a]ch. 29:3 [b]Gen. 39:14 [c]Ezek. 13:18 ′Heb. *the woman of a man, or, a mans wife*
31 [a]Ex. 22:1
32 [a]ch. 7:7 ′Heb. *heart*
35 ′Heb. *He will not accept the face of any ransom*
7:1 [a]ch. 2:1
2 [a]Lev. 18:5; ch. 4:4 [b]Deut. 32:10
3 [a]Deut. 6:8 & 11:18; ch. 3:3 & 6:21
5 [a]ch. 2:16 & 5:3; & 6:24
7 [a]ch. 6:32 & 9:4, 16 ′Heb. *the sons*
9 [a]Job 24:15 ′Heb. *in the evening of the day*

H *Pr 5:22* ◀▶ *Pr 9:18*
M *Pr 3:34* ◀▶ *Pr 14:16*

woman *with* the attire of an harlot, and
subtle of heart.
11 ([a]She *is* loud and stubborn; [b]her
feet abide not in her house:
12 Now *is she* without, now in the
streets, and lieth in wait at every corner.)
13 So she caught him, and kissed him,
and [1]with an impudent face said unto
him,
14 [1]*I have* peace offerings with me;
this day have I paid my vows.
15 Therefore came I forth to meet
thee, diligently to seek thy face, and I
have found thee.
16 I have decked my bed with coverings of tapestry, with carved *works,* with
[a]fine linen of Egypt.
17 I have perfumed my bed with
myrrh, aloes, and cinnamon.
18 Come, let us take our fill of love
until the morning: let us solace ourselves
with loves.
19 For the goodman *is* not at home, he
is gone a long journey:
20 He hath taken a bag of money [1]with
him, *and* will come home at [2]the day appointed.
21 With [a]her much fair speech she
caused him to yield, [b]with the flattering
of her lips she forced him.
22 He goeth after her [1]straightway, as
an ox goeth to the slaughter, or as a fool
to the correction of the stocks;
23 Till a dart strike through his liver;
[a]as a bird hasteth to the snare, and knoweth not that it *is* for his life.
24 ¶ Hearken unto me now therefore,
O ye children, and attend to the words of
my mouth.
25 Let not thine heart decline to her
ways, go not astray in her paths.
26 For she hath cast down many
wounded: yea, [a]many strong *men* have
been slain by her.
27 [a]Her house *is* the way to hell, going
down to the chambers of death.

The call of wisdom

8 DOTH NOT [a]wisdom cry? and understanding put forth her voice?
2 She standeth in the top of high
places, by the way in the places of the
paths.
3 She crieth at the gates, at the entry
of the city, at the coming in at the doors.
4 Unto you, O men, I call; and my
voice *is* to the sons of man.

11 [a]ch. 9:13 [b]1 Tim. 5:13; Tit. 2:5
13 [1]Heb. *she strengthened her face and said*
14 [1]Heb. *Peace offerings are upon me*
16 [a]Is. 19:9
20 [1]Heb. *in his hand* [2]Or, *the new moon*
21 [a]ch. 5:3 [b]Ps. 12:2
22 [1]Heb. *suddenly*
23 [a]Eccl. 9:12
26 [a]Neh. 13:26
27 [a]ch. 2:18 & 5:5 & 9:18
8:1 [a]ch. 1:20 & 9:3
6 [a]ch. 22:20
7 [1]Heb. *the abomination of my lips*
8 [1]Heb. *wreathed*
11 [a]Job 28:15; Ps. 19:10 & 119:127; ch. 3:14,15 & 4:5, 7 & 16:16
12 [1]Or, *subtlety*
13 [a]ch. 16:6 [b]ch. 6:17 [c]ch. 4:24
14 [a]Eccl. 7:19
15 [a]Dan. 2:21; Rom. 13:1
17 [a]1 Sam. 2:30; Ps. 91:14; John 14:21 [b]Jas. 1:5
18 [a]ch. 3:16; Mat. 6:33
19 [a]ver. 10; ch. 3:14
20 [1]Or, *walk*
22 [a]ch. 3:19
23 [a]Ps. 2:6

5 O ye simple, understand wisdom:
and, ye fools, be ye of an understanding
heart.
6 Hear; for I will speak of [a]excellent
things; and the opening of my lips *shall
be* right things.
7 For my mouth shall speak truth; and
wickedness *is* [1]an abomination to my
lips.
8 All the words of my mouth *are* in
righteousness; *there is* nothing [1]froward
or perverse in them.
9 They *are* all plain to him that understandeth, and right to them that find
knowledge.
10 Receive my instruction, and not silver; and knowledge rather than choice
gold.
11 [a]For wisdom *is* better than rubies;
and all the things that may be desired are
not to be compared to it.
12 I wisdom dwell with [1]prudence,
and find out knowledge of witty inventions.
13 [a]The fear of the LORD *is* to hate evil:
[b]pride, and arrogancy, and the evil way,
and [c]the froward mouth, do I hate.
14 Counsel *is* mine, and sound wisdom: I *am* understanding; [a]I have
strength.
15 [a]By me kings reign, and princes decree justice.
16 By me princes rule, and nobles,
even all the judges of the earth.
17 [a]I love them that love me; and L
[b]those that seek me early shall find me. N
18 [a]Riches and honour *are* with me; P
yea, durable riches and righteousness.
19 [a]My fruit *is* better than gold, yea,
than fine gold; and my revenue than
choice silver.
20 I [1]lead in the way of righteousness,
in the midst of the paths of judgment:
21 That I may cause those that love me
to inherit substance; and I will fill their
treasures.
22 [a]The LORD possessed me in the beginning of his way, before his works of
old.
23 [a]I was set up from everlasting, from
the beginning, or ever the earth was.
24 When *there were* no depths, I was

L *Ps 149:4* ◀▶ *Pr 28:13*
N *Pr 1:24–33* ◀▶ *Pr 14:16*
P *Pr 3:16* ◀▶ *Pr 10:22*

brought forth; when *there were* no fountains abounding with water.

25 [a]Before the mountains were settled, before the hills was I brought forth:

26 While as yet he had not made the earth, nor the [1]fields, nor [2]the highest part of the dust of the world.

27 When he prepared the heavens, I *was* there: when he set [1]a compass upon the face of the depth:

28 When he established the clouds above: when he strengthened the fountains of the deep:

29 [a]When he gave to the sea his decree, that the waters should not pass his commandment: when [b]he appointed the foundations of the earth:

30 [a]Then I was by him, *as* one brought up *with him:* [b]and I was daily *his* delight, rejoicing always before him;

31 Rejoicing in the habitable part of his earth; and [a]my delights *were* with the sons of men.

32 Now therefore hearken unto me, O ye children: for [a]blessed *are they that* keep my ways.

33 Hear instruction, and be wise, and refuse it not.

34 [a]Blessed *is* the man that heareth me, watching daily at my gates, waiting at the posts of my doors.

35 For whoso findeth me findeth life, and shall [a]obtain[1] favour of the LORD.

C 36 But he that sinneth against me [a]wrongeth his own soul: all they that hate me love death.

Wisdom and folly contrasted

9 WISDOM HATH [a]builded her house, she hath hewn out her seven pillars:

2 [a]She hath killed [1]her beasts; [b]she hath mingled her wine; she hath also furnished her table.

3 She hath [a]sent forth her maidens; [b]she crieth [c]upon the highest places of the city,

4 [a]Whoso *is* simple, let him turn in hither: *as for* him that wanteth understanding, she saith to him,

5 [a]Come, eat of my bread, and drink of the wine *which* I have mingled.

6 Forsake the foolish, and live; and go in the way of understanding.

7 He that reproveth a scorner getteth to himself shame: and he that rebuketh a wicked *man getteth* himself a blot.

8 [a]Reprove not a scorner, lest he hate thee: [b]rebuke a wise man, and he will love thee.

9 Give *instruction* to a wise *man,* and he will be yet wiser: teach a just *man,* [a]and he will increase in learning.

10 [a]The fear of the LORD *is* the beginning of wisdom: and the knowledge of the holy *is* understanding.

11 [a]For by me thy days shall be multiplied, and the years of thy life shall be increased. H

12 [a]If thou be wise, thou shalt be wise for thyself: but *if* thou scornest, thou alone shalt bear *it.*

13 ¶ [a]A foolish woman *is* clamorous: *she is* simple, and knoweth nothing.

14 For she sitteth at the door of her house, on a seat [a]in the high places of the city,

15 To call passengers who go right on their ways:

16 [a]Whoso *is* simple, let him turn in hither: and *as for* him that wanteth understanding, she saith to him,

17 [a]Stolen waters are sweet, and bread [1]*eaten* in secret is pleasant.

18 But he knoweth not that [a]the dead *are* there; *and that* her guests *are* in the depths of hell. H

Proverbs of Solomon

10 THE PROVERBS of Solomon. [a]A wise son maketh a glad father: but a foolish son *is* the heaviness of his mother.

2 [a]Treasures of wickedness profit nothing: [b]but righteousness delivereth from death.

3 [a]The LORD will not suffer the soul of the righteous to famish: but he casteth away [1]the substance of the wicked. F

4 [a]He becometh poor that dealeth *with* a slack hand: but [b]the hand of the diligent maketh rich.

5 He that gathereth in summer *is* a wise son: *but* he that sleepeth in harvest *is* [a]a son that causeth shame.

6 Blessings *are* upon the head of the U

25 [a]Job 15:7,8
26 [1]Or, *open places* [2]Or, *the chief part*
27 [1]Or, *a circle*
29 [a]Gen. 1:9,10; Job 38:10; Jer. 5:22 [b]Job 38:4
30 [a]John 1:1,2 [b]Mat. 3:17; Col. 1:13
31 [a]Ps. 16:3
32 [a]Ps. 119:1,2; Luke 11:28
34 [a]ch. 3:13,18
35 [a]ch. 12:2 [1]Heb. *bring forth*
36 [a]ch. 20:2
9:1 [a]Mat. 16:18; Eph. 2:20; 1 Pet. 2:5
2 [a]Mat. 22:4 [b]ch. 23:30 [1]Heb. *her killing*
3 [a]Rom. 10:15 [b]ch. 8:1,2 [c]ver. 14
4 [a]Ps. 19:7; ch. 6:32
5 [a]Sol. 5:1; Is. 55:1; John 6:27
8 [a]Mat. 7:6 [b]Ps. 141:5
9 [a]Mat. 13:12
10 [a]Job 28:28; ch. 1:7
11 [a]ch. 3:2,16
12 [a]Job 35:6,7; ch. 16:26
13 [a]ch. 7:11
14 [a]ver. 3
16 [a]ch. 7:7,8
17 [a]ch. 20:17 [1]Heb. *of secrecies*
18 [a]ch. 2:18
10:1 [a]ch. 15:20
2 [a]Ps. 49:6; Luke 12:20 [b]Dan. 4:27
3 [a]Ps. 10:14 [1]Or, *the wicked for* their *wickedness*
4 [a]ch. 19:15 [b]ch. 13:4
5 [a]ch. 19:26

C *Pr 5:22–23* ◀▶ *Pr 11:18*
H *Pr 4:22* ◀▶ *Pr 10:16*
H *Pr 6:15* ◀▶ *Pr 11:21*
F *Ps 147:14* ◀▶ *Pr 13:25*
U *Pr 4:18* ◀▶ *Pr 10:22*

just: but [a]violence covereth the mouth of the wicked.

7 [a]The memory of the just *is* blessed: but the name of the wicked shall rot.

8 The wise in heart will receive commandments: [a]but [1]a prating fool [2]shall fall.

9 [a]He that walketh uprightly walketh surely: but he that perverteth his ways shall be known.

10 [a]He that winketh with the eye causeth sorrow: [b]but a prating fool [1]shall fall.

11 [a]The mouth of a righteous *man is* a well of life: but [b]violence covereth the mouth of the wicked.

12 Hatred stirreth up strifes: but [a]love covereth all sins.

13 In the lips of him that hath understanding wisdom is found: but [a]a rod *is* for the back of him that is void of [1]understanding.

14 Wise *men* lay up knowledge: but [a]the mouth of the foolish *is* near destruction.

15 [a]The rich man's wealth *is* his strong city: the destruction of the poor *is* their poverty.

H 16 The labour of the righteous *tendeth* to life: the fruit of the wicked to sin.

17 He *is in* the way of life that keepeth instruction: but he that refuseth reproof [1]erreth.

18 He that hideth hatred *with* lying lips, and [a]he that uttereth a slander, *is* a fool.

19 [a]In the multitude of words there wanteth not sin: but [b]he that refraineth his lips *is* wise.

20 The tongue of the just *is as* choice silver: the heart of the wicked *is* little worth.

21 The lips of the righteous feed many: but fools die for want [1]of wisdom.

P 22 [a]The blessing of the LORD, it maketh
U rich, and he addeth no sorrow with it.

23 [a]*It is* as sport to a fool to do mischief: but a man of understanding hath wisdom.

H *Pr 9:11* ◀▶ *Pr 10:27*
P *Pr 8:18* ◀▶ *Pr 11:24–25*
U *Pr 10:6* ◀▶ *Pr 10:24*

6 [a]ver. 11
7 [a]Ps. 112:6; Eccl. 8:10
8 [a]ver. 10 [1]Heb. *a fool of lips* [2]Or, *shall be beaten*
9 [a]Ps. 23:4; ch. 28:18; Is. 33:15,16
10 [a]ch. 6:13 [b]ver. 8 [1]Or, *shall be beaten*
11 [a]Ps. 37:30 [b]Ps. 107:42
12 [a]1 Cor. 13:7; 1 Pet. 4:8
13 [a]ch. 26:3 [1]Heb. *heart*
14 [a]ch. 18:7
15 [a]Job 31:24; 1 Tim. 6:17
17 [1]Or, *causeth to err*
18 [a]Ps. 15:3
19 [a]Eccl. 5:3 [b]Jas. 3:2
21 [1]Heb. *of heart*
22 [a]Gen. 24:35; Ps. 37:22
23 [a]ch. 15:21
24 [a]Job 15:21 [b]Ps. 145:19; Mat. 5:6; 1 John 5:14
25 [a]Ps. 37:9,10 [b]Ps. 15:5; Mat:16:18
27 [a]ch. 9:11 [b]Job 15:32 [1]Heb. *addeth*
28 [a]Job 8:13
29 [a]Ps. 1:6
30 [a]Ps. 37:22
31 [a]Ps. 37:30
32 [1]Heb. *frowardnesses*
11:1 [a]Lev. 19:35; Deut. 25:13 [1]Heb. *Balances of deceit* [2]Heb. *a perfect stone*
2 [a]ch. 16:18
3 [a]ch. 13:6
4 [a]Ezek. 7:19; Zeph. 1:18 [b]Gen. 7:1
5 [1]Heb. *rectify*
6 [a]Eccl. 10:8
7 [a]ch. 10:28

24 [a]The fear of the wicked, it shall come upon him: but [b]the desire of the righteous shall be granted. U

25 As the whirlwind passeth, [a]so *is* the wicked no *more:* but [b]the righteous *is* an everlasting foundation.

26 As vinegar to the teeth, and as smoke to the eyes, so *is* the sluggard to them that send him.

27 [a]The fear of the LORD [1]prolongeth days: but [b]the years of the wicked shall be shortened. H

28 The hope of the righteous *shall be* gladness: but the [a]expectation of the wicked shall perish.

29 The way of the LORD *is* strength to the upright: [a]but destruction *shall be* to the workers of iniquity. S

30 [a]The righteous shall never be removed: but the wicked shall not inhabit the earth. N

31 [a]The mouth of the just bringeth forth wisdom: but the froward tongue shall be cut out.

32 The lips of the righteous know what is acceptable: but the mouth of the wicked *speaketh* [1]frowardness.

11 A [a]FALSE[1] balance *is* abomination to the LORD: but [2]a just weight *is* his delight.

2 [a]*When* pride cometh, then cometh shame: but with the lowly *is* wisdom.

3 [a]The integrity of the upright shall guide them: but the perverseness of transgressors shall destroy them.

4 [a]Riches profit not in the day of wrath: but [b]righteousness delivereth from death.

5 The righteousness of the perfect shall [1]direct his way: but the wicked shall fall by his own wickedness.

6 The righteousness of the upright shall deliver them: but [a]transgressors shall be taken in *their own* naughtiness. S

7 [a]When a wicked man dieth, *his* expectation shall perish: and the hope of unjust *men* perisheth.

U *Pr 10:22* ◀▶ *Pr 11:8*
H *Pr 10:16* ◀▶ *Pr 14:30*
S *Pr 4:27* ◀▶ *Pr 11:6*
N *Ps 104:5* ◀▶ *Ecc 1:4*
S *Pr 10:29–30* ◀▶ *Pr 14:9*

10:30 Solomon declared that the wicked will be destroyed and have no place in the coming millennial kingdom of Christ.

8 [a]The righteous is delivered out of trouble, and the wicked cometh in his stead.

9 An hypocrite with *his* mouth destroyeth his neighbour: but through knowledge shall the just be delivered.

10 [a]When it goeth well with the righteous, the city rejoiceth: and when the wicked perish, *there is* shouting.

11 [a]By the blessing of the upright the city is exalted: but it is overthrown by the mouth of the wicked.

12 He that is [1]void of wisdom despiseth his neighbour: but a man of understanding holdeth his peace.

13 [a]A[1] talebearer revealeth secrets: but he that is of a faithful spirit concealeth the matter.

14 [a]Where no counsel *is,* the people fall: but in the multitude of counsellors *there is* safety.

15 [a]He that is surety for a stranger [1]shall smart *for it:* and he that hateth [2]suretyship is sure.

16 [a]A gracious woman retaineth honour: and strong *men* retain riches.

17 [a]The merciful man doeth good to his own soul: but *he that is* cruel troubleth his own flesh.

18 The wicked worketh a deceitful work: but [a]to him that soweth righteousness *shall be* a sure reward.

19 As righteousness *tendeth* to life: so he that pursueth evil *pursueth it* to his own death.

20 They that are of a froward heart *are* abomination to the LORD: but *such as are* upright in *their* way *are* his delight.

21 [a]*Though* hand *join* in hand, the wicked shall not be unpunished: but [b]the seed of the righteous shall be delivered.

22 *As* a jewel of gold in a swine's snout, *so is* a fair woman which [1]is without discretion.

23 The desire of the righteous *is* only good: *but* the expectation of the wicked [a]*is* wrath.

24 There is that [a]scattereth, and yet increaseth; and *there is* that withholdeth more than is meet, but *it tendeth* to poverty.

25 [a]The[1] liberal soul shall be made fat: [b]and he that watereth shall be watered also himself.

26 [a]He that withholdeth corn, the people shall curse him: but [b]blessing *shall be* upon the head of him that selleth *it.*

27 He that diligently seeketh good procureth favour: [a]but he that seeketh mischief, it shall come unto him.

28 [a]He that trusteth in his riches shall fall: but [b]the righteous shall flourish as a branch.

29 He that troubleth his own house [a]shall inherit the wind: and the fool *shall be* servant to the wise of heart.

30 The fruit of the righteous *is* a tree of life; and [a]he that [1]winneth souls *is* wise.

31 [a]Behold, the righteous shall be recompensed in the earth: much more the wicked and the sinner.

12 WHOSO LOVETH instruction loveth knowledge: but he that hateth reproof *is* brutish.

2 A good *man* obtaineth favour of the LORD: but a man of wicked devices will he condemn.

3 A man shall not be established by wickedness: but the [a]root of the righteous shall not be moved.

4 [a]A virtuous woman *is* a crown to her husband: but she that maketh ashamed *is* [b]as rottenness in his bones.

5 The thoughts of the righteous *are* right: *but* the counsels of the wicked *are* deceit.

6 [a]The words of the wicked *are* to lie in wait for blood: [b]but the mouth of the upright shall deliver them.

7 [a]The wicked are overthrown, and *are* not: but the house of the righteous shall stand.

8 A man shall be commended according to his wisdom: [a]but he that is [1]of a perverse heart shall be despised.

9 [a]*He that is* despised, and hath a servant, *is* better than he that honoureth himself, and lacketh bread.

10 [a]A righteous *man* regardeth the life

8 [a]ch. 21:18
10 [a]Esth. 8:15
11 [a]ch. 29:8
12 [1]Heb. *destitute of heart*
13 [a]Lev. 19:16; ch. 20:19 [1]Heb. *He that walketh,* being *a talebearer*
14 [a]1 Ki. 12:1
15 [a]ch. 6:1 [1]Heb. *shall be sore broken* [2]Heb. *those that strike* hands
16 [a]ch. 31:30
17 [a]Mat. 5:7
18 [a]Hos. 10:12
21 [a]ch. 16:5 [b]Ps. 112:2
22 [1]Heb. *departeth from*
23 [a]Rom. 2:8,9
24 [a]Ps. 112:9
25 [a]2 Cor. 9:6 [b]Mat. 5:7 [1]Heb. *The soul of blessing*
26 [a]Amos 8:5,6 [b]Job 29:13
27 [a]Esth. 7:10; Ps. 7:15,16
28 [a]Job 31:24; Mark 10:24; Luke 12:21; 1 Tim. 6:17 [b]Ps. 1:3; Jer. 17:8
29 [a]Eccl. 5:16
30 [a]Dan. 12:3; Jas. 5:20 [1]Heb. *taketh*
31 [a]Jer. 25:29
12:3 [a]ch. 10:25
4 [a]1 Cor. 11:7 [b]ch. 14:30
6 [a]ch. 1:11,18 [b]ch. 14:3
7 [a]Ps. 37:36
8 [a]1 Sam. 25:17 [1]Heb. *perverse of heart*
9 [a]ch. 13:7
10 [a]Deut. 25:4

U *Pr 10:24* ◀▶ *Pr 11:20*
C *Pr 8:36* ◀▶ *Pr 12:5*
U *Pr 11:8* ◀▶ *Pr 11:24–25*
H *Pr 9:18* ◀▶ *Pr 13:6*
P *Pr 10:22* ◀▶ *Pr 13:22*
U *Pr 11:20* ◀▶ *Pr 11:28*
U *Pr 11:24–25* ◀▶ *Pr 11:31*
U *Pr 11:28* ◀▶ *Pr 12:1–3*
U *Pr 11:31* ◀▶ *Pr 12:13*
C *Pr 11:18* ◀▶ *Pr 13:15*

of his beast: but the ʹtender mercies of the wicked *are* cruel.

11 [a]He that tilleth his land shall be satisfied with bread: but he that followeth vain *persons* [b]*is* void of understanding.

12 The wicked desireth ʹthe net of evil *men:* but the root of the righteous yieldeth *fruit.*

U 13 [a]Theʹ wicked is snared by the
V transgression of *his* lips: [b]but the just shall come out of trouble.

14 [a]A man shall be satisfied with good by the fruit of *his* mouth: [b]and the recompence of a man's hands shall be rendered unto him.

15 [a]The way of a fool *is* right in his own eyes: but he that hearkeneth unto counsel *is* wise.

16 [a]A fool's wrath is ʹpresently known: but a prudent *man* covereth shame.

17 [a]*He that* speaketh truth showeth forth righteousness: but a false witness deceit.

18 [a]There is that speaketh like the piercings of a sword: but the tongue of the wise *is* health.

19 The lip of truth shall be established for ever: [a]but a lying tongue *is* but for a moment.

20 Deceit *is* in the heart of them that imagine evil: but to the counsellors of peace *is* joy.

A 21 There shall no evil happen to the just: but the wicked shall be filled with mischief.

22 [a]Lying lips *are* abomination to the LORD: but they that deal truly *are* his delight.

23 [a]A prudent man concealeth knowledge: but the heart of fools proclaimeth foolishness.

24 [a]The hand of the diligent shall bear rule: but the ʹslothful shall be under tribute.

25 [a]Heaviness in the heart of man maketh it stoop: but [b]a good word maketh it glad.

26 The righteous *is* more ʹexcellent than his neighbour: but the way of the wicked seduceth them.

27 The slothful *man* roasteth not that

10 ʹOr, *bowels*
11 [a]Gen. 3:19; ch. 28:19 [b]ch. 6:32
12 ʹOr, *the fortress*
13 [a]ch. 18:7 [b]2 Pet. 2:9 ʹHeb. *The snare of the wicked is in the transgression of lips*
14 [a]ch. 13:2 [b]Is. 3:10,11
15 [a]Luke 18:11
16 [a]ch. 29:11 ʹHeb. *in that day*
17 [a]ch. 14:5
18 [a]Ps. 57:4 & 64:3
19 [a]ch. 19:5,9
22 [a]Rev. 22:15
23 [a]ch. 13:16
24 [a]ch. 10:4 ʹOr, *deceitful*
25 [a]ch. 15:13 [b]Is. 50:4
26 ʹOr, *abundant*
13:1 [a]Is. 28:15
2 [a]ch. 12:14
3 [a]Ps. 39:1; ch. 21:23; Jas. 3:2
4 [a]ch. 10:4
6 [a]ch. 11:3,5,6 ʹHeb. *sin*
7 [a]ch. 12:9
9 [a]Job 18:5,6 & 21:17; ch. 24:20 ʹOr, *candle*
11 [a]ch. 10:2 & 20:21 ʹHeb. *with the hand*
12 [a]ver. 19
13 [a]2 Chr. 36:16 ʹOr, *shall be in peace*
14 [a]ch. 10:11 & 14:27 & 16:22 [b]2 Sam. 22:6
16 [a]ch. 12:23 & 15:2 ʹHeb. *spreadeth*

which he took in hunting: but the substance of a diligent man *is* precious.

28 In the way of righteousness *is* life; U
and *in* the pathway *thereof there is* no death.

13

A WISE son *heareth* his father's instruction: [a]but a scorner heareth not rebuke.

2 [a]A man shall eat good by the fruit of *his* mouth: but the soul of the transgressors *shall eat* violence.

3 [a]He that keepeth his mouth keepeth his life: *but* he that openeth wide his lips shall have destruction.

4 [a]The soul of the sluggard desireth, and *hath* nothing: but the soul of the diligent shall be made fat.

5 A righteous *man* hateth lying: but a wicked *man* is loathsome, and cometh to shame.

6 [a]Righteousness keepeth *him that is* H
upright in the way: but wickedness overthroweth ʹthe sinner.

7 [a]There is that maketh himself rich, yet *hath* nothing: *there is* that maketh himself poor, yet *hath* great riches.

8 The ransom of a man's life *are* his riches: but the poor heareth not rebuke.

9 The light of the righteous rejoiceth: H
[a]but the ʹlamp of the wicked shall be put out.

10 Only by pride cometh contention: but with the well advised *is* wisdom.

11 [a]Wealth *gotten* by vanity shall be diminished: but he that gathereth ʹby labour shall increase.

12 Hope deferred maketh the heart sick: but [a]*when* the desire cometh, *it is* a tree of life.

13 Whoso [a]despiseth the word shall be destroyed: but he that feareth the commandment ʹshall be rewarded.

14 [a]The law of the wise *is* a fountain of life, to depart from [b]the snares of death.

15 Good understanding giveth favour: C
but the way of transgressors *is* hard. H

16 [a]Every prudent *man* dealeth with knowledge: but a fool ʹlayeth open *his* folly.

U *Pr 12:1–3* ◀▶ *Pr 12:28*
V *Ps 138:7* ◀▶ *Pr 16:7*
A *Ps 121:7* ◀▶ *Pr 19:23*
U *Pr 12:13* ◀▶ *Pr 13:21*
H *Pr 11:21* ◀▶ *Pr 13:9*
H *Pr 13:6* ◀▶ *Pr 13:15*
C *Pr 12:5* ◀▶ *Pr 13:19*
H *Pr 13:9* ◀▶ *Pr 13:21*

17 A wicked messenger falleth into mischief: but [a]a[ʹ] faithful ambassador *is* health.

18 Poverty and shame *shall be to* him that refuseth instruction: but [a]he that regardeth reproof shall be honoured.

C 19 [a]The desire accomplished is sweet to the soul: but *it is* abomination to fools to depart from evil.

20 He that walketh with wise *men* shall be wise: but a companion of fools [ʹ]shall be destroyed.

H U 21 [a]Evil pursueth sinners: but to the righteous good shall be repaid.

P 22 A good *man* leaveth an inheritance to his children's children: and [a]the wealth of the sinner *is* laid up for the just.

23 [a]Much food *is in* the tillage of the poor: but there is *that is* destroyed for want of judgment.

24 [a]He that spareth his rod hateth his son: but he that loveth him chasteneth him betimes.

F 25 [a]The righteous eateth to the satisfying of his soul: but the belly of the wicked shall want.

14 EVERY WISE woman buildeth her house: but the foolish plucketh it down with her hands.

2 He that walketh in his uprightness feareth the LORD: [a]but *he that is* perverse in his ways despiseth him.

3 In the mouth of the foolish *is* a rod of pride: [a]but the lips of the wise shall preserve them.

4 Where no oxen *are,* the crib *is* clean: but much increase *is* by the strength of the ox.

5 [a]A faithful witness will not lie: but a false witness will utter lies.

6 A scorner seeketh wisdom, and *findeth it* not: but [a]knowledge *is* easy unto him that understandeth.

7 Go from the presence of a foolish man, when thou perceivest not *in him* the lips of knowledge.

8 The wisdom of the prudent *is* to understand his way: but the folly of fools *is* deceit.

C 9 [a]Fools make a mock at sin: but among the righteous *there is* favour. S

U 10 The heart knoweth [ʹ]his own bitterness; and a stranger doth not intermeddle with his joy.

U 11 [a]The house of the wicked shall be overthrown: but the tabernacle of the upright shall flourish.

H 12 [a]There is a way which seemeth right unto a man, but [b]the end thereof *are* the ways of death.

C 13 Even in laughter the heart is sorrowful; and [a]the end of that mirth *is* heaviness.

S 14 The backslider in heart shall be [a]filled with his own ways: and a good man *shall be satisfied* from himself.

15 The simple believeth every word: but the prudent *man* looketh well to his going.

C M N 16 [a]A wise *man* feareth, and departeth from evil: but the fool rageth, and is confident.

R 17 *He that is* soon angry dealeth foolishly: and a man of wicked devices is hated.

18 The simple inherit folly: but the prudent are crowned with knowledge.

19 The evil bow before the good; and the wicked at the gates of the righteous.

20 [a]The poor is hated even of his own neighbour: but [ʹ]the rich *hath* many friends.

21 He that despiseth his neighbour sinneth: [a]but he that hath mercy on the poor, happy *is* he.

22 Do they not err that devise evil? but mercy and truth *shall be* to them that devise good.

23 In all labour there is profit: but the talk of the lips *tendeth* only to penury.

24 The crown of the wise *is* their riches: *but* the foolishness of fools *is* folly.

25 [a]A true witness delivereth souls: but a deceitful *witness* speaketh lies.

26 In the fear of the LORD *is* strong

17 [a]ch. 25:13 [ʹ]Heb. *an ambassador of faithfulness*
18 [a]ch. 15:5,31
19 [a]ver. 12
20 [ʹ]Heb. *shall be broken*
21 [a]Ps. 32:10
22 [a]Job 27:17; ch. 28:8; Eccl. 2:26
23 [a]ch. 12:11
24 [a]ch. 19:18 & 22:15 & 23:13 & 29:15,17
25 [a]Ps. 34:10 & 37:3
14:2 [a]Rom. 2:4
3 [a]ch. 12:6
5 [a]ver. 25; Ex. 20:16 & 23:1; ch. 6:19 & 12:17
6 [a]ch. 8:9 & 17:24
9 [a]ch. 10:23
10 [ʹ]Heb. *the bitterness of his soul*
11 [a]Job 8:15
12 [a]ch. 16:25 [b]Rom. 6:21
13 [a]ch. 5:4; Eccl. 2:2
14 [a]ch. 1:31 & 12:14
16 [a]ch. 22:3
20 [a]ch. 19:7 [ʹ]Heb. *many are the lovers of the rich*
21 [a]Ps. 41:1 & 112:9
25 [a]ver. 5

C *Pr 13:15 ◀▶ Pr 14:9*
H *Pr 13:15 ◀▶ Pr 14:12*
U *Pr 12:28 ◀▶ Pr 14:9*
P *Pr 11:24–25 ◀▶ Pr 15:6*
F *Pr 10:3 ◀▶ Isa 1:19*

C *Pr 13:19 ◀▶ Pr 14:13*
S *Pr 11:6 ◀▶ Pr 14:14*
U *Pr 13:21 ◀▶ Pr 14:11*
U *Pr 14:9 ◀▶ Pr 14:32*
H *Pr 13:21 ◀▶ Pr 15:24*
C *Pr 14:9 ◀▶ Pr 14:16*
S *Pr 14:9 ◀▶ Pr 15:9*
C *Pr 14:13 ◀▶ Pr 14:34*
M *Pr 6:16–17 ◀▶ Pr 15:33*
N *Pr 8:17 ◀▶ Pr 14:32*
R *Pr 3:7 ◀▶ Pr 28:13*

confidence: and his children shall have a place of refuge.

27 [a]The fear of the LORD *is* a fountain of life, to depart from the snares of death.

28 In the multitude of people *is* the king's honour: but in the want of people *is* the destruction of the prince.

29 [a]*He that is* slow to wrath *is* of great understanding: but *he that is* ʹhasty of spirit exalteth folly.

H 30 A sound heart *is* the life of the flesh: but [a]envy [b]the rottenness of the bones.

31 [a]He that oppresseth the poor reproacheth [b]his Maker: but he that honoureth him hath mercy on the poor.

N 32 The wicked is driven away in his
U wickedness: but [a]the righteous hath hope in his death.

33 Wisdom resteth in the heart of him that hath understanding: but [a]*that which is* in the midst of fools is made known.

C 34 Righteousness exalteth a nation: but sin *is* a reproach ʹto any people.

35 [a]The king's favour *is* toward a wise servant: but his wrath is *against* him that causeth shame.

15 A [a]SOFT answer turneth away wrath: but [b]grievous words stir up anger.

2 The tongue of the wise useth knowledge aright: [a]but the mouth of fools ʹpoureth out foolishness.

E 3 [a]The eyes of the LORD *are* in every place, beholding the evil and the good.

4 ʹA wholesome tongue *is* a tree of life: but perverseness therein *is* a breach in the spirit.

5 [a]A fool despiseth his father's instruction: [b]but he that regardeth reproof is prudent.

P 6 In the house of the righteous *is* much treasure: but in the revenues of the wicked is trouble.

7 The lips of the wise disperse knowledge: but the heart of the foolish *doeth* not so.

C 8 [a]The sacrifice of the wicked *is* an
U abomination to the LORD: but the prayer of the upright *is* his delight.

9 The way of the wicked *is* an abomination unto the LORD: but he loveth him that [a]followeth after righteousness. S

10 ʹCorrection *is* [a]grievous unto him that forsaketh the way: *and* [b]he that hateth reproof shall die.

11 [a]Hell and destruction *are* before the LORD: how much more then [b]the hearts of the children of men? E

12 [a]A scorner loveth not one that reproveth him: neither will he go unto the wise.

13 [a]A merry heart maketh a cheerful countenance: but [b]by sorrow of the heart the spirit is broken.

14 The heart of him that hath understanding seeketh knowledge: but the mouth of fools feedeth on foolishness.

15 All the days of the afflicted *are* evil: [a]but he that is of a merry heart *hath* a continual feast.

16 [a]Better *is* little with the fear of the LORD than great treasure and trouble therewith.

17 [a]Better *is* a dinner of herbs where love is, than a stalled ox and hatred therewith.

18 [a]A wrathful man stirreth up strife: but *he that is* slow to anger appeaseth strife.

19 [a]The way of the slothful *man is* as an hedge of thorns: but the way of the righteous ʹ*is* made plain.

20 [a]A wise son maketh a glad father: but a foolish man despiseth his mother.

21 [a]Folly *is* joy to *him that is* ʹdestitute of wisdom: [b]but a man of understanding walketh uprightly.

22 [a]Without counsel purposes are disappointed: but in the multitude of counsellors they are established.

23 A man hath joy by the answer of his mouth: and [a]a word *spoken* ʹin due season, how good *is it!*

24 [a]The way of life *is* above to the wise, that he may depart from hell beneath. H

25 [a]The LORD will destroy the house of the proud: but [b]he will establish the border of the widow.

27 [a]ch. 13:14
29 [a]Jas. 1:19 ʹHeb. *short of spirit*
30 [a]Ps. 112:10 [b]ch. 12:4
31 [a]ch. 17:5; Mat. 25:40 [b]ch. 22:2
32 [a]Job 13:15; Ps. 23:4; 2 Cor. 1:9; 2 Tim. 4:18
33 [a]ch. 12:16
34 ʹHeb. *to nations*
35 [a]Mat. 24:45
15:1 [a]ch. 25:15 [b]1 Sam. 25:10
2 [a]ch. 12:23 ʹHeb. *belcheth,* or, *bubbleth*
3 [a]Job 34:21; Heb. 4:13
4 ʹHeb. *The healing of the tongue*
5 [a]ch. 10:1 [b]ch. 13:18
8 [a]Is. 1:11; Jer. 6:20; Amos 5:22
9 [a]ch. 21:21; 1 Tim. 6:11
10 [a]1 Ki. 22:8 [b]ch. 5:12 ʹOr, *Instruction*
11 [a]Job 26:6; Ps. 139:8 [b]2 Chr. 6:30; John 2:24
12 [a]Amos 5:10; 2 Tim. 4:3
13 [a]ch. 17:22 [b]ch. 12:25
15 [a]ch. 17:22
16 [a]Ps. 37:16; 1 Tim. 6:6
17 [a]ch. 17:1
18 [a]ch. 26:21
19 [a]ch. 22:5 ʹHeb. *is raised up*
20 [a]ch. 10:1
21 [a]ch. 10:23 [b]Eph. 5:15 ʹHeb. *void of heart*
22 [a]ch. 11:14
23 [a]ch. 25:11 ʹHeb. *in his season*
24 [a]Phil. 3:20; Col. 3:1,2
25 [a]ch. 12:7 [b]Ps. 68:5,6

H *Pr 10:27* ◀▶ *Pr 17:22*
N *Pr 14:16* ◀▶ *Pr 27:1*
U *Pr 14:11* ◀▶ *Pr 15:8–9*
C *Pr 14:16* ◀▶ *Pr 15:8–9*
E *Pr 5:21* ◀▶ *Pr 15:11*
P *Pr 13:22* ◀▶ *Pr 19:17*
C *Pr 14:34* ◀▶ *Pr 15:26*
U *Pr 14:32* ◀▶ *Pr 15:29*

S *Pr 14:14* ◀▶ *Pr 15:29*
E *Pr 15:3* ◀▶ *Pr 16:2*
H *Pr 14:12* ◀▶ *Pr 16:4–5*

C 26 [a]The thoughts of the wicked *are* an
abomination to the LORD: [b]but *the words*
of the pure *are* [1]pleasant words.
27 [a]He that is greedy of gain troubleth
his own house; but he that hateth gifts
shall live.
28 The heart of the righteous [a]studieth
to answer: but the mouth of the wicked
poureth out evil things.
C 29 [a]The LORD *is* far from the wicked:
S but [b]he heareth the prayer of the righ-
U teous.
30 The light of the eyes rejoiceth the
heart: *and* a good report maketh the
bones fat.
31 [a]The ear that heareth the reproof of
life abideth among the wise.
32 He that refuseth [1]instruction despiseth his own soul: but he that [2]hear-
eth reproof [3]getteth understanding.
M 33 [a]The fear of the LORD *is* the instruction of wisdom; and [b]before honour *is*
humility.

16 THE [a]PREPARATIONS[1] of the
heart in man, [b]and the answer of
the tongue, *is* from the LORD.
E 2 [a]All the ways of a man *are* clean in
G his own eyes; but [b]the LORD weigheth the
spirits.
3 [a]Commit[1] thy works unto the LORD,
and thy thoughts shall be established.
H 4 [a]The LORD hath made all *things* for
himself: [b]yea, even the wicked for the
day of evil.
M 5 [a]Every one *that is* proud in heart *is*
an abomination to the LORD: [b]*though*
hand *join* in hand, he shall not be [1]un-
punished.
S 6 [a]By mercy and truth iniquity is
purged: and [b]by the fear of the LORD *men*
depart from evil.

C *Pr 15:8–9 ◀▶ Pr 15:29*
C *Pr 15:26 ◀▶ Pr 21:16*
S *Pr 15:9 ◀▶ Pr 16:6*
U *Pr 15:8–9 ◀▶ Pr 16:7*
M *Pr 14:16 ◀▶ Pr 16:5*
E *Pr 15:11 ◀▶ Pr 17:3*
G *Pr 3:5–6 ◀▶ Pr 19:21*
H *Pr 15:24 ◀▶ Pr 16:18*
M *Pr 15:33 ◀▶ Pr 16:18*
S *Pr 15:29 ◀▶ Pr 16:17*

7 When a man's ways please the LORD, U
he maketh even his enemies to be at V
peace with him.
8 [a]Better *is* a little with righteousness
than great revenues without right.
9 [a]A man's heart deviseth his way:
[b]but the LORD directeth his steps.
10 [1]A divine sentence *is* in the lips of
the king: his mouth transgresseth not in
judgment.
11 [a]A just weight and balance *are* the
LORD'S: [1]all the weights of the bag *are* his
work.
12 *It is* an abomination to kings to
commit wickedness: for [a]the throne is established by righteousness.
13 [a]Righteous lips *are* the delight of
kings; and they love him that speaketh
right.
14 [a]The wrath of a king *is as* messengers of death: but a wise man will pac-
ify it.
15 In the light of the king's countenance *is* life; and [a]his favour *is* [b]as a
cloud of the latter rain.
16 [a]How much better *is it* to get wisdom than gold! and to get understanding
rather to be chosen than silver!
17 The highway of the upright *is* to de- S
part from evil: he that keepeth his way
preserveth his soul.
18 Pride *goeth* before destruction, and H
an haughty spirit before a fall. M
19 Better *it is to be* of an humble spirit
with the lowly, than to divide the spoil
with the proud.
20 [1]He that handleth a matter wisely
shall find good: and whoso [a]trusteth in
the LORD, happy *is* he.
21 The wise in heart shall be called
prudent: and the sweetness of the lips increaseth learning.
22 [a]Understanding *is* a wellspring of
life unto him that hath it: but the instruction of fools *is* folly.
23 The heart of the wise [1]teacheth his
mouth, and addeth learning to his lips.

U *Pr 15:29 ◀▶ Pr 21:21*
V *Pr 12:13 ◀▶ Pr 20:22*
S *Pr 16:6 ◀▶ Pr 17:15*
H *Pr 16:4–5 ◀▶ Pr 16:25*
M *Pr 16:5 ◀▶ Pr 18:12*

26 [a]ch. 6:16,18 [b]Ps. 37:30 [1]Heb. *words of pleasantness*
27 [a]Is. 5:8
28 [a]1 Pet. 3:15
29 [a]Ps. 10:1 & 34:16 [b]Ps. 145:18
31 [a]ver. 5
32 [1]Or, *correction* [2]Or, *obeyeth* [3]Heb. *possesseth an heart*
33 [a]ch. 1:7 [b]ch. 18:12
16:1 [a]Jer. 10:23 [b]Mat. 10:19 [1]Or, *disposings*
2 [a]ch. 21:2 [b]1 Sam. 16:7
3 [a]Ps. 37:5 [1]Heb. *Roll*
4 [a]Is. 43:7 [b]Job 21:30
5 [a]ch. 8:13 [b]ch. 11:21 [1]Heb. *held innocent*
6 [a]Dan. 4:27 [b]ch. 14:16
8 [a]Ps. 37:16
9 [a]ch. 19:21 [b]Jer. 10:23
10 [1]Heb. *Divination*
11 [a]Lev. 19:36 [1]Heb. *all the stones*
12 [a]ch. 25:5
13 [a]ch. 14:35
14 [a]ch. 19:12
15 [a]ch. 19:12 [b]Job 29:23
16 [a]ch. 8:11,19
20 [a]Ps. 34:8 [1]Or, *He that understandeth a matter*
22 [a]ch. 13:14
23 [1]Heb. *maketh wise*

16:6 When people repent of their sin in the fear of God and live their lives according to his law, God will forgive them. God, in his love and mercy, has provided a way to remove our iniquity and that is through the shed blood of Jesus Christ on the cross.

24 Pleasant words *are as* an honeycomb, sweet to the soul, and health to the bones.

H 25 [a]There is a way that seemeth right unto a man, but the end thereof *are* the ways of death.

26 [a]He[1] that laboureth laboureth for himself; for his mouth [2]craveth it of him.

27 [1]An ungodly man diggeth up evil: and in his lips *there is* as a burning fire.

28 [a]A froward man [1]soweth strife: and [b]a whisperer separateth chief friends.

29 A violent man [a]enticeth his neighbour, and leadeth him into the way *that is* not good.

30 He shutteth his eyes to devise froward things: moving his lips he bringeth evil to pass.

31 [a]The hoary head *is* a crown of glory, *if* it be found in the way of righteousness.

32 [a]*He that is* slow to anger *is* better than the mighty; and he that ruleth his spirit than he that taketh a city.

33 The lot is cast into the lap; but the whole disposing thereof *is* of the LORD.

17 BETTER *IS* [a]a dry morsel, and quietness therewith, than an house full of [1]sacrifices *with* strife.

2 A wise servant shall have rule over [a]a son that causeth shame, and shall have part of the inheritance among the brethren.

E T 3 The refining pot *is* for silver, and the furnace for gold: [a]but the LORD trieth the hearts.

4 A wicked doer giveth heed to false lips; *and* a liar giveth ear to a naughty tongue.

5 [a]Whoso mocketh the poor reproacheth his Maker: *and* he that is glad at calamities shall not be [1]unpunished.

6 Children's children *are* the crown of old men; and the glory of children *are* their fathers.

7 [1]Excellent speech becometh not a fool: much less do [2]lying lips a prince.

8 A gift *is as* [1]a precious stone in the eyes of him that hath it: whithersoever it turneth, it prospereth.

9 [a]He that covereth a transgression [1]seeketh love; but [b]he that repeateth a matter separateth *very* friends.

10 [1]A reproof entereth more into a wise man than an hundred stripes into a fool.

11 An evil *man* seeketh only rebellion: therefore a cruel messenger shall be sent against him.

12 Let [a]a bear robbed of her whelps meet a man, rather than a fool in his folly.

13 Whoso [a]rewardeth evil for good, evil shall not depart from his house.

14 The beginning of strife *is as* when one letteth out water: therefore [a]leave off contention, before it be meddled with.

15 [a]He that justifieth the wicked, and he that condemneth the just, even they both *are* abomination to the LORD. S

16 Wherefore *is there* a price in the hand of a fool to get wisdom, [a]seeing *he hath* no heart *to it?*

17 [a]A friend loveth at all times, and a brother is born for adversity.

18 [a]A man void of [1]understanding striketh hands, *and* becometh surety in the presence of his friend.

19 He loveth transgression that loveth strife: *and* [a]he that exalteth his gate seeketh destruction.

20 [1]He that hath a froward heart findeth no good: and he that hath [a]a perverse tongue falleth into mischief.

21 [a]He that begetteth a fool *doeth it* to his sorrow: and the father of a fool hath no joy.

22 [a]A merry heart doeth good [1]*like* a medicine: [b]but a broken spirit drieth the bones. H

23 A wicked *man* taketh a gift out of the bosom [a]to pervert the ways of judgment.

24 [a]Wisdom *is* before him that hath understanding; but the eyes of a fool *are* in the ends of the earth.

25 [a]A foolish son *is* a grief to his father, and bitterness to her that bare him.

26 Also [a]to punish the just *is* not good, *nor* to strike princes for equity.

27 [a]He that hath knowledge spareth his words: *and* a man of understanding is of [1]an excellent spirit.

28 [a]Even a fool, when he holdeth his peace, is counted wise: *and* he that shutteth his lips *is esteemed* a man of understanding.

25 [a]ch. 14:12
26 [a]Eccl. 6:7 [1]Heb. *The soul of him that laboureth* [2]Heb. *boweth unto him*
27 [1]Heb. *A man of Belial*
28 [a]ch. 15:18 [b]ch. 17:9 [1]Heb. *sendeth forth*
29 [a]ch. 1:10
31 [a]ch. 20:29
32 [a]ch. 19:11
17:1 [a]ch. 15:17 [1]Or, *good cheer*
2 [a]ch. 10:5
3 [a]Jer. 17:10
5 [a]ch. 14:31 [1]Heb. *held innocent*
7 [1]Heb. *A lip of excellency* [2]Heb. *a lip of lying*
8 [1]Heb. *a stone of grace*
9 [a]ch. 10:12 [b]ch. 16:28 [1]Or, *procureth*
10 [1]Or, *A reproof aweth more a wise man, than to strike a fool an hundred times*
12 [a]Hos. 13:8
13 [a]Ps. 109:4,5; Jer. 18:20
14 [a]ch. 20:3
15 [a]Ex. 23:7; Is. 5:23
16 [a]ch. 21:25,26
17 [a]Ruth 1:16
18 [a]ch. 6:1 [1]Heb. *heart*
19 [a]ch. 16:18
20 [a]Jas. 3:8 [1]Heb. *The froward of heart*
21 [a]ch. 10:1
22 [a]ch. 12:25 [b]Ps. 22:15 [1]Or, *to a medicine*
23 [a]Ex. 23:8
24 [a]Eccl. 2:14
25 [a]ch. 10:1
26 [a]ch. 18:5
27 [a]Jas. 1:19 [1]Or, *a cool spirit*
28 [a]Job 13:5

H *Pr 16:18* ◄► *Pr 18:12*
E *Pr 16:2* ◄► *Pr 21:2*
T *Pr 3:11–12* ◄► *Pr 25:4*
S *Pr 16:17* ◄► *Pr 21:16*
H *Pr 14:30* ◄► *Pr 19:23*

18

THROUGH [1]DESIRE a man, having separated himself, seeketh *and* intermeddleth with all wisdom.

2 A fool hath no delight in understanding, but that his heart may discover itself.

3 When the wicked cometh, *then* cometh also contempt, and with ignominy reproach.

4 [a]The words of a man's mouth *are as* deep waters, [b]*and* the wellspring of wisdom *as* a flowing brook.

5 [a]*It is* not good to accept the person of the wicked, to overthrow the righteous in judgment.

6 A fool's lips enter into contention, and his mouth calleth for strokes.

7 [a]A fool's mouth *is* his destruction, and his lips *are* the snare of his soul.

8 [a]The words of a [1]talebearer *are* [2]as wounds, and they go down into the [3]innermost parts of the belly.

9 He also that is slothful in his work is [a]brother to him that is a great waster.

S 10 [a]The name of the LORD *is* a strong tower: the righteous runneth into it, and [1]is safe.

11 [a]The rich man's wealth *is* his strong city, and as an high wall in his own conceit.

H M 12 [a]Before destruction the heart of man is haughty, and before honour *is* humility.

13 He that [1]answereth a matter [a]before he heareth *it,* it *is* folly and shame unto him.

14 The spirit of a man will sustain his infirmity; but a wounded spirit who can bear?

15 The heart of the prudent getteth knowledge; and the ear of the wise seeketh knowledge.

16 [a]A man's gift maketh room for him, and bringeth him before great men.

17 *He that is* first in his own cause *seemeth* just; but his neighbour cometh and searcheth him.

18 The lot causeth contentions to cease, and parteth between the mighty.

19 A brother offended *is harder to be won* than a strong city: and *their* contentions *are* like the bars of a castle.

20 [a]A man's belly shall be satisfied with the fruit of his mouth; *and* with the increase of his lips shall he be filled.

21 [a]Death and life *are* in the power of the tongue: and they that love it shall eat the fruit thereof.

22 [a]*Whoso* findeth a wife findeth a good *thing,* and obtaineth favour of the LORD.

23 The poor useth entreaties; but the rich answereth [a]roughly.

24 A man *that hath* friends must show himself friendly: [a]and there is a friend *that* sticketh closer than a brother. L

19

BETTER [a]*IS* the poor that walketh in his integrity, than *he that is* perverse in his lips, and is a fool.

2 Also, *that* the soul *be* without knowledge, *it is* not good; and he that hasteth with *his* feet sinneth.

3 The foolishness of man perverteth his way: [a]and his heart fretteth against the LORD.

4 [a]Wealth maketh many friends; but the poor is separated from his neighbour.

5 [a]A false witness shall not be [1]unpunished, and *he that* speaketh lies shall not escape.

6 [a]Many will entreat the favour of the prince: and [b]every man *is* a friend to [1]him that giveth gifts.

7 [a]All the brethren of the poor do hate him: how much more do his friends go [b]far from him? he pursueth *them with* words, *yet* they *are* wanting *to him.*

8 He that getteth [1]wisdom loveth his own soul: he that keepeth understanding [a]shall find good.

9 [a]A false witness shall not be unpunished, and *he that* speaketh lies shall perish.

10 Delight is not seemly for a fool; much less [a]for a servant to have rule over princes.

11 [a]The [1]discretion of a man deferreth his anger; [b]and *it is* his glory to pass over a transgression.

12 [a]The king's wrath *is* as the roaring of a lion; but his favour *is* [b]as dew upon the grass.

13 [a]A foolish son *is* the calamity of his father: [b]and the contentions of a wife *are* a continual dropping.

14 [a]House and riches *are* the inheritance of fathers: and [b]a prudent wife *is* from the LORD.

18:1 [1]Or, *He that separateth himself seeketh according to his desire and intermeddleth in every business*
4 [a]ch. 10:11 [b]Jas. 3:17
5 [a]Lev. 19:15
7 [a]ch. 10:14
8 [a]ch. 12:18 [1]Or, *whisperer* [2]Or, *like as when men are wounded* [3]Heb. *chambers*
9 [a]ch. 28:24
10 [a]2 Sam. 22:3 [1]Heb. *is set aloft*
11 [a]ch. 10:15
12 [a]ch. 16:18
13 [a]John 7:51 [1]Heb. *returneth a word*
16 [a]Gen. 32:20; 1 Sam. 25:27
20 [a]ch. 12:14
21 [a]Mat. 12:37
22 [a]ch. 31:10
23 [a]Jas. 2:3
24 [a]ch. 17:17
19:1 [a]ch. 28:6
3 [a]Ps. 37:7
4 [a]ch. 14:20
5 [a]Ex. 23:1 [1]Heb. *held innocent*
6 [a]ch. 29:26 [b]ch. 17:8 [1]Heb. *a man of gifts*
7 [a]ch. 14:20 [b]Ps. 38:11
8 [a]ch. 16:20 [1]Heb. *an heart*
9 [a]ver. 5
10 [a]ch. 30:22
11 [a]Jas. 1:19 [b]ch. 16:32 [1]Or, *prudence*
12 [a]ch. 16:14 [b]Hos. 14:5
13 [a]ch. 10:1 [b]ch. 21:9,19
14 [a]2 Cor. 12:14 [b]ch. 18:22

S *Pr 3:23–26* ◀▶ *Pr 29:25*
H *Pr 16:25* ◀▶ *Pr 22:3*
M *Pr 16:18* ◀▶ *Pr 26:12*
L *Pr 2:8* ◀▶ *SS 2:3–4*

15 [a]Slothfulness casteth into a deep sleep; and an idle soul shall [b]suffer hunger.

16 [a]He that keepeth the commandment keepeth his own soul; *but* he that despiseth his ways shall die.

P 17 [a]He that hath pity upon the poor lendeth unto the LORD; and [1]that which he hath given will he pay him again.

18 [a]Chasten thy son while there is hope, and let not thy soul spare [1]for his crying.

19 A man of great wrath shall suffer punishment: for if thou deliver *him,* yet thou must [1]do it again.

20 Hear counsel, and receive instruction, that thou mayest be wise [a]in thy latter end.

G 21 *There are* many devices in a man's
O heart; [a]nevertheless the counsel of the LORD, that shall stand.

22 The desire of a man *is* his kindness: and a poor man *is* better than a liar.

A 23 [a]The fear of the LORD *tendeth* to
H life: and *he that hath it* shall abide satisfied; he shall not be visited with evil.

24 [a]A slothful *man* hideth his hand in *his* bosom, and will not so much as bring it to his mouth again.

25 Smite a scorner, and the simple [a]will[1] beware: and [b]reprove one that hath understanding, *and* he will understand knowledge.

26 He that wasteth *his* father, *and* chaseth away *his* mother, *is* [a]a son that causeth shame, and bringeth reproach.

27 Cease, my son, to hear the instruction *that causeth* to err from the words of knowledge.

28 [1]An ungodly witness scorneth judgment: and [a]the mouth of the wicked devoureth iniquity.

29 Judgments are prepared for scorners, [a]and stripes for the back of fools.

20

WINE [a]*IS* a mocker, strong drink *is* raging: and whosoever is deceived thereby is not wise.

2 [a]The fear of a king *is* as the roaring of a lion: *whoso* provoketh him to anger [b]sinneth *against* his own soul.

3 [a]*It is* an honour for a man to cease from strife: but every fool will be meddling.

4 [a]The sluggard will not plow by reason of the [1]cold; [b]*therefore* shall he beg in harvest, and *have* nothing.

5 Counsel in the heart of man *is like* deep water; but a man of understanding will draw it out.

6 [a]Most men will proclaim every one his own [1]goodness: but [b]a faithful man who can find?

7 [a]The just *man* walketh in his integrity: [b]his children *are* blessed after him.

8 [a]A king that sitteth in the throne of judgment scattereth away all evil with his eyes.

9 [a]Who can say, I have made my heart A
clean, I am pure from my sin? G

10 [a]Divers[1] weights, *and* [2]divers measures, both of them *are* alike abomination to the LORD.

11 Even a child is [a]known by his doings, whether his work *be* pure, and whether *it be* right.

12 [a]The hearing ear, and the seeing eye, the LORD hath made even both of them.

13 [a]Love not sleep, lest thou come to poverty; open thine eyes, *and* thou shalt be satisfied with bread.

14 *It is* naught, *it is* naught, saith the buyer: but when he is gone his way, then he boasteth.

15 There is gold, and a multitude of rubies: but [a]the lips of knowledge *are* a precious jewel.

16 [a]Take his garment that is surety *for* a stranger: and take a pledge of him for a strange woman.

17 [a]Bread[1] of deceit *is* sweet to a man; but afterwards his mouth shall be filled with gravel.

18 [a]*Every* purpose is established by counsel: [b]and with good advice make war.

19 [a]He that goeth about *as* a talebearer revealeth secrets: therefore meddle not with him [b]that [1]flattereth with his lips.

20 [a]Whoso curseth his father or his mother, [b]his [1]lamp shall be put out in obscure darkness.

21 [a]An inheritance *may be* gotten hastily at the beginning; [b]but the end thereof shall not be blessed.

15 [a]ch. 6:9 [b]ch. 10:4
16 [a]Luke 10:28
17 [a]2 Cor. 9:6 [1]Or, *his deed*
18 [a]ch. 13:24 [1]Or, *to his destruction:* or, *to cause him to die*
19 [1]Heb. *add*
20 [a]Ps. 37:37
21 [a]Heb. 6:17
23 [a]1 Tim. 4:8
24 [a]ch. 15:19
25 [a]Deut. 13:11 [b]ch. 9:8 [1]Heb. *will be cunning*
26 [a]ch. 17:2
28 [a]Job 15:16 [1]Heb. *A witness of Belial*
29 [a]ch. 26:3
20:1 [a]Gen. 9:21
2 [a]ch. 19:12 [b]ch. 8:36
3 [a]ch. 17:14
4 [a]ch. 10:4 [b]ch. 19:15 [1]Or, *winter*
6 [a]Mat. 6:2; Luke 18:11 [b]Luke 18:8 [1]Or, *bounty*
7 [a]2 Cor. 1:12 [b]Ps. 37:26
8 [a]ver. 26
9 [a]1 Ki. 8:46
10 [a]Deut. 25:13 [1]Heb. *A stone and a stone* [2]Heb. *an ephah and an ephah*
11 [a]Mat. 7:16
12 [a]Ex. 4:11
13 [a]Rom. 12:11
15 [a]ch. 3:15
16 [a]ch. 22:26
17 [a]ch. 9:17 [1]Heb. *Bread of lying,* or, *falsehood*
18 [a]ch. 24:6 [b]Luke 14:31
19 [a]ch. 11:13 [b]Rom. 16:18 [1]Or, *enticeth*
20 [a]Mat. 15:4 [b]Job 18:5,6 [1]Or, *candle*
21 [a]ch. 28:20 [b]Hab. 2:6

P *Pr 15:6* ◀▶ *Pr 22:9*
G *Pr 16:2* ◀▶ *Pr 20:9*
O *Ps 127:1* ◀▶ *Ecc 7:13*
A *Pr 12:21* ◀▶ *Isa 58:11*
H *Pr 17:22* ◀▶ *Isa 35:3–6*

A *Ps 143:2* ◀▶ *Ecc 7:20*
G *Pr 19:21* ◀▶ *Pr 21:2*

V 22 [a]Say not thou, I will recompense evil; *but* [b]wait on the LORD, and he shall save thee.

23 [a]Divers weights *are* an abomination unto the LORD; and [1]a false balance *is* not good.

24 [a]Man's goings *are* of the LORD; how can a man then understand his own way?

25 *It is* a snare to the man *who* devoureth *that which is* holy, and [a]after vows to make inquiry.

26 [a]A wise king scattereth the wicked, and bringeth the wheel over them.

27 [a]The spirit of man *is* the [1]candle of the LORD, searching all the inward parts of the belly.

28 [a]Mercy and truth preserve the king: and his throne is upholden by mercy.

29 The glory of young men *is* their strength: and [a]the beauty of old men *is* the gray head.

30 The blueness of a wound [1]cleanseth away evil: so *do* stripes the inward parts of the belly.

21

THE KING'S heart *is* in the hand of the LORD, *as* the rivers of water: he turneth it whithersoever he will.

E 2 [a]Every way of a man *is* right in his
G own eyes: [b]but the LORD pondereth the hearts.

3 [a]To do justice and judgment *is* more acceptable to the LORD than sacrifice.

4 [a]An[1] high look, and a proud heart, *and* [2]the plowing of the wicked, *is* sin.

5 [a]The thoughts of the diligent *tend* only to plenteousness; but of every one *that is* hasty only to want.

6 [a]The getting of treasures by a lying tongue *is* a vanity tossed to and fro of them that seek death.

7 The robbery of the wicked shall [1]destroy them; because they refuse to do judgment.

8 The way of man *is* froward and strange: but *as for* the pure, his work *is* right.

9 *It is* better to dwell in a corner of the housetop, than with [1]a brawling woman in [2]a wide house.

10 [a]The soul of the wicked desireth evil: his neighbour [1]findeth no favour in his eyes.

V *Pr 16:7* ◀▶ *Isa 41:11–14*
E *Pr 17:3* ◀▶ *Pr 24:12*
G *Pr 20:9* ◀▶ *Pr 26:12*

22 [a]Rom. 12:17 [b]2 Sam. 16:12
23 [a]ver. 10 [1]Heb. *balances of deceit*
24 [a]Ps. 37:23
25 [a]Eccl. 5:4,5
26 [a]Ps. 101:8
27 [a]1 Cor. 2:11 [1]Or, *lamp*
28 [a]Ps. 101:1
29 [a]ch. 16:31
30 [1]Heb. *is a purging medicine against evil*
21:2 [a]ch. 16:2 [b]ch. 24:12; Luke 16:15
3 [a]1 Sam. 15:22
4 [a]ch. 6:17 [1]Heb. *Haughtiness of eyes* [2]Or, *the light of the wicked*
5 [a]ch. 10:4
6 [a]2 Pet. 2:3
7 [1]Heb. *saw them,* or, *dwell with them*
9 [1]Heb. *a woman of contentions* [2]Heb. *an house of society*
10 [a]Jas. 4:5 [1]Heb. *is not favoured*
11 [a]ch. 19:25
13 [a]Mat. 7:2
17 [1]Or, *sport*
19 [1]Heb. *in the land of the desert*
20 [a]Ps. 112:3; Mat. 25:3,4
21 [a]Mat. 5:6
22 [a]Eccl. 9:14
23 [a]ch. 12:13; Jas. 3:2
24 [1]Heb. *in the wrath of pride*
27 [a]Jer. 6:20 [1]Heb. *in wickedness?*
28 [1]Heb. *A witness of lies*

11 [a]When the scorner is punished, the simple is made wise: and when the wise is instructed, he receiveth knowledge.

12 The righteous *man* wisely considereth the house of the wicked: *but God* overthroweth the wicked for *their* wickedness.

13 [a]Whoso stoppeth his ears at the cry of the poor, he also shall cry himself, but shall not be heard.

14 A gift in secret pacifieth anger: and a reward in the bosom strong wrath.

15 *It is* joy to the just to do judgment: but destruction *shall be* to the workers of iniquity.

16 The man that wandereth out of the C
way of understanding shall remain in the S
congregation of the dead.

17 He that loveth [1]pleasure *shall be* a poor man: he that loveth wine and oil shall not be rich.

18 The wicked *shall be* a ransom for the righteous, and the transgressor for the upright.

19 *It is* better to dwell [1]in the wilderness, than with a contentious and an angry woman.

20 [a]*There is* treasure to be desired and oil in the dwelling of the wise; but a foolish man spendeth it up.

21 [a]He that followeth after righteous- U
ness and mercy findeth life, righteousness, and honour.

22 [a]A wise *man* scaleth the city of the mighty, and casteth down the strength of the confidence thereof.

23 [a]Whoso keepeth his mouth and his tongue keepeth his soul from troubles.

24 Proud *and* haughty scorner *is* his name, who dealeth [1]in proud wrath.

25 The desire of the slothful killeth him; for his hands refuse to labour.

26 He coveteth greedily all the day long: but the righteous giveth and spareth not.

27 [a]The sacrifice of the wicked *is* C
abomination: how much more, *when* he bringeth it [1]with a wicked mind?

28 [1]A false witness shall perish: but the man that heareth speaketh constantly.

29 A wicked man hardeneth his face:

C *Pr 15:29* ◀▶ *Pr 21:27*
S *Pr 17:15* ◀▶ *Pr 22:8*
U *Pr 16:7* ◀▶ *Pr 24:16*
C *Pr 21:16* ◀▶ *Pr 30:12–13*

but *as for* the upright, he [1]directeth his way.

30 [a]*There is* no wisdom nor understanding nor counsel against the LORD.

31 The horse *is* prepared against the day of battle: but [a]safety[1] *is* of the LORD.

22 A [a]*GOOD* name *is* rather to be chosen than great riches, *and* [1]loving favour rather than silver and gold.

2 The rich and poor meet together: the LORD *is* the maker of them all.

H 3 A prudent *man* foreseeth the evil, and hideth himself: but the simple pass on, and are punished.

4 [1]By humility *and* the fear of the LORD *are* riches, and honour, and life.

5 Thorns *and* snares *are* in the way of the froward: he that doth keep his soul shall be far from them.

6 [a]Train[1] up a child [2]in the way he should go: and when he is old, he will not depart from it.

7 The rich ruleth over the poor, and the borrower *is* servant [1]to the lender.

S 8 He that soweth iniquity shall reap vanity: [1]and the rod of his anger shall fail.

P 9 [a]He[1] that hath a bountiful eye shall be blessed; for he giveth of his bread to the poor.

10 [a]Cast out the scorner, and contention shall go out; yea, strife and reproach shall cease.

11 [a]He that loveth pureness of heart, [1]*for* the grace of his lips the king *shall be* his friend.

12 The eyes of the LORD preserve knowledge, and he overthroweth [1]the words of the transgressor.

13 [a]The slothful *man* saith, *There is* a lion without, I shall be slain in the streets.

14 [a]The mouth of strange women *is* a deep pit: [b]he that is abhorred of the LORD shall fall therein.

15 Foolishness *is* bound in the heart of a child; *but* [a]the rod of correction shall drive it far from him.

16 He that oppresseth the poor to increase his *riches, and* he that giveth to the rich, *shall* surely *come* to want.

Hear the words of the wise

17 Bow down thine ear, and hear the words of the wise, and apply thine heart unto my knowledge.

18 For *it is* a pleasant thing if thou keep them [1]within thee; they shall withal be fitted in thy lips.

19 That thy trust may be in the LORD, I have made known to thee this day, [1]even to thee.

20 Have not I written to thee excellent things in counsels and knowledge,

21 [a]That I might make thee know the certainty of the words of truth; [b]that thou mightest answer the words of truth [1]to them that send unto thee?

22 Rob not the poor, because he *is* poor: neither oppress the afflicted in the gate:

23 [a]For the LORD will plead their cause, and spoil the soul of those that spoiled them.

24 Make no friendship with an angry man; and with a furious man thou shalt not go:

25 Lest thou learn his ways, and get a snare to thy soul.

26 [a]Be not thou *one* of them that strike hands, *or* of them that are sureties for debts.

27 If thou hast nothing to pay, why should he take away thy bed from under thee?

28 [a]Remove not the ancient [1]landmark, which thy fathers have set.

29 Seest thou a man diligent in his business? he shall stand before kings; he shall not stand before [1]mean *men.*

23 WHEN THOU sittest to eat with a ruler, consider diligently what *is* before thee:

2 And put a knife to thy throat, if thou *be* a man given to appetite.

3 Be not desirous of his dainties: for they *are* deceitful meat.

4 [a]Labour not to be rich: [b]cease from thine own wisdom.

5 [1]Wilt thou set thine eyes upon that which is not? for *riches* certainly make themselves wings; they fly away as an eagle toward heaven.

6 Eat thou not the bread of *him that hath* [a]an evil eye, neither desire thou his dainty meats:

7 For as he thinketh in his heart, so *is* he: Eat and drink, [a]saith he to thee; but his heart *is* not with thee.

8 The morsel *which* thou hast eaten

29 [1]Or, *considereth*
30 [a]Is. 8:9,10; Jer. 9:23; Acts 5:39
31 [a]Ps. 3:8 [1]Or, *victory*
22:1 [a]Eccl. 7:1 [1]Or, *favour is better than*
4 [1]Or, *The reward of humility*
6 [a]Eph. 6:4; 2 Tim. 3:15 [1]Or, *Catechise* [2]Heb. *in his way*
7 [1]Heb. *to the man that lendeth*
8 [1]Or, *and with the rod of his anger he shall be consumed*
9 [a]2 Cor. 9:6 [1]Heb. *Good of eye*
10 [a]Ps. 101:5
11 [a]Ps. 101:6 [1]Or, and hath *grace in his lips*
12 [1]Or, *the matters*
13 [a]ch. 26:13
14 [a]ch. 2:16 & 5:3 & 7:5 [b]Eccl. 7:26
15 [a]ch. 13:24
18 [1]Heb. *in thy belly*
19 [1]Or, trust *thou also*
21 [a]Luke 1:3,4 [b]1 Pet. 3:15 [1]Or, *to those that send thee?*
23 [a]1 Sam. 24:12; Ps. 12:5
26 [a]ch. 11:15
28 [a]Deut. 19:14 [1]Or, *bound*
29 [1]Heb. *obscure* men
23:4 [a]1 Tim. 6:9 [b]Rom. 12:16
5 [1]Heb. *Wilt thou cause thine eyes to fly upon*
6 [a]Deut. 15:9
7 [a]Ps. 12:2

H *Pr 18:12* ◀ ▶ *Pr 23:14*
S *Pr 21:16* ◀ ▶ *Pr 24:12*
P *Pr 19:17* ◀ ▶ *Pr 28:8*

shalt thou vomit up, and lose thy sweet
words.
9 [a]Speak not in the ears of a fool: for
he will despise the wisdom of thy words.
10 Remove not the old [1]landmark; and
enter not into the fields of the fatherless:
K 11 [a]For their redeemer *is* mighty; he
shall plead their cause with thee.
12 Apply thine heart unto instruction,
and thine ears to the words of
knowledge.
13 [a]Withhold not correction from the
child: for *if* thou beatest him with the
rod, he shall not die.
H 14 Thou shalt beat him with the rod,
and shalt deliver his soul from hell.
15 My son, if thine heart be wise, my
heart shall rejoice, [1]even mine.
16 Yea, my reins shall rejoice, when
thy lips speak right things.
17 [a]Let not thine heart envy sinners:
but [b]*be thou* in the fear of the LORD all the
day long.
18 [a]For surely there is an [1]end; and
thine expectation shall not be cut off.
19 Hear thou, my son, and be wise,
and guide thine heart in the way.
20 [a]Be not among winebibbers; among
riotous eaters [1]of flesh:
21 For the drunkard and the glutton
shall come to poverty: and drowsiness
shall clothe *a man* with rags.
22 [a]Hearken unto thy father that begat
thee, and despise not thy mother when
she is old.
23 [a]Buy the truth, and sell *it* not; *also*
wisdom, and instruction, and understanding.
24 [a]The father of the righteous shall
greatly rejoice: and he that begetteth a
wise *child* shall have joy of him.
25 Thy father and thy mother shall be
glad, and she that bare thee shall rejoice.
26 My son, give me thine heart, and
let thine eyes observe my ways.
27 [a]For a whore *is* a deep ditch; and a
strange woman *is* a narrow pit.
28 [a]She also lieth in wait [1]as *for* a
prey, and increaseth the transgressors
among men.
29 [a]Who hath woe? who hath sorrow?
who hath contentions? who hath bab-
bling? who hath wounds without cause?
who [b]hath redness of eyes?
30 [a]They that tarry long at the wine;
they that go to seek [b]mixed wine.
31 Look not thou upon the wine when
it is red, when it giveth his colour in the
cup, *when* it moveth itself aright.
32 At the last it biteth like a serpent,
and stingeth like [1]an adder.
33 Thine eyes shall behold strange
women, and thine heart shall utter perverse things.
34 Yea, thou shalt be as he that lieth
down [1]in the midst of the sea, or as he
that lieth upon the top of a mast.
35 [a]They have stricken me, *shalt thou*
say, and I was not sick; they have beaten
me, *and* [b]I[1] felt *it* not: when shall I
awake? I will seek it yet again.

24 BE NOT thou [a]envious against
evil men, neither desire to be
with them.
2 For their heart studieth destruction,
and their lips talk of mischief.
3 Through wisdom is an house
builded; and by understanding it is established:
4 And by knowledge shall the chambers be filled with all precious and pleasant riches.
5 [a]A wise man [1]*is* strong; yea, a man of
knowledge [2]increaseth strength.
6 [a]For by wise counsel thou shalt make
thy war: and in multitude of counsellors
there is safety.
7 [a]Wisdom *is* too high for a fool: he
openeth not his mouth in the gate.
8 He that [a]deviseth to do evil shall be
called a mischievous person.
9 The thought of foolishness *is* sin: and
the scorner *is* an abomination to men.
10 *If* thou faint in the day of adversity,
thy strength *is* [1]small.
11 [a]If thou forbear to deliver *them that*
are drawn unto death, and *those that are*
ready to be slain;
12 If thou sayest, Behold, we knew it E
not; doth not [a]he that pondereth the S
heart consider *it?* and he that keepeth thy
soul, doth *not* he know *it?* and shall *not*
he render to *every* man [b]according to his
works?
13 My son, [a]eat thou honey, because *it*
is good; and the honeycomb, *which is*
sweet [1]to thy taste:
14 [a]So *shall* the knowledge of wisdom

9 [a]ch. 9:8; Mat. 7:6
10 [1]Or, *bound*
11 [a]ch. 22:23
13 [a]ch. 13:24
15 [1]Or, *even I* will rejoice
17 [a]Ps. 37:1 [b]ch. 28:14
18 [a]Ps. 37:37 [1]Or, *reward*
20 [a]Is. 5:22 [1]Heb. *of their flesh*
22 [a]ch. 1:8; Eph. 6:1,2
23 [a]Mat. 13:44
24 [a]ch. 10:1
27 [a]ch. 22:14
28 [a]ch. 7:12; Eccl. 7:26 [1]Or, *as a robber*
29 [a]Is. 5:11,22 [b]Gen. 49:12
30 [a]Eph. 5:18 [b]Ps. 75:8
32 [1]Or, *a cockatrice*
34 [1]Heb. *in the heart of the sea*
35 [a]Jer. 5:3 [b]Eph. 4:19 [1]Heb. *I knew it not*
24:1 [a]Ps. 37:1 & 73:3; ch. 3:31
5 [a]ch. 21:22 [1]Heb. *is in strength* [2]Heb. *strengtheneth might*
6 [a]Luke 14:31
7 [a]Ps. 10:5
8 [a]Rom. 1:30
10 [1]Heb. *narrow*
11 [a]Ps. 82:4; Is. 58:6,7; 1 John 3:16
12 [a]ch. 21:2 [b]Ps. 62:12
13 [a]Sol. 5:1 [1]Heb. *upon thy palate*
14 [a]Ps. 19:10

K *Ps 130:7* ◀▶ *Isa 1:18*
H *Pr 22:3* ◀▶ *Pr 24:20*
E *Pr 21:2* ◀▶ *Isa 29:15*
S *Pr 22:8* ◀▶ *Pr 24:20*

be unto thy soul: when thou hast found *it,* then there shall be a reward, and thy expectation shall not be cut off.

15 Lay not wait, O wicked *man,* against the dwelling of the righteous; spoil not his resting place:

U 16 [a]For a just *man* falleth seven times, and riseth up again: [b]but the wicked shall fall into mischief.

17 [a]Rejoice not when thine enemy falleth, and let not thine heart be glad when he stumbleth:

18 Lest the LORD see *it,* and [l]it displease him, and he turn away his wrath from him.

19 [a]Fret[l] not thyself because of evil *men,* neither be thou envious at the wicked;

H S 20 For there shall be no reward to the evil *man;* the [l]candle of the wicked shall be put out.

21 My son, [a]fear thou the LORD and the king: *and* meddle not with [l]them that are given to change:

22 For their calamity shall rise suddenly; and who knoweth the ruin of them both?

Sayings of the wise

23 These *things* also *belong* to the wise. [a]*It is* not good to have respect of persons in judgment.

S 24 [a]He that saith unto the wicked, Thou *art* righteous; him shall the people curse, nations shall abhor him:

25 But to them that rebuke *him* shall be delight, and [l]a good blessing shall come upon them.

26 *Every man* shall kiss *his* lips [l]that giveth a right answer.

27 [a]Prepare thy work without, and make it fit for thyself in the field; and afterwards build thine house.

28 [a]Be not a witness against thy neighbour without cause; and deceive *not* with thy lips.

29 [a]Say not, I will do so to him as he hath done to me: I will render to the man according to his work.

30 I went by the field of the slothful, and by the vineyard of the man void of understanding;

31 And, lo, [a]it was all grown over with thorns, *and* nettles had covered the face thereof, and the stone wall thereof was broken down.

32 Then I saw, *and* [l]considered *it* well: I looked upon *it, and* received instruction.

33 [a]*Yet* a little sleep, a little slumber, a little folding of the hands to sleep:

34 So shall thy poverty come *as* one that travelleth; and thy want as [l]an armed man.

More proverbs of Solomon

25

THESE[a] *ARE* also proverbs of Solomon, which the men of Hezekiah king of Judah copied out.

2 [a]*It is* the glory of God to conceal a thing: but the honour of kings *is* [b]to search out a matter.

3 The heaven for height, and the earth for depth, and the heart of kings [l]*is* unsearchable.

4 [a]Take away the dross from the silver, and there shall come forth a vessel for the refiner. T

5 [a]Take away the wicked *from* before the king, and [b]his throne shall be established in righteousness.

6 [l]Put not forth thyself in the presence of the king, and stand not in the place of great *men:*

7 [a]For better *it is* that it be said unto thee, Come up hither; than that thou shouldest be put lower in the presence of the prince whom thine eyes have seen.

8 [a]Go not forth hastily to strive, lest *thou know not* what to do in the end thereof, when thy neighbour hath put thee to shame.

9 [a]Debate thy cause with thy neighbour *himself;* and [l]discover not a secret to another:

10 Lest he that heareth *it* put thee to shame, and thine infamy turn not away.

11 [a]A word [l]fitly spoken *is like* apples of gold in pictures of silver.

12 *As* an earring of gold, and an ornament of fine gold, *so is* a wise reprover upon an obedient ear.

13 [a]As the cold of snow in the time of harvest, *so is* a faithful messenger to them that send him: for he refresheth the soul of his masters.

14 [a]Whoso boasteth himself [l]of a false

---

16 [a]Ps. 34:19; Mic. 7:8 [b]Esth. 7:10; Amos 5:2
17 [a]Job 31:29; Obad. 12
18 [l]Heb. *it be evil in his eyes*
19 [a]Ps. 37:1 [l]Or, *Keep not company with the wicked*
20 [l]Or, *lamp*
21 [a]Rom. 13:7; 1 Pet. 2:17 [l]Heb. *changers*
23 [a]Lev. 19:15; Deut. 16:19
24 [a]Is. 5:23
25 [l]Heb. *a blessing of good*
26 [l]Heb. *that answereth right words*
27 [a]1 Ki. 5:17
28 [a]Eph. 4:25
29 [a]Mat. 5:39
31 [a]Gen. 3:18
32 [l]Heb. *set my heart*
33 [a]ch. 6:9
34 [l]Heb. *a man of shield*
25:1 [a]1 Ki. 4:32
2 [a]Rom. 11:33 [b]Job 29:16
3 [l]Heb. there is *no searching*
4 [a]2 Tim. 2:21
5 [a]ch. 20:8 [b]ch. 16:12
6 [l]Heb. *Set not out thy glory*
7 [a]Luke 14:10
8 [a]Mat. 5:25
9 [a]Mat. 5:25 [l]Or, *discover not the secret of another*
11 [a]ch. 15:23 [l]Heb. *spoken upon his wheels*
13 [a]ch. 13:17
14 [a]ch. 20:6 [l]Heb. *in a gift of falsehood*

U *Pr 21:21* ◀▶ *Pr 25:21–22*
H *Pr 23:14* ◀▶ *Pr 26:10*
S *Pr 24:12* ◀▶ *Pr 24:24*
S *Pr 24:20* ◀▶ *Ecc 12:13–14*
T *Pr 17:3* ◀▶ *Ecc 7:14*

gift *is like* [b]clouds and wind without rain.

15 [a]By long forbearing is a prince persuaded, and a soft tongue breaketh the bone.

16 [a]Hast thou found honey? eat so much as is sufficient for thee, lest thou be filled therewith, and vomit it.

17 [1]Withdraw thy foot from thy neighbour's house; lest he be [2]weary of thee, and *so* hate thee.

18 [a]A man that beareth false witness against his neighbour *is* a maul, and a sword, and a sharp arrow.

19 Confidence in an unfaithful man in time of trouble *is like* a broken tooth, and a foot out of joint.

20 *As* he that taketh away a garment in cold weather, *and as* vinegar upon nitre, so *is* he that [a]singeth songs to an heavy heart.

U 21 [a]If thine enemy be hungry, give him bread to eat; and if he be thirsty, give him water to drink:

22 For thou shalt heap coals of fire upon his head, [a]and the LORD shall reward thee.

23 [a]The[1] north wind driveth away rain: so *doth* an angry countenance [b]a backbiting tongue.

24 [a]*It is* better to dwell in the corner of the housetop, than with a brawling woman and in a wide house.

25 *As* cold waters to a thirsty soul, so *is* good news from a far country.

26 A righteous man falling down before the wicked *is as* a troubled fountain, and a corrupt spring.

27 [a]*It is* not good to eat much honey: so *for men* [b]to search their own glory *is not* glory.

28 [a]He that *hath* no rule over his own spirit *is like* a city *that is* broken down, *and* without walls.

26

AS SNOW in summer, [a]and as rain in harvest, so honour is not seemly for a fool.

2 As the bird by wandering, as the swallow by flying, so [a]the curse causeless shall not come.

3 [a]A whip for the horse, a bridle for the ass, and a rod for the fool's back.

4 Answer not a fool according to his folly, lest thou also be like unto him.

5 [a]Answer a fool according to his folly, lest he be wise in [1]his own conceit.

6 He that sendeth a message by the hand of a fool cutteth off the feet, *and* drinketh [1]damage.

7 The legs of the lame [1]are not equal: so *is* a parable in the mouth of fools.

8 [1]As he that bindeth a stone in a sling, so *is* he that giveth honour to a fool.

9 *As* a thorn goeth up into the hand of a drunkard, so *is* a parable in the mouth of fools.

10 [1]The great *God* that formed all *things* both rewardeth the fool, and rewardeth transgressors. H

11 [a]As a dog returneth to his vomit, [b]*so* a fool [1]returneth to his folly.

12 [a]Seest thou a man wise in his own conceit? *there is* more hope of a fool than of him. G M

13 The slothful *man* saith, *There is* a lion in the way; a lion *is* in the streets.

14 *As* the door turneth upon his hinges, so *doth* the slothful upon his bed.

15 The slothful hideth his hand in *his* bosom; [1]it grieveth him to bring it again to his mouth.

16 The sluggard *is* wiser in his own conceit than seven men that can render a reason.

17 He that passeth by, *and* [1]meddleth with strife *belonging* not to him, *is like* one that taketh a dog by the ears.

18 As a mad *man* who casteth [1]firebrands, arrows, and death,

19 So *is* the man *that* deceiveth his neighbour, and saith, [a]Am not I in sport?

20 [1]Where no wood is, *there* the fire goeth out: so where *there is* no [2]talebearer, the strife [3]ceaseth.

21 [a]*As* coals *are* to burning coals, and wood to fire; so *is* a contentious man to kindle strife.

22 The words of a talebearer *are* as wounds, and they go down into the [1]innermost parts of the belly.

23 Burning lips and a wicked heart *are like* a potsherd covered with silver dross.

24 He that hateth [1]dissembleth with his lips, and layeth up deceit within him;

25 [a]When he [1]speaketh fair, believe him not: for *there are* seven abominations in his heart.

26 *Whose* [1]hatred is covered by deceit,

14 [b]Jude 12
15 [a]ch. 15:1
16 [a]ver. 27
17 [1]Or, *Let thy foot be seldom in thy neighbour's house* [2]Heb. *full of thee*
18 [a]Ps. 57:4
20 [a]Dan. 6:18
21 [a]Mat. 5:44
22 [a]2 Sam. 16:12
23 [a]Job 37:22 [b]Ps. 101:5 [1]Or, *The north wind bringeth forth rain: so doth a backbiting tongue an angry countenance*
24 [a]ch. 19:13
27 [a]ver. 16 [b]ch. 27:2
28 [a]ch. 16:32
26:1 [a]1 Sam. 12:17
2 [a]Deut. 23:5
3 [a]Ps. 32:9
5 [a]Mat. 16:1-4 [1]Heb. *his own eyes*
6 [1]Or, *violence*
7 [1]Heb. *are lifted up*
8 [1]Or, *As he that putteth a precious stone in an heap of stones*
10 [1]Or, *A great man grieveth all, and he hireth the fool, he hireth also transgressors*
11 [a]2 Pet. 2:22 [b]Ex. 8:15 [1]Heb. *iterateth his folly*
12 [a]Rev. 3:17
15 [1]Or, *he is weary*
17 [1]Or, *is enraged*
18 [1]Heb. *flames,* or, *sparks*
19 [a]Eph. 5:4
20 [1]Heb. *Without wood* [2]Or, *whisperer* [3]Heb. *is silent*
21 [a]ch. 15:18
22 [1]Heb. *chambers*
24 [1]Or, *is known*
25 [a]Ps. 28:3 [1]Heb. *maketh his voice gracious*
26 [1]Or, *hatred is covered in secret*

U *Pr 24:16* ◀ ▶ *Pr 28:10*

H *Pr 24:20* ◀ ▶ *Pr 27:12*
G *Pr 21:2* ◀ ▶ *Pr 28:26*
M *Pr 18:12* ◀ ▶ *Pr 29:1*

his wickedness shall be shown before the *whole* congregation.

27 [a]Whoso diggeth a pit shall fall therein: and he that rolleth a stone, it will return upon him.

28 A lying tongue hateth *those that are* afflicted by it; and a flattering mouth worketh ruin.

N **27** BOAST NOT thyself of [1]tomorrow; for thou knowest not what a day may bring forth.

2 Let another man praise thee, and not thine own mouth; a stranger, and not thine own lips.

3 A stone *is* [1]heavy, and the sand weighty; but a fool's wrath *is* heavier than them both.

4 [1]Wrath *is* cruel, and anger *is* outrageous; but who *is* able to stand before [2]envy?

5 Open rebuke *is* better than secret love.

6 Faithful *are* the wounds of a friend; but the kisses of an enemy *are* [1]deceitful.

7 The full soul [1]loatheth an honeycomb; but to the hungry soul every bitter thing is sweet.

8 As a bird that wandereth from her nest, so *is* a man that wandereth from his place.

9 Ointment and perfume rejoice the heart: so *doth* the sweetness of a man's friend [1]by hearty counsel.

10 Thine own friend, and thy father's friend, forsake not; neither go into thy brother's house in the day of thy calamity: *for* [a]better *is* a neighbour *that is* near than a brother far off.

11 My son, be wise, and make my heart glad, [a]that I may answer him that reproacheth me.

H 12 A prudent *man* foreseeth the evil, *and* hideth himself; *but* the simple pass on, *and* are punished.

13 Take his garment that is surety for a stranger, and take a pledge of him for a strange woman.

14 He that blesseth his friend with a loud voice, rising early in the morning, it shall be counted a curse to him.

15 A continual dropping in a very rainy day and a contentious woman are alike.

16 Whosoever hideth her hideth the wind, and the ointment of his right hand, *which* betrayeth *itself.*

17 Iron sharpeneth iron; so a man sharpeneth the countenance of his friend.

18 [a]Whoso keepeth the fig tree shall eat the fruit thereof: so he that waiteth on his master shall be honoured.

19 As in water face *answereth* to face, so the heart of man to man.

20 [a]Hell and destruction are [1]never full; so [b]the eyes of man are never satisfied.

21 [a]*As* the refining pot for silver, and the furnace for gold; so *is* a man to his praise.

22 [a]Though thou shouldest bray a fool in a mortar among wheat with a pestle, *yet* will not his foolishness depart from him.

23 Be thou diligent to know the state of thy flocks, *and* [1]look well to thy herds.

24 For [1]riches *are* not for ever: and doth the crown *endure* [2]to every generation?

25 [a]The hay appeareth, and the tender grass showeth itself, and herbs of the mountains are gathered.

26 The lambs *are* for thy clothing, and the goats *are* the price of the field.

27 And *thou shalt have* goats' milk enough for thy food, for the food of thy household, and *for* the [1]maintenance for thy maidens.

28 THE [a]WICKED flee when no man pursueth: but the righteous are bold as a lion.

2 For the transgression of a land many *are* the princes thereof: but [1]by a man of understanding *and* knowledge the state *thereof* shall be prolonged.

3 [a]A poor man that oppresseth the poor *is like* a sweeping rain [1]which leaveth no food.

4 [a]They that forsake the law praise the wicked: [b]but such as keep the law contend with them.

5 [a]Evil men understand not judgment: but [b]they that seek the LORD understand all *things.*

6 [a]Better *is* the poor that walketh in his uprightness, than *he that is* perverse *in his* ways, though he *be* rich.

7 [a]Whoso keepeth the law *is* a wise son: but he that [1]is a companion of riotous *men* shameth his father.

27 [a]Ps. 7:15
27:1 [1]Heb. *tomorrow day*
3 [1]Heb. *heaviness*
4 [1]Heb. *Wrath is cruelty, and anger an overflowing* [2]Or, *jealousy?*
6 [1]Or, *earnest,* or, *frequent*
7 [1]Heb. *treadeth under foot*
9 [1]Heb. *from the counsel of the soul*
10 [a]ch. 17:17
11 [a]Ps. 127:5
18 [a]1 Cor. 9:7
20 [a]Hab. 2:5 [b]Eccl. 1:8 [1]Heb. *not*
21 [a]ch. 17:3
22 [a]Jer. 5:3
23 [1]Heb. *set thy heart*
24 [1]Heb. *strength* [2]Heb. *to generation and generation?*
25 [a]Ps. 104:14
27 [1]Heb. *life*
28:1 [a]Ps. 53:5
2 [1]Or, *by men of understanding* and *wisdom shall they likewise be prolonged*
3 [a]Mat. 18:28 [1]Heb. *without food*
4 [a]Rom. 1:32 [b]1 Ki. 18:18
5 [a]Ps. 92:6 [b]John 7:17
6 [a]ch. 19:1
7 [a]ch. 29:3 [1]Or, *feedeth gluttons*

N *Pr 14:32* ◀▶ *Pr 29:1*
H *Pr 26:10* ◀▶ *Pr 29:1*

P 8 [a]He that by usury and 'unjust gain
increaseth his substance, he shall gather
it for him that will pity the poor.
9 He that turneth away his ear from
hearing the law, [a]even his prayer *shall be*
abomination.
U 10 [a]Whoso causeth the righteous to go
astray in an evil way, he shall fall himself
into his own pit: [b]but the upright shall
have good *things* in possession.
11 The rich man *is* wise 'in his own
conceit; but the poor that hath understanding searcheth him out.
12 [a]When righteous *men* do rejoice,
there is great glory: but when the wicked
rise, a man is 'hidden.
L 13 [a]He that covereth his sins shall not
R prosper: but whoso confesseth and forsaketh *them* shall have mercy.
14 Happy *is* the man [a]that feareth always: [b]but he that hardeneth his heart
shall fall into mischief.
15 [a]*As* a roaring lion, and a ranging
bear; [b]*so is* a wicked ruler over the poor
people.
16 The prince that wanteth understanding *is* also a great oppressor: *but* he
that hateth covetousness shall prolong *his*
days.
17 [a]A man that doeth violence to the
blood of *any* person shall flee to the pit;
let no man stay him.
18 [a]Whoso walketh uprightly shall be
saved: but [b]*he that is* perverse *in his*
ways shall fall at once.
19 [a]He that tilleth his land shall have
plenty of bread: but he that followeth after vain *persons* shall have poverty
enough.
U 20 A faithful man shall abound with
blessings: [a]but he that maketh haste to be
rich shall not be 'innocent.
21 [a]To have respect of persons *is* not
good: for [b]for a piece of bread *that* man
will transgress.
22 [a]He' that hasteth to be rich *hath* an
evil eye, and considereth not that poverty
shall come upon him.
23 [a]He that rebuketh a man afterwards
shall find more favour than he that flattereth with the tongue.

8 [a]ch. 13:22 'Heb. *by increase*
9 [a]Ps. 66:18
10 [a]ch. 26:27 [b]Mat. 6:33
11 'Heb. *in his eyes*
12 [a]ch. 11:10 'Or, *sought for*
13 [a]Ps. 32:3,5
14 [a]Ps. 16:8 [b]Rom. 2:5
15 [a]1 Pet. 5:8 [b]Mat. 2:16
17 [a]Gen. 9:6
18 [a]ch. 10:9,25 [b]ver. 6
19 [a]ch. 12:11
20 [a]1 Tim. 6:9 'Or, *unpunished*
21 [a]ch. 18:5 [b]Ezek. 13:19
22 [a]ver. 20 'Or, *He that hath an evil eye hasteth to be rich*
23 [a]ch. 27:5,6
24 [a]ch. 18:9 'Heb. *a man destroying*
25 [a]ch. 13:10 [b]1 Tim. 6:6
27 [a]Deut. 15:7
28 [a]ver. 12 [b]Job 24:4
29:1 [a]2 Chr. 36:16 'Heb. *A man of reproofs*
2 [a]Esth. 8:15 [b]Esth. 3:15 'Or, *increased*
3 [a]ch. 10:1 [b]Luke 15:13
4 'Heb. *a man of oblations*
7 [a]Job 29:16; Ps. 41:1
8 [a]ch. 11:11 [b]Ezek. 22:30 'Or, *set a city on fire*
9 [a]Mat. 11:17
10 [a]1 John 3:12 'Heb. *Men of blood*
11 [a]ch. 12:16
13 'Or, *the usurer*

24 Whoso robbeth his father or his
mother, and saith, *It is* no transgression;
the same [a]*is* the companion of 'a destroyer.
25 [a]He that is of a proud heart stirreth U
up strife: [b]but he that putteth his trust in
the LORD shall be made fat.
26 He that trusteth in his own heart is G
a fool: but whoso walketh wisely, he shall
be delivered.
27 [a]He that giveth unto the poor shall P
not lack: but he that hideth his eyes shall
have many a curse.
28 [a]When the wicked rise, [b]men hide
themselves: but when they perish, the
righteous increase.

29 HE,[a] ' THAT being often re- H
proved hardeneth *his* neck, shall M
suddenly be destroyed, and that without N
remedy.
2 [a]When the righteous are 'in authority, the people rejoice: but when the
wicked beareth rule, [b]the people mourn.
3 [a]Whoso loveth wisdom rejoiceth his
father: [b]but he that keepeth company
with harlots spendeth *his* substance.
4 The king by judgment establisheth
the land: but 'he that receiveth gifts overthroweth it.
5 A man that flattereth his neighbour
spreadeth a net for his feet.
6 In the transgression of an evil man
there is a snare: but the righteous doth
sing and rejoice.
7 [a]The righteous considereth the
cause of the poor: *but* the wicked regardeth not to know *it.*
8 [a]Scornful men 'bring a city into a
snare: but wise *men* [b]turn away wrath.
9 *If* a wise man contendeth with a foolish man, [a]whether he rage or laugh,
there is no rest.
10 [a]The' bloodthirsty hate the upright: but the just seek his soul.
11 A [a]fool uttereth all his mind: but a
wise *man* keepeth it in till afterwards.
12 If a ruler hearken to lies, all his servants *are* wicked.
13 The poor and 'the deceitful man

P *Pr 22:9* ◀ ▶ *Pr 28:27*
U *Pr 25:21–22* ◀ ▶ *Pr 28:20*
L *Pr 8:17* ◀ ▶ *Isa 1:18–19*
R *Pr 14:16* ◀ ▶ *Isa 1:16–17*
U *Pr 28:10* ◀ ▶ *Pr 28:25*
U *Pr 28:20* ◀ ▶ *Ecc 2:26*
G *Pr 26:12* ◀ ▶ *Ecc 1:14–15*
P *Pr 28:8* ◀ ▶ *Ecc 2:26*
H *Pr 27:12* ◀ ▶ *Ecc 8:11–13*
M *Pr 26:12* ◀ ▶ *Pr 30:12–13*
N *Pr 27:1* ◀ ▶ *Ecc 8:8*

meet together: [a]the LORD lighteneth both their eyes.

14 [a]The king that faithfully judgeth the poor, his throne shall be established for ever.

15 The rod and reproof give wisdom: but [a]a child left *to himself* bringeth his mother to shame.

16 When the wicked are multiplied, transgression increaseth: [a]but the righteous shall see their fall.

17 [a]Correct thy son, and he shall give thee rest; yea, he shall give delight unto thy soul.

18 [a]Where *there is* no vision, the people ǀperish: but [b]he that keepeth the law, happy *is* he.

19 A servant will not be corrected by words: for though he understand he will not answer.

20 Seest thou a man *that is* hasty ǀin his words? [a]*there is* more hope of a fool than of him.

21 He that delicately bringeth up his servant from a child shall have him become *his* son at the length.

22 [a]An angry man stirreth up strife, and a furious man aboundeth in transgression.

23 [a]A man's pride shall bring him low: but honour shall uphold the humble in spirit.

24 Whoso is partner with a thief hateth his own soul: [a]he heareth cursing, and betrayeth *it* not.

F 25 [a]The fear of man bringeth a snare:
W but whoso putteth his trust in the LORD
S ǀshall be safe.

26 [a]Many seek ǀthe ruler's favour; but *every* man's judgment *cometh* from the LORD.

27 An unjust man *is* an abomination to the just: and *he that is* upright in the way *is* abomination to the wicked.

Observations of Agur

30 THE WORDS of Agur the son of Jakeh, *even* the prophecy: the man spake unto Ithiel, even unto Ithiel and Ucal,

2 [a]Surely I *am* more brutish than *any* man, and have not the understanding of a man.

3 I neither learned wisdom, nor ǀhave the knowledge of the holy.

4 [a]Who hath ascended up into heaven, or descended? [b]who hath gathered the wind in his fists? who hath bound the waters in a garment? who hath established all the ends of the earth? what *is* his name, and what *is* his son's name, if thou canst tell?

5 [a]Every word of God *is* ǀpure: [b]he *is* a S
shield unto them that put their trust in him.

6 [a]Add thou not unto his words, lest he reprove thee, and thou be found a liar.

7 Two *things* have I required of thee; ǀdeny me *them* not before I die:

8 Remove far from me vanity and lies: give me neither poverty nor riches; [a]feed me with food ǀconvenient for me:

9 [a]Lest I be full, and ǀdeny *thee,* and say, Who *is* the LORD? or lest I be poor, and steal, and take the name of my God *in vain.*

10 ǀAccuse not a servant unto his master, lest he curse thee, and thou be found guilty.

11 *There is* a generation *that* curseth their father, and doth not bless their mother.

12 *There is* a generation [a]*that are* pure C
in their own eyes, and *yet* is not washed M
from their filthiness.

13 *There is* a generation, O how [a]lofty are their eyes! and their eyelids are lifted up.

14 [a]*There is* a generation, whose teeth *are as* swords, and their jaw teeth *as* knives, [b]to devour the poor from off the earth, and the needy from *among* men.

15 The horseleach hath two daughters, *crying,* Give, give. There are three *things that* are never satisfied, *yea,* four *things* say not, ǀ*It is* enough:

16 [a]The grave; and the barren womb; the earth *that* is not filled with water; and the fire *that* saith not, *It is* enough.

17 [a]The eye *that* mocketh at *his* father, and despiseth to obey *his* mother, the ravens of ǀthe valley shall pick it out, and the young eagles shall eat it.

18 There be three *things which* are too wonderful for me, yea, four which I know not:

13 [a]Mat. 5:45
14 [a]ch. 20:28
15 [a]ch. 17:21,25
16 [a]Ps. 37:36
17 [a]ch. 19:18
18 [a]1 Sam. 3:1; Amos 8:11 [b]John 13:17 ǀOr, *is made naked*
20 [a]ch. 26:12 ǀOr, *in his matters?*
22 [a]ch. 26:21
23 [a]Job 22:29; Is. 66:2; Dan. 4:30; Mat. 23:12
24 [a]Lev. 5:1
25 [a]Gen. 12:12 ǀHeb. *shall be set on high*
26 [a]Ps. 20:9 ǀHeb. *the face of a ruler*
30:2 [a]Ps. 73:22
3 ǀHeb. *know*
4 [a]John 3:13 [b]Job 38:4; Ps. 104:3; Is. 40:12
5 [a]Ps. 12:6 [b]Ps. 18:30 ǀHeb. *purified*
6 [a]Deut. 4:2; Rev. 22:18
7 ǀHeb. *withhold not from me*
8 [a]Mat. 6:11 ǀHeb. *of my allowance*
9 [a]Deut. 8:12 ǀHeb. *belie thee*
10 ǀHeb. *Hurt not with thy tongue*
12 [a]Luke 18:11
13 [a]Ps. 131:1; ch. 6:17
14 [a]Job 29:17; Ps. 52:2 [b]Ps. 14:4; Amos 8:4
15 ǀHeb. *Wealth*
16 [a]ch. 27:20; Hab. 2:5
17 [a]Gen. 9:22; Lev. 20:9; ch. 20:20 & 23:22 ǀOr, *the brook*

F *Ps 125:1* ◀▶ *Isa 7:9*
W *Ps 145:18* ◀▶ *Isa 1:18*
S *Pr 18:10* ◀▶ *Pr 30:5*

S *Pr 29:25* ◀▶ *Isa 32:18*
C *Pr 21:27* ◀▶ *Ecc 7:29*
M *Pr 29:1* ◀▶ *Isa 2:10–17*

19 The way of an eagle in the air; the way of a serpent upon a rock; the way of a ship in the [1]midst of the sea; and the way of a man with a maid.

20 Such *is* the way of an adulterous woman; she eateth, and wipeth her mouth, and saith, I have done no wickedness.

21 For three *things* the earth is disquieted, and for four *which* it cannot bear:

22 [a]For a servant when he reigneth; and a fool when he is filled with meat;

23 For an odious *woman* when she is married; and an handmaid that is heir to her mistress.

24 There be four *things which are* little upon the earth, but they *are* [1]exceeding wise:

25 [a]The ants *are* a people not strong, yet they prepare their meat in the summer;

26 [a]The conies *are but* a feeble folk, yet make they their houses in the rocks;

27 The locusts have no king, yet go they forth all of them [1]by bands;

28 The spider taketh hold with her hands, and is in kings' palaces.

29 There be three *things* which go well, yea, four are comely in going:

30 A lion *which is* strongest among beasts, and turneth not away for any;

31 A [1,2]greyhound; an he goat also; and a king, against whom *there is* no rising up.

32 If thou hast done foolishly in lifting up thyself, or if thou hast thought evil, [a]*lay* thine hand upon thy mouth.

33 Surely the churning of milk bringeth forth butter, and the wringing of the nose bringeth forth blood: so the forcing of wrath bringeth forth strife.

Words of king Lemuel

31 THE WORDS of king Lemuel, the prophecy that his mother taught him.

2 What, my son? and what, [a]the son of my womb? and what, the son of my vows?

3 [a]Give not thy strength unto women, nor thy ways [b]to that which destroyeth kings.

4 [a]*It is* not for kings, O Lemuel, *it is* not for kings to drink wine; nor for princes strong drink:

5 [a]Lest they drink, and forget the law, and [1]pervert the judgment [2]of any of the afflicted.

6 [a]Give strong drink unto him that is ready to perish, and wine unto those that be [1]of heavy hearts.

7 Let him drink, and forget his poverty, and remember his misery no more.

8 [a]Open thy mouth for the dumb in the cause of all [1]such as are appointed to destruction.

9 Open thy mouth, [a]judge righteously, and [b]plead the cause of the poor and needy.

The virtuous woman

10 ¶ [a]Who can find a virtuous woman? for her price *is* far above rubies.

11 The heart of her husband doth safely trust in her, so that he shall have no need of spoil.

12 She will do him good and not evil all the days of her life.

13 She seeketh wool, and flax, and worketh willingly with her hands.

14 She is like the merchants' ships; she bringeth her food from afar.

15 [a]She riseth also while it is yet night, and [b]giveth meat to her household, and a portion to her maidens.

16 She considereth a field, and [1]buyeth it: with the fruit of her hands she planteth a vineyard.

17 She girdeth her loins with strength, and strengtheneth her arms.

18 [1]She perceiveth that her merchandise *is* good: her candle goeth not out by night.

19 She layeth her hands to the spindle, and her hands hold the distaff.

20 [a]She[1] stretcheth out her hand to the poor; yea, she reacheth forth her hands to the needy.

21 She is not afraid of the snow for her household: for all her household *are* clothed with [1]scarlet.

22 She maketh herself coverings of tapestry; her clothing *is* silk and purple.

23 [a]Her husband is known in the gates, when he sitteth among the elders of the land.

24 She maketh fine linen, and selleth *it;* and delivereth girdles unto the merchant.

25 Strength and honour *are* her clothing; and she shall rejoice in time to come.

26 She openeth her mouth with wis-

19 [1]Heb. *heart*
22 [a]ch. 19:10; Eccl. 10:7
24 [1]Heb. *wise, made wise*
25 [a]ch. 6:6
26 [a]Ps. 104:18
27 [1]Heb. *gathered together*
31 [1]Or, *horse* [2]Heb. *girt in the loins*
32 [a]Job 21:5 & 40:4; Mic. 7:16
31:2 [a]Is. 49:15
3 [a]ch. 5:9 [b]Deut. 17:17; Neh. 13:26; ch. 7:26; Hos. 4:11
4 [a]Eccl. 10:17
5 [a]Hos. 4:11 [1]Heb. *alter* [2]Heb. *of all the sons of affliction*
6 [a]Ps. 104:15 [1]Heb. *bitter of soul*
8 [a]See Job 29:15, 16 [1]Heb. *the sons of destruction*
9 [a]Lev. 19:15; Deut. 1:16 [b]Job 29:12; Is. 1:17; Jer. 22:16
10 [a]ch. 12:4 & 18:22 & 19:14
15 [a]Rom. 12:11 [b]Luke 12:42
16 [1]Heb. *taketh*
18 [1]Heb. *She tasteth*
20 [a]Eph. 4:28; Heb. 13:16 [1]Heb. *She spreadeth*
21 [1]Or, *double garments*
23 [a]ch. 12:4

dom; and in her tongue *is* the law of kindness.

27 She looketh well to the ways of her household, and eateth not the bread of idleness.

28 Her children arise up, and call her blessed; her husband *also,* and he praiseth her.

29 Many daughters [l]have done virtuously, but thou excellest them all.

30 Favour *is* deceitful, and beauty *is* vain: *but* a woman *that* feareth the LORD, she shall be praised.

31 Give her of the fruit of her hands; and let her own works praise her in the gates.

29 [l]Or, *have gotten riches*

Ecclesiastes

Author: King Solomon

Theme: Only a life centered on God has meaning

Date of Writing: c. 950 B.C.

Outline of Ecclesiastes

I. Working for Gain Is Profitless (1:1–11)
II. Enjoy God's Gift of Life (1:12—11:6)
III. Enjoy Life While Young for God Will Judge (11:7—12:7)
IV. Reverently Trust and Obey God (12:8–14)

THE BOOK OF Ecclesiastes identifies its author as "the Teacher," a title derived from the Hebrew word *qoheleth*. When scholars of the Septuagint (the Greek translation of the OT) translated this book, they titled it *ecclesiastes*, which is the Greek word meaning "teacher." Most English translations use the Septuagint title. Because several passages strongly suggest that King Solomon was "the Teacher," Jewish and Christian scholars traditionally ascribe authorship to him (see 1:1; 2:4–9; 7:26–29). Several references to Aramaic and Phoenician customs also help place this book in Solomon's time.

Included in the Jewish megilloth (a five-book grouping read aloud in the Jewish synagogues) and annually read during the Feast of the Tabernacles, Ecclesiastes measures life as a whole to determine its worth and significance. Examining the "vanity" and futility of wisdom, education, knowledge, pleasure, happiness, power, influence and religion, the author concludes that life is meaningless unless it is centered on a proper respect and reverence for God. The mood of the book is sad, mournful and depressed, intimating that these are the philosophical and theological reflections of an older person whose life "under the sun" (1:3) was meaningless because he had not relied on God. While unequaled wisdom, vast wealth, pleasure in abundance and ideal working conditions all have temporary value, the Teacher declares that these blessings have lasting value only when life is lived in obedience to God.

Vanity of human wisdom

1 THE WORDS [a]of the Preacher, the son of David, king in Jerusalem.

2 [a]Vanity of vanities, saith the Preacher, vanity of vanities; [b]all *is* vanity.

3 [a]What profit hath a man of all his labour which he taketh under the sun?

N 4 *One* generation passeth away, and *another* generation cometh: [a]but the earth abideth for ever.

5 [a]The sun also ariseth, and the sun goeth down, and [1]hasteth to his place where he arose.

6 [a]The wind goeth toward the south, and turneth about unto the north; it whirleth about continually, and the wind returneth again according to his circuits.

7 [a]All the rivers run into the sea; yet the sea *is* not full; unto the place from whence the rivers come, thither they [1]return again.

8 All things *are* full of labour; man cannot utter *it:* [a]the eye is not satisfied with seeing, nor the ear filled with hearing.

9 [a]The thing that hath been, it *is that* which shall be; and that which is done *is* that which shall be done: and *there is* no new *thing* under the sun.

10 Is there *any* thing whereof it may be said, See, this *is* new? it hath been already of old time, which was before us.

11 *There is* no remembrance of former *things;* neither shall there be *any* remembrance of *things* that are to come with *those* that shall come after.

12 ¶ [a]I the Preacher was king over Israel in Jerusalem.

13 And I gave my heart to seek and search out by wisdom concerning all *things* that are done under heaven: [a]this sore travail hath God given to the sons of man [1]to be exercised therewith.

G 14 I have seen all the works that are done under the sun; and, behold, all *is* vanity and vexation of spirit.

N *Pr 10:30* ◀ ▶ *Isa 65:16–18*
G *Pr 28:26* ◀ ▶ *Isa 28:15–20*

1:1 [a]ver. 12; ch. 7:27 & 12:8-10
2 [a]Ps. 39:5,6 & 62:9 & 144:4; ch. 12:8 [b]Rom. 8:20
3 [a]ch. 2:22
4 [a]Ps. 104:5 & 119:90
5 [a]Ps. 19:4-6 [1]Heb. *panteth*
6 [a]John 3:8
7 [a]Ps. 104:8,9; Jer. 5:22 [1]Heb. *return to go*
8 [a]Prov. 27:20
9 [a]ch. 3:15
12 [a]ver. 1
13 [a]Gen. 3:19; ch. 3:10 [1]Or, *to afflict them*
15 [a]ch. 7:13 [1]Heb. *defect*
16 [a]1 Ki. 3:12,13 [1]Heb. *had seen much*
17 [a]ch. 2:3,12
18 [a]ch. 12:12
2:1 [a]Luke 12:19 [b]ch. 1:2
3 [a]ch. 1:17 [1]Heb. *to draw my flesh with wine* [2]Heb. *the number of the days of their life*
7 [1]Heb. *sons of my house*
8 [a]1 Ki. 9:28 & 10:10,14,21

15 [a]*That which is* crooked cannot be made straight: and [1]that which is wanting cannot be numbered.

16 I communed with mine own heart, saying, Lo, I am come to great estate, and have gotten [a]more wisdom than all *they* that have been before me in Jerusalem: yea, my heart [1]had great experience of wisdom and knowledge.

17 [a]And I gave my heart to know wisdom, and to know madness and folly: I perceived that this also is vexation of spirit.

18 For [a]in much wisdom *is* much grief: and he that increaseth knowledge increaseth sorrow.

Vanity of pleasure and wealth

2 I[a] SAID in mine heart, Go to now, I will prove thee with mirth, therefore enjoy pleasure: and, behold, [b]this also *is* vanity.

2 I said of laughter, *It is* mad: and of mirth, What doeth it?

3 [a]I sought in mine heart [1]to give myself unto wine, yet acquainting mine heart with wisdom; and to lay hold on folly, till I might see what *was* that good for the sons of men, which they should do under the heaven [2]all the days of their life.

4 I made me great works; I builded me houses; I planted me vineyards:

5 I made me gardens and orchards, and I planted trees in them of all *kind of* fruits:

6 I made me pools of water, to water therewith the wood that bringeth forth trees:

7 I got *me* servants and maidens, and had [1]servants born in my house; also I had great possessions of great and small cattle above all that were in Jerusalem before me:

8 [a]I gathered me also silver and gold, and the peculiar treasure of kings and of the provinces: I gat me men singers and women singers, and the delights of the

1:4 Solomon declared that "the earth abideth for ever," indicating that by contrast, humanity's lifespan is fleeting.

1:6 When Solomon described these circular wind patterns he was accurately describing the major patterns of global weather that scientists have only recently been able to verify with satellite photos—another marvelous confirmation of the divine inspiration of Scripture.

1:7 This verse describes the hydrological cycle that governs evaporation, cloud formation and precipitation. Even Job was familiar with this water cycle (see Job 26:27–33).

sons of men, *as* ʹmusical instruments, and that of all sorts.

9 So I was great, and increased more than all that were before me in Jerusalem: also my wisdom remained with me.

10 And whatsoever mine eyes desired I kept not from them, I withheld not my heart from any joy; for my heart rejoiced in all my labour: and [a]this was my portion of all my labour.

11 Then I looked on all the works that my hands had wrought, and on the labour that I had laboured to do: and, behold, all *was* [a]vanity and vexation of spirit, and *there was* no profit under the sun.

The fool and the wise must die

12 ¶ And I turned myself to behold wisdom, [a]and madness, and folly: for what *can* the man *do* that cometh after the king? ʹ*even* that which hath been already done.

13 Then I saw ʹthat wisdom excelleth folly, as far as light excelleth darkness.

14 [a]The wise man's eyes *are* in his head; but the fool walketh in darkness: and I myself perceived also that [b]one event happeneth to them all.

15 Then said I in my heart, As it happeneth to the fool, so it ʹhappeneth even to me; and why was I then more wise? Then I said in my heart, that this also *is* vanity.

16 For *there is* no remembrance of the wise more than of the fool for ever; seeing that which now *is* in the days to come shall all be forgotten. And how dieth the wise *man?* as the fool.

17 Therefore I hated life; because the work that is wrought under the sun *is* grievous unto me: for all *is* vanity and vexation of spirit.

The futility of labour

18 ¶ Yea, I hated all my labour which I had ʹtaken under the sun: because [a]I should leave it unto the man that shall be after me.

19 And who knoweth whether he shall be a wise *man* or a fool? yet shall he have rule over all my labour wherein I have laboured, and wherein I have shown myself wise under the sun. This *is* also vanity.

20 Therefore I went about to cause my heart to despair of all the labour which I took under the sun.

21 For there is a man whose labour *is* in wisdom, and in knowledge, and in equity; yet to a man that hath not laboured therein shall he ʹleave it *for* his portion. This also *is* vanity and a great evil.

22 [a]For what hath man of all his labour, and of the vexation of his heart, wherein he hath laboured under the sun?

23 For all his days *are* [a]sorrows, and his travail grief; yea, his heart taketh not rest in the night. This is also vanity.

24 ¶ [a]*There is* nothing better for a man, *than* that he should eat and drink, and *that* he ʹshould make his soul enjoy good in his labour. This also I saw, that it *was* from the hand of God.

25 For who can eat, or who else can hasten *hereunto,* more than I?

26 For *God* giveth to a man that *is* good ʹin his sight wisdom, and knowledge, and joy: but to the sinner he giveth travail, to gather and to heap up, that [a]he may give to *him that is* good before God. This also *is* vanity and vexation of spirit. P U

A time for everything

3 TO EVERY *thing there is* a season, and a [a]time to every purpose under the heaven:

2 A time ʹto be born, and [a]a time to die; a time to plant, and a time to pluck up *that which is* planted;

3 A time to kill, and a time to heal; a time to break down, and a time to build up;

4 A time to weep, and a time to laugh; a time to mourn, and a time to dance;

5 A time to cast away stones, and a time to gather stones together; a time to embrace, and [a]a time ʹto refrain from embracing;

6 A time to ʹget, and a time to lose; a time to keep, and a time to cast away;

7 A time to rend, and a time to sew; [a]a time to keep silence, and a time to speak;

8 A time to love, and a time to [a]hate; a time of war, and a time of peace.

9 [a]What profit hath he that worketh in that wherein he laboureth?

10 [a]I have seen the travail, which God hath given to the sons of men to be exercised in it.

11 He hath made every *thing* beautiful in his time: also he hath set the world in

8 ʹHeb. *musical instrument and instruments*
10 [a]ch. 3:22 & 5:18 & 9:9
11 [a]ch. 1:3,14
12 [a]ch. 1:17 & 7:25 ʹOr, *in those things which have been already done*
13 ʹHeb. *that there is an excellency in wisdom more than in folly*
14 [a]Prov. 17:24; ch. 8:1 [b]Ps. 49:10; ch. 9:2,3,11
15 ʹHeb. *happeneth to me, even to me*
18 [a]Ps. 49:10 ʹHeb. *laboured*
21 ʹHeb. *give*
22 [a]ch. 1:3 & 3:9
23 [a]Job 5:7 & 14:1
24 [a]ch. 3:12,13, 22 & 5:18 & 8:15 ʹOr, *delight his senses*
26 [a]Job 27:16,17; Prov. 28:8 ʹHeb. *before him*
3:1 [a]ver. 17; ch. 8:6
2 [a]Heb. 9:27 ʹHeb. *to bear*
5 [a]Joel 2:16; 1 Cor. 7:5 ʹHeb. *to be far from*
6 ʹOr, *seek*
7 [a]Amos 5:13
8 [a]Luke 14:26
9 [a]ch. 1:3
10 [a]ch. 1:13

P Pr 28:27 ◄► Ecc 5:19
U Pr 28:25 ◄► Ecc 7:18

their heart, so that [a]no man can find out
the work that God maketh from the beginning to the end.
12 I know that *there is* no good in
them, but for *a man* to rejoice, and to do
good in his life.
13 And also [a]that every man should
eat and drink, and enjoy the good of all
his labour, it *is* the gift of God.
14 I know that, whatsoever God doeth, it shall be for ever: [a]nothing can be
put to it, nor anything taken from it: and
God doeth *it*, that *men* should fear before
him.
15 [a]That which hath been is now; and
that which is to be hath already been;
and God requireth [1]that which is past.

The vanity of all life

16 ¶ And moreover [a]I saw under the
sun the place of judgment, *that* wickedness *was* there; and the place of righteousness, *that* iniquity *was* there.
J 17 I said in mine heart, [a]God shall
J judge the righteous and the wicked: for
there is [b]a time there for every purpose
and for every work.
18 I said in mine heart concerning the
estate of the sons of men, [1]that God
might manifest them, and that they might
see that they themselves are beasts.
19 [a]For that which befalleth the sons
of men befalleth beasts; even one thing
befalleth them: as the one dieth, so dieth
the other; yea, they have all one breath;
so that a man hath no preeminence above
a beast: for all *is* vanity.
20 All go unto one place; [a]all are of the
dust, and all turn to dust again.
21 [a]Who knoweth the spirit [1]of man
that [2]goeth upward, and the spirit of the
beast that goeth downward to the earth?
22 [a]Wherefore I perceive that *there is*
nothing better, than that a man should
rejoice in his own works; for [b]that *is* his
portion: [c]for who shall bring him to see
what shall be after him?
4 SO I returned, and considered all the
[a]oppressions that are done under the
sun: and behold the tears of *such as were*
oppressed, and they had no comforter;
and on the [1]side of their oppressors *there*
was power; but they had no comforter.
2 [a]Wherefore I praised the dead which
are already dead more than the living
which are yet alive.
3 [a]Yea, better *is he* than both they,
which hath not yet been, who hath not
seen the evil work that is done under the
sun.

Travail of the wise and foolish

4 ¶ Again, I considered all travail, and
[1]every right work, that [2]for this a man is
envied of his neighbour. This *is* also
vanity and vexation of spirit.
5 [a]The fool foldeth his hands together,
and eateth his own flesh.
6 [a]Better *is* an handful *with* quietness,
than both the hands full *with* travail and
vexation of spirit.
7 ¶ Then I returned, and I saw vanity
under the sun.
8 There is one *alone*, and *there is* not a
second; yea, he hath neither child nor
brother: yet *is there* no end of all his labour; neither is his [a]eye satisfied with
riches; [b]neither *saith he*, For whom do I
labour, and bereave my soul of good?
This *is* also vanity, yea, it *is* a sore travail.
9 ¶ Two *are* better than one; because
they have a good reward for their labour.
10 For if they fall, the one will lift up
his fellow: but woe to him *that is* alone
when he falleth; for *he hath* not another
to help him up.
11 Again, if two lie together, then they
have heat: but how can one be warm
alone?
12 And if one prevail against him, two
shall withstand him; and a threefold cord
is not quickly broken.
13 ¶ Better *is* a poor and a wise child
than an old and foolish king, [1]who will
no more be admonished.
14 For out of prison he cometh to
reign; whereas also *he that is* born in his
kingdom becometh poor.
15 I considered all the living which
walk under the sun, with the second
child that shall stand up in his stead.
16 *There is* no end of all the people,
even of all that have been before them:
they also that come after shall not rejoice
in him. Surely this also *is* vanity and vexation of spirit.

11 [a]ch. 8:17; Rom. 11:33
13 [a]ch. 2:24
14 [a]Jas. 1:17
15 [a]ch. 1:9 [1]Heb. *that which is driven away*
16 [a]ch. 5:8
17 [a]Rom. 2:6-8; 2 Cor. 5:10; 2 Thes. 1:6 [b]ver. 1
18 [1]Or, *that they might clear God, and see*
19 [a]Ps. 49:12,20 & 73:22; ch. 2:16
20 [a]Gen. 3:19
21 [a]ch. 12:7 [1]Heb. *of the sons of man* [2]Heb. *is ascending*
22 [a]ver. 12; ch. 2:24 & 5:18 & 11:9 [b]ch. 2:10 [c]ch. 6:12 & 8:7 & 10:14
4:1 [a]ch. 3:16 & 5:8 [1]Heb. *hand*
2 [a]Job 3:17
3 [a]Job 3:11,16,21; ch. 6:3
4 [1]Heb. *all the rightness of work* [2]Heb. *this is the envy of a man from his neighbour*
5 [a]Prov. 6:10 & 24:33
6 [a]Prov. 15:16,17 & 16:8
8 [a]Prov. 27:20; 1 John 2:16 [b]Ps. 39:6
13 [1]Heb. *who knoweth not to be admonished*

J *Ps 87:4–6* ◄► *Ecc 11:9*
J *Ps 98:9* ◄► *Ecc 11:9*

The vanity of vows

5 KEEP [a]THY foot when thou goest to the house of God, and be more ready to hear, [b]than to give the sacrifice of fools: for they consider not that they do evil.

2 Be not rash with thy mouth, and let not thine heart be hasty to utter *any* [1]thing before God: for God *is* in heaven, and thou upon earth: therefore let thy words [a]be few.

3 For a dream cometh through the multitude of business; and [a]a fool's voice *is known* by multitude of words.

4 [a]When thou vowest a vow unto God, defer not to pay it; for *he hath* no pleasure in fools: pay that which thou hast vowed.

5 [a]Better *is it* that thou shouldest not vow, than that thou shouldest vow and not pay.

6 Suffer not thy mouth to cause thy flesh to sin; [a]neither say thou before the angel, that it *was* an error: wherefore should God be angry at thy voice, and destroy the work of thine hands?

7 For in the multitude of dreams and many words *there are* also *divers* vanities: but [a]fear thou God.

The vanity of riches

8 ¶ If thou [a]seest the oppression of the poor, and violent perverting of judgment and justice in a province, marvel not [1]at the matter: for [b]*he that is* higher than the highest regardeth; and *there be* higher than they.

9 ¶ Moreover the profit of the earth is for all: the king *himself* is served by the field.

10 He that loveth silver shall not be satisfied with silver; nor he that loveth abundance with increase: this *is* also vanity.

11 When goods increase, they are increased that eat them: and what good *is there* to the owners thereof, saving the beholding *of them* with their eyes?

12 The sleep of a labouring man *is* sweet, whether he eat little or much: but the abundance of the rich will not suffer him to sleep.

13 [a]There is a sore evil *which* I have seen under the sun, *namely,* riches kept for the owners thereof to their hurt.

14 But those riches perish by evil travail: and he begetteth a son, and *there is* nothing in his hand.

15 [a]As he came forth of his mother's womb, naked shall he return to go as he came, and shall take nothing of his labour, which he may carry away in his hand.

16 And this also *is* a sore evil, *that* in all points as he came, so shall he go: and [a]what profit hath he [b]that hath laboured for the wind?

17 All his days also [a]he eateth in darkness, and *he hath* much sorrow and wrath with his sickness.

18 ¶ Behold *that* which I have seen: [a]*it*[1] *is* good and comely *for one* to eat and to drink, and to enjoy the good of all his labour that he taketh under the sun [2]all the days of his life, which God giveth him: [b]for it *is* his portion.

19 [a]Every man also to whom God hath given riches and wealth, and hath given him power to eat thereof, and to take his portion, and to rejoice in his labour; this *is* the gift of God. P

20 [1]For he shall not much remember the days of his life; because God answereth *him* in the joy of his heart.

6 THERE[a] IS an evil which I have seen under the sun, and it *is* common among men:

2 A man to whom God hath given riches, wealth, and honour, [a]so that he wanteth nothing for his soul of all that he desireth, [b]yet God giveth him not power to eat thereof, but a stranger eateth it: this *is* vanity, and it *is* an evil disease.

3 ¶ If a man beget an hundred *children,* and live many years, so that the days of his years be many, and his soul be not filled with good, and [a]also *that* he have no burial; I say, *that* [b]an untimely birth *is* better than he.

4 For he cometh in with vanity, and departeth in darkness, and his name shall be covered with darkness.

5 Moreover he hath not seen the sun, nor known *any thing:* this hath more rest than the other.

6 ¶ Yea, though he live a thousand years twice *told,* yet hath he seen no good: do not all go to one place?

7 [a]All the labour of man *is* for his mouth, and yet the [1]appetite is not filled.

8 For what hath the wise more than

5:1 [a]See Ex. 3:5; Is. 1:12 [b]1 Sam. 15:22; Ps. 50:8; Prov. 15:8 & 21:27; Hos. 6:6
2 [a]Prov. 10:19; Mat. 6:7 [1]Or, *word*
3 [a]Prov. 10:19
4 [a]Num. 30:2; Deut. 23:21
5 [a]Prov. 20:25; Acts 5:4
6 [a]1 Cor. 11:10
7 [a]ch. 12:13
8 [a]ch. 3:16 [b]Ps. 12:5 & 58:11 & 82:1 [1]Heb. *at the will,* or, *purpose*
13 [a]ch. 6:1
15 [a]Job 1:21; Ps. 49:17; 1 Tim. 6:7
16 [a]ch. 1:3 [b]Prov. 11:29
17 [a]Ps. 127:2
18 [a]ch. 2:24 & 3:12,13 & 9:7 & 11:9; 1 Tim. 6:17 [b]ch. 2:10 & 3:22 [1]Heb. there is a *good which is comely* [2]Heb. *the number of the days*
19 [a]ch. 2:24 & 3:13
20 [1]Or, *Though he give not much,* yet *he remembereth*
6:1 [a]ch. 5:13
2 [a]Job 21:10; Ps. 17:14 & 73:7 [b]Luke 12:20
3 [a]2 Ki. 9:35; Is. 14:19,20; Jer. 22:19 [b]Job 3:16; Ps. 58:8; ch. 4:3
7 [a]Prov. 16:26 [1]Heb. *soul*

the fool? what hath the poor, that knoweth to walk before the living?
9 ¶ Better *is* the sight of the eyes [l]than
the wandering of the desire: this *is* also
vanity and vexation of spirit.
10 That which hath been is named already, and it is known that it *is* man:
[a]neither may he contend with him that is
mightier than he.
11 ¶ Seeing there be many things that
increase vanity, what *is* man the better?
12 For who knoweth what *is* good for
man in *this* life, [l]all the days of his vain
life which he spendeth as [a]a shadow? for
[b]who can tell a man what shall be after
him under the sun?

Choosing wisdom

7 A [a]GOOD name *is* better than precious ointment; and the day of death
than the day of one's birth.
2 ¶ *It is* better to go to the house of
mourning, than to go to the house of
feasting: for that *is* the end of all men;
and the living will lay *it* to his heart.
3 [l]Sorrow *is* better than laughter: [a]for
by the sadness of the countenance the
heart is made better.
4 The heart of the wise *is* in the house
of mourning; but the heart of fools *is* in
the house of mirth.
5 [a]*It is* better to hear the rebuke of the
wise, than for a man to hear the song of
fools.
6 [a]For as the [l]crackling of thorns under a pot, so *is* the laughter of the fool:
this also *is* vanity.
7 ¶ Surely oppression maketh a wise
man mad; [a]and a gift destroyeth the
heart.
8 Better *is* the end of a thing than the
beginning thereof: *and* [a]the patient in
spirit *is* better than the proud in spirit.
9 [a]Be not hasty in thy spirit to be angry: for anger resteth in the bosom of
fools.
10 Say not thou, What is *the cause* that
the former days were better than these?
for thou dost not inquire [l]wisely concerning this.
11 ¶ Wisdom *is* [l]good with an inheritance: and *by it there is* profit [a]to them
that see the sun.
12 For wisdom *is* a [l]defence, *and*
money *is* a defence: but the excellency of
knowledge *is, that* wisdom giveth life to
them that have it.

9 [l]Heb. *than the walking of the soul*

10 [a]Job 9:32; Is. 45:9; Jer. 49:19

12 [a]Ps. 102:11 & 144:4; Jas. 4:14 [b]Ps. 39:6; ch. 8:7 [l]Heb. *the number of the days of the life of his vanity*

7:1 [a]Prov. 22:1

3 [a]2 Cor. 7:10 [l]Or, *Anger*

5 [a]Ps. 141:5; Prov. 15:31

6 [a]ch. 2:2 [l]Heb. *sound*

7 [a]Ex. 23:8; Deut. 16:19

8 [a]Prov. 14:29

9 [a]Prov. 14:17; Jas. 1:19

10 [l]Heb. *out of wisdom*

11 [a]ch. 11:7 [l]Or, *as good as an inheritance, yea, better too*

12 [l]Heb. *shadow*

13 [a]Job 12:14; ch. 1:15

14 [a]Deut. 28:47 [l]Heb. *made*

15 [a]ch. 8:14

16 [a]Prov. 25:16 [b]Rom. 12:3 [l]Heb. *be desolate?*

17 [a]Job 15:32; Ps. 55:23 [l]Heb. *not in thy time?*

19 [a]Prov. 21:22; ch. 9:16,18

20 [a]1 Ki. 8:46; 2 Chr. 6:36; Prov. 20:9; 1 John 1:8

21 [l]Heb. *give not thine heart*

23 [a]Rom. 1:22

24 [a]Job 28:12; 1 Tim. 6:16 [b]Rom. 11:33

25 [a]ch. 1:17 [l]Heb. *I and my heart compassed*

26 [a]Prov. 5:3,4 [l]Heb. he that is *good before God*

27 [a]ch. 1:1,2 [l]Or, *weighing one thing after another, to find out the reason*

13 Consider the work of God: for [a]who O
can make *that* straight, which he hath
made crooked?
14 [a]In the day of prosperity be joyful, T
but in the day of adversity consider: God
also hath [l]set the one over against the
other, to the end that man should find
nothing after him.
15 All *things* have I seen in the days of
my vanity: [a]there is a just *man* that perisheth in his righteousness, and there is a
wicked *man* that prolongeth *his life* in his
wickedness.
16 [a]Be not righteous over much; [b]nei-
ther make thyself over wise: why shouldest thou [l]destroy thyself?
17 Be not over much wicked, neither
be thou foolish: [a]why shouldest thou die
[l]before thy time?
18 *It is* good that thou shouldest take U
hold of this; yea, also from this withdraw
not thine hand: for he that feareth God
shall come forth of them all.
19 [a]Wisdom strengtheneth the wise
more than ten mighty *men* which are in
the city.
20 [a]For *there is* not a just man upon A
earth, that doeth good, and sinneth not.
21 Also [l]take no heed unto all words
that are spoken; lest thou hear thy servant curse thee:
22 For oftentimes also thine own heart
knoweth that thou thyself likewise hast
cursed others.
23 ¶ All this have I proved by wisdom:
[a]I said, I will be wise; but it *was* far
from me.
24 [a]That which is far off, and [b]exceed-
ing deep, who can find it out?
25 [a]I[l] applied mine heart to know,
and to search, and to seek out wisdom,
and the reason *of things,* and to know the
wickedness of folly, even of foolishness
and madness:
26 [a]And I find more bitter than death
the woman, whose heart *is* snares and
nets, *and* her hands *as* bands: [l]whoso
pleaseth God shall escape from her; but
the sinner shall be taken by her.
27 Behold, this have I found, saith [a]the
preacher, [l]counting one by one, to find
out the account:

O *Pr 19:21* ◀ ▶ *Isa 43:11*
T *Pr 25:4* ◀ ▶ *Isa 48:10*
U *Ecc 2:26* ◀ ▶ *Isa 1:19*
A *Pr 20:9* ◀ ▶ *Isa 53:6*

28 Which yet my soul seeketh, but I find not: [a]one man among a thousand have I found; but a woman among all those have I not found.

C 29 Lo, this only have I found, [a]that God hath made man upright; but [b]they have sought out many inventions.

Obedience to authority

8 WHO *IS* as the wise *man?* and who knoweth the interpretation of a thing? [a]a man's wisdom maketh his face to shine, and [b]the[/] boldness of his face shall be changed.

2 I *counsel thee* to keep the king's commandment, [a]and *that* in regard of the oath of God.

3 [a]Be not hasty to go out of his sight: stand not in an evil thing; for he doeth whatsoever pleaseth him.

4 Where the word of a king *is, there is* power: and [a]who may say unto him, What doest thou?

5 Whoso keepeth the commandment [/]shall feel no evil thing: and a wise man's heart discerneth both time and judgment.

6 ¶ Because [a]to every purpose there is time and judgment, therefore the misery of man *is* great upon him.

7 [a]For he knoweth not that which shall be: for who can tell him [/]when it shall be?

N 8 [a]*There is* no man that hath power over the spirit to retain the spirit; neither *hath he* power in the day of death: and *there is* no [/]discharge in *that* war; neither shall wickedness deliver those that are given to it.

9 All this have I seen, and applied my heart unto every work that is done under the sun: *there is* a time wherein one man ruleth over another to his own hurt.

10 And so I saw the wicked buried, who had come and gone from the place of the holy, and they were forgotten in the city where they had so done: this *is* also vanity.

C
H
N 11 [a]Because sentence against an evil work is not executed speedily, therefore the heart of the sons of men is fully set in them to do evil.

12 ¶ [a]Though a sinner do evil an hundred times, and his *days* be prolonged, yet surely I know that [b]it shall be well with them that fear God, which fear before him:

13 But it shall not be well with the wicked, neither shall he prolong *his* days, *which are* as a shadow; because he feareth not before God.

14 There is a vanity which is done upon the earth; that there be just *men,* unto whom it [a]happeneth according to the work of the wicked; again, there be wicked *men,* to whom it happeneth according to the work of the righteous: I said that this also *is* vanity.

15 [a]Then I commended mirth, because a man hath no better thing under the sun, than to eat, and to drink, and to be merry: for that shall abide with him of his labour the days of his life, which God giveth him under the sun.

16 ¶ When I applied mine heart to know wisdom, and to see the business that is done upon the earth: (for also *there is that* neither day nor night seeth sleep with his eyes:)

17 Then I beheld all the work of God, that [a]a man cannot find out the work that is done under the sun: because though a man labour to seek *it* out, yet he shall not find *it;* yea further; though a wise *man* think to know *it,* yet shall he not be able to find *it.*

Make the best of this life

9 FOR ALL this [/]I considered in my heart even to declare all this, [a]that the righteous, and the wise, and their works, *are* in the hand of God: no man knoweth either love or hatred *by* all *that is* before them.

2 [a]All *things come* alike to all: *there is* one event to the righteous, and to the wicked; to the good and to the clean, and to the unclean; to him that sacrificeth, and to him that sacrificeth not: as *is* the good, so *is* the sinner; *and* he that sweareth, as *he* that feareth an oath.

3 This *is* an evil among all *things* that are done under the sun, that *there is* one event unto all: yea, also the heart of the sons of men is full of evil, and madness *is* in their heart while they live, and after that *they go* to the dead. C

4 ¶ For to him that is joined to all the

C *Pr 30:12–13* ◀▶ *Ecc 8:11*
N *Pr 29:1* ◀▶ *Ecc 8:11–13*
C *Ecc 7:29* ◀▶ *Ecc 9:3*
H *Pr 29:1* ◀▶ *Ecc 9:12*
N *Ecc 8:8* ◀▶ *Ecc 9:10–12*

C *Ecc 8:11* ◀▶ *Ecc 9:18*

28 [a]Job 33:23; Ps. 12:1
29 [a]Gen. 1:27 [b]Gen. 3:6,7
8:1 [a]Prov. 4:8,9; Acts 6:15 [b]Deut. 28:50 [/]Heb. *the strength*
2 [a]1 Chr. 29:24; Ezek. 17:18
3 [a]ch. 10:4
4 [a]Job 34:18
5 [/]Heb. *shall know*
6 [a]ch. 3:1
7 [a]Prov. 24:22; ch. 6:12 & 9:12 & 10:14 [/]Or, *how it shall be?*
8 [a]Ps. 49:6,7 [/]Or, *casting off* weapons
11 [a]Ps. 10:6 & 50:21; Is. 26:10
12 [a]Is. 65:20; Rom. 2:5 [b]Ps. 37:11,18,19; Prov. 1:32,33; Is. 3:10, 11; Mat. 25:34,41
14 [a]Ps. 73:14; ch. 2:14 & 7:15 & 9:1-3
15 [a]ch. 2:24 & 3:12,22 & 5:18 & 9:7
17 [a]Job 5:9; ch. 3:11; Rom. 11:33
9:1 [a]ch. 8:14 [/]Heb. *I gave,* or, *set to my heart*
2 [a]Job 21:7; Ps. 73:3,12,13; Mal. 3:15

living there is hope: for a living dog is better than a dead lion.

5 For the living know that they shall die: but [a]the dead know not any thing, neither have they any more a reward; for [b]the memory of them is forgotten.

6 Also their love, and their hatred, and their envy, is now perished; neither have they any more a portion for ever in any *thing* that is done under the sun.

7 ¶ Go thy way, [a]eat thy bread with joy, and drink thy wine with a merry heart; for God now accepteth thy works.

8 Let thy garments be always white; and let thy head lack no ointment.

9 ʹLive joyfully with the wife whom thou lovest all the days of the life of thy vanity, which he hath given thee under the sun, all the days of thy vanity: [a]for that *is* thy portion in *this* life, and in thy labour which thou takest under the sun.

N 10 Whatsoever thy hand findeth to do, do *it* with thy might; for *there is* no work, nor device, nor knowledge, nor wisdom, in the grave, whither thou goest.

11 ¶ I returned, [a]and saw under the sun, that the race *is* not to the swift, nor the battle to the strong, neither yet bread to the wise, nor yet riches to men of understanding, nor yet favour to men of skill; but time and chance happeneth to them all.

H 12 For [a]man also knoweth not his time: as the fishes that are taken in an evil net, and as the birds that are caught in the snare; so *are* the sons of men [b]snared in an evil time, when it falleth suddenly upon them.

The wise man and the fool

13 ¶ This wisdom have I seen also under the sun, and it *seemed* great unto me:

14 [a]*There was* a little city, and few men within it; and there came a great king against it, and besieged it, and built great bulwarks against it:

15 Now there was found in it a poor wise man, and he by his wisdom delivered the city; yet no man remembered that same poor man.

16 [a]Then said I, Wisdom *is* better than strength: nevertheless [b]the poor man's wisdom *is* despised, and his words are not heard.

17 The words of wise *men are* heard in quiet more than the cry of him that ruleth among fools.

18 [a]Wisdom *is* better than weapons of war: but [b]one sinner destroyeth much good. C

10 DEAD ʹFLIES cause the ointment of the apothecary to send forth a stinking savour: *so doth* a little folly him that is in reputation for wisdom *and* honour.

2 A wise man's heart *is* at his right hand; but a fool's heart at his left.

3 Yea also, when he that is a fool walketh by the way, ʹhis wisdom faileth *him*, [a]and he saith to every one *that* he *is* a fool.

4 If the spirit of the ruler rise up against thee, [a]leave not thy place; for [b]yielding pacifieth great offences.

5 There is an evil *which* I have seen under the sun, as an error *which* proceedeth ʹfrom the ruler:

6 [a]Folly is set ʹin great dignity, and the rich sit in low place.

7 I have seen servants [a]upon horses, and princes walking as servants upon the earth.

8 [a]He that diggeth a pit shall fall into it; and whoso breaketh an hedge, a serpent shall bite him.

9 Whoso removeth stones shall be hurt therewith; *and* he that cleaveth wood shall be endangered thereby.

10 If the iron be blunt, and he do not whet the edge, then must he put to more strength: but wisdom *is* profitable to direct.

11 Surely the serpent will bite [a]without enchantment; and ʹa babbler is no better.

12 [a]The words of a wise man's mouth *are* ʹgracious; but [b]the lips of a fool will swallow up himself.

13 The beginning of the words of his mouth *is* foolishness: and the end of ʹhis talk *is* mischievous madness.

14 [a]A fool also ʹis full of words: a man cannot tell what shall be; and [b]what shall be after him, who can tell him?

15 The labour of the foolish wearieth every one of them, because he knoweth not how to go to the city.

5 [a]Job 14:21; Is. 63:16 [b]Job 7:8-10; Is. 26:14
7 [a]ch. 8:15
9 [a]ch. 2:10,24 & 3:13,22 & 5:18 ʹHeb. *See, or, Enjoy life*
11 [a]Amos 2:14,15; Jer. 9:23
12 [a]ch. 8:7 [b]Prov. 29:6; Luke 12:20, 39 & 17:26; 1 Thes. 5:3
14 [a]See 2 Sam. 20:16-22
16 [a]ver. 18; Prov. 21:22 & 24:5; ch. 7:19 [b]Mark 6:2
18 [a]ver. 16 [b]Josh. 7:1
10:1 ʹHeb. *Flies of death*
3 [a]Prov. 13:16 & 18:2 ʹHeb. *his heart*
4 [a]ch. 8:3 [b]1 Sam. 25:24; Prov. 25:15
5 ʹHeb. *from before*
6 [a]Esth. 3:1 ʹHeb. *in great heights*
7 [a]Prov. 19:10 & 30:22
8 [a]Ps. 7:15; Prov. 26:27
11 [a]Ps. 58:4,5; Jer. 8:17 ʹHeb. *the master of the tongue*
12 [a]Prov. 10:32 [b]Prov. 10:14 ʹHeb. *grace*
13 ʹHeb. *his mouth*
14 [a]Prov. 15:2 [b]ch. 3:22 & 8:7 ʹHeb. *multiplieth words*

N *Ecc 8:11–13* ◀▶ *Ecc 12:1*
H *Ecc 8:11–13* ◀▶ *Isa 1:24*
C *Ecc 9:3* ◀▶ *Isa 1:4–6*

16 ¶ [a]Woe to thee, O land, when thy king *is* a child, and thy princes eat in the morning!

17 Blessed *art* thou, O land, when thy king *is* the son of nobles, and [a]thy princes eat in due season, for strength, and not for drunkenness!

18 ¶ By much slothfulness the building decayeth; and through idleness of the hands the house droppeth through.

19 ¶ A feast is made for laughter, and [a]wine [1]maketh merry: but money answereth all *things*.

20 ¶ [a]Curse not the king, no not in thy [1]thought; and curse not the rich in thy bedchamber: for a bird of the air shall carry the voice, and that which hath wings shall tell the matter.

The investment of a life

P 11 CAST THY bread [a]upon [1] the waters: [b]for thou shalt find it after many days.

2 [a]Give a portion [b]to seven, and also to eight; [c]for thou knowest not what evil shall be upon the earth.

3 If the clouds be full of rain, they empty *themselves* upon the earth: and if the tree fall toward the south, or toward the north, in the place where the tree falleth, there it shall be.

4 He that observeth the wind shall not sow; and he that regardeth the clouds shall not reap.

5 As [a]thou knowest not what *is* the way of the spirit, [b]*nor* how the bones *do grow* in the womb of her that is with child: even so thou knowest not the works of God who maketh all.

6 In the morning sow thy seed, and in the evening withhold not thine hand: for thou knowest not whether [1]shall prosper, either this or that, or whether they both *shall be* alike good.

7 ¶ Truly the light *is* sweet, and a pleasant *thing it is* for the eyes [a]to behold the sun:

8 But if a man live many years, *and* rejoice in them all; yet let him remember the days of darkness; for they shall be many. All that cometh *is* vanity.

J 9 ¶ Rejoice, O young man, in thy
J youth; and let thy heart cheer thee in the days of thy youth, [a]and walk in the ways of thine heart, and in the sight of thine eyes: but know thou, that for all these *things* [b]God will bring thee into judgment.

10 Therefore remove [1]sorrow from thy heart, and [a]put away evil from thy flesh: [b]for childhood and youth *are* vanity.

The span of a life

12 REMEMBER [a]NOW thy Creator N
in the days of thy youth, while the evil days come not, nor the years draw nigh, [b]when thou shalt say, I have no pleasure in them;

2 While the sun, or the light, or the moon, or the stars, be not darkened, nor the clouds return after the rain:

3 In the day when the keepers of the house shall tremble, and the strong men shall bow themselves, and [1]the grinders cease because they are few, and those that look out of the windows be darkened,

4 And the doors shall be shut in the streets, when the sound of the grinding is low, and he shall rise up at the voice of the bird, and all [a]the daughters of music shall be brought low;

5 Also *when* they shall be afraid of *that which is* high, and fears *shall be* in the way, and the almond tree shall flourish, and the grasshopper shall be a burden, and desire shall fail: because man goeth to [a]his long home, and [b]the mourners go about the streets:

6 Or ever the silver cord be loosed, or the golden bowl be broken, or the pitcher be broken at the fountain, or the wheel broken at the cistern.

7 [a]Then shall the dust return to the earth as it was: [b]and the spirit shall return unto God [c]who gave it.

8 ¶ [a]Vanity of vanities, saith the preacher; all *is* vanity.

The whole duty of man

9 And [1]moreover, because the preacher was wise, he still taught the people knowledge; yea, he gave good heed, and sought out, *and* [a]set in order many proverbs.

10 The preacher sought to find out [1]acceptable words: and *that which was* written *was* upright, *even* words of truth.

16 [a]Is. 3:4,5 & 5:11
17 [a]Prov. 31:4
19 [a]Ps. 104:15 [1]Heb. *maketh glad the life*
20 [a]Ex. 22:28; Acts 23:5 [1]Or, *conscience*
11:1 [a]See Is. 32:20 [b]Deut. 15:10; Prov. 19:17; Mat. 10:42 [1]Heb. *upon the face of the waters*
2 [a]Ps. 112:9; 1 Tim. 6:18 [b]Mic. 5:5 [c]Eph. 5:16
5 [a]John 3:8 [b]Ps. 139:14
6 [1]Heb. *shall be right*
7 [a]ch. 7:11
9 [a]Num. 15:39 [b]ch. 12:14
10 [a]2 Cor. 7:1 [b]Ps. 39:5 [1]Or, *anger*
12:1 [a]Lam. 3:27 [b]2 Sam. 19:35
3 [1]Or, *the grinders fail, because they grind little*
4 [a]2 Sam. 19:35
5 [a]Job 17:13 [b]Jer. 9:17
7 [a]Gen. 3:19 [b]ch. 3:21 [c]Num. 16:22; Job 34:14; Zech. 12:1
8 [a]Ps. 62:9
9 [a]1 Ki. 4:32 [1]Or, *the more wise the preacher was*
10 [1]Heb. *words of delight*

P *Ecc 5:19* ◀▶ *Hos 2:8*
J *Ecc 3:17–18* ◀▶ *Ecc 12:14*
J *Ecc 3:17* ◀▶ *Ecc 12:14*
N *Ecc 9:10–12* ◀▶ *Isa 26:10–11*

11 The words of the wise *are* as goads,
and as nails fastened *by* the masters of
assemblies, *which* are given from one
shepherd.
12 And further, by these, my son, be
admonished: of making many books *there*
is no end; and [a]much [/]study *is* a weariness of the flesh.
S 13 ¶ [/]Let us hear the conclusion of the
whole matter: [a]Fear God, and keep his
commandments: for this *is* the whole
duty of man.
14 For [a]God shall bring every work J
into judgment, with every secret thing, J
whether *it be* good, or whether *it be*
evil.

12 [a]ch. 1:18 [/]Or, *reading*

13 [a]Deut. 10:12 [/]Or, *The end of the matter, even all that hath been heard,* is

14 [a]Mat. 12:36

S *Pr 24:24* ◀ ▶ *Isa 1:13–17*

J *Ecc 11:9* ◀ ▶ *Isa 10:33–34*
J *Ecc 11:9* ◀ ▶ *Da 7:9–10*

12:14 God will ultimately judge every act according to his righteousness.

Song of Solomon

Author: Uncertain; possibly Solomon

Theme: Marital love mirrors God's love for his people

Date of Writing: c. 965 B.C.

Outline of Song of Solomon

I. Courtship (1:1—3:5)
II. The Wedding Procession (3:6–11)
III. Declarations of Love (4:1—5:1)
IV. Conflict and Resolution (5:2—6:13)
V. More Loving Words (7:1—8:4)
VI. Conclusion (8:5–14)

THE TITLE IN Hebrew for this delightful love song is "Solomon's Song of Songs," meaning a great song by, for or about Solomon. After the opening verse, Solomon is mentioned five more times in the text (see 1:5; 3:9, 11; 8:11–12), adding credence to the early church recognition of Solomon's authorship of this short book. In addition, the numerous references to customs, local geography and nature fit the context of Solomon's day.

While there are no specific prophecies in the Song of Solomon, the book is nonetheless difficult to interpret. Some people view it literally, as a secular love song between Solomon and his bride, reflecting Solomon's actual experiences and expressing warm emotions of human love. This interpretation attaches little spiritual significance to the words or situations. Others understand the book to be a collection of love songs without a specific story to tell.

A third way to approach this love song is to view it allegorically, applying OT and NT types to each of the participants. In this way Solomon, the one who loves his chosen bride, is an OT type of God and a NT type of Christ, while the Shulamite bride, the one who resists her lover's advances, is an OT type of Israel and a NT type of the church. The whole love story becomes an allegory that depicts both God's love for Israel and Christ's love for the church. Scripture does treat Solomon as a type of Christ (see Ps 72; Mt 12:42) lending credence to this last interpretation. Yet whether interpreted by any of these means, the intent of the Song of Solomon is clear: Love is a precious gift that cannot be bought. "If a man would give all the substance of his house for love, it would utterly be contemned" (8:7).

1

THE [a]SONG of songs, which *is* Solomon's.

In the chambers of the king

2 Let him kiss me with the kisses of his mouth: [a]for [1]thy love *is* better than wine.

3 Because of the savour of thy good ointments thy name *is as* ointment poured forth, therefore do the virgins love thee.

H 4 [a]Draw me, [b]we will run after thee:
T the king [c]hath brought me into his chambers: we will be glad and rejoice in thee, we will remember thy love more than wine: [1]the upright love thee.

5 I *am* black, but comely, O ye daughters of Jerusalem, as the tents of Kedar, as the curtains of Solomon.

6 Look not upon me, because I *am* black, because the sun hath looked upon me: my mother's children were angry with me; they made me the keeper of the vineyards; *but* mine own vineyard have I not kept.

7 Tell me, O thou whom my soul loveth, where thou feedest, where thou makest *thy flock* to rest at noon: for why should I be [1]as one that turneth aside by the flocks of thy companions?

8 ¶ If thou know not, [a]O thou fairest among women, go thy way forth by the footsteps of the flock, and feed thy kids beside the shepherds' tents.

9 I have compared thee, [a]O my love, [b]to a company of horses in Pharaoh's chariots.

10 [a]Thy cheeks are comely with rows *of jewels,* thy neck with chains *of gold.*

11 We will make thee borders of gold with studs of silver.

12 ¶ While the king *sitteth* at his table, my spikenard sendeth forth the smell thereof.

13 A bundle of myrrh *is* my wellbeloved unto me; he shall lie all night betwixt my breasts.

14 My beloved *is* unto me *as* a cluster of [a]camphire[1] in the vineyards of Engedi.

15 [a]Behold, thou *art* fair, [1]my love; behold, thou *art* fair; thou *hast* doves' eyes.

16 Behold, thou *art* fair, my beloved, yea, pleasant: also our bed *is* green.

17 The beams of our house *are* cedar, *and* our [1]rafters of fir.

The rose of Sharon

2

I AM the rose of Sharon, *and* the lily of the valleys.

2 As the lily among thorns, so *is* my love among the daughters.

3 As the apple tree among the trees of M
the wood, so *is* my beloved among the L
sons. [1]I sat down under his shadow with great delight, [a]and his fruit *was* sweet to my [2]taste.

4 He brought me to the [1]banqueting H
house, and his banner over me *was* love.

5 Stay me with flagons, [1]comfort me with apples: for I *am* sick of love.

6 [a]His left hand *is* under my head, and L
his right hand doth embrace me.

7 [a]I[1] charge you, O ye daughters of Je- C
rusalem, by the roes, and by the hinds of the field, that ye stir not up, nor awake *my* love, till he please.

8 ¶ The voice of my beloved! behold, he cometh leaping upon the mountains, skipping upon the hills.

9 [a]My beloved is like a roe or a young hart: behold, he standeth behind our wall, he looketh forth at the windows, [1]showing himself through the lattice.

10 My beloved spake, and said unto T
me, [a]Rise up, my love, my fair one, and come away.

11 For, lo, the winter is past, the rain M
is over *and* gone;

12 The flowers appear on the earth; the time of the singing *of birds* is come, and the voice of the turtle is heard in our land;

13 The fig tree putteth forth her green figs, and the vines *with* the tender grape give a *good* smell. [a]Arise, my love, my fair one, and come away.

14 ¶ O my dove, *that art* in the clefts of the rock, in the secret *places* of the stairs, let me see thy countenance, [a]let me hear thy voice; for sweet *is* thy voice, and thy countenance *is* comely.

15 Take us [a]the foxes, the little foxes,

1:1 [a]1 Ki. 4:32
2 [a]ch. 4:10 [1]Heb. *thy loves*
4 [a]Hos. 11:4; John 6:44 & 12:32 [b]Phil. 3:12-14 [c]Ps. 45:14,15; John 14:2; Eph. 2:6 [1]Or, *they love thee uprightly*
7 [1]Or, *as one that is veiled*
8 [a]ch. 5:9
9 [a]ch. 2:2,10,13 & 4:1,7; John 15:14 [b]2 Chr. 1:16
10 [a]Ezek. 16:11
14 [a]ch. 4:13 [1]Or, *cypress*
15 [a]ch. 4:1 & 5:12 [1]Or, *my companion*
17 [1]Or, *galleries*
2:3 [a]Rev. 22:1,2 [1]Heb. *I delighted and sat down* [2]Heb. *palate*
4 [1]Heb. *house of wine*
5 [1]Heb. *straw me with apples*
6 [a]ch. 8:3
7 [a]ch. 3:5 & 8:4 [1]Heb. *I adjure you*
9 [a]ver. 17 [1]Heb. *flourishing*
10 [a]ver. 13
13 [a]ver. 10
14 [a]ch. 8:13
15 [a]Ps. 80:13; Ezek. 13:4; Luke 13:32

H *Ps 45:14–15* ◀▶ *SS 2:4*
T *Ps 45:14–15* ◀▶ *SS 2:10*

M *Ps 132:11–18* ◀▶ *SS 2:11–13*
L *Pr 18:24* ◀▶ *SS 2:6*
H *SS 1:4* ◀▶ *Isa 26:20–21*
L *SS 2:3–4* ◀▶ *SS 4:9–10*
C *Ps 109:8* ◀▶ *SS 2:17*
T *SS 1:4* ◀▶ *SS 6:10*
M *SS 2:3–6* ◀▶ *SS 4:16*

that spoil the vines: for our vines *have*
tender grapes.
16 ¶ [a]My beloved *is* mine, and I *am*
his: he feedeth among the lilies.
C 17 [a]Until the day break, and the shadows flee away, turn, my beloved, and be
thou [b]like a roe or a young hart upon the
mountains ʹof Bether.

The maiden's search

3 BY [a]NIGHT on my bed I sought him
whom my soul loveth: I sought him,
but I found him not.
2 I will rise now, and go about the city
in the streets, and in the broad ways I
will seek him whom my soul loveth: I
sought him, but I found him not.
3 [a]The watchmen that go about the
city found me: *to whom I said,* Saw ye
him whom my soul loveth?
4 *It was* but a little that I passed from
them, but I found him whom my soul loveth: I held him, and would not let him go,
until I had brought him into my mother's
house, and into the chamber of her that
conceived me.
5 [a]I charge you, O ye daughters of Jerusalem, by the roes, and by the hinds of
the field, that ye stir not up, nor awake
my love, till he please.
6 ¶ [a]Who *is* this that cometh out of
the wilderness like pillars of smoke, perfumed with myrrh and frankincense,
with all powders of the merchant?
7 Behold his bed, which *is* Solomon's;
threescore valiant men *are* about it, of
the valiant of Israel.
8 They all hold swords, *being* expert in
war: every man *hath* his sword upon his
thigh because of fear in the night.
9 King Solomon made himself ʹa chariot of the wood of Lebanon.
10 He made the pillars thereof *of* silver, the bottom thereof *of* gold, the covering of it *of* purple, the midst thereof
being paved *with* love, for the daughters
of Jerusalem.
11 Go forth, O ye daughters of Zion,
and behold king Solomon with the crown
wherewith his mother crowned him in
the day of his espousals, and in the day of
the gladness of his heart.

16 [a]ch. 6:3
17 [a]ch. 4:6 [b]ver. 9; ch. 8:14 ʹOr, *of division*
3:1 [a]Is. 26:9
3 [a]ch. 5:7
5 [a]ch. 2:7 & 8:4
6 [a]ch. 8:5
9 ʹOr, *a bed*
4:1 [a]ch. 1:15 & 5:12 [b]ch. 6:5 ʹOr, *that eat of*
2 [a]ch. 6:6
3 [a]ch. 6:7
4 [a]ch. 7:4 [b]Neh. 3:19
5 [a]See Prov. 5:19; ch. 7:3
6 [a]ch. 2:17 ʹHeb. *breathe*
7 [a]Eph. 5:27
8 [a]Deut. 3:9
9 ʹOr, *taken away my heart*
10 [a]ch. 1:2
11 [a]Prov. 24:13, 14; ch. 5:1 [b]Gen. 27:27; Hos. 14:6,7
12 ʹHeb. *barred*
13 ʹOr, *cypress*
15 [a]John 4:10 & 7:38

The king offers his love

4 BEHOLD, [a]THOU *art* fair, my love;
behold, thou *art* fair; thou *hast*
doves' eyes within thy locks: thy hair *is*
as a [b]flock of goats, ʹthat appear from
mount Gilead.
2 [a]Thy teeth *are* like a flock *of sheep*
that are even shorn, which came up from
the washing; whereof every one bear
twins, and none *is* barren among them.
3 Thy lips *are* like a thread of scarlet,
and thy speech *is* comely: [a]thy temples
are like a piece of a pomegranate within
thy locks.
4 [a]Thy neck *is* like the tower of David
builded [b]for an armoury, whereon there
hang a thousand bucklers, all shields of
mighty men.
5 [a]Thy two breasts *are* like two young
roes that are twins, which feed among
the lilies.
6 [a]Until the day ʹbreak, and the shad- C
ows flee away, I will get me to the mountain of myrrh, and to the hill of frankincense.
7 [a]Thou *art* all fair, my love; *there is*
no spot in thee.
8 ¶ Come with me from Lebanon, *my*
spouse, with me from Lebanon: look from
the top of Amana, from the top of Shenir
[a]and Hermon, from the lions' dens, from
the mountains of the leopards.
9 Thou hast ʹravished my heart, my L
sister, *my* spouse; thou hast ravished my
heart with one of thine eyes, with one
chain of thy neck.
10 How fair is thy love, my sister, *my*
spouse! [a]how much better is thy love
than wine! and the smell of thine ointments than all spices!
11 Thy lips, O *my* spouse, drop *as* the
honeycomb: [a]honey and milk *are* under
thy tongue; and the smell of thy garments
is [b]like the smell of Lebanon.
12 A garden ʹinclosed *is* my sister, *my*
spouse; a spring shut up, a fountain
sealed.
13 Thy plants *are* an orchard of pomegranates, with pleasant fruits; ʹcamphire,
with spikenard,
14 Spikenard and saffron; calamus and
cinnamon, with all trees of frankincense;
myrrh and aloes, with all the chief spices:
15 A fountain of gardens, a well of [a]liv-
ing waters, and streams from Lebanon.

C SS 2:7–8 ◀▶ SS 4:6

C SS 2:17 ◀▶ SS 5:8 L SS 2:6 ◀▶ Isa 32:2

M 16 ¶ Awake, O north wind; and come, thou south; blow upon my garden, *that* the spices thereof may flow out. [a]Let my beloved come into his garden, and eat his pleasant fruits.

5 I [a]AM come into my garden, my sister, *my* spouse: I have gathered my myrrh with my spice; [b]I have eaten my honeycomb with my honey; I have drunk my wine with my milk: eat, O [c]friends; drink, [l]yea, drink abundantly, O beloved.

The torment of separation

2 ¶ I sleep, but my heart waketh: *it is* the voice of my beloved [a]that knocketh, *saying,* Open to me, my sister, my love, my dove, my undefiled: for my head is filled with dew, *and* my locks with the drops of the night.

3 I have put off my coat; how shall I put it on? I have washed my feet; how shall I defile them?

4 My beloved put in his hand by the hole *of the door,* and my bowels were moved [l]for him.

5 I rose up to open to my beloved; and my hands dropped *with* myrrh, and my fingers *with* [l]sweetsmelling myrrh, upon the handles of the lock.

6 I opened to my beloved; but my beloved had withdrawn himself, *and* was gone: my soul failed when he spake: [a]I sought him, but I could not find him; I called him, but he gave me no answer.

7 [a]The watchmen that went about the city found me, they smote me, they wounded me; the keepers of the walls took away my veil from me.

C 8 I charge you, O daughters of Jerusalem, if ye find my beloved, [l]that ye tell him, that I *am* sick of love.

9 ¶ What *is* thy beloved more than *another* beloved, [a]O thou fairest among women? what *is* thy beloved more than *another* beloved, that thou dost so charge us?

10 My beloved *is* white and ruddy, [l]the chiefest among ten thousand.

11 His head *is as* the most fine gold, his locks *are* [l]bushy, *and* black as a raven.

12 [a]His eyes *are* as *the eyes* of doves by the rivers of waters, washed with milk, *and* [l]fitly set.

16 [a]ch. 5:1
5:1 [a]ch. 4:16 [b]ch. 4:11 [c]Luke 15:7,10 [l]Or, *and be drunken with loves*
2 [a]Rev. 3:20
4 [l]Or, (as some read) *in me*
5 [l]Heb. *passing,* or, *running about*
6 [a]ch. 3:1
7 [a]ch. 3:3
8 [l]Heb. *what*
9 [a]ch. 1:8
10 [l]Heb. *a standard bearer*
11 [l]Or, *curled*
12 [a]ch. 1:15 & 4:1 [l]Heb. *sitting in fulness,* i.e. *fitly placed, and set as a precious stone in the foil of a ring*
13 [l]Or, *towers of perfumes*
16 [l]Heb. *His palate*
6:1 [a]ch. 1:8
3 [a]ch. 2:16 & 7:10
4 [a]ver. 10
5 [a]ch. 4:1 [l]Or, *they have puffed me up*
6 [a]ch. 4:2
7 [a]ch. 4:3
10 [a]ver. 4
11 [a]ch. 7:12

13 His cheeks *are* as a bed of spices, *as* [l]sweet flowers: his lips *like* lilies, dropping sweetsmelling myrrh.

14 His hands *are as* gold rings set with the beryl: his belly *is as* bright ivory overlaid *with* sapphires.

15 His legs *are as* pillars of marble, set upon sockets of fine gold: his countenance *is* as Lebanon, excellent as the cedars.

16 [l]His mouth *is* most sweet: yea, he *is* altogether lovely. This *is* my beloved, and this *is* my friend, O daughters of Jerusalem.

6 WHITHER IS thy beloved gone, [a]O thou fairest among women? whither is thy beloved turned aside? that we may seek him with thee.

2 My beloved is gone down into his garden, to the beds of spices, to feed in the gardens, and to gather lilies.

3 [a]I *am* my beloved's, and my beloved *is* mine: he feedeth among the lilies.

The maiden's beauty

4 ¶ Thou *art* beautiful, O my love, as Tirzah, comely as Jerusalem, [a]terrible as *an army* with banners.

5 Turn away thine eyes from me, for [l]they have overcome me: thy hair is [a]as a flock of goats that appear from Gilead.

6 [a]Thy teeth *are* as a flock of sheep which go up from the washing, whereof every one beareth twins, and *there is* not one barren among them.

7 [a]As a piece of a pomegranate *are* thy temples within thy locks.

8 There are threescore queens, and fourscore concubines, and virgins without number.

9 My dove, my undefiled is *but* one; she *is* the *only* one of her mother, she *is* the choice *one* of her that bare her. The daughters saw her, and blessed her; *yea,* the queens and the concubines, and they praised her.

10 ¶ Who *is* she *that* looketh forth as the morning, fair as the moon, clear as the sun, [a]*and* terrible as *an army* with banners? T

11 I went down into the garden of nuts to see the fruits of the valley, *and* [a]to see whether the vine flourished, *and* the pomegranates budded. C

M *SS 2:11–13* ◀▶ *Isa 2:1–5*
C *SS 4:6* ◀▶ *SS 6:11–12*

T *SS 2:10* ◀▶ *Isa 26:20*
C *SS 5:8* ◀▶ *SS 7:8–9*

12 [1]Or ever I was aware, my soul [2]made me *like* the chariots of Amminadib.

13 Return, return, O Shulamite; return, return, that we may look upon thee. What will ye see in the Shulamite? As it were the company of two armies.

7 HOW BEAUTIFUL are thy feet with shoes, [a]O prince's daughter! the joints of thy thighs *are* like jewels, the work of the hands of a cunning workman.

2 Thy navel *is like* a round goblet, *which* wanteth not [1]liquor: thy belly *is like* an heap of wheat set about with lilies.

3 [a]Thy two breasts *are* like two young roes *that are* twins.

4 [a]Thy neck *is* as a tower of ivory; thine eyes *like* the fishpools in Heshbon, by the gate of Bath-rabbim: thy nose *is* as the tower of Lebanon which looketh toward Damascus.

5 Thine head upon thee *is* like [1]Carmel, and the hair of thine head like purple; the king *is* [2]held in the galleries.

6 How fair and how pleasant art thou, O love, for delights!

7 This thy stature is like to a palm tree, and thy breasts to clusters *of grapes*.

C 8 I said, I will go up to the palm tree, I will take hold of the boughs thereof: now also thy breasts shall be as clusters of the vine, and the smell of thy nose like apples;

9 And the roof of thy mouth like the best wine for my beloved, that goeth *down* [1]sweetly, causing the lips [2]of those that are asleep to speak.

The maiden desires her beloved

10 ¶ [a]I *am* my beloved's, and [b]his desire *is* toward me.

11 Come, my beloved, let us go forth into the field; let us lodge in the villages.

12 Let us get up early to the vineyards; let us [a]see if the vine flourish, *whether* the tender grape [1]appear, *and* the pomegranates bud forth: there will I give thee my loves.

13 The [a]mandrakes give a smell, and at our gates [b]*are* all manner of pleasant *fruits*, new and old, *which* I have laid up for thee, O my beloved.

8 O THAT thou *wert* as my brother, that sucked the breasts of my mother! *when* I should find thee without, I would kiss thee; yea, [1]I should not be despised.

2 I would lead thee, *and* bring thee into my mother's house, *who* would instruct me: I would cause thee to drink of [a]spiced wine of the juice of my pomegranate.

3 [a]His left hand *should be* under my head, and his right hand should embrace me.

4 [a]I charge you, O daughters of Jerusalem, [1]that ye stir not up, nor awake *my* love, until he please. C

5 [a]Who *is* this that cometh up from the wilderness, leaning upon her beloved? I raised thee up under the apple tree: there thy mother brought thee forth: there she brought thee forth *that* bare thee. D

6 ¶ [a]Set me as a seal upon thine heart, as a seal upon thine arm: for love *is* strong as death; jealousy *is* [1]cruel as the grave: the coals thereof *are* coals of fire, *which hath* a most vehement flame.

7 Many waters cannot quench love, neither can the floods drown it: [a]if a man would give all the substance of his house for love, it would utterly be contemned.

8 ¶ [a]We have a little sister, and she hath no breasts: what shall we do for our sister in the day when she shall be spoken for? G

9 If she *be* a wall, we will build upon her a palace of silver: and if she *be* a door, we will inclose her with boards of cedar.

10 I *am* a wall, and my breasts like towers: then was I in his eyes as one that found [1]favour.

11 Solomon had a vineyard at Baal-hamon; [a]he let out the vineyard unto keepers; every one for the fruit thereof was to bring a thousand *pieces* of silver.

12 My vineyard, which *is* mine, *is* before me: thou, O Solomon, *must have* a

12 [1]Heb. *I knew not* [2]Or, *set me on the chariots of my willing people*
7:1 [a]Ps. 45:13
2 [1]Heb. *mixture*
3 [a]ch. 4:5
4 [a]ch. 4:4
5 [1]Or, *crimson* [2]Heb. *bound*
9 [1]Heb. *straightly* [2]Or, *of the ancient*
10 [a]ch. 2:16 & 6:3 [b]Ps. 45:11
12 [a]ch. 6:11 [1]Heb. *open*
13 [a]Gen. 30:14 [b]Mat. 13:52
8:1 [1]Heb. *they should not despise me*
2 [a]Prov. 9:2
3 [a]ch. 2:6
4 [a]ch. 2:7 & 3:5 [1]Heb. *why should ye stir up*, or, *why*
5 [a]ch. 3:6
6 [a]Is. 49:16; Jer. 22:24; Hag. 2:23 [1]Heb. *hard*
7 [a]Prov. 6:35
8 [a]Ezek. 23:33
10 [1]Heb. *peace*
11 [a]Mat. 21:33

C *SS 6:11–12* ◀▶ *SS 8:4*

C *SS 7:8–9* ◀▶ *SS 8:14*
D *Ps 98:9* ◀▶ *Eze 43:1–2*
G *Dt 32:21* ◀▶ *Isa 65:1*

thousand, and those that keep the fruit
thereof two hundred.
13 Thou that dwellest in the gardens,
the companions hearken to thy voice:
[a]cause me to hear *it*.

13 [a]ch. 2:14

14 [a]See Rev. 22:17,20 [b]ch. 2:17 [/]Heb. *flee away*

14 ¶ [a]Make[/] haste, my beloved, and C
[b]be thou like to a roe or to a young hart
upon the mountains of spices.

C *SS 8:4* ◀ ▶ *Isa 64:1*

Isaiah

Author: Isaiah

Theme: God, the sovereign Lord, judge and redeemer

Date of Writing: c. 700–680 B.C.

Outline of Isaiah

I. God's Judgment and Promise (1:1—6:13)
II. Immanuel's Kingdom (7:1—12:6)
III. Judgment Against the Nations (13:1—23:18)
IV. Judgment of Israel and a Promise (24:1—27:13)
V. Warnings to Israel and Assyria (28:1—33:24)
VI. Judgment and Promise (34:1—35:10)
VII. The Assyrian Threat and Babylonian Exile (36:1—39:8)
VIII. Israel's Deliverance and Restoration (40:1—48:22)
IX. The Servant's Ministry (49:1—57:21)
X. Judgment and Everlasting Deliverance (58:1—66:24)

ISAIAH, THE SON of Amoz, was a prophet in the southern kingdom of Judah. Respected in royal circles despite his repeated warnings of the approaching judgment of God, Isaiah prophesied during a troublesome time in the life of Israel and Judah. Israel faced the threat of domination by the Assyrians. Isaiah warned that Judah too would face capture and captivity because of their sins unless they placed their total reliance on God, not on political alliances, religious ritual or material possessions. A contemporary of Amos, Hosea and Micah, Isaiah echoed their warnings of judgment. Yet his literary style, beautiful images and insights into God's character make Isaiah the greatest of the writing prophets and the most quoted OT prophet in the entire NT.

Isaiah began this book during King Uzziah's reign and continued his prophetic ministry for more than sixty years through the reigns of Jotham, Ahaz and Hezekiah. More than half of his written record concerns prophetic events. The time period covered in chapters 1—39 took place during Isaiah's ministry, including the prediction and fulfillment of the destruction of Jerusalem. Note that Jerusalem appears numerous times with different prophetic names in Isaiah's prophecies.

The remainder of the book focuses on events that were to happen centuries after Isaiah's time. Covering the deliverance of his people from the Babylonians and prefiguring the coming of the Messiah, these chapters may have been completed during Isaiah's later years. The predictions in these later chapters also describe the destiny of virtually every nation on earth. In addition, many of these prophecies directly relate to the Messiah's birth, lineage, ministry, death on a cross and plan of redemption as well as the establishment of the Messianic kingdom during the end times.

1 THE [a]VISION of Isaiah the son of
Amoz, which he saw concerning Ju-
dah and Jerusalem in the days of Uzziah,
Jotham, Ahaz, *and* Hezekiah, kings of
Judah.

Israel's rebellion

2 [a]Hear, O heavens, and give ear,
O earth: for the LORD hath spoken, I have
nourished and brought up children, and
they have rebelled against me.
3 [a]The ox knoweth his owner, and the
ass his master's crib: *but* Israel [b]doth not
know, my people doth not consider.
C 4 Ah sinful nation, a people [1]laden
with iniquity, [a]a seed of evildoers, children that are corrupters: they have forsaken the LORD, they have provoked the
Holy One of Israel unto anger, they are
[2]gone away backward.
5 ¶ [a]Why should ye be stricken any
more? ye will [1]revolt more and more: the
whole head is sick, and the whole heart
faint.
6 From the sole of the foot even unto
the head *there is* no soundness in it; *but*
wounds, and bruises, and putrifying
sores: they have not been closed, neither
bound up, neither mollified with
[1]ointment.
R 7 [a]Your country *is* desolate, your cities
are burned with fire: your land, strangers
devour it in your presence, and *it is* desolate, [1]as overthrown by strangers.
8 And the daughter of Zion is left [a]as a
cottage in a vineyard, as a lodge in a garden of cucumbers, [b]as a besieged city.
9 [a]Except the LORD of hosts had left
unto us a very small remnant, we should
have been as [b]Sodom, *and* we should
have been like unto Gomorrah.
10 ¶ Hear the word of the LORD, ye rulers [a]of Sodom; give ear unto the law of
our God, ye people of Gomorrah.
11 To what purpose *is* the multitude of
your [a]sacrifices unto me? saith the LORD: I
am full of the burnt offerings of rams, and
the fat of fed beasts; and I delight not in
the blood of bullocks, or of lambs, or of
[1]he goats.
12 When ye come [a]to[1] appear before
me, who hath required this at your hand,
to tread my courts?
13 Bring no more [a]vain oblations; in- S
cense is an abomination unto me; the
new moons and sabbaths, [b]the calling of
assemblies, I cannot away with; *it is* [1]in-
iquity, even the solemn meeting.
14 Your [a]new moons and your [b]ap-
pointed feasts my soul hateth: they are a
trouble unto me; [c]I am weary to bear
them.
15 And [a]when ye spread forth your
hands, I will hide mine eyes from you:
[b]yea, when ye [1]make many prayers, I will
not hear: your hands are full of [2]blood.

1:1 [a]Num. 12:6
2 [a]Jer. 2:12
3 [a]Jer. 8:7 [b]Jer. 9:3,6
4 [a]Mat. 3:7 [1]Heb. *of heaviness* [2]Heb. *alienated, or, separated*
5 [a]ch. 9:13 [1]Heb. *increase revolt*
6 [1]Or, *oil*
7 [a]Deut. 28:51 [1]Heb. *as the overthrow of strangers*
8 [a]Job 27:18 [b]Jer. 4:17
9 [a]Lam. 3:22 [b]Gen. 19:24
10 [a]Deut. 32:32
11 [a]1 Sam. 15:22 [1]Heb. *great he goats*
12 [a]Ex. 23:17 [1]Heb. *to be seen*
13 [a]Mat. 15:9 [b]Joel 1:14 [1]Or, *grief*
14 [a]Num. 28:11 [b]Lam. 2:6 [c]ch. 43:24
15 [a]Prov. 1:28; Mic. 3:4 [b]Ps. 66:18 [1]Heb. *multiply prayer* [2]Heb. *bloods*

C *Ecc 9:18* ◀▶ *Isa 3:9*
R *Ps 80:12–16* ◀▶ *Isa 1:21–22*
S *Ecc 12:13–14* ◀▶ *Isa 1:19*

1:7–9 Isaiah prophesied about God's rejection of Judah and Jerusalem due to their continued wickedness, describing their future destruction in the past tense to emphasize its certainty and noting that unless God showed mercy to a small remnant, the kingdom of Judah would be annihilated like Sodom and Gomorrah.

R 16 ¶ [a]Wash you, make you clean; put away the evil of your doings from before mine eyes; [b]cease to do evil;
17 Learn to do well; seek judgment, [1]relieve the oppressed, judge the fatherless, plead for the widow.
K 18 Come now, and [a]let us reason to-
L gether, saith the LORD: though your sins
W be as scarlet, [b]they shall be as white as snow; though they be red like crimson, they shall be as wool.
S 19 If ye be willing and obedient, ye
F shall eat the good of the land:
U 20 But if ye refuse and rebel, ye shall be devoured with the sword: [a]for the mouth of the LORD hath spoken *it*.
R 21 ¶ [a]How is the faithful city become an harlot! it was full of judgment; righteousness lodged in it; but now murderers.
22 [a]Thy silver is become dross, thy wine mixed with water:
23 [a]Thy princes *are* rebellious, and [b]companions of thieves: [c]every one loveth gifts, and followeth after rewards: they [d]judge not the fatherless, neither doth the cause of the widow come unto them.
P 24 Therefore saith the Lord, the LORD
H of hosts, the mighty One of Israel, Ah, [a]I will ease me of mine adversaries, and avenge me of mine enemies:

R *Pr 28:13* ◀▶ *Isa 55:7*
K *Pr 23:11* ◀▶ *Isa 1:25*
L *Pr 28:13* ◀▶ *Isa 1:25*
W *Pr 29:25* ◀▶ *Isa 42:3*
S *Isa 1:13–17* ◀▶ *Isa 1:27–28*
F *Pr 13:25* ◀▶ *Isa 33:16*
U *Ecc 7:18* ◀▶ *Isa 3:10*
R *Isa 1:7–9* ◀▶ *Isa 2:6*
P *Pr 2:21–22* ◀▶ *Isa 1:28*
H *Ecc 9:12* ◀▶ *Isa 1:28*

16 [a]Jer. 4:14 [b]Rom. 12:9
17 [1]Or, *righten*
18 [a]ch. 43:26 [b]Ps. 51:7; Rev. 7:14
20 [a]Tit. 1:2
21 [a]Jer. 2:20
22 [a]Jer. 6:28
23 [a]Hos. 9:15 [b]Prov. 29:24 [c]Jer. 22:17; Ezek. 22:12 [d]Jer. 5:28; Zech. 7:10
24 [a]Deut. 28:63
25 [a]Mal. 3:3 [1]Heb. *according to pureness*
26 [a]Jer. 33:7 [b]Zech. 8:3
27 [1]Or, *they that return of her*
28 [a]Job 31:3 [1]Heb. *breaking*
29 [a]ch. 57:5 [b]ch. 65:3
31 [a]Ezek. 32:21 [b]ch. 43:17 [1]Or, *and his work*
2:2 [a]Mic. 4:1 [b]Gen. 49:1; Jer. 23:20

25 ¶ And I will turn my hand upon I
thee, and [a]purely[1] purge away thy dross, K
and take away all thy tin: L
26 And I will restore thy judges [a]as at the first, and thy counsellors as at the beginning: afterward [b]thou shalt be called, The city of righteousness, the faithful city.
27 Zion shall be redeemed with judg- S
ment, and [1]her converts with righteousness.
28 ¶ And the [a]destruction[1] of the P
transgressors and of the sinners *shall be* H
together, and they that forsake the LORD shall be consumed.
29 For they shall be ashamed of [a]the oaks which ye have desired, [b]and ye shall be confounded for the gardens that ye have chosen.
30 For ye shall be as an oak whose leaf P
fadeth, and as a garden that hath no H
water.
31 [a]And the strong shall be [b]as tow, [1]and the maker of it as a spark, and they shall both burn together, and none shall quench *them*.

God's kingdom to triumph

2 THE WORD that Isaiah the son of I
Amoz saw concerning Judah and Je- M
rusalem.
2 And [a]it shall come to pass [b]in the last

I *Ps 147:2* ◀▶ *Isa 2:1–5*
K *Isa 1:18* ◀▶ *Isa 4:6*
L *Isa 1:18–19* ◀▶ *Isa 4:6*
S *Isa 1:19* ◀▶ *Isa 5:18*
P *Isa 1:24* ◀▶ *Isa 1:30–31*
H *Isa 1:24* ◀▶ *Isa 1:30–31*
P *Isa 1:28* ◀▶ *Isa 2:10–21*
H *Isa 1:28* ◀▶ *Isa 2:10–21*
I *Isa 1:25–27* ◀▶ *Isa 4:2–6*
M *SS 4:16* ◀▶ *Isa 4:5–6*

1:21–22 Using the imagery of an unfaithful harlot, God condemns Judah's compromise with evil and corruption.
1:24 God promised Judah that he would take vengeance against those nations that had helped turn Judah away from him.
1:25–28 God promises to cleanse his people of their sin and redeem them "with judgment" (1:27). This prophecy was initially fulfilled when Jerusalem fell in 586 B.C. to the Babylonians, but will find its fullest fulfillment during the great tribulation and the final judgment of God's people. At that time God will "restore thy judges as at the first" (1:26) under the Messiah, and Jerusalem will become "the faithful city" (1:26).
1:30–31 These verses likely refer to the destruction of the oak groves and gardens that were used in pagan idolatrous rituals.
2:1–6 Despite the certainty of God's approaching judgment, Isaiah also prophesied the final redemption of Israel and Judah in the millennial kingdom when the Lord will bring about the restoration of the nation and the rebuilding of the temple. Isaiah also prophesied that all the nations would come to Jerusalem to worship God during the Messiah's reign. Christ will then "teach us of his ways" (2:3) as he proclaims God's laws throughout the earth from his throne in Jerusalem. Isaiah therefore urged Judah to

days, [c]*that* the mountain of the LORD'S house shall be [1]established in the top of the mountains, and shall be exalted above the hills; [d]and all nations shall flow unto it.

3 And many people shall go and say, [a]Come ye, and let us go up to the mountain of the LORD, to the house of the God of Jacob; and he will teach us of his ways, and we will walk in his paths: [b]for out of Zion shall go forth the law, and the word of the LORD from Jerusalem.

U 4 And he shall judge among the nations, and shall rebuke many people: and [a]they shall beat their swords into plowshares, and their spears into [1]pruninghooks: nation shall not lift up sword against nation, [b]neither shall they learn war any more.

The day of the LORD

5 O house of Jacob, come ye, and let us [a]walk in the light of the LORD.

R 6 ¶ Therefore thou hast forsaken thy people the house of Jacob, because they be replenished [a]from[1] the east, and [b]*are* soothsayers like the Philistines, [c]and they [2]please themselves in the children of strangers.

7 [a]Their land also is full of silver and gold, neither *is there any* end of their treasures; their land is also full of horses, neither *is there any* end of their chariots:

8 [a]Their land also is full of idols; they worship the work of their own hands, that which their own fingers have made:

9 And the mean man boweth down, and the great man humbleth himself: therefore forgive them not.

P 10 ¶ [a]Enter into the rock, and hide
H thee in the dust, for fear of the LORD, and
M for the glory of his majesty.

11 The [a]lofty looks of man shall be humbled, and the haughtiness of men shall be bowed down, and the LORD alone shall be exalted [b]in that day.

12 For the day of the LORD of hosts *shall be* upon every *one that is* proud and lofty, and upon every *one that is* lifted up; and he shall be brought low:

13 And upon all [a]the cedars of Lebanon, *that are* high and lifted up, and upon all the oaks of Bashan,

14 And [a]upon all the high mountains, and upon all the hills *that are* lifted up,

15 And upon every high tower, and upon every fenced wall,

16 [a]And upon all the ships of Tarshish, and upon all [1]pleasant pictures.

17 [a]And the loftiness of man shall be bowed down, and the haughtiness of men shall be made low: and the LORD alone shall be exalted [b]in that day.

18 And [1]the idols he shall utterly abolish.

19 And they shall go into the [a]holes of the rocks, and into the caves of [1]the earth, [b]for fear of the LORD, and for the glory of his majesty, when he ariseth [c]to shake terribly the earth.

20 In that day a man shall cast [1]his idols of silver, and his idols of gold, [2]which they made *each one* for himself to worship, to the moles and to the bats;

21 [a]To go into the clefts of the rocks, and into the tops of the ragged rocks, [b]for fear of the LORD, and for the glory of his majesty, when he ariseth to shake terribly the earth.

22 [a]Cease ye from man, whose [b]breath *is* in his nostrils: for wherein is he to be accounted of?

The judgment of the LORD

3 FOR, BEHOLD, the Lord, the LORD of hosts, [a]doth take away from Jerusalem and from Judah [b]the stay and the staff, the whole stay of bread, and the whole stay of water, R

2 [a]The mighty man, and the man of war, the judge, and the prophet, and the prudent, and the ancient,

3 The captain of fifty, and [1]the honourable man, and the counsellor, and the cunning artificer, and the [2]eloquent orator.

4 And I will give [a]children *to be* their

U *Ps 72:7* ◀ ▶ *Isa 9:6*
R *Isa 1:21–22* ◀ ▶ *Isa 3:1–8*
P *Isa 1:30–31* ◀ ▶ *Isa 11:4*
H *Isa 1:30–31* ◀ ▶ *Isa 3:11*
M *Pr 30:12–13* ◀ ▶ *Isa 5:14–16*

R *Isa 2:6* ◀ ▶ *Isa 3:8*

2 [c]Ps. 68:15 [d]Ps. 72:8 [1]Or, *prepared*
3 [a]Jer. 50:5; Zech. 8:21 [b]Luke 24:47
4 [a]Ps. 46:9 [b]Ps. 72:3,7 [1]Or, *scythes*
5 [a]Eph. 5:8
6 [a]Num. 23:7 [b]Deut. 18:14 [c]Ps. 106:35; Jer. 10:2 [1]Or, *more than the east* [2]Or, *abound with the children*
7 [a]Deut. 17:16
8 [a]Jer. 2:28
10 [a]Rev. 6:15
11 [a]ch. 5:15 [b]Hos. 2:16; Zech. 9:16
13 [a]ch. 14:8; Ezek. 31:3; Zech. 11:1
14 [a]ch. 30:25
16 [a]1 Ki. 10:22 [1]Heb. *pictures of desire*
17 [a]ver. 11 [b]ver. 11
18 [1]Or, *the idols shall utterly pass away*
19 [a]Hos. 10:8; Rev. 9:6 [b]2 Thes. 1:9 [c]Hag. 2:6,21 [1]Heb. *the dust*
20 [1]Heb. *the idols of his silver* [2]Or, *which they made for him*
21 [a]ver. 19 [b]ver. 10,19
22 [a]Ps. 146:3 [b]Job 27:3
3:1 [a]Jer. 37:21 [b]Lev. 26:26
2 [a]2 Ki. 24:14
3 [1]Heb. *a man eminent in countenance* [2]Or, *skilful of speech*
4 [a]Eccl. 10:16

repent and "walk in the light of the LORD" (2:5).

2:10–21 Isaiah describes the desperate actions and fear that will afflict the world during the tribulation under the cruel rule of the antichrist before the Messiah's return.

princes, and babes shall rule over them.
5 And the people shall be oppressed,
every one by another, and every one by
his neighbour: the child shall behave
himself proudly against the ancient, and
the base against the honourable.
6 When a man shall take hold of his
brother of the house of his father, *saying,*
Thou hast clothing, be thou our ruler,
and *let* this ruin *be* under thy hand:
7 In that day shall he swear, saying, I
will not be an [1]healer; for in my house *is*
neither bread nor clothing: make me not
a ruler of the people.
R 8 For [a]Jerusalem is ruined, and Judah
is fallen: because their tongue and their
doings *are* against the LORD, to provoke
the eyes of his glory.
C 9 ¶ The show of their countenance
doth witness against them; and they declare their sin as [a]Sodom, they hide *it*
not. Woe unto their soul! for they have
rewarded evil unto themselves.
U 10 Say ye to the righteous, [a]that *it*
shall be well *with him:* [b]for they shall eat
the fruit of their doings.
H 11 Woe unto the wicked! [a]*it shall be* ill
with him: for the reward of his hands
shall be [1]given him.
12 ¶ *As for* my people, [a]children *are*
their oppressors, and women rule over
them. O my people, [b]they[1] which lead
thee cause *thee* to err, and [2]destroy the
way of thy paths.
13 The LORD standeth up [a]to plead, and
standeth to judge the people.
H 14 The LORD will enter into judgment
with the ancients of his people, and the
princes thereof: for ye have [1]eaten up
[a]the vineyard; the spoil of the poor *is* in
your houses.
15 What mean ye *that* ye [a]beat my
people to pieces, and grind the faces of
the poor? saith the Lord GOD of hosts.
16 ¶ Moreover the LORD saith, Because
the daughters of Zion are haughty, and

7 [1]Heb. *binder up*
8 [a]Mic. 3:12
9 [a]Gen. 13:13
10 [a]Eccl. 8:12 [b]Ps. 128:2
11 [a]Ps. 11:6 [1]Heb. *done to him*
12 [a]ver. 4 [b]ch. 9:16 [1]Or, *they which call thee blessed* [2]Heb. *swallow up*
13 [a]Mic. 6:2
14 [a]Mat. 21:33 [1]Or, *burnt*
15 [a]Mic. 3:2,3
16 [1]Heb. *deceiving with their eyes* [2]Or, *tripping nicely*
17 [a]Deut. 28:27 [b]Jer. 13:22 [1]Heb. *make naked*
18 [a]Judg. 8:21 [1]Or, *networks*
19 [1]Or, *sweet balls* [2]Or, *spangled ornaments*
20 [1]Heb. *houses of the soul*
24 [a]ch. 22:12
25 [1]Heb. *might*
26 [a]Jer. 14:2 [b]Lam. 2:10 [1]Or, *emptied* [2]Heb. *cleansed*
4:1 [a]ch. 2:11,17 [b]2 Thes. 3:12 [c]Luke 1:25 [1]Heb. *let thy name be called upon us* [2]Or, *take thou away*
2 [a]Jer. 23:5 [1]Heb. *beauty and glory* [2]Heb. *for the escaping of Israel*

walk with stretched forth necks and
[1]wanton eyes, walking and [2]mincing *as*
they go, and making a tinkling with their
feet:
17 Therefore the Lord will smite with
[a]a scab the crown of the head of the
daughters of Zion, and the LORD will [b]dis-
cover[1] their secret parts.
18 In that day the Lord will take away
the bravery of *their* tinkling ornaments
about their feet, and *their* [1]cauls, and
their [a]round tires like the moon,
19 The [1]chains, and the bracelets, and
the [2]mufflers,
20 The bonnets, and the ornaments of
the legs, and the headbands, and the
[1]tablets, and the earrings,
21 The rings, and nose jewels,
22 The changeable suits of apparel,
and the mantles, and the wimples, and
the crisping pins,
23 The glasses, and the fine linen, and
the hoods, and the veils.
24 And it shall come to pass, *that* in- H
stead of sweet smell there shall be stink;
and instead of a girdle a rent; and instead
of well set hair [a]baldness; and instead of
a stomacher a girding of sackcloth; *and*
burning instead of beauty.
25 Thy men shall fall by the sword,
and thy [1]mighty in the war.
26 [a]And her gates shall lament and R
mourn; and she *being* [1,2]desolate [b]shall
sit upon the ground.
4 AND [a]IN that day seven women
shall take hold of one man, saying,
We will [b]eat our own bread, and wear
our own apparel: only [1]let us be called by
thy name, [2]to take away [c]our reproach.

Blessings under the Messiah

2 In that day shall [a]the branch of the I
LORD be [1]beautiful and glorious, and the
fruit of the earth *shall be* excellent and
comely [2]for them that are escaped of
Israel.
3 And it shall come to pass, *that he* S

R *Isa 3:1–8* ◀▶ *Isa 3:26*
C *Isa 1:4–6* ◀▶ *Isa 5:18*
U *Isa 1:19* ◀▶ *Isa 32:17*
H *Isa 2:10–21* ◀▶ *Isa 3:14–15*
H *Isa 3:11* ◀▶ *Isa 3:24*

H *Isa 3:14–15* ◀▶ *Isa 8:15*
R *Isa 3:8* ◀▶ *Isa 5:1–10*
I *Isa 2:1–5* ◀▶ *Isa 9:1–4*
S *Ps 51:10* ◀▶ *Eze 11:19*

4:1–6 This unusual prophecy reveals that the unprecedented slaughter of humanity during the wars of the tribulation period will severely reduce the number of marriageable men. Yet when the Messiah returns, God's glory will provide a defense for the people, worship in the temple will resume and the temple will become a place of refuge for God's people.

that is left in Zion, and *he that* remaineth in Jerusalem, [a]shall be called holy, *even* every one that is [b]written [1]among the living in Jerusalem:

N P R 4 When [a]the Lord shall have washed away the filth of the daughters of Zion, and shall have purged the blood of Jerusalem from the midst thereof by the spirit of judgment, and by the spirit of burning.

M 5 And the LORD will create upon every dwellingplace of mount Zion, and upon her assemblies, [a]a cloud and smoke by day, and [b]the shining of a flaming fire by night: for [1]upon all the glory *shall be* [2]a defence.

K L 6 And there shall be a tabernacle for a shadow in the daytime from the heat, and [a]for a place of refuge, and for a covert from storm and from rain.

The parable of the vineyard

R **5** NOW WILL I sing to my wellbeloved a song of my beloved touching [a]his vineyard. My wellbeloved hath a vineyard in [1]a very fruitful hill:

2 And he [1]fenced it, and gathered out the stones thereof, and planted it with the choicest vine, and built a tower in the midst of it, and also [2]made a winepress therein: [a]and he looked that it should bring forth grapes, and it brought forth wild grapes.

3 And now, O inhabitants of Jerusalem, and men of Judah, [a]judge, I pray you, betwixt me and my vineyard.

4 What could have been done more to my vineyard, that I have not done in it? wherefore, when I looked that it should bring forth grapes, brought it forth wild grapes?

5 And now go to; I will tell you what I will do to my vineyard: [a]I will take away the hedge thereof, and it shall be eaten up; *and* break down the wall thereof, and it shall be [1]trodden down:

6 And I will lay it waste: it shall not be pruned, nor digged; but there shall come up briers and thorns: I will also command the clouds that they rain no rain upon it.

7 For the vineyard of the LORD of hosts *is* the house of Israel, and the men of Judah [1]his pleasant plant: and he looked for judgment, but behold [2]oppression; for righteousness, but behold a cry.

God's judgment against Judah

8 ¶ Woe unto them that join [a]house to house, *that* lay field to field, till *there be* no place, that [1]they may be placed alone in the midst of the earth!

9 [a]In [1] mine ears *said* the LORD of hosts, [2]Of a truth many houses shall be desolate, *even* great and fair, without inhabitant.

10 Yea, ten acres of vineyard shall yield one [a]bath, and the seed of an homer shall yield an ephah.

11 ¶ [a]Woe unto them that rise up early in the morning, *that* they may follow strong drink; that continue until night, *till* wine [1]inflame them!

12 And [a]the harp, and the viol, the tabret, and pipe, and wine, are in their feasts: but [b]they regard not the work of the LORD, neither consider the operation of his hands.

13 ¶ [a]Therefore my people are gone into captivity, because *they have* no knowledge: and [1]their honourable men *are* famished, and their multitude dried up with thirst.

14 Therefore hell hath enlarged herself, and opened her mouth without measure: and their glory, and their multitude, and their pomp, and he that rejoiceth, shall descend into it. M

15 And [a]the mean man shall be brought down, and the mighty man shall be humbled, and the eyes of the lofty shall be humbled:

16 But the LORD of hosts shall be exalted in judgment, and [1,2]God that is holy shall be sanctified in righteousness.

17 Then shall the lambs feed after

3 [a]ch. 60:21 [b]Phil. 4:3 [1]Or, *to life*
4 [a]Mal. 3:2,3
5 [a]Ex. 13:21 [b]Zech. 2:5 [1]Or, *above* [2]Heb. *a covering*
6 [a]ch. 25:4
5:1 [a]Ps. 80:8; Jer. 2:21; Mat. 21:33; Mark 12:1 [1]Heb. *the horn of the son of oil*
2 [a]Deut. 32:6 [1]Or, *made a wall about it* [2]Heb. *hewed*
3 [a]Rom. 3:4
5 [a]Ps. 80:12 [1]Heb. *for a treading*
7 [1]Heb. *plant of his pleasures* [2]Heb. *a scab*
8 [a]Mic. 2:2 [1]Heb. *ye*
9 [a]ch. 22:14 [1]Or, *This is in mine ears, saith the LORD* [2]Heb. *If not*
10 [a]Ezek. 45:11
11 [a]Prov. 23:29 [1]Or, *pursue them*
12 [a]Amos 6:5 [b]Job 34:27; Ps. 28:5
13 [a]Hos. 4:6 [1]Heb. *their glory are men of famine*
15 [a]ch. 2:9,11
16 [1]Or, *the holy God* [2]Heb. *the God the holy*

N *Ps 143:10* ◀▶ *Isa 11:2*
P *Pr 1:22–23* ◀▶ *Isa 32:15*
R *Ps 51:12–13* ◀▶ *Isa 61:1–3*
M *Isa 2:1–5* ◀▶ *Isa 9:6–7*
K *Isa 1:25* ◀▶ *Isa 25:4*
L *Isa 1:25* ◀▶ *Isa 9:2*
R *Isa 3:26* ◀▶ *Isa 5:25–30*
M *Isa 2:10–17* ◀▶ *Isa 5:21*

5:1–10 This passage reveals the judgment of God upon the nation as a result of their continued sin. Elsewhere in Scripture the nation is also pictured as a vineyard that yields evil fruit (see Ps 80:8–9; Jer 12:10; Mt 21:33–44; Mk 12:1–11; Lk 20:9–18).

their manner, and the waste places of [a]the fat ones shall strangers eat.

C S 18 Woe unto them that draw iniquity with cords of vanity, and sin as it were with a cart rope:

19 [a]That say, Let him make speed, *and* hasten his work, that we may see *it:* and let the counsel of the Holy One of Israel draw nigh and come, that we may know *it!*

C 20 ¶ Woe unto them that [1]call evil good, and good evil; that put darkness for light, and light for darkness; that put bitter for sweet, and sweet for bitter!

M 21 Woe unto *them that are* [a]wise in their own eyes, and prudent [1]in their own sight!

22 Woe unto *them that are* mighty to drink wine, and men of strength to mingle strong drink:

23 Which [a]justify the wicked for reward, and take away the righteousness of the righteous from him!

24 Therefore [a]as [1]the fire devoureth the stubble, and the flame consumeth the chaff, *so* [b]their root shall be as rottenness, and their blossom shall go up as dust: because they have cast away the law of the LORD of hosts, and despised the word of the Holy One of Israel.

R 25 [a]Therefore is the anger of the LORD kindled against his people, and he hath stretched forth his hand against them, and hath smitten them: and [b]the hills did tremble, and their carcases *were* [1]torn in the midst of the streets. [c]For all this his anger is not turned away, but his hand *is* stretched out still.

26 ¶ [a]And he will lift up an ensign to the nations from far, and will [b]hiss unto them from [c]the end of the earth: and, behold, [d]they shall come with speed swiftly:

27 None shall be weary nor stumble among them; none shall slumber nor sleep; neither [a]shall the girdle of their loins be loosed, nor the latchet of their shoes be broken:

28 [a]Whose arrows *are* sharp, and all their bows bent, their horses' hoofs shall be counted like flint, and their wheels like a whirlwind:

29 Their roaring *shall be* like a lion, they shall roar like young lions: yea, they shall roar, and lay hold of the prey, and shall carry *it* away safe, and none shall deliver *it.*

30 And in that day they shall roar against them like the roaring of the sea: and if *one* [a]look unto the land, behold darkness *and* [1]sorrow, [2]and the light is darkened in the heavens thereof.

Isaiah commissioned

6 IN THE year that king Uzziah died I [a]saw also the Lord sitting upon a throne, high and lifted up, and [1]his train filled the temple.

2 Above it stood the seraphims: each one had six wings; with twain he covered his face, and [a]with twain he covered his feet, and with twain he did fly.

3 And [1]one cried unto another, and said, [a]Holy, holy, holy, *is* the LORD of hosts: [b]the[2] whole earth *is* full of his glory.

4 And the posts of the [1]door moved at the voice of him that cried, and the house was filled with smoke.

5 ¶ Then said I, Woe *is* me! for I am [1]undone; because I *am* a man of unclean lips, and I dwell in the midst of a people of unclean lips: for mine eyes have seen the King, the LORD of hosts. C

6 Then flew one of the seraphims unto me, [1]having a live coal in his hand, *which*

17 [a]ch. 10:16
19 [a]Jer. 17:15; Amos 5:18
20 [1]Heb. *that say concerning evil,* It is *good*
21 [a]Rom. 1:22 [1]Heb. *before their face*
23 [a]Prov. 17:15
24 [a]Ex. 15:7 [b]Job 18:16 [1]Heb. *the tongue of fire*
25 [a]2 Ki. 22:13 [b]Jer. 4:24 [c]ch. 9:12,17 [1]Or, *as dung*
26 [a]ch. 11:12 [b]ch. 7:18 [c]Mal. 1:11 [d]Joel 2:7
27 [a]Dan. 5:6
28 [a]Jer. 5:16
30 [a]ch. 8:22 [1]Or, *distress* [2]Or, *when it is light, it shall be dark in the destructions thereof*
6:1 [a]John 12:41 [1]Or, *the skirts thereof*
2 [a]Ezek. 1:11
3 [a]Rev. 4:8 [b]Ps. 72:19 [1]Heb. *this cried to this* [2]Heb. *his glory is the fulness of the whole earth*
4 [1]Heb. *thresholds*
5 [1]Heb. *cut off*
6 [1]Heb. *and in his hand a live coal*

C *Isa 3:9* ◀▶ *Isa 5:20*
S *Isa 1:27–28* ◀▶ *Isa 32:17*
C *Isa 5:18* ◀▶ *Isa 6:5*
M *Isa 5:14–16* ◀▶ *Isa 10:15*
R *Isa 5:1–10* ◀▶ *Isa 6:9–13*

C *Isa 5:20* ◀▶ *Isa 6:9–10*

5:25 Isaiah declares God's determination to punish his people as a result of their continued rebellion.

5:30 God affirms his coming judgment at the hands of a destroying enemy due to the nation's rebellion.

6:1–8 This remarkable passage tells of a vision that Isaiah received when he went to the temple to pray. Isaiah saw God in all his majesty and glory, "high and lifted up" (6:1). In response to this vision Isaiah declared his sinfulness and the sinfulness of the nation too, so God sent an angel to cleanse Isaiah from his sin. Note that only after acknowledging his sin and receiving cleansing can Isaiah answer God's question "Whom shall I send?" with a firm "Here am I; send me" (6:8).

he had taken with the tongs from off [a]the
altar:
7 And he [a]laid[1] *it* upon my mouth, and
said, Lo, this hath touched thy lips; and
thine iniquity is taken away, and thy sin
purged.
8 Also I heard the voice of the Lord,
saying, Whom shall I send, and who will
go for [a]us? Then said I, [1]Here *am* I;
send me.
R 9 ¶ And he said, Go, and tell this peo-
C ple, Hear ye [1,2]indeed, but understand
not; and see ye [3]indeed, but perceive not.
10 Make [a]the heart of this people fat,
and make their ears heavy, and shut their
eyes; [b]lest they see with their eyes, and
hear with their ears, and understand with
their heart, and convert, and be healed.
11 Then said I, Lord, how long? And
he answered, [a]Until the cities be wasted
without inhabitant, and the houses without man, and the land be [1]utterly desolate,
12 [a]And the LORD have removed men
far away, and *there be* a great forsaking in
the midst of the land.
13 ¶ But yet in it *shall be* a tenth, [1]and
it shall return, and shall be eaten: as a teil
tree, and as an oak, whose [2]substance *is*
in them, when they cast *their leaves: so*
[a]the holy seed *shall be* the substance
thereof.

The sign of Immanuel

7 AND IT came to pass in the days of
Ahaz the son of Jotham, the son of
Uzziah, king of Judah, *that* Rezin the king
of Syria, and Pekah the son of Remaliah,
king of Israel, went up toward Jerusalem
to war against it, but could not prevail
against it.
2 And it was told the house of David,
saying, Syria [1]is confederate with
Ephraim. And his heart was moved, and
the heart of his people, as the trees of the
wood are moved with the wind.
3 Then said the LORD unto Isaiah, Go R
forth now to meet Ahaz, thou, and
[1]Shear-jashub thy son, at the end of the
conduit of the upper pool in the [2]high-
way of the fuller's field;
4 And say unto him, Take heed, and be
quiet; fear not, [1]neither be fainthearted
for the two tails of these smoking firebrands, for the fierce anger of Rezin with
Syria, and of the son of Remaliah.
5 Because Syria, Ephraim, and the son
of Remaliah, have taken evil counsel
against thee, saying,
6 Let us go up against Judah, and [1]vex
it, and let us make a breach therein for
us, and set a king in the midst of it, *even*
the son of Tabeal:
7 Thus saith the Lord GOD, [a]It shall not R
stand, neither shall it come to pass.
8 [a]For the head of Syria *is* Damascus,
and the head of Damascus *is* Rezin; and
within threescore and five years shall
Ephraim be broken, [1]that it be not a
people.
9 And the head of Ephraim *is* Samaria, F
and the head of Samaria *is* Remaliah's
son. [a]If[1] ye will not believe, surely ye
shall not be established.
10 ¶ [1]Moreover the LORD spake again
unto Ahaz, saying,
11 [a]Ask thee a sign of the LORD thy
God; [1]ask it either in the depth, or in the
height above.
12 But Ahaz said, I will not ask, neither will I tempt the LORD.
13 And he said, Hear ye now, O house B
of David; *Is it* a small thing for you to
weary men, but will ye weary my God
also?
14 Therefore the Lord himself shall

6 [a]Rev. 8:3
7 [a]Jer. 1:9 [1]Heb. *caused it to touch*
8 [a]Gen. 1:26 [1]Heb. *Behold me*
9 [1]Or, *without ceasing* [2]Heb. *hear ye in hearing* [3]Heb. *in seeing*
10 [a]Ps. 119:70 [b]Jer. 5:21
11 [a]Mic. 3:12 [1]Heb. *desolate with desolation*
12 [a]2 Ki. 25:21
13 [a]Ezra 9:2 [1]Or, *when it is returned, and hath been broused* [2]Or, *stock,* or, *stem*
7:2 [1]Heb. *resteth on Ephraim*
3 [1]i.e. *The remnant shall return* [2]Or, *causeway*
4 [1]Heb. *let not thy heart be tender*
6 [1]Or, *waken*
7 [a]ch. 8:10
8 [a]2 Sam. 8:6 [1]Heb. *from a people*
9 [a]2 Chr. 20:20 [1]Or, *Do ye not believe?* it is because ye *are not stable*
10 [1]Heb. *And the LORD added to speak*
11 [a]Mat. 12:38 [1]Or, *make thy petition deep*

R *Isa 5:25–30* ◀▶ *Isa 7:3–4*
C *Isa 6:5* ◀▶ *Isa 9:2*
R *Isa 6:9–13* ◀▶ *Isa 7:7–9*
R *Isa 7:3–4* ◀▶ *Isa 7:17*
F *Pr 29:25* ◀▶ *Isa 26:3–4*
B *Ps 22:1–18* ◀▶ *Isa 9:6–7*

6:9–13 God declared that those who received Isaiah's prophecy would fail to hear or understand his inspired words. Until the threatened destruction was fulfilled, the people would not understand God's warning.
7:3 Isaiah calls his son "Shearjashub" (7:3), which prophetically means "a remnant will return."
7:8–9 This fascinating prophecy was fulfilled 65 years later in 670 B.C. when the conquering Assyrian king settled Assyrian colonists in Israel. The intermarriage of theses colonists with the remaining Israelites who had not been exiled resulted in the people group called the Samaritans (see 2Ki 17:24–34) and marked the end of the tribe of Ephraim.
7:14 This prophecy is the clearest prediction of the virgin birth of the Messiah in the OT. It expands the earlier prophecy found in Genesis that the seed of the woman would defeat the seed of Satan

give you a sign; [a]Behold, a virgin shall conceive, and bear [b]a son, and shall call his name [c]Immanuel.

15 Butter and honey shall he eat, that he may know to refuse the evil, and choose the good.

16 [a]For before the child shall know to refuse the evil, and choose the good, the land that thou abhorrest shall be forsaken of [b]both her kings.

R 17 ¶ [a]The LORD shall bring upon thee, and upon thy people, and upon thy father's house, days that have not come, from the day that [b]Ephraim departed from Judah; *even* the king of Assyria.

R 18 And it shall come to pass in that day, *that* the LORD [a]shall hiss for the fly that *is* in the uttermost part of the rivers of Egypt, and for the bee that *is* in the land of Assyria.

19 And they shall come, and shall rest all of them in the desolate valleys, and in [a]the holes of the rocks, and upon all thorns, and upon all [ǀ]bushes.

20 In the same day shall the Lord shave with a [a]razor that is hired, *namely,* by them beyond the river, by the king of Assyria, the head, and the hair of the feet: and it shall also consume the beard.

21 And it shall come to pass in that day, *that* a man shall nourish a young cow, and two sheep;

22 And it shall come to pass, for the abundance of milk *that* they shall give he shall eat butter: for butter and honey shall every one eat that is left [ǀ]in the land.

R 23 And it shall come to pass in that day, *that* every place shall be, where there were a thousand vines at a thousand silverlings, [a]it shall *even* be for briers and thorns.

24 With arrows and with bows shall *men* come thither; because all the land shall become briers and thorns.

25 And *on* all hills that shall be digged with the mattock, there shall not come thither the fear of briers and thorns: but it shall be for the sending forth of oxen, and for the treading of lesser cattle.

R *Isa 7:7–9* ◀ ▶ *Isa 7:18–25*
R *Isa 7:17* ◀ ▶ *Isa 7:23–24*
R *Isa 7:18–25* ◀ ▶ *Isa 8:9–10*

The coming war and deliverer

8 MOREOVER THE LORD said unto me, Take thee a great roll, and [a]write in it with a man's pen concerning [ǀ]Maher-shalal-hash-baz.

2 And I took unto me faithful witnesses to record, [a]Uriah the priest, and Zechariah the son of Jeberechiah.

3 And I [ǀ]went unto the prophetess; and she conceived, and bare a son. Then said the LORD to me, Call his name Maher-shalal-hash-baz.

4 [a]For before the child shall have knowledge to cry, My father, and my mother, [b]the[ǀ] riches of Damascus and the spoil of Samaria shall be taken away before the king of Assyria.

5 ¶ The LORD spake also unto me again, saying,

6 Forasmuch as this people refuseth the waters of [a]Shiloah that go softly, and rejoice [b]in Rezin and Remaliah's son;

7 Now therefore, behold, the Lord bringeth up upon them the waters of the river, strong and many, *even* the king of Assyria, and all his glory: and he shall come up over all his channels, and go over all his banks:

8 And he shall pass through Judah; he shall overflow and go over, [a]he shall reach *even* to the neck; and [ǀ]the stretching out of his wings shall fill the breadth of thy land, O [b]Immanuel.

9 ¶ [a]Associate yourselves, O ye people, [ǀ]and ye shall be broken in pieces; and give ear, all ye of far countries: gird yourselves, and ye shall be broken in pieces; gird yourselves, and ye shall be broken in pieces. R

10 [a]Take counsel together, and it shall come to nought; speak the word, [b]and it shall not stand: [c]for God *is* with us.

11 ¶ For the LORD spake thus to me

R *Isa 7:23–24* ◀ ▶ *Isa 8:17*

14 [a]Mat. 1:23 [b]ch. 9:6 [c]ch. 8:8
16 [a]See ch. 8:4 [b]2 Ki. 15:30
17 [a]2 Chr. 28:19 [b]1 Ki. 12:16
18 [a]ch. 5:26
19 [a]Jer. 16:16 [ǀ]Or, *commendable trees*
20 [a]2 Ki. 16:7
22 [ǀ]Heb. *in the midst of the land*
23 [a]ch. 5:6
8:1 [a]Hab. 2:2 [ǀ]Heb. *In making speed to the spoil he hasteneth the prey,* or, *Make speed*
2 [a]2 Ki. 16:10
3 [ǀ]Heb. *approached unto*
4 [a]ch. 7:16 [b]2 Ki. 15:29 [ǀ]Or, he that *is before the king of Assyria shall take away the riches*
6 [a]John 9:7 [b]ch. 7:1,2
8 [a]ch. 30:28 [b]ch. 7:14 [ǀ]Heb. *the fulness of the breadth of thy land shall be the stretchings out of his wings*
9 [a]Joel 3:9 [ǀ]Or, *yet*
10 [a]Job 5:12 [b]ch. 7:7 [c]ch. 7:14; Rom. 8:31

(see Ge 3:15). By using the Hebrew word *almah* (translated "virgin") to denote an unmarried young woman as the mother of this child, Isaiah's prophecy declared that this miraculous conception and birth would be "a sign" from God, and that her miraculous son would be named Immanuel, which means "God with us" (Mt 1:23). Centuries later, the virgin Mary gave birth to the Christ-child Jesus in fulfillment of this extraordinary prophecy (see Lk 1:26–37).

7:23–24 Isaiah predicted that the fertility of the land of Palestine would turn to barrenness as a result of the nation's continued rebellion against God.

[1]with a strong hand, and instructed me that I should not walk in the way of this people, saying,

12 Say ye not, A confederacy, to all *them to* whom [a]this people shall say, A confederacy; [b]neither fear ye their fear, nor be afraid.

13 [a]Sanctify the LORD of hosts himself; and [b]*let* him *be* your fear, and *let* him *be* your dread.

14 And [a]he shall be for a sanctuary; but for [b]a stone of stumbling and for a rock of offence to both the houses of Israel, for a gin and for a snare to the inhabitants of Jerusalem.

H 15 And many among them shall [a]stumble, and fall, and be broken, and be snared, and be taken.

Command to trust the LORD

16 Bind up the testimony, seal the law among my disciples.

R 17 And I will wait upon the LORD, that [a]hideth his face from the house of Jacob, and I [b]will look for him.

18 [a]Behold, I and the children whom the LORD hath given me [b]*are* for signs and for wonders in Israel from the LORD of hosts, which dwelleth in mount Zion.

19 ¶ And when they shall say unto you, [a]Seek unto them that have familiar spirits, and unto wizards [b]that peep, and that mutter: should not a people seek unto their God? for the living [c]to the dead?

20 [a]To the law and to the testimony: if they speak not according to this word, *it is* because [b]*there is* [1]no light in them.

21 And they shall pass through it, hardly bestead and hungry: and it shall come to pass, that when they shall be hungry, they shall fret themselves, and [a]curse their king and their God, and look upward.

22 And [a]they shall look unto the earth; and behold trouble and darkness, [b]dimness of anguish; and *they shall be* driven to darkness.

The birth of the messianic king

9 NEVERTHELESS [a]THE dimness *shall* I
not *be* such as *was* in her vexation, when at the [b]first he lightly afflicted the land of Zebulun and the land of Naphtali, and [c]afterward did more grievously afflict *her by* the way of the sea, beyond Jordan, in Galilee [1]of the nations.

2 [a]The people that walked in darkness C
have seen a great light: they that dwell in L
the land of the shadow of death, upon them hath the light shined.

3 Thou hast multiplied the nation, *and* [1]not increased the joy: they joy before thee according to the joy in harvest, *and* as *men* rejoice [a]when they divide the spoil.

4 [1]For thou hast broken the yoke of his burden, and [a]the staff of his shoulder, the rod of his oppressor, as in the day of [b]Midian.

5 [1]For every battle of the warrior *is* with confused noise, and garments rolled in blood; [a]but[2] *this* shall be with burning *and* [3]fuel of fire.

6 [a]For unto us a child is born, unto us B
a [b]son is given: and [c]the government M
shall be upon his shoulder: and his name U
shall be called [d]Wonderful, Counsellor, V

11 [1]Heb. *in strength of hand*
12 [a]ch. 7:2 [b]1 Pet. 3:14
13 [a]Num. 20:12 [b]Ps. 76:7; Luke 12:5
14 [a]Ezek. 11:16 [b]Luke 2:34; Rom. 9:33; 1 Pet. 2:8
15 [a]Mat. 21:44; Luke 20:18; Rom. 11:25
17 [a]ch. 54:8 [b]Hab. 2:3; Luke 2:25
18 [a]Heb. 2:13 [b]Ps. 71:7; Zech. 3:8
19 [a]1 Sam. 28:8 [b]ch. 29:4 [c]Ps. 106:28
20 [a]Luke 16:29 [b]Mic. 3:6 [1]Heb. *no morning*
21 [a]Rev. 16:11
22 [a]ch. 5:30 [b]ch. 9:1
9:1 [a]ch. 8:22 [b]2 Ki. 15:29; 2 Chr. 16:4 [c]Lev. 26:24; 2 Ki. 17:5; 1 Chr. 5:26 [1]Or, *populous*
2 [a]Mat. 4:16; Eph. 5:8,14
3 [a]Judg. 5:30 [1]Or, *to him*
4 [a]ch. 10:5 [b]Judg. 7:22; Ps. 83:9 [1]Or, *When thou brakest*
5 [a]ch. 66:15 [1]Or, *When the whole battle of the warrior was* [2]Or, *and it was* [3]Heb. *meat*
6 [a]ch. 7:14; Luke 2:11 [b]John 3:16 [c]Mat. 28:18; 1 Cor. 15:25 [d]Judg. 13:18

H *Isa 3:24* ◀ ▶ *Isa 9:18*
R *Isa 8:9–10* ◀ ▶ *Isa 10:12*
I *Isa 4:2–6* ◀ ▶ *Isa 9:7*
C *Isa 6:9–10* ◀ ▶ *Isa 26:10–11*
L *Isa 4:6* ◀ ▶ *Isa 12:1–3*
B *Isa 7:13–16* ◀ ▶ *Isa 11:1–5*
M *Isa 4:5–6* ◀ ▶ *Isa 11:4–10*
U *Isa 2:4* ◀ ▶ *Isa 11:6–9*
V *Ps 110:1* ◀ ▶ *Isa 11:1–9*

9:1–2 This prophecy notes that though Zebulun and Naphtali were humbled by the Assyrians (see 2Ki 15:29), Galilee would be the center of the Messiah's ministry, bringing glory back to these humbled tribes. Many of the people of Galilee responded favorably to the message of Christ during his ministry there (see Mk 4:13–16), leaving their darkness for his "great light" (9:2).

9:6–7 Isaiah's famous prophecy of the Messiah points to Christ's ultimate establishment of his millennial kingdom. Christ will rule in those days as the Prince of Peace from David's throne in Zion. Isaiah predicts that this kingdom will increase forever. Some scholars believe that Christ will only rule during the Millennium for a period of a thousand years (see Rev 20:6). Other scholars suggest that this millennial rule is only one piece of God's plan following the Battle of Armageddon. These scholars contend that after Satan's final rebellion at the end of the Millennium, God's kingdom will continue forever on the new earth as Christians rule over the earth under the leadership of Christ the Messiah (see 2Ti 2:12; Rev 3:21; 22:5).

[e]The mighty God, The everlasting Father, [f]The Prince of Peace.

I 7 Of the increase of *his* government and peace [a]*there shall be* no end, upon the throne of David, and upon his kingdom, to order it, and to establish it with judgment and with justice from henceforth even for ever. The [b]zeal of the LORD of hosts will perform this.

The LORD's anger against Israel

8 ¶ The Lord sent a word into Jacob, and it hath lighted upon Israel.

9 And all the people shall know, *even* Ephraim and the inhabitant of Samaria, that say in the pride and stoutness of heart,

10 The bricks are fallen down, but we will build with hewn stones: the sycamores are cut down, but we will change *them into* cedars.

11 Therefore the LORD shall set up the adversaries of Rezin against him, and [1]join his enemies together;

12 The Syrians before, and the Philistines behind; and they shall devour Israel [1]with open mouth. [a]For all this his anger is not turned away, but his hand *is* stretched out still.

13 ¶ For [a]the people turneth not unto him that smiteth them, neither do they seek the LORD of hosts.

14 Therefore the LORD will cut off from Israel head and tail, branch and rush, [a]in one day.

15 The ancient and honourable, he *is* the head; and the prophet that teacheth lies, he *is* the tail.

16 For [a]the[1] leaders of this people cause *them* to err; and [2]*they that are* led of them *are* [3]destroyed.

17 Therefore the Lord [a]shall have no joy in their young men, neither shall have mercy on their fatherless and widows: for every one *is* an hypocrite and an evildoer, and every mouth speaketh [1]folly. [b]For all this his anger is not turned away, but his hand *is* stretched out still.

H 18 ¶ For wickedness [a]burneth as the fire: it shall devour the briers and thorns, and shall kindle in the thickets of the forest, and they shall mount up *like* the lifting up of smoke.

19 Through the wrath of the LORD of hosts is [a]the land darkened, and the people shall be as the [1]fuel of the fire: [b]no man shall spare his brother.

20 And he shall [1]snatch on the right hand, and be hungry; and he shall eat on the left hand, [a]and they shall not be satisfied: [b]they shall eat every man the flesh of his own arm:

21 Manasseh, Ephraim; and Ephraim, Manasseh: *and* they together *shall be* against Judah. [a]For all this his anger is not turned away, but his hand *is* stretched out still.

10 WOE UNTO them that [a]decree unrighteous decrees, and [1]that write grievousness *which* they have prescribed;

2 To turn aside the needy from judgment, and to take away the right from the poor of my people, that widows may be their prey, and *that* they may rob the fatherless!

3 And [a]what will ye do in [b]the day of visitation, and in the desolation *which* shall come from far? to whom will ye flee for help? and where will ye leave your glory?

4 Without me they shall bow down under the prisoners, and they shall fall under the slain. [a]For all this his anger is not turned away, but his hand *is* stretched out still.

Assyria to be destroyed

5 ¶ [1]O [2]Assyrian, [a]the rod of mine anger, [3]and the staff in their hand is mine indignation.

6 I will send him against [a]an hypocritical nation, and against the people of my wrath will I [b]give him a charge, to take the spoil, and to take the prey, and [1]to tread them down like the mire of the streets.

7 [a]Howbeit he meaneth not so, neither doth his heart think so; but *it is* in his heart to destroy and cut off nations not a few.

6 [e]Tit. 2:13 [f]Eph. 2:14
7 [a]Dan. 2:44; Luke 1:32 [b]ch. 37:32
11 [1]Heb. *mingle*
12 [a]Jer. 4:8 [1]Heb. *with whole mouth*
13 [a]Jer. 5:3
14 [a]Rev. 18:8
16 [a]ch. 3:12 [1]Or, *they that call them blessed* [2]Or, *they that are called blessed of them* [3]Heb. *swallowed up*
17 [a]Ps. 147:10 [b]ch. 5:25 [1]Or, *villany*
18 [a]Mal. 4:1
19 [a]ch. 8:22 [b]Mic. 7:2,6 [1]Heb. *meat*
20 [a]Lev. 26:26 [b]Jer. 19:9 [1]Heb. *cut*
21 [a]ver. 12,17
10:1 [a]Ps. 58:2 [1]Or, *to the writers that write grievousness*
3 [a]Job 31:14 [b]Hos. 9:7
4 [a]ch. 5:25
5 [a]Jer. 51:20 [1]Or, *Woe to the Assyrian* [2]Heb. *Asshur* [3]Or, *though*
6 [a]ch. 9:17 [b]Jer. 34:22 [1]Heb. *to lay them a treading*
7 [a]Gen. 50:20

I *Isa 9:1–4* ◄► *Isa 11:11–15*
H *Isa 8:15* ◄► *Isa 11:4*

10:5–6 This prediction referred initially to the Assyrian king whom God sent to judge his people. The prophetic title of the "Assyrian" (10:5) also refers to the antichrist, who will come against the nation of Israel in the last days during the tribulation.

The Prophecies of Christ's First Coming

THOUGH THE WRITINGS of other religious beliefs do not contain detailed, specific prophecies, one of the strongest evidences of the divine inspiration of Scripture can be attributed to the hundreds of verifiable, detailed prophecies spanning thousands of years and concerning various nations, events and individuals. When we examine the prophecies in the Bible, we find predictions of events which historians and archeologists verify have been fulfilled. God declared that these prophecies and their fulfillments are verification that the Bible is truly the inspired Word of God (see Isa 46:9–10).

Out of hundreds of Biblical prophecies concerning the promised Messiah's birth, life, death and resurrection, some are quite specific, including the eleven listed below. Note that the chart below suggests an estimate of the probability of each prophecy's fulfillment, with more commonplace customs showing a higher probability of occurrence and the more restrictive prophecies reflecting a lesser probability of occurrence. Though the odds assigned in this chart are arbitrary, they are presented to give the reader an indication of the preponderance of evidence for the divine inspiration of Scripture.

Note also that statistical theory holds that if the probability of one event occurring is one in five, and the probability of another event occurring is one in ten, then the probability of both events being fulfilled in sequence is one in fifty. The following eleven Messianic predictions were made more than four hundred years before they were fulfilled. If these arbitrarily assigned odds were statistically calculated, there is only one chance in 10^{19} that the prophets could have accurately predicted these eleven specific prophecies. Searching the Scriptures for the other specific prophecies regarding Christ's first coming and factoring in their mathematical probabilities reveal the virtual impossibility that these prophecies could be fulfilled by chance alone. God made these promises, and God kept his promises.

Eleven Predictions About the Promised Messiah

PREDICTION & PROBABILITY	OT PREDICTION	NT FULFILLMENT
1. **Be born in Bethlehem** *1 in 200*	But thou, Bethlehem Ephratah, though thou be little among the thousands of Judah, yet out of thee shall he come forth unto me that is to be ruler in Israel (Mic 5:2).	Jesus was born in Bethlehem of Judaea in the days of Herod the king (Mt 2:1).
2. **Be preceded by a messenger** *1 in 20*	The voice of him that crieth in the wilderness, "Prepare ye the way of the LORD, make straight in the desert a highway for our God" (Isa 40:3).	In those days came John the Baptist, preaching in the wilderness of Judaea, And saying, Repent ye: for the kingdom of heaven is at hand (Mt 3:1–2).

PREDICTION & PROBABILITY	OT PREDICTION	NT FULFILLMENT
3. Enter Jerusalem on a colt *1 in 50*	Rejoice greatly, O daughter of Zion; shout, O daughter of Jerusalem: behold, thy King cometh unto thee: he is just, and having salvation; lowly, and riding upon an ass, and upon a colt the foal of an ass (Zec 9:9).	And they cast their garments upon the colt, and they set Jesus thereon. And as he went, they spread their clothes in the way. And when he was come nigh, even now at the descent of the mount of Olives, the whole multitude of the disciples began to rejoice and praise God with a loud voice for all the mighty works that they had seen (Lk 19:35–37).
4. Be betrayed by a friend *1 in 10*	Yea, mine own familiar friend, in whom I trusted, which did eat of my bread, hath lifted up his heel against me (Ps 41:9).	And while he yet spake, lo, Judas, one of the twelve, came, and with him a great multitude with swords and staves, from the chief priests and elders of the people. Now he that betrayed him gave them a sign, saying, Whomsoever I shall kiss, that same is he; hold him fast . . . And Jesus said unto him, Friend, wherefore art thou come? (Mt 26:47–50)
5. Have his hands and feetpierced *1 in 100*	The assembly of the wicked have enclosed me: they pierced my hands and my feet (Ps 22:16).	When they were come to the place, which is called Calvary, there they crucified him, and the malefactors, one on the right hand, and the other on the left (Lk 23:33).
6. Be wounded and whipped by his enemies *1 in 25*	He was wounded for our transgressions, he was bruised for our iniquities: the chastisement of our peace was upon him; and with his stripes we are healed (Isa 53:5).	Then released he Barabbas unto them: and when he had scourged Jesus, he delivered him to be crucified (Mt 27:26).
7. Be sold for thirty pieces of silver *1 in 100*	I said unto them, If ye think good, give me my price; and if not, forbear. So they weighed for my price thirty pieces of silver (Zec 11:12).	What will ye give me, and I will deliver him unto you? And they covenanted with him for thirty pieces of silver (Mt 26:15).
8. Be spit upon and beaten *1 in 10*	I gave my back to the smiters, and my cheeks to them that plucked off the hair: I hid not my face from shame and spitting (Isa 50:6).	Then did they spit in his face, and buffeted him; and others smote him with the palms of their hands (Mt 26:67).
9. Have his betrayal money thrown in the temple and given for a potter's field *1 in 200*	And the LORD said unto me, Cast it unto the potter: a goodly price that I was prized at of them. And I took the thirty pieces of silver, and cast them to the potter in the house of the LORD (Zec 11:13).	He cast down the pieces of silver in the temple, and departed, and went and hanged himself. And the chief priests took the silver pieces, and said, It is not lawful for to put them into the treasury, because it is the price of blood. And they took counsel, and bought with them the potter's field, to bury strangers in (Mt 27:5–7).
10. Be silent before his accusers *1 in 100*	He was oppressed, and he was afflicted, yet he opened not his mouth: he is brought as a lamb to the slaughter, and as a sheep before her shearers is dumb, so he openeth not his mouth (Isa 53:7).	When he was accused of the chief priests and elders, he answered nothing. Then said Pilate unto him, Hearest thou not how many things they witness against thee? And he answered him never a word, insomuch that the governor marveled greatly (Mt 27:12–14).
11. Be crucified with thieves *1 in 100*	He hath poured out his soul unto death: and he was numbered with the transgressors; and he bare the sin of many, and made intercession for the transgressors (Isa 53:12).	Then were there two thieves crucified with him, one on the right hand, and another on the left (Mt 27:38).

8 [a]For he saith, *Are* not my princes altogether kings?

9 *Is* not [a]Calno [b]as Carchemish? *is* not Hamath as Arpad? *is* not Samaria [c]as Damascus?

10 As my hand hath found the kingdoms of the idols, and whose graven images did excel them of Jerusalem and of Samaria;

11 Shall I not, as I have done unto Samaria and her idols, so do to Jerusalem and her idols?

R 12 Wherefore it shall come to pass, *that* when the Lord hath performed his whole work [a]upon mount Zion and on Jerusalem, [b]I will [1]punish the fruit [2]of the stout heart of the king of Assyria, and the glory of his high looks.

13 [a]For he saith, By the strength of my hand I have done *it,* and by my wisdom; for I am prudent: and I have removed the bounds of the people, and have robbed their treasures, and I have put down the inhabitants [1]like a valiant *man:*

14 And [a]my hand hath found as a nest the riches of the people: and as one gathereth eggs *that are* left, have I gathered all the earth; and there was none that moved the wing, or opened the mouth, or peeped.

M 15 Shall [a]the axe boast itself against him that heweth therewith? *or* shall the saw magnify itself against him that shaketh it? [1]as if the rod should shake *itself* against them that lift it up, *or* as if the staff should lift up [2]*itself, as if it were* no wood.

R 16 Therefore shall the Lord, the Lord of hosts, send among his fat ones leanness; and under his glory he shall kindle a burning like the burning of a fire.

17 And the light of Israel shall be for a fire, and his Holy One for a flame: [a]and it shall burn and devour his thorns and his briers in one day;

18 And shall consume the glory of his forest, and of [a]his fruitful field, [1]both soul and body: and they shall be as when a standardbearer fainteth.

19 And the rest of the trees of his forest shall be [1]few, that a child may write them.

A remnant of Israel to be saved

20 ¶ And it shall come to pass in that day, *that* the remnant of Israel, and such as are escaped of the house of Jacob, [a]shall no more again stay upon him that smote them; but shall stay upon the LORD, the Holy One of Israel, in truth.

21 The remnant shall return, *even* the remnant of Jacob, unto the mighty God.

22 [a]For though thy people Israel be as the sand of the sea, [b]*yet* a remnant [1]of them shall return: the consumption decreed shall overflow [2]with righteousness. R

23 [a]For the Lord GOD of hosts shall make a consumption, even determined, in the midst of all the land.

24 ¶ Therefore thus saith the Lord GOD of hosts, O my people that dwellest in Zion, [a]be not afraid of the Assyrian: he shall smite thee with a rod, [1]and shall lift up his staff against thee, after the manner of [b]Egypt.

25 For yet a very little while, [a]and the indignation shall cease, and mine anger in their destruction.

26 And the LORD of hosts shall stir up [a]a scourge for him according to the slaughter of [b]Midian at the rock of Oreb: and [c]*as* his rod *was* upon the sea, so shall he lift it up after the manner of Egypt.

27 And it shall come to pass in that day, *that* his burden [1]shall be taken away from off thy shoulder, and his yoke from off thy neck, and the yoke shall be destroyed because of [a]the anointing.

R *Isa 8:17* ◀▶ *Isa 10:16–19*
M *Isa 5:21* ◀▶ *Isa 13:11*
R *Isa 10:12* ◀▶ *Isa 10:22–27*
R *Isa 10:16–19* ◀▶ *Isa 14:28–31*

8 [a]2 Ki. 19:10
9 [a]Amos 6:2 [b]2 Chr. 35:20 [c]2 Ki. 16:9
12 [a]2 Ki. 19:31 [b]Jer. 50:18 [1]Heb. *visit upon* [2]Heb. *of the greatness of the heart*
13 [a]Is. 37:24 [1]Or, *like many people*
14 [a]Job 31:25
15 [a]Jer. 51:20 [1]Or, *as if a rod should shake them that lift it up* [2]Or, that which is *not wood*
17 [a]ch. 9:18
18 [a]2 Ki. 19:23 [1]Heb. *from the soul, and even to the flesh*
19 [1]Heb. *number*
20 [a]2 Ki. 16:7
22 [a]Rom. 9:27 [b]ch. 6:13 [1]Heb. *in,* or, *among* [2]Or, *in*
23 [a]Dan. 9:27; Rom. 9:28
24 [a]ch. 37:6 [b]Ex. 14 [1]Or, *but he shall lift up his staff for thee*
25 [a]Dan. 11:36
26 [a]2 Ki. 19:35 [b]ch. 9:4 [c]Ex. 14:26
27 [a]Ps. 105:15; 1 John 2:20 [1]Heb. *shall remove*

10:12 This verse found its initial fulfillment in God's punishment of the nation of Assyria. Though God used this wicked nation to carry out his judgment on his people, Assyria was still punished for its misdeeds. The final punishment of the antichrist, "the king of Assyria" (10:12), will come at the end times.

10:21–23 Isaiah prophesied that although the nation of Israel would be dispersed throughout the nations, a remnant would return to establish their nation in the last days.

10:24–27 The prophet assured the people that God's judgment on Israel would come to an end and that God would punish the Assyrians for their part in Israel's judgment. Note also that this prophecy may be applied to the end times when the antichrist, prophetically called "the Assyrian," (10:24) will finally be destroyed by God.

28 He is come to Aiath, he is passed to
Migron; at Michmash he hath laid up his
carriages:
29 They are gone over [a]the passage:
they have taken up their lodging at Geba;
Ramah is afraid; [b]Gibeah of Saul is fled.
30 [/]Lift up thy voice, O daughter [a]of
Gallim: cause it to be heard unto [b]Laish,
O poor Anathoth.
31 [a]Madmenah is removed; the inhabitants of Gebim gather themselves to flee.
32 As yet shall he remain [a]at Nob that
day: he shall [b]shake his hand *against* the
mount of [c]the daughter of Zion, the hill
of Jerusalem.
J 33 Behold, the Lord, the LORD of hosts,
shall lop the bough with terror: and [a]the
high ones of stature *shall be* hewn down,
and the haughty shall be humbled.
34 And he shall cut down the thickets
of the forest with iron, and Lebanon shall
fall [/]by a mighty one.

The branch out of Jesse

B V 11 AND [a]THERE shall come forth a
rod out of the stem of [b]Jesse, and
[c]a Branch shall grow out of his roots:
B 2 [a]And the spirit of the LORD shall rest
G upon him, the spirit of wisdom and un-
M derstanding, the spirit of counsel and
N might, the spirit of knowledge and of the
T fear of the LORD;
3 And shall make him of [/]quick under-

J *Ecc 12:14 ◀▶ Isa 15:1–9*
B *Isa 9:6–7 ◀▶ Isa 50:6–9*
V *Isa 9:6–7 ◀▶ Isa 45:23*
B *Ps 51:12–13 ◀▶ Isa 42:1*
G *Pr 1:22–23 ◀▶ Isa 28:6*
M *Ps 139:7 ◀▶ Isa 28:6*
N *Isa 4:4 ◀▶ Isa 30:1*
T *Pr 1:22–23 ◀▶ Isa 28:6*

29 [a]1 Sam. 13:23 [b]1 Sam. 11:4
30 [a]1 Sam. 25:44 [b]Judg. 18:7 [/]Heb. *Cry shrill with thy voice*
31 [a]Josh. 15:31
32 [a]1 Sam. 21:1; Neh. 11:32 [b]ch. 13:2 [c]ch. 37:22
33 [a]Amos 2:9
34 [/]Or, *mightily*
11:1 [a]Zech. 6:12; Rev. 5:5 [b]Acts 13:23 [c]ch. 4:2
2 [a]ch. 61:1; John 1:32
3 [/]Heb. *scent,* or, *smell*
4 [a]Rev. 19:11 [b]Job 4:9; Mal. 4:6; 2 Thes. 2:8 [/]Or, *argue*
6 [a]Hos. 2:18
8 [/]Or, *adder's*
9 [a]Job 5:23 [b]Hab. 2:14
10 [a]ch. 2:11 [b]Rom. 15:12 [c]Rom. 15:10 [/]Heb. *glory*

standing in the fear of the LORD: and he
shall not judge after the sight of his eyes,
neither reprove after the hearing of his
ears:
4 But [a]with righteousness shall he M
judge the poor, and [/]reprove with equity P
for the meek of the earth: and he shall H
[b]smite the earth with the rod of his
mouth, and with the breath of his lips
shall he slay the wicked.
5 And righteousness shall be the girdle
of his loins, and faithfulness the girdle of
his reins.
6 [a]The wolf also shall dwell with the U
lamb, and the leopard shall lie down with
the kid; and the calf and the young lion
and the fatling together; and a little child
shall lead them.
7 And the cow and the bear shall
feed; their young ones shall lie down
together: and the lion shall eat straw
like the ox.
8 And the sucking child shall play on
the hole of the asp, and the weaned child
shall put his hand on the [/]cockatrice's
den.
9 [a]They shall not hurt nor destroy in K
all my holy mountain: for [b]the earth shall
be full of the knowledge of the LORD, as
the waters cover the sea.
10 ¶ [a]And in that day [b]there shall be a
root of Jesse, which shall stand for an
ensign of the people; to it shall the
[c]Gentiles seek: and his rest shall be
[/]glorious.

M *Isa 9:6–7 ◀▶ Isa 14:2*
P *Isa 2:10–21 ◀▶ Isa 13:1–22*
H *Isa 9:18 ◀▶ Isa 13:6–13*
U *Isa 9:6 ◀▶ Isa 32:17–18*
K *Ps 145:13 ◀▶ Jer 31:34*

11:1 This powerful prophecy described the coming Messiah as David's descendant, "a Branch," that would come from David's roots (see 4:2). This messianic title, "the Branch," is also mentioned by other OT prophets: "I will raise unto David a righteous Branch" (Jer 23:5) and "Behold the man whose name is The BRANCH" (Zec 6:12). Note that the Hebrew word for branch, *neser*, is also the root word for the city of Nazareth. Since Jesus came from that city, he is truly that Branch (see Mt 2:23).
11:2 Compare this prophecy with Zec 4:10. Note that Isaiah's prophecy described the anointing of the Messiah with seven characteristics of God: "the spirit of the LORD," the spirits of wisdom, understanding, counsel, might, knowledge and the spirit of the fear of the Lord.
11:3–5 Though the rulers of Isaiah's day lacked all of these qualities, the Messiah will possess God's understanding, allowing him to rule with perfect justice. His government will be characterized by righteousness for the poor and judgment for the wicked.
11:6–9 Isaiah described the future millennial reign of Christ as a time in which the curse of sin and violence will be lifted from the earth. Carnivorous animals will no longer kill to eat. Violence will be eliminated. This prediction is paralleled by other OT prophecies that confirm the peace and safety of the Messiah's rule (see Eze 34:25–28; Hos 2:18).
11:10 This prediction indicates the full acceptance of the Messiah by all nations.

I 11 And it shall come to pass in that
day, *that* the Lord shall set his hand again
the second time to recover the remnant
of his people, which shall be left, [a]from
Assyria, and from Egypt, and from Pathros, and from Cush, and from Elam,
and from Shinar, and from Hamath, and
from the islands of the sea.
12 And he shall set up an ensign for
the nations, and shall assemble the outcasts of Israel, and gather together the
[a]dispersed of Judah from the four [1]cor-
ners of the earth.
13 [a]The envy also of Ephraim shall depart, and the adversaries of Judah shall be
cut off: Ephraim shall not envy Judah, and
Judah shall not vex Ephraim.
14 But they shall fly upon the shoulders of the Philistines toward the west;
they shall spoil [1]them of the east together: [a]they[2] shall lay their hand upon
Edom and Moab; [3]and the children of
Ammon shall obey them.
15 And the LORD [a]shall utterly destroy
the tongue of the Egyptian sea; and with
his mighty wind shall he shake his hand
over the river, and shall smite it in the
seven streams, [b]and make *men* go over
[1]dryshod.
16 And [a]there shall be an highway for
the remnant of his people, which shall be
left, from Assyria; [b]like as it was to Israel
in the day that he came up out of the land
of Egypt.

I *Isa 9:7* ◀ ▶ *Isa 12:1–6*

11 [a]Zech. 10:10
12 [a]John 7:35 [1]Heb. *wings*
13 [a]Jer. 3:18; Ezek. 37:16,17,22
14 [a]Dan. 11:41 [1]Heb. *the children of the east* [2]Heb. *Edom and Moab* shall be *the laying on of their hand* [3]Heb. *the children of Ammon their obedience*
15 [a]Zech. 10:11 [b]Rev. 16:12 [1]Heb. *in shoes*
16 [a]ch. 19:23 [b]Ex. 14:29
12:1 [a]ch. 2:11
2 [a]Ps. 83:18 [b]Ex. 15:2; Ps. 118:14
3 [a]John 4:10
4 [a]1 Chr. 16:8; Ps. 105:1 [b]Ps. 145:4-6 [c]Ps. 34:3 [1]Or, *proclaim his name*
5 [a]Ex. 15:1; Ps. 98:1
6 [a]Zeph. 3:14 [b]Ps. 89:18 [1]Heb. *inhabitress*
13:1 [a]Jer. 50 & 51
2 [a]ch. 18:3 [b]Jer. 51:25

Thanksgiving for God's salvation

12 AND [a]IN that day thou shalt say, I
O LORD, I will praise thee: though L
thou wast angry with me, thine anger is
turned away, and thou comfortedst me.
2 Behold, God *is* my salvation; I will W
trust, and not be afraid: for the LORD
[a]JEHOVAH *is* my [b]strength and *my* song;
he also is become my salvation.
3 Therefore with joy shall ye draw S
[a]water out of the wells of salvation.
4 And in that day shall ye say, [a]Praise T
the LORD, [1]call upon his name, [b]declare
his doings among the people, make mention that his [c]name is exalted.
5 [a]Sing unto the LORD; for he hath done
excellent things: this *is* known in all the
earth.
6 [a]Cry out and shout, thou [1]inhabitant I
of Zion: for great *is* [b]the Holy One of Israel in the midst of thee.

The doom of Babylon

13 THE [a]BURDEN of Babylon, P
which Isaiah the son of Amoz did
see.
2 [a]Lift ye up a banner [b]upon the high
mountain, exalt the voice unto them,

I *Isa 11:11–15* ◀ ▶ *Isa 12:6*
L *Isa 9:2* ◀ ▶ *Isa 32:2*
W *Pr 1:33* ◀ ▶ *Isa 26:3–4*
S *Ps 16:11* ◀ ▶ *Isa 25:8*
T *Ps 145:10–12* ◀ ▶ *Isa 43:10*
I *Isa 12:1–6* ◀ ▶ *Isa 18:7*
P *Isa 11:4* ◀ ▶ *Isa 24:1*

11:11–12 At the second coming, Christ will bring about the return of all of the Jews to the promised land. Eight specific areas of the world are named in this passage. Note that this promised return "from the four corners of the earth" (11:12) does not mean that Isaiah taught that the earth was flat. Isaiah also refers to the earth as a sphere in other prophecies (see 40:22). Rather, this metaphor indicates that God will bring his people back from all over the world to resettle the promised land.

11:13–16 The division between the two kingdoms of Israel and Judah will be healed by the return of the Messiah. Aided by God's miraculous intervention, the armies of the reunited kingdom of Israel will march across former rivers to attack their surrounding enemies (see Rev 16:12). Isaiah also foresaw the peaceful millennial kingdom of the Messiah, and described a highway for the Jewish refugees who would return to the promised land.

12:1–6 This prophecy confidently foreshadowed Israel's final deliverance and reconciliation with God. Note also the final fulfillment of the role that God originally intended for his chosen people—to "declare his doings among the people" (12:4).

13:1–22 In this passage, Isaiah prophesied God's final judgment and destruction on Babylon that would occur during "the day of the LORD" (13:6). Though Babylon was initially destroyed by Cyrus the Persian in 539 B.C., its final destruction is announced here and in Rev 14:8; 16:19; 17—18. Paralleling Babylon's devastation with the destruction of Sodom and Gomorrah, Isaiah's words of doom signal the total victory of the Messiah over the satanic forces of the antichrist, prophetically called "the king of Babylon" (14:4).

Though for centuries Arab shepherds have used the region that formerly was the Babylonian empire as a grazing land, the ruins of the city of Babylon lay buried under desert sand and have only recently been discovered by archaeologists. Some Arab nations have begun to rebuild the city, however, in an attempt to restore Babylon to its glory. Isaiah's

[c]shake the hand, that they may go into
the gates of the nobles.
3 I have commanded my sanctified
ones, I have also called [a]my mighty ones
for mine anger, *even* them that [b]rejoice
in my highness.
4 The noise of a multitude in the
mountains, [1]like as of a great people; a
tumultuous noise of the kingdoms of nations gathered together: the LORD of hosts
mustereth the host of the battle.
5 They come from a far country, from
the end of heaven, *even* the LORD, and the
weapons of his indignation, to destroy
the whole land.
H 6 ¶ Howl ye; [a]for the day of the LORD *is*
at hand; [b]it shall come as a destruction
from the Almighty.
7 Therefore shall all hands [1]be faint,
and every man's heart shall melt:
8 And they shall be afraid: [a]pangs and
sorrows shall take hold of them; they
shall be in pain as a woman that travaileth: they shall [1]be amazed [2]one at another; their faces *shall be as* [3]flames.
9 Behold, [a]the day of the LORD cometh,
cruel both with wrath and fierce anger, to
lay the land desolate: and he shall destroy
[b]the sinners thereof out of it.
10 For the stars of heaven and the constellations thereof shall not give their
light: the sun shall be [a]darkened in his
going forth, and the moon shall not cause
her light to shine.
M 11 And I will punish the world for
their evil, and the wicked for their iniquity; [a]and I will cause the arrogancy of
the proud to cease, and will lay low the
haughtiness of the terrible.
12 I will make a man more precious
than fine gold; even a man than the
golden wedge of Ophir.

H *Isa 11:4* ◀▶ *Isa 24:17–23*
M *Isa 10:15* ◀▶ *Isa 46:12*

2 [c]ch. 10:32
3 [a]Joel 3:11 [b]Ps. 149:2
4 [1]Heb. *the likeness of*
6 [a]Zeph. 1:7; Rev. 6:17 [b]Job 31:23; Joel 1:15
7 [1]Or, *fall down*
8 [a]Ps. 48:6 [1]Heb. *wonder* [2]Heb. *every man at his neighbour* [3]Heb. *faces of the flames*
9 [a]Mal. 4:1 [b]Ps. 104:35; Prov. 2:22
10 [a]Ezek. 32:7; Joel 2:31; Mat. 24:29; Mark 13:24
11 [a]ch. 2:17
13 [a]Hag. 2:6 [b]Ps. 110:5; Lam. 1:12
14 [a]Jer. 50:16
16 [a]Ps. 137:9; Nah. 3:10; Zech. 14:2
17 [a]Jer. 51:11; Dan. 5:28
19 [a]ch. 14:4 [b]Gen. 19:24; Deut. 29:23; Jer. 50:40 [1]Heb *as the overthrowing*
20 [a]Jer. 50:3
21 [a]ch. 34:11 [1]Heb. *Ziim* [2]Heb. *Ochim* [3]Or, *ostriches* [4]Heb. *daughters of the owl*
22 [a]Jer. 51:33 [1]Heb. *Iim* [2]Or, *palaces*
14:1 [a]Ps. 102:13 [b]Zech. 1:17 [c]ch. 60:4,5,10

13 [a]Therefore I will shake the heavens, and the earth shall remove out of her
place, in the wrath of the LORD of hosts,
and in [b]the day of his fierce anger.
14 And it shall be as the chased roe,
and as a sheep that no man taketh up:
[a]they shall every man turn to his own
people, and flee every one into his own
land.
15 Every one that is found shall be
thrust through; and every one that is
joined *unto them* shall fall by the sword.
16 Their children also shall be [a]dashed
to pieces before their eyes; their houses
shall be spoiled, and their wives ravished.
17 [a]Behold, I will stir up the Medes
against them, which shall not regard silver; and *as for* gold, they shall not delight
in it.
18 *Their* bows also shall dash the
young men to pieces; and they shall have
no pity on the fruit of the womb; their
eye shall not spare children.
19 ¶ [a]And Babylon, the glory of kingdoms, the beauty of the Chaldees' excellency, shall be [1]as when God overthrew
[b]Sodom and Gomorrah.
20 [a]It shall never be inhabited, neither
shall it be dwelt in from generation to
generation: neither shall the Arabian
pitch tent there; neither shall the shepherds make their fold there.
21 [a]But [1]wild beasts of the desert shall
lie there; and their houses shall be full of
[2]doleful creatures; and [3,4]owls shall dwell
there, and satyrs shall dance there.
22 And [1]the wild beasts of the islands
shall cry in their [2]desolate houses, and
dragons in *their* pleasant palaces: [a]and
her time *is* near to come, and her days
shall not be prolonged.

14

FOR THE LORD [a]will have mercy
on Jacob, and [b]will yet choose Israel, and set them in their own land:
[c]and the strangers shall be joined with

---

prediction that no Arab will pitch a tent in that region (13:20) has not been fulfilled yet in history and therefore must refer to Babylon's final destruction when Christ returns to defeat the forces of Satan at Armageddon.

14:1–27 God promised that Babylon's fall would be linked to the nation's restoration. Despite their coming judgment and exile, God would ultimately "have mercy on Jacob"(14:1). In this taunt, Isaiah prophesied that the grave would welcome the wicked king of Babylon (14:9) as he is brought down at the hand of God. Isaiah also refers to this wicked ruler as "the Assyrian" (14:25), a title used earlier to refer to the antichrist (see 10:5).

Note also that the list of the sins of the king of Babylon can be directly attributed to Satan (14:13–14). Addressed as the "son of the morning" (14:12), Satan, the antichrist, desired to become like God and set his throne up "above the stars of God" (14:13). Satan's sinful pride is the essence of all sin—the desire to become as gods (see Ge 3:5).

them, and they shall cleave to the house of Jacob.

M 2 And the people shall take them, [a]and bring them to their place: and the house of Israel shall possess them in the land of the LORD for servants and handmaids: and they shall take them captives, [1]whose captives they were; [b]and they shall rule over their oppressors.

3 And it shall come to pass in the day that the LORD shall give thee rest from thy sorrow, and from thy fear, and from the hard bondage wherein thou wast made to serve,

4 ¶ That thou [a]shalt take up this [1]proverb against the king of Babylon, and say, How hath the oppressor ceased! the [b]golden[2] city ceased!

5 The LORD hath broken [a]the staff of the wicked, *and* the sceptre of the rulers.

6 He who smote the people in wrath with [1]a continual stroke, he that ruled the nations in anger, is persecuted, *and* none hindereth.

7 The whole earth is at rest, *and* is quiet: they break forth into singing.

8 [a]Yea, the fir trees rejoice at thee, *and* the cedars of Lebanon, *saying,* Since thou art laid down, no feller is come up against us.

9 [a]Hell[1] from beneath is moved for thee to meet *thee* at thy coming: it stirreth up the dead for thee, *even* all the [2,3]chief ones of the earth; it hath raised up from their thrones all the kings of the nations.

10 All they shall speak and say unto thee, Art thou also become weak as we? art thou become like unto us?

11 Thy pomp is brought down to the grave, *and* the noise of thy viols: the worm is spread under thee, and the worms cover thee.

12 [a]How art thou fallen from heaven, [1]O Lucifer, son of the morning! *how* art thou cut down to the ground, which didst weaken the nations!

13 For thou hast said in thine heart, [a]I will ascend into heaven, [b]I will exalt my throne above the stars of God: I will sit also upon the mount of the congregation, [c]in the sides of the north:

14 I will ascend above the heights of the clouds: [a]I will be like the most High.

15 Yet thou [a]shalt be brought down to hell, to the sides of the pit.

16 They that see thee shall narrowly look upon thee, *and* consider thee, *saying, Is* this the man that made the earth to tremble, that did shake kingdoms;

17 *That* made the world as a wilderness, and destroyed the cities thereof; *that* [1]opened not the house of his prisoners?

18 All the kings of the nations, *even* all of them, lie in glory, every one in his own house.

19 But thou art cast out of thy grave like an abominable branch, *and as* the raiment of those that are slain, thrust through with a sword, that go down to the stones of the pit; as a carcase trodden under feet.

20 Thou shalt not be joined with them in burial, because thou hast destroyed thy land, *and* slain thy people: [a]the seed of evildoers shall never be renowned.

21 Prepare slaughter for his children [a]for the iniquity of their fathers; that they do not rise, nor possess the land, nor fill the face of the world with cities.

22 For I will rise up against them, saith the LORD of hosts, and cut off from Babylon [a]the name, and [b]remnant, [c]and son, and nephew, saith the LORD.

23 [a]I will also make it a possession for the bittern, and pools of water: and I will sweep it with the besom of destruction, saith the LORD of hosts.

The overthrow of Assyria

24 ¶ The LORD of hosts hath sworn, saying, Surely as I have thought, so shall it come to pass; and as I have purposed, *so* shall it stand:

25 That I will break the Assyrian in my land, and upon my mountains tread him under foot: then shall [a]his yoke depart from off them, and his burden depart from off their shoulders.

26 This *is* the purpose that is purposed upon the whole earth: and this *is* the hand that is stretched out upon all the nations.

27 For the LORD of hosts hath [a]purposed, and who shall disannul *it?* and his hand *is* stretched out, and who shall turn it back?

2 [a]ch. 49:22 & 60:9 & 66:20 [b]ch. 60:14 [1]Heb. *that had taken them captives*
4 [a]ch. 13:19; Hab. 2:6 [b]Rev. 18:16 [1]Or, *taunting speech* [2]Or, *exactress of gold*
5 [a]Ps. 125:3
6 [1]Heb. *a stroke without removing*
8 [a]ch. 55:12; Ezek. 31:16
9 [a]Ezek. 32:21 [1]Or, *The grave* [2]Heb. *leaders* [3]Or, *great goats*
12 [a]ch. 34:4 [1]Or, *O day star*
13 [a]Mat. 11:23 [b]Dan. 8:10 [c]Ps. 48:2
14 [a]ch. 47:8; 2 Thes. 2:4
15 [a]Mat. 11:23
17 [1]Or, *did not let his prisoners loose homewards?*
20 [a]Job 18:19; Ps. 21:10 & 37:28 & 109:13
21 [a]Ex. 20:5; Mat. 23:35
22 [a]Prov. 10:7; Jer. 51:62 [b]1 Ki. 14:10 [c]Job 18:19
23 [a]ch. 34:11; Zeph. 2:14
25 [a]ch. 10:27
27 [a]2 Chr. 20:6; Job 9:12 & 23:13; Ps. 33:11; Prov. 19:21 & 21:30; ch. 43:13; Dan. 4:31, 35

A burden about Palestina

R 28 In the year that [a]king Ahaz died was this burden.

29 ¶ Rejoice not thou, whole Palestina, [a]because the rod of him that smote thee is broken: for out of the serpent's root shall come forth a [1]cockatrice, [b]and his fruit *shall be* a fiery flying serpent.

30 And the firstborn of the poor shall feed, and the needy shall lie down in safety: and I will kill thy root with famine, and he shall slay thy remnant.

31 Howl, O gate; cry, O city; thou, whole Palestina, *art* dissolved: for there shall come from the north a smoke, and [1]none *shall be* alone in his [2]appointed times.

32 What shall *one* then answer the messengers of the nation? That [a]the LORD hath founded Zion, and [b]the poor of his people shall [1]trust in it.

Moab's devastation

J **15** THE [a]BURDEN of Moab. Because in the night [b]Ar of Moab is laid waste, *and* [1]brought to silence; because in the night Kir of Moab is laid waste, *and* brought to silence;

2 He is gone up to Bajith, and to Dibon, the high places, to weep: Moab shall howl over Nebo, and over Medeba: [a]on all their heads *shall be* baldness, *and* every beard cut off.

3 In their streets they shall gird themselves with sackcloth: on the tops of their houses, and in their streets, every one shall howl, [1]weeping abundantly.

4 And Heshbon shall cry, and Elealeh: their voice shall be heard *even* unto Jahaz: therefore the armed soldiers of Moab shall cry out; his life shall be grievous unto him.

5 [a]My heart shall cry out for Moab; [1]his fugitives *shall flee* unto Zoar, an heifer of three years old: for [b]by the mounting up of Luhith with weeping shall they go it up; for in the way of Horonaim they shall raise up a cry of [2]destruction.

6 For the waters [a]of Nimrim shall be [1]desolate: for the hay is withered away, the grass faileth, there is no green thing.

7 Therefore the abundance they have gotten, and that which they have laid up, shall they carry away to the [1]brook of the willows.

8 For the cry is gone round about the borders of Moab; the howling thereof unto Eglaim, and the howling thereof unto Beer-elim.

9 For the waters of Dimon shall be full of blood: for I will bring [1]more upon Dimon, [a]lions upon him that escapeth of Moab, and upon the remnant of the land.

16 SEND [a]YE the lamb to the ruler of the land [b]from [1]Sela to the wilderness, unto the mount of the daughter of Zion.

2 For it shall be, *that,* as a wandering bird [1]cast out of the nest, *so* the daughters of Moab shall be at the fords of [a]Arnon.

3 [1]Take counsel, execute judgment; make thy shadow as the night in the midst of the noonday; hide the outcasts; betray not him that wandereth.

4 Let mine outcasts dwell with thee, Moab; be thou a covert to them from the face of the spoiler: for the [1]extortioner is at an end, the spoiler ceaseth, [2]the oppressors are consumed out of the land.

5 And in mercy [a]shall the throne be M [1]established: and he shall sit upon it in truth in the tabernacle of David, [b]judging, and seeking judgment, and hasting righteousness.

6 ¶ We have heard of the [a]pride of Moab; *he is* very proud: *even* of his haughtiness, and his pride, and his wrath: [b]*but* his lies *shall* not *be* so.

7 Therefore shall Moab [a]howl for

28 [a]2 Ki. 16:20
29 [a]2 Chr. 26:6 [b]2 Ki. 18:8 [1]Or, *adder*
31 [1]Or, he shall *not be alone* [2]Or, *assemblies*
32 [a]Ps. 87:1,5 [b]Zech. 11:11 [1]Or, *betake themselves unto it*
15:1 [a]Jer. 48:1 [b]Num. 21:28 [1]Or, *cut off*
2 [a]Lev. 21:5
3 [1]Heb. *descending into weeping,* or, *coming down with weeping*
5 [a]Jer. 48:31 [b]Jer. 48:5 [1]Or, *to the borders thereof, even to Zoar,* as an *heifer* [2]Heb. *breaking*
6 [a]Num. 32:36 [1]Heb. *desolations*
7 [1]Or, *valley of the Arabians*
9 [a]2 Ki. 17:25 [1]Heb. *additions*
16:1 [a]2 Ki. 3:4 [b]2 Ki. 14:7 [1]Or, Petra Heb. *A rock*
2 [a]Num. 21:13 [1]Or, *a nest forsaken*
3 [1]Heb. *Bring*
4 [1]Heb. *wringer* [2]Heb. *the treaders down*
5 [a]Luke 1:33 [b]Ps. 72:2 [1]Or, *prepared*
6 [a]Jer. 48:29 [b]ch. 28:15
7 [a]Jer. 48:20

R *Isa 10:22–27* ◀ ▶ *Isa 17:9–11*
J *Isa 10:33–34* ◀ ▶ *Isa 20:1–6*
M *Isa 14:2* ◀ ▶ *Isa 24:13–15*

14:29–31 Isaiah also predicted the coming judgment of God upon the wicked inhabitants of Palestine, involving famine and war with their northern enemies. This prophecy was fulfilled in a succession of Assyrian invasions of Israel under the Assyrian King Shalmaneser and his successor King Sargon (727–705 B.C.).

16:1–5 The immediate explanation of these verses concerned the nation of Moab. Sela was the fortified capital of Edom, situated on a cliff overlooking nearby Petra (see 42:11). Moabite refugees had settled in Sela and had requested asylum in Israel. The interpretation of this passage with a view to the future suggests that refugees will once again seek asylum in Israel and that Gentile nations will participate in the Millennium.

Moab, every one shall howl: for the foundations [b]of Kir-hareseth shall ye [l]mourn; surely *they are* stricken.

8 For [a]the fields of Heshbon languish, *and* [b]the vine of Sibmah: the lords of the heathen have broken down the principal plants thereof, they are come *even* unto Jazer, they wandered *through* the wilderness: her branches are [l]stretched out, they are gone over the sea.

9 ¶ Therefore I will bewail with the weeping of Jazer the vine of Sibmah: I will water thee with my tears, [a]O Heshbon, and Elealeh: for [l]the shouting for thy summer fruits and for thy harvest is fallen.

10 And [a]gladness is taken away, and joy out of the plentiful field; and in the vineyards there shall be no singing, neither shall there be shouting: the treaders shall tread out no wine in *their* presses; I have made *their vintage* shouting to cease.

11 Wherefore [a]my bowels shall sound like an harp for Moab, and mine inward parts for Kir-haresh.

12 ¶ And it shall come to pass, when it is seen that Moab is weary on [a]the high place, that he shall come to his sanctuary to pray; but he shall not prevail.

13 This *is* the word that the LORD hath spoken concerning Moab since that time.

14 But now the LORD hath spoken, saying, Within three years, [a]as the years of an hireling, and the glory of Moab shall be contemned, with all that great multitude; and the remnant *shall be* very small *and* [l]feeble.

Crushing of Damascus

17 THE [a]BURDEN of Damascus. Behold, Damascus is taken away from *being* a city, and it shall be a ruinous heap.

2 The cities of Aroer *are* forsaken: they shall be for flocks, which shall lie down, and [a]none shall make *them* afraid.

3 [a]The fortress also shall cease from Ephraim, and the kingdom from Damascus, and the remnant of Syria: they shall be as the glory of the children of Israel, saith the LORD of hosts.

4 And in that day it shall come to pass, *that* the glory of Jacob shall be made thin, and [a]the fatness of his flesh shall wax lean.

5 [a]And it shall be as when the harvestman gathereth the corn, and reapeth the ears with his arm; and it shall be as he that gathereth ears in the valley of Rephaim.

6 ¶ [a]Yet gleaning grapes shall be left in it, as the shaking of an olive tree, two *or* three berries in the top of the uppermost bough, four *or* five in the outmost fruitful branches thereof, saith the LORD God of Israel.

7 At that day shall a man [a]look to his Maker, and his eyes shall have respect to the Holy One of Israel.

8 And he shall not look to the altars, the work of his hands, neither shall respect *that* which his fingers have made, either the groves, or the [l]images.

9 ¶ In that day shall his strong cities be as a forsaken bough, and an uppermost branch, which they left because of the children of Israel: and there shall be desolation. **R**

10 Because thou hast forgotten [a]the God of thy salvation, and hast not been mindful of the rock of thy strength, therefore shalt thou plant pleasant plants, and shalt set it with strange slips:

11 In the day shalt thou make thy plant to grow, and in the morning shalt thou make thy seed to flourish: *but* the harvest *shall be* [l]a heap in the day of grief and of desperate sorrow.

12 ¶ Woe to the [l]multitude of many people, *which* make a noise [a]like the noise of the seas; and to the rushing of nations, *that* make a rushing like the rushing of [2]mighty waters!

13 The nations shall rush like the rushing of many waters: but *God* shall [a]rebuke them, and they shall flee far off, and [b]shall be chased as the chaff of the mountains before the wind, and like [l]a rolling thing before the whirlwind.

14 And behold at eveningtide trouble; *and* before the morning he *is* not. This *is*

R *Isa 14:28–31* ◄► *Isa 18:2*

7 [b]2 Ki. 3:25 [l]Or, *mutter*
8 [a]ch. 24:7 [b]ver. 9 [l]Or, *plucked up*
9 [a]ch. 15:4 [l]Or, *the alarm is fallen upon*
10 [a]ch. 24:8; Jer. 48:33
11 [a]Jer. 48:36
12 [a]ch. 15:2
14 [a]ch. 21:16 [l]Or, *not many*
17:1 [a]Jer. 49:23; Amos 1:3; Zech. 9:1
2 [a]Jer. 7:33
3 [a]ch. 7:16 & 8:4
4 [a]ch. 10:16
5 [a]Jer. 51:33
6 [a]ch. 24:13
7 [a]Mic. 7:7
8 [l]Or, *sun images*
10 [a]Ps. 68:19
11 [l]Or, *removed in the day of inheritance, and there shall be deadly sorrow*
12 [a]Jer. 6:23 [l]Or, *noise* [2]Or, *many*
13 [a]Ps. 9:5 [b]Ps. 88:13; Hos. 13:3 [l]Or, *thistledown*

17:1 Isaiah directed his prophecy to Damascus, the capital city of Syria, declaring that "it shall be a ruinous heap" (17:1). Compare this prophecy against the nation's enemy with Jer 49:27.

17:9–11 God declared that he would reject his people because of their sins.

the portion of them that spoil us, and the lot of them that rob us.

An oracle about Ethiopia

18 WOE [a]TO the land shadowing with wings, which *is* beyond the rivers of Ethiopia:

R 2 That sendeth ambassadors by the sea, even in vessels of bulrushes upon the waters, *saying,* Go, ye swift messengers, to [a]a nation [1]scattered and peeled, to a people terrible from their beginning hitherto; [2,3]a nation meted out and trodden down, [4]whose land the rivers have spoiled!

3 All ye inhabitants of the world, and dwellers on the earth, see ye, [a]when he lifteth up an ensign on the mountains; and when he bloweth a trumpet, hear ye.

4 For so the LORD said unto me, I will take my rest, and I will [1]consider in my dwellingplace like a clear heat [2]upon herbs, *and* like a cloud of dew in the heat of harvest.

5 For afore the harvest, when the bud is perfect, and the sour grape is ripening in the flower, he shall both cut off the sprigs with pruning hooks, and take away *and* cut down the branches.

6 They shall be left together unto the fowls of the mountains, and to the beasts of the earth: and the fowls shall summer upon them, and all the beasts of the earth shall winter upon them.

I 7 ¶ In that time [a]shall the present be brought unto the LORD of hosts of a people [b]scattered[1] and peeled, and from a people terrible from their beginning hitherto; a nation meted out and trodden under foot, whose land the rivers have spoiled, to the place of the name of the LORD of hosts, the mount Zion.

The doom of Egypt

19 THE [a]BURDEN of Egypt. Behold, the LORD [b]rideth upon a swift cloud, and shall come into Egypt: and [c]the idols of Egypt shall be moved at his presence, and the heart of Egypt shall melt in the midst of it.

2 And I will [a]set[1] the Egyptians against the Egyptians: and they shall fight every one against his brother, and every one against his neighbour; city against city, *and* kingdom against kingdom.

3 And the spirit of Egypt [1]shall fail in the midst thereof; and I will [2]destroy the counsel thereof: and they shall [a]seek to the idols, and to the charmers, and to them that have familiar spirits, and to the wizards.

4 And the Egyptians will I [1]give over [a]into the hand of a cruel lord; and a fierce king shall rule over them, saith the Lord, the LORD of hosts.

5 [a]And the waters shall fail from the sea, and the river shall be wasted and dried up.

6 And they shall turn the rivers far away; *and* the brooks [a]of defence shall be emptied and dried up: the reeds and flags shall wither.

7 The paper reeds by the brooks, by the mouth of the brooks, and every thing sown by the brooks, shall wither, be driven away, [1]and be no *more.*

8 The fishers also shall mourn, and all they that cast angle into the brooks shall lament, and they that spread nets upon the waters shall languish.

9 Moreover they that work in [a]fine flax, and they that weave [1]networks, shall be confounded.

10 And they shall be broken in the [1]purposes thereof, all that make sluices *and* ponds [2]for fish.

11 ¶ Surely the princes of [a]Zoan *are* fools, the counsel of the wise counsellors of Pharaoh is become brutish: how say ye unto Pharaoh, I *am* the son of the wise, the son of ancient kings?

12 [a]Where *are* they? where *are* thy wise *men?* and let them tell thee now, and let them know what the LORD of hosts hath purposed upon Egypt.

13 The princes of Zoan are become fools, [a]the princes of Noph are deceived; they have also seduced Egypt, *even*

18:1 [a]ch. 20:4,5; Ezek. 30:4,5,9; Zeph. 2:12 & 3:10
2 [a]ver. 7 [1]Or, *outspread and polished* [2]Or, *a nation that meteth out, and treadeth down* [3]Heb. *a nation of line, line, and treading under foot* [4]Or, *whose land the rivers despise*
3 [a]ch. 5:26
4 [1]Or, *regard my set dwelling* [2]Or, *after rain*
7 [a]See Ps. 68:31 & 72:10; ch. 16:1; Zeph. 3:10; Mal. 1:11 [b]ver. 2 [1]Or, *outspread and polished*
19:1 [a]Jer. 46:13; Ezek. 29 & 30 [b]Ps. 18:10 & 104:3 [c]Ex. 12:12; Jer. 43:12
2 [a]Judg. 7:22; 1 Sam. 14:16,20; 2 Chr. 20:23 [1]Heb. *mingle*
3 [a]ch. 8:19 & 47:12 [1]Heb. *shall be emptied* [2]Heb. *swallow up*
4 [a]ch. 20:4; Jer. 46:26; Ezek. 29:19 [1]Or, *shut up*
5 [a]Jer. 51:36; Ezek. 30:12
6 [a]2 Ki. 19:24
7 [1]Heb. *and shall not be*
9 [a]1 Ki. 10:28; Prov. 7:16 [1]Or, *white works*
10 [1]Heb. *foundations* [2]Heb. *of living things*
11 [a]Num. 13:22
12 [a]1 Cor. 1:20
13 [a]Jer. 2:16

R *Isa 17:9–11* ◀ ▶ *Isa 22:17–19*
I *Isa 12:6* ◀ ▶ *Isa 25:8–10*

18:2–4 The Cushites were an ancient Ethiopian dynasty established in Egypt c. 714 B.C. (This nation is not to be confused with modern-day Ethiopia that is further to the southeast than ancient Cush.) Some believe that the ark of the covenant survived Nebuchadnezzar's destruction of the temple and accompanied the remnant of Jews who fled to Egypt (Cush).

[1,2]*they that are* the stay of the tribes thereof.

14 The LORD hath mingled [a]a [1] perverse spirit in the midst thereof: and they have caused Egypt to err in every work thereof, as a drunken *man* staggereth in his vomit.

15 Neither shall there be *any* work for Egypt, which [a]the head or tail, branch or rush, may do.

16 In that day shall Egypt [a]be like unto women: and it shall be afraid and fear because of the shaking of the hand of the LORD of hosts, [b]which he shaketh over it.

17 And the land of Judah shall be a terror unto Egypt, every one that maketh mention thereof shall be afraid in himself, because of the counsel of the LORD of hosts, which he hath determined against it.

18 ¶ In that day shall five cities in the land of Egypt [a]speak [1]the language of Canaan, and swear to the LORD of hosts; one shall be called, The city [2]of destruction.

19 In that day [a]shall there be an altar to the LORD in the midst of the land of Egypt, and a pillar at the border thereof to the LORD.

20 And [a]it shall be for a sign and for a witness unto the LORD of hosts in the land of Egypt: for they shall cry unto the LORD because of the oppressors, and he shall send them a saviour, and a great one, and he shall deliver them.

21 And the LORD shall be known to Egypt, and the Egyptians shall know the LORD in that day, and [a]shall do sacrifice and oblation; yea, they shall vow a vow unto the LORD, and perform *it.*

22 And the LORD shall smite Egypt: he shall smite and heal *it:* and they shall return *even* to the LORD, and he shall be entreated of them, and shall heal them.

23 ¶ In that day [a]shall there be a highway out of Egypt to Assyria, and the Assyrian shall come into Egypt, and the Egyptian into Assyria, and the Egyptians shall serve with the Assyrians.

24 In that day shall Israel be the third with Egypt and with Assyria, *even* a blessing in the midst of the land:

25 Whom the LORD of hosts shall bless, saying, Blessed *be* Egypt my people, and Assyria [a]the work of my hands, and Israel mine inheritance.

20 IN THE year that [a]Tartan came unto Ashdod, (when Sargon the king of Assyria sent him,) and fought against Ashdod, and took it; J

2 At the same time spake the LORD [1]by Isaiah the son of Amoz, saying, Go and loose [a]the sackcloth from off thy loins, and put off thy shoe from thy foot. And he did so, [b]walking naked and barefoot.

3 And the LORD said, Like as my servant Isaiah hath walked naked and barefoot three years [a]*for* a sign and wonder upon Egypt and upon Ethiopia;

4 So shall the king of Assyria lead away [1]the Egyptians prisoners, and the Ethiopians captives, young and old, naked and barefoot, [a]even with *their* buttocks uncovered, to the [2]shame of Egypt.

5 [a]And they shall be afraid and ashamed of Ethiopia their expectation, and of Egypt their glory.

6 And the inhabitant of this [1]isle shall say in that day, Behold, such *is* our expectation, whither we flee for help to be delivered from the king of Assyria: and how shall we escape?

Elam and Media defeat Babylon

21 THE BURDEN of the desert of the sea. As [a]whirlwinds in the south pass through; *so* it cometh from the desert, from a terrible land.

2 A [1]grievous vision is declared unto me; [a]the treacherous dealer dealeth treacherously, and the spoiler spoileth. [b]Go up, O Elam: besiege, O Media; all the sighing thereof have I made to cease.

3 Therefore [a]are my loins filled with pain: [b]pangs have taken hold upon me, as the pangs of a woman that travaileth: I was bowed down at the hearing *of it;* I was dismayed at the seeing *of it.*

4 [1]My heart panted, fearfulness affrighted me: [a]the night of my pleasure hath he [2]turned into fear unto me.

5 [a]Prepare the table, watch in the

J *Isa 15:1–9* ◀ ▶ *Isa 21:13–16*

13 [1]Or, *governors* [2]Heb. *corners*
14 [a]1 Ki. 22:22; ch. 29:10 [1]Heb. *a spirit of perverseness*
15 [a]ch. 9:14
16 [a]Jer. 51:30; Nah. 3:13 [b]ch. 11:15
18 [a]Zeph. 3:9 [1]Heb. *the lip* [2]Or, *of Heres,* or, *of the sun*
19 [a]Gen. 28:18; Ex. 24:4; Josh. 22:10,26,27
20 [a]Josh. 4:20 & 22:27
21 [a]Mal. 1:11
23 [a]ch. 11:16
25 [a]Ps. 100:3; ch. 29:23; Hos. 2:23; Eph. 2:10
20:1 [a]2 Ki. 18:17
2 [a]Zech. 13:4 [b]1 Sam. 19:24; Mic. 1:8,11 [1]Heb. *by the hand of Isaiah*
3 [a]ch. 8:18
4 [a]2 Sam. 10:4; ch. 3:17; Jer. 13:22; Mic. 1:11 [1]Heb. *the captivity of Egypt* [2]Heb. *nakedness*
5 [a]2 Ki. 18:21
6 [1]Or, *country*
21:1 [a]Zech. 9:14
2 [a]ch. 33:1 [b]ch. 13:17; Jer. 49:34 [1]Heb. *hard*
3 [a]ch. 15:5 & 16:11 [b]ch. 13:8
4 [a]Deut. 28:67 [1]Or, *My mind wandered* [2]Heb. *put*
5 [a]Dan. 5:5

19:18 This prophecy suggested that the entire land of Egypt would one day worship the true God. The "city of destruction" was probably a reference to Heliopolis, the center of worship for the Egyptian sun god that was destroyed by Nebuchadnezzar (see Jer 43:12–13).

watchtower, eat, drink: arise, ye princes, *and* anoint the shield.

6 For thus hath the Lord said unto me, Go, set a watchman, let him declare what he seeth.

7 [a]And he saw a chariot *with* a couple of horsemen, a chariot of asses, *and* a chariot of camels; and he hearkened diligently with much heed:

8 And [1]he cried, A lion: My lord, I stand continually upon the [a]watchtower in the daytime, and I am set in my ward [2]whole nights:

9 And, behold, here cometh a chariot of men, *with* a couple of horsemen. And he answered and said, [a]Babylon is fallen, is fallen; and [b]all the graven images of her gods he hath broken unto the ground.

10 [a]O my threshing, and the [1]corn of my floor: that which I have heard of the LORD of hosts, the God of Israel, have I declared unto you.

11 ¶ [a]The burden of Dumah. He calleth to me out of Seir, Watchman, what of the night? Watchman, what of the night?

12 The watchman said, The morning cometh, and also the night: if ye will inquire, inquire ye: return, come.

J

13 ¶ [a]The burden upon Arabia. In the forest in Arabia shall ye lodge, O ye travelling companies [b]of Dedanim.

14 The inhabitants of the land of Tema [1]brought water to him that was thirsty, they prevented with their bread him that fled.

15 For they fled [1,2]from the swords, from the drawn sword, and from the bent bow, and from the grievousness of war.

16 For thus hath the Lord said unto me, Within a year, [a]according to the years of an hireling, and all the glory of [b]Kedar shall fail:

17 And the residue of the number of [1]archers, the mighty men of the children of Kedar, shall be diminished: for the LORD God of Israel hath spoken *it.*

A burden about Jerusalem

22 THE BURDEN of the valley of vision. What aileth thee now, that thou art wholly gone up to the housetops?

2 Thou that art full of stirs, a tumultuous city, [a]a joyous city: thy slain *men are* not slain with the sword, nor dead in battle.

3 All thy rulers are fled together, they are bound [1]by the archers: all that are found in thee are bound together, *which* have fled from far.

4 Therefore said I, Look away from me; [a]I[1] will weep bitterly, labour not to comfort me, because of the spoiling of the daughter of my people.

5 [a]For *it is* a day of trouble, and of treading down, and of perplexity [b]by the Lord GOD of hosts in the valley of vision, breaking down the walls, and of crying to the mountains.

6 [a]And Elam bare the quiver with chariots of men *and* horsemen, and [b]Kir [1]uncovered the shield.

7 And it shall come to pass, *that* [1]thy choicest valleys shall be full of chariots, and the horsemen shall set themselves in array [2]at the gate.

8 ¶ And he discovered the covering of Judah, and thou didst look in that day to the armour [a]of the house of the forest.

9 [a]Ye have seen also the breaches of the city of David, that they are many: and ye gathered together the waters of the lower pool.

10 And ye have numbered the houses of Jerusalem, and the houses have ye broken down to fortify the wall.

11 [a]Ye made also a ditch between the two walls for the water of the old pool: but ye have not looked unto the maker thereof, neither had respect unto him that fashioned it long ago.

12 And in that day did the Lord GOD of hosts [a]call to weeping, and to mourning, and [b]to baldness, and to girding with sackcloth:

13 And behold joy and gladness, slaying oxen, and killing sheep, eating flesh, and drinking wine: [a]let us eat and drink; for tomorrow we shall die.

14 [a]And it was revealed in mine ears by the LORD of hosts, Surely this iniquity [b]shall not be purged from you till ye die, saith the Lord GOD of hosts.

15 ¶ Thus saith the Lord GOD of hosts, Go, get thee unto this treasurer, *even* unto [a]Shebna, which *is* over the house, *and say,*

16 What hast thou here? and whom hast thou here, that thou hast hewed thee out a sepulchre here, [1]*as* he [a]that heweth him out a sepulchre on high, *and*

7 [a]ver. 9

8 [a]Hab. 2:1 [1]Or, *cried as a lion* [2]Or, *every night*

9 [a]Jer. 51:8; Rev. 14:8 & 18:2 [b]ch. 46:1; Jer. 50:2 & 51:44

10 [a]Jer. 51:33 [1]Heb. *son*

11 [a]1 Chr. 1:30; Jer. 49:7,8; Ezek. 35:2; Obad. 1

13 [a]Jer. 49:28 [b]1 Chr. 1:9

14 [1]Or, *bring ye*

15 [1]Or, *for fear* [2]Heb. *from the face*

16 [a]ch. 16:14 [b]Ps. 120:5; ch. 60:7

17 [1]Heb. *bows*

22:2 [a]ch. 32:13

3 [1]Heb. *of the bow*

4 [a]Jer. 4:19 [1]Heb. *I will be bitter in weeping*

5 [a]ch. 37:3 [b]Lam. 1:5

6 [a]Jer. 49:35 [b]ch. 15:1 [1]Heb. *made naked*

7 [1]Heb. *the choice of thy valleys* [2]Or, *toward*

8 [a]1 Ki. 7:2 & 10:17

9 [a]2 Ki. 20:20; 2 Chr. 32:4

11 [a]Neh. 3:16

12 [a]Joel 1:13 [b]See Ezra 9:3; ch. 15:2; Mic. 1:16

13 [a]ch. 56:12; 1 Cor. 15:32

14 [a]ch. 5:9 [b]1 Sam. 3:14; Ezek. 24:13

15 [a]2 Ki. 18:37; ch. 36:3

16 [a]See 2 Sam. 18:18; Mat. 27:60 [1]Or, *O he*

J *Isa 20:1–6* ◀ ▶ *Isa 23:1–17*

that graveth an habitation for himself in a rock?

R 17 Behold, [1]the LORD will carry thee away with [2]a mighty captivity, [a]and will surely cover thee.

18 He will surely violently turn and toss thee *like* a ball into a [1]large country: there shalt thou die, and there the chariots of thy glory *shall be* the shame of thy lord's house.

19 And I will drive thee from thy station, and from thy state shall he pull thee down.

20 ¶ And it shall come to pass in that day, that I will call my servant [a]Eliakim the son of Hilkiah:

21 And I will clothe him with thy robe, and strengthen him with thy girdle, and I will commit thy government into his hand: and he shall be a father to the inhabitants of Jerusalem, and to the house of Judah.

22 And the key of the house of David will I lay upon his shoulder; so he shall [a]open, and none shall shut; and he shall shut, and none shall open.

23 And I will fasten him *as* [a]a nail in a sure place; and he shall be for a glorious throne to his father's house.

24 And they shall hang upon him all the glory of his father's house, the offspring and the issue, all vessels of small quantity, from the vessels of cups, even to all the [1]vessels of flagons.

25 In that day, saith the LORD of hosts, shall the nail that is fastened in the sure place be removed, and be cut down, and fall; and the burden that *was* upon it shall be cut off: for the LORD hath spoken *it.*

A burden about Tyre

J **23** THE [a]BURDEN of Tyre. Howl, ye ships of Tarshish; for it is laid waste, so that there is no house, no entering in: [b]from the land of Chittim it is revealed to them.

2 Be [1]still, ye inhabitants of the isle; thou whom the merchants of Zidon, that pass over the sea, have replenished.

3 And by great waters the seed of Sihor, the harvest of the river, *is* her revenue; and [a]she is a mart of nations.

4 Be thou ashamed, O Zidon: for the sea hath spoken, *even* the strength of the sea, saying, I travail not, nor bring forth children, neither do I nourish up young men, *nor* bring up virgins.

5 [a]As at the report concerning Egypt, *so* shall they be sorely pained at the report of Tyre.

6 Pass ye over to Tarshish; howl, ye inhabitants of the isle.

7 *Is* this your [a]joyous *city,* whose antiquity *is* of ancient days? her own feet shall carry her [1]afar off to sojourn.

8 Who hath taken this counsel against Tyre, [a]the crowning *city,* whose merchants *are* princes, whose traffickers *are* the honourable of the earth?

9 The LORD of hosts hath purposed it, [1]to stain the pride of all glory, *and* to bring into contempt all the honourable of the earth.

10 Pass through thy land as a river, O daughter of Tarshish: *there is* no more [1]strength.

11 He stretched out his hand over the sea, he shook the kingdoms: the LORD hath given a commandment [1]against [2]the merchant *city,* to destroy the [3]strong holds thereof.

12 And he said, [a]Thou shalt no more rejoice, O thou oppressed virgin, daughter of Zidon: arise, [b]pass over to Chittim; there also shalt thou have no rest.

13 Behold the land of the Chaldeans; this people was not, *till* the Assyrian founded it for [a]them that dwell in the wilderness: they set up the towers thereof, they raised up the palaces thereof; *and* he brought it to ruin.

14 Howl, ye ships of Tarshish: for your strength is laid waste.

15 And it shall come to pass in that day, that Tyre shall be forgotten seventy years, according to the days of one king: after the end of seventy years [1]shall Tyre sing as an harlot.

16 Take an harp, go about the city, thou harlot that hast been forgotten; make sweet melody, sing many songs, that thou mayest be remembered.

17 ¶ And it shall come to pass after the

22:17 [a]Esth. 7:8 [1]Or, *the LORD who covered thee with an excellent covering, and clothed thee gorgeously, shall surely* [2]Heb. *the captivity of a man*
18 [1]Heb. *large of spaces*
20 [a]2 Ki. 18:18
22 [a]Job 12:14
23 [a]Ezra 9:8
24 [1]Or, *instruments of viols*
23:1 [a]Jer. 25:22 & 47:4; Ezek. 26 & 27 & 28; Amos 1:9; Zech. 9:2,4 [b]ver. 12
2 [1]Heb. *silent*
3 [a]Ezek. 27:3
5 [a]ch. 19:16
7 [a]ch. 22:2 [1]Heb. *from afar off*
8 [a]See Ezek. 28:2, 12
9 [1]Heb. *to pollute*
10 [1]Heb. *girdle*
11 [1]Or, *concerning a merchantman* [2]Heb. *Canaan* [3]Or, *strengths*
12 [a]Rev. 18:22 [b]ver. 1
13 [a]Ps. 72:9
15 [1]Heb. *it shall be unto Tyre as the song of an harlot*

R *Isa 18:2* ◄► *Isa 26:15–17*
J *Isa 21:13–16* ◄► *Isa 30:5–7*

22:17–19 This prophecy was spoken to one of the officials in Hezekiah's court who coveted a tomb worthy of a king (22:16; see 2Ch 16:14).

end of seventy years, that the LORD will
visit Tyre, and she shall turn to her hire,
and [a]shall commit fornication with all the
kingdoms of the world upon the face of
the earth.
18 And her merchandise and her hire
[a]shall be holiness to the LORD: it shall not
be treasured nor laid up; for her merchandise shall be for them that dwell before the LORD, to eat sufficiently, and for
[1]durable clothing.

Judgment for universal sin

P 24 BEHOLD, THE LORD maketh the
earth empty, and maketh it
waste, and [1]turneth it upside down, and
scattereth abroad the inhabitants thereof.
2 And it shall be, as with the people,
so with the [a]priest;[1] as with the servant,
so with his master; as with the maid,
so with her mistress; [b]as with the buyer, so
with the seller; as with the lender, so
with the borrower; as with the taker of
usury, so with the giver of usury to him.
P 3 The land shall be utterly emptied,
and utterly spoiled: for the LORD hath spoken this word.
4 The earth mourneth *and* fadeth
away, the world languisheth *and* fadeth
away, [1]the haughty people of the earth do
languish.
5 [a]The earth also is defiled under the
inhabitants thereof; because they have
transgressed the laws, changed the ordinance, broken the everlasting covenant.
P 6 Therefore hath [a]the curse devoured
the earth, and they that dwell therein are
desolate: therefore the inhabitants of the
earth are burned, and few men left.
7 [a]The new wine mourneth, the vine
languisheth, all the merryhearted do sigh.
8 The mirth [a]of tabrets ceaseth, the
noise of them that rejoice endeth, the joy
of the harp ceaseth.
9 They shall not drink wine with a
song; strong drink shall be bitter to them
that drink it.

P *Isa 13:1–22* ◀▶ *Isa 24:3*
P *Isa 24:1* ◀▶ *Isa 24:6*
P *Isa 24:3* ◀▶ *Isa 24:17–23*

17 [a]Rev. 17:2
18 [a]Zech. 14:20,21 [1]Heb. *old*
24:1 [1]Heb. *perverteth the face thereof*
2 [a]Hos. 4:9 [b]Ezek. 7:12,13 [1]Or, *prince*
4 [1]Heb. *the height of the people*
5 [a]Gen. 3:17; Num. 35:33
6 [a]Mal. 4:6
7 [a]ch. 16:8,9; Joel 1:10,12
8 [a]Jer. 7:34 & 16:9 & 25:10; Ezek. 26:13; Hos. 2:11; Rev. 18:22
13 [a]ch. 17:5,6
15 [a]Mal. 1:11 [1]Or, *valleys*
16 [a]Jer. 5:11 [1]Heb. *wing* [2]Heb. *Leanness to me*, or, *My secret to me*
17 [a]See Jer. 48:43, 44
18 [a]Gen. 7:11 [b]Ps. 18:7
19 [a]Jer. 4:23
20 [a]ch. 19:14
21 [a]Ps. 76:12 [1]Heb. *visit upon*

10 The city of confusion is broken
down: every house is shut up, that no
man may come in.
11 *There is* a crying for wine in the
streets; all joy is darkened, the mirth of
the land is gone.
12 In the city is left desolation, and the
gate is smitten with destruction.
13 ¶ When thus it shall be in the midst M
of the land among the people, [a]*there
shall be* as the shaking of an olive tree,
and as the gleaning grapes when the vintage is done.
14 They shall lift up their voice, they
shall sing for the majesty of the LORD, they
shall cry aloud from the sea.
15 Wherefore glorify ye the LORD in the
[1]fires, *even* [a]the name of the LORD God of
Israel in the isles of the sea.
16 ¶ From the [1]uttermost part of the
earth have we heard songs, *even* glory to
the righteous. But I said, [2]My leanness,
my leanness, woe unto me! [a]the treacherous dealers have dealt treacherously;
yea, the treacherous dealers have dealt
very treacherously.
17 [a]Fear, and the pit, and the snare, P
are upon thee, O inhabitant of the earth. H
18 And it shall come to pass, *that* he
who fleeth from the noise of the fear shall
fall into the pit; and he that cometh up
out of the midst of the pit shall be taken
in the snare: for [a]the windows from on
high are open, and [b]the foundations of
the earth do shake.
19 [a]The earth is utterly broken down,
the earth is clean dissolved, the earth is
moved exceedingly.
20 The earth shall [a]reel to and fro like
a drunkard, and shall be removed like a
cottage; and the transgression thereof
shall be heavy upon it; and it shall fall,
and not rise again.
21 And it shall come to pass in that
day, *that* the LORD shall [1]punish the host
of the high ones *that are* on high, [a]and
the kings of the earth upon the earth.

M *Isa 16:5* ◀▶ *Isa 24:23*
P *Isa 24:6* ◀▶ *Isa 26:20–21*
H *Isa 13:6–13* ◀▶ *Isa 26:20–21*

24:1, 3, 6 This prophecy foretells the great destruction of the earth's population during the tribulation period.

24:13–15 Isaiah foresaw the peace of the millennial kingdom.

24:17–23 Isaiah reveals the coming punishment of God upon his enemies during the tribulation period, ending in the complete destruction of the antichrist in the final conflict and the establishment of the glorious reign of the Messiah.

22 And they shall be gathered together, [1]*as* prisoners are gathered in the [2]pit, and shall be shut up in the prison, and after many days shall they be [3]visited.

M 23 Then the [a]moon shall be confounded, and the sun ashamed, when the LORD of hosts shall [b]reign in [c]mount Zion, and in Jerusalem, and [1]before his ancients gloriously.

Praise the LORD

25 O LORD, thou *art* my God; [a]I will exalt thee, I will praise thy name; [b]for thou hast done wonderful *things;* [c]*thy* counsels of old *are* faithfulness *and* truth.

2 For thou hast made [a]of a city an heap; *of* a defenced city a ruin: a palace of strangers to be no city; it shall never be built.

3 Therefore shall the strong people [a]glorify thee, the city of the terrible nations shall fear thee.

K 4 For thou hast been a strength to the poor, a strength to the needy in his distress, [a]a refuge from the storm, a shadow from the heat, when the blast of the terrible ones *is* as a storm *against* the wall.

5 Thou shalt bring down the noise of strangers, as the heat in a dry place; *even* the heat with the shadow of a cloud: the branch of the terrible ones shall be brought low.

M 6 ¶ And in [a]this mountain shall [b]the LORD of hosts make unto [c]all people a feast of fat things, a feast of wines on the lees, of fat things full of marrow, of wines on the lees well refined.

7 And he will [1]destroy in this mountain the face of the covering [2]cast over all people, and [a]the veil that is spread over all nations.

F I S 8 He will [a]swallow up death in victory; and the Lord GOD will [b]wipe away tears from off all faces; and the rebuke of his people shall he take away from off all the earth: for the LORD hath spoken *it.*

9 ¶ And it shall be said in that day, Lo, this *is* our God; [a]we have waited for him, and he will save us: this *is* the LORD; we have waited for him, [b]we will be glad and rejoice in his salvation.

10 For in this mountain shall the hand of the LORD rest, and Moab shall be [1]trodden down under him, even as straw is [2]trodden down for the dunghill.

11 And he shall spread forth his hands in the midst of them, as he that swimmeth spreadeth forth *his hands* to swim: and he shall bring down their pride together with the spoils of their hands.

12 And the [a]fortress of the high fort of thy walls shall he bring down, lay low, *and* bring to the ground, *even* to the dust.

Song of rejoicing in Judah

26 IN [a]THAT day shall this song be sung in the land of Judah; We have a strong city; [b]salvation will *God* appoint *for* walls and bulwarks. I M

2 [a]Open ye the gates, that the righteous nation which keepeth the [1]truth may enter in.

3 Thou wilt keep *him* in [1]perfect peace, *whose* [2]mind *is* stayed *on thee:* because he trusteth in thee. F K J

4 Trust ye in the LORD for ever: [a]for in the LORD JEHOVAH *is* [b]everlasting[1] strength: W

5 ¶ For he bringeth down them that dwell on high; [a]the lofty city, he layeth it low; he layeth it low, *even* to the ground; he bringeth it *even* to the dust.

6 The foot shall tread it down, *even* the feet of the poor, *and* the steps of the needy.

7 The way of the just *is* uprightness:

M *Isa 24:13–15* ◀▶ *Isa 25:6–10*
K *Isa 4:6* ◀▶ *Isa 26:3–4*
M *Isa 24:23* ◀▶ *Isa 26:1–2*
F *Ps 88:10–12* ◀▶ *Isa 26:19*
I *Isa 18:7* ◀▶ *Isa 26:1–2*
S *Isa 12:3* ◀▶ *Isa 35:10*

I *Isa 25:8–10* ◀▶ *Isa 26:12*
M *Isa 25:6–10* ◀▶ *Isa 29:17–24*
F *Isa 7:9* ◀▶ *Jer 17:7*
K *Isa 25:4* ◀▶ *Isa 28:16*
J *Pr 1:33* ◀▶ *Isa 51:12*
W *Isa 12:2–3* ◀▶ *Isa 32:17*

22 [1]Heb. *with the gathering of prisoners* [2]Or, *dungeon* [3]Or, *found wanting*
23 [a]ch. 13:10 & 60:19; Ezek. 32:7; Joel 2:31 & 3:15 [b]Rev. 19:4,6 [c]Heb. 12:22 [1]Or, there shall be *glory before his ancients*
25:1 [a]Ex. 15:2 [b]Ps. 98:1 [c]Num. 23:19
2 [a]ch. 21:9 & 23:13; Jer. 51:37
3 [a]Rev. 11:13
4 [a]ch. 4:6
6 [a]ch. 2:2,3 [b]Prov. 9:2; Mat. 22:4 [c]Dan. 7:14; Mat. 8:11
7 [a]2 Cor. 3:15; Eph. 4:18 [1]Heb. *swallow up* [2]Heb. *covered*
8 [a]Hos. 13:14; 1 Cor. 15:54 [b]Rev. 7:17 & 21:4
9 [a]Gen. 49:18; Tit. 2:13 [b]Ps. 20:5
10 [1]Or, *threshed* [2]Or, *threshed in Madmenah*
12 [a]ch. 26:5
26:1 [a]ch. 2:11 [b]ch. 60:18
2 [a]Ps. 118:19,20 [1]Heb. *truths*
3 [1]Heb. *peace, peace;* see ch. 57:19 [2]Or, *thought,* or, *imagination*
4 [a]ch. 45:17 [b]Deut. 32:4 [1]Heb. *the rock of ages*
5 [a]ch. 25:12 & 32:19

25:6 This prophecy will be ultimately fulfilled during the marriage supper of the Lamb (see Rev 19:9).
25:7–10 Isaiah prophesied the Lord's ultimate victory over death (compare with 1Co 15:54; Rev 21:4). This victory will be total and absolute, a complete fulfillment of the ancient prophecies.
26:1–2 This prophecy anticipates the victory of the Messiah as he ushers in the millennial kingdom and reconciles the nation to God.

[a]thou, most upright, dost weigh the path
of the just.
8 Yea, [a]in the way of thy judgments,
O LORD, have we waited for thee; the desire of *our* soul *is* to thy name, and to the
remembrance of thee.
9 [a]With my soul have I desired thee in
the night; yea, with my spirit within me
will I seek thee early: for when thy judgments *are* in the earth, the inhabitants of
the world will learn righteousness.
C 10 [a]Let favour be shown to the
N wicked, *yet* will he not learn righteousness: in [b]the land of uprightness will he
deal unjustly, and will not behold the
majesty of the LORD.
11 LORD, *when* thy hand is lifted up,
[a]they will not see: *but* they shall see, and
be ashamed for *their* envy [l]at the people;
yea, the fire of thine enemies shall devour them.
I 12 ¶ LORD, thou wilt ordain peace for
us: for thou also hast wrought all our
works [l]in us.
13 O LORD our God, [a]*other* lords beside
thee have had dominion over us: *but* by
thee only will we make mention of thy
name.
14 *They are* dead, they shall not live;
they are deceased, they shall not rise:
therefore hast thou visited and destroyed
them, and made all their memory to
perish.
R 15 Thou hast increased the nation,
O LORD, thou hast increased the nation:
thou art glorified: thou hadst removed *it*
far *unto* all the ends of the earth.
16 LORD, [a]in trouble have they visited
thee, they poured out a [l]prayer *when* thy
chastening *was* upon them.

C *Isa 9:2* ◀▶ *Isa 30:9–10*
N *Ecc 12:1* ◀▶ *Isa 28:12–13*
I *Isa 26:1–2* ◀▶ *Isa 26:19*
R *Isa 22:17–19* ◀▶ *Isa 28:13*

7 [a]Ps. 37:23
8 [a]ch. 64:5
9 [a]Ps. 63:6; Sol. 3:1
10 [a]Eccl. 8:12; Rom 2:4 [b]Ps. 143:10
11 [a]Job 34:27; Ps. 28:5; ch. 5:12 [l]Or, *toward* thy *people*
12 [l]Or, *for us*
13 [a]2 Chr. 12:8
16 [a]Hos. 5:15 [l]Heb. *secret speech*
17 [a]ch. 13:8; John 16:21
18 [a]Ps. 17:14
19 [a]Ezek. 37:1 [b]Dan. 12:2
20 [a]Ex. 12:22,23 [b]Ps. 30:5; ch. 54:7, 8; 2 Cor. 4:17
21 [a]Mic. 1:3; Jude 14 [l]Heb. *bloods*
27:1 [a]Ps. 74:13,14 [b]ch. 51:9; Ezek. 29:3 & 32:2 [l]Or, *crossing like a bar*
2 [a]ch. 5:1 [b]Ps. 80:8; Jer. 2:21
3 [a]Ps. 121:4,5

17 Like as [a]a woman with child, *that*
draweth near the time of her delivery, is
in pain, *and* crieth out in her pangs; so
have we been in thy sight, O LORD.
18 We have been with child, we have
been in pain, we have as it were brought
forth wind; we have not wrought any deliverance in the earth; neither have [a]the
inhabitants of the world fallen.
19 [a]Thy dead *men* shall live, *together* F
with my dead body shall they arise. I
[b]Awake and sing, ye that dwell in dust:
for thy dew *is as* the dew of herbs, and
the earth shall cast out the dead.
20 ¶ Come, my people, [a]enter thou H
into thy chambers, and shut thy doors P
about thee: hide thyself as it were [b]for a T
little moment, until the indignation be H
overpast.
21 For, behold, the LORD [a]cometh out
of his place to punish the inhabitants of
the earth for their iniquity: the earth also
shall disclose her [l]blood, and shall no
more cover her slain.

Israel to be delivered

27 IN THAT day the LORD with his
sore and great and strong sword
shall punish leviathan the [l]piercing serpent, [a]even leviathan that crooked serpent; and he shall slay [b]the dragon that *is*
in the sea.
2 In that day [a]sing ye unto her, [b]A I
vineyard of red wine.
3 [a]I the LORD do keep it; I will water it
every moment: lest *any* hurt it, I will
keep it night and day.
4 Fury *is* not in me: who would set

F *Isa 25:8* ◀▶ *Eze 37:12–14*
I *Isa 26:12* ◀▶ *Isa 27:2–6*
H *SS 2:4* ◀▶ *Mt 22:2–3*
P *Isa 24:17–23* ◀▶ *Isa 28:17–18*
T *SS 6:10* ◀▶ *Mt 3:12*
H *Isa 24:17–23* ◀▶ *Isa 28:15–18*
I *Isa 26:19* ◀▶ *Isa 27:12–13*

26:12 The final reward of true peace will be won by Israel's Messiah.
26:15–17 Isaiah likened the approaching crisis in the last days to a pregnant woman in labor, awaiting the delivery of her child.
26:19–21 Isaiah prophesied a word of reassurance to God's people by promising the future resurrection of the righteous (see Job 19:26; Da 12:2). Their oppression would end and God would avenge their deaths (see Ge 4:10; Rev 20:13).
27:2–6 Isaiah spoke another vineyard song (see 5:1–7) picturing the nation's lukewarm attitude toward God as not "briers and thorns" (27:4) but neither a relationship of complete trust. Yet when the Messiah comes "Israel shall blossom and bud and fill the face of the world with fruit" (27:6). This prophecy is being fulfilled in our generation as the returning Jews transform the landscape of Palestine. Where once there was desert, there are now farms. Where once there was desolation, there are now vineyards and orchards.

[a]the briers *and* thorns against me in battle? I would [/]go through them, I would burn them together.
5 Or let him take hold [a]of my strength,
that he may [b]make peace with me; *and* he shall make peace with me.
6 He shall cause them that come of Jacob [a]to take root: Israel shall blossom and bud, and fill the face of the world with fruit.
7 ¶ Hath he smitten him, [/]as he smote those that smote him? *or* is he slain according to the slaughter of them that are slain by him?
8 [a]In measure, [/]when it shooteth forth, thou wilt debate with it: [b]he[2] stayeth his rough wind in the day of the east wind.
9 By this therefore shall the iniquity of Jacob be purged; and this *is* all the fruit to take away his sin; when he maketh all the stones of the altar as chalkstones that are beaten in sunder, the groves and [/]images shall not stand up.
10 Yet the defenced city *shall be* desolate, *and* the habitation forsaken, and left like a wilderness: [a]there shall the calf feed, and there shall he lie down, and consume the branches thereof.
11 When the boughs thereof are withered, they shall be broken off: the women come, *and* set them on fire: for [a]it *is* a people of no understanding: therefore he that made them will not have mercy on them, and [b]he that formed them will show them no favour.
12 ¶ And it shall come to pass in that day, *that* the LORD shall beat off from the channel of the river unto the stream of Egypt, and ye shall be gathered one by one, O ye children of Israel.
13 [a]And it shall come to pass in that day, [b]*that* the great trumpet shall be blown, and they shall come which were ready to perish in the land of Assyria, and the outcasts in the land of Egypt, and shall worship the LORD in the holy mount at Jerusalem.

I *Isa 27:2–6* ◀ ▶ *Isa 28:5–6*

4 [a]2 Sam. 23:6; ch. 9:18 [/]Or, *march against*
5 [a]ch. 25:4 [b]Job 22:21
6 [a]ch. 37:31; Hos. 14:5,6
7 [/]Heb. *according to the stroke of those*
8 [a]Job 23:6; Ps. 6:1; Jer. 10:24 & 30:11 & 46:28; 1 Cor. 10:13 [b]Ps. 78:38 [/]Or, *when thou sendest it forth* [2]Or, *when he removeth it*
9 [/]Or, *sun images*
10 [a]See ch. 17:2 & 32:14
11 [a]Deut. 32:28; ch. 1:3; Jer. 8:7 [b]Deut. 32:18; ch. 43:1,7 & 44:2,21, 24
13 [a]ch. 2:11 [b]Mat. 24:31; Rev. 11:15
28:1 [a]ver. 3 [b]ver. 4 [/]Heb. *broken*
2 [a]ch. 30:30; Ezek. 13:11
3 [a]ver. 1 [/]Heb. *with feet*
4 [a]ver. 1 [/]Heb. *swalloweth*
7 [a]Prov. 20:1; Hos. 4:11 [b]ch. 56:10,12
9 [a]Jer. 6:10 [/]Heb. *the hearing?*
10 [/]Or, hath been
11 [a]1 Cor. 14:21 [/]Heb. *stammerings of lips* [2]Or, *he hath spoken*

Woe to Ephraim

28 WOE TO [a]the crown of pride, to the drunkards of Ephraim, whose [b]glorious beauty *is* a fading flower, which *are* on the head of the fat valleys of them that are [/]overcome with wine!
2 Behold, the Lord hath a mighty and strong one, [a]*which* as a tempest of hail *and* a destroying storm, as a flood of mighty waters overflowing, shall cast down to the earth with the hand.
3 [a]The crown of pride, the drunkards of Ephraim, shall be trodden [/]under feet:
4 And [a]the glorious beauty, which *is* on the head of the fat valley, shall be a fading flower, *and* as the hasty fruit before the summer; which *when* he that looketh upon it seeth, while it is yet in his hand he [/]eateth it up.
5 ¶ In that day shall the LORD of hosts be for a crown of glory, and for a diadem of beauty, unto the residue of his people, I
6 And for a spirit of judgment to him that sitteth in judgment, and for strength to them that turn the battle to the gate. G M T
7 ¶ But they also [a]have erred through wine, and through strong drink are out of the way; [b]the priest and the prophet have erred through strong drink, they are swallowed up of wine, they are out of the way through strong drink; they err in vision, they stumble *in* judgment.
8 For all tables are full of vomit *and* filthiness, *so that there is* no place *clean.*
9 ¶ [a]Whom shall he teach knowledge? and whom shall he make to understand [/]doctrine? *them that are* weaned from the milk, *and* drawn from the breasts.
10 For precept [/]*must be* upon precept, precept upon precept; line upon line, line upon line; here a little, *and* there a little:
11 For with [a]stammering[/] lips and another tongue [2]will he speak to this people.

I *Isa 27:12–13* ◀ ▶ *Isa 30:15*
G *Isa 11:2–3* ◀ ▶ *Isa 42:1*
M *Isa 11:2* ◀ ▶ *Isa 31:3*
T *Isa 11:2–3* ◀ ▶ *Isa 40:13*

27:12–13 This passage reconfirmed the return of the Jews to their homeland. Isaiah specifically refers to the blowing of a "trumpet" (27:13) in connection with this return of God's people from their captivity "in the land of Assyria" (27:13). The trumpet mentioned here is the shophar, a ram's horn used to call the troops together (see 1Sa 13:3).

28:5–6 Isaiah foresaw the future millennial rule of the coming Messiah who will be "a crown of glory" (28:5) for the nation. He will usher in a reign of righteousness and justice that the nation has anticipated for centuries.

N 12 To whom he said, This *is* the rest *wherewith* ye may cause the weary to rest; and this *is* the refreshing: yet they would not hear.

R 13 But the word of the LORD was unto them precept upon precept, precept upon precept; line upon line, line upon line; here a little, *and* there a little; that they might go, and fall backward, and be broken, and snared, and taken.

14 ¶ Wherefore hear the word of the LORD, ye scornful men, that rule this people which *is* in Jerusalem.

G H 15 Because ye have said, We have made a covenant with death, and with hell are we at agreement; when the overflowing scourge shall pass through, it shall not come unto us: [a]for we have made lies our refuge, and under falsehood have we hid ourselves:

K 16 ¶ Therefore thus saith the Lord GOD, Behold, I lay in Zion for a foundation [a]a stone, a tried stone, a precious corner *stone,* a sure foundation: he that believeth shall not make haste.

P 17 Judgment also will I lay to the line, and righteousness to the plummet: and the hail shall sweep away [a]the refuge of lies, and the waters shall overflow the hiding place.

18 ¶ And your covenant with death shall be disannulled, and your agreement with hell shall not stand; when the overflowing scourge shall pass through, then ye shall be [1]trodden down by it.

19 From the time that it goeth forth it shall take you: for morning by morning shall it pass over, by day and by night: and it shall be a vexation only [1]*to* understand the report.

20 For the bed is shorter than that *a man* can stretch himself *on it:* and the covering narrower than that he can wrap himself *in it.*

N *Isa 26:10–11* ◀▶ *Isa 40:6*
R *Isa 26:15–17* ◀▶ *Isa 29:4*
G *Ecc 1:14–15* ◀▶ *Isa 29:8*
H *Isa 26:20–21* ◀▶ *Isa 28:22*
K *Isa 26:3–4* ◀▶ *Isa 32:2*
P *Isa 26:20–21* ◀▶ *Isa 28:21–22*

15 [a]Amos 2:4
16 [a]Gen. 49:24; Ps. 118:22; Mat. 21:42; Acts 4:11; Rom. 9:33 & 10:11; Eph. 2:20; 1 Pet. 2:6-8
17 [a]ver. 15
18 [1]Heb. *a treading down to it*
19 [1]Or, *when he shall make you to understand doctrine*
21 [a]2 Sam. 5:20; 1 Chr. 14:11 [b]Josh. 10:10,12; 2 Sam. 5:25; 1 Chr. 14:16 [c]Lam. 3:33
22 [a]ch. 10:22; Dan 9:27
25 [1]Or, *the wheat in the principal* place, *and barley in the appointed* place [2]Or, *spelt* [3]Heb. *border?*
26 [1]Or, *And he bindeth it in such sort as his God doth teach him*
29 [a]Ps. 92:5; Jer. 32:19
29:1 [a]Ezek. 43:15, 16 [b]2 Sam. 5:9 [1]Or, *O Ariel,* i.e. *the lion of God* [2]Or, *of the city* [3]Heb. *cut off the heads*

21 For the LORD shall rise up as *in* mount [a]Perazim, he shall be wroth as *in* the valley of [b]Gibeon, that he may do his work, [c]his strange work; and bring to pass his act, his strange act. P

22 Now therefore be ye not mockers, lest your bands be made strong: for I have heard from the Lord GOD of hosts [a]a consumption, even determined upon the whole earth. H

23 ¶ Give ye ear, and hear my voice; hearken, and hear my speech.

24 Doth the plowman plow all day to sow? doth he open and break the clods of his ground?

25 When he hath made plain the face thereof, doth he not cast abroad the fitches, and scatter the cummin, and cast in [1]the principal wheat and the appointed barley and the [2]rie in their [3]place?

26 [1]For his God doth instruct him to discretion, *and* doth teach him.

27 For the fitches are not threshed with a threshing instrument, neither is a cart wheel turned about upon the cummin; but the fitches are beaten out with a staff, and the cummin with a rod.

28 Bread *corn* is bruised; because he will not ever be threshing it, nor break *it with* the wheel of his cart, nor bruise it *with* his horsemen.

29 This also cometh forth from the LORD of hosts, [a]*which* is wonderful in counsel, *and* excellent in working.

Doom to the city of Jerusalem

29 WOE [a]TO[1] Ariel, to Ariel, [2]the city [b]*where* David dwelt! add ye year to year; let them [3]kill sacrifices.

2 Yet I will distress Ariel, and there shall be heaviness and sorrow: and it shall be unto me as Ariel.

3 And I will camp against thee round

P *Isa 28:17–18* ◀▶ *Isa 29:20*
H *Isa 28:15–18* ◀▶ *Isa 30:30*

28:14–22 This prophecy reviled the unrighteous leaders of the nation who preferred to trust in their alliances "with death and with hell" (28:15), the nation's deadly enemies, rather than obey God. Isaiah predicted the staggering consequences that such alliances would bring about in the final conflict.

However, Isaiah also predicted that God would intervene to save the nation from total destruction, referring to Israel's deliverance from her enemies at the Battle of Armageddon (see Rev 19:21). Isaiah's words in 28:22 tie this prediction to Daniel's prophecy of the destruction of the antichrist and his armies in Da 9:24–27.

about, and will lay siege against thee with
a mount, and I will raise forts against
thee.
R 4 And thou shalt be brought down,
and shalt speak out of the ground, and
thy speech shall be low out of the dust,
and thy voice shall be, as of one that hath
a familiar spirit, [a]out of the ground, and
thy speech shall [/]whisper out of the dust.
5 Moreover the multitude of thy
[a]strangers shall be like small dust, and
the multitude of the terrible ones *shall be*
[b]as chaff that passeth away: yea, it shall
be [c]at an instant suddenly.
6 [a]Thou shalt be visited of the LORD of
hosts with thunder, and with earthquake,
and great noise, with storm and tempest,
and the flame of devouring fire.
7 ¶ [a]And the multitude of all the nations that fight against Ariel, even all that
fight against her and her munition, and
that distress her, shall be [b]as a dream of a
night vision.
G 8 [a]It shall even be as when an hungry
man dreameth, and, behold, he eateth;
but he awaketh, and his soul is empty: or
as when a thirsty man dreameth, and, behold, he drinketh; but he awaketh, and,
behold, *he is* faint, and his soul hath appetite: so shall the multitude of all the
nations be, that fight against mount Zion.
9 ¶ Stay yourselves, and wonder; [/]cry
ye out, and cry: [a]they are drunken, [b]but
not with wine; they stagger, but not with
strong drink.
10 For [a]the LORD hath poured out upon
you the spirit of deep sleep, and hath
[b]closed your eyes: the prophets and your
[/]rulers, [c]the seers hath he covered.
11 And the vision of all is become unto
you as the words of a [/]book [a]that is
sealed, which *men* deliver to one that is
learned, saying, Read this, I pray thee:
[b]and he saith, I cannot; for it *is* sealed:
12 And the book is delivered to him
that is not learned, saying, Read this, I

4 [a]ch. 8:19 [/]Heb. *peep,* or, *chirp*
5 [a]ch. 25:5 [b]Job 21:18; ch. 17:13 [c]ch. 30:13
6 [a]ch. 28:2 & 30:30
7 [a]ch. 37:36 [b]Job 20:8
8 [a]Ps. 73:20
9 [a]See ch. 28:7,8 [b]ch. 51:21 [/]Or, *take your pleasure, and riot*
10 [a]Rom. 11:8 [b]Ps. 69:23; ch. 6:10 [c]1 Sam. 9:9 [/]Heb. *heads*
11 [a]ch. 8:16 [b]Dan. 12:4; Rev. 5:1-5,9 [/]Or, *letter*
13 [a]Ezek. 33:31; Mat. 15:8,9; Mark 7:6,7 [b]Col. 2:22
14 [a]Hab. 1:5 [b]Jer. 49:7; Obad. 8; 1 Cor. 1:19 [/]Heb. *I will add*
15 [a]ch. 30:1 [b]Ps. 94:7
16 [a]ch. 45:9; Rom. 9:20
17 [a]ch. 32:15
18 [a]ch. 35:5
19 [a]ch. 61:1 [b]Jas. 2:5 [/]Heb. *shall add*
20 [a]ch. 28:14,22 [b]Mic. 2:1
21 [a]Amos 5:10,12 [b]Prov. 28:21
22 [a]Josh. 24:3

pray thee: and he saith, I am not learned.
13 ¶ Wherefore the Lord said, [a]Foras- R
much as this people draw near *me* with G
their mouth, and with their lips do honour me, but have removed their heart far
from me, and their fear toward me is
taught by [b]the precept of men:
14 [a]Therefore, behold, [/]I will proceed
to do a marvellous work among this people, *even* a marvellous work and a wonder: [b]for the wisdom of their wise *men*
shall perish, and the understanding of
their prudent *men* shall be hid.
15 [a]Woe unto them that seek deep to E
hide their counsel from the LORD, and
their works are in the dark, and [b]they
say, Who seeth us? and who knoweth us?
16 Surely your turning of things upside
down shall be esteemed as the potter's
clay: for shall the [a]work say of him that
made it, He made me not? or shall the
thing framed say of him that framed it,
He had no understanding?
17 *Is* it not yet a very little while, and M
[a]Lebanon shall be turned into a fruitful
field, and the fruitful field shall be esteemed as a forest?
18 ¶ And [a]in that day shall the deaf
hear the words of the book, and the eyes
of the blind shall see out of obscurity, and
out of darkness.
19 [a]The meek also [/]shall increase *their*
joy in the LORD, and [b]the poor among men
shall rejoice in the Holy One of Israel.
20 For the terrible one is brought to P
nought, and [a]the scorner is consumed,
and all that [b]watch for iniquity are cut
off:
21 That make a man an offender for a
word, and [a]lay a snare for him that reproveth in the gate, and turn aside the
just [b]for a thing of nought.
22 Therefore thus saith the LORD, [a]who

R *Isa 28:13* ◀ ▶ *Isa 29:13–14*
G *Isa 28:15–20* ◀ ▶ *Isa 29:13–14*

R *Isa 29:4* ◀ ▶ *Isa 30:13–14*
G *Isa 29:8* ◀ ▶ *Isa 30:1*
E *Pr 24:12* ◀ ▶ *Jer 11:20*
M *Isa 26:1–2* ◀ ▶ *Isa 32:1–4*
P *Isa 28:21–22* ◀ ▶ *Isa 30:27*

29:4 Isaiah indicated that Judah's alliance with death (see 28:15–18) would only bring about the nation's death.

29:13–14 In their insincere worship of God, the people rejected God's Word and followed the "precept of men" (29:13) instead. Note that Jesus quoted from this prophecy to illustrate the hypocrisy of the Pharisees (see Mt 15:8–9).

29:17–20 These wondrous prophecies saw an initial fulfillment when Jesus healed the deaf and the blind and will be completely fulfilled during the Millennium.

redeemed Abraham, concerning the house of Jacob, Jacob shall not now be ashamed, neither shall his face now wax pale.

23 But when he seeth his children, [a]the work of mine hands, in the midst of him, they shall sanctify my name, and sanctify the Holy One of Jacob, and shall fear the God of Israel.

24 They also [a]that erred in spirit [/]shall come to understanding, and they that murmured shall learn doctrine.

Rebellious Judah to be crushed

E 30 WOE TO the rebellious children,
N saith the LORD, [a]that take counsel,
W but not of me; and that cover with a cov-
G ering, but not of my spirit, [b]that they may
add sin to sin:

2 [a]That walk to go down into Egypt, and [b]have not asked at my mouth; to strengthen themselves in the strength of Pharaoh, and to trust in the shadow of Egypt!

3 [a]Therefore shall the strength of Pharaoh be your shame, and the trust in the shadow of Egypt *your* confusion.

4 For his princes were at [a]Zoan, and his ambassadors came to Hanes.

J 5 [a]They were all ashamed of a people *that* could not profit them, nor be an help nor profit, but a shame, and also a reproach.

6 [a]The burden of the beasts of the south: into the land of trouble and anguish, from whence *come* the young and old lion, [b]the viper and fiery flying serpent, they will carry their riches upon the shoulders of young asses, and their treasures upon the bunches of camels, to a people *that* shall not profit *them.*

7 [a]For the Egyptians shall help in vain, and to no purpose: therefore have I cried [/]concerning this, [b]Their strength *is* to sit still.

8 ¶ Now go, [a]write it before them in a table, and note it in a book, that it may be for [/]the time to come for ever and ever:

9 That [a]this *is* a rebellious people, lying children, children *that* will not hear the law of the LORD: C

10 [a]Which say to the seers, See not; and to the prophets, Prophesy not unto us right things, [b]speak unto us smooth things, prophesy deceits:

11 Get you out of the way, turn aside out of the path, cause the Holy One of Israel to cease from before us.

12 Wherefore thus saith the Holy One of Israel, Because ye despise this word, and trust in [/]oppression and perverseness, and stay thereon:

13 Therefore this iniquity shall be to you [a]as a breach ready to fall, swelling out in a high wall, whose breaking [b]cometh suddenly at an instant. R

14 And [a]he shall break it as the breaking of [/]the potters' vessel that is broken in pieces; he shall not spare: so that there shall not be found in the bursting of it a sherd to take fire from the hearth, or to take water *withal* out of the pit.

15 For thus saith the Lord GOD, the Holy One of Israel; [a]In returning and rest shall ye be saved; in quietness and in confidence shall be your strength: [b]and ye would not. I

16 But ye said, No; for we will flee upon horses; therefore shall ye flee: and, We will ride upon the swift; therefore shall they that pursue you be swift.

17 [a]One thousand *shall flee* at the rebuke of one; at the rebuke of five shall ye flee: till ye be left as [/]a beacon upon the top of a mountain, and as an ensign on an hill. R

23 [a]ch. 19:25 & 45:11 & 60:21; Eph. 2:10
24 [a]ch. 28:7 [/]Heb. *shall know understanding*
30:1 [a]ch. 29:15 [b]Deut. 29:19
2 [a]ch. 31:1 [b]Num. 27:21; Josh. 9:14; 1 Ki. 22:7; Jer. 21:2 & 42:2,20
3 [a]ch. 20:5; Jer. 37:5,7
4 [a]ch. 19:11
5 [a]Jer. 2:36
6 [a]ch. 57:9; Hos. 8:9 & 12:1 [b]Deut. 8:15
7 [a]Jer. 37:7 [b]ver. 15 [/]Or, *to her*
8 [a]Hab. 2:2 [/]Heb. *the latter day*
9 [a]Deut. 32:20; ch. 1:4
10 [a]Jer. 11:21; Amos 2:12; Mic. 2:6 [b]1 Ki. 22:13; Mic. 2:11
12 [/]Or, *fraud*
13 [a]Ps. 62:3 [b]ch. 29:5
14 [a]Ps. 2:9; Jer. 19:11 [/]Heb. *the bottle of potters*
15 [a]ch. 7:4 [b]Mat. 23:37
17 [a]Lev. 26:8; Deut. 28:25; Josh. 23:10 [/]Or, *a tree bereft of branches,* or, *boughs:* or, *a mast*

E *Ps 143:10* ◀▶ *Isa 34:16*
N *Isa 11:2* ◀▶ *Isa 40:7*
W *Pr 1:22–23* ◀▶ *Mic 2:7*
G *Isa 29:13–14* ◀▶ *Isa 50:11*
J *Isa 23:1–17* ◀▶ *Isa 48:14–15*
C *Isa 26:10–11* ◀▶ *Isa 43:8*
R *Isa 29:13–14* ◀▶ *Isa 30:17*
I *Isa 28:5–6* ◀▶ *Isa 30:18–26*
R *Isa 30:13–14* ◀▶ *Isa 32:10*

30:13–15 Though the people had allowed oppression and deceit to become their wall of security, Isaiah said it would be shattered. The only way to true security was through repentance.

30:17–27 Isaiah began this passage by foretelling the fear and terror that would afflict the Jews when their enemies would attack in the last days. Note his mention of the Battle of Armageddon (30:25) and the description of the intense burning of the sun and the moon (30:17, 26) indicating the supernatural judgments of God which will be displayed during the closing moments of the tribulation.

I 18 ¶ And therefore will the LORD wait, that he may be gracious unto you, and therefore will he be exalted, that he may have mercy upon you: for the LORD *is* a God of judgment: [a]blessed *are* all they that wait for him.

19 For the people [a]shall dwell in Zion at Jerusalem: thou shalt weep no more: he will be very gracious unto thee at the voice of thy cry; when he shall hear it, he will answer thee.

20 And *though* the Lord give you [a]the bread of adversity, and the water of [1]affliction, yet shall not [b]thy teachers be removed into a corner any more, but thine eyes shall see thy teachers:

21 And thine ears shall hear a word behind thee, saying, This *is* the way, walk ye in it, when ye [a]turn to the right hand, and when ye turn to the left.

22 [a]Ye shall defile also the covering of [1]thy graven images of silver, and the ornament of thy molten images of gold: thou shalt [2]cast them away as a menstruous cloth; [b]thou shalt say unto it, Get thee hence.

23 [a]Then shall he give the rain of thy seed, that thou shalt sow the ground withal; and bread of the increase of the earth, and it shall be fat and plenteous: in that day shall thy cattle feed in large pastures.

24 The oxen likewise and the young asses that ear the ground shall eat [1,2]clean provender, which hath been winnowed with the shovel and with the fan.

25 And there shall be [a]upon every high mountain, and upon every [1]high hill, rivers *and* streams of waters in the day of the great slaughter, when the towers fall.

26 Moreover [a]the light of the moon shall be as the light of the sun, and the light of the sun shall be sevenfold, as the light of seven days, in the day that the LORD bindeth up the breach of his people, and healeth the stroke of their wound.

I *Isa 30:15* ◄► *Isa 30:29*

18 [a]Ps. 2:12 & 34:8; Prov. 16:20; Jer. 17:7
19 [a]ch. 65:9
20 [a]1 Ki. 22:27; Ps. 127:2 [b]Ps. 74:9; Amos 8:11 [1]Or, *oppression*
21 [a]Josh. 1:7
22 [a]2 Chr. 31:1; ch. 31:7 [b]Hos. 14:8 [1]Heb. *the graven images of thy silver* [2]Heb. *scatter*
23 [a]Mat. 6:33; 1 Tim. 4:8
24 [1]Or, *savoury* [2]Heb. *leavened*
25 [a]ch. 2:14,15 [1]Heb. *lifted up*
26 [a]ch. 60:19,20
27 [1]Or, *and the grievousness of flame* [2]Heb. *heaviness*
28 [a]ch. 11:4 [b]ch. 8:8 [c]ch. 37:29
29 [a]ch. 2:3 [b]Deut. 32:4 [1]Heb. *Rock*
30 [a]ch. 29:6 [b]ch. 28:2 [1]Heb. *the glory of his voice*
31 [a]ch. 37:36 [b]ch. 10:5,24
32 [a]ch. 11:15 [1]Heb. *every passing of the rod founded* [2]Heb. *cause to rest upon him* [3]Or, *against them*
33 [a]Jer. 7:31 [1]Heb. *from yesterday*
31:1 [a]ch. 30:2 [b]Ps. 20:7

27 ¶ Behold, the name of the LORD cometh from far, burning *with* his anger, [1]and the burden *thereof is* [2]heavy: his lips are full of indignation, and his tongue as a devouring fire: P

28 And [a]his breath, as an overflowing stream, [b]shall reach to the midst of the neck, to sift the nations with the sieve of vanity: and *there shall be* [c]a bridle in the jaws of the people, causing *them* to err.

29 Ye shall have a song, as in the night *when* a holy solemnity is kept; and gladness of heart, as when one goeth with a pipe to come into [a]the mountain of the LORD, to the [b]mighty[1] One of Israel. I

30 [a]And the LORD shall cause [1]his glorious voice to be heard, and shall show the lighting down of his arm, with the indignation of *his* anger, and *with* the flame of a devouring fire, *with* scattering, and tempest, [b]and hailstones. P H

31 For [a]through the voice of the LORD shall the Assyrian be beaten down, [b]*which* smote with a rod.

32 And [1]*in* every place where the grounded staff shall pass, which the LORD shall [2]lay upon him, *it* shall be with tabrets and harps: and in battles of [a]shaking will he fight [3]with it.

33 [a]For Tophet *is* ordained [1]of old; yea, for the king it is prepared; he hath made *it* deep *and* large: the pile thereof *is* fire and much wood; the breath of the LORD, like a stream of brimstone, doth kindle it. H

The folly of reliance upon Egypt

31 WOE TO them [a]that go down to Egypt for help; and [b]stay on horses, and trust in chariots, because *they are* many; and in horsemen, because

P *Isa 29:20* ◄► *Isa 30:30*
I *Isa 30:18–26* ◄► *Isa 32:15–18*
P *Isa 30:27* ◄► *Isa 33:12*
H *Isa 28:22* ◄► *Isa 30:33*
H *Isa 30:30* ◄► *Isa 33:11–12*

30:30–33 This passage carries a double meaning: the wrath of God on the Assyrian army as well as God's judgment on the future antichrist, referred to in this passage as "the Assyrian" (30:31; see 14:25). Isaiah further declared that Tophet, which is a name for "hell," is prepared and ready for its king. Despite his satanic power, the antichrist will be utterly destroyed by Jesus Christ and cast into hell forever (see Rev 19:19–20).

they are very strong; but they look not unto the Holy One of Israel, [c]neither seek the LORD!

2 Yet he also *is* wise, and will bring evil, and [a]will not [1]call back his words: but will arise against the house of the evildoers, and against the help of them that work iniquity.

M 3 Now the Egyptians *are* men, and not God; and their horses flesh, and not spirit. When the LORD shall stretch out his hand, both he that helpeth shall fall, and he that is helped shall fall down, and they all shall fail together.

4 For thus hath the LORD spoken unto me, [a]Like as the lion and the young lion roaring on his prey, when a multitude of shepherds is called forth against him, *he* will not be afraid of their voice, nor abase himself for the [1]noise of them: so shall the LORD of hosts come down to fight for mount Zion, and for the hill thereof.

5 [a]As birds flying, so will the LORD of hosts defend Jerusalem; defending also he will deliver *it; and* passing over he will preserve *it.*

6 ¶ Turn ye unto *him from* whom the children of Israel have deeply revolted.

7 For in that day every man shall [a]cast away his idols of silver, and [1]his idols of gold, which your own hands have made unto you *for* [b]a sin.

8 ¶ Then shall the Assyrian [a]fall with the sword, not of a mighty man; and the sword, not of a mean man, shall devour him: but he shall flee [1]from the sword, and his young men shall be [2,3]discomfited.

9 And [a]he[1] shall pass over to [2]his strong hold for fear, and his princes shall be afraid of the ensign, saith the LORD, whose fire *is* in Zion, and his furnace in Jerusalem.

M *Isa 28:6* ◀▶ *Isa 32:15*

1 [c]Dan. 9:13

2 [a]Num. 23:19 [1]Heb. *remove*

4 [a]Amos 3:8 [1]Or, *multitude*

5 [a]Deut. 32:11

7 [a]ch. 2:20 [b]1 Ki. 12:30 [1]Heb. *the idols of his gold*

8 [a]2 Ki. 19:35,36 [1]Or, *for fear of the sword* [2]Or, *tributary* [3]Heb. *for melting,* or, *tribute*

9 [a]ch. 37:37 [1]Heb. *his rock shall pass away for fear* [2]Or, *his strength*

32:1 [a]Ps. 45:1

2 [a]ch. 4:6 [1]Heb. *heavy*

3 [a]ch. 29:18

4 [1]Heb. *hasty* [2]Or, *elegantly*

7 [1]Or, *when he speaketh against the poor in judgment*

8 [1]Or, *be established*

9 [a]Amos 6:1

10 [1]Heb. *Days above a year*

Israel's ultimate deliverance

32 BEHOLD, [a]A king shall reign in righteousness, and princes shall rule in judgment. M

2 And a man shall be as an hiding place from the wind, and [a]a covert from the tempest; as rivers of water in a dry place, as the shadow of a [1]great rock in a weary land. K L L

3 And [a]the eyes of them that see shall not be dim, and the ears of them that hear shall hearken.

4 The heart also of the [1]rash shall understand knowledge, and the tongue of the stammerers shall be ready to speak [2]plainly.

5 The vile person shall be no more called liberal, nor the churl said *to be* bountiful.

6 For the vile person will speak villany, and his heart will work iniquity, to practise hypocrisy, and to utter error against the LORD, to make empty the soul of the hungry, and he will cause the drink of the thirsty to fail.

7 The instruments also of the churl *are* evil: he deviseth wicked devices to destroy the poor with lying words, even [1]when the needy speaketh right.

8 But the liberal deviseth liberal things; and by liberal things shall he [1]stand.

After calamity, restoration

9 ¶ Rise up, ye women [a]that are at ease; hear my voice, ye careless daughters; give ear unto my speech.

10 [1]Many days and years shall ye be troubled, ye careless women: for the vintage shall fail, the gathering shall not come. R

M *Isa 29:17–24* ◀▶ *Isa 33:20–22*
K *Isa 28:16* ◀▶ *Isa 40:8*
L *Isa 12:1–3* ◀▶ *Isa 38:17*
L *SS 4:9–10* ◀▶ *Isa 41:10*
R *Isa 30:17* ◀▶ *Isa 32:13–14*

31:5 This prophecy likened God's protection of Jerusalem to a bird that hovers over its nest protecting its young from marauders. Note that the phrase "passing over" is the same word used of the destroying angel in Egypt at the first Passover (see Ex 12:12–13).

31:8–9 This passage may also carry a double meaning. The Assyrians that amassed against Hezekiah were defeated by a supernatural intervention of God (see 37:36) as an initial fulfillment of this prophecy. The final fulfillment may be realized at the final destruction of the antichrist, "the Assyrian," who will "fall with the sword" (31:8) of the Lord in the end times (see Rev 19:11–21).

32:1–4 The Messiah is again in view in this prophecy as Isaiah describes the rule and government that will be established in the Millennium when "a king shall reign in righteousness" (32:1).

11 Tremble, ye women that are at
ease; be troubled, ye careless ones: strip
you, and make you bare, and gird *sack-*
cloth upon *your* loins.
12 They shall lament for the teats, for
[l]the pleasant fields, for the fruitful vine.
R 13 [a]Upon the land of my people shall
come up thorns *and* briers; [l]Yea, upon all
the houses of joy *in* [b]the joyous city:
14 [a]Because the palaces shall be forsaken; the multitude of the city shall be
left; the [l]forts and towers shall be for
dens for ever, a joy of wild asses, a pasture of flocks;
I 15 Until [a]the spirit be poured upon us
M from on high, and [b]the wilderness be a
P fruitful field, and the fruitful field be
counted for a forest.
16 Then judgment shall dwell in the
wilderness, and righteousness remain in
the fruitful field.
U 17 [a]And the work of righteousness
S shall be peace; and the effect of righ-
U teousness quietness and assurance for
W ever.
S 18 And my people shall dwell in a
peaceable habitation, and in sure dwellings, and in quiet resting places;
19 [a]When it shall hail, coming down
[b]on the forest; [l]and the city shall be low
in a low place.
20 Blessed *are* ye that sow beside all
waters, that send forth *thither* the feet of
[a]the ox and the ass.

The distress of Judah

33 WOE TO thee [a]that spoilest, and
thou *wast* not spoiled; and dealest treacherously, and they dealt not
treacherously with thee! [b]when thou
shalt cease to spoil, thou shalt be spoiled;
and when thou shalt make an end to deal
treacherously, they shall deal treacherously with thee.
2 O LORD, be gracious unto us; [a]we
have waited for thee: be thou their arm
every morning, our salvation also in the
time of trouble.
3 At the noise of the tumult the people
fled; at the lifting up of thyself the nations
were scattered.
4 And your spoil shall be gathered *like*
the gathering of the caterpillar: as the
running to and fro of locusts shall he run
upon them.
5 [a]The LORD is exalted; for he dwelleth
on high: he hath filled Zion with judgment and righteousness.
6 And wisdom and knowledge shall be
the stability of thy times, *and* strength of
[l]salvation: the fear of the LORD *is* his
treasure.
7 Behold, their [l]valiant ones shall cry
without: [a]the ambassadors of peace shall
weep bitterly.
8 [a]The highways lie waste, the wayfaring man ceaseth: [b]he hath broken the
covenant, he hath despised the cities, he
regardeth no man.
9 [a]The earth mourneth *and* languisheth: Lebanon is ashamed *and* [l]hewn
down: Sharon is like a wilderness; and
Bashan and Carmel shake off *their fruits.*
10 [a]Now will I rise, saith the LORD;
now will I be exalted; now will I lift up
myself.
11 [a]Ye shall conceive chaff, ye shall H
bring forth stubble: your breath, *as* fire,
shall devour you.
12 And the people shall be *as* the P
burnings of lime: [a]*as* thorns cut up shall
they be burned in the fire.
13 ¶ Hear, [a]ye *that are* far off, what I
have done; and, ye *that are* near, acknowledge my might.
14 The sinners in Zion are afraid; fear- H
fulness hath surprised the hypocrites. S
Who among us shall dwell with the devouring fire? who among us shall dwell
with everlasting burnings?

12 [l]Heb. *the fields of desire*
13 [a]Hos. 9:6 [b]ch. 22:2 [l]Or, *burning upon*
14 [a]ch. 27:10 [l]Or, *clifts and watchtowers*
15 [a]Joel 2:28 [b]ch. 29:17
17 [a]Jas. 3:18
19 [a]ch. 30:30 [b]Zech. 11:2 [l]Or, *and the city shall be utterly abased*
20 [a]ch. 30:24
33:1 [a]ch. 21:2; Hab. 2:8 [b]Rev. 13:10
2 [a]ch. 25:9
5 [a]Ps. 97:9
6 [l]Heb. *salvations*
7 [a]2 Ki. 18:18,37 [l]Or, *messengers*
8 [a]Judg. 5:6 [b]2 Ki. 18:14-17
9 [a]ch. 24:4 [l]Or, *withered away*
10 [a]Ps. 12:5
11 [a]Ps. 7:14; ch. 59:4
12 [a]ch. 9:18
13 [a]ch. 49:1

R *Isa 32:10* ◀ ▶ *Isa 38:5*
I *Isa 30:29* ◀ ▶ *Isa 33:20–22*
M *Isa 31:3* ◀ ▶ *Isa 34:16*
P *Isa 4:4* ◀ ▶ *Isa 44:3–4*
U *Isa 11:6–9* ◀ ▶ *Isa 65:25*
S *Isa 5:18* ◀ ▶ *Isa 33:14–17*
U *Isa 3:10* ◀ ▶ *Isa 33:15–16*
W *Isa 26:3–4* ◀ ▶ *Jer 10:2*
S *Pr 30:5* ◀ ▶ *Isa 43:2*

H *Isa 30:33* ◀ ▶ *Isa 33:14*
P *Isa 30:30* ◀ ▶ *Isa 34:1–4*
H *Isa 33:11–12* ◀ ▶ *Isa 35:4*
S *Isa 32:17* ◀ ▶ *Isa 35:8–9*

32:13–18 This passage envisioned both the rejection of the nation by God (as judgment for their rebellion) as well as their future millennial blessing when they shall be restored to God's blessing under their Messiah.

U 15 He that [a]walketh [1]righteously, and speaketh [2]uprightly; he that despiseth the gain of [3]oppressions, that shaketh his hands from holding of bribes, that stoppeth his ears from hearing of [4]blood, and [b]shutteth his eyes from seeing evil;

F 16 He shall dwell on [1]high: his place of defence *shall be* the munitions of rocks: bread shall be given him; his waters *shall be* sure.

Safety and joy under the Messiah

17 Thine eyes shall see the king in his beauty: they shall behold [1]the land that is very far off.

18 Thine heart shall meditate terror. [a]Where *is* the scribe? where *is* the [1]receiver? where *is* he that counted the towers?

19 [a]Thou shalt not see a fierce people, [b]a people of a deeper speech than thou canst perceive; of a [1]stammering tongue, *that thou canst* not understand.

I M 20 [a]Look upon Zion, the city of our solemnities: thine eyes shall see [b]Jerusalem a quiet habitation, a tabernacle *that* shall not be taken down; [c]not one of [d]the stakes thereof shall ever be removed, neither shall any of the cords thereof be broken.

21 But there the glorious LORD *will be* unto us a place [1]of broad rivers *and* streams; wherein shall go no galley with oars, neither shall gallant ship pass thereby.

22 For the LORD *is* our judge, the LORD *is* our [a]lawgiver,[1] [b]the LORD *is* our king; he will save us.

23 [1]Thy tacklings are loosed; they could not well strengthen their mast, they could not spread the sail: then is the prey of a great spoil divided; the lame take the prey.

24 And the inhabitant shall not say, I am sick: [a]the people that dwell therein *shall be* forgiven *their* iniquity.

U *Isa 32:17* ◀ ▶ *Isa 55:2*
F *Isa 1:19* ◀ ▶ *Isa 41:17*
I *Isa 32:15–18* ◀ ▶ *Isa 37:31–32*
M *Isa 32:1–4* ◀ ▶ *Isa 35:1–10*

15 [a]Ps. 15:2 & 24:4 [b]Ps. 119:37 [1]Heb. *in righteousnesses* [2]Heb. *uprightnesses* [3]Or, *deceits* [4]Heb. *bloods*
16 [1]Heb. *heights,* or, *high places*
17 [1]Heb. *the land of far distances*
18 [a]1 Cor. 1:20 [1]Heb. *weigher?*
19 [a]2 Ki. 19:32 [b]Deut. 28:49,50; Jer. 5:15 [1]Or, *ridiculous*
20 [a]Ps. 48:12 [b]Ps. 46:5 & 125:1,2 [c]ch. 37:33 [d]ch. 54:2
21 [1]Heb. *broad of spaces,* or, *hands*
22 [a]Jas. 4:12 [b]Ps. 89:18 [1]Heb. *statutemaker*
23 [1]Or, *They have forsaken thy tacklings*
24 [a]Jer. 50:20
34:1 [a]Ps. 49:1 [b]Deut. 32:1 [1]Heb. *the fulness thereof*
3 [a]Joel 2:20
4 [a]Ps. 102:26; Ezek. 32:7,8; Joel 2:31; Mat. 24:29; 2 Pet. 3:10 [b]ch. 14:12 [c]Rev. 6:13
5 [a]Jer. 46:10 [b]Jer. 49:7; Mal. 1:4
6 [a]Zeph. 1:7
7 [1]Or, *rhinocerots* [2]Or, *drunken*
8 [a]ch. 63:4
9 [a]Deut. 29:23
10 [a]Rev. 14:11 & 18:18 & 19:3 [b]Mal. 1:4

The judgment on the nations

34 COME[a] NEAR, ye nations, to hear; and hearken, ye people: [b]let the earth hear, and [1]all that is therein; the world, and all things that come forth of it. P

2 For the indignation of the LORD *is* upon all nations, and *his* fury upon all their armies: he hath utterly destroyed them, he hath delivered them to the slaughter.

3 Their slain also shall be cast out, and [a]their stink shall come up out of their carcases, and the mountains shall be melted with their blood.

4 And [a]all the host of heaven shall be dissolved, and the heavens shall be rolled together as a scroll: [b]and all their host shall fall down, as the leaf falleth off from the vine, and as a [c]falling *fig* from the fig tree.

5 For [a]my sword shall be bathed in heaven: behold, it [b]shall come down upon Idumea, and upon the people of my curse, to judgment. P

6 The sword of the LORD is filled with blood, it is made fat with fatness, *and* with the blood of lambs and goats, with the fat of the kidneys of rams: for [a]the LORD hath a sacrifice in Bozrah, and a great slaughter in the land of Idumea.

7 And the [1]unicorns shall come down with them, and the bullocks with the bulls; and their land shall be [2]soaked with blood, and their dust made fat with fatness.

8 For *it is* the day of the LORD'S [a]vengeance, *and* the year of recompences for the controversy of Zion.

9 [a]And the streams thereof shall be turned into pitch, and the dust thereof into brimstone, and the land thereof shall become burning pitch.

10 It shall not be quenched night nor day; [a]the smoke thereof shall go up for ever: [b]from generation to generation it shall lie waste; none shall pass through it for ever and ever.

P *Isa 33:12* ◀ ▶ *Isa 34:5–17*
P *Isa 34:1–4* ◀ ▶ *Isa 40:24*

33:20–22 The prophet foresaw the Millennium when the nation would be restored to God's blessing and the Messiah would rule, ushering in peace and security.

34:1–4 This prophecy described the concluding judgments of God to be poured out upon the unrepentant nations during the final years of the tribulation period. See the judgments described in Rev 6.

11 ¶ [a]But the [1]cormorant and the bittern shall possess it; the owl also and the raven shall dwell in it: and [b]he shall stretch out upon it the line of confusion, and the stones of emptiness.

12 They shall call the nobles thereof to the kingdom, but none *shall be* there, and all her princes shall be nothing.

13 And [a]thorns shall come up in her palaces, nettles and brambles in the fortresses thereof: and [b]it shall be an habitation of dragons, *and* a court for [1,2]owls.

14 [1]The wild beasts of the desert shall also meet with [2]the wild beasts of the island, and the satyr shall cry to his fellow; the [3]screech owl also shall rest there, and find for herself a place of rest.

15 There shall the great owl make her nest, and lay, and hatch, and gather under her shadow: there shall the vultures also be gathered, every one with her mate.

E
M 16 ¶ Seek ye out of [a]the book of the LORD, and read: no one of these shall fail, none shall want her mate: for my mouth it hath commanded, and his spirit it hath gathered them.

17 And he hath cast the lot for them, and his hand hath divided it unto them by line: they shall possess it for ever, from generation to generation shall they dwell therein.

The return to Zion promised

M 35 THE [a]WILDERNESS and the solitary place shall be glad for them; and the desert shall rejoice, and blossom as the rose.

2 [a]It shall blossom abundantly, and rejoice even with joy and singing: the glory of Lebanon shall be given unto it, the excellency of Carmel and Sharon, they shall see the glory of the LORD, *and* the excellency of our God.

H 3 ¶ [a]Strengthen ye the weak hands, and confirm the feeble knees.

4 Say to them *that are* of a [1]fearful heart, Be strong, fear not: behold, your God will come *with* vengeance, *even* God *with* a recompence; he will come and save you. H

5 Then the [a]eyes of the blind shall be opened, and [b]the ears of the deaf shall be unstopped.

6 Then shall the [a]lame *man* leap as an hart, and the [b]tongue of the dumb sing: for in the wilderness shall [c]waters break out, and streams in the desert.

7 And the parched ground shall become a pool, and the thirsty land springs of water: in [a]the habitation of dragons, where each lay, *shall be* [1]grass with reeds and rushes.

8 And an highway shall be there, and a way, and it shall be called The way of holiness; [a]the unclean shall not pass over it; [1]but it *shall be* for those: the wayfaring men, though fools, shall not err *therein.* S

9 [a]No lion shall be there, nor *any* ravenous beast shall go up thereon, it shall not be found there; but the redeemed shall walk *there:*

10 And the [a]ransomed of the LORD shall return, and come to Zion with songs and everlasting joy upon their heads: they shall obtain joy and gladness, and [b]sorrow and sighing shall flee away. S

Sennacherib taunts Hezekiah

36 NOW [a]IT came to pass in the fourteenth year of king Hezekiah, *that* Sennacherib king of Assyria came up against all the defenced cities of Judah, and took them.

2 And the king of Assyria sent Rab-shakeh from Lachish to Jerusalem unto king Hezekiah with a great army. And he stood by the conduit of the upper pool in the highway of the fuller's field.

3 Then came forth unto him Eliakim, Hilkiah's son, which was over the house, and Shebna the [1]scribe, and Joah, Asaph's son, the recorder.

4 ¶ [a]And Rab-shakeh said unto them,

11 [a]ch. 14:23; Zeph. 2:14; Rev. 18:2 [b]2 Ki. 21:13; Lam. 2:8 [1]Or, *pelican*
13 [a]ch. 32:13; Hos. 9:6 [b]ch. 13:21 [1]Or, *ostriches* [2]Heb. *daughters of the owl*
14 [1]Heb. *Ziim* [2]Heb. *Ijim* [3]Or, *night monster*
16 [a]Mal. 3:16
35:1 [a]ch. 55:12
2 [a]ch. 32:15
3 [a]Job 4:3,4; Heb. 12:12
4 [1]Heb. *hasty*
5 [a]ch. 29:18; Mat. 9:27 & 11:5; John 9:6,7 [b]Mat. 11:5
6 [a]Mat. 11:5 & 15:30; John 5:8,9; Acts 8:7 [b]ch. 32:4; Mat. 9:32 & 12:22 [c]ch. 41:18; John 7:38
7 [a]ch. 34:13 [1]Or, *a court for reeds*
8 [a]ch. 52:1; Rev. 21:27 [1]Or, *for he shall be with them*
9 [a]Lev. 26:6; ch. 11:9; Ezek. 34:25
10 [a]ch. 51:11 [b]ch. 25:8; Rev. 7:17 & 21:4
36:1 [a]2 Ki. 18:13, 17; 2 Chr. 32:1
3 [1]Or, *secretary*
4 [a]2 Ki. 18:19

E *Isa 30:1* ◀ ▶ *Isa 40:7*
M *Isa 32:15* ◀ ▶ *Isa 40:7*
M *Isa 33:20–22* ◀ ▶ *Isa 40:4–5*
H *Pr 19:23* ◀ ▶ *Isa 38:16*

H *Isa 33:14* ◀ ▶ *Isa 59:18*
S *Isa 33:14–17* ◀ ▶ *Isa 48:22*
S *Isa 25:8* ◀ ▶ *Isa 51:11*

35:1–10 Isaiah prophesied the blessings of the millennial kingdom when the Messiah's rule is established. Notice the confirmations of the different parts of this prophecy throughout the book of Isaiah: the fertility of the land (see 41:18); peace within the animal kingdom (see 11:6–9); the return of the exiles from all over the world (see 11:11–16).

Say ye now to Hezekiah, Thus saith the
great king, the king of Assyria, What confidence *is* this wherein thou trustest?
5 I say, *sayest thou,* (but *they are but*
[1]vain words) [2]*I have* counsel and strength
for war: now on whom dost thou trust,
that thou rebellest against me?
6 Lo, thou trustest in the [a]staff of this
broken reed, on Egypt; whereon if a man
lean, it will go into his hand, and pierce
it: so *is* Pharaoh king of Egypt to all that
trust in him.
7 But if thou say to me, We trust in the
LORD our God: *is it* not he, whose high
places and whose altars Hezekiah hath
taken away, and said to Judah and to Jerusalem, Ye shall worship before this altar?
8 Now therefore give [1]pledges, I pray
thee, to my master the king of Assyria,
and I will give thee two thousand horses,
if thou be able on thy part to set riders
upon them.
9 How then wilt thou turn away the
face of one captain of the least of my master's servants, and put thy trust on Egypt
for chariots and for horsemen?
10 And am I now come up without the
LORD against this land to destroy it? the
LORD said unto me, Go up against this
land, and destroy it.
11 ¶ Then said Eliakim and Shebna
and Joah unto Rab-shakeh, Speak, I pray
thee, unto thy servants in the Syrian language; for we understand *it:* and speak
not to us in the Jews' language, in the
ears of the people that *are* on the wall.
12 ¶ But Rab-shakeh said, Hath my
master sent me to thy master and to thee
to speak these words? *hath he* not *sent*
me to the men that sit upon the wall, that
they may eat their own dung, and drink
their own piss with you?
13 Then Rab-shakeh stood, and cried
with a loud voice in the Jews' language,
and said, Hear ye the words of the great
king, the king of Assyria.
14 Thus saith the king, Let not Hezekiah deceive you: for he shall not be able
to deliver you.
15 Neither let Hezekiah make you
trust in the LORD, saying, The LORD will
surely deliver us: this city shall not be
delivered into the hand of the king of Assyria.
16 Hearken not to Hezekiah: for thus
saith the king of Assyria, [1,2]Make *an*
agreement with me *by* a present, and
come out to me: [a]and eat ye every one of
his vine, and every one of his fig tree, and
drink ye every one the waters of his own
cistern;
17 Until I come and take you away to a
land like your own land, a land of corn
and wine, a land of bread and vineyards.
18 *Beware* lest Hezekiah persuade
you, saying, The LORD will deliver us.
Hath any of the gods of the nations delivered his land out of the hand of the king
of Assyria?
19 Where *are* the gods of Hamath and
Arphad? where *are* the gods of Sepharvaim? and have they delivered Samaria
out of my hand?
20 Who *are they* among all the gods of
these lands, that have delivered their
land out of my hand, that the LORD should
deliver Jerusalem out of my hand?
21 But they held their peace, and answered him not a word: for the king's
commandment was, saying, Answer him
not.
22 ¶ Then came Eliakim, the son of
Hilkiah, that *was* over the household, and
Shebna the scribe, and Joah, the son of
Asaph, the recorder, to Hezekiah with
their clothes rent, and told him the words
of Rab-shakeh.

Isaiah's message to Hezekiah

37 AND [a]IT came to pass, when
king Hezekiah heard *it,* that he
rent his clothes, and covered himself
with sackcloth, and went into the house
of the LORD.
2 And he sent Eliakim, who *was* over
the household, and Shebna the scribe,
and the elders of the priests covered with
sackcloth, unto Isaiah the prophet the
son of Amoz.
3 And they said unto him, Thus saith
Hezekiah, This day *is* a day of trouble,
and of rebuke, and of [1]blasphemy: for the
children are come to the birth, and *there*
is not strength to bring forth.
4 It may be the LORD thy God will hear
the words of Rab-shakeh, whom the king
of Assyria his master hath sent to reproach the living God, and will reprove
the words which the LORD thy God hath
heard: wherefore lift up *thy* prayer for the
remnant that is [1]left.
5 So the servants of king Hezekiah
came to Isaiah.
6 ¶ And Isaiah said unto them, Thus

5 [1]Heb. *a word of lips* [2]Or, but *counsel and strength* are *for the war*

6 [a]Ezek. 29:6,7

8 [1]Or, *hostages*

16 [a]Zech. 3:10 [1]Or, *Seek my favour by a present* [2]Heb. *Make with me a blessing*

37:1 [a]2 Ki. 19:1

3 [1]Or, *provocation*

4 [1]Heb. *found*

shall ye say unto your master, Thus saith
the LORD, Be not afraid of the words that
thou hast heard, wherewith the servants
of the king of Assyria have blasphemed me.
7 Behold, I will [1]send a blast upon
him, and he shall hear a rumour, and return to his own land; and I will cause him
to fall by the sword in his own land.
8 ¶ So Rab-shakeh returned, and found
the king of Assyria warring against Libnah: for he had heard that he was departed from Lachish.
9 And he heard say concerning Tirhakah king of Ethiopia, He is come forth to
make war with thee. And when he heard
it, he sent messengers to Hezekiah,
saying,
10 Thus shall ye speak to Hezekiah
king of Judah, saying, Let not thy God, in
whom thou trustest, deceive thee, saying,
Jerusalem shall not be given into the
hand of the king of Assyria.
11 Behold, thou hast heard what the
kings of Assyria have done to all lands by
destroying them utterly; and shalt thou
be delivered?
12 Have the gods of the nations delivered them which my fathers have destroyed, *as* Gozan, and Haran, and Rezeph, and the children of Eden which
were in Telassar?
13 Where *is* the king of [a]Hamath, and
the king of Arphad, and the king of the
city of Sepharvaim, Hena, and Ivah?

Hezekiah's prayer to the LORD

14 ¶ And Hezekiah received the letter
from the hand of the messengers, and
read it: and Hezekiah went up unto the
house of the LORD, and spread it before
the LORD.
15 And Hezekiah prayed unto the
LORD, saying,
16 O LORD of hosts, God of Israel, that
dwellest *between* the cherubims, thou *art*
the God, *even* thou alone, of all the kingdoms of the earth: thou hast made
heaven and earth.
17 [a]Incline thine ear, O LORD, and
hear; open thine eyes, O LORD, and see:
and hear all the words of Sennacherib,
which hath sent to reproach the living
God.
18 Of a truth, LORD, the kings of Assyria have laid waste all the [1]nations, and
their countries,
19 And have [1]cast their gods into the
fire: for they *were* no gods, but the work
of men's hands, wood and stone: therefore they have destroyed them.
20 Now therefore, O LORD our God,
save us from his hand, that all the kingdoms of the earth may know that thou *art*
the LORD, *even* thou only.

The promise of deliverance

21 ¶ Then Isaiah the son of Amoz sent
unto Hezekiah, saying, Thus saith the
LORD God of Israel, Whereas thou hast
prayed to me against Sennacherib king of
Assyria:
22 This *is* the word which the LORD
hath spoken concerning him; The virgin,
the daughter of Zion, hath despised thee,
and laughed thee to scorn; the daughter
of Jerusalem hath shaken her head at
thee.
23 Whom hast thou reproached and
blasphemed? and against whom hast thou
exalted *thy* voice, and lifted up thine eyes
on high? *even* against the Holy One of
Israel.
24 [1]By thy servants hast thou reproached the Lord, and hast said, By the
multitude of my chariots am I come up to
the height of the mountains, to the sides
of Lebanon; and I will cut down [2]the tall
cedars thereof, *and* the choice fir trees
thereof: and I will enter into the height of
his border, *and* [3]the forest of his Carmel.
25 I have digged, and drunk water;
and with the sole of my feet have I dried
up all the rivers of the [1]besieged places.
26 [a]Hast[1] thou not heard long ago,
how I have done it; *and* of ancient times,
that I have formed it? now have I brought
it to pass, that thou shouldest be to lay
waste defenced cities *into* ruinous heaps.
27 Therefore their inhabitants *were*
[1]of small power, they were dismayed and
confounded: they were *as* the grass of the
field, and *as* the green herb, *as* the grass
on the housetops, and *as corn* blasted before it be grown up.
28 But I know thy [1]abode, and thy going out, and thy coming in, and thy rage
against me.
29 Because thy rage against me, and
thy tumult, is come up into mine ears,
therefore [a]will I put my hook in thy nose,
and my bridle in thy lips, and I will turn
thee back by the way by which thou
camest.

7 [1]Or, *put a spirit into him*
13 [a]Jer. 49:23
17 [a]Dan. 9:18
18 [1]Heb *lands*
19 [1]Heb. *given*
24 [1]Heb. *By the hand of thy servants* [2]Heb. *the tallness of the cedars thereof,* and *the choice of the fir trees thereof* [3]Or, *the forest* and *his fruitful field*
25 [1]Or, *fenced and closed*
26 [a]2 Ki. 19:25 [1]Or, *Hast thou not heard* how *I have made it long ago,* and *formed it of ancient times? should I now bring it to be laid waste,* and *defenced cities* to be *ruinous heaps?*
27 [1]Heb. *short of hand*
28 [1]Or, *sitting*
29 [a]ch. 30:28; Ezek. 38:4

30 And this *shall be* a sign unto thee, Ye shall eat *this* year such as groweth of itself; and the second year that which springeth of the same: and in the third year sow ye, and reap, and plant vineyards, and eat the fruit thereof.

I 31 And ʹthe remnant that is escaped of the house of Judah shall again take root downward, and bear fruit upward:

32 For out of Jerusalem shall go forth a remnant, and ʹthey that escape out of mount Zion: the [a]zeal of the LORD of hosts shall do this.

33 Therefore thus saith the LORD concerning the king of Assyria, He shall not come into this city, nor shoot an arrow there, nor come before it with ʹshields, nor cast a bank against it.

34 By the way that he came, by the same shall he return, and shall not come into this city, saith the LORD.

35 For I will [a]defend this city to save it for mine own sake, and for my servant David's sake.

36 Then the [a]angel of the LORD went forth, and smote in the camp of the Assyrians a hundred and fourscore and five thousand: and when they arose early in the morning, behold, they *were* all dead corpses.

37 ¶ So Sennacherib king of Assyria departed, and went and returned, and dwelt at Nineveh.

38 And it came to pass, as he was worshipping in the house of Nisroch his god, that Adrammelech and Sharezer his sons smote him with the sword; and they escaped into the land of ʹArmenia: and Esar-haddon his son reigned in his stead.

Hezekiah's sickness

E **38** IN [a]THOSE days was Hezekiah sick unto death. And Isaiah the prophet the son of Amoz came unto him, and said unto him, Thus saith the LORD, [b]Setʹ thine house in order: for thou shalt die, and not live.

2 Then Hezekiah turned his face toward the wall, and prayed unto the LORD,

3 And said, [a]Remember now, O LORD, I beseech thee, how I have walked before thee in truth and with a perfect heart, and have done *that which is* good in thy sight. And Hezekiah wept ʹsore.

4 ¶ Then came the word of the LORD to Isaiah, saying,

5 Go, and say to Hezekiah, Thus saith the LORD, the God of David thy father, I have heard thy prayer, I have seen thy tears: behold, I will add unto thy days fifteen years. R

6 And I will deliver thee and this city out of the hand of the king of Assyria: and [a]I will defend this city.

7 And this *shall be* [a]a sign unto thee from the LORD, that the LORD will do this thing that he hath spoken;

8 Behold, I will bring again the shadow of the degrees, which is gone down in the ʹsun dial of Ahaz, ten degrees backward. So the sun returned ten degrees, by which degrees it was gone down.

9 ¶ The writing of Hezekiah king of Judah, when he had been sick, and was recovered of his sickness:

10 I said in the cutting off of my days, I shall go to the gates of the grave; I am deprived of the residue of my years.

11 I said, I shall not see the LORD, *even* the LORD, [a]in the land of the living: I shall behold man no more with the inhabitants of the world.

12 [a]Mine age is departed, and is removed from me as a shepherd's tent: I have cut off like a weaver my life: he will cut me off ʹwith pining sickness: from day *even* to night wilt thou make an end of me.

13 I reckoned till morning, *that,* as a lion, so will he break all my bones: from day *even* to night wilt thou make an end of me.

14 Like a crane *or* a swallow, so did I chatter: [a]I did mourn as a dove: mine eyes fail *with looking* upward: O LORD, I am oppressed; ʹundertake for me.

15 What shall I say? he hath both spoken unto me, and himself hath done *it:* I shall go softly all my years [a]in the bitterness of my soul.

31 ʹHeb. *the escaping of the house of Judah that remaineth*
32 [a]2 Ki. 19:31; ch. 9:7 ʹHeb. *the escaping*
33 ʹHeb. *shield*
35 [a]2 Ki. 20:6; ch. 38:6
36 [a]2 Ki. 19:35
38 ʹHeb. *Ararat*
38:1 [a]2 Ki. 20:1; 2 Chr. 32:24 [b]2 Sam. 17:23 ʹHeb. *Give charge concerning thy house*
3 [a]Neh. 13:14 ʹHeb. *with great weeping*
6 [a]ch. 37:35
7 [a]2 Ki. 20:8; ch. 7:11
8 ʹHeb. *degrees by,* or, *with the sun*
11 [a]Ps. 27:13 & 116:9
12 [a]Job 7:6 ʹOr, *from the* thrum
14 [a]ch. 59:11 ʹOr, *ease me*
15 [a]Job 7:11

I *Isa 33:20–22* ◀ ▶ *Isa 40:1–2*
E *Ps 107:20* ◀ ▶ *Da 1:15*
R *Isa 32:13–14* ◀ ▶ *Isa 40:2*

37:31–32, 36 Isaiah prophesied to King Hezekiah that, despite the seemingly overwhelming military force of Assyria, God would save Judah from destruction. Isaiah's words record an astonishing miracle when God defeated the Assyrian army by destroying 185,000 Assyrian soldiers in one night.

H 16 O Lord, by these *things men* live,
and in all these *things is* the life of my
spirit: so wilt thou recover me, and make
me to live.

L 17 Behold, [1]for peace I had great bitterness: but [2]thou hast in love to my soul
delivered it from the pit of corruption:
for thou hast cast all my sins behind thy
back.

L 18 For [a]the grave cannot praise thee,
death can *not* celebrate thee: they that go
down into the pit cannot hope for thy
truth.

19 The living, the living, he shall
praise thee, as I *do* this day: [a]the father to
the children shall make known thy truth.

20 The LORD *was ready* to save me:
therefore we will sing my songs to the
stringed instruments all the days of our
life in the house of the LORD.

L 21 For [a]Isaiah had said, Let them take
a lump of figs, and lay *it* for a plaster upon
the boil, and he shall recover.

22 [a]Hezekiah also had said, What *is*
the sign that I shall go up to the house of
the LORD?

Hezekiah's folly and exile

39 AT [a]THAT time Merodach-baladan, the son of Baladan, king of
Babylon, sent letters and a present to
Hezekiah: for he had heard that he had
been sick, and was recovered.

2 [a]And Hezekiah was glad of them,
and showed them the house of his [1]pre-
cious things, the silver, and the gold, and
the spices, and the precious ointment,
and all the house of his [2,3]armour, and all
that was found in his treasures: there was
nothing in his house, nor in all his dominion, that Hezekiah showed them not.

3 ¶ Then came Isaiah the prophet unto
king Hezekiah, and said unto him, What
said these men? and from whence came
they unto thee? And Hezekiah said, They
are come from a far country unto me,
even from Babylon.

4 Then said he, What have they seen
in thine house? And Hezekiah answered,
All that *is* in mine house have they seen:
there is nothing among my treasures that
I have not shown them.

5 Then said Isaiah to Hezekiah, Hear
the word of the LORD of hosts:

6 Behold, the days come, [a]that all that
is in thine house, and *that* which thy fathers have laid up in store until this day,
shall be carried to Babylon: nothing shall
be left, saith the LORD.

7 And of thy sons that shall issue from
thee, which thou shalt beget, shall they
take away; and [1]they shall be eunuchs in
the palace of the king of Babylon.

8 Then said Hezekiah to Isaiah, [a]Good
is the word of the LORD which thou hast
spoken. He said moreover, For there shall
be peace and truth in my days.

Comfort for God's people

40 COMFORT YE, comfort ye my I
people, saith your God.

2 Speak ye [1]comfortably to Jerusalem, R
and cry unto her, that her [2]warfare is accomplished, that her iniquity is pardoned: [a]for she hath received of the
LORD'S hand double for all her sins.

3 ¶ [a]The voice of him that crieth in the
wilderness, [b]Prepare ye the way of the
LORD, [c]make straight in the desert a highway for our God.

4 Every valley shall be exalted, and ev- M
ery mountain and hill shall be made low:
[a]and the crooked shall be made [1]straight,
and the rough places [2]plain:

5 And the glory of the LORD shall be
revealed, and all flesh shall see *it* to-

17 [1]Or, *on my peace came great bitterness* [2]Heb. *thou hast loved my soul from the pit*
18 [a]Ps. 6:5 & 30:9 & 88:11 & 115:17; Eccl. 9:10
19 [a]Deut. 4:9 & 6:7; Ps. 78:3,4
21 [a]2 Ki. 20:7
22 [a]2 Ki. 20:8
39:1 [a]2 Ki. 20:12
2 [a]2 Chr. 32:31 [1]Or, *spicery* [2]Or, *jewels* [3]Heb. *vessels,* or, *instruments*
6 [a]Jer. 20:5
7 [1]Fulfilled in Dan. 1:2,3
8 [a]1 Sam. 3:18
40:2 [a]ch. 61:7 [1]Heb. *to the heart* [2]Or, *appointed time*
3 [a]Mat. 3:3 [b]Mal. 3:1 [c]Ps. 68:4
4 [a]ch. 45:2 [1]Or, *a straight place* [2]Or, *a plain place*

H *Isa 35:3–6* ◀ ▶ *Isa 40:29–31*
L *Isa 32:2* ◀ ▶ *Isa 42:6–7*
L *2Ch 34:28* ◀ ▶ *Isa 38:21–22*
L *Isa 38:18* ◀ ▶ *Isa 45:1–5*
I *Isa 37:31–32* ◀ ▶ *Isa 40:8–11*
R *Isa 38:5* ◀ ▶ *Isa 42:22–25*
M *Isa 35:1–10* ◀ ▶ *Isa 41:18–20*

39:5–7 Isaiah's tragic prophecy foretold the final destruction of Hezekiah's reign by the pagan Babylonians. Hezekiah's proud revelation of the treasures in his palace to the representatives of Babylon would ultimately cause Babylon to plunder all of Hezekiah's riches; "nothing shall be left" (39:6). Isaiah also prophesied the future castration of Hezekiah's sons—a procedure that would ensure no royal heir to usurp Babylonian authority.

40:1–11 This prophecy foreshadowed three events: the return from the exile (see 52:7–9); the first coming of Christ (see Mt 21:5); and the glorious blessing of the millennial kingdom when the Messiah will rule on earth (see 62:11; Rev 22:12). Note that the NT links the voice of John the Baptist with 40:3 (see Mt 3:3; Mk 1:3; Lk 3:4; Jn 1:23).

gether: for the mouth of the LORD hath
spoken *it.*
N 6 The voice said, Cry. And he said,
What shall I cry? [a]All flesh *is* grass, and
all the goodliness thereof *is* as the flower
of the field:
E 7 The grass withereth, the flower fad-
M eth: because the spirit of the LORD blow-
N eth upon it: surely the people *is* grass.
I 8 The grass withereth, the flower fad-
K eth: but [a]the word of our God shall stand
for ever.
9 ¶ [a]O[1] Zion, that bringest good tidings, get thee up into the high mountain;
[2]O Jerusalem, that bringest good tidings,
lift up thy voice with strength; lift *it* up,
be not afraid; say unto the cities of Judah,
Behold your God!
10 Behold, the Lord GOD will come
[1]with strong *hand,* and [a]his arm shall
rule for him: behold, [b]his reward *is* with
him, and [c]his[2] work before him.
11 He shall [a]feed his flock like a shepherd: he shall gather the lambs with his
arm, and carry *them* in his bosom, *and*
shall gently lead those [1]that are with
young.
12 ¶ [a]Who hath measured the waters
in the hollow of his hand, and meted out
heaven with the span, and comprehended the dust of the earth in [1]a measure, and weighed the mountains in
scales, and the hills in a balance?
D 13 [a]Who hath directed the spirit of the
M LORD, or *being* [1]his counsellor hath taught
T him?
14 With whom took he counsel, and
who [1]instructed him, and taught him in
the path of judgment, and taught him
knowledge, and showed to him the way
of [2]understanding?
15 Behold, the nations *are* as a drop of
a bucket, and are counted as the small
dust of the balance: behold, he taketh up
the isles as a very little thing.
16 And Lebanon *is* not sufficient to
burn, nor the beasts thereof sufficient for
a burnt offering.
17 All nations before him *are* as [a]noth-
ing; and [b]they are counted to him less
than nothing, and vanity.
18 ¶ To whom then will ye [a]liken
God? or what likeness will ye compare
unto him?
19 [a]The workman melteth a graven
image, and the goldsmith spreadeth it
over with gold, and casteth silver chains.
20 He that [1]*is* so impoverished that he
hath no oblation chooseth a tree *that* will
not rot; he seeketh unto him a cunning
workman [a]to prepare a graven image,
that shall not be moved.
21 [a]Have ye not known? have ye not
heard? hath it not been told you from the
beginning? have ye not understood from
the foundations of the earth?
22 [1]*It is* he that sitteth upon the circle
of the earth, and the inhabitants thereof
are as grasshoppers; that [a]stretcheth out
the heavens as a curtain, and spreadeth
them out as a tent to dwell in:
23 That bringeth the [a]princes to nothing; he maketh the judges of the earth as
vanity.
24 Yea, they shall not be planted; yea, P
they shall not be sown: yea, their stock
shall not take root in the earth: and he
shall also blow upon them, and they shall
wither, and the whirlwind shall take
them away as stubble.
25 [a]To whom then will ye liken me, or
shall I be equal? saith the Holy One.
26 Lift up your eyes on high, and behold who hath created these *things,* that
bringeth out their host by number: [a]he
calleth them all by names by the greatness of his might, for that *he is* strong in
power; not one faileth.
27 Why sayest thou, O Jacob, and I
speakest, O Israel, My way is hid from
the LORD, and my judgment is passed over
from my God?
28 ¶ Hast thou not known? hast thou

6 [a]Job 14:2
8 [a]John 12:34
9 [a]ch. 41:27 [1]Or, *O thou that tellest good tidings to Zion* [2]Or, *O thou that tellest good tidings to Jerusalem*
10 [a]ch. 59:16 [b]ch. 62:11 [c]ch. 49:4 [1]Or, *against the strong* [2]Or, *recompence for his work*
11 [a]Ezek. 34:23; John 10:11; Heb. 13:20; 1 Pet. 2:25 [1]Or, *that give suck*
12 [a]Prov. 30:4 [1]Heb. *a tierce*
13 [a]Job 21:22; 1 Cor. 2:16 [1]Heb. *man of his counsel*
14 [1]Heb. *made him understand* [2]Heb. *understandings?*
17 [a]Dan. 4:35 [b]Ps. 62:9
18 [a]ch. 46:5; Acts 17:29
19 [a]ch. 41:6,7 & 44:12; Jer. 10:3
20 [a]ch. 41:7; Jer. 10:4 [1]Heb. is *poor of oblation*
21 [a]Ps. 19:1; Acts 14:17; Rom. 1:19
22 [a]Job 9:8; Ps. 104:2; ch. 42:5 & 51:13; Jer. 10:12 [1]Or, *Him that sitteth*
23 [a]Job 12:21; Ps. 107:40
25 [a]ver. 18
26 [a]Ps. 147:4

N *Isa 28:12–13* ◀▶ *Isa 48:4*
E *Isa 34:16* ◀▶ *Isa 48:16*
M *Isa 34:16* ◀▶ *Isa 40:13*
N *Isa 30:1* ◀▶ *Isa 44:3–4*
I *Isa 40:1–2* ◀▶ *Isa 40:27–28*
K *Isa 32:2* ◀▶ *Isa 40:29*
D *Ps 139:7* ◀▶ *Mt 12:31–32*
M *Isa 40:7* ◀▶ *Isa 44:3–4*
T *Isa 28:6* ◀▶ *Isa 42:1*

P *Isa 34:5–17* ◀▶ *Isa 42:13–15*
I *Isa 40:8–11* ◀▶ *Isa 41:8–21*

40:27–28 The prophet confirms that God's understanding and purposes are beyond the understanding of those who do not listen to God's Spirit.

not heard, *that* the everlasting God, the LORD, the Creator of the ends of the earth, fainteth not, neither is weary? [a]*there is* no searching of his understanding.

K H 29 He giveth power to the faint; and to *them that have* no might he increaseth strength.

30 Even the youths shall faint and be weary, and the young men shall utterly fall:

K 31 But they that wait upon the LORD [a]shall [1]renew *their* strength; they shall mount up with wings as eagles; they shall run, and not be weary; *and* they shall walk, and not faint.

God will help Israel

41 KEEP[a] SILENCE before me, O islands; and let the people renew *their* strength: let them come near; then let them speak: let us come near together to judgment.

2 Who raised up [1]the righteous *man* [a]from the east, called him to his foot, [b]gave the nations before him, and made *him* rule over kings? he gave *them* as the dust to his sword, *and* as driven stubble to his bow.

3 He pursued them, *and* passed [1]safely; *even* by the way *that* he had not gone with his feet.

4 [a]Who hath wrought and done *it,* calling the generations from the beginning? I the LORD, the [b]first, and with the last; I *am* he.

5 The isles saw *it,* and feared; the ends of the earth were afraid, drew near, and came.

6 [a]They helped every one his neighbour; and *every one* said to his brother, [1]Be of good courage.

7 [a]So the carpenter encouraged the [1]goldsmith, *and* he that smootheth *with* the hammer [2]him that smote the anvil, [3]saying, It *is* ready for the soldering: and he fastened it with nails, [b]*that* it should not be moved.

I 8 But thou, Israel, *art* my servant, Jacob whom I have [a]chosen, the seed of Abraham my [b]friend.

9 *Thou* whom I have taken from the ends of the earth, and called thee from the chief men thereof, and said unto thee, Thou *art* my servant; I have chosen thee, and not cast thee away.

10 ¶ [a]Fear thou not; [b]for I *am* with thee: be not dismayed; for I *am* thy God: I will strengthen thee; yea, I will help thee; yea, I will uphold thee with the right hand of my righteousness. K L

11 Behold, all they that were incensed against thee shall be [a]ashamed and confounded: they shall be as nothing; and [1]they that strive with thee shall perish. V

12 Thou shalt seek them, and shalt not find them, *even* [1]them that contended with thee: [2]they that war against thee shall be as nothing, and as a thing of nought.

13 For I the LORD thy God will hold thy right hand, saying unto thee, Fear not; I will help thee. L

14 Fear not, thou worm Jacob, *and* ye [1]men of Israel; I will help thee, saith the LORD, and thy redeemer, the Holy One of Israel.

15 Behold, [a]I will make thee a new sharp threshing instrument having [1]teeth: thou shalt thresh the mountains, and beat *them* small, and shalt make the hills as chaff.

16 Thou shalt [a]fan them, and the wind shall carry them away, and the whirlwind shall scatter them: and thou shalt rejoice in the LORD, *and* [b]shalt glory in the Holy One of Israel.

17 *When* the poor and needy seek water, and *there is* none, *and* their tongue faileth for thirst, I the LORD will hear them, *I* the God of Israel will not forsake them. F

18 I will open [a]rivers in high places, and fountains in the midst of the valleys: I will make the [b]wilderness a pool of water, and the dry land springs of water. M

28 [a]Ps. 147:5; Rom. 11:33
31 [a]Ps. 103:5 [1]Heb. *change*
41:1 [a]Zech. 2:13
2 [a]ch. 46:11 [b]Gen. 14:14; ch. 45:1 [1]Heb. *righteousness*
3 [1]Heb. *in peace*
4 [a]ver. 26 [b]ch. 44:6; Rev. 1:17 & 22:13
6 [a]ch. 40:19 [1]Heb. *Be strong*
7 [a]ch. 40:19 [b]ch. 40:20 [1]Or, *founder* [2]Or, *the smiting* [3]Or, *saying of the soder, It is good*
8 [a]Deut. 7:6 & 10:15; Ps. 135:4; ch. 43:1 [b]2 Chr. 20:7; Jas. 2:23
10 [a]ver. 13,14; ch. 43:5 [b]Deut. 31:6
11 [a]Ex. 23:22; ch. 45:24 & 60:12; Zech. 12:3 [1]Heb. *the men of thy strife*
12 [1]Heb. *the men of thy contention* [2]Heb. *the men of thy war*
14 [1]Or, *few men*
15 [a]Mic. 4:13; 2 Cor. 10:4 [1]Heb. *mouths*
16 [a]Jer. 51:2 [b]ch. 45:25
18 [a]ch. 35:6,7 & 43:19 & 44:3 [b]Ps. 107:35

K *Isa 40:8* ◀ ▶ *Isa 40:31*
H *Isa 38:16* ◀ ▶ *Isa 53:4*
K *Isa 40:29* ◀ ▶ *Isa 41:10*
I *Isa 40:27–28* ◀ ▶ *Isa 42:16*
K *Isa 40:31* ◀ ▶ *Isa 48:18*
L *Isa 32:2* ◀ ▶ *Isa 41:13–14*
V *Pr. 20:22* ◀ ▶ *Isa 50:9*
L *Isa 41:10* ◀ ▶ *Isa 43:2*
F *Isa 33:16* ◀ ▶ *Isa 48:21*
M *Isa 40:4–5* ◀ ▶ *Isa 42:4*

41:8–20 God declares that he has chosen Israel as his servant and that he would not cast his people away. He promised, "Fear not; I will help thee" (41:13).

19 I will plant in the wilderness the
cedar, the shittah tree, and the myrtle,
and the oil tree; I will set in the desert
the fir tree, *and* the pine, and the box
tree together:
20 [a]That they may see, and know, and
consider, and understand together, that
the hand of the LORD hath done this, and
the Holy One of Israel hath created it.
21 [1]Produce your cause, saith the
LORD; bring forth your strong *reasons,*
saith the King of Jacob.
22 [a]Let them bring *them* forth, and
show us what shall happen: let them
show the former things, what they *be,*
that we may [1]consider them, and know
the latter end of them; or declare us
things for to come.
23 [a]Show the things that are to
come hereafter, that we may know that
ye *are* gods: yea, [b]do good, or do evil,
that we may be dismayed, and behold *it*
together.
24 Behold, [a]ye *are* [1]of nothing, and
your work [2]of nought: an abomination *is*
he that chooseth you.
25 I have raised up *one* from the
north, and he shall come: from the rising
of the sun [a]shall he call upon my name:
[b]and he shall come upon princes as
upon mortar, and as the potter treadeth
clay.
26 [a]Who hath declared from the beginning, that we may know? and beforetime, that we may say, *He is* righteous?
yea, *there is* none that showeth, yea,
there is none that declareth, yea, *there is*
none that heareth your words.
27 [a]The first [b]*shall say* to Zion,
Behold, behold them: and I will give
to Jerusalem one that bringeth good
tidings.
28 [a]For I beheld, and *there was* no
man; even among them, and *there was*
no counsellor, that, when I asked of
them, could [1]answer a word.
29 [a]Behold, they *are* all vanity; their
works *are* nothing: their molten images
are wind and confusion.

The mission of God's servant

42 BEHOLD [a]MY servant, whom I B
uphold; mine elect, *in whom* my G
soul [b]delighteth; [c]I have put my spirit T
upon him: he shall bring forth judgment
to the Gentiles.
2 He shall not cry, nor lift up, nor
cause his voice to be heard in the street.
3 A bruised reed shall he not break, W
and the [1]smoking flax shall he not
[2]quench: he shall bring forth judgment
unto truth.
4 He shall not fail nor be [1]discouraged, M
till he have set judgment in the earth:
[a]and the isles shall wait for his law.
5 ¶ Thus saith God the LORD, [a]he that
created the heavens, and stretched them
out; he that spread forth the earth, and
that which cometh out of it; [b]he that giveth breath unto the people upon it, and
spirit to them that walk therein:
6 [a]I the LORD have called thee in righ- L
teousness, and will hold thine hand, and
will keep thee, [b]and give thee for a covenant of the people, for [c]a light of the
Gentiles;
7 [a]To open the blind eyes, to [b]bring
out the prisoners from the prison, *and*
them that sit in [c]darkness out of the
prison house.
8 I *am* the LORD: that *is* my name: and
my [a]glory will I not give to another, neither my praise to graven images.
9 Behold, the former things are come
to pass, and new things do I declare: before they spring forth I tell you of them.

Song of praise to the LORD

10 [a]Sing unto the LORD a new song,
and his praise from the end of the earth,
[b]ye that go down to the sea, and [1]all that
is therein; the isles, and the inhabitants
thereof.
11 Let the wilderness and the cities

20 [a]Job 12:9
21 [1]Heb. *Cause to come near*
22 [a]ch. 45:21 [1]Heb. *set our heart upon them*
23 [a]ch. 42:9 & 44:7,8 & 45:3; John 13:19 [b]Jer. 10:5
24 [a]Ps. 115:8; ch. 44:9; 1 Cor. 8:4 [1]Or, worse *than nothing* [2]Or, worse *than of a viper*
25 [a]Ezra 1:2 [b]ver. 2
26 [a]ch. 43:9
27 [a]ver. 4 [b]ch. 40:9
28 [a]ch. 63:5 [1]Heb. *return*
29 [a]ver. 24
42:1 [a]ch. 43:10 & 49:3,6; Mat. 12:18; Phil. 2:7 [b]Mat. 3:17 & 17:5; Eph. 1:6 [c]ch. 11:2; John 3:34
3 [1]Or, *dimly burning* [2]Heb. *quench it*
4 [a]Gen. 49:10 [1]Heb. *broken*
5 [a]ch. 44:24; Zech. 12:1 [b]Acts 17:25
6 [a]ch. 43:1 [b]ch. 49:8 [c]ch. 49:6; Luke 2:32; Acts 13:47
7 [a]ch. 35:5 [b]ch. 61:1; Luke 4:18; 2 Tim. 2:26; Heb. 2:14 [c]ch. 9:2
8 [a]ch. 48:11
10 [a]Ps. 33:3 & 40:3 & 98:1 [b]Ps. 107:23 [1]Heb. *the fulness thereof*

B *Isa 11:2* ◀ ▶ *Isa 44:3*
G *Isa 28:6* ◀ ▶ *Isa 61:1*
T *Isa 40:13* ◀ ▶ *Isa 61:1*
W *Isa 1:18* ◀ ▶ *Isa 45:22*
M *Isa 41:18–20* ◀ ▶ *Isa 44:3–5*
L *Isa 38:17* ◀ ▶ *Isa 43:25*

41:21–24 God's prophet challenged the pagan idols to bring forth their predictions of future events to prove that they were truly powerful. Since the idols could neither predict nor perform powerful deeds, God declared that the idols were nothing and that the people who worshiped them were "an abomination" (41:24).

42:4 The prophet predicted a day when Jesus Christ, the Messiah, would return to establish his righteous judgment and law on earth.

thereof lift up *their voice,* the villages *that* Kedar doth inhabit: let the inhabitants of the rock sing, let them shout from the top of the mountains.

12 Let them give glory unto the LORD, and declare his praise in the islands.

P 13 The LORD shall go forth as a mighty man, he shall stir up jealousy like a man of war: he shall cry, [a]yea, roar; he shall [1]prevail against his enemies.

14 I have long time holden my peace; I have been still, *and* refrained myself: *now* will I cry like a travailing woman; I will destroy and [1]devour at once.

15 I will make waste mountains and hills, and dry up all their herbs; and I will make the rivers islands, and I will dry up the pools.

I 16 And I will bring the blind by a way *that* they knew not; I will lead them in paths *that* they have not known: I will make darkness light before them, and crooked things [1]straight. These things will I do unto them, and not forsake them.

17 ¶ They shall be [a]turned back, they shall be greatly ashamed, that trust in graven images, that say to the molten images, Ye *are* our gods.

The nation's sin and punishment

18 Hear, ye deaf; and look, ye blind, that ye may see.

19 [a]Who *is* blind, but my servant? or deaf, as my messenger *that* I sent? who *is* blind as *he that is* perfect, and blind as the LORD'S servant?

20 Seeing many things, [a]but thou observest not; opening the ears, but he heareth not.

21 The LORD is well pleased for his righteousness' sake; he will magnify the law, and make [1]*it* honourable.

R 22 But this *is* a people robbed and spoiled; [1]*they are* all of them snared in holes, and they are hid in prison houses: they are for a prey, and none delivereth; for [2]a spoil, and none saith, Restore.

23 Who among you will give ear to this? *who* will hearken and hear [1]for the time to come?

24 Who gave Jacob for a spoil, and Israel to the robbers? did not the LORD, he against whom we have sinned? for they would not walk in his ways, neither were they obedient unto his law.

25 Therefore he hath poured upon him the fury of his anger, and the strength of battle: [a]and it hath set him on fire round about, [b]yet he knew not; and it burned him, yet he laid *it* not to heart.

God will redeem his people

43 BUT NOW thus saith the LORD [a]that created thee, O Jacob, [b]and he that formed thee, O Israel, Fear not: [c]for I have redeemed thee, [d]I have called *thee* by thy name; thou *art* mine.

L S 2 [a]When thou passest through the waters, [b]I *will be* with thee; and through the rivers, they shall not overflow thee: when thou [c]walkest through the fire, thou shalt not be burned; neither shall the flame kindle upon thee.

3 For I *am* the LORD thy God, the Holy One of Israel, thy Saviour: [a]I gave Egypt *for* thy ransom, Ethiopia and Seba for thee.

4 Since thou wast precious in my sight, thou hast been honourable, and I have loved thee: therefore will I give men for thee, and people for thy [1]life.

I 5 [a]Fear not: for I *am* with thee: I will bring thy seed from the east, and gather thee from the west;

6 I will say to the north, Give up; and to the south, Keep not back: bring my

13 [a]ch. 31:4 [1]Or, *behave himself mightily*
14 [1]Heb. *swallow,* or, *sup up*
16 [1]Heb. *into straightness*
17 [a]Ps. 97:7; ch. 1:29 & 44:11 & 45:16
19 [a]ch. 43:8; Ezek. 12:2; See John 9:39,41
20 [a]Rom. 2:21
21 [1]Or, him
22 [1]Or, *in snaring all the young men of them* [2]Heb. *a treading*
23 [1]Heb. *for the after time?*
25 [a]2 Ki. 25:9 [b]Hos. 7:9
43:1 [a]ver. 7 [b]ver. 21; ch. 44:2,21 [c]ch. 44:6 [d]ch. 42:6 & 45:4
2 [a]Ps. 66:12 & 91:3 [b]Deut. 31:6 [c]Dan. 3:25
3 [a]Prov. 11:8 & 21:18
4 [1]Or, *person*
5 [a]ch. 41:10 & 44:2; Jer. 30:10 & 46:27,28

P *Isa 40:24* ◀ ▶ *Isa 45:23–24*
I *Isa 41:8–21* ◀ ▶ *Isa 43:5–7*
R *Isa 40:2* ◀ ▶ *Isa 43:27–28*

L *Isa 41:13–14* ◀ ▶ *Isa 46:3–4*
S *Isa 32:18* ◀ ▶ *Da 3:17*
I *Isa 42:16* ◀ ▶ *Isa 43:19–21*

42:13–16 Isaiah prophesied that when the Messiah returns he would display his supernatural power, defeat his enemies and establish his victorious millennial kingdom.

42:22–25 Israel was punished by God not because Babylon was stronger than the Lord, but because Israel had sinned. This punishment would give Israel a foretaste of the final day of the Lord.

43:5–7 This prophecy found its initial fulfillment in the return of Israel from exile in Babylon. In modern times, Jews from all over the world have been resettling in the promised land. At Christ's second coming this prophecy will be ultimately fulfilled when the Jews will return to Palestine from all parts of the earth.

sons from far, and my daughters from the ends of the earth;

7 *Even* every one that is [a]called by my name: for [b]I have created him for my glory, [c]I have formed him; yea, I have made him.

C 8 ¶ [a]Bring forth the blind people that have eyes, and the deaf that have ears.

9 Let all the nations be gathered together, and let the people be assembled: [a]who among them can declare this, and show us former things? let them bring forth their witnesses, that they may be justified: or let them hear, and say, *It is* truth.

T 10 [a]Ye *are* my witnesses, saith the LORD, [b]and my servant whom I have chosen: that ye may know and believe me, and understand that I *am* he: [c]before me there was ʹno God formed, neither shall there be after me.

O 11 I, *even* I, [a]*am* the LORD; and beside me *there is* no saviour.

T 12 I have declared, and have saved, and I have shown, when *there was* no [a]strange *god* among you: [b]therefore ye *are* my witnesses, saith the LORD, that I *am* God.

13 [a]Yea, before the day *was* I *am* he; and *there is* none that can deliver out of my hand: I will work, and who shall [b]letʹ it?

14 ¶ Thus saith the LORD, your redeemer, the Holy One of Israel; For your sake I have sent to Babylon, and have brought down all their ʹnobles, and the Chaldeans, whose cry *is* in the ships.

15 I *am* the LORD, your Holy One, the creator of Israel, your King.

16 Thus saith the LORD, which [a]maketh a way in the sea, and a [b]path in the mighty waters;

17 Which [a]bringeth forth the chariot and horse, the army and the power; they shall lie down together, they shall not rise: they are extinct, they are quenched as tow.

18 ¶ [a]Remember ye not the former things, neither consider the things of old.

19 Behold, I will do a [a]new thing; now it shall spring forth; shall ye not know it? [b]I will even make a way in the wilderness, *and* rivers in the desert. I

20 The beast of the field shall honour me, the dragons and the ʹ[1,2]owls: because [a]I give waters in the wilderness, *and* rivers in the desert, to give drink to my people, my chosen.

21 [a]This people have I formed for myself; they shall show forth my praise.

Israel's sin of ingratitude

22 ¶ But thou hast not called upon me, O Jacob; but thou [a]hast been weary of me, O Israel.

23 [a]Thou hast not brought me the ʹsmall cattle of thy burnt offerings; neither hast thou honoured me with thy sacrifices. I have not caused thee to serve with an offering, nor wearied thee with incense.

24 Thou hast bought me no sweet cane with money, neither hast thou ʹfilled me with the fat of thy sacrifices: but thou hast made me to serve with thy sins, thou hast [a]wearied me with thine iniquities.

25 I, *even* I, *am* he that [a]blotteth out thy transgressions [b]for mine own sake, and [c]will not remember thy sins. I L

26 Put me in remembrance: let us plead together: declare thou, that thou mayest be justified.

27 Thy first father hath sinned, and thy [a]teachersʹ have transgressed against me. R

28 Therefore [a]I have profaned the ʹprinces of the sanctuary, [b]and have given Jacob to the curse, and Israel to reproaches.

7 [a]ch. 63:19; Jas. 2:7 [b]Ps. 100:3; ch. 29:23; John 3:3,5; 2 Cor. 5:17; Eph. 2:10 [c]ver. 1
8 [a]ch. 6:9 & 42:19; Ezek. 12:2
9 [a]ch. 41:21,22,26
10 [a]ch. 44:8 [b]ch. 55:4 [c]ch. 44:6 ʹOr, *nothing formed of God*
11 [a]ch. 45:21; Hos. 13:4
12 [a]Deut. 32:16; Ps. 81:9 [b]ch. 44:8
13 [a]Ps. 90:2; John 8:58 [b]Job 9:12; ch. 14:27 ʹHeb. *turn it back?*
14 ʹHeb. *bars*
16 [a]Ex. 14:16; Ps. 77:19; ch. 51:10 [b]Josh. 3:13
17 [a]Ex. 14:4-9,25
18 [a]Jer. 16:14
19 [a]2 Cor. 5:17; Rev. 21:5 [b]Ex. 17:6; Num. 20:11; Deut. 8:15; Ps. 78:16
20 [a]ch. 48:21 ʹOr, *ostriches* [2]Heb. *daughters of the owl*
21 [a]Ps. 102:18; Eph. 1:5,6
22 [a]Mal. 1:13
23 [a]Amos 5:25 ʹHeb. *lambs*, or, *kids*
24 [a]ch. 1:14; Mal. 2:17 ʹHeb. *made me drunk*, or, *abundantly moistened*
25 [a]ch. 44:22; Jer. 50:20; Acts 3:19 [b]Ezek. 36:22 [c]ch. 1:18; Jer. 31:34
27 [a]Mal. 2:7,8 ʹHeb. *interpreters*
28 [a]ch. 47:6; Lam. 2:2,6 [b]Ps. 79:4; Jer. 24:9; Dan. 9:11; Zech. 8:13 ʹOr, *holy princes*

C *Isa 30:9–10* ◀▶ *Isa 44:18*
T *Isa 12:4* ◀▶ *Isa 43:12*
O *Ecc 7:13* ◀▶ *Isa 44:6*
T *Isa 43:10* ◀▶ *Isa 44:8*
I *Isa 43:5–7* ◀▶ *Isa 43:25*
I *Isa 43:19–21* ◀▶ *Isa 44:1–8*
L *Isa 42:6–7* ◀▶ *Isa 44:22*
R *Isa 42:22–25* ◀▶ *Isa 44:28*

43:19–21 Isaiah prophesied that the astonishing rebirth of the nation of Israel would be so wonderful as to make the other miracles of Israel's history seem as nothing.
43:25 In spite of the punishment God's people would suffer, Isaiah declared God's commitment to forgive their sins.
43:27–28 God declared that Abraham had sinned (see Ge 12:18; 20:9) and so had the priests and leaders, so destruction would come.

God's blessings upon the nation

I 44 YET NOW hear, [a]O Jacob my servant; and Israel, whom I have chosen:

2 Thus saith the LORD that made thee, [a]and formed thee from the womb, *which* will help thee; Fear not, O Jacob, my servant; and thou, [b]Jesurun, whom I have chosen.

M B J M N P 3 For I will [a]pour water upon him that is thirsty, and floods upon the dry ground: I will pour my spirit upon thy seed, and my blessing upon thine offspring:

4 And they shall spring up *as* among the grass, as willows by the water courses.

5 One shall say, I *am* the LORD'S; and another shall call *himself* by the name of Jacob; and another shall subscribe *with* his hand unto the LORD, and surname *himself* by the name of Israel.

Judgment upon idol worship

O 6 Thus saith the LORD the King of Israel, and his redeemer the LORD of hosts; [a]I *am* the first, and I *am* the last; and beside me *there is* no God.

7 And [a]who, as I, shall call, and shall declare it, and set it in order for me, since I appointed the ancient people? and the things that are coming, and shall come, let them show unto them.

O T 8 Fear ye not, neither be afraid: [a]have not I told thee from that time, and have declared *it?* [b]ye *are* even my witnesses. Is there a God beside me? yea, [c]*there is* no [ǀ]God; I know not *any.*

9 ¶ [a]They that make a graven image *are* all of them vanity; and their [ǀ]delectable things shall not profit; and they *are* their own witnesses; [b]they see not, nor know; that they may be ashamed.

10 Who hath formed a god, or molten a graven image [a]*that* is profitable for nothing?

11 Behold, all his fellows shall be [a]ashamed: and the workmen, they *are* of men: let them all be gathered together, let them stand up; *yet* they shall fear, *and* they shall be ashamed together.

12 [a]The smith [ǀ]with the tongs both worketh in the coals, and fashioneth it with hammers, and worketh it with the strength of his arms: yea, he is hungry, and his strength faileth: he drinketh no water, and is faint.

13 The carpenter stretcheth out *his* rule; he marketh it out with a line; he fitteth it with planes, and he marketh it out with the compass, and maketh it after the figure of a man, according to the beauty of a man; that it may remain in the house.

14 He heweth him down cedars, and taketh the cypress and the oak, which he [ǀ]strengtheneth for himself among the trees of the forest: he planteth an ash, and the rain doth nourish *it.*

15 Then shall it be for a man to burn: for he will take thereof, and warm himself; yea, he kindleth *it,* and baketh bread; yea, he maketh a god, and worshippeth *it;* he maketh it a graven image, and falleth down thereto.

16 He burneth part thereof in the fire; with part thereof he eateth flesh; he roasteth roast, and is satisfied: yea, he warmeth *himself,* and saith, Aha, I am warm, I have seen the fire:

17 And the residue thereof he maketh a god, *even* his graven image: he falleth down unto it, and worshippeth *it,* and prayeth unto it, and saith, Deliver me; for thou *art* my god.

18 [a]They have not known nor understood: for [b]he hath [ǀ]shut their eyes, that they cannot see; *and* their hearts, that they cannot understand. C

19 And none [a]considereth[ǀ] in his heart, neither *is there* knowledge nor understanding to say, I have burned part of it in the fire; yea, also I have baked bread upon the coals thereof; I have roasted flesh, and eaten *it:* and shall I make the

44:1 [a]ver. 21; Jer. 30:10 & 46:27,28
2 [a]ch. 43:1,7 [b]Deut. 32:15
3 [a]ch. 35:7; Joel 2:28; John 7:38; Acts 2:18
6 [a]ch. 41:4; Rev. 1:8,17 & 22:13
7 [a]ch. 41:4,22
8 [a]ch. 41:22 [b]ch. 43:10 [c]Deut. 4:35 & 32:39; 1 Sam. 2:2; 2 Sam. 22:32 [ǀ]Heb. *rock;* see Deut. 32:4
9 [a]ch. 41:24 [b]Ps. 115:4 [ǀ]Heb. *desirable*
10 [a]Jer. 10:5; Hab. 2:18
11 [a]Ps. 97:7; ch. 1:29 & 42:17
12 [a]ch. 40:19; Jer. 10:3 [ǀ]Or, *with an axe*
14 [ǀ]Or, *taketh courage*
18 [a]ch. 45:20 [b]2 Thes. 2:11 [ǀ]Heb. *daubed*
19 [a]ch. 46:8 [ǀ]Heb. *setteth to his heart*

I *Isa 43:25* ◀▶ *Isa 44:21–23*
M *Isa 42:4* ◀▶ *Isa 45:8*
B *Isa 42:1* ◀▶ *Isa 61:1*
J *Ps 51:12* ◀▶ *Isa 63:14*
M *Isa 40:13* ◀▶ *Isa 59:19*
N *Isa 40:7* ◀▶ *Eze 3:12*
P *Isa 32:15* ◀▶ *Eze 11:19*
O *Isa 43:11* ◀▶ *Isa 44:8*
O *Isa 44:6* ◀▶ *Isa 45:5–9*
T *Isa 43:12* ◀▶ *Jer 1:17*
C *Isa 43:8* ◀▶ *Isa 44:20*

44:1–8 Isaiah proclaimed that God alone knows the future and that he alone is God.

residue thereof an abomination? shall I fall down to [2]the stock of a tree?

C 20 He feedeth on ashes: [a]a deceived heart hath turned him aside, that he cannot deliver his soul, nor say, *Is there* not a lie in my right hand?

I 21 ¶ Remember these, O Jacob and Israel; for [a]thou *art* my servant: I have formed thee; thou *art* my servant: O Israel, thou shalt not be forgotten of me.

L 22 [a]I have blotted out, as a thick cloud, thy transgressions, and, as a cloud, thy sins: return unto me; for [b]I have redeemed thee.

23 [a]Sing, O ye heavens; for the LORD hath done *it:* shout, ye lower parts of the earth: break forth into singing, ye mountains, O forest, and every tree therein: for the LORD hath redeemed Jacob, and glorified himself in Israel.

Cyrus to restore Jerusalem

24 Thus saith the LORD, [a]thy redeemer, and [b]he that formed thee from the womb, I *am* the LORD that maketh all *things;* [c]that stretcheth forth the heavens alone; that spreadeth abroad the earth by myself;

25 That [a]frustrateth the tokens [b]of the liars, and maketh diviners mad; that turneth wise *men* backward, [c]and maketh their knowledge foolish;

I 26 [a]That confirmeth the word of his servant, and performeth the counsel of his messengers; that saith to Jerusalem, Thou shalt be inhabited; and to the cities of Judah, Ye shall be built, and I will raise up the [1]decayed places thereof:

27 [a]That saith to the deep, Be dry, and I will dry up thy rivers:

R 28 That saith of Cyrus, *He is* my shepherd, and shall perform all my pleasure: even saying to Jerusalem, [a]Thou shalt be built; and to the temple, Thy foundation shall be laid.

45

L THUS SAITH the LORD to his anointed, to Cyrus, whose [a]right hand I [1]have holden, [b]to subdue nations before him; and I will loose the loins of kings, to open before him the two leaved gates; and the gates shall not be shut;

2 I will go before thee, [a]and make the crooked places straight: [b]I will break in pieces the gates of brass, and cut in sunder the bars of iron:

3 And I will give thee the treasures of darkness, and hidden riches of secret places, [a]that thou mayest know that I, the LORD, which [b]call *thee* by thy name, *am* the God of Israel.

4 For [a]Jacob my servant's sake, and Israel mine elect, I have even called thee by thy name: I have surnamed thee, though thou hast not known me.

5 ¶ I [a]*am* the LORD, and [b]*there is* none else, *there is* no God beside me: [c]I girded thee, though thou hast not known me: O

6 [a]That they may know from the rising of the sun, and from the west, that *there is* none beside me. I *am* the LORD, and *there is* none else.

7 I form the light, and create darkness: I make peace, and [a]create evil: I the LORD do all these *things.*

8 [a]Drop down, ye heavens, from above, and let the skies pour down righteousness: let the earth open, and let them bring forth salvation, and let righteousness spring up together; I the LORD have created it. M

9 Woe unto him that striveth with [a]his Maker! *Let* the potsherd *strive* with the potsherds of the earth. [b]Shall the clay say to him that fashioneth it, What makest thou? or thy work, He hath no hands?

10 Woe unto him that saith unto *his* father, What begettest thou? or to the woman, What hast thou brought forth?

11 Thus saith the LORD, the Holy One

19 [2]Heb. *that which comes of a tree?*
20 [a]Hos. 4:12; Rom. 1:21; 2 Thes. 2:11
21 [a]ver. 1,2
22 [a]ch. 43:25 [b]ch. 43:1; 1 Cor. 6:20; 1 Pet. 1:18
23 [a]Ps. 69:34; ch. 42:10 & 49:13; Jer. 51:48; Rev. 18:20
24 [a]ch. 43:14 [b]ch. 43:1 [c]Job 9:8
25 [a]ch. 47:13 [b]Jer. 50:36 [c]1 Cor. 1:20
26 [a]Zech. 1:6 [1]Heb. *wastes*
27 [a]Jer. 50:38 & 51:32,36
28 [a]2 Chr. 36:22; Ezra 1:1; ch. 45:13
45:1 [a]ch. 41:13 [b]Dan. 5:30 [1]Or, *strengthened*
2 [a]ch. 40:4 [b]Ps. 107:16
3 [a]ch. 41:23 [b]Ex. 33:12
4 [a]ch. 44:1
5 [a]Deut. 4:35 & 32:39; ch. 44:8 [b]ver. 14,18 [c]Ps. 18:32
6 [a]Ps. 102:15; Mal. 1:11
7 [a]Amos 3:6
8 [a]Ps. 85:11
9 [a]ch. 64:8 [b]ch. 29:16; Jer. 18:6; Rom. 9:20

C *Isa 44:18* ◀▶ *Isa 48:4*
I *Isa 44:1–8* ◀▶ *Isa 44:26*
L *Isa 43:25* ◀▶ *Isa 45:22*
I *Isa 44:21–23* ◀▶ *Isa 45:17–19*
R *Isa 43:27–28* ◀▶ *Isa 50:1*
L *Isa 38:21–22* ◀▶ *Isa 45:13*
O *Isa 44:8* ◀▶ *Isa 45:18*
M *Isa 44:3–5* ◀▶ *Isa 45:23–24*

44:21–23 Israel's suffering has paved the way for God's forgiveness and the final restoration of his people in the millennial kingdom.
44:26–28 Isaiah predicted the return of the exiles under King Cyrus of Persia more than a hundred years before it happened. His words also foreshadow the final restoration of Jerusalem and the kingdom of Judah in the coming millennial kingdom, when the Messiah will reign from the throne of David.
45:8 This prophecy foreshadowed the abundance, deliverance, peace and justice under the millennial reign of Christ.

of Israel, and his Maker, Ask me of things to come concerning [a]my sons, and concerning [b]the work of my hands command ye me.

12 [a]I have made the earth, and [b]created man upon it: I, *even* my hands, have stretched out the heavens, and [c]all their host have I commanded.

L 13 [a]I have raised him up in righteousness, and I will [1]direct all his ways: he shall [b]build my city, and he shall let go my captives, [c]not for price nor reward, saith the LORD of hosts.

14 Thus saith the LORD, [a]The labour of Egypt, and merchandise of Ethiopia and of the Sabeans, men of stature, shall come over unto thee, and they shall be thine: they shall come after thee; [b]in chains they shall come over, and they shall fall down unto thee, they shall make supplication unto thee, *saying,* [c]Surely God *is* in thee; and [d]*there is* none else, *there is* no God.

15 Verily thou *art* a God [a]that hidest thyself, O God of Israel, the Saviour.

16 They shall be ashamed, and also confounded, all of them: they shall go to confusion together *that are* [a]makers of idols.

I 17 [a]*But* Israel shall be saved in the LORD with an everlasting salvation: ye shall not be ashamed nor confounded world without end.

O 18 For thus saith the LORD [a]that created the heavens; God himself that formed the earth and made it; he hath established it, he created it not in vain, he formed it to be inhabited: [b]I *am* the LORD; and *there is* none else.

19 I have not spoken in [a]secret, in a dark place of the earth: I said not unto the seed of Jacob, Seek ye me in vain: [b]I the LORD speak righteousness, I declare things that are right.

20 ¶ Assemble yourselves and come; draw near together, ye *that are* escaped of the nations: [a]they have no knowledge that set up the wood of their graven image, and pray unto a god *that* cannot save.

21 Tell ye, and bring *them* near; yea, let them take counsel together: [a]who hath declared this from ancient time? *who* hath told it from that time? *have* not I the LORD? [b]and *there is* no God else beside me; a just God and a Saviour; *there is* none beside me. O

22 [a]Look unto me, and be ye saved, all the ends of the earth: for I *am* God, and *there is* none else. L W

23 [a]I have sworn by myself, the word is gone out of my mouth *in* righteousness, and shall not return, That unto me every [b]knee shall bow, [c]every tongue shall swear. M P V

24 [1]Surely, shall *one* say, in the LORD have I [a]righteousness[2] and strength: *even* to him shall *men* come; and [b]all that are incensed against him shall be ashamed.

25 [a]In the LORD shall all the seed of Israel be justified, and [b]shall glory. I

Babylon's idols and the LORD

46 BEL [a]BOWETH down, Nebo stoopeth, their idols were upon the beasts, and upon the cattle: your carriages *were* heavy laden; [b]*they are* a burden to the weary *beast.*

2 They stoop, they bow down together; they could not deliver the burden, [a]but [1]themselves are gone into captivity.

3 ¶ Hearken unto me, O house of Jacob, and all the remnant of the house of Israel, [a]which are borne *by me* from the belly, which are carried from the womb: I L

L *Isa 45:1–5* ◀▶ *Jer 39:17–18*
I *Isa 44:26* ◀▶ *Isa 45:25*
O *Isa 45:5–9* ◀▶ *Isa 45:21–22*

O *Isa 45:18* ◀▶ *Isa 46:9*
L *Isa 44:22* ◀▶ *Isa 49:6*
W *Isa 42:3* ◀▶ *Isa 49:6*
M *Isa 45:8* ◀▶ *Isa 49:7–12*
P *Isa 42:13–15* ◀▶ *Isa 61:2*
V *Isa 11:1–9* ◀▶ *Jer 23:5–6*
I *Isa 45:17–19* ◀▶ *Isa 46:3–4*
I *Isa 45:25* ◀▶ *Isa 46:12–13*
L *Isa 43:2* ◀▶ *Isa 48:17*

11 [a]Jer. 31:9 [b]Is. 29:23
12 [a]ch. 42:5 [b]Gen. 1:26 [c]Gen. 2:1
13 [a]ch. 41:2 [b]2 Chr. 36:22 [c]Rom. 3:24 [1]Or, *make straight*
14 [a]Ps. 68:31; Zech. 8:22 [b]Ps. 149:8 [c]1 Cor. 14:25 [d]ver. 5
15 [a]Ps. 44:24; ch. 57:17
16 [a]ch. 44:11
17 [a]ch. 26:4
18 [a]ch. 42:5 [b]ver. 5
19 [a]Deut. 30:11 [b]Ps. 19:8
20 [a]ch. 46:7
21 [a]ch. 41:22 & 43:9 [b]ch. 44:8
22 [a]Ps. 22:27 & 65:5
23 [a]Heb. 6:13 [b]Phil. 2:10 [c]Ps. 63:11
24 [a]Jer. 23:5; 1 Cor. 1:30 [b]ch. 41:11 [1]Or, *Surely he shall say of me, In the LORD is all righteousness and strength* [2]Heb. *righteousnesses*
25 [a]ver. 17 [b]1 Cor. 1:31
46:1 [a]ch. 21:9; Jer. 50:2 [b]Jer. 10:5
2 [a]Jer. 48:7 [1]Heb. *their soul*
3 [a]Deut. 32:11; Ps. 71:6

45:17–19 God has repeatedly proclaimed that "Israel shall be saved in the LORD with an everlasting salvation" (45:17).

45:23–25 The apostle Paul quoted this prophecy to confirm Christ's exalted position (see Ro 14:11; Php 2:10–11). Note too that while those who love Jesus willingly bow to him as their Savior, even those who are unrepentant will be forced to bow their knee to him when he is revealed in all of his glory as the King of Kings.

46:3–4 Isaiah declared God's deliverance and power to carry Israel, echoing Moses' words in the desert: "the LORD thy God bare thee, as a man doth bear his son, in all the way that ye went" (Dt 1:31).

4 And *even* to *your* old age [a]I *am* he; and *even* to hoar hairs [b]will I carry *you:* I have made, and I will bear; even I will carry, and will deliver *you.*

5 ¶ [a]To whom will ye liken me, and make *me* equal, and compare me, that we may be like?

6 [a]They lavish gold out of the bag, and weigh silver in the balance, *and* hire a goldsmith; and he maketh it a god: they fall down, yea, they worship.

7 [a]They bear him upon the shoulder, they carry him, and set him in his place, and he standeth; from his place shall he not remove: yea, [b]*one* shall cry unto him, yet can he not answer, nor save him out of his trouble.

8 Remember this, and show yourselves men: [a]bring *it* again to mind, O ye transgressors.

O 9 [a]Remember the former things of old: for I *am* God, and [b]*there is* none else; *I am* God, and *there is* none like me,

10 [a]Declaring the end from the beginning, and from ancient times *the things* that are not *yet* done, saying, [b]My counsel shall stand, and I will do all my pleasure:

11 Calling a ravenous bird [a]from the east, [1]the man [b]that executeth my counsel from a far country: yea, [c]I have spoken *it,* I will also bring it to pass; I have purposed *it,* I will also do it.

I 12 ¶ Hearken unto me, ye [a]stout-
M hearted, [b]that *are* far from righteousness:

13 [a]I bring near my righteousness; it shall not be far off, and my salvation [b]shall not tarry: and I will place [c]salvation in Zion for Israel my glory.

Judgment against Babylon

47 COME [a]DOWN, and [b]sit in the dust, O virgin daughter of Babylon, sit on the ground: *there is* no throne, O daughter of the Chaldeans: for thou shalt no more be called tender and delicate.

2 [a]Take the millstones, and grind meal: uncover thy locks, make bare the leg, uncover the thigh, pass over the rivers.

3 [a]Thy nakedness shall be uncovered, yea, thy shame shall be seen: [b]I will take vengeance, and I will not meet *thee as* a man.

4 *As for* [a]our redeemer, the LORD of hosts *is* his name, the Holy One of Israel.

5 Sit thou [a]silent, and get thee into darkness, O daughter of the Chaldeans: [b]for thou shalt no more be called, The lady of kingdoms.

6 ¶ [a]I was wroth with my people, [b]I have polluted mine inheritance, and given them into thine hand: thou didst show them no mercy; [c]upon the ancient hast thou very heavily laid thy yoke.

7 ¶ And thou saidst, I shall be [a]a lady for ever: *so* that thou didst not [b]lay these *things* to thy heart, [c]neither didst remember the latter end of it.

8 Therefore hear now this, *thou that art* given to pleasures, that dwellest carelessly, that sayest in thine heart, [a]I *am,* and none else beside me; [b]I shall not sit *as* a widow, neither shall I know the loss of children:

9 But [a]these two *things* shall come to thee [b]in a moment in one day, the loss of children, and widowhood: they shall come upon thee in their perfection [c]for the multitude of thy sorceries, *and* for the great abundance of thine enchantments.

10 ¶ For thou [a]hast trusted in thy wickedness: [b]thou hast said, None seeth me. Thy wisdom and thy knowledge, it hath [1]perverted thee; [c]and thou hast said in thine heart, I *am,* and none else beside me.

11 ¶ Therefore shall evil come upon thee; thou shalt not know [1]from whence it riseth: and mischief shall fall upon thee; thou shalt not be able to [2]put it off: and [a]desolation shall come upon thee suddenly, *which* thou shalt not know.

12 Stand now with thine enchantments, and with the multitude of thy sorceries, wherein thou hast laboured from thy youth; if so be thou shalt be able to profit, if so be thou mayest prevail.

13 [a]Thou art wearied in the multitude of thy counsels. Let now [b]the [1]astrolo-

4 [a]Mal. 3:6 [b]Ps. 48:14
5 [a]ch. 40:18
6 [a]ch. 40:19 & 41:6; Jer. 10:3
7 [a]Jer. 10:5 [b]ch. 45:20
8 [a]ch. 44:19
9 [a]Deut. 32:7 [b]ch. 45:5,21
10 [a]ch. 45:21 [b]Ps. 33:11; Prov. 19:21; Acts 5:39; Heb. 6:17
11 [a]ch. 41:2,25 [b]ch. 44:28 [c]Num. 23:19 [1]Heb. *the man of my counsel*
12 [a]Ps. 76:5 [b]Rom. 10:3
13 [a]Rom. 1:17 [b]Hab. 2:3 [c]ch. 62:11
47:1 [a]Jer. 48:18 [b]ch. 3:26
2 [a]Ex. 11:5; Judg. 16:21; Mat. 24:41
3 [a]ch. 3:17 & 20:4; Jer. 13:22; Nah. 3:5 [b]Rom. 12:19
4 [a]Jer. 50:34
5 [a]1 Sam. 2:9 [b]Dan. 2:37
6 [a]See 2 Sam. 24:14; 2 Chr. 28:9; Zech. 1:15 [b]ch. 43:28 [c]Deut. 28:50
7 [a]Rev. 18:7 [b]ch. 46:8 [c]Deut. 32:29
8 [a]Zeph. 2:15 [b]Rev. 18:7
9 [a]ch. 51:19 [b]1 Thes. 5:3 [c]Nah. 3:4
10 [a]Ps. 52:7 [b]ch. 29:15; Ezek. 8:12 [c]ver. 8 [1]Or, *caused thee to turn away*
11 [a]1 Thes. 5:3 [1]Heb. *the morning thereof* [2]Heb. *expiate*
13 [a]ch. 57:10 [b]Dan. 2:2 [1]Heb. *viewers of the heavens*

O *Isa 45:21–22* ◀▶ *Isa 50:10–11*
I *Isa 46:3–4* ◀▶ *Isa 49:5–6*
M *Isa 13:11* ◀▶ *Isa 48:4*

46:9–10 Only God alone knows the details of future events before they occur, and only he can accurately predict the final end of events before they begin.

46:12–13 Isaiah declared that God would ultimately deliver his people Israel in the last days.

gers, the stargazers, [2]the monthly prog-
nosticators, stand up, and save thee from
these things that shall come upon thee.
14 Behold, they shall be [a]as stubble;
the fire shall burn them; they shall not
deliver [1]themselves from the power of
the flame: *there shall* not *be* a coal to
warm at, *nor* fire to sit before it.
15 Thus shall they be unto thee with
whom thou hast laboured, *even* [a]thy merchants, from thy youth: they shall wander
every one to his quarter; none shall save
thee.

Obstinate Israel

48 HEAR YE this, O house of Jacob,
which are called by the name of
Israel, and [a]are come forth out of the waters of Judah, [b]which swear by the name
of the LORD, and make mention of the
God of Israel, [c]*but* not in truth, nor in
righteousness.
2 For they call themselves [a]of the holy
city, and [b]stay themselves upon the God
of Israel; The LORD of hosts *is* his name.
3 [a]I have declared the former things
from the beginning; and they went forth
out of my mouth, and I showed them; I
did *them* suddenly, [b]and they came to
pass.
C 4 Because I knew that thou *art* [1]obsti-
M nate, and [a]thy neck *is* an iron sinew, and
N thy brow brass;
5 [a]I have even from the beginning declared *it* to thee; before it came to pass I
showed *it* thee: lest thou shouldest say,
Mine idol hath done them, and my
graven image, and my molten image,
hath commanded them.
6 Thou hast heard, see all this; and will
not ye declare *it?* I have shown thee new
things from this time, even hidden
things, and thou didst not know them.
7 They are created now, and not from
the beginning; even before the day when
thou heardest them not; lest thou shouldest say, Behold, I knew them.
8 Yea, thou heardest not; yea, thou
knewest not; yea, from that time *that*
thine ear was not opened: for I knew that
thou wouldest deal very treacherously,
and wast called [a]a transgressor from the
womb.
9 ¶ [a]For my name's sake [b]will I defer
mine anger, and for my praise will I refrain for thee, that I cut thee not off.
10 Behold, [a]I have refined thee, but T
not [1]with silver; I have chosen thee in
the furnace of affliction.
11 [a]For mine own sake, *even* for mine
own sake, will I do *it:* for [b]how should *my*
name be polluted? and [c]I will not give my
glory unto another.

The Redeemer of Israel

12 ¶ Hearken unto me, O Jacob and Is-
rael, my called; [a]I *am* he; I *am* the [b]first, I
also *am* the last.
13 [a]Mine hand also hath laid the foundation of the earth, and [1]my right hand
hath spanned the heavens: *when* [b]I call
unto them, they stand up together.
14 All ye, assemble yourselves, and J
hear; which among them hath declared
these *things?* [a]The LORD hath loved him:
[b]he will do his pleasure on Babylon, and
his arm *shall be on* the Chaldeans.
15 I, *even* I, have spoken; yea, [a]I have
called him: I have brought him, and he
shall make his way prosperous.
16 ¶ Come ye near unto me, hear ye E
this; [a]I have not spoken in secret from L
the beginning; from the time that it was,
there *am* I: and now [b]the Lord GOD, and
his spirit, hath sent me.
17 Thus saith [a]the LORD, thy Re- L
deemer, the Holy One of Israel; I *am* the
LORD thy God which teacheth thee to
profit, [b]which leadeth thee by the way
that thou shouldest go.
18 [a]O that thou hadst hearkened to K
my commandments! [b]then had thy peace
been as a river, and thy righteousness as
the waves of the sea:
19 [a]Thy seed also had been as the
sand, and the offspring of thy bowels like
the gravel thereof; his name should not
have been cut off nor destroyed from before me.
20 ¶ [a]Go ye forth of Babylon, flee ye
from the Chaldeans, with a voice of singing declare ye, tell this, utter it *even* to
the end of the earth; say ye, The LORD
hath [b]redeemed his servant Jacob.

13 [2]Heb. *that give knowledge concerning the months*
14 [a]Nah. 1:10; Mal. 4:1 [1]Heb. *their souls*
15 [a]Rev. 18:11
48:1 [a]Ps. 68:26 [b]Deut. 6:13; Zeph. 1:5 [c]Jer. 4:2
2 [a]ch. 52:1 [b]Mic. 3:11; Rom. 2:17
3 [a]ch. 44:7,8 [b]Josh. 21:45
4 [a]Ex. 32:9; Deut. 31:27 [1]Heb. *hard*
5 [a]ver. 3
8 [a]Ps. 58:3
9 [a]Ps. 79:9 & 106:8; Ezek. 20:9 [b]Ps. 78:38
10 [a]Ps. 66:10 [1]Or, *for silver;* see Ezek. 22:20-22
11 [a]ver. 9 [b]Deut. 32:26; Ezek. 20:9 [c]ch. 42:8
12 [a]Deut. 32:39 [b]ch. 44:6; Rev. 22:13
13 [a]Ps. 102:25 [b]ch. 40:26 [1]Or, *the palm of my right hand hath spread out*
14 [a]ch. 45:1 [b]ch. 44:28
15 [a]ch. 45:1,2
16 [a]ch. 45:19 [b]Zech. 2:8
17 [a]ch. 43:14 [b]Ps. 32:8
18 [a]Deut. 32:29; Ps. 81:13 [b]Ps. 119:165
19 [a]Gen. 22:17; Hos. 1:10
20 [a]Jer. 50:8 [b]Ex. 19:4-6

C *Isa 44:20* ◀▶ *Isa 48:22*
M *Isa 46:12* ◀▶ *Isa 57:15*
N *Isa 40:6* ◀▶ *Isa 55:6*
T *Ecc 7:14* ◀▶ *Da 12:10*
J *Isa 30:5–7* ◀▶ *Jer 1:13–16*
E *Isa 40:7* ◀▶ *Isa 59:21*
L *Ps 143:10* ◀▶ *Isa 63:14*
L *Isa 46:3–4* ◀▶ *Isa 49:15–16*
K *Isa 41:10* ◀▶ *Isa 50:2*

21 And they [a]thirsted not *when* he led them through the deserts: he [b]caused the waters to flow out of the rock for them: he clave the rock also, and the waters gushed out.

22 [a]*There is* no peace, saith the LORD, unto the wicked.

The servant's call

49 LISTEN, [a]O isles, unto me; and hearken, ye people, from far; [b]The LORD hath called me from the womb; from the bowels of my mother hath he made mention of my name.

2 And he hath made [a]my mouth like a sharp sword; [b]in the shadow of his hand hath he hid me, and made me [c]a polished shaft; in his quiver hath he hid me;

3 And said unto me, [a]Thou *art* my servant, O Israel, [b]in whom I will be glorified.

4 [a]Then I said, I have laboured in vain, I have spent my strength for nought, and in vain: *yet* surely my judgment *is* with the LORD, and [b]my[1] work with my God.

5 ¶ And now, saith the LORD [a]that formed me from the womb *to be* his servant, to bring Jacob again to him, [1]Though Israel [b]be not gathered, yet shall I be glorious in the eyes of the LORD, and my God shall be my strength.

6 And he said, [1]It is a light thing that thou shouldest be my servant to raise up the tribes of Jacob, and to restore the [2]preserved of Israel: I will also give thee for a [a]light to the Gentiles, that thou mayest be my salvation unto the end of the earth.

7 Thus saith the LORD, the Redeemer of Israel, *and* his Holy One, [a]to[1] him whom man despiseth, to him whom the nation abhorreth, to a servant of rulers, [b]Kings shall see and arise, princes also shall worship, because of the LORD that is faithful, *and* the Holy One of Israel, and he shall choose thee.

The restoration of Israel

8 Thus saith the LORD, [a]In an acceptable time have I heard thee, and in a day of salvation have I helped thee: and I will preserve thee, [b]and give thee for a covenant of the people, to [1]establish the earth, to cause to inherit the desolate heritages;

9 That thou mayest say [a]to the prisoners, Go forth; to them that *are* in darkness, Show yourselves. They shall feed in the ways, and their pastures *shall be* in all high places.

10 They shall not [a]hunger nor thirst; [b]neither shall the heat nor sun smite them: for he that hath mercy on them [c]shall lead them, even by the springs of water shall he guide them.

11 [a]And I will make all my mountains a way, and my highways shall be exalted.

12 Behold, [a]these shall come from far: and, lo, these from the north and from the west; and these from the land of Sinim.

13 ¶ [a]Sing, O heavens; and be joyful, O earth; and break forth into singing, O mountains: for the LORD hath comforted his people, and will have mercy upon his afflicted.

14 [a]But Zion said, The LORD hath forsaken me, and my Lord hath forgotten me.

15 [a]Can a woman forget her sucking child, [1]that she should not have compassion on the son of her womb? yea, they may forget, [b]yet will I not forget thee.

16 Behold, [a]I have graven thee upon the palms of *my* hands; thy walls *are* continually before me.

21 [a]ch. 41:17,18 [b]Ex. 17:6; Ps. 105:41
22 [a]ch. 57:21
49:1 [a]ch. 41:1 [b]Jer. 1:5; Mat. 1:20; John 10:36
2 [a]ch. 11:4; Hos. 6:5; Rev. 1:16 [b]ch. 51:16 [c]Ps. 45:5
3 [a]ch. 42:1; Zech. 3:8 [b]John 15:8; Eph. 1:6
4 [a]Ezek. 3:19 [b]ch. 40:10 [1]Or, *my reward*
5 [a]ver. 1 [b]Mat. 23:37 [1]Or, *That Israel may be gathered to him, and I may*
6 [a]Luke 2:32 [1]Or, Art thou *lighter than that thou shouldest* [2]Or, *desolations*
7 [a]Mat. 26:67 [b]Ps. 72:10 [1]Or, *to him that is despised in soul*
8 [a]Ps. 69:13; 2 Cor. 6:2 [b]ch. 42:6 [1]Or, *raise up*
9 [a]Zech. 9:12
10 [a]Rev. 7:16 [b]Ps. 121:6 [c]Ps. 23:2
11 [a]ch. 40:4
12 [a]ch. 43:5,6
13 [a]ch. 44:23
14 [a]ch. 40:27
15 [a]Ps. 103:13; Mal. 3:17; Mat. 7:11 [b]Rom. 11:29 [1]Heb. *from having compassion*
16 [a]Ex. 13:9; Sol. 8:6

F *Isa 41:17* ◀▶ *Isa 49:9–10*
C *Isa 48:4* ◀▶ *Isa 53:6*
S *Isa 35:8–9* ◀▶ *Isa 60:21*
I *Isa 46:12–13* ◀▶ *Isa 49:8–23*
L *Isa 45:22* ◀▶ *Isa 52:3*
W *Isa 45:22* ◀▶ *Isa 53:6*
M *Isa 45:23–24* ◀▶ *Isa 52:13*
I *Isa 49:5–6* ◀▶ *Isa 50:2*
F *Isa 48:21* ◀▶ *Isa 58:11*
L *Isa 48:17* ◀▶ *Isa 54:10*

49:5–6 God has promised that he will "restore the preserved of Israel" to "give thee for a light to the Gentiles" (49:6) indicating that the Messiah would be the light of the world during the last days. See also Ac 13:46–48; 26:23.

49:8–23 Compare 49:8 with 2Co 6:2. Isaiah prophesied that the return from exile would bring the same restoration of land for the people as the Year of Jubilee did (see Lev 25:10). Note that under Joshua the land had been divided among the tribes. When Israel is completely restored in the Millennium, the Messiah will justly reassign the promised land. Compare also the description of heaven with Rev 7:16–17.

17 Thy children shall make haste; [a]thy destroyers and they that made thee waste shall go forth of thee.

18 ¶ [a]Lift up thine eyes round about, and behold: all these gather themselves together, *and* come to thee. *As* I live, saith the LORD, thou shalt surely clothe thee with them all, [b]as with an ornament, and bind them *on thee,* as a bride *doeth.*

19 For thy waste and thy desolate places, and the land of thy destruction, [a]shall even now be too narrow by reason of the inhabitants, and they that swallowed thee up shall be far away.

20 [a]The children which thou shalt have, [b]after thou hast lost the other, shall say again in thine ears, The place *is* too strait for me: give place to me that I may dwell.

21 Then shalt thou say in thine heart, Who hath begotten me these, seeing I have lost my children, and am desolate, a captive, and removing to and fro? and who hath brought up these? Behold, I was left alone; these, where *had* they *been?*

22 [a]Thus saith the Lord GOD, Behold, I will lift up mine hand to the Gentiles, and set up my standard to the people: and they shall bring thy sons in *their* [1]arms, and thy daughters shall be carried upon *their* shoulders.

23 [a]And kings shall be thy [1]nursing fathers, and their [2]queens thy nursing mothers: they shall bow down to thee with *their* face toward the earth, and [b]lick up the dust of thy feet; and thou shalt know that I *am* the LORD: for [c]they shall not be ashamed that wait for me.

24 ¶ [a]Shall the prey be taken from the mighty, or [1]the lawful captive delivered?

25 But thus saith the LORD, Even the [1]captives of the mighty shall be taken away, and the prey of the terrible shall be delivered: for I will contend with him that contendeth with thee, and I will save thy children.

26 And I will [a]feed them that oppress thee with their own flesh; and they shall be drunken with their own [b]blood, as with [1]sweet wine: and all flesh [c]shall know that I the LORD *am* thy Saviour and thy Redeemer, the mighty One of Jacob.

Sin separates Israel from God

50 THUS SAITH the LORD, Where *is* R
[a]the bill of your mother's divorcement, whom I have put away? or which of my [b]creditors *is it* to whom I have sold you? Behold, for your iniquities [c]have ye sold yourselves, and for your transgressions is your mother put away.

2 Wherefore, when I came, *was there* I
no man? [a]when I called, *was there* none K
to answer? [b]Is my hand shortened at all, that it cannot redeem? or have I no power to deliver? behold, [c]at my rebuke I [d]dry up the sea, I make the [e]rivers a wilderness: [f]their fish stinketh, because *there is* no water, and dieth for thirst.

3 [a]I clothe the heavens with blackness, [b]and I make sackcloth their covering.

Obedient response of the servant

4 [a]The Lord GOD hath given me the tongue of the learned, that I should know how to speak a word in season to *him that is* [b]weary: he wakeneth morning by morning, he wakeneth mine ear to hear as the learned.

5 ¶ The Lord GOD [a]hath opened mine ear, and I was not [b]rebellious, neither turned away back.

6 [a]I gave my back to the smiters, and B
[b]my cheeks to them that plucked off the hair: I hid not my face from shame and spitting.

7 ¶ For the Lord GOD will help me; therefore shall I not be confounded: therefore have [a]I set my face like a flint, and I know that I shall not be ashamed.

8 [a]*He is* near that justifieth me; who will contend with me? let us stand together: who *is* [1]mine adversary? let him come near to me.

9 Behold, the Lord GOD will help me; V
who *is* he *that* shall condemn me? [a]lo, they all shall wax old as a garment; [b]the moth shall eat them up.

10 ¶ Who *is* among you that feareth K
the LORD, that obeyeth the voice of his O

17 [a]ver. 19
18 [a]ch. 60:4 [b]Prov. 17:6
19 [a]ch. 54:1,2; Zech. 10:10
20 [a]ch. 60:4 [b]Mat. 3:9; Rom. 11:11
22 [a]ch. 60:4 [1]Heb. *bosom*
23 [a]Ps. 72:11; ch. 52:15 & 60:16 [b]Ps. 72:9; Mic. 7:17 [c]Ps. 34:22; Rom. 5:5 & 9:33 [1]Heb. *nourishers* [2]Heb. *princesses*
24 [a]Mat. 12:29; Luke 11:21,22 [1]Heb. *the captivity of the just*
25 [1]Heb. *captivity*
26 [a]ch. 9:20 [b]Rev. 14:20 & 16:6 [c]Ps. 9:16; ch. 60:16 [1]Or, *new wine*
50:1 [a]Deut. 24:1; Jer. 3:8; Hos. 2:2 [b]2 Ki. 4:1; Mat. 18:25 [c]ch. 52:3
2 [a]Prov. 1:24; ch. 65:12; Jer. 35:15 [b]Num. 11:23 [c]Ps. 106:9; Nah. 1:4 [d]Ex. 14:21 [e]Josh. 3:16 [f]Ex. 7:18
3 [a]Ex. 10:21 [b]Rev. 6:12
4 [a]Ex. 4:11 [b]Mat. 11:28
5 [a]Ps. 40:6-8 [b]Mat. 26:39; John 14:31; Heb. 10:5
6 [a]Mat. 26:67 [b]Lam. 3:30
7 [a]Ezek. 3:8,9
8 [a]Rom. 8:32 [1]Heb. *the master of my cause?*
9 [a]Job 13:28; Ps. 102:26; ch. 51:6 [b]ch. 51:8

R *Isa 44:28* ◀▶ *Isa 51:17*
I *Isa 49:8–23* ◀▶ *Isa 51:3–4*
K *Isa 48:18* ◀▶ *Isa 50:10*
B *Isa 11:1–5* ◀▶ *Isa 52:13*
V *Isa 41:11–14* ◀▶ *Isa 54:15*
K *Isa 50:2* ◀▶ *Isa 51:6*
O *Isa 46:9* ◀▶ *Jer 2:13*

50:1 Isaiah's words reminded the people that their own disobedience led to their judgment before God.

servant, that [a]walketh *in* darkness, and hath no light? [b]let him trust in the name of the LORD, and stay upon his God.

G 11 Behold, all ye that kindle a fire, that compass *yourselves* about with sparks: walk in the light of your fire, and in the sparks *that* ye have kindled. [a]This shall ye have of mine hand; ye shall lie down [b]in sorrow.

The LORD will deliver his people

51 HEARKEN TO me, [a]ye that follow after righteousness, ye that seek the LORD: look unto the rock *whence* ye are hewn, and to the hole of the pit *whence* ye are digged.

2 [a]Look unto Abraham your father, and unto Sarah *that* bare you: [b]for I called him alone, and [c]blessed him, and increased him.

I 3 For the LORD [a]shall comfort Zion: he will comfort all her waste places; and he will make her wilderness like Eden, and her desert [b]like the garden of the LORD; joy and gladness shall be found therein, thanksgiving, and the voice of melody.

4 ¶ Hearken unto me, my people; and give ear unto me, O my nation: [a]for a law shall proceed from me, and I will make my judgment to rest [b]for a light of the people.

5 [a]My righteousness *is* near; my salvation is gone forth, [b]and mine arms shall judge the people; [c]the isles shall wait upon me, and [d]on mine arm shall they trust.

K 6 [a]Lift up your eyes to the heavens, and look upon the earth beneath: for [b]the heavens shall vanish away like smoke, [c]and the earth shall wax old like a garment, and they that dwell therein shall die in like manner: but my salvation shall be for ever, and my righteousness shall not be abolished.

7 ¶ [a]Hearken unto me, ye that know righteousness, the people [b]in whose heart *is* my law; [c]fear ye not the reproach of men, neither be ye afraid of their revilings.

8 For [a]the moth shall eat them up like a garment, and the worm shall eat them like wool: but my righteousness shall be for ever, and my salvation from generation to generation.

9 ¶ [a]Awake, awake, [b]put on strength, O arm of the LORD; awake, [c]as in the ancient days, in the generations of old. [d]*Art* thou not it that hath cut [e]Rahab, *and* wounded the [f]dragon? I

10 *Art* thou not it which hath [a]dried the sea, the waters of the great deep; that hath made the depths of the sea a way for the ransomed to pass over?

11 Therefore [a]the redeemed of the LORD shall return, and come with singing unto Zion; and everlasting joy *shall be* upon their head: they shall obtain gladness and joy; *and* sorrow and mourning shall flee away. I S

12 I, *even* I, *am* he [a]that comforteth you: who *art* thou, that thou shouldest be afraid [b]of a man *that* shall die, and of the son of man *which* shall be made [c]*as* grass; J

13 And forgettest the LORD thy maker, [a]that hath stretched forth the heavens, and laid the foundations of the earth; and hast feared continually every day because of the fury of the oppressor, as if he ʹwere ready to destroy? [b]and where *is* the fury of the oppressor?

14 The captive exile hasteneth that he may be loosed, [a]and that he should not die in the pit, nor that his bread should fail.

15 But I *am* the LORD thy God, that [a]divided the sea, whose waves roared: The LORD of hosts *is* his name. I

16 And [a]I have put my words in thy mouth, and [b]I have covered thee in the shadow of mine hand, [c]that I may plant the heavens, and lay the foundations of

10 [a]Ps. 23:4 [b]2 Chr. 20:20; Ps. 20:7
11 [a]John 9:39 [b]Ps. 16:4
51:1 [a]Rom. 9:30-32
2 [a]Rom. 4:1; Heb. 11:11 [b]Gen. 12:1 [c]Gen. 24:35
3 [a]ver. 12; ch. 52:9 [b]Gen. 13:10; Joel 2:3
4 [a]ch. 2:3 [b]ch. 42:6
5 [a]ch. 46:13; Rom. 1:16 [b]Ps. 67:4 [c]ch. 60:9 [d]Rom. 1:16
6 [a]ch. 40:26 [b]Ps. 102:26; Mat. 24:35; 2 Pet. 3:10 [c]ch. 50:9
7 [a]ver. 1 [b]Ps. 37:31 [c]Mat. 10:28; Acts 5:41
8 [a]ch. 50:9
9 [a]Ps. 44:23 [b]Ps. 93:1 [c]Ps. 44:1 [d]Job 26:12 [e]Ps. 87:4 & 89:10 [f]Ps. 74:13; Ezek. 29:3
10 [a]Ex. 14:21; ch. 43:16
11 [a]ch. 35:10
12 [a]2 Cor. 1:3 [b]Ps. 118:6 [c]1 Pet. 1:24
13 [a]Ps. 104:2 [b]Job 20:7 ʹOr, *made himself ready*
14 [a]Zech. 9:11
15 [a]Job 26:12; Ps. 74:13; Jer. 31:35
16 [a]Deut. 18:18; ch. 59:21; John 3:34 [b]ch. 49:2 [c]ch. 65:17

G *Isa 30:1* ◀▶ *Isa 64:6*
I *Isa 50:2* ◀▶ *Isa 51:9*
K *Isa 50:10* ◀▶ *Isa 53:5*

I *Isa 51:3–4* ◀▶ *Isa 51:11–12*
I *Isa 51:9* ◀▶ *Isa 51:15–17*
S *Isa 35:10* ◀▶ *Isa 61:3*
J *Isa 26:3* ◀▶ *Hab 3:17*
I *Isa 51:11–12* ◀▶ *Isa 51:22*

51:3–9 Israel prophesied Israel's ultimate restoration in these verses.
51:11 Note that this verse is the same as 35:10 and reconfirmed the same promise of comfort and blessing.
51:15–16 The prophet reaffirmed God's declaration of love and care for his people "in the shadow" (51:16) of his almighty hand.

the earth, and say unto Zion, Thou *art* my people.

The cup of God's fury

R 17 ¶ [a]Awake, awake, stand up, O Jerusalem, which [b]hast drunk at the hand of the LORD the cup of his fury; [c]thou hast drunken the dregs of the cup of trembling, *and* wrung *them* out.

18 *There is* none to guide her among all the sons *whom* she hath brought forth; neither *is there any* that taketh her by the hand of all the sons *that* she hath brought up.

R 19 [a]These two *things* [1]are come unto thee; who shall be sorry for thee? desolation, and [2]destruction, and the famine, and the sword: [b]by whom shall I comfort thee?

20 [a]Thy sons have fainted, they lie at the head of all the streets, as a wild bull in a net: they are full of the fury of the LORD, the rebuke of thy God.

21 ¶ Therefore hear now this, thou afflicted, and drunken, [a]but not with wine:

I 22 Thus saith thy Lord the LORD, and thy God [a]*that* pleadeth the cause of his people, Behold, I have taken out of thine hand the cup of trembling, *even* the dregs of the cup of my fury; thou shalt no more drink it again:

23 But [a]I will put it into the hand of them that afflict thee; [b]which have said to thy soul, Bow down, that we may go over: and thou hast laid thy body as the ground, and as the street, to them that went over.

God will restore Jerusalem

I 52 AWAKE, [a]AWAKE; put on thy strength, O Zion; put on thy beautiful garments, O Jerusalem, [b]the holy city: for [c]henceforth there shall no more come into thee the uncircumcised [d]and the unclean.

2 [a]Shake thyself from the dust; arise, *and* sit down, O Jerusalem: [b]loose thyself from the bands of thy neck, O captive daughter of Zion.

3 For thus saith the LORD, [a]Ye have sold yourselves for nought; and ye shall be redeemed without money. L

4 For thus saith the Lord GOD, My people went down aforetime into [a]Egypt to sojourn there; and the Assyrian oppressed them without cause.

5 Now therefore, what have I here, saith the LORD, that my people is taken away for nought? they that rule over them make them to howl, saith the LORD; and my name continually every day *is* [a]blasphemed.

6 Therefore my people shall know my name: therefore *they shall know* in that day that I *am* he that doth speak: behold, *it is* I. I

7 ¶ [a]How beautiful upon the mountains are the feet of him that bringeth good tidings, that publisheth peace; that bringeth good tidings of good, that publisheth salvation; that saith unto Zion, [b]Thy God reigneth!

8 Thy watchmen shall lift up the voice; with the voice together shall they sing: for they shall see eye to eye, when the LORD shall bring again Zion.

9 ¶ Break forth into joy, sing together, ye waste places of Jerusalem: for the LORD hath comforted his people, he hath redeemed Jerusalem.

10 [a]The LORD hath made bare his holy arm in the eyes of all the nations; and [b]all the ends of the earth shall see the salvation of our God.

11 ¶ [a]Depart ye, depart ye, go ye out from thence, touch no unclean *thing;* go ye out of the midst of her; [b]be ye clean, that bear the vessels of the LORD.

12 For [a]ye shall not go out with haste,

17 [a]ch. 52:1 [b]Job 21:20; Jer. 25:15 [c]See Deut. 28:28, 34; Ps. 60:3; Ezek. 23:32-34
19 [a]ch. 47:9 [b]Amos 7:2 [1]Heb. *happened* [2]Heb. *breaking*
20 [a]Lam. 2:11
21 [a]See ver. 17; Lam. 3:15
22 [a]Jer. 50:34
23 [a]Jer. 25:17; Zech. 12:2 [b]Ps. 66:11
52:1 [a]ch. 51:9,17 [b]Neh. 11:1; Mat. 4:5; Rev. 21:2 [c]Nah. 1:15 [d]Rev. 21:27
2 [a]ch. 3:26 [b]Zech. 2:7
3 [a]Ps. 44:12
4 [a]Gen. 46:6
5 [a]Ezek. 36:20
7 [a]Rom. 10:15 [b]Ps. 93:1
10 [a]Ps. 98:2,3 [b]Luke 3:6
11 [a]ch. 48:20 [b]Lev. 22:2
12 [a]Ex. 12:33

R *Isa 50:1* ◀▶ *Isa 51:19*
R *Isa 51:17* ◀▶ *Isa 54:4*
I *Isa 51:15–17* ◀▶ *Isa 52:1–3*
I *Isa 51:22* ◀▶ *Isa 52:6–9*
L *Isa 49:6* ◀▶ *Isa 53:4–6*
I *Isa 52:1–3* ◀▶ *Isa 54:1–14*

51:19–23 God promised that even though his people would suffer, that "cup of trembling" (51:22) would be removed and given instead to their enemies.

52:1–3 Isaiah prophesied that Israel would be delivered from the control of the "uncircumcised and the unclean" (52:1) Babylonians without having to pay any ransom.

52:6–9 Though the prophet declared these words as a promise that God's people would one day be returned to Jerusalem, the apostle Paul used this prophecy to describe the ministry of missionaries of the gospel (see Ro 10:15).

nor go by flight: [b]for the LORD will go before you; [c]and the God of Israel *will* [1]be
your rearward.

The servant of the LORD

B 13 ¶ Behold, [a]my servant shall [b]deal[1]
M prudently, [c]he shall be exalted and extolled, and be very high.
D 14 As many were astonied at thee; his
[a]visage was so marred more than any
man, and his form more than the sons of
men:
15 [a]So shall he sprinkle many nations;
the kings shall shut their mouths at him:
for *that* [b]which had not been told them
shall they see; and *that* which they had
not heard shall they consider.

53 WHO [a]HATH believed our [1,2]re-
port? and to whom is the arm of
the LORD revealed?
2 For he shall grow up before him as a
tender plant, and as a root out of a dry
ground: he hath no form nor comeliness;
and when we shall see him, *there is* no
beauty that we should desire him.
D 3 [a]He is despised and rejected of men;
a man of sorrows, and [b]acquainted with
grief: and [1,2]we hid as it were *our* faces
from him; he was despised, and [c]we esteemed him not.
L 4 ¶ Surely [a]he hath borne our griefs,
H and carried our sorrows: yet we did esteem him stricken, smitten of God, and
afflicted.
5 But he *was* [a]wounded[1] for our trans- K
gressions, *he was* bruised for our iniquities: the chastisement of our peace *was*
upon him; and with his [b]stripes[2] we are
healed.
6 All we like sheep have gone astray; A
we have turned every one to his own C
way; and the LORD [1]hath laid on him the W
iniquity of us all.
7 He was oppressed, and he was afflicted, yet [a]he opened not his mouth:
[b]he is brought as a lamb to the slaughter,
and as a sheep before her shearers is
dumb, so he openeth not his mouth.
8 [1]He was taken from prison and from
judgment: and who shall declare his generation? for [a]he was cut off out of the
land of the living: for the transgression of
my people [2]was he stricken.
9 [a]And he made his grave with the
wicked, and with the rich in his [1]death;
because he had done no violence, neither
was any [b]deceit in his mouth.
10 ¶ Yet it pleased the LORD to bruise
him; he hath put *him* to grief: [1]when
thou shalt make his soul [a]an offering for
sin, he shall see *his* seed, he shall prolong
his days, and the pleasure of the LORD
shall prosper in his hand.
11 He shall see of the travail of his K
soul, *and* shall be satisfied: by his knowl- L

12 [b]Mic. 2:13 [c]Ex. 14:19 [1]Heb. *gather you up*
13 [a]ch. 42:1 [b]Jer. 23:5 [c]Phil. 2:9 [1]Or, *prosper*
14 [a]Ps. 22:6,7
15 [a]Ezek. 36:25 [b]Eph. 3:5,9
53:1 [a]John 12:38; Rom. 10:16 [1]Or, *doctrine?* [2]Heb. *hearing?*
3 [a]Ps. 22:6 [b]Heb. 4:15 [c]John 1:10 [1]Or, *he hid as it were his face from us* [2]Heb. *as an hiding of faces from him,* or, *from us*
4 [a]Mat. 8:17; Heb. 9:28
5 [a]Rom. 4:25 [b]1 Pet. 2:24 [1]Or, *tormented* [2]Heb. *bruise*
6 [1]Heb. *hath made the iniquity of us all to meet on him*
7 [a]Mat. 26:63 [b]Acts 8:32
8 [a]Dan. 9:26 [1]Or, *He was taken away by distress and judgment: but* [2]Heb. was *the stroke upon him*
9 [a]Mat. 27:57 [b]1 John 3:5 [1]Heb. *deaths*
10 [a]2 Cor. 5:21 [1]Or, *when his soul shall make an offering*

B *Isa 50:6–9* ◀▶ *Isa 61:1–3*
M *Isa 49:7–12* ◀▶ *Isa 55:3*
D *Ps 69:22–21* ◀▶ *Isa 53:3–12*
D *Isa 52:14–15* ◀▶ *Eze 46:13*
L *Isa 52:3* ◀▶ *Isa 53:11–12*
H *Isa 40:29–31* ◀▶ *Jer 8:22*

K *Isa 51:6* ◀▶ *Isa 53:11*
A *Ecc 7:20* ◀▶ *Mt 12:30*
C *Isa 48:22* ◀▶ *Isa 55:2*
W *Isa 49:6* ◀▶ *Isa 55:1*
K *Isa 53:5* ◀▶ *Isa 55:7*
L *Isa 53:4–6* ◀▶ *Isa 55:1–3*

53:1–12 In this detailed prophecy, Isaiah describes God's suffering servant, Jesus Christ, including the revelation that God's own people would reject these words. Isaiah's prophecy details events in the life of Jesus seven centuries before his birth.

1. Isaiah prophesied that he would be "despised and rejected of men" (53:3). Jesus was rejected by his own people during his life and at his death.
2. Isaiah said that the servant would bear our griefs but we would consider him worthy of God's punishment (53:4). The majority of the Jews and Roman authorities rejected Jesus, desiring only his execution.
3. Isaiah portrayed the wounds that were laid on the servant (53:5), indicating the death Jesus would die on the cross for our sins.
4. Isaiah prophesied that the servant would be silent before his oppressors as "a sheep before her shearers is dumb" (53:7). Scripture records that when Jesus stood before his accusers "he answered nothing" (Mt 27:12).
5. Isaiah accurately predicted that Jesus would be "taken from prison" (53:8) and killed.
6. Isaiah declared that "he made his grave with the wicked, and with the rich in his death" (53:9), foreshadowing Jesus' burial in a rich man's tomb (Joseph of Arimathea).
7. Isaiah's prediction stated that God's servant would be "numbered with the transgressors" (53:12), a startling prophecy that affirmed Jesus' execution with sinners. At the crucifixion Jesus was executed with two criminals, exactly as prophesied in the book of Isaiah.

edge shall [a]my righteous [b]servant [c]justify many; for he shall bear their iniquities.

12 [a]Therefore will I divide him *a portion* with the great, [b]and he shall divide the spoil with the strong; because he hath poured out his soul unto death: and he was [c]numbered with the transgressors; and he bare the sin of many, and [d]made intercession for the transgressors.

Blessings through the servant

I 54 SING,[a] O barren, thou *that* didst not bear; break forth into singing, and cry aloud, thou *that* didst not travail with child: for [b]more *are* the children of the desolate than the children of the married wife, saith the LORD.

2 [a]Enlarge the place of thy tent, and let them stretch forth the curtains of thine habitations: spare not, lengthen thy cords, and strengthen thy stakes;

3 For thou shalt break forth on the right hand and on the left; [a]and thy seed shall inherit the Gentiles and make the desolate cities to be inhabited.

R 4 Fear not; for thou shalt not be ashamed: neither be thou confounded; for thou shalt not be put to shame: for thou shalt forget the shame of thy youth, and shalt not remember the reproach of thy widowhood any more.

5 [a]For thy Maker *is* thine husband; the [b]LORD of hosts *is* his name; and thy Redeemer the Holy One of Israel; [c]The God of the whole earth shall he be called.

R 6 For the LORD [a]hath called thee as a woman forsaken and grieved in spirit, and a wife of youth, when thou wast refused, saith thy God.

7 [a]For a small moment have I forsaken thee; but with great mercies will I gather thee.

8 In a little wrath I hid my face from thee for a moment; [a]but with everlasting kindness will I have mercy on thee, saith the LORD thy Redeemer.

9 For this *is as* the waters of [a]Noah unto me: for *as* I have sworn that the waters of Noah should no more go over

I *Isa 52:6–9* ◀ ▶ *Isa 54:17*
R *Isa 51:19* ◀ ▶ *Isa 54:6–8*
R *Isa 54:4* ◀ ▶ *Isa 54:11*

11 [a]1 John 2:1 [b]ch. 42:1 [c]Rom 5:18
12 [a]Ps. 2:8 [b]Col. 2:15 [c]Luke 22:37 [d]Luke 23:34
54:1 [a]Gal. 4:27 [b]1 Sam. 2:5
2 [a]ch. 49:19,20
3 [a]ch. 55:5
5 [a]Jer. 3:14 [b]Luke 1:32 [c]Zech. 14:9; Rom. 3:29
6 [a]ch. 62:4
7 [a]Ps. 30:5; ch. 26:20 & 60:10; 2 Cor. 4:17
8 [a]ch. 55:3; Jer. 31:3
9 [a]Gen. 8:21
10 [a]Ps. 46:2; ch. 51:6; Mat. 5:18 [b]Ps. 89:33
11 [a]1 Chr. 29:2; Rev. 21:18
13 [a]ch. 11:9; Jer. 31:34; John 6:45; 1 Cor. 2:10; 1 Thes. 4:9; 1 John 2:20 [b]Ps. 119:165
17 [a]ch. 45:24,25
55:1 [a]John 4:14 [b]Mat. 13:44; Rev. 3:18

the earth; so have I sworn that I would not be wroth with thee, nor rebuke thee.

10 For [a]the mountains shall depart, and the hills be removed; [b]but my kindness shall not depart from thee, neither shall the covenant of my peace be removed, saith the LORD that hath mercy on thee. L

11 ¶ O thou afflicted, tossed with tempest, *and* not comforted, behold, I will lay thy stones with [a]fair colours, and lay thy foundations with sapphires. R

12 And I will make thy windows of agates, and thy gates of carbuncles, and all thy borders of pleasant stones.

13 And all thy children *shall be* [a]taught of the LORD; and [b]great *shall be* the peace of thy children.

14 In righteousness shalt thou be established: thou shalt be far from oppression; for thou shalt not fear: and from terror; for it shall not come near thee.

15 Behold, they shall surely gather together, *but* not by me: whosoever shall gather together against thee shall fall for thy sake. V

16 Behold, I have created the smith that bloweth the coals in the fire, and that bringeth forth an instrument for his work; and I have created the waster to destroy.

17 ¶ No weapon that is formed against thee shall prosper; and every tongue *that* shall rise against thee in judgment thou shalt condemn. This *is* the heritage of the servants of the LORD, [a]and their righteousness *is* of me, saith the LORD. I V

The great invitation

55 HO, [a]EVERY one that thirsteth, come ye to the waters, and he that hath no money; [b]come ye, buy, and eat; yea, come, buy wine and milk without money and without price. L W

L *Isa 49:15–16* ◀ ▶ *Isa 63:9*
R *Isa 54:6–8* ◀ ▶ *Isa 59:2*
V *Isa 50:9* ◀ ▶ *Isa 54:17*
I *Isa 54:1–14* ◀ ▶ *Isa 55:5*
V *Isa 54:15* ◀ ▶ *Jer 1:19*
L *Isa 53:11–12* ◀ ▶ *Isa 55:6–7*
W *Isa 53:6* ◀ ▶ *Isa 55:6–7*

54:1–14, 17 This series of prophetic verses confirmed God's promise to make Israel a great nation (see note at Ge 15:4). Israel's descendants would finally "inherit the Gentiles" (54:3) and their lands in the coming millennial kingdom.

C 2 Wherefore do ye [1]spend money for
U *that which is* not bread? and your labour
for *that which* satisfieth not? hearken diligently unto me, and eat ye *that which is*
good, and let your soul delight itself in
fatness.
M 3 Incline your ear, and [a]come unto
me: hear, and your soul shall live; [b]and I
will make an everlasting covenant with
you, *even* the [c]sure mercies of David.
4 Behold, I have given him *for* [a]a witness to the people, [b]a leader and commander to the people.
I 5 [a]Behold, thou shalt call a nation *that*
thou knowest not, [b]and nations *that*
knew not thee shall run unto thee because of the LORD thy God, and for the
Holy One of Israel; [c]for he hath glorified
thee.
L 6 ¶ [a]Seek ye the LORD while he may be
N found, call ye upon him while he is near:
W 7 [a]Let the wicked forsake his way, and
K [1]the unrighteous man [b]his thoughts: and
R let him return unto the LORD, [c]and he will
have mercy upon him; and to our God,
for [2]he will abundantly pardon.
8 ¶ [a]For my thoughts *are* not your
thoughts, neither *are* your ways my ways,
saith the LORD.
9 [a]For *as* the heavens are higher than
the earth, so are my ways higher than
your ways, and my thoughts than your
thoughts.
10 For [a]as the rain cometh down, and
the snow from heaven, and returneth not
thither, but watereth the earth, and maketh it bring forth and bud, that it may
give seed to the sower, and bread to the
eater:
11 [a]So shall my word be that goeth
forth out of my mouth: it shall not return
unto me void, but it shall accomplish that
which I please, and it shall prosper *in the thing* whereto I sent it.
12 [a]For ye shall go out with joy, and be I
led forth with peace: the mountains and M
the hills shall [b]break forth before you into
singing, and [c]all the trees of the field
shall clap *their* hands.
13 [a]Instead of [b]the thorn shall come
up the fir tree, and instead of the brier
shall come up the myrtle tree: and it shall
be to the LORD [c]for a name, for an everlasting sign *that* shall not be cut off.

Strangers included in the blessing

56 THUS SAITH the LORD, Keep ye [1]judgment, and do justice: [a]for my salvation *is* near to come, and my righteousness to be revealed.
2 Blessed *is* the man *that* doeth this,
and the son of man *that* layeth hold on it;
[a]that keepeth the sabbath from polluting
it, and keepeth his hand from doing any
evil.
3 ¶ Neither let [a]the son of the
stranger, that hath joined himself to the
LORD, speak, saying, The LORD hath utterly
separated me from his people: neither let
the eunuch say, Behold, I *am* a dry tree.
4 For thus saith the LORD unto the eunuchs that keep my sabbaths, and choose
the things that please me, and take hold
of my covenant;
5 Even unto them will I give in [a]mine
house and within my walls a place [b]and a
name better than of sons and of daughters: I will give them an everlasting
name, that shall not be cut off.
6 Also the sons of the stranger, that
join themselves to the LORD, to serve him,
and to love the name of the LORD, to be
his servants, every one that keepeth the
sabbath from polluting it, and taketh hold
of my covenant;
7 Even them will I [a]bring to my holy
mountain, and make them joyful in my
house of prayer: [b]their burnt offerings
and their sacrifices *shall be* accepted
upon mine altar; for [c]mine house shall be
called an house of prayer [d]for all people.

2 [1]Heb. *weigh*
3 [a]Mat. 11:28 [b]ch. 54:8 & 61:8; Jer. 32:40 [c]2 Sam. 7:8; Ps. 89:28; Acts 13:34
4 [a]John 18:37; Rev. 1:5 [b]Jer. 30:9; Ezek. 34:23; Dan. 9:25; Hos. 3:5
5 [a]ch. 52:15; Eph. 2:11 [b]ch. 60:5 [c]ch. 60:9
6 [a]Ps. 32:6; Mat. 5:25 & 25:11; John 7:34 & 8:21; 2 Cor. 6:1; Heb. 3:13
7 [a]ch. 1:16 [b]Zech. 8:17 [c]Ps. 130:7; Jer. 3:12 [1]Heb. *the man of iniquity* [2]Heb. *he will multiply to pardon*
8 [a]2 Sam. 7:19
9 [a]Ps. 103:11
10 [a]Deut. 32:2
11 [a]ch. 54:9
12 [a]ch. 35:10 [b]Ps. 98:8 [c]1 Chr. 16:33
13 [a]ch. 41:19 [b]Mic. 7:4 [c]Jer. 13:11
56:1 [a]Mat. 4:17 [1]Or, *equity*
2 [a]ch. 58:13
3 [a]Acts 8:27
5 [a]1 Tim. 3:15 [b]1 John 3:1
7 [a]ch. 2:2 [b]Rom. 12:1; Heb. 13:15; 1 Pet. 2:5 [c]Mat. 21:13 [d]Mal. 1:11

C *Isa 53:6* ◀▶ *Isa 57:4*
U *Isa 33:15–16* ◀▶ *Isa 57:1–2*
M *Isa 52:13* ◀▶ *Isa 55:12–13*
I *Isa 54:17* ◀▶ *Isa 55:12–13*
L *Isa 55:1–3* ◀▶ *Isa 57:15–16*
N *Isa 48:4* ◀▶ *Isa 63:10*
W *Isa 55:1* ◀▶ *Isa 57:19*
K *Isa 53:11* ◀▶ *Isa 57:13*
R *Isa 1:16–17* ◀▶ *Isa 57:15*

I *Isa 55:5* ◀▶ *Isa 56:8*
M *Isa 55:3* ◀▶ *Isa 59:19*

55:5 Isaiah prophesied that nations would be attracted to Zion and the God of Israel in the last days because they would be restored both physically and spiritually.

55:12–13 The prophet gave the people a glimpse of life in the millennial kingdom when Jesus Christ will rule with power and peace, allowing the increased fertility of the land of Israel.

I 8 The Lord GOD [a]which gathereth the outcasts of Israel saith, [b]Yet will I gather *others* to him, [1]beside those that are gathered unto him.

The failure of Israel's leaders

9 ¶ [a]All ye beasts of the field, come to devour, *yea,* all ye beasts in the forest.

10 His watchmen *are* [a]blind: they are all ignorant, [b]they *are* all dumb dogs, they cannot bark; [1]sleeping, lying down, loving to slumber.

11 Yea, *they are* [a]greedy[1] dogs *which* [b]can[2] never have enough, and they *are* shepherds *that* cannot understand: they all look to their own way, every one for his gain, from his quarter.

12 Come ye, *say they,* I will fetch wine, and we will fill ourselves with strong drink; [a]and tomorrow shall be as this day, *and* much more abundant.

U 57 THE RIGHTEOUS perisheth, and no man layeth *it* to heart: and [a]merciful[1] men *are* taken away, [b]none considering that the righteous is taken away [2]from the evil *to come.*

2 He shall [a]enter[1] into peace: they shall rest in [b]their beds, *each one* walking [2]*in* his uprightness.

3 ¶ But draw near hither, [a]ye sons of the sorceress, the seed of the adulterer and the whore.

C 4 Against whom do ye sport yourselves? against whom make ye a wide mouth, *and* draw out the tongue? *are* ye not children of transgression, a seed of falsehood,

5 Enflaming yourselves [1]with idols [a]under every green tree, [b]slaying the children in the valleys under the clefts of the rocks?

6 Among the smooth *stones* of the stream *is* thy portion; they, they *are* thy lot: even to them hast thou poured a drink offering, thou hast offered a meat offering. Should I receive comfort in these?

7 [a]Upon a lofty and high mountain hast thou set [b]thy bed: even thither wentest thou up to offer sacrifice.

8 Behind the doors also and the posts hast thou set up thy remembrance: for thou hast discovered *thyself to another* than me, and art gone up; thou hast enlarged thy bed, and [1]made thee *a covenant* with them; [a]thou lovedst their bed [2]where thou sawest *it.*

9 And [a]thou[1] wentest to the king with ointment, and didst increase thy perfumes, and didst send thy messengers far off, and didst debase *thyself even* unto hell.

10 Thou art wearied in the greatness of thy way; [a]*yet* saidst thou not, There is no hope: thou hast found the [1]life of thine hand; therefore thou wast not grieved.

11 And [a]of whom hast thou been afraid or feared, that thou hast lied, and hast not remembered me, nor laid *it* to thy heart? [b]have not I held my peace even of old, and thou fearest me not?

12 I will declare thy righteousness, and thy works; for they shall not profit thee.

13 ¶ When thou criest, let thy compa- K
nies deliver thee; but the wind shall carry them all away; vanity shall take *them:* but he that putteth his trust in me shall possess the land, and shall inherit my holy mountain;

Compassion for the repentant

14 And shall say, [a]Cast ye up, cast ye up, prepare the way, take up the stumblingblock out of the way of my people.

15 For thus saith the high and lofty L
One that inhabiteth eternity, [a]whose M
name *is* Holy; [b]I dwell in the high and P
holy *place,* [c]with him also *that is* of a R
contrite and humble spirit, [d]to revive the spirit of the humble, and to revive the heart of the contrite ones.

16 [a]For I will not contend for ever, I

8 [a]ch. 11:12 [b]John 10:16 [1]Heb. *to his gathered*
9 [a]Jer. 12:9
10 [a]Mat. 15:14 [b]Phil. 3:2 [1]Or, *dreaming,* or, *talking in their sleep*
11 [a]Mic. 3:11 [b]Ezek. 34:2 [1]Heb. *strong of appetite* [2]Heb. *know not to be satisfied*
12 [a]Ps. 10:6; Prov. 23:35; Luke 12:19
57:1 [a]Ps. 12:1 [b]1 Ki. 14:13 [1]Heb. *men of kindness,* or, *godliness* [2]Or, *from that which is evil*
2 [a]Luke 2:29 [b]2 Chr. 16:14 [1]Or, *go in peace* [2]Or, *before him*
3 [a]Mat. 16:4
5 [a]2 Ki. 16:4 [b]Lev. 18:21; 2 Ki. 16:3; Jer. 7:31; Ezek. 16:20 [1]Or, *among the oaks*
7 [a]Ezek. 16:16 [b]Ezek. 23:41
8 [a]Ezek. 16:26 [1]Or, *hewed it for thyself* larger than *theirs* [2]Or, *thou providedst room*
9 [a]Hos. 7:11 [1]Or, *thou respectedst the king*
10 [a]Jer. 2:25 [1]Or, *living*
11 [a]ch. 51:12 [b]Ps. 50:21
14 [a]ch. 40:3
15 [a]Job 6:10; Luke 1:49 [b]Zech. 2:13 [c]Ps. 34:18 & 51:17 [d]Ps. 147:3; ch. 61:1
16 [a]Ps. 85:5 & 103:9; Mic. 7:18

I *Isa 55:12–13* ◀▶ *Isa 57:16–19*
U *Isa 55:2* ◀▶ *Isa 58:8*
C *Isa 55:2* ◀▶ *Isa 57:20–21*

K *Isa 55:7* ◀▶ *Isa 59:1*
L *Isa 55:6–7* ◀▶ *Isa 57:18–19*
M *Isa 48:4* ◀▶ *Isa 66:2*
P *Ps 78:38* ◀▶ *Jer 3:1*
R *Isa 55:7* ◀▶ *Isa 58:5–10*
I *Isa 56:8* ◀▶ *Isa 58:8–12*

56:8 Isaiah described the return of the Jewish exiles to Israel, as well as the Gentiles who will attach themselves to the Jewish people in recognition of their favored position with God in the millennial kingdom.

57:16–19 The prophet declared that God would

neither will I be always wroth: for the
spirit should fail before me, and the souls
[b]*which* I have made.
17 For the iniquity of [a]his covetousness was I wroth, and smote him: [b]I hid
me, and was wroth, [c]and he went on
[1]frowardly in the way of his heart.
L 18 I have seen his ways, and [a]will heal
him: I will lead him also, and restore
comforts unto him and to [b]his mourners.
W 19 I create [a]the fruit of the lips; Peace,
peace [b]to *him that is* far off, and to *him
that is* near, saith the LORD; and I will heal
him.
C 20 [a]But the wicked *are* like the troubled sea, when it cannot rest, whose waters cast up mire and dirt.
21 [a]*There is* no peace, saith my God,
to the wicked.

Right and wrong fasting

58 CRY [1]ALOUD, spare not, lift up
thy voice like a trumpet, and
show my people their transgression, and
the house of Jacob their sins.
2 Yet they seek me daily, and delight
to know my ways, as a nation that did
righteousness, and forsook not the ordinance of their God: they ask of me the
ordinances of justice; they take delight in
approaching to God.
3 ¶ [a]Wherefore have we fasted, *say
they,* and thou seest not? *wherefore* have
we [b]afflicted our soul, and thou takest no
knowledge? Behold, in the day of your
fast ye find pleasure, and exact all your
[1,2]labours.
4 [a]Behold, ye fast for strife and debate,
and to smite with the fist of wickedness:
[1]ye shall not fast as *ye do this* day, to
make your voice to be heard on high.
R 5 Is it [a]such a fast that I have chosen?
[b]a[1] day for a man to afflict his soul? *is it*
to bow down his head as a bulrush, and
[c]to spread sackcloth and ashes *under
him?* wilt thou call this a fast, and an acceptable day to the LORD?
6 *Is* not this the fast that I have chosen? to loose the bands of wickedness,
[a]to undo [1]the heavy burdens, and [b]to let
the [2]oppressed go free, and that ye break
every yoke?
7 *Is it* not [a]to deal thy bread to the
hungry, and that thou bring the poor that
are [1]cast out to thy house? [b]when thou
seest the naked, that thou cover him; and
that thou hide not thyself from [c]thine
own flesh?
8 ¶ [a]Then shall thy light break forth as I
the morning, and thine health shall U
spring forth speedily: and thy righteousness shall go before thee; [b]the glory of
the LORD [1]shall be thy rearward.
9 Then shalt thou call, and the LORD
shall answer; thou shalt cry, and he shall
say, Here I *am.* If thou take away from
the midst of thee the yoke, the putting
forth of the finger, and [a]speaking vanity;
10 And *if* thou draw out thy soul to the U
hungry, and satisfy the afflicted soul; then
shall thy light rise in obscurity, and thy
darkness *be* as the noonday:
11 And the LORD shall guide thee con- A
tinually, and satisfy thy soul in [1]drought, F
and make fat thy bones: and thou shalt be
like a watered garden, and like a spring of
water, whose waters [2]fail not.
12 And *they that shall be* of thee [a]shall
build the old waste places: thou shalt
raise up the foundations of many generations; and thou shalt be called, The re-
pairer of the breach, The restorer of paths
to dwell in.
13 ¶ If [a]thou turn away thy foot from
the sabbath, *from* doing thy pleasure on
my holy day; and call the sabbath a delight, the holy of the LORD, honourable;

16 [b]Num. 16:22; Job 34:14; Heb. 12:9
17 [a]Jer. 6:13 [b]ch. 8:17 & 45:15 [c]ch. 9:13 [1]Heb. *turning away*
18 [a]Jer. 3:22 [b]ch. 61:2
19 [a]Heb. 13:15 [b]Acts 2:39; Eph. 2:17
20 [a]Job 15:20; Prov. 4:16
21 [a]ch. 48:22
58:1 [1]Heb. *with the throat*
3 [a]Mal. 3:14 [b]Lev. 16:29 & 23:27 [1]Or, *things wherewith ye grieve others* [2]Heb. *griefs*
4 [a]1 Ki. 21:9 [1]Or, *ye fast not as this day*
5 [a]Zech. 7:5 [b]Lev. 16:29 [c]Esth. 4:3; Job 2:8; Dan. 9:3 [1]Or, *to afflict his soul for a day?*
6 [a]Neh. 5:10 [b]Jer. 34:9 [1]Heb. *the bundles of the yoke* [2]Heb. *broken*
7 [a]Ezek. 18:7; Mat. 25:35 [b]Job 31:19 [c]Gen. 29:14; Neh. 5:5 [1]Or, *afflicted*
8 [a]Job 11:17 [b]Ex. 14:19; ch. 52:12 [1]Heb. *shall gather thee up*
9 [a]Ps. 12:2
11 [1]Heb. *droughts* [2]Heb. *lie,* or, *deceive*
12 [a]ch. 61:4
13 [a]ch. 56:2

L *Isa 57:15–16* ◀▶ *Isa 59:1*
W *Isa 55:6–7* ◀▶ *Eze 18:23*
C *Isa 57:4* ◀▶ *Isa 59:2–3*
R *Isa 57:15* ◀▶ *Isa 66:2*

I *Isa 57:16–19* ◀▶ *Isa 58:14*
U *Isa 57:1–2* ◀▶ *Isa 58:10*
U *Isa 58:8* ◀▶ *Isa 58:14*
A *Pr 19:23* ◀▶ *Ro 8:28*
F *Isa 49:9–10* ◀▶ *Isa 65:13*

---

not punish his people forever for their rebellion but would finally heal them and restore them. This ultimate restoration and healing of Israel's sins is one of the unshakable covenant promises God made to Abraham and his descendants (see note at Ge 15:4).

58:8–12 This passage contained God's promises for his covenant people if they would follow his law, show justice to the oppressed, share with the poor and turn away from vain practices and sinful idolatry.

58:13–14 Isaiah reminded the people to keep God's Sabbath and thereby show their love for him and his law. Such obedience would bring blessings.

and shalt honour him, not doing thine
own ways, nor finding thine own pleasure, nor speaking *thine own* words:
I 14 [a]Then shalt thou delight thyself in
U the LORD; and I will cause thee to [b]ride
upon the high places of the earth, and
feed thee with the heritage of Jacob thy
father: [c]for the mouth of the LORD hath
spoken *it.*

Sin, confession and redemption

K 59 BEHOLD, THE LORD'S hand is not
L [a]shortened, that it cannot save;
neither his ear heavy, that it cannot hear:
R 2 But your iniquities have separated
C between you and your God, and your sins
[1]have hid *his* face from you, that he will
not hear.
3 For [a]your hands are defiled with
blood, and your fingers with iniquity;
your lips have spoken lies, your tongue
hath muttered perverseness.
4 None calleth for justice, nor *any*
pleadeth for truth: they trust in vanity,
and speak lies; [a]they conceive mischief,
and bring forth iniquity.
5 They hatch [1]cockatrice' eggs, and
weave the spider's web: he that eateth of
their eggs dieth, and [2]that which is
crushed breaketh out into a viper.
6 [a]Their webs shall not become garments, neither shall they cover themselves with their works: their works *are*
works of iniquity, and the act of violence
is in their hands.
7 [a]Their feet run to evil, and they
make haste to shed innocent blood: their
thoughts *are* thoughts of iniquity; wasting
and [1]destruction *are* in their paths.
C 8 The way of peace they know not; and
there is no [1]judgment in their goings:
[a]they have made them crooked paths:
whosoever goeth therein shall not know
peace.
9 ¶ Therefore is judgment far from us, R
neither doth justice overtake us: [a]we
wait for light, but behold obscurity; for
brightness, *but* we walk in darkness.
10 [a]We grope for the wall like the
blind, and we grope as if *we had* no eyes:
we stumble at noonday as in the night;
we are in desolate places as dead *men.*
11 We roar all like bears, and [a]mourn
sore like doves: we look for judgment,
but *there is* none; for salvation, *but* it is
far off from us.
12 For our transgressions are multi- C
plied before thee, and our sins testify
against us: for our transgressions *are* with
us; and *as for* our iniquities, we know
them;
13 In transgressing and lying against
the LORD, and departing away from our
God, speaking oppression and revolt,
conceiving and uttering [a]from the heart
words of falsehood.
14 And judgment is turned away backward, and justice standeth afar off: for
truth is fallen in the street, and equity
cannot enter.
15 Yea, truth faileth; and he *that* departeth from evil [1]maketh himself a prey:
and the LORD saw *it,* and [2]it displeased
him that *there was* no judgment.
16 ¶ [a]And he saw that *there was* no
man, and [b]wondered that *there was* no
intercessor: [c]therefore his arm brought
salvation unto him; and his righteousness, it sustained him.
17 [a]For he put on righteousness as a
breastplate, and an helmet of salvation
upon his head; and he put on the garments of vengeance *for* clothing, and was
clad with zeal as a cloak.
18 [a]According to *their* [1]deeds, accord- H

14 [a]Job 22:26 [b]Deut. 32:13 & 33:29 [c]ch. 1:20 & 40:5; Mic. 4:4
59:1 [a]Num. 11:23; ch. 50:2
2 [1]Or, *have made him hide*
3 [a]ch. 1:15
4 [a]Job 15:35; Ps. 7:14
5 [1]Or, *adders'* [2]Or, *that which is sprinkled* is as if *there brake out a viper*
6 [a]Job 8:14
7 [a]Prov. 1:16; Rom. 3:15 [1]Heb. *breaking*
8 [a]Ps. 125:5; Prov. 2:15 [1]Or, *right*
9 [a]Jer. 8:15
10 [a]Deut. 28:29; Job 5:14; Amos 8:9
11 [a]ch. 38:14; Ezek. 7:16
13 [a]Mat. 12:34
15 [1]Or, *is accounted mad* [2]Heb. *it was evil in his eyes*
16 [a]Ezek. 22:30 [b]Mark 6:6 [c]Ps. 98:1; ch. 63:5
17 [a]Eph. 6:14,17; 1 Thes. 5:8
18 [a]ch. 63:6 [1]Heb. *recompences*

I *Isa 58:8–12* ◀ ▶ *Isa 59:20*
U *Isa 58:10* ◀ ▶ *Isa 62:4*
K *Isa 57:13* ◀ ▶ *Isa 60:19–21*
L *Isa 57:18–19* ◀ ▶ *Isa 61:1–3*
R *Isa 54:11* ◀ ▶ *Isa 59:9–12*
C *Isa 57:20–21* ◀ ▶ *Isa 59:8*
C *Isa 59:2–3* ◀ ▶ *Isa 59:12*
R *Isa 59:2* ◀ ▶ *Isa 60:10*
C *Isa 59:8* ◀ ▶ *Isa 61:1*
H *Isa 35:4* ◀ ▶ *Isa 61:2*

59:2 Israel's sins were the reason for their alienation from God and his refusal to hear their cries.
59:9–12 Isaiah declared that the people could not find justice or light because their transgressions against God cut them off from his justice and blessings.
59:17–21 Despite Israel's past rebellion, God promised to send the Messiah as their deliverer who would bring "fury to his adversaries, recompense to his enemies" (59:18). This passage parallels other prophecies that confirm the powerful deliverance that Messiah will bring to his chosen people at Armageddon (see Jude 14–15; Rev 19:11–21). God has not rejected Israel forever, but rather has promised to save all "that turn from transgression in Jacob" (59:20).

ingly he will repay, fury to his adversaries, recompence to his enemies; to the islands he will repay recompence.

M M 19 [a]So shall they fear the name of the LORD from the west, and his glory from the rising of the sun. When the enemy shall come in [b]like a flood, the spirit of the LORD shall [1]lift up a standard against him.

I 20 ¶ And [a]the Redeemer shall come to Zion, and unto them that turn from transgression in Jacob, saith the LORD.

M E 21 [a]As for me, this *is* my covenant with them, saith the LORD; My spirit that *is* upon thee, and my words which I have put in thy mouth, shall not depart out of thy mouth, nor out of the mouth of thy seed, nor out of the mouth of thy seed's seed, saith the LORD, from henceforth and for ever.

The dawn of Zion's glory

I M **60** ARISE, [a]SHINE;[1] for thy light is come, and [b]the glory of the LORD is risen upon thee.

2 For, behold, the darkness shall cover the earth, and gross darkness the people: but the LORD shall arise upon thee, and his glory shall be seen upon thee.

3 And the [a]Gentiles shall come to thy light, and kings to the brightness of thy rising.

4 [a]Lift up thine eyes round about, and see: all they gather themselves together, [b]they come to thee: thy sons shall come from far, and thy daughters shall be nursed at *thy* side.

5 Then thou shalt see, and flow together, and thine heart shall fear, and be enlarged; because [a]the [1]abundance of the sea shall be converted unto thee, the [2]forces of the Gentiles shall come unto thee.

6 The multitude of camels shall cover thee, the dromedaries of Midian and [a]Ephah; all they from [b]Sheba shall come: they shall bring [c]gold and incense; and they shall show forth the praises of the LORD.

7 All the flocks of [a]Kedar shall be gathered together unto thee, the rams of Nebaioth shall minister unto thee: they shall come up with acceptance on mine altar, and [b]I will glorify the house of my glory.

8 Who *are* these *that* fly as a cloud, and as the doves to their windows?

9 [a]Surely the isles shall wait for me, and the ships of Tarshish first, [b]to bring thy sons from far, [c]their silver and their gold with them, [d]unto the name of the LORD thy God, and to the Holy One of Israel, [e]because he hath glorified thee.

10 And [a]the sons of strangers shall build up thy walls, [b]and their kings shall minister unto thee: for [c]in my wrath I smote thee, [d]but in my favour have I had mercy on thee. R

11 Therefore thy gates [a]shall be open continually; they shall not be shut day nor night; that *men* may bring unto thee the [1]forces of the Gentiles, and *that* their kings *may be* brought.

12 [a]For the nation and kingdom that will not serve thee shall perish; yea, *those* nations shall be utterly wasted.

13 [a]The glory of Lebanon shall come unto thee, the fir tree, the pine tree, and the box together, to beautify the place of my sanctuary; and I will make [b]the place of my feet glorious.

14 The sons also of them that afflicted thee shall come bending unto thee; and R

19 [a]Ps. 113:3; Mal. 1:11 [b]Rev. 12:15 [1]Or, *put him to flight*
20 [a]Rom. 11:26
21 [a]Heb. 8:10 & 10:16
60:1 [a]Eph. 5:14 [b]Mal. 4:2 [1]Or, *be enlightened; for thy light cometh*
3 [a]ch. 49:6,23; Rev. 21:24
4 [a]ch. 49:18 [b]ch. 49:20-22 & 66:12
5 [a]Rom. 11:25 [1]Or, *noise of the sea shall be turned toward thee* [2]Or, *wealth;* see ver. 11; ch. 61:6
6 [a]Gen. 25:4 [b]Ps. 72:10 [c]ch. 61:6; Mat. 2:11
7 [a]Gen. 25:13 [b]Hag. 2:7,9
9 [a]Ps. 72:10; ch. 51:5 [b]Gal. 4:26 [c]Ps. 68:30; Zech. 14:14 [d]Jer. 3:17 [e]ch. 55:5
10 [a]Zech. 6:15 [b]ch. 49:23; Rev. 21:24 [c]ch. 57:17 [d]ch. 54:7,8
11 [a]Rev. 21:25 [1]Or, *wealth;* see ver. 5
12 [a]Zech. 14:17; Mat. 21:44
13 [a]ch. 35:2 [b]1 Chr. 28:2; Ps. 132:7

M *Isa 55:12–13* ◀ ▶ *Isa 59:21*
M *Isa 44:3–4* ◀ ▶ *Eze 2:2–3*
I *Isa 58:14* ◀ ▶ *Isa 60:1–22*
M *Isa 59:19* ◀ ▶ *Isa 60:1–22*
E *Isa 48:16* ◀ ▶ *Isa 63:10–11*
I *Isa 59:20* ◀ ▶ *Isa 61:3*
M *Isa 59:21* ◀ ▶ *Isa 65:16–25*
R *Isa 59:9–12* ◀ ▶ *Isa 60:14–15*
R *Isa 60:10* ◀ ▶ *Isa 63:17*

60:1–18 Though this prophecy of restored blessing and God's favor was initially fulfilled when the exiles returned from Babylon, final fulfillment of these marvelous words will not be realized until the Messiah returns to defeat the enemies of his people and establish his millennial kingdom. At that time Israel will be acknowledged for its supremacy among the millennial nations and will receive both gifts and assistance from Gentile nations for rebuilding their land. In addition, Isaiah prophesied that God would severely punish any Gentile nation that failed to serve Israel (60:12).

Note too that the blessings on Israel and Jerusalem will not be limited by time but rather will be "a joy of many generations" (60:15), indicating God's eternal blessing for his chosen people. The peace of the millennial kingdom of the Messiah is assured with God's words, "Violence shall no more be heard in thy land" (60:18).

all they that despised thee shall [a]bow
themselves down at the soles of thy feet;
and they shall call thee, The city of the
LORD, [b]The Zion of the Holy One of Israel.
15 Whereas thou hast been forsaken
and hated, so that no man went through
thee, I will make thee an eternal excellency, a joy of many generations.
16 Thou shalt also suck the milk of the
Gentiles, [a]and shalt suck the breast of
kings: and thou shalt know that [b]I the
LORD *am* thy Saviour and thy Redeemer,
the mighty One of Jacob.
17 For brass I will bring gold, and for
iron I will bring silver, and for wood
brass, and for stones iron: I will also
make thy officers peace, and thine exac-
tors righteousness.
18 Violence shall no more be heard in
thy land, wasting nor destruction within
thy borders; but thou shalt call [a]thy walls
Salvation, and thy gates Praise.
K 19 The [a]sun shall be no more thy light
by day; neither for brightness shall the
moon give light unto thee: but the LORD
shall be unto thee an everlasting light,
and [b]thy God thy glory.
20 [a]Thy sun shall no more go down;
neither shall thy moon withdraw itself:
for the LORD shall be thine everlasting
light, and the days of thy mourning shall
be ended.
S 21 [a]Thy people also *shall be* all righteous: [b]they shall inherit the land for
ever, [c]the branch of my planting, [d]the
work of my hands, that I may be glorified.
22 [a]A little one shall become a thousand, and a small one a strong nation: I
the LORD will hasten it in his time.

K *Isa 59:1 ◀▶ Isa 63:1*
S *Isa 48:22 ◀▶ Jer 2:19*

14 [a]ch. 49:23; Rev. 3:9 [b]Heb. 12:22; Rev. 14:1
16 [a]ch. 49:23 & 61:6 [b]ch. 43:3
18 [a]ch. 26:1
19 [a]Rev. 21:23 [b]Zech. 2:5
20 [a]Amos 8:9
21 [a]ch. 52:1; ch. 52:1; Rev. 21:27 [b]Ps. 37:11; Mat. 5:5 [c]ch. 61:3; Mat. 15:13; John 15:2 [d]ch. 29:23; Eph. 2:10
22 [a]Mat. 13:31
61:1 [a]Luke 4:18; John 1:32 & 3:34 [b]Ps. 45:7 [c]Ps. 147:3; ch. 57:15 [d]ch. 42:7; Jer. 34:8
2 [a]Lev. 25:9 [b]ch. 34:8; Mal. 4:1,3; 2 Thes. 1:7 [c]ch. 57:18; Mat. 5:4
3 [a]Ps. 30:11 [b]ch. 60:21 [c]John 15:8
4 [a]ch. 49:8; Ezek. 36:33
5 [a]Eph. 2:12
6 [a]Ex. 19:6; ch. 60:17; 1 Pet. 2:5; Rev. 1:6 & 5:10

Good tidings of salvation

61 THE [a]SPIRIT of the Lord GOD *is* B
upon me; because the LORD [b]hath B
anointed me to preach good tidings unto G
the meek; he hath sent me [c]to bind up R
the brokenhearted, to proclaim [d]liberty T
to the captives, and the opening of the C
prison to *them that are* bound; L
2 [a]To proclaim the acceptable year of P
the LORD, and [b]the day of vengeance of H
our God; [c]to comfort all that mourn;
3 To appoint unto them that mourn in I
Zion, [a]to give unto them beauty for S
ashes, the oil of joy for mourning, the garment of praise for the spirit of heaviness;
that they might be called trees of righteousness, [b]the planting of the LORD, [c]that
he might be glorified.
4 ¶ And they shall [a]build the old
wastes, they shall raise up the former
desolations, and they shall repair the
waste cities, the desolations of many generations.
5 And [a]strangers shall stand and feed
your flocks, and the sons of the alien *shall
be* your plowmen and your vinedressers.
6 [a]But ye shall be named the Priests of

B *Isa 52:13 ◀▶ Jer 22:29–30*
B *Isa 44:3 ◀▶ Isa 63:11*
G *Isa 42:1 ◀▶ Da 4:8–9*
R *Isa 4:4 ◀▶ Eze 11:19*
T *Isa 42:1 ◀▶ Eze 8:3*
C *Isa 59:12 ◀▶ Isa 64:6*
L *Isa 59:1 ◀▶ Isa 63:9*
P *Isa 45:23–24 ◀▶ Isa 63:3–6*
H *Isa 59:18 ◀▶ Isa 63:3–4*
I *Isa 60:1–22 ◀▶ Isa 65:8–10*
S *Isa 51:11 ◀▶ Rev 7:17*

60:19–22 Isaiah's prophecy looked forward to the blessings of the new Jerusalem. There would be no need for the sun or moon since the Lamb will be the source of light (see Rev 21:23). There would be no more sorrow or nighttime (see Rev 21:4; 22:5) but only the light of joy and salvation. Only the redeemed would enter into those full blessings (see Rev 21:27).

61:1–3 The background for this prophecy is probably the Year of Jubilee (see Lev 25:10) because the restoration of Israel prophesied here is as significant as the restoration for the land during that year of liberty. Jesus began his public ministry in Nazareth by reading the first part of this prophecy in Isaiah and declaring that, "This day is this scripture fulfilled in your ears" (Lk 4:21). With this declaration Jesus claimed that he was the Messiah Isaiah had prophesied about centuries before. Some scholars believe that by dividing 61:2 in half with this reading in the synagogue, Jesus read only what applied to his ministry on earth at his first coming. These scholars contend that the remainder of this passage will find its fulfillment in Christ's second coming.

61:4–11 Isaiah continued with his description of the millennial kingdom's reign of the Messiah. Israel will be rebuilt with the assistance of the Gentiles and the Lord will rule with justice. Those living on the earth will prosper, have children and live in an atmosphere of righteousness and praise for God. Note that Isaiah also declares that nations will still exist in the Millennium (61:11). Compare this verse with John's prophecy in Rev 21:24–26.

the LORD: *men* shall call you the Ministers of our God: [b]ye shall eat the riches of the Gentiles, and in their glory shall ye boast yourselves.

7 ¶ [a]For your shame *ye shall have* double; and *for* confusion they shall rejoice in their portion: therefore in their land they shall possess the double: everlasting joy shall be unto them.

8 For [a]I the LORD love judgment, [b]I hate robbery for burnt offering; and I will direct their work in truth, [c]and I will make an everlasting covenant with them.

9 And their seed shall be known among the Gentiles, and their offspring among the people: all that see them shall acknowledge them, [a]that they *are* the seed *which* the LORD hath blessed.

10 [a]I will greatly rejoice in the LORD, my soul shall be joyful in my God; for [b]he hath clothed me with the garments of salvation, he hath covered me with the robe of righteousness, [c]as a bridegroom [1]decketh *himself* with ornaments, and as a bride adorneth *herself* with her jewels.

11 For as the earth bringeth forth her bud, and as the garden causeth the things that are sown in it to spring forth; so the Lord GOD will cause [a]righteousness and [b]praise to spring forth before all the nations.

The restoration of Zion

62 FOR ZION'S sake will I not hold my peace, and for Jerusalem's sake I will not rest, until the righteousness thereof go forth as brightness, and the salvation thereof as a lamp *that* burneth.

2 [a]And the Gentiles shall see thy righteousness, and all kings thy glory: [b]and thou shalt be called by a new name, which the mouth of the LORD shall name.

3 Thou shalt also be [a]a crown of glory in the hand of the LORD, and a royal diadem in the hand of thy God.

U 4 [a]Thou shalt no more be termed [b]Forsaken; neither shall thy land any more be termed [c]Desolate: but thou shalt be called [1]Hephzibah, and thy land [2]Beulah: for the LORD delighteth in thee, and thy land shall be married.

5 ¶ For *as* a young man marrieth a virgin, *so* shall thy sons marry thee: and [1]*as* the bridegroom rejoiceth over the bride, *so* [a]shall thy God rejoice over thee.

6 [a]I have set watchmen upon thy walls, O Jerusalem, *which* shall never hold their peace day nor night: [1]ye that make mention of the LORD, keep not silence,

7 And give him no [1]rest, till he establish, and till he make Jerusalem [a]a praise in the earth.

8 The LORD hath sworn by his right hand, and by the arm of his strength, [1]Surely I will no more [a]give thy corn *to be* meat for thine enemies; and the sons of the stranger shall not drink thy wine, for the which thou hast laboured:

9 But they that have gathered it shall eat it, and praise the LORD; and they that have brought it together shall drink it [a]in the courts of my holiness.

10 ¶ Go through, go through the gates; [a]prepare ye the way of the people; cast up, cast up the highway; gather out the stones; [b]lift up a standard for the people.

11 Behold, the LORD hath proclaimed unto the end of the world, [a]Say ye to the daughter of Zion, Behold, thy salvation cometh; behold, his [b]reward *is* with him, and his [1]work before him.

12 And they shall call them, The holy people, The redeemed of the LORD: and thou shalt be called, Sought out, A city [a]not forsaken.

Vengeance and redemption

63 WHO *IS* this that cometh from Edom, with dyed garments from Bozrah? this *that is* [1]glorious in his apparel, travelling in the greatness of his K

6 [b]ch. 60:5
7 [a]ch. 40:2; Zech. 9:12
8 [a]Ps. 11:7 [b]ch. 1:11,13 [c]ch. 55:3
9 [a]ch. 65:23
10 [a]Hab. 3:18 [b]Ps. 132:9,16 [c]ch. 49:18; Rev. 21:2 [1]Heb. *decketh as a priest*
11 [a]Ps. 72:3 & 85:11 [b]ch. 60:18 & 62:7
62:2 [a]ch. 60:3 [b]See ver. 4,12
3 [a]Zech. 9:16
4 [a]Hos. 1:10 [b]ch. 49:14 & 54:6,7 [c]ch. 54:1 [1]i.e. *My delight is in her* [2]i.e. *Married*
5 [a]ch. 65:19 [1]Heb. *with the joy of the bridegroom*
6 [a]Ezek. 3:17 [1]Or, *ye that are the LORD'S remembrancers*
7 [a]ch. 61:11; Zeph. 3:20 [1]Heb. *silence*
8 [a]Deut. 28:31; Jer. 5:17 [1]Heb. *If I give*
9 [a]See Deut. 12:12 & 14:23,26 & 16:11,14
10 [a]ch. 40:3 & 57:14 [b]ch. 11:12
11 [a]Zech. 9:9; Mat. 21:5; John 12:15 [b]ch. 40:10; Rev. 22:12 [1]Or, *recompence*
12 [a]ver. 4
63:1 [1]Heb. *decked*

U *Isa 58:14* ◄► *Isa 64:4–5*

K *Isa 60:19–21* ◄► *Jer 8:22*

62:1–12 God declares his commitment to defend his people and bring them salvation in the last days. He even promises to give Israel a new name. This prophecy of restoration affirmed that Israel's desolate condition would become a time of blessing and forgiveness both physically and spiritually.

63:1–3 Isaiah prophesied that the Messiah would come "from Edom" (63:1) with his garments covered with blood. Edom symbolized the world that hated God's people. Isaiah's imagery pictured Christ coming again in judgment (see Rev 14:17–20; 19:15) at the end of the great tribulation. Christ will return to save Israel from annihilation (see Mt 24:30; Jude 14–15; Rev 19:11–21).

strength? I that speak in righteousness, mighty to save.

2 Wherefore [a]*art thou* red in thine apparel, and thy garments like him that treadeth in the winevat?

P H 3 I have [a]trodden the winepress alone; and of the people *there was* none with me: for I will tread them in mine anger, and trample them in my fury; and their blood shall be sprinkled upon my garments, and I will stain all my raiment.

4 For the [a]day of vengeance *is* in mine heart, and the year of my redeemed is come.

5 [a]And I looked, and [b]*there was* none to help; and I wondered that *there was* none to uphold: therefore mine own [c]arm brought salvation unto me; and my fury, it upheld me.

6 And I will tread down the people in mine anger, and make them drunk in my fury, and I will bring down their strength to the earth.

Praise to the LORD

7 ¶ I will mention the lovingkindnesses of the LORD, *and* the praises of the LORD, according to all that the LORD hath bestowed on us, and the great goodness toward the house of Israel, which he hath bestowed on them according to his mercies, and according to the multitude of his lovingkindnesses.

8 For he said, Surely they *are* my people, children *that* will not lie: so he was their Saviour.

L L 9 [a]In all their affliction he was afflicted, [b]and the angel of his presence saved them: [c]in his love and in his pity he redeemed them; and [d]he bare them, and carried them all the days of old.

P *Isa 61:2* ◀ ▶ *Isa 64:2–3*
H *Isa 61:2* ◀ ▶ *Isa 65:6*
L *Isa 61:1–3* ◀ ▶ *Isa 65:2*
L *Isa 54:10* ◀ ▶ *Jer 31:3*

2 [a]Rev. 19:13
3 [a]Lam. 1:15; Rev. 14:19,20 & 19:15
4 [a]ch. 34:8 & 61:2
5 [a]ch. 41:28 & 59:16 [b]John 16:32 [c]Ps. 98:1; ch. 59:16
9 [a]Judg. 10:16; Acts 9:4 [b]Ex. 14:19; Acts 12:11 [c]Deut. 7:7 [d]Ex. 19:4
10 [a]Ex. 15:24; Ps. 95:9 [b]Ps. 78:40; Acts 7:51 [c]Ex. 23:21
11 [a]Ex. 14:30 [b]Ps. 77:20 [c]Num. 11:17 [1]Or, *shepherds*
12 [a]Ex. 15:6 [b]Josh. 3:16
13 [a]Ps. 106:9
14 [a]2 Sam. 7:23
15 [a]Deut. 26:15; Ps. 80:14 [b]Ps. 33:14 [c]Jer. 31:20; Hos. 11:8 [1]Or, *the multitude*
16 [a]Deut. 32:6 [b]Job 14:21 [1]Or, *our redeemer from everlasting is thy name*
17 [a]Ps. 119:10 [b]ch. 6:10 with John 12:40 [c]Ps. 90:13
18 [a]Deut. 7:6

10 ¶ But they [a]rebelled, and [b]vexed his holy spirit: [c]therefore he was turned to be their enemy, *and* he fought against them. E Q N

11 Then he remembered the days of old, Moses, *and* his people, *saying,* Where *is* he that [a]brought them up out of the sea with the [b]shepherd[1] of his flock? [c]where *is* he that put his holy spirit within him? B

12 That led *them* by the right hand of Moses [a]with his glorious arm, [b]dividing the water before them, to make himself an everlasting name?

13 [a]That led them through the deep, as an horse in the wilderness, *that* they should not stumble?

14 As a beast goeth down into the valley, the spirit of the LORD caused him to rest: so didst thou lead thy people, [a]to make thyself a glorious name. E F J L

Judah appeals to God

15 ¶ [a]Look down from heaven, and behold [b]from the habitation of thy holiness and of thy glory: where *is* thy zeal and thy strength, [1]the sounding [c]of thy bowels and of thy mercies toward me? are they restrained?

16 [a]Doubtless thou *art* our father, though Abraham [b]be ignorant of us, and Israel acknowledge us not: thou, O LORD, *art* our father, [1]our redeemer; thy name *is* from everlasting.

17 ¶ O LORD, why hast thou [a]made us to err from thy ways, *and* [b]hardened our heart from thy fear? [c]Return for thy servants' sake, the tribes of thine inheritance. R

18 [a]The people of thy holiness have

E *Isa 59:21* ◀ ▶ *Isa 63:14*
Q *Ps 51:11* ◀ ▶ *La 2:9*
N *Isa 55:6* ◀ ▶ *Isa 65:12*
B *Isa 61:1* ◀ ▶ *Eze 11:19*
E *Isa 63:10–11* ◀ ▶ *Eze 1:12*
F *Ps 51:12* ◀ ▶ *Ac 9:31*
J *Isa 44:3* ◀ ▶ *Mt 3:16*
L *Isa 48:16* ◀ ▶ *Eze 1:12*
R *Isa 60:14–15* ◀ ▶ *Isa 64:7*

63:4–6 Isaiah continued his prophecy with the words that Israel would find themselves in danger of total destruction with no allies to come to their aid. Christ would then return in wrath to judge Israel's unrighteous enemies. Compare these words with Isaiah's prophecy in 61:1–3.

63:16–19 Isaiah's words reaffirmed God's concern for his people when he stated that though human fathers might abandon Israel, God would not abandon them. Though all twelve tribes of Israel and Judah strayed from God's plan, God let them wander and then punished them with exile because of the hardness of their hearts; but he never stopped loving his chosen people.

possessed *it* but a little while: [b]our adversaries have trodden down thy sanctuary.
19 We are *thine:* thou never barest
rule over them; [l]they were not called by
thy name.

C **64** OH THAT thou wouldest [a]rend
the heavens, that thou wouldest
come down, that [b]the mountains might
flow down at thy presence,
P 2 As *when* [l]the melting fire burneth,
the fire causeth the waters to boil, to
make thy name known to thine adversaries, *that* the nations may tremble at thy
presence!
3 When [a]thou didst terrible things
which we looked not for, thou camest
down, the mountains flowed down at thy
presence.
C 4 For since the beginning of the world
U [a]*men* have not heard, nor perceived by
the ear, neither hath the eye [l]seen,
O God, beside thee, *what* he hath prepared for him that waiteth for him.
5 Thou meetest him that rejoiceth
[a]and worketh righteousness, [b]*those that*
remember thee in thy ways: behold, thou
art wroth; for we have sinned: [c]in those
is continuance, and we shall be saved.
C 6 But we are all as an unclean *thing,*
G and all [a]our righteousnesses *are* as filthy
rags; and we all do [b]fade as a leaf; and our
iniquities, like the wind, have taken us
away.
R 7 And *there is* none that calleth upon
thy name, that stirreth up himself to take
hold of thee: for thou hast hid thy face
from us, and hast [l]consumed us, because
of our iniquities.
8 [a]But now, O LORD, thou *art* our father; we *are* the clay, [b]and thou our potter; and we all *are* [c]the work of thy hand.
9 ¶ Be not [a]wroth very sore, O LORD, R
neither remember iniquity for ever: behold, see, we beseech thee, [b]we *are* all
thy people.
10 Thy holy cities are a wilderness,
Zion is a wilderness, [a]Jerusalem a desolation.
11 [a]Our holy and our beautiful house,
where our fathers praised thee, is burned
up with fire: and all [b]our pleasant things
are laid waste.
12 [a]Wilt thou refrain thyself for these R
things, O LORD? [b]wilt thou hold thy
peace, and afflict us very sore?

Judgment and salvation

65 I [a]AM sought of *them that* asked G
not *for me;* I am found of *them*
that sought me not: I said, Behold me,
behold me, unto a nation *that* [b]was not
called by my name.
2 [a]I have spread out my hands all the C
day unto a rebellious people, which walk- L
eth in a way *that was* not good, after their
own thoughts;
3 A people [a]that provoketh me to anger continually to my face; [b]that sacrificeth in gardens, and burneth incense
[l]upon altars of brick;
4 [a]Which remain among the graves,
and lodge in the monuments, [b]which eat
swine's flesh, and [l]broth of abominable
things is in their vessels;
5 [a]Which say, Stand by thyself, come
not near to me; for I am holier than thou.
These *are* a smoke in my [l]nose, a fire
that burneth all the day.
6 Behold, [a]*it is* written before me: [b]I H
will not keep silence, [c]but will recom-

18 [b]Ps. 74:7
19 [l]Or, *thy name was not called upon them*
64:1 [a]Ps. 144:5 [b]Mic. 1:4
2 [l]Heb. *the fire of meltings*
3 [a]Ex. 34:10; Ps. 68:8
4 [a]Ps. 31:19; 1 Cor. 2:9 [l]Or, *seen a God beside thee,* which *doeth* so *for him*
5 [a]Acts 10:35 [b]ch. 26:8 [c]Mal. 3:6
6 [a]Phil. 3:9 [b]Ps. 90:5,6
7 [l]Heb. *melted*
8 [a]ch. 63:16 [b]ch. 29:16 [c]Eph. 2:10
9 [a]Ps. 74:1,2 [b]Ps. 79:13
10 [a]Ps. 79:1
11 [a]Ps. 74:7 [b]Ezek. 24:21
12 [a]ch. 42:14 [b]Ps. 83:1
65:1 [a]Rom. 9:24; Eph. 2:12 [b]ch. 63:19
2 [a]Rom. 10:21
3 [a]Deut. 32:21 [b]ch. 1:29; Lev. 17:5 [l]Heb. *upon bricks*
4 [a]Deut. 18:11 [b]ch. 66:17 [l]Or, *pieces*
5 [a]Mat. 9:11; Luke 18:11; Jude 19 [l]Or, *anger*
6 [a]Deut. 32:34; Mal. 3:16 [b]Ps. 50:3 [c]Ps. 79:12; Jer. 16:18; Ezek. 11:21

C *SS 8:14* ◀▶ *Isa 64:4*
P *Isa 63:3–6* ◀▶ *Isa 66:5–6*
C *Isa 64:1* ◀▶ *Da 7:13*
U *Isa 62:4* ◀▶ *Isa 65:13–14*
C *Isa 61:1* ◀▶ *Isa 65:2*
G *Isa 50:11* ◀▶ *Jer 2:13*
R *Isa 63:17* ◀▶ *Isa 64:9–10*
R *Isa 64:7* ◀▶ *Isa 64:12*
R *Isa 64:9–10* ◀▶ *Jer 2:14–17*
G *SS 8:8–9* ◀▶ *Jer 16:19*
C *Isa 64:6* ◀▶ *Jer 2:19*
L *Isa 63:9* ◀▶ *Jer 3:1*
H *Isa 63:3–4* ◀▶ *Isa 65:13–14*

64:1–4 In this passage Isaiah prayed for God's intervention on behalf of Israel with the kind of prayer that Israel might pray during the tribulation period. Note the similarity of 64:4 with Paul's words in 1Co 2:9.

64:7–12 This prophecy revealed the "desolation" (64:10) that fell on Israel because of her sinfulness. Yet Isaiah reminds us that we are only clay and God is the potter (64:8); our lives and future are in God's hands.

65:1 Isaiah prophesied that the Gentile nations would find God because God would reveal himself to them. This prophecy found its fulfillment in the missionary effort of the early Christians in the first century (see Ac 10:19–45) and is still being fulfilled today.

pense, even recompense into their bosom,

7 Your iniquities, and [a]the iniquities of your fathers together, saith the LORD, [b]which have burned incense upon the mountains, [c]and blasphemed me upon the hills: therefore will I measure their former work into their bosom.

I 8 ¶ Thus saith the LORD, As the new wine is found in the cluster, and *one* saith, Destroy it not; for [a]a blessing *is* in it: so will I do for my servants' sakes, that I may not destroy them all.

9 And I will bring forth a seed out of Jacob, and out of Judah an inheritor of my mountains: and mine [a]elect shall inherit it, and my servants shall dwell there.

10 And [a]Sharon shall be a fold of flocks, and [b]the valley of Achor a place for the herds to lie down in, for my people that have sought me.

11 ¶ But ye *are* they that forsake the LORD, that forget [a]my holy mountain, that prepare [b]a table for that [1]troop, and that furnish the drink offering unto that [2]number.

N 12 Therefore will I number you to the sword, and ye shall all bow down to the slaughter: [a]because when I called, ye did not answer; when I spake, ye did not hear; but did evil before mine eyes, and did choose *that* wherein I delighted not.

H N 13 Therefore thus saith the Lord GOD, Behold, my servants shall eat, but ye shall be hungry: behold, my servants shall drink, but ye shall be thirsty: behold, my servants shall rejoice, but ye shall be ashamed:

14 Behold, my servants shall sing for joy of heart, but ye shall cry for sorrow of heart, and [a]shall howl for [1]vexation of spirit.

15 And ye shall leave your name [a]for a curse unto [b]my chosen: for the Lord GOD shall slay thee, and [c]call his servants by another name:

16 [a]That he who blesseth himself in the earth shall bless himself in the God of truth; and [b]he that sweareth in the earth shall swear by the God of truth; because the former troubles are forgotten, and because they are hid from mine eyes. I M N

The joy of the new age

17 ¶ For, behold, I create [a]new heavens and a new earth: and the former shall not be remembered, nor [1]come into mind.

18 But be ye glad and rejoice for ever *in that* which I create: for, behold, I create Jerusalem a rejoicing, and her people a joy.

19 And [a]I will rejoice in Jerusalem, and joy in my people: and the [b]voice of weeping shall be no more heard in her, nor the voice of crying.

20 There shall be no more thence an infant of days, nor an old man that hath not filled his days; for the child shall die

7 [a]Ex. 20:5 [b]Ezek. 18:6 [c]Ezek. 20:27
8 [a]Joel 2:14
9 [a]Mat. 24:22
10 [a]ch. 33:9 [b]Josh. 7:24; Hos. 2:15
11 [a]ch. 56:7 [b]Ezek. 23:41; 1 Cor. 10:21 [1]Or, *Gad* [2]Or, *Meni*
12 [a]2 Chr. 36:15, 16; Prov. 1:24; Jer. 7:13
14 [a]Mat. 8:12; Luke 13:28 [1]Heb. *breaking*
15 [a]Jer. 29:22; Zech. 8:13 [b]ver. 9, 22 [c]Acts 11:26
16 [a]Ps. 72:17; Jer. 4:2 [b]Deut. 6:13; Zeph. 1:5
17 [a]2 Pet. 3:13; Rev. 21:1 [1]Heb. *come upon the heart*
19 [a]ch. 62:5 [b]ch. 35:10; Rev. 7:17

I *Isa 61:3* ◀▶ *Isa 65:16–25*
N *Isa 63:10* ◀▶ *Isa 65:13–14*
H *Isa 65:6* ◀▶ *Isa 66:14–16*
N *Isa 65:12* ◀▶ *Isa 66:4*
F *Isa 58:11* ◀▶ *Hos 2:8*
U *Isa 64:4–5* ◀▶ *Jer 7:23*

I *Isa 65:8–10* ◀▶ *Isa 66:5–6*
M *Isa 60:1–22* ◀▶ *Isa 66:18–24*
N *Ecc 1:4* ◀▶ *Mt 5:5*

65:8–10 Despite the prophesied judgments against Israel, God promised to leave a remnant who would one day repossess the promised land under their Messiah.

65:16 Isaiah proclaimed that God's people needed nothing more than God; he is enough. Those who are concerned with worldly things bless themselves with the abundance of worldly things (see Ps 49:18; Lk 12:19). We who are God's children should bless ourselves in him for he alone is our strength (see 12:2). We should only swear by him and not false gods of power or materialism. We should honor him as the God of truth and covenant with him who is "the Amen, the faithful and true witness" (Rev 3:14).

65:17–19 The climax of Isaiah's prophecies was this promise that one day God would create "new heavens and a new earth" (65:17) where things that happened in the past will no longer be remembered. The inhabitants of this future world will not be robbed of the joy of heaven by the memories of past events. Notice also that the portrait of the new Jerusalem is painted in terms of rejoicing: "the voice of weeping shall be no more heard in her" (65:19).

65:20–24 Isaiah's prophecy includes a description of the Millennium that will precede these "new" things. While there will be no death or sin forever in the new heavens and new earth, there will be some degree of sin and punishment for sin during the Millennium (65:20). Infant mortality will no longer exist and people will live longer lives than we commonly experience today. The inhabitants of the Millennium will live in peace and security, able to "enjoy the work of their hands" (65:22) with no fear of war or

an hundred years old; [a]but the sinner *being* an hundred years old shall be accursed.

21 And they shall build houses, and inhabit *them;* and they shall plant vineyards, and eat the fruit of them.

22 They shall not build, and another inhabit; they shall not plant, and another eat: for [a]as the days of a tree *are* the days of my people, and [b]mine elect [1]shall long enjoy the work of their hands.

23 They shall not labour in vain, [a]nor bring forth for trouble; for [b]they *are* the seed of the blessed of the LORD, and their offspring with them.

24 And it shall come to pass, that [a]before they call, I will answer; and while they are yet speaking, I will hear.

25 The [a]wolf and the lamb shall feed together, and the lion shall eat straw like the bullock: [b]and dust *shall be* the serpent's meat. They shall not hurt nor destroy in all my holy mountain, saith the LORD.

Judgment and hope

66 THUS SAITH the LORD, [a]The heaven *is* my throne, and the earth *is* my footstool: where *is* the house that ye build unto me? and where *is* the place of my rest?

2 For all those *things* hath mine hand made, and all those *things* have been, saith the LORD: [a]but to this *man* will I look, [b]*even* to *him that is* poor and of a contrite spirit, and [c]trembleth at my word.

3 [a]He that killeth an ox *is as if* he slew a man; he that sacrificeth a [1]lamb, *as if* he [b]cut off a dog's neck; he that offereth an oblation, *as if he offered* swine's blood; he that [2]burneth incense, *as if* he blessed an idol. Yea, they have chosen their own ways, and their soul delighteth in their abominations.

4 I also will choose their [1]delusions, and will bring their fears upon them; [a]because when I called, none did answer; when I spake, they did not hear: but they did evil before mine eyes, and chose *that* in which I delighted not.

5 ¶ Hear the word of the LORD, [a]ye that tremble at his word; Your brethren that hated you, that cast you out for my name's sake, said, [b]Let the LORD be glorified: but [c]he shall appear to your joy, and they shall be ashamed.

6 A voice of noise from the city, a voice from the temple, a voice of the LORD that rendereth recompence to his enemies.

7 Before she travailed, she brought forth; before her pain came, she was delivered of a man child.

8 Who hath heard such a thing? who hath seen such things? Shall the earth be made to bring forth in one day? *or* shall a nation be born at once? for as soon as Zion travailed, she brought forth her children.

9 Shall I bring to the birth, and not [1]cause to bring forth? saith the LORD: shall I cause to bring forth, and shut *the womb?* saith thy God.

10 Rejoice ye with Jerusalem, and be glad with her, all ye that love her: rejoice for joy with her, all ye that mourn for her:

11 That ye may suck, and be satisfied with the breasts of her consolations; that

20 [a]Eccl. 8:12
22 [a]Ps. 92:12 [b]ver. 9,15 [1]Heb. *shall make them continue long,* or, *shall wear out*
23 [a]Hos. 9:12 [b]ch. 61:9
24 [a]Dan. 9:21
25 [a]ch. 11:6 [b]Gen. 3:14
66:1 [a]1 Ki. 8:27; 2 Chr. 6:18; Mat. 5:34; Acts 17:24
2 [a]ch. 57:15 & 61:1 [b]Ps. 34:18 & 51:17 [c]ver. 5; Ezra 9:4 & 10:3; Prov. 28:14
3 [a]ch. 1:11 [b]Deut. 23:18 [1]Or, *kid* [2]Heb. *maketh a memorial of;* see Lev. 2:2
4 [a]Prov. 1:24; ch. 65:12; Jer. 7:13 [1]Or, *devices*
5 [a]ver. 2 [b]ch. 5:19 [c]2 Thes. 1:10; Tit. 2:13
9 [1]Or, *beget?*

U *Isa 32:17–18* ◀ ▶ *Hos 2:18*
M *Isa 57:15* ◀ ▶ *Jer 2:35*
R *Isa 58:5–10* ◀ ▶ *Jer 3:12–13*
N *Isa 65:13–14* ◀ ▶ *Jer 2:27*
I *Isa 65:16–25* ◀ ▶ *Isa 66:8*
P *Isa 64:2–3* ◀ ▶ *Isa 66:14–17*
I *Isa 66:5–6* ◀ ▶ *Isa 66:10–14*
I *Isa 66:8* ◀ ▶ *Isa 66:18–24*

---

being cast out of their homes. Above all, the relationship between humanity and God will be so close that "before they call, I will answer" (65:24).

65:25 Isaiah included a final word about the remarkable transformation of the animal kingdom that will occur when Christ renews the earth from its curse of sin and death. When Christ returns, even the most ferocious beast will become a harmless vegetarian.

66:5–6 This prophecy declared that when the Messiah comes Israel's enemies would be repaid for their sarcasm and derision.

66:8–9 Isaiah predicted that the final restoration of Israel will be astonishing and complete and that the nation will "be born at once" (66:8) during a period of great travail. This prophecy found its partial fulfillment when Israel declared its independence on May 15, 1948, and will find its final fulfillment when Christ returns.

66:10–14 This prophecy confirmed Israel's blessings in the Millennium. She will finally experience the peace that has eluded her throughout history.

ye may milk out, and be delighted with
the [l]abundance of her glory.
12 For thus saith the LORD, Behold, [a]I
will extend peace to her like a river, and
the glory of the Gentiles like a flowing
stream: then shall ye [b]suck, ye shall be
[c]borne upon *her* sides, and be dandled
upon *her* knees.
13 As one whom his mother comforteth, so will I comfort you; and ye shall be
comforted in Jerusalem.
P 14 And when ye see *this,* your heart
H shall rejoice, and [a]your bones shall flourish like an herb: and the hand of the LORD
shall be known toward his servants, and
his indignation toward his enemies.
15 [a]For, behold, the LORD will come
with fire, and with his chariots like a
whirlwind, to render his anger with fury,
and his rebuke with flames of fire.
16 For by fire and by [a]his sword will
the LORD plead with all flesh: and the slain
of the LORD shall be many.
17 [a]They that sanctify themselves, and
purify themselves in the gardens [l]behind
one *tree* in the midst, eating swine's
flesh, and the abomination, and the
mouse, shall be consumed together, saith
the LORD.
I 18 For I *know* their works and their
M thoughts: it shall come, that I will gather
all nations and tongues; and they shall
come, and see my glory.

P *Isa 66:5–6* ◀ ▶ *Isa 66:24*
H *Isa 65:13–14* ◀ ▶ *Isa 66:24*
I *Isa 66:10–14* ◀ ▶ *Jer 3:14–19*
M *Isa 65:16–25* ◀ ▶ *Jer 3:17*

11 [l]Or, *brightness*
12 [a]ch. 48:18 & 60:5 [b]ch. 60:16 [c]ch. 49:22 & 60:4
14 [a]See Ezek. 37:1
15 [a]ch. 9:5
16 [a]ch. 27:1
17 [a]ch. 65:3,4 [l]Or, *one after another*
19 [a]Luke 2:34 [b]Mal. 1:11
20 [a]Rom. 15:16 [l]Or, *coaches*
21 [a]Ex. 19:6; ch. 61:6; 1 Pet. 2:9; Rev. 1:6
22 [a]ch. 65:17; 2 Pet. 3:13; Rev. 21:1
23 [a]Zech. 14:16 [b]Ps. 65:2 [l]Heb. *from new moon to his new moon, and from sabbath to his sabbath*
24 [a]ver. 16 [b]Mark 9:44,46,48

19 [a]And I will set a sign among them,
and I will send those that escape of them
unto the nations, *to* Tarshish, Pul, and
Lud, that draw the bow, *to* Tubal, and
Javan, *to* the isles afar off, that have not
heard my fame, neither have seen my
glory; [b]and they shall declare my glory
among the Gentiles.
20 And they shall bring all your brethren [a]*for* an offering unto the LORD out of
all nations upon horses, and in chariots,
and in [l]litters, and upon mules, and upon
swift beasts, to my holy mountain Jerusalem, saith the LORD, as the children of Israel bring an offering in a clean vessel
into the house of the LORD.
21 And I will also take of them for
[a]priests *and* for Levites, saith the LORD.
22 For as [a]the new heavens and the
new earth, which I will make, shall remain before me, saith the LORD, so shall
your seed and your name remain.
23 And [a]it shall come to pass, *that*
[l]from one new moon to another, and
from one sabbath to another, [b]shall all
flesh come to worship before me, saith
the LORD.
24 And they shall go forth, and look P
upon [a]the carcases of the men that have H
transgressed against me: for their [b]worm
shall not die, neither shall their fire be
quenched; and they shall be an abhorring
unto all flesh.

P *Isa 66:14–17* ◀ ▶ *Jer 10:10*
H *Isa 66:14–16* ◀ ▶ *Jer 4:4*

66:15–17 Isaiah declared that the Messiah would judge all sinners "by fire and by his sword" (66:16; see Rev 19:11–21). Whether their sins were public or committed in secret, God promised to punish "all flesh" (66:16).

66:18–21 Isaiah revealed that even the Gentiles would recognize God's glory and acknowledge his kingdom in the last days. God also promised to reestablish the priesthood and the Levites for leading worship in the rebuilt temple (see 2:1–3; Rev 11:1–2).

66:22–24 Isaiah concluded his prophecy with God's declaration that Israel would endure forever (66:22). Note the reference also to the continuation of a way to mark time (66:23). For further information about the passage of time in heaven, see the article on "Heaven," p. 1226.

Jeremiah

Author: Jeremiah

Theme: God's warning and subsequent judgment for Judah's sins

Date of Writing: c. 585–580 B.C.

Outline of Jeremiah

I. Jeremiah's Call (1:1–19)
II. Judah's Sinful Condition (2:1—12:17)
III. The Certainty of Captivity (13:1—29:32)
IV. The Promise of Restoration (30:1—33:26)
V. Disintegration Before Jerusalem Falls (34:1—35:19)
VI. Jeremiah Suffers (36:1—38:28)
VII. The Fall of Jerusalem (39:1—45:5)
VIII. Foreign Nations Judged (46:1—51:64)
IX. Historical Appendix (52:1–34)

JEREMIAH WAS A priest from the city of Anathoth. The book that bears his name is replete with personal details about Jeremiah's life, including his confessions of self-criticism and bold statements about his feelings toward God. His words of doom and woe earned Jeremiah a nickname as the "weeping prophet." Jeremiah's faithful secretary, Baruch, helped him compile the prophecies in this book. Since the messages in Jeremiah are not arranged chronologically, it is vital to read the books of Kings and Chronicles to bring Jeremiah's prophecies into historical perspective.

Jeremiah chronicles life in Judah from the time of King Josiah until Jerusalem's overthrow by Babylon in 586 B.C. Jeremiah repeatedly warned his listeners of impending destruction because of the people's continued wickedness. Though King Josiah instituted a religious reformation during his reign, Jeremiah's words failed to inspire lasting repentance. The people based their security on their possession of the law, God's covenant and the temple. Jeremiah warned that possessions, regardless of their religious significance, were not enough. God required obedience, or judgment would come.

Under King Josiah's rule Judah experienced religious revival. But following Josiah's death in 609 B.C., political and religious leaders returned to their wicked ways. Jeremiah faced constant opposition because of his continued warnings of God's impending judgment. He went into hiding, using Baruch to deliver his messages of doom. Yet the leaders refused to repent, and the kingdom continued to disintegrate. Finally in 586 B.C. the Babylonians under Nebuchadnezzar destroyed the city of Jerusalem and the temple. The remaining citizens of Judah fled to Egypt for safety, and Jeremiah went with them.

The book of Jeremiah offers profound prophetic insight into the conditions of the kingdom of Judah during its final forty years of existence. More than half of the book is concerned with prophetic messages, some of which were fulfilled in Jeremiah's lifetime. Other messages deal with prophecies about Judah's future, including the duration of the Babylonian captivity and its relation to Judah's failure to observe the Sabbath of the land (see 25:11; 2Ch 36:21).

The prophet's call

1 THE WORDS of Jeremiah the son of
Hilkiah, of the priests that *were* [a]in
Anathoth in the land of Benjamin:
2 To whom the word of the LORD came
in the days of Josiah the son of Amon
king of Judah, [a]in the thirteenth year of
his reign.
3 It came also in the days of Jehoiakim
the son of Josiah king of Judah, [a]unto the
end of the eleventh year of Zedekiah the
son of Josiah king of Judah, [b]unto the carrying away of Jerusalem captive [c]in the
fifth month.
4 Then the word of the LORD came
unto me, saying,
5 Before I [a]formed thee in the belly [b]I
knew thee; and before thou camest forth
out of the womb I [c]sanctified thee, *and* I
[/]ordained thee a prophet unto the nations.
6 Then said I, [a]Ah, Lord GOD! behold, I
cannot speak: for I *am* a child.
7 ¶ But the LORD said unto me, Say not,
I *am* a child: for thou shalt go to all that I
shall send thee, and [a]whatsoever I command thee thou shalt speak.
8 [a]Be not afraid of their faces: for [b]I *am*
with thee to deliver thee, saith the LORD.
9 Then the LORD put forth his hand,
and [a]touched my mouth. And the LORD
said unto me, Behold, I have [b]put my
words in thy mouth.
10 [a]See, I have this day set thee over
the nations and over the kingdoms, to
[b]root out, and to pull down, and to destroy, and to throw down, to build, and to
plant.
11 ¶ Moreover the word of the LORD
came unto me, saying, Jeremiah, what
seest thou? And I said, I see a rod of an
almond tree.
12 Then said the LORD unto me, Thou
hast well seen: for I will hasten my word
to perform it.
13 And the word of the LORD came J
unto me the second time, saying, What
seest thou? And I said, I see [a]a seething
pot; and the face thereof *is* [/]toward the
north.
14 Then the LORD said unto me, Out of
the [a]north an evil [/]shall break forth upon
all the inhabitants of the land.
15 For, lo, I will [a]call all the families of
the kingdoms of the north, saith the LORD;
and they shall come, and they shall [b]set
every one his throne at the entering of
the gates of Jerusalem, and against all the
walls thereof round about, and against all
the cities of Judah.
16 And I will utter my judgments
against them touching all their wickedness, [a]who have forsaken me, and have
burned incense unto other gods, and
worshipped the works of their own
hands.
17 ¶ Thou therefore [a]gird up thy loins, T
and arise, and speak unto them all that I
command thee: [b]be not dismayed at their
faces, lest I [/]confound thee before them.

J *Isa 48:14–15* ◀ ▶ *Jer 1:18–19*
T *Isa 44:8* ◀ ▶ *Joel 2:26*

1:1 [a]Josh. 21:18; 1 Chr. 6:60; ch. 32:7,8
2 [a]ch. 25:3
3 [a]ch. 39:2 [b]ch. 52:12 [c]2 Ki. 25:8
5 [a]Is. 49:1,5 [b]Ex. 33:12 [c]Luke 1:15; Gal. 1:15 [/]Heb. *gave*
6 [a]Ex. 4:10 & 6:12,30
7 [a]Num. 22:20,38; Mat. 28:20
8 [a]Ezek. 2:6 & 3:9 [b]Ex. 3:12; Deut. 31:6; Josh. 1:5; ch. 15:20; Acts 26:17; Heb. 13:6
9 [a]Is. 6:7 [b]Is. 51:16; ch. 5:14
10 [a]1 Ki. 19:17 [b]ch. 18:7; 2 Cor. 10:4
13 [a]Ezek. 11:3 & 24:3 [/]Heb. *from the face of the north*
14 [a]ch. 6:1 [/]Heb. *shall be opened*
15 [a]ch. 6:22 [b]ch. 39:3
16 [a]Deut. 28:20; ch. 17:13
17 [a]2 Ki. 4:29; Job 38:3; Luke 12:35; 1 Pet. 1:13 [b]Ex. 3:12; Ezek. 2:6 [/]Or, *break to pieces*

J 18 For, behold, I have made thee this day [a]a defenced city, and an iron pillar, and brasen walls against the whole land, against the kings of Judah, against the princes thereof, against the priests thereof, and against the people of the land.

V 19 And they shall fight against thee; but they shall not prevail against thee; [a]for I *am* with thee, saith the LORD, to deliver thee.

Israel's faithlessness

2 MOREOVER THE word of the LORD came to me, saying,

2 Go and cry in the ears of Jerusalem, saying, Thus saith the LORD; I remember 'thee, the kindness of thy [a]youth, the love of thine espousals, [b]when thou wentest after me in the wilderness, in a land *that was* not sown.

3 [a]Israel *was* holiness unto the LORD, *and* [b]the firstfruits of his increase: [c]all that devour him shall offend; evil shall come upon them, saith the LORD.

4 Hear ye the word of the LORD, O house of Jacob, and all the families of the house of Israel:

5 ¶ Thus saith the LORD, [a]What iniquity have your fathers found in me, that they are gone far from me, [b]and have walked after vanity, and are become vain?

6 Neither said they, Where *is* the LORD that [a]brought us up out of the land of Egypt, that led us through [b]the wilderness, through a land of deserts and of pits, through a land of drought, and of the shadow of death, through a land that no man passed through, and where no man dwelt?

7 And I brought you into [a]a' plentiful country, to eat the fruit thereof and the goodness thereof; but when ye entered, ye [b]defiled my land, and made mine heritage an abomination.

8 The priests said not, Where *is* the LORD? and they that handle the [a]law knew me not: the pastors also transgressed against me, [b]and the prophets prophesied by Baal, and walked after *things that* do not profit.

9 ¶ Wherefore [a]I will yet plead with you, saith the LORD, and with your children's children will I plead.

10 For pass 'over the isles of Chittim, and see; and send unto Kedar, and consider diligently, and see if there be such a thing.

11 [a]Hath a nation changed *their* gods, which *are* [b]yet no gods? [c]but my people have changed their glory for *that which* doth not profit.

12 Be astonished, O ye heavens, at this, and be horribly afraid, be ye very desolate, saith the LORD.

13 For my people have committed two evils; they have forsaken me the [a]fountain of living waters, *and* hewed them out cisterns, broken cisterns, that can hold no water. G O

14 ¶ *Is* Israel [a]a servant? *is* he a homeborn *slave?* why is he 'spoiled? R

15 [a]The young lions roared upon him, *and* 'yelled, and they made his land waste: his cities are burned without inhabitant.

16 Also the children of Noph and [a]Tahapanes 'have broken the crown of thy head.

17 [a]Hast thou not procured this unto thyself, in that thou hast forsaken the LORD thy God, when [b]he led thee by the way?

18 And now what hast thou to do [a]in the way of Egypt, to drink the waters of [b]Sihor? or what hast thou to do in the way of Assyria, to drink the waters of the river?

19 Thine own wickedness shall correct thee, and thy backslidings shall reprove thee: know therefore and see that *it is* an evil *thing* and bitter, that thou hast forsaken the LORD thy God, and that my fear *is* not in thee, saith the Lord GOD of hosts. C S

20 ¶ For of old time I have broken thy yoke, *and* burst thy bands; and [a]thou saidst, I will not 'transgress; when [b]upon

18 [a]Is. 50:7; ch. 6:27 & 15:20
19 [a]ver. 8
2:2 [a]Ezek. 16:8, 22,60 & 23:3,8; Hos. 2:15 [b]Deut. 2:7 'Or, *for thy sake*
3 [a]Ex. 19:5,6 [b]Jas. 1:18; Rev. 14:4 [c]ch. 12:14; See ch. 50:7
5 [a]Is. 5:4; Mic. 6:3 [b]2 Ki. 17:15; Jonah 2:8
6 [a]Is. 63:9 [b]Deut. 8:15
7 [a]Num. 13:27 [b]Num. 35:33 'Or, *the land of Carmel*
8 [a]Rom. 2:20 [b]ch. 23:13
9 [a]Ezek. 20:35,36; Mic. 6:2
10 'Or, *over to*
11 [a]Mic. 4:5 [b]Ps. 115:4; Is. 37:19 [c]Ps. 106:20; Rom. 1:23
13 [a]Ps. 36:9; John 4:14
14 [a]Ex. 4:22 'Heb. become *a spoil?*
15 [a]Is. 1:7 'Heb. *gave out their voice*
16 [a]ch. 43:7-9 'Or, *feed on thy crown*
17 [a]ch. 4:18 [b]Deut. 32:10
18 [a]Is. 30:1,2 [b]Josh. 13:3
20 [a]Judg. 10:16 [b]Deut. 12:2 'Or, *serve*

J *Jer 1:13–16* ◀▶ *Jer 9:26*
V *Isa 54:17* ◀▶ *Jer 15:20–21*

G *Isa 64:6* ◀▶ *Jer 2:22*
O *Isa 50:10–11* ◀▶ *Jer 2:22*
R *Isa 64:12* ◀▶ *Jer 3:8*
C *Isa 65:2* ◀▶ *Jer 2:32*
S *Isa 60:21* ◀▶ *Jer 3:8*

2:14–17 Jeremiah prophesied that Judah's approaching judgment was the direct result of their apostasy; they had "forsaken the LORD" (2:17).

every high hill and under every green
tree thou wanderest, [c]playing the harlot.
21 Yet I had [a]planted thee a noble
vine, wholly a right seed: how then art
thou turned into [b]the degenerate plant of
a strange vine unto me?
G 22 For though thou wash thee with
O nitre, and take thee much soap, *yet* thine
iniquity is marked before me, saith the
Lord GOD.
23 [a]How canst thou say, I am not polluted, I have not gone after Baalim? see
thy way in the valley, know what thou
hast done: [1]*thou art* a swift dromedary
traversing her ways;
24 [1]A wild ass [2]used to the wilderness,
that snuffeth up the wind at [3]her pleasure; in her occasion who can [4]turn her
away? all they that seek her will not
weary themselves; in her month they
shall find her.
25 Withhold thy foot from being un-
shod, and thy throat from thirst: but thou
saidst, [1]There is no hope: no; for I have
loved [a]strangers, and after them will I go.
26 As the thief is ashamed when he is
found, so is the house of Israel ashamed;
they, their kings, their princes, and their
priests, and their prophets,
N 27 Saying to a stock, Thou *art* my father; and to a stone, Thou hast [1]brought
me forth: for they have turned [2]*their* back
unto me, and not *their* face: but in the
time of their [a]trouble they will say, Arise,
and save us.
G 28 But [a]where *are* thy gods that thou
hast made thee? let them arise, if they
[b]can save thee in the time of thy [1]trou-
ble: for [c]*according to* the number of thy
cities are thy gods, O Judah.
29 Wherefore will ye plead with me?
ye all have transgressed against me, saith
the LORD.
30 In vain have I [a]smitten your children; they received no correction: your
own sword hath [b]devoured your prophets, like a destroying lion.
31 ¶ O generation, see ye the word of
the LORD. Have I been a wilderness unto
Israel? a land of darkness? wherefore say
my people, [1]We are lords; [a]we will come
no more unto thee?

G *Jer 2:13* ◀ ▶ *Jer 2:28*
O *Jer 2:13* ◀ ▶ *Jer 13:23*
N *Isa 66:4* ◀ ▶ *Jer 3:5*
G *Jer 2:22* ◀ ▶ *Jer 2:35*

20 [c]Ex. 34:15
21 [a]Ex. 15:17 [b]Is. 5:4
23 [a]Prov. 30:12 [1]Or, *O swift dromedary*
24 [1]Or, *O wild ass* [2]Heb. *taught* [3]Heb. *the desire of her heart* [4]Or, *reverse it?*
25 [a]ch. 3:13 [1]Or, *Is the case desperate?*
27 [a]Is. 26:16 [1]Or, *begotten me* [2]Heb. *the hinder part of the neck*
28 [a]Judg. 10:14 [b]Is. 45:20 [c]ch. 11:13 [1]Heb. *evil*
30 [a]Is. 9:13 [b]Acts 7:52
31 [a]Deut. 32:15 [1]Heb. *We have dominion*
32 [a]Ps. 106:21
34 [a]Ps. 106:38 [1]Heb. *digging*
35 [a]ver. 23,29 [b]ver. 9 [c]Prov. 28:13
36 [a]Hos. 12:1 [b]Is. 30:3 [c]2 Chr. 28:16
37 [a]2 Sam. 13:19
3:1 [a]Deut. 24:4 [b]ch. 2:7 [c]ch. 2:20; Ezek. 16:26 [d]Zech. 1:3 [1]Heb. *Saying*
2 [a]Deut. 12:2 [b]Prov. 23:28 [c]ch. 2:7
3 [a]Lev. 26:19 [b]Zeph. 3:5
4 [a]Prov. 2:17 [b]Hos. 2:15
5 [a]Ps. 103:9; Is. 57:16
6 [a]ch. 7:24

32 Can a maid forget her ornaments, C
or a bride her attire? yet my people [a]have
forgotten me days without number.
33 Why trimmest thou thy way to seek
love? therefore hast thou also taught the
wicked ones thy ways.
34 Also in thy skirts is found [a]the
blood of the souls of the poor innocents: I
have not found it by [1]secret search, but
upon all these.
35 [a]Yet thou sayest, Because I am in- G
nocent, surely his anger shall turn from M
me. Behold, [b]I will plead with thee, [c]be-
cause thou sayest, I have not sinned.
36 [a]Why gaddest thou about so much
to change thy way? [b]thou also shalt be
ashamed of Egypt, [c]as thou wast ashamed
of Assyria.
37 Yea, thou shalt go forth from him,
and [a]thine hands upon thine head: for
the LORD hath rejected thy confidences,
and thou shalt not prosper in them.
3 THEY [1]SAY, If a man put away his L
wife, and she go from him, and be- P
come another man's, [a]shall he return
unto her again? shall not that [b]land be
greatly polluted? but thou hast [c]played
the harlot with many lovers; [d]yet return
again to me, saith the LORD.
2 Lift up thine eyes unto [a]the high
places, and see where thou hast not been
lain with. [b]In the ways hast thou sat for
them, as the Arabian in the wilderness;
[c]and thou hast polluted the land with thy
whoredoms and with thy wickedness.
3 Therefore the [a]showers have been M
withholden, and there hath been no latter rain; and thou hadst a [b]whore's forehead, thou refusedst to be ashamed.
4 Wilt thou not from this time cry unto
me, My father, thou *art* [a]the guide of [b]my
youth?
5 [a]Will he reserve *his anger* for ever? N
will he keep *it* to the end? Behold, thou P
hast spoken and done evil things as thou
couldest.
6 ¶ The LORD said also unto me in the
days of Josiah the king, Hast thou seen
that which [a]backsliding Israel hath done?

C *Jer 2:19* ◀ ▶ *Jer 4:22*
G *Jer 2:28* ◀ ▶ *Jer 9:23–24*
M *Isa 66:2* ◀ ▶ *Jer 3:3*
L *Isa 65:2* ◀ ▶ *Jer 3:12*
P *Isa 57:15–19* ◀ ▶ *Jer 3:5*
M *Jer 2:35* ◀ ▶ *Jer 4:3–4*
N *Jer 2:27* ◀ ▶ *Jer 5:21–25*
P *Jer 3:1* ◀ ▶ *Jer 3:12–14*

she is [b]gone up upon every high mountain and under every green tree, and there hath played the harlot.

7 [a]And I said after she had done all these *things,* Turn thou unto me. But she returned not. And her treacherous [b]sister Judah saw *it.*

8 And I saw, when [a]for all the causes whereby backsliding Israel committed adultery I had [b]put her away, and given her a bill of divorce; [c]yet her treacherous sister Judah feared not, but went and played the harlot also.

9 And it came to pass through the [1]lightness of her whoredom, that she [a]defiled the land, and committed adultery with [b]stones and with stocks.

10 And yet for all this her treacherous sister Judah hath not turned unto me [a]with her whole heart, but [1]feignedly, saith the LORD.

11 And the LORD said unto me, [a]The backsliding Israel hath justified herself more than treacherous Judah.

12 ¶ Go and proclaim these words toward [a]the north, and say, Return, thou backsliding Israel, saith the LORD; *and* I will not cause mine anger to fall upon you: for I *am* [b]merciful, saith the LORD, *and* I will not keep *anger* for ever.

13 [a]Only acknowledge thine iniquity, that thou hast transgressed against the LORD thy God, and hast [b]scattered thy ways to the [c]strangers [d]under every green tree, and ye have not obeyed my voice, saith the LORD.

14 Turn, O backsliding children, saith the LORD; [a]for I am married unto you: and I will take you [b]one of a city, and two of a family, and I will bring you to Zion:

15 And I will give you [a]pastors according to mine heart, which shall [b]feed you with knowledge and understanding.

16 And it shall come to pass, when ye be multiplied and increased in the land, in those days, saith the LORD, they shall say no more, The ark of the covenant of the LORD: [a]neither shall it [1]come to mind: neither shall they remember it; neither shall they visit *it;* neither shall [2]*that* be done any more.

17 At that time they shall call Jerusalem the throne of the LORD; and all the nations shall be gathered unto it, [a]to the name of the LORD, to Jerusalem: neither shall they [b]walk any more after the [1]imagination of their evil heart.

18 In those days [a]the house of Judah shall walk [1]with the house of Israel, and they shall come together out of the land of [b]the north to [c]the land that I have [2]given for an inheritance unto your fathers.

19 But I said, How shall I put thee among the children, and give thee [a]a [1]pleasant land, [2]a goodly heritage of the hosts of nations? and I said, Thou shalt

6 [b]ch. 2:20
7 [a]2 Ki. 17:13 [b]Ezek. 16:46
8 [a]Ezek. 23:9 [b]2 Ki. 17:6 [c]Ezek. 23:11
9 [a]ch. 2:7 [b]ch. 2:27 [1]Or, *fame*
10 [a]Hos. 7:14 [1]Heb. *in falsehood*
11 [a]Ezek. 16:51
12 [a]2 Ki. 17:6 [b]Ps. 86:15
13 [a]Deut. 30:1 [b]Ezek. 16:15 [c]ch. 2:25 [d]Deut. 12:2
14 [a]Hos. 2:19 [b]Rom. 11:5
15 [a]Ezek. 34:23; Eph. 4:11 [b]Acts 20:28
16 [a]Is. 65:17 [1]Heb. *come upon the heart* [2]Or, *it be magnified*
17 [a]Is. 60:9 [b]ch. 11:8 [1]Or, *stubbornness*
18 [a]Is. 11:13; Hos. 1:11 [b]ch. 31:8 [c]Amos 9:15 [1]Or, *to* [2]Or, *caused your fathers to possess*
19 [a]Ps. 106:24 [1]Heb. *land of desire* [2]Heb. *an heritage of glory, or, beauty*

R *Jer 2:14–17* ◀▶ *Jer 4:20*
S *Jer 2:19* ◀▶ *Jer 4:14*
L *Jer 3:1* ◀▶ *Jer 3:14*
P *Jer 3:5* ◀▶ *Jer 3:20–22*
R *Isa 66:2* ◀▶ *Jer 4:1*

I *Isa 66:18–24* ◀▶ *Jer 12:14–17*
L *Jer 3:12* ◀▶ *Jer 3:22*
M *Isa 66:18–24* ◀▶ *Jer 23:5–6*

3:8 God condemned Judah's apostasy and spiritual adultery just as he condemned Israel's apostasy when he sent her into captivity to Assyria.

3:14–15 Jeremiah predicted that God would restore a remnant of his people and provide "pastors according to mine heart" (3:15). This prophecy was initially fulfilled when the exiles returned to their land to rebuild the temple under the godly leadership of Nehemiah and Ezra. In the last days, when the Messiah rules in the millennial kingdom, this prophecy will find its lasting fulfillment (see Rev 7; 14).

3:16–17 In this millennial prophecy God declared that after the return of all the Jews to the promised land people would no longer talk about, think about, remember or visit the ark of the covenant. Because the ark symbolized God's presence with his people, when the Messiah comes and rules on his throne this symbolic token will no longer be needed. Jeremiah also said that Jerusalem would be known as "the throne of the LORD; and all the nations shall be gathered unto it" (3:17). This places the fulfillment of this prophecy during the Millennium (see Zec 14:16–21).

Jeremiah's reference to the ark of the covenant in this passage raises some questions since the ark has been missing from the temple in Jerusalem since the reign of King Solomon. For Jeremiah to write these words about the ark may suggest that the ark may be found in the last days and play a role in the events of the end times.

3:18–19 Jeremiah confirmed the prophecies given by Isaiah and Ezekiel that the exiles from Israel will be joined to the exiles of Judah and returned to the promised land (see Isa 11:11–12; Eze 37:15–24).

call me, [b]My father; and shalt not turn
away [3]from me.
P 20 ¶ Surely *as* a wife treacherously departeth from her [1]husband, so [a]have ye
dealt treacherously with me, O house of
Israel, saith the LORD.
21 A voice was heard upon [a]the high
places, weeping *and* supplications of the
children of Israel: for they have perverted
their way, *and* they have forgotten the
LORD their God.
L 22 [a]Return, ye backsliding children,
and [b]I will heal your backslidings. Behold, we come unto thee; for thou *art* the
LORD our God.
23 [a]Truly in vain *is salvation hoped for*
from the hills, *and from* the multitude of
mountains: [b]truly in the LORD our God *is*
the salvation of Israel.
24 [a]For shame hath devoured the labour of our fathers from our youth; their
flocks and their herds, their sons and
their daughters.
25 We lie down in our shame, and our
confusion covereth us: [a]for we have
sinned against the LORD our God, we and
our fathers, from our youth even unto
this day, and [b]have not obeyed the voice
of the LORD our God.
P 4 IF THOU wilt return, O Israel, saith
R the LORD, [a]return unto me: and if
thou wilt put away thine abominations
out of my sight, then shalt thou not
remove.
2 [a]And thou shalt swear, The LORD liveth, [b]in truth, in judgment, and in righteousness; [c]and the nations shall bless
themselves in him, and in him shall they
[d]glory.
M 3 ¶ For thus saith the LORD to the men
of Judah and Jerusalem, [a]Break up your
fallow ground, and [b]sow not among
thorns.
H 4 [a]Circumcise yourselves to the LORD,
and take away the foreskins of your heart,
ye men of Judah and inhabitants of Jerusalem: lest my fury come forth like fire,
and burn that none can quench *it*, because of the evil of your doings.

P *Jer 3:12–14* ◄► *Jer 4:1*
L *Jer 3:14* ◄► *Jer 18:8*
P *Jer 3:20–22* ◄► *Jer 29:11–13*
R *Jer 3:12–13* ◄► *Jer 4:14*
M *Jer 3:3* ◄► *Jer 5:3*
H *Isa 66:24* ◄► *Jer 5:9*

19 [b]Is. 63:16 [3]Heb. *from after me*
20 [a]Is. 48:8 [1]Heb. *friend*
21 [a]Is. 15:2
22 [a]ver. 14; Hos. 14:1 [b]Hos. 6:1 & 14:4
23 [a]Ps. 121:1,2 [b]Ps. 3:8
24 [a]ch. 11:13; Hos. 9:10
25 [a]Ezra 9:7 [b]ch. 22:21
4:1 [a]ch. 3:1,22; Joel 2:12
2 [a]Deut. 10:20; Is. 45:23 & 65:16; See ch. 5:2 [b]Is. 48:1; Zech. 8:8 [c]Gen. 22:18; Ps. 72:17; Gal. 3:8 [d]1 Cor. 1:31
3 [a]Hos. 10:12 [b]Mat. 13:7
4 [a]Deut. 10:16; ch. 9:26; Rom. 2:28
5 [a]ch. 8:14
6 [a]ch. 1:13-15 & 6:1,22 [1]Or, *strengthen* [2]Heb. *breaking*
7 [a]2 Ki. 24:1; ch. 5:6; Dan. 7:4 [b]ch. 25:9 [c]Is. 1:7
8 [a]Is. 22:12
10 [a]Ezek. 14:9; 2 Thes. 2:11 [b]ch. 14:13
11 [a]ch. 51:1; Ezek. 17:10; Hos. 13:15
12 [a]ch. 1:16 [1]Or, *a fuller wind than those* [2]Heb. *utter judgments*
13 [a]Is. 5:28 [b]Deut. 28:49; Lam. 4:19; Hos. 8:1; Hab. 1:8
14 [a]Is. 1:16; Jas. 4:8
15 [a]ch. 8:16
17 [a]2 Ki. 25:1

Judgment from the north

5 Declare ye in Judah, and publish in
Jerusalem; and say, Blow ye the trumpet
in the land: cry, gather together, and say,
[a]Assemble yourselves, and let us go into
the defenced cities.
6 Set up the standard toward Zion: [1]re-
tire, stay not: for I will bring evil from the
[a]north, and a great [2]destruction.
7 [a]The lion is come up from his
thicket, and [b]the destroyer of the Gentiles is on his way; he is gone forth from
his place [c]to make thy land desolate; *and*
thy cities shall be laid waste, without an
inhabitant.
8 For this [a]gird you with sackcloth, lament and howl: for the fierce anger of the
LORD is not turned back from us.
9 And it shall come to pass at that day,
saith the LORD, *that* the heart of the king
shall perish, and the heart of the princes;
and the priests shall be astonished, and
the prophets shall wonder.
10 Then said I, Ah, Lord GOD! [a]surely
thou hast greatly deceived this people
and Jerusalem, [b]saying, Ye shall have
peace; whereas the sword reacheth unto
the soul.
11 At that time shall it be said to this
people and to Jerusalem, [a]A dry wind of
the high places in the wilderness toward
the daughter of my people, not to fan, nor
to cleanse,
12 *Even* [1]a full wind from those *places*
shall come unto me: now also [a]will I
[2]give sentence against them.
13 Behold, he shall come up as clouds,
and [a]his chariots *shall be* as a whirlwind:
[b]his horses are swifter than eagles. Woe
unto us! for we are spoiled.
14 O Jerusalem, [a]wash thine heart R
from wickedness, that thou mayest be S
saved. How long shall thy vain thoughts
lodge within thee?
15 For a voice declareth [a]from Dan,
and publisheth affliction from mount
Ephraim.
16 Make ye mention to the nations;
behold, publish against Jerusalem, *that*
watchers come from a far country, and
give out their voice against the cities of
Judah.
17 [a]As keepers of a field, are they
against her round about; because she

R *Jer 4:1* ◄► *Jer 7:3*
S *Jer 3:8* ◄► *Jer 7:9–11*

hath been rebellious against me, saith the LORD.

18 [a]Thy way and thy doings have procured these *things* unto thee; this *is* thy wickedness, because it is bitter, because it reacheth unto thine heart.

19 ¶ My [a]bowels, my bowels! I am pained at [/]my very heart; my heart maketh a noise in me; I cannot hold my peace, because thou hast heard, O my soul, the sound of the trumpet, the alarm of war.

R 20 [a]Destruction upon destruction is cried; for the whole land is spoiled: suddenly are [b]my tents spoiled, *and* my curtains in a moment.

21 How long shall I see the standard, *and* hear the sound of the trumpet?

C 22 For my people *is* foolish, they have not known me; they *are* sottish children, and they have none understanding: [a]they *are* wise to do evil, but to do good they have no knowledge.

R 23 I [a]beheld the earth, and, lo, *it was* [b]without form, and void; and the heavens, and they *had* no light.

24 [a]I beheld the mountains, and, lo, they trembled, and all the hills moved lightly.

25 I beheld, and, lo, *there was* no man, and [a]all the birds of the heavens were fled.

R 26 I beheld, and, lo, the fruitful place *was* a wilderness, and all the cities thereof were broken down at the presence of the LORD, *and* by his fierce anger.

27 For thus hath the LORD said, The whole land shall be desolate; [a]yet will I not make a full end.

28 For this [a]shall the earth mourn, and [b]the heavens above be black: because I have spoken *it,* I have purposed *it,* and [c]will not repent, neither will I turn back from it.

29 The whole city shall flee for the noise of the horsemen and bowmen; they shall go into thickets, and climb up upon the rocks: every city *shall be* forsaken, and not a man dwell therein.

30 And *when* thou *art* spoiled, what wilt thou do? Though thou clothest thyself with crimson, though thou deckest thee with ornaments of gold, [a]though thou rentest thy [/]face with painting, in vain shalt thou make thyself fair; [b]*thy* lovers will despise thee, they will seek thy life.

31 For I have heard a voice as of a woman in travail, *and* the anguish as of her that bringeth forth her first child, the voice of the daughter of Zion, *that* bewaileth herself, *that* [a]spreadeth her hands, *saying,* Woe *is* me now! for my soul is wearied because of murderers.

Futile search for an upright man

5 RUN YE to and fro through the streets of Jerusalem, and see now, and know, and seek in the broad places thereof, [a]if ye can find a man, [b]if there be *any* that executeth judgment, that seeketh the truth; [c]and I will pardon it.

2 And [a]though they say, [b]The LORD liveth; surely they [c]swear falsely.

3 O LORD, *are* not [a]thine eyes upon the truth? thou hast [b]stricken them, but they have not grieved; thou hast consumed them, *but* [c]they have refused to receive correction: they have made their faces harder than a rock; they have refused to return. R M

4 Therefore I said, Surely these *are* poor; they are foolish: for [a]they know not the way of the LORD, *nor* the judgment of their God. C

5 I will get me unto the great men, and will speak unto them; for [a]they have known the way of the LORD, *and* the judgment of their God: but these have altogether [b]broken the yoke, *and* burst the bonds.

6 Wherefore [a]a lion out of the forest shall slay them, [b]*and* a wolf of the [/]evenings shall spoil them, [c]a leopard shall watch over their cities: every one that go-

18 [a]Ps. 107:17; Is. 50:1; ch. 2:17,19
19 [a]Is. 15:5 & 16:11 & 21:3; See Luke 19:42 [/]Heb. *the walls of my heart*
20 [a]Ps. 42:7; Ezek. 7:26 [b]ch. 10:20
22 [a]Rom. 16:19
23 [a]Is. 24:19 [b]Gen. 1:2
24 [a]Is. 5:25; Ezek. 38:20
25 [a]Zeph. 1:3
27 [a]ch. 5:10,18 & 30:11 & 46:28
28 [a]Hos. 4:3 [b]Is. 5:30 & 50:3 [c]Num. 23:19; ch. 7:16
30 [a]2 Ki. 9:30 [b]ch. 22:20,22 [/]Heb. *eyes*
31 [a]Is. 1:15; Lam. 1:17
5:1 [a]Ezek. 22:30 [b]Gen. 18:23 [c]Gen. 18:26
2 [a]Tit. 1:16 [b]ch. 4:2 [c]ch. 7:9
3 [a]2 Chr. 16:9 [b]Is. 1:5 & 9:13; ch. 2:30 [c]ch. 7:28; Zeph. 3:2
4 [a]ch. 8:7
5 [a]Mic. 3:1 [b]Ps. 2:3
6 [a]ch. 4:7 [b]Ps. 104:20; Hab. 1:8; Zeph. 3:3 [c]Hos. 13:7 [/]Or, *deserts*

R *Jer 3:8* ◀▶ *Jer 4:23*
C *Jer 2:32* ◀▶ *Jer 5:4*
R *Jer 4:20* ◀▶ *Jer 4:26–28*
R *Jer 4:23* ◀▶ *Jer 5:3*

R *Jer 4:26–28* ◀▶ *Jer 5:9–10*
M *Jer 4:3–4* ◀▶ *Jer 6:15*
C *Jer 4:22* ◀▶ *Jer 5:21–25*

4:20 Jeremiah predicted the certainty of Judah's destruction.

4:26–28 God declared his resolve to punish his people for their sinful rebellion. Though he would make the land desolate, his punishment would not totally destroy the land.

5:3 Jeremiah noted the lack of repentance among the people in their refusal of God's "correction."

eth out thence shall be torn in pieces:
because their transgressions are many,
and their backslidings [2]are increased.
7 ¶ How shall I pardon thee for this?
thy children have forsaken me, and
[a]sworn by *them* [b]*that are* no gods: [c]when
I had fed them to the full, they then committed adultery, and assembled themselves by troops in the harlots' houses.
8 [a]They were *as* fed horses in the
morning: every one neighed after his
neighbour's wife.
R 9 [a]Shall I not visit for these *things?*
H saith the LORD: [b]and shall not my soul be
avenged on such a nation as this?
10 ¶ [a]Go ye up upon her walls, and
destroy; [b]but make not a full end: take
away her battlements; for they *are* not
the LORD'S.
11 For [a]the house of Israel and the
house of Judah have dealt very treacherously against me, saith the LORD.
12 [a]They have belied the LORD, and
said, [b]*It is* not he; neither shall evil come
upon us; [c]neither shall we see sword nor
famine:
13 And the prophets shall become
wind, and the word *is* not in them: thus
shall it be done unto them.
14 Wherefore thus saith the LORD God
of hosts, Because ye speak this word, [a]be-
hold, I will make my words in thy mouth
fire, and this people wood, and it shall
devour them.
15 Lo, I will bring a [a]nation upon you
[b]from far, O house of Israel, saith the
LORD: it *is* a mighty nation, it *is* an ancient
nation, a nation whose language thou
knowest not, neither understandest what
they say.
16 Their quiver *is* as an open sepulchre, they *are* all mighty men.
17 And they shall eat up thine [a]har-
vest, and thy bread, *which* thy sons and
thy daughters should eat: they shall eat
up thy flocks and thine herds: they shall
eat up thy vines and thy fig trees: they
shall impoverish thy fenced cities,

R *Jer 5:3* ◀ ▶ *Jer 5:19*
H *Jer 4:4* ◀ ▶ *Jer 5:29*

6 [2]Heb. *are strong*
7 [a]Josh. 23:7; Zeph. 1:5 [b]Deut. 32:21; Gal. 4:8 [c]Deut. 32:15
8 [a]Ezek. 22:11
9 [a]ver. 29; ch. 9:9 [b]ch. 44:22
10 [a]ch. 39:8 [b]ver. 18; ch. 4:27
11 [a]ch. 3:20
12 [a]2 Chr. 36:16; ch. 4:10 [b]Is. 28:15 [c]ch. 14:13
14 [a]ch. 1:9
15 [a]Deut. 28:49; Is. 5:26; ch. 1:15 & 6:22 [b]Is. 39:3; ch. 4:16
17 [a]Lev. 26:16; Deut. 28:31,33
18 [a]ch. 4:27
19 [a]Deut. 29:24; 1 Ki. 9:8,9; ch. 13:22 & 16:10 [b]ch. 2:13 [c]Deut. 28:48
21 [a]Is. 6:9; Ezek. 12:2; Mat. 13:14; John 12:40; Acts 28:26; Rom. 11:8 [1]Heb. *heart*
22 [a]Rev. 15:4 [b]Job 26:10; Prov. 8:29
24 [a]Ps. 147:8; Acts 14:17 [b]Joel 2:23 [c]Gen. 8:22
25 [a]ch. 3:3
26 [a]Prov. 1:11; Hab. 1:15 [1]Or, *they pry as fowlers lie in wait*
27 [1]Or, *coop*
28 [a]Deut. 32:15 [b]Is. 1:23; Zech. 7:10 [c]Job 12:6; Ps. 73:12

wherein thou trustedst, with the sword.
18 Nevertheless in those days, saith
the LORD, I [a]will not make a full end with
you.
19 ¶ And it shall come to pass, when R
ye shall say, [a]Wherefore doeth the LORD
our God all these *things* unto us? then
shalt thou answer them, Like as ye have
[b]forsaken me, and served strange gods in
your land, so [c]shall ye serve strangers in a
land *that is* not yours.
20 Declare this in the house of Jacob,
and publish it in Judah, saying,
21 Hear now this, O [a]foolish people, C
and without [1]understanding; which have N
eyes, and see not; which have ears, and
hear not:
22 [a]Fear ye not me? saith the LORD:
will ye not tremble at my presence,
which have placed the sand *for* the
[b]bound of the sea by a perpetual decree,
that it cannot pass it: and though the
waves thereof toss themselves, yet can
they not prevail; though they roar, yet
can they not pass over it?
23 But this people hath a revolting and
a rebellious heart; they are revolted and
gone.
24 Neither say they in their heart, Let
us now fear the LORD our God, [a]that giveth rain, both the [b]former and the latter,
in his season: [c]he reserveth unto us the
appointed weeks of the harvest.
25 ¶ [a]Your iniquities have turned
away these *things,* and your sins have
withholden good *things* from you.
26 For among my people are found
wicked *men:* [1]they [a]lay wait, as he that
setteth snares; they set a trap, they catch
men.
27 As a [1]cage is full of birds, so *are*
their houses full of deceit: therefore they
are become great, and waxen rich.
28 They are waxen [a]fat, they shine:
yea, they overpass the deeds of the
wicked: they judge not [b]the cause, the
cause of the fatherless, [c]yet they prosper;

R *Jer 5:9–10* ◀ ▶ *Jer 5:29*
C *Jer 5:4* ◀ ▶ *Jer 6:10*
N *Jer 3:5* ◀ ▶ *Jer 6:15–17*

5:9–10 Once again God declared his intention to deliver his vengeance upon unrepentant Judah.

5:19 As the judgments fall on the nation, people will ask Jeremiah for the reason for the punishments. God provided Jeremiah with a clear answer: because the people have rejected God and "served strange gods" God would exile them as slaves to a land of strangers.

and the right of the needy do they not judge.

R H 29 [a]Shall I not visit for these *things?* saith the LORD: shall not my soul be avenged on such a nation as this?

30 ¶ [/]A wonderful and [a]horrible thing is committed in the land;

31 The prophets prophesy [a]falsely, and the priests [/]bear rule by their means; and my people [b]love *to have it* so: and what will ye do in the end thereof?

Jerusalem under siege

6 O YE children of Benjamin, gather yourselves to flee out of the midst of Jerusalem, and blow the trumpet in Tekoa, and set up a sign of fire in [a]Beth-haccerem: [b]for evil appeareth out of the north, and great destruction.

2 I have likened the daughter of Zion to a [/]comely and delicate *woman.*

3 The shepherds with their flocks shall come unto her; [a]they shall pitch *their* tents against her round about; they shall feed every one in his place.

4 [a]Prepare ye war against her; arise, and let us go up [b]at noon. Woe unto us! for the day goeth away, for the shadows of the evening are stretched out.

5 Arise, and let us go by night, and let us destroy her palaces.

6 ¶ For thus hath the LORD of hosts said, Hew ye down trees, and [/]cast a mount against Jerusalem: this *is* the city to be visited; she *is* wholly oppression in the midst of her.

7 [a]As a fountain casteth out her waters, so she casteth out her wickedness: [b]violence and spoil is heard in her; before me continually *is* grief and wounds.

8 Be thou instructed, O Jerusalem, lest [a]my soul [/]depart from thee; lest I make thee desolate, a land not inhabited.

R 9 ¶ Thus saith the LORD of hosts, They shall thoroughly glean the remnant of Israel as a vine: turn back thine hand as a grapegatherer into the baskets.

C 10 To whom shall I speak, and give warning, that they may hear? behold, their [a]ear *is* uncircumcised, and they cannot hearken: behold, [b]the word of the LORD is unto them a reproach; they have no delight in it.

11 Therefore I am full of the fury of the LORD; [a]I am weary with holding in: I will pour it out [b]upon the children abroad, and upon the assembly of young men together: for even the husband with the wife shall be taken, the aged with *him that is* full of days. R

12 And [a]their houses shall be turned unto others, *with their* fields and wives together: for I will stretch out my hand upon the inhabitants of the land, saith the LORD.

13 For from the least of them even unto the greatest of them every one *is* given to [a]covetousness; and from the prophet even unto the priest every one dealeth falsely.

14 They have [a]healed also the [/]hurt *of the daughter* of my people slightly, [b]saying, Peace, peace; when *there is* no peace.

15 Were they [a]ashamed when they had committed abomination? nay, they were not at all ashamed, neither could they blush: therefore they shall fall among them that fall: at the time *that* I visit them they shall be cast down, saith the LORD. C M N

16 Thus saith the LORD, Stand ye in the ways, and see, and ask for the [a]old paths, where *is* the good way, and walk therein, and ye shall find [b]rest for your souls. But they said, We will not walk *therein.*

17 Also I set [a]watchmen over you, *saying,* Hearken to the sound of the trumpet. But they said, We will not hearken. C

18 ¶ Therefore hear, ye nations, and know, O congregation, what *is* among them.

R *Jer 5:19 ◄► Jer 6:9*
H *Jer 5:9 ◄► Jer 6:19*
R *Jer 5:29 ◄► Jer 6:11–12*
C *Jer 5:21–25 ◄► Jer 6:15*

R *Jer 6:9 ◄► Jer 6:19*
C *Jer 6:10 ◄► Jer 6:17*
M *Jer 5:3 ◄► Jer 8:12*
N *Jer 5:21–25 ◄► Jer 6:19*
C *Jer 6:15 ◄► Jer 6:28*

29 [a]Mal. 3:5
30 [a]Hos. 6:10 [/]Or, *Astonishment and filthiness*
31 [a]ch. 14:14 & 23:25,26; Ezek. 13:6 [b]Mic. 2:11 [/]Or, *take into their hands*
6:1 [a]Neh. 3:14 [b]ch. 4:6
2 [/]Or, *dwelling at home*
3 [a]2 Ki. 25:1
4 [a]Joel 3:9 [b]ch. 15:8
6 [/]Or, *pour out the engine of shot*
7 [a]Is. 57:20 [b]Ps. 55:9; ch. 20:8; Ezek. 7:11
8 [a]Hos. 9:12 [/]Heb. *be loosed,* or, *disjointed*
10 [a]Acts 7:51; See Ex. 6:12 [b]ch. 20:8
11 [a]ch. 20:9 [b]ch. 9:21
12 [a]Deut. 28:30; ch. 8:10
13 [a]Is. 56:11; ch. 8:10; Mic. 3:5,11
14 [a]ch. 8:11; Ezek. 13:10 [b]ch. 4:10 & 23:17 [/]Heb. *bruise,* or, *breach*
15 [a]ch. 3:3
16 [a]Is. 8:20; ch. 18:15; Mal. 4:4; Luke 16:29 [b]Mat. 11:29
17 [a]Is. 21:11 & 58:1; ch. 25:4; Ezek. 3:17; Hab. 2:1

5:29 God notes the justice of his decision to judge this rebellious nation.

6:11–12, 19 Jeremiah warns of God's coming judgment and explains that the reason for this judgment was Judah's refusal to obey God's Word.

R H N 19 [a]Hear, O earth: behold, I will bring evil upon this people, *even* [b]the fruit of their thoughts, because they have not hearkened unto my words, nor to my law, but rejected it.

20 [a]To what purpose cometh there to me incense [b]from Sheba, and the sweet cane from a far country? [c]your burnt offerings *are* not acceptable, nor your sacrifices sweet unto me.

21 Therefore thus saith the LORD, Behold, I will lay stumblingblocks before this people, and the fathers and the sons together shall fall upon them; the neighbour and his friend shall perish.

22 Thus saith the LORD, Behold, a people cometh from the [a]north country, and a great nation shall be raised from the sides of the earth.

23 They shall lay hold on bow and spear; they *are* cruel, and have no mercy; their voice [a]roareth like the sea; and they ride upon horses, set in array as men for war against thee, O daughter of Zion.

24 We have heard the fame thereof: our hands wax feeble: [a]anguish hath taken hold of us, *and* pain, as of a woman in travail.

25 Go not forth into the field, nor walk by the way; for the sword of the enemy *and* fear *is* on every side.

26 ¶ O daughter of my people, [a]gird *thee* with sackcloth, [b]and wallow thyself in ashes: [c]make thee mourning, *as for* an only son, most bitter lamentation: for the spoiler shall suddenly come upon us.

27 I have set thee *for* a tower *and* [a]a fortress among my people, that thou mayest know and try their way.

C 28 [a]They *are* all grievous revolters, [b]walking with slanders: *they are* [c]brass and iron; they *are* all corrupters.

29 The bellows are burned, the lead is consumed of the fire; the founder melteth in vain: for the wicked are not plucked away.

R C 30 [a]Reprobate[1] silver shall *men* call

R *Jer 6:11–12* ◀ ▶ *Jer 6:30*
H *Jer 5:29* ◀ ▶ *Jer 8:20*
N *Jer 6:15–17* ◀ ▶ *Jer 8:9*
C *Jer 6:17* ◀ ▶ *Jer 6:30*
R *Jer 6:19* ◀ ▶ *Jer 7:14–16*
C *Jer 6:28* ◀ ▶ *Jer 7:24*

19 [a]Is. 1:2 [b]Prov. 1:31
20 [a]Ps. 40:6 & 50:7-9; Is. 1:11 & 66:3; Amos 5:21; Mic. 6:6 [b]Is. 60:6 [c]ch. 7:21
22 [a]ch. 1:15 & 10:22
23 [a]Is. 5:30
24 [a]ch. 4:31 & 13:21 & 49:24 & 50:43
26 [a]ch. 4:8 [b]ch. 25:34; Mic. 1:10 [c]Zech. 12:10
27 [a]ch. 1:18 & 15:20
28 [a]ch. 5:23 [b]ch. 9:4 [c]Ezek. 22:18
30 [a]Is. 1:22 [1]Or, *Refuse silver*
7:2 [a]ch. 26:2
3 [a]ch. 18:11 & 26:13
4 [a]Mic. 3:11
5 [a]ch. 22:3
6 [a]Deut. 6:14,15 & 8:19; ch. 13:10
7 [a]Deut. 4:40 [b]ch. 3:18
8 [a]ver. 4 [b]ch. 5:31 & 14:13,14
9 [a]1 Ki. 18:21; Hos. 4:1,2; Zeph. 1:5 [b]Ex. 20:3
10 [a]Ezek. 23:39 [b]ver. 11,14; ch. 32:34 & 34:15 [1]Heb. *whereupon my name is called*
11 [a]Is. 56:7 [b]Mat. 21:13; Mark 11:17; Luke 19:46
12 [a]Josh. 18:1; Judg. 18:31 [b]Deut. 12:11 [c]1 Sam. 4:10; Ps. 78:60; ch. 26:6
13 [a]2 Chr. 36:15; ch. 11:7

them, because the LORD hath rejected them.

Judah's idolatry and immorality

7 THE WORD that came to Jeremiah from the LORD, saying,

2 [a]Stand in the gate of the LORD'S house, and proclaim there this word, and say, Hear the word of the LORD, all *ye of* Judah, that enter in at these gates to worship the LORD.

3 Thus saith the LORD of hosts, the God of Israel, [a]Amend your ways and your doings, and I will cause you to dwell in this place. R

4 [a]Trust ye not in lying words, saying, The temple of the LORD, The temple of the LORD, The temple of the LORD, *are* these.

5 For if ye thoroughly amend your ways and your doings; if ye thoroughly [a]execute judgment between a man and his neighbour; R

6 *If* ye oppress not the stranger, the fatherless, and the widow, and shed not innocent blood in this place, [a]neither walk after other gods to your hurt:

7 [a]Then will I cause you to dwell in this place, in [b]the land that I gave to your fathers, for ever and ever.

8 ¶ Behold, [a]ye trust in [b]lying words, that cannot profit.

9 [a]Will ye steal, murder, and commit adultery, and swear falsely, and burn incense unto Baal, and [b]walk after other gods whom ye know not; S

10 [a]And come and stand before me in this house, [b]which[1] is called by my name, and say, We are delivered to do all these abominations?

11 Is [a]this house, which is called by my name, become a [b]den of robbers in your eyes? Behold, even I have seen *it,* saith the LORD.

12 But go ye now unto [a]my place which *was* in Shiloh, [b]where I set my name at the first, and see [c]what I did to it for the wickedness of my people Israel.

13 And now, because ye have done all these works, saith the LORD, and I spake unto you, [a]rising up early and speaking,

R *Jer 4:14* ◀ ▶ *Jer 7:5–7*
R *Jer 7:3* ◀ ▶ *Jer 18:11*
S *Jer 4:14* ◀ ▶ *Jer 7:23*

6:30 God rejected his wicked people as a refiner rejects impure silver.

but ye heard not; and I [b]called you, but ye answered not;

R 14 Therefore will I do unto *this* house, which is called by my name, wherein ye trust, and unto the place which I gave to you and to your fathers, as I have done to [a]Shiloh.

15 And I will cast you out of my sight, [a]as I have cast out all your brethren, [b]*even* the whole seed of Ephraim.

16 Therefore [a]pray not thou for this people, neither lift up cry nor prayer for them, neither make intercession to me: [b]for I will not hear thee.

17 ¶ Seest thou not what they do in the cities of Judah and in the streets of Jerusalem?

18 [a]The children gather wood, and the fathers kindle the fire, and the women knead *their* dough, to make cakes to the [1]queen of heaven, and to [b]pour out drink offerings unto other gods, that they may provoke me to anger.

19 [a]Do they provoke me to anger? saith the LORD: *do they* not *provoke* themselves to the confusion of their own faces?

R 20 Therefore thus saith the Lord GOD; Behold, mine anger and my fury shall be poured out upon this place, upon man, and upon beast, and upon the trees of the field, and upon the fruit of the ground; and it shall burn, and shall not be quenched.

21 ¶ Thus saith the LORD of hosts, the God of Israel; [a]Put your burnt offerings unto your sacrifices, and eat flesh.

22 [a]For I spake not unto your fathers, nor commanded them in the day that I brought them out of the land of Egypt, [1]concerning burnt offerings or sacrifices:

S 23 But this thing commanded I them,
U saying, [a]Obey my voice, and [b]I will be your God, and ye shall be my people: and walk ye in all the ways that I have commanded you, that it may be well unto you.

C 24 [a]But they hearkened not, nor inclined their ear, but [b]walked in the counsels *and* in the [1]imagination of their evil heart, and [c]went[2] backward, and not forward.

25 Since the day that your fathers came forth out of the land of Egypt unto this day I have even [a]sent unto you all my servants the prophets, [b]daily rising up early and sending *them:*

C 26 [a]Yet they hearkened not unto me, nor inclined their ear, but [b]hardened their neck: [c]they did worse than their fathers.

27 Therefore [a]thou shalt speak all these words unto them; but they will not hearken to thee: thou shalt also call unto them; but they will not answer thee.

28 But thou shalt say unto them, This *is* a nation that obeyeth not the voice of the LORD their God, [a]nor receiveth [1]correction: [b]truth is perished, and is cut off from their mouth.

R 29 ¶ [a]Cut off thine hair, *O Jerusalem,* and cast *it* away, and take up a lamentation on high places; for the LORD hath rejected and forsaken the generation of his wrath.

The terrible days to come

30 For the children of Judah have done evil in my sight, saith the LORD: [a]they have set their abominations in the house which is called by my name, to pollute it.

31 And they have built the [a]high places of Tophet, which *is* in the valley of the son of Hinnom, to [b]burn their sons and their daughters in the fire; [c]which I commanded *them* not, neither [1]came it into my heart.

32 ¶ Therefore, behold, [a]the days come, saith the LORD, that it shall no more be called Tophet, nor the valley of the son of Hinnom, but the valley of slaugh-

13 [b]Prov. 1:24; Is. 65:12 & 66:4
14 [a]1 Sam. 4:10; Ps. 78:60
15 [a]2 Ki. 17:23 [b]Ps. 78:67
16 [a]Ex. 32:10 [b]ch. 15:1
18 [a]ch. 44:17 [b]ch. 19:13 [1]Or, *frame,* or, *workmanship of heaven*
19 [a]Deut. 32:16, 21
21 [a]Is. 1:11; Amos 5:21; Hos. 8:13
22 [a]1 Sam. 15:22; Ps. 51:16; Hos. 6:6 [1]Heb. *concerning the matter of*
23 [a]Ex. 15:26; Deut. 6:3 [b]Ex. 19:5; Lev. 26:12
24 [a]Ps. 81:11 [b]Ps. 81:12 [c]ch. 32:33 [1]Or, *stubbornness* [2]Heb. *were*
25 [a]2 Chr. 36:15 [b]ver. 13
26 [a]ch. 11:8 [b]Neh. 9:17 [c]ch. 16:12
27 [a]Ezek. 2:7
28 [a]ch. 5:3 [b]ch. 9:3 [1]Or, *instruction*
29 [a]Job 1:20; Is. 15:2; Mic 1:16
30 [a]2 Ki. 21:4; 2 Chr. 33:4; Ezek. 7:20; Dan. 9:27
31 [a]2 Ki. 23:10 [b]Ps. 106:38 [c]Deut. 17:3 [1]Heb. *came it upon my heart*
32 [a]ch. 19:6

R *Jer 6:30* ◀ ▶ *Jer 7:20*
R *Jer 7:14–16* ◀ ▶ *Jer 7:29*
S *Jer 7:9–11* ◀ ▶ *Jer 14:10*
U *Isa 65:13–14* ◀ ▶ *Jer 17:7–8*
C *Jer 6:30* ◀ ▶ *Jer 7:26*
C *Jer 7:24* ◀ ▶ *Jer 8:9*
R *Jer 7:20* ◀ ▶ *Jer 7:34*

7:14–16 The people had placed their trust in God's temple while openly rebelling against God's law. God said he would destroy the temple, the source of their confidence, and would cast them out of the land just as he had expelled the kingdom of Israel.

7:20 God's coming judgment would not be limited to the city, but would be poured upon everything in the whole land of Judah.

7:29 Jeremiah advised his listeners to cut their hair as a sign of mourning because of the coming judgment of God upon the rebellious nation.

ter: [b]for they shall bury in Tophet, till
there be no place.
33 And the [a]carcases of this people
shall be meat for the fowls of the heaven,
and for the beasts of the earth; and none
shall fray *them* away.
R 34 Then will I cause to [a]cease from the
cities of Judah, and from the streets of
Jerusalem, the voice of mirth, and the
voice of gladness, the voice of the bridegroom, and the voice of the bride: for
[b]the land shall be desolate.

8 AT THAT time, saith the LORD, they
shall bring out the bones of the kings
of Judah, and the bones of his princes,
and the bones of the priests, and the
bones of the prophets, and the bones of
the inhabitants of Jerusalem, out of their
graves:
2 And they shall spread them before
the sun, and the moon, and all the host
of heaven, whom they have loved, and
whom they have served, and after whom
they have walked, and whom they have
sought, and [a]whom they have worshipped: they shall not be gathered, [b]nor
be buried; they shall be for dung upon
the face of the earth.
3 And [a]death shall be chosen rather
than life by all the residue of them that
remain of this evil family, which remain
in all the places whither I have driven
them, saith the LORD of hosts.

Punishment of sinful Israel

4 ¶ Moreover thou shalt say unto
them, Thus saith the LORD; Shall they fall,
and not arise? shall he turn away, and not
return?
R 5 Why *then* is this people of Jerusalem
[a]slidden back by a perpetual backsliding?
[b]they hold fast deceit, [c]they refuse to
return.
6 [a]I hearkened and heard, *but* they
spake not aright: no man repented him
of his wickedness, saying, What have I
done? every one turned to his course, as
the horse rusheth into the battle.

R *Jer 7:29* ◀ ▶ *Jer 8:5–6*
R *Jer 7:34* ◀ ▶ *Jer 8:12–14*

7 Yea, [a]the stork in the heaven knoweth her appointed times; and [b]the turtle
and the crane and the swallow observe
the time of their coming; but [c]my people
know not the judgment of the LORD.
8 How do ye say, We *are* wise, [a]and
the law of the LORD *is* with us? Lo, certainly [b]in[1] vain made he *it;* the pen of the
scribes *is* in vain.
9 [a]The[1] wise *men* are ashamed, they C
are dismayed and taken: lo, they have re- N
jected the word of the LORD; and [2]what
wisdom *is* in them?
10 Therefore [a]will I give their wives
unto others, *and* their fields to them that
shall inherit *them:* for every one from the
least even unto the greatest is given to
[1]covetousness, from the prophet even
unto the priest every one dealeth falsely.
11 For they have [a]healed the hurt of
the daughter of my people slightly, saying, [b]Peace, peace; when *there is* no
peace.
12 Were they [a]ashamed when they R
had committed abomination? nay, they M
were not at all ashamed, neither could
they blush: therefore shall they fall
among them that fall: in the time of their
visitation they shall be cast down, saith
the LORD.
13 ¶ [1]I will surely consume them,
saith the LORD: *there shall be* no grapes
[a]on the vine, nor figs on the [b]fig tree, and
the leaf shall fade; and *the things that* I
have given them shall pass away from
them.
14 Why do we sit still? [a]assemble
yourselves, and let us enter into the defenced cities, and let us be silent there:
for the LORD our God hath put us to silence, and given us [b]water of [1]gall to
drink, because we have sinned against
the LORD.
15 We [a]looked for peace, but no good
came; and for a time of health, and behold trouble!

C *Jer 7:26* ◀ ▶ *Jer 9:3*
N *Jer 6:19* ◀ ▶ *Jer 8:20*
R *Jer 8:5–6* ◀ ▶ *Jer 9:9–22*
M *Jer 6:15* ◀ ▶ *Jer 13:15–17*

32 [b]2 Ki. 23:10; ch. 19:11
33 [a]Deut. 28:26
34 [a]Is. 24:7,8; Ezek. 26:13; Hos. 2:11; Rev. 18:23 [b]Lev. 26:33
8:2 [a]2 Ki. 23:5; Ezek. 8:16 [b]ch. 22:19
3 [a]Job 3:21 & 7:15,16; Rev. 9:6
5 [a]ch. 7:24 [b]ch. 9:6 [c]ch. 5:3
6 [a]2 Pet. 3:9
7 [a]Is. 1:3 [b]Sol. 2:12 [c]ch. 5:4,5
8 [a]Rom. 2:17 [b]Is. 10:1 [1]Or, *the false pen of the scribes worketh for falsehood*
9 [a]ch. 6:15 [1]Or, *Have they been ashamed* [2]Heb. *the wisdom of what thing*
10 [a]Zeph. 1:13 [1]Is. 56:11
11 [a]ch. 6:14 [b]Ezek. 13:10
12 [a]ch. 3:3
13 [a]Joel 1:7 [b]Mat. 21:19 [1]Or, *In gathering I will consume*
14 [a]ch. 4:5 [b]ch. 9:15 [1]Or, *poison*
15 [a]ch. 14:19

7:34 The happy sounds of life would be silenced in the coming desolation of the land.
8:5–6 Because of the people's "perpetual backsliding" (8:5) they refused to turn away from their course and rushed headlong to utter destruction "as the horse rusheth into the battle" (8:6).
8:12–14 Again God confirmed his determination to "surely consume them" (8:13) because of Judah's refusal to repent of their sin.

16 The snorting of his horses was heard from [a]Dan: the whole land trembled at the sound of the neighing of his [b]strong ones; for they are come, and have devoured the land, and [/]all that is in it; the city, and those that dwell therein.

17 For, behold, I will send serpents, cockatrices, among you, which *will* not *be* [a]charmed, and they shall bite you, saith the LORD.

18 ¶ *When* I would comfort myself against sorrow, my heart *is* faint [/]in me.

19 Behold the voice of the cry of the daughter of my people [/]because of them that dwell in [a]a far country: *Is* not the LORD in Zion? *is* not her king in her? Why have they provoked me to anger with their graven images, *and* with strange vanities?

H 20 The harvest is past, the summer is
N ended, and we are not saved.

21 [a]For the hurt of the daughter of my people am I hurt; I am [b]black; astonishment hath taken hold on me.

K 22 *Is there* no [a]balm in Gilead; *is there*
H no physician there? why then is not the health of the daughter of my people [/]recovered?

9

OH [a]THAT[/] my head were waters, and mine eyes a fountain of tears, that I might weep day and night for the slain of the daughter of my people!

2 Oh that I had in the wilderness a lodging place of wayfaring men; that I might leave my people, and go from them! for [a]they *be* all adulterers, an assembly of treacherous men.

C 3 And [a]they bend their tongues *like* their bow *for* lies: but they are not valiant for the truth upon the earth; for they proceed from evil to evil, and they [b]know not me, saith the LORD.

4 [a]Take ye heed every one of his [/]neighbour, and trust ye not in any brother: for every brother will utterly supplant, and every neighbour will [b]walk with slanders.

5 And they will [/]deceive every one his neighbour, and will not speak the truth: they have taught their tongue to speak lies, *and* weary themselves to commit iniquity.

6 Thine habitation *is* in the midst of deceit; through deceit they refuse to know me, saith the LORD.

7 Therefore thus saith the LORD of hosts, Behold, [a]I will melt them, and try them; [b]for how shall I do for the daughter of my people?

8 Their tongue *is as* an arrow shot out; it speaketh [a]deceit: *one* speaketh [b]peaceably to his neighbour with his mouth, but [c]in heart he layeth [/]his wait.

9 ¶ [a]Shall I not visit them for these R
things? saith the LORD: shall not my soul H
be avenged on such a nation as this?

10 For the mountains will I take up a weeping and wailing, and [a]for the [/]habitations of the wilderness a lamentation, because they are [2]burned up, so that none can pass through *them;* neither can *men* hear the voice of the cattle; [b]both[3] the fowl of the heavens and the beast are fled; they are gone.

11 And I will make Jerusalem [a]heaps, *and* [b]a den of dragons; and I will make the cities of Judah [/]desolate, without an inhabitant.

12 ¶ [a]Who *is* the wise man, that may understand this? and *who is he* to whom the mouth of the LORD hath spoken, that he may declare it, for what the land perisheth *and* is burned up like a wilderness, that none passeth through?

13 And the LORD saith, Because they have forsaken my law which I set before them, and have not obeyed my voice, neither walked therein;

14 But have [a]walked after the [b]imagination of their own heart, and after Baalim, [c]which their fathers taught them:

15 Therefore thus saith the LORD of hosts, the God of Israel; Behold, I will [a]feed them, *even* this people, [b]with wormwood, and give them water of gall to drink.

16 [a]ch. 4:15 [b]ch. 47:3 [/]Heb. *the fulness thereof*
17 [a]Ps. 58:4,5
18 [/]Heb. *upon*
19 [a]Is. 39:3 [/]Heb. *because of the country of them that are far off*
21 [a]ch. 9:1 [b]Joel 2:6
22 [a]ch. 46:11 [/]Heb. *gone up?*
9:1 [a]Is. 22:4 [/]Heb. *Who will give my head*
2 [a]ch. 5:7,8
3 [a]Ps. 64:3 [b]1 Sam. 2:12
4 [a]Mic. 7:5,6 [b]ch. 6:28 [/]Or, *friend*
5 [/]Or, *mock*
7 [a]Is. 1:25 [b]Hos. 11:8
8 [a]Ps. 12:2 [b]Ps. 55:21 [c]Heb. *in the midst of him* [/]Or, *wait for him*
9 [a]ch. 5:9,29
10 [a]Hos. 4:3 [b]ch. 4:25 [/]Or, *pastures* [2]Or, *desolate* [3]Heb. *from the fowl even to*
11 [a]Is. 25:2 [b]Is. 13:22 & 34:13 [/]Heb. *desolation*
12 [a]Hos. 14:9
14 [a]ch. 7:24 [b]Or, *stubbornness* [c]Gal. 1:14
15 [a]Ps. 80:5 [b]ch. 8:14; Lam. 3:19

H *Jer 6:19* ◀▶ *Jer 9:9*
N *Jer 8:9* ◀▶ *Jer 13:15–17*
K *Isa 63:1* ◀▶ *Jer 17:13–14*
H *Isa 53:4* ◀▶ *Jer 17:14*
C *Jer 8:9* ◀▶ *Jer 11:8*

R *Jer 8:12–14* ◀▶ *Jer 10:18*
H *Jer 8:20* ◀▶ *Jer 10:10*

9:9–22 Jeremiah announced God's declaration to utterly destroy Jerusalem "because they have forsaken my law which I set before them" (9:13) and warned that he would "scatter them also among the heathen" (9:22).

16 I will [a]scatter them also among the heathen, whom neither they nor their fathers have known: [b]and I will send a sword after them, till I have consumed them.

17 ¶ Thus saith the LORD of hosts, Consider ye, and call for [a]the mourning women, that they may come; and send for cunning *women,* that they may come:

18 And let them make haste, and take up a wailing for us, that [a]our eyes may run down with tears, and our eyelids gush out with waters.

19 For a voice of wailing is heard out of Zion, How are we spoiled! we are greatly confounded, because we have forsaken the land, because [a]our dwellings have cast *us* out.

20 Yet hear the word of the LORD, O ye women, and let your ear receive the word of his mouth, and teach your daughters wailing, and every one her neighbour lamentation.

21 For death is come up into our windows, *and* is entered into our palaces, to cut off [a]the children from without, *and* the young men from the streets.

22 Speak, Thus saith the LORD, Even the carcases of men shall fall [a]as dung upon the open field, and as the handful after the harvestman, and none shall gather *them.*

G 23 ¶ Thus saith the LORD, [a]Let not the
wise *man* glory in his wisdom, neither let
the mighty *man* glory in his might, let not
the rich *man* glory in his riches:

24 But [a]let him that glorieth glory in this, that he understandeth and knoweth me, that I *am* the LORD which exercise lovingkindness, judgment, and righteousness, in the earth: [b]for in these *things* I delight, saith the LORD.

25 ¶ Behold, the days come, saith the LORD, that [a]I will [1]punish all *them which are* circumcised with the uncircumcised;

J 26 Egypt, and Judah, and Edom, and
the children of Ammon, and Moab, and
all *that are* [1]in the [a]utmost corners, that
dwell in the wilderness: for all *these* nations
are uncircumcised, and all the house of Israel *are* [b]uncircumcised in the heart.

16 [a]Lev. 26:33; Deut. 28:64 [b]Lev. 26:33; ch. 44:27; Ezek. 5:2
17 [a]2 Chr. 35:25; Job 3:8; Eccl. 12:5; Amos 5:16; Mat. 9:23
18 [a]ch. 14:17
19 [a]Lev. 18:28
21 [a]ch. 6:11
22 [a]ch. 8:2
23 [a]Eccl. 9:11
24 [a]1 Cor. 1:31; 2 Cor. 10:17 [b]Mic. 7:18
25 [a]Rom. 2:8,9 [1]Heb. *visit upon*
26 [a]ch. 25:23 [b]Lev. 26:41; Ezek. 44:7; Rom. 2:28 [1]Heb. *cut off into corners,* or, *having the corners* of their hair *polled*
10:2 [a]Lev. 18:3
3 [a]Is. 40:19 & 45:20 [1]Heb. *statutes,* or, *ordinances are vanity*
4 [a]Is. 41:7
5 [a]Ps. 115:5; Hab. 2:19; 1 Cor. 12:2 [b]Ps. 115:7; Is. 46:1,7 [c]Is. 41:23
6 [a]Ex. 15:11; Ps. 86:8,10
7 [a]Rev. 15:4 [b]Ps. 89:6 [1]Or, *it liketh thee*
8 [a]Ps. 115:8; Hab. 2:18 [1]Heb. *in one, or, at once*
9 [a]Dan. 10:5 [b]Ps. 115:4
10 [a]Ps. 31:5 [b]1 Tim. 6:17 [c]Ps. 10:16 [1]Heb. *God of truth* [2]Heb. *king of eternity*
11 [a]Ps. 96:5 [b]Zech. 13:2 [1]Ver. 11 is in the Chaldean language
12 [a]Gen. 1:1,6; Ps. 136:5 [b]Ps. 93:1

The living God and dead gods

10 HEAR YE the word which the LORD speaketh unto you, O house of Israel:

2 Thus saith the LORD, [a]Learn not the W
way of the heathen, and be not dismayed
at the signs of heaven; for the heathen
are dismayed at them.

3 For the [1]customs of the people *are* vain: for [a]*one* cutteth a tree out of the forest, the work of the hands of the workman, with the axe.

4 They deck it with silver and with gold; they [a]fasten it with nails and with hammers, that it move not.

5 They *are* upright as the palm tree, [a]but speak not: they must needs be [b]borne, because they cannot go. Be not afraid of them; for [c]they cannot do evil, neither also *is it* in them to do good.

6 Forasmuch as *there is* none [a]like unto thee, O LORD; thou *art* great, and thy name *is* great in might.

7 [a]Who would not fear thee, O King of nations? for [1]to thee doth it appertain: forasmuch as [b]among all the wise *men* of the nations, and in all their kingdoms, *there is* none like unto thee.

8 But they are [1]altogether [a]brutish and foolish: the stock *is* a doctrine of vanities.

9 Silver spread into plates is brought from Tarshish, and [a]gold from Uphaz, the work of the workman, and of the hands of the founder: blue and purple *is* their clothing: they *are* all [b]the work of cunning *men.*

10 But the LORD *is* the [a]true [1] God, he P
is [b]the living God, and an [c]everlasting[2] H
king: at his wrath the earth shall tremble,
and the nations shall not be able to abide
his indignation.

11 [1]Thus shall ye say unto them, [a]The gods that have not made the heavens and the earth, *even* [b]they shall perish from the earth, and from under these heavens.

12 He [a]hath made the earth by his power, he hath [b]established the world by

G *Jer 2:35* ◀▶ *Jer 13:23*
J *Jer 1:18–19* ◀▶ *Jer 11:20*

W *Isa 32:17* ◀▶ *Mt 6:25–34*
P *Isa 66:24* ◀▶ *Jer 23:19–20*
H *Jer 9:9* ◀▶ *Jer 12:5*

10:10 Jeremiah declared that only God is the true and living God in contrast to the multitude of pagan idols worshiped by Judah's neighbors.

his wisdom, and [c]hath stretched out the heavens by his discretion.

13 [a]When he uttereth his voice, *there is* a [1]multitude of waters in the heavens, and [b]he causeth the vapours to ascend from the ends of the earth; he maketh lightnings [2]with rain, and bringeth forth the wind out of his treasures.

14 [a]Every man [1]is [b]brutish in *his* knowledge: [c]every founder is confounded by the graven image: [d]for his molten image *is* falsehood, and *there is* no breath in them.

15 They *are* vanity, *and* the work of errors: in the time of their visitation they shall perish.

16 [a]The portion of Jacob *is* not like them: for he *is* the former of all *things;* and [b]Israel *is* the rod of his inheritance: [c]The LORD of hosts *is* his name.

Coming distress

17 ¶ [a]Gather up thy wares out of the land, O [1]inhabitant of the fortress.

R 18 For thus saith the LORD, Behold, I will [a]sling out the inhabitants of the land at this once, and will distress them, [b]that they may find *it so.*

19 ¶ [a]Woe is me for my hurt! my wound is grievous: but I said, [b]Truly this *is* a grief, and [c]I must bear it.

R 20 [a]My tabernacle is spoiled, and all my cords are broken: my children are gone forth of me, and they *are* not: *there is* none to stretch forth my tent any more, and to set up my curtains.

21 For the pastors are become brutish, and have not sought the LORD: therefore they shall not prosper, and all their flocks shall be scattered.

22 Behold, the noise of the bruit is come, and a great commotion out of the [a]north country, to make the cities of Judah desolate, *and* a [b]den of dragons.

23 ¶ O LORD, I know that the [a]way of man *is* not in himself: *it is* not in man that walketh to direct his steps.

24 O LORD, [a]correct me, but with judgment; not in thine anger, lest thou [1]bring me to nothing.

R *Jer 9:9–22* ◀▶ *Jer 10:20–21*
R *Jer 10:18* ◀▶ *Jer 10:25*

12 [c]Job 9:8; Ps. 104:2; Is. 40:22
13 [a]Job 38:34 [b]Ps. 135:7 [1]Or, *noise* [2]Or, *for rain*
14 [a]ch. 51:17 [b]Prov. 30:2 [c]Is. 42:17 & 44:11 [d]Hab. 2:18 [1]Or, *is more brutish than to know*
16 [a]Lam. 3:24 [b]Deut. 32:9 [c]Is. 47:4 & 54:5
17 [a]ch. 6:1; Ezek. 12:3 [1]Heb. *inhabitress*
18 [a]1 Sam. 25:29 [b]Ezek. 6:10
19 [a]ch. 8:21 [b]Ps. 77:10 [c]Mic. 7:9
20 [a]ch. 4:20
22 [a]ch. 5:15 [b]ch. 9:11
23 [a]Prov. 16:1
24 [a]ch. 30:11 [1]Heb. *diminish me*
25 [a]Ps. 79:6 [b]Job 18:21 [c]ch. 8:16
11:3 [a]Deut. 27:26
4 [a]Deut. 4:20 [b]Lev. 26:12; ch. 7:23
5 [a]Deut. 7:12; Ps. 105:9 [1]Heb. *Amen*
6 [a]Rom. 2:13; Jas. 1:22
7 [a]ch. 35:15
8 [a]ch. 7:26 [b]ch. 9:14 [1]Or, *stubbornness*
9 [a]Ezek. 22:25
10 [a]Ezek. 20:18

25 [a]Pour out thy fury upon the heathen [b]that know thee not, and upon the families that call not on thy name: for they have eaten up Jacob, and [c]devoured him, and consumed him, and have made his habitation desolate. R

Judah has broken the covenant

11 THE WORD that came to Jeremiah from the LORD, saying,

2 Hear ye the words of this covenant, and speak unto the men of Judah, and to the inhabitants of Jerusalem;

3 And say thou unto them, Thus saith the LORD God of Israel; [a]Cursed *be* the man that obeyeth not the words of this covenant,

4 Which I commanded your fathers in the day *that* I brought them forth out of the land of Egypt, [a]from the iron furnace, saying, [b]Obey my voice, and do them, according to all which I command you: so shall ye be my people, and I will be your God:

5 That I may perform the [a]oath which I have sworn unto your fathers, to give them a land flowing with milk and honey, as *it is* this day. Then answered I, and said, [1]So be it, O LORD.

6 Then the LORD said unto me, Proclaim all these words in the cities of Judah, and in the streets of Jerusalem, saying, Hear ye the words of this covenant, [a]and do them.

7 For I earnestly protested unto your fathers in the day *that* I brought them up out of the land of Egypt, *even* unto this day, [a]rising early and protesting, saying, Obey my voice.

8 [a]Yet they obeyed not, nor inclined their ear, but [b]walked every one in the [1]imagination of their evil heart: therefore I will bring upon them all the words of this covenant, which I commanded *them* to do; but they did *them* not. C

9 And the LORD said unto me, [a]A conspiracy is found among the men of Judah, and among the inhabitants of Jerusalem.

10 They are turned back to [a]the iniquities of their forefathers, which refused to

R *Jer 10:20–21* ◀▶ *Jer 13:9–11*
C *Jer 9:3* ◀▶ *Jer 13:23*

10:18–25 Jeremiah spoke with despair of the unrighteous disobedience of Judah, the spoiling of the temple and her exile as consequences of her continued rebellion against God.

hear my words; and they went after other gods to serve them: the house of Israel and the house of Judah have broken my covenant which I made with their fathers.

11 ¶ Therefore thus saith the LORD, Behold, I will bring evil upon them, which they shall not be able [1]to escape; and [a]though they shall cry unto me, I will not hearken unto them.

12 Then shall the cities of Judah and inhabitants of Jerusalem go, and [a]cry unto the gods unto whom they offer incense: but they shall not save them at all in the time of their [1]trouble.

13 For *according to* the number of thy [a]cities were thy gods, O Judah; and *according to* the number of the streets of Jerusalem have ye set up altars to *that* [b]shameful[1] thing, *even* altars to burn incense unto Baal.

14 Therefore [a]pray not thou for this people, neither lift up a cry or prayer for them: for I will not hear *them* in the time that they cry unto me for their [1]trouble.

15 [a]What[1] hath my beloved to do in mine house, *seeing* she hath [b]wrought lewdness with many, and [c]the holy flesh is passed from thee? [2]when thou doest evil, then thou [d]rejoicest.

16 The LORD called thy name, [a]A green olive tree, fair, *and* of goodly fruit: with the noise of a great tumult he hath kindled fire upon it, and the branches of it are broken.

17 For the LORD of hosts, [a]that planted thee, hath pronounced evil against thee, for the evil of the house of Israel and of the house of Judah, which they have done against themselves to provoke me to anger in offering incense unto Baal.

The certainty of doom

18 ¶ And the LORD hath given me knowledge *of it,* and I know *it:* then thou showedst me their doings.

19 But I *was* like a lamb *or* an ox *that* is brought to the slaughter; and I knew not that they had devised devices against me, *saying,* Let us destroy [1]the tree with the fruit thereof, [a]and let us cut him off from [b]the land of the living, that his name may be no more remembered.

J E 20 But, O LORD of hosts, that judgest righteously, that [a]triest the reins and the heart, let me see thy vengeance on them: for unto thee have I revealed my cause.

21 Therefore thus saith the LORD of the men of Anathoth, [a]that seek thy life, saying, [b]Prophesy not in the name of the LORD, that thou die not by our hand:

22 Therefore thus saith the LORD of hosts, Behold, I will [1]punish them: the young men shall die by the sword; their sons and their daughters shall die by famine:

23 And there shall be no remnant of them: for I will bring evil upon the men of Anathoth, *even* [a]the year of their visitation.

Jeremiah's prayer

12 RIGHTEOUS [a]*ART* thou, O LORD, when I plead with thee: yet [1]let me talk with thee of *thy* judgments: [b]Wherefore doth the way of the wicked prosper? *wherefore* are all they happy that deal very treacherously?

2 Thou hast planted them, yea, they have taken root: [1]they grow, yea, they bring forth fruit: [a]thou *art* near in their mouth, and far from their reins.

3 But thou, O LORD, [a]knowest me: thou hast seen me, and [b]tried mine heart [1]toward thee: pull them out like sheep for the slaughter, and prepare them for [c]the day of slaughter.

4 How long shall [a]the land mourn, and the herbs of every field wither, [b]for the wickedness of them that dwell therein? [c]the beasts are consumed, and the birds; because they said, He shall not see our last end.

God's answer

5 ¶ If thou hast run with the footmen, and they have wearied thee, then how canst thou contend with horses? and *if* in the land of peace, *wherein* thou trustedst, *they wearied thee,* then how wilt thou do in [a]the swelling of Jordan? H

6 For even [a]thy brethren, and the house of thy father, even they have dealt treacherously with thee; yea, [1]they have called a multitude after thee: [b]believe them not, though they speak [2]fair words unto thee.

7 ¶ I have forsaken mine house, I have left mine heritage; I have given [1]the

11 [a]Ps. 18:41; Prov. 1:28 [1]Heb. *to go forth of*
12 [a]Deut. 32:37 [1]Heb. *evil*
13 [a]ch. 2:28 [b]ch. 3:24 [1]Heb. *shame*
14 [a]Ex. 32:10 [1]Heb. *evil*
15 [a]Ps. 50:16 [b]Ezek. 16:25 [c]Tit. 1:15 [d]Prov. 2:14 [1]Heb. *What is to my beloved in my house* [2]Or, *when thy evil is*
16 [a]Ps. 52:8
17 [a]Is. 5:2
19 [a]Ps. 83:4 [b]Ps. 27:13 [1]Heb. *the stalk with his bread*
20 [a]1 Chr. 28:9; Ps. 7:9
21 [a]ch. 12:5,6 [b]Mic. 2:6
22 [1]Heb. *visit upon*
23 [a]ch. 23:12
12:1 [a]Ps. 51:4 [b]Mal. 3:15 [1]Or, *let me reason the case with thee*
2 [a]Mat. 15:8 [1]Heb. *they go on*
3 [a]Ps. 17:3 [b]ch. 11:20 [c]Jas. 5:5 [1]Heb. *with thee*
4 [a]Hos. 4:3 [b]Ps. 107:34 [c]ch. 9:10
5 [a]Josh. 3:15; 1 Chr. 12:15
6 [a]ch. 9:4 [b]Prov. 26:25 [1]Or, *they cried after thee fully* [2]Heb. *good things*
7 [1]Heb. *the love*

J *Jer 9:26* ◀ ▶ *Jer 27:22*
E *Isa 29:15* ◀ ▶ *Jer 16:17*
H *Jer 10:10* ◀ ▶ *Jer 13:15–16*

dearly beloved of my soul into the hand of her enemies.

8 Mine heritage is unto me as a lion in the forest; it [1,2]crieth out against me: therefore have I hated it.

9 Mine heritage *is* unto me *as* a [1]speckled bird, the birds round about *are* against her; come ye, assemble all the beasts of the field, [a]come[2] to devour.

10 Many [a]pastors have destroyed [b]my vineyard, they have [c]trodden my portion under foot, they have made my [1]pleasant portion a desolate wilderness.

11 They have made it desolate, *and being* desolate [a]it mourneth unto me; the whole land is made desolate, because [b]no man layeth *it* to heart.

12 The spoilers are come upon all high places through the wilderness: for the sword of the LORD shall devour from the *one* end of the land even to the *other* end of the land: no flesh shall have peace.

13 [a]They have sown wheat, but shall reap thorns: they have put themselves to pain, *but* shall not profit: and [1]they shall be ashamed of your revenues because of the fierce anger of the LORD.

I 14 ¶ Thus saith the LORD against all mine evil neighbours, that [a]touch the inheritance which I have caused my people Israel to inherit; Behold, I will [b]pluck them out of their land, and pluck out the house of Judah from among them.

15 [a]And it shall come to pass, after that I have plucked them out I will return, and have compassion on them, [b]and will bring them again, every man to his heritage, and every man to his land.

16 And it shall come to pass, if they will diligently learn the ways of my people, [a]to swear by my name, The LORD liveth; as they taught my people to swear by Baal; then shall they be [b]built in the midst of my people.

17 But if they will not [a]obey, I will utterly pluck up and destroy that nation, saith the LORD.

I *Jer 3:14–19* ◀ ▶ *Jer 16:14–16*

8 [1]Or, *yelleth* [2]Heb. *giveth out his voice*

9 [a]Is. 56:9 [1]Or, *taloned* [2]Or, *cause them to come*

10 [a]ch. 6:3 [b]Is. 5:1,5 [c]Is. 63:18 [1]Heb. *portion of desire*

11 [a]ver. 4 [b]Is. 42:25

13 [a]Lev. 26:16; Deut. 28:38; Mic. 6:15; Hag. 1:6 [1]Or, *ye*

14 [a]Zech. 2:8 [b]Deut. 30:3; ch. 32:37

15 [a]Ezek. 28:25 [b]Amos 9:14

16 [a]ch. 4:2 [b]Eph. 2:20,21; 1 Pet. 2:5

17 [a]Is. 60:12

13:9 [a]Lev. 26:19

10 [a]ch. 9:14 & 11:8 & 16:12 [1]Or, *stubbornness*

11 [a]Ex. 19:5 [b]ch. 33:9

The parable of the girdle

13 THUS SAITH the LORD unto me, Go and get thee a linen girdle, and put it upon thy loins, and put it not in water.

2 So I got a girdle according to the word of the LORD, and put *it* on my loins.

3 And the word of the LORD came unto me the second time, saying,

4 Take the girdle that thou hast got, which *is* upon thy loins, and arise, go to Euphrates, and hide it there in a hole of the rock.

5 So I went, and hid it by Euphrates, as the LORD commanded me.

6 And it came to pass after many days, that the LORD said unto me, Arise, go to Euphrates, and take the girdle from thence, which I commanded thee to hide there.

7 Then I went to Euphrates, and digged, and took the girdle from the place where I had hid it: and, behold, the girdle was marred, it was profitable for nothing.

8 Then the word of the LORD came unto me, saying,

9 Thus saith the LORD, After this manner [a]will I mar the pride of Judah, and the great pride of Jerusalem. R

10 This evil people, which refuse to hear my words, which [a]walk in the [1]imagination of their heart, and walk after other gods, to serve them, and to worship them, shall even be as this girdle, which is good for nothing.

11 For as the girdle cleaveth to the loins of a man, so have I caused to cleave unto me the whole house of Israel and the whole house of Judah, saith the LORD; that [a]they might be unto me for a people, and [b]for a name, and for a praise, and for a glory: but they would not hear.

The parable of the bottles

12 ¶ Therefore thou shalt speak unto them this word; Thus saith the LORD God of Israel, Every bottle shall be filled with wine: and they shall say unto thee, Do we

R *Jer 10:25* ◀ ▶ *Jer 13:17–21*

12:15 Despite the terrible punishment and exile from the promised land, God promises that he will return his people to their land and "have compassion on them."

13:9–11 God had commanded Jeremiah to take a linen belt and bury it in a hole in a rock. When Jeremiah retrieved it some time later it was mildewed and rotten, symbolizing the useless, ruined nation of Judah that would soon be destroyed.

not certainly know that every bottle shall be filled with wine?

13 Then shalt thou say unto them, Thus saith the LORD, Behold, I will fill all the inhabitants of this land, even the kings that sit upon David's throne, and the priests, and the prophets, and all the inhabitants of Jerusalem, [a]with drunkenness.

14 And [a]I will dash them [1]one against another, even the fathers and the sons together, saith the LORD: I will not pity, nor spare, nor have mercy, [2]but destroy them.

The pride and shame of Jerusalem

H M N 15 ¶ Hear ye, and give ear; be not proud: for the LORD hath spoken.

16 Give glory to the LORD your God, before he cause [a]darkness, and before your feet stumble upon the dark mountains, and, while ye [b]look for light, he turn it into [c]the shadow of death, *and* make *it* gross darkness.

R 17 But if ye will not hear it, my soul shall weep in secret places for *your* pride; and [a]mine eye shall weep sore, and run down with tears, because the LORD'S flock is carried away captive.

18 Say unto [a]the king and to the queen, Humble yourselves, sit down: for your [1]principalities shall come down, *even* the crown of your glory.

19 The cities of the south shall be shut up, and none shall open *them:* Judah shall be carried away captive all of it, it shall be wholly carried away captive.

20 Lift up your eyes, and behold them [a]that come from the north: where *is* the flock *that* was given thee, thy beautiful flock?

21 What wilt thou say when he shall [1]punish thee? for thou hast taught them *to be* captains, *and* as chief over thee: shall not [a]sorrows take thee, as a woman in travail?

22 ¶ And if thou say in thine heart, [a]Wherefore come these things upon me? For the greatness of thine iniquity are [b]thy skirts discovered, *and* thy heels [1]made bare.

23 Can the Ethiopian change his skin, or the leopard his spots? *then* may ye also do good, that are [1]accustomed to do evil. C G O

24 Therefore will I scatter them [a]as the stubble that passeth away by the wind of the wilderness. R H

25 [a]This *is* thy lot, the portion of thy measures from me, saith the LORD; because thou hast forgotten me, and trusted in [b]falsehood.

26 Therefore [a]will I discover thy skirts upon thy face, that thy shame may appear.

27 I have seen thine adulteries, and thy [a]neighings, the lewdness of thy whoredom, *and* thine abominations [b]on the hills in the fields. Woe unto thee, O Jerusalem! wilt thou not be made clean? [1]when *shall it* once *be?*

Judah beyond deliverance

14 THE WORD of the LORD that came to Jeremiah concerning [1]the dearth.

2 Judah mourneth, and [a]the gates thereof languish; they are [b]black unto the ground; and [c]the cry of Jerusalem is gone up.

3 And their nobles have sent their little ones to the waters: they came to the pits, *and* found no water; they returned with their vessels empty; they were [a]ashamed and confounded, [b]and covered their heads.

4 Because the ground is chapt, for there was no rain in the earth, the plowmen were ashamed, they covered their heads.

5 Yea, the hind also calved in the field, and forsook *it,* because there was no grass.

6 And [a]the wild asses did stand in the high places, they snuffed up the wind like dragons; their eyes did fail, because *there was* no grass.

7 ¶ O LORD, though our iniquities tes-

13 [a]Is. 51:17,21 & 63:6; ch. 25:27 & 51:7
14 [a]Ps. 2:9 [1]Heb. *a man against his brother* [2]Heb. *from destroying them*
16 [a]Is. 5:30 & 8:22; Amos 8:9 [b]Is. 59:9 [c]Ps. 44:19
17 [a]ch. 9:1 & 14:17; Lam. 1:2,16 & 2:18
18 [a]2 Ki. 24:12; ch. 22:26 [1]Or, *head tires*
20 [a]ch. 6:22
21 [a]ch. 6:24 [1]Heb. *visit upon*
22 [a]ch. 16:10 [b]Is. 3:17 & 47:2,3; Ezek. 16:37-39; Nah. 3:5 [1]Or, *shall be violently taken away*
23 [1]Heb. *taught*
24 [a]Ps. 1:4; Hos. 13:3
25 [a]Job 20:29; Ps. 11:6 [b]ch. 10:14
26 [a]Lam. 1:8; Ezek. 16:37; Hos. 2:10
27 [a]ch. 5:8 [b]Is. 65:7; ch. 2:20 [1]Heb. *after when yet?*
14:1 [1]Heb. *the words of the dearths, or, restraints*
2 [a]Is. 3:26 [b]ch. 8:21 [c]1 Sam. 5:12
3 [a]Ps. 40:14 [b]2 Sam. 15:30
6 [a]ch. 2:24

H *Jer 12:5* ◀▶ *Jer 13:24*
M *Jer 8:12* ◀▶ *Jer 29:12–13*
N *Jer 8:20* ◀▶ *Jer 32:33*
R *Jer 13:9–11* ◀▶ *Jer 13:24*

C *Jer 11:8* ◀▶ *Jer 17:1*
G *Jer 9:23–24* ◀▶ *Jer 17:5*
O *Jer 2:22* ◀▶ *Jer 17:13–14*
R *Jer 13:17–21* ◀▶ *Jer 14:19*
H *Jer 13:15–16* ◀▶ *Jer 17:4*

13:17–21, 24 God told Jeremiah to warn the king and queen of Judah of the coming exile of their people and destruction of their cities because of their unconfessed sins.

tify against us, do thou *it* [a]for thy name's sake: for our backslidings are many; we have sinned against thee.

8 [a]O the hope of Israel, the saviour thereof in time of trouble, why shouldest thou be as a stranger in the land, and as a wayfaring man *that* turneth aside to tarry for a night?

9 Why shouldest thou be as a man astonied, as a mighty man [a]*that* cannot save? yet thou, O LORD, [b]*art* in the midst of us, and [l]we are called by thy name; leave us not.

S 10 ¶ Thus saith the LORD unto this people, [a]Thus have they loved to wander, they have not refrained their feet, therefore the LORD doth not accept them; [b]he will now remember their iniquity, and visit their sins.

11 Then said the LORD unto me, [a]Pray not for this people for *their* good.

12 [a]When they fast, I will not hear their cry; and [b]when they offer burnt offering and an oblation, I will not accept them: but [c]I will consume them by the sword, and by the famine, and by the pestilence.

13 ¶ [a]Then said I, Ah, Lord GOD! behold, the prophets say unto them, Ye shall not see the sword, neither shall ye have famine; but I will give you [l]assured peace in this place.

14 Then the LORD said unto me, [a]The prophets prophesy lies in my name: [b]I sent them not, neither have I commanded them, neither spake unto them: they prophesy unto you a false vision and divination, and a thing of nought, and the deceit of their heart.

15 Therefore thus saith the LORD concerning the prophets that prophesy in my name, and I sent them not, [a]yet they say, Sword and famine shall not be in this land; By sword and famine shall those prophets be consumed.

16 And the people to whom they prophesy shall be cast out in the streets of Jerusalem because of the famine and the sword; [a]and they shall have none to bury them, them, their wives, nor their sons, nor their daughters: for I will pour their wickedness upon them.

17 ¶ Therefore thou shalt say this word unto them; [a]Let mine eyes run down with tears night and day, and let them not cease: [b]for the virgin daughter of my people is broken with a great breach, with a very grievous blow.

18 If I go forth into [a]the field, then behold the slain with the sword! and if I enter into the city, then behold them that are sick with famine! yea, both the prophet and the priest [b]go [l] about into a land that they know not.

19 [a]Hast thou utterly rejected Judah? hath thy soul loathed Zion? why hast thou smitten us, and [b]*there is* no healing for us? [c]we looked for peace, and *there is* no good; and for the time of healing, and behold trouble! R

20 We acknowledge, O LORD, our wickedness, *and* the iniquity of our fathers: for [a]we have sinned against thee.

21 Do not abhor *us,* for thy name's sake, do not disgrace the throne of thy glory: [a]remember, break not thy covenant with us.

22 [a]Are there *any* among [b]the vanities of the Gentiles that can cause rain? or can the heavens give showers? [c]*art* not thou he, O LORD our God? therefore we will wait upon thee: for thou hast made all these *things.*

15 THEN SAID the LORD unto me, [a]Though [b]Moses and [c]Samuel stood before me, *yet* my mind *could* not *be* toward this people: cast *them* out of my sight, and let them go forth. R

2 And it shall come to pass, if they say unto thee, Whither shall we go forth? then thou shalt tell them, Thus saith the LORD; [a]Such as *are* for death, to death; and such as *are* for the sword, to the sword; and such as *are* for the famine, to the famine; and such as *are* for the captivity, to the captivity.

7 [a]Ps. 25:11
8 [a]ch. 17:13
9 [a]Is. 59:1 [b]Ex. 29:45; Lev. 26:11 [l]Heb. *thy name is called upon us*
10 [a]See ch. 2:23-25 [b]Hos. 8:13
11 [a]Ex. 32:10
12 [a]Prov. 1:28; Is. 1:15; Ezek. 8:18; Zech. 7:13 [b]ch. 6:20 [c]ch. 9:16
13 [a]ch. 4:10 [l]Heb. *peace of truth*
14 [a]ch. 27:10 [b]ch. 29:8,9
15 [a]ch. 5:12
16 [a]Ps. 79:3
17 [a]ch. 9:1 [b]ch. 8:21
18 [a]Ezek. 7:15 [b]ch. 5:31 [l]Or, *make merchandise against a land, and* men *acknowledge it not*
19 [a]Lam. 5:22 [b]ch. 15:18 [c]ch. 8:15
20 [a]Ps. 106:6; Dan. 9:8
21 [a]Ps. 106:45
22 [a]Zech. 10:1 [b]Deut. 32:21 [c]Ps. 135:7
15:1 [a]Ezek. 14:14 [b]Ex. 32:11; Ps. 99:6 [c]1 Sam. 7:9
2 [a]Ezek. 5:2; Zech. 11:9

S *Jer 7:23* ◀ ▶ *Jer 15:6*

R *Jer 13:24* ◀ ▶ *Jer 15:1–4*
R *Jer 14:19* ◀ ▶ *Jer 15:6–7*

14:19 Jeremiah prophesied that when the judgment and wrath of God fell upon Judah the people would finally awaken to their terrible fate.
15:1–7 Jeremiah said that even though Moses and Samuel had successfully interceded in the past to prevent God from destroying his people, the apostasy of Judah was so terrible that nothing would prevent the coming wrath of God. Jeremiah's prophecy declared four distinct judgments on Judah in addition to exile: death by sword, dogs, birds and beasts.

3 And I will [a]appoint over them four [l]kinds, saith the LORD: the sword to slay, and the dogs to tear, and [b]the fowls of the heaven, and the beasts of the earth, to devour and destroy.

4 And [l]I will cause them to be [a]removed into all kingdoms of the earth, because of [b]Manasseh the son of Hezekiah king of Judah, for *that* which he did in Jerusalem.

5 For who shall have pity upon thee, O Jerusalem? or who shall bemoan thee? or who shall go aside [l]to ask how thou doest?

R S 6 [a]Thou hast forsaken me, saith the LORD, thou art [b]gone backward: therefore will I stretch out my hand against thee, and destroy thee; [c]I am weary with repenting.

7 And I will fan them with a fan in the gates of the land; I will bereave *them* of [l]children, I will destroy my people, *since* they return not from their ways.

8 Their widows are increased to me above the sand of the seas: I have brought upon them [l]against the mother of the young men a spoiler at noonday: I have caused *him* to fall upon it suddenly, and terrors upon the city.

9 [a]She that hath borne seven languisheth: she hath given up the ghost; [b]her sun is gone down while *it was* yet day: she hath been ashamed and confounded: and the residue of them will I deliver to the sword before their enemies, saith the LORD.

10 ¶ [a]Woe is me, my mother, that thou hast borne me a man of strife and a man of contention to the whole earth! I have neither lent on usury, nor men have lent to me on usury; *yet* every one of them doth curse me.

11 The LORD said, Verily it shall be well with thy remnant; verily [l]I will cause [a]the enemy to entreat thee *well* in the time of evil and in the time of affliction.

12 Shall iron break the northern iron and the steel?

13 Thy substance and thy treasures will I give to the [a]spoil without price, and *that* for all thy sins, even in all thy borders.

14 And I will make *thee* to pass with thine enemies [a]into a land *which* thou knowest not: for a [b]fire is kindled in mine anger, *which* shall burn upon you.

15 ¶ O LORD, [a]thou knowest: remember me, and visit me, and [b]revenge me of my persecutors; take me not away in thy longsuffering: know that [c]for thy sake I have suffered rebuke.

16 Thy words were found, and I did [a]eat them; and [b]thy word was unto me the joy and rejoicing of mine heart: for [l]I am called by thy name, O LORD God of hosts.

17 [a]I sat not in the assembly of the mockers, nor rejoiced; I sat alone because of thy hand: for thou hast filled me with indignation.

18 Why is my [a]pain perpetual, and my wound incurable, *which* refuseth to be healed? wilt thou be altogether unto me [b]as a liar, *and as* waters *that* [l]fail?

19 ¶ Therefore thus saith the LORD, [a]If thou return, then will I bring thee again, *and* thou shalt [b]stand before me: and if thou [c]take forth the precious from the vile, thou shalt be as my mouth: let them return unto thee; but return not thou unto them.

20 And I will make thee unto this people a fenced brasen wall: and they shall fight against thee, but [a]they shall not prevail against thee: for I *am* with thee to save thee and to deliver thee, saith the LORD. V

21 And I will deliver thee out of the hand of the wicked, and I will redeem thee out of the hand of the terrible.

Punishment and promise

16 THE WORD of the LORD came also unto me, saying,

2 Thou shalt not take thee a wife, neither shalt thou have sons or daughters in this place.

3 For thus saith the LORD concerning the sons and concerning the daughters that are born in this place, and concerning their mothers that bare them, and concerning their fathers that begat them in this land;

4 They shall die of [a]grievous deaths; they shall not be [b]lamented; neither shall they be buried; *but* they shall be [c]as dung upon the face of the earth: and they shall be consumed by the sword, and by famine; and their [d]carcases shall be meat for

3 [a]Lev. 26:16 [b]Deut. 28:26 [l]Heb. *families*
4 [a]Deut. 28:25 [b]2 Ki. 24:3,4 [l]Heb. *I will give them for a removing*
5 [l]Heb. *to ask of thy peace?*
6 [a]ch. 2:13 [b]ch. 7:24 [c]Hos. 13:14
7 [l]Or, *whatsoever is dear*
8 [l]Or, *against the mother* city *a young man spoiling* or, *against the mother* and *the young men*
9 [a]1 Sam. 2:5 [b]Amos 8:9
10 [a]Job 3:1
11 [a]ch. 40:4,5 [l]Or, *I will entreat the enemy for thee*
13 [a]Ps. 44:12
14 [a]ch. 16:13 [b]Deut. 32:22
15 [a]ch. 12:3 [b]ch. 20:12 [c]Ps. 69:7
16 [a]Ezek. 3:1,3; Rev. 10:9 [b]Job 23:12; Ps. 119:72 [l]Heb. *thy name is called upon me*
17 [a]Ps. 26:4,5
18 [a]ch. 30:15 [b]ch. 1:18,19 [l]Heb. *be not sure?*
19 [a]Zech. 3:7 [b]ver. 1 [c]Ezek. 22:26
20 [a]ch. 20:11
16:4 [a]ch. 15:2 [b]ch. 22:18 & 25:33 [c]Ps. 83:10; ch. 8:2 & 9:22 [d]Ps. 79:2; ch. 7:33 & 34:20

R *Jer 15:1–4* ◄► *Jer 16:18*
S *Jer 14:10* ◄► *Jer 17:10*
V *Jer 1:19* ◄► *Jer 20:11*

the fowls of heaven, and for the beasts of the earth.

5 For thus saith the LORD, [a]Enter not into the house of [/]mourning, neither go to lament nor bemoan them: for I have taken away my peace from this people, saith the LORD, *even* lovingkindness and mercies.

6 Both the great and the small shall die in this land: they shall not be buried, [a]neither shall *men* lament for them, nor [b]cut themselves, nor [c]make themselves bald for them:

7 Neither shall *men* [a]tear[/] *themselves* for them in mourning, to comfort them for the dead; neither shall *men* give them the cup of consolation to [b]drink for their father or for their mother.

8 Thou shalt not also go into the house of feasting, to sit with them to eat and to drink.

9 For thus saith the LORD of hosts, the God of Israel; Behold, [a]I will cause to cease out of this place in your eyes, and in your days, the voice of mirth, and the voice of gladness, the voice of the bridegroom, and the voice of the bride.

10 ¶ And it shall come to pass, when thou shalt show this people all these words, and they shall say unto thee, [a]Wherefore hath the LORD pronounced all this great evil against us? or what *is* our iniquity? or what *is* our sin that we have committed against the LORD our God?

11 Then shalt thou say unto them, [a]Because your fathers have forsaken me, saith the LORD, and have walked after other gods, and have served them, and have worshipped them, and have forsaken me, and have not kept my law;

12 And ye have done [a]worse than your fathers; for, behold, [b]ye walk every one after the [/]imagination of his evil heart, that they may not hearken unto me:

13 [a]Therefore will I cast you out of this land [b]into a land that ye know not, *neither* ye nor your fathers; and there shall ye serve other gods day and night; where I will not show you favour.

14 ¶ Therefore, behold, the [a]days I
come, saith the LORD, that it shall no more be said, The LORD liveth, that brought up the children of Israel out of the land of Egypt;

15 But, The LORD liveth, that brought up the children of Israel from the land of the north, and from all the lands whither he had driven them: and [a]I will bring them again into their land that I gave unto their fathers.

16 ¶ Behold, I will send for many [a]fishers, saith the LORD, and they shall fish them; and after will I send for many hunters, and they shall hunt them from every mountain, and from every hill, and out of the holes of the rocks.

17 For mine [a]eyes *are* upon all their E
ways: they are not hid from my face, neither is their iniquity hid from mine eyes.

18 And first I will recompense their R
iniquity and their sin [a]double; because [b]they have defiled my land, they have filled mine inheritance with the carcases of their detestable and abominable things.

19 O LORD, [a]my strength, and my for- G
tress, and [b]my refuge in the day of affliction, the Gentiles shall come unto thee from the ends of the earth, and shall say, Surely our fathers have inherited lies, vanity, and *things* [c]wherein *there is* no profit.

20 Shall a man make gods unto himself, and [a]they *are* no gods?

21 Therefore, behold, I will this once cause them to know, I will cause them to know mine hand and my might; and they shall know that [a]my name *is* [/]The LORD.

5 [a]Ezek. 24:17,22,23 [/]Or, *mourning feast*
6 [a]ch. 22:18 [b]Lev. 19:28; Deut. 14:1; ch. 41:5 & 47:5 [c]Is. 22:12; ch. 7:29
7 [a]Ezek. 24:17; Hos. 9:4; See Deut. 26:14; Job 42:11 [b]Prov. 31:6 [/]Or, *break bread for them*
9 [a]Is. 24:7,8; Ezek. 26:13; Hos. 2:11; Rev. 18:23
10 [a]Deut. 29:24; ch. 5:19
11 [a]Deut. 29:25; ch. 22:9
12 [a]ch. 7:26 [b]ch. 13:10 [/]Or, *stubbornness*
13 [a]Deut. 4:26 & 28:36,63 [b]ch. 15:14
14 [a]Is. 43:18; ch. 23:7,8
15 [a]ch. 24:6 & 30:3 & 32:37
16 [a]Amos 4:2; Hab. 1:15
17 [a]Job 34:21; Prov. 5:21 & 15:3; ch. 32:19
18 [a]Is. 40:2; ch. 17:18 [b]Ezek. 43:7
19 [a]Ps. 18:2 [b]ch. 17:17 [c]Is. 44:10; ch. 10:5
20 [a]Is. 37:19; ch. 2:11; Gal. 4:8
21 [a]Ex. 15:3; ch. 33:2; Amos 5:8 [/]Or, *JEHOVAH;* see Ps. 83:18

I *Jer 12:14–17* ◀▶ *Jer 23:3–8*
E *Jer 11:20* ◀▶ *Jer 17:1*
R *Jer 15:6–7* ◀▶ *Jer 17:4*
G *Isa 65:1* ◀▶ *Da 2:28–45*

16:14–19 This prophecy recounted Israel's history from the exodus (c. 1446 B.C.) to the exile (586 B.C.) and to the promised return to their land (536 B.C.) while also foreshadowing the ultimate fulfillment of this prophecy in the last days. Note Jeremiah's use of the phrase "the land of the north" (16:15) to refer to Judah's destroyers (see 50:3; Zec 2:6–7). Jeremiah also declared that the people would honor God for delivering them from exile just as their ancestors had honored him for delivering them from Egypt. Note that 23:7–8 is almost quoted verbatim from 16:14–15, highlighting the importance of this event.

God, the hope of Israel

C **17** THE SIN of Judah *is* written with
E a [a]pen of iron, *and* with the
[/]point of a diamond: *it is* [b]graven upon
the table of their heart, and upon the
horns of your altars;
2 Whilst their children remember
their altars and their [a]groves by the green
trees upon the high hills.
3 O my mountain in the field, I will
give thy substance *and* all thy treasures to
the spoil, *and* thy high places for sin,
throughout all thy borders.
R 4 And thou, even [/]thyself, shalt dis-
H continue from thine heritage that I gave
thee; and I will cause thee to serve thine
enemies in [a]the land which thou knowest not: for [b]ye have kindled a fire in
mine anger, *which* shall burn for ever.
G 5 ¶ Thus saith the LORD; [a]Cursed *be*
the man that trusteth in man, and maketh [b]flesh his arm, and whose heart departeth from the LORD.
6 For he shall be [a]like the heath in the
desert, and [b]shall not see when good
cometh; but shall inhabit the parched
places in the wilderness, [c]*in* a salt land
and not inhabited.
F 7 [a]Blessed *is* the man that trusteth in
U the LORD, and whose hope the LORD is.
8 For he shall be [a]as a tree planted by
the waters, and *that* spreadeth out her
roots by the river, and shall not see when
heat cometh, but her leaf shall be green;
and shall not be careful in the year of
[/]drought, neither shall cease from yielding fruit.
C 9 ¶ The heart *is* deceitful above all
things, and desperately wicked: who can
know it?
E 10 I the LORD [a]search the heart, *I* try
S the reins, [b]even to give every man according to his ways, *and* according to the
fruit of his doings.
11 *As* the partridge [/]sitteth *on eggs,*
and hatcheth *them* not; *so* he that getteth
riches, and not by right, [a]shall leave them
in the midst of his days, and at his end
shall be [b]a fool.
12 ¶ A glorious high throne from the
beginning *is* the place of our sanctuary.
13 O LORD, [a]the hope of Israel, [b]all that K
forsake thee shall be ashamed, *and* they O
that depart from me shall be [c]written in S
the earth, because they have forsaken the
LORD, the [d]fountain of living waters.
14 Heal me, O LORD, and I shall be H
healed; save me, and I shall be saved: for
[a]thou *art* my praise.
15 ¶ Behold, they say unto me,
[a]Where *is* the word of the LORD? let it
come now.
16 As for me, [a]I have not hastened
from *being* a pastor [/]to follow thee: neither have I desired the woeful day; thou
knowest: that which came out of my lips
was *right* before thee.
17 Be not a terror unto me: [a]thou *art*
my hope in the day of evil.
18 [a]Let them be confounded that persecute me, but [b]let not me be confounded: let them be dismayed, but let
not me be dismayed: bring upon them
the day of evil, and [c]destroy[/] them with
double destruction.

Sabbath observance stressed

19 ¶ Thus said the LORD unto me; Go
and stand in the gate of the children of
the people, whereby the kings of Judah
come in, and by the which they go out,
and in all the gates of Jerusalem;
20 And say unto them, [a]Hear ye the
word of the LORD, ye kings of Judah, and
all Judah, and all the inhabitants of Jerusalem, that enter in by these gates:
21 Thus saith the LORD; [a]Take heed to
yourselves, and bear no burden on the
sabbath day, nor bring *it* in by the gates
of Jerusalem;
22 Neither carry forth a burden out of

17:1 [a]Job 19:24 [b]Prov. 3:3; 2 Cor. 3:3 [/]Heb. *nail*
2 [a]Judg. 3:7; 2 Chr. 24:18 & 33:3,19; ch. 2:20
4 [a]ch. 16:13 [b]ch. 15:14 [/]Heb. *in thyself*
5 [a]Is. 30:1,2 & 31:1 [b]See Is. 31:3
6 [a]ch. 48:6 [b]Job 20:17 [c]Deut. 29:23
7 [a]Ps. 2:12 & 34:8; Prov. 16:20; Is. 30:18
8 [a]Job 8:16; Ps. 1:3 [/]Or, *restraint*
10 [a]1 Sam. 16:7; 1 Chr. 28:9; Ps. 7:9 & 139:23,24; Prov. 17:3; ch. 20:12; Rom. 8:27; Rev. 2:23 [b]Ps. 62:12; ch. 32:19; Rom. 2:6
11 [a]Ps. 55:23 [b]Luke 12:20 [/]Or, *gathereth* young *which she hath not brought forth*
13 [a]ch. 14:8 [b]Ps. 73:27; Is. 1:28 [c]See Luke 10:20 [d]ch. 2:13
14 [a]Deut. 10:21; Ps. 109:1 & 148:14
15 [a]Is. 5:19; Ezek. 12:22; Amos 5:18; 2 Pet. 3:4
16 [a]ch. 1:4 [/]Heb. *after thee*
17 [a]ch. 16:19
18 [a]Ps. 35:4 & 70:2 [b]Ps. 25:2 [c]ch. 11:20 [/]Heb. *break them with a double breach*
20 [a]ch. 19:3
21 [a]Num. 15:32; Neh. 13:19

C *Jer 13:23* ◀ ▶ *Jer 17:9*
E *Jer 16:17* ◀ ▶ *Jer 17:10*
R *Jer 16:18* ◀ ▶ *Jer 18:16–17*
H *Jer 13:24* ◀ ▶ *Jer 20:11*
G *Jer 13:23* ◀ ▶ *Jer 18:13–15*
F *Isa 26:3–4* ◀ ▶ *Hab 2:4*
U *Jer 7:23* ◀ ▶ *Jer 35:19*
C *Jer 17:1* ◀ ▶ *Jer 23:12*
E *Jer 17:1* ◀ ▶ *Jer 20:12*
S *Jer 15:6* ◀ ▶ *Jer 17:13*

K *Jer 8:22* ◀ ▶ *Jer 24:7*
O *Jer 13:23* ◀ ▶ *La 3:37*
S *Jer 17:10* ◀ ▶ *Jer 23:21–22*
H *Jer 8:22* ◀ ▶ *Eze 34:16*

17:4 God declared that unrepentant Judah would serve their enemies in an unknown land as punishment for their sins.

your houses on the sabbath day, neither
do ye any work, but hallow ye the sabbath day, as I [a]commanded your fathers.
23 [a]But they obeyed not, neither inclined their ear, but made their neck stiff,
that they might not hear, nor receive instruction.
24 And it shall come to pass, if ye diligently hearken unto me, saith the LORD,
to bring in no burden through the gates
of this city on the sabbath day, but hallow
the sabbath day, to do no work therein;
25 [a]Then shall there enter into the
gates of this city kings and princes sitting
upon the throne of David, riding in chariots and on horses, they, and their
princes, the men of Judah, and the inhabitants of Jerusalem: and this city shall remain for ever.
26 And they shall come from the cities
of Judah, and from [a]the places about Jerusalem, and from the land of Benjamin,
and from [b]the plain, and from the mountains, and from [b]the south, bringing
burnt offerings, and sacrifices, and meat
offerings, and incense, and bringing [c]sac-
rifices of praise, unto the house of the
LORD.
27 But if ye will not hearken unto me
to hallow the sabbath day, and not to bear
a burden, even entering in at the gates of
Jerusalem on the sabbath day; then [a]will I
kindle a fire in the gates thereof, [b]and it
shall devour the palaces of Jerusalem, and
it shall not be quenched.

The parable of potter and clay

18 THE WORD which came to Jeremiah from the LORD, saying,
2 Arise, and go down to the potter's
house, and there I will cause thee to hear
my words.
3 Then I went down to the potter's
house, and, behold, he wrought a work
on the [1]wheels.
4 And the vessel [1]that he made of clay
was marred in the hand of the potter: so
he [2]made it again another vessel, as
seemed good to the potter to make *it.*
5 Then the word of the LORD came to
me, saying,
6 O house of Israel, [a]cannot I do with
you as this potter? saith the LORD. Behold,
[b]as the clay *is* in the potter's hand, so *are*
ye in mine hand, O house of Israel.
7 *At what* instant I shall speak concerning a nation, and concerning a kingdom, to [a]pluck up, and to pull down, and
to destroy *it;*
8 [a]If that nation, against whom I have L
pronounced, turn from their evil, [b]I will
repent of the evil that I thought to do
unto them.
9 And *at what* instant I shall speak concerning a nation, and concerning a kingdom, to build and to plant *it;*
10 If it do evil in my sight, that it obey
not my voice, then I will repent of the
good, wherewith I said I would benefit
them.
11 ¶ Now therefore go to, speak to the R
men of Judah, and to the inhabitants of
Jerusalem, saying, Thus saith the LORD;
Behold, I frame evil against you, and devise a device against you: [a]return ye now
every one from his evil way, and make
your ways and your doings good.
12 And they said, [a]There is no hope:
but we will walk after our own devices,
and we will every one do the imagination
of his evil heart.
13 Therefore thus saith the LORD; [a]Ask G
ye now among the heathen, who hath
heard such things: the virgin of Israel
hath done [b]a very horrible thing.
14 Will *a man* leave [1]the snow of Lebanon *which cometh* from the rock of the
field? *or* shall the cold flowing waters that
come from another place be forsaken?
15 Because my people hath forgotten
[a]me, they have burned incense to vanity,
and they have caused them to stumble in
their ways *from* the [b]ancient paths, to
walk in paths, *in* a way not cast up;
16 To make their land [a]desolate, *and* a R
perpetual [b]hissing; every one that passeth thereby shall be astonished, and wag
his head.
17 [a]I will scatter them [b]as with an east
wind before the enemy; [c]I will show

22 [a]Ex. 20:8 & 31:13; Ezek. 20:12
23 [a]ch. 7:24,26
25 [a]ch. 22:4
26 [a]ch. 33:13 [b]Zech. 7:7 [c]Ps. 107:22 & 116:17
27 [a]ch. 21:14; Lam. 4:11; Amos 1:4,7,10,12 [b]2 Ki. 25:9; ch. 52:13
18:3 [1]Or, *frames,* or, *seats*
4 [1]Or, *that he made was marred, as clay in the hand of the potter* [2]Heb. *returned and made*
6 [a]Is. 45:9; Rom. 9:20 [b]Is. 64:8
7 [a]ch. 1:10
8 [a]Ezek. 18:21 & 33:11 [b]ch. 26:3; Jonah 3:10
11 [a]2 Ki. 17:13; ch. 7:3
12 [a]ch. 2:25
13 [a]ch 2:10; 1 Cor. 5:1 [b]ch. 5:30
14 [1]Or, *my fields for a rock,* or for the *snow of Lebanon? shall the running waters be forsaken for the strange cold* waters?
15 [a]ch. 2:13,32 [b]ch. 6:16
16 [a]ch. 19:8 [b]1 Ki. 9:8; Lam. 2:15; Mic. 6:16
17 [a]ch. 13:24 [b]Ps. 48:7 [c]See ch. 2:27

L *Jer 3:22* ◀ ▶ *Jer 21:8*
R *Jer 7:5–7* ◀ ▶ *Jer 25:4–5*
G *Jer 17:5* ◀ ▶ *Jer 30:12*
R *Jer 17:4* ◀ ▶ *Jer 19:8*

18:16–17 Jeremiah prophesied that because Judah had turned her back on God by indulging in idolatry, God would show Judah his back instead of his face. To Judah, God's face symbolized blessing, but God's back stood for desolation and calamity.

them the back, and not the face, in the day of their calamity.

18 ¶ Then said they, [a]Come, and let us devise devices against Jeremiah; [b]for the law shall not perish from the priest, nor counsel from the wise, nor the word from the prophet. Come, and let us smite him ʹwith the tongue, and let us not give heed to any of his words.

19 Give heed to me, O LORD, and hearken to the voice of them that contend with me.

20 [a]Shall evil be recompensed for good? for [b]they have digged a pit for my soul. Remember that I stood before thee to speak good for them, *and* to turn away thy wrath from them.

21 Therefore [a]deliver up their children to the famine, and ʹpour out their *blood* by the force of the sword; and let their wives be bereaved of their children, and *be* widows; and let their men be put to death; *let* their young men *be* slain by the sword in battle.

22 Let a cry be heard from their houses, when thou shalt bring a troop suddenly upon them: for [a]they have digged a pit to take me, and hid snares for my feet.

23 Yet, LORD, thou knowest all their counsel against me ʹto slay *me:* [a]forgive not their iniquity, neither blot out their sin from thy sight, but let them be overthrown before thee; deal *thus* with them in the time of thine anger.

19 THUS SAITH the LORD, Go and get a potter's earthen bottle, and *take* of the ancients of the people, and of the ancients of the priests;

2 And go forth unto [a]the valley of the son of Hinnom, which *is* by the entry of ʹthe east gate, and proclaim there the words that I shall tell thee,

3 [a]And say, Hear ye the word of the LORD, O kings of Judah, and inhabitants of Jerusalem; Thus saith the LORD of hosts, the God of Israel; Behold, I will bring evil upon this place, the which whosoever heareth, his ears shall [b]tingle.

4 Because they [a]have forsaken me, and have estranged this place, and have burned incense in it unto other gods, whom neither they nor their fathers have known, nor the kings of Judah, and have filled this place with [b]the blood of innocents;

5 [a]They have built also the high places of Baal, to burn their sons with fire *for* burnt offerings unto Baal, [b]which I commanded not, nor spake *it,* neither came *it* into my mind:

6 Therefore, behold, the days come, saith the LORD, that this place shall no more be called Tophet, nor [a]The valley of the son of Hinnom, but The valley of slaughter.

7 And I will make void the counsel of Judah and Jerusalem in this place; [a]and I will cause them to fall by the sword before their enemies, and by the hands of them that seek their lives: and their [b]carcases will I give to be meat for the fowls of the heaven, and for the beasts of the earth.

8 And I will make this city [a]desolate, and an hissing; every one that passeth thereby shall be astonished and hiss because of all the plagues thereof. R

9 And I will cause them to eat the [a]flesh of their sons and the flesh of their daughters, and they shall eat every one the flesh of his friend in the siege and straitness, wherewith their enemies, and they that seek their lives, shall straiten them.

10 [a]Then shalt thou break the bottle in the sight of the men that go with thee,

11 And shalt say unto them, Thus saith the LORD of hosts; [a]Even so will I break this people and this city, as *one* breaketh a potter's vessel, that cannot ʹbe made whole again: and they shall [b]bury *them* in Tophet, till *there be* no place to bury.

12 Thus will I do unto this place, saith the LORD, and to the inhabitants thereof, and *even* make this city as Tophet:

13 And the houses of Jerusalem, and the houses of the kings of Judah, shall be defiled [a]as the place of Tophet, because of all the houses upon whose [b]roofs they have burned incense unto all the host of heaven, and [c]have poured out drink offerings unto other gods.

14 Then came Jeremiah from Tophet,

18 [a]ch. 11:19 [b]Lev. 10:11; Mal. 2:7; John 7:48 ʹOr, *for the tongue*
20 [a]Ps. 109:4 [b]ver. 22; Ps. 35:7
21 [a]Ps. 109:9 ʹHeb. *pour them out*
22 [a]ver. 20
23 [a]Ps. 35:4 & 109:14; ch. 11:20 ʹHeb. *for death*
19:2 [a]Josh. 15:8; 2 Ki. 23:10 ʹHeb. *the sun gate*
3 [a]ch. 17:20 [b]1 Sam. 3:11; 2 Ki. 21:12
4 [a]Deut. 28:20; Is. 65:11 [b]2 Ki. 21:16; ch. 2:34
5 [a]ch. 7:31 & 32:35 [b]Lev. 18:21
6 [a]Josh. 15:8
7 [a]Lev. 26:17; Deut. 28:25 [b]Ps. 79:2; ch. 7:33 & 16:4 & 34:20
8 [a]ch. 18:16 & 49:13 & 50:13
9 [a]Lev. 26:29; Deut. 28:53; Is. 9:20; Lam. 4:10
10 [a]ch. 51:63,64
11 [a]Ps. 2:9; Is. 30:14; Lam. 4:2 [b]ch. 7:32 ʹHeb. *be healed*
13 [a]2 Ki. 23:10 [b]2 Ki. 23:12; ch. 32:29; Zeph. 1:5 [c]ch. 7:18

R *Jer 18:16–17* ◀ ▶ *Jer 20:6*

19:8 God again declared that the city would be devastated and become an object of ridicule for everyone who passed by due because of the idolatry within Jerusalem's walls.

whither the LORD had sent him to prophesy; and he stood in [a]the court of the
LORD'S house; and said to all the people,
15 Thus saith the LORD of hosts, the
God of Israel; Behold, I will bring upon
this city and upon all her towns all the
evil that I have pronounced against it, because [a]they have hardened their necks,
that they might not hear my words.

Jeremiah and Pashur

20 NOW PASHUR the son of [a]Im-
mer the priest, who *was* also
chief governor in the house of the LORD,
heard that Jeremiah prophesied these
things.
2 Then Pashur smote Jeremiah the
prophet, and put him in the stocks that
were in the high gate of Benjamin, which
was by the house of the LORD.
3 And it came to pass on the morrow,
that Pashur brought forth Jeremiah out of
the stocks. Then said Jeremiah unto him,
The LORD hath not called thy name
Pashur, but [1]Magor-missabib.
4 For thus saith the LORD, Behold, I will
make thee a terror to thyself, and to all
thy friends: and they shall fall by the
sword of their enemies, and thine eyes
shall behold *it:* and I will give all Judah
into the hand of the king of Babylon, and
he shall carry them captive into Babylon,
and shall slay them with the sword.
5 Moreover I [a]will deliver all the
strength of this city, and all the labours
thereof, and all the precious things
thereof, and all the treasures of the kings
of Judah will I give into the hand of their
enemies, which shall spoil them, and
take them, and carry them to Babylon.
R 6 And thou, Pashur, and all that dwell
in thine house shall go into captivity: and
thou shalt come to Babylon, and there
thou shalt die, and shalt be buried there,
thou, and all thy friends, to whom thou
hast [a]prophesied lies.

Jeremiah complains to the LORD

7 ¶ O LORD, thou hast deceived me,
and I was [1]deceived: [a]thou art stronger
than I, and hast prevailed: [b]I am in derision daily, every one mocketh me.
8 For since I spake, I cried out, [a]I cried
violence and spoil; because the word of
the LORD was made a reproach unto me,
and a derision, daily.
9 Then I said, I will not make mention
of him, nor speak any more in his name.
But *his word* was in mine heart as a
[a]burning fire shut up in my bones, and I
was weary with forbearing, and [b]I could
not *stay.*
10 ¶ [a]For I heard the defaming of
many, fear on every side. Report, *say
they,* and we will report it. [b]All[1] my
familiars watched for my halting, *saying,*
Peradventure he will be enticed, and we
shall prevail against him, and we shall
take our revenge on him.
11 But the LORD *is* with me as a mighty H
terrible one: therefore my persecutors V
shall stumble, and they shall not [a]prevail:
they shall be greatly ashamed; for they
shall not prosper: *their* [b]everlasting confusion shall never be forgotten.
12 But, O LORD of hosts, that [a]triest the E
righteous, *and* seest the reins and the
heart, [b]let me see thy vengeance on
them: for unto thee have I opened my
cause.
13 Sing unto the LORD, praise ye the
LORD: for [a]he hath delivered the soul of
the poor from the hand of evildoers.
14 ¶ [a]Cursed *be* the day wherein I was
born: let not the day wherein my mother
bare me be blessed.
15 Cursed *be* the man who brought
tidings to my father, saying, A man child
is born unto thee; making him very glad.
16 And let that man be as the cities
which the LORD [a]overthrew, and repented
not: and let him [b]hear the cry in the
morning, and the shouting at noontide;
17 [a]Because he slew me not from the
womb; or that my mother might have
been my grave, and her womb *to be* always great *with me.*
18 [a]Wherefore came I forth out of the
womb to [b]see labour and sorrow, that my
days should be consumed with shame?

Zedekiah's prayer; God's answer

21 THE WORD which came unto
Jeremiah from the LORD, when
king Zedekiah sent unto him [a]Pashur the
son of Melchiah, and [b]Zephaniah the son
of Maaseiah the priest, saying,

14 [a]See 2 Chr. 20:5
15 [a]ch. 7:26 & 17:23
20:1 [a]1 Chr. 24:14
3 [1]i.e. *Fear round about;* see Ps. 31:13; ver. 10; ch. 6:25 & 46:5 & 49:29
5 [a]2 Ki. 20:17 & 24:12-16 & 25:13; ch. 3:24
6 [a]ch. 14:13,14 & 28:15 & 29:21
7 [a]ch. 1:6,7 [b]Lam. 3:14 [1]Or, *enticed*
8 [a]ch. 6:7
9 [a]Job 32:18,19; Ps. 39:3 [b]Job 32:18; Acts 18:5
10 [a]Ps. 31:13 [b]Job 19:19; Ps. 41:9 & 55:13,14; Luke 11:53,54 [1]Heb. *Every man of my peace*
11 [a]ch. 15:20 & 17:18 [b]ch. 23:40
12 [a]ch. 11:20 & 17:10 [b]Ps. 54:7 & 59:10
13 [a]Ps. 35:9,10 & 109:30,31
14 [a]Job 3:3; ch. 15:10
16 [a]Gen. 19:25 [b]ch. 18:22
17 [a]Job 3:10,11
18 [a]Job 3:20 [b]Lam. 3:1
21:1 [a]ch. 38:1 [b]2 Ki. 25:18; ch. 29:25 & 37:3

R *Jer 19:8* ◀▶ *Jer 21:7*
H *Jer 17:4* ◀▶ *Jer 23:12*
V *Jer 15:20–21* ◀▶ *Jer 39:17–18*
E *Jer 17:10* ◀▶ *Jer 23:23–24*

2 [a]Inquire, I pray thee, of the LORD for us; for Nebuchadrezzar king of Babylon maketh war against us; if so be that the LORD will deal with us according to all his wondrous works, that he may go up from us.

3 ¶ Then said Jeremiah unto them, Thus shall ye say to Zedekiah:

4 Thus saith the LORD God of Israel; Behold, I will turn back the weapons of war that *are* in your hands, wherewith ye fight against the king of Babylon, and *against* the Chaldeans, which besiege you without the walls, and [a]I will assemble them into the midst of this city.

5 And I myself will fight against you with an [a]outstretched hand and with a strong arm, even in anger, and in fury, and in great wrath.

D 6 And I will smite the inhabitants of this city, both man and beast: they shall die of a great pestilence.

R 7 And afterward, saith the LORD, [a]I will deliver Zedekiah king of Judah, and his servants, and the people, and such as are left in this city from the pestilence, from the sword, and from the famine, into the hand of Nebuchadrezzar king of Babylon, and into the hand of their enemies, and into the hand of those that seek their life: and he shall smite them with the edge of the sword; [b]he shall not spare them, neither have pity, nor have mercy.

L 8 ¶ And unto this people thou shalt say, Thus saith the LORD; Behold, [a]I set before you the way of life, and the way of death.

9 He that [a]abideth in this city shall die by the sword, and by the famine, and by the pestilence: but he that goeth out, and falleth to the Chaldeans that besiege you, he shall live, and [b]his life shall be unto him for a prey.

R 10 For I have [a]set my face against this city for evil, and not for good, saith the LORD: [b]it shall be given into the hand of the king of Babylon, and he shall [c]burn it with fire.

D Ps 106:29 ◀ ▶ Jer 44:13
R Jer 20:6 ◀ ▶ Jer 21:10
L Jer 18:8 ◀ ▶ Jer 26:13
R Jer 21:7 ◀ ▶ Jer 22:5

11 ¶ And touching the house of the king of Judah, *say,* Hear ye the word of the LORD;

12 O house of David, thus saith the LORD; [a]Execute[†] judgment [b]in the morning, and deliver *him that is* spoiled out of the hand of the oppressor, lest my fury go out like fire, and burn that none can quench *it,* because of the evil of your doings.

13 Behold, [a]I *am* against thee, O [†]inhabitant of the valley, *and* rock of the plain, saith the LORD; which say, [b]Who shall come down against us? or who shall enter into our habitations?

14 But I will [†]punish you according to the [a]fruit of your doings, saith the LORD: and I will kindle a fire in the forest thereof, and [b]it shall devour all things round about it.

A burden about evil kings

22 THUS SAITH the LORD; Go down to the house of the king of Judah, and speak there this word,

2 And say, [a]Hear the word of the LORD, O king of Judah, that sittest upon the throne of David, thou, and thy servants, and thy people that enter in by these gates:

3 Thus saith the LORD; [a]Execute ye judgment and righteousness, and deliver the spoiled out of the hand of the oppressor: and do no wrong, do no violence to the stranger, the fatherless, nor the widow, neither shed innocent blood in this place.

4 For if ye do this thing indeed, [a]then shall there enter in by the gates of this house kings sitting [†]upon the throne of David, riding in chariots and on horses, he, and his servants, and his people.

5 But if ye will not hear these words, [a]I swear by myself, saith the LORD, that this house shall become a desolation. R

6 For thus saith the LORD unto the king's house of Judah; Thou *art* Gilead unto me, *and* the head of Lebanon: *yet*

R Jer 21:10 ◀ ▶ Jer 22:10–12

2 [a]ch. 37:3,7
4 [a]Is. 13:4
5 [a]Ex. 6:6
7 [a]ch. 37:17 & 39:5 & 52:9 [b]Deut. 28:50; 2 Chr. 36:17
8 [a]Deut. 30:19
9 [a]ch. 38:2,17,18 [b]ch. 39:18 & 45:5
10 [a]Lev. 17:10; ch. 44:11; Amos 9:4 [b]ch. 38:3 [c]ch. 34:2,22 & 37:10 & 38:18,23 & 52:13
12 [a]ch. 22:3; Zech. 7:9 [b]Ps. 101:8 [†]Heb. *Judge*
13 [a]Ezek. 13:8 [b]ch. 49:4 [†]Heb. *inhabitress*
14 [a]Prov. 1:31; Is. 3:10,11 [b]2 Chr. 36:19; ch. 52:13 [†]Heb. *visit upon*
22:2 [a]ch. 17:20
3 [a]ch. 21:12
4 [a]ch. 17:25 [†]Heb. *for David upon his throne*
5 [a]Heb. 6:13,17

21:10 Jeremiah pronounced God's terrible verdict against the wickedness and evil of Jerusalem. The cruel, pagan king of Babylon would destroy the city and carry the people away as slaves.

22:3–5 God commanded the kings of Judah to carry out justice to all otherwise "this house shall become a desolation" (22:5).

surely I will make thee a wilderness; *and*
cities *which* are not inhabited.
7 And I will prepare destroyers against
thee, every one with his weapons: and
they shall cut down [a]thy choice cedars,
[b]and cast *them* into the fire.
8 And many nations shall pass by this
city, and they shall say every man to his
neighbour, [a]Wherefore hath the LORD
done thus unto this great city?
9 Then they shall answer, [a]Because
they have forsaken the covenant of the
LORD their God, and worshipped other
gods, and served them.
R 10 ¶ Weep ye not for [a]the dead, neither bemoan him: *but* weep sore for him
[b]that goeth away: for he shall return no
more, nor see his native country.
11 For thus saith the LORD touching
[a]Shallum the son of Josiah king of Judah,
which reigned instead of Josiah his father, [b]which went forth out of this place;
He shall not return thither any more:
12 But he shall die in the place
whither they have led him captive, and
shall see this land no more.
13 ¶ [a]Woe unto him that buildeth his
house by unrighteousness, and his chambers by wrong; [b]*that* useth his neighbour's service without wages, and giveth
him not for his work;
14 That saith, I will build me a wide
house and large chambers, and cutteth
him out [1]windows; and *it is* ceiled with
cedar, and painted with vermilion.
15 Shalt thou reign, because thou closest *thyself* in cedar? did not thy father eat
and drink, and do judgment and justice,
and then [a]*it was* well with him?
16 He judged the cause of the poor and
needy; then *it was* well *with him: was* not
this to know me? saith the LORD.
17 [a]But thine eyes and thine heart *are*
not but for thy covetousness, and for to
shed innocent blood, and for oppression,
and for [1]violence, to do *it*.

R *Jer 22:5* ◄► *Jer 22:18–19*

7 [a]Is. 37:24 [b]ch. 21:14
8 [a]Deut. 29:24,25; 1 Ki. 9:8,9
9 [a]2 Ki. 22:17; 2 Chr. 34:25
10 [a]2 Ki. 22:20 [b]ver. 11
11 [a]See 1 Chr. 3:15, with 2 Ki. 23:30 [b]2 Ki. 23:34
13 [a]ver. 18; 2 Ki. 23:35 [b]Lev. 19:13; Deut. 24:14,15; Mic. 3:10; Hab. 2:9; Jas. 5:4
14 [1]Or, *my windows*
15 [a]Ps. 128:2; Is. 3:10
17 [a]Ezek. 19:6 [1]Or, *incursion*
18 [a]ch. 16:4,6 [b]See 1 Ki. 13:30 Fulfilled
19 [a]2 Chr. 36:6; ch. 36:30
21 [a]ch. 3:25 & 7:23 [1]Heb. *prosperities*
22 [a]ch. 23:1
23 [a]ch. 6:24 [1]Heb. *inhabitress*
24 [a]See 2 Ki. 24:6, 8; 1 Chr. 3:16; ch. 37:1 [b]Sol. 8:6; Hag. 2:23
25 [a]ch. 34:20
26 [a]2 Ki. 24:15; 2 Chr. 36:10
27 [1]Heb. *lift up their mind*
28 [a]Ps. 31:12; ch. 48:38; Hos. 8:8

18 Therefore thus saith the LORD con- R
cerning Jehoiakim the son of Josiah king
of Judah; [a]They shall not lament for him,
saying, [b]Ah my brother! or, Ah sister!
they shall not lament for him, *saying*, Ah
lord! or, Ah his glory!
19 [a]He shall be buried with the burial
of an ass, drawn and cast forth beyond
the gates of Jerusalem.
20 ¶ Go up to Lebanon, and cry; and
lift up thy voice in Bashan, and cry from
the passages: for all thy lovers are destroyed.
21 I spake unto thee in thy [1]prosper-
ity; *but* thou saidst, I will not hear. [a]This
hath been thy manner from thy youth,
that thou obeyedst not my voice.
22 The wind shall eat up all [a]thy pastors, and thy lovers shall go into captivity:
surely then shalt thou be ashamed and
confounded for all thy wickedness.
23 O [1]inhabitant of Lebanon, that
makest thy nest in the cedars, how gracious shalt thou be when pangs come
upon thee, [a]the pain as of a woman in
travail!
24 *As* I live, saith the LORD, [a]though
Coniah the son of Jehoiakim king of Judah [b]were the signet upon my right
hand, yet would I pluck thee thence;
25 [a]And I will give thee into the hand
of them that seek thy life, and into the
hand *of them* whose face thou fearest,
even into the hand of Nebuchadrezzar
king of Babylon, and into the hand of the
Chaldeans.
26 [a]And I will cast thee out, and thy
mother that bare thee, into another country, where ye were not born; and there
shall ye die.
27 But to the land whereunto they
[1]desire to return, thither shall they not
return.
28 *Is* this man Coniah a despised broken idol? *is he* [a]a vessel wherein *is* no
pleasure? wherefore are they cast out, he

R *Jer 22:10–12* ◄► *Jer 23:39–40*

22:28–30 The name Coniah is a shortened form of Jeconiah (see Mt 1:11–12) and was an informal name for King Jehoiachin (see 22:24; 1Ch 3:15–17). Because none of Jehoiachin's children ever ruled in Jerusalem, Jeremiah's prophecy appears at first glance to contradict the Davidic covenant that guaranteed the throne to David's seed forever. However, this prophecy will be fulfilled, and the covenant with David upheld, when Jesus the Messiah rules from Jerusalem during the Millennium. When Jesus was born, the genealogical records preserved in the temple at that time would have proved his double right to rule from the throne of David—a legal descent through King Jehoiachin (see Mt 1:1–17) as well as his maternal descent from King David (see Lk 3:23–38).

and his seed, and are cast into a land which they know not?

B 29 [a]O earth, earth, earth, hear the word of the LORD.

30 Thus saith the LORD, Write ye this man [a]childless, a man *that* shall not prosper in his days: for no man of his seed shall prosper, [b]sitting upon the throne of David, and ruling any more in Judah.

The remnant and the true king

23 WOE [a]BE unto the pastors that destroy and scatter the sheep of my pasture! saith the LORD.

2 Therefore thus saith the LORD God of Israel against the pastors that feed my people; Ye have scattered my flock, and driven them away, and have not visited them: [a]behold, I will visit upon you the evil of your doings, saith the LORD.

I 3 And [a]I will gather the remnant of my flock out of all countries whither I have driven them, and will bring them again to their folds; and they shall be fruitful and increase.

4 And I will set up [a]shepherds over them which shall feed them: and they shall fear no more, nor be dismayed, neither shall they be lacking, saith the LORD.

M 5 ¶ Behold, [a]the days come, saith the
V LORD, that I will raise unto David a righteous Branch, and a King shall reign and prosper, [b]and shall execute judgment and justice in the earth.

6 [a]In his days Judah shall be saved, and Israel [b]shall dwell safely: and [c]this *is* his name whereby he shall be called, [1]THE LORD OUR RIGHTEOUSNESS.

7 Therefore, behold, [a]the days come, saith the LORD, that they shall no more say, The LORD liveth, which brought up the children of Israel out of the land of Egypt;

8 But, The LORD liveth, which brought up and which led the seed of the house of Israel out of the north country, [a]and from all countries whither I had driven them; and they shall dwell in their own land.

False prophets

9 ¶ Mine heart within me is broken because of the prophets; [a]all my bones shake; I am like a drunken man, and like a man whom wine hath overcome, because of the LORD, and because of the words of his holiness.

10 For [a]the land is full of adulterers; for [b]because of [1]swearing the land mourneth; [c]the pleasant places of the wilderness are dried up, and their [2]course is evil, and their force *is* not right.

11 For [a]both prophet and priest are profane; yea, [b]in my house have I found their wickedness, saith the LORD.

12 [a]Wherefore their way shall be unto them as slippery *ways* in the darkness: they shall be driven on, and fall therein: for I [b]will bring evil upon them, *even* the year of their visitation, saith the LORD. C H

13 And I have seen [1,2]folly in the prophets of Samaria; [a]they prophesied in Baal, and [b]caused my people Israel to err.

14 I have seen also in the prophets of Jerusalem [1]an horrible thing: [a]they commit adultery, and [b]walk in lies: they [c]strengthen also the hands of evildoers, that none doth return from his wickedness: they are all of them unto me as [d]Sodom, and the inhabitants thereof as Gomorrah.

15 Therefore thus saith the LORD of hosts concerning the prophets; Behold, I will feed them with [a]wormwood, and make them drink the water of gall: for from the prophets of Jerusalem is [1]profaneness gone forth into all the land.

16 Thus saith the LORD of hosts, Hearken not unto the words of the prophets that prophesy unto you: they make you vain: [a]they speak a vision of their

29 [a]Deut. 32:1; Is. 1:2 & 34:1; Mic. 1:2
30 [a]See 1 Chr. 3:16,17; Mat. 1:12 [b]ch. 36:30
23:1 [a]ch. 10:21; 22:22; Ezek. 34:2
2 [a]Ex. 32:34
3 [a]ch. 32:37; Ezek. 34:13
4 [a]ch. 3:15; Ezek. 34:23
5 [a]Is. 4:2 & 11:1 & 40:10,11; ch. 33:14; Dan. 9:24; Zech. 6:12; John 1:45 [b]Ps. 72:2; Is. 9:7 & 32:1,18
6 [a]Deut. 33:28; Zech. 14:11 [b]ch. 32:37 [c]ch. 33:16; 1 Cor. 1:30 [1]Heb. *Jehovah-tsidkenu*
7 [a]ch. 16:14
8 [a]Is. 43:5,6
9 [a]See Hab. 3:16
10 [a]ch. 9:2 [b]Hos. 4:2,3 [c]ch. 9:10 [1]Or, *cursing* [2]Or, *violence*
11 [a]Zeph. 3:4 [b]ch. 7:30; Ezek. 8:11 & 23:39
12 [a]Ps. 35:6; Prov. 4:19; ch. 13:16 [b]ch. 11:23
13 [a]ch. 2:8 [b]Is. 9:16 [1]Or, *an absurd thing* [2]Heb. *unsavoury*
14 [a]ch. 29:23 [b]ver. 26 [c]Ezek. 13:22 [d]Is. 1:9,10 [1]Or, *filthiness*
15 [a]ch. 9:15 [1]Or, *hypocrisy*
16 [a]ch. 14:14

B *Isa 61:1–3 ◀▶ Da 9:24–26*
I *Jer 16:14–16 ◀▶ Jer 25:12*
M *Jer 3:17 ◀▶ Jer 30:9*
V *Isa 45:23 ◀▶ Jer 31:34*
C *Jer 17:9 ◀▶ Jer 44:10*
H *Jer 20:11 ◀▶ Jer 23:17–19*

23:3–8 God stated his ultimate intent to judge the wicked of Judah yet also bring his people back to the promised land from their exile among the nations. Jeremiah foretold the great promise of the Messiah who will "execute judgment and justice in the earth" (22:5). Under the rule of the Messiah, Israel will finally espouse righteousness and experience safety. Jeremiah also declared that the people would honor God for delivering them from exile just as their ancestors had honored him for delivering them from Egypt. Note also that 23:7–8 is quoted almost verbatim from 16:14–15, indicating the significance of this event.

own heart, *and* not out of the mouth of the LORD.

H 17 They say still unto them that despise me, The LORD hath said, [a]Ye shall have peace; and they say unto every one that walketh after the [l]imagination of his own heart, [b]No evil shall come upon you.

18 For [a]who hath stood in the [l]counsel of the LORD, and hath perceived and heard his word? who hath marked his word, and heard *it*?

P 19 Behold, a [a]whirlwind of the LORD is gone forth in fury, even a grievous whirlwind: it shall fall grievously upon the head of the wicked.

20 The [a]anger of the LORD shall not return, until he have executed, and till he have performed the thoughts of his heart: [b]in the latter days ye shall consider it perfectly.

S 21 [a]I have not sent these prophets, yet they ran: I have not spoken to them, yet they prophesied.

22 But if they had [a]stood in my counsel, and had caused my people to hear my words, then they should have [b]turned them from their evil way, and from the evil of their doings.

E 23 *Am* I a God at hand, saith the LORD, and not a God afar off?

24 Can any [a]hide himself in secret places that I shall not see him? saith the LORD. [b]Do not I fill heaven and earth? saith the LORD.

25 I have heard what the prophets said, that prophesy lies in my name, saying, I have dreamed, I have dreamed.

26 How long shall *this* be in the heart of the prophets that prophesy lies? yea, *they are* prophets of the deceit of their own heart;

27 Which think to cause my people to forget my name by their dreams which they tell every man to his neighbour, [a]as their fathers have forgotten my name for Baal.

28 The prophet [l]that hath a dream, let him tell a dream; and he that hath my word, let him speak my word faithfully. What *is* the chaff to the wheat? saith the LORD.

29 *Is* not my word like as a fire? saith the LORD; and like a hammer *that* breaketh the rock in pieces?

30 Therefore, behold, [a]I *am* against the prophets, saith the LORD, that steal my words every one from his neighbour.

31 Behold, I *am* against the prophets, saith the LORD, [l]that use their tongues, and say, He saith.

32 Behold, I *am* against them that prophesy false dreams, saith the LORD, and do tell them, and cause my people to err by their lies, and by [a]their lightness; yet I sent them not, nor commanded them: therefore they shall not profit this people at all, saith the LORD.

The burden of the LORD

33 ¶ And when this people, or the prophet, or a priest, shall ask thee, saying, What *is* [a]the burden of the LORD? thou shalt then say unto them, What burden? [b]I will even forsake you, saith the LORD.

34 And *as for* the prophet, and the priest, and the people, that shall say, The burden of the LORD, I will even [l]punish that man and his house.

35 Thus shall ye say every one to his neighbour, and every one to his brother, What hath the LORD answered? and, What hath the LORD spoken?

36 And the burden of the LORD shall ye mention no more: for every man's word shall be his burden; for ye have perverted the words of the living God, of the LORD of hosts our God.

37 Thus shalt thou say to the prophet, What hath the LORD answered thee? and, What hath the LORD spoken?

38 But since ye say, The burden of the LORD; therefore thus saith the LORD; Because ye say this word, The burden of the LORD, and I have sent unto you, saying, Ye shall not say, The burden of the LORD;

39 Therefore, behold, I, even I, [a]will utterly forget you, and [b]I will forsake you, R

17 [a]ch. 8:11; Ezek. 13:10; Zech. 10:2 [b]Mic. 3:11 [l]Or, *stubbornness*
18 [a]Job 15:8; 1 Cor. 2:16 [l]Or, *secret*
19 [a]ch. 25:32 & 30:23
20 [a]ch. 30:24 [b]Gen. 49:1
21 [a]ch. 14:14
22 [a]ver. 18 [b]ch. 25:5
24 [a]Ps. 139:7; Amos 9:2,3 [b]1 Ki. 8:27; Ps. 139:7
27 [a]Judg. 3:7
28 [l]Heb. *with whom* is
30 [a]Deut. 18:20; ch. 14:14,15
31 [l]Or, *that smooth their tongues*
32 [a]Zeph. 3:4
33 [a]Mal. 1:1 [b]ver. 39
34 [l]Heb. *visit upon*
39 [a]Hos. 4:6 [b]ver. 33

H *Jer 23:12* ◀ ▶ *Jer 23:40*
P *Jer 10:10* ◀ ▶ *Jer 25:29–33*
S *Jer 17:13* ◀ ▶ *Jer 32:19*
E *Jer 20:12* ◀ ▶ *Jer 32:19*
R *Jer 22:18–19* ◀ ▶ *Jer 25:17–18*

23:19–20 Jeremiah's words portray a vivid picture of God's wrath in the last days during the tribulation period.

23:39–40 God again proclaimed his determination to punish Judah because of her continued rebellion against him.

and the city that I gave you and your fathers, *and cast you* out of my presence:

H 40 And I will bring [a]an everlasting reproach upon you, and a perpetual shame, which shall not be forgotten.

Sign of the good and evil figs

24 THE [a]LORD showed me, and, behold, two baskets of figs *were* set before the temple of the LORD, after that Nebuchadrezzar [b]king of Babylon had carried away captive [c]Jeconiah the son of Jehoiakim king of Judah, and the princes of Judah, with the carpenters and smiths, from Jerusalem, and had brought them to Babylon.

2 One basket *had* very good figs, *even* like the figs *that are* first ripe: and the other basket *had* very naughty figs, which could not be eaten, [l]they were so bad.

3 Then said the LORD unto me, What seest thou, Jeremiah? And I said, Figs; the good figs, very good; and the evil, very evil, that cannot be eaten, they are so evil.

4 ¶ Again the word of the LORD came unto me, saying,

5 Thus saith the LORD, the God of Israel; Like these good figs, so will I acknowledge [l]them that are carried away captive of Judah, whom I have sent out of this place into the land of the Chaldeans for *their* good.

6 For I will set mine eyes upon them for good, and [a]I will bring them again to this land: and [b]I will build them, and not pull *them* down; and I will plant them, and not pluck *them* up.

K 7 And I will give them [a]an heart to know me, that I *am* the LORD: and they shall be [b]my people, and I will be their God: for they shall return unto me [c]with their whole heart.

8 ¶ And as the evil [a]figs, which cannot be eaten, they are so evil; surely thus saith the LORD, So will I give Zedekiah the king of Judah, and his princes, and the residue of Jerusalem, that remain in this

H *Jer 23:17–19* ◀ ▶ *Jer 30:23–24*
K *Jer 17:13–14* ◀ ▶ *Jer 31:33–34*

40 [a]ch. 20:11

24:1 [a]Amos 7:1,4; & 8:1 [b]2 Ki. 24:12; 2 Chr. 36:10 [c]See ch. 22:24 & 29:2

2 [l]Heb. *for badness*

5 [l]Heb. *the captivity*

6 [a]ch. 12:15 & 29:10 [b]ch. 32:41 & 33:7 & 42:10

7 [a]Deut. 30:6; ch. 32:39; Ezek. 11:19 & 36:26,27 [b]ch. 30:22 & 31:33 & 32:38 [c]ch. 29:13

8 [a]ch. 29:17 [b]See ch. 43 & 44

9 [a]Deut. 28:25,37; 1 Ki. 9:7; 2 Chr. 7:20; ch. 15:4 & 29:18 & 34:17 [b]Ps. 44:13,14 [l]Heb. *for removing, or, vexation*

25:1 [a]ch 36:1

3 [a]ch. 1:2 [b]ch. 7:13 & 11:7,8,10

4 [a]ch. 7:13,25

5 [a]ch. 18:11; Jonah 3:8

7 [a]Deut. 32:21

9 [a]ch. 1:15

land, and [b]them that dwell in the land of Egypt:

9 And I will deliver them [l]to [a]be removed into all the kingdoms of the earth for *their* hurt, [b]*to be* a reproach and a proverb, a taunt and a curse, in all places whither I shall drive them.

10 And I will send the sword, the famine, and the pestilence, among them, till they be consumed from off the land that I gave unto them and to their fathers.

Judah's captivity

25 THE WORD that came to Jeremiah concerning all the people of Judah [a]in the fourth year of Jehoiakim the son of Josiah king of Judah, that *was* the first year of Nebuchadrezzar king of Babylon;

2 The which Jeremiah the prophet spake unto all the people of Judah, and to all the inhabitants of Jerusalem, saying,

3 [a]From the thirteenth year of Josiah the son of Amon king of Judah, even unto this day, that *is* the three and twentieth year, the word of the LORD hath come unto me, and I have spoken unto you, rising early and speaking; [b]but ye have not hearkened.

4 And the LORD hath sent unto you all his servants the prophets, [a]rising early and sending *them;* but ye have not hearkened, nor inclined your ear to hear. R

5 They said, [a]Turn ye again now every one from his evil way, and from the evil of your doings, and dwell in the land that the LORD hath given unto you and to your fathers for ever and ever:

6 And go not after other gods to serve them, and to worship them, and provoke me not to anger with the works of your hands; and I will do you no hurt.

7 Yet ye have not hearkened unto me, saith the LORD; that ye might [a]provoke me to anger with the works of your hands to your own hurt.

8 ¶ Therefore thus saith the LORD of hosts; Because ye have not heard my words,

9 Behold, I will send and take [a]all the

R *Jer 18:11* ◀ ▶ *Jer 26:13*

24:1–10 Jeremiah likened Judah to a basket of figs, a symbolic usage that occurs several times in Scripture (see 8:13; Mic 7:1; Na 3:12). The "good figs" symbolized people of Judah who repented of their sins while in captivity and who would be returned to their land. The "bad figs" symbolized the people who would not repent of their sins and who would "be consumed from off the land" (24:10).

families of the north, saith the LORD, and
Nebuchadrezzar the king of Babylon, [b]my
servant, and will bring them against this
land, and against the inhabitants thereof,
and against all these nations round about,
and will utterly destroy them, and [c]make
them an astonishment, and an hissing,
and perpetual desolations.
10 Moreover ′I will take from them
the [a]voice of mirth, and the voice of gladness, the voice of the bridegroom, and
the voice of the bride, [b]the sound of the
millstones, and the light of the candle.
11 And this whole land shall be a desolation, *and* an astonishment; and these
nations shall serve the king of Babylon
seventy years.
I 12 ¶ And it shall come to pass, [a]when
seventy years are accomplished, *that* I
will ′punish the king of Babylon, and that
nation, saith the LORD, for their iniquity,
and the land of the Chaldeans, [b]and will
make it perpetual desolations.
13 And I will bring upon that land all
my words which I have pronounced
against it, *even* all that is written in this
book, which Jeremiah hath prophesied
against all the nations.
14 [a]For many nations [b]and great kings
shall [c]serve themselves of them also:
[d]and I will recompense them according
to their deeds, and according to the
works of their own hands.

The cup of fury

15 ¶ For thus saith the LORD God of
Israel unto me; Take the [a]wine cup of
this fury at my hand, and cause all the
nations, to whom I send thee, to drink it.
16 And [a]they shall drink, and be
moved, and be mad, because of the
sword that I will send among them.
R 17 Then took I the cup at the LORD'S
hand, and made all the nations to drink,
unto whom the LORD had sent me:
18 *To wit,* Jerusalem, and the cities of
Judah, and the kings thereof, and the
princes thereof, to make them [a]a desolation, an astonishment, an hissing, and [b]a
curse; as *it is* this day;
19 Pharaoh king of Egypt, and his servants, and his princes, and all his people;
20 And all the mingled people, and all
the kings of [a]the land of Uz, and all the
kings of the land of the Philistines, and
Ashkelon, and Azzah, and Ekron, and
[b]the remnant of Ashdod,
21 [a]Edom, and Moab, and the children
of Ammon,
22 And all the kings of [a]Tyrus, and all
the kings of Zidon, and the kings of the
′isles which *are* beyond the [b]sea,
23 [a]Dedan, and Tema, and Buz, and all
′*that are* in the utmost corners,
24 And all the kings of Arabia, and all
the kings of the [a]mingled people that
dwell in the desert,
25 And all the kings of Zimri, and all
the kings of Elam, and all the kings of the
Medes,
26 [a]And all the kings of the north, far
and near, one with another, and all the
kingdoms of the world, which *are* upon
the face of the earth: and the king of She-
shach shall drink after them.
27 Therefore thou shalt say unto them,
Thus saith the LORD of hosts, the God of
Israel; [a]Drink ye, and [b]be drunken, and
spew, and fall, and rise no more, because
of the sword which I will send among
you.
28 And it shall be, if they refuse to
take the cup at thine hand to drink, then
shalt thou say unto them, Thus saith the
LORD of hosts; Ye shall certainly drink.
29 For, lo, [a]I begin to bring evil on the P
city [b]which′ is called by my name, and

9 [b]ch. 27:6; Is. 45:1 [c]ch. 18:16
10 [a]Is. 24:7; Hos. 2:11; Rev. 18:23 [b]Eccl. 12:4 ′Heb. *I will cause to perish from them*
12 [a]2 Chr. 36:21, 22; Ezra 1:1; Dan. 9:2 [b]Is. 21:1; ch. 50:3 ′Heb. *visit upon*
14 [a]ch. 50:9 & 51:27,28 [b]ch. 51:27 [c]ch. 27:7 [d]ch. 50:29 & 51:6, 24
15 [a]Job 21:20; Ps. 75:8; Is. 51:17; Rev. 14:10
16 [a]ch. 51:7; Ezek. 23:34; Nah. 3:11
18 [a]ver. 9,11 [b]ch. 24:9
20 [a]Job 1:1 [b]Is. 20:1
21 [a]ch. 49:7
22 [a]ch. 47:4 [b]ch. 49:23 ′Or, *region by the sea side*
23 [a]ch. 49:8 ′Heb. *cut off into corners,* or, *having the corners* of the hair *polled;* see ch. 9:26
24 [a]Ezek. 30:5
26 [a]ch. 50:9
27 [a]Hab. 2:16 [b]Is. 63:6
29 [a]Ezek. 9:6; Luke 23:31; 1 Pet. 4:17 [b]Dan. 9:18 ′Heb. *upon which my name is called*

I *Jer 23:3–8* ◀▶ *Jer 30:1–3*
R *Jer 23:39–40* ◀▶ *Jer 26:3*
P *Jer 23:19–20* ◀▶ *Jer 30:23–24*

25:11–13 Jeremiah delivered one of the most significant prophecies of the OT in this passage, clearly stating who would conquer Judah and how long Judah would be in exile. Since the nation had not followed God's command to let the land lie unplowed every seven years, the seventy-year captivity in Babylon would give the land its Sabbaths (see 2Ch 36:21). God also declared that following this seventy-year captivity he would punish the Babylonians for their pagan idolatry and savage treatment of his people. These prophecies were fulfilled when Nebuchadnezzar conquered Judah in 606 B.C. and when seventy years later Cyrus, the king of Persia, issued his proclamation allowing the exiles to return to the promised land (see Ezr 1:1–4; Da 9:2).
25:17–18 Jeremiah refers to "the cup" of punishment that God required him to offer to the kings, princes, the cities and Jerusalem itself.
25:29–33 The prophet looks forward to the end of this age when God will unleash his wrath from

should ye be utterly unpunished? Ye shall not be unpunished: for [c]I will call for a sword upon all the inhabitants of the earth, saith the LORD of hosts.

30 Therefore prophesy thou against them all these words, and say unto them, The LORD shall [a]roar from on high, and utter his voice from [b]his holy habitation; he shall mightily roar upon [c]his habitation; he shall give [d]a shout, as they that tread *the grapes,* against all the inhabitants of the earth.

31 A noise shall come *even* to the ends of the earth; for the LORD hath [a]a controversy with the nations, [b]he will plead with all flesh; he will give them *that are* wicked to the sword, saith the LORD.

32 Thus saith the LORD of hosts, Behold, evil shall go forth from nation to nation, and [a]a great whirlwind shall be raised up from the coasts of the earth.

33 [a]And the slain of the LORD shall be at that day from *one* end of the earth even unto the *other* end of the earth: they shall not be [b]lamented, [c]neither gathered, nor buried; they shall be dung upon the ground.

34 ¶ [a]Howl, ye shepherds, and cry; and wallow yourselves *in the ashes,* ye principal of the flock: for [1]the days of your slaughter and of your dispersions are accomplished; and ye shall fall like [2]a pleasant vessel.

35 And the shepherds shall have no way to flee, nor the principal of the flock to escape.

36 A voice of the cry of the shepherds, and an howling of the principal of the flock, *shall be heard:* for the LORD hath spoiled their pasture.

37 And the peaceable habitations are cut down because of the fierce anger of the LORD.

38 He hath forsaken his covert, as the lion: for their land is [1]desolate because of the fierceness of the oppressor, and because of his fierce anger.

29 [c]Ezek. 38:21
30 [a]Is. 42:13; Joel 3:16; Amos 1:2 [b]Ps. 11:4 [c]1 Ki. 9:3; Ps. 132:14 [d]Is. 16:9; ch. 48:33
31 [a]Hos. 4:1; Mic. 6:2 [b]Is. 66:16; Joel 3:2
32 [a]ch. 23:19 & 30:23
33 [a]Is. 66:16 [b]ch. 16:4,6 [c]Ps. 79:3; ch. 8:2; Rev. 11:9
34 [a]ch. 4:8 & 6:26 [1]Heb. *your days for slaughter* [2]Heb. *a vessel of desire*
38 [1]Heb. *a desolation*
26:2 [a]ch. 19:14 [b]Ezek. 3:10; Mat. 28:20 [c]Acts 20:27
3 [a]ch. 36:3 [b]ch. 18:8; Jonah 3:8,9
4 [a]Lev. 26:14; Deut. 28:15
5 [a]ch. 7:13,25 & 11:7 & 25:3,4
6 [a]1 Sam. 4:10,11; Ps. 78:60; ch. 7:12, 14 [b]Is. 65:15; ch. 24:9

Jeremiah arrested and released

26 IN THE beginning of the reign of Jehoiakim the son of Josiah king of Judah came this word from the LORD, saying,

2 Thus saith the LORD; Stand in [a]the court of the LORD'S house, and speak unto all the cities of Judah, which come to worship in the LORD'S house, [b]all the words that I command thee to speak unto them; [c]diminish not a word:

3 [a]If so be they will hearken, and turn every man from his evil way, that I may [b]repent me of the evil, which I purpose to do unto them because of the evil of their doings. R

4 And thou shalt say unto them, Thus saith the LORD; [a]If ye will not hearken to me, to walk in my law, which I have set before you,

5 To hearken to the words of my servants the prophets, [a]whom I sent unto you, both rising up early, and sending *them,* but ye have not hearkened;

6 Then will I make this house like [a]Shiloh, and will make this city [b]a curse to all the nations of the earth. R

7 So the priests and the prophets and all the people heard Jeremiah speaking these words in the house of the LORD.

8 ¶ Now it came to pass, when Jeremiah had made an end of speaking all that the LORD had commanded *him* to speak unto all the people, that the priests and the prophets and all the people took him, saying, Thou shalt surely die.

9 Why hast thou prophesied in the name of the LORD, saying, This house shall be like Shiloh, and this city shall be desolate without an inhabitant? And all the people were gathered against Jeremiah in the house of the LORD.

10 ¶ When the princes of Judah heard these things, then they came up from the king's house unto the house of the LORD,

R *Jer 25:17–18* ◀ ▶ *Jer 26:6*
R *Jer 26:3* ◀ ▶ *Jer 26:20*

---

heaven "against all the inhabitants of the earth" (25:30). Note the parallel between this prophecy and Isa 63:1–4. The slaughter during this tribulation will be horrific. Jeremiah states that the dead will cover the earth from one end to the other, indicating that there will be too many bodies to be buried in a timely manner (see Isa 66:16; Rev 19:14–21).

26:6 Shiloh, the former site of the tabernacle and once the home to the ark of the covenant, was only a ruin in Jeremiah's day because Israel's refusal to repent had brought about its destruction.

and sat down [l]in the entry of the new gate of the LORD'S *house.*

11 Then spake the priests and the prophets unto the princes and to all the people, saying, [l]This man *is* worthy to die; [a]for he hath prophesied against this city, as ye have heard with your ears.

12 ¶ Then spake Jeremiah unto all the princes and to all the people, saying, The LORD sent me to prophesy against this house and against this city all the words that ye have heard.

L R 13 Therefore now [a]amend your ways and your doings, and obey the voice of the LORD your God; and the LORD will [b]repent him of the evil that he hath pronounced against you.

14 As for me, behold, [a]I *am* in your hand: do with me [l]as seemeth good and meet unto you.

15 But know ye for certain, that if ye put me to death, ye shall surely bring innocent blood upon yourselves, and upon this city, and upon the inhabitants thereof: for of a truth the LORD hath sent me unto you to speak all these words in your ears.

16 ¶ Then said the princes and all the people unto the priests and to the prophets; This man *is* not worthy to die: for he hath spoken to us in the name of the LORD our God.

17 [a]Then rose up certain of the elders of the land, and spake to all the assembly of the people, saying,

18 [a]Micah the Morasthite prophesied in the days of Hezekiah king of Judah, and spake to all the people of Judah, saying, Thus saith the LORD of hosts; [b]Zion shall be plowed *like* a field, and Jerusalem shall become heaps, and the mountain of the house as the high places of a forest.

19 Did Hezekiah king of Judah and all Judah put him at all to death? [a]did he not fear the LORD, and besought [l]the LORD, and the LORD [b]repented him of the evil which he had pronounced against them? [c]Thus might we procure great evil against our souls.

20 And there was also a man that prophesied in the name of the LORD, Urijah the son of Shemaiah of Kirjath-jearim, who prophesied against this city and against this land according to all the words of Jeremiah: R

21 And when Jehoiakim the king, with all his mighty men, and all the princes, heard his words, the king sought to put him to death: but when Urijah heard it, he was afraid, and fled, and went into Egypt;

22 And Jehoiakim the king sent men into Egypt, *namely,* Elnathan the son of Achbor, and *certain* men with him into Egypt.

23 And they fetched forth Urijah out of Egypt, and brought him unto Jehoiakim the king; who slew him with the sword, and cast his dead body into the graves of the [l]common people.

24 Nevertheless [a]the hand of Ahikam the son of Shaphan was with Jeremiah, that they should not give him into the hand of the people to put him to death.

Nebuchadnezzar's victory

27 IN THE beginning of the reign of Jehoiakim the son of Josiah [a]king of Judah came this word unto Jeremiah from the LORD, saying,

2 Thus [l]saith the LORD to me; Make thee bonds and yokes, [a]and put them upon thy neck,

3 And send them to the king of Edom, and to the king of Moab, and to the king of the Ammonites, and to the king of Tyrus, and to the king of Zidon, by the hand of the messengers which come to Jerusalem unto Zedekiah king of Judah;

4 And command them [l]to say unto their masters, Thus saith the LORD of hosts, the God of Israel; Thus shall ye say unto your masters;

10 [l]Or, *at the door*
11 [a]ch. 38:4 [l]Heb. *The judgment of death* is *for this man*
13 [a]ch. 7:3 [b]ver. 3,19
14 [a]ch. 38:5 [l]Heb. *as it is good and right in your eyes*
17 [a]See Acts 5:34
18 [a]Mic. 1:1 [b]Mic. 3:12
19 [a]2 Chr. 32:26 [b]Ex. 32:14; 2 Sam. 24:16 [c]Acts 5:39 [l]Heb. *the face of the LORD*
23 [l]Heb. *sons of the people*
24 [a]2 Ki. 22:12,14; ch. 39:14
27:1 [a]See ver. 3, 12,20; ch. 28:1
2 [a]ch. 28:10,12; Ezek. 4:1 & 12:3 & 24:3 [l]Or, *hath the LORD said*
4 [l]Or, *concerning their masters, saying*

L *Jer 21:8* ◀ ▶ *Jer 29:13*
R *Jer 25:4–5* ◀ ▶ *Jer 29:12–13*
R *Jer 26:6* ◀ ▶ *Jer 30:7*

26:18–24 Some of the princes wanted to kill Jeremiah because of his predictions of coming judgment. Yet the more righteous leaders of the court reminded the people that Micah had prophesied in a similar manner during the reign of King Hezekiah. King Hezekiah and his people responded in repentance and God delayed their punishment. These leaders also pointed out that the prophet Urijah had also prophesied judgment on Judah, but King Jehoiakim had killed him. A righteous man named Ahikam, a friend of King Josiah, came to Jeremiah's defense and persuaded the princes to let Jeremiah live. Note that Ahikam's son later became Nebuchadnezzar's governor of Judah (see 40:5; 2Ki 22:12).

5 [a]I have made the earth, the man and the beast that *are* upon the ground, by my great power and by my outstretched arm, and [b]have given it unto whom it seemed meet unto me.

6 [a]And now have I given all these lands into the hand of Nebuchadnezzar the king of Babylon, [b]my servant; and [c]the beasts of the field have I given him also to serve him.

7 [a]And all nations shall serve him, and his son, and his son's son, [b]until the very time of his land come: [c]and then many nations and great kings shall serve themselves of him.

8 And it shall come to pass, *that* the nation and kingdom which will not serve the same Nebuchadnezzar the king of Babylon, and that will not put their neck under the yoke of the king of Babylon, that nation will I punish, saith the LORD, with the sword, and with the famine, and with the pestilence, until I have consumed them by his hand.

9 Therefore hearken not ye to your prophets, nor to your diviners, nor to your [/]dreamers, nor to your enchanters, nor to your sorcerers, which speak unto you, saying, Ye shall not serve the king of Babylon:

10 [a]For they prophesy a lie unto you, to remove you far from your land; and that I should drive you out, and ye should perish.

11 But the nations that bring their neck under the yoke of the king of Babylon, and serve him, those will I let remain still in their own land, saith the LORD; and they shall till it, and dwell therein.

12 ¶ I spake also to [a]Zedekiah king of Judah according to all these words, saying, Bring your necks under the yoke of the king of Babylon, and serve him and his people, and live.

13 [a]Why will ye die, thou and thy people, by the sword, by the famine, and by the pestilence, as the LORD hath spoken against the nation that will not serve the king of Babylon?

14 Therefore hearken not unto the words of the prophets that speak unto you, saying, Ye shall not serve the king of Babylon: for they prophesy [a]a lie unto you.

15 For I have not sent them, saith the LORD, yet they prophesy [/]a lie in my name; that I might drive you out, and that ye might perish, ye, and the prophets that prophesy unto you.

16 Also I spake to the priests and to all this people, saying, Thus saith the LORD; Hearken not to the words of your prophets that prophesy unto you, saying, Behold, [a]the vessels of the LORD'S house shall now shortly be brought again from Babylon: for they prophesy a lie unto you.

17 Hearken not unto them; serve the king of Babylon, and live: wherefore should this city be laid waste?

18 But if they *be* prophets, and if the word of the LORD be with them, let them now make intercession to the LORD of hosts, that the vessels which are left in the house of the LORD, and *in* the house of the king of Judah, and at Jerusalem, go not to Babylon.

19 ¶ For thus saith the LORD of hosts [a]concerning the pillars, and concerning the sea, and concerning the bases, and concerning the residue of the vessels that remain in this city,

20 Which Nebuchadnezzar king of Babylon took not, when he carried away [a]captive Jeconiah the son of Jehoiakim king of Judah from Jerusalem to Babylon, and all the nobles of Judah and Jerusalem;

21 Yea, thus saith the LORD of hosts, the God of Israel, concerning the vessels that remain *in* the house of the LORD, and *in* the house of the king of Judah and of Jerusalem;

22 They shall be [a]carried to Babylon, and there shall they be until the day that I [b]visit them, saith the LORD; then [c]will I bring them up, and restore them to this place. J

Jeremiah exposes Hananiah

28 AND [a]IT came to pass the same year, in the beginning of the reign of Zedekiah king of Judah, in the fourth year, *and* in the fifth month, *that* Hananiah the son of Azur the prophet, which *was* of Gibeon, spake unto me in the house of the LORD, in the presence of the priests and of all the people, saying,

2 Thus speaketh the LORD of hosts, the God of Israel, saying, I have broken [a]the yoke of the king of Babylon.

3 [a]Within [/]two full years will I bring again into this place all the vessels of the

5 [a]Ps. 115:15 & 146:6; Is. 45:12 [b]Ps. 115:16; Dan. 4:17,25,32
6 [a]ch. 28:14 [b]ch. 25:9 & 43:10; Ezek. 29:18,20 [c]ch. 28:14; Dan. 2:38
7 [a]2 Chr. 36:20 [b]ch. 25:12 & 50:27; Dan. 5:26 [c]ch. 25:14
9 [/]Heb. *dreams*
10 [a]ver. 14
12 [a]ch. 28:1 & 38:17
13 [a]Ezek. 18:31
14 [a]ch. 14:14 & 23:21 & 29:8,9
15 [/]Heb. *in a lie,* or, *lyingly*
16 [a]2 Chr. 36:7, 10; ch. 28:3; Dan. 1:2
19 [a]2 Ki. 25:13; ch. 52:17,20,21
20 [a]2 Ki. 24:14,15; ch. 24:1
22 [a]2 Ki. 25:13; 2 Chr. 36:18 [b]2 Chr. 36:21; ch. 29:10 & 32:5 [c]Ezra 1:7 & 7:19
28:1 [a]ch. 27:1
2 [a]ch. 27:12
3 [a]ch. 27:16 [/]Heb. *two years of days*

J *Jer 11:20* ◄ ► *Jer 28:16*

LORD'S house, that Nebuchadnezzar king
of Babylon took away from this place, and
carried them to Babylon:
4 And I will bring again to this place
Jeconiah the son of Jehoiakim king of Judah, with all the [l]captives of Judah, that
went into Babylon, saith the LORD: for I
will break the yoke of the king of
Babylon.
5 ¶ Then the prophet Jeremiah said
unto the prophet Hananiah in the presence of the priests, and in the presence of
all the people that stood in the house of
the LORD,
6 Even the prophet Jeremiah said,
[a]Amen: the LORD do so: the LORD perform
thy words which thou hast prophesied,
to bring again the vessels of the LORD'S
house, and all that is carried away captive, from Babylon into this place.
7 Nevertheless hear thou now this
word that I speak in thine ears, and in the
ears of all the people;
8 The prophets that have been before
me and before thee of old prophesied
both against many countries, and against
great kingdoms, of war, and of evil, and
of pestilence.
9 [a]The prophet which prophesieth of
peace, when the word of the prophet
shall come to pass, *then* shall the prophet
be known, that the LORD hath truly sent
him.
10 ¶ Then Hananiah the prophet took
the [a]yoke from off the prophet Jeremiah's
neck, and brake it.
11 And Hananiah spake in the presence of all the people, saying, Thus saith
the LORD; Even so will I break the yoke of
Nebuchadnezzar king of Babylon [a]from
the neck of all nations within the space of
two full years. And the prophet Jeremiah
went his way.
12 ¶ Then the word of the LORD came
unto Jeremiah *the prophet,* after that
Hananiah the prophet had broken the
yoke from off the neck of the prophet Jeremiah, saying,
13 Go and tell Hananiah, saying, Thus
saith the LORD; Thou hast broken the
yokes of wood; but thou shalt make for
them yokes of iron.
14 For thus saith the LORD of hosts, the
God of Israel; [a]I have put a yoke of iron
upon the neck of all these nations, that
they may serve Nebuchadnezzar king of
Babylon; and they shall serve him: and [b]I
have given him the beasts of the field
also.
15 ¶ Then said the prophet Jeremiah
unto Hananiah the prophet, Hear now,
Hananiah; The LORD hath not sent thee;
but [a]thou makest this people to trust in a
lie.
16 Therefore thus saith the LORD; Be- J
hold, I will cast thee from off the face of
the earth: this year thou shalt die, because thou hast taught [a]rebellion[l] against
the LORD.
17 So Hananiah the prophet died the
same year in the seventh month.

A letter to the captives

29 NOW THESE *are* the words of
the letter that Jeremiah the
prophet sent from Jerusalem unto the
residue of the elders which were carried
away captives, and to the priests, and to
the prophets, and to all the people whom
Nebuchadnezzar had carried away captive from Jerusalem to Babylon;
2 (After that [a]Jeconiah the king, and
the queen, and the [l]eunuchs, the princes
of Judah and Jerusalem, and the carpenters, and the smiths, were departed from
Jerusalem;)
3 By the hand of Elasah the son of Shaphan, and Gemariah the son of Hilkiah,
(whom Zedekiah king of Judah sent unto
Babylon to Nebuchadnezzar king of Babylon) saying,
4 Thus saith the LORD of hosts, the God
of Israel, unto all that are carried away
captives, whom I have caused to be carried away from Jerusalem unto Babylon;
5 [a]Build ye houses, and dwell *in them;*
and plant gardens, and eat the fruit of
them;
6 Take ye wives, and beget sons and
daughters; and take wives for your sons,
and give your daughters to husbands, that
they may bear sons and daughters; that
ye may be increased there, and not diminished.
7 And seek the peace of the city
whither I have caused you to be carried
away captives, [a]and pray unto the LORD
for it: for in the peace thereof shall ye
have peace.
8 ¶ For thus saith the LORD of hosts, the
God of Israel; Let not your prophets and
your diviners, that *be* in the midst of you,

4 [l]Heb. *captivity*
6 [a]1 Ki. 1:36
9 [a]Deut. 18:22
10 [a]ch. 27:2
11 [a]ch. 27:7
14 [a]Deut. 28:48; ch. 27:7 [b]ch. 27:6
15 [a]ch. 29:31; Ezek. 13:22
16 [a]Deut. 13:5; ch. 29:32 [l]Heb. *revolt*
29:2 [a]2 Ki. 24:12; ch. 22:26 & 28:4 [l]Or, *chamberlains*
5 [a]ver. 28
7 [a]Ezra 6:10; 1 Tim. 2:2

J *Jer 27:22* ◄ ► *Jer 29:21–22*

[a]deceive you, neither hearken to your
dreams which ye cause to be dreamed.
9 [a]For they prophesy [/]falsely unto you
in my name: I have not sent them, saith
the LORD.
10 ¶ For thus saith the LORD, That after
[a]seventy years be accomplished at Babylon I will visit you, and perform my good
word toward you, in causing you to return to this place.
P 11 For I know the thoughts that I think
toward you, saith the LORD, thoughts of
peace, and not of evil, to give you an [/]ex-
pected end.
M 12 Then shall ye [a]call upon me, and ye
R shall go and pray unto me, and I will
hearken unto you.
L 13 And [a]ye shall seek me, and find *me*,
when ye shall search for me [b]with all
your heart.
14 And [a]I will be found of you, saith
the LORD: and I will turn away your captivity, and [b]I will gather you from all the
nations, and from all the places whither I
have driven you, saith the LORD; and I will
bring you again into the place whence I
caused you to be carried away captive.
15 ¶ Because ye have said, The LORD
hath raised us up prophets in Babylon;
16 *Know* that thus saith the LORD of the
king that sitteth upon the throne of David, and of all the people that dwelleth in
this city, *and* of your brethren that are
not gone forth with you into captivity;
17 Thus saith the LORD of hosts; Behold, I will send upon them the sword,
the famine, and the pestilence, and will
make them like [a]vile figs, that cannot be
eaten, they are so evil.
18 And I will persecute them with the
sword, with the famine, and with the
pestilence, and [a]will deliver them to be
removed to all the kingdoms of the earth,
[/]to be [b]a curse, and an astonishment, and
an hissing, and a reproach, among all the
nations whither I have driven them:
19 Because they have not hearkened
to my words, saith the LORD, which [a]I
sent unto them by my servants the prophets, rising up early and sending *them;* but
ye would not hear, saith the LORD.
20 ¶ Hear ye therefore the word of the

P *Jer 4:1* ◀ ▶ *Jer 31:3*
M *Jer 13:15–17* ◀ ▶ *Jer 49:16*
R *Jer 26:13* ◀ ▶ *Jer 36:3*
L *Jer 26:13* ◀ ▶ *Jer 31:3*

8 [a]ch. 14:14 & 23:21 & 27:14,15; Eph. 5:6
9 [a]ver. 31 [/]Heb. *in a lie*
10 [a]2 Chr. 36:21, 22; Ezra 1:1; ch. 25:12 & 27:22; Dan. 9:2
11 [/]Heb. *end and expectation*
12 [a]Dan. 9:3
13 [a]Lev. 26:39,40; Deut. 30:1 [b]ch. 24:7
14 [a]Deut. 4:7; Ps. 32:6 & 46:1; Is. 55:6 [b]ch. 23:3,8 & 30:3 & 32:37
17 [a]ch. 24:8
18 [a]Deut. 28:25; 2 Chr. 29:8; ch. 15:4 & 24:9 & 34:17 [b]ch. 26:6 & 42:18 [/]Heb. *for a curse*
19 [a]ch. 25:4 & 32:33
22 [a]See Gen. 48:20; Is. 65:15 [b]Dan. 3:6
23 [a]ch. 23:14
24 [/]Or, *dreamer*
25 [a]2 Ki. 25:18; ch. 21:1
26 [a]ch. 20:1 [b]2 Ki. 9:11; Acts 26:24 [c]ch. 20:2
28 [a]ver. 5
31 [a]ch. 28:15

LORD, all ye of the captivity, whom I have
sent from Jerusalem to Babylon:
21 Thus saith the LORD of hosts, the J
God of Israel, of Ahab the son of Kolaiah,
and of Zedekiah the son of Maaseiah,
which prophesy a lie unto you in my
name; Behold, I will deliver them into
the hand of Nebuchadrezzar king of Babylon; and he shall slay them before your
eyes;
22 [a]And of them shall be taken up a
curse by all the captivity of Judah which
are in Babylon, saying, The LORD make
thee like Zedekiah and like Ahab, [b]whom
the king of Babylon roasted in the fire;
23 Because [a]they have committed vil-
lainy in Israel, and have committed adultery with their neighbours' wives, and
have spoken lying words in my name,
which I have not commanded them; even
I know, and *am* a witness, saith the LORD.

A letter to Shemaiah

24 ¶ *Thus* shalt thou also speak to Shemaiah the [/]Nehelamite, saying,
25 Thus speaketh the LORD of hosts,
the God of Israel, saying, Because thou
hast sent letters in thy name unto all the
people that *are* at Jerusalem, [a]and to
Zephaniah the son of Maaseiah the
priest, and to all the priests, saying,
26 The LORD hath made thee priest in
the stead of Jehoiada the priest, that ye
should be [a]officers in the house of the
LORD, for every man *that is* [b]mad, and
maketh himself a prophet, that thou
shouldest [c]put him in prison, and in the
stocks.
27 Now therefore why hast thou not
reproved Jeremiah of Anathoth, which
maketh himself a prophet to you?
28 For therefore he sent unto us *in*
Babylon, saying, This *captivity is* long:
[a]build ye houses, and dwell *in them;* and
plant gardens, and eat the fruit of them.
29 And Zephaniah the priest read this
letter in the ears of Jeremiah the prophet.
30 ¶ Then came the word of the LORD
unto Jeremiah, saying,
31 Send to all them of the captivity,
saying, Thus saith the LORD concerning
Shemaiah the Nehelamite; Because that
Shemaiah hath prophesied unto you,
[a]and I sent him not, and he caused you to
trust in a lie:

J *Jer 28:16* ◀ ▶ *Jer 29:32*

J 32 Therefore thus saith the LORD; Behold, I will punish Shemaiah the Nehelamite, and his seed: he shall not have a man to dwell among this people; neither shall he behold the good that I will do for my people, saith the LORD; [a]because he hath taught ʹrebellion against the LORD.

Restoration of Israel

I 30 THE WORD that came to Jeremiah from the LORD, saying,

2 Thus speaketh the LORD God of Israel, saying, Write thee all the words that I have spoken unto thee in a book.

3 For, lo, the days come, saith the LORD, that [a]I will bring again the captivity of my people Israel and Judah, saith the LORD: [b]and I will cause them to return to the land that I gave to their fathers, and they shall possess it.

4 ¶ And these *are* the words that the LORD spake concerning Israel and concerning Judah.

5 For thus saith the LORD; We have heard a voice of trembling, ʹof fear, and not of peace.

6 Ask ye now, and see whether ʹa man doth travail with child? wherefore do I see every man with his hands on his loins, [a]as a woman in travail, and all faces are turned into paleness?

I R 7 [a]Alas! for that day *is* great, [b]so that none *is* like it: it *is* even the time of Jacob's trouble; but he shall be saved out of it.

8 For it shall come to pass in that day, saith the LORD of hosts, *that* I will break his yoke from off thy neck, and will burst thy bonds, and strangers shall no more serve themselves of him:

M 9 But they shall serve the LORD their God, and [a]David their king, whom I will [b]raise up unto them.

10 ¶ Therefore [a]fear thou not, O my servant Jacob, saith the LORD; neither be dismayed, O Israel: for, lo, I will save thee from afar, and thy seed [b]from the land of their captivity; and Jacob shall return, and shall be in rest, and be quiet, and none shall make *him* afraid.

11 For I *am* with thee, saith the LORD, to save thee: [a]though I make a full end of all nations whither I have scattered thee, [b]yet will I not make a full end of thee: but I will correct thee [c]in measure, and will not leave thee altogether unpunished.

12 For thus saith the LORD, [a]Thy bruise *is* incurable, *and* thy wound *is* grievous. G

13 *There is* none to plead thy cause, ʹthat thou mayest be bound up: [a]thou hast no healing medicines.

14 [a]All thy lovers have forgotten thee; I they seek thee not; for I have wounded thee with the wound [b]of an enemy, with the chastisement [c]of a cruel one, for the multitude of thine iniquity; [d]*because* thy sins were increased.

15 Why [a]criest thou for thine affliction? thy sorrow *is* incurable for the multitude of thine iniquity: *because* thy sins were increased, I have done these things unto thee.

16 Therefore all they that devour thee [a]shall be devoured; and all thine adversaries, every one of them, shall go into captivity; and they that spoil thee shall be a spoil, and all that prey upon thee will I give for a prey.

17 [a]For I will restore health unto thee, I and I will heal thee of thy wounds, saith R the LORD; because they called thee an Outcast, *saying,* This *is* Zion, whom no man seeketh after.

18 ¶ Thus saith the LORD; Behold, [a]I

32 [a]ch. 28:16 ʹHeb. *revolt*
30:3 [a]ver. 18; ch. 32:44; Ezek. 39:25; Amos 9:14,15 [b]ch. 16:15
5 ʹOr, there is *fear, and not peace*
6 [a]ch. 4:31 & 6:24 ʹHeb. *a male*
7 [a]Joel 2:11,31; Amos 5:18; Zeph. 1:14 [b]Dan. 12:1
9 [a]Is. 55:3,4; Ezek. 34:23 & 37:24; Hos. 3:5 [b]Luke 1:69; Acts 2:30 & 13:23
10 [a]Is. 41:13 & 43:5 & 44:2; ch. 46:27,28 [b]ch. 3:18
11 [a]Amos 9:8 [b]ch. 4:27 [c]Ps. 6:1; Is. 27:8; ch. 10:24 & 46:28
12 [a]2 Chr. 36:16; ch. 15:18
13 [a]ch. 8:22 ʹHeb. *for binding up,* or, *pressing*
14 [a]Lam. 1:2 [b]Job 13:24 & 16:9 & 19:11 [c]Job 30:21 [d]ch. 5:6
15 [a]ch. 15:18
16 [a]Ex. 23:22; Is. 33:1 & 41:11; ch. 10:25
17 [a]ch. 33:6
18 [a]ver. 3; ch. 33:7,11

J Jer 29:21–22 ◀▶ Jer 44:30
I Jer 25:12 ◀▶ Jer 30:7–10
I Jer 30:1–3 ◀▶ Jer 30:14
R Jer 26:20 ◀▶ Jer 30:17
M Jer 23:5–6 ◀▶ Jer 33:15
G Jer 18:13–15 ◀▶ Jer 46:11
I Jer 30:7–10 ◀▶ Jer 30:17–22
I Jer 30:14 ◀▶ Jer 31:1
R Jer 30:7 ◀▶ Jer 34:22

30:1–3 Jeremiah recorded God's solemn promise to end the captivity of his people and bring them back to the land. Note God's promise that they would "possess" the land, reaffirming God's covenant with Abraham (see note at Ge 15:4).

30:7–11 In this prophetic passage, Jeremiah declared God's plan to redeem Israel in the last days. Despite "the time of Jacob's trouble" (30:7) and punishment for Israel's sins, Jeremiah prophesied that God would deliver his people and "not make a full end of thee" (30:11). God will remove the "yoke" of Israel's enemies and give Israel rest and safety under the rule of the Messiah.

30:17–24 Jeremiah prophesied that despite God's judgment on the sins of Judah, God would ultimately restore Jerusalem.

will bring again the captivity of Jacob's
tents, and [b]have mercy on his dwellingplaces; and the city shall be builded upon
her own [1]heap, and the palace shall remain after the manner thereof.
19 And [a]out of them shall proceed
thanksgiving and the voice of them that
make merry: [b]and I will multiply them,
and they shall not be few; I will also glorify them, and they shall not be small.
20 Their children also shall be [a]as
aforetime, and their congregation shall be
established before me, and I will punish
all that oppress them.
21 And their nobles shall be of themselves, [a]and their governor shall proceed
from the midst of them; and I will [b]cause
him to draw near, and he shall approach
unto me: for who *is* this that engaged his
heart to approach unto me? saith the
LORD.
22 And ye shall be [a]my people, and I
will be your God.
P 23 Behold, the [a]whirlwind of the LORD
H goeth forth with fury, a [1]continuing
whirlwind: it shall [2]fall with pain upon
the head of the wicked.
24 The fierce anger of the LORD shall
not return, until he have done *it,* and until he have performed the intents of his
heart: [a]in the latter days ye shall consider it.
I 31 AT [a]THE same time, saith the
LORD, [b]will I be the God of all the
families of Israel, and they shall be my
people.
2 Thus saith the LORD, The people
which were left of the sword found grace
in the wilderness; *even* Israel, when [a]I
went to cause him to rest.
I 3 The LORD hath appeared [1]of old unto
L
P
L

P *Jer 25:29–33* ◀▶ *Jer 45:5*
H *Jer 23:40* ◀▶ *Jer 36:7*
I *Jer 30:17–22* ◀▶ *Jer 31:3–14*
I *Jer 31:1* ◀▶ *Jer 31:28–29*
L *Jer 29:13* ◀▶ *Jer 31:20*
P *Jer 29:11–13* ◀▶ *Jer 31:20*
L *Isa 63:9* ◀▶ *Da 3:25*

18 [b]Ps. 102:13 [1]Or, *little hill*
19 [a]Is. 51:11 [b]Zech. 10:8
20 [a]Is. 1:26
21 [a]Gen. 49:10 [b]Num. 16:5
22 [a]ch. 31:1,33
23 [a]ch. 23:19 & 25:32 [1]Heb. *cutting* [2]Or, *remain*
24 [a]Gen. 49:1
31:1 [a]ch. 30:24 [b]ch. 30:22
2 [a]Num. 10:33; Deut. 1:33; Ps. 95:11; Is. 63:14
3 [a]Mal. 1:2 [b]Rom. 11:28 [c]Hos. 11:4 [1]Heb. *from afar* [2]Or, *have I extended lovingkindness unto thee*
4 [a]ch. 33:7 [b]Ex. 15:20; Judg. 11:34; Ps. 149:3 [1]Or, *timbrels*
5 [a]Is. 65:21; Amos 9:14 [b]Deut. 20:6 [1]Heb. *profane* them
6 [a]Is. 2:3; Mic. 4:2
7 [a]Is. 12:5,6
8 [a]ch. 3:12,18 & 23:8 [b]Ezek. 20:34, 41 & 34:13
9 [a]ch. 50:4 [b]Zech. 12:10 [c]Is. 35:8 & 43:19 & 49:10,11 [d]Ex. 4:22 [1]Or, *favours*
10 [a]Is. 40:11; Ezek. 34:12-14
11 [a]Is. 44:23 & 48:20 [b]Is. 49:24
12 [a]Ezek. 17:23 [b]Hos. 3:5 [c]Is. 58:11

me, *saying,* Yea, [a]I have loved thee with
[b]an everlasting love: therefore [2]with lovingkindness have I [c]drawn thee.
4 Again [a]I will build thee, and thou
shalt be built, O virgin of Israel: thou
shalt again be adorned with thy [b]tabrets,[1]
and shalt go forth in the dances of them
that make merry.
5 [a]Thou shalt yet plant vines upon the
mountains of Samaria: the planters shall
plant, and shall [b]eat[1] *them* as common
things.
6 For there shall be a day, *that* the
watchmen upon the mount Ephraim shall
cry, [a]Arise ye, and let us go up to Zion
unto the LORD our God.
7 For thus saith the LORD; [a]Sing with
gladness for Jacob, and shout among the
chief of the nations: publish ye, praise
ye, and say, O LORD, save thy people, the
remnant of Israel.
8 Behold, I will bring them [a]from the
north country, and [b]gather them from
the coasts of the earth, *and* with them
the blind and the lame, the woman with
child and her that travaileth with child
together: a great company shall return
thither.
9 [a]They shall come with weeping, and
with [b]supplications[1] will I lead them: I
will cause them to walk [c]by the rivers of
waters in a straight way, wherein they
shall not stumble: for I am a father to
Israel, and Ephraim *is* my [d]firstborn.
10 ¶ Hear the word of the LORD, O ye
nations, and declare *it* in the isles afar
off, and say, He that scattered Israel [a]will
gather him, and keep him, as a shepherd
doth his flock.
11 For [a]the LORD hath redeemed Jacob,
and ransomed him [b]from the hand of *him*
that was stronger than he.
12 Therefore they shall come and sing
in [a]the height of Zion, and shall flow together to [b]the goodness of the LORD, for
wheat, and for wine, and for oil, and for
the young of the flock and of the herd:
and their soul shall be as a [c]watered gar-

31:1 God promised that he would "be the God of all the families of Israel" when their chastening is finished and they are restored in the last days.

31:3–14 In this wonderful prophecy of restoration, God promises to gather his people from all parts of the world and bring them back to the promised land to fulfill his ancient covenants (see notes at Ge 15:4; Dt 30:1; 2Sa 7:16). God's promise is slowly being fulfilled in our century. Following World War I, Israel was given some territory along the Mediterranean Sea for use as their homeland. Many Jews from every continent have begun to return to this small territory even though some Arab nations continue to dispute the Jews' claim to this land.

den; [d]and they shall not sorrow any more at all.

13 Then shall the virgin rejoice in the dance, both young men and old together: for I will turn their mourning into joy, and will comfort them, and make them rejoice from their sorrow.

14 And I will satiate the soul of the priests with fatness, and my people shall be satisfied with my goodness, saith the LORD.

15 ¶ Thus saith the LORD; [a]A voice was heard in [b]Ramah, lamentation, *and* bitter weeping; Rahel weeping for her children refused to be comforted for her children, because [c]they *were* not.

16 Thus saith the LORD; Refrain thy voice from weeping, and thine eyes from tears: for thy work shall be rewarded, saith the LORD; and [a]they shall come again from the land of the enemy.

17 And there is hope in thine end, saith the LORD, that thy children shall come again to their own border.

18 ¶ I have surely heard Ephraim bemoaning himself *thus;* Thou hast chastised me, and I was chastised, as a bullock unaccustomed *to the yoke:* [a]turn thou me, and I shall be turned; for thou *art* the LORD my God.

19 Surely [a]after that I was turned, I repented; and after that I was instructed, I smote upon *my* thigh: I was ashamed, yea, even confounded, because I did bear the reproach of my youth.

L P 20 *Is* Ephraim my dear son? *is he* a pleasant child? for since I spake against him, I do earnestly remember him still: [a]therefore my bowels [l]are troubled for him; [b]I will surely have mercy upon him, saith the LORD.

21 Set thee up waymarks, make thee high heaps: [a]set thine heart toward the highway, *even* the way *which* thou wentest: turn again, O virgin of Israel, turn again to these thy cities.

22 ¶ How long wilt thou [a]go about, O thou [b]backsliding daughter? for the LORD hath created a new thing in the earth, A woman shall compass a man.

23 Thus saith the LORD of hosts, the God of Israel; As yet they shall use this speech in the land of Judah and in the cities thereof, when I shall bring again their captivity; [a]The LORD bless thee, O habitation of justice, *and* [b]mountain of holiness.

24 And there shall dwell in Judah itself, and [a]in all the cities thereof together, husbandmen, and they *that* go forth with flocks.

25 For I have satiated the weary soul, and I have replenished every sorrowful soul.

26 Upon this I awaked, and beheld; and my sleep was sweet unto me.

27 ¶ Behold, the days come, saith the LORD, that [a]I will sow the house of Israel and the house of Judah with the seed of man, and with the seed of beast.

28 And it shall come to pass, *that* like as I have [a]watched over them, [b]to pluck up, and to break down, and to throw down, and to destroy, and to afflict; so will I watch over them, [c]to build, and to plant, saith the LORD. I

29 [a]In those days they shall say no more, The fathers have eaten a sour grape, and the children's teeth are set on edge.

30 [a]But every one shall die for his own iniquity: every man that eateth the sour grape, his teeth shall be set on edge.

31 ¶ Behold, the [a]days come, saith the I

12 [d]Is. 35:10 & 65:19; Rev. 21:4
15 [a]Mat. 2:17,18 [b]Josh. 18:25 [c]Gen. 42:13
16 [a]ver. 4,5; Ezra 1:5; Hos. 1:11
18 [a]Lam. 5:21
19 [a]Deut. 30:2
20 [a]Deut. 32:36; Is. 63:15; Hos. 11:8 [b]Is. 57:18; Hos. 14:4 [l]Heb. *sound*
21 [a]ch. 50:5
22 [a]ch. 2:18,23,36 [b]ch. 3:6,8,11,12, 14,22
23 [a]Ps. 122:5-8; Is. 1:26 [b]Zech. 8:3
24 [a]ch. 33:12
27 [a]Ezek. 36:9-11
28 [a]ch. 44:27 [b]ch. 1:10 & 18:7 [c]ch. 24:6
29 [a]Ezek. 18:2,3
30 [a]Gal. 6:5,7
31 [a]ch. 32:40 & 33:14; Ezek. 37:26; Heb. 8:8-12 & 10:16,17

L *Jer 31:3* ◀▶ *Jer 31:34*
P *Jer 31:3* ◀▶ *Jer 33:6–8*

I *Jer 31:3–14* ◀▶ *Jer 31:31–34*
I *Jer 31:28–29* ◀▶ *Jer 31:38–40*

31:15–17 This unusual prophecy was partially fulfilled when evil King Herod sent his soldiers to kill all of the male children below the age of two in a vain attempt to kill the young King sought for by the wise men (see Mt 2:17–18). However, this prophecy will be finally fulfilled in the last days. Rachel prophetically symbolizes the mother of the entire nation of Israel. As many as two thirds of both Jews and Gentiles will die during the tribulation. Yet despite these horrible predictions, God still offers hope and promises that the Jews will return in peace to the promised land.

31:27–29 Jeremiah predicted that Israel would finally be restored, physically and spiritually, in the last days.

31:31–36 This astonishing prophecy revealed God's commitment to establish a new covenant relationship with his people based on his promise to place his law "in their inward parts, and write it in their hearts" (31:33). This covenant is not merely a restatement of older covenants, but a new covenant through Jesus Christ (see Heb 8:6–13). This new

LORD, that I will make a new covenant
with the house of Israel, and with the
house of Judah:
32 Not according to the covenant that
I made with their fathers in the day *that*
[a]I took them by the hand to bring them
out of the land of Egypt; which my covenant they brake, [1]although I was an husband unto them, saith the LORD:
K 33 [a]But this *shall be* the covenant that
I will make with the house of Israel; After
those days, saith the LORD, [b]I will put my
law in their inward parts, and write it in
their hearts; [c]and will be their God, and
they shall be my people.
K 34 And they shall teach no more every
V man his neighbour, and every man his
L brother, saying, Know the LORD: for [a]they
shall all know me, from the least of them
unto the greatest of them, saith the LORD:
for [b]I will forgive their iniquity, and I will
remember their sin no more.
35 ¶ Thus saith the LORD, [a]which giveth the sun for a light by day, *and* the
ordinances of the moon and of the stars
for a light by night, which divideth [b]the
sea when the waves thereof roar; [c]The
LORD of hosts *is* his name:
36 [a]If those ordinances depart from
before me, saith the LORD, *then* the seed
of Israel also shall cease from being a nation before me for ever.
37 Thus saith the LORD; [a]If heaven
above can be measured, and the foundations of the earth searched out beneath, I
will also cast off all the seed of Israel for
all that they have done, saith the LORD.
I 38 ¶ Behold, the days come, saith the
LORD, that the city shall be built to the

32 [a]Deut. 1:31 [1]*Or, should I have continued an husband unto them?*
33 [a]ch. 32:40 [b]Ps. 40:8; Ezek. 11:19 & 36:26,27 [c]ch. 24:7 & 30:22 & 32:38
34 [a]Is. 54:13; John 6:45; 1 Cor. 2:10; 1 John 2:20 [b]ch. 33:8 & 50:20; Mic. 7:18; Acts 10:43 & 13:39; Rom. 11:27
35 [a]Gen. 1:16; Ps. 72:5,17 & 89:2,36 & 119:91 [b]Is. 51:15 [c]ch. 10:16
36 [a]Ps. 148:6; Is. 54:9,10; ch. 33:20
37 [a]ch. 33:22
38 [a]Neh. 3:1; Zech. 14:10
39 [a]Ezek. 40:8; Zech. 2:1
40 [a]2 Chr. 23:15; Neh. 3:28 [b]Joel 3:17
32:1 [a]2 Ki. 25:1; ch. 39:1
2 [a]Neh. 3:25; ch. 33:1 & 37:21 & 39:14
3 [a]ch. 34:2
4 [a]ch. 34:3 & 38:18,23 & 39:5 & 52:9
5 [a]ch. 27:22 [b]ch. 21:4 & 33:5

LORD [a]from the tower of Hananeel unto
the gate of the corner.
39 And [a]the measuring line shall yet
go forth over against it upon the hill Gareb, and shall compass about to Goath.
40 And the whole valley of the dead
bodies, and of the ashes, and all the fields
unto the brook of Kidron, [a]unto the corner of the horse gate toward the east,
[b]*shall be* holy unto the LORD; it shall not
be plucked up, nor thrown down any
more for ever.

Jeremiah buys a field

32 THE WORD that came to Jeremiah from the LORD [a]in the tenth
year of Zedekiah king of Judah, which
was the eighteenth year of Nebuchadrezzar.
2 For then the king of Babylon's army
besieged Jerusalem: and Jeremiah the
prophet was shut up [a]in the court of the
prison, which *was* in the king of Judah's
house.
3 For Zedekiah king of Judah had shut
him up, saying, Wherefore dost thou
prophesy, and say, Thus saith the LORD,
[a]Behold, I will give this city into the hand
of the king of Babylon, and he shall
take it;
4 And Zedekiah king of Judah [a]shall
not escape out of the hand of the Chaldeans, but shall surely be delivered into the
hand of the king of Babylon, and shall
speak with him mouth to mouth, and his
eyes shall behold his eyes;
5 And he shall lead Zedekiah to Babylon, and there shall he be [a]until I visit
him, saith the LORD: [b]though ye fight with
the Chaldeans, ye shall not prosper.
6 ¶ And Jeremiah said, The word of
the LORD came unto me, saying,
7 Behold, Hanameel the son of Shallum thine uncle shall come unto thee,
saying, Buy thee my field that *is* in Ana-

K *Jer 24:7* ◀ ▶ *Jer 32:27*
K *Isa 11:9* ◀ ▶ *Da 7:13–14*
V *Jer 23:5–6* ◀ ▶ *Da 2:44*
L *Jer 31:20* ◀ ▶ *Jer 33:8*
I *Jer 31:31–34* ◀ ▶ *Jer 32:36–42*

covenant will be an everlasting covenant with the nation of Israel. God's commitment to Israel is unshakable and his plans for her extend into the events of the last days. The prophet Isaiah prophetically revealed Israel's role reminding them that God would "keep thee, and give thee for a covenant of the people, for a light of the Gentiles" (Isa 42:6) so that "thou mayest be my salvation unto the end of the earth" (Isa 49:6).

31:38–40 The rebuilding of the city of Jerusalem will be the first sign of the fulfillment of the new covenant in the last days. Jeremiah described specific details about the rebuilding project, indicating that the city will be restored in its entirety, beginning at the eastern and western ends of the northern wall. Following this prophecy in sequence and direction, history confirms the fulfillment of Jeremiah's words as the various neighborhoods of Jerusalem have been rebuilt in this exact order.

thoth: for the [a]right of redemption *is*
thine to buy *it.*
8 So Hanameel mine uncle's son came
to me in the court of the prison according
to the word of the LORD, and said unto
me, Buy my field, I pray thee, that *is* in
Anathoth, which *is* in the country of Benjamin: for the right of inheritance *is*
thine, and the redemption *is* thine; buy *it*
for thyself. Then I knew that this *was* the
word of the LORD.
9 And I bought the field of Hanameel
my uncle's son, that *was* in Anathoth,
and [a]weighed him the money, *even* [‖]sev-
enteen shekels of silver.
10 And I [‖]subscribed the evidence,
and sealed *it,* and took witnesses, and
weighed *him* the money in the balances.
11 So I took the evidence of the purchase, *both* that which was sealed *according* to the law and custom, and that
which was open:
12 And I gave the evidence of the purchase unto [a]Baruch the son of Neriah,
the son of Maaseiah, in the sight of
Hanameel mine uncle's *son,* and in the
presence of the [b]witnesses that sub-
scribed the book of the purchase, before
all the Jews that sat in the court of the
prison.
13 ¶ And I charged Baruch before
them, saying,
14 Thus saith the LORD of hosts, the
God of Israel; Take these evidences, this
evidence of the purchase, both which is
sealed, and this evidence which is open;
and put them in an earthen vessel, that
they may continue many days.
15 For thus saith the LORD of hosts, the
God of Israel; Houses and fields and vineyards [a]shall be possessed again in this
land.
16 ¶ Now when I had delivered the
evidence of the purchase unto Baruch the
son of Neriah, I prayed unto the LORD,
saying,
17 Ah Lord GOD! behold, [a]thou hast
made the heaven and the earth by thy
great power and stretched out arm, *and*
[b]there is nothing [‖]too hard for thee:
18 Thou showest [a]lovingkindness unto
thousands, and recompensest the iniquity
of the fathers into the bosom of their
children after them: the Great, [b]the
Mighty God, [c]the LORD of hosts, *is* his
name,
19 [a]Great in counsel, and mighty in E
[‖]work: for thine [b]eyes *are* open upon all S
the ways of the sons of men: [c]to give every one according to his ways, and according to the fruit of his doings:
20 Which hast set signs and wonders
in the land of Egypt, *even* unto this day,
and in Israel, and among *other* men; and
hast made thee [a]a name, as at this day;
21 And [a]hast brought forth thy people
Israel out of the land of Egypt with signs,
and with wonders, and with a strong
hand, and with a stretched out arm, and
with great terror;
22 And hast given them this land,
which thou didst swear to their fathers to
give them, [a]a land flowing with milk and
honey;
23 And they came in, and possessed it;
but [a]they obeyed not thy voice, neither
walked in thy law; they have done nothing of all that thou commandedst them to
do: therefore thou hast caused all this evil
to come upon them:
24 Behold the [a]mounts,[‖] they are
come unto the city to take it; and the city
[b]is given into the hand of the Chaldeans,
that fight against it, because of [c]the
sword, and of the famine, and of the pestilence: and what thou hast spoken is
come to pass; and, behold, thou seest *it.*
25 And thou hast said unto me, O Lord
GOD, Buy thee the field for money, and
take witnesses; [‖]for [a]the city is given into
the hand of the Chaldeans.
26 ¶ Then came the word of the LORD
unto Jeremiah, saying,
27 Behold, I *am* the LORD, the [a]God of K
all flesh: [b]is there any thing too hard
for me?
28 Therefore thus saith the LORD; Behold, [a]I will give this city into the hand
of the Chaldeans, and into the hand of
Nebuchadrezzar king of Babylon, and he
shall take it:
29 And the Chaldeans, that fight
against this city, shall come and [a]set fire
on this city, and burn it with the houses,
[b]upon whose roofs they have offered incense unto Baal, and poured out drink offerings unto other gods, to provoke me to
anger.
30 For the children of Israel and the

7 [a]Lev. 25:24,25, 32; Ruth 4:4
9 [a]Gen. 23:16; Zech. 11:12 [‖]Or, *seven shekels and ten pieces of silver*
10 [‖]Heb. *wrote in the book*
12 [a]ch. 36:4 [b]See Is. 8:2
15 [a]ver. 37,43
17 [a]2 Ki. 19:15 [b]ver. 27; Gen. 18:14; Luke 1:37 [‖]Or, *hid from thee*
18 [a]Ex. 20:6 & 34:7; Deut. 5:9,10 [b]Is. 9:6 [c]ch. 10:16
19 [a]Is. 28:29 [b]Job 34:21; Ps. 33:13; Prov. 5:21; ch. 16:17 [c]ch. 17:10 [‖]Heb. *doing*
20 [a]Ex. 9:16; 1 Chr. 17:21; Is. 63:12; Dan. 9:15
21 [a]Ex. 6:6; 2 Sam. 7:23; 1 Chr. 17:21; Ps. 136:11,12
22 [a]Ex. 3:8,17; ch. 11:5
23 [a]Neh. 9:26; ch. 11:8; Dan. 9:10-14
24 [a]ch. 33:4 [b]ver. 25,36 [c]ch. 14:12 [‖]Or, *engines of shot*
25 [a]ver. 24 [‖]Or, *though*
27 [a]Num. 16:22 [b]ver. 17
28 [a]ver. 3
29 [a]ch. 21:10 & 37:8,10 & 52:13 [b]ch. 19:13

E *Jer 23:23–24* ◀ ▶ *Eze 8:12*
S *Jer 23:21–22* ◀ ▶ *Eze 3:20–21*
K *Jer 31:33–34* ◀ ▶ *Jer 32:38–39*

children of Judah [a]have only done evil before me from their youth: for the children of Israel have only provoked me to anger with the work of their hands, saith the LORD.

31 For this city hath been to me *as* ′[a] provocation of mine anger and of my fury from the day that they built it even unto this day; [a]that I should remove it from before my face,

32 Because of all the evil of the children of Israel and of the children of Judah, which they have done to provoke me to anger, [a]they, their kings, their princes, their priests, and their prophets, and the men of Judah, and the inhabitants of Jerusalem.

N 33 And they have turned unto me the [a]back,′ and not the face: though I taught them, [b]rising up early and teaching *them,* yet they have not hearkened to receive instruction.

34 But they [a]set their abominations in the house, which is called by my name, to defile it.

35 And they built the high places of Baal, which *are* in the valley of the son of Hinnom, to [a]cause their sons and their daughters to pass through *the fire* unto [b]Molech; [c]which I commanded them not, neither came it into my mind, that they should do this abomination, to cause Judah to sin.

I 36 ¶ And now therefore thus saith the LORD, the God of Israel, concerning this city, whereof ye say, [a]It shall be delivered into the hand of the king of Babylon by the sword, and by the famine, and by the pestilence;

37 Behold, I will [a]gather them out of all countries, whither I have driven them in mine anger, and in my fury, and in great wrath; and I will bring them again unto this place, and I will cause them [b]to dwell safely:

K 38 And they shall be [a]my people, and I will be their God:

N *Jer 13:15–17* ◀ ▶ *Eze 3:7*
I *Jer 31:38–40* ◀ ▶ *Jer 32:44*
K *Jer 32:27* ◀ ▶ *Jer 33:8*

30 [a]ch. 2:7 & 3:25 & 7:22-26; Ezek. 20:28
31 [a]2 Ki. 24:3 ′Heb. *for my anger*
32 [a]Is. 1:4,6; Dan. 9:8
33 [a]ch. 2:27 & 7:24 [b]ch. 7:13 ′Heb. *neck*
34 [a]ch. 23:11; Ezek. 8:5,6
35 [a]ch. 7:31 & 19:5 [b]Lev. 18:21; 1 Ki. 11:33 [c]ch. 7:31
36 [a]ver. 24
37 [a]Deut. 30:3; ch. 23:3 & 29:14; Ezek. 37:21 [b]ch. 33:16
38 [a]ch. 24:7 & 30:22 & 31:33
39 [a]ch. 24:7; Ezek. 11:19 ′Heb. *all days*
40 [a]Is. 55:3; ch. 31:31 [b]ch. 31:33 ′Heb. *from after them*
41 [a]Deut. 30:9; Zeph. 3:17 [b]ch. 24:6 & 31:28; Amos 9:15 ′Heb. *in truth,* or, *stability*
42 [a]ch. 31:28
43 [a]ver. 15 [b]ch. 33:10
44 [a]ch. 17:26 [b]ch. 33:7,11
33:1 [a]ch. 32:2,3
2 [a]Is. 37:26 [b]Ex. 15:3; Amos 5:8 & 9:6 ′Or, *JEHOVAH*
3 [a]Ps. 91:15; ch. 29:12 [b]Is. 48:6 ′Or, *hidden*
4 [a]ch. 32:24
5 [a]ch. 32:5

39 And I will [a]give them one heart, and one way, that they may fear me ′for ever, for the good of them, and of their children after them:

40 And [a]I will make an everlasting covenant with them, that I will not turn away ′from them, to do them good; but [b]I will put my fear in their hearts, that they shall not depart from me.

41 Yea, [a]I will rejoice over them to do them good, and [b]I will plant them in this land ′assuredly with my whole heart and with my whole soul.

42 For thus saith the LORD; [a]Like as I have brought all this great evil upon this people, so will I bring upon them all the good that I have promised them.

43 And [a]fields shall be bought in this land, [b]whereof ye say, *It is* desolate without man or beast; it is given into the hand of the Chaldeans.

44 Men shall buy fields for money, and subscribe evidences, and seal *them,* and take witnesses in [a]the land of Benjamin, and in the places about Jerusalem, and in the cities of Judah, and in the cities of the mountains, and in the cities of the valley, and in the cities of the south: for [b]I will cause their captivity to return, saith the LORD. I

Promise of restoration

33 MOREOVER THE word of the LORD came unto Jeremiah the second time, while he was yet [a]shut up in the court of the prison, saying,

2 Thus saith the LORD the [a]maker thereof, the LORD that formed it, to establish it; [b]the′ LORD *is* his name; I

3 [a]Call unto me, and I will answer thee, and show thee great and [b]mighty′ things, which thou knowest not.

4 For thus saith the LORD, the God of Israel, concerning the houses of this city, and concerning the houses of the kings of Judah, which are thrown down by [a]the mounts, and by the sword;

5 [a]They come to fight with the Chalde-

I *Jer 32:36–42* ◀ ▶ *Jer 33:2–3*
I *Jer 32:44* ◀ ▶ *Jer 33:6–11*

32:36–44 While Jeremiah confirmed the coming destruction of Jerusalem by Babylon, he also delivered God's promise to bring the exiles back to Israel from the nations where their enemies would drive them. The prophet then described legal land transactions as proof that the Babylonian captivity would not be permanent.

33:2–3 God reassured Jeremiah that he was with him, even in prison, and would show Jeremiah incredible things.

ans, but *it is* to fill them with the dead
bodies of men, whom I have slain in
mine anger and in my fury, and for all
whose wickedness I have hid my face
from this city.
I 6 Behold, [a]I will bring it health and
P cure, and I will cure them, and will reveal unto them the abundance of peace
and truth.
7 And [a]I will cause the captivity of Judah and the captivity of Israel to return,
and will build them, [b]as at the first.
K 8 And I will [a]cleanse them from all
L their iniquity, whereby they have sinned
against me; and I will [b]pardon all their
iniquities, whereby they have sinned,
and whereby they have transgressed
against me.
9 ¶ [a]And it shall be to me a name of
joy, a praise and an honour before all the
nations of the earth, which shall hear all
the good that I do unto them: and they
shall [b]fear and tremble for all the goodness and for all the prosperity that I procure unto it.
10 Thus saith the LORD; Again there
shall be heard in this place, [a]which ye say
shall be desolate without man and without beast, *even* in the cities of Judah, and
in the streets of Jerusalem, that are desolate, without man, and without inhabitant, and without beast,
11 The [a]voice of joy, and the voice of
gladness, the voice of the bridegroom,
and the voice of the bride, the voice of
them that shall say, [b]Praise the LORD of
hosts: for the LORD *is* good; for his mercy
endureth for ever: *and* of them that shall
bring [c]the sacrifice of praise into the
house of the LORD. For [d]I will cause to
return the captivity of the land, as at the
first, saith the LORD.
12 Thus saith the LORD of hosts; [a]Again
in this place, which is desolate without
man and without beast, and in all the cities thereof, shall be an habitation of shepherds causing *their* flocks to lie down.
13 [a]In the cities of the mountains, in
the cities of the vale, and in the cities of
the south, and in the land of Benjamin,
and in the places about Jerusalem, and in
the cities of Judah, shall the flocks [b]pass
again under the hands of him that telleth
them, saith the LORD.
14 [a]Behold, the days come, saith the
LORD, that [b]I will perform that good thing
which I have promised unto the house of
Israel and to the house of Judah.
15 ¶ In those days, and at that time, I
will I cause the [a]Branch of righteousness M
to grow up unto David; and he shall execute judgment and righteousness in the
land.
16 In those days shall Judah be saved,
and Jerusalem shall dwell safely: and this
is the name wherewith she shall be
called, [f]The LORD our righteousness.
17 ¶ For thus saith the LORD; [f]David
shall never [a]want a man to sit upon the
throne of the house of Israel;
18 Neither shall the priests the Levites
want a man before me to [a]offer burnt offerings, and to kindle meat offerings, and
to do sacrifice continually.
19 ¶ And the word of the LORD came
unto Jeremiah, saying,
20 Thus saith the LORD; [a]if ye can
break my covenant of the day, and my
covenant of the night, and that there
should not be day and night in their
season;
21 *Then* may also [a]my covenant be
broken with David my servant, that he
should not have a son to reign upon his
throne; and with the Levites the priests,
my ministers.
22 As [a]the host of heaven cannot be
numbered, neither the sand of the sea
measured: so will I multiply the seed of

6 [a]ch. 30:17
7 [a]ch. 30:3 & 32:44 [b]Is. 1:26; ch. 24:6 & 30:20 & 31:4,28 & 42:10
8 [a]Ezek. 36:25; Zech. 13:1; Heb. 9:13,14 [b]ch. 31:34; Mic. 7:18
9 [a]Is. 62:7; ch. 13:11 [b]Is. 60:5
10 [a]ch. 32:43
11 [a]ch. 7:34 & 16:9 & 25:10; Rev. 18:23 [b]1 Chr. 16:8; 2 Chr. 5:13; Ezra 3:11; Ps. 136:1; Is. 12:4 [c]Lev. 7:12; Ps. 107:22 & 116:17 [d]ver. 7
12 [a]Is. 65:10; ch. 31:24 & 50:19
13 [a]ch. 17:26 & 32:44 [b]Lev. 27:32
14 [a]ch. 23:5 & 31:27,31 [b]ch. 29:10
15 [a]Is. 4:2 & 11:1; ch. 23:5
16 [f]Heb. *Jehovah-tsidkenu*
17 [a]2 Sam. 7:16; 1 Ki. 2:4; Ps. 89:29; Luke 1:32 [f]Heb. *There shall not be cut off from David*
18 [a]Rom. 12:1 & 15:16; 1 Pet. 2:5,9; Rev. 1:6
20 [a]ver. 25; Ps. 89:37; Is. 54:9; ch. 31:36
21 [a]Ps. 89:34
22 [a]Gen. 15:5

I *Jer 33:2–3* ◀ ▶ *Jer 33:15–16*
P *Jer 31:20* ◀ ▶ *Jer 36:3*
K *Jer 32:38–39* ◀ ▶ *Jer 50:20*
L *Jer 31:34* ◀ ▶ *Jer 36:3*
I *Jer 33:6–11* ◀ ▶ *Jer 35:18–19*
M *Jer 30:9* ◀ ▶ *Eze 21:26–27*

33:6–11 Just as God had promised the removal of the sounds of happiness in Judah (see 7:34), this prophecy stated that God's blessings and the sounds of happiness would be once again be restored to Judah.
33:15–16 Jeremiah prophesied the coming blessing in the millennial kingdom of the Messiah when Judah and Jerusalem would live in safety.
33:22 These words echo God's promises to Abraham (see note at Ge 15:4). These numerous descendants will be counted among the great throng who will reign with Christ and those who have been consecrated to be priests with him (see Ro 5:17; 1Co 6:3; 2Ti 2:12; 1Pe 2:5; Rev 1:6; 5:10; 22:5).

David my servant, and the Levites that minister unto me.

23 Moreover the word of the LORD came to Jeremiah, saying,

24 Considerest thou not what this people have spoken, saying, [a]The two families which the LORD hath chosen, he hath even cast them off ? thus they have despised my people, that they should be no more a nation before them.

25 Thus saith the LORD; If [a]my covenant *be* not with day and night, *and if* I have not [b]appointed the ordinances of heaven and earth;

26 [a]Then will I cast away the seed of Jacob, and David my servant, *so* that I will not take *any* of his seed *to be* rulers over the seed of Abraham, Isaac, and Jacob: for [b]I will cause their captivity to return, and have mercy on them.

Zedekiah's broken promise

34 THE WORD which came unto Jeremiah from the LORD, [a]when Nebuchadnezzar king of Babylon, and all his army, and [b]all the kingdoms of the earth [1]of his dominion, and all the people, fought against Jerusalem, and against all the cities thereof, saying,

2 Thus saith the LORD, the God of Israel; Go and speak to Zedekiah king of Judah, and tell him, Thus saith the LORD; Behold, [a]I will give this city into the hand of the king of Babylon, and [b]he shall burn it with fire:

3 And [a]thou shalt not escape out of his hand, but shalt surely be taken, and delivered into his hand; and thine eyes shall behold the eyes of the king of Babylon, and [1]he shall speak with thee mouth to mouth, and thou shalt go to Babylon.

4 Yet hear the word of the LORD, O Zedekiah king of Judah; Thus saith the LORD of thee, Thou shalt not die by the sword:

5 *But* thou shalt die in peace: and with [a]the burnings of thy fathers, the former kings which were before thee, [b]so shall they burn *odours* for thee; and [c]they will lament thee, *saying,* Ah lord! for I have pronounced the word, saith the LORD.

6 Then Jeremiah the prophet spake all these words unto Zedekiah king of Judah in Jerusalem,

7 When the king of Babylon's army fought against Jerusalem, and against all the cities of Judah that were left, against Lachish, and against Azekah: for [a]these defenced cities remained of the cities of Judah.

8 ¶ *This is* the word that came unto Jeremiah from the LORD, after that the king Zedekiah had made a covenant with all the people which *were* at Jerusalem, to proclaim [a]liberty unto them;

9 [a]That every man should let his manservant, and every man his maidservant, *being* an Hebrew or an Hebrewess, go free; [b]that none should serve himself of them, *to wit,* of a Jew his brother.

10 Now when all the princes, and all the people, which had entered into the covenant, heard that every one should let his manservant, and every one his maidservant, go free, that none should serve themselves of them any more, then they obeyed, and let *them* go.

11 But [a]afterward they turned, and caused the servants and the handmaids, whom they had let go free, to return, and brought them into subjection for servants and for handmaids.

Jeremiah warns of punishment

12 ¶ Therefore the word of the LORD came to Jeremiah from the LORD, saying,

13 Thus saith the LORD, the God of Israel; I made a covenant with your fathers in the day that I brought them forth out of the land of Egypt, out of the house of bondmen, saying,

14 At the end of [a]seven years let ye go every man his brother an Hebrew, which [1]hath been sold unto thee; and when he hath served thee six years, thou shalt let him go free from thee: but your fathers hearkened not unto me, neither inclined their ear.

15 And ye were [1]now turned, and had done right in my sight, in proclaiming liberty every man to his neighbour; and ye had [a]made a covenant before me [b]in the house [2]which is called by my name:

16 But ye turned and [a]polluted my name, and caused every man his servant, and every man his handmaid, whom ye had set at liberty at their pleasure, to return, and brought them into subjection, to be unto you for servants and for handmaids.

17 Therefore thus saith the LORD; Ye have not hearkened unto me, in proclaiming liberty, every one to his brother, and every man to his neighbour: [a]behold,

24 [a]ver. 21,22
25 [a]ver. 20; Gen. 8:22 [b]Ps. 74:16 & 104:19; ch. 31:35, 36
26 [a]ch. 31:37 [b]ver. 7,11; Ezra 2:1
34:1 [a]2 Ki. 25:1; ch. 39:1 & 52:4 [b]ch. 1:15 [1]Heb. *the dominion of his hand*
2 [a]ch. 21:10 & 32:3,28 [b]ver. 22; ch. 32:29
3 [a]ch. 32:4 [1]Heb. *his mouth shall speak to thy mouth*
5 [a]2 Chr. 16:14 & 21:19 [b]Dan. 2:46 [c]See ch. 22:18
7 [a]2 Ki. 18:13 & 19:8; 2 Chr. 11:5,9
8 [a]ver. 14; Ex. 21:2; Lev. 25:10
9 [a]Neh. 5:11 [b]Lev. 25:39-46
11 [a]See ver. 21; ch. 37:5
14 [a]Ex. 21:2 & 23:10; Deut. 15:12 [1]Or, *hath sold himself*
15 [a]2 Ki. 23:3; Neh. 10:29 [b]ch. 7:10 [1]Heb. *today* [2]Heb. *whereupon my name is called*
16 [a]Ex. 20:7; Lev. 19:12
17 [a]Mat. 7:2; Gal. 6:7; Jas. 2:13

I proclaim a liberty for you, saith the LORD, [b]to the sword, to the pestilence, and to the famine; and I will make you [†]to be [c]removed into all the kingdoms of the earth.

18 And I will give the men that have transgressed my covenant, which have not performed the words of the covenant which they had made before me, when [a]they cut the calf in twain, and passed between the parts thereof,

19 The princes of Judah, and the princes of Jerusalem, the eunuchs, and the priests, and all the people of the land, which passed between the parts of the calf;

20 I will even give them into the hand of their enemies, and into the hand of them that seek their life: and their [a]dead bodies shall be for meat unto the fowls of the heaven, and to the beasts of the earth.

21 And Zedekiah king of Judah and his princes will I give into the hand of their enemies, and into the hand of them that seek their life, and into the hand of the king of Babylon's army, [a]which are gone up from you.

R 22 [a]Behold, I will command, saith the LORD, and cause them to return to this city; and they shall fight against it, [b]and take it, and burn it with fire: and [c]I will make the cities of Judah a desolation without an inhabitant.

The Rechabites

35 THE WORD which came unto Jeremiah from the LORD in the days of Jehoiakim the son of Josiah king of Judah, saying,

2 Go unto the house of the [a]Rechabites, and speak unto them, and bring them into the house of the LORD, into one of [b]the chambers, and give them wine to drink.

3 Then I took Jaazaniah the son of Jeremiah, the son of Habaziniah, and his brethren, and all his sons, and the whole house of the Rechabites;

4 And I brought them into the house of the LORD, into the chamber of the sons of Hanan, the son of Igdaliah, a man of God, which *was* by the chamber of the princes, which *was* above the chamber of Maaseiah the son of Shallum, [a]the keeper of the [†]door:

5 And I set before the sons of the house of the Rechabites pots full of wine, and cups, and I said unto them, Drink ye wine.

6 But they said, We will drink no wine: for [a]Jonadab the son of Rechab our father commanded us, saying, Ye shall drink no wine, *neither* ye, nor your sons for ever:

7 Neither shall ye build house, nor sow seed, nor plant vineyard, nor have *any:* but all your days ye shall dwell in tents; [a]that ye may live many days in the land where ye *be* strangers.

8 Thus have we obeyed the voice of Jonadab the son of Rechab our father in all that he hath charged us, to drink no wine all our days, we, our wives, our sons, nor our daughters;

9 Nor to build houses for us to dwell in: neither have we vineyard, nor field, nor seed:

10 But we have dwelt in tents, and have obeyed, and done according to all that Jonadab our father commanded us.

11 But it came to pass, when Nebuchadrezzar king of Babylon came up into the land, that we said, Come, and let us go to Jerusalem for fear of the army of the Chaldeans, and for fear of the army of the Syrians: so we dwell at Jerusalem.

12 ¶ Then came the word of the LORD unto Jeremiah, saying,

13 Thus saith the LORD of hosts, the God of Israel; Go and tell the men of Judah and the inhabitants of Jerusalem, Will ye not [a]receive instruction to hearken to my words? saith the LORD.

14 The words of Jonadab the son of Rechab, that he commanded his sons not to drink wine, are performed; for unto this day they drink none, but obey their father's commandment: [a]notwithstanding I have spoken unto you, [b]rising early and speaking; but ye hearkened not unto me.

15 I have sent also unto you all my servants the prophets, rising up early and sending *them,* saying, [a]Return ye now ev-

17 [b]ch. 32:24,36 [c]Deut. 28:25,64; ch. 29:18 [†]Heb. *for a removing*
18 [a]See Gen. 15:10,17
20 [a]ch. 7:33 & 16:4 & 19:7
21 [a]See ch. 37:5, 11
22 [a]ch. 37:8,10 [b]ch. 38:3 & 39:1, 2,8 & 52:7,13 [c]ch. 9:11 & 44:2,6
35:2 [a]2 Ki. 10:15; 1 Chr. 2:55 [b]1 Ki. 6:5
4 [a]2 Ki. 12:9 & 25:18; 1 Chr. 9:18, 19 [†]Heb. *threshold,* or, *vessel*
6 [a]2 Ki. 10:15
7 [a]Ex. 20:12; Eph. 6:2,3
13 [a]ch. 32:33
14 [a]2 Chr. 36:15 [b]ch. 7:13 & 25:3
15 [a]ch. 18:11 & 25:5,6

R *Jer 30:17* ◄ ► *Jer 38:21–23*

34:22 God declared that the Babylonians would utterly destroy Jerusalem with fire and that the other cities of Judah would meet a similar fate.

ery man from his evil way, and amend your doings, and go not after other gods to serve them, and ye shall dwell in the land which I have given to you and to your fathers: but ye have not inclined your ear, nor hearkened unto me.

16 Because the sons of Jonadab the son of Rechab have performed the commandment of their father, which he commanded them; but this people hath not hearkened unto me:

17 Therefore thus saith the LORD God of hosts, the God of Israel; Behold, I will bring upon Judah and upon all the inhabitants of Jerusalem all the evil that I have pronounced against them: [a]because I have spoken unto them, but they have not heard; and I have called unto them, but they have not answered.

I 18 ¶ And Jeremiah said unto the house of the Rechabites, Thus saith the LORD of hosts, the God of Israel; Because ye have obeyed the commandment of Jonadab your father, and kept all his precepts, and done according unto all that he hath commanded you:

U 19 Therefore thus saith the LORD of hosts, the God of Israel; [/]Jonadab the son of Rechab shall not want a man to [a]stand before me for ever.

The reading of the roll

36 AND IT came to pass in the fourth year of Jehoiakim the son of Josiah king of Judah, *that* this word came unto Jeremiah from the LORD, saying,

2 Take thee a [a]roll of a book, and [b]write therein all the words that I have spoken unto thee against Israel, and against Judah, and against [c]all the nations, from the day I spake unto thee, from the days of [d]Josiah, even unto this day.

I Jer 33:15–16 ◀▶ Jer 46:27–28
U Jer 17:7–8 ◀▶ Eze 34:26–27

17 [a]Prov. 1:24; Is. 65:12 & 66:4; ch. 7:13

19 [a]ch. 15:19 [/]Heb. *There shall not a man be cut off from Jonadab the son of Rechab to stand*

36:2 [a]Is. 8:1; Ezek. 2:9; Zech. 5:1 [b]ch. 30:2 [c]ch. 25:15 [d]ch. 25:3

3 [a]ver. 7; ch. 26:3 [b]ch. 18:8; Jonah 3:8

4 [a]ch. 32:12 [b]See ch. 45:1

6 [a]Lev. 16:29 & 23:27-32; Acts 27:9

7 [a]ver. 3 [/]Heb. *their supplications shall fall*

10 [a]ch. 26:10 [/]Or, *door*

3 [a]It may be that the house of Judah will hear all the evil which I purpose to do unto them; that they may [b]return every man from his evil way; that I may forgive their iniquity and their sin. L P R

4 Then Jeremiah [a]called Baruch the son of Neriah: and [b]Baruch wrote from the mouth of Jeremiah all the words of the LORD, which he had spoken unto him, upon a roll of a book.

5 And Jeremiah commanded Baruch, saying, I *am* shut up; I cannot go into the house of the LORD:

6 Therefore go thou, and read in the roll, which thou hast written from my mouth, the words of the LORD in the ears of the people in the LORD'S house upon [a]the fasting day: and also thou shalt read them in the ears of all Judah that come out of their cities.

7 [a]It may be [/]they will present their supplication before the LORD, and will return every one from his evil way: for great *is* the anger and the fury that the LORD hath pronounced against this people. H

8 And Baruch the son of Neriah did according to all that Jeremiah the prophet commanded him, reading in the book the words of the LORD in the LORD'S house.

9 And it came to pass in the fifth year of Jehoiakim the son of Josiah king of Judah, in the ninth month, *that* they proclaimed a fast before the LORD to all the people in Jerusalem, and to all the people that came from the cities of Judah unto Jerusalem.

10 Then read Baruch in the book the words of Jeremiah in the house of the LORD, in the chamber of Gemariah the son of Shaphan the scribe, in the higher court, at the [a]entry[/] of the new gate of the LORD'S house, in the ears of all the people.

L Jer 33:8 ◀▶ Jer 50:20
P Jer 33:6–8 ◀▶ Eze 34:11–12
R Jer 29:12–13 ◀▶ La 3:40–41
H Jer 30:23–24 ◀▶ La 3:39

35:18–19 Jeremiah had set wine in front of the Rechabites, a tribe of Kenites (see 2Ki 10:15–16; 1Ch 2:55). Because of a vow their fathers had made to refrain from drinking wine, these Rechabites refused Jeremiah's offer. Jeremiah recorded this incident as an example to Judah of the choices that the people should make to follow the laws of God rather than succumb to temptation.

36:4 Baruch, the son of Neriah, was Jeremiah's personal secretary. We are not told why Baruch recorded these messages, but it is evident that Jeremiah trusted him with both his words and possessions (see 32:12).

11 ¶ When Michaiah the son of Gemariah, the son of Shaphan, had heard out of the book all the words of the LORD,

12 Then he went down into the king's house, into the scribe's chamber: and, lo, all the princes sat there, *even* Elishama the scribe, and Delaiah the son of Shemaiah, and Elnathan the son of Achbor, and Gemariah the son of Shaphan, and Zedekiah the son of Hananiah, and all the princes.

13 Then Michaiah declared unto them all the words that he had heard, when Baruch read the book in the ears of the people.

14 Therefore all the princes sent Jehudi the son of Nethaniah, the son of Shelemiah, the son of Cushi, unto Baruch, saying, Take in thine hand the roll wherein thou hast read in the ears of the people, and come. So Baruch the son of Neriah took the roll in his hand, and came unto them.

15 And they said unto him, Sit down now, and read it in our ears. So Baruch read *it* in their ears.

16 Now it came to pass, when they had heard all the words, they were afraid both one and other, and said unto Baruch, We will surely tell the king of all these words.

17 And they asked Baruch, saying, Tell us now, How didst thou write all these words at his mouth?

18 Then Baruch answered them, He pronounced all these words unto me with his mouth, and I wrote *them* with ink in the book.

19 Then said the princes unto Baruch, Go, hide thee, thou and Jeremiah; and let no man know where ye be.

20 ¶ And they went in to the king into the court, but they laid up the roll in the chamber of Elishama the scribe, and told all the words in the ears of the king.

21 So the king sent Jehudi to fetch the roll: and he took it out of Elishama the scribe's chamber. And Jehudi read it in the ears of the king, and in the ears of all the princes which stood beside the king.

22 Now the king sat in [a]the winterhouse in the ninth month: and *there was a fire* on the hearth burning before him.

23 And it came to pass, *that* when Jehudi had read three or four leaves, he cut it with the penknife, and cast *it* into the fire that *was* on the hearth, until all the roll was consumed in the fire that *was* on the hearth.

24 Yet they were not afraid, nor [a]rent their garments, *neither* the king, nor any of his servants that heard all these words.

25 Nevertheless Elnathan and Delaiah and Gemariah had made intercession to the king that he would not burn the roll: but he would not hear them.

26 But the king commanded Jerahmeel the son [1]of Hammelech, and Seraiah the son of Azriel, and Shelemiah the son of Abdeel, to take Baruch the scribe and Jeremiah the prophet: but the LORD hid them.

27 ¶ Then the word of the LORD came to Jeremiah, after that the king had burned the roll, and the words which Baruch wrote at the mouth of Jeremiah, saying,

28 Take thee again another roll, and write in it all the former words that were in the first roll, which Jehoiakim the king of Judah hath burned.

29 And thou shalt say to Jehoiakim king of Judah, Thus saith the LORD; Thou hast burned this roll, saying, Why hast thou written therein, saying, The king of Babylon shall certainly come and destroy this land, and shall cause to cease from thence man and beast?

30 Therefore thus saith the LORD of Jehoiakim king of Judah; [a]He shall have none to sit upon the throne of David: and his dead body shall be [b]cast out in the day to the heat, and in the night to the frost.

31 And I will [a]punish[1] him and his seed and his servants for their iniquity; and I will bring upon them, and upon the inhabitants of Jerusalem, and upon the men of Judah, all the evil that I have pronounced against them; but they hearkened not.

32 ¶ Then took Jeremiah another roll, and gave it to Baruch the scribe, the son of Neriah; who wrote therein from the mouth of Jeremiah all the words of the book which Jehoiakim king of Judah had burned in the fire: and there were added besides unto them many [1]like words.

Jeremiah's imprisonment

37 AND KING [a]Zedekiah the son of Josiah reigned instead of Coniah the son of Jehoiakim, whom Nebuchadrezzar king of Babylon made king in the land of Judah.

22 [a]See Amos 3:15
24 [a]2 Ki. 22:11; Is. 36:22 & 37:1
26 [1]Or, *of the king*
30 [a]ch. 22:30 [b]ch. 22:19
31 [a]ch. 23:34 [1]Heb. *visit upon*
32 [1]Heb. *as they*
37:1 [a]2 Ki. 24:17; 2 Chr. 36:10; ch. 22:24

2 [a]But neither he, nor his servants,
nor the people of the land, did hearken
unto the words of the LORD, which he
spake [l]by the prophet Jeremiah.
3 And Zedekiah the king sent Jehucal
the son of Shelemiah and [a]Zephaniah the
son of Maaseiah the priest to the prophet
Jeremiah, saying, Pray now unto the LORD
our God for us.
4 Now Jeremiah came in and went out
among the people: for they had not put
him into prison.
5 Then [a]Pharaoh's army was come
forth out of Egypt: [b]and when the Chaldeans that besieged Jerusalem heard tidings
of them, they departed from Jerusalem.
6 ¶ Then came the word of the LORD
unto the prophet Jeremiah, saying,
7 Thus saith the LORD, the God of Israel; Thus shall ye say to the king of Judah, [a]that sent you unto me to inquire of
me; Behold, Pharaoh's army, which is
come forth to help you, shall return to
Egypt into their own land.
8 [a]And the Chaldeans shall come
again, and fight against this city, and take
it, and burn it with fire.
9 Thus saith the LORD; Deceive not
[l]yourselves, saying, The Chaldeans shall
surely depart from us: for they shall not
depart.
10 [a]For though ye had smitten the
whole army of the Chaldeans that fight
against you, and there remained *but*
[l]wounded men among them, *yet* should
they rise up every man in his tent, and
burn this city with fire.
11 ¶ [a]And it came to pass, that when
the army of the Chaldeans was [l]broken
up from Jerusalem for fear of Pharaoh's
army,
12 Then Jeremiah went forth out of Jerusalem to go into the land of Benjamin,
[l]to separate himself thence in the midst
of the people.
13 And when he was in the gate of
Benjamin, a captain of the ward *was*
there, whose name *was* Irijah, the son of
Shelemiah, the son of Hananiah; and he
took Jeremiah the prophet, saying, Thou
fallest away to the Chaldeans.
14 Then said Jeremiah, *It is* [l]false; I
fall not away to the Chaldeans. But he
hearkened not to him: so Irijah took Jeremiah, and brought him to the princes.
15 Wherefore the princes were wroth
with Jeremiah, and smote him, [a]and put
him in prison in the house of Jonathan
the scribe: for they had made that the
prison.
16 ¶ When Jeremiah was entered into
[a]the dungeon, and into the [l]cabins, and
Jeremiah had remained there many days;
17 Then Zedekiah the king sent, and
took him out: and the king asked him secretly in his house, and said, Is there *any*
word from the LORD? And Jeremiah said,
There is: for, said he, thou shalt be delivered into the hand of the king of Babylon.
18 Moreover Jeremiah said unto king
Zedekiah, What have I offended against
thee, or against thy servants, or against
this people, that ye have put me in
prison?
19 Where *are* now your prophets
which prophesied unto you, saying, The
king of Babylon shall not come against
you, nor against this land?
20 Therefore hear now, I pray thee,
O my lord the king: [l]let my supplication,
I pray thee, be accepted before thee; that
thou cause me not to return to the house
of Jonathan the scribe, lest I die there.
21 Then Zedekiah the king commanded that they should commit Jeremiah [a]into the court of the prison, and
that they should give him daily a piece of
bread out of the bakers' street, [b]until all
the bread in the city were spent. Thus
Jeremiah remained in the court of the
prison.

The miry dungeon

38 THEN SHEPHATIAH the son of
Mattan, and Gedaliah the son of
Pashur, and [a]Jucal the son of Shelemiah,
and [b]Pashur the son of Malchiah, [c]heard
the words that Jeremiah had spoken unto
all the people, saying,
2 Thus saith the LORD, [a]He that remaineth in this city shall die by the
sword, by the famine, and by the pestilence: but he that goeth forth to the Chaldeans shall live; for he shall have his life
for a prey, and shall live.
3 Thus saith the LORD, [a]This city shall
surely be given into the hand of the king
of Babylon's army, which shall take it.
4 Therefore the princes said unto the
king, We beseech thee, [a]let this man be
put to death: for thus he weakeneth the
hands of the men of war that remain in
this city, and the hands of all the people,
in speaking such words unto them: for

2 [a]2 Chr. 36:12,14 [l]Heb. *by the hand of the prophet*
3 [a]ch. 21:1,2 & 29:25 & 52:24
5 [a]See 2 Ki. 24:7; Ezek. 17:15 [b]ver. 11; ch. 34:21
7 [a]ch. 21:2
8 [a]ch. 34:22
9 [l]Heb. *souls*
10 [a]ch. 21:4,5 [l]Heb. *thrust through*
11 [a]ver. 5 [l]Heb. *made to ascend*
12 [l]Or, *to slip away from thence in the midst of the people*
14 [l]Heb. *falsehood, or, a lie*
15 [a]ch. 38:26
16 [a]ch. 38:6 [l]Or, *cells*
20 [l]Heb. *let my supplication fall*
21 [a]ch. 32:2 & 38:13,28 [b]ch. 38:9 & 52:6
38:1 [a]ch. 37:3 [b]ch. 21:1 [c]ch. 21:8
2 [a]ch. 21:9
3 [a]ch. 21:10 & 32:3
4 [a]See ch. 26:11

this man seeketh not the [l]welfare of this people, but the hurt.

5 Then Zedekiah the king said, Behold, he *is* in your hand: for the king *is* not *he that* can do *any* thing against you.

6 [a]Then took they Jeremiah, and cast him into the dungeon of Malchiah the son [l]of Hammelech, that *was* in the court of the prison: and they let down Jeremiah with cords. And in the dungeon *there was* no water, but mire: so Jeremiah sunk in the mire.

7 ¶ [a]Now when Ebed-melech the Ethiopian, one of the eunuchs which was in the king's house, heard that they had put Jeremiah in the dungeon; the king then sitting in the gate of Benjamin;

8 Ebed-melech went forth out of the king's house, and spake to the king, saying,

9 My lord the king, these men have done evil in all that they have done to Jeremiah the prophet, whom they have cast into the dungeon; and [l]he is like to die for hunger in the place where he is: for *there is* no more bread in the city.

10 Then the king commanded Ebed-melech the Ethiopian, saying, Take from hence thirty men [l]with thee, and take up Jeremiah the prophet out of the dungeon, before he die.

11 So Ebed-melech took the men with him, and went into the house of the king under the treasury, and took thence old cast clouts and old rotten rags, and let them down by cords into the dungeon to Jeremiah.

12 And Ebed-melech the Ethiopian said unto Jeremiah, Put now *these* old cast clouts and rotten rags under thine armholes under the cords. And Jeremiah did so.

13 [a]So they drew up Jeremiah with cords, and took him up out of the dungeon: and Jeremiah remained [b]in the court of the prison.

Jeremiah's advice to Zedekiah

14 ¶ Then Zedekiah the king sent, and took Jeremiah the prophet unto him into the [l]third entry that *is* in the house of the LORD: and the king said unto Jeremiah, I will ask thee a thing; hide nothing from me.

15 Then Jeremiah said unto Zedekiah, If I declare *it* unto thee, wilt thou not surely put me to death? and if I give thee counsel, wilt thou not hearken unto me?

16 So Zedekiah the king sware secretly unto Jeremiah, saying, *As* the LORD liveth, [a]that made us this soul, I will not put thee to death, neither will I give thee into the hand of these men that seek thy life.

17 Then said Jeremiah unto Zedekiah, Thus saith the LORD, the God of hosts, the God of Israel; If thou wilt assuredly [a]go forth [b]unto the king of Babylon's princes, then thy soul shall live, and this city shall not be burned with fire; and thou shalt live, and thine house:

18 But if thou wilt not go forth to the king of Babylon's princes, then shall this city be given into the hand of the Chaldeans, and they shall burn it with fire, and [a]thou shalt not escape out of their hand.

19 And Zedekiah the king said unto Jeremiah, I am afraid of the Jews that are fallen to the Chaldeans, lest they deliver me into their hand, and they [a]mock me.

20 But Jeremiah said, They shall not deliver *thee.* Obey, I beseech thee, the voice of the LORD, which I speak unto thee: so it shall be well unto thee, and thy soul shall live.

21 But if thou refuse to go forth, this *is* the word that the LORD hath shown me: R

22 And, behold, all the women that are left in the king of Judah's house *shall be* brought forth to the king of Babylon's princes, and those *women* shall say, [l]Thy friends have set thee on, and have prevailed against thee: thy feet are sunk in the mire, *and* they are turned away back.

23 So they shall bring out all thy wives and [a]thy children to the Chaldeans: and thou shalt not escape out of their hand, but shalt be taken by the hand of the king of Babylon: and [l]thou shalt cause this city to be burned with fire.

24 ¶ Then said Zedekiah unto Jeremiah, Let no man know of these words, and thou shalt not die.

25 But if the princes hear that I have talked with thee, and they come unto thee, and say unto thee, Declare unto us now what thou hast said unto the king, hide it not from us, and we will not put thee to death; also what the king said unto thee:

26 Then thou shalt say unto them, [a]I presented my supplication before the king, that he would not cause me to re-

4 [l]Heb. *peace*
6 [a]ch. 37:21 [l]Or, *of the king*
7 [a]ch. 39:16
9 [l]Heb. *he will die*
10 [l]Heb. *in thine hand*
13 [a]ver. 6 [b]ch. 37:21
14 [l]Or, *principal*
16 [a]Is. 57:16
17 [a]2 Ki. 24:12 [b]ch. 39:3
18 [a]ver. 23; ch. 32:4 & 34:3
19 [a]1 Sam. 31:4
22 [l]Heb. *Men of thy peace*
23 [a]ch. 39:6 & 41:10 [l]Heb. *thou shalt burn*
26 [a]ch. 37:20

R *Jer 34:22* ◀▶ *Jer 44:2*

turn [b]to Jonathan's house, to die there.

27 Then came all the princes unto Jeremiah, and asked him: and he told them according to all these words that the king had commanded. So [l]they left off speaking with him; for the matter was not perceived.

28 So [a]Jeremiah abode in the court of the prison until the day that Jerusalem was taken: and he was *there* when Jerusalem was taken.

The fall of Jerusalem

39 IN THE [a]ninth year of Zedekiah king of Judah, in the tenth month, came Nebuchadrezzar king of Babylon and all his army against Jerusalem, and they besieged it.

2 *And* in the eleventh year of Zedekiah, in the fourth month, the ninth *day* of the month, the city was broken up.

3 [a]And all the princes of the king of Babylon came in, and sat in the middle gate, *even* Nergal-sharezer, Samgar-nebo, Sarsechim, Rabsaris, Nergal-sharezer, Rab-mag, with all the residue of the princes of the king of Babylon.

4 ¶ [a]And it came to pass, *that* when Zedekiah the king of Judah saw them, and all the men of war, then they fled, and went forth out of the city by night, by the way of the king's garden, by the gate betwixt the two walls: and he went out the way of the plain.

5 But the Chaldeans' army pursued after them, and [a]overtook Zedekiah in the plains of Jericho: and when they had taken him, they brought him up to Nebuchadnezzar king of Babylon to [b]Riblah in the land of Hamath, where he [l]gave judgment upon him.

6 Then the king of Babylon slew the sons of Zedekiah in Riblah before his eyes: also the king of Babylon slew all the nobles of Judah.

7 Moreover [a]he put out Zedekiah's eyes, and bound him [l]with chains, to carry him to Babylon.

8 ¶ [a]And the Chaldeans burned the king's house, and the houses of the people, with fire, and brake down the walls of Jerusalem.

26 [b]ch. 37:15
27 [l]Heb. *they were silent from him*
28 [a]ch. 37:21 & 39:14
39:1 [a]2 Ki. 25:1-4
3 [a]ch. 38:17
4 [a]2 Ki. 25:4; ch. 52:7
5 [a]ch. 32:4 & 38:18,23 [b]2 Ki. 23:33 [l]Heb. *spake with him judgments*
7 [a]Ezek. 12:13, compared with ch. 32:4 [l]Heb. *with two brasen chains, or, fetters*
8 [a]2 Ki. 25:9; ch. 38:18 & 52:13
9 [a]2 Ki. 25:11 [l]Or, *chief marshal*
10 [l]Heb. *in that day*
11 [l]Heb. *by the hand of*
12 [l]Heb. *set thine eyes upon him*
14 [a]ch. 38:28 [b]ch. 40:5 [c]ch. 26:24
16 [a]ch. 38:7,12 [b]Dan. 9:12
18 [a]ch. 21:9 & 45:5 [b]1 Chr. 5:20; Ps. 37:40

9 [a]Then Nebuzar-adan the [l]captain of the guard carried away captive into Babylon the remnant of the people that remained in the city, and those that fell away, that fell to him, with the rest of the people that remained.

10 But Nebuzar-adan the captain of the guard left of the poor of the people, which had nothing, in the land of Judah, and gave them vineyards and fields [l]at the same time.

11 ¶ Now Nebuchadrezzar king of Babylon gave charge concerning Jeremiah [l]to Nebuzar-adan the captain of the guard, saying,

12 Take him, and [l]look well to him, and do him no harm; but do unto him even as he shall say unto thee.

13 So Nebuzar-adan the captain of the guard sent, and Nebushasban, Rabsaris, and Nergal-sharezer, Rab-mag, and all the king of Babylon's princes;

14 Even they sent, [a]and took Jeremiah out of the court of the prison, and committed him [b]unto Gedaliah the son of [c]Ahikam the son of Shaphan, that he should carry him home: so he dwelt among the people.

15 ¶ Now the word of the LORD came unto Jeremiah, while he was shut up in the court of the prison, saying,

16 Go and speak to [a]Ebed-melech the Ethiopian, saying, Thus saith the LORD of hosts, the God of Israel; Behold, [b]I will bring my words upon this city for evil, and not for good; and they shall be *accomplished* in that day before thee.

17 But I will deliver thee in that day, saith the LORD: and thou shalt not be given into the hand of the men of whom thou *art* afraid. L V

18 For I will surely deliver thee, and thou shalt not fall by the sword, but [a]thy life shall be for a prey unto thee: [b]because thou hast put thy trust in me, saith the LORD.

L *Isa 45:13* ◀▶ *Da 2:28–32*
V *Jer 20:11* ◀▶ *Jer 51:36*

39:6–7 Jeremiah recorded that Nebuchadnezzar killed Zedekiah's sons right in front of him and then blinded him before taking him to Babylon in chains. The last thing Zedekiah saw, the last image indelibly imprinted on his mind, was the murder of his own children brought on by his own rebellion.

Jeremiah released

40 THE WORD that came to Jeremiah from the LORD, [a]after that Nebuzar-adan the captain of the guard had let him go from Ramah, when he had taken him being bound in [1]chains among all that were carried away captive of Jerusalem and Judah, which were carried away captive unto Babylon.

2 And the captain of the guard took Jeremiah, and [a]said unto him, The LORD thy God hath pronounced this evil upon this place.

3 Now the LORD hath brought *it,* and done according as he hath said: [a]because ye have sinned against the LORD, and have not obeyed his voice, therefore this thing is come upon you.

4 And now, behold, I loose thee this day from the chains which [1]*were* upon thine hand. [a]If it seem good unto thee to come with me into Babylon, come; and [2]I will look well unto thee: but if it seem ill unto thee to come with me into Babylon, forbear: behold, [b]all the land *is* before thee: whither it seemeth good and convenient for thee to go, thither go.

5 Now while he was not yet gone back, *he said,* Go back also to Gedaliah the son of Ahikam the son of Shaphan, [a]whom the king of Babylon hath made governor over the cities of Judah, and dwell with him among the people: or go wheresoever it seemeth convenient unto thee to go. So the captain of the guard gave him victuals and a reward, and let him go.

6 [a]Then went Jeremiah unto Gedaliah the son of Ahikam to [b]Mizpah; and dwelt with him among the people that were left in the land.

Gedaliah slain by Ishmael

7 ¶ [a]Now when all the captains of the forces which *were* in the fields, *even* they and their men, heard that the king of Babylon had made Gedaliah the son of Ahikam governor in the land, and had committed unto him men, and women, and children, and of [b]the poor of the land, of them that were not carried away captive to Babylon;

8 Then they came to Gedaliah to Mizpah, [a]even Ishmael the son of Nethaniah, and Johanan and Jonathan the sons of Kareah, and Seraiah the son of Tanhumeth, and the sons of Ephai the Netophathite, and Jezaniah the son of a Maachathite, they and their men.

9 And Gedaliah the son of Ahikam the son of Shaphan sware unto them and to their men, saying, Fear not to serve the Chaldeans: dwell in the land, and serve the king of Babylon, and it shall be well with you.

10 As for me, behold, I will dwell at Mizpah to serve the Chaldeans, which will come unto us: but ye, gather ye wine, and summer fruits, and oil, and put *them* in your vessels, and dwell in your cities that ye have taken.

11 Likewise when all the Jews that *were* in Moab, and among the Ammonites, and in Edom, and that *were* in all the countries, heard that the king of Babylon had left a remnant of Judah, and that he had set over them Gedaliah the son of Ahikam the son of Shaphan;

12 Even all the Jews returned out of all places whither they were driven, and came to the land of Judah, to Gedaliah, unto Mizpah, and gathered wine and summer fruits very much.

13 ¶ Moreover Johanan the son of Kareah, and all the captains of the forces that *were* in the fields, came to Gedaliah to Mizpah,

14 And said unto him, Dost thou certainly know that [a]Baalis the king of the Ammonites hath sent Ishmael the son of Nethaniah [1]to slay thee? But Gedaliah the son of Ahikam believed them not.

15 Then Johanan the son of Kareah spake to Gedaliah in Mizpah secretly, saying, Let me go, I pray thee, and I will slay Ishmael the son of Nethaniah, and no man shall know *it:* wherefore should he slay thee, that all the Jews which are gathered unto thee should be scattered, and the remnant in Judah perish?

16 But Gedaliah the son of Ahikam said unto Johanan the son of Kareah, Thou shalt not do this thing: for thou speakest falsely of Ishmael.

41 NOW IT came to pass in the seventh month, [a]*that* Ishmael the son of Nethaniah the son of Elishama, of the seed royal, and the princes of the king, even ten men with him, came unto Gedaliah the son of Ahikam to Mizpah; and there they did eat bread together in Mizpah.

2 Then arose Ishmael the son of Nethaniah, and the ten men that were with

---

40:1 [a]ch. 39:14 [1]Or, *manacles*

2 [a]ch 50:7

3 [a]Deut. 29:24,25; Dan. 9:11

4 [a]ch. 39:12 [b]Gen. 20:15 [1]Or, *are upon thine hand* [2]Heb. *I will set mine eye upon thee*

5 [a]See ch. 41:10

6 [a]ch. 39:14 [b]Judg. 20:1

7 [a]2 Ki. 25:23 [b]ch. 39:10

8 [a]ch. 41:1

14 [a]See ch. 41:10 [1]Heb. *to strike thee in soul?*

41:1 [a]2 Ki. 25:25; ch. 40:6,8

him, and [a]smote Gedaliah the son of Ahikam the son of Shaphan with the sword, and slew him, whom the king of Babylon had made governor over the land.

3 Ishmael also slew all the Jews that were with him, *even* with Gedaliah, at Mizpah, and the Chaldeans that were found there, *and* the men of war.

4 And it came to pass the second day after he had slain Gedaliah, and no man knew *it,*

5 That there came certain from Shechem, from Shiloh, and from Samaria, *even* fourscore men, [a]having their beards shaven, and their clothes rent, and having cut themselves, with offerings and incense in their hand, to bring *them* to [b]the house of the LORD.

6 And Ishmael the son of Nethaniah went forth from Mizpah to meet them, [1]weeping all along as he went: and it came to pass, as he met them, he said unto them, Come to Gedaliah the son of Ahikam.

7 And it was *so,* when they came into the midst of the city, that Ishmael the son of Nethaniah slew them, *and cast them* into the midst of the pit, he, and the men that *were* with him.

8 But ten men were found among them that said unto Ishmael, Slay us not: for we have treasures in the field, of wheat, and of barley, and of oil, and of honey. So he forbare, and slew them not among their brethren.

9 Now the pit wherein Ishmael had cast all the dead bodies of the men, whom he had slain [1,2]because of Gedaliah, *was* it [a]which Asa the king had made for fear of Baasha king of Israel: *and* Ishmael the son of Nethaniah filled it with *them that were* slain.

10 Then Ishmael carried away captive all the residue of the people that *were* in Mizpah, [a]*even* the king's daughters, and all the people that remained in Mizpah, [b]whom Nebuzar-adan the captain of the guard had committed to Gedaliah the son of Ahikam: and Ishmael the son of Nethaniah carried them away captive, and departed to go over to [c]the Ammonites.

11 ¶ But when Johanan the son of Kareah, and all [a]the captains of the forces that *were* with him, heard of all the evil that Ishmael the son of Nethaniah had done,

12 Then they took all the men, and went to fight with Ishmael the son of Nethaniah, and found him by [a]the great waters that *are* in Gibeon.

13 Now it came to pass, *that* when all the people which *were* with Ishmael saw Johanan the son of Kareah, and all the captains of the forces that *were* with him, then they were glad.

14 So all the people that Ishmael had carried away captive from Mizpah cast about and returned, and went unto Johanan the son of Kareah.

15 But Ishmael the son of Nethaniah escaped from Johanan with eight men, and went to the Ammonites.

16 Then took Johanan the son of Kareah, and all the captains of the forces that *were* with him, all the remnant of the people whom he had recovered from Ishmael the son of Nethaniah, from Mizpah, after *that* he had slain Gedaliah the son of Ahikam, *even* mighty men of war, and the women, and the children, and the eunuchs, whom he had brought again from Gibeon:

17 And they departed, and dwelt in the habitation of [a]Chimham, which is by Bethlehem, to go to enter into Egypt,

18 Because of the Chaldeans: for they were afraid of them, because Ishmael the son of Nethaniah had slain Gedaliah the son of Ahikam, [a]whom the king of Babylon made governor in the land.

The flight to Egypt

42 THEN ALL the captains of the forces, [a]and Johanan the son of Kareah, and Jezaniah the son of Hoshaiah, and all the people from the least even unto the greatest, came near,

2 And said unto Jeremiah the prophet, [1]Let, we beseech thee, our supplication be accepted before thee, and [a]pray for us unto the LORD thy God, *even* for all this remnant; (for we are left *but* [b]a few of many, as thine eyes do behold us:)

3 That the LORD thy God may show us [a]the way wherein we may walk, and the thing that we may do.

4 Then Jeremiah the prophet said unto them, I have heard *you;* behold, I will pray unto the LORD your God according to your words; and it shall come to pass, *that* [a]whatsoever thing the LORD shall answer you, I will declare *it* unto you; I will [b]keep nothing back from you.

5 Then they said to Jeremiah, [a]The

2 [a]2 Ki. 25:25
5 [a]Lev. 19:27,28; Deut. 14:1; Is. 15:2 [b]See 1 Sam. 1:7; 2 Ki. 25:9
6 [1]Heb. *in going and weeping*
9 [a]1 Ki. 15:22; 2 Chr. 16:6 [1]Or, *near Gedaliah* [2]Heb. *by the hand,* or, *by the side of Gedaliah*
10 [a]ch. 43:6 [b]ch. 40:7 [c]ch. 40:14
11 [a]ch. 40:7,8,13
12 [a]2 Sam. 2:13
17 [a]2 Sam. 19:37, 38
18 [a]ch. 40:5
42:1 [a]ch. 40:8,13 & 41:11
2 [a]1 Sam. 7:8 & 12:19; Is. 37:4; Jas. 5:16 [b]Lev. 26:22 [1]Or, *Let our supplication fall before thee*
3 [a]Ezra 8:21
4 [a]1 Ki. 22:14 [b]1 Sam. 3:18; Acts 20:20
5 [a]Gen. 31:50

LORD be a true and faithful witness between us, if we do not even according to
all things for the which the LORD thy God
shall send thee to us.
6 Whether *it be* good, or whether *it be*
evil, we will obey the voice of the LORD
our God, to whom we send thee; [a]that it
may be well with us, when we obey the
voice of the LORD our God.
7 ¶ And it came to pass after ten days,
that the word of the LORD came unto Jeremiah.
8 Then called he Johanan the son of
Kareah, and all the captains of the forces
which *were* with him, and all the people
from the least even to the greatest,
9 And said unto them, Thus saith the
LORD, the God of Israel, unto whom ye
sent me to present your supplication before him;
10 If ye will still abide in this land,
then [a]will I build you, and not pull *you*
down, and I will plant you, and not pluck
you up: for I [b]repent me of the evil that I
have done unto you.
11 Be not afraid of the king of Babylon,
of whom ye are afraid; be not afraid of
him, saith the LORD: [a]for I *am* with you to
save you, and to deliver you from his
hand.
12 And [a]I will show mercies unto you,
that he may have mercy upon you, and
cause you to return to your own land.
13 ¶ But if [a]ye say, We will not dwell
in this land, neither obey the voice of the
LORD your God,
14 Saying, No; but we will go into the
land of Egypt, where we shall see no war,
nor hear the sound of the trumpet, nor
have hunger of bread; and there will we
dwell:
15 And now therefore hear the word
of the LORD, ye remnant of Judah; Thus
saith the LORD of hosts, the God of Israel;
If ye [a]wholly set [b]your faces to enter into
Egypt, and go to sojourn there;
16 Then it shall come to pass, *that* the
sword, which ye feared, shall overtake
you there in the land of Egypt, and the
famine, whereof ye were afraid, [l]shall
follow close after you there in Egypt; and
there ye shall die.
17 [l]So shall it be with all the men that
set their faces to go into Egypt to sojourn
there; they shall die [a]by the sword, by
the famine, and by the pestilence: and
[b]none of them shall remain or escape
from the evil that I will bring upon them.
18 For thus saith the LORD of hosts, the
God of Israel; As mine anger and my fury
hath been [a]poured forth upon the inhabitants of Jerusalem; so shall my fury be
poured forth upon you, when ye shall enter into Egypt: and [b]ye shall be an execration, and an astonishment, and a curse,
and a reproach; and ye shall see this place
no more.
19 ¶ The LORD hath said concerning
you, O ye remnant of Judah; [a]Go ye not
into Egypt: know certainly that I have
[l]admonished you this day.
20 For [l]ye dissembled in your hearts,
when ye sent me unto the LORD your God,
saying, Pray for us unto the LORD our God;
and according unto all that the LORD our
God shall say, so declare unto us, and we
will do *it*.
21 And *now* I have this day declared *it*
to you; but ye have not obeyed the voice
of the LORD your God, nor any *thing* for
the which he hath sent me unto you.
22 Now therefore know certainly that
[a]ye shall die by the sword, by the famine,
and by the pestilence, in the place
whither ye desire [l]to go *and* to sojourn.

43 AND IT came to pass, *that* when
Jeremiah had made an end of
speaking unto all the people all the words
of the LORD their God, for which the LORD
their God had sent him to them, *even* all
these words,
2 [a]Then spake Azariah the son of Hoshaiah, and Johanan the son of Kareah,
and all the proud men, saying unto Jeremiah, Thou speakest falsely: the LORD our
God hath not sent thee to say, Go not
into Egypt to sojourn there:
3 But Baruch the son of Neriah setteth
thee on against us, for to deliver us into
the hand of the Chaldeans, that they
might put us to death, and carry us away
captives into Babylon.
4 So Johanan the son of Kareah, and all
the captains of the forces, and all the people, obeyed not the voice of the LORD, to
dwell in the land of Judah.
5 But Johanan the son of Kareah, and
all the captains of the forces, took [a]all the
remnant of Judah, that were returned
from all nations, whither they had been
driven, to dwell in the land of Judah;
6 *Even* men, and women, and children, [a]and the king's daughters, [b]and every person that Nebuzar-adan the captain

6 [a]Deut. 6:3; ch. 7:23
10 [a]ch. 24:6 & 31:28 & 33:7 [b]Deut. 32:36; ch. 18:8
11 [a]Is. 43:5; Rom. 8:31
12 [a]Ps. 106:45,46
13 [a]ch. 44:16
15 [a]Deut. 17:16; ch. 44:12-14 [b]Luke 9:51
16 [l]Heb. *shall cleave after you*
17 [a]ver. 22; ch. 24:10 [b]See ch. 44:14,28 [l]Heb. *So shall all the men be*
18 [a]ch. 7:20 [b]ch. 18:16 & 24:9 & 26:6 & 29:18,22 & 44:12; Zech. 8:13
19 [a]Deut. 17:16 [l]Heb. *testified against you*
20 [l]Or, *ye have used deceit against your souls*
22 [a]ver. 17; Ezek. 6:11 [l]Or, *to go to sojourn*
43:2 [a]ch. 42:1
5 [a]ch. 40:11,12
6 [a]ch. 41:10 [b]ch. 39:10 & 40:7

of the guard had left with Gedaliah the son of Ahikam the son of Shaphan, and Jeremiah the prophet, and Baruch the son of Neriah.

7 So they came into the land of Egypt: for they obeyed not the voice of the LORD: thus came they *even* to [a]Tahpanhes.

8 ¶ Then came the word of the LORD unto Jeremiah in Tahpanhes, saying,

9 Take great stones in thine hand, and hide them in the clay in the brickkiln, which *is* at the entry of Pharaoh's house in Tahpanhes, in the sight of the men of Judah;

10 And say unto them, Thus saith the LORD of hosts, the God of Israel; Behold, I will send and take Nebuchadrezzar the king of Babylon, [a]my servant, and will set his throne upon these stones that I have hid; and he shall spread his royal pavilion over them.

11 [a]And when he cometh, he shall smite the land of Egypt, *and deliver* [b]such *as are* for death to death; and such *as are* for captivity to captivity; and such *as are* for the sword to the sword.

12 And I will kindle a fire in the houses of [a]the gods of Egypt; and he shall burn them, and carry them away captives: and he shall array himself with the land of Egypt, as a shepherd putteth on his garment; and he shall go forth from thence in peace.

13 He shall break also the [1]images of [2]Beth-shemesh, that *is* in the land of Egypt; and the houses of the gods of the Egyptians shall he burn with fire.

The refugees rebuked

44 THE WORD that came to Jeremiah concerning all the Jews which dwell in the land of Egypt, which dwell at [a]Migdol, and at [b]Tahpanhes, and at [c]Noph, and in the country of Pathros, saying,

R 2 Thus saith the LORD of hosts, the God of Israel; Ye have seen all the evil that I have brought upon Jerusalem, and upon all the cities of Judah; and, behold, this

R *Jer 38:21–23* ◀▶ *Jer 44:6*

day they *are* [a]a desolation, and no man dwelleth therein,

3 Because of their wickedness which they have committed to provoke me to anger, in that they went [a]to burn incense, *and* to [b]serve other gods, whom they knew not, *neither* they, ye, nor your fathers.

4 Howbeit [a]I sent unto you all my servants the prophets, rising early and sending *them,* saying, Oh, do not this abominable thing that I hate.

5 But they hearkened not, nor inclined their ear to turn from their wickedness, to burn no incense unto other gods.

6 Wherefore my fury and mine anger R was poured forth, and was kindled in the cities of Judah and in the streets of Jerusalem; and they are wasted *and* desolate, as at this day.

7 Therefore now thus saith the LORD, the God of hosts, the God of Israel; Wherefore commit ye *this* great evil [a]against your souls, to cut off from you man and woman, child and suckling, [1]out of Judah, to leave you none to remain;

8 In that ye [a]provoke me unto wrath with the works of your hands, burning incense unto other gods in the land of Egypt, whither ye be gone to dwell, that ye might cut yourselves off, and that ye might be [b]a curse and a reproach among all the nations of the earth?

9 Have ye forgotten the [1]wickedness of your fathers, and the wickedness of the kings of Judah, and the wickedness of their wives, and your own wickedness, and the wickedness of your wives, which they have committed in the land of Judah, and in the streets of Jerusalem?

10 They are not [1]humbled *even* unto C this day, neither have they [a]feared, nor walked in my law, nor in my statutes, that I set before you and before your fathers.

11 ¶ Therefore thus saith the LORD of R hosts, the God of Israel; Behold, [a]I will

R *Jer 44:2* ◀▶ *Jer 44:11–12*
C *Jer 23:12* ◀▶ *La 3:19–20*
R *Jer 44:6* ◀▶ *Jer 44:22*

7 [a]ch. 2:16 & 44:1; called *Hanes,* Is. 30:4
10 [a]ch. 25:9 & 27:6; See Ezek. 29:18,20
11 [a]ch. 44:13 & 46:13 [b]ch. 15:2; Zech. 11:9
12 [a]ch. 46:25
13 [1]Heb. *statues,* or, *standing images* [2]Or, *The house of the sun*
44:1 [a]Ex. 14:2; ch. 46:14 [b]ch. 43:7 [c]Is. 19:13
2 [a]ch. 9:11 & 34:22
3 [a]ch. 19:4 [b]Deut. 13:6 & 32:17
4 [a]2 Chr. 36:15; ch. 7:25 & 25:4 & 26:5 & 29:19
7 [a]Num. 16:38; ch. 7:19 [1]Heb. *out of the midst of Judah*
8 [a]ch. 25:6,7 [b]ver. 12; ch. 42:18
9 [1]Heb. *wickednesses,* or, *punishments*
10 [a]Prov. 28:14 [1]Heb. *contrite;* see Ps. 51:17
11 [a]Lev. 17:10 & 20:5,6; ch. 21:10; Amos 9:4

44:2–6 God announced that his punishment upon Jerusalem was delivered and that Judah's cities and towns were no longer inhabited. There was no turning back from his judgment.
44:11–12 Many of the remnant of Judah that had escaped the first wave of exiles to Babylon now planned to escape to Egypt. But Jeremiah warned that God would destroy all those who tried to flee south to escape punishment.

set my face against you for evil, and to cut
off all Judah.
12 And I will take the remnant of Judah, that have set their faces to go into
the land of Egypt to sojourn there, and
[a]they shall all be consumed, *and* fall in
the land of Egypt; they shall *even* be consumed by the sword *and* by the famine:
they shall die, from the least even unto
the greatest, by the sword and by the
famine: and [b]they shall be an execration,
and an astonishment, and a curse, and a
reproach.
D 13 [a]For I will punish them that dwell
in the land of Egypt, as I have punished
Jerusalem, by the sword, by the famine,
and by the pestilence:
14 So that none of the remnant of Judah, which are gone into the land of
Egypt to sojourn there, shall escape or remain, that they should return into the
land of Judah, to the which they [1]have a
desire to return to dwell there: for [a]none
shall return but such as shall escape.
15 ¶ Then all the men which knew
that their wives had burned incense unto
other gods, and all the women that stood
by, a great multitude, even all the people
that dwelt in the land of Egypt, in Pathros, answered Jeremiah, saying,
16 *As for* the word that thou hast spoken unto us in the name of the LORD, [a]we
will not hearken unto thee.
17 But we will certainly do [a]whatso-
ever thing goeth forth out of our own
mouth, to burn incense unto the [b]queen[1]
of heaven, and to pour out drink offerings
unto her, as we have done, we, and our
fathers, our kings, and our princes, in the
cities of Judah, and in the streets of Jerusalem: for *then* had we plenty of [2]vict-
uals, and were well, and saw no evil.
18 But since we left off to burn incense to the queen of heaven, and to
pour out drink offerings unto her, we
have wanted all *things,* and have been
consumed by the sword and by the
famine.
19 [a]And when we burned incense to
the queen of heaven, and poured out
drink offerings unto her, did we make
her cakes to worship her, and pour out

12 [a]ch. 42:15-17, 22 [b]ch. 42:18
13 [a]ch. 43:11
14 [a]ver. 28 [1]Heb. *lift up their soul*
16 [a]ch. 6:16
17 [a]See ver. 25; Num. 30:12; Deut. 23:23; Judg. 11:36 [b]ch. 7:18 [1]Or, *frame of heaven* [2]Heb. *bread*
19 [a]ch. 7:18 [1]Or, *husbands?*
22 [a]ch. 25:11,18, 38 [b]ver. 6
23 [a]Dan. 9:11,12
24 [a]ver. 15; ch. 43:7
25 [a]ver. 15
26 [a]Gen. 22:16 [b]Ezek. 20:39
27 [a]ch. 1:10 & 31:28; Ezek. 7:6 [b]ver. 12
28 [a]ver. 14; Is. 27:13

drink offerings unto her, without our
[1]men?
20 ¶ Then Jeremiah said unto all the
people, to the men, and to the women,
and to all the people which had given
him *that* answer, saying,
21 The incense that ye burned in the
cities of Judah, and in the streets of Jerusalem, ye, and your fathers, your kings,
and your princes, and the people of the
land, did not the LORD remember them,
and came it *not* into his mind?
22 So that the LORD could no longer R
bear, because of the evil of your doings,
and because of the abominations which
ye have committed; therefore is your land
[a]a desolation, and an astonishment, and a
curse, without an inhabitant, [b]as at this
day.
23 Because ye have burned incense,
and because ye have sinned against the
LORD, and have not obeyed the voice of
the LORD, nor walked in his law, nor in
his statutes, nor in his testimonies;
[a]therefore this evil is happened unto you,
as at this day.
24 Moreover Jeremiah said unto all the
people, and to all the women, Hear the
word of the LORD, all Judah [a]that *are* in
the land of Egypt:
25 Thus saith the LORD of hosts, the
God of Israel, saying; [a]Ye and your wives
have both spoken with your mouths, and
fulfilled with your hand, saying, We will
surely perform our vows that we have
vowed, to burn incense to the queen of
heaven, and to pour out drink offerings
unto her: ye will surely accomplish your
vows, and surely perform your vows.
26 Therefore hear ye the word of the
LORD, all Judah that dwell in the land of
Egypt; Behold, [a]I have sworn by my great
name, saith the LORD, that [b]my name shall
no more be named in the mouth of any
man of Judah in all the land of Egypt, saying, The Lord GOD liveth.
27 [a]Behold, I will watch over them for
evil, and not for good: and all the men of
Judah that *are* in the land of Egypt [b]shall
be consumed by the sword and by the
famine, until there be an end of them.
28 Yet [a]a small number that escape the

D *Jer 21:6* ◄► *Eze 5:12*

R *Jer 44:11–12* ◄► *Jer 45:4*

44:22 Jeremiah declared that Judah's desolation was the result of their apostasy.

sword shall return out of the land of Egypt into the land of Judah, and all the remnant of Judah, that are gone into the land of Egypt to sojourn there, shall know whose [b]words shall stand, [1]mine, or theirs.

29 ¶ And this *shall be* a sign unto you, saith the LORD, that I will punish you in this place, that ye may know that my words shall surely stand against you for evil:

J 30 Thus saith the LORD; Behold, [a]I will give Pharaoh-hophra king of Egypt into the hand of his enemies, and into the hand of them that seek his life; as I gave [b]Zedekiah king of Judah into the hand of Nebuchadrezzar king of Babylon, his enemy, and that sought his life.

Encouragement to Baruch

45 THE [a]WORD that Jeremiah the prophet spake unto Baruch the son of Neriah, when he had written these words in a book at the mouth of Jeremiah, in the fourth year of Jehoiakim the son of Josiah king of Judah, saying,

2 Thus saith the LORD, the God of Israel, unto thee, O Baruch;

3 Thou didst say, Woe is me now! for the LORD hath added grief to my sorrow; I fainted in my sighing, and I find no rest.

R 4 ¶ Thus shalt thou say unto him, The LORD saith thus; Behold, [a]*that* which I have built will I break down, and that which I have planted I will pluck up, even this whole land.

P 5 And seekest thou great things for thyself? seek *them* not: for, behold, [a]I will bring evil upon all flesh, saith the LORD: but thy life will I give unto thee [b]for a prey in all places whither thou goest.

The prophecy about Egypt

46 THE WORD of the LORD which came to Jeremiah the prophet against [a]the Gentiles;

2 Against Egypt, [a]against the army of Pharaoh-necho king of Egypt, which was by the river Euphrates in Carchemish, which Nebuchadrezzar king of Babylon smote in the fourth year of Jehoiakim the son of Josiah king of Judah.

3 [a]Order ye the buckler and shield, and draw near to battle.

4 Harness the horses; and get up, ye horsemen, and stand forth with *your* helmets; furbish the spears, *and* put on the brigandines.

5 Wherefore have I seen them dismayed *and* turned away back? and their mighty ones are [1]beaten down, and are [2]fled apace, and look not back: *for* [a]fear *was* round about, saith the LORD.

6 Let not the swift flee away, nor the mighty man escape; they shall [a]stumble, and fall toward the north by the river Euphrates.

7 Who *is* this *that* cometh up [a]as a flood, whose waters are moved as the rivers?

8 Egypt riseth up like a flood, and *his* waters are moved like the rivers; and he saith, I will go up, *and* will cover the earth; I will destroy the city and the inhabitants thereof.

9 Come up, ye horses; and rage, ye chariots; and let the mighty men come forth; [1]the Ethiopians and [2]the Libyans, that handle the shield; and the Lydians, [a]that handle *and* bend the bow.

10 For this *is* [a]the day of the Lord GOD of hosts, a day of vengeance, that he may avenge him of his adversaries: and [b]the sword shall devour, and it shall be satiate and made drunk with their blood: for the Lord GOD of hosts [c]hath a sacrifice in the north country by the river Euphrates.

11 [a]Go up into Gilead, and take balm, [b]O virgin, the daughter of Egypt: in vain shalt thou use many medicines; *for* [c]thou[1] shalt not be cured. G

12 The nations have heard of thy shame, and thy cry hath filled the land: for the mighty man hath stumbled against the mighty, *and* they are fallen both together.

13 ¶ The word that the LORD spake to Jeremiah the prophet, how Nebuchadrez-

28 [b]ver. 17,25,26 [1]Heb. *from me, or them*
30 [a]ch. 46:25,26; Ezek. 29:3 & 30:21 [b]ch. 39:5
45:1 [a]ch. 36:1,4, 32
4 [a]Is. 5:5
5 [a]ch. 25:26 [b]ch. 21:9 & 38:2 & 39:18
46:1 [a]ch. 25:15
2 [a]2 Ki. 23:29; 2 Chr. 35:20 Fulfilled presently
3 [a]ch. 51:11,12; Nah. 2:1 & 3:14
5 [a]ch. 49:29 [1]Heb. *broken in pieces* [2]Heb. *fled a flight*
6 [a]Dan. 11:19
7 [a]Is. 8:7,8; ch. 47:2
9 [a]Is. 66:19 [1]Heb. *Cush* [2]Heb. *Put*
10 [a]Is. 13:6; Joel 1:15 [b]Deut. 32:42; Is. 34:6 [c]Is. 34:6; Zeph. 1:7; See Ezek. 39:17
11 [a]ch. 8:22 [b]Is. 47:1 [c]Ezek. 30:21 [1]Heb. *no cure shall be unto thee*

J *Jer 29:32* ◀▶ *Jer 46:26*
R *Jer 44:22* ◀▶ *La 1:1–2*
P *Jer 30:23–24* ◀▶ *Jer 48:47*
G *Jer 30:12* ◀▶ *Eze 13:10–14*

45:4–5 Though God had built up the land of Judah, he promised to tear it down because of its sins. Yet God is merciful. He promised to preserve Baruch "in all places whither thou goest" (45:5). Jewish tradition suggests that Baruch joined his people in exile and died in Babylon.

zar king of Babylon should come *and* [a]smite the land of Egypt.

14 Declare ye in Egypt, and publish in Migdol, and publish in Noph and in Tahpanhes: say ye, [a]Stand fast, and prepare thee; for [b]the sword shall devour round about thee.

15 Why are thy valiant *men* swept away? they stood not, because the LORD did drive them.

16 He [1]made many to fall, yea, [a]one fell upon another: and they said, Arise, and let us go again to our own people, and to the land of our nativity, from the oppressing sword.

17 They did cry there, Pharaoh king of Egypt *is but* a noise; he hath passed the time appointed.

18 *As* I live, saith the King, [a]whose name *is* the LORD of hosts, Surely as Tabor *is* among the mountains, and as Carmel by the sea, *so* shall he come.

19 O [a]thou daughter dwelling in Egypt, [1]furnish thyself [b]to go into captivity: for Noph shall be waste and desolate without an inhabitant.

20 Egypt *is like* a very fair [a]heifer, *but* destruction cometh; it cometh [b]out of the north.

21 Also her hired men *are* in the midst of her like [1]fatted bullocks; for they also are turned back, *and* are fled away together: they did not stand, because [a]the day of their calamity was come upon them, *and* the time of their visitation.

22 [a]The voice thereof shall go like a serpent; for they shall march with an army, and come against her with axes, as hewers of wood.

23 They shall [a]cut down her forest, saith the LORD, though it cannot be searched; because they are more than the [b]grasshoppers, and *are* innumerable.

24 The daughter of Egypt shall be confounded; she shall be delivered into the hand of [a]the people of the north.

25 The LORD of hosts, the God of Israel, saith; Behold, I will punish the [1,2]multitude of [a]No, and Pharaoh, and Egypt, [b]with their gods, and their kings: even Pharaoh, and *all* them that trust in him:

26 [a]And I will deliver them into the hand of those that seek their lives, and into the hand of Nebuchadrezzar king of Babylon, and into the hand of his servants: and [b]afterward it shall be inhabited, as in the days of old, saith the LORD. J

27 ¶ [a]But fear not thou, O my servant Jacob, and be not dismayed, O Israel: for, behold, I will save thee from afar off, and thy seed from the land of their captivity; and Jacob shall return, and be in rest and at ease, and none shall make *him* afraid. I

28 Fear thou not, O Jacob my servant, saith the LORD: for I *am* with thee; for I will make a full end of all the nations whither I have driven thee: but I will not make [a]a full end of thee, but correct thee in measure; yet will I [1]not leave thee wholly unpunished.

Prophecy about the Philistines

47 THE WORD of the LORD that came to Jeremiah the prophet [a]against the Philistines, [b]before that Pharaoh smote [1]Gaza.

2 Thus saith the LORD; Behold, [a]waters rise up [b]out of the north, and shall be an overflowing flood, and shall overflow the land, and [1]all that is therein; the city, and them that dwell therein: then the men shall cry, and all the inhabitants of the land shall howl.

3 At the [a]noise of the stamping of the hoofs of his strong *horses,* at the rushing of his chariots, *and at* the rumbling of his wheels, the fathers shall not look back to *their* children for feebleness of hands;

4 Because of the day that cometh to spoil all the Philistines, *and* to cut off from [a]Tyrus and Zidon every helper that remaineth: for the LORD will spoil the Philistines, [b]the remnant of [1]the country of [c]Caphtor.

5 [a]Baldness is come upon Gaza; [b]Ashkelon is cut off *with* the remnant of their valley: how long wilt thou cut thyself? J

13 [a]Is. 19:1; Ezek. 29 & 30 & 32
14 [a]ver. 3,4 [b]ver. 10
16 [a]Lev. 26:37 [1]Heb. *multiplied the faller*
18 [a]Is. 47:4; ch. 48:15
19 [a]ch. 48:18 [b]Is. 20:4 [1]Heb. *make thee instruments of captivity*
20 [a]Hos. 10:11 [b]ch. 1:14
21 [a]Ps. 37:13; ch. 50:27 [1]Heb. *bullocks of the stall*
22 [a]Is. 29:4
23 [a]Is. 10:34 [b]Judg. 6:5
24 [a]ch. 1:15
25 [a]Ezek. 30:14 [b]ch. 43:12 [1]Or, *nourisher* [2]Heb. *Amon*
26 [a]Ezek. 32:11 [b]Ezek. 29:11,13,14
27 [a]Is. 41:13
28 [a]ch. 10:24 [1]Or, *not utterly cut thee off*
47:1 [a]Zeph. 2:4 [b]Amos 1:6 [1]Heb. *Azzah*
2 [a]Is. 8:7 [b]ch. 1:14 [1]Heb. *the fulness thereof*
3 [a]ch. 8:16
4 [a]ch. 25:22 [b]Ezek. 25:16 [c]Gen. 10:14 [1]Heb. *the isle*
5 [a]Mic. 1:16 [b]ch. 25:20

J *Jer 44:30* ◀ ▶ *Jer 47:5*
I *Jer 35:18–19* ◀ ▶ *Jer 50:19–20*
J *Jer 46:26* ◀ ▶ *Eze 12:13*

46:27–28 Notice the similarity between this passage and 30:10–11. Jeremiah declared that despite the terrible punishment of captivity and exile, God would ultimately restore his people to the promised land. God would also destroy those nations that gloried in their victory over God's people. In fulfillment of this prophecy both the great empires of Assyria and Babylon were so totally destroyed that archeologists have only recently discovered the ruins of their vast cities.

6 O thou [a]sword of the LORD, how long *will it be* ere thou be quiet? [1]put up thyself into thy scabbard, rest, and be still.

7 [1]How can it be quiet, seeing the LORD hath [a]given it a charge against Ashkelon, and against the sea shore? there hath he [b]appointed it.

The prophecy against Moab

48 AGAINST [a]MOAB thus saith the LORD of hosts, the God of Israel; Woe unto [b]Nebo! for it is spoiled: [c]Kiriathaim is confounded *and* taken: [1]Misgab is confounded and dismayed.

2 [a]*There shall be* no more praise of Moab: in [b]Heshbon they have devised evil against it; come, and let us cut it off from *being* a nation. Also thou shalt [1]be cut down, O Madmen; the sword shall [2]pursue thee.

3 A voice of crying *shall be* from Horonaim, spoiling and great destruction.

4 Moab is destroyed; her little ones have caused a cry to be heard.

5 [a]For in the going up of Luhith [1]continual weeping shall go up; for in the going down of Horonaim the enemies have heard a cry of destruction.

6 Flee, save your lives, and be like [1]the [a]heath in the wilderness.

7 ¶ For because thou hast trusted in thy works and in thy treasures, thou shalt also be taken: and [a]Chemosh shall go forth into captivity *with* his [b]priests and his princes together.

8 And [a]the spoiler shall come upon every city, and no city shall escape: the valley also shall perish, and the plain shall be destroyed, as the LORD hath spoken.

9 [a]Give wings unto Moab, that it may flee and get away: for the cities thereof shall be desolate, without any to dwell therein.

10 [a]Cursed *be* he that doeth the work of the LORD [1]deceitfully, and cursed *be* he that keepeth back his sword from blood.

11 ¶ Moab hath been at ease from his youth, and he [a]hath settled on his lees, and hath not been emptied from vessel to vessel, neither hath he gone into captivity: therefore his taste [1]remained in him, and his scent is not changed.

12 Therefore, behold, the days come, saith the LORD, that I will send unto him wanderers, that shall cause him to wander, and shall empty his vessels, and break their bottles.

13 And Moab shall be ashamed of [a]Chemosh, as the house of Israel [b]was ashamed of [c]Beth-el their confidence.

14 ¶ How say ye, [a]We *are* mighty and strong men for the war?

15 [a]Moab is spoiled, and gone up *out of* her cities, and [1]his chosen young men are [b]gone down to the slaughter, saith [c]the King, whose name *is* the LORD of hosts.

16 The calamity of Moab *is* near to come, and his affliction hasteth fast.

17 All ye that are about him, bemoan him; and all ye that know his name, say, [a]How is the strong staff broken, *and* the beautiful rod!

18 [a]Thou daughter that dost inhabit [b]Dibon, come down from *thy* glory, and sit in thirst; for [c]the spoiler of Moab shall come upon thee, *and* he shall destroy thy strong holds.

19 O [1]inhabitant of [a]Aroer, [b]stand by the way, and espy; ask him that fleeth, and her that escapeth, *and* say, What is done?

20 Moab is confounded; for it is broken down: [a]howl and cry; tell ye it in [b]Arnon, that Moab is spoiled,

21 And judgment is come upon [a]the plain country; upon Holon, and upon Jahazah, and upon Mephaath,

22 And upon Dibon, and upon Nebo, and upon Beth-diblathaim,

23 And upon Kiriathaim, and upon Beth-gamul, and upon Beth-meon,

24 And upon [a]Kerioth, and upon Bozrah, and upon all the cities of the land of Moab, far or near.

25 [a]The horn of Moab is cut off, and his [b]arm is broken, saith the LORD.

26 ¶ [a]Make ye him drunken: for he magnified *himself* against the LORD: Moab also shall wallow in his vomit, and he also shall be in derision.

27 For [a]was not Israel a derision unto thee? [b]was he found among thieves? for since thou spakest of him, thou [1]skippedst for joy.

28 O ye that dwell in Moab, leave the cities, and [a]dwell in the rock, and be like [b]the dove *that* maketh her nest in the sides of the hole's mouth.

29 We have heard the [a]pride of Moab, (he is exceeding proud) his loftiness, and his arrogancy, and his pride, and the haughtiness of his heart.

30 I know his wrath, saith the LORD;

---

6 [a]Ezek. 21:3 [1]Heb. *gather thyself*

7 [a]Ezek. 14:17 [b]Mic. 6:9 [1]Heb. *How canst thou*

48:1 [a]Is. 15 & 16 [b]Is. 15:2 [c]Num. 32:37 [1]Or, *The high place*

2 [a]Is. 16:14 [b]Is. 15:4 [1]Or, *be brought to silence;* see Is. 15:1 [2]Heb. *go after thee*

5 [a]Is. 15:5 [1]Heb. *weeping with weeping*

6 [a]ch. 17:6 [1]Or, *a naked tree*

7 [a]Num. 21:29; Judg. 11:24; Is. 46:1,2 [b]ch. 49:3

8 [a]ch. 6:26

9 [a]Ps. 55:6

10 [a]Judg. 5:23; 1 Sam. 15:3; 1 Ki. 20:42 [1]Or, *negligently*

11 [a]Zeph. 1:12 [1]Heb. *stood*

13 [a]1 Ki. 11:7 [b]Hos. 10:6 [c]1 Ki. 12:29

14 [a]Is. 16:6

15 [a]ver. 8,9,18 [b]ch. 50:27 [c]ch. 46:18 [1]Heb. *the choice of*

17 [a]Is. 9:4 & 14:4, 5

18 [a]Is. 47:1 [b]Num. 21:30; Is. 15:2 [c]ver. 8

19 [a]Deut. 2:36 [b]1 Sam. 4:13 [1]Heb. *inhabitress*

20 [a]Is. 16:7 [b]Num. 21:13

21 [a]ver. 8

24 [a]Amos 2:2

25 [a]Ps. 75:10 [b]Ezek. 30:21

26 [a]ch. 25:15

27 [a]Zeph. 2:8 [b]ch. 2:26 [1]Or, *movedst thyself*

28 [a]Ps. 55:6,7 [b]Sol. 2:14

29 [a]Is. 16:6

but *it shall* not *be* so; [a]his[1] lies shall not so effect *it*.

31 Therefore [a]will I howl for Moab, and I will cry out for all Moab; *mine heart* shall mourn for the men of Kir-heres.

32 [a]O vine of Sibmah, I will weep for thee with the weeping of Jazer: thy plants are gone over the sea, they reach *even* to the sea of Jazer: the spoiler is fallen upon thy summer fruits and upon thy vintage.

33 And [a]joy and gladness is taken from the plentiful field, and from the land of Moab; and I have caused wine to fail from the winepresses: none shall tread with shouting; *their* shouting *shall be* no shouting.

34 [a]From the cry of Heshbon *even* unto Elealeh, *and even* unto Jahaz, have they uttered their voice, [b]from Zoar *even* unto Horonaim, *as* an heifer of three years old: for the waters also of Nimrim shall be [1]desolate.

35 Moreover I will cause to cease in Moab, saith the LORD, [a]him that offereth in the high places, and him that burneth incense to his gods.

36 Therefore [a]mine heart shall sound for Moab like pipes, and mine heart shall sound like pipes for the men of Kir-heres: because [b]the riches *that* he hath gotten are perished.

37 For [a]every head *shall be* bald, and every beard [1]clipped: upon all the hands *shall be* cuttings, and [b]upon the loins sackcloth.

38 *There shall be* lamentation generally upon all the housetops of Moab, and in the streets thereof: for I have broken Moab like [a]a vessel wherein *is* no pleasure, saith the LORD.

39 They shall howl, *saying,* How is it broken down! how hath Moab turned the [1]back with shame! so shall Moab be a derision and a dismaying to all them about him.

40 For thus saith the LORD; Behold, [a]he shall fly as an eagle. and shall [b]spread his wings over Moab.

41 [a]Kerioth[1] is taken, and the strong holds are surprised, and [b]the mighty men's hearts in Moab at that day shall be as the heart of a woman in her pangs.

42 And Moab shall be destroyed [a]from *being* a people, because he hath magnified *himself* against the LORD.

43 [a]Fear, and the pit, and the snare, *shall be* upon thee, O inhabitant of Moab, saith the LORD.

44 He that fleeth from the fear shall fall into the pit; and he that getteth up out of the pit shall be taken in the snare: for [a]I will bring upon it, *even* upon Moab, the year of their visitation, saith the LORD.

45 They that fled stood under the shadow of Heshbon because of the force: but [a]a fire shall come forth out of Heshbon, and a flame from the midst of Sihon, and [b]shall devour the corner of Moab, and the crown of the head of the [1]tumultuous ones.

46 [a]Woe be unto thee, O Moab! the people of Chemosh perisheth: for thy sons are taken [1]captives, and thy daughters captives.

47 ¶ Yet will I bring again the captivity P
of Moab [a]in the latter days, saith the LORD. Thus far *is* the judgment of Moab.

30 [a]Is. 16:6; ch. 50:36 [1]Or, *those on whom he stayeth* (Heb. *his bars) do not right*
31 [a]Is. 15:5
32 [a]Is. 16:8,9
33 [a]Is. 16:10; Joel 1:12
34 [a]Is. 15:4-6 [b]Is. 15:5,6 [1]Heb. *desolations*
35 [a]Is. 15:2 & 16:12
36 [a]Is. 15:5 & 16:11 [b]Is. 15:7
37 [a]Is. 15:2,3 [b]Gen. 37:34 [1]Heb. *diminished*
38 [a]ch. 22:28
39 [1]Heb. *neck*
40 [a]Deut. 28:49; Hab. 1:8 [b]Is. 8:8
41 [a]ver. 24 [b]Is. 13:8 & 21:3; Mic. 4:9 [1]Or, *The cities*
42 [a]Ps. 83:4
43 [a]Is. 24:17
44 [a]ch. 11:23
45 [a]Num. 21:28 [b]Num. 24:17 [1]Heb. *children of noise*
46 [a]Num 21:29 [1]Heb. *in captivity*
47 [a]ch. 49:6
49:1 [a]Ezek. 21:28 & 25:2; Amos 1:13; Zeph. 2:8,9 [b]Amos 1:13 [1]Or, *Against* [2]Or, *Melcom*
2 [a]Ezek. 25:5; Amos 1:14
3 [a]Is. 32:11 [1]Or, *Melcom; see* 1 Ki. 11:5

The prophecy against Ammon

49 CONCERNING[1] [a]THE Ammonites, thus saith the LORD; Hath Israel no sons? hath he no heir? why *then* doth [2]their king inherit [b]Gad, and his people dwell in his cities?

2 Therefore, behold, the days come, P
saith the LORD, that I will cause an alarm of war to be heard in [a]Rabbah of the Ammonites; and it shall be a desolate heap, and her daughters shall be burned with fire: then shall Israel be heir unto them that were his heirs, saith the LORD.

3 Howl, O Heshbon, for Ai is spoiled: cry, ye daughters of Rabbah, [a]gird you with sackcloth; lament, and run to and fro by the hedges; for [1]their king shall go

P *Jer 45:5* ◀▶ *Jer 49:2–6*
P *Jer 48:47* ◀▶ *Jer 49:23–27*

49:1–2, 6 This prophecy told of the destruction of the Ammonites (see Eze 25:1–7; Am 1:13–15; Zep 2:8–11). Ammon was located on the east side of the Jordan and north of Moab. Ammon joined forces with Moab and supplied troops to Nebuchadnezzar during the attack on Judah (see 2Ki 24:2). Yet Ammon apparently rebelled against Nebuchadnezzar's governor Gedaliah (see 40:13—41:3). Such treachery would have been punished by Babylon and probably led to an attack that virtually wiped out Ammon. Though Ammon was sentenced to destruction, note that God promised to restore them (49:6).

into captivity, *and* his [b]priests and his princes together.

4 Wherefore gloriest thou in the valleys, [1]thy flowing valley, O [a]backsliding daughter? that trusted in her treasures, [b]*saying,* Who shall come unto me?

5 Behold, I will bring a fear upon thee, saith the Lord GOD of hosts, from all those that be about thee; and ye shall be driven out every man right forth; and none shall gather up him that wandereth.

6 And [a]afterward I will bring again the captivity of the children of Ammon, saith the LORD.

The prophecy against Edom

7 ¶ [a]Concerning Edom, thus saith the LORD of hosts; [b]*Is* wisdom no more in Teman? [c]is counsel perished from the prudent? is their wisdom vanished?

8 [a]Flee ye, [1]turn back, dwell deep, O inhabitants of [b]Dedan; for I will bring the calamity of Esau upon him, the time *that* I will visit him.

9 If [a]grapegatherers come to thee, would they not leave *some* gleaning grapes? if thieves by night, they will destroy [1]till they have enough.

10 [a]But I have made Esau bare, I have uncovered his secret places, and he shall not be able to hide himself: his seed is spoiled, and his brethren, and his neighbours, and [b]he *is* not.

11 Leave thy fatherless children, I will preserve *them* alive; and let thy widows trust in me.

12 For thus saith the LORD; Behold, [a]they whose judgment *was* not to drink of the cup have assuredly drunken; and *art* thou he *that* shall altogether go unpunished? thou shalt not go unpunished, but thou shalt surely drink *of it.*

13 For [a]I have sworn by myself, saith the LORD, that [b]Bozrah shall become a desolation, a reproach, a waste, and a curse; and all the cities thereof shall be perpetual wastes.

14 I have heard a [a]rumour from the LORD, and an ambassador is sent unto the heathen, *saying,* Gather ye together, and come against her, and rise up to the battle.

3 [b]ch. 48:7
4 [a]ch. 3:14 [b]ch. 21:13 [1]Or, *thy valley floweth away*
6 [a]ver. 39; ch. 48:47
7 [a]Ezek. 25:12 [b]Obad. 8 [c]Is. 19:11
8 [a]ver. 30 [b]ch. 25:23 [1]Or, *they are turned back*
9 [a]Obad. 5 [1]Heb. *their sufficiency*
10 [a]Mal. 1:3 [b]Is. 17:14
12 [a]ch. 25:29; Obad. 16
13 [a]Gen. 22:16; Is. 45:23; Amos 6:8 [b]Is. 34:6 & 63:1
14 [a]Obad. 1-3
16 [a]Obad. 4 [b]Job 39:27 [c]Amos 9:2
17 [a]ch. 18:16 & 50:13
18 [a]Gen. 19:25; Deut. 29:23; ch. 50:40
19 [a]ch. 50:44 [b]ch. 12:5 [c]Ex. 15:11 [d]Job 41:10 [1]Or, *summon me in judgment*
20 [a]ch. 50:45
21 [a]ch. 50:46 [1]Heb. *Weedy sea*
22 [a]ch. 48:40,41
23 [a]Is. 17:1 & 37:13; Amos 1:3; Zech. 9:1,2 [b]Is. 57:20 [1]Heb. *melted* [2]Or, *as on the sea*

15 For, lo, I will make thee small among the heathen, *and* despised among men.

16 Thy terribleness hath deceived thee, *and* the pride of thine heart, O thou that dwellest in the clefts of the rock, that holdest the height of the hill: [a]though thou shouldest make thy [b]nest as high as the eagle, [c]I will bring thee down from thence, saith the LORD. M

17 Also Edom shall be a desolation: [a]every one that goeth by it shall be astonished, and shall hiss at all the plagues thereof.

18 [a]As in the overthrow of Sodom and Gomorrah and the neighbour *cities* thereof, saith the LORD, no man shall abide there, neither shall a son of man dwell in it.

19 [a]Behold, he shall come up like a lion from [b]the swelling of Jordan against the habitation of the strong: but I will suddenly make him run away from her: and who *is* a chosen *man, that* I may appoint over her? for [c]who *is* like me? and who will [1]appoint me the time? and [d]who *is* that shepherd that will stand before me?

20 [a]Therefore hear the counsel of the LORD, that he hath taken against Edom; and his purposes, that he hath purposed against the inhabitants of Teman: Surely the least of the flock shall draw them out: surely he shall make their habitations desolate with them.

21 [a]The earth is moved at the noise of their fall, at the cry the noise thereof was heard in the [1]Red sea.

22 Behold, [a]he shall come up and fly as the eagle, and spread his wings over Bozrah: and at that day shall the heart of the mighty men of Edom be as the heart of a woman in her pangs.

23 ¶ [a]Concerning Damascus. Hamath is confounded, and Arpad: for they have heard evil tidings: they are [1]fainthearted; [b]*there is* sorrow [2]on the sea; it cannot be quiet. P

24 Damascus is waxed feeble, *and*

M *Jer 29:12–13* ◀ ▶ *La 3:19–21*
P *Jer 49:2–6* ◀ ▶ *Jer 49:39*

49:23–27 Damascus was the capital of Syria, a frequent enemy of Israel. Note that this prophecy about a fire in the wall of Damascus parallels the prophecy found in Isa 17:1. These words may refer to Nebuchadnezzar's overthrow of Syria or may refer to Damascus' destruction in the end times.

turneth herself to flee, and fear hath
seized on *her:* [a]anguish and sorrows have
taken her, as a woman in travail.
25 How is [a]the city of praise not left,
the city of my joy!
26 [a]Therefore her young men shall fall
in her streets, and all the men of war
shall be cut off in that day, saith the LORD
of hosts.
27 And I will kindle a [a]fire in the wall
of Damascus, and it shall consume the
palaces of Ben-hadad.

The prophecy against Kedar

28 ¶ [a]Concerning Kedar, and concerning the kingdoms of Hazor, which Nebuchadrezzar king of Babylon shall smite,
thus saith the LORD; Arise ye, go up to
Kedar, and spoil [b]the men of the east.
29 Their [a]tents and their flocks shall
they take away: they shall take to themselves their curtains, and all their vessels,
and their camels; and they shall cry unto
them, [b]Fear *is* on every side.
30 ¶ [a]Flee, [/]get you far off, dwell deep,
O ye inhabitants of Hazor, saith the LORD;
for Nebuchadrezzar king of Babylon hath
taken counsel against you, and hath conceived a purpose against you.
31 Arise, get you up unto [a]the
[/]wealthy nation, that dwelleth without
care, saith the LORD, which have neither
gates nor bars, *which* [b]dwell alone.
32 And their camels shall be a booty,
and the multitude of their cattle a spoil:
and I will scatter into all winds them *that*
are [/]in the utmost corners; and I will
bring their calamity from all sides
thereof, saith the LORD.
33 And Hazor [a]shall be a dwelling for
dragons, *and* a desolation for ever: [b]there
shall no man abide there, nor *any* son of
man dwell in it.

The prophecy against Elam

34 ¶ The word of the LORD that came to
Jeremiah the prophet against [a]Elam in
the beginning of the reign of Zedekiah
king of Judah, saying,
35 Thus saith the LORD of hosts; Behold, I will break [a]the bow of Elam, the
chief of their might.
36 And upon Elam will I bring the four

24 [a]Is. 13:8; ch. 4:31 & 6:24 & 48:41
25 [a]ch. 33:9
26 [a]ch. 50:30
27 [a]Amos 1:4
28 [a]Is. 21:13 [b]Judg. 6:3; Job 1:3
29 [a]Ps. 120:5 [b]ch. 46:5
30 [a]ver. 8 [/]Heb. *flit greatly*
31 [a]Ezek. 38:11 [b]Num. 23:9; Deut. 33:28; Mic. 7:14 [/]Or, *that is at ease*
32 [/]Heb. *cut off into corners,* or, *that have the corners* of their hair *polled*
33 [a]ch. 9:11 & 10:22; Mal. 1:3 [b]ver. 18
34 [a]ch. 25:25
35 [a]Is. 22:6
36 [a]ver. 32
37 [a]ch. 9:16
38 [a]ch. 43:10
39 [a]ch. 48:47
50:1 [a]Is. 13:1 & 47:1 [/]Heb. *by the hand of Jeremiah*
2 [a]Is. 46:1; ch. 51:44 [b]See ch. 43:12,13 [/]Heb. *lift up*
3 [a]ch. 51:48 [b]Is. 13:17,18,20
4 [a]Hos. 1:11 [b]Ezra 3:12; ch. 31:9; Zech. 12:10 [c]Hos. 3:5
5 [a]ch. 31:31
6 [a]Is. 53:6; 1 Pet. 2:25 [b]ch. 2:20 & 3:6,23 [/]Heb. *place to lie down in*
7 [a]Ps. 79:7

winds from the four quarters of heaven,
and [a]will scatter them toward all those
winds; and there shall be no nation
whither the outcasts of Elam shall not
come.
37 For I will cause Elam to be dismayed before their enemies, and before
them that seek their life: and I will bring
evil upon them, *even* my fierce anger,
saith the LORD; [a]and I will send the sword
after them, till I have consumed them:
38 And I will [a]set my throne in Elam,
and will destroy from thence the king and
the princes, saith the LORD.
39 ¶ But it shall come to pass [a]in the P
latter days, *that* I will bring again the captivity of Elam, saith the LORD.

The prophecy against Babylon

50 THE WORD that the LORD spake
[a]against Babylon *and* against the
land of the Chaldeans [/]by Jeremiah the
prophet.
2 Declare ye among the nations, and
publish, and [/]set up a standard; publish,
and conceal not: say, Babylon is taken,
[a]Bel is confounded, Merodach is broken
in pieces; [b]her idols are confounded, her
images are broken in pieces.
3 [a]For out of the north there cometh
up [b]a nation against her, which shall
make her land desolate, and none shall
dwell therein: they shall remove, they
shall depart, both man and beast.
4 ¶ In those days, and in that time,
saith the LORD, the children of Israel shall
come, [a]they and the children of Judah together, [b]going and weeping: they shall
go, [c]and seek the LORD their God.
5 They shall ask the way to Zion with
their faces thitherward, *saying,* Come,
and let us join ourselves to the LORD in [a]a
perpetual covenant *that* shall not be forgotten.
6 My people hath been [a]lost sheep:
their shepherds have caused them to go
astray, they have turned them away *on*
[b]the mountains: they have gone from
mountain to hill, they have forgotten
their [/]restingplace.
7 All that found them have [a]devoured

P *Jer 49:23–27* ◀▶ *Eze 38:1–23*

50:1, 9–10 Jeremiah ultimately delivered this prophecy to Babylon itself (see 51:59–61), naming the nations who would come against this great empire and ultimately destroy it (see 51:27–28).

them: and [b]their adversaries said, [c]We
offend not, because they have sinned
against the LORD, [d]the habitation of justice, even the LORD, [e]the hope of their
fathers.
8 [a]Remove out of the midst of Babylon,
and go forth out of the land of the Chaldeans, and be as the he goats before the
flocks.
9 ¶ [a]For, lo, I will raise and cause to
come up against Babylon an assembly of
great nations from the north country: and
they shall set themselves in array against
her; from thence she shall be taken: their
arrows *shall be* as of a mighty [1]expert
man; [b]none shall return in vain.
10 And Chaldea shall be a spoil: [a]all
that spoil her shall be satisfied, saith the
LORD.
11 [a]Because ye were glad, because ye
rejoiced, O ye destroyers of mine heritage, because ye are grown [1]fat [b]as the
heifer at grass, and [2]bellow as bulls;
12 Your mother shall be sore confounded; she that bare you shall be
ashamed: behold, the hindermost of the
nations *shall be* a wilderness, a dry land,
and a desert.
13 Because of the wrath of the LORD it
shall not be inhabited, [a]but it shall be
wholly desolate: [b]every one that goeth by
Babylon shall be astonished, and hiss at
all her plagues.
14 [a]Put yourselves in array against
Babylon round about: all ye [b]that bend
the bow, shoot at her, spare no arrows:
for she hath sinned against the LORD.
15 Shout against her round about: she
hath [a]given her hand: her foundations
are fallen, [b]her walls are thrown down:
for [c]it *is* the vengeance of the LORD: take
vengeance upon her; as she hath done,
do unto her.
16 Cut off the sower from Babylon,
and him that handleth the [1]sickle in the
time of harvest: for fear of the oppressing
sword [a]they shall turn every one to his
people, and they shall flee every one to
his own land.
17 ¶ Israel *is* [a]a scattered sheep; [b]the
lions have driven *him* away: first [c]the
king of Assyria hath devoured him; and
last this [d]Nebuchadrezzar king of Babylon
hath broken his bones.
18 Therefore thus saith the LORD of
hosts, the God of Israel; Behold, I will
punish the king of Babylon and his land,
as I have punished the king of Assyria.
19 [a]And I will bring Israel again to his I
habitation, and he shall feed on Carmel
and Bashan, and his soul shall be satisfied
upon mount Ephraim and Gilead.
20 In those days, and in that time, K
saith the LORD, [a]the iniquity of Israel shall L
be sought for, and *there shall be* none;
and the sins of Judah, and they shall not
be found: for I will pardon them [b]whom I
reserve.
21 ¶ Go up against the land [1]of Mera-
thaim, *even* against it, and against the inhabitants of [a]Pekod: [2] waste and utterly
destroy after them, saith the LORD, and do
[b]according to all that I have commanded
thee.
22 [a]A sound of battle *is* in the land,
and of great destruction.
23 How is [a]the hammer of the whole
earth cut asunder and broken! how is
Babylon become a desolation among the
nations!
24 I have laid a snare for thee, and
thou art also taken, O Babylon, [a]and thou
wast not aware: thou art found, and also
caught, because thou hast striven against
the LORD.
25 The LORD hath opened his armoury,
and hath brought forth [a]the weapons of
his indignation: for this *is* the work of the
Lord GOD of hosts in the land of the Chaldeans.
26 Come against her [1]from the utmost
border, open her storehouses: [2]cast her
up as heaps, and destroy her utterly: let
nothing of her be left.
27 Slay all her [a]bullocks; let them go
down to the slaughter: woe unto them!
for their day is come, the time of [b]their
visitation.
28 The voice of them that flee and escape out of the land of Babylon, [a]to de-

7 [b]ch. 40:2,3; Zech. 11:5 [c]See ch. 2:3; Dan 9:16 [d]Ps. 90:1 & 91:1 [e]Ps. 22:4
8 [a]Is. 48:20; ch. 51:6,45; Zech. 2:6, 7; Rev. 18:4
9 [a]ch. 15:14 & 51:27 [b]2 Sam. 1:22 [1]Or, *destroyer*
10 [a]Rev. 17:16
11 [a]Is. 47:6 [b]Hos. 10:11 [1]Heb. *big,* or, *corpulent* [2]Or, *neigh as steeds*
13 [a]ch. 25:12 [b]ch. 49:17
14 [a]ch. 51:2 [b]ver. 29
15 [a]1 Chr. 29:24; 2 Chr. 30:8; Lam. 5:6; Ezek. 17:18 [b]ch. 51:58 [c]ch. 51:6,11
16 [a]Is. 13:14 [1]Or, *scythe*
17 [a]ver. 6 [b]ch. 2:15 [c]2 Ki. 17:6 [d]2 Ki. 24:10,14
19 [a]Is. 65:10; ch. 33:12; Ezek. 34:13
20 [a]ch. 31:34 [b]Is. 1:9
21 [a]Ezek. 23:23 [b]See 2 Sam. 16:11; 2 Ki. 18:25; 2 Chr. 36:23; Is. 10:6 & 44:28 & 48:14 [1]Or, *of the rebels* [2]Or, *Visitation*
22 [a]ch. 51:54
23 [a]Is. 14:6; ch. 51:20
24 [a]ch. 51:8,31; Dan. 5:30
25 [a]Is. 13:5
26 [1]Heb. *from the end* [2]Or, *tread her*
27 [a]Ps. 22:12; Is. 34:7; ch. 46:21 [b]ch. 48:44
28 [a]ch. 51:10

I *Jer 46:27–28* ◀▶ *Jer 51:5*
K *Jer 33:8* ◀▶ *Eze 11:19–20*
L *Jer 36:3* ◀▶ *La 3:25*

50:19–20 In the last days, when the Messiah returns and declares "I will pardon them whom I reserve" (50:20), the Jews will return to the promised land.

clare in Zion the vengeance of the LORD
our God, the vengeance of his temple.
29 Call together the archers against
Babylon: [a]all ye that bend the bow, camp
against it round about; let none thereof
escape: [b]recompense her according to
her work; according to all that she hath
done, do unto her: [c]for she hath been
proud against the LORD, against the Holy
One of Israel.
30 [a]Therefore shall her young men fall
in the streets, and all her men of war
shall be cut off in that day, saith the
LORD.
31 Behold, I *am* against thee, *O thou*
[1]most proud, saith the Lord GOD of hosts:
for [a]thy day is come, the time *that* I will
visit thee.
32 And [1]the most proud shall stumble
and fall, and none shall raise him up: and
[a]I will kindle a fire in his cities, and it
shall devour all round about him.
33 ¶ Thus saith the LORD of hosts; The
children of Israel and the children of Judah *were* oppressed together: and all that
took them captives held them fast; they
refused to let them go.
34 [a]Their Redeemer *is* strong; [b]the
LORD of hosts *is* his name: he shall thoroughly plead their cause, that he may
give rest to the land, and disquiet the inhabitants of Babylon.
35 ¶ A sword *is* upon the Chaldeans,
saith the LORD, and upon the inhabitants
of Babylon, and [a]upon her princes, and
upon [b]her wise *men.*
36 A sword *is* [a]upon the [1,2]liars; and
they shall dote: a sword *is* upon her
mighty men; and they shall be dismayed.
37 A sword *is* upon their horses, and
upon their chariots, and upon all [a]the
mingled people that *are* in the midst of
her; and [b]they shall become as women: a
sword *is* upon her treasures; and they
shall be robbed.
38 [a]A drought *is* upon her waters; and
they shall be dried up: for it *is* the land of
[b]graven images, and they are mad upon
their idols.
39 [a]Therefore the wild beasts of the
desert with the wild beasts of the islands
shall dwell *there,* and the owls shall dwell
therein: [b]and it shall be no more inhabited for ever; neither shall it be dwelt in
from generation to generation.
40 [a]As God overthrew Sodom and Gomorrah and the neighbour *cities* thereof,
saith the LORD; *so* shall no man abide
there, neither shall any son of man dwell
therein.
41 [a]Behold, a people shall come from
the north, and a great nation, and many
kings shall be raised up from the coasts of
the earth.
42 [a]They shall hold the bow and the
lance: [b]they *are* cruel, and will not show
mercy: [c]their voice shall roar like the sea,
and they shall ride upon horses, *every
one* put in array, like a man to the battle,
against thee, O daughter of Babylon.
43 The king of Babylon hath heard the
report of them, and his hands waxed feeble: anguish took hold of him, *and* pangs
as of a woman in travail.
44 [a]Behold, he shall come up like a
lion from the swelling of Jordan unto the
habitation of the strong: but I will make
them suddenly run away from her: and
who *is* a chosen *man, that* I may appoint
over her? for who *is* like me? and
who will [1]appoint me the time? and
[b]who *is* that shepherd that will stand
before me?
45 Therefore hear ye [a]the counsel of
the LORD, that he hath taken against Babylon; and his purposes, that he hath purposed against the land of the Chaldeans:
Surely the least of the flock shall draw
them out: surely he shall make *their* habitation desolate with them.
46 [a]At the noise of the taking of Babylon the earth is moved, and the cry is
heard among the nations.

51 THUS SAITH the LORD; Behold, I
will raise up against Babylon, and
against them that dwell in the [1]midst of
them that rise up against me, [a]a destroying wind;
2 And will send unto Babylon [a]fan-
ners, that shall fan her, and shall empty
her land: [b]for in the day of trouble they
shall be against her round about.
3 Against *him that* bendeth [a]let the archer bend his bow, and against *him that*
lifteth himself up in his brigandine: and
spare ye not her young men; [b]destroy ye
utterly all her host.
4 Thus the slain shall fall in the land of
the Chaldeans, [a]and *they that are* thrust
through in her streets.

29 [a]ver. 14 [b]ver. 15; ch. 51:56; Rev. 18:6 [c]Is. 47:10
30 [a]ch. 49:26 & 51:4
31 [a]ver. 27 [1]Heb. *pride*
32 [a]ch. 21:14 [1]Heb. *pride*
34 [a]Rev. 18:8 [b]Is. 47:4
35 [a]Dan. 5:30 [b]Is. 47:13
36 [a]Is. 44:25; ch. 48:30 [1]Or, *chief stays* [2]Heb. *bars*
37 [a]ch. 25:20; Ezek. 30:5 [b]ch. 51:30; Nah. 3:13
38 [a]Is. 44:27; ch. 51:36; Rev. 16:12 [b]ver. 2
39 [a]Is. 13:21,22 & 34:14; ch. 51:37; Rev. 18:2 [b]Is. 13:20; ch. 25:12
40 [a]Gen. 19:25; Is. 13:19; ch. 51:26
41 [a]ver. 9; ch. 6:22 & 25:14 & 51:27; Rev. 17:16
42 [a]ch. 6:23 [b]Is. 13:18 [c]Is. 5:30
44 [a]ch. 49:19 [b]Job 41:10; ch. 49:19 [1]Or, *summon me to plead?*
45 [a]Is. 14:24; ch. 51:11
46 [a]Rev. 18:9
51:1 [a]2 Ki. 19:7; ch. 4:11 [1]Heb. *heart*
2 [a]ch. 15:7 [b]ch. 50:14
3 [a]ch. 50:14 [b]ch. 50:21
4 [a]ch. 49:26 & 50:30,37

I 5 For Israel *hath* not *been* forsaken,
nor Judah of his God, of the LORD of hosts;
though their land was filled with sin
against the Holy One of Israel.
6 [a]Flee out of the midst of Babylon,
and deliver every man his soul: be not cut
off in her iniquity; for [b]this *is* the time of
the LORD'S vengeance; [c]he will render
unto her a recompence.
7 [a]Babylon *hath been* a golden cup in
the LORD'S hand, that made all the earth
drunken: [b]the nations have drunken of
her wine; therefore the nations [c]are mad.
8 Babylon is suddenly [a]fallen and destroyed: [b]howl for her; [c]take balm for her
pain, if so be she may be healed.
9 We would have healed Babylon, but
she is not healed: forsake her, and [a]let us
go every one into his own country: [b]for
her judgment reacheth unto heaven, and
is lifted up *even* to the skies.
10 The LORD hath [a]brought forth our
righteousness: come, and let us [b]declare
in Zion the work of the LORD our God.
11 [a]Make [1]bright the arrows; gather
the shields: [b]the LORD hath raised up the
spirit of the kings of the Medes: [c]for his
device *is* against Babylon, to destroy it;
because it *is* [d]the vengeance of the LORD,
the vengeance of his temple.
12 [a]Set up the standard upon the walls
of Babylon, make the watch strong, set up
the watchmen, prepare the [1]ambushes:
for the LORD hath both devised and done
that which he spake against the inhabitants of Babylon.
13 [a]O thou that dwellest upon many
waters, abundant in treasures, thine end
is come, *and* the measure of thy covetousness.
14 [a]The LORD of hosts hath sworn [1]by
himself, *saying,* Surely I will fill thee with
men, [b]as with caterpillars; and they shall
[2]lift [c]up a shout against thee.
15 [a]He hath made the earth by his
power, he hath established the world by
his wisdom, and [b]hath stretched out the
heaven by his understanding.
16 When he uttereth *his* voice, *there
is* a [1]multitude of waters in the heavens;
and [a]he causeth the vapours to ascend
from the ends of the earth: he maketh
lightnings with rain, and bringeth forth
the wind out of his treasures.
17 [a]Every man [1]is brutish by *his*
knowledge; every founder is confounded
by the graven image: [b]for his molten image *is* falsehood, and *there is* no breath in
them.
18 [a]They *are* vanity, the work of errors: in the time of their visitation they
shall perish.
19 [a]The portion of Jacob *is* not like
them; for he *is* the former of all things:
and *Israel is* the rod of his inheritance:
the LORD of hosts *is* his name.
20 [a]Thou *art* my battle axe *and* weapons of war: for [1]with thee will I break in
pieces the nations, and with thee will I
destroy kingdoms;
21 And with thee will I break in pieces
the horse and his rider; and with thee
will I break in pieces the chariot and his
rider;
22 With thee also will I break in pieces
man and woman; and with thee will I
break in pieces [a]old and young; and with
thee will I break in pieces the young man
and the maid;
23 I will also break in pieces with thee
the shepherd and his flock; and with thee
will I break in pieces the husbandman
and his yoke of oxen; and with thee will I
break in pieces captains and rulers.
24 [a]And I will render unto Babylon
and to all the inhabitants of Chaldea all
their evil that they have done in Zion in
your sight, saith the LORD.
25 Behold, I *am* against thee,
[a]O destroying mountain, saith the LORD,
which destroyest all the earth: and I will
stretch out mine hand upon thee, and
roll thee down from the rocks, [b]and will
make thee a burnt mountain.
26 And they shall not take of thee a
stone for a corner, nor a stone for foundations; [a]but thou shalt be [1]desolate for
ever, saith the LORD.
27 [a]Set ye up a standard in the land,
blow the trumpet among the nations,
[b]prepare the nations against her, call together against her [c]the kingdoms of Ararat, Minni, and Ashchenaz; appoint a captain against her; cause the horses to come
up as the rough caterpillars.
28 Prepare against her the nations

6 [a]ch. 50:8; Rev. 18:4 [b]ch. 50:15 [c]ch. 25:14
7 [a]Rev. 17:4 [b]Rev. 14:8 [c]ch. 25:16
8 [a]Is. 21:9; Rev. 14:8 & 18:2 [b]ch. 48:20; Rev. 18:9, 11,19 [c]ch. 46:11
9 [a]Is. 13:14; ch. 50:16 [b]Rev. 18:5
10 [a]Ps. 37:6 [b]ch. 50:28
11 [a]ch. 46:4 [b]ver. 28; Is. 13:17 [c]ch. 50:45 [d]ch. 50:28 [1]Heb. *pure*
12 [a]Nah. 2:1 & 3:14 [1]Heb. *liers in wait*
13 [a]Rev. 17:1,15
14 [a]ch. 49:13; Amos 6:8 [b]Nah. 3:15 [c]ch. 50:15 [1]Heb. *by his soul* [2]Heb. *utter*
15 [a]Gen. 1:1,6; ch. 10:12 [b]Job 9:8; Ps. 104:2; Is. 40:22
16 [a]Ps. 135:7 [1]Or, *noise*
17 [a]ch. 10:14 [b]ch. 50:2 [1]Or, *is more brutish than to know*
18 [a]ch. 10:15
19 [a]ch. 10:16
20 [a]Is. 10:5,15; ch. 50:23 [1]Or, *in thee, or, by thee*
22 [a]2 Chr. 36:17
24 [a]ch. 50:15
25 [a]Is. 13:2; Zech. 4:7 [b]Rev. 8:8
26 [a]ch. 50:40 [1]Heb. *everlasting desolations*
27 [a]Is. 13:2 [b]ch. 25:14 [c]ch. 50:41

I *Jer 50:19–20* ◀ ▶ *La 3:31*

51:5 God declared that his people have not been utterly forsaken.

with [a]the kings of the Medes, the captains thereof, and all the rulers thereof,
and all the land of his dominion.
29 And the land shall tremble and sorrow: for every purpose of the LORD shall
be performed against Babylon, [a]to make
the land of Babylon a desolation without
an inhabitant.
30 The mighty men of Babylon have
forborne to fight, they have remained in
their holds: their might hath failed; [a]they
became as women: they have burned her
dwellingplaces; [b]her bars are broken.
31 [a]One post shall run to meet another, and one messenger to meet another, to show the king of Babylon that
his city is taken at *one* end,
32 And that [a]the passages are stopped,
and the reeds they have burned with fire,
and the men of war are affrighted.
33 For thus saith the LORD of hosts, the
God of Israel; The daughter of Babylon *is*
[a]like a threshingfloor, [b]*it*[1] *is* time to
thresh her: yet a little while, [c]and the
time of her harvest shall come.
34 Nebuchadrezzar the king of Babylon hath [a]devoured me, he hath crushed
me, he hath made me an empty vessel,
he hath swallowed me up like a dragon,
he hath filled his belly with my deli-
cates, he hath cast me out.
35 [1]The violence done to me and to
my [2]flesh *be* upon Babylon, shall the [3]in-
habitant of Zion say; and my blood upon
the inhabitants of Chaldea, shall Jerusalem say.
V 36 Therefore thus saith the LORD; Behold, [a]I will plead thy cause, and take
vengeance for thee; [b]and I will dry up her
sea, and make her springs dry.
37 [a]And Babylon shall become heaps,
a dwellingplace for dragons, [b]an astonishment, and an hissing, without an inhabitant.
38 They shall roar together like lions:
they shall [1]yell as lions' whelps.
39 In their heat I will make their
feasts, and [a]I will make them drunken,
that they may rejoice, and sleep a perpetual sleep, and not wake, saith the
LORD.
40 I will bring them down like lambs
to the slaughter, like rams with he goats.
41 How is [a]Sheshach taken! and how
is [b]the praise of the whole earth surprised! how is Babylon become an astonishment among the nations!
42 [a]The sea is come up upon Babylon:
she is covered with the multitude of the
waves thereof.
43 [a]Her cities are a desolation, a dry
land, and a wilderness, a land wherein no
man dwelleth, neither doth *any* son of
man pass thereby.
44 [a]And I will punish Bel in Babylon,
and I will bring forth out of his mouth
that which he hath swallowed up: and
the nations shall not flow together any
more unto him: yea, [b]the wall of Babylon
shall fall.
45 [a]My people, go ye out of the midst
of her, and deliver ye every man his soul
from the fierce anger of the LORD.
46 And [1]lest your heart faint, and ye
fear [a]for the rumour that shall be heard
in the land; a rumour shall both come
one year, and after that in *another* year
shall come a rumour, and violence in the
land, ruler against ruler.
47 Therefore, behold, the days come,
that [a]I will [1]do judgment upon the graven
images of Babylon: and her whole land
shall be confounded, and all her slain
shall fall in the midst of her.
48 Then [a]the heaven and the earth,
and all that *is* therein, shall sing for Babylon: [b]for the spoilers shall come unto
her from the north, saith the LORD.
49 [1]As Babylon *hath caused* the slain
of Israel to fall, so at Babylon shall fall the
slain of all [2]the earth.
50 [a]Ye that have escaped the sword,
go away, stand not still: remember the
LORD afar off, and let Jerusalem come into
your mind.
51 [a]We are confounded, because we
have heard reproach: shame hath covered our faces: for strangers are come
into the sanctuaries of the LORD'S house.
52 Wherefore, behold, the days come,
saith the LORD, [a]that I will do judgment

28 [a]ver. 11
29 [a]ver. 43; ch. 50:13
30 [a]Is. 19:16; ch. 48:41 & 50:37 [b]Lam. 2:9; Amos 1:5; Nah. 3:13
31 [a]ch. 50:24
32 [a]ch. 50:38
33 [a]Is. 21:10; Amos 1:3; Mic. 4:13 [b]Is. 41:15; Hab. 3:12 [c]Is. 17:5; Hos. 6:11; Joel 3:13; Rev. 14:15 [1]Or, *in the time that he thresheth her*
34 [a]ch. 50:17
35 [1]Heb. *My violence* [2]Or, *remainder* [3]Heb. *inhabitress*
36 [a]ch. 50:34 [b]ch. 50:38
37 [a]Is. 13:22; ch. 50:39; Rev. 18:2 [b]ch. 25:9,18
38 [1]Or, *shake themselves*
39 [a]ver. 57
41 [a]ch. 25:26 [b]Is. 13:19
42 [a]See Is. 8:7
43 [a]ver. 29; ch. 50:39
44 [a]Is. 46:1 [b]ver. 58
45 [a]ver. 6; ch. 50:8; Rev. 18:4
46 [a]2 Ki. 19:7 [1]Or, *let not*
47 [a]ver. 52 [1]Heb. *visit upon*
48 [a]Is. 44:23 [b]ch. 50:3,41
49 [1]Or, *Both Babylon is to fall, O ye slain of Israel, and with Babylon* [2]Or, *the country*
50 [a]ch. 44:28
51 [a]Ps. 44:15 & 79:4
52 [a]ver. 47

V Jer 39:17–18 ◀▶ Da 11:32

51:37 Jeremiah prophesied that Babylon would meet her own fate and be totally destroyed. This prophecy was amply fulfilled when the Medes and Persians destroyed Babylon in 538 B.C. The city became a ruin that was ultimately covered by desert sand for almost two thousand years.

upon her graven images: and through all her land the wounded shall groan.

53 [a]Though Babylon should mount up to heaven, and though she should fortify the height of her strength, *yet* from me shall spoilers come unto her, saith the LORD.

54 [a]A sound of a cry *cometh* from Babylon, and great destruction from the land of the Chaldeans:

55 Because the LORD hath spoiled Babylon, and destroyed out of her the great voice; when her waves do roar like great waters, a noise of their voice is uttered:

56 Because the spoiler is come upon her, *even* upon Babylon, and her mighty men are taken, every one of their bows is broken: [a]for the LORD God of recompences shall surely requite.

57 [a]And I will make drunk her princes, and her wise *men,* her captains, and her rulers, and her mighty men: and they shall sleep a perpetual sleep, and not wake, saith [b]the King, whose name *is* the LORD of hosts.

58 Thus saith the LORD of hosts; [a]The [1] broad walls of Babylon shall be utterly [2]broken, and her high gates shall be burned with fire; and [b]the people shall labour in vain, and the folk in the fire, and they shall be weary.

59 ¶ The word which Jeremiah the prophet commanded Seraiah the son of Neriah, the son of Maaseiah, when he went [1]with Zedekiah the king of Judah into Babylon in the fourth year of his reign. And *this* Seraiah *was* a [2]quiet prince.

60 So Jeremiah wrote in a book all the evil that should come upon Babylon, *even* all these words that are written against Babylon.

61 And Jeremiah said to Seraiah, When thou comest to Babylon, and shalt see, and shalt read all these words;

62 Then shalt thou say, O LORD, thou hast spoken against this place, to cut it off, that [a]none shall remain in it, neither man nor beast, but that it shall be [1]desolate for ever.

63 And it shall be, when thou hast made an end of reading this book, [a]*that* thou shalt bind a stone to it, and cast it into the midst of Euphrates:

64 And thou shalt say, Thus shall Babylon sink, and shall not rise from the evil that I will bring upon her: [a]and they shall be weary. Thus far *are* the words of Jeremiah.

Downfall of Jerusalem

52 ZEDEKIAH *WAS* [a]one and twenty years old when he [1]began to reign, and he reigned eleven years in Jerusalem. And his mother's name *was* Hamutal the daughter of Jeremiah of Libnah.

2 And he did *that which was* evil in the eyes of the LORD, according to all that Jehoiakim had done.

3 For through the anger of the LORD it came to pass in Jerusalem and Judah, till he had cast them out from his presence, that Zedekiah rebelled against the king of Babylon.

4 ¶ And it came to pass in the [a]ninth year of his reign, in the tenth month, in the tenth *day* of the month, *that* Nebuchadrezzar king of Babylon came, he and all his army, against Jerusalem, and pitched against it, and built forts against it round about.

5 So the city was besieged unto the eleventh year of king Zedekiah.

6 And in the fourth month, in the ninth *day* of the month, the famine was sore in the city, so that there was no bread for the people of the land.

7 Then the city was broken up, and all the men of war fled, and went forth out of the city by night by the way of the gate between the two walls, which *was* by the king's garden; (now the Chaldeans *were* by the city round about:) and they went by the way of the plain.

8 ¶ But the army of the Chaldeans pursued after the king, and overtook Zedekiah in the plains of Jericho; and all his army was scattered from him.

9 [a]Then they took the king, and carried him up unto the king of Babylon to Riblah in the land of Hamath; where he gave judgment upon him.

10 [a]And the king of Babylon slew the sons of Zedekiah before his eyes: he slew also all the princes of Judah in Riblah.

11 Then he [1]put out the eyes of Zedekiah; and the king of Babylon bound him in [2]chains, and carried him to Babylon, and put him in [3]prison till the day of his death.

12 ¶ [a]Now in the fifth month, in the tenth *day* of the month, [b]which *was* the nineteenth year of Nebuchadrezzar king

---

53 [a]ch. 49:16; Amos 9:2; Obad. 4
54 [a]ch. 50:22
56 [a]ver. 24; Ps. 94:1; ch. 50:29
57 [a]ver. 39 [b]ch. 46:18 & 48:15
58 [a]ver. 44 [b]Hab. 2:13 [1]Or, *The walls of broad Babylon* [2]Or, *made naked*
59 [1]Or, *on the behalf of* [2]Or, *prince of Menucha,* or, *chief chamberlain*
62 [a]ver. 29; ch. 50:3,39 [1]Heb. *desolations*
63 [a]See Rev. 18:21
64 [a]ver. 58
52:1 [a]2 Ki. 24:18 [1]Heb. *reigned*
4 [a]2 Ki. 25:1-27; ch. 39:1; Zech. 8:19
9 [a]ch. 32:4
10 [a]Ezek. 12:13
11 [1]Heb. *blinded* [2]Or, *fetters* [3]Heb. *house of the wards*
12 [a]Zech. 7:5 & 8:19 [b]See ver. 29

of Babylon, [c]came Nebuzar-adan, [1]captain of the guard, *which* [2]served the king of Babylon, into Jerusalem,

13 And burned the house of the LORD, and the king's house; and all the houses of Jerusalem, and all the houses of the great *men,* burned he with fire:

14 And all the army of the Chaldeans, that *were* with the captain of the guard, brake down all the walls of Jerusalem round about.

15 [a]Then Nebuzar-adan the captain of the guard carried away captive *certain* of the poor of the people, and the residue of the people that remained in the city, and those that fell away, that fell to the king of Babylon, and the rest of the multitude.

16 But Nebuzar-adan the captain of the guard left *certain* of the poor of the land for vinedressers and for husbandmen.

17 [a]Also the [b]pillars of brass that *were* in the house of the LORD, and the bases, and the brasen sea that *was* in the house of the LORD, the Chaldeans brake, and carried all the brass of them to Babylon.

18 [a]The caldrons also, and the [1]shovels, and the snuffers, and the [2]bowls, and the spoons, and all the vessels of brass wherewith they ministered, took they away.

19 And the basins, and the [1]firepans, and the bowls, and the caldrons, and the candlesticks, and the spoons, and the cups; *that* which *was* of gold *in* gold, and *that* which *was* of silver *in* silver, took the captain of the guard away.

20 The two pillars, one sea, and twelve brasen bulls that *were* under the bases, which king Solomon had made in the house of the LORD: [a]the[1] brass of all these vessels was without weight.

21 And *concerning* the [a]pillars, the height of one pillar *was* eighteen cubits; and a [1]fillet of twelve cubits did compass it; and the thickness thereof *was* four fingers: *it was* hollow.

22 And a chapiter of brass *was* upon it; and the height of one chapiter *was* five cubits, with network and pomegranates upon the chapiters round about, all *of* brass. The second pillar also and the pomegranates *were* like unto these.

23 And there were ninety and six pomegranates on a side; *and* [a]all the pomegranates upon the network *were* an hundred round about.

24 ¶ And [a]the captain of the guard took Seraiah the chief priest, [b]and Zephaniah the second priest, and the three keepers of the [1]door:

25 He took also out of the city an eunuch, which had the charge of the men of war; and seven men of them that [1]were near the king's person, which were found in the city; and the [2]principal scribe of the host, who mustered the people of the land; and threescore men of the people of the land, that were found in the midst of the city.

26 So Nebuzar-adan the captain of the guard took them, and brought them to the king of Babylon to Riblah.

27 And the king of Babylon smote them, and put them to death in Riblah in the land of Hamath. Thus Judah was carried away captive out of his own land.

28 [a]This *is* the people whom Nebuchadrezzar carried away captive: in the [b]seventh year [c]three thousand Jews and three and twenty:

29 [a]In the eighteenth year of Nebuchadrezzar he carried away captive from Jerusalem eight hundred thirty and two [1]persons:

30 In the three and twentieth year of Nebuchadrezzar Nebuzar-adan the captain of the guard carried away captive of the Jews seven hundred forty and five persons: all the persons *were* four thousand and six hundred.

The honour given Jehoiachin

31 ¶ [a]And it came to pass in the seven and thirtieth year of the captivity of Jehoiachin king of Judah, in the twelfth month, in the five and twentieth *day* of the month, *that* Evil-merodach king of Babylon in the *first* year of his reign [b]lifted up the head of Jehoiachin king of Judah, and brought him forth out of prison,

32 And spake [1]kindly unto him, and set his throne above the throne of the kings that *were* with him in Babylon,

33 And changed his prison garments: [a]and he did continually eat bread before him all the days of his life.

34 And *for* his diet, there was a continual diet given him of the king of Babylon, [1]every day a portion until the day of his death, all the days of his life.

12 [c]ch. 39:9 [1]Or, *chief marshal* [2]Heb. *stood before*
15 [a]ch. 39:9
17 [a]ch. 27:19 [b]See 1 Ki. 7:15,23,27,50
18 [a]Ex. 27:3; 2 Ki. 25:14-16 [1]Or, *instruments to remove the ashes* [2]Or, *basins*
19 [1]Or, *censers*
20 [a]1 Ki. 7:47 [1]Heb. *their brass*
21 [a]1 Ki. 7:15; 2 Ki. 25:17; 2 Chr. 3:15 [1]Heb. *thread*
23 [a]See 1 Ki. 7:20
24 [a]2 Ki. 25:18 [b]ch. 21:1 & 29:5 [1]Heb. *threshold*
25 [1]Heb. *saw the face of the king* [2]Or, *scribe of the captain of the host*
28 [a]2 Ki. 24:2 [b]See 2 Ki. 24:12 [c]See 2 Ki. 24:14
29 [a]See ver. 12; ch. 39:9 [1]Heb. *souls*
31 [a]2 Ki. 25:27-30 [b]Gen. 40:13,20
32 [1]Heb. *good things with him*
33 [a]2 Sam. 9:13
34 [1]Heb. *the matter of the day in his day*

Lamentations

Author: Probably Jeremiah

Theme: Sadness over the fall of Jerusalem

Date of Writing: 586 B.C.

Outline of Lamentations

I. Jerusalem's Desolation (1:1–22)
II. God's Wrath Against the People (2:1–22)
III. The Reason for Comfort (3:1–66)
IV. Jerusalem's Past Glory and Present Misery (4:1–22)
V. A Prayer for God's Mercy (5:1–22)

THE BOOK OF Lamentations does not name its author but has traditionally been ascribed to the prophet Jeremiah. Since Jeremiah lived in Jerusalem, warned the people about the city's coming destruction and then witnessed this terrible judgment, is it assumed that Jeremiah authored this book. In addition, the similarity of vocabulary and style between the books of Lamentations and Jeremiah suggests one author for both books. The book's English title is derived from the Septuagint (the Greek translation of the OT) title that means "to cry aloud." Written as a reminder of the fall of Jerusalem and the destruction of the temple, Lamentations mournfully cries its sense of loss and anguish in its five funeral poems, or laments.

In the Hebrew text the first four chapters are acrostically arranged. Each of the twenty-two verses in chapters 1, 2 and 4 begin with a successive letter of the Hebrew alphabet. The third chapter divides its sixty-six verses into twenty-two groups and follows the same acrostic poem arrangement. The last chapter of the book is not alphabetic but still mirrors the somber mood of the previous four. This stylistic form reflects the meter used in funeral dirges and indicates that despite the passionate tone of these poems, they were composed with expert precision.

While other books in the OT contain community laments, this composition focuses on the terrible calamity that has befallen Jerusalem. The author recognizes that its destruction is the judgment of a righteous God and appeals to God for mercy. Note the similarity between the author's concern for Jerusalem and Jesus' words about the city (see Mt 23:37–38).

Jerusalem's desolation

R **1** HOW DOTH the city sit solitary, *that was* full of people! [a]*how* is she become as a widow! she *that was* great among the nations, *and* princess among the provinces, *how* is she become tributary!

2 She [a]weepeth sore in the [b]night, and her tears *are* on her cheeks: among all her lovers she hath none to comfort *her*: all her friends have dealt treacherously with her, they are become her enemies.

3 Judah is gone into captivity because of affliction, and [1]because of great servitude: [a]she dwelleth among the heathen, she findeth no rest: all her persecutors overtook her between the straits.

R 4 The ways of Zion do mourn, because none come to the solemn feasts: all her gates are desolate: her priests sigh, her virgins are afflicted, and she *is* in bitterness.

5 Her adversaries [a]are the chief, her enemies prosper; for the LORD hath afflicted her [b]for the multitude of her transgressions: her [c]children are gone into captivity before the enemy.

6 And from the daughter of Zion all her beauty is departed: her princes are become like harts *that* find no pasture, and they are gone without strength before the pursuer.

7 Jerusalem remembered in the days of her affliction and of her miseries all her [1]pleasant things that she had in the days of old, when her people fell into the hand of the enemy, and none did help her: the adversaries saw her, *and* did mock at her sabbaths.

8 [a]Jerusalem hath grievously sinned; therefore she [1]is removed: all that honoured her despise her, because [b]they have seen her nakedness: yea, she sigheth, and turneth backward.

9 Her filthiness *is* in her skirts; she [a]remembereth not her last end; therefore she came down wonderfully: [b]she had no comforter. O LORD, behold my affliction: for the enemy hath magnified *himself.*

10 The adversary hath spread out his hand upon [a]all her [1]pleasant things: for she hath seen *that* [b]the heathen entered into her sanctuary, whom thou didst command *that* [c]they should not enter into thy congregation.

11 All her people sigh, [a]they seek bread; they have given their pleasant things for meat [1]to relieve the soul: see, O LORD, and consider; for I am become vile.

12 ¶ [1]*Is it* nothing to you, all ye that [2]pass by? behold, and see [a]if there be any sorrow like unto my sorrow, which is done unto me, wherewith the LORD hath afflicted *me* in the day of his fierce anger. R

13 From above hath he sent fire into my bones, and it prevaileth against them: he hath [a]spread a net for my feet, he hath turned me back: he hath made me desolate *and* faint all the day.

14 [a]The yoke of my transgressions is bound by his hand: they are wreathed, *and* come up upon my neck: he hath made my strength to fall, the Lord hath delivered me into *their* hands, *from whom* I am not able to rise up.

15 The Lord hath trodden under foot all my mighty *men* in the midst of me: he hath called an assembly against me to crush my young men: [a]the Lord hath trodden [1]the virgin, the daughter of Judah, *as* in a winepress.

16 For these *things* I weep; [a]mine eye, mine eye runneth down with water, because [b]the comforter that should [1]relieve my soul is far from me: my children are desolate, because the enemy prevailed. R

17 [a]Zion spreadeth forth her hands, *and* [b]*there is* none to comfort her: the LORD hath commanded concerning Jacob, *that* his adversaries *should be* round about him: Jerusalem is as a menstruous woman among them.

R *Jer 45:4* ◀▶ *La 1:4–10*
R *La 1:1–2* ◀▶ *La 1:12*
R *La 1:4–10* ◀▶ *La 1:16–17*
R *La 1:12* ◀▶ *La 2:1–2*

1:1 [a]Is. 47:7,8
2 [a]Jer. 13:17 [b]Job 7:3
3 [a]ch. 2:9 [1]Heb. *for the greatness of servitude*
5 [a]Deut. 28:43 [b]Jer. 30:14; Dan. 9:7 [c]Jer. 52:28
7 [1]Or, *desirable*
8 [a]1 Ki. 8:46 [b]Jer. 13:22; Ezek. 16:37; Hos. 2:10 [1]Heb. *is become a removing,* or, *wandering*
9 [a]Deut. 32:29; Is. 47:7 [b]ver. 2,17,21
10 [a]ver. 7 [b]Jer. 51:51 [c]Deut. 23:3; Neh. 13:1 [1]Or, *desirable*
11 [a]Jer. 38:9 & 52:6 [1]Or, *to make the soul to come again*
12 [a]Dan. 9:12 [1]Or, It is *nothing* [2]Heb. *pass by the way?*
13 [a]Ezek. 12:13
14 [a]Deut. 28:48
15 [a]Is. 63:3; Rev. 14:19 [1]Or, *the winepress of the virgin*
16 [a]Jer. 13:17; ch. 2:18 [b]ver. 2,9 [1]Heb. *bring back*
17 [a]Jer. 4:31 [b]ver. 2,9

1:1 The prophet lamented over the destruction of Jerusalem which was once "great among the nations" but now is left desolate because of her destruction at the hands of Babylon.

1:4–12 Jeremiah lamented the utter destruction of his beloved city while recognizing that this is God's judgment for "the multitude of her transgressions" (1:5).

1:16–17 Jeremiah lamented that at the time of Jerusalem's desolation there was no one to help because God had sent enemies to surround the city.

18 ¶ The LORD is [a]righteous; for I have [b]rebelled against his ʹcommandment: hear, I pray you, all people, and behold my sorrow: my virgins and my young men are gone into captivity.

19 I called for my lovers, *but* [a]they deceived me: my priests and mine elders gave up the ghost in the city, [b]while they sought their meat to relieve their souls.

20 Behold, O LORD; for I *am* in distress: my [a]bowels are troubled; mine heart is turned within me; for I have grievously rebelled: [b]abroad the sword bereaveth, at home *there is* as death.

21 They have heard that I sigh: [a]*there is* none to comfort me: all mine enemies have heard of my trouble; they are glad that thou hast done *it:* thou wilt bring [b]the day *that* thou hast ʹcalled, and they shall be like unto me.

22 [a]Let all their wickedness come before thee; and do unto them, as thou hast done unto me for all my transgressions: for my sighs *are* many, and [b]my heart *is* faint.

The judgment of the LORD

R **2** HOW HATH the Lord covered the daughter of Zion with a cloud in his anger, [a]*and* cast down from heaven unto the earth [b]the beauty of Israel, and remembered not [c]his footstool in the day of his anger!

2 The Lord hath swallowed up all the habitations of Jacob, and hath not pitied: he hath thrown down in his wrath the strong holds of the daughter of Judah; he hath ʹbrought *them* down to the ground: [a]he hath polluted the kingdom and the princes thereof.

3 He hath cut off in *his* fierce anger all the horn of Israel: [a]he hath drawn back his right hand from before the enemy, [b]and he burned against Jacob like a flaming fire, *which* devoureth round about.

4 [a]He hath bent his bow like an enemy: he stood with his right hand as an adversary, and slew [b]allʹ *that were* pleasant to the eye in the tabernacle of the daughter of Zion: he poured out his fury like fire.

5 [a]The Lord was as an enemy: he hath swallowed up Israel, [b]he hath swallowed up all her palaces: he hath destroyed his strong holds, and hath increased in the daughter of Judah mourning and lamentation.

6 And he hath violently [a]taken away his ʹtabernacle, [b]as *if it were of* a garden: he hath destroyed his places of the assembly: [c]the LORD hath caused the solemn feasts and sabbaths to be forgotten in Zion, and hath despised in the indignation of his anger the king and the priest. R

7 The Lord hath cast off his altar, he hath abhorred his sanctuary, he hath ʹgiven up into the hand of the enemy the walls of her palaces; [a]they have made a noise in the house of the LORD, as in the day of a solemn feast.

8 The LORD hath purposed to destroy the wall of the daughter of Zion: [a]he hath stretched out a line, he hath not withdrawn his hand from ʹdestroying: therefore he made the rampart and the wall to lament; they languished together.

9 Her gates are sunk into the ground; he hath destroyed and [a]broken her bars: [b]her king and her princes *are* among the Gentiles: [c]the law *is* no *more;* her [d]prophets also find no vision from the LORD. Q

10 The elders of the daughter of Zion [a]sit upon the ground, *and* keep silence: they have [b]cast up dust upon their heads; they have [c]girded themselves with sackcloth: the virgins of Jerusalem hang down their heads to the ground.

11 [a]Mine eyes do fail with tears, [b]my bowels are troubled, [c]my liver is poured upon the earth, for the destruction of the daughter of my people; because [d]the children and the sucklings ʹswoon in the streets of the city.

12 They say to their mothers, Where *is* corn and wine? when they swooned as the wounded in the streets of the city,

1:18 [a]Neh. 9:33; Dan. 9:7,14 [b]1 Sam. 12:14 ʹHeb. *mouth*
19 [a]ver. 2; Jer. 30:14 [b]ver. 11
20 [a]Job 30:27; Is. 16:11; Jer. 4:19; Hos. 11:8 [b]Deut. 32:25; Ezek. 7:15
21 [a]ver. 2 [b]Is. 13; Jer. 46 ʹOr, *proclaimed*
22 [a]Ps. 109:15 [b]ch. 5:17
2:1 [a]Mat. 11:23 [b]2 Sam. 1:19 [c]1 Chr. 28:2; Ps. 99:5
2 [a]Ps. 89:39 ʹHeb. *made to touch*
3 [a]Ps. 74:11 [b]Ps. 89:46
4 [a]Is. 63:10 [b]Ezek. 24:25 ʹHeb. *all the desirable of the eye*
5 [a]Jer. 30:14 [b]2 Ki. 25:9; Jer. 52:13
6 [a]Ps. 80:12 & 89:40; Is. 5:5 [b]Is. 1:8 [c]ch. 1:4 ʹOr, *hedge*
7 [a]Ps. 74:4 ʹHeb. *shut up*
8 [a]2 Ki. 21:13; Is. 34:11 ʹHeb. *swallowing up*
9 [a]Jer. 51:30 [b]Deut. 28:36; 2 Ki. 24:15 [c]2 Chr. 15:3 [d]Ps. 74:9; Ezek. 7:26
10 [a]Job 2:13; Is. 3:26 [b]Job 2:12 [c]Is. 15:3
11 [a]ch. 3:48 [b]ch. 1:20 [c]Job 16:13; Ps. 22:14 [d]ch. 4:4 ʹOr, *faint*

R *La 1:16–17* ◀▶ *La 2:6*
R *La 2:1–2* ◀▶ *La 3:1–3*
Q *Isa 63:10* ◀▶ *Mic 3:6*

2:1–2 The image here is of a falling star (see Isa 14:12) being hurled from God's presence.
2:6 Destruction fell on the temple, the place where God met with his people, destroying the feasts and Sabbath remembrances, the kings and the priests.

when their soul was poured out into their
mothers' bosom.
13 What thing shall I take to witness
for thee? [a]what thing shall I liken to thee,
O daughter of Jerusalem? what shall I
equal to thee, that I may comfort thee,
O virgin daughter of Zion? for thy breach
is great like the sea: who can heal thee?
14 Thy [a]prophets have seen vain and
foolish things for thee: and they have not
[b]discovered thine iniquity, to turn away
thy captivity; but have seen for thee false
burdens and causes of banishment.
15 All that pass [/]by [a]clap *their* hands
at thee; they hiss [b]and wag their head at
the daughter of Jerusalem, *saying, Is* this
the city that *men* call [c]The perfection of
beauty, The joy of the whole earth?
16 [a]All thine enemies have opened
their mouth against thee: they hiss and
gnash the teeth: they say, [b]We have swallowed *her* up: certainly this *is* the day
that we looked for; we have found, [c]we
have seen *it.*
17 The LORD hath done *that* which he
had [a]devised; he hath fulfilled his word
that he had commanded in the days of
old: he hath thrown down, and hath not
pitied: and he hath caused *thine* enemy
to [b]rejoice over thee, he hath set up the
horn of thine adversaries.
18 Their heart cried unto the Lord,
O wall of the daughter of Zion, [a]let tears
run down like a river day and night: give
thyself no rest: let not the apple of thine
eye cease.
19 Arise, [a]cry out in the night: in the
beginning of the watches [b]pour out thine
heart like water before the face of the
Lord: lift up thy hands toward him for the
life of thy young children, that faint for
hunger [c]in the top of every street.
20 ¶ Behold, O LORD, and consider to
whom thou hast done this. [a]Shall the
women eat their fruit, *and* children [/]of a
span long? [b]shall the priest and the
prophet be slain in the sanctuary of the
Lord?
21 [a]The young and the old lie on the
ground in the streets: my virgins and my
young men are fallen by the sword; thou
hast slain *them* in the day of thine anger;
[b]thou hast killed, *and* not pitied.

13 [a]ch. 1:12; Dan. 9:12
14 [a]Jer. 2:8; Ezek. 13:2 [b]Is. 58:1
15 [a]Ezek. 25:6 [b]2 Ki. 19:21; Ps. 44:14 [c]Ps. 48:2 [/]Heb. *by the way*
16 [a]Job 16:9; ch. 3:46 [b]Ps. 56:2 [c]Ps. 35:21
17 [a]Lev. 26:16; Deut. 28:15 [b]Ps. 38:16
18 [a]Jer. 14:17
19 [a]Ps. 119:147 [b]Ps. 62:8 [c]Is. 51:20; Nah. 3:10
20 [a]Lev. 26:29; Deut. 28:53; Jer. 19:9; ch. 4:10 [b]ch. 4:13,16 [/]Or, *swaddled with their hands?*
21 [a]2 Chr. 36:17 [b]ch. 3:43
22 [a]Ps. 31:13; Jer. 6:25 & 46:5 [b]Hos. 9:12
3:4 [a]Job 16:8 [b]Ps. 51:8; Is. 38:13
6 [a]Ps. 88:5,6
7 [a]Hos. 2:6
8 [a]Job 30:20
10 [a]Is. 38:13; Hos. 5:14
11 [a]Hos. 6:1
12 [a]Job 7:20; Ps. 38:2
13 [a]Job 6:4 [/]Heb. *sons*
14 [a]Jer. 20:7 [b]Job 30:9; Ps. 69:12
15 [a]Jer. 9:15 [/]Heb. *bitternesses*
16 [a]Prov. 20:17 [/]Or, *rolled me in the ashes*
17 [/]Heb. *good*
18 [a]Ps. 31:22
19 [/]Or, *Remember*

22 Thou hast called as in a solemn day
[a]my terrors round about, so that in the
day of the LORD'S anger none escaped nor
remained: [b]those that I have swaddled
and brought up hath mine enemy consumed.

Lament and hope

3 I *AM* the man *that* hath seen afflic- R
tion by the rod of his wrath.
2 He hath led me, and brought *me into*
darkness, but not *into* light.
3 Surely against me is he turned; he
turneth his hand *against me* all the day.
4 [a]My flesh and my skin hath he made
old; he hath [b]broken my bones.
5 He hath builded against me, and
compassed *me* with gall and travail.
6 [a]He hath set me in dark places, as
they that be dead of old.
7 [a]He hath hedged me about, that I
cannot get out: he hath made my chain
heavy.
8 Also [a]when I cry and shout, he shutteth out my prayer.
9 He hath inclosed my ways with
hewn stone, he hath made my paths
crooked.
10 [a]He *was* unto me *as* a bear lying in
wait, *and as* a lion in secret places.
11 He hath turned aside my ways, and
[a]pulled me in pieces: he hath made me
desolate.
12 He hath bent his bow, and [a]set me
as a mark for the arrow.
13 He hath caused [a]the [/]arrows of his
quiver to enter into my reins.
14 I was a [a]derision to all my people;
and [b]their song all the day.
15 [a]He hath filled me with [/]bitterness,
he hath made me drunken with
wormwood.
16 He hath also broken my teeth [a]with
gravel stones, he hath [/]covered me with
ashes.
17 And thou hast removed my soul far
off from peace: I forgat [/]prosperity.
18 [a]And I said, My strength and my
hope is perished from the LORD:
19 [/]Remembering mine affliction and C
M

R *La 2:6* ◀▶ *La 3:45*
C *Jer 44:10* ◀▶ *Eze 2:4*
M *Jer 49:16* ◀▶ *Eze 3:7*

3:1–3 God had allowed his servant, the prophet, to witness this destruction of Jerusalem at the hands of Babylon.

my misery, [a]the wormwood and the gall.

20 My soul hath *them* still in remembrance, and is [1]humbled in me.

21 This I [1]recall to my mind, therefore have I hope.

22 ¶ [a]*It is of* the LORD's mercies that we are not consumed, because his compassions fail not.

23 *They are* new [a]every morning: great *is* thy faithfulness.

24 The LORD *is* my [a]portion, saith my soul; therefore will I hope in him.

L 25 The LORD *is* good unto them that [a]wait for him, to the soul *that* seeketh him.

26 *It is* good that *a man* should both hope [a]and quietly wait for the salvation of the LORD.

27 [a]*It is* good for a man that he bear the yoke in his youth.

28 [a]He sitteth alone and keepeth silence, because he hath borne *it* upon him.

29 [a]He putteth his mouth in the dust; if so be there may be hope.

30 [a]He giveth *his* cheek to him that smiteth him: he is filled full with reproach.

I 31 [a]For the Lord will not cast off for ever:

L 32 But though he cause grief, yet will he have compassion according to the multitude of his mercies.

33 For [a]he doth not afflict [1]willingly nor grieve the children of men.

34 To crush under his feet all the prisoners of the earth,

35 To turn aside the right of a man before the face of [1]the most High,

36 To subvert a man in his cause, [a]the Lord [1]approveth not.

O 37 ¶ Who *is* he [a]*that* saith, and it cometh to pass, *when* the Lord commandeth *it* not?

38 Out of the mouth of the most High proceedeth not [a]evil and good?

L *Jer 50:20* ◀ ▶ *La 3:32–33*
I *Jer 51:5* ◀ ▶ *Eze 4:4–6*
L *La 3:25* ◀ ▶ *Eze 18:21–23*
O *Jer 17:13–14* ◀ ▶ *Hos 13:4*

19 [a]Jer. 9:15
20 [1]Heb. *bowed*
21 [1]Heb. *make to return to my heart*
22 [a]Mal. 3:6
23 [a]Is. 33:2
24 [a]Ps. 16:5
25 [a]Is. 30:18; Mic. 7:7
26 [a]Ps. 37:7
27 [a]Ps. 94:12
28 [a]Jer. 15:17
29 [a]Job 42:6
30 [a]Is. 50:6; Mat. 5:39
31 [a]Ps. 94:14
33 [a]Ezek. 33:11 [1]Heb. *from his heart*
35 [1]Or, *a superior*
36 [a]Hab. 1:13 [1]Or, *seeth not*
37 [a]Ps. 33:9
38 [a]Job 2:10; Amos 3:6
39 [a]Prov. 19:3 [b]Mic. 7:9 [1]Or, *murmur*
41 [a]Ps. 86:4
42 [a]Dan. 9:5
44 [a]ver. 8
45 [a]1 Cor. 4:13
46 [a]ch. 2:16
47 [a]Is. 24:17 [b]Is. 51:19
48 [a]Jer. 4:19
49 [a]Ps. 77:2
50 [a]Is. 63:15
51 [1]Heb. *my soul* [2]Or, *more than all*
52 [a]Ps. 35:7
53 [a]Jer. 37:16 [b]Dan. 6:17
54 [a]Ps. 69:2 [b]Is. 38:10
55 [a]Ps. 130:1
56 [a]Ps. 3:4
57 [a]Jas. 4:8
58 [a]Ps. 35:1; Jer. 51:36 [b]Ps. 71:23
59 [a]Ps. 9:4

39 [a]Wherefore doth a living man [1]complain, [b]a man for the punishment of his sins? H

40 Let us search and try our ways, and turn again to the LORD. R

41 [a]Let us lift up our heart with *our* hands unto God in the heavens.

42 [a]We have transgressed and have rebelled: thou hast not pardoned.

43 Thou hast covered with anger, and persecuted us: thou hast slain, thou hast not pitied.

44 Thou hast covered thyself with a cloud, [a]that *our* prayer should not pass through.

45 Thou hast made us *as* the [a]offscouring and refuse in the midst of the people. R

46 [a]All our enemies have opened their mouths against us.

47 [a]Fear and a snare is come upon us, [b]desolation and destruction.

48 [a]Mine eye runneth down with rivers of water for the destruction of the daughter of my people.

49 [a]Mine eye trickleth down, and ceaseth not, without any intermission,

50 Till the LORD [a]look down, and behold from heaven.

51 Mine eye affecteth [1]mine heart [2]because of all the daughters of my city.

52 Mine enemies chased me sore, like a bird, [a]without cause.

53 They have cut off my life [a]in the dungeon, and [b]cast a stone upon me.

54 [a]Waters flowed over mine head; *then* [b]I said, I am cut off.

55 ¶ [a]I called upon thy name, O LORD, out of the low dungeon.

56 [a]Thou hast heard my voice: hide not thine ear at my breathing, at my cry.

57 Thou [a]drewest near in the day *that* I called upon thee: thou saidst, Fear not.

58 O Lord, thou hast [a]pleaded the causes of my soul; [b]thou hast redeemed my life.

59 O LORD, thou hast seen my wrong: [a]judge thou my cause.

H *Jer 36:7* ◀ ▶ *Eze 7:8*
R *Jer 36:3* ◀ ▶ *Eze 14:6*
R *La 3:1–3* ◀ ▶ *La 4:22*

3:31 Despite God's judgment, the people would not be cast away from God forever because of God's promise to Abraham (see note at Ge 15:4).

3:45 Jeremiah described the city as refuse because of God's terrible judgment fulfilled at the hands of the Babylonians. Moses had warned the people of such judgments for disobedience (see Dt 28:13; 28:37).

60 Thou hast seen all their vengeance *and* all their [a]imaginations against me.

61 Thou hast heard their reproach, O LORD, *and* all their imaginations against me;

62 The lips of those that rose up against me, and their device against me all the day.

63 Behold their [a]sitting down, and their rising up; I *am* their music.

64 ¶ [a]Render unto them a recompence, O LORD, according to the work of their hands.

65 Give them [ʹ]sorrow of heart, thy curse unto them.

66 Persecute and destroy them in anger [a]from under the [b]heavens of the LORD.

The punishment of Zion

4 HOW IS the gold become dim! *how* is the most fine gold changed! the stones of the sanctuary are poured out [a]in the top of every street.

2 The precious sons of Zion, comparable to fine gold, how are they esteemed [a]as earthen pitchers, the work of the hands of the potter!

3 Even the [ʹ]sea monsters draw out the breast, they give suck to their young ones: the daughter of my people *is become* cruel, [a]like the ostriches in the wilderness.

4 [a]The tongue of the sucking child cleaveth to the roof of his mouth for thirst: [b]the young children ask bread, *and* no man breaketh *it* unto them.

5 They that did feed delicately are desolate in the streets: they that were brought up in scarlet [a]embrace dunghills.

6 For the [ʹ]punishment of the iniquity of the daughter of my people is greater than the punishment of the sin of Sodom, that was [a]overthrown as in a moment, and no hands stayed on her.

7 Her Nazarites were purer than snow, they were whiter than milk, they were more ruddy in body than rubies, their polishing *was* of sapphire:

8 Their visage is [a]blacker[ʹ] than a coal; they are not known in the streets: [b]their skin cleaveth to their bones; it is withered, it is become like a stick.

9 *They that be* slain with the sword are better than *they that be* slain with hunger: for these [ʹ]pine away, stricken through for *want of* the fruits of the field.

10 [a]The hands of the [b]pitiful women have sodden their own children: they were their [c]meat in the destruction of the daughter of my people.

11 The LORD hath accomplished his fury; [a]he hath poured out his fierce anger, and [b]hath kindled a fire in Zion, and it hath devoured the foundations thereof.

12 The kings of the earth, and all the inhabitants of the world, would not have believed that the adversary and the enemy should have entered into the gates of Jerusalem.

13 ¶ [a]For the sins of her prophets, *and* the iniquities of her priests, [b]that have shed the blood of the just in the midst of her,

14 They have wandered *as* blind *men* in the streets, [a]they have polluted themselves with blood, [b]so[ʹ] that men could not touch their garments.

15 They cried unto them, Depart ye; [ʹ]*It is* [a]unclean; depart, depart, touch not: when they fled away and wandered, they said among the heathen, They shall no more sojourn *there.*

16 The [ʹ]anger of the LORD hath divided them; he will no more regard them: [a]they respected not the persons of the priests, they favoured not the elders.

17 As for us, [a]our eyes as yet failed for our vain help: in our watching we have watched for a nation *that* could not save *us.*

18 [a]They hunt our steps, that we cannot go in our streets: our end is near, our days are fulfilled; for [b]our end is come.

19 Our persecutors are [a]swifter than the eagles of the heaven: they pursued us upon the mountains, they laid wait for us in the wilderness.

20 The [a]breath of our nostrils, the anointed of the LORD, [b]was taken in their pits, of whom we said, Under his shadow we shall live among the heathen.

21 ¶ Rejoice and be glad, O daughter of Edom, that dwellest in the land of Uz; [a]the cup also shall pass through unto thee: thou shalt be drunken, and shalt make thyself naked.

60 [a]Jer. 11:19
63 [a]Ps. 139:2
64 [a]Ps. 28:4; Jer. 11:20
65 [ʹ]Or, *obstinacy of heart*
66 [a]Deut. 25:19; Jer. 10:11 [b]Ps. 8:3
4:1 [a]ch. 2:19
2 [a]Is. 30:14; Jer. 19:11
3 [a]Job 39:14 [ʹ]Or, *sea calves*
4 [a]Ps. 22:15 [b]See ch. 2:11,12
5 [a]Job 24:8
6 [a]Gen. 19:25 [ʹ]Or, *iniquity*
8 [a]ch. 5:10; Joel 2:6; Nah. 2:10 [b]Ps. 102:5 [ʹ]Heb. *darker than blackness*
9 [ʹ]Heb. *flow out*
10 [a]ch. 2:20 [b]Is. 49:15 [c]Deut. 28:57
11 [a]Jer. 7:20 [b]Deut. 32:22
13 [a]Jer. 6:13; Ezek. 22:26 [b]Mat. 23:31
14 [a]Jer. 2:34 [b]Num. 19:16 [ʹ]Or, *in that they could not but touch*
15 [a]Lev. 13:45 [ʹ]Or, *ye polluted*
16 [a]ch. 5:12 [ʹ]Or, *face*
17 [a]2 Ki. 24:7; Is. 20:5; Jer. 37:7
18 [a]2 Ki. 25:4 [b]Ezek 7:2,3
19 [a]Deut. 28:49
20 [a]Gen. 2:7 [b]Jer. 52:9; Ezek. 12:13
21 [a]Jer. 25:15; Obad. 10

R 22 ¶ [a]The[1] punishment of thine iniquity is accomplished, O daughter of Zion; he will no more carry thee away into captivity: [b]he will visit thine iniquity, O daughter of Edom; he will [2]discover thy sins.

A prayer for mercy

5 REMEMBER,[a] O LORD, what is come upon us: consider, and behold [b]our reproach.

2 [a]Our inheritance is turned to strangers, our houses to aliens.

3 We are orphans and fatherless, our mothers *are* as widows.

4 We have drunken our water for money; our wood [1]is sold unto us.

5 [a]Our[1] necks *are* under persecution: we labour, *and* have no rest.

6 [a]We have given the hand [b]*to* the Egyptians, *and to* the Assyrians, to be satisfied with bread.

7 [a]Our fathers have sinned, *and are* not; and we have borne their iniquities.

8 Servants have ruled over us: *there is* none that doth deliver *us* out of their hand.

9 We gat our bread with *the peril of* our lives because of the sword of the wilderness.

10 Our skin was black like an oven because of the [1]terrible famine.

11 They ravished the women in Zion, *and* the maids in the cities of Judah.

12 Princes are hanged up by their hand: the faces of elders were not honoured.

13 They took the young men to grind, and the children fell under the wood.

14 The elders have ceased from the gate, the young men from their music.

15 The joy of our heart is ceased; our dance is turned into mourning.

16 [a]The[1] crown is fallen *from* our head: woe unto us, that we have sinned!

17 For this our heart is faint; [a]for these *things* our eyes are dim.

18 Because of the mountain of Zion, which is desolate, the foxes walk upon it.

19 Thou, O LORD, [a]remainest for ever; [b]thy throne from generation to generation.

20 [a]Wherefore dost thou forget us for ever, *and* forsake us [1]so long time?

21 Turn thou us unto thee, O LORD, and we shall be turned; renew our days as of old.

22 [1]But thou hast utterly rejected us; thou art very wroth against us.

R *La 3:45* ◄ ► *Eze 5:3–4*

22 [a]Is. 40:2 [b]Ps. 137:7 [1]Or, *Thine iniquity* [2]Or, *carry* thee *captive for thy sins*

5:1 [a]Ps. 89:50 [b]Ps. 79:4; ch. 2:15

2 [a]Ps. 79:1

4 [1]Heb. *cometh for price*

5 [a]Jer. 28:14 [1]Heb. *On our necks are we persecuted*

6 [a]Gen. 24:2 [b]Hos. 12:1

7 [a]Jer. 31:29

10 [1]Or, *terrors,* or, *storms*

16 [a]Ps. 89:39 [1]Heb. *The crown of our head is fallen*

17 [a]Ps. 6:7

19 [a]Ps. 9:7 [b]Ps. 45:6

20 [a]Ps. 13:1 [1]Heb. *for length of days?*

22 [1]Or, *For wilt thou utterly reject us?*

4:22 The prophet declares that the savage defilement of Jerusalem and God's punishment of Judah will end. Once Israel is reestablished in the promised land they will never again be carried into captivity.

Ezekiel

Author: Ezekiel

Theme: God is active in the events of human history

Date of Writing: c. 571 B.C.

Outline of Ezekiel

I. Ezekiel's Call and Divine Commission (1:1—3:27)
II. Sinful Conditions and Promised Doom (4:1—19:14)
III. The Last Full Measure of Judgment (20:1—24:27)
IV. Judgment Against Foreign Nations (25:1—32:32)
V. Hope for Restoration (33:1—39:29)
VI. Restoration and Renewal (40:1—48:35)

THIS BOOK IS named after the prophet Ezekiel, whose name means "God is strong." Born into a priestly family who served in the temple, Ezekiel witnessed the wickedness of his people and was among the captives taken by Nebuchadnezzar into Babylonian exile in 597 B.C. While in Babylon, Ezekiel received God's call to the prophetic ministry (see 1:1) and shared God's messages concerning the destiny of Israel with his fellow exiles. Ezekiel's book contains more dates than any other Biblical record, indicating that his messages were given between 593–571 B.C. Jewish tradition suggests that Ezekiel, God's watchman of judgment, died during the Babylonian captivity.

Over half of this major prophetic book contains promises about Israel's future. During his early ministry, Ezekiel proclaimed the same message as Jeremiah—that the sinfulness and idolatry that prevailed in Jerusalem, even after Babylon's initial conquest, would finally result in God's abandonment and the city's destruction. The first twenty-four chapters of Ezekiel reflect this theme.

After the news reached Babylon that Jerusalem had actually been destroyed, Ezekiel's message became a message of hope and restoration. Ezekiel prophesied that God, the great Shepherd, would gather the exiles from the ends of the earth and establish them in their own land forever. Gentile nations who dared to challenge Israel's return to the promised land would face defeat and God's judgment. In addition, Ezekiel was given a vision of the millennial temple to be established by the Messiah for use in Israel's future worship.

The vision of the four creatures

1 NOW IT came to pass in the thirtieth
year, in the fourth *month,* in the fifth
day of the month, as I *was* among the
ʹcaptives [a]by the river of Chebar, *that*
[b]the heavens were opened, and I saw [c]vi-
sions of God.
2 In the fifth *day* of the month, which
was the fifth year of [a]king Jehoiachin's
captivity,
3 The word of the LORD came expressly
unto ʹEzekiel the priest, the son of Buzi,
in the land of the Chaldeans by the river
Chebar; and [a]the hand of the LORD was
there upon him.
4 ¶ And I looked, and, behold, [a]a
whirlwind came [b]out of the north, a great
cloud, and a fire ʹinfolding itself, and a
brightness *was* about it, and out of the
midst thereof as the colour of amber, out
of the midst of the fire.
5 [a]Also out of the midst thereof *came*
the likeness of four living creatures. And
[b]this *was* their appearance; they had [c]the
likeness of a man.
6 And every one had four faces, and
every one had four wings.
7 And their feet *were* ʹstraight feet;
and the sole of their feet *was* like the sole
of a calf's foot: and they sparkled [a]like the
colour of burnished brass.
8 [a]And *they had* the hands of a man
under their wings on their four sides; and
they four had their faces and their wings.
9 [a]Their wings *were* joined one to another; [b]they turned not when they went;
they went every one straight forward.
10 As for [a]the likeness of their faces,
they four [b]had the face of a man, [c]and the
face of a lion, on the right side: [d]and they
four had the face of an ox on the left side;
[e]they four also had the face of an eagle.
11 Thus *were* their faces: and their
wings *were* ʹstretched upward; two
wings of every one *were* joined one to
another, and [a]two covered their bodies.
12 And [a]they went every one straight
forward: [b]whither the spirit was to go,
they went; *and* they turned not when
they went.
13 As for the likeness of the living
creatures, their appearance *was* like
burning coals of fire, [a]*and* like the appearance of lamps: it went up and down
among the living creatures; and the fire
was bright, and out of the fire went forth
lightning.
14 And the living creatures ran and returned [a]as the appearance of a flash of
lightning.

The vision of the four wheels

15 ¶ Now as I beheld the living creatures, behold [a]one wheel upon the earth
by the living creatures, with his four
faces.
16 [a]The appearance of the wheels and
their work *was* [b]like unto the colour of a
beryl: and they four had one likeness: and
their appearance and their work *was* as it
were a wheel in the middle of a wheel.
17 When they went, they went upon
their four sides: [a]*and* they turned not
when they went.
18 As for their rings, they were so high
that they were dreadful; and their ʹrings
were [a]full of eyes round about them four.
19 And [a]when the living creatures
went, the wheels went by them: and
when the living creatures were lifted up
from the earth, the wheels were
lifted up.
20 [a]Whithersoever the spirit was to
go, they went, thither *was their* spirit to
go; and the wheels were lifted up over
against them: [b]for the spirit ʹof the living
creature *was* in the wheels.
21 [a]When those went, *these* went;
and when those stood, *these* stood; and

1:1 [a]ch. 3:15,23 [b]Mat. 3:16; Acts 7:56 [c]ch. 8:3 ʹHeb. *captivity*
2 [a]2 Ki. 24:12
3 [a]1 Ki. 18:46; ch. 3:14 ʹHeb. *Jehezkel*
4 [a]Jer. 23:19 & 25:32 [b]Jer. 1:14 ʹHeb. *catching itself*
5 [a]Rev. 4:6 [b]ch. 10:8 [c]ch. 10:14
7 [a]Dan. 10:6; Rev. 1:15 ʹHeb. *a straight foot*
8 [a]ch. 10:8
9 [a]ver. 11 [b]ver. 12
10 [a]Rev. 4:7 [b]Num. 2:10 [c]Num. 2:3 [d]Num. 2:18 [e]Num. 2:25
11 [a]Is. 6:2 ʹOr, *divided above*
12 [a]ch. 10:22 [b]ver. 20
13 [a]Rev. 4:5
14 [a]Mat. 24:27
15 [a]ch. 10:9
16 [a]ch. 10:9,10 [b]Dan. 10:6
17 [a]ver. 12
18 [a]ch. 10:12; Zech. 4:10 ʹOr, *strakes*
19 [a]ch. 10:16,17
20 [a]ver. 12 [b]ch. 10:17 ʹOr, *of life*
21 [a]ver. 19,20; ch. 10:17

E L (1:12)
E L (1:20)

E *Isa 63:14* ◄► *Eze 1:20*
L *Isa 63:14* ◄► *Eze 1:20*
E *Eze 1:12* ◄► *Eze 2:2–3*
L *Eze 1:12* ◄► *Eze 2:2–3*

1:1 This verse indicates that Ezekiel began to write his prophecy when he was approximately thirty years old, the age that a person entered the Levitical priesthood (see Nu 4:3). Ezekiel was from a priestly family but could not commence his service in the temple because he had been exiled to Babylon. God gave Ezekiel another commission—that of a prophet.
1:4–6, 10 Ezekiel's commission as God's prophet began with this vision of "four living creatures" (1:5). The four creatures represented all the facets of God's creation: "man" (1:5), God's ruler of creation; "lion" (1:10), the strongest of the wild animals; "ox" (1:10), the strongest domesticated animal; and "eagle" (1:10), the greatest bird. Compare this vision with Rev 4:7.

when those were lifted up from the earth, the wheels were lifted up over against them: for the spirit [l]of the living creature *was* in the wheels.

22 [a]And the likeness of the firmament upon the heads of the living creature *was* as the colour of the terrible crystal, stretched forth over their heads above.

23 And under the firmament *were* their wings straight, the one toward the other: every one had two, which covered on this side, and every one had two, which covered on that side, their bodies.

24 [a]And when they went, I heard the noise of their wings, [b]like the noise of great waters, as [c]the voice of the Almighty, the voice of speech, as the noise of an host: when they stood, they let down their wings.

25 And there was a voice from the firmament that *was* over their heads, when they stood, *and* had let down their wings.

26 ¶ [a]And above the firmament that *was* over their heads *was* the likeness of a throne, [b]as the appearance of a sapphire stone: and upon the likeness of the throne *was* the likeness as the appearance of a man above upon it.

27 [a]And I saw as the colour of amber, as the appearance of fire round about within it, from the appearance of his loins even upward, and from the appearance of his loins even downward, I saw as it were the appearance of fire, and it had brightness round about.

28 [a]As the appearance of the bow that is in the cloud in the day of rain, so *was* the appearance of the brightness round about. [b]This *was* the appearance of the likeness of the glory of the LORD. And when I saw *it*, [c]I fell upon my face, and I heard a voice of one that spake.

Ezekiel's commission

2 AND HE said unto me, Son of man, [a]stand upon thy feet, and I will speak unto thee.

E L M 2 And [a]the spirit entered into me when he spake unto me, and set me upon my feet, that I heard him that spake unto me.

3 And he said unto me, Son of man, I send thee to the children of Israel, to a rebellious [l]nation that hath rebelled against me: [a]they and their fathers have transgressed against me, *even* unto this very day.

4 [a]For *they are* [l]impudent children and stiffhearted. I do send thee unto them; and thou shalt say unto them, Thus saith the Lord GOD. C

5 [a]And they, whether they will hear, or whether they will forbear, (for they *are* a rebellious house,) yet [b]shall know that there hath been a prophet among them.

6 ¶ And thou, son of man, [a]be not afraid of them, neither be afraid of their words, though [b]briers[l] and thorns *be* with thee, and thou dost dwell among scorpions: [c]be not afraid of their words, nor be dismayed at their looks, [d]though they *be* a rebellious house. C

7 [a]And thou shalt speak my words unto them, [b]whether they will hear, or whether they will forbear: for they *are* [l]most rebellious.

8 But thou, son of man, hear what I say unto thee; Be not thou rebellious like that rebellious house: open thy mouth, and [a]eat that I give thee.

9 ¶ And when I looked, behold, [a]an hand *was* sent unto me; and, lo, [b]a roll of a book *was* therein;

10 And he spread it before me; and it *was* written within and without: and *there was* written therein lamentations, and mourning, and woe.

3 MOREOVER HE said unto me, Son of man, eat that thou findest; [a]eat this roll, and go speak unto the house of Israel.

2 So I opened my mouth, and he caused me to eat that roll.

3 And he said unto me, Son of man, cause thy belly to eat, and fill thy bowels with this roll that I give thee. Then did I [a]eat *it;* and it was in my mouth [b]as honey for sweetness.

4 ¶ And he said unto me, Son of man, go, get thee unto the house of Israel, and speak with my words unto them.

5 For thou *art* not sent to a people [l]of a strange speech and of an hard language, *but* to the house of Israel;

6 Not to many people [l]of a strange speech and of an hard language, whose words thou canst not understand.

21 [l]Or, *of life*
22 [a]ch. 10:1
24 [a]ch. 10:5 [b]ch. 43:2; Dan. 10:6; Rev. 1:15 [c]Job 37:4,5; Ps. 29:3,4 & 68:33
26 [a]ch. 10:1 [b]Ex. 24:10
27 [a]ch. 8:2
28 [a]Rev. 4:3 & 10:1 [b]ch. 3:23 & 8:4 [c]ch. 3:23; Dan. 8:17; Acts 9:4; Rev. 1:17
2:1 [a]Dan. 10:11
2 [a]ch. 3:24
3 [a]Jer. 3:25; ch. 20:18,21,30 [l]Heb. *nations*
4 [a]ch. 3:7 [l]Heb. *hard of face*
5 [a]ch. 3:11,26,27 [b]ch. 33:33
6 [a]Jer. 1:8,17; Luke 12:4 [b]Is. 9:18; Jer. 6:28; Mic. 7:4 [c]ch. 3:9; 1 Pet. 3:14 [d]ch. 3:9,26,27 [l]Or, *rebels*
7 [a]Jer. 1:7,17 [b]ver. 5 [l]Heb. *rebellion*
8 [a]Rev. 10:9
9 [a]Jer. 1:9; ch. 8:3 [b]ch. 3:1
3:1 [a]ch. 2:8,9
3 [a]Rev. 10:9; See Jer. 15:16 [b]Ps. 19:10 & 119:103
5 [l]Heb. *deep of lip, and heavy of tongue*
6 [l]Heb. *deep of lip, and heavy of language*

E *Eze 1:20* ◀ ▶ *Eze 3:12*
L *Eze 1:20* ◀ ▶ *Eze 3:14*
M *Isa 59:19* ◀ ▶ *Eze 3:12*

C *La 3:19–20* ◀ ▶ *Eze 2:6*
C *Eze 2:4* ◀ ▶ *Eze 3:7*

[2]Surely, [a]had I sent thee to them, they would have hearkened unto thee.

7 But the house of Israel will not hearken unto thee; [a]for they will not hearken unto me: [b]for all the house of Israel *are* [1]impudent and hardhearted.

8 Behold, I have made thy face strong against their faces, and thy forehead strong against their foreheads.

9 [a]As an adamant harder than flint have I made thy forehead: [b]fear them not, neither be dismayed at their looks, though they *be* a rebellious house.

10 Moreover he said unto me, Son of man, all my words that I shall speak unto thee receive in thine heart, and hear with thine ears.

11 And go, get thee to them of the captivity, unto the children of thy people, and speak unto them, and tell them, [a]Thus saith the Lord GOD; whether they will hear, or whether they will forbear.

12 Then [a]the spirit took me up, and I heard behind me a voice of a great rushing, *saying,* Blessed *be* the glory of the LORD from his place.

13 *I heard* also the noise of the wings of the living creatures that [1]touched one another, and the noise of the wheels over against them, and a noise of a great rushing.

14 So [a]the spirit lifted me up, and took me away, and I went [1]in bitterness, in the [2]heat of my spirit; but [b]the hand of the LORD was strong upon me.

15 ¶ Then I came to them of the captivity at Tel-abib, that dwelt by the river of Chebar, and [a]I sat where they sat, and remained there astonished among them seven days.

Warning to Israel

16 And it came to pass at the end of seven days, that the word of the LORD came unto me, saying,

17 [a]Son of man, I have made thee [b]a watchman unto the house of Israel: therefore hear the word at my mouth, and give them warning from me.

18 When I say unto the wicked, Thou shalt surely die; and thou givest him not warning, nor speakest to warn the wicked from his wicked way, to save his life; the same wicked *man* [a]shall die in his iniquity; but his blood will I require at thine hand.

19 Yet if thou warn the wicked, and he turn not from his wickedness, nor from his wicked way, he shall die in his iniquity; [a]but thou hast delivered thy soul.

20 Again, When a [a]righteous *man* doth turn from his [1]righteousness, and commit iniquity, and I lay a stumblingblock before him, he shall die: because thou hast not given him warning, he shall die in his sin, and his righteousness which he hath done shall not be remembered; but his blood will I require at thine hand.

21 Nevertheless if thou warn the righteous *man,* that the righteous sin not, and he doth not sin, he shall surely live, because he is warned; also thou hast delivered thy soul.

22 ¶ [a]And the hand of the LORD was there upon me; and he said unto me, Arise, go forth [b]into the plain, and I will there talk with thee.

23 Then I arose, and went forth into the plain: and, behold, [a]the glory of the LORD stood there, as the glory which I [b]saw by the river of Chebar: [a]and I fell on my face.

24 Then [a]the spirit entered into me, and set me upon my feet, and spake with me, and said unto me, Go, shut thyself within thine house.

25 But thou, O son of man, behold, [a]they shall put bands upon thee, and shall bind thee with them, and thou shalt not go out among them:

26 And [a]I will make thy tongue cleave to the roof of thy mouth, that thou shalt be dumb, and shalt not be to them [1]a reprover: [b]for they *are* a rebellious house.

27 [a]But when I speak with thee, I will open thy mouth, and thou shalt say unto them, [b]Thus saith the Lord GOD; He that heareth, let him hear; and he that for-

6 [a]Mat. 11:21 [2]Or, *If I had sent thee, &c., would they not have hearkened unto thee?*
7 [a]John 15:20 [b]ch. 2:4 [1]Heb. *stiff of forehead and hard of heart*
9 [a]Is. 50:7; Jer. 1:18; Mic. 3:8 [b]Jer. 1:8,17; ch. 2:6
11 [a]ch. 2:5,7
12 [a]ch. 8:3; 1 Ki. 18:12; Acts 8:39
13 [1]Heb. *kissed*
14 [a]ver. 12; ch. 8:3 [b]2 Ki. 3:15; ch. 1:3 & 8:1 [1]Heb. *bitter* [2]Heb. *hot anger*
15 [a]Job 2:13; Ps. 137:1
17 [a]ch. 33:7-9 [b]Is. 52:8 & 56:10; Jer. 6:17
18 [a]ch. 33:6; John 8:21
19 [a]Is. 49:4,5; Acts 20:26
20 [a]ch. 18:24 & 33:12,13 [1]Heb. *righteousnesses*
22 [a]ch. 1:3 [b]ch. 8:4
23 [a]ch. 1:28 [b]ch. 1:1
24 [a]ch. 2:2
25 [a]ch. 4:8
26 [a]ch. 24:27; Luke 1:20 [b]ch. 2:5-7 [1]Heb. *a man reproving*
27 [a]ch. 24:27 & 33:22 [b]ver. 11

C *Eze 2:6* ◀ ▶ *Eze 12:2*
M *La 3:19–21* ◀ ▶ *Da 9:3–5*
N *Jer 32:33* ◀ ▶ *Eze 33:4–5*
E *Eze 2:2–3* ◀ ▶ *Eze 3:14*
M *Eze 2:2–3* ◀ ▶ *Eze 3:14*
N *Isa 44:3–4* ◀ ▶ *Eze 3:14*
E *Eze 3:12* ◀ ▶ *Eze 3:24*
L *Eze 2:2–3* ◀ ▶ *Eze 3:24*
M *Eze 3:12* ◀ ▶ *Eze 3:24*
N *Eze 3:12* ◀ ▶ *Eze 8:3*

S *Jer 32:19* ◀ ▶ *Eze 9:4–6*
E *Eze 3:14* ◀ ▶ *Eze 8:3*
L *Eze 3:14* ◀ ▶ *Eze 11:1*
M *Eze 3:14* ◀ ▶ *Eze 36:27*

beareth, let him forbear: for they *are* a rebellious house.

Symbol of the siege and exile

4 THOU ALSO, son of man, take thee a tile, and lay it before thee, and portray upon it the city, *even* Jerusalem:

2 And lay siege against it, and build a fort against it, and cast a mount against it; set the camp also against it, and set [l]*battering* rams against it round about.

3 Moreover take thou unto thee [l]an iron pan, and set it *for* a wall of iron between thee and the city: and set thy face against it, and it shall be besieged, and thou shalt lay siege against it. [a]This *shall be* a sign to the house of Israel.

I 4 Lie thou also upon thy left side, and lay the iniquity of the house of Israel upon it: *according* to the number of the days that thou shalt lie upon it thou shalt bear their iniquity.

5 For I have laid upon thee the years of their iniquity, according to the number of the days, three hundred and ninety days: [a]so shalt thou bear the iniquity of the house of Israel.

6 And when thou hast accomplished them, lie again on thy right side, and thou shalt bear the iniquity of the house of Judah forty days: I have appointed thee [l]each day for a year.

7 Therefore thou shalt set thy face toward the siege of Jerusalem, and thine arm *shall be* uncovered, and thou shalt prophesy against it.

8 [a]And, behold, I will lay bands upon thee, and thou shalt not turn thee [l]from one side to another, till thou hast ended the days of thy siege.

9 ¶ Take thou also unto thee wheat, and barley, and beans, and lentils, and millet, and [l]fitches, and put them in one vessel, and make thee bread thereof, *according* to the number of the days that thou shalt lie upon thy side, three hundred and ninety days shalt thou eat thereof.

10 And thy meat which thou shalt eat *shall be* by weight, twenty shekels a day: from time to time shalt thou eat it.

11 Thou shalt drink also water by measure, the sixth part of an hin: from time to time shalt thou drink.

12 And thou shalt eat it *as* barley cakes, and thou shalt bake it with dung that cometh out of man, in their sight.

13 And the LORD said, Even thus [a]shall the children of Israel eat their defiled bread among the Gentiles, whither I will drive them.

14 Then said I, [a]Ah Lord GOD! behold, my soul hath not been polluted: for from my youth up even till now have I not eaten of [b]that which dieth of itself, or is torn in pieces; neither came there [c]abominable flesh into my mouth.

15 Then he said unto me, Lo, I have given thee cow's dung for man's dung, and thou shalt prepare thy bread therewith.

16 Moreover he said unto me, Son of man, behold, I will break the [a]staff of bread in Jerusalem: and they shall [b]eat bread by weight, and with care; and they shall [c]drink water by measure, and with astonishment:

17 That they may want bread and water, and be astonied one with another, and [a]consume away for their iniquity.

5 AND THOU, son of man, take thee a sharp knife, take thee a barber's razor, [a]and cause *it* to pass upon thine head and upon thy beard: then take thee balances to weigh, and divide the *hair.*

2 [a]Thou shalt burn with fire a third

I *La 3:31* ◄► *Eze 11:17–20*

4:2 [l]Or, *chief leaders;* see ch. 21:22
3 [a]ch. 12:6,11 & 24:24,27 [l]Or, *a flat plate,* or, *slice*
5 [a]Num. 14:34
6 [l]Heb. *a day for a year, a day for a year*
8 [a]ch. 3:25 [l]Heb. *from thy side to thy side*
9 [l]Or, *spelt*
13 [a]Hos. 9:3
14 [a]Acts 10:14 [b]Ex. 22:31; Lev. 11:40 & 17:15 [c]Deut. 14:3; Is. 65:4
16 [a]Lev. 26:26; Ps. 105:16; Is. 3:1; ch. 5:16 & 14:13 [b]ver. 10; ch. 12:19 [c]ver. 11
17 [a]Lev. 26:39; ch. 24:23
5:1 [a]See Lev. 21:5; Is. 7:20; ch. 44:20
2 [a]ver. 12

4:3–6 Jeremiah had prophesied that Judah would serve seventy years of captivity in Babylon. Ezekiel was serving that sentence when God gave him these additional time markers to symbolize Israel and Judah's sins and set a time for their punishment.

Lying on his left side while he prophesied for 390 days, Ezekiel faced north, symbolizing the northern kingdom of Israel. Lying on his right side for 40 days and facing south, Ezekiel symbolized the southern kingdom of Judah. Scripture records that each day represented one year (4:6).

Determining the actual events of these time periods has been difficult. The 40-year period may correspond to the long reign of wicked King Manasseh before he repented. Or it may refer to the time between the fall of Jerusalem and the defeat of Babylon by Persia. Some scholars believe that the 390 years refer to the time between Solomon's kingdom and the fall of Jerusalem. Others believe that this time period covers the years from the division of the kingdom until the emancipation from Babylon. Still others suggest that the 390 years calculate the rebirth of modern Israel as a nation.

5:1–4, 12 Ezekiel again acted out a specific

part in the midst of [b]the city, when [c]the days of the siege are fulfilled: and thou shalt take a third part, *and* smite about it with a knife: and a third part thou shalt scatter in the wind; and I will draw out a sword after them.

R 3 [a]Thou shalt also take thereof a few in number, and bind them in thy [l]skirts.

4 Then take of them again, and [a]cast them into the midst of the fire, and burn them in the fire; *for* thereof shall a fire come forth into all the house of Israel.

5 ¶ Thus saith the Lord GOD; This *is* Jerusalem: I have set it in the midst of the nations and countries *that are* round about her.

6 And she hath changed my judgments into wickedness more than the nations, and my statutes more than the countries that *are* round about her: for they have refused my judgments and my statutes, they have not walked in them.

7 Therefore thus saith the Lord GOD; Because ye multiplied more than the nations that *are* round about you, *and* have not walked in my statutes, neither have kept my judgments, [a]neither have done according to the judgments of the nations that *are* round about you;

8 Therefore thus saith the Lord GOD; Behold, I, even I, *am* against thee, and will execute judgments in the midst of thee in the sight of the nations.

9 [a]And I will do in thee that which I have not done, and whereunto I will not do any more the like, because of all thine abominations.

10 Therefore the fathers [a]shall eat the sons in the midst of thee, and the sons shall eat their fathers; and I will execute judgments in thee, and the whole remnant of thee will I [b]scatter into all the winds.

11 Wherefore, *as* I live, saith the Lord GOD; Surely, because thou hast [a]defiled my sanctuary with all thy [b]detestable things, and with all thine abominations, therefore will I also diminish *thee;* [c]neither shall mine eye spare, neither will I have any pity.

12 ¶ [a]A third part of thee shall die with the pestilence, and with famine shall they be consumed in the midst of thee: and a third part shall fall by the sword round about thee; and [b]I will scatter a third part into all the winds, and [c]I will draw out a sword after them. D

13 Thus shall mine anger [a]be accomplished, and I will [b]cause my fury to rest upon them, [c]and I will be comforted: [d]and they shall know that I the LORD have spoken *it* in my zeal, when I have accomplished my fury in them.

14 Moreover [a]I will make thee waste, and a reproach among the nations that *are* round about thee, in the sight of all that pass by. R

15 So it shall be a [a]reproach and a taunt, an instruction and an astonishment unto the nations that *are* round about thee, when I shall execute judgments in thee in anger and in fury and in [b]furious rebukes. I the LORD have spoken *it.*

16 When I shall [a]send upon them the evil arrows of famine, which shall be for *their* destruction, *and* which I will send to destroy you: and I will increase the famine upon you, and will break your [b]staff of bread:

17 So will I send upon you famine and [a]evil beasts, and they shall bereave thee; and [b]pestilence and blood shall pass through thee; and I will bring the sword upon thee. I the LORD have spoken *it.*

2 [b]ch. 4:1 [c]ch. 4:8,9
3 [a]Jer. 40:6 & 52:16 [l]Heb. *wings*
4 [a]Jer. 41:1,2 & 44:14
7 [a]Jer. 2:10,11; ch. 16:47
9 [a]Lam. 4:6; Dan. 9:12; Amos 3:2
10 [a]Lev. 26:29; Deut. 28:53; 2 Ki. 6:29; Jer. 19:9; Lam. 2:20 & 4:10 [b]Lev. 26:33; Deut. 28:64; ch. 12:14; Zech. 2:6
11 [a]2 Chr. 36:14; ch. 7:20 [b]ch. 11:21 [c]ch. 7:4,9
12 [a]Jer. 15:2 & 21:9; ch. 6:12 [b]Jer. 9:16 [c]ver. 2; Lev. 26:33; ch. 12:14
13 [a]Lam. 4:11; ch. 6:12 & 7:8 [b]ch. 21:17 [c]Deut. 32:36; Is. 1:24 [d]ch. 36:6 & 38:19
14 [a]Lev. 26:31; Neh. 2:17
15 [a]Deut. 28:37; 1 Ki. 9:7; Ps. 79:4; Jer. 24:9; Lam. 2:15 [b]ch. 25:17
16 [a]Deut. 32:23 [b]Lev. 26:26; ch. 4:16 & 14:13
17 [a]Lev. 26:22; Deut. 32:24; ch. 14:21 & 33:27 & 34:25 [b]ch. 38:22

R *La 4:22* ◀▶ *Eze 5:14–15*
D *Jer 44:13* ◀▶ *Eze 7:15*
R *Eze 5:3–4* ◀▶ *Eze 6:6*

---

prophecy of God. The hair from Ezekiel's head demonstrated the tragic fate of his people: one third destroyed in the city by famine and plague; one third consumed by battle; one third scattered into exile (5:12). Only a small remnant (5:3) would be spared.

5:15 God said that this destruction of Jerusalem would become a proverb among the nations as they recognized God's hand of judgment against his disobedient servants.

5:17 God declared that four specific judgments—famine, evil beasts, pestilence, the sword—represented his wrath against the sinful nation. Compare this prophecy with the four seals of Rev 6, noting that God's wrath will be poured out against unrepentant sinners during the tribulation.

The high places to be destroyed

6 AND THE word of the LORD came unto me, saying,

2 Son of man, [a]set thy face toward the [b]mountains of Israel, and prophesy against them,

3 And say, Ye mountains of Israel, hear the word of the Lord GOD; Thus saith the Lord GOD to the mountains, and to the hills, to the rivers, and to the valleys; Behold, I, *even* I, will bring a sword upon you, and [a]I will destroy your high places.

4 And your altars shall be desolate, and your ′images shall be broken: and [a]I will cast down your slain *men* before your idols.

5 And I will ′lay the dead carcases of the children of Israel before their idols; and I will scatter your bones round about your altars.

R 6 In all your dwellingplaces the cities shall be laid waste, and the high places shall be desolate; that your altars may be laid waste and made desolate, and your idols may be broken and cease, and your images may be cut down, and your works may be abolished.

7 And the slain shall fall in the midst of you, and [a]ye shall know that I *am* the LORD.

8 ¶ [a]Yet will I leave a remnant, that ye may have *some* that shall escape the sword among the nations, when ye shall be scattered through the countries.

9 And they that escape of you shall remember me among the nations whither they shall be carried captives, because [a]I am broken with their whorish heart, which hath departed from me, and [b]with their eyes, which go a-whoring after their idols: and [c]they shall loathe themselves for the evils which they have committed in all their abominations.

R 10 And they shall know that I *am* the LORD, *and that* I have not said in vain that I would do this evil unto them.

11 ¶ Thus saith the Lord GOD; Smite [a]with thine hand, and stamp with thy foot, and say, Alas for all the evil abominations of the house of Israel! [b]for they shall fall by the sword, by the famine, and by the pestilence.

12 He that is far off shall die of the pestilence; and he that is near shall fall by the sword; and he that remaineth and is besieged shall die by the famine: [a]thus will I accomplish my fury upon them.

13 Then [a]shall ye know that I *am* the LORD, when their slain *men* shall be among their idols round about their altars, [b]upon every high hill, [c]in all the tops of the mountains, and [d]under every green tree, and under every thick oak, the place where they did offer sweet savour to all their idols.

14 So will I [a]stretch out my hand upon them, and make the land desolate, yea, ′more desolate than the wilderness toward [b]Diblath, in all their habitations: and they shall know that I *am* the LORD.

An end is come

7 MOREOVER THE word of the LORD came unto me, saying, R

2 Also, thou son of man, thus saith the Lord GOD unto the land of Israel; [a]An end, the end is come upon the four corners of the land.

3 Now *is* the end *come* upon thee, and I will send mine anger upon thee, and will judge thee according to thy ways, and will ′recompense upon thee all thine abominations.

4 And [a]mine eye shall not spare thee, neither will I have pity: but I will recompense thy ways upon thee, and thine abominations shall be in the midst of thee: [b]and ye shall know that I *am* the LORD.

5 Thus saith the Lord GOD; An evil, an only evil, behold, is come.

6 An end is come, the end is come: it ′watcheth for thee; behold, it is come.

7 [a]The morning is come unto thee, O thou that dwellest in the land: [b]the time is come, the day of trouble *is* near, and not the ′sounding again of the mountains.

6:2 [a]ch. 20:46 & 21:2 & 25:2 [b]ch. 36:1
3 [a]Lev. 26:30
4 [a]Lev. 26:30 ′Or, *sun images*
5 ′Heb. *give*
7 [a]ver. 13; ch. 7:4, 9
8 [a]Jer. 44:28; ch. 5:2,12 & 12:16 & 14:22
9 [a]Ps. 78:40; Is. 7:13 & 43:24 [b]Num. 15:39; ch. 20:7,24 [c]Lev. 26:39; Job 42:6; ch. 20:43 & 36:31
11 [a]ch. 21:14 [b]ch. 5:12
12 [a]ch. 5:13
13 [a]ver. 7 [b]Jer. 2:20 [c]Hos. 4:13 [d]Is. 57:5
14 [a]Is. 5:25 [b]Num. 33:46; Jer. 48:22 ′Or, *desolate from the wilderness*
7:2 [a]Amos 8:2; Mat. 24:6,13,14
3 ′Heb. *give*
4 [a]ch. 5:11 [b]ch. 12:20
6 ′Heb. *awaketh against thee*
7 [a]ver. 10 [b]Zeph. 1:14,15 ′Or, *echo*

R *Eze 5:14–15* ◀ ▶ *Eze 6:10*
R *Eze 6:6* ◀ ▶ *Eze 7:1–2*
R *Eze 6:10* ◀ ▶ *Eze 9:4–5*

6:6 Ezekiel confirmed that God would destroy their cities, homes and places of idol worship.

6:10 The fulfillment of God's prophecies would prove his prophets' divine inspiration and God's determination to bring judgment on his people.

7:1–2 After centuries of warning, the time of judgment finally arrived.

H 8 Now will I shortly [a]pour out my fury upon thee, and accomplish mine anger upon thee: and I will judge thee according to thy ways, and will recompense thee for all thine abominations.

9 And mine eye shall not spare, neither will I have pity: I will recompense [1]thee according to thy ways and thine abominations *that* are in the midst of thee; and ye shall know that I *am* the LORD that smiteth.

10 Behold the day, behold, it is come: [a]the morning is gone forth; the rod hath blossomed, pride hath budded.

11 [a]Violence is risen up into a rod of wickedness: none of them *shall remain,* nor of their [1]multitude, nor of any of [2]theirs: [b]neither *shall there be* wailing for them.

12 The time is come, the day draweth near: let not the buyer rejoice, nor the seller mourn: for wrath *is* upon all the multitude thereof.

13 For the seller shall not return to that which is sold, [1]although they were yet alive: for the vision *is* touching the whole multitude thereof, *which* shall not return; neither shall any strengthen himself [2]in [3]the iniquity of his life.

14 They have blown the trumpet, even to make all ready; but none goeth to the battle: for my wrath *is* upon all the multitude thereof.

D 15 [a]The sword *is* without, and the pestilence and the famine within: he that *is* in the field shall die with the sword; and he that *is* in the city, famine and pestilence shall devour him.

16 ¶ But they that escape of them shall escape, and shall be on the mountains like doves of the valleys, all of them mourning, every one for his iniquity.

H 17 All [a]hands shall be feeble, and all knees shall [1]be weak *as* water.

18 They shall also [a]gird *themselves* with sackcloth, and horror shall cover them; and shame *shall be* upon all faces, and baldness upon all their heads.

19 They shall cast their silver in the streets, and their gold shall be [1]removed: their [a]silver and their gold shall not be able to deliver them in the day of the wrath of the LORD: they shall not satisfy their souls, neither fill their bowels: [2]because it is the stumblingblock of their iniquity.

20 ¶ As for the beauty of his ornament, he set it in majesty: [a]but they made the images of their abominations *and* of their detestable things therein: therefore have I [1]set it far from them.

21 And I will give it into the hands of the strangers for a prey, and to the wicked of the earth for a spoil; and they shall pollute it.

22 My face will I turn also from them, and they shall pollute my secret *place:* for the [1]robbers shall enter into it, and defile it.

23 ¶ Make a chain: for [a]the land is full of bloody crimes, and the city is full of violence.

24 Wherefore I will bring the worst of the heathen, and they shall possess their houses: I will also make the pomp of the strong to cease; and [1]their holy places shall be defiled.

25 [1]Destruction cometh; and they shall seek peace, and *there shall be* none.

26 [a]Mischief shall come upon mischief, and rumour shall be upon rumour; [b]then shall they seek a vision of the prophet; but the law shall perish from the priest, and counsel from the ancients.

27 The king shall mourn, and the prince shall be clothed with desolation, and the hands of the people of the land shall be troubled: I will do unto them after their way, and [1]according to their deserts will I judge them; and they shall know that I *am* the LORD.

An end is come

8 AND IT came to pass in the sixth year, in the sixth *month,* in the fifth *day* of the month, *as* I sat in mine house, and [a]the elders of Judah sat before me, that [b]the hand of the Lord GOD fell there upon me.

2 [a]Then I beheld, and lo a likeness as the appearance of fire: from the appearance of his loins even downward, fire; and from his loins even upward, as the appearance of brightness, [b]as the colour of amber.

E N T 3 And he [a]put forth the form of an

8 [a]ch. 20:8,21
9 [1]Heb. *upon thee*
10 [a]ver. 7
11 [a]Jer. 6:7 [b]Jer. 16:5,6; ch. 24:16, 22 [1]Or, *tumult* [2]Or, *their tumultuous persons*
13 [1]Heb. *though their life* were *yet among the living* [2]Or, *whose life is in his iniquity* [3]Heb. *his iniquity*
15 [a]Deut. 32:25; Lam. 1:20
17 [a]Is. 13:7; Jer. 6:24 [1]Heb. *go into water*
18 [a]Is. 3:24; Amos 8:10
19 [a]Prov. 11:4; Zeph. 1:18 [1]Heb. *for a separation,* or, *uncleanness* [2]Or, *because their iniquity is* their *stumblingblock*
20 [a]Jer. 7:30 [1]Or, *made it unto them an unclean thing*
22 [1]Or, *burglars*
23 [a]2 Ki. 21:16
24 [1]Or, *they shall inherit their holy places*
25 [1]Heb. *Cutting off*
26 [a]Deut. 32:23; Jer. 4:20 [b]Ps. 74:9; ch. 20:1,3
27 [1]Heb. *with their judgments*
8:1 [a]ch. 14:1 & 20:1 & 33:31 [b]ch. 1:3 & 3:22
2 [a]ch. 1:26,27 [b]ch. 1:4
3 [a]Dan. 5:5

H *La 3:39* ◀ ▶ *Eze 7:17–18*
D *Eze 5:12* ◀ ▶ *Eze 14:19*
H *Eze 7:8* ◀ ▶ *Eze 9:10*
E *Eze 3:24* ◀ ▶ *Eze 11:1*
N *Eze 3:14* ◀ ▶ *Eze 37:1*
T *Isa 61:1* ◀ ▶ *Eze 11:24*

hand, and took me by a lock of mine head; and [b]the spirit lifted me up between the earth and the heaven, and [c]brought me in the visions of God to Jerusalem, to the door of the inner gate that looketh toward the north; [d]where *was* the seat of the image of jealousy, which [e]provoketh to jealousy.

4 And, behold, the glory of the God of Israel *was* there, according to the vision that I [a]saw in the plain.

5 ¶ Then said he unto me, Son of man, lift up thine eyes now the way toward the north. So I lifted up mine eyes the way toward the north, and behold northward at the gate of the altar this image of jealousy in the entry.

6 He said furthermore unto me, Son of man, seest thou what they do? *even* the great abominations that the house of Israel committeth here, that I should go far off from my sanctuary? but turn thee yet again, *and* thou shalt see greater abominations.

7 ¶ And he brought me to the door of the court; and when I looked, behold a hole in the wall.

8 Then said he unto me, Son of man, dig now in the wall: and when I had digged in the wall, behold a door.

9 And he said unto me, Go in, and behold the wicked abominations that they do here.

10 So I went in and saw; and behold every form of creeping things, and abominable beasts, and all the idols of the house of Israel, portrayed upon the wall round about.

11 And there stood before them seventy men of the ancients of the house of Israel, and in the midst of them stood Jaazaniah the son of Shaphan, with every man his censer in his hand; and a thick cloud of incense went up.

E 12 Then said he unto me, Son of man, hast thou seen what the ancients of the house of Israel do in the dark, every man in the chambers of his imagery? for they say, [a]The LORD seeth us not; the LORD hath forsaken the earth.

13 ¶ He said also unto me, Turn thee yet again, *and* thou shalt see greater abominations that they do.

14 Then he brought me to the door of the gate of the LORD'S house which *was* toward the north; and, behold, there sat women weeping for Tammuz.

15 ¶ Then said he unto me, Hast thou seen *this,* O son of man? turn thee yet again, *and* thou shalt see greater abominations than these.

16 And he brought me into the inner court of the LORD'S house, and, behold, at the door of the temple of the LORD, [a]between the porch and the altar, [b]*were* about five and twenty men, [c]with their backs toward the temple of the LORD, and their faces toward the east; and they worshipped [d]the sun toward the east.

17 ¶ Then he said unto me, Hast thou seen *this,* O son of man? [1]Is it a light thing to the house of Judah that they commit the abominations which they commit here? for they have [a]filled the land with violence, and have returned to provoke me to anger: and, lo, they put the branch to their nose.

18 [a]Therefore will I also deal in fury: mine [b]eye shall not spare, neither will I have pity: and though they [c]cry in mine ears with a loud voice, *yet* will I not hear them.

The slaughter of the idolaters

9 HE CRIED also in mine ears with a loud voice, saying, Cause them that have charge over the city to draw near, even every man *with* his destroying weapon in his hand.

2 And, behold, six men came from the way of the higher gate, [1]which lieth toward the north, and every man [2]a slaughter weapon in his hand; [a]and one man among them *was* clothed with linen, with a writer's inkhorn [3]by his side: and they went in, and stood beside the brasen altar.

3 And [a]the glory of the God of Israel was gone up from the cherub, whereupon he was, to the threshold of the house. And he called to the man clothed with linen, which *had* the writer's inkhorn by his side;

4 And the LORD said unto him, Go R
through the midst of the city, through S
the midst of Jerusalem, and [1]set [a]a mark upon the foreheads of the men [b]that sigh and that cry for all the abominations that be done in the midst thereof.

3 [b]ch. 3:14 [c]ch. 11:1,24 & 40:2 [d]Jer. 7:30 & 32:34; ch. 5:11 [e]Deut. 32:16,21

4 [a]ch. 1:28 & 3:22,23

12 [a]ch. 9:9

16 [a]Joel 2:17 [b]ch. 11:1 [c]Jer. 2:27 & 32:33 [d]Deut. 4:19; 2 Ki. 23:5,11; Job 31:26; Jer. 44:17

17 [a]ch. 9:9 [1]Or, *Is there any thing lighter than to commit*

18 [a]ch. 5:13 & 16:42 & 24:13 [b]ch. 5:11 & 7:4,9 & 9:5,10 [c]Prov. 1:28; Is. 1:15; Jer. 11:11 & 14:12; Mic. 3:4; Zech. 7:13

9:2 [a]Lev. 16:4; ch. 10:2,6,7; Rev. 15:6 [1]Heb. *which is turned* [2]Heb. *a weapon of his breaking in pieces* [3]Heb. *upon his loins*

3 [a]See ch. 3:23 & 8:4 & 10:4,18 & 11:22,23

4 [a]Ex. 12:7; Rev. 7:3 & 9:4 & 13:16, 17 & 20:4 [b]Ps. 119:53,136; Jer. 13:17; 2 Cor. 12:21; 2 Pet. 2:8 [1]Heb. *mark a mark*

E *Jer 32:19* ◀ ▶ *Eze 9:9–10*

R *Eze 7:1–2* ◀ ▶ *Eze 11:10–12*

S *Eze 3:20–21* ◀ ▶ *Eze 11:19–21*

5 ¶ And to the others he said in [1]mine hearing, Go ye after him through the city, and smite: [a]let not your eye spare, neither have ye pity:

6 [a]Slay [1]utterly old *and* young, both maids, and little children, and women: but [b]come not near any man upon whom *is* the mark; and [c]begin at my sanctuary. [d]Then they began at the ancient men which *were* before the house.

7 And he said unto them, Defile the house, and fill the courts with the slain: go ye forth. And they went forth, and slew in the city.

8 ¶ And it came to pass, while they were slaying them, and I was left, that I [a]fell upon my face, and cried, and said, [b]Ah Lord GOD! wilt thou destroy all the residue of Israel in thy pouring out of thy fury upon Jerusalem?

E 9 Then said he unto me, The iniquity of the house of Israel and Judah *is* exceeding great, and [a]the land is [1]full of blood, and the city full of [2]perverseness: for they say, [b]The LORD hath forsaken the earth, and [c]the LORD seeth not.

H 10 And as for me also, mine [a]eye shall not spare, neither will I have pity, *but* [b]I will recompense their way upon their head.

11 And, behold, the man clothed with linen, which *had* the inkhorn by his side, [1]reported the matter, saying, I have done as thou hast commanded me.

The glory of the LORD

10 THEN I looked, and, behold, in the [a]firmament that was above the head of the cherubims there appeared over them as it were a sapphire stone, as the appearance of the likeness of a throne.

2 [a]And he spake unto the man clothed with linen, and said, Go in between the wheels, *even* under the cherub, and fill [1]thine hand with [b]coals of fire from between the cherubims, and [c]scatter *them* over the city. And he went in in my sight.

3 Now the cherubims stood on the right side of the house, when the man went in; and the cloud filled the inner court.

4 [a]Then the glory of the LORD [1]went up from the cherub, *and stood* over the threshold of the house; and [b]the house was filled with the cloud, and the court was full of the brightness of the LORD'S glory.

5 And the [a]sound of the cherubims' wings was heard *even* to the outer court, as [b]the voice of the Almighty God when he speaketh.

6 And it came to pass, *that* when he had commanded the man clothed with linen, saying, Take fire from between the wheels, from between the cherubims; then he went in, and stood beside the wheels.

7 And *one* cherub [1]stretched forth his hand from between the cherubims unto the fire that *was* between the cherubims, and took *thereof,* and put *it* into the hands of *him that was* clothed with linen: who took *it,* and went out.

8 ¶ [a]And there appeared in the cherubims the form of a man's hand under their wings.

9 [a]And when I looked, behold the four wheels by the cherubims, one wheel by one cherub, and another wheel by another cherub: and the appearance of the wheels *was* as the colour of a [b]beryl stone.

10 And *as for* their appearances, they four had one likeness, as if a wheel had been in the midst of a wheel.

11 [a]When they went, they went upon their four sides; they turned not as they went, but to the place whither the head looked they followed it; they turned not as they went.

12 And their whole [1]body, and their backs, and their hands, and their wings, and the wheels, *were* full of eyes round about, *even* the wheels that they four had.

13 As for the wheels, [1]it was cried unto them in my hearing, O wheel.

14 [a]And every one had four faces: the first face *was* the face of a cherub, and the second face *was* the face of a man, and the third the face of a lion, and the fourth the face of an eagle.

15 And the cherubims were lifted up. This *is* [a]the living creature that I saw by the river of Chebar.

16 [a]And when the cherubims went, the wheels went by them: and when the cherubims lifted up their wings to mount up from the earth, the same wheels also turned not from beside them.

5 [a]ver. 10; ch. 5:11 [1]Heb. *mine ears*

6 [a]2 Chr. 36:17 [b]Rev. 9:4 [c]Jer. 25:29; 1 Pet. 4:17 [d]ch. 8:11,12,16 [1]Heb. *to destruction*

8 [a]Num. 14:5 & 16:4,22,45; Josh. 7:6 [b]ch. 11:13

9 [a]2 Ki. 21:16; ch. 8:17 [b]ch. 8:12 [c]Ps. 10:11; Is. 29:15 [1]Heb. *filled with* [2]Or, *wresting of* judgment

10 [a]ch. 5:11 & 7:4 & 8:18 [b]ch. 11:21

11 [1]Heb. *returned the word*

10:1 [a]ch. 1:2,26

2 [a]ch. 9:2,3 [b]ch. 1:13 [c]See Rev. 8:5 [1]Heb. *the hollow of thine hand*

4 [a]See ver. 18; ch. 1:28 & 9:3 [b]1 Ki. 8:10; ch. 43:5 [1]Heb. *was lifted up*

5 [a]ch. 1:24 [b]Ps. 29:3

7 [1]Heb. *sent forth*

8 [a]ver. 21

9 [a]ch. 1:15 [b]ch. 1:16

11 [a]ch. 1:17

12 [1]Heb. *flesh*

13 [1]Or, *they were called in my hearing, wheel*

14 [a]ch. 1:6,10

15 [a]ch. 1:5

16 [a]ch. 1:19

E *Eze 8:12* ◀ ▶ *Eze 11:5*
H *Eze 7:17–18* ◀ ▶ *Eze 11:21*

17 [a]When they stood, *these* stood; and
when they were lifted up, *these* lifted up
themselves *also:* for the spirit [/]of the living creature *was* in them.
18 Then [a]the glory of the LORD [b]de-
parted from off the threshold of the
house, and stood over the cherubims.
19 And [a]the cherubims lifted up their
wings, and mounted up from the earth in
my sight: when they went out, the
wheels also *were* beside them, and *every
one* stood at the door of the east gate of
the LORD'S house; and the glory of the God
of Israel *was* over them above.
20 [a]This *is* the living creature that I
saw under the God of Israel [b]by the river
of Chebar; and I knew that they *were* the
cherubims.
21 [a]Every one had four faces apiece,
and every one four wings; and the likeness of the hands of a man *was* under
their wings.
22 And [a]the likeness of their faces *was*
the same faces which I saw by the river
of Chebar, their appearances and themselves: [b]they went every one straight
forward.

Ungodly rulers to be punished

E 11 MOREOVER [a]THE spirit lifted
L me up, and brought me unto [b]the
east gate of the LORD'S house, which looketh eastward: and behold [c]at the door of
the gate five and twenty men; among
whom I saw Jaazaniah the son of Azur,
and Pelatiah the son of Benaiah, princes
of the people.
2 Then said he unto me, Son of man,
these *are* the men that devise mischief,
and give wicked counsel in this city:
3 Which say, [/]*It is* not [a]near; let us
build houses: [b]this *city is* the caldron,
and we *be* the flesh.
4 ¶ Therefore prophesy against them,
prophesy, O son of man.

5 And [a]the spirit of the LORD fell upon E
me, and said unto me, Speak; Thus saith L
the LORD; Thus have ye said, O house of E
Israel: for I know the things that come
into your mind, *every one of* them.
6 [a]Ye have multiplied your slain in this
city, and ye have filled the streets thereof
with the slain.
7 Therefore thus saith the Lord GOD;
[a]Your slain whom ye have laid in the
midst of it, they *are* the flesh, and this
city is the caldron: [b]but I will bring you
forth out of the midst of it.
8 Ye have feared the sword; and I will
bring a sword upon you, saith the Lord
GOD.
9 And I will bring you out of the midst
thereof, and deliver you into the hands of
strangers, and [a]will execute judgments
among you.
10 [a]Ye shall fall by the sword; I will R
judge you in [b]the border of Israel; [c]and ye
shall know that I *am* the LORD.
11 [a]This *city* shall not be your caldron,
neither shall ye be the flesh in the midst
thereof; *but* I will judge you in the border
of Israel:
12 And [a]ye shall know that I *am* the
LORD: [/]for ye have not walked in my statutes, neither executed my judgments, but
[b]have done after the manners of the heathen that *are* round about you.

Hope for the remnant of Israel

13 ¶ And it came to pass, when I
prophesied, that [a]Pelatiah the son of Benaiah died. Then [b]fell I down upon my
face, and cried with a loud voice, and
said, Ah Lord GOD! wilt thou make a full
end of the remnant of Israel?
14 Again the word of the LORD came
unto me, saying,
15 Son of man, thy brethren, *even* thy
brethren, the men of thy kindred, and all

17 [a]ch. 1:12,20,21 [/]Or, *of life*
18 [a]ver. 4 [b]Hos. 9:12
19 [a]ch. 11:22
20 [a]ver. 15; ch. 1:22 [b]ch. 1:1
21 [a]ch. 1:6
22 [a]ch. 1:10 [b]ch. 1:12
11:1 [a]ver. 24; ch. 3:12,14 [b]ch. 10:19 [c]See ch. 8:16
3 [a]ch. 12:22,27; 2 Pet. 3:4 [b]See Jer. 1:13; ch. 24:3 [/]Or, It is *not* for us *to build houses near*
5 [a]ch. 2:2 & 3:24
6 [a]ch. 7:23
7 [a]ch. 24:3,6; Mic. 3:3 [b]ver. 9
9 [a]ch. 5:8
10 [a]2 Ki. 25:19-21; Jer. 39:6 & 52:10 [b]1 Ki. 8:65; 2 Ki. 14:25 [c]Ps. 9:16; ch. 6:7 & 13:9,14,21, 23
11 [a]See ver. 3
12 [a]ver. 10 [b]Lev. 18:3,24; Deut. 12:30,31; ch. 8:10, 14,16 [/]Or, *which have not walked*
13 [a]Acts 5:5 [b]ch. 9:8

E *Eze 8:3* ◀▶ *Eze 11:5*
L *Eze 3:24* ◀▶ *Eze 11:5*

E *Eze 11:1* ◀▶ *Eze 11:24*
L *Eze 11:1* ◀▶ *Eze 13:3*
E *Eze 9:9–10* ◀▶ *Da 2:22*
R *Eze 9:4–5* ◀▶ *Eze 11:16*

10:18–19 The glory of the Lord departed to the threshold of the temple (see 9:3) and then moved out of the temple to the east gate of the outer court (10:19). Some scholars believe that this was the gate Jesus used to enter the temple on Palm Sunday. Others state that this is the same site as the modern "Golden Gate" of Jerusalem that was sealed off centuries ago. Ezekiel later prophesies that the glory of the Lord will reenter the temple "by way of the gate whose prospect is toward the east" (43:4). The rebuilt temple will be cleansed (see Da 8:14) and the millennial kingdom of the Messiah will be ushered in.

the house of Israel wholly, *are* they unto whom the inhabitants of Jerusalem have said, Get you far from the LORD: unto us is this land given in possession.

16 Therefore say, Thus saith the Lord GOD; Although I have cast them far off among the heathen, and although I have scattered them among the countries, [a]yet will I be to them as a little sanctuary in the countries where they shall come.

17 Therefore say, Thus saith the Lord GOD; [a]I will even gather you from the people, and assemble you out of the countries where ye have been scattered, and I will give you the land of Israel.

18 And they shall come thither, and [a]they shall take away all the detestable things thereof and all the abominations thereof from thence.

19 And [a]I will give them one heart, and I will put [b]a new spirit within you; and I will take [c]the stony heart out of their flesh, and will give them an heart of flesh:

20 [a]That they may walk in my statutes, and keep mine ordinances, and do them: [b]and they shall be my people, and I will be their God.

21 But *as for them* whose heart walketh after the heart of their detestable things and their abominations, [a]I will recompense their way upon their own heads, saith the Lord GOD.

22 ¶ Then did the cherubims [a]lift up their wings, and the wheels beside them; and the glory of the God of Israel *was* over them above.

23 And [a]the glory of the LORD went up from the midst of the city, and stood [b]upon the mountain [c]which *is* on the east side of the city.

R *Eze 11:10–12* ◀▶ *Eze 12:15*
I *Eze 4:4–6* ◀▶ *Eze 16:53*
B *Isa 63:11* ◀▶ *Eze 36:26–27*
P *Isa 44:3–4* ◀▶ *Eze 36:26–27*
R *Isa 61:1–3* ◀▶ *Eze 36:25–27*
S *Isa 4:3–4* ◀▶ *Eze 36:25–27*
K *Jer 50:20* ◀▶ *Eze 12:25*
S *Eze 9:4–6* ◀▶ *Eze 13:22*
H *Eze 9:10* ◀▶ *Eze 13:14*

16 [a]Ps. 90:1 & 91:9; Is. 8:14
17 [a]Jer. 24:5; ch. 38:25 & 34:13
18 [a]ch. 37:23
19 [a]Jer. 32:39; ch. 36:26; See Zeph. 3:9 [b]Ps. 51:10; Jer. 31:33; ch. 18:31 [c]Zech. 7:12
20 [a]Ps. 105:45 [b]Jer. 24:7; ch. 14:11 & 36:28 & 37:27
21 [a]ch. 9:10 & 22:31
22 [a]ch. 1:19 & 10:19
23 [a]ch. 8:4 & 9:3; & 10:4,18 & 43:4 [b]See Zech. 14:4 [c]ch. 43:2
24 [a]ch. 8:3
12:2 [a]ch. 2:3,6-8 & 3:26,27 [b]Is. 6:9 & 42:20; Jer. 5:21; Mat. 13:13,14 [c]ch. 2:5
3 [l]Or, *instruments*
4 [l]Heb. *as the goings forth of captivity*
5 [l]Heb. *Dig for thee*
6 [a]ver. 11; Is. 8:18; ch. 4:3 & 24:24
7 [l]Heb. *digged for me*
9 [a]ch. 2:5 [b]ch. 17:12 & 24:19
10 [a]Mal. 1:1

24 ¶ Afterwards [a]the spirit took me up, and brought me in a vision by the spirit of God into Chaldea, to them of the captivity. So the vision that I had seen went up from me.

25 Then I spake unto them of the captivity all the things that the LORD had shown me.

Captivity symbolized

12 THE WORD of the LORD also came unto me, saying,

2 Son of man, thou dwellest in the midst of [a]a rebellious house, which [b]have eyes to see, and see not; they have ears to hear, and hear not: [c]for they *are* a rebellious house.

3 Therefore, thou son of man, prepare thee [l]stuff for removing, and remove by day in their sight; and thou shalt remove from thy place to another place in their sight: it may be they will consider, though they *be* a rebellious house.

4 Then shalt thou bring forth thy stuff by day in their sight, as stuff for removing: and thou shalt go forth at even in their sight, [l]as they that go forth into captivity.

5 [l]Dig thou through the wall in their sight, and carry out thereby.

6 In their sight shalt thou bear *it* upon *thy* shoulders, *and* carry *it* forth in the twilight: thou shalt cover thy face, that thou see not the ground: [a]for I have set thee *for* a sign unto the house of Israel.

7 And I did so as I was commanded: I brought forth my stuff by day, as stuff for captivity, and in the even I [l]digged through the wall with mine hand; I brought *it* forth in the twilight, *and* I bare *it* upon *my* shoulder in their sight.

8 ¶ And in the morning came the word of the LORD unto me, saying,

9 Son of man, hath not the house of Israel, [a]the rebellious house, said unto thee, [b]What doest thou?

10 Say thou unto them, Thus saith the Lord GOD; This [a]burden *concerneth* the

E *Eze 11:5* ◀▶ *Eze 13:3*
T *Eze 8:3* ◀▶ *Eze 13:3*
C *Eze 3:7* ◀▶ *Eze 22:18*

11:17–20 Ezekiel prophesied that God would bring all of the exiles back to the promised land. God will also transform the hearts of his chosen people so that they will willingly follow him and keep his laws.

prince in Jerusalem, and all the house of
Israel that *are* among them.
11 Say, [a]I *am* your sign: like as I have
done, so shall it be done unto them:
[b]they[1] shall remove *and* go into captivity.
12 And [a]the prince that *is* among them
shall bear upon *his* shoulder in the twilight, and shall go forth: they shall dig
through the wall to carry out thereby: he
shall cover his face, that he see not the
ground with *his* eyes.
J 13 My [a]net also will I spread upon
him, and he shall be taken in my snare:
and [b]I will bring him to Babylon *to* the
land of the Chaldeans; yet shall he not
see it, though he shall die there.
14 And [a]I will scatter toward every
wind all that *are* about him to help him,
and all his bands; and [b]I will draw out the
sword after them.
R 15 [a]And they shall know that I *am* the
LORD, when I shall scatter them among
the nations, and disperse them in the
countries.
16 [a]But I will leave [1]a few men of
them from the sword, from the famine,
and from the pestilence; that they may
declare all their abominations among the
heathen whither they come; and they
shall know that I *am* the LORD.
17 ¶ Moreover the word of the LORD
came to me, saying,
18 Son of man, [a]eat thy bread with
quaking, and drink thy water with trembling and with carefulness;
19 And say unto the people of the
land, Thus saith the Lord GOD of the inhabitants of Jerusalem, *and* of the land of
Israel; They shall eat their bread with
carefulness, and drink their water with
astonishment, that her land may [a]be desolate from [1]all that is therein, [b]because
of the violence of all them that dwell
therein.
R 20 And the cities that are inhabited
shall be laid waste, and the land shall be
desolate; and ye shall know that I *am* the
LORD.

J *Jer 47:5* ◀▶ *Eze 21:28–31*
R *Eze 11:16* ◀▶ *Eze 12:20*
R *Eze 12:15* ◀▶ *Eze 17:9–10*

11 [a]ver. 6 [b]2 Ki. 25:4,5,7 [1]Heb. *by removing go into captivity*
12 [a]Jer. 39:4
13 [a]Job 19:6; Jer. 52:9; Lam. 1:13; ch. 17:20 [b]2 Ki. 25:7; Jer. 52:11; ch. 17:16
14 [a]2 Ki. 25:4; ch. 5:10 [b]ch. 5:2,12
15 [a]ver. 16,20; Ps. 9:16; ch. 6:7,14 & 11:10
16 [a]ch. 6:8-10 [1]Heb. *men of number*
18 [a]ch. 4:16
19 [a]Zech. 7:14 [b]Ps. 107:34 [1]Heb. *the fulness thereof*
22 [a]ver. 27; ch. 11:3; Amos 6:3; 2 Pet. 3:4
23 [a]Joel 2:1; Zeph. 1:14
24 [a]ch. 13:23 [b]Lam. 2:14
25 [a]ver. 28; Is. 55:11; Dan. 9:12; Luke 21:33
27 [a]ver. 22
28 [a]ver. 23,25
13:2 [a]ver. 17 [b]Jer. 14:14 & 23:16,26 [1]Heb. *them that are prophets out of their own hearts*
3 [1]Heb. *walk after* [2]Or, *and things which they have not seen*
4 [a]Sol. 2:15
5 [a]Ps. 106:23,30; ch. 22:30 [1]Or, *breaches* [2]Heb. *hedged the hedge*

21 ¶ And the word of the LORD came
unto me, saying,
22 Son of man, what *is* that proverb
that ye have in the land of Israel, saying,
[a]The days are prolonged, and every vision faileth?
23 Tell them therefore, Thus saith the
Lord GOD; I will make this proverb to
cease, and they shall no more use it as a
proverb in Israel; but say unto them,
[a]The days are at hand, and the effect of
every vision.
24 For [a]there shall be no more any
[b]vain vision nor flattering divination
within the house of Israel.
25 For I *am* the LORD: I will speak, and K
[a]the word that I shall speak shall come to
pass; it shall be no more prolonged: for in
your days, O rebellious house, will I say
the word, and will perform it, saith the
Lord GOD.
26 ¶ Again the word of the LORD came
to me, saying,
27 [a]Son of man, behold, *they of* the
house of Israel say, The vision that he
seeth *is* for many days *to come,* and he
prophesieth of the times *that are* far off.
28 [a]Therefore say unto them, Thus
saith the Lord GOD; There shall none of
my words be prolonged any more, but
the word which I have spoken shall be
done, saith the Lord GOD.

Prophecy against false prophets

13 AND THE word of the LORD came
unto me, saying,
2 Son of man, prophesy against the
prophets of Israel that prophesy, and say
thou unto [a]them[1] that prophesy out of
their own [b]hearts, Hear ye the word of
the LORD;
3 Thus saith the Lord GOD; Woe unto E
the foolish prophets, that [1]follow their L
own spirit, [2]and have seen nothing! T
4 O Israel, thy prophets are [a]like the
foxes in the deserts.
5 Ye [a]have not gone up into the [1]gaps,
neither [2]made up the hedge for the house

K *Eze 11:19–20* ◀▶ *Eze 36:25–26*
E *Eze 11:24* ◀▶ *Eze 37:1*
L *Eze 11:5* ◀▶ *Eze 36:27*
T *Eze 11:24* ◀▶ *Eze 40:1–2*

12:15, 20 The phrase "they shall know that I *am* the LORD" occurs more than 20 times in Ezekiel to emphasize the fact that God is in control of everything, whether judgment or restoration.

of Israel to stand in the battle in the day of the LORD.

6 [a]They have seen vanity and lying divination, saying, The LORD saith: and the LORD hath not sent them: and they have made *others* to hope that they would confirm the word.

7 Have ye not seen a vain vision, and have ye not spoken a lying divination, whereas ye say, The LORD saith *it;* albeit I have not spoken?

8 Therefore thus saith the Lord GOD; Because ye have spoken vanity, and seen lies, therefore, behold, I *am* against you, saith the Lord GOD.

9 And mine hand shall be upon the prophets that see vanity, and that divine lies: they shall not be in the [1]assembly of my people, [a]neither shall they be written in the writing of the house of Israel, [b]neither shall they enter into the land of Israel; [c]and ye shall know that I *am* the Lord GOD.

G 10 ¶ Because, even because they have seduced my people, saying, [a]Peace; and *there was* no peace; and one built up [1]a wall, and, lo, others [b]daubed it with untempered *mortar:*

11 Say unto them which daub *it* with untempered *mortar,* that it shall fall: [a]there shall be an overflowing shower; and ye, O great hailstones, shall fall; and a stormy wind shall rend *it.*

12 Lo, when the wall is fallen, shall it not be said unto you, Where *is* the daubing wherewith ye have daubed *it?*

13 Therefore thus saith the Lord GOD; I will even rend *it* with a stormy wind in my fury; and there shall be an overflowing shower in mine anger, and great hailstones in *my* fury to consume *it.*

H 14 So will I break down the wall that ye have daubed with untempered *mortar,* and bring it down to the ground, so that the foundation thereof shall be discovered, and it shall fall, and ye shall be consumed in the midst thereof: [a]and ye shall know that I *am* the LORD.

15 Thus will I accomplish my wrath upon the wall, and upon them that have daubed it with untempered *mortar,* and will say unto you, The wall *is* no *more,* neither they that daubed it;

16 *To wit,* the prophets of Israel which prophesy concerning Jerusalem, and which [a]see visions of peace for her, and *there is* no peace, saith the Lord GOD.

17 ¶ Likewise, thou son of man, [a]set thy face against the daughters of thy people, [b]which prophesy out of their own heart; and prophesy thou against them,

18 And say, Thus saith the Lord GOD; Woe to the *women* that sew pillows to all [1]armholes, and make kerchiefs upon the head of every stature to hunt souls! Will ye [a]hunt the souls of my people, and will ye save the souls alive *that come* unto you?

19 And will ye pollute me among my people [a]for handfuls of barley and for pieces of bread, to slay the souls that should not die, and to save the souls alive that should not live, by your lying to my people that hear *your* lies?

20 Wherefore thus saith the Lord GOD; Behold, I *am* against your pillows, wherewith ye there hunt the souls [1]to make *them* fly, and I will tear them from your arms, and will let the souls go, *even* the souls that ye hunt to make *them* fly.

21 Your kerchiefs also will I tear, and deliver my people out of your hand, and they shall be no more in your hand to be hunted; [a]and ye shall know that I *am* the LORD.

22 Because with lies ye have made the heart of the righteous sad, whom I have not made sad; and [a]strengthened the hands of the wicked, that he should not return from his wicked way, [1,2]by promising him life: S

23 Therefore [a]ye shall see no more vanity, nor divine divinations: for I will deliver my people out of your hand: and ye shall know that I *am* the LORD.

Call to turn from idols

14 THEN [a]CAME certain of the elders of Israel unto me, and sat before me.

2 And the word of the LORD came unto me, saying,

3 Son of man, these men have set up their idols in their heart, and put [a]the stumblingblock of their iniquity before their face: [b]should I be inquired of at all by them?

4 Therefore speak unto them, and say unto them, Thus saith the Lord GOD; Ev-

6 [a]ver. 23; ch. 12:24 & 22:28
9 [a]Ezra 2:59,62; Neh. 7:5; Ps. 69:28 [b]ch. 20:38 [c]ch. 11:10,12 [1]Or, *secret,* or, *council*
10 [a]Jer. 6:14 & 8:11 [b]ch. 22:28 [1]Or, *a slight wall*
11 [a]ch. 38:22
14 [a]ver. 9,21,23; ch. 14:8
16 [a]Jer. 6:14 & 28:9
17 [a]ch. 20:46 & 21:2 [b]ver. 2
18 [a]2 Pet. 2:14 [1]Or, *elbows*
19 [a]See Prov. 28:21; Mic. 3:5
20 [1]Or, *into gardens*
21 [a]ver. 9
22 [a]Jer. 23:14 [1]Or, *that I should save his life* [2]Heb. *by quickening him*
23 [a]ver. 6; ch. 12:24; Mic. 3:6
14:1 [a]ch. 8:1 & 20:1 & 33:31
3 [a]ver. 4,7; ch. 7:19 [b]2 Ki. 3:13

G *Jer 46:11* ◀▶ *Eze 33:31*
H *Eze 11:21* ◀▶ *Eze 16:23*
S *Eze 11:19–21* ◀▶ *Eze 14:6–8*

ery man of the house of Israel that setteth
up his idols in his heart, and putteth the
stumblingblock of his iniquity before his
face, and cometh to the prophet; I the
LORD will answer him that cometh according to the multitude of his idols;
5 That I may take the house of Israel in
their own heart, because they are all estranged from me through their idols.
R 6 ¶ Therefore say unto the house of Is-
S rael, Thus saith the Lord GOD; Repent,
and turn [1]*yourselves* from your idols; and
turn away your faces from all your abominations.
7 For every one of the house of Israel,
or of the stranger that sojourneth in Israel, which separateth himself from me,
and setteth up his idols in his heart, and
putteth the stumblingblock of his iniquity
before his face, and cometh to a prophet
to inquire of him concerning me; I the
LORD will answer him by myself:
8 And [a]I will set my face against that
man, and will make him a [b]sign and a
proverb, and I will cut him off from the
midst of my people; [c]and ye shall know
that I *am* the LORD.
9 And if the prophet be deceived when
he hath spoken a thing, I the LORD [a]have
deceived that prophet, and I will stretch
out my hand upon him, and will destroy
him from the midst of my people Israel.
10 And they shall bear the punishment
of their iniquity: the punishment of the
prophet shall be even as the punishment
of him that seeketh *unto him;*
11 That the house of Israel may [a]go no
more astray from me, neither be polluted
any more with all their transgressions;
[b]but that they may be my people, and I
may be their God, saith the Lord GOD.

Deliverance through righteousness

12 ¶ The word of the LORD came again
to me, saying,
13 Son of man, when the land sinneth
against me by trespassing grievously,
then will I stretch out mine hand upon
it, and will break the [a]staff of the bread
thereof, and will send famine upon it,
and will cut off man and beast from it:
14 [a]Though these three men, Noah,
Daniel, and Job, were in it, they should
deliver *but* their own souls [b]by their righteousness, saith the Lord GOD.
15 ¶ If I cause [a]noisome beasts to pass
through the land, and they [1]spoil it, so
that it be desolate, that no man may pass
through because of the beasts:
16 [a]*Though* these three men *were* [1]in
it, *as* I live, saith the Lord GOD, they shall
deliver neither sons nor daughters; they
only shall be delivered, but the land shall
be desolate.
17 ¶ Or *if* [a]I bring a sword upon that
land, and say, Sword, go through the
land; so that I [b]cut off man and beast
from it:
18 [a]Though these three men *were* in
it, *as* I live, saith the Lord GOD, they shall
deliver neither sons nor daughters, but
they only shall be delivered themselves.
19 ¶ Or *if* I send [a]a pestilence into that D
land, and [b]pour out my fury upon it in
blood, to cut off from it man and beast:
20 [a]Though Noah, Daniel, and Job,
were in it, *as* I live, saith the Lord GOD,
they shall deliver neither son nor daughter; they shall *but* deliver their own souls
by their righteousness.
21 For thus saith the Lord GOD; [1]How D
much more when [a]I send my four sore
judgments upon Jerusalem, the sword,
and the famine, and the noisome beast,
and the pestilence, to cut off from it
man and beast?
22 ¶ [a]Yet, behold, therein shall be left
a remnant that shall be brought forth,
both sons and daughters: behold, they
shall come forth unto you, and [b]ye shall
see their way and their doings: and ye
shall be comforted concerning the evil
that I have brought upon Jerusalem, *even*
concerning all that I have brought
upon it.
23 And they shall comfort you, when
ye see their ways and their doings: and ye
shall know that I have not done [a]without

R *La 3:40–41* ◀▶ *Eze 18:21–23*
S *Eze 13:22* ◀▶ *Eze 18:4*

D *Eze 7:15* ◀▶ *Eze 14:21*
D *Eze 14:19* ◀▶ *Eze 28:23*

6 [1]Or, others
8 [a]Lev. 17:10 & 20:3,5,6; Jer. 44:11; ch. 15:7 [b]Num. 26:10; Deut. 28:37; ch. 5:15 [c]ch. 6:7
9 [a]1 Ki. 22:23; Job 12:16; Jer. 4:10; 2 Thes. 2:11
11 [a]2 Pet. 2:15 [b]ch. 11:20 & 37:27
13 [a]Lev. 26:26; Is. 3:1; ch. 4:16 & 5:16
14 [a]ver. 16,18,20; Jer. 15:1; See Jer. 7:16 & 11:14 & 14:11 [b]Prov. 11:4
15 [a]Lev. 26:22; ch. 5:17 [1]Or, *bereave*
16 [a]ver. 14,18,20 [1]Heb. *in the midst of it*
17 [a]Lev. 26:25; ch. 5:12 & 21:3,4 & 29:8 & 38:21 [b]ch. 25:13; Zeph. 1:3
18 [a]ver. 14
19 [a]2 Sam. 24:15; ch. 38:22 [b]ch. 7:8
20 [a]ver. 14
21 [a]ch. 5:17 & 33:27 [1]Or, *Also when*
22 [a]ch. 6:8 [b]ch. 20:43
23 [a]Jer. 22:8,9

14:21 Ezekiel described the wrath of God in terms of four severe judgments: sword, famine, wild beasts and plague. Compare these judgments with those listed in 5:17 and the judgments of the tribulation (see Rev 6:1–8).

cause all that I have done in it, saith the Lord GOD.

The parable of the vine

15 AND THE word of the LORD came unto me, saying,

2 Son of man, What is the vine tree more than any tree, *or than* a branch which is among the trees of the forest?

3 Shall wood be taken thereof to do any work? or will *men* take a pin of it to hang any vessel thereon?

4 Behold, [a]it is cast into the fire for fuel; the fire devoureth both the ends of it, and the midst of it is burned. [1]Is it meet for *any* work?

5 Behold, when it was whole, it was [1]meet for no work: how much less shall it be meet yet for *any* work, when the fire hath devoured it, and it is burned?

6 ¶ Therefore thus saith the Lord GOD; As the vine tree among the trees of the forest, which I have given to the fire for fuel, so will I give the inhabitants of Jerusalem.

7 And [a]I will set my face against them; [b]they shall go out from *one* fire, and *another* fire shall devour them; [c]and ye shall know that I *am* the LORD, when I set my face against them.

8 And I will make the land desolate, because they have [1]committed a trespass, saith the Lord GOD.

The judgment upon Israel

16 AGAIN THE word of the LORD came unto me, saying,

2 Son of man, [a]cause Jerusalem to know her abominations,

3 And say, Thus saith the Lord GOD unto Jerusalem; Thy [1]birth [a]and thy nativity *is* of the land of Canaan; [b]thy father *was* an Amorite, and thy mother an Hittite.

4 And *as for* thy nativity, [a]in the day thou wast born thy navel was not cut, neither wast thou washed in water [1]to supple *thee;* thou wast not salted at all, nor swaddled at all.

5 None eye pitied thee, to do any of these unto thee, to have compassion upon thee; but thou wast cast out in the open field, to the loathing of thy person, in the day that thou wast born.

6 ¶ And when I passed by thee, and saw thee [1]polluted in thine own blood, I said unto thee *when thou wast* in thy blood, Live; yea, I said unto thee *when thou wast* in thy blood, Live.

7 [a]I have [1]caused thee to multiply as the bud of the field, and thou hast increased and waxen great, and thou art come to [2]excellent ornaments: *thy* breasts are fashioned, and thine hair is grown, whereas thou *wast* naked and bare.

8 Now when I passed by thee, and looked upon thee, behold, thy time *was* the time of love; [a]and I spread my skirt over thee, and covered thy nakedness: yea, I sware unto thee, and entered into a covenant with thee, saith the Lord GOD, and [b]thou becamest mine.

9 Then washed I thee with water; yea, I thoroughly washed away thy [1]blood from thee, and I anointed thee with oil.

10 I clothed thee also with broidered work, and shod thee with badgers' skin, and I girded thee about with fine linen, and I covered thee with silk. C

11 I decked thee also with ornaments, and I [a]put bracelets upon thy hands, [b]and a chain on thy neck.

12 And I put a jewel on thy [1]forehead, and earrings in thine ears, and a beautiful crown upon thine head.

13 Thus wast thou decked with gold and silver; and thy raiment *was of* fine linen, and silk, and broidered work; [a]thou didst eat fine flour, and honey, and oil: and thou wast exceeding [b]beautiful, and thou didst prosper into a kingdom.

14 And [a]thy renown went forth among the heathen for thy beauty: for it *was* perfect through my comeliness, which I had put upon thee, saith the Lord GOD.

15 ¶ [a]But thou didst trust in thine own beauty, [b]and playedst the harlot because of thy renown, and pouredst out thy fornications on every one that passed by; his it was.

16 [a]And of thy garments thou didst take, and deckedst thy high places with divers colours, and playedst the harlot thereupon: *the like things* shall not come, neither shall it be *so.*

17 Thou hast also taken thy fair jewels of my gold and of my silver, which I had given thee, and madest to thyself images [1]of men, and didst commit whoredom with them,

18 And tookest thy broidered gar-

15:4 [a]John 15:6 [1]Heb. *Will it prosper?*
5 [1]Heb. *made* fit
7 [a]Lev. 17:10; ch. 14:8 [b]Is. 24:18 [c]ch. 7:4
8 [1]Heb. *trespassed a trespass*
16:2 [a]ch. 20:4 & 22:2
3 [a]ch. 21:30 [b]ver. 45 [1]Heb. *cutting out,* or, *habitation*
4 [a]Hos. 2:3 [1]Or, *when I looked* upon thee
6 [1]Or, *trodden under foot*
7 [a]Ex. 1:7 [1]Heb. *made thee a million* [2]Heb. *ornament of ornaments*
8 [a]Ruth 3:9 [b]Ex. 19:5; Jer. 2:2
9 [1]Heb. *bloods*
11 [a]Gen. 24:22 [b]Prov. 1:9
12 [1]Heb. *nose*
13 [a]Deut. 32:13, 14 [b]Ps. 48:2
14 [a]Lam. 2:15
15 [a]Deut. 32:15; Jer. 7:4; Mic. 3:11 [b]Is. 1:21 & 57:8; Jer. 2:20 & 3:2,6, 20; ch. 23:3,8
16 [a]2 Ki. 23:7; ch. 7:20; Hos. 2:8
17 [1]Heb. *of a male*

C Job 27:16–17 ◄ ► Mt 6:25–34

ments, and coveredst them: and thou
hast set mine oil and mine incense before
them.
19 [a]My meat also which I gave thee,
fine flour, and oil, and honey, *wherewith*
I fed thee, thou hast even set it before
them for ʹa sweet savour: and *thus* it
was, saith the Lord GOD.
20 [a]Moreover thou hast taken thy sons
and thy daughters, whom thou hast
borne unto me, and these hast thou sacrificed unto them ʹto be devoured. *Is this*
of thy whoredoms a small matter,
21 That thou hast slain my children,
and delivered them to cause them to pass
through *the fire* for them?
22 And in all thine abominations and
thy whoredoms thou hast not remembered the days of thy [a]youth, [b]when thou
wast naked and bare, *and* wast polluted
in thy blood.
H 23 And it came to pass after all thy
wickedness, (woe, woe unto thee! saith
the Lord GOD;)
24 *That* [a]thou hast also built unto thee
an ʹeminent place, and [b]hast made thee
an high place in every street.
25 Thou hast built thy high place [a]at
every head of the way, and hast made thy
beauty to be abhorred, and hast opened
thy feet to every one that passed by, and
multiplied thy whoredoms.
26 Thou hast also committed fornication with [a]the Egyptians thy neighbours,
great of flesh; and hast increased thy
whoredoms, to provoke me to anger.
27 Behold, therefore I have stretched
out my hand over thee, and have diminished thine ordinary *food,* and delivered
thee unto the will of them that hate thee,
[a]the ʹdaughters of the Philistines, which
are ashamed of thy lewd way.
28 Thou hast played the whore also
with the Assyrians, because thou wast
unsatiable; yea, thou hast played the harlot with them, and yet couldest not be
satisfied.
29 Thou hast moreover multiplied thy
fornication in the land of Canaan [a]unto
Chaldea; and yet thou wast not satisfied
herewith.
30 How weak is thine heart, saith the
Lord GOD, seeing thou doest all these
things, the work of an imperious whorish
woman;
31 ʹIn that [a]thou buildest thine eminent place in the head of every way, and
makest thine high place in every street;
and hast not been as an harlot, in that
thou scornest hire;
32 *But as* a wife that committeth adultery, *which* taketh strangers instead of
her husband!
33 They give gifts to all whores: but
[a]thou givest thy gifts to all thy lovers, and
ʹhirest them, that they may come unto
thee on every side for thy whoredom.
34 And the contrary is in thee from
other women in thy whoredoms,
whereas none followeth thee to commit
whoredoms: and in that thou givest a reward, and no reward is given unto thee,
therefore thou art contrary.
35 ¶ Wherefore, O harlot, hear the
word of the LORD:
36 Thus saith the Lord GOD; Because
thy filthiness was poured out, and thy nakedness discovered through thy whoredoms with thy lovers, and with all the
idols of thy abominations, and by [a]the
blood of thy children, which thou didst
give unto them;
37 Behold, therefore [a]I will gather all
thy lovers, with whom thou hast taken
pleasure, and all *them* that thou hast
loved, with all *them* that thou hast hated;
I will even gather them round about
against thee, and will discover thy nakedness unto them, that they may see all thy
nakedness.
38 And I will judge thee, ʹas [a]women
that break wedlock and [b]shed blood are
judged; and I will give thee blood in fury
and jealousy.
39 And I will also give thee into their
hand, and they shall throw down [a]thine
eminent place, and shall break down thy
high places: [b]they shall strip thee also of
thy clothes, and shall take ʹthy fair jewels, and leave thee naked and bare.
40 [a]They shall also bring up a company against thee, [b]and they shall stone
thee with stones, and thrust thee through
with their swords.
41 And they shall [a]burn thine houses
with fire, and [b]execute judgments upon
thee in the sight of many women: and I
will cause thee to [c]cease from playing the
harlot, and thou also shalt give no hire
any more.
42 So [a]will I make my fury toward
thee to rest, and my jealousy shall depart

19 [a]Hos. 2:8 ʹHeb. *a savour of rest*
20 [a]2 Ki. 16:3; Ps. 106:37; Is. 57:5; Jer. 7:31; ch. 20:26 ʹHeb. *to devour*
22 [a]ver. 43,60; Jer. 2:2; Hos. 11:1 [b]ver. 4,5,6
24 [a]ver. 31 [b]Is. 57:5,7; Jer. 2:20 & 3:2 ʹOr, *brothel house*
25 [a]Prov. 9:14
26 [a]ch. 8:10,14
27 [a]ver. 57; 2 Chr. 28:18 ʹOr, *cities*
29 [a]ch. 23:14
31 [a]ver. 24,39 ʹOr, *In thy daughters* is *thine*
33 [a]Is. 30:6; Hos. 8:9 ʹHeb. *bribest*
36 [a]ver. 20; Jer. 2:34
37 [a]Jer. 13:22,26; Lam. 1:8; ch. 23:9, 10,22,29; Hos. 2:10 & 8:10; Nah. 3:5
38 [a]Lev. 20:10; Deut. 22:22; ch. 23:45 [b]See ver. 20, 36; Gen. 9:6; Ex. 21:12 ʹHeb. *with judgments of*
39 [a]ver. 24,31 [b]ch. 23:26; Hos. 2:3 ʹHeb. *instruments of thine ornament*
40 [a]ch. 23:46 [b]John 8:5,7
41 [a]Deut. 13:16; 2 Ki. 25:9; Jer. 39:8 & 52:13 [b]ch. 5:8 & 23:10,48 [c]ch. 23:27
42 [a]ch. 5:13

H *Eze 13:14* ◀ ▶ *Eze 18:4*

from thee, and I will be quiet, and will be no more angry.

43 Because [a]thou hast not remembered the days of thy youth, but hast fretted me in all these *things;* behold, therefore [b]I also will recompense thy way upon *thine* head, saith the Lord GOD: and thou shalt not commit this lewdness above all thine abominations.

44 ¶ Behold, every one that useth proverbs shall use *this* proverb against thee, saying, As *is* the mother, *so is* her daughter.

45 Thou *art* thy mother's daughter, that loatheth her husband and her children; and thou *art* the sister of thy sisters, which loathed their husbands and their children: [a]your mother *was* an Hittite, and your father an Amorite.

46 And thine elder sister *is* Samaria, she and her daughters that dwell at thy left hand: and [a]thy[1] younger sister, that dwelleth at thy right hand, *is* Sodom and her daughters.

47 Yet hast thou not walked after their ways, nor done after their abominations: but, [1]as *if that were* a very little *thing,* [a]thou wast corrupted more than they in all thy ways.

48 *As* I live, saith the Lord GOD, [a]Sodom thy sister hath not done, she nor her daughters, as thou hast done, thou and thy daughters.

49 Behold, this was the iniquity of thy sister Sodom, pride, [a]fulness of bread, and abundance of idleness was in her and in her daughters, neither did she strengthen the hand of the poor and needy.

50 And they were haughty, and [a]committed abomination before me: therefore [b]I took them away as I saw *good.*

51 Neither hath Samaria committed half of thy sins; but thou hast multiplied thine abominations more than they, and [a]hast justified thy sisters in all thine abominations which thou hast done.

52 Thou also, which hast judged thy sisters, bear thine own shame for thy sins that thou hast committed more abominable than they: they are more righteous than thou: yea, be thou confounded also, and bear thy shame, in that thou hast justified thy sisters.

53 [a]When I shall bring again their captivity, [b]the captivity of Sodom and her daughters, and the captivity of Samaria and her daughters, then *will I bring again* the captivity of thy captives in the midst of them:

54 That thou mayest bear thine own shame, and mayest be confounded in all that thou hast done, in that thou art [a]a comfort unto them.

55 When thy sisters, Sodom and her daughters, shall return to their former estate, and Samaria and her daughters shall return to their former estate, then thou and thy daughters shall return to your former estate.

56 For thy sister Sodom was not [1]mentioned by thy mouth in the day of thy [2]pride,

57 Before thy wickedness was discovered, as at the time of *thy* [a]reproach of the daughters of [1]Syria, and all *that are* round about her, [b]the daughters of the Philistines, which [2]despise thee round about.

58 [a]Thou hast [1]borne thy lewdness and thine abominations, saith the LORD.

59 For thus saith the Lord GOD; I will even deal with thee as thou hast done, which hast [a]despised [b]the oath in breaking the covenant.

60 ¶ Nevertheless I will [a]remember my covenant with thee in the days of thy youth, and I will establish unto thee [b]an everlasting covenant.

61 Then [a]thou shalt remember thy ways, and be ashamed, when thou shalt receive thy sisters, thine elder and thy younger: and I will give them unto thee for [b]daughters, [c]but not by thy covenant.

62 [a]And I will establish my covenant with thee; and thou shalt know that I *am* the LORD:

63 That thou mayest remember, and be confounded, [a]and never open thy mouth any more because of thy shame,

43 [a]ver. 22; Ps. 78:42 [b]ch. 9:10 & 11:21 & 22:31
45 [a]ver. 3
46 [a]Deut. 32:32; Is. 1:10 [1]Heb. *lesser than thou*
47 [a]ver. 48,51; 2 Ki. 21:9; ch. 5:6,7 [1]Or, *that was loathed as a small thing*
48 [a]Mat. 10:15 & 11:24
49 [a]Gen. 13:10
50 [a]Gen. 13:13 & 18:20 & 19:5 [b]Gen. 19:24
51 [a]Jer. 3:11; Mat. 12:41
53 [a]See Is. 1:9 & ver. 60 [b]Jer. 20:16
54 [a]ch. 14:22
56 [1]Heb. *for a report,* or, *hearing* [2]Heb. *prides,* or, *excellencies*
57 [a]2 Ki. 16:5; 2 Chr. 28:18; Is. 7:1 & 14:28 [b]ver. 27 [1]Heb. *Aram* [2]Or, *spoil*
58 [a]ch. 23:49 [1]Heb. *borne them*
59 [a]ch. 17:13 [b]Deut. 29:12
60 [a]Ps. 106:45 [b]Jer. 32:40 & 50:5
61 [a]ch. 20:43 & 36:31 [b]Is. 54:1 & 60:4; Gal. 4:26 [c]Jer. 31:31
62 [a]Hos. 2:19
63 [a]Rom 3:19

Eze 11:17–20 ◄► *Eze 16:55*
Eze 16:53 ◄► *Eze 16:60–63*
Eze 16:55 ◄► *Eze 17:17*

16:53–63 The prophet declared that even though God would punish his people for their sin, God would restore the exiles to their promised land and fulfill his everlasting covenant with the descendants of Abraham.

when I am pacified toward thee for all that thou hast done, saith the Lord GOD.

The eagles and the cedar

17 AND THE word of the LORD came unto me, saying,
2 Son of man, put forth a riddle, and speak a parable unto the house of Israel;
3 And say, Thus saith the Lord GOD; [a]A great eagle with great wings, longwinged, full of feathers, which had [†]divers colours, came unto Lebanon, and [b]took the highest branch of the cedar:
4 He cropped off the top of his young twigs, and carried it into a land of traffic; he set it in a city of merchants.
5 He took also of the seed of the land, and [†]planted it in [a]a fruitful field; he placed *it* by great waters, *and* set it [b]*as* a willow tree.
6 And it grew, and became a spreading vine [a]of low stature, whose branches turned toward him, and the roots thereof were under him: so it became a vine, and brought forth branches, and shot forth sprigs.
7 There was also another great eagle with great wings and many feathers: and, behold, [a]this vine did bend her roots toward him, and shot forth her branches toward him, that he might water it by the furrows of her plantation.
8 It was planted in a good [†]soil by great waters, that it might bring forth branches, and that it might bear fruit, that it might be a goodly vine.
R 9 Say thou, Thus saith the Lord GOD; Shall it prosper? [a]shall he not pull up the roots thereof, and cut off the fruit thereof, that it wither? it shall wither in all the leaves of her spring, even without great power or many people to pluck it up by the roots thereof.
10 Yea, behold, *being* planted, shall it prosper? [a]shall it not utterly wither, when the east wind toucheth it? it shall wither in the furrows where it grew.
11 ¶ Moreover the word of the LORD came unto me, saying,
12 Say now to [a]the rebellious house, Know ye not what these *things mean?* tell *them,* Behold, [b]the king of Babylon is come to Jerusalem, and hath taken the king thereof, and the princes thereof, and led them with him to Babylon;
13 [a]And hath taken of the king's seed, and made a covenant with him, [b]and hath [†]taken an oath of him: he hath also taken the mighty of the land:
14 That the kingdom might be [a]base, that it might not lift itself up, [†]*but* that by keeping of his covenant it might stand.
15 But [a]he rebelled against him in sending his ambassadors into Egypt, [b]that they might give him horses and much people. [c]Shall he prosper? shall he escape that doeth such *things?* or shall he break the covenant, and be delivered?
16 *As* I live, saith the Lord GOD, surely [a]in the place *where* the king *dwelleth* that made him king, whose oath he despised, and whose covenant he brake, *even* with him in the midst of Babylon he shall die.
17 [a]Neither shall Pharaoh with *his* mighty army and great company make for him in the war, [b]by casting up mounts, and building forts, to cut off many persons:
18 Seeing he despised the oath by breaking the covenant, when, lo, he had [a]given his hand, and hath done all these *things,* he shall not escape.
19 Therefore thus saith the Lord GOD; *As* I live, surely mine oath that he hath despised, and my covenant that he hath broken, even it will I recompense upon his own head.
20 And I will [a]spread my net upon him, and he shall be taken in my snare, and I will bring him to Babylon, and [b]will plead with him there for his trespass that he hath trespassed against me.
21 And [a]all his fugitives with all his bands shall fall by the sword, and they that remain shall be scattered toward all winds: and ye shall know that I the LORD have spoken *it.*
22 ¶ Thus saith the Lord GOD; I will

17:3 [a]See ver. 12 [b]2 Ki. 24:12 [†]Heb. *embroidering*
5 [a]Deut. 8:7 [b]Is. 44:4 [†]Heb. *put it in a field of seed*
6 [a]ver. 14
7 [a]ver. 15
8 [†]Heb. *field*
9 [a]2 Ki. 25:7
10 [a]ch. 19:12; Hos. 13:15
12 [a]ch. 2:5 & 12:9 [b]ver. 3; 2 Ki. 24:11-16
13 [a]2 Ki. 24:17 [b]2 Chr. 36:13 [†]Heb. *brought him to an oath*
14 [a]ver. 6; ch. 29:14 [†]Heb. *to keep his covenant, to stand to it*
15 [a]2 Ki. 24:20; 2 Chr. 36:13 [b]Deut. 17:16; Is. 31:1,3 & 36:6,9 [c]ver. 9
16 [a]Jer. 32:5 & 34:3; ch. 12:13
17 [a]Jer. 37:7 [b]Jer. 52:4
18 [a]1 Chr. 29:24; Lam. 5:6
20 [a]ch. 12:13 [b]ch. 20:36
21 [a]ch. 12:14

R *Eze 12:20* ◀ ▶ *Eze 21:3*
| *Eze 16:60–63* ◀ ▶ *Eze 17:22–24*
| *Eze 17:17* ◀ ▶ *Eze 20:34–38*

17:10 In this verse, Ezekiel likened Nebuchadnezzar and his Babylonian army to the hot, dry winds from the east that withered all vegetation.

17:22–24 Though this Messianic promise used the same imagery of a branch, this prophecy used it

also take of the highest [a]branch of the high cedar, and will set *it;* I will crop off from the top of his young twigs [b]a tender one, and will [c]plant *it* upon an high mountain and eminent:

23 [a]In the mountain of the height of Israel will I plant it: and it shall bring forth boughs, and bear fruit, and be a goodly cedar: and [b]under it shall dwell all fowl of every wing; in the shadow of the branches thereof shall they dwell.

24 And all the trees of the field shall know that I the LORD [a]have brought down the high tree, have exalted the low tree, have dried up the green tree, and have made the dry tree to flourish: [b]I the LORD have spoken and have done *it.*

The soul that sinneth shall die

18 THE WORD of the LORD came unto me again, saying,

2 What mean ye, that ye use this proverb concerning the land of Israel, saying, The [a]fathers have eaten sour grapes, and the children's teeth are set on edge?

3 *As* I live, saith the Lord GOD, ye shall not have *occasion* any more to use this proverb in Israel.

H 4 Behold, all souls are mine; as the
S soul of the father, so also the soul of the son is mine: [a]the soul that sinneth, it shall die.

5 ¶ But if a man be just, and do [1]that which is lawful and right,

6 [a]*And* hath not eaten upon the mountains, neither hath lifted up his eyes to the idols of the house of Israel, neither hath [b]defiled his neighbour's wife, neither hath come near to [c]a menstruous woman,

7 And hath not [a]oppressed any, *but* hath restored to the debtor his [b]pledge, hath spoiled none by violence, hath [c]given his bread to the hungry, and hath covered the naked with a garment;

8 He *that* hath not given forth upon [a]usury, neither hath taken any increase, *that* hath withdrawn his hand from iniquity, [b]hath executed true judgment between man and man,

9 Hath walked in my statutes, and hath kept my judgments, to deal truly; he *is* just, he shall surely [a]live, saith the Lord GOD.

10 ¶ If he beget a son *that is* a [1]robber, [a]a shedder of blood, and [2]*that* doeth the like to *any* one of these *things,*

11 And that doeth not any of those *duties,* but even hath eaten upon the mountains, and defiled his neighbour's wife,

12 Hath oppressed the poor and needy, hath spoiled by violence, hath not restored the pledge, and hath lifted up his eyes to the idols, hath [a]committed abomination,

13 Hath given forth upon usury, and hath taken increase: shall he then live? he shall not live: he hath done all these abominations; he shall surely die; [a]his [1]blood shall be upon him.

14 ¶ Now, lo, *if* he beget a son, that seeth all his father's sins which he hath done, and considereth, and doeth not such like,

15 [a]*That* hath not eaten upon the mountains, neither hath lifted up his eyes to the idols of the house of Israel, hath not defiled his neighbour's wife,

16 Neither hath oppressed any, [1]hath not withholden the pledge, neither hath spoiled by violence, *but* hath given his bread to the hungry, and hath covered the naked with a garment,

17 *That* hath taken off his hand from the poor, *that* hath not received usury nor increase, hath executed my judgments, hath walked in my statutes; he shall not die for the iniquity of his father, he shall surely live.

18 *As for* his father, because he cruelly oppressed, spoiled his brother by violence, and did *that* which *is* not good among his people, lo, even [a]he shall die in his iniquity.

19 ¶ Yet say ye, Why? [a]doth not the son bear the iniquity of the father? When the son hath done that which is lawful and right, *and* hath kept all my statutes, and hath done them, he shall surely live.

20 [a]The soul that sinneth, it shall die. H
[b]The son shall not bear the iniquity of the S
father, neither shall the father bear the

22 [a]Is. 11:1; Jer. 23:5; Zech. 3:8 [b]Is. 53:2 [c]Ps. 2:6
23 [a]Is. 2:2,3 [b]See ch. 31:6; Dan. 4:12
24 [a]Luke 1:52 [b]ch. 22:14
18:2 [a]Jer. 31:29; Lam. 5:7
4 [a]Rom. 6:23
5 [1]Heb. *judgment and justice*
6 [a]ch. 22:9 [b]Lev. 18:20 & 20:10 [c]Lev. 18:19 & 20:18
7 [a]Ex. 22:21; Lev. 19:15 & 25:14 [b]Ex. 22:26; Deut. 24:12 [c]Deut. 15:7; Is. 58:7; Mat. 25:35
8 [a]Ex. 22:25; Lev. 25:36; Deut. 23:19; Neh. 5:7; Ps. 15:5 [b]Deut. 1:16; Zech. 8:16
9 [a]ch. 20:11; Amos 5:4
10 [a]Gen. 9:6; Ex. 21:12; Num. 35:31 [1]Or, *breaker up of an house* [2]Or, *that doeth to his brother besides any of these*
12 [a]ch. 8:6,17
13 [a]Lev. 20:9, 11-13,16,27; ch. 3:18; Acts 18:6 [1]Heb. *bloods*
15 [a]ver. 6
16 [1]Heb. *hath not pledged the pledge,* or, *taken to pledge*
18 [a]ch. 3:18
19 [a]Ex. 20:5; Deut. 5:9; 2 Ki. 23:26 & 24:3,4
20 [a]ver. 4 [b]Deut. 24:16; 2 Ki. 14:6; 2 Chr. 25:4; Jer. 31:29,30

H *Eze 16:23* ◄► *Eze 18:20*
S *Eze 14:6–8* ◄► *Eze 18:20–27*

H *Eze 18:4* ◄► *Eze 18:30*
S *Eze 18:4* ◄► *Eze 18:30–32*

---

in an unexpected way to describe the Messiah's rule in Jerusalem. Compare this prophecy with Isa 11:1; Jer 23:5; Zec 3:8; 6:12.

iniquity of the son: [c]the righteousness of the righteous shall be upon him, [d]and the wickedness of the wicked shall be upon him.

L R 21 But [a]if the wicked will turn from all his sins that he hath committed, and keep all my statutes, and do that which is lawful and right, he shall surely live, he shall not die.

22 [a]All his transgressions that he hath committed, they shall not be mentioned unto him: in his righteousness that he hath done he shall live.

W 23 [a]Have I any pleasure at all that the wicked should die? saith the Lord GOD: *and* not that he should return from his ways, and live?

24 ¶ But [a]when the righteous turneth away from his righteousness, and committeth iniquity, *and* doeth according to all the abominations that the wicked *man* doeth, shall he live? [b]All his righteousness that he hath done shall not be mentioned: in his trespass that he hath trespassed, and in his sin that he hath sinned, in them shall he die.

25 ¶ Yet ye say, [a]The way of the Lord is not equal. Hear now, O house of Israel; Is not my way equal? are not your ways unequal?

26 [a]When a righteous *man* turneth away from his righteousness, and committeth iniquity, and dieth in them; for his iniquity that he hath done shall he die.

L R 27 Again, [a]when the wicked *man* turneth away from his wickedness that he hath committed, and doeth that which is lawful and right, he shall save his soul alive.

28 Because he [a]considereth, and turneth away from all his transgressions that he hath committed, he shall surely live, he shall not die.

29 [a]Yet saith the house of Israel, The way of the Lord is not equal. O house of Israel, are not my ways equal? are not your ways unequal?

H R S 30 [a]Therefore I will judge you, O house of Israel, every one according to his ways, saith the Lord GOD. [b]Repent, and turn [1]*yourselves* from all your transgressions; so iniquity shall not be your ruin.

31 ¶ [a]Cast away from you all your transgressions, whereby ye have transgressed; and make you a [b]new heart and a new spirit: for why will ye die, O house of Israel?

32 For [a]I have no pleasure in the death of him that dieth, saith the Lord GOD: wherefore turn [1]*yourselves,* and live ye. L W

Lament for Israel's princes

19 MOREOVER [a]TAKE thou up a lamentation for the princes of Israel,

2 And say, What *is* thy mother? A lioness: she lay down among lions, she nourished her whelps among young lions.

3 And she brought up one of her whelps: [a]it became a young lion, and it learned to catch the prey; it devoured men.

4 The nations also heard of him; he was taken in their pit, and they brought him with chains unto the land of [a]Egypt.

5 Now when she saw that she had waited, *and* her hope was lost, then she took [a]another of her whelps, *and* made him a young lion.

6 [a]And he went up and down among the lions, [b]he became a young lion, and learned to catch the prey, *and* devoured men.

7 And he knew [1]their desolate palaces, and he laid waste their cities; and the land was desolate, and the fulness thereof, by the noise of his roaring.

8 [a]Then the nations set against him on every side from the provinces, and spread their net over him: [b]he was taken in their pit.

9 [a]And they put him in ward [1]in chains, and brought him to the king of Babylon: they brought him into holds, that his voice should no more be heard upon [b]the mountains of Israel.

10 ¶ Thy mother *is* [a]like a vine [1]in thy blood, planted by the waters: she was [b]fruitful and full of branches by reason of many waters.

11 And she had strong rods for the

L *La 3:32–33* ◀▶ *Eze 18:27–28*
R *Eze 14:6* ◀▶ *Eze 18:27–28*
W *Isa 57:19* ◀▶ *Eze 18:32*
L *Eze 18:21–23* ◀▶ *Eze 18:32*
R *Eze 18:21–23* ◀▶ *Eze 18:30–32*
H *Eze 18:20* ◀▶ *Eze 22:20–22*
R *Eze 18:27–28* ◀▶ *Eze 33:9*
S *Eze 18:20–27* ◀▶ *Eze 33:11–16*

L *Eze 18:27–28* ◀▶ *Eze 33:11–12*
W *Eze 18:23* ◀▶ *Eze 33:11*

20 [c]Is. 3:10,11 [d]Rom. 2:9
21 [a]ver. 27; ch. 33:12,19
22 [a]ch. 33:16
23 [a]ver. 32; ch. 33:11; 1 Tim. 2:4; 2 Pet. 3:9
24 [a]ch. 3:20 & 33:12,13,18 [b]2 Pet. 2:20
25 [a]ver. 29; ch. 33:17,20
26 [a]ver. 24
27 [a]ver. 21
28 [a]ver. 14
29 [a]ver. 25
30 [a]ch. 7:3 & 33:20 [b]Mat. 3:2; Rev. 2:5 [1]Or, others
31 [a]Eph. 4:22,23 [b]Jer. 32:39; ch. 11:19 & 36:26
32 [a]ver. 23; Lam. 3:33; ch. 33:11; 2 Pet. 3:9 [1]Or, others
19:1 [a]ch. 26:17 & 27:2
3 [a]ver. 6; 2 Ki. 23:31,32
4 [a]2 Ki. 23:33; 2 Chr. 36:4; Jer. 22:11,12
5 [a]2 Ki. 23:34
6 [a]Jer. 22:13-17 [b]ver. 3
7 [1]Or, *their widows*
8 [a]2 Ki. 24:2 [b]ver. 4
9 [a]2 Chr. 36:6; Jer. 22:18 [b]ch. 6:2 [1]Or, *in hooks*
10 [a]ch. 17:6 [b]Deut. 8:7-9 [1]Or, *in thy quietness,* or, *in thy likeness*

sceptres of them that bare rule, and her
[a]stature was exalted among the thick
branches, and she appeared in her height
with the multitude of her branches.
12 But she was plucked up in fury, she
was cast down to the ground, and the
[a]east wind dried up her fruit: her strong
rods were broken and withered; the fire
consumed them.
13 And now she *is* planted in the wilderness, in a dry and thirsty ground.
14 [a]And fire is gone out of a rod of her
branches, *which* hath devoured her fruit,
so that she hath no strong rod *to be* a
sceptre to rule. [b]This *is* a lamentation,
and shall be for a lamentation.

Israel's apostasy

20 AND IT came to pass in the seventh year, in the fifth *month,* the
tenth *day* of the month, *that* [a]certain of
the elders of Israel came to inquire of the
LORD, and sat before me.
2 Then came the word of the LORD
unto me, saying,
3 Son of man, speak unto the elders of
Israel, and say unto them, Thus saith the
Lord GOD; Are ye come to inquire of me?
As I live, saith the Lord GOD, [a]I will not
be inquired of by you.
4 Wilt thou [a]judge[ʹ] them, son of man,
wilt thou judge *them?* [b]cause them to
know the abominations of their fathers:
5 ¶ And say unto them, Thus saith the
Lord GOD; In the day when [a]I chose Israel, and [ʹ]lifted up mine hand unto the
seed of the house of Jacob, and made myself [b]known unto them in the land of
Egypt, when I lifted up mine hand unto
them, saying, [c]I *am* the LORD your God;
6 In the day *that* I lifted up mine hand
unto them, [a]to bring them forth of the
land of Egypt into a land that I had espied
for them, flowing with milk and honey,
[b]which *is* the glory of all lands:
7 Then said I unto them, [a]Cast ye
away every man [b]the abominations of his
eyes, and defile not yourselves with [c]the
idols of Egypt: I *am* the LORD your God.
8 But they rebelled against me, and
would not hearken unto me: they did not
every man cast away the abominations of
their eyes, neither did they forsake the
idols of Egypt: then I said, I will [a]pour out
my fury upon them, to accomplish my anger against them in the midst of the land
of Egypt.

9 [a]But I wrought for my name's sake,
that it should not be polluted before the
heathen, among whom they *were,* in
whose sight I made myself known unto
them, in bringing them forth out of the
land of Egypt.
10 ¶ Wherefore I [a]caused them to go
forth out of the land of Egypt, and
brought them into the wilderness.
11 [a]And I gave them my statutes, and
[ʹ]showed them my judgments, [b]which *if* a
man do, he shall even live in them.
12 Moreover also I gave them my [a]sab-
baths, to be a sign between me and them,
that they might know that I *am* the LORD
that sanctify them.
13 But the house of Israel [a]rebelled
against me in the wilderness: they
walked not in my statutes, and they [b]de-
spised my judgments, which *if* a man do,
he shall even live in them; and my sabbaths they greatly [c]polluted: then I said, I
would pour out my fury upon them in the
[d]wilderness, to consume them.
14 [a]But I wrought for my name's sake,
that it should not be polluted before the
heathen, in whose sight I brought them
out.
15 Yet also [a]I lifted up my hand unto
them in the wilderness, that I would not
bring them into the land which I had
given *them,* flowing with milk and
honey, [b]which *is* the glory of all lands;
16 [a]Because they despised my judgments, and walked not in my statutes,
but polluted my sabbaths: for [b]their heart
went after their idols.
17 [a]Nevertheless mine eye spared
them from destroying them, neither did I
make an end of them in the wilderness.
18 But I said unto their children in the
wilderness, Walk ye not in the statutes of
your fathers, neither observe their judgments, nor defile yourselves with their
idols:
19 I *am* the LORD your God; [a]walk in
my statutes, and keep my judgments, and
do them;
20 [a]And hallow my sabbaths; and they
shall be a sign between me and you, that
ye may know that I *am* the LORD your
God.
21 Notwithstanding [a]the children rebelled against me: they walked not in my
statutes, neither kept my judgments to do
them, [b]which *if* a man do, he shall even
live in them; they polluted my sabbaths:

11 [a]ch. 31:3; Dan. 4:11
12 [a]ch. 17:10; Hos. 13:15
14 [a]Judg. 9:15; 2 Ki. 24:20; ch. 17:18 [b]Lam. 4:20
20:1 [a]ch. 8:1
3 [a]ch. 14:3
4 [a]ch. 22:2 [b]ch. 16:2 [ʹ]Or, *plead for them*
5 [a]Ex. 6:7; Deut. 7:6 [b]Ex. 3:8 & 4:31; Deut. 4:34 [c]Ex. 20:2 [ʹ]Or, *sware*
6 [a]Ex. 3:8,17; Deut. 8:7-9; Jer. 32:22 [b]ver. 15; Ps. 48:2; Dan. 8:9; Zech. 7:14
7 [a]ch. 18:31 [b]2 Chr. 15:8 [c]Lev. 18:3; Deut. 29:16; Josh. 24:14
8 [a]ch. 7:8
9 [a]Num. 14:13; ch. 36:21,22
10 [a]Ex. 13:18
11 [a]Deut. 4:8; Neh. 9:13; Ps. 147:19 [b]Lev. 18:5; Rom. 10:5; Gal. 3:12 [ʹ]Heb. *made them to know*
12 [a]Ex. 20:8; Deut. 5:12; Neh. 9:14
13 [a]Num. 14:22; Ps. 78:40 & 95:8-10 [b]Prov. 1:25 [c]Ex. 16:27 [d]Num. 14:29; Ps. 106:23
14 [a]ver. 9,22
15 [a]Num. 14:28; Ps. 95:11 & 106:26 [b]ver. 6
16 [a]ver. 13,24 [b]Num. 15:39; Ps. 78:37; Amos 5:25; Acts 7:42
17 [a]Ps. 78:38
19 [a]Deut. 5:32 & chs. 6,7,8,10,11,12
20 [a]Jer. 17:22
21 [a]Num. 25:1; Deut. 9:23 [b]ver. 11,13

then I said, [c]I would pour out my fury
upon them, to accomplish my anger
against them in the wilderness.
22 [a]Nevertheless I withdrew mine
hand, and [b]wrought for my name's sake,
that it should not be polluted in the sight
of the heathen, in whose sight I brought
them forth.
23 I lifted up mine hand unto them
also in the wilderness, that [a]I would scatter them among the heathen, and disperse them through the countries;
24 [a]Because they had not executed my
judgments, but had despised my statutes,
and had polluted my sabbaths, and [b]their
eyes were after their fathers' idols.
25 Wherefore [a]I gave them also statutes *that were* not good, and judgments
whereby they should not live;
26 And I polluted them in their own
gifts, in that they caused to pass [a]through
the fire all that openeth the womb, that I
might make them desolate, to the end
that they [b]might know that I *am* the LORD.
27 ¶ Therefore, son of man, speak
unto the house of Israel, and say unto
them, Thus saith the Lord GOD; Yet in
this your fathers have [a]blasphemed me,
in that they have [l]committed a trespass
against me.
28 *For* when I had brought them into
the land, *for* the which I lifted up mine
hand to give it to them, then [a]they saw
every high hill, and all the thick trees,
and they offered there their sacrifices,
and there they presented the provocation
of their offering: there also they made
their [b]sweet savour, and poured out
there their drink offerings.
29 Then [l]I said unto them, What *is* the
high place whereunto ye go? And the
name thereof is called Bamah unto this
day.
30 Wherefore say unto the house of Israel, Thus saith the Lord GOD; Are ye polluted after the manner of your fathers?
and commit ye whoredom after their
abominations?
31 For when ye offer [a]your gifts, when

21 [c]ver. 8,13
22 [a]ver. 17 [b]ver. 9,14
23 [a]Lev. 26:33; Deut. 28:64; Ps. 106:27; Jer. 15:4
24 [a]ver. 13,16 [b]See ch. 6:9
25 [a]See Ps. 81:12; Rom. 1:24; 2 Thes. 2:11
26 [a]2 Ki. 17:17 & 21:6; 2 Chr. 28:3 & 33:6; Jer. 32:35; ch. 16:20 [b]ch. 6:7
27 [a]Rom. 2:24 [l]Heb. *trespassed a trespass*
28 [a]Is. 57:5; ch. 6:13 [b]ch. 16:19
29 [l]Or, *I told them what the high place* was, or, *Bamah*
31 [a]ver. 26
32 [a]ch. 11:5
33 [a]Jer. 21:5
35 [a]Jer. 2:9,35; ch. 17:20
36 [a]Num. 14:21-23,28
37 [a]Lev. 27:32; Jer. 33:13 [l]Or, *a delivering*
38 [a]ch. 34:17; Mat. 25:32 [b]Jer. 44:14
39 [a]Judg. 10:14; Ps. 81:12; Amos 4:4 [b]Is. 1:13; ch. 23:38
40 [a]Is. 2:2,3; ch. 17:23; Mic. 4:1

ye make your sons to pass through the
fire, ye pollute yourselves with all your
idols, even unto this day: and shall I be
inquired of by you, O house of Israel? *As* I
live, saith the Lord GOD, I will not be inquired of by you.

Israel purged and accepted

32 And that [a]which cometh into your
mind shall not be at all, that ye say, We
will be as the heathen, as the families
of the countries, to serve wood and
stone.
33 ¶ *As* I live, saith the Lord GOD,
surely with a mighty hand, and [a]with a
stretched out arm, and with fury poured
out, will I rule over you:
34 And I will bring you out from the
people, and will gather you out of the
countries wherein ye are scattered, with
a mighty hand, and with a stretched out
arm, and with fury poured out.
35 And I will bring you into the wilderness of the people, and there [a]will I
plead with you face to face.
36 [a]Like as I pleaded with your fathers
in the wilderness of the land of Egypt, so
will I plead with you, saith the Lord
GOD.
37 And I will cause you to [a]pass under
the rod, and I will bring you into [l]the
bond of the covenant:
38 And [a]I will purge out from among
you the rebels, and them that transgress
against me: I will bring them forth out of
the country where they sojourn, and
[b]they shall not enter into the land of Israel: and ye shall know that I *am* the
LORD.
39 As for you, O house of Israel, thus
saith the Lord GOD; [a]Go ye, serve ye every one his idols, and hereafter *also,* if ye
will not hearken unto me: [b]but pollute ye
my holy name no more with your gifts,
and with your idols.
40 For [a]in mine holy mountain, in the

Eze 17:22–24 ◀▶ *Eze 20:40–42*
Eze 20:34–38 ◀▶ *Eze 28:25–26*

20:34–38 The prophet announced that the exile would seem to the Israelites like a return to their ancestors' time in the desert (see Hos 2:14). Yet God promised to restore his people to their promised land after the completion of their exile. Note also that this passage foreshadows the coming judgment of the Jews in the tribulation period. Only those who follow the Messiah willingly will be allowed to live in his millennial kingdom.

20:40–42 Ezekiel prophesied that in the Millennium the returned Jews would willingly serve God and enjoy God's blessings in the promised land.

mountain of the height of Israel, saith the
Lord GOD, there shall all the house of Israel, all of them in the land, serve me:
there [b]will I accept them, and there will I
require your offerings, and the [l]firstfruits
of your oblations, with all your holy
things.
41 I will accept you with your [a]sweet[l]
savour, when I bring you out from the
people, and gather you out of the countries wherein ye have been scattered; and
I will be sanctified in you before the
heathen.
42 [a]And ye shall know that I *am* the
LORD, [b]when I shall bring you into the
land of Israel, into the country *for* the
which I lifted up mine hand to give it to
your fathers.
43 And [a]there shall ye remember your
ways, and all your doings, wherein ye
have been defiled; and [b]ye shall loathe
yourselves in your own sight for all your
evils that ye have committed.
44 [a]And ye shall know that I *am* the
LORD, when I have wrought with you [b]for
my name's sake, not according to your
wicked ways, nor according to your corrupt doings, O ye house of Israel, saith
the Lord GOD.

The prophecy against the south

45 ¶ Moreover the word of the LORD
came unto me, saying,
46 [a]Son of man, set thy face toward
the south, and drop *thy word* toward the
south, and prophesy against the forest of
the south field;
47 And say to the forest of the south,
Hear the word of the LORD; Thus saith the
Lord GOD; Behold, [a]I will kindle a fire in
thee, and it shall devour [b]every green
tree in thee, and every dry tree: the flaming flame shall not be quenched, and all
faces [c]from the south to the north shall
be burned therein.
48 And all flesh shall see that I the
LORD have kindled it: it shall not be
quenched.
49 Then said I, Ah Lord GOD! they say
of me, Doth he not speak parables?

40 [b]Is. 56:7 & 60:7; Zech. 8:20; Mal. 3:4; Rom. 12:1 [l]Or, *chief*
41 [a]Eph. 5:2; Phil. 4:18 [l]Heb. *savour of rest*
42 [a]ver. 38,44; ch. 36:23 & 38:23 [b]ch. 11:17 & 34:13 & 36:24
43 [a]ch. 16:61 [b]Lev. 26:39; ch. 6:9; Hos. 5:15
44 [a]ver. 38; ch. 24:24 [b]ch. 36:22
46 [a]ch. 21:2
47 [a]Jer. 21:14 [b]Luke 23:31 [c]ch. 21:4
21:2 [a]ch. 20:46 [b]Amos 7:16
3 [a]Job 9:22
4 [a]ch. 20:47
5 [a]Is. 45:23 & 55:11
6 [a]Is. 22:4
7 [a]ch. 7:17 [l]Heb. *shall go into water*
9 [a]ver. 15,28; Deut. 32:41
10 [l]Or, it is *the rod of my son, it despiseth every tree*
11 [a]ver. 19
12 [a]Jer. 31:19 [l]Or, *they are thrust down to the sword with my people*
13 [a]Job 9:23; 2 Cor. 8:2 [l]Or, *When the trial* hath been, *what then? shall they not also belong to the despising rod?*

The LORD's sword

21 AND THE word of the LORD came
unto me, saying,
2 [a]Son of man, set thy face toward Jerusalem, and [b]drop *thy word* toward the
holy places, and prophesy against the
land of Israel,
3 And say to the land of Israel, Thus R
saith the LORD; Behold, I *am* against thee,
and will draw forth my sword out of his
sheath, and will cut off from thee [a]the
righteous and the wicked.
4 Seeing then that I will cut off from
thee the righteous and the wicked, therefore shall my sword go forth out of his
sheath against all flesh [a]from the south to
the north:
5 That all flesh may know that I the
LORD have drawn forth my sword out of
his sheath: it [a]shall not return any more.
6 [a]Sigh therefore, thou son of man,
with the breaking of *thy* loins; and with
bitterness sigh before their eyes.
7 And it shall be, when they say unto
thee, Wherefore sighest thou? that thou
shalt answer, For the tidings; because it
cometh: and every heart shall melt, and
[a]all hands shall be feeble, and every spirit
shall faint, and all knees [l]shall be weak *as*
water: behold, it cometh, and shall be
brought to pass, saith the Lord GOD.
8 ¶ Again the word of the LORD came
unto me, saying,
9 Son of man, prophesy, and say, Thus
saith the LORD; Say, [a]A sword, a sword is
sharpened, and also furbished:
10 It is sharpened to make a sore
slaughter; it is furbished that it may glit-
ter: should we then make mirth? [l]it con-
temneth the rod of my son, *as* every tree.
11 And he hath given it to be furbished, that it may be handled: this
sword is sharpened, and it is furbished, to
give it into the hand of [a]the slayer.
12 Cry and howl, son of man: for it
shall be upon my people, it *shall be* upon
all the princes of Israel: [l]terrors by reason of the sword shall be upon my people: [a]smite therefore upon *thy* thigh.
13 [l]Because *it is* [a]a trial, and what if

R *Eze 17:9–10* ◀ ▶ *Eze 21:18–23*

21:3 This is the first of five oracles that involved the sword of the Lord's judgment (see 21:8–17, 18–24, 25–27, 28–32). God's judgment would come and no one, not even the righteous, would be able to escape.

the sword contemn even the rod? [b]it shall be no *more,* saith the Lord GOD.

14 Thou therefore, son of man, prophesy, and [a]smite *thine* [1]hands together, and let the sword be doubled the third time, the sword of the slain: it *is* the sword of the great *men that are* slain, which entereth into their [b]privy chambers.

15 I have set the [1]point of the sword against all their gates, that *their* heart may faint, and *their* ruins be multiplied: ah! [a]*it is* made bright, *it is* [2]wrapped up for the slaughter.

16 [a]Go thee one way or other, *either* on the right hand, [1]*or* on the left, whithersoever thy face *is* set.

17 I will also [a]smite mine hands together, and [b]I will cause my fury to rest: I the LORD have said *it.*

R 18 ¶ The word of the LORD came unto me again, saying,

19 Also, thou son of man, appoint thee two ways, that the sword of the king of Babylon may come: both twain shall come forth out of one land: and choose thou a place, choose *it* at the head of the way to the city.

20 Appoint a way, that the sword may come to [a]Rabbath of the Ammonites, and to Judah in Jerusalem the defenced.

21 For the king of Babylon stood at the [1]parting of the way, at the head of the two ways, to use divination: he made *his* [2]arrows bright, he consulted with [3]images, he looked in the liver.

22 At his right hand was the divination for Jerusalem, to appoint [1]captains, to open the mouth in the slaughter, to [a]lift up the voice with shouting, [b]to appoint *battering* rams against the gates, to cast a mount, *and* to build a fort.

23 And it shall be unto them as a false divination in their sight, [1]to them that [a]have sworn oaths: but he will call to remembrance the iniquity, that they may be taken.

24 Therefore thus saith the Lord GOD; Because ye have made your iniquity to be remembered, in that your transgressions are discovered, so that in all your doings your sins do appear; because, *I say,* that ye are come to remembrance, ye shall be taken with the hand.

25 ¶ And thou, [a]profane wicked prince of Israel, [b]whose day is come, when iniquity *shall have* an end,

26 Thus saith the Lord GOD; Remove M
the diadem, and take off the crown: this R
shall not *be* the same: [a]exalt *him that is* low, and abase *him that is* high.

27 [1]I will overturn, overturn, overturn, it: [a]and it shall be no *more,* until he come whose right it is; and I will give it *him.*

28 ¶ And thou, son of man, prophesy J
and say, Thus saith the Lord GOD [a]concerning the Ammonites, and concerning their reproach; even say thou, The sword, the sword *is* drawn: for the slaughter *it is* furbished, to consume because of the glittering:

29 Whiles they [a]see vanity unto thee, whiles they divine a lie unto thee, to bring thee upon the necks of *them that are* slain, of the wicked, [b]whose day is come, when their iniquity *shall have* an end.

30 [a]Shall[1] I cause *it* to return into his sheath? [b]I will judge thee in the place where thou wast created, [c]in the land of thy nativity.

31 And I will [a]pour out mine indignation upon thee, I will [b]blow against thee in the fire of my wrath, and deliver thee into the hand of [1]brutish men, *and* skilful to destroy.

32 Thou shalt be for fuel to the fire; thy blood shall be in the midst of the land; [a]thou shalt be no *more* remembered: for I the LORD have spoken *it.*

The indictment of Jerusalem

22 MOREOVER THE word of the LORD came unto me, saying,

2 Now, thou son of man, [a]wilt thou [1]judge, wilt thou judge [b]the [2]bloody city?

13 [b]ver. 27
14 [a]Num. 24:10 [b]1 Ki. 20:30 [1]Heb. *hand to hand*
15 [a]ver. 10,28 [1]Or, *glittering,* or, *fear* [2]Or, *sharpened*
16 [a]ch. 14:17 [1]Heb. *set thyself, take the left hand*
17 [a]ver. 14; ch. 22:13 [b]ch. 5:13
20 [a]Jer. 49:2; Amos 1:14
21 [1]Heb. *mother of the way* [2]Or, *knives* [3]Heb. *teraphim*
22 [a]Jer. 51:14 [b]ch. 4:2 [1]Or, battering *rams; see ch. 4:2*
23 [a]ch. 17:13 [1]Or, *for the oaths made unto them*
25 [a]Jer. 52:2 [b]ver. 29
26 [a]Luke 1:52
27 [a]Gen. 49:10; Luke 1:32 [1]Heb. *Perverted, perverted, perverted, will I make it*
28 [a]ch. 25:2,3
29 [a]ch. 12:24 [b]Job 18:20; Ps. 37:13
30 [a]Jer. 47:6,7 [b]Gen. 15:14 [c]ch. 16:3 [1]Or, *Cause it to return*
31 [a]ch. 7:8 [b]ch. 22:20 [1]Or, *burning*
32 [a]ch. 25:10
22:2 [a]ch. 20:4 [b]Nah. 3:1 [1]Or, *plead for* [2]Heb. *city of bloods?*

R *Eze 21:3* ◀▶ *Eze 21:26–27*

M *Jer 33:15* ◀▶ *Eze 34:23–29*
R *Eze 21:18–23* ◀▶ *Eze 22:4*
J *Eze 12:13* ◀▶ *Eze 24:21*

21:26–27 Ezekiel declared that because of Israel's continued wickedness, no Israelite king would rule until the coming of the rightful king, the Messiah, in the last days. As a sidelight, the coronation of former British monarchs has limited the length of the monarch's reign with Ezekiel's words: "until he come whose right it is" (21:27).

yea, thou shalt [3]show her all her abominations.

3 Then say thou, Thus saith the Lord GOD, The city sheddeth blood in the midst of it, that her time may come, and maketh idols against herself to defile herself.

R 4 Thou art become guilty in thy blood that thou hast [a]shed; and hast defiled thyself in thine idols which thou hast made; and thou hast caused thy days to draw near, and art come *even* unto thy years: [b]therefore have I made thee a reproach unto the heathen, and a mocking to all countries.

5 *Those that be* near, and *those that be* far from thee, shall mock thee, *which art* ‖infamous *and* much vexed.

6 Behold, [a]the princes of Israel, every one were in thee to their ‖power to shed blood.

7 In thee have they [a]set light by father and mother: in the midst of thee have they [b]dealt by ‖oppression with the stranger: in thee have they vexed the fatherless and the widow.

8 Thou hast despised mine holy things, and hast [a]profaned my sabbaths.

9 In thee are [a]men‖ that carry tales to shed blood: [b]and in thee they eat upon the mountains: in the midst of thee they commit lewdness.

10 In thee have they [a]discovered their fathers' nakedness: in thee have they humbled her that was [b]set apart for pollution.

11 And ‖one hath committed abomination [a]with his neighbour's wife; and ‖another [b]hath [2]lewdly defiled his daughter-in-law; and another in thee hath humbled his [c]sister, his father's daughter.

12 In thee [a]have they taken gifts to shed blood; [b]thou hast taken usury and increase, and thou hast greedily gained of thy neighbours by extortion, and [c]hast forgotten me, saith the Lord GOD.

13 ¶ Behold, therefore I have [a]smitten mine hand at thy dishonest gain which thou hast made, and at thy blood which hath been in the midst of thee.

14 [a]Can thine heart endure, or can thine hands be strong, in the days that I shall deal with thee? [b]I the LORD have spoken *it*, and will do *it*.

15 And [a]I will scatter thee among the heathen, and disperse thee in the countries, and [b]will consume thy filthiness out of thee. R

16 And thou ‖shalt take thine inheritance in thyself in the sight of the heathen, and [a]thou shalt know that I *am* the LORD.

17 And the word of the LORD came unto me, saying,

18 Son of man, [a]the house of Israel is to me become dross: all they *are* brass, and tin, and iron, and lead, in the midst of the furnace; they are *even* the ‖dross of silver. C

19 Therefore thus saith the Lord GOD; Because ye are all become dross, behold, therefore I will gather you into the midst of Jerusalem.

20 ‖*As* they gather silver, and brass, and iron, and lead, and tin, into the midst of the furnace, to blow the fire upon it, to melt *it;* so will I gather *you* in mine anger and in my fury, and I will leave *you there,* and melt you. H

21 Yea, I will gather you, and blow upon you in the fire of my wrath, and ye shall be melted in the midst thereof.

22 As silver is melted in the midst of the furnace, so shall ye be melted in the midst thereof; and ye shall know that I the LORD have [a]poured out my fury upon you.

23 ¶ And the word of the LORD came unto me, saying,

24 Son of man, say unto her, Thou *art* the land that is not cleansed, nor rained upon in the day of indignation.

25 [a]*There is* a conspiracy of her prophets in the midst thereof, like a roaring

2 [3]Heb. *make her know*
4 [a]2 Ki. 21:16 [b]Deut. 28:37; Dan. 9:16
5 ‖Heb. *polluted of name, much in vexation*
6 [a]Is. 1:23 ‖Heb. *arm*
7 [a]Deut. 27:16 [b]Ex. 22:21 ‖Or, *deceit*
8 [a]Lev. 19:30
9 [a]Lev. 19:16 [b]ch. 18:6,11 ‖Heb. *men of slanders*
10 [a]Lev. 18:7,8 [b]Lev. 18:19
11 [a]Lev. 18:20 [b]Lev. 18:15 [c]Lev. 18:9 ‖Or, *every one* [2]Or, *by lewdness*
12 [a]Ex. 23:8; Deut. 16:19 [b]Ex. 22:25 [c]Jer. 3:21
13 [a]ch. 21:17
14 [a]ch. 21:7 [b]ch. 17:24
15 [a]Deut. 4:27 [b]ch. 23:27
16 [a]Ps. 9:16 ‖Or, *shalt be profaned*
18 [a]Ps. 119:119; Is. 1:22; Jer. 6:28 ‖Heb. *drosses*
20 ‖Heb. *According to the gathering*
22 [a]ch. 20:8,33
25 [a]Hos. 6:9

R *Eze 21:26–27* ◀ ▶ *Eze 22:15*

R *Eze 22:4* ◀ ▶ *Eze 23:32–33*
C *Eze 12:2* ◀ ▶ *Da 9:5*
H *Eze 18:30* ◀ ▶ *Eze 25:17*

22:4 God detailed the grave sins that forced him to judge his people.

22:15 God's divine purpose for the exile of his people was to purge them from their idolatry and pagan religious practices. Though the Jews may have resisted the worship of stone statues and pagan rituals since their return from exile, they still face the temptations of idolatry manifested in materialism, power, status and position—the same idols that threaten to topple the faith of NT believers (see Mt 6:24 ; Col 3:1–2).

lion ravening the prey; they [b]have devoured souls; [c]they have taken the treasure and precious things; they have made
her many widows in the midst thereof.
26 [a]Her priests have [1]violated my law,
and have [b]profaned mine holy things:
they have put no [c]difference between the
holy and profane, neither have they
shown *difference* between the unclean
and the clean, and have hid their eyes
from my sabbaths, and I am profaned
among them.
27 Her [a]princes in the midst thereof
are like wolves ravening the prey, to shed
blood, *and* to destroy souls, to get dishonest gain.
28 And [a]her prophets have daubed
them with untempered *mortar,* [b]seeing
vanity, and divining lies unto them, saying, Thus saith the Lord GOD, when the
LORD hath not spoken.
29 The people of the land have used
[1]oppression, and exercised robbery, and
have vexed the poor and needy: yea, they
have [a]oppressed the stranger [2]wrong-
fully.
30 [a]And I sought for a man among
them, that should [b]make up the hedge,
and [c]stand in the gap before me for the
land, that I should not destroy it: but I
found none.
31 Therefore have I [a]poured out mine
indignation upon them; I have consumed
them with the fire of my wrath: [b]their
own way have I recompensed upon their
heads, saith the Lord GOD.

Two adulterous sisters

23 THE WORD of the LORD came
again unto me, saying,
2 Son of man, there were [a]two
women, the daughters of one mother:
3 And [a]they committed whoredoms in
Egypt; they committed whoredoms in
[b]their youth: there were their breasts
pressed, and there they bruised the teats
of their virginity.
4 And the names of them *were* Aholah
the elder, and Aholibah her sister: and
[a]they were mine, and they bare sons
and daughters. Thus *were* their names;
Samaria *is* [1]Aholah, and Jerusalem
[2]Aholibah.
5 And Aholah played the harlot when
she was mine; and she doted on her lovers, on [a]the Assyrians *her* neighbours,
6 *Which were* clothed with blue, captains and rulers, all of them desirable
young men, horsemen riding upon
horses.
7 Thus she [1]committed her whoredoms with them, with all them *that were*
[2]the chosen men of Assyria, and with all
on whom she doted: with all their idols
she defiled herself.
8 Neither left she her whoredoms
brought [a]from Egypt: for in her youth
they lay with her, and they bruised the
breasts of her virginity, and poured their
whoredom upon her.
9 Wherefore I have delivered her into
the hand of her lovers, into the hand of
the [a]Assyrians, upon whom she doted.
10 These discovered her nakedness:
they took her sons and her daughters,
and slew her with the sword: and she
became [1]famous among women; for they
had executed judgment upon her.
11 And [a]when her sister Aholibah saw
this, [b]she[1] was more corrupt in her inordinate love than she, and in her whoredoms [2]more than her sister in *her*
whoredoms.
12 She doted upon the [a]Assyrians *her*
neighbours, [b]captains and rulers clothed
most gorgeously, horsemen riding upon
horses, all of them desirable young men.
13 Then I saw that she was defiled,
that they *took* both one way,
14 And *that* she increased her whoredoms: for when she saw men portrayed
upon the wall, the images of the Chaldeans portrayed with vermilion,
15 Girded with girdles upon their
loins, exceeding in dyed attire upon their
heads, all of them princes to look to, after
the manner of the Babylonians of Chaldea, the land of their nativity:
16 [a]And [1]as soon as she saw them
with her eyes, she doted upon them, and
sent messengers unto them into Chaldea.
17 And the [1]Babylonians came to her
into the bed of love, and they defiled her
with their whoredom, and she was polluted with them, and [a]her mind was
[2]alienated from them.
18 So she discovered her whoredoms,
and discovered her nakedness: then [a]my
mind was alienated from her, like as my
mind was alienated from her sister.
19 Yet she multiplied her whoredoms,
in calling to remembrance the days of her
youth, [a]wherein she had played the harlot in the land of Egypt.

25 [b]Mat. 23:14 [c]Mic. 3:11
26 [a]Mal. 2:8 [b]1 Sam. 2:29 [c]Lev. 10:10 [1]Heb. *offered violence to*
27 [a]Is. 1:23; ch. 22:6
28 [a]ch. 13:10 [b]ch. 13:6,7
29 [a]Ex. 23:9; Lev. 19:33 [1]Or, *deceit* [2]Heb. *without right*
30 [a]Jer. 5:1 [b]ch. 13:5 [c]Ps. 106:23
31 [a]ver. 22 [b]ch. 9:10
23:2 [a]Jer. 3:7,8
3 [a]Lev. 17:7; Josh. 24:14 [b]ch. 16:22
4 [a]ch. 16:8,20 [1]i.e. *His tent,* or, *tabernacle* [2]i.e. *My tabernacle in her*
5 [a]Hos. 8:9
7 [1]Heb. *bestowed her whoredoms upon them* [2]Heb. *the choice of the children of Asshur*
8 [a]ver. 3
9 [a]2 Ki. 17:3
10 [1]Heb. *a name*
11 [a]Jer. 3:8 [b]Jer. 3:11 [1]Heb. *she corrupted her inordinate love more than* [2]Heb. *more than the whoredoms of her sister*
12 [a]2 Ki. 16:7 [b]ver. 6,23
16 [a]2 Ki. 24:1 [1]Heb. *at the sight of her eyes*
17 [a]ver. 22,28 [1]Heb. *children of Babel* [2]Heb. *loosed,* or, *disjointed*
18 [a]Jer. 6:8
19 [a]ver. 3

20 For she doted upon their paramours, whose flesh *is as* the flesh of asses, and whose issue *is like* the issue of horses.

21 Thus thou calledst to remembrance the lewdness of thy youth, in bruising thy teats by the Egyptians for the paps of thy youth.

22 ¶ Therefore, O Aholibah, thus saith the Lord GOD; [a]Behold, I will raise up thy lovers against thee, from whom thy mind is alienated, and I will bring them against thee on every side;

23 The Babylonians, and all the Chaldeans, [a]Pekod, and Shoa, and Koa, *and* all the Assyrians with them: [b]all of them desirable young men, captains and rulers, great lords and renowned, all of them riding upon horses.

24 And they shall come against thee with chariots, wagons, and wheels, and with an assembly of people, *which* shall set against thee buckler and shield and helmet round about: and I will set judgment before them, and they shall judge thee according to their judgments.

25 And I will set my jealousy against thee, and they shall deal furiously with thee: they shall take away thy nose and thine ears; and thy remnant shall fall by the sword: they shall take thy sons and thy daughters; and thy residue shall be devoured by the fire.

26 [a]They shall also strip thee out of thy clothes, and take away thy [ʹ]fair jewels.

27 Thus [a]will I make thy lewdness to cease from thee, and thy [b]whoredom *brought* from the land of Egypt: so that thou shalt not lift up thine eyes unto them, nor remember Egypt any more.

28 For thus saith the Lord GOD; Behold, I will deliver thee into the hand *of them* [a]whom thou hatest, into the hand *of them* [b]from whom thy mind is alienated:

29 And they shall deal with thee hatefully, and shall take away all thy labour, and [a]shall leave thee naked and bare: and the nakedness of thy whoredoms shall be discovered, both thy lewdness and thy whoredoms.

30 I will do these *things* unto thee, because thou hast [a]gone awhoring after the heathen, *and* because thou art polluted with their idols.

31 Thou hast walked in the way of thy sister; therefore will I give her [a]cup into thine hand.

32 Thus saith the Lord GOD; Thou shalt drink of thy sister's cup deep and large: [a]thou shalt be laughed to scorn and had in derision; it containeth much. R

33 Thou shalt be filled with drunkenness and sorrow, with the cup of astonishment and desolation, with the cup of thy sister Samaria.

34 Thou shalt [a]even drink it and suck *it* out, and thou shalt break the sherds thereof, and pluck off thine own breasts: for I have spoken *it,* saith the Lord GOD.

35 Therefore thus saith the Lord GOD; Because thou [a]hast forgotten me, and [b]cast me behind thy back, therefore bear thou also thy lewdness and thy whoredoms.

36 ¶ The LORD said moreover unto me; Son of man, wilt thou [a]judge[ʹ] Aholah and Aholibah? yea, [b]declare unto them their abominations;

37 That they have committed adultery, and [a]blood *is* in their hands, and with their idols have they committed adultery, and have also caused their sons, [b]whom they bare unto me, to pass for them through *the fire,* to devour *them.*

38 Moreover this they have done unto me: they have defiled my sanctuary in the same day, and [a]have profaned my sabbaths.

39 For when they had slain their children to their idols, then they came the same day into my sanctuary to profane it; and, lo, [a]thus have they done in the midst of mine house.

40 And furthermore, that ye have sent for men [ʹ]to come from far, [a]unto whom a messenger *was* sent; and, lo, they came: for whom thou didst [b]wash thyself, [c]paintedst thy eyes, and deckedst thyself with ornaments,

41 And satest upon a [ʹ]stately [a]bed, and a table prepared before it, [b]whereupon thou hast set mine incense and mine oil.

R *Eze 22:15* ◄► *Eze 24:13*

22 [a]ver. 28; ch. 16:37
23 [a]Jer. 50:21 [b]ver. 12
26 [a]ch. 16:39 [ʹ]Heb. *instruments of thy decking*
27 [a]ch. 16:41 & 22:15 [b]ver. 3,19
28 [a]ch. 16:37 [b]ver. 17
29 [a]ver. 26; ch. 16:39
30 [a]ch. 6:9
31 [a]Jer. 25:15
32 [a]ch. 22:4,5
34 [a]Ps. 75:8; Is. 51:17
35 [a]Jer. 2:32 & 3:21 & 13:25; ch. 22:12 [b]1 Ki. 14:9; Neh. 9:26
36 [a]ch. 20:4 & 22:2 [b]Is. 58:1 [ʹ]Or, *plead for*
37 [a]ver. 45; ch. 16:38 [b]ch. 16:20, 21,36,45 & 20:26, 31
38 [a]ch. 22:8
39 [a]2 Ki. 21:4
40 [a]Is. 57:9 [b]Ruth 3:3 [c]2 Ki. 9:30; Jer. 4:30 [ʹ]Heb. *coming*
41 [a]Esth. 1:6; Is. 57:7; Amos 2:8 & 6:4 [b]Prov. 7:17; ch. 16:18,19; Hos. 2:8 [ʹ]Heb. *honourable*

23:32–33 Ezekiel warned Judah that because of her continued failure to repent of her rebellion, Judah would experience the same fate of Israel—exile to a pagan nation.

42 And a voice of a multitude being at ease *was* with her: and with the men [1]of the common sort *were* brought [2]Sabeans from the wilderness, which put bracelets upon their hands, and beautiful crowns upon their heads.

43 Then said I unto *her that was* old in adulteries, Will they now commit [1]whoredoms with her, and she *with them?*

44 Yet they went in unto her, as they go in unto a woman that playeth the harlot: so went they in unto Aholah and unto Aholibah, the lewd women.

45 ¶ And the righteous men, they shall [a]judge them after the manner of adulteresses, and after the manner of women that shed blood; because they *are* adulteresses, and [b]blood *is* in their hands.

46 For thus saith the Lord GOD; [a]I will bring up a company upon them, and will give them [1]to be removed and spoiled.

47 [a]And the company shall stone them with stones, and [1]dispatch them with their swords; [b]they shall slay their sons and their daughters, and burn up their houses with fire.

48 Thus [a]will I cause lewdness to cease out of the land, [b]that all women may be taught not to do after your lewdness.

49 And they shall recompense your lewdness upon you, and ye shall [a]bear the sins of your idols: [b]and ye shall know that I *am* the Lord GOD.

The parable of the boiling pot

24 AGAIN IN the ninth year, in the tenth month, in the tenth *day* of the month, the word of the LORD come unto me, saying,

2 Son of man, write thee the name of the day, *even* of this same day: the king of Babylon set himself against Jerusalem [a]this same day.

3 [a]And utter a parable unto the rebellious house, and say unto them, Thus saith the Lord GOD; [b]Set on a pot, set *it* on, and also pour water into it:

4 Gather the pieces thereof into it, *even* every good piece, the thigh, and the shoulder; fill *it* with the choice bones.

5 Take the choice of the flock, and [1]burn also the bones under it, *and* make it boil well, and let them seethe the bones of it therein.

6 ¶ Wherefore thus saith the Lord GOD; Woe to [a]the bloody city, to the pot whose scum *is* therein, and whose scum is not gone out of it! bring it out piece by piece; let no [b]lot fall upon it.

7 For her blood is in the midst of her; she set it upon the top of a rock; [a]she poured it not upon the ground, to cover it with dust;

8 That it might cause fury to come up to take vengeance; [a]I have set her blood upon the top of a rock, that it should not be covered.

9 Therefore thus saith the Lord GOD; [a]Woe to the bloody city! I will even make the pile for fire great.

10 Heap on wood, kindle the fire, consume the flesh, and spice it well, and let the bones be burned.

11 Then set it empty upon the coals thereof, that the brass of it may be hot, and may burn, and *that* [a]the filthiness of it may be molten in it, *that* the scum of it may be consumed.

12 She hath wearied *herself* with lies, and her great scum went not forth out of her: her scum *shall be* in the fire.

13 In thy filthiness *is* lewdness: because I have purged thee, and thou wast not purged, thou shalt not be purged from thy filthiness any more, [a]till I have caused my fury to rest upon thee. **R**

14 [a]I the LORD have spoken *it:* it shall come to pass, and I will do *it;* I will not go back, [b]neither will I spare, neither will I repent; according to thy ways, and according to thy doings, shall they judge thee, saith the Lord GOD.

The death of Ezekiel's wife

15 ¶ Also the word of the LORD came unto me, saying,

16 Son of man, behold, I take away from thee the desire of thine eyes with a stroke: yet neither shalt thou mourn nor weep, neither shall thy tears [1]run down.

17 [1]Forbear to cry, [a]make no mourning for the dead, [b]bind the tire of thine

R *Eze 23:32–33* ◀ ▶ *Eze 33:28–29*

42 [1]Heb. *of the multitude of men* [2]Or, *drunkards*
43 [1]Heb. *her whoredoms*
45 [a]ch. 16:38 [b]ver. 37
46 [a]ch. 16:40 [1]Heb. *for a removing and spoil*
47 [a]ch. 16:40 [b]2 Chr. 36:17,19; ch. 24:21 [1]Or, *single them out*
48 [a]ch. 22:15 [b]Deut. 13:11; 2 Pet. 2:6
49 [a]ver. 35 [b]ch. 20:38,42,44 & 25:5
24:2 [a]2 Ki. 25:1; Jer. 39:1 & 52:4
3 [a]ch. 17:12 [b]See Jer. 1:13; ch. 11:3
5 [1]Or, *heap*
6 [a]ch. 22:3 [b]See 2 Sam. 8:2; Joel 3:3; Obad. 11 ; Nah. 3:10
7 [a]Lev. 17:13; Deut. 12:16
8 [a]Mat. 7:2
9 [a]ver. 6; Hab. 2:12
11 [a]ch. 22:15
13 [a]ch. 8:18
14 [a]1 Sam. 15:29 [b]ch. 5:11
16 [1]Heb. *go*
17 [a]Jer. 16:5 [b]See Lev. 10:6 & 21:10 [1]Heb. *Be silent*

24:13 Despite earlier judgments, Judah had refused to repent of her widespread idolatry, so God would purge her sin by exiling Judah to Babylon.

head upon thee, and [c]put on thy shoes
upon thy feet, and [d]cover not *thy* [e]lips,[2]
and eat not the bread of men.
18 So I spake unto the people in the
morning: and at even my wife died; and I
did in the morning as I was commanded.
19 ¶ And the people said unto me,
[a]Wilt thou not tell us what these *things*
are to us, that thou doest *so?*
20 Then I answered them, The word
of the LORD came unto me, saying,
J 21 Speak unto the house of Israel,
Thus saith the Lord GOD; Behold, [a]I will
profane my sanctuary, the excellency of
your strength, the desire of your eyes,
and [1]that which your soul pitieth; [b]and
your sons and your daughters whom ye
have left shall fall by the sword.
22 And ye shall do as I have done: [a]ye
shall not cover *your* lips, nor eat the
bread of men.
23 And your tires *shall be* upon your
heads, and your shoes upon your feet: [a]ye
shall not mourn nor weep; but [b]ye shall
pine away for your iniquities, and mourn
one toward another.
24 Thus [a]Ezekiel is unto you a sign:
according to all that he hath done shall
ye do: [b]and when this cometh, [c]ye shall
know that I *am* the Lord GOD.
J 25 Also, thou son of man, *shall it* not
be in the day when I take from them
[a]their strength, the joy of their glory, the
desire of their eyes, and [1]that whereupon
they set their minds, their sons and their
daughters,
26 *That* [a]he that escapeth in that day
shall come unto thee, to cause *thee* to
hear *it* with *thine* ears?
27 [a]In that day shall thy mouth be
opened to him which is escaped, and
thou shalt speak, and be no more dumb:
and thou shalt be a sign unto them; and
they shall know that I *am* the LORD.

Prophecy against Ammon

25 THE WORD of the LORD came
again unto me, saying,
2 Son of man, [a]set thy face [b]against the
Ammonites, and prophesy against them;
3 And say unto the Ammonites, Hear
the word of the Lord GOD; Thus saith the
Lord GOD; [a]Because thou saidst, Aha,
against my sanctuary, when it was profaned; and against the land of Israel,
when it was desolate; and against the
house of Judah, when they went into captivity;
4 Behold, therefore I will deliver thee
to the [1]men of the east for a possession,
and they shall set their palaces in thee,
and make their dwellings in thee: they
shall eat thy fruit, and they shall drink thy
milk.
5 And I will make [a]Rabbah [b]a stable
for camels, and the Ammonites a couching place for flocks: [c]and ye shall know
that I *am* the LORD.
6 For thus saith the Lord GOD; Because
thou [a]hast clapped *thine* [1]hands, and
stamped with the [2]feet, and [b]rejoiced in
[3]heart with all thy despite against the
land of Israel;
7 Behold, therefore I will [a]stretch out
mine hand upon thee, and will deliver
thee for [1]a spoil to the heathen; and I will
cut thee off from the people, and I will
cause thee to perish out of the countries:
I will destroy thee; and thou shalt know
that I *am* the LORD.

Prophecy against Moab

8 ¶ Thus saith the Lord GOD; Because
that [a]Moab and [b]Seir do say, Behold, the
house of Judah *is* like unto all the
heathen;
9 Therefore, behold, I will open the
[1]side of Moab from the cities, from his
cities *which are* on his frontiers, the glory
of the country, Beth-jeshimoth, Baal-
meon, and Kiriathaim,
10 [a]Unto the men of the east [1]with the
Ammonites, and will give them in possession, that the Ammonites [b]may not be
remembered among the nations.
11 And I will execute judgments upon
Moab; and they shall know that I *am* the
LORD.

Prophecy against Edom

12 ¶ Thus saith the Lord GOD; [a]Be-
cause that Edom hath dealt against the
house of Judah [1]by taking vengeance, and
hath greatly offended, and revenged himself upon them;
13 Therefore thus saith the Lord GOD;
I will also stretch out mine hand upon
Edom, and will cut off man and beast
from it; and I will make it desolate from
Teman; and [1]they of Dedan shall fall by
the sword.

17 [c]2 Sam. 15:30 [d]Mic. 3:7 [e]ver. 22; Lev. 13:45 [2]Heb. *upper lip*
19 [a]ch. 12:9 & 37:18
21 [a]Jer. 7:14; ch. 7:20 [b]ch. 23:47 [1]Heb. *the pity of your soul*
22 [a]ver. 17; Jer. 16:6,7
23 [a]Job 27:15; Ps. 78:64 [b]Lev. 26:39
24 [a]Is. 20:3; ch. 4:3 & 12:6,11 [b]Jer. 17:15; John 13:19 & 14:29 [c]ch. 6:7 & 25:5
25 [a]ver. 21 [1]Heb. *the lifting up of their soul*
26 [a]ch. 33:21
27 [a]ch. 3:26
25:2 [a]ch. 35:2 [b]Jer. 49:1; ch. 21:28; Zeph. 2:9
3 [a]Prov. 17:5; ch. 26:2
4 [1]Heb. *children*
5 [a]ch. 21:20 [b]Is. 17:2 [c]ch. 24:24
6 [a]Job 27:23; Lam. 2:15; Zeph. 2:15 [b]ch. 36:5 [1]Heb. *hand* [2]Heb. *foot* [3]Heb. *soul*
7 [a]ch. 35:3 [1]Or, *meat*
8 [a]Is. 15 & 16; Jer. 48:1; Amos 2:1 [b]ch. 35:2,5
9 [1]Heb. *shoulder of Moab*
10 [a]ver. 4 [b]ch. 21:32 [1]Or, *against the children of Ammon*
12 [a]2 Chr. 28:17; Ps. 137:7; Jer. 49:7, 8; Amos 1:11; Obad. 10 [1]Heb. *by revenging revengement*
13 [1]Or, *they shall fall by the sword unto Dedan*

J *Exe 21:28–31* ◀▶ *Eze 24:25–27*
J *Eze 24:21* ◀▶ *Eze 25:15–17*

14 And [a]I will lay my vengeance upon Edom by the hand of my people Israel: and they shall do in Edom according to mine anger and according to my fury; and they shall know my vengeance, saith the Lord GOD.

Prophecy against Philistia

J 15 ¶ Thus saith the Lord GOD; [a]Because [b]the Philistines have dealt by revenge, and have taken vengeance with a despiteful heart, to destroy *it* [l]for the old hatred;

16 Therefore thus saith the Lord GOD; Behold, [a]I will stretch out mine hand upon the Philistines, and I will cut off the [b]Cherethims, [c]and destroy the remnant of the [l]sea coast.

H 17 And I will [a]execute great [l]vengeance upon them with furious rebukes; [b]and they shall know that I *am* the LORD, when I shall lay my vengeance upon them.

Prophecy against Tyrus

J **26** AND IT came to pass in the eleventh year, in the first *day* of the month, *that* the word of the LORD came unto me, saying,

2 Son of man, [a]because that Tyrus hath said against Jerusalem, [b]Aha, she is broken *that was* the gates of the people: she is turned unto me: I shall be replenished, *now* she is laid waste:

3 Therefore thus saith the Lord GOD; Behold, I *am* against thee, O Tyrus, and will cause many nations to come up against thee, as the sea causeth his waves to come up.

4 And they shall destroy the walls of Tyrus, and break down her towers: I will also scrape her dust from her, and [a]make her like the top of a rock.

5 It shall be *a place for* the spreading of nets [a]in the midst of the sea: for I have spoken *it,* saith the Lord GOD: and it shall become a spoil to the nations.

6 And her daughters which *are* in the field shall be slain by the sword; [a]and they shall know that I *am* the LORD.

7 ¶ For thus saith the Lord GOD; Behold, I will bring upon Tyrus Nebuchadrezzar king of Babylon, [a]a king of kings, from the north, with horses, and with chariots, and with horsemen, and companies, and much people.

8 He shall slay with the sword thy daughters in the field: and he shall [a]make a fort against thee, and [l]cast a mount against thee, and lift up the buckler against thee.

9 And he shall set engines of war against thy walls, and with his axes he shall break down thy towers.

10 By reason of the abundance of his horses their dust shall cover thee: thy walls shall shake at the noise of the horsemen, and of the wheels, and of the chariots, when he shall enter into thy gates, [l]as men enter into a city wherein is made a breach.

11 With the hoofs of his horses shall he tread down all thy streets: he shall slay thy people by the sword, and thy strong garrisons shall go down to the ground.

12 And they shall make a spoil of thy riches, and make a prey of thy merchandise: and they shall break down thy walls, and destroy [l]thy pleasant houses: and they shall lay thy stones and thy timber and thy dust in the midst of the water. J

13 [a]And I will cause the noise of [b]thy songs to cease; and the sound of thy harps shall be no more heard.

14 And [a]I will make thee like the top of a rock: thou shalt be *a place* to spread nets upon; thou shalt be built no more: for I the LORD have spoken *it,* saith the Lord GOD.

15 ¶ Thus saith the Lord GOD to Tyrus; Shall not the isles [a]shake at the sound of thy fall, when the wounded cry, when the slaughter is made in the midst of thee?

16 Then all the [a]princes of the sea shall [b]come down from their thrones, and lay away their robes, and put off their broidered garments: they shall clothe themselves with [l]trembling; [c]they shall sit upon the ground, and [d]shall tremble at *every* moment, and [e]be astonished at thee.

17 And they shall take up a [a]lamentation for thee, and say to thee, How art thou destroyed, *that wast* inhabited [l]of seafaring men, the renowned city, which wast [b]strong in the sea, she and her inhabitants, which cause their terror *to be* on all that haunt it!

14 [a]Is. 11:14
15 [a]Jer. 25:20; Amos 1:6 [b]2 Chr. 28:18 [l]Or, *with perpetual hatred*
16 [a]Zeph. 2:4 [b]1 Sam. 30:14 [c]Jer. 47:4 [l]Or, *haven of the sea*
17 [a]ch. 5:15 [b]Ps. 9:16 [l]Heb. *vengeances*
26:2 [a]Is. 23; Jer. 25:22; Amos 1:9; Zech. 9:2 [b]ch. 25:3
4 [a]ver. 14
5 [a]ch. 27:32
6 [a]ch. 25:5
7 [a]Ezra 7:12; Dan. 2:37
8 [a]ch. 21:22 [l]Or, *pour out the engine of shot*
10 [l]Heb. *according to the enterings of a city broken up*
12 [l]Heb. *houses of thy desire*
13 [a]Is. 14:11 & 24:8; Jer. 7:34 & 25:10 [b]Is. 23:16; ch. 28:13; Rev. 18:22
14 [a]ver. 4,5
15 [a]ver. 18; Jer. 49:21; ch. 27:28
16 [a]Is. 23:8 [b]Jonah 3:6 [c]Job 2:13 [d]ch. 32:10 [e]ch. 27:35 [l]Heb. *tremblings*
17 [a]ch. 27:32; Rev. 18:9 [b]Is. 23:4 [l]Heb. *of the seas*

J *Eze 24:25–27* ◀ ▶ *Eze 26:1–5*
H *Eze 22:20–22* ◀ ▶ *Eze 33:11*
J *Eze 25:15–17* ◀ ▶ *Eze 26:12–21*
J *Eze 26:1–5* ◀ ▶ *Eze 28:20–24*

18 Now shall [a]the isles tremble in the day of thy fall; yea, the isles that *are* in the sea shall be troubled at thy departure.

19 For thus saith the Lord GOD; When I shall make thee a desolate city, like the cities that are not inhabited; when I shall bring up the deep upon thee, and great waters shall cover thee;

20 When I shall bring thee down [a]with them that descend into the pit, with the people of old time, and shall set thee in the low parts of the earth, in places desolate of old, with them that go down to the pit, that thou be not inhabited; and I shall set glory [b]in the land of the living;

21 [a]I will make thee [1]a terror, and thou *shalt be* no *more:* [b]though thou be sought for, yet shalt thou never be found again, saith the Lord GOD.

The lament for Tyrus

27 THE WORD of the LORD came again unto me, saying,

2 Now, thou son of man, [a]take up a lamentation for Tyrus;

3 And say unto Tyrus, [a]O thou that art situate at the entry of the sea, *which art* [b]a merchant of the people for many isles, Thus saith the Lord GOD; O Tyrus, thou hast said, [c]I *am* [1]of perfect beauty.

4 Thy borders *are* in the [1]midst of the seas, thy builders have perfected thy beauty.

5 They have [1]made all thy *ship* boards of fir trees of [a]Senir: they have taken cedars from Lebanon to make masts for thee.

6 *Of* the oaks of Bashan have they made thine oars; [1,2]the company of the Ashurites have made thy benches *of* ivory, *brought* out of [a]the isles of Chittim.

7 Fine linen with broidered work from Egypt was that which thou spreadest forth to be thy sail; [1]blue and purple from the isles of Elishah was that which covered thee.

8 The inhabitants of Zidon and Arvad were thy mariners: thy wise *men,* O Tyrus, *that* were in thee, were thy pilots.

9 The ancients of [a]Gebal and the wise *men* thereof were in thee thy [1,2]calkers: all the ships of the sea with their mariners were in thee to occupy thy merchandise.

18 [a]ver. 15
20 [a]ch. 32:18 [b]ch. 32:23
21 [a]ch. 28:19 [b]Ps. 37:36 [1]Heb. *terrors*
27:2 [a]ch. 26:17
3 [a]ch. 28:2 [b]Is. 23:3 [c]ch. 28:12 [1]Heb. *perfect of beauty*
4 [1]Heb. *heart*
5 [a]Deut. 3:9 [1]Heb. *built*
6 [a]Jer. 2:10 [1]Or, *they have made thy hatches of ivory well trodden* [2]Heb. *the daughter*
7 [1]Or, *purple and scarlet*
9 [a]1 Ki. 5:18; Ps. 83:7 [1]Or, *stoppers of chinks* [2]Heb. *strengtheners*
11 [a]ver. 3
12 [a]Gen. 10:4; 2 Chr. 20:36
13 [a]Gen. 10:2 [b]Rev. 18:13 [1]Or, *merchandise*
14 [a]ch. 38:6
15 [a]Gen. 10:7
16 [1]Heb. *thy works* [2]Heb. *chrysoprase*
17 [a]Judg. 11:33 [b]Jer. 8:22 [1]Or, *rosin*
19 [1]Or, *Meuzal*
20 [a]Gen. 25:3 [1]Heb. *clothes of freedom*
21 [a]Gen. 25:13; Is. 60:7 [1]Heb. *they* were *the merchants of thy hand*
22 [a]Gen. 10:7; 1 Ki. 10:1,2; Ps. 72:10; Is. 60:6
23 [a]Gen. 11:31; 2 Ki. 19:12 [b]Gen. 25:3
24 [1]Or, *excellent things* [2]Heb. *foldings*

10 They of Persia and of Lud and of Phut were in thine army, thy men of war: they hanged the shield and helmet in thee; they set forth thy comeliness.

11 The men of Arvad with thine army *were* upon thy walls round about, and the Gammadims were in thy towers: they hanged their shields upon thy walls round about; they have made [a]thy beauty perfect.

12 [a]Tarshish *was* thy merchant by reason of the multitude of all *kind of* riches; with silver, iron, tin, and lead, they traded in thy fairs.

13 [a]Javan, Tubal, and Meshech, they *were* thy merchants: they traded [b]the persons of men and vessels of brass in thy [1]market.

14 They of the house of [a]Togarmah traded in thy fairs with horses and horsemen and mules.

15 The men of [a]Dedan *were* thy merchants; many isles *were* the merchandise of thine hand: they brought thee *for* a present horns of ivory and ebony.

16 Syria *was* thy merchant by reason of the multitude of [1]the wares of thy making: they occupied in thy fairs with emeralds, purple, and broidered work, and fine linen, and coral, and [2]agate.

17 Judah, and the land of Israel, they *were* thy merchants: they traded in thy market wheat of [a]Minnith, and Pannag, and honey, and oil, and [b]balm.[1]

18 Damascus *was* thy merchant in the multitude of the wares of thy making, for the multitude of all riches; in the wine of Helbon, and white wool.

19 Dan also and Javan [1]going to and fro occupied in thy fairs: bright iron, cassia, and calamus, were in thy market.

20 [a]Dedan *was* thy merchant in [1]precious clothes for chariots.

21 Arabia, and all the princes of [a]Kedar, [1]they occupied with thee in lambs, and rams, and goats: in these *were they* thy merchants.

22 The merchants of [a]Sheba and Raamah, they *were* thy merchants: they occupied in thy fairs with chief of all spices, and with all precious stones, and gold.

23 [a]Haran, and Canneh, and Eden, the merchants of [b]Sheba, Asshur, *and* Chilmad, *were* thy merchants.

24 These *were* thy merchants in [1]all sorts *of things,* in blue [2]clothes, and broidered work, and in chests of rich apparel,

bound with cords, and made of cedar, among thy merchandise.

25 [a]The ships of Tarshish did sing of thee in thy market: and thou wast replenished, and made very glorious [b]in the midst of the seas.

26 ¶ Thy rowers have brought thee into great waters: [a]the east wind hath broken thee in the [1]midst of the seas.

27 Thy [a]riches, and thy fairs, thy merchandise, thy mariners, and thy pilots, thy calkers, and the occupiers of thy merchandise, and all thy men of war, that *are* in thee, [1]and in all thy company which *is* in the midst of thee, shall fall into the [2]midst of the seas in the day of thy ruin.

28 The [1]suburbs[a] shall shake at the sound of the cry of thy pilots.

29 And [a]all that handle the oar, the mariners, *and* all the pilots of the sea, shall come down from their ships, they shall stand upon the land;

30 And shall cause their voice to be heard against thee, and shall cry bitterly, and shall [a]cast up dust upon their heads, they [b]shall wallow themselves in the ashes:

31 And they shall [a]make themselves utterly bald for thee, and gird them with sackcloth, and they shall weep for thee with bitterness of heart *and* bitter wailing.

32 And in their wailing they shall [a]take up a lamentation for thee, and lament over thee, *saying,* [b]What *city is* like Tyrus, like the destroyed in the midst of the sea?

33 [a]When thy wares went forth out of the seas, thou filledst many people; thou didst enrich the kings of the earth with the multitude of thy riches and of thy merchandise.

34 In the time *when* [a]thou shalt be broken by the seas in the depths of the waters [b]thy merchandise and all thy company in the midst of thee shall fall.

35 [a]All the inhabitants of the isles shall be astonished at thee, and their kings shall be sore afraid, they shall be troubled in *their* countenance.

36 The merchants among the people [a]shall hiss at thee; [b]thou shalt be [1]a terror, and [2]never *shalt be* any more.

Tyrus' pride and ruin

28 THE WORD of the LORD came again unto me, saying,

2 Son of man, say unto the prince of Tyrus, Thus saith the Lord GOD; Because thine heart *is* lifted up, and [a]thou hast said, I *am* a God, I sit *in* the seat of God, [b]in the [1]midst of the seas; [c]yet thou *art* a man, and not God, though thou set thine heart as the heart of God:

3 Behold, [a]thou *art* wiser than Daniel; there is no secret that they can hide from thee:

4 With thy wisdom and with thine understanding thou hast gotten thee riches, and hast gotten gold and silver into thy treasures:

5 [a]By[1] thy great wisdom *and* by thy traffic hast thou increased thy riches, and thine heart is lifted up because of thy riches:

6 Therefore thus saith the Lord GOD; Because thou hast set thine heart as the heart of God;

7 Behold, therefore I will bring strangers upon thee, [a]the terrible of the nations: and they shall draw their swords against the beauty of thy wisdom, and they shall defile thy brightness.

8 They shall bring thee down to the pit, and thou shalt die the deaths of *them that are* slain in the midst of the seas.

25 [a]Ps. 48:7; Is. 2:16 [b]ver. 4
26 [a]Ps. 48:7 [1]Heb. *heart*
27 [a]Prov. 11:4 [1]Or, *even with all* [2]Heb. *heart*
28 [a]ch. 26:15 [1]Or, *waves*
29 [a]Rev. 18:17
30 [a]Job 2:12; Rev. 18:19 [b]Esth. 4:1,3; Jer. 6:26
31 [a]Jer. 16:6
32 [a]ch. 26:17 [b]Rev. 18:18
33 [a]Rev. 18:19
34 [a]ch. 26:19 [b]ver. 27
35 [a]ch. 26:15
36 [a]Jer. 18:16 [b]ch. 26:21 [1]Heb. *terrors* [2]Heb. shalt *not* be *for ever*
28:2 [a]ver. 9 [b]ch. 27:3,4 [c]Is. 31:3 [1]Heb. *heart*
3 [a]Zech. 9:2
5 [a]Ps. 62:10; Zech. 9:3 [1]Heb. *By the greatness of thy wisdom*
7 [a]ch. 30:11 & 31:12 & 32:12

28:1–19 This prophecy, like many in Ezekiel, contains a double meaning. Note that the prophecy is delivered against Tyre, and that the first part of the prophecy is directed at the "prince" of Tyre (28:2), while the latter part of the prophecy is directed against the "king" of Tyre (28:12). While some scholars view this entire prophecy in light of the end times and liken the prince of Tyre to the antichrist, other scholars suggest that the prince was probably the king of Tyre in Ezekiel's day—Ittobaal. Though this ruler was so proud of his accomplishments that he viewed himself as a god, his wickedness was merely an instrument of the "king"—Satan. Ezekiel reminded this ruler that he was merely a man and would "die the deaths of the uncircumcised by the hand of strangers" (28:10).

Ezekiel then turned his attention to the "king" of Tyre, describing his unique privileges in the garden of Eden as a created being (28:15) and recounting his sin and methods of violence that culminated in his removal from the "mountain of God" (28:16). Ezekiel's prophecy closed with a vivid description of Satan's judgment, indicating that these verses will not be completely fulfilled until Satan is forever cast into the lake of fire (see Rev 20:10).

Satan and the Fallen Angels

Angels are created, immortal beings who play significant roles in God's plan for humanity (see Ps 148:2, 5; Lk 20:36; Eph 3:10; Col 1:16). Present at pivotal points in the spiritual history of the world, God's angels are spiritual messengers, sent to minister to believers (see Heb 1:14). Because angels are spiritual beings, they may be visible to animals but are usually invisible to humans (see Nu 22:22–27). When angels do appear to people they take on human form and may encourage some type of action (see Ge 21:18; Jdg 6:14; Mt 2:13; Ac 8:26; 12:7). At other times God sends his angels to protect his people (see Ps 34:7; Da 3:21; 6:22). Angels are also sent to comfort or share a special message from God (see Mt 1:20; Lk 2:10–11; Ac 27:24). God's angels will return with Jesus Christ at the second coming to establish the Messianic kingdom (see Mt 16:27).

Yet some of these created spiritual beings chose to join Satan and rebel against God. These fallen angels display the same hate, anger, lust and pride that motivated Satan to exalt himself above God (see Isa 14:13–14). Referred to in Isaiah as "Lucifer, son of the morning" (Isa 14:12), Satan left heaven to wander "to and fro in the earth" (Job 2:2) with those angels who joined his rebellion. Many scholars also believe that Ezekiel's title "king of Tyrus" (Eze 28:12) refers to Satan when Ezekiel described this ruler as "the anointed cherub . . . perfect in thy ways from the day that thou wast created, till iniquity was found in thee" (Eze 28:14–15).

Scripture sheds abundant light on the role of Satan and his minions. The book of Job describes the scene of Satan appearing before the throne of God to accuse Job of a self-centered worship of God (see Job 1:6). Zechariah prophesied about Satan's resistance against the high priest Joshua and the angel of the Lord (see Zec 3:1). Paul warns that Satan often appears as "an angel of light" (2Co 11:14) to deceive believers. Jesus himself was tempted by Satan but did not sin (see Mt 4:1–10) and was likened by the Jewish leaders to one of Satan's servants (see Mt 12:24–28). Satan can even use well-meaning people to work his plans (see Mt 16:22–23; Rev 2:9, 13; 3:9).

The book of Revelation gives additional information about Satan's involvement in the last days. At that time Satan's angels will tempt the nations to resist God (see Rev 16:14). Because of this increased rebellion, Satan and his angels will be denied access to heaven by the archangel Michael and the angels of the Lord (see Rev 12:7–9). In retaliation, Satan will attempt to destroy the righteous during the perilous last half of the great tribulation. God will supernaturally intervene to protect his people, and Satan will be defeated by Jesus Christ at the Battle of Armageddon and be cast into the bottomless pit (see Rev 20:2).

Yet this imprisonment is not final. When Satan is released from his thousand-year imprisonment, he will be allowed to tempt humanity one last time. Those who choose to join

Satan and his angels in a last attempt to overthrow Christ's rule will find themselves destroyed. They will face a final judgment for their rebellion (see Jude 6) and be cast into "everlasting fire, prepared for the devil and his angels" (Mt 25:41; see Rev 20:10–15). Jesus Christ will destroy Satan because of his age-long opposition to God's kingdom. From that moment on there will be no possibility of sin or temptation in the universe. The holiness and justice of our Lord Jesus Christ will cover the earth as the waters cover the sea.

9 Wilt thou yet [a]say before him that slayeth thee, I *am* God? but thou *shalt be* a man, and no God, in the hand of him that [1]slayeth thee.

10 Thou shalt die the deaths of [a]the uncircumcised by the hand of strangers: for I have spoken *it,* saith the Lord GOD.

11 ¶ Moreover the word of the LORD came unto me, saying,

12 Son of man, [a]take up a lamentation upon the king of Tyrus, and say unto him, Thus saith the Lord GOD; [b]Thou sealest up the sum, full of wisdom, and perfect in beauty.

13 Thou hast been in [a]Eden the garden of God; every precious stone *was* thy covering, the [1]sardius, topaz, and the diamond, the [2]beryl, the onyx, and the jasper, the sapphire, the [3]emerald, and the carbuncle, and gold: the workmanship of [b]thy tabrets and of thy pipes was prepared in thee in the day that thou wast created.

14 Thou *art* the anointed [a]cherub that covereth; and I have set thee *so:* thou wast upon [b]the holy mountain of God; thou hast walked up and down in the midst of the stones of fire.

15 Thou *wast* perfect in thy ways from the day that thou wast created, till iniquity was found in thee.

16 By the multitude of thy merchandise they have filled the midst of thee with violence, and thou hast sinned: therefore I will cast thee as profane out of the mountain of God: and I will destroy thee, [a]O covering cherub, from the midst of the stones of fire.

17 [a]Thine heart was lifted up because of thy beauty, thou hast corrupted thy wisdom by reason of thy brightness: I will cast thee to the ground, I will lay thee before kings, that they may behold thee.

18 Thou hast defiled thy sanctuaries by the multitude of thine iniquities, by the iniquity of thy traffic; therefore will I bring forth a fire from the midst of thee, it shall devour thee, and I will bring thee to ashes upon the earth in the sight of all them that behold thee.

19 All they that know thee among the people shall be astonished at thee: [a]thou shalt be [1]a terror, and never *shalt* thou *be* any more.

9 [a]ver. 2 [1]Or, *woundeth*
10 [a]ch. 31:18 & 32:19,21,25,27
12 [a]ch. 27:2 [b]ver. 3; ch. 27:3
13 [a]ch. 31:8,9 [b]ch. 26:13 [1]Or, *ruby* [2]Or, *chrysolite* [3]Or, *chrysoprase*
14 [a]ver. 16; See Ex. 25:20 [b]ch. 20:40
16 [a]ver. 14
17 [a]ver. 2,5
19 [a]ch. 26:21 & 27:36 [1]Heb. *terrors*
21 [a]ch. 6:2 & 25:2 & 29:2 [b]Is. 23:4,12; Jer. 25:22 & 27:3; ch. 32:30
22 [a]Ex. 14:4,17; ch. 39:13 [b]Ps. 9:16 [c]ver. 25; ch. 20:41 & 36:23
23 [a]ch. 38:22
24 [a]Num. 33:55; Josh. 23:13
25 [a]Is. 11:12; ch. 11:17 & 20:41 & 34:13 & 37:21 [b]ver. 22
26 [a]Jer. 23:6; ch. 36:28 [b]Is. 65:21; Amos 9:14 [c]Jer. 31:5 [1]Or, *with confidence* [2]Or, *spoil*
29:2 [a]ch. 28:21 [b]Is. 19:1; Jer. 25:19 & 46:2,25

Zidon to perish

20 ¶ Again the word of the LORD came unto me, saying, J

21 Son of man, [a]set thy face [b]against Zidon, and prophesy against it,

22 And say, Thus saith the Lord GOD; [a]Behold, I *am* against thee, O Zidon; and I will be glorified in the midst of thee: and [b]they shall know that I *am* the LORD, when I shall have executed judgments in her, and shall be [c]sanctified in her.

23 [a]For I will send into her pestilence, and blood into her streets; and the wounded shall be judged in the midst of her by the sword upon her on every side; and they shall know that I *am* the LORD. D

24 ¶ And there shall be no more [a]a pricking brier unto the house of Israel, nor *any* grieving thorn of all *that are* round about them, that despised them; and they shall know that I *am* the Lord GOD.

25 Thus saith the Lord GOD; When I shall have [a]gathered the house of Israel from the people among whom they are scattered, and shall be [b]sanctified in them in the sight of the heathen, then shall they dwell in their land that I have given to my servant Jacob. I

26 And they shall [a]dwell [1]safely therein, and shall [b]build houses, and [c]plant vineyards; yea, they shall dwell with confidence, when I have executed judgments upon all those that [2]despise them round about them; and they shall know that I *am* the LORD their God.

Egypt's pride and desolation

29 IN THE tenth year, in the tenth *month,* in the twelfth *day* of the month, the word of the LORD came unto me, saying, J

2 Son of man, [a]set thy face against Pharaoh king of Egypt, and prophesy against him, and [b]against all Egypt:

3 Speak, and say, Thus saith the Lord

J *Eze 26:12–21* ◀ ▶ *Eze 29:1–6*
D *Eze 14:21* ◀ ▶ *Eze 33:27*
I *Eze 20:40–42* ◀ ▶ *Eze 34:11–16*
J *Eze 28:20–24* ◀ ▶ *Eze 29:19–20*

28:25–26 This passage confirmed the final restoration of God's people to safety and security in the promised land. This prophecy will be fulfilled in the Millennium after the return of the Messiah.

GOD; [a]Behold, I *am* against thee, Pharaoh king of Egypt, the great [b]dragon that lieth in the midst of his rivers, [c]which hath said, My river *is* mine own, and I have made *it* for myself.

4 But [a]I will put hooks in thy jaws, and I will cause the fish of thy rivers to stick unto thy scales, and I will bring thee up out of the midst of thy rivers, and all the fish of thy rivers shall stick unto thy scales.

5 And I will leave thee *thrown* into the wilderness, thee and all the fish of thy rivers: thou shalt fall upon the [1]open fields; [a]thou shalt not be brought together, nor gathered: [b]I have given thee for meat to the beasts of the field and to the fowls of the heaven.

6 And all the inhabitants of Egypt shall know that I *am* the LORD, because they have been a [a]staff of reed to the house of Israel.

7 [a]When they took hold of thee by thy hand, thou didst break, and rend all their shoulder: and when they leaned upon thee, thou brakest, and madest all their loins to be at a stand.

8 ¶ Therefore thus saith the Lord GOD; Behold, I will bring [a]a sword upon thee, and cut off man and beast out of thee.

9 And the land of Egypt shall be desolate and waste; and they shall know that I *am* the LORD: because he hath said, The river *is* mine, and I have made *it*.

10 Behold, therefore I *am* against thee, and against thy rivers, [a]and I will make the land of Egypt [1]utterly waste *and* desolate, [b]from[2] the tower of [3]Syene even unto the border of Ethiopia.

11 [a]No foot of man shall pass through it, nor foot of beast shall pass through it, neither shall it be inhabited forty years.

12 [a]And I will make the land of Egypt desolate in the midst of the countries *that are* desolate, and her cities among the cities *that are* laid waste shall be desolate forty years: and I will scatter the Egyptians among the nations, and will disperse them through the countries.

13 ¶ Yet thus saith the Lord GOD; At the [a]end of forty years will I gather the Egyptians from the people whither they were scattered:

14 And I will bring again the captivity of Egypt, and will cause them to return *into* the land of Pathros, into the land of their [1]habitation; and they shall be there a [a]base[2] kingdom.

15 It shall be the basest of the kingdoms; neither shall it exalt itself any more above the nations: for I will diminish them, that they shall no more rule over the nations.

16 And it shall be no more [a]the confidence of the house of Israel, which bringeth *their* iniquity to remembrance, when they shall look after them: but they shall know that I *am* the Lord GOD.

17 ¶ And it came to pass in the seven and twentieth year, in the first *month,* in the first *day* of the month, the word of the LORD came unto me, saying,

18 Son of man, [a]Nebuchadrezzar king of Babylon caused his army to serve a great service against Tyrus: every head *was* made bald, and every shoulder *was* peeled: yet had he no wages, nor his army, for Tyrus, for the service that he had served against it:

19 Therefore thus saith the Lord GOD; Behold, I will give the land of Egypt unto Nebuchadrezzar king of Babylon; and he shall take her multitude, and [1]take her spoil, and take her prey; and it shall be the wages for his army. J

20 I have given him the land of Egypt [1]*for* his labour wherewith he [a]served against it, because they wrought for me, saith the Lord GOD.

21 ¶ In that day [a]will I cause the horn of the house of Israel to bud forth, and I will give thee [b]the opening of the mouth in the midst of them; and they shall know that I *am* the LORD.

3 [a]ver. 10; Jer. 44:30; ch. 28:22 [b]Ps. 74:13,14; Is. 27:1 & 51:9; ch. 32:2 [c]See ch. 28:2
4 [a]Is. 37:29; ch. 38:4
5 [a]Jer. 8:2 & 16:4; & 25:33 [b]Jer. 7:33 & 34:20 [1]Heb. *face of the field*
6 [a]2 Ki. 18:21; Is. 36:6
7 [a]Jer. 37:5,7,11; ch. 17:17
8 [a]ch. 14:17 & 32:11-13
10 [a]ch. 30:12 [b]ch. 30:6 [1]Heb. *wastes of waste* [2]Or, *from Migdol to Syene;* see Ex. 14:2; Jer. 44:1 [3]Heb. *Seveneh*
11 [a]ch. 32:13
12 [a]ch. 30:7,26
13 [a]Is. 19:23; Jer. 46:26
14 [a]ch. 17:6,14 [1]Or, *birth* [2]Heb. *low*
16 [a]Is. 30:2,3 & 36:4,6
18 [a]Jer. 27:6; ch. 26:7,8
19 [1]Heb. *spoil her spoil, and prey her prey*
20 [a]Jer. 25:9 [1]Or, *for his hire*
21 [a]Ps. 132:17 [b]ch. 24:27

J *Eze 29:1–6* ◀ ▶ *Eze 35:1–15*

29:10–15 In this oracle against Egypt, Ezekiel declared God's intent to punish the nation of Egypt and make its land desolate and its cities ruined. Ezekiel also named Nebuchadnezzar as God's means to deliver this judgment (see 29:19). According to history, Nebuchadnezzar suffered such great losses in his attack on Tyre (585–572 B.C.) that he sent his troops to plunder Egypt and carry off thousands of Egyptians as slaves.

A lament for Egypt

30 THE WORD of the LORD came again unto me, saying,

2 Son of man, prophesy and say, Thus saith the Lord GOD; [a]Howl ye, Woe worth the day!

3 For [a]the day *is* near, even the day of the LORD *is* near, a cloudy day; it shall be the time of the heathen.

4 And the sword shall come upon Egypt, and great [1]pain shall be in Ethiopia, when the slain shall fall in Egypt, and they [a]shall take away her multitude, and [b]her foundations shall be broken down.

5 Ethiopia, and [1]Libya, and Lydia, and [a]all the mingled people, and Chub, and the [2]men of the land that is in league, shall fall with them by the sword.

6 Thus saith the LORD; They also that uphold Egypt shall fall; and the pride of her power shall come down: [a]from[1] the tower of Syene shall they fall in it by the sword, saith the Lord GOD.

7 [a]And they shall be desolate in the midst of the countries *that are* desolate, and her cities shall be in the midst of the cities *that are* wasted.

8 And they shall know that I *am* the LORD, when I have set a fire in Egypt, and *when* all her helpers shall be [1]destroyed.

9 In that day [a]shall messengers go forth from me in ships to make the careless Ethiopians afraid, and great pain shall come upon them, as in the day of Egypt: for, lo, it cometh.

10 Thus saith the Lord GOD; [a]I will also make the multitude of Egypt to cease by the hand of Nebuchadrezzar king of Babylon.

11 He and his people with him, [a]the terrible of the nations, shall be brought to destroy the land: and they shall draw their swords against Egypt, and fill the land with the slain.

12 And [a]I will make the rivers [1]dry, and [b]sell the land into the hand of the wicked: and I will make the land waste, and [2]all that is therein, by the hand of strangers: I the LORD have spoken *it.*

13 Thus saith the Lord GOD; I will also [a]destroy the idols, and I will cause *their* images to cease out of Noph; [b]and there shall be no more a prince of the land of Egypt: [c]and I will put a fear in the land of Egypt.

14 And I will make [a]Pathros desolate, and will set fire in [b]Zoan,[1] [c]and will execute judgments in No.

15 And I will pour my fury upon [1]Sin, the strength of Egypt; and [a]I will cut off the multitude of No.

16 And I will [a]set fire in Egypt: Sin shall have great pain, and No shall be rent asunder, and Noph *shall have* distresses daily.

17 The young men of [1]Aven and of [2]Pibeseth shall fall by the sword: and these *cities* shall go into captivity.

18 [a]At Tehaphnehes also the day shall be [1]darkened, when I shall break there the yokes of Egypt: and the pomp of her strength shall cease in her: as for her, a cloud shall cover her, and her daughters shall go into captivity.

19 Thus will I execute judgments in Egypt: and they shall know that I *am* the LORD.

20 ¶ And it came to pass in the eleventh year, in the first *month,* in the seventh *day* of the month, *that* the word of the LORD came unto me, saying,

21 Son of man, I have [a]broken the arm of Pharaoh king of Egypt; and, lo, [b]it shall not be bound up to be healed, to put a roller to bind it, to make it strong to hold the sword.

22 Therefore thus saith the Lord GOD; Behold, I *am* against Pharaoh king of Egypt, and will [a]break his arms, the strong, and that which was broken; and I will cause the sword to fall out of his hand.

23 [a]And I will scatter the Egyptians among the nations, and will disperse them through the countries.

24 And I will strengthen the arms of the king of Babylon, and put my sword in his hand: but I will break Pharaoh's arms, and he shall groan before him with the groanings of a deadly wounded *man.*

25 But I will strengthen the arms of the king of Babylon, and the arms of Pharaoh shall fall down; and [a]they shall know that I *am* the LORD, when I shall put my sword into the hand of the king of Babylon, and he shall stretch it out upon the land of Egypt.

26 [a]And I will scatter the Egyptians among the nations, and disperse them among the countries; and they shall know that I *am* the LORD.

30:2 [a]Is. 13:6
3 [a]ch. 7:7,12; Joel 2:1; Zeph. 1:7
4 [a]ch. 29:19 [b]Jer. 50:15 [1]Or, *fear*
5 [a]Jer. 25:20,24 [1]Heb. *Phut;* see ch. 27:10 [2]Heb. *children*
6 [a]ch. 29:10 [1]Or, *from Migdol to Syene*
7 [a]ch. 29:12
8 [1]Heb. *broken*
9 [a]Is. 18:1,2
10 [a]ch. 29:19
11 [a]ch. 28:7
12 [a]Is. 19:5,6 [b]Is. 19:4 [1]Heb. *drought* [2]Heb. *the fulness thereof*
13 [a]Is. 19:1; Jer. 43:12 & 46:25; Zech. 13:2 [b]Zech. 10:11 [c]Is. 19:16
14 [a]ch. 29:14 [b]Ps. 78:12,43 [c]Nah. 3:8-10 [1]Or, *Tanis*
15 [a]Jer. 46:25 [1]Or, *Pelusium*
16 [a]ver. 8
17 [1]Or, *Heliopolis* [2]Or, *Pubastum*
18 [a]Jer. 2:16 [1]Or, *restrained*
21 [a]Jer. 48:25 [b]Jer. 46:11
22 [a]Ps. 37:17
23 [a]ver. 26; ch. 29:12
25 [a]Ps. 9:16
26 [a]ver. 23; ch. 29:12

Parable of the cedar of Lebanon

31 AND IT came to pass in the eleventh year, in the third *month,* in
the first *day* of the month, *that* the word
of the LORD came unto me, saying,
2 Son of man, speak unto Pharaoh king
of Egypt, and to his multitude; [a]Whom
art thou like in thy greatness?
3 ¶ [a]Behold, the Assyrian *was* a cedar
in Lebanon [1]with fair branches, and with
a shadowing shroud, and of an high stature; and his top was among the thick
boughs.
4 [a]The waters [1]made him great, the
deep [2]set him up on high with her rivers
running round about his plants, and sent
out her [3]little rivers unto all the trees of
the field.
5 Therefore [a]his height was exalted
above all the trees of the field, and
his boughs were multiplied, and his
branches became long because of the
multitude of waters, [1]when he shot forth.
6 All the [a]fowls of heaven made their
nests in his boughs, and under his
branches did all the beasts of the field
bring forth their young, and under his
shadow dwelt all great nations.
7 Thus was he fair in his greatness, in
the length of his branches: for his root
was by great waters.
8 The cedars in the [a]garden of God
could not hide him: the fir trees were not
like his boughs, and the chestnut trees
were not like his branches; nor any tree
in the garden of God was like unto him in
his beauty.
9 I have made him fair by the multitude of his branches: so that all the trees
of Eden, that *were* in the garden of God,
envied him.
10 ¶ Therefore thus saith the Lord
GOD; Because thou hast lifted up thyself
in height, and he hath shot up his top
among the thick boughs, and [a]his heart is
lifted up in his height;
11 I have therefore delivered him into
the hand of the mighty one of the heathen; [1]he shall surely deal with him: I
have driven him out for his wickedness.
12 And strangers, [a]the terrible of the
nations, have cut him off, and have
left him: [b]upon the mountains and in all the
valleys his branches are fallen, and his
boughs are broken by all the rivers of the
land; and all the people of the earth are
gone down from his shadow, and have
left him.
13 [a]Upon his ruin shall all the fowls of
the heaven remain, and all the beasts of
the field shall be upon his branches:
14 To the end that none of all the trees
by the waters exalt themselves for their
height, neither shoot up their top among
the thick boughs, neither their trees
[1]stand up in their height, all that drink
water: for [a]they are all delivered unto
death, [b]to the nether parts of the earth,
in the midst of the children of men, with
them that go down to the pit.
15 Thus saith the Lord GOD; In the day
when he went down to the grave I
caused a mourning: I covered the deep
for him, and I restrained the floods
thereof, and the great waters were
stayed: and I caused Lebanon [1]to mourn
for him, and all the trees of the field
fainted for him.
16 I made the nations to [a]shake at the
sound of his fall, when I [b]cast him down
to hell with them that descend into the
pit: and [c]all the trees of Eden, the choice
and best of Lebanon, all that drink water,
[d]shall be comforted in the nether parts of
the earth.
17 They also went down into hell with
him unto *them that be* slain with the
sword; and *they that were* his arm, *that*
[a]dwelt under his shadow in the midst of
the heathen.
18 ¶ [a]To whom art thou thus like in
glory and in greatness among the trees of
Eden? yet shalt thou be brought down
with the trees of Eden unto the nether
parts of the earth: [b]thou shalt lie in the
midst of the uncircumcised with *them
that be* slain by the sword. This *is* Pharaoh and all his multitude, saith the Lord
GOD.

The lament for Pharaoh

32 AND IT came to pass in the
twelfth year, in the twelfth
month, in the first *day* of the month, *that*
the word of the LORD came unto me,
saying,
2 Son of man, [a]take up a lamentation
for Pharaoh king of Egypt, and say unto
him, [b]Thou art like a young lion of the
nations, [c]and thou *art* as a [1]whale in the
seas: and thou camest forth with thy rivers, and troubledst the waters with thy
feet, and [d]fouledst their rivers.

31:2 [a]ver. 18
3 [a]Dan. 4:10 [1]Heb. *fair of branches*
4 [a]Jer. 51:36 [1]Or, *nourished* [2]Or, *brought him up* [3]Or, *conduits*
5 [a]Dan. 4:11 [1]Or, *when it sent* them *forth*
6 [a]ch. 17:23; Dan. 4:12
8 [a]Gen. 2:8 & 13:10; ch. 28:13
10 [a]Dan. 5:20
11 [1]Heb. *in doing he shall do unto him*
12 [a]ch. 28:7 [b]ch. 32:5 & 35:8
13 [a]Is. 18:6; ch. 32:4
14 [a]Ps. 82:7 [b]ch. 32:18 [1]Or, *stand upon themselves for their height*
15 [1]Heb. *to be black*
16 [a]ch. 26:15 [b]Is. 14:15 [c]Is. 14:8 [d]ch. 32:31
17 [a]Lam. 4:20
18 [a]ver. 2; ch. 32:19 [b]ch. 28:10 & 32:19,21,24
32:2 [a]ver. 16; ch. 27:2 [b]ch. 19:3,6 & 38:13 [c]ch. 29:3 [d]ch. 34:18 [1]Or, *dragon*

3 Thus saith the Lord GOD; I will therefore [a]spread out my net over thee with a company of many people; and they shall bring thee up in my net.

4 Then [a]will I leave thee upon the land, I will cast thee forth upon the open field, and [b]will cause all the fowls of the heaven to remain upon thee, and I will fill the beasts of the whole earth with thee.

5 And I will lay thy flesh [a]upon the mountains, and fill the valleys with thy height.

6 I will also water with thy blood [1]the land wherein thou swimmest, *even* to the mountains; and the rivers shall be full of thee.

7 And when I shall [1]put thee out, [a]I will cover the heaven, and make the stars thereof dark; I will cover the sun with a cloud, and the moon shall not give her light.

8 All the [1]bright lights of heaven will I make [2]dark over thee, and set darkness upon thy land, saith the Lord GOD.

9 I will also [1]vex the hearts of many people, when I shall bring thy destruction among the nations, into the countries which thou hast not known.

10 Yea, I will make many people amazed at thee, and their kings shall be horribly afraid for thee, when I shall brandish my sword before them; and [a]they shall tremble at *every* moment, every man for his own life, in the day of thy fall.

11 ¶ [a]For thus saith the Lord GOD; The sword of the king of Babylon shall come upon thee.

12 By the swords of the mighty will I cause thy multitude to fall, [a]the terrible of the nations, all of them: and [b]they shall spoil the pomp of Egypt, and all the multitude thereof shall be destroyed.

13 I will destroy also all the beasts thereof from beside the great waters; [a]neither shall the foot of man trouble them any more, nor the hoofs of beasts trouble them.

14 Then will I make their waters deep, and cause their rivers to run like oil, saith the Lord GOD.

15 When I shall make the land of Egypt desolate, and the country shall be [1]destitute of that whereof it was full, when I shall smite all them that dwell therein, [a]then shall they know that I *am* the LORD.

16 This *is* the [a]lamentation wherewith they shall lament her: the daughters of the nations shall lament her: they shall lament for her, *even* for Egypt, and for all her multitude, saith the Lord GOD.

17 ¶ It came to pass also in the twelfth year, in the fifteenth *day* of the month, *that* the word of the LORD came unto me, saying,

18 Son of man, wail for the multitude of Egypt, and [a]cast them down, *even* her, and the daughters of the famous nations, unto the nether parts of the earth, with them that go down into the pit.

19 [a]Whom dost thou pass in beauty? [b]go down, and be thou laid with the uncircumcised.

20 They shall fall in the midst of *them that are* slain by the sword: [1]she is delivered to the sword: draw her and all her multitudes.

21 [a]The strong among the mighty shall speak to him out of the midst of hell with them that help him: they are [b]gone down, they lie uncircumcised, slain by the sword.

22 Asshur *is* there and all her company: his graves *are* about him: all of them slain, fallen by the sword:

23 [a]Whose graves are set in the sides of the pit, and her company is round about her grave: all of them slain, fallen by the sword, which [b]caused [1]terror in the land of the living.

24 There *is* [a]Elam and all her multitude round about her grave, all of them slain, fallen by the sword, which are [b]gone down uncircumcised into the nether parts of the earth, [c]which caused their terror in the land of the living; yet have they borne their shame with them that go down to the pit.

25 They have set her a bed in the midst of the slain with all her multitude: her graves *are* round about him: all of them uncircumcised, slain by the sword: though their terror was caused in the land of the living, yet have they borne their shame with them that go down to the pit: he is put in the midst of *them that be* slain.

26 There *is* [a]Meshech, Tubal, and all her multitude: her graves *are* round about him: all of them [b]uncircumcised,

3 [a]ch. 12:13 & 17:20; Hos. 7:12
4 [a]ch. 29:5 [b]ch. 31:13
5 [a]ch. 31:12
6 [1]Or, *the land of thy swimming*
7 [a]Is. 13:10; Joel 2:31 & 3:15; Amos 8:9; Mat. 24:29; Rev. 6:12,13 [1]Or, *extinguish*
8 [1]Heb. *lights of the light in heaven* [2]Heb. *them dark*
9 [1]Heb. *provoke to anger*, or, *grief*
10 [a]ch. 26:16
11 [a]Jer. 46:26; ch. 30:4
12 [a]ch. 28:7 [b]ch. 29:19
13 [a]ch. 29:11
15 [a]Ex. 7:5 & 14:4,18; Ps. 9:16; ch. 6:7 [1]Heb. *desolate from the fulness thereof*
16 [a]ver. 2; 2 Sam. 1:17; 2 Chr. 35:25; ch. 26:17
18 [a]ch. 26:20 & 31:14
19 [a]ch. 31:2,18 [b]ver. 21,24; ch. 28:10
20 [1]Or, *the sword is laid*
21 [a]ver. 27; Is. 1:31 & 14:9,10 [b]ver. 19,25
23 [a]Is. 14:15 [b]ver. 24-27,32 [1]Or, *dismaying*
24 [a]Jer. 49:34 [b]ver. 21 [c]ver. 23
26 [a]Gen. 10:2; ch. 27:13 [b]ver. 19,20

slain by the sword, though they caused their terror in the land of the living.

27 [a]And they shall not lie with the mighty *that are* fallen of the uncircumcised, which are gone down to hell [l]with their weapons of war: and they have laid their swords under their heads, but their iniquities shall be upon their bones, though *they were* the terror of the mighty in the land of the living.

28 Yea, thou shalt be broken in the midst of the uncircumcised, and shalt lie with *them that are* slain with the sword.

29 There *is* [a]Edom, her kings, and all her princes, which with their might are [l]laid by *them that were* slain by the sword: they shall lie with the uncircumcised, and with them that go down to the pit.

30 [a]There *be* the princes of the north, all of them, and all the [b]Zidonians, which are gone down with the slain; with their terror they are ashamed of their might; and they lie uncircumcised with *them that be* slain by the sword, and bear their shame with them that go down to the pit.

31 Pharaoh shall see them, and shall be [a]comforted over all his multitude, *even* Pharaoh and all his army slain by the sword, saith the Lord GOD.

32 For I have caused my terror in the land of the living: and he shall be laid in the midst of the uncircumcised with *them that are* slain with the sword, *even* Pharaoh and all his multitude, saith the Lord GOD.

Ezekiel as Israel's watchman

33 AGAIN THE word of the LORD came unto me, saying,

2 Son of man, speak to [a]the children of thy people, and say unto them, [b]When [l] I bring the sword upon a land, if the people of the land take a man of their coasts, and set him for their [c]watchman:

3 If when he seeth the sword come upon the land, he blow the trumpet, and warn the people;

N 4 Then [l]whosoever heareth the sound of the trumpet, and taketh not warning; if the sword come, and take him away, [a]his blood shall be upon his own head.

5 He heard the sound of the trumpet, and took not warning; his blood shall be upon him. But he that taketh warning shall deliver his soul.

6 But if the watchman see the sword come, and blow not the trumpet, and the people be not warned; if the sword come, and take *any* person from among them, [a]he is taken away in his iniquity; but his blood will I require at the watchman's hand.

7 ¶ [a]So thou, O son of man, I have set thee a watchman unto the house of Israel; therefore thou shalt hear the word at my mouth, and warn them from me.

8 When I say unto the wicked, O wicked *man,* thou shalt surely die; if thou dost not speak to warn the wicked from his way, that wicked *man* shall die in his iniquity; but his blood will I require at thine hand.

9 Nevertheless, if thou warn the wicked of his way to turn from it; if he do not turn from his way, he shall die in his iniquity; but thou hast delivered thy soul. N R

10 Therefore, O thou son of man, speak unto the house of Israel; Thus ye speak, saying, If our transgressions and our sins *be* upon us, and we [a]pine away in them, [b]how should we then live?

11 Say unto them, *As* I live, saith the Lord GOD, [a]I have no pleasure in the death of the wicked; but that the wicked turn from his way and live: turn ye, turn ye from your evil ways; for [b]why will ye die, O house of Israel? H L R S W

12 Therefore, thou son of man, say unto the children of thy people, The [a]righteousness of the righteous shall not deliver him in the day of his transgression: as for the wickedness of the wicked, [b]he shall not fall thereby in the day that he turneth from his wickedness; neither shall the righteous be able to live for his *righteousness* in the day that he sinneth.

13 When I shall say to the righteous, *that* he shall surely live; [a]if he trust to his own righteousness, and commit iniquity, all his righteousnesses shall not be remembered; but for his iniquity that he hath committed, he shall die for it. H

27 [a]ver. 21; Is. 14:18,19 [l]Heb. *with weapons of their war*
29 [a]ch. 25:12 [l]Heb. *given, or, put*
30 [a]ch. 38:6,15 & 39:2 [b]ch. 28:21
31 [a]ch. 31:16
33:2 [a]ch. 3:11 [b]ch. 14:17 [c]ver. 7; 2 Sam. 18:24,25; 2 Ki. 9:17; Hos. 9:8 [l]Heb. *A land when I bring a sword upon her*
4 [a]ch. 18:13 [l]Heb. *he that hearing heareth*
6 [a]ver. 8
7 [a]ch. 3:17
10 [a]ch. 24:23 [b]Is. 49:14
11 [a]2 Sam. 14:14; 2 Pet. 3:9 [b]ch. 18:31
12 [a]ch. 3:20 & 18:24,26 [b]2 Chr. 7:14
13 [a]ch. 3:20 & 18:24

N *Eze 3:7* ◀▶ *Eze 33:9*

N *Eze 33:4–5* ◀▶ *Eze 33:31*
R *Eze 18:30–32* ◀▶ *Eze 33:11–12*
H *Eze 25:17* ◀▶ *Eze 33:13*
L *Eze 18:32* ◀▶ *Eze 33:14–16*
R *Eze 33:9* ◀▶ *Eze 33:14–16*
S *Eze 18:30–32* ◀▶ *Eze 33:18*
W *Eze 18:32* ◀▶ *Mt 7:7–8*
H *Eze 33:11* ◀▶ *Eze 35:14*

L R 14 Again, [a]when I say unto the wicked, Thou shalt surely die; if he turn from his sin, and do [/]that which is lawful and right;

15 *If* the wicked [a]restore the pledge, [b]give again that he had robbed, walk in [c]the statutes of life, without committing iniquity; he shall surely live, he shall not die.

16 [a]None of his sins that he hath committed shall be mentioned unto him: he hath done that which is lawful and right; he shall surely live.

17 ¶ [a]Yet the children of thy people say, The way of the Lord is not equal: but as for them, their way is not equal.

S 18 [a]When the righteous turneth from his righteousness, and committeth iniquity, he shall even die thereby.

L R 19 But if the wicked turn from his wickedness, and do that which is lawful and right, he shall live thereby.

20 ¶ Yet ye say, [a]The way of the Lord is not equal. O ye house of Israel, I will judge you every one after his ways.

Jerusalem's fall

21 ¶ And it came to pass in the twelfth year [a]of our captivity, in the tenth *month,* in the fifth *day* of the month, [b]*that* one that had escaped out of Jerusalem came unto me, saying, [c]The city is smitten.

22 Now [a]the hand of the LORD was upon me in the evening, afore he that was escaped came; and had opened my mouth, until he came to me in the morning; [b]and my mouth was opened, and I was no more dumb.

23 Then the word of the LORD came unto me, saying,

24 Son of man, [a]they that inhabit those [b]wastes of the land of Israel speak, saying, [c]Abraham was one, and he inherited the land: [d]but we *are* many; the land is given us for inheritance.

25 Wherefore say unto them, Thus saith the Lord GOD; [a]Ye eat with the blood, and [b]lift up your eyes toward your idols, and [c]shed blood: and shall ye possess the land?

26 Ye stand upon your sword, ye work abomination, and ye [a]defile every one his neighbour's wife: and shall ye possess the land?

D 27 Say thou thus unto them, Thus saith the Lord GOD; *As* I live, surely [a]they that *are* in the wastes shall fall by the sword, and him that *is* in the open field [b]will I give to the beasts [/]to be devoured, and they that *be* in the forts and [c]in the caves shall die of the pestilence.

R 28 [a]For I will lay the land [/]most desolate, and the [b]pomp of her strength shall cease; and [c]the mountains of Israel shall be desolate, that none shall pass through.

29 Then shall they know that I *am* the LORD, when I have laid the land most desolate because of all their abominations which they have committed.

30 ¶ Also, thou son of man, the children of thy people still are talking [/]against thee by the walls and in the doors of the houses, and [a]speak one to another, every one to his brother, saying, Come, I pray you, and hear what is the word that cometh forth from the LORD.

G N S 31 And [a]they come unto thee [/]as the people cometh, and [2]they [b]sit before thee *as* my people, and they hear thy words, but they will not do them: [c]for with their mouth [3]they show much love, *but* [d]their heart goeth after their covetousness.

32 And, lo, thou *art* unto them as [/]a very lovely song of one that hath a pleasant voice, and can play well on an instrument: for they hear thy words, but they do them not.

33 [a]And when this cometh to pass, (lo, it will come,) then [b]shall they know that a prophet hath been among them.

14 [a]ch. 3:18,19 & 18:27 [/]Heb. *judgment and justice*
15 [a]ch. 18:7 [b]Ex. 22:1,4; Lev. 6:2,4,5 [c]Lev. 18:5; ch. 20:11,13,21
16 [a]ch. 18:22
17 [a]ver. 20; ch. 18:25,29
18 [a]ch. 18:26
20 [a]ver. 17; ch. 18:25
21 [a]ch. 1:2 [b]ch. 24:26 [c]2 Ki. 25:4
22 [a]ch. 1:3 [b]ch. 24:27
24 [a]ch. 34:2 [b]ver. 27; ch. 36:4 [c]Is. 51:2; Acts 7:5 [d]Mic. 3:11; Mat. 3:9; John 8:39
25 [a]Gen. 9:4; Lev. 3:17 & 7:26 & 17:10 & 19:26; Deut. 12:16 [b]ch. 18:6 [c]ch. 22:6,9
26 [a]ch. 18:6 & 22:11
27 [a]ver. 24 [b]ch. 39:4 [c]Judg. 6:2; 1 Sam. 13:6 [/]Heb. *to devour him*
28 [a]Jer. 44:2,6,22; ch. 36:34,35 [b]ch. 7:24 & 24:21 & 30:6,7 [c]ch. 6:2,3,6 [/]Heb. *desolation and desolation*
30 [a]Is. 29:13 [/]Or, *of thee*
31 [a]ch. 14:1 & 20:1 [b]ch. 8:1 [c]Ps. 78:36,37; Is. 29:13 [d]Mat. 13:22 [/]Heb. *according to the coming of the people* [2]Or, *my people sit before thee* [3]Heb. *they make loves,* or, *jests*
32 [/]Heb. *a song of loves*
33 [a]1 Sam. 3:20 [b]ch. 2:5

L *Eze 33:11–12* ◀▶ *Eze 33:19*
R *Eze 33:11–12* ◀▶ *Eze 33:19*
S *Eze 33:11–16* ◀▶ *Eze 33:31*
L *Eze 33:14–16* ◀▶ *Eze 34:11–12*
R *Eze 33:14–16* ◀▶ *Da 4:27*
D *Eze 28:23* ◀▶ *Eze 38:22*
R *Eze 24:13* ◀▶ *Eze 34:1–2*
G *Eze 13:10–14* ◀▶ *Zep 1:18*
N *Eze 33:9* ◀▶ *Da 5:1–6*
S *Eze 33:18* ◀▶ *Eze 36:25–27*

33:28–29 God declared that all nations would recognize that the desolation of Israel was due to their continued rebellion and apostasy against God.

Israel's shepherds

R **34** AND THE word of the LORD came
unto me, saying,
2 Son of man, prophesy against the
shepherds of Israel, prophesy, and say
unto them, Thus saith the Lord GOD unto
the shepherds; [a]Woe *be* to the shepherds
of Israel that do feed themselves! should
not the shepherds feed the flocks?
3 [a]Ye eat the fat, and ye clothe you
with the wool, ye kill them that are fed:
but ye feed not the flock.
4 [a]The diseased have ye not strengthened, neither have ye healed that which
was sick, neither have ye bound up *that
which was* broken, neither have ye
brought again that which was driven
away, neither have ye [b]sought that which
was lost; but with [c]force and with cruelty
have ye ruled them.
R 5 [a]And they were [b]scattered, [c]be-
cause[1] *there is* no shepherd: [d]and they
became meat to all the beasts of the field,
when they were scattered.
6 My sheep wandered through all the
mountains, and upon every high hill: yea,
my flock was scattered upon all the face
of the earth, and none did search or seek
after them.
7 ¶ Therefore, ye shepherds, hear the
word of the LORD;
8 *As* I live, saith the Lord GOD, surely
because my flock became a prey, and my
flock [a]became meat to every beast of the
field, because *there was* no shepherd,
neither did my shepherds search for my
flock, [b]but the shepherds fed themselves,
and fed not my flock;
9 Therefore, O ye shepherds, hear the
word of the LORD;
10 Thus saith the Lord GOD; Behold, I
am against the shepherds; and [a]I will require my flock at their hand, and cause
them to cease from feeding the flock; neither shall the shepherds [b]feed themselves any more; for I will deliver my
flock from their mouth, that they may not
be meat for them.

R *Eze 33:28–29* ◄► *Eze 34:5–10*
R *Eze 34:1–2* ◄► *Eze 36:3–7*

34:2 [a]Jer. 23:1; Zech. 11:17
3 [a]Is. 56:11; Zech. 11:16
4 [a]Zech. 11:16 [b]Luke 15:4 [c]1 Pet. 5:3
5 [a]ch. 33:21 [b]1 Ki. 22:17; Mat. 9:36 [c]ver. 8 [d]Is. 56:9; Jer. 12:9 [1]*Or, without a shepherd*
8 [a]ver. 5,6 [b]ver. 2, 10
10 [a]ch. 3:18; Heb. 13:17 [b]ver. 2,8
12 [a]ch. 30:3 [1]Heb. *According to the seeking*
13 [a]Is. 65:9,10; Jer. 23:3
14 [a]Ps. 23:2 [b]Jer. 33:12
16 [a]Is. 40:11; Mic. 4:6; Mat. 18:11; Luke 5:32 [b]Is. 10:16; Amos 4:1 [c]Jer. 10:24
17 [a]ch. 20:37; Mat. 25:32 [1]Heb. *small cattle of lambs and kids* [2]Heb. *great he goats*
20 [a]ver. 17

The LORD God is a shepherd

11 ¶ For thus saith the Lord GOD; Be- I
hold, I, *even* I, will both search my sheep, L
and seek them out. P
12 [1]As a shepherd seeketh out his
flock in the day that he is among his
sheep *that are* scattered; so will I seek out
my sheep, and will deliver them out of all
places where they have been scattered in
[a]the cloudy and dark day.
13 And [a]I will bring them out from the
people, and gather them from the countries, and will bring them to their own
land, and feed them upon the mountains
of Israel by the rivers, and in all the inhabited places of the country.
14 [a]I will feed them in a good pasture,
and upon the high mountains of Israel
shall their fold be: [b]there shall they lie in
a good fold, and *in* a fat pasture shall they
feed upon the mountains of Israel.
15 I will feed my flock, and I will cause
them to lie down, saith the Lord GOD.
16 [a]I will seek that which was lost, H
and bring again that which was driven
away, and will bind up *that which was*
broken, and will strengthen that which
was sick: but I will destroy [b]the fat and
the strong; I will feed them [c]with
judgment.
17 And *as for* you, O my flock, thus
saith the Lord GOD; [a]Behold, I judge between [1]cattle and cattle, between the
rams and the [2]he goats.
18 *Seemeth it* a small thing unto you to
have eaten up the good pasture, but ye
must tread down with your feet the residue of your pastures? and to have drunk
of the deep waters, but ye must foul the
residue with your feet?
19 And *as for* my flock, they eat that
which ye have trodden with your feet;
and they drink that which ye have fouled
with your feet.
20 ¶ Therefore thus saith the Lord GOD
unto them; [a]Behold, I, *even* I, will judge

I *Eze 28:25–26* ◄► *Eze 34:22*
L *Eze 33:19* ◄► *Eze 36:25*
P *Jer 36:3* ◄► *Da 9:9*
H *Jer 17:14* ◄► *Eze 47:12*

34:5–6 This image of Israel without a shepherd is used often in the Bible (see Mk 6:34).

34:11–16 Using the imagery of a shepherd and his flock, God declared his intent to care for his people when their punishment was finished. He would bring his people back to their land and restore their possessions. Compare this imagery with Isa 40:11 and Jn 10:11.

between the fat cattle and between the lean cattle.

21 Because ye have thrust with side and with shoulder, and pushed all the diseased with your horns, till ye have scattered them abroad;

I 22 Therefore will I save my flock, and they shall no more be a prey; and I will judge between cattle and cattle.

M 23 And I will set up one [a]shepherd over them, and he shall feed them, [b]*even* my servant David; he shall feed them, and he shall be their shepherd.

24 And [a]I the LORD will be their God, and my servant David [b]a prince among them; I the LORD have spoken *it.*

M 25 And [a]I will make with them a covenant of peace, and [b]will cause the evil beasts to cease out of the land: and they [c]shall dwell safely in the wilderness, and sleep in the woods.

B U 26 And I will make them and the places round about [a]my hill [b]a blessing; and I will [c]cause the shower to come down in his season; there shall be [d]showers of blessing.

27 And [a]the tree of the field shall yield her fruit, and the earth shall yield her increase, and they shall be safe in their land, and shall know that I *am* the LORD, when I have [b]broken the bands of their yoke, and delivered them out of the hand of those that [c]served themselves of them.

28 And they shall no more be a prey to the heathen, neither shall the beast of the land devour them; but [a]they shall dwell safely, and none shall make *them* afraid.

29 And I will raise up for them a [a]plant [1]of renown, and they shall be no more [2]consumed with hunger in the land, [b]neither bear the shame of the heathen any more.

30 Thus shall they know that [a]I the LORD their God *am* with them, and *that* they, *even* the house of Israel, *are* my people, saith the Lord GOD.

31 And ye my [a]flock, the flock of my pasture, *are* men, *and* I *am* your God, saith the Lord GOD.

I *Eze 34:11–16* ◀ ▶ *Eze 36:8–12*
M *Eze 21:26–27* ◀ ▶ *Eze 34:25–28*
M *Eze 34:23–29* ◀ ▶ *Eze 37:22–28*
B *Pr 3:9–10* ◀ ▶ *Eze 36:30*
U *Jer 35:19* ◀ ▶ *Da 1:15*

Prophecy against mount Seir

35 MOREOVER THE word of the LORD came unto me, saying, J

2 Son of man, set thy face against [a]mount Seir, and [b]prophesy against it,

3 And say unto it, Thus saith the Lord GOD; Behold, O mount Seir, I *am* against thee, and [a]I will stretch out mine hand against thee, and I will make thee [1]most desolate.

4 I will lay thy cities waste, and thou shalt be desolate, and thou shalt know that I *am* the LORD.

5 [a]Because thou hast had a [1]perpetual hatred, and hast [2]shed *the blood of* the children of Israel by the [3]force of the sword in the time of their calamity, [b]in the time *that their* iniquity *had* an end:

6 Therefore, *as* I live, saith the Lord GOD, I will prepare thee unto blood, and blood shall pursue thee: [a]since thou hast not hated blood, even blood shall pursue thee.

7 Thus will I make mount Seir [1]most desolate, and cut off from it [a]him that passeth out and him that returneth.

8 And I will fill his mountains with his slain *men:* in thy hills, and in thy valleys, and in all thy rivers, shall they fall that are slain with the sword.

9 [a]I will make thee perpetual desolations, and thy cities shall not return: [b]and ye shall know that I *am* the LORD.

10 Because thou hast said, These two nations and these two countries shall be mine, and we will [a]possess it; [1]whereas [b]the LORD was there:

11 Therefore, *as* I live, saith the Lord GOD, I will even do [a]according to thine anger, and according to thine envy which thou hast used out of thy hatred against them; and I will make myself known among them, when I have judged thee.

J *Eze 29:19–20* ◀ ▶ *Da 4:10–17*

23 [a]Is. 40:11; John 10:11; Heb. 13:20; 1 Pet. 2:25 [b]Jer. 30:9; Hos. 3:5
24 [a]Ex. 29:45 [b]ch. 37:22
25 [a]ch. 37:26 [b]Lev. 26:6; Is. 11:6-9; Hos. 2:18 [c]Jer. 23:6
26 [a]Is. 56:7 [b]Gen. 12:2; Is. 19:24; Zech. 8:13 [c]Lev. 26:4 [d]Ps. 68:9
27 [a]Lev. 26:4; Ps. 85:12; Is. 4:2 [b]Jer. 2:20 [c]Jer. 25:14
28 [a]Jer. 30:10
29 [a]Is. 11:1 [b]ch. 36:3,6 [1]Or, *for renown* [2]Heb. *taken away*
30 [a]ver. 24
31 [a]Ps. 100:3; John 10:11
35:2 [a]Deut. 2:5 [b]Amos 1:11
3 [a]ch. 6:14 [1]Heb. *desolation and desolation*
5 [a]ch. 25:12 [b]Ps. 137:7; Dan. 9:24 [1]Or, *hatred of old* [2]Heb. *poured out the children* [3]Heb. *hands*
6 [a]Ps. 109:17
7 [a]Judg. 5:6 [1]Heb. *desolation and desolation*
9 [a]Jer. 49:17 [b]ch. 36:11
10 [a]Ps. 83:4,12 [b]Ps. 48:1,3; ch. 48:35 [1]Or, *though the LORD was there*
11 [a]Mat. 7:2; Jas. 2:13

34:22–31 God promised to "set up one shepherd over them" (34:22), indicating that the Messiah, the Son of David, would finally rule over God's people in his peaceful millennial kingdom. Note that this prophecy involved a removal of the wild beasts (34:25, 28) that could kill the sheep. This imagery confirms that Israel will find peace, security and an absence of hostility when the Messiah rules in power and glory.

12 [a]And thou shalt know that I *am* the LORD, *and that* I have heard all thy blasphemies which thou hast spoken against the mountains of Israel, saying, They are laid desolate, they are given us [1]to consume.

13 Thus [a]with your mouth ye have [1]boasted against me, and have multiplied your words against me: I have heard *them.*

H 14 Thus saith the Lord GOD; [a]When the whole earth rejoiceth, I will make thee desolate.

15 [a]As thou didst rejoice at the inheritance of the house of Israel, because it was desolate, so will I do unto thee: thou shalt be desolate, O mount Seir, and all Idumea, *even* all of it: and they shall know that I *am* the LORD.

A prophecy to Israel

36 ALSO, THOU son of man, prophesy unto the [a]mountains of Israel, and say, Ye mountains of Israel, hear the word of the LORD:

2 Thus saith the Lord GOD; Because [a]the enemy hath said against you, Aha, [b]even the ancient high places [c]are ours in possession:

R 3 Therefore prophesy and say, Thus saith the Lord GOD; [1]Because they have made *you* desolate, and swallowed you up on every side, that ye might be a possession unto the residue of the heathen, [a]and [2]ye are taken up in the lips of talkers, and *are* an infamy of the people:

4 Therefore, ye mountains of Israel, hear the word of the Lord GOD; Thus saith the Lord GOD to the mountains, and to the hills, to the [1]rivers, and to the valleys, to the desolate wastes, and to the cities that are forsaken, which [a]became a prey and [b]derision to the residue of the heathen that *are* round about;

5 Therefore thus saith the Lord GOD; [a]Surely in the fire of my jealousy have I spoken against the residue of the heathen, and against all Idumea, [b]which have appointed my land into their possession with the joy of all *their* heart, with despiteful minds, to cast it out for a prey.

6 Prophesy therefore concerning the land of Israel, and say unto the mountains, and to the hills, to the rivers, and to the valleys, Thus saith the Lord GOD; Behold, I have spoken in my jealousy and in my fury, because ye have [a]borne the shame of the heathen:

7 Therefore thus saith the Lord GOD; I have [a]lifted up mine hand, Surely the heathen that *are* about you, they shall bear their shame.

8 ¶ But ye, O mountains of Israel, ye shall shoot forth your branches, and yield your fruit to my people of Israel; for they are at hand to come. I

9 For, behold, I *am* for you, and I will turn unto you, and ye shall be tilled and sown:

10 And I will multiply men upon you, all the house of Israel, *even* all of it: and the cities shall be inhabited, and [a]the wastes shall be builded:

11 And [a]I will multiply upon you man and beast; and they shall increase and bring fruit: and I will settle you after your old estates, and will do better *unto you* than at your beginnings: [b]and ye shall know that I *am* the LORD.

12 Yea, I will cause men to walk upon you, *even* my people Israel; [a]and they shall possess thee, and thou shalt be their inheritance, and thou shalt no more henceforth [b]bereave them *of men.*

13 Thus saith the Lord GOD; Because they say unto you, [a]Thou *land* devourest up men, and hast bereaved thy nations;

14 Therefore thou shalt devour men no more, neither [1]bereave thy nations any more, saith the Lord GOD.

15 [a]Neither will I cause *men* to hear in thee the shame of the heathen any more, neither shalt thou bear the reproach of the people any more, neither shalt thou cause thy nations to fall any more, saith the Lord GOD.

16 ¶ Moreover the word of the LORD came unto me, saying,

17 Son of man, when the house of Israel dwelt in their own land, [a]they de-

12 [a]Ps. 9:16 [1]Heb. *to devour*
13 [a]1 Sam. 2:3 [1]Heb. *magnified*
14 [a]Is. 65:13
15 [a]Obad. 12,15
36:1 [a]ch. 6:2,3
2 [a]ch. 25:3 [b]Deut. 32:13 [c]ch. 35:10
3 [a]Deut. 28:37 [1]Heb. *Because for because* [2]Or, *ye are made to come upon the lip of the tongue*
4 [a]ch. 34:28 [b]Ps. 79:4 [1]Or, *bottoms,* or, *dales*
5 [a]Deut. 4:24; ch. 38:19 [b]ch. 35:10, 12
6 [a]ver. 15; Ps. 123:3,4; ch. 34:29
7 [a]ch. 20:5
10 [a]ver. 33; Is. 58:12 & 61:4; Amos 9:14
11 [a]Jer. 31:27 & 33:12 [b]ch. 35:9 & 37:6,13
12 [a]Obad. 17 [b]See Jer. 15:7
13 [a]Num. 13:32
14 [1]Or, *cause to fall*
15 [a]ch. 34:29
17 [a]Lev. 18:25,27, 28; Jer. 2:7

H *Eze 33:13* ◀ ▶ *Da 5:1–6*
R *Eze 34:5–10* ◀ ▶ *Eze 36:18–19*
I *Eze 34:22* ◀ ▶ *Eze 37:1–28*

36:8–12 Despite God's imminent judgment, God promised restoration for his people, their cities and their land. In fact, their blessings in the last days will exceed their former blessings. Compare this promise with Job's account (see Job 42:10).

filed it by their own way and by their doings: their way was before me as [b]the uncleanness of a removed woman.

R 18 Wherefore I poured my fury upon them [a]for the blood that they had shed upon the land, and for their idols *wherewith* they had polluted it:

19 And I scattered them among the heathen, and they were dispersed through the countries: [a]according to their way and according to their doings I judged them.

20 And when they entered unto the heathen, whither they went, they [a]profaned my holy name, when they said to them, These *are* the people of the LORD, and are gone forth out of his land.

21 ¶ But I had pity [a]for mine holy name, which the house of Israel had profaned among the heathen, whither they went.

22 Therefore say unto the house of Israel, Thus saith the Lord GOD; I do not *this* for your sakes, O house of Israel, [a]but for mine holy name's sake, which ye have profaned among the heathen, whither ye went.

23 And I will sanctify my great name, which was profaned among the heathen, which ye have profaned in the midst of them; and the heathen shall know that I *am* the LORD, saith the Lord GOD, when I shall be [a]sanctified in you before [1]their eyes.

24 For [a]I will take you from among the heathen, and gather you out of all countries, and will bring you into your own land.

R S K L S 25 ¶ [a]Then will I sprinkle clean water upon you, and ye shall be clean: [b]from all your filthiness, and from all your idols, will I cleanse you.

26 A [a]new heart also will I give you, and a new spirit will I put within you: and I will take away the stony heart out of your flesh, and I will give you an heart of flesh. B P

27 And I will put my [a]spirit within you, and cause you to walk in my statutes, and ye shall keep my judgments, and do *them*. L M

28 [a]And ye shall dwell in the land that I gave to your fathers; [b]and ye shall be my people, and I will be your God.

29 I will also [a]save you from all your uncleannesses: and [b]I will call for the corn, and will increase it, and [c]lay no famine upon you. K L S

30 [a]And I will multiply the fruit of the tree, and the increase of the field, that ye shall receive no more reproach of famine among the heathen. B

31 Then [a]shall ye remember your own evil ways, and your doings that *were* not good, and [b]shall loathe yourselves in your own sight for your iniquities and for your abominations.

32 [a]Not for your sakes do I *this*, saith the Lord GOD, be it known unto you: be ashamed and confounded for your own ways, O house of Israel.

33 Thus saith the Lord GOD; In the day that I shall have cleansed you from all your iniquities I will also cause *you* to dwell in the cities, [a]and the wastes shall be builded. K

34 And the desolate land shall be

17 [b]Lev. 15:19
18 [a]ch. 16:36,38; & 23:37
19 [a]ch. 7:3 & 18:30 & 39:24
20 [a]Is. 52:5; Rom. 2:24
21 [a]ch. 20:9,14
22 [a]Ps. 106:8
23 [a]ch. 20:41 & 28:22 [1]Or, *your*
24 [a]ch. 34:13 & 37:21
25 [a]Is. 52:15; Heb. 10:22 [b]Jer. 33:8
26 [a]Jer. 32:39; ch. 11:19
27 [a]ch. 11:19 & 37:14
28 [a]ch. 28:25 & 37:25 [b]Jer. 30:22; ch. 11:20 & 37:27
29 [a]Mat. 1:21; Rom. 11:26 [b]See Ps. 105:16 [c]ch. 34:29
30 [a]ch. 34:27
31 [a]ch. 16:61,63 [b]Lev. 26:39; ch. 6:9 & 20:43
32 [a]ver. 22; Deut. 9:5
33 [a]ver. 10

R *Eze 36:3–7* ◀▶ *Eze 39:21–24*
R *Eze 11:19* ◀▶ *Lk 1:17*
S *Eze 11:19* ◀▶ *Mic 2:7*
K *Eze 12:25* ◀▶ *Eze 36:29*
L *Eze 34:11–12* ◀▶ *Eze 36:29*
S *Eze 33:31* ◀▶ *Eze 36:29*

B *Eze 11:19* ◀▶ *Eze 37:14*
P *Eze 11:19* ◀▶ *Joel 2:28–29*
L *Eze 13:3* ◀▶ *Mt 4:1*
M *Eze 3:24* ◀▶ *Eze 37:14*
K *Eze 36:25–26* ◀▶ *Eze 36:33*
L *Eze 36:25* ◀▶ *Da 9:9*
S *Eze 36:25–27* ◀▶ *Hos 10:2*
B *Eze 34:26–27* ◀▶ *Hos 2:21–22*
K *Eze 36:29* ◀▶ *Eze 37:23*

36:18–19 God declared that the Jews' exile was a direct result of their wickedness.

36:22–24 God's determination to restore his chosen people to their land was not because of anything they had done, but rather to show his holiness and faithfulness to them. When the nations witnessed this restoration then they would also "know that I am the LORD" (36:23).

36:25–38 The ritual of sprinkling water upon someone removed their religious depravity (see Ex 30:17–21; Lev 14:52; Nu 19:17–19). The outpouring of the Holy Spirit is also a sign of the Messiah's kingdom. In this prophecy God promised to cleanse his people, give them a new heart and fill them with his Spirit. Other millennial blessings include repossession of the land, renewed relationship with God, increased fertility in the land and the end of Israel's continued rebellion against God.

tilled, whereas it lay desolate in the sight
of all that passed by.
35 And they shall say, This land that
was desolate is become like the garden of
[a]Eden; and the waste and desolate and
ruined cities *are become* fenced, *and* are
inhabited.
36 Then the heathen that are left
round about you shall know that I the
LORD build the ruined *places, and* plant
that that was desolate: [a]I the LORD have
spoken *it,* and I will do *it.*
37 Thus saith the Lord GOD; [a]I will yet
for this be inquired of by the house of
Israel, to do *it* for them; I will [b]increase
them with men like a flock.
38 As the [l]holy flock, as the flock of
Jerusalem in her solemn feasts; so shall
the waste cities be filled with flocks of
men: and they shall know that I *am* the
LORD.

Vision of dry bones in the valley

I 37 THE [a]HAND of the LORD was
E upon me, and carried me out [b]in
N the spirit of the LORD, and set me down in
the midst of the valley which *was* full of
bones,
2 And caused me to pass by them
round about: and, behold, *there were*
very many in the open [l]valley; and, lo,
they were very dry.
3 And he said unto me, Son of man,
can these bones live? And I answered,
O Lord GOD, [a]thou knowest.
4 Again he said unto me, Prophesy
upon these bones, and say unto them,
O ye dry bones, hear the word of the
LORD.
5 Thus saith the Lord GOD unto these
bones; Behold, I will [a]cause breath to enter into you, and ye shall live:
6 And I will lay sinews upon you, and
will bring up flesh upon you, and cover
you with skin, and put breath in you, and
ye shall live; [a]and ye shall know that I *am*
the LORD.
7 So I prophesied as I was commanded: and as I prophesied, there was
a noise, and behold a shaking, and the
bones came together, bone to his bone.
8 And when I beheld, lo, the sinews
and the flesh came up upon them, and
the skin covered them above: but *there
was* no breath in them.
9 Then said he unto me, Prophesy
unto the [l]wind, prophesy, son of man,
and say to the wind, Thus saith the Lord
GOD; [a]Come from the four winds,
O breath, and breathe upon these slain,
that they may live.
10 So I prophesied as he commanded
me, [a]and the breath came into them, and
they lived, and stood up upon their feet,
an exceeding great army.
11 ¶ Then he said unto me, Son of
man, these bones are the whole house of
Israel: behold, they say, [a]Our bones are
dried, and our hope is lost: we are cut off
for our parts.
12 Therefore prophesy and say unto F
them, Thus saith the Lord GOD; Behold,
[a]O my people, I will open your graves,
and cause you to come up out of your
graves, and [b]bring you into the land of
Israel.
13 And ye shall know that I *am* the H
LORD, when I have opened your graves,
O my people, and brought you up out of
your graves,
14 And [a]shall put my spirit in you, and B
ye shall live, and I shall place you in your M
own land: then shall ye know that I the
LORD have spoken *it,* and performed *it,*
saith the LORD.

The parable of the two sticks

15 ¶ The word of the LORD came again
unto me, saying,

35 [a]Is. 51:3; ch. 28:13; Joel 2:3
36 [a]ch. 17:24 & 22:14 & 37:14
37 [a]See ch. 14:3 & 20:3,31 [b]ver. 10
38 [l]Heb. *flock of holy things*
37:1 [a]ch. 1:3 [b]ch. 3:14 & 8:3 & 11:24; Luke 4:1
2 [l]Or, *champaign*
3 [a]Deut. 32:39; 1 Sam. 2:6; John 5:21; Rom. 4:17; 2 Cor. 1:9
5 [a]ver. 9; Ps. 104:30
6 [a]ch. 6:7 & 35:12; Joel 2:27 & 3:17
9 [a]ver. 5; Ps. 104:30 [l]Or, *breath*
10 [a]Rev. 11:11
11 [a]Ps. 141:7; Is. 49:14
12 [a]Is. 26:19; Hos. 13:14 [b]ver. 25; ch. 36:24
14 [a]ch. 36:27

I *Eze 36:8–12* ◀ ▶ *Eze 38:8*
E *Eze 13:3* ◀ ▶ *Eze 43:5*
N *Eze 8:3* ◀ ▶ *Eze 43:4–5*

F *Isa 26:19* ◀ ▶ *Da 12:2*
H *Job 33:4* ◀ ▶ *Mt 12:28*
B *Eze 36:26–27* ◀ ▶ *Da 4:8–9*
M *Eze 36:27* ◀ ▶ *Da 4:8–9*

37:1–14 Though this is one of Ezekiel's major visions, no date is given in this passage. Israel was a hopeless nation, languishing like dry bones in a land of exile. Ezekiel's words gave immediate hope to the exiles that they would be restored to their land (37:14). Yet Ezekiel's words also foreshadowed the spiritual restoration of Israel at Christ's second coming. Israel's restoration would be God's proof of his power and rule.
37:15–28 The prophet indicated that in the last days God would finally restore the northern kingdom of Israel that was exiled in 721 B.C. and join them with the exiled kingdom of Judah so that they would never again "be divided into two kingdoms"

16 Moreover, thou son of man, [a]take thee one stick, and write upon it, For Judah, and for [b]the children of Israel his companions: then take another stick, and write upon it, For Joseph, the stick of Ephraim, and *for* all the house of Israel his companions:

17 And [a]join them one to another into one stick; and they shall become one in thine hand.

18 ¶ And when the children of thy people shall speak unto thee, saying, [a]Wilt thou not show us what thou *meanest* by these?

19 [a]Say unto them, Thus saith the Lord GOD; Behold, I will take [b]the stick of Joseph, which *is* in the hand of Ephraim, and the tribes of Israel his fellows, and will put them with him, *even* with the stick of Judah, and make them one stick, and they shall be one in mine hand.

20 ¶ And the sticks whereon thou writest shall be in thine hand [a]before their eyes.

21 And say unto them, Thus saith the Lord GOD; Behold, [a]I will take the children of Israel from among the heathen, whither they be gone, and will gather them on every side, and bring them into their own land:

M 22 And [a]I will make them one nation in the land upon the mountains of Israel; and [b]one king shall be king to them all: and they shall be no more two nations, neither shall they be divided into two kingdoms any more at all:

K 23 [a]Neither shall they defile themselves any more with their idols, nor with their detestable things, nor with any of their transgressions: but [b]I will save them out of all their dwellingplaces, wherein they have sinned, and will cleanse them: so shall they be my people, and I will be their God.

24 And [a]David my servant *shall be* king over them; and [b]they all shall have one shepherd: [c]they shall also walk in my judgments, and observe my statutes, and do them.

25 [a]And they shall dwell in the land that I have given unto Jacob my servant, wherein your fathers have dwelt; and they shall dwell therein, *even* they, and their children, and their children's children [b]for ever: and [c]my servant David *shall be* their prince for ever.

26 Moreover I will make a [a]covenant of peace with them; it shall be an everlasting covenant with them: and I will place them, and [b]multiply them, and will set my [c]sanctuary in the midst of them for evermore.

27 [a]My tabernacle also shall be with them: yea, I will be [b]their God, and they shall be my people.

28 [a]And the heathen shall know that I the LORD do [b]sanctify Israel, when my sanctuary shall be in the midst of them for evermore.

Prophecy against Gog

38 AND THE word of the LORD came P
unto me, saying,

2 [a]Son of man, [b]set thy face against [c]Gog, the land of Magog, [1]the chief prince of [d]Meshech and Tubal, and prophesy against him,

3 And say, Thus saith the Lord GOD; Behold, I *am* against thee, O Gog, the chief prince of Meshech and Tubal:

4 And [a]I will turn thee back, and put

16 [a]See Num. 17:2 [b]2 Chr. 11:12,13, 16 & 15:9 & 30:11,18
17 [a]See ver. 22,24
18 [a]ch. 12:9 & 24:19
19 [a]Zech. 10:6 [b]ver. 16,17
20 [a]ch. 12:3
21 [a]ch. 36:24
22 [a]Is. 11:13; Jer. 3:18; Hos. 1:11 [b]ch. 34:23; John 10:16
23 [a]ch. 36:25 [b]ch. 36:28
24 [a]Is. 40:11; Jer. 23:5; Luke 1:32 [b]John 10:16 [c]ch. 36:27
25 [a]ch. 36:28 [b]Is. 60:21; Joel 3:20; Amos 9:15 [c]John 12:34
26 [a]Ps. 89:3; Is. 55:3; Jer. 32:40 [b]ch. 36:10 [c]2 Cor. 6:16
27 [a]Lev. 26:11; John 1:14 [b]ch. 11:20
28 [a]ch. 36:23 [b]ch. 20:12
38:2 [a]ch. 39:1 [b]ch. 35:2,3 [c]Rev. 20:8 [d]ch. 32:26 [1]Or, *prince of the chief*
4 [a]2 Ki. 19:28; ch. 29:4

M *Eze 34:25–28* ◀ ▶ *Eze 43:5–7*
K *Eze 36:33* ◀ ▶ *Joel 2:32*
P *Jer 49:39* ◀ ▶ *Eze 39:1–22*

(37:22). James echoed this prophecy in his salutation to "the twelve tribes which are scattered abroad" (Jas 1:1). Though Jews of each tribe have begun to return to Palestine, a careful examination of Ezekiel's prophecy reveals that these words will not be completely fulfilled until the second coming of Christ.

Note also that this passage called the Messiah "David" because he would be a descendant of David and bring to Israel all the good aspects of David's rule—and much more (37:24).

38:1–7 Ezekiel prophesied that in the last days, after the return of the Jews to the promised land, a confederacy of nations would join together militarily to invade and destroy Palestine. Ezekiel called the leader of this alliance "Gog," who was "the chief prince of Meshech and Tubal" (38:2).

Ezekiel declared God's determination to stand against Gog and destroy the armies and leaders that attempt to destroy God's people. Though the alliance is strong, God is the one who will control the outcome of the battle and will lead Gog around like a beast with a bit in its mouth. For more information about Gog and Magog, see the article "The Battle of Gog and Magog," p. 930.

hooks into thy jaws, and I will bring thee
forth, and all thine army, horses and
horsemen, [b]all of them clothed with all
sorts *of armour, even* a great company
with bucklers and shields, all of them
handling swords:
5 Persia, Ethiopia, and [1]Libya with
them; all of them with shield and helmet:
6 [a]Gomer, and all his bands; the house
of [b]Togarmah of the north quarters, and
all his bands: *and* many people with thee.
7 [a]Be thou prepared, and prepare for
thyself, thou, and all thy company that
are assembled unto thee, and be thou a
guard unto them.
8 ¶ [a]After many days [b]thou shalt be
visited: in the latter years thou shalt
come into the land *that is* brought back
from the sword, [c]*and is* gathered out of
many people, against [d]the mountains of
Israel, which have been always waste:
but it is brought forth out of the nations,
and they shall [e]dwell safely all of them.
9 Thou shalt ascend and come [a]like a
storm, thou shalt be [b]like a cloud to cover
the land, thou, and all thy bands, and
many people with thee.
10 Thus saith the Lord GOD; It shall
also come to pass, *that* at the same time
shall things come into thy mind, and thou
shalt [1]think an evil thought:
11 And thou shalt say, I will go up to
the land of unwalled villages; I will [a]go to
them that are at rest, [b]that dwell [1]safely,
all of them dwelling without walls, and
having neither bars nor gates,
12 [a]To[1] take a spoil, and to take a
prey; to turn thine hand upon the deso-

Eze 37:1–28 ◀▶ *Eze 38:11–12*
Eze 38:8 ◀▶ *Eze 38:14*

4 [b]ch. 23:12
5 [1]Or, *Phut;* see ch. 27:10
6 [a]Gen. 10:2 [b]ch. 27:14
7 [a]Is. 8:9,10; Jer. 46:3,4
8 [a]ver. 16; Deut. 4:30 [b]Is. 29:6 [c]ch. 34:13 [d]ch. 36:1,4 [e]Jer. 23:6
9 [a]Is. 28:2 [b]Jer. 4:13
10 [1]Or, *conceive a mischievous purpose*
11 [a]Jer. 49:31 [b]ver. 8 [1]Or, *confidently*
12 [a]ch. 29:19 [b]ver. 8 [1]Heb. *To spoil the spoil, and to prey the prey* [2]Heb. *navel;* see Judg. 9:37
13 [a]ch. 27:22 [b]ch. 27:15 [c]ch. 27:12 [d]ch. 19:3,5
14 [a]Is. 4:1 [b]ver. 8
15 [a]ch. 39:2 [b]ver. 6
16 [a]ver. 9 [b]ver. 8
17 [1]Heb. *by the hands*

late places *that are now* inhabited, [b]and
upon the people *that are* gathered out of
the nations, which have gotten cattle and
goods, that dwell in the [2]midst of the
land.
13 [a]Sheba, and [b]Dedan, and the merchants [c]of Tarshish, with all [d]the young
lions thereof, shall say unto thee, Art
thou come to take a spoil? hast thou gathered thy company to take a prey? to carry
away silver and gold, to take away cattle
and goods, to take a great spoil?
14 ¶ Therefore, son of man, prophesy
and say unto Gog, Thus saith the Lord
GOD; [a]In that day when my people of Israel [b]dwelleth safely, shalt thou not
know *it?*
15 [a]And thou shalt come from thy
place out of the north parts, thou, [b]and
many people with thee, all of them riding
upon horses, a great company, and a
mighty army:
16 [a]And thou shalt come up against
my people of Israel, as a cloud to cover
the land; [b]it shall be in the latter days,
and I will bring thee against my land, that
the heathen may know me, when I shall
be sanctified in thee, O Gog, before their
eyes.
17 Thus saith the Lord GOD; *Art* thou
he of whom I have spoken in old time [1]by
my servants the prophets of Israel, which
prophesied in those days *many* years that
I would bring thee against them?
18 And it shall come to pass at the
same time when Gog shall come against
the land of Israel, saith the Lord GOD, *that*
my fury shall come up in my face.

Eze 38:11–12 ◀▶ *Eze 38:16*
Eze 38:14 ◀▶ *Eze 38:20*

38:8–16 The phrase "in the latter years" (38:8) designates the time when Gog will invade Israel. At this time in the future, the people of Israel are living in their own land (38:8) in relative safety (38:11). Their army has been strengthened, convincing the people of their ability to defeat all of their enemies. However, the size of the armies of the coalition and their sophisticated weapons will be overwhelming. This enemy alliance will invade Israel and "go up to the land of unwalled villages" (38:11) and swarm over them like "a cloud to cover the land" (38:16) and plunder Israel's wealth. Ezekiel's vision could well relate to our century or beyond because modern warfare with tanks, cruise missiles, bombers and paratroopers would find city walls and gates no hindrance to an invasion force.

Ezekiel's words about Sheba, Dedan and Tarshish, seem to reflect only a diplomatic complaint from these nations about this invasion, without any military response or aid being offered to Israel by these nations. Yet when God destroys Israel's enemies, he will forever demonstrate that he is the God of Israel. For more information about Gog and Magog, see the article "The Battle of Gog and Magog," p. 930.

38:17–23 Ezekiel prophesied that the destruction of Israel's enemies would come through divine intervention. When the coalition comes against Israel, God will send a great earthquake, plagues, rain, hail "fire and brimstone" (38:22) to destroy Israel's enemies and demonstrate his power and might.

The Battle of Gog and Magog

WHILE SOME SCHOLARS contend that Ezekiel's prophecy in chs. 38—39 is merely a symbol of the apocalyptic war between good and evil, specific details in Ezekiel's prophecy point to this event as a literal battle that will be waged sometime in the future. This war is referred to as the Battle of Gog and Magog.

The Identification of Gog and Magog

Ezekiel 38:3 describes Gog as the leader of a confederacy of northern nations. Described as a very strong leader, he will have the power to commit his allies to war. God will control Gog's mind and direct him to attack Israel (see 38:11). Gog will come from the land of Magog, a nation composed of three parts: Rosh, Meshech and Tubal. Therefore the identification of the land of Magog is of great interest to prophecy scholars.

Studying Genesis 10, scholars note that after the flood, Noah's descendants dispersed to various parts of Asia. Among them was Magog, a son of Japheth (see Ge 10:1–2). History indicates that Magog settled in what is now called the Caucasus region between the Black and Caspian Seas. The Greeks called Magog's descendants "Scythians." While some of these Scythians moved farther north into Europe, others remained in Asia and emigrated as far as the Urals, becoming the ancestors of the Tartars, Cossacks, Mongols and others. Thus identifying Magog with this area of southwest Russia seems feasible.

The Motive for the Battle

Ezekiel's prophecy indicates that Magog will attempt to destroy Israel and capture her land as a geographically strategic prize. This narrow strip of land has historically been fought over by any empire that wanted to dominate the world. Today, whoever controls this small strip of land along the Mediterranean controls the Middle East as well as the vital oil supplies that flow through it. Because of worldwide dependence on Middle East oil, this outcome of this strategic battle will affect the economies of all industrialized nations.

According to Ezekiel, Magog (Russia) will need help in acquiring the land of Israel and will form a confederation of nations to attack the promised land (see 38:1–6). Historians and Biblical scholars have identified these nations as modern-day Iran, some of the Arab states adjacent to Iran, Germany, Turkey and the central Asiatic peoples allied with Russia.

The Attack of the Confederation

The Bible describes several battles that will occur in the last days. The Battle of Gog and Magog will be the first major struggle against the land of Israel.

Biblical scholars generally agree that the battle described in Ezekiel will take place following an alliance between Magog (Russia) and its allies (38:2, 5–6). Though some nations will protest the invasion, it will proceed unhindered as Gog's armies marshal themselves in an open field (38:13; 39:5).

The Lord will unleash the greatest earthquake in history in response to the attack of Magog and the confederation. Other natural disasters will require seven months for Israel to bury the dead and seven years to burn up the confederation's weapons (39:4–12). God's intervention will cause many to repent (39:21–22). Even the Gentile nations will acknowledge God's power. Russia and her allies' military devastation will set the stage for the rebuilding of the temple in Jerusalem and the rise of antichrist.

The Time of the Battle

A final question in the minds of Bible scholars concerns the timing of this future battle. Scholars generally agree that this battle has not yet occurred because no invasion in Israel's history sufficiently fulfills the details of this prophecy. Though scholars agree that the conflict will occur at some point in the near future, before Armageddon, they differ on the exact timing of this battle. In fact, six different theories exist about its timing.

Some scholars believe this battle will occur either before, in the middle of, or after the tribulation. Others suggest that the battle will occur either at the beginning of or the end of the Millennium. Still others believe this conflict will occur prior to the rapture of the church. Because Scripture gives varying support to each of these theories, we cannot be dogmatic about the details.

However, this author subscribes to the belief that the battle will occur prior to the tribulation for several reasons. Note that Ezekiel's prophecy does not mention the antichrist, the seven-year treaty or Israel's expectation that anyone would protect them from an invading army. It seems inconsistent with the prophet to omit these details from his precise prediction if this invasion will occur during the seven-year period of peace between Israel and the antichrist. Note also that 38:11–12 indicates that Israel appears to be at peace. Ezekiel's vision does not suggest that Israel is living in total peace with her neighbors prior to the attack, but rather that Israel is secure in her position and not expecting an attack.

The results of this battle also help to place the event prior to the tribulation. Ezekiel prophesied that when the battle ends, only one-sixth of Magog's armies will remain (39:2). This massive destruction will profoundly alter the political and military balance of power, effectively removing Russia and her allies from a major role in future conflicts, and clearing the way for the antichrist's kingdom and final struggle at Armageddon.

19 For [a]in my jealousy [b]*and* in the fire
of my wrath have I spoken, [c]Surely in
that day there shall be a great shaking in
the land of Israel;
I 20 So that [a]the fishes of the sea, and
the fowls of the heaven, and the beasts
of the field, and all creeping things that
creep upon the earth, and all the men
that *are* upon the face of the earth, shall
shake at my presence, [b]and the mountains shall be thrown down, and the
[1]steep places shall fall, and every wall
shall fall to the ground.
21 And I will [a]call for [b]a sword against
him throughout all my mountains, saith
the Lord GOD: [c]every man's sword shall
be against his brother.
D 22 And I will [a]plead against him with
[b]pestilence and with blood; and [c]I will
rain upon him, and upon his bands, and
upon the many people that *are* with him,
an overflowing rain, and [d]great hailstones, fire, and brimstone.
23 Thus will I magnify myself, and
[a]sanctify myself; [b]and I will be known in
the eyes of many nations, and they shall
know that I *am* the LORD.
P 39 THEREFORE, [a]THOU son of
man, prophesy against Gog, and
say, Thus saith the Lord GOD; Behold, I
am against thee, O Gog, the chief prince
of Meshech and Tubal:
2 And I will turn thee back, and leave
but the sixth part of thee, [a]and will cause
thee to come up from [1]the north parts,
and will bring thee upon the mountains
of Israel:
3 And I will smite thy bow out of thy
left hand, and will cause thine arrows to
fall out of thy right hand.
4 [a]Thou shalt fall upon the mountains
of Israel, thou, and all thy bands, and the
people that *is* with thee: [b]I will give thee
unto the ravenous birds of every [1]sort,
and *to* the beasts of the field [2]to be devoured.
5 Thou shalt fall upon [1]the open field:
for I have spoken *it,* saith the Lord GOD.
6 [a]And I will send a fire on Magog, and
among them that dwell [1]carelessly in
[b]the isles: and they shall know that I *am*
the LORD.
7 [a]So will I make my holy name I
known in the midst of my people Israel;
and I will not *let them* [b]pollute my holy
name any more: [c]and the heathen shall
know that I *am* the LORD, the Holy One in
Israel.
8 ¶ [a]Behold, it is come, and it is done,
saith the Lord GOD; this *is* the day
[b]whereof I have spoken.
9 And they that dwell in the cities of
Israel shall go forth, and shall set on fire
and burn the weapons, both the shields
and the bucklers, the bows and the arrows, and the [1]handstaves, and the
spears, and they shall [2]burn them with
fire seven years:
10 So that they shall take no wood out
of the field, neither cut down *any* out of
the forests; for they shall burn the weapons with fire: [a]and they shall spoil those
that spoiled them, and rob those that
robbed them, saith the Lord GOD.
11 ¶ And it shall come to pass in that
day, *that* I will give unto Gog a place
there of graves in Israel, the valley of the
passengers on the east of the sea: and it
shall stop the [1]*noses* of the passengers:
and there shall they bury Gog and all his
multitude: and they shall call *it* The valley
of [2]Hamon-gog.
12 And seven months shall the house
of Israel be burying of them, [a]that they
may cleanse the land.
13 Yea, all the people of the land shall
bury *them;* and it shall be to them a renown the day that [a]I shall be glorified,
saith the Lord GOD.
14 And they shall sever out [1]men of
continual employment, passing through

19 [a]ch. 36:5,6 [b]Ps. 89:46 [c]Hag. 2:6,7; Rev. 16:18
20 [a]Hos. 4:3 [b]Jer. 4:24 [1]Or, *towers,* or, *stairs*
21 [a]Ps. 105:16 [b]ch. 14:17 [c]Judg. 7:22; 1 Sam. 14:20
22 [a]Is. 66:16; Jer. 25:31 [b]ch. 5:17 [c]Ps. 11:6; Is. 30:30 [d]Rev. 16:21
23 [a]ch. 36:23 [b]ch. 37:28
39:1 [a]ch. 38:2,3
2 [a]ch. 38:15 [1]Heb. *the sides of the north*
4 [a]ch. 38:21 [b]ch. 33:27 [1]Heb. *wing* [2]Heb. *to devour*
5 [1]Heb. *the face of the field*
6 [a]Amos 1:4 [b]Ps. 72:10 [1]Or, *confidently*
7 [a]ver. 22 [b]Lev. 18:21 [c]ch. 38:16
8 [a]Rev. 16:17 & 21:6 [b]ch. 38:17
9 [1]Or, *javelins* [2]Or, *make a fire of them*
10 [a]Is. 14:2
11 [1]Or, mouths [2]i.e., *The multitude of Gog*
12 [a]Deut. 21:23
13 [a]ch. 28:22
14 [1]Heb. *men of continuance*

I *Eze 38:16* ◄► *Eze 39:7–10*
D *Eze 33:27* ◄► *Mt 13:58*
P *Eze 38:1–23* ◄► *Da 12:1*

I *Eze 38:20* ◄► *Eze 39:25–29*

39:1–10 God declared that the destruction of Gog and his forces would be horrific, not only involving two-thirds of their armies but their homelands too. The amount of weapons gathered by Israel from this battle would also be so large that Israel would be able to use these weapons as fuel for their fires for seven years.

39:11–20 God declared he would provide a cemetery for the slain of Gog's armies. The number of dead bodies would be so extensive it would take seven months to bury them all. The slaughter would be so terrible that predatory animals and birds would gorge on the bodies of Gog's soldiers killed in this battle.

the land to bury with the passengers
those that remain upon the face of the
earth, [a]to cleanse it: after the end of
seven months shall they search.
15 And the passengers *that* pass
through the land, when *any* seeth a
man's bone, then shall he [1]set up a sign
by it, till the buriers have buried it in the
valley of Hamon-gog.
16 And also the name of the city *shall*
be [1]Hamonah. Thus shall they [a]cleanse
the land.
17 ¶ And, thou son of man, thus saith
the Lord GOD; [a]Speak [1]unto every feath-
ered fowl, and to every beast of the field,
[b]Assemble yourselves, and come; gather
yourselves on every side to my [2]sacrifice
that I do sacrifice for you, *even* a great
sacrifice [c]upon the mountains of Israel,
that ye may eat flesh, and drink blood.
18 [a]Ye shall eat the flesh of the
mighty, and drink the blood of the
princes of the earth, of rams, of lambs,
and of [1]goats, of bullocks, all of them [b]fat-
lings of Bashan.
19 And ye shall eat fat till ye be full,
and drink blood till ye be drunken, of my
sacrifice which I have sacrificed for you.
20 [a]Thus ye shall be filled at my table
with horses and chariots, [b]with mighty
men, and with all men of war, saith the
Lord GOD.
21 [a]And I will set my glory among the R
heathen, and all the heathen shall see my

14 [a]ver. 12
15 [1]Heb. *build*
16 [a]ver. 12 [1]i.e. *The multitude*
17 [a]Rev. 19:7 [b]Is. 18:6; Zeph. 1:7 [c]ver. 4 [1]Heb. *to the fowl of every wing* [2]Or, *slaughter*
18 [a]Rev. 19:18 [b]Deut. 32:14; Ps. 22:12 [1]Heb. *great goats*
20 [a]Ps. 76:6; ch. 38:4 [b]Rev. 19:18
21 [a]ch. 38:16,23

R *Eze 36:18–19* ◄ ► *Eze 39:26*

39:21–29 As a postscript to the horror of the battle, God declared his intent to graciously restore Israel in the last days so that the nations would acknowledge God's glory. God's visible presence and intervention in history would be a glorious display of his power to the heathen nations.

The Nations of Ezekiel 38—39

The War of Gog and Magog

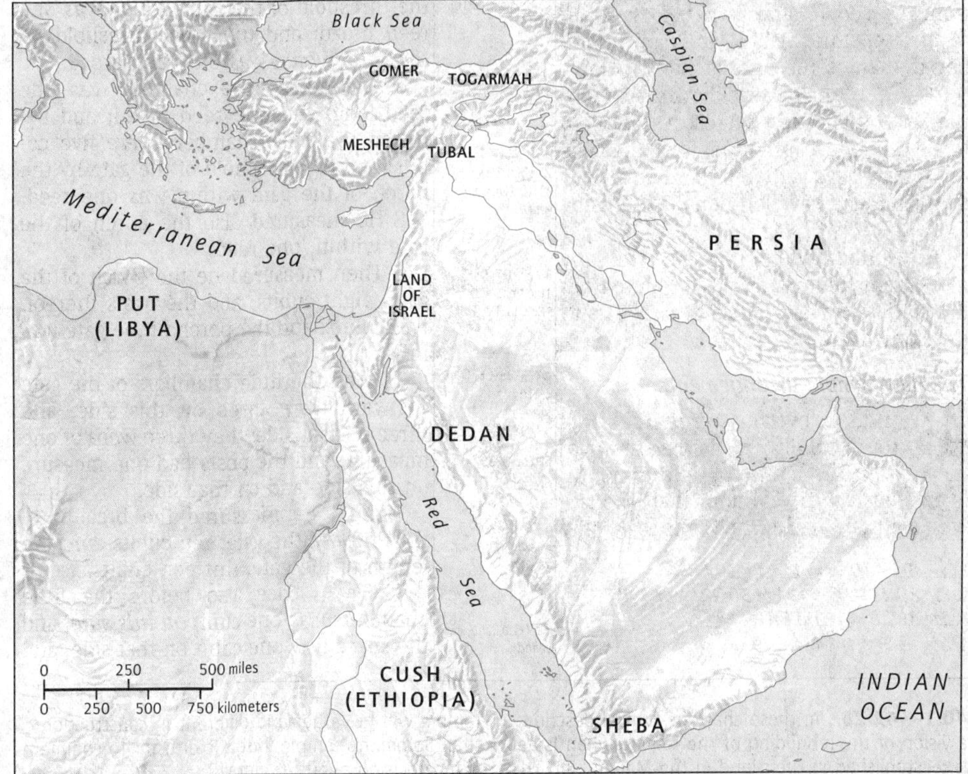

judgment that I have executed, and [b]my hand that I have laid upon them.

22 [a]So the house of Israel shall know that I *am* the LORD their God from that day and forward.

23 ¶ [a]And the heathen shall know that the house of Israel went into captivity for their iniquity: because they trespassed against me, therefore [b]hid I my face from them, and [c]gave them into the hand of their enemies: so fell they all by the sword.

24 [a]According to their uncleanness and according to their transgressions have I done unto them, and hid my face from them.

I 25 Therefore thus saith the Lord GOD; [a]Now will I bring again the captivity of Jacob, and have mercy upon the [b]whole house of Israel, and will be jealous for my holy name;

R 26 [a]After that they have borne their shame, and all their trespasses whereby they have trespassed against me, when they [b]dwelt safely in their land, and none made *them* afraid.

27 [a]When I have brought them again from the people, and gathered them out of their enemies' lands, and [b]am sanctified in them in the sight of many nations;

R 28 [a]Then shall they know that I *am* the LORD their God, [/]which caused them to be led into captivity among the heathen: but I have gathered them unto their own land, and have left none of them any more there.

29 [a]Neither will I hide my face any more from them: for I have [b]poured out my spirit upon the house of Israel, saith the Lord GOD.

The new temple arrangements

T 40 IN THE five and twentieth year of our captivity, in the beginning of the year, in the tenth *day* of the month, in the fourteenth year after that [a]the city was smitten, in the selfsame day [b]the hand of the LORD was upon me, and brought me thither.

2 [a]In the visions of God brought he me into the land of Israel, and [b]set me upon a very high mountain, [/]by which *was* as the frame of a city on the south.

3 And he brought me thither, and, behold, *there was* a man, whose appearance *was* [a]like the appearance of brass, [b]with a line of flax in his hand, [c]and a measuring reed; and he stood in the gate.

4 And the man said unto me, [a]Son of man, behold with thine eyes, and hear with thine ears, and set thine heart upon all that I shall show thee; for to the intent that I might show *them* unto thee *art* thou brought hither: [b]declare all that thou seest to the house of Israel.

5 And behold [a]a wall on the outside of the house round about, and in the man's hand a measuring reed of six cubits *long* by the cubit and an handbreadth: so he measured the breadth of the building, one reed; and the height, one reed.

6 ¶ Then came he unto the gate [/]which looketh toward the east, and went up the stairs thereof, and measured the threshold of the gate, *which was* one reed broad; and the other threshold *of the gate, which was* one reed broad.

7 And *every* little chamber *was* one reed long, and one reed broad; and between the little chambers *were* five cubits; and the threshold of the gate by the porch of the gate within *was* one reed.

8 He measured also the porch of the gate within, one reed.

9 Then measured he the porch of the gate, eight cubits; and the posts thereof, two cubits; and the porch of the gate *was* inward.

10 And the little chambers of the gate eastward *were* three on this side, and three on that side; they three *were* of one measure: and the posts had one measure on this side and on that side.

11 And he measured the breadth of the entry of the gate, ten cubits; *and* the length of the gate, thirteen cubits.

12 The [/]space also before the little chambers *was* one cubit *on this side,* and the space *was* one cubit on that side: and

21 [b]Ex. 7:4
22 [a]ver. 7,28
23 [a]ch. 36:18-20, **23** [b]Deut. 31:17; Is. 59:2 [c]Lev. 26:25
24 [a]ch. 36:19
25 [a]Jer. 30:3,18; ch. 34:13 & 36:24 [b]ch. 20:40; Hos. 1:11
26 [a]Dan. 9:16 [b]Lev. 26:5,6
27 [a]ch. 28:25,26 [b]ch. 36:23,24 & 38:16
28 [a]ver. 22; ch. 34:30 [/]Heb. *by my causing of them*
29 [a]Is. 54:8 [b]Joel 2:28; Zech. 12:10; Acts 2:17
40:1 [a]ch. 33:21 [b]ch. 1:3
2 [a]ch. 8:3 [b]Rev. 21:10 [/]Or, *upon which*
3 [a]ch. 1:7; Dan. 10:6 [b]ch. 47:3 [c]Rev. 11:1 & 21:15
4 [a]ch. 44:5 [b]ch. 43:10
5 [a]ch. 42:20
6 [/]Heb. *whose face was the way toward the east*
12 [/]Heb. *limit,* or, *bound*

I *Eze 39:7–10* ◀ ▶ *Eze 43:5–7*
R *Eze 39:21–24* ◀ ▶ *Eze 39:28*
R *Eze 39:26* ◀ ▶ *Da 8:11–14*
T *Eze 13:3* ◀ ▶ *Da 4:8–9*

40:1—42:20 In these chapters Ezekiel describes a vision of the rebuilding of the temple when Israel is reestablished in their land in the Millennium. This temple will be larger and different in construction than Solomon's temple, but it is difficult to comment with precision about its details.

Ezekiel's Temple

A. Wall (40:5,16-20)
B. East gate (40:6-14,16)
C. Portico (40:8)
D. Outer court (40:17)
E. Pavement (40:17)
F. Inner court (40:19)
G. North gate (40:20-22)
H. Inner court (40:23)
I. South gate (40:24-26)
J. South inner court (40:27)
K. Gateway (40:28-31)
L. Gateway (40:32-34)
M. Gateway (40:35-38)
N. Priests' rooms (40:44-45)
O. Court (40:47)
P. Temple portico (40:48-49)
Q. Outer sanctuary (41:1-2)
R. Most Holy Place (41:3-4)
S. Temple walls (41:5-7,9,11)
T. Base (41:8)
U. Open area (41:10)
V. West building (41:12)
W. Priests' rooms (42:1-10)
X. Altar (43:13-17)
AA. Rooms for preparing sacrifices (40:39-43)
BB. Ovens (46:19-20)
CC. Kitchens (46:21-24)

Ezekiel uses a long or "royal" cubit, 20.4 inches or 51.81 cm ("cubit and a handbreadth," Eze 40:5) as opposed to the standard Hebrew cubit of 17.6 inches or 44.7 cm.

Scripture describes a floor plan, but provides few height dimensions. This artwork shows an upward projection of the temple over the floor plan. This temple existed only in a vision of Ezekiel (Eze 40:2), and has never actually been built as were the temples of Solomon, Zerubbabel and Herod.

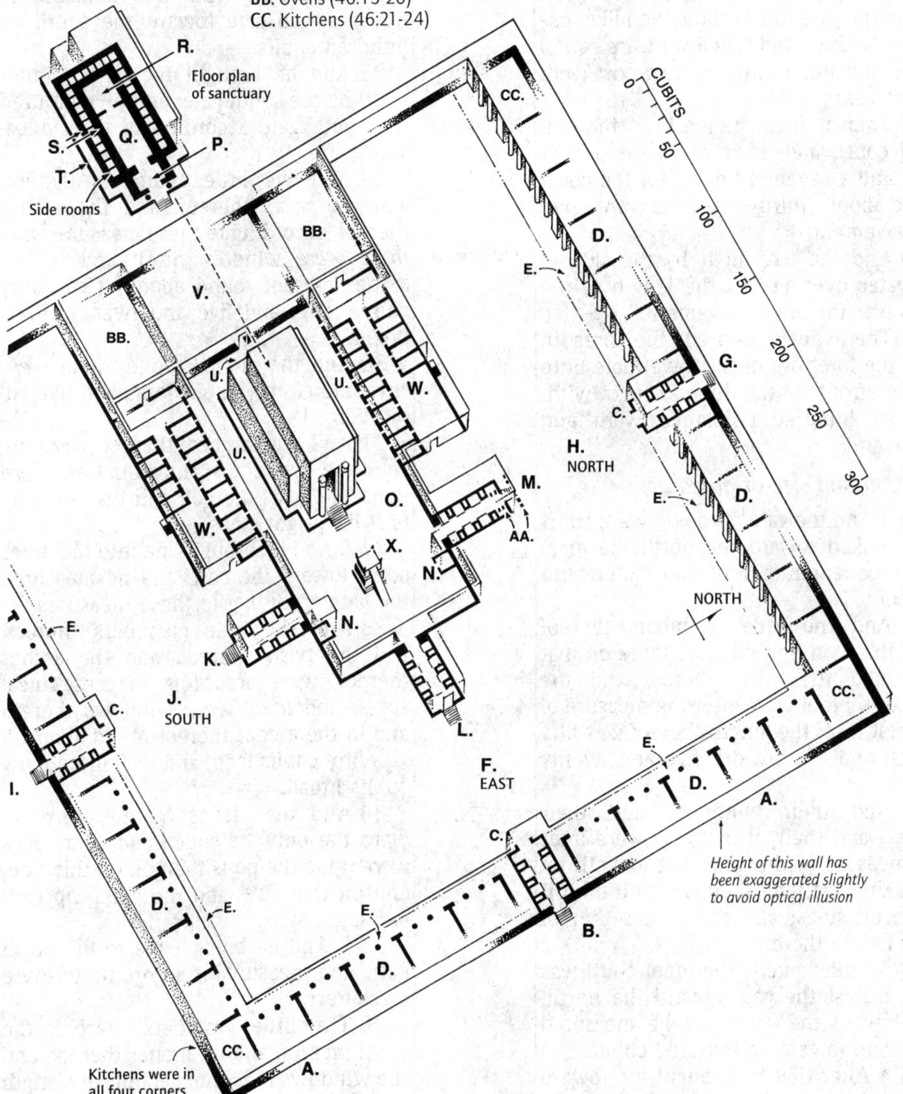

Plan adapted from the design given in *The Zondervan Pictorial Bible Dictionary*. Copyright © 1975 by The Zondervan Corporation. Used by permission.

the little chambers *were* six cubits on this
side, and six cubits on that side.
13 He measured then the gate from
the roof of *one* little chamber to the roof
of another: the breadth *was* five and
twenty cubits, door against door.
14 He made also posts of threescore
cubits, even unto the post of the court
round about the gate.
15 And from the face of the gate of the
entrance unto the face of the porch of the
inner gate *were* fifty cubits.
16 And *there were* [a]narrow[1] windows
to the little chambers, and to their posts
within the gate round about, and likewise
to the [2]arches: and windows *were* round
about [3]inward: and upon *each* post *were*
palm trees.
17 Then brought he me into [a]the outward court, and, lo, *there were* [b]cham-
bers, and a pavement made for the court
round about: [c]thirty chambers *were* upon
the pavement.
18 And the pavement by the side of
the gates over against the length of the
gates *was* the lower pavement.
19 Then he measured the breadth
from the forefront of the lower gate unto
the forefront of the inner court [1]with-
out, an hundred cubits eastward and
northward.

Location and size of gates

20 ¶ And the gate of the outward court
[1]that looked toward the north, he measured the length thereof, and the breadth
thereof.
21 And the little chambers thereof
were three on this side and three on that
side; and the posts thereof and the
[1]arches thereof were after the measure of
the first gate: the length thereof *was* fifty
cubits, and the breadth five and twenty
cubits.
22 And their windows, and their
arches, and their palm trees, *were* after
the measure of the gate that looketh toward the east; and they went up unto it
by seven steps; and the arches thereof
were before them.
23 And the gate of the inner court *was*
over against the gate toward the north,
and toward the east; and he measured
from gate to gate an hundred cubits.
24 ¶ After that he brought me toward
the south, and behold a gate toward the
south: and he measured the posts thereof
and the arches thereof according to these
measures.
25 And *there were* windows in it and
in the arches thereof round about, like
those windows: the length *was* fifty cubits, and the breadth five and twenty
cubits.
26 And *there were* seven steps to go
up to it, and the arches thereof *were* before them: and it had palm trees, one on
this side, and another on that side, upon
the posts thereof.
27 And *there was* a gate in the inner
court toward the south: and he measured
from gate to gate toward the south an
hundred cubits.
28 And he brought me to the inner
court by the south gate: and he measured
the south gate according to these measures;
29 And the little chambers thereof,
and the posts thereof, and the arches
thereof, according to these measures: and
there were windows in it and in the
arches thereof round about: *it was* fifty
cubits long, and five and twenty cubits
broad.
30 And the arches round about *were*
[a]five and twenty cubits long, and five cubits [1]broad.
31 And the arches thereof *were* toward the utter court; and palm trees *were*
upon the posts thereof: and the going up
to it *had* eight steps.
32 ¶ And he brought me into the inner
court toward the east: and he measured
the gate according to these measures.
33 And the little chambers thereof,
and the posts thereof, and the arches
thereof, *were* according to these measures: and *there were* windows therein
and in the arches thereof round about: *it
was* fifty cubits long, and five and twenty
cubits broad.
34 And the arches thereof *were* toward the outward court; and palm trees
were upon the posts thereof, on this side,
and on that side: and the going up to it
had eight steps.
35 ¶ And he brought me to the north
gate, and measured *it* according to these
measures;
36 The little chambers thereof, the
posts thereof, and the arches thereof, and
the windows to it round about: the length
was fifty cubits, and the breadth five and
twenty cubits.

16 [a]1 Ki. 6:4 [1]Heb. *closed* [2]Or, *galleries,* or, *porches* [3]Or, *within*

17 [a]Rev. 11:2 [b]1 Ki. 6:5 [c]ch. 45:5

19 [1]Or, *from without*

20 [1]Heb. *whose face* was

21 [1]Or, *galleries,* or, *porches*

30 [a]See ver. 21,25, 33,36 [1]Heb. *breadth*

37 And the posts thereof *were* toward the utter court; and palm trees *were* upon the posts thereof, on this side, and on that side: and the going up to it *had* eight steps.

The porch and its furnishings

38 And the chambers and the entries thereof *were* by the posts of the gates, where they washed the burnt offering.

39 ¶ And in the porch of the gate *were* two tables on this side, and two tables on that side, to slay thereon the burnt offering and [a]the sin offering and [b]the trespass offering.

40 And at the side without, [1]as one goeth up to the entry of the north gate, *were* two tables; and on the other side, which *was* at the porch of the gate, *were* two tables.

41 Four tables *were* on this side, and four tables on that side, by the side of the gate; eight tables, whereupon they slew *their sacrifices.*

42 And the four tables *were* of hewn stone for the burnt offering, of a cubit and an half long, and a cubit and an half broad, and one cubit high: whereupon also they laid the instruments wherewith they slew the burnt offering and the sacrifice.

43 And within *were* [1]hooks, an hand broad, fastened round about: and upon the tables *was* the flesh of the offering.

44 ¶ And without the inner gate *were* the chambers of [a]the singers in the inner court, which *was* at the side of the north gate; and their prospect *was* toward the south: one at the side of the east gate *having* the prospect toward the north.

45 And he said unto me, This chamber, whose prospect *is* toward the south, *is* for the priests, [a]the keepers of the [1]charge of the house.

46 And the chamber whose prospect *is* toward the north *is* for the priests, [a]the keepers of the charge of the altar: these *are* the sons of [b]Zadok among the sons of Levi, which come near to the LORD to minister unto him.

47 So he measured the court, an hundred cubits long, and an hundred cubits broad, foursquare; and the altar *that was* before the house.

48 ¶ And he brought me to the porch of the house, and measured *each* post of the porch, five cubits on this side, and five cubits on that side: and the breadth of the gate *was* three cubits on this side, and three cubits on that side.

49 [a]The length of the porch *was* twenty cubits, and the breadth eleven cubits; and *he brought me* by the steps whereby they went up to it: and *there were* [b]pillars by the posts, one on this side, and another on that side.

The temple and its walls

41 AFTERWARD HE brought me to the temple, and measured the posts, six cubits broad on the one side, and six cubits broad on the other side, *which was* the breadth of the tabernacle.

2 And the breadth of the [1]door *was* ten cubits; and the sides of the door *were* five cubits on the one side, and five cubits on the other side: and he measured the length thereof, forty cubits: and the breadth, twenty cubits.

3 Then went he inward, and measured the post of the door, two cubits; and the door, six cubits; and the breadth of the door, seven cubits.

4 So [a]he measured the length thereof, twenty cubits; and the breadth, twenty cubits, before the temple: and he said unto me, This *is* the most holy *place.*

5 After he measured the wall of the house, six cubits; and the breadth of *every* side chamber, four cubits, round about the house on every side.

6 [a]And the side chambers *were* three, [1]one over another, and [2]thirty in order; and they entered into the wall which *was* of the house for the side chambers round about, that they might [3]have hold, but they had not hold in the wall of the house.

7 And [a]*there*[1] *was* an enlarging, and a winding about still upward to the side chambers: for the winding about of the house went still upward round about the house: therefore the breadth of the house *was still* upward, and so increased *from* the lowest *chamber* to the highest by the midst.

8 I saw also the height of the house round about: the foundations of the side chambers *were* [a]a full reed of six great cubits.

9 The thickness of the wall, which *was* for the side chamber without, *was* five cubits: and *that* which *was* left *was* the

39 [a]Lev. 4:2,3 [b]Lev. 5:6 & 6:6 & 7:1
40 [1]Or, *at the step*
43 [1]Or, *endirons,* or, *the two hearthstones*
44 [a]1 Chr. 6:31
45 [a]Lev. 8:35; Num. 3:27,28,32, 38 & 18:5; 1 Chr. 9:23; 2 Chr. 13:11; Ps. 134:1 [1]Or, *ward,* or, *ordinance*
46 [a]Num. 18:5; ch. 44:15 [b]1 Ki. 2:35; ch. 43:19 & 44:15, 16
49 [a]1 Ki. 6:3 [b]1 Ki. 7:21
41:2 [1]Or, *entrance*
4 [a]1 Ki. 6:20; 2 Chr. 3:8
6 [a]1 Ki. 6:5,6 [1]Heb. *side chamber over side chamber* [2]Or, *three and thirty times,* or, *foot* [3]Heb. *be holden*
7 [a]1 Ki. 6:8 [1]Heb. *it was made broader, and went round*
8 [a]ch. 40:5

place of the side chambers that *were* within.

10 And between the chambers *was* the wideness of twenty cubits round about the house on every side.

11 And the doors of the side chambers *were* toward *the place that was* left, one door toward the north, and another door toward the south: and the breadth of the place that was left *was* five cubits round about.

12 Now the building that *was* before the separate place at the end toward the west *was* seventy cubits broad; and the wall of the building *was* five cubits thick round about, and the length thereof ninety cubits.

13 So he measured the house, an hundred cubits long; and the separate place, and the building, with the walls thereof, an hundred cubits long;

14 Also the breadth of the face of the house, and of the separate place toward the east, an hundred cubits.

15 And he measured the length of the building over against the separate place which *was* behind it, and the [1]galleries thereof on the one side and on the other side, an hundred cubits, with the inner temple, and the porches of the court;

16 The door posts, and [a]the narrow windows, and the galleries round about on their three stories, over against the door, [1]ceiled with wood round about, [2]and from the ground up to the windows, and the windows *were* covered;

17 To that above the door, even unto the inner house, and without, and by all the wall round about within and without, by [1]measure.

18 And *it was* made [a]with cherubims and palm trees, so that a palm tree *was* between a cherub and a cherub; and *every* cherub had two faces;

19 [a]So that the face of a man *was* toward the palm tree on the one side, and the face of a young lion toward the palm tree on the other side: *it was* made through all the house round about.

20 From the ground unto above the door *were* cherubims and palm trees made, and *on* the wall of the temple.

21 The [1]posts of the temple *were* squared, *and* the face of the sanctuary; the appearance *of the one* as the appearance *of the other.*

22 [a]The altar of wood *was* three cubits high, and the length thereof two cubits; and the corners thereof, and the length thereof, and the walls thereof, *were* of wood: and he said unto me, This *is* [b]the table that *is* [c]before the LORD.

23 [a]And the temple and the sanctuary had two doors.

24 And the doors had two leaves *apiece,* two turning leaves; two *leaves* for the one door, and two leaves for the other *door.*

25 And *there were* made on them, on the doors of the temple, cherubims and palm trees, like as *were* made upon the walls; and *there were* thick planks upon the face of the porch without.

26 And *there were* [a]narrow windows and palm trees on the one side and on the other side, on the sides of the porch, and *upon* the side chambers of the house, and thick planks.

The priests' chambers

42 THEN HE brought me forth into the utter court, the way toward the north: and he brought me into [a]the chamber that *was* over against the separate place, and which *was* before the building toward the north.

2 Before the length of an hundred cubits *was* the north door, and the breadth *was* fifty cubits.

3 Over against the twenty *cubits* which *were* for the inner court, and over against the pavement which *was* for the utter court, *was* [a]gallery against gallery in three *stories.*

4 And before the chambers *was* a walk of ten cubits breadth inward, a way of one cubit; and their doors toward the north.

5 Now the upper chambers *were* shorter: for the galleries [1]were higher than these, [2]than the lower, and than the middlemost of the building.

6 For they *were* in three *stories,* but had not pillars as the pillars of the courts: therefore *the building* was straitened more than the lowest and the middlemost from the ground.

7 And the wall that *was* without over against the chambers, toward the utter court on the forepart of the chambers, the length thereof *was* fifty cubits.

15 [1]Or, *several walks,* or, *walks with pillars*

16 [a]ver. 26; ch. 40:16 [1]Heb. *ceiling of wood* [2]Or, *and the ground unto the windows*

17 [1]Heb. *measures*

18 [a]1 Ki. 6:29

19 [a]See ch. 1:10

21 [1]Heb. *post*

22 [a]Ex. 30:1 [b]ch. 44:16; Mal. 1:7,12 [c]Ex. 30:8

23 [a]1 Ki. 6:31-35

26 [a]ver. 16; ch. 40:16

42:1 [a]ch. 41:12,15

3 [a]ch. 41:16

5 [1]Or, *did eat of these* [2]Or, *and the building consisted of the lower and the middlemost*

8 For the length of the chambers that *were* in the utter court *was* fifty cubits: and, lo, before the temple *were* an hundred cubits.

9 And [1]from under these chambers *was* [2]the entry on the east side, [3]as one goeth into them from the utter court.

10 The chambers *were* in the thickness of the wall of the court toward the east, over against the separate place, and over against the building.

11 And [a]the way before them *was* like the appearance of the chambers which *were* toward the north, as long as they, *and* as broad as they: and all their goings out *were* both according to their fashions, and according to their doors.

12 And according to the doors of the chambers that *were* toward the south *was* a door in the head of the way, *even* the way directly before the wall toward the east, as one entereth into them.

13 ¶ Then said he unto me, The north chambers *and* the south chambers, which *are* before the separate place, they *be* holy chambers, where the priests that approach unto the LORD [a]shall eat the most holy things: there shall they lay the most holy things, and [b]the meat offering, and the sin offering, and the trespass offering; for the place *is* holy.

14 [a]When the priests enter therein, then shall they not go out of the holy *place* into the utter court, but there they shall lay their garments wherein they minister; for they *are* holy; and shall put on other garments, and shall approach to *those things* which *are* for the people.

15 Now when he had made an end of measuring the inner house, he brought me forth toward the gate whose prospect *is* toward the east, and measured it round about.

16 He measured the east [1]side with the measuring reed, five hundred reeds, with the measuring reed round about.

17 He measured the north side, five hundred reeds, with the measuring reed round about.

9 [1]Or, *from the place* [2]Or, *he that brought me* [3]Or, *as he came*

11 [a]ver. 4

13 [a]Lev. 6:16,26; & 24:9 [b]Lev. 2:3, 10 & 6:14,17,25, 29

14 [a]ch. 44:19

16 [1]Heb. *wind*

20 [a]ch. 40:5 [b]ch. 45:2

43:1 [a]ch. 10:19 & 46:1

2 [a]ch. 11:23 [b]ch. 1:24; Rev. 1:15 & 14:2 [c]ch. 10:4; Rev. 18:1

3 [a]ch. 1:4,28 [b]See ch. 9:1 [c]Jer. 1:10 [d]ch. 3:23 [1]Or, *when I came to* prophesy *that the city should be destroyed*

4 [a]ch. 10:19

5 [a]ch. 3:12,14 & 8:3 [b]1 Ki. 8:10,11

6 [a]ch. 40:3

7 [a]Ps. 99:1 [b]1 Chr. 28:2; Ps. 99:5 [c]Ex. 29:45; Ps. 68:16 & 132:14; Joel 3:17; John 1:14; 2 Cor. 6:16 [d]ch. 39:7

18 He measured the south side, five hundred reeds, with the measuring reed.

19 ¶ He turned about to the west side, *and* measured five hundred reeds with the measuring reed.

20 He measured it by the four sides: [a]it had a wall round about, [b]five hundred *reeds* long, and five hundred broad, to make a separation between the sanctuary and the profane place.

The LORD's glory fills the temple

43 AFTERWARD HE brought me to the gate, *even* the gate [a]that looketh toward the east: D

2 [a]And, behold, the glory of the God of Israel came from the way of the east: and [b]his voice *was* like a noise of many waters: [c]and the earth shined with his glory.

3 And *it was* [a]according to the appearance of the vision which I saw, *even* according to the vision that I saw [b]when [1] I came [c]to destroy the city: and the visions *were* like the vision that I saw [d]by the river Chebar; and I fell upon my face.

4 [a]And the glory of the LORD came into D
the house by the way of the gate whose N
prospect *is* toward the east.

5 [a]So the spirit took me up, and I
brought me into the inner court; and, be- M
hold, [b]the glory of the LORD filled the E
house.

6 And I heard *him* speaking unto me out of the house; and [a]the man stood by me.

7 ¶ And he said unto me, Son of man, [a]the place of my throne, and [b]the place of the soles of my feet, [c]where I will dwell in the midst of the children of Israel for ever, and my holy name, shall the house of Israel [d]no more defile, *neither* they,

D SS 8:5 ◀▶ Eze 43:4–7
D Eze 43:1–2 ◀▶ Eze 44:1–2
N Eze 37:1 ◀▶ Da 5:12
I Eze 39:25–29 ◀▶ Eze 43:9
M Eze 37:22–28 ◀▶ Eze 47:1–21
E Eze 37:1 ◀▶ Da 4:8–9

43:1–9 Ezekiel saw in his vision the return of the Lord to the temple via the east gate, which was the gate through which he had earlier departed (see 10:18–19). God then declared his intent to "dwell in the midst of the children of Israel for ever" (43:7) and that his people would renounce their sins and receive transformed hearts.

nor their kings, by their whoredom, nor by [e]the carcases of their kings in their high places.

8 [a]In their setting of their threshold by my thresholds, and their post by my posts, [1]and the wall between me and them, they have even defiled my holy name by their abominations that they have committed: wherefore I have consumed them in mine anger.

9 Now let them put away their whoredom, and [a]the carcases of their kings, far from me, [a]and I will dwell in the midst of them for ever.

10 ¶ Thou son of man, [a]show the house to the house of Israel, that they may be ashamed of their iniquities: and let them measure the [1]pattern.

11 And if they be ashamed of all that they have done, show them the form of the house, and the fashion thereof, and the goings out thereof, and the comings in thereof, and all the forms thereof, and all the ordinances thereof, and all the forms thereof, and all the laws thereof: and write *it* in their sight, that they may keep the whole form thereof, and all the ordinances thereof, and do them.

12 This *is* the law of the house; Upon [a]the top of the mountain the whole limit thereof round about *shall be* most holy. Behold, this *is* the law of the house.

The size and use of the altar

13 ¶ And these *are* the measures of the altar after the cubits: [a]The cubit *is* a cubit and an handbreadth; even the [1]bottom *shall be* a cubit, and the breadth a cubit, and the border thereof by the [2]edge thereof round about *shall be* a span: and this *shall be* the higher place of the altar.

14 And from the bottom *upon* the ground *even* to the lower settle *shall be* two cubits, and the breadth one cubit; and from the lesser settle *even* to the greater settle *shall be* four cubits, and the breadth *one* cubit.

15 So [1]the altar *shall be* four cubits; and from [2]the altar and upward *shall be* four horns.

16 And the altar *shall be* twelve *cubits* long, twelve broad, square in the four squares thereof.

17 And the settle *shall be* fourteen *cubits* long and fourteen broad in the four squares thereof; and the border about it *shall be* half a cubit; and the bottom thereof *shall be* a cubit about; and [a]his stairs shall look toward the east.

18 ¶ And he said unto me, Son of man, thus saith the Lord GOD; These *are* the ordinances of the altar in the day when they shall make it, to offer burnt offerings thereon, and to [a]sprinkle blood thereon.

19 And thou shalt give to [a]the priests the Levites that be of the seed of Zadok, which approach unto me, to minister unto me, saith the Lord GOD, [b]a young bullock for a sin offering.

20 And thou shalt take of the blood thereof, and put *it* on the four horns of it, and on the four corners of the settle, and upon the border round about: thus shalt thou cleanse and purge it.

21 Thou shalt take the bullock also of the sin offering, and he [a]shall burn it in the appointed place of the house, [b]without the sanctuary.

22 And on the second day thou shalt offer a kid of the goats without blemish for a sin offering; and they shall cleanse the altar, as they did cleanse *it* with the bullock.

23 When thou hast made an end of cleansing *it,* thou shalt offer a young bullock without blemish, and a ram out of the flock without blemish.

24 And thou shalt offer them before the LORD, [a]and the priests shall cast salt upon them, and they shall offer them up *for* a burnt offering unto the LORD.

25 [a]Seven days shalt thou prepare every day a goat *for* a sin offering: they shall also prepare a young bullock, and a ram out of the flock, without blemish.

26 Seven days shall they purge the altar and purify it; and they shall [1]consecrate themselves.

27 [a]And when these days are expired, it shall be, *that* upon the eighth day, and *so* forward, the priests shall make your burnt offerings upon the altar, and your [1]peace offerings; and I will [b]accept you, saith the Lord GOD.

7 [e]Lev. 26:30; Jer. 16:18
8 [a]See 2 Ki. 16:14 & 21:4,5,7; ch. 8:3 & 23:39 & 44:7 [1]Or, *for* there was but *a wall between me and them*
9 [a]ver. 7
10 [a]ch. 40:4 [1]Or, *sum,* or, *number*
12 [a]ch. 40:2
13 [a]ch. 41:8 [1]Heb. *bosom* [2]Heb. *lip*
15 [1]Heb. *Harel,* i.e. *the mountain of God* [2]Heb. *Ariel,* i.e. *the lion of God*
17 [a]See Ex. 20:26
18 [a]Lev. 1:5
19 [a]ch. 44:15 [b]Ex. 29:10; Lev. 8:14; ch. 45:18
21 [a]Ex. 29:14 [b]Heb. 13:11
24 [a]Lev. 2:13
25 [a]Ex. 29:35; Lev. 8:33
26 [1]Heb. *fill their hands*
27 [a]Lev. 9:1 [b]ch. 20:40,41; Rom. 12:1; 1 Pet. 2:5 [1]Or, *thank offerings*

Eze 43:5–7 ◀ ▶ *Eze 45:1–2*

The use of the temple

D

44 THEN HE brought me back the way of the gate of the outward sanctuary [a]which looketh toward the east; and it *was* shut.

2 Then said the LORD unto me; This gate shall be shut, it shall not be opened, and no man shall enter in by it; [a]because the LORD, the God of Israel, hath entered in by it, therefore it shall be shut.

3 *It is* for the prince; the prince, he shall sit in it to [a]eat bread before the LORD; [b]he shall enter by the way of the porch of *that* gate, and shall go out by the way of the same.

4 ¶ Then brought he me the way of the north gate before the house: and I looked, and, [a]behold, the glory of the LORD filled the house of the LORD: [b]and I fell upon my face.

5 And the LORD said unto me, [a]Son of man, [1]mark well, and behold with thine eyes, and hear with thine ears all that I say unto thee concerning all the ordinances of the house of the LORD, and all the laws thereof; and mark well the entering in of the house, with every going forth of the sanctuary.

6 And thou shalt say to the [a]rebellious, *even* to the house of Israel, Thus saith the Lord GOD; O ye house of Israel, [b]let it suffice you of all your abominations,

7 [a]In that ye have brought *into my sanctuary* [b]strangers,[1] [c]uncircumcised in heart, and uncircumcised in flesh, to be in my sanctuary, to pollute it, *even* my house, when ye offer [d]my bread, [e]the fat and the blood, and they have broken my covenant because of all your abominations.

8 And ye have not [a]kept the charge of mine holy things: but ye have set keepers of my [1]charge in my sanctuary for yourselves.

9 ¶ Thus saith the Lord GOD; [a]No stranger, uncircumcised in heart, nor uncircumcised in flesh, shall enter into my sanctuary, of any stranger that *is* among the children of Israel.

10 [a]And the Levites that are gone away far from me, when Israel went astray, which went astray away from me after their idols; they shall even bear their iniquity.

11 Yet they shall be ministers in my sanctuary, [a]*having* charge at the gates of the house, and ministering to the house: [b]they shall slay the burnt offering and the sacrifice for the people, and [c]they shall stand before them to minister unto them.

12 Because they ministered unto them before their idols, and [a]caused[1] the house of Israel to fall into iniquity; therefore have I [b]lifted up mine hand against them, saith the Lord GOD, and they shall bear their iniquity.

13 [a]And they shall not come near unto me, to do the office of a priest unto me, nor to come near to any of my holy things, in the most holy *place:* but they shall [b]bear their shame, and their abominations which they have committed.

14 But I will make them [a]keepers of the charge of the house, for all the service thereof, and for all that shall be done therein.

15 ¶ [a]But the priests the Levites, [b]the sons of Zadok, that kept the charge of my sanctuary [c]when the children of Israel went astray from me, they shall come near to me to minister unto me, and they [d]shall stand before me to offer unto me [e]the fat and the blood, saith the Lord GOD:

16 They shall enter into my sanctuary, and they shall come near to [a]my table, to minister unto me, and they shall keep my charge.

17 ¶ And it shall come to pass, *that* when they enter in at the gates of the inner court, [a]they shall be clothed with linen garments; and no wool shall come upon them, whiles they minister in the gates of the inner court, and within.

44:1 [a]ch. 43:1
2 [a]ch. 43:4
3 [a]Gen. 31:54; 1 Cor. 10:18 [b]ch. 46:2,8
4 [a]ch. 3:23 [b]ch. 1:28
5 [a]ch. 40:4 [1]Heb. *set thine heart*
6 [a]ch. 2:5 [b]ch. 45:9; 1 Pet. 4:3
7 [a]ver. 9; ch. 43:8; Acts 21:28 [b]Lev. 22:25 [c]Lev. 26:41; Acts 7:51 [d]Lev. 21:17 [e]Lev. 3:16 [1]Heb. *children of a stranger*
8 [a]Lev. 22:2 [1]Or, *ward,* or, *ordinance*
9 [a]ver. 7
10 [a]2 Ki. 23:8; ch. 48:11
11 [a]1 Chr. 26:1 [b]2 Chr. 29:34 [c]Num. 16:9
12 [a]Is. 9:16; Mal. 2:8 [b]Ps. 106:26 [1]Heb. *were for a stumblingblock of iniquity unto;* see ch. 14:3,4
13 [a]Num. 18:3; 2 Ki. 23:9 [b]ch. 32:30
14 [a]Num. 18:4; 1 Chr. 23:28
15 [a]ch. 40:46 [b]1 Sam. 2:35 [c]ver. 10 [d]Deut. 10:8 [e]ver. 7
16 [a]ch. 41:22
17 [a]Ex. 28:39

D *Eze 43:4–7* ◀▶ *Zec 2:10*

44:1–2 Ezekiel's vision revealed that the Eastern Gate of the temple would be shut because the Lord entered through it. That the gate remained shut may reaffirm God's promise in 43:7 to dwell with his children forever, or it may merely signify its holy status since the Lord crossed its threshold.

Note that Jerusalem has many city gates. The Eastern (Golden) Gate in the old walled city which surrounds the Moslem area of Jerusalem has been walled shut since the sixteenth century, possibly as a result of a related Moslem tradition. Other city gates have suffered similar fates in order to control public access to Moslem mosques in that area.

18 [a]They shall have linen bonnets upon their heads, and shall have linen breeches upon their loins; they shall not gird *themselves* [1,2]with any thing that causeth sweat.

19 And when they go forth into the utter court, *even* into the utter court to the people, [a]they shall put off their garments wherein they ministered, and lay them in the holy chambers, and they shall put on other garments; and they shall [b]not sanctify the people with their garments.

20 [a]Neither shall they shave their heads, nor suffer their locks to grow long; they shall only poll their heads.

21 [a]Neither shall any priest drink wine, when they enter into the inner court.

22 Neither shall they take for their wives a [a]widow, nor her that is [1]put away: but they shall take maidens of the seed of the house of Israel, or a widow [2]that had a priest before.

23 And [a]they shall teach my people *the difference* between the holy and profane, and cause them to discern between the unclean and the clean.

24 And [a]in controversy they shall stand in judgment; *and* they shall judge it according to my judgments: and they shall keep my laws and my statutes in all mine assemblies; [b]and they shall hallow my sabbaths.

25 And they shall come at no dead person to defile themselves: but for father, or for mother, or for son, or for daughter, for brother, or for sister that hath had no husband, they may defile themselves.

26 And [a]after he is cleansed, they shall reckon unto him seven days.

27 And in the day that he goeth into the sanctuary, [a]unto the inner court, to minister in the sanctuary, [b]he shall offer his sin offering, saith the Lord GOD.

28 And it shall be unto them for an inheritance: I [a]*am* their inheritance: and ye shall give them no possession in Israel: I *am* their possession.

29 [a]They shall eat the meat offering, and the sin offering, and the trespass offering; and [b]every [1]dedicated thing in Israel shall be theirs.

18 [a]Ex. 28:40 & 39:28 [1]Or, *in sweating* places [2]Heb. *in,* or, *with sweat*

19 [a]ch. 42:14 [b]ch. 46:20; Ex. 30:29; Lev. 6:27; Mat. 23:17

20 [a]Lev. 21:5

21 [a]Lev. 10:9

22 [a]Lev. 21:7 [1]Heb. *thrust forth* [2]Heb. *from a priest*

23 [a]ch. 22:26; Mal. 2:7

24 [a]Deut. 17:8; 2 Chr. 19:8 [b]See ch. 22:26

26 [a]Num. 6:10 & 19:11

27 [a]ver. 17 [b]Lev. 4:3

28 [a]Num. 18:20; Deut. 10:9 & 18:1, 2; Josh. 13:14

29 [a]Lev. 7:6 [b]Lev. 27:21,28, compared with Num. 18:14 [1]Or, *devoted*

30 [a]Ex. 13:2 & 22:29 & 23:19; Num. 3:13 & 18:12 [b]Num. 15:20; Neh. 10:37 [c]Prov. 3:9; Mal. 3:10 [1]Or, *chief*

31 [a]Ex. 22:31; Lev. 22:8

45:1 [a]ch. 47:22 [b]ch. 48:8 [1]Heb. *when ye cause the land to fall* [2]Heb. *holiness*

2 [1]Or, *void places*

3 [a]ch. 48:10

4 [a]ver. 1; ch. 48:10

5 [a]ch. 48:13 [b]See ch. 40:17

6 [a]ch. 48:15

7 [a]ch. 48:21

30 And the [a]first[1] of all the firstfruits of all *things*, and every oblation of all, of every *sort* of your oblations, shall be the priest's: ye [b]shall also give unto the priest the first of your dough, [c]that he may cause the blessing to rest in thine house.

31 The priests shall not eat of any thing that is [a]dead of itself, or torn, whether it be fowl or beast.

Division of the land

45 MOREOVER, [1]WHEN ye shall [a]divide by lot the land for inheritance, ye shall [b]offer an oblation unto the LORD, [2]an holy portion of the land: the length *shall be* the length of five and twenty thousand *reeds*, and the breadth *shall be* ten thousand. This *shall be* holy in all the borders thereof round about.

2 Of this there shall be for the sanctuary five hundred *in length,* with five hundred *in breadth,* square round about; and fifty cubits round about for the [1]suburbs thereof.

3 And of this measure shalt thou measure the length of five and twenty thousand, and the breadth of ten thousand: [a]and in it shall be the sanctuary *and* the most holy *place*.

4 [a]The holy *portion* of the land shall be for the priests the ministers of the sanctuary, which shall come near to minister unto the LORD: and it shall be a place for their houses, and an holy place for the sanctuary.

5 [a]And the five and twenty thousand of length, and the ten thousand of breadth, shall also the Levites, the ministers of the house, have for themselves, for a possession for [b]twenty chambers.

6 ¶ [a]And ye shall appoint the possession of the city five thousand broad, and five and twenty thousand long, over against the oblation of the holy *portion:* it shall be for the whole house of Israel.

7 ¶ [a]And *a portion shall be* for the prince on the one side and on the other side of the oblation of the holy *portion,* and of the possession of the city, before the oblation of the holy *portion,* and before the possession of the city, from the

❙ *Eze 43:9* ◀▶ *Eze 45:8*

45:1–2 The prophet declared that in the Millennium the land of Israel would be divided by lot for purposes of inheritance and that a portion of the land would be set aside for the temple.

west side westward, and from the east side eastward: and the length *shall be* over against one of the portions, from the west border unto the east border.

8 In the land shall be his possession in Israel: and [a]my princes shall no more oppress my people; and *the rest of* the land shall they give to the house of Israel according to their tribes.

9 ¶ Thus saith the Lord GOD; [a]Let it suffice you, O princes of Israel: [b]remove violence and spoil, and execute judgment and justice, take away your [1]exactions from my people, saith the Lord GOD.

Laws about weights and offerings

10 Ye shall have just [a]balances, and a just ephah, and a just bath.

11 The ephah and the bath shall be of one measure, that the bath may contain the tenth part of an homer, and the ephah the tenth part of an homer: the measure thereof shall be after the homer.

12 And the [a]shekel *shall be* twenty gerahs: twenty shekels, five and twenty shekels, fifteen shekels, shall be your maneh.

13 This *is* the oblation that ye shall offer; the sixth part of an ephah of an homer of wheat, and ye shall give the sixth part of an ephah of an homer of barley:

14 Concerning the ordinance of oil, the bath of oil, *ye shall offer* the tenth part of a bath out of the cor, *which is* an homer of ten baths; for ten baths *are* an homer:

15 And one [1]lamb out of the flock, out of two hundred, out of the fat pastures of Israel; for a meat offering, and for a burnt offering, and for [2]peace offerings, [a]to make reconciliation for them, saith the Lord GOD.

16 All the people of the land [1]shall give this oblation [2]for the prince in Israel.

17 And it shall be the prince's part *to give* burnt offerings, and meat offerings, and drink offerings, in the feasts, and in the new moons, and in the sabbaths, in all solemnities of the house of Israel: he shall prepare the sin offering, and the meat offering, and the burnt offering, and the [1]peace offerings, to make reconciliation for the house of Israel.

18 Thus saith the Lord GOD; In the first *month,* in the first *day* of the month, thou shalt take a young bullock without blemish, and [a]cleanse the sanctuary:

19 [a]And the priest shall take of the blood of the sin offering, and put *it* upon the posts of the house, and upon the four corners of the settle of the altar, and upon the posts of the gate of the inner court.

20 And so thou shalt do the seventh *day* of the month [a]for every one that erreth, and for *him that is* simple: so shall ye reconcile the house.

21 [a]In the first *month,* in the fourteenth day of the month, ye shall have the passover, a feast of seven days; unleavened bread shall be eaten.

22 And upon that day shall the prince prepare for himself and for all the people of the land [a]a bullock *for* a sin offering.

23 And [a]seven days of the feast he shall prepare a burnt offering to the LORD, seven bullocks and seven rams without blemish daily the seven days; [b]and a kid of the goats daily *for* a sin offering.

24 [a]And he shall prepare a meat offering of an ephah for a bullock, and an ephah for a ram, and an hin of oil for an ephah.

25 In the seventh *month,* in the fifteenth day of the month, shall he do the like in the [a]feast of the seven days, according to the sin offering, according to the burnt offering, and according to the meat offering, and according to the oil.

46 THUS SAITH the Lord GOD; The gate of the inner court that looketh toward the east shall be shut the six working days; but on the sabbath it shall be opened, and in the day of the new moon it shall be opened.

2 [a]And the prince shall enter by the way of the porch of *that* gate without, and shall stand by the post of the gate, and the priests shall prepare his burnt offering and his peace offerings, and he shall worship at the threshold of the gate: then he shall go forth; but the gate shall not be shut until the evening.

3 Likewise the people of the land shall worship at the door of this gate before

8 [a]See Jer. 22:17; ch. 22:27 & 46:18
9 [a]ch. 44:6 [b]Jer. 22:3 [1]Heb. *expulsions*
10 [a]Lev. 19:35,36; Prov. 11:1
12 [a]Ex. 30:13; Lev. 27:25; Num. 3:47
15 [a]Lev. 1:4 [1]Or, *kid* [2]Or, *thank offerings*
16 [1]Heb. *shall be for* [2]Or, *with*
17 [1]Or, *thank offerings*
18 [a]Lev. 16:16
19 [a]ch. 43:20
20 [a]Lev. 4:27
21 [a]Ex. 12:18; Lev. 23:5,6; Num. 9:2,3 & 28:16,17; Deut. 16:1
22 [a]Lev. 4:14
23 [a]Lev. 23:8 [b]See Num. 28:15,22,30 & 29:5,11,16,19
24 [a]ch. 46:5,7
25 [a]Lev. 23:34; Num. 29:12; Deut. 16:13
46:2 [a]ver. 8; ch. 44:3

I *Eze 45:1–2* ◀▶ *Eze 47:1*

45:8 Ezekiel declared that the oppression of God's people by their own rulers would cease forever in the millennial kingdom.

the LORD in the sabbaths and in the new moons.

4 And the burnt offering that [a]the prince shall offer unto the LORD in the sabbath day *shall be* six lambs without blemish, and a ram without blemish.

5 [a]And the meat offering *shall be* an ephah for a ram, and the meat offering for the lambs [b]as[1] he shall be able to give, and an hin of oil to an ephah.

6 And in the day of the new moon *it shall be* a young bullock without blemish, and six lambs, and a ram: they shall be without blemish.

7 And he shall prepare a meat offering, an ephah for a bullock, and an ephah for a ram, and for the lambs according as his hand shall attain unto, and an hin of oil to an ephah.

8 [a]And when the prince shall enter, he shall go in by the way of the porch of *that* gate, and he shall go forth by the way thereof.

9 ¶ But when the people of the land [a]shall come before the LORD in the solemn feasts, he that entereth in by the way of the north gate to worship shall go out by the way of the south gate; and he that entereth by the way of the south gate shall go forth by the way of the north gate: he shall not return by the way of the gate whereby he came in, but shall go forth over against it.

10 And the prince in the midst of them, when they go in, shall go in; and when they go forth, shall go forth.

11 And in the feasts and in the solemnities [a]the meat offering shall be an ephah to a bullock, and an ephah to a ram, and to the lambs as he is able to give, and an hin of oil to an ephah.

12 Now when the prince shall prepare a voluntary burnt offering or peace offerings voluntarily unto the LORD, [a]*one* shall then open him the gate that looketh toward the east, and he shall prepare his burnt offering and his peace offerings, as he did on the sabbath day: then he shall go forth; and after his going forth *one* shall shut the gate.

D 13 [a]Thou shalt daily prepare a burnt offering unto the LORD *of* a lamb [1]of the first year without blemish: thou shalt prepare it [2]every morning.

14 And thou shalt prepare a meat offering for it every morning, the sixth part of an ephah, and the third part of an hin of oil, to temper with the fine flour; a meat offering continually by a perpetual ordinance unto the LORD.

15 Thus shall they prepare the lamb, and the meat offering, and the oil, every morning *for* a continual burnt offering.

16 ¶ Thus saith the Lord GOD; If the prince give a gift unto any of his sons, the inheritance thereof shall be his sons'; it *shall be* their possession by inheritance.

17 But if he give a gift of his inheritance to one of his servants, then it shall be his to [a]the year of liberty; after it shall return to the prince: but his inheritance shall be his sons' for them.

18 Moreover [a]the prince shall not take of the people's inheritance by oppression, to thrust them out of their possession; *but* he shall give his sons inheritance out of his own possession: that my people be not scattered every man from his possession.

19 ¶ After he brought me through the entry, which *was* at the side of the gate, into the holy chambers of the priests, which looked toward the north: and, behold, there *was* a place on the two sides westward.

20 Then said he unto me, This *is* the place where the priests shall [a]boil the trespass offering and the sin offering, where they shall [b]bake the meat offering; that they bear *them* not out into the utter court, [c]to sanctify the people.

21 Then he brought me forth into the utter court, and caused me to pass by the four corners of the court; and, behold, [1]in every corner of the court *there was* a court.

22 In the four corners of the court *there were* courts [1]joined of forty *cubits* long and thirty broad: these four [2]corners *were* of one measure.

23 And *there was* a row *of building* round about in them, round about them four, and *it was* made with boiling places under the rows round about.

24 Then said he unto me, These *are* the places of them that boil, where the ministers of the house shall [a]boil the sacrifice of the people.

4 [a]ch. 45:17
5 [a]ver. 7,11; ch. 45:24 [b]Deut. 16:17 [1]Heb. *the gift of his hand*
8 [a]ver. 2
9 [a]Ex. 23:14-17; Deut. 16:16
11 [a]ver. 5
12 [a]ver. 2; ch. 44:3
13 [a]Ex. 29:38; Num. 28:3 [1]Heb. *a son of his year* [2]Heb. *morning by morning*
17 [a]Lev. 25:10
18 [a]ch. 45:8
20 [a]2 Chr. 35:13 [b]Lev. 2:4,5,7 [c]ch. 44:19
21 [1]Heb. *a court in a corner of a court and a court in a corner of a court*
22 [1]Or, *made with chimneys* [2]Heb. *cornered*
24 [a]See ver. 20

D *Isa 53:3–12* ◀ ▶ *Da 9:24–26*

The river from the temple

I M **47** AFTERWARD HE brought me again unto the door of the house; and, behold, [a]waters issued out from under the threshold of the house eastward: for the forefront of the house *stood toward* the east, and the waters came down from under from the right side of the house, at the south *side* of the altar.

2 Then brought he me out of the way of the gate northward, and led me about the way without unto the utter gate by the way that looketh eastward; and, behold, there ran out waters on the right side.

3 And when [a]the man that had the line in his hand went forth eastward, he measured a thousand cubits, and he brought me through the waters; the [l]waters *were* to the ankles.

4 Again he measured a thousand, and brought me through the waters; the waters *were* to the knees. Again he measured a thousand, and brought me through; the waters *were* to the loins.

5 Afterward he measured a thousand; *and it was* a river that I could not pass over: for the waters were risen, [l]waters to swim in, a river that could not be passed over.

6 ¶ And he said unto me, Son of man, hast thou seen *this?* Then he brought me, and caused me to return to the brink of the river.

7 Now when I had returned, behold, at the [l]bank of the river *were* very many [a]trees on the one side and on the other.

8 Then said he unto me, These waters issue out toward the east country, and go down into the [l]desert, and go into the sea: *which being* brought forth into the sea, the waters shall be healed.

9 And it shall come to pass, *that* every thing that liveth, which moveth, whithersoever the [l]rivers shall come, shall live: and there shall be a very great multitude of fish, because these waters shall come thither: for they shall be healed; and every thing shall live whither the river cometh.

10 And it shall come to pass, *that* the fishers shall stand upon it from En-gedi even unto En-eglaim; they shall be a *place* to spread forth nets; their fish shall be according to their kinds, as the fish [a]of the great sea, exceeding many.

11 But the miry places thereof and the marshes thereof [l]shall not be healed; they shall be given to salt.

12 And [a]by the river upon the bank thereof, on this side and on that side, [l]shall grow all trees for meat, [b]whose leaf shall not fade, neither shall the fruit thereof be consumed: it shall bring forth [2]new fruit according to his months, because their waters they issued out of the sanctuary: and the fruit thereof shall be for meat, and the leaf thereof [3]for [c]medicine. H

The borders of the land

13 ¶ Thus saith the Lord GOD; This *shall be* the border, whereby ye shall inherit the land according to the twelve tribes of Israel: [a]Joseph *shall have two* portions.

14 And ye shall inherit it, one as well as another: *concerning* the which I [a]lifted[l] up mine hand to give it unto your fathers: and this land shall [b]fall unto you for inheritance.

15 And this *shall be* the border of the land toward the north side, from the great sea, [a]the way of Hethlon, as men go to [b]Zedad;

16 [a]Hamath, [b]Berothah, Sibraim, which *is* between the border of Damascus and the border of Hamath; [l]Hazar-hatticon, which *is* by the coast of Hauran.

17 And the border from the sea shall be [a]Hazar-enan, the border of Damascus, and the north northward, and the border of Hamath. And *this is* the north side.

18 And the east side ye shall measure [l]from Hauran, and from Damascus, and from Gilead, and from the land of Israel

47:1 [a]Joel 3:18; Zech. 13:1 & 14:8; Rev. 22:1
3 [a]ch. 40:3 [l]Heb. *waters of the ankles*
5 [l]Heb. *waters of swimming*
7 [a]ver. 12; Rev. 22:2 [l]Heb. *lip*
8 [l]Or, *plain;* see Deut. 3:17 & 4:49; Josh. 3:16
9 [l]Heb. *two rivers*
10 [a]Num. 34:3; Josh. 23:4; ch. 48:28
11 [l]Or, *and that* which *shall not be healed*
12 [a]ver. 7 [b]Job 8:16; Ps. 1:3; Jer. 17:8 [c]Rev. 22:2 [l]Heb. *shall come up* [2]Or, *principal* [3]Or, *for bruises and sores*
13 [a]Gen. 48:5; 1 Chr. 5:1; ch. 48:4,5
14 [a]Gen. 12:7 & 13:15 & 15:7 & 17:8 & 26:3 & 28:13; ch. 20:5,6, 28,42 [b]ch. 48:29 [l]Or, *swore*
15 [a]ch. 48:1 [b]Num. 34:8
16 [a]Num. 34:8 [b]2 Sam. 8:8 [l]Or, *the middle village*
17 [a]Num. 34:9; ch. 48:1
18 [l]Heb. *from between*

I *Eze 45:8* ◄ ► *Da 8:19*
M *Eze 43:5–7* ◄ ► *Eze 48:1–7*
H *Eze 34:16* ◄ ► *Mt 8:17*

47:1–23 Ezekiel's vision of the new temple concluded with a view of water flowing out from under the temple. This water would transform the barren landscape into fertile fields and refresh the Dead Sea so that it could support fish again. Note also that Ezekiel outlined the boundaries of Israel's kingdom during the Millennium (47:15–21), a reaffirmation of God's promise to restore all of the promised land to Israel's possession when the Messiah returns.

by Jordan, from the border unto the east
sea. And *this is* the east side.
19 And the south side southward,
from Tamar *even* to [a]the waters of [1]strife
in Kadesh, the [2]river to the great sea.
And *this is* [3]the south side southward.
20 The west side also *shall be* the great
sea from the border, till a man come over
against Hamath. This *is* the west side.
21 So shall ye divide this land unto you
according to the tribes of Israel.
22 ¶ And it shall come to pass, *that* ye
shall divide it by lot for an inheritance
unto you, [a]and to the strangers that sojourn among you, which shall beget children among you: [b]and they shall be unto
you as born in the country among the
children of Israel; they shall have inheritance with you among the tribes of Israel.
23 And it shall come to pass, *that* in
what tribe the stranger sojourneth, there
shall ye give *him* his inheritance, saith
the Lord GOD.

19 [a]Num. 20:13; Deut. 32:51; Ps. 81:7; ch. 48:28 [1]Or, *Meribah* [2]Or, *valley* [3]Or, *toward Teman*

22 [a]See Eph. 3:6; Rev. 7:9,10 [b]Rom. 10:12; Gal. 3:28; Col. 3:11

The division of the land

M 48 NOW THESE *are* the names of
the tribes. [a]From the north end
to the coast of the way of Hethlon, as one
goeth to Hamath, Hazar-enan, the border
of Damascus northward, to the coast of
Hamath; for these are his sides east *and*
west; [1]a *portion for* Dan.
2 And by the border of Dan, from the
east side unto the west side, a *portion for*
Asher.
3 And by the border of Asher, from the
east side even unto the west side, a *portion for* Naphtali.
4 And by the border of Naphtali, from
the east side unto the west side, a *portion
for* Manasseh.
5 And by the border of Manasseh, from
the east side unto the west side, a *portion
for* Ephraim.
6 And by the border of Ephraim, from
the east side even unto the west side, a
portion for Reuben.
7 And by the border of Reuben, from
the east side unto the west side, a *portion
for* Judah.
8 ¶ And by the border of Judah, from
the east side unto the west side, shall be
[a]the offering which ye shall offer of five
and twenty thousand *reeds in* breadth,
and *in* length as one of the *other* parts,
from the east side unto the west side: and
the sanctuary shall be in the midst of it.
9 The oblation that ye shall offer unto
the LORD *shall be* of five and twenty thousand in length, and of ten thousand in
breadth.
10 And for them, *even* for the priests, M
shall be *this* holy oblation; toward the
north five and twenty thousand *in length,*
and toward the west ten thousand in

48:1 [a]ch. 47:15 [1]Heb. *one* portion

8 [a]ch. 45:1-6

M *Eze 47:1–21* ◀▶ *Eze 48:10–35*

M *Eze 48:1–7* ◀▶ *Da 2:34–35*

48:1–29 Ezekiel then shared his vision of the disposition of the land during the Millennium for each of the tribes of Israel. Notice that these allotments differ slightly from Joshua's original apportionments as the tribes entered Canaan because Ezekiel's allotments run all the way from the eastern to the western borders of the land. See the map of Israel during the Millennium on p. 947.

The northernmost allotment went to the tribe of Dan, descendants of Rachel's maidservant Bilhah (see Ge 35:25). The other northern allotments went to Asher and Naphtali, sons of Leah's and Rachel's maidservants (see Ge 35:25–26), because the tribes descended from maidservants were placed farthest from the sanctuary. The furthest allotment to the south was given to the tribe of Gad, descendants of Zilpah, Leah's maidservant (see Ge 35:25) for the same reason.

Next in line from the north were Manasseh and Ephraim, Joseph's two sons who were adopted by Jacob (see Ge 48:17–20). Since the tribe of Levi received no land (see 44:28) Manasseh and Ephraim received the allotments for Joseph and Levi (48:4–5).

Reuben's allotment came next, and Judah occupied the most prestigious northern allotment alongside the holy portion that was set aside for the temple. Note that in Joshua's allotment of the land of Canaan the tribe of Judah settled in the south. Yet prophecy said that out of the tribe of Judah would come the Messiah (see Ge 49:8–12). Possibly settling the tribe of Judah with the northern tribes in the reunited Israel would signify that these northern tribes would finally have a "part in David" (2Sa 20:1; see 1Ki 12:16; 2Ch 10:16).

The central portion of the promised land included the area of Jerusalem and the area set aside as a sacred district to house the temple, the priests and Levites, and the prince.

Directly to the south of the sacred land was the allotment for the tribe of Benjamin, followed by the allotments for the tribes of Simeon, Issachar and Zebulun. Note that this arrangement is different from the allotments given in Joshua's day (see Jos 13—17).

breadth, and toward the east ten thousand in breadth, and toward the south five and twenty thousand in length: and the sanctuary of the LORD shall be in the midst thereof.

11 [a]*It*[1] *shall be* for the priests that are sanctified of the sons of Zadok; which have kept my [2]charge, which went not astray when the children of Israel went astray, [b]as the Levites went astray.

12 And *this* oblation of the land that is offered shall be unto them a thing most holy by the border of the Levites.

13 And over against the border of the priests the Levites *shall have* five and twenty thousand in length, and ten thousand in breadth: all the length *shall be* five and twenty thousand, and the breadth ten thousand.

14 [a]And they shall not sell of it, neither exchange, nor alienate the firstfruits of the land: for *it is* holy unto the LORD.

15 ¶ [a]And the five thousand, that are left in the breadth over against the five and twenty thousand, shall be [b]a profane *place* for the city, for dwelling, and for suburbs: and the city shall be in the midst thereof.

16 And these *shall be* the measures thereof; the north side four thousand and five hundred, and the south side four thousand and five hundred, and on the east side four thousand and five hundred, and the west side four thousand and five hundred.

17 And the suburbs of the city shall be toward the north two hundred and fifty, and toward the south two hundred and fifty, and toward the east two hundred and fifty, and toward the west two hundred and fifty.

18 And the residue in length over against the oblation of the holy *portion shall be* ten thousand eastward, and ten thousand westward: and it shall be over against the oblation of the holy *portion;* and the increase thereof shall be for food unto them that serve the city.

19 [a]And they that serve the city shall serve it out of all the tribes of Israel.

11 [a]ch. 44:15 [b]ch. 44:10 [1]Or, *The sanctified* portion shall be *for the priests* [2]Or, *ward,* or, *ordinance*

14 [a]Ex. 22:29; Lev. 27:10,28,33

15 [a]ch. 45:6 [b]ch. 42:20

19 [a]ch. 45:6

Division of the Land in the Millennium

Eze 47—48

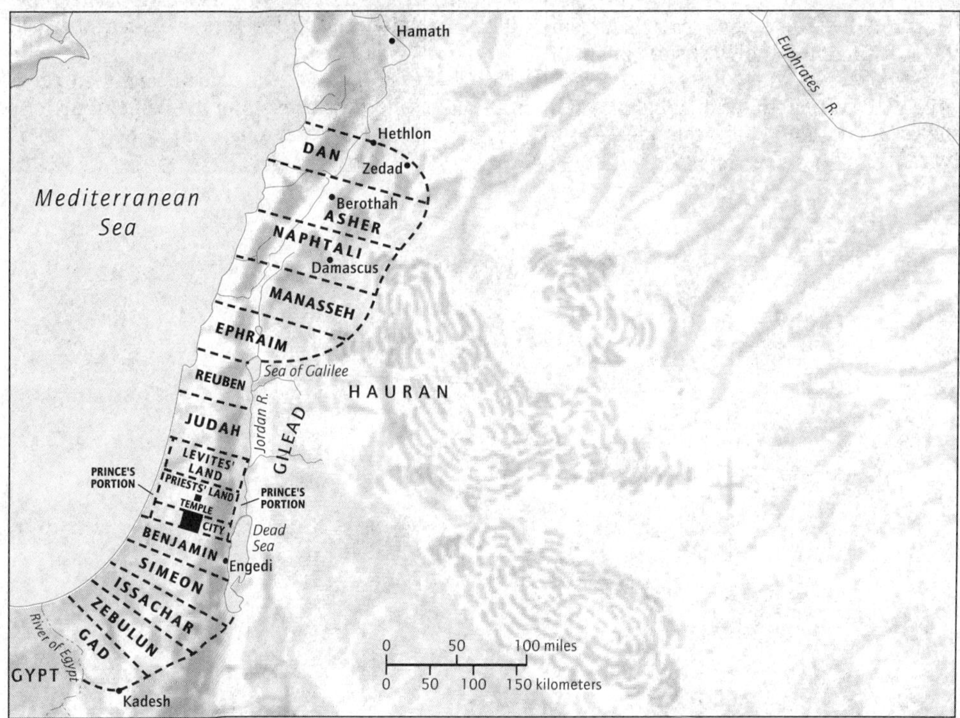

20 All the oblation *shall be* five and twenty thousand by five and twenty thousand: ye shall offer the holy oblation foursquare, with the possession of the city.

21 ¶ [a]And the residue *shall be* for the prince, on the one side and on the other of the holy oblation, and of the possession of the city, over against the five and twenty thousand of the oblation toward the east border, and westward over against the five and twenty thousand toward the west border, over against the portions for the prince: and it shall be the holy oblation; [b]and the sanctuary of the house *shall be* in the midst thereof.

22 Moreover from the possession of the Levites, and from the possession of the city, *being* in the midst *of that* which is the prince's, between the border of Judah and the border of Benjamin, shall be for the prince.

23 As for the rest of the tribes, from the east side unto the west side, Benjamin *shall have* ʹa *portion.*

24 And by the border of Benjamin, from the east side unto the west side, Simeon *shall have* a *portion.*

25 And by the border of Simeon, from the east side unto the west side, Issachar a *portion.*

26 And by the border of Issachar, from the east side unto the west side, Zebulun a *portion.*

27 And by the border of Zebulun, from the east side unto the west side, Gad a *portion.*

28 And by the border of Gad, at the south side southward, the border shall be even from Tamar *unto* [a]the waters of ʹstrife *in* Kadesh, *and* to the river toward the great sea.

29 [a]This *is* the land which ye shall divide by lot unto the tribes of Israel for inheritance, and these *are* their portions, saith the Lord GOD.

The name of the city

30 ¶ And these *are* the goings out of the city on the north side, four thousand and five hundred measures.

31 [a]And the gates of the city *shall be* after the names of the tribes of Israel: three gates northward; one gate of Reuben, one gate of Judah, one gate of Levi.

32 And at the east side four thousand and five hundred: and three gates; and one gate of Joseph, one gate of Benjamin, one gate of Dan.

33 And at the south side four thousand and five hundred measures: and three gates; one gate of Simeon, one gate of Issachar, one gate of Zebulun.

34 At the west side four thousand and five hundred, *with* their three gates; one gate of Gad, one gate of Asher, one gate of Naphtali.

35 *It was* round about eighteen thousand *measures:* [a]and the name of the city from *that* day *shall be,* [b]The ʹ LORD *is* there.

21 [a]ch. 45:7 [b]ver. 8,10

23 ʹHeb. *one portion*

28 [a]ch. 47:19 ʹHeb. *Meribah-kadesh*

29 [a]ch. 47:14,21, 22

31 [a]Rev. 21:12

35 [a]Jer. 33:16 [b]Jer. 3:17; Joel 3:21; Zech. 2:10; Rev. 21:3 & 22:3 ʹHeb. *Jehovah-shammah*

Daniel

Author: Daniel

Theme: God is sovereign over human governments

Date of Writing: c. 536–530 B.C.

Outline of Daniel

I. Background Information About Daniel (1:1–21)
II. The Nations Are in God's Hands (2:1—7:28)
  A. Nebuchadnezzar's Dreams, Idols and Madness (2:1—4:37)
  B. Belshazzar's Feast and Babylon's Fall (5:1–31)
  C. King Cyrus and the Lion's Den (6:1–28)
  D. Four World Empires (7:1–28)
III. Israel Is in God's Hands (8:1—12:13)
  A. The Vision of the Ram and Goat (8:1–27)
  B. Daniel's Messianic Vision of the Seventy Weeks (9:1–27)
  C. A Vision of Israel's Future and Final Victory (10:1—12:13)

THE BOOK OF Daniel takes its name from its author, a man of God who was granted a divine ability to see through time and describe the future. Taken captive to Babylon by Nebuchadnezzar after the destruction of Jerusalem in 605 B.C., Daniel rose from his position as the king's servant to a position as royal advisor for several Babylonian and Persian kings. As God's prophet, Daniel, whose name means "God is my judge," faithfully and wisely served the kings who had conquered his people. Through his book and ministry, Daniel demonstrates God's sovereign control over the destiny of all nations and brings a clearer understanding of God's plan to redeem the earth from sin's curse.

Scholars consider Daniel's prophecies fundamental to understanding the main themes of the end times. Apocalyptic in style, Daniel's predictions refer to future events using many figures of speech and symbols to convey God's message, sometimes even fixing the time when these events would occur. Because of this, ancient Jewish historians held Daniel's prophecies in highest honor in their theology of the Messiah. In addition, Daniel's predictions harmonize the prophetic details found in Mt 24, 2 Thessalonians, and Revelation. The most notable prophecies in Daniel concern the rise and fall of the four Gentile empires and the establishment of the millennial kingdom of the Messiah.

The book of Daniel also reaffirms the need for consistent holiness and bears out God's triumph over evil. Daniel's record of the persecution of his three companions and himself (chs. 3; 6) by their pagan conquerors foreshadows the persecution of the saints by the antichrist during the tribulation period. Also, King Nebuchadnezzar's statue and King Darius's prohibition of the worship of God warn of the attacks on the true worship of God during the conflict between the antichrist and God's children.

Despite attacks denying Daniel's divine inspiration concerning future events, Jesus confirmed Daniel's accuracy and inspiration by basing some of his prophetic words on Daniel's prophecies (see Mt 24:15). Recent archeological and scientific discoveries also confirm Daniel's divine visions.

The test of Daniel and his friends

1 IN THE third year of the reign of Jehoiakim king of Judah [a]came Nebuchadnezzar king of Babylon unto Jerusalem, and besieged it.
2 And the Lord gave Jehoiakim king of
Judah into his hand, with [a]part of the vessels of the house of God: which he carried [b]into the land of Shinar to the house
of his god; [c]and he brought the vessels
into the treasure house of his god.
3 ¶ And the king spake unto Ashpenaz
the master of his eunuchs, that he should
bring [l]*certain* of the children of Israel,
and of the king's seed, and of the princes;
4 Children [a]in whom *was* no blemish,
but wellfavoured, and skilful in all wisdom, and cunning in knowledge, and understanding science, and such as *had* ability in them to stand in the king's palace,
and [b]whom they might teach the learning
and the tongue of the Chaldeans.
5 And the king appointed them a daily
provision of the king's meat, and of [l]the
wine which he drank: so nourishing
them three years, that at the end thereof
they might [a]stand before the king.
6 Now among these were of the children of Judah, Daniel, Hananiah, Mishael, and Azariah:
7 [a]Unto whom the prince of the eu-

1:1 [a]2 Ki. 24:1; 2 Chr. 36:6
2 [a]Jer. 27:19 [b]Gen. 10:10; Zech. 5:11 [c]2 Chr. 36:7
3 [l]Foretold in 2 Ki. 20:17,18; Is. 39:7
4 [a]See Lev. 24:19, 20 [b]Acts 7:22
5 [a]ver. 19; Gen. 41:46; 1 Ki. 10:8 [l]Heb. *the wine of his drink*
7 [a]Gen. 41:45; 2 Ki. 24:17

1:1–2 The deportation referred to in this passage was the first in a series of deportations of Jewish exiles to Babylon located some 600 miles across the desert in what is now southwestern Iraq (see Jer 25:11). The prophet Ezekiel was taken captive in the second deportation in 598 B.C.

The Babylonian army under King Nebuchadnezzar also captured some of the temple vessels in fulfillment of Isaiah's prophecy to King Hezekiah (see Isa 39:1–6). Daniel recorded that Nebuchadnezzar placed them in "the treasure house of his god" (1:2), which was probably the temple of Marduk (Bel), the chief god of Babylon. However, some of the temple vessels in Jerusalem escaped this first desecration (see Jer 27:19–22).

1:3–4 The nobles and talented artisans of the exiles were taken to the capital of Babylon to be trained for service (see 2Ki 24:14). These captives were selected from the royal dynasty of the kingdom of Judah because they were still of a teachable age, possessed good health and were intelligent and wise. Babylonian history records that young teenage boys were often chosen for an intensive training period to ready them to serve the court as royal advisors.

1:6 Because of their royal standing, skills and abilities, Daniel and his three companions were chosen to join the king's staff.

1:7 It was customary in ancient pagan courts to rename foreign captives to further emphasize their subjection to the conquering king. The original Hebrew names of these Jewish captives honored the name of God in their construction and meaning. Their Babylonian names reflected Nebuchadnezzar's desire to honor his pagan god Bel (see note at 1:1–2).

Daniel's Hebrew name means "God is (my) Judge." His name was changed to *Belteshazzar*, which probably meant in Babylonian "Bel protect his life!" *Hananiah* was the Hebrew for "The LORD shows grace"; his changed name *Shadrach* probably meant "at the command of Aku." (Aku was a Sumerian moon-god.) *Mishael*, meaning "Who is what God is?" found his name changed to *Meshach*, which probably meant "Who is what Aku is?" And *Azariah*, meaning "The LORD helps," was renamed after another

nuchs gave names: [b]for he gave unto
Daniel *the name* of Belteshazzar; and to
Hananiah, of Shadrach; and to Mishael, of
Meshach; and to Azariah, of Abed-nego.
8 ¶ But Daniel purposed in his heart
that he would not defile himself [a]with
the portion of the king's meat, nor with
the wine which he drank: therefore he
requested of the prince of the eunuchs
that he might not defile himself.
9 Now [a]God had brought Daniel into
favour and tender love with the prince of
the eunuchs.
10 And the prince of the eunuchs said
unto Daniel, I fear my lord the king, who
hath appointed your meat and your drink:
for why should he see your faces [1]worse
liking than the children which *are* of your
[2]sort? then shall ye make *me* endanger
my head to the king.
11 Then said Daniel to [1]Melzar, whom
the prince of the eunuchs had set over
Daniel, Hananiah, Mishael, and Azariah,
12 Prove thy servants, I beseech thee,
ten days; and let them give us [1]pulse [2]to
eat, and water to drink.
13 Then let our countenances be
looked upon before thee, and the countenance of the children that eat of the portion of the king's meat: and as thou seest,
deal with thy servants.
14 So he consented to them in this
matter, and proved them ten days.
E 15 And at the end of ten days their
U countenances appeared fairer and fatter
in flesh than all the children which did
eat the portion of the king's meat.

E *Isa 38:1–22* ◀▶ *Hos 11:3*
U *Eze 34:26–27* ◀▶ *Da 10:12*

7 [b]ch. 4:8 & 5:12
8 [a]Deut. 32:38; Ezek. 4:13; Hos. 9:3
9 [a]See Gen. 39:21; Ps. 106:46; Prov. 16:7
10 [1]Heb. *sadder* [2]Or, *term*, or, *continuance?*
11 [1]Or, *The steward*
12 [1]Heb. *of pulse* [2]Heb. *that we may eat*
17 [a]1 Ki. 3:12; Jas. 1:5,17 [b]Acts 7:22 [c]Num. 12:6; 2 Chr. 26:5; ch. 5:11,12, 14 & 10:1 [1]Or, *he made Daniel understand*
19 [a]ver. 5; Gen. 41:46
20 [a]1 Ki. 10:1 [1]Heb. *wisdom of understanding*
21 [a]ch. 6:28 & 10:1
2:1 [a]Gen. 41:8; ch. 4:5 [b]Esth. 6:1; ch. 6:18
2 [a]Gen. 41:8; Ex. 7:11; ch. 5:7

16 Thus Melzar took away the portion
of their meat, and the wine that they
should drink; and gave them pulse.
17 ¶ As for these four children, [a]God
gave them [b]knowledge and skill in all
learning and wisdom: and [1]Daniel had
[c]understanding in all visions and dreams.
18 Now at the end of the days that the
king had said he should bring them in,
then the prince of the eunuchs brought
them in before Nebuchadnezzar.
19 And the king communed with
them; and among them all was found
none like Daniel, Hananiah, Mishael, and
Azariah: therefore [a]stood they before the
king.
20 [a]And in all matters of [1]wisdom *and*
understanding, that the king inquired of
them, he found them ten times better
than all the magicians *and* astrologers
that *were* in all his realm.
21 [a]And Daniel continued *even* unto
the first year of king Cyrus.

Nebuchadnezzar's dream

2 AND IN the second year of the reign
of Nebuchadnezzar, Nebuchadnezzar dreamed dreams, [a]wherewith his
spirit was troubled, and [b]his sleep brake
from him.
2 [a]Then the king commanded to call
the magicians, and the astrologers, and
the sorcerers, and the Chaldeans, for to
show the king his dreams. So they came
and stood before the king.
3 And the king said unto them, I have
dreamed a dream, and my spirit was troubled to know the dream.
4 Then spake the Chaldeans to the

Babylonian god when he was given the name *Abednego*, which probably meant "servant of Nego."
1:8 Daniel and his friends respectfully rejected the king's food because of their determination to follow God's dietary commands in the Law of Moses (see Lev 11:1–31). Note that Daniel's submissive attitude earned him favor in the eyes of his masters.
1:19–20 At the end of the training period, the king interviewed all of the young men. Daniel, Hananiah, Mishael and Azariah stood out from all the rest, exhibiting the wisdom of God (see Jas 1:5).
1:21 Daniel's remarkable career spanned the reign of several kings and different empires (605–539 B.C.) because of his resolve to obey God and honestly serve his masters.
2:1 The date of this verse could apply to the second year that Nebuchadnezzar ruled over Israel—604 B.C.—or it could refer to the Babylonian system of dating the years of a king's reign. The Babylonians did not count the year of a king's accession to the throne as a numbered year of that king's reign. Thus calculating the second year of Nebuchadnezzar's reign in the Babylonian way would mean that this dream coincided with Daniel's last year of training.
2:4 Since the king's advisors came from different racial backgrounds, they spoke to the king in Aramaic (Syriac), a language that was familiar to everyone. This language was the accepted language for commerce and politics in the Babylonian and Persian empires. Note that in the original manuscript chapters 2—7 of Daniel were written in Aramaic since the information included in these chapters was important for the Gentile nations of the Near East to

king in Syriac, [a]O king, live for ever: tell
thy servants the dream, and we will show
the interpretation.
5 The king answered and said to the
Chaldeans, The thing is gone from me: if
ye will not make known unto me the
dream, with the interpretation thereof,
ye shall be [a]cut[/] in pieces, and your
houses shall be made a dunghill.
6 [a]But if ye show the dream, and the
interpretation thereof, ye shall receive of
me gifts and [b]rewards[/] and great honour:
therefore show me the dream, and the
interpretation thereof.
7 They answered again and said, Let
the king tell his servants the dream, and
we will show the interpretation of it.
8 The king answered and said, I know

4 [a] 1 Ki. 1:31; ch. 3:9 & 5:10 & 6:6, 21

5 [a] 2 Ki. 10:27; Ezra 6:11; ch. 3:29 [/] Chald. *made pieces*

6 [a] ch. 5:16 [b] ver. 48; ch. 5:17 [/] Or, *fee*

11 [a] ch. 5:11

of certainty that ye would gain the time,
because ye see the thing is gone from me.
9 But if ye will not make known unto
me the dream, *there is but* one decree for
you: for ye have prepared lying and corrupt words to speak before me, till the
time be changed: therefore tell me the
dream, and I shall know that ye can show
me the interpretation thereof.
10 ¶ The Chaldeans answered before
the king, and said, There is not a man
upon the earth that can show the king's
matter: therefore *there is* no king, lord,
nor ruler, *that* asked such things at any
magician, or astrologer, or Chaldean.
11 And *it is* a rare thing that the king
requireth, and there is none other that
can show it before the king, [a]except the

understand too. The latter chapters of Daniel revert to Hebrew text since that material is primarily directed to God's chosen people.
2:5–11 The king demanded something extraordinary: that the wise men describe his forgotten dream and then interpret it for him. The wise men declared correctly that no one could fulfill the king's command "except the gods" (2:11).

The Four Gentile World Empires

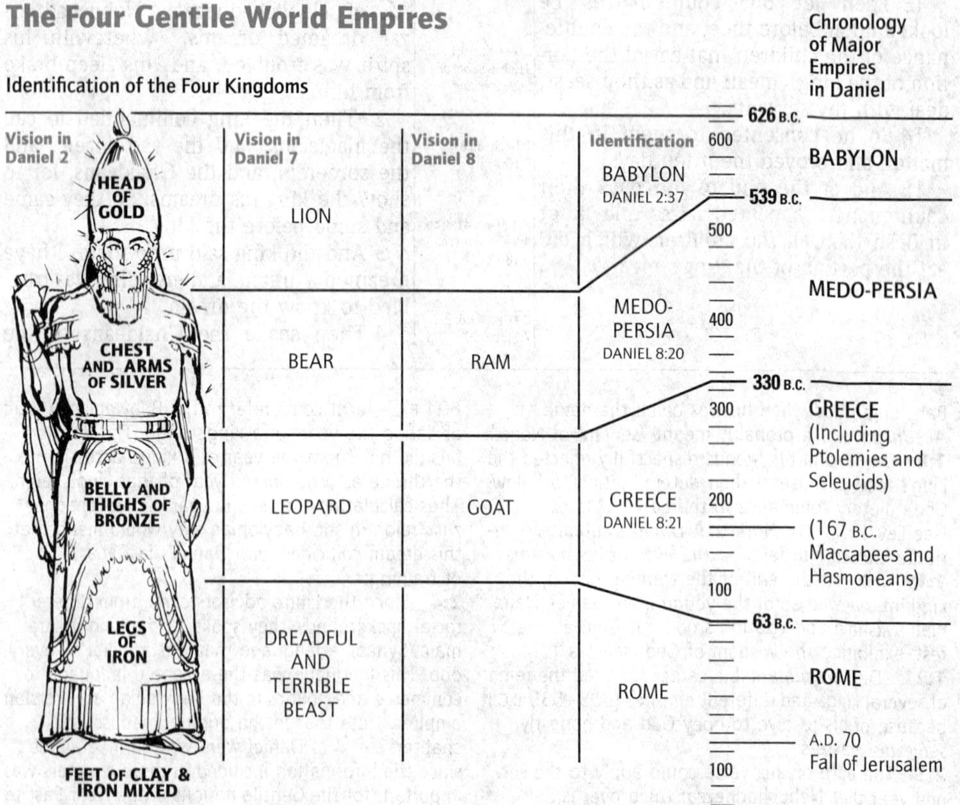

gods, whose dwelling is not with flesh.

12 For this cause the king was angry and very furious, and commanded to destroy all the wise *men* of Babylon.

13 And the decree went forth that the wise *men* should be slain; and they sought Daniel and his fellows to be slain.

14 ¶ Then Daniel [1]answered with counsel and wisdom to Arioch the [2,3]captain of the king's guard, which was gone forth to slay the wise *men* of Babylon:

15 He answered and said to Arioch the king's captain, Why *is* the decree *so* hasty from the king? Then Arioch made the thing known to Daniel.

16 Then Daniel went in, and desired of the king that he would give him time, and that he would show the king the interpretation.

17 Then Daniel went to his house, and made the thing known to Hananiah, Mishael, and Azariah, his companions:

18 [a]That they would desire mercies [1]of the God of heaven concerning this secret; [2]that Daniel and his fellows should not perish with the rest of the wise *men* of Babylon.

19 ¶ Then was the secret revealed unto Daniel [a]in a night vision. Then Daniel blessed the God of heaven.

20 Daniel answered and said, [a]Blessed be the name of God for ever and ever: [b]for wisdom and might are his:

21 And he changeth [a]the times and the seasons: [b]he removeth kings, and setteth up kings: [c]he giveth wisdom unto the wise, and knowledge to them that know understanding:

E 22 [a]He revealeth the deep and secret things: [b]he knoweth what *is* in the darkness, and [c]the light dwelleth with him.

23 I thank thee, and praise thee, O thou God of my fathers, who hast given me wisdom and might, and hast made known unto me now what we [a]desired of thee: for thou hast *now* made known unto us the king's matter.

E *Eze 11:5* ◀▶ *Da 5:27*

Daniel interprets the dream

24 ¶ Therefore Daniel went in unto Arioch, whom the king had ordained to destroy the wise *men* of Babylon: he went and said thus unto him; Destroy not the wise *men* of Babylon: bring me in before the king, and I will show unto the king the interpretation.

25 Then Arioch brought in Daniel before the king in haste, and said thus unto him, [1]I have found a man of the [2]captives of Judah, that will make known unto the king the interpretation.

26 The king answered and said to Daniel, whose name *was* Belteshazzar, Art thou able to make known unto me the dream which I have seen, and the interpretation thereof?

27 Daniel answered in the presence of the king, and said, The secret which the king hath demanded cannot the wise *men*, the astrologers, the magicians, the soothsayers, show unto the king;

28 [a]But there is a God in heaven that G
revealeth secrets, and [1]maketh known to L
the king Nebuchadnezzar [b]what shall be in the latter days. Thy dream, and the visions of thy head upon thy bed, are these;

29 As for thee, O king, thy thoughts [1]came *into thy mind* upon thy bed, what should come to pass hereafter: [a]and he that revealeth secrets maketh known to thee what shall come to pass.

30 [a]But as for me, this secret is not revealed to me for *any* wisdom that I have more than any living, [1]but for *their* sakes that shall make known the interpretation to the king, [b]and that thou mightest know the thoughts of thy heart.

31 ¶ Thou, O king, [1]sawest, and be-

G *Jer 16:19* ◀▶ *Da 7:2–28*
L *Jer 39:17–18* ◀▶ *Jnh 2:4*

14 [1]Chald. *returned* [2]Or, *chief marshal* [3]Chald. *chief of the executioners,* or, *slaughtermen*

18 [a]Mat. 18:19 [1]Chald. *from before God* [2]Or, *that they should not destroy Daniel*

19 [a]Num. 12:6; Job 33:15

20 [a]Ps. 113:2 [b]Jer. 32:19

21 [a]Esth. 1:13 [b]Job 12:18; Ps. 75:6,7; Jer. 27:5 [c]Jas. 1:5

22 [a]Job 12:22; Ps. 25:14 [b]Ps. 139:11; Heb. 4:13 [c]ch. 5:11,14

23 [a]ver. 18

25 [1]Chald. *That I have found* [2]Chald. *children of the captivity of Judah*

28 [a]Gen. 40:8; Amos 4:13 [b]Gen. 49:1 [1]Chald. *hath made known*

29 [a]ver. 22,28 [1]Chald. *came up*

30 [a]Acts 3:12 [b]ver. 47 [1]Or, *but for the intent that the interpretation may be made known to the king*

31 [1]Chald. *wast seeing*

2:17–27 Rather than take personal credit for this revelation, Daniel repeatedly affirmed that only God "revealeth the deep and secret things" (2:22).

2:28 Daniel affirmed that God alone knew the future and could reveal the secrets of the future through his prophets (see Ge 40:8; 41:16; Isa 46:9–10).

2:31 Daniel interpreted the king's dream, describing a great, metallic image that represented the future course of Gentile world rule through four successive world empires. King Nebuchadnezzar's curiosity about the future of his empire and those that would follow was answered with this divinely inspired prophetic dream that outlined the course of world history. Note that both the beginning and end of these Gentile world empires are marked by the setting up of a pagan image (see Da 2:31; 3:1; Rev 13:14–15).

The Four World Empires

King Nebuchadnezzar of Babylon meditated on what course history would follow after his death and received a vision from God of a great metallic image. God gave the young prophet Daniel the interpretation to this vision. Daniel told the king that the dream symbolized the great world kingdoms that would follow after Nebuchadnezzar's death. Daniel described the great metallic image as a man's body with a head of gold, a chest of silver, an abdomen of bronze, legs of iron and feet and toes made of a mixture of iron and clay. In Nebuchadnezzar's vision, a stone "cut out without hands" (2:34) suddenly destroyed this magnificent statue, pulverizing the iron and clay feet and grinding the rest of the metals in the image into dust. The stone grew to become a great mountain and filled the entire earth.

Daniel interpreted this curious dream as a clear prophecy of the four future world empires that would rule the earth from Nebuchadnezzar's death until the Messiah sets up his kingdom. True to Daniel's prophecy, the four empires appeared in the exact order that Daniel said they would. And despite repeated efforts, no single nation has succeeded in establishing a fifth world empire to replace ancient Rome. The final world empire will be the kingdom of the Messiah. Nebuchadnezzar's vision is described in the table below.

The Great Image of Daniel 2

THE SYMBOL	THE EMPIRE	THE PROPHECY
Head of gold	Babylon	"Thou art this head of gold" (2:38).
Chest of silver	Medo-Persia	"After thee shall arise another kingdom inferior to thee" (2:39).
Belly of brass	Greece	"And another third kingdom of brass, which shall bear rule over all the earth" (2:39).
Legs of iron	Rome	"The fourth kingdom shall be strong as iron . . . iron breaketh in pieces and subdueth all things" (2:40).
Toes of iron and clay	Ten Nations	"The kingdom shall be divided . . . partly strong, and partly broken" (2:41–42).
Stone cut without hands	Messianic Kingdom	"In the days of these kings shall the God of heaven set up a kingdom, which shall never be destroyed" (2:44).

In 608 B.C. the Babylonian empire under King Nebuchadnezzar was strong, powerful and wealthy, aptly fulfilling the position as the image's head of god. Yet, as predicted by Jeremiah (see Jer 25:12), Babylon was destroyed within seventy years by the rise of Medo-Persia under the rule of King Cyrus. In one night the Medes and Persians conquered the kingdom of Babylon while Babylon's king Belshazzar feasted in his palace. Using the vessels from the temple in Jerusalem for profane purposes, Belshazzar was shaken from his revelry when the finger of God wrote a verdict of judgment on the wall of the palace. Daniel, now an old man and probably forgotten by the new rulers after Nebuchadnezzar's death, was called upon by the queen mother to interpret the writing. Daniel declared to Belshazzar God's judgment: God had decided to finish Belshazzar's reign; Belshazzar had been judged and "found wanting" (5:27) and Belshazzar's kingdom would be "divided, and given to the Medes and Persians" (5:28).

The Euphrates River cut through the mighty city of Babylon. Waterways were guarded with gates of strong brass. While Belshazzar feasted, the rebel Medo-Persian army under the leadership of Darius diverted the Euphrates River so that when the riverbed emptied, the Medo-Persian soldiers could slip right under the river gates into the heart of the city. Though Daniel was promoted to the third most powerful position in the kingdom of Babylon, he held that position for only a few hours before the city fell to Darius the Mede (see 5:30).

Nebuchadnezzar's image symbolized the second empire as a chest of silver. This indicated that the next empire would be stronger since silver is a stronger metal than gold but of inferior value. True to Nebuchadnezzar's vision, the Medo-Persians raised enormous armies and were powerful in battle, yet they lacked the nobility and wealth of Babylon. The Medo-Persian empire lasted only 207 years until it was destroyed by the swiftly moving armies of Alexander the Great in a climactic battle in 331 B.C.

The third world empire was symbolized by brass, a stronger metal than silver but a metal of less value. The Greek empire, based on the democratic governments of the Greek city-states, broke its world empire into four divisions led by Alexander's four generals. In a supplementary vision of a rapidly moving male goat that is recorded in ch. 8, Daniel predicted that the Greek empire would destroy Medo-Persia (represented by a ram). History records that the aggressive Alexander the Great exacted his revenge on the Persians for the Persian king Xerxes' earlier attack on Greece. The young Alexander conquered the known world from the Mediterranean to India with only 32,000 men in less than ten years.

Alexander's rule in Greece was short but full of conquests. After conquering the ancient seaport of Tyre in 332 B.C. he moved on, intending to destroy the city of Jerusalem because the Jews had resisted his demands. As Alexander approached the city, he was met by the high priest of the temple and informed that God had revealed to the prophet Daniel more than 300 years earlier that a great king would arise from Greece and subdue the entire world. When the priest showed Alexander the exact prophecies in the ancient Scriptures, Alexander was so moved that he worshiped in the temple and gave orders not to destroy Jerusalem or the land of Israel.

Yet Daniel had also prophesied that at the peak of Alexander's power the male goat's great horn would be broken and instead up would come "four notable ones toward the four winds of heaven" (8:8). When Alexander died suddenly at a young age, he left was no heir as successor. The huge empire was divided among his top four generals, just as Daniel had predicted 300 years earlier.

In this fourfold state, Greece continued to rule from the borders of India to Europe from 331 B.C. until the year 63 B.C. when the Roman army under General Pompey successfully attacked the independent kingdom of Israel and captured the temple. Pompey entered the Holy of Holies and installed his Roman garrisons throughout Palestine, occupying the fortress north of the temple that was later named the Tower of Antonia after Mark Antony.

Pompey's occupation of Palestine marked the end of the Greek empire. The fourth world empire of Nebuchadnezzar's vision was represented as two strong legs of iron that broke in pieces all which stood before it. This fourth world empire was Rome. One of the characteristics of the Roman empire was its incredible military might, and Rome transformed the various parts of its empire into an enormous military machine. Combining strength with an efficient police and judicial system, Rome completely supplanted the three preceding kingdoms. Rome's influence was so pervasive that even today, after two thousand years, many of our governmental institutions, bureaucracy, judicial codes and languages are based on the systems used in the Roman empire.

The fourth world empire of Nebuchadnezzar's vision ruled the known world longer than any of the other three. Exactly as foretold, the Roman empire split into two portions after the rule of Emperor Constantine. The western arm of the empire was based in Rome, and the eastern arm of the empire ruled from Constantinople (today's Istanbul, Turkey). Barbarians destroyed Rome's influence in the west in A.D. 476, while the eastern arm of the Roman empire became known as the Byzantine empire and continued its rule until its defeat by the Turks in A.D. 1453.

The last part of Nebuchadnezzar's dream concerned the final stage of the world's empires represented by the ten toes of iron and clay. God clearly predicted that in the days immediately before the establishment of the Messianic kingdom of the stone "cut out of the mountain without hands" (2:45), there would be a final revival of the Roman empire consisting of ten nations united together in a confederacy. Since Israel's rebirth as a nation in 1948 Europe has begun to come together more and more as a united federation for economic, trade and security reasons.

In 1948 the North Atlantic Treaty Organization (NATO) was formed to defend Europe against the threat of the massed armies of Communist Russia. In 1957 many European nations banded together in a confederation of economic and trade relationships. In 1992 European nations gathered to discuss future moves toward full integration of member economies, utilizing one economic system, a common monetary system as well as a common defense capability and foreign policy. Today, fifteen member states belong to the European Union, creating one of the largest economic, political and military powers in the western world. Daniel prophesied about a united federation under the revived Roman empire. For the first time in two thousand years, a united Europe would be able to fulfill this specific prophecy.

hold a great image. This great image, whose brightness *was* excellent, stood before thee; and the form thereof *was* terrible.

32 [a]This image's head *was* of fine gold, his breast and his arms of silver, his belly and his [l]thighs of brass,

33 His legs of iron, his feet part of iron and part of clay.

M 34 Thou sawest till that a stone was cut out [a]without hands, which smote the image upon his feet *that were* of iron and clay, and brake them to pieces.

35 Then was the iron, the clay, the brass, the silver, and the gold, broken to pieces together, and became [a]like the chaff of the summer threshingfloors; and the wind carried them away, that [b]no place was found for them: and the stone that smote the image [c]became a great mountain, [d]and filled the whole earth.

36 ¶ This *is* the dream; and we will tell the interpretation thereof before the king.

37 [a]Thou, O king, *art* a king of kings: [b]for the God of heaven hath given thee a kingdom, power, and strength, and glory.

38 [a]And wheresoever the children of men dwell, the beasts of the field and the fowls of the heaven hath he given into thine hand, and hath made thee ruler over them all. [b]Thou *art* this head of gold.

39 And after thee shall arise [a]another kingdom [b]inferior to thee, and another third kingdom of brass, which shall bear rule over all the earth.

40 And [a]the fourth kingdom shall be strong as iron: forasmuch as iron breaketh in pieces and subdueth all *things:* and as iron that breaketh all these, shall it break in pieces and bruise.

41 And whereas thou sawest the feet and toes, part of potters' clay, and part of iron, the kingdom shall be divided; but there shall be in it of the strength of the iron, forasmuch as thou sawest the iron mixed with miry clay.

42 And *as* the toes of the feet *were* part of iron, and part of clay, *so* the kingdom shall be partly strong, and partly [l]broken.

43 And whereas thou sawest iron mixed with miry clay, they shall mingle themselves with the seed of men: but they shall not cleave [l]one to another, even as iron is not mixed with clay.

44 And in [l]the days of these kings M V

32 [a]See ver. 38 [l]Or, *sides*
34 [a]Zech. 4:6; 2 Cor. 5:1; Heb. 9:24
35 [a]Hos. 13:3 [b]Ps. 37:10,36 [c]Is. 2:2,3 [d]Ps. 80:9
37 [a]Ezra 7:12; Is. 47:5; Jer. 27:6,7; Ezek. 26:7; Hos. 8:10 [b]Ezra 1:2
38 [a]ch. 4:21,22; Jer. 27:6 [b]ver. 32
39 [a]ch. 5:28,31 [b]ver. 32
40 [a]ch. 7:7,23
42 [l]Or, *brittle*
43 [l]Chald. *this with this*
44 [l]Chald. *their days*

M *Eze 48:10–35* ◄► *Da 2:44–45*

M *Da 2:34–35* ◄► *Da 7:13–14*
V *Jer 31:34* ◄► *Da 7:14*

2:34–35 The stone "cut out without hands" (2:34) represented Jesus Christ who would utterly destroy the Gentile world empires with a sudden blow at the Battle of Armageddon. This vivid imagery does not evoke a gradual conquest but rather suggests full-scale destruction of the fourth world kingdom (see Rev 16:13–16; 19:17). This destruction is immediately followed by the establishment of the kingdom of the "stone"—the kingdom of Christ.

This vision clearly foreshadowed Christ's ultimate victory with the defeat of the antichrist during the last days. Note also that the stone (rock) is used elsewhere in Scripture as a symbol for the Messiah (see Ge 49:24; Isa 8:14; 28:16; Zec 3:9).

2:37–40 The four metals of the great statue symbolized four Gentile world empires (Babylon, Medo-Persia, Greece and Rome) that would dominate the world from the time of Daniel (606 B.C.) until the end of this age. Note that the diminishing value of the metals from gold to silver to bronze to iron represented the decreasing grandeur and individual power of the successive kings and their empires. Yet each successive metal was stronger than the previous, indicating that each succeeding empire would last longer than the previous one.

Note that of all the empires the fourth and final world power (Rome) would be divided. The two legs of the image would ultimately become the divided Roman empire with its eastern (Byzantine) territory and its western (Roman) region. The ten toes of the image were also forged of iron and also represented the Roman influence. At the end of this age this last portion of Nebuchadnezzar's image will rise as a new Roman confederacy of ten nations. See the article on "The Four World Empires," p. 954.

2:38 The golden head of the image represented the kingdom of Babylon. God had given Nebuchadnezzar the authority to rule over all the nations of the known world at that time.

2:41 The feet and toes of the image were a composite blend of iron and clay symbolizing both strong and weak people. The ten toes symbolized ten confederate nations that will rule the earth during the last years of this age.

2:44 The ten kings of the confederated kingdoms (symbolized by the ten toes of Nebuchadnezzar's image) will be in existence when Christ comes again. These ten kings did not exist during the time of Christ's first coming, nor at any other time since Christ's ascension into heaven, but will be in power when Christ returns to deliver his people and establish his millennial kingdom (Ps 2:1–9; Zec 14:1–9).

[a]shall the God of heaven set up a kingdom, [b]which shall never be destroyed:
and the [2]kingdom shall not be left to
other people, [c]*but* it shall break in pieces
and consume all these kingdoms, and it
shall stand for ever.
45 [a]Forasmuch as thou sawest that the
stone was cut out of the mountain [1]with-
out hands, and that it brake in pieces the
iron, the brass, the clay, the silver, and
the gold; the great God hath made known
to the king what shall come to pass [2]here-
after: and the dream *is* certain, and the
interpretation thereof sure.
46 ¶ [a]Then the king Nebuchadnezzar
fell upon his face, and worshipped Daniel, and commanded that they should offer an oblation [b]and sweet odours unto
him.
47 The king answered unto Daniel,
and said, Of a truth *it is*, that your God *is*
a God of gods, and a Lord of kings, and a
revealer of secrets, seeing thou couldest
reveal this secret.
48 Then the king made Daniel a great
man, [a]and gave him many great gifts, and
made him ruler over the whole province
of Babylon, and [b]chief of the governors
over all the wise *men* of Babylon.
49 Then Daniel requested of the king,
[a]and he set Shadrach, Meshach, and
Abed-nego, over the affairs of the province of Babylon: but Daniel [b]*sat* in the
gate of the king.

The fiery furnace

3 NEBUCHADNEZZAR THE king
made an image of gold, whose height
was threescore cubits, *and* the breadth
thereof six cubits: he set it up in the plain
of Dura, in the province of Babylon.
2 Then Nebuchadnezzar the king sent
to gather together the princes, the governors, and the captains, the judges, the
treasurers, the counsellors, the sheriffs,
and all the rulers of the provinces, to
come to the dedication of the image
which Nebuchadnezzar the king had
set up.
3 Then the princes, the governors, and
captains, the judges, the treasurers, the
counsellors, the sheriffs, and all the rulers of the provinces, were gathered together unto the dedication of the image
that Nebuchadnezzar the king had set up;
and they stood before the image that
Nebuchadnezzar had set up.
4 Then an herald cried [1]aloud, To you
[2]it is commanded, [a]O people, nations,
and languages,
5 *That* at what time ye hear the sound
of the cornet, flute, harp, sackbut, psaltery, [1,2]dulcimer, and all kinds of music,
ye fall down and worship the golden image that Nebuchadnezzar the king hath
set up:
6 And whoso falleth not down and
worshippeth shall the same hour [a]be cast
into the midst of a burning fiery furnace.
7 Therefore at that time, when all the
people heard the sound of the cornet,
flute, harp, sackbut, psaltery, and all
kinds of music, all the people, the nations, and the languages, fell down *and*
worshipped the golden image that Nebuchadnezzar the king had set up.
8 ¶ Wherefore at that time certain
Chaldeans [a]came near, and accused the
Jews.
9 They spake and said to the king Nebuchadnezzar, [a]O king, live for ever.
10 Thou, O king, hast made a decree,
that every man that shall hear the sound
of the cornet, flute, harp, sackbut, psaltery, and dulcimer, and all kinds of music, shall fall down and worship the
golden image:
11 And whoso falleth not down and
worshippeth, *that* he should be cast into
the midst of a burning fiery furnace.
12 [a]There are certain Jews whom thou
hast set over the affairs of the province of
Babylon, Shadrach, Meshach, and Abed-
nego; these men, O king, [1]have not regarded thee: they serve not thy gods, nor
worship the golden image which thou
hast set up.

44 [a]ver. 28 [b]ch. 4:3,34 & 6:26 & 7:14,27; Mic. 4:7; Luke 1:32,33 [c]Ps. 2:9; Is. 60:12; 1 Cor. 15:24 [2]Chald. *kingdom thereof*
45 [a]ver. 35; Is. 28:16 [1]Or, *which* was *not in hand* [2]Chald. *after this*
46 [a]See Acts 10:25 & 14:13 & 28:6 [b]Ezra 6:10
48 [a]ver. 6 [b]ch. 4:9 & 5:11
49 [a]ch. 3:12 [b]Esth. 2:19,21 & 3:2
3:4 [a]ch. 4:1 & 6:25 [1]Chald. *with might* [2]Chald. *they command*
5 [1]Or, *singing* [2]Chald. *symphony*
6 [a]Jer. 29:22; Rev. 13:15
8 [a]ch. 6:12
9 [a]ch. 2:4 & 5:10 & 6:6,21
12 [a]ch. 2:49 [1]Chald. *have set no regard upon thee*

3:1 The inauguration of the first Gentile empire of Nebuchadnezzar's vision was marked by the enforced public worship of a golden image created by King Nebuchadnezzar. This golden image may have been human in form, though probably not a likeness of the king himself. Its measurements (90′ x 9′) probably included a lofty pedestal. Notice that the last empire in Nebuchadnezzar's vision will also enforce the worship of an idolatrous image during the great tribulation (see Rev 13:14–15).

3:6 This command to worship required the recognition of Nebuchadnezzar's gods (see 3:12).

13 ¶ Then Nebuchadnezzar in *his* rage
and fury commanded to bring Shadrach,
Meshach, and Abed-nego. Then they
brought these men before the king.
14 Nebuchadnezzar spake and said
unto them, *Is it* [1]true, O Shadrach, Meshach, and Abed-nego, do not ye serve
my gods, nor worship the golden image
which I have set up?
15 Now if ye be ready that at what
time ye hear the sound of the cornet,
flute, harp, sackbut, psaltery, and dulcimer, and all kinds of music, ye fall down
and worship the image which I have
made; [a]*well:* but if ye worship not, ye
shall be cast the same hour into the midst
of a burning fiery furnace; [b]and who *is*
that God that shall deliver you out of my
hands?
16 Shadrach, Meshach, and Abed-
nego, answered and said to the king,
O Nebuchadnezzar, [a]we *are* not careful
to answer thee in this matter.
S 17 If it be *so*, our God whom we serve
is able to deliver us from the burning fiery furnace, and he will deliver *us* out of
thine hand, O king.
18 But if not, be it known unto thee,
O king, that we will not serve thy gods,
nor worship the golden image which
thou hast set up.
19 ¶ Then was Nebuchadnezzar [1]full
of fury, and the form of his visage was
changed against Shadrach, Meshach, and
Abed-nego: *therefore* he spake, and commanded that they should heat the furnace
one seven times more than it was wont
to be heated.
20 And he commanded the [1]most
mighty men that *were* in his army to bind
Shadrach, Meshach, and Abed-nego, *and*
to cast *them* into the burning fiery
furnace.

S *Isa 43:2* ◄► *Da 3:24–25*

14 [1]Or, *of purpose*
15 [a]As Ex. 32:32; Luke 13:9 [b]Ex. 5:2; 2 Ki. 18:35
16 [a]Mat. 10:19
19 [1]Chald. *filled*
20 [1]Chald. *mighty of strength*
21 [1]Or, *mantles* [2]Or, *turbans*
22 [1]Chald. *word* [2]Or, *spark*
24 [1]Or, *governors*
25 [a]Is. 43:2 [b]ver. 28; Job 1:6 & 38:7; Ps. 34:7 [1]Chald. *there is no hurt in them*
26 [1]Chald. *door*
27 [a]Heb. 11:34

21 Then these men were bound in
their [1]coats, their hosen, and their [2]hats,
and their *other* garments, and were cast
into the midst of the burning fiery
furnace.
22 Therefore because the king's [1]com-
mandment was urgent, and the furnace
exceeding hot, the [2]flame of the fire slew
those men that took up Shadrach, Meshach, and Abed-nego.
23 And these three men, Shadrach,
Meshach, and Abed-nego, fell down
bound into the midst of the burning fiery
furnace.
24 Then Nebuchadnezzar the king was S
astonied, and rose up in haste, *and* spake,
and said unto his [1]counsellors, Did not
we cast three men bound into the midst
of the fire? They answered and said unto
the king, True, O king.
25 He answered and said, Lo, I see L
four men loose, [a]walking in the midst of
the fire, and [1]they have no hurt; and
the form of the fourth is like [b]the Son
of God.
26 ¶ Then Nebuchadnezzar came near
to the [1]mouth of the burning fiery furnace, *and* spake, and said, Shadrach, Meshach, and Abed-nego, ye servants of the
most high God, come forth, and come
hither. Then Shadrach, Meshach, and
Abed-nego, came forth of the midst of the
fire.
27 And the princes, governors, and S
captains, and the king's counsellors, being gathered together, saw these men,
[a]upon whose bodies the fire had no
power, nor was an hair of their head
singed, neither were their coats changed,
nor the smell of fire had passed on
them.

S *Da 3:17* ◄► *Da 3:27*
L *Jer 31:3* ◄► *Da 6:22*
S *Da 3:24–25* ◄► *Da 6:22–23*

3:17 The faithfulness of Daniel's three companions is an inspiration to all believers to stand fast in the day of trial. Whether they received deliverance or martyrdom, Daniel's friends left their lives in God's hands. In the coming tribulation, millions will be martyred for their faith (see Rev 7:14–17).

3:25 There are different interpretations regarding the identity of the fourth person visible in the furnace. Some suggest it was an angel, for angels are referred to in Scripture as God's messengers and ministers (see Heb 1:14), and God used an angel to deliver Daniel (see 6:22). Others think that this person was Jesus, the eternal Son of God, and not a created angel. Nebuchadnezzar, with his limited, pagan polytheism was unsure of this person's identity too, referring to him as "the Son of God" (3:25) and as God's "angel" (3:28). The important thing is that the king recognized that this being was mightier than any of the Babylonian gods because he was able to rescue the three men from the fire.

28 *Then* Nebuchadnezzar spake, and
said, Blessed *be* the God of Shadrach, Meshach, and Abed-nego, who hath sent his
angel, and delivered his servants that
[a]trusted in him, and have changed the
king's word, and yielded their bodies,
that they might not serve nor worship
any god, except their own God.
29 [a]Therefore [1]I make a decree, That
every people, nation, and language,
which speak [2]any thing amiss against the
God of Shadrach, Meshach, and Abed-
nego, shall be [b]cut[3] in pieces, and their
houses shall be made a dunghill: [c]be-
cause there is no other God that can deliver after this sort.
30 Then the king [1]promoted Shadrach,
Meshach, and Abed-nego, in the province of Babylon.

The king's dream

4 NEBUCHADNEZZAR THE king,
[a]unto all people, nations, and languages, that dwell in all the earth; Peace
be multiplied unto you.
2 [1]I thought it good to show the signs
and wonders [a]that the high God hath
wrought toward me.
3 [a]How great *are* his signs! and how
mighty *are* his wonders! his kingdom *is*
[b]an everlasting kingdom, and his dominion *is* from generation to generation.
4 ¶ I Nebuchadnezzar was at rest in
mine house, and flourishing in my
palace:
5 I saw a dream which made me afraid,
[a]and the thoughts upon my bed and the
visions of my head [b]troubled me.
6 Therefore made I a decree to bring in
all the wise *men* of Babylon before me,
that they might make known unto me the
interpretation of the dream.
7 [a]Then came in the magicians, the astrologers, the Chaldeans, and the soothsayers: and I told the dream before them;
but they did not make known unto me
the interpretation thereof.
8 ¶ But at the last Daniel came in be- B
fore me, [a]whose name *was* Belteshazzar, E
according to the name of my god, [b]and in G
whom *is* the spirit of the holy gods: and M
before him I told the dream, *saying,* T
9 O Belteshazzar, [a]master of the magicians, because I know that the spirit of
the holy gods *is* in thee, and no secret
troubleth thee, tell me the visions of my
dream that I have seen, and the interpretation thereof.
10 Thus *were* the visions of mine head J
in my bed; [1]I saw, and behold [a]a tree in
the midst of the earth, and the height
thereof *was* great.
11 The tree grew, and was strong, and
the height thereof reached unto heaven,
and the sight thereof to the end of all the
earth:
12 The leaves thereof *were* fair, and
the fruit thereof much, and in it *was* meat
for all: [a]the beasts of the field had shadow
under it, and the fowls of the heaven
dwelt in the boughs thereof, and all flesh
was fed of it.
13 I saw in the visions of my head
upon my bed, and, behold, [a]a watcher
and [b]an holy one came down from
heaven;
14 He cried [1]aloud, and said thus,
[a]Hew down the tree, and cut off his
branches, shake off his leaves, and scatter
his fruit: [b]let the beasts get away from
under it, and the fowls from his
branches:
15 Nevertheless leave the stump of his
roots in the earth, even with a band of
iron and brass, in the tender grass of the
field; and let it be wet with the dew of
heaven, and *let* his portion *be* with the
beasts in the grass of the earth:

28 [a]Ps. 34:7,8; Jer. 17:7; ch. 6:22,23
29 [a]ch. 6:26 [b]ch. 2:5 [c]ch. 6:27 [1]Chald. *a decree is made by me* [2]Chald. *error* [3]Chald. *made pieces*
30 [1]Chald. *made to prosper*
4:1 [a]ch. 3:4 & 6:25
2 [a]ch. 3:26 [1]Chald. *It was seemly before me*
3 [a]ch. 6:27 [b]ver. 34; ch. 2:44 & 6:26
5 [a]ch. 2:28,29 [b]ch. 2:1
7 [a]ch. 2:2
8 [a]ch. 1:7 [b]ver. 18; Is. 63:11; ch. 2:11 & 5:11,14
9 [a]ch. 2:48 & 5:11
10 [a]ver. 20; Ezek. 31:3 [1]Chald. *I was seeing*
12 [a]Ezek. 17:23 & 31:6; See Lam. 4:20
13 [a]ver. 17,23 [b]Deut. 33:2; ch. 8:13; Zech. 14:5; Jude 14
14 [a]Mat. 3:10 [b]Ezek. 31:12 [1]Chald. *with might*

B *Eze 37:14* ◀ ▶ *Da 4:18*
E *Eze 43:5* ◀ ▶ *Da 4:18*
G *Isa 61:1* ◀ ▶ *Da 4:18*
M *Eze 37:14* ◀ ▶ *Da 4:18*
T *Eze 40:1–2* ◀ ▶ *Da 4:18*
J *Eze 35:1–15* ◀ ▶ *Da 4:20–26*

4:1 This chapter is a public decree written by King Nebuchadnezzar that acknowledged God's greatness over the king and all humanity. The seven years of madness likely occurred during the last ten years of Nebuchadnezzar's reign.

4:13 This mysterious messenger may refer to one of the special angels charged with oversight over the affairs of a particular nation (see 10:13, 20–21; 12:1). This idea of angels overseeing the affairs of the nations finds its roots in ancient Persian angelology and would have been taught to Daniel during his training. The concept does not contradict any Scriptural teaching, however, and might have comforted the exiled Jews.

16 Let his heart be changed from man's, and let a beast's heart be given unto him; and let seven [a]times pass over him.

17 This matter *is* by the decree of the watchers, and the demand by the word of the holy ones: to the intent [a]that the living may know [b]that the most High ruleth in the kingdom of men, and giveth it to whomsoever he will, and setteth up over it the basest of men.

B 18 This dream I king Nebuchadnezzar
E have seen. Now thou, O Belteshazzar, de-
G clare the interpretation thereof, [a]foras-
M much as all the wise *men* of my kingdom
T are not able to make known unto me the
interpretation: but thou *art* able; [b]for the spirit of the holy gods *is* in thee.

The interpretation and warning

19 ¶ Then Daniel, [a]whose name *was* Belteshazzar, was astonied for one hour, and his thoughts troubled him. The king spake, and said, Belteshazzar, let not the dream, or the interpretation thereof, trouble thee. Belteshazzar answered and said, My lord, [b]the dream *be* to them that hate thee, and the interpretation thereof to thine enemies.

J 20 [a]The tree that thou sawest, which grew, and was strong, whose height reached unto the heaven, and the sight thereof to all the earth;

21 Whose leaves *were* fair, and the fruit thereof much, and in it *was* meat for all; under which the beasts of the field dwelt, and upon whose branches the fowls of the heaven had their habitation:

22 [a]It *is* thou, O king, that art grown and become strong: for thy greatness is grown, and reacheth unto heaven, [b]and thy dominion to the end of the earth.

23 [a]And whereas the king saw a watcher and an holy one coming down from heaven, and saying, Hew the tree down, and destroy it; yet leave the stump of the roots thereof in the earth, even with a band of iron and brass, in the tender grass of the field; and let it be wet with the dew of heaven, [b]and *let* his portion *be* with the beasts of the field, till seven times pass over him;

24 This *is* the interpretation, O king, and this *is* the decree of the most High, which is come upon my lord the king:

25 That they shall [a]drive thee from men, and thy dwelling shall be with the beasts of the field, and they shall make thee [b]to eat grass as oxen, and they shall wet thee with the dew of heaven, and seven times shall pass over thee, [c]till thou know that the most High ruleth in the kingdom of men, and [d]giveth it to whomsoever he will.

26 And whereas they commanded to leave the stump of the tree roots; thy kingdom shall be sure unto thee, after that thou shalt have known that the [a]heavens do rule.

27 Wherefore, O king, let my counsel be acceptable unto thee, and [a]break off thy sins by righteousness, and thine iniquities by showing mercy to the poor; [b]if it may be [c]a [1] lengthening of thy tranquillity. R

The dream is fulfilled

28 ¶ All this came upon the king Nebuchadnezzar.

29 At the end of twelve months he walked [1]in the palace of the kingdom of Babylon.

30 The king [a]spake, and said, Is not this great Babylon, that I have built for the house of the kingdom by the might

16 [a]ch. 11:13 & 12:7
17 [a]Ps. 9:16 [b]ver. 25,32; ch. 2:21 & 5:21
18 [a]Gen. 41:8,15; ch. 5:8,15 [b]ver. 8
19 [a]ver. 8 [b]See 2 Sam. 18:32; Jer. 29:7
20 [a]ver. 10,11,12
22 [a]ch. 2:38 [b]Jer. 27:6-8
23 [a]ver. 13 [b]ch. 5:21
25 [a]ver. 32; ch. 5:21 [b]Ps. 106:20 [c]ver. 17,32; Ps. 83:18 [d]Jer. 27:5
26 [a]Mat. 21:25; Luke 15:18
27 [a]1 Pet. 4:8 [b]Ps. 41:1 [c]1 Ki. 21:29 [1]Or, *an healing of thine error*
29 [1]Or, *upon*
30 [a]Prov. 16:18; ch. 5:20

B *Da 4:8–9* ◀ ▶ *Da 5:11–12*
E *Da 4:8–9* ◀ ▶ *Da 5:11–12*
G *Da 4:8–9* ◀ ▶ *Da 5:11–12*
M *Da 4:8–9* ◀ ▶ *Da 5:11–12*
T *Da 4:8–9* ◀ ▶ *Da 5:11–12*
J *Da 4:10–17* ◀ ▶ *Da 4:31–32*
R *Eze 33:19* ◀ ▶ *Hos 5:15*

4:16 God condemned Nebuchadnezzar to seven years of madness because of Nebuchadnezzar's sinful boasting of his accomplishments without acknowledging God's blessings. Note that Nebuchadnezzar, the defiler of the temple in Jerusalem, was struck with madness for same period of time it took King Solomon to build the temple—seven years.
4:17 God ultimately chooses who will rule the kingdoms of this earth, and he will one day deliver the direct rule of all the nations of this world to the Messiah, Jesus Christ (see Rev 11:15–17).

4:29 Despite God's clear warning issued one year earlier, Nebuchadnezzar proudly boasted about his own accomplishments, and God instantly inflicted the prophesied judgment of seven years of insanity.

of my power, and for the honour of my majesty?

J 31 [a]While the word *was* in the king's mouth, there fell [b]a voice from heaven, *saying,* O king Nebuchadnezzar, to thee it is spoken; The kingdom is departed from thee.

32 And [a]they shall drive thee from men, and thy dwelling *shall be* with the beasts of the field: they shall make thee to eat grass as oxen, and seven times shall pass over thee, until thou know that the most High ruleth in the kingdom of men, and giveth it to whomsoever he will.

33 The same hour was the thing fulfilled upon Nebuchadnezzar: and he was driven from men, and did eat grass as oxen, and his body was wet with the dew of heaven, till his hairs were grown like eagles' *feathers,* and his nails like birds' *claws.*

34 And [a]at the end of the days I Nebuchadnezzar lifted up mine eyes unto heaven, and mine understanding returned unto me, and I blessed the most High, and I praised and honoured him [b]that liveth for ever, whose dominion *is* [c]an everlasting dominion, and his kingdom *is* from generation to generation:

35 And [a]all the inhabitants of the earth *are* reputed as nothing: and [b]he doeth according to his will in the army of heaven, and *among* the inhabitants of the earth: and [c]none can stay his hand, or say unto him, [d]What doest thou?

36 At the same time my reason returned unto me; [a]and for the glory of my kingdom, mine honour and brightness returned unto me; and my counsellors and my lords sought unto me; and I was established in my kingdom, and excellent majesty was [b]added unto me.

37 Now I Nebuchadnezzar praise and extol and honour the King of heaven, [a]all whose works *are* truth, and his ways judgment: [b]and those that walk in pride he is able to abase.

The handwriting on the wall

5 BELSHAZZAR THE king [a]made a great feast to a thousand of his lords, and drank wine before the thousand. H N

2 Belshazzar, whiles he tasted the wine, commanded to bring the golden and silver vessels [a]which his [1]father Nebuchadnezzar had [2]taken out of the temple which *was* in Jerusalem; that the king, and his princes, his wives, and his concubines, might drink therein.

3 Then they brought the golden vessels that were taken out of the temple of the house of God which *was* at Jerusalem; and the king, and his princes, his wives, and his concubines, drank in them.

4 They drank wine, [a]and praised the gods of gold, and of silver, of brass, of iron, of wood, and of stone.

5 ¶ [a]In the same hour came forth fingers of a man's hand, and wrote over against the candlestick upon the plaster of the wall of the king's palace: and the king saw the part of the hand that wrote. J

6 Then the king's countenance was changed, and his thoughts troubled him, so that the [a][1]joints of his loins were loosed, and his [b]knees smote one against another.

7 [a]The king cried [1]aloud to bring in [b]the astrologers, the Chaldeans, and the soothsayers. *And* the king spake, and said to the wise *men* of Babylon, Whosoever shall read this writing, and show me the interpretation thereof, shall be clothed with [2]scarlet, and *have* a chain of gold

31 [a]ch. 5:5; Luke 12:20 [b]ver. 24
32 [a]ver. 25
34 [a]ver. 26 [b]ch. 12:7; Rev. 4:10 [c]Ps. 10:16; ch. 2:44; Mic. 4:7; Luke 1:33
35 [a]Is. 40:15 [b]Ps. 115:3 & 135:6 [c]Job 34:29 [d]Job 9:12; Is. 45:9; Rom. 9:20
36 [a]ver. 26 [b]Job 42:12; Prov. 22:4; Mat. 6:33
37 [a]Ps. 33:4; Rev. 15:3 [b]Ex. 18:11; ch. 5:20
5:1 [a]Esth. 1:3
2 [a]ch. 1:2; Jer. 52:19 [1]Or, *grandfather* [2]Chald. *brought forth*
4 [a]Rev. 9:20
5 [a]ch. 4:31
6 [a]Is. 5:27 [b]Nah. 2:10 [1]Or, *girdles*
7 [a]ch. 4:6 [b]Is. 47:13 [1]Chald. *with might* [2]Or, *purple*

J *Da 4:20–26* ◀ ▶ *Da 5:5*

H *Eze 35:14* ◀ ▶ *Da 12:1*
N *Eze 33:31* ◀ ▶ *Hos 4:17*
J *Da 4:31–32* ◀ ▶ *Da 5:24–28*

4:34 Following his horrible experience of seven years of insanity, King Nebuchadnezzar recovered his right mind and acknowledged that God's kingdom was far superior in power and duration to any human kingdom.

5:2 The Aramaic word for "father" in this verse indicates a direct ancestor such as a grandson, descendant or successor, but not necessarily an immediate father. In a similar manner, the NT refers to Jesus as David's son (see Mt 1:1; Lk 1:32).

5:3 The king's wives did not usually attend public festivals with the king (see Est 1:9). Belshazzar's decision to include women in his feast while defiling the holy temple vessels was another indication of his contempt for the God of Israel.

5:5 God instantly responded to Belshazzar's blasphemy with a message of judgment supernaturally written on the wall of Belshazzar's palace.

about his neck, [c]and shall be the third
ruler in the kingdom.
8 Then came in all the king's wise
men: [a]but they could not read the writing, nor make known to the king the interpretation thereof.
9 Then was king Belshazzar greatly
[a]troubled, and his [1]countenance was
changed in him, and his lords were astonied.
10 ¶ *Now* the queen, by reason of the
words of the king and his lords, came into
the banquet house: *and* the queen spake
and said, O king, live for ever: let not thy
thoughts trouble thee, nor let thy countenance be changed:
B 11 [a]There is a man in thy kingdom, in
E whom *is* the spirit of the holy gods; and
G in the days of thy [1]father light and under-
M standing and wisdom, like the wisdom of
T the gods, was found in him; whom the
king Nebuchadnezzar thy [2]father, the
king, *I say,* thy father, made [b]master of
the magicians, astrologers, Chaldeans,
and soothsayers;
N 12 [a]Forasmuch as an excellent spirit,
and knowledge, and understanding, [1]in-
terpreting of dreams, and showing of
hard sentences, and [2]dissolving of
[3]doubts, were found in the same Daniel,
[b]whom the king named Belteshazzar:
now let Daniel be called, and he will
show the interpretation.
13 Then was Daniel brought in before
the king. *And* the king spake and said
unto Daniel, *Art* thou that Daniel, which
art of the children of the captivity of Judah, whom the king my [1]father brought
out of Jewry?

B Da 4:18 ◀ ▶ Da 5:14
E Da 4:18 ◀ ▶ Da 5:14
G Da 4:18 ◀ ▶ Da 5:14
M Da 4:18 ◀ ▶ Da 5:14
T Da 4:18 ◀ ▶ Da 5:14
N Eze 43:4–5 ◀ ▶ Da 6:3

7 [c]ch. 6:2
8 [a]ch. 2:27
9 [a]ch. 2:1 [1]Chald. *brightnesses*
11 [a]ch. 2:48 & 4:8,9,18 [b]ch. 4:9 [1]Or, *grandfather* [2]Or, *grandfather;* ver. 2
12 [a]ch. 6:3 [b]ch. 1:7 [1]Or, *of an interpreter* [2]Or, *of a dissolver* [3]Chald. *knots*
13 [1]Or, *grandfather*
14 [a]ver. 11,12
15 [a]ver. 7,8
16 [a]ver. 7 [1]Chald. *interpret*
17 [a]ch. 2:6 [1]Or, *fee*
18 [a]ch. 2:37,38 & 4:17,22,25
19 [a]Jer. 27:7; ch. 3:4
20 [a]ch. 4:30,37 [1]Chald. *made to come down*
21 [a]ch. 4:32 [1]Or, *he made his heart equal*

14 I have even heard of thee, that [a]the B
spirit of the gods *is* in thee, and *that* light E
and understanding and excellent wisdom G
is found in thee. M
15 And now [a]the wise *men,* the astrol- T
ogers, have been brought in before me,
that they should read this writing, and
make known unto me the interpretation
thereof: but they could not show the interpretation of the thing:
16 And I have heard of thee, that thou
canst [1]make interpretations, and dissolve
doubts: [a]now if thou canst read the writing, and make known to me the interpretation thereof, thou shalt be clothed with
scarlet, and *have* a chain of gold about thy
neck, and shalt be the third ruler in the
kingdom.
17 ¶ Then Daniel answered and said
before the king, Let thy gifts be to thyself,
and give thy [a]rewards[1] to another; yet I
will read the writing unto the king, and
make known to him the interpretation.
18 O thou king, [a]the most high God
gave Nebuchadnezzar thy father a kingdom, and majesty, and glory, and honour:
19 And for the majesty that he gave
him, [a]all people, nations, and languages,
trembled and feared before him: whom
he would he slew; and whom he would
he kept alive; and whom he would he set
up; and whom he would he put down.
20 [a]But when his heart was lifted up,
and his mind hardened in pride, he was
[1]deposed from his kingly throne, and
they took his glory from him:
21 And he was [a]driven from the sons
of men; and [1]his heart was made like the
beasts, and his dwelling *was* with the

B Da 5:11–12 ◀ ▶ Da 6:3
E Da 5:11–12 ◀ ▶ Da 6:3
G Da 5:11–12 ◀ ▶ Joel 2:28–29
M Da 5:11–12 ◀ ▶ Da 6:3
T Da 5:11–12 ◀ ▶ Joel 2:28–29

5:12 Daniel's official Babylonian name "Belteshazzar" replaced his Jewish name whenever he appeared at court or served in an advisor's position.
5:16 The third in command of the Babylonian kingdom would be like a prime minister. Nabonidus was the king ex officio, Belshazzar occupied the throne and Daniel would be elevated to the chief advisor to the king or prime minister's position.
5:18 Many kings ruled Babylon during Daniel's life. Recent archeological discoveries have confirmed the chronology of the last rulers of Babylon: Nebuchadnezzar died in 562 B.C. and was succeeded on the throne by his son Evil-Merodach (see Jer 52:31). Evil-Merodach was soon murdered and succeeded by Nergal-Sharezer in 560 B.C. (see Jer 39:3, 13). Though his son Labash-Merodach succeeded him in 556 B.C., rebels immediately assassinated this son and crowned Nabonidus as king from 556–539 B.C. When King Nabonidus retired to Tema in the province of Arabia, he left his son Belshazzar in charge of Babylon. In that very year Babylon fell to the Medo-Persians.

wild asses: they fed him with grass like
oxen, and his body was wet with the dew
of heaven; [b]till he knew that the most
high God ruled in the kingdom of men,
and *that* he appointeth over it whomsoever he will.
22 And thou his son, O Belshazzar,
[a]hast not humbled thine heart, though
thou knewest all this;
23 [a]But hast lifted up thyself against
the Lord of heaven; and they have
brought the vessels of his house before
thee, and thou, and thy lords, thy wives,
and thy concubines, have drunk wine in
them; and thou hast praised the gods of
silver, and gold, of brass, iron, wood, and
stone, [b]which see not, nor hear, nor
know: and the God in whose hand thy
breath *is,* [c]and whose *are* all thy ways,
hast thou not glorified:
J 24 Then was the part of the hand sent
from him; and this writing was written.
25 ¶ And this *is* the writing that
was written, MENE, MENE, TEKEL,
UPHARSIN.
26 This *is* the interpretation of the
thing: MENE; God hath numbered thy
kingdom, and finished it.
E 27 TEKEL; [a]Thou art weighed in the
balances, and art found wanting.
28 PERES; Thy kingdom is divided,
and given to the [a]Medes and [b]Persians.
29 Then commanded Belshazzar, and
they clothed Daniel with scarlet, and *put*
a chain of gold about his neck, and made
a proclamation concerning him, [a]that he
should be the third ruler in the kingdom.

J *Da 5:5 ◀▶ Da 7:10–11*
E *Da 2:22 ◀▶ Hos 7:2*

21 [b]ch. 4:17,25
22 [a]2 Chr. 33:23 & 36:12
23 [a]ver. 3,4 [b]Ps. 115:5,6 [c]Jer. 10:23
27 [a]Job 31:6; Ps. 62:9; Jer. 6:30
28 [a]Foretold Is. 21:2; ver. 31; ch. 9:1 [b]ch. 6:28
29 [a]ver. 7
30 [a]Jer. 51:31,39, 57
31 [a]ch. 9:1 [1]Chald. he as *the son of* [2]Or, *now*
6:3 [a]ch. 5:12
4 [a]Eccl. 4:4
6 [a]ver. 21; Neh. 2:3; ch. 2:4 [1]Or, *came tumultuously*

30 ¶ [a]In that night was Belshazzar the
king of the Chaldeans slain.
31 [a]And Darius the Median took the
kingdom, [1]*being* [2]about threescore and
two years old.

Daniel in the den of lions

6 IT PLEASED Darius to set over the
kingdom an hundred and twenty
princes, which should be over the whole
kingdom;
2 And over these three presidents; of
whom Daniel *was* first: that the princes
might give accounts unto them, and the
king should have no damage.
3 Then this Daniel was preferred B
above the presidents and princes, [a]be- E
cause an excellent spirit *was* in him; and M
the king thought to set him over the N
whole realm.
4 ¶ [a]Then the presidents and princes
sought to find occasion against Daniel
concerning the kingdom; but they could
find none occasion nor fault; forasmuch
as he *was* faithful, neither was there any
error or fault found in him.
5 Then said these men, We shall not
find any occasion against this Daniel, except we find *it* against him concerning
the law of his God.
6 Then these presidents and princes
[1]assembled together to the king, and said
thus unto him, [a]King Darius, live for
ever.
7 All the presidents of the kingdom,
the governors, and the princes, the counsellors, and the captains, have consulted

B *Da 5:14 ◀▶ Joel 2:28–29*
E *Da 5:14 ◀▶ Mic 3:8*
M *Da 5:14 ◀▶ Joel 2:28*
N *Da 5:12 ◀▶ Zec 6:8*

5:25 The finger wrote upon the wall of the Babylonian palace these fateful Aramaic words: *MENE, MENE, TEKEL, UPHARSIN.* Because Aramaic was a common language among the Babylonians (see note at 2:4) Belshazzar should have been able to interpret it. Possibly this message was written as an acrostic. Or, since written Aramaic follows the written Hebrew style of omitting vowels, this message may have seemed to be disconnected letters without a clear meaning. Daniel's divine interpretation of God's judgment upon this Gentile empire reverberates down through the ages upon all kingdoms that reject the laws of God.

5:30 God's judgment announced by the writing on the wall was immediately fulfilled. The decadent King Belshazzar was killed that night and the kingdom of Babylon was given to Darius the Mede exactly as God foretold (see Jer 25:12).

5:31 Darius the Mede might be another name for Gubaru, referred to in some Babylonian inscriptions as the governor assigned by Cyrus to rule newly conquered Babylon. Or, Darius the Mede may be the official court name for Cyrus who ruled Babylon from 539–530 B.C. This interchange of names was common in the ancient political world to reflect the different languages of the conquered nations (see 1Ch 5:26). Note that Darius the Mede is not the same individual as King Darius who ruled Persia from 521–486 B.C. (see Ezr 4:5).

together to establish a royal statute, and
to make a firm [l]decree, that whosoever
shall ask a petition of any God or man for
thirty days, save of thee, O king, he shall
be cast into the den of lions.
8 Now, O king, establish the decree,
and sign the writing, that it be not
changed, according to the [a]law of the
Medes and Persians, which [l]altereth not.
9 Wherefore king Darius signed the
writing and the decree.
10 ¶ Now when Daniel knew that the
writing was signed, he went into his
house; and his windows being open in
his chamber [a]toward Jerusalem, he
kneeled upon his knees [b]three times a
day, and prayed, and gave thanks before
his God, as he did aforetime.
11 Then these men assembled, and
found Daniel praying and making supplication before his God.
12 [a]Then they came near, and spake
before the king concerning the king's decree; Hast thou not signed a decree, that
every man that shall ask *a petition* of any
God or man within thirty days, save of
thee, O king, shall be cast into the den of
lions? The king answered and said, The
thing *is* true, [b]according to the law of the
Medes and Persians, which altereth not.
13 Then answered they and said before the king, That Daniel, [a]which *is* of
the children of the captivity of Judah, [b]re-
gardeth not thee, O king, nor the decree
that thou hast signed, but maketh his petition three times a day.
14 Then the king, when he heard
these words, [a]was sore displeased with
himself, and set *his* heart on Daniel to
deliver him: and he laboured till the going down of the sun to deliver him.
15 Then these men assembled unto
the king, and said unto the king, Know,
O king, that [a]the law of the Medes and
Persians *is*, That no decree nor statute
which the king establisheth may be
changed.
16 Then the king commanded, and
they brought Daniel, and cast *him* into
the den of lions. *Now* the king spake and

7 [l]Or, *interdict*
8 [a]ver. 12,15; Esth. 1:19 & 8:8 [l]Chald. *passeth not*
10 [a]1 Ki. 8:44,48; Ps. 5:7; Jonah 2:4 [b]Ps. 55:17; Acts 2:1,2,15 & 3:1 & 10:9
12 [a]ch. 3:8 [b]ver. 8
13 [a]ch. 1:6 & 5:13 [b]ch. 3:12
14 [a]Mark 6:26
15 [a]ver. 8
17 [a]Lam. 3:53 [b]Mat. 27:66
18 [a]ch. 2:1 [l]Or, *table*
20 [a]ch. 3:15
21 [a]ch. 2:4
22 [a]ch. 3:28 [b]Heb. 11:33
23 [a]Heb. 11:33
24 [a]Deut. 19:19 [b]Esth. 9:10; See Deut. 24:16; 2 Ki. 14:6
25 [a]ch. 4:1
26 [a]ch. 3:29 [b]Ps. 99:1 [c]ch. 4:34

said unto Daniel, Thy God whom thou
servest continually, he will deliver thee.
17 [a]And a stone was brought, and laid
upon the mouth of the den; [b]and the king
sealed it with his own signet, and with
the signet of his lords; that the purpose
might not be changed concerning Daniel.
18 ¶ Then the king went to his palace,
and passed the night fasting: neither
were [l]instruments of music brought before him: [a]and his sleep went from him.
19 Then the king arose very early in
the morning, and went in haste unto the
den of lions.
20 And when he came to the den, he
cried with a lamentable voice unto Daniel: *and* the king spake and said to Daniel,
O Daniel, servant of the living God, [a]is
thy God, whom thou servest continually,
able to deliver thee from the lions?
21 Then said Daniel unto the king,
[a]O king, live for ever.
22 [a]My God hath sent his angel, and L
hath [b]shut the lions' mouths, that they S
have not hurt me: forasmuch as before
him innocency was found in me; and also
before thee, O king, have I done no hurt.
23 Then was the king exceeding glad
for him, and commanded that they
should take Daniel up out of the den. So
Daniel was taken up out of the den, and
no manner of hurt was found upon him,
[a]because he believed in his God.
24 ¶ And the king commanded, [a]and
they brought those men which had accused Daniel, and they cast *them* into the
den of lions, them, [b]their children, and
their wives; and the lions had the mastery of them, and brake all their bones in
pieces or ever they came at the bottom of
the den.
25 ¶ [a]Then king Darius wrote unto all
people, nations, and languages, that
dwell in all the earth; Peace be multiplied
unto you.
26 [a]I make a decree, That in every dominion of my kingdom men [b]tremble and
fear before the God of Daniel: [c]for he *is*

L Da 3:25 ◀▶ Da 9:23
S Da 3:27 ◀▶ Jnh 1:17

6:10 Scripture indicates that Daniel "kneeled upon his knees three times a day, and prayed." Both King Solomon and Ezra used this same posture in their prayers (see 1Ki 8:54; Ezr 9:5). While kneeling in prayer has fallen out of favor among many modern-day Jews and Christians, this humble posture is a symbol of reverence and submission to God and an indication of our reliance on him for our very lives.

the living God, and stedfast for ever, and
his kingdom *that* which shall not be [d]de-
stroyed, and his dominion *shall be even*
unto the end.
27 He delivereth and rescueth, [a]and
he worketh signs and wonders in heaven
and in earth, who hath delivered Daniel
from the [1]power of the lions.
28 So this Daniel prospered in the
reign of Darius, [a]and in the reign of [b]Cy-
rus the Persian.

Daniel's dream of four beasts

7 IN THE first year of Belshazzar king
of Babylon [a]Daniel [1]had a dream and
[b]visions of his head upon his bed: then
he wrote the dream, *and* told the sum of
the [2]matters.
G 2 Daniel spake and said, I saw in my
vision by night, and, behold, the four
winds of the heaven strove upon the
great sea.
3 And four great beasts [a]came up from
the sea, diverse one from another.
4 The first *was* [a]like a lion, and had
eagle's wings: I beheld till the wings
thereof were plucked, [1]and it was lifted
up from the earth, and made stand upon
the feet as a man, and a man's heart was
given to it.

G *Da 2:28–45* ◀ ▶ *Da 8:1–26*

26 [d]ch. 2:44 & 4:3,34; Luke 1:33

27 [a]ch. 4:3 [1]Heb. *hand*

28 [a]ch. 1:21 [b]Ezra 1:1,2

7:1 [a]Num. 12:6; Amos 3:7 [b]ch. 2:28 [1]Chald. *saw* [2]Or, *words*

3 [a]Rev. 13:1

4 [a]Deut. 28:49; 2 Sam. 1:23; Jer. 48:40; Ezek. 17:3; Hab. 1:8 [1]Or, *wherewith*

5 [a]ch. 2:39 [1]Or, *it raised up one dominion*

6 [a]ch. 8:8,22

7 [a]ch. 2:40 [b]ch. 2:41; Rev. 13:1

8 [a]ch. 8:9 [b]Rev. 9:7 [c]Ps. 12:3; Rev. 13:5

9 [a]Rev. 20:4 [b]Ps. 90:2 [c]Ps. 104:2; Rev. 1:14

5 [a]And behold another beast, a second, like to a bear, and [1]it raised up itself
on one side, and *it had* three ribs in the
mouth of it between the teeth of it: and
they said thus unto it, Arise, devour
much flesh.
6 After this I beheld, and lo another,
like a leopard, which had upon the back
of it four wings of a fowl; the beast had
also [a]four heads; and dominion was given
to it.
7 After this I saw in the night visions,
and behold [a]a fourth beast, dreadful and
terrible, and strong exceedingly; and it
had great iron teeth: it devoured and
brake in pieces, and stamped the residue
with the feet of it: and it *was* diverse
from all the beasts that *were* before it;
[b]and it had ten horns.
8 I considered the horns, and, behold,
[a]there came up among them another little horn, before whom there were three
of the first horns plucked up by the roots:
and, behold, in this horn *were* eyes like
the eyes [b]of man, [c]and a mouth speaking
great things.
9 ¶ [a]I beheld till the thrones were cast J
down, and [b]the Ancient of days did sit,
[c]whose garment *was* white as snow, and

J *Ecc 12:14* ◀ ▶ *Am 4:12*

6:28 The overthrow of the Babylonian empire by the Medo-Persians fulfilled the second stage of Nebuchadnezzar's vision of the metallic image (see Da 2:31–40). King Cyrus, monarch of Medo-Persia, ruled in Babylon from 538–530 B.C. Note that more than one hundred years earlier this Persian king was mentioned by Isaiah as the king who would release the Jewish exiles (see Isa 44:28; 45:13; see also Ezr 1:1–4).
7:1 Since the events of ch. 7 precede the events described in ch. 5, Daniel's vision of the four beasts probably occurred in 553 B.C.
7:2 The large sea was used to indicate the multitudes, the great political world (see Isa 60:5; Rev 13:1).
7:3 Daniel's vision of the four beasts paralleled Nebuchadnezzar's vision of the metallic image recorded in Da 2 as they both foreshadowed the future course of the Gentile world empires that would precede the kingdom of the Messiah. However, while King Nebuchadnezzar noted the glory and power of these empires, Daniel's vision concentrated on the true spiritual character of the four empires that would rule the known world until the end of this age. Note that each of the four beasts were predatory and violent, indicating that these empires would rule by force, greed and war.
7:5 The three ribs in the bear's mouth may refer to the three provincial territories that were conquered by the Medo-Persians: Lydia (546 B.C.), Babylon (539 B.C.) and Egypt (525 B.C.). The Medo-Persian empire ultimately encompassed twenty-seven provinces from northern Africa to India—every nation in the known world at that time.
7:6 The leopard with four wings referred to the empire of Alexander the Great from Greece. The greatest general of the ancient world, Alexander conquered the nations from India to Africa in less than ten years.
7:7–8 The fourth creature in Daniel's vision represented the Roman empire. The ten little horns corresponded to the metallic image's ten toes (see 2:40–42) and indicated the totality of the beast's sphere of authority. Some interpret these ten horns as ten kingdoms, a revived Roman empire, that will arise in the last days (see 7:24–25; Rev 17:12). The smaller horn that appeared in the middle of the other horns is believed to represent the antichrist (see 7:25; 11:36; 12:11; 2Th 2:3, 4, 8; Rev 13:5–6). Daniel describes the antichrist's evil rule in Da 8:23–26 and 11:36–45.
7:9 This title "the Ancient of days" refers to Jesus

the hair of his head like the pure wool:
his throne *was like* the fiery flame, [d]*and*
his wheels *as* burning fire.
J 10 [a]A fiery stream issued and came
forth from before him: [b]thousand thousands ministered unto him, and ten thousand times ten thousand stood before
him: [c]the judgment was set, and the
books were opened.
11 I beheld then because of the voice
of the great words which the horn spake:
[a]I beheld *even* till the beast was slain,
and his body destroyed, and given to the
burning flame.
12 As concerning the rest of the
beasts, they had their dominion taken
away: yet [l]their lives were prolonged for
a season and time.
C 13 I saw in the night visions, and, be-
K hold, [a]*one* like the Son of man came with
M the clouds of heaven, and came to the
Ancient of days, and they brought him
near before him.
V 14 [a]And there was given him dominion, and glory, and a kingdom, that all
[b]people, nations, and languages, should
serve him: his dominion *is* [c]an everlasting dominion, which shall not pass away,
and his kingdom *that* which shall not be
destroyed.

The dream explained

15 ¶ I Daniel was grieved in my spirit
in the midst of *my* [l]body, and the visions
of my head troubled me.

9 [d]Ezek. 1:15
10 [a]Ps. 50:3; Is. 30:33 & 66:15 [b]1 Ki. 22:19; Ps. 68:17; Rev. 5:11 [c]Rev. 20:4
11 [a]Rev. 19:20
12 [l]Chald. *a prolonging in life was given them*
13 [a]Ezek. 1:26; Mat. 24:30; Rev. 1:7
14 [a]Ps. 2:6-8; Mat. 28:18; John 3:35; 1 Cor. 15:27; Eph. 1:22 [b]ch. 3:4 [c]Ps. 145:13; Mic. 4:7; Luke 1:33; John 12:34; Heb. 12:28
15 [l]Chald. *sheath*
18 [a]Is. 60:12; 2 Tim. 2:11; Rev. 2:26 [l]Chald. *high ones*, i.e. *things*, or, *places*
19 [l]Chald. *from all those*
21 [a]Rev. 17:14
22 [a]Rev. 1:6
23 [a]ch. 2:40
24 [a]Rev. 17:12

16 I came near unto one of them that
stood by, and asked him the truth of all
this. So he told me, and made me know
the interpretation of the things.
17 These great beasts, which are four,
are four kings, *which* shall arise out of the
earth.
18 But [a]the saints of the [l]most High M
shall take the kingdom, and possess the
kingdom for ever, even for ever and ever.
19 Then I would know the truth of the
fourth beast, which was diverse [l]from all
the others, exceeding dreadful, whose
teeth *were of* iron, and his nails *of* brass;
which devoured, brake in pieces, and
stamped the residue with his feet;
20 And of the ten horns that *were* in
his head, and *of* the other which came
up, and before whom three fell; even *of*
that horn that had eyes, and a mouth that
spake very great things, whose look *was*
more stout than his fellows.
21 I beheld, [a]and the same horn made
war with the saints, and prevailed against
them;
22 Until the Ancient of days came, M
[a]and judgment was given to the saints of
the most High; and the time came that
the saints possessed the kingdom.
23 Thus he said, The fourth beast shall
be [a]the fourth kingdom upon earth,
which shall be diverse from all kingdoms,
and shall devour the whole earth, and
shall tread it down, and break it in
pieces.
24 [a]And the ten horns out of this kingdom *are* ten kings *that* shall arise: and
another shall rise after them; and he shall

J *Da 5:24–28* ◀▶ *Zep 2:4–15*
C *Isa 64:4* ◀▶ *Hag 2:6–7*
K *Jer 31:34* ◀▶ *Hab 2:14*
M *Da 2:44–45* ◀▶ *Da 7:18*
V *Da 2:44* ◀▶ *Zec 9:10*
M *Da 7:13–14* ◀▶ *Da 7:22*
M *Da 7:18* ◀▶ *Da 7:27*

Christ who is God eternal and the righteous judge of the world (see Isa 57:15).

7:11 Compare this verse with Rev 19:20. Daniel witnessed the ultimate defeat of Satan's antichrist, destroyed by Jesus Christ when he returns from heaven to establish his kingdom. Though the antichrist's body will die, his spirit will be consigned to the lake of fire (hell) for eternity.

7:13–14 This passage is the first reference to the Messiah as the "Son of man" (7:13), a title that Jesus often used for himself (see Mt 8:20; 9:6; 10:23; 12:40; Mk 14:41; Lk 6:5). This prophecy clearly foretells the Messiah's coronation and rule over all nations forever in justice and peace. See also note at 7:9.

7:17 The four great beasts represented the kings of the four empires that would rule the world until the return of Jesus the Messiah.

7:18 The "saints" of God are Christ's followers who will enjoy exalted privileges during the Messianic kingdom (see Mt 19:28–29; Lk 22:29–30). John records God's promise to the saints who participate in the first resurrection that they will "reign with him a thousand years" (Rev 20:6). Other NT passages confirm that Christ's followers will rule over the Gentiles and Jews living on the new earth following the Millennium (see Ro 8:17; 2Ti 2:10–12; Rev 3:21; 5:10).

7:24 The other horn referred to here is the antichrist, the "little horn" of 7:7–8. For additional information about the antichrist, see the notes on Rev 13:1–18.

be diverse from the first, and he shall subdue three kings.

25 [a]And he shall speak *great* words against the most High, and shall [b]wear out the saints of the most High, and [c]think to change times and laws: and [d]they shall be given into his hand [e]until a time and times and the dividing of time.

26 [a]But the judgment shall sit, and they shall take away his dominion, to consume and to destroy *it* unto the end.

M 27 And the [a]kingdom and dominion, and the greatness of the kingdom under the whole heaven, shall be given to the people of the saints of the most High, [b]whose kingdom *is* an everlasting kingdom, [c]and all [1]dominions shall serve and obey him.

28 Hitherto *is* the end of the matter. As for me Daniel, [a]my cogitations much troubled me, and my countenance changed in me: but I [b]kept the matter in my heart.

Vision of the ram, goat and horn

G 8 IN THE third year of the reign of king Belshazzar a vision appeared unto me, *even unto* me Daniel, after that which appeared unto me [a]at the first.

2 And I saw in a vision; and it came to pass, when I saw, that I *was* at [a]Shushan *in* the palace, which *is* in the province of Elam; and I saw in a vision, and I was by the river of Ulai.

3 Then I lifted up mine eyes, and saw, and, behold, there stood before the river a ram which had *two* horns: and the *two* horns *were* high; but one *was* higher than [1]the other, and the higher came up last.

4 I saw the ram pushing westward, and northward, and southward; so that no beasts might stand before him, neither *was there any* that could deliver out of his hand; [a]but he did according to his will, and became great.

5 And as I was considering, behold, an he goat came from the west on the face of the whole earth, and [1]touched not the ground: and the goat *had* [2]a notable horn between his eyes.

6 And he came to the ram that had *two* horns, which I had seen standing before the river, and ran unto him in the fury of his power.

7 And I saw him come close unto the ram, and he was moved with choler against him, and smote the ram, and brake his two horns: and there was no power in the ram to stand before him, but he cast him down to the ground, and stamped upon him: and there was none that could deliver the ram out of his hand.

8 Therefore the he goat waxed very

M *Da 7:22 ◀ ▶ Hos 2:18*
G *Da 7:2–28 ◀ ▶ Da 9:26–27*

25 [a]Is. 37:23 [b]Rev. 17:6 [c]ch. 2:21 [d]Rev. 13:7 [e]Rev. 12:14
26 [a]ver. 10,22
27 [a]ver. 14,18 [b]Luke 1:33; John 12:34; Rev. 11:15 [c]Is. 60:12 [1]Or, *rulers*
28 [a]ch. 8:27 [b]Luke 2:19
8:1 [a]ch. 7:1
2 [a]Esth. 1:2
3 [1]Heb. *the second*
4 [a]ch. 5:19
5 [1]Or, *none touched* him *in the earth* [2]Heb. *a horn of sight*

7:25 The antichrist will "wear out the saints of the most High" indicating the severe persecution of the Jewish and Gentile tribulation saints. The antichrist will also "think to change times and laws," which may mean that he may introduce new laws restricting the worship of God while promoting his own glorification. The antichrist may also create a new calendar that will no longer acknowledge the role of Jesus Christ in history. Even now such discussions are under way in an attempt to circumvent the technological difficulties raised by the current calendar system.

Note the expression "time and times and the dividing of time." Found in Daniel and Revelation (see 12:7; Rev 12:14), this expression referred to a three-and-a-half-year period that will occur during the last seven-year tribulation period (Daniel's seventieth week). Jesus referred to this time as the great tribulation (see Mt 24:21).

7:26 This verse foretells the final defeat of the antichrist and the ten-nation confederacy of the fourth beast (v. 7). This will occur at the Battle of Armageddon (see Rev 16:16–19; 19:14–21).

8:1–7 Daniel received this vision of the ram (8:3) two years after the vision in chapter 7 and just prior to the destruction of Babylon. Daniel described the Medes and Persians as a ram with two horns (see 8:20). The first horn represented the Medes who dominated the empire during the first few years, but the second horn, the highest, reflected the predominant position and superior strength of Persia. Daniel also saw a male goat that came from the west. It too had a horn on its head. This goat charged at the ram with great speed and power, breaking the ram's horns. The goat symbolized the Greek empire under the rule of Alexander the Great. True to Daniel's vision, Alexander's armies, utilizing brilliant military strategy and awesome courage, swiftly invaded Persia and destroyed it.

8:8 Daniel's vision prophesied the early death of Alexander the Great (the image of the broken goat horn) and prophetically described the breakup of Alexander's empire into four kingdoms. True to this prophecy, Alexander died at the age of 32, and the empire was divided among his four generals—Cassander, Lysimachus, Seleucus and Ptolemy. See

great: and when he was strong, the great
horn was broken; and for it came up
[a]four notable ones toward the four winds
of heaven.
9 [a]And out of one of them came forth a
little horn, which waxed exceeding great,
[b]toward the south, and toward the east,
and toward the [c]pleasant *land.*
10 [a]And it waxed great, *even* [1]to [b]the
host of heaven; and [c]it cast down *some* of
the host and of the stars to the ground,
and stamped upon them.
R 11 Yea, [a]he magnified *himself* even [1]to
[b]the prince of the host, [c]and [2]by him
[d]the daily *sacrifice* was taken away,
and the place of his sanctuary was cast
down.
12 And [a]an[1] host was given *him*
against the daily *sacrifice* by reason of
transgression, and it cast down [b]the truth
to the ground; and it [c]practised, and prospered.
13 ¶ Then I heard [a]one saint speaking,
and another saint said unto [1,2]that certain
saint which spake, How long *shall be* the
vision *concerning* the daily *sacrifice,* and
the transgression [b]of[3] desolation, to give
both the sanctuary and the host to be
trodden under foot?
14 And he said unto me, Unto two
thousand and three hundred [1]days; then
shall the sanctuary be [2]cleansed.

R *Eze 39:28* ◄► *Da 8:19*

Gabriel explains the vision

15 ¶ And it came to pass, when I, *even*
I Daniel, had seen the vision, and [a]sought
for the meaning, then, behold, there
stood before me [b]as the appearance of a
man.
16 And I heard a man's voice [a]be-
tween *the banks of* Ulai, which called,
and said, [b]Gabriel, make this *man* to understand the vision.
17 So he came near where I stood: and
when he came, I was afraid, and [a]fell
upon my face: but he said unto me, Understand, O son of man: for at the time of
the end *shall be* the vision.
18 [a]Now as he was speaking with me,
I was in a deep sleep on my face toward
the ground: [b]but he touched me, and [1]set
me upright.
19 And he said, Behold, I will make I
thee know what shall be in the last end R
of the indignation: [a]for at the time appointed the end *shall be.*
20 The ram which thou sawest having
two horns *are* the kings of Media and
Persia.
21 And the rough goat *is* the king of

I *Eze 47:1* ◄► *Da 12:1*
R *Da 8:11–14* ◄► *Da 8:24*

8 [a]ver. 22
9 [a]ch. 11:21 [b]ch. 11:25 [c]Ps. 48:2
10 [a]ch. 11:28 [b]Is. 14:13 [c]Rev. 12:4 [1]Or, *against the host*
11 [a]ch. 11:36 [b]Josh. 5:14 [c]ch. 11:31 [d]Ex. 29:38 [1]Or, *against* [2]Or, *from him*
12 [a]ch. 11:31 [b]Ps. 119:43; Is. 59:14 [c]ver. 4 [1]Or, *the host was given over for the transgression against the daily* sacrifice
13 [a]ch. 4:13; 1 Pet. 1:12 [b]ch. 11:31 [1]Or, *the numberer of secrets,* or, *the wonderful numberer* [2]Heb. *Palmoni* [3]Or, *making desolate*
14 [1]Heb. *evening morning* [2]Heb. *justified*
15 [a]1 Pet. 1:10 [b]Ezek. 1:26
16 [a]ch. 12:6,7 [b]Luke 1:19
17 [a]Ezek. 1:28; Rev. 1:17
18 [a]Luke 9:32 [b]Ezek. 2:2 [1]Heb. *made me stand upon my standing*
19 [a]Hab. 2:3

---

notes at 8:22 and 11:4.

8:9 Daniel's prophecy envisioned a "little horn" growing up from the territory of one of the four horns. Note that this "little horn" arises from the remnants of the third world empire and is a different person than the "little horn" of 7:8 who will arise from the fourth world empire. Though both of these small horns hate the Jews and would profane the temple at Jerusalem, they are different individuals.

The small horn in this passage found fulfillment in Antiochus Epiphanes. During the last years of his reign in 171–165 B.C., Antiochus Epiphanes attempted to eradicate the Jewish faith by persecuting the Palestinian Jews and defiling the temple. He even set himself up to be the equal of God (see 8:11) and ordered an end to daily sacrifices in the temple. Antiochus Epiphanes was finally overthrown when Judas Maccabeus recaptured Jerusalem and rededicated the temple in 165 B.C.

8:13 Daniel used the word "desolation" many times in this book. The first desolation (8:13) predicted the defilement of the sanctuary by Antiochus Epiphanes. The second desolation (see 9:17) occurred when Nebuchadnezzar destroyed Solomon's temple. The word was used again to describe the condition of Palestine during its occupation by its enemies (see 9:18). The fourth desolation occurred when the Messiah was cut off and Jerusalem and the temple were destroyed by Rome in A.D. 70 (see 9:26). Daniel also used the word "desolation" three more times to describe the future defilement of the temple by the "beast," the future antichrist.

8:14 This prediction of the 2300 days was fulfilled during the bitter persecution under Antiochus Epiphanes, beginning when peaceful relations ended between the Jews and this Syrian king in 171 B.C. and ending with the cleansing of the temple in Jerusalem by Judas Maccabeus in 165 B.C. Yet this prophecy also foreshadows the future tribulation of the last days. When Christ returns the sanctuary will be cleansed and the antichrist destroyed.

8:17–26 This prophecy concerning "the time of the end" (see also 12:4) seems to be one of double fulfillment. Initially fulfilled when Medo-Persia was destroyed by Alexander the Great and by the cruel reign of Antiochus Epiphanes, the second and final fulfillment of this prophecy will occur when the Gentile kingdoms will be replaced by the Messianic kingdom of Christ (see Lk 21:24–25; Rev 16:19).

The Antichrist

THOUGH WE ARE often unaware of the spiritual warfare going on around us, from the time of Satan's rebellion against God this spiritual battle has affected every life on earth. Satan's emissary, the antichrist, will ultimately do battle with Jesus Christ in the last days to put an end to the war against good and evil. This antichrist will be a liar and a deceiver because he is Satan's tool (see 1 Jn 2:22). Some suggest that he may be a Jew who is either a eunuch or a homosexual since Daniel warned that he would have no regard for "the God of his fathers, nor the desire of women" (11:37). Both the OT and NT use various names and titles to describe this satanic deceiver's career, nature and ultimate defeat by the Messiah.

The Antichrist in the Old Testament

Satan's Seed The Bible's first prophecy describes the antichrist as Satan's seed because he will attempt to do the will of his father, Satan, the father of all lies (see Ge 3:15; Jn 8:44).

The King of Babylon He is called the "king of Babylon" (Isa 14:4) because he will make the rebuilt city of Babylon one of his capitals during his brief reign.

Prince of Tyrus Ezekiel called the antichrist the "prince of Tyrus" (Eze 28:2) declaring that though he would be possessed by Satan, he was still a man and not a god. The antichrist will exalt himself to be worshiped, exactly as Satan wanted the worship of the fallen angels.

The Little Horn Daniel calls him a "little horn" (7:8) in contrast to the ten horns that represent ten nations arising out of the revived Roman empire. Endowed with satanic powers, he will be a powerful speaker, able to impress people with his brilliant speech.

A King of Fierce Countenance The antichrist will be "a king of fierce countenance" (8:23), a leader with a striking appearance and great charisma.

The Prince That Shall Come Daniel 9:26 says that a people would come to destroy Jerusalem and the temple. The Romans fulfilled this prophecy in A.D. 70. Therefore the "prince that shall come" (9:26) will come from the revived Roman empire.

The Willful King Jesus came to do his Father's will (see Lk 2:49). In total contrast, the antichrist will "do according to his will" (Da 11:36).

The Assyrian Prior to 608 B.C. ancient Assyria occupied the same geographic area as

Babylon. Isaiah's words may identify the antichrist as "the Assyrian" (Isa 10:24) because of his future role in Babylon.

The Idol Shepherd The antichrist is called the "idol shepherd" (Zec 11:17) because his purpose is to use, abandon and destroy God's flock for Satan's benefit. This title may also be applied to the antichrist because he will make an image of himself in the rebuilt temple and require people to worship it (see Rev 13:14–15).

The Spoiler and the Extortioner Isaiah describes the antichrist as "the spoiler" and "the extortioner" (Isa 16:4) because he will attempt to destroy all who resist his claims to be a god while using coercion to gain great riches.

The Wicked The apostle Paul describes the antichrist as "that Wicked" (2Th 2:8) because he will give himself entirely to Satan's evil designs to destroy God's people and purposes.

The Antichrist in the New Testament

The Man of Sin Paul tells us that the antichrist will not appear until there has been a falling away first. Then "that man of sin" (2Th 2:3) will be revealed after God has removed his restraining Spirit (see 2Th 2:6–7).

The Son of Perdition Paul calls the antichrist "the son of perdition" (2Th 2:3) because the antichrist is destined to destroy and be destroyed by God. Judas Iscariot was also referred to by this name (see Jn 17:12).

Antichrist The title "antichrist" (1Jn 2:18) is the most common one used to describe this last enemy of humanity. The antichrist will appear to emulate Jesus but will be a counterfeit.

The First Beast The antichrist is identified as "the beast" (Rev 11:7) that rises "up out of the sea" (Rev 13:1). The sea usually depicts Gentile nations so this title indicates the antichrist's power within the ten-nation kingdom.

The One Who Comes in His Own Name Though people rejected Jesus' claim to be the Messiah who came in the name of his Father, the Jews will one day accept the antichrist who "shall come in his own name" (Jn 5:43).

The Defilement of the Temple

Daniel and Paul both mention the defilement of the rebuilt temple when the antichrist will enter the Holy of Holies (see 9:27; 2Th 2:4). What he will do there is uncertain, but this act will surely qualify as "the abomination of desolation" (Mt 24:15) that Jesus warned his disciples to flee (see Mt 24:15–17). God's wrath will be instantly poured out when the antichrist defiles the temple half way through the seven-year treaty period. This will usher in the final great tribulation.

Many Jews will recognize that the antichrist is the false Messiah when he defiles the temple. As these Jews rebel, Satan will empower the antichrist to supernaturally fight the righteous and attack Israel as she flees into the wilderness seeking God's power and protection (see Rev 12:17).

The Worship of the Antichrist

The antichrist will suffer a deadly wound but will be miraculously healed and restored (see Rev 13:12–13). After this miracle, the false prophet will convince the world that the antichrist is the long-awaited Messiah. The false prophet will force everyone under the jurisdiction of his world government to worship the antichrist. From that point on it will be spiritual and physical warfare for three and a half years for those who choose to serve God.

The Destruction of the Antichrist

In the final years of the tribulation the kings of the east will mobilize a vast army to rebel against the tyranny of the antichrist (see Rev 9:16). They will march across Asia killing one third of humanity as they move towards Armageddon (see Rev 9:18). When they approach the Euphrates River it will dry up to allow their army to march across its dry riverbed to the final Battle of Armageddon (see Rev 9:14–15; 16:12).

When the enormous armies of the kings of the east, north, south and the ten-nation federation of the antichrist join battle, Jesus Christ will descend with his heavenly army of saints to defeat the antichrist and his allies (see Rev 19:19–21). The antichrist and the false prophet will be thrown into the lake of fire, while the sword of the Lord will kill their allies. A remnant of the antichrist's armies will escape and invade Jerusalem a few days later, taking the population captive. Jesus will descend to Jerusalem to destroy the last of the wicked armies and save all of the Jews who repent (see Zec 12:8-11; 14:1-5). Christ will then enter the rebuilt temple through the newly opened eastern gate and usher in the millennial kingdom (see Eze 43:1-5).

Grecia: and the great horn that *is* between his eyes [a]*is* the first king.
22 [a]Now that being broken, whereas
four stood up for it, four kingdoms shall
stand up out of the nation, but not in his
power.
23 And in the latter time of their kingdom, when the transgressors /are come
to the full, a king [a]of fierce countenance,
and understanding dark sentences, shall
stand up.
R 24 And his power shall be mighty,
[a]but not by his own power: and he shall
destroy wonderfully, [b]and shall prosper,
and practise, [c]and shall destroy the
mighty and the /holy people.
25 And [a]through his policy also he
shall cause craft to prosper in his hand;
[b]and he shall magnify *himself* in his
heart, and by /peace shall destroy many:
[b]he shall also stand up against the Prince
of princes; but he shall be [c]broken without hand.
26 And the vision of the evening and
the morning which was told *is* true:
[a]wherefore shut thou up the vision; for it
shall be for many days.
27 [a]And I Daniel fainted, and was sick
certain days; afterward I rose up, and did
the king's business; and I was astonished
at the vision, but none understood *it.*

Daniel's prayer for the people

9 IN THE first year [a]of Darius the son
of Ahasuerus, of the seed of the
Medes, /which was made king over the
realm of the Chaldeans;
2 In the first year of his reign I Daniel R
understood by books the number of the
years, whereof the word of the LORD came
to [a]Jeremiah the prophet, that he would
accomplish seventy years in the desolations of Jerusalem.
3 ¶ [a]And I set my face unto the Lord M
God, to seek by prayer and supplications,
with fasting, and sackcloth, and ashes:
4 And I prayed unto the LORD my God,
and made my confession, and said,
O [a]Lord, the great and dreadful God,
keeping the covenant and mercy to them

R *Da 8:19 ◀▶ Da 9:2*

R *Da 8:24 ◀▶ Da 9:16–18*
M *Eze 3:7 ◀▶ Da 9:20–21*

21 [a]ch. 11:3
22 [a]ch. 11:4
23 [a]Deut. 28:50 /Heb. *are accomplished*
24 [a]Rev. 17:13 [b]ch. 11:36 [c]ch. 7:25 /Heb. *people of the holy ones*
25 [a]ch. 11:21 [b]ch. 11:36 [c]Job 34:20; Lam. 4:6 /Or, *prosperity*
26 [a]Ezek. 12:27; Rev. 22:10
27 [a]ch. 7:28
9:1 [a]ch. 1:21 /Or, *in which he*
2 [a]2 Chr. 36:21; Jer. 25:11
3 [a]Neh. 1:4; Jer. 29:12; ch. 6:10
4 [a]Ex. 20:6; Deut. 7:9

8:22 The four separate subkingdoms of the Greek empire—Macedonia, Syria, Egypt, Asia Minor—were ruled by four generals following the death of Alexander the Great in 323 B.C.

8:23 This verse viewed Antiochus Epiphanes as a symbol of the satanic power of the future antichrist that will arise in the end times. Evil will abound in the last days "when the transgressors are come to the full," and the antichrist will be fearsome in appearance and deeply involved in satanic practices and occult rituals.

8:24 Though the details of this verse can be applied directly to Antiochus Epiphanes, the final fulfillment of this prophecy will come in the end times when the antichrist will be strong in battle (see Rev 13:4) and find success in his endeavors (see Rev 13:16–18). His power will come from Satan (see Rev 13:2), and he will also oppress "the holy people" during the final great tribulation as is suggested in 12:1 and Rev 12:6–17.

8:25 This verse found initial fulfillment in the reign of Antiochus Epiphanes. Through deceit, intrigue and treachery, Antiochus brought great wealth to his kingdom. But he also oppressed God's people and was ultimately destroyed by an unexplained illness in 164 B.C. The final fulfillment of Daniel's words revolves around the rule of the antichrist. Daniel stated that this antichrist would experience an economic success that would solidify his popularity (see 11:39). The antichrist would boastfully "magnify himself in his heart" and deceitfully offer a false peace to destroy his enemies. Daniel also prophesied that the antichrist would oppose Jesus Christ, "the Prince of princes; but he shall be broken without hand" at the Battle of Armageddon (see Rev 16:16).

8:26 The angel Gabriel confirmed that this prophecy would be completely fulfilled at the final end of this age.

8:27 Daniel admitted that he was astonished at the vision, but unable to understand it. We, too, can only understand the prophetic outline of God's plan for history when we harmonize the predictions of Daniel with the prophecies of Mt 24, 2 Thessalonians and Revelation.

9:1–19 In his prayer, Daniel repented for the nation of Israel for the sins that led to the destruction of Jerusalem. Daniel understood that Israel's punishment was the fulfillment of Solomon's prayer (see 1Ki 8:33–36). Daniel's prayer expressed his deep adoration of God (9:4), his confession of Israel's sins (9:5–15) and his heartfelt petition that God would forgive and limit Israel's desolation to seventy years (9:16–19; see also Jer 25:11–12). Daniel's life reminds us that our study of the deep truths of prophecy should lead us to a deeper spiritual life.

9:2 Daniel declared that the time had come for the ending of the Jews' seventy-year captivity in Babylon as prophesied by Jeremiah (see Jer 25:11–12).

that love him, and to them that keep his commandments;

C 5 [a]We have sinned, and have committed iniquity, and have done wickedly, and have rebelled, even by departing from thy precepts and from thy judgments:

6 [a]Neither have we hearkened unto thy servants the prophets, which spake in thy name to our kings, our princes, and our fathers, and to all the people of the land.

7 O Lord, [a]righteousness [1]*belongeth* unto thee, but unto us confusion of faces, as at this day; to the men of Judah, and to the inhabitants of Jerusalem, and unto all Israel, *that are* near, and *that are* far off, through all the countries whither thou hast driven them, because of their trespass that they have trespassed against thee.

8 O Lord, to us *belongeth* confusion of face, to our kings, to our princes, and to our fathers, because we have sinned against thee.

L P 9 [a]To the Lord our God *belong* mercies and forgivenesses, though we have rebelled against him;

10 Neither have we obeyed the voice of the LORD our God, to walk in his laws, which he set before us by his servants the prophets.

11 Yea, [a]all Israel have transgressed thy law, even by departing, that they might not obey thy voice; therefore the curse is poured upon us, and the oath that *is* written in the [b]law of Moses the servant of God, because we have sinned against him.

12 And he hath [a]confirmed his words, which he spake against us, and against our judges that judged us, by bringing upon us a great evil: [b]for under the whole heaven hath not been done as hath been done upon Jerusalem.

13 [a]As *it is* written in the law of Moses, all this evil is come upon us: [b]yet [1]made we not our prayer before the LORD our God, that we might turn from our iniquities, and understand thy truth.

14 Therefore hath the LORD [a]watched upon the evil, and brought it upon us: for [b]the LORD our God *is* righteous in all his works which he doeth: for we obeyed not his voice.

15 And now, O Lord our God, [a]that hast brought thy people forth out of the land of Egypt with a mighty hand, and hast [1]gotten thee [b]renown, as at this day; we have sinned, we have done wickedly.

16 ¶ O Lord, [a]according to all thy righteousness, I beseech thee, let thine anger and thy fury be turned away from thy city Jerusalem, [b]thy holy mountain: because for our sins, [c]and for the iniquities of our fathers, [d]Jerusalem and thy people [e]*are become* a reproach to all *that are* about us. R

17 Now therefore, O our God, hear the prayer of thy servant, and his supplications, [a]and cause thy face to shine upon thy sanctuary [b]that is desolate, [c]for the Lord's sake.

18 [a]O my God, incline thine ear, and hear; open thine eyes, [b]and behold our desolations, and the city [c]which[1] is called by thy name: for we do not [2]present our supplications before thee for our righteousnesses, but for thy great mercies.

19 O Lord, hear; O Lord, forgive; O Lord, hearken and do; defer not, for thine own sake, O my God: for thy city and thy people are called by thy name.

The meaning of the seventy weeks

20 ¶ And whiles I *was* speaking, and praying, and confessing my sin and the sin of my people Israel, and presenting my supplication before the LORD my God for the holy mountain of my God; M

21 Yea, whiles I *was* speaking in prayer, even the man [a]Gabriel, whom I had seen in the vision at the beginning, being caused to fly [1]swiftly, touched me about the time of the evening oblation.

22 And he informed *me,* and talked with me, and said, O Daniel, I am now come forth [1]to give thee skill and understanding.

23 At the beginning of thy supplications the [1]commandment came forth, and I am come to show *thee;* for thou *art* [2]greatly beloved: therefore [a]understand the matter, and consider the vision. L

5 [a]1 Ki. 8:47; Ps. 106:6; Jer. 14:7
6 [a]2 Chr. 36:15
7 [a]Neh. 9:33 [1]Or, *thou* hast
9 [a]Ps. 130:4,7
11 [a]Is. 1:4-6 [b]Lev. 26:14; Deut. 27:15; Lam. 2:17
12 [a]Zech. 1:6 [b]Lam. 1:12; Ezek. 5:9; Amos 3:2
13 [a]Deut. 28:15; Lam. 2:17 [b]Is. 9:13; Jer. 2:30; Hos. 7:7 [1]Heb. *entreated we not the face of the*
14 [a]Jer. 31:28 [b]Neh. 9:33
15 [a]Ex. 32:11; 1 Ki. 8:51; Neh. 1:10 [b]Ex. 14:18; Neh. 9:10; Jer. 32:20 [1]Heb. *made thee a name*
16 [a]1 Sam. 12:7; Ps. 31:1; Mic. 6:4,5 [b]Zech. 8:3 [c]Ex. 20:5 [d]Lam. 2:16 [e]Ps. 79:4
17 [a]Num. 6:25 [b]Lam. 5:18 [c]John 16:24
18 [a]Is. 37:17 [b]Ex. 3:7 [c]Jer. 25:29 [1]Heb. *whereupon thy name is called* [2]Heb. *cause to fall*
21 [a]ch. 8:16 [1]Heb. *with weariness,* or, *flight*
22 [1]Heb. *to make thee skilful of understanding*
23 [a]Mat. 24:15 [1]Heb. *word* [2]Heb. *a* man *of desires*

C *Eze 22:18* ◀▶ *Hos 1:9*
L *Eze 36:29* ◀▶ *Hos 6:3*
P *Eze 34:11–12* ◀▶ *Hos 6:1*
R *Da 9:2* ◀▶ *Da 9:26–27*
M *Da 9:3–5* ◀▶ *Hos 10:12*
L *Da 6:22* ◀▶ *Joel 2:27–28*

B 24 Seventy weeks are determined
D upon thy people and upon thy holy city,
[1]to finish the transgression, and [2]to make
an end of sins, [a]and to make reconciliation for iniquity, [b]and to bring in everlasting righteousness, and to seal up the vision and [3]prophecy, [c]and to anoint the
most Holy.
25 Know therefore and understand,
that from the going forth of the commandment to restore and to build Jerusalem unto [a]the Messiah [b]the Prince *shall*
be seven weeks, and threescore and two
weeks: the street shall be built again, and
the wall, even in troublous times.
26 And after threescore and two G
weeks [a]shall Messiah be cut off, [b]but[1] R
not for himself: [2]and [c]the people of the
prince that shall come [d]shall destroy the
city and the sanctuary; and the end
thereof *shall be* with a flood, and unto
the end of the war desolations are determined.
27 And he shall confirm [a]the[1] cov-

24 [a]Is. 53:10 [b]Rev. 14:6 [c]Ps. 45:7 [1]*Or, to restrain* [2]*Or, to seal up* [3]*Heb. prophet*

25 [a]John 1:41 [b]Is. 55:4

26 [a]Is. 53:8 [b]1 Pet. 2:21 [c]Mat. 22:7 [d]Luke 19:44 [1]*Or, and shall have nothing* [2]*Or, and [the Jews] they shall be no more his people, ch. 11:17, or, and the prince's [Messiah's, ver. 25] future people*

27 [a]Is. 42:6 [1]*Or, a*

B *Jer 22:29–30* ◀▶ *Mic 5:1–4*
D *Eze 46:13* ◀▶ *Zec 12:10*

G *Da 8:1–26* ◀▶ *Da 10:1*
R *Da 9:16–18* ◀▶ *Da 11:2*

9:24–27 Careful study of Daniel's prophecy of the "seventy weeks" is essential to a proper understanding of the unfolding of end time events. This prophecy of the seventy weeks, or "sevens" (NIV), provides an outline of history from the time between the command to rebuild the walls of Jerusalem to the coming of the Messiah and the final establishment of his kingdom. Though the interpretation of these verses varies among scholars, most agree that each "week" symbolizes the passage of seven years. (For the Biblical usage of a "week" referring to a period of seven years, see Ge 29:26–28.) Daniel's seventy weeks of years are then subdivided into three distinct units: 49 years (corresponding to the "seven weeks" of 9:25), 434 years (corresponding to the "threescore and two weeks" of 9:26) and 7 more years (corresponding to "the week" of 9:27).

Note that the focus of this prophecy is on the Jews and Jerusalem. Daniel fixed the date of the beginning of his vision from the time of the decree to rebuild Jerusalem (9:25). Though various edicts were issued to rebuild the temple, history records only one decree issued in 445 B.C. that authorized the rebuilding of the city (see Ne 2:1–8).

Daniel also noted that the Messiah would come "seven weeks, and threescore and two weeks" (9:25) after this historic decree. Yet Daniel indicated that the Messiah would "be cut off" (9:26). This portion of Daniel's prophecy was fulfilled precisely 483 years later when Jesus entered Jerusalem on a donkey on Palm Sunday, was rejected by the Jews, and crucified by the Romans. Note too that Daniel recorded the future destruction of Jerusalem by "the prince that shall come" (9:26), referring to the "little horn" of 7:8. Many scholars agree that this prophecy was fulfilled when Rome destroyed Jerusalem in A.D. 70.

There appears to be a period of time between the conclusion of the sixty-ninth week and the beginning of the seventieth week in Daniel's prophecy. This time period will encompass certain "desolations" (9:26) that are not described here.

9:27 Though some scholars feel that this verse found its fulfillment during the reign of Antiochus Epiphanes and his oppression of the Jews, other scholars suggest that this last "week" of Daniel's prophecy refers to the end times. This futurist view suggests that the last "week" covers the seven-year tribulation period that will occur in the end times, with the second half of those seven years referred to as "a time and times and the dividing of time" (Da 7:25; Rev 12:14). According to futurist scholars, during this "week" the antichrist (the "little horn" in 7:8) will make a covenant between himself and the Jews. At the midpoint of this "week," after only

Daniel's Vision of the Seventy Weeks

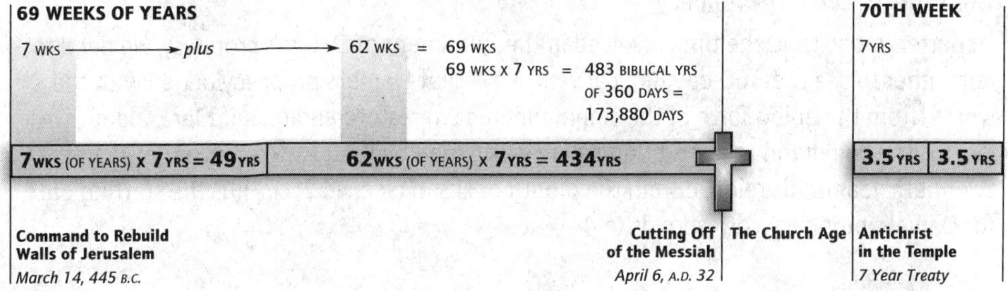

The Vision of the Seventy Weeks

DANIEL'S VISION OF the seventy weeks contains a brief outline of the future history of the world (see 9:24-27). The prophet Jeremiah had declared that Israel's captivity in Babylon would last seventy years (see Jer 25:11). Daniel was aware of Jeremiah's prediction and realized in 538 B.C. that the seventy years of Israel's Babylonian captivity were about to end. Daniel asked God to show him what would happen to the Jews after their captivity. God responded by giving Daniel this astonishing vision that foretold Israel's rejection of their promised Messiah and the rise of an evil ruler who would ally himself with Israel in the last days.

The Length of a Year

An important but often ignored factor in determining the chronology of prophecy is determining the length of a year. Our solar year of 365.25 days was unknown to ancient civilizations. The ancient Jews followed the Chaldean lunar-solar year. This method of marking time recognized four distinct seasons and determined the length of months by the course of the moon. Four full seasons and twelve lunar months of 30 days each totaled 360 days or one year in ancient Jewish records.

Abraham followed this method of marking years when he migrated to Canaan from Ur. The Bible also confirms the use of the 30-day month in the record of the flood. Noah and his family were shut up in the ark on the seventeenth day of the second month and did not land on the mountain until five months later on the seventeenth day of the seventh month. Scripture says that the elapsed time was a total of 150 days, indicating that each month contained 30 days each (see Ge 7:11; 7:24; 8:3–4). In the book of Revelation, John indicated that the last half of the great tribulation would last 1260 days (see Rev 12:6). This period also corresponds to the "time, and times, and half a time" (Rev 12:14) and the "forty and two months" (Rev 13:5)—all references to three and a half Biblical years of 360 days each.

The Years of Daniel's Prophecy

To better understand the time involved in the fulfillment of Daniel's prophecy, we need to remember to use the 360-day Biblical year. Note that Daniel's prophecy began with the words "from the going forth of the commandment to restore and to build Jerusalem" (9:25). The command to restore Jerusalem was issued by King Artaxerxes of Persia in the twentieth year of his reign, during the month of Nisan (see Ne 2:1). Thus the starting date for Daniel's prophecy corresponds to 444 B.C.

Most scholars agree that Daniel's vision of weeks describes the passage of years; seven weeks are equivalent to seven years. Thus seven Biblical years are equivalent to 2520 days. Understanding these basics makes calculating the remainder of Daniel's prophecy fairly simple, since Daniel divides his prophecy into different sections.

The time period from the decree of Artaxerxes "to build Jerusalem unto the Messiah the Prince shall be seven weeks, and threescore and two weeks" (9:25)—a total of 483 Biblical years. A careful calculation reveals that exactly 483 Biblical years from the beginning of Daniel's prophecy in 444 B.C., Jesus Christ entered Jerusalem through the Eastern Gate on Palm Sunday and presented himself to Israel as their promised Messiah. Yet according to Daniel's prophecy, at the end of the sixty-nine weeks (483 years) the Messiah would be cut off (9:26). The first sixty-nine weeks of Daniel's vision of the seventy weeks were precisely fulfilled because, just a few days later, Jesus Christ the Messiah was cut off and crucified on the cross, rose from the grave and ascended to heaven.

The Seventieth Week

The seventieth "week" of Daniel's prophecy has yet to be fulfilled. When Israel rejected Jesus Christ as their promised Messiah at the conclusion of Daniel's sixty-ninth week, God's prophetic clock for Israel stopped ticking. As a consequence of Israel's rejection of the Messiah, God postponed Israel's prophesied kingdom for almost two thousand years. During the interval between Daniel's sixty-ninth and seventieth weeks, God has instituted a church of believers from all nations to witness to the world of his offer of salvation.

Daniel prophesied that the full seventy weeks were decreed for the Jews (9:24). In fact, the central focus of this final week will be God's dealing with his chosen people. This final week of years will culminate with the tyranny of the antichrist, the terror of the tribulation and the mark of the beast. Until then, wars and desolations will continue until the end of the age.

The seventieth will begin when the antichrist signs a seven-year treaty, or covenant, with Israel (9:27). The preceding verse helps identify this antichrist as "the prince that shall come" from the people who will "destroy the city and the sanctuary" (9:26). History reveals that the Romans destroyed Jerusalem and the temple in A.D. 70. Therefore, the antichrist, "the prince," must rise out of the territories and nations of the Roman empire. In the last days this antichrist will lead his armies in a relentless campaign to conquer the nations of the whole earth.

After three and a half years, the antichrist will break his treaty with Israel, halt the daily sacrifices in the rebuilt temple and defile the Holy of Holies, claiming his own divinity. This defilement of the temple is referred to as "the abomination of desolation" (Mk 13:14).

The Abomination of Desolation

The strange phrase "the abomination of desolation" is mentioned by Jesus in Mt 24:15 as part of Daniel's prophecy of the seventy weeks. Jesus warned his disciples to watch for the events that will transpire during the countdown to the Battle of Armageddon and to "flee into the mountains" (Mt 24:16) if they saw these things occur. Jesus confirmed Daniel's prediction that the antichrist would defile the temple and commit an act of supreme spiritual defiance against heaven by entering the Holy of Holies. Paul called this antichrist a "man of sin" and a "son of perdition" (2Th 2:3) who would exalt himself above God and sit in the temple accepting worship like a god. But the antichrist will not go unchallenged. The seventieth week will end when Jesus Christ descends from heaven to defeat the antichrist's armies at the Battle of Armageddon.

enant with [b]many for one week: and in
the midst of the week he shall cause the
sacrifice and the oblation to cease, and
for the overspreading of abominations he
shall make *it* desolate, [c]even until the
consummation, and that determined shall
be poured upon the desolate.

Daniel's vision of an angel

G 10 IN THE third year of Cyrus king
of Persia a thing was revealed
unto Daniel, whose name was called Belteshazzar; and the thing *was* true, but the
time appointed *was* [1]long: and he understood the thing, and had understanding of
the vision.
2 In those days I Daniel was mourning
three [1]full weeks.
3 I ate no [1]pleasant bread, neither
came flesh nor wine in my mouth, neither did I anoint myself at all, till three
whole weeks were fulfilled.
4 And in the four and twentieth day of
the first month, as I was by the side of the
great river, which *is* Hiddekel;
5 Then I lifted up mine eyes, and
looked, and behold [1]a certain man
clothed in linen, whose loins *were*
[a]girded with fine gold of Uphaz:
6 His body also *was* like the beryl, and
his face as the appearance of lightning,
and his eyes as lamps of fire, and his arms
and his feet like in colour to polished
brass, [a]and the voice of his words like the
voice of a multitude.
7 And I Daniel alone saw the vision:
for the men that were with me saw not

G *Da 9:26–27* ◄► *Da 10:14*

27 [b]Mat. 26:28 [c]ch. 11:36
10:1 [1]Heb. *great*
2 [1]Heb. *weeks of days*
3 [1]Heb. *bread of desires*
5 [a]Rev. 1:13 [1]Heb. *one man*
6 [a]Rev. 1:15
8 [1]Or, *vigour*
10 [a]ch. 9:21 [1]Heb. *moved*
11 [a]ch. 9:23 [1]Heb. *a man of desires* [2]Heb. *stand upon thy standing*
12 [a]Rev. 1:17 [b]ch. 9:3,4,22,23; Acts 10:4
13 [a]ver. 20 [b]ver. 21; ch. 12:1; Jude 9; Rev. 12:7 [1]Or, *the first*
14 [a]Gen. 49:1; ch. 2:28 [b]ver. 1; ch. 8:26; Hab. 2:3

the vision; but a great quaking fell upon
them, so that they fled to hide themselves.
8 Therefore I was left alone, and saw
this great vision, and there remained no
strength in me: for my [1]comeliness was
turned in me into corruption, and I retained no strength.
9 Yet heard I the voice of his words:
and when I heard the voice of his words,
then was I in a deep sleep on my face,
and my face toward the ground.
10 ¶ [a]And, behold, an hand touched
me, which [1]set me upon my knees and
upon the palms of my hands.
11 And he said unto me, O Daniel, [a]a[1]
man greatly beloved, understand the
words that I speak unto thee, and [2]stand
upright: for unto thee am I now sent. And
when he had spoken this word unto me, I
stood trembling.
12 Then said he unto me, [a]Fear not, U
Daniel: for from the first day that thou
didst set thine heart to understand, and
to chasten thyself before thy God, [b]thy
words were heard, and I am come for thy
words.
13 [a]But the prince of the kingdom of
Persia withstood me one and twenty
days: but, lo, [b]Michael, [1]one of the chief
princes, came to help me; and I remained
there with the kings of Persia.
14 Now I am come to make thee un- G
derstand what shall befall thy people [a]in
the latter days: [b]for yet the vision *is* for
many days.

U *Da 1:15* ◄► *Da 10:19*
G *Da 10:1* ◄► *Da 10:20*

---

3 1/2 years, the antichrist will break this covenant, interrupt Jewish worship in the temple, defile the sanctuary and begin to persecute the Jews. For further information on the futurist interpretation of prophecy, refer to the article entitled "Introduction to Prophecy," p. vi.

Jesus' words seem to confirm that this final "week" is still in the future and that these events will transpire just prior to his second coming (see Mt 24:6–15) thus placing several centuries between the sixty-ninth week and the seventieth week of Daniel's prophecy. When Christ returns, he will destroy the antichrist at the end of the seventieth week and introduce a time of "everlasting righteousness" (9:24). Note Daniel's reference to the anointing of the Messiah when he comes again to rule. (Compare this verse with 1Sa 16:13.) The oil used for anointing a king was made from special ingredients (see Ex 30:25–26). A sample of this oil was discovered in recent archeological digs near the Dead Sea.

10:2–3 Daniel mourned for 21 days, "three full weeks" (10:2). This reference to "weeks" is clearly differentiated from the "weeks" of 9:24–27. Daniel was probably mourning the destruction of Jerusalem and the exile of his people to Babylon.

10:10–17 While Daniel prayed, an angel came to strengthen him and give him additional prophetic information. Note that the angel's reason for delay was because of demonic interference (10:13). This seems to indicate that demonic spirits or fallen angels have been given authority under the direction of Satan to disturb the affairs of the nations (see 10:20).

The Tribulation

JESUS REFERRED SEVERAL times to the terrible persecution that would occur before his return, intimating that it would be worse than anything that has happened since the beginning of the world (see Mt 24:21). This time of persecution is called the tribulation, derived from a root word that means "squeeze" or "press." Prophecy about the tribulation begins in the OT and runs through the entire NT, providing substantial information about this important eschatological doctrine.

The exact timing of this period of suffering is uncertain. Those who teach the preterist view of prophecy suggest that the predictions concerning the tribulation were fulfilled during the destruction of Jerusalem in A.D. 70. However, the futurist view contends that the tribulation period will occur just prior to Christ's second coming and will coincide with what Scripture calls the great day of the Lord. Though the tribulation will last only seven years, the great day of the Lord will continue until the end of the Millennium (see 2Pe 3:10).

The involvement that believers will play in the tribulation is also a matter of some debate. Some scholars feel that believers will be translated to heaven before the beginning of the tribulation. Using a literal method of the interpretation of the Bible, these pretribulation scholars believe that the passages of Scripture that deal with the tribulation relate only to God's interaction with Israel; therefore the church will not be a participant in it. Others suggest that believers will be raptured to heaven during the tribulation. These midtribulation scholars believe the church will endure the first half of this period of suffering but will be raptured to heaven before the full outpouring of God's wrath. Still other scholars subscribe to a posttribulation view of the rapture, basing their belief on the Scriptures that state the church will have to go through a period of testing and tribulation. Because of the varied opinions about the church's role in the tribulation it is vital to understand the events that will transpire. (For additional information about the translation of believers to heaven, see the article entitled "The Rapture" on p. 1370.)

Commencing when the antichrist signs a seven-year treaty with Israel (9:27), the tribulation will continue until the return of Jesus Christ to defeat the antichrist at Armageddon. The seven years of tribulation will be a time of unparalleled evil, war, persecution and martyrdom (see Rev 12:12). The Bible indicates that as many as four billion people will die as the wrath of God is poured out during the judgments of the great tribulation. Unrepentant sinners in that day will still defy God, and the consequences will be catastrophic (see Rev 9:20–21).

God's wrath will be poured out during the tribulation in a sevenfold series of judgments from heaven that begin with the seven seals (see Rev 6:1–17). The first four seals are opened by the Lord and handed over for implementation to the four horsemen of the apocalypse: The white horseman represents false peace; the red horseman symbolizes war; the black horseman stands for famine; the pale horseman represents death. The remaining seals are opened and symbolize the martyrdom of the tribulation saints and the convulsions of the whole earth and the heavens. When the seventh seal is opened, silence falls in heaven for half an hour (see Rev 8:1) as the world waits for the beginning of the seven trumpet judgments.

The seven trumpet judgments begin in the middle of the tribulation and continue to its end, unleashing the wrath of God upon the earth, sea, waters and heavens (see Rev 8:7–13). As these judgments continue, demonic spirits released from the bottomless pit will torment humanity for five months, four angels from the Euphrates River will marshal the armies of the East to attack and the final crisis will lead to Christ's return (see Rev 9:1–19; 11:15). There are also seven vial judgments described in Revelation that will occur just before Armageddon (see Rev 16:1–21). Though similar to the trumpet judgments, these judgments occur at the end of the tribulation and are primarily directed against unbelievers.

At the beginning of the tribulation, the treaty between the antichrist and Israel will be in effect. Though initially allied with only ten nations, the antichrist will bring more nations under his power until the whole world allies with his kingdom. At the midpoint of the seven-year treaty, Satan will be expelled from heaven, and the antichrist will suffer a mortal wound that will be miraculously healed (see Rev 13:3). This miracle will convince many that he is the Messiah. The antichrist will capitalize on this miracle and consciously try to fulfill the ancient prophetic expectations of the Jews. The false prophet will introduce the system of the mark of the beast that will continue until the Battle of Armageddon and will also force people to worship a statue of the antichrist or face death (see Rev 13:14).

Though many Jews will be constrained to accept the antichrist as their Messiah, when the antichrist violates the Holy of Holies, many righteous Jews in Israel will realize that he is not their true Messiah. They will attempt to break with the antichrist for the remainder of the tribulation and will also reject the false prophet's words (see Rev 12:6). Other nations will follow Israel and attempt to rebel against the antichrist. As nation after nation tries to throw off the yoke of the antichrist, the entire tribulation will be filled with war and famine.

The antichrist will establish a military base in Israel. The kings of the northern alliance and the king of the south will attack the antichrist's forces in Palestine, but he will defeat their armies (see Da 11:40). As the antichrist reinforces his military position near Jerusalem, the nations of the east will realize that they must act immediately if they wish to throw off the chains of the world dictator. The final focus of their rebellion will result in the Battle of Armageddon and will involve all the armies of the world (see 11:44; see Rev 16:16).

The armies will fight all across Asia, killing one third of humanity, but the final war will center on the Valley of Jezreel in a place called Armageddon. Whether through the miraculous intervention of God or through a complete closure of the spillways of the Ataturk Dam in Turkey, the Euphrates River will dry up, allowing the army of the east to cross into northern Israel (see Rev 16:12).

Despite the antichrist's huge military and satanic forces, he will be defeated (see Da 11:45). Jesus Christ, with his army of saints from heaven, will return to defeat the antichrist and his powerful armies, throwing this prince of darkness into the lake of fire (see 8:25; Rev 19:11–14; 19–20). The tribulation will conclude and Jesus Christ will establish his millennial kingdom.

15 And when he had spoken such words unto me, [a]I set my face toward the ground, and I became dumb.

16 And, behold, [a]*one* like the similitude of the sons of men [b]touched my lips: then I opened my mouth, and spake, and said unto him that stood before me, O my lord, by the vision [c]my sorrows are turned upon me, and I have retained no strength.

17 For how can [1]the servant of this my lord talk with this my lord? for as for me, straightway there remained no strength in me, neither is there breath left in me.

18 Then there came again and touched me *one* like the appearance of a man, and he strengthened me,

U 19 [a]And said, O man greatly beloved, [b]fear not: peace *be* unto thee, be strong, yea, be strong. And when he had spoken unto me, I was strengthened, and said, Let my lord speak; for thou hast strengthened me.

G 20 Then said he, Knowest thou wherefore I come unto thee? and now will I return to fight [a]with the prince of Persia: and when I am gone forth, lo, the prince of Grecia shall come.

21 But I will show thee that which is noted in the scripture of truth: and *there is* none that [1]holdeth with me in these things, [a]but Michael your prince.

U *Da 10:12* ◀▶ *Da 12:3*
G *Da 10:14* ◀▶ *Da 11:31*

15 [a]ver. 9; ch. 8:18
16 [a]ch. 8:15 [b]ver. 10; Jer. 1:9 [c]ver. 8
17 [1]Or, *this servant of my lord*
19 [a]ver. 11 [b]Judg. 6:23
20 [a]ver. 13
21 [a]ver. 13; Jude 9; Rev. 12:7 [1]Heb. *strengtheneth himself*
11:1 [a]ch. 9:1 [b]ch. 5:31
3 [a]ch. 7:6 & 8:5 [b]ver. 16,36; ch. 8:4
4 [a]ch. 8:8 [b]ch. 8:22
6 [1]Heb. *shall associate themselves* [2]Heb. *rights* [3]Or, *whom she brought forth*

11 ALSO I [a]in the first year of [b]Darius the Mede, *even* I, stood to confirm and to strengthen him.

Conflict between north and south

2 And now will I show thee the truth. Behold, there shall stand up yet three kings in Persia; and the fourth shall be far richer than *they* all: and by his strength through his riches he shall stir up all against the realm of Grecia. R

3 And [a]a mighty king shall stand up, that shall rule with great dominion, and [b]do according to his will.

4 And when he shall stand up, [a]his kingdom shall be broken, and shall be divided toward the four winds of heaven; and not to his posterity, [b]nor according to his dominion which he ruled: for his kingdom shall be plucked up, even for others beside those.

5 ¶ And the king of the south shall be strong, and *one* of his princes; and he shall be strong above him, and have dominion; his dominion *shall be* a great dominion.

6 And in the end of years they [1]shall join themselves together; for the king's daughter of the south shall come to the king of the north to make [2]an agreement: but she shall not retain the power of the arm; neither shall he stand, nor his arm: but she shall be given up, and they that brought her, and [3]he that begat her, and

R *Da 9:26–27* ◀▶ *Da 11:31*

11:1 The series of predictions found in this chapter refer to the complex events that transpired following the death of Alexander the Great. The details concerning personal, political and military events of the reign of Antiochus Epiphanes are remarkable for their accuracy, correctly predicting the wars between the Seleucids of Syria and the Ptolemies of Egypt and their struggle to rule the Holy Land between 323–165 B.C. Only a divinely inspired prophecy could be this accurate.

11:2–35 The prophecies in the first part of this chapter concern the future of the Medo-Persian and Greek empires. Daniel's vision revealed that four kings would rule Medo-Persia in quick succession. These kings were probably Cambyses (530–522 B.C.), Pseudo-Smerdis (522–521 B.C.), Darius I Hystaspes (521–486 B.C.; see Ezr 5—6) and Xerxes I, also known as Ahasuerus (486–465 B.C.; see Ezr 4:6). Despite these rulers, Persia would fall to Greece, and this Greek empire would quickly be divided into four parts (see 8:22). The complicated history of the battles between the Syrian and Egyptian kingdoms is outlined with precision between 11:5–20.

11:3 The "mighty king" referred to in this verse is Alexander the Great, who ruled Greece from 330–323 B.C. See also 7:6; 8:5–8, 21–22.

11:4 After the untimely death of Alexander the Great in 323 B.C., the Greek empire was quickly divided into four kingdoms ruled by Alexander's four generals. Cassander became king of Macedonia, the original kingdom in Alexander's empire. Lysimachus ruled Asia Minor and Thrace. Ptolemy and his successors ruled the kingdom of Egypt and her territories for three centuries. Seleucus and his descendants ruled Syria and the surrounding territories of the Middle East until the Roman conquest in 65 B.C.

11:5 This "king of the south" is Ptolemy I Soter of Egypt (323–285 B.C.).

11:6 This "king of the south" is probably Ptolemy II Philadelphus who ruled Egypt from 285–246 B.C. His daughter was named Berenice.

he that strengthened her in *these* times.

7 But out of a branch of her roots shall *one* stand up [a]in[1] his estate, which shall come with an army, and shall enter into the fortress of the king of the north, and shall deal against them, and shall prevail:

8 And shall also carry captives into Egypt their gods, with their princes, *and* with [1]their precious vessels of silver and of gold; and he shall continue *more* years than the king of the north.

9 So the king of the south shall come into *his* kingdom, and shall return into his own land.

10 But his sons [1]shall be stirred up, and shall assemble a multitude of great forces: and *one* shall certainly come, [a]and overflow, and pass through: [2]then shall he return, and be stirred up, [b]*even* to his fortress.

11 And the king of the south shall be moved with choler, and shall come forth and fight with him, *even* with the king of the north: and he shall set forth a great multitude; but the multitude shall be given into his hand.

12 *And* when he hath taken away the multitude, his heart shall be lifted up; and he shall cast down *many* ten thousands: but he shall not be strengthened *by it.*

13 For the king of the north shall return, and shall set forth a multitude greater than the former, and shall certainly come [1]after certain years with a great army and with much riches.

14 And in those times there shall many stand up against the king of the south: also [1]the robbers of thy people shall exalt themselves to establish the vision; but they shall fall.

15 So the king of the north shall come, and cast up a mount, and take [1]the most fenced cities: and the arms of the south shall not withstand, neither [2]his chosen people, neither *shall there be any* strength to withstand.

16 But he that cometh against him [a]shall do according to his own will, and [b]none shall stand before him: and he shall stand in [1]the [2]glorious land, which by his hand shall be consumed.

17 He shall also [a]set his face to enter with the strength of his whole kingdom, and [1]upright ones with him; thus shall he do: and he shall give him the daughter of women, [2]corrupting her: but she shall not stand *on his side,* [b]neither be for him.

18 After this shall he turn his face unto the isles, and shall take many: but a prince [1]for his own behalf shall cause [2]the reproach offered by him to cease; without his own reproach he shall cause *it* to turn upon him.

19 Then he shall turn his face toward the fort of his own land: but he shall stumble and fall, [a]and not be found.

20 Then shall stand up [1]in his estate [2]a raiser of taxes *in* the glory of the kingdom: but within few days he shall be destroyed, neither in [3]anger, nor in battle.

21 And [1]in his estate [a]shall stand up a vile person, to whom they shall not give the honour of the kingdom: but he shall come in peaceably, and obtain the kingdom by flatteries.

22 And with the arms of a flood shall they be overflown from before him, and shall be broken; [a]yea, also the prince of the covenant.

23 And after the league *made* with him [a]he shall work deceitfully: for he shall come up, and shall become strong with a small people.

24 He shall enter [1]peaceably even upon the fattest places of the province; and he shall do *that* which his fathers have not done, nor his fathers' fathers; he shall scatter among them the prey, and spoil, and riches: *yea,* and he shall [2]fore-

7 [a]ver. 20 [1]Or, *in his place,* or, *office*
8 [1]Heb. *vessels of their desire*
10 [a]Is. 8:8; ch. 9:26 [b]ver. 7 [1]Or, *shall war* [2]Or, *then shall he be stirred up again*
13 [1]Heb. *at the end of times, even years;* see ch. 4:16 & 12:7
14 [1]Heb. *the children of robbers*
15 [1]Heb. *the city of munitions* [2]Heb. *the people of his choices*
16 [a]ch. 8:4,7 [b]Josh. 1:5 [1]Heb. *the land of ornament* [2]Or, *goodly*
17 [a]2 Chr. 20:3 [b]ch. 9:26 [1]Or, *much uprightness:* or, *equal conditions* [2]Heb. *to corrupt*
18 [1]Heb. *for him* [2]Heb. *his*
19 [a]Ps. 37:36
20 [1]Or, *in his place* [2]Heb. *one that causeth an exacter to pass over* [3]Heb. *angers*
21 [a]ch. 7:8 [1]Or, *in his place*
22 [a]ch. 8:10,11
23 [a]ch. 8:25
24 [1]Or, *into the peaceable and fat* [2]Heb. *think his thoughts*

11:7–9 Berenice's brother, Ptolemy III Euergetes (246–221 B.C.) engineered the death of Laodice, Antiochus II Theos' wife who had attempted to murder Berenice.

11:10 The sons mentioned in this verse refer to two of the Seleucids: Seleucus III Ceraunus (226–223 B.C.) and Antiochus III the Great (223–187 B.C.).

11:11 This "king of the south" was Ptolemy IV Philopator (221–203 B.C.) of Egypt.

11:14 This "king of the south" was Ptolemy V Epiphanes (203–181 B.C.) of Egypt.

11:15 This "king of the north" was Seleucus IV Philopator (187–175 B.C.) of Syria.

11:21 The northern king described here is clearly Antiochus IV Epiphanes who ruled in Syria from 175–164 B.C. Antiochus Epiphanes (the "little horn" of 8:9) oppressed the Jews, defiled the temple and typifies the future antichrist who will rule the earth at the end of the age.

cast his devices against the strong holds, even for a time.

25 And he shall stir up his power and his courage against the king of the south with a great army; and the king of the south shall be stirred up to battle with a very great and mighty army; but he shall not stand: for they shall forecast devices against him.

26 Yea, they that feed of the portion of his meat shall destroy him, and his army shall overflow: and many shall fall down slain.

27 And both these kings' [1]hearts *shall be* to do mischief, and they shall speak lies at one table; but it shall not prosper: for yet the end *shall be* at the time appointed.

28 Then shall he return into his land with great riches; and his heart *shall be* against the holy covenant; and he shall do *exploits,* and return to his own land.

29 At the time appointed he shall return, and come toward the south; but it shall not be as the former, or as the latter.

30 ¶ [a]For the ships of Chittim shall come against him: therefore he shall be grieved, and return, and have indignation against the holy covenant: so shall he do; he shall even return, and have intelligence with them that forsake the holy covenant.

31 And arms shall stand on his part, [a]and they shall pollute the sanctuary of strength, and shall take away the daily *sacrifice,* and they shall place the abomination that [1]maketh desolate.

32 And such as do wickedly against the covenant shall he [1]corrupt by flatteries: but the people that do know their God shall be strong, and do *exploits.*

33 And they that understand among the people shall instruct many: yet they shall fall by the sword, and by flame, by captivity, and by spoil, *many* days.

34 Now when they shall fall, they shall be helped with a little help: but many shall cleave to them with flatteries.

35 And *some* of them of understanding shall fall, [a]to try [1]them, and to purge, and to make *them* white, *even* to the time of the end: because *it is* yet for a time appointed.

The power of the northern king

36 And the king shall do according to his will; and he shall [a]exalt himself, and magnify himself above every god, and shall speak marvellous things against the God of gods, and shall prosper till the indignation be accomplished: for that that is determined shall be done.

37 Neither shall he regard the God of his fathers, nor the desire of women, [a]nor regard any god: for he shall magnify himself above all.

38 But [1]in his [2]estate shall he honour the God of [3,4]forces: and a god whom his fathers knew not shall he honour with gold, and silver, and with precious stones, and [5]pleasant things.

39 Thus shall he do in the [1]most strong holds with a strange god, whom he shall acknowledge *and* increase with glory: and he shall cause them to rule over many, and shall divide the land for [2]gain.

40 And at the time of the end shall the

27 [1]Heb. *their hearts*
30 [a]Jer. 2:10
31 [a]ch. 8:11 [1]Or, *astonisheth*
32 [1]Or, *cause to dissemble*
35 [a]ch. 12:10 [1]Or, *by them*
36 [a]ch. 7:8,25
37 [a]Is. 14:13
38 [1]Heb. *as for the almighty God, in his seat he shall honour, yea, he shall honour a god, whom* [2]Or, *stead* [3]Or, *munitions* [4]Heb. *Mauzzim,* or, *God's protectors* [5]Heb. *things desired*
39 [1]Heb. *fortresses of munitions* [2]Heb. *a price*

G *Da 10:20* ◀▶ *Da 12:6–7*
R *Da 11:2* ◀▶ *Da 11:36*
V *Jer 51:36* ◀▶ *Zec 4:6*
R *Da 11:31* ◀▶ *Da 12:7*

11:25–28 This passage prophesied a series of military expeditions by Antiochus Epiphanes against the kingdom of Egypt.

11:30 Roman ships under the command of Gaius Popilius Laenas challenged Antiochus Epiphanes to cease his attacks toward Egypt.

11:31–35 This passage prophesied the defilement of the temple in Jerusalem by the Antiochus Epiphanes (the "little horn" of ch. 8). In 168 B.C. Antiochus Epiphanes erected a statue of Zeus in the Holy Place of the temple. This defilement of the temple prefigured the abomination that Jesus predicted would occur in the end times (see Mt 24:15; Lk 21:20).

11:36–45 Some scholars suggest that the willful king in this passage is Antiochus Epiphanes, the same individual described in ch. 8 as the "little horn." The reign of Antiochus Epiphanes was marked by satanic ritual and cruel attacks on God's chosen people. However, other scholars suggest that the prophetic details revealed about this willful king (11:36–45) describe the antichrist, the future head of the revived Roman empire.

11:37 This willful king will have no respect for religion or religious practices and will utterly disregard Israel's God. In addition, this willful king will only worship himself.

king of the south push at him: and the king of the north shall come against him [a]like a whirlwind, with chariots, [b]and with horsemen, and with many ships; and he shall enter into the countries, and shall overflow and pass over.

41 He shall enter also into the [1,2]glorious land, and many *countries* shall be overthrown: but these shall escape out of his hand, [a]*even* Edom, and Moab, and the chief of the children of Ammon.

42 He shall [1]stretch forth his hand also upon the countries: and the land of Egypt shall not escape.

43 But he shall have power over the treasures of gold and of silver, and over all the precious things of Egypt: and the Libyans and the Ethiopians *shall be* [a]at his steps.

44 But tidings out of the east and out of the north shall trouble him: therefore he shall go forth with great fury to destroy, and utterly to make away many.

45 And he shall plant the tabernacles of his palace between the seas in [a]the [1,2]glorious holy mountain; [b]yet he shall come to his end, and none shall help him.

The time of great trouble

I P H 12 AND AT that time shall Michael stand up, the great prince which standeth for the children of thy people: [a]and there shall be a time of trouble, such as never was since there was a nation *even* to that same time: and at that time thy people [b]shall be delivered, every one that shall be found [c]written in the book.

F W 2 And many of them that sleep in the dust of the earth shall awake, [a]some to everlasting life, and some to shame [b]*and* everlasting contempt.

U 3 And they that be [1]wise shall [a]shine as the brightness of the firmament; [b]and they that turn many to righteousness [c]as the stars for ever and ever.

E 4 But thou, O Daniel, [a]shut up the words, and seal the book, *even* to the time of the end: many shall run to and fro, and knowledge shall be increased.

5 ¶ Then I Daniel looked, and, behold, there stood other two, the one on this side of the [1]bank of the river, and the other on that side of the bank [a]of the river.

G 6 And *one* said to the man clothed in linen, which *was* [1]upon the waters of the river, [a]How long *shall it be to* the end of these wonders?

R 7 And I heard the man clothed in linen, which *was* upon the waters of the river, when he [a]held up his right hand and his left hand unto heaven, and sware by him [b]that liveth for ever [c]that *it shall be* for a time, times, and [1]an half; [d]and when he shall have accomplished to scatter the power of [e]the holy people, all these *things* shall be finished.

8 And I heard, but I understood not: then said I, O my Lord, what *shall be* the end of these *things?*

E 9 And he said, Go thy way, Daniel: for

40 [a]Is. 21:1 [b]Ezek. 38:4; Rev. 9:16
41 [a]Is. 11:14 [1]Or, *goodly land* [2]Heb. *land of delight,* or, *ornament*
42 [1]Heb. *send forth*
43 [a]Ex. 11:8
45 [a]Ps. 48:2 [b]Rev. 19:20 [1]Or, *goodly* [2]Heb. *mountain of delight of holiness*
12:1 [a]Is. 26:20; Jer. 30:7; Rev. 16:18 [b]Rom. 11:26 [c]Ex. 32:32; Ps. 56:8
2 [a]Mat. 25:46; John 5:28; Acts 24:15 [b]Is. 66:24; Rom. 9:21
3 [a]Mat. 13:43 [b]Jas. 5:20 [c]1 Cor. 15:41 [1]Or, *teachers*
4 [a]Rev. 22:10
5 [a]ch. 10:4 [1]Heb. *lip*
6 [a]ch. 8:13 [1]Or, *from above*
7 [a]Deut. 32:40 [b]ch. 4:34 [c]ch. 7:25 [d]Luke 21:24 [e]ch. 8:24 [1]Or, *part*

I *Da 8:19* ◀▶ *Hos 1:10–11*
P *Eze 39:1–22* ◀▶ *Joel 1:15*
H *Da 5:1–6* ◀▶ *Hos 8:7*

F *Eze 37:12–14* ◀▶ *Da 12:13*
W ▶ *Jn 5:25–29*
U *Da 10:19* ◀▶ *Hag 2:15–19*
E ▶ *Da 12:9–10*
G *Da 11:31* ◀▶ *Da 12:11–12*
R *Da 11:36* ◀▶ *Da 12:11–12*
E *Da 12:4* ◀▶ *Mt 16:3*

11:45 Despite his powerful armies and success in battle, the antichrist will be defeated at the second coming of Christ and the Battle of Armageddon (see Rev 13:11–18).

12:2 This verse is the clearest confirmation in the OT of God's promise of the physical resurrection of his saints "to everlasting life" and the resurrection of unrepentant sinners "to shame and everlasting contempt." This final resurrection will occur at the end of the seven-year tribulation period. The participants in this resurrection will be those who accept Christ during the tribulation. The resurrection of the saints of the church, known as the rapture, will occur before the signing of the seven-year covenant with the antichrist. For further information on the resurrection of the body and the rapture of the saints, see the articles on pp. 1206 and 1370.

12:4 Note the similarity between this verse and 8:17–19; 9:26; 11:35, 40, 45; 12:4, 6, 9. Daniel was to seal the scroll, indicating that the words of the prophecy were complete as given and should be kept unaltered until the predictions were fulfilled.

12:7 The angel declared that until all these things would be finished would be a period of 3 1/2 years (see 7:25; 12:7; Rev.13:5). This same period of time was referred to by Jesus as the "great tribulation, such as was not since the beginning of the world to this time" (Mt 24:21).

the words *are* closed up and sealed till
the time of the end.
T 10 [a]Many shall be purified, and made
white, and tried; [b]but the wicked shall do
wickedly: and none of the wicked shall
understand; but [c]the wise shall understand.
G 11 And from the time *that* the daily
R

sacrifice shall be taken away, and [1]the
abomination that [2]maketh desolate set
up, *there shall be* a thousand two hundred and ninety days.
12 Blessed *is* he that waiteth, and cometh to the thousand three hundred and
five and thirty days.
13 But go thou thy way till the end *be:* F
[a]for[1] thou shalt rest, [b]and stand in thy lot
at the end of the days.

T *Isa 48:10* ◄► *Hag 1:5–11*
G *Da 12:6–7* ◄► *Zec 1:18–21*
R *Da 12:7* ◄► *Hos 1:4*

F *Da 12:2* ◄► *Hos 13:14*

10 [a]Zech. 13:9 [b]Hos. 14:9 [c]John 8:47

11 [1]Heb. *to set up the abomination* [2]Or, *astonisheth*

13 [a]Rev. 14:13 [b]Ps. 1:5 [1]Or, *and thou*

12:11–12 These verses represent further calculations for the end times. Beginning at the time of the desecration of the temple, the midpoint of Daniel's seventieth week (see 9:27; Mt 24:14–15; 2Th 2:4), there will be 1,290 days until the end of the tribulation and the judgments after Christ's second coming. This 3 1/2-year period marks the great tribulation. The 1,335 days corresponds to an additional 45 days beyond the Battle of Armageddon and must mark the final state of millennial blessing. The additional 75 extra days may be needed to prepare the earth for the blessings that will be revealed when Jesus Christ rules the earth.

12:13 The angel's promise to Daniel suggested that Daniel would be resurrected in the last days to witness the final victory of Jesus Christ over the kingdoms of this world.

Hosea

Author: Hosea

Theme: God's undying love for his people

Date of Writing: c. 715 B.C.

Outline of Hosea

I. Hosea's Life and God's Relationship With Israel (1:1—3:5)
II. Israel's Wickedness (4:1—6:3)
III. Israel's Punishment (6:4—10:15)
IV. God's Unchanging Love (11:1—13:8)
V. Israel's Final Restoration (13:9—14:9)

THIS BOOK TAKES its name from the prophet whose message it records. Hosea, meaning "salvation," prophesied during the final days of the kingdom of Israel, beginning with the reign of King Jeroboam II and continuing until the Assyrian destruction of Israel. Hosea's ministry coincided with that of the prophet Amos, also a prophet to Israel, and with Isaiah and Micah, who prophesied to Judah. Scripture records that Hosea was the "son of Beeri" (1:1). Some Jewish scholars believe this was the same man referred to in 1 Chronicles 5:6 who was a "prince of the Reubenites" carried into captivity by Tilgath-pilneser of Assyria. Such a heritage would have made this book's message of God's unchanging love for Israel especially meaningful to Hosea and to the NT writers who borrow from his writings (see Mt 2:15; 9:13; 12:7; Ro 9:25–26; 1Pe 2:10).

Hosea's prophecies warn of God's imminent judgment due to Israel's evil lifestyle of open idolatry. Hosea's wife's infidelity serves as a vivid symbol of Israel's spiritual unfaithfulness in her covenant relationship with God. Instead of responding in gratitude and love to God's grace, the Israelites offered worship to pagan idols.

Hosea's three children also bear names that symbolize the breakdown of Israel's relationship with God. Hosea's oldest son was named Jezreel, meaning "God sows," as a forewarning of the great slaughter to befall Israel's evil king, a descendant of Jehu (see 2Ki 10:1–14). Hosea's daughter was named Lo-ruhamah, meaning "not pitied, not favored." Such a name indicated that God would no longer show mercy to Israel as he had in the past. Hosea's third child, a son, was named Lo-ammi. His name meant "not my people" and symbolized God's rejection of his people because of their wickedness. Despite the sins of the people and the certainty of judgment, Hosea ends his message with the reassurance of God's undying love and Israel's future restoration.

1 THE [a]WORD of the LORD that came
unto Hosea, the son of Beeri, in the
days of Uzziah, Jotham, Ahaz, *and* Hezekiah, kings of Judah, and in the days of
Jeroboam the son of Joash, king of Israel.

Hosea's wife and children

2 The beginning of the word of the
LORD by Hosea. And the LORD said to Hosea, [a]Go, take unto thee a wife of whoredoms and children of whoredoms: for
[b]the land hath committed great whoredom, *departing* from the LORD.
3 So he went and took Gomer the
daughter of Diblaim; which conceived,
and bare him a son.
R 4 And the LORD said unto him, Call his
name Jezreel; for yet a little *while,* [a]and I
will [1]avenge the blood of Jezreel upon
the house of Jehu, [b]and will cause to
cease the kingdom of the house of Israel.
5 [a]And it shall come to pass at that
day, that I will break the bow of Israel in
the valley of Jezreel.
R 6 ¶ And she conceived again, and bare
a daughter. And *God* said unto him, Call
her name [1]Lo-ruhamah: [a]for [2]I will no
more have mercy upon the house of Israel; [3]but I will utterly take them away.
7 [a]But I will have mercy upon the
house of Judah, and will save them by the
LORD their God, and [b]will not save them
by bow, nor by sword, nor by battle, by
horses, nor by horsemen.
R 8 ¶ Now when she had weaned Lo-ruhamah, she conceived, and bare a son.
C 9 Then said *God,* Call his name [1]Lo-

R *Da 12:11–12 ◀▶ Hos 1:6*
R *Hos 1:4 ◀▶ Hos 1:8–9*
R *Hos 1:6 ◀▶ Hos 2:1–3*
C *Da 9:5 ◀▶ Hos 6:4*

1:1 [a]2 Pet. 1:21
2 [a]ch. 3:1 [b]Deut. 31:16; Ps. 73:27; Jer. 2:13; Ezek. 23:3
4 [a]2 Ki. 10:11 [b]2 Ki. 15:10 [1]Heb. *visit*
5 [a]2 Ki. 15:29
6 [a]2 Ki. 17:6 [1]i.e. *Not having obtained mercy* [2]Heb. *I will not add any more to* [3]Or, *that I should altogether pardon them*
7 [a]2 Ki. 19:35 [b]Zech. 4:6
9 [1]i.e. *Not my people*
10 [a]Gen. 32:12 [b]1 Pet. 2:10 [c]John 1:12 [1]Or, *instead of that*
11 [a]Is. 11:12
2:1 [1]i.e. *My people* [2]i.e. *Having obtained mercy*
2 [a]Is. 50:1 [b]Ezek. 16:25
3 [a]Jer. 13:22 [b]Ezek. 16:4 [c]Amos 8:11
4 [a]John 8:41
5 [a]ver. 8,12 [1]Heb. *drinks*
6 [a]Lam. 3:7,9

ammi: for ye *are* not my people, and I will
not be your *God.*
10 ¶ Yet [a]the number of the children I
of Israel shall be as the sand of the sea,
which cannot be measured nor num-
bered; [b]and it shall come to pass, *that* [1]in
the place where it was said unto them, Ye
are not my people, *there* it shall be said
unto them, *Ye are* [c]the sons of the living
God.
11 [a]Then shall the children of Judah
and the children of Israel be gathered together, and appoint themselves one head,
and they shall come up out of the land:
for great *shall be* the day of Jezreel.
2 SAY YE unto your brethren, [1]Ammi; R
and to your sisters, [2]Ruhamah.

Gomer punished and restored

2 Plead with your mother, plead: for
[a]she *is* not my wife, neither *am* I her
husband: let her therefore put away her
[b]whoredoms out of her sight, and
her adulteries from between her breasts;
3 Lest [a]I strip her naked, and set her as
in the day that she was [b]born, and make
her as a wilderness, and set her like a dry
land, and slay her with [c]thirst.
4 And I will not have mercy upon her
children; for they *be* the [a]children of
whoredoms.
5 For their mother hath played the harlot: she that conceived them hath done
shamefully: for she said, I will go after my
lovers, [a]that give *me* my bread and my
water, my wool and my flax, mine oil and
my [1]drink.
6 ¶ Therefore, behold, [a]I will hedge up R

I *Da 12:1 ◀▶ Hos 2:7*
R *Hos 1:8–9 ◀▶ Hos 2:6*
R *Hos 2:1–3 ◀▶ Hos 2:11–12*

1:4 God commanded Hosea to name his son *Jezreel* meaning "God scatters." This conveyed God's warning that Israel's period of grace was almost expired. Note that the valley named Jezreel has witnessed more significant battles than any other place in the Middle East and is named as the site of the Battle of Armageddon (see Zec 12:11; Rev 16:16).

1:6 Israel's coming judgment was indicated by naming Hosea's daughter *Lo-ruhamah,* which means, "not loved." This name symbolized God's withdrawal of his mercy from Israel.

1:8–11 Hosea's third child, a son, was named *Lo-ammi* which meant "not my people." This name indicated a break in the covenant relationship between the Lord and Israel. God would reject Israel as his people for a time because of their continual idolatry. However, the prophet recorded God's promise that judgment would be tempered with mercy. The covenant would be restored and the people would be reconciled to God. The future population of Israel would be "as the sand of the sea" (1:10). Furthermore, the Lord promised that the restoration of his people would include the reconciliation and reunion of the ten tribes of Israel and the two tribes of Judah into one united nation under "one head," the Messiah (1:11).

2:1–6 Hosea urged Israel to reject her sinful ways as he plead with his unfaithful wife to turn from her infidelities.

thy way with thorns, and [1]make a wall, that she shall not find her paths.

I 7 And she shall follow after her lovers, but she shall not overtake them; and she shall seek them, but shall not find *them:* then shall she say, [a]I will go and return to my [b]first husband; for then *was it* better with me than now.

F P 8 For she did not [a]know that I gave her corn, and [1]wine, and oil, and multiplied her silver and gold, [2]*which* they prepared for Baal.

9 Therefore will I return, and take away my corn in the time thereof, and my wine in the season thereof, and will [1]recover my wool and my flax *given* to cover her nakedness.

10 And now [a]will I discover her [1]lewdness in the sight of her lovers, and none shall deliver her out of mine hand.

R 11 [a]I will also cause all her mirth to cease, her feast days, her new moons, and her sabbaths, and all her solemn feasts.

12 And I will [1]destroy her vines and her fig trees, whereof she hath said, These *are* my rewards that my lovers have given me: and I will make them a forest, and the beasts of the field shall eat them.

13 And I will visit upon her the days of Baalim, wherein she burned incense to them, and she decked herself with her earrings and her jewels, and she went after her lovers, and forgat me, saith the LORD.

I *Hos 1:10–11* ◀ ▶ *Hos 2:14–16*
F *Isa 65:13* ◀ ▶ *Hos 11:4*
P *Ecc 11:1* ◀ ▶ *Mal 3:10–11*
R *Hos 2:6* ◀ ▶ *Hos 3:2–4*

6 [1]Heb. *wall a wall*
7 [a]Luke 15:18 [b]Ezek. 16:8
8 [a]Is. 1:3 [1]Heb. *new wine* [2]Or, wherewith *they made Baal*
9 [1]Or, *take away*
10 [a]Ezek. 16:37 [1]Heb. *folly,* or, *villany*
11 [a]Amos 8:10
12 [1]Heb. *make desolate*
14 [1]Or, *friendly* [2]Heb. *to her heart*
15 [a]Josh. 7:26 [b]Jer. 2:2; Ezek. 16:8 [c]Ex. 15:1
16 [1]i.e. *My husband* [2]i.e. *My lord*
17 [a]Ex. 23:13; Ps. 16:4
18 [a]Job 5:23 [b]Is. 2:4 [c]Lev. 26:5; Jer. 23:6
20 [a]Jer. 31:33; John 17:3
21 [a]Zech. 8:12

14 ¶ Therefore, behold, I will allure her, and bring her into the wilderness, and speak [1,2]comfortably unto her. I

15 And I will give her her vineyards from thence, and [a]the valley of Achor for a door of hope: and she shall sing there, as in [b]the days of her youth, and [c]as in the day when she came up out of the land of Egypt.

16 And it shall be at that day, saith the LORD, *that* thou shalt call me [1]Ishi; and shalt call me no more [2]Baali.

17 For [a]I will take away the names of Baalim out of her mouth, and they shall no more be remembered by their name.

18 And in that day will I make a [a]covenant for them with the beasts of the field, and with the fowls of heaven, and *with* the creeping things of the ground: and [b]I will break the bow and the sword and the battle out of the earth, and will make them to [c]lie down safely. I M U

19 And I will betroth thee unto me for ever; yea, I will betroth thee unto me in righteousness, and in judgment, and in lovingkindness, and in mercies.

20 I will even betroth thee unto me in faithfulness: and [a]thou shalt know the LORD.

21 And it shall come to pass in that day, [a]I will hear, saith the LORD, I will hear the heavens, and they shall hear the earth; M B

22 And the earth shall hear the corn,

I *Hos 2:7* ◀ ▶ *Hos 2:18–23*
I *Hos 2:14–16* ◀ ▶ *Hos 3:5*
M *Da 7:27* ◀ ▶ *Hos 2:21–22*
U *Isa 65:25* ◀ ▶ *Mic 4:3–4*
M *Hos 2:18* ◀ ▶ *Hos 3:5*
B *Eze 36:30* ◀ ▶ *Joel 2:22*

2:7 Hosea prophesied that Israel would eventually desire to return to God once she recognized the hopelessness of her relationship with pagan gods.
2:11–12 God promised Israel that judgment would fall on her for her idolatry.
2:14–16 This passage prophesied Israel's final reconciliation to the Lord. Note the symbolism as Israel calls God *Ishi* (2:16), which means "my husband," instead of addressing him as *Baali* (2:16), a pagan term which meant "my master."
2:18–23 This curious prophecy revealed that God would make a covenant with the beasts, birds and creeping things on the earth. Where before they had been instruments of destruction (see 2:12), all the animals, birds and insects would no longer threaten life. Every created thing would live in peace. This peaceful creation is confirmed in Isa 11:6–9; 65:25. Contrast this peaceful scene, however, with the tribulation judgment of the fourth horseman of the apocalypse (see Rev 6:8). Wild animals with no fear of people will become instruments of judgment and death on one fourth of the earth.

Note also that the Lord promised to restore his eternal covenant with his people: "I will betroth thee unto me for ever" (2:19). God's unshakable promise of ultimate reconciliation with the children of Abraham is expressed in his prophetic declaration: "Thou art my people; and they shall say, Thou art my God" (2:23).

and the wine, and the oil; and they shall hear Jezreel.

23 And [a]I will sow her unto me in the earth; [b]and I will have mercy upon her that had not obtained mercy; and I [c]will say to *them which were* not my people, Thou *art* my people; and they shall say, *Thou art* my God.

Israel will return to God

3 THEN SAID the LORD unto me, [a]Go yet, love a woman beloved of *her* [b]friend, yet an adulteress, according to the love of the LORD toward the children of Israel, who look to other gods, and love flagons [1]of wine.

R 2 So I bought her to me for fifteen *pieces* of silver, and *for* an homer of barley, and an [1]half homer of barley:

3 And I said unto her, Thou shalt [a]abide for me many days; thou shalt not play the harlot, and thou shalt not be for *another* man: so *will* I also *be* for thee.

R 4 For the children of Israel shall abide many days [a]without a king, and without a prince, and without a sacrifice, and without [1]an image, and without an [b]ephod, and *without* [c]teraphim:

I M 5 Afterward shall the children of Israel return, and [a]seek the LORD their God, and [b]David their king; and shall fear the LORD and his goodness in the [c]latter days.

Israel's immorality

4 HEAR THE word of the LORD, ye children of Israel: for the LORD hath a [a]controversy with the inhabitants of the land, because *there is* no truth, nor mercy, nor [b]knowledge of God in the land.

2 By swearing, and lying, and killing, and stealing, and committing adultery, they break out, and [1]blood toucheth blood.

3 Therefore [a]shall the land mourn, and [b]every one that dwelleth therein shall languish, with the beasts of the field, and with the fowls of heaven; yea, the fishes of the sea also shall be taken away. R

4 Yet let no man strive, nor reprove another: for thy people *are* as they [a]that strive with the priest.

5 Therefore shalt thou fall [a]in the day, and the prophet also shall fall with thee in the night, and I will [1]destroy thy mother.

6 ¶ [a]My people are [1]destroyed for lack of knowledge: because thou hast rejected knowledge, I will also reject thee, that thou shalt be no priest to me: seeing thou hast forgotten the law of thy God, I will also forget thy children. R

7 As they were increased, so they sinned against me: [a]*therefore* will I change their glory into shame.

8 They eat up the sin of my people, and they [1]set their heart on their iniquity.

9 And there shall be, [a]like people, like priest: and I will [1]punish them for their ways, and [2]reward them their doings. R

10 For [a]they shall eat, and not have enough: they shall commit whoredom, and shall not increase: because they have left off to take heed to the LORD.

11 Whoredom and wine and new wine [a]take away the heart.

12 ¶ My people ask counsel at their [a]stocks, and their staff declareth unto them: for [b]the spirit of whoredoms hath caused *them* to err, and they have gone a-whoring from under their God.

13 [a]They sacrifice upon the tops of the mountains, and burn incense upon the

R *Hos 2:11–12 ◀ ▶ Hos 3:4*
R *Hos 3:2–4 ◀ ▶ Hos 4:3*
I *Hos 2:18–23 ◀ ▶ Hos 6:1–3*
M *Hos 2:21–22 ◀ ▶ Joel 3:4*

R *Hos 3:4 ◀ ▶ Hos 4:6*
R *Hos 4:3 ◀ ▶ Hos 4:9*
R *Hos 4:6 ◀ ▶ Hos 5:5*

23 [a]Jer. 31:27 [b]ch. 1:6 [c]ch. 1:10
3:1 [a]ch. 1:2 [b]Jer. 3:20 [1]Heb. *of grapes*
2 [1]Heb. *lethech*
3 [a]Deut. 21:13
4 [a]ch. 10:3 [b]Ex. 28:6 [c]Judg. 17:5 [1]Heb. *a standing,* or, *statue,* or, *pillar*
5 [a]ch. 5:6 [b]Jer. 30:9; Ezek. 34:23, 24 [c]Is. 2:2; Jer. 30:24; Ezek. 38:8
4:1 [a]Is. 1:18 [b]Jer. 4:22
2 [1]Heb. *bloods*
3 [a]Amos 5:16 [b]Zeph. 1:3
4 [a]Deut. 17:12
5 [a]Jer. 15:8 [1]Heb. *cut off*
6 [a]Is. 5:13 [1]Heb. *cut off*
7 [a]1 Sam. 2:30; Mal. 2:9
8 [1]Heb. *lift up their soul to their iniquity*
9 [a]Is. 24:2; Jer. 5:31 [1]Heb. *visit upon* [2]Heb. *cause to return*
10 [a]Lev. 26:26; Mic. 6:14
11 [a]Is. 28:7
12 [a]Jer. 2:27 [b]Is. 44:20
13 [a]Is. 1:29; Ezek. 6:13

3:4–5 Hosea's prophecy was precisely fulfilled. While these verses picture the exile and Israel's return to their homeland, this passage also foreshadows the centuries following the Jews' rejection of Jesus as Messiah. Even today the Jews remain scattered among the Gentile nations, without their beloved temple or a king. However, Hosea prophesied the final restoration of Israel "in the latter days" (3:5) when the Jews would return to the promised land, seeking the Lord and David's descendant.

4:3–9 This passage sternly warned the priests against passing blame for Israel's judgment on the people. Hosea proceeded to charge the priests with their guilt for not instructing the people in the correct way to worship. Israel's judgment was directly related to her "lack of knowledge" (4:6) and obedience to God's law. Hosea's indictment, "like people, like priest" (4:9), conveyed God's judgment on Israel's people and her leaders. The land, too, would suffer and be left desolate during the time of judgment.

hills, under oaks and poplars and elms,
because the shadow thereof *is* good:
[b]therefore your daughters shall commit
whoredom, and your spouses shall commit adultery.
14 [1]I will not punish your daughters
when they commit whoredom, nor your
spouses when they commit adultery: for
themselves are separated with whores,
and they sacrifice with harlots: therefore
the people *that* doth not understand shall
[2]fall.
15 ¶ Though thou, Israel, play the harlot, *yet* let not Judah offend; [a]and come
not ye unto Gilgal, neither go ye up to
[b]Beth-aven, [c]nor swear, The LORD liveth.
16 For Israel [a]slideth back as a backsliding heifer: now the LORD will feed
them as a lamb in a large place.
N 17 Ephraim *is* joined to idols: [a]let him
alone.
18 Their drink [1]is sour: they have
committed whoredom continually: [a]her
rulers *with* shame do love, Give ye.
19 [a]The wind hath bound her up in
her wings, and [b]they shall be ashamed
because of their sacrifices.

God's severity toward Israel

5 HEAR YE this, O priests; and
hearken, ye house of Israel; and give
ye ear, O house of the king; for judgment
is toward you, because [a]ye have been a
snare on Mizpah, and a net spread upon
Tabor.
2 And the revolters are [a]profound to
make slaughter, [1]though I *have been* [2]a
rebuker of them all.
3 [a]I know Ephraim, and Israel is not
hid from me: for now, O Ephraim, [b]thou
committest whoredom, *and* Israel is defiled.
4 [1]They will not frame their doings to
turn unto their God: for [a]the spirit of
whoredoms *is* in the midst of them, and
they have not known the LORD.
R 5 And the pride of Israel doth testify
to his face: therefore shall Israel and
Ephraim fall in their iniquity; Judah also
shall fall with them.
6 [a]They shall go with their flocks and
with their herds to seek the LORD; but
they shall not find *him;* he hath withdrawn himself from them.
7 They have [a]dealt treacherously
against the LORD: for they have begotten
strange children: now shall a month devour them with their portions.
8 [a]Blow ye the cornet in Gibeah, *and*
the trumpet in Ramah: [b]cry aloud *at*
[c]Beth-aven, after thee, O Benjamin.
9 Ephraim shall be desolate in the day R
of rebuke: among the tribes of Israel have
I made known that which shall surely be.
10 The princes of Judah were like
them that [a]remove the bound: *therefore* I
will pour out my wrath upon them like
water.
11 Ephraim *is* [a]oppressed *and* broken
in judgment, because he willingly walked
after [b]the commandment.
12 Therefore *will* I *be* unto Ephraim as R
a moth, and to the house of Judah [a]as
[1]rottenness.
13 When Ephraim saw his sickness,
and Judah *saw* his [a]wound, then went
Ephraim [b]to the Assyrian, and sent [1]to
king Jareb: yet could he not heal you, nor
cure you of your wound.
14 For [a]I *will be* unto Ephraim as a R
lion, and as a young lion to the house of
Judah: [b]I, *even* I, will tear and go away; I
will take away, and none shall rescue
him.
15 ¶ I will go *and* return to my place, R
[1]till they acknowledge their offence, and
seek my face: in their affliction they will
seek me early.
6 COME, AND let us return unto the I
LORD: for [a]he hath torn, and [b]he will P
heal us; he hath smitten, and he will bind
us up.

13 [b]Amos 7:17; Rom. 1:28
14 [1]Or, *Shall I not* [2]Or, *be punished*
15 [a]ch. 9:15 [b]1 Ki. 12:29 [c]Amos 8:14
16 [a]Jer. 3:6
17 [a]Mat. 15:14
18 [a]Mic. 3:11 [1]Heb. *is gone*
19 [a]Jer. 51:1 [b]Is. 1:29
5:1 [a]ch. 6:9
2 [a]Is. 29:15 [1]Or, *and* [2]Heb. *a correction*
3 [a]Amos 3:2 [b]ch. 4:17
4 [a]ch. 4:12 [1]Or, *Their doings will not suffer* them
6 [a]Prov. 1:28
7 [a]Jer. 3:20
8 [a]Joel 2:1 [b]Is. 10:30 [c]Josh. 7:2
10 [a]Deut. 19:14
11 [a]Deut. 28:33 [b]Mic. 6:16
12 [a]Prov. 12:4 [1]Or, *a worm*
13 [a]Jer. 30:12 [b]2 Ki. 15:19 [1]Or, *to the king of Jareb,* or, *to the king* that *should plead*
14 [a]Lam. 3:10 [b]Ps. 50:22
15 [1]Heb. *till they be guilty*
6:1 [a]Deut. 32:39 [b]Jer. 30:17

N *Da 5:1–6* ◀▶ *Joel 3:14*
R *Hos 4:9* ◀▶ *Hos 5:9*
R *Hos 5:5* ◀▶ *Hos 5:12*
R *Hos 5:9* ◀▶ *Hos 5:14*
R *Hos 5:12* ◀▶ *Hos 6:11*
R *Da 4:27* ◀▶ *Hos 10:12*
I *Hos 3:5* ◀▶ *Hos 12:9*
P *Da 9:9* ◀▶ *Hos 14:1–2*

5:5–14 Hosea predicted that God would judge both Israel and Judah for their proud rebellion. Ephraim (Israel) would be desolate and Judah would be rotten, and no one would be able to rescue them from the certainty of God's impending judgment.

6:1–3 This passage contains one of the greatest OT prophecies of the Messiah. God urged Israel to repent and return to him knowing that he would heal their wounds. God's wrath would only be temporary, lasting only a figurative two or three days

2 [a]After two days will he revive us: in the third day he will raise us up, and we shall live in his sight.

L 3 [a]Then shall we know, *if* we follow on to know the LORD: his going forth is prepared [b]as the morning; and [c]he shall come unto us [d]as the rain, as the latter *and* former rain unto the earth.

Israel's unfaithfulness

C 4 ¶ O Ephraim, what shall I do unto thee? O Judah, what shall I do unto thee? for your [1]goodness *is* as a morning cloud, and as the early dew it goeth away.

5 Therefore have I hewed *them* by the prophets; I have slain them by [a]the words of my mouth: [1]and thy judgments *are as* the light *that* goeth forth.

6 For I desired [a]mercy, and [b]not sacrifice; and the [c]knowledge of God more than burnt offerings.

7 But they [1]like men have transgressed the covenant: there have they dealt treacherously against me.

8 Gilead *is* a city of them that work iniquity, *and is* [1]polluted with blood.

9 And as troops of robbers wait for a man, *so* the company of priests murder in the way [1]by consent: for they commit [2]lewdness.

10 I have seen an horrible thing in the house of Israel: there *is* the whoredom of Ephraim, Israel is defiled.

R 11 Also, O Judah, he hath set an harvest for thee, when I returned the captivity of my people.

7 WHEN I would have healed Israel, then the iniquity of Ephraim was discovered, and the [1]wickedness of Samaria: for [a]they commit falsehood; and the thief cometh in, *and* the troop of robbers [2]spoileth without.

E 2 And they [1]consider not in their hearts *that* I [a]remember all their wickedness: now their own doings have beset them about; they are before my face.

3 They make the king glad with their wickedness, and the princes [a]with their lies.

4 [a]They *are* all adulterers, as an oven heated by the baker, [1]*who* ceaseth [2]from raising after he hath kneaded the dough, until it be leavened.

5 In the day of our king the princes have made *him* sick [1]with bottles of wine; he stretched out his hand with scorners.

6 For they have [1]made ready their heart like an oven, whiles they lie in wait: their baker sleepeth all the night; in the morning it burneth as a flaming fire.

7 They are all hot as an oven, and have devoured their judges; all their kings are fallen: [a]*there is* none among them that calleth unto me.

8 Ephraim, he [a]hath mixed himself among the people; Ephraim is a cake not turned.

9 [a]Strangers have devoured his strength, and he knoweth *it* not: yea, gray hairs are [1]here and there upon him, yet he knoweth not.

10 And the [a]pride of Israel testifieth to his face: and [b]they do not return to the LORD their God, nor seek him for all this.

11 ¶ [a]Ephraim also is like a silly dove without heart: [b]they call to Egypt, they go to Assyria.

12 When they shall go, I will spread my net upon them; I will bring them down as the fowls of the heaven; I will chastise them, [a]as their congregation hath heard.

13 Woe unto them! for they have fled from me: [1]destruction unto them! because they have transgressed against me: though [a]I have redeemed them, yet they have spoken lies against me.

14 [a]And they have not cried unto me with their heart, when they howled upon their beds: they assemble themselves for corn and wine, *and* they rebel against me.

15 Though I [1]have bound *and* strengthened their arms, yet do they imagine mischief against me.

16 They return, *but* not to the most High: [a]they are like a deceitful bow: their princes shall fall by the sword for the

2 [a]1 Cor. 15:4
3 [a]Is. 54:13 [b]2 Sam. 23:4 [c]Ps. 72:6 [d]Job 29:23
4 [1]Or, *mercy,* or, *kindness*
5 [a]Jer. 23:29 [1]Or, *that thy judgments might be*
6 [a]Mat. 9:13 [b]Is. 1:11 [c]John 17:3
7 [1]Or, *like Adam;* see Job 31:33
8 [1]Or, *cunning for blood*
9 [1]Heb. *with one shoulder,* or, *to Shechem* [2]Or, *enormity*
7:1 [a]ch. 5:1 [1]Heb. *evils* [2]Heb. *strippeth*
2 [a]Jer. 17:1 [1]Heb. *say not to*
3 [a]Rom. 1:32
4 [a]Jer. 9:2 [1]Or, *the raiser will cease* [2]Or, *from waking*
5 [1]Or, *with heat through wine*
6 [1]Or, *applied*
7 [a]Is. 64:7
8 [a]Ps. 106:35
9 [a]ch. 8:7 [1]Heb. *sprinkled*
10 [a]ch. 5:5 [b]Is. 9:13
11 [a]ch. 11:11 [b]ch. 5:13
12 [a]Lev. 26:14; Deut. 28:15; 2 Ki. 17:13
13 [a]Mic. 6:4 [1]Heb. *spoil*
14 [a]Job 35:9; Jer. 3:10; Zech. 7:5
15 [1]Or, *chastened*
16 [a]Ps. 78:57

L *Da 9:9* ◀▶ *Hos 13:9*
C *Hos 1:9* ◀▶ *Hos 10:1–2*
R *Hos 5:14* ◀▶ *Hos 8:8*
E *Da 5:27* ◀▶ *Am 8:7*

(see Lk 13:32–33). Israel would be restored when Christ returns (see Ro 11:26). As surely as the seasonal rains fell and revived the earth, God's favor would return and restore Israel (see Joel 2:23; Zec 10:1).

[b]rage of their tongue: this *shall be* their derision [c]in the land of Egypt.

God's sentence

8 *SET* THE trumpet to ′thy mouth. *He shall come* [a]as an eagle against the house of the LORD, because they have transgressed my covenant, and trespassed against my law.

2 [a]Israel shall cry unto me, My God, [b]we know thee.

3 Israel hath cast off *the thing that is* good: the enemy shall pursue him.

4 [a]They have set up kings, but not by me: they have made princes, and I knew *it* not: of their silver and their gold have they made them idols, that they may be cut off.

5 ¶ Thy calf, O Samaria, hath cast *thee* off; mine anger is kindled against them: [a]how long *will it be* ere they attain to innocency?

6 For from Israel *was* it also: the workman made it; therefore it *is* not God: but the calf of Samaria shall be broken in pieces.

H 7 For [a]they have sown the wind, and they shall reap the whirlwind: it hath no ′stalk: the bud shall yield no meal: if so be it yield, the strangers shall swallow it up.

R 8 [a]Israel is swallowed up: now shall they be among the Gentiles [b]as a vessel wherein *is* no pleasure.

9 For they are gone up to Assyria, [a]a wild ass alone by himself: Ephraim [b]hath hired ′lovers.

10 Yea, though they have hired among the nations, now [a]will I gather them, and they shall ′sorrow a little for the burden of [b]the king of princes.

11 Because Ephraim hath made many altars to sin, altars shall be unto him to sin.

12 I have written to him [a]the great things of my law, *but* they were counted as a strange thing.

H *Da 12:1* ◀▶ *Hos 13:3*
R *Hos 6:11* ◀▶ *Hos 9:3*

16 [b]Ps. 73:9 [c]ch. 9:3,6

8:1 [a]Deut. 28:49; Jer. 4:13 ′Heb. *the roof of thy mouth*

2 [a]Ps. 78:34 [b]Tit. 1:16

4 [a]2 Ki. 15:13,17, 25, Shallum, Menahem, Pekahiah

5 [a]Jer. 13:27

7 [a]Prov. 22:8 ′Or, *standing corn*

8 [a]2 Ki. 17:6 [b]Jer. 22:28

9 [a]Jer. 2:24 [b]Ezek. 16:33,34 ′Heb. *loves*

10 [a]Ezek. 16:37 [b]Is. 10:8; Ezek. 26:7; Dan. 2:37 ′Or, *begin*

12 [a]Deut. 4:6,8; Ps. 119:18

13 [a]Zech. 7:6 [b]Jer. 14:10 ′Or, *In the sacrifices of mine offerings they*

14 [a]Deut. 32:18 [b]Is. 29:23 [c]Jer. 17:27

9:1 [a]Jer. 44:17 ′Or, *in*

2 ′Or, *winevat*

3 [a]Lev. 25:23; Jer. 2:7 [b]ch. 8:13 [c]Ezek. 4:13

4 [a]Jer. 6:20

6 ′Heb. *spoil* [2]Or, *their silver shall be desired, the nettle* [3]Heb. *the desire*

7 [a]Mic. 2:11 ′Heb. *man of the spirit*

8 ′Or, *against*

13 [a]They′ sacrifice flesh *for* the sacrifices of mine offerings, and eat *it;* [b]*but* the LORD accepteth them not; now will he remember their iniquity, and visit their sins: they shall return to Egypt.

14 [a]For Israel hath forgotten [b]his Maker, and buildeth temples; and Judah hath multiplied fenced cities: but [c]I will send a fire upon his cities, and it shall devour the palaces thereof.

Israel's punishment

9 REJOICE NOT, O Israel, for joy, as *other* people: for thou hast gone a-whoring from thy God, thou hast loved a [a]reward ′upon every cornfloor.

2 The floor and the ′winepress shall not feed them, and the new wine shall fail in her.

3 They shall not dwell in [a]the LORD'S land; [b]but Ephraim shall return to Egypt, and [c]they shall eat unclean *things* in Assyria. R

4 They shall not offer wine *offerings* to the LORD, [a]neither shall they be pleasing unto him: their sacrifices *shall be* unto them as the bread of mourners; all that eat thereof shall be polluted: for their bread for their soul shall not come into the house of the LORD.

5 What will ye do in the solemn day, and in the day of the feast of the LORD?

6 For, lo, they are gone because of ′destruction: Egypt shall gather them up, Memphis shall bury them: [2,3]the pleasant *places* for their silver, nettles shall possess them: thorns *shall be* in their tabernacles. R

7 The days of visitation are come, the days of recompence are come; Israel shall know *it:* the prophet *is* a fool, [a]the ′spiritual man *is* mad, for the multitude of thine iniquity, and the great hatred.

8 The watchman of Ephraim *was* with my God: *but* the prophet *is* a snare of a fowler in all his ways, *and* hatred ′in the house of his God.

R *Hos 8:8* ◀▶ *Hos 9:6*
R *Hos 9:3* ◀▶ *Hos 9:12*

8:8 The prophet confirmed the exile of Israel as God's judgment upon his people for their apostasy.
9:3–17 This woeful passage promised punishment for Israel that would include exile from their beloved land into Egypt and Assyria. In fulfillment of this prophecy, Assyria conquered Israel in 721 B.C. and carried her people away captive. God further warned that Israel would be "wanderers among the nations" (9:17). This prophecy too has been tragically fulfilled as millions of Jews have searched for a peaceful life over the centuries in nation after nation without finding refuge.

9 [a]They have deeply corrupted *themselves,* as in the days of [b]Gibeah: *therefore* he will remember their iniquity, he will visit their sins.

10 I found Israel like grapes in the wilderness; I saw your fathers as the firstripe in the fig tree at her first time: *but* they went to [a]Baal-peor, and separated themselves unto *that* shame; [b]and *their* abominations were according as they loved.

11 *As for* Ephraim, their glory shall fly away like a bird, from the birth, and from the womb, and from the conception.

R 12 Though they bring up their children, yet will I bereave them, *that there shall* not *be* a man *left:* yea, [a]woe also to them when I depart from them!

13 Ephraim, [a]as I saw Tyrus, *is* planted in a pleasant place: but Ephraim shall bring forth his children to the murderer.

14 Give them, O LORD: what wilt thou give? give them [a]a [1]miscarrying womb and dry breasts.

15 All their wickedness *is* in Gilgal: for there I hated them: for the wickedness of their doings I will drive them out of mine house, I will love them no more: [a]all their princes *are* revolters.

16 Ephraim is smitten, their root is dried up, they shall bear no fruit: yea, though they bring forth, yet will I slay *even* [a]the[1] beloved *fruit* of their womb.

R 17 My God will cast them away, because they did not hearken unto him: and they shall be wanderers among the nations.

C 10 ISRAEL *IS* [a]an[1] empty vine, he bringeth forth fruit unto himself: according to the multitude of his fruit [b]he hath increased the altars; according to the goodness of his land they have made goodly [2]images.

S 2 [1]Their heart is [a]divided; now shall they be found faulty: he shall [2]break down their altars, he shall spoil their images.

3 For now they shall say, We have no king, because we feared not the LORD; what then should a king do to us?

4 They have spoken words, swearing falsely in making a covenant: thus judgment springeth up [a]as hemlock in the furrows of the field.

5 The inhabitants of Samaria shall fear because of the calves of Beth-aven: for the people thereof shall mourn over it, and [a]the[1] priests thereof *that* rejoiced on it, for the glory thereof, because it is departed from it.

6 It shall be also carried unto Assyria *for* a present to king Jareb: Ephraim shall receive shame, and Israel shall be ashamed of his own counsel.

7 *As for* Samaria, her king is cut off as R
the foam upon [1]the water.

8 The high places also of Aven, [a]the sin of Israel, shall be destroyed: the thorn and the thistle shall come up on their altars; [b]and they shall say to the mountains, Cover us; and to the hills, Fall on us.

9 O Israel, thou hast sinned from the days of Gibeah: there they stood: the battle in Gibeah against the children of iniquity did not overtake them.

10 *It is* in my desire that I should chas- R
tise them; and [a]the people shall be gathered against them, [1]when they shall bind themselves in their two furrows.

11 And Ephraim *is as* [a]an heifer *that is* taught, *and* loveth to tread out *the corn;* but I passed over upon [1]her fair neck: I will make Ephraim to ride; Judah shall plow, *and* Jacob shall break his clods.

12 Sow to yourselves in righteousness, M
reap in mercy; [a]break up your fallow R
ground: for *it is* time to seek the LORD, till he come and rain righteousness upon you.

13 [a]Ye have plowed wickedness, ye C
have reaped iniquity; ye have eaten the fruit of lies: because thou didst trust in thy way, in the multitude of thy mighty men.

14 Therefore shall a tumult arise

9 [a]ch. 10:9 [b]Judg. 19:22
10 [a]Num. 25:3; Ps. 106:28 [b]Ps. 81:12
12 [a]Deut. 31:17
13 [a]Ezek. 26 & 27 & 28
14 [a]Luke 23:29 [1]Heb. *that casteth the fruit*
15 [a]Is. 1:23
16 [a]Ezek. 24:21 [1]Heb. *the desires*
10:1 [a]Nah. 2:2 [b]ch. 8:11 [1]Or, *a vine emptying the fruit which it giveth* [2]Heb. *statues,* or, *standing images*
2 [a]1 Ki. 18:21; Mat. 6:24 [1]Or, *he hath divided their heart* [2]Heb. *behead*
4 [a]Amos 5:7
5 [a]2 Ki. 23:5 [1]Or, *Chemarim*
7 [1]Heb. *the face of the water*
8 [a]Deut. 9:21 [b]Is. 2:19; Luke 23:30
10 [a]Jer. 16:16 [1]Or, *when I shall bind them for their two transgressions,* or, *in their two habitations*
11 [a]Mic. 4:13 [1]Heb. *the beauty of her neck*
12 [a]Jer. 4:3
13 [a]Prov. 22:8; Gal. 6:7,8

R *Hos 9:6* ◀ ▶ *Hos 9:17*
R *Hos 9:12* ◀ ▶ *Hos 10:7*
C *Hos 6:4* ◀ ▶ *Hos 10:13*
S *Eze 36:29* ◀ ▶ *Hos 12:6*

R *Hos 9:17* ◀ ▶ *Hos 10:10*
R *Hos 10:7* ◀ ▶ *Hos 12:2*
M *Da 9:20–21* ◀ ▶ *Joel 2:13*
R *Hos 5:15* ◀ ▶ *Joel 2:12–13*
C *Hos 10:1–2* ◀ ▶ *Hos 13:3*

10:7–10 Hosea predicted the death of the king of Samaria and the chastening of Israel. This prophecy was fulfilled when Assyria conquered Israel in 721 B.C.

among thy people, and all thy fortresses shall be spoiled, as Shalman spoiled Beth-arbel in the day of battle: the mother was dashed in pieces upon *her* children.

15 So shall Beth-el do unto you because of [1]your great wickedness: in a morning shall the king of Israel utterly be cut off.

God's compassion toward Israel

11

WHEN ISRAEL *was* a child, then I loved him, and [a]called my [b]son out of Egypt.

2 *As* they called them, so they went from them: they sacrificed unto Baalim, and burned incense to graven images.

E 3 [a]I taught Ephraim also to go, taking them by their arms; but they knew not that [b]I healed them.

F 4 I drew them with cords of a man, with bands of love: and [a]I was to them as they that [1]take off the yoke on their jaws, and [b]I laid meat unto them.

5 ¶ He shall not return into the land of Egypt, but the Assyrian shall be his king, because they refused to return.

6 And the sword shall abide on his cities, and shall consume his branches, and devour *them,* because of their own counsels.

7 And my people are bent to [a]backsliding from me: though they called them to the most High, [1]none at all would exalt *him.*

8 [a]How shall I give thee up, Ephraim? *how* shall I deliver thee, Israel? how shall I make thee as [b]Admah? *how* shall I set thee as Zeboim? mine heart is turned within me, my repentings are kindled together.

9 I will not execute the fierceness of mine anger, I will not return to destroy Ephraim: [a]for I *am* God, and not man; the Holy One in the midst of thee: and I will not enter into the city.

10 They shall walk after the LORD: [a]he shall roar like a lion: when he shall roar, then the children shall tremble from the west.

11 They shall tremble as a bird out of Egypt, [a]and as a dove out of the land of Assyria: [b]and I will place them in their houses, saith the LORD.

Israel's sin

12 Ephraim compasseth me about with lies, and the house of Israel with deceit: but Judah yet ruleth with God, and is faithful [1]with the saints.

12

EPHRAIM FEEDETH on wind, and followeth after the east wind: he daily increaseth lies and desolation; [a]and they do make a covenant with the Assyrians, and [b]oil is carried into Egypt.

2 [a]The LORD hath also a controversy with Judah, and will [1]punish Jacob according to his ways; according to his doings will he recompense him. R

3 ¶ He took his brother [a]by the heel in the womb, and by his strength he [b]had [1] power with God:

4 Yea, he had power over the angel, and prevailed: he wept, and made supplication unto him: he found him *in* [a]Beth-el, and there he spake with us;

5 Even the LORD God of hosts; the LORD *is* his [a]memorial.

6 [a]Therefore turn thou to thy God: keep mercy and judgment, and wait on thy God continually. S

7 ¶ *He is* [1]a merchant, [a]the balances of deceit *are* in his hand: he loveth to [2]oppress.

8 And Ephraim said, [a]Yet I am become rich, I have found me out substance: [1]*in* all my labours they shall find none iniquity in me [2]that *were* sin.

9 And I *that am* the LORD thy God from the land of Egypt [a]will yet make thee to dwell in tabernacles, as in the days of the solemn feast. I

15 [1]Heb. *the evil of your evil*
11:1 [a]Mat. 2:15 [b]Ex. 4:22
3 [a]Deut. 1:31 [b]Ex. 15:26
4 [a]Lev. 26:13 [b]Ps. 78:25 [1]Heb. *lift up*
7 [a]Jer. 3:6 [1]Heb. *together they exalted not*
8 [a]Jer. 9:7 [b]Gen. 14:8
9 [a]Num. 23:19
10 [a]Joel 3:16
11 [a]Is. 60:8 [b]Ezek. 28:25,26
12 [1]Or, *with the most holy*
12:1 [a]2 Ki. 17:4 [b]Is. 30:6
2 [a]Mic. 6:2 [1]Heb. *visit upon*
3 [a]Gen. 25:26 [b]Gen. 32:28 [1]Heb. *was a prince,* or, *behaved himself princely*
4 [a]Gen. 28:12
5 [a]Ex. 3:15
6 [a]Mic. 6:8
7 [a]Amos 8:5 [1]Or, *Canaan* [2]Or, *deceive*
8 [a]Rev. 3:17 [1]Or, *all my labours suffice me not:* he shall have *punishment of iniquity in whom is sin* [2]Heb. *which*
9 [a]Lev. 23:42

E *Da 1:15* ◀▶ *Mt 4:23–25*
F *Hos 2:8* ◀▶ *Hos 13:5–6*
R *Hos 10:10* ◀▶ *Hos 13:3*
S *Hos 10:2* ◀▶ *Hos 14:1*
I *Hos 6:1–3* ◀▶ *Hos 13:14*

12:2 The prophet likened Judah to her father Jacob, a deceiver and schemer. Because of Judah's deceit, God would judge the nation and exile the people from the promised land.

12:9 God reminded Israel that he had delivered them from the slavery of Egypt and would "yet make thee to dwell in tabernacles." This promise will be fulfilled in the last days when the Messiah returns to establish his glorious and eternal kingdom in the land of Israel.

10 [a]I have also spoken by the prophets, and I have multiplied visions, and used similitudes, [l]by the ministry of the prophets.

11 *Is there* iniquity *in* Gilead? surely they are vanity: they sacrifice bullocks in Gilgal; yea, their altars *are* as heaps in the furrows of the fields.

12 And Jacob [a]fled into the country of Syria, and Israel served for a wife, and for a wife he kept *sheep.*

13 [a]And by a prophet the LORD brought Israel out of Egypt, and by a prophet was he preserved.

14 Ephraim provoked *him* to anger [l]most bitterly: therefore shall he leave his [2]blood upon him, [a]and his reproach shall his Lord return unto him.

Ephraim's doom

13 WHEN EPHRAIM spake trembling, he exalted himself in Israel; but when he offended in Baal, he died.

2 And now [l]they sin more and more, and have made them molten images of their silver, *and* idols according to their own understanding, all of it the work of the craftsmen: they say of them, Let [2]the men that sacrifice kiss the calves.

R C H 3 Therefore they shall be as the morning cloud, and as the early dew that passeth away, [a]as the chaff *that* is driven with the whirlwind out of the floor, and as the smoke out of the chimney.

O 4 Yet [a]I *am* the LORD thy God from the land of Egypt, and thou shalt know no god but me: for [a]*there is* no saviour beside me.

F 5 ¶ [a]I did know thee in the wilderness, [b]in the land of [l]great drought.

6 [a]According to their pasture, so were they filled; they were filled, and their heart was exalted; therefore have they forgotten me.

7 Therefore [a]I will be unto them as a lion: as [b]a leopard by the way will I observe *them:*

8 I will meet them [a]as a bear *that is* bereaved *of her whelps,* and will rend the caul of their heart, and there will I devour them like a lion: [l]the wild beast shall tear them.

9 ¶ O Israel, thou hast destroyed thyself; but in me [l]*is* thine help. L

10 [l]I will be thy king: [a]where *is any other* that may save thee in all thy cities? and thy judges of whom [b]thou saidst, Give me a king and princes?

11 [a]I gave thee a king in mine anger, and took *him* away in my wrath.

12 [a]The iniquity of Ephraim *is* bound up; his sin *is* hid.

13 [a]The sorrows of a travailing woman shall come upon him: he *is* an unwise son; for he should not stay [l]long in *the place of* the breaking forth of children. R

14 I will ransom them from [l]the power of the grave; I will redeem them from death: [a]O death, I will be thy plagues; O grave, I will be thy destruction: [b]repentance shall be hid from mine eyes. F I

15 ¶ Though he be fruitful among *his* brethren, [a]an east wind shall come, the wind of the LORD shall come up from the wilderness, and his spring shall become dry, and his fountain shall be dried up: he shall spoil the treasure of all [l]pleasant vessels.

16 Samaria shall become desolate; for she hath rebelled against her God: [a]they shall fall by the sword: their infants shall be dashed in pieces, and their women with child shall be ripped up. R

10 [a]2 Ki. 17:13 [l]Heb. *by the hand*
12 [a]Gen. 28:5
13 [a]Ex. 12:50
14 [a]Dan. 11:18 [l]Heb. *with bitternesses* [2]Heb. *bloods*
13:2 [l]Heb. *they add to sin* [2]Or, *the sacrificers of men*
3 [a]Dan. 2:35
4 [a]Is. 43:11
5 [a]Deut. 2:7 [b]Deut. 8:15 [l]Heb. *droughts*
6 [a]Deut. 8:12
7 [a]Lam. 3:10 [b]Jer. 5:6
8 [a]2 Sam. 17:8 [l]Heb. *the beast of the field*
9 [l]Heb. *in thy help*
10 [a]Deut. 32:38 [b]1 Sam. 8:5 [l]Rather, *Where is thy king?* King Hoshea being then in prison; see 2 Ki. 17:4
11 [a]1 Sam. 8:7
12 [a]Deut. 32:34
13 [a]Is. 13:8 [l]Heb. *a time*
14 [a]1 Cor. 15:54 [b]Jer. 15:6 [l]Heb. *the hand*
15 [a]Jer. 4:11 [l]Heb. *vessels of desire*
16 [a]2 Ki. 8:12

R *Hos 12:2* ◀▶ *Hos 13:13*
C *Hos 10:13* ◀▶ *Am 5:7*
H *Hos 8:7* ◀▶ *Joel 1:15*
O *La 3:37* ◀▶ *Jnh 2:9*
F *Hos 11:4* ◀▶ *Joel 2:19*
L *Hos 6:3* ◀▶ *Hos 14:4*
R *Hos 13:3* ◀▶ *Hos 13:16*
F *Da 12:13* ◀▶ *Mt 22:30–32*
I *Hos 12:9* ◀▶ *Hos 14:4–8*
R *Hos 13:13* ◀▶ *Hos 14:1*

13:3–4 God likened the future existence of the rebellious nation of Israel to short-lived and vaporous clouds and dust, indicating that Ephraim (Israel) would soon vanish as a nation when they were carried into captivity. God also reminded Israel that only he was their God and Savior.

13:12–16 In this passage Hosea prophesied God's certain judgment upon Ephraim (Israel) for her wickedness. This prophecy was fulfilled in 721 B.C. when the armies of Assyria overwhelmed Israel's armies, destroying the capital city and the kingdom.

The call to repent

R P S 14 O ISRAEL, [a]return unto the LORD thy God; for thou hast fallen by thine iniquity.

2 Take with you words, and turn to the LORD: say unto him, Take away all iniquity, and [1]receive *us* graciously: so will we render the [a]calves of our lips.

3 Asshur shall not save us; [a]we will not ride upon horses: neither will we say any more to the work of our hands, *Ye are* our gods: [b]for in thee the fatherless findeth mercy.

I L P 4 ¶ I will heal their backsliding, I will love them freely: for mine anger is turned away from him.

5 I will be as [a]the dew unto Israel: he shall [1]grow as the lily, and [2]cast forth his roots as Lebanon.

6 His branches [1]shall spread, and [a]his beauty shall be as the olive tree, and [b]his smell as Lebanon.

7 [a]They that dwell under his shadow shall return; they shall revive *as* the corn, and [1]grow as the vine: the [2]scent thereof *shall be* as the wine of Lebanon.

8 Ephraim *shall say,* What have I to do any more with idols? I have heard *him,* and observed him: I *am* like a green fir tree. From me is thy fruit found.

9 Who *is* wise, and he shall understand these *things?* prudent, and he shall know them? for [a]the ways of the LORD *are* right, and the just shall walk in them: but the transgressors shall fall therein.

R *Hos 13:16* ◄► *Joel 1:4*
P *Hos 6:1* ◄► *Hos 14:4*
S *Hos 12:6* ◄► *Am 3:3*
I *Hos 13:14* ◄► *Joel 2:21*
L *Hos 13:9* ◄► *Joel 2:13*
P *Hos 14:1–2* ◄► *Joel 2:12–13*

14:1 [a]Joel 2:13
2 [a]Heb. 13:15 [1]Or, *give good*
3 [a]Ps. 33:17 [b]Ps. 10:14
5 [a]Prov. 19:12 [1]Or, *blossom* [2]Heb. *strike*
6 [a]Ps. 52:8 [b]Gen. 27:27 [1]Heb. *shall go*
7 [a]Ps. 91:1 [1]Or, *blossom* [2]Or, *memorial*
9 [a]Prov. 10:29

14:1 Hosea warned Israel to repent of her rebellion because of the judgment about to fall on her.
14:4–8 The prophet ended his predictions by delivering God's promise to restore Israel once again, likening the final restoration of Israel to a flourishing olive tree. Israel will ultimately be purged of its sin and experience God's full forgiveness and restoration under the coming Messiah.

Joel

Author: Joel

Theme: A locust plague foreshadows the day of the Lord

Date of Writing: c. 830 B.C.

Outline of Joel

I. The Plague of Locusts (1:1–12)
II. Joel's Admonition (1:13–20)
III. Joel's Five Visions (2:1–32)
IV. Judgment and Restoration (3:1–21)

THIS PROPHECY WAS written by Joel, a common OT name that means "Jehovah is God." Joel is mentioned only in this short book and again in Acts (see Ac 2:16); little is known about the personal life of Joel except that he was the son of Pethuel and probably lived in Judah. In addition, the political and social conditions reflected in Joel's book mirror those of the ninth century B.C. during the early years of King Joash while the high priest Jehoiada ruled in his stead (see 2Ki 11:4).

The majority of Joel's message is an apocalyptic prophecy that uses symbolic visions and language to emphasize impending judgment. A severe locust plague that devastated the land of Judah and the burning drought which followed prompted Joel's warning to the people of Judah to repent and return to God. Joel warned that these occurrences were only symbols of the great judgment that would come at the terrible "day of the LORD" (2:31). Joel also prophesied that before the fulfillment of this judgment, God would send his Holy Spirit to grant extended blessing (see 2:28–32). In the NT, on the day of Pentecost, Peter refers to a partial fulfillment of this prophecy (see Ac 2:16).

1 THE WORD of the LORD that came to
Joel the son of Pethuel.

The plague of insects

2 Hear this, ye old men, and give ear,
all ye inhabitants of the land. [a]Hath this
been in your days, or even in the days of
your fathers?
3 [a]Tell ye your children of it, and *let*
your children *tell* their children, and
their children another generation.
R 4 [a]That′ which the palmerworm hath
left hath the locust eaten; and that which
the locust hath left hath the cankerworm
eaten; and that which the cankerworm
hath left hath the caterpillar eaten.
5 Awake, ye drunkards, and weep; and
howl, all ye drinkers of wine, because of
the new wine; [a]for it is cut off from your
mouth.
6 For [a]a nation is come up upon my
land, strong, and without number,
[b]whose teeth *are* the teeth of a lion, and
he hath the cheek teeth of a great lion.
R 7 He hath [a]laid my vine waste, and
′barked my fig tree: he hath made it
clean bare, and cast *it* away; the branches
thereof are made white.
8 ¶ [a]Lament like a virgin girded with
sackcloth for [b]the husband of her youth.
9 [a]The meat offering and the drink offering is cut off from the house of the
LORD; the priests, the LORD'S ministers,
mourn.
10 The field is wasted, [a]the land
mourneth; for the corn is wasted: [b]the
new wine is ′dried up, the oil languisheth.
11 [a]Be ye ashamed, O ye husbandmen; howl, O ye vinedressers, for the
wheat and for the barley; because the
harvest of the field is perished.
12 [a]The vine is dried up, and the fig
tree languisheth; the pomegranate tree,
the palm tree also, and the apple tree,

1:2 [a]ch. 2:2
3 [a]Ps. 78:4
4 [a]Deut. 28:38 ′Heb. *The residue of the palmerworm*
5 [a]Is. 32:10
6 [a]Prov. 30:23 [b]Rev. 9:8
7 [a]Is. 5:6 ′Heb. laid *my fig tree for a barking*
8 [a]Is. 22:12 [b]Prov. 2:17; Jer. 3:4
9 [a]ch. 2:14
10 [a]Jer. 12:11 [b]Is. 24:7 ′Or, *ashamed*
11 [a]Jer. 14:3,4
12 [a]ver. 10 [b]Is. 24:11; Jer. 48:33
13 [a]Jer. 4:8
14 [a]2 Chr. 20:3 [b]Lev. 23:36 [c]2 Chr. 20:13 ′Or, day of *restraint*
15 [a]Jer. 30:7 [b]Is. 13:6,9
16 [a]See Deut. 12:6,7
17 ′Heb. *grains*
18 [a]Hos. 4:3
19 [a]Ps. 50:15 [b]Jer. 9:10 ′Or, *habitations*
20 [a]Job 38:41; Ps. 104:21 [b]1 Ki. 17:7
2:1 [a]Jer. 4:5 [b]Num. 10:5 [c]Obad. 15; Zeph. 1:14 ′Or, *cornet*
2 [a]Amos 5:18

even all the trees of the field, are withered: because [b]joy is withered away from
the sons of men.
13 [a]Gird yourselves, and lament, ye
priests: howl, ye ministers of the altar:
come, lie all night in sackcloth, ye ministers of my God: for the meat offering and
the drink offering is withholden from the
house of your God.
14 ¶ [a]Sanctify ye a fast, call [b]a ′solemn
assembly, gather the elders *and* [c]all the
inhabitants of the land *into* the house of
the LORD your God, and cry unto the LORD.
15 [a]Alas for the day! for [b]the day of the P
LORD *is* at hand, and as a destruction from H
the Almighty shall it come.
16 Is not the meat cut off before our
eyes, *yea,* [a]joy and gladness from the
house of our God?
17 The ′seed is rotten under their
clods, the garners are laid desolate, the
barns are broken down; for the corn is
withered.
18 How do [a]the beasts groan! the
herds of cattle are perplexed, because
they have no pasture; yea, the flocks of
sheep are made desolate.
19 O LORD, [a]to thee will I cry: for [b]the
fire hath devoured the ′pastures of the
wilderness, and the flame hath burned all
the trees of the field.
20 The beasts of the field [a]cry also
unto thee: for [b]the rivers of waters are
dried up, and the fire hath devoured the
pastures of the wilderness.

The coming day of the LORD

2 BLOW[a] YE the ′trumpet in Zion, and P
[b]sound an alarm in my holy moun- H
tain: let all the inhabitants of the land
tremble: for [c]the day of the LORD cometh,
for *it is* nigh at hand;
2 [a]A day of darkness and of gloomi-

R *Hos 14:1* ◀▶ *Joel 1:7*
R *Joel 1:4* ◀▶ *Joel 3:2*
P *Da 12:1* ◀▶ *Joel 2:1–11*
H *Hos 13:3* ◀▶ *Joel 2:1–2*
P *Joel 1:15* ◀▶ *Joel 2:19–32*
H *Joel 1:15* ◀▶ *Joel 2:6*

1:4–7 Using the occasion of a devastating plague of locusts as a prophetic type, Joel warned the people that God's judgment would certainly fall and leave the nation of Judah desolate.
1:15 Joel warned of the certainty of God's judgment when "the day of the LORD" finally comes and enemy armies invade the land.
2:1–11 The trumpet mentioned in this passage was not the silver trumpet used for feasts and festivals (see Nu 10:10). The silver trumpet's notes signified rejoicing or a call to worship. Joel instead indicated that the trumpet to be blown would be the shophar, a ram's or bull's horn used to assemble the army (see Jdg 3:27; 1Sa 13:3), to sound an attack (see Job 39:24–25) or to sound an alarm (see Jer 6:1; Hos 5:8; Am 3:6). The fearsome noise of

ness, a day of clouds and of thick darkness, as the morning spread upon the
mountains: [b]a great people and a strong;
[c]there hath not been ever the like, neither shall be any more after it, *even* to
the years [ǀ]of many generations.
3 A fire devoureth before them; and
behind them a flame burneth: the land *is*
as [a]the garden of Eden before them, [b]and
behind them a desolate wilderness; yea,
and nothing shall escape them.
4 [a]The appearance of them *is* as the
appearance of horses; and as horsemen,
so shall they run.
5 [a]Like the noise of chariots on the
tops of mountains shall they leap, like the
noise of a flame of fire that devoureth
the stubble, as a strong people set in
battle array.
H 6 Before their face the people shall be
much pained: [a]all faces shall gather
[ǀ]blackness.
7 They shall run like mighty men; they
shall climb the wall like men of war; and
they shall march every one on his ways,
and they shall not break their ranks:
8 Neither shall one thrust another;
they shall walk every one in his path: and
when they fall upon the [ǀ]sword, they
shall not be wounded.
9 They shall run to and fro in the city;
they shall run upon the wall, they shall
climb up upon the houses; they shall [a]en-
ter in at the windows [b]like a thief.
H 10 [a]The earth shall quake before
them; the heavens shall tremble: [b]the

H *Joel 2:1–2* ◀▶ *Joel 2:10–11*
H *Joel 2:6* ◀▶ *Joel 2:31*

2 [b]ch. 1:6 [c]Ex. 10:14 [ǀ]Heb. *of generation and generation*
3 [a]Gen. 2:8; Is. 51:3 [b]Zech. 7:14
4 [a]Rev. 9:7
5 [a]Rev. 9:9
6 [a]Jer. 8:21; Lam. 4:8; Nah. 2:10 [ǀ]Heb. *pot*
8 [ǀ]Or, *dart*
9 [a]Jer. 9:21 [b]John 10:1
10 [a]Ps. 18:7 [b]Is. 13:10; Mat. 24:29
11 [a]Jer. 25:30 [b]Jer. 50:34; Rev. 18:8 [c]Jer. 30:7; Amos 5:18; Zeph. 1:15 [d]Mal. 3:2
12 [a]Jer. 4:1; Hos. 12:6
13 [a]Ps. 34:18 [b]Gen. 37:34; 2 Sam. 1:11; Job 1:20 [c]Ex. 34:6
14 [a]Josh. 14:12; 2 Ki. 19:4 [b]Hag. 2:19 [c]ch. 1:9,13
15 [a]Num. 10:3 [b]ch. 1:14
16 [a]Ex. 19:10 [b]1 Cor. 7:5
17 [a]Ezek. 8:16; Mat. 23:35 [b]Ex. 32:11,12

sun and the moon shall be dark, and the
stars shall withdraw their shining:
11 [a]And the LORD shall utter his voice
before his army: for his camp *is* very
great: [b]for *he is* strong that executeth his
word: for the [c]day of the LORD *is* great and
very terrible; and [d]who can abide it?

The call to repentance

12 ¶ Therefore also now, saith the P
LORD, [a]turn ye *even* to me with all your R
heart, and with fasting, and with weeping, and with mourning:
13 And [a]rend your heart, and not L
[b]your garments, and turn unto the LORD M
your God: for he *is* [c]gracious and merciful, slow to anger, and of great kindness,
and repenteth him of the evil.
14 [a]Who knoweth *if* he will return and
repent, and leave [b]a blessing behind him;
even [c]a meat offering and a drink offering
unto the LORD your God?
15 ¶ [a]Blow the trumpet in Zion, [b]sanc-
tify a fast, call a solemn assembly:
16 Gather the people, [a]sanctify the
congregation, assemble the elders, gather
the children, and those that suck the
breasts: [b]let the bridegroom go forth of
his chamber, and the bride out of her
closet.
17 Let the priests, the ministers of the
LORD, weep [a]between the porch and the
altar, and let them say, [b]Spare thy people,
O LORD, and give not thine heritage to re-

P *Hos 14:4* ◀▶ *Am 5:4*
R *Hos 10:12* ◀▶ *Jnh 3:5–10*
L *Hos 14:4* ◀▶ *Jnh 3:10*
M *Hos 10:12* ◀▶ *Ob 3–4*

---

the shophar could be heard from a great distance (see Ex 19:16) and signaled approaching danger. Joel prophesied that all who heard the sound of the shophar would tremble at that awful day.

Note also that Joel described the invaders as "horsemen" (2:4), indicating their swiftness as they crush their enemies. The sound of the invaders was "like the noise of chariots" (2:5), possibly suggesting modern tanks or armored vehicles. However, Joel promised that God's wrath would be revealed through earthquakes and the darkening of the sun and moon. This parallels Revelation's description of God's final judgment when "the sun became black as sackcloth of hair, and the moon became as blood" (Rev 6:12).

Joel's prophecy indicated that God would raise up an army to fight these invaders (2:11; see also Jude 14–15). This prophecy will be fulfilled at the Battle of Armageddon when the armies of the antichrist will be defeated and Jesus Christ will set up his Messianic kingdom of peace (see Rev 9:13–19; 16:12–16; 19:11–16).

2:15–16 In this passage, Joel called for the sounding of the *chatsotseroth*, the trumpets used in sacred assembly. He urged all of the people to assemble, fast and repent. No one was exempt (see Dt 24:5).

2:17 Joel gave specific instructions to the priests who were to offer prayers of intercession. The location for these prayers "between the porch and the altar" was the customary place in the temple for priestly intercession (see 1Ki 8:22; Eze 8:16). Though Joel's words were directed to the priests in his day, this prophecy prefigures the temple that will be rebuilt in the last days in Jerusalem (see Eze 40; 2Th. 2:4).

proach, that the heathen should [1]rule
over them: [c]wherefore should they say
among the people, Where *is* their God?

Deliverance to follow repentance

18 ¶ Then will the LORD [a]be jealous for
his land, [b]and pity his people.
P 19 Yea, the LORD will answer and say
F unto his people, Behold, I will send you
[a]corn, and wine, and oil, and ye shall be
satisfied therewith: and I will no more
make you a reproach among the heathen:
20 But [a]I will remove far off from you
[b]the northern *army*, and will drive him
into a land barren and desolate, with his
face toward the east sea, and his hinder
part [c]toward the utmost sea, and his stink
shall come up, and his ill savour shall
come up, because [1]he hath done great
things.
I 21 ¶ Fear not, O land; be glad and rejoice: for the LORD will do great things.
B 22 Be not afraid, ye beasts of the field:
for [a]the pastures of the wilderness do
spring, for the tree beareth her fruit, the
fig tree and the vine do yield their
strength.
23 Be glad then, ye children of Zion,
and [a]rejoice in the LORD your God: for he
hath given you [1]the former rain [2]moder-
ately, and he [b]will cause to come down
for you the rain, the former rain, and the
latter rain in the first *month*.

P *Joel 2:1–11* ◀▶ *Joel 3:1–2*
F *Hos 13:5–6* ◀▶ *Joel 2:24–26*
I *Hos 14:4–8* ◀▶ *Joel 3:16–18*
B *Hos 2:21–22* ◀▶ *Joel 2:24–26*

17 [c]Ps. 42:10 [1]Or, *use a byword against them*
18 [a]Zech. 1:14 [b]Is. 60:10
19 [a]ch. 1:10; Mal. 3:10
20 [a]Ex. 10:19 [b]Jer. 1:14 [c]Deut. 11:24 [1]Heb. *he hath magnified to do*
22 [a]ch. 1:19
23 [a]Is. 41:16; Hab. 3:18; Zech. 10:7 [b]Lev. 26:4; Deut. 11:14 [1]Or, *a teacher of righteousness* [2]Heb. *according to righteousness*
25 [a]ch. 1:4
26 [a]Lev. 26:5
27 [a]Lev. 26:11 [b]Is. 45:5
28 [a]Ezek. 39:29 [b]Zech. 12:10 [c]Is. 54:13 [d]Acts 21:9
29 [a]Gal. 3:28
30 [a]Mat. 24:29; Mark 13:24; Luke 21:11

24 And the floors shall be full of B
wheat, and the vats shall overflow with F
wine and oil.
25 And I will restore to you the years
[a]that the locust hath eaten, the cankerworm, and the caterpillar, and the palmerworm, my great army which I sent
among you.
26 And ye shall [a]eat in plenty, and be T
satisfied, and praise the name of the LORD
your God, that hath dealt wondrously
with you: and my people shall never be
ashamed.
27 And ye shall know that I *am* [a]in the L
midst of Israel, and *that* [b]I *am* the LORD
your God, and none else: and my people
shall never be ashamed.

Promised outpouring of the Spirit

28 ¶ [a]And it shall come to pass after- B
ward, *that* I [b]will pour out my spirit upon G
all flesh; [c]and your sons and [d]your daugh- M
ters shall prophesy, your old men shall P
dream dreams, your young men shall see T
visions:
29 And also upon [a]the servants and
upon the handmaids in those days will I
pour out my spirit.
30 And [a]I will show wonders in the

B *Joel 2:22* ◀▶ *Hag 2:15–19*
F *Joel 2:19* ◀▶ *Hab 3:17–18*
T *Jer 1:17* ◀▶ *Mal 3:16–17*
L *Da 9:23* ◀▶ *Zec 2:8*
B *Da 6:3* ◀▶ *Mic 3:8*
G *Da 5:14* ◀▶ *Mic 3:8*
M *Da 6:3* ◀▶ *Mic 2:7*
P *Eze 36:26–27* ◀▶ *Zec 12:10*
T *Da 5:14* ◀▶ *Mt 10:19–20*

2:18 Joel's focus shifted from the destruction on the land to the blessings that God will give to those who repent.

2:20 Joel's vision accurately detailed an actual plague of locusts that devastated the land of Judah in his day. When the locusts died, the stench from their dead bodies was horrible. Because Israel's most powerful enemies were located geographically to the north of the promised land, this verse also foreshadows the destruction of the army from the north during the tribulation (see Eze 39:2). God will supernaturally defeat this army of the antichrist at the Battle of Armageddon. The expression "his stink shall come up" suggests the magnitude of the devastation that will follow God's judgment. Compare this verse with Rev 19:17–21.

2:21–27 Joel prophesied that God would restore Israel to its place of peace and prosperity in the promised land. The land would produce an agricultural abundance and the people would "be satisfied, and praise the name of the LORD" (2:26). Joel also prophesied that God would never desert them again so that his "people shall never be ashamed" (2:27).

2:28–29 God promised that in the last days he would "pour out my spirit upon all flesh" (2:28). The apostle Peter referred to this prophecy at the outpouring of the Holy Spirit on the day of Pentecost (see Ac 2:16–21). This was a partial fulfillment of the final outpouring of God's Spirit on Israel in the last days. This final outpouring of the Holy Spirit will transform the hearts of Israel in preparation to meet their Messiah.

2:30–32 The cosmic events noted here will accompany the day of the Lord. Joel's words are confirmed in Rev 6. As these signs occur in the heavens, the whole world will be aware of the coming judgment and wrath of God. Yet God promised mercy to a remnant of Israel who would "call on the name of

heavens and in the earth, blood, and fire, and pillars of smoke.

H 31 [a]The sun shall be turned into darkness, and the moon into blood, [b]before the great and the terrible day of the LORD come.

K 32 And it shall come to pass, *that* [a]whosoever shall call on the name of the LORD shall be delivered: for [b]in mount Zion and in Jerusalem shall be deliverance, as the LORD hath said, and in [c]the remnant whom the LORD shall call.

Judgment of Judah's enemies

P 3 FOR, BEHOLD, [a]in those days, and in that time, when I shall bring again the captivity of Judah and Jerusalem,

R 2 [a]I will also gather all nations, and will bring them down into the valley of Jehoshaphat, and [b]will plead with them there for my people and *for* my heritage Israel, whom they have scattered among the nations, and parted my land.

3 And they have [a]cast lots for my people; and have given a boy for an harlot, and sold a girl for wine, that they might drink.

M 4 Yea, and what have ye to do with me, [a]O Tyre, and Zidon, and all the coasts of Palestine? will ye render me a recompense? and if ye recompense me, swiftly *and* speedily will I return your recompense upon your own head;

5 Because ye have taken my silver and my gold, and have carried into your temples my goodly [a]pleasantʹ things:

6 The children also of Judah and the children of Jerusalem have ye sold unto ʹthe Grecians, that ye might remove them far from their border.

7 Behold, [a]I will raise them out of the place whither ye have sold them, and will return your recompense upon your own head:

8 And I will sell your sons and your daughters into the hand of the children of Judah, and they shall sell them to the [a]Sabeans, to a people [b]far off: for the LORD hath spoken *it.*

9 ¶ [a]Proclaim ye this among the Gentiles; ʹPrepare war, wake up the mighty men, let all the men of war draw near; let them come up: P

10 [a]Beat your plowshares into swords, and your ʹpruning hooks into spears: [b]let the weak say, I *am* strong.

11 Assemble yourselves, and come, all ye heathen, and gather yourselves together round about: thither ʹcause [a]thy mighty ones to come down, O LORD.

12 Let the heathen be wakened, and come up to the valley of Jehoshaphat: for there will I sit to [a]judge all the heathen round about.

13 [a]Put ye in the sickle, for [b]the harvest is ripe: come, get you down; for the [c]press is full, the vats overflow; for their wickedness *is* great. H

14 Multitudes, multitudes in the valley of ʹdecision: for [a]the day of the LORD *is* near in the valley of decision. N

15 The sun and the moon shall be darkened, and the stars shall withdraw their shining.

16 The LORD also shall roar out of Zion, and utter his voice from Jerusalem; and the heavens and the earth shall shake: [a]but the LORD *will be* the ʹhope of his people, and the strength of the children of Israel. I

31 [a]Is. 13:9,10 [b]Mal. 4:5
32 [a]Rom. 10:13 [b]Is. 46:13; Rom. 11:26 [c]Is. 11:11; Jer. 31:7; Mic. 4:7; Rom. 9:27
3:1 [a]Jer. 30:3; Ezek. 38:14
2 [a]Zech. 14:2 [b]Is. 66:16; Ezek. 38:22
3 [a]Obad. 11; Nah. 3:10
4 [a]Amos 1:6
5 [a]Dan. 11:38 ʹHeb. *desirable*
6 ʹHeb. *the sons of the Grecians*
7 [a]Is. 43:5,6; Jer. 23:8
8 [a]Ezek. 23:42 [b]Jer. 6:20
9 [a]Ezek. 38:7 ʹHeb. *Sanctify*
10 [a]Is. 2:4; Mic. 4:3 [b]Zech. 12:8 ʹOr, *scythes*
11 [a]Ps. 103:20; Is. 13:3 ʹOr, *the LORD shall bring down*
12 [a]Ps. 96:13; Is. 2:4
13 [a]Mat. 13:39; Rev. 14:15 [b]Jer. 51:33 [c]Is. 63:3; Rev. 14:19
14 [a]ch. 2:1 ʹOr, *concision,* or, *threshing*
16 [a]Is. 51:5,6 ʹHeb. *place of repair,* or, *harbour*

H *Joel 2:10–11* ◀▶ *Joel 3:13–14*
K *Eze 37:23* ◀▶ *Am 5:4*
P *Joel 2:19–32* ◀▶ *Joel 3:9–17*
R *Joel 1:7* ◀▶ *Am 2:1–6*
M *Hos 3:5* ◀▶ *Joel 3:18–20*

P *Joel 3:1–2* ◀▶ *Am 1:2–15*
H *Joel 2:31* ◀▶ *Am 2:14–16*
N *Hos 4:17* ◀▶ *Am 4:12*
I *Joel 2:21* ◀▶ *Joel 3:20–21*

---

the LORD" (2:32; see also Zec 12:10).

3:1–2 God declared that at the time of Israel's final redemption he would bring his people back from captivity and judge the nations who had gathered against Jerusalem. This judgment would take place in the Valley of Jehoshaphat. Note that this valley near Jerusalem was the site of one of the Lord's historic victories over the nations during the reign of King Jehoshaphat (see 2Ch 20:1–30).

3:9–16 Joel prophetically proclaimed God's command to the Gentiles to prepare for war, for God would bring his heavenly army against them and bring them into judgment (see Eze 38—39; Rev 19). Despite all of the talk about peace, God promised their sure destruction (see 1Th 5:3). Joel called the location of this climactic battle as "the valley of decision" (3:14). Note the parallel prophecy in Isa 34:2–8 and Am 1:2.

Eternal blessing for God's people

17 So shall ye know that I *am* the LORD
your God dwelling in Zion, my holy
mountain: then shall Jerusalem be [l]holy,
and there shall no strangers pass through
her any more.
M 18 ¶ And it shall come to pass in that
day, *that* the mountains shall drop down
new wine, and the hills shall flow with
milk, and all the rivers of Judah shall
[l]flow with waters, and a fountain shall
come forth of the house of the LORD, and
shall water the valley of Shittim.
19 Egypt shall be a desolation, and
Edom shall be a desolate wilderness, for
the violence *against* the children of Judah,
because they have shed innocent
blood in their land.
20 But Judah shall [l]dwell for ever, and I
Jerusalem from generation to generation.
21 For I will [a]cleanse their blood *that* I
have not cleansed: [l]for the LORD dwelleth
in Zion.

17 [l]Heb. *holiness*
18 [l]Heb. *go*
20 [l]Or, *abide*
21 [a]Is. 4:4 [l]Or, *even I the LORD that dwelleth in Zion*

M *Joel 3:4* ◀ ▶ *Mic 4:3–4*

I *Joel 3:16–18* ◀ ▶ *Am 9:11–15*

3:17–18 This prophecy will be fulfilled when Jesus rules from Jerusalem and establishes his Messianic kingdom. Compare with 2:27; Ps 46:4; Rev 21:3. Though strangers have ruled Jerusalem for centuries, the city will be freed from her captors and filled with God's abiding presence. Only then will Jerusalem be holy and invincible. Streams of blessing will flow from God's presence, refreshing his people. The land will no longer be barren, but well-watered and lush. Note the parallels between this passage and Zec 13:1 as well as Ezekiel's prediction of the millennial kingdom (see Eze 47:1–8).

3:19 Joel prophesied judgment against Egypt and Edom because of their violence against God's people.

3:20–21 Joel's prophecy ends on an encouraging note: God promises that Judah and Jerusalem will dwell in peace forever under the rule of the Messiah.

Amos

Author: Amos

Theme: God will judge injustice

Date of Writing: c. 760–750 B.C.

Outline of Amos

I. The Nations Denounced (1:1—2:5)
II. Israel's Guilt (2:6—6:14)
III. Five Visions of Divine Retribution (7:1—9:10)
IV. The Promise of Restoration (9:11–15)

AMOS WAS A shepherd or herdsman from Tekoa, a village southeast of Bethlehem, in Judah. Though he lived in the kingdom of Judah, Amos delivered God's messages to the northern kingdom of Israel, warning rulers and people alike of the danger of spiritual apathy and social injustice. Prophesying during the reigns of King Jeroboam II of Israel and King Uzziah of Judah, Amos urged the leaders to return to God and enforce justice or suffer the coming judgment of God.

Both Israel and Judah enjoyed a period of peace and prosperity during Amos's day that was marked by widespread social corruption, idolatry, injustice and rampant materialism. God was repulsed by these attitudes and actions among his people and sent Amos to warn this self-satisfied generation of impending judgment. Israel had neglected God's Word, and Amos promised that God would punish Israel if they did not "hate the evil, and love the good, and establish judgment in the gate" (5:15). Yet Amos also prophesied the future re-establishment of the kingdom of David under the rule of the Messiah.

1 THE WORDS of Amos, who was among the herdmen of [a]Tekoa, which he saw concerning Israel in the days of Uzziah king of Judah, and in the days of [b]Jeroboam the son of Joash king of Israel, two years before the [c]earthquake.

P 2 And he said, the LORD will [a]roar from Zion, and utter his voice from Jerusalem; and the habitations of the shepherds shall mourn, and the top of [b]Carmel shall wither.

Judgment on the nations

3 Thus saith the LORD; For three transgressions of [a]Damascus, [1]and for four, I will not [2]turn away *the punishment* thereof; because they have threshed Gilead with threshing instruments of iron:

4 [a]But I will send a fire into the house of Hazael, which shall devour the palaces of Ben-hadad.

5 I will break also the [a]bar of Damascus, and cut off the inhabitant from [1]the plain of Aven, and him that holdeth the sceptre from [2]the house of Eden: and the people of Syria shall go into captivity unto Kir, saith the LORD.

6 ¶ Thus saith the LORD; For three transgressions of [a]Gaza, and for four, I will not turn away *the punishment* thereof; because they [1]carried away captive the whole captivity, to deliver *them* up to Edom:

7 [a]But I will send a fire on the wall of Gaza, which shall devour the palaces thereof:

8 And I will cut off the inhabitant [a]from Ashdod, and him that holdeth the sceptre from Ashkelon, and I will [b]turn mine hand against Ekron: and [c]the remnant of the Philistines shall perish, saith the Lord GOD.

9 ¶ Thus saith the LORD; For three transgressions of [a]Tyrus, and for four, I will not turn away *the punishment* thereof; because they delivered up the whole captivity to Edom, and remembered not [b]the[1] brotherly covenant:

10 But I will send a fire on the wall of Tyrus, which shall devour the palaces thereof.

11 ¶ Thus saith the LORD; For three transgressions of [a]Edom, and for four, I will not turn away *the punishment* thereof; because he did pursue his brother with the sword, and [1]did cast off all pity, and his anger did tear perpetually, and he kept his wrath for ever:

12 But [a]I will send a fire upon Teman, which shall devour the palaces of Bozrah.

13 ¶ Thus saith the LORD; For three transgressions of [a]the children of Ammon, and for four, I will not turn away *the punishment* thereof; because they have [1]ripped up the women with child of Gilead, that they might enlarge their border:

14 But I will kindle a fire in the wall of [a]Rabbah, and it shall devour the palaces thereof, [b]with shouting in the day of battle, with a tempest in the day of the whirlwind:

15 And [a]their king shall go into captivity, he and his princes together, saith the LORD.

2 THUS SAITH the LORD; For three transgressions of Moab, and for four, I will not turn away *the punishment* thereof; because he [a]burned the bones of the king of Edom into lime: R

2 But I will send a fire upon Moab, and it shall devour the palaces of [a]Kirioth: and Moab shall die with tumult, with shouting, *and* with the sound of the trumpet:

3 And I will cut off [a]the judge from the midst thereof, and will slay all the princes thereof with him, saith the LORD.

4 ¶ Thus saith the LORD; For three transgressions of Judah, and for four, I will not turn away *the punishment* thereof; [a]because they have despised the law of the LORD, and have not kept his commandments, and [b]their lies caused them to err, [c]after the which their fathers have walked:

1:1 [a]2 Sam. 14:2 [b]ch. 7:10 [c]Zech. 14:5
2 [a]Joel 3:16 [b]1 Sam. 25:2; Is. 33:9
3 [a]Is. 8:4 [1]Or, *yea, for four* [2]Or, *convert it,* or, *let it be quiet*
4 [a]Jer. 17:27
5 [a]Jer. 51:30 [1]Or, *Bikath-aven* [2]Or, *Beth-eden*
6 [a]Jer. 47:4,5 [1]Or, *carried them away with an entire captivity*
7 [a]Jer. 47:1
8 [a]Zeph. 2:4 [b]Ps. 81:14 [c]Ezek. 25:16
9 [a]Is. 23:1 [b]1 Ki. 5:1 [1]Heb. *the covenant of brethren*
11 [a]Is. 21:11; Jer. 49:8 [1]Heb. *corrupted his compassions*
12 [a]Obad. 9,10
13 [a]Jer. 49:1; Ezek. 25:2 [1]Or, *divided the mountains*
14 [a]Deut. 3:11 [b]ch. 2:2
15 [a]Jer. 49:3
2:1 [a]2 Ki. 3:27
2 [a]Jer. 48:41
3 [a]Num. 24:17; Jer. 48:7
4 [a]Lev. 26:14 [b]Is. 28:15; Jer. 16:19 [c]Ezek. 20:13,16,18

P *Joel 3:9–17 ◀ ▶ Ob 1–10*

R *Joel 3:2 ◀ ▶ Am 7:9*

1:2 Note the parallel between this verse and Joel 3:16.

1:3–5 Amos prophesied the coming judgment upon Damascus, the ancient capital of Syria, for repeated acts of rebellion. Isaiah had also prophesied the final destruction of Damascus (see Isa 17:1, 3).

1:6–7 Amos declared that the ancient Philistine city of Gaza would be consumed by fire because of God's judgment.

1:9–10 Despite Tyre's economic prosperity and virtual inaccessibility on a rocky island, Amos pronounced God's judgment on this boastful city.

5 [a]But I will send a fire upon Judah, and it shall devour the palaces of Jerusalem.

Prophecy against Israel

6 ¶ Thus saith the LORD; For three transgressions of Israel, and for four, I will not turn away *the punishment* thereof; because [a]they sold the righteous for silver, and the poor for a pair of shoes;

7 That pant after the dust of the earth on the head of the poor, and [a]turn aside the way of the meek: [b]and a man and his father will go in unto the *same* [1]maid, [c]to profane my holy name:

8 And they lay *themselves* down upon clothes [a]laid to pledge [b]by every altar, and they drink the wine of [1]the condemned *in* the house of their god.

9 ¶ Yet destroyed I the [a]Amorite before them, whose height *was* like the height of the cedars, and he *was* strong as the oaks; yet I [b]destroyed his fruit from above, and his roots from beneath.

10 Also [a]I brought you up from the land of Egypt, and [b]led you forty years through the wilderness, to possess the land of the Amorite.

11 And I raised up of your sons for prophets, and of your young men for [a]Nazarites. *Is it* not even thus, O ye children of Israel? saith the LORD.

12 But ye gave the Nazarites wine to drink; and commanded the prophets, [a]saying, Prophesy not.

13 [a]Behold, [1]I am pressed under you, as a cart is pressed *that is* full of sheaves.

H 14 [a]Therefore the flight shall perish from the swift, and the strong shall not strengthen his force, [b]neither shall the mighty deliver [1]himself:

15 Neither shall he stand that handleth the bow; and *he that is* swift of foot shall not deliver *himself:* neither shall he that rideth the horse deliver himself.

16 And *he that is* [1]courageous among the mighty shall flee away naked in that day, saith the LORD.

H *Joel 3:13–14* ◀▶ *Am 4:12*

The relation of Israel to God

3 HEAR THIS word that the LORD hath spoken against you, O children of Israel, against the whole family which I brought up from the land of Egypt, saying,

2 [a]You only have I known of all the families of the earth: [b]therefore I will [1]punish you for all your iniquities.

3 Can two walk together, except they S
be agreed?

4 Will a lion roar in the forest, when he hath no prey? will a young lion [1]cry out of his den, if he have taken nothing?

5 Can a bird fall in a snare upon the earth, where no gin *is* for him? shall *one* take up a snare from the earth, and have taken nothing at all?

6 Shall a trumpet be blown in the city, and the people [1]not be afraid? [a]shall there be evil in a city, [2]and the LORD hath not done *it?*

7 Surely the Lord GOD will do nothing, but [a]he revealeth his secret unto his servants the prophets.

8 The lion hath roared, who will not fear? the Lord GOD hath spoken, [a]who can but prophesy?

9 ¶ Publish in the palaces at Ashdod, and in the palaces in the land of Egypt, and say, Assemble yourselves upon the mountains of Samaria, and behold the great tumults in the midst thereof, and the [1]oppressed in the midst thereof.

10 For they [a]know not to do right, saith the LORD, who store up violence and [1]robbery in their palaces.

11 Therefore thus saith the Lord GOD; An adversary *there shall be* even round about the land; and he shall bring down thy strength from thee, and thy palaces shall be spoiled.

12 Thus saith the LORD; As the shepherd [1]taketh out of the mouth of the lion two legs, or a piece of an ear; so shall the children of Israel be taken out that dwell in Samaria in the corner of a bed, and [2]in Damascus *in* a couch.

13 Hear ye, and testify in the house of

S *Hos 14:1* ◀▶ *Am 6:12*

5 [a]Jer. 17:27; Hos. 8:14
6 [a]Is. 29:21
7 [a]ch. 5:12 [b]Ezek. 22:11 [c]Lev. 20:3 [1]Or, *young woman*
8 [a]Ex. 22:26 [b]1 Cor. 8:10 [1]Or, *such as have fined,* or, *mulcted*
9 [a]Num. 21:24; Deut. 2:31 [b]Is. 5:24; Mal. 4:1
10 [a]Ex. 12:51 [b]Deut. 2:7
11 [a]Num. 6:2; Judg. 13:5
12 [a]Is. 30:10; Jer. 11:21; Mic. 2:6
13 [a]Is. 1:14 [1]Or, *I will press your place, as a cart full of sheaves presseth*
14 [a]Jer. 9:23 [b]Ps. 33:16 [1]Heb. *his soul,* or *life*
16 [1]Heb. *strong of his heart*
3:2 [a]Deut. 7:6; Ps. 147:19 [b]Mat. 11:22; Rom. 2:9 [1]Heb. *visit upon*
4 [1]Heb. *give forth his voice*
6 [a]Is. 45:7 [1]Or, *not run together?* [2]Or, *and shall not the LORD do somewhat?*
7 [a]Gen. 6:13; John 15:15
8 [a]Acts 4:20
9 [1]Or, *oppressions*
10 [a]Jer. 4:22 [1]Or, *spoil*
12 [1]Heb. *delivereth* [2]Or, *on the bed's feet*

3:7 Amos declared that God had warned the people through his prophets of his intentions, yet the people refused to listen and told the prophets to be quiet (see 2:12). Even today God desires to reveal his prophetic truth to those who seek to understand his Word.

Jacob, saith the Lord GOD, the God of
hosts,
14 That in the day that I shall [1]visit the
transgressions of Israel upon him I will
also visit the altars of Beth-el: and the
horns of the altar shall be cut off, and fall
to ground.
15 And I will smite [a]the winter house
with [b]the summer house; and [c]the
houses of ivory shall perish, and the great
houses shall have an end, saith the LORD.
4 HEAR THIS word, ye [a]kine of Bashan, that *are* in the mountain of Samaria, which oppress the poor, which
crush the needy, which say to their masters, Bring, and let us drink.
2 [a]The Lord GOD hath sworn by his holiness, that, lo, the days shall come upon
you, that he will take you away [b]with
hooks, and your posterity with fishhooks.
3 And [a]ye shall go out at the breaches,
every *cow at that which is* before her;
and [1]ye shall cast *them* into the palace,
saith the LORD.

Israel's failure to return to God

4 ¶ [a]Come to Beth-el, and transgress;
at [b]Gilgal multiply transgression; and
[c]bring your sacrifices every morning,
[d]*and* your tithes after [1]three years:
5 [a]And [1]offer a sacrifice of thanksgiving with leaven, and proclaim *and* publish [b]the free offerings: for [2]this liketh
you, O ye children of Israel, saith the
Lord GOD.
6 ¶ And I also have given you cleanness of teeth in all your cities, and want
of bread in all your places: [a]yet have ye
not returned unto me, saith the LORD.
7 And also I have withholden the rain
from you, when *there were* yet three
months to the harvest: and I caused it to
rain upon one city, and caused it not to
rain upon another city: one piece was
rained upon, and the piece whereupon it
rained not withered.
8 So two *or* three cities wandered unto
one city, to drink water; but they were
not satisfied: yet have ye not returned
unto me, saith the LORD.
9 [a]I have smitten you with blasting
and mildew: [1]when your gardens and
your vineyards and your fig trees and
your olive trees increased, [b]the palmerworm devoured *them:* yet have ye not returned unto me, saith the LORD.
10 I have sent among you the pestilence [a]after[1] the manner of Egypt: your
young men have I slain with the sword,
[b]and[2] have taken away your horses; and I
have made the stink of your camps to
come up unto your nostrils: yet have ye
not returned unto me, saith the LORD.
11 I have overthrown *some* of you, as
God overthrew [a]Sodom and Gomorrah,
and ye were as a firebrand plucked out of
the burning: yet have ye not returned
unto me, saith the LORD.
12 Therefore thus will I do unto thee, H
O Israel: *and* because I will do this unto J
thee, [a]prepare to meet thy God, O Israel. N
13 For, lo, he that formeth the mountains, and createth the [1]wind, [a]and declareth unto man what *is* his thought,
that maketh the morning darkness, [b]and
treadeth upon the high places of the
earth, [c]The LORD, The God of hosts, *is* his
name.
5 HEAR YE this word which I [a]take up
against you, *even* a lamentation,
O house of Israel.
2 The virgin of Israel is fallen; she shall
no more rise: she is forsaken upon her
land; *there is* none to raise her up.
3 For thus saith the Lord GOD; The city
that went out *by* a thousand shall leave an
hundred, and that which went forth *by*
an hundred shall leave ten, to the house
of Israel.

The call to repentance

4 ¶ For thus saith the LORD unto the K
house of Israel, [a]Seek ye me, [b]and ye P
shall live:
5 But seek not [a]Beth-el, nor enter into
Gilgal, and pass not to [b]Beer-sheba: for
Gilgal shall surely go into captivity, and
[c]Beth-el shall come to nought.
6 Seek the LORD, and ye shall live; lest K
he break out like fire in the house of Joseph, and devour *it,* and *there be* none to
quench *it* in Beth-el.
7 Ye who [a]turn judgment to worm- C
wood, and leave off righteousness in the
earth,
8 *Seek him* that maketh the [a]seven
stars and Orion, and turneth the shadow

14 [1]Or, *punish Israel for*
15 [a]Jer. 36:22 [b]Judg. 3:20 [c]1 Ki. 22:39
4:1 [a]Ps. 22:12; Ezek. 39:18
2 [a]Ps. 89:35 [b]Jer. 16:16; Hab. 1:15
3 [a]Ezek. 12:5 [1]Or, *ye shall cast away the things of the palace*
4 [a]Ezek. 20:39 [b]Hos. 4:15 [c]Num. 28:3 [d]Deut. 14:28 [1]Heb. *three years of days*
5 [a]Lev. 7:13 [b]Lev. 22:18; Deut. 12:6 [1]Heb. *offer by burning* [2]Heb. *so ye love*
6 [a]Is. 26:11; Jer. 5:3; Hag. 2:17
9 [a]Deut. 28:22; Hag. 2:17 [b]Joel 1:4 [1]Or, *the multitude of your gardens, &c. did the palmerworm*
10 [a]Ex. 9:3,6; Deut. 28:27; Ps. 78:50 [b]2 Ki. 13:7 [1]Or, *in the way* [2]Heb. *with the captivity of your horses*
11 [a]Gen. 19:24; Is. 13:19
12 [a]Ezek. 13:5
13 [a]Ps. 139:2; Dan. 2:28 [b]Mic. 1:3 [c]Is. 47:4; Jer. 10:16 [1]Or, *spirit*
5:1 [a]Jer. 7:29
4 [a]Jer. 29:13 [b]Is. 55:3
5 [a]ch. 4:4 [b]ch. 8:14 [c]Hos. 4:15
7 [a]ch. 6:12
8 [a]Job 9:9

H *Am 2:14–16* ◀ ▶ *Am 5:16–20*
J *Da 7:9–10* ◀ ▶ *Mt 7:1–2*
N *Joel 3:14* ◀ ▶ *Zec 1:4–5*
K *Joel 2:32* ◀ ▶ *Am 5:6*
P *Joel 2:12–13* ◀ ▶ *Mic 7:18–19*
K *Am 5:4* ◀ ▶ *Ob 17*
C *Hos 13:3* ◀ ▶ *Am 6:12*

of death into the morning, [b]and maketh the day dark with night: that [c]calleth for the waters of the sea, and poureth them out upon the face of the earth: [d]The LORD *is* his name:

9 That strengtheneth the [1]spoiled against the strong, so that the spoiled shall come against the fortress.

10 [a]They hate him that rebuketh in the gate, and they [b]abhor him that speaketh uprightly.

11 Forasmuch therefore as your treading *is* upon the poor, and ye take from him burdens of wheat: [a]ye have built houses of hewn stone, but ye shall not dwell in them; ye have planted [1]pleasant vineyards, but ye shall not drink wine of them.

12 For I know your manifold transgressions and your mighty sins: [a]they afflict the just, they take [1]a bribe, and they [b]turn aside the poor in the gate *from their right.*

13 Therefore [a]the prudent shall keep silence in that time; for it *is* an evil time.

14 Seek good, and not evil, that ye may live: and so the LORD, the God of hosts, shall be with you, [a]as ye have spoken.

15 [a]Hate the evil, and love the good, and establish judgment in the gate: [b]it may be that the LORD God of hosts will be gracious unto the remnant of Joseph.

H 16 Therefore the LORD, the God of hosts, the Lord, saith thus; Wailing *shall be* in all streets; and they shall say in all the highways, Alas! alas! and they shall call the husbandman to mourning, and [a]such as are skilful of lamentation to wailing.

17 And in all vineyards *shall be* wailing: for [a]I will pass through thee, saith the LORD.

The day of the LORD

18 [a]Woe unto you that desire the day of the LORD! to what end *is* it for you? [b]the day of the LORD *is* darkness, and not light.

19 [a]As if a man did flee from a lion, and a bear met him; or went into the house, and leaned his hand on the wall, and a serpent bit him.

20 *Shall* not the day of the LORD *be* darkness, and not light? even very dark, and no brightness in it?

21 ¶ [a]I hate, I despise your feast days, and [b]I will not [1]smell in your solemn assemblies.

22 [a]Though ye offer me burnt offerings and your meat offerings, I will not accept *them:* neither will I regard the [1]peace offerings of your fat beasts.

23 Take thou away from me the noise of thy songs; for I will not hear the melody of thy viols.

24 [a]But let judgment [1]run down as waters, and righteousness as a mighty stream.

25 [a]Have ye offered unto me sacrifices and offerings in the wilderness forty years, O house of Israel?

26 But ye have borne [1]the tabernacle [a]of your Moloch and Chiun your images, the star of your god, which ye made to yourselves.

27 Therefore will I cause you to go into captivity [a]beyond Damascus, saith the LORD, [b]whose name *is* The God of hosts.

Captivity inevitable

6 WOE [a]TO them *that* [1]*are* at ease in Zion, and trust in the mountain of Samaria, *which are* named [b]chief[2] of the nations, to whom the house of Israel came!

2 [a]Pass ye unto [b]Calneh, and see; and from thence go ye to [c]Hamath the great: then go down to Gath of the Philistines: [d]*be they* better than these kingdoms? or their border greater than your border?

3 Ye that [a]put far away the [b]evil day, [c]and cause [d]the [1]seat of violence to come near;

4 That lie upon beds of ivory, and [1]stretch themselves upon their couches, and eat the lambs out of the flock, and the calves out of the midst of the stall;

5 [a]That [1]chant to the sound of the viol, *and* invent to themselves instruments of music, [b]like David;

6 That drink [1]wine in bowls, and anoint themselves with the chief ointments: [a]but they are not grieved for the [2]affliction of Joseph.

7 ¶ Therefore now shall they go captive with the first that go captive, and the banquet of them that stretched themselves shall be removed.

8 [a]The Lord GOD hath sworn by himself, saith the LORD the God of hosts, I abhor [b]the excellency of Jacob, and hate

8 [b]Ps. 104:20 [c]Job 38:34 [d]ch. 4:13
9 [1]Heb. *spoil*
10 [a]Is. 29:21 [b]1 Ki. 22:8
11 [a]Mic. 6:15 [1]Heb. *vineyards of desire*
12 [a]ch. 2:6 [b]Is. 29:21 [1]Or, *a ransom*
13 [a]ch. 6:10
14 [a]Mic. 3:11
15 [a]Rom. 12:9 [b]Joel 2:14
16 [a]Jer. 9:17
17 [a]Ex. 12:12
18 [a]Is. 5:19; Jer. 17:15 [b]Joel 2:2
19 [a]Jer. 48:44
21 [a]Is. 1:11-16 [b]Lev. 26:31 [1]Or, *smell your holy days*
22 [a]Is. 66:3; Mic. 6:6,7 [1]Or, *thank offerings*
24 [a]Hos. 6:6; Mic. 6:8 [1]Heb. *roll*
25 [a]Deut. 32:17; Josh. 24:14; Is. 43:23
26 [a]1 Ki. 11:33 [1]Or, *Siccuth your king*
27 [a]2 Ki. 17:6 [b]ch. 4:13
6:1 [a]Luke 6:24 [b]Ex. 19:5 [1]Or, *are secure* [2]Or, *firstfruits*
2 [a]Jer. 2:10 [b]Is. 10:9 [c]2 Ki. 18:34 [d]Nah. 3:8
3 [a]Ezek. 12:27 [b]ch. 5:18 [c]ch. 5:12 [d]Ps. 94:20 [1]Or, *habitation*
4 [1]Or, *abound with superfluities*
5 [a]Is. 5:12 [b]1 Chr. 23:5 [1]Or, *quaver*
6 [a]Gen. 37:25 [1]Or, *in bowls of wine* [2]Heb. *breach*
8 [a]Jer. 51:14 [b]Ps. 47:4; Ezek. 24:21

H *Am 4:12* ◀▶ *Am 8:7*

his palaces: therefore will I deliver up the city with all [l]that is therein.

Oppression and desolation

9 And it shall come to pass, if there remain ten men in one house, that they shall die.

10 And a man's uncle shall take him up, and he that burneth him, to bring out the bones out of the house, and shall say unto him that *is* by the sides of the house, *Is there* yet *any* with thee? and he shall say, No. Then shall he say, [a]Hold thy tongue: [b]for [l]we may not make mention of the name of the LORD.

11 For, behold, [a]the LORD commandeth, [b]and he will smite the great house with [l]breaches, and the little house with clefts.

C 12 ¶ Shall horses run upon the rock?
S will *one* plow *there* with oxen? for [a]ye
have turned judgment into gall, and the
fruit of righteousness into hemlock:

13 Ye which rejoice in a thing of nought, which say, Have we not taken to us horns by our own strength?

14 But, behold, [a]I will raise up against you a nation, O house of Israel, saith the LORD the God of hosts; and they shall afflict you from the [b]entering in of Hemath unto the [l]river of the wilderness.

Two plagues

7 THUS HATH the Lord GOD shown unto me; and, behold, he formed [l]grasshoppers in the beginning of the shooting up of the latter growth; and, lo, *it was* the latter growth after the king's mowings.

2 And it came to pass, *that* when they had made an end of eating the grass of the land, then I said, O Lord GOD, forgive, I beseech thee: [a]by[l] whom shall Jacob arise? for he *is* small.

3 [a]The LORD repented for this: It shall not be, saith the LORD.

4 ¶ Thus hath the Lord GOD shown unto me: and, behold, the Lord GOD called to contend by fire, and it devoured the great deep, and did eat up a part.

5 Then said I, O Lord GOD, cease, I beseech thee: [a]by whom shall Jacob arise? for he *is* small.

6 The LORD repented for this: This also shall not be, saith the Lord GOD.

The vision of the plumbline

7 ¶ Thus he showed me: and, behold, the Lord stood upon a wall *made* by a plumbline, with a plumbline in his hand.

8 And the LORD said unto me, Amos, what seest thou? And I said, A plumbline. Then said the Lord, Behold, [a]I will set a plumbline in the midst of my people Israel: [b]I will not again pass by them any more:

9 [a]And the high places of Isaac shall R
be desolate, and the sanctuaries of Israel
shall be laid waste; and [b]I will rise against
the house of Jeroboam with the sword.

10 ¶ Then Amaziah [a]the priest of Beth-el sent to [b]Jeroboam king of Israel, saying, Amos hath conspired against thee in the midst of the house of Israel: the land is not able to bear all his words.

11 For thus Amos saith, Jeroboam shall die by the sword, and Israel shall surely be led away captive out of their own land.

12 Also Amaziah said unto Amos, O thou seer, go, flee thee away into the land of Judah, and there eat bread, and prophesy there:

13 But [a]prophesy not again any more at Beth-el: [b]for it *is* the king's [l]chapel, and it *is* the [2]king's court.

14 ¶ Then answered Amos, and said to Amaziah, I *was* no prophet, neither *was* I [a]a prophet's son; [b]but I *was* an herdman, and a gatherer of [l]sycamore fruit:

15 And the LORD took me [l]as I followed the flock, and the LORD said unto me, Go, prophesy unto my people Israel.

16 ¶ Now therefore hear thou the R
word of the LORD: Thou sayest, Prophesy
not against Israel, and [a]drop not *thy word*
against the house of Isaac.

17 [a]Therefore thus saith the LORD; [b]Thy wife shall be an harlot in the city, and thy sons and thy daughters shall fall by the sword, and thy land shall be di-

8 [l]Heb. *the fulness thereof*
10 [a]ch. 5:13 [b]ch. 8:3 [l]Or, *they will not, or, have not*
11 [a]Is. 55:11 [b]ch. 3:15 [l]Or, *droppings*
12 [a]Hos. 10:4
14 [a]Jer. 5:15 [b]1 Ki. 8:65 [l]Or, *valley*
7:1 [l]Or, *green worms*
2 [a]Is. 51:19 [l]Or, *who of (or, for) Jacob shall stand?*
3 [a]Deut. 32:36; Jonah 3:10; Jas. 5:16
5 [a]ver. 2,3
8 [a]See 2 Ki. 21:13; Is. 28:17; Lam. 2:8 [b]Mic. 7:18
9 [a]Beer-sheba Gen. 26:23 & 46:1; ch. 5:5 & 8:14 [b]Fulfilled 2 Ki. 15:10
10 [a]1 Ki. 12:32 [b]2 Ki. 14:23
13 [a]ch. 2:12 [b]1 Ki. 12:32 [l]Or, *sanctuary* [2]Heb. *house of the kingdom*
14 [a]1 Ki. 20:35; 2 Ki. 2:5 [b]Zech. 13:5 [l]Or, *wild figs*
15 [l]Heb. *from behind*
16 [a]Ezek. 21:2; Mic. 2:6
17 [a]Jer. 28:12 & 29:21,32 [b]Is. 13:16; Lam. 5:11; Hos. 4:13; Zech. 14:2

C *Am 5:7* ◀▶ *Hab 2:4*
S *Am 3:3* ◀▶ *Ob 17*

R *Am 2:1–6* ◀▶ *Am 7:16–17*
R *Am 7:9* ◀▶ *Am 8:2*

7:9 Amos prophesied that the centers of religious and self-righteous pride would be destroyed. Note that while Amos's words in the previous chapters were spoken to Israel's leadership as a whole, this verse is directed to one man, King Jeroboam.

vided by line; and thou shalt die in a polluted land: and Israel shall surely go into captivity forth of his land.

The vision of Israel's ruin

8 THUS HATH the Lord GOD shown unto me: and behold a basket of summer fruit.

R 2 And he said, Amos, what seest thou? And I said, A basket of summer fruit. Then said the LORD unto me, [a]The end is come upon my people of Israel; [b]I will not again pass by them any more.

3 And [a]the songs of the temple [1]shall be howlings in that day, saith the Lord GOD: *there shall be* many dead bodies in every place; [b]they shall cast *them* forth [2]with silence.

4 ¶ Hear this, O ye that [a]swallow up the needy, even to make the poor of the land to fail,

5 Saying, When will the [1]new moon be gone, that we may sell corn? and [a]the sabbath, that we may [2]set forth wheat, [b]making the ephah small, and the shekel great, and [3]falsifying the balances by deceit?

6 That we may buy the poor for [a]silver, and the needy for a pair of shoes; *yea,* and sell the refuse of the wheat?

E H 7 The LORD hath sworn by [a]the excellency of Jacob, Surely [b]I will never forget any of their works.

8 [a]Shall not the land tremble for this, and every one mourn that dwelleth therein? and it shall rise up wholly as a flood; and it shall be cast out and drowned, [b]as *by* the flood of Egypt.

9 And it shall come to pass in that day, saith the Lord GOD, [a]that I will cause the sun to go down at noon, and I will darken the earth in the clear day:

10 And I will turn your feasts into mourning, and all your songs into lamentation; [a]and I will bring up sackcloth upon all loins, and baldness upon every head; [b]and I will make it as the mourning of an only *son,* and the end thereof as a bitter day.

11 ¶ Behold, the days come, saith the Lord GOD, that I will send a famine in the land, not a famine of bread, nor a thirst for water, but [a]of hearing the words of the LORD:

12 And they shall wander from sea to sea, and from the north even to the east, they shall run to and fro to seek the word of the LORD, and shall not find *it.*

13 In that day shall the fair virgins and young men faint for thirst.

14 They that [a]swear by [b]the sin of Samaria, and say, Thy god, O Dan, liveth; and, The [1]manner of [c]Beer-sheba liveth; even they shall fall, and never rise up again.

The destruction of the sanctuary

9 I SAW the Lord standing upon the altar: and he said, Smite the [1]lintel of the door, that the posts may shake: and [a]cut[2] them in the head, all of them; and I will slay the last of them with the sword: [b]he that fleeth of them shall not flee away, and he that escapeth of them shall not be delivered. H

2 [a]Though they dig into hell, thence shall mine hand take them; [b]though they climb up to heaven, thence will I bring them down:

3 And though they hide themselves in the top of Carmel, I will search and take them out thence; and though they be hid from my sight in the bottom of the sea, thence will I command the serpent, and he shall bite them:

4 And though they go into captivity before their enemies, [a]thence will I command the sword, and it shall slay them: and [b]I will set mine eyes upon them for evil, and not for good.

5 And the Lord GOD of hosts *is* he that toucheth the land, and it shall [a]melt, [b]and all that dwell therein shall mourn: and it shall rise up wholly like a flood; R

R *Am 7:16–17 ◀ ▶ Am 9:5*
E *Hos 7:2 ◀ ▶ Zec 4:10*
H *Am 5:16–20 ◀ ▶ Am 9:1–4*

H *Am 8:7 ◀ ▶ Ob 15*
R *Am 8:2 ◀ ▶ Am 9:8–10*

8:2 [a]Ezek. 7:2 [b]ch. 7:8
3 [a]ch. 5:23 [b]ch. 6:9,10 [1]Heb. *shall howl* [2]Heb. *be silent*
4 [a]Ps. 14:4; Prov. 30:14
5 [a]Neh. 13:15 [b]Mic. 6:10 [1]Or, *month* [2]Heb. *open* [3]Heb. *perverting the balances of deceit*
6 [a]ch. 2:6
7 [a]ch. 6:8 [b]Hos. 8:13
8 [a]Hos. 4:3 [b]ch. 9:5
9 [a]Job 5:14; Is. 13:10 & 59:9,10; Jer. 15:9; Mic. 3:6
10 [a]Is. 15:2,3; Jer. 48:37; Ezek. 27:31 [b]Jer. 6:26; Zech. 12:10
11 [a]1 Sam. 3:1; Ps. 74:9; Ezek. 7:26
14 [a]Hos. 4:15 [b]Deut. 9:21 [c]ch. 5:5 [1]Heb. *way*
9:1 [a]Ps. 68:21; Hab. 3:13 [b]ch. 2:14 [1]Or, *chapiter,* or, *knob* [2]Or, *wound them*
2 [a]Ps. 139:8 [b]Jer. 51:53
4 [a]Lev. 26:33 [b]Lev. 17:10
5 [a]Mic. 1:4 [b]ch. 8:8

8:2 Ripe fruit must be eaten quickly; its shelf life is short. This metaphor indicated that Israel's judgment would come soon.

9:5 Note the similarity between this verse and 8:8. Because of heavy seasonal rains, the Nile River would rise as much as 20 feet over its banks, flooding the surrounding valley and depositing large amounts of topsoil on the land. Amos notes that God controls even these natural events.

and shall be drowned, as *by* the flood of
Egypt.
6 *It is* he that buildeth his [a]stories [1,2] in
the heaven, and hath founded his [3]troop
in the earth; he that [b]calleth for the waters of the sea, and poureth them out
upon the face of the earth: [c]The LORD *is*
his name.
7 *Are* ye not as children of the Ethiopians unto me, O children of Israel? saith
the LORD. Have not I brought up Israel out
of the land of Egypt? and the [a]Philistines
from [b]Caphtor, and the Syrians from
[c]Kir?
R 8 Behold, [a]the eyes of the Lord GOD
are upon the sinful kingdom, and I [b]will
destroy it from off the face of the earth;
saving that I will not utterly destroy the
house of Jacob, saith the LORD.
9 For, lo, I will command, and I will
[1]sift the house of Israel among all nations, like as *corn* is sifted in a sieve, yet
shall not the least [2]grain fall upon the
earth.
10 All the sinners of my people shall
die by the sword, [a]which say, The evil
shall not overtake nor prevent us.

R *Am 9:5* ◀ ▶ *Mic 1:6*

6 [a]Ps. 104:3 [b]ch. 5:8 [c]ch. 4:13 [1]Or, *spheres* [2]Heb. *ascensions* [3]Or, *bundle*

7 [a]Jer. 47:4 [b]Deut. 2:23; Jer. 47:4 [c]ch. 1:5

8 [a]ver. 4 [b]Jer. 30:11; Obad. 16,17

9 [1]Heb. *cause to move* [2]Heb. *stone*

10 [a]ch. 6:3

11 [a]Acts 15:16 [1]Heb. *hedge*, or, *wall*

12 [a]Obad. 19 [b]Num. 24:18 [1]Heb. *upon whom my name is called*

13 [a]Lev. 26:5 [b]Joel 3:18 [1]Heb. *draweth forth* [2]Or, *new wine*

14 [a]Jer. 30:3 [b]Is. 61:4

15 [a]Ezek. 34:28

Israel's fortunes to be restored

11 ¶ [a]In that day will I raise up the I
tabernacle of David that is fallen, and
[1]close up the breaches thereof; and I will
raise up his ruins, and I will build it as in
the days of old:
12 [a]That they may possess the remnant of [b]Edom, and of all the heathen,
[1]which are called by my name, saith the
LORD that doeth this.
13 Behold, [a]the days come, saith the
LORD, that the plowman shall overtake the
reaper, and the treader of grapes him that
[1]soweth seed; [b]and the mountains shall
drop [2]sweet wine, and all the hills shall
melt.
14 [a]And I will bring again the captivity
of my people of Israel, and [b]they shall
build the waste cities, and inhabit *them;*
and they shall plant vineyards, and drink
the wine thereof; they shall also make
gardens, and eat the fruit of them.
15 And I will plant them upon their
land, and [a]they shall no more be pulled
up out of their land which I have given
them, saith the LORD thy God.

I *Joel 3:20–21* ◀ ▶ *Ob 17*

9:8–10 Amos prophesied that God would judge Israel. Sinners would die for their persistent rebellion, but God would graciously spare a remnant of the faithful.

9:11 This Messianic prophecy echoes the hope that underlies Amos's words—God will bring blessing after judgment and will ultimately restore Israel. Note that the reference to the restoration of David's "tabernacle" refers to the reinstatement of David's rule through Jesus the Messiah (see Ac 15:15–17).

9:12–15 After all of the promises of destruction and death, Amos prophesied the return of the Jewish exiles to the promised land in the last days. Note the promised prosperity and fertility of the land so that harvesting and planting will run simultaneously. The Messiah will reign over this land and even over Israel's former enemies, and Israel will never again be destroyed.

Obadiah

Author: Obadiah

Theme: God's judgment on proud Edom

Date of Writing: Disputed; possibly c. 853–841 B.C. or 605–586 B.C.

Outline of Obadiah

I. Edom's Doom (1–9)
II. Edom's Attitude Toward Jerusalem (10–14)
III. Edom in the Day of the Lord (15–21)

ALTHOUGH THE NAME "Obadiah" is frequently found in the OT and means "servant (or worshiper) of the LORD," nothing specific is known about this prophet beyond his identification with this short book. Even the date of this composition is obscure. Verses 11–14 contain the only datable pieces in the book and may apply to two different times in Israel's history. If these verses pertain to the invasion of Jerusalem by the Philistines during the reign of Jehoram (see 2Ki 8:20–22; 2Ch 21:8–20), the prophet Obadiah would have prophesied alongside Elisha (853–841 B.C.). However, if these verses pertain to the Babylonian destruction of Jerusalem, Obadiah would have been a contemporary of Jeremiah (605–586 B.C.). Since there are some parallels between the book of Obadiah and Jer 49:7–22 this exilic date seems more likely.

The book of Obadiah is the shortest book in the whole OT. Covering the period of judgment upon the nation of Judah, Obadiah predicts the total annihilation of the kingdom of Edom. The Edomites, who were the descendants of Esau, proudly held the mountain strongholds of Mt. Seir, the area to the south of the Dead Sea, and maliciously mocked the people of Judah when they were invaded by their enemies. The Edomites themselves participated in at least four plunderings of Jerusalem. Yet God's promised destruction of Edom was fulfilled. Following the destruction of Jerusalem in A.D. 70, the Edomites have never been heard of again.

Edom's destruction

P 1 THE VISION of Obadiah. Thus saith the Lord GOD [a]concerning Edom; We [b]have heard a rumour from the LORD, and an ambassador is sent among the heathen, Arise ye, and let us rise up against her in battle.

2 Behold, I have made thee small among the heathen: thou art greatly despised.

M 3 ¶ The pride of thine heart hath deceived thee, thou that dwellest in the clefts of the rock, whose habitation *is* high; [a]that saith in his heart, Who shall bring me down to the ground?

4 [a]Though thou exalt *thyself* as the eagle, and though thou [b]set thy nest among the stars, thence will I bring thee down, saith the LORD.

5 If [a]thieves came to thee, if robbers by night, (how art thou cut off!) would they not have stolen till they had enough? if the grapegatherers came to thee, [b]would they not leave [1]*some* grapes?

6 How are *the things* of Esau searched out! *how* are his hidden things sought up!

7 All the men of thy confederacy have brought thee *even* to the border: [a]the[1] men that were at peace with thee have deceived thee, *and* prevailed against thee; [2]*they that eat* thy bread have laid a wound under thee: [b]*there is* none understanding [3]in him.

8 [a]Shall I not in that day, saith the LORD, even destroy the wise *men* out of Edom, and understanding out of the mount of Esau?

9 And thy [a]mighty *men*, O [b]Teman, shall be dismayed, to the end that every one of the mount of Esau may be cut off by slaughter.

10 ¶ For *thy* [a]violence against thy brother Jacob shame shall cover thee, and [b]thou shalt be cut off for ever.

11 In the day that thou stoodest on the other side, in the day that the strangers [1]carried away captive his forces, and foreigners entered into his gates, and [a]cast lots upon Jerusalem, even thou *wast* as one of them.

12 But [1]thou shouldest not have [a]looked on the day of thy brother in the day that he became a stranger; neither shouldest thou have [b]rejoiced over the children of Judah in the day of their destruction; neither shouldest thou have [2]spoken proudly in the day of distress.

13 Thou shouldest not have entered into the gate of my people in the day of their calamity; yea, thou shouldest not have looked on their affliction in the day of their calamity, nor have laid *hands* on their [1]substance in the day of their calamity;

14 Neither shouldest thou have stood in the crossway, to cut off those of his that did escape; neither shouldest thou have [1]delivered up those of his that did remain in the day of distress.

Judgment upon the nations

15 [a]For the day of the LORD *is* near P
upon all the heathen: [b]as thou hast done, H
it shall be done unto thee: thy reward shall return upon thine own head.

16 [a]For as ye have drunk upon my holy mountain, *so* shall all the heathen drink continually, yea, they shall drink, and they shall [1]swallow down, and they shall be as though they had not been.

Deliverance in Zion

17 ¶ But upon mount Zion [a]shall be I
[1]deliverance, and [2]there shall be holi- K
ness; and the house of Jacob shall possess S
their possessions.

1:1 [a]Is. 21:11; Ezek. 25:12; Joel 3:19; Mal. 1:3 [b]Jer. 49:14
3 [a]Is. 14:13-15; Rev. 18:7
4 [a]Job 20:6 [b]Hab. 2:9
5 [a]Jer. 49:9 [b]Deut. 24:21 [1]Or, *gleanings?*
7 [a]Jer. 38:22 [b]Is. 19:11 [1]Heb. *the men of thy peace* [2]Heb. the men *of thy bread* [3]Or, *of it*
8 [a]Job 5:12; Is. 29:14
9 [a]Ps. 76:5 [b]Jer. 49:7
10 [a]Gen. 27:41 [b]Ezek. 35:9
11 [a]Nah. 3:10 [1]Or, *carried away his substance*
12 [a]Mic. 4:11 [b]Prov. 17:5 [1]Or, *do not behold* [2]Heb. *magnified thy mouth*
13 [1]Or, *forces*
14 [1]Or, *shut up;* see Ps. 31:8
15 [a]Ezek. 30:3 [b]Hab. 2:8
16 [a]Joel 3:17 [1]Or, *sup up*
17 [a]Amos 9:8 [1]Or, *they that escape* [2]Or, *it shall be holy*

P *Am 1:2–15* ◀ ▶ *Ob 15–16*
M *Joel 2:13* ◀ ▶ *Jnh 3:5–10*

P *Ob 1–10* ◀ ▶ *Mic 1:3–7*
H *Am 9:1–4* ◀ ▶ *Mic 5:15*
I *Am 9:11–15* ◀ ▶ *Mic 2:12*
K *Am 5:6* ◀ ▶ *Jnh 2:9*
S *Am 6:12* ◀ ▶ *Jnh 2:8*

1–4 Despite the invincibility of Edom's mountain fortresses atop the cliffs, God declared that he would cut Edom down to size and destroy it. This prophecy was fulfilled when Petra was destroyed in A.D. 629–32 by the Moslems and never inhabited again.
10 Despite the natural economic and defensive advantages of the ancient nation of Edom, this prophecy has been fulfilled in totality. The powerful, rich kingdom of Edom has totally disappeared from the scene of human history, exactly as Obadiah divinely prophesied.
17 Obadiah prophesied God's deliverance and blessing of his chosen people and his judgment on their enemies. The Messiah's kingdom is in view when Obadiah declares that Jerusalem will no longer be occupied by her enemies; Mount Zion would once again be holy to the Lord in the last days of history (see Rev 11:15).

18 And the house of Jacob [a]shall be a
fire, and the house of Joseph a flame, and
the house of Esau for stubble, and they
shall kindle in them, and devour them;
and there shall not be *any* remaining of
the house of Esau; for the LORD hath spoken *it.*
19 And *they of* the south shall possess
the mount of Esau; [a]and *they of* the plain
the Philistines: and they shall possess the
fields of Ephraim, and the fields of Samaria: and Benjamin *shall possess*
Gilead.
20 And the captivity of this host of the
children of Israel *shall possess* that of the
Canaanites, *even* [a]unto Zarephath; and
the captivity of Jerusalem, [/]which *is* in
Sepharad, [b]shall possess the cities of the
south.
21 And [a]saviours shall come up on
mount Zion to judge the mount of Esau;
and the [b]kingdom shall be the LORD'S.

18 [a]Zech. 12:6
19 [a]Zeph. 2:7
20 [a]1 Ki. 17:9 [b]Jer. 32:44 [/]Or, shall possess *that which is in Sepharad*
21 [a]Jas. 5:20 [b]Rev. 11:15

Jonah

Author: Jonah

Theme: God's love and forgiveness is for everyone

Date of Writing: c. 785–750 B.C.

Outline of Jonah

I. Jonah Runs Away From God's Commission (1:1–17)
II. Jonah's Repentance and Deliverance (2:1–10)
III. Jonah's Mission to Nineveh (3:1–10)
IV. Jonah's Disappointment in God's Mercy (4:1–11)

The book of Jonah is named after its main character, a prophet and the son of Amittai. This Jonah is probably the same prophet mentioned in 2Ki 14:25, thus dating Jonah's mission to Nineveh during the latter part of King Jeroboam II's reign. Since the author is not identified in the text, others may have written this book a century or two after Jonah's trip to Nineveh. While some scholars have rejected the literal record found in Jonah, most conservative scholars acknowledge the historical truth found in its pages. Jesus also acknowledged the historical truth of Jonah's book in several direct references (see Mt 12:39–41; 16:4; Lk 11:29–32).

Jonah was given a divine commission to warn the people of Nineveh, the capital city of Assyria, of their coming judgment. Jonah did not want God to show mercy to Israel's most feared and hated enemy even if they repented, so he ran in the other direction. Through a series of supernatural events, Jonah finally relented, went to Nineveh and preached to the city. When the people of Nineveh repented, God extended his mercy to them and delayed his promised judgment against them for more than a century. As successive generations of Ninevites fell back into gross wickedness, God's judgment was finally enacted and Nineveh was destroyed.

Though only five verses of Jonah contain predictive matter, this prophetic narrative conveys a strong theme of God's forgiveness for all who repent of their sins. The prophetic sign of the three days that Jonah spent in the big fish corresponds to the three days Jesus Christ spent in the grave. Note also that while Jonah was only one witness to the Gentiles, during the seven-year tribulation Israel will win millions to Christ in the closing years leading to Armageddon.

Jonah flees to Tarshish

1 NOW THE word of the LORD came unto [1]Jonah the son of Amittai, saying,

2 Arise, go to Nineveh, that [a]great city, and cry against it; for [b]their wickedness is come up before me.

3 But Jonah rose up to flee unto Tarshish from the presence of the LORD, and went down to [a]Joppa; and he found a ship going to Tarshish: so he paid the fare thereof, and went down into it, to go with them unto Tarshish [b]from the presence of the LORD.

4 ¶ But [a]the LORD [1]sent out a great wind into the sea, and there was a mighty tempest in the sea, so that the ship was [2]like to be broken.

5 Then the mariners were afraid, and cried every man unto his god, and cast forth the wares that *were* in the ship into the sea, to lighten *it* of them. But Jonah was gone down [a]into the sides of the ship; and he lay, and was fast asleep.

6 So the shipmaster came to him, and said unto him, What meanest thou, O sleeper? arise, [a]call upon thy God, [b]if so be that God will think upon us, that we perish not.

7 And they said every one to his fellow, Come, and let us [a]cast lots, that we may know for whose cause this evil *is* upon us. So they cast lots, and the lot fell upon Jonah.

8 Then said they unto him, [a]Tell us, we pray thee, for whose cause this evil *is* upon us; What *is* thine occupation? and whence comest thou? what *is* thy country? and of what people *art* thou?

9 And he said unto them, I *am* an Hebrew; and I fear [1]the LORD, the God of heaven, [a]which hath made the sea and the dry *land*.

10 Then were the men [1]exceedingly afraid, and said unto him, Why hast thou done this? For the men knew that he fled from the presence of the LORD, because he had told them.

11 ¶ Then said they unto him, What shall we do unto thee, that the sea [1]may be calm unto us? for the sea [2,3]wrought, and was tempestuous.

12 And he said unto them, [a]Take me up, and cast me forth into the sea; so shall the sea be calm unto you: for I know that for my sake this great tempest *is* upon you.

13 Nevertheless the men [1]rowed hard to bring *it* to the land; [a]but they could not: for the sea wrought, and was tempestuous against them.

14 Wherefore they cried unto the LORD, and said, We beseech thee, O LORD, we beseech thee, let us not perish for this man's life, and [a]lay not upon us innocent blood: for thou, O LORD, [b]hast done as it pleased thee.

15 So they took up Jonah, and cast him forth into the sea: [a]and the sea [1]ceased from her raging.

16 Then the men [a]feared the LORD exceedingly, and [1]offered a sacrifice unto the LORD, and made vows.

17 ¶ Now the LORD had prepared a great fish to swallow up Jonah. And [a]Jonah was in the [1]belly of the fish three days and three nights. S

Prayer and deliverance of Jonah

2 THEN JONAH prayed unto the LORD his God out of the fish's belly,

2 And said, I [a]cried [1]by reason of mine affliction unto the LORD, [b]and he heard me; out of the belly of [c]hell[2] cried I, *and* thou heardest my voice.

3 [a]For thou hadst cast me into the deep, in the [1]midst of the seas; and the

S *Da 6:22–23* ◀ ▶ *Jnh 2:10*

1 [1]Called *Jonas* in Mat. 12:39
2 [a]Gen. 10:11 [b]Gen. 18:20
3 [a]Josh. 19:46 [b]Gen. 4:16
4 [a]Ps. 107:25 [1]Heb. *cast forth* [2]Heb. *thought to be broken*
5 [a]1 Sam. 24:3
6 [a]Ps. 107:28 [b]Joel 2:14
7 [a]Josh. 7:14; 1 Sam. 14:41
8 [a]Josh. 7:19
9 [a]Ps. 146:6; Acts 17:24 [1]Or, *JEHOVAH*
10 [1]Heb. *with great fear*
11 [1]Heb. *may be silent from us* [2]Or, *grew more and more tempestuous* [3]Heb. *went*
12 [a]John 11:50
13 [a]Prov. 21:30 [1]Heb. *digged*
14 [a]Deut. 21:8 [b]Ps. 115:3
15 [a]Ps. 89:9; Luke 8:24 [1]Heb. *stood*
16 [a]Mark 4:41; Acts 5:11 [1]Heb. *sacrificed a sacrifice unto the LORD, and vowed vows*
17 [a]Mat. 12:40; Luke 11:30 [1]Heb. *bowels*
2:2 [a]Ps. 120:1; Lam. 3:55 [b]Ps. 65:2 [c]Is. 14:9 [1]Or, *out of mine affliction* [2]Or, *the grave*
3 [a]Ps. 88:6 [1]Heb. *heart*

1:1–3 Despite God's clear command, Jonah did not want to preach a message of repentance to the hated city of Nineveh, deciding instead to run away.
1:12 Jonah told the sailors that the storm would cease if they threw him into the sea. As soon as Jonah was thrown overboard, the sea became calm (see 1:15).
1:17 God sovereignly provided a "great fish" to swallow Jonah so that he would survive and fulfill his divine mission to preach to the Ninevites. This verse notes the duration of Jonah's ordeal as "three days and three nights." While westerners calculate a day based on a full 24-hour period, ancient middle easterners calculated a day as any portion of that day. Thus the phrase "three days and three nights" probably meant any portion of the first day, plus a full second day, plus any portion of the third day for a total time of as little as 26 hours. In a similar manner this inclusive method of reckoning time helps reconcile the 36–40 hours from Christ's burial on Friday afternoon until his supernatural resurrection on Sunday morning as "three days" (see Mt 12:40).

The Prophets in Palestine

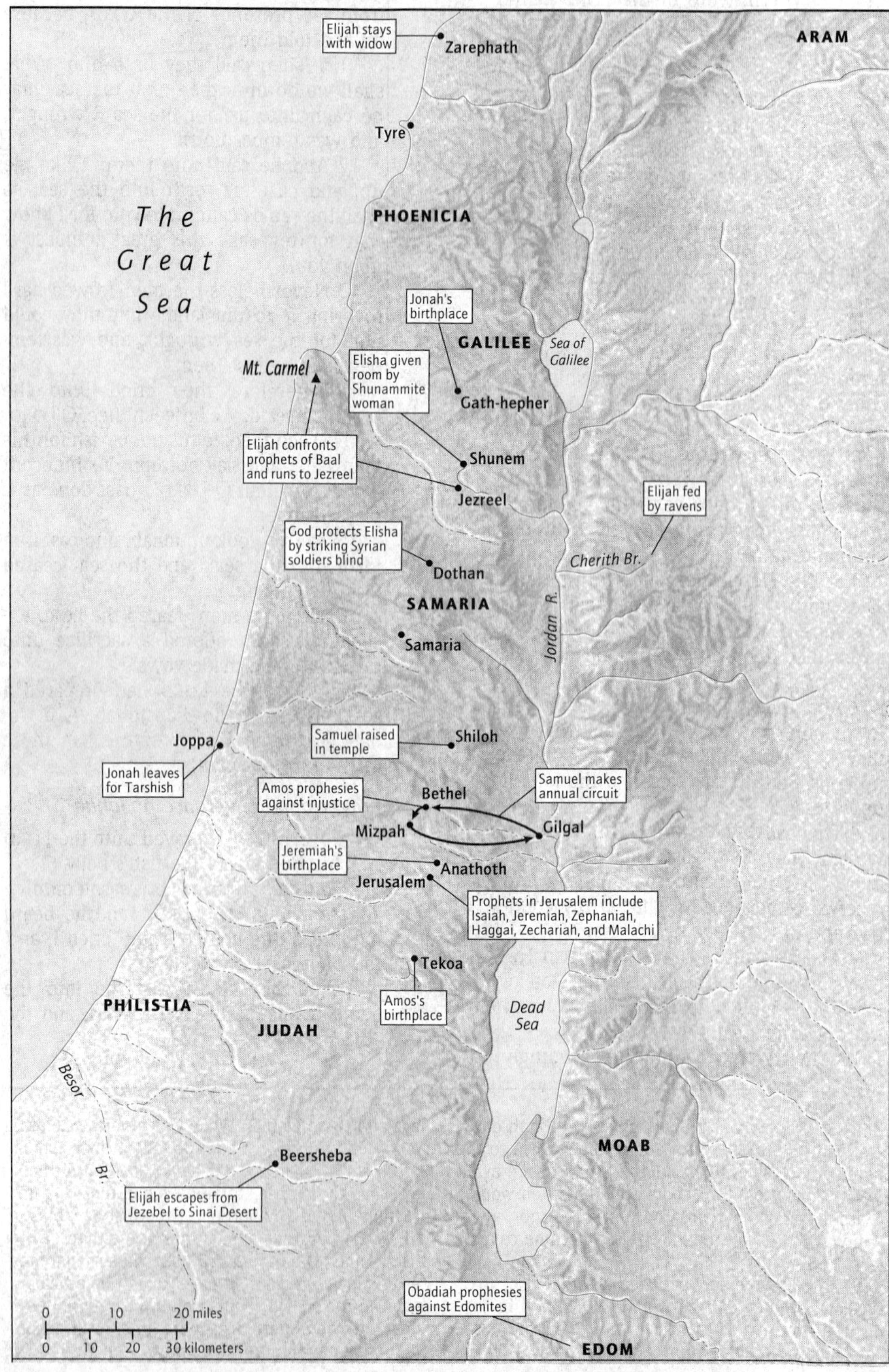
Elijah stays with widow
Zarephath
ARAM
Tyre
The Great Sea
PHOENICIA
Jonah's birthplace
GALILEE
Sea of Galilee
Mt. Carmel
Elisha given room by Shunammite woman
Gath-hepher
Elijah confronts prophets of Baal and runs to Jezreel
Shunem
Jezreel
Elijah fed by ravens
God protects Elisha by striking Syrian soldiers blind
Cherith Br.
Dothan
SAMARIA
Samaria
Jordan R.
Joppa
Samuel raised in temple
Shiloh
Jonah leaves for Tarshish
Amos prophesies against injustice
Bethel
Samuel makes annual circuit
Mizpah
Gilgal
Jeremiah's birthplace
Anathoth
Jerusalem
Prophets in Jerusalem include Isaiah, Jeremiah, Zephaniah, Haggai, Zechariah, and Malachi
Tekoa
Amos's birthplace
Dead Sea
PHILISTIA
JUDAH
Besor Br.
MOAB
Beersheba
Elijah escapes from Jezebel to Sinai Desert
Obadiah prophesies against Edomites
0 10 20 miles
0 10 20 30 kilometers
EDOM

floods compassed me about: [b]all thy billows and thy waves passed over me.
L 4 [a]Then I said, I am cast out of thy
sight; yet I will look again [b]toward thy
holy temple.
5 The [a]waters compassed me about,
even to the soul: the depth closed me
round about, the weeds were wrapped
about my head.
6 I went down to the [1]bottoms of the
mountains; the earth with her bars *was*
about me for ever: yet hast thou brought
up my life [a]from [2]corruption, O LORD my
God.
7 When my soul fainted within me I
remembered the LORD: [a]and my prayer
came in unto thee, into thine holy
temple.
S 8 They that observe [a]lying vanities forsake their own mercy.
K 9 But I will [a]sacrifice unto thee with
O the voice of thanksgiving; I will pay *that*
that I have vowed. [b]Salvation *is* of the
LORD.
S 10 ¶ And the LORD spake unto the fish,
and it vomited out Jonah upon the dry
land.

Jonah preaches at Nineveh

3 AND THE word of the LORD came
unto Jonah the second time, saying,
2 Arise, go unto Nineveh, that great
city, and preach unto it the preaching
that I bid thee.
3 So Jonah arose, and went unto Nineveh, according to the word of the LORD.
Now Nineveh was an exceeding great
city of three days' journey.
4 And Jonah began to enter into the
city a day's journey, and [a]he cried, and
said, Yet forty days, and Nineveh shall be
overthrown.

5 ¶ So the people of Nineveh [a]believed M
God, and proclaimed a fast, and put on R
sackcloth, from the greatest of them even
to the least of them.
6 For word came unto the king of Nineveh, and he arose from his throne, and
he laid his robe from him, and covered
him with sackcloth, [a]and sat in ashes.
7 [a]And he caused *it* to be proclaimed
and [1]published through Nineveh by the
decree of the king and his [2]nobles, saying, Let neither man nor beast, herd nor
flock, taste any thing: let them not feed,
nor drink water:
8 But let man and beast be covered
with sackcloth, and cry mightily unto
God: yea, [a]let them turn every one from
his evil way, and from [b]the violence that
is in their hands.
9 [a]Who can tell *if* God will turn and
repent, and turn away from his fierce anger, that we perish not?

Sparing of the city angers Jonah

10 ¶ [a]And God saw their works, that L
they turned from their evil way; and God
repented of the evil, that he had said that
he would do unto them; and he did *it* not.
4 BUT IT displeased Jonah exceedingly, and he was very angry.
2 And he prayed unto the LORD, and L
said, I pray thee, O LORD, *was* not this my
saying, when I was yet in my country?
Therefore I [a]fled before unto Tarshish:
for I knew that thou *art* a [b]gracious God,
and merciful, slow to anger, and of great
kindness, and repentest thee of the evil.
3 [a]Therefore now, O LORD, take, I beseech thee, my life from me; for [b]*it is*
better for me to die than to live.
4 ¶ Then said the LORD, [1]Doest thou
well to be angry?
5 So Jonah went out of the city, and sat
on the east side of the city, and there

3 [b]Ps. 42:7
4 [a]Ps. 31:22 [b]1 Ki. 8:38
5 [a]Ps. 69:1; Lam. 3:54
6 [a]Ps. 16:10 [1]Heb. *cuttings off* [2]Or, *the pit*
7 [a]Ps. 18:6
8 [a]2 Ki. 17:15; Jer. 10:8
9 [a]Ps. 50:14; Hos. 14:2 [b]Ps. 3:8
3:4 [a]Deut. 18:22
5 [a]Mat. 12:41; Luke 11:32
6 [a]Job 2:8
7 [a]2 Chr. 20:3; Joel 2:15 [1]Heb. *said* [2]Heb. *great men*
8 [a]Is. 58:6 [b]Is. 59:6
9 [a]2 Sam. 12:22; Joel 2:14
10 [a]Jer. 18:8; Amos 7:3,6
4:2 [a]ch. 1:3 [b]Ex. 34:6; Ps. 86:5; Joel 2:13
3 [a]1 Ki. 19:4 [b]ver. 8
4 [1]Or, *Art thou greatly angry?*

L *Da 2:28–32* ◀ ▶ *Mt 10:17–23*
S *Ob 17* ◀ ▶ *Mic 6:7–8*
K *Ob 17* ◀ ▶ *Zec 13:1*
O *Hos 13:4* ◀ ▶ *Mt 7:26–27*
S *Jnh 1:17* ◀ ▶ *Na 1:7*

M *Ob 3–4* ◀ ▶ *Hab 2:4*
R *Joel 2:12–13* ◀ ▶ *Mt 3:2*
L *Joel 2:13* ◀ ▶ *Jnh 4:2*
L *Jnh 3:10* ◀ ▶ *Mic 6:6–8*

3:4–10 Jonah arrived in Nineveh and obediently proclaimed God's coming judgment. However, the people repented and God delayed his judgment in response to their unprecedented repentance. In fact, God's judgment was delayed for over a century. When the next generation of Assyrians fell back into wickedness, God's judgment was finally carried out.

3:9 The king of Assyria hoped that God would forgive. Although "the wages of sin is death" (Ro 6:23), the unchanging promise of God is that "if we confess our sins, he is faithful and just to forgive us our sins, and to cleanse us from all unrighteousness" (1Jn 1:9).

made him a booth, and sat under it in the
shadow, till he might see what would become of the city.

The unlimited mercy of God

6 And the LORD God prepared a
[1,2]gourd, and made *it* to come up over
Jonah, that it might be a shadow over his
head, to deliver him from his grief. So
Jonah [3]was exceeding glad of the gourd.
7 But God prepared a worm when the
morning rose the next day, and it smote
the gourd that it withered.
8 And it came to pass, when the sun
did arise, that God prepared a [1]vehement
east wind; and the sun beat upon the
head of Jonah, that he fainted, and
wished in himself to die, and said, [a]*It is*
better for me to die than to live.
9 And God said to Jonah, [1]Doest thou
well to be angry for the gourd? And he
said, [2]I do well to be angry, *even* unto
death.
10 Then said the LORD, Thou hast [1]had
pity on the gourd, for the which thou hast
not laboured, neither madest it grow;
which [2]came up in a night, and perished
in a night:
11 And should not I spare Nineveh,
[a]that great city, wherein are more than
sixscore thousand persons [b]that cannot
discern between their right hand and
their left hand; and *also* much [c]cattle?

6 [1]Or, *palmcrist* [2]Heb. *Kikajon* [3]Heb. *rejoiced with great joy*
8 [a]ver. 3 [1]Or, *silent*
9 [1]Or, *Art thou greatly angry?* [2]Or, *I am greatly angry*
10 [1]Or, *spared* [2]Heb. *was the son of the night*
11 [a]ch. 1:2 & 3:2, 3 [b]Deut. 1:39 [c]Ps. 36:6 & 145:9

4:11 Jonah's great prophecy ends with a heartfelt expression of a God who takes "no pleasure in the death of the wicked" (Eze 33:11) but rather offers grace and mercy to all.

Micah

Author: Micah

Theme: The lives of God's children should reflect God's standards

Date of Writing: c. 740–710 B.C.

Outline of Micah

I. Samaria and Jerusalem Under Judgment (1:1–16)
II. Guilty Leaders and Wicked Oppressors (2:1—3:12)
III. The Promise of Divine Restoration (4:1—5:15)
IV. God's Judgment and Mercy (6:1—7:20)

A MAN NAMED Micah from Moresheth, a small village southwest of Jerusalem, wrote this sixth book of the Minor Prophets. Though Micah was a common name in OT times that meant "Who is like the LORD?" few additional details are known about this man of God. Ministering in Judah during the reigns of King Ahaz and King Hezekiah (see Jer 26:18), Micah was a contemporary of the prophets Isaiah (1:1; see Isa 1:1), Amos and Hosea. Warning of the impending judgment of God on unrepentant Israel and Judah, Micah's words parallel the prophecies of Isaiah (see 4:1–5; Isa 2:2–4). Jesus also quoted Micah's words when instructing his disciples (see 7:6; Mt 10:35–36).

Micah's warnings are primarily directed toward the leaders of Judah and Israel in their capital cities of Jerusalem and Samaria. The prophet warns the people of Judah against their false assumption of protection from God's coming judgment simply because they possess his temple. Micah prophesied that both capitals faced certain destruction unless the people and leaders of the kingdoms repented of their sin, predicting God's use of the Assyrians as his instrument of wrath. The people, however, refused to listen to Micah's warnings, and the powerful Assyrian armies invaded the kingdom of Israel and destroyed its capital city, Samaria, in 722 B.C.

Micah concludes his prophecy by predicting the future glory of God's Messiah and his just rule. This promise of final restoration provides hope for all who put their trust in God. Jerusalem will become the center of a universal kingdom where absolute peace and justice prevail. The Messiah, whose birthplace is identified in Micah's prophecy as Bethlehem in Judah, will establish a kingdom that will last forever (see 5:2).

1 THE WORD of the LORD that came to [a]Micah the Morasthite in the days of Jotham, Ahaz, *and* Hezekiah, kings of Judah, which he saw concerning Samaria and Jerusalem.

Samaria and Judah

2 [1]Hear, all ye people; hearken, O earth, and all that therein is: and let the Lord GOD be witness against you, the Lord from [a]his holy temple.

P 3 For, behold, the LORD cometh forth out of his place, and will come down, and tread upon the high places of the earth.

4 And [a]the mountains shall be molten under him, and the valleys shall be cleft, as wax before the fire, *and* as the waters *that are* poured down [1]a steep place.

5 For the transgression of Jacob *is* all this, and for the sins of the house of Israel. What *is* the transgression of Jacob? *is it* not Samaria? and what *are* the high places of Judah? *are they* not Jerusalem?

R 6 Therefore I will make Samaria [a]as an heap of the field, *and* as plantings of a vineyard: and I will pour down the stones thereof into the valley, and I will [b]discover the foundations thereof.

7 And all the graven images thereof shall be beaten to pieces, and all the [a]hires thereof shall be burned with the fire, and all the idols thereof will I lay desolate: for she gathered *it* of the hire of an harlot, and they shall return to the hire of an harlot.

The lament of the prophet

8 Therefore I will wail and howl, I will go stripped and naked: [a]I will make a wailing like the dragons, and mourning as the [1]owls.

P 9 For [1]her wound *is* incurable; for [a]it is come unto Judah; he is come unto the gate of my people, *even* to Jerusalem.

10 ¶ [a]Declare ye *it* not at Gath, weep ye not at all: in the house of [1]Aphrah roll thyself in the dust.

11 Pass ye away, [1]thou [2]inhabitant of Saphir, having thy shame naked: the inhabitant of [3]Zaanan came not forth in the mourning of [4]Beth-ezel; he shall receive of you his standing.

12 For the inhabitant of Maroth [1]waited carefully for good: but [a]evil came down from the LORD unto the gate of Jerusalem.

13 O thou inhabitant of [a]Lachish, bind the chariot to the swift beast: she *is* the beginning of the sin to the daughter of Zion: for the transgressions of Israel were found in thee.

14 Therefore shalt thou [a]give presents [1]to Moresheth-gath: the houses of [b]Achzib[2] *shall be* a lie to the kings of Israel.

15 Yet will I bring an heir unto thee, O inhabitant of [a]Mareshah: [1]he shall come unto [b]Adullam the glory of Israel.

16 Make thee [a]bald, and poll thee for thy [b]delicate children; enlarge thy baldness as the eagle; for they are gone into captivity from thee.

Wicked deeds of the rich

2 WOE TO them that devise iniquity, and work evil upon their beds! when the morning is light, they practice it, because it is in the power of their hand.

2 And they covet fields, and take *them* by violence; and houses, and take *them* away: so they [1]oppress a man and his house, even a man and his heritage.

3 Therefore thus saith the LORD; Behold, against this family do I devise an evil, from which ye shall not remove your necks; neither shall ye go haughtily: for this time *is* evil.

4 ¶ In that day shall *one* take up a para- R

1:1 [a]Jer. 26:18
2 [a]Ps. 11:4 [1]Heb. *Hear, ye people, all of them*
4 [a]Amos 9:5 [1]Heb. *a descent*
6 [a]2 Ki. 19:25 [b]Ezek. 13:14
7 [a]Hos. 2:5
8 [a]Ps. 102:6 [1]Heb. *daughters of the owl*
9 [a]2 Ki. 18:13 [1]Or, she is *grievously sick of her wounds*
10 [a]2 Sam. 1:20 [1]i.e. *Dust*
11 [1]Or, *thou that dwellest fairly* [2]Heb. *inhabitress* [3]Or, *the country of flocks* [4]Or, *a place near*
12 [a]Amos 3:6 [1]Or, *was grieved*
13 [a]2 Ki. 18:14
14 [a]2 Sam. 8:2; 2 Ki. 18:14 [b]Josh. 15:44 [1]Or, *for* [2]i.e. *a lie*
15 [a]Josh. 15:44 [b]2 Chr. 11:7 [1]Or, *the glory of Israel shall come*
16 [a]Job 1:20; Is. 15:2; Jer. 7:29 [b]Lam. 4:5
2:2 [1]Or, *defraud*

P *Ob 15–16* ◀▶ *Mic 1:9*
R *Am 9:8–10* ◀▶ *Mic 2:4*
P *Mic 1:3–7* ◀▶ *Mic 5:5*
R *Mic 1:6* ◀▶ *Mic 3:12*

1:1–6 Micah declared that God had called him to prophesy to Samaria and Jerusalem because of their continued wickedness. Though directed to the two capital cities, Micah's words applied to their people as well as he prophesied their coming destruction.
1:7–16 In these verses Micah described the coming destruction of Samaria at the hands of the Assyrians (see 2Ki 17:1–18). The wealth that Israel had gained from her idolatry would be taken by Assyria and turned over for use in idol worship. Micah may have actually acted out part of this prophecy, stripped to his loincloth and wailing through the city streets. His vivid prophecy was fulfilled in 721 B.C. when the people of Israel were taken in exile to Assyria. Note that Micah also warned Jerusalem of impending doom (1:9).
2:4 Micah predicted that the rich people would feel the brunt of God's judgment when the treacher-

ble against you, and [a]lament[1] with a doleful lamentation, *and* say, We be utterly spoiled: he hath changed the portion of my people: how hath he removed *it* from me! [2]turning away he hath divided our fields.

5 Therefore thou shalt have none that shall cast a cord by lot in the congregation of the LORD.

6 [1]Prophesy ye not, *say they to them that* prophesy: they shall not prophesy to them, *that* they shall not take shame.

M S W 7 ¶ O *thou that art* named the house of Jacob, is the spirit of the LORD [1]straitened? *are* these his doings? do not my words do good to him that walketh [2]uprightly?

8 Even [1]of late my people is risen up as an enemy: ye pull off the robe [2]with the garment from them that pass by securely as men averse from war.

9 The [1]women of my people have ye cast out from their pleasant houses; from their children have ye taken away my glory for ever.

10 Arise ye, and depart; for this *is* not *your* [a]rest: because it is [b]polluted, it shall destroy *you,* even with a sore destruction.

11 If a man [1]walking in the spirit and falsehood do lie, *saying,* I will prophesy unto thee of wine and of strong drink; he shall even be the prophet of this people.

The remnant regathered

I 12 ¶ [a]I will surely assemble, O Jacob, all of thee; I will surely gather the remnant of Israel; I will put them together [b]as the sheep of Bozrah, as the flock in the midst of their fold: [c]they shall make great noise by reason of *the multitude of* men.

13 The breaker is come up before them: they have broken up, and have passed through the gate, and are gone out by it: and [a]their king shall pass before them, [b]and the LORD on the head of them.

4 [a]2 Sam. 1:17 [1]Heb. *with a lamentation of lamentations* [2]Or, *instead of restoring*

6 [1]Or, *Prophesy not as they prophesy*

7 [1]Or, *shortened?* [2]Heb. *upright?*

8 [1]Heb. *yesterday* [2]Heb. *over against a garment*

9 [1]Or, *wives*

10 [a]Deut. 12:9 [b]Lev. 18:25; Jer. 3:2

11 [1]Or, *walk with the wind, and lie falsely*

12 [a]ch. 4:6,7 [b]Jer. 31:10 [c]Ezek. 36:37

13 [a]Hos. 3:5 [b]Is. 52:12

3:1 [a]Jer. 5:4,5

3 [a]Ps. 14:4 [b]Ezek. 11:3

4 [a]Ps. 18:41; Prov. 1:28; Is. 1:15

5 [a]Is. 56:10,11; Ezek. 13:10 [b]Mat. 7:15 [c]Ezek. 13:18

6 [a]Is. 8:20; Ezek. 13:23 [b]Amos 8:9 [1]Heb. *from a vision* [2]Heb. *from divining*

7 [a]Amos 8:11 [1]Heb. *upper lip*

8 [a]Is. 58:1

Israel's sins denounced

3 AND I said, Hear, I pray you, O heads of Jacob, and ye princes of the house of Israel; [a]*Is it* not for you to know judgment?

2 Who hate the good, and love the evil; who pluck off their skin from off them, and their flesh from off their bones;

3 Who also [a]eat the flesh of my people, and flay their skin from off them; and they break their bones, and chop them in pieces, as for the pot, and [b]as flesh within the caldron.

4 Then [a]shall they cry unto the LORD, but he will not hear them: he will even hide his face from them at that time, as they have behaved themselves ill in their doings.

5 ¶ Thus saith the LORD [a]concerning the prophets that make my people err, that [b]bite with their teeth, and cry, Peace; and [c]he that putteth not into their mouths, they even prepare war against him.

6 [a]Therefore night *shall be* unto you, [1]that ye shall not have a vision; and it shall be dark unto you, [2]that ye shall not divine; [b]and the sun shall go down over the prophets, and the day shall be dark over them. Q

7 Then shall the seers be ashamed, and the diviners confounded: yea, they shall all cover their [1]lips; [a]for *there is* no answer of God.

8 ¶ But truly I am full of power by the spirit of the LORD, and of judgment, and of might, [a]to declare unto Jacob his transgression, and to Israel his sin. B C E G M

Destruction of Jerusalem foretold

9 Hear this, I pray you, ye heads of the house of Jacob, and princes of the house of Israel, that abhor judgment, and pervert all equity.

M *Joel 2:28* ◀ ▶ *Mic 3:8*
S *Eze 36:25–27* ◀ ▶ *Lk 1:17*
W *Isa 30:1* ◀ ▶ *Zec 4:6*
I *Ob 17* ◀ ▶ *Mic 4:1–4*

Q *La 2:9* ◀ ▶ *Zec 6:8*
B *Joel 2:28–29* ◀ ▶ *Mal 3:10*
C *Ps 139:7* ◀ ▶ *Zec 12:10*
E *Da 6:3* ◀ ▶ *Hag 2:5*
G *Joel 2:28–29* ◀ ▶ *Mt 10:19–20*
M *Mic 2:7* ◀ ▶ *Zec 4:6*

ous Assyrians conquered the land.

2:12 Despite the doom pronounced upon the wickedness of Judah and Israel, the prophet interrupted his discourse promising the ultimate restoration of "the remnant of Israel."

10 [a]They build up Zion with [b]blood, [l]
and Jerusalem with iniquity.
11 [a]The heads thereof judge for reward, and [b]the priests thereof teach for
hire, and the prophets thereof divine for
money: [c]yet will they lean upon the LORD,
[l]and say, *Is* not the LORD among us? none
evil can come upon us.
R 12 Therefore shall Zion for your sake
be [a]plowed *as* a field, [b]and Jerusalem
shall become heaps, and [c]the mountain
of the house as the high places of the
forest.

The coming of law and peace

I 4 BUT [a]IN the last days it shall come to
pass, *that* the mountain of the house
of the LORD shall be established in the top
of the mountains, and it shall be exalted
above the hills; and people shall flow
unto it.
2 And many nations shall come, and
say, Come, and let us go up to the mountain of the LORD, and to the house of the
God of Jacob; and he will teach us of his
ways, and we will walk in his paths: for
the law shall go forth of Zion, and the
word of the LORD from Jerusalem.
M 3 ¶ And he shall judge among many
U people, and rebuke strong nations afar
off; and they shall beat their swords into
[a]plowshares, and their spears into
[l]pruninghooks: nation shall not lift up a
sword against nation, [b]neither shall they
learn war any more.
4 [a]But they shall sit every man under
his vine and under his fig tree; and none
shall make *them* afraid: for the mouth of
the LORD of hosts hath spoken *it*.

5 For all people will walk every one in
the name of his god, and [a]we will walk in
the name of the LORD our God for ever
and ever.

The LORD reigns in Zion

6 In that day, saith the LORD, [a]will I I
assemble her that halteth, [b]and I will
gather her that is driven out, and her that
I have afflicted;
7 And I will make her that halted a
[a]remnant, and her that was cast far off a
strong nation: and the LORD [b]shall reign
over them in mount Zion from henceforth, even for ever.
8 ¶ And thou, O tower of [l]the flock,
the strong hold of the daughter of Zion,
unto thee shall it come, even the first dominion; the kingdom shall come to the
daughter of Jerusalem.
9 Now why dost thou cry out aloud?
[a]*is there* no king in thee? is thy counsellor perished? for [b]pangs have taken thee
as a woman in travail.
10 Be in pain, and labour to bring
forth, O daughter of Zion, like a woman
in travail: for now shalt thou go forth out
of the city, and thou shalt dwell in the
field, and thou shalt go *even* to Babylon;
there shalt thou be delivered; there the
LORD shall redeem thee from the hand of
thine enemies.
11 ¶ [a]Now also many nations are gath- R
ered against thee, that say, Let her be defiled, and let our eye [b]look upon Zion.
12 But they know not [a]the thoughts of I
the LORD, neither understand they his
counsel: for he shall gather them [b]as the
sheaves into the floor.
13 [a]Arise and thresh, O daughter of

10 [a]Jer. 22:13 [b]Ezek. 22:27; Zeph. 3:3 [l]Heb. *bloods*
11 [a]Is. 1:23; Ezek. 22:12 [b]Jer. 6:13 [c]Is. 48:2; Jer. 7:4 [l]Heb. *saying*
12 [a]Jer. 26:18 [b]Ps. 79:1 [c]ch. 4:2
4:1 [a]Ezek. 17:22
3 [a]Is. 2:4; Joel 3:10 [b]Ps. 72:7 [l]Or, *scythes*
4 [a]1 Ki. 4:25; Zech. 3:10
5 [a]Zech. 10:12
6 [a]Ezek. 34:16 [b]Ps. 147:2; Ezek. 34:13
7 [a]ch. 2:12 [b]Is. 9:6; Dan. 7:14; Luke 1:33; Rev. 11:15
8 [l]Or, *Edar;* see Gen. 35:21
9 [a]Jer. 8:19 [b]Is. 13:8; Jer. 30:6
11 [a]Lam. 2:16 [b]Obad. 12
12 [a]Is. 55:8 [b]Is. 21:10
13 [a]Jer. 51:33

R *Mic 2:4* ◀ ▶ *Mic 4:11*
I *Mic 2:12* ◀ ▶ *Mic 4:6–8*
M *Joel 3:18–20* ◀ ▶ *Mic 5:2*
U *Hos 2:18* ◀ ▶ *Zec 9:10*

I *Mic 4:1–4* ◀ ▶ *Mic 4:12–13*
R *Mic 3:12* ◀ ▶ *Mic 6:13*
I *Mic 4:6–8* ◀ ▶ *Mic 5:2*

3:12 God prophesied that Jerusalem would be utterly destroyed because of her continued wickedness. Every wall would fall and Jerusalem's enemies would plough up the foundations to signal the city's total defeat.

4:1–8 Note the similarity of this passage and Isa 2:2–4. In these verses Micah described the blessings of the millennial kingdom. Despite the certainty of God's judgment, the last days would bring a time of peace and justice. The temple would be rebuilt and the Messiah would justly "judge among many people" (4:3) from his throne in Jerusalem. Peace would exist between nations and they would no longer "learn war any more" (4:3). Fear would be a thing of the past (4:4), and the kingdom of David would be reunited and restored under the glorious reign of the Messiah (4:8).

4:11–13 These verses contain Micah's prophecy of God's judgment against the nations who laughed at Israel's devastation. Hidden within this passage is the promise of Israel's ultimate restoration in the last days when Israel will miraculously defeat her enemies. This prophecy foreshadows the supernatural deliverance of God's people at the Battle of Armageddon (see Rev 16:13–16).

Zion: for I will make thine horn iron, and
I will make thy hoofs brass: and thou
shalt [b]beat in pieces many people: [c]and I
will consecrate their gain unto the LORD,
and their substance unto [d]the Lord of the
whole earth.

The coming ruler and his reign

B 5 NOW GATHER thyself in troops,
O daughter of troops: he hath laid
siege against us: they shall [a]smite the
judge of Israel with a rod upon the cheek.
I 2 But thou, [a]Bethlehem Ephratah,
M *though* thou be little [b]among the [c]thou-
sands of Judah, *yet* out of thee shall he
come forth unto me *that is* to be [d]ruler
in Israel; [e]whose goings forth *have been*
from of old, from [1]everlasting.
3 Therefore will he give them up, until
the time *that* [a]she which travaileth hath
brought forth: then [b]the remnant of his
brethren shall return unto the children of
Israel.
4 ¶ And he shall stand and [a]feed[1] in
the strength of the LORD, in the majesty of
the name of the LORD his God; and they
shall abide: for now [b]shall he be great
unto the ends of the earth.
P 5 And this *man* [a]shall be the peace,
when the Assyrian shall come into our
land: and when he shall tread in our palaces, then shall we raise against him
seven shepherds, and eight [1]principal
men.
6 And they shall [1]waste the land of Assyria with the sword, and the land of
[a]Nimrod [2]in the entrances thereof: thus
shall he [b]deliver *us* from the Assyrian,
when he cometh into our land, and when
he treadeth within our borders.
7 And [a]the remnant of Jacob shall be
in the midst of many people [b]as a dew
from the LORD, as the showers upon the
grass, that tarrieth not for man, nor waiteth for the sons of men.
8 ¶ And the remnant of Jacob shall be
among the Gentiles in the midst of many
people as a lion among the beasts of the
forest, as a young lion among the flocks
of [1]sheep: who, if he go through, both
treadeth down, and teareth in pieces, and
none can deliver.
9 Thine hand shall be lifted up upon
thine adversaries, and all thine enemies
shall be cut off.

Idols and weapons destroyed

10 [a]And it shall come to pass in that
day, saith the LORD, that I will cut off thy
horses out of the midst of thee, and I will
destroy thy chariots:
11 And I will cut off the cities of thy
land, and throw down all thy strong
holds:
12 And I will cut off witchcrafts out of
thine hand; and thou shalt have no *more*
[a]soothsayers:
13 [a]Thy graven images also will I cut
off, and thy [1]standing images out of the
midst of thee; and thou shalt [b]no more
worship the work of thine hands.
14 And I will pluck up thy groves out
of the midst of thee: so will I destroy thy
[1]cities.

13 [b]Dan. 2:44 [c]Is. 18:7 [d]Zech. 4:14
5:1 [a]Lam. 3:30
2 [a]Mat. 2:6; John 7:42 [b]1 Sam. 23:23 [c]Ex. 18:25 [d]Gen. 49:10; Is. 9:6 [e]Ps. 90:2; John 1:1 [1]Heb. *the days of eternity*
3 [a]ch. 4:10 [b]ch. 4:7
4 [a]Is. 40:11; Ezek. 34:23 [b]Ps. 72:8; Is. 52:13; Zech. 9:10 [1]Or, *rule*
5 [a]Ps. 72:7; Is. 9:6 [1]Heb. *princes of men*
6 [a]Gen. 10:8 [b]Luke 1:71 [1]Heb. *eat up* [2]Or, *with her own naked swords*
7 [a]ver. 3 [b]Deut. 32:2; Ps. 72:6
8 [1]Or, *goats*
10 [a]Zech. 9:10
12 [a]Is. 2:6
13 [a]Zech. 13:2 [b]Is. 2:8 [1]Or, *statues*
14 [1]Or, *enemies*

B *Da 9:24–26* ◀▶ *Hag 2:9*
I *Mic 4:12–13* ◀▶ *Mic 7:7–9*
M *Mic 4:3–4* ◀▶ *Hab 2:14*
P *Mic 1:9* ◀▶ *Mic 5:15*

5:1 To strike a ruler on the cheek was a supreme insult. Micah used this metaphor to indicate that Jerusalem's ability to resist destruction was gone. The city would be besieged and the kings seized and taken captive. This prophecy was fulfilled when Babylon carried Zedekiah into exile (see 2Ki 25:7).

5:2–3 Once again Micah makes a shift from words of doom to words of hope. This well-known prophecy clearly predicted nearly seven hundred years before its fulfillment that the town of Bethlehem in the region of Ephratah would become the birthplace of the Messiah. This prophecy also indicated that Israel would be abandoned to the discretion of their enemies until the birth of the Messiah and the reuniting of the nation once more (see Isa 7:14).

5:4–6 Micah prophesied the future rule of the Messiah, who will rule "in the majesty of the name of the LORD" (5:4) and will defeat "the Assyrian" (5:5), a symbol of all of the enemies of God's people. Note that this title is also sometimes applied to the antichrist because of his role as the King of Babylon (see note at Isa 10:5; 14:4, 25). The antichrist will invade the promised land and will be defeated by the Messiah at the Battle of Armageddon (see Da 11:36–45; Rev 19:14–21). The reference to "seven shepherds, and eight principal men" (5:5) may refer to a group of great military leaders who will resist the antichrist's invasion of Israel toward the end of the seven-year tribulation period.

5:11–15 In the Messianic kingdom God's people will no longer rely on weapons of war or pagan idols. God will be the source of the people's success and strength and will bring destruction on those nations who disobey him.

P H 15 And I will [a]execute vengeance in anger and fury upon the heathen, such as they have not heard.

God's complaint

6 HEAR YE now what the LORD saith; Arise, contend thou [1]before the mountains, and let the hills hear thy voice.

2 [a]Hear ye, O mountains, [b]the LORD'S controversy, and ye strong foundations of the earth: for [c]the LORD hath a controversy with his people, and he will plead with Israel.

3 O my people, [a]what have I done unto thee? and wherein have I wearied thee? testify against me.

4 [a]For I brought thee up out of the land of Egypt, and redeemed thee out of the house of servants; and I sent before thee Moses, Aaron, and Miriam.

5 O my people, remember now what [a]Balak king of Moab consulted, and what Balaam the son of Beor answered him from [b]Shittim unto Gilgal; that ye may know [c]the righteousness of the LORD.

L 6 ¶ Wherewith shall I come before the LORD, *and* bow myself before the high God? shall I come before him with burnt offerings, with calves [1]of a year old?

S 7 [a]Will the LORD be pleased with thousands of rams, *or* with ten thousands of [b]rivers of oil? [c]shall I give my firstborn *for* my transgression, the fruit of my [1]body *for* the sin of my soul?

8 He hath [a]shown thee, O man, what *is* good; and what doth the LORD require of thee, but [b]to do justly, and to love mercy, and to [1]walk humbly with thy God?

The corruption of Israel

9 The LORD'S voice crieth unto the city, and [1]*the man of* wisdom shall see thy name: hear ye the rod, and who hath appointed it.

15 [a]2 Thes. 1:8
6:1 [1]Or, *with*
2 [a]Ps. 50:1,4 [b]Hos. 12:2 [c]Is. 1:18
3 [a]Jer. 2:5,31
4 [a]Deut. 4:20
5 [a]Num. 22:5; Josh. 24:9 [b]Num. 25:1 [c]Judg. 5:11
6 [1]Heb. *sons of a year?*
7 [a]Ps. 50:9; Is. 1:11 [b]Job 29:6 [c]2 Ki. 16:3; Ezek. 23:37 [1]Heb. *belly*
8 [a]Deut. 10:12; 1 Sam. 15:22 [b]Gen. 18:19; Is. 1:17 [1]Heb. *humble thyself to walk*
9 [1]Or, *thy name shall see that which is*
10 [a]Amos 8:5 [1]Or, Is there *yet unto every man an house of the wicked* [2]Heb. *measure of leanness*
11 [a]Hos. 12:7 [1]Or, *Shall I be pure with*
12 [a]Jer. 9:3,5
13 [a]Lev. 26:16; Ps. 107:17
14 [a]Lev. 26:26
15 [a]Amos 5:11
16 [a]1 Ki. 16:25 [b]Hos. 5:11 [c]Is. 25:8 [1]Or, *he doth much keep the* [2]Or, *astonishment*
7:1 [a]Is. 17:6 [b]Is. 28:4 [1]Heb. *the gatherings of summer*
2 [a]Ps. 12:1; Is. 57:1 [b]Hab. 1:15 [1]Or, *godly,* or, *merciful*
3 [1]Heb. *the mischief of his soul*

10 ¶ [1]Are there yet the treasures of wickedness in the house of the wicked, and the [a]scant[2] measure *that is* abominable?

11 [1]Shall I count *them* pure with [a]the wicked balances, and with the bag of deceitful weights?

12 For the rich men thereof are full of violence, and the inhabitants thereof have spoken lies, and [a]their tongue *is* deceitful in their mouth.

13 Therefore also will I [a]make *thee* sick in smiting thee, in making *thee* desolate because of thy sins. R H

14 [a]Thou shalt eat, but not be satisfied; and thy casting down *shall be* in the midst of thee; and thou shalt take hold, but shalt not deliver; and *that* which thou deliverest will I give up to the sword.

15 Thou shalt [a]sow, but thou shalt not reap; thou shalt tread the olives, but thou shalt not anoint thee with oil; and sweet wine, but shalt not drink wine.

16 ¶ For [1]the statutes of [a]Omri are [b]kept, and all the works of the house of Ahab, and ye walk in their counsels; that I should make thee a [2]desolation, and the inhabitants thereof an hissing: therefore ye shall bear the [c]reproach of my people. R

The counsel of despair

7 WOE IS me! for I am as [1]when they have gathered the summer fruits, as [a]the grapegleanings of the vintage: *there is* no cluster to eat: [b]my soul desired the firstripe fruit. R

2 The [a]good[1] *man* is perished out of the earth: and *there is* none upright among men: they all lie in wait for blood; [b]they hunt every man his brother with a net.

3 ¶ That they may do evil with both hands earnestly, the prince asketh, and the judge *asketh* for a reward; and the great *man*, he uttereth [1]his mischievous desire: so they wrap it up.

P *Mic 5:5* ◀▶ *Na 1:2*
H *Ob 15* ◀▶ *Mic 6:13*
L *Jnh 4:2* ◀▶ *Mic 7:18–19*
S *Jnh 2:8* ◀▶ *Na 1:3*

R *Mic 4:11* ◀▶ *Mic 6:16*
H *Mic 5:15* ◀▶ *Na 1:2–3*
R *Mic 6:13* ◀▶ *Mic 7:1*
R *Mic 6:16* ◀▶ *Na 2:2*

6:13 Micah's words indicate that God has already begun to destroy Israel with sickness and desolation as part of his judgment for their sins.
6:16 Micah indicted the leaders of Israel with following the practices of the most evil kings of Israel (see 1Ki 16:25, 30). God promised their ultimate ruin and scorn.
7:1 Micah complained that looking for the godly in Israel was like looking for fruit after the harvest is over (see Jer 8:20).

4 The best of them [a]*is* as a brier: the most upright *is sharper* than a thorn hedge: the day of thy watchmen *and* thy visitation cometh; now shall be their perplexity.

5 ¶ Trust ye not in a friend, put ye not confidence in a guide: keep the doors of thy mouth from her that lieth in thy bosom.

6 For [a]the son dishonoureth the father, the daughter riseth up against her mother, the daughter-in-law against her mother-in-law; a man's enemies *are* the men of his own house.

Trust in God's salvation

I 7 Therefore I will look unto the LORD; I will wait for the God of my salvation: my God will hear me.

8 ¶ [a]Rejoice not against me, O mine enemy: [b]when I fall, I shall arise; when I sit in darkness, the LORD *shall be* a light unto me.

9 [a]I will bear the indignation of the LORD, because I have sinned against him, until he plead my cause, and execute judgment for me: he will bring me forth to the light, *and* I shall behold his righteousness.

I 10 [1]Then *she that is* mine enemy shall see *it,* and [a]shame shall cover her which said unto me, [b]Where is the LORD thy God? mine eyes shall behold her: now [2]shall she be trodden down as the mire of the streets.

I 11 *In* the day that thy walls are to be built, *in* that day shall the decree be far removed.

12 *In* that day *also* [a]he shall come even to thee from Assyria, [1]and *from* the fortified cities, and from the fortress even to the river, and from sea to sea, and *from* mountain to mountain.

13 [1]Notwithstanding the land shall be desolate because of them that dwell therein, [a]for the fruit of their doings.

14 ¶ [a]Feed[1] thy people with thy rod, the flock of thine heritage, which dwell solitarily *in* [b]the wood, in the midst of Carmel: let them feed *in* Bashan and Gilead, as in the days of old.

God's pardon and love

15 [a]According to the days of thy coming out of the land of Egypt will I show unto him marvellous *things.*

16 ¶ The nations [a]shall see and be confounded at all their might: [b]they shall lay *their* hand upon *their* mouth, their ears shall be deaf.

17 They shall lick the [a]dust like a serpent, [b]they shall move out of their holes like [1]worms of the earth: they shall be afraid of the LORD our God, and shall fear because of thee.

18 [a]Who *is* a God like unto thee, that L
[b]pardoneth iniquity, and passeth by the P
transgression of [c]the remnant of his heritage? [d]he retaineth not his anger for ever, because he delighteth *in* mercy.

19 He will turn again, he will have compassion upon us; he will subdue our iniquities; and thou wilt cast all their sins into the depths of the sea.

20 [a]Thou wilt perform the truth to Jacob, *and* the mercy to Abraham, [b]which thou hast sworn unto our fathers from the days of old.

4 [a]Ezek. 2:6; Is. 55:13
6 [a]Mat. 10:21
8 [a]Prov. 24:17 [b]Ps. 37:24; Prov. 24:16
9 [a]Lam. 3:39
10 [a]Ps. 35:26 [b]Ps. 42:3 [1]Or, *And thou wilt see her that is mine enemy, and cover her with shame* [2]Heb. *she shall be for a treading down*
12 [a]Is. 11:16 [1]Or, *even to*
13 [a]Jer. 21:14 [1]Or, *After that it hath been*
14 [a]Ps. 28:9 [b]Is. 37:24 [1]Or, *Rule*
15 [a]Ps. 68:22
16 [a]Is. 26:11 [b]Job 21:5
17 [a]Ps. 72:9; Is. 49:23 [b]Ps. 18:45 [1]Or, *creeping things*
18 [a]Ex. 15:11 [b]Ex. 34:6; Jer. 50:20 [c]ch. 4:7 [d]Ps. 103:9; Is. 57:16
20 [a]Luke 1:72 [b]Ps. 105:9

I *Mic 5:2* ◀▶ *Mic 7:10*
I *Mic 7:7–9* ◀▶ *Mic 7:11–20*
I *Mic 7:10* ◀▶ *Na 1:12*
L *Mic 6:6–8* ◀▶ *Zec 1:3*
P *Am 5:4* ◀▶ *Zec 1:3*

7:7–20 Though this passage begins on a note of judgment and doom, it ends with a statement of hope. Micah clearly understood that God's judgment would come on his people for their persistent wickedness, yet he looked forward hopefully "for the God of my salvation" (7:7) with supreme confidence that God would hear the prayers of the godly. Micah warned his enemies not to laugh at Israel's fall into judgment, for though God would make the land desolate for a time, he would also show mercy to Israel and deliver them from their enemies. Micah ended his words with a powerful reminder to the people of God's mercy and forgiveness (7:18) that was built on the covenantal promises made to Abraham and Jacob "from the days of old" (7:20).

Nahum

Author: Nahum

Theme: God will judge Nineveh

Date of Writing: c. 626–585 B.C.

Outline of Nahum

I. God's Anger Against Nineveh (1:1–15)
II. The Fall of the Assyrian Capital (2:1–13)
III. Woe to Nineveh (3:1–19)

THE BOOK OF Nahum is like a sequel to the book of Jonah as it predicts the final fall of the powerful city of Nineveh, the great Assyrian capital. Written by Nahum the Elkoshite, a contemporary of the prophets Zephaniah, Jeremiah and Habakkuk, this book incorporates the purity of classical, poetic language with the forcefulness of prophetic imagery to convey the theme of Assyria's approaching doom. Though most of his words were directed to the Assyrians, Nahum briefly encouraged his people to observe their religious feasts, promising that the Assyrians would never again threaten Jerusalem (see 1:15).

Composed after the Assyrian conquest of Samaria in 721 B.C., Nahum's book vividly describes the ruthless subjugation of Assyria's enemies. Though the Assyrians had formerly been granted mercy because of their repentance under Jonah's ministry, Nahum stated that their return to cruelty and gross wickedness would ensure their destruction. Nahum warned that God's righteousness would not tolerate Nineveh's brutal cruelty forever. He graphically portrays the final siege and fall of the Assyrian capital. This prophecy against Assyria was ultimately fulfilled in 612 B.C. when the Babylonians invaded Assyria and destroyed Nineveh.

God's vengeance and goodness

1 THE BURDEN [a]of Nineveh. The
book of the vision of Nahum the Elkoshite.
P 2 [1]God *is* [a]jealous, and the LORD re-
H vengeth; the LORD revengeth, and [2]*is* furious; the LORD will take vengeance on his
adversaries, and he reserveth *wrath* for
his enemies.
S 3 The LORD *is* [a]slow to anger, and
[b]great in power, and will not at all acquit
the wicked: [c]the LORD *hath* his way in
the whirlwind and in the storm, and the
clouds *are* the dust of his feet.
4 [a]He rebuketh the sea, and maketh it
dry, and drieth up all the rivers: [b]Bashan
languisheth, and Carmel, and the flower
of Lebanon languisheth.
P 5 The mountains quake at him, and
H the hills melt, and the earth is burned at
his presence, yea, the world, and all that
dwell therein.
6 Who can stand before his indignation? and [a]who can [1]abide in the fierceness of his anger? his fury is poured out
like fire, and the rocks are thrown down
by him.
S 7 [a]The LORD *is* good, a [1]strong hold in
the day of trouble; and he knoweth them
that trust in him.
8 But with an overrunning flood he
will make an utter end of the place
thereof, and darkness shall pursue his enemies.
9 [a]What do ye imagine against the
LORD? [b]he will make an utter end: affliction shall not rise up the second time.
10 For while *they be* folden together
[a]*as* thorns, [b]and while they are drunken
as drunkards, [c]they shall be devoured as
stubble fully dry.
11 There is *one* come out of thee, that
imagineth evil against the LORD, [1]a
wicked counsellor.
12 Thus saith the LORD; [1]Though *they* I
be quiet, and likewise many, yet thus
shall they be [2]cut down, when he shall
pass through. Though I have afflicted
thee, I will afflict thee no more.
13 For now will I break his yoke from
off thee, and will burst thy bonds in
sunder.
14 And the LORD hath given a commandment concerning thee, *that* no
more of thy name be sown: out of the
house of thy gods will I cut off the graven
image and the molten image: I will make
thy grave; for thou art vile.
15 Behold upon the mountains the feet I
of him that bringeth good tidings, that P
publisheth peace! O Judah, [1]keep thy solemn feasts, perform thy vows: for [2]the
wicked shall no more pass through thee;
he is utterly cut off.

The siege of Nineveh

2 HE [1]THAT dasheth in pieces is come
up before thy face: keep the munition, watch the way, make *thy* loins
strong, fortify *thy* power mightily.
2 For the LORD hath turned away [1]the R
excellency of Jacob, as the excellency of
Israel: for the emptiers have emptied

1:1 [a]Zeph. 2:13
2 [a]Ex. 20:5; Deut. 4:24; Josh. 24:19 [1]Or, *The LORD is a jealous God, and a revenger* [2]Heb. *that hath fury*
3 [a]Ex. 34:6,7; Neh. 9:17 [b]Job 9:4 [c]Ps. 18:7
4 [a]Mat. 8:26 [b]Is. 33:9
6 [a]Mal. 3:2 [1]Heb. *stand up*
7 [a]Jer. 33:11 [1]Or, *strength*
9 [a]Ps. 2:1 [b]1 Sam. 3:12
10 [a]2 Sam. 23:6 [b]ch. 3:11 [c]Mal. 4:1
11 [1]Heb. *a counsellor of Belial*
12 [1]Or, *If they would have been at peace, so should they have been many, and so should they have been shorn, and he should have passed away* [2]Heb. *shorn*
15 [1]Heb. *feast* [2]Heb. *Belial*
2:1 [1]Or, *The disperser,* or, *hammer*
2 [1]Or, *the pride of Jacob as the pride of Israel*

P *Mic 5:15 ◀ ▶ Na 1:5–12*
H *Mic 6:13 ◀ ▶ Na 1:5–6*
S *Mic 6:7–8 ◀ ▶ Zep 1:6–7*
P *Na 1:2 ◀ ▶ Na 1:15*
H *Na 1:2–3 ◀ ▶ Na 2:10*
S *Jnh 2:10 ◀ ▶ Mt 4:6*

I *Mic 7:11–20 ◀ ▶ Na 1:15*
I *Na 1:12 ◀ ▶ Zep 3:9–20*
P *Na 1:5–12 ◀ ▶ Hab 3:3–16*
R *Mic 7:1 ◀ ▶ Hab 1:5–12*

1:1–3 Nahum announced that his prophecy against Nineveh was a "burden" or "oracle." In Hebrew this term relates to a word meaning "to lift up or carry" and may be understood as lifting up one's voice or carrying a burden of a message of doom. Nahum was conscious of the coming judgment of God upon Nineveh, and his words reflected the heaviness he felt in his heart as he delivered God's sentence of judgment.

In Nahum's time Nineveh was the greatest city in the world, defended by powerful armies and surrounded by reinforced walls. As the capital city of Assyria, Nineveh enjoyed an economic prosperity and military invincibility that led to arrogance and inhumanity to its enemies. Prisoners of war were cruelly tortured before they were killed. Nahum promised that God "will not at all acquit the wicked" (1:3).

1:5–12 This prophecy of Nineveh's destruction was fulfilled in 612 B.C. when the invading armies of the Medes, the Babylonians and the Scythians overthrew this powerful city (see Eze 32:22–23).

1:15 Nahum's prophecy in this verse carried a double meaning. The direct reference here was to the good news of Judah's deliverance from the threat of the Assyrians. Yet Paul used this same imagery to announce the eternal deliverance from sin (see Ro 10:15). See also Isa 52:7.

them out, and marred their vine
branches.
3 The shield of his mighty men is
made red, the valiant men *are* [1]in scarlet:
the chariots *shall be* with [2]flaming
torches in the day of his preparation, and
the fir trees shall be terribly shaken.
4 The chariots shall rage in the streets,
they shall justle one against another in
the broad ways: [1]they shall seem like
torches, they shall run like the lightnings.
5 He shall recount his [1]worthies: they
shall stumble in their walk; they shall
make haste to the wall thereof, and the
[2]defence shall be prepared.
6 The gates of the rivers shall be
opened, and the palace shall be [1]dis-
solved.
7 And [1]Huzzab shall be [2]led away captive, she shall be brought up, and her
maids shall lead *her* as with the voice of
doves, tabering upon their breasts.
8 But Nineveh *is* [1]of old like a pool of
water: yet they shall flee away. Stand,
stand, *shall they cry;* but none shall [2]look
back.
9 Take ye the spoil of silver, take the
spoil of gold: [1]for *there is* none end of the
store *and* glory out of all the [2]pleasant
furniture.
H 10 She is empty, and void, and waste:
and the heart melteth, and the knees
smite together, and much pain *is* in all
loins, and the faces of them all gather
blackness.
11 Where *is* the dwelling of the lions,
and the feedingplace of the young lions,
where the lion, *even* the old lion, walked,
and the lion's whelp, and none made
them afraid?
12 The lion did tear in pieces enough
for his whelps, and strangled for his lion-
esses, and filled his holes with prey, and
his dens with ravin.
13 Behold, I *am* against thee, saith the
LORD of hosts, and I will burn her chariots
in the smoke, and the sword shall devour
thy young lions: and I will cut off thy prey
from the earth, and the voice of thy messengers shall no more be heard.

H *Na 1:5–6* ◀ ▶ *Zep 1:6–8*

The sure destruction

3 WOE TO the [1]bloody city! it *is* all full
of lies *and* robbery; the prey departeth not;
2 The noise of a whip, and the noise
of the rattling of the wheels, and of the
prancing horses, and of the jumping
chariots.
3 The horseman lifteth up both [1]the
bright sword and the glittering spear: and
there is a multitude of slain, and a great
number of carcases; and *there is* none
end of *their* corpses; they stumble upon
their corpses:
4 Because of the multitude of the
whoredoms of the wellfavoured harlot,
[a]the mistress of witchcrafts, that selleth
nations through her whoredoms, and
families through her witchcrafts.
5 [a]Behold, I *am* against thee, saith the
LORD of hosts; and [b]I will discover thy
skirts upon thy face, and I will show the
nations thy nakedness, and the kingdoms
thy shame.
6 And I will cast abominable filth upon
thee, and make thee vile, and will set
thee as [a]a gazingstock.
7 And it shall come to pass, *that* all
they that look upon thee [a]shall flee from
thee, and say, Nineveh is laid waste:
[b]who will bemoan her? whence shall I
seek comforters for thee?
8 [a]Art thou better than [1,2]populous
[b]No, that was situate among the rivers,
that had the waters round about it,
whose rampart *was* the sea, *and* her wall
was from the sea?
9 Ethiopia and Egypt *were* her
strength, and *it was* infinite; Put and
Lubim were [1]thy helpers.
10 Yet *was* she carried away, she went
into captivity: [a]her young children also
were dashed in pieces [b]at the top of all
the streets: and they [c]cast lots for her
honourable men, and all her great men
were bound in chains.

3 [1]Or, *dyed* [2]Or, *fiery*
4 [1]Heb. *their show*
5 [1]Or, *gallants* [2]Heb. *covering,* or, *coverer*
6 [1]Or, *molten*
7 [1]Or, *that which was established,* or, *there was a stand made* [2]Or, *discovered*
8 [1]Or, *from the days* that *she* hath been [2]Or, *cause* them *to turn*
9 [1]Or, *and* their *infinite store* [2]Heb. *vessels of desire*
3:1 [1]Heb. *city of bloods*
3 [1]Heb. *the flame of the sword, and the lightning of the spear*
4 [a]Is. 47:9,12
5 [a]ch. 2:13 [b]Is. 47:2,3
6 [a]Heb. 10:33
7 [a]Rev. 18:10 [b]Jer. 15:5
8 [a]Amos 6:2 [b]Jer. 46:25 [1]Or, *nourishing* [2]Heb. *No Amon*
9 [1]Heb. *in thy help*
10 [a]Ps. 137:9; Is. 13:16; Hos. 13:16 [b]Lam. 2:19 [c]Joel 3:3; Obad. 11

3:7 Nahum declared that no one would feel sympathy when God's ultimate judgment fell upon the wicked city of Nineveh.

3:9–10 In this passage, Nahum compared Nineveh's arrogance to the arrogance of Thebes, one of the cities captured by the Assyrians. Both cities were located on rivers. Both cities thought they were invincible. Both cities had strong allies. But what the Assyrians did to Thebes would soon happen to Nineveh. Nineveh had reached the time of her final judgment by the hand of God. There was no escape.

11 Thou also shalt be [a]drunken: thou
shalt be hid, thou also shalt seek strength
because of the enemy.
12 All thy strong holds *shall be like*
[a]fig trees with the firstripe figs: if they
be shaken, they shall even fall into the
mouth of the eater.
13 Behold, [a]thy people in the midst of
thee *are* women: the gates of thy land
shall be set wide open unto thine enemies: the fire shall devour thy [b]bars.
14 Draw thee waters for the siege,
[a]fortify thy strong holds: go into clay, and
tread the mortar, make strong the
brickkiln.
15 There shall the fire devour thee;
the sword shall cut thee off, it shall eat
thee up like [a]the cankerworm: make thyself many as the cankerworm, make thyself many as the locusts.
16 Thou hast multiplied thy merchants
above the stars of heaven: the cankerworm ʹspoileth, and flieth away.
17 [a]Thy crowned *are* as the locusts,
and thy captains as the great grasshoppers, which camp in the hedges in the
cold day, *but* when the sun ariseth they
flee away, and their place is not known
where they *are.*
18 [a]Thy shepherds slumber, O [b]king
of Assyria: thy ʹnobles shall dwell *in the*
dust: thy people is [c]scattered upon the
mountains, and no man gathereth
them.
19 *There is* no ʹhealing of thy bruise;
[a]thy wound is grievous: [b]all that hear the
bruit of thee shall clap the hands over
thee: for upon whom hath not thy wickedness passed continually?

11 [a]Jer. 25:17; ch. 1:10
12 [a]Rev. 6:13
13 [a]Jer. 50:37 [b]Ps. 147:13; Jer. 51:30
14 [a]ch. 2:1
15 [a]Joel 1:4
16 ʹOr, *spreadeth himself*
17 [a]Rev. 9:7
18 [a]Ex. 15:16; Ps. 76:6 [b]Jer. 50:18; Ezek. 31:3 [c]1 Ki. 22:17 ʹOr, *valiant ones*
19 [a]Mic. 1:9 [b]Lam. 2:15; Zeph. 2:15 ʹHeb. *wrinkling*

3:11–15 Nahum's prophecy was fulfilled with chilling accuracy. Archeologists have confirmed that Nineveh was sacked and burned when the Medes, Babylonians and Scythians overran it in 612 B.C.

3:19 Nahum's prophecy revealed that God's judgment on Nineveh was irreversible. In fulfillment of this grave pronouncement, Nineveh was so totally destroyed that it was never rebuilt and the shifting desert sand covered its ruins.

Habakkuk

Author: Habakkuk

Theme: God's role in the face of evil and injustice

Date of Writing: c. 610–605 B.C.

Outline of Habakkuk

I. Habakkuk's First Question and God's Answer (1:1–11)
II. Habakkuk's Second Question and God's Answer (1:12—2:20)
III. Habakkuk's Prayer of Thanksgiving (3:1–19)

LITTLE IS KNOWN about Habakkuk beyond his calling as a prophet of God. His name is unusual and comes from a Hebrew word meaning "to clasp or embrace," an appropriate name for a prophet who held to his vigorous faith in a time of national crisis. Certain statements in Habakkuk help date this prophecy to the time of King Jehoiakim and make Habakkuk a contemporary of Jeremiah. Habakkuk probably lived to see the initial fulfillment of his words when Jerusalem fell to the Babylonians in 597 B.C.

The book of Habakkuk consists of an ongoing conversation with God. The prophet recognized that the political and religious leaders of Judah had oppressed the poor and questioned why God would allow the wicked to prosper despite their obvious sins. God's answer to Habakkuk that the Babylonians would soon punish Judah led the prophet to question God's justice in allowing the Babylonians, who were more wicked than Judah's leaders, to bring judgment upon God's chosen people. God's reply silenced further questions when he reminded Habakkuk that the godly should have confidence in God's justice and mercy. Habakkuk was then assured that the Babylonians would be judged in God's time. Habakkuk closes his book with a psalm of praise that confirmed his acceptance of God's plan and his recognition of God's justice.

Wrong judgment prevails

1 THE BURDEN which Habakkuk the prophet did see.

2 O LORD, how long shall I cry, [a]and thou wilt not hear! *even* cry out unto thee *of* violence, and thou wilt not save!

3 Why dost thou show me iniquity, and cause *me* to behold grievance? for spoiling and violence *are* before me: and there are *that* raise up strife and contention.

4 Therefore the law is slacked, and judgment doth never go forth: for the [a]wicked doth compass about the righteous; therefore [1]wrong judgment proceedeth.

Punishment by the Chaldeans

R 5 ¶ [a]Behold ye among the heathen, and regard, and wonder marvellously: for *I* will work a work in your days, *which* ye will not believe, though it be told *you.*

6 For, lo, [1]I raise up the Chaldeans, *that* bitter and hasty nation, which shall march through the [2]breadth of the land, to possess the dwellingplaces *that are* not theirs.

7 They *are* terrible and dreadful: [1]their judgment and their dignity shall proceed of themselves.

8 Their horses also are swifter than the leopards, and are more [1]fierce than the evening wolves: and their horsemen shall spread themselves, and their horsemen shall come from far; they shall fly as the eagle *that* hasteth to eat.

9 They shall come all for violence: [1,2]their faces shall sup up *as* the east wind, and they shall gather the captivity as the sand.

10 And they shall scoff at the kings, and the princes shall be a scorn unto them: they shall deride every strong hold; for they shall heap dust, and take it.

11 Then shall *his* mind change, and he shall pass over, and offend, [a]*imputing* this his power unto his god.

The wicked destroy the righteous

12 ¶ *Art* thou not from everlasting, O LORD my God, mine Holy One? we shall not die. O LORD, [a]thou hast ordained them for judgment; and, O [1]mighty God, thou hast [2]established them for correction.

13 *Thou art* of purer eyes than to behold evil, and canst not look on [1]iniquity: wherefore lookest thou upon them that deal treacherously, *and* holdest thy tongue when the wicked devoureth *the man that is* more righteous than he?

14 And makest men as the fishes of the sea, as the [1]creeping things, *that have* no ruler over them?

15 They take up all of them with the angle, they catch them in their net, and gather them in their [1]drag: therefore they rejoice and are glad.

16 Therefore [a]they sacrifice unto their net, and burn incense unto their drag; because by them their portion *is* fat, and their meat [1,2]plenteous.

17 Shall they therefore empty their net, and not spare continually to slay the nations?

Life to the just

2 I WILL [a]stand upon my watch, and set me upon the [1]tower, and will watch to see what he will say [2]unto me, and what I shall answer [3,4]when I am reproved.

2 And the LORD answered me, and said, [a]Write the vision, and make *it* plain upon tables, that he may run that readeth it.

3 For [a]the vision *is* yet for an appointed time, but at the end it shall speak, and not lie: though it tarry, wait for it; because it will [b]surely come, it will not tarry.

4 Behold, his soul *which* is lifted up is C
not upright in him: but the [a]just shall live F
by his faith. M

5 ¶ [1]Yea also, because he transgresseth by wine, *he is* a proud man, neither keepeth at home, who enlargeth his desire as hell, and *is* as death, and cannot be satisfied, but gathereth unto him all nations, and heapeth unto him all people:

Woe to the unrighteous

6 Shall not all these take up a parable R
against him, and a taunting proverb against him, and say, [1]Woe to him that increaseth *that which is* not his! how long? and to him that ladeth himself with thick clay!

7 Shall they not rise up suddenly that

1:2 [a]Lam. 3:8
4 [a]Jer. 12:1 [1]Or, *wrested*
5 [a]Is. 29:14
6 [1]Fulfilled in 2 Chr. 36:6 [2]Heb. *breadths*
7 [1]Or, *from them shall proceed the judgment of these, and the captivity of these*
8 [1]Heb. *sharp*
9 [1]Or, *the supping up of their faces,* or, *their faces shall look toward the east* [2]Heb. *the opposition of their faces toward the east*
11 [a]Dan. 5:4
12 [a]Is. 10:5-7 [1]Heb. *rock* [2]Heb. *founded*
13 [1]Or, *grievance*
14 [1]Or, *moving*
15 [1]Or, *flue net*
16 [a]Deut. 8:17 [1]Or, *dainty* [2]Heb. *fat*
2:1 [a]Is. 21:8,11 [1]Heb. *fenced place* [2]Or, *in me* [3]Or, *when I am argued with* [4]Heb. *upon my reproof,* or, *arguing*
2 [a]Is. 8:1
3 [a]Dan. 10:14 [b]Heb. 10:37
4 [a]John 3:36
5 [1]Or, *How much more*
6 [1]Or, *Ho, he*

R *Na 2:2* ◀▶ *Hab 2:6–13*

C *Am 6:12* ◀▶ *Zep 1:12*
F *Jer 17:7* ◀▶ *Mt 11:12*
M *Jnh 3:5–10* ◀▶ *Zep 2:2–3*
R *Hab 1:5–12* ◀▶ *Hab 2:15–19*

shall bite thee, and awake that shall vex thee, and thou shalt be for booties unto them?

8 [a]Because thou hast spoiled many nations, all the remnant of the people shall spoil thee; because of men's [1]blood, and *for* the violence of the land, of the city, and of all that dwell therein.

9 ¶ Woe to him that [1]coveteth an evil covetousness to his house, that he may [a]set his nest on high, that he may be delivered from the [2]power of evil!

10 Thou hast consulted shame to thy house by cutting off many people, and hast sinned *against* thy soul.

11 For the stone shall cry out of the wall, and the [1]beam out of the timber shall [2]answer it.

12 ¶ Woe to him that buildeth a town with [1]blood, and stablisheth a city by iniquity!

13 Behold, *is it* not of the LORD of hosts that the people shall labour in the very fire, and the people shall weary themselves [1]for very vanity?

K 14 For the earth shall be filled [1]with
M the knowledge of the glory of the LORD, as the waters cover the sea.

R 15 ¶ Woe unto him that giveth his neighbour drink, that puttest thy [a]bottle to *him,* and makest *him* drunken also, that thou mayest look on their nakedness!

16 Thou art filled [1]with shame for glory: drink thou also, and let thy foreskin be uncovered: the cup of the LORD'S right hand shall be turned unto thee, and shameful spewing *shall be* on thy glory.

17 For the violence of Lebanon shall cover thee, and the spoil of beasts, *which* made them afraid, because of men's blood, and for the violence of the land, of the city, and of all that dwell therein.

18 ¶ What profiteth the graven image that the maker thereof hath graven it; the molten image, and a teacher of lies, that [1]the maker of his work trusteth therein, to make dumb idols?

19 Woe unto him that saith to the wood, Awake; to the dumb stone, Arise, it shall teach! Behold, it *is* laid over with gold and silver, and *there is* no breath at all in the midst of it.

20 But the LORD *is* in his holy temple: M
[1]let all the earth keep silence before him.

Habakkuk's prayer

3 A PRAYER of Habakkuk the prophet [1]upon Shigionoth.

2 O LORD, I have heard [1]thy speech, *and* was afraid: O LORD, [2]revive thy work in the midst of the years, in the midst of the years make known; in wrath remember mercy.

3 God came from [1]Teman, and the P
Holy One from mount Paran. Selah. His

8 [a]Is. 33:1 [1]Heb. *bloods*
9 [a]Obad. 4 [1]Or, *gaineth an evil gain* [2]Heb. *palm of the hand*
11 [1]Or, *piece,* or, *fastening* [2]Or, *witness against it*
12 [1]Heb. *bloods*
13 [1]Or, *in vain?*
14 [1]Or, *by knowing the glory of the LORD*
15 [a]Hos. 7:5
16 [1]Or, *more with shame than with glory*
18 [1]Heb. *the fashioner of his fashion*
20 [1]Heb. *be silent all the earth before him*
3:1 [1]Or, *according to variable songs,* or, *tunes,* called in Hebrew, *Shigionoth*
2 [1]Heb. *thy report,* or, *thy hearing* [2]Or, *preserve alive*
3 [1]Or, *the south*

K *Da 7:13–14* ◀▶ *Zec 14:9*
M *Mic 5:2* ◀▶ *Hab 2:20*
R *Hab 2:6–13* ◀▶ *Zep 1:2–4*

M *Hab 2:14* ◀▶ *Hag 2:23*
P *Na 1:15* ◀▶ *Zep 1:14–18*

2:14 Habakkuk's words hold a double meaning. When Babylon was destroyed by the Medo-Persians, Babylon's glory paled in comparison to God's glory. In the millennial kingdom of the Messiah, Habakkuk's words will take on their full meaning. God's glory will outshine the glory of the nations, and all of humanity will know the truth of God.

2:20 Just as stone idols maintained their silence before their worshipers, humanity will stand in silence before the Judge of all the earth (see Isa 41:1; Zep 1:7; Zec 2:13).

3:2 Habakkuk remembered God's miraculous works among his ancestors and asked God to intercede again in such a way. Note that Habakkuk acknowledged that God's ways are merciful even if not completely comprehensible.

3:3–16 In this passage Habakkuk recalled the events of the deliverance from Egypt, God's miraculous provision in the Sinai and the overwhelming victories of the conquest of Canaan. Habakkuk referenced well-known miracles and historical happenings such as plagues (3:5; see Ex 7—12), earthquakes (3:6; see Ex 19:18), military victories (3:8; see Jos 2:9–10), natural phenomena (3:11; see Jos 10:12–13) and the miracle at the Red Sea (3:14–15; see Ex 14:15–31). Though Habakkuk recognized the imminent judgment of God upon the people of Israel, these past events and miraculous interventions set the precedent for God's ultimate deliverance of his people.

Though Israel experienced partial restoration after their return from Babylonian exile, the final fulfillment of Israel's deliverance and restoration will not take place until Christ returns and sets up his millennial kingdom. Just as God used supernatural happenings in the past to signal his intervention in Israel's deliverance, these supernatural occurrences will also take place in the end times (see Joel 2:10; Mt 24:7, 14–15, 29; Mk 13:24; Lk 21:25; Rev 6:8).

glory covered the heavens, and the earth
was full of his praise.
4 And *his* brightness was as the light;
he had [1]horns *coming* out of his hand:
and there *was* the hiding of his power.
5 Before him went the pestilence, and
[1]burning coals went forth at his feet.
6 He stood, and measured the earth:
he beheld, and drove asunder the nations; [a]and the everlasting mountains
were scattered, the perpetual hills did
bow: his ways *are* everlasting.
7 I saw the tents of [1]Cushan [2]in affliction: *and* the curtains of the land of Midian did tremble.
8 Was the LORD displeased against the
rivers? *was* thine anger against the rivers? *was* thy wrath against the sea, that
thou didst ride upon thine horses *and*
[1]thy chariots of salvation?
9 Thy bow was made quite naked, *according* to the oaths of the tribes, *even
thy* word. Selah. [1]Thou didst cleave the
earth with rivers.
10 The mountains saw thee, *and* they
trembled: the overflowing of the water
passed by: the deep uttered his voice,
and [a]lifted up his hands on high.
11 The sun *and* moon stood still in
their habitation: [1]at the light of thine arrows they went, *and* at the shining of thy
glittering spear.
12 Thou didst march through the land
in indignation, thou didst thresh the heathen in anger.
13 Thou wentest forth for the salvation
of thy people, *even* for salvation with
thine anointed; thou woundedst the head
out of the house of the wicked, [1]by dis-
covering the foundation unto the neck.
Selah.
14 Thou didst strike through with his
staves the head of his villages: they
[1]came out as a whirlwind to scatter me:
their rejoicing *was* as to devour the poor
secretly.
15 [a]Thou didst walk through the sea
with thine horses, *through* the [1]heap of
great waters.
16 When I heard, [a]my belly trembled;
my lips quivered at the voice: rottenness
entered into my bones, and I trembled in
myself, that I might rest in the day of
trouble: when he cometh up unto the
people, he will [1]invade them with his
troops.
17 ¶ Although the fig tree shall not F
blossom, neither *shall* fruit *be* in the J
vines; the labour of the olive shall [1]fail,
and the fields shall yield no meat; the
flock shall be cut off from the fold, and
there shall be no herd in the stalls:
18 Yet I will rejoice in the LORD, I will
joy in the God of my salvation.
19 The LORD God *is* my strength, and
he will make my feet like [a]hinds' *feet,*
and he will make me to [b]walk upon mine
high places. To the chief singer on my
[1]stringed instruments.

4 [1]Or, *bright beams out of his side*
5 [1]Or, *burning diseases*
6 [a]Nah. 1:5
7 [1]Or, *Ethiopia* [2]Or, *under affliction,* or, *vanity*
8 [1]Or, *thy chariots were salvation?*
9 [1]Or, *Thou didst cleave the rivers of the earth*
10 [a]Ex. 14:22
11 [1]Or, *thine arrows walked in the light*
13 [1]Heb. *making naked*
14 [1]Heb. *were tempestuous*
15 [a]Ps. 77:19 [1]Or, *mud*
16 [a]Ps. 119:120 [1]Or, *cut them in pieces*
17 [1]Heb. *lie*
19 [a]2 Sam. 22:34 [b]Deut. 32:13 [1]Heb. *Neginoth;* see Ps. 4, title

F *Joel 2:24–26* ◀ ▶ *Mt 4:11*
J *Isa 51:12* ◀ ▶ *Mt 5:11–12*

3:13 The latter half of this verse forms a curious prophecy that has a double meaning. When the Israelites entered Canaan and began to conquer it, God gave them victory over the heads of many ruling princes and kings, razing their family line to the foundation. This prophecy may also be applied to the victory of the Messiah over the armies of the antichrist in the end times (see Ps 110:6).

3:19 Habakkuk concluded his prophecy with a declaration of God's blessing and help despite trouble and hard times. Note the metaphor Habakkuk used is that of a deer. These sure-footed animals can walk securely on high, rocky ledges. Similarly, Habakkuk purposed to follow in the footsteps of God, knowing that God's way was the only secure way to go. We, too, should purpose to follow Christ, confident to "walk upon mine high places" because we will be following in his footsteps.

Zephaniah

Author: Zephaniah

Theme: The coming day of the Lord

Date of Writing: c. 635–630 B.C.

Outline of Zephaniah

I. The Day of the Lord Is Coming (1:1–18)
II. God's Judgment on the Nations (2:1—3:8)
III. Redemption and the Coming Kingdom (3:9–20)

THE PROPHET ZEPHANIAH, whose name means "The Lord hides (or protects)," wrote this prophecy of God's approaching judgment on Judah. His prophetic ministry is specifically dated to the reign of King Josiah (see 1:1), making him a contemporary of Jeremiah, Nahum and possibly Habakkuk. Zephaniah's words show a familiarity with royal and political issues, lending credence to the Hebrew tradition that Zephaniah may have been a descendant of King Hezekiah.

The book of Zephaniah records the warning that the "day of the LORD" will come and bring judgment upon Judah and Jerusalem. With vivid details Zephaniah describes this coming day of judgment, using the term "day of the LORD" repeatedly. This prophecy probably referred to the invasion of the Babylonians in 605–586 B.C. Though Zephaniah urged the nation of Judah to seek righteousness so that they would "be hid in the day of the LORD's anger" (2:3), the people refused to listen and God's promised judgment was carried out.

After calling Judah to repent, Zephaniah also foresaw the future judgment on foreign nations (see 2:13) and the final restoration of Israel under the Messiah, the future King of Israel, who will rule forever in Zion. Though Judah's guilt was certain and her punishment was inevitable, God's promise of restoration is assured too.

1 THE WORD of the LORD which came unto Zephaniah the son of Cushi, the son of Gedaliah, the son of Amariah, the son of Hizkiah, in the days of Josiah the son of Amon, king of Judah.

Judgment upon Jerusalem

R 2 ′I will utterly consume all *things* from off ²the land, saith the LORD.

3 [a]I will consume man and beast; I will consume the fowls of the heaven, and the fishes of the sea, and the ′stumblingblocks with the wicked; and I will cut off man from off the land, saith the LORD.

4 I will also stretch out mine hand upon Judah, and upon all the inhabitants of Jerusalem; and I will cut off the remnant of Baal from this place, *and* the name of [a]the Chemarims with the priests;

5 And them [a]that worship the host of heaven upon the housetops; and them that worship *and* that swear ′by the LORD, and that swear [b]by Malcham;

H S 6 And [a]them that are turned back from the LORD; and *those* that [b]have not sought the LORD, nor inquired for him.

7 [a]Hold thy peace at the presence of the Lord GOD: [b]for the day of the LORD *is* at hand: for [c]the LORD hath prepared a sacrifice, he hath ′bid his guests.

8 And it shall come to pass in the day of the LORD'S sacrifice, that I will ′punish [a]the princes, and the king's children, and all such as are clothed with strange apparel.

9 In the same day also will I punish all those that leap on the threshold, which fill their masters' houses with violence and deceit.

10 And it shall come to pass in that day, saith the LORD, *that there shall be* the noise of a cry from [a]the fish gate, and an howling from the second, and a great crashing from the hills.

R *Hab 2:15–19* ◀▶ *Zec 1:12–15*
H *Na 2:10* ◀▶ *Zep 1:12*
S *Na 1:3* ◀▶ *Zep 2:3*

1:2 ′Heb. *By taking away I will make an end* ²Heb. *the face of the land*
3 [a]Hos. 4:3 ′Or, *idols*
4 [a]Hos. 10:5
5 [a]2 Ki. 23:12 [b]Josh. 23:7 ′Or, *to the LORD*
6 [a]Is. 1:4; Jer. 2:13 [b]Hos. 7:7
7 [a]Hab. 2:20; Zech. 2:13 [b]Is. 13:6 [c]Is. 34:6; Jer. 46:10 ′Heb. *sanctified*, or, *prepared*
8 [a]Jer. 39:6 ′Heb. *visit upon*
10 [a]2 Chr. 33:14
11 [a]Jas. 5:1
12 [a]Jer. 48:11 [b]Ps. 94:7 ′Heb. *curded*, or, *thickened*
13 [a]Amos 5:11 [b]Mic. 6:15
14 [a]Joel 2:1,11
15 [a]Is. 22:5; Jer. 30:7
16 [a]Jer. 4:19
17 [a]Deut. 28:29 [b]Ps. 79:3 [c]Jer. 9:22
18 [a]Ezek. 7:19 [b]ch. 3:8 [c]ver. 2,3

11 [a]Howl, ye inhabitants of Maktesh, for all the merchant people are cut down; all they that bear silver are cut off.

12 And it shall come to pass at that time, *that* I will search Jerusalem with candles, and punish the men that are [a]settled′ on their lees: [b]that say in their heart, The LORD will not do good, neither will he do evil. C H

13 Therefore their goods shall become a booty, and their houses a desolation: they shall also build houses, but [a]not inhabit *them;* and they shall plant vineyards, but [b]not drink the wine thereof.

The day of wrath

14 [a]The great day of the LORD *is* near, *it is* near, and hasteth greatly, *even* the voice of the day of the LORD: the mighty man shall cry there bitterly. P H

15 [a]That day *is* a day of wrath, a day of trouble and distress, a day of wasteness and desolation, a day of darkness and gloominess, a day of clouds and thick darkness,

16 A day of [a]the trumpet and alarm against the fenced cities, and against the high towers.

17 And I will bring distress upon men, that they shall [a]walk like blind men, because they have sinned against the LORD: and [b]their blood shall be poured out as dust, and their flesh [c]as the dung. H

18 [a]Neither their silver nor their gold shall be able to deliver them in the day of the LORD'S wrath; but the whole land shall be [b]devoured by the fire of his jealousy: for [c]he shall make even a speedy riddance of all them that dwell in the land. G

C *Hab 2:4* ◀▶ *Mal 3:13–14*
H *Zep 1:6–8* ◀▶ *Zep 1:14–15*
P *Hab 3:3–16* ◀▶ *Zep 3:8*
H *Zep 1:12* ◀▶ *Zep 1:17–18*
H *Zep 1:14–15* ◀▶ *Zep 2:2–3*
G *Eze 33:31* ◀▶ *Mt 5:20*

1:2–4 Zephaniah described the terrible judgment of God during the tribulation when all living things would experience God's unprecedented wrath. This sweeping destruction mirrors the destruction of the flood (see Ge 6:7), but this judgment will be carried out with fire (see 1:18; 3:8).

1:14–18 Zephaniah warned about the imminent "great day of the LORD" (1:14). With dramatic imagery Zephaniah described the worldwide destruction that would accompany this "day of wrath" (1:15). Neither wealth nor position would protect the wicked from this time of desolation and trouble.

The call to repentance

2 GATHER[a] YOURSELVES together, yea, gather together, O nation [1]not desired;

H M 2 Before the decree bring forth, *before* the day pass [a]as the chaff, before [b]the fierce anger of the LORD come upon you, before the day of the LORD's anger come upon you.

S 3 [a]Seek ye the LORD, [b]all ye meek of the earth, which have wrought his judgment; seek righteousness, seek meekness: [c]it may be ye shall be hid in the day of the LORD's anger.

J 4 ¶ For [a]Gaza shall be forsaken, and Ashkelon a desolation: they shall drive out Ashdod [b]at the noon day, and Ekron shall be rooted up.

The woe upon the nations

5 Woe unto the inhabitants of [a]the sea coast, the nation of the Cherethites! the word of the LORD *is* against you; O [b]Canaan, the land of the Philistines, I will even destroy thee, that there shall be no inhabitant.

6 And the sea coast shall be dwellings *and* cottages for shepherds, [a]and folds for flocks.

7 And the coast shall be for [a]the remnant of the house of Judah; they shall feed thereupon: in the houses of Ashkelon shall they lie down in the evening: [1]for the LORD their God shall [b]visit them, and [c]turn away their captivity.

8 ¶ [a]I have heard the reproach of Moab, and [b]the revilings of the children of Ammon, whereby they have reproached my people, and [c]magnified *themselves* against their border.

9 Therefore *as* I live, saith the LORD of hosts, the God of Israel, Surely [a]Moab shall be as Sodom, and [b]the children of Ammon as Gomorrah, [c]*even* the breeding of nettles, and saltpits, and a perpetual desolation: [d]the residue of my people shall spoil them, and the remnant of my people shall possess them.

10 This shall they have [a]for their pride, because they have reproached and magnified *themselves* against the people of the LORD of hosts.

11 The LORD *will be* terrible unto them: for he will [1]famish all the gods of the earth; [a]and *men* shall worship him, every one from his place, *even* all [b]the isles of the heathen.

12 ¶ [a]Ye Ethiopians also, ye *shall be* slain by [b]my sword.

13 And he will stretch out his hand against the north, and [a]destroy Assyria; and will make Nineveh a desolation, *and* dry like a wilderness.

14 And [a]flocks shall lie down in the midst of her, all [b]the beasts of the nations: both the [c]cormorant[1] and the bittern shall lodge in the [2]upper lintels of it; *their* voice shall sing in the windows; desolation *shall be* in the thresholds: [3]for he shall uncover the [d]cedar work.

15 This *is* the rejoicing city [a]that dwelt carelessly, [b]that said in her heart, I *am*, and *there is* none beside me: how is she become a desolation, a place for beasts to lie down in! every one that passeth by her [c]shall hiss, *and* [d]wag his hand.

The future of Jerusalem

3 WOE TO [1,2]her that is filthy and polluted, to the oppressing city!

2 She [a]obeyed not the voice; she [b]received not [1]correction; she trusted not in the LORD; she drew not near to her God.

3 [a]Her princes within her *are* roaring lions; her judges *are* [b]evening wolves; they gnaw not the bones till the morrow.

4 Her [a]prophets *are* light *and* treacher-

H *Zep 1:17–18* ◀ ▶ *Zep 3:8*
M *Hab 2:4* ◀ ▶ *Mal 3:13*
S *Zep 1:6–7* ◀ ▶ *Zec 7:9–10*
J *Da 7:10–11* ◀ ▶ *Mt 10:15*

2:1 [a]Joel 2:16 [1]Or, *not desirous*
2 [a]Job 21:18; Is. 17:13 [b]2 Ki. 23:26
3 [a]Amos 5:6 [b]Ps. 76:9 [c]Amos 5:15
4 [a]Zech. 9:5,6 [b]Jer. 6:4
5 [a]Ezek. 25:16 [b]Josh. 13:3
6 [a]Is. 17:2
7 [a]Mic. 5:7,8 [b]Luke 1:68 [c]Jer. 29:14 [1]Or, *when*
8 [a]Jer. 48:27 [b]Ezek. 25:3 [c]Jer. 49:1
9 [a]Is. 15 [b]Amos 1:13 [c]Deut. 29:33 [d]ver. 7
10 [a]Is. 16:6; Jer. 48:29
11 [a]Mal. 1:11; John 4:21 [b]Gen. 10:5 [1]Heb. *make lean*
12 [a]Is. 18:1; Jer. 46:9 [b]Ps. 17:13
13 [a]Is. 10:12; Nah. 1:1
14 [a]ver. 6 [b]Is. 13:21 [c]Is. 34:11 [d]Jer. 22:14 [1]Or, *pelican* [2]Or, *knobs,* or, *chapiters* [3]Or, *when he hath uncovered*
15 [a]Is. 47:8 [b]Rev. 18:7 [c]Lam. 2:15 [d]Nah. 3:19
3:1 [1]Or, *gluttonous* [2]Heb. *craw*
2 [a]Jer. 22:21 [b]Jer. 5:3 [1]Or, *instruction*
3 [a]Ezek. 22:27; Mic. 3:9 [b]Hab. 1:8
4 [a]Hos. 9:7

2:1–3 Zephaniah warned his people to repent of their wickedness in order that his people would "be hid in the day of the LORD's anger" (2:3).

2:4 This prophecy of judgment declared doom on four of the five great Philistine cities, indicating the extent of the destruction of this nation. Throughout the centuries following this prophecy, these ancient cities of Philistia have been conquered, rebuilt and conquered again. History records that the conquest of Gaza by Alexander the Great in 332 B.C. took over two months because of Gaza's strong defenses. When Alexander finally took the city, he killed all the male survivors and sold the women and children into slavery.

ous persons: her priests have polluted the sanctuary, they have done [b]violence to the law.

5 [a]The just LORD [b]*is* in the midst thereof; he will not do iniquity: [/]every morning doth he bring his judgment to light, he faileth not; but [c]the unjust knoweth no shame.

6 I have cut off the nations: their [/]towers are desolate; I made their streets waste, that none passeth by: their cities are destroyed, so that there is no man, that there is none inhabitant.

7 [a]I said, Surely thou wilt fear me, thou wilt receive instruction; so their dwelling should not be cut off, howsoever I punished them: but they rose early, *and* [b]corrupted all their doings.

P 8 ¶ Therefore [a]wait ye upon me, saith
H the LORD, until the day that I rise up to the prey: for my determination *is* to [b]gather the nations, that I may assemble the kingdoms, to pour upon them mine indignation, *even* all my fierce anger: for all the earth [c]shall be devoured with the fire of my jealousy.

I 9 For then will I turn to the people [a]a pure [/]language, that they may all call upon the name of the LORD, to serve him with one [2]consent.

10 [a]From beyond the rivers of Ethiopia my suppliants, *even* the daughter of my dispersed, shall bring mine offering.

11 In that day shalt thou not be ashamed for all thy doings, wherein thou hast transgressed against me: for then I will take away out of the midst of thee them that [a]rejoice in thy pride, and thou shalt no more be haughty [/]because of my holy mountain.

12 I will also leave in the midst of thee [a]an afflicted and poor people, and they shall trust in the name of the LORD.

13 [a]The remnant of Israel [b]shall not do iniquity, [c]nor speak lies; neither shall a deceitful tongue be found in their mouth: for [d]they shall feed and lie down, and none shall make *them* afraid.

14 ¶ [a]Sing, O daughter of Zion; shout, O Israel; be glad and rejoice with all the heart, O daughter of Jerusalem.

15 The LORD hath taken away thy judgments, he hath cast out thine enemy: [a]the king of Israel, *even* the LORD, [b]*is* in the midst of thee: thou shalt not see evil any more.

16 In that day [a]it shall be said to Jerusalem, Fear thou not: *and to* Zion, [b]Let not thine hands be [/]slack.

17 The LORD thy God [a]in the midst of thee *is* mighty; he will save, [b]he will rejoice over thee with joy; [/]he will rest in his love, he will joy over thee with singing.

18 I will gather *them that* [a]*are* sorrowful for the solemn assembly, *who* are of thee, *to whom* [/]the reproach of it *was* a burden.

19 Behold, at that time I will undo all that afflict thee: and I will save her that

4 [b]Ezek. 22:26
5 [a]Deut. 32:4 [b]Mic. 3:11 [/]Heb. *morning by morning* [c]Jer. 3:3
6 [/]Or, *corners*
7 [a]Jer. 8:6 [b]Gen. 6:12
8 [a]Prov. 20:22 [b]Joel 3:2 [c]ch. 1:18
9 [a]Is. 19:18 [/]Heb. *lip* [2]Heb. *shoulder*
10 [a]Ps. 68:31; Acts 8:27
11 [a]Mat. 3:9 [/]Heb. *in my holy*
12 [a]Is. 14:32
13 [a]Mic. 4:7 [b]Is. 60:21 [c]Rev. 14:5 [d]Ezek. 34:28
14 [a]Is. 12:6
15 [a]John 1:49 [b]Ezek. 48:35; Rev. 7:15
16 [a]Is. 35:3,4 [b]Heb. 12:12 [/]Or, *faint*
17 [a]ver. 15 [b]Is. 62:5; Jer. 32:41 [/]Heb. *he will be silent*
18 [a]Lam. 2:6 [/]Heb. *the burden upon it was reproach*

P *Zep 1:14–18* ◄► *Hag 2:22*
H *Zep 2:2–3* ◄► *Zec 3:2*
I *Na 1:15* ◄► *Hag 2:7*

3:8 This prophecy looks forward to the tribulation and the final Battle of Armageddon when Jesus Christ will destroy the armies of the antichrist and his allies. God will then judge the nations and "pour upon them mine indignation." Compare this verse with Joel 3:2; Mt 25:31–32; Rev 16:14.
3:9 Though some view this verse as a prophecy regarding the reestablishment of ancient Hebrew as the language of millennial Jerusalem, others understand this verse as a prophecy of the purification of the nations. God's judgment in the last days will impact the nations so much that they will turn from their idols and worship him in both word and deed. They will call on his name and honor him and honor his chosen people. Compare this verse with Isa 6:5 and Hos 2:17.
3:10 Cush is believed to be the area of southern Egypt, Sudan and northern Ethiopia. Exiled Jews have made this part of the world their home for centuries, with some Ethiopians claiming King Solomon as their ancestor. Though some of these Jews are slowly returning to the promised land, Zephaniah's words promised that all of the Jews who were widely scattered to the far ends of the world would be restored to their homeland when the Messiah returns.
3:11–20 God promised that his people would be fully restored to Jerusalem and the promised land in the last days. There would be joy in the city, no more lying, no unrighteousness, an abundance of peace and security because the Messiah would be in their midst. Zephaniah encouraged the people to take heart because of God's assurance of restoration. In contrast to the messages of doom and judgment on Israel, this prophecy promised blessing and God's intent to make Israel "a praise among all the people of the earth" (3:20).

[a]halteth, and gather her that was driven
out; and [1]I will get them praise and fame
in every land [2]where they have been put
to shame.
20 At that time [a]will I bring you *again,*
even in the time that I gather you: for I
will make you a name and a praise among
all people of the earth, when I turn back
your captivity before your eyes, saith the
LORD.

19 [a]Ezek. 34:16; Mic. 4:6,7 [1]Heb. *I will set them for a praise* [2]Heb. *of their shame*
20 [a]Is. 11:12; Ezek. 28:25

Haggai

Author: Haggai

Theme: The blessing in rebuilding

Date of Writing: c. 520 B.C.

Outline of Haggai

I. The People Stirred to Action (1:1–15)
II. Hopes for the New Temple (2:1–9)
III. Promised Blessings (2:10–19)
IV. God's Final Triumph (2:20–23)

THIS VERY SHORT book takes its name from the prophet Haggai, who ministered during the reign of King Darius to the returned exiles in Jerusalem. A contemporary of Zechariah, Haggai noticed that the exiles who had returned from Babylon had not rebuilt the temple because they were too busy rebuilding their own homes. In four distinct messages Haggai vehemently reproved his people and demanded that they obey God's command to rebuild his temple in Jerusalem. Haggai is one of the few prophets who saw a positive response to his urgings.

The Babylonian exiles had been granted permission to return to the promised land to rebuild God's temple. Though the people started the project with enthusiasm, they soon turned their attention to their own needs, and God withdrew his blessing from them. Haggai assured the people that if they would give priority to God's work they would prosper. His words roused the people to action under the leadership of Zerubbabel, governor of Judea, and Joshua the high priest. As the rebuilding project resumed, many of the older exiles were saddened that the rebuilt temple was not as magnificent as Solomon's temple had been before its destruction in 586 B.C. Haggai reassured them that even though the building might be less impressive, the glory of this rebuilt temple would be greater than that of the former.

The call to rebuild the temple

1 IN [a]THE second year of Darius the king, in the sixth month, in the first day of the month, came the word of the LORD [/]by Haggai the prophet unto [b]Zerubbabel the son of Shealtiel, [2]governor of Judah, and to [c]Joshua the son of [d]Josedech, the high priest, saying,

2 Thus speaketh the LORD of hosts, saying, This people say, The time is not come, the time that the LORD'S house should be built.

3 Then came the word of the LORD [a]by Haggai the prophet, saying,

4 [a]*Is it* time for you, O ye, to dwell in your ceiled houses, and this house *lie* waste?

T 5 Now therefore thus saith the LORD of hosts; [a]Consider[/] your ways.

6 Ye have [a]sown much, and bring in little; ye eat, but ye have not enough; ye drink, but ye are not filled with drink; ye clothe you, but there is none warm; and [b]he that earneth wages earneth wages *to put it* into a bag [/]with holes.

7 ¶ Thus saith the LORD of hosts; Consider your ways.

8 Go up to the mountain, and bring wood, and build the house; and I will take pleasure in it, and I will be glorified, saith the LORD.

9 [a]Ye looked for much, and, lo, *it came* to little; and when ye brought *it* home, [b]I did [/]blow upon it. Why? saith the LORD of hosts. Because of mine house that *is* waste, and ye run every man unto his own house.

10 Therefore [a]the heaven over you is stayed from dew, and the earth is stayed *from* her fruit.

11 And I [a]called for a drought upon the land, and upon the mountains, and upon the corn, and upon the new wine, and upon the oil, and upon *that* which the ground bringeth forth, and upon men, and upon cattle, and [b]upon all the labour of the hands.

12 ¶ [a]Then Zerubbabel the son of Shealtiel, and Joshua the son of Josedech, the high priest, with all the remnant of the people, obeyed the voice of the LORD their God, and the words of Haggai the prophet, as the LORD their God had sent him, and the people did fear before the LORD.

13 Then spake Haggai the LORD'S messenger in the LORD'S message unto the people, saying, [a]I *am* with you, saith the LORD.

14 And [a]the LORD stirred up the spirit of Zerubbabel the son of Shealtiel, [b]governor of Judah, and the spirit of Joshua the son of Josedech, the high priest, and the spirit of all the remnant of the people; [c]and they came and did work in the house of the LORD of hosts, their God,

15 In the four and twentieth day of the sixth month, in the second year of Darius the king.

Comfort and hope from God

2 IN THE seventh *month,* in the one and twentieth *day* of the month, came the word of the LORD [/]by the prophet Haggai, saying,

2 Speak now to Zerubbabel the son of Shealtiel, governor of Judah, and to Joshua the son of Josedech, the high priest, and to the residue of the people, saying,

3 [a]Who *is* left among you that saw this house in her first glory? and how do ye see it now? [b]*is it* not in your eyes in comparison of it as nothing?

4 Yet now [a]be strong, O Zerubbabel, saith the LORD; and be strong, O Joshua, son of Josedech, the high priest; and be strong, all ye people of the land, saith the LORD, and work: for I *am* with you, saith the LORD of hosts:

5 [a]*According to* the word that I covenanted with you when ye came out of Egypt, so [b]my spirit remaineth among you: fear ye not. E

6 For thus saith the LORD of hosts; [a]Yet once, it *is* a little while, and [b]I will shake the heavens, and the earth, and the sea, and the dry *land;* C

T *Da 12:10* ◀▶ *Hag 2:15–19*

E *Mic 3:8* ◀▶ *Zec 4:6*
C *Da 7:13* ◀▶ *Mt 16:27–28*

1:1 [a]Ezra 4:24 [b]1 Chr. 3:17 [c]Ezra 5:2 [d]1 Chr. 6:15 [/]Heb. *by the hand of Haggai* [2]Or, *captain*
3 [a]Ezra 5:1
4 [a]2 Sam. 7:2
5 [a]Lam. 3:40 [/]Heb. *Set your heart on your ways*
6 [a]Deut. 28:38 [b]Zech. 8:10 [/]Heb. *pierced through*
9 [a]ch. 2:16 [b]ch. 2:17 [/]Or, *blow it away*
10 [a]Lev. 26:19; Deut. 28:23; 1 Ki. 8:35
11 [a]1 Ki. 17:1; 2 Ki. 8:1 [b]ch. 2:17
12 [a]Ezra 5:2
13 [a]Mat. 28:20; Rom. 8:31
14 [a]2 Chr. 36:22; Ezra 1:1 [b]ch. 2:21 [c]Ezra 5:2,8
2:1 [/]Heb. *by the hand of*
3 [a]Ezra 3:12 [b]Zech. 4:10
4 [a]Zech. 8:9
5 [a]Ex. 29:45,46 [b]Neh. 9:20; Is. 63:11
6 [a]ver. 21; Heb. 12:26 [b]Joel 3:16

2:6 God's promise to "shake the heavens, and the earth" was initially fulfilled when Persia fell to Alexander the Great (333–330 B.C.). That tumultuous overthrow foreshadowed the judgment of the nations at the second coming of Christ. Compare this verse with Heb 12:26–27.

I 7 And I will shake all nations, [a]and the desire of all nations shall come: and I will fill this house with glory, saith the LORD of hosts.
8 The silver *is* mine, and the gold *is* mine, saith the LORD of hosts.

I *Zep 3:9–20* ◀ ▶ *Zec 1:12*

7 [a]Gen. 49:10; Mal. 3:1
9 [a]John 1:14 [b]Ps. 85:8,9; Luke 2:14; Eph. 2:14

9 [a]The glory of this latter house shall be greater than of the former, saith the LORD of hosts: and in this place will I give [b]peace, saith the LORD of hosts. B

Holiness and uncleanness

10 ¶ In the four and twentieth *day* of

B *Mic 5:1–4* ◀ ▶ *Zec 9:9*

2:7 The Hebrew phrasing in this verse allows for a variety of translations. Some feel this verse refers to the coming of the Messiah (see Mal 3:1). Others feel this verse refers to articles of wealth and value such as King Darius's contribution to the temple (see Ezr 6:8) and thus foreshadows the offerings that the nations will bring to the millennial temple. The word "glory" in this verse could refer either to material splendor (see Isa 60:7, 13) or to God's presence (see 1Ki 8:10–11; Lk 2:27, 32).

2:9 This verse may have different interpretations. The reference to the two different temples may be a comparison between Zerubbabel's temple and Herod's temple, or it may reflect a comparison between the current temple and the one to be built during the millennium. The peace that God would grant might refer to the peace brought by Christ in his first coming and death on the cross or it may refer to the world peace of Christ's millennial reign. Either interpretation is prophetic and wonderful in its scope.

Zerubbabel's Temple

536–516 B.C.

Temple source materials are subject to academic interpretation, and subsequent art reconstructions vary.

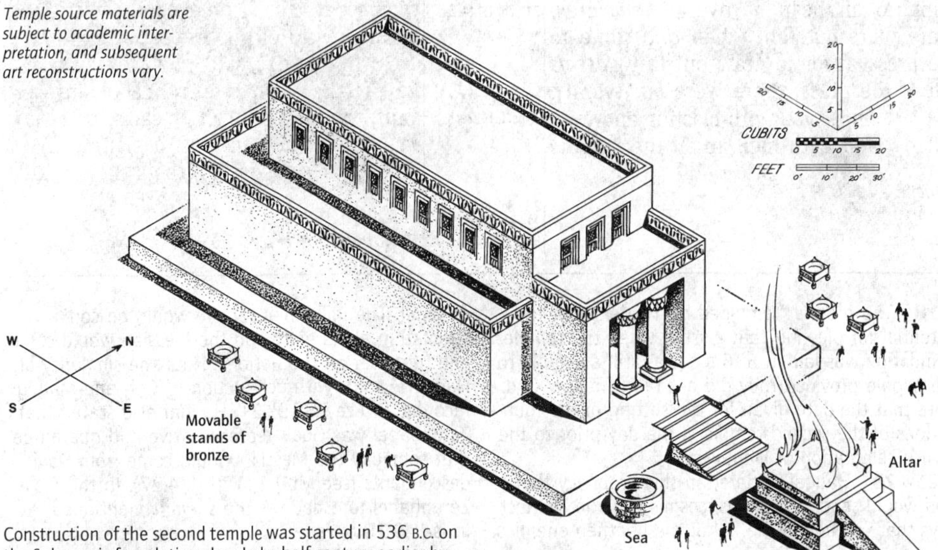

©1981 Hugh Claycombe

Construction of the second temple was started in 536 B.C. on the Solomonic foundations leveled a half-century earlier by the Babylonians. People who remembered the earlier temple wept at the comparison (Ezr 3:12). Not until 516 B.C., the 6th year of the Persian emperor Darius I (522-486), was the temple finally completed at the urging of Haggai and Zechariah (Ezr 6:13-15).

Archaeological evidence confirms that the Persian period in Palestine was a comparatively impoverished one in terms of material culture. Later Aramaic documents from Elephantine in Upper Egypt illustrate the official process of gaining permission to construct a Jewish place of worship, and the opposition engendered by the presence of various foes during this period.

Of the temple and its construction, little is known. Among the few contemporary buildings, the Persian palace at Lachish and the Tobiad monument at Iraq el-Amir may be compared in terms of technique.

Unlike the more famous structures razed in 586 B.C. and A.D. 70, the temple begun by Zerubbabel suffered no major hostile destruction, but was gradually repaired and reconstructed over a long period. Eventually it was replaced entirely by Herod's magnificent edifice.

the ninth *month,* in the second year of
Darius, came the word of the LORD by
Haggai the prophet, saying,
11 Thus saith the LORD of hosts; [a]Ask
now the priests *concerning* the law,
saying,
12 If one bear holy flesh in the skirt of
his garment, and with his skirt do touch
bread, or pottage, or wine, or oil, or any
meat, shall it be holy? And the priests
answered and said, No.
13 Then said Haggai, If *one that is* [a]un-
clean by a dead body touch any of these,
shall it be unclean? And the priests answered and said, It shall be unclean.
14 Then answered Haggai, and said,
[a]So *is* this people, and so *is* this nation
before me, saith the LORD; and so *is* every
work of their hands; and that which they
offer there *is* unclean.
B 15 And now, I pray you, [a]consider
T from this day and upward, from before a
U stone was laid upon a stone in the temple
of the LORD:
16 Since those *days* were, [a]when *one*
came to an heap of twenty *measures,*
there were *but* ten: when *one* came to
the pressvat for to draw out fifty *vessels*
out of the press, there were *but* twenty.
17 [a]I smote you with blasting and with
mildew and with hail [b]in all the labours
of your hands; [c]yet ye *turned* not to me,
saith the LORD.
18 Consider now from this day and upward, from the four and twentieth day of
the ninth *month, even* from [a]the day that
the foundation of the LORD'S temple was
laid, consider *it.*
19 [a]Is the seed yet in the barn? yea, as
yet the vine, and the fig tree, and the
pomegranate, and the olive tree, hath not
brought forth: from this day will I bless
you.

Zerubbabel chosen by the LORD

20 ¶ And again the word of the LORD
came unto Haggai in the four and twentieth *day* of the month, saying,
21 Speak to Zerubbabel, [a]governor of
Judah, saying, [b]I will shake the heavens
and the earth;
22 And [a]I will overthrow the throne of P
kingdoms, and I will destroy the strength
of the kingdoms of the heathen; and [b]I
will overthrow the chariots, and those
that ride in them; and the horses and
their riders shall come down, every one
by the sword of his brother.
23 In that day, saith the LORD of hosts, M
will I take thee, O Zerubbabel, my servant, the son of Shealtiel, saith the LORD,
[a]and will make thee as a signet: for [b]I
have chosen thee, saith the LORD of hosts.

11 [a]Lev. 10:10,11; Deut. 33:10; Mal. 2:7
13 [a]Num. 19:11
14 [a]Tit. 1:15
15 [a]ch. 1:5
16 [a]ch. 1:6,9; Zech. 8:10
17 [a]Deut. 28:22; 1 Ki. 8:37; Amos 4:9; ch. 1:9 [b]ch. 1:11 [c]Jer. 5:3; Amos 4:6,8-11
18 [a]Zech. 8:9
19 [a]Zech. 8:12
21 [a]ch. 1:14 [b]ver. 6,7
22 [a]Dan. 2:44 [b]Mic. 5:10; Zech. 9:10
23 [a]Sol. 8:6; Jer. 22:24 [b]Is. 42:1 & 43:10

B *Joel 2:24–26* ◄► *Zec 8:12*
T *Hag 1:5–11* ◄► *1Co 11:32*
U *Da 12:3* ◄► *Mal 2:5*
P *Zep 3:8* ◄► *Zec 9:2*
M *Hab 2:20* ◄► *Zec 2:5*

2:18 The prophet reminded his readers that the potential for blessing that existed when the temple foundation was laid in 536 B.C. was still available to the people provided they did not fail to follow God. Note that the date given for the setting of the foundations of the second temple is the day prior to the Jewish celebration of Hanukkah.

2:21–23 Haggai declared in this prophecy that God would send miraculous, cosmic signs in the last days that will herald the fall of the heathen enemies of Israel. The millennial temple would be constructed in all its glory and the Messiah would come and rule over all the nations. Note the similarity of Haggai's words with destruction of Gog and Magog recorded in Eze 38:19–21. Haggai also stated that Zerubbabel was God's representative and guarantee that someday the Messiah would come from David's descendants (see Mt 1:1, 12; Ac 4:27). In this way Zerubbabel foreshadows the servant mentioned in Isa 42:10.

Zechariah

Author: Zechariah

Theme: Rebuilding the temple and the nation of Judah

Date of Writing: c. 520 B.C.

Outline of Zechariah

I. The Call to Obedience (1:1–6)
II. Eight Visions (1:7—6:8)
III. Crowning the High Priest (6:9–15)
IV. Obedience Versus Legalism (7:1—8:23)
V. The King Rejected (9:1—11:17)
VI. The King Enthroned (12:1–14:21)

THIS BOOK WAS written by the prophet Zechariah, whose name means "The LORD remembers." Zechariah belonged to a priestly family (see 1:1, 7) and was a young man when he accompanied those who returned from Babylon in 538 B.C. Zechariah began his ministry during the reign of King Darius of Persia, about the same time as the prophet Haggai delivered his first message to the returned exiles. The duration of Zechariah's ministry is uncertain, but it is possible that he witnessed the rise of Greece as a major power (see 9:13), suggesting that he ministered to the returned exiles for almost forty years.

In his opening message, Zechariah admonished the people to learn from their ancestors' mistakes. Zechariah maintained that the Jews needed to listen to God's message through his prophets and renew their covenant relationship with God lest they fall again under his judgment. Zechariah then recorded a series of night visions meant to encourage the rebuilders of the temple. Though the exiles faced opposition to their rebuilding program (see Ezr 5—6), Zechariah's visions reminded the Jews that God was ultimately in control of everything and had a long-range plan for Israel.

The book of Zechariah, as one of the closing prophetic books of the OT, parallels the book of Revelation, the NT's last revelation of God. Both books contain apocalyptic prophecies that summarize and expand the prophecies found in the other books. Note the similarity between Zechariah's visions and those recorded in Revelation of the four horsemen (see 1:1–17; Rev 6:4), the measuring of Jerusalem (see 2:1–13; Rev 21:15–17) and the flying roll (see 5:1–4; Rev 5:1–14).

Call for national repentance

1 IN THE eighth month, [a]in the second year of Darius, came the word of the LORD [b]unto Zechariah, the son of Berechiah, the son of Iddo the prophet, saying,

2 The LORD hath been ʹsore displeased with your fathers.

L 3 Therefore say thou unto them, Thus
P saith the LORD of hosts; Turn [a]ye unto me, saith the LORD of hosts, and I will turn unto you, saith the LORD of hosts.

N 4 Be ye not as your fathers, [a]unto whom the former prophets have cried, saying, Thus saith the LORD of hosts; [b]Turn ye now from your evil ways, and *from* your evil doings: but they did not hear, nor hearken unto me, saith the LORD.

5 Your fathers, where *are* they? and the prophets, do they live for ever?

6 But [a]my words and my statutes, which I commanded my servants the prophets, did they not ʹtake hold of your fathers? and they returned and said, [b]Like as the LORD of hosts thought to do unto us, according to our ways, and according to our doings, so hath he dealt with us.

The horsemen among the myrtles

7 ¶ Upon the four and twentieth day of the eleventh month, which *is* the month Sebat, in the second year of Darius, came the word of the LORD unto Zechariah, the son of Berechiah, the son of Iddo the prophet, saying,

8 I saw by night, and behold [a]a man riding upon a red horse, and he stood among the myrtle trees that *were* in the bottom; and behind him *were there* [b]red horses, ʹspeckled, and white.

9 Then said I, O my lord, what *are* these? And the angel that talked with me said unto me, I will show thee what these *be*.

10 And the man that stood among the myrtle trees answered and said, [a]These *are they* whom the LORD hath sent to walk to and fro through the earth.

11 [a]And they answered the angel of the LORD that stood among the myrtle trees, and said, We have walked to and fro through the earth, and, behold, all the earth sitteth still, and is at rest.

12 ¶ Then the angel of the LORD an- I
swered and said, O LORD of hosts, how R
long wilt thou not have mercy on Jerusalem and on the cities of Judah, against which thou hast had indignation [a]these threescore and ten years?

13 And the LORD answered the angel that talked with me *with* [a]good words *and* comfortable words.

14 So the angel that communed with me said unto me, Cry thou, saying, Thus saith the LORD of hosts; I am [a]jealous for Jerusalem and for Zion with a great jealousy.

15 And I am very sore displeased with the heathen *that are* at ease: for [a]I was but a little displeased, and they helped forward the affliction.

16 Therefore thus saith the LORD; [a]I am returned to Jerusalem with mercies: my house shall be built in it, saith the LORD of hosts, and [b]a line shall be stretched forth upon Jerusalem.

17 Cry yet, saying, Thus saith the LORD of hosts; My cities through ʹprosperity shall yet be spread abroad; [a]and the LORD shall yet comfort Zion, and [b]shall yet choose Jerusalem.

Four horns and four carpenters

18 ¶ Then lifted I up mine eyes, and G
saw, and behold four horns. R

1:1 [a]Ezra 4:24; Hag. 1:1 [b]Ezra 5:1; Mat. 23:35
2 ʹHeb. *with displeasure*
3 [a]Jer. 25:5 & 35:15; Mic. 7:19; Mal. 3:7; Luke 15:20; Jas. 4:8
4 [a]2 Chr. 36:15,16 [b]Is. 31:6; Jer 3:12 & 18:11; Ezek. 18:30; Hos. 14:1
6 [a]Is. 55:1 [b]Lam. 1:18 & 2:17 ʹOr, *overtake*
8 [a]Josh. 5:13; Rev. 6:4 [b]ch. 6:2-7 ʹOr, *bay*
10 [a]Heb. 1:14
11 [a]Ps. 103:20,21
12 [a]Jer. 25:11,12; Dan. 9:2; ch. 7:5
13 [a]Jer. 29:10
14 [a]Joel 2:18; ch. 8:2
15 [a]Is. 47:6
16 [a]Is. 12:1 & 54:8; ch. 2:10 & 8:3 [b]ch. 2:1,2
17 [a]Is. 51:3 [b]Is. 14:1; ch. 2:12 & 3:2 ʹHeb. *good*

L *Mic 7:18–19* ◀▶ *Zec 3:1–5*
P *Mic 7:18–19* ◀▶ *Mal 3:7*
N *Am 4:12* ◀▶ *Zec 7:11–12*

I *Hag 2:7* ◀▶ *Zec 2:1–5*
R *Zep 1:2–4* ◀▶ *Zec 1:18–21*
G *Da 12:11–12* ◀▶ *Mal 1:11*
R *Zec 1:12–15* ◀▶ *Zec 3:3–4*

1:8–17 Zechariah saw eight visions in one night. His first vision involved a man among the myrtle trees and four horses. The imagery of this vision indicated that though Israel suffered and their oppressors were successful, God is concerned about his people and will restore them and their temple. God called Zechariah to look beyond his circumstances to God's eternal promises. The significance of the different colored horses is uncertain.

1:18–21 Zechariah saw four horns in his second vision. These horns prophetically represented four empires, probably referring to Assyria, Egypt, Babylonia and Medo-Persia. These powerful nations had devastated Israel, and God promised that they in turn would be destroyed. The four craftsmen, probably Egypt, Babylonia, Medo-Persia and Greece,

19 And I said unto the angel that talked with me, What *be* these? And he answered me, [a]These *are* the horns which have scattered Judah, Israel, and Jerusalem.

20 And the LORD showed me four carpenters.

21 Then said I, What come these to do? And he spake, saying, These *are* the horns which have scattered Judah, so that no man did lift up his head: but these are come to fray them, to cast out the horns of the Gentiles, which [a]lifted up *their* horn over the land of Judah to scatter it.

The measuring line of Jerusalem

I **2** I LIFTED up mine eyes again, and looked, and behold [a]a man with a measuring line in his hand.

2 Then said I, Whither goest thou? And he said unto me, [a]To measure Jerusalem, to see what *is* the breadth thereof, and what *is* the length thereof.

3 And, behold, the angel that talked with me went forth, and another angel went out to meet him,

4 And said unto him, Run, speak to this young man, saying, [a]Jerusalem shall be inhabited *as* towns without walls for the multitude of men and cattle therein:

M 5 For I, saith the LORD, will be unto her [a]a wall of fire round about, [b]and will be the glory in the midst of her.

6 ¶ Ho, ho, *come forth,* and flee [a]from the land of the north, saith the LORD: for I have [b]spread you abroad as the four winds of the heaven, saith the LORD.

7 [a]Deliver thyself, O Zion, that dwellest *with* the daughter of Babylon.

L 8 For thus saith the LORD of hosts; After the glory hath he sent me unto the nations which spoiled you: for he that [a]toucheth you toucheth the apple of his eye.

9 For, behold, I will [a]shake mine hand upon them, and they shall be a spoil to their servants: and [b]ye shall know that the LORD of hosts hath sent me.

D I M 10 ¶ [a]Sing and rejoice, O daughter of Zion: for, lo, I come, and I [b]will dwell in the midst of thee, saith the LORD.

11 [a]And many nations shall be joined to the LORD [b]in that day, and shall be [c]my people: and I will dwell in the midst of thee, and [d]thou shalt know that the LORD of hosts hath sent me unto thee.

12 And the LORD shall [a]inherit Judah his portion in the holy land, and [b]shall choose Jerusalem again.

13 [a]Be silent, O all flesh, before the LORD: for he is raised up [b]out of [1]his holy habitation.

Joshua cleansed and reclothed

L **3** AND HE showed me [a]Joshua the high priest standing before the angel of the LORD, and [b]Satan[1] standing at his right hand [2]to resist him.

I H 2 And the LORD said unto Satan, [a]The LORD rebuke thee, O Satan; even the LORD that [b]hath chosen Jerusalem rebuke thee: [c]*is* not this a brand plucked out of the fire?

R 3 Now Joshua was clothed with [a]filthy garments, and stood before the angel.

4 And he answered and spake unto those that stood before him, saying, Take away the filthy garments from him. And unto him he said, Behold, I have caused

I *Zec 1:12* ◄► *Zec 2:10–13*
M *Hag 2:23* ◄► *Zec 2:10–13*
L *Joel 2:27–28* ◄► *Mal 3:16–17*

D *Eze 44:1–2* ◄► *Zec 14:4–7*
I *Zec 2:1–5* ◄► *Zec 3:2–5*
M *Zec 2:5* ◄► *Zec 6:11–15*
L *Zec 1:3* ◄► *Zec 13:1*
I *Zec 2:10–13* ◄► *Zec 3:9–10*
H *Zep 3:8* ◄► *Mal 1:4*
R *Zec 1:18–21* ◄► *Zec 7:14*

19 [a]Ezra 4:1,4,7 & 5:3
21 [a]Ps. 75:4,5
2:1 [a]Ezek. 40:3
2 [a]Rev. 11:1
4 [a]Jer. 31:27; Ezek. 36:10
5 [a]Is. 26:1 [b]Is. 60:19
6 [a]Is. 48:20 [b]Deut. 28:64; Ezek. 17:21
7 [a]Rev. 18:4
8 [a]Deut. 32:10
9 [a]Is. 19:16 [b]ch. 4:9
10 [a]Is. 12:6 [b]Lev. 26:12
11 [a]Is. 2:2,3 [b]ch. 3:10 [c]Ex. 12:49 [d]Ezek. 33:33
12 [a]Deut. 32:9 [b]ch. 1:17
13 [a]Hab. 2:20 [b]Ps. 68:5; Is. 57:15 [1]Heb. *the habitation of his holiness*
3:1 [a]Hag. 1:1 [b]Ps. 109:6 [1]i.e. *an adversary* [2]Heb. *to be his adversary*
2 [a]Jude 9 [b]Rom. 8:33 [c]Amos 4:11; Rom. 11:5
3 [a]Is. 64:6

---

would come against the four horns and destroy them. This vision clearly stated that all of Judah's enemies would ultimately be defeated.

2:1–13 This third vision promised a full restoration of Jerusalem, the temple and the people during the last days when the Messiah will rule from the throne of David in the millennial kingdom. Though Jerusalem will expand beyond its walls, it will experience peace and security because of God's protection.

3:1–10 Zechariah envisioned Joshua the high priest, standing in opposition to Satan before God's angel. Just as the angel of the Lord required the cleansing of Joshua, so God required the cleansing of Israel and the removal of their sin so that they might be restored to a priestly position before God. This vision also symbolized the future cleansing of the nation of Israel at the second coming of Christ and foreshadowed the Messiah with several different symbols and titles: "servant" (3:8; see Isa 41:8–9), "BRANCH" (3:8; see Isa 4:2; 11:1), and "stone" (3:9; see Isa 8:13–15; 28:16).

thine iniquity to pass from thee, [a]and I will clothe thee with change of raiment.

5 And I said, Let them set a fair [a]mitre upon his head. So they set a fair mitre upon his head, and clothed him with garments. And the angel of the LORD stood by.

6 And the angel of the LORD protested unto Joshua, saying,

7 Thus saith the LORD of hosts; If thou wilt walk in my ways, and if thou wilt [a]keep my [1]charge, then thou shalt also [b]judge my house, and shalt also keep my courts, and I will give thee [2]places to walk among these that [c]stand by.

8 Hear now, O Joshua the high priest, thou, and thy fellows that sit before thee: for they *are* [a]men[1] wondered at: for, behold, I will bring forth [b]my servant the [c]BRANCH.

I 9 For behold the stone that I have laid before Joshua; [a]upon one stone *shall be* [b]seven eyes: behold, I will engrave the graving thereof, saith the LORD of hosts, and [c]I will remove the iniquity of that land in one day.

10 [a]In that day, saith the LORD of hosts, shall ye call every man his neighbour [b]under the vine and under the fig tree.

The candlestick and two olive trees

4 AND [a]THE angel that talked with me came again, and waked me, [b]as a man that is wakened out of his sleep,

2 And said unto me, What seest thou? And I said, I have looked, and behold [a]a candlestick all *of* gold, [1]with a bowl upon the top of it, [b]and his seven lamps thereon, and [2]seven pipes to the seven lamps, which *are* upon the top thereof:

I *Zec 3:2–5* ◄► *Zec 8:1–3*

4 [a]Is. 61:10; Luke 15:22
5 [a]Ex. 29:6
7 [a]Lev. 8:35; Ezek. 44:16 [b]Deut. 17:9 [c]ch. 4:14 [1]Or, *ordinance* [2]Heb. *walks*
8 [a]Ps. 71:7; Is. 8:18 [b]Is. 42:1; Ezek. 34:23 [c]Is. 11:1; ch. 6:12 [1]Heb. *men of wonder,* or, *sign*
9 [a]Ps. 118:22; Is. 28:16 [b]Rev. 5:6 [c]Jer. 31:34; Mic. 7:18
10 [a]ch. 2:11 [b]Is. 36:16; Mic. 4:4
4:1 [a]ch. 2:3 [b]Dan. 8:18
2 [a]Rev. 1:12 [b]Rev. 4:5 [1]Heb. *with her bowl* [2]Or, *seven several pipes to the lamps*
3 [a]Rev. 11:4
6 [a]Hos. 1:7 [1]Or, *army*
7 [a]Jer. 51:25; Mat. 21:21 [b]Ps. 118:22 [c]Ezra 3:11,13
9 [a]Ezra 3:10 [b]Ezra 6:15 [c]ch. 2:9,11 & 6:15 [d]Is. 48:16; ch. 2:8
10 [a]Hag. 2:3 [b]2 Chr. 16:9; Prov. 15:3; ch. 3:9 [1]Or, *since the seven eyes of the LORD shall rejoice* [2]Heb. *stone of tin*
11 [a]ver. 3

3 [a]And two olive trees by it, one upon the right *side* of the bowl, and the other upon the left *side* thereof.

4 So I answered and spake to the angel that talked with me, saying, What *are* these, my lord?

5 Then the angel that talked with me answered and said unto me, Knowest thou not what these be? And I said, No, my lord.

6 Then he answered and spake unto E
me, saying, This *is* the word of the LORD M
unto Zerubbabel, saying, [a]Not by [1]might, W
nor by power, but by my spirit, saith the V
LORD of hosts.

7 Who *art* thou, [a]O great mountain? before Zerubbabel *thou shalt become* a plain: and he shall bring forth [b]the headstone *thereof* [c]*with* shoutings, *crying,* Grace, grace unto it.

8 Moreover the word of the LORD came unto me, saying,

9 The hands of Zerubbabel [a]have laid the foundation of this house; his hands [b]shall also finish it; and [c]thou shalt know that the [d]LORD of hosts hath sent me unto you.

10 For who hath despised the day of E
[a]small things? [1]for they shall rejoice, and shall see the [2]plummet in the hand of Zerubbabel *with* those seven; [b]they *are* the eyes of the LORD, which run to and fro through the whole earth.

11 ¶ Then answered I, and said unto him, What *are* these [a]two olive trees

E *Hag 2:5* ◄► *Zec 6:8*
M *Mic 3:8* ◄► *Zec 6:8*
W *Mic 2:7* ◄► *Lk 24:49*
V *Da 11:32* ◄► *Zec 12:8*
E *Am 8:7* ◄► *Mt 9:4*

3:9 The prophet described this "stone" as a prophetic representation of the Messiah (see Ps 118:22–23; 1Pe 2:6–8). The "seven eyes" (see 4:10) may represent infinite intelligence or may refer to the seven spirits or characteristics of God (see Isa 11:2; 1Co 12:4–11; Rev 3:1; 4:5; 5:6).

3:10 Zechariah described a vision of the messianic era of world peace and security (see 1Ki 4:25; Isa 36:16; Mic 4:4). This was a traditional Jewish image of the future messianic kingdom.

4:1–14 Zechariah's vision of the candlestick with its seven lamps depicted the divine resources available to God's people. The light from the lamps represents God's glory among his people and is made possible only by the oil that is the power of God's Spirit. Note the parallel between this vision and Christ among the seven golden candles in Rev 1:12.

4:3–14 The symbolism of the two olive trees contains a double meaning. Its initial fulfillment depicted the priestly and royal offices occupied by Joshua and Zerubbabel. The continuous supply of oil indicated God's empowering for these two men to stand as God's witnesses to oversee the reconstruction of the temple. In the last days these verses will be completely fulfilled when two mighty witnesses arise during the tribulation just prior to the Battle of Armageddon. These witnesses will be empowered by the Holy Spirit for an astonishing ministry in the last days (see Rev 11:3–12).

upon the right *side* of the candlestick and upon the left *side* thereof?

12 And I answered again, and said unto him, What *be these* two olive branches which [1]through the two golden pipes [2]empty [3]the golden *oil* out of themselves?

13 And he answered me and said, Knowest thou not what these *be?* And I said, No, my lord.

14 Then said he, [a]These *are* the two [1]anointed ones, [b]that stand by [c]the Lord of the whole earth.

The flying roll

5 THEN I turned, and lifted up mine eyes, and looked, and behold a flying [a]roll.

2 And he said unto me, What seest thou? And I answered, I see a flying roll; the length thereof *is* twenty cubits, and the breadth thereof ten cubits.

3 Then said he unto me, This *is* the [a]curse that goeth forth over the face of the whole earth: for [1]every one that stealeth shall be cut off *as* on this side according to it; and every one that sweareth shall be cut off *as* on that side according to it.

4 I will bring it forth, saith the LORD of hosts, and it shall enter into the house of the thief, and into the house of [a]him that sweareth falsely by my name: and it shall remain in the midst of his house, and [b]shall consume it with the timber thereof and the stones thereof.

The ephah of iniquity

5 ¶ Then the angel that talked with me went forth, and said unto me, Lift up now thine eyes, and see what *is* this that goeth forth.

6 And I said, What *is* it? And he said, This *is* an ephah that goeth forth. He said moreover, This *is* their resemblance through all the earth.

7 And, behold, there was lifted up a [1]talent of lead: and this *is* a woman that sitteth in the midst of the ephah.

8 And he said, This *is* wickedness. And he cast it into the midst of the ephah; and he cast the weight of lead upon the mouth thereof.

9 Then lifted I up mine eyes, and looked, and, behold, there came out two women, and the wind *was* in their wings; for they had wings like the wings of a stork: and they lifted up the ephah between the earth and the heaven.

10 Then said I to the angel that talked with me, Whither do these bear the ephah?

11 And he said unto me, To [a]build it an house in [b]the land of Shinar: and it shall be established, and set there upon her own base.

Four chariots of divine judgment

6 AND I turned, and lifted up mine eyes, and looked, and, behold, there came four chariots out from between two mountains; and the mountains *were* mountains of brass.

2 In the first chariot *were* [a]red horses; and in the second chariot [b]black horses;

3 And in the third chariot white horses; and in the fourth chariot grisled and [1]bay horses.

4 Then I answered [a]and said unto the angel that talked with me, What *are* these, my lord?

5 And the angel answered and said unto me, [a]These *are* the four [1]spirits of the heavens, which go forth from [b]standing before the Lord of all the earth.

6 The black horses which *are* therein go forth into [a]the north country; and the white go forth after them; and the grisled go forth toward the south country.

7 And the bay went forth, and sought to go that they might [a]walk to and fro through the earth: and he said, Get you hence, walk to and fro through the earth. So they walked to and fro through the earth.

12 [1]Heb. *by the hand* [2]Or, *empty oil into the gold* [3]Heb. *the gold*

14 [a]Rev. 11:4 [b]ch. 3:7 [c]See Josh. 3:11, 13; ch. 6:5 [1]Heb. *sons of oil*

5:1 [a]Ezek. 2:9

3 [a]Mal. 4:6 [1]Or, *every one of this people that stealeth holdeth* himself *guiltless, as it* doth

4 [a]Lev. 19:12; ch. 8:17; Mal. 3:5 [b]See Lev. 14:45

7 [1]Or, *weighty piece*

11 [a]Jer. 29:5,28 [b]Gen. 10:10

6:2 [a]ch. 1:8 [b]Rev. 6:5

3 [1]Or, *strong*

4 [a]ch. 5:10

5 [a]Ps. 104:4; Heb. 1:7,14 [b]1 Ki. 22:19; Dan. 7:10; ch. 4:14; Luke 1:19 [1]Or, *winds*

6 [a]Jer. 1:14

7 [a]Gen. 13:17; ch. 1:10

5:1–4 This passage marks Zechariah's sixth night vision by describing an enormous scroll that lists the curses that God has pronounced upon his people because of their sins of dishonesty, stealing and swearing.

5:5–11 Zechariah's seventh vision illustrated that the persistent wickedness of Israel would be removed from the land and deposited in Babylon. The overall message of the vision was that the whole system of evil present in Israel would be divinely removed.

6:1–8 This final night vision described four horses and chariots that represented the watchful spirit of God that overlooks the affairs of those who follow him.

E M N Q 8 Then cried he upon me, and spake unto me, saying, Behold, these that go toward the north country have quieted my [a]spirit in the north country.

The crowning of Joshua

9 ¶ And the word of the LORD came unto me, saying,

10 Take of *them of* the captivity, *even* of Heldai, of Tobijah, and of Jedaiah, which are come from Babylon, and come thou the same day, and go into the house of Josiah the son of Zephaniah;

M 11 Then take silver and gold, and make [a]crowns, and set *them* upon the head of Joshua the son of Josedech, the high priest;

12 And speak unto him, saying, Thus speaketh the LORD of hosts, saying, Behold [a]the man whose name *is* The [b]BRANCH; and he shall [1]grow up out of his place, [c]and he shall build the temple of the LORD:

13 Even he shall build the temple of the LORD; and he [a]shall bear the glory, and shall sit and rule upon his throne; and [b]he shall be a priest upon his throne: and the counsel of peace shall be between them both.

14 And the crowns shall be to Helem, and to Tobijah, and to Jedaiah, and to Hen the son of Zephaniah, [a]for a memorial in the temple of the LORD.

15 And [a]they *that are* far off shall come and build in the temple of the LORD, and ye shall know that the LORD of hosts hath sent me unto you. And *this* shall come to pass, if ye will diligently obey the voice of the LORD your God.

Hearts of stone

7 AND IT came to pass in the fourth year of king Darius, *that* the word of the LORD came unto Zechariah in the fourth *day* of the ninth month, *even* in Chisleu;

2 When they had sent unto the house of God Sherezer and Regem-melech, and their men, [a]to[1] pray before the LORD,

3 *And* to [a]speak unto the priests which *were* in the house of the LORD of hosts, and to the prophets, saying, Should I weep in [b]the fifth month, separating myself, as I have done these so many years?

4 ¶ Then came the word of the LORD of hosts unto me, saying,

5 Speak unto all the people of the land, and to the priests, saying, When ye [a]fasted and mourned in the fifth [b]and seventh *month,* [c]even those seventy years, did ye at all fast [d]unto me, *even* to me?

6 And when ye did eat, and when ye did drink, [1]did not ye eat *for yourselves,* and drink *for yourselves?*

7 [1]*Should ye* not *hear* the words which the LORD hath cried [2]by the former prophets, when Jerusalem was inhabited and in prosperity, and the cities thereof round about her, when *men* inhabited [a]the south and the plain?

8 ¶ And the word of the LORD came unto Zechariah, saying,

9 Thus speaketh the LORD of hosts, saying, [a]Execute[1] true judgment, and show mercy and compassions every man to his brother: S

10 And [a]oppress not the widow, nor the fatherless, the stranger, nor the poor; [b]and let none of you imagine evil against his brother in your heart.

11 But they refused to hearken, and [a]pulled[1] away the shoulder, and [b]stopped[2] their ears, that they should not hear. N

12 Yea, they made their [a]hearts *as* an adamant stone, [b]lest they should hear the law, and the words which the LORD of hosts hath sent in his spirit [1]by the former prophets: [c]therefore came a great wrath from the LORD of hosts. E

13 Therefore it is come to pass, *that* as he cried, and they would not hear; so [a]they cried, and I would not hear, saith the LORD of hosts:

---

8 [a]Eccl. 10:4

11 [a]Ex. 29:6

12 [a]Luke 1:78; John 1:45 [b]ch. 3:8 [c]Mat. 16:18; Eph. 2:20; Heb. 3:3 [1]Or, *branch up from under him*

13 [a]Is. 22:24 [b]Ps. 110:4; Heb. 3:1

14 [a]Ex. 12:14; Mark 14:9

15 [a]Is. 57:19; Eph. 2:13

7:2 [a]1 Sam. 13:12 [1]Heb. *to entreat the face of the LORD*

3 [a]Deut. 17:9; Mal. 2:7 [b]ch. 8:19

5 [a]Is. 58:5 [b]Jer. 41:1 [c]ch. 1:12 [d]Rom. 14:6

6 [1]Or, be *not ye they that*

7 [a]Jer. 17:26 [1]Or, Are *not these the words* [2]Heb. *by the hand of*

9 [a]Is. 58:6,7; Jer. 7:23 [1]Heb. *Judge judgment of truth*

10 [a]Ex. 22:21; Is. 1:17; Jer. 5:28 [b]Ps. 36:4; Mic. 2:1

11 [a]Neh. 9:29 [b]Acts 7:57 [1]Heb. *they gave a backsliding shoulder* [2]Heb. *made heavy*

12 [a]Ezek. 11:19 [b]Neh. 9:29 [c]2 Chr. 36:16; Dan. 9:11 [1]Heb. *by the hand of*

13 [a]Prov. 1:24; Is. 1:15; Mic. 3:4

E *Zec 4:6* ◀ ▶ *Zec 7:12*
M *Zec 4:6* ◀ ▶ *Mt 3:11*
N *Da 6:3* ◀ ▶ *Zec 12:10*
Q *Mic 3:6* ◀ ▶ *Mt 12:31–32*
M *Zec 2:10–13* ◀ ▶ *Zec 8:3–8*
S *Zep 2:3* ◀ ▶ *Zec 8:16–17*
N *Zec 1:4–5* ◀ ▶ *Mal 2:2*
E *Zec 6:8* ◀ ▶ *Mt 1:18*

6:11–15 The crowning of Joshua symbolized the crowning of the Messiah who will unite the priestly and kingly roles into one divine office. Zechariah prophesied that the Messiah would rebuild God's temple during the Millennium with the help of the Gentile nations (see Eze 40—48).

R 14 But [a]I scattered them with a whirlwind among all the nations whom they
knew not. Thus the land was desolate after them, that no man passed through nor
returned: for they laid the ˈpleasant land
desolate.

God's intent to restore Jerusalem

I **8** AGAIN THE word of the LORD of
R hosts came *to me,* saying,
2 Thus saith the LORD of hosts; [a]I was
jealous for Zion with great jealousy, and I
was jealous for her with great fury.
M 3 Thus saith the LORD; I am returned
unto Zion, and will dwell in the midst of
Jerusalem: and Jerusalem [a]shall be called
a city of truth; and [b]the mountain of the
LORD of hosts [c]the holy mountain.
4 Thus saith the LORD of hosts; [a]There
shall yet old men and old women dwell in
the streets of Jerusalem, and every man
with his staff in his hand ˈfor very age.
5 And the streets of the city shall be
full of boys and girls playing in the streets
thereof.
6 Thus saith the LORD of hosts; If it be
ˈmarvellous in the eyes of the remnant of
this people in these days, [a]should it also
be marvellous in mine eyes? saith the
LORD of hosts.
I 7 Thus saith the LORD of hosts; Behold,
[a]I will save my people from the east
country, and from [b]theˈ west country;
8 And I will bring them, and they shall
dwell in the midst of Jerusalem: [a]and
they shall be my people, and I will be
their God, [b]in truth and in righteousness.
9 ¶ Thus saith the LORD of hosts; [a]Let
your hands be strong, ye that hear in
these days these words by the mouth of
[b]the prophets, which *were* in [c]the day
that the foundation of the house of the
LORD of hosts was laid, that the temple
might be built.
10 For before these days ˈthere was no
[a]hire for man, nor any hire for beast; neither *was there any* peace to him that
went out or came in because of the affliction: for I set all men every one against
his neighbour.
11 But now I *will* not *be* unto the residue of this people as in the former days,
saith the LORD of hosts.
12 [a]For the seed *shall be* ˈprosperous; B
the vine shall give her fruit, and [b]the
ground shall give her increase, and [c]the
heavens shall give their dew; and I will
cause the remnant of this people to possess all these *things.*
13 And it shall come to pass, *that* as
ye were [a]a curse among the heathen,
O house of Judah, and house of Israel; so
will I save you, and [b]ye shall be a blessing: fear not, *but* let your hands be
strong.
14 For thus saith the LORD of hosts; [a]As
I thought to punish you, when your fathers provoked me to wrath, saith the
LORD of hosts, [b]and I repented not:
15 So again have I thought in these
days to do well unto Jerusalem and to the
house of Judah: fear ye not.
16 ¶ These *are* the things that ye shall S
do; [a]Speak ye every man the truth to his
neighbour; ˈexecute the judgment of
truth and peace in your gates:
17 [a]And let none of you imagine evil
in your hearts against his neighbour; and
love no false oath: for all these *are things*
that I hate, saith the LORD.
18 ¶ And the word of the LORD of hosts
came unto me, saying,
19 Thus saith the LORD of hosts; [a]The
fast of the fourth *month,* [b]and the fast of
the fifth, [c]and the fast of the seventh,
[d]and the fast of the tenth, shall be to the
house of Judah [e]joy and gladness, and
cheerful ˈfeasts; [f]therefore love the truth
and peace.
20 Thus saith the LORD of hosts; *It shall* I
M

R *Zec 3:3–4 ◀ ▶ Zec 8:1–2*
I *Zec 3:9–10 ◀ ▶ Zec 8:7–8*
R *Zec 7:14 ◀ ▶ Zec 11:9–10*
M *Zec 6:11–15 ◀ ▶ Zec 8:20–23*
I *Zec 8:1–3 ◀ ▶ Zec 8:20–23*

B *Hag 2:15–19 ◀ ▶ Mal 3:11–12*
S *Zec 7:9–10 ◀ ▶ Mal 1:6*
I *Zec 8:7–8 ◀ ▶ Zec 9:9–10*
M *Zec 8:3–8 ◀ ▶ Zec 9:9–10*

14 [a]Deut. 28:64 ˈHeb. *land of desire*
8:2 [a]Nah. 1:2
3 [a]Is. 1:21 [b]Is. 2:2, 3 [c]Jer. 31:23
4 [a]1 Sam. 2:31; Is. 65:20 ˈHeb. *for multitude of days*
6 [a]Gen. 18:14; Luke 1:37 ˈOr, *hard, or, difficult*
7 [a]Is. 11:11; Ezek. 37:21 [b]See Ps. 50:1 ˈHeb. *the country of the going down of the sun*
8 [a]Jer. 31:1,33 [b]Jer. 4:2
9 [a]Hag. 2:4 [b]Ezra 5:1,2 [c]Hag. 2:18
10 [a]Hag. 1:6,9 ˈOr, *the hire of man became nothing*
12 [a]Joel 2:22 [b]Ps. 67:6 [c]Hag. 1:10 ˈHeb. *of peace*
13 [a]Jer. 42:18 [b]Gen. 12:2; Ruth 4:11
14 [a]Jer. 31:28 [b]2 Chr. 36:16
16 [a]Eph. 4:25 ˈHeb. *judge truth, and the judgment of peace*
17 [a]Prov. 3:29
19 [a]Jer. 52:6 [b]Jer. 52:12 [c]2 Ki. 25:25; Jer. 41:1,2 [d]Jer. 52:4 [e]Esth. 8:17 [f]ver. 16 ˈOr, *solemn,* or *set times*

7:14 The prophet revealed that God had scattered his people throughout the world in judgment for their sins.
8:1–5 Although God purposed to judge his people for their sins, he also promised to redeem them and restore Jerusalem and the temple. Such peace and security will pervade the city that the streets will be filled with old men and women and children at play.
8:7–8 God promised to restore his people and return them to their land in the last days.
8:20–23 Zechariah's vision of the millennial king-

yet *come to pass,* that there shall come people, and the inhabitants of many cities:

21 And the inhabitants of one *city* shall go to another, saying, [a]Let us go [1,2]speedily [3]to pray before the LORD, and to seek the LORD of hosts: I will go also.

22 Yea, [a]many people and strong nations shall come to seek the LORD of hosts in Jerusalem, and to pray before the LORD.

23 Thus saith the LORD of hosts; In those days *it shall come to pass,* that ten men shall [a]take hold out of all languages of the nations, even shall take hold of the skirt of him that is a Jew, saying, We will go with you: for we have heard [b]*that* God *is* with you.

The coming of the king

9 THE [a]BURDEN of the word of the LORD in the land of Hadrach, and [b]Damascus *shall be* the rest thereof: when [c]the eyes of man, as of all the tribes of Israel, *shall be* toward the LORD.

P 2 And [a]Hamath also shall border thereby; [b]Tyrus, and [c]Zidon, though it be very [d]wise.

3 And Tyrus did build herself a strong hold, and heaped up silver as the dust, and fine gold as the mire of the streets.

4 Behold, [a]the Lord will cast her out, and he will smite [b]her power in the sea; and she shall be devoured with fire.

P 5 Ashkelon shall see *it,* and fear; Gaza also *shall see it,* and be very sorrowful, and Ekron; for her expectation shall be ashamed; and the king shall perish from Gaza, and Ashkelon shall not be inhabited.

6 And a bastard shall dwell [a]in Ashdod, and I will cut off the pride of the Philistines.

P *Hag 2:22* ◀ ▶ *Zec 9:5–8*
P *Zec 9:2* ◀ ▶ *Zec 9:12–16*

21 [a]Is. 2:3; Mic. 4:1,2 [1]Or, *continually* [2]Heb. *going* [3]Heb. *to entreat the face of the LORD*
22 [a]Is. 60:3
23 [a]Is. 3:6 [b]1 Cor. 14:25
9:1 [a]Jer. 23:33 [b]Amos 1:3 [c]2 Chr. 20:12; Ps. 145:15
2 [a]Jer. 49:23 [b]Is. 23; Ezek. 26 [c]1 Ki. 17:9 [d]Ezek. 28:3
4 [a]Is. 23:1 [b]Ezek. 26:17
6 [a]Amos 1:8
7 [1]Heb. *bloods*
8 [a]Ps. 34:7
9 [a]ch. 2:10 [b]Jer. 23:5; Luke 19:38 [1]Or, *saving himself*
10 [a]Hos. 1:7; Mic. 5:10
11 [a]Ex. 24:8 [b]Is. 42:7 [1]Or, *whose covenant is by blood*
12 [a]Is. 49:9
14 [a]Ps. 18:14

7 And I will take away his [1]blood out of his mouth, and his abominations from between his teeth: but he that remaineth, even he, *shall be* for our God, and he shall be as a governor in Judah, and Ekron as a Jebusite.

8 And [a]I will encamp about mine house because of the army, because of him that passeth by, and because of him that returneth: and no oppressor shall pass through them any more: for now have I seen with mine eyes.

9 ¶ [a]Rejoice greatly, O daughter of Zion; shout, O daughter of Jerusalem: behold, [b]thy King cometh unto thee: he *is* just, and [1]having salvation; lowly, and riding upon an ass, and upon a colt the foal of an ass. B I M

10 And I [a]will cut off the chariot from Ephraim, and the horse from Jerusalem, and the battle bow shall be cut off: and he shall speak peace unto the heathen: and his dominion *shall be* from sea *even* to sea, and from the river *even* to the ends of the earth. U V

11 As for thee also, [a]by[1] the blood of thy covenant I have sent forth thy [b]prisoners out of the pit wherein *is* no water.

12 ¶ Turn you to the strong hold, [a]ye prisoners of hope: even today do I declare *that* I will render double unto thee; P

13 When I have bent Judah for me, filled the bow with Ephraim, and raised up thy sons, O Zion, against thy sons, O Greece, and made thee as the sword of a mighty man.

14 And the LORD shall be seen over them, and [a]his arrow shall go forth as the lightning: and the Lord GOD shall blow

B *Hag 2:9* ◀ ▶ *Zec 11:12–13*
I *Zec 8:20–23* ◀ ▶ *Zec 10:6–8*
M *Zec 8:20–23* ◀ ▶ *Zec 14:9*
U *Mic 4:3–4* ◀ ▶ *Mt 5:9*
V *Da 7:14* ◀ ▶ *Mt 22:44*
P *Zec 9:5–8* ◀ ▶ *Zec 11:8*

---

dom foretold a time when the Gentiles would seek the Lord (see Isa 2:2–4; Mic 4:1–5). Zechariah prophesied that the Jews would be recognized as God's chosen people and that the Gentiles would choose to come and worship their Messiah.

9:9–10 Over five hundred years before the birth of Jesus, Zechariah saw this vision of the Messiah riding royally into Jerusalem on a donkey just as David and his sons had ridden centuries before (see 2Sa 18:9; 1Ki 1:33). This prophecy was completely fulfilled when Christ entered Jerusalem on Palm Sunday, proving he was Israel's Messiah (see Mt 21:4–5; Jn 12:15). This triumphal entry concluded the period of the 69 weeks of years prophesied by Daniel (see Da 9:24–26). For a detailed examination of this prophecy, see the chart on "Daniel's Vision of the Seventy Weeks," p. 975. Because Israel rejected Christ at his first advent, God's mercy and the time of world peace will not be realized until the second coming of Christ in the last days.

the trumpet, and shall go [b]with whirlwinds of the south.

15 The LORD of hosts shall defend them; and they shall devour, and [1]subdue with sling stones; and they shall drink, *and* make a noise as through wine; and they [2]shall be filled like bowls, *and* as the corners of the altar.

16 And the LORD their God shall save them in that day as the flock of his people: for [a]*they shall be as* the stones of a crown, [b]lifted up as an ensign upon his land.

17 For [a]how great *is* his goodness, and how great *is* his beauty! [b]corn shall make the young men [1]cheerful, and new wine the maids.

The redemption of God's people

10 ASK YE [a]of the LORD [b]rain [c]in the time of the latter rain; *so* the LORD shall make [1]bright clouds, and give them showers of rain, to every one grass in the field.

2 For the [a]idols[1] have spoken vanity, and the diviners have seen a lie, and have told false dreams; they [b]comfort in vain: therefore they went their way as a flock, they [2]were troubled, [c]because *there was* no shepherd.

3 Mine anger was kindled against the shepherds, [a]and I [1]punished the goats: for the LORD of hosts [b]hath visited his flock the house of Judah, and [c]hath made them as his goodly horse in the battle.

4 Out of him came forth [a]the corner, out of him [b]the nail, out of him the battle bow, out of him every oppressor together.

5 ¶ And they shall be as mighty *men,* which [a]tread down *their enemies* in the mire of the streets in the battle: and they shall fight, because the LORD *is* with them, and [1]the riders on horses shall be confounded.

6 And I will strengthen the house of Judah, and I will save the house of Joseph, and [a]I will bring them again to place them; for I [b]have mercy upon them: and they shall be as though I had not cast them off: for I *am* the LORD their God, and [c]will hear them.

7 And *they of* Ephraim shall be like a mighty *man,* and their [a]heart shall rejoice as through wine: yea, their children shall see *it,* and be glad; their heart shall rejoice in the LORD.

8 I will [a]hiss for them, and gather them; for I have redeemed them: [b]and they shall increase as they have increased.

9 And [a]I will sow them among the people: and they shall [b]remember me in far countries; and they shall live with their children, and turn again.

10 [a]I will bring them again also out of the land of Egypt, and gather them out of Assyria; and I will bring them into the land of Gilead and Lebanon; and [b]*place* shall not be found for them.

11 [a]And he shall pass through the sea with affliction, and shall smite the waves in the sea, and all the deeps of the river shall dry up: and [b]the pride of Assyria shall be brought down, and [c]the sceptre of Egypt shall depart away.

12 And I will strengthen them in the LORD; and [a]they shall walk up and down in his name, saith the LORD.

The rejection of the king

11 OPEN [a]THY doors, O Lebanon, that the fire may devour thy cedars.

2 Howl, fir tree; for the cedar is fallen; because the [1]mighty are spoiled: howl, O ye oaks of Bashan; [a]for [2]the forest of the vintage is come down.

3 ¶ *There is* a voice of the howling of the shepherds; for their glory is spoiled: a voice of the roaring of young lions; for the pride of Jordan is spoiled.

4 Thus saith the LORD my God; Feed the flock of the slaughter;

5 Whose possessors slay them, and [a]hold themselves not guilty: and they that sell them [b]say, Blessed *be* the LORD; for I am rich: and their own shepherds pity them not.

6 For I will no more pity the inhabitants of the land, saith the LORD: but, lo, I will [1]deliver the men every one into his neighbour's hand, and into the hand of

14 [b]Is. 21:1
15 [1]Or, *subdue the stones of the sling* [2]Or, *shall fill both the bowls*
16 [a]Is. 62:3; Mal. 3:17 [b]Is. 11:12
17 [a]Ps. 31:19 [b]Joel 3:18 [1]Or, *grow,* or, *speak*
10:1 [a]Jer. 14:22 [b]Deut. 11:14 [c]Joel 2:23 [1]Or, *lightnings*
2 [a]Jer. 10:8; Hab. 2:18 [b]Job 13:4 [c]Ezek. 34:5 [1]Heb. *teraphims; see Judg. 17:5* [2]Or, *answered that*
3 [a]Ezek. 34:17 [b]Luke 1:68 [c]Sol. 1:9 [1]Heb. *visited upon*
4 [a]Is. 28:16 [b]Is. 22:23
5 [a]Ps. 18:42 [1]Or, *they shall make the riders on horses ashamed*
6 [a]Jer. 3:18; Ezek. 37:21 [b]Hos. 1:7 [c]ch. 13:9
7 [a]Ps. 104:15
8 [a]Is. 5:26 [b]Is. 49:19; Ezek. 36:37
9 [a]Hos. 2:23 [b]Deut. 30:1
10 [a]Is. 11:11; Hos. 11:11 [b]Is. 49:20
11 [a]Is. 11:15 [b]Is. 14:25 [c]Ezek. 30:13
12 [a]Mic. 4:5
11:1 [a]ch. 10:10
2 [a]Is. 32:19 [1]Or, *gallants* [2]Or, *the defenced forest*
5 [a]Jer. 2:3 & 50:7 [b]Deut. 29:19; Hos. 12:8
6 [1]Heb. *make to be found*

I *Zec 9:9–10* ◀ ▶ *Zec 12:8*

10:6–8 This prophecy declared that God would "strengthen" both Judah and Israel by reuniting them as one nation. God's mercy would bring them back together.

his king: and they shall smite the land, and out of their hand I will not deliver *them.*

7 And I will feed the flock of slaughter, [1]*even* you, [a]O poor of the flock. And I took unto me two staves; the one I called Beauty, and the other I called [2]Bands; and I fed the flock.

P 8 Three shepherds also I cut off [a]in one month; and my soul [1]loathed them, and their soul also abhorred me.

R 9 Then said I, I will not feed you: [a]that that dieth, let it die; and that that is to be cut off, let it be cut off; and let the rest eat every one the flesh [1]of another.

10 ¶ And I took my staff, *even* Beauty, and cut it asunder, that I might break my covenant which I had made with all the people.

11 And it was broken in that day: and [1]so [a]the poor of the flock that waited upon me knew that it *was* the word of the LORD.

B 12 And I said unto them, [1]If ye think good, give *me* my price; and if not, forbear. So they [a]weighed for my price thirty *pieces* of silver.

13 And the LORD said unto me, Cast it unto the [a]potter: a goodly price that I was prised at of them. And I took the thirty *pieces* of silver, and cast them to the potter in the house of the LORD.

14 Then I cut asunder mine other staff, *even* [1]Bands, that I might break the brotherhood between Judah and Israel. R

The false shepherd described

15 ¶ And the LORD said unto me, [a]Take unto thee yet the instruments of a foolish shepherd.

16 For, lo, I will raise up a shepherd in the land, *which* shall not visit those that be [1]cut off, neither shall seek the young one, nor heal that that is broken, nor [2]feed that that standeth still: but he shall eat the flesh of the fat, and tear their claws in pieces.

17 [a]Woe to the idol shepherd that leaveth the flock! the sword *shall be* upon his arm, and upon his right eye: his arm shall be clean dried up, and his right eye shall be utterly darkened.

12

THE BURDEN of the word of the LORD for Israel, saith the LORD, [a]which stretcheth forth the heavens, and layeth the foundation of the earth, and [b]formeth the spirit of man within him.

2 Behold, I will make Jerusalem [a]a cup P

7 [a]Zeph. 3:12; Mat. 11:5 [1]Or, *verily the poor* [2]Or, *Binders*
8 [a]Hos. 5:7 [1]Heb. *was straitened for them*
9 [a]Jer. 15:2 [1]Heb. *of his fellow,* or, *neighbour*
11 [a]Zeph. 3:12 [1]Or, *the poor of the flock, &c. certainly knew*
12 [a]Mat. 26:15; Ex. 21:32 [1]Heb. *If it be good in your eyes*
13 [a]Mat. 27:9
14 [1]Or, *Binders*
15 [a]Ezek. 34:2
16 [1]Or, *hidden* [2]Or, *bear*
17 [a]Jer. 23:1; Ezek. 34:2; John 10:12
12:1 [a]Is. 42:5 & 44:24 [b]Num. 16:22; Eccl. 12:7; Is. 57:16
2 [a]Is. 51:17

P *Zec 9:12–16* ◄► *Zec 12:2–6*
R *Zec 8:1–2* ◄► *Zec 11:14*
B *Zec 9:9* ◄► *Mt 1:21–23*
R *Zec 11:9–10* ◄► *Mt 10:6*
P *Zec 11:8* ◄► *Zec 12:9–14*

11:9–10 Zechariah declared that God would terminate his care for the people because of their rejection of the Messiah. His words "let the rest eat every one the flesh of another" (11:9) foreshadowed the horror of the cannibalism the occurred during the Roman siege of Jerusalem in A.D. 70. Though God had held back the nations from oppressing Israel, because of Israel's rejection of the Messiah God would let enemies to conquer his people. This prophecy found its fulfillment in the brutal conquest of Israel by Rome.

11:12–13 Thirty pieces of silver was the price of an Israelite slave (see Ex 21:32) and was an insult to the shepherd to be of so little value. Yet this was the exact amount paid to Judas Iscariot for Christ's betrayal (see Mt 26:14–16). Note that Zechariah predicted that this money would be thrown into the potter's house. In the NT, Matthew records that the betrayal money that Judas returned to the chief priests was used to buy "the potter's field" (Mt 27:7).

11:15–17 Because Israel refused its good shepherd, the Messiah, a foolish, greedy, corrupt shepherd would replace him. This worthless shepherd is a picture of the antichrist who will neither heal nor feed God's people. The antichrist is the exact opposite of Jesus Christ, the good shepherd, who gave his life for his sheep (see Jn 10:11).

The last verse in this passage notes the wounds that will be inflicted on the antichrist. His arm will lose its strength and his eye will lose its sight symbolizing the removal of his power and insight into world affairs. This loss of eyesight may be the mysterious wound that John refers to in Rev 13:3. Some suggest that the wounds may be the result of an assassination attempt, while others state that these will be the first death blows inflicted on the antichrist.

12:2–9 Zechariah prophesied that God's wrath would fall on those who lay siege to Jerusalem during the last days. At the Battle of Armageddon God will cut all of Israel's enemies in pieces even though "all the people of the earth be gathered together against it" (12:3). God will defend his people and bring supernatural forces to bear against Israel's enemies. Even the weakest inhabitants of Jerusalem will be empowered with strength so that they "shall be as David" (12:8).

of [1]trembling unto all the people round
about, [2]when they shall be in the siege
both against Judah *and* against Jerusalem.
3 ¶ [a]And in that day will I make Jerusalem [b]a burdensome stone for all people: all that burden themselves with
it shall be cut in pieces, though all the
people of the earth be gathered together
against it.
4 In that day, saith the LORD, [a]I will
smite every horse with astonishment,
and his rider with madness: and I will
open mine eyes upon the house of Judah,
and will smite every horse of the people
with blindness.
5 And the governors of Judah shall say
in their heart, [1]The inhabitants of Jerusalem *shall be* my strength in the LORD of
hosts their God.
6 ¶ In that day will I make the governors of Judah [a]like an hearth of fire
among the wood, and like a torch of fire
in a sheaf; and they shall devour all the
people round about, on the right hand
and on the left: and Jerusalem shall be
inhabited again in her own place, *even* in
Jerusalem.
7 The LORD also shall save the tents of
Judah first, that the glory of the house of
David and the glory of the inhabitants
of Jerusalem do not magnify *themselves*
against Judah.
I 8 In that day shall the LORD defend the
V inhabitants of Jerusalem; and he that is
[1,2]feeble among them at that day shall be
as David; and the house of David *shall be*
as God, as the angel of the LORD before
them.
P 9 ¶ And it shall come to pass in that
day, *that* I will seek to [a]destroy all the
nations that come against Jerusalem.

I *Zec 10:6–8 ◀ ▶ Zec 13:9*
V *Zec 4:6 ◀ ▶ Lk 21:18*
P *Zec 12:2–6 ◀ ▶ Zec 13:7–9*

2 [1]Or, *slumber, or, poison* [2]Or, *and also against Judah shall* he be *which shall be in siege against Jerusalem*

3 [a]ver. 4,6,8 & ch. 13:1 [b]Mat. 21:44

4 [a]Ps. 76:6; Ezek. 38:4

5 [1]Or, There is *strength to me* and *to the inhabitants*

6 [a]Obad. 18

8 [1]Or, *abject* [2]Heb. *fallen*

9 [a]Hag. 2:22

10 [a]Jer. 31:9 & 50:4; Ezek. 39:29; Joel 2:28 [b]John 19:34; Rev. 1:7 [c]Jer. 6:26; Amos 8:10

11 [a]Acts 2:37 [b]2 Ki. 23:29

12 [a]Rev. 1:7 [b]Luke 3:31 [1]Heb. *families, families*

13 [1]Or, *of Simeon,* as LXX

13:1 [a]Heb. 9:14 [1]Heb. *separation for uncleanness*

2 [a]Ex. 23:13 [b]2 Pet. 2:1

The compassion of Jerusalem

10 [a]And I will pour upon the house of C
David, and upon the inhabitants of Jeru- N
salem, the spirit of grace and of supplica- P
tions: and they shall [b]look upon me D
whom they have pierced, and they shall
mourn for him, [c]as one mourneth for *his*
only *son,* and shall be in bitterness for
him, as one that is in bitterness for *his*
firstborn.
11 In that day shall there be a great
[a]mourning in Jerusalem, [b]as the mourning of Hadadrimmon in the valley of Me-
giddon.
12 [a]And the land shall mourn, [1]every
family apart; the family of the house of
David apart, and their wives apart; the
family of the house of [b]Nathan apart, and
their wives apart;
13 The family of the house of Levi
apart, and their wives apart; the family
[1]of Shimei apart, and their wives apart;
14 All the families that remain, every
family apart, and their wives apart.
13 IN THAT day there shall be [a]a D
fountain opened to the house of K
David and to the inhabitants of Jerusalem L
for sin and for [1]uncleanness.
2 ¶ And it shall come to pass in that
day, saith the LORD of hosts, *that* I will
[a]cut off the names of the idols out of the
land, and they shall no more be remembered: and also I will cause [b]the prophets
and the unclean spirit to pass out of the
land.
3 And it shall come to pass, *that* when
any shall yet prophesy, then his father
and his mother that begat him shall say
unto him, Thou shalt not live; for thou
speakest lies in the name of the LORD: and
his father and his mother that begat him

C *Mic 3:8 ◀ ▶ Lk 1:15–17*
N *Zec 6:8 ◀ ▶ Mt 3:11*
P *Joel 2:28–29 ◀ ▶ Mt 3:11*
D *Da 9:24–26 ◀ ▶ Zec 13:1*
D *Zec 12:10 ◀ ▶ Mal 1:8*
K *Jnh 2:9 ◀ ▶ Mt 1:21*
L *Zec 3:1–5 ◀ ▶ Mal 3:7*

12:10–14 In this passage Zechariah prophesied that Israel's eyes would be opened when Christ returns. The Jews would recognize Jesus of Nazareth as their true Messiah and would realize that their ancestors had crucified him. Contrition and mourning would be felt from the highest leader to the most ordinary person and be so heartfelt that it would resemble the mourning of the ancient Israelites over the death of King Josiah in the plain of Megiddo.

13:1 Zechariah proclaimed that in the days following the victory over the antichrist's armies at the Battle of Armageddon, God would cleanse his people from their sins (see Ro 11:26–27).

[a]shall thrust him through when he prophesieth.

4 And it shall come to pass in that day, *that* [a]the prophets shall be ashamed every one of his vision, when he hath prophesied; neither shall they wear [b]a[1] rough garment [2]to deceive:

5 [a]But he shall say, I *am* no prophet, I *am* an husbandman; for man taught me to keep cattle from my youth.

6 And *one* shall say unto him, What *are* these wounds in thine hands? Then he shall answer, *Those* with which I was wounded *in* the house of my friends.

Israel chastened

P 7 ¶ Awake, O sword, against [a]my shepherd, and against the man [b]*that is* my fellow, saith the LORD of hosts: [c]smite the shepherd, and the sheep shall be scattered: and I will turn mine hand upon [d]the little ones.

8 And it shall come to pass, *that* in all the land, saith the LORD, two parts therein shall be cut off *and* die; [a]but the third shall be left therein.

I 9 And I will bring the third part [a]through the fire, and will [b]refine them as silver is refined, and will try them as gold is tried: [c]they shall call on my name, and I will hear them: [d]I will say, It *is* my people: and they shall say, The LORD *is* my God.

P *Zec 12:9–14* ◄► *Mal 3:2–5*
I *Zec 12:8* ◄► *Zec 14:8–11*

3 [a]Deut. 18:20
4 [a]Mic. 3:6,7 [b]2 Ki. 1:8 [1]Heb. *a garment of hair* [2]Heb. *to lie*
5 [a]Amos 7:14
7 [a]Is. 40:11 [b]John 10:30 [c]Mat. 26:31 [d]Luke 12:32
8 [a]Rom. 11:5
9 [a]Is. 48:10 [b]1 Pet. 1:6 [c]Ps. 50:15 [d]Jer. 30:22
14:1 [a]Is. 13:9
2 [a]Joel 3:2
4 [a]Ezek. 11:23 [b]Joel 3:12
5 [a]Amos 1:1 [b]Mat. 24:30 [c]Joel 3:11 [1]Or, *my mountains* [2]Or, *when he shall touch the valley of the mountains to the place he separated*
6 [1]*i.e.* it shall not be clear in some places, and dark in other places of the world [2]Heb. *precious* [3]Heb. *thickness*
7 [a]Mat. 24:36 [1]Or, *the day shall be one*

Judah's king supreme

14 BEHOLD, [a]THE day of the LORD cometh, and thy spoil shall be divided in the midst of thee.

2 For [a]I will gather all nations against Jerusalem to battle; and the city shall be taken, and the houses rifled, and the women ravished; and half of the city shall go forth into captivity, and the residue of the people shall not be cut off from the city.

3 Then shall the LORD go forth, and fight against those nations, as when he fought in the day of battle.

4 ¶ And his feet shall stand in that day D [a]upon the mount of Olives, which *is* before Jerusalem on the east, and the mount of Olives shall cleave in the midst thereof toward the east and toward the west, [b]*and there shall be* a very great valley; and half of the mountain shall remove toward the north, and half of it toward the south.

5 And ye shall flee *to* the valley of [1]the mountains; [2]for the valley of the mountains shall reach unto Azal: yea, ye shall flee, like as ye fled from before the [a]earthquake in the days of Uzziah king of Judah: [b]and the LORD my God shall come, *and* [c]all the saints with thee.

6 And it shall come to pass in that day, [1]*that* the light shall not be [2]clear, *nor* [3]dark:

7 But [1]it shall be one day [a]which shall

D *Zec 2:10* ◄► *Zec 14:14–20*

13:8–9 This passage indicates that God's judgment at Christ's second coming will destroy two-thirds of the Jewish people (see Isa 48:10). Only a small remnant will be left from this refining to be saved (see Ro 11:26).

14:1–5 The "day of the LORD" (14:1) is the focus of Zechariah's remaining prophecies. In this concluding vision, the prophet described the Battle of Armageddon and the final battle for Jerusalem when the armies of the antichrist would lay siege to Jerusalem in the days following their defeat at Armageddon (see Rev 19:11–21). Though many captives will be taken, Jesus and his army will descend from heaven to rescue Israel from certain destruction, and the evil nations will be supernaturally destroyed. In light of Zechariah's earlier prophecy regarding Israel's repentance after the Battle of Armageddon (see 12:10–14) it is possible that these events will be spread over a period of several days, rather than a one-day battle as some commentators have suggested.

Note that Zechariah intimated that the return of Christ would cause the Mount of Olives to split in two, revealing a valley from the Dead Sea to the Mediterranean. This valley would offer a way of escape for those survivors fleeing Jerusalem. Yet God's victory over his enemies is assured. This vision parallels the prophetic visions of Joel 3:11; Jude 14; and Rev 11—14.

14:7–11 Zechariah declared that only God knows the actual day of Christ's second coming. Note that supernatural changes will occur in the topography and political arenas when Christ returns. Zechariah indicated that the flow of water would be affected (see Eze 47:1–12), all of the land surrounding Jerusalem would be leveled, and Jerusalem would be raised to new prominence (see Isa 2:2–4). Christ will be crowned "king over all the earth in that day" (14:9) as the peaceful, worldwide millennial kingdom of the Messiah is established. Security will be the hallmark of his reign, and the city of Jerusalem will know true peace for the first time.

be known to the LORD, not day, nor night: but it shall come to pass, *that* at [b]evening time it shall be light.

I 8 And it shall be in that day, *that* living [a]waters shall go out from Jerusalem; half of them toward the [1]former sea, and half of them toward the hinder sea: in summer and in winter shall it be.

K M 9 And the LORD shall be [a]king over all the earth: in that day shall there be [b]one LORD, and his name one.

10 All the land shall be [1]turned as a plain from Geba to Rimmon south of Jerusalem: and it shall be lifted up, and [a]inhabited[2] in her place, from Benjamin's gate unto the place of the first gate, unto the corner gate, [b]and *from* the tower of Hananeel unto the king's winepresses.

11 And *men* shall dwell in it, and there shall be [a]no more utter destruction; [b]but Jerusalem [1]shall be safely inhabited.

12 ¶ And this shall be the plague wherewith the LORD will smite all the people that have fought against Jerusalem; Their flesh shall consume away while they stand upon their feet, and their eyes shall consume away in their holes, and their tongue shall consume away in their mouth.

13 And it shall come to pass in that day, *that* [a]a great tumult from the LORD shall be among them; and they shall lay hold every one on the hand of his neighbour, and [b]his hand shall rise up against the hand of his neighbour.

D 14 And [1]Judah also shall fight [2]at Jerusalem; [a]and the wealth of all the heathen round about shall be gathered together, gold, and silver, and apparel, in great abundance.

15 And [a]so shall be the plague of the horse, of the mule, of the camel, and of the ass, and of all the beasts that shall be in these tents, as this plague.

16 ¶ And it shall come to pass, *that* every one that is left of all the nations which came against Jerusalem shall even [a]go up from year to year to worship the King, the LORD of hosts, and to keep [b]the feast of tabernacles. I

17 [a]And it shall be, *that* whoso will not come up of *all* the families of the earth unto Jerusalem to worship the King, the LORD of hosts, even upon them shall be no rain.

18 And if the family of Egypt go not up, and come not, [a]that[1] *have* no *rain;* there shall be the plague, wherewith the LORD will smite the heathen that come not up to keep the feast of tabernacles.

19 This shall be the [1]punishment of Egypt, and the punishment of all nations that come not up to keep the feast of tabernacles.

20 ¶ In that day shall there be upon the [1]bells of the horses, [a]HOLINESS UNTO THE LORD; and the pots in the LORD's house shall be like the bowls before the altar.

21 Yea, every pot in Jerusalem and in Judah shall be holiness unto the LORD of hosts: and all they that sacrifice shall come and take of them, and seethe therein: and in that day there shall be no more the [a]Canaanite in [b]the house of the LORD of hosts.

7 [b]Is. 30:26
8 [a]Ezek. 47:1 [1]Or, *eastern;* see Joel 2:20
9 [a]Rev. 11:15 [b]Eph. 4:5,6
10 [a]ch. 12:6 [b]Neh. 3:1 [1]Or, *compassed* [2]Or, *shall abide*
11 [a]Jer. 31:40 [b]Jer. 23:6 [1]Or, *shall abide*
13 [a]1 Sam. 14:15, 20 [b]Judg. 7:22; 2 Chr. 20:23; Ezek. 38:21
14 [a]Ezek. 39:10,17 [1]Or, *thou also, O Judah, shalt* [2]Or, *against*
15 [a]ver. 12
16 [a]Is. 60:6 & 66:23 [b]Lev. 23:34; Neh. 8:14; Hos. 12:9; John 7:2
17 [a]Is. 60:12
18 [a]Deut. 11:10 [1]Heb. *upon whom there is not*
19 [1]Or, *sin*
20 [a]Is. 23:18 [1]Or, *bridles*
21 [a]Is. 35:8; Joel 3:17; Rev. 21:27 & 22:15 [b]Eph. 2:19-22

I Zec 13:9 ◀ ▶ Zec 14:16–21
K Hab 2:14 ◀ ▶ Mt 6:10
M Zec 9:9–10 ◀ ▶ Mal 1:4–5
D Zec 14:4–7 ◀ ▶ Mt 25:31
I Zec 14:8–11 ◀ ▶ Mal 3:2–4

14:12–15 Zechariah described terrible plagues and pestilence that will affect Israel's enemies during the final battle against Jerusalem. The prophet's graphic description of the death of the soldiers of the antichrist accurately depicts the devastation of an overexposure to radiation or biological weapons. Massive amounts of gamma rays literally melt the flesh off of living beings while leaving buildings and machinery unharmed.

14:16–21 The prophet revealed that the representatives of the nations of the world would celebrate the feast of tabernacles. Those nations that refused to celebrate this joyous feast would experience drought. Because the timing of this celebration in Zechariah's prophecy falls so close to the prophecies of the establishment of the Messiah's kingdom, some believe that the antichrist's defeat might coincide with the earlier feast of trumpets. Only God knows for sure; and only time will tell.

Malachi

Author: Malachi

Theme: Only repentance can remove skepticism and indifference

Date of Writing: c. 433–430 B.C.

Outline of Malachi

I. God Proclaims His Love for Israel (1:1–5)
II. Israel Offends God (1:6—2:17)
III. God's Requirements (3:1–15)
IV. The Righteous and the Wicked (3:16—4:6)

THIS BOOK IS attributed to Malachi, a contemporary of Ezra and Nehemiah. Since the Hebrew word *malachi* translates as "my messenger," some scholars suggest that this is a title rather than a name for an individual. Though this matter is uncertain, it is still possible that the title bears the author's name. The content of this book—religious apathy, intermarriage with foreign women, neglect of paying the tithe—are similar to the conditions in Nehemiah's time and places Malachi's active ministry during the time of the rebuilding of the temple (see Ne 13:6).

Malachi's chief concern was his people's relationship with God. In his short book, Malachi recorded several significant prophecies concerning the Messiah as he urged the exiles to repent and prepare their hearts for his coming kingdom. The people had begun to doubt God's love. They neglected God by robbing him of his tithe and failing to obey the commands of his covenant with them. Consequently, God's judgment awaited them. Yet Malachi assured the people that those who feared God and followed his ways would enjoy God's salvation forever.

Fall of Edom shows God's love

1 THE BURDEN of the word of the
LORD to Israel [1]by Malachi.
2 [a]I have loved you, saith the LORD. Yet
ye say, Wherein hast thou loved us? *Was*
not Esau Jacob's brother? saith the LORD:
yet [b]I loved Jacob,
3 And I hated Esau, and [a]laid his
mountains and his heritage waste for the
dragons of the wilderness.
M 4 Whereas Edom saith, We are impov-
H erished, but we will return and build the
desolate places; thus saith the LORD of
hosts, They shall build, but I will throw
down; and they shall call them, The border of wickedness, and, The people
against whom the LORD hath indignation
for ever.
5 And your eyes shall see, and ye shall
say, [a]The LORD will be magnified [1,2]from
the border of Israel.

The sins of the priesthood

S 6 ¶ A son [a]honoureth *his* father, and a
servant his master: [b]if then I *be* a father,
where *is* mine honour? and if I *be* a master, where *is* my fear? saith the LORD of
hosts unto you, O priests, that despise my
name. [c]And ye say, Wherein have we despised thy name?
7 [1]Ye offer [a]polluted bread upon mine
altar; and ye say, Wherein have we polluted thee? In that ye say, [b]The table of
the LORD *is* contemptible.
D 8 And [a]if ye offer the blind [1]for sacrifice, *is it* not evil? and if ye offer the lame
and sick, *is it* not evil? offer it now unto
thy governor; will he be pleased with
thee, or [b]accept thy person? saith the
LORD of hosts.
9 And now, I pray you, beseech [1]God
that he will be gracious unto us: [a]this
hath been [2]by your means: will he regard
your persons? saith the LORD of hosts.
10 Who *is there* even among you that
would shut the doors *for nought?* [a]nei-
ther do ye kindle *fire* on mine altar for
nought. I have no pleasure in you, saith
the LORD of hosts, [b]neither will I accept
an offering at your hand.
11 For [a]from the rising of the sun even G
unto the going down of the same my
name *shall be* great [b]among the Gentiles;
[c]and in every place [d]incense *shall be* offered unto my name, and a pure offering:
[e]for my name *shall be* great among the
heathen, saith the LORD of hosts.
12 ¶ But ye have profaned it, in that ye
say, [a]The table of the LORD *is* polluted;
and the fruit thereof, *even* his meat, *is*
contemptible.
13 Ye said also, Behold, what a weari- D
ness *is it!* [1]and ye have snuffed at it, saith
the LORD of hosts; and ye brought *that*
which was torn, and the lame, and the
sick; thus ye brought an offering: [a]should
I accept this of your hand? saith the LORD.
14 But cursed *be* [a]the deceiver,
[1]which hath in his flock a male, and vow-
eth, and sacrificeth unto the Lord a corrupt thing: for [b]I *am* a great King, saith
the LORD of hosts, and my name *is* dreadful among the heathen.

The warning to the priesthood

2 AND NOW, O ye priests, this commandment *is* for you.
2 [a]If ye will not hear, and if ye will H
not lay *it* to heart, to give glory unto my N
name, saith the LORD of hosts, I will even
send a curse upon you, and I will curse
your blessings: yea, I have cursed them
already, because ye do not lay *it* to heart.
3 Behold, I will [1]corrupt your seed,
and [2]spread dung upon your faces, *even*
the dung of your solemn feasts; and [3]*one*
shall [a]take you away with it.
4 And ye shall know that I have sent
this commandment unto you, that my
covenant might be with Levi, saith the
LORD of hosts.
5 [a]My covenant was with him of life U
and peace; and I gave them to him [b]*for*
the fear wherewith he feared me, and
was afraid before my name.
6 [a]The law of truth was in his mouth,

1:1 [1]Heb. *by the hand of Malachi*
2 [a]Deut. 7:8 & 10:15 [b]Rom. 9:13
3 [a]Jer. 49:18; Ezek. 35:3; Obad. 10
5 [a]Ps. 35:27 [1]Or, *upon* [2]Heb. *from upon*
6 [a]Ex. 20:12 [b]Luke 6:46 [c]ch. 2:14
7 [a]Deut. 15:21 [b]Ezek. 41:22 [1]Or, *Bring unto*
8 [a]Lev. 22:22 [b]Job 42:8 [1]Heb. *to sacrifice*
9 [a]Hos. 13:9 [1]Heb. *the face of God* [2]Heb. *from your hand*
10 [a]1 Cor. 9:13 [b]Is. 1:11
11 [a]Is. 59:19 [b]Is. 60:3,5 [c]1 Tim. 2:8 [d]Rev. 8:3 [e]Is. 66:19
12 [a]ver. 7
13 [a]Lev. 22:20 [1]*Or, whereas ye might have blown it away*
14 [a]ver. 8 [b]Ps. 47:2; 1 Tim. 6:15 [1]Or, *in whose flock is*
2:2 [a]Deut. 28:15
3 [a]1 Ki. 14:10 [1]Or, *reprove* [2]Heb. *scatter* [3]Or, *it shall take you away to it*
5 [a]Num. 25:12; Ezek. 34:25 [b]Deut. 33:9
6 [a]Deut. 33:10

M *Zec 14:9 ◀▶ Mal 3:1*
H *Zec 3:2 ◀▶ Mal 2:2*
S *Zec 8:16–17 ◀▶ Mal 2:17*
D *Zec 13:1 ◀▶ Mal 1:13–14*
G *Zec 1:18–21 ◀▶ Mt 21:41*
D *Mal 1:8 ◀▶ Mt 1:21*
H *Mal 1:4 ◀▶ Mal 3:2*
N *Zec 7:11–12 ◀▶ Mt 10:14–15*
U *Hag 2:15–19 ◀▶ Mal 3:10*

1:11 Despite the universal paganism of his day, Malachi prophesied that a day would come in the kingdom of the Messiah when everyone on earth would worship God.

and iniquity was not found in his lips: he walked with me in peace and equity, and did [b]turn many away from iniquity.

7 [a]For the priest's lips should keep knowledge, and they should seek the law at his mouth: [b]for he *is* the messenger of the LORD of hosts.

8 But ye are departed out of the way; ye [a]have caused many to [1]stumble at the law; [b]ye have corrupted the covenant of Levi, saith the LORD of hosts.

9 Therefore [a]have I also made you contemptible and base before all the people, according as ye have not kept my ways, but [1,2]have been partial in the law.

The warning to the unfaithful

10 [a]Have we not all one father? [b]hath not one God created us? why do we deal treacherously every man against his brother, by profaning the covenant of our fathers?

11 ¶ Judah hath dealt treacherously, and an abomination is committed in Israel and in Jerusalem; for Judah hath profaned the holiness of the LORD which he [1]loved, [a]and hath married the daughter of a strange god.

12 The LORD will cut off the man that doeth this, [1]the master and the scholar, out of the tabernacles of Jacob, [a]and him that offereth an offering unto the LORD of hosts.

13 And this have ye done again, covering the altar of the LORD with tears, with weeping, and with crying out, insomuch that he regardeth not the offering any more, or receiveth *it* with good will at your hand.

14 ¶ Yet ye say, Wherefore? Because the LORD hath been witness between thee and [a]the wife of thy youth, against whom thou hast dealt treacherously: [b]yet *is* she thy companion, and the wife of thy covenant.

15 And [a]did not he make one? Yet had he the [1]residue of the spirit. And wherefore one? That he might seek [b]a[2] godly seed. Therefore take heed to your spirit, and let none deal [3]treacherously against the wife of his youth.

16 For [a]the LORD, the God of Israel, saith [1]that he hateth [2]putting away: for *one* covereth violence with his garment, saith the LORD of hosts: therefore take heed to your spirit, that ye deal not treacherously.

The sending of the Messiah

17 ¶ [a]Ye have wearied the LORD with S
your words. Yet ye say, Wherein have we
wearied *him?* When ye say, Every one
that doeth evil *is* good in the sight of the
LORD, and he delighteth in them; or,
Where *is* the God of judgment?

3 BEHOLD, [a]I will send my messen- M
ger, and he shall [b]prepare the way
before me: and the Lord, whom ye seek,
shall suddenly come to his temple, [c]even
the messenger of the covenant, whom ye
delight in: behold, [d]he shall come, saith
the LORD of hosts.

2 But who may abide [a]the day of his I
coming? and [b]who shall stand when he P
appeareth? for [c]he *is* like a refiner's fire, H
and like fullers' soap:

3 And [a]he shall sit *as* a refiner and purifier of silver: and he shall purify the sons of Levi, and purge them as gold and silver, that they may [b]offer unto the LORD an offering in righteousness.

4 Then [a]shall the offering of Judah and Jerusalem be pleasant unto the LORD, as in the days of old, and as in [1]former years.

5 And I will come near to you to judg- H
ment; and I will be a swift witness against
the sorcerers, and against the adulterers,
[a]and against false swearers, and against

6 [b]Jer. 23:22; Jas. 5:20
7 [a]Deut. 17:9 [b]Gal. 4:14
8 [a]Jer. 18:15 [b]Neh. 13:29 [1]Or, *fall in the law*
9 [a]1 Sam. 2:30 [1]Or, *lifted up the face against* [2]Heb. *accepted faces*
10 [a]1 Cor. 8:6 [b]Job 31:15
11 [a]Ezra 9:1; Neh. 13:23 [1]Or, *ought to love*
12 [a]Neh. 13:29 [1]Or, *him that waketh, and him that answereth*
14 [a]Prov. 5:18 [b]Prov. 2:17
15 [a]Mat. 19:4 [b]Ezra 9:2; 1 Cor. 7:14 [1]Or, *excellency* [2]Heb. *a seed of God* [3]Or, *unfaithfully*
16 [a]Deut. 24:1; Mat. 5:32 [1]Or, *if he hate her, put her away* [2]Heb. *to put away*
17 [a]Is. 43:24
3:1 [a]Mat. 11:10; Luke 1:76 [b]Is. 40:3 [c]Is. 63:9 [d]Hag. 2:7
2 [a]ch. 4:1 [b]Rev. 6:17 [c]Is. 4:4; Mat. 3:10
3 [a]Is. 1:25 [b]1 Pet. 2:5
4 [a]ch. 1:11 [1]Or, *ancient*
5 [a]Zech. 5:4; Jas. 5:4

S *Mal 1:6* ◀▶ *Mal 3:18*
M *Mal 1:4–5* ◀▶ *Mal 3:17–18*
I *Zec 14:16–21* ◀▶ *Mt 2:2*
P *Zec 13:7–9* ◀▶ *Mal 4:1*
H *Mal 2:2* ◀▶ *Mal 3:5*
H *Mal 3:2* ◀▶ *Mal 4:1*

3:1–5 Note that the first verse of this prophecy carries a double meaning. Initially fulfilled in the earthly ministry of John the Baptist (see Isa 40:3; Mt 11:10), this prophecy will be completely fulfilled in the last days. The Lord will mercifully send witnesses before him to prepare his people (see Rev 11:3–12) prior to his appearance at the Battle of Armageddon.

Malachi also revealed that the "day of his coming" (3:2) would be a time of affliction for God to refine and purify his people. This cleansing would begin with the tribe of Levi since the priests were supposed to be God's messengers but had instead become messengers of pagan idols and unfaithfulness. When the Lord returns he will purify the Levites and judge the people of their sins of sorcery, oppression, adultery and perjury.

those that [1]oppress the hireling in *his* wages, the widow, and the fatherless, and that turn aside the stranger *from his right,* and fear not me, saith the LORD of hosts.

The sins of the people

6 For I *am* the LORD, [a]I change not; [b]therefore ye sons of Jacob are not consumed.

L P 7 ¶ Even from the days of [a]your fathers ye are gone away from mine ordinances, and have not kept *them.* [b]Return unto me, and I will return unto you, saith the LORD of hosts. [c]But ye said, Wherein shall we return?

8 ¶ Will a man rob God? Yet ye have robbed me. But ye say, Wherein have we robbed thee? [a]In tithes and offerings.

9 Ye *are* cursed with a curse: for ye have robbed me, *even* this whole nation.

B P U 10 [a]Bring ye all the tithes into [b]the storehouse, that there may be meat in mine house, and prove me now herewith, saith the LORD of hosts, if I will not open you the [c]windows of heaven, and [d]pour[1] you out a blessing, that *there shall* not *be room* enough *to receive it.*

B 11 And I will rebuke [a]the devourer for your sakes, and he shall not [1]destroy the fruits of your ground; neither shall your vine cast her fruit before the time in the field, saith the LORD of hosts.

12 And all nations shall call you blessed: for ye shall be [a]a delightsome land, saith the LORD of hosts.

C M 13 ¶ [a]Your words have been stout against me, saith the LORD. Yet ye say, What have we spoken *so much* against thee?

14 [a]Ye have said, It *is* vain to serve God: and what profit *is it* that we have kept [1]his ordinance, and that we have walked [2]mournfully before the LORD of hosts?

15 And now [a]we call the proud happy; yea, they that work wickedness [1]are set up; yea, *they that* [b]tempt God are even delivered.

16 ¶ Then they [a]that feared the LORD [b]spake often one to another: and the LORD hearkened, and heard *it,* and [c]a book of remembrance was written before him for them that feared the LORD, and that thought upon his name. T L

17 And [a]they shall be mine, saith the LORD of hosts, in that day when I make up my [b]jewels;[1] and [c]I will spare them, as a man spareth his own son that serveth him. M

18 [a]Then shall ye return, and discern between the righteous and the wicked, between him that serveth God and him that serveth him not. S

The coming day of the LORD

4 FOR, BEHOLD, [a]the day cometh, that shall burn as an oven; and all [b]the proud, yea, and all that do wickedly, shall be [c]stubble: and the day that cometh shall burn them up, saith the LORD of hosts, that it shall [d]leave them neither root nor branch. P H M

2 ¶ But unto you that [a]fear my name shall the [b]Sun of righteousness arise with healing in his wings; and ye shall go M

5 [1]Or, *defraud*
6 [a]Num. 23:19; Rom. 11:29; Jas. 1:17 [b]Lam. 3:22
7 [a]Acts 7:51 [b]Zech. 1:3 [c]ch. 1:6
8 [a]Neh. 13:10
10 [a]Prov. 3:9 [b]1 Chr. 26:20; 2 Chr. 31:11; Neh. 10:38 [c]Gen. 7:11; 2 Ki. 7:2 [d]2 Chr. 31:10 [1]Heb. *empty out*
11 [a]Amos 4:9 [1]Heb. *corrupt*
12 [a]Dan. 8:9
13 [a]ch. 2:17
14 [a]Job 21:14 [1]Heb. *his observation* [2]Heb. *in black*
15 [a]Ps. 73:12 [b]Ps. 95:9 [1]Heb. *are built*
16 [a]Ps. 66:16 [b]Heb. 3:13 [c]Ps. 56:8; Is. 65:6; Rev. 20:12
17 [a]Ex. 19:5; Deut. 7:6; Ps. 135:4 [b]Is. 62:3 [c]Ps. 103:13 [1]Or, *special treasure*
18 [a]Ps. 58:11
4:1 [a]Joel 2:31; 2 Pet. 3:7 [b]ch. 3:18 [c]Obad. 18 [d]Amos 2:9
2 [a]ch. 3:16 [b]Luke 1:78; Eph. 5:14; Rev. 2:28

L *Zec 1:3:1 ◀ ▶ Mt 1:21*
P *Zec 1:3 ◀ ▶ Mt 10:6*
B *Mic 3:8 ◀ ▶ Mt 3:11*
P *Hos 2:8 ◀ ▶ Mt 6:31–33*
U *Mal 2:5 ◀ ▶ Mt 5:5–12*
B *Zec 8:12 ◀ ▶ 2Co 9:10*
C *Zep 1:12 ◀ ▶ Mt 3:7*
M *Zep 2:2–3 ◀ ▶ Mal 4:1*

T *Joel 2:26 ◀ ▶ Mt 10:32–33*
L *Zec 2:8 ◀ ▶ Mt 6:8*
M *Mal 3:1 ◀ ▶ Mal 4:2–3*
S *Mal 2:17 ◀ ▶ Mt 1:21*
P *Mal 3:2–5 ◀ ▶ Mal 4:3*
H *Mal 3:5 ◀ ▶ Mal 4:3*
M *Mal 3:13 ◀ ▶ Mt 5:3–5*
M *Mal 3:17–18 ◀ ▶ Mt 2:2*

3:16–18 Malachi declared that God kept a record of the ones who remained faithful to him despite the widespread complaining against the Lord. This book of remembrance is similar to the records that earthly kings kept of the deeds of valor performed by their faithful subjects (see Est 6:1–3; Isa 4:3; Da 7:10; 12:1). God feels a tender love for those who love and fear him, referring to them as his "jewels" (3:17). Yet Malachi warned the people that God would return and judge "between the righteous and the wicked" (3:18) because God knows what is in every heart.

4:1–3 Malachi warned that God's purifying fire will utterly destroy the proud and the wicked. Yet God promised his people hope, healing and true peace under the coming Messiah's rule. This prophecy parallels the message in Revelation that foretells Christ's victory over the forces of the antichrist at the Battle of Armageddon (see Rev 19:11–21).

forth, and grow up as calves of the
stall.
P 3 [a]And ye shall tread down the
H wicked; for they shall be ashes under the
soles of your feet in the day that I shall do
this, saith the LORD of hosts.
4 ¶ Remember ye the [a]law of Moses
my servant, which I commanded unto
him [b]in Horeb for all Israel, *with* [c]the
statutes and judgments.
5 ¶ Behold, I will send you [a]Elijah the P
prophet [b]before the coming of the great
and dreadful day of the LORD:
6 And he shall turn the heart of the
fathers to the children, and the heart of
the children to their fathers, lest I come
and [a]smite the earth with [b]a curse.

P *Mal 4:1* ◀ ▶ *Mal 4:5*
H *Mal 4:1* ◀ ▶ *Mt 3:7*

P *Mal 4:3* ◀ ▶ *Mt 3:12*

3 [a]Mic. 7:10
4 [a]Ex. 20:3 [b]Deut. 4:10 [c]Ps. 147:19
5 [a]Mat. 11:14; Luke 1:17 [b]Joel 2:31
6 [a]Zech. 14:12 [b]Zech. 5:3

4:4–6 Malachi ended his OT prophecy with a warning to repent because of the certainty of God's judgment. Yet Malachi also delivered a promise of salvation and hope to all who love God and obey his commands. He said that God would send Elijah to prepare the people for the Lord's coming. Note too that Malachi said that a return to God would result in a restoration of familial love. This prophecy was initially fulfilled in John the Baptist who ministered "in the spirit and power of Elias" (Lk 1:17). This prophecy will be ultimately fulfilled by the return of Elijah as one of the two witnesses during the tribulation (see Rev 11:3). For further information, see the article "The Two Witnesses," p. 1462.

NEW TESTAMENT

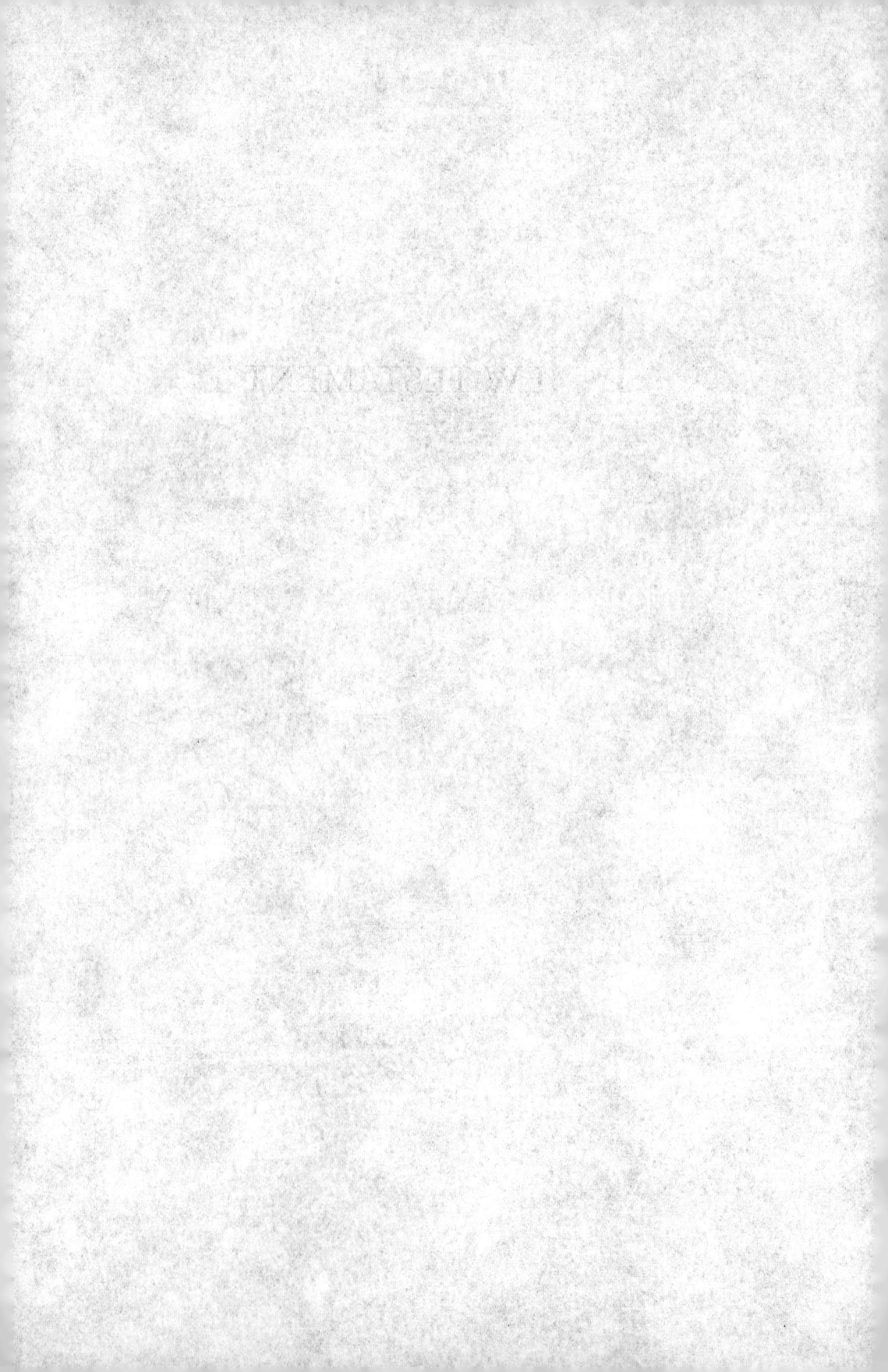

Matthew

Author: Matthew

Theme: The long-awaited Messiah has come

Date of Writing: c. A.D. 70–80

Outline of Matthew

I. Background and Early Years (1:1—2:23)
II. Preparation for Ministry (3:1—4:11)
III. The Galilean Ministry (4:12—18:35)
  A. The calling of the first disciples (4:12–25)
  B. The Sermon on the Mount (5:1—7:29)
  C. The ministry through miracles (8:1—11:1)
  D. Teaching through parables (11:2—13:53)
  E. Opposition and withdrawal (13:54—16:12)
  F. Jesus as the Son of God (16:13—18:3)
IV. The Final Period (19:1—28:20)
  1. Toward Jerusalem (19:1—20:34)
  2. The triumphal entry (21:1–16)
  3. Jesus as teacher (21:17—25:46)
  4. Trial, death and burial (26:1—27:66)
  5. Resurrection (28:1–20)

Though this book is anonymous, Matthew, one of the twelve disciples, is credited with the authorship of the book that bears his name. Because of the Jewish nature of the material included in this book, it seems likely that Matthew originally wrote it in Hebrew; a later Greek edition was widely known and circulated. Most scholars suggest that Matthew wrote his Gospel shortly before the destruction of Jerusalem in A.D. 70 and that he penned it from Antioch in Syria, a leading center of Christianity in the first century. It was in Antioch that the followers of Jesus were first called "Christians" (see Ac 11:26).

Although Matthew's Gospel has much in common with the books written by Mark and Luke, there are certain characteristics that are peculiar to Matthew's own account. His approach in sharing the good news of Jesus demonstrated that Jesus is the true Messiah of Israel. Often describing Jesus as the "Son of David," Matthew repeatedly referred to the OT prophecies and illustrated how Jesus' birth, life and resurrection fulfilled them (see 1:23; 2:6, 15, 18, 23; 3:3; 4:15–16; 8:17; 12:18–21; 13:35; 21:5; 26:56). Matthew also used the phrase "kingdom of heaven" with frequency throughout his book, emphasizing the ethical and spiritual principles of the coming Messianic kingdom by acknowledging the kingdom's present existence as well as its future manifestation in the last days.

Matthew also demonstrated a strong concern for the Gentiles and their salvation (see 13:38; 28:18–20). In fact, his is the only Gospel to record the visit of non-Jewish Magi to worship the infant Jesus (see 2:1–12). Note also Matthew's mention of the teaching ministry of Jesus, particularly apparent in five sections (see 5:3—7:27; 10:5–42; 13:3–52; 18:3–35; 24:4—25:46).

The genealogy of Jesus

1 THE BOOK of the [a]generation of Jesus Christ, [b]the son of David, [c]the son of Abraham.

2 [a]Abraham begat Isaac; and [b]Isaac begat Jacob; and [c]Jacob begat Judas and his brethren;

3 And [a]Judas begat Phares and Zara of Thamar; and [b]Phares begat Esrom; and Esrom begat Aram;

4 And Aram begat Aminadab; and Aminadab begat Naasson; and Naasson begat Salmon;

5 And Salmon begat Booz of Rachab; and Booz begat Obed of Ruth; and Obed begat Jesse;

6 And [a]Jesse begat David the king; and [b]David the king begat Solomon of her *that had been the wife* of Urias;

7 And [a]Solomon begat Roboam; and Roboam begat Abia; and Abia begat Asa;

8 And Asa begat Josaphat; and Josaphat begat Joram; and Joram begat Ozias;

9 And Ozias begat Joatham; and Joatham begat Achaz; and Achaz begat Ezekias;

10 And [a]Ezekias begat Manasses; and Manasses begat Amon; and Amon begat Josias;

11 And [a]Josias[l] begat Jechonias and his brethren, about the time they were [b]carried away to Babylon:

12 And after they were brought to Babylon, [a]Jechonias begat Salathiel; and Salathiel begat [b]Zorobabel;

13 And Zorobabel begat Abiud; and Abiud begat Eliakim; and Eliakim begat Azor;

14 And Azor begat Sadoc; and Sadoc begat Achim; and Achim begat Eliud;

15 And Eliud begat Eleazar; and Eleazar begat Matthan; and Matthan begat Jacob;

16 And Jacob begat Joseph the husband of Mary, of whom was born Jesus, who is called Christ.

17 So all the generations from Abraham to David *are* fourteen generations; and from David until the carrying away into Babylon *are* fourteen generations; and from the carrying away into Babylon unto Christ *are* fourteen generations.

The birth of Jesus

18 ¶ Now the [a]birth of Jesus Christ E
was on this wise: When as his mother Mary was espoused to Joseph, before they came together, she was found with child [b]of the Holy Ghost.

19 Then Joseph her husband, being a just *man,* and not willing [a]to make her a public example, was minded to put her away privily.

20 But while he thought on these E
things, behold, the angel of the Lord appeared unto him in a dream, saying, Joseph, thou son of David, fear not to take unto thee Mary thy wife: [a]for that which is [l]conceived in her is of the Holy Ghost.

E *Zec 7:12* ◄► *Mt 1:20*
E *Mt 1:18* ◄► *Mt 3:16*

1:1 [a]Luke 3:23 [b]Ps. 132:11; Is. 11:1; Jer. 23:5; ch. 22:42; John 7:42; Acts 2:30; Rom. 1:3 [c]Gen. 12:3
2 [a]Gen. 21:2 [b]Gen. 25:26 [c]Gen. 29:35
3 [a]Gen. 38:27 [b]Ruth 4:18; 1 Chr. 2:5
6 [a]1 Sam. 16:1 & 17:12 [b]2 Sam. 12:24
7 [a]1 Chr. 3:10
10 [a]2 Ki. 20:21; 1 Chr. 3:13
11 [a]See 1 Chr. 3:15,16 [b]2 Ki. 24:14-16 & 25:11; 2 Chr. 36:10; Jer. 27:20 & 52:11,15; Dan. 1:2 [l]Some read *Josias begat Jakim, and Jakim begat Jechonias*
12 [a]1 Chr. 3:17 [b]Ezra 3:2; Neh. 12:1; Hag. 1:1
18 [a]Luke 1:27 [b]Luke 1:35
19 [a]Deut. 24:1
20 [a]Luke 1:35 [l]Gk. *begotten*

B 21 [a]And she shall bring forth a son,
D and thou shalt call his name ʹJESUS: for
K [b]he shall save his people from their sins.
L 22 Now all this was done, that it might
S be fulfilled which was spoken of the Lord
by the prophet, saying,
23 [a]Behold, a virgin shall be with
child, and shall bring forth a son, and
ʹthey shall call his name Emmanuel,
which being interpreted is, God with us.
24 Then Joseph being raised from
sleep did as the angel of the Lord had
bidden him, and took unto him his wife:
25 And knew her not till she had
brought forth [a]her firstborn son: and he
called his name JESUS.

The coming of the wise men

2 NOW WHEN [a]Jesus was born in
Bethlehem of Judaea in the days of
Herod the king, behold, there came wise
men [b]from the east to Jerusalem,
I 2 Saying, [a]Where is he that is born
M King of the Jews? for we have seen [b]his
star in the east, and are come to worship
him.
3 When Herod the king had heard
these things, he was troubled, and all Jerusalem with him.
4 And when he had gathered all [a]the
chief priests and [b]scribes of the people
together, [c]he demanded of them where
Christ should be born.
5 And they said unto him, In Bethlehem of Judaea: for thus it is written by
the prophet,
6 [a]And thou Bethlehem, *in* the land of I
Judah, art not the least among the princes M
of Judah: for out of thee shall come a Governor, [b]that shall ʹrule my people Israel.
7 Then Herod, when he had privily
called the wise men, inquired of them diligently what time the star appeared.
8 And he sent them to Bethlehem, and
said, Go and search diligently for the
young child; and when ye have found
him, bring me word again, that I may
come and worship him also.
9 When they had heard the king, they
departed; and, lo, the star, which they
saw in the east, went before them, till it
came and stood over where the young
child was.

21 [a]Luke 1:31 [b]Acts 4:12 & 5:31 & 13:23,38 ʹi.e. *Saviour*
23 [a]Is. 7:14 ʹOr, *his name shall be called*
25 [a]Ex:13:2; Luke 2:7,21
2:1 [a]Luke 2:4,6 [b]Gen. 25:6; 1 Ki. 4:30
2 [a]Luke 2:11 [b]Num. 24:17; Is. 60:3
4 [a]2 Chr. 36:14 [b]2 Chr. 34:13 [c]Mal. 2:7
6 [a]John 7:42 [b]Rev. 2:27 ʹOr, *feed*

B *Zec 11:12–13* ◀ ▶ *Mt 2:14–15*
D *Mal 1:13–14* ◀ ▶ *Mt 20:28*
K *Zec 13:1* ◀ ▶ *Mt 6:13*
L *Mal 3:7* ◀ ▶ *Mt 4:16*
S *Mal 3:18* ◀ ▶ *Mt 3:10*
I *Mal 3:2–4* ◀ ▶ *Mt 2:6*
M *Mal 4:2–3* ◀ ▶ *Mt 2:6*

I *Mt 2:2* ◀ ▶ *Mt 19:28*
M *Mt 2:2* ◀ ▶ *Mt 6:10*

1:21 The first prophecy in the NT refers to the greatest promise God ever gave to humanity. The angel of the Lord came to Joseph and instructed him to marry Mary since the child in her womb had been conceived supernaturally by the power of God. Furthermore, the angel told Joseph to name the child "JESUS: for he shall save his people from their sins." The name *Jesus* means "Jehovah is salvation." What an appropriate name for one whose purpose was "to give his life a ransom for many" (Mt 20:28).

1:22–23 Matthew reveals that this supernatural birth of Jesus to the virgin Mary would fulfill the prophecy made by Isaiah over seven hundred years earlier: "Behold, a virgin shall conceive, and bear a son, and shall call his name Immanuel" (Isa 7:14).

Isaiah used the Hebrew word *almah* in this verse to refer to the child's mother. Because *almah* refers to an unmarried, young woman and does not definitely translate as "virgin," some scholars deny the possibility of the virgin birth. However, the Hebrew word *almah* carries with it an implication of morality, so that a young, unmarried woman would be expected to still be a virgin. Consider also that this prophecy was to be a supernatural sign. If *almah* did not mean a virgin, how would the birth of a son to a sexually active young woman be a prophetic sign from God since such births happen every day? Obviously, the meaning of Isaiah's prophecy signaled a virgin birth. Jesus came to humanity, revealed as God, descended from his heavenly throne, taking human flesh through the miracle of the incarnation.

2:2 The wise men were guided to Jerusalem and Bethlehem by a supernatural celestial object. Some suggest that this may have been a super nova or an unusual alignment of the constellations. Though the Bible does not give the exact details of this phenomenon, it was spectacular enough to cause these scholars to seek out the birthplace of the promised Messiah. Note that the words of the Magi, or wise men, were prophetic of Christ's final victory over Satan when Jesus will be universally acknowledged as the "King of the Jews" and rule in Jerusalem during the Millennium.

2:6 The chief priests and scribes told the wise men where to look for the Messiah because of Micah's words that "thou, Bethlehem Ephrathah, though thou be little among the thousands of Judah, yet out of thee shall he come forth unto me that is to be ruler in Israel" (Mic 5:2).

10 When they saw the star, they rejoiced with exceeding great joy.

11 ¶ And when they were come into the house, they saw the young child with Mary his mother, and fell down, and worshipped him: and when they had opened their treasures, [a]they [1]presented unto him gifts; gold, and frankincense, and myrrh.

12 And being warned of God [a]in a dream that they should not return to Herod, they departed into their own country another way.

The flight into Egypt

13 And when they were departed, behold, the angel of the Lord appeareth to Joseph in a dream, saying, Arise, and take the young child and his mother, and flee into Egypt, and be thou there until I bring thee word: for Herod will seek the young child to destroy him.

B 14 When he arose, he took the young child and his mother by night, and departed into Egypt:

15 And was there until the death of Herod: that it might be fulfilled which was spoken of the Lord by the prophet, saying, [a]Out of Egypt have I called my son.

16 ¶ Then Herod, when he saw that he was mocked of the wise men, was exceeding wroth, and sent forth, and slew all the children that were in Bethlehem, and in all the coasts thereof, from two years old and under, according to the time which he had diligently inquired of the wise men.

17 Then was fulfilled that which was spoken by [a]Jeremy the prophet, saying,

18 In Rama was there a voice heard, lamentation, and weeping, and great mourning, Rachel weeping *for* her children, and would not be comforted, because they are not.

B *Mt 1:21–23* ◀ ▶ *Mt 2:23*

From Egypt to Nazareth

19 ¶ But when Herod was dead, behold, an angel of the Lord appeareth in a dream to Joseph in Egypt,

20 Saying, Arise, and take the young child and his mother, and go into the land of Israel: for they are dead which sought the young child's life.

21 And he arose, and took the young child and his mother, and came into the land of Israel.

22 But when he heard that Archelaus did reign in Judaea in the room of his father Herod, he was afraid to go thither: notwithstanding, being warned of God in a dream, he turned aside [a]into the parts of Galilee:

23 And he came and dwelt in a city called [a]Nazareth: that it might be fulfilled [b]which was spoken by the prophets, He shall be called a Nazarene. B

John the Baptist

3 IN THOSE days came [a]John the Baptist, preaching [b]in the wilderness of Judaea,

2 And saying, Repent ye: for [a]the kingdom of heaven is at hand. R

3 For this is he that was spoken of by the prophet Esaias, saying, [a]The voice of one crying in the wilderness, [b]Prepare ye the way of the Lord, make his paths straight. B

4 And [a]the same John [b]had his raiment of camel's hair, and a leathern girdle about his loins; and his meat was [c]locusts and [d]wild honey.

B *Mt 2:14–15* ◀ ▶ *Mt 3:3*
R *Jnh 3:5–10* ◀ ▶ *Mt 3:8*
B *Mt 2:23* ◀ ▶ *Mt 4:13–15*

11 [a]Ps. 72:10; Is. 60:6 [1]Or, *offered*
12 [a]ch. 1:20
15 [a]Hos. 11:1
17 [a]Jer. 31:15
22 [a]ch. 3:13; Luke 2:39
23 [a]John 1:45 [b]Judg. 13:5; 1 Sam. 1:11
3:1 [a]Mark 1:4,15; Luke 3:2,3; John 1:28 [b]Josh. 14:10
2 [a]Dan. 2:44; ch. 4:17 & 10:7
3 [a]Is. 40:3; Mark 1:3; Luke 3:4; John 1:23 [b]Luke 1:76
4 [a]Mark 1:6 [b]2 Ki. 1:8; Zech. 13:4 [c]Lev. 11:22 [d]1 Sam. 14:25,26

2:14–15 Though this quotation from Hosea originally applied to the Israelites' exodus from Egypt under Moses, Matthew applies it also to Jesus. History does not record exactly how long Jesus and his family stayed in Egypt.

2:23 Though the exact words of this prophecy do not exist in the OT, note that Matthew indicated that the prophetical words were spoken by more than one prophet. When several of the OT prophecies are viewed together (especially Ps 22:6; Isa 11:1; and 53:3), the Messiah is pictured as someone who was despised or referred to as a branch. The Hebrew word for branch is *neser*, the root word for the name "Nazareth." In Jesus' day Nazareth was an obscure town with a bad reputation. Inhabitants of this town were despised by most of the other Jews. For both of these reasons, Jesus was "called a Nazarene."

3:3 John the Baptist preached about the need for the Jews to repent of their sins in preparation for the coming of the Messiah. John called upon the people to "Prepare ye the way of the Lord," echoing the words of Isa 40:3.

5 [a]Then went out to him Jerusalem,
and all Judaea, and all the region round
about Jordan,
6 [a]And were baptized of him in Jordan, confessing their sins.
7 ¶ But when he saw many of the
Pharisees and Sadducees come to his baptism, he said unto them, [a]O generation of
vipers, who hath warned you to flee from
[b]the wrath to come?
8 Bring forth therefore fruits [1]meet for
repentance:
9 And think not to say within yourselves, [a]We have Abraham to *our* father:
for I say unto you, that God is able of
these stones to raise up children unto
Abraham.
10 And now also the axe is laid unto
the root of the trees: [a]therefore every
tree which bringeth not forth good fruit is
hewn down, and cast into the fire.
11 [a]I indeed baptize you with water
unto repentance: but he that cometh after me is mightier than I, whose shoes I
am not worthy to bear: [b]he shall baptize
you with the Holy Ghost, and *with* fire:
12 [a]Whose fan *is* in his hand, and he
will thoroughly purge his floor, and
gather his wheat into the garner; but he
will [b]burn up the chaff with unquenchable fire.

The baptism of Jesus

13 ¶ [a]Then cometh Jesus [b]from Galilee
to Jordan unto John, to be baptized of
him.
14 But John forbad him, saying, I have

C *Mal 3:13–14* ◀▶ *Mt 3:12*
H *Mal 4:3* ◀▶ *Mt 3:10*
R *Mt 3:2* ◀▶ *Mt 4:17*
H *Mt 3:7* ◀▶ *Mt 3:12*
S *Mt 1:21* ◀▶ *Mt 5:8*
B *Mal 3:10* ◀▶ *Mt 3:16*
M *Zec 6:8* ◀▶ *Mt 12:28*
N *Zec 12:10* ◀▶ *Mt 3:16*
P *Zec 12:10* ◀▶ *Mk 1:8*
P *Mal 4:5* ◀▶ *Mt 13:27–30*
T *Isa 26:20* ◀▶ *Mt 13:30*
C *Mt 3:7* ◀▶ *Mt 4:16*
H *Mt 3:10* ◀▶ *Mt 5:22*

need to be baptized of thee, and comest
thou to me?
15 And Jesus answering said unto him,
Suffer *it to be so* now: for thus it becometh us to fulfil all righteousness. Then he
suffered him.
16 [a]And Jesus, when he was baptized,
went up straightway out of the water:
and, lo, the heavens were opened unto
him, and he saw [b]the Spirit of God descending like a dove, and lighting upon
him:
17 [a]And lo a voice from heaven, saying, [b]This is my beloved Son, in whom I
am well pleased.

The temptation in the wilderness

4 THEN WAS [a]Jesus led up of [b]the
Spirit into the wilderness to be
tempted of the devil.
2 And when he had fasted forty days
and forty nights, he was afterward an
hungered.
3 And when the tempter came to him,
he said, If thou be the Son of God, command that these stones be made bread.
4 But he answered and said, It is written, [a]Man shall not live by bread alone,
but by every word that proceedeth out of
the mouth of God.
5 Then the devil taketh him up [a]into
the holy city, and setteth him on a pinnacle of the temple,
6 And saith unto him, If thou be the
Son of God, cast thyself down: for it is
written, [a]He shall give his angels charge
concerning thee: and in *their* hands they
shall bear thee up, lest at any time thou
dash thy foot against a stone.
7 Jesus said unto him, It is written
again, [a]Thou shalt not tempt the Lord thy
God.
8 Again, the devil taketh him up into

B *Mt 3:11* ◀▶ *Mt 12:18*
E *Mt 1:20* ◀▶ *Mt 4:1*
J *Isa 63:14* ◀▶ *Mk 1:10*
N *Mt 3:11* ◀▶ *Mk 1:10*
E *Mt 3:16* ◀▶ *Mt 12:28*
L *Eze 36:27* ◀▶ *Mt 10:19–20*
S *Na 1:7* ◀▶ *Mk 4:40*

5 [a]Mark 1:5; Luke 3:7
6 [a]Acts 19:4,18
7 [a]ch. 12:34 & 23:33; Luke 3:7-9 [b]Rom. 5:9; 1 Thes. 1:10
8 [1]Or, *answerable to amendment of life*
9 [a]John 8:33,39; Acts 13:26; Rom. 4:1,11,16
10 [a]ch. 7:19; Luke 13:7,9; John 15:6
11 [a]Mark 1:8; Luke 3:16; John 1:15,26, 33; Acts 1:5 & 11:16 & 19:4 [b]Is 4:4 & 44:3; Mal. 3:2; Acts 2:3,4; 1 Cor. 12:13
12 [a]Mal. 3:3 [b]Mal. 4:1; ch. 13:30
13 [a]Mark 1:9; Luke 3:21 [b]ch. 2:22
16 [a]Mark 1:10 [b]Is. 11:2 & 42:1; Luke 3:22; John 1:32
17 [a]John 12:28 [b]Ps. 2:7; Is. 42:1; ch. 17:5; Mark 1:11; Luke 9:35; Eph. 1:6; Col. 1:13; 2 Pet. 1:17
4:1 [a]Mark 1:12; Luke 4:1 [b]See 1 Ki. 18:12; Ezek. 3:14 & 8:3 & 11:1,24 & 40:2 & 43:5; Acts 8:39
4 [a]Deut. 8:3
5 [a]Neh. 11:1; Is. 48:2 & 52:1; ch. 27:53; Rev. 11:2
6 [a]Ps. 91:11,12
7 [a]Deut. 6:16

3:11–12 Matthew records John's prophecy that Jesus would "baptize you with the Holy Ghost and with fire" (3:11). This prophecy was fulfilled after Christ's resurrection on the day of Pentecost when the Holy Spirit empowered the early disciples and strengthened them to accomplish Christ's great commission (see Ac 2:1–4). However, this prophecy also looks forward to the last days when Christ will finally judge the nations and "burn up the chaff with unquenchable fire" (3:12).

an exceeding high mountain, and showeth him all the kingdoms of the world, and the glory of them;

9 And saith unto him, All these things will I give thee, if thou wilt fall down and worship me.

10 Then saith Jesus unto him, Get thee hence, Satan: for it is written, [a]Thou shalt worship the Lord thy God, and him only shalt thou serve.

F 11 Then the devil leaveth him, and, behold, [a]angels came and ministered unto him.

The beginning of Jesus' ministry

12 ¶ [a]Now when Jesus had heard that John was [/]cast into prison, he departed into Galilee;

B 13 And leaving Nazareth, he came and dwelt in Capernaum, which is upon the sea coast, in the borders of Zabulon and Nephthalim:

14 That it might be fulfilled which was spoken by Esaias the prophet, saying,

15 [a]The land of Zabulon, and the land of Nephthalim, *by* the way of the sea, beyond Jordan, Galilee of the Gentiles;

C L 16 [a]The people which sat in darkness saw great light; and to them which sat in the region and shadow of death light is sprung up.

R 17 ¶ [a]From that time Jesus began to preach, and to say, [b]Repent: for the kingdom of heaven is at hand.

Jesus calls four disciples

18 ¶ [a]And Jesus, walking by the sea of Galilee, saw two brethren, Simon [b]called Peter, and Andrew his brother, casting a net into the sea: for they were fishers.

19 And he saith unto them, Follow me, and [a]I will make you fishers of men.

20 [a]And they straightway left *their* nets, and followed him.

21 [a]And going on from thence, he saw other two brethren, James *the son* of Zebedee, and John his brother, in a ship with Zebedee their father, mending their nets; and he called them.

22 And they immediately left the ship and their father, and followed him.

23 ¶ And Jesus went about all Galilee, E [a]teaching in their synagogues, and preaching [b]the gospel of the kingdom, [c]and healing all manner of sickness and all manner of disease among the people.

24 And his fame went throughout all Syria: and they brought unto him all sick people that were taken with divers diseases and torments, and those which were possessed with devils, and those which were lunatic, and those that had the palsy; and he healed them.

25 [a]And there followed him great multitudes of people from Galilee, and *from* Decapolis, and *from* Jerusalem, and *from* Judaea, and *from* beyond Jordan.

The Beatitudes

5 AND SEEING the multitudes, [a]he went up into a mountain: and when he was set, his disciples came unto him:

2 And he opened his mouth, and taught them, saying,

3 [a]Blessed *are* the poor in spirit: for theirs is the kingdom of heaven. M

4 [a]Blessed *are* they that mourn: for they shall be comforted.

5 [a]Blessed *are* the meek: for [b]they shall inherit the earth. N L

6 Blessed *are* they which do hunger U

10 [a]Deut. 6:13 & 10:20; Josh. 24:14; 1 Sam. 7:3
11 [a]Heb. 1:14
12 [a]Mark 1:14; Luke 3:20 & 4:14, 31; John 4:43 [/]Or, *delivered up*
15 [a]Is. 9:1,2
16 [a]Is. 42:7; Luke 2:32
17 [a]Mark 1:14 [b]ch. 3:2 & 10:7
18 [a]Mark 1:16-18; Luke 5:2 [b]John 1:42
19 [a]Luke 5:10
20 [a]Mark 10:28; Luke 18:28
21 [a]Mark 1:19; Luke 5:10
23 [a]ch. 9:35; Mark 1:21,39; Luke 4:15, 44 [b]ch. 24:14; Mark 1:14 [c]Mark 1:34
25 [a]Mark 3:7
5:1 [a]Mark 3:13
3 [a]Luke 6:20; See Ps. 51:17; Prov. 16:19 & 29:23; Is. 57:15 & 66:2
4 [a]Is. 61:2,3; Luke 6:21; John 16:20; 2 Cor. 1:7; Rev. 21:4
5 [a]Ps. 37:11 [b]Rom. 4:13

F *Hab 3:17–18* ◀ ▶ *Mt 6:11*
B *Mt 3:3* ◀ ▶ *Mt 12:40–41*
C *Mt 3:12* ◀ ▶ *Mt 6:23*
L *Mt 1:21* ◀ ▶ *Mt 5:5*
R *Mt 3:8* ◀ ▶ *Mt 6:12*

E *Hos 11:3* ◀ ▶ *Mt 7:22*
M *Mal 4:1* ◀ ▶ *Mt 18:1–4*
N *Isa 65:16–18* ◀ ▶ *Heb 1:10–12*
L *Mt 4:16* ◀ ▶ *Mt 6:14*
U *Mal 3:10* ◀ ▶ *Mt 6:4*

4:13–16 Matthew refers to Christ's ministry in Capernaum, near Zabulon and Nephthalim, as the fulfillment of Isaiah's words that "the people that walked in darkness have seen a great light" (Isa 9:2). Capernaum was the home of Peter and became Jesus' base of operations during his ministry in the largely Gentile area of Galilee (see Mk 2:1; 9:33). The Jews showed disdain for anyone who came from this region, claiming that "out of Galilee ariseth no prophet" (Jn 7:52). Yet their contempt was misdirected because one of Israel's greatest prophets (Jonah) had come from a town in Galilee (see 2Ki 14:25).

5:5 Jesus' words echo the psalmist in this passage as he spoke this prophecy which will be fulfilled in the last days. In the millennial kingdom "the meek shall inherit the earth" (Ps 37:11) when Christ eliminates all violence (see Isa 11:4–6) and people live humbly before God in the new earth (see Rev 21:1).

and thirst after righteousness: [a]for they shall be filled.

7 Blessed *are* the merciful: [a]for they shall obtain mercy.

S 8 [a]Blessed *are* the pure in heart: for [b]they shall see God.

U 9 Blessed *are* the peacemakers: for they shall be called the children of God.

10 [a]Blessed *are* they which are persecuted for righteousness' sake: for theirs is the kingdom of heaven.

J 11 [a]Blessed are ye, when *men* shall revile you, and persecute *you,* and shall say all manner of [b]evil against you [l]falsely, for my sake.

12 [a]Rejoice, and be exceeding glad: for great *is* your reward in heaven: for [b]so persecuted they the prophets which were before you.

Teaching about salt and light

S 13 ¶ Ye are the salt of the earth: [a]but if the salt have lost his savour, wherewith shall it be salted? it is thenceforth good for nothing, but to be cast out, and to be trodden under foot of men.

14 [a]Ye are the light of the world. A city that is set on an hill cannot be hid.

15 Neither do men [a]light a candle, and put it under [l]a bushel, but on a candlestick; and it giveth light unto all that are in the house.

16 Let your light so shine before men, [a]that they may see your good works, and [b]glorify your Father which is in heaven.

The higher righteousness

17 ¶ [a]Think not that I am come to destroy the law, or the prophets: I am not come to destroy, but to fulfil.

18 For verily I say unto you, [a]Till heaven and earth pass, one jot or one tittle shall in no wise pass from the law, till all be fulfilled.

19 [a]Whosoever therefore shall break one of these least commandments, and shall teach men so, he shall be called the least in the kingdom of heaven: but whosoever shall do and teach *them,* the same shall be called great in the kingdom of heaven.

20 For I say unto you, That except your righteousness shall exceed [a]*the righteousness* of the scribes and Pharisees, ye shall in no case enter into the kingdom of heaven. G

Anger and reconciliation

21 ¶ Ye have heard that it was said [l]by them of old time, [a]Thou shalt not kill; and whosoever shall kill shall be in danger of the judgment:

22 But I say unto you, That [a]whosoever is angry with his brother without a cause shall be in danger of the judgment: and whosoever shall say to his brother, [b]Raca,[l] shall be in danger of the council: but whosoever shall say, Thou fool, shall be in danger of hell fire. H

23 Therefore [a]if thou bring thy gift to the altar, and there rememberest that thy brother hath aught against thee;

24 [a]Leave there thy gift before the altar, and go thy way; first be reconciled to thy brother, and then come and offer thy gift.

25 [a]Agree with thine adversary quickly, [b]whiles thou art in the way with him; lest at any time the adversary deliver thee to the judge, and the judge deliver thee to the officer, and thou be cast into prison.

26 Verily I say unto thee, Thou shalt by no means come out thence, till thou hast paid the uttermost farthing.

Adultery and divorce

27 ¶ Ye have heard that it was said by them of old time, [a]Thou shalt not commit adultery:

28 But I say unto you, That whosoever [a]looketh on a woman to lust after her hath committed adultery with her already in his heart.

29 [a]And if thy right eye [l]offend thee, H
[b]pluck it out, and cast *it* from thee: for it S

6 [a]Is. 55:1 & 65:13
7 [a]Ps. 41:1; Mark 11:25
8 [a]Ps. 15:2; Heb. 12:14 [b]1 Cor. 13:12
10 [a]2 Cor. 4:17; 1 Pet. 3:14
11 [a]Luke 6:22 [b]1 Pet. 4:14 [l]Gk. *lying*
12 [a]Luke 6:23; Acts 5:41; 1 Pet. 4:13 [b]Neh. 9:26; Acts 7:52
13 [a]Mark 9:50; Luke 14:34
14 [a]Prov. 4:18; Phil. 2:15
15 [a]Mark 4:21; Luke 8:16 [l]The word in the original signifieth *a measure containing about a pint less than a peck*
16 [a]1 Pet. 2:12 [b]John 15:8; 1 Cor. 14:25
17 [a]Rom. 10:4
18 [a]Luke 16:17
19 [a]Jas. 2:10
20 [a]Rom. 10:3
21 [a]Ex. 20:13 [l]Or, *to them*
22 [a]1 John 3:15 [b]Jas. 2:20 [l]i.e. *Vain fellow*
23 [a]ch. 8:4
24 [a]Job 42:8; 1 Tim. 2:8; 1 Pet. 3:7
25 [a]Prov. 25:8; Luke 12:58 [b]Ps. 32:6; Is. 55:6
27 [a]Ex. 20:14; Deut. 5:18
28 [a]Job 31:1; Prov. 6:25
29 [a]Mark 9:43 [b]Col. 3:5 [l]Or, *do cause thee to offend*

S *Mt 3:10* ◀ ▶ *Mt 5:13*
U *Zec 9:10* ◀ ▶ *Lk 2:14*
J *Hab 3:17* ◀ ▶ *Lk 6:22–23*
S *Mt 5:8* ◀ ▶ *Mt 5:29–30*

G *Zep 1:18* ◀ ▶ *Mt 7:26–27*
H *Mt 3:12* ◀ ▶ *Mt 5:29–30*
H *Mt 5:22* ◀ ▶ *Mt 7:13*
S *Mt 5:13* ◀ ▶ *Mt 5:48*

5:9 Jesus blessed the peacemakers, those who strive to promote peace (see Ro 12:18), for those are the ones who truly reflect the character of God. Perfect peace will one day exist throughout the earth when Christ will reign forever as the "Prince of Peace" (Isa 9:6).

is profitable for thee that one of thy members should perish, and not *that* thy
whole body should be cast into hell.
30 And if thy right hand offend thee,
cut it off, and cast *it* from thee: for it is
profitable for thee that one of thy members should perish, and not *that* thy
whole body should be cast into hell.
31 It hath been said, [a]Whosoever shall
put away his wife, let him give her a writing of divorcement:
32 But I say unto you, That [a]whoso-
ever shall put away his wife, saving for
the cause of fornication, causeth her to
commit adultery: and whosoever shall
marry her that is divorced committeth
adultery.

Oaths and retaliation

33 ¶ Again, ye have heard that [a]it hath
been said by them of old time, [b]Thou
shalt not forswear thyself, but [c]shalt perform unto the Lord thine oaths:
34 But I say unto you, [a]Swear not at
all; neither by heaven; for it is [b]God's
throne:
35 Nor by the earth; for it is his footstool: neither by Jerusalem; for it is [a]the
city of the great King.
36 Neither shalt thou swear by thy
head, because thou canst not make one
hair white or black.
37 [a]But let your communication be,
Yea, yea; Nay, nay: for whatsoever is
more than these cometh of evil.
38 ¶ Ye have heard that it hath been
said, [a]An eye for an eye, and a tooth for a
tooth:
39 But I say unto you, [a]That ye resist
not evil: but [b]whosoever shall smite thee
on thy right cheek, turn to him the other
also.
40 And if any man will sue thee at the
law, and take away thy coat, let him have
thy cloak also.
41 And whosoever [a]shall compel thee
to go a mile, go with him twain.
42 Give to him that asketh thee, and
[a]from him that would borrow of thee
turn not thou away.

Neighbours and enemies

43 ¶ Ye have heard that it hath been
said, [a]Thou shalt love thy neighbour,
[b]and hate thine enemy.
44 But I say unto you, [a]Love your enemies, bless them that curse you, do good
to them that hate you, and pray [b]for them
which despitefully use you, and persecute you;
45 That ye may be the children of your
Father which is in heaven: for [a]he maketh his sun to rise on the evil and on the
good, and sendeth rain on the just and on
the unjust.
46 [a]For if ye love them which love
you, what reward have ye? do not even
the publicans the same?
47 And if ye salute your brethren only,
what do ye more *than others?* do not
even the publicans so?
48 [a]Be ye therefore perfect, even [b]as S
your Father which is in heaven is perfect.

Piety and almsgiving

6 TAKE HEED that ye do not your
[1]alms before men, to be seen of
them: otherwise ye have no reward [2]of
your Father which is in heaven.
2 Therefore [a]when thou doest *thine*
alms, [1]do not sound a trumpet before
thee, as the hypocrites do in the synagogues and in the streets, that they may
have glory of men. Verily I say unto you,
They have their reward.
3 But when thou doest alms, let not
thy left hand know what thy right hand
doeth:
4 That thine alms may be in secret: U
and thy Father which seeth in secret himself [a]shall reward thee openly.

Prayer and fasting

5 ¶ And when thou prayest, thou shalt
not be as the hypocrites *are:* for they love
to pray standing in the synagogues and in
the corners of the streets, that they may
be seen of men. Verily I say unto you,
They have their reward.
6 But thou, when thou prayest, [a]enter U
into thy closet, and when thou hast shut
thy door, pray to thy Father which is in
secret; and thy Father which seeth in secret shall reward thee openly.
7 But when ye pray, [a]use not vain
repetitions, as the heathen *do:* [b]for they
think that they shall be heard for their
much speaking.
8 Be not ye therefore like unto them: L

31 [a]Deut. 24:1; Jer. 3:1; Mark 10:2
32 [a]Luke 16:18; Rom. 7:3
33 [a]ch. 23:16 [b]Ex. 20:7; Lev. 19:12 [c]Deut. 23:23
34 [a]ch. 23:16; Jas. 5:12 [b]Is. 66:1
35 [a]Ps. 48:2
37 [a]Col. 4:6; Jas. 5:12
38 [a]Ex. 21:24; Lev. 24:20; Deut. 19:21
39 [a]Prov. 20:22; Luke 6:29; Rom. 12:17; 1 Cor. 6:7; 1 Pet. 3:9 [b]Is. 50:6; Lam. 3:30
41 [a]ch. 27:32
42 [a]Deut. 15:8; Luke 6:30
43 [a]Lev. 19:18 [b]Deut. 23:6; Ps. 41:10
44 [a]Luke 6:27; Rom. 12:14 [b]Luke 23:34; Acts 7:60; 1 Cor. 4:12; 1 Pet. 2:23
45 [a]Job 25:3
46 [a]Luke 6:32
48 [a]Gen. 17:1; Lev. 11:44 & 19:2; Luke 6:36; Col. 1:28 & 4:12; Jas. 1:4; 1 Pet. 1:15 [b]Eph. 5:1
6:1 [1]Or, *righteousness;* Deut. 24:13; Ps. 112:9; Dan. 4:27; 2 Cor. 9:9 [2]Or, *with*
2 [a]Rom. 12:8 [1]Or, *cause not a trumpet to be sounded*
4 [a]Luke 14:14
6 [a]2 Ki. 4:33
7 [a]Eccl. 5:2 [b]1 Ki. 18:26

S *Mt 5:29–30* ◄► *Mt 6:21–24*
U *Mt 5:5–12* ◄► *Mt 6:6*
U *Mt 6:4* ◄► *Mt 6:18*
L *Mal 3:16–17* ◄► *Mt 6:25–34*

for your Father knoweth what things ye
have need of, before ye ask him.
9 After this manner therefore pray ye:
[a]Our Father which art in heaven, Hallowed be thy name.
K 10 Thy kingdom come. [a]Thy will be
M done in earth, [b]as *it is* in heaven.
F 11 Give us this day our [a]daily bread.
R 12 And [a]forgive us our debts, as we
forgive our debtors.
M 13 [a]And lead us not into temptation,
K but [b]deliver us from evil: [c]For thine is the
kingdom, and the power, and the glory,
for ever. Amen.
L 14 [a]For if ye forgive men their tres-
R passes, your heavenly Father will also forgive you:
15 But [a]if ye forgive not men their
trespasses, neither will your Father forgive your trespasses.
16 ¶ Moreover [a]when ye fast, be not,
as the hypocrites, of a sad countenance:
for they disfigure their faces, that they
may appear unto men to fast. Verily I say
unto you, They have their reward.
17 But thou, when thou fastest,
[a]anoint thine head, and wash thy face;
U 18 That thou appear not unto men to
fast, but unto thy Father which is in secret: and thy Father, which seeth in secret, shall reward thee openly.

Possessions and masters

19 ¶ [a]Lay not up for yourselves treasures upon earth, where moth and rust
doth corrupt, and where thieves break
through and steal:
20 [a]But lay up for yourselves treasures
in heaven, where neither moth nor rust
doth corrupt, and where thieves do not
break through nor steal:

K *Zec 14:9* ◀ ▶ *Mt 13:33*
M *Mt 2:6* ◀ ▶ *Mt 6:13*
F *Mt 4:11* ◀ ▶ *Mt 6:25–34*
R *Mt 4:17* ◀ ▶ *Mt 6:14–15*
M *Mt 6:10* ◀ ▶ *Mt 13:31–33*
K *Mt 1:21* ◀ ▶ *Mt 7:24–25*
L *Mt 5:5* ◀ ▶ *Mt 7:7–8*
R *Mt 6:12* ◀ ▶ *Mt 18:35*
U *Mt 6:6* ◀ ▶ *Mt 6:33*

9 [a]Luke 11:2
10 [a]ch. 26:39; Acts 21:14 [b]Ps. 103:20
11 [a]See Job 23:12; Prov. 30:8
12 [a]ch. 18:21
13 [a]ch. 26:41; 1 Cor. 10:13; 2 Pet. 2:9; Rev. 3:10 [b]John 17:15 [c]1 Chr. 29:11
14 [a]Mark 11:25; Eph. 4:32; Col 3:13
15 [a]ch. 18:35; Jas. 2:13
16 [a]Is. 58:5
17 [a]Ruth 3:3; Dan. 10:3
19 [a]Prov. 23:4; 1 Tim. 6:17; Heb. 13:5; Jas. 5:1
20 [a]ch. 19:21; Luke 12:33 & 18:22; 1 Tim. 6:19; 1 Pet. 1:4
22 [a]Luke 11:34
24 [a]Luke 16:13 [b]Gal. 1:10; 1 Tim. 6:17; Jas. 4:4; 1 John 2:15
25 [a]Ps. 55:22; Luke 12:22; Phil. 4:6; 1 Pet. 5:7
26 [a]Job 38:41; Ps. 147:9; Luke 12:24

21 For where your treasure is, there S
will your heart be also.
22 [a]The light of the body is the eye: if
therefore thine eye be single, thy whole
body shall be full of light.
23 But if thine eye be evil, thy whole C
body shall be full of darkness. If therefore
the light that is in thee be darkness, how
great *is* that darkness!
24 ¶ [a]No man can serve two masters:
for either he will hate the one, and love
the other; or else he will hold to the one,
and despise the other. [b]Ye cannot serve
God and mammon.

Anxiety and God's kingdom

25 Therefore I say unto you, [a]Take no C
thought for your life, what ye shall eat, F
or what ye shall drink; nor yet for your L
body, what ye shall put on. Is not the life W
more than meat, and the body than
raiment?
26 [a]Behold the fowls of the air: for
they sow not, neither do they reap, nor
gather into barns; yet your heavenly Father feedeth them. Are ye not much better than they?
27 Which of you by taking thought can
add one cubit unto his stature?
28 And why take ye thought for raiment? Consider the lilies of the field,
how they grow; they toil not, neither do
they spin:
29 And yet I say unto you, That even
Solomon in all his glory was not arrayed
like one of these.
30 Wherefore, if God so clothe the
grass of the field, which today is, and tomorrow is cast into the oven, *shall he*
not much more *clothe* you, O ye of little
faith?
31 Therefore take no thought, saying, P
What shall we eat? or, What shall we

S *Mt 5:48* ◀ ▶ *Mt 7:13–14*
C *Mt 4:16* ◀ ▶ *Mt 7:16–20*
C *Eze 16:10* ◀ ▶ *Lk 12:22–31*
F *Mt 6:11* ◀ ▶ *Mt 14:15–21*
L *Mt 6:8* ◀ ▶ *Mt 7:7–11*
W *Jer 10:2* ◀ ▶ *Mt 8:26*
P *Mal 3:10–11* ◀ ▶ *Mt 17:27*

6:10, 13 In this prayer, Jesus highlights a present reality as well as a future prophecy. God's kingdom is present with us now (see Lk 17:21; Ro 14:17) yet we can still look ahead to a time when God's kingdom will be fully established on earth (see Lk 21:31). Jesus will rule from the throne of David in Jerusalem, and the peace and justice of heaven will exist on earth forever.

drink? or, Wherewithal shall we be clothed?

32 (For after all these things do the Gentiles seek:) for your heavenly Father knoweth that ye have need of all these things.

U 33 But [a]seek ye first the kingdom of God, and his righteousness; and all these things shall be added unto you.

34 Take therefore no thought for the morrow: for the morrow shall take thought for the things of itself. Sufficient unto the day *is* the evil thereof.

Judging and hypocrisy

J 7 JUDGE[a] NOT, that ye be not judged.
2For with what judgment ye judge, ye shall be judged: [a]and with what measure ye mete, it shall be measured to you again.

3 [a]And why beholdest thou the mote that is in thy brother's eye, but considerest not the beam that is in thine own eye?

4 Or how wilt thou say to thy brother, Let me pull out the mote out of thine eye; and, behold, a beam *is* in thine own eye?

5 Thou hypocrite, first cast out the beam out of thine own eye; and then shalt thou see clearly to cast out the mote out of thy brother's eye.

6 ¶ [a]Give not that which is holy unto the dogs, neither cast ye your pearls before swine, lest they trample them under their feet, and turn again and rend you.

Prayer and the Golden Rule

L 7 ¶ [a]Ask, and it shall be given you;
W seek, and ye shall find; knock, and it shall
L be opened unto you:

8 For [a]every one that asketh receiveth; and he that seeketh findeth; and to him that knocketh it shall be opened.

9 [a]Or what man is there of you, whom if his son ask bread, will he give him a stone?

10 Or if he ask a fish, will he give him a serpent?

11 If ye then, [a]being evil, know how to give good gifts unto your children, how much more shall your Father which is in heaven give good things to them that ask him?

12 Therefore all things [a]whatsoever ye would that men should do to you, do ye even so to them: for [b]this is the law and the prophets.

The strait and wide gates

13 ¶ [a]Enter ye in at the strait gate: for H
wide *is* the gate, and broad *is* the way, S
that leadeth to destruction, and many there be which go in thereat:

14 [I]Because strait *is* the gate, and narrow *is* the way, which leadeth unto life, and few there be that find it.

The test of false prophets

15 ¶ [a]Beware of false prophets, [b]which come to you in sheep's clothing, but inwardly they are [c]ravening wolves.

16 [a]Ye shall know them by their fruits. C
[b]Do men gather grapes of thorns, or figs S
of thistles?

17 Even so [a]every good tree bringeth forth good fruit; but a corrupt tree bringeth forth evil fruit.

18 A good tree cannot bring forth evil fruit, neither *can* a corrupt tree bring forth good fruit.

19 [a]Every tree that bringeth not forth H
good fruit is hewn down, and cast into the fire.

20 Wherefore by their fruits ye shall know them.

21 ¶ Not every one that saith unto me, [a]Lord, Lord, shall enter into the kingdom of heaven; but he that doeth the will of my Father which is in heaven.

22 Many will say to me in that day, E
Lord, Lord, have we [a]not prophesied in thy name? and in thy name have cast out devils? and in thy name done many wonderful works?

23 And [a]then will I profess unto them, I never knew you: [b]depart from me, ye that work iniquity.

The wise and foolish builders

24 ¶ Therefore [a]whosoever heareth K
W

33 [a]See 1 Ki. 3:13; Ps. 37:25; Mark 10:30; Luke 12:31; 1 Tim. 4:8
7:1 [a]Luke 6:37; Rom. 14:3; 1 Cor. 4:3; Jas. 4:11
2 [a]Mark 4:24; Luke 6:38
3 [a]Luke 6:41
6 [a]Prov. 9:7,8 & 23:9; Acts 13:45
7 [a]ch. 21:22; Mark 11:24; Luke 11:9 & 18:1; John 14:13 & 15:7 & 16:23,24; Jas. 1:5,6; 1 John 3:22 & 5:14,15
8 [a]Prov. 8:17; Jer. 29:12
9 [a]Luke 11:11
11 [a]Gen. 6:5 & 8:21
12 [a]Luke 6:31 [b]Lev. 19:18; ch. 22:40; Rom. 13:8; Gal. 5:14; 1 Tim. 1:5
13 [a]Luke 13:24
14 [I]Or, *How*
15 [a]Deut. 13:3; Jer. 23:16; ch. 24:4, 5; Mark 13:22; Rom. 16:17; Eph. 5:6; Col. 2:8; 2 Pet. 2:1; 1 John 4:1 [b]Mic. 3:5; 2 Tim. 3:5 [c]Acts 20:29
16 [a]ver. 20 [b]Luke 6:43
17 [a]Jer. 11:19; ch. 12:33
19 [a]ch. 3:10; Luke 3:9; John 15:2
21 [a]Hos. 8:2; ch. 25:11; Luke 6:46 & 13:25; Acts 19:13; Rom. 2:13; Jas. 1:22
22 [a]Num. 24:4; John 11:51; 1 Cor. 13:2
23 [a]ch. 25:12; Luke 13:25; 2 Tim. 2:19 [b]Ps. 5:5 & 6:8; ch. 25:41
24 [a]Luke 6:47

U *Mt 6:18* ◀▶ *Mt 19:29*
J *Am 4:12* ◀▶ *Mt 10:15*
L *Mt 6:14* ◀▶ *Mt 9:12–13*
W *Eze 33:11* ◀▶ *Mt 7:24*
L *Mt 6:25–34* ◀▶ *Mt 8:26*
H *Mt 5:29–30* ◀▶ *Mt 7:19*
S *Mt 6:21–24* ◀▶ *Mt 7:16–24*
C *Mt 6:23* ◀▶ *Mt 7:26–27*
S *Mt 7:13–14* ◀▶ *Mt 10:22*
H *Mt 7:13* ◀▶ *Mt 7:26–27*
E *Mt 4:23–25* ◀▶ *Mt 8:2–3*
K *Mt 6:13* ◀▶ *Mt 9:6*
W *Mt 7:7–8* ◀▶ *Mt 10:32*

these sayings of mine, and doeth them, I will liken him unto a wise man, which built his house upon a rock:

25 And the rain descended, and the floods came, and the winds blew, and beat upon that house; and it fell not: for it was founded upon a rock.

C 26 And every one that heareth these
G sayings of mine, and doeth them not,
H shall be likened unto a foolish man,
O which built his house upon the sand:

27 And the rain descended, and the floods came, and the winds blew, and beat upon that house; and it fell: and great was the fall of it.

28 And it came to pass, when Jesus had ended these sayings, [a]the people were astonished at his doctrine:

29 [a]For he taught them as *one* having authority, and not as the scribes.

The leper cleansed

8 WHEN HE was come down from the mountain, great multitudes followed him.

E 2 [a]And, behold, there came a leper and worshipped him, saying, Lord, if thou wilt, thou canst make me clean.

3 And Jesus put forth *his* hand, and touched him, saying, I will; be thou clean. And immediately his leprosy was cleansed.

4 And Jesus saith unto him, [a]See thou tell no man; but go thy way, show thyself to the priest, and offer the gift that [b]Moses commanded, for a testimony unto them.

The centurion's servant healed

E 5 ¶ [a]And when Jesus was entered into Capernaum, there came unto him a centurion, beseeching him,

6 And saying, Lord, my servant lieth at home sick of the palsy, grievously tormented.

7 And Jesus saith unto him, I will come and heal him.

8 The centurion answered and said, Lord, [a]I am not worthy that thou shouldest come under my roof: but [b]speak the word only, and my servant shall be healed.

9 For I am a man under authority, having soldiers under me: and I say to this *man,* Go, and he goeth; and to another, Come, and he cometh; and to my servant, Do this, and he doeth *it.*

10 When Jesus heard *it,* he marvelled, and said to them that followed, Verily I say unto you, I have not found so great faith, no, not in Israel.

11 And I say unto you, That [a]many shall come from the east and west, and shall sit down with Abraham, and Isaac, and Jacob, in the kingdom of heaven.

12 But [a]the children of the kingdom H
[b]shall be cast out into outer darkness: there shall be weeping and gnashing of teeth.

13 And Jesus said unto the centurion, Go thy way; and as thou hast believed, *so* be it done unto thee. And his servant was healed in the selfsame hour.

Peter's mother-in-law healed

14 ¶ [a]And when Jesus was come into Peter's house, he saw [b]his wife's mother laid, and sick of a fever.

15 And he touched her hand, and the fever left her: and she arose, and ministered unto them.

16 ¶ [a]When the even was come, they brought unto him many that were possessed with devils: and he cast out the spirits with *his* word, and healed all that were sick:

17 That it might be fulfilled which was H
spoken by Esaias the prophet, saying, [a]Himself took our infirmities, and bare *our* sicknesses.

C *Mt 7:16–20* ◀▶ *Mt 8:22*
G *Mt 5:20* ◀▶ *Mt 15:8–9*
H *Mt 7:19* ◀▶ *Mt 8:12*
O *Jnh 2:9* ◀▶ *Mt 10:32–33*
E *Mt 7:22* ◀▶ *Mt 8:5–17*
E *Mt 8:2–3* ◀▶ *Mt 8:28–32*

H *Mt 7:26–27* ◀▶ *Mt 10:14–15*
H *Eze 47:12* ◀▶ *Mt 10:7–8*

28 [a]ch. 13:54; Mark 1:22 & 6:2; Luke 4:32
29 [a]John 7:46
8:2 [a]Mark 1:40; Luke 5:12
4 [a]ch. 9:30; Mark 5:43 [b]Lev. 14:3,4, 10; Luke 5:14
5 [a]Luke 7:1
8 [a]Luke 15:19,21 [b]Ps. 107:20
11 [a]Gen. 12:3; Is. 2:2,3 & 11:10; Mal. 1:11; Luke 13:29; Acts 10:45 & 11:18 & 14:27; Rom. 15:9; Eph. 3:6
12 [a]ch. 21:43 [b]ch. 13:42,50 & 22:13 & 24:51 & 25:30; Luke 13:28; 2 Pet. 2:17; Jude 13
14 [a]Mark 1:29-31; Luke 4:38,39 [b]1 Cor. 9:5
16 [a]Mark 1:32; Luke 4:40,41
17 [a]Is. 53:4; 1 Pet. 2:24

8:11–12 Matthew's words are directed to all people as he records Jesus' prophecy of the great Messianic feast that will follow Christ's victory over the antichrist at Armageddon (see Isa 25:6–9). The Gentile nations "from the east and west" (8:11) will be invited to join the Jews and celebrate the establishment of the rule of the Messiah. Jesus warns that those Jews who thought their heritage was enough to get them into the kingdom (see 3:9–10) will find themselves "cast out into outer darkness" (8:12).

Teaching about discipleship

18 ¶ Now when Jesus saw great multitudes about him, he gave commandment to depart unto the other side.

19 [a]And a certain scribe came, and said unto him, Master, I will follow thee whithersoever thou goest.

20 And Jesus saith unto him, The foxes have holes, and the birds of the air *have* nests; but the Son of man hath not where to lay *his* head.

21 [a]And another of his disciples said unto him, Lord, [b]suffer me first to go and bury my father.

C 22 But Jesus said unto him, Follow me; and let the dead bury their dead.

The storm stilled

23 ¶ And when he was entered into a ship, his disciples followed him.

24 [a]And, behold, there arose a great tempest in the sea, insomuch that the ship was covered with the waves: but he was asleep.

25 And his disciples came to *him,* and awoke him, saying, Lord, save us: we perish.

L W 26 And he saith unto them, Why are ye fearful, O ye of little faith? Then [a]he arose, and rebuked the winds and the sea; and there was a great calm.

27 But the men marvelled, saying, What manner of man is this, that even the winds and the sea obey him!

Devils cast out

E 28 ¶ [a]And when he was come to the other side into the country of the Gergesenes, there met him two possessed with devils, coming out of the tombs, exceeding fierce, so that no man might pass by that way.

29 And, behold, they cried out, saying, What have we to do with thee, Jesus, thou Son of God? art thou come hither to torment us before the time?

30 And there was a good way off from them an herd of many swine feeding.

31 So the devils besought him, saying, If thou cast us out, suffer us to go away into the herd of swine.

32 And he said unto them, Go. And when they were come out, they went into the herd of swine: and, behold, the whole herd of swine ran violently down a steep place into the sea, and perished in the waters.

33 And they that kept them fled, and went their ways into the city, and told every thing, and what was befallen to the possessed of the devils.

34 And, behold, the whole city came out to meet Jesus: and when they saw him, [a]they besought *him* that he would depart out of their coasts.

A man with palsy healed

9 AND HE entered into a ship, and passed over, [a]and came into his own city.

2 [a]And, behold, they brought to him a man sick of the palsy, lying on a bed: [b]and Jesus seeing their faith said unto the sick of the palsy; Son, be of good cheer; thy sins be forgiven thee. E

3 And, behold, certain of the scribes said within themselves, This *man* blasphemeth.

4 And Jesus [a]knowing their thoughts said, Wherefore think ye evil in your hearts? E

5 For whether is easier, to say, *Thy sins be forgiven thee;* or to say, Arise, and walk?

6 But that ye may know that the Son of man hath power on earth to forgive sins, (then saith he to the sick of the palsy,) Arise, take up thy bed, and go unto thine house. K

7 And he arose, and departed to his house.

8 But when the multitudes saw *it,* they marvelled, and glorified God, which had given such power unto men.

Matthew called

9 ¶ [a]And as Jesus passed forth from thence, he saw a man, named Matthew, sitting at the receipt of custom: and he saith unto him, Follow me. And he arose, and followed him.

10 ¶ [a]And it came to pass, as Jesus sat at meat in the house, behold, many publicans and sinners came and sat down with him and his disciples.

11 And when the Pharisees saw *it,*

19 [a]Luke 9:57,58
21 [a]Luke 9:59,60 [b]See 1 Ki. 19:20
24 [a]Mark 4:37; Luke 8:23
26 [a]Ps. 65:7 & 89:9 & 107:29
28 [a]Mark 5:1; Luke 8:26
34 [a]See Deut. 5:25; 1 Ki. 17:18; Luke 5:8; Acts 16:39
9:1 [a]ch. 4:13
2 [a]Mark 2:3; Luke 5:18 [b]ch. 8:10
4 [a]Ps. 139:2; ch. 12:25; Mark 12:15; Luke 5:22 & 6:8 & 9:47 & 11:17
9 [a]Mark 2:14; Luke 5:27
10 [a]Mark 2:15; Luke 5:29

C *Mt 7:26–27* ◀ ▶ *Mt 9:12*
L *Mt 7:7–11* ◀ ▶ *Mt 10:29–31*
W *Mt 6:25–34* ◀ ▶ *Mk 4:40*
E *Mt 8:5–17* ◀ ▶ *Mt 9:2–8*
E *Mt 8:28–32* ◀ ▶ *Mt 9:18–35*
E *Zec 4:10* ◀ ▶ *Mt 12:25*
K *Mt 7:24–25* ◀ ▶ *Mt 11:28–29*

they said unto his disciples, Why eateth your Master with [a]publicans and [b]sinners?

C 12 But when Jesus heard *that,* he said
L unto them, They that be whole need not a physician, but they that are sick.

13 But go ye and learn what *that* meaneth, [a]I will have mercy, and not sacrifice: for I am not come to call the righteous, [b]but sinners to repentance.

The question about fasting

14 ¶ Then came to him the disciples of John, saying, [a]Why do we and the Pharisees fast oft, but thy disciples fast not?

15 And Jesus said unto them, Can [a]the children of the bridechamber mourn, as long as the bridegroom is with them? but the days will come, when the bridegroom shall be taken from them, and [b]then shall they fast.

16 No man putteth a piece of [/]new cloth unto an old garment, for that which is put in to fill it up taketh from the garment, and the rent is made worse.

17 Neither do men put new wine into old bottles: else the bottles break, and the wine runneth out, and the bottles perish: but they put new wine into new bottles, and both are preserved.

A ruler's daughter raised

E 18 ¶ [a]While he spake these things unto them, behold, there came a certain ruler, and worshipped him, saying, My daughter is even now dead: but come and lay thy hand upon her, and she shall live.

19 And Jesus arose, and followed him, and *so did* his disciples.

20 ¶ [a]And, behold, a woman, which was diseased with an issue of blood twelve years, came behind *him,* and touched the hem of his garment:

21 For she said within herself, If I may but touch his garment, I shall be whole.

22 But Jesus turned him about, and when he saw her, he said, Daughter, be of good comfort; [a]thy faith hath made thee whole. And the woman was made whole from that hour.

C *Mt 8:22* ◀ ▶ *Mt 10:6*
L *Mt 7:7–8* ◀ ▶ *Mt 11:28–29*
E *Mt 9:2–8* ◀ ▶ *Mt 10:1*

11 [a]ch. 11:19; Luke 5:30 & 15:2 [b]Gal. 2:15
13 [a]Hos. 6:6; Mic. 6:6-8; ch. 12:7 [b]1 Tim. 1:15
14 [a]Mark 2:18; Luke 5:33 & 18:12
15 [a]John 3:29 [b]Acts 13:2,3 & 14:23; 1 Cor. 7:5
16 [/]Or, *raw,* or, *unwrought cloth*
18 [a]Mark 5:22; Luke 8:41
20 [a]Mark 5:25; Luke 8:43
22 [a]Luke 7:50 & 8:48 & 17:19 & 18:42
23 [a]Mark 5:38; Luke 8:51 [b]See 2 Chr. 35:25
24 [a]Acts 20:10
26 [/]Or, *this fame*
27 [a]ch. 15:22; Mark 10:47; Luke 18:38
30 [a]ch. 8:4; Luke 5:14
31 [a]Mark 7:36
32 [a]ch. 12:22; Luke 11:14
34 [a]ch. 12:24; Luke 11:15
35 [a]ch. 4:23
36 [a]Mark 6:34 [b]Num. 27:17; 1 Ki. 22:17 [/]Or, *were tired and lay down*

23 [a]And when Jesus came into the ruler's house, and saw [b]the minstrels and the people making a noise,

24 He said unto them, [a]Give place: for the maid is not dead, but sleepeth. And they laughed him to scorn.

25 But when the people were put forth, he went in, and took her by the hand, and the maid arose.

26 And [/]the fame hereof went abroad into all that land.

27 ¶ And when Jesus departed thence, two blind men followed him, crying, and saying, [a]*Thou* Son of David, have mercy on us.

28 And when he was come into the house, the blind men came to him: and Jesus saith unto them, Believe ye that I am able to do this? They said unto him, Yea, Lord.

29 Then touched he their eyes, saying, According to your faith be it unto you.

30 And their eyes were opened; and Jesus straitly charged them, saying, [a]See *that* no man know *it.*

31 [a]But they, when they were departed, spread abroad his fame in all that country.

32 ¶ [a]As they went out, behold, they brought to him a dumb man possessed with a devil.

33 And when the devil was cast out, the dumb spake: and the multitudes marvelled, saying, It was never so seen in Israel.

34 But the Pharisees said, [a]He casteth out devils through the prince of the devils.

The need for labourers

35 And Jesus went about all the cities and villages, [a]teaching in their synagogues, and preaching the gospel of the kingdom, and healing every sickness and every disease among the people.

36 ¶ [a]But when he saw the multitudes, he was moved with compassion on them, because they [/]fainted, and were scattered abroad, [b]as sheep having no shepherd.

9:15 When John's disciples complained that Jesus' disciples did not fast as often as they did, Jesus replied by predicting a future time when he would be taken away from his followers, causing them to fast.

37 Then saith he unto his disciples,
[a]The harvest truly *is* plenteous, but the
labourers *are* few;
38 [a]Pray ye therefore the Lord of the
harvest, that he will send forth labourers
into his harvest.

The mission of the Twelve

E 10 AND [a]WHEN he had called unto
him his twelve disciples, he gave
them power ʹ*against* unclean spirits, to
cast them out, and to heal all manner of
sickness and all manner of disease.
2 Now the names of the twelve apostles are these; The first, Simon, [a]who is
called Peter, and Andrew his brother;
James *the son* of Zebedee, and John his
brother;
3 Philip, and Bartholomew; Thomas,
and Matthew the publican; James *the son*
of Alphaeus, and Lebbaeus, whose surname was Thaddaeus;
4 [a]Simon the Canaanite, and Judas [b]Is-
cariot, who also betrayed him.
5 These twelve Jesus sent forth, and
commanded them, saying, [a]Go not into
the way of the Gentiles, and into *any* city
of [b]the Samaritans enter ye not:
R 6 [a]But go rather to the [b]lost sheep of
C the house of Israel.
P 7 [a]And as ye go, preach, saying, [b]The
E kingdom of heaven is at hand.
H 8 Heal the sick, cleanse the lepers,
raise the dead, cast out devils: [a]freely ye
have received, freely give.
9 [a]Provideʹ neither gold, nor silver,
nor [b]brass in your purses,
10 Nor scrip for *your* journey, neither
two coats, neither shoes, nor yet ʹstaves:
[a]for the workman is worthy of his meat.
11 [a]And into whatsoever city or town

E *Mt 9:18–35 ◀▶ Mt 10:7–8*
R *Zec 11:14 ◀▶ Mt 15:23–27*
C *Mt 9:12 ◀▶ Mt 12:30*
P *Mal 3:7 ◀▶ Mt 18:11–14*
E *Mt 10:1 ◀▶ Mt 11:4–5*
H *Mt 8:17 ◀▶ Mk 9:23*

37 [a]Luke 10:2; John 4:35
38 [a]2 Thes. 3:1
10:1 [a]Mark 3:13; Luke 6:13 ʹOr, over
2 [a]John 1:42
4 [a]Luke 6:15; Acts 1:13 [b]John 13:26
5 [a]ch. 4:15 [b]2 Ki. 17:24; John 4:9
6 [a]ch. 15:24; Acts 13:46 [b]Is. 53:6; Jer. 50:6; Ezek. 34:5; 1 Pet. 2:25
7 [a]Luke 9:2 [b]ch. 3:2; Luke 10:9
8 [a]Acts 8:18
9 [a]1 Sam. 9:7; Mark 6:8; Luke 9:3 & 10:4 [b]Mark 6:8 ʹOr, *Get*
10 [a]Luke 10:7; 1 Cor. 9:7; 1 Tim. 5:18 ʹGk. *a staff*
11 [a]Luke 10:8
13 [a]Luke 10:5 [b]Ps. 35:13
14 [a]Mark 6:11; Luke 9:5 & 10:10, 11 [b]Neh. 5:13; Acts 13:51
15 [a]ch. 11:22
16 [a]Luke 10:3 [b]Rom. 16:19; Eph. 5:15 [c]Phil. 2:15 ʹOr, *simple*
17 [a]Mark 13:9; Luke 12:11 [b]Acts 5:40
18 [a]Acts 12:1 & 25:7,23; 2 Tim. 4:16
19 [a]Luke 21:14 [b]Ex. 4:12; Jer. 1:7
20 [a]2 Sam. 23:2; 2 Tim. 4:17
21 [a]Mic. 7:6; Luke 21:16

ye shall enter, inquire who in it is worthy; and there abide till ye go thence.
12 And when ye come into an house,
salute it.
13 [a]And if the house be worthy, let
your peace come upon it: [b]but if it be not
worthy, let your peace return to you.
14 [a]And whosoever shall not receive H
you, nor hear your words, when ye de- N
part out of that house or city, [b]shake off
the dust of your feet.
15 Verily I say unto you, [a]It shall be J
more tolerable for the land of Sodom and J
Gomorrha in the day of judgment, than
for that city.
16 ¶ [a]Behold, I send you forth as sheep
in the midst of wolves: [b]be ye therefore
wise as serpents, and [c]harmlessʹ as
doves.
17 But beware of men: for [a]they will L
deliver you up to the councils, and [b]they
will scourge you in their synagogues;
18 And [a]ye shall be brought before
governors and kings for my sake, for a
testimony against them and the Gentiles.
19 [a]But when they deliver you up, G
take no thought how or what ye shall L
speak: for [b]it shall be given you in that T
same hour what ye shall speak.
20 [a]For it is not ye that speak, but the
Spirit of your Father which speaketh in
you.
21 [a]And the brother shall deliver up
the brother to death, and the father the
child: and the children shall rise up
against *their* parents, and cause them to
be put to death.

H *Mt 8:12 ◀▶ Mt 10:28*
N *Mal 2:2 ◀▶ Mt 11:20–24*
J *Zep 2:4–15 ◀▶ Mt 11:22*
J *Mt 7:1–2 ◀▶ Mt 11:22*
L *Jnh 2:4 ◀▶ Mt 26:13*
G *Mic 3:8 ◀▶ Mk 13:11*
L *Mt 4:1 ◀▶ Mk 1:12*
T *Joel 2:28–29 ◀▶ Mt 22:43–44*

9:37–38 The metaphor of the harvest is often used in the NT to refer to the end times. In this passage, Jesus instructs his disciples to pray to God to send workers to bring in the spiritual harvest of souls. How great that opportunity still is as we see the prophetic signs of Christ's second coming fulfilled in this generation.

10:14–15 When the NT Pharisees left a Gentile area they shook the dust off their sandals to symbolize ridding themselves of any contamination from anything "unclean." This command to the disciples to "shake off the dust of your feet" (10:14) is a solemn warning to those who utterly reject the message of Christ (see Lk 9:5; Ac 13:51; 18:6). Those who reject Christ will receive a worse punishment than Sodom and Gomorrah received. Scripture promises that all unrepentant sinners will be individually judged and endure hell forever (see Rev 20:12).

S 22 And [a]ye shall be hated of all *men*
for my name's sake: [b]but he that endureth to the end shall be saved.
23 But [a]when they persecute you in
this city, flee ye into another: for verily I
say unto you, Ye shall not [1]have gone
over the cities of Israel, [b]till the Son of
man be come.
24 [a]The disciple is not above *his* master, nor the servant above his lord.
25 It is enough for the disciple that he
be as his master, and the servant as his
lord. If [a]they have called the master of
the house [1]Beelzebub, how much more
shall they call them of his household?
26 Fear them not therefore: [a]for there
is nothing covered, that shall not be revealed; and hid, that shall not be known.
27 What I tell you in darkness, *that*
speak ye in light: and what ye hear in the
ear, *that* preach ye upon the housetops.
H 28 [a]And fear not them which kill the
body, but are not able to kill the soul: but
rather fear him which is able to destroy
both soul and body in hell.
L 29 Are not two sparrows sold for a
[1]farthing? and one of them shall not fall
on the ground without your Father.
30 [a]But the very hairs of your head are
all numbered.
31 Fear ye not therefore, ye are of
more value than many sparrows.
O 32 [a]Whosoever therefore shall confess
T me before men, [b]him will I confess also
W before my Father which is in heaven.
33 [a]But whosoever shall deny me before men, him will I also deny before my
Father which is in heaven.

S *Mt 7:16–24* ◀▶ *Mt 10:37–38*
H *Mt 10:14–15* ◀▶ *Mt 11:20–24*
L *Mt 8:26* ◀▶ *Mt 18:5–6*
O *Mt 7:26–27* ◀▶ *Mt 15:13*
T *Mal 3:16–17* ◀▶ *Mk 5:19*
W *Mt 7:24* ◀▶ *Mt 11:28–29*

22 [a]Luke 21:17 [b]Dan. 12:12; Mark 13:13
23 [a]ch. 2:13; Acts 8:1 [b]ch. 16:28 [1]Or, *end,* or, *finish*
24 [a]Luke 6:40; John 15:20
25 [a]Mark 3:22; John 8:48 [1]Gk. *Beelzebul*
26 [a]Mark 4:22; Luke 8:17 & 12:2,3
28 [a]Is. 8:12,13; Luke 12:4; 1 Pet. 3:14
29 [1]A farthing is a small amount of money, worth approximately one cent.
30 [a]1 Sam. 14:45; Luke 21:18; Acts 27:34
32 [a]Luke 12:8; Rom. 10:9 [b]Rev. 3:5
33 [a]Luke 9:26; 2 Tim. 2:12
34 [a]Luke 12:49
35 [a]Mic. 7:6
36 [a]Ps. 41:9 & 55:13; John 13:18
37 [a]Luke 14:26
38 [a]Mark 8:34
39 [a]Luke 17:33; John 12:25
40 [a]Luke 9:48; John 12:44; Gal. 4:14
41 [a]1 Ki. 17:10; 2 Ki. 4:8
42 [a]ch. 25:40; Mark 9:41; Heb. 6:10
11:2 [a]Luke 7:18 [b]ch. 14:3

34 [a]Think not that I am come to send
peace on earth: I came not to send peace,
but a sword.
35 For I am come to set a man at variance [a]against his father, and the daughter
against her mother, and the daughter-in-
law against her mother-in-law.
36 And [a]a man's foes *shall be* they of
his own household.
37 [a]He that loveth father or mother S
more than me is not worthy of me: and
he that loveth son or daughter more than
me is not worthy of me.
38 [a]And he that taketh not his cross,
and followeth after me, is not worthy
of me.
39 [a]He that findeth his life shall lose it:
and he that loseth his life for my sake
shall find it.
40 ¶ [a]He that receiveth you receiveth
me, and he that receiveth me receiveth
him that sent me.
41 [a]He that receiveth a prophet in the
name of a prophet shall receive a
prophet's reward; and he that receiveth a
righteous man in the name of a righteous
man shall receive a righteous man's
reward.
42 [a]And whosoever shall give to drink
unto one of these little ones a cup of cold
water only in the name of a disciple,
verily I say unto you, he shall in no wise
lose his reward.
11 AND IT came to pass, when Jesus
had made an end of commanding
his twelve disciples, he departed thence
to teach and to preach in their cities.

Tribute to John the Baptist

2 [a]Now when John had heard [b]in the
prison the works of Christ, he sent two of
his disciples,

S *Mt 10:22* ◀▶ *Mt 12:33–37*

10:22 Matthew records Jesus' prophecy of the persecution of believers. This persecution began immediately following Christ's resurrection and has continued unabated for centuries. Worldwide persecution will increase in the last days during the tribulation. Those who stand firm against the antichrist during the years before the Battle of Armageddon and Christ's return will experience a terrible time of trial. But Jesus promised that those who stand firm "to the end shall be saved."

11:2–5 John's words here do not question Jesus' role as the Messiah, a fact that John clearly acknowledged (see 3:13–17; Mk 1:9–11; Lk 3:21; Jn 1:29). John was more concerned about Jesus' methods. The OT prophecies about the Messiah described a compassionate servant, a just judge, a powerful king and a mighty warrior (see Isa 9:6–8; 53:1–12; 61:1–2; Mic 5:2; Zec 9:9). The reports John heard while he languished in prison indicated that while Jesus was compassionate, he was not behaving like a warrior or a judge or a king. Jesus' response to John linked his mission to the prophetic words of Isaiah given seven centuries earlier: The Messiah would open blind eyes, deaf ears and preach good tidings to the

Hell

ALL OF THOSE who reject God's offer of salvation will be confronted with his judgment—an eternity in hell experiencing "the lake of fire and brimstone" (Rev 20:10; see Mt 25:41, 46; Rev 21:8). The Bible declares that hell is absolutely real, that it will be unpleasant and that it will last forever (see Mt 13:42; Rev 14:10). Some theologians have attempted to escape Scripture's clear teaching about the terrors of hell by assuming that it will involve the annihilation of the sinner's soul and consciousness. Jesus' words contradict this teaching and indicate that those who spend an eternity in hell will do so fully conscious with much "weeping and gnashing of teeth" (Mt 8:12).

The Bible's Description of Hell

The Bible describes hell as a "lake of fire" (Rev 20:10; see Mk 9:47) that cannot be destroyed. Several terms are used throughout Scripture when referring to hell: *Sheol, hades, gehenna* and *tartarus*. In the OT the most common word for "hell" is *Sheol*. Though the exact translation of *Sheol* is unknown, the OT often equates it with the grave (see Ge 37:35; 1Sa 2:6; Job 7:9; 14:13; Ps 6:5; 49:14; Isa 14:11) and also translates *Sheol* as "hell" (see Dt 32:22; Ps 9:17; 18:5; Isa 14:9; Am 9:2). Believed to be a shadowy underground region inhabited by disembodied souls (see Ge 37:35; Nu 16:30, 33; Job 11:8; Ps 9:17; Is 38:10; Am 9:2), Sheol became a synonym for the abode of the wretched dead. Even though God is present in Sheol (see Ps 139:8), the believer's hope for the future is ultimate deliverance from Sheol and restoration to a life in God's presence in heaven (see Job 14:13–15; 19:25–27; Ps 16:10–11; 17:15; 49:15; 73:24–26; Ac 2:27).

The NT uses the word *hades* as the Greek equivalent of *Sheol*, though *hades* rarely refers to the "grave" (see Ac 2:31). Its most common usage refers to the world of future punishment (see Mt 11:23; 16:18; Ac 2:31; Rev 1:18; 6:8; 20:13–14), describing a place where wicked spirits await the day of judgment at the end of the Millennium. Yet Scripture indicates that before Christ's death, resurrection and ascension *hades* was divided into two portions and separated by a great gulf (see Lk 16:22–26). One side of *hades* was a pleasant place known as "Abraham's bosom" (Lk 16:22), the repository of those righteous souls who died during the OT. Those souls who had rejected God's truth were confined to the other part of *hades* known as "the place of torment" (Lk 16:28).

Another word associated with hell is the word *tartarus*, which is found in only one place in Scripture (see 2Pe 2:4). This verse indicates that there is a special place in hell where God will imprison fallen angels "in everlasting chains under darkness unto the judgment of the great day" (Jude 6).

The final word translated "hell" in the Bible is the word *gehenna.* This word occurs repeatedly in the NT (see Mt 5:22–30; Mk 9:43–47). In the Valley of Hinnom outside the walls of Jerusalem was a horrible, burning garbage pit whose fire never ceased. The bodies of criminals were thrown into this garbage pit to rot and burn. Significantly, the Scriptures liken this pit to *gehenna* and paint a graphic visual image of pain, torment and punishment in every passage in the NT where the word *gehenna* appears.

The Punished and Their Punishment

Scripture assures us of God's perfect justice (see Ge 18:25). God's holiness demands a just judgment of all sinners. Every sinner from Cain to the last rebel at the end of the Millennium will appear before the great white throne in heaven to be judged individually by God (see Rev 20:11–14). Since everyone who appears at this judgment before God's throne is an unrepentant sinner, there would be no need for this special judgment unless individual sentences were to be handed out. Though all those who enter hell will endure its flames forever, when "the books" (Rev 20:12) are opened there will be different degrees of punishment meted out in hell to reflect the evil deeds of those who reject Jesus Christ (see Ecc 12:14; Jer 17:10; 32:19; Ro 2:6; Rev 20:13). (For further information on this final judgment, see the article on "The Great White Throne Judgment" on p. 1484.)

Hell will be filled with untold billions of sinners. Their resurrected bodies will never die in hell but will feel every pain and torment of their eternal punishment. These sinners in hell will curse God and rage against his justice, desiring to avenge themselves against God, but they will not succeed (see Rev 14:11; 16:10–11).

In their frustration they may vent their anger on their weaker companions in hell. Hell has no guards or bars to protect a weaker prisoner from the cruelty of a stronger, wicked prisoner. The most a sinner could hope for in this life would be a swift death. However, in hell there will be no death. Those who reject salvation will spend eternity in hell as companions to every murderer, rapist, abuser and vile person who ever lived.

Though some liberal theologians accept the reality of hell, many seek to minimize hell's horror by suggesting that those who enter damnation will finally emerge at some point in the future to take their part among the blessed of the Lord. Others suggest that a loving God would rather annihilate the souls of those who reject Christ's salvation instead of condemning them to eternal torment. Both of these viewpoints are repudiated in Scripture. The judgment and punishment of hell will last forever (see Mt 25:41, 46; Rev 14:10), and the souls of those who reject Christ's mercy will not be annihilated but will be conscious in their eternity of torment (see Lk 16:22–28).

Final Justice

In the book of Ecclesiastes, King Solomon, the wisest man who ever lived, described the lack of justice in human life. He questioned the fact that evil deeds appear to go unpunished in this life while the righteous often have trouble all their days (see Ecc 8:11–12). God, in his mercy, often delays the punishment for sin, allowing a time for repentance and salvation (see 2Pe 3:9). And sometimes, Satan, in his cunning attempt to destroy humanity, delays the consequences of sin, leading people deeper and deeper into the whirlpool of depravity. If sin immediately resulted in painful and embarrassing consequences, many people would turn from their sinful path. However, when someone seems to "get away with it," this apparent lack of consequences leads step by step to a life lived against God's plan. Solomon's inspired conclusion was that God's justice, though delayed, would finally be revealed and God would "bring every work into judgment, with every secret thing, whether it be good, or whether it be evil"(Ecc 12:14). That final judgment will bring about the just punishment of hell.

3 And said unto him, Art thou [a]he that
should come, or do we look for another?
E 4 Jesus answered and said unto them,
Go and show John again those things
which ye do hear and see:
5 [a]The blind receive their sight, and
the lame walk, the lepers are cleansed,
and the deaf hear, the dead are raised up,
and [b]the poor have the gospel preached
to them.
6 And blessed is *he,* whosoever shall
not [a]be offended in me.
7 ¶ [a]And as they departed, Jesus began
to say unto the multitudes concerning
John, What went ye out into the wilderness to see? [b]A reed shaken with the
wind?
8 But what went ye out for to see? A
man clothed in soft raiment? behold, they
that wear soft *clothing* are in kings'
houses.
9 But what went ye out for to see? A
prophet? yea, I say unto you, [a]and more
than a prophet.
10 For this is *he,* of whom it is written,
[a]Behold, I send my messenger before thy
face, which shall prepare thy way before
thee.
11 Verily I say unto you, Among them
that are born of women there hath not
risen a greater than John the Baptist: notwithstanding he that is least in the kingdom of heaven is greater than he.
F 12 [a]And from the days of John the Baptist until now the kingdom of heaven
[1]suffereth violence, and the violent take
it by force.
13 [a]For all the prophets and the law
prophesied until John.
14 And if ye will receive *it,* this is
[a]Elias, which was for to come.
15 [a]He that hath ears to hear, let him
hear.
16 ¶ [a]But whereunto shall I liken this
generation? It is like unto children sitting
in the markets, and calling unto their
fellows,
17 And saying, We have piped unto
you, and ye have not danced; we have
mourned unto you, and ye have not lamented.
18 For John came neither eating nor
drinking, and they say, He hath a devil.
19 The Son of man came eating and
drinking, and they say, Behold a man
gluttonous, and a winebibber, [a]a friend of
publicans and sinners. [b]But wisdom is
justified of her children.

The judgment of the unrepentant

20 ¶ [a]Then began he to upbraid the H
cities wherein most of his mighty works N
were done, because they repented not:
21 Woe unto thee, Chorazin! woe
unto thee, Bethsaida! for if the mighty
works, which were done in you, had
been done in Tyre and Sidon, they would
have repented long ago [a]in sackcloth and
ashes.

3 [a]Gen. 49:10; Num. 24:17; Dan. 9:24; John 6:14
5 [a]Is. 29:18 & 35:4-6; John 2:23 [b]Ps. 22:26; Is. 61:1; Luke 4:18; Jas. 2:5
6 [a]Is. 8:14,15; Rom. 9:32; 1 Pet. 2:8
7 [a]Luke 7:24 [b]Eph. 4:14
9 [a]Luke 1:76
10 [a]Mal. 3:1; Mark 1:2; Luke 1:76
12 [a]Luke 16:16 [1]*Or, is gotten by force, and they that thrust men*
13 [a]Mal. 4:6
14 [a]Mal. 4:5; Luke 1:17
15 [a]ch. 13:9; Luke 8:8; Rev. 2:7,11,17, 29 & 3:6,13
16 [a]Luke 7:31
19 [a]ch. 9:10 [b]Luke 7:35
20 [a]Luke 10:13
21 [a]Jonah 3:7

E *Mt 10:7–8* ◀▶ *Mt 12:9–13*
F *Hab 2:4* ◀▶ *Mt 21:31–32*
H *Mt 10:28* ◀▶ *Mt 13:30*
N *Mt 10:14–15* ◀▶ *Mt 12:41–42*

---

poor (see Isa 35:5; 61:1). In this way Jesus told John to trust his mission even if his methods were not completely comprehensible.

Of the signs that Jesus used to prove his claim as Messiah, the healing of the blind is one of the most significant. When Jesus healed a blind boy (see Jn 9:1–38) it was the first time in the Jews' recorded history that anyone born blind was healed. With this miracle Jesus uniquely fulfilled a qualification of the Messiah outlined in several OT prophecies (see Ps 146:8; Isa 29:18; 42:7); he opened blind eyes for the first time in history.

11:21–24 Jesus chastens the unrepentant people of the cities of Chorazin and Bethsaida, declaring that because of their refusal to repent they would be judged by God more harshly than the wicked Phoenician cities of Tyre and Sidon. Capernaum's indictment is more severe since it was Jesus' base of operations while he ministered in Galilee. Capernaum had its own synagogue where Jesus often taught (see Mk 1:21; Lk 4:31; Jn 6:59). Jesus also performed many miracles of healing in Capernaum: the centurion's servant (see 8:5; Lk 7:1–2), Peter's mother-in-law (see 8:14; Mk 1:30; Lk 4:38), the paralytic (see 9:1–2; Mk 2:1–3) and the demon-possessed man (see Mk 1:32; Lk 4:33). Yet the citizens of Capernaum still rejected Jesus' call to follow him.

The prophecy of judgment spoken against these three cities has been completely fulfilled. Though Chorazin was a place of some importance during the ministry of Jesus, by the end of the first century it was already deserted and desolate with only a few carved stones to mark its existence. Because the destruction of the other two cities was so complete, archeologists are not even sure of the exact location of these cities that figured so prominently in Jesus' ministry.

22 But I say unto you, [a]It shall be more tolerable for Tyre and Sidon at the day of judgment, than for you.

23 And thou, Capernaum, [a]which art exalted unto heaven, shalt be brought down to hell: for if the mighty works, which have been done in thee, had been done in Sodom, it would have remained until this day.

24 But I say unto you, [a]That it shall be more tolerable for the land of Sodom in the day of judgment, than for thee.

Jesus reveals the Father

25 ¶ [a]At that time Jesus answered and said, I thank thee, O Father, Lord of heaven and earth, because [b]thou hast hid these things from the wise and prudent, [c]and hast revealed them unto babes.

26 Even so, Father: for so it seemed good in thy sight.

27 [a]All things are delivered unto me of my Father: and no man knoweth the Son, but the Father; [b]neither knoweth any man the Father, save the Son, and *he* to whomsoever the Son will reveal *him.*

28 ¶ Come unto me, all *ye* that labour and are heavy laden, and I will give you rest.

29 Take my yoke upon you, [a]and learn of me; for I am meek and [b]lowly in heart: [c]and ye shall find rest unto your souls.

30 [a]For my yoke *is* easy, and my burden is light.

Jesus the Lord of the Sabbath

12 AT THAT time [a]Jesus went on the sabbath day through the corn; and his disciples were an hungered, and began to pluck the ears of corn, and to eat.

2 But when the Pharisees saw *it,* they said unto him, Behold, thy disciples do that which is not lawful to do upon the sabbath day.

3 But he said unto them, Have ye not read [a]what David did, when he was an hungered, and they that were with him;

4 How he entered into the house of God, and did eat [a]the showbread, which was not lawful for him to eat, neither for them which were with him, [b]but only for the priests?

5 Or have ye not read in the [a]law, how that on the sabbath days the priests in the temple profane the sabbath, and are blameless?

6 But I say unto you, That in this place is [a]*one* greater than the temple.

7 But if ye had known what *this* meaneth, [a]I will have mercy, and not sacrifice, ye would not have condemned the guiltless.

8 For the Son of man is Lord even of the sabbath day.

9 [a]And when he was departed thence, he went into their synagogue:

10 ¶ And, behold, there was a man which had *his* hand withered. And they asked him, saying, [a]Is it lawful to heal on the sabbath days? that they might accuse him.

11 And he said unto them, What man shall there be among you, that shall have one sheep, and if [a]it fall into a pit on the sabbath day, will he not lay hold on it, and lift *it* out?

12 How much then is a man better than a sheep? Wherefore it is lawful to do well on the sabbath days.

13 Then saith he to the man, Stretch forth thine hand. And he stretched *it* forth; and it was restored whole, like as the other.

14 ¶ Then [a]the Pharisees went out, and [1]held a council against him, how they might destroy him.

Jesus heals many

15 But when Jesus knew *it,* [a]he withdrew himself from thence: [b]and great multitudes followed him, and he healed them all;

16 And [a]charged them that they should not make him known:

17 That it might be fulfilled which was spoken by Esaias the prophet, saying,

18 [a]Behold my servant, whom I have chosen; my beloved, [b]in whom my soul is well pleased: I will put my spirit upon him, and he shall show judgment to the Gentiles.

19 He shall not strive, nor cry; neither

22 [a]ver. 24; ch. 10:15
23 [a]See Is. 14:13; Lam. 2:1
24 [a]ch. 10:15
25 [a]Luke 10:21 [b]Ps. 8:2; 1 Cor. 1:19 & 2:8; 2 Cor. 3:14 [c]ch. 16:17
27 [a]ch. 28:18; Luke 10:22; John 3:35 & 13:3 & 17:2; 1 Cor. 15:27 [b]John 1:18 & 6:46 & 10:15
29 [a]John 13:15; Phil. 2:5; 1 Pet. 2:21; 1 John 2:6 [b]Zech. 9:9; Phil. 2:7,8 [c]Jer. 6:16
30 [a]1 John 5:3
12:1 [a]Deut. 23:25; Mark 2:23; Luke 6:1
3 [a]1 Sam. 21:6
4 [a]Ex. 25:30; Lev. 24:5 [b]Ex. 29:32; Lev. 8:31 & 24:9
5 [a]Num. 28:9; John 7:22
6 [a]2 Chr. 6:18; Mal. 3:1
7 [a]Hos. 6:6; Mic. 6:6-8; ch. 9:13
9 [a]Mark 3:1; Luke 6:6
10 [a]Luke 13:14 & 14:3; John 9:16
11 [a]See Ex. 23:4,5; Deut. 22:4
14 [a]ch. 27:1; Mark 3:6; Luke 6:11; John 5:18 & 10:39 & 11:53 [1]Or, *took counsel*
15 [a]See ch. 10:23; Mark 3:7 [b]ch. 19:2
16 [a]ch. 9:30
18 [a]Is. 42:1 [b]ch. 3:17 & 17:5

J *Mt 10:15* ◀▶ *Mt 11:24*
J *Mt 10:15* ◀▶ *Mt 11:24*
J *Mt 11:22* ◀▶ *Mt 12:36*
J *Mt 11:22* ◀▶ *Mt 12:36*
K *Mt 9:6* ◀▶ *Mt 19:26*
L *Mt 9:12–13* ◀▶ *Mt 12:20*
W *Mt 10:32* ◀▶ *Mt 12:20*
E *Mt 11:4–5* ◀▶ *Mt 12:15*
E *Mt 12:9–13* ◀▶ *Mt 12:22–29*
B *Mt 3:16* ◀▶ *Mk 1:8*

shall any man hear his voice in the streets.

20 A bruised reed shall he not break, and smoking flax shall he not quench, till he send forth judgment unto victory.

21 And in his name shall the Gentiles trust.

The Pharisees' slander

22 ¶ [a]Then was brought unto him one possessed with a devil, blind, and dumb: and he healed him, insomuch that the blind and dumb both spake and saw.

23 And all the people were amazed, and said, Is not this the son of David?

24 [a]But when the Pharisees heard *it,* they said, This *fellow* doth not cast out devils, but by [l]Beelzebub the prince of the devils.

25 And Jesus [a]knew their thoughts, and said unto them, Every kingdom divided against itself is brought to desolation; and every city or house divided against itself shall not stand:

26 And if Satan cast out Satan, he is divided against himself; how shall then his kingdom stand?

27 And if I by Beelzebub cast out devils, by whom do your children cast *them* out? therefore they shall be your judges.

28 But if I cast out devils by the Spirit of God, then [a]the kingdom of God is come unto you.

29 [a]Or else how can one enter into a strong man's house, and spoil his goods, except he first bind the strong man? and then he will spoil his house.

L *Mt 11:28–29* ◀ ▶ *Mt 12:31–32*
W *Mt 11:28–29* ◀ ▶ *Mt 20:1–16*
E *Mt 12:15* ◀ ▶ *Mt 14:14*
E *Mt 9:4* ◀ ▶ *Lk 6:8*
E *Mt 4:1* ◀ ▶ *Mt 22:43*
H *Eze 37:13–14* ◀ ▶ *Jn 3:3–8*
M *Mt 3:11* ◀ ▶ *Mk 13:11*

22 [a]See ch. 9:32; Mark 3:11; Luke 11:14
24 [a]ch. 9:34; Mark 3:22; Luke 11:15 [l]Gk. *Beelzebul;* also ver. 27
25 [a]ch. 9:4; John 2:25; Rev. 2:23
28 [a]Dan. 2:44 & 7:14; Luke 1:33 & 11:20 & 17:20,21
29 [a]Is. 49:24; Luke 11:21-23
31 [a]Mark 3:28; Luke 12:10; Heb. 6:4 & 10:26,29; 1 John 5:16 [b]Acts 7:51
32 [a]ch. 11:19 & 13:55; John 7:12,52 [b]1 Tim. 1:13
33 [a]ch. 7:17; Luke 6:43
34 [a]ch. 3:7 & 23:33 [b]Luke 6:45
38 [a]ch. 16:1; Mark 8:11; Luke 11:16; John 2:18; 1 Cor. 1:22

30 He that is not with me is against me; and he that gathereth not with me scattereth abroad.

31 ¶ Wherefore I say unto you, [a]All manner of sin and blasphemy shall be forgiven unto men: [b]but the blasphemy *against* the *Holy* Ghost shall not be forgiven unto men.

32 And whosoever [a]speaketh a word against the Son of man, [b]it shall be forgiven him: but whosoever speaketh against the Holy Ghost, it shall not be forgiven him, neither in this world, neither in the *world* to come.

33 Either make the tree good, and [a]his fruit good; or else make the tree corrupt, and his fruit corrupt: for the tree is known by *his* fruit.

34 O [a]generation of vipers, how can ye, being evil, speak good things? [b]for out of the abundance of the heart the mouth speaketh.

35 A good man out of the good treasure of the heart bringeth forth good things: and an evil man out of the evil treasure bringeth forth evil things.

36 But I say unto you, That every idle word that men shall speak, they shall give account thereof in the day of judgment.

37 For by thy words thou shalt be justified, and by thy words thou shalt be condemned.

Warning against seeking signs

38 ¶ [a]Then certain of the scribes and of the Pharisees answered, saying, Master, we would see a sign from thee.

39 But he answered and said unto

A *Isa 53:6* ◀ ▶ *Mt 22:11–14*
C *Mt 10:6* ◀ ▶ *Mt 13:14–15*
D *Isa 40:13* ◀ ▶ *Mt 28:19*
Q *Zec 6:8* ◀ ▶ *Mk 3:29*
L *Mt 12:20* ◀ ▶ *Mt 18:11–14*
S *Mt 10:37–38* ◀ ▶ *Mt 12:50*
J *Mt 11:24* ◀ ▶ *Mt 12:42*
J *Mt 11:24* ◀ ▶ *Mt 12:41–42*

12:36–37 Jesus warns that all of us will be judged by our words in the final judgment. All of our words, even those carelessly spoken, are important (see 5:22; 2Co 12:20; 1Ti 1:10; Jas 3:6; Rev 21:8). Scripture clearly states that our words impact our eternal lives because "with the mouth confession is made unto salvation" (Ro 10:10). For further information, see the article on "The Great White Throne Judgment" on p. 1484.

12:39–40 Jesus' words confirm the historical reality of Jonah's experience in the belly of the great fish. The "three days and three nights" (12:40) that Jonah spent in the great fish signify the same length of time that Jesus would be "in the heart of the earth" (12:40). Since the ancient Jews measured time inclusively, this time period is probably much shorter than three, full 24-hour periods. Though we calculate a day as 24 full hours, ancient Jews calculated any portion of one day as a full day. Thus this phrase "three days and three nights" meant any por-

them, An evil and [a]adulterous generation seeketh after a sign; and there shall no sign be given to it, but the sign of the prophet Jonas:

B 40 [a]For as Jonas was three days and three nights in the whale's belly; so shall the Son of man be three days and three nights in the heart of the earth.

J 41 [a]The men of Nineveh shall rise in
N judgment with this generation, and [b]shall
condemn it: [c]because they repented at the preaching of Jonas; and, behold, a greater than Jonas *is* here.

J 42 [a]The queen of the south shall rise up in the judgment with this generation, and shall condemn it: for she came from the uttermost parts of the earth to hear the wisdom of Solomon; and, behold, a greater than Solomon *is* here.

43 [a]When the unclean spirit is gone out of a man, [b]he walketh through dry places, seeking rest, and findeth none.

44 Then he saith, I will return into my house from whence I came out; and when he is come, he findeth *it* empty, swept, and garnished.

45 Then goeth he, and taketh with himself seven other spirits more wicked than himself, and they enter in and dwell there: [a]and the last *state* of that man is worse than the first. Even so shall it be also unto this wicked generation.

Jesus' true family

46 ¶ While he yet talked to the people, [a]behold, *his* mother and [b]his brethren stood without, desiring to speak with him.

47 Then one said unto him, Behold, thy mother and thy brethren stand without, desiring to speak with thee.

48 But he answered and said unto him that told him, Who is my mother? and who are my brethren?

B *Mt 4:13–15* ◀ ▶ *Mt 27:9–10*
J *Mt 12:36* ◀ ▶ *Mt 25:31–46*
N *Mt 11:20–24* ◀ ▶ *Mt 13:13–15*
J *Mt 12:36* ◀ ▶ *Mt 25:19*

39 [a]Is. 57:3; ch. 16:4; Mark 8:38; John 4:48
40 [a]Jonah 1:17
41 [a]Luke 11:32 [b]See Jer. 3:11; Ezek. 16:51; Rom. 2:27 [c]Jonah 3:5
42 [a]1 Ki. 10:1; 2 Chr. 9:1; Luke 11:31
43 [a]Luke 11:24 [b]Job 1:7; 1 Pet. 5:8
45 [a]Heb. 6:4 & 10:26; 2 Pet. 2:20-22
46 [a]Mark 3:31; Luke 8:19-21 [b]ch. 13:55; Mark 6:3; John 2:12 & 7:3,5; Acts 1:14; 1 Cor. 9:5; Gal. 1:19
50 [a]See John 15:14; Gal. 5:6 & 6:15; Col. 3:11; Heb. 2:11
13:1 [a]Mark 4:1
2 [a]Luke 8:4 [b]Luke 5:3
3 [a]Luke 8:5
8 [a]Gen. 26:12
9 [a]ch. 11:15; Mark 4:9
11 [a]ch. 11:25 & 16:17; Mark 4:11; 1 Cor. 2:10; 1 John 2:27
12 [a]ch. 25:29; Mark 4:25; Luke 8:18 & 19:26

49 And he stretched forth his hand toward his disciples, and said, Behold my mother and my brethren!

50 For [a]whosoever shall do the will of S
my Father which is in heaven, the same is my brother, and sister, and mother.

The parable of the sower

13 THE SAME day went Jesus out of the house, [a]and sat by the sea side.

2 [a]And great multitudes were gathered together unto him, so that [b]he went into a ship, and sat; and the whole multitude stood on the shore.

3 And he spake many things unto them in parables, saying, [a]Behold, a sower went forth to sow;

4 And when he sowed, some *seeds* fell by the way side, and the fowls came and devoured them up:

5 Some fell upon stony places, where S
they had not much earth: and forthwith they sprung up, because they had no deepness of earth:

6 And when the sun was up, they were scorched; and because they had no root, they withered away.

7 And some fell among thorns; and the thorns sprung up, and choked them:

8 But other fell into good ground, and brought forth fruit, some [a]an hundredfold, some sixtyfold, some thirtyfold.

9 [a]Who hath ears to hear, let him hear.

10 And the disciples came, and said unto him, Why speakest thou unto them in parables?

11 He answered and said unto them, Because [a]it is given unto you to know the mysteries of the kingdom of heaven, but to them it is not given.

12 [a]For whosoever hath, to him shall be given, and he shall have more abundance: but whosoever hath not, from him shall be taken away even that he hath.

S *Mt 12:33–37* ◀ ▶ *Mt 13:5–8*
S *Mt 12:50* ◀ ▶ *Mt 13:20–22*

---

tion of the first day, plus all of the second day, plus any portion of the third day. In a similar manner, Christ's burial late Friday afternoon until his resurrection on Sunday morning occupied the same amount of time that the prophet Jonah was in the great fish.

12:42 Matthew's "queen of the south" is probably the "queen of Sheba" from 1Ki 10:1. Just as this pagan queen stood in Solomon's presence and recognized God's touch on his life, so Matthew rebukes the scribes and Pharisees for their refusal to repent despite the overwhelming evidence of the life and ministry of Jesus Christ.

N 13 Therefore speak I to them in parables: because they seeing see not; and hearing they hear not, neither do they understand.

C 14 And in them is fulfilled the prophecy of Esaias, which saith, [a]By hearing ye shall hear, and shall not understand; and seeing ye shall see, and shall not perceive:

15 For this people's heart is waxed gross, and *their* ears [a]are dull of hearing, and their eyes they have closed; lest at any time they should see with *their* eyes, and hear with *their* ears, and should understand with *their* heart, and should be converted, and I should heal them.

16 But [a]blessed *are* your eyes, for they see: and your ears, for they hear.

17 For verily I say unto you, [a]That many prophets and righteous *men* have desired to see *those things* which ye see, and have not seen *them;* and to hear *those things* which ye hear, and have not heard *them*.

18 ¶ [a]Hear ye therefore the parable of the sower.

19 When any one heareth the word [a]of the kingdom, and understandeth *it* not, then cometh the wicked *one,* and catcheth away that which was sown in his heart. This is he which received seed by the way side.

S 20 But he that received the seed into stony places, the same is he that heareth the word, and anon [a]with joy receiveth it;

21 Yet hath he not root in himself, but dureth for a while: for when tribulation or persecution ariseth because of the word, by and by [a]he is offended.

N *Mt 12:41–42* ◀▶ *Mt 21:44*
C *Mt 12:30* ◀▶ *Mt 13:38*
S *Mt 13:5–8* ◀▶ *Mt 16:24*

14 [a]Is. 6:9; Ezek. 12:2; Mark 4:12; Luke 8:10; John 12:40; Acts 28:26, 27; Rom. 11:8; 2 Cor. 3:14,15
15 [a]Heb. 5:11
16 [a]ch. 16:17; Luke 10:23,24; John 20:29
17 [a]Heb. 11:13; 1 Pet. 1:10,11
18 [a]Mark 4:14; Luke 8:11
19 [a]ch. 4:23
20 [a]Is. 58:2; Ezek. 33:31,32; John 5:35
21 [a]ch. 11:6; 2 Tim. 1:15
22 [a]ch. 19:23; Mark 10:23; Luke 18:24; 1 Tim. 6:9; 2 Tim. 4:10 [b]Jer. 4:3
30 [a]ch. 3:12

22 [a]He also that received seed [b]among the thorns is he that heareth the word; and the care of this world, and the deceitfulness of riches, choke the word, and he becometh unfruitful.

23 But he that received seed into the good ground is he that heareth the word, and understandeth *it;* which also beareth fruit, and bringeth forth, some an hundredfold, some sixty, some thirty.

Parables about the kingdom

24 ¶ Another parable put he forth unto them, saying, The kingdom of heaven is likened unto a man which sowed good seed in his field:

25 But while men slept, his enemy came and sowed tares among the wheat, and went his way.

26 But when the blade was sprung up, and brought forth fruit, then appeared the tares also.

27 So the servants of the householder P
came and said unto him, Sir, didst not thou sow good seed in thy field? from whence then hath it tares?

28 He said unto them, An enemy hath done this. The servants said unto him, Wilt thou then that we go and gather them up?

29 But he said, Nay; lest while ye gather up the tares, ye root up also the wheat with them.

30 Let both grow together until the T
harvest: and in the time of harvest I will H
say to the reapers, Gather ye together first the tares, and bind them in bundles to burn them: but [a]gather the wheat into my barn.

31 ¶ Another parable put he forth unto M

P *Mt 3:12* ◀▶ *Mt 13:39–42*
T *Mt 3:12* ◀▶ *Mt 24:31*
H *Mt 11:20–24* ◀▶ *Mt 13:38–42*
M *Mt 6:13* ◀▶ *Mt 13:43*

13:27–30 Some weeds resemble wheat when both plants are young. This made it very difficult to eradicate the weeds before the grain was ripe. Farmers would allow the wheat and weeds to grow together until the final harvest when the two plants would be easily distinguishable.

Jesus explains that this parable prophetically points to the final judgment when the angels of God will "gather out of his kingdom all things that offend, and them which do iniquity" (13:41). After the seven-year tribulation and the Battle of Armageddon, Christ will judge the nations and usher in his millennial kingdom. The weeds (sinners) will be gathered to judgment (see 13:41–42; 25:31–33) but God will command that the reapers place the wheat (believers) in his barn (13:30). The raptured saints will return with Christ (see Rev 19:11–14) where they will be "priests of God and of Christ, and shall reign with him a thousand years" (Rev 20:6).

13:31–32 The parable of the mustard seed foreshadows the amazing growth of the kingdom throughout the centuries, from the first disciples to the world dominion of the last days (see Da 2:35,

them, saying, [a]The kingdom of heaven is like to a grain of mustard seed, which a man took, and sowed in his field:

32 Which indeed is the least of all seeds: but when it is grown, it is the greatest among herbs, and becometh a tree, so that the birds of the air come and lodge in the branches thereof.

K 33 ¶ [a]Another parable spake he unto them; The kingdom of heaven is like unto leaven, which a woman took, and hid in three [l]measures of meal, till the whole was leavened.

34 [a]All these things spake Jesus unto the multitude in parables; and without a parable spake he not unto them:

35 That it might be fulfilled which was spoken by the prophet, saying, [a]I will open my mouth in parables; [b]I will utter things which have been kept secret from the foundation of the world.

Parable of the tares explained

36 Then Jesus sent the multitude away, and went into the house: and his disciples came unto him, saying, Declare unto us the parable of the tares of the field.

37 He answered and said unto them, He that soweth the good seed is the Son of man;

C 38 [a]The field is the world; the good
H seed are the children of the kingdom; but
the tares are [b]the children of the wicked
one;

P 39 The enemy that sowed them is the devil; [a]the harvest is the end of the world; and the reapers are the angels.

40 As therefore the tares are gathered and burned in the fire; so shall it be in the end of this world.

41 The Son of man shall send forth his angels, [a]and they shall gather out of his kingdom all [l]things that offend, and them which do iniquity;

42 [a]And shall cast them into a furnace of fire: [b]there shall be wailing and gnashing of teeth.

43 [a]Then shall the righteous shine M
forth as the sun in the kingdom of their Father. [b]Who hath ears to hear, let him hear.

Further parables of the kingdom

44 ¶ Again, the kingdom of heaven is like unto treasure hid in a field; the which when a man hath found, he hideth, and for joy thereof goeth and [a]selleth all that he hath, and [b]buyeth that field.

45 ¶ Again, the kingdom of heaven is like unto a merchant man, seeking goodly pearls:

46 Who, when he had found [a]one H
pearl of great price, went and sold all that he had, and bought it.

47 ¶ Again, the kingdom of heaven is P
like unto a net, that was cast into the sea, and [a]gathered of every kind:

48 Which, when it was full, they drew to shore, and sat down, and gathered the good into vessels, but cast the bad away.

49 So shall it be at the end of the world: the angels shall come forth, and [a]sever the wicked from among the just,

50 And shall cast them into the furnace of fire: there shall be wailing and gnashing of teeth.

51 Jesus saith unto them, Have ye understood all these things? They say unto him, Yea, Lord.

52 Then said he unto them, Therefore every scribe *which is* instructed unto the kingdom of heaven is like unto a man

31 [a]Is. 2:2,3; Mic. 4:1; Mark 4:30; Luke 13:18
33 [a]Luke 13:20 [l]*The word in the Greek is a measure containing about a peck and a half, wanting a little more than a pint*
34 [a]Mark 4:33
35 [a]Ps. 78:2 [b]Rom. 16:25,26; 1 Cor. 2:7; Eph. 3:9; Col. 1:26
38 [a]ch. 24:14 & 28:19; Mark 16:15; Luke 24:47; Rom. 10:18; Col. 1:6 [b]Gen. 3:15; John 8:44; Acts 13:10; 1 John 3:8
39 [a]Joel 3:13; Rev. 14:15
41 [a]ch. 18:7; 2 Pet. 2:1,2 [l]*Or, scandals*
42 [a]ch. 3:12; Rev. 19:20 & 20:10 [b]ver. 50; ch. 8:12
43 [a]Dan. 12:3; 1 Cor. 15:42,43,58 [b]ver. 9
44 [a]Phil. 3:7,8 [b]Is. 55:1; Rev. 3:18
46 [a]Prov. 2:4 & 3:14,15 & 8:10,19
47 [a]ch. 22:10
49 [a]ch. 25:32

K *Mt 6:10* ◀ ▶ *Mt 16:18–20*
C *Mt 13:14–15* ◀ ▶ *Mt 15:14*
H *Mt 13:30* ◀ ▶ *Mt 13:46–50*
P *Mt 13:27–30* ◀ ▶ *Mt 13:47–50*

M *Mt 13:31–33* ◀ ▶ *Mt 19:28*
H *Mt 13:38–42* ◀ ▶ *Mt 15:13–14*
P *Mt 13:39–42* ◀ ▶ *Mt 24:50–51*

44–45; 4:21; 7:27; Rev 11:15).

13:33 It was a common practice for a baker to retain a small lump of leavened bread dough to place within a new batch of dough to raise it thoroughly. Since the Bible usually speaks of leaven as a symbol of sin and iniquity, some scholars view this parable as an indication of the growth of sin and corruption within the kingdom of heaven (see 1Co 5:6–9; Gal 5:9; 1Ti 4:1; 2Ti 4:3–4; Jude 12). Others view the meaning of leaven in this passage in a positive sense, symbolizing the growth of the kingdom of heaven because of the powerful message of the gospel.

13:47–50 The parable of the net prophetically confirms the same general lesson as the parable of the weeds and wheat: The Lord will eventually judge between the righteous and the wicked. Those who have not genuinely repented of their sins will associate with the church for various reasons, but they will finally be identified and judged in the last days.

that is an householder, which bringeth forth out of his treasure [a]*things* new and old.

Jesus rejected at Nazareth

53 ¶ And it came to pass, *that* when Jesus had finished these parables, he departed thence.

54 [a]And when he was come into his own country, he taught them in their synagogue, insomuch that they were astonished, and said, Whence hath this *man* this wisdom, and *these* mighty works?

55 [a]Is not this the carpenter's son? is not his mother called Mary? and [b]his brethren, [c]James, and Joses, and Simon, and Judas?

56 And his sisters, are they not all with us? Whence then hath this *man* all these things?

57 And they [a]were offended in him. But Jesus said unto them, [b]A prophet is not without honour, save in his own country, and in his own house.

D 58 And [a]he did not many mighty works there because of their unbelief.

Death of John the Baptist

14 AT THAT time [a]Herod the tetrarch heard of the fame of Jesus,

2 And said unto his servants, This is John the Baptist; he is risen from the dead; and therefore mighty works [/]do show forth themselves in him.

3 ¶ [a]For Herod had laid hold on John, and bound him, and put *him* in prison for Herodias' sake, his brother Philip's wife.

4 For John said unto him, [a]It is not lawful for thee to have her.

5 And when he would have put him to death, he feared the multitude, [a]because they counted him as a prophet.

6 But when Herod's birthday was kept, the daughter of Herodias danced [/]before them, and pleased Herod.

7 Whereupon he promised with an oath to give her whatsoever she would ask.

D Eze 38:22 ◄ ► Mk 6:5–6

52 [a]Sol. 7:13
54 [a]ch. 2:23; Mark 6:1; Luke 4:16
55 [a]Is. 49:7; Mark 6:3; Luke 3:23; John 6:42 [b]ch. 12:46 [c]Mark 15:40
57 [a]ch. 11:6; Mark 6:3,4 [b]Luke 4:24; John 4:44
58 [a]Mark 6:5,6
14:1 [a]Mark 6:14; Luke 9:7
2 [/]Or, *are wrought by him*
3 [a]Mark 6:17; Luke 3:19,20
4 [a]Lev. 18:16 & 20:21
5 [a]ch. 21:26; Luke 20:6
6 [/]Gk. *in the midst*
13 [a]ch. 10:23 & 12:15; Mark 6:32; Luke 9:10; John 6:1,2
14 [a]ch. 9:36; Mark 6:34
15 [a]Mark 6:35; Luke 9:12; John 6:5
19 [a]ch. 15:36

8 And she, being before instructed of her mother, said, Give me here John Baptist's head in a charger.

9 And the king was sorry: nevertheless for the oath's sake, and them which sat with him at meat, he commanded *it* to be given *her.*

10 And he sent, and beheaded John in the prison.

11 And his head was brought in a charger, and given to the damsel: and she brought *it* to her mother.

12 And his disciples came, and took up the body, and buried it, and went and told Jesus.

The five thousand fed

13 ¶ [a]When Jesus heard *of it,* he departed thence by ship into a desert place apart: and when the people had heard *thereof,* they followed him on foot out of the cities.

14 And Jesus went forth, and saw a great multitude, and [a]was moved with compassion toward them, and he healed their sick. E

15 ¶ [a]And when it was evening, his disciples came to him, saying, This is a desert place, and the time is now past; send the multitude away, that they may go into the villages, and buy themselves victuals. F

16 But Jesus said unto them, They need not depart; give ye them to eat.

17 And they say unto him, We have here but five loaves, and two fishes.

18 He said, Bring them hither to me.

19 And he commanded the multitude to sit down on the grass, and took the five loaves, and the two fishes, and looking up to heaven, [a]he blessed, and brake, and gave the loaves to *his* disciples, and the disciples to the multitude.

20 And they did all eat, and were filled: and they took up of the fragments that remained twelve baskets full.

E Mt 12:22–29 ◄ ► Mt 14:34–36
F Mt 6:25–34 ◄ ► Mt 15:32–38

13:55–57 In this passage Jesus recognizes the truth of the adage "familiarity breeds contempt." Because Jesus' neighbors had known him since he was a child, they believed they knew him well. Yet when Jesus displayed wisdom and understanding that went beyond their preconceived notions about him, the people of Nazareth rejected his words, his works and ultimately Jesus himself.

21 And they that had eaten were about five thousand men, beside women and children.

Jesus walks on the sea

22 ¶ And straightway Jesus constrained his disciples to get into a ship, and to go before him unto the other side, while he sent the multitudes away.

23 [a]And when he had sent the multitudes away, he went up into a mountain apart to pray: [b]and when the evening was come, he was there alone.

24 But the ship was now in the midst of the sea, tossed with waves: for the wind was contrary.

25 And in the fourth watch of the night Jesus went unto them, walking on the sea.

26 And when the disciples saw him [a]walking on the sea, they were troubled, saying, It is a spirit; and they cried out for fear.

27 But straightway Jesus spake unto them, saying, Be of good cheer; it is I; be not afraid.

28 And Peter answered him and said, Lord, if it be thou, bid me come unto thee on the water.

29 And he said, Come. And when Peter was come down out of the ship, he walked on the water, to go to Jesus.

30 But when he saw the wind [/]boisterous, he was afraid; and beginning to sink, he cried, saying, Lord, save me.

31 And immediately Jesus stretched forth *his* hand, and caught him, and said unto him, O thou of little faith, wherefore didst thou doubt?

32 And when they were come into the ship, the wind ceased.

33 Then they that were in the ship came and worshipped him, saying, Of a truth [a]thou art the Son of God.

E 34 ¶ [a]And when they were gone over, they came into the land of Gennesaret.

35 And when the men of that place had knowledge of him, they sent out into all that country round about, and brought unto him all that were diseased;

36 And besought him that they might only touch the hem of his garment: and [a]as many as touched were made perfectly whole.

E *Mt 14:14* ◄► *Mt 15:21–28*

23 [a]Mark 6:46 [b]John 6:16
26 [a]Job 9:8
30 [/]Or, *strong*
33 [a]Ps. 2:7; ch. 16:16 & 26:63; Mark 1:1; Luke 4:41; John 1:49 & 6:69 & 11:27; Acts 8:37; Rom. 1:4
34 [a]Mark 6:53
36 [a]ch. 9:20; Mark 3:10; Luke 6:19; Acts 19:12
15:1 [a]Mark 7:1
2 [a]Mark 7:5
4 [a]Ex. 20:12; Lev. 19:3; Deut. 5:16; Prov. 23:22; Eph. 6:2 [b]Ex. 21:17; Lev. 20:9; Deut. 27:16; Prov. 20:20 & 30:17
5 [a]Mark 7:11,12
7 [a]Mark 7:6
8 [a]Is. 29:13; Ezek. 33:31
9 [a]Is. 29:13; Col. 2:18-22; Tit. 1:14
10 [a]Mark 7:14
11 [a]Acts 10:15; Rom. 14:14,17,20; 1 Tim. 4:4; Tit. 1:15
13 [a]John 15:2; 1 Cor. 3:12
14 [a]Is 9:16; Mal. 2:8; ch. 23:16; Luke 6:39
15 [a]Mark 7:17
16 [a]ch. 16:9; Mark 7:18

What defiles a man

15 THEN [a]CAME to Jesus scribes and Pharisees, which were of Jerusalem, saying,

2 [a]Why do thy disciples transgress the tradition of the elders? for they wash not their hands when they eat bread.

3 But he answered and said unto them, Why do ye also transgress the commandment of God by your tradition?

4 For God commanded, saying, [a]Honour thy father and mother: and, [b]He that curseth father or mother, let him die the death.

5 But ye say, Whosoever shall say to *his* father or *his* mother, [a]*It is* a gift, by whatsoever thou mightest be profited by me;

6 And honour not his father or his mother, *he shall be free*. Thus have ye made the commandment of God of none effect by your tradition.

7 *Ye* [a]hypocrites, well did Esaias prophesy of you, saying,

8 [a]This people draweth nigh unto me G with their mouth, and honoureth me with *their* lips; but their heart is far from me.

9 But in vain they do worship me, [a]teaching *for* doctrines the commandments of men.

10 ¶ [a]And he called the multitude, and said unto them, Hear, and understand:

11 [a]Not that which goeth into the mouth defileth a man; but that which cometh out of the mouth, this defileth a man.

12 Then came his disciples, and said unto him, Knowest thou that the Pharisees were offended, after they heard this saying?

13 But he answered and said, [a]Every H plant, which my heavenly Father hath O not planted, shall be rooted up.

14 Let them alone: [a]they be blind lead- C ers of the blind. And if the blind lead the blind, both shall fall into the ditch.

15 [a]Then answered Peter and said unto him, Declare unto us this parable.

16 And Jesus said, [a]Are ye also yet without understanding?

17 Do not ye yet understand, that

G *Mt 7:26–27* ◄► *Mt 22:11–14*
H *Mt 13:46–50* ◄► *Mt 16:26–27*
O *Mt 10:32–33* ◄► *Mt 16:19*
C *Mt 13:38* ◄► *Mt 15:18–19*

[a]whatsoever entereth in at the mouth goeth into the belly, and is cast out into the draught?

C 18 But [a]those things which proceed out of the mouth come forth from the heart; and they defile the man.

19 [a]For out of the heart proceed evil thoughts, murders, adulteries, fornications, thefts, false witness, blasphemies:

20 These are *the things* which defile a man: but to eat with unwashen hands defileth not a man.

The faith of a Canaanite woman

E 21 ¶ [a]Then Jesus went thence, and departed into the coasts of Tyre and Sidon.

22 And, behold, a woman of Canaan came out of the same coasts, and cried unto him, saying, Have mercy on me, O Lord, *thou* Son of David; my daughter is grievously vexed with a devil.

R 23 But he answered her not a word. And his disciples came and besought him, saying, Send her away; for she crieth after us.

24 But he answered and said, [a]I am not sent but unto the lost sheep of the house of Israel.

25 Then came she and worshipped him, saying, Lord, help me.

26 But he answered and said, It is not meet to take the children's bread, and to cast *it* to [a]dogs.

27 And she said, Truth, Lord: yet the dogs eat of the crumbs which fall from their masters' table.

28 Then Jesus answered and said unto her, O woman, great *is* thy faith: be it unto thee even as thou wilt. And her daughter was made whole from that very hour.

The four thousand fed

29 [a]And Jesus departed from thence, and came nigh [b]unto the sea of Galilee; and went up into a mountain, and sat down there.

30 [a]And great multitudes came unto him, having with them *those that were* lame, blind, dumb, maimed, and many others, and cast them down at Jesus' feet; and he healed them: E

31 Insomuch that the multitude wondered, when they saw the dumb to speak, the maimed to be whole, the lame to walk, and the blind to see: and they glorified the God of Israel.

32 ¶ [a]Then Jesus called his disciples *unto him,* and said, I have compassion on the multitude, because they continue with me now three days, and have nothing to eat: and I will not send them away fasting, lest they faint in the way. F

33 [a]And his disciples say unto him, Whence should we have so much bread in the wilderness, as to fill so great a multitude?

34 And Jesus saith unto them, How many loaves have ye? And they said, Seven, and a few little fishes.

35 And he commanded the multitude to sit down on the ground.

36 And [a]he took the seven loaves and the fishes, and [b]gave thanks, and brake *them,* and gave to his disciples, and the disciples to the multitude.

37 And they did all eat, and were filled: and they took up of the broken *meat* that was left seven baskets full.

38 And they that did eat were four thousand men, beside women and children.

39 [a]And he sent away the multitude, and took ship, and came into the coasts of Magdala.

Pharisees ask for a sign

16 THE [a]PHARISEES also with the Sadducees came, and tempting desired him that he would show them a sign from heaven.

2 He answered and said unto them, When it is evening, ye say, *It will be* fair weather: for the sky is red.

17 [a] 1 Cor. 6:13
18 [a] Jas. 3:6
19 [a] Gen. 6:5 & 8:21; Prov. 6:14; Jer. 17:9; Mark 7:21
21 [a] Mark 7:24
24 [a] ch. 10:5,6
26 [a] ch. 7:6; Phil. 3:2
29 [a] Mark 7:31 [b] ch. 4:18
30 [a] Is. 35:5,6; ch. 11:5; Luke 7:22
32 [a] Mark 8:1
33 [a] 2 Ki. 4:43
36 [a] ch. 14:19 [b] 1 Sam. 9:13; Luke 22:19
39 [a] Mark 8:10
16:1 [a] ch. 12:38; Mark 8:11; Luke 11:16 & 12:54-56; 1 Cor. 1:22

C *Mt 15:14* ◀▶ *Mt 18:11–14*
E *Mt 14:34–36* ◀▶ *Mt 15:30–31*
R *Mt 10:6* ◀▶ *Mt 21:41*
E *Mt 15:21–28* ◀▶ *Mt 17:14–21*
F *Mt 14:15–21* ◀▶ *Mt 16:5–10*

15:22–27 This passage reveals that Jesus' original mission was directed to "the lost sheep of the house of Israel" (15:24). Yet this foreigner was willing to settle for "crumbs," so Jesus rewarded her persistence and great faith. It was only after the Jews had rejected Christ's claims as their Messiah that Jesus gave his disciples the command to go "and teach all nations, baptizing them in the name of the Father, and of the Son, and of the Holy Ghost" (28:19).

E 3 And in the morning, *It will be* foul weather today: for the sky is red and lowering. O *ye* hypocrites, ye can discern the face of the sky; but can ye not *discern* the signs of the times?

4 [a]A wicked and adulterous generation seeketh after a sign; and there shall no sign be given unto it, but the sign of the prophet Jonas. And he left them, and departed.

F 5 And [a]when his disciples were come to the other side, they had forgotten to take bread.

6 ¶ Then Jesus said unto them, [a]Take heed and beware of the leaven of the Pharisees and of the Sadducees.

7 And they reasoned among themselves, saying, *It is* because we have taken no bread.

8 *Which* when Jesus perceived, he said unto them, O ye of little faith, why reason ye among yourselves, because ye have brought no bread?

9 [a]Do ye not yet understand, neither remember the five loaves of the five thousand, and how many baskets ye took up?

10 [a]Neither the seven loaves of the four thousand, and how many baskets ye took up?

11 How is it that ye do not understand that I spake *it* not to you concerning bread, that ye should beware of the leaven of the Pharisees and of the Sadducees?

12 Then understood they how that he bade *them* not beware of the leaven of bread, but of the doctrine of the Pharisees and of the Sadducees.

Peter's confession of faith

13 ¶ When Jesus came into the coasts of Caesarea Philippi, he asked his disciples, saying, [a]Whom do men say that I the Son of man am?

14 And they said, [a]Some *say that thou art* John the Baptist: some, Elias; and others, Jeremias, or one of the prophets.

15 He saith unto them, But whom say ye that I am?

16 And Simon Peter answered and said, [a]Thou art the Christ, the Son of the living God.

17 And Jesus answered and said unto him, Blessed art thou, Simon Bar-jona: [a]for flesh and blood hath not revealed *it* unto thee, but [b]my Father which is in heaven.

18 And I say also unto thee, That [a]thou K
art Peter, and [b]upon this rock I will build my church; and [c]the gates of hell shall not prevail against it.

19 [a]And I will give unto thee the keys O
of the kingdom of heaven: and whatsoever thou shalt bind on earth shall be bound in heaven: and whatsoever thou shalt loose on earth shall be loosed in heaven.

20 [a]Then charged he his disciples that they should tell no man that he was Jesus the Christ.

4 [a]ch. 12:39
5 [a]Mark 8:14
6 [a]Luke 12:1
9 [a]ch. 14:17; John 6:9
10 [a]ch. 15:34
13 [a]Mark 8:27; Luke 9:18
14 [a]ch. 14:2; Luke 9:7-9
16 [a]ch. 14:33; Mark 8:29; Luke 9:20; John 6:69 & 11:27; Acts 8:37 & 9:20; Heb. 1:2,5; 1 John 4:15
17 [a]Eph. 2:8 [b]1 Cor. 2:10; Gal. 1:16
18 [a]John 1:42 [b]Eph. 2:20; Rev. 21:14 [c]Job 38:17; Ps. 9:13 & 107:18; Is. 38:10
19 [a]ch. 18:18; John 20:23
20 [a]ch. 17:9; Luke 9:21

E Da 12:9–10 ◄► Mt 24:3–6
F Mt 15:32–38 ◄► Mk 1:13.
K Mt 13:33 ◄► Mk 4:26–28
O Mt 15:13 ◄► Mt 18:3

16:3–4 Jesus criticized the religious leaders of Israel for their ability to read weather signs but their inability to read and understand the spiritual signs from the Scriptures concerning the promised Messiah. Though the leaders wanted a supernatural manifestation to prove Jesus' claim as the Messiah, Jesus warned that the only sign they would receive was the sign of Jonah's three days and three nights, words that foreshadowed his crucifixion and resurrection from the dead.

16:18 Though Jesus renamed his disciple *Peter,* which means "stone," and said that he would build his church on a "rock," the teaching of the NT is clear that the church is built solely on Jesus Christ himself. While some scholars have theorized that the church was built on Peter and his direct successors, Peter himself describes Jesus Christ as the cornerstone and foundation of the church (see 1Pe 2:4–8).

16:19 This verse does not suggest that Peter and his apostolic successors in some manner control the gates of heaven. The "keys" referred to here probably signify the authority conferred on the apostles to share the gospel message. In this way the apostles would open the kingdom to those who would believe the gospel and close the kingdom to those who would not receive Christ (see Isa 22:22; Rev 3:7).

The history of the church described in Acts defines this authority of the "keys." Peter declared the need for repentance of the Jews on the day of Pentecost (see Ac 2:38–39). Peter also was the first to accept Christ's command to preach the gospel to the Gentiles after the vision he received directed him to the house of Cornelius (see Ac 10:34–35, 45; 15:7–11). In the church council it was James, the brother of Jesus, who exercised final authority and issued the decision as to what would be required of Gentile converts to Christianity.

Future events foretold

21 ¶ From that time forth began Jesus [a]to show unto his disciples, how that he must go unto Jerusalem, and suffer many things of the elders and chief priests and scribes, and be killed, and be raised again the third day.

22 Then Peter took him, and began to rebuke him, saying, [/]Be it far from thee, Lord: this shall not be unto thee.

23 But he turned, and said unto Peter, Get thee behind me, [a]Satan: [b]thou art an offence unto me: for thou savourest not the things that be of God, but those that be of men.

S 24 ¶ [a]Then said Jesus unto his disciples, If any *man* will come after me, let him deny himself, and take up his cross, and follow me.

25 For [a]whosoever will save his life shall lose it: and whosoever will lose his life for my sake shall find it.

H 26 For what is a man profited, if he shall gain the whole world, and lose his own soul? or [a]what shall a man give in exchange for his soul?

C 27 For [a]the Son of man shall come in
S the glory of his Father [b]with his angels; [c]and then he shall reward every man according to his works.

28 Verily I say unto you, [a]There be some standing here, which shall not taste of death, till they see the Son of man coming in his kingdom.

The transfiguration

17 AND [a]AFTER six days Jesus taketh Peter, James, and John his brother, and bringeth them up into an high mountain apart,

2 And was transfigured before them: and his face did shine as the sun, and his raiment was white as the light.

3 And, behold, there appeared unto them Moses and Elias talking with him.

S *Mt 13:20–22* ◀ ▶ *Mt 16:27*
H *Mt 15:13–14* ◀ ▶ *Mt 18:6–9*
C *Hag 2:6–7* ◀ ▶ *Mt 24:3*
S *Mt 16:24* ◀ ▶ *Mt 18:8–9*

21 [a]ch. 20:17; Mark 8:31 & 9:31 & 10:33; Luke 9:22 & 18:31 & 24:6,7
22 [/]Gk. *Pity thyself*
23 [a]See 2 Sam. 19:22 [b]Rom. 8:7
24 [a]Mark 8:34; Luke 9:23 & 14:27; Acts 14:22; 1 Thes. 3:3; 2 Tim. 3:12
25 [a]Luke 17:33; John 12:25
26 [a]Ps. 49:7,8
27 [a]ch. 26:64; Mark 8:38; Luke 9:26 [b]Dan. 7:10; Zech. 14:5; ch. 25:31; Jude 14 [c]Job 34:11; Ps. 62:12; Prov. 24:12; Jer. 17:10 & 32:19; Rom. 2:6; 1 Cor. 3:8; 2 Cor. 5:10; 1 Pet. 1:17; Rev. 2:23 & 22:12
28 [a]Mark 9:1; Luke 9:27
17:1 [a]Mark 9:2; Luke 9:28
5 [a]2 Pet. 1:17 [b]ch. 3:17; Mark 1:11; Luke 3:22 [c]Is. 42:1 [d]Deut. 18:15,19; Acts 3:22,23
6 [a]2 Pet. 1:18
7 [a]Dan. 8:18 & 9:21 & 10:10,18
9 [a]ch. 16:20; Mark 8:30 & 9:9
10 [a]Mal. 4:5; ch. 11:14; Mark 9:11
11 [a]Mal. 4:6; Luke 1:16,17; Acts 3:21
12 [a]ch. 11:14; Mark 9:12,13 [b]ch. 14:3,10 [c]ch. 16:21
13 [a]ch. 11:14
14 [a]Mark 9:14; Luke 9:37

4 Then answered Peter, and said unto Jesus, Lord, it is good for us to be here: if thou wilt, let us make here three tabernacles; one for thee, and one for Moses, and one for Elias.

5 [a]While he yet spake, behold, a bright cloud overshadowed them: and behold a voice out of the cloud, which said, [b]This is my beloved Son, [c]in whom I am well pleased; [d]hear ye him.

6 [a]And when the disciples heard *it,* they fell on their face, and were sore afraid.

7 And Jesus came and [a]touched them, and said, Arise, and be not afraid.

8 And when they had lifted up their eyes, they saw no man, save Jesus only.

9 And as they came down from the mountain, [a]Jesus charged them, saying, Tell the vision to no man, until the Son of man be risen again from the dead.

10 And his disciples asked him, saying, [a]Why then say the scribes that Elias must first come?

11 And Jesus answered and said unto them, Elias truly shall first come, and [a]restore all things.

12 [a]But I say unto you, That Elias is come already, and they knew him not, but [b]have done unto him whatsoever they listed. Likewise [c]shall also the Son of man suffer of them.

13 [a]Then the disciples understood that he spake unto them of John the Baptist.

A demoniac boy healed

14 ¶ [a]And when they were come to the multitude, there came to him a *certain* man, kneeling down to him, and saying, E

15 Lord, have mercy on my son: for he is lunatic, and sore vexed: for ofttimes he falleth into the fire, and oft into the water.

16 And I brought him to thy disciples, and they could not cure him.

17 Then Jesus answered and said, O faithless and perverse generation, how

E *Mt 15:30–31* ◀ ▶ *Mt 19:1–2*

16:21 Jesus told his disciples the details of the remainder of his mission: his journey to Jerusalem, his trial, death and resurrection on "the third day" (see Mt 27:63; 28:1).

16:27 Jesus will return from heaven with his angelic army to defeat the antichrist and the kings of the east at the Battle of Armageddon. After his victory he will establish his Messianic millennial kingdom on earth and "reward every man according to his works." Compare this promised judgment with 25:31–46 and Eze 20:36–38.

long shall I be with you? how long shall I suffer you? bring him hither to me.

18 And Jesus rebuked the devil; and he departed out of him: and the child was cured from that very hour.

19 Then came the disciples to Jesus apart, and said, Why could not we cast him out?

20 And Jesus said unto them, Because of your unbelief: for verily I say unto you, [a]If ye have faith as a grain of mustard seed, ye shall say unto this mountain, Remove hence to yonder place; and it shall remove; and nothing shall be impossible unto you.

21 Howbeit this kind goeth not out but by prayer and fasting.

22 ¶ [a]And while they abode in Galilee, Jesus said unto them, The Son of man shall be betrayed into the hands of men:

23 And they shall kill him, and the third day he shall be raised again. And they were exceeding sorry.

The money in the fish's mouth

24 ¶ And [a]when they were come to Capernaum, they that received [b]tribute/ *money* came to Peter, and said, Doth not your master pay tribute?

25 He saith, Yes. And when he was come into the house, Jesus prevented him, saying, What thinkest thou, Simon? of whom do the kings of the earth take custom or tribute? of their own children, or of strangers?

26 Peter saith unto him, Of strangers. Jesus saith unto him, Then are the children free.

P 27 Notwithstanding, lest we should offend them, go thou to the sea, and cast an hook, and take up the fish that first cometh up; and when thou hast opened his mouth, thou shalt find /a piece of money: that take, and give unto them for me and thee.

The greatest in the kingdom

M 18 AT [a]THE same time came the disciples unto Jesus, saying, Who is the greatest in the kingdom of heaven?

2 And Jesus called a little child unto him, and set him in the midst of them,

O 3 And said, Verily I say unto you, [a]Except ye be converted, and become as little children, ye shall not enter into the kingdom of heaven.

4 [a]Whosoever therefore shall humble himself as this little child, the same is greatest in the kingdom of heaven.

5 And [a]whoso shall receive one such little child in my name receiveth me. L

6 [a]But whoso shall offend one of these little ones which believe in me, it were better for him that a millstone were hanged about his neck, and *that* he were drowned in the depth of the sea. H

7 ¶ Woe unto the world because of offences! for [a]it must needs be that offences come; but [b]woe to that man by whom the offence cometh!

8 [a]Wherefore if thy hand or thy foot offend thee, cut them off, and cast *them* from thee: it is better for thee to enter into life halt or maimed, rather than having two hands or two feet to be cast into everlasting fire. S

9 And if thine eye offend thee, pluck it out, and cast *it* from thee: it is better for thee to enter into life with one eye, rather than having two eyes to be cast into hell fire.

The parable of the lost sheep

10 Take heed that ye despise not one of these little ones; for I say unto you, That in heaven [a]their angels do always [b]behold the face of my Father which is in heaven. L

11 [a]For the Son of man is come to save that which was lost. C L

12 [a]How think ye? if a man have an hundred sheep, and one of them be gone astray, doth he not leave the ninety and nine, and goeth into the mountains, and seeketh that which is gone astray? P

13 And if so be that he find it, verily I say unto you, he rejoiceth more of that *sheep*, than of the ninety and nine which went not astray.

14 Even so it is not the will of your Father which is in heaven, that one of these little ones should perish.

---

20 [a]ch. 21:21; Mark 11:23; Luke 17:6; 1 Cor. 12:9 & 13:2
22 [a]ch. 16:21 & 20:17; Mark 8:31 & 9:30,31 & 10:33; Luke 9:22,44 & 18:31 & 24:6,7
24 [a]Mark 9:33 [b]Ex. 30:13 & 38:26 /Called in the original, *didrachma,* worth about 32 cents or 2 days' wages for a laborer
27 /Or, *a stater,* worth about 64 cents or 4 days' wages for a laborer
18:1 [a]Mark 9:33; Luke 9:46 & 22:24
3 [a]Ps. 131:2; ch. 19:14; Mark 10:14; Luke 18:16; 1 Cor. 14:20; 1 Pet. 2:2
4 [a]ch. 20:27 & 23:11
5 [a]ch. 10:42; Luke 9:48
6 [a]Mark 9:42; Luke 17:1,2
7 [a]Luke 17:1; 1 Cor. 11:19 [b]ch. 26:24
8 [a]ch. 5:29,30; Mark 9:43,45
10 [a]Ps. 34:7; Zech. 13:7; Heb. 1:14 [b]Esth. 1:14; Luke 1:19
11 [a]Luke 9:56 & 19:10; John 3:17 & 12:47
12 [a]Luke 15:4

P *Mt 6:31–33* ◀▶ *Lk 22:35*
M *Mt 5:3–5* ◀▶ *Mt 18:26–27*
O *Mt 16:19* ◀▶ *Mt 18:18*
L *Mt 10:29–31* ◀▶ *Mt 18:10*
H *Mt 16:26–27* ◀▶ *Mt 21:44*
S *Mt 16:27* ◀▶ *Mt 18:17*
L *Mt 18:5–6* ◀▶ *Mt 18:19–20*
C *Mt 15:18–19* ◀▶ *Mt 22:11–14*
L *Mt 12:31–32* ◀▶ *Mt 18:26–27*
P *Mt 10:6* ◀▶ *Lk 15:3–32*

Sin and forgiveness

15 ¶ Moreover [a]if thy brother shall trespass against thee, go and tell him his fault between thee and him alone: if he shall hear thee, [b]thou hast gained thy brother.

16 But if he will not hear *thee, then* take with thee one or two more, that in [a]the mouth of two or three witnesses every word may be established.

S 17 And if he shall neglect to hear them, tell *it* unto the church: but if he neglect to hear the church, let him be unto thee as an [a]heathen man and a publican.

O 18 Verily I say unto you, [a]Whatsoever ye shall bind on earth shall be bound in heaven: and whatsoever ye shall loose on earth shall be loosed in heaven.

L 19 [a]Again I say unto you, That if two of you shall agree on earth as touching any thing that they shall ask, [b]it shall be done for them of my Father which is in heaven.

20 For where two or three are gathered together in my name, there am I in the midst of them.

21 ¶ Then came Peter to him, and said, Lord, how oft shall my brother sin against me, and I forgive him? [a]till seven times?

22 Jesus saith unto him, I say not unto thee, Until seven times: [a]but, Until seventy times seven.

Parable of the unforgiving servant

S 23 ¶ Therefore is the kingdom of heaven likened unto a certain king, which would take account of his servants.

24 And when he had begun to reckon, one was brought unto him, which owed him ten thousand [I]talents.

25 But forasmuch as he had not to pay, his lord commanded him [a]to be sold, and his wife, and children, and all that he had, and payment to be made.

L 26 The servant therefore fell down,
M and [I]worshipped him, saying, Lord, have patience with me, and I will pay thee all.

27 Then the lord of that servant was moved with compassion, and loosed him, and forgave him the debt.

28 But the same servant went out, and found one of his fellowservants, which owed him an hundred [I]pence: and he laid hands on him, and took *him* by the throat, saying, Pay me that thou owest.

29 And his fellowservant fell down at his feet, and besought him, saying, Have patience with me, and I will pay thee all.

30 And he would not: but went and cast him into prison, till he should pay the debt.

31 So when his fellowservants saw what was done, they were very sorry, and came and told unto their lord all that was done.

32 Then his lord, after that he had called him, said unto him, O thou wicked servant, I forgave thee all that debt, because thou desiredst me:

33 Shouldest not thou also have had compassion on thy fellowservant, even as I had pity on thee?

34 And his lord was wroth, and delivered him to the tormentors, till he should pay all that was due unto him.

35 [a]So likewise shall my heavenly Father do also unto you, if ye from your R
hearts forgive not every one his brother their trespasses.

Marriage and divorce

19 AND IT came to pass, [a]*that* when E
Jesus had finished these sayings, he departed from Galilee, and came into the coasts of Judaea beyond Jordan;

2 [a]And great multitudes followed him; and he healed them there.

3 ¶ The Pharisees also came unto him, tempting him, and saying unto him, Is it lawful for a man to put away his wife for every cause?

4 And he answered and said unto them, Have ye not read, [a]that he which made *them* at the beginning made them male and female,

5 And said, [a]For this cause shall a man leave father and mother, and shall cleave to his wife: and [b]they twain shall be one flesh?

6 Wherefore they are no more twain, but one flesh. What therefore God hath

---

15 [a]Lev. 19:17; Luke 17:3 [b]Jas. 5:20; 1 Pet. 3:1
16 [a]Deut. 17:6 & 19:15; John 8:17; 2 Cor. 13:1; Heb. 10:28
17 [a]Rom. 16:17; 1 Cor. 5:9; 2 Thes. 3:6,14; 2 John 10
18 [a]ch. 16:19; John 20:23; 1 Cor. 5:4
19 [a]ch. 5:24 [b]1 John 3:22 & 5:14
21 [a]Luke 17:4
22 [a]ch. 6:14; Mark 11:25; Col. 3:13
24 [I]Ten thousand talents are equivalent to several million dollars
25 [a]2 Ki. 4:1; Neh. 5:8
26 [I]Or, *besought him*
28 [I]A hundred pence are equivalent to a few dollars
35 [a]Prov. 21:13; ch. 6:12; Mark 11:26; Jas. 2:13
19:1 [a]Mark 10:1; John 10:40
2 [a]ch. 12:15
4 [a]Gen. 1:27 & 5:2; Mal. 2:15
5 [a]Gen. 2:24; Mark 10:5-9; Eph. 5:31 [b]1 Cor. 6:16 & 7:2

S *Mt 18:8–9* ◀ ▶ *Mt 18:23–35*
O *Mt 18:3* ◀ ▶ *Mt 22:11–14*
L *Mt 18:10* ◀ ▶ *Mt 21:22*
S *Mt 18:17* ◀ ▶ *Mt 19:16–21*
L *Mt 18:11–14* ◀ ▶ *Mt 20:1–14*
M *Mt 18:1–4* ◀ ▶ *Mt 19:14*
R *Mt 6:14–15* ◀ ▶ *Mt 21:28–32*
E *Mt 17:14–21* ◀ ▶ *Mt 20:30–34*

joined together, let not man put asunder.

7 They say unto him, [a]Why did Moses then command to give a writing of divorcement, and to put her away?

8 He saith unto them, Moses because of the hardness of your hearts suffered you to put away your wives: but from the beginning it was not so.

9 [a]And I say unto you, Whosoever shall put away his wife, except *it be* for fornication, and shall marry another, committeth adultery: and whoso marrieth her which is put away doth commit adultery.

10 ¶ His disciples say unto him, [a]If the case of the man be so with *his* wife, it is not good to marry.

11 But he said unto them, [a]All *men* cannot receive this saying, save *they* to whom it is given.

12 For there are some eunuchs, which were so born from *their* mother's womb: and there are some eunuchs, which were made eunuchs of men: and [a]there be eunuchs, which have made themselves eunuchs for the kingdom of heaven's sake. He that is able to receive *it,* let him receive *it.*

Jesus blesses the little children

13 ¶ [a]Then were there brought unto him little children, that he should put *his* hands on them, and pray: and the disciples rebuked them.

M 14 But Jesus said, Suffer little children, and forbid them not, to come unto me: for [a]of such is the kingdom of heaven.

15 And he laid *his* hands on them, and departed thence.

The rich young ruler

S 16 ¶ [a]And, behold, one came and said unto him, [b]Good Master, what good thing shall I do, that I may have eternal life?

17 And he said unto him, Why callest thou me good? *there is* none good but one, *that is,* God: but if thou wilt enter into life, keep the commandments.

18 He saith unto him, Which? Jesus said, [a]Thou shalt do no murder, Thou shalt not commit adultery, Thou shalt not steal, Thou shalt not bear false witness,

19 [a]Honour thy father and *thy* mother: and, [b]Thou shalt love thy neighbour as thyself.

20 The young man saith unto him, All these things have I kept from my youth up: what lack I yet?

21 Jesus said unto him, If thou wilt be perfect, [a]go *and* sell that thou hast, and give to the poor, and thou shalt have treasure in heaven: and come *and* follow me.

22 But when the young man heard that saying, he went away sorrowful: for he had great possessions.

23 ¶ Then said Jesus unto his disciples, M
Verily I say unto you, That [a]a rich man shall hardly enter into the kingdom of heaven.

24 And again I say unto you, It is easier for a camel to go through the eye of a needle, than for a rich man to enter into the kingdom of God.

25 When his disciples heard *it,* they were exceedingly amazed, saying, Who then can be saved?

26 But Jesus beheld *them,* and said K
unto them, With men this is impossible; but [a]with God all things are possible.

27 ¶ Then answered Peter and said unto him, Behold, [a]we have forsaken all, and followed thee; what shall we have therefore?

28 And Jesus said unto them, Verily I I
say unto you, That ye which have fol- M
lowed me, in the regeneration when the Son of man shall sit in the throne of his glory, [a]ye also shall sit upon twelve

M *Mt 18:26–27* ◀ ▶ *Mt 19:23–24*
S *Mt 18:23–35* ◀ ▶ *Mt 21:28–31*

M *Mt 19:14* ◀ ▶ *Mt 23:12*
K *Mt 11:28–29* ◀ ▶ *Mt 24:35*
I *Mt 2:6* ◀ ▶ *Mt 21:5*
M *Mt 13:43* ◀ ▶ *Mt 20:20–21*

7 [a]Deut. 24:1; ch. 5:31
9 [a]ch. 5:32; Mark 10:11; Luke 16:18; 1 Cor. 7:10
10 [a]Prov. 21:19
11 [a]1 Cor. 7:2,7,9, 17
12 [a]1 Cor. 7:32 & 9:5,15
13 [a]Mark 10:13; Luke 18:15
14 [a]ch. 18:3
16 [a]Mark 10:17; Luke 18:18 [b]Luke 10:25
18 [a]Ex. 20:13; Deut. 5:17
19 [a]ch. 15:4 [b]Lev. 19:18; ch. 22:39; Rom. 13:9; Gal. 5:14; Jas. 2:8
21 [a]ch. 6:20; Luke 12:33 & 16:9; Acts 2:45 & 4:34,35; 1 Tim. 6:18,19
23 [a]ch. 13:22; Mark 10:24; 1 Cor. 1:26; 1 Tim. 6:9
26 [a]Gen. 18:14; Job 42:2; Jer. 32:17; Zech. 8:6; Luke 1:37 & 18:27
27 [a]Deut. 33:9; ch. 4:20; Luke 5:11
28 [a]ch. 10:21; Luke 22:28-30; 1 Cor. 6:2; Rev. 2:26

19:28 This fascinating prophecy confirms the restoration of the kingdom of Israel during the Millennium (see Eze 37:12–22) and foresees the day when the twelve disciples of Jesus will govern the twelve tribes of Israel. Ezekiel adds that the twelve tribes will receive land allotments in the promised land during the Millennium (see Eze 47—48). Both these prophecies will necessitate the restoration of the individualities of the twelve tribes. While some Jews are able to trace their tribal identity through their family name, many Jews today are uncertain of their ancestry. These prophecies indicate that God will reveal the tribal identity of all the Jews in the last days.

thrones, judging the twelve tribes of Israel.

U 29 [a]And every one that hath forsaken houses, or brethren, or sisters, or father, or mother, or wife, or children, or lands, for my name's sake, shall receive an hundredfold, and shall inherit everlasting life.

30 [a]But many *that are* first shall be last; and the last *shall be* first.

The worker in the vineyard

L W 20 FOR THE kingdom of heaven is like unto a man *that is* an householder, which went out early in the morning to hire labourers into his vineyard.

2 And when he had agreed with the labourers for a [l]penny a day, he sent them into his vineyard.

3 And he went out about the third hour, and saw others standing idle in the marketplace,

4 And said unto them; Go ye also into the vineyard, and whatsoever is right I will give you. And they went their way.

5 Again he went out about the sixth and ninth hour, and did likewise.

6 And about the eleventh hour he went out, and found others standing idle, and saith unto them, Why stand ye here all the day idle?

7 They say unto him, Because no man hath hired us. He saith unto them, Go ye also into the vineyard; and whatsoever is right, *that* shall ye receive.

8 So when even was come, the lord of the vineyard saith unto his steward, Call the labourers, and give them *their* hire, beginning from the last unto the first.

9 And when they came that *were hired* about the eleventh hour, they received every man a penny.

10 But when the first came, they supposed that they should have received more; and they likewise received every man a penny.

11 And when they had received *it*, they murmured against the goodman of the house,

12 Saying, These last [l]have wrought *but* one hour, and thou hast made them equal unto us, which have borne the burden and heat of the day.

13 But he answered one of them, and said, Friend, I do thee no wrong: didst not thou agree with me for a penny?

14 Take *that* thine *is*, and go thy way: I will give unto this last, even as unto thee.

15 [a]Is it not lawful for me to do what I will with mine own? [b]Is thine eye evil, because I am good?

16 [a]So the last shall be first, and the first last: [b]for many be called, but few chosen.

Jesus foretells his death

17 ¶ [a]And Jesus going up to Jerusalem took the twelve disciples apart in the way, and said unto them,

18 [a]Behold, we go up to Jerusalem; and the Son of man shall be betrayed unto the chief priests and unto the scribes, and they shall condemn him to death,

19 [a]And shall deliver him to the Gentiles to mock, and to scourge, and to crucify *him*: and the third day he shall rise again.

The ambition of James and John

20 ¶ [a]Then came to him the mother of [b]Zebedee's children with her sons, worshipping *him*, and desiring a certain thing of him. M

21 And he said unto her, What wilt thou? She saith unto him, Grant that these my two sons [a]may sit, the one on thy right hand, and the other on the left, in thy kingdom.

22 But Jesus answered and said, Ye know not what ye ask. Are ye able to drink of [a]the cup that I shall drink of, and to be baptized with [b]the baptism that I am baptized with? They say unto him, We are able.

23 And he saith unto them, [a]Ye shall drink indeed of my cup, and be baptized with the baptism that I am baptized with: but to sit on my right hand, and on my left, is not mine to [b]give, but *it shall be given to them* for whom it is prepared of my Father.

29 [a]Mark 10:29,30; Luke 18:29,30
30 [a]ch. 20:16 & 21:31,32; Mark 10:31; Luke 13:30
20:2 [l]The penny, worth about 16 cents, was the usual day's wage for a laborer
12 [l]Or, *have continued one hour only*
15 [a]Rom. 9:21 [b]Deut. 15:9; Prov. 23:6; ch. 6:23
16 [a]ch. 19:30 [b]ch. 22:14
17 [a]Mark 10:32; Luke 18:31; John 12:12
18 [a]ch. 16:21
19 [a]ch. 27:2; Mark 15:1,16; Luke 23:1; John 18:28; Acts 3:13
20 [a]Mark 10:35 [b]ch. 4:21
21 [a]ch. 19:28
22 [a]ch. 26:39,42; Mark 14:36; Luke 22:42; John 18:11 [b]Luke 12:50
23 [a]Acts 12:2; Rom. 8:17; 2 Cor. 1:7; Rev. 1:9 [b]ch. 25:34

U *Mt 6:33* ◀ ▶ *Mk 10:28–30*
L *Mt 18:26–27* ◀ ▶ *Mt 21:31–32*
W *Mt 12:20* ◀ ▶ *Mt 22:1–10*
M *Mt 19:28* ◀ ▶ *Mt 21:5*

20:20–21 The mother of two of Christ's disciples, James and John, requested cabinet positions in the future millennial kingdom, believing that Jesus would establish his kingdom immediately.

24 [a]And when the ten heard *it,* they
were moved with indignation against the
two brethren.
25 But Jesus called them *unto him,*
and said, Ye know that the princes of the
Gentiles exercise dominion over them,
and they that are great exercise authority
upon them.
26 But [a]it shall not be so among you:
but [b]whosoever will be great among you,
let him be your minister;
27 [a]And whosoever will be chief
among you, let him be your servant:
D 28 [a]Even as the [b]Son of man came not
to be ministered unto, [c]but to minister,
and [d]to give his life a ransom [e]for many.

Healing of two blind men

29 [a]And as they departed from Jericho,
a great multitude followed him.
E 30 ¶ And, behold, [a]two blind men sitting by the way side, when they heard
that Jesus passed by, cried out, saying,
Have mercy on us, O Lord, *thou* Son of
David.
31 And the multitude rebuked them,
because they should hold their peace: but
they cried the more, saying, Have mercy
on us, O Lord, *thou* Son of David.
32 And Jesus stood still, and called
them, and said, What will ye that I shall
do unto you?
33 They say unto him, Lord, that our
eyes may be opened.
34 So Jesus had compassion *on them,*
and touched their eyes: and immediately
their eyes received sight, and they followed him.

D *Mt 1:21 ◀ ▶ Mt 26:26–28*
E *Mt 19:1–2 ◀ ▶ Mt 21:14*

24 [a]Mark 10:41; Luke 22:24,25
26 [a]1 Pet. 5:3 [b]ch. 23:11; Mark 9:35 & 10:43
27 [a]ch. 18:4
28 [a]John 13:4 [b]Phil. 2:7 [c]Luke 22:27; John 13:14 [d]Is. 53:10,11; Dan. 9:24,26; John 11:51,52; 1 Tim. 2:6; Tit. 2:14; 1 Pet. 1:19 [e]ch. 26:28; Rom. 5:15, 19; Heb. 9:28
29 [a]Mark 10:46; Luke 18:35
30 [a]ch. 9:27
21:1 [a]Mark 11:1; Luke 19:29 [b]Zech. 14:4
5 [a]Is. 62:11; Zech. 9:9; John 12:15
6 [a]Mark 11:4
7 [a]2 Ki. 9:13
8 [a]See Lev. 23:40; John 12:13
9 [a]Ps. 118:25 [b]Ps. 118:26; ch. 23:39
10 [a]Mark 11:15; Luke 19:45; John 2:13,15
11 [a]ch. 2:23; Luke 7:16; John 6:14 & 7:40 & 9:17

The triumphal entry

21 AND [a]WHEN they drew nigh
unto Jerusalem, and were come
to Bethphage, unto [b]the mount of Olives,
then sent Jesus two disciples,
2 Saying unto them, Go into the village
over against you, and straightway ye shall
find an ass tied, and a colt with her: loose
them, and bring *them* unto me.
3 And if any *man* say aught unto you,
ye shall say, The Lord hath need of them;
and straightway he will send them.
4 All this was done, that it might be
fulfilled which was spoken by the
prophet, saying,
5 [a]Tell ye the daughter of Zion, Be- I
hold, thy King cometh unto thee, meek, M
and sitting upon an ass, and a colt the foal
of an ass.
6 [a]And the disciples went, and did as
Jesus commanded them,
7 And brought the ass, and the colt,
and [a]put on them their clothes, and they
set *him* thereon.
8 And a very great multitude spread
their garments in the way; [a]others cut
down branches from the trees, and
strawed *them* in the way.
9 And the multitudes that went before,
and that followed, cried, saying, [a]Ho-
sanna to the son of David: [b]Blessed *is* he
that cometh in the name of the Lord; Hosanna in the highest.
10 [a]And when he was come into Jerusalem, all the city was moved, saying,
Who is this?
11 And the multitude said, This is
Jesus [a]the prophet of Nazareth of Galilee.

I *Mt 19:28 ◀ ▶ Mt 27:11*
M *Mt 20:20–21 ◀ ▶ Mt 21:38*

21:5 Jesus quotes the prophecy of Zec 9:9 that foretold his Messianic entrance into Jerusalem through the eastern gate in fulfillment of Da 9:24–26. See the article on "The Vision of the Seventy Weeks" on p. 976.

The Four Temples in Israel's History

Solomon's Temple	Zerubbabel's Temple		Tribulation Temple	Millennial Temple
1	2		3	4
1000 B.C. (1000–587 B.C.)	*536 B.C. (516 B.C.–A.D. 70)*	*A.D. 32 Crucifixion*	*The 7 year Tribulation Period*	*Following Battle of Armageddon*

Cleansing of the temple

12 ¶ [a]And Jesus went into the temple of God, and cast out all them that sold and bought in the temple, and overthrew the tables of the [b]moneychangers, and the seats of them that sold doves,

13 And said unto them, It is written, [a]My house shall be called the house of prayer; [b]but ye have made it a den of thieves.

E 14 And the blind and the lame came to him in the temple; and he healed them.

15 And when the chief priests and scribes saw the wonderful things that he did, and the children crying in the temple, and saying, Hosanna to the son of David; they were sore displeased,

16 And said unto him, Hearest thou what these say? And Jesus saith unto them, Yea; have ye never read, [a]Out of the mouth of babes and sucklings thou hast perfected praise?

17 ¶ And he left them, and went out of the city into [a]Bethany; and he lodged there.

The barren fig tree

18 [a]Now in the morning as he returned into the city, he hungered.

19 [a]And when he saw [1]a fig tree in the way, he came to it, and found nothing thereon, but leaves only, and said unto it, Let no fruit grow on thee henceforward for ever. And presently the fig tree withered away.

20 [a]And when the disciples saw *it,* they marvelled, saying, How soon is the fig tree withered away!

21 Jesus answered and said unto them, Verily I say unto you, [a]If ye have faith, and [b]doubt not, ye shall not only do this *which is done* to the fig tree, [c]but also if ye shall say unto this mountain, Be thou removed, and be thou cast into the sea; it shall be done.

L 22 And [a]all things, whatsoever ye shall ask in prayer, believing, ye shall receive.

Jesus' authority challenged

23 ¶ [a]And when he was come into the temple, the chief priests and the elders of the people came unto him as he was teaching, and [b]said, By what authority doest thou these things? and who gave thee this authority?

24 And Jesus answered and said unto them, I also will ask you one thing, which if ye tell me, I in like wise will tell you by what authority I do these things.

25 The baptism of John, whence was it? from heaven, or of men? And they reasoned with themselves, saying, If we shall say, From heaven; he will say unto us, Why did ye not then believe him?

26 But if we shall say, Of men; we fear the people; [a]for all hold John as a prophet.

27 And they answered Jesus, and said, We cannot tell. And he said unto them, Neither tell I you by what authority I do these things.

The parable of the two sons

28 ¶ But what think ye? A *certain* man R
had two sons; and he came to the first, S
and said, Son, go work today in my vineyard.

29 He answered and said, I will not: but afterward he repented, and went.

30 And he came to the second, and said likewise. And he answered and said, I *go,* sir: and went not.

31 Whether of them twain did the will F
of *his* father? They say unto him, The L
first. Jesus saith unto them, [a]Verily I say unto you, That the publicans and the harlots go into the kingdom of God before you.

32 For [a]John came unto you in the way of righteousness, and ye believed him not: [b]but the publicans and the harlots believed him: and ye, when ye had seen *it,* repented not afterward, that ye might believe him.

The parable of the husbandmen

33 ¶ Hear another parable: There was a certain householder, [a]which planted a vineyard, and hedged it round about, and digged a winepress in it, and built a tower, and let it out to husbandmen, and [b]went into a far country:

34 And when the time of the fruit S
drew near, he sent his servants to the

12 [a]Mark 11:11; Luke 19:45; John 2:15 [b]Deut. 14:25
13 [a]Is. 56:7 [b]Jer. 7:11; Mark 11:17; Luke 19:46
16 [a]Ps. 8:2
17 [a]Mark 11:11; John 11:18
18 [a]Mark 11:12
19 [a]Mark 11:13 [1]Gk. *one fig tree*
20 [a]Mark 11:20
21 [a]ch. 17:20 [b]Jas. 1:6 [c]1 Cor. 13:2
22 [a]ch. 7:7; Mark 11:24; Luke 11:9; Jas. 5:16; 1 John 3:22 & 5:14
23 [a]Mark 11:27; Luke 20:1 [b]Ex. 2:14; Acts 4:7 & 7:27
26 [a]ch. 14:5; Mark 6:20; Luke 20:6
31 [a]Luke 7:29,50
32 [a]ch. 3:1 [b]Luke 3:12,13
33 [a]Ps. 80:9; Sol. 8:11; Is. 5:1; Jer. 2:21; Mark 12:1; Luke 20:9 [b]ch. 25:14

E *Mt 20:30–34* ◀▶ *Mk 1:23–34*
L *Mt 18:19–20* ◀▶ *Mt 28:20*

R *Mt 18:35* ◀▶ *Mt 26:75*
S *Mt 19:16–21* ◀▶ *Mt 21:34*
F *Mt 11:12* ◀▶ *Mk 1:15*
L *Mt 20:1–14* ◀▶ *Mt 22:9–10*
S *Mt 21:28–31* ◀▶ *Mt 21:41*

husbandmen, [a]that they might receive the fruits of it.

35 [a]And the husbandmen took his servants, and beat one, and killed another, and stoned another.

36 Again, he sent other servants more than the first: and they did unto them likewise.

37 But last of all he sent unto them his son, saying, They will reverence my son.

M 38 But when the husbandmen saw the son, they said among themselves, [a]This is the heir; [b]come, let us kill him, and let us seize on his inheritance.

39 [a]And they caught him, and cast *him* out of the vineyard, and slew *him.*

40 When the lord therefore of the vineyard cometh, what will he do unto those husbandmen?

G R S 41 [a]They say unto him, [b]He will miserably destroy those wicked men, [c]and will let out *his* vineyard unto other husbandmen, which shall render him the fruits in their seasons.

42 Jesus saith unto them, [a]Did ye never read in the scriptures, The stone which the builders rejected, the same is become the head of the corner: this is the Lord's doing, and it is marvellous in our eyes?

G R 43 Therefore say I unto you, [a]The kingdom of God shall be taken from you, and given to a nation bringing forth the fruits thereof.

H N 44 And whosoever [a]shall fall on this stone shall be broken: but on whomsoever it shall fall, [b]it will grind him to powder.

45 And when the chief priests and Pharisees had heard his parables, they perceived that he spake of them.

46 But when they sought to lay hands on him, they feared the multitude, because [a]they took him for a prophet.

The marriage dinner

22 AND JESUS answered [a]and spake unto them again by parables, and said, N W

2 The kingdom of heaven is like unto a certain king, which made a marriage for his son, H

3 And sent forth his servants to call them that were bidden to the wedding: and they would not come.

4 Again, he sent forth other servants, saying, Tell them which are bidden, Behold, I have prepared my dinner: [a]my oxen and *my* fatlings *are* killed, and all things *are* ready: come unto the marriage.

5 But they made light of *it,* and went their ways, one to his farm, another to his merchandise:

6 And the remnant took his servants, and entreated *them* spitefully, and slew *them.*

7 But when the king heard *thereof,* he was wroth: and he sent forth [a]his armies, and destroyed those murderers, and burned up their city. R H

8 Then saith he to his servants, The wedding is ready, but they which were bidden were not [a]worthy. H

9 Go ye therefore into the highways, G L

34 [a]Sol. 8:11,12
35 [a]2 Chr. 24:21; & 36:16; Neh. 9:26; ch. 5:12 & 23:34, 37; Acts 7:52; 1 Thes. 2:15; Heb. 11:36,37
38 [a]Ps. 2:8; Heb. 1:2 [b]Ps. 2:2; ch. 26:3 & 27:1; John 11:53; Acts 4:27
39 [a]ch. 26:50; Mark 14:46; Luke 22:54; John 18:12; Acts 2:23
41 [a]Luke 20:16 [b]Luke 21:24; Heb. 2:3 [c]Acts 13:46 & 15:7 & 18:6 & 28:28; Rom. 9 & 10 & 11
42 [a]Ps. 118:22; Is. 28:16; Mark 12:10; Luke 20:17; Acts 4:11; Eph. 2:20; 1 Pet. 2:6,7
43 [a]ch. 8:12
44 [a]Is. 8:14,15; Zech. 12:3; Luke 20:18; Rom. 9:33; 1 Pet. 2:8 [b]Is. 60:12; Dan. 2:44
46 [a]ver. 11; Luke 7:16; John 7:40
22:1 [a]Luke 14:16; Rev. 19:7,9
4 [a]Prov. 9:2
7 [a]Dan. 9:26; Luke 19:27
8 [a]ch. 10:11; Acts 13:46

M *Mt 21:5* ◀ ▶ *Mt 22:44*
G *Mal 1:11* ◀ ▶ *Mt 21:43*
R *Mt 15:23–27* ◀ ▶ *Mt 21:43*
S *Mt 21:34* ◀ ▶ *Mt 22:36–40*
G *Mt 21:41* ◀ ▶ *Mt 22:9–10*
R *Mt 21:41* ◀ ▶ *Mt 22:7–8*
H *Mt 18:6–9* ◀ ▶ *Mt 22:7*
N *Mt 13:13–15* ◀ ▶ *Mt 22:1–7*
N *Mt 21:44* ◀ ▶ *Mt 23:37–38*
W *Mt 20:1–16* ◀ ▶ *Mk 3:28*
H *Isa 26:20–21* ◀ ▶ *Mt 22:8–10*
R *Mt 21:43* ◀ ▶ *Mt 23:37–39*
H *Mt 21:44* ◀ ▶ *Mt 22:11–13*
H *Mt 22:2–3* ◀ ▶ *Mt 22:14*
G *Mt 21:43* ◀ ▶ *Mk 12:9*
L *Mt 21:31–32* ◀ ▶ *Mt 23:37*

21:37–43 This prophetic parable foretells the rejection and crucifixion of the Messiah by the people of Israel. Jesus said that God would respond to Israel's rejection of his Son by rejecting Israel for a time and turning his kingdom over to "other husbandmen" (21:41)—a reference to the church, which is composed mainly of Gentiles.

22:2–14 Jesus continues his prophetic parables about the kingdom of heaven by comparing it to a marriage supper given for the son of a great king. Those who received the king's invitation "made light of it, and went their ways" (22:5). The king destroyed those who held his invitation in such contempt and sent his servants to invite "as many as ye shall find" (22:9) to attend the marriage supper. Clearly this parable illustrates that God turned from Israel when they rejected his Son and instead offered the "marriage supper of the Lamb" (Rev 19:9) to all who would repent of their sins and trust in Christ for their salvation.

and as many as ye shall find, bid to the
marriage.
10 So those servants went out into the
highways, and [a]gathered together all as
many as they found, both bad and good:
and the wedding was furnished with
guests.
A 11 ¶ And when the king came in to see
C the guests, he saw there a man [a]which
G had not on a wedding garment:
H 12 And he saith unto him, Friend, how
O camest thou in hither not having a wedding garment? And he was speechless.
13 Then said the king to the servants,
Bind him hand and foot, and take him
away, and cast *him* [a]into outer darkness;
there shall be weeping and gnashing of
teeth.
H 14 [a]For many are called, but few *are*
chosen.

Tribute money to Caesar

15 ¶ [a]Then went the Pharisees, and
took counsel how they might entangle
him in *his* talk.
16 And they sent out unto him their
disciples with the Herodians, saying,
Master, we know that thou art true, and
teachest the way of God in truth, neither
carest thou for any *man:* for thou regardest not the person of men.
17 Tell us therefore, What thinkest
thou? Is it lawful to give tribute unto Caesar, or not?
18 But Jesus perceived their wickedness, and said, Why tempt ye me, *ye* hypocrites?
19 Show me the tribute money. And
they brought unto him a [l]penny.
20 And he saith unto them, Whose *is*
this image and [l]superscription?

A *Mt 12:30 ◀▶ Lk 11:23*
C *Mt 18:11–14 ◀▶ Mt 23:17*
G *Mt 15:8–9 ◀▶ Mt 25:3*
H *Mt 22:7 ◀▶ Mt 22:44*
O *Mt 18:18 ◀▶ Mt 25:1–12*
H *Mt 22:8–10 ◀▶ Mt 25:1–13*

10 [a]ch. 13:38
11 [a]2 Cor. 5:3; Eph. 4:24; Col. 3:10,12; Rev. 3:4 & 16:15 & 19:8
13 [a]ch. 8:12
14 [a]ch. 20:16
15 [a]Mark 12:13; Luke 20:20
19 [l]The penny, worth about 16 cents, was the usual day's wage for a laborer
20 [l]Or, *inscription?*
21 [a]ch. 17:25; Rom. 13:7
23 [a]Mark 12:18; Luke 20:27 [b]Acts 23:8
24 [a]Deut. 25:5
26 [l]Gk. *seven*
29 [a]John 20:9
30 [a]1 John 3:2
32 [a]Ex. 3:6,16; Mark 12:26; Luke 20:37; Acts 7:32; Heb. 11:16
33 [a]ch. 7:28

21 They say unto him, Caesar's. Then
saith he unto them, [a]Render therefore
unto Caesar the things which are Caesar's; and unto God the things that are
God's.
22 When they had heard *these words,*
they marvelled, and left him, and went
their way.

Sadducees and the resurrection

23 ¶ [a]The same day came to him the
Sadducees, [b]which say that there is no
resurrection, and asked him,
24 Saying, Master, [a]Moses said, If a
man die, having no children, his brother
shall marry his wife, and raise up seed
unto his brother.
25 Now there were with us seven
brethren: and the first, when he had married a wife, deceased, and having no issue, left his wife unto his brother:
26 Likewise the second also, and the
third, unto the [l]seventh.
27 And last of all the woman died also.
28 Therefore in the resurrection
whose wife shall she be of the seven? for
they all had her.
29 Jesus answered and said unto them,
Ye do err, [a]not knowing the scriptures,
nor the power of God.
30 For in the resurrection they neither F
marry, nor are given in marriage, but [a]are
as the angels of God in heaven.
31 But as touching the resurrection of
the dead, have ye not read that which
was spoken unto you by God, saying,
32 [a]I am the God of Abraham, and the
God of Isaac, and the God of Jacob? God
is not the God of the dead, but of the
living.
33 And when the multitude heard
this, [a]they were astonished at his doctrine.

F *Hos 13:14 ◀▶ Mk 12:24–25*

22:29–32 The Sadducees denied the possibility of bodily resurrection, taught the annihilation of the soul at death and rejected any portion of Scripture except the five books of Moses. Jesus answered their question about the resurrection by quoting Moses' words from Ex 3:6 that affirmed the spiritual existence of Abraham, Isaac and Jacob centuries after their physical deaths.

The Sadducees then asked a hypothetical question about a woman who died after marrying and being widowed by a series of seven brothers (see Dt 25:5). Their question concerned the law of levirate marriage that assured the preservation of both inherited land and the lineage of a departed brother. Jesus answered their specific question by declaring that marriage will not exist in the resurrection, either for angels or for believers.

The great commandment

34 ¶ [a]But when the Pharisees had heard that he had put the Sadducees to silence, they were gathered together.

35 Then one of them, *which was* [a]a lawyer, asked *him a question,* tempting him, and saying,

S 36 Master, which *is* the great commandment in the law?

37 Jesus said unto him, [a]Thou shalt love the Lord thy God with all thy heart, and with all thy soul, and with all thy mind.

38 This is the first and great commandment.

39 And the second *is* like unto it, [a]Thou shalt love thy neighbour as thyself.

40 [a]On these two commandments hang all the law and the prophets.

The question about David's son

41 ¶ [a]While the Pharisees were gathered together, Jesus asked them,

42 Saying, What think ye of Christ? whose son is he? They say unto him, *The son* of David.

E 43 He saith unto them, How then doth
T David in spirit call him Lord, saying,
M 44 [a]The LORD said unto my Lord, Sit
V thou on my right hand, till I make thine
H enemies thy footstool?

45 If David then call him Lord, how is he his son?

46 [a]And no man was able to answer him a word, [b]neither durst any *man* from that day forth ask him any more *questions.*

The woes upon the Pharisees

23 THEN SPAKE Jesus to the multitude, and to his disciples,

2 Saying, [a]The scribes and the Pharisees sit in Moses' seat:

S *Mt 21:41* ◀ ▶ *Mt 24:13*
E *Mt 12:28* ◀ ▶ *Mk 1:10*
T *Mt 10:19–20* ◀ ▶ *Mk 12:36*
M *Mt 21:38* ◀ ▶ *Mt 25:21*
V *Zec 9:10* ◀ ▶ *Mk 12:36*
H *Mt 22:11–13* ◀ ▶ *Mt 23:14–15*

3 All therefore whatsoever they bid you observe, *that* observe and do; but do not ye after their works: for [a]they say, and do not.

4 [a]For they bind heavy burdens and grievous to be borne, and lay *them* on men's shoulders; but they *themselves* will not move them with one of their fingers.

5 But [a]all their works they do for to be seen of men: [b]they make broad their phylacteries, and enlarge the borders of their garments,

6 [a]And love the uppermost rooms at feasts, and the chief seats in the synagogues,

7 And greetings in the markets, and to be called of men, Rabbi, Rabbi.

8 [a]But be not ye called Rabbi: for one is your Master, *even* Christ; and all ye are brethren.

9 And call no *man* your father upon the earth: [a]for one is your Father, which is in heaven.

10 Neither be ye called masters: for one is your Master, *even* Christ.

11 But [a]he that is greatest among you shall be your servant.

12 [a]And whosoever shall exalt himself shall be abased; and he that shall humble himself shall be exalted. M

13 ¶ But [a]woe unto you, scribes and Pharisees, hypocrites! for ye shut up the kingdom of heaven against men: for ye neither go in *yourselves,* neither suffer ye them that are entering to go in.

14 Woe unto you, scribes and Pharisees, hypocrites! [a]for ye devour widows' houses, and for a pretence make long prayer: therefore ye shall receive the greater damnation. H

15 Woe unto you, scribes and Pharisees, hypocrites! for ye compass sea and land to make one proselyte, and when he is made, ye make him twofold more the child of hell than yourselves.

16 Woe unto you, [a]*ye* blind guides,

M *Mt 19:23–24* ◀ ▶ *Mk 10:14–15*
H *Mt 22:44* ◀ ▶ *Mt 23:33*

34 [a]Mark 12:28
35 [a]Luke 10:25
37 [a]Deut. 6:5 & 10:12 & 30:6; Luke 10:27
39 [a]Lev. 19:18; ch. 19:19; Mark 12:31; Luke 10:27; Rom. 13:9; Gal. 5:14; Jas. 2:8
40 [a]ch. 7:12; 1 Tim. 1:5
41 [a]Mark 12:35; Luke 20:41
44 [a]Ps. 110:1; Acts 2:34; 1 Cor. 15:25; Heb. 1:13 & 10:12, 13
46 [a]Luke 14:6 [b]Mark 12:34; Luke 20:40
23:2 [a]Neh. 8:4,8; Mal. 2:7; Mark 12:38; Luke 20:45
3 [a]Rom. 2:19
4 [a]Luke 11:46; Acts 15:10; Gal. 6:13
5 [a]ch. 6:1,2,5,16 [b]Num. 15:38; Deut. 6:8 & 22:12; Prov. 3:3
6 [a]Mark 12:38,39; Luke 11:43 & 20:46; 3 John 9
8 [a]Jas. 3:1; See 2 Cor. 1:24; 1 Pet. 5:3
9 [a]Mal. 1:6
11 [a]ch. 20:26,27
12 [a]Job 22:29; Prov. 15:33 & 29:23; Luke 14:11 & 18:14; Jas. 4:6; 1 Pet. 5:5
13 [a]Luke 11:52
14 [a]Mark 12:40; Luke 20:47; 2 Tim. 3:6; Tit. 1:11
16 [a]ver. 24; ch. 15:14

22:44 Jesus asked the Pharisees a question about the Messiah that they were unable to answer. He did so to demonstrate that the Messiah is both the Son of David and the Son of God at the same time, thus revealing the divine nature of the Messiah. King David acknowledged that God the Father told the Messiah (Jesus Christ) to "sit thou at my right hand, until I make thine enemies thy footstool" (Ps 110:1). This prophecy also foreshadows the final triumph of the Messiah over all his enemies in the millennial kingdom following the Battle of Armageddon.

which say, [b]Whosoever shall swear by the temple, it is nothing; but whosoever shall swear by the gold of the temple, he is a debtor!

C 17 *Ye* fools and blind: for whether is greater, the gold, [a]or the temple that sanctifieth the gold?

18 And, Whosoever shall swear by the altar, it is nothing; but whosoever sweareth by the gift that is upon it, he is [l]guilty.

C 19 *Ye* fools and blind: for whether *is* greater, the gift, or [a]the altar that sanctifieth the gift?

20 Whoso therefore shall swear by the altar, sweareth by it, and by all things thereon.

21 And whoso shall swear by the temple, sweareth by it, and by [a]him that dwelleth therein.

22 And he that shall swear by heaven, sweareth by [a]the throne of God, and by him that sitteth thereon.

23 Woe unto you, scribes and Pharisees, hypocrites! [a]for ye pay tithe of mint and [l]anise and cummin, and [b]have omitted the weightier *matters* of the law, judgment, mercy, and faith: these ought ye to have done, and not to leave the other undone.

24 *Ye* blind guides, which strain at a gnat, and swallow a camel.

C 25 Woe unto you, scribes and Pharisees, hypocrites! [a]for ye make clean the outside of the cup and of the platter, but within they are full of extortion and excess.

26 *Thou* blind Pharisee, cleanse first that *which is* within the cup and platter, that the outside of them may be clean also.

27 Woe unto you, scribes and Pharisees, hypocrites! [a]for ye are like unto whited sepulchres, which indeed appear beautiful outward, but are within full of

C *Mt 22:11–14* ◀▶ *Mt 23:19*
C *Mt 23:17* ◀▶ *Mt 23:25–28*
C *Mt 23:19* ◀▶ *Mt 23:33*

16 [b]ch. 5:33,34
17 [a]Ex. 30:29
18 [l]Or, *debtor*, or, *bound*
19 [a]Ex. 29:37
21 [a]1 Ki. 8:13; 2 Chr. 6:2; Ps. 26:8 & 132:14
22 [a]Ps. 11:4; ch. 5:34; Acts 7:49
23 [a]Luke 11:42 [b]1 Sam. 15:22; Hos. 6:6; Mic. 6:8; ch. 9:13 & 12:7 [l]Or, *dill*
25 [a]Mark 7:4; Luke 11:39
27 [a]Luke 11:44; Acts 23:3
29 [a]Luke 11:47
31 [a]Acts 7:51,52; 1 Thes. 2:15
32 [a]Gen. 15:16; 1 Thes. 2:16
33 [a]ch. 3:7 & 12:34
34 [a]ch. 21:34,35; Luke 11:49 [b]Acts 5:40 & 7:58,59 & 22:19 [c]ch. 10:17; 2 Cor. 11:24,25
35 [a]Rev. 18:24 [b]Gen. 4:8; 1 John 3:12 [c]2 Chr. 24:20, 21
37 [a]Luke 13:34 [b]2 Chr. 24:21 [c]Deut. 32:11,12 [d]Ps. 17:8 & 91:4

dead *men's* bones, and of all uncleanness.

28 Even so ye also outwardly appear righteous unto men, but within ye are full of hypocrisy and iniquity.

29 [a]Woe unto you, scribes and Pharisees, hypocrites! because ye build the tombs of the prophets, and garnish the sepulchres of the righteous,

30 And say, If we had been in the days of our fathers, we would not have been partakers with them in the blood of the prophets.

31 Wherefore ye be witnesses unto yourselves, that [a]ye are the children of them which killed the prophets.

32 [a]Fill ye up then the measure of your fathers.

33 *Ye* serpents, *ye* [a]generation of vipers, how can ye escape the damnation of hell? C H

34 ¶ [a]Wherefore, behold, I send unto you prophets, and wise men, and scribes: and [b]*some* of them ye shall kill and crucify; and [c]*some* of them shall ye scourge in your synagogues, and persecute *them* from city to city:

35 [a]That upon you may come all the righteous blood shed upon the earth, [b]from the blood of righteous Abel unto [c]the blood of Zacharias son of Barachias, whom ye slew between the temple and the altar.

36 Verily I say unto you, All these things shall come upon this generation.

37 [a]O Jerusalem, Jerusalem, *thou* that killest the prophets, [b]and stonest them which are sent unto thee, how often would [c]I have gathered thy children together, even as a hen gathereth her chickens [d]under *her* wings, and ye would not! R L N

38 Behold, your house is left unto you desolate.

C *Mt 23:25–28* ◀▶ *Mt 25:2–3*
H *Mt 23:14–15* ◀▶ *Mt 24:21*
R *Mt 22:7–8* ◀▶ *Mt 24:1–3*
L *Mt 22:9–10* ◀▶ *Mk 2:17*
N *Mt 22:1–7* ◀▶ *Mt 24:43–44*

23:37–39 As Jesus came to the close of his earthly ministry, he pronounced a terrible prophecy on Jerusalem that was tragically fulfilled when the Roman legions burned the temple and city to the ground in A.D. 70. Jesus also announced that the Jews would not see him again until they repented of their sins and acknowledged the return of their Messiah. This prophecy will be fulfilled when Christ triumphantly returns to save Israel from the antichrist at the Battle of Armageddon. Zechariah confirmed this prophetic picture of the repentance of Israel and says their eyes will finally be opened to see Jesus as their true Messiah (see Zec 12:9–11).

39 For I say unto you, Ye shall not see me henceforth, till ye shall say, [a]Blessed *is* he that cometh in the name of the Lord.

Signs of the end of this age

R 24 AND [a]JESUS went out, and departed from the temple: and his disciples came to *him* for to show him the buildings of the temple.

2 And Jesus said unto them, See ye not all these things? verily I say unto you, [a]There shall not be left here one stone upon another, that shall not be thrown down.

C 3 ¶ And as he sat upon the mount of
E Olives, [a]the disciples came unto him privately, saying, [b]Tell us, when shall these things be? and what *shall be* the sign of thy coming, and of the end of the world?

4 And Jesus answered and said unto them, [a]Take heed that no man deceive you.

5 For [a]many shall come in my name, saying, I am Christ; [b]and shall deceive many.

6 And ye shall hear of wars and rumours of wars: see that ye be not troubled: for all *these things* must come to pass, but the end is not yet.

7 For [a]nation shall rise against nation, and kingdom against kingdom: and there shall be famines, and pestilences, and earthquakes, in divers places.

8 All these *are* the beginning of sorrows.

9 [a]Then shall they deliver you up to be

R *Mt 23:37–39* ◀▶ *Mt 24:15–22*
C *Mt 16:27–28* ◀▶ *Mt 24:26–27*
E *Mt 16:3* ◀▶ *Mt 24:32–33*

39 [a]Ps. 118:26; ch. 21:9
24:1 [a]Mark 13:1; Luke 21:5
2 [a]1 Ki. 9:7; Jer. 26:18; Mic. 3:12; Luke 19:44
3 [a]Mark 13:3 [b]1 Thes. 5:1
4 [a]Eph. 5:6; Col. 2:8,18; 2 Thes. 2:3; 1 John 4:1
5 [a]ver. 24; Jer. 14:14 & 23:21,25; John 5:43 [b]ver. 11
7 [a]2 Chr. 15:6; Is. 19:2; Hag. 2:22; Zech. 14:13
9 [a]ch. 10:17; Luke 21:12; John 16:2; Acts 4:2,3

24:1–3 Jesus left the temple, knowing that it was destined to certain destruction within that generation because the Jews had rejected Jesus as their Messiah. The disciples wondered aloud when this terrible judgment would fall on the temple. Jesus gave a clear answer that was recorded in Lk 21:20–24. Then the disciples asked Jesus two additional questions regarding the signs of his second coming and the signs of the end of the world. The balance of Mt 24 reveals Jesus' detailed answer to these questions.

In order to understand the meaning of Jesus' prophetic signs in this chapter we must remember that this discourse occurred before the crucifixion. The Gentile church of believers did not exist yet. Jesus was speaking primarily to his Jewish followers and warning of the prophetic signs that would occur just prior to his second coming.

24:4–5 Significantly, the first sign of Christ's return is the rise of false Christs who "shall deceive many" (24:5). Throughout history impostors and delusional fanatics have arisen and claimed to be the Messiah. In our generation alone we have seen an explosion of those claiming to be Jesus Christ, including David Koresh, Sun Myung Moon and the Lord Maitreya.

24:6 Jesus also warned about the increase of wars before his second coming (see Joel 3:9–10). Statistics show that over the centuries our planet has endured 13 years of war for every year of peace. Despite the numerous peace and disarmament treaties enacted since 1945, we have not known a single day of worldwide peace but rather have experienced more wars than any other generation in history. Despite the growing dangers of war, Jesus told his followers not to be troubled because "the end is not yet."

24:7–8 Jesus also warned that a series of cataclysmic natural phenomena would characterize his imminent return. Famine, pestilence and earthquakes would not only increase in frequency in the last days; they would also occur in different or unusual places. Note the following statistics that herald the fulfillment of this prophecy.

Famine: Millions are at risk of famine in this decade in central Africa, India, North Korea and China. Many other nations are unable to properly feed their people due to the decreasing amounts of agricultural lands, increasing amounts of deserts and the soaring growth of their populations. Diminished food resources will be overwhelmed during the tribulation when worldwide famine destroys millions of lives (see Rev 6:5–6).

Earthquakes: Killer earthquakes (6.5 or higher on the Richter scale) occurred only once every decade during the 1800s. According to current statistics, the number of these major earthquakes has increased to over 100 in this decade alone.

Pestilence: Worldwide pestilence would also signal Jesus' return. In the past twenty years, according to the World Health Organization (WHO), health professionals have diagnosed more than 25 infectious diseases with no known treatment or cure. These have come about as a result of the ease of travel between nations, poor sanitation, growing urbanization and overpopulation. Sexually transmitted diseases are increasing, causing sterility and death. Recent studies predict that AIDS may wipe out as much as one quarter of the global population (see Rev 6:8).

Jesus warns that these terrible judgments will only set the stage for the terrible judgments of the tribulation.

24:9–12 Jesus warned that his followers would be subject to extreme persecution and martyrdom because of a profound hatred of Jesus by the reli-

afflicted, and shall kill you: and ye shall
be hated of all nations for my name's
sake.
10 And then shall many [a]be offended,
and shall betray one another, and shall
hate one another.
11 And [a]many false prophets shall rise,
and [b]shall deceive many.
12 And because iniquity shall abound,
the love of many shall wax cold.
S 13 [a]But he that shall endure unto the
end, the same shall be saved.
14 And this [a]gospel of the kingdom
[b]shall be preached in all the world for a
witness unto all nations; and then shall
the end come.
R 15 [a]When ye therefore shall see the
abomination of desolation, spoken of by
[b]Daniel the prophet, stand in the holy
place, ([c]whoso readeth, let him understand:)

S *Mt 22:36–40* ◀▶ *Mt 24:48–51*
R *Mt 24:1–3* ◀▶ *Mk 12:9*

10 [a]2 Tim. 1:15 & 4:10,16
11 [a]Acts 20:29; 2 Pet. 2:1 [b]1 Tim. 4:1
13 [a]ch. 10:22; Mark 13:13; Rev. 2:10
14 [a]ch. 4:23 [b]Rom. 10:18; Col. 1:6,23
15 [a]Mark 13:14; Luke 21:20 [b]Dan. 9:27 & 12:11 [c]Dan. 9:23
19 [a]Luke 23:29
21 [a]Dan. 9:26; Joel 2:2
22 [a]Is. 65:8,9; Zech. 14:2
23 [a]Mark 13:21; Luke 17:23 & 21:8

16 Then let them which be in Judaea
flee into the mountains:
17 Let him which is on the housetop
not come down to take any thing out of
his house:
18 Neither let him which is in the field
return back to take his clothes.
19 And [a]woe unto them that are with
child, and to them that give suck in those
days!
20 But pray ye that your flight be not
in the winter, neither on the sabbath day:
21 For [a]then shall be great tribulation, H
such as was not since the beginning of
the world to this time, no, nor ever
shall be.
22 And except those days should be
shortened, there should no flesh be
saved: [a]but for the elect's sake those days
shall be shortened.
23 [a]Then if any man shall say unto

H *Mt 23:33* ◀▶ *Mt 24:50–51*

---

gious authorities. This prophecy was initially fulfilled during the first wave of persecution by the Jewish authorities during the first century but will find its final fulfillment in the terrible persecution of the tribulation.

Because of this persecution in the last days, many will turn from their faith and betray other believers. Jesus also warned of the proliferation of false prophets and the tragic alienation of affection between people. In our generation we have seen an astonishing rise of false prophets, telepaths and cults. The growing litany of child abuse, spousal battery and abuse of the elderly reflects the widespread iniquity of our time.

24:13–14 Despite the coming trials and persecutions, Jesus promised that those who remained faithful would be saved. The generation of the last days would witness the gospel being preached in an unprecedented way throughout the world. Only then would the end come. The spectacular growth of the church in our generation is one of the great signs of the nearness of Christ's return. Some studies indicate that one person in ten of the world's population today is a Christian. "Even so, come, Lord Jesus" (Rev 22:20).

24:15–19 At the beginning of the great tribulation, when the antichrist breaks his seven-year treaty with Israel, defiles the rebuilt temple and establishes the mark of the beast, Jesus will give his followers a warning sign, the sign of the prophet Daniel (see Da 9:27; 12:11). When believers become aware of the antichrist's abomination, Jesus warns them to quickly run into the hills of Judea because the terrible wrath of God will soon be poured out on unrepentant sinners.

24:20 If this abomination occurred during the winter or on the Sabbath, escape would be much more difficult. The ancient Jews observed an orthodox ritual that prohibited travel on the Sabbath to no more than 1000 yards beyond the walls of Jerusalem lest they violate the injunction against working on the Sabbath (see Ex 16:29). This distance was considered a "sabbath day's journey" (Ac 1:12). This verse carries added weight today as orthodox Jews become more powerful in the Israeli government and urge the reinstitution of stringent Sabbath laws to restrict Sabbath-day activities of the people.

24:21–22 Jesus warned that the tribulation to come would be unprecedented in its terror and destructiveness. All of humanity would be destroyed unless those days were shortened for the sake of the people of God. These are the tribulation saints saved during the period that follows the rapture of the church. The OT usage of the word for these "elect" ones clearly applies to the Jews in Isa 45:4; 65:9; 65:22.

24:23–27 Jesus warned against anyone believing another's claim that they had seen Christ. This prophetic warning should alert anyone to the claims of false messiahs. Jesus warned that these false Christs would produce deceptive signs that would be so amazing that they could even deceive, "if it were possible" (24:24), the people of God. When Jesus truly returns, his coming will be as spectacular and unmistakable as lightning. He will appear in the sky exactly as he ascended almost 2000 years ago (see Ac 1:11).

you, Lo, here *is* Christ, or there; believe
it not.
24 For [a]there shall arise false Christs,
and false prophets, and shall show great
signs and wonders; insomuch that, [b]if *it*
were possible, they shall deceive the very
elect.
25 Behold, I have told you before.
C 26 Wherefore if they shall say unto
you, Behold, he is in the desert; go not
forth: behold, *he is* in the secret chambers; believe *it* not.
27 [a]For as the lightning cometh out of
the east, and shineth even unto the west;
so shall also the coming of the Son of
man be.
28 [a]For wheresoever the carcase is,
there will the eagles be gathered together.
C 29 ¶ [a]Immediately after the tribulation
of those days [b]shall the sun be darkened,
and the moon shall not give her light, and
the stars shall fall from heaven, and the
powers of the heavens shall be shaken:
30 [a]And then shall appear the sign of
the Son of man in heaven: [b]and then
shall all the tribes of the earth mourn,
[c]and they shall see the Son of man coming in the clouds of heaven with power
and great glory.
31 [a]And he shall send his angels [l]with T
a great sound of a trumpet, and they shall
gather together his elect from the four
winds, from one end of heaven to the
other.
32 Now learn [a]a parable of the fig tree; E
When his branch is yet tender, and putteth forth leaves, ye know that summer *is*
nigh:
33 So likewise ye, when ye shall see all
these things, know [a]that [l]it is near, *even*
at the doors.
34 Verily I say unto you, [a]This generation shall not pass, till all these things be
fulfilled.
35 [a]Heaven and earth shall pass away, K
but my words shall not pass away.
36 ¶ [a]But of that day and hour know- C
eth no *man,* no, not the angels of heaven,
[b]but my Father only.
37 But as the days of Noe *were,* so

24 [a]Deut. 13:1; 2 Thes. 2:9; Rev. 13:13 [b]John 6:37 & 10:28,29; Rom. 8:28; 2 Tim. 2:19
27 [a]Luke 17:24
28 [a]Job 39:30; Luke 17:37
29 [a]Dan. 7:11 [b]Ezek. 32:7; Joel 2:10; Amos 8:9; Mark 13:24; Acts 2:20
30 [a]Dan. 7:13 [b]Zech. 12:12 [c]Mark 13:26; Rev. 1:7
31 [a]1 Cor. 15:52; 1 Thes. 4:16 [l]Or, *with a trumpet, and a great voice*
32 [a]Luke 21:29
33 [a]Jas. 5:9 [l]Or, *he*
34 [a]ch. 16:28; Mark 13:30; Luke 21:32
35 [a]Ps. 102:26; Is. 51:6; Jer. 31:35; Mark 13:31; Luke 21:33
36 [a]Mark 13:32; Acts 1:7; 1 Thes. 5:2; 2 Pet. 3:10 [b]Zech. 14:7

C *Mt 24:3* ◀▶ *Mt 24:29–33*
C *Mt 24:26–27* ◀▶ *Mt 24:36–51*
T *Mt 13:30* ◀▶ *Lk 17:34–36*
E *Mt 24:3–6* ◀▶ *Mk 13:5–13*
K *Mt 19:26* ◀▶ *Mt 28:18*
C *Mt 24:29–33* ◀▶ *Mt 25:1–13*

24:28 This prophecy may refer to the terrible aftermath of Armageddon when God will gather the birds of prey to eat the bodies of the dead (see Rev 19:17–18 and Job 39:30).

24:31 When Christ comes, he will send his angels to gather the "elect" from all over the world. These "elect" ones are the saints who come to faith in Christ during the terrible persecution of the tribulation. This gathering of the "elect" is a different event from the translation of the saints described by Paul in 1Co 15:51. Note that the angels gather these "elect," while the rapture that Paul describes indicates that the saints will rise in their resurrection bodies to meet Christ in the air (see 1Th 4:16–17). Also note that this gathering in Mt 24:31 does not mention any change in anyone's physical bodies, but the transformation to a resurrection body occurs at the rapture of the church saints prior to the tribulation.

The purposes of these two gatherings are different too. Christ will gather the "elect" to protect the tribulation saints from the wrath of God that is about to be poured out from heaven upon unrepentant sinners. The purpose of the rapture is to clothe the Christian saints, living and departed, with a glorious resurrection body like the body Jesus had when he rose from the dead (see Ro 8:22–23; Php 3:20–21; 1Jn 3:2).

24:32–35 The example of the fig tree reminded Jesus' followers to stay alert and observant. Just as the fig tree indicated the seasons by its foliage, so God's people could recognize the imminence of Christ's return by the fulfillment of these signs.

Jesus' use of the phrase "this generation shall not pass" (24:34) has caused some discussion among scholars about the length of time in a "generation." In the OT, Scripture uses this term to indicate time periods of about 40 years (illustrated by the reigns of Saul, David and Solomon), 100 years (see Ge 15:13–14) and 70–80 years (a natural lifetime; Ps 90:10). The NT most often uses this term to refer to a group of people living at one particular time. The understanding in this passage is that the generation alive to witness the rebirth of Israel will still be alive when Jesus returns to establish his kingdom. Jesus also affirms that his words are more certain than the existence of the universe.

24:36 Jesus declared that only the Father knew when Christ would return. Jesus voluntarily limited his supernatural knowledge while incarnated in his human body during his earthly ministry. Yet Jesus, the Holy Spirit and the Father are three persons of the one God. Therefore, after Jesus' ascent to heaven, he possesses the knowledge of the time of his return.

24:37–51 The balance of this prophetic dis-

shall also the coming of the Son of
man be.
38 [a]For as in the days that were before
the flood they were eating and drinking,
marrying and giving in marriage, until
the day that Noe entered into the ark,
39 And knew not until the flood came,
and took them all away; so shall also the
coming of the Son of man be.
40 [a]Then shall two be in the field; the
one shall be taken, and the other left.
41 Two *women shall be* grinding at the
mill; the one shall be taken, and the other
left.
42 ¶ [a]Watch therefore: for ye know
not what hour your Lord doth come.
N 43 [a]But know this, that if the goodman
of the house had known in what watch
the thief would come, he would have
watched, and would not have suffered his
house to be broken up.
44 [a]Therefore be ye also ready: for in
such an hour as ye think not the Son of
man cometh.

Faithful and unfaithful servants

45 [a]Who then is a faithful and wise
servant, whom his lord hath made ruler
over his household, to give them meat in
due season?
46 [a]Blessed *is* that servant, whom his
lord when he cometh shall find so doing.
47 Verily I say unto you, That [a]he shall
make him ruler over all his goods.

N *Mt 23:37–38 ◀ ▶ Mt 24:50–51*

38 [a]Gen. 6:3-5; Luke 17:26; 1 Pet. 3:20
40 [a]Luke 17:34
42 [a]ch. 25:13; Luke 21:36
43 [a]Luke 12:39; 1 Thes. 5:2; Rev. 3:3
44 [a]1 Thes. 5:6
45 [a]Luke 12:42; Acts 20:28
46 [a]Rev. 16:15
47 [a]ch. 25:21,23; Luke 22:29
51 [a]ch. 8:12 & 25:30 ǀOr, *cut him off*
25:1 [a]Eph. 5:29, 30; Rev. 19:7 & 21:2,9
2 [a]ch. 13:47 & 22:10
5 [a]1 Thes. 5:6
6 [a]ch. 24:31; 1 Thes. 4:16

48 But and if that evil servant shall say S
in his heart, My lord delayeth his coming;
49 And shall begin to smite *his* fellowservants, and to eat and drink with the
drunken;
50 The lord of that servant shall come P
in a day when he looketh not for *him*, H
and in an hour that he is not aware of, N
51 And shall ǀcut him asunder, and
appoint *him* his portion with the hypocrites: [a]there shall be weeping and gnashing of teeth.

The parable of the ten virgins

25 THEN SHALL the kingdom of C
heaven be likened unto ten vir- H
gins, which took their lamps, and went O
forth to meet [a]the bridegroom.
2 [a]And five of them were wise, and C
five *were* foolish.
3 They that *were* foolish took their G
lamps, and took no oil with them:
4 But the wise took oil in their vessels
with their lamps.
5 While the bridegroom tarried, [a]they
all slumbered and slept.
6 And at midnight [a]there was a cry

S *Mt 24:13 ◀ ▶ Mt 25:24–30*
P *Mt 13:47–50 ◀ ▶ Lk 12:45–47*
H *Mt 24:21 ◀ ▶ Mt 25:30–46*
N *Mt 24:43–44 ◀ ▶ Mt 25:10–11*
C *Mt 24:36–51 ◀ ▶ Mt 25:19*
H *Mt 22:14 ◀ ▶ Lk 14:16*
O *Mt 22:11–14 ◀ ▶ Mk 8:38*
C *Mt 23:33 ◀ ▶ Mk 2:17*
G *Mt 22:11–14 ◀ ▶ Mk 7:6–7*

---

course describes the conditions in the last days and Jesus' instructions to his followers. Jesus warns that, just as in Noah's day, widespread violence, corruption and evil will characterize life on earth. As humanity rejected God's prophetic warnings from Noah, our generation has dismissed the warnings associated with Christ's return. Jesus warned that his judgment would separate the wicked from the repentant, without warning, like the unexpected appearance of a thief. Jesus challenged his followers to stay alert and faithful to the Master. Those who forget the Lord's coming will be cast into hell.

25:1–13 This parable prophetically urges Israel and the tribulation saints to remain vigilant and watchful for Christ's return during the coming tribulation. Jesus details an ancient Jewish wedding to portray the varied spiritual condition of the Jewish tribulation saints prior to Christ's return at Armageddon.

Scholars differ on the interpretation of various pieces in this parable. Note that all ten virgins initially had oil. The mistake of the five foolish virgins was neglecting to take an extra supply of oil. While some contend that the "oil" in this story is symbolic of the Holy Spirit, this is highly unlikely because the Holy Spirit's presence can neither be bought, sold nor shared. Other scholars have suggested that the ten virgins represent the church. This interpretation seems inconsistent with the parable because the virgins mentioned in the text were friends of the bride who were supposed to join the procession heading for the wedding supper. Also, just as the bridegroom had only one bride, so Christ has only one bride—his church. Note that the ten virgins are waiting for the call to go to the home of the bridegroom (heaven) to attend the wedding supper (see Rev 19:7–9). The message in this parable clearly is to be watchful and in constant readiness because no one knows when Christ will return.

Signs of the Second Coming

DURING THE EARLY centuries following the ascension of Jesus into heaven, Christians often greeted one another by saying, "Maranatha." This Aramaic expression means "Come, O Lord" and echoed the believers' cry for the imminent return of Christ (see 1Co 16:22). Warning signs will herald his return (see Lk 21:28). The fulfillment of several of these signs in our generation points to the imminent return of Jesus Christ.

False Christs and Rumors of War

The first prophetic sign that will signal Christ's second coming involves the rise of false Christs and false prophets in the last days (see Mt 24:4–5). Though there are no historical references to any false messiahs prior to the resurrection of Jesus, many false messiahs have appeared throughout the centuries following his ascension. In our generation alone these imposters have included Charles Manson, Rev. Sun Myung Moon, Jim Jones and David Koresh. This rising number of false messiahs will pave the way for the worship of the antichrist during the last days.

The Lord also warned that prior to his second coming we would "hear of wars and rumours of wars" (24:6). Since the end of World War II the number of wars in our world has increased dramatically. New nations have demanded independence as old empires disintegrate. Though there have been numerous peace treaties, the world has not known a single day without some nation at war with another somewhere on earth. Today's standing armies of the world comprise millions of soldiers. The continuing arms buildup among superpowers and lesser third world nations is even now setting the stage for the final Battle of Armageddon, a war that will drench the world in blood.

Famine and Pestilence

Another prophetic warning sign of Christ's imminent return is the increase of devastating, widespread famine (see 24:7). In our generation we are faced with severe drought and famine conditions throughout portions of Africa, India and Southeast Asia. Many nations in these areas are already unable to properly feed their populations. Because of severe drought, millions of acres of fertile, agricultural land have been transformed into arid wasteland. Large quantities of precious topsoil are lost each year. Tropical rain forests, which contribute significant amounts of our planet's oxygen and water supply, are shrinking every year. Compounding these problems are the staggering statistics concerning the growth rate of the world's population. Every day more than 225,000 people are added to the earth's population with the largest percentage born in third world nations where food supplies are already compromised.

Plagues and epidemics typically follow famine and war, compounding their terrors. Jesus warned that worldwide pestilence would signify his imminent return (see 24:7). During the coming holocaust of the tribulation, these epidemics will decimate one-fourth of the world's population (see Rev 6:8).

In our generation, health officials have discovered more than 20 new infectious diseases for which there are no known cures or treatments. Growing urbanization, poor sanitation and the increase in air travel have all helped to spread these deadly diseases throughout our world. Though we try to protect ourselves with antibiotic drugs, health officials now find that we may have compounded the problem. Increasing numbers of diseases are showing resistance to traditional antibiotics. Many diseases of the past—bubonic plague, smallpox, diphtheria, yellow fever, malaria—are reemerging as strains that are resistant to standard treatments and are becoming deadly threats to human populations. Sexually transmitted diseases are also on the rise. Of these, the AIDS virus is the most dangerous plague in history.

Toxic substances are also proliferating in our environment. Untested chemicals created in laboratories every year are casually introduced into the earth's biosphere without adequate tests of their effects on humans, animals or plant life. Scientists readily recognize that a large percentage of cancers and cancerous tumors are caused by exposure to hazardous substances in our environment. In addition, the pestilence of pesticides has created an emergence of a new strain of germs highly resistant to chemical eradication.

Earthquakes

Both Jesus Christ and the OT prophets prophesied that the last days would see an increase in the number and severity of earthquakes (see Isa 29:6; Mt 24:7; Rev 11:13). Jesus also indicated that earthquakes would occur in strange places (see Mt 24:7). In our century, we have experienced an unparalleled increase in the frequency and intensity of "killer" earthquakes that register 6.5 or higher on the Richter scale. The reported number of severe earthquakes between 1900–1970 totaled only 37. The decade immediately following reported 56 occurrences, and the 1980s witnessed 74 major earthquakes. Yet the first half of the 1990s has posted a record of 125 killer earthquakes worldwide, a significant jump in the geological annals. While better reporting has influenced the total count of earthquakes per year, earthquakes of 6.5 or more on the Richter scale have always been so destructive that historical records note these killer quakes.

Increased Hatred and Alienation

While nations have always found reasons to hate one another, Jesus warned of a worldwide hatred of the Jews that would signal his impending return (see 24:9). The genocide of the Jews during Hitler's reign, the vile anti-Semitic propaganda and persecution throughout Russia and modern Arab nations, and the terrorist attacks against Jewish synagogues and cemeteries worldwide points to the fulfillment of this sign.

Note that Jesus also indicated that this hatred would extend from between nations to between families and individuals. Jesus warned that a denial of natural love would be a condition of the end times prior to his return (see 24:10–12). Familial alienation and breakdown are a common tragedy in our society. Economic and social forces bear down on families, wreaking havoc on the "normal" nuclear family unit of two parents and their own children. Such a nuclear family is now a minority in North America. Transitory relationships are the norm for many. Divorces exceed marriages in numerous communities. Many western hospitals even register more abortions than live births, exceeding one million abortions every year in North America alone.

Worldwide Evangelism

We have never seen such an astonishing move of God as we are witnessing today. Millions in Indonesia, Africa and Southeast Asia have become followers of Jesus Christ. This growth of evangelism throughout the globe during our generation is another sign of the near return of Christ (see 24:14). Statisticians in Lausanne, Switzerland, are recording an explosive growth in the number of Christians worldwide, noting that while only 1 person in 32 claimed an affiliation with Christianity in the 1940s, statistics indicate that 1 person in 10 in 1997 claimed to be a Christian.

Church membership throughout the world is on the rise, too, growing at twice the rate of the overall population growth. The evangelical church worldwide has grown from only 41 million in 1934 to 540 million today, with the greatest increase seen in the underground church in communist China. Christian radio broadcasts now reach almost half of the world's major languages. Every year more than 300 million Bibles, New Testaments and Scripture portions are distributed throughout the world. The gospel is definitely being preached to all nations. As expectant believers we must be aware of these signs, for when these signs are fulfilled "then shall the end come" (24:14).

Stay Alert

Other prophecies in the Bible herald Christ's return and the beginning of the last days. Israel's rebirth as a nation in 1948 fulfilled Isaiah's words of a nation being born in one day (see Isa 66:8). Joel refers to signs and "wonders in the heavens" (Joel 2:30; see Rev 6:12–17). Even Jesus reminded his disciples to be watchful and alert, to see the signs and recognize their fulfillment, just as they knew that when a fig tree's "branch is yet tender, and putteth forth leaves" (Mt 24:32) summer was at hand. As believers we should also be alert, knowing his coming could be at any time. In light of the fulfillment of prophecies in our generation we need to heed Jesus' words to "look up, and lift up your heads; for your redemption draweth nigh" (Lk 21:28). Although we may not know "the day nor the hour wherein the Son of man cometh" (Mt 25:13), the fulfillment of these specific prophecies in our lifetime indicates that Jesus Christ's second coming may occur at any time. "Even so, come, Lord Jesus" (Rev 22:20). Maranatha!

made, Behold, the bridegroom cometh; go ye out to meet him.

7 Then all those virgins arose, and [a]trimmed their lamps.

8 And the foolish said unto the wise, Give us of your oil; for our lamps are [l]gone out.

9 But the wise answered, saying, *Not so;* lest there be not enough for us and you: but go ye rather to them that sell, and buy for yourselves.

N 10 And while they went to buy, the bridegroom came; and they that were ready went in with him to the marriage: and [a]the door was shut.

11 Afterward came also the other virgins, saying, [a]Lord, Lord, open to us.

12 But he answered and said, Verily I say unto you, [a]I know you not.

13 [a]Watch therefore, for ye know neither the day nor the hour wherein the Son of man cometh.

The parable of the talents

14 ¶ [a]For *the kingdom of heaven is* [b]as a man travelling into a far country, *who* called his own servants, and delivered unto them his goods.

15 And unto one he gave five [l]talents, to another two, and to another one; [a]to every man according to his several ability; and straightway took his journey.

16 Then he that had received the five talents went and traded with the same, and made *them* other five talents.

17 And likewise he that *had received* two, he also gained other two.

18 But he that had received one went and digged in the earth, and hid his lord's money.

C J 19 After a long time the lord of those servants cometh, and reckoneth with them.

20 And so he that had received five talents came and brought other five talents, saying, Lord, thou deliveredst unto me five talents: behold, I have gained beside them five talents more.

21 His lord said unto him, Well done, *thou* good and faithful servant: thou hast been faithful over a few things, [a]I will make thee ruler over many things: enter thou into [b]the joy of thy lord. M

22 He also that had received two talents came and said, Lord, thou deliveredst unto me two talents: behold, I have gained two other talents beside them.

23 His lord said unto him, [a]Well done, good and faithful servant; thou hast been faithful over a few things, I will make thee ruler over many things: enter thou into the joy of thy lord. M

24 Then he which had received the one talent came and said, Lord, I knew thee that thou art an hard man, reaping where thou hast not sown, and gathering where thou hast not strawed: S

25 And I was afraid, and went and hid thy talent in the earth: lo, *there* thou hast *that is* thine.

26 His lord answered and said unto him, *Thou* wicked and slothful servant, thou knewest that I reap where I sowed not, and gather where I have not strawed:

27 Thou oughtest therefore to have put my money to the exchangers, and *then* at my coming I should have received mine own with usury.

28 Take therefore the talent from him, and give *it* unto him which hath ten talents.

29 [a]For unto every one that hath shall be given, and he shall have abundance: but from him that hath not shall be taken away even that which he hath.

30 And cast ye the unprofitable servant [a]into outer darkness: there shall be weeping and gnashing of teeth. H

7 [a]Luke 12:35
8 [l]Or, *going out*
10 [a]Luke 13:25
11 [a]ch. 7:21-23
12 [a]Ps. 5:5; Hab. 1:13; John 9:31
13 [a]ch. 24:42,44; Mark 13:33,35; Luke 21:36
14 [a]Luke 19:12 [b]ch. 21:33
15 [a]Rom. 12:6; 1 Cor. 12:7,11,29; Eph. 4:11 [l]The talent was worth more than a thousand dollars
21 [a]ver. 34,46; ch. 24:47; Luke 12:44 & 22:29,30 [b]2 Tim. 2:12; Heb. 12:2; 1 Pet. 1:8
23 [a]ver. 21
29 [a]ch. 13:12; Mark 4:25; Luke 8:18 & 19:26; John 15:2
30 [a]ch. 8:12 & 24:51

N *Mt 24:50–51* ◀▶ *Mk 6:11*
C *Mt 25:1–13* ◀▶ *Mt 26:64*
J *Mt 12:42* ◀▶ *Mt 25:31–46*
M *Mt 22:44* ◀▶ *Mt 25:23*
M *Mt 25:21* ◀▶ *Mt 27:11*
S *Mt 24:48–51* ◀▶ *Mt 25:34–36*
H *Mt 24:50–51* ◀▶ *Mt 26:24*

25:14–30 This parable stresses the need for good stewardship of the resources that God places in our hands during our earthly life. Just as the master held each servant responsible for what he had done with the talents entrusted to him, in the final judgment our Lord will also reward his servants for their faithfulness or lack of service. Our spiritual rewards and responsibilities in the millennial kingdom will reflect our use of the talents Christ entrusted to us on this earth. Those who are faithful will be given cities to govern under the leadership of Jesus the Messiah during his millennial kingdom.

The judgment

D 31 ¶ [a]When the Son of man shall come
J in his glory, and all the holy angels with
J him, then shall he sit upon the throne of
his glory:
32 And [a]before him shall be gathered
all nations: and [b]he shall separate them
one from another, as a shepherd divideth
his sheep from the goats:
33 And he shall set the sheep on his
right hand, but the goats on the left.
S 34 Then shall the King say unto them
on his right hand, Come, ye blessed of
my Father, [a]inherit the kingdom [b]pre-
pared for you from the foundation of the
world:
35 [a]For I was an hungered, and ye
gave me meat: I was thirsty, and ye gave
me drink: [b]I was a stranger, and ye took
me in:
36 [a]Naked, and ye clothed me: I was
sick, and ye visited me: [b]I was in prison,
and ye came unto me.
37 Then shall the righteous answer
him, saying, Lord, when saw we thee an
hungered, and fed *thee?* or thirsty, and
gave *thee* drink?
38 When saw we thee a stranger, and
took *thee* in? or naked, and clothed *thee?*
39 Or when saw we thee sick, or in
prison, and came unto thee?
40 And the King shall answer and say
unto them, Verily I say unto you, [a]Inas-
much as ye have done *it* unto one of the
least of these my brethren, ye have done
it unto me.
S 41 Then shall he say also unto them
on the left hand, [a]Depart from me, ye
cursed, [b]into everlasting fire, prepared
for [c]the devil and his angels:
42 For I was an hungered, and ye gave
me no meat; I was thirsty, and ye gave
me no drink:
43 I was a stranger, and ye took me
not in: naked, and ye clothed me not:
sick, and in prison, and ye visited me not.
44 Then shall they also answer him,
saying, Lord, when saw we thee an hungered, or athirst, or a stranger, or naked,
or sick, or in prison, and did not minister
unto thee?
45 Then shall he answer them, saying,
Verily I say unto you, [a]Inasmuch as ye
did *it* not to one of the least of these, ye
did *it* not to me.
46 And [a]these shall go away into everlasting punishment: but the righteous
into life eternal.

The plot to kill Jesus

26 AND IT came to pass, when Jesus
had finished all these sayings, he
said unto his disciples,
2 [a]Ye know that after two days is *the
feast of* the passover, and the Son of man
is betrayed to be crucified.
3 [a]Then assembled together the chief
priests, and the scribes, and the elders of
the people, unto the palace of the high
priest, who was called Caiaphas,
4 And consulted that they might take
Jesus by subtlety, and kill *him.*
5 But they said, Not on the feast *day,*
lest there be an uproar among the people.

Anointing of Jesus at Bethany

6 ¶ [a]Now when Jesus was in [b]Bethany,
in the house of Simon the leper,
7 There came unto him a woman having an alabaster box of very precious ointment, and poured it on his head, as he sat
at meat.

31 [a]Zech. 14:5; ch. 16:27 & 19:28; Mark 8:38; Acts 1:11; 1 Thes. 4:16; 2 Thes. 1:7; Jude 14; Rev. 1:7
32 [a]Rom. 14:10; 2 Cor. 5:10; Rev. 20:12 [b]Ezek. 20:38
34 [a]Rom. 8:17; 1 Pet. 1:4,9 & 3:9; Rev. 21:7 [b]ch. 20:23; Mark 10:40; 1 Cor. 2:9; Heb. 11:16
35 [a]Is. 58:7; Ezek. 18:7; Jas. 1:27 [b]Heb. 13:2; 3 John 5
36 [a]Jas. 2:15,16 [b]2 Tim. 1:16
40 [a]Prov. 14:31 & 19:17; ch. 10:42; Mark 9:41; Heb. 6:10
41 [a]Ps. 6:8; ch. 7:23; Luke 13:27 [b]ch. 13:40,42 [c]2 Pet. 2:4; Jude 6
45 [a]Prov. 14:31 & 17:5; Zech. 2:8; Acts 9:5
46 [a]Dan 12:2; John 5:29; Rom. 2:7
26:2 [a]Mark 14:1; Luke 22:1; John 13:1
3 [a]Ps. 2:2; John 11:47; Acts 4:25
6 [a]Mark 14:3; John 11:1,2 & 12:3 [b]ch. 21:17

D *Zec 14:14–20* ◀ ▶ *Mk 13:26*
J *Mt 25:19* ◀ ▶ *Mk 6:11*
J *Mt 12:41–42* ◀ ▶ *Mk 6:11*
S *Mt 25:24–30* ◀ ▶ *Mt 25:41–43*
S *Mt 25:34–36* ◀ ▶ *Mt 28:20*

25:31–46 Jesus Christ will judge the Gentile nations following the Battle of Armageddon and his return to earth in all his glory (see Rev 19:19–21). (Note that there is no resurrection of bodies connected with this judgment, so this reckoning is not the great white throne judgment.) The nations will be judged and separated into two categories: the sheep and the goats.

The sheep represent those saved Gentiles who cared for God's chosen people during the tribulation. These Gentiles will be invited to enter the kingdom of the Messiah, and with the saved Jews of Israel, will make up the core population of the millennial kingdom.

The goats symbolize the unsaved Gentiles who provided no aid to God's people but rather participated in their persecution. Jesus will separate these "goats" from his faithful "sheep" and condemn the unsaved Gentiles to hell. Note that this prophetic passage reveals that hell was originally "prepared for the devil and his angels" (25:41). Because unrepentant people chose to rebel against God as Satan did, unrepentant people will also suffer the same punishment as Satan.

8 [a]But when his disciples saw *it,* they had indignation, saying, To what purpose *is* this waste?

9 For this ointment might have been sold for much, and given to the poor.

10 When Jesus understood *it,* he said unto them, Why trouble ye the woman? for she hath wrought a good work upon me.

11 [a]For ye have the poor always with you; but [b]me ye have not always.

12 For in that she hath poured this ointment on my body, she did *it* for my burial.

L 13 Verily I say unto you, Wheresoever this gospel shall be preached in the whole world, *there* shall also this, that this woman hath done, be told for a memorial of her.

The bargain of Judas Iscariot

14 ¶ [a]Then one of the twelve, called [b]Judas Iscariot, went unto the chief priests,

15 And said *unto them,* [a]What will ye give me, and I will deliver him unto you? And they covenanted with him for thirty pieces of silver.

16 And from that time he sought opportunity to betray him.

The last supper

17 ¶ [a]Now the first *day* of the *feast of* unleavened bread the disciples came to Jesus, saying unto him, Where wilt thou that we prepare for thee to eat the passover?

18 And he said, Go into the city to such a man, and say unto him, The Master saith, My time is at hand; I will keep the passover at thy house with my disciples.

19 And the disciples did as Jesus had appointed them; and they made ready the passover.

20 [a]Now when the even was come, he sat down with the twelve.

21 And as they did eat, he said, Verily I say unto you, that one of you shall betray me.

22 And they were exceeding sorrowful, and began every one of them to say unto him, Lord, is it I?

23 And he answered and said, [a]He that dippeth *his* hand with me in the dish, the same shall betray me.

24 The Son of man goeth [a]as it is written of him: but [b]woe unto that man by whom the Son of man is betrayed! it had been good for that man if he had not been born. H

25 Then Judas, which betrayed him, answered and said, Master, is it I? He said unto him, Thou hast said.

26 ¶ [a]And as they were eating, [b]Jesus took bread, and [†]blessed *it,* and brake *it,* and gave *it* to the disciples, and said, Take, eat; [c]this is my body. D

27 And he took the cup, and gave thanks, and gave *it* to them, saying, [a]Drink ye all of it;

28 For [a]this is my blood [b]of the new testament, which is shed [c]for many for the remission of sins.

29 But [a]I say unto you, I will not drink henceforth of this fruit of the vine, [b]until that day when I drink it new with you in my Father's kingdom.

30 [a]And when they had sung an [†]hymn, they went out into the mount of Olives.

31 Then saith Jesus unto them, [a]All ye shall [b]be offended because of me this night: for it is written, [c]I will smite the shepherd, and the sheep of the flock shall be scattered abroad.

32 But after I am risen again, [a]I will go before you into Galilee.

33 Peter answered and said unto him, Though all *men* shall be offended because of thee, *yet* will I never be offended.

34 Jesus said unto him, [a]Verily I say unto thee, That this night, before the cock crow, thou shalt deny me thrice.

35 Peter said unto him, Though I

8 [a]John 12:4
11 [a]Deut. 15:11; John 12:8 [b]See ch. 18:20 & 28:20; John 13:33 & 14:19 & 16:5,28 & 17:11
14 [a]Mark 14:10; Luke 22:3; John 13:2,30 [b]ch. 10:4
15 [a]Zech. 11:12; ch. 27:3
17 [a]Ex. 12:6,18; Mark 14:12; Luke 22:7
20 [a]Mark 14:17-21; Luke 22:14; John 13:21
23 [a]Ps. 41:9; Luke 22:21; John 13:18
24 [a]Ps. 22; Is. 53; Dan. 9:26; Mark 9:12; Luke 24:25, 26,46; Acts 17:2,3 & 26:22,23; 1 Cor. 15:3 [b]John 17:12
26 [a]Mark 14:22; Luke 22:19 [b]1 Cor. 11:23 [c]1 Cor. 10:16 [†]Many Greek copies have, *gave thanks;* see Mark 6:41
27 [a]Mark 14:23
28 [a]See Ex. 24:8; Lev. 17:11 [b]Jer. 31:31 [c]ch. 20:28; Rom. 5:15; Heb. 9:22
29 [a]Mark 14:25; Luke 22:18 [b]Acts 10:41
30 [a]Mark 14:26 [†]Or, *psalm*
31 [a]Mark 14:27; John 16:32 [b]ch. 11:6 [c]Zech. 13:7
32 [a]ch. 28:7,10; Mark 14:28 & 16:7
34 [a]Mark 14:30; Luke 22:34; John 13:38

L *Mt 10:17–23* ◀
H *Mt 25:30–46* ◀ ▶ *Mk 6:11*
D *Mt 20:28* ◀ ▶ *Mk 10:45*

26:29 Jesus prophesied to his disciples that he would not drink wine again until they were all reunited in heaven (see Rev 19:7–9). This proves that our resurrected bodies will be able to eat and drink with our Lord to celebrate our union with him forever.

26:32 Jesus prophesied that he would meet his disciples in Galilee after his resurrection from the grave. This prophecy was fulfilled in Mt 28:16–20.

should die with thee, yet will I not deny thee. Likewise also said all the disciples.

Jesus' agony in Gethsemane

36 ¶ [a]Then cometh Jesus with them unto a place called Gethsemane, and saith unto the disciples, Sit ye here, while I go and pray yonder.

37 And he took with him Peter and [a]the two sons of Zebedee, and began to be sorrowful and very heavy.

38 Then saith he unto them, [a]My soul is exceeding sorrowful, even unto death: tarry ye here, and watch with me.

39 And he went a little farther, and fell on his face, and [a]prayed, saying, [b]O my Father, if it be possible, [c]let this cup pass from me: nevertheless [d]not as I will, but as thou *wilt.*

40 And he cometh unto the disciples, and findeth them asleep, and saith unto Peter, What, could ye not watch with me one hour?

41 [a]Watch and pray, that ye enter not into temptation: the spirit indeed *is* willing, but the flesh *is* weak.

42 He went away again the second time, and prayed, saying, O my Father, if this cup may not pass away from me, except I drink it, thy will be done.

43 And he came and found them asleep again: for their eyes were heavy.

44 And he left them, and went away again, and prayed the third time, saying the same words.

45 Then cometh he to his disciples, and saith unto them, Sleep on now, and take *your* rest: behold, the hour is at hand, and the Son of man is betrayed into the hands of sinners.

46 Rise, let us be going: behold, he is at hand that doth betray me.

Jesus' betrayal and arrest

47 ¶ And [a]while he yet spake, lo, Judas, one of the twelve, came, and with him a great multitude with swords and staves, from the chief priests and elders of the people.

48 Now he that betrayed him gave them a sign, saying, Whomsoever I shall kiss, that same is he: hold him fast.

49 And forthwith he came to Jesus, and said, Hail, master; [a]and kissed him.

36 [a] Mark 14:32-35; Luke 22:39; John 18:1

37 [a] ch. 4:21

38 [a] John 12:27

39 [a] Mark 14:36; Luke 22:42; Heb. 5:7 [b] John 12:27 [c] ch. 20:22 [d] John 5:30 & 6:38; Phil. 2:8

41 [a] Mark 13:33 & 14:38; Luke 22:40, 46; Eph. 6:18

47 [a] Mark 14:43; Luke 22:47; John 18:3; Acts 1:16

49 [a] 2 Sam. 20:9

50 [a] Ps. 41:9 & 55:13

51 [a] John 18:10

52 [a] Gen. 9:6; Rev. 13:10

53 [a] 2 Ki. 6:17; Dan. 7:10

54 [a] ver. 24; Is. 53:7; Luke 24:25, 44,46

56 [a] Lam. 4:20 [b] See John 18:15

57 [a] Mark 14:53; Luke 22:54; John 18:12,13,24

60 [a] Ps. 27:12 & 35:11; Mark 14:55; Acts 6:13 [b] Deut. 19:15

61 [a] ch. 27:40; John 2:19

62 [a] Mark 14:60

63 [a] Is. 53:7; ch. 27:12 [b] Lev. 5:1; 1 Sam. 14:24,26

50 And Jesus said unto him, [a]Friend, wherefore art thou come? Then came they, and laid hands on Jesus, and took him.

51 And, behold, [a]one of them which were with Jesus stretched out *his* hand, and drew his sword, and struck a servant of the high priest's, and smote off his ear.

52 Then said Jesus unto him, Put up again thy sword into his place: [a]for all they that take the sword shall perish with the sword.

53 Thinkest thou that I cannot now pray to my Father, and he shall presently give me [a]more than twelve legions of angels?

54 But how then shall the scriptures be fulfilled, [a]that thus it must be?

55 In that same hour said Jesus to the multitudes, Are ye come out as against a thief with swords and staves for to take me? I sat daily with you teaching in the temple, and ye laid no hold on me.

56 But all this was done, that the [a]scriptures of the prophets might be fulfilled. Then [b]all the disciples forsook him, and fled.

Jesus before Caiaphas

57 ¶ [a]And they that had laid hold on Jesus led *him* away to Caiaphas the high priest, where the scribes and the elders were assembled.

58 But Peter followed him afar off unto the high priest's palace, and went in, and sat with the servants, to see the end.

59 Now the chief priests, and elders, and all the council, sought false witness against Jesus, to put him to death;

60 But found none: yea, though [a]many false witnesses came, *yet* found they none. At the last came [b]two false witnesses,

61 And said, This *fellow* said, [a]I am able to destroy the temple of God, and to build it in three days.

62 [a]And the high priest arose, and said unto him, Answerest thou nothing? *what is it which* these witness against thee?

63 But [a]Jesus held his peace. And the high priest answered and said unto him, [b]I adjure thee by the living God, that

thou tell us whether thou be the Christ, the Son of God.

C 64 Jesus saith unto him, Thou hast said: nevertheless I say unto you, [a]Hereafter shall ye see the Son of man [b]sitting on the right hand of power, and coming in the clouds of heaven.

65 [a]Then the high priest rent his clothes, saying, He hath spoken blasphemy; what further need have we of witnesses? behold, now ye have heard his blasphemy.

66 What think ye? They answered and said, [a]He is guilty of death.

67 [a]Then did they spit in his face, and buffeted him; and [b]others smote *him* with [1]the palms of their hands,

68 Saying, [a]Prophesy unto us, thou Christ, Who is he that smote thee?

Peter's denial of Jesus

69 ¶ [a]Now Peter sat without in the palace: and a damsel came unto him, saying, Thou also wast with Jesus of Galilee.

70 But he denied before *them* all, saying, I know not what thou sayest.

71 And when he was gone out into the porch, another *maid* saw him, and said unto them that were there, This *fellow* was also with Jesus of Nazareth.

72 And again he denied with an oath, I do not know the man.

73 And after a while came unto *him* they that stood by, and said to Peter, Surely thou also art *one* of them; for thy [a]speech betrayeth thee.

74 Then [a]began he to curse and to swear, *saying,* I know not the man. And immediately the cock crew.

R 75 And Peter remembered the word of Jesus, which said unto him, [a]Before the cock crow, thou shalt deny me thrice. And he went out, and wept bitterly.

C *Mt 25:19* ◀▶ *Mk 4:29*
R *Mt 21:28–32* ◀▶ *Mk 1:15*

64 [a]Dan. 7:13; ch. 16:27 & 24:30 & 25:31; Luke 21:27; John 1:51; Rom. 14:10; 1 Thes. 4:16; Rev. 1:7 [b]Ps. 110:1; Acts 7:55
65 [a]2 Ki. 18:37
66 [a]Lev. 24:16; John 19:7
67 [a]Is. 50:6 & 53:3; ch. 27:30 [b]Luke 22:63 [1]Or, *rods*
68 [a]Mark 14:65; Luke 22:64
69 [a]Mark 14:66; Luke 22:55; John 18:16,17,25
73 [a]Luke 22:59
74 [a]Mark 14:71
75 [a]ver. 34; Luke 22:61; John 13:38
27:1 [a]Ps. 2:2; Mark 15:1; Luke 22:66 & 23:1; John 18:28
2 [a]ch. 20:19; Acts 3:13
3 [a]ch. 26:14
5 [a]2 Sam. 17:23; Acts 1:18
8 [a]Acts 1:19
9 [a]Zech. 11:12 [1]Or, *whom they bought of the children of Israel*
11 [a]Mark 15:2; Luke 23:3; John 18:33 [b]John 18:37; 1 Tim. 6:13
12 [a]ch. 26:63; John 19:9

The death of Judas Iscariot

27 WHEN THE morning was come, [a]all the chief priests and elders of the people took counsel against Jesus to put him to death:

2 And when they had bound him, they led *him* away, and [a]delivered him to Pontius Pilate the governor.

3 ¶ [a]Then Judas, which had betrayed him, when he saw that he was condemned, repented himself, and brought again the thirty pieces of silver to the chief priests and elders,

4 Saying, I have sinned in that I have betrayed the innocent blood. And they said, What *is that* to us? see thou *to that.*

5 And he cast down the pieces of silver in the temple, [a]and departed, and went and hanged himself.

6 And the chief priests took the silver pieces, and said, It is not lawful for to put them into the treasury, because it is the price of blood.

7 And they took counsel, and bought with them the potter's field, to bury strangers in.

8 Wherefore that field was called, [a]The field of blood, unto this day.

9 Then was fulfilled that which was spoken by Jeremy the prophet, saying, [a]And they took the thirty pieces of silver, the price of him that was valued, [1]whom they of the children of Israel did value; B

10 And gave them for the potter's field, as the Lord appointed me.

Jesus before Pontius Pilate

11 And Jesus stood before the governor: [a]and the governor asked him, saying, Art thou the King of the Jews? And Jesus said unto him, [b]Thou sayest. I M

12 And when he was accused of the chief priests and elders, [a]he answered nothing.

B *Mt 12:40–41* ◀▶ *Mt 27:51*
I *Mt 21:5* ◀▶ *Mt 27:29*
M *Mt 25:23* ◀▶ *Mt 27:29*

26:64 Jesus' answer to the high priest was a prophecy about his ultimate glorious return as "the Son of man sitting on the right hand of power." This prophecy will be fulfilled when Jesus returns at the Battle of Armageddon to save his people.

27:11, 29, 37, 42 When Jesus was taken before the Roman governor Pontius Pilate, Pilate asked Jesus about his identity as "the King of the Jews" (27:11). Jesus not only affirmed his claim to that title, but also by his affirmation foreshadowed his return to rule from the throne of David in Jerusalem following the Battle of Armageddon. Though the Roman soldiers, the unrepentant thief and the people standing near the cross mocked his royal position, Jesus will one day be acclaimed the true King of the Jews.

13 Then said Pilate unto him, [a]Hearest thou not how many things they witness against thee?

14 And he answered him to never a word; insomuch that the governor marvelled greatly.

15 [a]Now at *that* feast the governor was wont to release unto the people a prisoner, whom they would.

16 And they had then a notable prisoner, called Barabbas.

17 Therefore when they were gathered together, Pilate said unto them, Whom will ye that I release unto you? Barabbas, or Jesus which is called Christ?

18 For he knew that for envy they had delivered him.

19 ¶ When he was set down on the judgment seat, his wife sent unto him, saying, Have thou nothing to do with that just man: for I have suffered many things this day in a dream because of him.

20 [a]But the chief priests and elders persuaded the multitude that they should ask Barabbas, and destroy Jesus.

21 The governor answered and said unto them, Whether of the twain will ye that I release unto you? They said, Barabbas.

22 Pilate saith unto them, What shall I do then with Jesus which is called Christ? *They* all say unto him, Let him be crucified.

23 And the governor said, Why, what evil hath he done? But they cried out the more, saying, Let him be crucified.

24 ¶ When Pilate saw that he could prevail nothing, but *that* rather a tumult was made, he [a]took water, and washed *his* hands before the multitude, saying, I am innocent of the blood of this just person: see ye *to it.*

25 Then answered all the people, and said, [a]His blood *be* on us, and on our children.

26 ¶ Then released he Barabbas unto them: and when [a]he had scourged Jesus, he delivered *him* to be crucified.

Jesus crowned with thorns

27 [a]Then the soldiers of the governor took Jesus into the [1]common hall, and gathered unto him the whole band *of soldiers.*

28 And they stripped him, and [a]put on him a scarlet robe.

13 [a]ch. 26:62; John 19:10
15 [a]Mark 15:6; Luke 23:17; John 18:39
20 [a]Mark 15:11; Luke 23:18; John 18:40; Acts 3:14
24 [a]Deut. 21:6
25 [a]Deut. 19:10; Josh. 2:19; 2 Sam. 1:16; 1 Ki. 2:32; Acts 5:28
26 [a]Is. 53:5; Mark 15:15; Luke 23:16, 24,25; John 19:1,16
27 [a]Mark 15:16; John 19:2 [1]Or, *governor's house*
28 [a]Luke 23:11
29 [a]Ps. 69:19; Is. 53:3
30 [a]Is. 50:6; ch. 26:67
31 [a]Is. 53:7
32 [a]Num. 15:35; 1 Ki. 21:13; Acts 7:58; Heb. 13:12 [b]Mark 15:21; Luke 23:26
33 [a]Mark 15:22; Luke 23:33; John 19:17
34 [a]See ver. 48; Ps. 69:21
35 [a]Mark 15:24; Luke 23:34; John 19:24 [b]Ps. 22:18
36 [a]ver. 54
37 [a]Mark 15:26; Luke 23:38; John 19:19
38 [a]Is. 53:12; Mark 15:27; Luke 23:32,33; John 19:18
39 [a]Ps. 22:7 & 109:25; Mark 15:29; Luke 23:35
40 [a]ch. 26:61; John 2:19 [b]ch. 26:63
43 [a]Ps. 22:8

29 ¶ [a]And when they had plaited a crown of thorns, they put *it* upon his head, and a reed in his right hand: and they bowed the knee before him, and mocked him, saying, Hail, King of the Jews! I M

30 And [a]they spit upon him, and took the reed, and smote him on the head.

31 And after that they had mocked him, they took the robe off from him, and put his own raiment on him, [a]and led him away to crucify *him.*

Jesus crucified

32 [a]And as they came out, [b]they found a man of Cyrene, Simon by name: him they compelled to bear his cross.

33 [a]And when they were come unto a place called Golgotha, that is to say, a place of a skull,

34 ¶ [a]They gave him vinegar to drink mingled with gall: and when he had tasted *thereof,* he would not drink.

35 [a]And they crucified him, and parted his garments, casting lots: that it might be fulfilled which was spoken by the prophet, [b]They parted my garments among them, and upon my vesture did they cast lots.

36 [a]And sitting down they watched him there;

37 And [a]set up over his head his accusation written, THIS IS JESUS THE KING OF THE JEWS. I M

38 [a]Then were there two thieves crucified with him, one on the right hand, and another on the left.

39 ¶ And [a]they that passed by reviled him, wagging their heads,

40 And saying, [a]Thou that destroyest the temple, and buildest *it* in three days, save thyself. [b]If thou be the Son of God, come down from the cross.

41 Likewise also the chief priests mocking *him,* with the scribes and elders, said,

42 He saved others; himself he cannot save. If he be the King of Israel, let him now come down from the cross, and we will believe him. I M

43 [a]He trusted in God; let him deliver

I *Mt 27:11* ◄► *Mt 27:37*
M *Mt 27:11* ◄► *Mt 27:37*
I *Mt 27:29* ◄► *Mt 27:42*
M *Mt 27:29* ◄► *Mt 27:42*
I *Mt 27:37* ◄► *Mk 11:10*
M *Mt 27:37* ◄► *Mk 4:30–32*

him now, if he will have him: for he said, I am the Son of God.

44 [a]The thieves also, which were crucified with him, cast the same in his teeth.

The death of Jesus

45 [a]Now from the sixth hour there was darkness over all the land unto the ninth hour.

46 And about the ninth hour [a]Jesus cried with a loud voice, saying, Eli, Eli, lama sabachthani? that is to say, [b]My God, my God, why hast thou forsaken me?

47 Some of them that stood there, when they heard *that,* said, This *man* calleth for Elias.

48 And straightway one of them ran, and took a sponge, [a]and filled *it* with vinegar, and put *it* on a reed, and gave him to drink.

49 The rest said, Let be, let us see whether Elias will come to save him.

50 ¶ [a]Jesus, when he had cried again with a loud voice, yielded up the ghost.

B 51 And, behold, the [a]veil of the temple was rent in twain from the top to the bottom; and the earth did quake, and the rocks rent;

52 And the graves were opened; and many bodies of the saints which slept arose,

53 And came out of the graves after his resurrection, and went into the holy city, and appeared unto many.

54 [a]Now when the centurion, and they that were with him, watching Jesus, saw the earthquake, and those things that were done, they feared greatly, saying, Truly this was the Son of God.

55 And many women were there beholding afar off, [a]which followed Jesus from Galilee, ministering unto him:

56 [a]Among which was Mary Magdalene, and Mary the mother of James and Joses, and the mother of Zebedee's children.

B *Mt 27:9–10* ◄ ► *Mk 1:7*

44 [a]Mark 15:32; Luke 23:39
45 [a]Amos 8:9; Mark 15:33; Luke 23:44
46 [a]Heb. 5:7 [b]Ps. 22:1
48 [a]Ps. 69:21; Mark 15:36; Luke 23:36; John 19:29
50 [a]Mark 15:37; Luke 23:46
51 [a]Ex. 26:31; 2 Chr. 3:14; Mark 15:38; Luke 23:45
54 [a]ver. 36; Mark 15:39; Luke 23:47
55 [a]Luke 8:2,3
56 [a]Mark 15:40
57 [a]Mark 15:42; Luke 23:50; John 19:38
60 [a]Is. 53:9
63 [a]ch. 16:21 & 17:23 & 20:19 & 26:61; Mark 8:31 & 10:34; Luke 9:22 & 18:33 & 24:6,7; John 2:19
66 [a]Dan. 6:17
28:1 [a]Mark 16:1; Luke 24:1; John 20:1 [b]ch. 27:56
2 [a]See Mark 16:5; Luke 24:4; John 20:12 [1]Or, *had been*

Jesus laid in the sepulchre

57 [a]When the even was come, there came a rich man of Arimathaea, named Joseph, who also himself was Jesus' disciple:

58 He went to Pilate, and begged the body of Jesus. Then Pilate commanded the body to be delivered.

59 And when Joseph had taken the body, he wrapped it in a clean linen cloth,

60 And [a]laid it in his own new tomb, which he had hewn out in the rock: and he rolled a great stone to the door of the sepulchre, and departed.

61 And there was Mary Magdalene, and the other Mary, sitting over against the sepulchre.

The sepulchre guarded

62 ¶ Now the next day, that followed the day of the preparation, the chief priests and Pharisees came together unto Pilate,

63 Saying, Sir, we remember that that deceiver said, while he was yet alive, [a]After three days I will rise again.

64 Command therefore that the sepulchre be made sure until the third day, lest his disciples come by night, and steal him away, and say unto the people, He is risen from the dead: so the last error shall be worse than the first.

65 Pilate said unto them, Ye have a watch: go your way, make *it* as sure as ye can.

66 So they went, and made the sepulchre sure, [a]sealing the stone, and setting a watch.

The resurrection of Jesus

28 IN THE [a]end of the sabbath, as it began to dawn toward the first *day* of the week, came Mary Magdalene [b]and the other Mary to see the sepulchre.

2 And, behold, there [1]was a great earthquake: for [a]the angel of the Lord descended from heaven, and came and

---

27:52–53 Though Matthew is the only author to record this unusual resurrection, this passage indicates that these resurrected saints went into Jerusalem and appeared to many people. The exact reason for this supernatural event is uncertain, but these resurrections proved Christ's power to defeat death and raise from the dead all those who trust in him. It is even possible that this supernatural event helped spread the truth of Christ's resurrection throughout the Roman empire. See the article on "The Resurrection of the Body" on p. 1206.

rolled back the stone from the door, and sat upon it.

3 [a]His countenance was like lightning, and his raiment white as snow:

4 And for fear of him the keepers did shake, and became as dead *men.*

5 And the angel answered and said unto the women, Fear not ye: for I know that ye seek Jesus, which was crucified.

6 He is not here: for he is risen, [a]as he said. Come, see the place where the Lord lay.

7 And go quickly, and tell his disciples that he is risen from the dead; and, behold, [a]he goeth before you into Galilee; there shall ye see him: lo, I have told you.

8 And they departed quickly from the sepulchre with fear and great joy; and did run to bring his disciples word.

9 ¶ And as they went to tell his disciples, behold, [a]Jesus met them, saying, All hail. And they came and held him by the feet, and worshipped him.

10 Then said Jesus unto them, Be not afraid: go tell [a]my brethren that they go into Galilee, and there shall they see me.

The bribing of the soldiers

11 ¶ Now when they were going, behold, some of the watch came into the city, and showed unto the chief priests all the things that were done.

12 And when they were assembled with the elders, and had taken counsel, they gave large money unto the soldiers,

13 Saying, Say ye, His disciples came by night, and stole him *away* while we slept.

14 And if this come to the governor's ears, we will persuade him, and secure you.

15 So they took the money, and did as they were taught: and this saying is commonly reported among the Jews until this day.

The Great Commission

16 ¶ Then the eleven disciples went away into Galilee, into a mountain [a]where Jesus had appointed them.

17 And when they saw him, they worshipped him: but some doubted.

18 And Jesus came and spake unto them, saying, [a]All power is given unto me in heaven and in earth. K

19 ¶ [a]Go ye therefore, and [b]teach[/] all nations, baptizing them in the name of the Father, and of the Son, and of the Holy Ghost: D

20 [a]Teaching them to observe all things whatsoever I have commanded you: and, lo, I am with you always, *even* unto the end of the world. Amen. S L

K *Mt 24:35* ◀ ▶ *Mk 2:10*
D *Mt 12:31–32* ◀ ▶ *Mk 3:29*
S *Mt 25:41–43* ◀ ▶ *Mk 3:35*
L *Mt 21:22* ◀ ▶ *Mk 9:42*

3 [a]Dan. 10:6
6 [a]ch. 12:40 & 16:21 & 17:23 & 20:19
7 [a]ch. 26:32; Mark 16:7
9 [a]See Mark 16:9; John 20:14
10 [a]See John 20:17; Rom. 8:29; Heb. 2:11
16 [a]ver. 7; ch. 26:32
18 [a]Dan. 7:13,14; ch. 11:27 & 16:28; Luke 1:32 & 10:22; John 3:35 & 5:22 & 13:3 & 17:2; Acts 2:36; Rom. 14:9; 1 Cor. 15:27; Eph. 1:10,21; Phil. 2:9, 10; Heb. 1:2 & 2:8; 1 Pet. 3:22; Rev. 17:14
19 [a]Mark 16:15 [b]Is. 52:10; Luke 24:47; Acts 2:38, 39; Rom. 10:18; Col. 1:23 [/]Or, *make disciples,* or, *Christians of all nations*
20 [a]Acts 2:42

Mark

Author: Mark

Theme: Jesus is God's Son, the Messiah

Date of Writing: c. A.D. 50–70

Outline of Mark

I. Background and Preparation (1:1–13)
II. Public Ministry of Healing and Teaching (1:14—8:26)
III. Jesus and His Disciples (8:27—10:45)
IV. Jericho and Jerusalem (10:46—13:37)
V. The Passion and Death of Jesus (14:1—15:47)
VI. The Resurrection of Jesus (16:1–20)

Most scholars agree that the author of this book is Mary's son John Mark (see Ac 12:12), the cousin of Barnabas (see Col 4:10). Mary's home in Jerusalem was a center for the early church. Mark's close association with Jesus, Peter and other disciples in this house church setting would have facilitated his recording the life of Jesus according to his own and Peter's eyewitness accounts. In fact, Peter's sermon in Acts 10:34–43 is remarkably similar to an outline of Mark's Gospel. Mark likely wrote this Gospel record toward the end of Peter's lifetime or just after Peter's death.

Though surrounded by strong witnesses for Christ, Mark let fear govern his missionary zeal when he was a young man. Though he traveled with Barnabas to Antioch (see Ac 4:36–37; 12:25) and started out with Paul on his first missionary journey, Mark deserted them both in the middle of the trip and returned to Jerusalem (see Ac 13:13). Mark's immaturity led Paul to reject him as a traveling companion on his next journey to Asia, but Barnabas traveled with Mark to Cyprus. Apparently this second chance was what Mark needed to solidify his Christian witness because ten years later Mark joined Paul in Rome (see 2Ti 4:11; Col 4:10). Peter also referred to Mark as "my son" (1Pe 5:13), suggesting that in later years Mark may have served as Peter's close associate.

Mark's terse writing style is directed toward a Roman audience. Latin words and phrases occur with frequency, sometimes used to help explain the Greek terms. On the other hand, Jewish laws and customs are rarely emphasized in Mark's account. Dealing with precise facts, Mark records the most vivid gospel account we possess of the life of Christ. Mark presents Jesus as a man of action and frequently records the reactions of the crowds to Jesus' ministry (see 1:27; 2:7; 4:41; 7:37).

John the Baptist

1 THE BEGINNING of the gospel of
Jesus Christ, [a]the Son of God;
2 As it is written in the prophets, [a]Be-
hold, I send my messenger before thy
face, which shall prepare thy way before
thee.
3 [a]The voice of one crying in the wilderness, Prepare ye the way of the Lord,
make his paths straight.
4 [a]John did baptize in the wilderness,
and preach the baptism of repentance
′for the remission of sins.
5 [a]And there went out unto him all the
land of Judaea, and they of Jerusalem, and
were all baptized of him in the river of
Jordan, confessing their sins.
6 And John was [a]clothed with camel's
hair, and with a girdle of a skin about his
loins; and he did eat locusts and wild
honey;
B 7 And preached, saying, [a]There cometh one mightier than I after me, the
latchet of whose shoes I am not worthy to
stoop down and unloose.
B 8 [a]I indeed have baptized you with wa-
P ter: but he shall baptize you [b]with the
Holy Ghost.

Baptism and temptation of Jesus

9 [a]And it came to pass in those days,
that Jesus came from Nazareth of Galilee,
and was baptized of John in Jordan.
B 10 [a]And straightway coming up out of
E the water, he saw the heavens ′opened,
J and the Spirit like a dove descending
N upon him:
11 And there came a voice from
heaven, *saying,* [a]Thou art my beloved
Son, in whom I am well pleased.
E 12 [a]And immediately the Spirit driveth
L him into the wilderness.
F 13 And he was there in the wilderness
forty days, tempted of Satan; and was
with the wild beasts; [a]and the angels
ministered unto him.
14 [a]Now after that John was put in
prison, Jesus came into Galilee, [b]preach-
ing the gospel of the kingdom of God,
15 And saying, [a]The time is fulfilled, F
and [b]the kingdom of God is at hand: re- R
pent ye, and believe the gospel.

Jesus calls four disciples

16 [a]Now as he walked by the sea of
Galilee, he saw Simon and Andrew his
brother casting a net into the sea: for they
were fishers.
17 And Jesus said unto them, Come ye
after me, and I will make you to become
fishers of men.
18 And straightway [a]they forsook their
nets, and followed him.
19 [a]And when he had gone a little farther thence, he saw James the *son* of
Zebedee, and John his brother, who also
were in the ship mending their nets.
20 And straightway he called them:
and they left their father Zebedee in the
ship with the hired servants, and went
after him.

The unclean spirit cast out

21 [a]And they went into Capernaum;
and straightway on the sabbath day he
entered into the synagogue, and taught.
22 [a]And they were astonished at his
doctrine: for he taught them as one that
had authority, and not as the scribes.
23 And there was in their synagogue a E
man with an unclean spirit; and he cried
out,
24 Saying, Let *us* alone; [a]what have
we to do with thee, thou Jesus of Nazareth? art thou come to destroy us? I know
thee who thou art, the Holy One of God.
25 And Jesus [a]rebuked him, saying,
Hold thy peace, and come out of him.
26 And when the unclean spirit [a]had
torn him, and cried with a loud voice, he
came out of him.
27 And they were all amazed, insomuch that they questioned among
themselves, saying, What thing is this?
what new doctrine *is* this? for with authority commandeth he even the unclean
spirits, and they do obey him.
28 And immediately his fame spread
abroad throughout all the region round
about Galilee.

1:1 [a]Mat. 14:33; Luke 1:35; John 1:34
2 [a]Mal. 3:1; Mat. 11:10; Luke 7:27
3 [a]Is. 40:3; Mat. 3:3; Luke 3:4; John 1:15,23
4 [a]Mat. 3:1; Luke 3:3; John 3:23 ′Or, *unto*
5 [a]Mat. 3:5
6 [a]Mat. 3:4
7 [a]Mat. 3:11; John 1:27; Acts 13:25
8 [a]Acts 1:5 & 11:16 & 19:4 [b]Is. 44:3; Joel 2:28; Acts 2:4 & 10:45 & 11:15,16; 1 Cor. 12:13
9 [a]Mat. 3:13; Luke 3:21
10 [a]Mat. 3:16; John 1:32 ′Or, *cloven, or, rent*
11 [a]Ps. 2:7; Mat. 3:17; ch. 9:7
12 [a]Mat. 4:1; Luke 4:1
13 [a]Mat. 4:11
14 [a]Mat. 4:12 [b]Mat. 4:23
15 [a]Dan. 9:25; Gal. 4:4; Eph. 1:10 [b]Mat. 3:2 & 4:17
16 [a]Mat. 4:18; Luke 5:4
18 [a]Mat. 19:27; Luke 5:11
19 [a]Mat. 4:21
21 [a]Mat. 4:13; Luke 4:31
22 [a]Mat. 7:28
24 [a]Mat. 8:29
25 [a]ver. 34
26 [a]ch. 9:20

B *Mt 27:51* ◀▶ *Mk 8:31*
B *Mt 12:18* ◀▶ *Mk 1:10*
P *Mt 3:11* ◀▶ *Lk 3:16*
B *Mk 1:8* ◀▶ *Lk 1:15*
E *Mt 22:43* ◀▶ *Mk 1:12*
J *Mt 3:16* ◀▶ *Lk 3:22*
N *Mt 3:16* ◀▶ *Lk 3:16*
E *Mk 1:10* ◀▶ *Mk 12:36*
L *Mt 10:19–20* ◀▶ *Mk 12:36*
F *Mt 16:5–10* ◀▶ *Mk 6:33–44*

F *Mt 21:31–32* ◀▶ *Mk 16:16*
R *Mt 26:75* ◀▶ *Mk 6:12*
E *Mt 21:14* ◀▶ *Mk 1:39–45*

The sick healed; devils cast out

29 [a]And forthwith, when they were come out of the synagogue, they entered into the house of Simon and Andrew, with James and John.

30 But Simon's wife's mother lay sick of a fever, and anon they tell him of her.

31 And he came and took her by the hand, and lifted her up; and immediately the fever left her, and she ministered unto them.

32 [a]And at even, when the sun did set, they brought unto him all that were diseased, and them that were possessed with devils.

33 And all the city was gathered together at the door.

34 And he healed many that were sick of divers diseases, and cast out many devils; and [a]suffered not the devils [1]to speak, because they knew him.

Jesus preaches in Galilee

35 And [a]in the morning, rising up a great while before day, he went out, and departed into a solitary place, and there prayed.

36 And Simon and they that were with him followed after him.

37 And when they had found him, they said unto him, All *men* seek for thee.

38 And he said unto them, [a]Let us go into the next towns, that I may preach there also: for [b]therefore came I forth.

E 39 [a]And he preached in their synagogues throughout all Galilee, and cast out devils.

The leper cleansed

40 [a]And there came a leper to him, beseeching him, and kneeling down to him, and saying unto him, If thou wilt, thou canst make me clean.

41 And Jesus, moved with compassion, put forth *his* hand, and touched him, and saith unto him, I will; be thou clean.

42 And as soon as he had spoken, immediately the leprosy departed from him, and he was cleansed.

43 And he straitly charged him, and forthwith sent him away;

44 And saith unto him, See thou say nothing to any man: but go thy way,

E *Mk 1:23–34* ◀ ▶ *Mk 2:3–12*

29 [a]Mat. 8:14; Luke 4:38
32 [a]Mat. 8:16; Luke 4:40
34 [a]ch. 3:12; Luke 4:41; See Acts 16:17,18 [1]Or, *to say that they knew him*
35 [a]Luke 4:42
38 [a]Luke 4:43 [b]Is. 61:1; John 16:28 & 17:4
39 [a]Mat. 4:23; Luke 4:44
40 [a]Mat. 8:2; Luke 5:12
44 [a]Lev. 14:3,4,10
45 [a]Luke 5:15 [b]ch. 2:13
2:1 [a]Mat. 9:1
7 [a]Job 14:4; Is. 43:25
9 [a]Mat. 9:5

show thyself to the priest, and offer for thy cleansing those things [a]which Moses commanded, for a testimony unto them.

45 [a]But he went out, and began to publish *it* much, and to blaze abroad the matter, insomuch that Jesus could no more openly enter into the city, but was without in desert places: [b]and they came to him from every quarter.

A man with palsy healed

2 AND AGAIN [a]he entered into Capernaum after *some* days; and it was noised that he was in the house.

2 And straightway many were gathered together, insomuch that there was no room to receive *them,* no, not so much as about the door: and he preached the word unto them.

3 And they come unto him, bringing one sick of the palsy, which was borne of four. E

4 And when they could not come nigh unto him for the press, they uncovered the roof where he was: and when they had broken *it* up, they let down the bed wherein the sick of the palsy lay.

5 When Jesus saw their faith, he said unto the sick of the palsy, Son, thy sins be forgiven thee.

6 But there were certain of the scribes sitting there, and reasoning in their hearts,

7 Why doth this *man* thus speak blasphemies? [a]who can forgive sins but God only?

8 And immediately when Jesus perceived in his spirit that they so reasoned within themselves, he said unto them, Why reason ye these things in your hearts?

9 [a]Whether is it easier to say to the sick of the palsy, *Thy* sins be forgiven thee; or to say, Arise, and take up thy bed, and walk?

10 But that ye may know that the Son of man hath power on earth to forgive sins, (he saith to the sick of the palsy,) K

11 I say unto thee, Arise, and take up thy bed, and go thy way into thine house.

12 And immediately he arose, took up the bed, and went forth before them all; insomuch that they were all amazed, and

E *Mk 1:39–45* ◀ ▶ *Mk 3:1–5*
K *Mt 28:18* ◀ ▶ *Mk 10:27*

glorified God, saying, We never saw it on this fashion.

Matthew called

13 [a]And he went forth again by the sea side; and all the multitude resorted unto him, and he taught them.

14 [a]And as he passed by, he saw Levi the *son* of Alphaeus sitting ʹat the receipt of custom, and said unto him, Follow me. And he arose and followed him.

15 [a]And it came to pass, that, as Jesus sat at meat in his house, many publicans and sinners sat also together with Jesus and his disciples: for there were many, and they followed him.

16 And when the scribes and Pharisees saw him eat with publicans and sinners, they said unto his disciples, How is it that he eateth and drinketh with publicans and sinners?

C L 17 When Jesus heard *it,* he saith unto them, [a]They that are whole have no need of the physician, but they that are sick: I came not to call the righteous, but sinners to repentance.

The question about fasting

18 [a]And the disciples of John and of the Pharisees used to fast: and they come and say unto him, Why do the disciples of John and of the Pharisees fast, but thy disciples fast not?

19 And Jesus said unto them, Can the children of the bridechamber fast, while the bridegroom is with them? as long as they have the bridegroom with them, they cannot fast.

20 But the days will come, when the bridegroom shall be taken away from them, and then shall they fast in those days.

21 No man also seweth a piece of ʹnew cloth on an old garment: else the new piece that filled it up taketh away from the old, and the rent is made worse.

22 And no man putteth new wine into old bottles: else the new wine doth burst the bottles, and the wine is spilled, and the bottles will be marred: but new wine must be put into new bottles.

Jesus the Lord of the Sabbath

23 [a]And it came to pass, that he went through the corn fields on the sabbath day; and his disciples began, as they went, [b]to pluck the ears of corn.

24 And the Pharisees said unto him, Behold, why do they on the sabbath day that which is not lawful?

25 And he said unto them, Have ye never read [a]what David did, when he had need, and was an hungered, he, and they that were with him?

26 How he went into the house of God in the days of Abiathar the high priest, and did eat the showbread, [a]which is not lawful to eat but for the priests, and gave also to them which were with him?

27 And he said unto them, The sabbath was made for man, and not man for the sabbath:

28 Therefore [a]the Son of man is Lord also of the sabbath.

3 AND [a]HE entered again into the synagogue; and there was a man there which had a withered hand. E

2 And they watched him, whether he would heal him on the sabbath day; that they might accuse him.

3 And he saith unto the man which had the withered hand, ʹStand forth.

4 And he saith unto them, Is it lawful to do good on the sabbath days, or to do evil? to save life, or to kill? But they held their peace.

5 And when he had looked round about on them with anger, being grieved for the ʹhardness of their hearts, he saith unto the man, Stretch forth thine hand. And he stretched *it* out: and his hand was restored whole as the other.

6 [a]And the Pharisees went forth, and straightway took counsel with [b]the Herodians against him, how they might destroy him.

Jesus heals many by the sea

7 But Jesus withdrew himself with his disciples to the sea: and a great multitude from Galilee followed him, [a]and from Judaea,

8 And from Jerusalem, and from Idumaea, and *from* beyond Jordan; and they about Tyre and Sidon, a great multitude, when they had heard what great things he did, came unto him.

9 And he spake to his disciples, that a small ship should wait on him because of

13 [a]Mat. 9:9
14 [a]Mat. 9:9; Luke 5:27 ʹOr, *at the place where the custom was received*
15 [a]Mat. 9:10
17 [a]Mat. 9:12,13; & 18:11; Luke 5:31, 32 & 19:10; 1 Tim. 1:15
18 [a]Mat. 9:14; Luke 5:33
21 ʹOr, *raw,* or, *unwrought*
23 [a]Mat. 12:1; Luke 6:1 [b]Deut. 23:25
25 [a]1 Sam. 21:6
26 [a]Ex. 29:32,33; Lev. 24:9
28 [a]Mat. 12:8
3:1 [a]Mat. 12:9; Luke 6:6
3 ʹGk. *Arise,* stand forth *in the midst*
5 ʹOr, *blindness*
6 [a]Mat. 12:14 [b]Mat. 22:16
7 [a]Luke 6:17

C *Mt 25:2–3* ◄► *Mk 4:12*
L *Mt 23:37* ◄► *Mk 3:28*
E *Mk 2:3–12* ◄► *Mk 3:10–12*

the multitude, lest they should throng him.

E 10 For he had healed many; insomuch that they [/]pressed upon him for to touch him, as many as had plagues.

11 [a]And unclean spirits, when they saw him, fell down before him, and cried, saying, [b]Thou art the Son of God.

12 And [a]he straitly charged them that they should not make him known.

The Twelve ordained

13 [a]And he goeth up into a mountain, and calleth *unto him* whom he would: and they came unto him.

E 14 And he ordained twelve, that they should be with him, and that he might send them forth to preach,

15 And to have power to heal sicknesses, and to cast out devils:

16 And Simon [a]he surnamed Peter;

17 And James the *son* of Zebedee, and John the brother of James; and he surnamed them Boanerges, which is, The sons of thunder:

18 And Andrew, and Philip, and Bartholomew, and Matthew, and Thomas, and James the *son* of Alphaeus, and Thaddaeus, and Simon the Canaanite,

19 And Judas Iscariot, which also betrayed him: and they went [/]into an house.

The Pharisees' slander

20 And the multitude cometh together again, [a]so that they could not so much as eat bread.

21 And when his [/]friends heard *of it,* they went out to lay hold on him: [a]for they said, He is beside himself.

E 22 ¶ And the scribes which came down from Jerusalem said, [a]He hath Beelzebub, and by the prince of the devils casteth he out devils.

23 [a]And he called them *unto him,* and said unto them in parables, How can Satan cast out Satan?

24 And if a kingdom be divided against itself, that kingdom cannot stand.

25 And if a house be divided against itself, that house cannot stand.

26 And if Satan rise up against himself, and be divided, he cannot stand, but hath an end.

27 [a]No man can enter into a strong man's house, and spoil his goods, except he will first bind the strong man; and then he will spoil his house.

28 [a]Verily I say unto you, All sins shall be forgiven unto the sons of men, and blasphemies wherewith soever they shall blaspheme: L W

29 But he that shall blaspheme against the Holy Ghost hath never forgiveness, but is in danger of eternal damnation: D Q

30 Because they said, He hath an unclean spirit.

Jesus' true family

31 ¶ [a]There came then his brethren and his mother, and, standing without, sent unto him, calling him.

32 And the multitude sat about him, and they said unto him, Behold, thy mother and thy brethren without seek for thee.

33 And he answered them, saying, Who is my mother, or my brethren?

34 And he looked round about on them which sat about him, and said, Behold my mother and my brethren!

35 For whosoever shall do the will of God, the same is my brother, and my sister, and mother. S

The parable of the sower

4 AND [a]HE began again to teach by the sea side: and there was gathered unto him a great multitude, so that he entered into a ship, and sat in the sea; and the whole multitude was by the sea on the land.

2 And he taught them many things by parables, [a]and said unto them in his doctrine,

3 Hearken; Behold, there went out a sower to sow:

4 And it came to pass, as he sowed, some fell by the way side, and the fowls of the air came and devoured it up.

5 And some fell on stony ground, where it had not much earth; and immediately it sprang up, because it had no depth of earth: S

6 But when the sun was up, it was

10 [/]Or, *rushed*
11 [a]ch. 1:23,24; Luke 4:41 [b]Mat. 14:33; ch. 1:1
12 [a]Mat. 12:16; ch. 1:25,34
13 [a]Mat. 10:1; Luke 6:12 & 9:1
16 [a]John 1:42
19 [/]Or, *home*
20 [a]ch. 6:31
21 [a]John 7:5 & 10:20 [/]Or, *kinsmen*
22 [a]Mat. 9:34 & 10:25; Luke 11:15; John 7:20 & 8:48, 52 & 10:20
23 [a]Mat. 12:25
27 [a]Is. 49:24; Mat. 12:29
28 [a]Mat. 12:31; Luke 12:10; 1 John 5:16
31 [a]Mat. 12:46; Luke 8:19
4:1 [a]Mat. 13:1; Luke 8:4
2 [a]ch. 12:38

E *Mk 3:1–5* ◀▶ *Mk 3:14–15*
E *Mk 3:10–12* ◀▶ *Mk 3:22–27*
E *Mk 3:14–15* ◀▶ *Mk 5:1–20*

L *Mk 2:17* ◀▶ *Lk 1:77–79*
W *Mt 22:1–10* ◀▶ *Mk 16:15–16*
D *Mt 28:19* ◀▶ *Ac 5:4*
Q *Mt 12:31–32* ◀▶ *Lk 12:10*
S *Mt 28:20* ◀▶ *Mk 4:5–8*
S *Mk 3:35* ◀▶ *Mk 4:16–20*

scorched; and because it had no root, it withered away.

7 And some fell among thorns, and the thorns grew up, and choked it, and it yielded no fruit.

8 And other fell on good ground, [a]and did yield fruit that sprang up and increased; and brought forth, some thirty, and some sixty, and some an hundred.

9 And he said unto them, He that hath ears to hear, let him hear.

10 [a]And when he was alone, they that were about him with the twelve asked of him the parable.

11 And he said unto them, Unto you it is given to know the mystery of the kingdom of God: but unto [a]them that are without, all *these* things are done in parables:

C 12 [a]That seeing they may see, and not perceive; and hearing they may hear, and not understand; lest at any time they should be converted, and *their* sins should be forgiven them.

13 And he said unto them, Know ye not this parable? and how then will ye know all parables?

14 ¶ [a]The sower soweth the word.

15 And these are they by the way side, where the word is sown; but when they have heard, Satan cometh immediately, and taketh away the word that was sown in their hearts.

S 16 And these are they likewise which are sown on stony ground; who, when they have heard the word, immediately receive it with gladness;

17 And have no root in themselves, and so endure but for a time: afterward, when affliction or persecution ariseth for the word's sake, immediately they are offended.

18 And these are they which are sown among thorns; such as hear the word,

19 And the cares of this world, [a]and the deceitfulness of riches, and the lusts of other things entering in, choke the word, and it becometh unfruitful.

20 And these are they which are sown on good ground; such as hear the word, and receive *it,* and bring forth fruit, some thirtyfold, some sixty, and some an hundred.

Parables about the kingdom

21 ¶ [a]And he said unto them, Is a candle brought to be put under a [l]bushel, or under a bed? and not to be set on a candlestick?

22 [a]For there is nothing hid, which shall not be manifested; neither was any thing kept secret, but that it should come abroad.

23 [a]If any man have ears to hear, let him hear.

24 And he said unto them, Take heed what ye hear: [a]with what measure ye mete, it shall be measured to you: and unto you that hear shall more be given.

25 [a]For he that hath, to him shall be given: and he that hath not, from him shall be taken even that which he hath.

26 ¶ And he said, [a]So is the kingdom of God, as if a man should cast seed into the ground; K

27 And should sleep, and rise night and day, and the seed should spring and grow up, he knoweth not how.

28 For the earth bringeth forth fruit of herself; first the blade, then the ear, after that the full corn in the ear.

29 But when the fruit is [l]brought forth, immediately [a]he putteth in the sickle, because the harvest is come. C

30 ¶ And he said, [a]Whereunto shall we liken the kingdom of God? or with what comparison shall we compare it? M

31 *It is* like a grain of mustard seed, which, when it is sown in the earth, is less than all the seeds that be in the earth:

32 But when it is sown, it groweth up, and becometh greater than all herbs, and shooteth out great branches; so that the fowls of the air may lodge under the shadow of it.

33 [a]And with many such parables

8 [a]John 15:5; Col. 1:6
10 [a]Mat. 13:10; Luke 8:9
11 [a]1 Cor. 5:12; Col. 4:5; 1 Thes. 4:12; 1 Tim. 3:7
12 [a]Is. 6:9; Mat. 13:14; Luke 8:10; John 12:40; Acts 28:26; Rom. 11:8
14 [a]Mat. 13:19
19 [a]1 Tim. 6:9,17
21 [a]Mat. 5:15; Luke 8:16 & 11:33 [l]The word in the original signifies a less measure; see Mat. 5:15
22 [a]Mat. 10:26
23 [a]ver. 9; Mat. 11:15
24 [a]Mat. 7:2; Luke 6:38
25 [a]Mat. 13:12 & 25:29; Luke 8:18 & 19:26
26 [a]Mat. 13:24
29 [a]Rev. 14:15 [l]Or, *ripe*
30 [a]Mat. 13:31; Luke 13:18; Acts 2:41 & 4:4 & 5:14 & 19:20
33 [a]Mat. 13:34; John 16:12

C *Mk 2:17* ◀ ▶ *Lk 1:79*
S *Mk 4:5–8* ◀ ▶ *Mk 8:34*
K *Mt 16:18–20* ◀ ▶ *Mk 9:1*
C *Mt 26:64* ◀ ▶ *Mk 8:38*
M *Mt 27:42* ◀ ▶ *Mk 10:37*

4:30–32 The parable of the mustard seed reveals the prophetic nature of the kingdom of God. This kingdom began with only twelve disciples and has grown throughout the last two thousand years to include more than 600 million Christians around the world today.

spake he the word unto them, as they were able to hear *it.*

34 But without a parable spake he not unto them: and when they were alone, he expounded all things to his disciples.

The storm stilled

35 [a]And the same day, when the even was come, he saith unto them, Let us pass over unto the other side.

36 And when they had sent away the multitude, they took him even as he was in the ship. And there were also with him other little ships.

37 And there arose a great storm of wind, and the waves beat into the ship, so that it was now full.

38 And he was in the hinder part of the ship, asleep on a pillow: and they awake him, and say unto him, Master, carest thou not that we perish?

39 And he arose, and rebuked the wind, and said unto the sea, Peace, be still. And the wind ceased, and there was a great calm.

S W 40 And he said unto them, Why are ye so fearful? how is it that ye have no faith?

41 And they feared exceedingly, and said one to another, What manner of man is this, that even the wind and the sea obey him?

Devils cast out

E 5 AND [a]THEY came over unto the other side of the sea, into the country of the Gadarenes.

2 And when he was come out of the ship, immediately there met him out of the tombs a man with an unclean spirit,

3 Who had *his* dwelling among the tombs; and no man could bind him, no, not with chains:

4 Because that he had been often bound with fetters and chains, and the chains had been plucked asunder by him, and the fetters broken in pieces: neither could any *man* tame him.

5 And always, night and day, he was in the mountains, and in the tombs, crying, and cutting himself with stones.

6 But when he saw Jesus afar off, he ran and worshipped him,

7 And cried with a loud voice, and said, What have I to do with thee, Jesus, *thou* Son of the most high God? I adjure thee by God, that thou torment me not.

8 For he said unto him, Come out of the man, *thou* unclean spirit.

9 And he asked him, What *is* thy name? And he answered, saying, My name *is* Legion: for we are many.

10 And he besought him much that he would not send them away out of the country.

11 Now there was there nigh unto the mountains a great herd of swine feeding.

12 And all the devils besought him, saying, Send us into the [a]swine, that we may enter into them.

13 And forthwith Jesus gave them leave. And the unclean spirits went out, and entered into the swine: and the herd ran violently down a steep place into the sea, (they were about two thousand;) and were choked in the sea.

14 And they that fed the swine fled, and told *it* in the city, and in the country. And they went out to see what it was that was done.

15 And they come to Jesus, and see him that was possessed with the devil, and had the legion, sitting, and clothed, and in his right mind: and they were afraid.

16 And they that saw *it* told them how it befell to him that was possessed with the devil, and *also* concerning the swine.

17 And [a]they began to pray him to depart out of their coasts.

18 And when he was come into the ship, [a]he that had been possessed with the devil prayed him that he might be with him.

19 Howbeit Jesus suffered him not, but saith unto him, Go home to thy friends, T
and tell them how great things the Lord hath done for thee, and hath had compassion on thee.

20 And he departed, and began to publish in Decapolis how great things Jesus had done for him: and all *men* did marvel.

Jairus' daughter raised

21 [a]And when Jesus was passed over again by ship unto the other side, much people gathered unto him: and he was nigh unto the sea.

35 [a]Mat. 8:18,23; Luke 8:22
5:1 [a]Mat. 8:28; Luke 8:26
12 [a]Lev. 11:7; Deut. 14:8; Is. 65:4; Luke 15:15
17 [a]Mat. 8:34; Acts 16:39
18 [a]Luke 8:38
21 [a]Mat. 9:1; Luke 8:40

S *Mt 4:6* ◀ ▶ *Lk 21:18*
W *Mt 8:26* ◀ ▶ *Lk 8:24–25*
E *Mk 3:22–27* ◀ ▶ *Mk 5:22–43*

T *Mt 10:32–33* ◀ ▶ *Mk 8:38*

E 22 [a]And, behold, there cometh one of the rulers of the synagogue, Jairus by name; and when he saw him, he fell at his feet,

23 And besought him greatly, saying, My little daughter lieth at the point of death: *I pray thee,* come and lay thy hands on her, that she may be healed; and she shall live.

24 And *Jesus* went with him; and much people followed him, and thronged him.

25 And a certain woman, [a]which had an issue of blood twelve years,

26 And had suffered many things of many physicians, and had spent all that she had, and was nothing bettered, but rather grew worse,

27 When she had heard of Jesus, came in the press behind, and touched his garment.

28 For she said, If I may touch but his clothes, I shall be whole.

29 And straightway the fountain of her blood was dried up; and she felt in *her* body that she was healed of that plague.

30 And Jesus, immediately knowing in himself that [a]virtue had gone out of him, turned him about in the press, and said, Who touched my clothes?

31 And his disciples said unto him, Thou seest the multitude thronging thee, and sayest thou, Who touched me?

32 And he looked round about to see her that had done this thing.

33 But the woman fearing and trembling, knowing what was done in her, came and fell down before him, and told him all the truth.

34 And he said unto her, Daughter, [a]thy faith hath made thee whole; go in peace, and be whole of thy plague.

35 [a]While he yet spake, there came from the ruler of the synagogue's *house certain* which said, Thy daughter is dead: why troublest thou the Master any further?

36 As soon as Jesus heard the word that was spoken, he saith unto the ruler of the synagogue, Be not afraid, only believe.

37 And he suffered no man to follow him, save Peter, and James, and John the brother of James.

38 And he cometh to the house of the ruler of the synagogue, and seeth the tumult, and them that wept and wailed greatly.

39 And when he was come in, he saith unto them, Why make ye this ado, and weep? the damsel is not dead, but [a]sleepeth.

40 And they laughed him to scorn. [a]But when he had put them all out, he taketh the father and the mother of the damsel, and them that were with him, and entereth in where the damsel was lying.

41 And he took the damsel by the hand, and said unto her, Talitha cumi; which is, being interpreted, Damsel, I say unto thee, arise.

42 And straightway the damsel arose, and walked; for she was *of the age* of twelve years. And they were astonished with a great astonishment.

43 And [a]he charged them straitly that no man should know it; and commanded that something should be given her to eat.

Jesus rejected at Nazareth

6 AND [a]HE went out from thence, and came into his own country; and his disciples follow him.

2 And when the sabbath day was come, he began to teach in the synagogue: and many hearing *him* were astonished, saying, [a]From whence hath this *man* these things? and what wisdom *is* this which is given unto him, that even such mighty works are wrought by his hands?

3 Is not this the carpenter, the son of Mary, [a]the brother of James, and Joses, and of Judah, and Simon? and are not his sisters here with us? And they [b]were offended at him.

4 But Jesus said unto them, [a]A prophet is not without honour, but in his own country, and among his own kin, and in his own house.

5 [a]And he could there do no mighty work, save that he laid his hands upon a few sick folk, and healed *them*. D E

6 And [a]he marvelled because of their unbelief. [b]And he went round about the villages, teaching.

22 [a]Mat. 9:18; Luke 8:41
25 [a]Lev. 15:25; Mat. 9:20
30 [a]Luke 6:19 & 8:46
34 [a]Mat. 9:22; ch. 10:52; Acts 14:9
35 [a]Luke 8:49
39 [a]John 11:11
40 [a]Acts 9:40
43 [a]Mat. 8:4 & 9:30 & 12:16 & 17:19; ch. 3:12; Luke 5:14
6:1 [a]Mat. 13:54; Luke 4:16
2 [a]John 6:42
3 [a]See Mat. 12:46; Gal. 1:19 [b]Mat. 11:6
4 [a]Mat. 13:57; John 4:44
5 [a]See Gen. 19:22; & 32:25; Mat. 13:58; ch. 9:23
6 [a]Is. 59:16 [b]Mat. 9:35; Luke 13:22

E *Mk 5:1–20* ◀ ▶ *Mk 6:5*
D *Mt 13:58* ◀ ▶ *Lk 1:20*
E *Mk 5:22–43* ◀ ▶ *Mk 6:7*

The mission of the Twelve

E 7 ¶ [a]And he called *unto him* the
twelve, and began to send them forth by
two and two; and gave them power over
unclean spirits;
8 And commanded them that they
should take nothing for *their* journey,
save a staff only; no scrip, no bread, no
[l]money in *their* purse:
9 But [a]*be* shod with sandals; and not
put on two coats.
10 [a]And he said unto them, In what
place soever ye enter into an house, there
abide till ye depart from that place.
J 11 [a]And whosoever shall not receive
H you, nor hear you, when ye depart
J thence, [b]shake off the dust under your
N feet for a testimony against them. Verily I
say unto you, It shall be more tolerable
for Sodom [l]and Gomorrha in the day of
judgment, than for that city.
R 12 And they went out, and preached
that men should repent.
E 13 And they cast out many devils, [a]and
anointed with oil many that were sick,
and healed *them*.

Death of John the Baptist

14 [a]And king Herod heard *of him;* (for
his name was spread abroad:) and he
said, That John the Baptist was risen from
the dead, and therefore mighty works do
show forth themselves in him.
15 [a]Others said, That it is Elias. And
others said, That it is a prophet, or as one
of the prophets.
16 [a]But when Herod heard *thereof,* he
said, It is John, whom I beheaded: he is
risen from the dead.
17 For Herod himself had sent forth
and laid hold upon John, and bound him
in prison for Herodias' sake, his brother
Philip's wife: for he had married her.
18 For John had said unto Herod, [a]It is
not lawful for thee to have thy brother's
wife.
19 Therefore Herodias had [l]a quarrel
against him, and would have killed him;
but she could not:
20 For Herod [a]feared John, knowing
that he was a just man and an holy, and
[l]observed him; and when he heard him,
he did many things, and heard him
gladly.
21 [a]And when a convenient day was
come, that Herod [b]on his birthday made a
supper to his lords, high captains, and
chief *estates* of Galilee;
22 And when the daughter of the said
Herodias came in, and danced, and
pleased Herod and them that sat with
him, the king said unto the damsel, Ask
of me whatsoever thou wilt, and I will
give *it* thee.
23 And he sware unto her, [a]Whatso-
ever thou shalt ask of me, I will give *it*
thee, unto the half of my kingdom.
24 And she went forth, and said unto
her mother, What shall I ask? And she
said, The head of John the Baptist.
25 And she came in straightway with
haste unto the king, and asked, saying, I
will that thou give me by and by in a
charger the head of John the Baptist.
26 [a]And the king was exceeding sorry;
yet for his oath's sake, and for their sakes
which sat with him, he would not reject
her.
27 And immediately the king sent [l]an
executioner, and commanded his head to
be brought: and he went and beheaded
him in the prison,
28 And brought his head in a charger,
and gave it to the damsel: and the damsel
gave it to her mother.
29 And when his disciples heard *of it,*
they came and took up his corpse, and
laid it in a tomb.

The five thousand fed

30 [a]And the apostles gathered themselves together unto Jesus, and told him
all things, both what they had done, and
what they had taught.
31 [a]And he said unto them, Come ye
yourselves apart into a desert place, and

7 [a]Mat. 10:1; ch. 3:13,14; Luke 9:1
8 [l]The word signifies *a piece of brass money,* worth about one cent, Mat. 10:9: but here it is taken in general for *money,* Luke 9:3
9 [a]Acts 12:8
10 [a]Mat. 10:11; Luke 9:4 & 10:7,8
11 [a]Mat. 10:14; Luke 10:10 [b]Acts 13:51 & 18:6 [l]Gk. *or*
13 [a]Jas. 5:14
14 [a]Mat. 14:1; Luke 9:7
15 [a]Mat. 16:14; ch. 8:28
16 [a]Mat. 14:2; Luke 3:19
18 [a]Lev. 18:16 & 20:21
19 [l]Or, *an inward grudge*
20 [a]Mat. 14:5 & 21:26 [l]Or, *kept him,* or *saved him*
21 [a]Mat. 14:6 [b]Gen. 40:20
23 [a]Esth. 5:3,6 & 7:2
26 [a]Mat. 14:9
27 [l]Or, *one of his guard*
30 [a]Luke 9:10
31 [a]Mat. 14:13

E *Mk 6:5* ◀▶ *Mk 6:13*
J *Mt 25:31–46* ◀▶ *Lk 10:12*
H *Mt 26:24* ◀▶ *Mk 8:36–38*
J *Mt 25:31–46* ◀▶ *Lk 10:12–14*
N *Mt 25:10–11* ◀▶ *Mk 16:15–16*
R *Mk 1:15* ◀▶ *Mk 11:25–26*
E *Mk 6:7* ◀▶ *Mk 6:54–56*

6:11 Jesus prophesied that those who reject the offer of salvation preached by his disciples will be judged accordingly. Though these unrepentant sinners received a much greater chance to respond than the ancient cities of Sodom and Gomorrah, they still rejected salvation.

rest a while: for [b]there were many coming and going, and they had no leisure so much as to eat.

32 [a]And they departed into a desert place by ship privately.

F 33 And the people saw them departing, and many knew him, and ran afoot thither out of all cities, and outwent them, and came together unto him.

34 [a]And Jesus, when he came out, saw much people, and was moved with compassion toward them, because they were as sheep not having a shepherd: and [b]he began to teach them many things.

35 [a]And when the day was now far spent, his disciples came unto him, and said, This is a desert place, and now the time *is* far passed:

36 Send them away, that they may go into the country round about, and into the villages, and buy themselves bread: for they have nothing to eat.

37 He answered and said unto them, Give ye them to eat. And they say unto him, [a]Shall we go and buy two hundred [†]pennyworth of bread, and give them to eat?

38 He saith unto them, How many loaves have ye? go and see. And when they knew, they say, [a]Five, and two fishes.

39 And he commanded them to make all sit down by companies upon the green grass.

40 And they sat down in ranks, by hundreds, and by fifties.

41 And when he had taken the five loaves and the two fishes, he looked up to heaven, [a]and blessed, and brake the loaves, and gave *them* to his disciples to set before them; and the two fishes divided he among them all.

42 And they did all eat, and were filled.

43 And they took up twelve baskets full of the fragments, and of the fishes.

44 And they that did eat of the loaves were about five thousand men.

Jesus walks on the sea

45 [a]And straightway he constrained his disciples to get into the ship, and to go to the other side before [†]unto Bethsaida, while he sent away the people.

46 And when he had sent them away, he departed into a mountain to pray.

47 [a]And when even was come, the ship was in the midst of the sea, and he alone on the land.

48 And he saw them toiling in rowing; for the wind was contrary unto them: and about the fourth watch of the night he cometh unto them, walking upon the sea, and [a]would have passed by them.

49 But when they saw him walking upon the sea, they supposed it had been a spirit, and cried out:

50 For they all saw him, and were troubled. And immediately he talked with them, and saith unto them, Be of good cheer: it is I; be not afraid.

51 And he went up unto them into the ship; and the wind ceased: and they were sore amazed in themselves beyond measure, and wondered.

52 For [a]they considered not *the miracle* of the loaves: for their [b]heart was hardened.

53 [a]And when they had passed over, they came into the land of Gennesaret, and drew to the shore.

54 And when they were come out of the ship, straightway they knew him, E

55 And ran through that whole region round about, and began to carry about in beds those that were sick, where they heard he was.

56 And whithersoever he entered, into villages, or cities, or country, they laid the sick in the streets, and besought him that [a]they might touch if it were but the border of his garment: and as many as touched [†]him were made whole.

What defiles a man

7 THEN [a]CAME together unto him the Pharisees, and certain of the scribes, which came from Jerusalem.

2 And when they saw some of his disciples eat bread with [†]defiled, that is to say, with unwashen, hands, they found fault.

3 For the Pharisees, and all the Jews, except they wash *their* hands [†]oft, eat not, holding the tradition of the elders.

4 And *when they come* from the market, except they wash, they eat not. And many other things there be, which they have received to hold, *as* the washing of

31 [b]ch. 3:20
32 [a]Mat. 14:13
34 [a]Mat. 9:36 & 14:14 [b]Luke 9:11
35 [a]Mat. 14:15; Luke 9:12
37 [a]Num. 11:13, 22; 2 Ki. 4:43 [†]The penny, worth about 16 cents, was the usual day's wage for a laborer
38 [a]Mat. 14:17; Luke 9:13; John 6:9; See Mat. 15:34; ch:8:5
41 [a]1 Sam. 9:13; Mat. 26:26
45 [a]Mat. 14:22; John 6:17 [†]Or, *over against Bethsaida*
47 [a]Mat. 14:23; John 6:16,17
48 [a]See Luke 24:28
52 [a]ch. 8:17,18 [b]ch. 3:5 & 16:14
53 [a]Mat. 14:34
56 [a]Mat. 9:20; ch. 5:27,28; Acts 19:12 [†]Or, *it*
7:1 [a]Mat. 15:1
2 [†]Or, *common*
3 [†]Or, *diligently:* in the original, *with the fist* Theophylact, *up to the elbow*

F *Mk 1:13* ◀▶ *Mk 8:1–9*
E *Mk 6:13* ◀▶ *Mk 7:25–37*

cups, and [1]pots, brasen vessels, and of [2]tables.

5 [a]Then the Pharisees and scribes asked him, Why walk not thy disciples according to the tradition of the elders, but eat bread with unwashen hands?

G 6 He answered and said unto them, Well hath Esaias prophesied of you hypocrites, as it is written, [a]This people honoureth me with *their* lips, but their heart is far from me.

7 Howbeit in vain do they worship me, teaching *for* doctrines the commandments of men.

8 For laying aside the commandment of God, ye hold the tradition of men, *as* the washing of pots and cups: and many other such like things ye do.

9 And he said unto them, Full well ye [1]reject the commandment of God, that ye may keep your own tradition.

10 For Moses said, [a]Honour thy father and thy mother; and, [b]Whoso curseth father or mother, let him die the death:

11 But ye say, If a man shall say to his father or mother, *It is* [a]Corban, that is to say, a gift, by whatsoever thou mightest be profited by me; *he shall be free.*

12 And ye suffer him no more to do aught for his father or his mother;

13 Making the word of God of none effect through your tradition, which ye have delivered: and many such like things do ye.

14 ¶ [a]And when he had called all the people *unto him*, he said unto them, Hearken unto me every one *of you*, and understand:

15 There is nothing from without a man, that entering into him can defile him: but the things which come out of him, those are they that defile the man.

16 [a]If any man have ears to hear, let him hear.

17 [a]And when he was entered into the house from the people, his disciples asked him concerning the parable.

18 And he saith unto them, Are ye so without understanding also? Do ye not perceive, that whatsoever thing from without entereth into the man, *it* cannot defile him;

19 Because it entereth not into his heart, but into the belly, and goeth out into the draught, purging all meats?

20 And he said, That which cometh out of the man, that defileth the man.

21 [a]For from within, out of the heart of men, proceed evil thoughts, adulteries, fornications, murders,

22 Thefts, [1]covetousness, wickedness, deceit, lasciviousness, an evil eye, blasphemy, pride, foolishness:

23 All these evil things come from within, and defile the man.

A Greek woman's faith

24 ¶ [a]And from thence he arose, and went into the borders of Tyre and Sidon, and entered into an house, and would have no man know *it:* but he could not be hid.

25 For a *certain* woman, whose young daughter had an unclean spirit, heard of him, and came and fell at his feet: E

26 The woman was a [1]Greek, a Syrophenician by nation; and she besought him that he would cast forth the devil out of her daughter.

27 But Jesus said unto her, Let the children first be filled: for it is not meet to take the children's bread, and to cast *it* unto the dogs.

28 And she answered and said unto him, Yes, Lord: yet the dogs under the table eat of the children's crumbs.

29 And he said unto her, For this saying go thy way; the devil is gone out of thy daughter.

30 And when she was come to her house, she found the devil gone out, and her daughter laid upon the bed.

A deaf mute healed

31 ¶ [a]And again, departing from the coasts of Tyre and Sidon, he came unto the sea of Galilee, through the midst of the coasts of Decapolis.

32 And [a]they bring unto him one that was deaf, and had an impediment in his speech; and they beseech him to put his hand upon him.

33 And he took him aside from the multitude, and put his fingers into his ears, and [a]he spit, and touched his tongue;

34 And [a]looking up to heaven, [b]he sighed, and saith unto him, Ephphatha, that is, Be opened.

35 [a]And straightway his ears were

4 [1]Sextarius is about a pint and a half [2]Or, *beds*
5 [a]Mat. 15:2
6 [a]Is. 29:13
9 [1]Or, *frustrate*
10 [a]Ex. 20:12; Deut. 5:16; Mat. 15:4 [b]Ex. 21:17; Lev. 20:9; Prov. 20:20
11 [a]Mat. 15:5 & 23:18
14 [a]Mat. 15:10
16 [a]Mat. 11:15
17 [a]Mat. 15:15
21 [a]Gen. 6:5 & 8:21; Mat. 15:19
22 [1]Gk. *covetousnesses, wickednesses*
24 [a]Mat. 15:21
26 [1]Or, *Gentile*
31 [a]Mat. 15:29
32 [a]Mat. 9:32; Luke 11:14
33 [a]ch. 8:23; John 9:6
34 [a]ch. 6:41; John 11:41 & 17:1 [b]John 11:33,38
35 [a]Is. 35:5,6

opened, and the string of his tongue was loosed, and he spake plain.

36 And [a]he charged them that they should tell no man: but the more he charged them, so much the more a great deal they published *it;*

37 And were beyond measure astonished, saying, He hath done all things well: he maketh both the deaf to hear, and the dumb to speak.

The four thousand fed

F 8 IN THOSE days [a]the multitude being very great, and having nothing to eat, Jesus called his disciples *unto him,* and saith unto them,

2 I have compassion on the multitude, because they have now been with me three days, and have nothing to eat:

3 And if I send them away fasting to their own houses, they will faint by the way: for divers of them came from far.

4 And his disciples answered him, From whence can a man satisfy these *men* with bread here in the wilderness?

5 [a]And he asked them, How many loaves have ye? And they said, Seven.

6 And he commanded the people to sit down on the ground: and he took the seven loaves, and gave thanks, and brake, and gave to his disciples to set before *them;* and they did set *them* before the people.

7 And they had a few small fishes: and [a]he blessed, and commanded to set them also before *them.*

8 So they did eat, and were filled: and they took up of the broken *meat* that was left seven baskets.

9 And they that had eaten were about four thousand: and he sent them away.

10 ¶ And [a]straightway he entered into a ship with his disciples, and came into the parts of Dalmanutha.

Pharisees ask for a sign

11 [a]And the Pharisees came forth, and began to question with him, seeking of him a sign from heaven, tempting him.

12 And he sighed deeply in his spirit, and saith, Why doth this generation seek after a sign? verily I say unto you, There shall no sign be given unto this generation.

13 And he left them, and entering into the ship again departed to the other side.

14 ¶ [a]Now *the disciples* had forgotten to take bread, neither had they in the ship with them more than one loaf. F

15 [a]And he charged them, saying, Take heed, beware of the leaven of the Pharisees, and *of* the leaven of Herod.

16 And they reasoned among themselves, saying, *It is* because we have no bread.

17 And when Jesus knew *it,* he saith unto them, Why reason ye, because ye have no bread? [a]perceive ye not yet, neither understand? have ye your heart yet hardened?

18 Having eyes, see ye not? and having ears, hear ye not? and do ye not remember?

19 [a]When I brake the five loaves among five thousand, how many baskets full of fragments took ye up? They say unto him, Twelve.

20 And [a]when the seven among four thousand, how many baskets full of fragments took ye up? And they said, Seven.

21 And he said unto them, How is it that [a]ye do not understand?

A blind man healed

22 ¶ And he cometh to Bethsaida; and they bring a blind man unto him, and besought him to touch him. E

23 And he took the blind man by the hand, and led him out of the town; and when [a]he had spit on his eyes, and put his hands upon him, he asked him if he saw aught.

24 And he looked up, and said, I see men as trees, walking.

25 After that he put *his* hands again upon his eyes, and made him look up: and he was restored, and saw every man clearly.

26 And he sent him away to his house, saying, Neither go into the town, [a]nor tell *it* to any in the town.

Peter's confession of faith

27 ¶ [a]And Jesus went out, and his disciples, into the towns of Caesarea Philippi: and by the way he asked his disciples, saying unto them, Whom do men say that I am?

36 [a]ch. 5:43
8:1 [a]Mat. 15:32
5 [a]Mat. 15:34; See ch. 6:38
7 [a]Mat. 14:19; ch. 6:41
10 [a]Mat. 15:39
11 [a]Mat. 12:38 & 16:1; John 6:30
14 [a]Mat. 16:5
15 [a]Mat. 16:6; Luke 12:1
17 [a]ch. 6:52
19 [a]Mat. 14:20; ch. 6:43; Luke 9:17; John 6:13
20 [a]ver. 8; Mat. 15:37
21 [a]ver. 17; ch. 6:52
23 [a]ch. 7:33
26 [a]Mat. 8:4; ch. 5:43
27 [a]Mat. 16:13; Luke 9:18

F *Mk 6:33–44* ◄► *Mk 8:14–21*
F *Mk 8:1–9* ◄► *Lk 4:25–26*
E *Mk 7:25–37* ◄► *Mk 9:14–29*

28 And they answered, [a]John the Baptist: but some *say,* Elias; and others, One of the prophets.

29 And he saith unto them, But whom say ye that I am? And Peter answereth and saith unto him, [a]Thou art the Christ.

30 [a]And he charged them that they should tell no man of him.

Future events foretold

B 31 And [a]he began to teach them, that the Son of man must suffer many things, and be rejected of the elders, and *of* the chief priests, and scribes, and be killed, and after three days rise again.

32 And he spake that saying openly. And Peter took him, and began to rebuke him.

33 But when he had turned about and looked on his disciples, he rebuked Peter, saying, Get thee behind me, Satan: for thou savourest not the things that be of God, but the things that be of men.

S 34 ¶ And when he had called the people *unto him* with his disciples also, he said unto them, [a]Whosoever will come after me, let him deny himself, and take up his cross, and follow me.

35 For [a]whosoever will save his life shall lose it; but whosoever shall lose his life for my sake and the gospel's, the same shall save it.

H 36 For what shall it profit a man, if he shall gain the whole world, and lose his own soul?

37 Or what shall a man give in exchange for his soul?

C 38 [a]Whosoever therefore [b]shall be
O ashamed of me and of my words in this
T adulterous and sinful generation; of him also shall the Son of man be ashamed, when he cometh in the glory of his Father with the holy angels.

B *Mk 1:7 ◀ ▶ Mk 14:18–21*
S *Mk 4:16–20 ◀ ▶ Mk 9:43–50*
H *Mk 6:11 ◀ ▶ Mk 9:42–49*
C *Mk 4:29 ◀ ▶ Mk 13:26*
O *Mt 25:1–12 ◀ ▶ Mk 10:15*
T *Mk 5:19 ◀ ▶ Lk 6:45*

9 AND HE said unto them, [a]Verily I say unto you, That there be some of them that stand here, which shall not taste of death, till they have seen [b]the kingdom of God come with power. K

The transfiguration

2 ¶ [a]And after six days Jesus taketh *with him* Peter, and James, and John, and leadeth them up into an high mountain apart by themselves: and he was transfigured before them.

3 And his raiment became shining, exceeding [a]white as snow; so as no fuller on earth can white them.

4 And there appeared unto them Elias with Moses: and they were talking with Jesus.

5 And Peter answered and said to Jesus, Master, it is good for us to be here: and let us make three tabernacles; one for thee, and one for Moses, and one for Elias.

6 For he wist not what to say; for they were sore afraid.

7 And there was a cloud that overshadowed them: and a voice came out of the cloud, saying, This is my beloved Son: hear him.

8 And suddenly, when they had looked round about, they saw no man any more, save Jesus only with themselves.

9 [a]And as they came down from the mountain, he charged them that they should tell no man what things they had seen, till the Son of man were risen from the dead.

10 And they kept that saying with themselves, questioning one with another what the rising from the dead should mean.

11 ¶ And they asked him, saying, Why say the scribes [a]that Elias must first come?

12 And he answered and told them, Elias verily cometh first, and restoreth all things; and [a]how it is written of the Son of man, that he must suffer many things, and [b]be set at nought.

13 But I say unto you, That [a]Elias is

K *Mk 4:26–28 ◀ ▶ Lk 11:2*

28 [a]Mat. 14:2
29 [a]Mat. 16:16; John 6:69 & 11:27
30 [a]Mat. 16:20
31 [a]Mat. 16:21 & 17:22; Luke 9:22
34 [a]Mat. 10:38 & 16:24; Luke 9:23 & 14:27
35 [a]John 12:25
38 [a]Mat. 10:33; Luke 9:26 & 12:9 [b]See Rom. 1:16; 2 Tim. 1:8 & 2:12
9:1 [a]Mat. 16:28; Luke 9:27 [b]Mat. 24:30
2 [a]Mat. 17:1; Luke 9:28
3 [a]Dan. 7:9
9 [a]Mat. 17:9
11 [a]Mal. 4:5; Mat. 17:10
12 [a]Ps. 22:6; Is. 53:2; Dan. 9:26 [b]Luke 23:11; Phil. 2:7
13 [a]Mat. 11:14 & 17:12; Luke 1:17

8:38 Jesus warned that those who deny their faith in him and his words will be rejected when he returns. When we face persecution for our Christian faith, we need to remember this warning and ask ourselves, "For what shall it profit a man, if he shall gain the whole world, and lose his own soul?" (Mk 8:36).

indeed come, and they have done unto him whatsoever they listed, as it is written of him.

The demoniac boy cured

E 14 ¶ [a]And when he came to *his* disciples, he saw a great multitude about them, and the scribes questioning with them.

15 And straightway all the people, when they beheld him, were greatly amazed, and running to *him* saluted him.

16 And he asked the scribes, What question ye ′with them?

17 And [a]one of the multitude answered and said, Master, I have brought unto thee my son, which hath a dumb spirit;

18 And wheresoever he taketh him, he ′teareth him: and he foameth, and gnasheth with his teeth, and pineth away: and I spake to thy disciples that they should cast him out; and they could not.

19 He answereth him, and saith, O faithless generation, how long shall I be with you? how long shall I suffer you? bring him unto me.

20 And they brought him unto him: and [a]when he saw him, straightway the spirit tare him; and he fell on the ground, and wallowed foaming.

21 And he asked his father, How long is it ago since this came unto him? And he said, Of a child.

22 And ofttimes it hath cast him into the fire, and into the waters, to destroy him: but if thou canst do any thing, have compassion on us, and help us.

H 23 Jesus said unto him, [a]If thou canst believe, all things *are* possible to him that believeth.

24 And straightway the father of the child cried out, and said with tears, Lord, I believe; help thou mine unbelief.

25 When Jesus saw that the people came running together, he rebuked the foul spirit, saying unto him, *Thou* dumb and deaf spirit, I charge thee, come out of him, and enter no more into him.

26 And *the spirit* cried, and rent him sore, and came out of him: and he was as one dead; insomuch that many said, He is dead.

E *Mk 8:22–26* ◀ ▶ *Mk 9:38–39*
H *Mt 10:7–8* ◀ ▶ *Mk 16:17–18*

27 But Jesus took him by the hand, and lifted him up; and he arose.

28 [a]And when he was come into the house, his disciples asked him privately, Why could not we cast him out?

29 And he said unto them, This kind can come forth by nothing, but by prayer and fasting.

30 ¶ And they departed thence, and passed through Galilee; and he would not that any man should know *it.*

31 [a]For he taught his disciples, and said unto them, The Son of man is delivered into the hands of men, and they shall kill him; and after that he is killed, he shall rise the third day.

32 But they understood not that saying, and were afraid to ask him.

True discipleship

33 ¶ [a]And he came to Capernaum: and being in the house he asked them, What was it that ye disputed among yourselves by the way?

34 But they held their peace: for by the way they had disputed among themselves, who *should be* the greatest.

35 And he sat down, and called the twelve, and saith unto them, [a]If any man desire to be first, *the same* shall be last of all, and servant of all.

36 And [a]he took a child, and set him in the midst of them: and when he had taken him in his arms, he said unto them,

37 Whosoever shall receive one of such children in my name, receiveth me: and [a]whosoever shall receive me, receiveth not me, but him that sent me.

38 ¶ [a]And John answered him, saying, Master, we saw one casting out devils in thy name, and he followeth not us: and we forbad him, because he followeth not us. E

39 But Jesus said, Forbid him not: [a]for there is no man which shall do a miracle in my name, that can lightly speak evil of me.

40 For [a]he that is not against us is on our part.

41 [a]For whosoever shall give you a cup of water to drink in my name, because ye belong to Christ, verily I say unto you, he shall not lose his reward.

E *Mk 9:14–29* ◀ ▶ *Mk 10:46–52*

14 [a]Mat. 17:14; Luke 9:37
16 ′Or, *among yourselves?*
17 [a]Mat. 17:14; Luke 9:38
18 ′Or, *dasheth him*
20 [a]ch. 1:26; Luke 9:42
23 [a]Mat. 17:20; ch. 11:23; Luke 17:6; John 11:40
28 [a]Mat. 17:19
31 [a]Mat. 17:22; Luke 9:44
33 [a]Mat. 18:1; Luke 9:46 & 22:24
35 [a]Mat. 20:26,27; ch. 10:43
36 [a]Mat. 18:2; ch. 10:16
37 [a]Mat. 10:40; Luke 9:48
38 [a]Num. 11:28; Luke 9:49
39 [a]1 Cor. 12:3
40 [a]See Mat. 12:30
41 [a]Mat. 10:42

H **L** 42 [a]And whosoever shall offend one of *these* little ones that believe in me, it is better for him that a millstone were hanged about his neck, and he were cast into the sea.

S 43 [a]And if thy hand [1]offend thee, cut it off: it is better for thee to enter into life maimed, than having two hands to go into hell, into the fire that never shall be quenched:

44 [a]Where their worm dieth not, and the fire is not quenched.

45 And if thy foot offend thee, cut it off: it is better for thee to enter halt into life, than having two feet to be cast into hell, into the fire that never shall be quenched:

46 Where their worm dieth not, and the fire is not quenched.

47 And if thine eye offend thee, pluck it out: it is better for thee to enter into the kingdom of God with one eye, than having two eyes to be cast into hell fire:

48 Where their worm dieth not, and the fire is not quenched.

49 For every one shall be salted with fire, [a]and every sacrifice shall be salted with salt.

50 [a]Salt *is* good: but if the salt have lost his saltness, wherewith will ye season it? [b]Have salt in yourselves, and [c]have peace one with another.

Marriage and divorce

10 AND [a]HE arose from thence, and cometh into the coasts of Judaea by the farther side of Jordan: and the people resort unto him again; and, as he was wont, he taught them again.

2 ¶ [a]And the Pharisees came to him, and asked him, Is it lawful for a man to put away *his* wife? tempting him.

3 And he answered and said unto them, What did Moses command you?

4 And they said, [a]Moses suffered to write a bill of divorcement, and to put *her* away.

5 And Jesus answered and said unto them, For the hardness of your heart he wrote you this precept.

6 But from the beginning of the creation [a]God made them male and female.

7 [a]For this cause shall a man leave his father and mother, and cleave to his wife;

8 And they twain shall be one flesh: so then they are no more twain, but one flesh.

9 What therefore God hath joined together, let not man put asunder.

10 And in the house his disciples asked him again of the same *matter.*

11 And he saith unto them, [a]Whosoever shall put away his wife, and marry another, committeth adultery against her.

12 And if a woman shall put away her husband, and be married to another, she committeth adultery.

Jesus blesses the little children

13 ¶ [a]And they brought young children to him, that he should touch them: and *his* disciples rebuked those that brought *them.*

14 But when Jesus saw *it,* he was **M** much displeased, and said unto them, Suffer the little children to come unto me, and forbid them not: for [a]of such is the kingdom of God.

15 Verily I say unto you, [a]Whosoever **O** shall not receive the kingdom of God as a little child, he shall not enter therein.

16 And he took them up in his arms, put *his* hands upon them, and blessed them.

The rich young ruler

17 ¶ [a]And when he was gone forth **G** into the way, there came one running, and kneeled to him, and asked him, Good Master, what shall I do that I may inherit eternal life?

18 And Jesus said unto him, Why callest thou me good? *there is* none good but one, *that is,* God.

19 Thou knowest the commandments, [a]Do not commit adultery, Do not kill, Do not steal, Do not bear false witness, Defraud not, Honour thy father and mother.

20 And he answered and said unto him, Master, all these have I observed from my youth.

21 Then Jesus beholding him loved him, and said unto him, One thing thou lackest: go thy way, sell whatsoever thou hast, and give to the poor, and thou shalt have [a]treasure in heaven: and come, take up the cross, and follow me.

42 [a]Mat. 18:6; Luke 17:1
43 [a]Deut. 13:6; Mat. 5:29 & 18:8 [1]Or, *cause thee to offend;* also ver. 45,47
44 [a]Is. 66:24
49 [a]Lev. 2:13; Ezek. 43:24
50 [a]Mat. 5:13; Luke 14:34 [b]Eph. 4:29; Col. 4:6 [c]Rom. 12:18 & 14:19; 2 Cor. 13:11; Heb. 12:14
10:1 [a]Mat. 19:1; John 10:40 & 11:7
2 [a]Mat. 19:3
4 [a]Deut. 24:1; Mat. 5:31 & 19:7
6 [a]Gen. 1:27 & 5:2
7 [a]Gen. 2:24; 1 Cor. 6:16; Eph. 5:31
11 [a]Mat. 5:32 & 19:9; Luke 16:18; Rom. 7:3; 1 Cor. 7:10,11
13 [a]Mat. 19:13; Luke 18:15
14 [a]1 Cor. 14:20; 1 Pet. 2:2
15 [a]Mat. 18:3
17 [a]Mat. 19:16; Luke 18:18
19 [a]Ex. 20; Rom. 13:9
21 [a]Mat. 6:19,20; & 19:21; Luke 12:33 & 16:9

H *Mk 8:36–38* ◀▶ *Mk 12:36–40*
L *Mt 28:20* ◀▶ *Mk 11:24*
S *Mk 8:34* ◀▶ *Mk 12:2*
M *Mt 23:12* ◀▶ *Mk 10:23–25*
O *Mk 8:38* ◀▶ *Mk 12:28–34*
G *Mk 7:6–7* ◀▶ *Lk 18:9–14*

22 And he was sad at that saying, and went away grieved: for he had great possessions.

M 23 ¶ [a]And Jesus looked round about, and saith unto his disciples, How hardly shall they that have riches enter into the kingdom of God!

24 And the disciples were astonished at his words. But Jesus answereth again, and saith unto them, Children, how hard is it for them [a]that trust in riches to enter into the kingdom of God!

25 It is easier for a camel to go through the eye of a needle, than for a rich man to enter into the kingdom of God.

26 And they were astonished out of measure, saying among themselves, Who then can be saved?

K 27 And Jesus looking upon them saith, With men *it is* impossible, but not with God: for [a]with God all things are possible.

U 28 ¶ [a]Then Peter began to say unto him, Lo, we have left all, and have followed thee.

29 And Jesus answered and said, Verily I say unto you, There is no man that hath left house, or brethren, or sisters, or father, or mother, or wife, or children, or lands, for my sake, and the gospel's,

30 [a]But he shall receive an hundredfold now in this time, houses, and brethren, and sisters, and mothers, and children, and lands, with persecutions; and in the world to come eternal life.

31 [a]But many *that are* first shall be last; and the last first.

Jesus again foretells his death

32 ¶ [a]And they were in the way going up to Jerusalem; and Jesus went before them: and they were amazed; and as they followed, they were afraid. [b]And he took again the twelve, and began to tell them what things should happen unto him,

33 *Saying,* Behold, we go up to Jerusalem; and the Son of man shall be delivered unto the chief priests, and unto the scribes; and they shall condemn him to death, and shall deliver him to the Gentiles:

34 And they shall mock him, and shall scourge him, and shall spit upon him, and shall kill him: and the third day he shall rise again.

The ambition of James and John

35 ¶ [a]And James and John, the sons of Zebedee, come unto him, saying, Master, we would that thou shouldest do for us whatsoever we shall desire.

36 And he said unto them, What would ye that I should do for you?

37 They said unto him, Grant unto us that we may sit, one on thy right hand, and the other on thy left hand, in thy glory. M

38 But Jesus said unto them, Ye know not what ye ask: can ye drink of the cup that I drink of? and be baptized with the baptism that I am baptized with?

39 And they said unto him, We can. And Jesus said unto them, Ye shall indeed drink of the cup that I drink of; and with the baptism that I am baptized withal shall ye be baptized: M

40 But to sit on my right hand and on my left hand is not mine to give; but *it shall be given to them* for whom it is prepared.

41 [a]And when the ten heard *it,* they began to be much displeased with James and John.

42 But Jesus called them *to him,* and saith unto them, [a]Ye know that they which [I]are accounted to rule over the Gentiles exercise lordship over them; and their great ones exercise authority upon them.

43 [a]But so shall it not be among you: but whosoever will be great among you, shall be your minister:

44 And whosoever of you will be the chiefest, shall be servant of all.

23 [a]Mat. 19:23; Luke 18:24
24 [a]Job 31:24; Ps. 52:7 & 62:10; 1 Tim. 6:17
27 [a]Jer. 32:17; Mat. 19:26; Luke 1:37
28 [a]Mat. 19:27; Luke 18:28
30 [a]2 Chr. 25:9; Luke 18:30
31 [a]Mat. 19:30 & 20:16; Luke 13:30
32 [a]Mat. 20:17; Luke 18:31 [b]ch. 8:31 & 9:31; Luke 9:22 & 18:31
35 [a]Mat. 20:20
41 [a]Mat. 20:24
42 [a]Luke 22:25 [I]Or, *think good*
43 [a]Mat. 20:26,28; ch. 9:35; Luke 9:48

M *Mk 10:14–15* ◀▶ *Lk 6:20–21*
K *Mk 2:10* ◀▶ *Mk 13:31*
U *Mt 19:29* ◀▶ *Lk 12:31*

M *Mk 4:30–32* ◀▶ *Mk 10:39–40*
M *Mk 10:37* ◀▶ *Mk 11:10*

10:37 The desire of James and John to attain cabinet positions in the coming kingdom of Jesus Christ reveals the physical reality of Christ's millennial kingdom. While many scholars have dismissed these ambitious disciples, we need to remember that even though these men did not understand that Jesus would die before returning to establish his millennial kingdom, they did understand that they had been promised the right to rule over the twelve tribes of Israel (see Mt 19:28).

D 45 For even [a]the Son of man came not to be ministered unto, but to minister, and [b]to give his life a ransom for many.

Bartimaeus receives his sight

E 46 ¶ [a]And they came to Jericho: and as he went out of Jericho with his disciples and a great number of people, blind Bartimaeus, the son of Timaeus, sat by the highway side begging.

47 And when he heard that it was Jesus of Nazareth, he began to cry out, and say, Jesus, *thou* son of David, have mercy on me.

48 And many charged him that he should hold his peace: but he cried the more a great deal, *Thou* son of David, have mercy on me.

49 And Jesus stood still, and commanded him to be called. And they call the blind man, saying unto him, Be of good comfort, rise; he calleth thee.

50 And he, casting away his garment, rose, and came to Jesus.

51 And Jesus answered and said unto him, What wilt thou that I should do unto thee? The blind man said unto him, Lord, that I might receive my sight.

52 And Jesus said unto him, Go thy way; [a]thy faith hath [/]made thee whole. And immediately he received his sight, and followed Jesus in the way.

The triumphal entry

11 AND [a]WHEN they came nigh to Jerusalem, unto Bethphage and Bethany, at the mount of Olives, he sendeth forth two of his disciples,

2 And saith unto them, Go your way into the village over against you: and as soon as ye be entered into it, ye shall find a colt tied, whereon never man sat; loose him, and bring *him.*

3 And if any man say unto you, Why do ye this? say ye that the Lord hath need of him; and straightway he will send him hither.

4 And they went their way, and found the colt tied by the door without in a place where two ways met; and they loose him.

5 And certain of them that stood there said unto them, What do ye, loosing the colt?

6 And they said unto them even as Jesus had commanded: and they let them go.

7 And they brought the colt to Jesus, and cast their garments on him; and he sat upon him.

8 [a]And many spread their garments in the way: and others cut down branches off the trees, and strawed *them* in the way.

9 And they that went before, and they that followed, cried, saying, [a]Hosanna; Blessed *is* he that cometh in the name of the Lord:

10 Blessed *be* the kingdom of our fa- I
ther David, that cometh in the name of M
the Lord: [a]Hosanna in the highest.

11 [a]And Jesus entered into Jerusalem, and into the temple: and when he had looked round about upon all things, and now the eventide was come, he went out unto Bethany with the twelve.

The cleansing of the temple

12 ¶ [a]And on the morrow, when they were come from Bethany, he was hungry:

13 [a]And seeing a fig tree afar off having leaves, he came, if haply he might find any thing thereon: and when he came to it, he found nothing but leaves; for the time of figs was not *yet.*

14 And Jesus answered and said unto it, No man eat fruit of thee hereafter for ever. And his disciples heard *it.*

15 ¶ [a]And they come to Jerusalem: and Jesus went into the temple, and began to

45 [a]John 13:14; Phil. 2:7 [b]Mat. 20:28; 1 Tim. 2:6; Tit. 2:14
46 [a]Mat. 20:29; Luke 18:35
52 [a]Mat. 9:22; ch. 5:34 [/]Or, *saved thee*
11:1 [a]Mat. 21:1; Luke 19:29; John 12:14
8 [a]Mat. 21:8
9 [a]Ps. 118:26
10 [a]Ps. 148:1
11 [a]Mat. 21:12
12 [a]Mat. 21:18
13 [a]Mat. 21:19
15 [a]Mat. 21:12; Luke 19:45; John 2:14

D *Mt 26:26–28* ◀ ▶ *Mk 14:22–24*
E *Mk 9:38–39* ◀ ▶ *Mk 16:9*
I *Mt 27:42* ◀ ▶ *Mk 15:2*
M *Mk 10:39–40* ◀ ▶ *Mk 12:36*

11:10 The disciples and the people that joined this procession acknowledged Jesus' legal right to be acclaimed Israel's Messiah and loudly announced his coming kingdom.

11:13–14, 20–21 The symbol of the fig tree appears numerous times in the OT in reference to Israel (see Jdg 9:10–11; 1Ki 4:25; Isa 36:16; Mic 4:4; Zec 3:10). Jesus withered this barren fig tree because it did not bear fruit for its Creator, symbolizing that Israel had not borne spiritual fruit. God promised that Israel would produce great spiritual fruit in the last days (see Ro 11:25–29). Jesus foretold that when we see the fig tree flourishing again—Israel reborn as a nation—we will know that the end times are "near, even at the doors" (Mt 24:33).

cast out them that sold and bought in the temple, and overthrew the tables of the moneychangers, and the seats of them that sold doves;

16 And would not suffer that any man should carry *any* vessel through the temple.

17 And he taught, saying unto them, Is it not written, [a]My house shall be called [l]of all nations the house of prayer? but [b]ye have made it a den of thieves.

18 And [a]the scribes and chief priests heard *it,* and sought how they might destroy him: for they feared him, because [b]all the people was astonished at his doctrine.

19 And when even was come, he went out of the city.

The power of faith

20 ¶ [a]And in the morning, as they passed by, they saw the fig tree dried up from the roots.

21 And Peter calling to remembrance saith unto him, Master, behold, the fig tree which thou cursedst is withered away.

22 And Jesus answering saith unto them, [l]Have faith in God.

23 For [a]verily I say unto you, That whosoever shall say unto this mountain, Be thou removed, and be thou cast into the sea; and shall not doubt in his heart, but shall believe that those things which he saith shall come to pass; he shall have whatsoever he saith.

L 24 Therefore I say unto you, [a]What things soever ye desire, when ye pray, believe that ye receive *them,* and ye shall have *them.*

R 25 And when ye stand praying, [a]forgive, if ye have aught against any: that your Father also which is in heaven may forgive you your trespasses.

26 But [a]if ye do not forgive, neither will your Father which is in heaven forgive your trespasses.

Jesus' authority challenged

27 ¶ And they come again to Jerusalem: [a]and as he was walking in the temple, there come to him the chief priests, and the scribes, and the elders,

17 [a]Is. 56:7 [b]Jer. 7:11 [l]Or, *an house of prayer for all nations?*

18 [a]Mat. 21:45,46; Luke 19:47 [b]Mat. 7:28; ch. 1,22; Luke 4:32

20 [a]Mat. 21:19

22 [l]Or, *Have the faith of God*

23 [a]Mat. 17:20 & 21:21; Luke 17:6

24 [a]Mat. 7:7; Luke 11:9; John 14:13 & 15:7 & 16:24; Jas. 1:5,6

25 [a]Mat. 6:14; Col. 3:13

26 [a]Mat. 18:35

27 [a]Mat. 21:23; Luke 20:1

29 [l]Or, *thing*

32 [a]Mat. 3:5 & 14:5; ch. 6:20

12:1 [a]Mat. 21:33; Luke 20:9

28 And say unto him, By what authority doest thou these things? and who gave thee this authority to do these things?

29 And Jesus answered and said unto them, I will also ask of you one [l]question, and answer me, and I will tell you by what authority I do these things.

30 The baptism of John, was *it* from heaven, or of men? answer me.

31 And they reasoned with themselves, saying, If we shall say, From heaven; he will say, Why then did ye not believe him?

32 But if we shall say, Of men; they feared the people: for [a]all *men* counted John, that he was a prophet indeed.

33 And they answered and said unto Jesus, We cannot tell. And Jesus answering saith unto them, Neither do I tell you by what authority I do these things.

The parable of the husbandmen

12 AND [a]HE began to speak unto them by parables. A *certain* man planted a vineyard, and set an hedge about *it,* and digged *a place for* the winefat, and built a tower, and let it out to husbandmen, and went into a far country.

2 And at the season he sent to the husbandmen a servant, that he might receive from the husbandmen of the fruit of the vineyard. S

3 And they caught *him,* and beat him, and sent *him* away empty.

4 And again he sent unto them another servant; and at him they cast stones, and wounded *him* in the head, and sent *him* away shamefully handled.

5 And again he sent another; and him they killed, and many others; beating some, and killing some.

6 Having yet therefore one son, his wellbeloved, he sent him also last unto them, saying, They will reverence my son.

7 But those husbandmen said among themselves, This is the heir; come, let us kill him, and the inheritance shall be ours.

8 And they took him, and killed *him,* and cast *him* out of the vineyard.

L *Mk 9:42* ◀ ▶ *Lk 4:10–11*
R *Mk 6:12* ◀ ▶ *Lk 3:8*
S *Mk 9:43–50* ◀ ▶ *Mk 13:13*

G R 9 What shall therefore the lord of the vineyard do? he will come and destroy the husbandmen, and will give the vineyard unto others.

10 And have ye not read this scripture; [a]The stone which the builders rejected is become the head of the corner:

11 This was the Lord's doing, and it is marvellous in our eyes?

12 [a]And they sought to lay hold on him, but feared the people: for they knew that he had spoken the parable against them: and they left him, and went their way.

Tribute to Caesar

13 ¶ [a]And they send unto him certain of the Pharisees and of the Herodians, to catch him in *his* words.

14 And when they were come, they say unto him, Master, we know that thou art true, and carest for no man: for thou regardest not the person of men, but teachest the way of God in truth: Is it lawful to give tribute to Caesar, or not?

15 Shall we give, or shall we not give? But he, knowing their hypocrisy, said unto them, Why tempt ye me? bring me a [l]penny, that I may see *it.*

16 And they brought *it.* And he saith unto them, Whose *is* this image and superscription? And they said unto him, Caesar's.

17 And Jesus answering said unto them, Render to Caesar the things that are Caesar's, and to God the things that are God's. And they marvelled at him.

Saddducees and the resurrection

18 ¶ [a]Then come unto him the Sadducees, [b]which say there is no resurrection; and they asked him, saying,

19 Master, [a]Moses wrote unto us, If a man's brother die, and leave *his* wife *behind him,* and leave no children, that his brother should take his wife, and raise up seed unto his brother.

20 Now there were seven brethren: and the first took a wife, and dying left no seed.

21 And the second took her, and died, neither left he any seed: and the third likewise.

22 And the seven had her, and left no seed: last of all the woman died also.

23 In the resurrection therefore, when they shall rise, whose wife shall she be of them? for the seven had her to wife.

24 And Jesus answering said unto them, Do ye not therefore err, because ye know not the scriptures, neither the power of God? F

25 For when they shall rise from the dead, they neither marry, nor are given in marriage; but [a]are as the angels which are in heaven.

26 And as touching the dead, that they rise: have ye not read in the book of Moses, how in the bush God spake unto him, saying, [a]I *am* the God of Abraham, and the God of Isaac, and the God of Jacob?

27 He is not the God of the dead, but the God of the living: ye therefore do greatly err.

The Great Commandment

28 ¶ [a]And one of the scribes came, and having heard them reasoning together, and perceiving that he had answered them well, asked him, Which is the first commandment of all? O

29 And Jesus answered him, The first of all the commandments *is,* [a]Hear, O Israel; The Lord our God is one Lord:

30 And thou shalt love the Lord thy God with all thy heart, and with all thy soul, and with all thy mind, and with all thy strength: this *is* the first commandment.

31 And the second *is* like, *namely* this, [a]Thou shalt love thy neighbour as thyself. There is none other commandment greater than these.

32 And the scribe said unto him, Well, Master, thou hast said the truth: for there

10 [a]Ps. 118:22
12 [a]Mat. 21:45,46; ch. 11:18; John 7:25,30,44
13 [a]Mat. 22:15; Luke 20:20
15 [l]The penny, worth about 16 cents, was the usual day's wage for a laborer
18 [a]Mat. 22:23; Luke 20:27 [b]Acts 23:8
19 [a]Deut. 25:5
25 [a]1 Cor. 15:42, 49,52
26 [a]Ex. 3:6
28 [a]Mat. 22:35
29 [a]Deut. 6:4; Luke 10:27
31 [a]Lev. 19:18; Mat. 22:39; Rom. 13:9; Gal. 5:14; Jas. 2:8

G *Mt 22:9–10* ◀▶ *Lk 14:21*
R *Mt 24:15–22* ◀▶ *Mk 13:1–2*
F *Mt 22:30–32* ◀▶ *Lk 14:13–14*
O *Mk 10:15* ◀▶ *Mk 16:15–16*

12:9 In this prophetic parable, Jesus taught that God as "the lord of the vineyard" would destroy the generation of unrepentant Jews who rejected Jesus' claims as their Messiah. Jesus' words foreshadowed the creation of the church, composed of both Gentiles and Jews, who would accept his claims as Messiah and inherit the spiritual kingdom of heaven because of their faith in him.

12:24–25 See study note at Mt 22:29–32.

is one God; [a]and there is none other
but he:
33 And to love him with all the heart,
and with all the understanding, and with
all the soul, and with all the strength, and
to love *his* neighbour as himself, [a]is more
than all whole burnt offerings and sacrifices.
34 And when Jesus saw that he answered discreetly, he said unto him,
Thou art not far from the kingdom of
God. [a]And no man after that durst ask
him *any question.*

The question about David's son

35 ¶ [a]And Jesus answered and said,
while he taught in the temple, How say
the scribes that Christ is the son of
David?
M 36 For David himself said [a]by the Holy
V Ghost, [b]The LORD said to my Lord, Sit
E thou on my right hand, till I make thine
L enemies thy footstool.
T 37 David therefore himself calleth him
H Lord; and whence is he *then* his son?
And the common people heard him
gladly.
38 ¶ And [a]he said unto them in his
doctrine, [b]Beware of the scribes, which
love to go in long clothing, and [c]*love* salutations in the marketplaces,
39 And the chief seats in the synagogues, and the uppermost rooms at
feasts:
40 [a]Which devour widows' houses,
and for a pretence make long prayers:
these shall receive greater damnation.

The widow's mite

41 ¶ [a]And Jesus sat over against the
treasury, and beheld how the people cast
[ℓ]money [b]into the treasury: and many that
were rich cast in much.
42 And there came a certain poor
widow, and she threw in two [ℓ]mites,
which make a farthing.
43 And he called *unto him* his disciples, and saith unto them, Verily I say
unto you, That [a]this poor widow hath
cast more in, than all they which have
cast into the treasury:
44 For all *they* did cast in of their abundance; but she of her want did cast in all
that she had, [a]*even* all her living.

Signs of the end of this age

13 AND [a]AS he went out of the tem- R
ple, one of his disciples saith
unto him, Master, see what manner of
stones and what buildings *are here!*
2 And Jesus answering said unto him,
Seest thou these great buildings? [a]there
shall not be left one stone upon another,
that shall not be thrown down.
3 And as he sat upon the mount of Olives over against the temple, Peter and
James and John and Andrew asked him
privately,
4 [a]Tell us, when shall these things be?
and what *shall be* the sign when all these
things shall be fulfilled?
5 And Jesus answering them began to E
say, [a]Take heed lest any *man* deceive
you:
6 For many shall come in my name,

32 [a]Deut. 4:39; Is. 45:6,14 & 46:9
33 [a]1 Sam. 15:22; Hos. 6:6; Mic. 6:6-8
34 [a]Mat. 22:46
35 [a]Mat. 22:41; Luke 20:41
36 [a]2 Sam. 23:2 [b]Ps. 110:1
38 [a]ch. 4:2 [b]Mat. 23:1; Luke 20:46 [c]Luke 11:43
40 [a]Mat. 23:14
41 [a]Luke 21:1 [b]2 Ki. 12:9 [ℓ]*A piece of brass money,* worth about one cent; see Mark 6:8
42 [ℓ]Two mites were worth only a fraction of a cent
43 [a]2 Cor. 8:12
44 [a]Deut. 24:6; 1 John 3:17
13:1 [a]Mat. 24:1; Luke 21:5
2 [a]Luke 19:44
4 [a]Mat. 24:3; Luke 21:7
5 [a]Jer. 29:8; Eph. 5:6; 1 Thes. 2:3

M *Mk 11:10* ◀ ▶ *Mk 15:2*
V *Mt 22:44* ◀ ▶ *Lk 1:33*
E *Mk 1:12* ◀ ▶ *Lk 1:15–17*
L *Mk 1:12* ◀ ▶ *Mk 13:11*
T *Mt 22:43–44* ◀ ▶ *Mk 13:11*
H *Mk 9:42–49* ◀ ▶ *Mk 13:19*

R *Mk 12:9* ◀ ▶ *Mk 13:14–20*
E *Mt 24:32–33* ◀ ▶ *Mk 13:22*

12:35–36 See study note at Mt 22:44.

13:1–2 This chapter records Christ's prophetic discourse to his disciples on the mount of Olives several days before his crucifixion (see Mt 24). Note that this discourse occurred before the crucifixion and before the establishment of the NT church.

As Jesus sat on the mount of Olives he prophesied that the temple would be totally destroyed so that "there shall not be left one stone upon another, that shall not be thrown down" (13:2). This detailed prophecy was precisely fulfilled when the Romans burned the temple to the ground in A.D. 70. The fire melted the gold that was inlaid on the walls of the sanctuary so that it flowed down into the cracks between the huge stones. When the fire subsided, Roman soldiers and scavengers pried the stones apart to recover the valuable gold. In complete fulfillment of this prophecy, not one stone was left on top of another.

13:4 This verse records the questions of Christ's disciples regarding the coming destruction of the temple and the final signs that will indicate the return of Jesus Christ in the last days. See the study notes for Mt 24:1–3 for additional information.

13:6–7 The first prophetic sign of Christ's return will be the rise of false Christs. Though there have always been those who claimed to be the Messiah, the incidence of such claims is increasingly on the

saying, I am *Christ;* and shall deceive
many.
7 And when ye shall hear of wars and
rumours of wars, be ye not troubled: for
such things must needs be; but the end
shall not *be* yet.
8 For nation shall rise against nation,
and kingdom against kingdom: and there
shall be earthquakes in divers places, and
there shall be famines and troubles:
[a]these *are* the beginnings of [l]sorrows.
9 ¶ But [a]take heed to yourselves: for
they shall deliver you up to councils; and
in the synagogues ye shall be beaten: and
ye shall be brought before rulers
and kings for my sake, for a testimony
against them.
10 And [a]the gospel must first be published among all nations.
G 11 [a]But when they shall lead *you,* and
L deliver you up, take no thought before-
M hand what ye shall speak, neither do ye
T premeditate: but whatsoever shall be
given you in that hour, that speak ye: for
it is not ye that speak, [b]but the Holy
Ghost.
12 Now [a]the brother shall betray the
brother to death, and the father the son;
and children shall rise up against *their*
parents, and shall cause them to be put to
death.
S 13 [a]And ye shall be hated of all *men*
for my name's sake: but [b]he that shall
endure unto the end, the same shall be
saved.

G *Mt 10:19–20 ◀ ▶ Mk 16:17–18*
L *Mk 12:36 ◀ ▶ Lk 2:27*
M *Mt 12:28 ◀ ▶ Lk 1:15–17*
T *Mk 12:36 ◀ ▶ Mk 16:17*
S *Mk 12:2 ◀ ▶ Lk 3:9*

8 [a]Mat. 24:8 [l]The word in the original importeth *the pains of a woman in travail*
9 [a]Mat. 10:17,18; & 24:9; Rev. 2:10
10 [a]Mat. 24:14
11 [a]Mat. 10:19; Luke 12:11 & 21:14 [b]Acts 2:4 & 4:8,31
12 [a]Mic. 7:6; Mat. 10:21 & 24:10; Luke 21:16
13 [a]Mat. 24:9; Luke 21:17 [b]Dan. 12:12; Mat. 10:22 & 24:13; Rev. 2:10
14 [a]Mat. 24:15 [b]Dan. 9:27 [c]Luke 21:21
17 [a]Luke 21:23
19 [a]Dan. 9:26 & 12:1; Joel 2:2; Mat. 24:21
21 [a]Mat. 24:23; Luke 17:23 & 21:8
23 [a]2 Pet. 3:17
24 [a]Dan. 7:10; Zeph. 1:15; Mat. 24:29

14 ¶ [a]But when ye shall see the abomi- R
nation of desolation, [b]spoken of by Daniel
the prophet, standing where it ought not,
(let him that readeth understand,) then
[c]let them that be in Judaea flee to the
mountains:
15 And let him that is on the housetop
not go down into the house, neither enter *therein,* to take any thing out of his
house:
16 And let him that is in the field not
turn back again for to take up his
garment.
17 [a]But woe to them that are with
child, and to them that give suck in those
days!
18 And pray ye that your flight be not
in the winter.
19 [a]For *in* those days shall be afflic- H
tion, such as was not from the beginning
of the creation which God created unto
this time, neither shall be.
20 And except that the Lord had shortened those days, no flesh should be
saved: but for the elect's sake, whom he
hath chosen, he hath shortened the days.
21 [a]And then if any man shall say to
you, Lo, here *is* Christ; or, lo, *he is* there;
believe *him* not:
22 For false Christs and false prophets E
shall rise, and shall show signs and wonders, to seduce, if *it were* possible, even
the elect.
23 But [a]take ye heed: behold, I have
foretold you all things.
24 ¶ [a]But in those days, after that trib- E

R *Mk 13:1–2 ◀ ▶ Lk 13:3*
H *Mk 12:36–40 ◀ ▶ Mk 14:21*
E *Mk 13:5–13 ◀ ▶ Mk 13:24*
E *Mk 13:22 ◀ ▶ Mk 13:27*

---

rise. Jesus also warned that "wars and rumours of wars" (13:7) would be another prophetic sign of his imminent return. Since 1945, we have endured more wars than any other generation in history (see Joel 3:9–10). See the study notes for Mt 24:4–8.

13:8 Jesus also warned that several cataclysmic signs in nature would signal his return. See the study notes for Mt 24:4–8.

13:9–10 Jesus prophesied that his followers would be subject to extreme persecution by the religious authorities. Initially fulfilled during the first century, this prophecy will find its final fulfillment during the tribulation. See the study notes for Mt 24:9–14.

13:14–20 Compare this passage with Mt 24:20–22 and refer to the study notes for more information.

13:21–25 This prophetic warning should alert anyone to the claims of false Christs who produce deceptive signs. Note the expression "if it were possible" (13:22) reveals the impossibility of deceiving the elect about the true identity of the Messiah. See the study notes for Mt 24:23–27.

13:24–27 Many cataclysmic events will occur in both nature and politics just after the tribulation. Then Christ will return "in the clouds with great power and glory" (13:26). His angels will gather the "elect" from all over the world. These "elect" are the saints who come to faith in Christ during the terrible persecution of the tribulation. This gathering is not the rapture described by the apostle Paul in

ulation, the sun shall be darkened, and the moon shall not give her light,

25 And the stars of heaven shall fall, and the powers that are in heaven shall be shaken.

C 26 [a]And then shall they see the Son of
D man coming in the clouds with great power and glory.

E 27 And then shall he send his angels, and shall gather together his elect from the four winds, from the uttermost part of the earth to the uttermost part of heaven.

28 [a]Now learn a parable of the fig tree; When her branch is yet tender, and putteth forth leaves, ye know that summer is near:

29 So ye in like manner, when ye shall see these things come to pass, know that it is nigh, *even* at the doors.

30 Verily I say unto you, that this generation shall not pass, till all these things be done.

E 31 Heaven and earth shall pass away:
K but [a]my words shall not pass away.

C 32 ¶ But of that day and *that* hour knoweth no man, no, not the angels which are in heaven, neither the Son, but the Father.

33 [a]Take ye heed, watch and pray: for ye know not when the time is.

34 [a]*For the Son of man is* as a man taking a far journey, who left his house, and gave authority to his servants, and to every man his work, and commanded the porter to watch.

35 [a]Watch ye therefore: for ye know not when the master of the house cometh, at even, or at midnight, or at the cockcrowing, or in the morning:

36 Lest coming suddenly he find you sleeping.

37 And what I say unto you I say unto all, Watch.

C *Mk 8:38* ◀ ▶ *Mk 13:32–37*
D *Mt 25:31* ◀ ▶ *1Th 3:13*
E *Mk 13:24* ◀ ▶ *Mk 13:31–32*
E *Mk 13:27* ◀ ▶ *Lk 17:26–30*
K *Mk 10:27* ◀ ▶ *Mk 14:36*
C *Mk 13:26* ◀ ▶ *Mk 14:62*

26 [a]Dan. 7:13,14; Mat. 16:27 & 24:30; ch. 14:62; Acts 1:11; 1 Thes. 4:16; 2 Thes. 1:7, 10; Rev. 1:7
28 [a]Mat. 24:32; Luke 21:29
31 [a]Is. 40:8
33 [a]Mat. 24:42 & 25:13; Luke 12:40 & 21:34; Rom. 13:11; 1 Thes. 5:6
34 [a]Mat. 24:45 & 25:14
35 [a]Mat. 24:42,44
14:1 [a]Mat. 26:2; Luke 22:1; John 11:55 & 13:1
3 [a]Mat. 26:6; John 12:1,3; See Luke 7:37 [1]Or, *pure nard,* or, *liquid nard*
5 [a]Mat. 18:28; ch. 12:15
10 [a]Mat. 26:14; Luke 22:3,4
12 [a]Mat. 26:17; Luke 22:7 [1]Or, *sacrificed*

Anointing of Jesus at Bethany

14 AFTER [a]TWO days was *the feast of* the passover, and of unleavened bread: and the chief priests and the scribes sought how they might take him by craft, and put *him* to death.

2 But they said, Not on the feast *day,* lest there be an uproar of the people.

3 ¶ [a]And being in Bethany in the house of Simon the leper, as he sat at meat, there came a woman having an alabaster box of ointment of [1]spikenard very precious; and she brake the box, and poured *it* on his head.

4 And there were some that had indignation within themselves, and said, Why was this waste of the ointment made?

5 For it might have been sold for more than three hundred [a]pence, and have been given to the poor. And they murmured against her.

6 And Jesus said, Let her alone; why trouble ye her? she hath wrought a good work on me.

7 For ye have the poor with you always, and whensoever ye will ye may do them good: but me ye have not always.

8 She hath done what she could: she is come aforehand to anoint my body to the burying.

9 Verily I say unto you, Wheresoever this gospel shall be preached throughout the whole world, *this* also that she hath done shall be spoken of for a memorial of her.

10 ¶ [a]And Judas Iscariot, one of the twelve, went unto the chief priests, to betray him unto them.

11 And when they heard *it,* they were glad, and promised to give him money. And he sought how he might conveniently betray him.

The last supper

12 ¶ [a]And the first day of unleavened bread, when they [1]killed the passover, his disciples said unto him, Where wilt thou that we go and prepare that thou mayest eat the passover?

13 And he sendeth forth two of his disciples, and saith unto them, Go ye into

---

1Co 15:51 and 1Th 4:16–17. See the study note at Mt 24:31 for further information.

13:28–37 The parable of the fig tree predicts the generation when the Son of man will return. This prophetic passage commands the saints to "watch" (13:34) for his return. See the study note for Mt 24:32–35.

the city, and there shall meet you a man bearing a pitcher of water: follow him.

14 And wheresoever he shall go in, say ye to the goodman of the house, The Master saith, Where is the guestchamber, where I shall eat the passover with my disciples?

15 And he will show you a large upper room furnished *and* prepared: there make ready for us.

16 And his disciples went forth, and came into the city, and found as he had said unto them: and they made ready the passover.

17 [a]And in the evening he cometh with the twelve.

B 18 And as they sat and did eat, Jesus said, Verily I say unto you, One of you which eateth with me shall betray me.

19 And they began to be sorrowful, and to say unto him one by one, *Is* it I? and another *said, Is* it I?

20 And he answered and said unto them, *It is* one of the twelve, that dippeth with me in the dish.

H 21 [a]The Son of man indeed goeth, as it is written of him: but woe to that man by whom the Son of man is betrayed! good were it for that man if he had never been born.

D 22 ¶ [a]And as they did eat, Jesus took bread, and blessed, and brake *it,* and gave to them, and said, Take, eat: this is my body.

23 And he took the cup, and when he had given thanks, he gave *it* to them: and they all drank of it.

24 And he said unto them, This is my blood of the new testament, which is shed for many.

25 Verily I say unto you, I will drink no more of the fruit of the vine, until that day that I drink it new in the kingdom of God.

Peter's denial foretold

26 ¶ [a]And when they had sung an [I]hymn, they went out into the mount of Olives.

B 27 [a]And Jesus saith unto them, All ye shall be offended because of me this night: for it is written, [b]I will smite the shepherd, and the sheep shall be scattered.

28 But [a]after that I am risen, I will go before you into Galilee.

29 [a]But Peter said unto him, Although all shall be offended, yet *will* not I.

30 And Jesus saith unto him, Verily I say unto thee, That this day, *even* in this night, before the cock crow twice, thou shalt deny me thrice. B

31 But he spake the more vehemently, If I should die with thee, I will not deny thee in any wise. Likewise also said they all.

Jesus' agony in Gethsemane

32 [a]And they came to a place which was named Gethsemane: and he saith to his disciples, Sit ye here, while I shall pray.

33 And he taketh with him Peter and James and John, and began to be sore amazed, and to be very heavy;

34 And saith unto them, [a]My soul is exceeding sorrowful unto death: tarry ye here, and watch.

35 And he went forward a little, and fell on the ground, and prayed that, if it were possible, the hour might pass from him.

36 And he said, [a]Abba, Father, [b]all things *are* possible unto thee; take away this cup from me: [c]nevertheless not what I will, but what thou wilt. K

37 And he cometh, and findeth them sleeping, and saith unto Peter, Simon, sleepest thou? couldest not thou watch one hour?

38 Watch ye and pray, lest ye enter into temptation. [a]The spirit truly *is* ready, but the flesh *is* weak.

39 And again he went away, and prayed, and spake the same words.

40 And when he returned, he found them asleep again, (for their eyes were heavy,) neither wist they what to answer him.

41 And he cometh the third time, and saith unto them, Sleep on now, and take *your* rest: it is enough, [a]the hour is come; behold, the Son of man is betrayed into the hands of sinners.

17 [a]Mat. 26:20
21 [a]Mat. 26:24; Luke 22:22
22 [a]Mat. 26:26; Luke 22:19; 1 Cor. 11:23
26 [a]Mat. 26:30 [I]Or, *psalm*
27 [a]Mat. 26:31 [b]Zech. 13:7
28 [a]ch. 16:7
29 [a]Mat. 26:33,34; Luke 22:33,34; John 13:37,38
32 [a]Mat. 26:36; Luke 22:39; John 18:1
34 [a]John 12:27
36 [a]Rom. 8:15; Gal. 4:6 [b]Heb. 5:7 [c]John 5:30 & 6:38
38 [a]Rom. 7:23; Gal. 5:17
41 [a]John 13:1

B *Mk 8:31* ◀▶ *Mk 14:27–28*
H *Mk 13:19* ◀▶ *Mk 16:16*
D *Mk 10:45* ◀▶ *Lk 22:17–20*
B *Mk 14:18–21* ◀▶ *Mk 14:30*

B *Mk 14:27–28* ◀▶ *Mk 14:42*
K *Mk 13:31* ◀▶ *Lk 1:37*

B 42 [a]Rise up, let us go; lo, he that betrayeth me is at hand.

Jesus' betrayal and arrest

43 ¶ [a]And immediately, while he yet spake, cometh Judas, one of the twelve, and with him a great multitude with swords and staves, from the chief priests and the scribes and the elders.

44 And he that betrayed him had given them a token, saying, Whomsoever I shall kiss, that same is he; take him, and lead *him* away safely.

45 And as soon as he was come, he goeth straightway to him, and saith, Master, master; and kissed him.

46 ¶ And they laid their hands on him, and took him.

47 And one of them that stood by drew a sword, and smote a servant of the high priest, and cut off his ear.

48 [a]And Jesus answered and said unto them, Are ye come out, as against a thief, with swords and *with* staves to take me?

49 I was daily with you in the temple teaching, and ye took me not: but [a]the scriptures must be fulfilled.

50 [a]And they all forsook him, and fled.

51 And there followed him a certain young man, having a linen cloth cast about *his* naked *body;* and the young men laid hold on him:

52 And he left the linen cloth, and fled from them naked.

Jesus before Caiaphas

53 ¶ [a]And they led Jesus away to the high priest: and with him were assembled all the chief priests and the elders and the scribes.

54 And Peter followed him afar off, even into the palace of the high priest: and he sat with the servants, and warmed himself at the fire.

55 [a]And the chief priests and all the council sought for witness against Jesus to put him to death; and found none.

56 For many bare false witness against him, but their witness agreed not together.

57 And there arose certain, and bare false witness against him, saying,

42 [a]Mat. 26:46; John 18:1,2
43 [a]Mat. 26:47; Luke 22:47; John 18:3
48 [a]Mat. 26:55; Luke 22:52
49 [a]Ps. 22:6; Is. 53:7; Luke 22:37 & 24:44
50 [a]ver. 27; Ps. 88:8
53 [a]Mat. 26:57; Luke 22:54; John 18:13
55 [a]Mat. 26:59
58 [a]ch. 15:29; John 2:19
60 [a]Mat. 26:62
61 [a]Is. 53:7 [b]Mat. 26:63
62 [a]Mat. 24:30 & 26:64; Luke 22:69
66 [a]Mat. 26:58,69; Luke 22:55; John 18:16
69 [a]Mat. 26:71; Luke 22:58; John 18:25
70 [a]Mat. 26:73; Luke 22:59; John 18:26 [b]Acts 2:7

58 We heard him say, [a]I will destroy this temple that is made with hands, and within three days I will build another made without hands.

59 But neither so did their witness agree together.

60 [a]And the high priest stood up in the midst, and asked Jesus, saying, Answerest thou nothing? what *is it which* these witness against thee?

61 But [a]he held his peace, and answered nothing. [b]Again the high priest asked him, and said unto him, Art thou the Christ, the Son of the Blessed?

62 And Jesus said, I am: [a]and ye shall see the Son of man sitting on the right hand of power, and coming in the clouds of heaven. C

63 Then the high priest rent his clothes, and saith, What need we any further witnesses?

64 Ye have heard the blasphemy: what think ye? And they all condemned him to be guilty of death.

65 And some began to spit on him, and to cover his face, and to buffet him, and to say unto him, Prophesy: and the servants did strike him with the palms of their hands.

Peter's denial of Jesus

66 ¶ [a]And as Peter was beneath in the palace, there cometh one of the maids of the high priest:

67 And when she saw Peter warming himself, she looked upon him, and said, And thou also wast with Jesus of Nazareth.

68 But he denied, saying, I know not, neither understand I what thou sayest. And he went out into the porch; and the cock crew.

69 [a]And a maid saw him again, and began to say to them that stood by, This is *one* of them.

70 And he denied it again. [a]And a little after, they that stood by said again to Peter, Surely thou art *one* of them: [b]for thou art a Galilaean, and thy speech agreeth *thereto.*

71 But he began to curse and to swear,

B *Mk 14:30 ◄► Lk 1:30–35*

C *Mk 13:32–37 ◄► Lk 9:26*

14:62 These prophetic words addressed to the high priest will be fulfilled when Christ returns at Armageddon to save his people.

saying, I know not this man of whom ye speak.

72 [a]And the second time the cock crew. And Peter called to mind the word that Jesus said unto him, Before the cock crow twice, thou shalt deny me thrice. And [l]when he thought thereon, he wept.

Jesus before Pontius Pilate

15 AND [a]STRAIGHTWAY in the morning the chief priests held a consultation with the elders and scribes and the whole council, and bound Jesus, and carried *him* away, and delivered *him* to Pilate.

I 2 [a]And Pilate asked him, Art thou the
M King of the Jews? And he answering said unto him, Thou sayest *it.*

3 And the chief priests accused him of many things: but he answered nothing.

4 [a]And Pilate asked him again, saying, Answerest thou nothing? behold how many things they witness against thee.

5 [a]But Jesus yet answered nothing; so that Pilate marvelled.

6 Now [a]at *that* feast he released unto them one prisoner, whomsoever they desired.

7 And there was *one* named Barabbas, *which lay* bound with them that had made insurrection with him, who had committed murder in the insurrection.

8 And the multitude crying aloud began to desire *him to do* as he had ever done unto them.

I 9 But Pilate answered them, saying,
M Will ye that I release unto you the King of the Jews?

10 For he knew that the chief priests had delivered him for envy.

11 But [a]the chief priests moved the people, that he should rather release Barabbas unto them.

I *Mk 11:10* ◀▶ *Mk 15:9*
M *Mk 12:36* ◀▶ *Mk 15:9*
I *Mk 15:2* ◀▶ *Mk 15:12*
M *Mk 15:2* ◀▶ *Mk 15:12*

72 [a]Mat. 26:75 [l]Or, *he wept abundantly,* or, *he began to weep*
15:1 [a]Ps. 2:2; Mat. 27:1; Luke 22:66 & 23:1; John 18:28; Acts 3:13 & 4:26
2 [a]Mat. 27:11
4 [a]Mat. 27:13
5 [a]Is. 53:7; John 19:9
6 [a]Mat. 27:15; Luke 23:17; John 18:39
11 [a]Mat. 27:20; Acts 3:14
15 [a]Mat. 27:26; John 19:1,16
16 [a]Mat. 27:27
21 [a]Mat. 27:32; Luke 23:26
22 [a]Mat. 27:33; Luke 23:33; John 19:17
23 [a]Mat. 27:34
24 [a]Ps. 22:18; Luke 23:34; John 19:23

12 And Pilate answered and said again I
unto them, What will ye then that I shall M
do *unto him* whom ye call the King of the Jews?

13 And they cried out again, Crucify him.

14 Then Pilate said unto them, Why, what evil hath he done? And they cried out the more exceedingly, Crucify him.

15 ¶ [a]And *so* Pilate, willing to content the people, released Barabbas unto them, and delivered Jesus, when he had scourged *him,* to be crucified.

Jesus crowned with thorns

16 [a]And the soldiers led him away into the hall, called Praetorium; and they call together the whole band.

17 And they clothed him with purple, I
and plaited a crown of thorns, and put it M
about his *head,*

18 And began to salute him, Hail, King of the Jews!

19 And they smote him on the head with a reed, and did spit upon him, and bowing *their* knees worshipped him.

20 And when they had mocked him, they took off the purple from him, and put his own clothes on him, and led him out to crucify him.

Jesus crucified

21 [a]And they compel one Simon a Cyrenian, who passed by, coming out of the country, the father of Alexander and Rufus, to bear his cross.

22 [a]And they bring him unto the place Golgotha, which is, being interpreted, The place of a skull.

23 [a]And they gave him to drink wine mingled with myrrh: but he received *it* not.

24 And when they had crucified him, [a]they parted his garments, casting lots upon them, what every man should take.

I *Mk 15:9* ◀▶ *Mk 15:17–18*
M *Mk 15:9* ◀▶ *Mk 15:17–18*
I *Mk 15:12* ◀▶ *Mk 15:26*
M *Mk 15:12* ◀▶ *Mk 15:26*

15:2–18, 26 Pontius Pilate asked Jesus, "Art thou the King of the Jews?" (15:2). Jesus' positive response not only affirmed his claim to be Israel's Messiah and king, but foreshadowed that future day following Armageddon when he will take his position on the throne of David in Jerusalem as the King of the whole world. The Roman soldiers that mocked his royalty, the accusation affixed to the cross and the personal accusation of the unrepentant thief all unwittingly acknowledged the prophetic truth that Jesus will one day be acclaimed "KING OF THE JEWS" (15:26).

25 And [a]it was the third hour, and they crucified him.

I M 26 And [a]the superscription of his accusation was written over, THE KING OF THE JEWS.

27 And [a]with him they crucify two thieves; the one on his right hand, and the other on his left.

28 And the scripture was fulfilled, which saith, [a]And he was numbered with the transgressors.

29 And [a]they that passed by railed on him, wagging their heads, and saying, Ah, [b]thou that destroyest the temple, and buildest *it* in three days,

30 Save thyself, and come down from the cross.

31 Likewise also the chief priests mocking said among themselves with the scribes, He saved others; himself he cannot save.

I M 32 Let Christ the King of Israel descend now from the cross, that we may see and believe. And [a]they that were crucified with him reviled him.

The death of Jesus

33 And [a]when the sixth hour was come, there was darkness over the whole land until the ninth hour.

34 And at the ninth hour Jesus cried with a loud voice, saying, [a]Eloi, Eloi, lama sabachthani? which is, being interpreted, My God, my God, why hast thou forsaken me?

35 And some of them that stood by, when they heard *it,* said, Behold, he calleth Elias.

36 And [a]one ran and filled a sponge full of vinegar, and put *it* on a reed, and [b]gave him to drink, saying, Let alone; let us see whether Elias will come to take him down.

37 [a]And Jesus cried with a loud voice, and gave up the ghost.

38 And [a]the veil of the temple was rent in twain from the top to the bottom.

39 ¶ And [a]when the centurion, which stood over against him, saw that he so cried out, and gave up the ghost, he said, Truly this man was the Son of God.

40 [a]There were also women looking on [b]afar off: among whom was Mary Magdalene, and Mary the mother of James the less and of Joses, and Salome;

41 (Who also, when he was in Galilee, [a]followed him, and ministered unto him;) and many other women which came up with him unto Jerusalem.

Jesus laid in the tomb

42 ¶ [a]And now when the even was come, because it was the preparation, that is, the day before the sabbath,

43 Joseph of Arimathaea, an honourable counsellor, which also [a]waited for the kingdom of God, came, and went in boldly unto Pilate, and craved the body of Jesus. M

44 And Pilate marvelled if he were already dead: and calling *unto him* the centurion, he asked him whether he had been any while dead.

45 And when he knew *it* of the centurion, he gave the body to Joseph.

46 [a]And he bought fine linen, and took him down, and wrapped him in the linen, and laid him in a sepulchre which was hewn out of a rock, and rolled a stone unto the door of the sepulchre.

47 And Mary Magdalene and Mary *the mother* of Joses beheld where he was laid.

The resurrection of Jesus

16 AND [a]WHEN the sabbath was past, Mary Magdalene, and Mary the *mother* of James, and Salome, [b]had bought sweet spices, that they might come and anoint him.

2 [a]And very early in the morning the first *day* of the week, they came unto the sepulchre at the rising of the sun.

3 And they said among themselves, Who shall roll us away the stone from the door of the sepulchre?

4 And when they looked, they saw that the stone was rolled away: for it was very great.

5 [a]And entering into the sepulchre, they saw a young man sitting on the right

25 [a]See Mat. 27:45; Luke 23:44; John 19:14
26 [a]Mat. 27:37; John 19:19
27 [a]Mat. 27:38
28 [a]Is. 53:12; Luke 22:37
29 [a]Ps. 22:7 [b]ch. 14:58; John 2:19
32 [a]Mat. 27:44; Luke 23:39
33 [a]Mat. 27:45; Luke 23:44
34 [a]Ps. 22:1; Mat. 27:46
36 [a]Mat. 27:48; John 19:29 [b]Ps. 69:21
37 [a]Mat. 27:50; Luke 23:46; John 19:30
38 [a]Mat. 27:51; Luke 23:45
39 [a]Mat. 27:54; Luke 23:47
40 [a]Mat. 27:55; Luke 23:49 [b]Ps. 38:11
41 [a]Luke 8:2,3
42 [a]Mat. 27:57; Luke 23:50; John 19:38
43 [a]Luke 2:25,38
46 [a]Mat. 27:59,60; Luke 23:53; John 19:40
16:1 [a]Mat. 28:1; Luke 24:1; John 20:1 [b]Luke 23:56
2 [a]Luke 24:1; John 20:1
5 [a]Luke 24:3; John 20:11

I *Mk 15:17–18* ◀▶ *Mk 15:32*
M *Mk 15:17–18* ◀▶ *Mk 15:32*
I *Mk 15:26* ◀▶ *Lk 1:32–33*
M *Mk 15:26* ◀▶ *Mk 15:43*
M *Mk 15:32* ◀▶ *Lk 1:32–33*

15:43 Joseph of Arimathaea acknowledged Jesus' claim as the Son of man who would rule in the millennial "kingdom of God" (15:43).

side, clothed in a long white garment; and they were affrighted.

6 [a]And he saith unto them, Be not affrighted: Ye seek Jesus of Nazareth, which was crucified: he is risen; he is not here: behold the place where they laid him.

7 But go your way, tell his disciples and Peter that he goeth before you into Galilee: there shall ye see him, [a]as he said unto you.

8 And they went out quickly, and fled from the sepulchre; for they trembled and were amazed: [a]neither said they any thing to any *man;* for they were afraid.

E 9 ¶ Now when *Jesus* was risen early the first *day* of the week, he appeared first to Mary Magdalene, [a]out of whom he had cast seven devils.

10 [a]*And* she went and told them that had been with him, as they mourned and wept.

11 [a]And they, when they had heard that he was alive, and had been seen of her, believed not.

12 ¶ After that he appeared in another form [a]unto two of them, as they walked, and went into the country.

13 And they went and told *it* unto the residue: neither believed they them.

14 ¶ [a]Afterward he appeared unto the eleven as they sat [1]at meat, and upbraided them with their unbelief and hardness of heart, because they believed not them which had seen him after he was risen.

15 [a]And he said unto them, Go ye into N
all the world, [b]and preach the gospel to O
every creature. W

16 [a]He that believeth and is baptized F
shall be saved; [b]but he that believeth not H
shall be damned.

17 And these signs shall follow them G
that believe; [a]In my name shall they cast T
out devils; [b]they shall speak with new H
tongues;

18 [a]They shall take up serpents; and if they drink any deadly thing, it shall not hurt them; [b]they shall lay hands on the sick, and they shall recover.

19 ¶ So then [a]after the Lord had spoken unto them, he was [b]received up into heaven, and [c]sat on the right hand of God.

20 And they went forth, and preached every where, the Lord working with *them,* [a]and confirming the word with signs following. Amen.

6 [a]Mat. 28:5
7 [a]Mat. 26:32; ch. 14:28
8 [a]Mat. 28:8; Luke 24:9
9 [a]Luke 8:2
10 [a]Luke 24:10; John 20:18
11 [a]Luke 24:11
12 [a]Luke 24:13
14 [a]Luke 24:36; John 20:19; 1 Cor. 15:5 [1]Or, *together*
15 [a]Mat. 28:19; John 15:16 [b]Col. 1:23
16 [a]John 3:18; Acts 2:38 & 16:30-32; Rom. 10:9; 1 Pet. 3:21 [b]John 12:48
17 [a]Luke 10:17; Acts 5:16 [b]Acts 2:4; 1 Cor. 12:10
18 [a]Luke 10:19; Acts 28:5 [b]Acts 5:15; Jas. 5:14
19 [a]Acts 1:2,3 [b]Luke 24:51 [c]Ps. 110:1; Acts 7:55
20 [a]Acts 5:12; 1 Cor. 2:4,5; Heb. 2:4

E *Mk 10:46–52* ◀▶ *Lk 1:18*

N *Mk 6:11* ◀▶ *Lk 10:10–16*
O *Mk 12:28–34* ◀▶ *Lk 6:47–49*
W *Mk 3:28* ◀▶ *Lk 2:10–11*
F *Mk 1:15* ◀▶ *Lk 7:50*
H *Mk 14:21* ◀▶ *Lk 3:7*
G *Mk 13:11* ◀▶ *Lk 1:17*
T *Mk 13:11* ◀▶ *Lk 1:41–42*
H *Mk 9:23* ◀▶ *Lk 4:18*

Luke

Author: Luke

Theme: The Savior of the world is Jesus

Date of Writing: c. A.D. 59–63

Outline of Luke

I. Prologue (1:1–4)
II. Jesus' Birth (1:5—2:52)
III. Ministry of John the Baptist (3:1–20)
IV. Jesus Is Publicly Introduced (3:21—4:44)
V. Jesus' Ministry in Galilee (5:1—6:16)
VI. Jesus Teaches and Heals (6:17—9:50)
VII. Jesus Ministers in Judea and Perea (9:51—18:30)
VIII. Suffering and Crucifixion (18:31—23:56)
IX. The Triumphal Resurrection (24:1–53)

This Gospel is a companion volume to the book of Acts and was written by Luke, "the beloved physician" (Col 4:14). A traveling companion and fellow worker with Paul (see 2Ti 4:11; Phm 24), Luke accompanied Paul on his last trip to Rome (see Ac 21:1–17; 27:28) and probably wrote this account shortly after Paul's death.

The book of Luke is the longest and most literary of the Gospels and was written primarily for Greek believers. Emphasizing the perfect humanity of Jesus while acknowledging him as God incarnate in human flesh, Luke traces Jesus' ancestry back to Adam. Along with its presentation of Jesus as the Son of Man, this book reveals Jesus' concern for a lost humanity and the gift of salvation for all as recorded in the parables of the lost sheep, the lost coin and the lost son (see 15:3–32). Luke's association with Paul is evident in the theological perspective of the work of the Holy Spirit in Jesus' life (see 1:15; 3:22; 4:1, 14; 10:21). Note also that Luke tells about Jesus' boyhood and reveals more of his prayer life than the other gospel narratives.

Luke's record of Jesus' life and ministry also contains the medical terms and trained observations of a physician as well as a doctor's compassion and concern for all types of people. With the narrative of the birth and infancy of Jesus presented from the point of view of Jesus' mother, Luke shows a concern for women, children and the poor that is unparalleled in any other NT account. This Gospel also identifies by name many of the women who ministered to Jesus and stresses Jesus' sympathy for the brokenhearted, the sick and the bereaved.

Preface

1 FORASMUCH AS many have taken
in hand to set forth in order a declaration of those things which are most
surely believed among us,
2 [a]Even as they delivered them unto
us, which [b]from the beginning were eyewitnesses, and ministers of the word;
3 [a]It seemed good to me also, having
had perfect understanding of all things
from the very first, to write unto thee [b]in
order, [c]most excellent Theophilus,
4 [a]That thou mightest know the certainty of those things, wherein thou hast
been instructed.

Birth of John foretold

5 ¶ There was [a]in the days of Herod,
the king of Judaea, a certain priest named
Zacharias, [b]of the course of Abia: and his
wife *was* of the daughters of Aaron, and
her name *was* Elisabeth.
6 And they were both [a]righteous before God, walking in all the commandments and ordinances of the Lord
blameless.
7 And they had no child, because that
Elisabeth was barren, and they both were
now well stricken in years.
8 And it came to pass, that while he
executed the priest's office before God
[a]in the order of his course,
9 According to the custom of the
priest's office, his lot was [a]to burn incense when he went into the temple of
the Lord.
10 [a]And the whole multitude of the
people were praying without at the time
of incense.
11 And there appeared unto him an
angel of the Lord standing on the right
side of [a]the altar of incense.
12 And when Zacharias saw *him,* [a]he
was troubled, and fear fell upon him.

1:2 [a]Heb. 2:3; 1 Pet. 5:1; 2 Pet. 1:16 [b]Mark 1:1; John 15:27
3 [a]Acts 15:19; 1 Cor. 7:40 [b]Acts 11:4 [c]Acts 1:1
4 [a]John 20:31
5 [a]Mat. 2:1 [b]1 Chr. 24:10; Neh. 12:4
6 [a]Gen. 7:1; 1 Ki. 9:4; 2 Ki. 20:3
8 [a]1 Chr. 24:19; 2 Chr. 8:14
9 [a]Ex. 30:7,8; 1 Chr. 23:13; 2 Chr. 29:11
10 [a]Lev. 16:17
11 [a]Ex. 30:1
12 [a]Judg. 6:22 & 13:22; Dan. 10:8; ch. 2:9; Acts 10:4; Rev. 1:17
13 [a]ver. 60,63
14 [a]ver. 58
15 [a]Num. 6:3; Judg. 13:4; ch. 7:33 [b]Jer. 1:5; Gal. 1:15
16 [a]Mal. 4:5,6
17 [a]Mal. 4:5; Mat. 11:14; Mark 9:12 [l]Or, *by*
18 [a]Gen. 17:17
19 [a]Dan. 8:16 & 9:21-23; Mat. 18:10; Heb. 1:14
20 [a]Ezek. 3:26 & 24:27

13 But the angel said unto him, Fear R
not, Zacharias: for thy prayer is heard;
and thy wife Elisabeth shall bear thee a
son, and [a]thou shalt call his name John.
14 And thou shalt have joy and gladness; and [a]many shall rejoice at his birth.
15 For he shall be great in the sight of B
the Lord, and [a]shall drink neither wine C
nor strong drink; and he shall be filled E
with the Holy Ghost, [b]even from his M
mother's womb.
16 [a]And many of the children of Israel
shall he turn to the Lord their God.
17 [a]And he shall go before him in the G
spirit and power of Elias, to turn the R
hearts of the fathers to the children, and S
the disobedient [l]to the wisdom of the
just; to make ready a people prepared for
the Lord.
18 And Zacharias said unto the angel, E
[a]Whereby shall I know this? for I am an
old man, and my wife well stricken in
years.
19 And the angel answering said unto
him, I am [a]Gabriel, that stand in the presence of God; and am sent to speak unto
thee, and to show thee these glad tidings.
20 And, behold, [a]thou shalt be dumb, D
and not able to speak, until the day that
these things shall be performed, because
thou believest not my words, which shall
be fulfilled in their season.
21 And the people waited for Zacharias, and marvelled that he tarried so long
in the temple.
22 And when he came out, he could
not speak unto them: and they perceived

R *Ps 144:12* ◄ **B** *Mk 1:10* ◄► *Lk 1:41*
C *Zec 12:10* ◄► *Jn 16:7–11*
E *Mk 12:36* ◄► *Lk 1:41*
M *Mk 13:11* ◄► *Lk 1:80*
G *Mk 16:17–18* ◄► *Lk 1:67*
R *Eze 36:25–27* ◄► *Jn 3:3–8*
S *Mic 2:7* ◄► *Ac 15:8–9*
E *Mk 16:9* ◄► *Lk 1:36–37*
D *Mk 6:5–6* ◄► *Lk 4:23–27*

1:13–17 The first prophecy in the book of Luke concerns the prediction given to the priest Zacharias that his wife Elisabeth would bear a son. This son was to be named John, and he would give joy to many. The angel predicted that John would become a Nazirite (see Jdg 13:5–7; 16:17; Nu 6; Am 2:11–12) and be filled with the Holy Spirit in his mother's womb. He would also fulfill Malachi's prophecies about Elias (Elijah) as he prepared Israel for the Lord's appearance (see Mal 3:1; 4:5–6).

Note that the angel foretold that John would accomplish only one part of Malachi's prophecy to "turn the hearts of the fathers to the children" (1:17). By omitting Malachi's words about the "great and dreadful day of the LORD" (Mal 4:5) the angel revealed that John would not fulfill the totality of Malachi's prophecy. This final fulfillment will occur in the last days with the rise of the two witnesses and Elijah the prophet (see Rev 11:3–12).

that he had seen a vision in the temple: for he beckoned unto them, and remained speechless.

23 And it came to pass, that as soon as [a]the days of his ministration were accomplished, he departed to his own house.

24 And after those days his wife Elisabeth conceived, and hid herself five months, saying,

25 Thus hath the Lord dealt with me in the days wherein he looked on *me,* to [a]take away my reproach among men.

The birth of Jesus foretold

26 And in the sixth month the angel Gabriel was sent from God unto a city of Galilee, named Nazareth,

27 To a virgin [a]espoused to a man whose name was Joseph, of the house of David; and the virgin's name *was* Mary.

28 And the angel came in unto her, and said, [a]Hail, *thou that art* [1]highly favoured, [b]the Lord *is* with thee: blessed *art* thou among women.

29 And when she saw *him,* [a]she was troubled at his saying, and cast in her mind what manner of salutation this should be.

B 30 And the angel said unto her, Fear
not, Mary: for thou hast found favour
with God.

31 [a]And, behold, thou shalt conceive
in thy womb, and bring forth a son, and
[b]shalt call his name JESUS.

I 32 He shall be great, [a]and shall be
M called the Son of the Highest: and [b]the
Lord God shall give unto him the throne
of his father David:

V 33 [a]And he shall reign over the house
of Jacob for ever; and of his kingdom
there shall be no end.

34 Then said Mary unto the angel, How shall this be, seeing I know not a man?

35 And the angel answered and said unto her, [a]The Holy Ghost shall come upon thee, and the power of the Highest shall overshadow thee: therefore also that holy thing which shall be born of thee shall be called [b]the Son of God.

36 And, behold, thy cousin Elisabeth, E
she hath also conceived a son in her old
age: and this is the sixth month with her,
who was called barren.

37 For [a]with God nothing shall be im- K
possible.

38 And Mary said, Behold the handmaid of the Lord; be it unto me according to thy word. And the angel departed from her.

Mary visits Elisabeth

39 And Mary arose in those days, and went into the hill country with haste, [a]into a city of Judah;

40 And entered into the house of Zacharias, and saluted Elisabeth.

41 And it came to pass, that, when B
Elisabeth heard the salutation of Mary, E
the babe leaped in her womb; and Elisa- T
beth was filled with the Holy Ghost:

42 And she spake out with a loud voice, and said, [a]Blessed *art* thou among women, and blessed *is* the fruit of thy womb.

43 And whence *is* this to me, that the mother of my Lord should come to me?

44 For, lo, as soon as the voice of thy salutation sounded in mine ears, the babe leaped in my womb for joy.

45 And blessed *is* she [1]that believed: for there shall be a performance of those things which were told her from the Lord.

The song of Mary

46 And Mary said, [a]My soul doth magnify the Lord,

47 And my spirit hath rejoiced in God my Saviour.

48 For [a]he hath regarded the low es-

23 [a]2 Ki. 11:5; 1 Chr. 9:25
25 [a]Gen. 30:23; Is. 4:1 & 54:1,4
27 [a]Mat. 1:18; ch. 2:4,5
28 [a]Dan. 9:23 & 10:19 [b]Judg. 6:12 [1]*Or, graciously accepted,* or, *much graced;* see ver. 30
29 [a]ver. 12
31 [a]Is. 7:14; Mat. 1:21 [b]ch. 2:21
32 [a]Mark 5:7 [b]2 Sam. 7:11; Ps. 132:11; Is. 9:6,7 & 16:5; Jer. 23:5; Rev. 3:7
33 [a]Dan. 2:44 & 7:14,27; Obad. 21; Mic. 4:7; John 12:34; Heb. 1:8
35 [a]Mat. 1:20 [b]Mat. 14:33 & 26:63,64; Mark 1:1; John 1:34 & 20:31; Acts 8:37; Rom. 1:4
37 [a]Gen. 18:14; Jer. 32:17; Zech. 8:6; Mat. 19:26; Mark 10:27; ch. 18:27; Rom. 4:21
39 [a]Josh. 21:9
42 [a]Judg. 5:24
45 [1]*Or, which believed that there*
46 [a]1 Sam. 2:1; Ps. 34:2,3; Hab. 3:18
48 [a]1 Sam. 1:11; Ps. 138:6

B *Mk 14:42* ◀ ▶ *Lk 2:30–32*
I *Mk 15:32* ◀ ▶ *Lk 1:68–79*
M *Mk 15:43* ◀ ▶ *Lk 2:26*
V *Mk 12:36* ◀ ▶ *Lk 20:42–43*
E *Lk 1:18* ◀ ▶ *Lk 4:23–27*
K *Mk 14:36* ◀ ▶ *Lk 2:10–11*
B *Lk 1:15* ◀ ▶ *Lk 1:67*
E *Lk 1:15–17* ◀ ▶ *Lk 1:67*
T *Mk 16:17* ◀ ▶ *Lk 1:67*

1:30–35 The angel prophesied that Mary would supernaturally conceive the Christ-child who would be named Jesus. The prediction included the words that Jesus would be "called the Son of the Highest" (1:32) and that, as the true Messiah, he would receive the "throne of his father David" (1:32). Finally, the angel prophesied that his kingdom would never end and that this child would be divine and be called "the Son of God" (1:35).

tate of his handmaiden: for, behold, from
henceforth [b]all generations shall call me
blessed.
49 For he that is mighty [a]hath done to
me great things; and [b]holy *is* his name.
50 And [a]his mercy *is* on them that fear
him from generation to generation.
51 [a]He hath shown strength with his
arm; [b]he hath scattered the proud in the
imagination of their hearts.
52 [a]He hath put down the mighty from
their seats, and exalted them of low
degree.
53 [a]He hath filled the hungry with
good things; and the rich he hath sent
empty away.
54 He hath helped his servant Israel,
[a]in remembrance of *his* mercy;
55 [a]As he spake to our fathers, to
Abraham, and to his seed for ever.
56 And Mary abode with her about
three months, and returned to her own
house.

The birth of John the Baptist

57 Now Elisabeth's full time came that
she should be delivered; and she brought
forth a son.
58 And her neighbours and her cous-
ins heard how the Lord had shown great
mercy upon her; and they rejoiced with
her.
59 And it came to pass, that [a]on the
eighth day they came to circumcise the
child; and they called him Zacharias, after
the name of his father.
60 And his mother answered and said,
[a]Not *so;* but he shall be called John.
61 And they said unto her, There is
none of thy kindred that is called by this
name.
62 And they made signs to his father,
how he would have him called.
63 And he asked for a writing table,
and wrote, saying, His name is John. And
they marvelled all.
64 And his mouth was opened immediately, and his tongue *loosed,* and he
spake, and praised God.
65 And fear came on all that dwelt
round about them: and all these [1]sayings
were noised abroad throughout all the
hill country of Judaea.
66 And all they that heard *them* [a]laid
them up in their hearts, saying, What
manner of child shall this be! And [b]the
hand of the Lord was with him.

The song of Zacharias

67 And his father Zacharias [a]was filled B
with the Holy Ghost, and prophesied, E
saying, G
68 [a]Blessed *be* the Lord God of Israel; T
for [b]he hath visited and redeemed his I
people,
69 [a]And hath raised up an horn of salvation for us in the house of his servant
David;
70 [a]As he spake by the mouth of his
holy prophets, which have been since the
world began:
71 That we should be saved from our
enemies, and from the hand of all that
hate us;
72 [a]To perform the mercy *promised* to
our fathers, and to remember his holy
covenant;
73 [a]The oath which he sware to our
father Abraham,
74 That he would grant unto us, that
we being delivered out of the hand of our
enemies might [a]serve him without fear,
75 [a]In holiness and righteousness before him, all the days of our life.
76 And thou, child, shalt be called the
prophet of the Highest: for [a]thou shalt go
before the face of the Lord to prepare his
ways;
77 To give knowledge of salvation unto L
his people [a]by[1] the remission of their
sins,
78 Through the [1]tender mercy of our
God; whereby the [2]dayspring from on
high hath visited us,
79 [a]To give light to them that sit in C

48 [b]ch. 11:27
49 [a]Ps. 71:19 & 126:2,3 [b]Ps. 111:9
50 [a]Gen. 17:7; Ex. 20:6; Ps. 103:17
51 [a]Ps. 98:1 & 118:15; Is. 40:10 [b]Ps. 33:10; 1 Pet. 5:5
52 [a]1 Sam. 2:6; Job 5:11; Ps. 113:6
53 [a]1 Sam. 2:5; Ps. 34:10
54 [a]Ps. 98:3; Jer. 31:3
55 [a]Gen. 17:19; Ps. 132:11; Gal. 3:16
59 [a]Gen. 17:12; Lev. 12:3
60 [a]ver. 13
65 [1]Or, *things*
66 [a]ch. 2:19 [b]Gen. 39:2; Ps. 80:17; Acts 11:21
67 [a]Joel 2:28
68 [a]1 Ki. 1:48; Ps. 41:13 [b]Ex. 3:16; Ps. 111:9; ch. 7:16
69 [a]Ps. 132:17
70 [a]Jer. 23:5; Dan. 9:24
72 [a]Lev. 26:42; Ezek. 16:60
73 [a]Gen. 12:3; Heb. 6:13
74 [a]Rom. 6:18; Heb. 9:14
75 [a]Jer. 32:39; Eph. 4:24; 2 Thes. 2:13
76 [a]Is. 40:3; Mal. 3:1; Mat. 11:10
77 [a]Mark 1:4 [1]Or, *for*
78 [1]Or, *bowels of the mercy* [2]Or, *sunrising,* or, *branch;* Num. 24:17; Is. 11:1
79 [a]Is. 9:2; Mat. 4:16

B *Lk 1:41* ◀ ▶ *Lk 3:16*
E *Lk 1:41* ◀ ▶ *Lk 1:80*
G *Lk 1:17* ◀ ▶ *Lk 2:40*
T *Lk 1:41–42* ◀ ▶ *Lk 2:40*
I *Lk 1:32–33* ◀ ▶ *Lk 2:25–26*
L *Mk 3:28* ◀ ▶ *Lk 2:10–11*
C *Mk 4:12* ◀ ▶ *Lk 3:7*

1:67–79 Zacharias, filled with the Holy Spirit, gave this prophecy about the role his son John the Baptist would play as "the prophet of the Highest" (1:76), who would prepare the people for the coming of the Messiah and "give knowledge of salvation unto his people" (1:77).

darkness and *in* the shadow of death, to guide our feet into the way of peace.

E M 80 And [a]the child grew, and waxed strong in spirit, and [b]was in the deserts till the day of his showing unto Israel.

The birth of Jesus

2 AND IT came to pass in those days, that there went out a decree from Caesar Augustus, that all the world should be [/]taxed.

2 ([a]*And* this taxing was first made when Cyrenius was governor of Syria.)

3 And all went to be taxed, every one into his own city.

4 And Joseph also went up from Galilee, out of the city of Nazareth, into Judaea, unto [a]the city of David, which is called Bethlehem; ([b]because he was of the house and lineage of David:)

5 To be taxed with Mary [a]his espoused wife, being great with child.

6 And so it was, that, while they were there, the days were accomplished that she should be delivered.

7 And [a]she brought forth her firstborn son, and wrapped him in swaddling clothes, and laid him in a manger; because there was no room for them in the inn.

The angels and the shepherds

8 And there were in the same country shepherds abiding in the field, keeping [/]watch over their flock by night.

9 And, lo, the angel of the Lord came upon them, and the glory of the Lord shone round about them: [a]and they were sore afraid.

K L W 10 And the angel said unto them, Fear not: for, behold, I bring you good tidings of great joy, [a]which shall be to all people.

11 [a]For unto you is born this day in the city of David [b]a Saviour, [c]which is Christ the Lord.

12 And this *shall be* a sign unto you; Ye shall find the babe wrapped in swaddling clothes, lying in a manger.

13 [a]And suddenly there was with the angel a multitude of the heavenly host praising God, and saying,

14 [a]Glory to God in the highest, and on earth [b]peace, [c]good will toward men. U

15 And it came to pass, as the angels were gone away from them into heaven, [/]the shepherds said one to another, Let us now go even unto Bethlehem, and see this thing which is come to pass, which the Lord hath made known unto us.

16 And they came with haste, and found Mary, and Joseph, and the babe lying in a manger.

17 And when they had seen *it,* they made known abroad the saying which was told them concerning this child.

18 And all they that heard *it* wondered at those things which were told them by the shepherds.

19 [a]But Mary kept all these things, and pondered *them* in her heart.

20 And the shepherds returned, glorifying and praising God for all the things that they had heard and seen, as it was told unto them.

Jesus presented in the temple

21 [a]And when eight days were accomplished for the circumcising of the child, his name was called [b]JESUS, which was so named of the angel before he was conceived in the womb.

22 And when [a]the days of her purification according to the law of Moses were accomplished, they brought him to Jerusalem, to present *him* to the Lord;

23 (As it is written in the law of the Lord, [a]Every male that openeth the womb shall be called holy to the Lord;)

24 And to offer a sacrifice according to [a]that which is said in the law of the Lord, A pair of turtledoves, or two young pigeons.

25 And, behold, there was a man in I E

80 [a]ch. 2:40 [b]Mat. 3:1
2:1 [/]Or, *enrolled*
2 [a]Acts 5:37
4 [a]1 Sam. 16:1; John 7:42 [b]Mat. 1:16
5 [a]Mat. 1:18
7 [a]Mat. 1:25
8 [/]Or, *the night watches*
9 [a]ch. 1:12
10 [a]Gen. 12:3; Mat. 28:19; Mark 1:15; Col. 1:23
11 [a]Is. 9:6 [b]Mat. 1:21 [c]Mat. 1:16 & 16:16; Acts 2:36; Phil. 2:11
13 [a]Gen. 28:12; Ps. 103:20 & 148:2; Dan. 7:10; Heb. 1:14; Rev. 5:11
14 [a]ch. 19:38; Eph. 1:6 [b]Is. 57:19; Rom. 5:1; Eph. 2:17; Col. 1:20 [c]John 3:16; Eph. 2:4,7; 2 Thes. 2:16; 1 John 4:9
15 [/]Gk. *the men the shepherds*
19 [a]Gen. 37:11; ch. 1:66
21 [a]Gen. 17:12; Lev. 12:3; ch. 1:59 [b]Mat. 1:21,25; ch. 1:31
22 [a]Lev. 12:2
23 [a]Ex. 13:2 & 22:29; Num. 3:13
24 [a]Lev. 12:2

E *Lk 1:67* ◀ ▶ *Lk 2:25–27*
M *Lk 1:15–17* ◀ ▶ *Lk 2:40*
K *Lk 1:37* ◀ ▶ *Lk 5:24*
L *Lk 1:77–79* ◀ ▶ *Lk 4:4*
W *Mk 16:15–16* ◀ ▶ *Lk 11:9–10*
U *Mt 5:9* ◀ **I** *Lk 1:68–79* ◀ ▶ *Lk 2:38*
E *Lk 1:80* ◀ ▶ *Lk 2:40*

2:14 The angelic host prophesied the assurance of peace to those who please God.

2:25–32 Luke describes a just and devoted man named Simeon who was "waiting for the consolation of Israel" (2:25; see Isa 25:9; 40:1–2). The Holy Spirit had confirmed to Simeon that he would see the Christ before his death. When the child was brought to the temple, Simeon was there, directed to come "by the Spirit into the temple" (2:27). Simeon immediately recognized Jesus as the fulfillment of

Jerusalem, whose name *was* Simeon; and
the same man *was* just and devout, [a]wait-
ing for the consolation of Israel: and the
Holy Ghost was upon him.
M 26 And it was revealed unto him by
the Holy Ghost, that he should not [a]see
death, before he had seen the Lord's
Christ.
L 27 And he came [a]by the Spirit into the
temple: and when the parents brought in
the child Jesus, to do for him after the
custom of the law,
28 Then took he him up in his arms,
and blessed God, and said,
29 Lord, [a]now lettest thou thy servant
depart in peace, according to thy word:
B 30 For mine eyes [a]have seen thy salvation,
31 Which thou hast prepared before
the face of all people;
32 [a]A light to lighten the Gentiles, and
the glory of thy people Israel.
33 And Joseph and his mother marvelled at those things which were spoken
of him.
B 34 And Simeon blessed them, and said
unto Mary his mother, Behold, this *child*
is set for the [a]fall and rising again of many
in Israel; and for [b]a sign which shall be
spoken against;
35 (Yea, [a]a sword shall pierce through
thy own soul also,) that the thoughts of
many hearts may be revealed.
36 And there was one Anna, a prophetess, the daughter of Phanuel, of the
tribe of Aser: she was of a great age, and
had lived with an husband seven years
from her virginity;
37 And she *was* a widow of about fourscore and four years, which departed not
from the temple, but served *God* with
fastings and prayers [a]night and day.
I 38 And she coming in that instant gave
thanks likewise unto the Lord, and spake

25 [a]ver. 38; Is. 40:1; Mark 15:43
26 [a]Ps. 89:48; Heb. 11:5
27 [a]Mat. 4:1
29 [a]Gen. 46:30; Phil. 1:23
30 [a]Is. 52:10
32 [a]Is. 9:2 & 42:6 & 49:6 & 60:1-3; Mat. 4:16; Acts 13:47 & 28:28
34 [a]Is. 8:14; Hos. 14:9; Mat. 21:44; Rom. 9:32; 1 Cor. 1:23; 2 Cor. 2:16; 1 Pet. 2:7,8 [b]Acts 28:22
35 [a]Ps. 42:10; John 19:25
37 [a]Acts 26:7; 1 Tim. 5:5
38 [a]ver. 25; Mark 15:43; ch. 24:21 [1]Or, *Israel*
40 [a]ver. 52; ch. 1:80
41 [a]Ex. 23:15,17; & 34:23; Deut. 16:1,16
47 [a]Mat. 7:28; Mark 1:22; ch. 4:22,32; John 7:15, 46
49 [a]John 2:16
50 [a]ch. 9:45 & 18:34

of him to all them that [a]looked for redemption in [1]Jerusalem.
39 And when they had performed all
things according to the law of the Lord,
they returned into Galilee, to their own
city Nazareth.
40 [a]And the child grew, and waxed E
strong in spirit, filled with wisdom: and G
the grace of God was upon him. M T

The boy Jesus in the temple

41 Now his parents went to Jerusalem
[a]every year at the feast of the passover.
42 And when he was twelve years old,
they went up to Jerusalem after the custom of the feast.
43 And when they had fulfilled the
days, as they returned, the child Jesus tarried behind in Jerusalem; and Joseph and
his mother knew not *of it.*
44 But they, supposing him to have
been in the company, went a day's journey; and they sought him among *their*
kinsfolk and acquaintance.
45 And when they found him not, they
turned back again to Jerusalem, seeking
him.
46 And it came to pass, that after three
days they found him in the temple, sitting
in the midst of the doctors, both hearing
them, and asking them questions.
47 And [a]all that heard him were astonished at his understanding and answers.
48 And when they saw him, they were
amazed: and his mother said unto him,
Son, why hast thou thus dealt with us?
behold, thy father and I have sought thee
sorrowing.
49 And he said unto them, How is it
that ye sought me? wist ye not that I must
be about [a]my Father's business?
50 And [a]they understood not the saying which he spake unto them.
51 And he went down with them, and
came to Nazareth, and was subject unto

M *Lk 1:32–33* ◀▶ *Lk 3:5–6*
L *Mk 13:11* ◀▶ *Lk 4:1*
B *Lk 1:30–35* ◀▶ *Lk 2:34–35*
B *Lk 2:30–32* ◀▶ *Lk 3:16*
I *Lk 2:25–26* ◀▶ *Lk 23:2–3*

E *Lk 2:25–27* ◀▶ *Lk 3:22*
G *Lk 1:67* ◀▶ *Lk 12:11–12*
M *Lk 1:80* ◀▶ *Lk 3:16*
T *Lk 1:67* ◀▶ *Lk 4:18*

Isaiah's prophecies of the Messiah (see Isa 9:2; 42:6–7; 49:6; 60:1–3) and blessed God for his faithfulness in fulfilling his word.

2:38 There were a number of righteous Jews who anticipated the imminent arrival of the Messiah. The righteous widow Anna was one of these who knew that the Messiah was about to appear on earth. As she entered the temple, she instantly recognized Jesus as the Messiah and shared her finding with those Jews who "looked for redemption in Jerusalem" at that time.

them: but his mother [a]kept all these sayings in her heart.

52 And Jesus [a]increased in wisdom and [1]stature, and in favour with God and man.

John the Baptist

3 NOW IN the fifteenth year of the reign of Tiberius Caesar, Pontius Pilate being governor of Judaea, and Herod being tetrarch of Galilee, and his brother Philip tetrarch of Ituraea and of the region of Trachonitis, and Lysanias the tetrarch of Abilene,

2 [a]Annas and Caiaphas being the high priests, the word of God came unto John the son of Zacharias in the wilderness.

3 [a]And he came into all the country about Jordan, preaching the baptism of repentance [b]for the remission of sins;

4 As it is written in the book of the words of Esaias the prophet, saying, [a]The voice of one crying in the wilderness, Prepare ye the way of the Lord, make his paths straight.

M 5 Every valley shall be filled, and every mountain and hill shall be brought low; and the crooked shall be made straight, and the rough ways *shall be* made smooth;

6 And [a]all flesh shall see the salvation of God.

C H 7 Then said he to the multitude that came forth to be baptized of him, [a]O generation of vipers, who hath warned you to flee from the wrath to come?

R 8 Bring forth therefore fruits [1]worthy of repentance, and begin not to say within yourselves, We have Abraham to *our* father: for I say unto you, That God is able of these stones to raise up children unto Abraham.

H S 9 And now also the axe is laid unto the root of the trees: [a]every tree therefore which bringeth not forth good fruit is hewn down, and cast into the fire.

10 And the people asked him, saying, [a]What shall we do then?

11 He answereth and saith unto them, [a]He that hath two coats, let him impart to him that hath none; and he that hath meat, let him do likewise.

12 Then [a]came also publicans to be baptized, and said unto him, Master, what shall we do?

13 And he said unto them, [a]Exact no more than that which is appointed you.

14 And the soldiers likewise demanded of him, saying, And what shall we do? And he said unto them, [1]Do violence to no man, [a]neither accuse *any* falsely; and be content with your [2]wages.

15 And as the people were [1]in expectation, and all men [2]mused in their hearts of John, whether he were the Christ, or not;

16 John answered, saying unto *them* all, [a]I indeed baptize you with water; but one mightier than I cometh, the latchet of whose shoes I am not worthy to unloose: he shall baptize you with the Holy Ghost and with fire: B B M N P

17 Whose fan *is* in his hand, and he will thoroughly purge his floor, and [a]will gather the wheat into his garner; but the chaff he will burn with fire unquenchable.

18 And many other things in his exhortation preached he unto the people.

19 [a]But Herod the tetrarch, being reproved by him for Herodias his brother Philip's wife, and for all the evils which Herod had done,

20 Added yet this above all, that he shut up John in prison.

The baptism of Jesus

21 Now when all the people were baptized, [a]it came to pass, that Jesus also be- B

51 [a]ver. 19; Dan. 7:28
52 [a]ver. 40; 1 Sam. 2:26 [1]Or, *age*
3:2 [a]John 11:49, 51 & 18:13; Acts 4:6
3 [a]Mat. 3:1; Mark 1:4 [b]ch. 1:77
4 [a]Is. 40:3; Mat. 3:3; Mark 1:3; John 1:23
6 [a]Ps. 98:2; Is. 52:10; ch. 2:10
7 [a]Mat. 3:7
8 [1]Or, *meet for*
9 [a]Mat. 7:19
10 [a]Acts 2:37
11 [a]ch. 11:41; 2 Cor. 8:14; Jas. 2:15,16; 1 John 3:17 & 4:20
12 [a]Mat. 21:32; ch. 7:29
13 [a]ch. 19:8
14 [a]Ex. 23:1; Lev. 19:11 [1]Or, *Put no man in fear* [2]Or, *allowance*
15 [1]Or, *in suspense* [2]Or, *reasoned*, or, *debated*
16 [a]Mat. 3:11
17 [a]Mic. 4:12; Mat. 13:30
19 [a]Mat. 14:3; Mark 6:17
21 [a]Mat. 3:13; John 1:32

M *Lk 2:26* ◀▶ *Lk 11:2*
C *Lk 1:79* ◀▶ *Lk 5:31*
H *Mk 16:16* ◀▶ *Lk 3:9*
R *Mk 11:25–26* ◀▶ *Lk 6:37*
H *Lk 3:7* ◀▶ *Lk 6:25*
S *Mk 13:13* ◀▶ *Lk 6:43–49*

B *Lk 2:34–35* ◀▶ *Lk 9:22*
B *Lk 1:67* ◀▶ *Lk 3:21–22*
M *Lk 2:40* ◀▶ *Lk 4:14*
N *Mk 1:10* ◀▶ *Lk 3:22*
P *Mk 1:8* ◀▶ *Lk 11:9–13*
B *Lk 3:16* ◀▶ *Lk 4:18*

3:4–6 John the Baptist was the forerunner of the Messiah, preparing people to accept the appearance of Jesus of Nazareth as the promised Messiah (see Isa 40:3). The final fulfillment of this prophecy will occur at the second coming when literally "all flesh shall see the salvation of God" (3:6; see Zec 12:10; Mt 24:30).

ing baptized, and praying, the heaven was opened,

22 And the Holy Ghost descended in a bodily shape like a dove upon him, and a voice came from heaven, which said, Thou art my beloved Son; in thee I am well pleased.

The genealogy of Jesus

23 And Jesus himself began to be [a]about thirty years of age, being (as was supposed) [b]the son of Joseph, which was *the son* of Heli,

24 Which was *the son* of Matthat, which was *the son* of Levi, which was *the son* of Melchi, which was *the son* of Janna, which was *the son* of Joseph,

25 Which was *the son* of Mattathias, which was *the son* of Amos, which was *the son* of Naum, which was *the son* of Esli, which was *the son* of Nagge,

26 Which was *the son* of Maath, which was *the son* of Mattathias, which was *the son* of Semei, which was *the son* of Joseph, which was *the son* of Judah,

27 Which was *the son* of Joanna, which was *the son* of Rhesa, which was *the son* of Zorobabel, which was *the son* of Salathiel, which was *the son* of Neri,

28 Which was *the son* of Melchi, which was *the son* of Addi, which was *the son* of Cosam, which was *the son* of Elmodam, which was *the son* of Er,

29 Which was *the son* of Jose, which was *the son* of Eliezer, which was *the son* of Jorim, which was *the son* of Matthat, which was *the son* of Levi,

30 Which was *the son* of Simeon, which was *the son* of Judah, which was *the son* of Joseph, which was *the son* of Jonan, which was *the son* of Eliakim,

31 Which was *the son* of Melea, which was *the son* of Menan, which was *the son* of Mattatha, which was *the son* of [a]Nathan, [b]which was *the son* of David,

32 [a]Which was *the son* of Jesse, which was *the son* of Obed, which was *the son* of Booz, which was *the son* of Salmon, which was *the son* of Naasson,

33 Which was *the son* of Aminadab, which was *the son* of Aram, which was *the son* of Esrom, which was *the son* of Phares, which was *the son* of Judah,

34 Which was *the son* of Jacob, which was *the son* of Isaac, which was *the son* of Abraham, [a]which was *the son* of Thara, which was *the son* of Nachor,

35 Which was *the son* of Saruch, which was *the son* of Ragau, which was *the son* of Phalec, which was *the son* of Heber, which was *the son* of Sala,

36 [a]Which was *the son* of Cainan, which was *the son* of Arphaxad, [b]which was *the son* of Sem, which was *the son* of Noe, which was *the son* of Lamech,

37 Which was *the son* of Mathusala, which was *the son* of Enoch, which was *the son* of Jared, which was *the son* of Maleleel, which was *the son* of Cainan,

38 Which was *the son* of Enos, which was *the son* of Seth, which was *the son* of Adam, [a]which was *the son* of God.

The temptation in the wilderness

4 AND [a]JESUS being full of the Holy Ghost returned from Jordan, and [b]was led by the Spirit into the wilderness,

2 Being forty days tempted of the devil. And [a]in those days he did eat nothing: and when they were ended, he afterward hungered.

3 And the devil said unto him, If thou be the Son of God, command this stone that it be made bread.

4 And Jesus answered him, saying, [a]It is written, That man shall not live by bread alone, but by every word of God.

5 And the devil, taking him up into an high mountain, showed unto him all the kingdoms of the world in a moment of time.

6 And the devil said unto him, All this power will I give thee, and the glory of them: for [a]that is delivered unto me; and to whomsoever I will I give it.

7 If thou therefore wilt [1]worship me, all shall be thine.

8 And Jesus answered and said unto him, Get thee behind me, Satan: for [a]it is written, Thou shalt worship the Lord thy God, and him only shalt thou serve.

9 [a]And he brought him to Jerusalem, and set him on a pinnacle of the temple, and said unto him, If thou be the Son of God, cast thyself down from hence:

3:23 [a]See Num. 4:3, 35,39,43,47 [b]Mat. 13:55; John 6:42
31 [a]Zech. 12:12 [b]2 Sam. 5:14; 1 Chr. 3:5
32 [a]Ruth 4:18; 1 Chr. 2:10
34 [a]Gen. 11:24,26
36 [a]See Gen. 11:12 [b]Gen. 5:6 & 11:10
38 [a]Gen. 5:12
4:1 [a]Mat. 4:1; Mark 1:12 [b]ver. 14; ch. 2:27
2 [a]Ex. 34:28; 1 Ki. 19:8
4 [a]Deut. 8:3
6 [a]John 12:31 & 14:30; Rev. 13:2,7
7 [1]Or, *fall down before me*
8 [a]Deut. 6:13 & 10:20
9 [a]Mat. 4:5

E *Lk 2:40* ◀▶ *Lk 4:1*
J *Mk 1:10* ◀▶ *Jn 1:32*
N *Lk 3:16* ◀▶ *Jn 1:32*
E *Lk 3:22* ◀▶ *Lk 4:14*
L *Lk 2:27* ◀▶ *Lk 4:14*
L *Lk 2:10–11* ◀▶ *Lk 4:18–19*

L 10 For [a]it is written, He shall give his angels charge over thee, to keep thee:

11 And in *their* hands they shall bear thee up, lest at any time thou dash thy foot against a stone.

12 And Jesus answering said unto him, [a]It is said, Thou shalt not tempt the Lord thy God.

13 And when the devil had ended all the temptation, he departed from him [a]for a season.

E L M 14 ¶ [a]And Jesus returned [b]in the power of the Spirit into [c]Galilee: and there went out a fame of him through all the region round about.

15 And he taught in their synagogues, being glorified of all.

Jesus rejected at Nazareth

16 ¶ And he came to [a]Nazareth, where he had been brought up: and, as his custom was, [b]he went into the synagogue on the sabbath day, and stood up for to read.

17 And there was delivered unto him the book of the prophet Esaias. And when he had opened the book, he found the place where it was written,

B T L H 18 [a]The Spirit of the Lord *is* upon me, because he hath anointed me to preach the gospel to the poor; he hath sent me to heal the brokenhearted, to preach deliverance to the captives, and recovering of sight to the blind, to set at liberty them that are bruised,

19 To preach the acceptable year of the Lord.

20 And he closed the book, and he gave *it* again to the minister, and sat down. And the eyes of all them that were in the synagogue were fastened on him.

21 And he began to say unto them, This day is this scripture fulfilled in your ears.

22 And all bare him witness, and [a]wondered at the gracious words which proceeded out of his mouth. And they said, [b]Is not this Joseph's son?

L *Mk 11:24* ◀ ▶ *Lk 12:6–7*
E *Lk 4:1* ◀ ▶ *Jn 1:32–33*
L *Lk 4:1* ◀ ▶ *Lk 12:11–12*
M *Lk 3:16* ◀ ▶ *Lk 21:14–15*
B *Lk 3:21–22* ◀ ▶ *Lk 24:49*
T *Lk 2:40* ◀ ▶ *Lk 12:11–12*
L *Lk 4:4* ◀ ▶ *Lk 5:31–32*
H *Mk 16:17–18* ◀ ▶ *Eph 6:2–3*

10 [a]Ps. 91:11
12 [a]Deut. 6:16
13 [a]John 14:30; Heb. 4:15
14 [a]Mat. 4:12; John 4:43 [b]ver. 1 [c]Acts 10:37
16 [a]Mat. 2:23 & 13:54; Mark 6:1 [b]Acts 13:14 & 17:2
18 [a]Is. 61:1
22 [a]Ps. 45:2; Mat. 13:54; Mark 6:2; ch. 2:47 [b]John 6:42
23 [a]Mat. 4:13 & 11:23 [b]Mat. 13:54; Mark 6:1
24 [a]Mat. 13:57; Mark 6:4; John 4:44
25 [a]1 Ki. 17:9 & 18:1; Jas. 5:17
27 [a]2 Ki. 5:14
29 [/]Or, *edge*
30 [a]John 8:59 & 10:39
31 [a]Mat. 4:13; Mark 1:21
32 [a]Mat. 7:28,29
33 [a]Mark 1:23
34 [a]ver. 41 [b]Ps. 16:10; Dan. 9:24; ch. 1:35 [/]Or, *Away*

D E 23 And he said unto them, Ye will surely say unto me this proverb, Physician, heal thyself: whatsoever we have heard done in [a]Capernaum, do also here in [b]thy country.

24 And he said, Verily I say unto you, No [a]prophet is accepted in his own country.

F 25 But I tell you of a truth, [a]many widows were in Israel in the days of Elias, when the heaven was shut up three years and six months, when great famine was throughout all the land;

26 But unto none of them was Elias sent, save unto Sarepta, *a city* of Sidon, unto a woman *that was* a widow.

27 [a]And many lepers were in Israel in the time of Eliseus the prophet; and none of them was cleansed, saving Naaman the Syrian.

28 And all they in the synagogue, when they heard these things, were filled with wrath,

29 And rose up, and thrust him out of the city, and led him unto the [/]brow of the hill whereon their city was built, that they might cast him down headlong.

30 But he [a]passing through the midst of them went his way,

The unclean spirit cast out

31 And [a]came down to Capernaum, a city of Galilee, and taught them on the sabbath days.

32 And they were astonished at his doctrine: [a]for his word was with power.

E 33 ¶ [a]And in the synagogue there was a man, which had a spirit of an unclean devil, and cried out with a loud voice,

34 Saying, [/]Let *us* alone; what have we to do with thee, *thou* Jesus of Nazareth? art thou come to destroy us? [a]I know thee who thou art; [b]the Holy One of God.

35 And Jesus rebuked him, saying, Hold thy peace, and come out of him. And when the devil had thrown him in the midst, he came out of him, and hurt him not.

36 And they were all amazed, and spake among themselves, saying, What a word *is* this! for with authority and

D *Lk 1:20* ◀ ▶ *Lk 13:16*
E *Lk 1:36–37* ◀ ▶ *Lk 4:33–41*
F *Mk 8:14–21* ◀ ▶ *Lk 5:4–9*
E *Lk 4:23–27* ◀ ▶ *Lk 5:12–26*

power he commandeth the unclean spirits, and they come out.

37 And the fame of him went out into every place of the country round about.

The sick healed; devils cast out

38 ¶ [a]And he arose out of the synagogue, and entered into Simon's house. And Simon's wife's mother was taken with a great fever; and they besought him for her.

39 And he stood over her, and rebuked the fever; and it left her: and immediately she arose and ministered unto them.

40 ¶ [a]Now when the sun was setting, all they that had any sick with divers diseases brought them unto him; and he laid his hands on every one of them, and healed them.

41 [a]And devils also came out of many, crying out, and saying, Thou art Christ the Son of God. And [b]he rebuking *them* suffered them not [/]to speak: for they knew that he was Christ.

42 [a]And when it was day, he departed and went into a desert place: and the people sought him, and came unto him, and stayed him, that he should not depart from them.

43 And he said unto them, I must preach the kingdom of God to other cities also: for therefore am I sent.

44 [a]And he preached in the synagogues of Galilee.

The call of the first disciples

5 AND [a]IT came to pass, that, as the people pressed upon him to hear the word of God, he stood by the lake of Gennesaret,

2 And saw two ships standing by the lake: but the fishermen were gone out of them, and were washing *their* nets.

3 And he entered into one of the ships, which was Simon's, and prayed him that he would thrust out a little from the land. And he sat down, and taught the people out of the ship.

F 4 Now when he had left speaking, he said unto Simon, [a]Launch out into the deep, and let down your nets for a draught.

5 And Simon answering said unto him, Master, we have toiled all the night, and have taken nothing: nevertheless at thy word I will let down the net.

6 And when they had this done, they inclosed a great multitude of fishes: and their net brake.

7 And they beckoned unto *their* partners, which were in the other ship, that they should come and help them. And they came, and filled both the ships, so that they began to sink.

8 When Simon Peter saw *it,* he fell down at Jesus' knees, saying, [a]Depart from me; for I am a sinful man, O Lord.

9 For he was astonished, and all that were with him, at the draught of the fishes which they had taken:

10 And so *was* also James, and John, the sons of Zebedee, which were partners with Simon. And Jesus said unto Simon, Fear not; [a]from henceforth thou shalt catch men.

11 And when they had brought their ships to land, [a]they forsook all, and followed him.

The leper cleansed

12 ¶ [a]And it came to pass, when he was in a certain city, behold a man full of leprosy: who seeing Jesus fell on *his* face, and besought him, saying, Lord, if thou wilt, thou canst make me clean. E

13 And he put forth *his* hand, and touched him, saying, I will: be thou clean. And immediately the leprosy departed from him.

14 [a]And he charged him to tell no man: but go, and show thyself to the priest, and offer for thy cleansing, [b]according as Moses commanded, for a testimony unto them.

15 But so much the more went there a fame abroad of him: [a]and great multitudes came together to hear, and to be healed by him of their infirmities.

16 ¶ [a]And he withdrew himself into the wilderness, and prayed.

A man with palsy healed

17 And it came to pass on a certain day, as he was teaching, that there were Pharisees and doctors of the law sitting by, which were come out of every town of Galilee, and Judaea, and Jerusalem: and the power of the Lord was *present* to heal them.

38 [a]Mat. 8:14; Mark 1:29
40 [a]Mat. 8:16; Mark 1:32
41 [a]Mark 1:34 & 3:11 [b]ver. 34,35; Mark 1:25,34 [/]Or, *to say that they knew him to be Christ*
42 [a]Mark 1:35
44 [a]Mark 1:39
5:1 [a]Mat. 4:18; Mark 1:16
4 [a]John 21:6
8 [a]2 Sam. 6:9; 1 Ki. 17:8
10 [a]Mat. 4:19; Mark 1:17
11 [a]Mat. 4:20 & 19:27; Mark 1:18; ch. 18:28
12 [a]Mat. 8:2; Mark 1:40
14 [a]Mat. 8:4 [b]Lev. 14:4,10,21,22
15 [a]Mat. 4:25; Mark 3:7; John 6:2
16 [a]Mat. 14:23; Mark 6:46

F Lk 4:25–26 ◀▶ Lk 9:12–17
E Lk 4:33–41 ◀▶ Lk 6:6–11

18 ¶ [a]And, behold, men brought in a bed a man which was taken with a palsy: and they sought *means* to bring him in, and to lay *him* before him.

19 And when they could not find by what *way* they might bring him in because of the multitude, they went upon the housetop, and let him down through the tiling with *his* couch into the midst before Jesus.

20 And when he saw their faith, he said unto him, Man, thy sins are forgiven thee.

21 [a]And the scribes and the Pharisees began to reason, saying, Who is this which speaketh blasphemies? [b]Who can forgive sins, but God alone?

22 But when Jesus perceived their thoughts, he answering said unto them, What reason ye in your hearts?

23 Whether is easier, to say, Thy sins be forgiven thee; or to say, Rise up and walk?

K 24 But that ye may know that the Son of man hath power upon earth to forgive sins, (he said unto the sick of the palsy,) I say unto thee, Arise, and take up thy couch, and go into thine house.

25 And immediately he rose up before them, and took up that whereon he lay, and departed to his own house, glorifying God.

26 And they were all amazed, and they glorified God, and were filled with fear, saying, We have seen strange things today.

The call of Levi

27 ¶ [a]And after these things he went forth, and saw a publican, named Levi, sitting at the receipt of custom: and he said unto him, Follow me.

28 And he left all, rose up, and followed him.

29 [a]And Levi made him a great feast in his own house: and [b]there was a great company of publicans and of others that sat down with them.

30 But their scribes and Pharisees murmured against his disciples, saying, Why do ye eat and drink with publicans and sinners?

C L 31 And Jesus answering said unto them, They that are whole need not a physician; but they that are sick.

32 [a]I came not to call the righteous, but sinners to repentance.

The question about fasting

33 ¶ And they said unto him, [a]Why do the disciples of John fast often, and make prayers, and likewise *the disciples* of the Pharisees; but thine eat and drink?

34 And he said unto them, Can ye make the children of the bridechamber fast, while the bridegroom is with them?

35 But the days will come, when the bridegroom shall be taken away from them, and then shall they fast in those days.

36 ¶ [a]And he spake also a parable unto them; No man putteth a piece of a new garment upon an old; if otherwise, then both the new maketh a rent, and the piece that was *taken* out of the new agreeth not with the old.

37 And no man putteth new wine into old bottles; else the new wine will burst the bottles, and be spilled, and the bottles shall perish.

38 But new wine must be put into new bottles; and both are preserved.

39 No man also having drunk old *wine* straightway desireth new: for he saith, The old is better.

Jesus the Lord of the Sabbath

6 AND [a]IT came to pass on the second sabbath after the first, that he went through the corn fields; and his disciples plucked the ears of corn, and did eat, rubbing *them* in *their* hands.

2 And certain of the Pharisees said unto them, Why do ye that [a]which is not lawful to do on the sabbath days?

3 And Jesus answering them said, Have ye not read so much as this, [a]what David did, when himself was an hungered, and they which were with him.

4 How he went into the house of God, and did take and eat the showbread, and gave also to them that were with him; [a]which it is not lawful to eat but for the priests alone?

5 And he said unto them, That the Son of man is Lord also of the sabbath.

6 [a]And it came to pass also on another sabbath, that he entered into the syna- E

18 [a]Mat. 9:2; Mark 2:3
21 [a]Mat. 9:3; Mark 2:6,7 [b]Ps. 32:5; Is. 43:25
27 [a]Mat. 9:9; Mark 2:13,14
29 [a]Mat. 9:10; Mark 2:15 [b]ch. 15:1
32 [a]Mat. 9:13; 1 Tim. 1:15
33 [a]Mat. 9:14; Mark 2:18
36 [a]Mat. 9:16,17; Mark 2:21,22
6:1 [a]Mat. 12:1; Mark 2:23
2 [a]Ex. 20:10
3 [a]1 Sam. 21:6
4 [a]Lev. 24:9
6 [a]Mat. 12:9; Mark 3:1; See ch. 13:14 & 14:3; John 9:16

K *Lk 2:10–11* ◀ ▶ *Lk 6:47–48*
C *Lk 3:7* ◀ ▶ *Lk 6:39*
L *Lk 4:18–19* ◀ ▶ *Lk 6:37*
E *Lk 5:12–26* ◀ ▶ *Lk 6:17–19*

gogue and taught: and there was a man
whose right hand was withered.
7 And the scribes and Pharisees
watched him, whether he would heal on
the sabbath day; that they might find an
accusation against him.
E 8 But he knew their thoughts, and said
to the man which had the withered hand,
Rise up, and stand forth in the midst. And
he arose and stood forth.
9 Then said Jesus unto them, I will ask
you one thing; Is it lawful on the sabbath
days to do good, or to do evil? to save life,
or to destroy *it?*
10 And looking round about upon
them all, he said unto the man, Stretch
forth thy hand. And he did so: and his
hand was restored whole as the other.
11 And they were filled with madness;
and communed one with another what
they might do to Jesus.

The choosing of the Twelve

12 And it came to pass in those days,
that he went out into a mountain to pray,
and continued all night in prayer to God.
13 ¶ And when it was day, he called
unto him his disciples: [a]and of them he
chose twelve, whom also he named
apostles;
14 Simon, ([a]whom he also named Peter,) and Andrew his brother, James and
John, Philip and Bartholomew,
15 Matthew and Thomas, James the
son of Alphaeus, and Simon called
Zelotes,
16 And Judas [a]*the brother* of James,
and Judas Iscariot, which also was the
traitor.

Beatitudes and woes

E 17 ¶ And he came down with them,
and stood in the plain, and the company
of his disciples, [a]and a great multitude of
people out of all Judaea and Jerusalem,
and from the sea coast of Tyre and Sidon,
which came to hear him, and to be
healed of their diseases;
18 And they that were vexed with unclean spirits: and they were healed.
19 And the whole multitude [a]sought
to touch him: for [b]there went virtue out
of him, and healed *them* all.
M 20 ¶ And he lifted up his eyes on his
disciples, and said, [a]Blessed *be ye* poor:
for yours is the kingdom of God.
21 [a]Blessed *are ye* that hunger now:
for ye shall be filled. [b]Blessed *are ye* that
weep now: for ye shall laugh.
22 [a]Blessed are ye, when men shall J
hate you, and when they [b]shall separate
you *from their company,* and shall reproach *you,* and cast out your name as
evil, for the Son of man's sake.
23 [a]Rejoice ye in that day, and leap for
joy: for, behold, your reward *is* great in
heaven: for [b]in the like manner did their
fathers unto the prophets.
24 [a]But woe unto you [b]that are rich!
for [c]ye have received your consolation.
25 [a]Woe unto you that are full! for ye H
shall hunger. [b]Woe unto you that laugh
now! for ye shall mourn and weep.
26 [a]Woe unto you, when all men shall
speak well of you! for so did their fathers
to the false prophets.

The law of love

27 ¶ [a]But I say unto you which hear,
Love your enemies, do good to them
which hate you,
28 Bless them that curse you, and
[a]pray for them which despitefully use
you.
29 [a]And unto him that smiteth thee on
the *one* cheek offer also the other; [b]and
him that taketh away thy cloak forbid not
to take thy coat also.
30 [a]Give to every man that asketh of
thee; and of him that taketh away thy
goods ask *them* not again.
31 [a]And as ye would that men should
do to you, do ye also to them likewise.
32 [a]For if ye love them which love
you, what thank have ye? for sinners also
love those that love them.
33 And if ye do good to them which do
good to you, what thank have ye? for sinners also do even the same.
34 [a]And if ye lend *to them* of whom ye
hope to receive, what thank have ye? for
sinners also lend to sinners, to receive as
much again.
35 But [a]love ye your enemies, and do
good, and [b]lend, hoping for nothing
again; and your reward shall be great, and
[c]ye shall be the children of the Highest:

13 [a]Mat. 10:1
14 [a]John 1:42
16 [a]Jude 1
17 [a]Mat. 4:25; Mark 3:7
19 [a]Mat. 14:36 [b]Mark 5:30; ch. 8:46
20 [a]Mat. 5:3 & 11:5; Jas. 2:5
21 [a]Is. 55:1 & 65:13; Mat. 5:6 [b]Is. 61:3; Mat. 5:4
22 [a]Mat. 5:11; 1 Pet. 2:19 & 3:14 & 4:14 [b]John 16:2
23 [a]Mat. 5:12; Acts 5:41; Col. 1:24; Jas. 1:2 [b]Acts 7:51
24 [a]Amos 6:1; Jas. 5:1 [b]ch. 12:21 [c]Mat. 6:2,5,16; ch. 16:25
25 [a]Is. 65:13 [b]Prov. 14:13
26 [a]John 15:19; 1 John 4:5
27 [a]ver. 35; Ex. 23:4; Prov. 25:21; Mat. 5:44; Rom. 12:20
28 [a]ch. 23:34; Acts 7:60
29 [a]Mat. 5:39 [b]1 Cor. 6:7
30 [a]Deut. 15:7,8, 10; Prov. 21:26; Mat. 5:42
31 [a]Mat. 7:12
32 [a]Mat. 5:46
34 [a]Mat. 5:42
35 [a]ver. 27 [b]ver. 30; Ps. 37:26 [c]Mat. 5:45

E *Mt 12:25* ◀ ▶ *Lk 12:2–3*
E *Lk 6:6–11* ◀ ▶ *Lk 7:1–22*
M *Mk 10:23–25* ◀ ▶ *Lk 10:13–15*
J *Mt 5:11–12* ◀ ▶ *Jn 16:33*
H *Lk 3:9* ◀ ▶ *Lk 6:39*

for he is kind unto the unthankful and *to* the evil.

36 [a]Be ye therefore merciful, as your Father also is merciful.

Judging others

L 37 [a]Judge not, and ye shall not be
R judged: condemn not, and ye shall not be condemned: forgive, and ye shall be forgiven:

38 [a]Give, and it shall be given unto you; good measure, pressed down, and shaken together, and running over, shall men give into your [b]bosom. For [c]with the same measure that ye mete withal it shall be measured to you again.

C 39 And he spake a parable unto them,
H [a]Can the blind lead the blind? shall they not both fall into the ditch?

40 [a]The disciple is not above his master: but every one [l]that is perfect shall be as his master.

41 [a]And why beholdest thou the mote that is in thy brother's eye, but perceivest not the beam that is in thine own eye?

42 Either how canst thou say to thy brother, Brother, let me pull out the mote that is in thine eye, when thou thyself beholdest not the beam that is in thine own eye? Thou hypocrite, cast out first the beam out of thine own eye, and then shalt thou see clearly to pull out the mote that is in thy brother's eye.

C 43 [a]For a good tree bringeth not forth
S corrupt fruit; neither doth a corrupt tree bring forth good fruit.

44 For [a]every tree is known by his own fruit. For of thorns men do not gather figs, nor of a bramble bush gather they [l]grapes.

T 45 [a]A good man out of the good treasure of his heart bringeth forth that which is good; and an evil man out of the evil treasure of his heart bringeth forth that which is evil: for [b]of the abundance of the heart his mouth speaketh.

The wise and foolish builders

46 ¶ [a]And why call ye me, Lord, Lord, and do not the things which I say?

L *Lk 5:31–32 ◀ ▶ Lk 7:41–42*
R *Lk 3:8 ◀ ▶ Lk 11:4*
C *Lk 5:31 ◀ ▶ Lk 6:43–45*
H *Lk 6:25 ◀ ▶ Lk 6:49*
C *Lk 6:39 ◀ ▶ Lk 6:49*
S *Lk 3:9 ◀ ▶ Lk 8:6–8*
T *Mk 8:38 ◀ ▶ Lk 9:25–26*

36 [a]Mat. 5:48
37 [a]Mat. 7:1
38 [a]Prov. 19:17 [b]Ps. 79:12 [c]Mat. 7:2; Mark 4:24; Jas. 2:13
39 [a]Mat. 15:14
40 [a]Mat. 10:24; John 13:16 & 15:20 [l]Or, *shall be perfected as his master*
41 [a]Mat. 7:3
43 [a]Mat. 7:16,17
44 [a]Mat. 12:33 [l]Gk. *a grape*
45 [a]Mat. 12:35 [b]Mat. 12:34
46 [a]Mal. 1:6; Mat. 7:21 & 25:11; ch. 13:25
47 [a]Mat. 7:24
7:1 [a]Mat. 8:5
8 [l]Gk. *this man*

47 [a]Whosoever cometh to me, and heareth my sayings, and doeth them, I will show you to whom he is like: K O

48 He is like a man which built an house, and digged deep, and laid the foundation on a rock: and when the flood arose, the stream beat vehemently upon that house, and could not shake it: for it was founded upon a rock.

49 But he that heareth, and doeth not, C
is like a man that without a foundation H
built an house upon the earth; against which the stream did beat vehemently, and immediately it fell; and the ruin of that house was great.

The centurion's servant healed

7 NOW WHEN he had ended all his sayings in the audience of the people, [a]he entered into Capernaum. E

2 And a certain centurion's servant, who was dear unto him, was sick, and ready to die.

3 And when he heard of Jesus, he sent unto him the elders of the Jews, beseeching him that he would come and heal his servant.

4 And when they came to Jesus, they besought him instantly, saying, That he was worthy for whom he should do this:

5 For he loveth our nation, and he hath built us a synagogue.

6 Then Jesus went with them. And when he was now not far from the house, the centurion sent friends to him, saying unto him, Lord, trouble not thyself: for I am not worthy that thou shouldest enter under my roof:

7 Wherefore neither thought I myself worthy to come unto thee: but say in a word, and my servant shall be healed.

8 For I also am a man set under authority, having under me soldiers, and I say unto [l]one, Go, and he goeth; and to another, Come, and he cometh; and to my servant, Do this, and he doeth *it.*

9 When Jesus heard these things, he marvelled at him, and turned him about, and said unto the people that followed him, I say unto you, I have not found so great faith, no, not in Israel.

10 And they that were sent, returning

K *Lk 5:24 ◀ ▶ Jn 1:4*
O *Mk 16:15–16 ◀ ▶ Lk 10:25–28*
C *Lk 6:43–45 ◀ ▶ Lk 11:23*
H *Lk 6:39 ◀ ▶ Lk 9:25–26*
E *Lk 6:17–19 ◀ ▶ Lk 8:26–56*

to the house, found the servant whole that had been sick.

The raising of the widow's son

11 ¶ And it came to pass the day after, that he went into a city called Nain; and many of his disciples went with him, and much people.

12 Now when he came nigh to the gate of the city, behold, there was a dead man carried out, the only son of his mother, and she was a widow: and much people of the city was with her.

13 And when the Lord saw her, he had compassion on her, and said unto her, Weep not.

14 And he came and touched the [1]bier: and they that bare *him* stood still. And he said, Young man, I say unto thee, [a]Arise.

15 And he that was dead sat up, and began to speak. And he delivered him to his mother.

16 [a]And there came a fear on all: and they glorified God, saying, [b]That a great prophet is risen up among us; and, [c]That God hath visited his people.

17 And this rumour of him went forth throughout all Judaea, and throughout all the region round about.

Tribute to John the Baptist

18 [a]And the disciples of John showed him of all these things.

19 ¶ And John calling *unto him* two of his disciples sent *them* to Jesus, saying, Art thou he that should come? or look we for another?

20 When the men were come unto him, they said, John Baptist hath sent us unto thee, saying, Art thou he that should come? or look we for another?

21 And in that same hour he cured many of *their* infirmities and plagues, and of evil spirits; and unto many *that were* blind he gave sight.

22 [a]Then Jesus answering said unto them, Go your way, and tell John what things ye have seen and heard; [b]how that the blind see, the lame walk, the lepers are cleansed, the deaf hear, the dead are raised, [c]to the poor the gospel is preached.

23 And blessed is *he,* whosoever shall not be offended in me.

24 ¶ [a]And when the messengers of John were departed, he began to speak unto the people concerning John, What went ye out into the wilderness for to see? A reed shaken with the wind?

25 But what went ye out for to see? A man clothed in soft raiment? Behold, they which are gorgeously apparelled, and live delicately, are in kings' courts.

26 But what went ye out for to see? A prophet? Yea, I say unto you, and much more than a prophet.

27 This is *he,* of whom it is written, [a]Behold, I send my messenger before thy face, which shall prepare thy way before thee.

28 For I say unto you, Among those that are born of women there is not a greater prophet than John the Baptist: but he that is least in the kingdom of God is greater than he.

29 And all the people that heard *him,* and the publicans, justified God, [a]being baptized with the baptism of John.

30 But the Pharisees and lawyers [1]rejected [a]the counsel of God [2]against themselves, being not baptized of him.

31 ¶ And the Lord said, [a]Whereunto then shall I liken the men of this generation? and to what are they like?

32 They are like unto children sitting in the marketplace, and calling one to another, and saying, We have piped unto you, and ye have not danced; we have mourned to you, and ye have not wept.

33 For [a]John the Baptist came neither eating bread nor drinking wine; and ye say, He hath a devil.

34 The Son of man is come eating and drinking; and ye say, Behold a gluttonous man, and a winebibber, a friend of publicans and sinners!

35 But [a]wisdom is justified of all her children.

Jesus forgives a sinful woman

36 ¶ [a]And one of the Pharisees desired him that he would eat with him. And he went into the Pharisee's house, and sat down to meat.

37 And, behold, a woman in the city, which was a sinner, when she knew that *Jesus* sat at meat in the Pharisee's house, brought an alabaster box of ointment,

38 And stood at his feet behind *him* weeping, and began to wash his feet with tears, and did wipe *them* with the hairs of her head, and kissed his feet, and anointed *them* with the ointment.

14 [a]ch. 8:54; John 11:43; Acts 9:40; Rom. 4:17 [1]Or, *coffin*
16 [a]ch. 1:65 [b]ch. 24:19; John 4:19 & 6:14 & 9:17 [c]ch. 1:68
18 [a]Mat. 11:2
22 [a]Mat. 11:4 [b]Is. 35:5 [c]ch. 4:18
24 [a]Mat. 11:7
27 [a]Mal. 3:1
29 [a]Mat. 3:5; ch. 3:12
30 [a]Acts 20:27 [1]Or, *frustrated* [2]Or, *within themselves*
31 [a]Mat. 11:16
33 [a]Mat. 3:4; Mark 1:6; ch. 1:15
35 [a]Mat. 11:19
36 [a]Mat. 26:6; Mark 14:3; John 11:2

39 Now when the Pharisee which had bidden him saw *it,* he spake within himself, saying, [a]This man, if he were a prophet, would have known who and what manner of woman *this is* that toucheth him: for she is a sinner.

40 And Jesus answering said unto him, Simon, I have somewhat to say unto thee. And he saith, Master, say on.

L 41 There was a certain creditor which had two debtors: the one owed five hundred [l]pence, and the other fifty.

42 And when they had nothing to pay, he frankly forgave them both. Tell me therefore, which of them will love him most?

43 Simon answered and said, I suppose that *he,* to whom he forgave most. And he said unto him, Thou hast rightly judged.

44 And he turned to the woman, and said unto Simon, Seest thou this woman? I entered into thine house, thou gavest me no water for my feet: but she hath washed my feet with tears, and wiped *them* with the hairs of her head.

45 Thou gavest me no kiss: but this woman since the time I came in hath not ceased to kiss my feet.

46 [a]My head with oil thou didst not anoint: but this woman hath anointed my feet with ointment.

L 47 [a]Wherefore I say unto thee, Her sins, which are many, are forgiven; for she loved much: but to whom little is forgiven, *the same* loveth little.

48 And he said unto her, [a]Thy sins are forgiven.

49 And they that sat at meat with him began to say within themselves, [a]Who is this that forgiveth sins also?

F 50 And he said to the woman, [a]Thy faith hath saved thee; go in peace.

The parable of the sower

8 AND IT came to pass afterward, that he went throughout every city and village, preaching and showing the glad tidings of the kingdom of God: and the twelve *were* with him,

2 And [a]certain women, which had been healed of evil spirits and infirmities, Mary called Magdalene, [b]out of whom went seven devils,

3 And Joanna the wife of Chuza Herod's steward, and Susanna, and many others, which ministered unto him of their substance.

4 ¶ [a]And when much people were gathered together, and were come to him out of every city, he spake by a parable:

5 A sower went out to sow his seed: and as he sowed, some fell by the way side; and it was trodden down, and the fowls of the air devoured it.

6 And some fell upon a rock; and as soon as it was sprung up, it withered away, because it lacked moisture. S

7 And some fell among thorns; and the thorns sprang up with it, and choked it.

8 And other fell on good ground, and sprang up, and bare fruit an hundredfold. And when he had said these things, he cried, He that hath ears to hear, let him hear.

9 [a]And his disciples asked him, saying, What might this parable be?

10 And he said, Unto you it is given to know the mysteries of the kingdom of God: but to others in parables; [a]that seeing they might not see, and hearing they might not understand.

11 [a]Now the parable is this: The seed is the word of God.

12 Those by the way side are they that hear; then cometh the devil, and taketh away the word out of their hearts, lest they should believe and be saved. F

13 They on the rock *are they,* which, when they hear, receive the word with joy; and these have no root, which for a while believe, and in time of temptation fall away. S

14 And that which fell among thorns are they, which, when they have heard, go forth, and are choked with cares and riches and pleasures of *this* life, and bring no fruit to perfection.

15 But that on the good ground are they, which in an honest and good heart, having heard the word, keep *it,* and bring forth fruit with patience.

16 ¶ [a]No man, when he hath lighted a candle, covereth it with a vessel, or putteth *it* under a bed; but setteth *it* on a

39 [a]ch. 15:2
41 [l]See Mat. 20:2
46 [a]Ps. 23:5
47 [a]1 Tim. 1:14
48 [a]Mat. 9:2; Mark 2:5
49 [a]Mat. 9:3; Mark 2:7
50 [a]Mat. 9:22; Mark 5:34 & 10:52; ch. 8:48 & 18:42
8:2 [a]Mat. 27:55,56 [b]Mark 16:9
4 [a]Mat. 13:2; Mark 4:1
9 [a]Mat. 13:10; Mark 4:10
10 [a]Is. 6:9; Mark 4:12
11 [a]Mat. 13:18; Mark 4:14
16 [a]Mat. 5:15; Mark 4:21; ch. 11:33

L *Lk 6:37* ◀▶ *Lk 7:47*
L *Lk 7:41–42* ◀▶ *Lk 9:56*
F *Mk 16:16* ◀▶ *Lk 8:12*
S *Lk 6:43–49* ◀▶ *Lk 8:13–15*
F *Lk 7:50* ◀▶ *Jn 1:12*
S *Lk 8:6–8* ◀▶ *Lk 8:21*

candlestick, that they which enter in may see the light.

17 [a]For nothing is secret, that shall not be made manifest; neither *any thing* hid, that shall not be known and come abroad.

18 Take heed therefore how ye hear: [a]for whosoever hath, to him shall be given; and whosoever hath not, from him shall be taken even that which he [1]seemeth to have.

Jesus' true family

19 ¶ [a]Then came to him *his* mother and his brethren, and could not come at him for the press.

20 And it was told him *by certain* which said, Thy mother and thy brethren stand without, desiring to see thee.

S 21 And he answered and said unto them, My mother and my brethren are these which hear the word of God, and do it.

The storm stilled

22 ¶ [a]Now it came to pass on a certain day, that he went into a ship with his disciples: and he said unto them, Let us go over unto the other side of the lake. And they launched forth.

23 But as they sailed he fell asleep: and there came down a storm of wind on the lake; and they were filled *with water,* and were in jeopardy.

W 24 And they came to him, and awoke him, saying, Master, master, we perish. Then he arose, and rebuked the wind and the raging of the water: and they ceased, and there was a calm.

25 And he said unto them, Where is your faith? And they being afraid wondered, saying one to another, What manner of man is this! for he commandeth even the winds and water, and they obey him.

Devils cast out

E 26 ¶ [a]And they arrived at the country of the Gadarenes, which is over against Galilee.

27 And when he went forth to land, there met him out of the city a certain man, which had devils long time, and ware no clothes, neither abode in *any* house, but in the tombs.

28 When he saw Jesus, he cried out, and fell down before him, and with a loud voice said, What have I to do with thee, Jesus, *thou* Son of God most high? I beseech thee, torment me not.

29 (For he had commanded the unclean spirit to come out of the man. For oftentimes it had caught him: and he was kept bound with chains and in fetters; and he brake the bands, and was driven of the devil into the wilderness.)

30 And Jesus asked him, saying, What is thy name? And he said, Legion: because many devils were entered into him.

31 And they besought him that he would not command them to go out [a]into the deep.

32 And there was there an herd of many swine feeding on the mountain: and they besought him that he would suffer them to enter into them. And [a]he suffered them.

33 Then went the devils out of the man, and entered into the swine: and the herd ran violently down a steep place into the lake, and were choked.

34 When they that fed *them* saw what was done, they fled, and went and told *it* in the city and in the country.

35 Then they went out to see what was done; and came to Jesus, and found the man, out of whom the devils were departed, sitting at the feet of Jesus, clothed, and in his right mind: and they were afraid.

36 They also which saw *it* told them by what means he that was possessed of the devils was healed.

37 ¶ [a]Then the whole multitude of the country of the Gadarenes round about [b]besought him to depart from them; for they were taken with great fear: and he went up into the ship, and returned back again.

38 Now [a]the man out of whom the devils were departed besought him that he might be with him: but Jesus sent him away, saying,

39 Return to thine own house, and show how great things God hath done unto thee. And he went his way, and published throughout the whole city how great things Jesus had done unto him.

17 [a]Mat. 10:26; ch. 12:2
18 [a]Mat. 13:12 & 25:29; ch. 19:26 [1]Or, *thinketh that he hath*
19 [a]Mat. 12:46; Mark 3:31
22 [a]Mat. 8:23; Mark 4:35
26 [a]Mat. 8:28; Mark 5:1
31 [a]Rev. 20:3
32 [a]Job 1:12 & 12:16; Rev. 20:7
37 [a]Mat. 8:34 [b]Acts 16:39
38 [a]Mark 5:18

S *Lk 8:13–15* ◀ ▶ *Lk 9:23*
W *Mk 4:40* ◀ ▶ *Lk 12:22–32*
E *Lk 7:1–22* ◀ ▶ *Lk 9:1–2*

A ruler's daughter raised

40 And it came to pass, that, when Jesus was returned, the people *gladly* received him: for they were all waiting for him.

41 ¶ [a]And, behold, there came a man named Jairus, and he was a ruler of the synagogue: and he fell down at Jesus' feet, and besought him that he would come into his house:

42 For he had one only daughter, about twelve years of age, and she lay a dying. But as he went the people thronged him.

43 ¶ [a]And a woman having an issue of blood twelve years, which had spent all her living upon physicians, neither could be healed of any,

44 Came behind *him,* and touched the border of his garment: and immediately her issue of blood stanched.

45 And Jesus said, Who touched me? When all denied, Peter and they that were with him said, Master, the multitude throng thee and press *thee,* and sayest thou, Who touched me?

46 And Jesus said, Somebody hath touched me: for I perceive that [a]virtue is gone out of me.

47 And when the woman saw that she was not hid, she came trembling, and falling down before him, she declared unto him before all the people for what cause she had touched him, and how she was healed immediately.

48 And he said unto her, Daughter, be of good comfort: thy faith hath made thee whole; go in peace.

49 ¶ [a]While he yet spake, there cometh one from the ruler of the synagogue's *house,* saying to him, Thy daughter is dead; trouble not the Master.

50 But when Jesus heard *it,* he answered him, saying, Fear not: believe only, and she shall be made whole.

51 And when he came into the house, he suffered no man to go in, save Peter, and James, and John, and the father and the mother of the maiden.

52 And all wept, and bewailed her: but he said, Weep not; she is not dead, [a]but sleepeth.

53 And they laughed him to scorn, knowing that she was dead.

54 And he put them all out, and took her by the hand, and called, saying, Maid, [a]arise.

55 And her spirit came again, and she arose straightway: and he commanded to give her meat.

56 And her parents were astonished: but [a]he charged them that they should tell no man what was done.

The mission of the Twelve

9 THEN [a]HE called his twelve disciples together, and gave them power and authority over all devils, and to cure diseases.

2 And [a]he sent them to preach the kingdom of God, and to heal the sick.

3 [a]And he said unto them, Take nothing for *your* journey, neither staves, nor scrip, neither bread, neither money; neither have two coats apiece.

4 [a]And whatsoever house ye enter into, there abide, and thence depart.

5 [a]And whosoever will not receive you, when ye go out of that city, [b]shake off the very dust from your feet for a testimony against them.

6 [a]And they departed, and went through the towns, preaching the gospel, and healing every where.

7 ¶ [a]Now Herod the tetrarch heard of all that was done by him: and he was perplexed, because that it was said of some, that John was risen from the dead;

8 And of some, that Elias had appeared; and of others, that one of the old prophets was risen again.

9 And Herod said, John have I beheaded: but who is this, of whom I hear such things? [a]And he desired to see him.

The five thousand fed

10 ¶ [a]And the apostles, when they were returned, told him all that they had done. [b]And he took them, and went aside privately into a desert place belonging to the city called Bethsaida.

11 And the people, when they knew *it,* followed him: and he received them, and spake unto them of the kingdom of God, and healed them that had need of healing.

12 [a]And when the day began to wear away, then came the twelve, and said

41 [a]Mat. 9:18; Mark 5:22
43 [a]Mat. 9:20
46 [a]Mark 5:30; ch. 6:19
49 [a]Mark 5:35
52 [a]John 11:11,13
54 [a]ch. 7:14; John 11:43
56 [a]Mat. 8:4 & 9:30; Mark 5:43
9:1 [a]Mat. 10:1; Mark 3:13 & 6:7
2 [a]Mat. 10:7,8; Mark 6:12; ch. 10:1,9
3 [a]Mat. 10:9; Mark 6:8; ch. 10:4 & 22:35
4 [a]Mat. 10:11; Mark 6:10
5 [a]Mat. 10:14 [b]Acts 13:51
6 [a]Mark 6:12
7 [a]Mark 14:1; Mark 6:14
9 [a]ch. 23:8
10 [a]Mark 6:30 [b]Mat. 14:13
12 [a]Mat. 14:15; Mark 6:35; John 6:1,5

E *Lk 8:26–56* ◄► *Lk 9:6*
E *Lk 9:1–2* ◄► *Lk 9:11*
E *Lk 9:6* ◄► *Lk 9:37–43*
F *Lk 5:4–9* ◄► *Lk 11:3*

unto him, Send the multitude away, that they may go into the towns and country round about, and lodge, and get victuals: for we are here in a desert place.

13 But he said unto them, Give ye them to eat. And they said, We have no more but five loaves and two fishes; except we should go and buy meat for all this people.

14 For they were about five thousand men. And he said to his disciples, Make them sit down by fifties in a company.

15 And they did so, and made them all sit down.

16 Then he took the five loaves and the two fishes, and looking up to heaven, he blessed them, and brake, and gave to the disciples to set before the multitude.

17 And they did eat, and were all filled: and there was taken up of fragments that remained to them twelve baskets.

Peter's confession of faith

18 ¶ [a]And it came to pass, as he was alone praying, his disciples were with him: and he asked them, saying, Whom say the people that I am?

19 They answering said, [a]John the Baptist; but some *say,* Elias; and others *say,* that one of the old prophets is risen again.

20 He said unto them, But whom say ye that I am? [a]Peter answering said, The Christ of God.

21 [a]And he straitly charged them, and commanded *them* to tell no man that thing;

22 Saying, [a]The Son of man must suffer many things, and be rejected of the elders and chief priests and scribes, and be slain, and be raised the third day. B

23 ¶ [a]And he said to *them* all, If any *man* will come after me, let him deny himself, and take up his cross daily, and follow me. S

24 For whosoever will save his life shall lose it: but whosoever will lose his life for my sake, the same shall save it.

25 [a]For what is a man advantaged, if he gain the whole world, and lose himself, or be cast away? H T

26 [a]For whosoever shall be ashamed of me and of my words, of him shall the Son of man be ashamed, when he shall come in his own glory, and *in his* Father's, and of the holy angels. C

27 [a]But I tell you of a truth, there be some standing here, which shall not taste of death, till they see the kingdom of God.

The transfiguration

28 ¶ [a]And it came to pass about an eight days after these [1]sayings, he took Peter and John and James, and went up into a mountain to pray. Q

29 And as he prayed, the fashion of his countenance was altered, and his raiment *was* white *and* glistering.

30 And, behold, there talked with him

18 [a]Mat. 16:13; Mark 8:27
19 [a]ver. 7,8; Mat. 14:2
20 [a]Mat. 16:16; John 6:69
21 [a]Mat. 16:20
22 [a]Mat. 16:21 & 17:22
23 [a]Mat. 10:38 & 16:24; Mark 8:34; ch. 14:27
25 [a]Mat. 16:26; Mark 8:36
26 [a]Mat. 10:33; Mark 8:38; 2 Tim. 2:12
27 [a]Mat. 16:28; Mark 9:1
28 [a]Mat. 17:1; Mark 9:2 [1]Or, *things*

B *Lk 3:16 ◀▶ Jn 1:29*
S *Lk 8:21 ◀▶ Lk 9:62*
H *Lk 6:49 ◀▶ Lk 10:12–15*
T *Lk 6:45 ◀▶ Lk 12:8–9*
C *Mk 14:62 ◀▶ Lk 12:35–47*
Q *Jdg 2:10 ◀▶ Lk 16:23–25*

9:26 Jesus warned that anyone who was ashamed of him and his words in this life would receive a similar response from Christ when he returns in glory at his second coming.

9:27 This prophetic statement has puzzled many, but there are two commonly accepted explanations. Some believe that this verse refers to Christ's authority and kingly reign over the kingdom of his post-resurrection church. The book of Acts confirms the disciples' participation in this growth of the early church.

Yet the context surrounding this verse seems to favor the view that this was a prediction of the transfiguration. Scholars who subscribe to this view state that the disciples experienced the kingdom of God when they were privileged to witness Jesus' supernatural appearance with Elijah and Moses on the Mount of Transfiguration only a few days later (see Mt 17:1; Mk 9:2).

9:28–33 This transfiguration visibly displayed Jesus' glory as the Son of God and prefigured his revelation in glory at his second coming at Armageddon. The fact that Elijah and Moses appeared in recognizable forms confirms that we will be recognized in heaven as ourselves and will be able to recognize other saints as well (see 2Sa 12:23). Though there appears to be a contradiction in the three gospel accounts regarding the timing of this event, Matthew and Mark counted the duration between the events exclusively while Luke counted both the initial day in which Jesus predicted the event, as well as the final day of its fulfillment as part of his eight days (see Mt 17:1–8; Mk 9:2–8).

two men, which were Moses and Elias:

31 Who appeared in glory, and spake of his decease which he should accomplish at Jerusalem.

32 But Peter and they that were with him [a]were heavy with sleep: and when they were awake, they saw his glory, and the two men that stood with him.

33 And it came to pass, as they departed from him, Peter said unto Jesus, Master, it is good for us to be here: and let us make three tabernacles; one for thee, and one for Moses, and one for Elias: not knowing what he said.

34 While he thus spake, there came a cloud, and overshadowed them: and they feared as they entered into the cloud.

35 And there came a voice out of the cloud, saying, [a]This is my beloved Son: [b]hear him.

36 And when the voice was past, Jesus was found alone. [a]And they kept *it* close, and told no man in those days any of those things which they had seen.

A demoniac boy healed

E 37 ¶ [a]And it came to pass, that on the next day, when they were come down from the hill, much people met him.

38 And, behold, a man of the company cried out, saying, Master, I beseech thee, look upon my son: for he is mine only child.

39 And, lo, a spirit taketh him, and he suddenly crieth out; and it teareth him that he foameth again, and bruising him hardly departeth from him.

40 And I besought thy disciples to cast him out; and they could not.

41 And Jesus answering said, O faithless and perverse generation, how long shall I be with you, and suffer you? Bring thy son hither.

42 And as he was yet a-coming, the devil threw him down, and tare *him.* And Jesus rebuked the unclean spirit, and healed the child, and delivered him again to his father.

43 ¶ And they were all amazed at the mighty power of God. But while they wondered every one at all things which Jesus did, he said unto his disciples,

44 [a]Let these sayings sink down into your ears: for the Son of man shall be delivered into the hands of men.

45 [a]But they understood not this saying, and it was hid from them, that they perceived it not: and they feared to ask him of that saying.

True discipleship

46 ¶ [a]Then there arose a reasoning among them, which of them should be greatest.

47 And Jesus, perceiving the thought of their heart, took a child, and set him by him,

48 And said unto them, [a]Whosoever shall receive this child in my name receiveth me: and whosoever shall receive me receiveth him that sent me: [b]for he that is least among you all, the same shall be great.

49 ¶ [a]And John answered and said, E
Master, we saw one casting out devils in thy name; and we forbad him, because he followeth not with us.

50 And Jesus said unto him, Forbid *him* not: for [a]he that is not against us is for us.

James and John rebuked

51 ¶ And it came to pass, when the time was come that [a]he should be received up, he stedfastly set his face to go to Jerusalem,

52 And sent messengers before his face: and they went, and entered into a village of the Samaritans, to make ready for him.

53 And [a]they did not receive him, because his face was as though he would go to Jerusalem.

54 And when his disciples James and John saw *this,* they said, Lord, wilt thou that we command fire to come down from heaven, and consume them, even as [a]Elias did?

55 But he turned, and rebuked them, and said, Ye know not what manner of spirit ye are of.

56 For [a]the Son of man is not come to L
destroy men's lives, but to save *them.* And they went to another village.

The teaching about discipleship

57 ¶ [a]And it came to pass, that, as they went in the way, a certain *man* said unto him, Lord, I will follow thee whithersoever thou goest.

32 [a]Dan. 8:18 & 10:9
35 [a]Mat. 3:17 [b]Acts 3:22
36 [a]Mat. 17:9
37 [a]Mat. 17:14; Mark 9:14,17
44 [a]Mat. 17:22
45 [a]Mark 9:32; ch. 2:50 & 18:34
46 [a]Mat. 18:1; Mark 9:34
48 [a]Mat. 10:40 & 18:5; Mark 9:37; John 12:44 & 13:20 [b]Mat. 23:11, 12
49 [a]Mark 9:38; See Num. 11:28
50 [a]See Mat. 12:30; ch. 11:23
51 [a]Mark 16:19; Acts 1:2
53 [a]John 4:4,9
54 [a]2 Ki. 1:10,12
56 [a]John 3:17 & 12:47
57 [a]Mat. 8:19

E *Lk 9:11* ◀▶ *Lk 9:49–50*
E *Lk 9:37–43* ◀▶ *Lk 10:9*
L *Lk 7:47* ◀▶ *Lk 11:9–10*

58 And Jesus said unto him, Foxes
have holes, and birds of the air *have*
nests; but the Son of man hath not where
to lay *his* head.
59 [a]And he said unto another, Follow
me. But he said, Lord, suffer me first to
go and bury my father.
60 Jesus said unto him, Let the dead
bury their dead: but go thou and preach
the kingdom of God.
61 And another also said, Lord, [a]I will
follow thee; but let me first go bid them
farewell, which are at home at my house.
S 62 And Jesus said unto him, No man,
having put his hand to the plough, and
looking back, is fit for the kingdom of
God.

The mission of the seventy

10 AFTER THESE things the Lord
appointed other seventy also, and
[a]sent them two and two before his face
into every city and place, whither he
himself would come.
2 Therefore said he unto them, [a]The
harvest truly *is* great, but the labourers
are few: [b]pray ye therefore the Lord of
the harvest, that he would send forth labourers into his harvest.
3 Go your ways: [a]behold, I send you
forth as lambs among wolves.
4 [a]Carry neither purse, nor scrip, nor
shoes: and [b]salute no man by the way.
5 [a]And into whatsoever house ye enter, first say, Peace *be* to this house.
6 And if the son of peace be there,
your peace shall rest upon it: if not, it
shall turn to you again.
7 [a]And in the same house remain,
[b]eating and drinking such things as they
give: for [c]the labourer is worthy of his
hire. Go not from house to house.
8 And into whatsoever city ye enter,
and they receive you, eat such things as
are set before you:
E 9 [a]And heal the sick that are therein,

S *Lk 9:23* ◀▶ *Lk 10:25–28*
E *Lk 9:49–50* ◀▶ *Lk 10:17–20*

59 [a]Mat. 8:21
61 [a]See 1 Ki. 19:20
10:1 [a]Mat. 10:1; Mark 6:7
2 [a]Mat. 9:37; John 4:35 [b]2 Thes. 3:1
3 [a]Mat. 10:16
4 [a]Mat. 10:9; Mark 6:8; ch. 9:3 [b]2 Ki. 4:29
5 [a]Mat. 10:12
7 [a]Mat. 10:11 [b]1 Cor. 10:27 [c]Mat. 10:10; 1 Cor. 9:4; 1 Tim. 5:18
9 [a]ch. 9:2 [b]ver. 11; Mat. 3:2 & 4:17 & 10:7
11 [a]Mat. 10:14; ch. 9:5; Acts 13:51 & 18:6
12 [a]Mat. 10:15; Mark 6:11
13 [a]Mat. 11:21 [b]Ezek. 3:6
15 [a]Mat. 11:23 [b]See Gen. 11:4; Deut. 1:28; Is. 14:13; Jer. 51:53 [c]See Ezek. 26:20 & 32:18
16 [a]Mat. 10:40; Mark 9:37; John 13:20 [b]1 Thes. 4:8 [c]John 5:23
17 [a]ver. 1
18 [a]John 12:31 & 16:11; Rev. 9:1 & 12:8,9
19 [a]Mark 16:18; Acts 28:5
20 [a]Ex. 32:32; Ps. 69:28; Is. 4:3; Dan. 12:1; Phil. 4:3; Heb. 12:23; Rev. 13:8 & 20:12

and say unto them, [b]The kingdom of God
is come nigh unto you.
10 But into whatsoever city ye enter, N
and they receive you not, go your ways
out into the streets of the same, and say,
11 [a]Even the very dust of your city,
which cleaveth on us, we do wipe off
against you: notwithstanding be ye sure
of this, that the kingdom of God is come
nigh unto you.
12 But I say unto you, that [a]it shall be J
more tolerable in that day for Sodom, H
than for that city. J
13 [a]Woe unto thee, Chorazin! woe M
unto thee, Bethsaida! [b]for if the mighty
works had been done in Tyre and Sidon,
which have been done in you, they had a
great while ago repented, sitting in sackcloth and ashes.
14 But it shall be more tolerable for J
Tyre and Sidon at the judgment, than for
you.
15 [a]And thou, Capernaum, which art
[b]exalted to heaven, [c]shalt be thrust down
to hell.
16 [a]He that heareth you heareth me;
and [b]he that despiseth you despiseth me;
[c]and he that despiseth me despiseth him
that sent me.
17 ¶ And [a]the seventy returned again E
with joy, saying, Lord, even the devils are
subject unto us through thy name.
18 And he said unto them, [a]I beheld
Satan as lightning fall from heaven.
19 Behold, [a]I give unto you power to
tread on serpents and scorpions, and over
all the power of the enemy: and nothing
shall by any means hurt you.
20 Notwithstanding in this rejoice not,
that the spirits are subject unto you; but
rather rejoice, because [a]your names are
written in heaven.

N *Mk 16:15–16* ◀▶ *Lk 11:23*
J *Mk 6:11* ◀▶ *Lk 10:14*
H *Lk 9:25–26* ◀▶ *Lk 12:4–5*
J *Mk 6:11* ◀▶ *Lk 11:31–32*
M *Lk 6:20–21* ◀▶ *Lk 14:11*
J *Lk 10:12* ◀▶ *Lk 11:31–32*
E *Lk 10:9* ◀▶ *Lk 11:14–26*

10:10–15 Jesus prophesied that those cities that willfully rejected his salvation would face ultimate judgment before the throne of God. The Galilean cities of Capernaum, Chorazin and Bethsaida where Jesus ministered will be judged more harshly than the wicked cities of Sodom, Sidon and Tyre because of the opportunity these people had to respond positively to the message of Jesus Christ. This prophecy confirms that individuals will be punished according to their sins, and whether they reject or receive the truth of Christ.

21 ¶ [a]In that hour Jesus rejoiced in spirit, and said, I thank thee, O Father, Lord of heaven and earth, that thou hast hid these things from the wise and prudent, and hast revealed them unto babes: even so, Father; for so it seemed good in thy sight.

22 [a]All′ things are delivered to me of my Father: and [b]no man knoweth who the Son is, but the Father; and who the Father is, but the Son, and *he* to whom the Son will reveal *him.*

23 ¶ And he turned him unto *his* disciples, and said privately, [a]Blessed *are* the eyes which see the things that ye see:

24 For I tell you, [a]that many prophets and kings have desired to see those things which ye see, and have not seen *them;* and to hear those things which ye hear, and have not heard *them.*

The good Samaritan

O 25 ¶ And, behold, a certain lawyer
S stood up, and tempted him, saying, [a]Master, what shall I do to inherit eternal life?

26 He said unto him, What is written in the law? how readest thou?

27 And he answering said, [a]Thou shalt love the Lord thy God with all thy heart, and with all thy soul, and with all thy strength, and with all thy mind; and [b]thy neighbour as thyself.

28 And he said unto him, Thou hast answered right: this do, and [a]thou shalt live.

29 But he, willing to [a]justify himself, said unto Jesus, And who is my neighbour?

30 And Jesus answering said, A certain *man* went down from Jerusalem to Jericho, and fell among thieves, which stripped him of his raiment, and wounded *him,* and departed, leaving *him* half dead.

31 And by chance there came down a certain priest that way: and when he saw him, [a]he passed by on the other side.

32 And likewise a Levite, when he was at the place, came and looked *on him,* and passed by on the other side.

O *Lk 6:47–49* ◀ ▶ *Lk 12:8–9*
S *Lk 9:62* ◀ ▶ *Lk 11:28*

21 [a]Mat. 11:25
22 [a]Mat. 28:18; John 3:35 & 5:27 & 17:2 [b]John 1:18 & 6:44,46 ′Many ancient copies add these words, *And turning to his disciples, he said*
23 [a]Mat. 13:16
24 [a]1 Pet. 1:10
25 [a]Mat. 19:16 & 22:35
27 [a]Deut. 6:5 [b]Lev. 19:18
28 [a]Lev. 18:5; Neh. 9:29; Ezek. 20:11,13,21; Rom. 10:5
29 [a]ch. 16:15
31 [a]Ps. 38:11
33 [a]John 4:9
35 ′See Mat. 20:2
38 [a]John 11:1 & 12:2,3
39 [a]1 Cor. 7:32 [b]ch. 8:35; Acts 22:3
42 [a]Ps. 27:4
11:2 [a]Mat. 6:9

33 But a certain [a]Samaritan, as he journeyed, came where he was: and when he saw him, he had compassion *on him,*

34 And went to *him,* and bound up his wounds, pouring in oil and wine, and set him on his own beast, and brought him to an inn, and took care of him.

35 And on the morrow when he departed, he took out two ′pence, and gave *them* to the host, and said unto him, Take care of him; and whatsoever thou spendest more, when I come again, I will repay thee.

36 Which now of these three, thinkest thou, was neighbour unto him that fell among the thieves?

37 And he said, He that showed mercy on him. Then said Jesus unto him, Go, and do thou likewise.

Jesus visits Mary and Martha

38 ¶ Now it came to pass, as they went, that he entered into a certain village: and a certain woman named [a]Martha received him into her house.

39 And she had a sister called Mary, [a]which also [b]sat at Jesus' feet, and heard his word.

40 But Martha was cumbered about much serving, and came to him, and said, Lord, dost thou not care that my sister hath left me to serve alone? bid her therefore that she help me.

41 And Jesus answered and said unto her, Martha, Martha, thou art careful and troubled about many things:

42 But [a]one thing is needful: and Mary hath chosen that good part, which shall not be taken away from her.

Jesus' teaching on prayer

11 AND IT came to pass, that, as he was praying in a certain place, when he ceased, one of his disciples said unto him, Lord, teach us to pray, as John also taught his disciples.

2 And he said unto them, When ye K
pray, say, [a]Our Father which art in M
heaven, Hallowed be thy name. Thy kingdom come. Thy will be done, as in heaven, so in earth.

K *Mk 9:1* ◀ ▶ *Ac 3:21*
M *Lk 3:5–6* ◀ ▶ *Lk 12:32*

11:2 When Jesus taught his disciples to pray, his words included the prophecy of the coming Millennium when God's kingdom will truly come on earth.

F 3 Give us ʹday by day our daily bread.
R 4 And forgive us our sins; for we also
forgive every one that is indebted to us.
And lead us not into temptation; but deliver us from evil.
5 And he said unto them, Which of
you shall have a friend, and shall go unto
him at midnight, and say unto him,
Friend, lend me three loaves;
6 For a friend of mine ʹin his journey
is come to me, and I have nothing to set
before him?
7 And he from within shall answer and
say, Trouble me not: the door is now
shut, and my children are with me in
bed; I cannot rise and give thee.
8 I say unto you, [a]Though he will not
rise and give him, because he is his
friend, yet because of his importunity he
will rise and give him as many as he
needeth.
A 9 [a]And I say unto you, Ask, and it shall
P be given you; seek, and ye shall find;
L knock, and it shall be opened unto you.
W 10 For every one that asketh receiveth;
and he that seeketh findeth; and to him
that knocketh it shall be opened.
11 [a]If a son shall ask bread of any of
you that is a father, will he give him a
stone? or if *he ask* a fish, will he for a fish
give him a serpent?
12 Or if he shall ask an egg, will he
ʹoffer him a scorpion?
13 If ye then, being evil, know how to
give good gifts unto your children: how
much more shall *your* heavenly Father
give the Holy Spirit to them that ask him?

The Pharisees' slander

E 14 ¶ [a]And he was casting out a devil,
and it was dumb. And it came to pass,
when the devil was gone out, the dumb
spake; and the people wondered.
15 But some of them said, [a]He casteth
out devils through ʹBeelzebub the chief
of the devils.
16 And others, tempting *him,* [a]sought
of him a sign from heaven.
17 [a]But [b]he, knowing their thoughts,
said unto them, Every kingdom divided
against itself is brought to desolation; and
a house *divided* against a house falleth.
18 If Satan also be divided against himself, how shall his kingdom stand? because ye say that I cast out devils through
Beelzebub.
19 And if I by Beelzebub cast out
devils, by whom do your sons cast *them*
out? therefore shall they be your judges.
20 But if I [a]with the finger of God cast
out devils, no doubt the kingdom of God
is come upon you.
21 [a]When a strong man armed keepeth his palace, his goods are in peace:
22 But [a]when a stronger than he shall
come upon him, and overcome him, he
taketh from him all his armour wherein
he trusted, and divideth his spoils.
23 [a]He that is not with me is against A
me: and he that gathereth not with me C
scattereth. N
24 [a]When the unclean spirit is gone
out of a man, he walketh through dry
places, seeking rest; and finding none,
he saith, I will return unto my house
whence I came out.
25 And when he cometh, he findeth *it*
swept and garnished.
26 Then goeth he, and taketh *to him*
seven other spirits more wicked than
himself; and they enter in, and dwell
there: and [a]the last *state* of that man is
worse than the first.
27 ¶ And it came to pass, as he spake
these things, a certain woman of the
company lifted up her voice, and said
unto him, [a]Blessed *is* the womb that bare
thee, and the paps which thou hast
sucked.
28 But he said, Yea [a]rather, blessed S
are they that hear the word of God, and
keep it.

Warning against seeking signs

29 ¶ [a]And when the people were gathered thick together, he began to say, This
is an evil generation: they seek a sign;
and there shall no sign be given it, but
the sign of Jonas the prophet.
30 For as [a]Jonas was a sign unto the
Ninevites, so shall also the Son of man be
to this generation.

3 ʹOr, *for the day*
6 ʹOr, *out of his way*
8 [a]ch. 18:1
9 [a]Mat. 7:7 & 21:22; Mark 11:24; John 15:7; Jas. 1:6; 1 John 3:22
11 [a]Mat. 7:9
12 ʹGk. *give*
14 [a]Mat. 9:32 & 12:22
15 [a]Mat. 9:34 & 12:24 ʹGk. *Beelzebul;* also ver. 18,19
16 [a]Mat. 12:38 & 16:1
17 [a]Mat. 12:25; Mark 3:24 [b]John 2:25
20 [a]Ex. 8:19
21 [a]Mat. 12:29; Mark 3:27
22 [a]Is. 53:12; Col. 2:15
23 [a]Mat. 12:30
24 [a]Mat. 12:43
26 [a]John 5:14; Heb. 6:4 & 10:26; 2 Pet. 2:20
27 [a]ch. 1:28,48
28 [a]Mat. 7:21; ch. 8:21; Jas. 1:25
29 [a]Mat. 12:38,39
30 [a]Jonah 1:17 & 2:10

F *Lk 9:12–17* ◀ ▶ *Lk 12:22–31*
R *Lk 6:37* ◀ ▶ *Lk 13:3*
A *Ps 51:10–13* ◀ ▶ *Jn 4:10*
P *Lk 3:16* ◀ ▶ *Lk 24:29*
L *Lk 9:56* ◀ ▶ *Lk 13:34*
W *Lk 2:10–11* ◀ ▶ *Lk 12:8*
E *Lk 10:17–20* ◀ ▶ *Lk 13:11–17*
A *Mt 22:11–14* ◀ ▶ *Jn 3:18*
C *Lk 6:49* ◀ ▶ *Lk 11:34–35*
N *Lk 10:10–16* ◀ ▶ *Lk 11:31–32*
S *Lk 10:25–28* ◀ ▶ *Lk 11:34*

J 31 [a]The queen of the south shall rise
J up in the judgment with the men of this
N generation, and condemn them: for she
came from the utmost parts of the earth
to hear the wisdom of Solomon; and, behold, a greater than Solomon *is* here.
32 The men of Nineve shall rise up in
the judgment with this generation, and
shall condemn it: for [a]they repented at
the preaching of Jonas; and, behold, a
greater than Jonas *is* here.

The parable of the lighted candle

33 [a]No man, when he hath lighted a
candle, putteth *it* in a secret place, neither under a [l]bushel, but on a candlestick, that they which come in may see
the light.
C 34 [a]The light of the body is the eye:
S therefore when thine eye is single, thy
whole body also is full of light; but when
thine eye is evil, thy body also *is* full of
darkness.
35 Take heed therefore that the light
which is in thee be not darkness.
36 If thy whole body therefore *be* full
of light, having no part dark, the whole
shall be full of light, as when [l]the bright
shining of a candle doth give thee light.

The warning against Pharisaism

37 ¶ And as he spake, a certain Pharisee besought him to dine with him: and
he went in, and sat down to meat.
38 And [a]when the Pharisee saw *it,* he
marvelled that he had not first washed
before dinner.
39 [a]And the Lord said unto him, Now
do ye Pharisees make clean the outside of
the cup and the platter; but [b]your inward
part is full of ravening and wickedness.
40 *Ye* fools, did not he that made that
which is without make that which is
within also?
41 [a]But rather give alms [l]of such
things as ye have; and, behold, all things
are clean unto you.
42 [a]But woe unto you, Pharisees! for
ye tithe mint and rue and all manner of
herbs, and pass over judgment and the
love of God: these ought ye to have done,
and not to leave the other undone.
43 [a]Woe unto you, Pharisees! for ye
love the uppermost seats in the synagogues, and greetings in the markets.
44 [a]Woe unto you, scribes and Pharisees, hypocrites! [b]for ye are as graves
which appear not, and the men that walk
over *them* are not aware *of them.*
45 ¶ Then answered one of the lawyers, and said unto him, Master, thus saying thou reproachest us also.
46 And he said, Woe unto you also, *ye*
lawyers! [a]for ye lade men with burdens
grievous to be borne, and ye yourselves
touch not the burdens with one of your
fingers.
47 [a]Woe unto you! for ye build the
sepulchres of the prophets, and your fathers killed them.
48 Truly ye bear witness that ye allow
the deeds of your fathers: for they indeed
killed them, and ye build their sepulchres.
49 Therefore also said the wisdom of
God, [a]I will send them prophets and
apostles, and *some* of them they shall slay
and persecute:
50 That the blood of all the prophets,
which was shed from the foundation of
the world, may be required of this generation;
51 [a]From the blood of Abel unto [b]the
blood of Zacharias, which perished between the altar and the temple: verily I
say unto you, It shall be required of this
generation.
52 [a]Woe unto you, lawyers! for ye
have taken away the key of knowledge:
ye entered not in yourselves, and them
that were entering in ye [l]hindered.
53 And as he said these things unto
them, the scribes and the Pharisees began to urge *him* vehemently, and to provoke him to speak of many things:

31 [a]1 Ki. 10:1
32 [a]Jonah 3:5
33 [a]Mat. 5:15; Mark 4:21; ch. 8:16 [l]See Mat. 5:15
34 [a]Mat. 6:22
36 [l]Gk. *a candle by its bright shining*
38 [a]Mark 7:3
39 [a]Mat. 23:25 [b]Tit. 1:15
41 [a]Is. 58:7; Dan. 4:27; ch. 12:33 [l]Or, *as you are able*
42 [a]Mat. 23:23
43 [a]Mat. 23:6; Mark 12:38,39
44 [a]Mat. 23:27 [b]Ps. 5:9
46 [a]Mat. 23:4
47 [a]Mat. 23:29
49 [a]Mat. 23:34
51 [a]Gen. 4:8 [b]2 Chr. 24:20,21
52 [a]Mat. 23:13 [l]Or, *forbad*

J *Lk 10:14* ◀▶ *Jn 12:48*
J *Lk 10:12–14* ◀▶ *Jn 12:48*
N *Lk 11:23* ◀▶ *Lk 12:16–21*
C *Lk 11:23* ◀▶ *Lk 12:16–21*
S *Lk 11:28* ◀▶ *Lk 13:9*

11:31–32 The opportunities to repent are so overwhelming and numerous that the kingdom of the queen of Sheba and the ancient Ninevites will condemn the Israelites for their unrepentant hearts. Both the queen of Sheba and the city of Nineveh repented with far less spiritual revelation than those of first-century Judea who experienced and rejected the ministry of Jesus. This prophecy confirms that those condemned to eternity in hell will be judged by their own evil deeds.

54 Laying wait for him, and [a]seeking to catch something out of his mouth, that they might accuse him.

The value of life

12 IN [a]THE mean time, when there were gathered together an innumerable multitude of people, insomuch that they trode one upon another, he began to say unto his disciples first of all, [b]Beware ye of the leaven of the Pharisees, which is hypocrisy.

E 2 [a]For there is nothing covered, that shall not be revealed; neither hid, that shall not be known.

3 Therefore whatsoever ye have spoken in darkness shall be heard in the light; and that which ye have spoken in the ear in closets shall be proclaimed upon the housetops.

H 4 [a]And I say unto you [b]my friends, Be not afraid of them that kill the body, and after that have no more that they can do.

5 But I will forewarn you whom ye shall fear: Fear him, which after he hath killed hath power to cast into hell; yea, I say unto you, Fear him.

L 6 Are not five sparrows sold for two [l]farthings, and not one of them is forgotten before God?

7 But even the very hairs of your head are all numbered. Fear not therefore: ye are of more value than many sparrows.

O T W 8 [a]Also I say unto you, Whosoever shall confess me before men, him shall the Son of man also confess before the angels of God:

9 But he that denieth me before men shall be denied before the angels of God.

Q 10 And [a]whosoever shall speak a word against the Son of man, it shall be forgiven him: but unto him that blasphemeth against the Holy Ghost it shall not be forgiven.

G L T 11 [a]And when they bring you unto the synagogues, and *unto* magistrates, and powers, take ye no thought how or what thing ye shall answer, or what ye shall say:

12 For the Holy Ghost shall teach you in the same hour what ye ought to say.

The parable of the rich fool

13 ¶ And one of the company said unto him, Master, speak to my brother, that he divide the inheritance with me.

14 And he said unto him, [a]Man, who made me a judge or a divider over you?

15 And he said unto them, [a]Take heed, and beware of covetousness: for a man's life consisteth not in the abundance of the things which he possesseth.

16 And he spake a parable unto them, saying, The ground of a certain rich man brought forth plentifully: C N

17 And he thought within himself, saying, What shall I do, because I have no room where to bestow my fruits?

18 And he said, This will I do: I will pull down my barns, and build greater; and there will I bestow all my fruits and my goods.

19 And I will say to my soul, [a]Soul, thou hast much goods laid up for many years; take thine ease, eat, drink, *and* be merry.

20 But God said unto him, *Thou* fool, this night [a]thy[l] soul shall be required of thee: [b]then whose shall those things be, which thou hast provided? H

21 So *is* he that layeth up treasure for himself, [a]and is not rich toward God.

The teaching about anxiety

22 ¶ And he said unto his disciples, Therefore I say unto you, [a]Take no thought for your life, what ye shall eat; neither for the body, what ye shall put on. C F L W

23 The life is more than meat, and the body *is more* than raiment.

24 Consider the ravens: for they neither sow nor reap; which neither have storehouse nor barn; and [a]God feedeth them: how much more are ye better than the fowls?

25 And which of you with taking

54 [a]Mark 12:13
12:1 [a]Mat 16:6; Mark 8:15 [b]Mat. 16:12
2 [a]Mat. 10:26; Mark 4:22; ch. 8:17
4 [a]Is. 51:7,8,12,13; Jer. 1:8; Mat. 10:28 [b]John 15:14,15
6 [l]See Mat. 10:29
8 [a]Mat. 10:32; Mark 8:38; 2 Tim. 2:12; 1 John 2:23
10 [a]Mat. 12:31,32; Mark 3:28; 1 John 5:16
11 [a]Mat. 10:19; Mark 13:11
14 [a]John 18:36
15 [a]1 Tim. 6:7
19 [a]Eccl. 11:9; 1 Cor. 15:32; Jas. 5:5
20 [a]Job 20:22 & 27:8; Ps. 52:7; Jas. 4:14 [b]Ps. 39:6; Jer. 17:11 [l]*Or, do they require thy soul*
21 [a]ver. 33; Mat. 6:20; 1 Tim. 6:18, 19; Jas. 2:5
22 [a]Mat. 6:25
24 [a]Job 38:41; Ps. 147:9

E *Lk 6:8* ◀▶ *Lk 16:15*
H *Lk 10:12–15* ◀▶ *Lk 12:20–21*
L *Lk 4:10–11* ◀▶ *Lk 12:22–32*
O *Lk 10:25–28* ◀▶ *Lk 18:16–17*
T *Lk 9:25–26* ◀▶ *Jn 12:42–43*
W *Lk 11:9–10* ◀▶ *Lk 14:16–23*
Q *Mk 3:29* ◀▶ *Ac 5:3–4*
G *Lk 2:40* ◀▶ *Lk 21:14–15*
L *Lk 4:14* ◀▶ *Lk 21:14–15*
T *Lk 4:18* ◀▶ *Lk 21:14–15*

C *Lk 11:34–35* ◀▶ *Lk 15:24*
N *Lk 11:31–32* ◀▶ *Lk 12:39–40*
H *Lk 12:4–5* ◀▶ *Lk 12:46–48*
C *Mt 6:25–34* ◀▶ *Lk 22:35*
F *Lk 11:3* ◀▶ *Lk 22:35*
L *Lk 12:6–7* ◀▶ *Lk 17:2*
W *Lk 8:24–25* ◀▶ *Lk 18:1*

thought can add to his stature one cubit?
26 If ye then be not able to do that
thing which is least, why take ye thought
for the rest?
27 Consider the lilies how they grow:
they toil not, they spin not; and yet I say
unto you, that Solomon in all his glory
was not arrayed like one of these.
28 If then God so clothe the grass,
which is today in the field, and tomorrow
is cast into the oven; how much more
will he clothe you, O ye of little faith?
29 And seek not ye what ye shall eat,
or what ye shall drink, [I]neither be ye of
doubtful mind.
30 For all these things do the nations
of the world seek after: and your Father
knoweth that ye have need of these
things.
U 31 ¶ [a]But rather seek ye the kingdom
of God; and all these things shall be
added unto you.
M 32 Fear not, little flock; for [a]it is your
Father's good pleasure to give you the
kingdom.
33 [a]Sell that ye have, and give alms;
[b]provide yourselves bags which wax not
old, a treasure in the heavens that faileth
not, where no thief approacheth, neither
moth corrupteth.
34 For where your treasure is, there
will your heart be also.

Parable of the watching servants

C 35 [a]Let your loins be girded about, and
[b]*your* lights burning;
36 And ye yourselves like unto men
that wait for their lord, when he will return from the wedding; that when he
cometh and knocketh, they may open
unto him immediately.
37 [a]Blessed *are* those servants, whom
the lord when he cometh shall find
watching: verily I say unto you, that he
shall gird himself, and make them to sit

29 [I]Or, *live not in careful suspense*
31 [a]Mat. 6:33
32 [a]Mat. 11:25,26
33 [a]Mat. 19:21; Acts 2:45 & 4:34 [b]Mat. 6:20; ch. 16:9; 1 Tim. 6:19
35 [a]Eph. 6:14; 1 Pet. 1:13 [b]Mat. 25:1
37 [a]Mat. 24:46
39 [a]Mat. 24:43; 1 Thes. 5:2; 2 Pet. 3:10; Rev. 3:3 & 16:15
40 [a]Mat. 24:44 & 25:13; Mark 13:33; ch. 21:34,36; 1 Thes. 5:6; 2 Pet. 3:12
42 [a]Mat. 24:45 & 25:21; 1 Cor. 42
44 [a]Mat. 24:47
45 [a]Mat. 24:48
46 [I]Or, *cut him off*
47 [a]Num. 15:30; Deut. 25:2; John 9:41 & 15:22; Acts 17:30; Jas. 4:17
48 [a]Lev. 5:17; 1 Tim. 1:13

down to meat, and will come forth and
serve them.
38 And if he shall come in the second
watch, or come in the third watch, and
find *them* so, blessed are those servants.
39 [a]And this know, that if the good- N
man of the house had known what hour
the thief would come, he would have
watched, and not have suffered his house
to be broken through.
40 [a]Be ye therefore ready also: for the
Son of man cometh at an hour when ye
think not.
41 ¶ Then Peter said unto him, Lord,
speakest thou this parable unto us, or
even to all?
42 And the Lord said, [a]Who then is
that faithful and wise steward, whom *his*
lord shall make ruler over his household,
to give *them their* portion of meat in due
season?
43 Blessed *is* that servant, whom his
lord when he cometh shall find so doing.
44 [a]Of a truth I say unto you, that he
will make him ruler over all that he hath.
45 [a]But and if that servant say in his P
heart, My lord delayeth his coming; and
shall begin to beat the menservants and
maidens, and to eat and drink, and to be
drunken;
46 The lord of that servant will come H
in a day when he looketh not for *him,* N
and at an hour when he is not aware, and
will [I]cut him in sunder, and will appoint
him his portion with the unbelievers.
47 And [a]that servant, which knew his
lord's will, and prepared not *himself,* neither did according to his will, shall be
beaten with many *stripes.*
48 [a]But he that knew not, and did
commit things worthy of stripes, shall be
beaten with few *stripes.* For unto whomsoever much is given, of him shall be
much required: and to whom men have

U *Mk 10:28–30* ◀▶ *Lk 18:29–30*
M *Lk 11:2* ◀▶ *Lk 13:19*
C *Lk 9:26* ◀▶ *Lk 17:23–24*
N *Lk 12:16–21* ◀▶ *Lk 12:46–47*
P *Mt 24:50–51* ◀▶ *Lk 17:26–30*
H *Lk 12:20–21* ◀▶ *Lk 13:5*
N *Lk 12:39–40* ◀▶ *Lk 13:24–25*

12:32 Jesus prophesied that God has promised to deliver the millennial kingdom to the saints in the future as well as "righteousness, and peace, and joy in the Holy Ghost" (Ro 14:17) each day.
12:35–47 Jesus warned his followers and servants to be watchful for his return. The Lord will come in an hour when the wicked servants are not watchful, and catch them unawares as a thief who breaks into a house. Jesus' followers must be ready at any time for his return "for the Son of man cometh at an hour when ye think not" (12:40). Those servants who obediently watch for his return, even if it is delayed, will be rewarded; those who are not prepared will be judged.

committed much, of him they will ask the more.

Jesus the divider

49 ¶ [a]I am come to send fire on the earth; and what will I, if it be already kindled?

50 But [a]I have a baptism to be baptized with; and how am I [/]straitened till it be accomplished!

51 [a]Suppose ye that I am come to give peace on earth? I tell you, Nay; [b]but rather division:

52 [a]For from henceforth there shall be five in one house divided, three against two, and two against three.

53 The father shall be divided against the son, and the son against the father; the mother against the daughter, and the daughter against the mother; the mother-in-law against her daughter-in-law, and the daughter-in-law against her mother-in-law.

Interpreting the present time

54 ¶ And he said also to the people, [a]When ye see a cloud rise out of the west, straightway ye say, There cometh a shower; and so it is.

55 And when *ye see* the south wind blow, ye say, There will be heat; and it cometh to pass.

56 *Ye* hypocrites, ye can discern the face of the sky and of the earth; but how is it that ye do not discern this time?

57 Yea, and why even of yourselves judge ye not what is right?

58 ¶ [a]When thou goest with thine adversary to the magistrate, [b]*as thou art* in the way, give diligence that thou mayest be delivered from him; lest he hale thee to the judge, and the judge deliver thee to the officer, and the officer cast thee into prison.

59 I tell thee, thou shalt not depart thence, till thou hast paid the very last [/]mite.

Jesus' call to repentance

13 THERE WERE present at that season some that told him of the Galilaeans, whose blood Pilate had mingled with their sacrifices.

2 And Jesus answering said unto them, Suppose ye that these Galilaeans were sinners above all the Galilaeans, because they suffered such things?

3 I tell you, Nay: but, except ye repent, R
ye shall all likewise perish. R

4 Or those eighteen, upon whom the tower in Siloam fell, and slew them, think ye that they were [/]sinners above all men that dwelt in Jerusalem?

5 I tell you, Nay: but, except ye repent, R
ye shall all likewise perish. H

6 ¶ He spake also this parable; [a]A cer- R
tain *man* had a fig tree planted in his vineyard; and he came and sought fruit thereon, and found none.

7 Then said he unto the dresser of his vineyard, Behold, these three years I come seeking fruit on this fig tree, and find none: cut it down; why cumbereth it the ground?

8 And he answering said unto him, Lord, let it alone this year also, till I shall dig about it, and dung *it:*

9 And if it bear fruit, *well:* and if not, H
then after that thou shalt cut it down. S

A woman healed on the Sabbath

10 And he was teaching in one of the synagogues on the sabbath.

11 ¶ And, behold, there was a woman E
which had a spirit of infirmity eighteen years, and was bowed together, and could in no wise lift up *herself.*

12 And when Jesus saw her, he called *her to him,* and said unto her, Woman, thou art loosed from thine infirmity.

13 [a]And he laid *his* hands on her: and immediately she was made straight, and glorified God.

14 And the ruler of the synagogue answered with indignation, because that Jesus had healed on the sabbath day, and said unto the people, [a]There are six days in which men ought to work: in them therefore come and be healed, and [b]not on the sabbath day.

49 [a]ver. 51
50 [a]Mat. 20:22; Mark 10:38 [/]Or, *pained*
51 [a]ver. 49; Mat. 10:34 [b]Mic. 7:6; John 7:43 & 9:16 & 10:19
52 [a]Mat. 10:35
54 [a]Mat. 16:2
58 [a]Prov. 25:8; Mat. 5:25 [b]See Ps. 32:6; Is. 55:6
59 [/]See Mark 12:42
13:4 [/]Or, *debtors;* see Mat. 18:24; Luke 11:4
6 [a]Is. 5:2; Mat. 21:19
13 [a]Mark 16:18; Acts 9:17
14 [a]Ex. 20:9 [b]Mat. 12:10; Mark 3:2; ch. 6:7 & 14:3

R *Mk 13:14–20* ◀▶ *Lk 13:5*
R *Lk 11:4* ◀▶ *Lk 13:5*
R *Lk 13:3* ◀▶ *Lk 13:34–35*
H *Lk 12:46–48* ◀▶ *Lk 13:9*
R *Lk 13:3* ◀▶ *Lk 15:7*
H *Lk 13:5* ◀▶ *Lk 13:24–28*
S *Lk 11:34* ◀▶ *Lk 13:23–28*
E *Lk 11:14–26* ◀▶ *Lk 13:32–33*

13:3–5 Jesus points out that all sinners who refuse to repent will perish.

15 The Lord then answered him, and said, *Thou* hypocrite, [a]doth not each one of you on the sabbath loose his ox or *his* ass from the stall, and lead *him* away to watering?

D 16 And ought not this woman, [a]being a daughter of Abraham, whom Satan hath bound, lo, these eighteen years, be loosed from this bond on the sabbath day?

17 And when he had said these things, all his adversaries were ashamed: and all the people rejoiced for all the glorious things that were done by him.

Parables about the kingdom

18 ¶ [a]Then said he, Unto what is the kingdom of God like? and whereunto shall I resemble it?

M 19 It is like a grain of mustard seed, which a man took, and cast into his garden; and it grew, and waxed a great tree; and the fowls of the air lodged in the branches of it.

20 And again he said, Whereunto shall I liken the kingdom of God?

M 21 It is like leaven, which a woman took and hid in three [l]measures of meal, till the whole was leavened.

The strait gate

22 [a]And he went through the cities and villages, teaching, and journeying toward Jerusalem.

S 23 Then said one unto him, Lord, are there few that be saved? And he said unto them,

H 24 ¶ [a]Strive to enter in at the strait
N gate: for [b]many, I say unto you, will seek to enter in, and shall not be able.

D *Lk 4:23–27* ◀ ▶ *Jn 5:14*
M *Lk 12:32* ◀ ▶ *Lk 13:21*
M *Lk 13:19* ◀ ▶ *Lk 19:11–26*
S *Lk 13:9* ◀ ▶ *Lk 14:26–27*
H *Lk 13:9* ◀ ▶ *Lk 14:24*
N *Lk 12:46–47* ◀ ▶ *Lk 13:34–35*

15 [a]ch. 14:5
16 [a]ch. 19:9
18 [a]Mat. 13:31; Mark 4:30
21 [l]See Mat. 13:33
22 [a]Mat. 9:35; Mark 6:6
24 [a]Mat. 7:13 [b]See John 7:34 & 8:21 & 13:33; Rom. 9:31
25 [a]Ps. 32:6; Is. 55:6 [b]Mat. 25:10 [c]ch. 6:46 [d]Mat. 7:23 & 25:12
27 [a]ver. 25; Mat. 7:23 & 25:41 [b]Ps. 6:8; Mat. 25:41
28 [a]Mat. 8:12 & 13:42 & 24:51 [b]Mat. 8:11
30 [a]Mat. 19:30 & 20:16; Mark 10:31
32 [a]Heb. 2:10
34 [a]Mat. 23:37

25 [a]When once the master of the house is risen up, and [b]hath shut to the door, and ye begin to stand without, and to knock at the door, saying, [c]Lord, Lord, open unto us; and he shall answer and say unto you, [d]I know you not whence ye are:

26 Then shall ye begin to say, We have eaten and drunk in thy presence, and thou hast taught in our streets.

27 [a]But he shall say, I tell you, I know you not whence ye are; [b]depart from me, all *ye* workers of iniquity.

28 [a]There shall be weeping and gnashing of teeth, [b]when ye shall see Abraham, and Isaac, and Jacob, and all the prophets, in the kingdom of God, and you *yourselves* thrust out.

29 And they shall come from the east, and *from* the west, and from the north, and *from* the south, and shall sit down in the kingdom of God.

30 [a]And, behold, there are last which shall be first, and there are first which shall be last.

The lament over Jerusalem

31 ¶ The same day there came certain of the Pharisees, saying unto him, Get thee out, and depart hence: for Herod will kill thee.

32 And he said unto them, Go ye, and tell that fox, Behold, I cast out devils, and I do cures today and tomorrow, and the third *day* [a]I shall be perfected. E

33 Nevertheless I must walk today, and tomorrow, and the *day* following: for it cannot be that a prophet perish out of Jerusalem.

34 [a]O Jerusalem, Jerusalem, which killest the prophets, and stonest them R L N

E *Lk 13:11–17* ◀ ▶ *Lk 14:1–6*
R *Lk 13:5* ◀ ▶ *Lk 14:24*
L *Lk 11:9–10* ◀ ▶ *Lk 14:21–23*
N *Lk 13:24–25* ◀ ▶ *Lk 14:16–24*

13:19 Jesus likens the kingdom of God to a "grain of mustard seed" which is almost invisible, yet grows into "a great tree." The church has grown from twelve disciples into a global church of over 600 million believers.

13:21 Jesus also compared the kingdom of God to the "leaven" that causes the whole amount of bread to rise. This comparison indicated the prophetic destiny of the church to influence the entire world with the teachings of Christ.

13:34–35 Jesus warned of God's approaching judgment on the city of Jerusalem and the temple because of the Jews refusal to repent and their rejection of Jesus as their Messiah. Jesus also warned that he would not see them again until their repentance at his second coming at Armageddon. At the conclusion of the savage persecution under the antichrist, the Jews will finally accept their Messiah who "cometh in the name of the Lord" (13:35; see Zec 12:1–14).

that are sent unto thee; how often would I have gathered thy children together, as a hen *doth gather* her brood under *her* wings, and ye would not!

35 Behold, [a]your house is left unto you desolate: and verily I say unto you, Ye shall not see me, until *the time* come when ye shall say, [b]Blessed *is* he that cometh in the name of the Lord.

Jesus heals on the Sabbath

E 14 AND IT came to pass, as he went into the house of one of the chief Pharisees to eat bread on the sabbath day, that they watched him.

2 And, behold, there was a certain man before him which had the dropsy.

3 And Jesus answering spake unto the lawyers and Pharisees, saying, [a]Is it lawful to heal on the sabbath day?

4 And they held their peace. And he took *him,* and healed him, and let him go;

5 And answered them, saying, [a]Which of you shall have an ass or an ox fallen into a pit, and will not straightway pull him out on the sabbath day?

6 And they could not answer him again to these things.

The honoured place

7 ¶ And he put forth a parable to those which were bidden, when he marked how they chose out the chief rooms; saying unto them,

8 When thou art bidden of any *man* to a wedding, sit not down in the highest room; lest a more honourable man than thou be bidden of him;

9 And he that bade thee and him come and say to thee, Give this man place; and thou begin with shame to take the lowest room.

10 [a]But when thou art bidden, go and sit down in the lowest room; that when he that bade thee cometh, he may say unto thee, Friend, go up higher: then shalt thou have worship in the presence of them that sit at meat with thee.

11 [a]For whosoever exalteth himself shall be abased; and he that humbleth himself shall be exalted. M

12 ¶ Then said he also to him that bade him, When thou makest a dinner or a supper, call not thy friends, nor thy brethren, neither thy kinsmen, nor *thy* rich neighbours; lest they also bid thee again, and a recompence be made thee.

13 But when thou makest a feast, call [a]the poor, the maimed, the lame, the blind: F

14 And thou shalt be blessed; for they cannot recompense thee: for thou shalt be recompensed at the resurrection of the just.

The parable of the great supper

15 ¶ And when one of them that sat at meat with him heard these things, he said unto him, [a]Blessed *is* he that shall eat bread in the kingdom of God.

16 [a]Then said he unto him, A certain man made a great supper, and bade many: H N W

17 And [a]sent his servant at supper time to say to them that were bidden, Come; for all things are now ready.

18 And they all with one *consent* began to make excuse. The first said unto him, I have bought a piece of ground, and I must needs go and see it: I pray thee have me excused.

19 And another said, I have bought five yoke of oxen, and I go to prove them: I pray thee have me excused.

20 And another said, I have married a wife, and therefore I cannot come.

21 So that servant came, and showed G L

35 [a]Lev. 26:31,32; Ps. 69:25; Is. 1:7; Dan. 9:27; Mic. 3:12 [b]Ps. 118:26; Mat. 21:9; Mark 11:10; ch. 19:38; John 12:13
14:3 [a]Mat. 12:10
5 [a]Ex. 23:5; Deut. 22:4; ch. 13:15
10 [a]Prov. 25:6,7
11 [a]Job 22:29; Ps. 18:27; Prov. 29:23; Mat. 23:12; ch. 18:14; Jas. 4:6; 1 Pet. 5:5
13 [a]Neh. 8:10,12
15 [a]Rev. 19:9
16 [a]Mat. 22:2
17 [a]Prov. 9:2,5

E *Lk 13:32–33* ◀ ▶ *Lk 17:11–19*

M *Lk 10:13–15* ◀ ▶ *Lk 18:9–14*
F *Mk 12:24–25* ◀ ▶ *Lk 20:34–38*
H *Mt 25:1–13* ◀ ▶ *Lk 22:16*
N *Lk 13:34–35* ◀ ▶ *Lk 16:30–31*
W *Lk 12:8* ◀ ▶ *Lk 15:7*
G *Mk 12:9* ◀ ▶ *Lk 20:16*
L *Lk 13:34* ◀ ▶ *Lk 15:3–24*

14:14 Jesus promised that everyone would receive just recompense for their actions at the first "resurrection of the just."

14:16–24 This prophetic parable illustrates the spiritual truth that God offered salvation and his kingdom to the people of Israel two thousand years ago. They rejected his offer and crucified his Son. In this parable when the first guests rejected the invitation, the master told his servants to go into the streets and invite strangers and the poor to join the feast. Likewise, Jesus turned from unrepentant Israel and offered salvation and God's kingdom to anyone, Jew or Gentile, who would repent of their sins and trust in his salvation.

his lord these things. Then the master of the house being angry said to his servant, Go out quickly into the streets and lanes of the city, and bring in hither the poor, and the maimed, and the halt, and the blind.

22 And the servant said, Lord, it is done as thou hast commanded, and yet there is room.

23 And the lord said unto the servant, Go out unto the highways and hedges, and compel *them* to come in, that my house may be filled.

R 24 For I say unto you, [a]That none of
H those men which were bidden shall taste of my supper.

The cost of discipleship

25 ¶ And there went great multitudes with him: and he turned, and said unto them,

S 26 [a]If any *man* come to me, [b]and hate not his father, and mother, and wife, and children, and brethren, and sisters, [c]yea, and his own life also, he cannot be my disciple.

27 And [a]whosoever doth not bear his cross, and come after me, cannot be my disciple.

28 For [a]which of you, intending to build a tower, sitteth not down first, and counteth the cost, whether he have *sufficient* to finish *it?*

29 Lest haply, after he hath laid the foundation, and is not able to finish *it,* all that behold *it* begin to mock him,

30 Saying, This man began to build, and was not able to finish.

31 Or what king, going to make war against another king, sitteth not down first, and consulteth whether he be able with ten thousand to meet him that cometh against him with twenty thousand?

32 Or else, while the other is yet a great way off, he sendeth an ambassage, and desireth conditions of peace.

S 33 So likewise, whosoever he be of you that forsaketh not all that he hath, he cannot be my disciple.

34 ¶ [a]Salt *is* good: but if the salt have lost his savour, wherewith shall it be seasoned?

R *Lk 13:34–35* ◄► *Lk 19:41–44*
H *Lk 13:24–28* ◄► *Lk 16:19–31*
S *Lk 13:23–28* ◄► *Lk 14:33–35*
S *Lk 14:26–27* ◄► *Lk 16:13*

24 [a]Mat. 21:43 & 22:8; Acts 13:46
26 [a]Deut. 13:6 & 33:9; Mat. 10:37 [b]Rom. 9:13 [c]Rev. 12:11
27 [a]Mat. 16:24; Mark 8:34; ch. 9:23; 2 Tim. 3:12
28 [a]Prov. 24:27
34 [a]Mat. 5:13; Mark 9:50
15:1 [a]Mat. 9:10
2 [a]Acts 11:3; Gal. 2:12
4 [a]Mat. 18:12
6 [a]1 Pet. 2:10,25
7 [a]ch. 5:32
8 [1]*Drachma,* here translated *a piece of silver,* was the usual day's wage for a laborer
12 [a]Mark 12:44

35 It is neither fit for the land, nor yet for the dunghill; *but* men cast it out. He that hath ears to hear, let him hear.

15 THEN [a]DREW near unto him all the publicans and sinners for to hear him.

2 And the Pharisees and scribes murmured, saying, This man receiveth sinners, [a]and eateth with them.

The parable of the lost sheep

3 ¶ And he spake this parable unto them, saying, L P

4 [a]What man of you, having an hundred sheep, if he lose one of them, doth not leave the ninety and nine in the wilderness, and go after that which is lost, until he find it?

5 And when he hath found *it,* he layeth *it* on his shoulders, rejoicing.

6 And when he cometh home, he calleth together *his* friends and neighbours, saying unto them, Rejoice with me; for I have found my sheep [a]which was lost.

7 I say unto you, that likewise joy shall R
be in heaven over one sinner that repent- W
eth, [a]more than over ninety and nine just persons, which need no repentance.

The lost piece of silver

8 ¶ Either what woman having ten [1]pieces of silver, if she lose one piece, doth not light a candle, and sweep the house, and seek diligently till she find *it?*

9 And when she hath found *it,* she calleth *her* friends and *her* neighbours together, saying, Rejoice with me; for I have found the piece which I had lost.

10 Likewise, I say unto you, there is R
joy in the presence of the angels of God over one sinner that repenteth.

The parable of the lost son

11 ¶ And he said, A certain man had two sons:

12 And the younger of them said to *his* father, Father, give me the portion of goods that falleth *to me.* And he divided unto them [a]*his* living.

13 And not many days after the younger son gathered all together, and took his journey into a far country, and there

L *Lk 14:21–23* ◄► *Lk 15:32*
P *Mt 18:11–14* ◄► *Ro 10:21*
R *Lk 13:5* ◄► *Lk 15:10*
W *Lk 14:16–23* ◄► *Lk 19:10*
R *Lk 15:7* ◄► *Lk 15:18–22*

wasted his substance with riotous living.

14 And when he had spent all, there arose a mighty famine in that land; and he began to be in want.

15 And he went and joined himself to a citizen of that country; and he sent him into his fields to feed swine.

16 And he would fain have filled his belly with the husks that the swine did eat: and no man gave unto him.

17 And when he came to himself, he said, How many hired servants of my father's have bread enough and to spare, and I perish with hunger!

R 18 I will arise and go to my father, and will say unto him, Father, I have sinned against heaven, and before thee,

19 And am no more worthy to be called thy son: make me as one of thy hired servants.

20 And he arose, and came to his father. But [a]when he was yet a great way off, his father saw him, and had compassion, and ran, and fell on his neck, and kissed him.

21 And the son said unto him, Father, I have sinned against heaven, [a]and in thy sight, and am no more worthy to be called thy son.

22 But the father said to his servants, Bring forth the best robe, and put *it* on him; and put a ring on his hand, and shoes on *his* feet:

23 And bring hither the fatted calf, and kill *it;* and let us eat, and be merry:

C 24 [a]For this my son was dead, and is alive again; he was lost, and is found. And they began to be merry.

25 Now his elder son was in the field: and as he came and drew nigh to the house, he heard music and dancing.

26 And he called one of the servants, and asked what these things meant.

27 And he said unto him, Thy brother is come; and thy father hath killed the fatted calf, because he hath received him safe and sound.

28 And he was angry, and would not go in: therefore came his father out, and entreated him.

29 And he answering said to *his* father, Lo, these many years do I serve thee, neither transgressed I at any time thy commandment: and yet thou never gavest me a kid, that I might make merry with my friends:

30 But as soon as this thy son was come, which hath devoured thy living with harlots, thou hast killed for him the fatted calf.

31 And he said unto him, Son, thou art ever with me, and all that I have is thine.

32 It was meet that we should make merry, and be glad: [a]for this thy brother was dead, and is alive again; and was lost, and is found. C L

The unrighteous steward

16 AND HE said also unto his disciples, There was a certain rich man, which had a steward; and the same was accused unto him that he had wasted his goods.

2 And he called him, and said unto him, How is it that I hear this of thee? give an [a]account of thy stewardship; for thou mayest be no longer steward.

3 Then the steward said within himself, What shall I do? for my lord taketh away from me the stewardship: I cannot dig; to beg I am ashamed.

4 I am resolved what to do, that, when I am put out of the stewardship, they may receive me into their houses.

5 So he called every one of his lord's debtors *unto him,* and said unto the first, How much owest thou unto my lord?

6 And he said, An hundred [l]measures of oil. And he said unto him, Take thy bill, and sit down quickly, and write fifty.

7 Then said he to another, And how much owest thou? And he said, An hundred [l]measures of wheat. And he said unto him, Take thy bill, and write fourscore.

8 And the lord commended the unjust steward, because he had done wisely: for the children of this world are in their generation wiser than [a]the children of light.

9 And I say unto you, [a]Make to yourselves friends of the [l]mammon of unrighteousness; that, when ye fail, they may receive you into everlasting habitations.

10 [a]He that is faithful in that which is least is faithful also in much: and he that is unjust in the least is unjust also in much.

20 [a]Acts 2:39; Eph. 2:13,17
21 [a]Ps. 51:4
24 [a]ver. 32
32 [a]ver. 24
16:2 [a]Eccl. 11:9, 10; Rom. 14:12; 2 Cor. 5:10; 1 Pet. 4:5
6 [l]The word *Batus* in the original contains nine gallons three quarts
7 [l]The word here interpreted *a measure* in the original contains about fourteen bushels.
8 [a]John 12:36; Eph. 5:8; 1 Thes. 5:5
9 [a]Dan. 4:27; Mat. 6:19 & 19:21; ch. 11:41; 1 Tim. 6:17-19 [l]Or, *riches*
10 [a]Mat. 25:21; ch. 19:17

R *Lk 15:10* ◄► *Lk 18:13–14*
C *Lk 12:16–21* ◄► *Lk 15:32*
C *Lk 15:24* ◄► *Lk 19:10*
L *Lk 15:3–24* ◄► *Lk 16:19–22*

11 If therefore ye have not been faithful in the unrighteous [l]mammon, who will commit to your trust the true *riches*?

12 And if ye have not been faithful in that which is another man's, who shall give you that which is your own?

S 13 ¶ [a]No servant can serve two masters: for either he will hate the one, and love the other; or else he will hold to the one, and despise the other. Ye cannot serve God and mammon.

14 And the Pharisees also, [a]who were covetous, heard all these things: and they derided him.

E 15 And he said unto them, Ye are they which [a]justify yourselves before men; but [b]God knoweth your hearts: for [c]that which is highly esteemed among men is abomination in the sight of God.

16 [a]The law and the prophets *were* until John: since that time the kingdom of God is preached, and every man presseth into it.

17 [a]And it is easier for heaven and earth to pass, than one tittle of the law to fail.

18 [a]Whosoever putteth away his wife, and marrieth another, committeth adultery: and whosoever marrieth her that is put away from *her* husband committeth adultery.

The rich man and Lazarus

H
L 19 ¶ There was a certain rich man, which was clothed in purple and fine linen, and fared sumptuously every day:

20 And there was a certain beggar named Lazarus, which was laid at his gate, full of sores,

21 And desiring to be fed with the crumbs which fell from the rich man's table: moreover the dogs came and licked his sores.

22 And it came to pass, that the beggar died, and was carried by the angels into Abraham's bosom: the rich man also died, and was buried;

23 And in hell he lift up his eyes, being in torments, and seeth Abraham afar off, and Lazarus in his bosom. Q

24 And he cried and said, Father Abraham, have mercy on me, and send Lazarus, that he may dip the tip of his finger in water, and [a]cool my tongue; for I [b]am tormented in this flame.

25 But Abraham said, Son, [a]remember that thou in thy lifetime receivedst thy good things, and likewise Lazarus evil things: but now he is comforted, and thou art tormented.

26 And beside all this, between us and you there is a great gulf fixed: so that they which would pass from hence to you cannot; neither can they pass to us, that *would come* from thence.

27 Then he said, I pray thee therefore, father, that thou wouldest send him to my father's house:

28 For I have five brethren; that he may testify unto them, lest they also come into this place of torment.

29 Abraham saith unto him, [a]They have Moses and the prophets; let them hear them.

30 And he said, Nay, father Abraham: N
but if one went unto them from the dead, they will repent.

31 And he said unto him, If they hear not Moses and the prophets, [a]neither will they be persuaded, though one rose from the dead.

Faith and forgiveness

17 THEN SAID he unto the disciples, [a]It is impossible but that offences will come: but woe *unto him,* through whom they come! H

2 It were better for him that a millstone were hanged about his neck, and L

11 [l]Or, *riches*
13 [a]Mat. 6:24
14 [a]Mat. 23:14
15 [a]ch. 10:29 [b]Ps. 7:9 [c]1 Sam. 16:7
16 [a]Mat. 4:17 & 11:12,13; ch. 7:29
17 [a]Ps. 102:26,27; Is. 40:8 & 51:6; Mat. 5:18; 1 Pet. 1:25
18 [a]Mat. 5:32 & 19:9; Mark 10:11; 1 Cor. 7:10,11
24 [a]Zech. 14:12 [b]Is. 66:24; Mark 9:44
25 [a]Job 21:13; ch. 6:24
29 [a]Is. 8:20 & 34:16; John 5:39, 45; Acts 15:21 & 17:11
31 [a]John 12:10,11
17:1 [a]Mat. 18:6,7; Mark 9:42; 1 Cor. 11:19

S *Lk 14:33–35* ◀▶ *Lk 17:32*
E *Lk 12:2–3* ◀▶ *Jn 2:24–25*
H *Lk 14:24* ◀▶ *Lk 17:1–2*
L *Lk 15:32* ◀▶ *Lk 18:9–14*
Q *Lk 9:28–33* ◀▶ *1Co 13:12*
N *Lk 14:16–24* ◀▶ *Lk 17:26–30*
H *Lk 16:19–31* ◀▶ *Lk 17:26–30*
L *Lk 12:22–32* ◀▶ *Lk 18:7–8*

16:23–25 Jesus' prophetic parable of the rich man illustrates that God judges the spiritual heart of people, not their outward condition. This parable also indicates that the conscious memory of loved ones and concern for family members continues for all the dead who are in hell awaiting the final judgment. These are aware of those who need to repent, conscious of their need for salvation and desirous that someone should warn them that there will be no second chances, but are tormented by their inability to communicate their discoveries with the living.

he cast into the sea, than that he should offend one of these little ones.

3 ¶ Take heed to yourselves: [a]If thy brother trespass against thee, [b]rebuke him; and if he repent, forgive him.

4 And if he trespass against thee seven times in a day, and seven times in a day turn again to thee, saying, I repent; thou shalt forgive him.

5 And the apostles said unto the Lord, Increase our faith.

6 [a]And the Lord said, If ye had faith as a grain of mustard seed, ye might say unto this sycamine tree, Be thou plucked up by the root, and be thou planted in the sea; and it should obey you.

7 But which of you, having a servant plowing or feeding cattle, will say unto him by and by, when he is come from the field, Go and sit down to meat?

8 And will not rather say unto him, Make ready wherewith I may sup, and gird thyself, [a]and serve me, till I have eaten and drunken; and afterward thou shalt eat and drink?

9 Doth he thank that servant because he did the things that were commanded him? I trow not.

10 So likewise ye, when ye shall have done all those things which are commanded you, say, We are [a]unprofitable servants: we have done that which was our duty to do.

The healing of the ten lepers

E 11 ¶ And it came to pass, [a]as he went to Jerusalem, that he passed through the midst of Samaria and Galilee.

12 And as he entered into a certain village, there met him ten men that were lepers, [a]which stood afar off:

13 And they lifted up *their* voices, and said, Jesus, Master, have mercy on us.

14 And when he saw *them,* he said unto them, [a]Go show yourselves unto the priests. And it came to pass, that, as they went, they were cleansed.

15 And one of them, when he saw that he was healed, turned back, and with a loud voice glorified God,

16 And fell down on *his* face at his feet, giving him thanks: and he was a Samaritan.

17 And Jesus answering said, Were there not ten cleansed? but where *are* the nine?

18 There are not found that returned to give glory to God, save this stranger.

19 [a]And he said unto him, Arise, go thy way: thy faith hath made thee whole.

The coming of the kingdom

20 ¶ And when he was demanded of the Pharisees, when the kingdom of God should come, he answered them and said, The kingdom of God cometh not [1]with observation:

21 [a]Neither shall they say, Lo here! or, lo there! for, behold, [b]the kingdom of God is [1]within you.

22 And he said unto the disciples, [a]The days will come, when ye shall desire to see one of the days of the Son of man, and ye shall not see *it.*

23 [a]And they shall say to you, See here; or, see there: go not after *them,* nor follow *them.* C

24 [a]For as the lightning, that lighteneth out of the one *part* under heaven, shineth unto the other *part* under heaven; so shall also the Son of man be in his day.

25 [a]But first must he suffer many things, and be rejected of this generation.

26 [a]And as it was in the days of Noe, so shall it be also in the days of the Son of man. C E P

27 They did eat, they drank, they married wives, they were given in marriage, until the day that Noe entered into the ark, and the flood came, and destroyed them all. H N

3 [a]Mat. 18:15,21 [b]Lev. 19:17; Prov. 17:10; Jas. 5:19
6 [a]Mat. 17:20 & 21:21; Mark 9:23 & 11:23
8 [a]ch. 12:37
10 [a]Job 22:3 & 35:7; Ps. 16:2; Mat. 25:30; Rom. 3:12 & 11:35; 1 Cor. 9:16, 17; Philem. 11
11 [a]ch. 9:51,52; John 4:4
12 [a]Lev. 13:46
14 [a]Lev. 13:2 & 14:2; Mat. 8:4; ch. 5:14
19 [a]Mat. 9:22; Mark 5:34 & 10:52; ch. 7:50 & 8:48 & 18:42
20 [1]Or, *with outward show*
21 [a]ver. 23 [b]Rom. 14:17 [1]Or, *among you;* cf. John 1:26
22 [a]See Mat. 9:15; John 17:12
23 [a]Mat. 24:23; Mark 13:21; ch. 21:8
24 [a]Mat. 24:27
25 [a]Mark 8:31 & 9:31 & 10:33; ch. 9:22
26 [a]Gen. 7; Mat. 24:37

E *Lk 14:1–6* ◀▶ *Lk 18:35–43*

C *Lk 12:35–47* ◀▶ *Lk 17:26–30*
C *Lk 17:23–24* ◀▶ *Lk 17:34–37*
E *Mk 13:31–32* ◀▶ *Lk 21:25–31*
P *Lk 12:45–47* ◀▶ *Lk 18:7–8*
H *Lk 17:1–2* ◀▶ *Lk 19:27*
N *Lk 16:30–31* ◀▶ *Lk 20:18*

17:24–30 Jesus prophesied about the signs leading up to his return. His second coming will be as spectacular as the lightning in the sky. Spiritual conditions will mirror the violence, corruption, hatred of God and rejection of God's warnings as in the days of Noe (Noah). Even the warning of Lot and Sodom will be rejected prior to Christ's return. The tribulation judgment will fall almost immediately following the supernatural removal of all living believers to heaven.

The Intermediate State

SOME SCHOLARS INTIMATE that the truth of the resurrection of the body was unknown to the OT Hebrews. Scripture indicates otherwise. Passages throughout the OT teach the reality of a bodily resurrection and a final judgment before God (see Job 19:25–26; Da 12:2). At issue, rather, is the temporary location of the souls of both believers and nonbelievers from the moment of death until their final arrival in heaven or hell. Genesis records Abraham's death and indicates that he "was gathered to his people" (Ge 25:8), intimating an intermediate state or place to await the final judgment. Yet the teachings regarding this intermediate state in the NT are not always clear. Different theories and conclusions have been suggested and are noted below. Of interest is the common agreement among scholars that although the OT speaks of *hades* and the grave as the destination of all departed souls, the Bible indicates that the experience of sinners and saints is quite different even before God's final judgment.

Hades

The word *Sheol* is the Hebrew equivalent of the Greek word *hades*. This term appears sixty-five times in the OT and is translated half of the time as "hell" and half of the time as "the grave." In the NT, the Greek usage of *hades* clearly refers to the abode of the dead. Many people speak as though unrepentant sinners immediately go to hell once they die. However, the Bible declares that these unrepentant souls descend into *hades* and are separated from the saved by a great chasm (see Lk 16:19–31). In their unjudged condition, these sinners suffer torment in this intermediate state of *hades*, awaiting the final great white throne judgment at the end of the Millennium when *hades* will surrender the wicked to God's judgment and the lake of fire (see Rev 20:13–14). Thus during the present age, the wicked who die await resurrection from *hades*, but this resurrection will only bring judgment and condemnation. For further information, see the article on "Hell" on p. 1080.

Abraham's Bosom

Scripture reveals a different end for the souls of those who died as believers in God before Christ's death and resurrection. All of the OT believers went to a place of waiting and comfort known as "Abraham's bosom" (Lk 16:22). Scripture indicates that though people in *hades* were aware of those in "Abraham's bosom," it was impossible for anyone to cross from one place to the other (see 16:26). From Abraham's bosom these righteous souls would be resurrected to heaven.

Some of these righteous souls, however, were resurrected early, immediately following Christ's resurrection (see Mt 27:52–53). This tremendous miracle of resurrecting these OT saints helped spread the truth of the resurrection of Christ and proved Christ's power over sin and death forever. Just as he resurrected those saints, someday soon he will resurrect the bodies of all living and departed believers when the church is raptured.

Paradise

A great transformation occurred in the spiritual world when Christ defeated Satan and "led captivity captive" (Eph 4:8). From the time of Christ's death on the cross, the souls of believers who die go immediately to a place called *paradise* to enjoy the presence of Jesus Christ forever (see Lk 23:43). Though the word *paradise* occurs only three times in the NT and never in Christ's public teaching, scholars have suggested various ideas about its location and characteristics.

Since the word *paradise* is of Persian origin and suggests an orchard, park or garden, some Jewish and Christian scholars believe that it is a place much like the Garden of Eden before the fall. Others suggest that paradise is merely a state of bliss that awaits the righteous after death and is an indication of the destiny of the redeemed (see Rev 22:2, 14). Still others equate paradise with the new Jerusalem, the city of God in heaven, and base their assumption on Paul's vision when "he was caught up into paradise, and heard unspeakable words, which it is not lawful for a man to utter" (2Co 12:4). That this viewpoint has merit is strengthened by Christ's own declaration that the tree of life exists "in the midst of the paradise of God" (Rev 2:7).

Believers who have died are with Jesus now in paradise, enjoying his presence and the presence of other saints as they all await the rapture. During this time the apostle Paul intimates that the souls of believers are conscious but merely resting in Christ (see 2Co 5:1–8; 1Th 4:14), clearly declaring that though believers are "absent from the body" they will be "present with the Lord" (2Co 5:8). When the rapture occurs, the departed souls of these righteous ones will receive their immortal, incorruptible resurrection bodies so that they can participate in all the experiences of heaven and join with Christ to rule the nations.

Different Lives, Different Conditions

The Bible teaches that the soul is neither annihilated at death nor does it sleep. In his story about the rich man and the beggar, Jesus Christ taught that the man who died in sin was alive, fully conscious and able to use his mental faculties. The sinful rich man was also tormented and unable to affect the destiny of his brothers, who faced similar punishments. There could be no change in his abode or the state of his soul. He was condemned to *hades*, and his soul would wait there until his ultimate judgment before God's great white throne. At that time all the unrepentant souls from *hades* will be resurrected to be judged for their unconfessed sins and evil works (see Rev 20:11–14). For further information, see the article on "The Great White Throne Judgment" on p. 1484.

Though some scholars subscribe to the teaching of soul sleep, Scripture clearly indicates that believers who die are alive and aware, but their souls are at rest until God resurrects them to a new immortal form for eternity. Scripture states that believers immediately join Christ's presence at the moment of death (see 2Co 5:8). In fact, Jesus promised that the thief on the cross would be with him that very day in paradise (see 23:42–43). Though a believer's body may reside in the grave where "there is no work, nor device, nor knowledge, nor wisdom, in the grave, whither thou goest" (Ecc 9:10), at the rapture the believer's "spirit shall return unto God who gave it" (Ecc 12:7).

28 [a]Likewise also as it was in the days
of Lot; they did eat, they drank, they bought,
they sold, they planted, they builded;
29 But [a]the same day that Lot went
out of Sodom it rained fire and brimstone
from heaven, and destroyed *them* all.
30 Even thus shall it be in the day
when the Son of man [a]is revealed.
31 In that day, he [a]which shall be
upon the housetop, and his stuff in the
house, let him not come down to take it
away: and he that is in the field, let him
likewise not return back.
S 32 [a]Remember Lot's wife.
33 [a]Whosoever shall seek to save his
life shall lose it; and whosoever shall lose
his life shall preserve it.
C 34 [a]I tell you, in that night there shall
T be two *men* in one bed; the one shall be
taken, and the other shall be left.
35 Two *women* shall be grinding together;
the one shall be taken, and the
other left.
36 [†]Two *men* shall be in the field; the
one shall be taken, and the other left.
37 And they answered and said unto
him, [a]Where, Lord? And he said unto
them, Wheresoever the body *is,* thither
will the eagles be gathered together.

The widow and the judge

W 18 AND HE spake a parable unto
them *to this end,* that men ought
[a]always to pray, and not to faint;
2 Saying, There was [†]in a city a judge,
which feared not God, neither regarded
man:
3 And there was a widow in that city;
and she came unto him, saying, Avenge
me of mine adversary.
4 And he would not for a while: but
afterward he said within himself, Though
I fear not God, nor regard man;
5 [a]Yet because this widow troubleth
me, I will avenge her, lest by her continual
coming she weary me.
6 And the Lord said, Hear what the unjust
judge saith.
7 And [a]shall not God avenge his own P
elect, which cry day and night unto him, L
though he bear long with them?
8 I tell you [a]that he will avenge them C
speedily. Nevertheless when the Son of
man cometh, shall he find faith on the
earth?

The Pharisee and the publican

9 And he spake this parable unto certain G
[a]which trusted in themselves [†]that L
they were righteous, and despised others: M
10 Two men went up into the temple
to pray; the one a Pharisee, and the other
a publican.
11 The Pharisee [a]stood and prayed thus
with himself, [b]God, I thank thee, that I
am not as other men *are,* extortioners,
unjust, adulterers, or even as this publican.
12 I fast twice in the week, I give
tithes of all that I possess.
13 And the publican, standing afar off, R
would not lift up so much as *his* eyes
unto heaven, but smote upon his breast,
saying, God be merciful to me a sinner.
14 I tell you, this man went down to
his house justified *rather* than the other:
[a]for every one that exalteth himself shall
be abased; and he that humbleth himself
shall be exalted.

Jesus and the little children

15 [a]And they brought unto him also
infants, that he would touch them: but
when *his* disciples saw *it,* they rebuked
them.

28 [a]Gen. 19
29 [a]Gen. 19:16,24
30 [a]2 Thes. 1:7
31 [a]Mat. 24:17; Mark 13:15
32 [a]Gen. 19:26
33 [a]Mat. 10:39 & 16:25; Mark 8:35; ch. 9:24; John 12:25
34 [a]Mat. 24:40,41; 1 Thes. 4:17
36 [†]This 36th verse is wanting in most of the Greek copies
37 [a]Job 39:30; Mat. 24:28
18:1 [a]ch. 11:5 & 21:36; Rom. 12:12; Eph. 6:18; Col. 4:2; 1 Thes. 5:17
2 [†]Gk. *in a certain city*
5 [a]ch. 11:8
7 [a]Rev. 6:10
8 [a]Heb. 10:37; 2 Pet. 3:8,9
9 [a]ch. 10:29 & 16:15 [†]Or, *as being righteous*
11 [a]Ps. 135:2 [b]Is. 1:15 & 58:2; Rev. 3:17
14 [a]Job 22:29; Mat. 23:12; ch. 14:11; Jas. 4:6; 1 Pet. 5:5
15 [a]Mat. 19:13; Mark 10:13

S *Lk 16:13* ◀▶ *Lk 20:10*
C *Lk 17:26–30* ◀▶ *Lk 18:8*
T *Mt 24:31* ◀▶ *Jn 3:8*
W *Lk 12:22–32* ◀▶ *Jn 14:1*

P *Lk 17:26–30* ◀▶ *Lk 19:27*
L *Lk 17:2* ◀▶ *Lk 21:18*
C *Lk 17:34–37* ◀▶ *Lk 19:15*
G *Mk 10:17–22* ◀▶ *Lk 18:16–22*
L *Lk 16:19–22* ◀▶ *Lk 19:10*
M *Lk 14:11* ◀▶ *Lk 18:24–25*
R *Lk 15:18–22* ◀▶ *Lk 19:8–9*

17:34–37 Jesus reveals that, at the end of the seven-year tribulation at Armageddon, God will send his angels to separate the believers and the unbelievers (see Mt 13:24–30; 24:40–42). The curious expression "thither will the eagles be gathered together" (17:37) may refer to the terrible aftermath of Armageddon when God will gather the birds of prey to eat the bodies of the dead (see Rev 19:17–18; see also Job 39:30).

18:7–8 Jesus warned that God would finally avenge himself against the enemies of the "elect"—the tribulation saints who resist the antichrist. Jesus

G 16 But Jesus called them *unto him,*
O and said, Suffer little children to come
unto me, and forbid them not: for [a]of
such is the kingdom of God.
17 [a]Verily I say unto you, Whosoever
shall not receive the kingdom of God as a
little child shall in no wise enter therein.

The rich young ruler

18 [a]And a certain ruler asked him, saying, Good Master, what shall I do to inherit eternal life?
19 And Jesus said unto him, Why callest thou me good? none *is* good, save
one, *that is,* God.
20 Thou knowest the commandments,
[a]Do not commit adultery, Do not kill, Do
not steal, Do not bear false witness,
[b]Honour thy father and thy mother.
21 And he said, All these have I kept
from my youth up.
22 Now when Jesus heard these
things, he said unto him, Yet lackest thou
one thing: [a]sell all that thou hast, and distribute unto the poor, and thou shalt have
treasure in heaven: and come, follow me.
23 And when he heard this, he was
very sorrowful: for he was very rich.
M 24 And when Jesus saw that he was
very sorrowful, he said, [a]How hardly
shall they that have riches enter into the
kingdom of God!
25 For it is easier for a camel to go
through a needle's eye, than for a rich
man to enter into the kingdom of God.
26 And they that heard *it* said, Who
then can be saved?
27 And he said, [a]The things which are
impossible with men are possible with God.
28 [a]Then Peter said, Lo, we have left
all, and followed thee.
U 29 And he said unto them, Verily I say

G *Lk 18:9–14 ◀ ▶ Jn 1:12–13*
O *Lk 12:8–9 ◀ ▶ Jn 3:3*
M *Lk 18:9–14 ◀ ▶ Jn 9:39*
U *Lk 12:31 ◀ ▶ Jn 12:25–26*

16 [a]1 Cor. 14:20; 1 Pet. 2:2
17 [a]Mark 10:15
18 [a]Mat. 19:16; Mark 10:17
20 [a]Ex. 20:12,16; Deut. 5:16-20; Rom. 13:9 [b]Eph. 6:2; Col. 3:20
22 [a]Mat. 6:19,20; & 19:21; 1 Tim. 6:19
24 [a]Prov. 11:28; Mat. 19:23; Mark 10:23
27 [a]Jer. 32:17; Zech. 8:6; Mat. 19:26; ch. 1:37
28 [a]Mat. 19:27
29 [a]Deut. 33:9
30 [a]Job 42:10
31 [a]Mat. 16:21 & 17:22 & 20:17; Mark 10:32 [b]Ps. 22; Is. 53
32 [a]Mat. 27:2; ch. 23:1; John 18:28; Acts 3:13
34 [a]Mark 9:32; ch. 2:50 & 9:45; John 10:6 & 12:16
35 [a]Mat. 20:29; Mark 10:46

unto you, [a]There is no man that hath left
house, or parents, or brethren, or wife, or
children, for the kingdom of God's sake,
30 [a]Who shall not receive manifold
more in this present time, and in the
world to come life everlasting.

Jesus again foretells his death

31 ¶ [a]Then he took *unto him* the
twelve, and said unto them, Behold, we
go up to Jerusalem, and all things [b]that
are written by the prophets concerning
the Son of man shall be accomplished.
32 For [a]he shall be delivered unto the
Gentiles, and shall be mocked, and spitefully entreated, and spitted on:
33 And they shall scourge *him,* and put
him to death: and the third day he shall
rise again.
34 [a]And they understood none of
these things: and this saying was hid
from them, neither knew they the things
which were spoken.

A blind man healed

35 ¶ [a]And it came to pass, that as he E
was come nigh unto Jericho, a certain
blind man sat by the way side begging:
36 And hearing the multitude pass by,
he asked what it meant.
37 And they told him, that Jesus of
Nazareth passeth by.
38 And he cried, saying, Jesus, *thou*
son of David, have mercy on me.
39 And they which went before rebuked him, that he should hold his
peace: but he cried so much the more,
Thou son of David, have mercy on me.
40 And Jesus stood, and commanded
him to be brought unto him: and when
he was come near, he asked him,
41 Saying, What wilt thou that I shall
do unto thee? And he said, Lord, that I
may receive my sight.

E *Lk 17:11–19 ◀ ▶ Lk 22:50–51*

---

prophesied that the antichrist would wage a devastating war against the followers of Christ during the tribulation (see Da 7:21; Rev 13:5–8), leaving very few believers alive during the final days leading up to the Battle of Armageddon. Millions of tribulation saints who become believers after the rapture will suffer martyrdom during the first half of the tribulation. Millions more will die following the persecution related to the antichrist's mark of the beast during the latter half of the tribulation (see Rev 17:5–6).

Though some contend that the church will win the world's population to Christ as a preparation for his return as Messiah, this prophecy suggests the opposite. When Jesus returns, spiritual decline and persecution will be so prevalent that those who model a faith that perseveres will be difficult to find. When all seems hopeless, Jesus will return, defeat the antichrist and cast Satan into the bottomless pit for a thousand years (see Rev 19:11–21).

42 And Jesus said unto him, Receive thy sight: [a]thy faith hath saved thee.

43 And immediately he received his sight, and followed him, [a]glorifying God: and all the people, when they saw *it,* gave praise unto God.

The conversion of Zacchaeus

19 AND *JESUS* entered and passed through Jericho.

2 And, behold, *there was* a man named Zacchaeus, which was the chief among the publicans, and he was rich.

3 And he sought to see Jesus who he was; and could not for the press, because he was little of stature.

4 And he ran before, and climbed up into a sycamore tree to see him: for he was to pass that *way.*

5 And when Jesus came to the place, he looked up, and saw him, and said unto him, Zacchaeus, make haste, and come down; for today I must abide at thy house.

6 And he made haste, and came down, and received him joyfully.

7 And when they saw *it,* they all murmured, saying, [a]That he was gone to be guest with a man that is a sinner.

R 8 And Zacchaeus stood, and said unto the Lord; Behold, Lord, the half of my goods I give to the poor; and if I have taken any thing from any man by [a]false accusation, [b]I restore *him* fourfold.

9 And Jesus said unto him, This day is salvation come to this house, forsomuch as [a]he also is [b]a son of Abraham.

C 10 [a]For the Son of man is come to seek
L and to save that which was lost.

W
The parable of the pounds

M 11 And as they heard these things, he added and spake a parable, because he was nigh to Jerusalem, and because [a]they thought that the kingdom of God should immediately appear.

12 [a]He said therefore, A certain nobleman went into a far country to receive for himself a kingdom, and to return.

13 And he called his ten servants, and delivered them ten [1]pounds, and said unto them, Occupy till I come.

14 [a]But his citizens hated him, and sent a message after him, saying, We will not have this *man* to reign over us.

15 And it came to pass, that when he C
was returned, having received the kingdom, then he commanded these servants to be called unto him, to whom he had given the [1]money, that he might know how much every man had gained by trading.

16 Then came the first, saying, Lord, thy pound hath gained ten pounds.

17 And he said unto him, Well, thou good servant: because thou hast been [a]faithful in a very little, have thou authority over ten cities.

18 And the second came, saying, Lord, thy pound hath gained five pounds.

19 And he said likewise to him, Be thou also over five cities.

20 And another came, saying, Lord, behold, *here is* thy pound, which I have kept laid up in a napkin:

21 [a]For I feared thee, because thou art an austere man: thou takest up that thou layedst not down, and reapest that thou didst not sow.

22 And he saith unto him, [a]Out of thine own mouth will I judge thee, *thou* wicked servant. [b]Thou knewest that I was an austere man, taking up that I laid not down, and reaping that I did not sow:

23 Wherefore then gavest not thou my C
money into the bank, that at my coming I might have required mine own with usury?

24 And he said unto them that stood by, Take from him the pound, and give *it* to him that hath ten pounds.

R *Lk 18:13–14 ◀ ▶ Lk 22:62*
C *Lk 15:32 ◀ ▶ Jn 3:19–20*
L *Lk 18:9–14 ◀ ▶ Lk 19:41–42*
W *Lk 15:7 ◀ ▶ Jn 1:7*
M *Lk 13:21 ◀ ▶ Lk 19:27*

C *Lk 18:8 ◀ ▶ Lk 19:23*
C *Lk 19:15 ◀ ▶ Lk 21:27–31*

42 [a]ch. 17:19
43 [a]ch. 5:26; Acts 4:21 & 11:18
19:7 [a]Mat. 9:11; ch. 5:30
8 [a]ch. 3:14 [b]Ex. 22:1; 1 Sam. 12:3; 2 Sam. 12:6
9 [a]Rom. 4:11,12, 16; Gal. 3:7 [b]ch. 13:16
10 [a]Mat. 18:11; See Mat. 10:6 & 15:24
11 [a]Acts 1:6
12 [a]Mat. 25:14; Mark 13:34
13 [1]*Mina,* here translated *pound,* was worth about 16 dollars or three months' wages for a laborer
14 [a]John 1:11
15 [1]Gk. *silver;* also ver. 23
17 [a]Mat. 25:21; ch. 16:10
21 [a]Mat. 25:24
22 [a]2 Sam. 1:16; Job 15:6; Mat. 12:37 [b]Mat. 25:26

19:11–19, 23 With this parable, Jesus wanted to correct the disciples' mistaken notion that God's kingdom would appear immediately. His story illustrated that he would be away from them in heaven for a long time. This parable confirms other statements that Jesus made about the long passage of time before the establishment of his Messianic kingdom. This parable contradicts the Preterist view of prophecy that states that all of the prophecies of Jesus' second coming were fulfilled in the destruction of Jerusalem in A.D. 70. See the information on the theories of prophetic interpretation in the article "Introduction to Prophecy" on p. vi.

25 (And they said unto him, Lord, he
hath ten pounds.)
26 For I say unto you, [a]That unto every
one which hath shall be given; and from
him that hath not, even that he hath shall
be taken away from him.
M 27 But those mine enemies, which
P would not that I should reign over them,
H bring hither, and slay *them* before me.

The triumphal entry

28 ¶ And when he had thus spoken,
[a]he went before, ascending up to Jerusalem.
29 [a]And it came to pass, when he was
come nigh to Bethphage and Bethany, at
the mount called *the mount* of Olives, he
sent two of his disciples,
30 Saying, Go ye into the village over
against *you;* in the which at your entering
ye shall find a colt tied, whereon yet
never man sat: loose him, and bring *him*
hither.
31 And if any man ask you, Why do ye
loose *him?* thus shall ye say unto him,
Because the Lord hath need of him.
32 And they that were sent went their
way, and found even as he had said unto
them.
33 And as they were loosing the colt,
the owners thereof said unto them, Why
loose ye the colt?
34 And they said, The Lord hath need
of him.
35 And they brought him to Jesus:
[a]and they cast their garments upon the
colt, and they set Jesus thereon.
36 And as he went, they spread their
clothes in the way.
37 And when he was come nigh, even
now at the descent of the mount of Olives, the whole multitude of the disciples
began to rejoice and praise God with a
loud voice for all the mighty works that
they had seen;
38 Saying, [a]Blessed *be* the King that
cometh in the name of the Lord: [b]peace
in heaven, and glory in the highest.
39 And some of the Pharisees from
among the multitude said unto him, Master, rebuke thy disciples.
40 And he answered and said unto
them, I tell you that, if these should hold
their peace, [a]the stones would immediately cry out.
41 ¶ And when he was come near, he R
beheld the city, and [a]wept over it, L
42 Saying, If thou hadst known, even
thou, at least in this thy day, the things
which belong unto thy peace! but now
they are hid from thine eyes.
43 For the days shall come upon thee,
that thine enemies shall [a]cast a trench
about thee, and compass thee round, and
keep thee in on every side,
44 And [a]shall lay thee even with the
ground, and thy children within thee;
and [b]they shall not leave in thee one
stone upon another; [c]because thou knewest not the time of thy visitation.

The cleansing of the temple

45 [a]And he went into the temple, and
began to cast out them that sold therein,
and them that bought;
46 Saying unto them, [a]It is written,
My house is the house of prayer: but [b]ye
have made it a den of thieves.
47 And he taught daily in the temple.
But [a]the chief priests and the scribes and
the chief of the people sought to destroy
him,
48 And could not find what they might

26 [a]Mat. 13:12 & 25:29; Mark 4:25; ch. 8:18
28 [a]Mark 10:32
29 [a]Mat. 21:1; Mark 11:1
35 [a]2 Ki. 9:13; Mat. 21:7; Mark 11:7; John 12:14
38 [a]Ps. 118:26; ch. 13:35 [b]ch. 2:14; Eph. 2:14
40 [a]Hab. 2:11
41 [a]John 11:35
43 [a]Is. 29:3,4; Jer. 6:3,6; ch. 21:20
44 [a]1 Ki. 9:7,8; Mic. 3:12 [b]Mat. 24:2; Mark 13:2; ch. 21:6 [c]Dan. 9:24; ch. 1:68,78; 1 Pet. 2:12
45 [a]Mat. 21:12; Mark 11:11,15; John 2:14,15
46 [a]Is. 56:7 [b]Jer. 7:11
47 [a]Mark 11:18; John 7:19 & 8:37

M *Lk 19:11–26* ◀▶ *Lk 20:14*
P *Lk 18:7–8* ◀▶ *Lk 21:5–7*
H *Lk 17:26–30* ◀▶ *Lk 20:18*
R *Lk 14:24* ◀▶ *Lk 20:9–16*
L *Lk 19:10* ◀▶ *Lk 23:42–43*

19:30–38 This remarkable passage records the public presentation of Jesus as Israel's Messiah on Palm Sunday, A.D. 32, when Christ approached the eastern gate to the temple. Despite the widespread rejoicing and acclamation by "the whole multitude of his disciples" (19:37), the Jewish and Roman leaders rejected Jesus' claim to be Israel's Messiah and had him crucified less than one week later, fulfilling Daniel's prophecy about the cutting off of the Messiah (see Da 9:24–27).

19:40–44 Jesus confirmed that this special day was the fulfillment of Daniel's prophecy (see Da 9:24–27) and mourned that Jerusalem did not recognize "the time of thy visitation" (19:44). The day when Jesus presented himself as Messiah to Jerusalem was Israel's last chance to accept his claim and avoid the coming judgment of God. See the article on "The Vision of the Seventy Weeks" on p. 976. Compare also the totality of the destruction of the city mentioned in this passage with Mt 24 and the study notes at Mk 13:1–2.

do: for all the people were very attentive to hear him.

Jesus' authority challenged

20 AND [a]IT came to pass, *that* on one of those days, as he taught the people in the temple, and preached the gospel, the chief priests and the scribes came upon *him* with the elders,

2 And spake unto him, saying, Tell us, [a]by what authority doest thou these things? or who is he that gave thee this authority?

3 And he answered and said unto them, I will also ask you one thing; and answer me:

4 The baptism of John, was it from heaven, or of men?

5 And they reasoned with themselves, saying, If we shall say, From heaven; he will say, Why then believed ye him not?

6 But and if we say, Of men; all the people will stone us: [a]for they be persuaded that John was a prophet.

7 And they answered, that they could not tell whence *it was.*

8 And Jesus said unto them, Neither tell I you by what authority I do these things.

The parable of the husbandmen

R 9 Then began he to speak to the people this parable; [a]A certain man planted a vineyard, and let it forth to husbandmen, and went into a far country for a long time.

S 10 And at the season he sent a servant to the husbandmen, that they should give him of the fruit of the vineyard: but the husbandmen beat him, and sent *him* away empty.

11 And again he sent another servant: and they beat him also, and entreated *him* shamefully, and sent *him* away empty.

12 And again he sent a third: and they wounded him also, and cast *him* out.

13 Then said the lord of the vineyard, What shall I do? I will send my beloved son: it may be they will reverence *him* when they see him.

14 But when the husbandmen saw him, they reasoned among themselves, saying, This is the heir: come, let us kill him, that the inheritance may be ours. M

15 So they cast him out of the vineyard, and killed *him.* What therefore shall the lord of the vineyard do unto them?

16 He shall come and destroy these husbandmen, and shall give the vineyard to others. And when they heard *it,* they said, God forbid. G

17 And he beheld them, and said, What is this then that is written, [a]The stone which the builders rejected, the same is become the head of the corner?

18 Whosoever shall fall upon that stone shall be broken; but [a]on whomsoever it shall fall, it will grind him to powder. H N

Tribute to Caesar

19 ¶ And the chief priests and the scribes the same hour sought to lay hands on him; and they feared the people: for they perceived that he had spoken this parable against them.

20 [a]And they watched *him,* and sent forth spies, which should feign themselves just men, that they might take hold of his words, that so they might deliver him unto the power and authority of the governor.

21 And they asked him, saying, [a]Master, we know that thou sayest and teachest rightly, neither acceptest thou the person *of any,* but teachest the way of God [ǀ]truly:

22 Is it lawful for us to give tribute unto Caesar, or no?

23 But he perceived their craftiness, and said unto them, Why tempt ye me?

24 Show me a [ǀ]penny. Whose image and superscription hath it? They answered and said, Caesar's.

25 And he said unto them, Render therefore unto Caesar the things which

20:1 [a]Mat. 21:23
2 [a]Acts 4:7 & 7:27
6 [a]Mat. 14:5 & 21:26; ch. 7:29
9 [a]Mat. 21:33; Mark 12:1
17 [a]Ps. 118:22; Mat. 21:42
18 [a]Dan. 2:34,35; Mat. 21:44
20 [a]Mat. 22:15
21 [a]Mat. 22:16; Mark 12:14 [ǀ]Or, *of a truth*
24 [ǀ]See Mat. 20:2

R *Lk 19:41–44* ◀ ▶ *Lk 21:20–24*
S *Lk 17:32* ◀ ▶ *Jn 4:23–24*

M *Lk 19:27* ◀ ▶ *Lk 20:42–43*
G *Lk 14:21* ◀ ▶ *Lk 21:24*
H *Lk 19:27* ◀ ▶ *Lk 20:42–43*
N *Lk 17:26–30* ◀ ▶ *Jn 3:18–20*

20:9–16 This prophetic parable teaches about God's dealings with Israel over the centuries and their rejection of God's prophets and the crucifixion of his Son. This story of the vineyard parallels Isa 5:1–7.

be Caesar's, and unto God the things which be God's.

26 And they could not take hold of his words before the people: and they marvelled at his answer, and held their peace.

Sadducees and the resurrection

27 ¶ [a]Then came to *him* certain of the Sadducees, [b]which deny that there is any resurrection; and they asked him,

28 Saying, Master, Moses wrote unto us, If any man's brother die, having a wife, and he die without children, that his brother should take his wife, and raise up seed unto his brother.

29 There were therefore seven brethren: and the first took a wife, and died without children.

30 And the second took her to wife, and he died childless.

31 And the third took her; and in like manner the seven also: and they left no children, and died.

32 Last of all the woman died also.

33 Therefore in the resurrection whose wife of them is she? for seven had her to wife.

F 34 And Jesus answering said unto them, The children of this world marry, and are given in marriage:

35 But they which shall be accounted worthy to obtain that world, and the resurrection from the dead, neither marry, nor are given in marriage:

36 Neither can they die any more: for [a]they are equal unto the angels; and are the children of God, [b]being the children of the resurrection.

37 Now that the dead are raised, [a]even Moses showed at the bush, when he calleth the Lord the God of Abraham, and the God of Isaac, and the God of Jacob.

38 For he is not a God of the dead, but of the living: for [a]all live unto him.

F *Lk 14:13–14 ◀ ▶ Jn 5:25–29*

27 [a]Mat. 22:23; Mark 12:18 [b]Acts 23:6,8
36 [a]1 Cor. 15:42, 49,52; 1 John 3:2 [b]Rom. 8:23
37 [a]Ex. 3:6
38 [a]Rom. 6:10,11
41 [a]Mat. 22:42; Mark 12:35
42 [a]Ps. 110:1; Acts 2:34
45 [a]Mat. 23:1; Mark 12:38
46 [a]Mat. 23:5 [b]ch. 11:43
47 [a]Mat. 23:14
21:1 [a]Mark 12:41
2 [l]See Mark 12:42
3 [a]2 Cor. 8:12
5 [a]Mat. 24:1; Mark 13:1

39 ¶ Then certain of the scribes answering said, Master, thou hast well said.

40 And after that they durst not ask him any *question at all.*

The question about David's son

41 And he said unto them, [a]How say they that Christ is David's son?

42 And David himself saith in the book of Psalms, [a]The LORD said unto my Lord, Sit thou on my right hand, M V H

43 Till I make thine enemies thy footstool.

44 David therefore calleth him Lord, how is he then his son?

45 ¶ [a]Then in the audience of all the people he said unto his disciples,

46 [a]Beware of the scribes, which desire to walk in long robes, and [b]love greetings in the markets, and the highest seats in the synagogues, and the chief rooms at feasts;

47 [a]Which devour widows' houses, and for a show make long prayers: the same shall receive greater damnation. H

The widow's offering

21 AND HE looked up, [a]and saw the rich men casting their gifts into the treasury.

2 And he saw also a certain poor widow casting in thither two [l]mites.

3 And he said, Of a truth I say unto you, [a]that this poor widow hath cast in more than they all:

4 For all these have of their abundance cast in unto the offerings of God: but she of her penury hath cast in all the living that she had.

Signs of the end of this age

5 ¶ [a]And as some spake of the temple, P

M *Lk 20:14 ◀ ▶ Lk 22:29–30*
V *Lk 1:33 ◀ ▶ Ac 2:34–35*
H *Lk 20:18 ◀ ▶ Lk 20:47*
H *Lk 20:42–43 ◀ ▶ Lk 21:25–26*
P *Lk 19:27 ◀ ▶ Lk 21:9–11*

20:34–38 The Sadducees were a group of wealthy religious teachers who denied the Scriptural teaching of bodily resurrection and taught the annihilation of the soul at death. They only accepted the authority of the five books of Moses. Jesus answered their question by affirming the spiritual existence of the patriarchs. See the study notes at Mt 22:29–32 for further information.

20:41–43 Jesus took the opportunity to ask the Pharisees a question about the Messiah to demonstrate the truth that the Messiah is both the Son of David and the Son of God at the same time. In this statement, King David acknowledged that God the Father told the Messiah (Jesus Christ) to "sit thou at my right hand, until I make thine enemies thy footstool" (Ps 110:1), revealing the final triumph of the Messiah over his enemies in the millennial kingdom following the Battle of Armageddon.

how it was adorned with goodly stones
and gifts, he said,
6 *As for* these things which ye behold,
the days will come, in the which [a]there
shall not be left one stone upon another,
that shall not be thrown down.
7 And they asked him, saying, Master,
but when shall these things be? and what
sign *will there be* when these things shall
come to pass?
8 And he said, [a]Take heed that ye be
not deceived: for many shall come in my
name, saying, I am *Christ;* [/]and the time
draweth near: go ye not therefore after
them.
P 9 But when ye shall hear of wars and
commotions, be not terrified: for these
things must first come to pass; but the
end *is* not by and by.
10 [a]Then said he unto them, Nation
shall rise against nation, and kingdom
against kingdom:
11 And great earthquakes shall be in
divers places, and famines, and pestilences;
and fearful sights and great signs
shall there be from heaven.
12 [a]But before all these, they shall lay
their hands on you, and persecute *you,*

P *Lk 21:5–7* ◀▶ *Lk 21:25–26*

6 [a]ch. 19:44

8 [a]Mat. 24:4; Mark 13:5; Eph. 5:6; 2 Thes. 2:3 [/]Or, *and, The time;* see Mat. 3:2 & 4:17

10 [a]Mat. 24:7

12 [a]Mark 13:9; Rev. 2:10 [b]Acts 4:3 & 5:18 & 12:4 & 16:24 [c]Acts 25:23 [d]1 Pet. 2:13

13 [a]Phil. 1:28; 2 Thes. 1:5

14 [a]Mat. 10:19; Mark 13:11; ch. 12:11

15 [a]Acts 6:10

16 [a]Mic. 7:6; Mark 13:12 [b]Acts 7:59 & 12:2

17 [a]Mat. 10:22

18 [a]Mat. 10:30

20 [a]Mat. 24:15; Mark 13:14

delivering *you* up to the synagogues, and
[b]into prisons, [c]being brought before
kings and rulers [d]for my name's sake.
13 And [a]it shall turn to you for a testimony.
14 [a]Settle *it* therefore in your hearts, G
not to meditate before what ye shall L
answer: M
15 For I will give you a mouth and wis- T
dom, [a]which all your adversaries shall
not be able to gainsay nor resist.
16 [a]And ye shall be betrayed both by
parents, and brethren, and kinsfolks, and
friends; and [b]*some* of you shall they
cause to be put to death.
17 And [a]ye shall be hated of all *men*
for my name's sake.
18 [a]But there shall not an hair of your L
head perish. S
19 In your patience possess ye your V
souls.
20 [a]And when ye shall see Jerusalem R

G *Lk 12:11–12* ◀▶ *Lk 24:49*
L *Lk 12:11–12* ◀▶ *Jn 4:23–24*
M *Lk 4:14* ◀▶ *Lk 24:49*
T *Lk 12:11–12* ◀▶ *Jn 3:34*
L *Lk 18:7–8* ◀▶ *Lk 22:31–32*
S *Mk 4:40* ◀▶ *Ac 18:10*
V *Zec 12:8* ◀▶ *Ac 5:19*
R *Lk 20:9–16* ◀▶ *Lk 23:28*

21:6–7 Jesus prophesied to his disciples that the temple would be destroyed in that generation because of Israel's rejection of Jesus as their Messiah. His disciples wondered aloud when this terrible judgment would occur and how would they know when "these things shall come to pass?" (21:7). The first portion of this chapter provides Jesus' detailed answer about the prophetic signs pointing to his second coming. Compare this passage with Mt 24 and Mk 13.

21:7 To understand the prophetic signs of Lk 21, we must remember that this discourse was given before the crucifixion and prior to the existence of the church. Jesus' words were directed to Jewish Christians of the first century and warned of the signs that would occur when he returns.

21:8 The first prophetic sign of Jesus' return is the widespread deception surrounding the proliferation of false Christs. Many charlatans and false Christs have arisen in almost every century including Simeon Bar Kochba (A.D. 135), Moses of Crete (5th century), Abraham Abulafia (A.D. 1296) and Shabbethai Zebi (17th century). Yet the number of impostors claiming to be Jesus Christ are on the rise, including David Koresh, Sun Myung Moon and the Lord Maitreya in the last two decades alone.

21:9–10 Jesus also warned that the increase in wars would signal his imminent return (see Joel 3:9–10). Despite thousands of peace treaties, our generation has endured more wars than any other generation in history. Many nations are actively acquiring nuclear, biological and chemical weapons of mass destruction. The prediction of devastating ethnic strife, civil wars and conflicts are being fulfilled in our century.

21:11 Jesus also warned that a cataclysmic upheaval in the natural world would foreshadow his return. Earthquakes, famine, pestilence and unusual signs in the heavens would alert Jesus' followers to his imminent return (see Joel 2:10; Mt 24:29–30). See the study notes at Mt 24:7–8 for further details.

21:12–17 The Jewish believers would experience persecution and martyrdom at the hands of the religious authorities who hated Jesus. This prophecy will also be fulfilled during the seven-year tribulation when all of Jesus' followers will "be hated of all men for my name's sake" (21:17).

21:20–26 This passage focuses on Jesus' prophetic words concerning the destruction of the temple and Jerusalem in A.D. 70. The Roman armies burned the city and took Jewish survivors into captivity in chains. Jesus also warned about the pervading sense of fear because of the shaking of the heavens. This may refer to use of powerful nuclear

compassed with armies, then know that the desolation thereof is nigh.

21 Then let them which are in Judaea flee to the mountains; and let them which are in the midst of it depart out; and let not them that are in the countries enter thereinto.

22 For these be the days of vengeance, that [a]all things which are written may be fulfilled.

23 [a]But woe unto them that are with child, and to them that give suck, in those days! for there shall be great distress in the land, and wrath upon this people.

G 24 And they shall fall by the edge of the sword, and shall be led away captive into all nations: and Jerusalem shall be trodden down of the Gentiles, [a]until the times of the Gentiles be fulfilled.

E P H 25 ¶ [a]And there shall be signs in the sun, and in the moon, and in the stars; and upon the earth distress of nations, with perplexity; the sea and the waves roaring;

26 Men's hearts failing them for fear, and for looking after those things which are coming on the earth: [a]for the powers of heaven shall be shaken.

C 27 And then shall they see the Son of man [a]coming in a cloud with power and great glory.

28 And when these things begin to come to pass, then look up, and lift up your heads; for [a]your redemption draweth nigh.

G *Lk 20:16* ◄► *Jn 10:16*
E *Lk 17:26–30* ◄► *Ac 2:17*
P *Lk 21:9–11* ◄► *Lk 21:36*
H *Lk 20:47* ◄► *Lk 23:30*
C *Lk 19:23* ◄► *Lk 21:34–36*

22 [a]Dan. 9:26,27; Zech. 11:1
23 [a]Mat. 24:19
24 [a]Dan. 9:27 & 12:7; Rom. 11:25
25 [a]Mat. 24:29; Mark 13:24; 2 Pet. 3:10,12
26 [a]Mat. 24:29
27 [a]Mat. 24:30; Rev. 1:7 & 14:14
28 [a]Rom. 8:19,23
29 [a]Mat. 24:32; Mark 13:28
33 [a]Mat. 24:35
34 [a]Rom. 13:13; 1 Thes. 5:6; 1 Pet. 4:7
35 [a]1 Thes. 5:2; 2 Pet. 3:10; Rev. 3:3 & 16:15
36 [a]Mat. 24:42 & 25:13; Mark 13:33 [b]ch. 18:1 [c]Ps. 1:5; Eph. 6:13
37 [a]John 8:1,2 [b]ch. 22:39
22:1 [a]Mat. 26:2; Mark 14:1
2 [a]Ps. 2:2; John 11:47; Acts 4:27

29 [a]And he spake to them a parable; Behold the fig tree, and all the trees;

30 When they now shoot forth, ye see and know of your own selves that summer is now nigh at hand.

31 So likewise ye, when ye see these things come to pass, know ye that the kingdom of God is nigh at hand.

32 Verily I say unto you, This generation shall not pass away, till all be fulfilled.

33 [a]Heaven and earth shall pass away: but my words shall not pass away.

34 ¶ And [a]take heed to yourselves, lest at any time your hearts be overcharged with surfeiting, and drunkenness, and cares of this life, and *so* that day come upon you unawares. C

35 For [a]as a snare shall it come on all them that dwell on the face of the whole earth.

36 [a]Watch ye therefore, and [b]pray always, that ye may be accounted worthy to escape all these things that shall come to pass, and [c]to stand before the Son of man. P

37 [a]And in the day time he was teaching in the temple; and [b]at night he went out, and abode in the mount that is called *the mount* of Olives.

38 And all the people came early in the morning to him in the temple, for to hear him.

The plot to kill Jesus

22 NOW [a]THE feast of unleavened bread drew nigh, which is called the Passover.

2 And [a]the chief priests and scribes

C *Lk 21:27–31* ◄► *Jn 21:22–23*
P *Lk 21:25–26* ◄► *Ac 2:19–20*

---

weapons in the last days.
21:27–28 This passage confirms the way in which Christ will return: "in a cloud with power and great glory" (21:27; see Ac 1:9–11; Rev 1:7). Rather than being frightened or feeling despair when these signs appear, Jesus said that the fulfillment of these signs should point believers toward a positive anticipation of the glorious day when Jesus will take his place as God's Messiah and the true King of the coming millennial kingdom.
21:29–36 This parable of the fig tree points to the time when the Son of man will return. The fig tree appears in many places throughout Scripture, appearing repeatedly in the OT as a symbol of Israel's security and blessing (see 1Ki 4:25; Isa 36:16; Mic 4:4; Zec 3:10). In the NT, Jesus withered away a barren fig tree to symbolize Israel's barren spiritual life. However, Jesus promised that Israel would produce great spiritual fruit in the last days (see Ro 11:25–29). Jesus said that when the fig tree flourishes again—when Israel is reborn as a nation—God's kingdom would be close at hand. In light of the certainty of Christ's return, Jesus said his followers should wait with watchfulness for the fulfillment of these signs. Careful Bible students who observe the changes in political, social and military structures in this generation have witnessed the fulfillment of more prophecies than any other generation since the life of Jesus.

sought how they might kill him; for they feared the people.

3 ¶ [a]Then entered Satan into Judas surnamed Iscariot, being of the number of the twelve.

4 And he went his way, and communed with the chief priests and captains, how he might betray him unto them.

5 And they were glad, and [a]covenanted to give him money.

6 And he promised, and sought opportunity to betray him unto them ʹin the absence of the multitude.

The last supper

7 ¶ [a]Then came the day of unleavened bread, when the passover must be killed.

8 And he sent Peter and John, saying, Go and prepare us the passover, that we may eat.

9 And they said unto him, Where wilt thou that we prepare?

10 And he said unto them, Behold, when ye are entered into the city, there shall a man meet you, bearing a pitcher of water; follow him into the house where he entereth in.

11 And ye shall say unto the goodman of the house, The Master saith unto thee, Where is the guestchamber, where I shall eat the passover with my disciples?

12 And he shall show you a large upper room furnished: there make ready.

13 And they went, and found as he had said unto them: and they made ready the passover.

14 [a]And when the hour was come, he sat down, and the twelve apostles with him.

15 And he said unto them, ʹWith desire I have desired to eat this passover with you before I suffer:

H 16 For I say unto you, I will not any more eat thereof, [a]until it be fulfilled in the kingdom of God.

D 17 And he took the cup, and gave thanks, and said, Take this, and divide *it* among yourselves:

18 For [a]I say unto you, I will not drink of the fruit of the vine, until the kingdom of God shall come.

19 ¶ [a]And he took bread, and gave thanks, and brake *it,* and gave unto them, saying, This is my body which is given for you: [b]this do in remembrance of me.

20 Likewise also the cup after supper, saying, [a]This cup *is* the new testament in my blood, which is shed for you.

21 ¶ [a]But, behold, the hand of him that betrayeth me *is* with me on the table.

22 [a]And truly the Son of man goeth, [b]as it was determined: but woe unto that man by whom he is betrayed!

23 [a]And they began to inquire among themselves, which of them it was that should do this thing.

24 ¶ [a]And there was also a strife among them, which of them should be accounted the greatest.

25 [a]And he said unto them, The kings of the Gentiles exercise lordship over them; and they that exercise authority upon them are called benefactors.

26 [a]But ye *shall* not *be* so: [b]but he that is greatest among you, let him be as the younger; and he that is chief, as he that doth serve.

27 [a]For whether *is* greater, he that sitteth at meat, or he that serveth? *is* not he that sitteth at meat? but [b]I am among you as he that serveth.

28 Ye are they which have continued with me in [a]my temptations.

29 And [a]I appoint unto you a kingdom, as my Father hath appointed unto me; M

30 That [a]ye may eat and drink at my table in my kingdom, [b]and sit on thrones judging the twelve tribes of Israel.

31 ¶ And the Lord said, Simon, Simon, behold, [a]Satan hath desired *to have* you, that he may [b]sift *you* as wheat: L

32 But [a]I have prayed for thee, that thy

3 [a]Mat. 26:14; Mark 14:10; John 13:2,27
5 [a]Zech. 11:12
6 ʹOr, *without tumult*
7 [a]Mat. 26:17; Mark 14:12
14 [a]Mat. 26:20; Mark 14:17
15 ʹOr, *I have heartily desired*
16 [a]ch. 14:15; Acts 10:41; Rev. 19:9
18 [a]Mat. 26:29; Mark 14:25
19 [a]Mat. 26:26; Mark 14:22 [b]1 Cor. 11:24
20 [a]1 Cor. 10:16
21 [a]Ps. 41:9; Mat. 26:21,23; Mark 14:18; John 13:21, 26
22 [a]Mat. 26:24 [b]Acts 2:23 & 4:28
23 [a]Mat. 26:22; John 13:22,25
24 [a]Mark 9:34; ch. 9:46
25 [a]Mat. 20:25; Mark 10:42
26 [a]Mat. 20:26; 1 Pet. 5:3 [b]ch. 9:48
27 [a]ch. 12:37 [b]Mat. 20:28; John 13:13,14; Phil. 2:7
28 [a]Heb. 4:15
29 [a]Mat. 24:47; ch. 12:32
30 [a]Mat. 8:11; ch. 14:15; Rev. 19:9 [b]Ps. 49:14; Mat. 19:28; 1 Cor. 6:2; Rev. 3:21
31 [a]1 Pet. 5:8 [b]Amos 9:9
32 [a]John 17:9,11, 15

H *Lk 14:16* ◀▶ *Eph 1:10*
D *Mk 14:22–24* ◀▶ *Jn 1:29*
M *Lk 20:42–43* ◀▶ *Lk 23:2–3*
L *Lk 21:18* ◀▶ *Lk 22:35*

22:29–30 Jesus prophesies about the coming millennial kingdom that will be established following the Battle of Armageddon. His followers will enter into the blessings of his kingdom and rule and reign with him for a thousand years. Jesus specifically promised his disciples the privilege of ruling over the twelve tribes of Israel. This prophecy confirms that God will restore the lost tribes to their land and place of honor in God's millennial kingdom (see Eze 47—48).

faith fail not: and when thou art converted, strengthen thy brethren.

33 And he said unto him, Lord, I am ready to go with thee, both into prison, and to death.

34 [a]And he said, I tell thee, Peter, the cock shall not crow this day, before that thou shalt thrice deny that thou knowest me.

C 35 [a]And he said unto them, When I
F sent you without purse, and scrip, and
L shoes, lacked ye any thing? And they
P said, Nothing.

36 Then said he unto them, But now, he that hath a purse, let him take *it,* and likewise *his* scrip: and he that hath no sword, let him sell his garment, and buy one.

37 For I say unto you, that this that is written must yet be accomplished in me, [a]And he was reckoned among the transgressors: for the things concerning me have an end.

38 And they said, Lord, behold, here *are* two swords. And he said unto them, It is enough.

Jesus' agony in Gethsemane

39 ¶ [a]And he came out, and [b]went, as he was wont, to the mount of Olives; and his disciples also followed him.

40 [a]And when he was at the place, he said unto them, Pray that ye enter not into temptation.

41 [a]And he was withdrawn from them about a stone's cast, and kneeled down, and prayed,

42 Saying, Father, if thou be [/]willing, remove this cup from me: nevertheless [a]not my will, but thine, be done.

43 And there appeared [a]an angel unto him from heaven, strengthening him.

44 [a]And being in an agony he prayed more earnestly: and his sweat was as it were great drops of blood falling down to the ground.

45 And when he rose up from prayer, and was come to his disciples, he found them sleeping for sorrow,

46 And said unto them, Why sleep ye? rise and [a]pray, lest ye enter into temptation.

C *Lk 12:22–31* ◄
F *Lk 12:22–31* ◄ ► *Jn 6:5–14*
L *Lk 22:31–32* ◄ ► *Jn 10:3–4*
P *Mt 17:27* ◄ ► *2Co 9:6–11*

34 [a]Mat. 26:34; Mark 14:30; John 13:38
35 [a]Mat. 10:9; ch. 9:3 & 10:4
37 [a]Is. 53:12; Mark 15:28
39 [a]Mat. 26:36; Mark 14:32; John 18:1 [b]ch. 21:37
40 [a]ver. 46; Mat. 6:13 & 26:41; Mark 14:38
41 [a]Mat. 26:39; Mark 14:35
42 [a]John 5:30 & 6:38 [/]Gk. *willing to remove*
43 [a]Mat. 4:11
44 [a]John 12:27; Heb. 5:7
46 [a]ver. 40
47 [a]Mat. 26:47; Mark 14:43; John 18:3
50 [a]Mat. 26:51; Mark 14:47
52 [a]Mat. 26:55; Mark 14:48
53 [a]John 12:27
54 [a]Mat. 26:57 [b]Mat. 26:58; John 18:15
55 [a]Mat. 26:69; Mark 14:66; John 18:17,18
58 [a]Mat. 26:71; Mark 14:69; John 18:25
59 [a]Mat. 26:73; Mark 14:70; John 18:26
61 [a]Mat. 26:75; Mark 14:72

Jesus' betrayal and arrest

47 ¶ And while he yet spake, [a]behold a multitude, and he that was called Judas, one of the twelve, went before them, and drew near unto Jesus to kiss him.

48 But Jesus said unto him, Judas, betrayest thou the Son of man with a kiss?

49 When they which were about him saw what would follow, they said unto him, Lord, shall we smite with the sword?

50 ¶ And [a]one of them smote the servant of the high priest, and cut off his right ear. E

51 And Jesus answered and said, Suffer ye thus far. And he touched his ear, and healed him.

52 [a]Then Jesus said unto the chief priests, and captains of the temple, and the elders, which were come to him, Be ye come out, as against a thief, with swords and staves?

53 When I was daily with you in the temple, ye stretched forth no hands against me: [a]but this is your hour, and the power of darkness.

Peter's denial of Jesus

54 ¶ [a]Then took they him, and led *him,* and brought him into the high priest's house. [b]And Peter followed afar off.

55 [a]And when they had kindled a fire in the midst of the hall, and were set down together, Peter sat down among them.

56 But a certain maid beheld him as he sat by the fire, and earnestly looked upon him, and said, This man was also with him.

57 And he denied him, saying, Woman, I know him not.

58 And [a]after a little while another saw him, and said, Thou art also of them. And Peter said, Man, I am not.

59 [a]And about the space of one hour after another confidently affirmed, saying, Of a truth this *fellow* also was with him: for he is a Galilaean.

60 And Peter said, Man, I know not what thou sayest. And immediately, while he yet spake, the cock crew.

61 And the Lord turned, and looked upon Peter. [a]And Peter remembered the word of the Lord, how he had said unto

E *Lk 18:35–43* ◄ ► *Jn 4:46–54*

him, [b]Before the cock crow, thou shalt deny me thrice.

R 62 And Peter went out, and wept bitterly.

63 ¶ [a]And the men that held Jesus mocked him, and smote *him.*

64 And when they had blindfolded him, they struck him on the face, and asked him, saying, Prophesy, who is it that smote thee?

65 And many other things blasphemously spake they against him.

Jesus before Pontius Pilate

66 ¶ [a]And as soon as it was day, [b]the elders of the people and the chief priests and the scribes came together, and led him into their council, saying,

67 [a]Art thou the Christ? tell us. And he said unto them, If I tell you, ye will not believe:

68 And if I also ask *you,* ye will not answer me, nor let *me* go.

69 [a]Hereafter shall the Son of man sit on the right hand of the power of God.

70 Then said they all, Art thou then the Son of God? And he said unto them, [a]Ye say that I am.

71 [a]And they said, What need we any further witness? for we ourselves have heard of his own mouth.

23 AND [a]THE whole multitude of them arose, and led him unto Pilate.

I 2 And they began to accuse him, say-
M ing, We found this *fellow* [a]perverting the nation, and [b]forbidding to give tribute to Caesar, saying [c]that he himself is Christ a King.

3 [a]And Pilate asked him, saying, Art thou the King of the Jews? And he answered him and said, Thou sayest *it.*

4 Then said Pilate to the chief priests and *to* the people, [a]I find no fault in this man.

5 And they were the more fierce, saying, He stirreth up the people, teaching

R *Lk 19:8–9* ◀ ▶ *Lk 24:47*
I *Lk 2:38* ◀ ▶ *Lk 23:37–38*
M *Lk 22:29–30* ◀ ▶ *Lk 23:37–38*

61 [b]Mat. 26:34,75; John 13:38
63 [a]Mat. 26:67,68; Mark 14:65
66 [a]Mat. 27:1 [b]Acts 4:26; See Acts 22:5
67 [a]Mat. 26:63; Mark 14:61
69 [a]Mat 26:64; Mark 14:62; Heb. 1:3 & 8:1
70 [a]Mat. 26:64; Mark 14:62
71 [a]Mat. 26:65; Mark 14:63
23:1 [a]Mat. 27:2; Mark 15:1; John 18:28
2 [a]Acts 17:7 [b]See Mat. 17:27 & 22:21; Mark 12:17 [c]John 19:12
3 [a]Mat. 27:11; 1 Tim. 6:13
4 [a]1 Pet. 2:22
7 [a]ch. 3:1
8 [a]ch. 9:9 [b]Mat. 14:1; Mark 6:14
11 [a]Is 53:3
12 [a]Acts 4:27
13 [a]Mat. 27:23; Mark 15:14; John 18:38 & 19:4
14 [a]ver. 1,2 [b]ver. 4
16 [a]Mat. 27:26; John 19:1
17 [a]Mat. 27:15; Mark 15:6; John 18:39
18 [a]Acts 3:14

throughout all Jewry, beginning from Galilee to this place.

6 When Pilate heard of Galilee, he asked whether the man were a Galilaean.

7 And as soon as he knew that he belonged unto [a]Herod's jurisdiction, he sent him to Herod, who himself also was at Jerusalem at that time.

8 ¶ And when Herod saw Jesus, he was exceeding glad: for [a]he was desirous to see him of a long *season,* because [b]he had heard many things of him; and he hoped to have seen some miracle done by him.

9 Then he questioned with him in many words; but he answered him nothing.

10 And the chief priests and scribes stood and vehemently accused him.

11 [a]And Herod with his men of war set him at nought, and mocked *him,* and arrayed him in a gorgeous robe, and sent him again to Pilate.

12 ¶ And the same day [a]Pilate and Herod were made friends together: for before they were at enmity between themselves.

13 ¶ [a]And Pilate, when he had called together the chief priests and the rulers and the people,

14 Said unto them, [a]Ye have brought this man unto me, as one that perverteth the people: and, behold, [b]I, having examined *him* before you, have found no fault in this man touching those things whereof ye accuse him:

15 No, nor yet Herod: for I sent you to him; and, lo, nothing worthy of death is done unto him.

16 [a]I will therefore chastise him, and release *him.*

17 [a](For of necessity he must release one unto them at the feast.)

18 And [a]they cried out all at once, saying, Away with this *man,* and release unto us Barabbas:

19 (Who for a certain sedition made in the city, and for murder, was cast into prison.)

20 Pilate therefore, willing to release Jesus, spake again to them.

23:3 When Jesus was taken before Pontius Pilate, the Roman governor asked Jesus to affirm his position as "the King of the Jews." Jesus' positive declaration affirmed his divine claim to be both Israel's Messiah and King. Jesus will one day rule from the throne of David in Jerusalem as the King of the Jews and King of the whole world after his victory at Armageddon.

21 But they cried, saying, Crucify *him,* crucify him.

22 And he said unto them the third time, Why, what evil hath he done? I have found no cause of death in him: I will therefore chastise him, and let *him* go.

23 And they were instant with loud voices, requiring that he might be crucified. And the voices of them and of the chief priests prevailed.

24 And [a]Pilate [b]gave[l] sentence that it should be as they required.

25 And he released unto them him that for sedition and murder was cast into prison, whom they had desired; but he delivered Jesus to their will.

Jesus crucified

26 [a]And as they led him away, they laid hold upon one Simon, a Cyrenian, coming out of the country, and on him they laid the cross, that he might bear *it* after Jesus.

27 ¶ And there followed him a great company of people, and of women, which also bewailed and lamented him.

R 28 But Jesus turning unto them said, Daughters of Jerusalem, weep not for me, but weep for yourselves, and for your children.

29 [a]For, behold, the days are coming, in the which they shall say, Blessed *are* the barren, and the wombs that never bare, and the paps which never gave suck.

H 30 [a]Then shall they begin to say to the mountains, Fall on us; and to the hills, Cover us.

31 [a]For if they do these things in a green tree, what shall be done in the dry?

R *Lk 21:20–24 ◀▶ Ro 9:25–29*
H *Lk 21:25–26 ◀▶ Jn 3:16–19*

32 [a]And there were also two other, malefactors, led with him to be put to death.

33 And [a]when they were come to the place, which is called [l]Calvary, there they crucified him, and the malefactors, one on the right hand, and the other on the left.

34 ¶ Then said Jesus, Father, [a]forgive them; for [b]they know not what they do. And [c]they parted his raiment, and cast lots.

35 And [a]the people stood beholding. And the [b]rulers also with them derided *him,* saying, He saved others; let him save himself, if he be Christ, the chosen of God.

36 And the soldiers also mocked him, coming to him, and offering him vinegar,

37 And saying, If thou be the king of the Jews, save thyself. I M

38 [a]And a superscription also was written over him in letters of Greek, and Latin, and Hebrew, THIS IS THE KING OF THE JEWS.

39 ¶ [a]And one of the malefactors which were hanged railed on him, saying, If thou be Christ, save thyself and us.

40 But the other answering rebuked him, saying, Dost not thou fear God, seeing thou art in the same condemnation?

41 And we indeed justly; for we receive the due reward of our deeds: but this man hath done nothing amiss.

42 And he said unto Jesus, Lord, remember me when thou comest into thy kingdom. M L

43 And Jesus said unto him, Verily I

I *Lk 23:2–3 ◀▶ Lk 24:21*
M *Lk 23:2–3 ◀▶ Lk 23:42*
M *Lk 23:37–38 ◀▶ Lk 23:51*
L *Lk 19:41–42 ◀▶ Lk 24:46–47*

24 [a]Mat:27:26; Mark 15:15; John 19:16 [b]Ex. 23:2 [l]*Or, assented*
26 [a]Mat. 27:32; Mark 15:21; See John 19:17
29 [a]Mat. 24:19; ch. 21:23
30 [a]Is. 2:19; Hos. 10:8; Rev. 6:16 & 9:6
31 [a]Prov. 11:31; Jer. 25:29; Ezek. 20:47 & 21:3,4; 1 Pet. 4:17
32 [a]Is. 53:12; Mat. 27:38
33 [a]Mat. 27:33; Mark 15:22; John 19:17,18 [l]*Or, The place of a skull*
34 [a]Mat. 5:44; Acts 7:60; 1 Cor. 4:12 [b]Acts 3:17 [c]Mat. 27:35; Mark 15:24; John 19:23
35 [a]Ps. 22:17; Zech. 12:10 [b]Mat. 27:39; Mark 15:29
38 [a]Mat. 27:37; Mark 15:26; John 19:19
39 [a]Mat. 27:44; Mark 15:32

23:28 Jesus warned those who rejected his earthly ministry to "weep for yourselves, and for your children." Tragically, this prophecy was fulfilled thirty-eight years later during the Roman siege of Jerusalem. Starvation and famine were so intense that parents literally ate their children in a vain attempt to stay alive while the Roman legions tightened their death grip on the city of Jerusalem.

23:37–38 The Roman soldiers hung a sign above the cross as a mockery of Jesus' royalty. Yet their derision was actually an acknowledgment of the prophetic truth that Jesus will be ultimately be acclaimed "King of the Jews" (23:3).

23:42–43 The thief on the cross acknowledged Jesus' authority and was rewarded with the immediate promise of paradise. Jesus' declaration confirms that the moment a believer dies, they will be with Jesus consciously and joyfully in heaven (see 2Co 5:8). The departed saints will then await the glorious day of the rapture when they will receive a new resurrection body like the body Jesus had when he arose from the dead (see 1Co 15:52; 1Th 4:16).

say unto thee, Today shalt thou be with
me in paradise.

The death of Jesus

44 [a]And it was about the sixth hour,
and there was a darkness over all the
[l]earth until the ninth hour.
45 And the sun was darkened, and
[a]the veil of the temple was rent in the
midst.
46 ¶ And when Jesus had cried with a
loud voice, he said, [a]Father, into thy
hands I commend my spirit: [b]and having
said thus, he gave up the ghost.
47 [a]Now when the centurion saw
what was done, he glorified God, saying,
Certainly this was a righteous man.
48 And all the people that came together to that sight, beholding the things
which were done, smote their breasts,
and returned.
49 [a]And all his acquaintance, and the
women that followed him from Galilee,
stood afar off, beholding these things.

Jesus laid in the sepulchre

50 ¶ [a]And, behold, *there was* a man
named Joseph, a counsellor; *and he was* a
good man, and a just:
M 51 (The same had not consented to the
counsel and deed of them;) *he was* of Arimathaea, a city of the Jews: [a]who also
himself waited for the kingdom of God.
52 This *man* went unto Pilate, and
begged the body of Jesus.
53 [a]And he took it down, and wrapped
it in linen, and laid it in a sepulchre that
was hewn in stone, wherein never man
before was laid.
54 And that day was [a]the preparation,
and the sabbath drew on.
55 And the women also, [a]which came

M *Lk 23:42* ◄► *Jn 10:16*

44 [a]Mat. 27:45; Mark 15:33 [l]Or, *land*
45 [a]Mat. 27:51; Mark 15:38
46 [a]Ps. 31:5; 1 Pet. 2:23 [b]Mat. 27:50; Mark 15:37; John 19:30
47 [a]Mat. 27:54; Mark 15:39
49 [a]Ps. 38:11; Mat. 27:55; Mark 15:40; See John 19:25
50 [a]Mat. 27:57; Mark 15:42; John 19:38
51 [a]Mark 15:43; ch. 2:25,38
53 [a]Mat. 27:59; Mark 15:46
54 [a]Mat. 27:62
55 [a]ch. 8:2 [b]Mark 15:47
56 [a]Mark 16:1 [b]Ex. 20:10
24:1 [a]Mat. 28:1; Mark 16:1; John 20:1 [b]ch. 23:56
2 [a]Mat. 28:2; Mark 16:4
3 [a]ver. 23; Mark 16:5
4 [a]John 20:12; Acts 1:10
5 [l]Or, *him that liveth*
6 [a]Mat. 16:21 & 17:23; Mark 8:31 & 9:31; ch. 9:22
8 [a]John 2:22
9 [a]Mat. 28:8; Mark 16:10
10 [a]ch. 8:3
11 [a]ver. 25
12 [a]John 20:3

with him from Galilee, followed after,
and [b]beheld the sepulchre, and how his
body was laid.
56 And they returned, and [a]prepared
spices and ointments: and rested the sabbath day [b]according to the commandment.

The resurrection of Jesus

24 NOW [a]UPON the first *day* of the
week, very early in the morning,
they came unto the sepulchre, [b]bringing
the spices which they had prepared, and
certain *others* with them.
2 [a]And they found the stone rolled
away from the sepulchre.
3 [a]And they entered in, and found not
the body of the Lord Jesus.
4 And it came to pass, as they were
much perplexed thereabout, [a]behold,
two men stood by them in shining garments:
5 And as they were afraid, and bowed
down *their* faces to the earth, they said
unto them, Why seek ye [l]the living
among the dead?
6 He is not here, but is risen: [a]remem-
ber how he spake unto you when he was
yet in Galilee,
7 Saying, The Son of man must be delivered into the hands of sinful men, and
be crucified, and the third day rise again.
8 And [a]they remembered his words,
9 [a]And returned from the sepulchre,
and told all these things unto the eleven,
and to all the rest.
10 It was Mary Magdalene, and [a]Jo-
anna, and Mary *the mother* of James, and
other *women that were* with them,
which told these things unto the apostles.
11 [a]And their words seemed to them
as idle tales, and they believed them not.
12 [a]Then arose Peter, and ran unto the
sepulchre; and stooping down, he beheld

23:44–45 Luke records an extraordinary miracle of worldwide darkness on the day of Jesus Christ's crucifixion. For three hours God supernaturally darkened the sky because of the terrible sacrifice of his only begotten Son on the cross. Ancient secular historians record that there was an unexplained darkness on the Feast of Passover in the spring of A.D. 32. Since the Feast of the Passover was always celebrated during a full moon, the position of the earth, sun and moon made an eclipse physically impossible. Therefore, we can conclude that this "darkness" was a true miracle and a marvelous confirmation of the truthfulness of the Gospel account of the crucifixion of Jesus Christ.

23:51 Joseph of Arimathaea was a member of the Sanhedrin who followed Christ and who provided the tomb for Jesus' body. Joseph believed the prophecies of the OT and "waited for the kingdom of God." As one of the ruling religious leaders, Joseph was undoubtedly familiar with the prophecy of Daniel's seventy weeks (see Da 9:24–27) and would have anticipated the appearance of the Messiah during his lifetime.

the linen clothes laid by themselves, and
departed, wondering in himself at that
which was come to pass.

The walk to Emmaus

13 ¶ [a]And, behold, two of them went
that same day to a village called Emmaus,
which was from Jerusalem *about* threescore furlongs.
14 And they talked together of all
these things which had happened.
15 And it came to pass, that, while
they communed *together* and reasoned,
[a]Jesus himself drew near, and went with
them.
16 But [a]their eyes were holden that
they should not know him.
17 And he said unto them, What manner of communications *are* these that ye
have one to another, as ye walk, and are
sad?
18 And the one of them, [a]whose name
was Cleopas, answering said unto him,
Art thou only a stranger in Jerusalem,
and hast not known the things which are
come to pass there in these days?
19 And he said unto them, What
things? And they said unto him, Concerning Jesus of Nazareth, [a]which was a
prophet [b]mighty in deed and word before
God and all the people:
20 [a]And how the chief priests and our
rulers delivered him to be condemned to
death, and have crucified him.
I 21 But we trusted [a]that it had been he
which should have redeemed Israel: and
beside all this, today is the third day since
these things were done.
22 Yea, and [a]certain women also of
our company made us astonished, which
were early at the sepulchre;
23 And when they found not his body,
they came, saying, that they had also
seen a vision of angels, which said that
he was alive.
24 And [a]certain of them which were
with us went to the sepulchre, and found
it even so as the women had said: but
him they saw not.
25 Then he said unto them, O fools,
and slow of heart to believe all that the
prophets have spoken:
26 [a]Ought not Christ to have suffered
these things, and to enter into his glory?
27 [a]And beginning at [b]Moses and [c]all
the prophets, he expounded unto them
in all the scriptures the things concerning
himself.
28 And they drew nigh unto the village, whither they went: and [a]he made as
though he would have gone further.
29 But [a]they constrained him, saying, P
Abide with us: for it is toward evening,
and the day is far spent. And he went in
to tarry with them.
30 And it came to pass, as he sat at
meat with them, [a]he took bread, and
blessed *it,* and brake, and gave to them.
31 And their eyes were opened, and
they knew him; and he [1]vanished out of
their sight.
32 And they said one to another, Did
not our heart burn within us, while he
talked with us by the way, and while he
opened to us the scriptures?
33 And they rose up the same hour,
and returned to Jerusalem, and found the
eleven gathered together, and them that
were with them,
34 Saying, The Lord is risen indeed,
and [a]hath appeared to Simon.
35 And they told what things *were*
done in the way, and how he was known
of them in breaking of bread.

Jesus appears to the ten

36 ¶ [a]And as they thus spake, Jesus
himself stood in the midst of them, and
saith unto them, Peace *be* unto you.
37 But they were terrified and affrighted, and supposed that they had seen
[a]a spirit.
38 And he said unto them, Why are ye
troubled? and why do thoughts arise in
your hearts?
39 Behold my hands and my feet, that
it is I myself: [a]handle me, and see; for a
spirit hath not flesh and bones, as ye see
me have.

13 [a]Mark 16:12
15 [a]Mat. 18:20
16 [a]John 20:14 & 21:4
18 [a]John 19:25
19 [a]Mat. 21:11; ch. 7:16; John 3:2 & 4:19 & 6:14; Acts 2:22 [b]Acts 7:22
20 [a]ch. 23:1; Acts 13:27
21 [a]ch. 1:68 & 2:38; Acts 1:6
22 [a]ver. 9,10; Mat. 28:8; Mark 16:10; John 20:18
24 [a]ver. 12
26 [a]Acts 17:3; 1 Pet. 1:11
27 [a]ver. 45 [b]Gen. 3:15 & 22:18 & 26:4 & 49:10; Num. 21:9; Deut. 18:15 [c]Ps. 16:9,10 & 22 & 132:11; Is. 7:14 & 9:6 & 40:10,11 & 50:6; Jer. 23:5 & 33:14, 15; Ezek. 34:23 & 37:25; Dan. 9:24; Mic. 7:20; Mal. 3:1 & 4:2; See John 1:45
28 [a]Gen. 32:26 & 42:7; Mark 6:48
29 [a]Gen. 19:3; Acts 16:15
30 [a]Mat. 14:19
31 [1]Or, *ceased to be seen of them*
34 [a]1 Cor. 15:5
36 [a]Mark 16:14; John 20:19; 1 Cor. 15:5
37 [a]Mark 6:49
39 [a]John 20:20

I *Lk 23:37–38* ◀ ▶ *Jn 1:49*

P *Lk 11:9–13* ◀ ▶ *Jn 1:33*

24:13–21 This remarkable passage records the event of the two disciples who unknowingly met Jesus on the road to Emmaus. Their words revealed that they had believed that Jesus was Israel's long awaited Messiah who would redeem Israel from sin and the oppression of Rome.

40 And when he had thus spoken, he
showed them *his* hands and *his* feet.
41 And while they yet believed not
[a]for joy, and wondered, he said unto
them, [b]Have ye here any meat?
42 And they gave him a piece of a
broiled fish, and of an honeycomb.
43 [a]And he took *it,* and did eat before
them.
44 And he said unto them, [a]These *are*
the words which I spake unto you, while
I was yet with you, that all things must be
fulfilled, which were written in the law
of Moses, and *in* the prophets, and *in* the
psalms, concerning me.
45 Then [a]opened he their understanding, that they might understand the scriptures,
L 46 And said unto them, [a]Thus it is
written, and thus it behooved Christ to
suffer, and to rise from the dead the third
day:
R 47 And that repentance and [a]remis-
sion of sins should be preached in his
name [b]among all nations, beginning at Jerusalem.
48 And [a]ye are witnesses of these
things.
49 ¶ [a]And, behold, I send the promise B
of my Father upon you: but tarry ye in the G
city of Jerusalem, until ye be endued with M
power from on high. W

Jesus' ascension

50 ¶ And he led them out [a]as far as to
Bethany, and he lifted up his hands, and
blessed them.
51 [a]And it came to pass, while he
blessed them, he was parted from them,
and carried up into heaven.
52 [a]And they worshipped him, and returned to Jerusalem with great joy:
53 And were continually [a]in the temple, praising and blessing God. Amen.

L *Lk 23:42–43* ◀▶ *Jn 1:7*
R *Lk 22:62* ◀▶ *Ac 2:37–38*

41 [a]Gen. 45:26 [b]John 21:5
43 [a]Acts 10:41
44 [a]ver. 6; Mat. 16:21 & 17:22 & 20:18; Mark 8:31; ch. 9:22 & 18:31
45 [a]Acts 16:14
46 [a]Ps. 22; Acts 17:3
47 [a]Dan. 9:24; Acts 13:38 [b]Ps. 22:27; Jer. 31:34; Mic. 4:2
48 [a]Acts 1:8
49 [a]Is. 44:3; Joel 2:28
50 [a]Acts 1:12
51 [a]Mark 16:19
52 [a]Mat. 28:9
53 [a]Acts 2:46

B *Lk 4:18* ◀▶ *Jn 1:32–33*
G *Lk 21:14–15* ◀▶ *Jn 3:34*
M *Lk 21:14–15* ◀▶ *Jn 7:38–39*
W *Zec 4:6* ◀▶ *Jn 4:23–24*

John

Author: John

Theme: Jesus gives abundant life

Date of Writing: C. A.D. 80–95

Outline of John

I. Prologue and Theme (1:1–18)
II. Introduction of Jesus (1:19—4:54)
III. Jesus' Ministry as God's Son (5:1—10:42)
IV. In Jerusalem (11:1—12:50)
V. Jesus With His disciples (13:1—17:26)
VI. Trial, Death and Burial (18:1—19:42)
VII. Resurrection and Conclusion (20:1—21:25)

JOHN, THE SON of Zebedee, composed this book before the destruction of Jerusalem in A.D. 70. John and his brother James were Galilean fishermen when Jesus called them to join him as disciples (see Mk 1:19–20). Because of their impetuosity and quick tempers, both men were given the nickname "the sons of thunder" (Mk 3:17), yet John became one of Jesus' closest disciples and was one of the three witnesses to Jesus' transfiguration experience. Known as the disciple "whom Jesus loved" (13:23), John participated in many of the events he records, explaining Jewish feasts and customs for Greek readers who were unfamiliar with the Jewish ways of religious life.

The book of John is very different in structure and style from the other three gospel accounts. Written in simple Greek language with precise details and profound observations, John records several miracles that are not mentioned elsewhere and stresses Jesus' ministry in Judea and Jerusalem while only touching on his Galilean ministry. John also highlights many personal interviews, such as the late-night visit with Nicodemus (see 3:1–18), to stress the importance of individual relationships with Jesus.

Throughout his book John presents Jesus as God's Son (see 1:34, 49), reporting the supernatural signs that accompanied Jesus' ministry so that John's readers might believe and receive eternal life (see 20:30–31). The word "believe" occurs repeatedly in John's Gospel. Introducing Jesus as the essence of God's revelation to humanity, John portrays Jesus as the "Lamb of God" (1:29) who offers salvation to all who will repent of their sins and trust in him.

John's Gospel is the only account that records Jesus' "I am" messages. Jesus identifies himself as "the bread of life" (6:35), "the light of the world" (8:12; 9:5), " the door" (10:7), "the good shepherd" (10:11, 14), "the resurrection, and the life" (11:25), "the way, the truth, and the life" (14:6) and "the true vine" (15:1).

The Word became flesh

1 IN THE beginning [a]was the Word,
and the Word was [b]with God, [c]and
the Word was God.
2 [a]The same was in the beginning
with God.
3 [a]All things were made by him; and
without him was not any thing made that
was made.
K 4 [a]In him was life; and [b]the life was
the light of men.
5 And [a]the light shineth in darkness;
and the darkness comprehended it
not.
6 ¶ [a]There was a man sent from God,
whose name *was* John.
L 7 [a]The same came for a witness, to
W bear witness of the Light, that all *men*
through him might believe.
8 He was not that Light, but *was sent*
to bear witness of that Light.
W 9 [a]*That* was the true Light, which
lighteth every man that cometh into the
world.
10 He was in the world, and [a]the
world was made by him, and the world
knew him not.
11 [a]He came unto his own, and his
own received him not.

K *Lk 6:47–48* ◀▶ *Jn 1:12*
L *Lk 24:46–47* ◀▶ *Jn 1:12*
W *Lk 19:10* ◀▶ *Jn 1:9*
W *Jn 1:7* ◀▶ *Jn 1:12*

1:1 [a]Prov. 8:22; 1 John 1:1 [b]Prov. 8:30; ch. 17:5 [c]1 John 5:7
2 [a]Gen. 1:1
3 [a]Ps. 33:6; Eph. 3:9; Col. 1:16
4 [a]1 John 5:11 [b]ch. 8:12
5 [a]ch. 3:19
6 [a]Mal. 3:1; Mat. 3:1; Luke 3:2
7 [a]Acts 19:4
9 [a]Is. 49:6
10 [a]Heb. 1:2
11 [a]Luke 19:14
12 [a]Gal. 3:26 [l]Or, *the right*, or, *privilege*
13 [a]1 Pet. 1:23
14 [a]Mat. 1:16; Luke 1:31 [b]Gal. 4:4 [c]Heb. 2:11 [d]Is. 40:5 [e]Col. 1:19
15 [a]ch. 3:32 [b]Mat. 3:11; Mark 1:7; Luke 3:16 [c]Col. 1:17
16 [a]Col. 1:19
17 [a]Ex. 20:1 [b]Rom. 5:21 [c]ch. 8:32
18 [a]Ex. 33:20; Mat. 11:27; 1 Tim. 6:16 [b]1 John 4:9
19 [a]ch. 5:33
20 [a]Luke 3:15; Acts 13:25

12 But [a]as many as received him, to F
them gave he [l]power to become the sons G
of God, *even* to them that believe on his K
name: L
13 [a]Which were born, not of blood, W
nor of the will of the flesh, nor of the will
of man, but of God.
14 [a]And the Word [b]was made [c]flesh,
and dwelt among us, (and [d]we beheld his
glory, the glory as of the only begotten of
the Father,) [e]full of grace and truth.
15 ¶ [a]John bare witness of him, and
cried, saying, This was he of whom I
spake, [b]He that cometh after me is preferred before me: [c]for he was before me.
16 And of his [a]fulness have all we received, and grace for grace.
17 For [a]the law was given by Moses,
but [b]grace and [c]truth came by Jesus
Christ.
18 [a]No man hath seen God at any
time; [b]the only begotten Son, which is in
the bosom of the Father, he hath declared
him.

John's witness to himself

19 ¶ And this is [a]the record of John,
when the Jews sent priests and Levites
from Jerusalem to ask him, Who art thou?
20 And [a]he confessed, and denied not;
but confessed, I am not the Christ.
21 And they asked him, What then?

F *Lk 8:12* ◀▶ *Jn 3:14–18*
G *Lk 18:16–22* ◀▶ *Jn 3:3*
K *Jn 1:4* ◀▶ *Jn 1:29* **L** *Jn 1:7* ◀▶ *Jn 1:29*
W *Jn 1:9* ◀▶ *Jn 1:29*

1:15 John's declaration foreshadows the day when Jesus will be acknowledged by everyone as the true Messiah, the King of Israel (see Zep 3:15; Rev 1:7). Also note that John the Baptist's ministry would precede the earthly ministry of Jesus of Nazareth.

1:21 The people believed that Elijah would return

Art thou [a]Elias? And he saith, I am not. Art thou [b]that[1] prophet? And he answered, No.

22 Then said they unto him, Who art thou? that we may give an answer to them that sent us. What sayest thou of thyself ?

23 [a]He said, I *am* the voice of one crying in the wilderness, Make straight the way of the Lord, as [b]said the prophet Esaias.

24 And they which were sent were of the Pharisees.

25 And they asked him, and said unto him, Why baptizest thou then, if thou be not that Christ, nor Elias, neither that prophet?

26 John answered them, saying, [a]I baptize with water: [b]but there standeth one among you, whom ye know not;

27 [a]He it is, who coming after me is preferred before me, whose shoe's latchet I am not worthy to unloose.

28 These things were done [a]in Bethabara beyond Jordan, where John was baptizing.

John's witness to Jesus

B D K L W 29 ¶ The next day John seeth Jesus coming unto him, and saith, Behold [a]the Lamb of God, [b]which [1]taketh away the sin of the world.

30 [a]This is he of whom I said, After me cometh a man which is preferred before me: for he was before me.

31 And I knew him not: but that he should be made manifest to Israel, [a]therefore am I come baptizing with water.

B E J N 32 [a]And John bare record, saying, I saw the Spirit descending from heaven like a dove, and it abode upon him.

B *Lk 9:22* ◀▶ *Jn 1:33*
D *Lk 22:17–20* ◀▶ *Jn 3:14–17*
K *Jn 1:12* ◀▶ *Jn 3:14–18*
L *Jn 1:12* ◀▶ *Jn 3:14–17*
W *Jn 1:12* ◀▶ *Jn 3:14–18*
B *Lk 24:49* ◀▶ *Jn 3:34*
E *Lk 4:14* ◀▶ *Jn 3:34*
J *Lk 3:22* ◀▶ *Jn 14:16–17*
N *Lk 3:22* ◀▶ *Jn 3:5*

21 [a]Mal. 4:5 [b]Deut. 18:15 [1]Or, *a prophet?*
23 [a]Mat. 3:3 [b]Is. 40:3
26 [a]Mat. 3:11 [b]Mal. 3:1
27 [a]Acts 19:4
28 [a]Judg. 7:24; ch. 10:40
29 [a]Ex. 12:3; Is. 53:7; Acts 8:32; 1 Pet. 1:19; Rev. 5:6 [b]Is. 53:11; 1 Cor. 15:3; Gal. 1:4; Heb. 1:3 & 2:17 & 9:28; 1 Pet. 2:24 & 3:18; 1 John 2:2 & 3:5; Rev. 1:5 [1]Or, *beareth*
30 [a]ver. 15,27
31 [a]Mal. 3:1; Mat. 3:6; Luke 1:17,76, 77 & 3:3,4
32 [a]Mat. 3:16; Mark 1:10; ch. 5:32
33 [a]Mat. 3:11; Acts 2:4 & 10:44
36 [a]ver. 29
38 [1]Or, *abidest*
39 [1]*That was two hours before night*
41 [1]Or, *the Anointed*
42 [a]Mat. 16:18 [1]Or, *Peter*
44 [a]ch. 12:21
45 [a]ch. 21:2 [b]Gen. 3:15 & 49:10; Deut. 18:18; See Luke 24:27 [c]Is. 4:2 & 7:14 & 9:6; Mic. 5:2; Zech. 6:12; See more on Luke 24:27

33 And I knew him not: but he that sent me to baptize with water, the same said unto me, Upon whom thou shalt see the Spirit descending, and remaining on him, [a]the same is he which baptizeth with the Holy Ghost. B P

34 And I saw, and bare record that this is the Son of God.

Andrew and Peter follow Jesus

35 ¶ Again the next day after John stood, and two of his disciples;

36 And looking upon Jesus as he walked, he saith, [a]Behold the Lamb of God!

37 And the two disciples heard him speak, and they followed Jesus.

38 Then Jesus turned, and saw them following, and saith unto them, What seek ye? They said unto him, Rabbi, (which is to say, being interpreted, Master,) where [1]dwellest thou?

39 He saith unto them, Come and see. They came and saw where he dwelt, and abode with him that day: for it was [1]about the tenth hour.

40 One of the two which heard John *speak,* and followed him, was Andrew, Simon Peter's brother.

41 He first findeth his own brother Simon, and saith unto him, We have found the Messias, which is, being interpreted, [1]the Christ.

42 And he brought him to Jesus. And when Jesus beheld him, he said, Thou art Simon the son of Jona: [a]thou shalt be called Cephas, which is by interpretation, [1]A stone.

Philip and Nathanael follow Jesus

43 ¶ The day following Jesus would go forth into Galilee, and findeth Philip, and saith unto him, Follow me.

44 Now [a]Philip was of Bethsaida, the city of Andrew and Peter.

45 Philip findeth [a]Nathanael, and saith unto him, We have found him, of whom [b]Moses in the law, and the [c]prophets,

B *Jn 1:29* ◀▶ *Jn 2:19*
P *Lk 24:29* ◀▶ *Jn 7:37–39*

---

to announce the end times. John emphatically denied that he was Elijah and instead pointed people back to Jesus Christ as the place for their focus and attention.

1:29 John's bold declaration foreshadowed the glorious salvation won by Christ's sacrifice on the cross. As "the Lamb of God" (1:29), Jesus defeated sin and death forever and grants salvation to all who repent.

did write, Jesus [d]of Nazareth, the son of Joseph.

46 And Nathanael said unto him, [a]Can there any good thing come out of Nazareth? Philip saith unto him, Come and see.

47 Jesus saw Nathanael coming to him, and saith of him, Behold [a]an Israelite indeed, in whom is no guile!

48 Nathanael saith unto him, Whence knowest thou me? Jesus answered and said unto him, Before that Philip called thee, when thou wast under the fig tree, I saw thee.

I 49 Nathanael answered and saith unto him, Rabbi, [a]thou art the Son of God; thou art [b]the King of Israel.

50 Jesus answered and said unto him, Because I said unto thee, I saw thee under the fig tree, believest thou? thou shalt see greater things than these.

51 And he saith unto him, Verily, verily, I say unto you, [a]Hereafter ye shall see heaven open, and the angels of God ascending and descending upon the Son of man.

Water made into wine

2 AND THE third day there was a marriage in [a]Cana of Galilee; and the mother of Jesus was there:

2 And both Jesus was called, and his disciples, to the marriage.

3 And when they wanted wine, the mother of Jesus saith unto him, They have no wine.

4 Jesus saith unto her, [a]Woman, [b]what have I to do with thee? [c]mine hour is not yet come.

5 His mother saith unto the servants, Whatsoever he saith unto you, do *it*.

6 And there were set there six waterpots of stone, [a]after the manner of the purifying of the Jews, containing two or three firkins apiece.

7 Jesus saith unto them, Fill the waterpots with water. And they filled them up to the brim.

8 And he saith unto them, Draw out now, and bear unto the governor of the feast. And they bare *it*.

I *Lk 24:21* ◀ ▶ *Jn 12:13–15*

45 [d]Mat. 2:23; Luke 2:4
46 [a]ch. 7:41,42
47 [a]Ps. 32:2 & 73:1; ch. 8:39; Rom. 2:28 & 9:6
49 [a]Mat. 14:33 [b]Mat. 21:5; ch. 18:37
51 [a]Gen. 28:12; Mat. 4:11; Luke 2:9,13 & 22:43; Acts 1:10
2:1 [a]See Josh. 19:28
4 [a]ch. 19:26 [b]2 Sam. 16:10 [c]ch. 7:6
6 [a]Mark 7:3
9 [a]ch. 4:46
11 [a]ch. 1:14
12 [a]Mat. 12:46
13 [a]Ex. 12:14; Deut. 16:1; ch. 5:1
14 [a]Mat. 21:12; Mark 11:15; Luke 19:45
16 [a]Luke 2:49
17 [a]Ps. 69:9
18 [a]Mat. 12:38; ch. 6:30
19 [a]Mat. 26:61 & 27:40; Mark 14:58 & 15:29
21 [a]Col. 2:9; Heb. 8:2; 1 Cor. 3:16 & 6:19; 2 Cor. 6:16
22 [a]Luke 24:8

9 When the ruler of the feast had tasted [a]the water that was made wine, and knew not whence it was: (but the servants which drew the water knew;) the governor of the feast called the bridegroom,

10 And saith unto him, Every man at the beginning doth set forth good wine; and when men have well drunk, then that which is worse: *but* thou hast kept the good wine until now.

11 This beginning of miracles did Jesus in Cana of Galilee, [a]and manifested forth his glory; and his disciples believed on him.

12 ¶ After this he went down to Capernaum, he, and his mother, and [a]his brethren, and his disciples: and they continued there not many days.

The cleansing of the temple

13 ¶ [a]And the Jews' passover was at hand, and Jesus went up to Jerusalem,

14 [a]And found in the temple those that sold oxen and sheep and doves, and the changers of money sitting:

15 And when he had made a scourge of small cords, he drove them all out of the temple, and the sheep, and the oxen; and poured out the changers' money, and overthrew the tables;

16 And said unto them that sold doves, Take these things hence; make not [a]my Father's house an house of merchandise.

17 And his disciples remembered that it was written, [a]The zeal of thine house hath eaten me up.

18 ¶ Then answered the Jews and said unto him, [a]What sign showest thou unto us, seeing that thou doest these things?

19 Jesus answered and said unto them, [a]Destroy this temple, and in three days I will raise it up. B

20 Then said the Jews, Forty and six years was this temple in building, and wilt thou rear it up in three days?

21 But he spake [a]of the temple of his body.

22 When therefore he was risen from the dead, [a]his disciples remembered that he had said this unto them; and they be-

B *Jn 1:33* ◀ ▶ *Jn 3:14*

1:49 When Jesus called Nathanael (also known as Bartholomew) to be his disciple, Nathanael acknowledged Christ's right to rule from the throne of David.

lieved the scripture, and the word which
Jesus had said.
23 ¶ Now when he was in Jerusalem at
the passover, in the feast *day,* many believed in his name, when they saw the
miracles which he did.
E 24 But Jesus did not commit himself
unto them, because he knew all *men,*
25 And needed not that any should
testify of man: for [a]he knew what was in
man.

Nicodemus visits Jesus

3 THERE WAS a man of the Pharisees,
named Nicodemus, a ruler of the
Jews:
2 [a]The same came to Jesus by night,
and said unto him, Rabbi, we know that
thou art a teacher come from God: for
[b]no man can do these miracles that thou
doest, except [c]God be with him.
H 3 Jesus answered and said unto him,
R Verily, verily, I say unto thee, [a]Except a
G man be born [1]again, he cannot see the
O kingdom of God.
4 Nicodemus saith unto him, How can
a man be born when he is old? can he
enter the second time into his mother's
womb, and be born?
N 5 Jesus answered, Verily, verily, I say
G unto thee, [a]Except a man be born of wa-
O ter and *of* the Spirit, he cannot enter into
the kingdom of God.
6 That which is born of the flesh is
flesh; and that which is born of the Spirit
is spirit.
7 Marvel not that I said unto thee, Ye
must be born [1]again.
T 8 [a]The wind bloweth where it listeth,
N and thou hearest the sound thereof, but
canst not tell whence it cometh, and
whither it goeth: so is every one that is
born of the Spirit.

9 Nicodemus answered and said unto
him, [a]How can these things be?
10 Jesus answered and said unto him,
Art thou a master of Israel, and knowest
not these things?
11 [a]Verily, verily, I say unto thee, We
speak that we do know, and testify that
we have seen; and [b]ye receive not our
witness.
12 If I have told you earthly things,
and ye believe not, how shall ye believe,
if I tell you *of* heavenly things?
13 And [a]no man hath ascended up to
heaven, but he that came down from
heaven, *even* the Son of man which is
in heaven.
14 ¶ [a]And as Moses lifted up the ser- B
pent in the wilderness, even so [b]must the D
Son of man be lifted up: F
15 That whosoever believeth in him K
should not perish, but [a]have eternal L
life. W
16 ¶ [a]For God so loved the world, that H
he gave his only begotten Son, that whosoever believeth in him should not perish, but have everlasting life.
17 [a]For God sent not his Son into the
world to condemn the world; but that the
world through him might be saved.
18 ¶ [a]He that believeth on him is not A
condemned: but he that believeth not is N
condemned already, because he hath not O
believed in the name of the only begotten
Son of God.
19 And this is the condemnation, [a]that C
light is come into the world, and men
loved darkness rather than light, because
their deeds were evil.
20 For [a]every one that doeth evil hateth the light, neither cometh to the light,
lest his deeds should be [1]reproved.
21 But he that doeth truth cometh to

25 [a] 1 Sam. 16:7; 1 Chr. 28:9; Mat. 9:4; Mark 2:8; ch. 6:64 & 16:30; Acts 1:24; Rev. 2:23
3:2 [a] ch. 7:50 & 19:39 [b] ch. 9:16,33; Acts 2:22 [c] Acts 10:38
3 [a] ch. 1:13; Gal. 6:15; Tit. 3:5; Jas. 1:18; 1 Pet. 1:23; 1 John 3:9 [1] Or, *from above*
5 [a] Mark 16:16; Acts 2:38
7 [1] Or, *from above*
8 [a] Eccl. 11:5; 1 Cor. 2:11
9 [a] ch. 6:52,60
11 [a] Mat. 11:27; ch. 1:18 & 7:16 & 8:28 [b] ver. 32
13 [a] Prov. 30:4; ch. 6:33,38; Acts 2:34; 1 Cor. 15:47; Eph. 4:9
14 [a] Num. 21:9 [b] ch. 8:28 & 12:32
15 [a] ver. 36; ch. 6:47
16 [a] Rom. 5:8; 1 John 4:9
17 [a] Luke 9:56; ch. 5:45 & 8:15 & 12:47; 1 John 4:14
18 [a] ch. 5:24 & 6:40,47 & 20:31
19 [a] ch. 1:4,9-11 & 8:12
20 [a] Job 24:13; Eph. 5:13 [1] Or, *discovered*

E *Lk 16:15* ◀▶ *Jn 4:29*
H *Mt 12:28* ◀▶ *Jn 6:63*
R *Lk 1:17* ◀▶ *Jn 6:63*
G *Jn 1:12–13* ◀▶ *Jn 3:5*
O *Lk 18:16–17* ◀▶ *Jn 3:5*
N *Jn 1:32* ◀▶ *Jn 3:8*
G *Jn 3:3* ◀▶ *Jn 6:28–29*
O *Jn 3:3* ◀▶ *Jn 3:18–19*
T *Lk 17:34–36* ◀▶ *Ro 8:17–18*
N *Jn 3:5* ◀▶ *Jn 3:34*

B *Jn 2:19* ◀▶ *Jn 7:42*
D *Jn 1:29* ◀▶ *Jn 6:51–56*
F *Jn 1:12* ◀▶ *Jn 3:36*
K *Jn 1:29* ◀▶ *Jn 4:10*
L *Jn 1:29* ◀▶ *Jn 3:36*
W *Jn 1:29* ◀▶ *Jn 3:36*
H *Lk 23:30* ◀▶ *Jn 3:36*
A *Lk 11:23* ◀▶ *Ro 3:9–12*
N *Lk 20:18* ◀▶ *Jn 3:36*
O *Jn 3:5* ◀▶ *Jn 3:36*
C *Lk 19:10* ◀▶ *Jn 8:34*

3:8 This verse indicates the sovereignty of the Holy Spirit. He works as he pleases when he renews human hearts.

the light, that his deeds may be made manifest, that they are wrought in God.

22 ¶ After these things came Jesus and his disciples into the land of Judaea; and there he tarried with them, [a]and baptized.

23 ¶ And John also was baptizing in Aenon near to [a]Salim, because there was much water there: [b]and they came, and were baptized.

24 For [a]John was not yet cast into prison.

John's testimony to Jesus

25 ¶ Then there arose a question between *some* of John's disciples and the Jews about purifying.

26 And they came unto John, and said unto him, Rabbi, he that was with thee beyond Jordan, [a]to whom thou barest witness, behold, the same baptizeth, and all *men* come to him.

27 John answered and said, [a]A man can [1]receive nothing, except it be given him from heaven.

28 Ye yourselves bear me witness, that I said, [a]I am not the Christ, but [b]that I am sent before him.

29 [a]He that hath the bride is the bridegroom: but [b]the friend of the bridegroom, which standeth and heareth him, rejoiceth greatly because of the bridegroom's voice: this my joy therefore is fulfilled.

30 He must increase, but I *must* decrease.

31 [a]He that cometh from above [b]is above all: [c]he that is of the earth is earthly, and speaketh of the earth: [d]he that cometh from heaven is above all.

32 And [a]what he hath seen and heard, that he testifieth; and no man receiveth his testimony.

33 He that hath received his testimony [a]hath set to his seal that God is true.

B E G N T 34 [a]For he whom God hath sent speaketh the words of God: for God giveth not the Spirit [b]by measure *unto him.*

35 [a]The Father loveth the Son, and hath given all things into his hand.

B *Jn 1:32–33* ◀▶ *Jn 7:37–39*
E *Jn 1:32–33* ◀▶ *Jn 20:22*
G *Lk 24:49* ◀▶ *Jn 14:26*
N *Jn 3:8* ◀▶ *Jn 7:37–39*
T *Lk 21:14–15* ◀▶ *Jn 14:26*

22 [a]ch. 4:2
23 [a]1 Sam. 9:4 [b]Mat. 3:5,6
24 [a]Mat. 14:3
26 [a]ch. 1:7,15,27, 34
27 [a]1 Cor. 4:7; Heb. 5:4; Jas. 1:17 [1]Or, *take unto himself*
28 [a]ch. 1:20,27 [b]Mal. 3:1; Mark 1:2; Luke 1:17
29 [a]Mat. 22:2; 2 Cor. 11:2; Eph. 5:25,27; Rev. 21:9 [b]Sol. 5:1
31 [a]ver. 13; ch. 8:23 [b]Mat. 28:18; ch. 1:15,27; Rom. 9:5 [c]1 Cor. 15:47 [d]ch. 6:33; 1 Cor. 15:47; Eph. 1:21; Phil. 2:9
32 [a]ver. 11; ch. 8:26 & 15:15
33 [a]Rom. 3:4; 1 John 5:10
34 [a]ch. 7:16 [b]ch. 1:16
35 [a]Mat. 11:27 & 28:18; Luke 10:22; ch. 5:20,22 & 13:3 & 17:2; Heb. 2:8
36 [a]ver. 15,16; ch. 1:12 & 6:47; Rom. 1:17; 1 John 5:10
4:1 [a]ch. 3:22,26
5 [a]Gen. 33:19 & 48:22; Josh. 24:32
9 [a]2 Ki. 17:24; Luke 9:52,53; Acts 10:28
10 [a]Is. 12:3 & 44:3; Jer. 2:13; Zech. 13:1 & 14:8

36 [a]He that believeth on the Son hath everlasting life: and he that believeth not the Son shall not see life; but the wrath of God abideth on him. F H L N O W

The woman of Samaria

4 WHEN THEREFORE the Lord knew how the Pharisees had heard that Jesus made and [a]baptized more disciples than John,

2 (Though Jesus himself baptized not, but his disciples,)

3 He left Judaea, and departed again into Galilee.

4 And he must needs go through Samaria.

5 Then cometh he to a city of Samaria, which is called Sychar, near to the parcel of ground [a]that Jacob gave to his son Joseph.

6 Now Jacob's well was there. Jesus therefore, being wearied with *his* journey, sat thus on the well: *and* it was about the sixth hour.

7 There cometh a woman of Samaria to draw water: Jesus saith unto her, Give me to drink.

8 (For his disciples were gone away unto the city to buy meat.)

9 Then saith the woman of Samaria unto him, How is it that thou, being a Jew, askest drink of me, which am a woman of Samaria? for [a]the Jews have no dealings with the Samaritans.

10 Jesus answered and said unto her, If thou knewest the gift of God, and who it is that saith to thee, Give me to drink; thou wouldest have asked of him, and he would have given thee [a]living water. A K L

11 The woman saith unto him, Sir, thou hast nothing to draw with, and the well is deep: from whence then hast thou that living water?

12 Art thou greater than our father Jacob, which gave us the well, and drank thereof himself, and his children, and his cattle?

F *Jn 3:14–18* ◀▶ *Jn 5:24*
H *Jn 3:16–19* ◀▶ *Jn 5:29*
L *Jn 3:14–17* ◀▶ *Jn 4:10*
N *Jn 3:18–20* ◀▶ *Jn 8:24*
O *Jn 3:18–19* ◀▶ *Jn 6:53*
W *Jn 3:14–18* ◀▶ *Jn 4:42*
A *Lk 11:9–13* ◀▶ *Ac 4:29–31*
K *Jn 3:14–18* ◀▶ *Jn 4:13–14*
L *Jn 3:36* ◀▶ *Jn 4:42*

K 13 Jesus answered and said unto her, Whosoever drinketh of this water shall thirst again:

14 But [a]whosoever drinketh of the water that I shall give him shall never thirst; but the water that I shall give him [b]shall be in him a well of water springing up into everlasting life.

15 [a]The woman saith unto him, Sir, give me this water, that I thirst not, neither come hither to draw.

16 Jesus saith unto her, Go, call thy husband, and come hither.

17 The woman answered and said, I have no husband. Jesus said unto her, Thou hast well said, I have no husband:

18 For thou hast had five husbands; and he whom thou now hast is not thy husband: in that saidst thou truly.

19 The woman saith unto him, Sir, [a]I perceive that thou art a prophet.

20 Our fathers worshipped in [a]this mountain; and ye say, that in [b]Jerusalem is the place where men ought to worship.

21 Jesus saith unto her, Woman, believe me, the hour cometh, [a]when ye shall neither in this mountain, nor yet at Jerusalem, worship the Father.

22 Ye worship [a]ye know not what: we know what we worship: for [b]salvation is of the Jews.

L 23 But the hour cometh, and now is,
W when the true worshippers shall worship
S the Father in [a]spirit [b]and in truth: for the Father seeketh such to worship him.

24 [a]God *is* a Spirit: and they that worship him must worship *him* in spirit and in truth.

25 The woman saith unto him, I know that Messias cometh, which is called Christ: when he is come, [a]he will tell us all things.

26 Jesus saith unto her, [a]I that speak unto thee am *he.*

27 ¶ And upon this came his disciples, and marvelled that he talked with the woman: yet no man said, What seekest thou? or, Why talkest thou with her?

28 The woman then left her waterpot, and went her way into the city, and saith to the men,

29 Come, see a man, [a]which told me all things that ever I did: is not this the Christ? E

30 Then they went out of the city, and came unto him.

31 ¶ In the mean while his disciples prayed him, saying, Master, eat.

32 But he said unto them, I have meat to eat that ye know not of.

33 Therefore said the disciples one to another, Hath any man brought him *aught* to eat?

34 Jesus saith unto them, [a]My meat is to do the will of him that sent me, and to finish his work.

35 Say not ye, There are yet four months, and *then* cometh harvest? behold, I say unto you, Lift up your eyes, and look on the fields; [a]for they are white already to harvest.

36 [a]And he that reapeth receiveth wages, and gathereth fruit unto life eternal: that both he that soweth and he that reapeth may rejoice together.

37 And herein is that saying true, One soweth, and another reapeth.

38 I sent you to reap that whereon ye bestowed no labour: other men laboured, and ye are entered into their labours.

The conversion of Samaritans

39 ¶ And many of the Samaritans of that city believed on him [a]for the saying of the woman, which testified, He told me all that ever I did.

40 So when the Samaritans were come unto him, they besought him that he would tarry with them: and he abode there two days.

41 And many more believed because of his own word;

42 And said unto the woman, Now we K
believe, not because of thy saying: for L
[a]we have heard *him* ourselves, and know W
that this is indeed the Christ, the Saviour of the world.

43 ¶ Now after two days he departed thence, and went into Galilee.

44 For [a]Jesus himself testified, that a prophet hath no honour in his own country.

45 Then when he was come into Gali-

14 [a]ch. 6:35,58 [b]ch. 7:38
15 [a]ch. 6:34 & 17:2,3; Rom. 6:23; 1 John 5:20
19 [a]Luke 7:16 & 24:19; ch. 6:14
20 [a]Judg. 9:7 [b]Deut. 12:5,11; 1 Ki. 9:3; 2 Chr. 7:12
21 [a]Mal. 1:11; 1 Tim. 2:8
22 [a]2 Ki. 17:29 [b]Is. 2:3; Luke 24:47; Rom. 9:4,5
23 [a]Phil. 3:3 [b]ch. 1:17
24 [a]2 Cor. 3:17
25 [a]ver. 29,39
26 [a]Mat. 26:63,64; Mark 14:61,62
29 [a]ver. 25
34 [a]Job 23:12; ch. 6:38 & 17:4 & 19:30
35 [a]Mat. 9:37; Luke 10:2
36 [a]Dan. 12:3
39 [a]ver. 29
42 [a]ch. 17:8; 1 John 4:14
44 [a]Mat. 13:57

K *Jn 4:10* ◀ ▶ *Jn 4:42*
L *Lk 21:14–15* ◀ ▶ *Jn 16:13*
W *Lk 24:49* ◀ ▶ *Jn 6:63*
S *Lk 20:10* ◀ ▶ *Jn 5:14*

E *Jn 2:24–25* ◀ ▶ *Jn 6:64*
K *Jn 4:13–14* ◀ ▶ *Jn 5:24*
L *Jn 4:10* ◀ ▶ *Jn 5:24*
W *Jn 3:36* ◀ ▶ *Jn 5:24*

lee, the Galilaeans received him, [a]having seen all the things that he did at Jerusalem at the feast: [b]for they also went unto the feast.

The healing of the nobleman's son

E 46 So Jesus came again into Cana of Galilee, [a]where he made the water wine. And there was a certain ʹnobleman, whose son was sick at Capernaum.

47 When he heard that Jesus was come out of Judaea into Galilee, he went unto him, and besought him that he would come down, and heal his son: for he was at the point of death.

48 Then said Jesus unto him, [a]Except ye see signs and wonders, ye will not believe.

49 The nobleman saith unto him, Sir, come down ere my child die.

50 Jesus saith unto him, Go thy way; thy son liveth. And the man believed the word that Jesus had spoken unto him, and he went his way.

51 And as he was now going down, his servants met him, and told *him,* saying, Thy son liveth.

52 Then inquired he of them the hour when he began to amend. And they said unto him, Yesterday at the seventh hour the fever left him.

53 So the father knew that *it was* at the same hour, in the which Jesus said unto him, Thy son liveth: and himself believed, and his whole house.

54 This *is* again the second miracle *that* Jesus did, when he was come out of Judaea into Galilee.

Jesus heals on the Sabbath

E 5 AFTER [a]THIS there was a feast of the Jews; and Jesus went up to Jerusalem.

2 Now there is at Jerusalem [a]by the sheep ʹ*market* a pool, which is called in the Hebrew tongue Bethesda, having five porches.

3 In these lay a great multitude of impotent folk, of blind, halt, withered, waiting for the moving of the water.

4 For an angel went down at a certain season into the pool, and troubled the water: whosoever then first after the troubling of the water stepped in was made whole of whatsoever disease he had.

5 And a certain man was there, which had an infirmity thirty and eight years.

6 When Jesus saw him lie, and knew that he had been now a long time *in that case,* he saith unto him, Wilt thou be made whole?

7 The impotent man answered him, Sir, I have no man, when the water is troubled, to put me into the pool: but while I am coming, another steppeth down before me.

8 Jesus saith unto him, [a]Rise, take up thy bed, and walk.

9 And immediately the man was made whole, and took up his bed, and walked: and [a]on the same day was the sabbath.

10 ¶ The Jews therefore said unto him that was cured, It is the sabbath day: [a]it is not lawful for thee to carry *thy* bed.

11 He answered them, He that made me whole, the same said unto me, Take up thy bed, and walk.

12 Then asked they him, What man is that which said unto thee, Take up thy bed, and walk?

13 And he that was healed wist not who it was: for Jesus had conveyed himself away, ʹa multitude being in *that* place.

14 Afterward Jesus findeth him in the temple, and said unto him, Behold, thou art made whole: [a]sin no more, lest a worse thing come unto thee. S D

15 The man departed, and told the Jews that it was Jesus, which had made him whole.

16 And therefore did the Jews persecute Jesus, and sought to slay him, because he had done these things on the sabbath day.

17 ¶ But Jesus answered them, [a]My Father worketh hitherto, and I work.

18 Therefore the Jews [a]sought the more to kill him, because he not only had broken the sabbath, but said also that God was his Father, [b]making himself equal with God.

The Son's witness to the Father

19 Then answered Jesus and said unto them, Verily, verily, I say unto you, [a]The Son can do nothing of himself, but what

45 [a] ch. 2:23 & 3:2 [b] Deut. 16:16
46 [a] ch. 2:1,11 ʹOr, *courtier,* or, *ruler*
48 [a] 1 Cor. 1:22
5:1 [a] Lev. 23:2; Deut. 16:1; ch. 2:13
2 [a] Neh. 3:1 & 12:39 ʹOr, *gate*
8 [a] Mat. 9:6; Mark 2:11; Luke 5:24
9 [a] ch. 9:14
10 [a] Ex. 20:10; Neh. 13:19; Jer. 17:21; Mat. 12:2; Mark 2:24; Luke 6:2
13 ʹOr, *from the multitude that was*
14 [a] Mat. 12:45; ch. 8:11
17 [a] ch. 9:4 & 14:10
18 [a] ch. 7:19 [b] ch. 10:30; Phil. 2:6
19 [a] ver. 30; ch. 8:28 & 9:4

E *Lk 22:50–51* ◄ ► *Jn 5:1–16*
E *Jn 4:46–54* ◄ ► *Jn 6:2*
S *Jn 4:23–24* ◄ ► *Jn 5:29*
D *Lk 13:16* ◄ ► *Jn 9:1–3*

he seeth the Father do: for what things soever he doeth, these also doeth the Son likewise.

20 For [a]the Father loveth the Son, and showeth him all things that himself doeth: and he will show him greater works than these, that ye may marvel.

21 For as the Father raiseth up the dead, and quickeneth *them;* [a]even so the Son quickeneth whom he will.

22 For the Father judgeth no man, but [a]hath committed all judgment unto the Son:

23 That all *men* should honour the Son, even as they honour the Father. [a]He that honoureth not the Son honoureth not the Father which hath sent him.

F 24 Verily, verily, I say unto you, [a]He
K that heareth my word, and believeth on
L him that sent me, hath everlasting life,
W and shall not come into condemnation;
[b]but is passed from death unto life.

F 25 Verily, verily, I say unto you, The
W hour is coming, and now is, when [a]the
dead shall hear the voice of the Son of
God: and they that hear shall live.

26 For as the Father hath life in himself; so hath he given to the Son to have life in himself;

27 And [a]hath given him authority to execute judgment also, [b]because he is the Son of man.

28 Marvel not at this: for the hour is coming, in the which all that are in the graves shall hear his voice,

H 29 [a]And shall come forth; [b]they that
S have done good, unto the resurrection of
life; and they that have done evil, unto the resurrection of damnation.

F *Jn 3:36* ◀▶ *Jn 6:28–29*
K *Jn 4:42* ◀▶ *Jn 6:27*
L *Jn 4:42* ◀▶ *Jn 6:35*
W *Jn 4:42* ◀▶ *Jn 6:35*
F *Lk 20:34–38* ◀▶ *Jn 6:39–40*
W *Da 12:2* ◀▶ *Ac 24:15*
H *Jn 3:36* ◀▶ *Jn 12:48*
S *Jn 5:14* ◀▶ *Jn 8:11–12*

The Father's witness to the Son

30 [a]I can of mine own self do nothing: as I hear, I judge: and my judgment is just; because [b]I seek not mine own will, but the will of the Father which hath sent me.

31 [a]If I bear witness of myself, my witness is not true.

32 ¶ [a]There is another that beareth witness of me; and I know that the witness which he witnesseth of me is true.

33 Ye sent unto John, [a]and he bare witness unto the truth.

34 But I receive not testimony from man: but these things I say, that ye might be saved.

35 He was a burning and [a]a shining light: and [b]ye were willing for a season to rejoice in his light.

36 ¶ But [a]I have greater witness than *that* of John: for [b]the works which the Father hath given me to finish, the same works that I do, bear witness of me, that the Father hath sent me.

37 And the Father himself, which hath sent me, [a]hath borne witness of me. Ye have neither heard his voice at any time, [b]nor seen his shape.

38 And ye have not his word abiding in you: for whom he hath sent, him ye believe not.

39 ¶ [a]Search the scriptures; for in them ye think ye have eternal life: and [b]they are they which testify of me.

40 [a]And ye will not come to me, that ye might have life.

41 [a]I receive not honour from men.

42 But I know you, that ye have not the love of God in you.

43 I am come in my Father's name, and ye receive me not: if another shall come in his own name, him ye will receive.

20 [a]Mat. 3:17; ch. 3:35
21 [a]Luke 7:14 & 8:54; ch. 11:25
22 [a]Mat. 11:27 & 28:18; ch. 3:35 & 17:2; Acts 17:31; 1 Pet. 4:5
23 [a]1 John 2:23
24 [a]ch. 3:16,18 & 6:40,47 & 8:51 [b]1 John 3:14
25 [a]Eph. 2:1,5 & 5:14; Col 2:13
27 [a]Acts 10:42 & 17:31 [b]Dan. 7:13
29 [a]Is. 26:19; 1 Cor. 15:52 [b]Dan. 12:2; Mat. 25:32, 33,46
30 [a]ver. 19 [b]Mat. 26:39; ch. 4:34 & 6:38
31 [a]ch. 8:14; Rev. 3:14
32 [a]Mat. 3:17 & 17:5; ch. 8:18; 1 John 5:6
33 [a]ch. 1:15,19, 27,32
35 [a]2 Pet. 1:19 [b]Mat. 13:20; Mark 6:20
36 [a]1 John 5:9 [b]ch. 3:2 & 10:25 & 15:24
37 [a]Mat. 3:17 & 17:5; ch. 6:27 & 8:18 [b]Deut. 4:12; ch. 1:18; 1 Tim. 1:17; 1 John 4:12
39 [a]ver. 46; Is. 8:20 & 34:16; Luke 16:29; Acts 17:11 [b]Deut. 18:15,18; Luke 24:27
40 [a]ch. 1:11 & 3:19
41 [a]ver. 34; 1 Thes. 2:6

5:25–29 This passage has been interpreted in different ways. Some feel that it refers to the future resurrection of the dead to judgment. Others believe Jesus' words refer to the spiritually dead who hear him, repent and receive life from him. Still others believe that this passage is a prediction of Jesus' descent into hell following his death on the cross. Those who subscribe to this belief suggest that this prophecy of resurrection also foreshadowed the day of Jesus' resurrection when many of the OT saints rose from the dead (see Mt 27:52–53) proving the truth of Christ's power over sin and the grave.

5:43 Jesus declared that, although he came in his "Father's name," many rejected him while "another shall come in his own name" (the antichrist) and be willingly received. This prophecy will find its tragic fulfillment during the tribulation when many will be deceived and accept the claim of the antichrist as their Messiah (see Rev 13:3–8).

44 [a]How can ye believe, which receive honour one of another, and seek not [b]the honour that *cometh* from God only?

45 Do not think that I will accuse you to the Father: [a]there is *one* that accuseth you, *even* Moses, in whom ye trust.

46 For had ye believed Moses, ye would have believed me: [a]for he wrote of me.

47 But if ye believe not his writings, how shall ye believe my words?

The five thousand fed

6

AFTER [a]THESE things Jesus went over the sea of Galilee, which is *the sea* of Tiberias.

E 2 And a great multitude followed him, because they saw his miracles which he did on them that were diseased.

3 And Jesus went up into a mountain, and there he sat with his disciples.

4 [a]And the passover, a feast of the Jews, was nigh.

F 5 ¶ [a]When Jesus then lifted up *his* eyes, and saw a great company come unto him, he saith unto Philip, Whence shall we buy bread, that these may eat?

6 And this he said to prove him: for he himself knew what he would do.

7 Philip answered him, [a]Two hundred pennyworth of bread is not sufficient for them, that every one of them may take a little.

8 One of his disciples, Andrew, Simon Peter's brother, saith unto him,

9 There is a lad here, which hath five barley loaves, and two small fishes: [a]but what are they among so many?

10 And Jesus said, Make the men sit down. Now there was much grass in the place. So the men sat down, in number about five thousand.

11 And Jesus took the loaves; and when he had given thanks, he distributed to the disciples, and the disciples to them that were set down; and likewise of the fishes as much as they would.

12 When they were filled, he said unto his disciples, Gather up the fragments that remain, that nothing be lost.

13 Therefore they gathered *them* together, and filled twelve baskets with the fragments of the five barley loaves, which remained over and above unto them that had eaten.

14 Then those men, when they had seen the miracle that Jesus did, said, This is of a truth [a]that prophet that should come into the world.

Jesus walks on the sea

15 ¶ When Jesus therefore perceived that they would come and take him by force, to make him a king, he departed again into a mountain himself alone.

16 [a]And when even was *now* come, his disciples went down unto the sea,

17 And entered into a ship, and went over the sea toward Capernaum. And it was now dark, and Jesus was not come to them.

18 And the sea arose by reason of a great wind that blew.

19 So when they had rowed about five and twenty or thirty furlongs, they see Jesus walking on the sea, and drawing nigh unto the ship: and they were afraid.

20 But he saith unto them, It is I; be not afraid.

21 Then they willingly received him into the ship: and immediately the ship was at the land whither they went.

Jesus the bread of life

22 ¶ The day following, when the people which stood on the other side of the sea saw that there was none other boat there, save that one whereinto his disciples were entered, and that Jesus went not with his disciples into the boat, but *that* his disciples were gone away alone;

23 (Howbeit there came other boats from Tiberias nigh unto the place where they did eat bread, after that the Lord had given thanks:)

24 When the people therefore saw that Jesus was not there, neither his disciples, they also took shipping, and came to Capernaum, seeking for Jesus.

25 And when they had found him on the other side of the sea, they said unto him, Rabbi, when camest thou hither?

26 Jesus answered them and said, Verily, verily, I say unto you, Ye seek me, not because ye saw the miracles, but because ye did eat of the loaves, and were filled.

27 [1]Labour not for the meat which K

44 [a]ch. 12:43 [b]Rom. 2:29
45 [a]Rom. 2:12
46 [a]Gen. 3:15 & 12:3 & 18:18 & 22:18 & 49:10; Deut. 18:15,18; ch. 1:45; Acts 26:22
6:1 [a]Mat. 14:15; Mark 6:35; Luke 9:10,12
4 [a]Lev. 23:5,7; Deut. 16:1; ch. 2:13 & 5:1
5 [a]Mat. 14:14; Mark 6:35; Luke 9:12
7 [a]See Num. 11:21,22
9 [a]2 Ki. 4:43
14 [a]Gen. 49:10; Deut. 18:15,18; Mat. 11:3; ch. 1:21 & 4:19,25 & 7:40
16 [a]Mat. 14:23; Mark 6:47
27 [1]Or, *Work not*

E *Jn 5:1–16* ◀ ▶ *Jn 7:23*
F *Lk 22:35* ◀ ▶ *Jn 6:31–32*
K *Jn 5:24* ◀ ▶ *Jn 6:33–35*

The Resurrection of the Body

THE HISTORICAL TRUTH about the resurrection of Jesus Christ is the essential bedrock upon which the Christian faith stands (see 1Co 15:14, 20–23). The Gospel accounts of the life, death and resurrection of Jesus were written and distributed within thirty-five years of the occurrence of these events. Those who witnessed Jesus' appearances after his resurrection were alive to verify the facts in these widely distributed documents. Secular historians also record events that prove the historicity of Jesus' death and resurrection.

Despite Christ's victory over the grave, some people refuse to believe in a final resurrection for all human beings. Those who have rejected God seek a false comfort in believing that they will never have to face God as their judge. They believe that all life ceases after death. Yet the German philosopher and poet Goethe said, "I am fully convinced that our spirit is a being of a nature quite indestructible, and its activity continues from eternity to eternity."

The Bible clearly teaches that there is life after death. Our bodies will undergo a transformation and a transition to prepare us for eternity. The body will die, but the soul and spirit will live on.

The Two Resurrections

All people, saved and unsaved, will rise again after death. However, since the Bible describes two different resurrections, there is a great difference between the destiny of these two groups. The first resurrection leads to life whereas the second brings about spiritual death (see Jn 5:28–29; Rev 20:6).

The first resurrection involves all those who repent of their sin and accept the pardon of God. The Bible uses the word "firstfruits" to describe this first resurrection. In Israel, the Feast of Firstfruits happened in the spring of the year to celebrate the first gathering of the harvest (see Ex 23:16–19). As the Jews brought tokens of the coming harvest to God, they acknowledged that he was the provider of the harvest. In the NT, this word "firstfruits" was initially applied to Jesus Christ, who became "the firstfruits of them that slept" (1Co 15:20). This term was thereafter applied to the resurrected saints as a token of the great harvest when Jesus, the Lord of the harvest, will come to gather the saints to meet him in the air (see 1Co 15:23; 1Th 4:14–17; Rev 14:4). These raptured believers are the firstfruits of the first resurrection, "the resurrection of life" (Jn 5:29). All who participate in this first resurrection to life are saved and will enjoy life in heaven forever.

This first resurrection has several different stages. Some of the OT saints participated in the first stage of this first resurrection two thousand years ago when they were called up from the grave at Christ's resurrection and appeared to many in Jerusalem (see Mt 27:52–53). With their resurrection, the Lord proved forever his claim to be the Messiah and affirmed his power over death, providing a resurrection to eternal life for all who would receive his offer of salvation.

Also included in this first resurrection is the future rapture of believers (see 1Th 4:14–17). (For further information on this, see the article on "The Rapture" on p. 1370.) After this rapture a group of Jewish and Gentile tribulation saints will also be resurrected when Christ returns at Armageddon (see study note at Rev 6:9–11). Whether an OT saint, a church-age believer or a tribulation convert, those who participate in this first resurrection will be blessed and "be priests of God and of Christ, and shall reign with him a thousand years" (Rev 20:6).

The second resurrection involves those who reject God's pardon and die in their sin. There will be an interval of one thousand years between the believers' resurrection to spiritual life in heaven and the final resurrection of the wicked dead to spiritual death in hell (see 20:4–11). The wicked will rise in that last day to stand in their resurrected bodies before God's great white throne (see 20:11). All those who participate in this tragic second resurrection will experience spiritual death for eternity, for "this is the second death" (20:14).

Whether the wicked have died on land or sea, the Bible declares that the wicked dead will be resurrected to stand before God and face judgment (see 20:13). All wicked sinners who have waited in torment in *hades* will finally be judged after the Millennium. Even *hades* itself will be "cast into the lake of fire" (20:14). Those who reject God's mercy will possess both their soul and body in "everlasting punishment" (Mt 25:46) in hell forever (see Mt 10:28). For further information, see the article on "The Great White Throne Judgment" on p. 1484.

Some believe these judgments of the saved and the sinners will occur at the same moment. Because of Daniel's prophecy that "many of them that sleep in the dust of the earth shall awake, some to everlasting life, and some to shame and everlasting contempt" (Da 12:2), these scholars contend that there will only be one final judgment of both the evil and the righteous. However, a careful reading of this passage reveals that Daniel is not declaring that the two resurrections will take place simultaneously. Daniel's words simply confirm the fact that two different groups will be resurrected and judged, and each will receive eternal consequences.

Our Resurrection Bodies

The clearest indication we have of our resurrection body was shown in the resurrection body of Jesus Christ. Because Jesus understood the human tendency to view bodies from the afterlife as some eerie, ghostly existence (see Lk 24:36–43), Jesus proved the reality of our future body by appearing to his disciples and his followers on many occasions after he rose from the grave. Scripture promises that our resurrection bodies will be like his body (see Php 3:21).

When Jesus rose from the dead and appeared to his disciples, his resurrected body was similar to, yet different from, his mortal body before his death on the cross. He still had flesh and bones, and his hands and feet carried the scars from the cross (see Lk 24:39). Jesus invited Thomas to put his finger on the scars in Jesus' hands and his hand on the scar on Jesus' side (see Jn 20:27). Jesus even ate and drank with his disciples after his resurrection (see Jn 21:12–14). Yet there was an indefinable quality about Christ's resurrected appearance that was different. His body was changed enough for Mary and his disciples to fail to recognize him at first glance (see 21:4). However, after being with him for a little while or hearing his voice or observing his actions, those who had known him recognized him.

As Jesus' body was changed, so shall ours be. Since our bodies will be like his, we shall have bodies of flesh and bone that are incorruptible, will never wear out, decay or die. Our resurrected bodies will never again experience pain. And our real, spiritual bodies will be able to transcend space and time. Jesus was able to enter locked rooms and disappear quickly from one place only to reappear in another (see Mt 28:10; Mk 16:11–12; Lk 24:31). In our resurrected bodies we too will have this supernatural control over matter.

Our Resurrection Mind

In the same way that our resurrected bodies will resemble Christ's, our minds and emotions and personalities will be affected by this new reality too. The Bible clearly shows that after his resurrection Jesus retained his love for his disciples, his concern for the welfare of his followers and an interest in their feelings. In our resurrection bodies we, too, will still feel the same love for our friends and families. We will experience a rich emotional life full of joy, peace, love and thanksgiving. Though Jesus said that marriage would not exist in heaven (see Mt 22:30), the spiritual essence of a pure, holy love will find its highest expression in an eternal cherishing of our loved ones.

Many assume that once we obtain our resurrection bodies and enter heaven we will automatically become bland, neutral saints without distinctive features of personality. Not so! In eternity we shall manifest the perfected form of the character we are building today. Christ will remove the sin in our lives, but we will still have those characteristics that make us unique as individuals. This diversity of personalities will provide one of the great joys of our future life and will make us recognizable to one another (see Mt 17:2–4).

Other believers have expressed the fear that once they have acquired their resurrection bodies and are residents of heaven they will not be able to enjoy the activities that they enjoy on earth. They are afraid that they will lose all knowledge and awareness of earthly relationships and interests. Why should we? Heaven is a place we will enjoy. Our creative talents will most probably flourish, and we will know and understand the vast secrets of our universe. We will be able to satisfy our curiosity about creation, history or science, and we will finally understand why certain things happened as they did. We will have greater vision and awareness because our current barriers of time and space will no longer limit us. In heaven we shall use all the faculties and gifts which our Creator has given us. And we shall do so to give him glory (see Rev 7:12).

perisheth, but [a]for that meat which endureth unto everlasting life, which the
Son of man shall give unto you: [b]for him
hath God the Father sealed.
F 28 Then said they unto him, What
G shall we do, that we might work the
works of God?
29 Jesus answered and said unto them,
[a]This is the work of God, that ye believe
on him whom he hath sent.
30 They said therefore unto him,
[a]What sign showest thou then, that we
may see, and believe thee? what dost
thou work?
F 31 [a]Our fathers did eat manna in the
desert; as it is written, [b]He gave them
bread from heaven to eat.
32 Then Jesus said unto them, Verily,
verily, I say unto you, Moses gave you not
that bread from heaven; but my Father
giveth you the true bread from heaven.
K 33 For the bread of God is he which
cometh down from heaven, and giveth
life unto the world.
34 [a]Then said they unto him, Lord,
evermore give us this bread.
F 35 And Jesus said unto them, [a]I am the
L bread of life: [b]he that cometh to me shall
W never hunger; and he that believeth on
me shall never thirst.
36 [a]But I said unto you, That ye also
have seen me, and believe not.
L 37 [a]All that the Father giveth me shall
W come to me; and [b]him that cometh to me
I will in no wise cast out.
38 For I came down from heaven, [a]not
to do mine own will, [b]but the will of him
that sent me.
F 39 And this is the Father's will which
K hath sent me, [a]that of all which he hath

F *Jn 5:24* ◀ ▶ *Jn 6:35* **G** *Jn 3:5* ◀ ▶ *Jn 9:39*
F *Jn 6:5–14* ◀ ▶ *Jn 21:8–13*
K *Jn 6:27* ◀ ▶ *Jn 6:39–40*
F *Jn 6:28–29* ◀ ▶ *Jn 6:40*
L *Jn 5:24* ◀ ▶ *Jn 6:37*
W *Jn 5:24* ◀ ▶ *Jn 6:37*
L *Jn 6:35* ◀ ▶ *Jn 6:40*
W *Jn 6:35* ◀ ▶ *Jn 6:40*
F *Jn 5:25–29* ◀ ▶ *Jn 6:44*
K *Jn 6:33–35* ◀ ▶ *Jn 6:50–51*

27 [a]ch. 4:14 [b]Mat. 3:17 & 17:5; Mark 1:11 & 9:7; Luke 3:22 & 9:35; ch. 5:37; Acts 2:22; 2 Pet. 1:17
29 [a]1 John 3:23
30 [a]Mat. 12:38 & 16:1; Mark 8:11; 1 Cor. 1:22
31 [a]Ex. 16:15; Num. 11:7; Neh. 9:15; 1 Cor. 10:3 [b]Ps. 78:24
34 [a]See ch. 4:15
35 [a]ver. 48,58 [b]ch. 4:14 & 7:37
36 [a]ver. 26,64
37 [a]ver. 45 [b]Mat. 24:24; ch. 10:28, 29; 2 Tim. 2:19; 1 John 2:19
38 [a]Mat. 26:39; ch. 5:30 [b]ch. 4:34
39 [a]ch. 10:28 & 17:12 & 18:9
40 [a]ver. 27,47,54; ch. 3:15,16 & 4:14
42 [a]Mat. 13:55; Mark 6:3; Luke 4:22
44 [a]ver. 65; Sol. 1:4
45 [a]Is. 54:13; Jer. 31:34; Mic. 4:2; Heb. 8:10 [b]ver. 37
46 [a]ch. 1:18 [b]Mat. 11:27; Luke 10:22; ch. 7:29
47 [a]ch. 3:16,18
48 [a]ver. 33,35
49 [a]ver. 31
50 [a]ver. 51,58
51 [a]ch. 3:13 [b]Heb. 10:5
52 [a]ch. 7:43 & 9:16 & 10:19

given me I should lose nothing, but
should raise it up again at the last day.
40 And this is the will of him that sent F
me, [a]that every one which seeth the Son, L
and believeth on him, may have everlast- W
ing life: and I will raise him up at the last
day.
41 The Jews then murmured at him,
because he said, I am the bread which
came down from heaven.
42 And they said, [a]Is not this Jesus,
the son of Joseph, whose father and
mother we know? how is it then that he
saith, I came down from heaven?
43 Jesus therefore answered and said
unto them, Murmur not among yourselves.
44 [a]No man can come to me, except F
the Father which hath sent me draw him:
and I will raise him up at the last day.
45 [a]It is written in the prophets, And
they shall be all taught of God. [b]Every
man therefore that hath heard, and hath
learned of the Father, cometh unto me.
46 [a]Not that any man hath seen the
Father, [b]save he which is of God, he hath
seen the Father.
47 Verily, verily, I say unto you, [a]He F
that believeth on me hath everlasting life. L
48 [a]I am that bread of life. W
49 [a]Your fathers did eat manna in the
wilderness, and are dead.
50 [a]This is the bread which cometh K
down from heaven, that a man may eat
thereof, and not die.
51 I am the living bread [a]which came D
down from heaven: if any man eat of this
bread, he shall live for ever: and [b]the
bread that I will give is my flesh, which I
will give for the life of the world.
52 The Jews therefore [a]strove among

F *Jn 6:35* ◀ ▶ *Jn 6:47*
L *Jn 6:37* ◀ ▶ *Jn 6:47*
W *Jn 6:37* ◀ ▶ *Jn 6:47*
F *Jn 6:39–40* ◀ ▶ *Jn 6:54*
F *Jn 6:40* ◀ ▶ *Jn 7:38*
L *Jn 6:40* ◀ ▶ *Jn 7:37*
W *Jn 6:40* ◀ ▶ *Jn 7:37*
K *Jn 6:39–40* ◀ ▶ *Jn 6:54–58*
D *Jn 3:14–17* ◀ ▶ *Jn 10:11*

6:39–40 Jesus' words reveal that those who trust in him can trust in their salvation when they die. If we are among those who "believeth on him" (6:40), we have confidence that we will "have everlasting life" (6:40) and participate in the resurrection in the last day.

6:44 This prophecy confirms humanity's response to God's sovereign grace. Those who respond positively to God are promised resurrection with him "at the last day."

themselves, saying, How can this man give us *his* flesh to eat?

O 53 Then Jesus said unto them, Verily, verily, I say unto you, Except [a]ye eat the flesh of the Son of man, and drink his blood, ye have no life in you.

F K 54 [a]Whoso eateth my flesh, and drinketh my blood, hath eternal life; and I will raise him up at the last day.

55 For my flesh is meat indeed, and my blood is drink indeed.

56 He that eateth my flesh, and drinketh my blood, [a]dwelleth in me, and I in him.

57 As the living Father hath sent me, and I live by the Father: so he that eateth me, even he shall live by me.

58 [a]This is that bread which came down from heaven: not as your fathers did eat manna, and are dead: he that eateth of this bread shall live for ever.

59 These things said he in the synagogue, as he taught in Capernaum.

The questioning disciples

60 [a]Many therefore of his disciples, when they had heard *this,* said, This is an hard saying; who can hear it?

61 When Jesus knew in himself that his disciples murmured at it, he said unto them, Doth this offend you?

62 [a]*What* and if ye shall see the Son of man ascend up where he was before?

H R W K 63 [a]It is the spirit that quickeneth; the flesh profiteth nothing: the words that I speak unto you, *they* are spirit, and *they* are life.

E 64 But [a]there are some of you that believe not. For [b]Jesus knew from the beginning who they were that believed not, and who should betray him.

65 And he said, Therefore [a]said I unto you, that no man can come unto me, except it were given unto him of my Father.

O *Jn 3:36* ◀▶ *Jn 8:24*
F *Jn 6:44* ◀▶ *Jn 11:23–25*
K *Jn 6:50–51* ◀▶ *Jn 6:63*
H *Jn 3:3–8* ◀▶ *Ro 1:4*
R *Jn 3:3–8* ◀▶ *Ro 8:1–16*
W *Jn 4:23–24* ◀▶ *Jn 14:16–17*
K *Jn 6:54–58* ◀▶ *Jn 6:68*
E *Jn 4:29* ◀▶ *Jn 16:30*

53 [a]Mat. 26:16
54 [a]ver. 27,40; ch. 4:14
56 [a]1 John 3:24 & 4:15,16
58 [a]ver. 49-51
60 [a]ver. 66; Mat. 11:6
62 [a]Mark 16:19; ch. 3:13; Acts 1:9; Eph. 4:8
63 [a]2 Cor. 3:6
64 [a]ver. 36 [b]ch. 2:24,25 & 13:11
65 [a]ver. 44,45
66 [a]ver. 60
68 [a]Acts 5:20
69 [a]Mat. 16:16; Mark 8:29; Luke 9:20; ch. 1:49 & 11:27
70 [a]Luke 6:13 [b]ch. 13:27
7:1 [a]ch. 5:16,18
2 [a]Lev. 23:34
3 [a]Mat. 12:46; Mark 3:31; Acts 1:14
5 [a]Mark 3:21
6 [a]ch. 2:4 & 8:20
7 [a]ch. 15:19 [b]ch. 3:19
8 [a]ch. 8:20

66 ¶ [a]From that *time* many of his disciples went back, and walked no more with him.

67 Then said Jesus unto the twelve, Will ye also go away?

68 Then Simon Peter answered him, Lord, to whom shall we go? thou hast [a]the words of eternal life. K

69 [a]And we believe and are sure that thou art that Christ, the Son of the living God.

70 Jesus answered them, [a]Have not I chosen you twelve, [b]and one of you is a devil?

71 He spake of Judas Iscariot *the son* of Simon: for he it was that should betray him, being one of the twelve.

Jesus at the feast of tabernacles

7 AFTER THESE things Jesus walked in Galilee: for he would not walk in Jewry, [a]because the Jews sought to kill him.

2 [a]Now the Jews' feast of tabernacles was at hand.

3 [a]His brethren therefore said unto him, Depart hence, and go into Judaea, that thy disciples also may see the works that thou doest.

4 For *there is* no man *that* doeth any thing in secret, and he himself seeketh to be known openly. If thou do these things, show thyself to the world.

5 For [a]neither did his brethren believe in him.

6 Then Jesus said unto them, [a]My time is not yet come: but your time is always ready.

7 [a]The world cannot hate you; but me it hateth, [b]because I testify of it, that the works thereof are evil.

8 Go ye up unto this feast: I go not up yet unto this feast; [a]for my time is not yet full come.

9 When he had said these words unto them, he abode *still* in Galilee.

10 ¶ But when his brethren were gone up, then went he also up unto the feast, not openly, but as it were in secret.

K *Jn 6:63* ◀▶ *Jn 7:17*

6:54 Jesus is not teaching that the sacrament of communion is necessary for salvation, but rather indicates that without a personal appropriation of Christ one cannot have eternal life or be raised up with him in the last days.

11 Then [a]the Jews sought him at the feast, and said, Where is he?

12 And [a]there was much murmuring among the people concerning him: for [b]some said, He is a good man: others said, Nay; but he deceiveth the people.

13 Howbeit no man spake openly of him [a]for fear of the Jews.

Jesus teaches in the temple

14 ¶ Now about the midst of the feast Jesus went up into the temple, and taught.

15 [a]And the Jews marvelled, saying, How knoweth this man [/]letters, having never learned?

16 Jesus answered them, and said, [a]My doctrine is not mine, but his that sent me.

K 17 [a]If any man will do his will, he shall know of the doctrine, whether it be of God, or *whether* I speak of myself.

18 [a]He that speaketh of himself seeketh his own glory: but he that seeketh his glory that sent him, the same is true, and no unrighteousness is in him.

19 [a]Did not Moses give you the law, and *yet* none of you keepeth the law? [b]Why go ye about to kill me?

20 The people answered and said, [a]Thou hast a devil: who goeth about to kill thee?

21 Jesus answered and said unto them, I have done one work, and ye all marvel.

22 [a]Moses therefore gave unto you circumcision; (not because it is of Moses, [b]but of the fathers;) and ye on the sabbath day circumcise a man.

E 23 If a man on the sabbath day receive circumcision, [/]that the law of Moses should not be broken; are ye angry at me, because [a]I have made a man every whit whole on the sabbath day?

24 [a]Judge not according to the appearance, but judge righteous judgment.

25 Then said some of them of Jerusalem, Is not this he, whom they seek to kill?

26 But, lo, he speaketh boldly, and they say nothing unto him. [a]Do the rulers know indeed that this is the very Christ?

27 [a]Howbeit we know this man whence he is: but when Christ cometh, no man knoweth whence he is.

K *Jn 6:68* ◀ ▶ *Jn 8:12*
E *Jn 6:2* ◀ ▶ *Jn 9:1–7*

28 Then cried Jesus in the temple as he taught, saying, [a]Ye both know me, and ye know whence I am: and [b]I am not come of myself, but he that sent me [c]is true, [d]whom ye know not.

29 But [a]I know him: for I am from him, and he hath sent me.

30 Then [a]they sought to take him: but [b]no man laid hands on him, because his hour was not yet come.

31 And [a]many of the people believed on him, and said, When Christ cometh, will he do more miracles than these which this *man* hath done?

32 ¶ The Pharisees heard that the people murmured such things concerning him; and the Pharisees and the chief priests sent officers to take him.

33 Then said Jesus unto them, [a]Yet a little while am I with you, and *then* I go unto him that sent me.

34 Ye [a]shall seek me, and shall not find *me:* and where I am, *thither* ye cannot come.

35 Then said the Jews among themselves, Whither will he go, that we shall not find him? will he go unto [a]the dispersed among the [/]Gentiles, and teach the Gentiles?

36 What *manner of* saying is this that he said, Ye shall seek me, and shall not find *me:* and where I am, *thither* ye cannot come?

The last day of the feast

37 [a]In the last day, that great *day* of the feast, Jesus stood and cried, saying, [b]If any man thirst, let him come unto me, and drink. B N P L

38 [a]He that believeth on me, as the scripture hath said, [b]out of his belly shall flow rivers of living water. W M F

39 ([a]But this spake he of the Spirit, which they that believe on him should receive: for the Holy Ghost was not yet *given;* because that Jesus was not yet [b]glorified.)

40 ¶ Many of the people therefore, when they heard this saying, said, Of a truth this is [a]the Prophet.

B *Jn 3:34* ◀ ▶ *Jn 14:16–17*
N *Jn 3:34* ◀ ▶ *Jn 14:16–17*
P *Jn 1:33* ◀ ▶ *Jn 14:16–17*
L *Jn 6:47* ◀ ▶ *Jn 8:11–12*
W *Jn 6:47* ◀ ▶ *Jn 11:26*
M *Lk 24:49* ◀ ▶ *Jn 14:26*
F *Jn 6:47* ◀ ▶ *Jn 11:25–26*

11 [a]ch. 11:56
12 [a]ch. 9:16 & 10:19 [b]ver. 40; Mat. 21:46; Luke 7:16; ch. 6:14
13 [a]ch. 9:22 & 12:42 & 19:38
15 [a]Mat. 13:54; Mark 6:2; Luke 4:22; Acts 2:7 [/]Or, *learning*
16 [a]ch. 3:11 & 8:28 & 12:49 & 14:10,24
17 [a]ch. 8:43
18 [a]ch. 5:41 & 8:50
19 [a]Ex. 24:3; Deut. 33:4; ch. 1:17; Acts 7:38 [b]Mat. 12:14; Mark 3:6; ch. 5:16, 18 & 10:31,39 & 11:53
20 [a]ch. 8:48,52 & 10:20
22 [a]Lev. 12:3 [b]Gen. 17:10
23 [a]ch. 5:8,9,16 [/]Or, *without breaking the law of Moses*
24 [a]Deut. 1:16; Prov. 24:23; ch. 8:15; Jas. 2:1
26 [a]ver. 48
27 [a]Mat. 13:55; Mark 6:3; Luke 4:22
28 [a]ch. 8:14 [b]ch. 5:43 & 8:42 [c]ch. 5:32 & 8:26; Rom. 3:4 [d]ch. 1:18 & 8:55
29 [a]Mat. 11:27; ch. 10:15
30 [a]Mark 11:18; Luke 19:47 & 20:19; ch. 8:37 [b]ver. 44
31 [a]Mat. 12:23; ch. 3:2 & 8:30
33 [a]ch. 13:33 & 16:16
34 [a]Hos. 5:6; ch. 8:21 & 13:33
35 [a]Is. 11:12; Jas. 1:1; 1 Pet. 1:1 [/]Or, *Greeks*
37 [a]Lev. 23:36 [b]Is. 55:1; ch. 6:35; Rev. 22:17
38 [a]Deut. 18:15 [b]Prov. 18:4; Is. 12:3 & 44:3; ch. 4:14
39 [a]Is. 44:3; Joel 2:28; ch. 16:7; Acts 2:17,33,38 [b]ch. 12:16 & 16:7
40 [a]Deut. 18:15; ch. 1:21 & 6:14

41 Others said, [a]This is the Christ. But some said, Shall Christ come [b]out of Galilee?

B 42 [a]Hath not the scripture said, That Christ cometh of the seed of David, and out of the town of Bethlehem, [b]where David was?

43 So [a]there was a division among the people because of him.

44 And [a]some of them would have taken him; but no man laid hands on him.

45 ¶ Then came the officers to the chief priests and Pharisees; and they said unto them, Why have ye not brought him?

46 The officers answered, Never man spake like this man.

47 Then answered them the Pharisees, Are ye also deceived?

48 [a]Have any of the rulers or of the Pharisees believed on him?

49 But this people who knoweth not the law are cursed.

50 Nicodemus saith unto them, ([a]he that came [/]to Jesus by night, being one of them,)

51 [a]Doth our law judge *any* man, before it hear him, and know what he doeth?

52 They answered and said unto him, Art thou also of Galilee? Search, and look: for [a]out of Galilee ariseth no prophet.

53 And every man went unto his own house.

The woman caught in adultery

8 JESUS WENT unto the mount of Olives.

2 And early in the morning he came again into the temple, and all the people came unto him; and he sat down, and taught them.

3 And the scribes and Pharisees brought unto him a woman taken in adultery; and when they had set her in the midst,

4 They say unto him, Master, this woman was taken in adultery, in the very act.

5 [a]Now Moses in the law commanded us, that such should be stoned: but what sayest thou?

6 This they said, tempting him, that they might have to accuse him. But Jesus stooped down, and with *his* finger wrote on the ground, *as though he heard them not.*

7 So when they continued asking him, he lifted up himself, and said unto them, [a]He that is without sin among you, let him first cast a stone at her.

8 And again he stooped down, and wrote on the ground.

9 And they which heard *it,* [a]being convicted by *their own* conscience, went out one by one, beginning at the eldest, *even* unto the last: and Jesus was left alone, and the woman standing in the midst.

10 When Jesus had lifted up himself, and saw none but the woman, he said unto her, Woman, where are those thine accusers? hath no man condemned thee?

11 She said, No man, Lord. And Jesus L
said unto her, [a]Neither do I condemn S
thee: go, and [b]sin no more.

Jesus the light of the world

12 ¶ Then spake Jesus again unto K
them, saying, [a]I am the light of the world: he that followeth me shall not walk in darkness, but shall have the light of life.

13 The Pharisees therefore said unto him, [a]Thou bearest record of thyself; thy record is not true.

14 Jesus answered and said unto them, Though I bear record of myself, *yet* my record is true: for I know whence I came, and whither I go; but [a]ye cannot tell whence I come, and whither I go.

15 [a]Ye judge after the flesh; [b]I judge no man.

16 And yet if I judge, my judgment is true: for [a]I am not alone, but I and the Father that sent me.

17 [a]It is also written in your law, that the testimony of two men is true.

41 [a]ch. 4:42 & 6:69 [b]ver. 52; ch. 1:46
42 [a]Ps. 132:11; Jer. 23:5; Mic. 5:2; Mat. 2:5; Luke 2:4 [b]1 Sam. 16:1,4
43 [a]ver. 12; ch. 9:16 & 10:19
44 [a]ver. 30
48 [a]ch. 12:42; Acts 6:7; 1 Cor. 1:20,26 & 2:8
50 [a]ch. 3:2 [/]Gk. *to him*
51 [a]Deut 1:17 & 17:8 & 19:15
52 [a]ver. 41; Is. 9:1,2; Mat. 4:15; ch. 1:46
8:5 [a]Lev. 20:10; Deut. 22:22
7 [a]Deut. 17:7; Rom. 2:1
9 [a]Rom. 2:22
11 [a]Luke 9:56 & 12:14; ch. 3:17 [b]ch. 5:14
12 [a]ch. 1:4,5,9 & 3:19 & 9:5 & 12:35,36,46
13 [a]ch. 5:31
14 [a]ch. 7:28 & 9:29
15 [a]ch. 7:24 [b]ch. 3:17 & 12:47 & 18:36
16 [a]ch. 16:32
17 [a]Deut. 17:6 & 19:15; Mat. 18:16; 2 Cor. 13:1; Heb. 10:28

B *Jn 3:14* ◀▶ *Jn 19:24*
L *Jn 7:37* ◀▶ *Jn 9:39*
S *Jn 5:29* ◀▶ *Jn 8:31*
K *Jn 7:17* ◀▶ *Jn 8:36*

7:52 The Pharisees and religious leaders challenged Jesus' claims by declaring that prophets did not come from Galilee. In this statement the religious leaders erred. The OT clearly records that the prophet Jonah arose from the region of Galilee before his dramatically successful missionary journey to Nineveh, the capital city of Assyria (see 2Ki 14:25).

18 I am one that bear witness of myself, and [a]the Father that sent me beareth witness of me.

19 Then said they unto him, Where is thy Father? Jesus answered, [a]Ye neither know me, nor my Father: [b]if ye had known me, ye should have known my Father also.

20 These words spake Jesus in [a]the treasury, as he taught in the temple: and [b]no man laid hands on him; for [c]his hour was not yet come.

Jesus warns against unbelief

21 Then said Jesus again unto them, I go my way, and [a]ye shall seek me, and [b]shall die in your sins: whither I go, ye cannot come.

22 Then said the Jews, Will he kill himself? because he saith, Whither I go, ye cannot come.

23 And he said unto them, [a]Ye are from beneath; I am from above: [b]ye are of this world; I am not of this world.

N 24 [a]I said therefore unto you, that ye
O shall die in your sins: [b]for if ye believe
not that I am *he,* ye shall die in your sins.

25 Then said they unto him, Who art thou? And Jesus saith unto them, Even *the same* that I said unto you from the beginning.

26 I have many things to say and to judge of you: but [a]he that sent me is true; and [b]I speak to the world those things which I have heard of him.

27 They understood not that he spake to them of the Father.

28 Then said Jesus unto them, When ye have [a]lifted up the Son of man, [b]then shall ye know that I am *he,* and [c]*that* I do nothing of myself; but [d]as my Father hath taught me, I speak these things.

29 And [a]he that sent me is with me: [b]the Father hath not left me alone; [c]for I do always those things that please him.

30 As he spake these words, [a]many believed on him.

The true children of Abraham

S 31 Then said Jesus to those Jews
which believed on him, If ye continue in
my word, *then* are ye my disciples
indeed;

18 [a]ch. 5:37
19 [a]ch. 16:3 [b]ch. 14:7
20 [a]Mark 12:41 [b]ch. 7:30 [c]ch. 7:8
21 [a]ch. 7:34 & 13:33 [b]ver. 24
23 [a]ch. 3:31 [b]ch. 15:19 & 17:16; 1 John 4:5
24 [a]ver. 21 [b]Mark 16:16
26 [a]ch. 7:28 [b]ch. 3:32 & 15:15
28 [a]ch. 3:14 & 12:32 [b]Rom. 1:4 [c]ch. 5:19,30 [d]ch. 3:11
29 [a]ch. 14:10 [b]ver. 16 [c]ch. 4:34 & 5:30 & 6:38
30 [a]ch. 7:31 & 10:42 & 11:45
32 [a]Rom. 6:14,18, 22; Jas. 1:25 & 2:12
33 [a]Lev. 25:42; Mat. 3:9
34 [a]Rom 6:16; 2 Pet. 2:19
35 [a]Gal. 4:30
36 [a]Rom. 8:2; Gal. 5:1
37 [a]ch. 7:19
38 [a]ch. 3:32 & 5:19,30 & 14:10, 24
39 [a]Mat. 3:9 [b]Rom. 2:28 & 9:7; Gal. 3:7,29
40 [a]ver. 37 [b]ver. 26
41 [a]Is. 63:16 & 64:8; Mal. 1:6
42 [a]1 John 5:1 [b]ch. 16:27 & 17:8, 25 [c]ch. 5:43 & 7:28,29
43 [a]ch. 7:17
44 [a]Mat. 13:38; 1 John 3:8 [b]Jude 6
47 [a]ch. 10:26; 1 John 4:6

32 And ye shall know the truth, and [a]the truth shall make you free.

33 ¶ They answered him, [a]We be Abraham's seed, and were never in bondage to any man: how sayest thou, Ye shall be made free?

34 Jesus answered them, Verily, C
verily, I say unto you, [a]Whosoever com- S
mitteth sin is the servant of sin.

35 And [a]the servant abideth not in the house for ever: *but* the Son abideth ever.

36 [a]If the Son therefore shall make you K
free, ye shall be free indeed.

37 I know that ye are Abraham's seed; but [a]ye seek to kill me, because my word hath no place in you.

38 [a]I speak that which I have seen with my Father: and ye do that which ye have seen with your father.

39 They answered and said unto him, [a]Abraham is our father. Jesus saith unto them, [b]If ye were Abraham's children, ye would do the works of Abraham.

40 [a]But now ye seek to kill me, a man that hath told you the truth, [b]which I have heard of God: this did not Abraham.

41 Ye do the deeds of your father. Then said they to him, We be not born of fornication; [a]we have one Father, *even* God.

42 Jesus said unto them, [a]If God were your Father, ye would love me: [b]for I proceeded forth and came from God; [c]neither came I of myself, but he sent me.

43 [a]Why do ye not understand my speech? *even* because ye cannot hear my word.

44 [a]Ye are of *your* father the devil, and C
the lusts of your father ye will do. He was a murderer from the beginning, and [b]abode not in the truth, because there is no truth in him. When he speaketh a lie, he speaketh of his own: for he is a liar, and the father of it.

45 And because I tell *you* the truth, ye believe me not.

46 Which of you convinceth me of sin? And if I say the truth, why do ye not believe me?

47 [a]He that is of God heareth God's N

N *Jn 3:36* ◀ ▶ *Jn 8:47*
O *Jn 6:53* ◀ ▶ *Jn 10:1*
S *Jn 8:11–12* ◀ ▶ *Jn 8:34–35*

C *Jn 3:19–20* ◀ ▶ *Jn 8:44*
S *Jn 8:31* ◀ ▶ *Jn 14:15*
K *Jn 8:12* ◀ ▶ *Jn 8:51*
C *Jn 8:34* ◀ ▶ *Ac 7:51*
N *Jn 8:24* ◀ ▶ *Jn 9:39–41*

words: ye therefore hear *them* not, because ye are not of God.

Controversy with the Jews

48 Then answered the Jews, and said unto him, Say we not well that thou art a Samaritan, and [a]hast a devil?

49 Jesus answered, I have not a devil; but I honour my Father, and ye do dishonour me.

50 And [a]I seek not mine own glory: there is one that seeketh and judgeth.

K 51 Verily, verily, I say unto you, [a]If a man keep my saying, he shall never see death.

52 Then said the Jews unto him, Now we know that thou hast a devil. [a]Abraham is dead, and the prophets; and thou sayest, If a man keep my saying, he shall never taste of death.

53 Art thou greater than our father Abraham, which is dead? and the prophets are dead: whom makest thou thyself ?

54 Jesus answered, If I honour myself, my honour is nothing: [a]it is my Father that honoureth me; of whom ye say, that he is your God:

55 Yet [a]ye have not known him; but I know him: and if I should say, I know him not, I shall be a liar like unto you: but I know him, and keep his saying.

56 Your father Abraham [a]rejoiced to see my day: [b]and he saw *it,* and was glad.

57 Then said the Jews unto him, Thou art not yet fifty years old, and hast thou seen Abraham?

58 Jesus said unto them, Verily, verily, I say unto you, Before Abraham was, [a]I am.

59 Then [a]took they up stones to cast at him: but Jesus hid himself, and went out of the temple, [b]going through the midst of them, and so passed by.

Jesus heals the man born blind

D
E 9 AND AS *Jesus* passed by, he saw a man which was blind from *his* birth.

2 And his disciples asked him, saying, Master, [a]who did sin, this man, or his parents, that he was born blind?

3 Jesus answered, Neither hath this man sinned, nor his parents: [a]but that the works of God should be made manifest in him.

4 [a]I must work the works of him that sent me, while it is day: the night cometh, when no man can work.

5 As long as I am in the world, [a]I am the light of the world. K

6 When he had thus spoken, [a]he spat on the ground, and made clay of the spittle, and he [1]anointed the eyes of the blind man with the clay,

7 And said unto him, Go, wash [a]in the pool of Siloam, (which is by interpretation, Sent.) [b]He went his way therefore, and washed, and came seeing.

8 ¶ The neighbours therefore, and they which before had seen him that he was blind, said, Is not this he that sat and begged?

9 Some said, This is he: others *said,* He is like him: *but* he said, I am *he.*

10 Therefore said they unto him, How were thine eyes opened?

11 He answered and said, [a]A man that is called Jesus made clay, and anointed mine eyes, and said unto me, Go to the pool of Siloam, and wash: and I went and washed, and I received sight.

12 Then said they unto him, Where is he? He said, I know not.

Pharisees question the healed man

13 ¶ They brought to the Pharisees him that aforetime was blind.

14 And it was the sabbath day when Jesus made the clay, and opened his eyes.

15 Then again the Pharisees also asked him how he had received his sight. He said unto them, He put clay upon mine eyes, and I washed, and do see.

16 Therefore said some of the Pharisees, This man is not of God, because he keepeth not the sabbath day. Others said, [a]How can a man that is a sinner do such miracles? And [b]there was a division among them.

17 They say unto the blind man again, What sayest thou of him, that he hath opened thine eyes? He said, [a]He is a prophet.

18 But the Jews did not believe concerning him, that he had been blind, and received his sight, until they called the parents of him that had received his sight.

19 And they asked them, saying, Is

48 [a]ver. 52; ch. 7:20 & 10:20
50 [a]ch. 5:41 & 7:18
51 [a]ch. 5:24 & 11:26
52 [a]Zech. 1:5; Heb. 11:13
54 [a]ch. 5:41 & 16:14 & 17:1; Acts 3:13
55 [a]ch. 7:28,29
56 [a]Luke 10:24 [b]Heb. 11:13
58 [a]Ex. 3:14; Is. 43:13; ch. 17:5,24; Col. 1:17; Rev. 1:8
59 [a]ch. 10:31,39; & 11:8 [b]Luke 4:30
9:2 [a]ver. 34
3 [a]ch. 11:4
4 [a]ch. 4:34 & 5:19,36 & 11:9 & 12:35 & 17:4
5 [a]ch. 1:5,9 & 3:19 & 8:12 & 12:35,46
6 [a]Mark 7:33 & 8:23 [1]Or, *spread the clay upon the eyes of the blind man*
7 [a]Neh. 3:15 [b]See 2 Ki. 5:14
11 [a]ver. 6,7
16 [a]ver. 33; ch. 3:2 [b]ch. 7:12,43 & 10:19
17 [a]ch. 4:19 & 6:14

K *Jn 8:36* ◄► *Jn 9:5*
D *Jn 5:14* ◄► *Jn 11:4*
E *Jn 7:23* ◄► *Jn 11:39–46*
K *Jn 8:51* ◄► *Jn 10:7*

this your son, who ye say was born blind? how then doth he now see?

20 His parents answered them and said, We know that this is our son, and that he was born blind:

21 But by what means he now seeth, we know not; or who hath opened his eyes, we know not: he is of age; ask him: he shall speak for himself.

22 These *words* spake his parents, because [a]they feared the Jews: for the Jews had agreed already, that if any man did confess that he was Christ, he [b]should be put out of the synagogue.

23 Therefore said his parents, He is of age; ask him.

24 Then again called they the man that was blind, and said unto him, [a]Give God the praise: [b]we know that this man is a sinner.

25 He answered and said, Whether he be a sinner *or no,* I know not: one thing I know, that, whereas I was blind, now I see.

26 Then said they to him again, What did he to thee? how opened he thine eyes?

27 He answered them, I have told you already, and ye did not hear: wherefore would ye hear *it* again? will ye also be his disciples?

28 Then they reviled him, and said, Thou art his disciple; but we are Moses' disciples.

29 We know that God spake unto Moses: *as for* this *fellow,* [a]we know not from whence he is.

30 The man answered and said unto them, [a]Why herein is a marvellous thing, that ye know not from whence he is, and *yet* he hath opened mine eyes.

31 Now we know that [a]God heareth not sinners: but if any man be a worshipper of God, and doeth his will, him he heareth.

32 Since the world began was it not heard that any man opened the eyes of one that was born blind.

33 [a]If this man were not of God, he could do nothing.

34 They answered and said unto him, [a]Thou wast altogether born in sins, and dost thou teach us? And they [1]cast him out.

Jesus talks to the healed man

35 Jesus heard that they had cast him out; and when he had found him, he said unto him, Dost thou believe on [a]the Son of God?

36 He answered and said, Who is he, Lord, that I might believe on him?

37 And Jesus said unto him, Thou hast both seen him, and [a]it is he that talketh with thee.

38 And he said, Lord, I believe. And he worshipped him.

39 ¶ And Jesus said, [a]For judgment I G
am come into this world, [b]that they L
which see not might see; and that they M
which see might be made blind. N

40 And *some* of the Pharisees which were with him heard these words, [a]and said unto him, Are we blind also?

41 Jesus said unto them, [a]If ye were blind, ye should have no sin: but now ye say, We see; therefore your sin remaineth.

Jesus the good shepherd

10 VERILY, VERILY, I say unto you, G
He that entereth not by the door O
into the sheepfold, but climbeth up some other way, the same is a thief and a robber.

2 But he that entereth in by the door is the shepherd of the sheep.

22 [a]ch. 7:13 & 12:42 & 19:38; Acts 5:13 [b]ver. 34; ch. 16:2
24 [a]Josh. 7:19; 1 Sam. 6:5 [b]ver. 16
29 [a]ch. 8:14
30 [a]ch. 3:10
31 [a]Job 27:9 & 35:12; Ps. 18:41 & 34:15 & 66:18; Prov. 1:28 & 15:29 & 28:9; Is. 1:15; Jer. 11:11 & 14:12; Ezek. 8:18; Mic. 3:4; Zech. 7:13
33 [a]ver. 16
34 [a]ver. 2 [1]Or, *excommunicated him;* see ver. 22
35 [a]Mat. 14:33 & 16:16; Mark 1:1; ch. 10:36; 1 John 5:13
37 [a]ch. 4:26
39 [a]ch. 5:22,27; See ch. 3:17 & 12:47 [b]Mat. 13:13
40 [a]Rom. 2:19
41 [a]ch. 15:22,24

G *Jn 6:28–29 ◀▶ Jn 10:1*
L *Jn 8:11–12 ◀▶ Jn 11:25–26*
M *Lk 18:24–25 ◀▶ Ac 7:51*
N *Jn 8:47 ◀▶ Jn 10:26–27*
G *Jn 9:39 ◀▶ Ro 3:20*
O *Jn 8:24 ◀▶ Jn 14:6*

9:32–33 The man who made this statement had been blind from birth, and his words were literally true. From the creation of Adam to that point in time, not one person born blind had ever been healed enough to allow them to see. Then Jesus came and healed this man. Isaiah had predicted that one of the miraculous signs of the Messiah was his ability to "open the blind eyes" (Isa 42:7). This explains why the priests so vehemently rejected the possibility that the man had been truly blind (see 9:18–19). These leaders knew the prophecies about the Messiah, that only the Messiah could open the eyes of one born blind. This extraordinary miracle of healing provided supernatural proof that Jesus was the Messiah—proof that the religious leaders did not want to accept.

L 3 To him the porter openeth; and the
sheep hear his voice: and he calleth his
own sheep by name, and leadeth them
out.
4 And when he putteth forth his own
sheep, he goeth before them, and the
sheep follow him: for they know his
voice.
5 And a stranger will they not follow,
but will flee from him: for they know not
the voice of strangers.
6 This parable spake Jesus unto them:
but they understood not what things they
were which he spake unto them.
K 7 Then said Jesus unto them again,
Verily, verily, I say unto you, I am the
door of the sheep.
8 All that ever came before me are
thieves and robbers: but the sheep did
not hear them.
K 9 [a]I am the door: by me if any man
L enter in, he shall be saved, and shall go in
and out, and find pasture.
10 The thief cometh not, but for to
steal, and to kill, and to destroy: I am
come that they might have life, and that
they might have *it* more abundantly.
D 11 [a]I am the good shepherd: the good
shepherd giveth his life for the sheep.
12 But he that is an hireling, and not
the shepherd, whose own the sheep are
not, seeth the wolf coming, and [a]leaveth
the sheep, and fleeth: and the wolf catcheth them, and scattereth the sheep.
13 The hireling fleeth, because he is
an hireling, and careth not for the sheep.
L 14 I am the good shepherd, and [a]know
my *sheep,* and am known of mine.
D 15 [a]As the Father knoweth me, even
so know I the Father: [b]and I lay down my
life for the sheep.
G 16 And [a]other sheep I have, which are
M not of this fold: them also I must bring,
and they shall hear my voice; [b]and there
shall be one fold, *and* one shepherd.
17 Therefore doth my Father love me,
[a]because I lay down my life, that I might
take it again.
18 No man taketh it from me, but I lay
it down of myself. I have power to lay it
down, and I [a]have power to take it again.
[b]This commandment have I received of
my Father.
19 ¶ [a]There was a division therefore
again among the Jews for these sayings.
20 And many of them said, [a]He hath a
devil, and is mad; why hear ye him?
21 Others said, These are not the
words of him that hath a devil. [a]Can a
devil [b]open the eyes of the blind?

The Jews try to arrest Jesus

22 ¶ And it was at Jerusalem the feast
of the dedication, and it was winter.
23 And Jesus walked in the temple [a]in
Solomon's porch.
24 Then came the Jews round about
him, and said unto him, How long dost
thou [/]make us to doubt? If thou be the
Christ, tell us plainly.
25 Jesus answered them, I told you,
and ye believed not: [a]the works that I do
in my Father's name, they bear witness
of me.
26 But [a]ye believe not, because ye are N
not of my sheep, as I said unto you.
27 [a]My sheep hear my voice, and I L
know them, and they follow me:
28 And I give unto them eternal life; K
and they shall never perish, neither shall
any *man* pluck them out of my hand.
29 [a]My Father, [b]which gave *them* me,
is greater than all; and no *man* is able to
pluck *them* out of my Father's hand.
30 [a]I and *my* Father are one.
31 Then [a]the Jews took up stones
again to stone him.
32 Jesus answered them, Many good
works have I shown you from my Father;
for which of those works do ye stone me?
33 The Jews answered him, saying,
For a good work we stone thee not; but

10:9 [a]ch. 14:6; Eph. 2:18
11 [a]Is. 40:11; Ezek. 34:12,23 & 37:24; Heb. 13:20; 1 Pet. 2:25 & 5:4
12 [a]Zech. 11:16,17
14 [a]2 Tim. 2:19
15 [a]Mat. 11:27 [b]ch. 15:13
16 [a]Is. 56:8 [b]Ezek. 37:22; Eph. 2:14; 1 Pet. 2:25
17 [a]Is. 53:7,8,12; Heb. 2:9
18 [a]ch. 2:19 [b]ch. 6:38 & 15:10; Acts 2:24,32
19 [a]ch. 7:43 & 9:16
20 [a]ch. 7:20 & 8:48,52
21 [a]Ex. 4:11; Ps. 94:9 & 146:8 [b]ch. 9:6,7,32,33
23 [a]Acts 3:11 & 5:12
24 [/]Or, *hold us in suspense?*
25 [a]ver. 38; ch. 3:2 & 5:36
26 [a]ch. 8:47
27 [a]ver. 4,14
29 [a]ch. 14:28 [b]ch. 17:2,6
30 [a]ch. 17:11,22
31 [a]ch. 8:59

L *Lk 22:35 ◀▶ Jn 10:9–11*
K *Jn 9:5 ◀▶ Jn 10:9–10*
K *Jn 10:7 ◀▶ Jn 10:28–29*
L *Jn 10:3–4 ◀▶ Jn 10:14–15*
D *Jn 6:51–56 ◀▶ Jn 10:15*
L *Jn 10:9–11 ◀▶ Jn 10:27–29*
D *Jn 10:11 ◀▶ Jn 11:49–52*
G *Lk 21:24 ◀▶ Ac 10:15*
M *Lk 23:51 ◀▶ Jn 12:13–15*
N *Jn 9:39–41 ◀▶ Jn 12:35–36*
L *Jn 10:14–15 ◀▶ Jn 14:13–14*
K *Jn 10:9–10 ◀▶ Jn 11:25–26*

10:16 This prophecy predicts that Jesus' offer of salvation would extend from his original offer to the Jews to include all of the Gentiles who would repent of their sins and accept God's offer of salvation.

for blasphemy; and because that thou, being a man, [a]makest thyself God.
34 Jesus answered them, [a]Is it not
written in your law, I said, Ye are gods?
35 If he called them gods, [a]unto whom
the word of God came, and the scripture
cannot be broken;
36 Say ye of him, [a]whom the Father
hath sanctified, and [b]sent into the world,
Thou blasphemest; [c]because I said, I am
[d]the Son of God?
37 [a]If I do not the works of my Father,
believe me not.
38 But if I do, though ye believe not
me, [a]believe the works: that ye may
know, and believe, [b]that the Father *is* in
me, and I in him.
39 [a]Therefore they sought again to
take him: but he escaped out of their
hand,
40 And went away again beyond Jordan into the place [a]where John at first
baptized; and there he abode.
41 And many resorted unto him, and
said, John did no miracle: [a]but all things
that John spake of this man were true.
42 [a]And many believed on him there.

Jesus hears of Lazarus' death

11 NOW A certain *man* was sick,
named Lazarus, of Bethany, the
town of [a]Mary and her sister Martha.
2 ([a]It was *that* Mary which anointed
the Lord with ointment, and wiped his
feet with her hair, whose brother Lazarus
was sick.)
3 Therefore his sisters sent unto him,
saying, Lord, behold, he whom thou lovest is sick.
D 4 When Jesus heard *that,* he said, This
sickness is not unto death, [a]but for the
glory of God, that the Son of God might
be glorified thereby.
5 Now Jesus loved Martha, and her sister, and Lazarus.
6 When he had heard therefore that he
was sick, [a]he abode two days still in the
same place where he was.
7 Then after that saith he to *his* disciples, Let us go into Judaea again.

8 *His* disciples say unto him, Master,
[a]the Jews of late sought to stone thee;
and goest thou thither again?
9 Jesus answered, Are there not twelve
hours in the day? [a]If any man walk in the
day, he stumbleth not, because he seeth
the light of this world.
10 But [a]if a man walk in the night, he
stumbleth, because there is no light in
him.
11 These things said he: and after that
he saith unto them, Our friend Lazarus
[a]sleepeth; but I go, that I may awake him
out of sleep.
12 Then said his disciples, Lord, if he
sleep, he shall do well.
13 Howbeit Jesus spake of his death:
but they thought that he had spoken of
taking of rest in sleep.
14 Then said Jesus unto them plainly,
Lazarus is dead.
15 And I am glad for your sakes that I
was not there, to the intent ye may believe; nevertheless let us go unto him.
16 Then said Thomas, which is called
Didymus, unto his fellowdisciples, Let us
also go, that we may die with him.

Jesus the resurrection and the life

17 Then when Jesus came, he found
that he had *lain* in the grave four days
already.
18 Now Bethany was nigh unto Jerusalem, [f]about fifteen furlongs off:
19 And many of the Jews came to Martha and Mary, to comfort them concerning their brother.
20 Then Martha, as soon as she heard
that Jesus was coming, went and met
him: but Mary sat *still* in the house.
21 Then said Martha unto Jesus, Lord,
if thou hadst been here, my brother had
not died.
22 But I know, that even now, [a]what-
soever thou wilt ask of God, God will give
it thee.
23 Jesus saith unto her, Thy brother F
shall rise again.
24 Martha saith unto him, [a]I know

33 [a]ch. 5:18
34 [a]Ps. 82:6
35 [a]Rom. 13:1
36 [a]ch. 6:27 [b]ch. 3:17 & 5:36,37 & 8:42 [c]ver. 30; ch. 5:17,18 [d]Luke 1:35; ch. 9:35,37
37 [a]ch. 15:24
38 [a]ch. 5:36 & 14:10,11 [b]ch. 14:10,11 & 17:21
39 [a]ch. 7:30,44 & 8:59
40 [a]ch. 1:28
41 [a]ch. 3:30
42 [a]ch. 8:30 & 11:45
11:1 [a]Luke 10:38, 39
2 [a]Mat. 26:7; Mark 14:3; ch. 12:3
4 [a]ver. 40; ch. 9:3
6 [a]ch. 10:40
8 [a]ch. 10:31
9 [a]ch. 9:4
10 [a]ch. 12:35
11 [a]Deut. 31:16; Dan. 12:2; Mat. 9:24; Acts 7:60; 1 Cor. 15:18,51
18 [f]i.e. *about two miles*
22 [a]ch. 9:31
24 [a]Luke 14:14; ch. 5:29

D Jn 9:1–3 ◀ ▶ Ac 9:8–9

F Jn 6:54 ◀ ▶ Ac 17:18

11:23–26 Jesus predicted the imminent resurrection from the dead of his friend Lazarus. When Martha affirmed the known OT teaching of the resurrection of the righteous dead, Jesus responded by affirming, "I am the resurrection, and the life: he that believeth in me, though he were dead, yet shall he live" (11:25). Jesus then added an astonishing new revelation that no one had ever heard before:

that he shall rise again in the resurrection at the last day.

25 Jesus said unto her, I am [a]the resurrection, and the life: [b]he that believeth in me, though he were dead, yet shall he live:

26 And whosoever liveth and believeth in me shall never die. Believest thou this?

27 She saith unto him, Yea, Lord: [a]I believe that thou art the Christ, the Son of God, which should come into the world.

28 And when she had so said, she went her way, and called Mary her sister secretly, saying, The Master is come, and calleth for thee.

29 As soon as she heard *that,* she arose quickly, and came unto him.

30 Now Jesus was not yet come into the town, but was in that place where Martha met him.

31 [a]The Jews then which were with her in the house, and comforted her, when they saw Mary, that she rose up hastily and went out, followed her, saying, She goeth unto the grave to weep there.

32 Then when Mary was come where Jesus was, and saw him, she fell down at his feet, saying unto him, [a]Lord, if thou hadst been here, my brother had not died.

33 When Jesus therefore saw her weeping, and the Jews also weeping which came with her, he groaned in the spirit, and [l]was troubled,

34 And said, Where have ye laid him? They said unto him, Lord, come and see.

35 [a]Jesus wept.

36 Then said the Jews, Behold how he loved him!

37 And some of them said, Could not this man, [a]which opened the eyes of the

F *Jn 7:38* ◄ ► *Jn 12:46*
K *Jn 10:28–29* ◄ ► *Jn 12:46*
L *Jn 9:39* ◄ ► *Jn 12:32*
W *Jn 7:37* ◄ ► *Jn 12:32*

25 [a]ch. 5:21 & 6:39,40,44 [b]ch. 3:36; 1 John 5:10
27 [a]Mat. 16:16; ch. 4:42 & 6:14,69
31 [a]ver. 19
32 [a]ver. 21
33 [l]Gk. *he troubled himself*
35 [a]Luke 19:41
37 [a]ch. 9:6
40 [a]ver. 4,23
42 [a]ch. 12:30
44 [a]ch. 20:7
45 [a]ch. 2:23 & 10:42 & 12:11,18
47 [a]Ps. 2:2; Mat. 26:3; Mark 14:1; Luke 22:2 [b]ch. 12:19; Acts 4:16

blind, have caused that even this man should not have died?

Jesus raises Lazarus

38 Jesus therefore again groaning in himself cometh to the grave. It was a cave, and a stone lay upon it.

39 Jesus said, Take ye away the stone. Martha, the sister of him that was dead, saith unto him, Lord, by this time he stinketh: for he hath been *dead* four days.

40 Jesus saith unto her, Said I not unto thee, that, if thou wouldest believe, thou shouldest [a]see the glory of God?

41 Then they took away the stone *from the place* where the dead was laid. And Jesus lifted up *his* eyes, and said, Father, I thank thee that thou hast heard me.

42 And I knew that thou hearest me always: but [a]because of the people which stand by I said *it,* that they may believe that thou hast sent me.

43 And when he thus had spoken, he cried with a loud voice, Lazarus, come forth.

44 And he that was dead came forth, bound hand and foot with graveclothes: and [a]his face was bound about with a napkin. Jesus saith unto them, Loose him, and let him go.

Pharisees plot to kill Jesus

45 Then many of the Jews which came to Mary, [a]and had seen the things which Jesus did, believed on him.

46 But some of them went their ways to the Pharisees, and told them what things Jesus had done.

47 ¶ [a]Then gathered the chief priests and the Pharisees a council, and said, [b]What do we? for this man doeth many miracles.

48 If we let him thus alone, all *men* will believe on him: and the Romans shall come and take away both our place and nation.

E *Jn 9:1–7* ◄ ► *Jn 12:9–11*

"whosoever liveth and believeth in me shall never die" (11:26). Some feel that this statement means that those saints who are alive at Jesus' second coming will never die because they will be raptured in the air with him at his return (see 1Th 4:16–17). Others believe that this verse refers to the never-ending spiritual fellowship that exists between believers and God. Jesus conveys life to believers so that they will always triumph over death. The fact that this statement of Jesus was something totally new is affirmed by his question: "Believest thou this?" (11:26).

D 49 And one of them, *named* [a]Caiaphas, being the high priest that same year, said unto them, Ye know nothing at all,

50 [a]Nor consider that it is expedient for us, that one man should die for the people, and that the whole nation perish not.

51 And this spake he not of himself: but being high priest that year, he prophesied that Jesus should die for that nation;

52 And [a]not for that nation only, [b]but that also he should gather together in one the children of God that were scattered abroad.

53 Then from that day forth they took counsel together for to put him to death.

54 Jesus [a]therefore walked no more openly among the Jews; but went thence unto a country near to the wilderness, into a city called [b]Ephraim, and there continued with his disciples.

55 ¶ [a]And the Jews' passover was nigh at hand: and many went out of the country up to Jerusalem before the passover, to purify themselves.

56 [a]Then sought they for Jesus, and spake among themselves, as they stood in the temple, What think ye, that he will not come to the feast?

57 Now both the chief priests and the Pharisees had given a commandment, that, if any man knew where he were, he should show *it,* that they might take him.

Jesus anointed at Bethany

12 THEN JESUS six days before the passover came to Bethany, [a]where Lazarus was which had been dead, whom he raised from the dead.

2 [a]There they made him a supper; and Martha served: but Lazarus was one of them that sat at the table with him.

3 Then took [a]Mary a pound of ointment of spikenard, very costly, and anointed the feet of Jesus, and wiped his feet with her hair: and the house was filled with the odour of the ointment.

4 Then saith one of his disciples, Judas Iscariot, Simon's *son,* which should betray him,

5 Why was not this ointment sold for three hundred pence, and given to the poor?

6 This he said, not that he cared for the poor; but because he was a thief, and [a]had the bag, and bare what was put therein.

7 Then said Jesus, Let her alone: against the day of my burying hath she kept this.

8 For [a]the poor always ye have with you; but me ye have not always.

9 Much people of the Jews therefore knew that he was there: and they came not for Jesus' sake only, but that they might see Lazarus also, [a]whom he had raised from the dead. E

10 ¶ [a]But the chief priests consulted that they might put Lazarus also to death;

11 [a]Because that by reason of him many of the Jews went away, and believed on Jesus.

The triumphal entry

12 ¶ [a]On the next day much people that were come to the feast, when they heard that Jesus was coming to Jerusalem,

13 Took branches of palm trees, and went forth to meet him, and cried, [a]Hosanna: Blessed *is* the King of Israel that cometh in the name of the Lord. I M

14 [a]And Jesus, when he had found a young ass, sat thereon; as it is written,

15 [a]Fear not, daughter of Zion: behold, thy King cometh, sitting on an ass's colt.

16 These things [a]understood not his disciples at the first: [b]but when Jesus was glorified, [c]then remembered they that these things were written of him, and *that* they had done these things unto him.

17 The people therefore that was with him when he called Lazarus out of his grave, and raised him from the dead, bare record. E

49 [a]Luke 3:2; ch. 18:14; Acts 4:6
50 [a]ch. 18:14
52 [a]Is. 49:6; 1 John 2:2 [b]ch. 10:16; Eph. 2:14-17
54 [a]ch. 4:1,3 & 7:1 [b]See 2 Chr. 13:19
55 [a]ch. 2:13 & 5:1 & 6:4
56 [a]ch. 7:11
12:1 [a]ch. 11:1,43
2 [a]Mat. 26:6; Mark 14:3
3 [a]Luke 10:38,39; ch. 11:2
6 [a]ch. 13:29
8 [a]Mat. 26:11; Mark 14:7
9 [a]ch. 11:43,44
10 [a]Luke 16:31
11 [a]ver. 18; ch. 11:45
12 [a]Mat. 21:8; Mark 11:8; Luke 19:35,36
13 [a]Ps. 118:25,26
14 [a]Mat. 21:7
15 [a]Zech. 9:9
16 [a]Luke 18:34 [b]ch. 7:39 [c]ch. 14:26

D *Jn 10:15* ◀▶ *Ac 8:32–35*

E *Jn 11:39–46* ◀▶ *Jn 12:17–19*
I *Jn 1:49* ◀▶ *Jn 18:33–37*
M *Jn 10:16* ◀▶ *Jn 18:33–37*
E *Jn 12:9–11* ◀▶ *Ac 3:1–16*

12:13–15 John records that many of Jesus' disciples "took branches of palm trees . . . and cried, Hosanna: Blessed is the King of Israel" (12:13), when Jesus rode into Jerusalem on Palm Sunday. This fulfilled Zechariah's prophecy made more than five centuries earlier (see Zec 9:9).

18 [a]For this cause the people also met him, for that they heard that he had done this miracle.

19 The Pharisees therefore said among themselves, [a]Perceive ye how ye prevail nothing? behold, the world is gone after him.

Jesus sought by the Gentiles

20 ¶ And there [a]were certain Greeks among them [b]that came up to worship at the feast:

21 The same came therefore to Philip, [a]which was of Bethsaida of Galilee, and desired him, saying, Sir, we would see Jesus.

22 Philip cometh and telleth Andrew: and again Andrew and Philip tell Jesus.

23 ¶ And Jesus answered them, saying, [a]The hour is come, that the Son of man should be glorified.

24 Verily, verily, I say unto you, [a]Except a corn of wheat fall into the ground and die, it abideth alone: but if it die, it bringeth forth much fruit.

U 25 [a]He that loveth his life shall lose it; and he that hateth his life in this world shall keep it unto life eternal.

26 If any man serve me, let him follow me; and [a]where I am, there shall also my servant be: if any man serve me, him will *my* Father honour.

27 [a]Now is my soul troubled; and what shall I say? Father, save me from this hour: [b]but for this cause came I unto this hour.

28 Father, glorify thy name. [a]Then came there a voice from heaven, *saying,* I have both glorified *it,* and will glorify *it* again.

29 The people therefore, that stood by, and heard *it,* said that it thundered: others said, An angel spake to him.

30 Jesus answered and said, [a]This voice came not because of me, but for your sakes.

31 Now is the judgment of this world: now shall [a]the prince of this world be cast out.

L 32 And I, [a]if I be lifted up from the
W earth, will draw [b]all *men* unto me.

33 [a]This he said, signifying what death he should die.

U *Lk 18:29–30* ◀▶ *Jn 14:21*
L *Jn 11:25–26* ◀▶ *Jn 12:46–47*
W *Jn 11:26* ◀▶ *Jn 12:46*

18 [a]ver. 11
19 [a]ch. 11:47,48
20 [a]Acts 17:4 [b]1 Ki. 8:41,42; Acts 8:27
21 [a]ch. 1:44
23 [a]ch. 13:32 & 17:1
24 [a]1 Cor. 15:36
25 [a]Mat. 10:39 & 16:25; Mark 8:35; Luke 9:24 & 17:33
26 [a]ch. 14:3 & 17:24; 1 Thes. 4:17
27 [a]Mat. 26:38,39; Luke 12:50; ch. 13:21 [b]Luke 22:53; ch. 18:37
28 [a]Mat. 3:17
30 [a]ch. 11:42
31 [a]Mat. 12:29; Luke 10:18; ch. 14:30 & 16:11; Acts 26:18; 2 Cor. 4:4; Eph. 2:2 & 6:12
32 [a]ch. 3:14 & 8:28 [b]Rom. 5:18; Heb. 2:9
33 [a]ch. 18:32
34 [a]Ps. 89:36,37; & 110:4; Is. 9:7 & 53:8; Ezek. 37:25; Dan. 2:44 & 7:14, 27; Mic. 4:7
35 [a]ch. 1:9 & 8:12 & 9:5 [b]Jer. 13:16; Eph. 5:8 [c]ch. 11:10; 1 John 2:11
36 [a]Luke 16:8; Eph. 5:8; 1 Thes. 5:5; 1 John 2:9-11 [b]ch. 8:59 & 11:54
38 [a]Is. 53:1; Rom. 10:16
40 [a]Is. 6:9,10; Mat. 13:14
41 [a]Is. 6:1
42 [a]ch. 7:13 & 9:22
43 [a]ch. 5:44
44 [a]Mark 9:37; 1 Pet. 1:21
45 [a]ch. 14:9
46 [a]ver. 35,36; ch. 3:19 & 9:5,39

34 The people answered him, [a]We have heard out of the law that Christ abideth for ever: and how sayest thou, The Son of man must be lifted up? who is this Son of man?

35 Then Jesus said unto them, Yet a N
little while [a]is the light with you. [b]Walk while ye have the light, lest darkness come upon you: for [c]he that walketh in darkness knoweth not whither he goeth.

36 While ye have light, believe in the light, that ye may be [a]the children of light. These things spake Jesus, and departed, and [b]did hide himself from them.

The cause of unbelief

37 ¶ But though he had done so many miracles before them, yet they believed not on him:

38 That the saying of Esaias the prophet might be fulfilled, which he spake, [a]Lord, who hath believed our report? and to whom hath the arm of the Lord been revealed?

39 Therefore they could not believe, because that Esaias said again,

40 [a]He hath blinded their eyes, and hardened their heart; that they should not see with *their* eyes, nor understand with *their* heart, and be converted, and I should heal them.

41 [a]These things said Esaias, when he saw his glory, and spake of him.

42 ¶ Nevertheless among the chief rul- T
ers also many believed on him; but [a]because of the Pharisees they did not confess *him,* lest they should be put out of the synagogue:

43 [a]For they loved the praise of men more than the praise of God.

A summary of Jesus' claims

44 ¶ Jesus cried and said, [a]He that believeth on me, believeth not on me, but on him that sent me.

45 And [a]he that seeth me seeth him that sent me.

46 [a]I am come a light into the world, F
that whosoever believeth on me should K
not abide in darkness. L

47 And if any man hear my words, and W

N *Jn 10:26–27* ◀▶ *Jn 12:48*
T *Lk 12:8–9* ◀▶ *Ro 1:16*
F *Jn 11:25–26* ◀▶ *Jn 20:29*
K *Jn 11:25–26* ◀▶ *Jn 12:50*
L *Jn 12:32* ◀▶ *Jn 15:13*
W *Jn 12:32* ◀▶ *Ac 2:21*

believe not, [a]I judge him not: for [b]I came not to judge the world, but to save the world.

J 48 [a]He that rejecteth me, and receiv-
H eth not my words, hath one that judgeth
J him: [b]the word that I have spoken, the
N same shall judge him in the last day.

49 For [a]I have not spoken of myself; but the Father which sent me, he gave me a commandment, [b]what I should say, and what I should speak.

K 50 And I know that his commandment is life everlasting: whatsoever I speak therefore, even as the Father said unto me, so I speak.

Washing the disciples' feet

13 NOW [a]BEFORE the feast of the passover, when Jesus knew that [b]his hour was come that he should depart out of this world unto the Father, having loved his own which were in the world, he loved them unto the end.

2 And supper being ended, [a]the devil having now put into the heart of Judas Iscariot, Simon's *son,* to betray him;

3 Jesus knowing [a]that the Father had given all things into his hands, and that he was come from God, and went to God;

4 [a]He riseth from supper, and laid aside his garments; and took a towel, and girded himself.

5 After that he poureth water into a basin, and began to wash the disciples' feet, and to wipe *them* with the towel wherewith he was girded.

6 Then cometh he to Simon Peter: and [/]Peter saith unto him, Lord, [a]dost thou wash my feet?

7 Jesus answered and said unto him, What I do thou knowest not now; [a]but thou shalt know hereafter.

8 Peter saith unto him, Thou shalt never wash my feet. Jesus answered him, [a]If I wash thee not, thou hast no part with me.

9 Simon Peter saith unto him, Lord, not my feet only, but also *my* hands and *my* head.

10 Jesus saith to him, He that is washed needeth not save to wash *his* feet, but is clean every whit: and [a]ye are clean, but not all.

11 For [a]he knew who should betray him; therefore said he, Ye are not all clean.

12 So after he had washed their feet, and had taken his garments, and was set down again, he said unto them, Know ye what I have done to you?

13 [a]Ye call me Master and Lord: and ye say well; for *so* I am.

14 [a]If I then, *your* Lord and Master, have washed your feet; [b]ye also ought to wash one another's feet.

15 For [a]I have given you an example, that ye should do as I have done to you.

16 [a]Verily, verily, I say unto you, The servant is not greater than his lord; neither he that is sent greater than he that sent him.

17 [a]If ye know these things, happy are ye if ye do them.

18 ¶ I speak not of you all: I know whom I have chosen: but that the scripture may be fulfilled, [a]He that eateth bread with me hath lifted up his heel against me.

19 [a]Now[/] I tell you before it come, that, when it is come to pass, ye may believe that I am *he.*

20 [a]Verily, verily, I say unto you, He that receiveth whomsoever I send receiveth me; and he that receiveth me receiveth him that sent me.

Jesus dismisses Judas

21 [a]When Jesus had thus said, [b]he was troubled in spirit, and testified, and said, Verily, verily, I say unto you, that [c]one of you shall betray me.

22 Then the disciples looked one on another, doubting of whom he spake.

23 Now [a]there was leaning on Jesus' bosom one of his disciples, whom Jesus loved.

24 Simon Peter therefore beckoned to him, that he should ask who it should be of whom he spake.

47 [a]ch. 5:45 & 8:15,26 [b]ch. 3:17
48 [a]Luke 10:16 [b]Deut. 18:19; Mark 16:16
49 [a]ch. 8:38 & 14:10 [b]Deut. 18:18
13:1 [a]Mat. 26:2 [b]ch. 12:23 & 17:1, 11
2 [a]Luke 22:3
3 [a]Mat. 11:27 & 28:18; ch. 3:35 & 17:2; Acts 2:36; 1 Cor. 15:27; Heb. 2:8
4 [a]Luke 22:27; Phil. 2:7,8
6 [a]Mat. 3:14 [/]Gk. *he*
7 [a]ver. 12
8 [a]ch. 3:5; 1 Cor. 6:11; Eph. 5:26; Tit. 3:5; Heb. 10:22
10 [a]ch. 15:3
11 [a]ch. 6:64
13 [a]Mat. 23:8; Luke 6:46; 1 Cor. 8:6 & 12:3; Phil. 2:11
14 [a]Luke 22:27 [b]Rom. 12:10; Gal. 6:1,2; 1 Pet. 5:5
15 [a]Mat. 11:29; Phil. 2:5; 1 Pet. 2:21; 1 John 2:6
16 [a]Mat. 10:24; Luke 6:40; ch. 15:20
17 [a]Jas. 1:25
18 [a]ver. 21; Ps. 41:9; Mat. 26:23
19 [a]ch. 14:29 & 16:4 [/]Or, *From henceforth*
20 [a]Mat. 10:40 & 25:40; Luke 10:16
21 [a]Mat. 26:21; Mark 14:18; Luke 22:21 [b]ch. 12:27 [c]Acts 1:17; 1 John 2:19
23 [a]ch. 19:26 & 20:2 & 21:7,20

J *Lk 11:31–32 ◀▶ Ac 17:31*
H *Jn 5:29 ◀▶ Jn 15:2*
J *Lk 11:31–32 ◀▶ Ac 10:42*
N *Jn 12:35–36 ◀▶ Ac 3:22–23*
K *Jn 12:46 ◀▶ Jn 14:6*

12:48 Jesus prophesied that those who rejected him and his words of salvation would be judged in the last days on the basis of Christ's own words.

The Judgments of God

THE VAST CHASM between God's holiness and humanity's sinfulness is highlighted by God's judgments. The Bible describes eight separate judgments of God.

The Judgment of a Believer's Sin

The Bible confirms that "the wages of sin is death" (Ro 6:23). God's holy law judges every sin and requires the mandatory sentence. Therefore it was necessary for Jesus Christ to die on the cross and bear the eternal punishment for sin. Thus the basis of this judgment of the believer's sin is the completed, perfect atoning work of Christ on the cross.

The Judgment of a Believer's Walk

There is a continuing judgment in a believer's daily walk of faith (see 1Co 11:31–32). The Holy Spirit awakens our conscience to an active obedience to God's will. God's chastening signals his love for us and directs us to a closer walk with him. While we sometimes resent this chastening, God corrects us because of his profound love for us and a desire for our best interests. Though not enjoyable, chastening will yield righteousness if we will learn from it (see Heb 12:1).

The Judgment of Israel

Israel's destiny as God's chosen people has truly been a two-edged sword. Blessed with God's Word, Israel bore a greater responsibility for obedience and a higher standard of spirituality than the pagan nations that surrounded her. In addition, God promised that Israel would face persecution and tribulation because of her rebellion against God's prophets and her rejection of God's commands and the Messiah. Tragically, Israel has reaped the fulfillment of this promised judgment over the centuries. Yet Israel's judgment has not come to an end.

The prophets foretold that just before the return of Jesus Christ the world would go through a time of terrible persecution under the antichrist. While this great tribulation will involve the whole world, its horrors will be focused upon Israel during the last three and one-half years before the Battle of Armageddon. God will still provide a witness for Israel and souls will be saved, beginning in Israel, during this tribulation period. Those who repent and survive through this prophesied period of trouble will be saved and blessed for eternity. Twenty-five centuries ago, the prophet Zechariah prophesied that despite the massive slaughter the Messiah would come and save Israel from her enemies (see Zec 13:1–9). At that time Israel will finally enjoy the great blessings and prosperity that have been the hope of the chosen people for centuries. For further information, see the article on "The Tribulation" on p. 980.

The Judgment of the Gentile Nations

In the last days, all the nations of the world will take part in a titanic struggle for world supremacy. Following the Battle of Armageddon, these nations will be judged by Jesus Christ based on their treatment of both Jewish and Gentile believers (see Mt 25:31–46). Those nations that have protected God's people will be preserved to enjoy the blessings of the millennial kingdom. Those nations who have despised and persecuted the people of God will be cast onto the dust heap of history.

Some have assumed that national distinctions will cease to exist once Jesus sets up his eternal kingdom on earth. However, God specifically described the future of humanity in terms of the continuation of both Israel and those nations that have blessed God's people during the tribulation. The Bible clearly states that the nations will be ruled by the saints during and after the Millennium (see Rev 5:10). After the earth is renewed, John describes a wonderful future in which the new Jerusalem will descend from heaven and Israel, the nations and Christ's kingdom will enjoy peace forever. For further information, see the article on "The New Jerusalem" on p. 1492.

The Judgment at the Great White Throne

John revealed that at the end of the Battle of Armageddon Satan would be chained in the bottomless pit for a period of one thousand years. People would enjoy peace and prosperity in God's kingdom during this Millennium. However, after the Millennium, Satan will be released to lead a final rebellion against God. The judgment at God's great white throne will occur after this rebellion. All unrepentant people who have ever lived will stand before God's throne, be judged for their wickedness and thrown into the lake of fire (see Rev 20:11–15). Note that Mt 25:41 says that the lake of fire was originally prepared for the devil and his angels. If people had never rebelled against God or stayed in their unrepentant state, they would never have been consigned to hell. For further information about this judgment, see the article on p. 1484.

The Judgment of Fallen Angels

Satan and all his rebellious angels will finally stand before Christ at the great white throne. Some say these wicked angels may have cohabited with women during the time of the flood, producing a race of wicked giants (see study note at Ge 6:1–4). Others contend that these evil angels rebelled with Satan against God before Adam and Eve sinned in the garden. In either case, these angels were chained by God in a special prison until the day of this judgment (see 2Pe 2:4; Jude 6). On this final judgment day these wicked angels will be imprisoned forever with Satan in the lake of everlasting fire (see Mt 25:41). For further information, see the article on "Satan and the Fallen Angels" on p. 914.

The Judgment of the Wicked Dead

The great white throne judgment will provide every person with a fair trial before the God of the universe. The souls of all people who have refused to repent will receive their resurrected bodies and appear before God on that ultimate judgment day. The grave and the sea will give up their dead, and even hell will surrender its souls to stand before God. All wicked persons who appear there will be judged by the works of their lives (see Rev 20:12). Many will claim to be Christians. They will point to their public religious life, but God will point to their heart and declare that their names were never entered in the book of life because they had never accepted the pardon of Jesus Christ. The only cure and deliverance from our sin and guilt is the miraculous transformation wrought by the blood of Jesus Christ.

The Bema Judgment

The apostle Paul uses the Greek word *bema* in 2Co 5:10 in reference to a judgment that will take place before Jesus Christ in heaven involving all Christians who have ever lived. A *bema* was "a raised space or bench, the official seat of a judge." Paul indicates that all believers will appear before this judgment seat of Christ to have their lives judged by Jesus on the basis of their righteous works. This *bema* judgment will occur after the resurrection of the saints and will involve the gain or loss of rewards for our service to God. Those who lived godly lives of work and service will withstand God's scrutiny and be blessed with eternal rewards in heaven; those whose works do not meet God's standards will not be rewarded (see 1Co 3:12–15). The blood of Christ will still save those who repent. For further information, see the article on "Crowns and Rewards" on p. 1318.

To reign and rule with Christ is part of the reward that will belong to faithful believers in the Millennium. Jesus Christ will rule as King of kings in Jerusalem (see Rev 19:16), and King David will be resurrected to serve as Christ's regent (see Isa 55:3–4; Jer 30:9; 33:15; Eze 34:23–24; Hos 3:5; Am 9:11). The twelve disciples will rule the twelve tribes of Israel (see Mt 19:28), and many believers will rule various cities throughout the earth (see Isa 40:10; Zec 3:7; Lk 19:12–28).

25 He then lying on Jesus' breast saith unto him, Lord, who is it?

26 Jesus answered, He it is, to whom I shall give a [l]sop, when I have dipped *it.* And when he had dipped the sop, he gave *it* to Judas Iscariot, *the son* of Simon.

27 [a]And after the sop Satan entered into him. Then said Jesus unto him, That thou doest, do quickly.

28 Now no man at the table knew for what intent he spake this unto him.

29 For some *of them* thought, because [a]Judas had the bag, that Jesus had said unto him, Buy *those things* that we have need of against the feast; or, that he should give something to the poor.

30 He then having received the sop went immediately out: and it was night.

31 ¶ Therefore, when he was gone out, Jesus said, [a]Now is the Son of man glorified, and [b]God is glorified in him.

32 If God be glorified in him, God shall also glorify him in himself, and [a]shall straightway glorify him.

33 Little children, yet a little while I am with you. Ye shall seek me: [a]and as I said unto the Jews, Whither I go, ye cannot come; so now I say to you.

34 [a]A new commandment I give unto you, That ye love one another; as I have loved you, that ye also love one another.

35 [a]By this shall all *men* know that ye are my disciples, if ye have love one to another.

Peter's denial foretold

36 ¶ Simon Peter said unto him, Lord, whither goest thou? Jesus answered him, Whither I go, thou canst not follow me now; but [a]thou shalt follow me afterwards.

37 Peter said unto him, Lord, why cannot I follow thee now? I will [a]lay down my life for thy sake.

38 Jesus answered him, Wilt thou lay down thy life for my sake? Verily, verily, I say unto thee, The cock shall not crow, till thou hast denied me thrice.

The way, the truth, and the life

W 14 LET [a]NOT your heart be troubled: ye believe in God, believe also in me.

2 In my Father's house are many mansions: if *it were* not *so,* I would have told you. [a]I go to prepare a place for you.

3 And if I go and prepare a place for you, [a]I will come again, and receive you unto myself; that [b]where I am, *there* ye may be also.

4 And whither I go ye know, and the way ye know.

5 Thomas saith unto him, Lord, we know not whither thou goest; and how can we know the way?

6 Jesus saith unto him, I am [a]the way, K
[b]the truth, and [c]the life: [d]no man cometh O
unto the Father, but by me.

7 [a]If ye had known me, ye should have known my Father also: and from henceforth ye know him, and have seen him.

8 Philip saith unto him, Lord, show us the Father, and it sufficeth us.

9 Jesus saith unto him, Have I been so long time with you, and yet hast thou not known me, Philip? [a]he that hath seen me hath seen the Father; and how sayest thou *then,* Show us the Father?

10 Believest thou not that [a]I am in the Father, and the Father in me? the words that I speak unto you [b]I speak not of myself: but the Father that dwelleth in me, he doeth the works.

11 Believe me that I *am* in the Father, and the Father in me: [a]or else believe me for the very works' sake.

12 [a]Verily, verily, I say unto you, He that believeth on me, the works that I do shall he do also; and greater *works* than these shall he do; because I go unto my Father.

13 [a]And whatsoever ye shall ask in my name, that will I do, that the Father may be glorified in the Son. L

14 If ye shall ask any thing in my name, I will do *it.*

The promise of the Spirit

15 ¶ [a]If ye love me, keep my commandments. S

26 [l]Or, *morsel*
27 [a]Luke 22:3; ch. 6:70
29 [a]ch. 12:6
31 [a]ch. 12:23 [b]ch. 14:13; 1 Pet. 4:11
32 [a]ch. 12:23
33 [a]ch. 8:21
34 [a]Lev. 19:18; ch. 15:12,17; Eph. 5:2; 1 Thes. 4:9; Jas. 2:8; 1 Pet. 1:22; 1 John 2:7 & 3:11, 23
35 [a]1 John 2:5 & 4:20
36 [a]ch. 21:18; 2 Pet. 1:14
37 [a]Mat. 26:33; Mark 14:29; Luke 22:33
14:1 [a]ver. 27
2 [a]ch. 13:33
3 [a]Acts 1:11 [b]ch. 12:26 & 17:24; 1 Thes. 4:17
6 [a]Heb. 9:8 [b]ch. 8:32 [c]ch. 11:25 [d]ch. 10:9
7 [a]ch. 8:19
9 [a]ch. 12:45; Col. 1:15; Heb. 1:3
10 [a]ch. 10:38 & 17:21,23 [b]ch. 5:19 & 8:28
11 [a]ch. 10:38
12 [a]Mat. 21:21; Mark 16:17; Luke 10:17
13 [a]Mat. 7:7 & 21:22; Mark 11:24; Luke 11:9; ch. 15:7, 16 & 16:23,24; Jas. 1:5; 1 John 3:22 & 5:14
15 [a]ver. 21,23; ch. 15:10; 1 John 5:3

W *Lk 18:1* ◀▶ *Jn 14:27*

K *Jn 12:50* ◀▶ *Jn 17:3*
O *Jn 10:1* ◀▶ *Jn 20:23*
L *Jn 10:27–29* ◀▶ *Jn 16:24*
S *Jn 8:34–35* ◀▶ *Jn 14:21*

Heaven

THOUGH THE BIBLE does not reveal the exact location of heaven, Scripture tells us that heaven is the home of God and his angelic host.

Heaven in the Old Testament

The OT makes reference to heaven in several ways. The opening chapters of Genesis describe the physical, astronomical heavens. According to the OT prophets, God's coming judgment will be announced in the astronomical heavens (see Isa 13:10; Joel 2:30–31).

However, the spiritual reality of heaven is described in other OT passages as God's abode (see Ps 11:4). This view of heaven is presented throughout the OT as the hope of the saints. Few details are given other than the fact that the saints will be "gathered unto their fathers" (Jdg 2:10) and that in this place they will dwell in the presence of God.

Heaven in the New Testament

Because of the advent of Christ and his teaching about God's kingdom, the NT contains many references to heaven that shed light on this glorious place. Note that occasionally a NT author may use the word *heaven* as a synonym for God to avoid the casual use of God's holy name (see Mt 23:22; Lk 15:21). Yet the majority of the NT Scriptures that deal with heaven refer to a specific place for believers. The apostle Paul suggests that heaven is full of unspeakable wonders for those who trust God (see 1Co 2:9). Fortunately, a number of NT passages describe enough details of heaven to awaken a sense of wonder and anticipation for those who long to see our Lord face to face. Many of these passages deal with references to a new heaven and a new earth that will exist after the Millennium. Cleansed by fire and housing the new Jerusalem, this eternal new heaven and new earth will no longer be subject to sin and its effects (see Rev 12:10). For further information, see the article on "A New Heaven and a New Earth" on p. 1488.

The Heavenly City

The largest percentage of teaching about heaven in the NT consists of information about the heavenly city, the new Jerusalem. This capital city of heaven is filled with God's glory and glows with an internal light, "even like a jasper stone, clear as crystal" (Rev 21:11). New Jerusalem is an enormous city—1,500 miles long along each side. Its foundation wall is over 216 feet high, and it is full of gates, mansions, streets and inhabitants (see 21:16–18). New Jerusalem's enormous size would easily accommodate more than a billion mansions larger and grander than any palace on earth today.

The dimensions of the new Jerusalem indicate that it will also be of an unusual shape, quite possibly pyramidal. The Bible indicates that 12 layers of stone support the foundation, and each layer contains "the names of the twelve apostles of the Lamb" (21:14). The walls have three pearl gates on each side; and the 12 layers of the foundations of the walls are made of precious stones like jasper, sapphire, emerald, topaz, amethyst and others (see 21:19–20). The streets in the new Jerusalem are made of pure gold, transparent like glass (see 21:21).

There will be no need of the sun or moon to provide light in the new Jerusalem because God's presence will light the whole city (see 21:23–24). His glory shines so brightly that "there shall be no night there" (21:25) and no danger of an enemy or a need to shut the gates. There will be no rust or decay because sin and its effects on the universe will have ceased.

Only the redeemed, those whose names "are written in the Lamb's book of life" (21:27), will inhabit the new Jerusalem. The faithful, ever since Abel, have been longing for this city (see Heb 11). The ultimate goal of every believer is to join the Savior in the new Jerusalem, the heavenly city of God. For further information, see the article on "The New Jerusalem" on p. 1492.

Although the new Jerusalem will be the final home of all believers, we will not be restricted to it. As God's children we will be able to explore the new earth and the new heaven, able to come and go, ruling and reigning with Christ. We will have access to the "pure river of water of life, clear as crystal, proceeding out of the throne of God and of the Lamb" (Rev 22:1) and be able to partake freely of the tree of life (see 22:2). We have Jesus' promise that he is preparing heaven for us right now and will one day "come again, and receive you unto myself; that where I am, there ye may be also" (Jn 14:3). What a wonder heaven will be!

16 And I will pray the Father, and [a]he
shall give you another Comforter, that he
may abide with you for ever;
17 *Even* [a]the Spirit of truth; [b]whom
the world cannot receive, because it
seeth him not, neither knoweth him: but
ye know him; for he dwelleth with you,
[c]and shall be in you.
18 [a]I will not leave you [1]comfortless:
[b]I will come to you.
19 Yet a little while, and the world
seeth me no more; but [a]ye see me: [b]be-
cause I live, ye shall live also.
20 At that day ye shall know that [a]I *am*
in my Father, and ye in me, and I in you.
21 [a]He that hath my commandments,
and keepeth them, he it is that loveth
me: and he that loveth me shall be loved
of my Father, and I will love him, and will
manifest myself to him.
22 [a]Judas saith unto him, not Iscariot,
Lord, how is it that thou wilt manifest
thyself unto us, and not unto the world?
23 Jesus answered and said unto him,
If a man love me, he will keep my words:
and my Father will love him, [a]and we
will come unto him, and make our abode
with him.
24 He that loveth me not keepeth not
my sayings: and [a]the word which ye hear
is not mine, but the Father's which
sent me.
25 These things have I spoken unto
you, being *yet* present with you.

B *Jn 7:37–39* ◀ ▶ *Jn 14:26*
J *Jn 1:32* ◀ ▶ *Jn 14:26*
N *Jn 7:37–39* ◀ ▶ *Jn 15:26*
P *Jn 7:37–39* ◀ ▶ *Jn 14:26*
W *Jn 6:63* ◀ ▶ *Jn 16:7*
S *Jn 14:15* ◀ ▶ *Jn 15:2*
U *Jn 12:25–26* ◀ ▶ *Jn 15:7*

16 [a]ch. 15:26 & 16:7; Rom. 8:15
17 [a]ch. 15:26 & 16:13; 1 John 4:6 [b]1 Cor. 2:14 [c]1 John 2:27
18 [a]Mat. 28:20 [b]ver. 3,28 [1]Or, *orphans*
19 [a]ch. 16:16 [b]1 Cor. 15:20
20 [a]ch. 10:38
21 [a]1 John 2:5 & 5:3
22 [a]Luke 6:16
23 [a]1 John 2:24; Rev. 3:20
24 [a]ch. 5:19
26 [a]Luke 24:49; ch. 15:26 [b]ch. 2:22 & 12:16; 1 John 2:20
27 [a]Phil. 4:7; Col. 3:15
28 [a]ver. 3,18 [b]ch. 16:16 & 20:17 [c]ch. 5:18 & 10:30; Phil. 2:6
29 [a]ch. 13:19 & 16:4
30 [a]ch. 12:31 & 16:11
31 [a]ch. 10:18; Phil. 2:8; Heb. 5:8
15:2 [a]Mat. 15:13

26 But [a]the Comforter, *which is* the
Holy Ghost, whom the Father will send
in my name, [b]he shall teach you all
things, and bring all things to your remembrance, whatsoever I have said unto
you.
27 [a]Peace I leave with you, my peace I
give unto you: not as the world giveth,
give I unto you. Let not your heart be
troubled, neither let it be afraid.
28 Ye have heard how [a]I said unto
you, I go away, and come *again* unto you.
If ye loved me, ye would rejoice, because
I said, [b]I go unto the Father: for [c]my Father is greater than I.
29 And [a]now I have told you before it
come to pass, that, when it is come to
pass, ye might believe.
30 Hereafter I will not talk much with
you: [a]for the prince of this world cometh,
and hath nothing in me.
31 But that the world may know that I
love the Father; and [a]as the Father gave
me commandment, even so I do. Arise,
let us go hence.

Jesus the true vine

15 I AM the true vine, and my Father is the husbandman.
2 [a]Every branch in me that beareth not
fruit he taketh away: and every *branch*

B *Jn 14:16–17* ◀ ▶ *Jn 15:26*
G *Jn 3:34* ◀ ▶ *Jn 16:13–15*
J *Jn 14:16–17* ◀ ▶ *Jn 15:26*
M *Jn 7:38–39* ◀ ▶ *Jn 16:7–15*
P *Jn 14:16–17* ◀ ▶ *Jn 15:26*
T *Jn 3:34* ◀ ▶ *Jn 15:26*
W *Jn 14:1* ◀ ▶ *Php 3:1*
H *Jn 12:48* ◀ ▶ *Jn 15:6*
S *Jn 14:21* ◀ ▶ *Jn 15:6*

14:16–18 This prophecy that God would send the Holy Spirit to empower believers was fulfilled on the day of Pentecost (see Ac 2:1–20). Note that Jesus promised that he would "not leave you comfortless" (14:18). This ongoing relationship of the Holy Spirit and the church will continue until the saints are resurrected to heaven when the Holy Spirit is removed in his role on earth as the restrainer of the antichrist (see 2Th 2:5–9). Satan will then be allowed to bring forth the first beast of Rev 13.

14:26 Jesus promised that the Holy Spirit would "teach you all things and bring all things to your remembrance, whatsoever I have said unto you" (14:26). This prophecy was fulfilled on Pentecost when the disciples received the Holy Spirit.

This prophecy also guarantees the accuracy of the NT accounts of Christ's teaching because the Holy Spirit enabled the disciples to correctly recall the words of Jesus and allowed them to accurately record his messages to his believers through the NT Scriptures. Though there are minute differences in phrasing between the Gospel authors on a few occasions, the divine inspiration of the accounts is indisputable. John also indicates that "there are also many other things which Jesus did, the which, if they should be written every one, I suppose that even the world itself could not contain the books that should be written" (21:25).

that beareth fruit, he purgeth it, that it may bring forth more fruit.

3 [a]Now ye are clean through the word which I have spoken unto you.

4 [a]Abide in me, and I in you. As the branch cannot bear fruit of itself, except it abide in the vine; no more can ye, except ye abide in me.

5 I am the vine, ye *are* the branches: He that abideth in me, and I in him, the same bringeth forth much [a]fruit: for [/]without me ye can do nothing.

H S 6 If a man abide not in me, [a]he is cast forth as a branch, and is withered; and men gather them, and cast *them* into the fire, and they are burned.

U 7 If ye abide in me, and my words abide in you, [a]ye shall ask what ye will, and it shall be done unto you.

8 [a]Herein is my Father glorified, that ye bear much fruit; [b]so shall ye be my disciples.

9 As the Father hath loved me, so have I loved you: continue ye in my love.

S 10 [a]If ye keep my commandments, ye shall abide in my love; even as I have kept my Father's commandments, and abide in his love.

U 11 These things have I spoken unto you, that my joy might remain in you, and [a]*that* your joy might be full.

12 [a]This is my commandment, That ye love one another, as I have loved you.

L 13 [a]Greater love hath no man than this, that a man lay down his life for his friends.

S 14 [a]Ye are my friends, if ye do whatsoever I command you.

15 Henceforth I call you not servants; for the servant knoweth not what his lord doeth: but I have called you friends; [a]for all things that I have heard of my Father I have made known unto you.

16 [a]Ye have not chosen me, but I have chosen you, and [b]ordained you, that ye should go and bring forth fruit, and *that* your fruit should remain: that [c]whatsoever ye shall ask of the Father in my name, he may give it you.

H *Jn 15:2* ◀▶ *Ac 1:25*
S *Jn 15:2* ◀▶ *Jn 15:10*
U *Jn 14:21* ◀▶ *Jn 15:11*
S *Jn 15:6* ◀▶ *Jn 15:14*
U *Jn 15:7* ◀▶ *Ro 8:28*
L *Jn 12:46–47* ◀▶ *Ac 3:19*
S *Jn 15:10* ◀▶ *Jn 17:15–20*

17 These things I command you, that ye love one another.

The hatred of the world

18 [a]If the world hate you, ye know that it hated me before *it hated* you.

19 [a]If ye were of the world, the world would love his own: but [b]because ye are not of the world, but I have chosen you out of the world, therefore the world hateth you.

20 Remember the word that I said unto you, [a]The servant is not greater than his lord. If they have persecuted me, they will also persecute you; [b]if they have kept my saying, they will keep yours also.

21 But [a]all these things will they do unto you for my name's sake, because they know not him that sent me.

22 [a]If I had not come and spoken unto them, they had not had sin: [b]but now they have no [/]cloak for their sin.

23 [a]He that hateth me hateth my Father also.

24 If I had not done among them [a]the works which none other man did, they had not had sin: but now have they both seen and hated both me and my Father.

25 But *this cometh to pass,* that the word might be fulfilled that is written in their law, [a]They hated me without a cause.

26 [a]But when the Comforter is come, whom I will send unto you from the Father, *even* the Spirit of truth, which proceedeth from the Father, [b]he shall testify of me: B J N P T

27 And [a]ye also shall bear witness, because [b]ye have been with me from the beginning.

16

THESE THINGS have I spoken unto you, that ye [a]should not be offended.

2 [a]They shall put you out of the synagogues: yea, the time cometh, [b]that whosoever killeth you will think that he doeth God service.

3 And [a]these things will they do unto you, because they have not known the Father, nor me.

4 But [a]these things have I told you, that when the time shall come, ye may

B *Jn 14:26* ◀▶ *Jn 16:7*
J *Jn 14:26* ◀▶ *Jn 16:7*
N *Jn 14:16–17* ◀▶ *Ac 2:2–4*
P *Jn 14:26* ◀▶ *Jn 16:7–15*
T *Jn 14:26* ◀▶ *Jn 16:7–15*

3 [a]ch. 13:10; Eph. 5:26; 1 Pet. 1:22
4 [a]Col. 1:23; 1 John 2:6
5 [a]Hos. 14:8; Phil. 1:11 & 4:13 [/]Or, *severed from me;* see Acts 4:12
6 [a]Mat. 3:10 & 7:19
7 [a]ch. 16:23
8 [a]Mat. 5:16; Phil. 1:11 [b]ch. 8:31
10 [a]ch. 14:15
11 [a]ch. 16:24 & 17:13; 1 John 1:4
12 [a]ch. 13:34; 1 Thes. 4:9; 1 Pet. 4:8; 1 John 3:11
13 [a]ch. 10:11; Rom. 5:7,8; Eph. 5:2; 1 John 3:16
14 [a]Mat. 12:50; ch. 14:15
15 [a]Gen. 18:17; ch. 17:26
16 [a]ch. 6:70 & 13:18; 1 John 4:10 [b]Mat. 28:19; Mark 16:15; Col. 1:6 [c]ver. 7
18 [a]1 John 3:13
19 [a]1 John 4:5 [b]ch. 17:14
20 [a]Mat. 10:24; Luke 6:40 [b]Ezek. 3:7
21 [a]Mat. 10:22 & 24:9
22 [a]ch. 9:41 [b]Rom. 1:20; Jas. 4:17 [/]Or, *excuse*
23 [a]1 John 2:23
24 [a]ch. 3:2
25 [a]Ps. 35:19 & 69:4
26 [a]Luke 24:49; ch. 14:17; Acts 2:33 [b]1 John 5:6
27 [a]Luke 24:48; Acts 1:21 & 2:32 & 3:15 & 4:20,33 & 5:32 & 10:39 & 13:31; 1 Pet. 5:1; 2 Pet. 1:16 [b]Luke 1:2; 1 John 1:1
16:1 [a]Mat. 11:6 & 24:10 & 26:31
2 [a]ch. 9:22 [b]Acts 8:1 & 9:1 & 26:9, 10
3 [a]ch. 15:21; Rom. 10:2; 1 Cor. 2:8; 1 Tim. 1:13
4 [a]ch. 13:19 & 14:29

remember that I told you of them. And these things I said not unto you at the beginning, because I was with you.

The coming of the Spirit

5 But now [a]I go my way to him that sent me; and none of you asketh me, Whither goest thou?

6 But because I have said these things unto you, sorrow hath filled your heart.

7 Nevertheless I tell you the truth; It is expedient for you that I go away: for if I go not away, [a]the Comforter will not come unto you; but [b]if I depart, I will send him unto you.

8 And when he is come, he will ʹreprove the world of sin, and of righteousness, and of judgment:

9 [a]Of sin, because they believe not on me;

10 [a]Of righteousness, [b]because I go to my Father, and ye see me no more;

11 [a]Of judgment, because [b]the prince of this world is judged.

12 I have yet many things to say unto you, [a]but ye cannot bear them now.

13 Howbeit when he, [a]the Spirit of truth, is come, [b]he will guide you into all truth: for he shall not speak of himself; but whatsoever he shall hear, *that* shall he speak: and he will show you things to come.

14 He shall glorify me: for he shall receive of mine, and shall show *it* unto you.

15 [a]All things that the Father hath are mine: therefore said I, that he shall take of mine, and shall show *it* unto you.

Jesus' farewell to his disciples

16 A little while, and ye shall not see me: and again, a little while, and ye shall see me, [a]because I go to the Father.

17 Then said *some* of his disciples among themselves, What is this that he saith unto us, A little while, and ye shall not see me: and again, a little while, and ye shall see me: and, Because I go to the Father?

18 They said therefore, What is this that he saith, A little while? we cannot tell what he saith.

19 Now Jesus knew that they were desirous to ask him, and said unto them, Do ye inquire among yourselves of that I said, A little while, and ye shall not see me: and again, a little while, and ye shall see me?

20 Verily, verily, I say unto you, That ye shall weep and lament, but the world shall rejoice: and ye shall be sorrowful, but your sorrow shall be turned into joy.

21 [a]A woman when she is in travail hath sorrow, because her hour is come: but as soon as she is delivered of the child, she remembereth no more the anguish, for joy that a man is born into the world.

22 And ye now therefore have sorrow: but I will see you again, and [a]your heart shall rejoice, and your joy no man taketh from you.

23 And in that day ye shall ask me nothing. [a]Verily, verily, I say unto you, Whatsoever ye shall ask the Father in my name, he will give *it* you.

24 Hitherto have ye asked nothing in my name: ask, and ye shall receive, [a]that your joy may be full.

25 These things have I spoken unto you in ʹproverbs: but the time cometh, when I shall no more speak unto you in proverbs, but I shall show you plainly of the Father.

26 At that day ye shall ask in my name: and I say not unto you, that I will pray the Father for you:

27 [a]For the Father himself loveth you,

B *Jn 15:26* ◀ ▶ *Jn 16:13*
C *Lk 1:15–17* ◀ ▶ *Ac 11:24*
J *Jn 15:26* ◀ ▶ *Jn 20:21–22*
M *Jn 14:26* ◀ ▶ *Ac 1:8*
P *Jn 15:26* ◀ ▶ *Ac 1:4–5*
T *Jn 15:26* ◀ ▶ *Ac 1:2*
W *Jn 14:16–17* ◀ ▶ *Ac 1:4–5*
B *Jn 16:7* ◀ ▶ *Ac 1:4–5*
G *Jn 14:26* ◀ ▶ *Ac 1:8*
L *Jn 4:23–24* ◀ ▶ *Ac 1:2*

L *Jn 14:13–14* ◀ ▶ *Ro 8:31–39*

5 [a]ch. 7:33 & 14:28
7 [a]ch. 7:39 & 14:16,26 & 15:26 [b]Acts 2:33; Eph. 4:8
8 ʹOr, *convince*
9 [a]Acts 2:22
10 [a]Acts 2:32 [b]ch. 5:32
11 [a]Acts 26:18 [b]Luke 10:18; Eph. 2:2; Col. 2:15; Heb. 2:14
12 [a]Mark 4:33; 1 Cor. 3:2; Heb. 5:12
13 [a]ch. 14:17 [b]ch. 14:26; 1 John 2:20
15 [a]Mat. 11:27; ch. 3:35
16 [a]ch. 13:3
21 [a]Is. 26:17
22 [a]Luke 24:41; ch. 14:1,27 & 20:20; Acts 2:46 & 13:52; 1 Pet. 1:8
23 [a]Mat. 7:7; ch. 14:13 & 15:16
24 [a]ch. 15:11
25 ʹOr, *parables*
27 [a]ch. 14:21

16:7–11 Jesus predicted that after his ascension to heaven he would send the Holy Spirit to "reprove the world of sin, and of righteousness, and of judgment" (16:8). The Holy Spirit also restrains "the prince of this world" (16:11) during this age of grace until the tribulation when he will be released to fulfill his prophesied role (see 2Th 2:6–9).

16:16 Jesus prophesied that he would leave his disciples soon, but he also foretold that he would physically return from heaven so that they would see him.

because ye have loved me, and [b]have believed that I came out from God.

28 [a]I came forth from the Father, and am come into the world: again, I leave the world, and go to the Father.

29 His disciples said unto him, Lo, now speakest thou plainly, and speakest no [l]proverb.

E 30 Now are we sure that [a]thou knowest all things, and needest not that any man should ask thee: by this [b]we believe that thou camest forth from God.

31 Jesus answered them, Do ye now believe?

32 [a]Behold, the hour cometh, yea, is now come, that ye shall be scattered, [b]every man to [l]his own, and shall leave me alone: and [c]yet I am not alone, because the Father is with me.

J 33 These things I have spoken unto you, that [a]in me ye might have peace. [b]In the world ye shall have tribulation: but be of good cheer; [c]I have overcome the world.

The prayer to be glorified

17 THESE WORDS spake Jesus, and lifted up his eyes to heaven, and said, Father, [a]the hour is come; glorify thy Son, that thy Son also may glorify thee:

2 [a]As thou hast given him power over all flesh, that he should give eternal life to as many [b]as thou hast given him.

K 3 And [a]this is life eternal, that they might know thee [b]the only true God, and Jesus Christ, [c]whom thou hast sent.

4 [a]I have glorified thee on the earth: [b]I have finished the work [c]which thou gavest me to do.

5 And now, O Father, glorify thou me with thine own self with the glory [a]which I had with thee before the world was.

The prayer for the disciples

6 [a]I have manifested thy name unto the men [b]which thou gavest me out of the world: thine they were, and thou gavest them me; and they have kept thy word.

7 Now they have known that all things whatsoever thou hast given me are of thee.

8 For I have given unto them the words [a]which thou gavest me; and they have received *them,* [b]and have known surely that I came out from thee, and they have believed that thou didst send me.

9 I pray for them: [a]I pray not for the world, but for them which thou hast given me; for they are thine.

10 And all mine are thine, and [a]thine are mine; and I am glorified in them.

11 [a]And now I am no more in the world, but these are in the world, and I come to thee. Holy Father, [b]keep through thine own name those whom thou hast given me, that they may be one, [c]as we *are.* K

12 While I was with them in the world, [a]I kept them in thy name: those that thou gavest me I have kept, and [b]none of them is lost, [c]but the son of perdition; [d]that the scripture might be fulfilled.

13 And now come I to thee; and these things I speak in the world, that they might have my joy fulfilled in themselves.

14 I have given them thy word; [a]and the world hath hated them, because they are not of the world, [b]even as I am not of the world.

15 I pray not that thou shouldest take them out of the world, but [a]that thou shouldest keep them from the evil. S

16 They are not of the world, even as I am not of the world.

17 [a]Sanctify them through thy truth: [b]thy word is truth.

18 [a]As thou hast sent me into the world, even so have I also sent them into the world.

19 And [a]for their sakes I sanctify my-

27 [b]ch. 3:13
28 [a]ch. 13:3
29 [l]Or, *parable*
30 [a]ch. 21:17 [b]ch. 17:8
32 [a]Mat. 26:31; Mark 14:27 [b]ch. 20:10 [c]ch. 8:29 [l]Or, *his own home*
33 [a]Is. 9:6; Rom. 5:1; Eph. 2:14 [b]2 Tim. 3:12 [c]Rom. 8:37; 1 John 4:4
17:1 [a]ch. 12:23
2 [a]Dan. 7:14; Mat. 11:27; ch. 3:35; Phil. 2:10; Heb. 2:8 [b]ver. 6,9,24; ch. 6:37
3 [a]Is. 53:11; Jer. 9:24 [b]1 Cor. 8:4; 1 Thes. 1:9 [c]ch. 3:34
4 [a]ch. 13:31 [b]ch. 4:34 [c]ch. 14:31
5 [a]Phil. 2:6; Col. 1:15; Heb. 1:3
6 [a]Ps. 22:22 [b]ch. 6:37
8 [a]ch. 8:28 [b]ch. 16:27
9 [a]1 John 5:19
10 [a]ch. 16:15
11 [a]ch. 13:1 [b]1 Pet. 1:5; Jude 1 [c]ch. 10:30
12 [a]Heb. 2:13 [b]1 John 2:19 [c]ch. 6:70 [d]Ps. 109:8; Acts 1:20
14 [a]1 John 3:13 [b]ch. 8:23
15 [a]Mat. 6:13; Gal. 1:4; 1 John 5:18
17 [a]Acts 15:9; Eph. 5:26; 1 Pet. 1:22 [b]Ps. 119:142, 151
18 [a]ch. 20:21
19 [a]1 Cor. 1:2; 1 Thes. 4:7; Heb. 10:10

E *Jn 6:64* ◀ ▶ *Jn 21:17*
J *Lk 6:22–23* ◀ ▶ *Ac 5:41*
K *Jn 14:6* ◀ ▶ *Jn 17:11–12*

K *Jn 17:3* ◀ ▶ *Jn 20:23*
S *Jn 15:14* ◀ ▶ *Ac 3:26*

16:33 While Jesus warned his followers of the persecution that would afflict them, he also told them to take heart because he is the one who overcomes the world. Though the church will undergo persecution because of its faith, Christians can rejoice in the certainty that Jesus has won total victory over sin, death and Satan (see Mt 24:9–10).

self, that they also might be [l]sanctified through the truth.

The prayer for the church

20 Neither pray I for these alone, but for them also which shall believe on me through their word;

21 [a]That they all may be one; as [b]thou, Father, *art* in me, and I in thee, that they also may be one in us: that the world may believe that thou hast sent me.

22 And the glory which thou gavest me I have given them; [a]that they may be one, even as we are one:

23 I in them, and thou in me, [a]that they may be made perfect in one; and that the world may know that thou hast sent me, and hast loved them, as thou hast loved me.

24 [a]Father, I will that they also, whom thou hast given me, be with me where I am; that they may behold my glory, which thou hast given me: [b]for thou lovedst me before the foundation of the world.

25 O righteous Father, [a]the world hath not known thee: but [b]I have known thee, and [c]these have known that thou hast sent me.

26 [a]And I have declared unto them thy name, and will declare *it:* that the love [b]wherewith thou hast loved me may be in them, and I in them.

Jesus' betrayal and arrest

18 WHEN JESUS had spoken these words, [a]he went forth with his disciples over [b]the brook Cedron, where was a garden, into the which he entered, and his disciples.

2 And Judas also, which betrayed him, knew the place: [a]for Jesus ofttimes resorted thither with his disciples.

3 [a]Judas then, having received a band *of men* and officers from the chief priests and Pharisees, cometh thither with lanterns and torches and weapons.

4 Jesus therefore, knowing all things that should come upon him, went forth, and said unto them, Whom seek ye?

5 They answered him, Jesus of Nazareth. Jesus saith unto them, I am *he.* And Judas also, which betrayed him, stood with them.

6 As soon then as he had said unto them, I am *he,* they went backward, and fell to the ground.

7 Then asked he them again, Whom seek ye? And they said, Jesus of Nazareth.

8 Jesus answered, I have told you that I am *he:* if therefore ye seek me, let these go their way:

9 That the saying might be fulfilled, which he spake, [a]Of them which thou gavest me have I lost none.

10 [a]Then Simon Peter having a sword drew it, and smote the high priest's servant, and cut off his right ear. The servant's name was Malchus.

11 Then said Jesus unto Peter, Put up thy sword into the sheath: [a]the cup which my Father hath given me, shall I not drink it?

Jesus before Jewish authorities

12 Then the band and the captain and officers of the Jews took Jesus, and bound him,

13 And [a]led him away to [b]Annas first; for he was father-in-law to Caiaphas, which was the high priest that same year.

14 [a]Now Caiaphas was he, which gave counsel to the Jews, that it was expedient that one man should die for the people.

15 ¶ [a]And Simon Peter followed Jesus, and *so did* another disciple: that disciple was known unto the high priest, and went in with Jesus into the palace of the high priest.

16 [a]But Peter stood at the door without. Then went out that other disciple, which was known unto the high priest, and spake unto her that kept the door, and brought in Peter.

17 Then saith the damsel that kept the door unto Peter, Art not thou also *one* of this man's disciples? He saith, I am not.

18 And the servants and officers stood there, who had made a fire of coals; for it was cold: and they warmed themselves: and Peter stood with them, and warmed himself.

19 ¶ The high priest then asked Jesus of his disciples, and of his doctrine.

20 Jesus answered him, [a]I spake openly to the world; I ever taught in the synagogue, and in the temple, whither the Jews always resort; and in secret have I said nothing.

21 Why askest thou me? ask them which heard me, what I have said unto them: behold, they know what I said.

22 And when he had thus spoken, one of the officers which stood by [a]struck

---

19 [l]Or, *truly sanctified*

21 [a]ch. 10:16; Rom. 12:5; Gal. 3:28 [b]ch. 10:38

22 [a]ch. 14:20; 1 John 1:3

23 [a]Col. 3:14

24 [a]ch. 12:26; 1 Thes. 4:17 [b]ver. 5

25 [a]ch. 15:21 & 16:3 [b]ch. 7:29 & 8:55 & 10:15 [c]ver. 8; ch. 16:27

26 [a]ver. 6; ch. 15:15 [b]ch. 15:9

18:1 [a]Mat. 26:36; Mark 14:32; Luke 22:39 [b]2 Sam. 15:23

2 [a]Luke 21:37 & 22:39

3 [a]Mat. 26:47; Mark 14:43; Luke 22:47; Acts 1:16

9 [a]ch. 17:12

10 [a]Mat. 26:51; Mark 14:47; Luke 22:49,50

11 [a]Mat. 20:22 & 26:39,42

13 [a]See Mat. 26:57 [b]Luke 3:2

14 [a]ch. 11:50

15 [a]Mat. 26:58; Mark 14:54; Luke 22:54

16 [a]Mat. 26:69; Mark 14:66; Luke 22:54

20 [a]Mat. 26:55; Luke 4:15; ch. 7:14, 26,28 & 8:2

22 [a]Jer. 20:2; Acts 23:2

Jesus ′with the palm of his hand, saying, Answerest thou the high priest so?

23 Jesus answered him, If I have spoken evil, bear witness of the evil: but if well, why smitest thou me?

24 [a]Now Annas had sent him bound unto Caiaphas the high priest.

25 And Simon Peter stood and warmed himself. [a]They said therefore unto him, Art not thou also *one* of his disciples? He denied *it,* and said, I am not.

26 One of the servants of the high priest, being *his* kinsman whose ear Peter cut off, saith, Did not I see thee in the garden with him?

27 Peter then denied again: and [a]immediately the cock crew.

Jesus before Pontius Pilate

28 ¶ [a]Then led they Jesus from Caiaphas unto [b]the′ hall of judgment: and it was early; [c]and they themselves went not into the judgment hall, lest they should be defiled; but that they might eat the passover.

29 Pilate then went out unto them, and said, What accusation bring ye against this man?

30 They answered and said unto him, If he were not a malefactor, we would not have delivered him up unto thee.

31 Then said Pilate unto them, Take ye him, and judge him according to your law. The Jews therefore said unto him, It is not lawful for us to put any man to death:

32 [a]That the saying of Jesus might be fulfilled, which he spake, signifying what death he should die.

I M 33 [a]Then Pilate entered into the judgment hall again, and called Jesus, and said unto him, Art thou the King of the Jews?

34 Jesus answered him, Sayest thou this thing of thyself, or did others tell it thee of me?

35 Pilate answered, Am I a Jew? Thine own nation and the chief priests have delivered thee unto me: what hast thou done?

36 [a]Jesus answered, [b]My kingdom is not of this world: if my kingdom were of this world, then would my servants fight, that I should not be delivered to the Jews: but now is my kingdom not from hence.

37 Pilate therefore said unto him, Art thou a king then? Jesus answered, Thou sayest that I am a king. To this end was I born, and for this cause came I into the world, that I should bear witness unto the truth. Every one that [a]is of the truth heareth my voice.

38 Pilate saith unto him, What is truth? And when he had said this, he went out again unto the Jews, and saith unto them, [a]I find in him no fault *at all.*

39 [a]But ye have a custom, that I should release unto you one at the passover: will ye therefore that I release unto you the King of the Jews? I M

40 [a]Then cried they all again, saying, Not this man, but Barabbas. [b]Now Barabbas was a robber.

Jesus crowned with thorns

19 THEN [a]PILATE therefore took Jesus, and scourged *him.*

2 And the soldiers plaited a crown of thorns, and put *it* on his head, and they put on him a purple robe, I

3 And said, Hail, King of the Jews! and they smote him with their hands.

4 Pilate therefore went forth again, and saith unto them, Behold, I bring him forth to you, [a]that ye may know that I find no fault in him.

5 Then came Jesus forth, wearing the crown of thorns, and the purple robe. And *Pilate* saith unto them, Behold the man!

6 [a]When the chief priests therefore and officers saw him, they cried out, saying, Crucify *him,* crucify *him.* Pilate saith unto them, Take ye him, and crucify *him:* for I find no fault in him.

7 The Jews answered him, [a]We have a law, and by our law he ought to die, because [b]he made himself the Son of God.

8 ¶ When Pilate therefore heard that saying, he was the more afraid;

22 ′Or, *with a rod*
24 [a]Mat. 26:57
25 [a]Mat. 26:69,71; Mark 14:69; Luke 22:58
27 [a]Mat. 26:74; Mark 14:72; Luke 22:60; ch. 13:38
28 [a]Mat. 27:2; Mark 15:1; Luke 23:1; Acts 3:13 [b]Mat. 27:27 [c]Acts 10:28 & 11:3 ′Or, *Pilate's house*
32 [a]Mat. 20:19; ch. 12:32,33
33 [a]Mat. 27:11
36 [a]1 Tim. 6:13 [b]Dan. 2:44 & 7:14; Luke 12:14; ch. 6:15 & 8:15
37 [a]ch. 8:47; 1 John 3:19 & 4:6
38 [a]Mat. 27:24; Luke 23:4; ch. 19:4, 6
39 [a]Mat. 27:15; Mark 15:6; Luke 23:17
40 [a]Acts 3:14 [b]Luke 23:19
19:1 [a]Mat. 20:19; & 27:26; Mark 15:15; Luke 18:33
4 [a]ver. 6; ch. 18:38
6 [a]Acts 3:13
7 [a]Lev. 24:16 [b]Mat. 26:65; ch. 5:18 & 10:33

I *Jn 12:13–15* ◀▶ *Jn 18:39*
M *Jn 12:13–15* ◀▶ *Jn 18:39*

I *Jn 18:33–37* ◀▶ *Jn 19:2–3*
M *Jn 18:33–37* ◀▶ *Jn 19:12–15*
I *Jn 18:39* ◀▶ *Jn 19:12–15*

18:33–37, 39 Pilate unknowingly acknowledged Jesus as the "King of the Jews" (18:33). Jesus acknowledged, "To this end was I born" (18:37).

19:2–3 The soldiers contemptuously hailed Jesus as "King of the Jews" (19:3) without knowing the truth of their statement.

9 And went again into the judgment hall, and saith unto Jesus, Whence art thou? [a]But Jesus gave him no answer.

10 Then saith Pilate unto him, Speakest thou not unto me? knowest thou not that I have power to crucify thee, and have power to release thee?

11 Jesus answered, [a]Thou couldest have no power *at all* against me, except it were given thee from above: therefore he that delivered me unto thee hath the greater sin.

I 12 And from thenceforth Pilate sought
M to release him: but the Jews cried out, saying, [a]If thou let this man go, thou art not Caesar's friend: [b]whosoever maketh himself a king speaketh against Caesar.

13 ¶ When Pilate therefore heard that saying, he brought Jesus forth, and sat down in the judgment seat in a place that is called the Pavement, but in the Hebrew, Gabbatha.

14 And [a]it was the preparation of the passover, and about the sixth hour: and he saith unto the Jews, Behold your King!

15 But they cried out, Away with *him,* away with *him,* crucify him. Pilate saith unto them, Shall I crucify your King? The chief priests answered, [a]We have no king but Caesar.

16 [a]Then delivered he him therefore unto them to be crucified. And they took Jesus, and led *him* away.

Jesus crucified

17 [a]And he bearing his cross [b]went forth into a place called *the place* of a skull, which is called in the Hebrew Golgotha:

18 Where they crucified him, and two other with him, on either side one, and Jesus in the midst.

I 19 ¶ [a]And Pilate wrote a title, and put
M *it* on the cross. And the writing was, JESUS OF NAZARETH THE KING OF THE JEWS.

20 This title then read many of the Jews: for the place where Jesus was crucified was nigh to the city: and it was written in Hebrew, *and* Greek, *and* Latin.

21 Then said the chief priests of the Jews to Pilate, Write not, The King of the Jews; but that he said, I am King of the Jews.

22 Pilate answered, What I have written I have written.

23 ¶ [a]Then the soldiers, when they had crucified Jesus, took his garments, and made four parts, to every soldier a part; and also *his* coat: now the coat was without seam, [1]woven from the top throughout.

24 They said therefore among them- B
selves, Let us not rend it, but cast lots for it, whose it shall be: that the scripture might be fulfilled, which saith, [a]They parted my raiment among them, and for my vesture they did cast lots. These things therefore the soldiers did.

25 ¶ [a]Now there stood by the cross of Jesus his mother, and his mother's sister, Mary the *wife* of [b]Cleophas,[1] and Mary Magdalene.

26 When Jesus therefore saw his mother, and [a]the disciple standing by, whom he loved, he saith unto his mother, [b]Woman, behold thy son!

27 Then saith he to the disciple, Behold thy mother! And from that hour that disciple took her [a]unto his own *home.*

The death of Jesus

28 ¶ After this, Jesus knowing that all things were now accomplished, [a]that the scripture might be fulfilled, saith, I thirst.

29 Now there was set a vessel full of vinegar: and [a]they filled a sponge with vinegar, and put *it* upon hyssop, and put *it* to his mouth.

30 When Jesus therefore had received the vinegar, he said, [a]It is finished: and he bowed his head, and gave up the ghost.

31 The Jews therefore, [a]because it was the preparation, [b]that the bodies should not remain upon the cross on the sabbath day, (for that sabbath day was an high

I *Jn 19:2–3* ◀▶ *Jn 19:19–22*
M *Jn 18:39* ◀▶ *Jn 19:19–22*
I *Jn 19:12–15* ◀▶ *Ac 1:6–7*
M *Jn 19:12–15* ◀▶ *Ac 2:29–31*

B *Jn 7:42* ◀▶ *Jn 19:36–37*

9 [a]Is. 53:7; Mat. 27:12,14
11 [a]Luke 22:53; ch. 7:30
12 [a]Luke 23:2 [b]Acts 17:7
14 [a]Mat. 27:62
15 [a]Gen. 49:10
16 [a]Mat. 27:26,31; Mark 15:15; Luke 23:24
17 [a]Mat. 27:31,33; Mark 15:21,22; Luke 23:26,33 [b]Num. 15:36; Heb. 13:12
19 [a]Mat. 27:37; Mark 15:26; Luke 23:38
23 [a]Mat. 27:35; Mark 15:24; Luke 23:34 [1]Or, *wrought*
24 [a]Ps. 22:18
25 [a]Mat. 27:55; Mark 15:40; Luke 23:49 [b]Luke 24:18 [1]Or, *Clopas*
26 [a]ch. 13:23 & 20:2 & 21:7,20,24 [b]ch. 2:4
27 [a]ch. 1:11 & 16:32
28 [a]Ps. 69:21
29 [a]Mat. 27:48
30 [a]ch. 17:4
31 [a]ver. 42; Mark 15:42 [b]Deut. 21:23

19:12–15, 19–22 This account of Pilate's interaction with Jesus revealed his unknowing acknowledgment of Jesus' true position as Israel's king. Though the religious leaders challenged the title "The King of the Jews" (19:21), Pilate refused to back down and responded, "What I have written I have written" (19:22).

day,) besought Pilate that their legs might be broken, and *that* they might be taken away.

32 Then came the soldiers, and brake the legs of the first, and of the other which was crucified with him.

33 But when they came to Jesus, and saw that he was dead already, they brake not his legs:

34 But one of the soldiers with a spear pierced his side, and forthwith [a]came there out blood and water.

35 And he that saw *it* bare record, and his record is true: and he knoweth that he saith true, that ye might believe.

B 36 For these things were done, [a]that the scripture should be fulfilled, A bone of him shall not be broken.

37 And again another scripture saith, [a]They shall look on him whom they pierced.

Jesus laid in the sepulchre

38 ¶ [a]And after this Joseph of Arimathaea, being a disciple of Jesus, but secretly [b]for fear of the Jews, besought Pilate that he might take away the body of Jesus: and Pilate gave *him* leave. He came therefore, and took the body of Jesus.

39 And there came also [a]Nicodemus, which at the first came to Jesus by night, and brought a mixture of myrrh and aloes, about an hundred pound *weight.*

40 Then took they the body of Jesus, and [a]wound it in linen clothes with the spices, as the manner of the Jews is to bury.

41 Now in the place where he was crucified there was a garden; and in the garden a new sepulchre, wherein was never man yet laid.

42 [a]There laid they Jesus therefore [b]because of the Jews' preparation *day;* for the sepulchre was nigh at hand.

The resurrection of Jesus

20 THE [a]FIRST *day* of the week cometh Mary Magdalene early, when it was yet dark, unto the sepulchre, and seeth the stone taken away from the sepulchre.

2 Then she runneth, and cometh to Simon Peter, and to the [a]other disciple, whom Jesus loved, and saith unto them, They have taken away the Lord out of the sepulchre, and we know not where they have laid him.

3 [a]Peter therefore went forth, and that other disciple, and came to the sepulchre.

4 So they ran both together: and the other disciple did outrun Peter, and came first to the sepulchre.

5 And he stooping down, *and looking in,* saw [a]the linen clothes lying; yet went he not in.

6 Then cometh Simon Peter following him, and went into the sepulchre, and seeth the linen clothes lie,

7 And [a]the napkin, that was about his head, not lying with the linen clothes, but wrapped together in a place by itself.

8 Then went in also that other disciple, which came first to the sepulchre, and he saw, and believed.

9 For as yet they knew not the [a]scripture, that he must rise again from the dead.

10 Then the disciples went away again unto their own home.

Jesus appears to the disciples

11 ¶ [a]But Mary stood without at the sepulchre weeping: and as she wept, she stooped down, *and looked* into the sepulchre,

12 And seeth two angels in white sitting, the one at the head, and the other at the feet, where the body of Jesus had lain.

13 And they say unto her, Woman, why weepest thou? She saith unto them, Because they have taken away my Lord, and I know not where they have laid him.

14 [a]And when she had thus said, she turned herself back, and saw Jesus standing, and [b]knew not that it was Jesus.

15 Jesus saith unto her, Woman, why weepest thou? whom seekest thou? She, supposing him to be the gardener, saith unto him, Sir, if thou have borne him hence, tell me where thou hast laid him, and I will take him away.

16 Jesus saith unto her, Mary. She turned herself, and saith unto him, Rabboni; which is to say, Master.

17 Jesus saith unto her, Touch me not; for I am not yet ascended to my Father: but go to [a]my brethren, and say unto them, [b]I ascend unto my Father, and your Father; and *to* [c]my God, and your God.

34 [a]1 John 5:6,8
36 [a]Ex. 12:46; Num. 9:12; Ps. 34:20
37 [a]Ps. 22:16,17; Zech. 12:10; Rev. 1:7
38 [a]Mat. 27:57; Mark 15:42; Luke 23:50 [b]ch. 9:22 & 12:42
39 [a]ch. 3:1,2 & 7:50
40 [a]Acts 5:6
42 [a]Is. 53:9 [b]ver. 31
20:1 [a]Mat. 28:1; Mark 16:1; Luke 24:1
2 [a]ch. 13:23 & 19:26 & 21:7,20, 24
3 [a]Luke 24:12
5 [a]ch. 19:40
7 [a]ch. 11:44
9 [a]Ps. 16:10; Acts 2:25-31 & 13:34, 35
11 [a]Mark 16:5
14 [a]Mat. 28:9; Mark 16:9 [b]Luke 24:16,31; ch. 21:4
17 [a]Ps. 22:22; Mat. 28:10; Rom. 8:29; Heb. 2:11 [b]ch. 16:28 [c]Eph. 1:17

B Jn 19:24 ◀ ▶ Ac 7:37–38

18 [a]Mary Magdalene came and told the disciples that she had seen the Lord, and *that* he had spoken these things unto her.

19 ¶ [a]Then the same day at evening, being the first *day* of the week, when the doors were shut where the disciples were assembled for fear of the Jews, came Jesus and stood in the midst, and saith unto them, Peace *be* unto you.

20 And when he had so said, he showed unto them *his* hands and his side. [a]Then were the disciples glad, when they saw the Lord.

J 21 Then said Jesus to them again, Peace *be* unto you: [a]as *my* Father hath sent me, even so send I you.

E 22 And when he had said this, he breathed on *them,* and saith unto them, Receive ye the Holy Ghost:

K 23 [a]Whosesoever sins ye remit, they
O are remitted unto them; *and* whosesoever *sins* ye retain, they are retained.

Thomas' doubt and belief

24 ¶ But Thomas, one of the twelve, [a]called Didymus, was not with them when Jesus came.

25 The other disciples therefore said unto him, We have seen the Lord. But he said unto them, Except I shall see in his hands the print of the nails, and put my finger into the print of the nails, and thrust my hand into his side, I will not believe.

26 ¶ And after eight days again his disciples were within, and Thomas with them: *then* came Jesus, the doors being shut, and stood in the midst, and said, Peace *be* unto you.

27 Then saith he to Thomas, Reach hither thy finger, and behold my hands; and [a]reach hither thy hand, and thrust *it* into my side: and be not faithless, but believing.

28 And Thomas answered and said unto him, My Lord and my God.

F 29 Jesus saith unto him, Thomas, because thou hast seen me, thou hast believed: [a]blessed *are* they that have not seen, and *yet* have believed.

30 ¶ [a]And many other signs truly did Jesus in the presence of his disciples, which are not written in this book:

31 [a]But these are written, that ye F
might believe that Jesus is the Christ, the Son of God; [b]and that believing ye might have life through his name.

The appearance beside the sea

21 AFTER THESE things Jesus showed himself again to the disciples at the sea of Tiberias; and on this wise showed he *himself.*

2 There were together Simon Peter, and Thomas called Didymus, and [a]Nathanael of Cana in Galilee, and [b]the *sons* of Zebedee, and two other of his disciples.

3 Simon Peter saith unto them, I go a-fishing. They say unto him, We also go with thee. They went forth, and entered into a ship immediately; and that night they caught nothing.

4 But when the morning was now come, Jesus stood on the shore: but the disciples [a]knew not that it was Jesus.

5 Then [a]Jesus saith unto them, [l]Children, have ye any meat? They answered him, No.

6 And he said unto them, [a]Cast the net on the right side of the ship, and ye shall find. They cast therefore, and now they were not able to draw it for the multitude of fishes.

7 Therefore [a]that disciple whom Jesus loved saith unto Peter, It is the Lord. Now when Simon Peter heard that it was the Lord, he girt *his* fisher's coat *unto him,* (for he was naked,) and did cast himself into the sea.

8 And the other disciples came in a lit- F
tle ship; (for they were not far from land, but as it were two hundred cubits,) dragging the net with fishes.

9 As soon then as they were come to land, they saw a fire of coals there, and fish laid thereon, and bread.

10 Jesus saith unto them, Bring of the fish which ye have now caught.

11 Simon Peter went up, and drew the net to land full of great fishes, an hundred and fifty and three: and for all there were so many, yet was not the net broken.

12 Jesus saith unto them, [a]Come *and* dine. And none of the disciples durst ask

18 [a]Mat. 28:10; Luke 24:10
19 [a]Mark 16:14; Luke 24:36; 1 Cor. 15:5
20 [a]ch. 16:22
21 [a]Mat. 28:18; ch. 17:18,19; 2 Tim. 2:2; Heb. 3:1
23 [a]Mat. 16:10 & 18:18
24 [a]ch. 11:16
27 [a]1 John 1:1
29 [a]2 Cor. 5:7; 1 Pet 1:8
30 [a]ch. 21:25
31 [a]Luke 1:4 [b]ch. 3:15,16 & 5:24; 1 Pet. 1:8,9
21:2 [a]ch. 1:45 [b]Mat. 4:21
4 [a]ch. 20:14
5 [a]Luke 24:41 [l]Or, *Sirs*
6 [a]Luke 5:4,6,7
7 [a]ch. 13:23 & 20:2
12 [a]Acts 10:41

J *Jn 16:7* ◀▶ *Ac 9:31*
E *Jn 3:34* ◀▶ *Ac 1:2*
K *Jn 17:11–12* ◀▶ *Ac 3:26*
O *Jn 14:6* ◀▶ *Ac 3:22–23*
F *Jn 12:46* ◀▶ *Jn 20:31*

F *Jn 20:29* ◀▶ *Ac 8:37*
F *Jn 6:31–32* ◀▶ *2Co 9:10*

him, Who art thou? knowing that it was
the Lord.
13 Jesus then cometh, and taketh
bread, and giveth them, and fish likewise.
14 This is now [a]the third time that
Jesus showed himself to his disciples, after that he was risen from the dead.

Jesus questions Peter

15 ¶ So when they had dined, Jesus
saith to Simon Peter, Simon, *son* of Jonas,
lovest thou me more than these? He saith
unto him, Yea, Lord; thou knowest that I
love thee. He saith unto him, Feed my
lambs.
16 He saith to him again the second
time, Simon, *son* of Jonas, lovest thou
me? He saith unto him, Yea, Lord; thou
knowest that I love thee. [a]He saith unto
him, Feed my sheep.
E 17 He saith unto him the third time,
Simon, *son* of Jonas, lovest thou me? Peter was grieved because he said unto him
the third time, Lovest thou me? And he
said unto him, Lord, [a]thou knowest all
things; thou knowest that I love thee.
Jesus saith unto him, Feed my sheep.
18 [a]Verily, verily, I say unto thee,
When thou wast young, thou girdedst
thyself, and walkedst whither thou
wouldest: but when thou shalt be old,

E *Jn 16:30* ◄► *Ac 1:24*

14 [a]See ch. 20:19, 26
16 [a]Acts 20:28; Heb. 13:20; 1 Pet. 2:25 & 5:2,4
17 [a]ch. 2:24,25 & 16:30
18 [a]ch. 13:36; Acts 12:3,4
19 [a]2 Pet. 1:14
20 [a]ch. 13:23,25; & 20:2
22 [a]Mat. 16:27,28; & 25:31; 1 Cor. 4:5 & 11:26; Rev. 2:25 & 3:11 & 22:7,20
24 [a]ch. 19:35; 3 John 12
25 [a]ch. 20:30 [b]Amos 7:10

thou shalt stretch forth thy hands, and
another shall gird thee, and carry *thee*
whither thou wouldest not.
19 This spake he, signifying [a]by what
death he should glorify God. And when
he had spoken this, he saith unto him,
Follow me.
20 Then Peter, turning about, seeth
the disciple [a]whom Jesus loved following;
which also leaned on his breast at supper,
and said, Lord, which is he that betrayeth
thee?
21 Peter seeing him saith to Jesus,
Lord, and what *shall* this man *do?*
22 Jesus saith unto him, If I will that C
he tarry [a]till I come, what *is that* to thee?
follow thou me.
23 Then went this saying abroad
among the brethren, that that disciple
should not die: yet Jesus said not unto
him, He shall not die; but, If I will that he
tarry till I come, what *is that* to thee?
24 This is the disciple which testifieth
of these things, and wrote these things:
and [a]we know that his testimony is true.
25 [a]And there are also many other
things which Jesus did, the which, if they
should be written every one, [b]I suppose
that even the world itself could not contain the books that should be written.
Amen.

C *Lk 21:34–36* ◄► *Ac 1:11*

21:22–23 In this curious passage Jesus affirms the certainty of his second coming. It could occur at any time, and could theoretically, but not necessarily, occur before John's death. Jesus was simply affirming to his disciples that they should be watchfully waiting until he returns. After almost two thousand years the church still waits expectantly for Christ to come. The fulfillments of the prophecies that signal his coming point directly to the soon return of Jesus for his church.

Harmony of the Gospels

	MATTHEW	MARK	LUKE	JOHN
A PREVIEW OF WHO JESUS IS				
Luke's purpose in writing a gospel			1:1–4	
John's prologue: Jesus Christ, the preexistent Word incarnate				1:1–18
Jesus' legal lineage through Joseph and natural lineage through Mary	1:1–17		3:23b–38	
THE EARLY YEARS OF JOHN THE BAPTIST				
John's birth foretold to Zechariah			1:5–25	
Jesus' birth foretold to Mary			1:26–38	
Mary's visit to Elizabeth and Elizabeth's song			1:39–45	
Mary's song of joy			1:46–56	
John's birth			1:57–66	
Zechariah's prophetic song			1:67–79	
John's growth and early life			1:80	
THE EARLY YEARS OF JESUS CHRIST				
Circumstances of Jesus' birth explained to Joseph	1:18–25			
Birth of Jesus			2:1–7	
Praise of the angels and witness of the shepherds			2:8–20	
Circumcision of Jesus			2:21	
Jesus presented in the temple with the homage of Simeon and Anna			2:22–38	
Visit of the Magi	2:1–12			
Escape into Egypt and murder of boys in Bethlehem	2:13–18			
Return to Nazareth	2:19–23		2:39	
Growth and early life of Jesus			2:40	
Jesus' first Passover in Jerusalem			2:41–50	
Jesus' growth to adulthood			2:51–52	
THE PUBLIC MINISTRY OF JOHN THE BAPTIST				
His ministry launched		1:1	3:1–2	
His person, proclamation, and baptism	3:1–6	1:2–6	3:3–6	
His messages to the Pharisees, Sadducees, crowds, tax collectors, and soldiers	3:7–10		3:7–14	
His description of Christ	3:11–12	1:7–8	3:15–18	
THE END OF JOHN'S MINISTRY AND THE BEGINNING OF CHRIST'S PUBLIC MINISTRY				
Jesus' baptism by John	3:13–17	1:9–11	3:21–23a	
Jesus' temptation in the desert	4:1–11	1:12–13	4:1–13	
John's testimony about himself to the priests and Levites				1:19–28
John's testimony to Jesus as the Son of God				1:29–34
Jesus' first followers				1:35–51
Jesus' first miracle: water becomes wine				2:1–11
Jesus' first stay in Capernaum with his relatives and early disciples				2:12
First cleansing of the temple at the Passover				2:13–22
Early response to Jesus' miracles				2:23–25
Nicodemus's interview with Jesus				3:1–21
John superseded by Jesus				3:22–36
Jesus' departure from Judea	4:12	1:14a	3:19–20; 4:14a	4:1–4
Discussion with a Samaritan woman				4:5–26
Challenge of a spiritual harvest				4:27–38
Evangelization of Sychar				4:39–42
Arrival in Galilee				4:43–45

Harmony of the Gospels

	MATTHEW	MARK	LUKE	JOHN
THE MINISTRY OF CHRIST IN GALILEE				
Opposition at Home and a New Headquarters				
Nature of the Galilean ministry	4:17	1:14b–15	4:14b–15	
Child at Capernaum healed by Jesus while at Cana				4:46–54
Ministry and rejection at Nazareth			4:16–31a	
Move to Capernaum	4:13–16			
Disciples Called and Ministry Throughout Galilee				
Call of the four	4:18–22	1:16–20	5:1–11	
Teaching in the synagogue of Capernaum authenticated by healing a demoniac		1:21–28	4:31b–37	
Peter's mother-in-law and others healed	8:14–17	1:29–34	4:38–41	
Tour of Galilee with Simon and others	4:23–25	1:35–39	4:42–44	
Cleansing of a man with leprosy, followed by much publicity	8:2–4	1:40–45	5:12–16	
Forgiving and healing of a paralytic	9:1–8	2:1–12	5:17–26	
Call of Matthew	9:9	2:13–14	5:27–28	
Banquet at Matthew's house	9:10–13	2:15–17	5:29–32	
Jesus defends his disciples for feasting instead of fasting with three parables	9:14–17	2:18–22	5:33–39	
Sabbath Controversies and Withdrawals				
Jesus heals an invalid on the Sabbath				5:1–9
Effort to kill Jesus for breaking the Sabbath and saying he was equal with God				5:10–18
Discourse demonstrating the Son's equality with the Father				5:19–47
Controversy over disciples' picking grain on the Sabbath	12:1–8	2:23–28	6:1–5	
Healing of a man's shriveled hand on the Sabbath	12:9–14	3:1–6	6:6–11	
Withdrawal to the Sea of Galilee with large crowds from many places	12:15–21	3:7–12		
Appointment of the Twelve and Sermon on the Mount				
Twelve apostles chosen		3:13–19	6:12–16	
Setting of the Sermon	5:1–2		6:17–19	
Blessings of those who inherit the kingdom and woes to those who do not	5:3–12		6:20–26	
Responsibility while awaiting the kingdom	5:13–16			
Law, righteousness, and the kingdom	5:17–20			
Six contrasts in interpreting the law	5:21–48		6:27–30, 32–36	
Three hypocritical "acts of righteousness" to be avoided	6:1–18			
Three prohibitions against avarice, harsh judgment, and unwise exposure of sacred things	6:19–7:6		6:37–42	
Application and conclusion	7:7–27		6:31, 43–49	
Reaction of the crowds	7:28–8:1			
Growing Fame and Emphasis on Repentance				
A centurion's faith and the healing of his servant	8:5–13		7:1–10	
A widow's son raised at Nain			7:11–17	
John the Baptist's relationship to the kingdom	11:2–19		7:18–35	
Woes upon Korazin and Bethsaida for failure to repent	11:20–30			
Christ's feet anointed by a sinful but contrite woman			7:36–50	
First Public Rejection by Jewish Leaders				
A tour with the Twelve and other followers			8:1–3	

Harmony of the Gospels

	MATTHEW	MARK	LUKE	JOHN
Blasphemous accusation by the teachers of the law and Pharisees	12:22–37	3:20–30		
Request for a sign refused	12:38–45			
Announcement of new spiritual kinship	12:46–50	3:31–35	8:19–21	
Secrets About the Kingdom Given in Parables				
To the Crowds by the Sea				
The setting of the parables	13:1–3a	4:1–2	8:4	
The parable of the soils	13:3b–23	4:3–25	8:5–18	
The parable of the seed's spontaneous growth		4:26–29		
The parable of the weeds	13:24–30			
The parable of the mustard tree	13:31–32	4:30–32		
The parable of the leavened loaf	13:33–35	4:33–34		
To the Disciples in the House				
The parable of the weeds explained	13:36–43			
The parable of the hidden treasure	13:44			
The parable of the valuable pearl	13:45–46			
The parable of the net	13:47–50			
The parable of the house owner	13:51–53			
Continuing Opposition				
Crossing the lake and calming the storm	8:18, 23–27	4:35–41	8:22–25	
Healing the Gerasene demoniacs and resultant opposition	8:28–34	5:1–20	8:26–39	
Return to Galilee, healing of a woman who touched Jesus' garment, and raising of Jairus's daughter	9:18–26	5:21–43	8:40–56	
Three miracles of healing and another blasphemous accusation	9:27–34			
Final visit to unbelieving Nazareth	13:54–58	6:1–6a		
Final Galilean Campaign				
Shortage of workers	9:35–38	6:6b		
Commissioning of the Twelve	10:1–42	6:7–11	9:1–5	
Workers sent out	11:1	6:12–13	9:6	
Antipas's mistaken identification of Jesus	14:1–2	6:14–16	9:7–9	
Earlier imprisonment and beheading of John the Baptist	14:3–12	6:17–29		
THE MINISTRY OF CHRIST AROUND GALILEE				
Lesson on the Bread of Life				
Return of the workers		6:30	9:10a	
Withdrawal from Galilee	14:13–14	6:31–34	9:10b–11	6:1–3
Feeding the five thousand	14:15–21	6:35–44	9:12–17	6:4–13
A premature attempt to make Jesus king blocked	14:22–23	6:45–46		6:14–15
Walking on the water during a storm on the lake	14:24–33	6:47–52		6:16–21
Healings at Gennesaret	14:34–36	6:53–56		
Discourse on the true bread of life				6:22–59
Defection among the disciples				6:60–71
Lesson on the Leaven of the Pharisees, Sadducees, and Herodians				
Conflict over the tradition of ceremonial uncleanness	15:1–3a, 7–9b, 3b–6, 10–20	7:1–23		7:1
Ministry to a believing Greek woman in Tyre and Sidon	15:21–28	7:24–30		
Healings in Decapolis	15:29–31	7:31–37		
Feeding the four thousand in Decapolis	15:32–38	8:1–9a		
Return to Galilee and encounter with the Pharisees and Sadducees	15:39–16:4	8:9b–12		

Harmony of the Gospels

	MATTHEW	MARK	LUKE	JOHN
Warning about the error of the Pharisees, Sadducees, and Herodians	16:5–12	8:13–21		
Healing a blind man at Bethsaida		8:22–26		
Lesson of Messiahship Learned and Confirmed				
Peter's identification of Jesus as the Christ and first prophecy of the church	16:13–20	8:27–30	9:18–21	
First direct prediction of the rejection, crucifixion, and resurrection	16:21–26	8:31–37	9:22–25	
Coming of the Son of Man and judgment	16:27–28	8:38—9:1	9:26–27	
Transfiguration of Jesus	17:1–8	9:2–8	9:28–36a	
Discussion of resurrection, Elijah, and John the Baptist	17:9–13	9:9–13	9:36b	
Lessons on Responsibility to Others				
Healing of demoniac boy and unbelief rebuked	17:14–20	9:14–29	9:37–43a	
Second prediction of Jesus' death and resurrection	17:22–23	9:30–32	9:43b–45	
Payment of temple tax	17:24–27			
Rivalry over greatness in the kingdom	18:1–5	9:33–37	9:46–48	
Warning against causing believers to sin	18:6–14	9:38–50	9:49–50	
Treatment and forgiveness of a sinning brother	18:15–35			
Journey to Jerusalem for the Feast of Tabernacles				
Complete commitment required of followers	8:19–22		9:57–62	
Ridicule by Jesus' half-brothers				7:2–9
Journey through Samaria			9:51–56	7:10
THE LATER JUDEAN MINISTRY OF CHRIST				
Ministry Beginning at the Feast of Tabernacles				
Mixed reaction to Jesus' teaching and miracles				7:11–31
Frustrated attempt to arrest Jesus				7:32–52
Jesus' forgiveness of a woman caught in adultery				[7:53—8:11]
Conflict over Jesus' claim to be the light of the world				8:12–20
Jesus' relationship to God the Father				8:21–30
Jesus' relationship to Abraham, and attempted stoning				8:31–59
Healing of a man born blind				9:1–7
Response of the blind man's neighbors				9:8–12
Examination and excommunication of the blind man by the Pharisees				9:13–34
Jesus' identification of himself to the blind man				9:35–38
Spiritual blindness of the Pharisees				9:39–41
Allegory of the good shepherd and the thief				10:1–18
Further division among the Jews				10:19–21
Private Lessons on Loving Service and Prayer				
Commissioning of the seventy			10:1–16	
Return of the seventy			10:17–24	
Story of the good Samaritan			10:25–37	
Jesus' visit with Mary and Martha			10:38–42	
Lesson on how to pray and parable of the bold friend			11:1–13	
Second Debate with the Teachers of the Law and the Pharisees				
A third blasphemous accusation and a second debate			11:14–36	
Woes to the Pharisees and the teachers of the law while eating with a Pharisee			11:37–54	
Warning the disciples about hypocrisy			12:1–12	
Warning about greed and trust in wealth			12:13–34	

Harmony of the Gospels

	MATTHEW	MARK	LUKE	JOHN
Warning against being unprepared for the Son of Man's coming				12:35–48
Warning about the coming division			12:49–53	
Warning against failing to discern the present time			12:54–59	
Two alternatives: repent or perish			13:1–9	
Opposition from a synagogue ruler for healing a woman on the Sabbath			13:10–21	
Another attempt to stone or arrest Jesus for blasphemy at the Feast of Dedication				10:22–39
THE MINISTRY OF CHRIST IN AND AROUND PEREA				
Principles of Discipleship				
From Jerusalem to Perea				10:40–42
Question about salvation and entering the kingdom			13:22–30	
Anticipation of Jesus' coming death and his sorrow over Jerusalem			13:31–35	
Healing of a man with dropsy while eating with a prominent Pharisee on the Sabbath, and three parables suggested by the occasion			14:1–24	
Cost of discipleship			14:25–35	
Parables in defense of association with sinners			15:1–32	
Parable to teach the proper use of money			16:1–13	
Story to teach the danger of wealth			16:14–31	
Four lessons on discipleship			17:1–10	
Sickness and death of Lazarus				11:1–16
Lazarus raised from the dead				11:17–44
Decision of the Sanhedrin to put Jesus to death				11:45–54
Teaching While on Final Journey to Jerusalem				
Healing of ten lepers while passing through Samaria and Galilee			17:11–21	
Instructions regarding the Son of Man's coming			17:22–37	
Two parables on prayer: the persistent widow, and the Pharisee and the tax collector			18:1–14	
Conflict with Pharisaic teaching on divorce	19:1–12	10:1–12		
Example of little children in relation to the kingdom	19:13–15	10:13–16	18:15–17	
Riches and the kingdom	19:16–30	10:17–31	18:18–30	
Parable of the landowner's sovereignty	20:1–16			
Third prediction of Jesus' death and resurrection	20:17–19	10:32–34	18:31–34	
Warning against ambitious pride	20:20–28	10:35–45		
Healing of blind Bartimaeus and his companion	20:29–34	10:46–52	18:35–43	
Salvation of Zacchaeus			19:1–10	
Parable to teach responsibility while the kingdom is delayed			19:11–28	
THE FORMAL PRESENTATION OF CHRIST TO ISRAEL AND THE RESULTING CONFLICT				
Triumphal Entry and the Fig Tree				
Arrival at Bethany				11:55—12:1, 9–11
Triumphal entry into Jerusalem	21:1–3, 6–7, 4–5, 8–11, 14–17	11:1–11	19:29–44	12:12–19
Cursing of the fig tree having leaves but no figs	21:18–19a	11:12–14		
Second cleansing of the temple	21:12–13	11:15–18	19:45–48	
Request of some Greeks to see Jesus and necessity of the Son of Man's being lifted up				12:20–36a

Harmony of the Gospels

	MATTHEW	MARK	LUKE	JOHN
Different responses to Jesus and Jesus' response to the crowds				12:36b–50
Withered fig tree and the lesson on faith	21:19b–22	11:19–25	21:37–38	
Official Challenge to Christ's Authority				
Questioning of Jesus' authority by the chief priests, teachers of the law, and elders	21:23–27	11:27–33	20:1–8	
Jesus' response with his own question and three parables	21:28—22:14	12:1–12	20:9–19	
Attempts by Pharisees and Herodians to trap Jesus with a question about paying taxes to Caesar	22:15–22	12:13–17	20:20–26	
Sadducees' puzzling question about the resurrection	22:23–33	12:18–27	20:27–40	
A Pharisee's legal question	22:34–40	12:28–34		
Christ's Response to His Enemies' Challenges				
Christ's relationship to David as son and Lord	22:41–46	12:35–37	20:41–44	
Seven woes against the teachers of the law and Pharisees	23:1–36	12:38–40	20:45–47	
Jesus' sorrow over Jerusalem	23:37–39			
A poor widow's gift of all she had		12:41–44	21:1–4	
PROPHECIES IN PREPARATION FOR THE DEATH OF CHRIST				
The Olivet Discourse: Jesus Speaks Prophetically About the Temple and His Own Second Coming				
Setting of the discourse	24:1–3	13:1–4	21:5–7	
Beginning of birth pains	24:4–14	13:5–13	21:8–19	
Abomination of desolation and subsequent distress	24:15–28	13:14–23	21:20–24	
Coming of the Son of Man	24:29–31	13:24–27	21:25–27	
Signs of nearness but unknown time	24:32–41	13:28–32	21:28–33	
Five parables to teach watchfulness and faithfulness	24:42—25:30	13:33–37	21:34–36	
Judgment at the Son of Man's coming	25:31–46			
Arrangements for Betrayal				
Plot by the Sanhedrin to arrest and kill Jesus	26:1–5	14:1–2	22:1–2	
Mary's anointing of Jesus for burial	26:6–13	14:3–9		12:2–8
Judas' agreement to betray Jesus	26:14–16	14:10–11	22:3–6	
The Last Supper				
Preparation for the Passover meal	26:17–19	14:12–16	22:7–13	
Beginning of the Passover meal and dissension among the disciples over greatness	26:20	14:17	22:14–16, 24–30	
Washing the disciples' feet				13:1–20
Identification of the betrayer	26:21–25	14:18–21	22:21–23	13:21–30
Prediction of Peter's denial	26:31–35	14:27–31	22:31–38	13:31–38
Conclusion of the meal and the Lord's Supper instituted (1 Cor. 11:23–26)	26:26–29	14:22–25	22:17–20	
Discourse and Prayers from the Upper Room to Gethsemane				
Questions about his destination, the Father, and the Holy Spirit answered				14:1–31
The vine and the branches				15:1–17
Opposition from the world				15:18—16:4
Coming and ministry of the Spirit				16:5–15
Prediction of joy over his resurrection				16:16–22
Promise of answered prayer and peace				16:23–33
Jesus' prayer for his disciples and all who believe				17:1–26
Jesus' three agonizing prayers in Gethsemane	26:30, 36–46	14:26, 32–42	22:39–46	18:1

Harmony of the Gospels

	MATTHEW	MARK	LUKE	JOHN
THE DEATH OF CHRIST				
Betrayal and Arrest				
Jesus betrayed, arrested, and forsaken	26:47–56	14:43–52	22:47–53	18:2–12
Trial				
First Jewish phase, before Annas				18:13–14, 19–23
Second Jewish phase, before Caiaphas and the Sanhedrin	26:57, 59–68	14:53, 55–65	22:54a, 63–65	18:24
Peter's denials	26:58, 69–75	14:54, 66–72	22:54b–62	18:15–18, 25–27
Third Jewish phase, before the Sanhedrin	27:1	15:1a	22:66–71	
Remorse and suicide of Judas Iscariot (Acts 1:18–19)	27:3–10			
First Roman phase, before Pilate	27:2, 11–14	15:1b–5	23:1–5	18:28–38
Second Roman phase, before Herod Antipas			23:6–12	
Third Roman phase, before Pilate	27:15–26	15:6–15	23:13–25	18:39—19:16a
Crucifixion				
Mockery by the Roman soldiers	27:27–30	15:16–19		
Journey to Golgotha	27:31–34	15:20–23	23:26–33a	19:16b–17
First three hours of crucifixion	27:35–44	15:24–32	23:33b–43	19:18, 23–24, 19–22, 25–27
Last three hours of crucifixion	27:45–50	15:33–37	23:44–45a, 46	19:28–30
Witness of Jesus' death	27:51–56	15:38–41	23:45b, 47–49	
Burial				
Certification of Jesus' death and procurement of his body	27:57–58	15:42–45	23:50–52	19:31–38
Jesus' body placed in a tomb	27:59–60	15:46	23:53–54	19:39–42
The tomb watched by the women and guarded by the soldiers	27:61–66	15:47	23:55–56	
THE RESURRECTION AND ASCENSION OF CHRIST				
The Empty Tomb				
The tomb visited by the women	28:1	16:1		
The stone rolled away	28:2–4			
The tomb found to be empty by the women	28:5–8	16:2–8	24:1–8	20:1
The tomb found to be empty by Peter and John			24:9–12	20:2–10
The Post Resurrection Appearances				
Appearance to Mary Magdalene		[16:9–11]		20:11–18
Appearance to the other women	28:9–10			
Report of the soldiers to the Jewish authorities	28:11–15			
Appearance to the two disciples traveling to Emmaus		[16:12–13]	24:13–32	
Report of the two disciples to the rest (1 Cor. 15:5a)			24:33–35	
Appearance to the ten assembled disciples		[16:14]	24:36–43	20:19–25
Appearance to the eleven assembled disciples (1 Cor. 15:5b)				20:26–31
Appearance to the seven disciples while fishing				21:1–25
Appearance to the Eleven in Galilee (1 Cor. 15:6)	28:16–20	[16:15–18]		
Appearance to James, Jesus' brother (1 Cor. 15:7)				
Appearance to the disciples in Jerusalem (Acts 1:3–8)			24:44–49	
The Ascension				
Christ's parting blessing and departure (Acts 1:9–12)		[16:19–20]	24:50–53	

Major Archaelogical Finds Relating to the NT

SITE OR ARTIFACT	LOCATION	RELATING SCRIPTURE
	ISRAEL	
Herod's temple	Jerusalem	Lk 1:9
Herod's winter palace	Jericho	Mt 2:4
The Herodium (possible site of Herod's tomb)	Near Bethlehem	Mt 2:19
Masada	Southwest of Dead Sea	Cf. Lk 21:20
Early synagogue	Capernaum	Mk 1:21
Pool of Siloam	Jerusalem	Jn 9:7
Pool of Bethesda	Jerusalem	Jn 5:2
Pilate inscription	Caesarea	Lk 3:1
Inscription: Gentile entrance of temple sanctuary	Jerusalem	Ac 21:27–29
Skeletal remains of crucified man	Jerusalem	Lk 23:33
Peter's house	Capernaum	Mt 8:14
Jacob's well	Nablus	Jn 4:5–6
	ASIA MINOR	
Derbe inscription	Kerti Hüyük	Ac 14:20
Sergius Paulus inscription	Antioch in Pisidia	Ac 13:6–7
Zeus altar (Satan's throne?)	Pergamum	Rev 2:13
Fourth-century B.C. walls	Assos	Ac 20:13–14
Artemis temple and altar	Ephesus	Ac 19:27–28
Ephesian theater	Ephesus	Ac 19:29
Silversmith shops	Ephesus	Ac 19:24
Artemis statues	Ephesus	Ac 19:35
	GREECE	
Erastus inscription	Corinth	Ro 16:23
Synagogue inscription	Corinth	Ac 18:4
Meat market inscription	Corinth	1Co 10:25
Cult dining rooms (in Asklepius and Demeter temples)	Corinth	1Co 8:10
Court (*bema*)	Corinth	Ac 18:12
Marketplace (*bema*)	Philippi	Ac 16:19
Starting gate for races	Isthmia	1Co 9:24,26
Gallio inscription	Delphi	Ac 18:12
Egnatian Way	Kavalla (Neapolis), Philippi, Apollonia, Thessalonica	Cf. Ac 16:11–12; 17:1
Politarch inscription	Thessalonica	Ac 17:6
	ITALY	
Tomb of Augustus	Rome	Lk 2:1
Mamertime Prison	Rome	2Ti 1:16–17; 2:9; 4:6–8
Appian Way	Puteoli to Rome	Ac 28:13–16
Golden House of Nero	Rome	Cf. Ac 25:10; 1Pe 2:13
Arch of Titus	Rome	Cf. Lk 19:43–44; 21:6,20

Acts

Author: Luke

Theme: The church is established worldwide as the gospel spreads

Date of Writing: c. A.D. 63–70

Outline of Acts

I. Jesus' Final Instructions (1:1–11)
II. The Church in Palestine (1:12—12:25)
  A. From Judea to Galilee and Samaria (1:12—9:31)
  B. From Phoenicia to Cyprus and Antioch (9:32—12:25)
III. The Church Expands to Rome (13:1—28:31)
  A. From Phrygia to Galatia (13:1—15:35)
    1. Paul's first missionary journey (13:1—14:28)
    2. The meeting at Jerusalem (15:1–35)
  B. Paul goes to Macedonia (15:36—21:16)
    1. Paul's second missionary journey (15:36—18:22)
    2. Paul's third missionary journey (18:23—20:2)
    3. Paul's work in Caesarea (20:3—21:16)
IV. Paul's Mission in Rome (21:17—28:31)

ALTHOUGH THE AUTHOR of the book of Acts is anonymous, inferences from the book and from outside Scripture point to Luke as the author of this companion volume to the Gospel of Luke. Luke personally participated in many of the events recorded in this book and would have learned about other events through firsthand reports from Paul, Peter and the other disciples. With his extensive knowledge of the laws and customs of the first-century Romans, Luke's account of the spread of Christianity in the book of Acts rings with historical accuracy. Luke probably completed this account while Paul was still a prisoner in Rome.

Addressed to Theophilus, the book of Acts provides the only chronological account in the NT that shows the spread of Christianity after the crucifixion of Christ. This pivotal book traces the growth of the church throughout the Roman empire and records early stories of evangelism, ways to defend our faith, the work of the Holy Spirit and the foundational doctrines of Christianity. Although the disciples are referred to in the first chapter, the focus of Acts quickly turns to the apostle Peter's role in the Jerusalem church and Paul's emergence as the leader of the missionary effort to bring the gospel to the Gentiles.

Though the book of Acts is concerned with the expansion of the church, doctrinal messages permeate the book too. While recording specific fulfillment of prophecies about the early church, Luke places tremendous emphasis on the work of the Holy Spirit to empower the church to reach a lost world. Peter's sermon on the day of Pentecost (see 2:14–40) and Paul's sermon at Antioch (see 13:16–42) stress the resurrection of Jesus as well as his standing as the Messiah who fulfilled the words of the OT prophets (see 17:1–3). The doctrinal background of Acts forms the basis for the teaching found in the remainder of the NT epistles.

The ascension

1 THE FORMER treatise have I made,
O [a]Theophilus, of all that Jesus began both to do and teach,
E 2 [a]Until the day in which he was taken
L up, after that he through the Holy Ghost
T [b]had given commandments unto the
apostles whom he had chosen:
3 [a]To whom also he showed himself
alive after his passion by many infallible
proofs, being seen of them forty days, and
speaking of the things pertaining to the
kingdom of God:
B 4 [a]And, [/]being assembled together
P with *them,* commanded them that they
W should not depart from Jerusalem, but
wait for the promise of the Father,
[b]which, *saith he,* ye have heard of me.
5 [a]For John truly baptized with water;
[b]but ye shall be baptized with the Holy
Ghost not many days hence.
6 When they therefore were come to- I
gether, they asked of him, saying, [a]Lord,
wilt thou at this time [b]restore again the
kingdom to Israel?
7 And he said unto them, [a]It is not for
you to know the times or the seasons,
which the Father hath put in his own
power.
8 [a]But ye shall receive [/]power, [b]after B
that the Holy Ghost is come upon you: G
and [c]ye shall be witnesses unto me both M
in Jerusalem, and in all Judaea, and in P

1:1 [a]Luke 1:3
2 [a]Mark 16:19; 1 Tim. 3:16 [b]Mat. 28:19; John 20:21
3 [a]Mark 16:14
4 [a]Luke 24:43 [b]Luke 24:49; John 14:16 [/]*Or, eating together with them*
5 [a]Mat. 3:11 [b]Joel 3:18
6 [a]Mat. 24:3 [b]Is. 1:26
7 [a]1 Thes. 5:1
8 [a]ch. 2:1,4 [b]Luke 24:49 [c]Luke 24:48 [/]*Or, the power of the Holy Ghost coming upon you*

E *Jn 20:22* ◀▶ *Ac 1:16*
L *Jn 16:13* ◀▶ *Ac 2:4*
T *Jn 16:7–15* ◀▶ *Ac 1:16*
B *Jn 16:13* ◀▶ *Ac 1:8*
P *Jn 16:7–15* ◀▶ *Ac 1:8*
W *Jn 16:7* ◀▶ *Ac 6:3*

I *Jn 19:19–22* ◀▶ *Ac 2:29–31*
B *Ac 1:4–5* ◀▶ *Ac 2:1–18*
G *Jn 16:13–15* ◀▶ *Ac 2:3–18*
M *Jn 16:7–15* ◀▶ *Ac 2:1–18*
P *Ac 1:4–5* ◀▶ *Ac 2:15–18*

1:4–8 The first prophecy in Acts is Christ's prophecy to his disciples concerning the baptism with the Holy Spirit. His followers seemed more interested in when he would defeat the brutal persecution of Rome and establish his Messianic kingdom. They knew the OT prophets had clearly predicted the Messiah's victory over Rome (see Da 2:44–45). Following his supernatural victory over death, the disciples wondered aloud if Jesus would now restore the kingdom. Though Jesus did not berate them for their anticipation of a restored kingdom, they mistakenly assumed that he would establish his kingdom immediately. Jesus' words to them are a warning to all believers to avoid useless speculation about the precise time of his return.

Instead, Jesus directed their thoughts to a spiritual kingdom. He promised that they would be supernaturally empowered to evangelize the entire world and prophesied that they would "be witnesses unto me both in Jerusalem, and in all Judea, and in Samaria, and unto the uttermost part of the earth" (1:8). By these words Jesus predicted the unprecedented growth and penetration of the gospel message to every nation and tribe on earth. Two thousand years later we are witnesses to the nearly complete fulfillment of these words as every major language group in the world has the gospel message in its native tongue.

Samaria, and unto the uttermost part of
the earth.
9 [a]And when he had spoken these
things, while they beheld, [b]he was taken
up; and a cloud received him out of their
sight.
10 And while they looked stedfastly toward heaven as he went up, behold, two
men stood by them [a]in white apparel;
C 11 Which also said, [a]Ye men of Galilee, why stand ye gazing up into heaven?
this same Jesus, which is taken up from
you into heaven, [b]shall so come in like
manner as ye have seen him go into
heaven.

Matthias chosen to replace Judas

12 [a]Then returned they unto Jerusalem from the mount called Olivet, which
is from Jerusalem a sabbath day's
journey.
13 And when they were come in, they
went up [a]into an upper room, where
abode both [b]Peter, and James, and John,
and Andrew, Philip, and Thomas, Bartholomew, and Matthew, James *the son*
of Alphaeus, and [c]Simon Zelotes, and [d]Ju-
das *the brother* of James.
14 [a]These all continued with one accord in prayer and supplication, with
[b]the women, and Mary the mother of
Jesus, and with [c]his brethren.
15 ¶ And in those days Peter stood up
in the midst of the disciples, and said,
(the number [a]of names together were
about an hundred and twenty,)
E 16 Men *and* brethren, this scripture
T must needs have been fulfilled, [a]which
the Holy Ghost by the mouth of David
spake before concerning Judas, [b]which
was guide to them that took Jesus.
17 For [a]he was numbered with us, and
had obtained part of [b]this ministry.
18 [a]Now this man purchased a field

C *Jn 21:22–23* ◀▶ *1Co 1:7–8*
E *Ac 1:2* ◀▶ *Ac 2:1–18*
T *Ac 1:2* ◀▶ *Ac 2:1–18*

9 [a]Luke 24:51 [b]ver. 2
10 [a]Mat. 28:3; Mark 16:5; Luke 24:4; John 20:12; ch. 10:3,30
11 [a]ch. 2:7 & 13:31 [b]Dan. 7:13; Mat. 24:30; Mark 13:26; Luke 21:27; John 14:3; 1 Thes. 1:10 & 4:16; 2 Thes. 1:10; Rev. 1:7
12 [a]Luke 24:52
13 [a]ch. 9:37,39 & 20:8 [b]Mat. 10:2-4 [c]Luke 6:15 [d]Jude 1
14 [a]ch. 2:1,46 [b]Luke 23:49,55 [c]Mat. 13:55
15 [a]Rev. 3:4
16 [a]Ps. 41:9; John 13:18 [b]Luke 22:47; John 18:3
17 [a]Mat. 10:4; Luke 6:16 [b]ver. 25; ch. 12:25 & 20:24 & 21:19
18 [a]Mat. 27:5,7,8 [b]Mat. 26:15; 2 Pet. 2:15
20 [a]Ps. 69:25 [b]Ps. 109:8 [1]Or, *office*, or, *charge*
22 [a]ver. 9 [b]ver. 8; John 15:27; ch. 4:33
23 [a]ch. 15:22
24 [a]1 Sam. 16:7; 1 Chr. 28:9 & 29:17; Jer. 11:20 & 17:10; ch. 15:8; Rev. 2:23
25 [a]ver. 17
2:1 [a]Lev. 23:15; Deut. 16:9; ch. 20:16 [b]ch. 1:14

with [b]the reward of iniquity; and falling
headlong, he burst asunder in the midst,
and all his bowels gushed out.
19 And it was known unto all the
dwellers at Jerusalem; insomuch as that
field is called in their proper tongue,
Aceldama, that is to say, The field of
blood.
20 For it is written in the book of
Psalms, [a]Let his habitation be desolate,
and let no man dwell therein: and [b]his
[1]bishopric let another take.
21 Wherefore of these men which
have companied with us all the time that
the Lord Jesus went in and out among us,
22 Beginning from the baptism of
John, unto that same day that [a]he was
taken up from us, must one be ordained
[b]to be a witness with us of his resurrection.
23 And they appointed two, Joseph
called [a]Barsabas, who was surnamed Justus, and Matthias.
24 And they prayed, and said, Thou, E
Lord, [a]which knowest the hearts of all
men, show whether of these two thou
hast chosen,
25 [a]That he may take part of this min- H
istry and apostleship, from which Judas
by transgression fell, that he might go to
his own place.
26 And they gave forth their lots; and
the lot fell upon Matthias; and he was
numbered with the eleven apostles.

The gift of the Holy Spirit

2 AND WHEN [a]the day of Pentecost B
was fully come, [b]they were all with E
one accord in one place. M
2 And suddenly there came a sound T
from heaven as of a rushing mighty wind, N

E *Jn 21:17* ◀▶ *Ac 15:8*
H *Jn 15:6* ◀▶ *Ac 2:34–35*
B *Ac 1:8* ◀▶ *Ac 2:33*
E *Ac 1:16* ◀▶ *Ac 2:33*
M *Ac 1:8* ◀▶ *Ac 4:29–31*
T *Ac 1:16* ◀▶ *Ac 6:3*
N *Jn 15:26* ◀▶ *Ac 2:33*

1:10–11 These two men in white clothing were angels sent by God to instruct the disciples. These angels indicated that Jesus was taken away from them up into heaven, but declared that he "shall so come in like manner as ye have seen him go into heaven" (1:11). Jesus will return from heaven to earth following the Battle of Armageddon just as he ascended—in full sight of his followers.

2:1 *Dispensation of the Church.* This dispensation corresponds to the church age, beginning at the cross and continuing until the resurrection of the saints (see 1Th 4:13–17). During this time period, the continuing revelation of the previous dispensations combines with the gospel message to emphasize humanity's utter sinfulness. Only through the completed work of Christ can humanity be saved by

and [a]it filled all the house where they were sitting.

G 3 And there appeared unto them cloven tongues like as of fire, and it sat upon each of them.

L 4 And [a]they were all filled with the Holy Ghost, and began [b]to speak with other tongues, as the Spirit gave them utterance.

5 And there were dwelling at Jerusalem Jews, devout men, out of every nation under heaven.

6 Now [1]when this was noised abroad, the multitude came together, and were [2]confounded, because that every man heard them speak in his own language.

7 And they were all amazed and marvelled, saying one to another, Behold, are not all these which speak [a]Galilaeans?

8 And how hear we every man in our own tongue, wherein we were born?

9 Parthians, and Medes, and Elamites, and the dwellers in Mesopotamia, and in Judaea, and Cappadocia, in Pontus, and Asia,

10 Phrygia, and Pamphylia, in Egypt, and in the parts of Libya about Cyrene, and strangers of Rome, Jews and proselytes,

11 Cretes and Arabians, we do hear them speak in our tongues the wonderful works of God.

12 And they were all amazed, and were in doubt, saying one to another, What meaneth this?

13 Others mocking said, These men are full of new wine.

Peter's Pentecostal sermon

14 ¶ But Peter, standing up with the eleven, lifted up his voice, and said unto them, Ye men of Judaea, and all *ye* that dwell at Jerusalem, be this known unto you, and hearken to my words:

15 For these are not drunken, as ye P
suppose, [a]seeing it is *but* the third hour of the day.

16 But this is that which was spoken by the prophet Joel;

17 [a]And it shall come to pass in the E
last days, saith God, [b]I will pour out of my Spirit upon all flesh: and your sons and [c]your daughters shall prophesy, and your young men shall see visions, and your old men shall dream dreams:

18 And on my servants and on my handmaidens I will pour out in those days of my Spirit; [a]and they shall prophesy:

19 [a]And I will show wonders in E
P

2 [a]ch. 4:31
4 [a]ch. 1:5 [b]Mark 16:17; ch. 10:46 & 19:6; 1 Cor. 12:10, 28,30 & 13:1 & 14:2
6 [1]Gk. *when this voice was made* [2]Or, *troubled in mind*
7 [a]ch. 1:11
15 [a]1 Thes. 5:7
17 [a]Is. 44:3; Ezek. 11:19; Joel 2:28; Zech. 12:10; John 7:38 [b]ch. 10:45 [c]ch. 21:9
18 [a]ch. 21:4,9; 1 Cor. 12:10 & 14:1
19 [a]Joel 2:30

G *Ac 1:8* ◄► *Ac 6:3* L *Ac 1:2* ◄► *Ac 4:8*
P *Ac 1:8* ◄► *Ac 2:38–39*
E *Lk 21:25–31* ◄► *Ac 2:19–20*
E *Ac 2:17* ◄► *1Th 5:1–4*
P *Lk 21:36* ◄► *1Co 16:22*

grace though faith (see Jn 14:6; Ro 3:21–26; Eph 2:8–9; 1Ti 4:10; Heb 11:6). Those who do trust and believe in Christ are to fulfill the Lord's command to preach the Gospel to the entire world (see Mk 16:15; Lk 24:46–48). During this time many will reject Christ or pretend to believe in him and introduce false doctrines into the church, thereby hindering its growth (see 1Ti 4:1–3). This dispensation of the church concludes with the translation of the true believers from the earth to heaven as they meet the Lord in the air when he returns (see 1Th 4:17) prior to the judgments of Daniel's seventieth week (see Da 9:24–27; Rev 7:14).

The seven dispensations revealed in Scripture are the dispensations of innocence (Ge 1:28), conscience (Ge 3:7), human government (Ge 8:15), promise (Ge 12:1), law (Ex 19:1), the church (Ac 2:1) and the kingdom (Rev 20:4). For further information on dispensations, see the article on "The Seven Dispensations" on p. 4.

2:2–6 Christ's earlier prophecy that God would send "another Comforter" (Jn 14:16) was fulfilled on the day of Pentecost. The Holy Spirit supernaturally filled the disciples with power from heaven, allowing them to miraculously "speak with other tongues, as the Spirit gave them utterance" (2:4). These other languages were the languages spoken by foreigners of that day. Remarkably, on the day of Pentecost, thousands of Jews from every nation in the known world had made the long journey to the temple in Jerusalem to celebrate a required annual feast. Jerusalem was filled with thousands of people representing every language in the known world. These visiting Jews heard the disciples "speak in his own language" (2:6). This miracle would have been avidly discussed everywhere as these Jewish pilgrims eventually returned to their distant homelands.

2:16–20 When some doubters suggested that the commotion could be explained by drunkenness, the apostle Peter declared that this supernatural event was a partial fulfillment of the great prophecy of Joel (see Joel 2:28–32). This prophecy will be completed in the last days when God will again pour his Spirit out on the righteous people of Israel and "they shall prophesy" (2:18). Peter's words confirmed that this supernatural evidence of the Holy Spirit would be identical to what will occur in the last days.

heaven above, and signs in the earth beneath; blood, and fire, and vapour of
smoke:
20 [a]The sun shall be turned into darkness, and the moon into blood, before
that great and notable day of the Lord
come:
W 21 And it shall come to pass, *that*
[a]whosoever shall call on the name of the
Lord shall be saved.
22 Ye men of Israel, hear these words;
Jesus of Nazareth, a man approved of God
among you [a]by miracles and wonders and
signs, which God did by him in the midst
of you, as ye yourselves also know:
23 Him, [a]being delivered by the deter-
minate counsel and foreknowledge of
God, [b]ye have taken, and by wicked
hands have crucified and slain:
24 [a]Whom God hath raised up, having
loosed the pains of death: because it was
not possible that he should be holden
of it.
25 For David speaketh concerning
him, [a]I foresaw the Lord always before
my face, for he is on my right hand, that I
should not be moved:
26 Therefore did my heart rejoice, and
my tongue was glad; moreover also my
flesh shall rest in hope:
27 Because thou wilt not leave my soul
in hell, neither wilt thou suffer thine
Holy One to see corruption.
28 Thou hast made known to me the
ways of life; thou shalt make me full of
joy with thy countenance.
I 29 Men *and* brethren, [1]let me freely
M

W *Jn 12:46* ◀▶ *Ac 10:34–35*
I *Ac 1:6–7* ◀▶ *Ro 9:4*
M *Jn 19:19–22* ◀▶ *Ac 2:34–35*

20 [a]Mat. 24:29; Mark 13:24; Luke 21:25
21 [a]Rom. 10:13
22 [a]John 3:2 & 14:10,11; ch. 10:38; Heb. 2:4
23 [a]Mat. 26:24; Luke 22:22; ch. 3:18 [b]ch. 5:30
24 [a]Rom. 8:11; 1 Cor. 6:14; 2 Cor. 4:14; Eph. 1:20; Col. 2:12; 1 Thes. 1:10; Heb. 13:20
25 [a]Ps. 16:8
29 [a]ch. 13:36 [1]Or, *I may*
30 [a]2 Sam. 7:12; Ps. 132:11; Luke 1:32; Rom. 1:3; 2 Tim. 2:8
31 [a]Ps. 16:10
32 [a]ver. 24 [b]ch. 1:8
33 [a]Phil. 2:9; Heb. 10:12 [b]John 14:26 & 16:7,13 [c]ch. 10:45; Eph. 4:8
34 [a]Ps. 110:1; Mat. 22:44; 1 Cor. 15:25; Eph. 1:20; Heb. 1:13
37 [a]Zech. 12:10; Luke 3:10; ch. 9:6

speak unto you [a]of the patriarch David,
that he is both dead and buried, and his
sepulchre is with us unto this day.
30 Therefore being a prophet, [a]and
knowing that God had sworn with an
oath to him, that of the fruit of his loins,
according to the flesh, he would raise up
Christ to sit on his throne;
31 He seeing this before spake of the
resurrection of Christ, [a]that his soul was
not left in hell, neither his flesh did see
corruption.
32 [a]This Jesus hath God raised up,
[b]whereof we all are witnesses.
33 Therefore [a]being by the right hand B
of God exalted, and [b]having received of E
the Father the promise of the Holy Ghost, N
he [c]hath shed forth this, which ye now
see and hear.
34 For David is not ascended into the M
heavens: but he saith himself, [a]The LORD V
said unto my Lord, Sit thou on my right H
hand,
35 Until I make thy foes thy footstool.
36 Therefore let all the house of Israel
know assuredly, that God hath made that
same Jesus, whom ye have crucified, both
Lord and Christ.

The community of the believers

37 ¶ Now when they heard *this,* [a]they R
were pricked in their heart, and said unto

B *Ac 2:1–18* ◀▶ *Ac 2:38–39*
E *Ac 2:1–18* ◀▶ *Ac 4:8*
N *Ac 2:2–4* ◀▶ *Ac 4:31*
M *Ac 2:29–31* ◀▶ *Ac 3:19–21*
V *Lk 20:42–43* ◀▶ *1Co 15:24–26*
H *Ac 1:25* ◀▶ *Ac 3:23*
R *Lk 24:47* ◀▶ *Ac 3:19*

2:22–35 Peter addressed his remarks to the "men of Israel" (2:22) as he recounted the well-known history of Christ's ministry, death and resurrection. Peter reminded them that they were all witnesses of his resurrection (see 2:32) and argued that the resurrection of Jesus proved his claim to be the Messiah because Jesus fulfilled the OT prophecies about rising from the dead. This argument would have been futile unless Peter knew that his audience in Jerusalem was well aware of Christ's resurrection; only ten days earlier Jesus had ascended to heaven in the sight of his disciples.

Peter reminded his listeners that David had predicted that God would raise up one of David's descendants "to sit on his throne" (2:30). Before the temple was burned in A.D. 70, genealogical records in the temple could be examined by anyone to trace their lineage. These genealogical records proved that Jesus was legally "the son of David" and thus had the right to "sit on his throne" (2:30). However, since the destruction of the temple, it has been impossible for anyone else to ever prove that they were legally descended from King David and thus able to meet these Messianic qualifications. Jesus is the first, last and only person to prove his legal right to the throne of David as the Messiah.

2:27 Peter taught that Jesus is the true Messiah by referring to King David's prophecy of Christ's resurrection (see Ps 16:10). Peter affirmed the prediction and fulfillment when Jesus supernaturally rose from the grave on the third day without his body suffering physical decay.

Peter and to the rest of the apostles, Men *and* brethren, what shall we do?

B P 38 Then Peter said unto them, [a]Repent, and be baptized every one of you in the name of Jesus Christ for the remission of sins, and ye shall receive the gift of the Holy Ghost.

39 For the promise is unto you, and [a]to your children, and [b]to all that are afar off, *even* as many as the Lord our God shall call.

40 And with many other words did he testify and exhort, saying, Save yourselves from this untoward generation.

41 ¶ Then they that gladly received his word were baptized: and the same day there were added *unto them* about three thousand souls.

42 [a]And they continued stedfastly in the apostles' doctrine and fellowship, and in breaking of bread, and in prayers.

43 And fear came upon every soul: and [a]many wonders and signs were done by the apostles.

44 And all that believed were together, and [a]had all things common;

45 And sold their possessions and goods, and [a]parted them to all *men,* as every man had need.

46 [a]And they, continuing daily with one accord [b]in the temple, and [c]breaking bread [l]from house to house, did eat their meat with gladness and singleness of heart,

47 Praising God, and [a]having favour with all the people. And [b]the Lord added to the church daily such as should be saved.

The healing of the lame man

E **3** NOW PETER and John went up together [a]into the temple at the hour of prayer, [b]*being* the ninth *hour.*

2 And [a]a certain man lame from his mother's womb was carried, whom they laid daily at the gate of the temple which is called Beautiful, [b]to ask alms of them that entered into the temple;

3 Who seeing Peter and John about to go into the temple asked an alms.

4 And Peter, fastening his eyes upon him with John, said, Look on us.

5 And he gave heed unto them, expecting to receive something of them.

6 Then Peter said, Silver and gold have I none; but such as I have give I thee: [a]In the name of Jesus Christ of Nazareth rise up and walk.

7 And he took him by the right hand, and lifted *him* up: and immediately his feet and ankle bones received strength.

8 And he [a]leaping up stood, and walked, and entered with them into the temple, walking, and leaping, and praising God.

9 [a]And all the people saw him walking and praising God:

10 And they knew that it was he which [a]sat for alms at the Beautiful gate of the temple: and they were filled with wonder and amazement at that which had happened unto him.

Peter's sermon

11 And as the lame man which was healed held Peter and John, all the people ran together unto them in the porch [a]that is called Solomon's, greatly wondering.

12 ¶ And when Peter saw *it,* he answered unto the people, Ye men of Israel, why marvel ye at this? or why look ye so earnestly on us, as though by our own power or holiness we had made this man to walk?

13 [a]The God of Abraham, and of Isaac, and of Jacob, the God of our fathers, [b]hath glorified his Son Jesus; whom ye [c]delivered up, and [d]denied him in the presence of Pilate, when he was determined to let *him* go.

14 But ye denied [a]the Holy One [b]and the Just, and desired a murderer to be granted unto you;

15 And killed the [a]Prince[l] of life, [b]whom God hath raised from the dead; [c]whereof we are witnesses.

16 [a]And his name through faith in his name hath made this man strong, whom ye see and know: yea, the faith which is by him hath given him this perfect soundness in the presence of you all.

17 And now, brethren, I wot that [a]through ignorance ye did *it,* as *did* also your rulers.

38 [a]Luke 24:47; ch. 3:19
39 [a]Joel 2:28; ch. 3:25 [b]ch. 11:15,18; Eph. 2:13
42 [a]ch. 1:14; Rom. 12:12; Eph. 6:18; Col. 4:2; Heb. 10:25
43 [a]Mark 16:17; ch. 5:12
44 [a]ch. 4:32,34
45 [a]Is. 58:7
46 [a]ch. 1:14 [b]Luke 24:53 [c]ch. 20:7 [l]Or, *at home*
47 [a]ch. 4:33; Rom. 14:18 [b]ch. 5:14
3:1 [a]ch. 2:46 [b]Ps. 55:17
2 [a]ch. 14:8 [b]John 9:8
6 [a]ch. 4:10
8 [a]Is. 35:6
9 [a]ch. 4:16,21
10 [a]Like John 9:8
11 [a]John 10:23; ch. 5:12
13 [a]ch. 5:30 [b]John 7:39 & 12:16 & 17:1 [c]Mat. 27:2 [d]Mat 27:20; Mark 15:11; Luke 23:18; John 18:40 & 19:15; ch. 13:28
14 [a]Ps. 16:10; Mark 1:24; Luke 1:35; ch. 2:27 & 4:27 [b]ch. 7:52 & 22:14
15 [a]1 John 5:11 [b]ch. 2:24 [c]ch. 2:32 [l]Or, *Author;* Heb. 2:10 & 5:9
16 [a]Mat. 9:22; ch. 4:10 & 14:9
17 [a]Luke 23:34; John 16:3; ch. 13:27; 1 Cor. 2:8; 1 Tim. 1:13

B *Ac 2:33* ◀ ▶ *Ac 4:31*
P *Ac 2:15–18* ◀ ▶ *Ac 11:16*
E *Jn 12:17–19* ◀ ▶ *Ac 4:8–10*

18 But [a]those things, which God before had shown [b]by the mouth of all his
prophets, that Christ should suffer, he
hath so fulfilled.
M 19 ¶ [a]Repent ye therefore, and be con-
L verted, that your sins may be blotted out,
R when the times of refreshing shall come
from the presence of the Lord;
20 And he shall send Jesus Christ,
which before was preached unto you:
K 21 [a]Whom the heaven must receive
until the times of [b]restitution of all
things, [c]which God hath spoken by the
mouth of all his holy prophets since the
world began.
N 22 For Moses truly said unto the fa-
O thers, [a]A prophet shall the Lord your
God raise up unto you of your brethren,
like unto me; him shall ye hear in all
things whatsoever he shall say unto
you.
H 23 And it shall come to pass, *that* every soul, which will not hear that
prophet, shall be destroyed from among
the people.
24 Yea, and all the prophets from Samuel and those that follow after, as many as
have spoken, have likewise foretold of
these days.
K 25 [a]Ye are the children of the prophets, and of the covenant which God made
with our fathers, saying unto Abraham,
[b]And in thy seed shall all the kindreds of
the earth be blessed.

M *Ac 2:34–35* ◀▶ *Ac 17:7*
L *Jn 15:13* ◀▶ *Ac 3:26*
R *Ac 2:37–38* ◀▶ *Ac 8:22*
K *Lk 11:2* ◀▶ *Ac 3:25*
N *Jn 12:48* ◀▶ *Ac 4:11–12*
O *Jn 20:23* ◀▶ *Ac 4:11–12*
H *Ac 2:34–35* ◀▶ *Ac 13:41*
K *Ac 3:21* ◀▶ *1Co 15:24–28*

18 [a]Luke 24:44; ch. 26:22 [b]Ps. 22; Is. 50:6 & 53:5; Dan. 9:26; 1 Pet. 1:10
19 [a]ch. 2:38
21 [a]ch. 1:11 [b]Mat. 17:11 [c]Luke 1:70
22 [a]Deut. 18:15, 18,19; ch. 7:37
25 [a]ch. 2:39; Rom. 9:4,8 & 15:8; Gal. 3:26 [b]Gen. 12:3 & 18:18 & 22:18 & 26:4 & 28:14; Gal. 3:8
26 [a]Mat. 10:5 & 15:24; Luke 24:47; ch. 13:32,33,46 [b]ver. 22 [c]Mat. 1:21
4:1 [a]Luke 22:4; ch. 5:24 [*l*]Or, *ruler*
6 [a]Luke 3:2; John 11:49 & 18:13
7 [a]Ex. 2:14; Mat. 21:23; ch. 7:27
8 [a]Luke 12:11,12

26 [a]Unto you first God, having raised K
up his Son Jesus, [b]sent him to bless you, L
[c]in turning away every one of you from S
his iniquities.

Peter and John arrested

4 AND AS they spake unto the people,
the priests, and the [a]captain[*l*] of the
temple, and the Sadducees, came upon
them,
2 Being grieved that they taught the
people, and preached through Jesus the
resurrection from the dead.
3 And they laid hands on them, and
put *them* in hold unto the next day: for it
was now eventide.
4 Howbeit many of them which heard
the word believed; and the number of the
men was about five thousand.
5 ¶ And it came to pass on the morrow, that their rulers, and elders, and
scribes,
6 And [a]Annas the high priest, and Caiaphas, and John, and Alexander, and as
many as were of the kindred of the high
priest, were gathered together at Jerusalem.
7 And when they had set them in the
midst, they asked, [a]By what power, or by
what name, have ye done this?
8 [a]Then Peter, filled with the Holy E
Ghost, said unto them, Ye rulers of the L
people, and elders of Israel, E
9 If we this day be examined of the
good deed done to the impotent man, by
what means he is made whole;
10 Be it known unto you all, and to all

K *Jn 20:23* ◀▶ *Ac 5:31*
L *Ac 3:19* ◀▶ *Ac 5:31*
S *Jn 17:15–20* ◀▶ *Ac 14:22*
E *Ac 2:33* ◀▶ *Ac 4:31*
L *Ac 2:4* ◀▶ *Ac 6:10*
E *Ac 3:1–16* ◀▶ *Ac 4:14–22*

3:18–21 Peter referred to the prophecies of the suffering of the Messiah (see Ps 22:1–18; Isa 52:13—53:12). These prophecies were perfectly fulfilled in the trial and cruel death of Jesus on the cross. Peter urged his listeners to repent in light of the promise of the "times of refreshing" (3:19) at the return of Christ in the last days. Peter also made reference to the prophecy that the righteous remnant of the Jews will repent just prior to the Millennium after Christ's return in glory (see Zec 12:10–14). While some individuals followed Christ, the majority of Israel generally rejected Peter's invitation to accept Jesus as their Messiah. Because of the lack of national repentance, the prophesied judgments against Jerusalem and the temple were fulfilled a few decades later when Rome destroyed the temple and the city of Jerusalem in A.D. 70.

3:22–23 Moses prophesied that God would raise up a prophet "like unto me" (Dt 18:15). This prophecy was precisely fulfilled; Jesus was more like Moses in his ministry and life than any other man in history. Peter also reminded his listeners of Moses' stern warning that "every soul, which will not hear that prophet, shall be destroyed from among the people" (3:23). For further information, see the article "A Prophet Like Unto Moses" on p. 242.

the people of Israel, [a]that by the name of Jesus Christ of Nazareth, whom ye crucified, [b]whom God raised from the dead, *even* by him doth this man stand here before you whole.

N O 11 [a]This is the stone which was set at nought of you builders, which is become the head of the corner.

12 [a]Neither is there salvation in any other: for there is none other name under heaven given among men, whereby we must be saved.

13 ¶ Now when they saw the boldness of Peter and John, [a]and perceived that they were unlearned and ignorant men, they marvelled; and they took knowledge of them, that they had been with Jesus.

E 14 And beholding the man which was healed [a]standing with them, they could say nothing against it.

15 But when they had commanded them to go aside out of the council, they conferred among themselves,

16 Saying, [a]What shall we do to these men? for that indeed a notable miracle hath been done by them *is* [b]manifest to all them that dwell in Jerusalem; and we cannot deny *it.*

17 But that it spread no further among the people, let us straitly threaten them, that they speak henceforth to no man in this name.

18 [a]And they called them, and commanded them not to speak at all nor teach in the name of Jesus.

19 But Peter and John answered and said unto them, [a]Whether it be right in the sight of God to hearken unto you more than unto God, judge ye.

20 [a]For we cannot but speak the things which [b]we have seen and heard.

21 So when they had further threatened them, they let them go, finding nothing how they might punish them, [a]because of the people: for all *men* glorified God for [b]that which was done.

22 For the man was above forty years old, on whom this miracle of healing was shown.

The report to the believers

23 ¶ And being let go, [a]they went to their own company, and reported all that the chief priests and elders had said unto them.

24 And when they heard that, they lifted up their voice to God with one accord, and said, Lord, [a]thou *art* God, which hast made heaven, and earth, and the sea, and all that in them is:

25 Who by the mouth of thy servant David hast said, [a]Why did the heathen rage, and the people imagine vain things?

26 The kings of the earth stood up, and the rulers were gathered together against the Lord, and against his Christ.

27 For [a]of a truth against [b]thy holy child Jesus, [c]whom thou hast anointed, both Herod, and Pontius Pilate, with the Gentiles, and the people of Israel, were gathered together,

28 [a]For to do whatsoever thy hand and thy counsel determined before to be done.

29 And now, Lord, behold their threatenings: and grant unto thy servants, [a]that with all boldness they may speak thy word, A M

30 By stretching forth thine hand to heal; [a]and that signs and wonders may be done [b]by the name of [c]thy holy child Jesus.

31 ¶ And when they had prayed, [a]the place was shaken where they were assembled together; and they were all filled with the Holy Ghost, [b]and they spake the word of God with boldness. B E N

The community of possessions

32 And the multitude of them that believed [a]were of one heart and of one soul: [b]neither said any *of them* that aught of the things which he possessed was his own; but they had all things common.

33 And with [a]great power gave the apostles [b]witness of the resurrection of the Lord Jesus: and [c]great grace was upon them all.

34 Neither was there any among them that lacked: [a]for as many as were possessors of lands or houses sold them, and brought the prices of the things that were sold,

35 [a]And laid *them* down at the apostles' feet: [b]and distribution was made

10 [a]ch. 3:6,16 [b]ch. 2:24
11 [a]Ps. 118:22; Is. 28:16; Mat. 21:42
12 [a]Mat. 1:21; ch. 10:43; 1 Tim. 2:5,6
13 [a]Mat. 11:25; 1 Cor. 1:27
14 [a]ch. 3:11
16 [a]John 11:47 [b]ch. 3:9,10
18 [a]Again, ch. 5:40
19 [a]ch. 5:29
20 [a]ch. 1:8 & 2:32 [b]ch. 22:15; 1 John 1:1,3
21 [a]Mat. 21:26; Luke 20:6,19 & 22:2; ch. 5:26 [b]ch. 3:7,8
23 [a]ch. 12:12
24 [a]2 Ki. 19:15
25 [a]Ps. 2:1
27 [a]Mat. 26:3; Luke 22:2 & 23:1,8 [b]Luke 1:35 [c]Luke 4:18; John 10:36
28 [a]ch. 2:23 & 3:18
29 [a]ver. 13,31; ch. 9:27 & 13:46 & 14:3 & 19:8 & 26:26; Eph. 6:19
30 [a]ch. 2:43 & 5:12 [b]ch. 3:6,16 [c]ver. 27
31 [a]ch. 2:2,4 & 16:26 [b]ver. 29
32 [a]ch. 5:12; Rom. 15:5,6; 2 Cor. 13:11; Phil. 1:27 & 2:2; 1 Pet. 3:8 [b]ch. 2:44
33 [a]ch. 1:8 [b]ch. 1:22 [c]ch. 2:45
34 [a]ch. 2:45
35 [a]ver. 37; ch. 5:2 [b]ch. 2:45 & 6:1

N *Ac 3:22–23* ◄► *Ac 7:51–53*
O *Ac 3:22–23* ◄► *Ro 8:9*
E *Ac 4:8–10* ◄► *Ac 5:14–16*

A *Jn 4:10* ◄► *Ac 8:14–17*
M *Ac 2:1–18* ◄► *Ac 6:8–10*
B *Ac 2:38–39* ◄► *Ac 5:32*
E *Ac 4:8* ◄► *Ac 5:3*
N *Ac 2:33* ◄► *Ac 8:39*

unto every man according as he had need.

36 And Joses, who by the apostles was surnamed Barnabas, (which is, being interpreted, The son of consolation,) a Levite, *and* of the country of Cyprus,

37 [a]Having land, sold *it,* and brought the money, and laid *it* at the apostles' feet.

Ananias and Sapphira punished

5 BUT A certain man named Ananias, with Sapphira his wife, sold a possession,

2 And kept back *part* of the price, his wife also being privy *to it,* and brought a certain part, and laid *it* at the apostles' feet.

E Q 3 [a]But Peter said, Ananias, why hath [b]Satan filled thine heart ʼto lie to the Holy Ghost, and to keep back *part* of the price of the land?

D 4 Whiles it remained, was it not thine own? and after it was sold, was it not in thine own power? why hast thou conceived this thing in thine heart? thou hast not lied unto men, but unto God.

5 And Ananias hearing these words [a]fell down, and gave up the ghost: and great fear came on all them that heard these things.

6 And the young men arose, [a]wound him up, and carried *him* out, and buried *him.*

7 And it was about the space of three hours after, when his wife, not knowing what was done, came in.

8 And Peter answered unto her, Tell me whether ye sold the land for so much? And she said, Yea, for so much.

E Q 9 Then Peter said unto her, How is it that ye have agreed together [a]to tempt the Spirit of the Lord? behold, the feet of them which have buried thy husband *are* at the door, and shall carry thee out.

10 [a]Then fell she down straightway at his feet, and yielded up the ghost: and the young men came in, and found her dead, and, carrying *her* forth, buried *her* by her husband.

11 [a]And great fear came upon all the

37 [a]ver. 34,35; ch. 5:1,2
5:3 [a]Num. 30:2; Deut. 23:21; Eccl. 5:4 [b]Luke 22:3 ʼOr, *to deceive*
5 [a]ver. 10,11
6 [a]John 19:40
9 [a]ver. 3; Mat. 4:7
10 [a]ver. 5
11 [a]ver. 5; ch. 2:43 & 19:17
12 [a]ch. 2:43 & 14:3 & 19:11; Rom. 15:19; 2 Cor. 12:12; Heb. 2:4 [b]ch. 3:11 & 4:32
13 [a]John 9:22 & 12:42 & 19:38 [b]ch. 2:47 & 4:21
15 [a]Mat. 9:21 & 14:36; ch. 19:12 ʼOr, *in every street*
16 [a]Mark 16:17, 18; John 14:12
17 [a]ch. 4:1,2,6 ʼOr, *envy*
18 [a]Luke 21:12
19 [a]ch. 12:7 & 16:26
20 [a]John 6:68 & 17:3; 1 John 5:11
21 [a]ch. 4:5,6
24 [a]Luke 22:4; ch. 4:1

church, and upon as many as heard these things.

12 ¶ And [a]by the hands of the apostles were many signs and wonders wrought among the people; ([b]and they were all with one accord in Solomon's porch.

13 And [a]of the rest durst no man join himself to them: [b]but the people magnified them.

14 And believers were the more added to the Lord, multitudes both of men and women.) E

15 Insomuch that they brought forth the sick ʼinto the streets, and laid *them* on beds and couches, [a]that at the least the shadow of Peter passing by might overshadow some of them.

16 There came also a multitude *out* of the cities round about unto Jerusalem, bringing [a]sick folks, and them which were vexed with unclean spirits: and they were healed every one.

The apostles imprisoned

17 ¶ [a]Then the high priest rose up, and all they that were with him, (which is the sect of the Sadducees,) and were filled with ʼindignation,

18 [a]And laid their hands on the apostles, and put them in the common prison.

19 But [a]the angel of the Lord by night opened the prison doors, and brought them forth, and said, V

20 Go, stand and speak in the temple to the people [a]all the words of this life.

21 And when they heard *that,* they entered into the temple early in the morning, and taught. [a]But the high priest came, and they that were with him, and called the council together, and all the senate of the children of Israel, and sent to the prison to have them brought.

22 But when the officers came, and found them not in the prison, they returned, and told,

23 Saying, The prison truly found we shut with all safety, and the keepers standing without before the doors: but when we had opened, we found no man within.

24 Now when the high priest and [a]the captain of the temple and the chief priests heard these things, they doubted of them whereunto this would grow.

E *Ac 4:31* ◀▶ *Ac 5:9*
Q *Lk 12:10* ◀▶ *Ac 5:9*
D *Mk 3:29* ◀▶ *1Co 3:16–17*
E *Ac 5:3* ◀▶ *Ac 5:32*
Q *Ac 5:3–4* ◀▶ *Ac 7:51*

E *Ac 4:14–22* ◀▶ *Ac 8:6–7*
V *Lk 21:18* ◀▶ *Ac 5:38–39*

25 Then came one and told them, saying, Behold, the men whom ye put in prison are standing in the temple, and teaching the people.

26 Then went the captain with the officers, and brought them without violence: [a]for they feared the people, lest they should have been stoned.

27 And when they had brought them, they set *them* before the council: and the high priest asked them,

28 Saying, [a]Did not we straitly command you that ye should not teach in this name? and, behold, ye have filled Jerusalem with your doctrine, [b]and intend to bring this man's [c]blood upon us.

29 ¶ Then Peter and the *other* apostles answered and said, [a]We ought to obey God rather than men.

30 [a]The God of our fathers raised up Jesus, whom ye slew and [b]hanged on a tree.

K L 31 [a]Him hath God exalted with his right hand *to be* [b]a Prince and [c]a Saviour, [d]for to give repentance to Israel, and forgiveness of sins.

B E 32 And [a]we are his witnesses of these things; and *so is* also the Holy Ghost, [b]whom God hath given to them that obey him.

The counsel of Gamaliel

33 ¶ [a]When they heard *that,* they were cut *to the heart,* and took counsel to slay them.

34 Then stood there up one in the council, a Pharisee, named [a]Gamaliel, a doctor of the law, had in reputation among all the people, and commanded to put the apostles forth a little space;

35 And said unto them, Ye men of Israel, take heed to yourselves what ye intend to do as touching these men.

36 For before these days rose up Theudas, boasting himself to be somebody; to whom a number of men, about four hundred, joined themselves: who was slain; and all, as many as [l]obeyed him, were scattered, and brought to nought.

37 After this man rose up Judas of Galilee in the days of the taxing, and drew away much people after him: he also perished; and all, *even* as many as obeyed him, were dispersed.

V 38 And now I say unto you, Refrain from these men, and let them alone: [a]for if this counsel or this work be of men, it will come to nought:

39 [a]But if it be of God, ye cannot overthrow it; lest haply ye be found even [b]to fight against God.

40 And to him they agreed: and when they had [a]called the apostles, [b]and beaten *them,* they commanded that they should not speak in the name of Jesus, and let them go.

J 41 ¶ And they departed from the presence of the council, [a]rejoicing that they were counted worthy to suffer shame for his name.

42 And daily [a]in the temple, and in every house, [b]they ceased not to teach and preach Jesus Christ.

The appointment of the seven

6 AND IN those days, [a]when the number of the disciples was multiplied, there arose a murmuring of the [b]Grecians against the Hebrews, because their widows were neglected [c]in the daily ministration.

2 Then the twelve called the multitude of the disciples *unto them,* and said, [a]It is not reason that we should leave the word of God, and serve tables.

B E G T 3 Wherefore, brethren, [a]look ye out among you seven men of honest report, full of the Holy Ghost and wisdom, whom we may appoint over this business.

W 4 But we [a]will give ourselves continually to prayer, and to the ministry of the word.

B E 5 ¶ And the saying pleased the whole multitude: and they chose Stephen, [a]a man full of faith and of the Holy Ghost, and [b]Philip, and Prochorus, and Nicanor, and Timon, and Parmenas, and [c]Nicolas a proselyte of Antioch:

6 Whom they set before the apostles:

26 [a]Mat. 21:26
28 [a]ch. 4:18 [b]ch. 2:23,36 & 3:15 & 7:52 [c]Mat. 23:35 & 27:25
29 [a]ch. 4:19
30 [a]ch. 3:13,15 & 22:14 [b]ch. 10:39 & 13:29; Gal. 3:13; 1 Pet. 2:24
31 [a]ch. 2:33,36; Phil. 2:9; Heb. 2:10 & 12:2 [b]ch. 3:15 [c]Mat. 1:21 [d]Luke 24:47; ch. 3:26 & 13:38; Eph. 1:7; Col. 1:14
32 [a]John 15:26,27 [b]ch. 2:4 & 10:44
33 [a]ch. 2:37 & 7:54
34 [a]ch. 22:3
36 [l]Or, *believed*
38 [a]Prov. 21:30; Is. 8:10; Mat. 15:13
39 [a]Luke 21:15; 1 Cor. 1:25 [b]ch. 7:51 & 9:5 & 23:9
40 [a]ch. 4:18 [b]Mat. 10:17 & 23:34; Mark 13:9
41 [a]Mat. 5:12; Rom. 5:3; 2 Cor. 12:10; Phil. 1:29; Heb. 10:34; Jas. 1:2; 1 Pet. 4:13,16
42 [a]ch. 2:46 [b]ch. 4:20,29
6:1 [a]ch. 2:41 & 4:4 & 5:14 & ver. 7 [b]ch. 9:29 & 11:20 [c]ch. 4:35
2 [a]Ex. 18:17
3 [a]Deut. 1:13; ch. 1:21 & 16:2; 1 Tim. 3:7
4 [a]ch. 2:42
5 [a]ch. 11:24 [b]ch. 8:5,26 & 21:8 [c]Rev. 2:6,15

K Ac 3:26 ◀ ▶ Ac 10:43
L Ac 3:26 ◀ ▶ Ac 10:43
B Ac 4:31 ◀ ▶ Ac 6:3
E Ac 5:9 ◀ ▶ Ac 6:3
V Ac 5:19 ◀ ▶ Ac 12:7–11
J Jn 16:33 ◀ ▶ Ac 6:15
B Ac 5:32 ◀ ▶ Ac 6:5
E Ac 5:32 ◀ ▶ Ac 6:5
G Ac 2:3–18 ◀ ▶ Ac 6:8–10
T Ac 2:1–18 ◀ ▶ Ac 6:9–10
W Ac 1:4–5 ◀ ▶ Ac 7:51
B Ac 6:3 ◀ ▶ Ac 8:14–21
E Ac 6:3 ◀ ▶ Ac 6:8–10

and [a]when they had prayed, [b]they laid *their* hands on them.

7 And [a]the word of God increased; and the number of the disciples multiplied in Jerusalem greatly; and a great company [b]of the priests were obedient to the faith.

The arrest of Stephen

E 8 And Stephen, full of faith and power,
G did great wonders and miracles among
M the people.
T 9 ¶ Then there arose certain of the synagogue, which is called *the synagogue* of the Libertines, and Cyrenians, and Alexandrians, and of them of Cilicia and of Asia, disputing with Stephen.
L 10 And [a]they were not able to resist the wisdom and the spirit by which he spake.

11 [a]Then they suborned men, which said, We have heard him speak blasphemous words against Moses, and *against* God.

12 And they stirred up the people, and the elders, and the scribes, and came upon *him,* and caught him, and brought *him* to the council,

13 And set up false witnesses, which said, This man ceaseth not to speak blasphemous words against this holy place, and the law:

14 [a]For we have heard him say, that this Jesus of Nazareth shall [b]destroy this place, and shall change the [1]customs which Moses delivered us.

M 15 And all that sat in the council, look-
J ing stedfastly on him, saw his face as it had been the face of an angel.

The defence of Stephen

7 THEN SAID the high priest, Are these things so?

2 And he said, [a]Men, brethren, and fathers, hearken; The God of glory appeared unto our father Abraham, when he was in Mesopotamia, before he dwelt in Charran,

3 And said unto him, [a]Get thee out of thy country, and from thy kindred, and come into the land which I shall show thee.

4 Then [a]came he out of the land of the Chaldaeans, and dwelt in Charran: and from thence, when his father was dead, he removed him into this land, wherein ye now dwell.

5 And he gave him none inheritance in it, no, not *so much as* to set his foot on: [a]yet he promised that he would give it to him for a possession, and to his seed after him, when *as yet* he had no child.

6 And God spake on this wise, [a]That his seed should sojourn in a strange land; and that they should bring them into bondage, and entreat *them* evil [b]four hundred years.

7 And the nation to whom they shall be in bondage will I judge, said God: and after that shall they come forth, and [a]serve me in this place.

8 [a]And he gave him the covenant of circumcision: [b]and so *Abraham* begat Isaac, and circumcised him the eighth day; [c]and Isaac *begat* Jacob; and [d]Jacob *begat* the twelve patriarchs.

9 [a]And the patriarchs, moved with envy, sold Joseph into Egypt: [b]but God was with him,

10 And delivered him out of all his afflictions, [a]and gave him favour and wisdom in the sight of Pharaoh king of Egypt; and he made him governor over Egypt and all his house.

11 [a]Now there came a dearth over all the land of Egypt and Chanaan, and great affliction: and our fathers found no sustenance.

12 [a]But when Jacob heard that there was corn in Egypt, he sent out our fathers first.

13 [a]And at the second *time* Joseph was made known to his brethren; and Joseph's kindred was made known unto Pharaoh.

14 [a]Then sent Joseph, and called his father Jacob to *him,* and [b]all his kindred, threescore and fifteen souls.

15 [a]So Jacob went down into Egypt, [b]and died, he, and our fathers,

16 And [a]were carried over into Sychem, and laid in [b]the sepulchre that Abraham bought for a sum of money of the sons of Emmor *the father* of Sychem.

17 But when [a]the time of the promise drew nigh, which God had sworn to

6 [a]ch. 1:24 [b]ch. 8:17 & 9:17 & 13:3; 1 Tim. 4:14 & 5:22; 2 Tim. 1:6
7 [a]ch. 12:24 & 19:20; Col. 1:6 [b]John 12:42
10 [a]Luke 21:15; ch. 5:39; See Ex. 4:12; Is. 54:17
11 [a]1 Ki. 21:10,13; Mat. 26:59,60
14 [a]ch. 25:8 [b]Dan. 9:26 [1]Or, *rites*
7:2 [a]ch. 22:1
3 [a]Gen. 12:1
4 [a]Gen. 11:31 & 12:4,5
5 [a]Gen. 12:7 & 13:15 & 15:3,18 & 17:8 & 26:3
6 [a]Gen. 15:13,16 [b]Ex. 12:40; Gal. 3:17
7 [a]Ex. 3:12
8 [a]Gen. 17:9-11 [b]Gen. 21:2-4 [c]Gen. 25:26 [d]Gen. 29:31 & 30:5 & 35:18,23
9 [a]Gen. 37:4,11, 28; Ps. 105:17 [b]Gen. 39:2,21,23
10 [a]Gen. 41:37 & 42:6
11 [a]Gen. 41:54
12 [a]Gen. 42:1
13 [a]Gen. 45:4,16
14 [a]Gen. 45:9,27 [b]Gen. 46:27; Deut. 10:22
15 [a]Gen. 46:5 [b]Gen. 49:33; Ex. 1:6
16 [a]Ex. 13:19; Josh. 24:32 [b]Gen. 23:16 & 33:19
17 [a]ver. 6; Gen. 15:13

E *Ac 6:5* ◀▶ *Ac 7:51*
G *Ac 6:3* ◀▶ *Ac 10:38*
M *Ac 4:29–31* ◀▶ *Ac 6:15*
T *Ac 6:3* ◀▶ *Ac 7:55*
L *Ac 4:8* ◀▶ *Ac 8:29*
M *Ac 6:8–10* ◀▶ *Ac 10:38*
J *Ac 5:41* ◀▶ *Ro 5:3*

Abraham, [b]the people grew and multiplied in Egypt,
18 Till another king arose, which
knew not Joseph.
19 The same dealt subtly with our kindred, and evil entreated our fathers, [a]so
that they cast out their young children, to
the end they might not live.
20 [a]In which time Moses was born,
and [b]was [/]exceeding fair, and nourished
up in his father's house three months:
21 And [a]when he was cast out, Pharaoh's daughter took him up, and nourished him for her own son.
22 And Moses was learned in all the
wisdom of the Egyptians, and was
[a]mighty in words and in deeds.
23 [a]And when he was full forty years
old, it came into his heart to visit his
brethren the children of Israel.
24 And seeing one *of them* suffer
wrong, he defended *him,* and avenged
him that was oppressed, and smote the
Egyptian:
25 [/]For he supposed his brethren
would have understood how that God by
his hand would deliver them: but they
understood not.
26 And the next day he showed himself unto them as they strove, and would
have set them at one again, saying, Sirs,
ye are brethren; why do ye wrong one to
another?
27 But he that did his neighbour
wrong thrust him away, saying, [a]Who
made thee a ruler and a judge over us?
28 Wilt thou kill me, as thou diddest
the Egyptian yesterday?
29 [a]Then fled Moses at this saying,
and was a stranger in the land of Madian,
where he begat two sons.
30 [a]And when forty years were expired, there appeared to him in the wilderness of mount Sina an angel of the
Lord in a flame of fire in a bush.
31 When Moses saw *it,* he wondered
at the sight: and as he drew near to behold *it,* the voice of the Lord came unto
him,
32 *Saying,* [a]I *am* the God of thy fathers, the God of Abraham, and the God

17 [b]Ex. 1:7-9; Ps. 105:24,25
19 [a]Ex. 1:22
20 [a]Ex. 2:2 [b]Heb. 11:23 [/]Or, *fair to God*
21 [a]Ex. 2:3-10
22 [a]Luke 24:19
23 [a]Ex. 2:11,12
25 [/]Or, *Now*
27 [a]See Luke 12:14; ch. 4:7
29 [a]Ex. 2:15,22 & 4:20 & 18:3,4
30 [a]Ex. 3:2
32 [a]Mat. 22:32; Heb. 11:16
33 [a]Ex. 3:5; Josh. 5:15
34 [a]Ex. 3:7
35 [a]Ex. 14:19; Num. 20:16
36 [a]Ex. 12:41 & 33:1 [b]Ex. 7 & 8 & 9 & 10; Ps. 105:27 [c]Ex. 14:21 [d]Ex. 16:1
37 [a]Deut. 18:15 [b]Mat. 17:5 [/]Or, *as myself*
38 [a]Ex. 19:3 [b]Is. 63:9; Gal. 3:19; Heb. 2:2 [c]Ex. 21:1; Deut. 5:27; John 1:17 [d]Rom. 3:2
40 [a]Ex. 32:1
41 [a]Deut. 9:16; Ps. 106:19
42 [a]Ps. 81:12; 2 Thes. 2:11 [b]Deut. 4:19; 2 Ki. 21:3 [c]Amos 5:25

of Isaac, and the God of Jacob. Then Moses trembled, and durst not behold.
33 [a]Then said the Lord to him, Put off
thy shoes from thy feet: for the place
where thou standest is holy ground.
34 [a]I have seen, I have seen the affliction of my people which is in Egypt, and I
have heard their groaning, and am come
down to deliver them. And now come, I
will send thee into Egypt.
35 This Moses whom they refused,
saying, Who made thee a ruler and a
judge? the same did God send *to be* a
ruler and a deliverer [a]by the hand of the
angel which appeared to him in the bush.
36 [a]He brought them out, after that he
had [b]shown wonders and signs in the
land of Egypt, [c]and in the Red sea, [d]and
in the wilderness forty years.
37 ¶ This is that Moses, which said B
unto the children of Israel, [a]A prophet
shall the Lord your God raise up unto you
of your brethren, [/]like unto me; [b]him
shall ye hear.
38 [a]This is he, that was in the church
in the wilderness with [b]the angel which
spake to him in the mount Sina, and *with*
our fathers: [c]who received the lively [d]or-
acles to give unto us:
39 To whom our fathers would not
obey, but thrust *him* from them, and in
their hearts turned back again into Egypt,
40 [a]Saying unto Aaron, Make us gods
to go before us: for *as for* this Moses,
which brought us out of the land of
Egypt, we wot not what is become of
him.
41 [a]And they made a calf in those
days, and offered sacrifice unto the idol,
and rejoiced in the works of their own
hands.
42 Then [a]God turned, and gave them
up to worship [b]the host of heaven; as it
is written in the book of the prophets,
[c]O ye house of Israel, have ye offered to
me slain beasts and sacrifices *by the
space of* forty years in the wilderness?
43 Yea, ye took up the tabernacle of
Moloch, and the star of your god Rem-
phan, figures which ye made to worship

B *Jn 19:36–37* ◀▶ *Ac 26:23*

7:37–38 In Stephen's last message he reminds the people that Moses had specifically prophesied that God would raise up a prophet "like unto me" (Dt 18:15). For further information, see the article "A Prophet Like Unto Moses" on p. 242.

them: and I will carry you away beyond
Babylon.
44 Our fathers had the tabernacle of
witness in the wilderness, as he had appointed, [l]speaking unto Moses, [a]that he
should make it according to the fashion
that he had seen.
45 [a]Which also our fathers [l]that came
after brought in with Jesus into the possession of the Gentiles, [b]whom God
drave out before the face of our fathers,
unto the days of David;
46 [a]Who found favour before God, and
[b]desired to find a tabernacle for the God
of Jacob.
47 [a]But Solomon built him an house.
48 Howbeit [a]the most High dwelleth
not in temples made with hands; as saith
the prophet,
49 [a]Heaven *is* my throne, and earth *is*
my footstool: what house will ye build
me? saith the Lord: or what *is* the place
of my rest?
50 Hath not my hand made all these
things?
E 51 ¶ Ye [a]stiffnecked and [b]uncircum-
Q cised in heart and ears, ye do always re-
W sist the Holy Ghost: as your fathers *did,*
C so *do* ye.
M 52 [a]Which of the prophets have not
N your fathers persecuted? and they have
slain them which showed before of the
coming of [b]the Just One; of whom ye
have been now the betrayers and murderers:
53 [a]Who have received the law by the
disposition of angels, and have not
kept *it.*

The stoning of Stephen

54 ¶ [a]When they heard these things,
they were cut to the heart, and they
gnashed on him with *their* teeth.
E 55 But he, [a]being full of the Holy
T Ghost, looked up stedfastly into heaven,
and saw the glory of God, and Jesus
standing on the right hand of God,
56 And said, Behold, [a]I see the heav-

E *Ac 6:8–10* ◀▶ *Ac 7:55*
Q *Ac 5:9* ◀▶ *Eph 4:30*
W *Ac 6:3* ◀▶ *Ac 8:14–15*
C *Jn 8:44* ◀▶ *Ac 8:23*
M *Jn 9:39* ◀▶ *Ac 8:22*
N *Ac 4:11–12* ◀▶ *Ac 24:25*
E *Ac 7:51* ◀▶ *Ac 8:14–21*
T *Ac 6:9–10* ◀▶ *Ac 10:46*

44 [a]Ex. 25:40; Heb. 8:5 [l]*Or, who spake*
45 [a]Josh. 3:14 [b]Neh. 9:24; Ps. 44:2 [l]*Or, having received*
46 [a]2 Sam. 7:1; Ps. 89:19 [b]1 Chr. 22:7
47 [a]1 Ki. 8:20
48 [a]1 Ki. 8:27; 2 Chr. 2:6
49 [a]Is. 66:1,2; Mat. 5:34
51 [a]Ex. 32:9 [b]Lev. 26:41; Deut. 10:16; Jer. 4:4
52 [a]2 Chr. 36:16; Mat. 21:35; 1 Thes. 2:15 [b]ch. 3:14
53 [a]Ex. 20:1; Gal. 3:19
54 [a]ch. 5:33
55 [a]ch. 6:5
56 [a]Mat. 3:16 [b]Dan. 7:13
58 [a]Luke 4:29; Heb. 13:12 [b]Lev. 24:16 [c]Deut. 13:9
59 [a]ch. 9:14 [b]Ps. 31:5; Luke 23:46
60 [a]ch. 9:40 [b]Mat. 5:44; Luke 6:28
8:1 [a]ch. 7:58 [b]ch. 11:19
2 [a]Gen. 23:2 & 50:10; 2 Sam. 3:31
3 [a]ch. 7:58; 1 Cor. 15:9; Gal. 1:13; Phil. 3:6; 1 Tim. 1:13
4 [a]Mat. 10:23
5 [a]ch. 6:5
7 [a]Mark 16:17
9 [a]ch. 13:6 [b]ch. 5:36

ens opened, and the [b]Son of man standing on the right hand of God.
57 Then they cried out with a loud
voice, and stopped their ears, and ran
upon him with one accord,
58 And [a]cast *him* out of the city, [b]and
stoned *him:* and [c]the witnesses laid down
their clothes at a young man's feet,
whose name was Saul.
59 And they stoned Stephen, [a]calling
upon *God,* and saying, Lord Jesus, [b]re-
ceive my spirit.
60 And he [a]kneeled down, and cried
with a loud voice, [b]Lord, lay not this sin
to their charge. And when he had said
this, he fell asleep.

The persecution of the church

8 AND [a]SAUL was consenting unto his
death. And at that time there was a
great persecution against the church
which was at Jerusalem; and [b]they were
all scattered abroad throughout the regions of Judaea and Samaria, except the
apostles.
2 And devout men carried Stephen *to
his burial,* and [a]made great lamentation
over him.
3 As for Saul, [a]he made havoc of the
church, entering into every house, and
haling men and women committed *them*
to prison.

Philip at Samaria

4 Therefore [a]they that were scattered
abroad went every where preaching the
word.
5 Then [a]Philip went down to the city
of Samaria, and preached Christ unto
them.
6 And the people with one accord gave E
heed unto those things which Philip
spake, hearing and seeing the miracles
which he did.
7 For [a]unclean spirits, crying with loud
voice, came out of many that were possessed *with them:* and many taken with
palsies, and that were lame, were healed.
8 And there was great joy in that city.

Conversion of Simon the sorcerer

9 But there was a certain man, called
Simon, which beforetime in the same city
[a]used sorcery, and bewitched the people
of Samaria, [b]giving out that himself was
some great one:

E *Ac 5:14–16* ◀▶ *Ac 9:12*

10 To whom they all gave heed, from the least to the greatest, saying, This man is the great power of God.

11 And to him they had regard, because that of long time he had bewitched them with sorceries.

12 But when they believed Philip preaching the things [a]concerning the kingdom of God, and the name of Jesus Christ, they were baptized, both men and women.

13 Then Simon himself believed also: and when he was baptized, he continued with Philip, and wondered, beholding the [l]miracles and signs which were done.

A B E W 14 Now when the apostles which were at Jerusalem heard that Samaria had received the word of God, they sent unto them Peter and John:

15 Who, when they were come down, prayed for them, [a]that they might receive the Holy Ghost:

16 (For [a]as yet he was fallen upon none of them: only [b]they were baptized in [c]the name of the Lord Jesus.)

17 Then [a]laid they *their* hands on them, and they received the Holy Ghost.

18 And when Simon saw that through laying on of the apostles' hands the Holy Ghost was given, he offered them money,

19 Saying, Give me also this power, that on whomsoever I lay hands, he may receive the Holy Ghost.

20 But Peter said unto him, Thy money perish with thee, because [a]thou hast thought that [b]the gift of God may be purchased with money.

21 Thou hast neither part nor lot in this matter: for thy heart is not right in the sight of God.

M R 22 Repent therefore of this thy wickedness, and pray God, [a]if perhaps the thought of thine heart may be forgiven thee.

C 23 For I perceive that thou art in [a]the gall of bitterness, and *in* the bond of iniquity.

24 Then answered Simon, and said, [a]Pray ye to the Lord for me, that none of these things which ye have spoken come upon me.

25 And they, when they had testified and preached the word of the Lord, returned to Jerusalem, and preached the gospel in many villages of the Samaritans.

Conversion of the Ethiopian

26 And the angel of the Lord spake unto Philip, saying, Arise, and go toward the south unto the way that goeth down from Jerusalem unto Gaza, which is desert.

27 And he arose and went: and, behold, [a]a man of Ethiopia, an eunuch of great authority under Candace queen of the Ethiopians, who had the charge of all her treasure, and [b]had come to Jerusalem for to worship,

28 Was returning, and sitting in his chariot read Esaias the prophet.

29 Then the Spirit said unto Philip, Go near, and join thyself to this chariot. E L

30 And Philip ran thither to *him,* and heard him read the prophet Esaias, and said, Understandest thou what thou readest?

31 And he said, How can I, except some man should guide me? And he desired Philip that he would come up and sit with him.

32 The place of the scripture which he read was this, [a]He was led as a sheep to the slaughter; and like a lamb dumb before his shearer, so opened he not his mouth: D

33 In his humiliation his judgment was taken away: and who shall declare his generation? for his life is taken from the earth.

34 And the eunuch answered Philip, and said, I pray thee, of whom speaketh the prophet this? of himself, or of some other man?

35 Then Philip opened his mouth, [a]and began at the same scripture, and preached unto him Jesus.

36 And as they went on *their* way, they came unto a certain water: and the eunuch said, See, *here is* water; [a]what doth hinder me to be baptized?

37 And Philip said, [a]If thou believest F

12 [a]ch. 1:3
13 [l]Gk. *signs and great miracles*
15 [a]ch. 2:38
16 [a]ch. 19:2 [b]Mat. 28:19; ch. 2:38 [c]ch. 10:48 & 19:5
17 [a]ch. 6:6 & 19:6; Heb. 6:2
20 [a]Mat. 10:8; See 2 Ki. 5:16 [b]ch. 2:38 & 10:45 & 11:17
22 [a]Dan. 4:27; 2 Tim. 2:25
23 [a]Heb. 12:15
24 [a]Gen. 20:7,17; Ex. 8:8; Num. 21:7; 1 Ki. 13:6; Job 42:8; Jas. 5:16
27 [a]Zeph. 3:10 [b]John 12:20
32 [a]Is. 53:7,8
35 [a]Luke 24:27; ch. 18:28
36 [a]ch. 10:47
37 [a]Mat. 28:19; Mark 16:16

A *Ac 4:29–31* ◀▶ *Eph 1:16–17*
B *Ac 6:5* ◀▶ *Ac 9:17*
E *Ac 7:55* ◀▶ *Ac 8:29*
W *Ac 7:51* ◀▶ *Ac 9:17*
M *Ac 7:51* ◀▶ *Ro 12:16*
R *Ac 3:19* ◀▶ *Ac 11:18*
C *Ac 7:51* ◀▶ *Ac 26:18*

E *Ac 8:14–21* ◀▶ *Ac 8:39*
L *Ac 6:10* ◀▶ *Ac 8:39*
D *Jn 11:49–52* ◀▶ *Ac 20:28*
F *Jn 20:31* ◀▶ *Ac 10:43*

with all thine heart, thou mayest. And he
answered and said, [b]I believe that Jesus
Christ is the Son of God.
38 And he commanded the chariot to
stand still: and they went down both into
the water, both Philip and the eunuch;
and he baptized him.
E 39 And when they were come up out
L of the water, [a]the Spirit of the Lord
N caught away Philip, that the eunuch saw
him no more: and he went on his way
rejoicing.
40 But Philip was found at Azotus: and
passing through he preached in all the
cities, till he came to Caesarea.

Conversion of Saul

9 AND [a]SAUL, yet breathing out
threatenings and slaughter against
the disciples of the Lord, went unto the
high priest,
2 And desired of him letters to Damascus to the synagogues, that if he found
any [a]of[1] this way, whether they were
men or women, he might bring them
bound unto Jerusalem.
3 And [a]as he journeyed, he came near
Damascus: and suddenly there shined
round about him a light from heaven:
4 And he fell to the earth, and heard a
voice saying unto him, Saul, Saul, [a]why
persecutest thou me?
5 And he said, Who art thou, Lord?
And the Lord said, I am Jesus whom thou
persecutest: *it is* hard for thee to kick
against the pricks.
6 And he trembling and astonished
said, Lord, [a]what wilt thou have me to
do? And the Lord *said* unto him, Arise,
and go into the city, and it shall be told
thee what thou must do.
7 And [a]the men which journeyed with
him stood speechless, hearing a voice,
but seeing no man.
D 8 And Saul arose from the earth; and
when his eyes were opened, he saw no
man: but they led him by the hand, and
brought *him* into Damascus.
9 And he was three days without sight,
and neither did eat nor drink.
10 ¶ And there was a certain disciple
at Damascus, [a]named Ananias; and to
him said the Lord in a vision, Ananias.
And he said, Behold, I *am here,* Lord.
11 And the Lord *said* unto him, Arise,
and go into the street which is called
Straight, and inquire in the house of Judas for *one* called Saul, [a]of Tarsus: for,
behold, he prayeth,
12 And hath seen in a vision a man E
named Ananias coming in, and putting
his hand on him, that he might receive
his sight.
13 Then Ananias answered, Lord, I
have heard by many of this man, [a]how
much evil he hath done to thy saints at
Jerusalem:
14 And here he hath authority from
the chief priests to bind all [a]that call on
thy name.
15 But the Lord said unto him, Go thy
way: for [a]he is a chosen vessel unto me,
to bear my name before [b]the Gentiles,
and [c]kings, and the children of Israel:
16 For [a]I will show him how great
things he must suffer for my name's sake.
17 [a]And Ananias went his way, and B
entered into the house; and [b]putting his E
hands on him said, Brother Saul, the W
Lord, *even* Jesus, that appeared unto thee E
in the way as thou camest, hath sent me,
that thou mightest receive thy sight, and
[c]be filled with the Holy Ghost.
18 And immediately there fell from his
eyes as it had been scales: and he received sight forthwith, and arose, and
was baptized.
19 And when he had received meat,
he was strengthened. [a]Then was Saul
certain days with the disciples which
were at Damascus.

Paul preaches at Damascus

20 And straightway he preached
Christ in the synagogues, that he is the
Son of God.
21 But all that heard *him* were
amazed, and said; [a]Is not this he that destroyed them which called on this name
in Jerusalem, and came hither for that intent, that he might bring them bound
unto the chief priests?
22 But Saul increased the more in
strength, [a]and confounded the Jews

37 [b]Mat. 16:16; John 6:69 & 9:35, 38 & 11:27; ch. 9:20; 1 John 4:15 & 5:5,13
39 [a]1 Ki. 18:12; 2 Ki. 2:16; Ezek. 3:12,14
9:1 [a]ch. 8:3; Gal. 1:13; 1 Tim. 1:13
2 [a]ch. 19:9,23 [1]Gk. *of the way*
3 [a]ch. 22:6 & 26:12; 1 Cor. 15:8
4 [a]Mat. 25:40
6 [a]Luke 3:10; ch 2:37 & 16:30
7 [a]Dan. 10:7; See ch. 22:9 & 26:13
10 [a]ch. 22:12
11 [a]ch. 21:39 & 22:3
13 [a]ver. 1
14 [a]ver. 21; ch. 7:59; 1 Cor. 1:2; 2 Tim. 2:22
15 [a]ch. 13:2 & 22:21; Rom. 1:1; 1 Cor. 15:10; Gal. 1:15; Eph. 3:7,8; 1 Tim. 2:7; 2 Tim. 1:11 [b]Rom. 1:5 & 11:13; Gal. 2:7,8 [c]ch. 25:22,23 & 26:1
16 [a]ch. 20:23 & 21:11; 2 Cor. 11:23
17 [a]ch. 22:12,13 [b]ch. 8:17 [c]ch. 2:4 & 4:31 & 8:17 & 13:52
19 [a]ch. 26:20
21 [a]ver. 1; ch. 8:3; Gal. 1:13,23
22 [a]ch. 18:28

E *Ac 8:29* ◀▶ *Ac 9:17*
L *Ac 8:29* ◀▶ *Ac 9:31*
N *Ac 4:31* ◀▶ *Ac 10:45*
D *Jn 11:4* ◀▶ *Ac 10:38*
E *Ac 8:6–7* ◀▶ *Ac 9:17*
B *Ac 8:14–21* ◀▶ *Ac 10:44–47*
E *Ac 8:39* ◀▶ *Ac 10:19*
W *Ac 8:14–15* ◀▶ *Ac 19:2*
E *Ac 9:12* ◀▶ *Ac 9:32–35*

which dwelt at Damascus, proving that this is very Christ.

Paul escapes to Jerusalem

23 ¶ And after that many days were fulfilled, [a]the Jews took counsel to kill him:

24 [a]But their laying await was known of Saul. And they watched the gates day and night to kill him.

25 Then the disciples took him by night, and [a]let *him* down by the wall in a basket.

26 And [a]when Saul was come to Jerusalem, he assayed to join himself to the disciples: but they were all afraid of him, and believed not that he was a disciple.

27 [a]But Barnabas took him, and brought *him* to the apostles, and declared unto them how he had seen the Lord in the way, and that he had spoken to him, [b]and how he had preached boldly at Damascus in the name of Jesus.

28 And [a]he was with them coming in and going out at Jerusalem.

29 And he spake boldly in the name of the Lord Jesus, and disputed against the [a]Grecians: [b]but they went about to slay him.

30 *Which* when the brethren knew, they brought him down to Caesarea, and sent him forth to Tarsus.

F 31 [a]Then had the churches rest
J throughout all Judaea and Galilee and Sa-
L maria, and were edified; and walking in
the fear of the Lord, and in the comfort of
the Holy Ghost, were multiplied.

Aeneas and Tabitha

E 32 ¶ And it came to pass, as Peter passed [a]throughout all *quarters,* he came down also to the saints which dwelt at Lydda.

33 And there he found a certain man named Aeneas, which had kept his bed eight years, and was sick of the palsy.

34 And Peter said unto him, Aeneas, [a]Jesus Christ maketh thee whole: arise, and make thy bed. And he arose immediately.

35 And all that dwelt at Lydda and [a]Saron saw him, and [b]turned to the Lord.

36 ¶ Now there was at Joppa a certain disciple named Tabitha, which by interpretation is called [1]Dorcas: this woman was full [a]of good works and almsdeeds which she did.

37 And it came to pass in those days, that she was sick, and died: whom when they had washed, they laid *her* in [a]an upper chamber.

38 And forasmuch as Lydda was nigh to Joppa, and the disciples had heard that Peter was there, they sent unto him two men, desiring *him* that he would not [1]delay to come to them.

39 Then Peter arose and went with them. When he was come, they brought him into the upper chamber: and all the widows stood by him weeping, and showing the coats and garments which Dorcas made, while she was with them.

40 But Peter [a]put them all forth, and [b]kneeled down, and prayed; and turning *him* to the body [c]said, Tabitha, arise. And she opened her eyes: and when she saw Peter, she sat up.

41 And he gave her *his* hand, and lifted her up, and when he had called the saints and widows, presented her alive.

42 And it was known throughout all Joppa; [a]and many believed in the Lord.

43 And it came to pass, that he tarried many days in Joppa with one [a]Simon a tanner.

Cornelius' vision

10 THERE WAS a certain man in Caesarea called Cornelius, a centurion of the band called the Italian *band,*

2 [a]*A* devout *man,* and one that [b]feared God with all his house, which gave much alms to the people, and prayed to God always.

3 [a]He saw in a vision evidently about the ninth hour of the day an angel of God coming in to him, and saying unto him, Cornelius.

4 And when he looked on him, he was afraid, and said, What is it, Lord? And he said unto him, Thy prayers and thine alms are come up for a memorial before God.

5 And now send men to Joppa, and call for *one* Simon, whose surname is Peter:

6 He lodgeth with one [a]Simon a tanner, whose house is by the sea side: [b]he shall tell thee what thou oughtest to do.

7 And when the angel which spake unto Cornelius was departed, he called

23 [a]ch. 23:12; 2 Cor. 11:26
24 [a]2 Cor. 11:32
25 [a]Josh. 2:15; 1 Sam. 19:12
26 [a]ch. 22:17; Gal. 1:17,18
27 [a]ch. 4:36 & 13:2 [b]ver. 20,22
28 [a]Gal. 1:18
29 [a]ch. 6:1 & 11:20 [b]ver. 23; 2 Cor. 11:26
31 [a]See ch. 8:1
32 [a]ch. 8:14
34 [a]ch. 3:6,16 & 4:10
35 [a]1 Chr. 5:16 [b]ch. 11:21
36 [a]1 Tim. 2:10; Tit. 3:8 [1]Or, *Doe,* or, *Roe*
37 [a]ch. 1:13
38 [1]Or, *be grieved*
40 [a]Mat. 9:25 [b]ch. 7:60 [c]Mark 5:41, 42; John 11:43
42 [a]John 11:45
43 [a]ch. 10:6
10:2 [a]ver. 22; ch. 8:2 & 22:12 [b]ver. 35
3 [a]ver. 30; ch. 11:13
6 [a]ch. 9:43 [b]ch. 11:14

F *Isa 63:14* ◄ ► *Ac 13:52*
J *Jn 20:21–22* ◄ ► *Ac 13:52*
L *Ac 8:39* ◄ ► *Ac 10:19–20*
E *Ac 9:17* ◄ ► *Ac 10:38*

two of his household servants, and a devout soldier of them that waited on him continually;

8 And when he had declared all *these* things unto them, he sent them to Joppa.

Peter's vision

9 ¶ On the morrow, as they went on their journey, and drew nigh unto the city, [a]Peter went up upon the housetop to pray about the sixth hour:

10 And he became very hungry, and would have eaten: but while they made ready, he fell into a trance,

11 And [a]saw heaven opened, and a certain vessel descending unto him, as it had been a great sheet knit at the four corners, and let down to the earth:

12 Wherein were all manner of fourfooted beasts of the earth, and wild beasts, and creeping things, and fowls of the air.

13 And there came a voice to him, Rise, Peter; kill, and eat.

14 But Peter said, Not so, Lord; [a]for I have never eaten any thing that is common or unclean.

G 15 And the voice *spake* unto him again the second time, [a]What God hath cleansed, *that* call not thou common.

16 This was done thrice: and the vessel was received up again into heaven.

Peter's visit to Cornelius

17 Now while Peter doubted in himself what this vision which he had seen should mean, behold, the men which were sent from Cornelius had made inquiry for Simon's house, and stood before the gate,

18 And called, and asked whether Simon, which was surnamed Peter, were lodged there.

E L 19 ¶ While Peter thought on the vision, [a]the Spirit said unto him, Behold, three men seek thee.

20 [a]Arise therefore, and get thee down, and go with them, doubting nothing: for I have sent them.

21 Then Peter went down to the men which were sent unto him from Cornelius; and said, Behold, I am he whom ye seek: what *is* the cause wherefore ye are come?

22 And they said, Cornelius the centurion, a just man, and one that feareth God, and [a]of good report among all the nation of the Jews, was warned from God by an holy angel to send for thee into his house, and to hear words of thee.

23 Then called he them in, and lodged *them*. And on the morrow Peter went away with them, [a]and certain brethren from Joppa accompanied him.

24 And the morrow after they entered into Caesarea. And Cornelius waited for them, and had called together his kinsmen and near friends.

25 And as Peter was coming in, Cornelius met him, and fell down at his feet, and worshipped *him*.

26 But Peter took him up, saying, [a]Stand up; I myself also am a man.

27 And as he talked with him, he went in, and found many that were come together.

28 And he said unto them, Ye know how [a]that it is an unlawful thing for a man that is a Jew to keep company, or come unto one of another nation; but [b]God hath shown me that I should not call any man common or unclean.

29 Therefore came I *unto you* without gainsaying, as soon as I was sent for: I ask therefore for what intent ye have sent for me?

30 And Cornelius said, Four days ago I was fasting until this hour; and at the ninth hour I prayed in my house, and, behold, [a]a man stood before me [b]in bright clothing,

31 And said, Cornelius, [a]thy prayer is heard, [b]and thine alms are had in remembrance in the sight of God.

32 Send therefore to Joppa, and call hither Simon, whose surname is Peter; he is lodged in the house of *one* Simon a

9 [a]ch. 11:5
11 [a]ch. 7:56; Rev. 19:11
14 [a]Lev. 11:4 & 20:25; Deut. 14:3, 7; Ezek. 4:14
15 [a]ver. 28; Mat. 15:11; Rom. 14:14, 17,20; 1 Cor. 10:25; 1 Tim. 4:4; Tit. 1:15
19 [a]ch. 11:12
20 [a]ch. 15:7
22 [a]ch. 22:12
23 [a]ch. 11:12
26 [a]ch. 14:14
28 [a]John 4:9 & 18:28; ch. 11:3; Gal. 2:12 [b]ch. 15:8, 9; Eph. 3:6
30 [a]ch. 1:10 [b]Mat. 28:3; Mark 16:5; Luke 24:4
31 [a]Dan. 10:12 [b]Heb. 6:10

G *Jn 10:16* ◀ ▶ *Ac 10:45*
E *Ac 9:17* ◀ ▶ *Ac 10:44–47*
L *Ac 9:31* ◀ ▶ *Ac 11:12*

10:15 The Holy Spirit came to Peter to instruct him that he was to preach the Gospel to the Gentiles as well as the Jews. Using a vivid illustration, God showed Peter that the ancient laws demanding a separation from the Gentiles to insure ritual cleanliness were no longer required. The doors of salvation were now open to anyone who would sincerely repent and follow Jesus (see Mk 7:14–19).

tanner by the sea side: who, when he cometh, shall speak unto thee.
33 Immediately therefore I sent to thee; and thou hast well done that thou art come. Now therefore are we all here present before God, to hear all things that are commanded thee of God.
34 ¶ Then Peter opened *his* mouth, and said, [a]Of a truth I perceive that God is no respecter of persons:
35 But [a]in every nation he that feareth him, and worketh righteousness, is accepted with him.
36 The word which *God* sent unto the children of Israel, [a]preaching peace by Jesus Christ: ([b]he is Lord of all:)
37 That word, *I say,* ye know, which was published throughout all Judaea, and [a]began from Galilee, after the baptism which John preached;
38 How [a]God anointed Jesus of Nazareth with the Holy Ghost and with power: who went about doing good, and healing all that were oppressed of the devil; [b]for God was with him.
39 And [a]we are witnesses of all things which he did both in the land of the Jews, and in Jerusalem; [b]whom they slew and hanged on a tree:
40 Him [a]God raised up the third day, and showed him openly;
41 [a]Not to all the people, but unto witnesses chosen before of God, *even* to us, [b]who did eat and drink with him after he rose from the dead.
42 And [a]he commanded us to preach unto the people, and to testify [b]that it is he which was ordained of God *to be* the Judge [c]of quick and dead.
43 [a]To him give all the prophets witness, that through his name [b]whosoever believeth in him shall receive remission of sins.

W Ac 2:21 ◀▶ Ac 10:43
G Ac 6:8–10 ◀▶ Ac 10:46
M Ac 6:15 ◀▶ Ac 10:46
D Ac 9:8–9 ◀▶ Ac 13:11
E Ac 9:32–35 ◀▶ Ac 14:3
J Jn 12:48 ◀▶ Ac 17:31
F Ac 8:37 ◀▶ Ac 13:38–39
K Ac 5:31 ◀▶ Ac 13:23
L Ac 5:31 ◀▶ Ac 11:18
W Ac 10:34–35 ◀▶ Ac 13:26

34 [a]Deut. 10:17; 2 Chr. 19:7; Job 34:19; Rom. 2:11; Gal. 2:6; Eph. 6:9; Col. 3:25; 1 Pet. 1:17
35 [a]ch. 15:9; Rom. 2:13 & 3:22 & 10:12,13; 1 Cor. 12:13; Gal. 3:28; Eph. 2:13
36 [a]Is. 57:19; Eph. 2:14; Col. 1:20 [b]Mat. 28:18; Rom. 10:12; 1 Cor. 15:27; Eph. 1:20; 1 Pet. 3:22; Rev. 17:14
37 [a]Luke 4:14
38 [a]Luke 4:18; Heb. 1:9 [b]John 3:2
39 [a]ch. 2:32 [b]ch. 5:30
40 [a]ch. 2:24
41 [a]John 14:17,22; ch. 13:31 [b]Luke 24:30; John 21:13
42 [a]Mat. 28:19; ch. 1:8 [b]John 5:22; ch. 17:31 [c]Rom. 14:9; 2 Cor. 5:10; 2 Tim. 4:1; 1 Pet. 4:5
43 [a]Is. 53:11; Jer. 31:34; Dan. 9:24; Mic. 7:18; Zech. 13:1; Mal. 4:2 [b]ch. 26:18; Rom. 10:11; Gal. 3:22
44 [a]ch. 4:31
45 [a]ver. 23 [b]ch. 11:18; Gal. 3:14
47 [a]ch. 11:17
48 [a]1 Cor. 1:17 [b]ch. 2:38 & 8:16
11:2 [a]ch. 10:45
3 [a]ch. 10:28 [b]Gal. 2:12
4 [a]Luke 1:3
5 [a]ch. 10:9

Gentiles receive the Holy Ghost

44 ¶ While Peter yet spake these words, [a]the Holy Ghost fell on all them which heard the word.
45 [a]And they of the circumcision which believed were astonished, as many as came with Peter, [b]because that on the Gentiles also was poured out the gift of the Holy Ghost.
46 For they heard them speak with tongues, and magnify God. Then answered Peter,
47 Can any man forbid water, that these should not be baptized, which have received the Holy Ghost [a]as well as we?
48 [a]And he commanded them to be baptized [b]in the name of the Lord. Then prayed they him to tarry certain days.

11 AND THE apostles and brethren that were in Judaea heard that the Gentiles had also received the word of God.
2 And when Peter was come up to Jerusalem, [a]they that were of the circumcision contended with him,
3 Saying, [a]Thou wentest in to men uncircumcised, [b]and didst eat with them.
4 But Peter rehearsed *the matter* from the beginning, and expounded *it* [a]by order unto them, saying,
5 [a]I was in the city of Joppa praying: and in a trance I saw a vision, A certain vessel descend, as it had been a great sheet, let down from heaven by four corners; and it came even to me:
6 Upon the which when I had fastened mine eyes, I considered, and saw fourfooted beasts of the earth, and wild beasts, and creeping things, and fowls of the air.

B Ac 9:17 ◀▶ Ac 11:15–17
E Ac 10:19 ◀▶ Ac 11:12
G Ac 10:15 ◀▶ Ac 11:18
N Ac 8:39 ◀▶ Ro 1:4
G Ac 10:38 ◀▶ Ac 11:27–28
M Ac 10:38 ◀▶ Ac 11:24
T Ac 7:55 ◀▶ Ac 11:28

10:44—11:1 The Jews found it hard to believe that God had opened the door of salvation to the Gentiles. Their lifelong training had confirmed that they alone were God's chosen people. Yet, when they saw the gift of the Holy Spirit poured out on the Gentiles, they realized that the church would be composed of people from every race.

7 And I heard a voice saying unto me,
Arise, Peter; slay and eat.
8 But I said, Not so, Lord: for nothing
common or unclean hath at any time entered into my mouth.
9 But the voice answered me again
from heaven, What God hath cleansed,
that call not thou common.
10 And this was done three times: and
all were drawn up again into heaven.
11 And, behold, immediately there
were three men already come unto the
house where I was, sent from Caesarea
unto me.
E 12 And [a]the Spirit bade me go with
L them, nothing doubting. Moreover
[b]these six brethren accompanied me, and
we entered into the man's house:
13 [a]And he showed us how he had
seen an angel in his house, which stood
and said unto him, Send men to Joppa,
and call for Simon, whose surname is
Peter;
14 Who shall tell thee words, whereby
thou and all thy house shall be saved.
B 15 And as I began to speak, the Holy
E Ghost fell on them, [a]as on us at the beginning.
P 16 Then remembered I the word of
the Lord, how that he said, [a]John indeed
baptized with water; but [b]ye shall be baptized with the Holy Ghost.
17 [a]Forasmuch then as God gave them
the like gift as *he did* unto us, who believed on the Lord Jesus Christ; [b]what
was I, that I could withstand God?
G 18 When they heard these things, they
L held their peace, and glorified God, say-
R ing, [a]Then hath God also to the Gentiles
granted repentance unto life.

The church at Antioch

19 ¶ [a]Now they which were scattered
abroad upon the persecution that arose
about Stephen travelled as far as Phenice,
and Cyprus, and Antioch, preaching the
word to none but unto the Jews only.
20 And some of them were men of Cyprus and Cyrene, which, when they were
come to Antioch, spake unto [a]the Grecians, preaching the Lord Jesus.
21 And [a]the hand of the Lord was with
them: and a great number believed, and
[b]turned unto the Lord.
22 ¶ Then tidings of these things came
unto the ears of the church which was in
Jerusalem: and they sent forth [a]Barnabas,
that he should go as far as Antioch.
23 Who, when he came, and had seen
the grace of God, was glad, and [a]exhorted
them all, that with purpose of heart they
would cleave unto the Lord.
24 For he was a good man, and [a]full of B
the Holy Ghost and of faith: [b]and much C
people was added unto the Lord. M
25 Then departed Barnabas to [a]Tarsus,
for to seek Saul:
26 And when he had found him, he
brought him unto Antioch. And it came
to pass, that a whole year they assembled
themselves [l]with the church, and taught
much people. And the disciples were
called Christians first in Antioch.
27 ¶ And in these days came [a]prophets G
from Jerusalem unto Antioch.
28 And there stood up one of them E
named [a]Agabus, and signified by the T
Spirit that there should be great dearth
throughout all the world: which came to
pass in the days of Claudius Caesar.
29 Then the disciples, every man according to his ability, determined to send
[a]relief unto the brethren which dwelt in
Judaea:
30 [a]Which also they did, and sent it to
the elders by the hands of Barnabas and
Saul.

Peter delivered from prison

12 NOW ABOUT that time Herod
the king [l]stretched forth *his*
hands to vex certain of the church.
2 And he killed James [a]the brother of
John with the sword.
3 And because he saw it pleased the
Jews, he proceeded further to take Peter
also. (Then were [a]the days of unleavened
bread.)
4 And [a]when he had apprehended
him, he put *him* in prison, and delivered

12 [a]John 16:13; ch. 10:19 & 15:7 [b]ch. 10:23
13 [a]ch. 10:30
15 [a]ch. 2:4
16 [a]Mat. 3:11; John 1:26,33; ch. 1:5 & 19:4 [b]Is. 44:3; Joel 2:28 & 3:18
17 [a]ch. 15:8,9 [b]ch. 10:47
18 [a]Rom. 10:12, 13 & 15:9,16
19 [a]ch. 8:1
20 [a]ch. 6:1 & 9:29
21 [a]Luke 1:66; ch. 2:47 [b]ch. 9:35
22 [a]ch. 9:27
23 [a]ch. 13:43 & 14:22
24 [a]ch. 6:5 [b]ver. 21; ch. 5:14
25 [a]ch. 9:30
26 [l]Or, *in the church*
27 [a]ch. 2:17 & 13:1 & 15:32 & 21:9; 1 Cor. 12:28; Eph. 4:11
28 [a]ch. 21:10
29 [a]Rom. 15:26; 1 Cor. 16:1; 2 Cor. 9:1
30 [a]ch. 12:25
12:1 [l]Or, *began*
2 [a]Mat. 4:21 & 20:23
3 [a]Ex. 12:14,15 & 23:15
4 [a]John 21:18

E *Ac 10:44–47* ◀ ▶ *Ac 11:15–17*
L *Ac 10:19–20* ◀ ▶ *Ac 13:2*
B *Ac 10:44–47* ◀ ▶ *Ac 11:24*
E *Ac 11:12* ◀ ▶ *Ac 11:28*
P *Ac 2:38–39* ◀ ▶ *Gal 3:14*
G *Ac 10:45* ◀ ▶ *Ac 13:46–48*
L *Ac 10:43* ◀ ▶ *Ac 13:38–39*
R *Ac 8:22* ◀ ▶ *Ac 17:30*

B *Ac 11:15–17* ◀ ▶ *Ac 13:52*
C *Jn 16:7–11* ◀ ▶ *Eph 6:17*
M *Ac 10:46* ◀ ▶ *Ac 19:6*
G *Ac 10:46* ◀ ▶ *Ac 19:6*
E *Ac 11:15–17* ◀ ▶ *Ac 13:2*
T *Ac 10:46* ◀ ▶ *Ac 19:6*

him to four quaternions of soldiers to
keep him; intending after Easter to bring
him forth to the people.
5 Peter therefore was kept in prison:
but [a]prayer[1] was made without ceasing of
the church unto God for him.
6 And when Herod would have
brought him forth, the same night Peter
was sleeping between two soldiers,
bound with two chains: and the keepers
before the door kept the prison.
V 7 And, behold, [a]the angel of the Lord
came upon *him,* and a light shined in the
prison: and he smote Peter on the side,
and raised him up, saying, Arise up
quickly. And his chains fell off from *his*
hands.
8 And the angel said unto him, Gird
thyself, and bind on thy sandals. And so
he did. And he saith unto him, Cast thy
garment about thee, and follow me.
9 And he went out, and followed him;
and [a]wist not that it was true which was
done by the angel; but thought [b]he saw a
vision.
10 When they were past the first and
the second ward, they came unto the iron
gate that leadeth unto the city; [a]which
opened to them of his own accord: and
they went out, and passed on through
one street; and forthwith the angel departed from him.
11 And when Peter was come to himself, he said, Now I know of a surety, that
[a]the Lord hath sent his angel, and [b]hath
delivered me out of the hand of Herod,
and *from* all the expectation of the people
of the Jews.
12 And when he had considered *the
thing,* [a]he came to the house of Mary the
mother of [b]John, whose surname was
Mark; where many were gathered together [c]praying.
13 And as Peter knocked at the door
of the gate, a damsel came [1]to hearken,
named Rhoda.
14 And when she knew Peter's voice,
she opened not the gate for gladness, but
ran in, and told how Peter stood before
the gate.
15 And they said unto her, Thou art
mad. But she constantly affirmed that it
was even so. Then said they, [a]It is his
angel.
16 But Peter continued knocking: and
when they had opened *the door,* and saw
him, they were astonished.
17 But he, [a]beckoning unto them with
the hand to hold their peace, declared
unto them how the Lord had brought him
out of the prison. And he said, Go show
these things unto James, and to the brethren. And he departed, and went into another place.

The death of Herod

18 Now as soon as it was day, there
was no small stir among the soldiers,
what was become of Peter.
19 And when Herod had sought for
him, and found him not, he examined
the keepers, and commanded that *they*
should be put to death. And he went
down from Judaea to Caesarea, and *there*
abode.
20 ¶ And Herod [1]was highly displeased with them of Tyre and Sidon: but
they came with one accord to him, and,
having made Blastus [2]the king's chamberlain their friend, desired peace; because
[a]their country was nourished by the
king's *country.*
21 And upon a set day Herod, arrayed
in royal apparel, sat upon his throne, and
made an oration unto them.
22 And the people gave a shout, *saying, It is* the voice of a god, and not of a
man.
23 And immediately the angel of the
Lord [a]smote him, because [b]he gave not
God the glory: and he was eaten of
worms, and gave up the ghost.
24 ¶ But [a]the word of God grew and
multiplied.
25 And Barnabas and Saul returned
from Jerusalem, when they had fulfilled
their [1]ministry, and [a]took with them
[b]John, whose surname was Mark.

Paul and Barnabas on Cyprus

13 NOW THERE were [a]in the
church that was at Antioch cer-
tain prophets and teachers; as [b]Barnabas,
and Simeon that was called Niger, and
[c]Lucius of Cyrene, and Manaen, [1]which
had been brought up with Herod the tetrarch, and Saul.
2 As they ministered to the Lord, and E
fasted, the Holy Ghost said, [a]Separate me L

5 [a]2 Cor. 1:11; Eph. 6:18; 1 Thes. 5:17 [1]Or, *instant and earnest prayer was made*
7 [a]ch. 5:19
9 [a]Ps. 126:1 [b]ch. 10:3,17 & 11:5
10 [a]ch. 16:26
11 [a]Ps. 34:7; Dan. 3:28 & 6:22; Heb. 1:14 [b]Job 5:19; Ps. 33:18,19 & 34:22 & 41:2 & 97:10; 2 Cor. 1:10; 2 Pet. 2:9
12 [a]ch. 4:23 [b]ch. 15:37 [c]ver. 5
13 [1]Or, *to ask who was there*
15 [a]Gen. 48:16; Mat. 18:10
17 [a]ch. 13:16 & 19:33 & 21:40
20 [a]1 Ki. 5:9,11; Ezek. 27:17 [1]Or, *bare an hostile mind, intending war* [2]Gk. *that was over the king's bedchamber*
23 [a]1 Sam. 25:38; 2 Sam. 24:17 [b]Ps. 115:1
24 [a]Is. 55:11; ch. 6:7 & 19:20; Col. 1:6
25 [a]ch. 13:5,13 & 15:37 [b]ver. 12 [1]Or, *charge;* see ch. 11:29,30
13:1 [a]ch. 14:26 [b]ch. 11:22 [c]Rom. 16:21 [1]Or, *Herod's fosterbrother*
2 [a]Num. 8:14; ch. 9:15 & 22:21; Rom. 1:1; Gal. 1:15 & 2:9

V Ac 5:38–39 ◀▶ Ac 14:19–20
E Ac 11:28 ◀▶ Ac 13:9
L Ac 11:12 ◀▶ Ac 13:9

Barnabas and Saul for the work [b]where-
unto I have called them.
3 And [a]when they had fasted and
prayed, and laid *their* hands on them,
they sent *them* away.
4 ¶ So they, being sent forth by the
Holy Ghost, departed unto Seleucia; and
from thence they sailed to [a]Cyprus.
5 And when they were at Salamis,
[a]they preached the word of God in the
synagogues of the Jews: and they had also
[b]John to *their* minister.
6 And when they had gone through
the isle unto Paphos, they found [a]a certain sorcerer, a false prophet, a Jew,
whose name *was* Bar-jesus:
7 Which was with the deputy of the
country, Sergius Paulus, a prudent man;
who called for Barnabas and Saul, and desired to hear the word of God.
8 But [a]Elymas the sorcerer (for so is
his name by interpretation) withstood
them, seeking to turn away the deputy
from the faith.
E 9 Then Saul, (who also *is called* Paul,)
L [a]filled with the Holy Ghost, set his eyes
on him,
10 And said, O full of all subtlety and
all mischief, [a]*thou* child of the devil, *thou*
enemy of all righteousness, wilt thou not
cease to pervert the right ways of the
Lord?
D 11 And now, behold, [a]the hand of the
Lord *is* upon thee, and thou shalt be
blind, not seeing the sun for a season.
And immediately there fell on him a mist
and a darkness; and he went about seeking some to lead him by the hand.
12 Then the deputy, when he saw
what was done, believed, being astonished at the doctrine of the Lord.

Preaching in Perga and Antioch

13 Now when Paul and his company
loosed from Paphos, they came to Perga
in Pamphylia: and [a]John departing from
them returned to Jerusalem.
14 ¶ But when they departed from
Perga, they came to Antioch in Pisidia,
and [a]went into the synagogue on the sabbath day, and sat down.
15 And [a]after the reading of the law
and the prophets the rulers of the synagogue sent unto them, saying, *Ye* men
and brethren, if ye have [b]any word of exhortation for the people, say on.
16 Then Paul stood up, and beckoning
with *his* hand said, Men of Israel, and [a]ye
that fear God, give audience.
17 The God of this people of Israel
[a]chose our fathers, and exalted the people [b]when they dwelt as strangers in the
land of Egypt, and with an high arm
brought he them out of it.
18 And [a]about the time of forty years
[1]suffered he their manners in the wilderness.
19 And when he had destroyed seven
nations in the land of Chanaan, [a]he divided their land to them by lot.
20 And after that [a]he gave *unto them*
judges about the space of four hundred
and fifty years, [b]until Samuel the
prophet.
21 [a]And afterward they desired a king:
and God gave unto them Saul the son of
Cis, a man of the tribe of Benjamin, by
the space of forty years.
22 And [a]when he had removed him,
[b]he raised up unto them David to be their
king; to whom also he gave testimony,
and said, [c]I have found David the *son* of
Jesse, [d]a man after mine own heart,
which shall fulfil all my will.
23 [a]Of this man's seed hath God ac- K
cording [b]to *his* promise raised unto Israel
[c]a Saviour, Jesus:
24 [a]When John had first preached before his coming the baptism of repentance to all the people of Israel.
25 And as John fulfilled his course, he
said, [a]Whom think ye that I am? I am not
he. But, behold, there cometh one after
me, whose shoes of *his* feet I am not worthy to loose.
26 Men *and* brethren, children of the W
stock of Abraham, and whosoever among
you feareth God, [a]to you is the word of
this salvation sent.
27 For they that dwell at Jerusalem,
and their rulers, [a]because they knew him
not, nor yet the voices of the prophets
which are read every sabbath day, they
have fulfilled *them* in condemning *him*.
28 [a]And though they found no cause of
death *in him*, yet desired they Pilate that
he should be slain.

2 [b]Mat. 9:38; ch. 14:26; Rom. 10:15; Eph. 3:7,8; 1 Tim. 2:7; 2 Tim. 1:11; Heb. 5:4
3 [a]ch. 6:6
4 [a]ch. 4:36
5 [a]ver. 46 [b]ch. 12:25 & 15:37
6 [a]ch. 8:9
8 [a]Ex. 7:11; 2 Tim. 3:8
9 [a]ch. 4:8
10 [a]Mat. 13:38; 1 John 3:8
11 [a]1 Sam. 5:6
13 [a]ch. 15:38
14 [a]ch. 16:13
15 [a]Luke 4:16 [b]Heb. 13:22
16 [a]ch. 10:35
17 [a]Deut. 7:6,7 [b]ch. 7:17
18 [a]Ex. 16:35 [1]Gk. *bore, or, fed them, as a nurse beareth,* or, *feedeth her child,* Deut. 1:31; according to the LXX and so Chrysostom
19 [a]Josh. 14:1
20 [a]Judg. 2:16 [b]1 Sam. 3:20
21 [a]1 Sam. 8:5
22 [a]1 Sam. 15:23 [b]1 Sam. 16:13 [c]Ps. 89:20 [d]1 Sam. 13:14
23 [a]Is. 11:1 [b]Ps. 132:11 [c]Mat. 1:21
24 [a]Mat. 3:1; Luke 3:3
25 [a]Mark 1:7
26 [a]Mat. 10:6
27 [a]Luke 23:34
28 [a]Mat. 27:22

E *Ac 13:2* ◀▶ *Ac 13:52*
L *Ac 13:2* ◀▶ *Ac 15:28*
D *Ac 10:38* ◀▶ *1Co 10:8*
K *Ac 10:43* ◀▶ *Ac 13:38–39*
W *Ac 10:43* ◀▶ *Ac 13:38–39*

29 [a]And when they had fulfilled all
that was written of him, [b]they took *him*
down from the tree, and laid *him* in a
sepulchre.
30 [a]But God raised him from the dead:
31 And [a]he was seen many days of
them which came up with him from Galilee to Jerusalem, who are his witnesses
unto the people.
32 And we declare unto you glad tidings, how that [a]the promise which was
made unto the fathers,
33 God hath fulfilled the same unto us
their children, in that he hath raised up
Jesus again; as it is also written in the
second psalm, [a]Thou art my Son, this day
have I begotten thee.
34 And as concerning that he raised
him up from the dead, *now* no more to
return to corruption, he said on this wise,
[a]I will give you the sure [l]mercies of
David.
35 Wherefore he saith also in another
psalm, [a]Thou shalt not suffer thine Holy
One to see corruption.
36 For David, [l]after he had served his
own generation by the will of God, [a]fell
on sleep, and was laid unto his fathers,
and saw corruption:
37 But he, whom God raised again,
saw no corruption.
F 38 ¶ Be it known unto you therefore,
K men *and* brethren, that [a]through this
L man is preached unto you the forgiveness
W of sins:
39 And [a]by him all that believe are
justified from all things, from which ye
could not be justified by the law of
Moses.
40 Beware therefore, lest that come
upon you, which is spoken of in [a]the
prophets;
H 41 Behold, ye despisers, and wonder,

F *Ac 10:43* ◀ ▶ *Ac 16:30–31*
K *Ac 13:23* ◀ ▶ *Ac 13:47*
L *Ac 11:18* ◀ ▶ *Ac 13:47*
W *Ac 13:26* ◀ ▶ *Ac 17:27*
H *Ac 3:23* ◀ ▶ *Ro 1:18*

29 [a]Luke 18:31 [b]Mat. 27:59
30 [a]Mat. 28:6
31 [a]Mat. 28:16
32 [a]Gen. 3:15
33 [a]Heb. 1:5
34 [a]Is. 55:3 [l]Gk. *holy,* or, *just things:* which word the LXX both in the place of Is. 55:3, and in many others, use for that which is in the Hebrew, *mercies*
35 [a]Ps. 16:10
36 [a]ch. 2:29 [l]Or, *after he had in his own age served the will of God;* see ver. 22
38 [a]Jer. 31:34
39 [a]Is. 53:11
40 [a]Hab. 1:5
42 [l]Gk. *in the week between,* or, *in the sabbath between*
43 [a]ch. 11:23 & 14:22 [b]Tit. 2:11; Heb. 12:15; 1 Pet. 5:12
45 [a]ch. 18:6; 1 Pet. 4:4; Jude 10
46 [a]ver. 26; Mat. 10:6; ch. 3:26; Rom. 1:16 [b]Ex. 32:10; Deut. 32:21; Is. 55:5; Mat. 21:43; Rom. 10:19 [c]ch. 18:6 & 28:28
47 [a]Is. 42:6 & 49:6; Luke 2:32
48 [a]ch. 2:47
50 [a]2 Tim. 3:11
51 [a]Mat. 10:14; Mark 6:11; Luke 9:5; ch. 18:6

and perish: for I work a work in your
days, a work which ye shall in no wise
believe, though a man declare it unto
you.
42 And when the Jews were gone out
of the synagogue, the Gentiles besought
that these words might be preached to
them [l]the next sabbath.
43 Now when the congregation was
broken up, many of the Jews and religious proselytes followed Paul and Barnabas: who, speaking to them, [a]persuaded
them to continue in [b]the grace of God.
44 ¶ And the next sabbath day came
almost the whole city together to hear
the word of God.
45 But when the Jews saw the multitudes, they were filled with envy, and
[a]spake against those things which were
spoken by Paul, contradicting and blas-
pheming.
46 Then Paul and Barnabas waxed G
bold, and said, [a]It was necessary that the
word of God should first have been spoken to you: but [b]seeing ye put it from
you, and judge yourselves unworthy of
everlasting life, lo, [c]we turn to the Gentiles.
47 For so hath the Lord commanded K
us, *saying,* [a]I have set thee to be a light of L
the Gentiles, that thou shouldest be for
salvation unto the ends of the earth.
48 And when the Gentiles heard this,
they were glad, and glorified the word of
the Lord: [a]and as many as were ordained
to eternal life believed.
49 And the word of the Lord was published throughout all the region.
50 But the Jews stirred up the devout
and honourable women, and the chief
men of the city, and [a]raised persecution
against Paul and Barnabas, and expelled
them out of their coasts.
51 [a]But they shook off the dust of their

G *Ac 11:18* ◀ ▶ *Ac 14:27*
K *Ac 13:38–39* ◀ ▶ *Ac 16:31*
L *Ac 13:38–39* ◀ ▶ *Ac 15:11*

13:46–48 Paul and Barnabas declared that since the Jews who persecuted them wanted nothing to do with their message about Christ and had judged themselves "unworthy of everlasting life" (13:46), Paul and Barnabas would take their message to the Gentiles. Paul said they were going to the Gentiles in fulfillment of Isaiah's prophecy to be "a light to the Gentiles, that thou mayest be my salvation unto the end of the earth" (Isa 49:6). Israel had failed to fulfill this command by ignoring the Gentile nations. Paul's outreach to the Gentiles proved that God's mercy extended to include "as many as were ordained to eternal life" (13:48).

feet against them, and came unto Iconium.

52 And the disciples [a]were filled with joy, and with the Holy Ghost.

Preaching at Iconium

14 AND IT came to pass in Iconium, that they went both together into the synagogue of the Jews, and so spake, that a great multitude both of the Jews and also of the Greeks believed.

2 But the unbelieving Jews stirred up the Gentiles, and made their minds evil affected against the brethren.

3 Long time therefore abode they speaking boldly in the Lord, [a]which gave testimony unto the word of his grace, and granted signs and wonders to be done by their hands.

4 But the multitude of the city was divided: and part held with the Jews, and part with the [a]apostles.

5 And when there was an assault made both of the Gentiles, and also of the Jews with their rulers, [a]to use *them* despitefully, and to stone them,

6 They were ware of *it,* and [a]fled unto Lystra and Derbe, cities of Lycaonia, and unto the region that lieth round about:

7 And there they preached the gospel.

Preaching at Lystra

8 ¶ [a]And there sat a certain man at Lystra, impotent in his feet, being a cripple from his mother's womb, who never had walked:

9 The same heard Paul speak: who stedfastly beholding him, and perceiving that he had faith to be healed,

10 Said with a loud voice, [a]Stand upright on thy feet. And he leaped and walked.

11 And when the people saw what Paul had done, they lifted up their voices, saying in the speech of Lycaonia, [a]The gods are come down to us in the likeness of men.

12 And they called Barnabas, Jupiter; and Paul, Mercurius, because he was the chief speaker.

13 Then the priest of Jupiter, which was before their city, brought oxen and garlands unto the gates, [a]and would have done sacrifice with the people.

14 *Which* when the apostles, Barnabas and Paul, heard *of,* [a]they rent their clothes, and ran in among the people, crying out,

15 And saying, Sirs, [a]why do ye these things? [b]We also are men of like passions with you, and preach unto you that ye should turn from [c]these vanities [d]unto the living God, [e]which made heaven, and earth, and the sea, and all things that are therein:

16 [a]Who in times past suffered all nations to walk in their own ways.

17 [a]Nevertheless he left not himself without witness, in that he did good, and [b]gave us rain from heaven, and fruitful seasons, filling our hearts with food and gladness.

18 And with these sayings scarce restrained they the people, that they had not done sacrifice unto them.

The return to Antioch

19 ¶ [a]And there came thither *certain* Jews from Antioch and Iconium, who persuaded the people, [b]and, having stoned Paul, drew *him* out of the city, supposing he had been dead.

20 Howbeit, as the disciples stood round about him, he rose up, and came into the city: and the next day he departed with Barnabas to Derbe.

21 And when they had preached the gospel to that city, [a]and [1]had taught many, they returned again to Lystra, and *to* Iconium, and Antioch,

22 Confirming the souls of the disciples, *and* [a]exhorting them to continue in the faith, and that [b]we must through much tribulation enter into the kingdom of God.

23 And when they had [a]ordained them elders in every church, and had prayed with fasting, they commended them to the Lord, on whom they believed.

24 And after they had passed throughout Pisidia, they came to Pamphylia.

25 And when they had preached the word in Perga, they went down into Attalia:

52 [a]Mat. 5:12; John 16:22; ch. 2:46
14:3 [a]Mark 16:20; Heb. 2:4
4 [a]ch. 13:2,3
5 [a]2 Tim. 3:11
6 [a]Mat. 10:23
8 [a]ch. 3:2
10 [a]Is. 35:6
11 [a]ch. 8:10 & 28:6
13 [a]Dan. 2:46
14 [a]Mat. 26:65
15 [a]ch. 10:26 [b]Jas. 5:17; Rev. 19:10 [c]1 Sam. 12:21; 1 Ki. 16:13; Jer. 14:22; Amos 2:4; 1 Cor. 8:4 [d]1 Thes. 1:9 [e]Gen. 1:1; Ps. 33:6 & 146:6; Rev. 14:7
16 [a]Ps. 81:12; ch. 17:30; 1 Pet. 4:3
17 [a]ch. 17:27; Rom. 1:20 [b]Lev. 26:4; Deut. 11:14 & 28:12; Job 5:10; Ps. 65:10 & 68:9 & 147:8; Jer. 14:22; Mat. 5:45
19 [a]ch. 13:45 [b]2 Cor. 11:25; 2 Tim. 3:11
21 [a]Mat. 28:19 [1]Gk. *had made many disciples*
22 [a]ch. 11:23 & 13:43 [b]Mat. 10:38 & 16:24; Luke 22:28; Rom. 8:17; 2 Tim. 2:12 & 3:12
23 [a]Tit. 1:5

B *Ac 11:24 ◀▶ Ac 15:8*
E *Ac 13:9 ◀▶ Ac 15:8*
F *Ac 9:31 ◀▶ Ro 5:5* **J** *Ac 9:31 ◀▶ Ro 5:5*
E *Ac 10:38 ◀▶ Ac 14:8–10*
E *Ac 14:3 ◀▶ Ac 14:19–20*
E *Ac 14:8–10 ◀▶ Ac 16:16–18*
V *Ac 12:7–11 ◀▶ Ac 16:26*
S *Ac 3:26 ◀▶ Ro 1:18*

26 And thence sailed to Antioch, [a]from whence they had been [b]recommended to the grace of God for the work which they fulfilled.

G 27 And when they were come, and had gathered the church together, [a]they rehearsed all that God had done with them, and how he had [b]opened the door of faith unto the Gentiles.

28 And there they abode long time with the disciples.

The council at Jerusalem

15 AND [a]CERTAIN men which came down from Judaea taught the brethren, *and said,* [b]Except ye be circumcised [c]after the manner of Moses, ye cannot be saved.

2 When therefore Paul and Barnabas had no small dissension and disputation with them, they determined that [a]Paul and Barnabas, and certain other of them, should go up to Jerusalem unto the apostles and elders about this question.

G 3 And [a]being brought on their way by the church, they passed through Phenice and Samaria, [b]declaring the conversion of the Gentiles: and they caused great joy unto all the brethren.

4 And when they were come to Jerusalem, they were received of the church, and *of* the apostles and elders, and [a]they declared all things that God had done with them.

5 But there [/]rose up certain of the sect of the Pharisees which believed, saying, [a]That it was needful to circumcise them, and to command *them* to keep the law of Moses.

G *Ac 13:46–48* ◀▶ *Ac 15:3*
G *Ac 14:27* ◀▶ *Ac 15:7–9*

26 [a]ch. 13:1,3 [b]ch. 15:40
27 [a]ch. 15:4,12 & 21:19 [b]1 Cor. 16:9; 2 Cor. 2:12; Col. 4:3; Rev. 3:8
15:1 [a]Gal. 2:12 [b]ver. 5; John 7:22; Gal. 5:2; Phil. 3:2; Col. 2:8,11,16 [c]Gen. 17:10; Lev. 12:3
2 [a]Gal. 2:1
3 [a]Rom. 15:24; 1 Cor. 16:6,11 [b]ch. 14:27
4 [a]ver. 12; ch. 14:27
5 [a]ver. 1 [/]Or, *rose up,* said they, *certain*
7 [a]ch. 10:20 & 11:12
8 [a]1 Chr. 28:9; ch. 1:24 [b]ch. 10:44
9 [a]Rom. 10:12 [b]ch. 10:15,28; 1 Cor. 1:2; 1 Pet. 1:22
10 [a]Mat. 23:4; Gal. 5:1
11 [a]Rom. 3:24; Eph. 2:8; Tit. 2:11 & 3:4,5
12 [a]ch. 14:27
13 [a]ch. 12:17
14 [a]ver. 7

6 ¶ And the apostles and elders came together for to consider of this matter.

7 And when there had been much disputing, Peter rose up, and said unto them, [a]Men *and* brethren, ye know how that a good while ago God made choice among us, that the Gentiles by my mouth should hear the word of the gospel, and believe. G

8 And God, [a]which knoweth the hearts, bare them witness, [b]giving them the Holy Ghost, even as *he did* unto us; B E S

9 [a]And put no difference between us and them, [b]purifying their hearts by faith. E

10 Now therefore why tempt ye God, [a]to put a yoke upon the neck of the disciples, which neither our fathers nor we were able to bear?

11 But [a]we believe that through the grace of the Lord Jesus Christ we shall be saved, even as they. L

12 ¶ Then all the multitude kept silence, and gave audience to Barnabas and Paul, declaring what miracles and wonders God had [a]wrought among the Gentiles by them. G

13 ¶ And after they had held their peace, [a]James answered, saying, Men *and* brethren, hearken unto me:

14 [a]Simeon hath declared how God at the first did visit the Gentiles, to take out of them a people for his name.

15 And to this agree the words of the prophets; as it is written,

G *Ac 15:3* ◀▶ *Ac 15:12*
B *Ac 13:52* ◀▶ *Ac 19:1–7*
E *Ac 13:52* ◀▶ *Ac 15:28*
S *Lk 1:17* ◀▶ *Ro 1:4*
E *Ac 1:24* ◀▶ *Ac 15:18*
L *Ac 13:47* ◀▶ *Ac 17:27*
G *Ac 15:7–9* ◀▶ *Ac 18:6*

14:27 When the church was gathered together, they discussed Isaiah's prophecies and God's offer of salvation extended to the Gentiles. This was a radical change for the Jewish believers because the Gentiles were now entering the fellowship of God on the same basis as the Jews—their repentance from sin.

15:3 The believers rejoiced when they heard that the church would include converted Gentiles.

15:7–12 The first council of the church at Jerusalem established guidelines for the proper response toward Gentile believers who accepted faith in Jesus and wished to join the church. Some Jewish believers, called Judaizers, wanted to force the Gentile converts to be circumcised and to follow the ancient Jewish law before they could be accepted as legitimate followers of Jesus. This fundamental dispute could have destroyed the early church unless it was resolved properly. Peter affirmed that God had offered salvation to the Gentiles and confirmed his gift by freely giving the Gentiles the gift of the Holy Spirit as well. "To put a yoke upon the neck" (5:10) of these new believers was not what God intended. Salvation was free, therefore acceptance and fellowship should be also.

15:15–20 The first bishop of the church in Jerusalem was James, the brother of Jesus. He replied to Peter and Paul's messages by reminding his audience that the prophet Amos had predicted that God would reach out to the Gentiles in the last days (see Am 9:11–12) and would reinstate David's rule

16 [a]After this I will return, and will build again the tabernacle of David, which is fallen down; and I will build again the ruins thereof, and I will set it up:

17 That the residue of men might seek after the Lord, and all the Gentiles, upon whom my name is called, saith the Lord, who doeth all these things.

E 18 Known unto God are all his works from the beginning of the world.

19 Wherefore [a]my sentence is, that we trouble not them, which from among the Gentiles [b]are turned to God:

20 But that we write unto them, that they abstain [a]from pollutions of idols, and [b]*from* fornication, and *from* things strangled, [c]and *from* blood.

21 For Moses of old time hath in every city them that preach him, [a]being read in the synagogues every sabbath day.

Letters sent to the Gentiles

22 Then pleased it the apostles and elders, with the whole church, to send chosen men of their own company to Antioch with Paul and Barnabas; *namely,* Judas surnamed [a]Barsabas, and Silas, chief men among the brethren:

23 And they wrote *letters* by them after this manner; The apostles and elders and brethren *send* greeting unto the brethren which are of the Gentiles in Antioch and Syria and Cilicia:

24 Forasmuch as we have heard, that [a]certain which went out from us have troubled you with words, subverting your souls, saying, *Ye must* be circumcised, and keep the law: to whom we gave no *such* commandment:

E *Ac 15:8* ◀▶ *Ro 8:27*

16 [a] Amos 9:11
19 [a] See ver. 23 [b] 1 Thes. 1:9
20 [a] Gen. 35:2; Ex. 20:3,23; Ezek. 20:30; 1 Cor. 8:1 & 10:20,28; Rev. 2:14 [b] 1 Cor. 6:9; Gal. 5:19; Eph. 5:3; Col. 3:5; 1 Thes. 4:3; 1 Pet. 4:3 [c] Gen. 9:4; Lev. 3:17; Deut. 12:16
21 [a] ch. 13:15,27
22 [a] ch. 1:23
24 [a] ver. 1; Gal. 2:4 & 5:12; Tit. 1:10,11
26 [a] ch. 13:50
27 [l] Gk. *word*
29 [a] ver. 20; ch. 21:25; Rev. 2:14,20 [b] Lev. 17:14
31 [l] Or, *exhortation*
32 [a] ch. 14:22 & 18:23
33 [a] 1 Cor. 16:11; Heb. 11:31
35 [a] ch. 13:1

25 It seemed good unto us, being assembled with one accord, to send chosen men unto you with our beloved Barnabas and Paul,

26 [a]Men that have hazarded their lives for the name of our Lord Jesus Christ.

27 We have sent therefore Judas and Silas, who shall also tell *you* the same things by [l]mouth.

28 For it seemed good to the Holy E
Ghost, and to us, to lay upon you no L
greater burden than these necessary things;

29 [a]That ye abstain from meats offered to idols, and [b]from blood, and from things strangled, and from fornication: from which if ye keep yourselves, ye shall do well. Fare ye well.

30 So when they were dismissed, they came to Antioch: and when they had gathered the multitude together, they delivered the epistle:

31 *Which* when they had read, they rejoiced for the [l]consolation.

32 And Judas and Silas, being prophets also themselves, [a]exhorted the brethren with many words, and confirmed *them.*

33 And after they had tarried *there* a space, they were let [a]go in peace from the brethren unto the apostles.

34 Notwithstanding it pleased Silas to abide there still.

35 [a]Paul also and Barnabas continued in Antioch, teaching and preaching the word of the Lord, with many others also.

Separation of Paul and Barnabas

36 ¶ And some days after Paul said unto Barnabas, Let us go again and visit

E *Ac 15:8* ◀▶ *Ac 16:6–7*
L *Ac 13:9* ◀▶ *Ac 16:6–7*

---

through Jesus the Messiah.

James' authoritative conclusion to this debate was that the Gentile converts should be given only four specific requirements: (1) they must abstain from food that had been polluted by, or offered to, idols (see 1Co 8:7–13; 10:18–22); (2) they should abstain from fornication and sexual immorality such as adultery, incest, prostitution and homosexuality; (3) Gentile converts must not eat anything strangled; and (4) these new converts were not permitted to eat blood. These last two restrictions were prudent commands for the Gentile believers because of Moses' restriction for God's people to abstain from association with any people who ate blood (see Lev 17:12). This declaration of the church settled forever that Gentiles believers did not need to become Jews or become circumcised or follow any other special Jewish legal regulation. Salvation is dependent entirely upon the atonement for sins based on the blood of Jesus Christ, not on any person's righteous works.

Note that the apostles did not demand that Gentile believers must worship on the Sabbath day (Saturday). The Gentile believers joined the Jewish believers and worshiped on the Lord's day (Sunday) in celebration of Christ's resurrection from the dead. While Jewish and Gentile believers worshiped Jesus on Sunday, many of the Jewish believers continued to celebrate the Sabbath day too and visit the temple in Jerusalem (see Ac 21:20–26).

our brethren [a]in every city where we have preached the word of the Lord, *and see* how they do.

37 And Barnabas determined to take with them [a]John, whose surname was Mark.

38 But Paul thought not good to take him with them, [a]who departed from them from Pamphylia, and went not with them to the work.

39 And the contention was so sharp between them, that they departed asunder one from the other: and so Barnabas took Mark, and sailed unto Cyprus;

40 And Paul chose Silas, and departed, [a]being recommended by the brethren unto the grace of God.

41 And he went through Syria and Cilicia, [a]confirming the churches.

The selection of Timothy

16 THEN CAME he to [a]Derbe and Lystra: and, behold, a certain disciple was there, [b]named Timotheus, [c]the son of a certain woman, which was a Jewess, and believed; but his father *was* a Greek:

2 Which [a]was well reported of by the brethren that were at Lystra and Iconium.

3 Him would Paul have to go forth with him; and [a]took and circumcised him because of the Jews which were in those quarters: for they knew all that his father was a Greek.

4 And as they went through the cities, they delivered them the decrees for to keep, [a]that were ordained of the apostles and elders which were at Jerusalem.

5 And [a]so were the churches established in the faith, and increased in number daily.

The Macedonian call

E L 6 Now when they had gone throughout Phrygia and the region of Galatia, and were forbidden of the Holy Ghost to preach the word in Asia,

7 After they were come to Mysia, they assayed to go into Bithynia: but the Spirit suffered them not.

8 And they passing by Mysia [a]came down to Troas.

9 And a vision appeared to Paul in the night; There stood a [a]man of Macedonia, and prayed him, saying, Come over into Macedonia, and help us.

10 And after he had seen the vision, immediately we endeavoured to go [a]into Macedonia, assuredly gathering that the Lord had called us for to preach the gospel unto them.

The conversion of Lydia

11 Therefore loosing from Troas, we came with a straight course to Samothracia, and the next *day* to Neapolis;

12 And from thence to [a]Philippi, which is [l]the chief city of that part of Macedonia, *and* a colony: and we were in that city abiding certain days.

13 And on the [l]sabbath we went out of the city by a river side, where prayer was wont to be made; and we sat down, and spake unto the women which resorted *thither.*

14 ¶ And a certain woman named Lydia, a seller of purple, of the city of Thyatira, which worshipped God, heard *us:* whose [a]heart the Lord opened, that she attended unto the things which were spoken of Paul.

15 And when she was baptized, and her household, she besought *us,* saying, If ye have judged me to be faithful to the Lord, come into my house, and abide *there.* And [a]she constrained us.

Paul and Silas imprisoned

16 ¶ And it came to pass, as we went to prayer, a certain damsel [a]possessed with a spirit [l]of divination met us, which brought her masters [b]much gain by soothsaying: E

17 The same followed Paul and us, and cried, saying, These men are the servants of the most high God, which show unto us the way of salvation.

18 And this did she many days. But Paul, [a]being grieved, turned and said to the spirit, I command thee in the name of Jesus Christ to come out of her. [b]And he came out the same hour.

19 ¶ And [a]when her masters saw that the hope of their gains was gone, they caught Paul and Silas, and [b]drew *them* into the [l]marketplace unto the rulers,

20 And brought them to the magis-

36 [a]ch. 13:4,13, 14,51 & 14:1,6,24, 25
37 [a]ch. 12:12,25 & 13:5; Col. 4:10; 2 Tim. 4:11; Philem. 24
38 [a]ch. 13:13
40 [a]ch. 14:26
41 [a]ch. 16:5
16:1 [a]ch. 14:6 [b]ch. 19:22; Rom. 16:21; 1 Cor. 4:17; Phil. 2:19; 1 Thes. 3:2; 1 Tim. 1:2; 2 Tim. 1:2 [c]2 Tim. 1:5
2 [a]ch. 6:3
3 [a]1 Cor. 9:20; Gal. 2:3; See Gal. 5:2
4 [a]ch. 15:28,29
5 [a]ch. 15:41
8 [a]2 Cor. 2:12; 2 Tim. 4:13
9 [a]ch. 10:30
10 [a]2 Cor. 2:13
12 [a]Phil. 1:1 [l]Or, *the first*
13 [l]Gk. *sabbath day*
14 [a]Luke 24:45
15 [a]Gen. 19:3 & 33:11; Judg. 19:21; Luke 24:29; Heb. 13:2
16 [a]1 Sam. 28:7 [b]ch. 19:24 [l]Or, *of Python*
18 [a]See Mark 1:25, 34 [b]Mark 16:17
19 [a]ch. 19:25,26 [b]Mat. 10:18 [l]Or, *court*

E *Ac 15:28* ◀ ▶ *Ac 18:5*
L *Ac 15:28* ◀ ▶ *Ac 18:5*
E *Ac 14:19–20* ◀ ▶ *Ac 19:11–12*

trates, saying, These men, being Jews,
[a]do exceedingly trouble our city,
21 And teach customs, which are not
lawful for us to receive, neither to observe, being Romans.
22 And the multitude rose up together
against them: and the magistrates rent off
their clothes, [a]and commanded to beat
them.
23 And when they had laid many
stripes upon them, they cast *them* into
prison, charging the jailer to keep them
safely:
24 Who, having received such a
charge, thrust them into the inner prison,
and made their feet fast in the stocks.
25 ¶ And at midnight Paul and Silas
prayed, and sang praises unto God: and
the prisoners heard them.
V 26 [a]And suddenly there was a great
earthquake, so that the foundations of the
prison were shaken: and immediately [b]all
the doors were opened, and every one's
bands were loosed.
27 And the keeper of the prison awak-
ing out of his sleep, and seeing the prison
doors open, he drew out his sword, and
would have killed himself, supposing that
the prisoners had been fled.
28 But Paul cried with a loud voice,
saying, Do thyself no harm: for we are all
here.
29 Then he called for a light, and
sprang in, and came trembling, and fell
down before Paul and Silas,
F 30 And brought them out, and said,
[a]Sirs, what must I do to be saved?
K 31 And they said, [a]Believe on the Lord
Jesus Christ, and thou shalt be saved, and
thy house.
32 And they spake unto him the word
of the Lord, and to all that were in his
house.
33 And he took them the same hour of
the night, and washed *their* stripes; and
was baptized, he and all his, straightway.
34 And when he had brought them

V *Ac 14:19–20* ◀ ▶ *Ac 18:10*
F *Ac 13:38–39* ◀ ▶ *Ac 20:21*
K *Ac 13:47* ◀ ▶ *Ac 20:32*

20 [a]1 Ki. 18:17; ch. 17:6
22 [a]2 Cor. 6:5 & 11:23,25; 1 Thes. 2:2
26 [a]ch. 4:31 [b]ch. 5:19 & 12:7,10
30 [a]Luke 3:10; ch. 2:37 & 9:6
31 [a]John 3:16,36; & 6:47; 1 John 5:10
34 [a]Luke 5:29 & 19:6
37 [a]ch. 22:25
39 [a]Mat. 8:34
40 [a]ver. 14
17:2 [a]Luke 4:16; ch. 9:20 & 13:5,14 & 14:1 & 16:13 & 19:8
3 [a]Luke 24:26,46; ch. 18:28; Gal. 3:1 [1]Or, *whom,* said he, *I preach*
4 [a]ch. 28:24 [b]ch. 15:22,27,32,40
5 [a]Rom. 16:21

into his house, [a]he set meat before them,
and rejoiced, believing in God with all his
house.
35 And when it was day, the magistrates sent the sergeants, saying, Let
those men go.
36 And the keeper of the prison told
this saying to Paul, The magistrates have
sent to let you go: now therefore depart,
and go in peace.
37 But Paul said unto them, They have
beaten us openly uncondemned, [a]being
Romans, and have cast *us* into prison;
and now do they thrust us out privily?
nay verily; but let them come themselves
and fetch us out.
38 And the sergeants told these words
unto the magistrates: and they feared,
when they heard that they were Romans.
39 And they came and besought them,
and brought *them* out, and [a]desired *them*
to depart out of the city.
40 And they went out of the prison,
[a]and entered into *the house of* Lydia: and
when they had seen the brethren, they
comforted them, and departed.

Paul at Thessalonica

17 NOW WHEN they had passed
through Amphipolis and Apollo-
nia, they came to Thessalonica, where
was a synagogue of the Jews:
2 And Paul, as his manner was, [a]went
in unto them, and three sabbath days reasoned with them out of the scriptures,
3 Opening and alleging, [a]that Christ
must needs have suffered, and risen again
from the dead; and that this Jesus,
[1]whom I preach unto you, is Christ.
4 [a]And some of them believed, and
consorted with Paul and [b]Silas; and of the
devout Greeks a great multitude, and of
the chief women not a few.
5 ¶ But the Jews which believed not,
moved with envy, took unto them certain
lewd fellows of the baser sort, and gathered a company, and set all the city on an
uproar, and assaulted the house of [a]Jason,
and sought to bring them out to the
people.
6 And when they found them not, they

17:6–7 The envious Jews who did not believe Paul's message accused the believers of preaching insurrection against Rome. Distorting the spiritual teachings that Jesus would ultimately be the Messiah, these enemies of the gospel intimated that Paul and Silas were encouraging resistance to Rome.

drew Jason and certain brethren unto the rulers of the city, crying, [a]These that have turned the world upside down are come hither also;

M 7 Whom Jason hath received: and these all do contrary to the decrees of Caesar, [a]saying that there is another king, *one* Jesus.

8 And they troubled the people and the rulers of the city, when they heard these things.

9 And when they had taken security of Jason, and of the other, they let them go.

Paul at Berea

10 ¶ And [a]the brethren immediately sent away Paul and Silas by night unto Berea: who coming *thither* went into the synagogue of the Jews.

11 These were more noble than those in Thessalonica, in that they received the word with all readiness of mind, and [a]searched the scriptures daily, whether those things were so.

12 Therefore many of them believed; also of honourable women which were Greeks, and of men, not a few.

13 But when the Jews of Thessalonica had knowledge that the word of God was preached of Paul at Berea, they came thither also, and stirred up the people.

14 [a]And then immediately the brethren sent away Paul to go as it were to the sea: but Silas and Timotheus abode there still.

15 And they that conducted Paul brought him unto Athens: and [a]receiving a commandment unto Silas and Timotheus for to come to him with all speed, they departed.

Paul at Athens

16 ¶ Now while Paul waited for them at Athens, [a]his spirit was stirred in him, when he saw the city [l]wholly given to idolatry.

17 Therefore disputed he in the synagogue with the Jews, and with the devout persons, and in the market daily with them that met with him.

F 18 Then certain philosophers of the Epicureans, and of the Stoics, encountered him. And some said, What will this [l]babbler say? other some, He seemeth to be a setter forth of strange gods: because he preached unto them Jesus, and the resurrection.

19 And they took him, and brought him unto [l]Areopagus, saying, May we know what this new doctrine, whereof thou speakest, *is?*

20 For thou bringest certain strange things to our ears: we would know therefore what these things mean.

21 (For all the Athenians and strangers which were there spent their time in nothing else, but either to tell, or to hear some new thing.)

22 ¶ Then Paul stood in the midst of [l]Mars' hill, and said, *Ye* men of Athens, I perceive that in all things ye are too superstitious.

23 For as I passed by, and beheld your [l]devotions, I found an altar with this inscription, TO THE UNKNOWN GOD. Whom therefore ye ignorantly worship, him declare I unto you.

24 [a]God that made the world and all things therein, seeing that he is [b]Lord of heaven and earth, [c]dwelleth not in temples made with hands;

25 Neither is worshipped with men's hands, [a]as though he needed any thing, seeing [b]he giveth to all life, and breath, and all things;

26 And hath made of one blood all nations of men for to dwell on all the face of the earth, and hath determined the times before appointed, and [a]the bounds of their habitation;

27 [a]That they should seek the Lord, if haply they might feel after him, and find him, [b]though he be not far from every one of us: L W

28 For [a]in him we live, and move, and have our being; [b]as certain also of your own poets have said, For we are also his offspring.

29 Forasmuch then as we are the offspring of God, [a]we ought not to think that the Godhead is like unto gold, or silver, or stone, graven by art and man's device.

6 [a]ch. 16:20
7 [a]Luke 23:2; John 19:12; 1 Pet. 2:13
10 [a]ver. 14; ch. 9:25
11 [a]Is. 34:16; Luke 16:29; John 5:39
14 [a]Mat. 10:23
15 [a]ch. 18:5
16 [a]2 Pet. 2:8 [l]Or, *full of idols*
18 [l]Or, *base fellow*
19 [l]Or, *Mars hill.* It was the highest court in Athens
22 [l]Or, *the court of the Areopagites*
23 [l]Or, *gods that ye worship;* see 2 Thes. 2:4
24 [a]ch. 14:15 [b]Mat. 11:25 [c]ch. 7:48
25 [a]Ps. 50:8 [b]Gen. 2:7; Num. 16:22; Job 12:10 & 27:3 & 33:4; Is. 42:5 & 57:16; Zech. 12:1
26 [a]Deut. 32:8
27 [a]Rom. 1:20 [b]ch. 14:17
28 [a]Col. 1:17; Heb. 1:3 [b]Tit. 1:12
29 [a]Is. 40:18

M *Ac 3:19–21* ◀▶ *Ro 4:13*
F *Jn 11:23–25* ◀▶ *Ac 23:6*
L *Ac 15:11* ◀▶ *Ac 26:17–18*
W *Ac 13:38–39* ◀▶ *Ro 1:16*

R 30 And [a]the times of this ignorance God winked at; but [b]now commandeth all men every where to repent:

J J 31 Because he hath appointed a day, in the which [a]he will judge the world in righteousness by *that* man whom he hath ordained; *whereof* he hath [/]given assurance unto all *men,* in that [b]he hath raised him from the dead.

32 ¶ And when they heard of the resurrection of the dead, some mocked: and others said, We will hear thee again of this *matter.*

33 So Paul departed from among them.

34 Howbeit certain men clave unto him, and believed: among the which *was* Dionysius the Areopagite, and a woman named Damaris, and others with them.

Paul at Corinth

18 AFTER THESE things Paul departed from Athens, and came to Corinth:

2 And found a certain Jew named [a]Aquila, born in Pontus, lately come from Italy, with his wife Priscilla; (because that Claudius had commanded all Jews to depart from Rome:) and came unto them.

3 And because he was of the same craft, he abode with them, [a]and wrought: for by their occupation they were tentmakers.

4 [a]And he reasoned in the synagogue every sabbath, and persuaded the Jews and the Greeks.

E L 5 And [a]when Silas and Timotheus were come from Macedonia, Paul was [b]pressed in the spirit, and testified to the Jews *that* Jesus [/]*was* Christ.

G 6 And [a]when they opposed themselves, and blasphemed, [b]he shook *his* raiment, and said unto them, [c]Your blood *be* upon your own heads; [d]I *am* clean: [e]from henceforth I will go unto the Gentiles.

7 And he departed thence, and entered into a certain *man's* house, named Justus, *one* that worshipped God, whose house joined hard to the synagogue.

8 [a]And Crispus, the chief ruler of the synagogue, believed on the Lord with all his house; and many of the Corinthians hearing believed, and were baptized.

9 Then [a]spake the Lord to Paul in the night by a vision, Be not afraid, but speak, and hold not thy peace:

10 [a]For I am with thee, and no man shall set on thee to hurt thee: for I have much people in this city. S V

11 And he [/]continued *there* a year and six months, teaching the word of God among them.

12 ¶ And when Gallio was the deputy of Achaia, the Jews made insurrection with one accord against Paul, and brought him to the judgment seat,

13 Saying, This *fellow* persuadeth men to worship God contrary to the law.

14 And when Paul was now about to open *his* mouth, Gallio said unto the Jews, [a]If it were a matter of wrong or wicked lewdness, O *ye* Jews, reason would that I should bear with you:

15 But if it be a question of words and names, and *of* your law, look ye *to it;* for I will be no judge of such *matters.*

16 And he drave them from the judgment seat.

17 Then all the Greeks took [a]Sosthenes, the chief ruler of the synagogue, and beat *him* before the judgment seat. And Gallio cared for none of those things.

Paul returns to Antioch

18 ¶ And Paul *after this* tarried *there* yet a good while, and then took his leave of the brethren, and sailed thence into Syria, and with him Priscilla and Aquila; having [a]shorn *his* head in [b]Cenchrea: for he had a vow.

19 And he came to Ephesus, and left them there: but he himself entered into the synagogue, and reasoned with the Jews.

30 [a]ch. 14:16; Rom. 3:25 [b]Luke 24:47; Tit. 2:11,12; 1 Pet. 1:14 & 4:3
31 [a]ch. 10:42; Rom. 2:16 & 14:10 [b]ch. 2:24 [/]Or, *offered faith*
18:2 [a]Rom. 16:3; 1 Cor. 16:19; 2 Tim. 4:19
3 [a]ch. 20:34; 1 Cor. 4:12; 1 Thes. 2:9; 2 Thes. 3:8
4 [a]ch. 17:2
5 [a]ch. 17:14,15 [b]ver. 28; Job 32:18; ch. 17:3 [/]Or, *is the Christ*
6 [a]ch. 13:45 [b]Neh. 5:13; Mat. 10:14; ch. 13:51 [c]Lev. 20:9,11,12; 2 Sam. 1:16; Ezek. 18:13 & 33:4 [d]Ezek. 3:18, 19 & 33:9; ch. 20:26 [e]ch. 13:46 & 28:28
8 [a]1 Cor. 1:14
9 [a]ch. 23:11
10 [a]Jer. 1:18,19
11 [/]Gk. *sat* there
14 [a]ch. 23:29 & 25:11,19
17 [a]1 Cor. 1:1
18 [a]Num. 6:18; ch. 21:24 [b]Rom. 16:1

R *Ac 11:18* ◀ ▶ *Ac 19:18–20*
J *Jn 12:48* ◀ ▶ *Ro 2:5*
J *Ac 10:42* ◀ ▶ *Ac 24:25*
E *Ac 16:6–7* ◀ ▶ *Ac 19:1–7*
L *Ac 16:6–7* ◀ ▶ *Ac 20:22–23*
G *Ac 15:12* ◀ ▶ *Ac 28:28*
S *Lk 21:18* ◀ ▶ *Ac 23:11*
V *Ac 16:26* ◀ ▶ *Ro 8:31*

17:30–31 Paul reminded his listeners that God's judgment is certain and will occur on an appointed day. He emphasized that God commands repentance because of sin and because of this approaching judgment.

18:6 After preaching Christ to these Jews that so vigorously rejected his teaching, Paul gave up on them and turned to preach to the Gentiles.

20 When they desired *him* to tarry longer time with them, he consented not;

21 But bade them farewell, saying, [a]I must by all means keep this feast that cometh in Jerusalem: but I will return again unto you, [b]if God will. And he sailed from Ephesus.

22 And when he had landed at Caesarea, and gone up, and saluted the church, he went down to Antioch.

23 And after he had spent some time *there,* he departed, and went over *all* the country of [a]Galatia and Phrygia in order, [b]strengthening all the disciples.

Apollos' preaching at Ephesus

24 ¶ [a]And a certain Jew named Apollos, born at Alexandria, an eloquent man, *and* mighty in the scriptures, came to Ephesus.

25 This man was instructed in the way of the Lord; and being [a]fervent in the spirit, he spake and taught diligently the things of the Lord, [b]knowing only the baptism of John.

26 And he began to speak boldly in the synagogue: whom when Aquila and Priscilla had heard, they took him unto *them,* and expounded unto him the way of God more perfectly.

27 And when he was disposed to pass into Achaia, the brethren wrote, exhorting the disciples to receive him: who, when he was come, [a]helped them much which had believed through grace:

28 For he mightily convinced the Jews, *and that* publicly, [a]showing by the scriptures that Jesus [1]was Christ.

Paul's work in Ephesus

B E **19** AND IT came to pass, that, while [a]Apollos was at Corinth, Paul having passed through the upper coasts came to Ephesus: and finding certain disciples,

W 2 He said unto them, Have ye received the Holy Ghost since ye believed? And they said unto him, [a]We have not so much as heard whether there be any Holy Ghost.

3 And he said unto them, Unto what then were ye baptized? And they said, [a]Unto John's baptism.

4 Then said Paul, [a]John verily baptized with the baptism of repentance, saying unto the people, that they should believe on him which should come after him, that is, on Christ Jesus.

5 When they heard *this,* they were baptized [a]in the name of the Lord Jesus.

6 And when Paul had [a]laid *his* hands G
upon them, the Holy Ghost came on M
them; and [b]they spake with tongues, and T
prophesied.

7 And all the men were about twelve.

8 [a]And he went into the synagogue, and spake boldly for the space of three months, disputing and persuading the things [b]concerning the kingdom of God.

9 But [a]when divers were hardened, and believed not, but spake evil [b]of that way before the multitude, he departed from them, and separated the disciples, disputing daily in the school of one Tyrannus.

10 And [a]this continued by the space of two years; so that all they which dwelt in Asia heard the word of the Lord Jesus, both Jews and Greeks.

11 And [a]God wrought special miracles E
by the hands of Paul:

12 [a]So that from his body were brought unto the sick handkerchiefs or aprons, and the diseases departed from them, and the evil spirits went out of them.

13 ¶ [a]Then certain of the vagabond Jews, exorcists, [b]took upon them to call over them which had evil spirits the name of the Lord Jesus, saying, We adjure you by Jesus whom Paul preacheth.

14 And there were seven sons of *one* Sceva, a Jew, *and* chief of the priests, which did so.

15 And the evil spirit answered and said, Jesus I know, and Paul I know; but who are ye?

16 And the man in whom the evil spirit was leaped on them, and overcame them, and prevailed against them, so that they fled out of that house naked and wounded.

17 And this was known to all the Jews and Greeks also dwelling at Ephesus; and [a]fear fell on them all, and the name of the Lord Jesus was magnified.

21 [a]ch. 19:21 & 20:16 [b]1 Cor. 4:19; Heb. 6:3; Jas. 4:15
23 [a]Gal. 1:2 & 4:14 [b]ch. 14:22 & 15:32,41
24 [a]1 Cor. 1:12 & 3:5,6 & 4:6; Tit. 3:13
25 [a]Rom. 12:11 [b]ch. 19:3
27 [a]1 Cor. 3:6
28 [a]ver. 5; ch. 9:22 & 17:3 [1]Or, *is the Christ*

19:1 [a]1 Cor. 1:12; & 3:5,6
2 [a]ch. 8:16; See 1 Sam. 3:7
3 [a]ch. 18:25
4 [a]Mat. 3:11; John 1:15,27,30; ch. 1:5 & 11:16 & 13:24, 25
5 [a]ch. 8:16
6 [a]ch. 6:6 & 8:17 [b]ch. 2:4 & 10:46
8 [a]ch. 17:2 & 18:4 [b]ch. 1:3 & 28:23
9 [a]2 Tim. 1:15; 2 Pet. 2:2; Jude 10 [b]ver. 23; See ch. 9:2 & 22:4 & 24:14
10 [a]See ch. 20:31
11 [a]Mark 16:20; ch. 14:3
12 [a]See 2 Ki. 4:29; ch. 5:15
13 [a]Mat. 12:27 [b]See Mark 9:38; Luke 9:49
17 [a]Luke 1:65 & 7:16; ch. 2:43 & 5:5,11

B *Ac 15:8* ◀▶ *Ro 8:23*
E *Ac 18:5* ◀▶ *Ac 20:22–23*
W *Ac 9:17* ◀▶ *Ro 1:11*

G *Ac 11:27–28* ◀▶ *Ac 20:28*
M *Ac 11:24* ◀▶ *Ro 1:4*
T *Ac 11:28* ◀▶ *Ac 20:23*
E *Ac 16:16–18* ◀▶ *Ac 20:9–12*

R 18 And many that believed came, and [a]confessed, and showed their deeds.

19 Many of them also which used curious arts brought their books together, and burned them before all *men:* and they counted the price of them, and found *it* fifty thousand *pieces* of silver.

20 [a]So mightily grew the word of God and prevailed.

21 ¶ [a]After these things were ended, Paul [b]purposed in the spirit, when he had passed through Macedonia and Achaia, to go to Jerusalem, saying, After I have been there, [c]I must also see Rome.

22 So he sent into Macedonia two of them that ministered unto him, Timotheus and [a]Erastus; but he himself stayed in Asia for a season.

The riot at Ephesus

23 And [a]the same time there arose no small stir about [b]that way.

24 For a certain *man* named Demetrius, a silversmith, which made silver shrines for Diana, brought [a]no small gain unto the craftsmen;

25 Whom he called together with the workmen of like occupation, and said, Sirs, ye know that by this craft we have our wealth.

26 Moreover ye see and hear, that not alone at Ephesus, but almost throughout all Asia, this Paul hath persuaded and turned away much people, saying that [a]they be no gods, which are made with hands:

27 So that not only this our craft is in danger to be set at nought; but also that the temple of the great goddess Diana should be despised, and her magnificence should be destroyed, whom all Asia and the world worshippeth.

28 And when they heard *these sayings,* they were full of wrath, and cried out, saying, Great *is* Diana of the Ephesians.

29 And the whole city was filled with confusion: and having caught [a]Gaius and [b]Aristarchus, men of Macedonia, Paul's companions in travel, they rushed with one accord into the theatre.

30 And when Paul would have entered in unto the people, the disciples suffered him not.

31 And certain of the chief of Asia, which were his friends, sent unto him, desiring *him* that he would not adventure himself into the theatre.

32 Some therefore cried one thing, and some another: for the assembly was confused; and the more part knew not wherefore they were come together.

33 And they drew Alexander out of the multitude, the Jews putting him forward. And [a]Alexander [b]beckoned with the hand, and would have made his defence unto the people.

34 But when they knew that he was a Jew, all with one voice about the space of two hours cried out, Great *is* Diana of the Ephesians.

35 And when the townclerk had appeased the people, he said, *Ye* men of Ephesus, what man is there that knoweth not how that the city of the Ephesians is [1]a worshipper of the great goddess Diana, and of the *image* which fell down from Jupiter?

36 Seeing then that these things cannot be spoken against, ye ought to be quiet, and to do nothing rashly.

37 For ye have brought hither these men, which are neither robbers of churches, nor yet blasphemers of your goddess.

38 Wherefore if Demetrius, and the craftsmen which are with him, have a matter against any man, [1]the law is open, and there are deputies: let them implead one another.

39 But if ye inquire any thing concerning other matters, it shall be determined in a [1]lawful assembly.

40 For we are in danger to be called in question for this day's uproar, there being no cause whereby we may give an account of this concourse.

41 And when he had thus spoken, he dismissed the assembly.

Macedonia and Greece

20 AND AFTER the uproar was ceased, Paul called unto *him* the disciples, and embraced *them,* and [a]departed for to go into Macedonia.

2 And when he had gone over those parts, and had given them much exhortation, he came into Greece,

3 And *there* abode three months. And [a]when the Jews laid wait for him, as he was about to sail into Syria, he purposed to return through Macedonia.

18 [a]Mat. 3:6
20 [a]ch. 6:7 & 12:24
21 [a]Rom. 15:25; Gal. 2:1 [b]ch. 20:22 [c]ch. 18:21 & 23:11; Rom. 15:24-28
22 [a]Rom. 16:23; 2 Tim. 4:20
23 [a]2 Cor. 1:8 [b]See ch. 9:2
24 [a]ch. 16:16,19
26 [a]Ps. 115:4; Is. 44:10-20; Jer. 10:3
29 [a]Rom. 16:23; 1 Cor. 1:14 [b]ch. 20:4 & 27:2; Col. 4:10; Philem. 24
33 [a]1 Tim. 1:20; 2 Tim. 4:14 [b]ch. 12:17
35 [1]Gk. *the temple keeper*
38 [1]Or, *the court days are kept*
39 [1]Or, *ordinary*
20:1 [a]1 Cor. 16:5; 1 Tim. 1:3
3 [a]ch. 9:23 & 23:12 & 25:3; 2 Cor. 11:26

4 And there accompanied him into Asia Sopater of Berea; and of the Thessalonians, [a]Aristarchus and Secundus; and [b]Gaius of Derbe, and [c]Timotheus; and of Asia, [d]Tychicus and [e]Trophimus.

From Philippi to Miletus

5 These going before tarried for us at Troas.

6 And we sailed away from Philippi after [a]the days of unleavened bread, and came unto them [b]to Troas in five days; where we abode seven days.

7 And upon [a]the first *day* of the week, when the disciples came together [b]to break bread, Paul preached unto them, ready to depart on the morrow; and continued his speech until midnight.

8 And there were many lights [a]in the upper chamber, where they were gathered together.

E 9 And there sat in a window a certain young man named Eutychus, being fallen into a deep sleep: and as Paul was long preaching, he sunk down with sleep, and fell down from the third loft, and was taken up dead.

10 And Paul went down, and [a]fell on him, and embracing *him* said, [b]Trouble not yourselves; for his life is in him.

11 When he therefore was come up again, and had broken bread, and eaten, and talked a long while, even till break of day, so he departed.

12 And they brought the young man alive, and were not a little comforted.

13 ¶ And we went before to ship, and sailed unto Assos, there intending to take in Paul: for so had he appointed, minding himself to go afoot.

14 And when he met with us at Assos, we took him in, and came to Mitylene.

15 And we sailed thence, and came the next *day* over against Chios; and the next *day* we arrived at Samos, and tarried at Trogyllium; and the next *day* we came to Miletus.

16 For Paul had determined to sail by Ephesus, because he would not spend the time in Asia: for [a]he hasted, if it were possible for him, [b]to be at Jerusalem [c]the day of Pentecost.

Paul and the Ephesian elders

17 ¶ And from Miletus he sent to Ephesus, and called the elders of the church.

18 And when they were come to him, he said unto them, Ye know, [a]from the first day that I came into Asia, after what manner I have been with you at all seasons,

19 Serving the Lord with all humility of mind, and with many tears, and temptations, which befell me [a]by the lying in wait of the Jews:

20 *And* how [a]I kept back nothing that was profitable *unto you,* but have shown you, and have taught you publicly, and from house to house,

21 [a]Testifying both to the Jews, and also to the Greeks, [b]repentance toward God, and faith toward our Lord Jesus Christ. F R

22 And now, behold, [a]I go bound in the spirit unto Jerusalem, not knowing the things that shall befall me there: E L

23 Save that [a]the Holy Ghost witnesseth in every city, saying that bonds and afflictions [1]abide me. T

24 But [a]none of these things move me, neither count I my life dear unto myself, [b]so that I might finish my course with joy, [c]and the ministry, [d]which I have received of the Lord Jesus, to testify the gospel of the grace of God.

25 And now, behold, [a]I know that ye all, among whom I have gone preaching the kingdom of God, shall see my face no more.

26 Wherefore I take you to record this day, that I *am* [a]pure from the blood of all *men.*

27 For [a]I have not shunned to declare unto you all [b]the counsel of God.

28 ¶ [a]Take heed therefore unto yourselves, and to all the flock, over the which the Holy Ghost [b]hath made you overseers, to feed the church of God, [c]which he hath purchased [d]with his own blood. E G L D

29 For I know this, that after my departing [a]shall grievous wolves enter in among you, not sparing the flock.

4 [a]ch. 19:29 & 27:2; Col. 4:10 [b]ch. 19:29 [c]ch. 16:1 [d]Eph. 6:21; Col. 4:7; 2 Tim. 4:12; Tit. 3:12 [e]ch. 21:29; 2 Tim. 4:20
6 [a]Ex. 12:14,15 & 23:15 [b]ch. 16:8; 2 Cor. 2:12; 2 Tim. 4:13
7 [a]1 Cor. 16:2; Rev. 1:10 [b]ch. 2:42,46; 1 Cor. 10:16 & 11:20
8 [a]ch. 1:13
10 [a]1 Ki. 17:21; 2 Ki. 4:34 [b]Mat. 9:24
16 [a]ch. 18:21 & 19:21 & 21:4,12 [b]ch. 24:17 [c]ch. 2:1; 1 Cor. 16:8
18 [a]ch. 18:19 & 19:1,10
19 [a]ver. 3
20 [a]ver. 27
21 [a]ch. 18:5 [b]Mark 1:15; Luke 24:27; ch. 2:38
22 [a]ch. 19:21
23 [a]ch. 21:4,11; 1 Thes. 3:3 [1]Or, *wait for me*
24 [a]ch. 21:13; Rom. 8:35; 2 Cor. 4:16 [b]2 Tim. 4:7 [c]ch. 1:17; 2 Cor. 4:1 [d]Gal. 1:1; Tit. 1:3
25 [a]ver. 38; Rom. 15:23
26 [a]ch. 18:6; 2 Cor. 7:2
27 [a]ver. 20 [b]Luke 7:30; John 15:15; Eph. 1:11
28 [a]1 Tim. 4:16; 1 Pet. 5:2 [b]1 Cor. 12:28 [c]Eph. 1:7,14; Col. 1:14; Heb. 9:12; 1 Pet. 1:19; Rev. 5:9 [d]See Heb. 9:14
29 [a]Mat. 7:15; 2 Pet. 2:1

E *Ac 19:11–12* ◀▶ *Ac 22:11–13*

F *Ac 16:30–31* ◀▶ *Ro 1:16*
R *Ac 19:18–20* ◀▶ *Ac 26:20*
E *Ac 19:1–7* ◀▶ *Ac 20:28*
L *Ac 18:5* ◀▶ *Ac 20:28*
T *Ac 19:6* ◀▶ *Ac 21:4*
E *Ac 20:22–23* ◀▶ *Ac 21:4*
G *Ac 19:6* ◀▶ *Ro 1:11*
L *Ac 20:22–23* ◀▶ *Ac 21:4*
D *Ac 8:32–35* ◀▶ *Ro 3:24–25*

30 Also [a]of your own selves shall men arise, speaking perverse things, to draw away disciples after them.

31 Therefore watch, and remember, that [a]by the space of three years I ceased not to warn every one night and day with tears.

K 32 And now, brethren, I commend you to God, and [a]to the word of his grace, which is able [b]to build you up, and to give you [c]an inheritance among all them which are sanctified.

33 [a]I have coveted no man's silver, or gold, or apparel.

34 Yea, ye yourselves know, [a]that these hands have ministered unto my necessities, and to them that were with me.

35 I have shown you all things, [a]how that so labouring ye ought to support the weak, and to remember the words of the Lord Jesus, how he said, It is more blessed to give than to receive.

36 ¶ And when he had thus spoken, he [a]kneeled down, and prayed with them all.

37 And they all wept sore, and [a]fell on Paul's neck, and kissed him,

38 Sorrowing most of all for the words [a]which he spake, that they should see his face no more. And they accompanied him unto the ship.

Paul travels to Caesarea

21 AND IT came to pass, that after we were gotten from them, and had launched, we came with a straight course unto Coos, and the *day* following unto Rhodes, and from thence unto Patara:

2 And finding a ship sailing over unto Phenicia, we went aboard, and set forth.

3 Now when we had discovered Cyprus, we left it on the left hand, and sailed into Syria, and landed at Tyre: for there the ship was to unlade her burden.

E L T 4 And finding disciples, we tarried there seven days: [a]who said to Paul through the Spirit, that he should not go up to Jerusalem.

5 And when we had accomplished those days, we departed and went our way; and they all brought us on our way, with wives and children, till *we were* out of the city: and [a]we kneeled down on the shore, and prayed.

6 And when we had taken our leave one of another, we took ship; and they returned [a]home again.

7 And when we had finished *our* course from Tyre, we came to Ptolemais, and saluted the brethren, and abode with them one day.

8 And the next *day* we that were of Paul's company departed, and came unto Caesarea: and we entered into the house of Philip [a]the evangelist, [b]which was *one* of the seven; and abode with him.

9 And the same man had four daughters, virgins, [a]which did prophesy.

10 And as we tarried *there* many days, there came down from Judaea a certain prophet, named [a]Agabus.

11 And when he was come unto us, he took Paul's girdle, and bound his own hands and feet, and said, Thus saith the Holy Ghost, [a]So shall the Jews at Jerusalem bind the man that owneth this girdle, and shall deliver *him* into the hands of the Gentiles. E T

12 And when we heard these things, both we, and they of that place, besought him not to go up to Jerusalem.

13 Then Paul answered, [a]What mean ye to weep and to break mine heart? for I am ready not to be bound only, but also to die at Jerusalem for the name of the Lord Jesus.

14 And when he would not be persuaded, we ceased, saying, [a]The will of the Lord be done.

Paul in Jerusalem

15 And after those days we took up our carriages, and went up to Jerusalem.

16 There went with us also *certain* of the disciples of Caesarea, and brought with them one Mnason of Cyprus, an old disciple, with whom we should lodge.

17 [a]And when we were come to Jerusalem, the brethren received us gladly.

18 And the *day* following Paul went in with us unto [a]James; and all the elders were present.

19 And when he had saluted them, [a]he declared particularly what things God

30 [a] 1 Tim. 1:20; 1 John 2:19
31 [a] ch. 19:10
32 [a] Heb. 13:9 [b] ch. 9:31 [c] ch. 26:18; Eph. 1:18; Col. 1:12 & 3:24; Heb. 9:15; 1 Pet. 1:4
33 [a] 1 Sam. 12:3; 1 Cor. 9:12; 2 Cor. 7:2 & 11:9 & 12:17
34 [a] ch. 18:3; 1 Cor. 4:12; 1 Thes. 2:9; 2 Thes. 3:8
35 [a] Rom. 15:1; 1 Cor. 9:12; 2 Cor. 11:9,12 & 12:13; Eph. 4:28; 1 Thes. 4:11 & 5:14; 2 Thes. 3:8
36 [a] ch. 7:60 & 21:5
37 [a] Gen. 45:14 & 46:29
38 [a] ver. 25
21:4 [a] ver. 12; ch. 20:23
5 [a] ch. 20:36
6 [a] John 1:11
8 [a] Eph. 4:11; 2 Tim. 4:5 [b] ch. 6:5 & 8:26,40
9 [a] Joel 2:28; ch. 2:17
10 [a] ch. 11:28
11 [a] ver. 33; ch. 20:23
13 [a] ch. 20:24
14 [a] Mat. 6:10 & 26:42; Luke 11:2 & 22:42
17 [a] ch. 15:4
18 [a] ch. 15:13; Gal. 1:19 & 2:9
19 [a] ch. 15:4,12; Rom. 15:18,19

K *Ac 16:31* ◀▶ *Ro 1:16*
E *Ac 20:28* ◀▶ *Ac 21:11*
L *Ac 20:28* ◀▶ *Ro 7:6*
T *Ac 20:23* ◀▶ *Ac 21:11*
E *Ac 21:4* ◀▶ *Ac 28:25*
T *Ac 21:4* ◀▶ *Ac 28:25*

had wrought among the Gentiles [b]by his
ministry.
20 And when they heard *it,* they glorified the Lord, and said unto him, Thou
seest, brother, how many thousands of
Jews there are which believe; and they
are all [a]zealous of the law:
21 And they are informed of thee, that
thou teachest all the Jews which are
among the Gentiles to forsake Moses,
saying that they ought not to circumcise
their children, neither to walk after the
customs.
22 What is it therefore? the multitude
must needs come together: for they will
hear that thou art come.
23 Do therefore this that we say to
thee: We have four men which have a
vow on them;
24 Them take, and purify thyself with
them, and be at charges with them, that
they may [a]shave *their* heads: and all may
know that those things, whereof they
were informed concerning thee, are
nothing; but *that* thou thyself also walkest orderly, and keepest the law.
25 As touching the Gentiles which believe, [a]we have written *and* concluded
that they observe no such thing, save
only that they keep themselves from
things offered to idols, and from blood,
and from strangled, and from fornication.
26 Then Paul took the men, and the
next day purifying himself with them
[a]entered into the temple, [b]to signify the
accomplishment of the days of purification, until that an offering should be offered for every one of them.

Paul's arrest

27 And when the seven days were almost ended, [a]the Jews which were of
Asia, when they saw him in the temple,
stirred up all the people, and [b]laid hands
on him,
28 Crying out, Men of Israel, help:
This is the man, [a]that teacheth all *men*
every where against the people, and the
law, and this place: and further brought
Greeks also into the temple, and hath polluted this holy place.
29 (For they had seen before with him
in the city [a]Trophimus an Ephesian,
whom they supposed that Paul had
brought into the temple.)
30 And [a]all the city was moved, and
the people ran together: and they took

19 [b]ch. 1:17 & 20:24
20 [a]ch. 22:3; Rom. 10:2; Gal. 1:14
24 [a]Num. 6:2,13, 18; ch. 18:18
25 [a]ch. 15:20,29
26 [a]ch. 24:18 [b]Num. 6:13
27 [a]ch. 24:18 [b]ch. 26:21
28 [a]ch. 24:5,6
29 [a]ch. 20:4
30 [a]ch. 26:21
32 [a]ch. 23:27 & 24:7
33 [a]ver. 11; ch. 20:23
36 [a]Luke 23:18; John 19:15; ch. 22:22
38 [a]See ch. 5:36
39 [a]ch. 9:11 & 22:3
40 [a]ch. 12:17
22:1 [a]ch. 7:2
3 [a]ch. 21:39; 2 Cor. 11:22; Phil. 3:5 [b]Deut. 33:3 [c]ch. 5:34 [d]ch. 26:5 [e]ch. 21:20; Gal. 1:14 [f]Rom. 10:2

Paul, and drew him out of the temple:
and forthwith the doors were shut.
31 And as they went about to kill him,
tidings came unto the chief captain of the
band, that all Jerusalem was in an uproar.
32 [a]Who immediately took soldiers
and centurions, and ran down unto them:
and when they saw the chief captain and
the soldiers, they left beating of Paul.
33 Then the chief captain came near,
and took him, and [a]commanded *him* to
be bound with two chains; and demanded who he was, and what he had
done.
34 And some cried one thing, some another, among the multitude: and when
he could not know the certainty for the
tumult, he commanded him to be carried
into the castle.
35 And when he came upon the stairs,
so it was, that he was borne of the soldiers for the violence of the people.
36 For the multitude of the people followed after, crying, [a]Away with him.

Paul's defence

37 And as Paul was to be led into the
castle, he said unto the chief captain,
May I speak unto thee? Who said, Canst
thou speak Greek?
38 [a]Art not thou that Egyptian, which
before these days madest an uproar, and
leddest out into the wilderness four thousand men that were murderers?
39 But Paul said, [a]I am a man *which
am* a Jew of Tarsus, *a city* in Cilicia, a
citizen of no mean city: and, I beseech
thee, suffer me to speak unto the people.
40 And when he had given him licence, Paul stood on the stairs, and
[a]beckoned with the hand unto the people. And when there was made a great
silence, he spake unto *them* in the Hebrew tongue, saying,
22 MEN, [a]BRETHREN, and fathers,
hear ye my defence *which I make*
now unto you.
2 (And when they heard that he spake
in the Hebrew tongue to them, they kept
the more silence: and he saith,)
3 [a]I am verily a man *which am* a Jew,
born in Tarsus, *a city* in Cilicia, yet
brought up in this city [b]at the feet of [c]Ga-
maliel, *and* taught [d]according to the perfect manner of the law of the fathers, and
[e]was zealous toward God, [f]as ye all are
this day.

4 [a]And I persecuted this way unto the death, binding and delivering into prisons both men and women.

5 As also the high priest doth bear me witness, and [a]all the estate of the elders: [b]from whom also I received letters unto the brethren, and went to Damascus, to bring them which were there bound unto Jerusalem, for to be punished.

6 And [a]it came to pass, that, as I made my journey, and was come nigh unto Damascus about noon, suddenly there shone from heaven a great light round about me.

7 And I fell unto the ground, and heard a voice saying unto me, Saul, Saul, why persecutest thou me?

8 And I answered, Who art thou, Lord? And he said unto me, I am Jesus of Nazareth, whom thou persecutest.

9 And [a]they that were with me saw indeed the light, and were afraid; but they heard not the voice of him that spake to me.

10 And I said, What shall I do, Lord? And the Lord said unto me, Arise, and go into Damascus; and there it shall be told thee of all things which are appointed for thee to do.

E 11 And when I could not see for the glory of that light, being led by the hand of them that were with me, I came into Damascus.

12 And [a]one Ananias, a devout man according to the law, [b]having a good report of all the [c]Jews which dwelt *there,*

13 Came unto me, and stood, and said unto me, Brother Saul, receive thy sight. And the same hour I looked up upon him.

14 And he said, [a]The God of our fathers [b]hath chosen thee, that thou shouldest know his will, and [c]see [d]that Just One, and [e]shouldest hear the voice of his mouth.

15 [a]For thou shalt be his witness unto all men of [b]what thou hast seen and heard.

16 And now why tarriest thou? arise, and be baptized, [a]and wash away thy sins, [b]calling on the name of the Lord.

17 And [a]it came to pass, that, when I was come again to Jerusalem, even while I prayed in the temple, I was in a trance;

18 And [a]saw him saying unto me, [b]Make haste, and get thee quickly out of Jerusalem: for they will not receive thy testimony concerning me.

19 And I said, Lord, [a]they know that I imprisoned and [b]beat in every synagogue them that believed on thee:

20 [a]And when the blood of thy martyr Stephen was shed, I also was standing by, and [b]consenting unto his death, and kept the raiment of them that slew him.

21 And he said unto me, Depart: [a]for I will send thee far hence unto the Gentiles.

22 And they gave him audience unto this word, and *then* lifted up their voices, and said, [a]Away with such a *fellow* from the earth: for it is not fit that [b]he should live.

23 And as they cried out, and cast off *their* clothes, and threw dust into the air,

24 The chief captain commanded him to be brought into the castle, and bade that he should be examined by scourging; that he might know wherefore they cried so against him.

25 And as they bound him with thongs, Paul said unto the centurion that stood by, [a]Is it lawful for you to scourge a man that is a Roman, and uncondemned?

26 When the centurion heard *that,* he went and told the chief captain, saying, Take heed what thou doest: for this man is a Roman.

27 Then the chief captain came, and said unto him, Tell me, art thou a Roman? He said, Yea.

28 And the chief captain answered, With a great sum obtained I this freedom. And Paul said, But I was *free* born.

29 Then straightway they departed from him which should have [f]examined him: and the chief captain also was afraid, after he knew that he was a Roman, and because he had bound him.

Before the Sanhedrin

30 On the morrow, because he would have known the certainty wherefore he was accused of the Jews, he loosed him from *his* bands, and commanded the chief priests and all their council to appear, and brought Paul down, and set him before them.

23 AND PAUL, earnestly beholding the council, said, Men *and* brethren, [a]I have lived in all good conscience before God until this day.

2 And the high priest Ananias com-

4 [a]ch. 8:3 & 26:9-11; Phil. 3:6; 1 Tim. 1:13
5 [a]Luke 22:66; ch. 4:5 [b]ch. 9:2 & 26:10,12
6 [a]ch. 9:3 & 26:12,13
9 [a]Dan. 10:7; ch. 9:7
12 [a]ch. 9:17 [b]ch. 10:22 [c]1 Tim. 3:7
14 [a]ch. 3:13 & 5:30 [b]ch. 9:15 & 26:16 [c]1 Cor. 9:1 & 15:8 [d]ch. 3:14 & 7:52 [e]1 Cor. 11:23; Gal. 1:12
15 [a]ch. 23:11 [b]ch. 4:20 & 26:16
16 [a]ch. 2:38; Heb. 10:22 [b]ch. 9:14; Rom. 10:13
17 [a]ch. 9:26; 2 Cor. 12:2
18 [a]ver. 14 [b]Mat. 10:14
19 [a]ver. 4; ch. 8:3 [b]Mat. 10:17
20 [a]ch. 7:58 [b]Luke 11:48; ch. 8:1; Rom. 1:32
21 [a]ch. 9:15 & 13:2,46,47 & 18:6 & 26:17; Rom. 1:5 & 11:13 & 15:16; Gal. 1:15,16 & 2:7, 8; Eph. 3:7,8; 1 Tim. 2:7; 2 Tim. 1:11
22 [a]ch. 21:36 [b]ch. 25:24
25 [a]ch. 16:37
29 [f]Or, *tortured him*
23:1 [a]ch. 24:16; 1 Cor. 4:4; 2 Cor. 1:12 & 4:2; 2 Tim. 1:3; Heb. 13:18

E Ac 20:9–12 ◀ ▶ Ac 28:3–9

manded them that stood by him [a]to smite him on the mouth.

3 Then said Paul unto him, God shall smite thee, *thou* whited wall: for sittest thou to judge me after the law, and [a]commandest me to be smitten contrary to the law?

4 And they that stood by said, Revilest thou God's high priest?

5 Then said Paul, [a]I wist not, brethren, that he was the high priest: for it is written, [b]Thou shalt not speak evil of the ruler of thy people.

F 6 But when Paul perceived that the one part were Sadducees, and the other Pharisees, he cried out in the council, Men *and* brethren, [a]I am a Pharisee, the son of a Pharisee: [b]of the hope and resurrection of the dead I am called in question.

7 And when he had so said, there arose a dissension between the Pharisees and the Sadducees: and the multitude was divided.

F 8 [a]For the Sadducees say that there is no resurrection, neither angel, nor spirit: but the Pharisees confess both.

9 And there arose a great cry: and the scribes *that were* of the Pharisees' part arose, and strove, saying, [a]We find no evil in this man: but [b]if a spirit or an angel hath spoken to him, [c]let us not fight against God.

10 And when there arose a great dissension, the chief captain, fearing lest Paul should have been pulled in pieces of them, commanded the soldiers to go down, and to take him by force from among them, and to bring *him* into the castle.

S 11 And [a]the night following the Lord stood by him, and said, Be of good cheer, Paul: for as thou hast testified of me in Jerusalem, so must thou bear witness also at Rome.

The plot to kill Paul

12 And when it was day, [a]certain of the Jews banded together, and bound themselves [I]under a curse, saying that they would neither eat nor drink till they had killed Paul.

13 And they were more than forty which had made this conspiracy.

14 And they came to the chief priests and elders, and said, We have bound ourselves under a great curse, that we will eat nothing until we have slain Paul.

15 Now therefore ye with the council signify to the chief captain that he bring him down unto you tomorrow, as though ye would inquire something more perfectly concerning him: and we, or ever he come near, are ready to kill him.

16 And when Paul's sister's son heard of their lying in wait, he went and entered into the castle, and told Paul.

17 Then Paul called one of the centurions unto *him,* and said, Bring this young man unto the chief captain: for he hath a certain thing to tell him.

18 So he took him, and brought *him* to the chief captain, and said, Paul the prisoner called me unto *him,* and prayed me to bring this young man unto thee, who hath something to say unto thee.

19 Then the chief captain took him by the hand, and went *with him* aside privately, and asked *him,* What is that thou hast to tell me?

20 And he said, [a]The Jews have agreed to desire thee that thou wouldest bring down Paul tomorrow into the council, as though they would inquire somewhat of him more perfectly.

21 But do not thou yield unto them: for there lie in wait for him of them more than forty men, which have bound themselves with an oath, that they will neither eat nor drink till they have killed him: and now are they ready, looking for a promise from thee.

22 So the chief captain *then* let the young man depart, and charged *him, See thou* tell no man that thou hast shown these things to me.

Paul taken to Caesarea

23 And he called unto *him* two centurions, saying, Make ready two hundred soldiers to go to Caesarea, and horsemen threescore and ten, and spearmen two hundred, at the third hour of the night;

2 [a]1 Ki. 22:24; Jer. 20:2; John 18:22
3 [a]Lev. 19:35; Deut. 25:1,2; John 7:51
5 [a]ch. 24:17 [b]Ex. 22:28; Eccl. 10:20; 2 Pet. 2:10; Jude 8
6 [a]ch. 26:5; Phil. 3:5 [b]ch. 24:15,21 & 26:6 & 28:20
8 [a]Mat. 22:23; Mark 12:18; Luke 20:27
9 [a]ch. 25:25 & 26:31 [b]ch. 22:7,17,18 [c]ch. 5:39
11 [a]ch. 18:9 & 27:23,24
12 [a]ver. 21,30; ch. 25:3 [I]Or, *with an oath of execration*
20 [a]ver. 12; ch. 20:3

F *Ac 17:18* ◀ ▶ *Ac 23:8*
F *Ac 23:6* ◀ ▶ *Ac 24:15*
S *Ac 18:10* ◀ ▶ *Ac 27:23–24*

23:6–8 Paul affirmed the Biblical truth of the resurrection from the dead. The Pharisees believed this doctrine, but the Sadducees, who rejected all but the first five books of the OT, rejected this teaching too.

24 And provide *them* beasts, that they may set Paul on, and bring *him* safe unto Felix the governor.

25 And he wrote a letter after this manner:

26 Claudius Lysias unto the most excellent governor Felix *sendeth* greeting.

27 [a]This man was taken of the Jews, and should have been killed of them: then came I with an army, and rescued him, having understood that he was a Roman.

28 [a]And when I would have known the cause wherefore they accused him, I brought him forth into their council:

29 Whom I perceived to be accused [a]of questions of their law, [b]but to have nothing laid to his charge worthy of death or of bonds.

30 And [a]when it was told me how that the Jews laid wait for the man, I sent straightway to thee, and [b]gave commandment to his accusers also to say before thee what *they had* against him. Farewell.

31 Then the soldiers, as it was commanded them, took Paul, and brought *him* by night to Antipatris.

32 On the morrow they left the horsemen to go with him, and returned to the castle:

33 Who, when they came to Caesarea, and delivered the epistle to the governor, presented Paul also before him.

34 And when the governor had read *the letter,* he asked of what province he was. And when he understood that *he was* of [a]Cilicia;

35 [a]I will hear thee, said he, when thine accusers are also come. And he commanded him to be kept in [b]Herod's judgment hall.

Paul tried before Felix

24 AND AFTER [a]five days [b]Ananias the high priest descended with the elders, and *with* a certain orator *named* Tertullus, who informed the governor against Paul.

2 And when he was called forth, Tertullus began to accuse *him,* saying, Seeing that by thee we enjoy great quietness, and that very worthy deeds are done unto this nation by thy providence,

3 We accept *it* always, and in all places, most noble Felix, with all thankfulness.

4 Notwithstanding, that I be not further tedious unto thee, I pray thee that thou wouldest hear us of thy clemency a few words.

5 [a]For we have found this man *a* pestilent *fellow,* and a mover of sedition among all the Jews throughout the world, and a ringleader of the sect of the Nazarenes:

6 [a]Who also hath gone about to profane the temple: whom we took, and would [b]have judged according to our law.

7 [a]But the chief captain Lysias came *upon us,* and with great violence took *him* away out of our hands,

8 [a]Commanding his accusers to come unto thee: by examining of whom thyself mayest take knowledge of all these things, whereof we accuse him.

9 And the Jews also assented, saying that these things were so.

10 Then Paul, after that the governor had beckoned unto him to speak, answered, Forasmuch as I know that thou hast been of many years a judge unto this nation, I do the more cheerfully answer for myself:

11 Because that thou mayest understand, that there are yet but twelve days since I went up to Jerusalem [a]for to worship.

12 [a]And they neither found me in the temple disputing with any man, neither raising up the people, neither in the synagogues, nor in the city:

13 Neither can they prove the things whereof they now accuse me.

14 But this I confess unto thee, that after [a]the way which they call heresy, so worship I the [b]God of my fathers, believing all things which are written in [c]the law and in the prophets:

15 And [a]have hope toward God, F W

F *Ac 23:8* ◀ ▶ *Ac 24:21*
W *Jn 5:25–29* ◀ ▶ *1Co 15:21–26*

27 [a]ch. 21:33 & 24:7
28 [a]ch. 22:30
29 [a]ch. 18:15 & 25:19 [b]ch. 26:31
30 [a]ver. 20 [b]ch. 24:8 & 25:6
34 [a]ch. 21:39
35 [a]ch. 24:1,10 & 25:16 [b]Mat. 27:27
24:1 [a]ch. 21:27 [b]ch. 23:2,30,35 & 25:2
5 [a]Luke 23:2; ch. 6:13 & 16:20 & 17:6 & 21:28; 1 Pet. 2:12,15
6 [a]ch. 21:28 [b]John 18:31
7 [a]ch. 21:33
8 [a]ch. 23:30
11 [a]ver. 17; ch. 21:26
12 [a]ch. 25:8 & 28:17
14 [a]See Amos 8:14; ch. 9:2 [b]2 Tim. 1:3 [c]ch. 26:22 & 28:23
15 [a]ch. 23:6 & 26:6,7 & 28:20

24:15, 21 Paul again confirmed the doctrine of the physical resurrection from the dead for the just and the unjust and affirmed the Pharisees' belief in this doctrine too.

which they themselves also allow, [b]that there shall be a resurrection of the dead, both of the just and unjust.

16 And [a]herein do I exercise myself, to have always a conscience void of offence toward God, and *toward* men.

17 Now after many years [a]I came to bring alms to my nation, and offerings.

18 [a]Whereupon certain Jews from Asia found me purified in the temple, neither with multitude, nor with tumult.

19 [a]Who ought to have been here before thee, and object, if they had aught against me.

20 Or else let these same *here* say, if they have found any evil doing in me, while I stood before the council,

F 21 Except it be for this one voice, that I cried standing among them, [a]Touching the resurrection of the dead I am called in question by you this day.

22 And when Felix heard these things, having more perfect knowledge of *that* way, he deferred them, and said, When [a]Lysias the chief captain shall come down, I will know the uttermost of your matter.

23 And he commanded a centurion to keep Paul, and to let *him* have liberty, and [a]that he should forbid none of his acquaintance to minister or come unto him.

24 And after certain days, when Felix came with his wife Drusilla, which was a Jewess, he sent for Paul, and heard him concerning the faith in Christ.

J N 25 And as he reasoned of righteousness, temperance, and judgment to come, Felix trembled, and answered, Go thy way for this time; when I have a convenient season, I will call for thee.

26 He hoped also that [a]money should have been given him of Paul, that he might loose him: wherefore he sent for him the oftener, and communed with him.

27 But after two years Porcius Festus came into Felix' room: and Felix, [a]willing to show the Jews a pleasure, left Paul bound.

15 [b]Dan. 12:2; John 5:28,29
16 [a]ch. 23:1
17 [a]ch. 11:29,30; & 20:16; Rom. 15:25; 2 Cor. 8:4; Gal. 2:10
18 [a]ch. 21:26,27; & 26:21
19 [a]ch. 23:30 & 25:16
21 [a]ch. 23:6 & 28:20
22 [a]ver. 7
23 [a]ch. 27:3 & 28:16
26 [a]Ex. 23:8
27 [a]Ex. 23:2; ch. 12:3 & 25:9,14
25:2 [a]ver. 15; ch. 24:1
3 [a]ch. 23:12,15
5 [a]ver. 18; ch. 18:14
6 [1]Or, as some copies read, *no more than eight or ten days*
7 [a]Mark 15:3; Luke 23:2,10; ch. 24:5, 13
8 [a]ch. 6:13 & 24:12 & 28:17
9 [a]ch. 24:27 [b]ver. 20
11 [a]ver. 25; ch. 18:14 & 23:29 & 26:31 [b]ch. 26:32 & 28:19

Paul tried before Festus

25 NOW WHEN Festus was come into the province, after three days he ascended from Caesarea to Jerusalem.

2 [a]Then the high priest and the chief of the Jews informed him against Paul, and besought him,

3 And desired favour against him, that he would send for him to Jerusalem, [a]laying wait in the way to kill him.

4 But Festus answered, that Paul should be kept at Caesarea, and that he himself would depart shortly *thither.*

5 Let them therefore, said he, which among you are able, go down with *me,* and accuse this man, [a]if there be any wickedness in him.

6 And when he had tarried among them [1]more than ten days, he went down unto Caesarea; and the next day sitting on the judgment seat commanded Paul to be brought.

7 And when he was come, the Jews which came down from Jerusalem stood round about, [a]and laid many and grievous complaints against Paul, which they could not prove.

8 While he answered for himself, [a]Neither against the law of the Jews, neither against the temple, nor yet against Caesar, have I offended any thing at all.

9 But Festus, [a]willing to do the Jews a pleasure, answered Paul, and said, [b]Wilt thou go up to Jerusalem, and there be judged of these things before me?

10 Then said Paul, I stand at Caesar's judgment seat, where I ought to be judged: to the Jews have I done no wrong, as thou very well knowest.

11 [a]For if I be an offender, or have committed any thing worthy of death, I refuse not to die: but if there be none of these things whereof these accuse me, no man may deliver me unto them. [b]I appeal unto Caesar.

12 Then Festus, when he had conferred with the council, answered, Hast thou appealed unto Caesar? unto Caesar shalt thou go.

Paul's case discussed

13 And after certain days king Agrippa and Bernice came unto Caesarea to salute Festus.

14 And when they had been there many days, Festus declared Paul's cause

F *Ac 24:15* ◀▶ *Ac 26:6–8*
J *Ac 17:31* ◀▶ *Ro 2:2–13*
N *Ac 7:51–53* ◀▶ *Ac 26:28–29*

unto the king, saying, [a]There is a certain man left in bonds by Felix:

15 [a]About whom, when I was at Jerusalem, the chief priests and the elders of the Jews informed *me,* desiring *to have* judgment against him.

16 [a]To whom I answered, It is not the manner of the Romans to deliver any man to die, before that he which is accused have the accusers face to face, and have licence to answer for himself concerning the crime laid against him.

17 Therefore, when they were come hither, [a]without any delay on the morrow I sat on the judgment seat, and commanded the man to be brought forth.

18 Against whom when the accusers stood up, they brought none accusation of such things as I supposed:

19 [a]But had certain questions against him of their own superstition, and of one Jesus, which was dead, whom Paul affirmed to be alive.

20 And because [/]I doubted of such manner of questions, I asked *him* whether he would go to Jerusalem, and there be judged of these matters.

21 But when Paul had appealed to be reserved unto the [/]hearing of Augustus, I commanded him to be kept till I might send him to Caesar.

22 Then [a]Agrippa said unto Festus, I would also hear the man myself. Tomorrow, said he, thou shalt hear him.

23 And on the morrow, when Agrippa was come, and Bernice, with great pomp, and was entered into the place of hearing, with the chief captains, and principal men of the city, at Festus' commandment Paul was brought forth.

24 And Festus said, King Agrippa, and all men which are here present with us, ye see this man, about whom [a]all the multitude of the Jews have dealt with me, both at Jerusalem, and *also* here, crying that he ought [b]not to live any longer.

25 But when I found that [a]he had committed nothing worthy of death, [b]and that he himself hath appealed to Augustus, I have determined to send him.

26 Of whom I have no certain thing to write unto my lord. Wherefore I have brought him forth before you, and specially before thee, O king Agrippa, that, after examination had, I might have somewhat to write.

27 For it seemeth to me unreasonable to send a prisoner, and not withal to signify the crimes *laid* against him.

Paul tried before Agrippa

26 THEN AGRIPPA said unto Paul, Thou art permitted to speak for thyself. Then Paul stretched forth the hand, and answered for himself:

2 I think myself happy, king Agrippa, because I shall answer for myself this day before thee touching all the things whereof I am accused of the Jews:

3 Especially *because I know* thee to be expert in all customs and questions which are among the Jews: wherefore I beseech thee to hear me patiently.

4 My manner of life from my youth, which was at the first among mine own nation at Jerusalem, know all the Jews;

5 Which knew me from the beginning, if they would testify, that after [a]the most straitest sect of our religion I lived a Pharisee.

6 [a]And now I stand and am judged for the hope of [b]the promise made of God unto our fathers: F

7 Unto which *promise* [a]our twelve tribes, instantly serving *God* [b]day[/] and night, [c]hope to come. For which hope's sake, king Agrippa, I am accused of the Jews.

8 Why should it be thought a thing incredible with you, that God should raise the dead?

9 [a]I verily thought with myself, that I ought to do many things contrary to the name of Jesus of Nazareth.

10 [a]Which thing I also did in Jerusalem: and many of the saints did I shut up in prison, having received authority [b]from the chief priests; and when they were put to death, I gave my voice against *them.*

11 [a]And I punished them oft in every synagogue, and compelled *them* to blas-

14 [a]ch. 24:27
15 [a]ver. 2,3
16 [a]ver. 4,5
17 [a]ver. 6
19 [a]ch. 18:15 & 23:29
20 [/]Or, *I was doubtful how to inquire hereof*
21 [/]Or, *judgment*
22 [a]See ch. 9:15
24 [a]ver. 2,3,7 [b]ch. 22:22
25 [a]ch. 23:9,29 & 26:31 [b]ver. 11,12
26:5 [a]ch. 22:3 & 23:6 & 24:15,21; Phil. 3:5
6 [a]ch. 23:6 [b]Gen. 3:15 & 22:18 & 26:4 & 49:10; Deut. 18:15; 2 Sam. 7:12; Ps. 132:11; Is. 4:2 & 7:14 & 9:6 & 40:10; Jer. 23:5 & 33:14-16; Ezek. 34:23 & 37:24; Dan. 9:24; ch. 13:32; Rom. 15:8; Tit. 2:13
7 [a]Jas. 1:1 [b]Luke 2:37; 1 Thes. 3:10; 1 Tim. 5:5 [c]Phil. 3:11 [/]Gk. *night and day*
9 [a]John 16:2; 1 Tim. 1:13
10 [a]ch. 8:3; Gal. 1:13 [b]ch. 9:14,21 & 22:5
11 [a]ch. 22:19

F *Ac 24:21* ◄► *Ac 28:20*

26:6–8 When called to defend his case before King Agrippa, Paul said that the crux of the controversy between the Jewish leaders and Paul revolved around the truth of the resurrection. Paul also reminded the king that the twelve tribes of Israel had always believed this doctrine.

pheme; and being exceedingly mad against them, I persecuted *them* even unto strange cities.

12 [a]Whereupon as I went to Damascus with authority and commission from the chief priests,

13 At midday, O king, I saw in the way a light from heaven, above the brightness of the sun, shining round about me and them which journeyed with me.

14 And when we were all fallen to the earth, I heard a voice speaking unto me, and saying in the Hebrew tongue, Saul, Saul, why persecutest thou me? *it is* hard for thee to kick against the pricks.

15 And I said, Who art thou, Lord? And he said, I am Jesus whom thou persecutest.

16 But rise, and stand upon thy feet: for I have appeared unto thee for this purpose, [a]to make thee a minister and a witness both of these things which thou hast seen, and of those things in the which I will appear unto thee;

L 17 Delivering thee from the people, and *from* the Gentiles, [a]unto whom now I send thee,

C 18 [a]To open their eyes, *and* [b]to turn *them* from darkness to light, and *from* the power of Satan unto God, [c]that they may receive forgiveness of sins, and [d]inheritance among them which are [e]sanctified by faith that is in me.

19 Whereupon, O king Agrippa, I was not disobedient unto the heavenly vision:

R 20 But [a]showed first unto them of Damascus, and at Jerusalem, and throughout all the coasts of Judaea, and *then* to the Gentiles, that they should repent and turn to God, and do [b]works meet for repentance.

21 For these causes [a]the Jews caught me in the temple, and went about to kill *me.*

22 Having therefore obtained help of God, I continue unto this day, witnessing both to small and great, saying none other things than those [a]which the prophets and [b]Moses did say should come:

B 23 [a]That Christ should suffer, *and* [b]that he should be the first that should rise from the dead, and [c]should show light unto the people, and to the Gentiles.

24 And as he thus spake for himself, Festus said with a loud voice, Paul, [a]thou art beside thyself; much learning doth make thee mad.

25 But he said, I am not mad, most noble Festus; but speak forth the words of truth and soberness.

26 For the king knoweth of these things, before whom also I speak freely: for I am persuaded that none of these things are hidden from him; for this thing was not done in a corner.

27 King Agrippa, believest thou the prophets? I know that thou believest.

28 Then Agrippa said unto Paul, Almost thou persuadest me to be a Christian. N

29 And Paul said, [a]I would to God, that not only thou, but also all that hear me this day, were both almost, and altogether such as I am, except these bonds.

30 And when he had thus spoken, the king rose up, and the governor, and Bernice, and they that sat with them:

31 And when they were gone aside, they talked between themselves, saying, [a]This man doeth nothing worthy of death or of bonds.

32 Then said Agrippa unto Festus, This man might have been set at liberty, [a]if he had not appealed unto Caesar.

Paul sent to Rome

27 AND WHEN [a]it was determined that we should sail into Italy, they delivered Paul and certain other prisoners unto *one* named Julius, a centurion of Augustus' band.

2 And entering into a ship of Adramyttium, we launched, meaning to sail by the coasts of Asia; *one* [a]Aristarchus, a Macedonian of Thessalonica, being with us.

3 And the next *day* we touched at Sidon. And Julius [a]courteously entreated Paul, and gave *him* liberty to go unto his friends to refresh himself.

4 And when we had launched from thence, we sailed under Cyprus, because the winds were contrary.

5 And when we had sailed over the sea of Cilicia and Pamphylia, we came to Myra, *a city* of Lycia.

12 [a]ch. 9:3 & 22:6
16 [a]ch. 22:15
17 [a]ch. 22:21
18 [a]Is. 35:5 & 42:7; Luke 1:79; John 8:12; 2 Cor. 4:4; Eph. 1:18; 1 Thes. 5:5 [b]2 Cor. 6:14; Eph. 4:18 & 5:8; Col. 1:13; 1 Pet. 2:9 [c]Luke 1:77 [d]Eph. 1:11; Col. 1:12 [e]ch. 20:32
20 [a]ch. 9:20,22 & 11:26 & chs. 13, 14 & 16-21 [b]Mat. 3:8
21 [a]ch. 21:30
22 [a]Luke 24:27; ch. 24:14 & 28:23; Rom. 3:21 [b]John 5:46
23 [a]Luke 24:26 [b]1 Cor. 15:20; Col. 1:18; Rev. 1:5 [c]Luke 2:32
24 [a]2 Ki. 9:11; John 10:20; 1 Cor. 1:23 & 2:13,14 & 4:10
29 [a]1 Cor. 7:7
31 [a]ch. 23:9,29 & 25:25
32 [a]ch. 25:11
27:1 [a]ch. 25:12,25
2 [a]ch. 19:29
3 [a]ch. 24:23 & 28:16

L *Ac 17:27* ◀▶ *Ac 28:28*
C *Ac 8:23* ◀▶ *Ac 28:26–27*
R *Ac 20:21* ◀▶ *2Co 7:9–10*
B *Ac 7:37–38* ◀
N *Ac 24:25* ◀▶ *Ro 1:20–22*

6 And there the centurion found a ship of Alexandria sailing into Italy; and he put us therein.

7 And when we had sailed slowly many days, and scarce were come over against Cnidus, the wind not suffering us, we sailed under [l]Crete, over against Salmone;

8 And, hardly passing it, came unto a place which is called The fair havens; nigh whereunto was the city *of* Lasea.

9 Now when much time was spent, and when sailing was now dangerous, [a]because the fast was now already past, Paul admonished *them,*

10 And said unto them, Sirs, I perceive that this voyage will be with [l]hurt and much damage, not only of the lading and ship, but also of our lives.

11 Nevertheless the centurion believed the master and the owner of the ship, more than those things which were spoken by Paul.

12 And because the haven was not commodious to winter in, the more part advised to depart thence also, if by any means they might attain to Phenice, *and there* to winter; *which is* an haven of Crete, and lieth toward the south west and north west.

The storm at sea

13 And when the south wind blew softly, supposing that they had obtained *their* purpose, loosing *thence,* they sailed close by Crete.

14 But not long after there [l]arose against it a tempestuous wind, called Euroclydon.

15 And when the ship was caught, and could not bear up into the wind, we let *her* drive.

16 And running under a certain island which is called Clauda, we had much work to come by the boat:

17 Which when they had taken up, they used helps, undergirding the ship; and, fearing lest they should fall into the quicksands, strake sail, and so were driven.

18 And we being exceedingly tossed with a tempest, the next *day* they lightened the ship;

19 And the third *day* [a]we cast out with our own hands the tackling of the ship.

20 And when neither sun nor stars in many days appeared, and no small tempest lay on *us,* all hope that we should be saved was then taken away.

21 But after long abstinence Paul stood forth in the midst of them, and said, Sirs, ye should have hearkened unto me, and not have loosed from Crete, and to have gained this harm and loss.

22 And now I exhort you to be of good cheer: for there shall be no loss of *any man's* life among you, but of the ship.

23 [a]For there stood by me this night the angel of God, whose I am, and [b]whom I serve, S

24 Saying, Fear not, Paul; thou must be brought before Caesar: and, lo, God hath given thee all them that sail with thee.

25 Wherefore, sirs, be of good cheer: [a]for I believe God, that it shall be even as it was told me.

26 Howbeit [a]we must be cast upon a certain island.

The shipwreck

27 But when the fourteenth night was come, as we were driven up and down in Adria, about midnight the shipmen deemed that they drew near to some country;

28 And sounded, and found *it* twenty fathoms: and when they had gone a little further, they sounded again, and found *it* fifteen fathoms.

29 Then fearing lest we should have fallen upon rocks, they cast four anchors out of the stern, and wished for the day.

30 And as the shipmen were about to flee out of the ship, when they had let down the boat into the sea, under colour as though they would have cast anchors out of the foreship,

31 Paul said to the centurion and to the soldiers, Except these abide in the ship, ye cannot be saved.

32 Then the soldiers cut off the ropes of the boat, and let her fall off.

33 And while the day was coming on, Paul besought *them* all to take meat, saying, This day is the fourteenth day that ye have tarried and continued fasting, having taken nothing.

34 Wherefore I pray you to take *some* meat: for this is for your health: for [a]there shall not an hair fall from the head of any of you.

7 [l]Or, *Candy*
9 [a]The fast was on the tenth day of the seventh month Lev. 23:27,29
10 [l]Or, *injury*
14 [l]Or, *beat*
19 [a]Jonah 1:5
23 [a]ch. 23:11 [b]Dan. 6:16; Rom. 1:9; 2 Tim. 1:3
25 [a]Luke 1:45; Rom. 4:20,21; 2 Tim. 1:12
26 [a]ch. 28:1
34 [a]1 Ki. 1:52; Mat. 10:30; Luke 12:7 & 21:18

S Ac 23:11 ◄► Ro 8:31

35 And when he had thus spoken, he took bread, and [a]gave thanks to God in presence of them all: and when he had broken *it,* he began to eat.

36 Then were they all of good cheer, and they also took *some* meat.

37 And we were in all in the ship two hundred threescore and sixteen [a]souls.

38 And when they had eaten enough, they lightened the ship, and cast out the wheat into the sea.

39 And when it was day, they knew not the land: but they discovered a certain creek with a shore, into the which they were minded, if it were possible, to thrust in the ship.

40 And when they had [l]taken up the anchors, they committed *themselves* unto the sea, and loosed the rudder bands, and hoisted up the mainsail to the wind, and made toward shore.

41 And falling into a place where two seas met, [a]they ran the ship aground; and the forepart stuck fast, and remained unmoveable, but the hinderpart was broken with the violence of the waves.

42 And the soldiers' counsel was to kill the prisoners, lest any of them should swim out, and escape.

43 But the centurion, willing to save Paul, kept them from *their* purpose; and commanded that they which could swim should cast *themselves* first *into the sea,* and get to land:

44 And the rest, some on boards, and some on *broken pieces* of the ship. And so it came to pass, [a]that they escaped all safe to land.

The stopover at Melita

28 AND WHEN they were escaped, then they knew that [a]the island was called Melita.

2 And the [a]barbarous people showed us no little kindness: for they kindled a fire, and received us every one, because of the present rain, and because of the cold.

E 3 And when Paul had gathered a bundle of sticks, and laid *them* on the fire, there came a viper out of the heat, and fastened on his hand.

4 And when the barbarians saw the *venomous* beast hang on his hand, they said among themselves, No doubt this man is a murderer, whom, though he hath escaped the sea, yet vengeance suffereth not to live.

5 And he shook off the beast into the fire, and [a]felt no harm.

6 Howbeit they looked when he should have swollen, or fallen down dead suddenly: but after they had looked a great while, and saw no harm come to him, they changed their minds, and [a]said that he was a god.

7 In the same quarters were possessions of the chief man of the island, whose name was Publius; who received us, and lodged us three days courteously.

8 And it came to pass, that the father of Publius lay sick of a fever and of a bloody flux: to whom Paul entered in, and [a]prayed, and [b]laid his hands on him, and healed him.

9 So when this was done, others also, which had diseases in the island, came, and were healed:

10 Who also honoured us with many [a]honours; and when we departed, they laded *us* with such things as were necessary.

11 And after three months we departed in a ship of Alexandria, which had wintered in the isle, whose sign was Castor and Pollux.

12 And landing at Syracuse, we tarried *there* three days.

13 And from thence we fetched a compass, and came to Rhegium: and after one day the south wind blew, and we came the next day to Puteoli:

14 Where we found brethren, and were desired to tarry with them seven days: and so we went toward Rome.

15 And from thence, when the brethren heard of us, they came to meet us as far as Appiiforum, and The three taverns: whom when Paul saw, he thanked God, and took courage.

16 And when we came to Rome, the centurion delivered the prisoners to the captain of the guard: but [a]Paul was suffered to dwell by himself with a soldier that kept him.

35 [a]1 Sam. 9:13; Mat. 15:36; Mark 8:6; John 6:11; 1 Tim. 4:3,4
37 [a]ch. 2:41 & 7:14; Rom. 13:1; 1 Pet. 3:20
40 [l]Or, *cut the anchors, they left them in the sea*
41 [a]2 Cor. 11:25
44 [a]ver:22
28:1 [a]ch. 27:26
2 [a]Rom. 1:14; 1 Cor. 14:11; Col. 3:11
5 [a]Mark 16:18; Luke 10:19
6 [a]ch. 14:11
8 [a]Jas. 5:14,15 [b]Mark 6:5 & 7:32 & 16:18; Luke 4:40; ch. 19:11,12; 1 Cor. 12:9,28
10 [a]Mat. 15:6; 1 Tim. 5:17
16 [a]ch. 24:25 & 27:3

E Ac 22:11–13 ◄► Ro 15:18–19

The arrival at Rome

17 And it came to pass, that after three days Paul called the chief of the Jews together: and when they were come together, he said unto them, Men *and* brethren, [a]though I have committed nothing against the people, or customs of our fathers, yet [b]was I delivered prisoner from Jerusalem into the hands of the Romans.

18 Who, [a]when they had examined me, would have let *me* go, because there was no cause of death in me.

19 But when the Jews spake against *it,* [a]I was constrained to appeal unto Caesar; not that I had aught to accuse my nation of.

F 20 For this cause therefore have I called for you, to see *you,* and to speak with *you:* because that [a]for the hope of Israel I am bound with [b]this chain.

21 And they said unto him, We neither received letters out of Judaea concerning thee, neither any of the brethren that came showed or spake any harm of thee.

22 But we desire to hear of thee what thou thinkest: for as concerning this sect, we know that every where [a]it is spoken against.

23 And when they had appointed him a day, there came many to him into *his* lodging; [a]to whom he expounded and testified the kingdom of God, persuading them concerning Jesus, [b]both out of the law of Moses, and *out of* the prophets, from morning till evening.

F *Ac 26:6–8* ◄► *Ro 8:11*

17 [a]ch. 24:12,13 [b]ch. 21:33
18 [a]ch. 22:24 & 24:10 & 25:8
19 [a]ch. 25:11
20 [a]ch. 26:6,7 [b]ch. 26:29; Eph. 3:1 & 4:1 & 6:20; 2 Tim. 1:16; Philem. 10,13
22 [a]Luke 2:34; ch. 24:5,14; 1 Pet. 2:12 & 4:14
23 [a]Luke 24:27; ch. 17:3 & 19:8 [b]See ch. 26:6,22
24 [a]ch. 14:4 & 19:9
26 [a]Is. 6:9; Jer. 5:21; Ezek. 12:2; Mat. 13:14; Mark 4:12; Luke 8:10; John 12:40; Rom. 11:8
28 [a]Mat. 21:41; ch. 13:46 & 18:6 & 26:17,18; Rom. 11:11
31 [a]ch. 4:31; Eph. 6:19

24 And [a]some believed the things which were spoken, and some believed not.

25 And when they agreed not among themselves, they departed, after that Paul had spoken one word, Well spake the Holy Ghost by Esaias the prophet unto our fathers, E T

26 Saying, [a]Go unto this people, and say, Hearing ye shall hear, and shall not understand; and seeing ye shall see, and not perceive: C

27 For the heart of this people is waxed gross, and their ears are dull of hearing, and their eyes have they closed; lest they should see with *their* eyes, and hear with *their* ears, and understand with *their* heart, and should be converted, and I should heal them.

28 Be it known therefore unto you, that the salvation of God is sent [a]unto the Gentiles, and *that* they will hear it. G L

29 And when he had said these words, the Jews departed, and had great reasoning among themselves.

30 And Paul dwelt two whole years in his own hired house, and received all that came in unto him,

31 [a]Preaching the kingdom of God, and teaching those things which concern the Lord Jesus Christ, with all confidence, no man forbidding him.

E *Ac 21:11* ◄► *Ro 1:4*
T *Ac 21:11* ◄► *Ro 12:6–8*
C *Ac 26:18* ◄► *Ro 1:20–21*
G *Ac 18:6* ◄► *Ro 9:30*
L *Ac 26:17–18* ◄► *Ro 3:21–30*

28:17–20 Paul wanted the "chief of the Jews" (28:17) in Rome to understand the truth about the accusations that were made against himself and other believers regarding "the hope of Israel" (28:20), that is, the hope of the resurrection from the dead.

28:28 The final prophecy in the book of Acts confirms that God would send the gospel to the Gentiles because the majority of Jews had rejected the claim of Jesus of Nazareth as their promised Messiah.

Romans

Author: Paul

Theme: Justification with God through faith in Christ

Date of Writing: A.D. 57

Outline of Romans

I. Introduction and Theme (1:1–17)
II. All People Are Unrighteous (1:18—3:20)
III. Righteousness Through Christ (3:21—5:21)
IV. Sanctification (6:1—8:39)
V. Israel's Rejection (9:1—11:36)
VI. Righteous Living (12:1—15:13)
VII. Conclusion, Commendation and Greetings (15:14—16:27)

PAUL ADDRESSED THIS letter to the believers in the Roman church. This church was made up primarily of Gentiles and may have been started by visitors from Rome who were present in Jerusalem on the day of Pentecost (see Ac 2:1, 10). Anticipating a visit to Rome (see Ro 15:24, 28, 32), Paul probably wrote this letter while in Corinth at the end of his third missionary journey and sent it to Rome with Phebe (see 16:1), a helper in the church of Cenchrea, a city near Corinth.

Although the introduction and the conclusion identify Romans as a Pauline letter, this book does not display the personal character of Paul that is seen in his other epistles. Instead, Paul's words to the Roman church are instructional, revealing an orderly, doctrinal presentation of the good news of Jesus Christ. This letter to the Romans forms one of the most complete NT expositions of the key doctrines of Christianity by following a systematic presentation of God's revelation of his righteousness to humanity through Christ. Since all humanity, Jews and Gentiles, are guilty before God (see 3:19, 23), Paul is determined to make all of his readers aware of God's offer of salvation through the substitutionary death and resurrection of Jesus Christ. Paul's extensive knowledge of, and quotations from, the OT support his words that our justification from sin is received solely through our faith in Christ (see 3:28) and that our ability to live in righteousness comes only through the supernatural power of the Holy Spirit.

Throughout this letter to the Romans, Paul clearly demonstrates his gratitude, purpose and mission in life. Recognizing humanity's lost condition without Christ, Paul gratefully acknowledges God's crediting of Christ's righteousness to Paul's life as the foundation for Paul's boldness in proclaiming the gospel. In the final portion of this letter, Paul develops the practical application of these key doctrines as a way to encourage the believers' daily walk of faith.

1 PAUL, A servant of Jesus Christ,
[a]called *to be* an apostle, [b]separated
unto the gospel of God,
2 ([a]Which he had promised afore [b]by
his prophets in the holy scriptures,)
3 Concerning his Son Jesus Christ our
Lord, which was [a]made of the seed of
David according to the flesh;
E 4 And [a]declared[/] *to be* the Son of God
H with power, according [b]to the spirit of
M holiness, by the resurrection from the
N dead:
S 5 By whom [a]we have received grace
and apostleship, [/]for [b]obedience to the
faith among all nations, [c]for his name:
6 Among whom are ye also the called
of Jesus Christ:
7 To all that be in Rome, beloved of
God, [a]called *to be* saints: [b]Grace to you
and peace from God our Father, and the
Lord Jesus Christ.

Thanksgiving and prayers

8 First, [a]I thank my God through Jesus
Christ for you all, that [b]your faith is spoken of throughout the whole world.
9 For [a]God is my witness, [b]whom I
serve [/]with my spirit in the gospel of his
Son, that [c]without ceasing I make mention of you always in my prayers;
10 Making request, if by any means
now at length I might have a prosperous
journey by the will of God to come unto
you.
E 11 For I long to see you, that [a]I may
impart unto you some spiritual gift, to the
end ye may be established;
12 That is, that I may be comforted together [/]with you by [a]the mutual faith
both of you and me.
13 Now I would not have you ignorant, brethren, that oftentimes I purposed
to come unto you, (but [a]was let hitherto,)
that I might have some [b]fruit [/]among you
also, even as among other Gentiles.
14 I am debtor both to the Greeks, and
to the Barbarians; both to the wise, and
to the unwise.
15 So, as much as in me is, I am ready
to preach the gospel to you that are at
Rome also.
16 For [a]I am not ashamed of the gospel F
of Christ: for [b]it is the power of God unto K
salvation to every one that believeth; [c]to T
the Jew first, and also to the Greek. W
17 For [a]therein is the righteousness of
God revealed from faith to faith: as it is
written, [b]The just shall live by faith.

The Gentiles: guilty before God

18 [a]For the wrath of God is revealed H
from heaven against all ungodliness and S
unrighteousness of men, who hold the
truth in unrighteousness;
19 Because [a]that which may be known
of God is manifest [/]in them; for [b]God
hath shown *it* unto them.
20 For [a]the invisible things of him C
from the creation of the world are clearly N
seen, being understood by the things that
are made, *even* his eternal power and

1:1 [a]1 Tim. 1:11 [b]Acts 9:15
2 [a]Acts 26:6 [b]Gal. 3:8
3 [a]Gal. 4:4
4 [a]Acts 13:33 [b]Heb. 9:14 [/]Gk. *determined*
5 [a]Eph. 3:8 [b]Acts 6:7 [c]Acts 9:15 [/]Or, *to the obedience of faith*
7 [a]1 Cor. 1:2 [b]1 Cor. 1:3
8 [a]1 Cor. 1:4 [b]ch. 16:19
9 [a]ch. 9:1 [b]Acts 27:23 [c]1 Thes. 3:10 [/]Or, *in my spirit*
11 [a]ch. 15:29
12 [a]Tit. 1:4 [/]Or, *in you*
13 [a]1 Thes. 2:18 [b]Phil. 4:17 [/]Or, *in you*
16 [a]Ps. 40:9,10; Mark 8:38 [b]1 Cor. 1:18 [c]Luke 2:30; Acts 13:26
17 [a]ch. 3:21 [b]Hab. 2:4; John 3:36; Gal. 3:11
18 [a]Acts 17:30; Eph. 5:6
19 [a]Acts 14:17 [b]John 1:9 [/]Or, *to them*
20 [a]Ps. 19:1; Acts 14:17

G
M
W

E *Ac 28:25* ◀▶ *Ro 1:11*
H *Jn 6:63* ◀▶ *Ro 8:2*
M *Ac 19:6* ◀▶ *Ro 1:11*
N *Ac 10:45* ◀▶ *1Co 2:11*
S *Ac 15:8–9* ◀▶ *Ro 8:1–16*
E *Ro 1:4* ◀▶ *Ro 5:5*
G *Ac 20:28* ◀▶ *Ro 12:6–8*
M *Ro 1:4* ◀▶ *Ro 8:2*
W *Ac 19:2* ◀▶ *Ro 7:6*

F *Ac 20:21* ◀▶ *Ro 3:21–30*
K *Ac 20:32* ◀▶ *Ro 3:3–4*
T *Jn 12:42–43* ◀▶ *Ro 10:8–10*
W *Ac 17:27* ◀▶ *Ro 3:21–24*
H *Ac 13:41* ◀▶ *Ro 2:2–13*
S *Ac 14:22* ◀▶ *Ro 2:6–13*
C *Ac 28:26–27* ◀▶ *Ro 1:24*
N *Ac 26:28–29* ◀▶ *Ro 2:5*

Godhead; [1]so that they are without
excuse:
21 Because that, when they knew
God, they glorified *him* not as God, neither were thankful; but [a]became vain in
their imaginations, and their foolish heart
was darkened.
22 [a]Professing themselves to be wise,
they became fools,
23 And changed the glory of the uncor-
ruptible [a]God into an image made like to
corruptible man, and to birds, and fourfooted beasts, and creeping things.
C 24 [a]Wherefore God also gave them up
to uncleanness through the lusts of their
own hearts, [b]to dishonour their own bodies [c]between themselves:
25 Who changed [a]the truth of God
[b]into a lie, and worshipped and served
the creature [1]more than the Creator,
who is blessed for ever. Amen.
C 26 For this cause God gave them up
unto [a]vile affections: for even their
women did change the natural use into
that which is against nature:
27 And likewise also the men, leaving
the natural use of the woman, burned in
their lust one toward another; men with
men working that which is unseemly,
and receiving in themselves that recompence of their error which was meet.
C 28 And even as they did not like [1]to
retain God in *their* knowledge, God gave
them over to [2]a reprobate mind, to do
those things [a]which are not convenient;
29 Being filled with all unrighteousness, fornication, wickedness, covetousness, maliciousness; full of envy, murder,
debate, deceit, malignity; whisperers,
30 Backbiters, haters of God, despiteful, proud, boasters, inventors of evil
things, disobedient to parents,
31 Without understanding, covenant-
breakers, [1]without natural affection, im-
placable, unmerciful:
32 Who [a]knowing the judgment of
God, that they which commit such things
[b]are worthy of death, not only do the
same, but [c]have[1] pleasure in them that
do them.

God's principles of judgment

2 THEREFORE THOU art [a]inexcusa-
ble, O man, whosoever thou art that
judgest: [b]for wherein thou judgest another, thou condemnest thyself; for thou
that judgest doest the same things.
2 But we are sure that the judgment of H
God is according to truth against them J
which commit such things.
3 And thinkest thou this, O man, that
judgest them which do such things, and
doest the same, that thou shalt escape the
judgment of God?
4 Or despisest thou [a]the riches of his
goodness and [b]forbearance and [c]longsuf-
fering; [d]not knowing that the goodness of
God leadeth thee to repentance?
5 But after thy hardness and impeni- J
tent heart [a]treasurest up unto thyself N
wrath against the day of wrath and revelation of the righteous judgment of God;
6 [a]Who will render to every man ac- S
cording to his deeds:
7 To them who by patient continuance
in well doing seek for glory and honour
and immortality, eternal life:
8 But unto them that are contentious,
and [a]do not obey the truth, but obey unrighteousness, indignation and wrath,
9 Tribulation and anguish, upon every
soul of man that doeth evil, of the Jew
[a]first, and also of the [1]Gentile;
10 [a]But glory, honour, and peace, to
every man that worketh good, to the Jew
first, and also to the [1]Gentile:
11 For [a]there is no respect of persons
with God.
12 For as many as have sinned without
law shall also perish without law: and as
many as have sinned in the law shall be
judged by the law;
13 (For [a]not the hearers of the law *are*
just before God, but the doers of the law
shall be justified.
14 For when the Gentiles, which have

20 [1]Or, *that they may be*
21 [a]2 Ki. 17:15; Jer. 2:5; Eph. 4:17
22 [a]Jer. 10:14
23 [a]Deut. 4:16; Ps. 106:20; Is. 40:18
24 [a]Ps. 81:12; Acts 7:42; Eph. 4:18 [b]1 Cor. 6:18; 1 Thes. 4:4 [c]Lev. 18:22
25 [a]1 Thes. 1:9; 1 John 5:20 [b]Is. 44:20; Jer. 10:14 [1]Or, *rather*
26 [a]Lev. 18:22; Eph. 5:12
28 [a]Eph. 5:4 [1]Or, *to acknowledge* [2]Or, *a mind void of judgment*
31 [1]Or, *unsociable*
32 [a]ch. 2:2 [b]ch. 6:21 [c]Ps. 50:18; Hos. 7:3 [1]Or, *consent with them*
2:1 [a]ch. 1:20 [b]2 Sam. 12:5; Mat. 7:1,2; John 8:9
4 [a]Eph. 1:7 [b]ch. 3:25 [c]Ex. 34:6 [d]Is. 30:18; 2 Pet. 3:9
5 [a]Deut. 32:34; Jas. 5:3
6 [a]Job 34:11; Ps. 62:12; Prov. 24:12; Jer. 17:10; 2 Cor. 5:10
8 [a]Job 24:13; 2 Thes. 1:8
9 [a]Amos 3:2; Luke 12:47; 1 Pet. 4:17 [1]Gk. *Greek*
10 [a]1 Pet. 1:7 [1]Gk. *Greek*
11 [a]Deut. 10:17; Job 34:19; Acts 10:34; Eph. 6:9
13 [a]Jas. 1:22; 1 John 3:7

C *Ro 1:20–21* ◀▶ *Ro 1:26*
C *Ro 1:24* ◀▶ *Ro 1:28–32*
C *Ro 1:26* ◀▶ *Ro 3:9–12*

H *Ro 1:18* ◀▶ *Ro 3:8*
J *Ac 24:25* ◀▶ *Ro 2:16*
J *Ac 17:31* ◀▶ *Ro 2:16*
N *Ro 1:20–22* ◀▶ *1Co 1:18*
S *Ro 1:18* ◀▶ *Ro 6:1–2*

2:5 Paul warns his readers that their hardness of heart has prepared them for God's wrath, revealed in the last day in "the righteous judgment of God" (2:5).

not the law, do by nature the things contained in the law, these, having not the law, are a law unto themselves:

15 Which show the work of the law written in their hearts, [1]their conscience also bearing witness, and *their* thoughts [2]the mean while accusing or else excusing one another;)

J 16 [a]In the day when God shall judge
J the secrets of men [b]by Jesus Christ [c]according to my gospel.

The Jews: guilty before God

17 Behold, [a]thou art called a Jew, and [b]restest in the law, [c]and makest thy boast of God,

18 And [a]knowest *his* will, and [b]approvest[1] the things that are more excellent, being instructed out of the law;

19 And [a]art confident that thou thyself art a guide of the blind, a light of them which are in darkness,

20 An instructor of the foolish, a teacher of babes, [a]which hast the form of knowledge and of the truth in the law.

21 [a]Thou therefore which teachest another, teachest thou not thyself? thou that preachest a man should not steal, dost thou steal?

22 Thou that sayest a man should not commit adultery, dost thou commit adultery? thou that abhorrest idols, [a]dost thou commit sacrilege?

23 Thou that [a]makest thy boast of the law, through breaking the law dishonourest thou God?

24 For the name of God is blasphemed among the Gentiles through you, as it is [a]written.

25 [a]For circumcision verily profiteth, if thou keep the law: but if thou be a breaker of the law, thy circumcision is made uncircumcision.

26 Therefore [a]if the uncircumcision keep the righteousness of the law, shall not his uncircumcision be counted for circumcision?

27 And shall not uncircumcision which is by nature, if it fulfil the law, [a]judge thee, who by the letter and circumcision dost transgress the law?

28 For [a]he is not a Jew, which is one outwardly; neither *is that* circumcision, which is outward in the flesh:

29 But he *is* a Jew, [a]which is one inwardly; and [b]circumcision *is that* of the heart, [c]in the spirit, *and* not in the letter; [d]whose praise *is* not of men, but of God.

3 WHAT ADVANTAGE then hath the Jew? or what profit *is there* of circumcision?

2 Much every way: chiefly, because that [a]unto them were committed the oracles of God.

3 For what if [a]some did not believe? K
[b]shall their unbelief make the faith of God without effect?

4 [a]God forbid: yea, let [b]God be true, but [c]every man a liar; as it is written, [d]That thou mightest be justified in thy sayings, and mightest overcome when thou art judged.

5 But if our unrighteousness commend the righteousness of God, what shall we say? *Is* God unrighteous who taketh vengeance? ([a]I speak as a man)

6 God forbid: for then [a]how shall God J
judge the world?

7 For if the truth of God hath more abounded through my lie unto his glory; why yet am I also judged as a sinner?

8 And not *rather,* (as we be slander- H
ously reported, and as some affirm that we say,) [a]Let us do evil, that good may come? whose damnation is just.

The world: guilty before God

9 What then? are we better *than they?* A
No, in no wise: for we have before C
[1]proved both Jews and Gentiles, that [a]they are all under sin;

10 As it is written, [a]There is none righteous, no, not one:

11 There is none that understandeth, there is none that seeketh after God.

12 They are all gone out of the way, they are together become unprofitable;

J *Ro 2:5 ◀ ▶ 1Co 4:5*
J *Ro 2:2–13 ◀ ▶ Ro 3:6*

K *Ro 1:16 ◀ ▶ Ro 3:24–25*
J *Ro 2:16 ◀ ▶ Ro 14:10–12*
H *Ro 2:2–13 ◀ ▶ Ro 6:23*
A *Jn 3:18 ◀ ▶ Ro 3:19*
C *Ro 1:28–32 ◀ ▶ Ro 3:17–20*

15 [1]Or, *the conscience witnessing with them* [2]Or, *between themselves*
16 [a]Eccl. 12:14; Mat. 25:31; Rev. 20:12 [b]John 5:22; Acts 10:42 [c]1 Tim. 1:11
17 [a]Mat. 3:9; John 8:33 [b]Mic. 3:11 [c]Is. 48:2
18 [a]Deut. 4:8 [b]Phil. 1:10 [1]Or, *triest the things that differ*
19 [a]Mat. 15:14; John 9:34
20 [a]2 Tim. 3:5
21 [a]Ps. 50:16; Mat. 23:3
22 [a]Mal. 3:8
23 [a]ver. 17
24 [a]2 Sam. 12:14; Is. 52:5; Ezek. 36:20
25 [a]Gal. 5:3
26 [a]Acts 10:34
27 [a]Mat. 12:41
28 [a]Mat. 3:9; John 8:39; Gal. 6:15
29 [a]1 Pet. 3:4 [b]Phil. 3:3 [c]ch. 7:6 [d]1 Cor. 4:5; 2 Cor. 10:18; 1 Thes. 2:4
3:2 [a]Deut. 4:7; Ps. 147:19
3 [a]Heb. 4:2 [b]Num. 23:19; 2 Tim. 2:13
4 [a]Job 40:8 [b]John 3:33 [c]Ps. 62:9 [d]Ps. 51:4
5 [a]Gal. 3:15
6 [a]Gen. 18:25
8 [a]ch. 5:20
9 [a]Gal. 3:22 [1]Gk. *charged*
10 [a]Ps. 14:1-3

2:16 God will judge humanity in the final judgment day at the end of the Millennium (see Rev 20:11–15).

there is none that doeth good, no, not
one.
13 [a]Their throat *is* an open sepulchre;
with their tongues they have used deceit;
[b]the poison of asps *is* under their lips:
14 [a]Whose mouth *is* full of cursing and
bitterness:
15 [a]Their feet *are* swift to shed blood:
16 Destruction and misery *are* in their
ways:
C 17 And the way of peace have they not
known:
18 [a]There is no fear of God before
their eyes.
A 19 Now we know that what things soever [a]the law saith, it saith to them who
are under the law: that [b]every mouth
may be stopped, and [c]all the world may
become [1]guilty before God.
G 20 Therefore [a]by the deeds of the law
there shall no flesh be justified in his
sight: for [b]by the law *is* the knowledge of
sin.

Faith: the means of salvation

F 21 But now [a]the righteousness of God
L without the law is manifested, [b]being
W witnessed by the law [c]and the prophets;
A 22 Even the righteousness of God
which is [a]by faith of Jesus Christ unto all
and upon all them that believe: for [b]there
is no difference:
A 23 For [a]all have sinned, and come
short of the glory of God;
D 24 Being justified freely [a]by his grace
K [b]through the redemption that is in Christ
Jesus:
25 Whom God hath [1]set forth [a]*to be* a
propitiation through faith [b]in his blood,
to declare his righteousness for the [2]re-
mission of [c]sins that are past, through the
forbearance of God;
26 To declare, *I say,* at this time his
righteousness: that he might be just, and
the justifier of him which believeth in
Jesus.

13 [a]Ps. 5:9; Jer. 5:16 [b]Ps. 140:3
14 [a]Ps. 10:7
15 [a]Prov. 1:16; Is. 59:7,8
18 [a]Ps. 36:1
19 [a]John 10:34 [b]Job 5:16; Ps. 107:42 [c]ch. 2:2 [1]Or, *subject to the judgment of God*
20 [a]Ps. 143:2; Acts 13:39; Gal. 2:16 [b]ch. 7:7
21 [a]Acts 15:11; ch. 1:17 [b]John 5:46 [c]1 Pet. 1:10
22 [a]ch. 4 [b]ch. 10:12; Gal. 3:28; Col. 3:11
23 [a]ch. 11:32; Gal. 3:22
24 [a]ch. 4:16; Eph. 2:8; Tit. 3:5,7 [b]Mat. 20:28; Eph. 1:7; Col. 1:14; 1 Tim. 2:6; Heb. 9:12; 1 Pet. 1:18
25 [a]Lev. 16:15; 1 John 2:2 & 4:10 [b]Col. 1:20 [c]Acts 17:30; Heb. 9:15 [1]Or, *foreordained* [2]Or, *passing over*
27 [a]ch. 2:17,23; 1 Cor. 1:29; Eph. 2:9
28 [a]ver. 20-22; Gal. 2:16
30 [a]ch. 10:12; Gal. 3:8,20
4:1 [a]Is. 51:2; Mat. 3:9; John 8:33; 2 Cor. 11:22
2 [a]ch. 3:20,27
3 [a]Gen. 15:6; Gal. 3:6; Jas. 2:23
4 [a]ch. 11:6
5 [a]Josh. 24:2
7 [a]Ps. 32:1,2
11 [a]Gen. 17:10 [b]ver. 12,16; Luke 19:9; Gal. 3:7

27 [a]Where *is* boasting then? It is ex- G
cluded. By what law? of works? Nay: but
by the law of faith.
28 Therefore we conclude [a]that a man W
is justified by faith without the deeds of
the law.
29 *Is he* the God of the Jews only? *is
he* not also of the Gentiles? Yes, of the
Gentiles also:
30 Seeing [a]*it is* one God, which shall
justify the circumcision by faith, and uncircumcision through faith.
31 Do we then make void the law
through faith? God forbid: yea, we establish the law.

Abraham saved by faith

4 WHAT SHALL we say then that G
[a]Abraham our father, as pertaining
to the flesh, hath found?
2 For if Abraham were [a]justified by
works, he hath *whereof* to glory; but not
before God.
3 For what saith the scripture? [a]Abra- F
ham believed God, and it was counted
unto him for righteousness.
4 Now [a]to him that worketh is the reward not reckoned of grace, but of debt.
5 But to him that worketh not, but believeth on him that justifieth [a]the ungodly, his faith is counted for righteousness.
6 Even as David also describeth the L
blessedness of the man, unto whom God
imputeth righteousness without works,
7 *Saying,* [a]Blessed *are* they whose iniquities are forgiven, and whose sins are
covered.
8 Blessed *is* the man to whom the Lord
will not impute sin.
9 *Cometh* this blessedness then upon
the circumcision *only,* or upon the uncircumcision also? for we say that faith was
reckoned to Abraham for righteousness.
10 How was it then reckoned? when
he was in circumcision, or in uncircumcision? Not in circumcision, but in uncircumcision.
11 And [a]he received the sign of circumcision, a seal of the righteousness of
the faith which *he had yet* being uncircumcised: that [b]he might be the father of

C *Ro 3:9–12* ◀▶ *Ro 6:16–17*
A *Ro 3:9–12* ◀▶ *Ro 3:22*
G *Jn 10:1* ◀▶ *Ro 3:27*
F *Ro 1:16* ◀▶ *Ro 4:3*
L *Ac 28:28* ◀▶ *Ro 4:6*
W *Ro 1:16* ◀▶ *Ro 3:28–30*
A *Ro 3:19* ◀▶ *Ro 3:23*
A *Ro 3:22* ◀▶ *Ro 5:12*
D *Ac 20:28* ◀▶ *Ro 8:32*
K *Ro 3:3–4* ◀▶ *Ro 5:1–2*

G *Ro 3:20* ◀▶ *Ro 4:1–4*
W *Ro 3:21–24* ◀▶ *Ro 5:18*
G *Ro 3:27* ◀▶ *Ro 4:14*
F *Ro 3:21–30* ◀▶ *Ro 4:16*
L *Ro 3:21–30* ◀▶ *Ro 4:12*

...n them that believe, though they be not circumcised; that righteousness might be imputed unto them also:

L 12 And the father of circumcision to them who are not of the circumcision only, but who also walk in the steps of that faith of our father Abraham, which *he had* being *yet* uncircumcised.

M 13 For the promise, that he should be the [a]heir of the world, *was* not to Abraham, or to his seed, through the law, but through the righteousness of faith.

G 14 For [a]if they which are of the law *be* heirs, faith is made void, and the promise made of none effect:

15 Because [a]the law worketh wrath: for where no law is, *there is* no transgression.

F 16 Therefore *it is* of faith, that *it might*
L *be* [a]by grace; [b]to the end the promise might be sure to all the seed; not to that only which is of the law, but to that also which is of the faith of Abraham; [c]who is the father of us all,

17 (As it is written, [a]I have made thee a father of many nations,) [ʼ]before him whom he believed, *even* God, [b]who quickeneth the dead, and calleth those [c]things which be not as though they were.

18 Who against hope believed in hope, that he might become the father of many nations, according to that which was spoken, [a]So shall thy seed be.

19 And being not weak in faith, [a]he considered not his own body now dead, when he was about an hundred years old, neither yet the deadness of Sarah's womb:

20 He staggered not at the promise of God through unbelief; but was strong in faith, giving glory to God;

21 And being fully persuaded that, what he had promised, [a]he was able also to perform.

L *Ro 4:6* ◀▶ *Ro 4:16*
M *Ac 17:7* ◀▶ *Ro 8:17–18*
G *Ro 4:1–4* ◀▶ *Ro 8:9*
F *Ro 4:3* ◀▶ *Ro 4:23–24*
L *Ro 4:12* ◀▶ *Ro 4:22–24*

13 [a]Gen. 17:4; Gal. 3:29
14 [a]Gal. 3:18
15 [a]ch. 3:20 & 7:8,10,11; 1 Cor. 15:56; 2 Cor. 3:7,9; Gal. 3:10; 1 John 3:4
16 [a]ch. 3:24 [b]Gal. 3:22 [c]Is. 51:2; ch. 9:8
17 [a]Gen. 17:5 [b]ch. 8:11; Eph. 2:1,5 [c]ch. 9:26; 1 Cor. 1:28; 1 Pet. 2:10 [ʼ]Or, *like unto him*
18 [a]Gen. 15:5
19 [a]Gen. 17:17 & 18:11; Heb. 11:11
21 [a]Ps. 115:3; Luke 1:37; Heb. 11:19
23 [a]ch. 15:4; 1 Cor. 10:6
24 [a]Acts 2:24
25 [a]Is. 53:5,6; ch. 3:25; Gal. 1:4; Heb. 9:28 [b]1 Cor. 15:17; 1 Pet. 1:21
5:1 [a]Is. 32:17; John 16:33 [b]Eph. 2:14
2 [a]John 10:9; Eph. 2:18 [b]1 Cor. 15:1 [c]Heb. 3:6
3 [a]Mat. 5:11; Acts 5:41; 2 Cor. 12:10; Phil. 2:17; Jas. 1:2 [b]Jas. 1:3
4 [a]Jas. 1:12
5 [a]Phil. 1:20 [b]2 Cor. 1:22; Eph. 1:13
6 [a]ch. 4:25 [ʼ]Or, *according to the time*
8 [a]John 15:13
9 [a]Eph. 2:13; 1 John 1:7 [b]1 Thes. 1:10
10 [a]ch. 8:32 [b]2 Cor. 5:18; Eph. 2:16

22 And therefore it was imputed to him for righteousness. L

23 Now [a]it was not written for his sake alone, that it was imputed to him; F

24 But for us also, to whom it shall be imputed, if we believe [a]on him that raised up Jesus our Lord from the dead;

25 [a]Who was delivered for our offences, and [b]was raised again for our justification.

Results of justification by faith

5 THEREFORE [a]BEING justified by F
faith, we have [b]peace with God K
through our Lord Jesus Christ: L

2 [a]By whom also we have access by faith into this grace [b]wherein we stand, and [c]rejoice in hope of the glory of God.

3 And not only *so,* but [a]we glory in J
tribulations also: [b]knowing that tribulation worketh patience;

4 [a]And patience, experience; and experience, hope:

5 [a]And hope maketh not ashamed; E
[b]because the love of God is shed abroad F
in our hearts by the Holy Ghost which is J
given unto us.

6 For when we were yet without L
strength, [ʼ]in due time [a]Christ died for the ungodly.

7 For scarcely for a righteous man will one die: yet peradventure for a good man some would even dare to die.

8 But [a]God commendeth his love toward us, in that, while we were yet sinners, Christ died for us.

9 Much more then, being now justified K
[a]by his blood, we shall be saved [b]from wrath through him.

10 For [a]if, when we were enemies, [b]we were reconciled to God by the death

L *Ro 4:16* ◀▶ *Ro 5:1*
F *Ro 4:16* ◀▶ *Ro 5:1–2*
F *Ro 4:23–24* ◀▶ *Ro 8:24*
K *Ro 3:24–25* ◀▶ *Ro 5:9–11*
L *Ro 4:22–24* ◀▶ *Ro 5:6–21*
J *Ac 6:15* ◀▶ *Ro 12:12*
E *Ro 1:11* ◀▶ *Ro 8:2*
F *Ac 13:52* ◀▶ *Ro 8:6*
J *Ac 13:52* ◀▶ *Ro 8:1*
L *Ro 5:1* ◀▶ *Ro 8:32*
K *Ro 5:1–2* ◀▶ *Ro 5:15–21*

4:13 Abraham was promised abundant offspring and given the land as his inheritance, not because of the law, but because of his faith in God (see Ge 15:4). This verse acknowledges God's promise made to Abraham and foresees the deliverance of the whole world into the hands of Jesus Christ as Messiah and "heir of the world" (4:13).

of his Son, much more, being reconciled, we shall be saved [c]by his life.

11 And not only *so,* but we also [a]joy in God through our Lord Jesus Christ, by whom we have now received the [1]atonement.

Christ the basis of our salvation

A 12 Wherefore, as [a]by one man sin entered into the world, and [b]death by sin; and so death passed upon all men, [1]for that all have sinned:

13 (For until the law sin was in the world: but [a]sin is not imputed when there is no law.

14 Nevertheless death reigned from Adam to Moses, even over them that had not sinned after the similitude of Adam's transgression, [a]who is the figure of him that was to come.

K 15 But not as the offence, so also *is* the free gift. For if through the offence of one many be dead, much more the grace of God, and the gift by grace, *which is* by one man, Jesus Christ, hath abounded [a]unto many.

16 And not as *it was* by one that sinned, *so is* the gift: for the judgment *was* by one to condemnation, but the free gift *is* of many offences unto justification.

17 For if [1]by one man's offence death reigned by one; much more they which receive abundance of grace and of the gift of righteousness shall reign in life by one, Jesus Christ.)

W 18 Therefore as [1]by the offence of one *judgment came* upon all men to condemnation; even so [2]by the righteousness of one *the free gift came* [a]upon all men unto justification of life.

19 For as by one man's disobedience many were made sinners, so by the obedience of one shall many be made righteous.

20 Moreover [a]the law entered, that the offence might abound. But where sin abounded, grace did much [b]more abound:

21 That as sin hath reigned unto death, even so might grace reign through righteousness unto eternal life by Jesus Christ our Lord.

Believers dead to sin

6 WHAT SHALL we say then? [a]Shall we continue in sin, that grace may abound? S

2 God forbid. How shall we, that are [a]dead to sin, live any longer therein?

3 Know ye not, that [a]so many of us as [1]were baptized into Jesus Christ [b]were baptized into his death?

4 Therefore we are [a]buried with him by baptism into death: that [b]like as Christ was raised up from the dead by [c]the glory of the Father, [d]even so we also should walk in newness of life.

5 [a]For if we have been planted together in the likeness of his death, we shall be also *in the likeness* of *his* resurrection:

6 Knowing this, that [a]our old man is crucified with *him,* that [b]the body of sin might be destroyed, that henceforth we should not serve sin. S

7 For [a]he that is dead is [1]freed from sin.

8 Now [a]if we be dead with Christ, we believe that we shall also live with him:

9 Knowing that [a]Christ being raised from the dead dieth no more; death hath no more dominion over him.

10 For in that he died, [a]he died unto sin once: but in that he liveth, [b]he liveth unto God.

11 Likewise reckon ye also yourselves to be [a]dead indeed unto sin, but [b]alive unto God through Jesus Christ our Lord. S

12 [a]Let not sin therefore reign in your mortal body, that ye should obey it in the lusts thereof.

13 Neither yield ye your [a]members *as* [1]instruments of unrighteousness unto sin: but [b]yield yourselves unto God, as those that are alive from the dead, and your members *as* instruments of righteousness unto God.

14 For [a]sin shall not have dominion over you: for ye are not under the law, but under grace.

Slaves to righteousness

15 What then? shall we sin, [a]because we are not under the law, but under grace? God forbid.

10 [c]John 14:19
11 [a]Gal. 4:9 [1]Or, *reconciliation*
12 [a]Gen. 3:6; 1 Cor. 15:21 [b]Gen. 2:17 [1]Or, *in whom*
13 [a]1 John 3:4
14 [a]1 Cor. 15:21
15 [a]Is. 53:11
17 [1]Or, *by one offence*
18 [a]John 12:32; Heb. 2:9 [1]Or, *by one offence* [2]Or, *by one righteousness*
20 [a]John 15:22; Gal. 3:19 [b]Luke 7:47
6:1 [a]ch. 3:8
2 [a]Gal. 2:19; Col. 3:3
3 [a]Gal. 3:27 [b]1 Cor. 15:29 [1]Or, *are*
4 [a]Col. 2:12 [b]ch. 8:11; 1 Cor. 6:14 [c]John 2:11 [d]Gal. 6:15
5 [a]Phil. 3:10
6 [a]Gal. 2:20 [b]Col. 2:11
7 [a]1 Pet. 4:1 [1]Gk. *justified*
8 [a]2 Tim. 2:11
9 [a]Rev. 1:18
10 [a]Heb. 9:27 [b]Luke 20:38
11 [a]ver. 2 [b]Gal. 2:19
12 [a]Ps. 19:13
13 [a]ch. 7:5; Col. 3:5; Jas. 4:1 [b]ch. 12:1; 1 Pet. 2:24 & 4:2 [1]Gk. *arms,* or, *weapons*
14 [a]ch. 7:4,6 & 8:2; Gal. 5:18
15 [a]1 Cor. 9:21

A *Ro 3:23* ◀ ▶ *Ro 8:5–9*
K *Ro 5:9–11* ◀ ▶ *Ro 7:24–25*
W *Ro 3:28–30* ◀ ▶ *Ro 9:33*
S *Ro 2:6–13* ◀ ▶ *Ro 6:6*
S *Ro 6:1–2* ◀ ▶ *Ro 6:11–23*
S *Ro 6:6* ◀ ▶ *Ro 7:4*

C 16 Know ye not, that [a]to whom ye yield yourselves servants to obey, his servants ye are to whom ye obey; whether of sin unto death, or of obedience unto righteousness?

17 But God be thanked, that ye were the servants of sin, but ye have obeyed from the heart [a]that form of doctrine [1]which was delivered you.

18 Being then [a]made free from sin, ye became the servants of righteousness.

19 I speak after the manner of men because of the infirmity of your flesh: for as ye have yielded your members servants to uncleanness and to iniquity unto iniquity; even so now yield your members servants to righteousness unto holiness.

C 20 For when ye were [a]the servants of sin, ye were free [1]from righteousness.

21 [a]What fruit had ye then in those things whereof ye are now ashamed? for [b]the end of those things *is* death.

22 But now [a]being made free from sin, and become servants to God, ye have your fruit unto holiness, and the end everlasting life.

H 23 For [a]the wages of sin *is* death; but [b]the gift of God *is* eternal life through Jesus Christ our Lord.

Married to Christ

7 KNOW YE not, brethren, (for I speak to them that know the law,) how that the law hath dominion over a man as long as he liveth?

2 For [a]the woman which hath an husband is bound by the law to *her* husband so long as he liveth; but if the husband be dead, she is loosed from the law of *her* husband.

3 So then [a]if, while *her* husband liveth, she be married to another man, she shall be called an adulteress: but if her husband be dead, she is free from that law; so that she is no adulteress, though she be married to another man.

S 4 Wherefore, my brethren, ye also are become [a]dead to the law by the body of Christ; that ye should be married to another, *even* to him who is raised from the dead, that we should [b]bring forth fruit unto God.

5 For when we were in the flesh, the [1]motions of sins, which were by the law, [a]did work in our members [b]to bring forth fruit unto death. C

6 But now we are delivered from the law, [1]that being dead wherein we were held; that we should serve [a]in newness of spirit, and not *in* the oldness of the letter. L W

The Christian struggle

7 What shall we say then? *Is* the law sin? God forbid. Nay, [a]I had not known sin, but by the law: for I had not known [1]lust, except the law had said, [b]Thou shalt not covet.

8 But [a]sin, taking occasion by the commandment, wrought in me all manner of concupiscence. For [b]without the law sin *was* dead.

9 For I was alive without the law once: but when the commandment came, sin revived, and I died. C

10 And the commandment, [a]which *was ordained* to life, I found *to be* unto death.

11 For sin, taking occasion by the commandment, deceived me, and by it slew *me*.

12 Wherefore [a]the law *is* holy, and the commandment holy, and just, and good.

13 Was then that which is good made death unto me? God forbid. But sin, that it might appear sin, working death in me by that which is good; that sin by the commandment might become exceeding sinful.

14 For we know that the law is spiritual: but I am carnal, [a]sold under sin. C

15 For that which I do I [1]allow not: for [a]what I would, that do I not; but what I hate, that do I.

16 If then I do that which I would not, I consent unto the law that *it is* good.

17 Now then it is no more I that do it, but sin that dwelleth in me.

18 For I know that [a]in me (that is, in my flesh,) dwelleth no good thing: for to will is present with me; but *how* to perform that which is good I find not.

19 For the good that I would I do not: but the evil which I would not, that I do.

20 Now if I do that I would not, it is no

16 [a]Mat. 6:24; John 8:34; 2 Pet. 2:19
17 [a]2 Tim. 1:13 [1]Gk. *whereto ye were delivered*
18 [a]John 8:32; 1 Cor. 7:22; Gal. 5:1; 1 Pet. 2:16
20 [a]John 8:34 [1]Gk. *to righteousness*
21 [a]ch. 7:5 [b]ch. 1:32
22 [a]John 8:32
23 [a]Gen. 2:17; ch. 5:12; Jas. 1:15 [b]ch. 2:7; 1 Pet. 1:4
7:2 [a]1 Cor. 7:39
3 [a]Mat. 5:32
4 [a]Gal. 2:19 & 5:18; Col. 2:14 [b]Gal. 5:22
5 [a]ch. 6:13 [b]ch. 6:21; Gal. 5:19; Jas. 1:15 [1]Gk. *passions*
6 [a]ch. 2:29; 2 Cor. 3:6 [1]Or, *being dead to that;* see ver. 4; ch. 6:2
7 [a]ch. 3:20 [b]Ex. 20:17; Deut. 5:21; Acts 20:33 [1]Or, *concupiscence*
8 [a]ch. 4:15 [b]1 Cor. 15:56
10 [a]Lev. 18:5; Ezek. 20:11,13,21; 2 Cor. 3:7
12 [a]Ps. 19:8 & 119:38; 1 Tim. 1:8
14 [a]2 Ki. 17:17
15 [a]Gal. 5:17 [1]Gk. *know;* see Ps. 1:6
18 [a]Gen. 6:5 & 8:21

C *Ro 3:17–20* ◀▶ *Ro 6:20*
C *Ro 6:16–17* ◀▶ *Ro 7:5*
H *Ro 3:8* ◀▶ *Ro 9:22*
S *Ro 6:11–23* ◀▶ *Ro 8:1–14*

C *Ro 6:20* ◀▶ *Ro 7:9–11*
L *Ac 21:4* ◀▶ *Ro 8:1–14*
W *Ro 1:11* ◀▶ *Ro 8:1–16*
C *Ro 7:5* ◀▶ *Ro 7:14–25*
C *Ro 7:9–11* ◀▶ *Ro 8:5–8*

more I that do it, but sin that dwelleth in me.

21 I find then a law, that, when I would do good, evil is present with me.

22 For I [a]delight in the law of God after [b]the inward man:

23 But [a]I see another law in [b]my members, warring against the law of my mind, and bringing me into captivity to the law of sin which is in my members.

K 24 O wretched man that I am! who shall deliver me from [1]the body of this death?

25 [a]I thank God through Jesus Christ our Lord. So then with the mind I myself serve the law of God; but with the flesh the law of sin.

Life in the Spirit

J L R S W K S E H M **8** *THERE IS* therefore now no condemnation to them which are in Christ Jesus, who [a]walk not after the flesh, but after the Spirit.

2 For [a]the law of [b]the Spirit of life in Christ Jesus hath made me free from [c]the law of sin and death.

3 For [a]what the law could not do, in that it was weak through the flesh, [b]God sending his own Son in the likeness of sinful flesh, and [1]for sin, condemned sin in the flesh:

4 That the righteousness of the law might be fulfilled in us, [a]who walk not after the flesh, but after the Spirit.

A C 5 For [a]they that are after the flesh do mind the things of the flesh; but they that are after the Spirit [b]the things of the Spirit.

6 For [a]to[1] be carnally minded *is* death; but [2]to be spiritually minded *is* life and peace. F

7 Because [a]the[1] carnal mind *is* enmity against God: for it is not subject to the law of God, [b]neither indeed can be.

8 So then they that are in the flesh cannot please God.

9 But ye are not in the flesh, but in the Spirit, if so be that the Spirit of God dwell in you. Now if any man have not [a]the Spirit of Christ, he is none of his. G O

10 And if Christ *be* in you, the body *is* dead because of sin; but the Spirit *is* life because of righteousness.

11 But if the Spirit of [a]him that raised up Jesus from the dead dwell in you, [b]he that raised up Christ from the dead shall also quicken your mortal bodies [1]by his Spirit that dwelleth in you. F H

12 [a]Therefore, brethren, we are debtors, not to the flesh, to live after the flesh.

13 For [a]if ye live after the flesh, ye shall die: but if ye through the Spirit do [b]mortify the deeds of the body, ye shall live.

14 For [a]as many as are led by the Spirit of God, they are the sons of God. O

15 For [a]ye have not received the spirit of bondage again [b]to fear; but ye have received the [c]Spirit of adoption, whereby we cry, [d]Abba, Father. E J

16 [a]The Spirit itself beareth witness with our spirit, that we are the children of God:

22 [a]Ps. 1:2 [b]2 Cor. 4:16; Eph. 3:16; Col. 3:9,10
23 [a]Gal. 5:17 [b]ch. 6:13,19
24 [1]Or, *this body of death*
25 [a]1 Cor. 15:57
8:1 [a]Gal. 5:16
2 [a]ch. 6:18,22 [b]1 Cor. 15:45 [c]ch. 7:24,25
3 [a]Acts 13:39; Heb. 7:18 [b]2 Cor. 5:21; Gal. 3:13 [1]Or, *by a sacrifice for sin*
4 [a]ver. 1
5 [a]John 3:6 [b]Gal. 5:22
6 [a]Gal. 6:8 [1]Gk. *the minding of the flesh* [2]Gk. *the minding of the Spirit*
7 [a]Jas. 4:4 [b]1 Cor. 2:14 [1]Gk. *the minding of the flesh*
9 [a]John 3:34; Gal. 4:6
11 [a]Acts 2:24 [b]1 Cor. 6:14; 2 Cor. 4:14 [1]Or, *because of his Spirit*
12 [a]ch. 6:7,14
13 [a]Gal. 6:8 [b]Eph. 4:22
14 [a]Gal. 5:18
15 [a]1 Cor. 2:12; Heb. 2:15 [b]2 Tim. 1:7; 1 John 4:18 [c]Is. 56:5 [d]Mark 14:36
16 [a]Eph. 1:13

K *Ro 5:15–21* ◀▶ *Ro 8:1–4*
J *Ro 5:5* ◀▶ *Ro 8:15*
L *Ro 7:6* ◀▶ *Ro 8:26–27*
R *Jn 6:63* ◀▶ *1Co 6:11*
S *Ro 1:4* ◀▶ *Ro 12:1–2*
W *Ro 7:6* ◀▶ *Ro 12:6–8*
K *Ro 7:24–25* ◀▶ *Ro 8:33–39*
S *Ro 7:4* ◀▶ *Ro 11:20–22*
E *Ro 5:5* ◀▶ *Ro 8:15*
H *Ro 1:4* ◀▶ *Ro 8:11*
M *Ro 1:11* ◀▶ *Ro 8:26–27*
A *Ro 5:12* ◀▶ *2Co 5:14*
C *Ro 7:14–25* ◀▶ *1Co 2:14*

F *Ro 5:5* ◀▶ *Ro 8:23*
G *Ro 4:14* ◀▶ *Ro 9:15–16*
O *Ac 4:11–12* ◀▶ *Ro 8:14*
F *Ac 28:20* ◀▶ *Ro 8:17–25*
H *Ro 8:2* ◀▶ *Ro 15:19*
O *Ro 8:9* ◀▶ *Ro 9:15–16*
E *Ro 8:2* ◀▶ *Ro 8:23*
J *Ro 8:1* ◀▶ *Ro 14:17*

8:11 This prophetic statement affirms the resurrection of our bodies because of the indwelling of the Holy Spirit.

8:16–25 Paul affirms that "we are the children of God" (8:16) because of our identification with Jesus Christ. Whatever sufferings we may face cannot compare to "the glory which shall be revealed in us" (8:18). Paul then tells us that the whole of creation awaits the day of renewal and deliverance from sin's effects. This renewal for believers will come with "the redemption of our body" (8:23) when Jesus raptures the saints to heaven and changes the bodies of the living and the departed saints into their glorious resurrection bodies—bodies like Jesus had after his resurrection from the grave (see 1Co 15:52).

F M T 17 And if children, then heirs; [a]heirs of God, and joint-heirs with Christ; [b]if so be that we suffer with *him,* that we may be also glorified together.

The future glory

18 For I reckon that [a]the sufferings of this present time *are* not worthy *to be compared* with the glory which shall be revealed in us.

19 For [a]the earnest expectation of the creature waiteth for the manifestation of the sons of God.

20 For [a]the creature was made subject to vanity, not willingly, but by reason of him who hath subjected *the same* in hope,

21 Because the creature itself also shall be delivered from the bondage of corruption into the glorious liberty of the children of God.

22 For we know that [1]the whole creation [a]groaneth and travaileth in pain together until now.

B E F 23 And not only *they,* but ourselves also, which have [a]the firstfruits of the Spirit, [b]even we ourselves groan within ourselves, [c]waiting for the adoption, *to wit,* the [d]redemption of our body.

F 24 For we are saved by hope: but [a]hope that is seen is not hope: for what a man seeth, why doth he yet hope for?

25 But if we hope for that we see not, *then* do we with patience wait for *it.*

E L M 26 Likewise the Spirit also helpeth our infirmities: for [a]we know not what we should pray for as we ought: but [b]the Spirit itself maketh intercession for us with groanings which cannot be uttered.

E 27 And [a]he that searcheth the hearts knoweth what *is* the mind of the Spirit, [1]because he maketh intercession for the saints [b]according to *the will of* God.

A U 28 And we know that all things work together for good to them that love God, to them [a]who are the called according to *his* purpose.

29 For whom [a]he did foreknow, [b]he also did predestinate [c]*to be* conformed to the image of his Son, [d]that he might be the firstborn among many brethren.

30 Moreover whom he did predestinate, them he also [a]called: and whom he called, them he also [b]justified: and whom he justified, them he also [c]glorified.

L S V 31 What shall we then say to these things? [a]If God *be* for us, who *can be* against us?

D L 32 [a]He that spared not his own Son, but [b]delivered him up for us all, how shall he not with him also freely give us all things?

K 33 Who shall lay any thing to the charge of God's elect? [a]*It is* God that justifieth.

34 [a]Who *is* he that condemneth? *It is* Christ that died, yea rather, that is risen again, [b]who is even at the right hand of God, [c]who also maketh intercession for us.

V 35 Who shall separate us from the love of Christ? *shall* tribulation, or distress, or persecution, or famine, or nakedness, or peril, or sword?

36 As it is written, [a]For thy sake we are killed all the day long; we are accounted as sheep for the slaughter.

37 [a]Nay, in all these things we are more than conquerors through him that loved us.

38 For I am persuaded, that neither death, nor life, nor angels, nor [a]principalities, nor powers, nor things present, nor things to come,

39 Nor height, nor depth, nor any other creature, shall be able to separate us from the love of God, which is in Christ Jesus our Lord.

17 [a]Acts 26:18 [b]Phil. 1:29
18 [a]2 Cor. 4:17; 1 Pet. 1:6
19 [a]2 Pet. 3:13
20 [a]Gen. 3:19
22 [a]Jer. 12:11 [1]Or, *every creature*
23 [a]2 Cor. 5:5; Eph. 1:14 [b]2 Cor. 5:2 [c]Luke 20:36 [d]Luke 21:28; Eph. 4:30
24 [a]2 Cor. 5:7; Heb. 11:1
26 [a]Mat. 20:22; Jas. 4:3 [b]Eph. 6:18
27 [a]1 Chr. 28:9; Acts 1:24 [b]1 John 5:14 [1]Or, *that*
28 [a]2 Tim. 1:9
29 [a]2 Tim. 2:19 [b]Eph. 1:5 [c]2 Cor. 3:18; 1 John 3:2 [d]Col. 1:15; Heb. 1:6
30 [a]1 Pet. 2:9 [b]1 Cor. 6:11 [c]John 17:22; Eph. 2:6
31 [a]Num. 14:9; Ps. 118:6
32 [a]ch. 5:6,10 [b]ch. 4:25
33 [a]Is. 50:8,9; Rev. 12:10
34 [a]Job 34:29 [b]Mark 16:19; Col. 3:1; Heb. 1:3 [c]Heb. 7:25 & 9:24; 1 John 2:1
36 [a]Ps. 44:22; 2 Cor. 4:11
37 [a]1 Cor. 15:57; 1 John 4:4
38 [a]Eph. 1:21

F *Ro 8:11* ◀▶ *1Co 6:14*
M *Ro 4:13* ◀▶ *Ro 14:11*
T *Jn 3:8* ◀▶ *1Co 15:50–55*
B *Ac 19:1–7* ◀▶ *Ro 15:13*
E *Ro 8:15* ◀▶ *Ro 8:26–27*
F *Ro 8:6* ◀▶ *Ro 14:17*
F *Ro 5:1–2* ◀▶ *Ro 9:30–33*
E *Ro 8:23* ◀▶ *Ro 9:1*
L *Ro 8:1–14* ◀▶ *Ro 9:1*
M *Ro 8:2* ◀▶ *Ro 15:13*
E *Ac 15:18* ◀▶ *1Co 4:5*

A *Isa 58:11* ◀▶ *1Th 5:18*
U *Jn 15:11* ◀▶ *1Co 2:9*
L *Jn 16:24* ◀▶ *1Co 10:13*
S *Ac 27:23–24* ◀▶ *Heb 11:33–34*
V *Ac 18:10* ◀▶ *Ro 8:35–39*
D *Ro 3:24–25* ◀▶ *1Co 5:7*
L *Ro 5:6–21* ◀▶ *Ro 10:4–13*
K *Ro 8:1–4* ◀▶ *Ro 9:15*
V *Ro 8:31* ◀▶ *1Co 15:57*

God's righteousness and mercy

9 I [a]SAY the truth in Christ, I lie not, my conscience also bearing me witness in the Holy Ghost,

2 [a]That I have great heaviness and continual sorrow in my heart.

3 For [a]I could wish that myself were [1]accursed from Christ for my brethren, my kinsmen according to the flesh:

4 Who are Israelites; [a]to whom *pertaineth* the adoption, and [b]the glory, and [c]the [1]covenants, and [d]the giving of the law, and [e]the service *of God,* and [f]the promises;

5 [a]Whose *are* the fathers, and [b]of whom as concerning the flesh Christ *came,* [c]who is over all, God blessed for ever. Amen.

6 [a]Not as though the word of God hath taken none effect. For [b]they *are* not all Israel, which are of Israel:

7 [a]Neither, because they are the seed of Abraham, *are they* all children: but, In [b]Isaac shall thy seed be called.

8 That is, They which are the children of the flesh, these *are* not the children of God: but [a]the children of the promise are counted for the seed.

9 For this *is* the word of promise, [a]At this time will I come, and Sarah shall have a son.

10 And not only *this;* but when [a]Rebecca also had conceived by one, *even* by our father Isaac;

11 (For *the children* being not yet born, neither having done any good or evil, that the purpose of God according to election might stand, not of works, but of [a]him that calleth;)

12 It was said unto her, [a]The [1]elder shall serve the [2]younger.

13 As it is written, [a]Jacob have I loved, but Esau have I hated.

14 What shall we say then? [a]*Is there* unrighteousness with God? God forbid.

E *Ro 8:26–27* ◀▶ *Ro 15:18–19*
L *Ro 8:26–27* ◀▶ *Ro 12:6–8*
I *Ac 2:29–31* ◀▶ *Ro 9:25–28*

9:1 [a]2 Cor. 1:23; Gal. 1:20; 1 Tim. 2:7
2 [a]ch. 10:1
3 [a]Ex. 32:32 [1]Or, *separated*
4 [a]Ex. 4:22; Deut. 14:1 [b]1 Sam. 4:21; 1 Ki. 8:11 [c]Acts 3:25 [d]Ps. 147:19 [e]Heb. 9:1 [f]Acts 13:32; Eph. 2:12 [1]Or, *testaments*
5 [a]Deut. 10:15 [b]Luke 3:23 [c]Jer. 23:6; Heb. 1:8
6 [a]Num. 23:19 [b]John 8:39; Gal. 6:16
7 [a]Gal. 4:23 [b]Gen. 21:12
8 [a]Gal. 4:28
9 [a]Gen. 18:10
10 [a]Gen. 25:21
11 [a]ch. 4:17
12 [a]Gen. 25:23 [1]Or, *greater* [2]Or, *lesser*
13 [a]Mal. 1:2,3; Mat. 10:37
14 [a]Deut. 32:4; Job 8:3
15 [a]Ex. 33:19
17 [a]Gal. 3:8 [b]Ex. 9:16
19 [a]2 Chr. 20:6; Dan. 4:35
20 [a]Is. 29:16 [1]Or, *answerest again,* or, *disputest with God?*
21 [a]Prov. 16:4 [b]2 Tim. 2:20
22 [a]1 Thes. 5:9 [b]1 Pet. 2:8 [1]Or, *made up*
23 [a]Col. 1:27 [b]ch. 8:28-30
24 [a]ch. 3:29
25 [a]Hos. 2:23
26 [a]Hos. 1:10

15 For he saith to Moses, [a]I will have mercy on whom I will have mercy, and I will have compassion on whom I will have compassion.

16 So then *it is* not of him that willeth, nor of him that runneth, but of God that showeth mercy.

17 For [a]the scripture saith unto Pharaoh, [b]Even for this same purpose have I raised thee up, that I might show my power in thee, and that my name might be declared throughout all the earth.

18 Therefore hath he mercy on whom he will *have mercy,* and whom he will he hardeneth.

19 Thou wilt say then unto me, Why doth he yet find fault? For [a]who hath resisted his will?

20 Nay but, O man, who art thou that [1]repliest against God? [a]Shall the thing formed say to him that formed *it,* Why hast thou made me thus?

21 Hath not the [a]potter power over the clay, of the same lump to make [b]one vessel unto honour, and another unto dishonour?

22 *What* if God, willing to show *his* wrath, and to make his power known, endured with much longsuffering [a]the vessels of wrath [b]fitted[1] to destruction:

23 And that he might make known [a]the riches of his glory on the vessels of mercy, which he had [b]afore prepared unto glory,

24 Even us, whom he hath called, [a]not of the Jews only, but also of the Gentiles?

25 As he saith also in Osee, [a]I will call them my people, which were not my people; and her beloved, which was not beloved.

26 [a]And it shall come to pass, *that* in the place where it was said unto them, Ye

G *Ro 8:9* ◀▶ *Ro 9:31–32*
K *Ro 8:33–39* ◀▶ *Ro 9:18*
O *Ro 8:14* ◀▶ *Ro 10:3–4*
K *Ro 9:15* ◀▶ *Ro 9:21*
K *Ro 9:18* ◀▶ *Ro 9:23*
H *Ro 6:23* ◀▶ *Ro 11:20–22*
K *Ro 9:21* ◀▶ *Ro 10:4*
I *Ro 9:4* ◀▶ *Ro 10:21*
R *Lk 23:28* ◀▶ *Ro 11:1–5*

9:25–30 Paul reaffirms Hosea's prophecies of Israel's rebirth as a nation in the last days (see Hos 2:23), declaring that, after repentance, Israel shall be "called the children of the living God" (9:26). He also refers to the prophecies of Isaiah who declared that only a small remnant of Israel would be saved and return (see Isa 10:22).

are not my people; there shall they be called the children of the living God.

27 Esaias also crieth concerning Israel, [a]Though the number of the children of Israel be as the sand of the sea, [b]a remnant shall be saved:

28 For he will finish [1]the work, and cut *it* short in righteousness: [a]because a short work will the Lord make upon the earth.

29 And as Esaias said before, [a]Except the Lord of Sabaoth had left us a seed, [b]we had been as Sodoma, and been made like unto Gomorrha.

The gospel offered to the Jews

G F 30 What shall we say then? [a]That the Gentiles, which followed not after righteousness, have attained to righteousness, [b]even the righteousness which is of faith.

G 31 But Israel, [a]which followed after the law of righteousness, [b]hath not attained to the law of righteousness.

32 Wherefore? Because *they sought it* not by faith, but as it were by the works of the law. For [a]they stumbled at that stumblingstone;

W 33 As it is written, [a]Behold, I lay in Zion a stumblingstone and rock of offence: and [b]whosoever believeth on him shall not be [1]ashamed.

G 10 BRETHREN, MY heart's desire and prayer to God for Israel is, that they might be saved.

2 For I bear them record [a]that they have a zeal of God, but not according to knowledge.

O 3 For they being ignorant of [a]God's righteousness, and going about to establish their own [b]righteousness, have not submitted themselves unto the righteousness of God.

F K L 4 For [a]Christ *is* the end of the law for righteousness to every one that believeth.

W 5 For Moses describeth the righteousness which is of the law, [a]That the man which doeth those things shall live by them.

6 But the righteousness which is of faith speaketh on this wise, [a]Say not in thine heart, Who shall ascend into heaven? (that is, to bring Christ down *from above:*) F W

7 Or, Who shall descend into the deep? (that is, to bring up Christ again from the dead.)

8 But what saith it? [a]The word is nigh thee, *even* in thy mouth, and in thy heart: that is, the word of faith, which we preach; T

9 That [a]if thou shalt confess with thy mouth the Lord Jesus, and shalt believe in thine heart that God hath raised him from the dead, thou shalt be saved.

10 For with the heart man believeth unto righteousness; and with the mouth confession is made unto salvation.

11 For the scripture saith, [a]Whosoever believeth on him shall not be ashamed. K

12 For [a]there is no difference between the Jew and the Greek: for [b]the same Lord over all [c]is rich unto all that call upon him.

13 [a]For whosoever shall call [b]upon the name of the Lord shall be saved.

14 How then shall they call on him in whom they have not believed? and how shall they believe in him of whom they have not heard? and how shall they hear [a]without a preacher?

15 And how shall they preach, except they be sent? as it is written, [a]How beautiful are the feet of them that preach the gospel of peace, and bring glad tidings of good things!

16 But they have not all obeyed the gospel. For Esaias saith, [a]Lord, who hath believed [1]our [2]report?

17 So then faith *cometh* by hearing, and hearing by the word of God.

18 But I say, Have they not heard? Yes verily, [a]their sound went into all the earth, [b]and their words unto the ends of the world.

27 [a]Is. 10:22 [b]ch. 11:5
28 [a]Is. 28:22 [1]Or, *the account*
29 [a]Is. 1:9; Lam. 3:22 [b]Is. 13:19; Jer. 50:40
30 [a]ch. 4:11 [b]ch. 1:17
31 [a]ch. 10:2 [b]Gal. 5:4
32 [a]Luke 2:34; 1 Cor. 1:23
33 [a]Ps. 118:22; Is. 8:14 & 28:16; Mat. 21:42; 1 Pet. 2:6-8 [b]ch. 10:11 [1]Or, *confounded*
10:2 [a]Acts 21:20; & 22:3; ch. 9:31; Gal. 1:14
3 [a]ch. 1:17 [b]Phil. 3:9
4 [a]Mat. 5:17; Gal. 3:24
5 [a]Lev. 18:5; Neh. 9:29; Ezek. 20:11; Gal. 3:12
6 [a]Deut. 30:12
8 [a]Deut. 30:14
9 [a]Mat. 10:32; Luke 12:8; Acts 8:37
11 [a]Is. 28:16 & 49:23; Jer. 17:7
12 [a]Acts 15:9; ch. 3:22 [b]Acts 10:36; 1 Tim. 2:5 [c]Eph. 1:7 & 2:4,7
13 [a]Joel 2:32; Acts 2:21 [b]Acts 9:14
14 [a]Tit. 1:3
15 [a]Is. 52:7; Nah. 1:15
16 [a]Is. 53:1; John 12:38 [1]Gk. *the hearing of us* [2]Or, *preaching?*
18 [a]Ps. 19:4; Mat. 24:14; Mark 16:15; Col. 1:6,23 [b]1 Ki. 18:10; Mat. 4:8

G *Ac 28:28* ◄► *Ro 10:19–20*
F *Ro 8:24* ◄► *Ro 10:4*
G *Ro 9:15–16* ◄► *Ro 10:1–3*
W *Ro 5:18* ◄► *Ro 10:4*
G *Ro 9:31–32* ◄► *Ro 11:5–6*
O *Ro 9:15–16* ◄► *1Co 3:11*
F *Ro 9:30–33* ◄► *Ro 10:6–11*
K *Ro 9:23* ◄► *Ro 10:11*
L *Ro 8:32* ◄► *Ro 10:21*
W *Ro 9:33* ◄► *Ro 10:6–13*

F *Ro 10:4* ◄► *Ro 11:23*
W *Ro 10:4* ◄► *2Co 5:14–15*
T *Ro 1:16* ◄► *1Co 14:24–25*
K *Ro 10:4* ◄► *Ro 16:25*

G 19 But I say, Did not Israel know? First Moses saith, [a]I will provoke you to jealousy by *them that are* no people, *and* by a [b]foolish nation I will anger you.

20 But Esaias is very bold, and saith, [a]I was found of them that sought me not; I was made manifest unto them that asked not after me.

I L P 21 But to Israel he saith, [a]All day long I have stretched forth my hands unto a disobedient and gainsaying people.

The remnant of Israel

R **11** I SAY then, [a]Hath God cast away his people? God forbid. For [b]I also am an Israelite, of the seed of Abraham, *of* the tribe of Benjamin.

2 God hath not cast away his people which [a]he foreknew. Wot ye not what the scripture saith [l]of Elias? how he maketh intercession to God against Israel, saying,

3 [a]Lord, they have killed thy prophets, and digged down thine altars; and I am left alone, and they seek my life.

4 But what saith the answer of God unto him? [a]I have reserved to myself seven thousand men, who have not bowed the knee to *the image of* Baal.

G 5 [a]Even so then at this present time also there is a remnant according to the election of grace.

6 And [a]if by grace, then *is it* no more of works: otherwise grace is no more grace. But if *it be* of works, then is it no more grace: otherwise work is no more work.

R 7 What then? [a]Israel hath not obtained that which he seeketh for; but the election hath obtained it, and the rest were [l]blinded

8 (According as it is written, [a]God hath given them the spirit of [l]slumber, [b]eyes that they should not see, and ears that they should not hear;) unto this day.

9 And David saith, [a]Let their table be made a snare, and a trap, and a stumblingblock, and a recompence unto them:

10 [a]Let their eyes be darkened, that they may not see, and bow down their back always.

Israel's future salvation

G 11 I say then, Have they stumbled that they should fall? God forbid: but *rather* [a]through their fall salvation *is come* unto the Gentiles, for to provoke them to jealousy.

I 12 Now if the fall of them *be* the riches of the world, and the [l]diminishing of them the riches of the Gentiles; how much more their fulness?

13 For I speak to you Gentiles, inasmuch as [a]I am the apostle of the Gentiles, I magnify mine office:

14 If by any means I may provoke to emulation *them which are* my flesh, and [a]might save some of them.

G I R 15 For if the casting away of them *be* the reconciling of the world, what *shall*

19 [a]ch. 11:11 [b]Tit. 3:3
20 [a]Is. 65:1
21 [a]Is. 65:2
11:1 [a]1 Sam. 12:22; Jer. 31:37 [b]2 Cor. 11:22; Phil. 3:5
2 [a]ch. 8:29 [l]Gk. *in Elias?*
3 [a]1 Ki. 19:10
4 [a]1 Ki. 19:18
5 [a]ch. 9:27
6 [a]ch. 4:4,5; Deut. 9:4,5; Gal. 5:4
7 [a]ch. 9:31 [l]Or, *hardened*
8 [a]Is. 29:10 [b]Deut. 29:4; Is. 6:9; Jer. 5:21; Ezek. 12:2; Mat. 13:14; John 12:40; Acts 28:26 [l]Or, *remorse*
9 [a]Ps. 69:22
10 [a]Ps. 69:23
11 [a]Acts 13:46 & 18:6; ch. 10:19
12 [l]Or, *decay,* or, *loss*
13 [a]Acts 9:15; Gal. 1:16; Eph. 3:8; 1 Tim. 2:7
14 [a]1 Cor. 9:22; 1 Tim. 4:16; Jas. 5:20

G *Ro 9:30* ◀▶ *Ro 11:11–12*
I *Ro 9:25–28* ◀▶ *Ro 11:12*
L *Ro 10:4–13* ◀▶ *1Co 6:9–11*
P *Lk 15:3–32* ◀▶ *Ro 11:23–24*
R *Ro 9:25–29* ◀▶ *Ro 11:7–12*
G *Ro 10:1–3* ◀▶ *1Co 1:18–21*
R *Ro 11:1–5* ◀▶ *Ro 11:15*
G *Ro 10:19–20* ◀▶ *Ro 11:15–29*
I *Ro 10:21* ◀▶ *Ro 11:15–29*
G *Ro 11:11–12* ◀▶ *Ro 15:12*
I *Ro 11:12* ◀▶ *Ro 11:32*
R *Ro 11:7–12* ◀▶ *Ro 11:17–28*

10:19–21 Paul says that because God provoked Israel to jealousy, many Gentiles had accepted the Messiah that the Jews had rejected, exactly as Isaiah had prophesied centuries earlier (see Isa 65:1).

11:1–5 Paul deals with a profound question regarding Israel's salvation. Despite the widespread rejection of Christ by the Jews, Paul says that some of the Jews secretly accepted faith in him as "a remnant according to the election of grace" (11:5). These were like the faithful Israelites in the days of wicked King Ahab, who refused to worship Baal and secretly worshiped God (see 1Ki 19:18).

11:7–12 Paul discusses the mystery of Israel's rejection of the Gospel. They were spiritually "blinded" (11:7) so that in God's ultimate plan, Christ's rejection by Israel would lead to the salvation of the Gentiles.

11:15–29, 32 Paul affirms that Israel's rejection of Christ as Messiah led ultimately to the reconciling of the Gentiles because of their acceptance of salvation through the atonement of Christ on the cross. Yet Paul warns the Gentiles against pride because even though God gave them Israel's chance for salvation, Israel is still "beloved for the fathers' sakes" (11:28). Paul confirms God's eternal covenant with Israel. Although individual Jews will be judged for their rejection of Christ's salvation, the nation of Israel is still a part of God's eternal plan to bring light to the Gentiles (see Isa 42:6; Ac 13:47).

the receiving *of them be,* but life from the dead?

16 For if [a]the firstfruit *be* holy, the lump *is* also *holy:* and if the root *be* holy, so *are* the branches.

R 17 And if [a]some of the branches be broken off, [b]and thou, being a wild olive tree, wert grafted in ʹamong them, and with them partakest of the root and fatness of the olive tree;

18 [a]Boast not against the branches. But if thou boast, thou bearest not the root, but the root thee.

19 Thou wilt say then, The branches were broken off, that I might be grafted in.

H 20 Well; because of unbelief they were
S broken off, and thou standest by faith. [a]Be not highminded, but [b]fear:

21 For if God spared not the natural branches, *take heed* lest he also spare not thee.

22 Behold therefore the goodness and severity of God: on them which fell, severity; but toward thee, goodness, [a]if thou continue in *his* goodness: otherwise [b]thou also shalt be cut off.

F 23 And they also, [a]if they abide not
P still in unbelief, shall be grafted in: for God is able to graft them in again.

24 For if thou wert cut out of the olive tree which is wild by nature, and wert grafted contrary to nature into a good olive tree: how much more shall these, which be the natural *branches,* be grafted into their own olive tree?

25 For I would not, brethren, that ye should be ignorant of this mystery, lest ye should be [a]wise in your own conceits; that [b]blindness ʹ in part is happened to Israel, [c]until the fulness of the Gentiles be come in.

26 And so all Israel shall be saved: as it is written, [a]There shall come out of Zion the Deliverer, and shall turn away ungodliness from Jacob:

27 [a]For this *is* my covenant unto them, when I shall take away their sins.

28 As concerning the gospel, *they are* enemies for your sakes: but as touching the election, *they are* [a]beloved for the fathers' sakes.

29 For the gifts and calling of God *are* [a]without repentance.

30 For as ye [a]in times past have not ʹbelieved God, yet have now obtained mercy through their unbelief:

31 Even so have these also now not ʹbelieved, that through your mercy they also may obtain mercy.

32 For [a]God hath ʹconcluded them all I
in unbelief, that he might have mercy upon all.

33 O the depth of the riches both of the wisdom and knowledge of God! [a]how unsearchable *are* his judgments, and [b]his ways past finding out!

34 [a]For who hath known the mind of the Lord? or [b]who hath been his counsellor?

35 Or [a]who hath first given to him, and it shall be recompensed unto him again?

36 For [a]of him, and through him, and to him, *are* all things: [b]to ʹwhom *be* glory for ever. Amen.

Christian conduct

12 I [a]BESEECH you therefore, S
brethren, by the mercies of God, S
[b]that ye [c]present your bodies [d]a living sacrifice, holy, acceptable unto God, *which is* your reasonable service.

2 And [a]be not conformed to this world: but [b]be ye transformed by the renewing of your mind, that ye may [c]prove what *is* that good, and acceptable, and perfect, will of God.

3 For I say, [a]through the grace given unto me, to every man that is among you, [b]not to think *of himself* more highly than he ought to think; but to think ʹsoberly, according as God hath dealt [c]to every man the measure of faith.

4 For [a]as we have many members in one body, and all members have not the same office:

5 So [a]we, *being* many, are one body in Christ, and every one members one of another.

16 [a]Lev. 23:10; Jas. 1:18
17 [a]Jer. 11:16 [b]Acts 2:39; Eph. 2:12 ʹOr, *for them*
18 [a]1 Cor. 10:12
20 [a]ch. 12:16 [b]Prov. 28:14; Is. 66:2
22 [a]1 Cor. 15:2; Heb. 3:6 [b]John 15:2
23 [a]2 Cor. 3:16
25 [a]ch. 12:16 [b]2 Cor. 3:14 [c]Luke 21:24; Rev. 7:9 ʹOr, *hardness*
26 [a]Ps. 14:7; Is. 59:20
27 [a]Is. 27:9; Jer. 31:31; Heb. 8:8
28 [a]Deut. 7:8
29 [a]Num. 23:19
30 [a]Eph. 2:2; Col. 3:7 ʹOr, *obeyed*
31 ʹOr, *obeyed*
32 [a]ch. 3:9 ʹOr, *shut them all up together*
33 [a]Ps. 36:6 [b]Job 11:7; Ps. 92:5
34 [a]Job 15:8; Is. 40:13; Jer. 23:18 [b]Job 36:22
35 [a]Job 35:7
36 [a]Col. 1:16 [b]Heb. 13:21; Rev. 1:6 ʹGk. *him*
12:1 [a]2 Cor. 10:1 [b]1 Pet. 2:5 [c]ch. 6 [d]Heb. 10:20
2 [a]1 John 2:15 [b]Eph. 4:23; Col. 3:10 [c]1 Thes. 4:3
3 [a]Gal. 2:9 [b]Prov. 25:27 [c]Eph. 4:7 ʹGk. *to sobriety*
4 [a]1 Cor. 12:12; Eph. 4:16
5 [a]1 Cor. 10:17; Eph. 1:23

R *Ro 11:15* ◀ ▶ *1Th 2:16*
H *Ro 9:22* ◀ ▶ *Ro 12:19*
S *Ro 8:1–14* ◀ ▶ *Ro 12:1–2*
F *Ro 10:6–11* ◀ ▶ *Ro 15:13*
P *Ro 10:21* ◀ ▶ *Jas 5:19–20*

I *Ro 11:15–29* ◀
S *Ro 8:1–16* ◀ ▶ *Ro 15:16*
S *Ro 11:20–22* ◀ ▶ *Ro 12:21*

6 [a]Having then gifts differing [b]according to the grace that is given to us, whether [c]prophecy, *let us prophesy* according to the proportion of faith;

7 Or ministry, *let us wait* on *our* ministering: or [a]he that teacheth, on teaching;

8 Or [a]he that exhorteth, on exhortation: [b]he that [1]giveth, *let him do it* [2]with simplicity; [c]he that ruleth, with diligence; he that showeth mercy, [d]with cheerfulness.

9 [a]*Let* love be without dissimulation. [b]Abhor that which is evil; cleave to that which is good.

10 [a]*Be* kindly affectioned one to another [1]with brotherly love; [b]in honour preferring one another;

11 Not slothful in business; fervent in spirit; serving the Lord;

12 [a]Rejoicing in hope; [b]patient in tribulation; [c]continuing instant in prayer;

13 [a]Distributing to the necessity of saints; [b]given to hospitality.

14 [a]Bless them which persecute you: bless, and curse not.

15 [a]Rejoice with them that do rejoice, and weep with them that weep.

16 [a]*Be* of the same mind one toward another. [b]Mind not high things, but [1]condescend to men of low estate. [c]Be not wise in your own conceits.

17 [a]Recompense to no man evil for evil. [b]Provide things honest in the sight of all men.

18 If it be possible, as much as lieth in you, [a]live peaceably with all men.

19 Dearly beloved, [a]avenge not yourselves, but *rather* give place unto wrath: for it is written, [b]Vengeance *is* mine; I will repay, saith the Lord.

20 [a]Therefore if thine enemy hunger, feed him; if he thirst, give him drink: for in so doing thou shalt heap coals of fire on his head.

21 Be not overcome of evil, but overcome evil with good.

G *Ro 1:11* ◀ ▶ *Ro 15:19*
L *Ro 9:1* ◀ ▶ *1Co 7:40*
T *Ac 28:25* ◀ ▶ *1Co 2:4–16*
W *Ro 8:1–16* ◀ ▶ *Ro 14:17*
J *Ro 5:3* ◀ ▶ *2Co 1:3–10*
M *Ac 8:22* ◀ ▶ *Ro 14:11*
H *Ro 11:20–22* ◀ ▶ *1Co 1:18*

6 [a]1 Cor. 12:4 [b]ver. 3 [c]Acts 11:27
7 [a]Eph. 4:11
8 [a]Acts 15:32 [b]Mat. 6:1-3 [c]Acts 20:28 [d]2 Cor. 9:7 [1]Or, *imparteth* [2]Or, *liberally*
9 [a]1 Tim. 1:5 [b]Ps. 34:14
10 [a]Heb. 13:1 [b]Phil. 2:3 [1]Or, *in the love of the brethren*
12 [a]Luke 10:20 [b]Luke 21:19 [c]Luke 18:1
13 [a]1 Cor. 16:1 [b]1 Tim. 3:2
14 [a]Mat. 5:44
15 [a]1 Cor. 12:26
16 [a]Phil. 2:2 [b]Jer. 45:5 [c]Prov. 3:7 [1]Or, *be contented with mean things*
17 [a]Mat. 5:39 [b]2 Cor. 8:21
18 [a]Heb. 12:14
19 [a]Lev. 19:18 [b]Deut. 32:35
20 [a]Mat. 5:44
13:1 [a]1 Pet. 2:13 [b]Dan. 2:21 [1]Or, *ordered*
2 [a]Tit. 3:1
3 [a]1 Pet. 2:14
5 [a]Eccl. 8:2 [b]1 Pet. 2:19
7 [a]Mat. 22:21; Luke 20:25
8 [a]Gal. 5:14; 1 Tim. 1:5
9 [a]Ex. 20:13; Mat. 19:18 [b]Lev. 19:18; Mark 12:31; Jas. 2:8
10 [a]Mat. 22:40
11 [a]1 Cor. 15:34; Eph. 5:14
12 [a]Eph. 5:11

13

LET EVERY soul [a]be subject unto the higher powers. For [b]there is no power but of God: the powers that be are [1]ordained of God.

2 Whosoever therefore resisteth [a]the power, resisteth the ordinance of God: and they that resist shall receive to themselves damnation.

3 For rulers are not a terror to good works, but to the evil. Wilt thou then not be afraid of the power? [a]do that which is good, and thou shalt have praise of the same:

4 For he is the minister of God to thee for good. But if thou do that which is evil, be afraid; for he beareth not the sword in vain: for he is the minister of God, a revenger to *execute* wrath upon him that doeth evil.

5 Wherefore [a]*ye* must needs be subject, not only for wrath, [b]but also for conscience sake.

6 For for this cause pay ye tribute also: for they are God's ministers, attending continually upon this very thing.

7 [a]Render therefore to all their dues: tribute to whom tribute *is due;* custom to whom custom; fear to whom fear; honour to whom honour.

8 Owe no man any thing, but to love one another: for [a]he that loveth another hath fulfilled the law.

9 For this, [a]Thou shalt not commit adultery, Thou shalt not kill, Thou shalt not steal, Thou shalt not bear false witness, Thou shalt not covet; and if *there be* any other commandment, it is briefly comprehended in this saying, namely, [b]Thou shalt love thy neighbour as thyself.

10 Love worketh no ill to his neighbour: therefore [a]love *is* the fulfilling of the law.

11 And that, knowing the time, that now *it is* high time [a]to awake out of sleep: for now *is* our salvation nearer than when we believed.

12 The night is far spent, the day is at hand: [a]let us therefore cast off the works

S *Ro 12:1–2* ◀ ▶ *Ro 13:14*

13:11–12 Paul declares that because "the day is at hand" (13:12), believers must awaken to their true situation and prepare for spiritual warfare.

of darkness, and [b]let us put on the armour of light.

13 [a]Let us walk ʹhonestly, as in the day; [b]not in rioting and drunkenness, [c]not in chambering and wantonness, [d]not in strife and envying.

S 14 But [a]put ye on the Lord Jesus Christ, and [b]make not provision for the flesh, to *fulfil* the lusts *thereof.*

The weak and the strong

14 HIM THAT [a]is weak in the faith receive ye, *but* ʹnot to doubtful disputations.

2 For one believeth that he [a]may eat all things: another, who is weak, eateth herbs.

3 Let not him that eateth despise him that eateth not; and [a]let not him which eateth not judge him that eateth: for God hath received him.

4 [a]Who art thou that judgest another man's servant? to his own master he standeth or falleth. Yea, he shall be holden up: for God is able to make him stand.

5 [a]One man esteemeth one day above another: another esteemeth every day *alike.* Let every man be ʹfully persuaded in his own mind.

6 He that [a]regardethʹ the day, regardeth *it* unto the Lord; and he that regardeth not the day, to the Lord he doth not regard *it.* He that eateth, eateth to the Lord, for [b]he giveth God thanks; and he that eateth not, to the Lord he eateth not, and giveth God thanks.

7 For [a]none of us liveth to himself, and no man dieth to himself.

8 For whether we live, we live unto the Lord; and whether we die, we die unto the Lord: whether we live therefore, or die, we are the Lord's.

9 For [a]to this end Christ both died, and rose, and revived, that he might be [b]Lord both of the dead and living.

J S 10 But why dost thou judge thy brother? or why dost thou set at nought thy brother? for [a]we shall all stand before the judgment seat of Christ.

M M 11 For it is written, [a]*As* I live, saith the Lord, every knee shall bow to me, and every tongue shall confess to God.

12 So then [a]every one of us shall give account of himself to God.

13 Let us not therefore judge one another any more: but judge this rather, that [a]no man put a stumblingblock or an occasion to fall in *his* brother's way.

14 I know, and am persuaded by the Lord Jesus, [a]that *there is* nothing ʹunclean of itself: but [b]to him that esteemeth any thing to be ʹunclean, to him *it is* unclean.

15 But if thy brother be grieved with *thy* meat, now walkest thou not ʹcharitably. [a]Destroy not him with thy meat, for whom Christ died. S

16 [a]Let not then your good be evil spoken of:

17 [a]For the kingdom of God is not meat and drink; but righteousness, and peace, and joy in the Holy Ghost. F J W

18 For he that in these things serveth Christ [a]*is* acceptable to God, and approved of men.

19 [a]Let us therefore follow after the things which make for peace, and things wherewith [b]one may edify another.

20 [a]For meat destroy not the work of God. [b]All things indeed *are* pure; [c]but *it is* evil for that man who eateth with offence.

21 *It is* good neither to eat [a]flesh, nor to drink wine, nor *any thing* whereby thy brother stumbleth, or is offended, or is made weak.

22 Hast thou faith? have *it* to thyself before God. [a]Happy *is* he that condemneth not himself in that thing which he alloweth.

23 And he that ʹdoubteth is damned if he eat, because *he eateth* not of faith: for [a]whatsoever *is* not of faith is sin.

15 WE [a]THEN that are strong ought to bear the [b]infirmities of the weak, and not to please ourselves.

2 [a]Let every one of us please *his* neighbour for *his* good [b]to edification.

3 [a]For even Christ pleased not himself; but, as it is written, The [b]reproaches of them that reproached thee fell on me.

4 For [a]whatsoever things were written

12 [b]Eph. 6:13
13 [a]Phil. 4:8 [b]Prov. 23:20 [c]1 Cor. 6:9 [d]Jas. 3:14 ʹOr, *decently*
14 [a]Gal. 3:27; Eph. 4:24 [b]Gal. 5:16
14:1 [a]1 Cor. 8:9 ʹOr, *not to judge* his *doubtful thoughts*
2 [a]1 Cor. 10:25; Tit. 1:15
3 [a]Col. 2:16
4 [a]Jas. 4:12
5 [a]Gal. 4:10 ʹOr, *fully assured*
6 [a]Gal. 4:10 [b]1 Cor. 10:31; 1 Tim. 4:3 ʹOr, *observeth*
7 [a]1 Cor. 6:19; Gal. 2:20; 1 Thes. 5:10; 1 Pet. 4:2
9 [a]2 Cor. 5:15 [b]Acts 10:36
10 [a]Mat. 25:31; 2 Cor. 5:10
11 [a]Is. 45:23
12 [a]Mat. 12:36; Gal. 6:5; 1 Pet. 4:5
13 [a]1 Cor. 8:9
14 [a]1 Cor. 10:25 [b]1 Cor. 8:7 ʹGk. *common*
15 [a]1 Cor. 8:11 ʹGk. *according to charity*
16 [a]ch. 12:17
17 [a]1 Cor. 8:8
18 [a]2 Cor. 8:21
19 [a]ch. 12:18 [b]1 Cor. 14:12; 1 Thes. 5:11
20 [a]ver. 15 [b]Mat. 15:11 [c]1 Cor. 8:9
21 [a]1 Cor. 8:13
22 [a]1 John 3:21
23 [a]Tit. 1:15 ʹOr, *discerneth and putteth a difference between meats*
15:1 [a]Gal. 6:1 [b]ch. 14:1
2 [a]1 Cor. 10:33 [b]ch. 14:19
3 [a]Mat. 26:39 [b]Ps. 69:9
4 [a]1 Cor. 10:11

S *Ro 12:21* ◄► *Ro 14:10–12*
J *Ro 3:6* ◄► *1Co 4:4–5*
S *Ro 13:14* ◄► *Ro 14:15–18*
M *Ro 8:17–18* ◄► *Ro 15:10*
M *Ro 12:16* ◄► *1Co 10:12*

S *Ro 14:10–12* ◄► *1Co 3:17*
F *Ro 8:23* ◄► *Ro 15:13*
J *Ro 8:15* ◄► *Ro 15:13*
W *Ro 12:6–8* ◄► *1Co 2:14*

aforetime were written for our learning, that we through patience and comfort of the scriptures might have hope.

5 [a]Now the God of patience and consolation grant you to be likeminded one toward another [l]according to Christ Jesus:

6 That ye may [a]with one mind *and* one mouth glorify God, even the Father of our Lord Jesus Christ.

7 Wherefore [a]receive ye one another, [b]as Christ also received us to the glory of God.

8 Now I say that [a]Jesus Christ was a minister of the circumcision for the truth of God, [b]to confirm the promises *made* unto the fathers:

9 And [a]that the Gentiles might glorify God for *his* mercy; as it is written, [b]For this cause I will confess to thee among the Gentiles, and sing unto thy name.

M 10 And again he saith, [a]Rejoice, ye Gentiles, with his people.

11 And again, [a]Praise the Lord, all ye Gentiles; and laud him all ye people.

G M 12 And again, Esaias saith, [a]There shall be a root of Jesse, and he that shall rise to reign over the Gentiles; in him shall the Gentiles trust.

B F J M F 13 Now the God of hope fill you with all [a]joy and peace in believing, that ye may abound in hope, through the power of the Holy Ghost.

Paul's reason for writing

14 And [a]I myself also am persuaded of you, my brethren, that ye also are full of goodness, [b]filled with all knowledge, able also to admonish one another.

15 Nevertheless, brethren, I have written the more boldly unto you in some sort, as putting you in mind, [a]because of the grace that is given to me of God,

G B S 16 That [a]I should be the minister of Jesus Christ to the Gentiles, ministering the gospel of God, that the [b]offering[l] up of the Gentiles might be acceptable, being sanctified by the Holy Ghost.

17 I have therefore whereof I may glory through Jesus Christ [a]in those things which pertain to God.

E E 18 For I will not dare to speak of any of those things [a]which Christ hath not wrought by me, [b]to make the Gentiles obedient, by word and deed,

G H M 19 [a]Through mighty signs and wonders, by the power of the Spirit of God; so that from Jerusalem, and round about unto Illyricum, I have fully preached the gospel of Christ.

20 Yea, so have I strived to preach the gospel, not where Christ was named, [a]lest I should build upon another man's foundation:

21 But as it is written, [a]To whom he was not spoken of, they shall see: and they that have not heard shall understand.

Paul's future plans

22 For which cause also [a]I have been [l]much hindered from coming to you.

23 But now having no more place in these parts, and [a]having a great desire these many years to come unto you;

24 Whensoever I take my journey into Spain, I will come to you: for I trust to see you in my journey, [a]and to be brought on my way thitherward by you, if first I be somewhat filled [b]with[l] your *company.*

25 But now [a]I go unto Jerusalem to minister unto the saints.

26 For [a]it hath pleased them of Macedonia and Achaia to make a certain contribution for the poor saints which are at Jerusalem.

5 [a]1 Cor. 1:10 [l]Or, *after the example of*
6 [a]Acts 4:24
7 [a]ch. 14:1,3 [b]ch. 5:2
8 [a]Mat. 15:24; John 1:11; Acts 3:25 [b]2 Cor. 1:20
9 [a]John 10:16 [b]Ps. 18:49
10 [a]Deut. 32:43
11 [a]Ps. 117:1
12 [a]Is. 11:1; Rev. 5:5
13 [a]ch. 12:12
14 [a]2 Pet. 1:12; 1 John 2:21 [b]1 Cor. 8:1
15 [a]ch. 1:5 & 12:3; Gal. 1:15; Eph. 3:7,8
16 [a]ch. 11:13; Gal. 2:7-9; 1 Tim. 2:7; 2 Tim. 1:11 [b]Is. 66:20; Phil. 2:17 [l]Or, *sacrificing*
17 [a]Heb. 5:1
18 [a]Acts 21:19; Gal. 2:8 [b]ch. 1:5 & 16:26
19 [a]Acts 19:11; 2 Cor. 12:12
20 [a]2 Cor. 10:13, 15,16
21 [a]Is. 52:15
22 [a]ch. 1:13; 1 Thes. 2:17 [l]Or, *many ways,* or, *oftentimes*
23 [a]Acts 19:21; ch. 1:11
24 [a]Acts 15:3 [b]ver. 32 [l]Gk. *with you*
25 [a]Acts 19:21 & 24:17
26 [a]1 Cor. 16:1; 2 Cor. 8:1

M *Ro 14:11 ◀▶ Ro 15:12*
G *Ro 11:15–29 ◀▶ Ro 15:16*
M *Ro 15:10 ◀▶ Ro 16:20*
B *Ro 8:23 ◀▶ Ro 15:16*
F *Ro 14:17 ◀▶ Ro 15:30*
J *Ro 14:17 ◀▶ 2Co 3:17*
M *Ro 8:26–27 ◀▶ Ro 15:19*
F *Ro 11:23 ◀▶ 1Co 1:21*

G *Ro 15:12 ◀▶ Ro 15:27*
B *Ro 15:13 ◀▶ 1Co 6:11*
S *Ro 12:1–2 ◀▶ 1Co 3:1*
E *Ro 9:1 ◀▶ Ro 15:30*
E *Ac 28:3–9 ◀▶ 1Co 12:9*
G *Ro 12:6–8 ◀▶ 1Co 1:4–7*
H *Ro 8:11 ◀▶ 1Co 12:9*
M *Ro 15:13 ◀▶ 1Co 2:4–10*

15:12 Paul quotes the ancient prophecy of Isaiah 11:10. The genealogies of Matthew and Luke confirm Jesus' claim to be the Messiah, the legitimate "son of David" (Mt 1:1) prophesied by the OT prophets (see Rev 5:5; 22:16).

15:16 The apostle affirms his role among the Gentiles and cites the Holy Spirit's sanctification as his source of power for his life and ministry.

G 27 It hath pleased them verily; and
their debtors they are. For [a]if the Gentiles have been made partakers of their
spiritual things, [b]their duty is also to minister unto them in carnal things.
28 When therefore I have performed
this, and have sealed to them [a]this fruit, I
will come by you into Spain.
29 [a]And I am sure that, when I come
unto you, I shall come in the fulness of
the blessing of the gospel of Christ.
E 30 Now I beseech you, brethren, for
F the Lord Jesus Christ's sake, and [a]for the
love of the Spirit, [b]that ye strive together
with me in *your* prayers to God for me;
31 [a]That I may be delivered from them
that [l]do not believe in Judaea; and that
[b]my service which *I have* for Jerusalem
may be accepted of the saints;
32 [a]That I may come unto you with joy
[b]by the will of God, and may with you
[c]be refreshed.
33 Now [a]the God of peace *be* with you
all. Amen.

Commendations and greetings

16 I COMMEND unto you Phebe
our sister, which is a servant of
the church which is at [a]Cenchrea;
2 [a]That ye receive her in the Lord, as
becometh saints, and that ye assist her in
whatsoever business she hath need of
you: for she hath been a succourer of
many, and of myself also.
3 Greet [a]Priscilla and Aquila my helpers in Christ Jesus:
4 Who have for my life laid down their
own necks: unto whom not only I give
thanks, but also all the churches of the
Gentiles.
5 Likewise *greet* [a]the church that is in
their house. Salute my wellbeloved Epae-
netus, who is [b]the firstfruits of Achaia
unto Christ.
6 Greet Mary, who bestowed much labour on us.
7 Salute Andronicus and Junia, my
kinsmen, and my fellowprisoners, who
are of note among the apostles, who also
[a]were in Christ before me.
8 Greet Amplias my beloved in the
Lord.
9 Salute Urbane, our helper in Christ,
and Stachys my beloved.
10 Salute Apelles approved in Christ.
Salute them which are of Aristobulus'
[l]*household*.
11 Salute Herodion my kinsman. Greet
them that be of the [l]*household* of Narcis-
sus, which are in the Lord.
12 Salute Tryphena and Tryphosa,
who labour in the Lord. Salute the beloved Persis, which laboured much in the
Lord.
13 Salute Rufus [a]chosen in the Lord,
and his mother and mine.
14 Salute Asyncritus, Phlegon, Her-
mas, Patrobas, Hermes, and the brethren
which are with them.
15 Salute Philologus, and Julia, Ne-
reus, and his sister, and Olympas, and all
the saints which are with them.
16 [a]Salute one another with an holy
kiss. The churches of Christ salute you.
17 Now I beseech you, brethren, mark
them [a]which cause divisions and offences contrary to the doctrine which ye
have learned; and [b]avoid them.
18 For they that are such serve not our
Lord Jesus Christ, but [a]their own belly;
and [b]by good words and fair speeches deceive the hearts of the simple.
19 For [a]your obedience is come abroad
unto all *men*. I am glad therefore on your
behalf: but yet I would have you [b]wise
unto that which is good, and [l]simple concerning evil.
20 And [a]the God of peace [b]shall M
[l]bruise Satan under your feet shortly.
[c]The grace of our Lord Jesus Christ *be*
with you. Amen.
21 [a]Timotheus my workfellow, and
[b]Lucius, and [c]Jason, and [d]Sosipater, my
kinsmen, salute you.

27 [a]ch. 11:17 [b]1 Cor. 9:11; Gal. 6:6
28 [a]Phil. 4:17
29 [a]ch. 1:11
30 [a]Phil. 2:1 [b]2 Cor. 1:11; Col. 4:12
31 [a]2 Thes. 3:2 [b]2 Cor. 8:4 [l]Or, *are disobedient*
32 [a]ch. 1:10 [b]Acts 18:21; 1 Cor. 4:19; Jas. 4:15 [c]1 Cor. 16:18; 2 Cor. 7:13; 2 Tim. 1:16; Philem. 7,20
33 [a]ch. 16:20; 1 Cor. 14:33; 2 Cor. 13:11; Phil. 4:9; 1 Thes. 5:23; 2 Thes. 3:16; Heb. 13:20
16:1 [a]Acts 18:18
2 [a]Phil. 2:29; 3 John 5,6
3 [a]Acts 18:2,18,26
5 [a]1 Cor. 16:19; Col. 4:15; Philem. 2 [b]1 Cor. 16:15
7 [a]Gal. 1:22
10 [l]Or, friends
11 [l]Or, friends
13 [a]2 John 1
16 [a]1 Cor. 16:20; 2 Cor. 13:12
17 [a]Acts 15:1 [b]1 Cor. 5:9; 2 Tim. 3:5
18 [a]Phil. 3:19; 1 Tim. 6:5 [b]Col. 2:4; 2 Tim. 3:6
19 [a]ch. 1:8 [b]Mat. 10:16 [l]Or, *harmless*
20 [a]ch. 15:33 [b]Gen. 3:15 [c]1 Cor. 16:23 [l]Or, *tread*
21 [a]Acts 16:1; Heb. 13:23 [b]Acts 13:1 [c]Acts 17:5 [d]Acts 20:4

G *Ro 15:16* ◀▶ *Rev 11:2*
E *Ro 15:18–19* ◀▶ *1Co 2:4–16*
F *Ro 15:13* ◀▶ *2Co 13:14*
M *Ro 15:12* ◀▶ *1Co 6:2–3*

15:27 Paul affirms that because the Jews' spiritual blessings, especially Christ and the gospel message, have been shared with the Gentiles, the Gentiles have a duty to share their material blessings with their Jewish brethren (see 1Co 16:1–4; 2Co 8—9).

16:20 The apostle Paul confirms the prophetic truth that God will ultimately defeat the antichrist and Satan (see Ge 3:15). After the Battle of Armageddon, the antichrist and false prophet will be thrown into hell, and Satan will be cast into the bottomless pit (see Rev 19:20; 20:2–3).

22 I Tertius, who wrote *this* epistle, salute you in the Lord.

23 [a]Gaius mine host, and of the whole church, saluteth you. [b]Erastus the chamberlain of the city saluteth you, and Quartus a brother.

24 [a]The grace of our Lord Jesus Christ *be* with you all. Amen.

K 25 Now [a]to him that is of power to stablish you [b]according to my gospel, and the preaching of Jesus Christ, [c]according to the revelation of the mystery, [d]which was kept secret since the world began,

26 But [a]now is made manifest, and by the scriptures of the prophets, according to the commandment of the everlasting God, made known to all nations for [b]the obedience of faith:

27 To [a]God only wise, *be* glory through Jesus Christ for ever. Amen.

K *Ro 10:11* ◀▶ *1Co 1:25*

23 [a]1 Cor. 1:14 [b]Acts 19:22
24 [a]1 Thes. 5:28
25 [a]Eph. 3:20 [b]ch. 2:16 [c]Eph. 1:9 [d]Col. 1:26
26 [a]Eph. 1:9 [b]Acts 6:7
27 [a]Jude 25

1 Corinthians

Author: Paul

Theme: Living the Christian life in a sinful world

Date of Writing: C. A.D. 54–55

Outline of 1 Corinthians

I. Greetings and Introduction (1:1–9)
II. Strife Within the Church (1:10—4:21)
III. Moral and Ethical Behavior (5:1—6:20)
IV. Marriage and Celibacy (7:1–40)
V. Rights and Responsibility (8:1—11:1)
VI. Proper Public Worship (11:2—14:40)
  A. Worshipful behavior (11:2–16)
  B. The Lord's Supper (11:17–34)
  C. Spiritual gifts (12:1—14:40)
VII. Teaching About the Resurrection (15:1–58)
VIII. Conclusion (16:1–24)

PAUL WROTE THIS letter to the Corinthian church during his third missionary journey and toward the end of his ministry at Ephesus. Paul had visited Corinth previously on his second missionary journey. This wealthy trading city on the Mediterranean coast contained a diverse population of Greeks, Jews and Romans. Though Paul's ministry was rejected by the Jews in Corinth, a successful house church was established among the Gentiles (see Ac 18:6–8). Paul remained with the Corinthian believers for a year and a half (see Ac 18:11), supporting himself by making tents. From Corinth, Paul continued on in his missionary journeys, accompanied by Priscilla and Aquila. During his absence, other teachers came to Corinth preaching a message that differed from Paul's words. These teachings caused confusion among the Corinthian believers. When some of the Corinthians brought a contribution to Paul, they also shared their questions and problems. The letter of 1 Corinthians contains Paul's reply to these questions.

Because of the varied makeup of the population of Corinth, the Corinthian believers were subjected to worldly influences that had affected their Christian walk. This epistle to the Corinthians addresses societal problems such as lawsuits, immorality and marriage as well as the pagan influences of idolatry and the mishandling of the sacraments. Paul also instructed the leaders on theological issues such as church finances, doctrinal divisions, disorder during worship, the gifts of the Holy Spirit, Paul's apostleship and the resurrection. Conversational in style, Paul's letter logically persuades, critiques and scolds the believers as Paul instructs them on how to apply the gospel to the challenges of everyday life in a pagan society.

Paul's thanksgiving

1 PAUL, [a]CALLED *to be* an apostle of Jesus Christ [b]through the will of God, and Sosthenes *our* brother,

2 Unto the church of God which is at Corinth, to them that [a]are sanctified in Christ Jesus, [b]called *to be* saints, with all that in every place call upon the name of Jesus Christ [c]our Lord, [d]both theirs and ours:

3 [a]Grace *be* unto you, and peace, from God our Father, and *from* the Lord Jesus Christ.

G 4 [a]I thank my God always on your behalf, for the grace of God which is given you by Jesus Christ;

5 That in every thing ye are enriched by him, [a]in all utterance, and *in* all knowledge;

6 Even as [a]the testimony of Christ was confirmed in you:

C 7 So that ye come behind in no gift; [a]waiting for the [/]coming of our Lord Jesus Christ:

8 [a]Who shall also confirm you unto the end, [b]*that ye may be* blameless in the day of our Lord Jesus Christ.

9 [a]God *is* faithful, by whom ye were called unto [b]the fellowship of his Son Jesus Christ our Lord.

An appeal for unity

10 Now I beseech you, brethren, by the name of our Lord Jesus Christ, [a]that ye all speak the same thing, and *that* there be no [/]divisions among you; but *that* ye be perfectly joined together in the same mind and in the same judgment.

11 For it hath been declared unto me of you, my brethren, by them *which are of the house* of Chloe, that there are contentions among you.

12 Now this I say, [a]that every one of you saith, I am of Paul; and I of [b]Apollos; and I of [c]Cephas; and I of Christ.

13 [a]Is Christ divided? was Paul crucified for you? or were ye baptized in the name of Paul?

14 I thank God that I baptized none of you, but [a]Crispus and [b]Gaius;

15 Lest any should say that I had baptized in mine own name.

16 And I baptized also the household of [a]Stephanas: besides, I know not whether I baptized any other.

17 For Christ sent me not to baptize, but to preach the gospel: [a]not with wisdom of [/]words, lest the cross of Christ should be made of none effect.

Christ, God's power and wisdom

18 For the preaching of the cross is to [a]them that perish [b]foolishness; but unto us [c]which are saved it is the [d]power of God. G H N

19 For it is written, [a]I will destroy the wisdom of the wise, and will bring to

1:1 [a]Rom. 1:1 [b]2 Cor. 1:1
2 [a]Acts 15:9 [b]Rom. 1:7 [c]ch. 8:6 [d]Rom. 3:22
3 [a]Rom. 1:7; 2 Cor. 1:2
4 [a]Rom. 1:8
5 [a]ch. 12:8
6 [a]2 Tim. 1:8; Rev. 1:2
7 [a]Phil. 3:20; Tit. 2:13; 2 Pet. 3:12 [/]Gk. *revelation*
8 [a]1 Thes. 3:13 [b]Col. 1:22
9 [a]Is. 49:7; 1 Thes. 5:24 [b]John 15:4
10 [a]2 Cor. 13:11; 1 Pet. 3:8 [/]Gk. *schisms*
12 [a]ch. 3:4 [b]Acts 18:24 [c]John 1:42
13 [a]2 Cor. 11:4
14 [a]Acts 18:8 [b]Rom. 16:23
16 [a]ch. 16:15
17 [a]ch. 2:4 [/]Or, *speech*
18 [a]2 Cor. 2:15 [b]Acts 17:18 [c]ch. 15:2 [d]Rom. 1:16
19 [a]Is. 29:14

G *Ro 15:19* ◀▶ *1Co 2:4–15*
C *Ac 1:11* ◀▶ *1Co 10:11*

G *Ro 11:5–6* ◀▶ *1Co 1:26–31*
H *Ro 12:19* ◀▶ *1Co 3:17*
N *Ro 2:5* ◀▶ *2Co 2:15–16*

1:7–8 Paul affirms the importance of anticipating the return of Jesus Christ. The Greek word that Paul uses in this passage for Christ's return is *apokalupsis* meaning "revelation." In this passage, it is clearly used in the context of Christ coming in the air for his church (see 1Th 4:16–17).

nothing the understanding of the prudent.

20 [a]Where *is* the wise? where *is* the scribe? where *is* the disputer of this world? [b]hath not God made foolish the wisdom of this world?

F 21 [a]For after that in the wisdom of God the world by wisdom knew not God, it pleased God by the foolishness of preaching to save them that believe.

22 For the [a]Jews require a sign, and the Greeks seek after wisdom:

23 But we preach Christ crucified, [a]unto the Jews a stumblingblock, and unto the Greeks [b]foolishness;

24 But unto them which are called, both Jews and Greeks, Christ [a]the power of God, and [b]the wisdom of God.

K 25 Because the foolishness of God is wiser than men; and the weakness of God is stronger than men.

G 26 For ye see your calling, brethren, how that [a]not many wise men after the flesh, not many mighty, not many noble, *are called:*

27 But [a]God hath chosen the foolish things of the world to confound the wise; and God hath chosen the weak things of the world to confound the things which are mighty;

28 And base things of the world, and things which are despised, hath God chosen, *yea,* and [a]things which are not, [b]to bring to nought things that are:

29 [a]That no flesh should glory in his presence.

K 30 But of him are ye in Christ Jesus, who of God is made unto us [a]wisdom, and [b]righteousness, and [c]sanctification, and [d]redemption:

31 That, according as it is written, [a]He that glorieth, let him glory in the Lord.

2 AND I, brethren, when I came to you, [a]came not with excellency of speech or of wisdom, declaring unto you [b]the testimony of God.

2 For I determined not to know any thing among you, [a]save Jesus Christ, and him crucified.

3 And [a]I was with you [b]in weakness, and in fear, and in much trembling.

4 And my speech and my preaching [a]*was* not with [1]enticing words of man's wisdom, [b]but in demonstration of the Spirit and of power: E G M T

5 That your faith should not [1]stand in the wisdom of men, but [a]in the power of God.

True wisdom the gift of God

6 Howbeit we speak wisdom among them [a]that are perfect: yet not [b]the wisdom of this world, nor of the princes of this world, [c]that come to nought:

7 But we speak the wisdom of God in a mystery, *even* the hidden *wisdom,* [a]which God ordained before the world unto our glory:

8 [a]Which none of the princes of this world knew: for [b]had they known *it,* they would not have crucified the Lord of glory.

9 But as it is written, [a]Eye hath not seen, nor ear heard, neither have entered into the heart of man, the things which God hath prepared for them that love him. U

10 But [a]God hath revealed *them* unto us by his Spirit: for the Spirit searcheth all things, yea, the deep things of God.

11 For what man knoweth the things of a man, [a]save the spirit of man which is in him? [b]even so the things of God knoweth no man, but the Spirit of God. N

12 Now we have received, not the spirit of the world, but [a]the spirit which is of God; that we might know the things that are freely given to us of God.

13 Which things also we speak, not in the words which man's wisdom teacheth, but which the Holy Ghost teacheth; comparing spiritual things with spiritual.

14 [a]But the natural man receiveth not the things of the Spirit of God: [b]for they are foolishness unto him: [c]neither can he know *them,* because they are spiritually discerned. W C

15 [a]But he that is spiritual [1]judgeth all things, yet he himself is [2]judged of no man.

20 [a]Is. 33:18 [b]Job 12:17; Is. 44:25; Rom. 1:22
21 [a]Mat. 11:25; Luke 10:21; Rom. 1:20
22 [a]Mat. 12:38; Mark 8:11; John 4:48
23 [a]Is. 8:14; Luke 2:34; John 6:60; Gal. 5:11 [b]ch. 2:14
24 [a]Rom. 1:4 [b]Col. 2:3
26 [a]John 7:48
27 [a]Mat. 11:25
28 [a]Rom. 4:17 [b]ch. 2:6
29 [a]Rom. 3:27; Eph. 2:9
30 [a]ver. 24 [b]Jer. 23:5; Rom. 4:25; 2 Cor. 5:21 [c]John 17:19 [d]Eph. 1:7
31 [a]Jer. 9:23
2:1 [a]ch. 1:17 [b]ch. 1:6
2 [a]Gal. 6:14; Phil. 3:8
3 [a]Acts 18:1 [b]2 Cor. 4:7
4 [a]2 Pet. 1:16 [b]Rom. 15:19 [1]Or, *persuasible*
5 [a]2 Cor. 4:7 [1]Gk. *be*
6 [a]ch. 14:20; Heb. 5:14 [b]2 Cor. 1:12 [c]ch. 1:28
7 [a]Eph. 3:5; Col. 1:26
8 [a]Mat. 11:25 [b]Luke 23:34
9 [a]Is. 64:4
10 [a]Mat. 13:11
11 [a]Prov. 20:27; Jer. 17:9 [b]Rom. 11:33
12 [a]Rom. 8:15
14 [a]Mat. 16:23 [b]ch. 1:18,23 [c]Jude 19
15 [a]1 John 4:1 [1]Or, *discerneth* [2]Or, *discerned*

F *Ro 15:13* ◀▶ *Gal 2:16*
K *Ro 16:25* ◀▶ *1Co 1:30*
G *1Co 1:18–21* ◀▶ *1Co 3:11*
K *1Co 1:25* ◀▶ *1Co 6:9–11*

E *Ro 15:30* ◀▶ *1Co 3:1*
G *1Co 1:4–7* ◀▶ *1Co 3:1–2*
M *Ro 15:19* ◀▶ *1Co 3:1*
T *Ro 12:6–8* ◀▶ *1Co 7:40*
U *Ro 8:28* ◀▶ *2Co 5:1*
N *Ro 1:4* ◀▶ *1Co 12:1–13*
W *Ro 14:17* ◀▶ *1Co 3:1–2*
C *Ro 8:5–8* ◀▶ *2Co 4:3–4*

16 [a]For who hath known the mind of the Lord, that he [1]may instruct him? [b]But we have the mind of Christ.

Fellow labourers for God

E G M S W **3** AND I, brethren, could not speak unto you as unto [a]spiritual, but as unto [b]carnal, *even* as unto [c]babes in Christ.

2 I have fed you with [a]milk, and not with meat: [b]for hitherto ye were not able *to bear it,* neither yet now are ye able.

3 For ye are yet carnal: for [a]whereas *there is* among you envying, and strife, and [1]divisions, are ye not carnal, and walk [2]as men?

4 For while one saith, I am of Paul; and another, I *am* of Apollos; are ye not carnal?

5 Who then is Paul, and who *is* Apollos, but [a]ministers by whom ye believed, [b]even as the Lord gave to every man?

6 [a]I have planted, [b]Apollos watered; [c]but God gave the increase.

7 So then [a]neither is he that planteth any thing, neither he that watereth; but God that giveth the increase.

8 Now he that planteth and he that watereth are one: [a]and every man shall receive his own reward according to his own labour.

9 For [a]we are labourers together with God: ye are God's [1]husbandry, *ye are* [b]God's building.

10 [a]According to the grace of God which is given unto me, as a wise masterbuilder, I have laid [b]the foundation, and another buildeth thereon. But let every man take heed how he buildeth thereupon.

G O 11 For other foundation can no man lay than [a]that is laid, [b]which is Jesus Christ.

12 Now if any man build upon this foundation gold, silver, precious stones, wood, hay, stubble;

13 Every man's work shall be made manifest: for the day [a]shall declare it, because [b]it [1]shall be revealed by fire; and the fire shall try every man's work of what sort it is.

14 If any man's work abide which he hath built thereupon, he shall receive a reward.

15 If any man's work shall be burned, he shall suffer loss: but he himself shall be saved; yet so as by fire.

16 [a]Know ye not that ye are the temple of God, and *that* the Spirit of God dwelleth in you? D E S

17 If any man [1]defile the temple of God, him shall God destroy; for the temple of God is holy, which *temple* ye are. H S

18 [a]Let no man deceive himself. If any man among you seemeth to be wise in this world, let him become a fool, that he may be wise.

19 For the wisdom of this world is foolishness with God. For it is written, [a]He taketh the wise in their own craftiness. G

20 And again, [a]The Lord knoweth the thoughts of the wise, that they are vain.

21 Therefore let no man glory in men. For [a]all things are yours;

22 Whether Paul, or Apollos, or Cephas, or the world, or life, or death, or things present, or things to come; all are yours;

23 And [a]ye are Christ's; and Christ *is* God's.

Apostles of Christ

4 LET A man so account of us, as of [a]the ministers of Christ, [b]and stewards of the mysteries of God.

2 Moreover it is required in stewards, that a man be found faithful.

3 But with me it is a very small thing that I should be judged of you, or of man's [1]judgment: yea, I judge not mine own self.

4 For I know nothing by myself; yet am I not hereby justified: but he that judgeth me is the Lord. J

16 [a]Job 15:8 [b]John 15:15 [1]Gk. *shall*
3:1 [a]ch. 2:15 [b]ch. 2:14 [c]Heb. 5:13
2 [a]Heb. 5:12; 1 Pet. 2:2 [b]John 16:12
3 [a]Gal. 5:20; Jas. 3:16 [1]Or, *factions* [2]Gk. *according to man?*
5 [a]2 Cor. 3:3 [b]Rom. 12:3; 1 Pet. 4:11
6 [a]Acts 18:4; 2 Cor. 10:14 [b]Acts 18:24 & 19:1 [c]2 Cor. 3:5
7 [a]2 Cor. 12:11; Gal. 6:3
8 [a]Ps. 62:12; Rom. 2:6; Gal. 6:4,5
9 [a]Acts 15:4; 2 Cor. 6:1 [b]Eph. 2:20; Col. 2:7; Heb. 3:3,4 [1]Or, *tillage*
10 [a]Rom. 1:5 & 12:3 [b]ch. 4:15
11 [a]Is. 28:16; Mat. 16:18; 2 Cor. 11:4 [b]Eph. 2:20
13 [a]1 Pet. 1:7 [b]Luke 2:35 [1]Gk. *is revealed*
16 [a]2 Cor. 6:16
17 [1]Or, *destroy*
18 [a]Prov. 3:7
19 [a]Job 5:13
20 [a]Ps. 94:11
21 [a]2 Cor. 4:5
23 [a]Rom. 14:8; 2 Cor. 10:7; Gal. 3:29
4:1 [a]Mat. 24:45; Col. 1:25 [b]Luke 12:42; Tit. 1:7
3 [1]Gk. *day;* see ch. 3:13

E *1Co 2:4–16* ◀▶ *1Co 3:16*
G *1Co 2:4–15* ◀▶ *1Co 7:7*
M *1Co 2:4–10* ◀▶ *2Co 3:5–18*
S *Ro 15:16* ◀▶ *1Co 3:16–17*
W *1Co 2:14* ◀▶ *1Co 12:1–11*
G *1Co 1:26–31* ◀▶ *1Co 3:19–20*
O *Ro 10:3–4* ◀▶ *2Co 10:17–18*

D *Ac 5:4* ◀▶ *2Co 3:17*
E *1Co 3:1* ◀▶ *1Co 6:11*
S *1Co 3:1* ◀▶ *1Co 6:11*
H *1Co 1:18* ◀▶ *1Co 6:9–10*
S *Ro 14:15–18* ◀▶ *1Co 6:9–11*
G *1Co 3:11* ◀▶ *2Co 10:18*
J *Ro 14:10–12* ◀▶ *2Co 5:10*

J E 5 [a]Therefore judge nothing before the time, until the Lord come, who both will bring to light the hidden things of darkness, and will make manifest the counsels of the hearts: and [b]then shall every man have praise of God.

6 And these things, brethren, [a]I have in a figure transferred to myself and *to* Apollos for your sakes; [b]that ye might learn in us not to think *of men* above that which is written, that no one of you [c]be puffed up for one against another.

7 For who [1]maketh thee to differ *from another?* and [a]what hast thou that thou didst not receive? now if thou didst receive *it,* why dost thou glory, as if thou hadst not received *it?*

8 Now ye are full, [a]now ye are rich, ye have reigned as kings without us: and I would to God ye did reign, that we also might reign with you.

9 For I think that God hath set forth [1]us the apostles last, [a]as it were appointed to death: for [b]we are made a [2]spectacle unto the world, and to angels, and to men.

10 [a]We *are* [b]fools for Christ's sake, but ye *are* wise in Christ; [c]we *are* weak, but ye *are* strong; ye *are* honourable, but we *are* despised.

11 [a]Even unto this present hour we both hunger, and thirst, and [b]are naked, and [c]are buffeted, and have no certain dwellingplace;

12 [a]And labour, working with our own hands: [b]being reviled, we bless; being persecuted, we suffer it:

13 Being defamed, we entreat: [a]we are made as the filth of the world, *and are* the offscouring of all things unto this day.

14 I write not these things to shame you, but [a]as my beloved sons I warn *you.*

15 For though ye have ten thousand instructors in Christ, yet *have ye* not many fathers: for [a]in Christ Jesus I have begotten you through the gospel.

16 Wherefore I beseech you, [a]be ye followers of me.

17 For this cause have I sent unto you [a]Timotheus, [b]who is my beloved son, and faithful in the Lord, who shall bring you [c]into remembrance of my ways which be in Christ, as I [d]teach every where [e]in every church.

18 [a]Now some are puffed up, as though I would not come to you.

19 [a]But I will come to you shortly, [b]if the Lord will, and will know, not the speech of them which are puffed up, but the power.

20 For [a]the kingdom of God *is* not in word, but in power.

21 What will ye? [a]shall I come unto you with a rod, or in love, and *in* the spirit of meekness?

Judgment of the immoral

5 IT IS reported commonly *that there is* fornication among you, and such fornication as is not so much as [a]named among the Gentiles, [b]that one should have his [c]father's wife.

2 [a]And ye are puffed up, and have not rather [b]mourned, that he that hath done this deed might be taken away from among you.

3 [a]For I verily, as absent in body, but present in spirit, have [1]judged already, as though I were present, *concerning* him that hath so done this deed,

4 In the name of our Lord Jesus Christ, when ye are gathered together, and my spirit, [a]with the power of our Lord Jesus Christ,

5 [a]To deliver such an one unto [b]Satan for the destruction of the flesh, that the spirit may be saved in the day of the Lord Jesus.

6 [a]Your glorying *is* not good. Know ye not that [b]a little leaven leaveneth the whole lump?

7 Purge out therefore the old leaven, that ye may be a new lump, as ye are unleavened. For even [a]Christ our [b]passover [1]is sacrificed for us: D

8 Therefore [a]let us keep [1]the feast, [b]not with old leaven, neither [c]with the

5 [a]Mat. 7:1; Rom. 2:1; Rev. 20:12 [b]Rom. 2:29; 2 Cor. 5:10
6 [a]ch. 1:12 [b]Rom. 12:3 [c]ch. 3:21
7 [a]John 3:27 [1]Gk. *distinguisheth thee*
8 [a]Rev. 3:17
9 [a]Ps. 44:22 [b]Heb. 10:33 [1]Or, *us the last apostles, as* [2]Gk. *theatre*
10 [a]ch. 2:3 [b]Acts 17:18 [c]2 Cor. 13:9
11 [a]Phil. 4:12 [b]Rom. 8:35 [c]Acts 23:2
12 [a]Acts 18:3 & 20:34; 1 Thes. 2:9; 2 Thes. 3:8; 1 Tim. 4:10 [b]Mat. 5:44; Luke 6:28 & 23:34; Acts 7:60; Rom. 12:14
13 [a]Lam. 3:45
14 [a]1 Thes. 2:11
15 [a]Acts 18:11; Gal. 4:19; Jas. 1:18
16 [a]ch. 11:1; 1 Thes. 1:6
17 [a]Acts 19:22; Phil. 2:19 [b]1 Tim. 1:2; 2 Tim. 1:2 [c]ch. 11:2 [d]ch. 7:17 [e]ch. 14:33
18 [a]ch. 5:2
19 [a]Acts 19:21; 2 Cor. 1:15 [b]Acts 18:21; Heb. 6:3; Jas. 4:15
20 [a]1 Thes. 1:5
21 [a]2 Cor. 10:2
5:1 [a]Eph. 5:3 [b]Lev. 18:8 [c]2 Cor. 7:12
2 [a]ch. 4:18 [b]2 Cor. 7:7
3 [a]Col. 2:5 [1]Or, *determined*
4 [a]Mat. 16:19; John 20:23; 2 Cor. 2:10
5 [a]Ps. 109:6; 1 Tim. 1:20 [b]Acts 26:18
6 [a]ch. 3:21 [b]Gal. 5:9; 2 Tim. 2:17
7 [a]Is. 53:7; 1 Pet. 1:19 [b]John 19:14 [1]Or, *is slain*
8 [a]Ex. 12:15 [b]Deut. 16:3 [c]Mat. 16:6; Mark 8:15; Luke 12:1 [1]Or, *holyday*

J *Ro 2:16* ◀ ▶ *2Co 5:9–11*
E *Ro 8:27* ◀ ▶ *1Th 2:4*
D *Ro 8:32* ◀ ▶ *1Co 6:20*

4:5 Paul warns Christians not to pass judgment on fellow believers' behavior or motives because Christ himself is our true judge. The final judgment of believers will occur in heaven after the rapture at "the judgment seat of Christ" (Ro 14:10). This judgment is concerned with the giving of crowns and rewards, not with punishment for sin (see 2Co 5:10; 2Ti 4:8; Rev 22:12). Those who truly repent and follow Jesus as their Lord and Savior have already had their sins judged forever at the cross.

leaven of malice and wickedness; but with the unleavened *bread* of sincerity and truth.

9 I wrote unto you in an epistle [a]not to company with fornicators:

10 [a]Yet not altogether with the fornicators [b]of this world, or with the covetous, or extortioners, or with idolaters; for then must ye needs go [c]out of the world.

11 But now I have written unto you not to keep company, [a]if any man that is called a brother be a fornicator, or covetous, or an idolater, or a railer, or a drunkard, or an extortioner; with such an one [b]no not to eat.

12 For what have I to do to judge [a]them also that are without? do not ye judge [b]them that are within?

13 But them that are without God judgeth. Therefore [a]put away from among yourselves that wicked person.

Lawsuits among brethren

6 DARE ANY of you, having a matter against another, go to law before the unjust, and not before the saints?

M 2 Do ye not know that [a]the saints shall judge the world? and if the world shall be judged by you, are ye unworthy to judge the smallest matters?

3 Know ye not that we shall [a]judge angels? how much more things that pertain to this life?

4 [a]If then ye have judgments of things pertaining to this life, set them to judge who are least esteemed in the church.

5 I speak to your shame. Is it so, that there is not a wise man among you? no, not one that shall be able to judge between his brethren?

6 But brother goeth to law with brother, and that before the unbelievers.

M *Ro 16:20* ◀▶ *1Co 15:24–28*

9 [a]2 Cor. 6:14; Eph. 5:11
10 [a]ch. 10:27 [b]ch. 1:20 [c]John 17:15; 1 John 5:19
11 [a]Mat. 18:17; Rom. 16:17; 2 John 10 [b]Gal. 2:12
12 [a]Mark 4:11; Col. 4:5; 1 Thes. 4:12 [b]ch. 6:1-4
13 [a]Deut. 13:5
6:2 [a]Ps. 49:14; Dan. 7:22; Mat. 19:28; Luke 22:30
3 [a]2 Pet. 2:4
4 [a]ch. 5:12
7 [a]Prov. 20:22; Mat. 5:39; Luke 6:29
8 [a]1 Thes. 4:6
9 [a]Gal. 5:21; Eph. 5:5; 1 Tim. 1:9
11 [a]ch. 12:2 [b]Heb. 10:22
12 [a]ch. 10:23 [1]Or, *profitable*
13 [a]Mat. 15:17; Rom. 14:17; Col. 2:22 [b]1 Thes. 4:3 [c]Eph. 5:23
14 [a]Rom. 6:5,8; 2 Cor. 4:14 [b]Eph. 1:19
15 [a]Rom. 12:5; Eph. 4:12 & 5:30

7 Now therefore there is utterly a fault among you, because ye go to law one with another. [a]Why do ye not rather take wrong? why do ye not rather *suffer yourselves to* be defrauded?

8 Nay, ye do wrong, and defraud, [a]and that *your* brethren.

God to be glorified in the body

9 Know ye not that the unrighteous H
shall not inherit the kingdom of God? Be K
not deceived: [a]neither fornicators, nor L
idolaters, nor adulterers, nor effeminate, S
nor abusers of themselves with mankind,

10 Nor thieves, nor covetous, nor drunkards, nor revilers, nor extortioners, shall inherit the kingdom of God.

11 And such were [a]some of you: [b]but B
ye are washed, but ye are sanctified, but E
ye are justified in the name of the Lord R
Jesus, and by the Spirit of our God. S

12 [a]All things are lawful unto me, but all things are not [1]expedient: all things are lawful for me, but I will not be brought under the power of any.

13 [a]Meats for the belly, and the belly for meats: but God shall destroy both it and them. Now the body *is* not for fornication, but [b]for the Lord; [c]and the Lord for the body.

14 And [a]God hath both raised up the F
Lord, and will also raise up us [b]by his own power.

15 Know ye not that [a]your bodies are the members of Christ? shall I then take

H *1Co 3:17* ◀▶ *1Co 10:5–12*
K *1Co 1:30* ◀▶ *1Co 15:56–57*
L *Ro 10:21* ◀▶ *1Co 7:23*
S *1Co 3:17* ◀▶ *1Co 6:20*
B *Ro 15:16* ◀▶ *1Co 12:1–11*
E *1Co 3:16* ◀▶ *1Co 6:19*
R *Ro 8:1–16* ◀▶ *1Co 12:13*
S *1Co 3:16–17* ◀▶ *2Co 3:18*
F *Ro 8:17–25* ◀▶ *1Co 15:20–26*

6:1–3 Paul warns believers against taking their disputes into the law courts of the unbelievers. Believers view things from a godly point of view; the law courts of unbelievers do not have that same vantage point. Paul reminds Christians that because we will judge the world with Christ in the Millennium, we ought to be competent enough to judge cases between Christians on this earth. Paul specifically notes that the church will participate in Christ's final judgment of the nations (see Da 7:22; Mt 19:28) as well as the judgment of the wicked angels that fell during Satan's rebellion (see 2Pe 2:4; Jude 6). In light of God's promise of our future ruling status we should deal with claims against each other internally, according to Biblical principles.

6:14 In this verse, the apostle prophesies about the first resurrection from the dead for believers and affirms that God has the power to raise all of his followers from the grave. The historical reality of the resurrection of Christ was powerfully confirmed through eyewitness evidence (see 15:4–6; Mk 16:14; Lk 24:23–40). His resurrection provides proof that God has the power to resurrect all believers.

the members of Christ, and make *them* the members of an harlot? God forbid.

16 What? know ye not that he which is joined to an harlot is one body? for [a]two, saith he, shall be one flesh.

17 [a]But he that is joined unto the Lord is one spirit.

18 [a]Flee fornication. Every sin that a man doeth is without the body; but he that committeth fornication sinneth [b]against his own body.

E 19 What? [a]know ye not that your body is the temple of the Holy Ghost *which is* in you, which ye have of God, [b]and ye are not your own?

D S 20 For [a]ye are bought with a price: therefore glorify God in your body, and in your spirit, which are God's.

Marriage

7 NOW CONCERNING the things whereof ye wrote unto me: [a]*It is* good for a man not to touch a woman.

2 Nevertheless, *to avoid* fornication, let every man have his own wife, and let every woman have her own husband.

3 [a]Let the husband render unto the wife due benevolence: and likewise also the wife unto the husband.

4 The wife hath not power of her own body, but the husband: and likewise also the husband hath not power of his own body, but the wife.

5 [a]Defraud ye not one the other, except *it be* with consent for a time, that ye may give yourselves to fasting and prayer; and come together again, that [b]Satan tempt you not for your incontinency.

6 But I speak this by permission, [a]*and* not of commandment.

G 7 For [a]I would that all men were [b]even as I myself. But [c]every man hath his proper gift of God, one after this manner, and another after that.

8 I say therefore to the unmarried and widows, [a]It is good for them if they abide even as I.

9 But [a]if they cannot contain, let them marry: for it is better to marry than to burn.

10 And unto the married I command, *yet* not I, but the Lord, [a]Let not the wife depart from *her* husband:

11 But and if she depart, let her remain unmarried, or be reconciled to *her* husband: and let not the husband put away *his* wife.

12 But to the rest speak I, not the Lord: If any brother hath a wife that believeth not, and she be pleased to dwell with him, let him not put her away.

13 And the woman which hath an husband that believeth not, and if he be pleased to dwell with her, let her not leave him.

14 For the unbelieving husband is sanctified by the wife, and the unbelieving wife is sanctified by the husband: else [a]were your children unclean; but now are they holy.

15 But if the unbelieving depart, let him depart. A brother or a sister is not under bondage in such *cases:* but God hath called us [a]to[′] peace.

16 For what knowest thou, O wife, whether thou shalt [a]save *thy* husband? or [′]how knowest thou, O man, whether thou shalt save *thy* wife?

17 But as God hath distributed to every man, as the Lord hath called every one, so let him walk. And [a]so ordain I in all churches.

18 Is any man called being circumcised? let him not become uncircumcised. Is any called in uncircumcision? [a]let him not be circumcised.

19 [a]Circumcision is nothing, and uncircumcision is nothing, but [b]the keeping of the commandments of God.

20 Let every man abide in the same calling wherein he was called.

21 Art thou called *being* a servant? care not for it: but if thou mayest be made free, use *it* rather.

22 For he that is called in the Lord, *being* a servant, is [a]the Lord's [′]freeman: likewise also he that is called, *being* free, is [b]Christ's servant.

23 [a]Ye are bought with a price; be not ye the servants of men. D L

24 Brethren, let every man, wherein he is called, therein abide with God.

25 Now concerning virgins [a]I have no commandment of the Lord: yet I give my

6:16 [a]Gen. 2:24; Mat. 19:5; Eph. 5:31
17 [a]John 17:21; Eph. 4:4
18 [a]Rom. 6:12; Heb. 13:4 [b]Rom. 1:24; 1 Thes. 4:4
19 [a]2 Cor. 6:16 [b]Rom. 14:7
20 [a]Acts 20:28; Gal. 3:13; Heb. 9:12; 1 Pet. 1:18; 2 Pet. 2:1; Rev. 5:9
7:1 [a]ver. 8,26
3 [a]Ex. 21:10; 1 Pet. 3:7
5 [a]Joel 2:16; Zech. 7:3; See Ex. 19:15; 1 Sam. 21:4 [b]1 Thes. 3:5
6 [a]2 Cor. 8:8 & 11:17
7 [a]Acts 26:29 [b]ch. 9:5 [c]ch. 12:11
8 [a]ver. 1,26
9 [a]1 Tim. 5:14
10 [a]Mal. 2:14; Mat. 5:32 & 19:6, 9; Mark 10:11; Luke 16:18
14 [a]Mal. 2:15
15 [a]Rom. 12:18 & 14:19; ch. 14:33 [′]Gk. *in peace*
16 [a]1 Pet. 3:1 [′]Gk. *what*
17 [a]ch. 4:17
18 [a]Acts 15:1; Gal. 5:2
19 [a]Gal. 5:6 [b]John 15:14; 1 John 2:3 & 3:24
22 [a]John 8:36; Rom. 6:18; Philem. 16 [b]ch. 9:21; Gal. 5:13; Eph. 6:6; 1 Pet. 2:16 [′]Gk. *made free*
23 [a]1 Pet. 1:18; See Lev. 25:42
25 [a]2 Cor. 8:8

E *1Co 6:11* ◀▶ *1Co 7:40*
D *1Co 5:7* ◀▶ *1Co 7:23*
S *1Co 6:9–11* ◀▶ *1Co 9:24–27*
G *1Co 3:1–2* ◀▶ *1Co 12:1–31*

D *1Co 6:20* ◀▶ *1Co 11:23–25*
L *1Co 6:9–11* ◀▶ *1Co 15:3*

judgment, as one [b]that hath obtained mercy of the Lord [c]to be faithful.

26 I suppose therefore that this is good for the present [1]distress, *I say,* [a]that *it is* good for a man so to be.

27 Art thou bound unto a wife? seek not to be loosed. Art thou loosed from a wife? seek not a wife.

28 But and if thou marry, thou hast not sinned; and if a virgin marry, she hath not sinned. Nevertheless such shall have trouble in the flesh: but I spare you.

29 But [a]this I say, brethren, the time *is* short: it remaineth, that both they that have wives be as though they had none;

30 And they that weep, as though they wept not; and they that rejoice, as though they rejoiced not; and they that buy, as though they possessed not;

31 And they that use this world, as not [a]abusing *it:* for [b]the fashion of this world passeth away.

32 But I would have you without carefulness. [a]He that is unmarried careth for the things [1]that belong to the Lord, how he may please the Lord:

33 But he that is married careth for the things that are of the world, how he may please *his* wife.

34 There is difference *also* between a wife and a virgin. The unmarried woman [a]careth for the things of the Lord, that she may be holy both in body and in spirit: but she that is married careth for the things of the world, how she may please *her* husband.

35 And this I speak for your own profit; not that I may cast a snare upon you, but for that which is comely, and that ye may attend upon the Lord without distraction.

36 But if any man think that he behaveth himself uncomely toward his virgin, if she pass the flower of *her* age, and need so require, let him do what he will, he sinneth not: let them marry.

37 Nevertheless he that standeth stedfast in his heart, having no necessity, but hath power over his own will, and hath so decreed in his heart that he will keep his virgin, doeth well.

38 [a]So then he that giveth *her* in marriage doeth well; but he that giveth *her* not in marriage doeth better.

39 [a]The wife is bound by the law as long as her husband liveth; but if her husband be dead, she is at liberty to be married to whom she will; [b]only in the Lord.

40 But she is happier if she so abide, [a]after my judgment: and [b]I think also that I have the Spirit of God.

Food offered to idols

8 NOW [a]AS touching things offered unto idols, we know that we all have [b]knowledge. [c]Knowledge puffeth up, but charity edifieth.

2 And [a]if any man think that he knoweth any thing, he knoweth nothing yet as he ought to know.

3 But if any man love God, [a]the same is known of him.

4 As concerning therefore the eating of those things that are offered in sacrifice unto idols, we know that [a]an idol *is* nothing in the world, [b]and that *there is* none other God but one.

5 For though there be that are [a]called gods, whether in heaven or in earth, (as there be gods many, and lords many,)

6 But [a]to us *there is but* one God, the Father, [b]of whom *are* all things, and we [1]in him; and [c]one Lord Jesus Christ, [d]by whom *are* all things, and we by him.

7 Howbeit *there is* not in every man that knowledge: for some [a]with conscience of the idol unto this hour eat *it* as a thing offered unto an idol; and their conscience being weak is [b]defiled.

8 But [a]meat commendeth us not to God: for neither, if we eat, [1]are we the better; neither, if we eat not, [2]are we the worse.

9 But [a]take heed lest by any means this [1]liberty of yours become [b]a stumblingblock to them that are weak.

10 For if any man see thee which hast knowledge sit at meat in the idol's temple, shall not [a]the conscience of him which is weak be [1]emboldened to eat those things which are offered to idols;

11 And [a]through thy knowledge shall the weak brother perish, for whom Christ died?

12 But [a]when ye sin so against the brethren, and wound their weak conscience, ye sin against Christ.

13 Wherefore, [a]if meat make my brother to offend, I will eat no flesh while

E L T

25 [b] 1 Tim. 1:16 [c] 1 Tim. 1:12
26 [a] ver. 1,8 [1] Or, *necessity*
29 [a] Rom. 13:11; 1 Pet. 4:7; 2 Pet. 3:8,9
31 [a] ch. 9:18 [b] Ps. 39:6; Jas. 1:10 & 4:14; 1 Pet. 1:24 & 4:7; 1 John 2:17
32 [a] 1 Tim. 5:5 [1] Gk. *of the Lord* as ver. 34
34 [a] Luke 10:40
38 [a] Heb. 13:4
39 [a] Rom. 7:2 [b] 2 Cor. 6:14
40 [a] ver. 25 [b] 1 Thes. 4:8
8:1 [a] Acts 15:20; ch. 10:19 [b] Rom. 14:14 [c] Rom. 14:3
2 [a] ch. 13:8,9; Gal. 6:3; 1 Tim. 6:4
3 [a] Ex. 33:12; Nah. 1:7; Mat. 7:23; Gal. 4:9
4 [a] Is. 41:24 [b] Deut. 4:39 & 6:4; Is. 44:8; Mark 12:29; Eph. 4:6; 1 Tim. 2:5
5 [a] John 10:34
6 [a] Mal. 2:10; Eph. 4:6 [b] Acts 17:28; Rom. 11:36 [c] John 13:13; Acts 2:36; Eph. 4:5; Phil. 2:11 [d] John 1:3; Col. 1:16; Heb. 1:2 [1] Or, *for him*
7 [a] ch. 10:28 [b] Rom. 14:14
8 [a] Rom. 14:17 [1] Or, *have we the more* [2] Or, *have we the less*
9 [a] Gal. 5:13 [b] Rom. 14:13 [1] Or, *power*
10 [a] ch. 10:28 [1] Gk. *edified*
11 [a] Rom. 14:15
12 [a] Mat. 25:40
13 [a] Rom. 14:21; 2 Cor. 11:29

E *1Co 6:19* ◀ ▶ *1Co 12:1–13*
L *Ro 12:6–8* ◀ ▶ *1Co 12:3*
T *1Co 2:4–16* ◀ ▶ *1Co 12:3*

the world standeth, lest I make my brother to offend.

Christian rights

9 AM[a] I not an apostle? am I not free? [b]have I not seen Jesus Christ our Lord? [c]are not ye my work in the Lord?

2 If I be not an apostle unto others, yet doubtless I am to you: for [a]the seal of mine apostleship are ye in the Lord.

3 Mine answer to them that do examine me is this,

4 [a]Have we not power to eat and to drink?

5 Have we not power to lead about a sister, a [1]wife, as well as other apostles, and *as* [a]the brethren of the Lord, and [b]Cephas?

6 Or I only and Barnabas, [a]have not we power to forbear working?

7 Who [a]goeth a warfare any time at his own charges? who [b]planteth a vineyard, and eateth not of the fruit thereof? or who [c]feedeth a flock, and eateth not of the milk of the flock?

8 Say I these things as a man? or saith not the law the same also?

9 For it is written in the law of Moses, [a]Thou shalt not muzzle the mouth of the ox that treadeth out the corn. Doth God take care for oxen?

10 Or saith he *it* altogether for our sakes? For our sakes, no doubt, *this* is written: that [a]he that ploweth should plow in hope; and that he that thresheth in hope should be partaker of his hope.

11 [a]If we have sown unto you spiritual things, *is it* a great thing if we shall reap your carnal things?

12 If others be partakers of *this* power over you, *are* not we rather? [a]Nevertheless we have not used this power; but suffer all things, [b]lest we should hinder the gospel of Christ.

13 [a]Do ye not know that they which minister about holy things [1]live *of the things* of the temple? and they which wait at the altar are partakers with the altar?

14 Even so [a]hath the Lord ordained [b]that they which preach the gospel should live of the gospel.

15 But [a]I have used none of these things: neither have I written these things, that it should be so done unto me: for [b]*it were* better for me to die, than that any man should make my glorying void.

16 For though I preach the gospel, I have nothing to glory of: for [a]necessity is laid upon me; yea, woe is unto me, if I preach not the gospel!

17 For if I do this thing willingly, [a]I have a reward: but if against my will, [b]a dispensation *of the gospel* is committed unto me.

18 What is my reward then? *Verily* that, [a]when I preach the gospel, I may make the gospel of Christ without charge, that I [b]abuse not my power in the gospel.

19 For though I be [a]free from all *men,* yet have [b]I made myself servant unto all, [c]that I might gain the more.

20 And [a]unto the Jews I became as a Jew, that I might gain the Jews; to them that are under the law, as under the law, that I might gain them that are under the law;

21 [a]To [b]them that are without law, as without law, ([c]being not without law to God, but under the law to Christ,) that I might gain them that are without law.

22 [a]To the weak became I as weak, that I might gain the weak: [b]I am made all things to all *men,* [c]that I might by all means save some.

23 And this I do for the gospel's sake, that I might be partaker thereof with *you.*

24 Know ye not that they which run S
in a race run all, but one receiveth the prize? [a]So run, that ye may obtain.

25 And every man that striveth for the mastery is temperate in all things. Now they *do it* to obtain a corruptible crown; but we [a]an incorruptible.

26 I therefore so run, [a]not as uncertainly; so fight I, not as one that beateth the air:

27 [a]But I keep under my body, and [b]bring *it* into subjection: lest that by any means, when I have preached to others, I myself should be [c]a castaway.

The idolatry in the wilderness

10 MOREOVER, BRETHREN, I would not that ye should be ignorant, how that all our fathers were under [a]the cloud, and all passed through [b]the sea;

2 And were all baptized unto Moses in the cloud and in the sea;

S *1Co 6:20* ◄► *1Co 10:11–12*

9:1 [a]Acts 9:15 & 13:2 & 26:17; 2 Cor. 12:12; Gal. 2:7,8; 1 Tim. 2:7; 2 Tim. 1:11 [b]Acts 9:3,17 & 18:9 & 22:14,18; ch. 15:8 [c]ch. 3:6
2 [a]2 Cor. 12:12
4 [a]1 Thes. 2:6
5 [a]Mat. 13:55; Gal. 1:19 [b]Mat. 8:14 [1]Or, *woman*
6 [a]2 Thes. 3:8
7 [a]2 Cor. 10:4; 1 Tim. 1:18 [b]Deut. 20:6 [c]John 21:15; 1 Pet. 5:2
9 [a]Deut. 25:4; 1 Tim. 5:18
10 [a]2 Tim. 2:6
11 [a]Rom. 15:27; Gal. 6:6
12 [a]Acts 20:33; 1 Thes. 2:6 [b]2 Cor. 11:12
13 [a]Lev. 6:16 [1]Or, *feed*
14 [a]Mat. 10:10; Luke 10:7 [b]Gal. 6:6
15 [a]Acts 18:3 [b]2 Cor. 11:10
16 [a]Rom. 1:14
17 [a]ch. 3:8,14 [b]Gal. 2:7; Col. 1:25
18 [a]ch. 10:33 [b]ch. 7:31
19 [a]ver. 1 [b]Gal. 5:13 [c]Mat. 18:15; 1 Pet. 3:1
20 [a]Acts 16:3 & 18:18
21 [a]Gal. 3:2 [b]Rom. 2:12 [c]ch. 7:22
22 [a]Rom. 15:1; 2 Cor. 11:29 [b]ch. 10:33 [c]Rom. 11:14
24 [a]Gal. 2:2; 2 Tim. 4:7
25 [a]Jas. 1:12; Rev. 2:10
26 [a]2 Tim. 2:5
27 [a]Rom. 8:13; Col. 3:5 [b]Rom. 6:18 [c]Jer. 6:30; 2 Cor. 13:5
10:1 [a]Ex. 13:21 [b]Ex. 14:22; Ps. 78:13

3 And did all eat the same [a]spiritual meat;

4 And did all drink the same [a]spiritual drink: for they drank of that spiritual Rock that [l]followed them: and that Rock was Christ.

H 5 But with many of them God was not well pleased: for they [a]were overthrown in the wilderness.

6 Now these things were [l]our examples, to the intent we should not lust after evil things, as [a]they also lusted.

7 [a]Neither be ye idolaters, as *were* some of them; as it is written, [b]The people sat down to eat and drink, and rose up to play.

D 8 [a]Neither let us commit fornication, as some of them committed, and [b]fell in one day three and twenty thousand.

9 Neither let us tempt Christ, as [a]some of them also tempted, and [b]were destroyed of serpents.

10 Neither murmur ye, as [a]some of them also murmured, and [b]were destroyed of [c]the destroyer.

C S 11 Now all these things happened unto them for [l]examples: and [a]they are written for our admonition, [b]upon whom the ends of the world are come.

M 12 Wherefore [a]let him that thinketh he standeth take heed lest he fall.

L 13 There hath no temptation taken you but such as is [l]common to man: but [a]God *is* faithful, [b]who will not suffer you to be tempted above that ye are able; but will with the temptation also make a way to escape, that ye may be able to bear *it.*

Prohibition of idol feasts

14 Wherefore, my dearly beloved, [a]flee from idolatry.

15 I speak as to [a]wise men; judge ye what I say.

16 [a]The cup of blessing which we bless, is it not the communion of the blood of Christ? [b]The bread which we break, is it not the communion of the body of Christ?

17 For [a]we *being* many are one bread, *and* one body: for we are all partakers of that one bread.

H *1Co 6:9–10* ◄► *1Co 11:32*
D *Ac 13:11* ◄► *1Co 11:29–32*
C *1Co 1:7–8* ◄► *1Co 11:26*
S *1Co 9:24–27* ◄► *1Co 10:31*
M *Ro 14:11* ◄► *1Co 14:24–25*
L *Ro 8:31–39* ◄► *Php 4:19*

3 [a]Ex. 16:15; Ps. 78:24
4 [a]Ex. 17:6; Ps. 78:15 [l]Or, *went with them*
5 [a]Num. 14:29; Ps. 106:26
6 [a]Num. 11:4 [l]Gk. *our figures*
7 [a]ver. 14 [b]Ex. 32:6
8 [a]Rev. 2:14 [b]Ps. 106:29
9 [a]Ex. 17:2,7 [b]Num. 21:6
10 [a]Ex. 16:2 [b]Num. 14:37 [c]Ex. 12:23
11 [a]Rom. 15:4 [b]Phil. 4:5; Heb. 10:25 [l]Or, *types*
12 [a]Rom. 11:20
13 [a]ch. 1:9 [b]Ps. 125:3; 2 Pet. 2:9 [l]Or, *moderate*
14 [a]2 Cor. 6:17
15 [a]ch. 8:1
16 [a]Mat. 26:26 [b]Acts 2:42
17 [a]ch. 12:27
18 [a]Rom. 4:12 [b]Rom. 4:1; 2 Cor. 11:18 [c]Lev. 3:3
19 [a]ch. 8:4
20 [a]Lev. 17:7; Deut. 32:17; Ps. 106:37
21 [a]2 Cor. 6:15 [b]Deut. 32:38
22 [a]Deut. 32:21 [b]Ezek. 22:14
23 [a]ch. 6:12
24 [a]Rom. 15:1,2; ch. 13:5
25 [a]1 Tim. 4:4
26 [a]Ex. 19:5; Ps. 24:1
27 [a]Luke 10:7
28 [a]ch. 8:10,12 [b]Deut. 10:14; Ps. 24:1
29 [a]Rom. 14:16
30 [a]Rom. 14:6; 1 Tim. 4:3,4 [l]Or, *thanksgiving*
31 [a]Col. 3:17; 1 Pet. 4:11
32 [a]Rom. 14:13; ch. 8:13 [b]Acts 20:28; 1 Tim. 3:5 [l]Gk. *Greeks*
33 [a]Rom. 15:2 [b]ver. 24

18 Behold [a]Israel [b]after the flesh: [c]are not they which eat of the sacrifices partakers of the altar?

19 What say I then? [a]that the idol is any thing, or that which is offered in sacrifice to idols is any thing?

20 But *I say,* that the things which the Gentiles [a]sacrifice, they sacrifice to devils, and not to God: and I would not that ye should have fellowship with devils.

21 [a]Ye cannot drink the cup of the Lord, and [b]the cup of devils: ye cannot be partakers of the Lord's table, and of the table of devils.

22 Do we [a]provoke the Lord to jealousy? [b]are we stronger than he?

Do all to the glory of God

23 [a]All things are lawful for me, but all things are not expedient: all things are lawful for me, but all things edify not.

24 [a]Let no man seek his own, but every man another's *wealth.*

25 [a]Whatsoever is sold in the shambles, *that* eat, asking no question for conscience sake:

26 For [a]the earth *is* the Lord's, and the fulness thereof.

27 If any of them that believe not bid you *to a feast,* and ye be disposed to go; [a]whatsoever is set before you, eat, asking no question for conscience sake.

28 But if any man say unto you, This is offered in sacrifice unto idols, eat not [a]for his sake that showed it, and for conscience sake: for [b]the earth *is* the Lord's, and the fulness thereof:

29 Conscience, I say, not thine own, but of the other: for [a]why is my liberty judged of another *man's* conscience?

30 For if I by [l]grace be a partaker, why am I evil spoken of for that [a]for which I give thanks?

31 [a]Whether therefore ye eat, or drink, or whatsoever ye do, do all to the glory of God. S

32 [a]Give none offence, neither to the Jews, nor to the [l]Gentiles, nor to [b]the church of God:

33 Even as [a]I please all *men* in all *things,* [b]not seeking mine own profit, but the *profit* of many, that they may be saved.

S *1Co 10:11–12* ◄► *1Co 11:27–32*

Crowns and Rewards

THE LORD ADVISES believers to walk in righteousness and earn "treasures in heaven, where neither moth nor rust doth corrupt, and where thieves do not break through nor steal" (Mt 6:20). These "treasures" are also referred to in other passages of the NT as "crowns." Jesus promises that when he returns, he will reward us with the crowns that we have earned and urges us to "hold that fast which thou hast, that no man take thy crown" (Rev 3:11). The NT highlights five special crowns for believers.

Crown of Glory: For Faithful Servants

"And when the chief Shepherd shall appear, ye shall receive a crown of glory that fadeth not away" (1Pe 5:4).

Those who have served Jesus Christ as elders and pastors in the church will receive their reward from God. Though they have often given thanklessly of their time and resources here, in heaven they shall receive a crown of glory.

Crown of Rejoicing: For Soul Winners

"For what is our hope, or joy, or crown of rejoicing? Are not even ye in the presence of our Lord Jesus Christ at his coming?" (1Th 2:19).

Those who have won others to faith in Jesus Christ as their Savior will experience joy because these new believers are their spiritual children. Because others have been converted under their ministry they are promised this special reward in heaven.

Crown of Righteousness: For Those Who Love His Return

"Henceforth there is laid up for me a crown of righteousness, which the Lord, the righteous judge, shall give me at that day: and not to me only, but unto all them also that love his appearing" (2Ti 4:8).

This crown will be given to all believers who long for the return of Christ. Throughout the NT, Christians are reminded to be watchful for the imminent return of their Lord. We must live active, vital lives as though we have a hundred years until he returns, while at the same time live in anticipation and holiness as though he will return today.

Incorruptible Crown: For Victorious Lives of Purity

"Every man that striveth for the mastery is temperate in all things. Now they do it to obtain a corruptible crown; but we an incorruptible" (1Co 9:25).

Borrowing imagery from athletic contests, Paul tells us that we must exercise discipline—spiritual discipline—if we are to experience victory in Christ. To be prepared for such spiritual discipline, Paul encourages us to daily "put on the whole armour of God" (Eph 6:11). Accordingly, those Christians who are victorious in their daily spiritual struggle will receive an incorruptible crown.

Crown of Life: For Christian Martyrs

"Fear none of those things which thou shalt suffer: behold, the devil shall cast some of you into prison, that ye may be tried; and ye shall have tribulation ten days: be thou faithful unto death, and I will give thee a crown of life" (Rev 2:10).

Christ promises a crown of life for all of those saints through the ages that have suffered martyrdom for their faith in him. His followers have experienced persecution in every century. Even today hundreds of thousands of Christians die throughout the world as martyrs for their faith.

11 BE [a]YE followers of me, even as I also *am* of Christ.

The covering of women's heads

2 Now I praise you, brethren, [a]that ye remember me in all things, and [b]keep the ʹordinances, as I delivered *them* to you.

3 But I would have you know, that [a]the head of every man is Christ; and [b]the head of the woman *is* the man; and [c]the head of Christ *is* God.

4 Every man praying or [a]prophesying, having *his* head covered, dishonoureth his head.

5 But [a]every woman that prayeth or prophesieth with *her* head uncovered dishonoureth her head: for that is even all one as if she were [b]shaven.

6 For if the woman be not covered, let her also be shorn: but if it be [a]a shame for a woman to be shorn or shaven, let her be covered.

7 For a man indeed ought not to cover *his* head, forasmuch as [a]he is the image and glory of God: but the woman is the glory of the man.

8 For [a]the man is not of the woman; but the woman of the man.

9 [a]Neither was the man created for the woman; but the woman for the man.

10 For this cause ought the woman [a]to have ʹpower on *her* head [b]because of the angels.

11 Nevertheless [a]neither is the man without the woman, neither the woman without the man, in the Lord.

12 For as the woman *is* of the man, even so *is* the man also by the woman; but all things of God.

13 Judge in yourselves: is it comely that a woman pray unto God uncovered?

14 Doth not even nature itself teach you, that, if a man have long hair, it is a shame unto him?

15 But if a woman have long hair, it is a glory to her: for *her* hair is given her for a ʹcovering.

16 But [a]if any man seem to be contentious, we have no such custom, [b]neither the churches of God.

The Lord's supper

17 Now in this that I declare *unto you* I praise *you* not, that ye come together not for the better, but for the worse.

18 For first of all, when ye come together in the church, [a]I hear that there be ʹdivisions among you; and I partly believe it.

19 For [a]there must be also ʹheresies among you, [b]that they which are approved may be made manifest among you.

20 When ye come together therefore into one place, ʹ*this* is not to eat the Lord's supper.

21 For in eating every one taketh before *other* his own supper: and one is hungry, and [a]another is drunken.

22 What? have ye not houses to eat and to drink in? or despise ye [a]the church of God, and [b]shame ʹthem that have not? What shall I say to you? shall I praise you in this? I praise *you* not.

23 For [a]I have received of the Lord that which also I delivered unto you, [b]That the Lord Jesus the *same* night in which he was betrayed took bread: **D**

24 And when he had given thanks, he brake *it,* and said, Take, eat: this is my body, which is broken for you: this do ʹin remembrance of me.

25 After the same manner also *he took* the cup, when he had supped, saying, This cup is the new testament in my blood: this do ye, as oft as ye drink *it,* in remembrance of me.

26 For as often as ye eat this bread, and drink this cup, ʹye do show the Lord's death [a]till he come. **C**

27 [a]Wherefore whosoever shall eat this bread, and drink *this* cup of the Lord, unworthily, shall be guilty of the body and blood of the Lord. **S**

28 But [a]let a man examine himself, and so let him eat of *that* bread, and drink of *that* cup.

D *1Co 7:23* ◀▶ *1Co 15:3*
C *1Co 10:11* ◀▶ *2Co 1:14*
S *1Co 10:31* ◀▶ *1Co 13:1–7*

11:1 [a]Eph. 5:1; Phil. 3:17
2 [a]ch. 4:17 [b]ch. 7:17 ʹ*Or, traditions*
3 [a]Eph. 5:23 [b]Gen. 3:16; 1 Tim. 2:11 [c]John 14:28; Phil. 2:7-9
4 [a]ch. 12:10
5 [a]Acts 21:9 [b]Deut. 21:12
6 [a]Num. 5:18
7 [a]Gen. 1:26
8 [a]Gen. 2:21
9 [a]Gen. 2:18
10 [a]Gen. 24:65 [b]Eccl. 5:6 ʹ*i.e. a covering, in sign that she is under the power of her husband*
11 [a]Gal. 3:28
15 ʹ*Or, veil*
16 [a]1 Tim. 6:4 [b]ch. 7:17
18 [a]ch. 1:10,11 ʹ*Or, schisms*
19 [a]Mat. 18:7; Luke 17:1; 1 Tim. 4:1 [b]Luke 2:35; 1 John 2:19 ʹ*Or, sects*
20 ʹ*Or, ye cannot eat*
21 [a]2 Pet. 2:13; Jude 12
22 [a]ch. 10:32 [b]Jas. 2:6 ʹ*Or, them that are poor?*
23 [a]ch. 15:3 [b]Mat. 26:26; Luke 22:19
24 ʹ*Or, for a remembrance*
26 [a]John 14:3; Acts 1:11 ʹ*Or, show ye*
27 [a]John 6:51
28 [a]2 Cor. 13:5

11:26 Our participation in the Lord's communion supper not only affirms our belief in his death and resurrection from the grave, but also confirms our belief in his second coming. Paul reminds us to commemorate his death and resurrection "till he come." Then we will participate in the glorious "marriage supper of the Lamb" (Rev 19:9) in heaven, celebrating our spiritual marriage to Christ forever.

D 29 For he that eateth and drinketh unworthily, eateth and drinketh ′damna-
tion to himself, not discerning the Lord's
body.
30 For this cause many *are* weak and
sickly among you, and many sleep.
31 For [a]if we would judge ourselves,
we should not be judged.
H 32 But when we are judged, [a]we are
T chastened of the Lord, that we should not
be condemned with the world.
33 Wherefore, my brethren, when ye
come together to eat, tarry one for another.
34 And if any man hunger, let him eat
at home; that ye come not together unto
′condemnation. And the rest [a]will I set
in order when [b]I come.

The diversities of gifts

B 12 NOW [a]CONCERNING spiritual
E *gifts,* brethren, I would not have
G you ignorant.
N 2 Ye know [a]that ye were Gentiles, car-
W ried away unto these [b]dumb idols, even
as ye were led.
L 3 Wherefore I give you to understand,
T [a]that no man speaking by the Spirit of
God calleth Jesus ′accursed: and [b]*that* no
man can say that Jesus is the Lord, but by
the Holy Ghost.
4 Now [a]there are diversities of gifts,
but [b]the same Spirit.
5 [a]And there are differences of ′ad-
ministrations, but the same Lord.
6 And there are diversities of operations, but it is the same God [a]which
worketh all in all.
7 [a]But the manifestation of the Spirit is
given to every man to profit withal.
T 8 For to one is given by the Spirit [a]the
word of wisdom; to another [b]the word of
knowledge by the same Spirit;
H 9 [a]To another faith by the same Spirit;
E

29 ′Or, *judgment*

31 [a]Ps. 32:5; 1 John 1:9

32 [a]Ps. 94:12

34 [a]Tit. 1:5 [b]ch. 4:19 ′Or, *judgment*

12:1 [a]ch. 14:1,37

2 [a]Eph. 2:11; 1 Thes. 1:9; 1 Pet. 4:3 [b]Ps. 115:5

3 [a]Mark 9:39; 1 John 4:2 [b]Mat. 16:17; John 15:26 ′Or, *anathema*

4 [a]Rom. 12:4; 1 Pet. 4:10 [b]Eph. 4:4

5 [a]Rom. 12:6; Eph. 4:11 ′Or, *ministries*

6 [a]Eph. 1:23

7 [a]Rom. 12:6; Eph. 4:7

8 [a]ch. 2:6,7 [b]2 Cor. 8:7

9 [a]Mat. 17:19; 2 Cor. 4:13 [b]Mark 16:18; Jas. 5:14

10 [a]Mark 16:17; Gal. 3:5 [b]Rom. 12:6 [c]1 John 4:1 [d]Acts 2:4

11 [a]Rom. 12:6; 2 Cor. 10:13 [b]John 3:8

12 [a]Rom. 12:4,5; Eph. 4:4 [b]Gal. 3:16

13 [a]Rom. 6:5 [b]Gal. 3:28; Col. 3:11 [c]John 6:63 ′Gk. *Greeks*

18 [a]ver. 28 [b]Rom. 12:3

23 ′Or, *put on*

25 ′Or, *division*

to another [b]the gifts of healing by the
same Spirit;
10 [a]To another the working of mira- T
cles; to another [b]prophecy; [c]to another
discerning of spirits; to another [d]*divers*
kinds of tongues; to another the interpretation of tongues:
11 But all these worketh that one and
the selfsame Spirit, [a]dividing to every
man severally [b]as he will.
12 For [a]as the body is one, and hath
many members, and all the members of
that one body, being many, are one body:
[b]so also *is* Christ.
13 For [a]by one Spirit are we all bap- R
tized into one body, [b]whether *we be* Jews
or ′Gentiles, whether *we be* bond or free;
and [c]have been all made to drink into
one Spirit.
14 For the body is not one member,
but many.
15 If the foot shall say, Because I am
not the hand, I am not of the body; is it
therefore not of the body?
16 And if the ear shall say, Because I
am not the eye, I am not of the body; is it
therefore not of the body?
17 If the whole body *were* an eye,
where *were* the hearing? If the whole
were hearing, where *were* the smelling?
18 But now hath [a]God set the members every one of them in the body, [b]as it
hath pleased him.
19 And if they were all one member,
where *were* the body?
20 But now *are they* many members,
yet but one body.
21 And the eye cannot say unto the
hand, I have no need of thee: nor again
the head to the feet, I have no need of
you.
22 Nay, much more those members of
the body, which seem to be more feeble,
are necessary:
23 And those *members* of the body,
which we think to be less honourable,
upon these we ′bestow more abundant
honour; and our uncomely *parts* have
more abundant comeliness.
24 For our comely *parts* have no need:
but God hath tempered the body together, having given more abundant honour to that *part* which lacked:
25 That there should be no ′schism in

D *1Co 10:8* ◀ ▶ *2Co 12:7–10*
H *1Co 10:5–12* ◀ ▶ *1Co 15:25*
T *Hag 2:15–19* ◀ ▶ *2Co 1:6–9*
B *1Co 6:11* ◀ ▶ *2Co 1:21–22*
E *1Co 7:40* ◀ ▶ *1Co 12:28–31*
G *1Co 7:7* ◀ ▶ *1Co 13:1–2*
N *1Co 2:11* ◀ ▶ *2Co 3:17*
W *1Co 3:1–2* ◀ ▶ *1Co 12:31*
L *1Co 7:40* ◀ ▶ *1Co 14:15*
T *1Co 7:40* ◀ ▶ *1Co 12:8*
T *1Co 12:3* ◀ ▶ *1Co 12:10*
H *Ro 15:19* ◀ ▶ *1Co 15:44–54*
E *Ro 15:18–19* ◀ ▶ *1Co 12:28*
T *1Co 12:8* ◀ ▶ *1Co 14:30*
R *1Co 6:11* ◀ ▶ *2Co 3:3*

the body; but *that* the members should
have the same care one for another.
26 And whether one member suffer,
all the members suffer with it; or one
member be honoured, all the members
rejoice with it.
27 Now [a]ye are the body of Christ, and
[b]members in particular.
E 28 And [a]God hath set some in the
E church, first [b]apostles, secondarily
[c]prophets, thirdly teachers, after that
[d]miracles, then [e]gifts of healings, [f]helps,
[g]governments, [/]diversities of tongues.
29 *Are* all apostles? *are* all prophets?
are all teachers? *are* all [/]workers of miracles?
30 Have all the gifts of healing? do all
speak with tongues? do all interpret?
W 31 But [a]covet earnestly the best gifts:
and yet show I unto you a more excellent
way.

The way of love

G 13 THOUGH I speak with the
S tongues of men and of angels,
and have not charity, I am become *as*
sounding brass, or a tinkling cymbal.
2 And though I have *the gift of* [a]proph-
ecy, and understand all mysteries, and all
knowledge; and though I have all faith,
[b]so that I could remove mountains, and
have not charity, I am nothing.
3 And [a]though I bestow all my goods
to feed *the poor,* and though I give my
body to be burned, and have not charity,
it profiteth me nothing.
4 [a]Charity suffereth long, *and* is kind;
charity envieth not; charity [/]vaunteth not
itself, is not puffed up,
5 Doth not behave itself unseemly,
[a]seeketh not her own, is not easily provoked, thinketh no evil;
6 [a]Rejoiceth not in iniquity, but [b]re-
joiceth [/]in the truth;
7 [a]Beareth all things, believeth all

27 [a]Rom. 12:5; Eph. 1:23 & 4:12 & 5:23,30; Col. 1:24 [b]Eph. 5:30
28 [a]Eph. 4:11 [b]Eph. 2:20 & 3:5 [c]Acts 13:1; Rom. 12:6 [d]ver. 10 [e]ver. 9 [f]Num. 11:17 [g]Rom. 12:8; 1 Tim. 5:17; Heb. 13:17, 24 [/]Or, *kinds;* ver. 10
29 [/]Or, *powers*
31 [a]ch. 14:1,39
13:2 [a]ch. 12:8-10, 28 & 14:1; See Mat. 7:22 [b]Mat. 17:20; Mark 11:23; Luke 17:6
3 [a]Mat. 6:1,2
4 [a]Prov. 10:12; 1 Pet. 4:8 [/]Or, *is not rash*
5 [a]ch. 10:24; Phil. 2:4
6 [a]Ps. 10:3; Rom. 1:32 [b]2 John 4 [/]Or, *with the truth*
7 [a]Rom. 15:1; Gal. 6:2; 2 Tim. 2:24
9 [a]ch. 8:2
11 [/]Or, *reasoned*
12 [a]2 Cor. 3:18 & 5:7; Phil. 3:12 [b]Mat. 18:10; 1 John 3:2 [/]Gk. *in a riddle*
14:1 [a]ch. 12:31 [b]Num. 11:25,29
2 [a]Acts 2:4 & 10:46 [/]Gk. *heareth;* see Acts 22:9

things, hopeth all things, endureth all
things.
8 Charity never faileth: but whether G
there be prophecies, they shall fail;
whether *there be* tongues, they shall
cease; whether *there be* knowledge, it
shall vanish away.
9 [a]For we know in part, and we prophesy in part.
10 But when that which is perfect is
come, then that which is in part shall be
done away.
11 When I was a child, I spake as a
child, I understood as a child, I [/]thought
as a child: but when I became a man, I
put away childish things.
12 For [a]now we see through a glass, Q
[/]darkly; but then [b]face to face: now I
know in part; but then shall I know even
as also I am known.
13 And now abideth faith, hope,
charity, these three; but the greatest of
these *is* charity.

Prophecy and tongues

14 FOLLOW AFTER charity, and G
[a]desire spiritual *gifts,* [b]but rather W
that ye may prophesy.
2 For he that [a]speaketh in an *unknown*
tongue speaketh not unto men, but unto
God: for no man [/]understandeth *him;*
howbeit in the spirit he speaketh mysteries.
3 But he that prophesieth speaketh
unto men *to* edification, and exhortation,
and comfort.
4 He that speaketh in an *unknown*
tongue edifieth himself; but he that
prophesieth edifieth the church.
5 I would that ye all spake with W
tongues, but rather that ye prophesied:
for greater *is* he that prophesieth than he
that speaketh with tongues, except he interpret, that the church may receive edifying.

E *1Co 12:1–13* ◀ ▶ *2Co 1:21–22*
E *1Co 12:9* ◀ ▶ *Php 2:27*
W *1Co 12:1–11* ◀ ▶ *1Co 14:1*
G *1Co 12:1–31* ◀ ▶ *1Co 13:8*
S *1Co 11:27–32* ◀ ▶ *1Co 15:2*

G *1Co 13:1–2* ◀ ▶ *1Co 14:1–40*
Q *Lk 16:23–25* ◀
G *1Co 13:8* ◀ ▶ *Eph 1:16–19*
W *1Co 12:31* ◀ ▶ *1Co 14:5*
W *1Co 14:1* ◀ ▶ *1Co 14:15*

13:8–13 Paul reminds us that because of our earthly limitations we can only know and understand part of God's purposes. When Jesus Christ comes again, our limited knowledge and understanding will be removed, and our spiritual eyes will be opened. When we receive our glorious resurrection bodies, we will no longer need "prophecies" (13:8) because we will finally see Jesus Christ "face to face" (13:12) and know everything there is to know about him just as he already knows everything about us.

6 Now, brethren, if I come unto you speaking with tongues, what shall I profit you, except I shall speak to you either by [a]revelation, or by knowledge, or by prophesying, or by doctrine?

7 And even things without life giving sound, whether pipe or harp, except they give a distinction in the [l]sounds, how shall it be known what is piped or harped?

8 For if the trumpet give an uncertain sound, who shall prepare himself to the battle?

9 So likewise ye, except ye utter by the tongue words [l]easy to be understood, how shall it be known what is spoken? for ye shall speak into the air.

10 There are, it may be, so many kinds of voices in the world, and none of them *is* without signification.

11 Therefore if I know not the meaning of the voice, I shall be unto him that speaketh a barbarian, and he that speaketh *shall be* a barbarian unto me.

12 Even so ye, forasmuch as ye are zealous [l]of spiritual *gifts,* seek that ye may excel to the edifying of the church.

13 Wherefore let him that speaketh in an *unknown* tongue pray that he may interpret.

14 For if I pray in an *unknown* tongue, my spirit prayeth, but my understanding is unfruitful.

L W 15 What is it then? I will pray with the spirit, and I will pray with the understanding also: [a]I will sing with the spirit, and I will sing [b]with the understanding also.

16 Else when thou shalt bless with the spirit, how shall he that occupieth the room of the unlearned say Amen [a]at thy giving of thanks, seeing he understandeth not what thou sayest?

17 For thou verily givest thanks well, but the other is not edified.

18 I thank my God, I speak with tongues more than ye all:

19 Yet in the church I had rather speak five words with my understanding, that *by my voice* I might teach others also, than ten thousand words in an *unknown* tongue.

20 Brethren, [a]be not children in understanding: howbeit in malice [b]be ye children, but in understanding be [l]men.

21 [a]In the law it is [b]written, With *men of* other tongues and other lips will I speak unto this people; and yet for all that will they not hear me, saith the Lord.

22 Wherefore tongues are for a sign, not to them that believe, but to them that believe not: but prophesying *serveth* not for them that believe not, but for them which believe.

23 If therefore the whole church be come together into one place, and all speak with tongues, and there come in *those that are* unlearned, or unbelievers, [a]will they not say that ye are mad?

24 But if all prophesy, and there come in one that believeth not, or *one* unlearned, he is convinced of all, he is judged of all: M T

25 And thus are the secrets of his heart made manifest; and so falling down on *his* face he will worship God, and report [a]that God is in you of a truth.

The use of spiritual gifts

26 How is it then, brethren? when ye come together, every one of you hath a psalm, [a]hath a doctrine, hath a tongue, hath a revelation, hath an interpretation. [b]Let all things be done unto edifying.

27 If any man speak in an *unknown* tongue, *let it be* by two, or at the most *by* three, and *that* by course; and let one interpret.

28 But if there be no interpreter, let him keep silence in the church; and let him speak to himself, and to God.

29 Let the prophets speak two or three, and [a]let the other judge.

30 If *any thing* be revealed to another that sitteth by, [a]let the first hold his peace. L T

31 For ye may all prophesy one by one, that all may learn, and all may be comforted.

32 And [a]the spirits of the prophets are subject to the prophets.

33 For God is not *the author* of [l]confusion, but of peace, [a]as in all churches of the saints.

34 [a]Let your women keep silence in the churches: for it is not permitted unto

6 [a]ver. 26
7 [l]Or, *tunes*
9 [l]Gk. *significant*
12 [l]Gk. *of spirits*
15 [a]Eph. 5:19; Col. 3:16 [b]Ps. 47:7
16 [a]ch. 11:24
20 [a]Ps. 131:2; Mat. 11:25 & 18:3 & 19:14; Rom. 16:19; ch. 3:1; Eph. 4:14; Heb. 5:12,13 [b]Mat. 18:3; 1 Pet. 2:2 [l]Gk. *perfect,* or, *of a ripe age;* see ch. 2:6
21 [a]John 10:34 [b]Is. 28:11,12
23 [a]Acts 2:13
25 [a]Is. 45:14; Zech. 8:23
26 [a]ver. 6; ch. 12:8-10 [b]ch. 12:7; 2 Cor. 12:19; Eph. 4:12
29 [a]ch. 12:10
30 [a]1 Thes. 5:19, 20
32 [a]1 John 4:1
33 [a]ch. 11:16 [l]Gk. *tumult,* or, *unquietness*
34 [a]1 Tim. 2:11,12

L *1Co 12:3* ◄► *1Co 14:30*
W *1Co 14:5* ◄► *2Co 3:6–11*
M *1Co 10:12* ◄► *Col 2:18*
T *Ro 10:8–10* ◄► *2Ti 1:8*
L *1Co 14:15* ◄► *2Co 12:18*
T *1Co 12:10* ◄► *Eph 1:17–19*

them to speak; but *they are commanded*
to be under obedience, as also saith the
[b]law.
35 And if they will learn any thing, let
them ask their husbands at home: for it
is a shame for women to speak in the
church.
36 What? came the word of God out
from you? or came it unto you only?
37 [a]If any man think himself to be a
prophet, or spiritual, let him acknowledge that the things that I write unto you
are the commandments of the Lord.
38 But if any man be ignorant, let him
be ignorant.
39 Wherefore, brethren, [a]covet to
prophesy, and forbid not to speak with
tongues.
40 [a]Let all things be done decently and
in order.

The resurrection

15 MOREOVER, BRETHREN, I declare unto you the gospel [a]which
I preached unto you, which also ye have
received, and [b]wherein ye stand;
S 2 [a]By which also ye are saved, if ye
[1]keep in memory [2]what I preached unto
you, unless [b]ye have believed in vain.
D 3 For [a]I delivered unto you first of all
L that [b]which I also received, how that
Christ died for our sins [c]according to the
scriptures;
4 And that he was buried, and that he
rose again the third day [a]according to the
scriptures:
5 [a]And that he was seen of Cephas,
then [b]of the twelve:
6 After that, he was seen of above five
hundred brethren at once; of whom the
greater part remain unto this present, but
some are fallen asleep.
7 After that, he was seen of James;
then [a]of all the apostles.
8 [a]And last of all he was seen of me
also, as of [1]one born out of due time.
9 For I am [a]the least of the apostles,
that am not meet to be called an apostle,
because [b]I persecuted the church of God.
10 But [a]by the grace of God I am what
I am: and his grace which *was bestowed*
upon me was not in vain; but [b]I laboured
more abundantly than they all: [c]yet not I,
but the grace of God which was with me.
11 Therefore whether *it were* I or
they, so we preach, and so ye believed.
12 Now if Christ be preached that he
rose from the dead, how say some among
you that there is no resurrection of the
dead?
13 But if there be no resurrection of
the dead, [a]then is Christ not risen:
14 And if Christ be not risen, then *is*
our preaching vain, and your faith *is* also
vain.
15 Yea, and we are found false witnesses of God; because [a]we have testified
of God that he raised up Christ: whom he
raised not up, if so be that the dead rise
not.
16 For if the dead rise not, then is not
Christ raised:
17 And if Christ be not raised, your
faith *is* vain; [a]ye are yet in your sins.
18 Then they also which are fallen
asleep in Christ are perished.
19 [a]If in this life only we have hope in
Christ, we are of all men most miserable.
20 But now [a]is Christ risen from the F

34 [b]Gen. 3:16
37 [a]2 Cor. 10:7; 1 John 4:6
39 [a]ch. 12:31; 1 Thes. 5:20
40 [a]ver. 33
15:1 [a]Gal. 1:11 [b]Rom. 5:2
2 [a]Rom. 1:16; ch. 1:21 [b]Gal. 3:4 [1]Or, *hold fast* [2]Gk. *by what speech*
3 [a]ch. 11:2,23 [b]Gal. 1:12 [c]Ps. 22:15; Is. 53:5,6; Dan. 9:26; Zech. 13:7; Luke 24:26, 46; Acts 3:18 & 26:23; 1 Pet. 1:11 & 2:24
4 [a]Ps. 16:10; Is. 53:10; Hos. 6:2; Luke 24:26; Acts 2:25; 1 Pet. 1:11
5 [a]Luke 24:34 [b]Mat. 28:17; Mark 16:14; Luke 24:36; John 20:19
7 [a]Luke 24:50; Acts 1:3,4
8 [a]Acts 9:4 & 22:14,18 [1]Or, *an abortive*
9 [a]Eph. 3:8 [b]Acts 8:3; Phil. 3:6
10 [a]Eph. 3:7,8 [b]2 Cor. 11:23 & 12:11 [c]Mat. 10:20; Rom. 15:18; 2 Cor. 3:5; Gal. 2:8; Eph. 3:7; Phil. 2:13
13 [a]1 Thes. 4:14
15 [a]Acts 2:24 & 4:10,33
17 [a]Rom. 4:25
19 [a]2 Tim. 3:12
20 [a]1 Pet. 1:3

S *1Co 13:1–7* ◀▶ *1Co 15:33–34*
D *1Co 11:23–25* ◀▶ *2Co 5:14–15*
L *1Co 7:23* ◀▶ *2Co 5:18–21*
F *1Co 6:14* ◀▶ *1Co 15:35–55*

15:4–6 Paul confirms the fulfillment of the prophecies that Christ would rise from the dead on the third day (see Mt 12:40; Jn 2:19–22) and confirms Christ's appearance to many of the disciples after the resurrection. These appearances to different persons at different times over a period of forty days proves that Jesus truly rose from the grave in his glorious resurrection body (see Mt 28:9, 16; Mk 16:9; Lk 24:13–31, 34; Jn 20:19, 26; 21:1–22; 1Co 15:5–7).

15:17–19 Paul admits that if Jesus' body still lay in the grave, our faith would be in vain. The physical resurrection of Jesus' body from death to life is the most fundamental fact upon which the faith of Christianity rests. Ancient Gnostics and modern-day liberals who denied the physical resurrection of Jesus have denied the most basic and fundamental truth of Christianity. This is why the NT writers described the events of Christ's trial, crucifixion, resurrection and appearances after the resurrection with such detail. They knew that Christianity would be nothing if Jesus had not been resurrected as prophesied.

15:20–28 Paul declares God's promise of the coming harvest of believers when all those who follow Christ will participate in the bodily resurrection to eternal life in heaven. At the Feast of Firstfruits, a sheaf of grain from the first cutting of the harvest was waved by a priest in the temple before the Lord

dead, *and* become [b]the firstfruits of them
that slept.
W 21 For [a]since by man *came* death, [b]by
man *came* also the resurrection of the
dead.
22 For as in Adam all die, even so in
Christ shall all be made alive.
23 But [a]every man in his own order:
Christ the firstfruits; afterward they that
are Christ's at his coming.
K 24 Then *cometh* the end, when he
M shall have delivered up [a]the kingdom to
V God, even the Father; when he shall have
put down all rule and all authority and
power.
H 25 For he must reign, [a]till he hath put
all enemies under his feet.
26 [a]The last enemy *that* shall be destroyed *is* death.
27 For he [a]hath put all things under
his feet. But when he saith all things are
put under *him, it is* manifest that he is
excepted, which did put all things under
him.
28 [a]And when all things shall be subdued unto him, then [b]shall the Son also
himself be subject unto him that put all
things under him, that God may be all in
all.
29 Else what shall they do which are
baptized for the dead, if the dead rise not
at all? why are they then baptized for the
dead?
30 And [a]why stand we in jeopardy every hour?
31 I protest by [a]your[/] rejoicing which
I have in Christ Jesus our Lord, [b]I die
daily.
32 If [/]after the manner of men [a]I have
fought with beasts at Ephesus, what ad-
vantageth it me, if the dead rise not? [b]let
us eat and drink: for tomorrow we die.
33 Be not deceived: [a]evil communica- S
tions corrupt good manners.
34 [a]Awake to righteousness, and sin
not; [b]for some have not the knowledge of
God: [c]I speak *this* to your shame.
35 But some *man* will say, [a]How are F
the dead raised up? and with what body
do they come?
36 *Thou* fool, [a]that which thou sowest
is not quickened, except it die:
37 And that which thou sowest, thou
sowest not that body that shall be, but
bare grain, it may chance of wheat, or of
some other *grain:*

20 [b]Acts 26:23; Rev. 1:5
21 [a]Rom. 5:12 [b]John 11:25; Rom. 6:23
23 [a]1 Thes. 4:15
24 [a]Dan. 7:14
25 [a]Ps. 110:1; Acts 2:34; Eph. 1:22
26 [a]2 Tim. 1:10; Rev. 20:14
27 [a]Ps. 8:6
28 [a]Phil. 3:21 [b]ch. 3:23 & 11:3
30 [a]2 Cor. 11:26; Gal. 5:11
31 [a]1 Thes. 2:19 [b]Rom. 8:36; 2 Cor. 4:10 [/]Some read, *our*
32 [a]2 Cor. 1:8 [b]Eccl. 2:24; Is. 22:13; Luke 12:19 [/]Or, to speak *after the manner of men*
33 [a]ch. 5:6
34 [a]Rom. 13:11; Eph. 5:14 [b]1 Thes. 4:5 [c]ch. 6:5
35 [a]Ezek. 37:3
36 [a]John 12:24

W *Ac 24:15* ◀▶ *Rev 20:5–6*
K *Ac 3:25* ◀▶ *Rev 11:15*
M *1Co 6:2–3* ◀▶ *Php 2:9–11*
V *Ac 2:34–35* ◀▶ *Eph 1:21–22*
H *1Co 11:32* ◀▶ *1Co 16:22*
S *1Co 15:2* ◀▶ *2Co 5:10*
F *1Co 15:20–26* ◀▶ *2Co 1:9*

---

as a grateful acknowledgment of the full harvest that would follow (see Lev 23:10–11). Jesus Christ's resurrection from death is the "firstfruits" (15:20) of the final resurrection of all believers.

Paul also explains that the resurrection of believers will involve several phases. The first step occurred when Jesus Christ rose from the grave, quite possibly on the day of the Feast of Firstfruits. The apostle then refers to the resurrection or rapture of the living and departed believers, both OT and NT, raised to eternal life in Christ. The final stage is the end of all things when Christ "shall have delivered up the kingdom to God, even the Father" (15:24) by defeating the antichrist and the rulers of the nations at Armageddon. Then Christ will reign on earth from the throne of David in Jerusalem for the Millennium and through eternity.

There will also be a physical resurrection of all of the wicked dead at the end of the Millennium just before the great white throne judgment of God (see Rev 21:11–15). As Adam's sin brought death to all people, the resurrection power of Jesus Christ will raise all humanity from the dead—the righteous to eternal life in heaven and the unrighteous for eternal judgment in hell (see Mt 25:34–46). For further information, see the article on "The Resurrection of the Body" on p. 1206.

15:35–50 Paul deals in this passage with questions about the resurrection body that believers will receive at Christ's coming in the air (see 1Th 4:16–17). A common error assumed that the resurrection body was identical to the dead body, only resuscitated like Lazarus was when he rose from the grave. The second error supposed that the resurrection body was a new creation, unrelated to the dead body. Paul indicates that the resurrection body is definitely related to the old body (15:36, 38), but that it will be transformed into a spiritual, celestial body with new capabilities (15:39–44) like the body that Jesus had when he rose from the grave (see Php 3:21; 1Jn 3:2). Our earthly bodies are prone to sin, corruption and disease and unfit for heaven's glory (15:50). But our resurrection bodies will be perfect, without sin, pain, disease or death so that we might enjoy the totality of heaven's glory and reign on the earth with Christ in the Millennium (see Rev 5:10). For further information, see the article on "The Resurrection of the Body" on p. 1206.

38 But God giveth it a body as it hath
pleased him, and to every seed his own
body.
39 All flesh *is* not the same flesh: but
there is one *kind of* flesh of men, another
flesh of beasts, another of fishes, *and* another of birds.
40 *There are* also celestial bodies, and
bodies terrestrial: but the glory of the celestial *is* one, and the *glory* of the terrestrial *is* another.
41 *There is* one glory of the sun, and
another glory of the moon, and another
glory of the stars: for *one* star differeth
from *another* star in glory.
42 [a]So also *is* the resurrection of the
dead. It is sown in corruption; it is raised
in incorruption:
43 [a]It is sown in dishonour; it is raised
in glory: it is sown in weakness; it is
raised in power:
H 44 It is sown a natural body; it is raised
a spiritual body. There is a natural body,
and there is a spiritual body.
45 And so it is written, The first man
Adam [a]was made a living soul; [b]the last
Adam *was made* [c]a quickening spirit.
46 Howbeit that *was* not first which is
spiritual, but that which is natural; and
afterward that which is spiritual.
47 [a]The first man *is* of the earth,
[b]earthy: the second man *is* the Lord
[c]from heaven.
48 As *is* the earthy, such *are* they also

H *1Co 12:9* ◀ ▶ *2Co 3:6*

42 [a]Dan. 12:3; Mat. 13:43
43 [a]Phil. 3:21
45 [a]Gen. 2:7 [b]Rom. 5:14 [c]John 5:21; Phil. 3:21; Col. 3:4
47 [a]John 3:31 [b]Gen. 3:19 [c]John 3:13
48 [a]Phil. 3:20
49 [a]Gen. 5:3 [b]Rom. 8:29; 2 Cor. 3:18; Phil. 3:21; 1 John 3:2
50 [a]Mat. 16:17; John 3:3,5
51 [a]1 Thes. 4:15 [b]Phil. 3:21
52 [a]Zech. 9:14; Mat. 24:31; John 5:25
53 [a]2 Cor. 5:4
54 [a]Is. 25:8; Rev. 20:14
55 [a]Hos. 13:14 [1]Or, *hell*
56 [a]Rom. 4:15
57 [a]Rom. 7:25 [b]1 John 5:4
58 [a]2 Pet. 3:14

that are earthy: [a]and as *is* the heavenly,
such *are* they also that are heavenly.
49 And [a]as we have borne the image
of the earthy, [b]we shall also bear the image of the heavenly.
50 Now this I say, brethren, that [a]flesh T
and blood cannot inherit the kingdom of
God; neither doth corruption inherit incorruption.
51 Behold, I show you a mystery; [a]We
shall not all sleep, [b]but we shall all be
changed,
52 In a moment, in the twinkling of an
eye, at the last trump: [a]for the trumpet
shall sound, and the dead shall be raised
incorruptible, and we shall be changed.
53 For this corruptible must put on incorruption, and [a]this mortal *must* put on
immortality.
54 So when this corruptible shall have
put on incorruption, and this mortal shall
have put on immortality, then shall be
brought to pass the saying that is written,
[a]Death is swallowed up in victory.
55 [a]O death, where *is* thy sting?
O [1]grave, where *is* thy victory?
56 The sting of death *is* sin; and [a]the K
strength of sin *is* the law.
57 [a]But thanks *be* to God, which giv- V
eth us [b]the victory through our Lord
Jesus Christ.
58 [a]Therefore, my beloved brethren,

T *Ro 8:17–18* ◀ ▶ *Php 3:21*
K *1Co 6:9–11* ◀ ▶ *2Co 1:20*
V *Ro 8:35–39* ◀ ▶ *2Co 2:14*

15:51–54 Paul reveals the "mystery" (15:51) of the rapture in this passage, that moment when all believers in Christ will be caught up into the air to receive the "redemption of our body" (Ro 8:23). Paul acknowledges that not every Christian will suffer death prior to this event. When Jesus returns in the air, there will be a group of living believers on earth at that moment. That generation of believers will pass from life to life eternal without ever experiencing the pangs of death. Their natural corruptible bodies will be instantaneously transformed into glorious, supernatural resurrection bodies, and they will be caught up to meet with the Lord in the air (see 1Th 4:17). At that point the rapture will signal the fulfillment of Isaiah's Messianic prophecy because "death is swallowed up in victory" (15:54; see Isa 25:8).

Note Paul's use of the phrase "at the last trump" (15:52). Some scholars have suggested that this means that the resurrection of the saints will take place when the last of the seven trumpet judgments of Revelation is sounded (see Rev 11:15). However, Scripture clearly shows that this trumpet in 15:52 sounds *before* God's wrath descends, whereas the seventh trumpet blown in Revelation is sounded at the *end* of God's wrath. Note also that the trumpet that summons the church is called "the trump of God" (1Th 4:16), while the seventh trumpet in Revelation is an angel's trumpet (see Rev 18:13).

It is more likely that in this verse Paul was referring to the last trumpet blasts that were given when the Israelites were traveling through the Sinai desert (see Nu 10:2–10). When the first trumpet blast sounded, the leaders gathered to Moses, and the people prepared to set out. Additional blasts were given to signal the movement for each tribe. When the last trumpet blast was sounded, this signified that the whole camp was on the move. Paul probably used this metaphor to symbolize God's signal to his people to be prepared to move out at the rapture.

be ye stedfast, unmoveable, always abounding in the work of the Lord, forasmuch as ye know [b]that your labour is not in vain in the Lord.

The collection for the poor

16 NOW CONCERNING [a]the collection for the saints, as I have given order to the churches of Galatia, even so do ye.

2 [a]Upon the first *day* of the week let every one of you lay by him in store, as *God* hath prospered him, that there be no gatherings when I come.

3 And when I come, [a]whomsoever ye shall approve by *your* letters, them will I send to bring your [l]liberality unto Jerusalem.

4 [a]And if it be meet that I go also, they shall go with me.

Paul's itinerary

5 Now I will come unto you, [a]when I shall pass through Macedonia: for I do pass through Macedonia.

6 And it may be that I will abide, yea, and winter with you, that ye may [a]bring me on my journey whithersoever I go.

7 For I will not see you now by the way; but I trust to tarry a while with you, [a]if the Lord permit.

8 But I will tarry at Ephesus until Pentecost.

9 For [a]a great door and effectual is opened unto me, and [b]*there are* many adversaries.

10 Now [a]if Timotheus come, see that he may be with you without fear: for [b]he worketh the work of the Lord, as I also *do.*

11 [a]Let no man therefore despise him: but conduct him forth [b]in peace, that he may come unto me: for I look for him with the brethren.

58 [b]ch. 3:8
16:1 [a]Acts 11:29; Gal. 2:10
2 [a]Acts 20:7
3 [a]2 Cor. 8:19 [l]Gk. *gift;* see 2 Cor. 8:4
4 [a]2 Cor. 8:19
5 [a]Acts 19:21; 2 Cor. 1:16
6 [a]Acts 15:3; Rom. 15:24
7 [a]Acts 18:21; Jas. 4:15
9 [a]Acts 14:27; 2 Cor. 2:12; Col. 4:3 [b]Acts 19:9
10 [a]Acts 19:22 [b]Phil. 2:20; 1 Thes. 3:2
11 [a]1 Tim. 4:12 [b]Acts 15:33
12 [a]ch. 1:12
13 [a]Mat. 24:42; 1 Thes. 5:6; 1 Pet. 5:8 [b]Phil. 1:27; 1 Thes. 3:8; 2 Thes. 2:15 [c]Eph. 6:10; Col. 1:11
14 [a]1 Pet. 4:8
15 [a]ch. 1:16 [b]Rom. 16:5 [c]2 Cor. 8:4; Heb. 6:10
16 [a]Heb. 13:17 [b]Heb. 6:10
17 [a]2 Cor. 11:9; Phil. 2:30
18 [a]Col. 4:8 [b]Phil. 2:29
19 [a]Rom. 16:5
20 [a]Rom. 16:16
21 [a]Col. 4:18
22 [a]Eph. 6:24 [b]Gal. 1:8,9 [c]Jude 14,15
23 [a]Rom. 16:20

12 As touching *our* brother [a]Apollos, I greatly desired him to come unto you with the brethren: but his will was not at all to come at this time; but he will come when he shall have convenient time.

Concluding message

13 [a]Watch ye, [b]stand fast in the faith, quit you like men, [c]be strong.

14 [a]Let all your things be done with charity.

15 I beseech you, brethren, (ye know [a]the house of Stephanas, that it is [b]the firstfruits of Achaia, and *that* they have addicted themselves to [c]the ministry of the saints,)

16 [a]That ye submit yourselves unto such, and to every one that helpeth with *us,* and [b]laboureth.

17 I am glad of the coming of Stephanas and Fortunatus and Achaicus: [a]for that which was lacking on your part they have supplied.

18 [a]For they have refreshed my spirit and yours: therefore [b]acknowledge ye them that are such.

19 The churches of Asia salute you. Aquila and Priscilla salute you much in the Lord, [a]with the church that is in their house.

20 All the brethren greet you. [a]Greet ye one another with an holy kiss.

21 [a]The salutation of *me* Paul with mine own hand.

22 If any man [a]love not the Lord Jesus **P**
Christ, [b]let him be Anathema **H**
[c]Maranatha.

23 [a]The grace of our Lord Jesus Christ *be* with you.

24 My love *be* with you all in Christ Jesus. Amen.

P *Ac 2:19–20* ◀ ▶ *1Th 5:3*
H *1Co 15:25* ◀ ▶ *2Co 2:15–16*

16:2 The early Christians (including Jewish and Gentile believers) worshiped on Sunday, "the first day of the week" (16:2), in commemoration of Christ's resurrection on that day.

16:22 Paul calls attention to the fact that he wrote these closing remarks with his own hand (16:21). The end of 16:22 is actually three words, not two. The first word is the Greek word *anathema,* which means, "cursed with a great curse." The next two words, *Maran* and *Atha*, are Aramaic, the language of familiarity in the NT world. *Maran* simply means "Lord." And *Atha* translates "come." The intent, then, of Paul's last words to the Corinthians is a warning that those who reject Christ's offer of salvation are accursed because they remain dead in their sins (see Jn 3:18–20). Yet Paul's words ring with the affirmation of the imminent return of Christ to take his church home to heaven as Paul cries "Lord, come!"

2 Corinthians

Author: Paul

Theme: God's strength in our weakness

Date of Writing: C. A.D. 55

Outline of 2 Corinthians

I. Introduction (1:1–11)
II. Paul as God's Messenger (1:12—7:16)
III. Stewardship in Giving (8:1—9:15)
IV. Paul as an Apostle (10:1—13:10)
V. Conclusion (13:11–14)

THE APOSTLE PAUL probably wrote the epistle known as 2 Corinthians a few months after his first letter to the Corinthian church. The problems that had occasioned Paul's first letter to this church were still present at the time this second letter was composed. Some of the members of the Corinthian church were unrepentant, and Paul was anxious about the welfare of the church. Reaching Macedonia, Paul was greatly relieved when Titus brought him the good news that a revival had broken out in the Corinthian church. Paul then wrote his second letter to the Corinthians, commending them for their repentance, encouraging their faithful giving to the poor and reestablishing his apostolic authority in his messages to them.

While the book of 2 Corinthians contains very few prophecies, the letter is filled with a variety of personal matters regarding Paul's feelings, obligations, ambitions and responsibilities. Containing more personal glimpses into Paul's life than any other letter, this epistle shares Paul's personal career with the Corinthian believers and deals with the attacks against his leadership (see 3:1, 8:20–23; 10:2, 8–10, 15; 11:5; 12:11–12, 16). Paul also shares some of the most significant teaching on giving, ministry and our Christian hope in this autobiographical letter.

The God of all comfort

1 PAUL, [a]AN apostle of Jesus Christ by the will of God, and Timothy *our* brother, unto the church of God which is at Corinth, [b]with all the saints which are in all Achaia:

2 [a]Grace *be* to you and peace from God our Father, and *from* the Lord Jesus Christ.

J 3 [a]Blessed *be* God, even the Father of our Lord Jesus Christ, the Father of mercies, and the God of all comfort;

4 Who comforteth us in all our tribulation, that we may be able to comfort them which are in any trouble, by the comfort wherewith we ourselves are comforted of God.

5 For as [a]the sufferings of Christ abound in us, so our consolation also aboundeth by Christ.

T 6 And whether we be afflicted, [a]*it is* for your consolation and salvation, which ʹis effectual in the enduring of the same sufferings which we also suffer: or whether we be comforted, *it is* for your consolation and salvation.

7 And our hope of you *is* stedfast, knowing, that [a]as ye are partakers of the sufferings, so *shall ye be* also of the consolation.

8 For we would not, brethren, have you ignorant of [a]our trouble which came to us in Asia, that we were pressed out of measure, above strength, insomuch that we despaired even of life:

F 9 But we had the ʹsentence of death in ourselves, that we should [a]not trust in ourselves, but in God which raiseth the dead:

10 [a]Who delivered us from so great a death, and doth deliver: in whom we trust that he will yet deliver *us;*

11 Ye also [a]helping together by prayer for us, that [b]for the gift *bestowed* upon us by the means of many persons thanks may be given by many on our behalf.

Paul's change of plans

12 For our rejoicing is this, the testimony of our conscience, that in simplicity and [a]godly sincerity, [b]not with fleshly wisdom, but by the grace of God, we have had our conversation in the world, and more abundantly to you-ward.

13 For we write none other things unto you, than what ye read or acknowledge; and I trust ye shall acknowledge even to the end;

14 As also ye have acknowledged us in part, [a]that we are your rejoicing, even as [b]ye also *are* ours in the day of the Lord Jesus. C

15 And in this confidence [a]I was minded to come unto you before, that ye might have [b]a second ʹbenefit;

16 And to pass by you into Macedonia, and [a]to come again out of Macedonia unto you, and of you to be brought on my way toward Judaea.

17 When I therefore was thus minded, did I use lightness? or the things that I purpose, do I purpose [a]according to the flesh, that with me there should be yea yea, and nay nay?

18 But *as* God *is* true, our ʹword toward you was not yea and nay.

19 For [a]the Son of God, Jesus Christ, who was preached among you by us, *even* by me and Silvanus and Timotheus, was not yea and nay, [b]but in him was yea.

20 [a]For all the promises of God in him *are* yea, and in him Amen, unto the glory of God by us. K

21 Now he which stablisheth us with you in Christ, and [a]hath anointed us, *is* God; B E

22 Who [a]hath also sealed us, and

1:1 [a]1 Cor. 1:1; Eph. 1:1; Col. 1:1; 1 Tim. 1:1; 2 Tim. 1:1 [b]Phil. 1:1; Col. 1:2
2 [a]Rom. 1:7; 1 Cor. 1:3; Gal. 1:3; Phil. 1:2; Col. 1:2; 1 Thes. 1:1; 2 Thes. 1:2
3 [a]Eph. 1:3; 1 Pet. 1:3
5 [a]Acts 9:4; ch. 4:10
6 [a]ch. 4:15 ʹOr, *is wrought*
7 [a]Rom. 8:17; 2 Tim. 2:12
8 [a]Acts 19:23; 1 Cor. 15:32 & 16:9
9 [a]Jer. 17:5,7 ʹOr, *answer*
10 [a]2 Pet. 2:9
11 [a]Rom. 15:30; Phil. 1:19; Philem. 22 [b]ch. 4:15
12 [a]ch. 2:17 [b]1 Cor. 2:4
14 [a]ch. 5:12 [b]Phil. 2:16; 1 Thes. 2:19
15 [a]1 Cor. 4:19 [b]Rom. 1:11 ʹOr, *grace*
16 [a]1 Cor. 16:5,6
17 [a]ch. 10:2
18 ʹOr, *preaching*
19 [a]Mark 1:1; Luke 1:35; Acts 9:20 [b]Heb. 13:8
20 [a]Rom. 15:8
21 [a]1 John 2:20
22 [a]Eph. 4:30; 2 Tim. 2:19; Rev. 2:17

J *Ro 12:12* ◀▶ *2Co 2:14*
T *1Co 11:32* ◀▶ *2Co 4:10–11*
F *1Co 15:35–55* ◀▶ *2Co 4:14*

C *1Co 11:26* ◀▶ *Php 1:6*
K *1Co 15:56–57* ◀▶ *2Co 2:14*
B *1Co 12:1–11* ◀▶ *2Co 5:5*
E *1Co 12:28–31* ◀▶ *2Co 3:3*

1:9 All of us carry the sentence of death in our bodies because we are descendants of Adam and because of our individual rebellion against our Creator. Yet Paul reminds us that our hope is not based in ourselves, but resides in Christ's victory on the cross over death and sin.

1:14 Paul rejoices in their mutual salvation in Jesus Christ and confidently awaits "the day of the Lord Jesus" when all believers will leave their mortal, corrupt bodies behind and receive glorious, resurrection bodies like Jesus had when he rose from the grave (see 1Co 15:42–44).

[b]given the earnest of the Spirit in our hearts.

23 Moreover [a]I call God for a record upon my soul, [b]that to spare you I came not as yet unto Corinth.

24 Not for [a]that we have dominion over your faith, but are helpers of your joy: for [b]by faith ye stand.

2 BUT I determined this with myself, [a]that I would not come again to you in heaviness.

2 For if I make you sorry, who is he then that maketh me glad, but the same which is made sorry by me?

3 And I wrote this same unto you, lest, when I came, [a]I should have sorrow from them of whom I ought to rejoice; [b]having confidence in you all, that my joy is *the joy* of you all.

4 For out of much affliction and anguish of heart I wrote unto you with many tears; [a]not that ye should be grieved, but that ye might know the love which I have more abundantly unto you.

Forgiveness of an offender

5 But [a]if any have caused grief, he hath not [b]grieved me, but in part: that I may not overcharge you all.

6 Sufficient to such a man *is* this [1]punishment, which *was inflicted* [a]of many.

7 [a]So that contrariwise ye *ought* rather to forgive *him,* and comfort *him,* lest perhaps such a one should be swallowed up with overmuch sorrow.

8 Wherefore I beseech you that ye would confirm *your* love toward him.

9 For to this end also did I write, that I might know the proof of you, whether ye be [a]obedient in all things.

10 To whom ye forgive any thing, I *forgive* also: for if I forgave any thing, to whom I forgave *it,* for your sakes *forgave I it* [1]in the person of Christ;

11 Lest Satan should get an advantage of us: for we are not ignorant of his devices.

Ministers of the new testament

12 Furthermore, [a]when I came to Troas to *preach* Christ's gospel, and [b]a door was opened unto me of the Lord,

13 [a]I had no rest in my spirit, because I found not Titus my brother: but taking my leave of them, I went from thence into Macedonia.

14 Now thanks *be* unto God, which al- K
ways causeth us to triumph in Christ, J
and maketh manifest [a]the savour of his V
knowledge by us in every place.

15 For we are unto God a sweet savour H
of Christ, [a]in them that are saved, and N
[b]in them that perish:

16 [a]To the one *we are* the savour of death unto death; and to the other the savour of life unto life. And [b]who *is* sufficient for these things?

17 For we are not as many, which [a]corrupt[1] the word of God: but as [b]of sincerity, but as of God, in the sight of God speak we [2]in Christ.

3 DO [a]WE begin again to commend ourselves? or need we, as some *others,* [b]epistles of commendation to you, or *letters* of commendation from you?

2 [a]Ye are our epistle written in our hearts, known and read of all men:

3 *Forasmuch as ye are* manifestly de- E
clared to be the epistle of Christ [a]minis- R
tered by us, written not with ink, but with the Spirit of the living God; not [b]in tables of stone, but [c]in fleshy tables of the heart.

4 And such trust have we through Christ to God-ward:

5 [a]Not that we are sufficient of our- M
selves to think any thing as of ourselves; but [b]our sufficiency *is* of God;

6 Who also hath made us able [a]minis- E
ters of [b]the new testament; not [c]of the H
letter, but of the spirit: for [d]the letter kill- W
eth, [e]but the spirit [1]giveth life.

A ministry of glory

7 But if [a]the ministration of death, [b]written *and* engraven in stones, was glorious, [c]so that the children of Israel could not stedfastly behold the face of Moses for the glory of his countenance; which *glory* was to be done away:

8 How shall not [a]the ministration of the spirit be rather glorious?

22 [b]ch. 5:5; Eph. 1:14
23 [a]Rom. 1:9; ch. 11:31; Gal. 1:20; Phil. 1:8 [b]1 Cor. 4:21; ch. 2:3 & 12:20 & 13:2,10
24 [a]1 Cor. 3:5; 1 Pet. 5:3 [b]Rom. 11:20; 1 Cor. 15:1
2:1 [a]ch. 1:23
3 [a]ch. 12:21 [b]ch. 8:22; Gal. 5:10
4 [a]ch. 7:8,9
5 [a]1 Cor. 5:1 [b]Gal. 4:12
6 [a]1 Cor. 5:4,5; 1 Tim. 5:20 [1]Or, *censure*
7 [a]Gal. 6:1
9 [a]ch. 10:6
10 [1]Or, *in the sight*
12 [a]Acts 16:8 [b]1 Cor. 16:9
13 [a]ch. 7:5,6
14 [a]Sol. 1:3
15 [a]1 Cor. 1:18 [b]ch. 4:3
16 [a]Luke 2:34; John 9:39; 1 Pet. 2:7 [b]1 Cor. 15:10
17 [a]2 Pet. 2:3 [b]ch. 1:12 [1]Or, *deal deceitfully with* [2]Or, *of*
3:1 [a]ch. 5:12 [b]Acts 18:27
2 [a]1 Cor. 9:2
3 [a]1 Cor. 3:5 [b]Ex. 24:12 [c]Ps. 40:8; Ezek. 11:19; Heb. 8:10
5 [a]John 15:5 [b]1 Cor. 15:10
6 [a]1 Cor. 3:5; Eph. 3:7; Col. 1:25 [b]Jer. 31:31; Mat. 26:28; Heb. 8:6,8 [c]Rom. 2:27 [d]Rom. 3:20; Gal. 3:10 [e]John 6:63; Rom. 8:2 [1]Or, *quickeneth*
7 [a]Rom. 7:10 [b]Ex. 34:1; Deut. 10:1 [c]Ex. 34:29
8 [a]Gal. 3:5

K *2Co 1:20* ◀ ▶ *2Co 9:8*
J *2Co 1:3–10* ◀ ▶ *2Co 4:8–10*
V *1Co 15:57* ◀ ▶ *2Ti 4:18*
H *1Co 16:22* ◀ ▶ *2Co 4:3*
N *1Co 1:18* ◀ ▶ *2Co 4:3–4*
E *2Co 1:21–22* ◀ ▶ *2Co 3:6–18*
R *1Co 12:13* ◀ ▶ *Gal 3:2–3*
M *1Co 3:1* ◀ ▶ *Gal 3:5*
E *2Co 3:3* ◀ ▶ *Gal 3:2–3*
H *1Co 15:44–54* ◀ ▶ *Heb 2:4*
W *1Co 14:15* ◀ ▶ *2Co 3:17–18*

9 For if the ministration of condemnation *be* glory, much more doth the ministration [a]of righteousness exceed in glory.

10 For even that which was made glorious had no glory in this respect, by reason of the glory that excelleth.

11 For if that which is done away *was* glorious, much more that which remaineth *is* glorious.

12 Seeing then that we have such hope, [a]we use great [I]plainness of speech:

13 And not as Moses, [a]*which* put a veil over his face, that the children of Israel could not stedfastly look to [b]the end of that which is abolished:

14 But [a]their minds were blinded: for until this day remaineth the same veil untaken away in the reading of the old testament; which *veil* is done away in Christ.

15 But even unto this day, when Moses is read, the veil is upon their heart.

16 Nevertheless [a]when it shall turn to the Lord, [b]the veil shall be taken away.

17 Now [a]the Lord is that Spirit: and where the Spirit of the Lord *is,* there *is* liberty.

18 But we all, with open face beholding [a]as in a glass [b]the glory of the Lord, [c]are changed into the same image from glory to glory, *even* as [I]by the Spirit of the Lord.

An honest and tried ministry

4 THEREFORE SEEING we have [a]this ministry, [b]as we have received mercy, we faint not;

2 But have renounced the hidden things of [I]dishonesty, not walking in craftiness, [a]nor handling the word of God deceitfully; but [b]by manifestation of the truth [c]commending ourselves to every man's conscience in the sight of God.

3 But if our gospel be hid, [a]it is hid to them that are lost:

4 In whom [a]the god of this world [b]hath blinded the minds of them which believe not, lest [c]the light of the glorious gospel of Christ, [d]who is the image of God, should shine unto them.

5 [a]For we preach not ourselves, but Christ Jesus the Lord; and [b]ourselves your servants for Jesus' sake.

6 For God, [a]who commanded the light to shine out of darkness, [I]hath [b]shined in our hearts, to *give* [c]the light of the knowledge of the glory of God in the face of Jesus Christ.

7 But we have this treasure in [a]earthen vessels, [b]that the excellency of the power may be of God, and not of us.

8 *We are* [a]troubled on every side, yet not distressed; *we are* perplexed, but [I]not in despair;

9 Persecuted, but not forsaken; [a]cast down, but not destroyed;

10 [a]Always bearing about in the body the dying of the Lord Jesus, [b]that the life also of Jesus might be made manifest in our body.

11 For we which live [a]are always delivered unto death for Jesus' sake, that the life also of Jesus might be made manifest in our mortal flesh.

12 So then [a]death worketh in us, but life in you.

13 We having [a]the same spirit of faith, according as it is written, [b]I believed, and therefore have I spoken; we also believe, and therefore speak;

14 Knowing that [a]he which raised up the Lord Jesus shall raise up us also by Jesus, and shall present *us* with you.

15 For [a]all things *are* for your sakes, that [b]the abundant grace might through the thanksgiving of many redound to the glory of God.

16 For which cause we faint not; but though our outward man perish, yet [a]the inward *man* is renewed day by day.

17 For [a]our light affliction, which is but for a moment, worketh for us a far

9 [a]Rom. 1:17
12 [a]ch. 7:4; Eph. 6:19 [I]Or, *boldness*
13 [a]Ex. 34:33 [b]Rom. 10:4; Gal. 3:23
14 [a]Is. 6:10; Acts 28:26
16 [a]Ex. 34:34; Rom. 11:23 [b]Is. 25:7
17 [a]1 Cor. 15:45
18 [a]1 Cor. 13:12 [b]ch. 4:4,6 [c]Rom. 8:29 [I]Or, *of the Lord the Spirit*
4:1 [a]ch. 3:6 [b]1 Cor. 7:25
2 [a]ch. 2:17 [b]ch. 6:4,7 [c]ch. 5:11 [I]Gk. *shame*
3 [a]1 Cor. 1:18
4 [a]Eph. 6:12 [b]John 12:40 [c]ch. 3:8,9 [d]John 1:18; Heb. 1:3
5 [a]1 Cor. 1:13 & 10:33 [b]1 Cor. 9:19
6 [a]Gen. 1:3 [b]2 Pet. 1:19 [c]1 Pet. 2:9 [I]Gk. is he *who hath*
7 [a]ch. 5:1 [b]1 Cor. 2:5
8 [a]ch. 7:5 [I]Or, *not altogether without help, or, means*
9 [a]Ps. 37:24
10 [a]Phil. 3:10 [b]Rom. 8:17
11 [a]Rom. 8:36
12 [a]ch. 13:9
13 [a]2 Pet. 1:1 [b]Ps. 116:10
14 [a]Rom. 8:11; 1 Cor. 6:14
15 [a]Col. 1:24; 2 Tim. 2:10 [b]ch. 1:11
16 [a]Rom. 7:22; Col. 3:10
17 [a]Mat. 5:12; Rom. 8:18; 1 Pet. 1:6

D *1Co 3:16–17* ◀▶ *2Co 6:16*
J *Ro 15:13* ◀▶ *Gal 5:22*
N *1Co 12:1–13* ◀▶ *2Co 11:4*
W *2Co 3:6–11* ◀▶ *2Co 6:6*
S *1Co 6:11* ◀▶ *Gal 5:16*
C *1Co 2:14* ◀▶ *2Co 5:14*
H *2Co 2:15–16* ◀▶ *2Co 5:10–11*
N *2Co 2:15–16* ◀▶ *2Co 6:2*

J *2Co 2:14* ◀▶ *2Co 4:16–18*
T *2Co 1:6–9* ◀▶ *2Co 4:17*
F *2Co 1:9* ◀▶ *Php 3:11–15*
J *2Co 4:8–10* ◀▶ *2Co 7:4*
T *2Co 4:10–11* ◀▶ *2Co 12:7–10*

4:14 Paul reminds us that God raised Jesus from the dead and will also resurrect us. Paul also indicates that there will be a presentation of some kind, possibly after the rapture at the glorious marriage supper of the Lamb in heaven (see Rev 19:7–9).

more exceeding *and* eternal weight of glory;

18 [a]While we look not at the things which are seen, but at the things which are not seen: for the things which are seen *are* temporal; but the things which are not seen *are* eternal.

A confident ministry

U **5** FOR WE know that if [a]our earthly house of *this* tabernacle were dissolved, we have a building of God, an house not made with hands, eternal in the heavens.

2 For in this [a]we groan, earnestly desiring to be clothed upon with our house which is from heaven:

3 If so be that [a]being clothed we shall not be found naked.

4 For we that are in *this* tabernacle do groan, being burdened: not for that we would be unclothed, but [a]clothed upon, that mortality might be swallowed up of life.

B 5 Now [a]he that hath wrought us for the selfsame thing *is* God, who also [b]hath given unto us the earnest of the Spirit.

6 Therefore *we are* always confident, knowing that, whilst we are at home in the body, we are absent from the Lord:

7 (For [a]we walk by faith, not by sight:)

8 We are confident, *I say,* and [a]willing rather to be absent from the body, and to be present with the Lord.

J 9 Wherefore we [ʼ]labour, that, whether present or absent, we may be accepted of him.

U *1Co 2:9* ◀▶ *2Co 6:17*
B *2Co 1:21–22* ◀▶ *Gal 3:5*
J *1Co 4:5* ◀▶ *Heb 9:27*

18 [a]Rom. 8:24; Heb. 11:1
5:1 [a]Job 4:19
2 [a]Rom. 8:23
3 [a]Rev. 3:18
4 [a]1 Cor. 15:53
5 [a]Is. 29:23; Eph. 2:10 [b]Rom. 8:23; Eph. 1:14
7 [a]Rom. 8:24; Heb. 11:1
8 [a]Phil. 1:23
9 [ʼ]Or, *endeavour*
10 [a]Rom. 14:10 [b]Gal. 6:7; Eph. 6:8; Rev. 22:12
11 [a]Heb. 10:31; Jude 23 [b]ch. 4:2
12 [a]ch. 3:1 [b]ch. 1:14 [ʼ]Gk. *in the face*
13 [a]ch. 11:1,16
14 [a]Rom. 5:15
15 [a]Rom. 6:11; 1 Cor. 6:19; Gal. 2:20
16 [a]Mat. 12:50; Col. 3:11 [b]John 6:63
17 [a]Rom. 8:9 [b]Gal. 5:6 [c]Is. 65:17; Eph. 2:15; Rev. 21:5 [ʼ]Or, let him be

10 [a]For we must all appear before the judgment seat of Christ; [b]that every one may receive the things *done* in *his* body, according to that he hath done, whether *it be* good or bad. H J S

A reconciling ministry

11 Knowing therefore [a]the terror of the Lord, we persuade men; but [b]we are made manifest unto God; and I trust also are made manifest in your consciences.

12 For [a]we commend not ourselves again unto you, but give you occasion [b]to glory on our behalf, that ye may have somewhat to *answer* them which glory [ʼ]in appearance, and not in heart.

13 For [a]whether we be beside ourselves, *it is* to God: or whether we be sober, *it is* for your cause.

14 For the love of Christ constraineth us; because we thus judge, that [a]if one died for all, then were all dead: A C D

15 And *that* he died for all, [a]that they which live should not henceforth live unto themselves, but unto him which died for them, and rose again. W S

16 [a]Wherefore henceforth know we no man after the flesh: yea, though we have known Christ after the flesh, [b]yet now henceforth know we *him* no more.

17 Therefore if any man [a]*be* in Christ, [ʼ]*he is* [b]a new creature: [c]old things are

H *2Co 4:3* ◀▶ *2Co 11:15*
J *1Co 4:4–5* ◀▶ *2Ti 4:1*
S *1Co 15:33–34* ◀▶ *2Co 5:15*
A *Ro 8:5–9* ◀▶ *2Co 13:5*
C *2Co 4:3–4* ◀▶ *Gal 5:19–21*
D *1Co 15:3* ◀▶ *2Co 5:18–21*
W *Ro 10:6–13* ◀▶ *Gal 3:6–9*
S *2Co 5:10* ◀▶ *2Co 6:14*

5:1–2 This passage teaches that our heavenly home and resurrection body will replace the "earthly house of this tabernacle" (5:1) because "this corruptible must put on incorruption, and this mortal must put on immortality" (1Co 15:53). Paul also says that our spirits inwardly long for this change.

5:8 Paul affirms the clear teaching of Scripture that the moment a believer dies their spirit is taken joyfully into the presence of Jesus Christ in heaven (Paradise). Though our bodies "sleep" in the grave, our spirits do not sleep but are consciously joined with Christ in heaven (see Lk 23:43).

5:9–11 All believers should strive to live righteously because of our love for Christ. In addition, God promises rewards to faithful believers after they are raptured and stand at the judgment seat of Christ (5:10). This accounting has nothing to do with sin and justification. The payment for the penalty for sin is credited to a believer fully and forever through faith in Christ. This judgment refers to the things we have done with our lives while we are Christians (see 1Co 3:11–15). As believers we are given certain responsibilities, and this judgment will address our faithfulness to Christ's commands. God knows our hearts and motives, and this should motivate us to persuade others to faith in Christ while there is still time to repent. See the article on "The Judgments of God" on p. 1222.

passed away; behold, all things are become new.

D L 18 And all things *are* of God, [a]who hath reconciled us to himself by Jesus Christ, and hath given to us the ministry of reconciliation;

19 To wit, that [a]God was in Christ, reconciling the world unto himself, not imputing their trespasses unto them; and hath [/]committed unto us the word of reconciliation.

20 Now then we are [a]ambassadors for Christ, as [b]though God did beseech *you* by us: we pray *you* in Christ's stead, be ye reconciled to God.

21 For [a]he hath made him *to be* sin for us, who knew no sin; that we might be made [b]the righteousness of God in him.

A suffering ministry

6 WE THEN, *as* [a]workers together *with him,* [b]beseech *you* also [c]that ye receive not the grace of God in vain.

L N 2 (For he saith, [a]I have heard thee in a time accepted, and in the day of salvation have I succoured thee: behold, now *is* the accepted time; behold, now *is* the day of salvation.)

3 [a]Giving no offence in any thing, that the ministry be not blamed:

4 But in all *things* [/]approving ourselves [a]as the ministers of God, in much patience, in afflictions, in necessities, in distresses,

5 [a]In stripes, in imprisonments, [/]in tumults, in labours, in watchings, in fastings;

W 6 By pureness, by knowledge, by longsuffering, by kindness, by the Holy Ghost, by love unfeigned,

7 [a]By the word of truth, by [b]the power of God, by [c]the armour of righteousness on the right hand and on the left,

8 By honour and dishonour, by evil report and good report: as deceivers, and *yet* true;

9 As unknown, and [a]*yet* well known; [b]as dying, and, behold, we live; as [c]chastened, and not killed;

10 As sorrowful, yet always rejoicing; as poor, yet making many rich; as having nothing, and *yet* possessing all things.

11 O *ye* Corinthians, our mouth is open unto you, [a]our heart is enlarged.

12 Ye are not straitened in us, but [a]ye are straitened in your own bowels.

13 Now for a recompence in the same, ([a]I speak as unto *my* children,) be ye also enlarged.

Believers are the temple of God

14 [a]Be ye not unequally yoked together with unbelievers: for [b]what fellowship hath righteousness with unrighteousness? and what communion hath light with darkness? S

15 And what concord hath Christ with Belial? or what part hath he that believeth with an infidel?

16 And what agreement hath the temple of God with idols? for [a]ye are the temple of the living God; as God hath said, [b]I will dwell in them, and walk in *them;* and I will be their God, and they shall be my people. D

17 [a]Wherefore come out from among them, and be ye separate, saith the Lord, and touch not the unclean *thing;* and I will receive you, U

18 [a]And will be a Father unto you, and ye shall be my sons and daughters, saith the Lord Almighty.

7 HAVING [a]THEREFORE these promises, dearly beloved, let us cleanse ourselves from all filthiness of the flesh and spirit, perfecting holiness in the fear of God. S

2 Receive us; we have wronged no man, we have corrupted no man, [a]we have defrauded no man.

3 I speak not *this* to condemn *you:* for [a]I have said before, that ye are in our hearts to die and live with *you.*

4 [a]Great *is* my boldness of speech toward you, [b]great *is* my glorying of you: [c]I am filled with comfort, I am exceeding joyful in all our tribulation. J

The joy of good news

5 For, [a]when we were come into Macedonia, our flesh had no rest, but [b]we were troubled on every side; [c]without *were* fightings, within *were* fears.

18 [a]Rom. 5:10; Eph. 2:16; Col. 1:20
19 [a]Rom. 3:24 [/]Gk. *put in us*
20 [a]Job 33:23; Mal. 2:7; Eph. 6:20 [b]ch. 6:1
21 [a]Is. 53:6,9; Gal. 3:13; 1 Pet. 2:22; 1 John 3:5 [b]Rom. 1:17 & 10:3
6:1 [a]1 Cor. 3:9 [b]ch. 5:20 [c]Heb. 12:15
2 [a]Is. 49:8
3 [a]Rom. 14:13; 1 Cor. 9:12 & 10:32
4 [a]1 Cor. 4:1 [/]Gk. *commending; see* ch. 4:2
5 [a]ch. 11:23 [/]Or, *in tossings to and fro*
7 [a]ch. 7:14 [b]1 Cor. 2:4 [c]ch. 10:4; Eph. 6:11; 2 Tim. 4:7
9 [a]ch. 4:2 & 5:11 [b]1 Cor. 4:9; ch. 1:9 & 4:10,11 [c]Ps. 118:18
11 [a]ch. 7:3
12 [a]ch. 12:15
13 [a]1 Cor. 4:14
14 [a]Deut. 7:2,3; 1 Cor. 5:9 [b]1 Sam. 5:2,3; 1 Ki. 18:21; 1 Cor. 10:21; Eph. 5:7,11
16 [a]1 Cor. 3:16 & 6:19; Eph. 2:21; Heb. 3:6 [b]Ex. 29:45; Lev. 26:12; Jer. 31:33 & 32:38; Ezek. 11:20; Zech. 13:9
17 [a]Is. 52:11; Rev. 18:4
18 [a]Jer. 31:1,9; Rev. 21:7
7:1 [a]1 John 3:3
2 [a]Acts 20:33
3 [a]ch. 6:11,12
4 [a]ch. 3:12 [b]1 Cor. 1:4 [c]Phil. 2:17; Col. 1:24
5 [a]ch. 2:13 [b]ch. 4:8 [c]Deut. 32:35

D *2Co 5:14–15* ◀▶ *2Co 9:15*
L *1Co 15:3* ◀▶ *2Co 6:2*
L *2Co 5:18–21* ◀▶ *2Co 9:15*
N *2Co 4:3–4* ◀▶ *1Th 5:2–3*
W *2Co 3:17–18* ◀▶ *2Co 13:14*

S *2Co 5:15* ◀▶ *2Co 7:1*
D *2Co 3:17* ◀▶ *2Co 13:14*
U *2Co 5:1* ◀▶ *Gal 6:16*
S *2Co 6:14* ◀▶ *2Co 13:11*
J *2Co 4:16–18* ◀▶ *2Co 8:1–2*

6 Nevertheless [a]God, that comforteth those that are cast down, comforted us by [b]the coming of Titus;

7 And not by his coming only, but by the consolation wherewith he was comforted in you, when he told us your earnest desire, your mourning, your fervent mind toward me; so that I rejoiced the more.

8 For though I made you sorry with a letter, I do not repent, [a]though I did repent: for I perceive that the same epistle hath made you sorry, though *it were* but for a season.

R 9 Now I rejoice, not that ye were made sorry, but that ye sorrowed to repentance: for ye were made sorry [']after a godly manner, that ye might receive damage by us in nothing.

10 For [a]godly sorrow worketh repentance to salvation not to be repented of: [b]but the sorrow of the world worketh death.

11 For behold this selfsame thing, that ye sorrowed after a godly sort, what carefulness it wrought in you, yea, *what* clearing of yourselves, yea, *what* indignation, yea, *what* fear, yea, *what* vehement desire, yea, *what* zeal, yea, *what* revenge! In all *things* ye have approved yourselves to be clear in this matter.

12 Wherefore, though I wrote unto you, *I did it* not for his cause that had done the wrong, nor for his cause that suffered wrong, [a]but that our care for you in the sight of God might appear unto you.

13 Therefore we were comforted in your comfort: yea, and exceedingly the more joyed we for the joy of Titus, because his spirit [a]was refreshed by you all.

14 For if I have boasted any thing to him of you, I am not ashamed; but as we spake all things to you in truth, even so our boasting, which *I made* before Titus, is found a truth.

15 And his [']inward affection is more abundant toward you, whilst he remembereth [a]the obedience of you all, how with fear and trembling ye received him.

16 I rejoice therefore that [a]I have confidence in you in all *things.*

6 [a]ch. 1:4 [b]See ch. 2:13
8 [a]ch. 2:4
9 [']Or, *according to God*
10 [a]2 Sam. 12:13; Mat. 26:75 [b]Prov. 17:22
12 [a]ch. 2:4
13 [a]Rom. 15:32
15 [a]ch. 2:9; Phil. 2:12 [']Gk. *bowels;* see ch. 6:12
16 [a]2 Thes. 3:4; Philem. 8,21
8:2 [a]Mark 12:44 [']Gk. *simplicity;* see also ch. 9:11
4 [a]Acts 11:29 & 24:17; Rom. 15:25, 26; 1 Cor. 16:1,3,4; ch. 9:1
6 [a]ver. 17; ch. 12:18 [']Or, *gift;* also ver. 4,19
7 [a]1 Cor. 1:5 & 12:13 [b]ch. 9:8
8 [a]1 Cor. 7:6
9 [a]Mat. 8:20; Luke 9:58; Phil. 2:6,7
10 [a]1 Cor. 7:25 [b]Prov. 19:17; Mat. 10:42; 1 Tim. 6:18, 19; Heb. 13:16 [c]ch. 9:2 [']Gk. *willing*
12 [a]Mark 12:43, 44; Luke 21:3
15 [a]Ex. 16:18

The giving of the Macedonians

8 MOREOVER, BRETHREN, we do you to wit of the grace of God bestowed on the churches of Macedonia; J

2 How that in a great trial of affliction the abundance of their joy and [a]their deep poverty abounded unto the riches of their [']liberality.

3 For to *their* power, I bear record, yea, and beyond *their* power *they were* willing of themselves;

4 Praying us with much entreaty that we would receive the gift, and *take upon us* [a]the fellowship of the ministering to the saints.

5 And *this they did,* not as we hoped, but first gave their own selves to the Lord, and unto us by the will of God.

6 Insomuch that [a]we desired Titus, that as he had begun, so he would also finish in you the same [']grace also.

7 Therefore, as [a]ye abound in every *thing, in* faith, and utterance, and knowledge, and *in* all diligence, and *in* your love to us, *see* [b]that ye abound in this grace also.

The example of Jesus

8 [a]I speak not by commandment, but by occasion of the forwardness of others, and to prove the sincerity of your love.

9 For ye know the grace of our Lord Jesus Christ, [a]that, though he was rich, yet for your sakes he became poor, that ye through his poverty might be rich.

10 And herein [a]I give *my* advice: for [b]this is expedient for you, who have begun before, not only to do, but also to be [c]forward['] a year ago.

11 Now therefore perform the doing *of it;* that as *there was* a readiness to will, so *there may be* a performance also out of that which ye have.

12 For [a]if there be first a willing mind, *it is* accepted according to that a man hath, *and* not according to that he hath not.

13 For *I mean* not that other men be eased, and ye burdened:

14 But by an equality, *that* now at this time your abundance *may be a supply* for their want, that their abundance also may be *a supply* for your want: that there may be equality:

15 As it is written, [a]He that *had gath-*

ered much had nothing over; and he that *had gathered* little had no lack.

Coming of Titus

16 But thanks *be* to God, which put the same earnest care into the heart of Titus for you.

17 For indeed he accepted [a]the exhortation; but being more forward, of his own accord he went unto you.

18 And we have sent with him [a]the brother, whose praise *is* in the gospel throughout all the churches;

19 And not *that* only, but who was also [a]chosen of the churches to travel with us with this [1]grace, which is administered by us [b]to the glory of the same Lord, and *declaration of* your ready mind:

20 Avoiding this, that no man should blame us in this abundance which is administered by us:

21 [a]Providing for honest things, not only in the sight of the Lord, but also in the sight of men.

22 And we have sent with them our brother, whom we have oftentimes proved diligent in many things, but now much more diligent, upon the great confidence which [1]*I have* in you.

23 Whether *any do inquire* of Titus, *he is* my partner and fellow-helper concerning you: or our brethren *be inquired of, they are* [a]the messengers of the churches, *and* the glory of Christ.

24 Wherefore show ye to them, and before the churches, the proof of your love, and of our [a]boasting on your behalf.

9 FOR AS touching [a]the ministering to the saints, it is superfluous for me to write to you:

2 For I know [a]the forwardness of your mind, [b]for which I boast of you to them of Macedonia, that [c]Achaia was ready a year ago; and your zeal hath provoked very many.

3 [a]Yet have I sent the brethren, lest our boasting of you should be in vain in this behalf; that, as I said, ye may be ready:

4 Lest haply if they of Macedonia come with me, and find you unprepared, we (that we say not, ye) should be ashamed in this same confident boasting.

5 Therefore I thought it necessary to exhort the brethren, that they would go before unto you, and make up beforehand your [1]bounty, [2]whereof ye had notice before, that the same might be ready, as *a matter of* bounty, and not as *of* covetousness.

God loveth a cheerful giver

6 [a]But this *I say,* He which soweth sparingly shall reap also sparingly; and he which soweth bountifully shall reap also bountifully. P

7 Every man according as he purposeth in his heart, *so let him give;* [a]not grudgingly, or of necessity: for [b]God loveth a cheerful giver.

8 [a]And God *is* able to make all grace abound toward you; that ye, always having all sufficiency in all *things,* may abound to every good work: K

9 (As it is written, [a]He hath dispersed abroad; he hath given to the poor: his righteousness remaineth for ever.

10 Now he that [a]ministereth seed to the sower both minister bread for *your* food, and multiply your seed sown, and increase the fruits of your [b]righteousness;) B F

11 Being enriched in every thing to all [1,2]bountifulness, [a]which causeth through us thanksgiving to God.

12 For the administration of this service not only [a]supplieth the want of the saints, but is abundant also by many thanksgivings unto God;

13 Whiles by the experiment of this ministration they [a]glorify God for your professed subjection unto the gospel of Christ, and for *your* liberal [b]distribution unto them, and unto all *men;*

14 And by their prayer for you, which long after you for the exceeding [a]grace of God in you.

15 Thanks *be* unto God [a]for his unspeakable gift. D L

Paul defends his ministry

10 NOW [a]I Paul myself beseech you by the meekness and gentleness of Christ, [b]who [1]in presence *am* base among you, but being absent am bold toward you:

2 But I beseech *you,* [a]that I may not be bold when I am present with that confidence, wherewith I think to be bold

17 [a]ver. 6
18 [a]ch. 12:18
19 [a]1 Cor. 16:3,4 [b]ch. 4:15 [1]Or, *gift;* also ver. 4,6,7; ch. 9:8
21 [a]Rom. 12:17; Phil. 4:8; 1 Pet. 2:12
22 [1]Or, he hath
23 [a]Phil. 2:25
24 [a]ch. 7:14 & 9:2
9:1 [a]Acts 11:29; Rom. 15:26; 1 Cor. 16:1; ch. 8:4; Gal. 2:10
2 [a]ch. 8:19 [b]ch. 8:24 [c]ch. 8:10
3 [a]ch. 8:6,17
5 [1]Gk. *blessing;* see Gen. 33:11; 1 Sam. 25:27; 2 Ki. 5:15 [2]Or, *which hath been so much spoken of before*
6 [a]Prov. 11:24
7 [a]Deut. 15:7 [b]Ex. 35:5; Prov. 11:25; Rom. 12:8; ch. 8:12
8 [a]Prov. 11:24; Phil. 4:19
9 [a]Ps. 112:9
10 [a]Is. 55:10 [b]Hos. 10:12; Mat. 6:1
11 [a]ch. 1:11 [1]Or, *liberality* [2]Gk. *simplicity*
12 [a]ch. 8:14
13 [a]Mat. 5:16 [b]Heb. 13:16
14 [a]ch. 8:1
15 [a]Jas. 1:17
10:1 [a]Rom. 12:1 [b]ch. 12:5 [1]Or, *in outward appearance*
2 [a]1 Cor. 4:21; ch. 13:2,10

P *Lk 22:35* ◄ ► *Php 4:19*
K *2Co 2:14* ◄ ► *Eph 1:7*
B *Mal 3:11–12* ◄ **F** *Jn 21:8–13* ◄
D *2Co 5:18–21* ◄ ► *Gal 1:4*
L *2Co 6:2* ◄ ► *Gal 1:4*

against some, which [/]think of us as if we walked according to the flesh.

3 For though we walk in the flesh, we do not war after the flesh:

4 ([a]For the weapons [b]of our warfare *are* not carnal, but [c]mighty [/]through God [d]to the pulling down of strong holds;)

5 [a]Casting down [/]imaginations, and every high thing that exalteth itself against the knowledge of God, and bringing into captivity every thought to the obedience of Christ;

6 [a]And having in a readiness to revenge all disobedience, when [b]your obedience is fulfilled.

7 [a]Do ye look on things after the outward appearance? [b]If any man trust to himself that he is Christ's, let him of himself think this again, that, as he *is* Christ's, even so *are* [c]we Christ's.

8 For though I should boast somewhat more [a]of our authority, which the Lord hath given us for edification, and not for your destruction, [b]I should not be ashamed:

9 That I may not seem as if I would terrify you by letters.

10 For *his* letters, [/]say they, *are* weighty and powerful; but [a]*his* bodily presence *is* weak, and *his* [b]speech contemptible.

11 Let such an one think this, that, such as we are in word by letters when we are absent, such *will we be* also in deed when we are present.

12 [a]For we dare not make ourselves of the number, or compare ourselves with some that commend themselves: but they measuring themselves by themselves, and comparing themselves among themselves, [/]are not wise.

13 [a]But we will not boast of things without *our* measure, but according to the measure of the [/]rule which God hath distributed to us, a measure to reach even unto you.

14 For we stretch not ourselves beyond *our measure,* as though we reached not unto you: [a]for we are come as far as to you also in *preaching* the gospel of Christ:

15 Not boasting of things without *our* measure, *that is,* [a]of other men's labours; but having hope, when your faith is increased, that we shall be [/]enlarged by you according to our rule abundantly,

16 To preach the gospel in the *regions* beyond you, *and* not to boast in another man's [/]line of things made ready to our hand.

17 [a]But he that glorieth, let him glory O
in the Lord.

18 For [a]not he that commendeth him- G
self is approved, but [b]whom the Lord commendeth.

Paul's fear of false teachers

11 WOULD TO God ye could bear with me a little in [a]*my* folly: and indeed [/]bear with me.

2 For I am [a]jealous over you with godly jealousy: for [b]I have espoused you to one husband, [c]that I may present *you* [d]*as* a chaste virgin to Christ.

3 But I fear, lest by any means, as [a]the serpent beguiled Eve through his subtlety, so your minds [b]should be corrupted from the simplicity that is in Christ.

4 For if he that cometh preacheth an- N
other Jesus, whom we have not preached, or *if* ye receive another spirit, which ye have not received, or [a]another gospel, which ye have not accepted, ye might well bear [/]with *him.*

5 For I suppose [a]I was not a whit behind the very chiefest apostles.

6 But though [a]*I be* rude in speech, yet not [b]in knowledge; but [c]we have been thoroughly made manifest among you in all things.

7 Have I committed an offence in abasing myself that ye might be exalted, because I have preached to you the gospel of God freely?

8 I robbed other churches, taking wages *of them,* to do you service.

9 And when I was present with you, and wanted, [a]I was chargeable to no man: for that which was lacking to me [b]the brethren which came from Macedonia supplied: and in all *things* I have kept myself [c]from being burdensome unto you, and *so* will I keep *myself.*

10 [a]As the truth of Christ is in me, [b]no[/] man shall stop me of this boasting in the regions of Achaia.

11 Wherefore? [a]because I love you not? God knoweth.

12 But what I do, that I will do, [a]that I may cut off occasion from them which

2 [/]*Or, reckon*
4 [a]Eph. 6:13; 1 Thes. 5:8 [b]1 Tim. 1:18; 2 Tim. 2:3 [c]Acts 7:22; 1 Cor. 2:5 [d]Jer. 1:10 [/]*Or, to God*
5 [a]1 Cor. 1:19 [/]*Or, reasonings*
6 [a]ch. 13:2,10 [b]ch. 7:15
7 [a]John 7:24 [b]1 Cor. 14:37; 1 John 4:6 [c]1 Cor. 3:23; ch. 11:23
8 [a]ch. 13:10 [b]ch. 7:14
10 [a]1 Cor. 2:3,4; Gal. 4:13 [b]1 Cor. 1:17 [/]*Gk. saith he*
12 [a]ch. 5:12 [/]*Or, understand it not*
13 [a]ver. 15 [/]*Or, line*
14 [a]1 Cor. 3:5
15 [a]Rom. 15:20 [/]*Or, magnified in you*
16 [/]*Or, rule*
17 [a]Is. 65:16; Jer. 9:24; 1 Cor. 1:31
18 [a]Prov. 27:2 [b]Rom. 2:29; 1 Cor. 4:5
11:1 [a]ver. 16; ch. 5:13 [/]*Or, ye do bear with me*
2 [a]Gal. 4:17 [b]Hos. 2:19; 1 Cor. 4:15 [c]Col. 1:28 [d]Lev. 21:13
3 [a]Gen. 3:4; John 8:44 [b]Eph. 6:24; Col. 2:4,8; 1 Tim. 1:3
4 [a]Gal. 1:7,8 [/]*Or, with me*
5 [a]1 Cor. 15:10
6 [a]1 Cor. 1:17 [b]Eph. 3:4 [c]ch. 12:12
9 [a]Acts 20:33; 1 Thes. 2:9 [b]Phil. 4:10 [c]ch. 12:14
10 [a]Rom. 9:1 [b]1 Cor. 9:15 [/]*Gk. this boasting shall not be stopped in me*
11 [a]ch. 6:11
12 [a]1 Cor. 9:12

O *1Co 3:11* ◀▶ *2Co 13:5*
G *1Co 3:19–20* ◀▶ *Gal 2:16*
N *2Co 3:17* ◀▶ *Gal 5:18*

desire occasion; that wherein they glory,
they may be found even as we.
13 For such [a]*are* false apostles, [b]deceit-
ful workers, transforming themselves
into the apostles of Christ.
14 And no marvel; for Satan himself is
transformed into [a]an angel of light.
H 15 Therefore *it is* no great thing if his
ministers also be transformed as the ministers of righteousness; [a]whose end shall
be according to their works.

Paul's rightful boasting

16 I say again, Let no man think me a
fool; if otherwise, yet as a fool [I]receive
me, that I may boast myself a little.
17 That which I speak, [a]I speak *it* not
after the Lord, but as it were foolishly, in
this confidence of boasting.
18 Seeing that many glory after the
flesh, I will glory also.
19 For ye suffer fools gladly, [a]seeing ye
yourselves are wise.
20 For ye suffer, [a]if a man bring you
into bondage, if a man devour *you,* if a
man take *of you,* if a man exalt himself, if
a man smite you on the face.
21 I speak as concerning reproach, [a]as
though we had been weak. Howbeit
[b]whereinsoever any is bold, (I speak foolishly,) I am bold also.
22 Are they Hebrews? [a]so *am* I. Are
they Israelites? so *am* I. Are they the seed
of Abraham? so *am* I.
23 Are they ministers of Christ? (I
speak as a fool) I *am* more; [a]in labours
more abundant, [b]in stripes above measure, in prisons more frequent, [c]in
deaths oft.
24 Of the Jews five times received I
[a]forty *stripes* save one.
25 Thrice was I [a]beaten with rods,
[b]once was I stoned, thrice I [c]suffered
shipwreck, a night and a day I have been
in the deep;

H *2Co 5:10–11* ◀▶ *Gal 5:19–21*

13 [a] Acts 15:24; Rom. 16:18; Gal. 1:7; Phil. 1:15; 2 Pet. 2:1; Rev. 2:2 [b] Phil. 3:2; Tit. 1:10
14 [a] Gal. 1:8
15 [a] Phil. 3:19
16 [I] Or, *suffer*
17 [a] 1 Cor. 7:6
19 [a] 1 Cor. 4:10
20 [a] Gal. 2:4
21 [a] ch. 10:10 [b] Phil. 3:4
22 [a] Acts 22:3; Rom. 11:1; Phil. 3:5
23 [a] 1 Cor. 15:10 [b] Acts 9:16 [c] 1 Cor. 15:30
24 [a] Deut. 25:3
25 [a] Acts 16:22 [b] Acts 14:19 [c] Acts 27:41
26 [a] Acts 9:23 [b] Acts 14:5
27 [a] Acts 20:31 [b] 1 Cor. 4:11
28 [a] Acts 20:18; Rom. 1:14
29 [a] 1 Cor. 8:13
30 [a] ch. 12:5
31 [a] Rom. 1:9; Gal. 1:20; 1 Thes. 2:5 [b] Rom. 9:5
32 [a] Acts 9:24
12:1 [I] Gk. *For I will come*
2 [a] Rom. 16:7; Gal. 1:22 [b] Acts 22:17
4 [a] Luke 23:43 [I] Or, *possible*
5 [a] ch. 11:30
6 [a] ch. 11:16

26 *In* journeyings often, *in* perils of
waters, *in* perils of robbers, [a]*in* perils by
mine own countrymen, [b]*in* perils by the
heathen, *in* perils in the city, *in* perils in
the wilderness, *in* perils in the sea, *in*
perils among false brethren;
27 In weariness and painfulness, [a]in
watchings often, [b]in hunger and thirst, in
fastings often, in cold and nakedness.
28 Beside those things that are without, that which cometh upon me daily,
[a]the care of all the churches.
29 [a]Who is weak, and I am not weak?
who is offended, and I burn not?
30 If I must needs glory, [a]I will glory
of the things which concern mine infirmities.
31 [a]The God and Father of our Lord
Jesus Christ, [b]which is blessed for evermore, knoweth that I lie not.
32 [a]In Damascus the governor under
Aretas the king kept the city of the Dama-
scenes with a garrison, desirous to apprehend me:
33 And through a window in a basket
was I let down by the wall, and escaped
his hands.

Paul's visions of the Lord

12 IT IS not expedient for me doubtless to glory. [I]I will come to visions and revelations of the Lord.
2 I knew a man [a]in Christ above fourteen years ago, (whether in the body, I
cannot tell; or whether out of the body, I
cannot tell: God knoweth;) such an one
[b]caught up to the third heaven.
3 And I knew such a man, (whether in
the body, or out of the body, I cannot tell:
God knoweth;)
4 How that he was caught up into [a]par-
adise, and heard unspeakable words,
which it is not [I]lawful for a man to utter.
5 Of such an one will I glory: [a]yet of
myself I will not glory, but in mine infirmities.
6 For [a]though I would desire to glory, I

12:2–4 Fourteen years previous to this point Paul was given a profound vision in which he was taken up to "the third heaven" (12:2), "paradise" (12:4), the abode of God. Unsure whether he was physically taken to the third heaven to see these remarkable things or whether only his spirit was taken in vision to that place, Paul heard things in his vision that he was forbidden to reveal to the church.

The Bible reveals that there are three heavens. The atmospheric heavens include the high clouds and the sky of our atmosphere (see Ge 1:8; Ps 77:17–18). The second heaven involves outer space beyond our atmosphere that is the abode of the galaxies visible to great telescopes (see Ge 15:5). The third heaven is the heaven where the throne of God exists (see Isa 14:12–14; Eph 4:10; Rev 4:1–11).

shall not be a fool; for I will say the truth: but *now* I forbear, lest any man should think of me above that which he seeth me *to be,* or *that* he heareth of me.

D 7 And lest I should be exalted above
T measure through the abundance of the revelations, there was given to me a [a]thorn in the flesh, [b]the messenger of Satan to buffet me, lest I should be exalted above measure.

8 [a]For this thing I besought the Lord thrice, that it might depart from me.

9 And he said unto me, My grace is sufficient for thee: for my strength is made perfect in weakness. Most gladly therefore [a]will I rather glory in my infirmities, [b]that the power of Christ may rest upon me.

J 10 Therefore [a]I take pleasure in infirmities, in reproaches, in necessities, in persecutions, in distresses for Christ's sake: [b]for when I am weak, then am I strong.

The signs of a true apostle

11 I am become [a]a fool in glorying; ye have compelled me: for I ought to have been commended of you: for [b]in nothing am I behind the very chiefest apostles, though [c]I be nothing.

12 [a]Truly the signs of an apostle were wrought among you in all patience, in signs, and wonders, and mighty deeds.

13 [a]For what is it wherein ye were inferior to other churches, except *it be* that [b]I myself was not burdensome to you? forgive me [c]this wrong.

14 [a]Behold, the third time I am ready to come to you; and I will not be burdensome to you: for [b]I seek not yours, but you: [c]for the children ought not to lay up for the parents, but the parents for the children.

15 And I will very gladly spend and be spent [a]for [1]you, though [b]the more abundantly I love you, the less I be loved.

16 But be it so, [a]I did not burden you: nevertheless, being crafty, I caught you with guile.

17 [a]Did I make a gain of you by any of them whom I sent unto you?

L 18 [a]I desired Titus, and with *him* I sent a [b]brother. Did Titus make a gain of you? walked we not in the same spirit? *walked we* not in the same steps?

The appeal for repentance

19 [a]Again, think ye that we excuse ourselves unto you? [b]we speak before God in Christ: [c]but *we do* all things, dearly beloved, for your edifying.

20 For I fear, lest, when I come, I shall not find you such as I would, and *that* [a]I shall be found unto you such as ye would not: lest *there be* debates, envyings, wraths, strifes, backbitings, whisperings, swellings, tumults:

21 *And* lest, when I come again, my God [a]will humble me among you, and *that* I shall bewail many [b]which have sinned already, and have not repented of the uncleanness and [c]fornication and lasciviousness which they have committed.

13

THIS *IS* [a]the third *time* I am coming to you. [b]In the mouth of two or three witnesses shall every word be established.

2 [a]I told you before, and foretell you, as if I were present, the second time; and being absent now I write to them [b]which heretofore have sinned, and to all other, that, if I come again, [c]I will not spare:

3 Since ye seek a proof of Christ [a]speaking in me, which to you-ward is not weak, but is mighty [b]in you.

4 [a]For though he was crucified through weakness, yet [b]he liveth by the power of God. For [c]we also are weak [1]in him, but we shall live with him by the power of God toward you.

5 Examine yourselves, whether ye be A
in the faith; prove your own selves. Know O
ye not your own selves, [a]how that Jesus Christ is in you, except ye be [b]reprobates?

6 But I trust that ye shall know that we are not reprobates.

7 Now I pray to God that ye do no evil; not that we should appear approved, but that ye should do that which is honest, though [a]we be as reprobates.

8 For we can do nothing against the truth, but for the truth.

9 For we are glad, [a]when we are weak, and ye are strong: and this also we wish, [b]*even* your perfection.

7 [a]See Ezek. 28:24; Gal. 4:13 [b]Job 2:7; Luke 13:16
8 [a]Deut. 3:23; Mat. 26:44
9 [a]ch. 11:30 [b]1 Pet. 4:14
10 [a]Rom. 5:3; ch. 7:4 [b]ch. 13:4
11 [a]ch. 11:1,16 [b]ch. 11:5; Gal. 2:6-8 [c]1 Cor. 3:7; Eph. 3:8
12 [a]Rom. 15:18; 1 Cor. 9:2; ch. 4:2
13 [a]1 Cor. 1:7 [b]1 Cor. 9:12; ch. 11:9 [c]ch. 11:7
14 [a]ch. 13:1 [b]Acts 20:33; 1 Cor. 10:33 [c]1 Cor. 4:14
15 [a]John 10:11; ch. 1:6; Col. 1:24; 2 Tim. 2:10 [b]ch. 6:12,13 [1]Gk. *your souls*
16 [a]ch. 11:9
17 [a]ch. 7:2
18 [a]ch. 8:6,16 [b]ch. 8:18
19 [a]ch. 5:12 [b]Rom. 9:1; ch. 11:31 [c]1 Cor. 10:33
20 [a]1 Cor. 4:21; ch. 13:2,10
21 [a]ch. 2:1,4 [b]ch. 13:2 [c]1 Cor. 5:1
13:1 [a]ch. 12:14 [b]Num. 35:30; Deut. 17:6; Mat. 18:16; John 8:17; Heb. 10:28
2 [a]ch. 10:2 [b]ch. 12:21 [c]ch. 1:23
3 [a]Mat. 10:20; 1 Cor. 5:4 [b]1 Cor. 9:2
4 [a]Phil. 2:7,8; 1 Pet. 3:18 [b]Rom. 6:4 [c]ch. 10:3,4 [1]Or, *with him*
5 [a]Rom. 8:10; Gal. 4:19 [b]1 Cor. 9:27
7 [a]ch. 6:9
9 [a]1 Cor. 4:10; ch. 11:30 [b]1 Thes. 3:10

D *1Co 11:29–32* ◀ ▶ *Php 2:30*
T *2Co 4:17* ◀ ▶ *Heb 5:8*
J *2Co 8:1–2* ◀ ▶ *Eph 5:20*
L *1Co 14:30* ◀ ▶ *Gal 5:5*

A *2Co 5:14* ◀ ▶ *Gal 3:22*
O *2Co 10:17–18* ◀ ▶ *Gal 1:8–9*

10 [a]Therefore I write these things being absent, lest being present I should use sharpness, according to the power which the Lord hath given me to edification, and not to destruction.

Farewell and benediction

S 11 Finally, brethren, farewell. Be perfect, be of good comfort, [a]be of one mind, live in peace; and the God of love [b]and peace shall be with you.

S *2Co 7:1* ◀ ▶ *Gal 2:17–18*

10 [a]1 Cor. 4:21; ch. 12:20,21
11 [a]Rom. 12:16,18 [b]Rom. 15:33
12 [a]Rom. 16:16; 1 Cor. 16:20; 1 Thes. 5:26; 1 Pet. 5:14
14 [a]Rom. 16:24 [b]Phil. 2:1

12 [a]Greet one another with an holy kiss.

13 All the saints salute you.

14 [a]The grace of the Lord Jesus Christ, and the love of God, and [b]the communion of the Holy Ghost, *be* with you all. Amen. D F W

D *2Co 6:16* ◀ ▶ *Eph 2:22*
F *Ro 15:30* ◀ ▶ *Gal 5:22–23*
W *2Co 6:6* ◀ ▶ *Gal 3:3*

Galatians

Author: Paul

Theme: Justification comes by faith alone

Date of Writing: c. A.D. 48–53

Outline of Galatians

I. Introduction (1:1–9)
II. The Gospel Paul Preached (1:10—2:21)
III. Legalism and God's Grace (3:1—4:31)
IV. The Gospel in Practice (5:1—6:10)
V. Conclusion (6:11–18)

MOST SCHOLARS AGREE that Paul wrote this epistle to the Galatians, but the date and particular destination of this letter have been the subject of much discussion. Some scholars contend that Paul addressed this letter to the churches in north central Asia Minor while he was on his journey to Troas in A.D. 53. These scholars believe that these churches were established during Paul's third missionary journey (see Ac 18:23).

Others contend that this letter is the earliest of Paul's epistles, written about A.D. 48–49, before the Jerusalem council, and addressed to the churches in the southern area of Galatia—Antioch in Pisidia, Iconium, Lystra and Derbe. These were the churches Paul had established on his first missionary journey (see Ac 13—14). Accepting this view would explain the lack of reference to the Jerusalem council's discussion about keeping the Jewish law and having faith in Christ—the very problem that Paul dealt with in this letter. Still others date this book between A.D. 51–53 and suggest that it was written in Corinth or Syrian Antioch.

When Paul wrote this letter, some Jewish Christians were teaching that a number of the Jewish laws and ceremonial practices were still binding on Gentile believers. In response to this argument, Paul pointedly declares that a person is saved by faith in Jesus Christ alone. Carefully summarizing the gospel message in this letter to the Galatians, Paul stresses that salvation comes by the grace of God alone through faith in Christ's completed work on the cross and not through the Law. To support his contention, Paul notes that Abraham was saved by his faith in God alone centuries before the law was revealed through Moses. Paul encourages his readers to "stand fast therefore in the liberty wherewith Christ hath made us free" (5:1) and rather "by love serve one another" (5:13).

No other gospel

1 PAUL, AN apostle, (not of men, neither by man, but [a]by Jesus Christ,
and God the Father, [b]who raised him
from the dead;)
2 And all the brethren [a]which are with
me, [b]unto the churches of Galatia:
3 [a]Grace *be* to you and peace from
God the Father, and *from* our Lord Jesus
Christ,
D 4 [a]Who gave himself for our sins, that
L he might deliver us [b]from this present
evil world, according to the will of God
and our Father:
5 To whom *be* glory for ever and ever.
Amen.
6 I marvel that ye are so soon removed
[a]from him that called you into the grace
of Christ unto another gospel:
7 [a]Which is not another; but there be
some [b]that trouble you, and would pervert the gospel of Christ.
O 8 But though [a]we, or an angel from
heaven, preach any other gospel unto you
than that which we have preached unto
you, let him be accursed.
9 As we said before, so say I now
again, If any *man* preach any other gospel
unto you [a]than that ye have received, let
him be accursed.
10 For [a]do I now [b]persuade men, or
God? or [c]do I seek to please men? for if I
yet pleased men, I should not be the servant of Christ.

Paul's authority of divine origin

11 [a]But I certify you, brethren, that
the gospel which was preached of me is
not after man.
12 For [a]I neither received it of man,
neither was I taught *it,* but [b]by the revelation of Jesus Christ.
13 For ye have heard of my conversation in time past in the Jews' religion,
how that [a]beyond measure I persecuted
the church of God, and [b]wasted it:
14 And profited in the Jews' religion
above many my [l]equals in mine own nation, [a]being more exceedingly zealous [b]of
the traditions of my fathers.
15 But when it pleased God, [a]who separated me from my mother's womb, and
called *me* by his grace,
16 [a]To reveal his Son in me, that [b]I
might preach him among the heathen;
immediately I conferred not with [c]flesh
and blood:
17 Neither went I up to Jerusalem to
them which were apostles before me; but
I went into Arabia, and returned again
unto Damascus.
18 Then after three years [a]I [l]went up
to Jerusalem to see Peter, and abode with
him fifteen days.
19 But [a]other of the apostles saw I
none, save [b]James the Lord's brother.
20 Now the things which I write unto
you, [a]behold, before God, I lie not.
21 [a]Afterwards I came into the regions
of Syria, and Cilicia;
22 And was unknown by face [a]unto
the churches of Judaea which [b]were in
Christ:
23 But they had heard only, That he
which persecuted us in times past now
preacheth the faith which once he destroyed.
24 And they glorified God in me.

Paul accepted by the church

2 THEN FOURTEEN years after [a]I
went up again to Jerusalem with Barnabas, and took Titus with *me* also.
2 And I went up by revelation, [a]and
communicated unto them that gospel
which I preach among the Gentiles, but
[l]privately to them which were of reputation, lest by any means [b]I should run, or
had run, in vain.
3 But neither Titus, who was with me,
being a Greek, was compelled to be circumcised:
4 And that because of [a]false brethren
unawares brought in, who came in privily
to spy out our [b]liberty which we have in

1:1 [a]Acts 9:6; Tit. 1:3 [b]Acts 2:24
2 [a]Phil. 2:22 [b]1 Cor. 16:1
3 [a]1 Thes. 1:1
4 [a]Mat. 20:28; Rom. 4:25; Tit. 2:14 [b]Heb. 2:5; 1 John 5:19
6 [a]ch. 5:8
7 [a]2 Cor. 11:4 [b]Acts 15:1; 2 Cor. 2:17
8 [a]1 Cor. 16:22
9 [a]Deut. 4:2; Prov. 30:6; Rev. 22:18
10 [a]1 Thes. 2:4 [b]1 Sam. 24:7; Mat. 28:14 [c]1 Thes. 2:4; Jas. 4:4
11 [a]1 Cor. 15:1
12 [a]1 Cor. 15:1 [b]Eph. 3:3
13 [a]Acts 9:1; 1 Tim. 1:13 [b]Acts 8:3
14 [a]Acts 26:9; Phil. 3:6 [b]Jer. 9:14; Mat. 15:2; Mark 7:5 [l]Gk. *equals in years*
15 [a]Is. 49:1,5
16 [a]2 Cor. 4:6 [b]Acts 9:15; Eph. 3:8 [c]Mat. 16:17; Eph. 6:12
18 [a]Acts 9:26 [l]Or, *returned*
19 [a]1 Cor. 9:5 [b]Mat. 13:55
20 [a]Rom. 9:1
21 [a]Acts 9:30
22 [a]1 Thes. 2:14 [b]Rom. 16:7
2:1 [a]Acts 15:2
2 [a]Acts 15:12 [b]Phil. 2:16; 1 Thes. 3:5 [l]Or, *severally*
4 [a]Acts 15:1; 2 Cor. 11:26 [b]ch. 3:25

D *2Co 9:15* ◀▶ *Gal 2:20*
L *2Co 9:15* ◀▶ *Gal 2:21*
O *2Co 13:5* ◀▶ *Gal 2:16*

1:8–9 Paul's warning prophetically foreshadows the rise of false cults and religions that would attack the church, claiming that God had given them an additional revelation to supplement the teachings of the Bible. These cults, as diverse as the first-century Gnostics to the modern-day Mormons, have claimed that these new messages came from angels. Note that Paul specifically warned against those who would claim an angel visitant provided a new "gospel." Paul's condemnation of such a claimant was clear: "let him be accursed" (1:9).

Christ Jesus, [c]that they might bring us into bondage:

5 To whom we gave place by subjection, no, not for an hour; that [a]the truth of the gospel might continue with you.

6 But of these [a]who seemed to be somewhat, (whatsoever they were, it maketh no matter to me: [b]God accepteth no man's person:) for they who seemed *to be somewhat* [c]in conference added nothing to me:

7 But contrariwise, [a]when they saw that the gospel of the uncircumcision [b]was committed unto me, as *the gospel* of the circumcision *was* unto Peter;

8 (For he that wrought effectually in Peter to the apostleship of the circumcision, [a]the same was [b]mighty in me toward the Gentiles:)

9 And when James, Cephas, and John, who seemed to be [a]pillars, perceived [b]the grace that was given unto me, they gave to me and Barnabas the right hands of fellowship; that we *should go* unto the heathen, and they unto the circumcision.

10 Only *they would* that we should remember the poor; [a]the same which I also was forward to do.

Paul's opposition to Peter

11 [a]But when Peter was come to Antioch, I withstood him to the face, because he was to be blamed.

12 For before that certain came from James, [a]he did eat with the Gentiles: but when they were come, he withdrew and separated himself, fearing them which were of the circumcision.

13 And the other Jews dissembled likewise with him; insomuch that Barnabas also was carried away with their dissimulation.

14 But when I saw that they walked not uprightly according to [a]the truth of the gospel, I said unto Peter [b]before *them* all, [c]If thou, being a Jew, livest after the manner of Gentiles, and not as do the Jews, why compellest thou the Gentiles to live as do the Jews?

15 [a]We *who are* Jews by nature, and not [b]sinners of the Gentiles,

F G O 16 [a]Knowing that a man is not justified by the works of the law, but [b]by the faith of Jesus Christ, even we have believed in Jesus Christ, that we might be justified by the faith of Christ, and not by the works of the law: for [c]by the works of the law shall no flesh be justified.

17 But if, while we seek to be justified by Christ, we ourselves also are found [a]sinners, *is* therefore Christ the minister of sin? God forbid. S

18 For if I build again the things which I destroyed, I make myself a transgressor.

19 For I [a]through the law [b]am dead to the law, that I might [c]live unto God.

20 I am [a]crucified with Christ: nevertheless I live; yet not I, but Christ liveth in me: and the life which I now live in the flesh [b]I live by the faith of the Son of God, [c]who loved me, and gave himself for me. D S

21 I do not frustrate the grace of God: for [a]if righteousness *come* by the law, then Christ is dead in vain. G L

Receiving the Spirit by faith

3 O FOOLISH Galatians, [a]who hath bewitched you, that ye should not obey [b]the truth, before whose eyes Jesus Christ hath been evidently set forth, crucified among you?

2 This only would I learn of you, Received ye [a]the Spirit by the works of the law, [b]or by the hearing of faith? E R

3 Are ye so foolish? [a]having begun in the Spirit, are ye now made perfect by [b]the flesh? W

4 [a]Have ye suffered [1]so many things in vain? if *it be* yet in vain.

5 He therefore that ministereth to you the Spirit, and worketh miracles among you, *doeth he it* by the works of the law, or by the hearing of faith? B E M

6 Even as [a]Abraham believed God, and it was [1]accounted to him for righteousness. F W

4 [c]ch. 4:3,9
5 [a]ver. 14
6 [a]ch. 6:3 [b]Acts 10:34; Rom. 2:11 [c]2 Cor. 12:11
7 [a]Acts 13:46; Rom. 11:13; 2 Tim. 1:11 [b]1 Thes. 2:4
8 [a]Acts 9:15; 1 Cor. 15:10 [b]ch. 3:5
9 [a]Mat. 16:18; Rev. 21:14 [b]Rom. 1:5; 1 Cor. 15:10; Eph. 3:8
10 [a]Acts 11:30; Rom. 15:25
11 [a]Acts 15:35
12 [a]Acts 10:28
14 [a]ver. 5 [b]1 Tim. 5:20 [c]Acts 10:28
15 [a]Acts 15:10 [b]Mat. 9:11; Eph. 2:3
16 [a]Acts 13:38 [b]Rom. 1:17; ch. 3:24 [c]Ps. 143:2; Rom. 3:20
17 [a]1 John 3:8
19 [a]Rom. 8:2 [b]Rom. 6:14 [c]Rom. 6:11; 2 Cor. 5:15; Heb. 9:14
20 [a]Rom. 6:6 [b]2 Cor. 5:15; 1 Pet. 4:2 [c]Eph. 5:2; Tit. 2:14
21 [a]Heb. 7:11; Rom. 11:6
3:1 [a]ch. 5:7 [b]ch. 2:14
2 [a]Acts 2:38; Eph. 1:13; Heb. 6:4 [b]Rom. 10:16
3 [a]ch. 4:9 [b]Heb. 7:16
4 [a]Heb. 10:35; 2 John 8 [1]Or, *so great*
6 [a]Gen. 15:6; Rom. 4:3,9; Jas. 2:23 [1]Or, *imputed*

F *1Co 1:21* ◀▶ *Gal 3:6–9*
G *2Co 10:18* ◀▶ *Gal 2:21*
O *Gal 1:8–9* ◀▶ *1Ti 2:5*

S *2Co 13:11* ◀▶ *Gal 2:20*
D *Gal 1:4* ◀▶ *Gal 3:13*
S *Gal 2:17–18* ◀▶ *Gal 5:6*
G *Gal 2:16* ◀▶ *Gal 3:10–12*
L *Gal 1:4* ◀▶ *Gal 3:8*
E *2Co 3:6–18* ◀▶ *Gal 3:5*
R *2Co 3:3* ◀▶ *Gal 4:6*
W *2Co 13:14* ◀▶ *Gal 3:14*
B *2Co 5:5* ◀▶ *Eph 1:13–14*
E *Gal 3:2–3* ◀▶ *Gal 4:6*
M *2Co 3:5–18* ◀▶ *Eph 1:17–19*
F *Gal 2:16* ◀▶ *Gal 3:11*
W *2Co 5:14–15* ◀▶ *Gal 3:22*

7 Know ye therefore that [a]they which are of faith, the same are the children of Abraham.

L 8 And [a]the scripture, foreseeing that God would justify the heathen through faith, preached before the gospel unto Abraham, *saying,* [b]In thee shall all nations be blessed.

9 So then they which be of faith are blessed with faithful Abraham.

G 10 For as many as are of the works of the law are under the curse: for it is written, [a]Cursed *is* every one that continueth not in all things which are written in the book of the law to do them.

F 11 But [a]that no man is justified by the law in the sight of God, *it is* evident: for, [b]The just shall live by faith.

12 And [a]the law is not of faith: but, [b]The man that doeth them shall live in them.

D 13 [a]Christ hath redeemed us from the curse of the law, being made a curse for us: for it is written, [b]Cursed *is* every one that hangeth on a tree:

P W 14 [a]That the blessing of Abraham might come on the Gentiles through Jesus Christ; that we might receive [b]the promise of the Spirit through faith.

15 Brethren, I speak after the manner of men; [a]Though *it be* but a man's ʼcovenant, yet *if it be* confirmed, no man disannulleth, or addeth thereto.

16 Now [a]to Abraham and his seed were the promises made. He saith not, And to seeds, as of many; but as of one, And to thy seed, which is [b]Christ.

17 And this I say, *that* the covenant, that was confirmed before of God in Christ, the law, [a]which was four hundred and thirty years after, cannot disannul, [b]that it should make the promise of none effect.

18 For if [a]the inheritance *be* of the law, [b]*it is* no more of promise: but God gave *it* to Abraham by promise.

The function of the law

19 Wherefore then *serveth* the law? [a]It was added because of transgressions, till the seed should come to whom the promise was made; *and it was* [b]ordained by angels in the hand [c]of a mediator.

20 Now a mediator is not *a mediator* of one, [a]but God is one.

21 *Is* the law then against the promises of God? God forbid: for if there had been a law given which could have given life, verily righteousness should have been by the law. G

22 But the scripture hath concluded [a]all under sin, [b]that the promise by faith of Jesus Christ might be given to them that believe. A F L W

23 But before faith came, we were kept under the law, shut up unto the faith which should afterwards be revealed.

24 Wherefore [a]the law was our schoolmaster *to bring us* unto Christ, [b]that we might be justified by faith. F

25 But after that faith is come, we are no longer under a schoolmaster.

26 For ye [a]are all the children of God by faith in Christ Jesus. L

27 For [a]as many of you as have been baptized into Christ [b]have put on Christ.

28 [a]There is neither Jew nor Greek, there is neither bond nor free, there is neither male nor female: for ye are all [b]one in Christ Jesus.

29 And [a]if ye *be* Christ's, then are ye Abraham's seed, and [b]heirs according to the promise.

Do not return to bondage

4 NOW I say, *That* the heir, as long as he is a child, differeth nothing from a servant, though he be lord of all;

2 But is under tutors and governors until the time appointed of the father.

3 Even so we, when we were children, [a]were in bondage under the ʼelements of the world:

4 But [a]when the fulness of the time was come, God sent forth his Son, [b]made [c]of a woman, [d]made under the law, D

7 [a]John 8:39
8 [a]Rom. 9:17 [b]Gen. 12:3; Acts 3:25
10 [a]Deut. 27:26; Jer. 11:3
11 [a]ch. 2:16 [b]Hab. 2:4; Rom. 1:17; Heb. 10:38
12 [a]Rom. 4:4,5 [b]Lev. 18:5; Rom. 10:5
13 [a]Rom. 8:3; 2 Cor. 5:21 [b]Deut. 21:23
14 [a]Rom. 4:9 [b]Is. 32:15; Ezek. 11:19; Acts 2:33
15 [a]Heb. 9:17 ʼOr, *testament*
16 [a]Gen. 12:3 [b]1 Cor. 12:12
17 [a]Ex. 12:40 [b]Rom. 4:13
18 [a]Rom. 8:17 [b]Rom. 4:14
19 [a]John 15:22; Rom. 4:15 [b]Acts 7:53 [c]Ex. 20:19; John 1:17
20 [a]Rom. 3:29
22 [a]Rom. 11:32 [b]Rom. 4:11
24 [a]Rom. 10:4 [b]Acts 13:39
26 [a]John 1:12; Rom. 8:14
27 [a]Rom. 6:3 [b]Rom. 13:14
28 [a]Rom. 10:12 [b]John 10:16; Eph. 2:14
29 [a]Gen. 21:10; Heb. 11:18 [b]Rom. 8:17
4:3 [a]Col. 2:8; Heb. 9:10 ʼOr, *rudiments*
4 [a]Gen. 49:10; Mark 1:15 [b]John 1:14; Heb. 2:14 [c]Gen. 3:15; Is. 7:14; Mat. 1:23 [d]Mat. 5:17; Luke 2:27

L *Gal 2:21* ◀▶ *Gal 3:22*
G *Gal 2:21* ◀▶ *Gal 3:21*
F *Gal 3:6–9* ◀▶ *Gal 3:22*
D *Gal 2:20* ◀▶ *Gal 4:4–5*
P *Ac 11:16* ◀ **W** *Gal 3:3* ◀▶ *Gal 5:16*

G *Gal 3:10–12* ◀▶ *Gal 5:4*
A *2Co 13:5* ◀▶ *Eph 2:1–3*
F *Gal 3:11* ◀▶ *Gal 3:24–26*
L *Gal 3:8* ◀▶ *Gal 3:26*
W *Gal 3:6–9* ◀▶ *Eph 2:17–18*
F *Gal 3:22* ◀▶ *Eph 2:8*
L *Gal 3:22* ◀▶ *Eph 1:6–7*
D *Gal 3:13* ◀▶ *Eph 1:6–7*

5 [a]To redeem them that were under the law, [b]that we might receive the adoption of sons.

E R 6 And because ye are sons, God hath sent forth [a]the Spirit of his Son into your hearts, crying, Abba, Father.

7 Wherefore thou art no more a servant, but a son; [a]and if a son, then an heir of God through Christ.

8 Howbeit then, [a]when ye knew not God, [b]ye did service unto them which by nature are no gods.

9 But now, [a]after that ye have known God, or rather are known of God, [b]how turn ye [1]again to [c]the weak and beggarly [2]elements, whereunto ye desire again to be in bondage?

10 [a]Ye observe days, and months, and times, and years.

11 I am afraid of you, [a]lest I have bestowed upon you labour in vain.

Paul's concern for the Galatians

12 Brethren, I beseech you, be as I *am;* for I *am* as ye *are:* [a]ye have not injured me at all.

13 Ye know how [a]through infirmity of the flesh I preached the gospel unto you at the first.

14 And my temptation which was in my flesh ye despised not, nor rejected; but received me [a]as an angel of God, [b]*even* as Christ Jesus.

15 [1]Where is then the blessedness ye spake of? for I bear you record, that, if *it had been* possible, ye would have plucked out your own eyes, and have given them to me.

16 Am I therefore become your enemy, because I tell you the truth?

17 They [a]zealously affect you, *but* not well; yea, they would exclude [1]you, that ye might affect them.

18 But *it is* good to be zealously affected always in *a* good *thing,* and not only when I am present with you.

19 [a]My little children, of whom I travail in birth again until Christ be formed in you,

20 I desire to be present with you now, and to change my voice; for [1]I stand in doubt of you.

The allegory of Abraham

21 Tell me, ye that desire to be under the law, do ye not hear the law?

22 For it is written, that Abraham had two sons, [a]the one by a bondmaid, [b]the other by a freewoman.

23 But he *who was* of the bondwoman [a]was born after the flesh; [b]but he of the freewoman *was* by promise.

24 Which things are an allegory: for these are the two [1]covenants; the one from the mount [a]Sinai,[2] which gendereth to bondage, which is Agar.

25 For this Agar is mount Sinai in Arabia, and [1]answereth to Jerusalem which now is, and is in bondage with her children.

26 But [a]Jerusalem which is above is free, which is the mother of us all.

27 For it is written, [a]Rejoice, *thou* barren that bearest not; break forth and cry, thou that travailest not: for the desolate hath many more children than she which hath an husband.

28 Now we, brethren, as Isaac was, are [a]the children of promise.

29 But as then [a]he that was born after the flesh persecuted him *that was born* after the Spirit, [b]even so *it is* now. R

30 Nevertheless what saith [a]the scripture? [b]Cast out the bondwoman and her son: for [c]the son of the bondwoman shall not be heir with the son of the freewoman.

31 So then, brethren, we are not children of the bondwoman, [a]but of the free.

Liberty threatened by legalism

5 STAND FAST therefore in [a]the liberty wherewith Christ hath made us free, and be not entangled again [b]with the yoke of bondage.

2 Behold, I Paul say unto you, that [a]if ye be circumcised, Christ shall profit you nothing.

3 For I testify again to every man that is circumcised, [a]that he is a debtor to do the whole law.

4 [a]Christ is become of no effect unto you, whosoever of you are justified by the law; [b]ye are fallen from grace. G

5 [a]Mat. 20:28; Heb. 9:12 [b]John 1:12; Eph. 1:5
6 [a]Rom. 5:5
7 [a]Rom. 8:16
8 [a]Eph. 2:12; 1 Thes. 4:5 [b]Rom. 1:25; 1 Cor. 12:2; 1 Thes. 1:9
9 [a]1 Cor. 8:3 [b]Col. 2:20 [c]Heb. 7:18 [1]Or, *back* [2]Or, *rudiments*
10 [a]Rom. 14:5
11 [a]1 Thes. 3:5
12 [a]2 Cor. 2:5
13 [a]1 Cor. 2:3
14 [a]Mal. 2:7 [b]Luke 10:16
15 [1]Or, *What was then*
17 [a]Rom. 10:2 [1]Or, *us*
19 [a]1 Cor. 4:15
20 [1]Or, *I am perplexed for you*
22 [a]Gen. 16:15 [b]Gen. 21:2
23 [a]Rom. 9:7,8 [b]Heb. 11:11
24 [a]Deut. 33:2 [1]Or, *testaments* [2]Gk. *Sina*
25 [1]Or, *is in the same rank with*
26 [a]Is. 2:2
27 [a]Is. 54:1
28 [a]Acts 3:25
29 [a]Gen. 21:9 [b]ch. 5:11
30 [a]ch. 3:8,22 [b]Gen. 21:10 [c]John 8:35
31 [a]John 8:36
5:1 [a]Rom. 6:18 [b]Acts 15:10
2 [a]Acts 15:1
3 [a]ch. 3:10
4 [a]Rom. 9:31 [b]Heb. 12:15

E *Gal 3:5* ◀▶ *Gal 5:5*
R *Gal 3:2–3* ◀▶ *Gal 4:29*
R *Gal 4:6* ◀▶ *Eph 1:13–14*
G *Gal 3:21* ◀▶ *Eph 2:5*

5 For we through the Spirit [a]wait for the hope of righteousness by faith.

6 For [a]in Jesus Christ neither circumcision availeth any thing, nor uncircumcision; but [b]faith which worketh by love.

7 Ye [a]did run well; [b]who [/]did hinder you that ye should not obey the truth?

8 This persuasion *cometh* not of him [a]that calleth you.

9 [a]A little leaven leaveneth the whole lump.

10 [a]I have confidence in you through the Lord, that ye will be none otherwise minded: but [b]he that troubleth you [c]shall bear his judgment, whosoever he be.

11 [a]And I, brethren, if I yet preach circumcision, [b]why do I yet suffer persecution? then is [c]the offence of the cross ceased.

12 [a]I would they were even cut off [b]which trouble you.

Liberty defined

13 For, brethren, ye have been called unto liberty; only [a]*use* not liberty for an occasion to the flesh, but [b]by love serve one another.

14 For [a]all the law is fulfilled in one word, *even* in this; [b]Thou shalt love thy neighbour as thyself.

15 But if ye bite and devour one another, take heed that ye be not consumed one of another.

16 *This* I say then, [a]Walk in the Spirit, and [/]ye shall not fulfil the lust of the flesh.

17 For [a]the flesh lusteth against the Spirit, and the Spirit against the flesh: and these are contrary the one to the other: [b]so that ye cannot do the things that ye would.

18 But [a]if ye be led of the Spirit, ye are not under the law.

19 Now [a]the works of the flesh are manifest, which are *these;* Adultery, fornication, uncleanness, lasciviousness,

20 Idolatry, witchcraft, hatred, variance, emulations, wrath, strife, seditions, heresies,

21 Envyings, murders, drunkenness, revellings, and such like: of the which I tell you before, as I have also told *you* in time past, that [a]they which do such things shall not inherit the kingdom of God.

22 But [a]the fruit of the Spirit is love, joy, peace, longsuffering, [b]gentleness, [c]goodness, [d]faith,

23 Meekness, temperance: [a]against such there is no law.

24 And they that are Christ's [a]have crucified the flesh with the [/]affections and lusts.

Fulfilling the law of Christ

25 [a]If we live in the Spirit, let us also walk in the Spirit.

26 [a]Let us not be desirous of vain glory, provoking one another, envying one another.

6 BRETHREN, [a]IF [/] a man be overtaken in a fault, ye [b]which are spiritual, restore such an one [c]in the spirit of meekness; considering thyself, [d]lest thou also be tempted.

2 [a]Bear ye one another's burdens, and so fulfil [b]the law of Christ.

3 For [a]if a man think himself to be something, when [b]he is nothing, he deceiveth himself.

4 But [a]let every man prove his own work, and then shall he have rejoicing in himself alone, and [b]not in another.

5 For [a]every man shall bear his own burden.

6 [a]Let him that is taught in the word

5 [a]Rom. 8:24
6 [a]Col. 3:11 [b]1 Thes. 1:3
7 [a]1 Cor. 9:24 [b]ch. 3:1 [/]*Or, who did drive you back*
8 [a]ch. 1:6
9 [a]1 Cor. 5:6
10 [a]2 Cor. 2:3 [b]ch. 1:7 [c]2 Cor. 10:6
11 [a]ch. 6:12 [b]1 Cor. 15:30 [c]1 Cor. 1:23
12 [a]Josh. 7:25 [b]Acts 15:1,2
13 [a]1 Cor. 8:9; 1 Pet. 2:16 [b]1 Cor. 9:19
14 [a]Mat. 7:12; Jas. 2:8 [b]Mat. 22:39
16 [a]Rom. 6:12; 1 Pet. 2:11 [/]*Or, fulfil not*
17 [a]Rom. 7:23 [b]Rom. 7:15
18 [a]Rom. 6:14
19 [a]Eph. 5:3
21 [a]1 Cor. 6:9
22 [a]John 15:2; Eph. 5:9 [b]Col. 3:12 [c]Rom. 15:14 [d]1 Cor. 13:7
23 [a]1 Tim. 1:9
24 [a]Rom. 6:6; 1 Pet. 2:11 [/]*Or, passions*
25 [a]Rom. 8:4,5
26 [a]Phil. 2:3
6:1 [a]Rom. 14:1 [b]1 Cor. 2:15 [c]1 Cor. 4:21 [d]1 Cor. 7:5 [/]*Or, although*
2 [a]Rom. 15:1; 1 Thes. 5:14 [b]Jas. 2:8
3 [a]Rom. 12:3; 1 Cor. 8:2 [b]2 Cor. 3:5
4 [a]1 Cor. 11:28 [b]Luke 18:11
5 [a]Rom. 2:6; 1 Cor. 3:8
6 [a]1 Cor. 9:11

E *Gal 4:6* ◀▶ *Gal 6:1*
L *2Co 12:18* ◀▶ *Gal 5:16–18*
S *Gal 2:20* ◀▶ *Gal 5:19–25*
L *Gal 5:5* ◀▶ *Gal 5:22–25*
S *2Co 3:18* ◀▶ *1Th 4:7–8*
W *Gal 3:14* ◀▶ *Gal 5:25*
N *2Co 11:4* ◀▶ *Eph 2:18*
C *2Co 5:14* ◀▶ *Eph 2:1–3*
H *2Co 11:15* ◀▶ *Gal 6:7–8*
S *Gal 5:6* ◀▶ *Gal 6:7–9*
F *2Co 13:14* ◀▶ *Eph 1:3*
J *2Co 3:17* ◀▶ *1Th 1:6*
L *Gal 5:16–18* ◀▶ *Gal 6:8*
W *Gal 5:16* ◀▶ *Eph 1:16–17*
E *Gal 5:5* ◀▶ *Eph 1:3*

5:5 Paul says that we who are in the Spirit "wait for the hope of righteousness by faith." This verse refers to our faith and hope of the coming resurrection when Jesus will return in the air to translate the bodies of his saints to glorious resurrection bodies fit for eternity that we might enjoy the new Jerusalem and "reign on the earth" (Rev 5:10).

communicate unto him that teacheth in
all good things.
H 7 [a]Be not deceived; [b]God is not
S mocked: for [c]whatsoever a man soweth,
that shall he also reap.
L 8 [a]For he that soweth to his flesh shall
of the flesh reap corruption; but he that
soweth to the Spirit shall of the Spirit
reap life everlasting.
9 And [a]let us not be weary in well doing: for in due season we shall reap, [b]if
we faint not.
10 [a]As we have therefore opportunity,
[b]let us do good unto all *men,* especially
unto them who are of [c]the household of
faith.

Paul's personal benediction

11 Ye see how large a letter I have
written unto you with mine own hand.
12 As many as desire to make a fair
show in the flesh, [a]they constrain you to
be circumcised; [b]only lest they should
[c]suffer persecution for the cross of
Christ.
13 For neither they themselves who
are circumcised keep the law; but desire
to have you circumcised, that they may
glory in your flesh.
14 [a]But God forbid that I should glory, S
save in the cross of our Lord Jesus Christ,
[1]by whom the world is [b]crucified unto
me, and I unto the world.
15 For [a]in Christ Jesus neither circumcision availeth any thing, nor uncircumcision, but [b]a new creature.
16 [a]And as many as walk [b]according to U
this rule, peace *be* on them, and mercy,
and upon [c]the Israel of God.
17 From henceforth let no man trouble
me: for [a]I bear in my body the marks of
the Lord Jesus.
18 Brethren, [a]the grace of our Lord
Jesus Christ *be* with your spirit. Amen.

7 [a] 1 Cor. 6:9 [b] Job 13:9 [c] Rom. 2:6; 2 Cor. 9:6
8 [a] Job 4:8
9 [a] 1 Cor. 15:58 [b] Mat. 24:13; Rev. 2:10
10 [a] John 9:4 [b] Tit. 3:8 [c] Eph. 2:19
12 [a] ch. 2:3,14 [b] Phil. 3:18 [c] ch. 5:11
14 [a] Phil. 3:3,7 [b] Rom. 6:6 [1] Or, *whereby*
15 [a] 1 Cor. 7:19 [b] 2 Cor. 5:17
16 [a] Ps. 125:5 [b] Phil. 3:16 [c] Rom. 2:29
17 [a] 2 Cor. 1:5
18 [a] 2 Tim. 4:22

H *Gal 5:19–21* ◀ ▶ *Eph 5:5–6*
S *Gal 5:19–25* ◀ ▶ *Gal 6:14–16*
L *Gal 5:22–25* ◀ ▶ *Eph 4:3–4*

S *Gal 6:7–9* ◀ ▶ *Eph 2:10*
U *2Co 6:17* ◀ ▶ *1Ti 4:8*

Ephesians

Author: Paul

Theme: Life in Christ

Date of Writing: C. A.D. 60–62

Outline of Ephesians

I. Salutation (1:1–2)
II. Christ Is the Head of the Church (1:3–23)
III. The Church Is the Body of Christ (2:1—3:21)
IV. The Conduct of Believers (4:1—6:9)
V. Spiritual Warfare (6:10–20)
VI. Conclusion (6:21–24)

IN ALL LIKELIHOOD Paul wrote this epistle during his two-year imprisonment in Rome, about A.D. 60. During this time Paul was at liberty to preach the gospel freely (see Ac 28). It is probable that Ephesians, Colossians and Philemon were all written at this same time and place too. Paul also had many companions with him at this time—Aristarchus, Epaphras, Luke, Demas, Mark, Onesimus and Tychicus (see Ac 20:4; Phm 23). Tychicus served as Paul's messenger to deliver this letter to the Ephesians (see 6:21).

Because this letter lacks personal greetings or references to specific problems or situations some scholars believe that this epistle may have been intended for a number of churches in the general area surrounding Ephesus. Embracing a broad perspective in this letter, Paul repeatedly uses the word "church" to refer to the whole body of believers. His teaching underscores the role of the church as the body of Christ as Paul reveals that God's plan and eternal purpose through redemption in Christ involved the establishment of the church.

The first portion of Paul's letter addresses the situation of the believer in Christ, contrasting the believer's conduct as a member of the body of Christ with the believer's former life of sin. The power of the Holy Spirit sets believers apart from the world and enables believers to live "in Christ." The second portion of the letter addresses a believer's conduct toward the church—not a building, but members of the body of Christ.

1 PAUL, AN apostle of Jesus Christ [a]by the will of God, [b]to the saints which are at Ephesus, [c]and to the faithful in Christ Jesus:

2 [a]Grace *be* to you, and peace, from God our Father, and *from* the Lord Jesus Christ.

Spiritual blessings in Christ

E F 3 [a]Blessed *be* the God and Father of our Lord Jesus Christ, who hath blessed us with all spiritual blessings in heavenly [1]*places* in Christ:

4 According as [a]he hath chosen us in him [b]before the foundation of the world, that we should [c]be holy and without blame before him in love:

5 [a]Having predestinated us unto [b]the adoption of children by Jesus Christ to himself, [c]according to the good pleasure of his will,

D L 6 To the praise of the glory of his grace, [a]wherein he hath made us accepted in [b]the beloved.

K 7 [a]In whom we have redemption through his blood, the forgiveness of sins, according to [b]the riches of his grace;

8 Wherein he hath abounded toward us in all wisdom and prudence;

9 [a]Having made known unto us the mystery of his will, according to his good pleasure [b]which he hath purposed in himself:

H 10 That in the dispensation of [a]the fulness of times [b]he might gather together in one [c]all things in Christ, both which are in [1]heaven, and which are on earth; *even* in him:

11 [a]In whom also we have obtained an inheritance, [b]being predestinated according to [c]the purpose of him who worketh all things after the counsel of his own will:

12 [a]That we should be to the praise of his glory, [b]who first [1]trusted in Christ.

B E R 13 In whom ye also *trusted,* after that ye heard [a]the word of truth, the gospel of your salvation: in whom also after that ye believed, [b]ye were sealed with that holy Spirit of promise,

14 [a]Which is the earnest of our inheritance [b]until the redemption of [c]the purchased possession, [d]unto the praise of his glory.

Prayer for wisdom and knowledge

15 Wherefore I also, [a]after I heard of your faith in the Lord Jesus, and love unto all the saints,

A G 16 [a]Cease not to give thanks for you, making mention of you in my prayers;

W M T 17 That [a]the God of our Lord Jesus Christ, the Father of glory, [b]may give unto you the spirit of wisdom and revelation [1]in the knowledge of him:

18 [a]The eyes of your understanding being enlightened; that ye may know what is [b]the hope of his calling, and what the riches of the glory of his inheritance in the saints,

19 And what *is* the exceeding greatness of his power to us-ward who believe, [a]according to the working [1]of his mighty power,

20 Which he wrought in Christ, when [a]he raised him from the dead, and [b]set *him* at his own right hand in the heavenly *places,*

V 21 [a]Far above all [b]principality, and

1:1 [a]2 Cor. 1:1 [b]Rom. 1:7; 2 Cor. 1:1 [c]1 Cor. 4:17
2 [a]Gal. 1:3
3 [a]2 Cor. 1:3 [1]Or, things
4 [a]Rom. 8:28 [b]1 Pet. 1:2 [c]Luke 1:75
5 [a]Rom. 8:29 [b]John 1:12 [c]1 Cor. 1:21
6 [a]Rom. 3:24 [b]Mat. 3:17
7 [a]Heb. 9:12 [b]Rom. 3:24
9 [a]Rom. 16:25 [b]2 Tim. 1:9
10 [a]Gal. 4:4 [b]1 Cor. 3:22 [c]Col. 1:20 [1]Gk. *the heavens*
11 [a]Rom. 8:17 [b]ver. 5 [c]Is. 46:10
12 [a]2 Thes. 2:13 [b]Jas. 1:18 [1]Or, *hoped*
13 [a]John 1:17 [b]2 Cor. 1:22
14 [a]2 Cor. 5:5 [b]Rom. 8:23 [c]Acts 20:28 [d]1 Pet. 2:9
15 [a]Col. 1:4
16 [a]Rom. 1:9
17 [a]John 20:17 [b]Col. 1:9 [1]Or, *for the acknowledgment*
18 [a]Acts 26:18 [b]ch. 2:12
19 [a]Col. 2:12 [1]Gk. *of the might of his power*
20 [a]Acts 2:24 [b]Ps. 110:1
21 [a]Phil. 2:9,10 [b]Rom. 8:38

E *Gal 6:1* ◀▶ *Eph 1:13–14*
F *Gal 5:22–23* ◀▶ *Eph 4:3*
D *Gal 4:4–5* ◀▶ *Eph 2:13–18*
L *Gal 3:26* ◀▶ *Eph 2:1–9*
K *2Co 9:8* ◀▶ *Eph 3:20*
H *Lk 22:16* ◀▶ *Eph 5:27*

B *Gal 3:5* ◀▶ *Eph 3:16*
E *Eph 1:3* ◀▶ *Eph 2:18*
R *Gal 4:29* ◀▶ *Eph 2:18*
A *Ac 8:14–17* ◀▶ *Eph 3:14–19*
G *1Co 14:1–40* ◀▶ *Eph 3:2–5*
W *Gal 5:25* ◀▶ *Eph 2:22*
M *Gal 3:5* ◀▶ *Eph 3:2–5*
T *1Co 14:30* ◀▶ *Eph 3:2–5*
V *1Co 15:24–26* ◀▶ *Php 2:9–10*

1:10 The word "dispensation" refers to a period of time in which someone is spiritually required to obey a certain revelation of truth. In this verse Paul mentions the "dispensation of the fulness of times," referring to the first advent of Christ. This dispensation of the gospel was instituted to draw people to Christ. Compare this verse with Gal 4:4.

1:21–22 God has established his Son, Jesus Christ, far above any power or name in the universe, placing everything in subjection to him (see Ps 8:5–6; Heb 2:6–9). This prophecy will be ultimately fulfilled following the defeat of Satan at Armageddon (see Rev 11:15).

power, and might, and dominion, and every name that is named, not only in this
world, but also in that which is to come:
22 And [a]hath put all *things* under his
feet, and gave him [b]*to be* the head over
all *things* to the church,
23 [a]Which is his body, [b]the fulness of
him [c]that filleth all in all.

New life with Christ

A 2 AND [a]YOU *hath he quickened,*
C [b]who were dead in trespasses and
L sins;
2 [a]Wherein in time past ye walked according to the course of this world, according to [b]the prince of the power of the
air, the spirit that now worketh in [c]the
children of disobedience:
3 [a]Among whom also we all had our
conversation in times past in [b]the lusts
of our flesh, fulfilling [/]the desires of the
flesh and of the mind; and [c]were by nature the children of wrath, even as
others.
4 But God, [a]who is rich in mercy, for
his great love wherewith he loved us,
G 5 [a]Even when we were dead in sins,
hath [b]quickened us together with Christ,
([/]by grace ye are saved;)
6 And hath raised *us* up together, and
made *us* sit together [a]in heavenly *places*
in Christ Jesus:
7 That in the ages to come he might
show the exceeding riches of his grace in
[a]*his* kindness toward us through Christ
Jesus.
F 8 [a]For by grace are ye saved [b]through
G faith; and that not of yourselves: [c]*it is* the
gift of God:
9 Not of works, lest any man should
boast.
S 10 For we are [a]his workmanship, created in Christ Jesus unto good works,
which God hath before [/]ordained that we
should walk in them.

The household of God

11 Wherefore remember, that ye *be-* L
ing in time past Gentiles in the flesh,
who are called Uncircumcision by that
which is called [a]the Circumcision in the
flesh made by hands;
12 [a]That at that time ye were without C
Christ, [b]being aliens from the common-
wealth of Israel, and strangers from [c]the
covenants of promise, [d]having no hope,
[e]and without God in the world:
13 [a]But now in Christ Jesus ye who D
sometimes were [b]far off are made nigh by
the blood of Christ.
14 For [a]he is our peace, [b]who hath
made both one, and hath broken down
the middle wall of partition *between us;*
15 [a]Having abolished [b]in his flesh the
enmity, *even* the law of commandments
contained in ordinances; for to make in
himself of twain one [c]new man, *so* making peace;
16 And that he might [a]reconcile both
unto God in one body by the cross, [b]hav-
ing slain the enmity [/]thereby:
17 And came [a]and preached peace to W
you which were afar off, and to [b]them
that were nigh.
18 For [a]through him we both have ac- E
cess [b]by one Spirit unto the Father. N
19 Now therefore ye are no more R
strangers and foreigners, but [a]fellowciti-
zens with the saints, and of [b]the household of God;
20 And are [a]built [b]upon the foundation of the [c]apostles and prophets, Jesus
Christ himself being [d]the chief corner
stone;
21 In whom all the building fitly
framed together groweth unto [a]an holy
temple in the Lord:
22 [a]In whom ye also are builded to- D
gether for an habitation of God through E
the Spirit. W

22 [a]Mat. 28:18 [b]Heb. 2:7
23 [a]Rom. 12:5 [b]Col. 2:9 [c]1 Cor. 12:6
2:1 [a]Col. 2:13 [b]ch. 4:18
2 [a]Col. 1:21 [b]ch. 6:12 [c]Col. 3:6
3 [a]1 Pet. 4:3 [b]Gal. 5:16 [c]Ps. 51:5 [/]Gk. *the wills*
4 [a]Rom. 10:12
5 [a]Rom. 5:6,8 [b]Rom. 6:4,5 [/]Or, *by whose grace*
6 [a]ch. 1:20
7 [a]Tit. 3:4
8 [a]2 Tim. 1:9 [b]Rom. 4:16 [c]Mat. 16:17
10 [a]Is. 19:25 [/]Or, *prepared*
11 [a]Col. 2:11
12 [a]Col. 1:21 [b]Ezek. 13:9 [c]Rom. 9:4,8 [d]1 Thes. 4:13 [e]Gal. 4:8
13 [a]Gal. 3:28 [b]Acts 2:39
14 [a]Mic. 5:5 [b]John 10:16
15 [a]Col. 2:14 [b]Col. 1:22 [c]Gal. 6:15
16 [a]Col. 1:20-22 [b]Rom. 6:6 [/]Or, *in himself*
17 [a]Is. 57:19 [b]Ps. 148:14
18 [a]John 10:9 [b]1 Cor. 12:13
19 [a]Phil. 3:20 [b]Gal. 6:10
20 [a]1 Pet. 2:4 [b]Mat. 16:18 [c]1 Cor. 12:28 [d]Ps. 118:22
21 [a]1 Cor. 3:17
22 [a]1 Pet. 2:5

A *Gal 3:22* ◀▶ *Jas 2:10*
C *Gal 5:19–21* ◀▶ *Eph 2:12*
L *Eph 1:6–7* ◀▶ *Eph 2:11–18*
G *Gal 5:4* ◀▶ *Eph 2:8–9*
F *Gal 3:24–26* ◀▶ *Php 3:9*
G *Eph 2:5* ◀▶ *Php 3:3–10*
S *Gal 6:14–16* ◀▶ *Eph 4:1*

L *Eph 2:1–9* ◀▶ *Eph 4:32*
C *Eph 2:1–3* ◀▶ *Eph 4:18*
D *Eph 1:6–7* ◀▶ *Eph 5:2*
W *Gal 3:22* ◀▶ *1Ti 1:15*
E *Eph 1:13–14* ◀▶ *Eph 2:22*
N *Gal 5:18* ◀▶ *Eph 3:16*
R *Eph 1:13–14* ◀▶ *Tit 3:5*
D *2Co 13:14* ◀▶ *Eph 4:4*
E *Eph 2:18* ◀▶ *Eph 3:2–5*
W *Eph 1:16–17* ◀▶ *Eph 3:14–19*

Paul, apostle to the Gentiles

3 FOR THIS cause I Paul, [a]the prisoner of Jesus Christ [b]for you Gentiles,

2 If ye have heard of [a]the dispensation of the grace of God [b]which is given me to you-ward:

3 [a]How that by revelation [b]he made known unto me the mystery; (as I wrote [/]afore in few words,

4 Whereby, when ye read, ye may understand my knowledge in the mystery of Christ)

5 [a]Which in other ages was not made known unto the sons of men, as it is now revealed unto his holy apostles and prophets by the Spirit;

6 That the Gentiles [a]should be fellowheirs, and of the same body, and partakers of his promise in Christ by the gospel:

7 [a]Whereof I was made a minister, [b]according to the gift of the grace of God given unto me by [c]the effectual working of his power.

8 Unto me, [a]who am less than the least of all saints, is this grace given, that I should preach among the Gentiles [b]the unsearchable riches of Christ;

9 And to make all *men* see what *is* the fellowship of the mystery, [a]which from the beginning of the world hath been hid in God, [b]who created all things by Jesus Christ:

10 [a]To the intent that now [b]unto the principalities and powers in heavenly *places* [c]might be known by the church the manifold wisdom of God,

11 According to the eternal purpose which he purposed in Christ Jesus our Lord:

12 In whom we have boldness and access [a]with confidence by the faith of him.

13 [a]Wherefore I desire that ye faint not at my tribulations for you, [b]which is your glory.

E *Eph 2:22* ◀▶ *Eph 4:3*
G *Eph 1:16–19* ◀▶ *Eph 3:7*
M *Eph 1:17–19* ◀▶ *Eph 3:14–19*
T *Eph 1:17–19* ◀▶ *Eph 3:16–19*
G *Eph 3:2–5* ◀▶ *Eph 3:14–19*

Strength through the Spirit

14 For this cause I bow my knees unto the Father of our Lord Jesus Christ,

15 Of whom [a]the whole family in heaven and earth is named,

16 That he would grant you, [a]according to the riches of his glory, [b]to be strengthened with might by his Spirit in [c]the inner man;

17 [a]That Christ may dwell in your hearts by faith; that ye, [b]being rooted and grounded in love,

18 [a]May be able to comprehend with all saints [b]what *is* the breadth, and length, and depth, and height;

19 And to know the love of Christ, which passeth knowledge, that ye might be filled [a]with all the fulness of God.

20 Now [a]unto him that is able to do exceeding abundantly [b]above all that we ask or think, [c]according to the power that worketh in us,

21 [a]Unto him *be* glory in the church by Christ Jesus throughout all ages, world without end. Amen.

The unity of the Spirit

4 I THEREFORE, [a]the prisoner [/]of the Lord, beseech you that ye [b]walk worthy of the vocation wherewith ye are called,

2 [a]With all lowliness and meekness, with longsuffering, forbearing one another in love;

3 Endeavouring to keep the unity of the Spirit [a]in the bond of peace.

4 [a]*There is* one body, and one Spirit,

A *Eph 1:16–17* ◀▶ *Col 1:9*
G *Eph 3:7* ◀▶ *Eph 4:7–8*
M *Eph 3:2–5* ◀▶ *Php 1:19*
W *Eph 2:22* ◀▶ *Eph 4:3–4*
B *Eph 1:13–14* ◀▶ *Eph 4:8*
N *Eph 2:18* ◀▶ *Eph 4:4*
T *Eph 3:2–5* ◀▶ *Eph 6:17*
K *Eph 1:7* ◀▶ *Eph 5:14*
S *Eph 2:10* ◀▶ *Eph 4:20–24*
E *Eph 3:2–5* ◀▶ *Eph 4:7–8*
F *Eph 1:3* ◀▶ *Eph 5:9*
L *Gal 6:8* ◀▶ *Eph 5:18–19*
W *Eph 3:14–19* ◀▶ *Eph 5:9*
D *Eph 2:22* ◀▶ *Heb 9:14*
N *Eph 3:16* ◀▶ *Eph 5:18*

3:1 [a]Acts 21:33 [b]Col. 1:24
2 [a]Rom. 1:5 [b]Acts 9:15
3 [a]Acts 22:17 [b]Rom. 16:25 [/]*Or, a little before*
5 [a]Rom. 16:25
6 [a]Gal. 3:28
7 [a]Rom. 15:16 [b]Rom. 1:5 [c]Rom. 15:18
8 [a]1 Cor. 15:9 [b]Col. 1:27
9 [a]Rom. 16:25 [b]Ps. 33:6
10 [a]1 Pet. 1:12 [b]Col. 1:16 [c]1 Tim. 3:16
12 [a]Heb. 4:16
13 [a]Phil. 1:14 [b]2 Cor. 1:6
15 [a]ch. 1:10
16 [a]Phil. 4:19 [b]Col. 1:11 [c]Rom. 7:22
17 [a]John 14:23 [b]Col. 1:23
18 [a]ch. 1:18 [b]Rom. 10:3
19 [a]ch. 1:23
20 [a]Rom. 16:25 [b]1 Cor. 2:9 [c]Col. 1:29
21 [a]Rom. 11:36
4:1 [a]Philem. 1,9 [b]Phil. 1:27 [/]*Or, in the Lord*
2 [a]Acts 20:19
3 [a]Col. 3:14
4 [a]Rom. 12:5

3:2–6 To the Jewish mind it was remarkable that God should freely offer salvation to the Gentiles who would repent and believe in Christ. God's offer to the Gentiles to become part "of the same body, and partakers of his promise in Christ" (3:6) revealed God's great mercy and love for all people.

even as ye are called in one hope of your calling;

5 [a]One Lord, [b]one faith, [c]one baptism,

6 [a]One God and Father of all, who *is* above all, and [b]through all, and in you all.

E 7 But [a]unto every one of us is given
G grace according to the measure of the gift of Christ.

B 8 Wherefore he saith, [a]When he ascended up on high, [b]he led [1]captivity captive, and gave gifts unto men.

9 [a](Now that he ascended, what is it but that he also descended first into the lower parts of the earth?

10 He that descended is the same also [a]that ascended up far above all heavens, [b]that he might [1]fill all things.)

G 11 [a]And he gave some, apostles; and some, prophets; and some, [b]evangelists; and some, [c]pastors and [d]teachers;

12 [a]For the perfecting of the saints, for the work of the ministry, [b]for the edifying of [c]the body of Christ:

13 Till we all come [1]in the unity of the faith, and [a]of the knowledge of the Son of God, unto [b]a perfect man, unto the measure of the [2]stature of the fulness of Christ:

14 That we *henceforth* be no more [a]children, [b]tossed to and fro, and carried about with every [c]wind of doctrine, by the sleight of men, *and* cunning craftiness, [d]whereby they lie in wait to deceive;

15 But [a]speaking[1] the truth in love, [b]may grow up into him in all things, [c]which is the head, *even* Christ:

16 [a]From whom the whole body fitly joined together and compacted by that which every joint supplieth, according to the effectual working in the measure of every part, maketh increase of the body unto the edifying of itself in love.

The old life and the new

17 This I say therefore, and testify in the Lord, that [a]ye henceforth walk not as other Gentiles walk, [b]in the vanity of their mind,

C 18 [a]Having the understanding darkened, [b]being alienated from the life of God through the ignorance that is in them, because of the [c]blindness[1] of their heart:

19 [a]Who being past feeling [b]have given themselves over unto lasciviousness, to work all uncleanness with greediness.

20 But ye have not so learned Christ; S

21 If so be that ye have heard him, and have been taught by him, as the truth is in Jesus:

22 That ye [a]put off concerning [b]the former conversation the old man, which is corrupt according to the deceitful lusts;

23 And [a]be renewed in the spirit of your mind;

24 And that ye [a]put on the new man, which after God is created in righteousness and [1]true holiness.

25 Wherefore putting away lying, [a]speak every man truth with his neighbour: for [b]we are members one of another.

26 [a]Be ye angry, and sin not: let not the sun go down upon your wrath:

27 [a]Neither give place to the devil.

28 Let him that stole steal no more: but rather [a]let him labour, working with *his* hands the thing which is good, that he may have [1]to give [b]to him that needeth.

29 [a]Let no corrupt communication proceed out of your mouth, but [b]that which is good [1]to the use of edifying, [c]that it may minister grace unto the hearers.

30 And [a]grieve not the holy Spirit of E
God, whereby ye are sealed unto the day Q
of [b]redemption.

31 [a]Let all bitterness, and wrath, and anger, and clamour, and [b]evil speaking, be put away from you, [c]with all malice:

32 And [a]be ye kind one to another, L
tenderhearted, [b]forgiving one another, even as God for Christ's sake hath forgiven you.

The works of light and darkness

5 BE [a]YE therefore followers of God, as dear children;

2 And [a]walk in love, [b]as Christ also D
hath loved us, and hath given himself for

4:5 [a]1 Cor. 1:13 [b]Jude 3 [c]Heb. 6:6
6 [a]Mal. 2:10 [b]Rom. 11:36
7 [a]1 Cor. 12:11
8 [a]Ps. 68:18 [b]Judg. 5:12 [1]Or, *a multitude of captives*
9 [a]John 3:13
10 [a]Acts 1:9 [b]Acts 2:33 [1]Or, *fulfil*
11 [a]1 Cor. 12:28 [b]Acts 21:8 [c]Acts 20:28 [d]Rom. 12:7
12 [a]1 Cor. 12:7 [b]1 Cor. 14:26 [c]Col. 1:24
13 [a]Col. 2:2 [b]1 Cor. 14:20 [1]Or, *into the unity* [2]Or, *age*
14 [a]Is. 28:9 [b]Heb. 13:9 [c]Mat. 11:7 [d]Rom. 16:18
15 [a]2 Cor. 4:2 [b]ch. 1:22 [c]Col. 1:18 [1]Or, *being sincere*
16 [a]Col. 2:19
17 [a]Col. 3:7 [b]Rom. 1:21
18 [a]Acts 26:18 [b]1 Thes. 4:5 [c]Rom. 1:21 [1]Or, *hardness*
19 [a]1 Tim. 4:2 [b]1 Pet. 4:3
22 [a]Col. 2:11 [b]Col. 3:7
23 [a]Col. 3:10
24 [a]Rom. 6:4 [1]Or, *holiness of truth*
25 [a]Zech. 8:16 [b]Rom. 12:5
26 [a]Ps. 37:8
27 [a]1 Pet. 5:9
28 [a]Acts 20:35 [b]Luke 3:11 [1]Or, *to distribute*
29 [a]Col. 3:8 [b]1 Thes. 5:11 [c]Col. 3:16 [1]Or, *to edify profitably*
30 [a]Is. 7:13 [b]Luke 21:28
31 [a]Col. 3:8,19 [b]Jas. 4:11 [c]Tit. 3:3
32 [a]2 Cor. 2:10 [b]Mark 11:25
5:1 [a]Luke 6:36
2 [a]1 Thes. 4:9 [b]Gal. 1:4

E *Eph 4:3* ◀▶ *Eph 4:30*
G *Eph 3:14–19* ◀▶ *Eph 4:11–14*
B *Eph 3:16* ◀▶ *Eph 5:18*
G *Eph 4:7–8* ◀▶ *Col 1:9*
C *Eph 2:12* ◀▶ *Eph 5:14*
S *Eph 4:1* ◀▶ *Eph 5:5–6*
E *Eph 4:7–8* ◀▶ *Php 3:3*
Q *Ac 7:51* ◀▶ *1Th 5:19*
L *Eph 2:11–18* ◀▶ *Eph 5:14*
D *Eph 2:13–18* ◀▶ *Eph 5:25*

us an offering and a sacrifice to God [c]for a
sweetsmelling savour.
3 But [a]fornication, and all uncleanness, or covetousness, [b]let it not be once
named among you, as becometh saints;
4 [a]Neither filthiness, nor foolish talking, nor jesting, [b]which are not convenient: but rather giving of thanks.
H 5 For this ye know, that [a]no whore-
S monger, nor unclean person, nor covetous man, [b]who is an idolater, [c]hath any
inheritance in the kingdom of Christ and
of God.
6 [a]Let no man deceive you with vain
words: for because of these things [b]com-
eth the wrath of God upon the children of
ǀdisobedience.
7 Be not ye therefore partakers with
them.
8 [a]For ye were sometimes darkness,
but now [b]*are ye* light in the Lord: walk as
[c]children of light:
F 9 (For [a]the fruit of the Spirit *is* in all
W goodness and righteousness and truth;)
10 [a]Proving what is acceptable unto
the Lord.
11 And have no fellowship with [a]the
unfruitful works of darkness, but rather
[b]reprove *them.*
12 [a]For it is a shame even to speak of
those things which are done of them in
secret.
13 But [a]all things that are ǀreproved
are made manifest by the light: for whatsoever doth make manifest is light.
C 14 Wherefore ǀhe saith, [a]Awake thou
K that sleepest, and [b]arise from the dead,
L and Christ shall give thee light.
15 [a]See then that ye walk circum-
spectly, not as fools, but as wise,
16 [a]Redeeming the time, [b]because the
days are evil.

H *Gal 6:7–8* ◀▶ *Php 1:28*
S *Eph 4:20–24* ◀▶ *Eph 5:25–27*
F *Eph 4:3* ◀▶ *Php 2:1*
W *Eph 4:3–4* ◀▶ *Eph 5:18*
C *Eph 4:18* ◀▶ *Php 2:21*
K *Eph 3:20* ◀▶ *Php 4:13*
L *Eph 4:32* ◀▶ *Col 1:13–14*

2 [c]2 Cor. 2:15
3 [a]Rom. 6:13 [b]1 Cor. 5:1
4 [a]Mat. 12:35 [b]Rom. 1:28
5 [a]1 Cor. 6:9 [b]Col. 3:5 [c]Rev. 22:15
6 [a]Jer. 29:8 [b]Rom. 1:18 ǀOr, *unbelief*
8 [a]Is. 9:2 [b]2 Cor. 3:18 [c]Luke 16:8
9 [a]Gal. 5:22
10 [a]Rom. 12:2
11 [a]Rom. 6:21 [b]1 Tim. 5:20
12 [a]Rom. 1:24
13 [a]John 3:20 ǀOr, *discovered*
14 [a]Is. 60:1 [b]John 5:25 ǀOr, *it*
15 [a]Col. 4:5
16 [a]Col. 4:5 [b]Eccl. 11:2
17 [a]Col. 4:5 [b]Rom. 12:2 [c]1 Thes. 4:3
18 [a]Prov. 20:1
19 [a]Acts 16:25
20 [a]Ps. 34:1 [b]1 Pet. 2:5
21 [a]Phil. 2:3
22 [a]Gen. 3:16 [b]ch. 6:5
23 [a]1 Cor. 11:3 [b]Col. 1:18 [c]ch. 1:23
24 [a]Tit. 2:9
25 [a]Col. 3:19 [b]Acts 20:28
26 [a]John 3:5
27 [a]Col. 1:22 [b]Sol. 4:7

17 [a]Wherefore be ye not unwise, but
[b]understanding [c]what the will of the
Lord *is.*
18 And [a]be not drunk with wine, B
wherein is excess; but be filled with the L
Spirit; N
19 Speaking to yourselves [a]in psalms W
and hymns and spiritual songs, singing
and making melody in your heart to the
Lord;
20 [a]Giving thanks always for all things J
unto God and the Father [b]in the name of
our Lord Jesus Christ;

Analogy of family and church

21 [a]Submitting yourselves one to another in the fear of God.
22 [a]Wives, submit yourselves unto
your own husbands, [b]as unto the Lord.
23 For [a]the husband is the head of
the wife, even as [b]Christ is the head of
the church: and he is the saviour of [c]the
body.
24 Therefore as the church is subject
unto Christ, so *let* the wives *be* to their
own husbands [a]in every thing.
25 [a]Husbands, love your wives, even D
as Christ also loved the church, and [b]gave S
himself for it;
26 That he might sanctify and cleanse
it [a]with the washing of water by the
word,
27 [a]That he might present it to himself H
a glorious church, [b]not having spot, or
wrinkle, or any such thing; but that it
should be holy and without blemish.
28 So ought men to love their wives as
their own bodies. He that loveth his wife
loveth himself.
29 For no man ever yet hated his own

B *Eph 4:8* ◀▶ *Tit 3:5–6*
L *Eph 4:3–4* ◀▶ *Eph 6:18*
N *Eph 4:4* ◀▶ *Heb 9:14*
W *Eph 5:9* ◀▶ *Php 3:3*
J *2Co 12:10* ◀▶ *Php 1:28–29*
D *Eph 5:2* ◀▶ *Col 1:14*
S *Eph 5:5–6* ◀▶ *Php 2:12*
H *Eph 1:10* ◀▶ *Rev 7:9–17*

5:26–27 Paul's words foreshadow the marriage supper of the Lamb which will occur in heaven following the rapture of the church (see Rev 19:7–9). Jesus expresses his profound love for the church by perfecting and sanctifying it through the application of his atoning blood to the souls of those who repent of their sins. Though some believe that the church must endure the persecution of the tribulation as a means of purification, this passage clearly states that only the blood of Christ cleanses the church.

flesh; but nourisheth and cherisheth it,
even as the Lord the church:
30 For [a]we are members of his body,
of his flesh, and of his bones.
31 [a]For this cause shall a man leave his
father and mother, and shall be joined
unto his wife, and they [b]two shall be one
flesh.
32 This is a great mystery: but I speak
concerning Christ and the church.
33 Nevertheless [a]let every one of you
in particular so love his wife even as himself; and the wife *see* that she [b]reverence
her husband.

6 CHILDREN, [a]OBEY your parents in
the Lord: for this is right.
H 2 [a]Honour thy father and mother;
which is the first commandment with
promise;
3 That it may be well with thee, and
thou mayest live long on the earth.
4 And, [a]ye fathers, provoke not your
children to wrath: but [b]bring them up in
the nurture and admonition of the Lord.
5 [a]Servants, be obedient to them that
are *your* masters according to the flesh,
[b]with fear and trembling, [c]in singleness
of your heart, as unto Christ;
6 [a]Not with eyeservice, as menpleasers; but as the servants of Christ, doing
the will of God from the heart;
7 With good will doing service, as to
the Lord, and not to men:
8 [a]Knowing that whatsoever good
thing any man doeth, the same shall he
receive of the Lord, [b]whether *he be* bond
or free.
9 And, ye [a]masters, do the same things
unto them, [1]forbearing threatening:
knowing that [2]your Master also is in
heaven; [b]neither is there respect of persons with him.

The whole armour of God

10 Finally, my brethren, be strong in
the Lord, and in the power of his might.
11 [a]Put on the whole armour of God,
that ye may be able to stand against the
wiles of the devil.

H *Lk 4:18* ◀▶ *Jas 5:13–18*

30 [a]Gen. 2:23
31 [a]Mat. 19:5 [b]1 Cor. 6:16
33 [a]Col. 3:19 [b]1 Pet. 3:6
6:1 [a]Col. 3:20
2 [a]Ex. 20:12
4 [a]Col. 3:21 [b]Gen. 18:19
5 [a]1 Tim. 6:1 [b]2 Cor. 7:15; Phil. 2:12 [c]1 Chr. 29:17; Col. 3:22
6 [a]Col. 3:22
8 [a]Rom. 2:6; Col. 3:24 [b]Gal. 3:28
9 [a]Col. 4:1 [b]Rom. 2:11 [1]Or, *moderating* [2]Some read, *both your and their Master*
11 [a]2 Cor. 6:7
12 [a]Rom. 8:38 [b]Luke 22:53 [1]Gk. *blood and flesh* [2]Or, *wicked spirits* [3]Or, *heavenly*
13 [a]2 Cor. 10:4 [b]ch. 5:16 [1]Or, *having overcome all*
14 [a]Is. 11:5; 1 Pet. 1:13 [b]Is. 59:17
15 [a]Is. 52:7
16 [a]1 John 5:4
17 [a]1 Thes. 5:8 [b]Heb. 4:12
18 [a]Luke 18:1 [b]Mat. 26:41 [c]Phil. 1:4
19 [a]Acts 4:29 [b]2 Cor. 3:12
20 [a]2 Cor. 5:20 [b]Phil. 1:20 [1]Or, *in a chain* [2]Or, *thereof*
21 [a]Acts 20:4
22 [a]Col. 4:8
23 [a]1 Pet. 5:14
24 [1]Or, *with incorruption*

12 For we wrestle not against [1]flesh
and blood, but against [a]principalities,
against powers, against [b]the rulers of the
darkness of this world, against [2]spiritual
wickedness in [3]high *places.*
13 [a]Wherefore take unto you the
whole armour of God, that ye may be
able to withstand [b]in the evil day, and
[1]having done all, to stand.
14 Stand therefore, [a]having your loins
girt about with truth, and [b]having on the
breastplate of righteousness;
15 [a]And your feet shod with the preparation of the gospel of peace;
16 Above all, taking [a]the shield of
faith, wherewith ye shall be able to
quench all the fiery darts of the wicked.
17 And [a]take the helmet of salvation, C
and [b]the sword of the Spirit, which is the T
word of God:
18 [a]Praying always with all prayer and L
supplication in the Spirit, and [b]watching
thereunto with all perseverance and
[c]supplication for all saints;
19 [a]And for me, that utterance may be
given unto me, that I may open my
mouth [b]boldly, to make known the mystery of the gospel,
20 For which [a]I am an ambassador [1]in
bonds: that [2]therein [b]I may speak boldly,
as I ought to speak.

Concluding benediction

21 But that ye also may know my affairs, *and* how I do, [a]Tychicus, a beloved
brother and faithful minister in the Lord,
shall make known to you all things:
22 [a]Whom I have sent unto you for the
same purpose, that ye might know our
affairs, and *that* he might comfort your
hearts.
23 [a]Peace *be* to the brethren, and love
with faith, from God the Father and the
Lord Jesus Christ.
24 Grace *be* with all them that love
our Lord Jesus Christ [1]in sincerity.
Amen.

C *Ac 11:24* ◀▶ *Rev 22:17*
T *Eph 3:16–19* ◀▶ *1Th 1:5*
L *Eph 5:18–19* ◀▶ *Php 3:3*

Philippians

Author: Paul

Theme: There is joy in a relationship with Jesus

Date of Writing: c. A.D. 60–62

Outline of Philippians

I. Introduction (1:1–11)
II. Paul's Circumstances and Concern (1:12–30)
III. Serving as Christ Served (2:1–18)
IV. Paul's Messenger (2:19–30)
V. Warnings and Exhortations (3:1—4:20)
VI. Conclusion (4:21–23)

The apostle Paul wrote this letter to the Philippians during his first imprisonment in Rome (A.D. 59–61). References to Caesar's household (see 4:22) and to the praetorian guard (see 1:13) confirm this letter's origin and classify it as a "Prison Epistle," along with Ephesians, Colossians and Philemon. The believers at Philippi had sent a gift to Paul while he was in prison. The messenger who delivered the gift, Epaphroditus (see 4:18), became ill and was forced to stay with Paul while he recovered. Paul then sent this letter back to Philippi with Epaphroditus in gratitude for the Philippians' love and help.

Paul founded the church at Philippi on his second missionary journey to Macedonia. This thriving city became Paul's base of operations for several days, and many Gentiles were converted. Yet after delivering a slave girl from demons Paul found himself in the Philippian jail. A miraculous earthquake released Paul from his chains and his Philippian jailer was converted (see Ac 16:14–34). Composed primarily of Gentiles (see Ac 16:12–15), the church at Philippi grew and became a special delight to Paul because of its generous response to his pleas to aid the church in Jerusalem. Though Paul never showed favoritism to a particular church, Paul and the believers at Philippi developed a bond of love that is evoked in this personal letter as Paul shares his gratitude and Christian experience with his dear friends.

Throughout this letter Paul talks about the importance of the gospel in his ministry (see 1:5, 7, 12, 16, 27; 2:22; 4:3). Although Paul was writing from prison, various forms of the words "joy" or "rejoice" occur repeatedly in this letter, reminding the Philippians that

God's peace brings joy despite adverse circumstances (see 4:4–7). This letter also includes a warning against pride and a self-seeking attitude, reminding the believers to follow Christ's example through one of the most profound statements of the incarnation found in the NT (2:5–11).

1 PAUL AND Timotheus, the servants of Jesus Christ, to all the saints [a]in Christ Jesus which are at Philippi, with the bishops and deacons:

2 [a]Grace *be* unto you, and peace, from God our Father, and *from* the Lord Jesus Christ.

Prayer of thankfulness

3 [a]I thank my God upon every [1]remembrance of you,

4 Always in every prayer of mine for you all making request with joy,

5 [a]For your fellowship in the gospel from the first day until now;

6 Being confident of this very thing, that he which hath begun [a]a good work in you [1]will perform *it* until the day of Jesus Christ:

7 Even as it is meet for me to think this of you all, because [1]I have you in my heart; inasmuch as both in my bonds, and in the defence and confirmation of the gospel, ye all are [2]partakers of my grace.

8 For [a]God is my record, how greatly I long after you all in the bowels of Jesus Christ.

9 And this I pray, that your love may abound yet more and more in knowledge and *in* all [1]judgment;

10 That [a]ye may [1]approve things that [2]are excellent; [b]that ye may be sincere and without offence [c]till the day of Christ;

11 Being filled with the fruits of righteousness, [a]which are by Jesus Christ, [b]unto the glory and praise of God.

C 2Co 1:14 ◀ ▶ Php 1:10
C Php 1:6 ◀ ▶ Php 2:16

1:1 a 1 Cor. 1:2
2 a 1 Pet. 1:2
3 a 1 Cor. 1:4 1 Or, *mention*
5 a Rom. 12:13
6 a John 6:29 1 Or, *will finish* it
7 1 Or, *ye have me in your heart* 2 Or, *partakers with me of grace*
8 a Rom. 1:9; Gal. 1:20
9 1 Or, *sense*
10 a Rom. 12:2 b Acts 24:16 c 1 Cor. 1:8 1 Or, *try* 2 Or, *differ*
11 a Eph. 2:10; Col. 1:6 b John 15:8
13 a ch. 4:22 1 Or, *for Christ* 2 Or, *Caesar's court* 3 Or, *to all others*
15 a ch. 2:3
19 a 2 Cor. 1:11
20 a Rom. 8:19 b Rom. 5:5 c Eph. 6:19

Paul's boldness in prison

12 But I would ye should understand, brethren, that the things *which happened* unto me have fallen out rather unto the furtherance of the gospel;

13 So that my bonds [1]in Christ are manifest [a]in all [2]the palace, and [3]in all other *places;*

14 And many of the brethren in the Lord, waxing confident by my bonds, are much more bold to speak the word without fear.

15 Some indeed preach Christ even of envy and [a]strife; and some also of good will:

16 The one preach Christ of contention, not sincerely, supposing to add affliction to my bonds:

17 But the other of love, knowing that I am set for the defence of the gospel.

18 What then? notwithstanding, every way, whether in pretence, or in truth, Christ is preached; and I therein do rejoice, yea, and will rejoice.

19 For I know that this shall turn to my salvation [a]through your prayer, and the supply of the Spirit of Jesus Christ,

20 According to my [a]earnest expectation and *my* hope, that [b]in nothing I shall be ashamed, but *that* [c]with all boldness, as always, *so* now also Christ shall be magnified in my body, whether *it be* by life, or by death.

21 For to me to live *is* Christ, and to die *is* gain.

22 But if I live in the flesh, this *is* the

M Eph 3:14–19 ◀ ▶ Col 1:9–11

1:6 Paul's reference to "the day of Jesus Christ" foreshadows the day of Christ's second coming in glory.

1:10 Paul again references "the day of Christ" as Christ's second coming when believers will give an account of their life lived toward the goal of excellency, sincerity and blamelessness (see 2Co 5:10).

fruit of my labour: yet what I shall choose
I wot not.
23 For [a]I am in a strait betwixt two,
having a desire to [b]depart, and to be with
Christ; which is far better:
24 Nevertheless to abide in the flesh *is*
more needful for you.
25 And [a]having this confidence, I
know that I shall abide and continue with
you all for your furtherance and joy of
faith;
26 That [a]your rejoicing may be more
abundant in Jesus Christ for me by my
coming to you again.

The example of Christ

27 Only [a]let your conversation be as it
becometh the gospel of Christ: that
whether I come and see you, or else be
absent, I may hear of your affairs, that ye
stand fast in one spirit, [b]with one mind
striving together for the faith of the
gospel;
H 28 And in nothing terrified by your ad-
J versaries: [a]which is to them an evident
token of perdition, [b]but to you of salvation, and that of God.
29 For unto you [a]it is given in the behalf of Christ, [b]not only to believe on
him, but also to suffer for his sake;
30 [a]Having the same conflict [b]which
ye saw in me, and now hear *to be* in me.
F 2 IF *THERE be* therefore any consolation in Christ, if any comfort of love,
[a]if any fellowship of the Spirit, if any
[b]bowels and mercies,
2 [a]Fulfil ye my joy, [b]that ye be likeminded, having the same love, *being* of
one accord, of one mind.
3 [a]*Let* nothing *be done* through strife
or vainglory; but [b]in lowliness of mind
let each esteem other better than themselves.
4 [a]Look not every man on his own
things, but every man also on the things
of others.

H *Eph 5:5–6* ◀▶ *Php 3:19*
J *Eph 5:20* ◀▶ *Php 2:17*
F *Eph 5:9* ◀▶ *Col 1:8*

23 [a]2 Cor. 5:8 [b]2 Tim. 4:6
25 [a]ch. 2:24
26 [a]2 Cor. 1:14
27 [a]Eph. 4:1; 1 Thes. 2:12 [b]1 Cor. 1:10; Acts 2:36
28 [a]2 Thes. 1:5 [b]Rom. 8:17
29 [a]Rom. 5:3 [b]Eph. 2:8
30 [a]Col. 2:1 [b]Acts 16:19; 1 Thes. 2:2
2:1 [a]2 Cor. 13:14 [b]Col. 3:12
2 [a]John 3:29 [b]Rom. 12:16; 1 Cor. 1:10
3 [a]Gal. 5:26; Jas. 3:14 [b]Rom. 12:10; 1 Pet. 5:5
4 [a]1 Cor. 13:5
5 [a]Mat. 11:29; 1 Pet. 2:21
6 [a]2 Cor. 4:4; Col. 1:15
7 [a]Ps. 22:6; Is. 53:3; Dan. 9:26; Mark 9:12 [b]Is. 42:1; Ezek. 34:23; Zech. 3:8; Mat. 20:28; Luke 22:27 [c]John 1:14; Rom. 1:3; Gal. 4:4 [1]Or, *habit*
8 [a]Mat. 26:39; Heb. 5:8
9 [a]Acts 2:33; Heb. 2:9 [b]Heb. 1:4
10 [a]Is. 45:23; Mat. 28:18
11 [a]John 13:13; Acts 2:36
12 [a]ch. 1:5 [b]Eph. 6:5
13 [a]2 Cor. 3:5
14 [a]1 Pet. 4:9 [b]Rom. 14:1
15 [a]Mat. 5:45; Eph. 5:1 [b]1 Pet. 2:12 [c]Deut. 32:5 [d]Eph. 5:8 [1]Or, *sincere* [2]Or, *shine ye*
16 [a]2 Cor. 1:14; 1 Thes. 2:19 [b]Gal. 2:2

5 [a]Let this mind be in you, which was
also in Christ Jesus:
6 Who, [a]being in the form of God,
thought it not robbery to be equal with
God:
7 [a]But made himself of no reputation,
and took upon him the form [b]of a servant, and [c]was made in the [1]likeness of
men:
8 And being found in fashion as a man,
he humbled himself, and [a]became obedient unto death, even the death of the
cross.
9 Wherefore God also [a]hath highly ex- M
alted him, and [b]given him a name which V
is above every name:
10 [a]That at the name of Jesus every
knee should bow, of *things* in heaven,
and *things* in earth, and *things* under the
earth;
11 And [a]*that* every tongue should confess that Jesus Christ *is* Lord, to the glory
of God the Father.

Obligations of Christians

12 Wherefore, my beloved, [a]as ye S
have always obeyed, not as in my presence only, but now much more in my
absence, work out your own salvation
with [b]fear and trembling.
13 For [a]it is God which worketh in
you both to will and to do of *his* good
pleasure.
14 Do all things [a]without murmurings
and [b]disputings:
15 That ye may be blameless and S
[1]harmless, [a]the sons of God, without rebuke, [b]in the midst of [c]a crooked and
perverse nation, among whom [d]ye[2] shine
as lights in the world;
16 Holding forth the word of life; that C
[a]I may rejoice in the day of Christ, that [b]I
have not run in vain, neither laboured in
vain.

M *1Co 15:24–28* ◀▶ *1Ti 6:15*
V *Eph 1:21–22* ◀▶ *2Th 2:8*
S *Eph 5:25–27* ◀▶ *Php 2:15*
S *Php 2:12* ◀▶ *Php 3:18*
C *Php 1:10* ◀▶ *Php 3:20–21*

2:9–11 Paul prophesied of a day after the second coming of Christ when the universe will acknowledge Christ's supremacy. Every spiritual being in heaven, earth or hell will recognize Jesus Christ as their divine King. Paul's prophetic revelation reminds us that while the return of Jesus will be the most joyful event in history for those who love him, Christ's return will produce fear among all those who have refused to repent of their sins (see Mal 3:2; Mt 24:30).

J 17 Yea, and if [a]I be [′]offered upon the sacrifice [b]and service of your faith, [c]I joy, and rejoice with you all.

18 For the same cause also do ye joy, and rejoice with me.

Timothy and Epaphroditus

19 [′]But I trust in the Lord Jesus to send [a]Timotheus shortly unto you, that I also may be of good comfort, when I know your state.

20 For I have no man [a]likeminded,[′] who will naturally care for your state.

C 21 For all [a]seek their own, not the things which are Jesus Christ's.

22 But ye know the proof of him, [a]that, as a son with the father, he hath served with me in the gospel.

23 Him therefore I hope to send presently, so soon as I shall see how it will go with me.

24 But [a]I trust in the Lord that I also myself shall come shortly.

25 Yet I supposed it necessary to send to you [a]Epaphroditus, my brother, and companion in labour, and [b]fellowsoldier, [c]but your messenger, and [d]he that ministered to my wants.

26 [a]For he longed after you all, and was full of heaviness, because that ye had heard that he had been sick.

E 27 For indeed he was sick nigh unto death: but God had mercy on him; and not on him only, but on me also, lest I should have sorrow upon sorrow.

28 I sent him therefore the more carefully, that, when ye see him again, ye may rejoice, and that I may be the less sorrowful.

29 Receive him therefore in the Lord with all gladness; and [a]hold[′] such in reputation:

D 30 Because for the work of Christ he was nigh unto death, not regarding his life, [a]to supply your lack of service toward me.

J *Php 1:28–29* ◀▶ *Php 3:8*
C *Eph 5:14* ◀▶ *Php 3:18–19*
E *1Co 12:28* ◀▶ *Heb 11:11–12*
D *2Co 12:7–10* ◀▶ *Heb 12:5–13*

17 [a]2 Tim. 4:6 [b]Rom. 15:16 [c]2 Cor. 7:4; Col. 1:24 [′]*Gk. poured forth*
19 [a]Rom. 16:21 [′]*Or, Moreover*
20 [a]Ps. 55:13 [′]*Or, so dear unto me*
21 [a]1 Cor. 10:24; & 13:5; 2 Tim. 4:10
22 [a]1 Cor. 4:17; 1 Tim. 1:2
24 [a]ch. 1:25
25 [a]ch. 4:18 [b]Philem. 2 [c]2 Cor. 8:23 [d]2 Cor. 11:9
26 [a]ch. 1:8
29 [a]1 Cor. 16:18; 1 Thes. 5:12; 1 Tim. 5:17 [′]*Or, honour such*
30 [a]1 Cor. 16:17
3:1 [a]2 Cor. 13:11; 1 Thes. 5:16
2 [a]Gal. 5:15 [b]Rom. 2:28
3 [a]Deut. 30:6; Jer. 4:4 [b]Rom. 7:6 [c]Gal. 6:14
4 [a]2 Cor. 11:18
5 [a]Rom. 11:1 [b]2 Cor. 11:22 [c]Acts 23:6
6 [a]Acts 22:3 [b]Rom. 10:5 [c]Luke 1:6
7 [a]Mat. 13:44
8 [a]Is. 53:11
9 [a]Rom. 10:3 [b]Rom. 1:17
10 [a]Rom. 6:3-5 & 8:17
11 [a]Acts 26:7

The example of Paul

3 FINALLY, MY brethren, [a]rejoice in the Lord. To write the same things to you, to me indeed *is* not grievous, but for you *it is* safe. W

2 [a]Beware of dogs, beware of evil workers, [b]beware of the concision.

3 For we are [a]the circumcision, [b]which worship God in the spirit, and [c]rejoice in Christ Jesus, and have no confidence in the flesh. E L W G

4 Though [a]I might also have confidence in the flesh. If any other man thinketh that he hath whereof he might trust in the flesh, I more:

5 Circumcised the eighth day, of the stock of Israel, [a]*of* the tribe of Benjamin, [b]an Hebrew of the Hebrews; as touching the law, [c]a Pharisee;

6 [a]Concerning zeal, persecuting the church; [b]touching the righteousness which is in the law, [c]blameless.

7 But [a]what things were gain to me, those I counted loss for Christ.

8 Yea doubtless, and I count all things *but* loss [a]for the excellency of the knowledge of Christ Jesus my Lord: for whom I have suffered the loss of all things, and do count them *but* dung, that I may win Christ, J

9 And be found in him, not having [a]mine own righteousness, which is of the law, but [b]that which is through the faith of Christ, the righteousness which is of God by faith: F

10 That I may know him, and the power of his resurrection, and [a]the fellowship of his sufferings, being made conformable unto his death;

11 If by any means I might [a]attain unto the resurrection of the dead. F

W *Jn 14:27* ◀▶ *Php 4:4*
E *Eph 4:30* ◀▶ *Col 1:8*
L *Eph 6:18* ◀▶ *1Th 5:19*
W *Eph 5:18* ◀▶ *Col 1:9*
G *Eph 2:8–9* ◀▶ *1Ti 6:17*
J *Php 2:17* ◀▶ *Heb 13:6*
F *Eph 2:8* ◀▶ *Heb 3:18–19*
F *2Co 4:14* ◀▶ *Php 3:21*

3:11–15 Paul anxiously anticipates the coming "resurrection of the dead" (3:11), admitting that he is not "perfect" (3:12). Although Paul was a mature believer, he still recognized that Christ was continuing the process of daily sanctification in his life. Paul explains that he has not yet achieved the final goal of perfection, but he will keep on toward that goal to win the prize that will be his in heaven with Christ (see 2Co 5:10). Paul then admonishes his readers to "press toward the mark" (3:14).

The high calling of God

12 Not as though I had already [a]attained, either were already [b]perfect: but I follow after, if that I may apprehend that for which also I am apprehended of Christ Jesus.

13 Brethren, I count not myself to have apprehended: but *this* one thing *I do,* [a]forgetting those things which are behind, and [b]reaching forth unto those things which are before,

14 [a]I press toward the mark for the prize of [b]the high calling of God in Christ Jesus.

15 Let us therefore, as many as be [a]perfect, [b]be thus minded: and if in any thing ye be otherwise minded, God shall reveal even this unto you.

16 Nevertheless, whereto we have already attained, [a]let us walk [b]by the same rule, let us mind the same thing.

17 Brethren, [a]be followers together of me, and mark them which walk so as [b]ye have us for an example.

C 18 (For many walk, of whom I have
S told you often, and now tell you even
weeping, *that they are* [a]the enemies of
the cross of Christ:
H 19 [a]Whose end *is* destruction, [b]whose
God *is their* belly, and [c]*whose* glory *is* in
their shame, [d]who mind earthly things.)
C 20 For [a]our conversation is in heaven;
[b]from whence also we [c]look for the Saviour, the Lord Jesus Christ:
F 21 [a]Who shall change our vile body,
T that it may be fashioned like unto his
glorious body, [b]according to the working
whereby he is able [c]even to subdue all things unto himself.

C *Php 2:21 ◀ ▶ Col 1:13*
S *Php 2:15 ◀ ▶ Col 1:10*
H *Php 1:28 ◀ ▶ Col 3:5–6*
C *Php 2:16 ◀ ▶ Php 4:5*
F *Php 3:11–15 ◀ ▶ 1Th 4:13–18*
T *1Co 15:50–55 ◀ ▶ 1Th 4:15–18*

12 [a]1 Tim. 6:12 [b]Heb. 12:23
13 [a]Luke 9:62 [b]Heb. 6:1
14 [a]2 Tim. 4:7 [b]Heb. 3:1
15 [a]1 Cor. 2:6 [b]Gal. 5:10
16 [a]Rom. 12:16 & 15:6 [b]Gal. 6:16
17 [a]1 Cor. 11:1; 1 Thes. 1:6 [b]1 Pet. 5:3
18 [a]Gal. 1:7 & 2:21
19 [a]2 Cor. 11:15 [b]1 Tim. 6:5; Tit. 1:11 [c]Hos. 4:7; Gal. 6:13 [d]Rom. 8:5
20 [a]Eph. 2:6; Col. 3:1,3 [b]Acts 1:11 [c]1 Cor. 1:7; 1 Thes. 1:10
21 [a]1 Cor. 15:43; Col. 3:4 [b]Eph. 1:19 [c]1 Cor. 15:26
4:1 [a]ch. 1:8 [b]2 Cor. 1:14; ch. 2:16 [c]ch. 1:27
2 [a]ch. 3:16
3 [a]Rom. 16:3 [b]Ex. 32:32; Ps. 69:28; Dan. 12:1
4 [a]Rom. 12:12; 1 Thes. 5:16; 1 Pet. 4:13
5 [a]Heb. 10:25; 1 Pet. 4:7
6 [a]Ps. 55:22; Prov. 16:3; Mat. 6:25
7 [a]John 14:27; Rom. 5:1; Col. 3:15
8 [a]1 Thes. 5:22 [1]Or, *venerable*
9 [a]ch. 3:17 [b]Rom. 15:33
10 [a]2 Cor. 11:9

Appeal to rejoice in the Lord

4 THEREFORE, MY brethren dearly beloved and [a]longed for, [b]my joy and crown, so [c]stand fast in the Lord, *my* dearly beloved.

2 I beseech Euodias, and beseech Syntyche, [a]that they be of the same mind in the Lord.

3 And I entreat thee also, true yokefellow, help those women which [a]laboured with me in the gospel, with Clement also, and *with* other my fellowlabourers, whose names *are* in [b]the book of life.

4 [a]Rejoice in the Lord always: *and* W
again I say, Rejoice.
5 Let your moderation be known unto C
all men. [a]The Lord *is* at hand.
6 [a]Be careful for nothing; but in every W
thing by prayer and supplication with thanksgiving let your requests be made known unto God.

7 And [a]the peace of God, which passeth all understanding, shall keep your hearts and minds through Christ Jesus.

8 Finally, brethren, whatsoever things are true, whatsoever things *are* [1]honest, whatsoever things *are* just, whatsoever things *are* pure, whatsoever things *are* lovely, [a]whatsoever things *are* of good report; if *there be* any virtue, and if *there be* any praise, think on these things.

9 [a]Those things, which ye have both learned, and received, and heard, and seen in me, do: and [b]the God of peace shall be with you.

The Philippian gifts

10 But I rejoiced in the Lord greatly, that now at the last [a]your care of me

W *Php 3:1 ◀ ▶ Php 4:6–7*
C *Php 3:20–21 ◀ ▶ Col 3:4*
W *Php 4:4 ◀ ▶ Php 4:11–13*

3:20–21 Paul encourages believers to focus on their future in heaven and reminds us that, at the resurrection, we will receive a body like the body Jesus had after he rose from the dead. Christ's resurrection body was immortal and incorruptible, able to travel instantaneously over great distances and able to appear and disappear at will (see Mt 28:10; Mk 16:11–12; Lk 24:31). Yet this body was identical in appearance to his natural body—solidly material, capable of touch and able to take sustenance (see Lk 24:38–43).

4:5 Our daily walk before the Lord should be lived in constant expectation that he could return at any moment. He has delayed his coming so that sinners could be saved and "come unto the knowledge of the truth" (1Ti 2:4; see 2Pe 3:9). Therefore, as believers we must witness and live in holiness, knowing that he may return at any time, but working to fulfill his great commission even if it means another century until he returns.

[1]hath flourished again; wherein ye were
also careful, but ye lacked opportunity.
W 11 Not that I speak in respect of want:
for I have learned, in whatsoever state I
am, [a]*therewith* to be content.
12 [a]I know both how to be abased, and
I know how to abound: every where and
in all things I am instructed both to be
full and to be hungry, both to abound and
to suffer need.
K 13 I can do all things [a]through Christ
which strengtheneth me.
14 Notwithstanding ye have well
done, that [a]ye did communicate with my
affliction.
15 Now ye Philippians know also, that
in the beginning of the gospel, when I
departed from Macedonia, [a]no church
communicated with me as concerning
giving and receiving, but ye only.
16 For even in Thessalonica ye sent
once and again unto my necessity.

W *Php 4:6–7* ◀▶ *Col 3:15*
K *Eph 5:14* ◀▶ *Php 4:19*

10 [1]Or, *is revived*
11 [a]1 Tim. 6:6
12 [a]1 Cor. 4:11
13 [a]John 15:5
14 [a]ch. 1:7
15 [a]2 Cor. 11:8
17 [a]Tit. 3:14
18 [a]ch. 2:25 [b]Heb. 13:16 [c]2 Cor. 9:12 [1]Or, *I have received all*
19 [a]Ps. 23:1 [b]Eph. 1:7
20 [a]Rom. 16:27
21 [a]Gal. 1:2
22 [a]ch. 1:13
23 [a]Rom. 16:24

17 Not because I desire a gift: but I
desire [a]fruit that may abound to your account.
18 But [1]I have all, and abound: I am
full, having received [a]of Epaphroditus the
things *which were sent* from you, [b]an
odour of a sweet smell, [c]a sacrifice acceptable, wellpleasing to God.
19 But my God [a]shall supply all your K
need [b]according to his riches in glory by L
Christ Jesus. P
20 [a]Now unto God and our Father *be*
glory for ever and ever. Amen.

Concluding benediction

21 Salute every saint in Christ Jesus.
The brethren [a]which are with me greet
you.
22 All the saints salute you, [a]chiefly
they that are of Caesar's household.
23 [a]The grace of our Lord Jesus Christ
be with you all. Amen.

K *Php 4:13* ◀▶ *Col 1:14*
L *1Co 10:13* ◀▶ *1Ti 6:17*
P *2Co 9:6–11* ◀▶ *1Ti 4:8*

Colossians

Author: Paul

Theme: The preeminence and glory of Christ as God's eternal Son

Date of Writing: c. A.D. 60–62

Outline of Colossians

I. Greetings and Appreciation (1:1–8)
II. Jesus Christ and the Believer (1:9—2:7)
III. Dangerous Doctrines (2:8—3:4)
IV. Practical Living (3:5—4:6)
V. Greetings and Conclusion (4:7–18)

PAUL WROTE THIS epistle to the Colossians at about the same time as his epistle to the Ephesians. The content of the two letters, in fact, is very similar, earning Colossians the nickname as the twin epistle of Ephesians. Because Paul was imprisoned in Rome, Tychicus delivered this letter to the struggling Colossian church (see 4:7).

Colosse was located about one hundred miles east of Ephesus near modern-day Turkey. During Paul's ministry in Ephesus, Epaphras was converted and had subsequently carried the gospel message to Colosse. The small church that resulted from Epaphras's witness was under attack by false teachers. Epaphras brought news of this attack to Paul, who ultimately penned this letter in response.

Philosophers and false teachers who fused religion and Greek philosophy had attempted to modify the gospel message in the Colossian church by challenging the preeminence of Christ, relying on human wisdom and tradition, worshiping angels and encouraging severe asceticism and ceremonialism in addition to faith in Christ. Paul defends the gospel by setting forth the clear doctrine of the nature of Christ and his preeminence in the church. Paul also warns against the danger of legalism, requiring instead that ethical demands and intellectual standards be properly integrated into the pattern of Christian living.

Salutation and thanksgiving

1 PAUL, [a]AN apostle of Jesus Christ by
the will of God, and Timotheus *our*
brother,
2 To the saints [a]and faithful brethren
in Christ which are at Colosse: [b]Grace *be*
unto you, and peace, from God our Father and the Lord Jesus Christ.
3 [a]We give thanks to God and the Father of our Lord Jesus Christ, praying always for you,
4 [a]Since we heard of your faith in
Christ Jesus, and of [b]the love *which ye*
have to all the saints,
5 For the hope [a]which is laid up for
you in heaven, whereof ye heard before
in the word of the truth of the gospel;
6 Which is come unto you, [a]as *it is* in
all the world; and bringeth forth fruit, as
it doth also in you, since the day ye heard
of it, and knew [b]the grace of God in
truth:
7 As ye also learned of [a]Epaphras our
dear fellowservant, who is for you [b]a
faithful minister of Christ;
E 8 Who also declared unto us your [a]love
F in the Spirit.

Paul's prayer for the Colossians

A 9 [a]For this cause we also, since the day
G we heard *it,* do not cease to pray for you,
M and to desire [b]that ye might be filled with
W [c]the knowledge of his will [d]in all wisdom
and spiritual understanding;
S 10 [a]That ye might walk worthy of the
Lord [b]unto all pleasing, [c]being fruitful in
every good work, and increasing in the
knowledge of God;
11 [a]Strengthened with all might, according to his glorious power, [b]unto all
patience and longsuffering [c]with joyfulness;
12 [a]Giving thanks unto the Father,
which hath made us meet to be partakers
of [b]the inheritance of the saints in light:
C 13 Who hath delivered us from [a]the
L power of darkness, [b]and hath translated
us into the kingdom of [1]his dear Son:

14 [a]In whom we have redemption D
through his blood, *even* the forgiveness of K
sins:

Christ's preeminence

15 Who is [a]the image of the invisible
God, [b]the firstborn of every creature:
16 For [a]by him were all things created,
that are in heaven, and that are in earth,
visible and invisible, whether *they be*
thrones, or [b]dominions, or principalities,
or powers: all things were created [c]by
him, and for him:
17 [a]And he is before all things, and by
him all things consist.
18 And [a]he is the head of the body,
the church: who is the beginning, [b]the
firstborn from the dead; that [1]in all *things*
he might have the preeminence.
19 For it pleased *the Father* that [a]in L
him should all fulness dwell;
20 And, [a]having[1] made peace through D
the blood of his cross, [b]by him to reconcile [c]all things unto himself; by him, *I*
say, whether *they be* things in earth, or
things in heaven.
21 And you, [a]that were sometime C
alienated and enemies [1]in *your* mind [b]by S
wicked works, yet now hath he reconciled
22 [a]In the body of his flesh through
death, [b]to present you holy and unblameable and unreproveable in his sight:
23 If ye continue in the faith
[a]grounded and settled, and *be* [b]not
moved away from the hope of the gospel,
which ye have heard, [c]*and* which was
preached to every creature which is under heaven; [d]whereof I Paul am made a
minister;

The ministry of Paul

24 [a]Who now rejoice in my sufferings
[b]for you, and fill up [c]that which is behind
of the afflictions of Christ in my flesh for
[d]his body's sake, which is the church:
25 Whereof I am made a minister, according to [a]the dispensation of God
which is given to me for you, [1]to fulfil the
word of God;
26 *Even* [a]the mystery which hath been

1:1 [a]Eph. 1:1
2 [a]1 Cor. 4:17 [b]Gal. 1:3
3 [a]1 Cor. 1:4; Eph. 1:16; Phil. 1:3
4 [a]Eph. 1:15 [b]Heb. 6:10
5 [a]1 Pet. 1:4
6 [a]Mat. 24:14 [b]Eph. 3:2; Tit. 2:11
7 [a]Philem. 23 [b]2 Cor. 11:23; 1 Tim. 4:6
8 [a]Rom. 15:30
9 [a]Eph. 1:15 [b]1 Cor. 1:5 [c]Rom. 12:2 [d]Eph. 1:8
10 [a]Phil. 1:27 [b]1 Thes. 4:1 [c]Heb. 13:21
11 [a]Eph. 3:16 [b]Eph. 4:2 [c]Acts 5:41
12 [a]Eph. 5:20 [b]Eph. 1:11
13 [a]Eph. 6:12 [b]2 Pet. 1:11 [1]Gk. *the Son of his love*
14 [a]Eph. 1:7
15 [a]2 Cor. 4:4 [b]Rev. 3:14
16 [a]Heb. 1:2 [b]Eph. 1:21 [c]Heb. 2:10
17 [a]John 17:5
18 [a]1 Cor. 11:3 [b]Rev. 1:5 [1]Or, *among*
19 [a]John 1:16
20 [a]Eph. 2:14 [b]2 Cor. 5:18 [c]Eph. 1:10 [1]Or, *making*
21 [a]Eph. 2:1 [b]Tit. 1:15 [1]Or, *by your mind in*
22 [a]Eph. 2:15 [b]Eph. 5:27
23 [a]Eph. 3:17 [b]John 15:6 [c]Rom. 10:18 [d]Acts 1:17
24 [a]2 Cor. 7:4 [b]Eph. 3:1,13 [c]2 Cor. 1:5 [d]Eph. 1:23
25 [a]Gal. 2:7 [1]Or, *fully to preach*
26 [a]1 Cor. 2:7

E *Php 3:3 ◀▶ Col 2:5*
F *Php 2:1 ◀▶ 1Th 1:6*
A *Eph 3:14–19 ◀*
G *Eph 4:11–14 ◀▶ 1Th 5:20*
M *Php 1:19 ◀▶ 1Th 1:5*
W *Php 3:3 ◀▶ 1Th 4:7–8*
S *Php 3:18 ◀▶ Col 1:21–23*
C *Php 3:18–19 ◀▶ Col 1:21*
L *Eph 5:14 ◀▶ Col 1:19–22*
D *Eph 5:25 ◀▶ Col 1:20–22*
K *Php 4:19 ◀▶ 1Th 5:9–10*
L *Col 1:13–14 ◀▶ Col 2:13*
D *Col 1:14 ◀▶ 1Th 5:9–10*
C *Col 1:13 ◀▶ Col 2:13*
S *Col 1:10 ◀▶ Col 2:6*

hid from ages and from generations, [b]but
now is made manifest to his saints:
27 [a]To whom God would make known
what *is* [b]the riches of the glory of this
mystery among the Gentiles; which is
Christ [1]in you, [c]the hope of glory:
28 Whom we preach, [a]warning every
man, and teaching every man in all wisdom; [b]that we may present every man
perfect in Christ Jesus:
29 [a]Whereunto I also labour, [b]striving
[c]according to his working, which worketh in me mightily.

2 FOR I would that ye knew what
great [a]conflict[1] I have for you, and
for them at Laodicea, and *for* as many as
have not seen my face in the flesh;
2 [a]That their hearts might be comforted, [b]being knit together in love, and
unto all riches of the full assurance of understanding, [c]to the acknowledgement of
the mystery of God, and of the Father,
and of Christ;
3 [a]In[1] whom are hid all the treasures
of wisdom and knowledge.
4 And this I say, [a]lest any man should
beguile you with enticing words.
E 5 For [a]though I be absent in the flesh,
yet am I with you in the spirit, joying and
beholding [b]your order, and the [c]stedfastness of your faith in Christ.
S 6 [a]As ye have therefore received
Christ Jesus the Lord, *so* walk ye in him:
7 [a]Rooted and built up in him, and
stablished in the faith, as ye have been
taught, abounding therein with thanksgiving.

The sufficiency of Christ

8 Beware lest any man spoil you
through philosophy and vain deceit, after
[a]the tradition of men, after the [b]rudiments[1] of the world, and not after Christ.
9 For [a]in him dwelleth all the fulness
of the Godhead bodily.
10 And ye are complete in him,
[a]which is the head of all [b]principality and
power:
S 11 In whom also ye are [a]circumcised
with the circumcision made without
hands, in [b]putting off the body of the sins
of the flesh by the circumcision of Christ:
12 Buried with him in baptism,
wherein also ye are risen with *him*
through [a]the faith of the operation of
God, [b]who hath raised him from the
dead.
13 And you, being dead in your sins C
and the uncircumcision of your flesh, L
hath he quickened together with him,
having forgiven you all trespasses;
14 [a]Blotting out the handwriting of ordinances that was against us, which was
contrary to us, and took it out of the way,
nailing it to his cross;
15 *And* [a]having spoiled [b]principalities
and powers, he made a show of them
openly, triumphing over them [1]in it.
16 Let no man therefore [a]judge you
[b]in[1] meat, or in drink, or [2]in respect [c]of
an holyday, or of the new moon, or of the
sabbath *days:*
17 [a]Which are a shadow of things to
come; but the body *is* of Christ.
18 Let no man [1]beguile you of your reward [2]in a voluntary humility and worshipping of angels, intruding into those M
things which he hath not seen, vainly
puffed up by his fleshly mind,
19 And not holding [a]the Head, from
which all the body by joints and bands
having nourishment ministered, and knit
together, increaseth with the increase of
God.
20 Wherefore if ye be [a]dead with
Christ from the [1]rudiments of the world,
[b]why, as though living in the world, are
ye subject to ordinances,
21 ([a]Touch not; taste not; handle not;
22 Which all are to perish with the using;) [a]after the commandments and doctrines of men?
23 [a]Which things have indeed a show
of wisdom in will-worship. and humility,
and [1]neglecting of the body; not in any
honour to the satisfying of the flesh.

The true center of Christian life

3 IF YE then be risen with Christ, seek
those things which are above, where
[a]Christ sitteth on the right hand of God.
2 Set your [1]affection on things above,
not on things on the earth.
3 [a]For ye are dead, [b]and your life is hid
with Christ in God.

26 [b]2 Tim. 1:10
27 [a]2 Cor. 2:14 [b]Rom. 9:23 [c]1 Tim. 1:1 [1]Or, *among*
28 [a]Acts 20:20 [b]Eph. 5:27
29 [a]1 Cor. 15:10 [b]ch. 2:1 [c]Eph. 1:19
2:1 [a]Phil. 1:30 [1]Or, *care*
2 [a]2 Cor. 1:6 [b]ch. 3:14 [c]Phil. 3:8
3 [a]1 Cor. 1:24 [1]Or, *Wherein*
4 [a]Rom. 16:18
5 [a]1 Thes. 2:17 [b]1 Cor. 14:40 [c]1 Pet. 5:9
6 [a]1 Thes. 4:1
7 [a]Eph. 2:21
8 [a]Gal. 1:14 [b]Gal. 4:3,9 [1]Or, *elements*
9 [a]John 1:14
10 [a]1 Pet. 3:22 [b]ch. 1:16
11 [a]Deut. 10:16 [b]Rom. 6:6
12 [a]Eph. 1:19 [b]Acts 2:24
14 [a]Eph. 2:15
15 [a]Is. 53:12 [b]Eph. 6:12 [1]Or, *in himself*
16 [a]Rom. 14:3 [b]Rom. 14:2 [c]Rom. 14:5 [1]Or, *for eating and drinking* [2]Or, *in part*
17 [a]Heb. 8:5
18 [1]Or, *judge against you* [2]Gk. *being a voluntary in humility*
19 [a]Eph. 4:15
20 [a]Rom. 6:3,5 [b]Gal. 4:3,9 [1]Or, *elements*
21 [a]1 Tim. 4:3
22 [a]Tit. 1:14
23 [a]1 Tim. 4:8 [1]Or, *punishing,* or, *not sparing*
3:1 [a]Eph. 1:20
2 [1]Or, *mind*
3 [a]Rom. 6:2 [b]2 Cor. 5:7

E *Col 1:8 ◀▶ 1Th 1:5–6*
S *Col 1:21–23 ◀▶ Col 2:11*
S *Col 2:6 ◀▶ Col 3:17*
C *Col 1:21 ◀▶ Col 3:5–7*
L *Col 1:19–22 ◀▶ 1Th 5:9–10*
M *1Co 14:24–25 ◀▶ 1Ti 6:3–4*

C 4 [a]When Christ, *who is* [b]our life, shall appear, then shall ye also appear with him [c]in glory.

C H 5 [a]Mortify therefore [b]your members which are upon the earth; [c]fornication, uncleanness, inordinate affection, evil concupiscence, and covetousness, [d]which is idolatry:

6 [a]For which things' sake the wrath of God cometh on [b]the children of disobedience:

7 [a]In the which ye also walked some time, when ye lived in them.

8 [a]But now ye also put off all these; anger, wrath, malice, blasphemy, [b]filthy communication out of your mouth.

9 [a]Lie not one to another, [b]seeing that ye have put off the old man with his deeds;

10 And have put on the new *man,* which [a]is renewed in knowledge [b]after the image of him that [c]created him:

11 Where there is neither [a]Greek nor Jew, circumcision nor uncircumcision, Barbarian, Scythian, bond *nor* free: [b]but Christ *is* all, and in all.

12 Put on therefore, [a]as the elect of God, holy and beloved, [b]bowels of mercies, kindness, humbleness of mind, meekness, longsuffering;

13 [a]Forbearing one another, and forgiving one another, if any man have a [/]quarrel against any: even as Christ forgave you, so also *do* ye.

14 [a]And above all these things [b]*put on* charity, which is the [c]bond of perfectness.

W 15 And let [a]the peace of God rule in your hearts, [b]to the which also ye are called [c]in one body; and be ye thankful.

16 Let the word of Christ dwell in you richly in all wisdom; teaching and admonishing one another [a]in psalms and hymns and spiritual songs, singing with grace in your hearts to the Lord.

S 17 And [a]whatsoever ye do in word or deed, *do* all in the name of the Lord

C *Php 4:5* ◄► *1Th 1:10*
C *Col 2:13* ◄► *1Th 4:13*
H *Php 3:19* ◄► *Col 3:25*
W *Php 4:11–13* ◄► *1Th 5:16*
S *Col 2:11* ◄► *Col 3:23–25*

4 [a]1 John 3:2 [b]John 14:6 [c]1 Cor. 15:43
5 [a]Rom. 8:13 [b]Rom. 6:13 [c]Eph. 5:3 [d]Eph. 5:5
6 [a]Rev. 22:15 [b]Eph. 2:2
7 [a]1 Cor. 6:11
8 [a]Eph. 4:22 [b]Eph. 4:29
9 [a]Eph. 4:25 [b]Eph. 4:22
10 [a]Rom. 12:2 [b]Eph. 4:23 [c]Eph. 2:10
11 [a]Gal. 3:28 [b]Eph. 1:23
12 [a]1 Pet. 1:2 [b]Gal. 5:22
13 [a]Mark 11:25 [/]Or, *complaint*
14 [a]1 Pet. 4:8 [b]1 Cor. 13 [c]Eph. 4:3
15 [a]Phil. 4:7 [b]1 Cor. 7:15 [c]Eph. 4:4
16 [a]Eph. 5:19
17 [a]1 Cor. 10:31
18 [a]1 Pet. 3:1 [b]Eph. 5:3
19 [a]Eph. 5:25 [b]Eph. 4:31
20 [a]Eph. 6:1 [b]Eph. 5:24
21 [a]Eph. 6:4
22 [a]Eph. 6:5; 1 Tim. 6:1; Tit. 2:9; 1 Pet. 2:18 [b]ver. 20 [c]Philem. 16
23 [a]Eph. 6:6,7
24 [a]Eph. 6:8 [b]1 Cor. 7:22
25 [a]Rom. 2:11; Eph. 6:9; 1 Pet. 1:17; Deut. 10:17
4:1 [a]Eph. 6:9
2 [a]Luke 18:1; Rom. 12:12 [b]ch. 2:7
3 [a]Eph. 6:19 [b]1 Cor. 16:9; 2 Cor. 2:12 [c]Eph. 6:20; Phil. 1:7
5 [a]Eph. 5:15 [b]Eph. 5:16
6 [a]Eccl. 10:12 [b]Mark 9:50 [c]1 Pet. 3:15
8 [a]Eph. 6:22

Jesus, giving thanks to God and the Father by him.

The Christian family

18 [a]Wives, submit yourselves unto your own husbands, [b]as it is fit in the Lord.

19 [a]Husbands, love *your* wives, and be not [b]bitter against them.

20 [a]Children, obey *your* parents [b]in all things: for this is wellpleasing unto the Lord.

21 [a]Fathers, provoke not your children *to anger,* lest they be discouraged.

22 [a]Servants, obey [b]in all things *your* masters [c]according to the flesh; not with eyeservice, as menpleasers; but in singleness of heart, fearing God:

23 [a]And whatsoever ye do, do *it* heartily, as to the Lord, and not unto men; S

24 [a]Knowing that of the Lord ye shall receive the reward of the inheritance: [b]for ye serve the Lord Christ.

25 But he that doeth wrong shall receive for the wrong which he hath done: and [a]there is no respect of persons. H

4 MASTERS,[a] GIVE unto *your* servants that which is just and equal; knowing that ye also have a Master in heaven.

2 [a]Continue in prayer, and watch in the same [b]with thanksgiving;

3 [a]Withal praying also for us, that God would [b]open unto us a door of utterance, to speak [a]the mystery of Christ, [c]for which I am also in bonds:

4 That I may make it manifest, as I ought to speak.

5 [a]Walk in wisdom toward them that are without, [b]redeeming the time.

6 Let your speech *be* always [a]with grace, [b]seasoned with salt, [c]that ye may know how ye ought to answer every man.

Tychicus and Onesimus

7 All my state shall Tychicus declare unto you, *who is* a beloved brother, and a faithful minister and fellowservant in the Lord:

8 [a]Whom I have sent unto you for the

S *Col 3:17* ◄► *1Th 4:3*
H *Col 3:5–6* ◄► *1Th 1:10*

3:4 Paul foreshadows the second coming in this verse as he pictures Christ's glorious appearance. This passage also suggests that the raptured saints will also share in that visible, manifested glory. This prophecy echoes Paul's words in Romans regarding this glorious manifestation (see Ro 8:18–19).

same purpose, that he might know your estate, and comfort your hearts;

9 With [a]Onesimus, a faithful and beloved brother, who is *one* of you. They shall make known unto you all things which *are done* here.

Greetings and final instructions

10 [a]Aristarchus my fellowprisoner saluteth you, and [b]Marcus, sister's son to Barnabas, (touching whom ye received commandments: if he come unto you, receive him;)

11 And Jesus, which is called Justus, who are of the circumcision. These only *are my* fellowworkers unto the kingdom of God, which have been a comfort unto me.

12 [a]Epaphras, who is *one* of you, a servant of Christ, saluteth you, always [b]labouring[1] fervently for you in prayers, that ye may stand [c]perfect and [2]complete in all the will of God.

13 For I bear him record, that he hath a great zeal for you, and them *that are* in Laodicea, and them in Hierapolis.

14 [a]Luke, the beloved physician, and [b]Demas, greet you.

15 Salute the brethren which are in Laodicea, and Nymphas, and [a]the church which is in his house.

16 And when [a]this epistle is read among you, cause that it be read also in the church of the Laodiceans; and that ye likewise read the *epistle* from Laodicea.

17 And say to [a]Archippus, Take heed to [b]the ministry which thou hast received in the Lord, that thou fulfil it.

18 [a]The salutation by the hand of me Paul. [b]Remember my bonds. [c]Grace *be* with you. Amen.

9 [a]Philem. 10

10 [a]Acts 19:29 [b]Acts 15:37; 2 Tim. 4:11

12 [a]Philem. 23 [b]Rom. 15:30 [c]Mat. 5:48; 1 Cor. 2:6 [1]Or, *striving* [2]Or, *filled*

14 [a]2 Tim. 4:11 [b]2 Tim. 4:10

15 [a]Rom. 16:5; 1 Cor. 16:19

16 [a]1 Thes. 5:27

17 [a]Philem. 2 [b]1 Tim. 4:6

18 [a]1 Cor. 16:21; 2 Thes. 3:17 [b]Heb. 13:3 [c]Heb. 13:25

1 Thessalonians

Author: Paul

Theme: The doctrine of the return of Christ

Date of Writing: c. A.D. 50–51

Outline of 1 Thessalonians

I. Introduction and Thanksgiving (1:1–10)
II. Paul Defends His Actions (2:1—3:13)
III. Practical Problems About Church Life (4:1—5:22)
IV. Conclusion (5:23–28)

THIS LETTER IS among the earliest of Paul's writings, written while Paul ministered in the city of Corinth during his second missionary journey. While on this missionary journey, Paul had taught in the seaport of Thessalonica for three weeks. Many Greeks believed in Christ, but Paul was forced to leave suddenly for Berea because of opposition from the Jews (see Ac 17). Paul's recent converts in Thessalonica were left with little support amid much persecution. Subsequently, Timothy brought Paul a report concerning the spiritual conditions in the church at Thessalonica. Paul's letter to this young church commends the Thessalonians for their courageous behavior in the face of persecution.

There are varied themes in this letter, but the subject of the second coming is referred to in all five chapters of this epistle. The believers had raised some questions about the return of the Lord, so Paul answers these questions by focusing their hope in Christ's return, offering comfort and encouragement for those facing the death of loved ones. Paul's discussion of eschatology is concentrated in 4:13–18, but there are many predictions about the rapture and the end times unveiled throughout this brief letter. Paul also supplements his former teaching concerning the problems that these new believers faced in living the Christian life.

Salutation and thanksgiving

1 PAUL, AND [a]Silvanus, and Timotheus, unto the church of the Thessalonians *which is* in God the Father and *in* the Lord Jesus Christ: [b]Grace *be* unto you, and peace, from God our Father, and the Lord Jesus Christ.

2 [a]We give thanks to God always for you all, making mention of you in our prayers;

3 [a]Remembering without ceasing [b]your work of faith, [c]and labour of love, and patience of hope in our Lord Jesus Christ, in the sight of God and our Father;

4 Knowing, brethren [/]beloved, [a]your election of God.

E 5 For [a]our gospel came not unto you in
M word only, but also in power, and [b]in the
T Holy Ghost, [c]and in much assurance; as
ye know what manner of men we were
among you for your sake.
F 6 And [a]ye became followers of us, and
J of the Lord, having received the word in
much affliction, [b]with joy of the Holy
Ghost:

7 So that ye were examples to all that believe in Macedonia and Achaia.

8 For from you [a]sounded out the word of the Lord not only in Macedonia and Achaia, but also [b]in every place your faith to God-ward is spread abroad; so that we need not to speak any thing.

9 For they themselves show of us [a]what manner of entering in we had unto you, [b]and how ye turned to God from idols to serve the living and true God;

10 And [a]to wait for his Son [b]from C
heaven, [c]whom he raised from the dead, H
even Jesus, which delivered us [d]from the
wrath to come.

Paul's work in Thessalonica

2 FOR [a]YOURSELVES, brethren, know our entrance in unto you, that it was not in vain:

2 But even after that we had suffered before, and were shamefully entreated, as ye know, at [a]Philippi, [b]we were bold in our God to speak unto you the gospel of God [c]with much contention.

3 [a]For our exhortation *was* not of deceit, nor of uncleanness, nor in guile:

4 But as [a]we were allowed of God [b]to E
be put in trust with the gospel, even so
we speak; [c]not as pleasing men, but God,
[d]which trieth our hearts.

5 For [a]neither at any time used we flattering words, as ye know, nor a cloak of covetousness; [b]God *is* witness:

6 [a]Nor of men sought we glory, neither of you, nor *yet* of others, when [b]we might have [/]been [c]burdensome, [d]as the apostles of Christ.

7 But [a]we were gentle among you, even as a nurse cherisheth her children:

8 So being affectionately desirous of you, we were willing [a]to have imparted unto you, not the gospel of God only, but also [b]our own souls, because ye were dear unto us.

9 For ye remember, brethren, our labour and travail: for [a]labouring night and day, [b]because we would not be chargeable unto any of you, we preached unto you the gospel of God.

10 [a]Ye *are* witnesses, and God *also,*

1:1 [a] 1 Pet. 5:12 [b] Eph. 1:2
2 [a] Rom. 1:8
3 [a] ch. 2:13 [b] John 6:29 [c] Rom. 16:6
4 [a] Col. 3:12 [/] Or, *beloved of God, your election*
5 [a] Mark 16:20 [b] 2 Cor. 6:6 [c] Heb. 2:3
6 [a] 1 Cor. 4:16; Phil. 3:17 [b] Acts 5:41; Heb. 10:34
8 [a] Rom. 10:18 [b] Rom. 1:8; 2 Thes. 1:4
9 [a] ch. 2:1 [b] 1 Cor. 12:2; Gal. 4:8
10 [a] Rom. 2:7; 2 Pet. 3:12 [b] Acts 1:11 [c] Acts 2:24 [d] Rom. 5:9
2:1 [a] ch. 1:5,9
2 [a] Acts 16:22 [b] ch. 1:5 [c] Phil. 1:30
3 [a] 2 Cor. 7:2
4 [a] 1 Cor. 7:25 [b] Tit. 1:3 [c] Gal. 1:10 [d] Prov. 17:3
5 [a] 2 Cor. 2:17 [b] Rom. 1:9
6 [a] 1 Tim. 5:17 [b] 1 Cor. 9:4 [c] 2 Cor. 11:9 [d] 1 Cor. 9:1 [/] Or, *used authority*
7 [a] 1 Cor. 2:3
8 [a] Rom. 1:11 & 15:29 [b] 2 Cor. 12:15
9 [a] Acts 20:34; 2 Thes. 3:8 [b] 2 Cor. 12:13
10 [a] ch. 1:5

E *Col 2:5 ◀ ▶ 1Th 4:8*
M *Col 1:9–11 ◀ ▶ 2Ti 1:7*
T *Eph 6:17 ◀ ▶ 1Ti 4:1*
F *Col 1:8 ◀ ▶ 2Ti 1:7*
J *Gal 5:22 ◀ ▶ Heb 1:9*

C *Col 3:4 ◀ ▶ 1Th 2:19*
H *Col 3:25 ◀ ▶ 1Th 5:3*
E *1Co 4:5 ◀ ▶ Heb 4:12–13*

1:10 Paul instructs believers to confidently and expectantly wait for the second coming of Christ because Jesus has been raised from the dead. Our hope and expectation are shaped by the Bible's promise that Jesus will deliver us "from the wrath to come." While some interpret this reference of "wrath" as the punishment of hell, this interpretation seems untenable in this case because believers have already been delivered from the wrath of hell by their repentance and belief in Christ. Other scholars suggest that the "wrath" referred to here is the great white throne judgment of God. However, Revelation clearly states that that final judgment is reserved for the wicked dead (see Rev 20:11–15) and Paul appears to be addressing believers in this verse in 1 Thessalonians.

Still other scholars believe that this verse refers to a future period of tribulation, called "wrath" in Rev 6:16. Since the language of this verse indicates that Christ's return is imminent, these scholars contend that the "wrath to come" must refer to the coming wrath of God during the tribulation. Christ will deliver the Christian saints before the wrath of God is poured out on an unrepentant humanity. For further discussion of this topic, see the article on "Reasons for a Pretribulation Rapture" on p. 1378.

[b]how holily and justly and unblameably we behaved ourselves among you that believe:

11 As ye know how we exhorted and comforted and charged every one of you, as a father *doth* his children,

12 [a]That ye would walk worthy of God, [b]who hath called you unto his kingdom and glory.

Paul's reception in Thessalonica

13 For this cause also thank we God [a]without ceasing, because, when ye received the word of God which ye heard of us, ye received *it* [b]not *as* the word of men, but as it is in truth, the word of God, which effectually worketh also in you that believe.

14 For ye, brethren, became followers [a]of the churches of God which in Judaea are in Christ Jesus: for [b]ye also have suffered like things of your own countrymen, even as they *have* of the Jews:

15 [a]Who both killed the Lord Jesus, and [b]their own prophets, and have [/]persecuted us; and they please not God, [c]and are contrary to all men:

R 16 [a]Forbidding us to speak to the Gentiles that they might be saved, [b]to fill up their sins always: [c]for the wrath is come upon them to the uttermost.

17 But we, brethren, being taken from you for a short time [a]in presence, not in heart, endeavoured the more abundantly [b]to see your face with great desire.

18 Wherefore we would have come unto you, even I Paul, once and again; but [a]Satan hindered us.

C 19 For [a]what *is* our hope, or joy, or [b]crown of [/]rejoicing? *Are* not even ye in the presence of our Lord Jesus Christ [c]at his coming?

20 For ye are our glory and joy.

R *Ro 11:17–28* ◀ ▶ *Rev 12:1–6*
C *1Th 1:10* ◀ ▶ *1Th 3:13*

10 [b]2 Cor. 7:2
12 [a]Col. 1:10 [b]1 Cor. 1:9; 2 Thes. 2:14
13 [a]ch. 1:3 [b]Gal. 4:14
14 [a]Gal. 1:22 [b]Acts 17:5
15 [a]Acts 2:23 [b]Mat. 5:12 [c]Esth. 3:8 [/]Or, *chased us out*
16 [a]Luke 11:52; Acts 13:50 [b]Gen. 15:16; Mat. 23:32 [c]Mat. 24:6
17 [a]1 Cor. 5:3; Col. 2:5 [b]ch. 3:10
18 [a]Rom. 1:13
19 [a]2 Cor. 1:14 [b]Prov. 16:31 [c]1 Cor. 15:23 [/]Or, *glorying?*
3:1 [a]ver. 5 [b]Acts 17:15
2 [a]Rom. 16:21; 1 Cor. 16:10
3 [a]Eph. 3:13 [b]Acts 9:16; 1 Cor. 4:9; 2 Tim. 3:12
4 [a]Acts 20:24
5 [a]ver. 1 [b]1 Cor. 7:5; 2 Cor. 11:3 [c]Gal. 2:2
6 [a]Acts 18:1 [b]Phil. 1:8
7 [a]2 Cor. 1:4
8 [a]Phil. 4:1
9 [a]ch. 1:2
10 [a]Acts 26:7 [b]Rom. 15:32 [c]ch. 2:17 [d]Col. 4:12

Timothy's visit and report

3 WHEREFORE [a]WHEN we could no longer forbear, [b]we thought it good to be left at Athens alone;

2 And sent [a]Timotheus, our brother, and minister of God, and our fellowlabourer in the gospel of Christ, to establish you, and to comfort you concerning your faith:

3 [a]That no man should be moved by these afflictions: for yourselves know that [b]we are appointed thereunto.

4 [a]For verily, when we were with you, we told you before that we should suffer tribulation; even as it came to pass, and ye know.

5 For this cause, [a]when I could no longer forbear, I sent to know your faith, [b]lest by some means the tempter have tempted you, and [c]our labour be in vain.

6 [a]But now when Timotheus came from you unto us, and brought us good tidings of your faith and charity, and that ye have good remembrance of us always, desiring greatly to see us, [b]as we also *to see* you:

7 Therefore, brethren, [a]we were comforted over you in all our affliction and distress by your faith:

8 For now we live, if ye [a]stand fast in the Lord.

9 [a]For what thanks can we render to God again for you, for all the joy wherewith we joy for your sakes before our God;

10 [a]Night and day [b]praying exceedingly [c]that we might see your face, [d]and might perfect that which is lacking in your faith?

2:16 Paul predicts that the wrath of God will fall upon those Jews who persecuted the early church. The fulfillment of this prophecy occurred only twenty years later when the Roman legions invaded Israel, destroyed Jerusalem and burned the temple in A.D. 70.

2:19 Paul's joy and "crown of rejoicing" were those believers that he had won to the Lord, those who would be in Christ's presence at his second coming. Since Christ's coming will be the time when the outcome of our works for the Lord will be made manifest (see 1Co 3:14; 2Co 5:10), Paul's joy will be his spiritual children (see 2Co 1:14; Php 2:16).

Note that Paul declares the certainty that his spiritual children will be in Christ's presence at the second coming. Such a positive expression might suggest that Paul saw the coming of Jesus as our deliverance from the coming wrath of God during "the time of Jacob's trouble" (Jer 30:7) and believed that Christians would be delivered from the tribulation and the untimely martyrdom of the wicked rule of the antichrist.

3:3–4 Paul reminds the church that though it will face opposition and persecution, these afflictions will help advance God's purposes (see Ac 11:19; Ro 5:3; 2Co 4:17).

11 Now God himself and our Father, and our Lord Jesus Christ, [a]direct[1] our way unto you.

12 And the Lord [a]make you to increase and abound in love one toward another, and toward all *men,* even as we *do* toward you:

13 To the end he may [a]stablish your hearts unblameable in holiness before God, even our Father, at the coming of our Lord Jesus Christ [b]with all his saints.

Living to please God

4 FURTHERMORE THEN we [1]beseech you, brethren, and [2]exhort *you* by the Lord Jesus, [a]that as ye have received of us [b]how ye ought to walk [c]and to please God, *so* ye would abound more and more.

2 For ye know what commandments we gave you by the Lord Jesus.

3 For this is [a]the will of God, *even* [b]your sanctification, [c]that ye should abstain from fornication:

4 [a]That every one of you should know how to possess his vessel in sanctification and honour;

5 [a]Not in the lust of concupiscence, [b]even as the Gentiles [c]which know not God:

6 That no *man* go beyond and [1]defraud his brother [2]in *any* matter: because that the Lord [a]*is* the avenger of all such, as we also have forewarned you and testified.

7 For God hath not called us unto uncleanness, [a]but unto holiness.

8 [a]He therefore that [1]despiseth, despiseth not man, but God, [b]who hath also given unto us his holy Spirit.

9 But as touching brotherly love [a]ye need not that I write unto you: for [b]ye yourselves are taught of God [c]to love one another.

10 [a]And indeed ye do it toward all the brethren which are in all Macedonia: but we beseech you, brethren, [b]that ye increase more and more;

11 And that ye study to be quiet, and [a]to do your own business, and [b]to work with your own hands, as we commanded you;

12 [a]That ye may walk honestly toward them that are without, and *that* ye may have lack [1]of nothing.

The sudden coming of the Lord

13 But I would not have you to be ignorant, brethren, concerning them which are asleep, that ye sorrow not, [a]even as others [b]which have no hope.

14 For [a]if we believe that Jesus died and rose again, even so [b]them also which sleep in Jesus will God bring with him.

15 For this we say unto you [a]by the word of the Lord, that [b]we which are alive *and* remain unto the coming of the

3:11 [a]Mark 1:3 [1]Or, *guide*
3:12 [a]ch. 4:10
3:13 [a]1 Cor. 1:8; Phil. 1:10 [b]Zech. 14:5
4:1 [a]Phil. 1:27 [b]ch. 2:12 [c]Col. 1:10 [1]Or, *request* [2]Or, *beseech*
3 [a]Rom. 12:2 [b]Eph. 5:27 [c]Col. 3:5
4 [a]Rom 6:19
5 [a]Col. 3:5 [b]Eph. 4:17 [c]1 Cor. 15:34
6 [a]2 Thes. 1:8 [1]Or, *oppress, or, overreach* [2]Or, *in the matter*
7 [a]Lev. 11:44
8 [a]Luke 10:16 [b]1 Cor. 2:10 [1]Or, *rejecteth*
9 [a]ch. 5:1 [b]Jer. 31:34 [c]Mat. 22:39
10 [a]ch. 1:7 [b]ch. 3:12
11 [a]2 Thes. 3:11 [b]Acts 20:35; Eph. 4:28
12 [a]Rom. 13:13 [1]Or, *of no man*
13 [a]Lev. 19:28; 2 Sam. 12:20 [b]Eph. 2:12
14 [a]1 Cor. 15:13 [b]1 Cor. 15:23
15 [a]1 Ki. 13:17 [b]1 Cor. 15:51

C *1Th 2:19* ◀▶ *1Th 4:14*
D *Mk 13:26* ◀▶ *Rev 3:12*
S *Col 3:23–25* ◀▶ *1Th 4:6–7*
S *1Th 4:3* ◀▶ *1Th 5:22–23*
S *Gal 5:16* ◀▶ *2Th 2:13*
W *Col 1:9* ◀▶ *2Th 2:13*
E *1Th 1:5–6* ◀▶ *2Th 2:13*
F *Php 3:21* ◀▶ *1Ti 6:13*
C *Col 3:5–7* ◀▶ *1Th 5:6*
C *1Th 3:13* ◀▶ *1Th 5:23*
T *Php 3:21* ◀

3:13 Christ will complete the process of sanctification in the life of the believers so that they will be holy before God when Christ returns (see 1Co 1:8; Php 1:6). This verse frames a clear reference to the first resurrection of the saints when Jesus comes in the air (see 4:16–17). While some scholars have suggested that the word "saints" may mean angels, this verse seems to use this word to mean the departed saints who will return with Jesus.

4:13–14 In these verses, Paul begins a major teaching about the resurrection of the saints. The believers in Thessalonica were concerned that those saints who had died might miss out on Christ's second coming. Paul assures them that they should not be concerned about the departed saints because they will participate in the rapture together with the believers that are still alive when Christ returns. Paul's words affirm Jesus' meaning to the thief on the cross when he promised, "Today shalt thou be with me in paradise" (Lk 23:43). Though the body of a believer "sleeps" until the resurrection, their soul is instantly transformed to "paradise." Paul says that the souls of departed believers will come with Jesus at the rapture to receive their eternal, resurrection bodies from God.

4:15–18 Paul reveals that Christians living at the moment Christ returns would not hinder the resurrection of the departed saints. The "dead in Christ shall rise first" (4:16) to receive their resurrection bodies a moment before the living believers are transformed into their new spiritual bodies. All believers shall then be gathered together in the clouds to meet Christ and remain with him forever.

The expression "caught up" (4:17) is the only place in the NT where a "rapture" is clearly referred to. This sudden raising up of a person or object

Lord shall not prevent them which are
asleep.
16 For [a]the Lord himself shall descend
from heaven with a shout, with the voice
of the archangel, and with [b]the trump of
God: [c]and the dead in Christ shall rise
first:
17 [a]Then we which are alive *and* remain shall be caught up together with
them [b]in the clouds, to meet the Lord in
the air: and so [c]shall we ever be with the
Lord.
18 [a]Wherefore [1]comfort one another
with these words.
E 5 BUT OF [a]the times and the seasons,
brethren, [b]ye have no need that I
write unto you.
N 2 For yourselves know perfectly that
[a]the day of the Lord so cometh as a thief
in the night.
P 3 For when they shall say, Peace and
H safety; then [a]sudden destruction cometh
upon them, [b]as travail upon a woman
with child; and they shall not escape.
P 4 [a]But ye, brethren, are not in darkness, that that day should overtake you as
a thief.
5 Ye are all [a]the children of light, and
the children of the day: we are not of the
night, nor of darkness.

E *Ac 2:19–20* ◀▶ *2Th 2:1–9*
N *2Co 6:2* ◀▶ *2Th 1:7–8*
P *1Co 16:22* ◀▶ *1Th 5:4*
H *1Th 1:10* ◀▶ *2Th 1:5–9*
P *1Th 5:3* ◀▶ *1Th 5:9*

16 [a]Mat. 24:30; Acts 1:11 [b]1 Cor. 15:52 [c]1 Cor. 15:23
17 [a]1 Cor. 15:51 [b]Acts 1:9 [c]John 17:24
18 [a]ch. 5:11 [1]Or, *exhort*
5:1 [a]Mat. 24:3 [b]ch. 4:9
2 [a]2 Pet. 3:10
3 [a]Is. 13:6-9 [b]Hos. 13:13
4 [a]Rom. 13:12
5 [a]Eph. 5:8
6 [a]Mat. 25:5 [b]1 Pet. 5:8
7 [a]Luke 21:34 [b]Acts 2:15
8 [a]Eph. 6:14
9 [a]Rom. 9:22 [b]2 Thes. 2:13
10 [a]2 Cor. 5:15
11 [a]ch. 4:18 [1]Or, *exhort*
12 [a]1 Cor. 16:18
13 [a]Mark 9:50
14 [a]2 Thes. 3:11 [b]Heb. 12:12 [c]Rom. 14:1 [d]Gal. 5:22 [1]Or, *beseech* [2]Or, *disorderly*
15 [a]Lev. 19:18

6 [a]Therefore let us not sleep, as *do* C
others; but [b]let us watch and be sober.
7 For [a]they that sleep sleep in the
night; and they that be drunken [b]are
drunken in the night.
8 But let us, who are of the day, be
sober, [a]putting on the breastplate of faith
and love; and for an helmet, the hope of
salvation.
9 For [a]God hath not appointed us to P
wrath, [b]but to obtain salvation by our D
Lord Jesus Christ, K
10 [a]Who died for us, that, whether we L
wake or sleep, we should live together
with him.
11 [a]Wherefore [1]comfort yourselves together, and edify one another, even as
also ye do.
12 And we beseech you, brethren, [a]to
know them which labour among you, and
are over you in the Lord, and admonish
you;
13 And to esteem them very highly in
love for their work's sake. [a]*And* be at
peace among yourselves.
14 Now we [1]exhort you, brethren,
[a]warn them that are [2]unruly, [b]comfort
the feebleminded, [c]support the weak,
[d]be patient toward all *men.*
15 [a]See that none render evil for evil

C *1Th 4:13* ◀▶ *2Th 1:8*
P *1Th 5:4* ◀▶ *2Th 1:5–9*
D *Col 1:20–22* ◀▶ *1Ti 2:5–6*
K *Col 1:14* ◀▶ *2Th 3:3*
L *Col 2:13* ◀▶ *1Ti 1:15*

---

describes the supernatural action of Christ to physically lift the resurrected bodies of the saints into the air to return to heaven with him as prophesied. This rapture of reunited believers will occur as Christ returns in the air (see Ac 1:11) just prior to the tribulation (see Rev 3:10). In light of this glorious resurrection, the believers should take comfort and comfort one another.

5:1–8 Paul encourages the believers to be watchful for the Lord's return. His return will be unexpected and sudden for unbelievers, appearing like "a thief in the night" (5:2). Unbelievers will not pay attention to the prophetic signs of his coming or the fulfillment of the prophecies in their day. The apostle warns that these unbelievers will perceive that all is "peace and safety" (5:3) and when destruction suddenly comes, they will not be able to escape.

While Paul did not want the Thessalonians trying to fix a specific date for Christ's return (see Ac 1:17), he did want them to be aware of the fulfillment of the prophetic signs so that Christ's return will be a joy. Watchful believers will understand the fulfillment of the prophetic signs that point to the imminent return of Christ because such believers are "the children of light, and the children of the day" (5:5). Paul says that the fulfillment of the prophecies of the second coming should motivate the saints to watch for the Lord's return and be prepared for the last days.

5:9–11 Despite persecution, Paul promises the saints that God has not chosen his children for wrath, but rather "to obtain salvation by our Lord Jesus Christ" (5:9). These are two opposing spiritual destinies—wrath and salvation. If the church is granted salvation, we can conclude that the church will not experience the "wrath" of God during the coming tribulation and wicked rule of the antichrist (see Rev 6:17). Paul further says that because of Christ's death and resurrection we can be comforted with the promise that whether we live or die, we will "live together with him" (5:10).

The Rapture

The English word *rapture* comes from the Latin *rapere*, which means "to snatch away; to be caught up." The OT notes two instances of this snatching or catching away of individuals. Genesis records that a righteous man named Enoch never died, "for God took him" (Ge 5:24). Later, the Bible tells us that the prophet Elijah also escaped death when "Elijah went up by a whirlwind into heaven" (2Ki 2:11).

However, when Bible scholars today talk about the rapture they are usually referring to the resurrection of the church, a concept that is clearly taught in several different passages of Scripture. Although the word *rapture* does not appear in English translations of the Bible, it is an excellent word that describes what the Bible declares will happen to all believers who are alive at the moment when Christ calls his church home to heaven (see 1Th 4:16–17).

Jesus and Paul Teach About the Rapture

Some scholars suggest that the first mention of the rapture and resurrection of the church in the NT occurred when Jesus comforted Martha after the death of her brother, Lazarus. Jesus promised that Lazarus would rise again. These scholars contend that Jesus was talking about more than the resurrection of those who are physically dead. They believe instead that Jesus' words in this passage indicate the first clear teaching in the NT about the translation of the church when Christ returns.

Note that Jesus appears to repeat himself when he claims that whosoever "believeth in me, though he were dead, yet shall he live: And whosoever liveth and believeth in me shall never die" (Jn 11:25–26). Some scholars suggest that Jesus is not being redundant but rather talking about two distinct groups of Christians. These scholars believe that the first group is composed of those Christians who have died and are buried before Christ's second coming, hence the words "though he were dead, yet shall he live" (11:25). These scholars further contend that the second group in this passage is composed of believers who are alive when Christ returns. These believers are the ones to whom Jesus refers in Jn 11:26 as those who live and believe in him and never die. This second group represents a whole generation of believers who will not have to pass through death to reach eternal life but will instead be "caught up together . . . to meet the Lord in the air" (1Th 4:17).

The apostle Paul sheds additional light on the rapture in his first letters to the Thessalonians and the Corinthians (see 1Th 4:15–18; 1Co 15:51–54). In these letters, Paul lists several components of the rapture: (1) Not all Christians will die (see 1Th 4:17; 1Co 15:51). Many will be alive in the final generation when Christ returns. They will pass from this earthly life to life eternal without passing through the portals of death. (2) Before those who are alive are translated to heaven, Christ will resurrect the bodies of those believers who have died (see 1Th 4:16; 1Co 15:52). (3) This rapture will be instantaneous (see 1Co 15:52). (4) The rapture will be accompanied by the blowing of the last trumpet (see 1Th 4:16; 1Co 15:52). (5) All believers, dead or alive, will be changed (see 1Co 15:51). Their mortal, corruptible, earthly bodies will be transformed into incorruptible, immortal, heavenly bodies fit for eternity.

The Purpose of the Rapture

Since God is a God of order there must be some reason for this rapture of the believers. Scripture clearly provides the reason for the rapture of the church. The apostle Paul reminds us that we cannot enter an incorruptible heaven in a corruptible body that is subject to decay and death, so "this corruptible must put on incorruption, and this mortal must put on immortality" (1Co 15:53). The rapture provides that transformation and changes our earthly bodies into new resurrection bodies that will be like Christ's resurrected body—incorruptible and immortal. The apostle John reminds us that when Christ returns "we shall be like him; for we shall see him as he is" (1Jn 3:2). For further information on our resurrection bodies, see the article "The Resurrection of the Body" on p. 1206.

If believers were not raptured and transformed, we would have to spend eternity in heaven without a body. Yet we must receive a new spiritual body to enjoy all that Christ has prepared for us in heaven. Therefore, the promise to the church is that we will all be transformed, the living and the dead, at the moment of his coming. Those Christians who have died in the faith will receive their new transformed bodies as they rise to meet Christ in the air, and those who are living will simultaneously be changed as they are raptured from the earth. Those who take part in the rapture will then appear before Christ's judgment seat to "receive the things done in his body, according to that he hath done, whether it be good or bad" (2Co 5:10). Then, as God's transformed children, we shall see Jesus face to face and "so shall we ever be with the Lord" (1Th 4:17).

The Timing of the Rapture

If the Bible had included one simple statement about the exact sequence of events of the rapture and the return of Christ, all confusion about the timing of these events would have been removed forever. Since there is no such clear statement in Scripture, there is a certain degree of ambiguity about the timing of the rapture. As a result, many excellent and sincere Bible teachers have formed differing conclusions regarding the timing of the rapture. Many believe that the rapture will precede the great tribulation. Others favor a midtribulation rapture. Still other scholars suggest that a posttribulation rapture will occur at the glorious return of Christ at the Battle of Armageddon. Other scholars contend that the timing of the rapture is unimportant. Whether or not the church will have to experience the mass martyrdom of the tribulation is a matter of serious study and some concern. However, the Bible urges believers to place their primary focus on Christ's return, not on their possible martyrdom or suffering.

Part of the confusion surrounding the timing of the rapture is caused by the lack of specific prophecies that reveal when it will occur. Jesus clearly said that the time of the future resurrection of the saints had been specifically hidden from everyone but God the Father (see Mt 24:36). It is therefore our responsibility as believers to wait in watchful expectation "for his Son from heaven, whom he raised from the dead, even Jesus, which delivered us from the wrath to come" (1 Th 1:10).

As we await Christ's return and our translation to heaven we are forced to live in a paradox. We are to be watchful and waiting, yet busy and witnessing since we do not know when Christ will return. This sense of spiritual tension has helped keep the church alive and focused. If Christ had clearly stated that his return would not occur for centuries, the church might have lost its sense of urgency and mission to go and "teach all nations, baptizing them in the name of the Father, and of the Son, and of the Holy Ghost" (Mt 28:19).

During the last two hundred years, this belief in the imminent return of Christ has been a strong motivator behind much of today's missionary outreach. A strong belief in the literal return of Christ will continue to spur us on to win more souls to Christ so that we all will be ready for his shout, the archangel's voice and God's trumpet calling us to meet him "in the clouds" (1 Th 4:17).

The Rapture and the Tribulation Period

THE PRETRIBULATION RAPTURE

The Church Age — *Rapture-Resurrection*

The 7 Year Tribulation Period

The Millennium — *Christ Descends to Defeat Antichrist*

3.5 YRS (1260 DAYS) | **3.5 YRS** (1260 DAYS) | **1000 YRS**

Antichrist Signs 7 Year Treaty with Israel

Antichrist Defiles Temple

Battle of Armageddon

THE MIDTRIBULATION RAPTURE

The Church Age

The 7 Year Tribulation Period — *Rapture-Resurrection*

The Millennium — *Christ Descends to Defeat Antichrist*

3.5 YRS (1260 DAYS) | **3.5 YRS** (1260 DAYS) | **1000 YRS**

Antichrist Signs 7 Year Treaty with Israel

Antichrist Defiles Temple

Battle of Armageddon

THE PREWRATH RAPTURE THEORY

The Church Age

The 7 Year Tribulation Period — *Rapture-Resurrection*

The Millennium — *Christ Descends to Defeat Antichrist*

3.5 YRS (1260 DAYS) | **3.5 YRS** (1260 DAYS) | **1000 YRS**

Antichrist Signs 7 Year Treaty with Israel

Antichrist Defiles Temple

Battle of Armageddon

THE POSTTRIBULATION THEORY

The Church Age

The 7 Year Tribulation Period — *Christ Descends to Defeat Antichrist* / *Rapture-Resurrection*

The Millennium

3.5 YRS (1260 DAYS) | **3.5 YRS** (1260 DAYS) | **1000 YRS**

Antichrist Signs 7 Year Treaty with Israel

Antichrist Defiles Temple

Battle of Armageddon

unto any *man;* but ever [b]follow that
which is good, both among yourselves,
and to all *men.*
W 16 [a]Rejoice evermore.
17 [a]Pray without ceasing.
A 18 In every thing give thanks: for this
W is the will of God in Christ Jesus concerning you.
L 19 [a]Quench not the Spirit.
Q 20 [a]Despise not prophesyings.
G 21 [a]Prove all things; [b]hold fast that
which is good.
S 22 [a]Abstain from all appearance of
evil.

W *Col 3:15* ◀▶ *1Th 5:18* A *Ro 8:28* ◀
W *1Th 5:16* ◀▶ *1Ti 6:6*
L *Php 3:3* ◀▶ *Heb 9:14*
Q *Eph 4:30* ◀▶ *Heb 10:29*
G *Col 1:9* ◀▶ *1Ti 4:14*
S *1Th 4:6–7* ◀▶ *2Th 3:6*

15 [b]Gal. 6:10
16 [a]2 Cor. 6:10
17 [a]Eph. 6:18
19 [a]Eph. 4:30
20 [a]1 Cor. 14:1
21 [a]1 John 4:1 [b]Phil. 4:8
22 [a]ch. 4:12
23 [a]Phil. 4:9 [b]ch. 3:13 [c]1 Cor. 1:8
24 [a]1 Cor. 1:9
25 [a]Col. 4:3
26 [a]Rom. 16:16
27 [a]Col. 4:16 [l]Or, *adjure*
28 [a]Rom. 16:20

Conclusion

23 And [a]the very God of peace [b]sanctify you wholly; and *I pray God* your C
whole spirit and soul and body [c]be preserved blameless unto the coming of our
Lord Jesus Christ.
24 [a]Faithful *is* he that calleth you, who
also will do *it.*
25 Brethren, [a]pray for us.
26 [a]Greet all the brethren with an
holy kiss.
27 I [l]charge you by the Lord that [a]this
epistle be read unto all the holy brethren.
28 [a]The grace of our Lord Jesus Christ
be with you. Amen.

C *1Th 4:14* ◀▶ *2Th 1:7*

5:23 Paul concludes his prophetic passage with a benediction for the total sanctification and purification of the church "unto the coming of our Lord Jesus Christ," indicating that the promise of his second coming was a major focus for this young church.

2 Thessalonians

Author: Paul

Theme: The revelation of Jesus Christ at his second coming

Date of Writing: c. A.D. 51–52

Outline of 2 Thessalonians

I. Paul's Greetings and Prayer (1:1–12)
II. Teaching About the Day of the Lord (2:1–17)
III. Exhortation and Instruction for the Believers (3:1–15)
IV. Final Greetings and Benediction (3:16–18)

PAUL WROTE THIS second epistle to the church at Thessalonica shortly after his first letter to these believers. Paul was ministering in Corinth during his second missionary journey when news reached him that some of the believers in the church at Thessalonica had misunderstood the message about the second coming that he had shared in his first letter. These believers mistakenly concluded that the second coming of Christ was so imminent that they failed to live with a balanced perspective. Paul attempted to correct their unbalanced view by reminding the believers to obey Christ's command to reach the world while still maintaining an attitude of expectation for his imminent return.

In this brief letter Paul reminds the believers in Thessalonica of what he had taught in his first letter to them and severely reprimands those who remain indifferent to Christ's second coming. Filled with references to the end times, this letter reiterates the prophetic signs that will prevail just before the return of the Lord. Paul urges the believers at Thessalonica to redeem the time they are given, working with their hands and keeping busy, while understanding that Christ may delay his return or may return at any moment.

Thanksgiving and prayer

1 PAUL, [a]AND Silvanus, and Timotheus, unto the church of the Thessalonians [b]in God our Father and the Lord
Jesus Christ:
2 [a]Grace unto you, and peace, from
God our Father and the Lord Jesus Christ.
3 [a]We are bound to thank God always
for you, brethren, as it is meet, because
that your faith groweth exceedingly, and
the charity of every one of you all toward
each other aboundeth;
4 So that [a]we ourselves glory in you in
the churches of God [b]for your patience
and faith [c]in all your persecutions and
tribulations that ye endure:
P 5 *Which is* [a]a manifest token of the
H righteous judgment of God, that ye may
be counted worthy of the kingdom of
God, [b]for which ye also suffer:
6 [a]Seeing *it is* a righteous thing with
God to recompense tribulation to them
that trouble you;
C 7 And to you who are troubled [a]rest
N with us, when [b]the Lord Jesus shall be
revealed from heaven with [/]his mighty
angels,
C 8 [a]In flaming fire [/]taking vengeance
on them [b]that know not God, and [c]that
obey not the gospel of our Lord Jesus
Christ:

P *1Th 5:9 ◀ ▶ 2Th 2:8–9*
H *1Th 5:3 ◀ ▶ 2Th 2:8*
C *1Th 5:23 ◀ ▶ 2Th 1:10*
N *1Th 5:2–3 ◀ ▶ 2Th 2:10–12*
C *1Th 5:6 ◀ ▶ 2Th 2:10–12*

1:1 [a]2 Cor. 1:19 [b]1 Thes. 1:1
2 [a]1 Cor. 1:3
3 [a]1 Thes. 1:2; ch. 2:13
4 [a]2 Cor. 7:14; 1 Thes. 2:19 [b]1 Thes. 1:3 [c]1 Thes. 2:14
5 [a]Phil. 1:28 [b]1 Thes. 2:14
6 [a]Rev. 6:10
7 [a]Rev. 14:13 [b]1 Thes. 4:16; Jude 14 [/]Gk. *the angels of his power*
8 [a]Heb. 12:29; 2 Pet. 3:7; Rev. 21:8 [b]Ps. 79:6 [c]Rom. 2:8 [/]Or, *yielding*
9 [a]Phil. 3:19; 2 Pet. 3:7 [b]Deut. 33:2; Is. 2:19
10 [a]Ps. 89:7 [b]Ps. 68:35
11 [a]ver. 5 [b]1 Thes. 1:3 [/]Or, *vouchsafe*
12 [a]1 Pet. 1:7
2:1 [a]1 Thes. 4:16 [b]Mat. 24:31; Mark 13:27
2 [a]Mat. 24:4; Eph. 5:6
3 [a]Mat. 24:4; Eph. 5:6 [b]1 Tim. 4:1 [c]Dan. 7:25; Rev. 13:11 [d]John 17:12
4 [a]Is. 14:13; Rev. 13:6

9 [a]Who shall be punished with everlasting destruction from the presence of
the Lord, and [b]from the glory of his
power;
10 [a]When he shall come to be glorified C
in his saints, [b]and to be admired in all
them that believe (because our testimony
among you was believed) in that day.
11 Wherefore also we pray always for
you, that our God would [a]count[/] you
worthy of *this* calling, and fulfil all the
good pleasure of *his* goodness, and [b]the
work of faith with power:
12 [a]That the name of our Lord Jesus
Christ may be glorified in you, and ye in
him, according to the grace of our God
and the Lord Jesus Christ.

The man of sin

2 NOW WE beseech you, brethren, C
[a]by the coming of our Lord Jesus E
Christ, [b]and *by* our gathering together
unto him,
2 [a]That ye be not soon shaken in
mind, or be troubled, neither by spirit,
nor by word, nor by letter as from us, as
that the day of Christ is at hand.
3 [a]Let no man deceive you by any
means: for *that day shall not come,* [b]ex-
cept there come a falling away first, and
[c]that man of sin be revealed, [d]the son of
perdition;
4 Who opposeth and [a]exalteth himself

C *2Th 1:7 ◀ ▶ 2Th 2:1–3*
C *2Th 1:10 ◀ ▶ 2Th 3:5*
E *1Th 5:1–4 ◀ ▶ 1Ti 4:1–3*

1:7–10 Paul advises the believers who were facing persecution to take heart because Paul understood the pressures they were facing (see 1Th 1:6; 2:14–18). They will all be granted relief when Christ returns in judgment against those "that know not God, and that obey not the gospel of our Lord Jesus Christ" (1:8).

2:1–3 In these verses Paul corrects a misunderstanding held by some of the Thessalonians that they had somehow missed the resurrection because the day of the Lord had already begun. Paul's words clarify his earlier teaching and give a clear order of events concerning the rise of antichrist to power during the tribulation:

1. The forces of lawlessness were already at work in Paul's day (2:7).
2. Paul reveals that there will be a "falling away first" (2:3). Note that though the majority of scholars believe this is an aggressive rebellion against the things of God (see Mt 24:10–12; 1Ti 4:1), a small group contend that the Greek word *apostasia* used here refers to the rapture. In Greek, the word *apostasia* means "the departure away from something or someone." While traditionally this has been applied to a departure *from* the beliefs of the church, some Bible students say that this word may refer to the departure *of* the church or its rapture from the earth. Since this interpretation is not well supported by the context of the surrounding verses, the majority of scholars believe that the concept of religious apostasy and rebellion against God is the intent of this Greek word and its English translation.
3. The "man of sin" (2:3) will not be revealed until the Holy Spirit, who is restraining the antichrist's appearance, is taken out of the way (2:7).

2:4–9 Paul warns that this "son of perdition" (2:3) will set himself up above every god and everything

[b]above all that is called God, or that is
worshipped; so that he as God sitteth in
the temple of God, showing himself that
he is God.
5 Remember ye not, that, when I was
yet with you, I told you these things?
6 And now ye know what [/]withhold-
eth that he might be revealed in his time.
7 For [a]the mystery of iniquity doth already work: only he who now letteth *will
let,* until he be taken out of the way.
P 8 And then shall that Wicked be re-
V vealed, [a]whom the Lord shall consume
H [b]with the spirit of his mouth, and shall
destroy [c]with the brightness of his
coming:
9 *Even him,* whose coming is [a]after
the working of Satan with all power and
[b]signs and lying wonders,
C 10 And with all deceivableness of un-
N righteousness in [a]them that perish; because they received not the love of the
truth, that they might be saved.
H 11 And [a]for this cause God shall send
them strong delusion, [b]that they should
believe a lie:
12 That they all might be damned who
believed not the truth, but [a]had pleasure
in unrighteousness.

Thanksgiving and appeal

E 13 But [a]we are bound to give thanks
S
W

P *2Th 1:5–9* ◀▶ *2Pe 3:10–12*
V *Php 2:9–10* ◀▶ *1Ti 6:15*
H *2Th 1:5–9* ◀▶ *2Th 2:11–12*
C *2Th 1:8* ◀▶ *1Ti 4:2*
N *2Th 1:7–8* ◀▶ *1Ti 4:2*
H *2Th 2:8* ◀▶ *1Ti 6:9*
E *1Th 4:8* ◀▶ *1Ti 3:16*
S *1Th 4:7–8* ◀▶ *Heb 10:14–15*
W *1Th 4:7–8* ◀▶ *1Ti 4:12*

4 [b]1 Cor. 8:5
6 [/]Or, *holdeth*
7 [a]1 John 2:18
8 [a]Dan. 7:10 [b]Is. 11:4 [c]Heb. 10:27
9 [a]John 8:41; Rev. 18:23 [b]Deut. 13:1; Rev. 19:20
10 [a]2 Cor. 2:15
11 [a]Rom. 1:24 [b]1 Tim. 4:1
12 [a]Rom. 1:32
13 [a]ch. 1:3 [b]1 Thes. 1:4 [c]Eph. 1:4 [d]1 Pet. 1:2
14 [a]1 Pet. 5:10
15 [a]1 Cor. 16:13 [b]1 Cor. 11:2
16 [a]ch. 1:1,2 [b]Rev. 1:5 [c]1 Pet. 1:3
17 [a]1 Cor. 1:8
3:1 [a]Eph. 6:19 [/]Gk. *may run*
2 [a]Rom. 15:31 [b]Acts 28:24; Rom. 10:16 [/]Gk. *absurd*
3 [a]1 Cor. 1:9 [b]John 17:15; 2 Pet. 2:9
4 [a]2 Cor. 7:16
5 [a]1 Chr. 29:18 [/]Or, *the patience of Christ*

always to God for you, brethren beloved
of the Lord, because God [b]hath [c]from
the beginning chosen you to salvation
[d]through sanctification of the Spirit and
belief of the truth:
14 Whereunto he called you by our
gospel, to [a]the obtaining of the glory of
our Lord Jesus Christ.
15 Therefore, brethren, [a]stand fast,
and hold [b]the traditions which ye have
been taught, whether by word, or our
epistle.
16 [a]Now our Lord Jesus Christ himself, and God, even our Father, [b]which
hath loved us, and hath given *us* everlasting consolation and [c]good hope through
grace,
17 Comfort your hearts, [a]and stablish
you in every good word and work.

Appeals for prayer and labour

3 FINALLY, BRETHREN, [a]pray for us,
that the word of the Lord [/]may have
free course, and be glorified, even as *it is*
with you:
2 And [a]that we may be delivered from
[/]unreasonable and wicked men: [b]for all
men have not faith.
3 But [a]the Lord is faithful, who shall K
stablish you, and [b]keep *you* from evil.
4 And [a]we have confidence in the
Lord touching you, that ye both do and
will do the things which we command
you.
5 And [a]the Lord direct your hearts into C
the love of God, and into [/]the patient
waiting for Christ.
6 Now we command you, brethren, in S

K *1Th 5:9–10* ◀▶ *1Ti 4:8*
C *2Th 2:1–3* ◀▶ *1Ti 6:14*
S *1Th 5:22–23* ◀▶ *1Ti 1:19*

---

associated with the worship of the true God. He will make his blasphemous pronouncements from the temple in Jerusalem (see Da 9:27; 11:36–45; 12:11; Mt 24:15; Rev 13:1–15), defiling the Holy of Holies.

Yet this antichrist will not be revealed until the Holy Spirit, who is restraining the antichrist's appearance, is taken out of the way (2:7). As long as the church is on earth, the indwelling Holy Spirit will continue to restrain the antichrist. However, when the saints are raptured, the Holy Spirit will be "taken out of the way" (2:7) to allow Satan to bring forth the antichrist. It is important to note that the Holy Spirit will not be removed from the earth but will still convict the world of sin (see Jn 16:7–8). Even during the tribulation millions will become believers and face martyrdom for their faith.

The apostle calls the antichrist the "Wicked" (2:8) but promises that he will be destroyed when Jesus Christ returns. Paul warns that the antichrist will deceive many because of his signs and wonders, but that the antichrist's power is all "after the working of Satan" (2:9).

3:5 Paul concludes this prophetic exhortation by urging the believers to focus on God's love and wait patiently for Christ's return (see Mk 13:33). In our waiting we are to walk in holiness as though Christ might return at any moment yet continue to work for his kingdom even if he tarries for another century.

Reasons for a Pretribulation Rapture

DIFFERENT METHODS IN the interpretation of prophecy affect the conclusions that are drawn from prophetic passages. Those who view prophetic Scripture as a figurative compilation of apocalyptic literature will draw different conclusions from those who view Scripture from a literal point of view. If one interprets Scripture literally and consistently one arrives at the conclusion that the church, the body of Christ, will be removed from the earth before any part of the tribulation begins. Several passages of Scripture support this interpretation of the pretribulation rapture of the church.

In Christ's messages to the seven churches in the opening chapters of Revelation the church is mentioned nineteen times as being on earth. However, the central chapters of Revelation (chs. 4—19), which describe the tribulation period in great detail, make no mention of the church's presence on earth during that time of wrath. Instead, throughout this section of Revelation the church is described as participating in the marriage supper of the Lamb (see Rev 19:7–9) and standing before the judgment seat of Christ in heaven (see 2Co 5:10).

Note also that Rev 6:17 and 7:1–8 prophesy that before the great day of God's wrath, the angels will hold back their judgment until they have "sealed the servants of our God in their foreheads" (Rev 7:3). John's account then describes the angels sealing "an hundred and forty and four thousand of all the tribes of the children of Israel" (7:4), describing each of the tribes of Israel by name and noting the number of each tribe that is sealed for divine protection. Because of God's great love for believers, the omission of a reference to any protection extended to the church strongly indicates that the church is already safely in heaven at this time.

John's vision in Rev 4 provides another supporting reason for a pretribulation rapture. When John was taken up to heaven to stand before the throne, he saw 24 elders with crowns on their heads. Scripture indicates that believers will be given crowns in heaven for specific behaviors and actions performed on earth. (For additional information, see the article on "Crowns and Rewards" on p. 1318.) Paul indicates that these crowns will be awarded by "the Lord, the righteous judge" (2Ti 4:8) after Christ's return. He also indicates that all believers must "appear before the judgment seat of Christ; that every one may receive the things done in his body, according to that he hath done, whether it be good or bad" (2Co 5:10). This judgment will take place following the resurrection of all believers. Therefore John's vision of the 24 crowned elders lends great credence to the belief that these elders represent the church and that the rapture of the church must have already occurred. It is only after John sees these 24 elders that he is granted the vision of the sequential series of judgments of the tribulation.

The book of Matthew also records the events of the tribulation and focuses on Israel's participation in this time of wrath while omitting any reference to the church (see Mt 24). Specifically, those in Judea are told to flee to the hills (see 24:26); there is no mention of any other country or persons told to flee. Jesus' words also indicate that the Jews should pray that this devastation does not occur on the Sabbath (see 24:20). Jewish rabbis had interpreted God's prohibition of work on the Sabbath in Ex 16:29 to include a restriction prohibiting a Jew from walking (or fleeing) more than two thousand cubits (one thousand yards) on the Sabbath. Only the Jews would be bound by the rabbinical restriction of this "sabbath day's journey" (Ac 1:12), so Jesus' concern would have no meaning for Christians. Obviously, Jesus was referring to the Jews enduring the tribulation, not the church.

Paul also supports the pretribulation rapture when he tells the Thessalonians that "God hath not appointed us to wrath, but to obtain salvation by our Lord Jesus Christ" (1Th 5:9). Notice that Paul contrasts two separate destinies in this verse. He reminds the church that their destiny is salvation, not God's wrath. When compared with his words earlier in this letter, Paul clearly says that Christians are to "wait for his Son from heaven, whom he raised from the dead, even Jesus, which delivered us from the wrath to come" (1Th 1:10). Though some contend that this coming wrath refers to the punishment of hell, Scripture clearly states that we are delivered from hell by Christ's first coming and death on the cross, not by his second coming in the clouds. This "wrath to come" of 1Th 1:10 must refer to the tribulation, and this verse, therefore, is a clear declaration that Christ's return for his church (see 1Th 4:16–17) is the event that will deliver us from the tribulations' wrath.

The strongest proof that the rapture will precede the tribulation is found in the book of 2 Thessalonians. The church at Thessalonica was apprehensive that the great day of the Lord could occur at any moment. Paul reminded the believers of his teaching about "the coming of our Lord Jesus Christ, and by our gathering together unto him" (2Th 2:1). He told them not to be confused about the incorrect teaching that Armageddon awaits the church and very specifically points out that Armageddon would not come "except there come a falling away first, and that man of sin be revealed, the son of perdition" (2:3). This man of sin is the antichrist.

Daniel clearly prophesied that the antichrist will not be revealed until he seizes power over the ten nations of revived Rome and makes a seven-year treaty with Israel (see Da 9:27). Paul declares that the antichrist will be revealed only at his appointed time (see 2Th 2:6), but until then he is restrained by supernatural powers until God releases him (see 2:7). Only then will this wicked antichrist be revealed: "Even him, whose coming is after the working of Satan with all power and signs and lying wonders" (2:9). For further information, see the study notes on Da 7—9 and the article on "The Vision of the Seventy Weeks" on p. 976.

Scholars have tried to identify the restrainer of the antichrist. Some believe that this restrainer is the system of human government, but that suggestion is disproved by the fact that governments and kingdoms will continue after antichrist is revealed (see Rev 13:7);

they will not be taken away. Others have suggested that the church is the antichrist's restrainer; however, nowhere else in Scripture is the church referred to with the masculine pronoun "he," nor does the church ever exhibit any supernatural power except that which God manifests through it.

Most probably, therefore, the restrainer of the antichrist is God's Holy Spirit. This determination further supports the pretribulation rapture of the church because of the Holy Spirit's ministry among believers. Prior to Christ's ascension to heaven, Jesus promised his disciples that the Holy Spirit would come to empower the church (see Ac 1:8). Jesus had promised earlier that the Holy Spirit would abide in the church forever in his role as the comforter (see Jn 14:16), but that the Holy Spirit could not come until Jesus had ascended (see Jn 16:7). Unless the Holy Spirit is removed from his role as the restrainer, the antichrist will not be revealed. Therefore, because of Jesus' promise to believers of the abiding presence of the Holy Spirit, when the Holy Spirit is removed as the restrainer of the antichrist, it is because the church has already been raptured and is now in heaven at the marriage supper of the Lamb. Note that though the Holy Spirit will be removed from his role as the restrainer and comforter of the raptured church, the third person of the Trinity was, is now and always will be omnipresent. He will continue to convict sinners and thereby save a great multitude out of the tribulation (see Rev 7:9–14).

The day is coming when God will call every believer, living or dead, to meet him in the air and return home to heaven to the great marriage supper of the Lamb. Since we know not the exact time, this rapture of the church could happen without warning at any moment. It has not occurred yet, and Scripture indicates that it will occur before the tribulation begins. Until that time, "beloved, seeing that ye look for such things, be diligent that ye may be found of him in peace, without spot, and blameless" (2Pe 3:14).

the name of our Lord Jesus Christ, [a]that
ye withdraw yourselves [b]from every
brother that walketh [c]disorderly, and not
after [d]the tradition which he received
of us.
7 For yourselves know [a]how ye ought
to follow us: for [b]we behaved not ourselves disorderly among you;
8 Neither did we eat any man's bread
for nought; but [a]wrought with labour and
travail night and day, that we might not
be chargeable to any of you:
9 [a]Not because we have not power,
but to make [b]ourselves an example unto
you to follow us.
10 For even when we were with you,
this we commanded you, [a]that if any
would not work, neither should he eat.
11 For we hear that there are some
[a]which walk among you disorderly,
[b]working not at all, but are busybodies.
12 [a]Now them that are such we com-

6 [a]Rom. 16:17 [b]1 Cor. 5:11 [c]1 Thes. 4:11 [d]ch. 2:15
7 [a]1 Cor. 4:16 [b]1 Thes. 2:10
8 [a]Acts 18:3; 2 Cor. 11:9
9 [a]1 Cor. 9:6 [b]ver. 7
10 [a]1 Thes. 4:11
11 [a]ver. 6 [b]1 Tim. 5:13
12 [a]1 Thes. 4:11 [b]Eph. 4:28
13 [a]Gal. 6:9 [1]Or, *faint not*
14 [a]Mat. 18:17 [1]Or, *signify that man by an epistle*
15 [a]Lev. 19:17 [b]Tit. 3:10
16 [a]Rom. 15:33
17 [a]1 Cor. 16:21
18 [a]Rom. 16:24

mand and exhort by our Lord Jesus
Christ, [b]that with quietness they work,
and eat their own bread.
13 But ye, brethren, [a]be[1] not weary in
well doing.
14 And if any man obey not our word
[1]by this epistle, note that man, and [a]have
no company with him, that he may be
ashamed.
15 [a]Yet count *him* not as an enemy,
[b]but admonish *him* as a brother.

Benediction

16 Now [a]the Lord of peace himself
give you peace always by all means. The
Lord *be* with you all.
17 [a]The salutation of Paul with mine
own hand, which is the token in every
epistle: so I write.
18 [a]The grace of our Lord Jesus Christ
be with you all. Amen.

1 Timothy

Author: Paul

Theme: Instructions for a faithful ministry

Date of Writing: C. A.D. 63–65

Outline of 1 Timothy

I. Warning Against False Teachers (1:1–17)
II. Instructions for the Church (1:18—3:16)
III. Instructions for Leaders (4:1—6:2)
IV. Salutations (6:3–21)

THOUGH THE BOOKS of the NT do not always offer a clear chronology of the growth of Christianity, references in the book of Acts and the epistles help us to trace some of Paul's journeys. After Paul's first imprisonment in Rome, Paul revisited the churches in the province of Asia. On his journey to Macedonia, Paul left Timothy behind to minister at Ephesus (see 1:3) while Paul traveled on to Crete to minister there for a time. When Paul realized that he might not be able to return to Ephesus in the near future, he wrote the book of 1 Timothy to help his young protégé lead this growing congregation.

Timothy was born in Lystra, a city near Ephesus, and was converted under Paul's ministry. Timothy's mother and grandmother were apparently converted at or about that same time (see 2Ti 1:5). These women made sure that Timothy had a strong foundation in God's Word (see 2Ti 3:15)—a background that Timothy would rely on heavily in his ministry at Ephesus. When Paul came to Lystra on his second missionary journey (see Ac 16:1–3) he asked Timothy to join his mission. Timothy remained a loyal disciple of Paul throughout his ministry and even suffered imprisonment for his faith (see Heb 13:23).

This letter to Timothy is both personal and conversational as Paul instructs Timothy in the duties and qualifications of church leaders. False teachers were prevalent in Ephesus, so Paul offers guidance to Timothy as a pastor, reminding him of his duties as well as his obligations to "fight the good fight of faith" (6:12).

1 PAUL, AN apostle of Jesus Christ [a]by the commandment [b]of God our Saviour, and Lord Jesus Christ, [c]*which is* our hope;

2 Unto [a]Timothy, [b]*my* own son in the faith: [c]Grace, mercy, *and* peace, from God our Father and Jesus Christ our Lord.

The problem of unsound doctrine

3 As I besought thee to abide still at Ephesus, [a]when I went into Macedonia, that thou mightest charge some [b]that they teach no other doctrine,

4 [a]Neither give heed to fables and endless genealogies, [b]which minister questions, rather than godly edifying which is in faith: *so do.*

5 Now [a]the end of the commandment is charity [b]out of a pure heart, and *of* a good conscience, and *of* faith unfeigned:

6 From which some [/]having swerved have turned aside unto [a]vain jangling;

7 Desiring to be teachers of the law; [a]understanding neither what they say, nor whereof they affirm.

8 But we know that [a]the law *is* good, if a man use it lawfully;

9 [a]Knowing this, that the law is not made for a righteous man, but for the lawless and disobedient, for the ungodly and for sinners, for unholy and profane, for murderers of fathers and murderers of mothers, for manslayers,

10 For whoremongers, for them that defile themselves with mankind, for menstealers, for liars, for perjured persons, and if there be any other thing that is contrary [a]to sound doctrine;

11 According to the glorious gospel of the blessed God, [a]which was committed to my trust.

The testimony of Paul

12 And I thank Christ Jesus our Lord, [a]who hath enabled me, [b]for that he counted me faithful, [c]putting me into the ministry;

13 [a]Who was before a blasphemer, and a persecutor, and injurious: but I obtained mercy, because [b]I did *it* ignorantly in unbelief.

14 [a]And the grace of our Lord was exceeding abundant [b]with faith [c]and love which is in Christ Jesus.

15 [a]This *is* a faithful saying, and wor- L
thy of all acceptation, that [b]Christ Jesus W
came into the world to save sinners; of
whom I am chief.

16 Howbeit for this cause [a]I obtained mercy, that in me first Jesus Christ might show forth all longsuffering, [b]for a pattern to them which should hereafter believe on him to life everlasting.

17 Now unto [a]the King eternal, [b]immortal, [c]invisible, [d]the only wise God, [e]*be* honour and glory for ever and ever. Amen.

18 This charge [a]I commit unto thee, son Timothy, [b]according to the prophecies which went before on thee, that thou by them mightest [c]war a good warfare;

19 Holding faith, and a good con- S
science; which some having put away
concerning faith have made shipwreck:

20 Of whom is [a]Hymenaeus and [b]Alexander; whom I have [c]delivered unto Satan, that they may learn not to [d]blaspheme.

Prayer and sobriety

2 I [/]EXHORT therefore, that, first of all, supplications, prayers, intercessions, *and* giving of thanks, be made for all men;

2 [a]For kings, and [b]*for* all that are in [/]authority; that we may lead a quiet and peaceable life in all godliness and honesty.

3 For this *is* [a]good and acceptable in L
the sight [b]of God our Saviour; W

4 [a]Who will have all men to be saved,
[b]and to come unto the knowledge of the
truth.

5 [a]For *there is* one God, and [b]one me- D
diator between God and men, the man O
Christ Jesus;

6 [a]Who gave himself a ransom for all,
[b]to[/] be testified [c]in due time.

7 [a]Whereunto I am ordained a preacher, and an apostle, ([b]I speak the truth in Christ, *and* lie not;) [c]a teacher of the Gentiles in faith and verity.

8 I will therefore that men pray [a]every

1:1 [a]Acts 9:15 [b]Tit. 1:3 [c]Col. 1:27
2 [a]Acts 16:1 [b]Tit. 1:4 [c]Gal. 1:3
3 [a]Acts 20:1 [b]Gal. 1:6,7
4 [a]Tit. 1:14 [b]ch. 6:4
5 [a]Rom. 13:8; Gal. 5:14 [b]2 Tim. 2:22
6 [a]ch. 6:4,20 [/]Or, *not aiming at*
7 [a]ch. 6:4
8 [a]Rom. 7:12
9 [a]Gal. 3:19
10 [a]2 Tim. 4:3; Tit. 1:9
11 [a]1 Cor. 9:17; Gal. 2:7; Col. 1:25
12 [a]2 Cor. 12:9 [b]1 Cor. 7:25 [c]2 Cor. 3:5
13 [a]Acts 8:3 [b]John 4:21
14 [a]Rom. 5:20 [b]2 Tim. 1:13 [c]Luke 7:47
15 [a]2 Tim. 2:11 [b]Mat. 9:13
16 [a]2 Cor. 4:1 [b]Acts 13:39
17 [a]Ps. 10:16 [b]Rom. 1:23 [c]Heb. 11:27 [d]Rom. 16:27 [e]1 Chr. 29:11
18 [a]2 Tim. 2:2 [b]ch. 4:14 [c]2 Tim. 2:3
20 [a]2 Tim. 2:17 [b]2 Tim. 4:14 [c]1 Cor. 5:5 [d]Acts 13:45
2:1 [/]Or, *desire*
2 [a]Ezra 6:10 [b]Rom. 13:1 [/]Or, *eminent place*
3 [a]Rom. 12:2 [b]2 Tim. 1:9
4 [a]Ezek. 18:23; Tit. 2:11 [b]John 17:3; 2 Tim. 2:25
5 [a]Gal. 3:20 [b]Heb. 9:15
6 [a]Mark 10:45 [b]1 Cor. 1:6; 2 Tim. 1:8 [c]Rom. 5:6; Eph. 1:9 [/]Or, *a testimony*
7 [a]Eph. 3:7,8 [b]Rom. 9:1 [c]Gal. 1:16
8 [a]Luke 23:34

L *1Th 5:9–10* ◀▶ *1Ti 2:3–4*
W *Eph 2:17–18* ◀▶ *1Ti 2:3–6*
S *2Th 3:6* ◀▶ *1Ti 4:16*
L *1Ti 1:15* ◀▶ *1Ti 4:10*
W *1Ti 1:15* ◀▶ *1Ti 4:10*
D *1Th 5:9–10* ◀▶ *Tit 2:14*
O *Gal 2:16* ◀▶ *2Ti 2:11–12*

where, [b]lifting up holy hands, without wrath and doubting.

9 In like manner also, that [a]women adorn themselves in modest apparel, with shamefacedness and sobriety; not with [/]braided hair, or gold, or pearls, or costly array;

10 [a]But (which becometh women professing godliness) with good works.

11 Let the woman learn in silence with all subjection.

12 But [a]I suffer not a woman to teach, nor to usurp authority over the man, but to be in silence.

13 For [a]Adam was first formed, then Eve.

14 And [a]Adam was not deceived, but the woman being deceived was in the transgression.

15 Notwithstanding she shall be saved in childbearing, if they continue in faith and charity and holiness with sobriety.

Bishops and deacons

3 THIS *IS* a true saying, If a man desire the office of a bishop, he desireth a good work.

2 [a]A bishop then must be blameless, the husband of one wife, vigilant, sober, [/]of good behaviour, given to hospitality, [b]apt to teach;

3 [/]Not given to wine, [a]no striker, [b]not greedy of filthy lucre; but patient, not a brawler, not covetous;

4 One that ruleth well his own house, [a]having his children in subjection with all gravity;

5 (For if a man know not how to rule his own house, how shall he take care of the church of God?)

6 Not [/]a novice, lest being lifted up with pride he fall into the condemnation of the devil.

7 Moreover he must have a good report [a]of them which are without; lest he fall into reproach [b]and the snare of the devil.

8 Likewise *must* [a]the deacons *be* grave, not doubletongued, [b]not given to much wine, not greedy of filthy lucre;

9 [a]Holding the mystery of the faith in a pure conscience.

10 And let these also first be proved; then let them use the office of a deacon, being *found* blameless.

11 [a]Even so *must their* wives *be* grave, not slanderers, sober, faithful in all things.

12 Let the deacons be the husbands of one wife, ruling their children and their own houses well.

13 For [a]they that have [/]used the office of a deacon well purchase to themselves a good degree, and great boldness in the faith which is in Christ Jesus.

14 These things write I unto thee, hoping to come unto thee shortly:

15 But if I tarry long, that thou mayest know how thou oughtest to behave thyself [a]in the house of God, which is the church of the living God, the pillar and [/]ground of the truth.

16 And without controversy great is the mystery of godliness: [a]God was [/]manifest in the flesh, [b]justified in the Spirit, [c]seen of angels, [d]preached unto the Gentiles, [e]believed on in the world, [f]received up into glory. E

Instructions for godly living

4 NOW THE Spirit [a]speaketh expressly, that [b]in the latter times some shall depart from the faith, giving heed [c]to seducing spirits, [d]and doctrines of devils; E E T

2 [a]Speaking lies in hypocrisy; [b]having their conscience seared with a hot iron; C N

3 [a]Forbidding to marry, [b]*and commanding* to abstain from meats, which God hath created [c]to be received [d]with

8 [b]Ps. 134:2
9 [a]1 Pet. 3:3 [/]Or, *plaited*
10 [a]1 Pet. 3:4
12 [a]1 Cor. 14:34
13 [a]Gen. 1:27; 1 Cor. 11:8
14 [a]Gen. 3:6; 2 Cor. 11:3
3:2 [a]Tit. 1:6 [b]2 Tim. 2:24 [/]Or, *modest*
3 [a]2 Tim. 2:24 [b]1 Pet. 5:2 [/]Or, *Not ready to quarrel, and offer wrong, as one in wine*
4 [a]Tit. 1:6
6 [/]Or, *one newly come to the faith*
7 [a]Acts 22:12; 1 Cor. 5:12 [b]2 Tim. 2:26
8 [a]Acts 6:3 [b]Ezek. 44:21
9 [a]ch. 1:19
11 [a]Tit. 2:3
13 [a]Mat. 25:21 [/]Or, *ministered*
15 [a]Eph. 2:21; 2 Tim. 2:20 [/]Or, *stay*
16 [a]John 1:14; 1 John 1:2 [b]Mat. 3:16; Rom. 1:4 [c]Mat. 28:2; Mark 16:5 [d]Acts 10:34; Rom. 10:18 [e]Col. 1:6,23 [f]Luke 24:51 [/]Gk. *manifested*
4:1 [a]John 16:13; 2 Thes. 2:3; 2 Tim. 3:1 [b]1 Pet. 1:20 [c]2 Tim. 3:13; Rev. 16:14 [d]Dan. 11:35; Rev. 9:20
2 [a]Mat. 7:15 [b]Eph. 4:19
3 [a]1 Cor. 7:28 [b]Rom. 14:3 [c]Gen. 1:29 [d]Rom. 14:6

E *2Th 2:13* ◀▶ *1Ti 4:1*
E *2Th 2:1–9* ◀▶ *2Ti 3:1–9*
E *1Ti 3:16* ◀▶ *1Ti 4:14*
T *1Th 1:5* ◀▶ *2Ti 3:16*
C *2Th 2:10–12* ◀▶ *1Ti 5:6*
N *2Th 2:10–12* ◀▶ *2Ti 4:3–4*

4:1–3 Paul clearly says that there will be those in the last days that will openly deny the fundamental doctrines of the divinity of Jesus and the reality of his resurrection. Paul warned that these heresies would be inspired by demons and hypocritical liars. Paul's prophecy foreshadowed the cultic practices of our generation that include the acceptance of immorality and the widespread requirement to abstain from certain types of foods. In addition, liberal theologians have openly denied the fundamental doctrines of the Bible and continue to propagate these heresies both in the pulpit and in seminary classrooms.

thanksgiving of them which believe and know the truth.

4 For [a]every creature of God *is* good, and nothing to be refused, if it be received with thanksgiving:

5 For it is sanctified by the word of God and prayer.

6 If thou put the brethren in remembrance of these things, thou shalt be a good minister of Jesus Christ, [a]nourished up in the words of faith and of good doctrine, whereunto thou hast attained.

7 But [a]refuse profane and old wives' fables, and [b]exercise thyself *rather* unto godliness.

K P U 8 For [a]bodily exercise profiteth [I]little: [b]but godliness is profitable unto all things, [c]having promise of the life that now is, and of that which is to come.

9 This *is* a faithful saying and worthy of all acceptation.

L W 10 For therefore [a]we both labour and suffer reproach, because we trust in the living God, [b]who is the Saviour of all men, specially of those that believe.

11 These things command and teach.

W 12 Let no man despise thy youth; but [a]be thou an example of the believers, in word, in conversation, in charity, in spirit, in faith, in purity.

13 Till I come, give attendance to reading, to exhortation, to doctrine.

E G 14 [a]Neglect not the gift that is in thee, which was given thee [b]by prophecy, [c]with the laying on of the hands of the presbytery.

15 Meditate upon these things; give thyself wholly to them; that thy profiting may appear [I]to all.

S 16 [a]Take heed unto thyself, and unto the doctrine; continue in them: for in doing this thou shalt both [b]save thyself, and them that hear thee.

5 REBUKE [a]NOT an elder, but entreat *him* as a father; *and* the younger men as brethren;

2 The elder women as mothers; the younger as sisters, with all purity.

K *2Th 3:3 ◀ ▶ 2Ti 1:12*
P *Php 4:19 ◀ ▶ Heb 6:10*
U *Gal 6:16 ◀ ▶ 1Pe 3:12*
L *1Ti 2:3–4 ◀ ▶ 2Ti 1:9*
W *1Ti 2:3–6 ◀ ▶ Tit 2:11*
W *2Th 2:13 ◀ ▶ 1Pe 1:2*
E *1Ti 4:1 ◀ ▶ 2Ti 1:6–7*
G *1Th 5:20 ◀ ▶ 2Ti 1:6–7*
S *1Ti 1:19 ◀ ▶ 1Ti 6:12*

4 [a]Rom. 14:14
6 [a]2 Tim. 3:14
7 [a]2 Tim. 2:16; Tit. 1:14 [b]Heb. 5:14
8 [a]1 Cor. 8:8 [b]ch. 6:6 [c]Ps. 37:4 [I]Or, *for a little time*
10 [a]1 Cor. 4:11 [b]Ps. 36:6
12 [a]Tit. 2:7
14 [a]2 Tim. 1:6 [b]ch. 1:18 [c]Acts 6:6
15 [I]Or, *in all things*
16 [a]Acts 20:28 [b]Ezek. 33:9
5:1 [a]Lev. 19:32
4 [a]Gen. 45:10; Mat. 15:4; Eph. 6:1, 2 [I]Or, *kindness*
5 [a]1 Cor. 7:32 [b]Luke 2:37 [c]Acts 26:7
6 [a]Jas. 5:5 [I]Or, *delicately*
8 [a]Is. 58:7; Gal. 6:10 [b]2 Tim. 3:5; Tit. 1:16 [c]Mat. 18:17 [I]Or, *kindred*
9 [I]Or, *chosen*
10 [a]Acts 16:15; Heb. 13:2; 1 Pet. 4:9 [b]Gen. 19:2
13 [a]2 Thes. 3:11
14 [a]1 Cor. 7:9 [b]Tit. 2:8 [I]Gk. *for their railing*
16 [a]ver. 3,5
17 [a]Phil. 2:29 [b]Acts 28:10
18 [a]Deut. 25:4; 1 Cor. 9:9

Pastoral duties

3 Honour widows that are widows indeed.

4 But if any widow have children or nephews, let them learn first to show [I]piety at home, and [a]to requite their parents: for that is good and acceptable before God.

5 [a]Now she that is a widow indeed, and desolate, trusteth in God, and [b]continueth in supplications and prayers [c]night and day.

6 [a]But she that liveth [I]in pleasure is dead while she liveth. C

7 And these things give in charge, that they may be blameless.

8 But if any provide not for his own, [a]and specially for those of his own [I]house, [b]he hath denied the faith, [c]and is worse than an infidel.

9 Let not a widow be [I]taken into the number under threescore years old, having been the wife of one man,

10 Well reported of for good works; if she have brought up children, if she have [a]lodged strangers, if she have [b]washed the saints' feet, if she have relieved the afflicted, if she have diligently followed every good work.

11 But the younger widows refuse: for when they have begun to wax wanton against Christ, they will marry;

12 Having damnation, because they have cast off their first faith.

13 [a]And withal they learn *to be* idle, wandering about from house to house; and not only idle, but tattlers also and busybodies, speaking things which they ought not.

14 [a]I will therefore that the younger women marry, bear children, guide the house, [b]give none occasion to the adversary [I]to speak reproachfully.

15 For some are already turned aside after Satan.

16 If any man or woman that believeth have widows, let them relieve them, and let not the church be charged; that it may relieve [a]them that are widows indeed.

17 [a]Let the elders that rule well [b]be counted worthy of double honour, especially they who labour in the word and doctrine.

18 For the scripture saith, [a]Thou shalt not muzzle the ox that treadeth out the

C *1Ti 4:2 ◀ ▶ 2Ti 2:26*

corn. And, [b]The labourer *is* worthy of his reward.

19 Against an elder receive not an accusation, but [a]before[/] two or three witnesses.

20 [a]Them that sin rebuke before all, [b]that others also may fear.

21 [a]I charge *thee* before God, and the Lord Jesus Christ, and the elect angels, that thou observe these things [/]without preferring one before another, doing nothing by partiality.

22 [a]Lay hands suddenly on no man, [b]neither be partaker of other men's sins: keep thyself pure.

23 Drink no longer water, but use a little wine [a]for thy stomach's sake and thine often infirmities.

24 [a]Some men's sins are open beforehand, going before to judgment; and some *men* they follow after.

25 Likewise also the good works *of some* are manifest beforehand; and they that are otherwise cannot be hid.

6 LET AS many [a]servants as are under the yoke count their own masters worthy of all honour, [b]that the name of God and *his* doctrine be not blasphemed.

2 And they that have believing masters, let them not despise *them,* [a]because they are brethren; but rather do *them* service, because they are [/]faithful and beloved, partakers of the benefit. These things teach and exhort.

The use of wealth

M 3 If any man teach otherwise, and consent [a]not to wholesome words, *even* the words of our Lord Jesus Christ, [b]and to the doctrine which is according to godliness;

4 He is [/]proud, [a]knowing nothing, but [2]doting about questions and strifes of words, whereof cometh envy, strife, railings, evil surmisings,

5 [a]Perverse[/] disputings of men of corrupt minds, and destitute of the truth, [b]supposing that gain is godliness: [c]from such withdraw thyself.

6 But [a]godliness with contentment is great gain. W

7 For [a]we brought nothing into *this* world, *and it is* certain we can carry nothing out.

8 And [a]having food and raiment let us be therewith content. W

9 But [a]they that will be rich fall into temptation and a snare, and *into* many foolish and hurtful lusts, [b]which drown men in destruction and perdition. H

10 [a]For the love of money is the root of all evil: which while some coveted after, they have [/]erred from the faith, and pierced themselves through with many sorrows.

The good fight of faith

11 [a]But thou, [b]O man of God, flee these things; and follow after righteousness, godliness, faith, love, patience, meekness.

12 [a]Fight the good fight of faith, [b]lay hold on eternal life, whereunto thou art also called, [c]and hast professed a good profession before many witnesses. S

13 [a]I give thee charge in the sight of God, [b]who quickeneth all things, and *before* Christ Jesus, [c]who before Pontius Pilate witnessed a good [/]confession; F

14 That thou keep *this* commandment without spot, unrebukeable, [a]until the appearing of our Lord Jesus Christ: C

M *Col 2:18 ◀▶ Jas 4:6–10*

W *1Th 5:18 ◀▶ 1Ti 6:8*
W *1Ti 6:6 ◀▶ Heb 13:5–6*
H *2Th 2:11–12 ◀▶ Heb 2:2–3*
S *1Ti 4:16 ◀▶ 2Ti 2:19*
F *1Th 4:13–18 ◀▶ 2Ti 2:17–18*
C *2Th 3:5 ◀▶ 2Ti 4:8*

18 [b]Lev. 19:13; Deut. 24:14; Mat. 10:10
19 [a]Deut. 19:15 [/]Or, *under*
20 [a]Tit. 1:13 [b]Deut. 13:11
21 [a]ch. 6:13; 2 Tim. 2:14 [/]Or, *without prejudice*
22 [a]Acts 6:6; 2 Tim. 1:6 [b]2 John 11
23 [a]Ps. 104:15
24 [a]Gal. 5:19
6:1 [a]Eph. 6:5; Col. 3:22; Tit. 2:9; 1 Pet. 2:18 [b]Is. 52:5; Rom. 2:24; Tit. 2:5,8
2 [a]Col. 4:1 [/]Or, *believing*
3 [a]2 Tim. 1:13; Tit. 1:9 [b]Tit. 1:1
4 [a]1 Cor. 8:2 [/]Or, *a fool* [2]Or, *sick*
5 [a]1 Cor. 11:16 [b]2 Pet. 2:3 [c]Rom. 16:17 [/]Or, *Gallings one of another*
6 [a]Ps. 37:16; Heb. 13:5
7 [a]Job 1:21
8 [a]Gen. 28:20; Heb. 13:5
9 [a]Prov. 15:27 [b]ch. 1:19
10 [a]Deut. 16:19 [/]Or, *been seduced*
11 [a]2 Tim. 2:22 [b]Deut. 33:1
12 [a]ch. 1:18 [b]Phil. 3:12 [c]Heb. 13:23
13 [a]ch. 5:21 [b]1 Sam. 2:6 [c]John 18:37 [/]Or, *profession*
14 [a]Phil. 1:6

6:13 The expression "who quickeneth all things," refers to Jesus Christ's power to resurrect the dead.
6:14–15 Paul commands Timothy to follow Christ's commandments until the Lord returns, revealing his earnest expectation of the imminence of Christ's return for the saints. This concept of imminence accepts that Jesus could return without warning at any moment for his saints (see 1Th 4:13–17), yet recognizes that it is also possible that the signs of Ezekiel (see Eze 39) and Jesus (see Mt 24) will occur before the resurrection of the saints.

The apostle reminds us that just as Jesus' first advent occurred when God wanted (see Gal 4:4), so also Christ's return will come at the precise moment God chooses. In his first advent Jesus came in humility as the Christ-child, the wonderful teacher, the healer, the Lamb sacrificed for our sins and risen from the dead. When he returns at his second coming, however, Jesus Christ will be revealed in all of his glory and power as "the King of kings, and Lord of lords" (6:15; see Rev 19:16).

M V 15 Which in his times he shall show,
who is [a]the blessed and only Potentate,
the King of kings, and Lord of lords;
16 Who only hath immortality, dwelling in the light which no man can approach unto; [a]whom no man hath seen,
nor can see: [b]to whom *be* honour and
power everlasting. Amen.
G L 17 Charge them that are rich in this
world, that they be not highminded, [a]nor
trust in [b]uncertain[1] riches, but in [c]the
living God, [d]who giveth us richly all
things to enjoy;

M *Php 2:9–11* ◄► *2Ti 2:12*
V *2Th 2:8* ◄► *Heb 1:2*
G *Php 3:3–10* ◄► *2Ti 1:9*
L *Php 4:19* ◄► *Heb 1:14*

15 [a]ch. 1:11,17
16 [a]John 6:46 [b]Eph. 3:21
17 [a]Luke 12:21 [b]Prov. 23:5 [c]1 Thes. 1:9 [d]Acts 14:17 [1]Gk. *uncertainty of riches*
18 [a]Jas. 2:5 [b]Rom. 12:13 [c]Gal. 6:6 [1]Or, *sociable*
19 [a]Mat. 6:20
20 [a]2 Tim. 1:14 [b]Tit. 1:14
21 [a]2 Tim. 2:18

18 That they do good, that [a]they be
rich in good works, [b]ready to distribute,
[c]willing[1] to communicate;
19 [a]Laying up in store for themselves
a good foundation against the time to
come, that they may lay hold on eternal
life.

Final charge and benediction

20 O Timothy, [a]keep that which is
committed to thy trust, [b]avoiding profane
and vain babblings, and oppositions of
science falsely so called:
21 Which some professing [a]have erred
concerning the faith. Grace *be* with thee.
Amen.

2 Timothy

Author: Paul

Theme: Timothy encouraged to stand firm in the faith

Date of Writing: c. A.D. 66–67

Outline of 2 Timothy

I. Salutation (1:1–2)
II. Faithfulness Is Essential in Service (1:3—2:13)
III. True and False Teachings (2:14—3:17)
IV. Paul's Charge to Timothy (4:1–8)
V. Conclusion (4:9–22)

After Paul's fourth missionary journey, Emperor Nero imprisoned Paul in Rome. Chained in a cold dungeon like a common criminal, Paul sensed that his opportunities for preaching the gospel were coming to an end. He wrote this second letter to Timothy while in prison in an attempt to ease his own loneliness while encouraging Timothy to stand firm in his faith.

In this letter Paul senses the great task facing Timothy. Paul also realizes that his own death is imminent and seeks to strengthen his young assistant with his last words. Paul longs to see Timothy again and asks him to bring the books and parchments Paul had left behind in Troas. Paul also calls Timothy's attention to those who have deserted Paul in his time of need. Charging Timothy to maintain sound doctrine, Paul expresses his personal confidence and faith in Christ as he urges Timothy to stand firm in his faith despite persecution. Paul ultimately died in prison in Rome as a martyr to his faith in Christ.

1 PAUL, [a]AN apostle of Jesus Christ by the will of God, according to [b]the promise of life which is in Christ Jesus,

2 [a]To Timothy, *my* dearly beloved son: Grace, mercy, *and* peace, from God the Father and Christ Jesus our Lord.

Appeal for faithfulness

3 [a]I thank God, [b]whom I serve from *my* forefathers with pure conscience, that [c]without ceasing I have remembrance of thee in my prayers night and day;

4 [a]Greatly desiring to see thee, being mindful of thy tears, that I may be filled with joy;

5 When I call to remembrance [a]the unfeigned faith that is in thee, which dwelt first in thy grandmother Lois, and [b]thy mother Eunice; and I am persuaded that in thee also.

6 Wherefore I put thee in remembrance [a]that thou stir up the gift of God, which is in thee by the putting on of my hands.

7 For [a]God hath not given us the spirit of fear; [b]but of power, and of love, and of a sound mind.

8 [a]Be not thou therefore ashamed of [b]the testimony of our Lord, nor of me [c]his prisoner: [d]but be thou partaker of the afflictions of the gospel according to the power of God;

9 [a]Who hath saved us, and [b]called *us* with an holy calling, [c]not according to our works, but [d]according to his own purpose and grace, which was given us in Christ Jesus [e]before the world began,

10 But [a]is now made manifest by the appearing of our Saviour Jesus Christ, [b]who hath abolished death, and hath brought life and immortality to light through the gospel:

11 [a]Whereunto I am appointed a preacher, and an apostle, and a teacher of the Gentiles.

12 [a]For the which cause I also suffer these things: nevertheless I am not ashamed: [b]for I know whom I have [1]believed, and am persuaded that he is able to [c]keep that which I have committed unto him against that day.

13 [a]Hold fast [b]the form of [c]sound words, which thou hast heard of me, [d]in faith and love which is in Christ Jesus.

14 That good thing which was committed unto thee keep by the Holy Ghost [a]which dwelleth in us.

15 This thou knowest, that [a]all they which are in Asia be turned away from me; of whom are Phygellus and Hermogenes.

16 The Lord [a]give mercy unto the house of Onesiphorus; [b]for he oft refreshed me, and was not ashamed of [c]my chain:

17 But, when he was in Rome, he sought me out very diligently, and found *me.*

18 The Lord grant unto him that he may find mercy of the Lord [a]in that day: and in how many things he [b]ministered unto me at Ephesus, thou knowest very well.

2 THOU THEREFORE, [a]my son, [b]be strong in the grace that is in Christ Jesus.

2 And the things that thou hast heard of me [1]among many witnesses, the same commit thou to faithful men, who shall be able to teach others also.

3 Thou therefore endure hardness, [a]as a good soldier of Jesus Christ.

4 [a]No man that warreth entangleth himself with the affairs of *this* life; that he may please him who hath chosen him to be a soldier.

5 And [a]if a man also strive for masteries, *yet* is he not crowned, except he strive lawfully.

6 [1]The husbandman that laboureth must be first partaker of the fruits.

7 Consider what I say; and the Lord give thee understanding in all things.

8 Remember that Jesus Christ [a]of the seed of David [b]was raised from the dead [c]according to my gospel:

9 [a]Wherein I suffer trouble, as an evildoer, [b]*even* unto bonds; [c]but the word of God is not bound.

10 Therefore [a]I endure all things for the elect's sakes, [b]that they may also obtain the salvation which is in Christ Jesus with eternal glory.

1:1 [a]2 Cor. 1:1 [b]Eph. 3:6; Heb. 9:15
2 [a]1 Tim. 1:2
3 [a]Rom. 1:8; Eph. 1:16 [b]Acts 22:3; Rom. 1:9 [c]1 Thes. 1:2
4 [a]ch. 4:9,21
5 [a]1 Tim. 1:5 [b]Acts 16:1
6 [a]1 Tim. 4:14
7 [a]Rom. 8:15 [b]Acts 1:8
8 [a]Rom. 1:16 [b]1 Tim. 2:6 [c]Eph. 3:1 [d]Col. 1:24
9 [a]1 Tim. 1:1 [b]Heb. 3:1 [c]Rom. 3:20 [d]Rom. 8:28 [e]Rom. 16:25
10 [a]Eph. 1:9 [b]1 Cor. 15:54
11 [a]Acts 9:15; 1 Tim. 2:7
12 [a]Eph. 3:1 [b]1 Pet. 4:19 [c]1 Tim. 6:20 [1]Or, *trusted*
13 [a]Tit. 1:9; Heb. 10:23 [b]Rom. 2:20 [c]1 Tim. 6:3 [d]1 Tim. 1:14
14 [a]Rom. 8:11
15 [a]Acts 19:10
16 [a]Mat. 5:7 [b]Philem. 7 [c]Acts 28:20
18 [a]2 Thes. 1:10 [b]Heb. 6:10
2:1 [a]1 Tim. 1:2 [b]Eph. 6:10
2 [1]Or, *by*
3 [a]1 Tim. 1:18
4 [a]1 Cor. 9:25
5 [a]1 Cor. 9:25
6 [1]Or, *The husbandman, labouring first, must be partaker of the fruits*
8 [a]Rom. 1:3,4 [b]1 Cor. 15:1 [c]Rom. 2:16
9 [a]Acts 9:16 [b]Eph. 3:1 [c]Acts 28:31; Eph. 6:19
10 [a]Eph. 3:13 [b]2 Cor. 1:6

E *1Ti 4:14* ◀▶ *2Ti 1:14*
G *1Ti 4:14* ◀▶ *2Ti 1:14*
F *1Th 1:6* ◀▶ *Heb 1:9*
M *1Th 1:5* ◀▶ *Heb 2:4*
T *1Co 14:24–25* ◀▶ *2Ti 2:12*
G *1Ti 6:17* ◀▶ *Tit 3:5*
L *1Ti 4:10* ◀▶ *Tit 2:11*
K *1Ti 4:8* ◀▶ *Tit 2:11*

E *2Ti 1:6–7* ◀▶ *Tit 3:5–6*
G *2Ti 1:6–7* ◀▶ *2Ti 3:16*

O 11 *It is* a faithful saying: For [a]if we be dead with *him,* we shall also live with *him:*

M 12 [a]If we suffer, we shall also reign
T with *him:* [b]if we deny *him,* he also will deny us:

13 [a]If we believe not, *yet* he abideth faithful: [b]he cannot deny himself.

A workman approved unto God

14 Of these things put *them* in remembrance, [a]charging *them* before the Lord that they strive not about words to no profit, *but* to the subverting of the hearers.

15 Study to show thyself approved unto God, a workman that needeth not to be ashamed, rightly dividing the word of truth.

16 But [a]shun profane *and* vain babblings: for they will increase unto more ungodliness.

F 17 And their word will eat as doth a [1]canker: of whom is Hymenaeus and Philetus;

18 Who concerning the truth have erred, [a]saying that the resurrection is past already; and overthrow the faith of some.

S 19 Nevertheless [a]the foundation of God standeth [1]sure, having this seal, The Lord [b]knoweth them that are his. And, Let every one that nameth the name of Christ depart from iniquity.

20 But in a great house there are not only vessels of gold and of silver, but also of wood and of earth; [a]and some to honour, and some to dishonour.

21 [a]If a man therefore purge himself from these, he shall be a vessel unto honour, sanctified, and meet for the master's use, *and* [b]prepared unto every good work.

22 Flee also youthful lusts: but follow righteousness, faith, charity, peace, with them that [a]call on the Lord [b]out of a pure heart.

23 But [a]foolish and unlearned questions avoid, knowing that they do gender strifes.

24 And [a]the servant of the Lord must not strive; but be gentle unto all *men,* [b]apt to teach, [1]patient,

25 [a]In meekness instructing those that oppose themselves; [b]if God peradventure will give them repentance [c]to the acknowledging of the truth;

26 And *that* they may [1]recover them- C
selves [a]out of the snare of the devil, who are [2]taken captive by him at his will.

The coming apostasy

3 THIS KNOW also, that [a]in the last E
days perilous times shall come. C

2 For men shall be [a]lovers of their own selves, [b]covetous, [c]boasters, [d]proud,

O *1Ti 2:5* ◀ ▶ *Heb 9:22*
M *1Ti 6:15* ◀ ▶ *2Ti 4:1*
T *2Ti 1:8* ◀ ▶ *Phm 6*
F *1Ti 6:13* ◀ ▶ *Heb 6:2*
S *1Ti 6:12* ◀ ▶ *Tit 1:16*

C *1Ti 5:6* ◀ ▶ *2Ti 3:1–5*
E *1Ti 4:1–3* ◀ ▶ *2Ti 4:3–4*
C *2Ti 2:26* ◀ ▶ *2Ti 3:8*

11 [a]Rom. 6:5,8
12 [a]Rom. 8:17; 1 Pet. 4:13 [b]Mat. 10:33; Mark 8:38
13 [a]Rom. 3:3 [b]Num. 23:19
14 [a]1 Tim. 5:21
16 [a]1 Tim. 4:7
17 [1]Or, *gangrene*
18 [a]1 Cor. 15:12
19 [a]Mat. 24:24 [b]Nah. 1:7; John 10:14 [1]Or, *steady*
20 [a]Rom. 9:21
21 [a]Is. 52:11 [b]ch. 3:17
22 [a]Acts 9:14; 1 Cor. 1:2 [b]1 Tim. 1:5
23 [a]1 Tim. 1:4
24 [a]Tit. 3:2 [b]Tit. 1:9 [1]Or, *forbearing*
25 [a]Gal. 6:1; 1 Tim. 6:11 [b]Acts 8:22 [c]1 Tim. 2:4
26 [a]1 Tim. 3:7 [1]Gk. *awake* [2]Gk. *taken alive*
3:1 [a]1 Tim. 4:1
2 [a]Phil. 2:21 [b]2 Pet. 2:3 [c]Jude 16 [d]1 Tim. 6:4

2:11–12 Paul's words here indicate that we died with Christ in the past when he died for us on the cross. Therefore we are promised that we will have eternal life in heaven with him. Paul also says that faithfully suffering in this life for our faith will result in our reigning with Christ in the coming kingdom of God on earth (see Rev 20:4). Yet Paul also warns that those who deny Jesus Christ in this life will be denied by him when they stand in judgment in the last days.

2:17–18 Two teachers were causing great confusion in the early church by denying the future bodily resurrection and teaching that the only resurrection was a symbolic resurrection that occurred at conversion (see 1Co 15:12–14). This teaching was devastating to the faith of those early believers who succumbed to this Gnostic heresy.

3:1–7 This prophecy describes the sinful attitudes and behaviors that will be manifest in the world from the time of Paul until the last days of this age.

1. *Self-centered.* This self-centered generation openly boasts of their dedication to personal pleasure, rather than to God or family.
2. *Covetous.* A value system that honors money and possessions elevates greed to a virtue in a corrupt and sinful society.
3. *Boastful and proud.* Self-promotion is emulated, boasting is widespread, and pride is no longer despised.
4. *Blasphemous.* Those who habitually use coarse, crude and blasphemous language are tolerated and even admired (see Eze 39:7).
5. *Disobedient.* Widespread disobedience to parents is an accepted practice despite its ban in the Ten Commandments (see Ex 20:12).
6. *Ungrateful and unholy.* An unprecedented lack of gratitude and widespread contempt for righteousness pervades society.

[e]blasphemers, [f]disobedient to parents,
unthankful, unholy,
3 [a]Without natural affection, [a]truce-
breakers, [/]false accusers, [b]incontinent,
fierce, despisers of those that are good,
4 [a]Traitors, heady, highminded, [b]lov-
ers of pleasures more than lovers of God;
5 Having a form of godliness, but [a]de-
nying the power thereof: [b]from such turn
away.
6 For [a]of this sort are they which creep
into houses, and lead captive silly women
laden with sins, led away with divers
lusts,
7 Ever learning, and never able [a]to
come to the knowledge of the truth.
C 8 [a]Now as Jannes and Jambres withstood Moses, so do these also resist the
truth: [b]men of corrupt minds, [c]repro-
bate[/] concerning the faith.
9 But they shall proceed no further: for
their folly shall be manifest unto all *men,*
[a]as theirs also was.

The defence of the faith

10 [a]But [/]thou hast fully known my
doctrine, manner of life, purpose, faith,
longsuffering, charity, patience,
11 Persecutions, afflictions, which
came unto me [a]at Antioch, [b]at Iconium,
[c]at Lystra; what persecutions I endured:
but [d]out of *them* all the Lord delivered me.
12 Yea, and [a]all that will live godly in
Christ Jesus shall suffer persecution.
C 13 [a]But evil men and seducers shall
wax worse and worse, deceiving, and being deceived.

C *2Ti 3:1–5* ◀▶ *2Ti 3:13*
C *2Ti 3:8* ◀▶ *2Ti 4:4*

2 [e]1 Tim. 1:20 [f]Rom. 1:30
3 [a]Rom. 1:31 [b]2 Pet. 3:3 [/]Or, *troublemakers*
4 [a]2 Pet. 2:10 [b]Phil. 3:19
5 [a]1 Tim. 5:8 [b]1 Tim. 6:5
6 [a]Mat. 23:14; Tit. 1:11
7 [a]1 Tim. 2:4
8 [a]Ex. 7:11 [b]1 Tim. 6:5 [c]Rom. 1:28 [/]Or, *of no judgment*
9 [a]Ex. 7:12
10 [a]1 Tim. 4:6 [/]Or, *thou hast been a diligent follower of*
11 [a]Acts 13:45 [b]Acts 14:2 [c]Acts 14:19 [d]Ps. 34:19
12 [a]Ps. 34:19
13 [a]2 Thes. 2:11
14 [a]ch. 1:13
15 [a]John 5:39
16 [a]2 Pet. 1:20 [b]Rom. 15:4
17 [a]1 Tim. 6:11 [b]ch. 2:21 [/]Or, *perfected*
4:1 [a]1 Tim. 5:21 [b]Acts 10:42
2 [a]1 Tim. 5:20; Tit. 1:13 [b]1 Tim. 4:13
3 [a]ch. 3:1 [b]1 Tim. 1:10 [c]ch. 3:6
4 [a]1 Tim. 1:4
5 [a]ch. 1:8 [b]Acts 21:8 [c]Rom. 15:19 [/]Or, *fulfil*
6 [a]Phil. 2:17

14 But [a]continue thou in the things
which thou hast learned and hast been
assured of, knowing of whom thou hast
learned *them;*
15 And that from a child thou hast
known [a]the holy scriptures, which are
able to make thee wise unto salvation
through faith which is in Christ Jesus.
16 [a]All scripture *is* given by inspira- G
tion of God, [b]and *is* profitable for doc- T
trine, for reproof, for correction, for instruction in righteousness:
17 [a]That the man of God may be perfect, [b]thoroughly[/] furnished unto all good
works.

4 I [a]CHARGE *thee* therefore before M
God, and the Lord Jesus Christ, J
[b]who shall judge the quick and the dead
at his appearing and his kingdom;
2 Preach the word; be instant in season, out of season; reprove, [a]rebuke, [b]ex-
hort with all longsuffering and doctrine.
3 [a]For the time will come when they E
will not endure [b]sound doctrine; [c]but af- N
ter their own lusts shall they heap to
themselves teachers, having itching ears;
4 And they shall turn away *their* ears C
from the truth, and [a]shall be turned unto
fables.
5 But watch thou in all things, [a]endure
afflictions, do the work of [b]an evangelist,
[c]make[/] full proof of thy ministry.
6 For [a]I am now ready to be offered,

G *2Ti 1:14* ◀▶ *Heb 2:4*
T *1Ti 4:1* ◀▶ *Heb 3:7*
M *2Ti 2:12* ◀▶ *2Ti 4:8*
J *2Co 5:10* ◀▶ *Heb 9:27*
E *2Ti 3:1–9* ◀▶ *Jas 5:1*
N *1Ti 4:2* ◀▶ *Heb 2:2–3*
C *2Ti 3:13* ◀▶ *Tit 1:16*

---

7. *Sexually perverted.* Public displays of immorality, sexual perversion and indecency are common and readily overlooked by society.
8. *Dishonest behavior.* The breakdown in personal righteousness and the loss of respect for honesty results in false accusers and contract breakers. The growing toleration for cheating on taxes, excessive litigation and white-collar crime shows the open contempt expressed for honest behavior.
9. *Bankrupt values.* Loving pleasure more than loving God. A value system that appears to embrace godly ideas, but has no spiritual center. A society willing to betray itself and its beliefs for worthless pleasure or goods.

Paul warned Timothy to turn away from people in his day that exemplified this sinful lifestyle. Today, we also must turn away from those who profess Christianity but deny the virgin birth, the miracles, prophecies and the resurrection of Jesus while openly endorsing sexual perversion. These are the ones that Paul says are "ever learning, and never able to come to the knowledge of the truth" (3:7).

4:1–4 Paul charges Timothy to preach the word until Jesus returns. We should heed Paul's words to Timothy and reach our world with the gospel message while we still have the chance. Many in the western world have had access to the Scriptures for generations and have rejected its message due to spiritual pride and arrogance. These have turned their ears from Biblical truth in favor of modern cults and religions, fulfilling this prophecy in a tragic way.

and the time of [b]my departure is at hand.

7 [a]I have fought a good fight, I have finished *my* course, I have kept the faith:

8 Henceforth there is laid up for me [a]a crown of righteousness, which the Lord, the righteous judge, shall give me [b]at that day: and not to me only, but unto all them also that love his appearing.

Greetings and benediction

9 Do thy diligence to come shortly unto me:

10 For [a]Demas hath forsaken me, [b]having loved this present world, and is departed unto Thessalonica; Crescens to Galatia, Titus unto Dalmatia.

11 [a]Only [b]Luke is with me. Take [c]Mark, and bring him with thee: for he is profitable to me for the ministry.

12 And [a]Tychicus have I sent to Ephesus.

13 The cloak that I left at Troas with Carpus, when thou comest, bring *with thee,* and the books, *but* especially the parchments.

14 [a]Alexander the coppersmith did me much evil: [b]the Lord reward him according to his works:

C *1Ti 6:14* ◀▶ *Tit 2:13*
M *2Ti 4:1* ◀▶ *2Ti 4:18*

15 Of whom be thou ware also; for he hath greatly withstood [1]our words.

16 At my first answer no man stood with me, but all *men* forsook me: [a]*I pray God* that it may not be laid to their charge.

17 [a]Notwithstanding the Lord stood with me, and strengthened me; [b]that by me the preaching might be fully known, and *that* all the Gentiles might hear: and I was delivered [c]out of the mouth of the lion.

18 [a]And the Lord shall deliver me from every evil work, and will preserve *me* unto his heavenly kingdom: [b]to whom *be* glory for ever and ever. Amen.

19 Salute [a]Prisca and Aquila, and the household of Onesiphorus.

20 [a]Erastus abode at Corinth: but [b]Trophimus have I left at Miletum sick.

21 [a]Do thy diligence to come before winter. Eubulus greeteth thee, and Pudens, and Linus, and Claudia, and all the brethren.

22 [a]The Lord Jesus Christ *be* with thy spirit. Grace *be* with you. Amen.

M *2Ti 4:8* ◀▶ *Heb 1:8*
V *2Co 2:14* ◀▶ *Heb 11:32–35*

6 [b]Phil. 1:23; 2 Pet. 1:14
7 [a]Phil. 3:14; Heb. 12:1
8 [a]Jas. 1:12 [b]ch. 1:12
10 [a]Col. 4:14 [b]1 John 2:15
11 [a]ch. 1:15 [b]Col. 4:14 [c]Acts 12:25
12 [a]Acts 20:4; Eph. 6:21
14 [a]Acts 19:33 [b]2 Sam. 3:39; Ps. 28:4
15 [1]Or, *our preachings*
16 [a]Acts 7:60
17 [a]Acts 23:11 [b]Acts 9:15 [c]Ps. 22:21
18 [a]Ps. 121:7 [b]Rom. 11:36; Gal. 1:5; Heb. 13:21
19 [a]Acts 18:2; Rom. 16:3
20 [a]Acts 19:22; Rom. 16:23 [b]Acts 20:4
21 [a]ver. 9
22 [a]Gal. 6:18; Philem. 25

4:8 As Paul contemplates his approaching martyrdom in Rome, he considers what lies ahead for the early church. Paul refers to that future day at the coming judgment seat of Christ (see Ro 14:10) when every believer who longs for Christ's return will win "a crown of righteousness." Paul's prophecy confirms the importance of the doctrine of the second coming and reveals that God will reward all who both believe and long for Christ's return with a glorious crown, an honor that will be theirs forever in the new Jerusalem.

Titus

Author: Paul

Theme: The need for order in the church

Date of Writing: c. A.D. 63–65

Outline of Titus

I. Introduction (1:1–4)
II. Duties of Elders and Deacons (1:5–16)
III. Pastoral Responsibilities (2:1—3:11)
IV. Conclusion (3:12–15)

PAUL WROTE THIS pastoral letter to his associate Titus shortly after Paul had left him in charge of the believers on the island of Crete. Titus had been Paul's trusted fellow worker for many years (see 2Co 7—8), sharing Paul's love for the believers in Corinth and assisting in his ministry throughout Asia. Though Titus was a Greek convert, he accompanied Paul and Barnabas to the Jerusalem council (see Gal 2:1–3). After Paul's first imprisonment in Rome, Titus accompanied the apostle on his missionary journeys, working with him closely on the island of Crete. Paul determined to continue his journey, but appointed Titus to stay behind and finish establishing the church. Paul may have been in Corinth when he wrote this instructional letter to Titus about church order and government.

Because the young church in Crete was disorganized and uninformed, the emphasis of this letter is similar to Paul's words in 1 Timothy. Many of the believers on Crete needed additional instruction and admonition concerning the necessity of order in the church. Paul carefully describes the qualifications for elders in the church, stresses the need for ethical behavior, strongly warns against false teachers and emphasizes the need for sound, doctrinal teaching. Paul repeatedly urges the believers to be obedient and strive to do good works. Outlining the essential elements of Christianity, this letter to Titus forms the clearest declaration in all of his writings of Paul's statement of faith.

1 PAUL, A servant of God, and an apostle of Jesus Christ, according to the faith of God's elect, and [a]the acknowledging of the truth [b]which is after godliness;

2 [a]In[1] hope of eternal life, which God, [b]that cannot lie, promised [c]before the world began;

3 [a]But hath in due times manifested his word through preaching, [b]which is committed unto me according to the commandment of God our Saviour;

4 To [a]Titus, *mine* own son after the common faith: [b]Grace, mercy, *and* peace, from God the Father and the Lord Jesus Christ our Saviour.

Qualifications for elders

5 For this cause left I thee in Crete, that thou shouldest [a]set in order the things that are [1]wanting, and ordain elders in every city, as I had appointed thee:

6 [a]If any be blameless, the husband of one wife, [b]having faithful children not accused of riot or unruly.

7 For a bishop must be blameless, as [a]the steward of God; not self-willed, not soon angry, [b]not given to wine, no striker, not given to filthy lucre;

8 [a]But a lover of hospitality, a lover of [1]good men, sober, just, holy, temperate;

9 Holding fast the faithful word [1]as he hath been taught, that he may be able [a]by sound doctrine both to exhort and to convince the gainsayers.

Dealing with false teachers

10 For [a]there are many unruly and vain talkers and deceivers, [b]specially they of the circumcision:

11 Whose mouths must be stopped, [a]who subvert whole houses, teaching things which they ought not, [b]for filthy lucre's sake.

12 [a]One of themselves, *even* a prophet of their own, said, The Cretians *are* always liars, evil beasts, slow bellies.

13 This witness is true. [a]Wherefore rebuke them sharply, that they may be [b]sound in the faith;

14 [a]Not giving heed to Jewish fables, and [b]commandments of men, that turn from the truth.

15 [a]Unto the pure all things *are* pure: but unto them that are defiled and unbelieving *is* nothing pure; but even their mind and conscience is defiled.

16 They profess that they know God; but [a]in works they deny *him,* being abominable, and disobedient, [b]and unto every good work [1]reprobate. C S

Christian doctrine and conduct

2 BUT SPEAK thou the things which become [a]sound doctrine:

2 That the aged men be [1]sober, grave, temperate, sound in faith, in charity, in patience.

3 The aged women likewise, that *they be* in behaviour as becometh [1]holiness, not [2]false accusers, not given to much wine, teachers of good things;

4 That they may teach the young women to be [1]sober, to love their husbands, to love their children,

5 *To be* discreet, chaste, keepers at home, good, [a]obedient to their own husbands, [b]that the word of God be not blasphemed.

6 Young men likewise exhort to be [1]sober minded.

7 [a]In all things showing thyself a pattern of good works: in doctrine *showing* uncorruptness, gravity, [b]sincerity,

8 [a]Sound speech, that cannot be condemned; [b]that he that is of the contrary part may be ashamed, having no evil thing to say of you.

9 *Exhort* [a]servants to be obedient unto their own masters, *and* to please *them* well [b]in all *things;* not [1]answering again;

10 Not purloining, but showing all good fidelity; [a]that they may adorn the doctrine of God our Saviour in all things.

11 For [a]the grace of God [1]that bringeth salvation [b]hath appeared to all men, K L

12 Teaching us [a]that, denying ungodliness [b]and worldly lusts, we should live soberly, righteously, and godly, in this present world; S W

C *2Ti 4:4* ◀▶ *Tit 3:3*
S *2Ti 2:19* ◀▶ *Tit 2:11–14*
K *2Ti 1:12* ◀▶ *Heb 2:18*
L *2Ti 1:9* ◀▶ *Tit 3:3–5*
S *Tit 1:16* ◀▶ *Tit 3:8*
W *1Ti 4:10* ◀▶ *Heb 2:9*

1:1 [a]2 Tim. 2:25 [b]1 Tim. 3:16
2 [a]2 Tim. 1:1 [b]2 Tim. 2:13 [c]Rom. 16:25 [1]Or, *For*
3 [a]2 Tim. 1:10 [b]1 Thes. 2:4
4 [a]2 Cor. 2:13 [b]Eph. 1:2
5 [a]1 Cor. 11:34 [1]Or, *left undone*
6 [a]1 Tim. 3:2 [b]1 Tim. 3:4
7 [a]Mat. 24:45 [b]Lev. 10:9
8 [a]1 Tim. 3:2 [1]Or, *good things*
9 [a]1 Tim. 1:10 [1]Or, *in teaching*
10 [a]1 Tim. 1:6 [b]Acts 15:1
11 [a]2 Tim. 3:6 [b]1 Tim. 6:5
12 [a]Acts 17:28
13 [a]2 Cor. 13:10 [b]ch. 2:2
14 [a]1 Tim. 1:4 [b]Is. 29:13
15 [a]1 Cor. 6:12
16 [a]2 Tim. 3:5 [b]Rom. 1:28 [1]Or, *void of judgment*
2:1 [a]1 Tim. 1:10
2 [1]Or, *vigilant*
3 [1]Or, *holy women* [2]Or, *troublemakers*
4 [1]Or, *wise*
5 [a]1 Cor. 14:34 [b]Rom. 2:24
6 [1]Or, *discreet*
7 [a]1 Tim. 4:12 [b]Eph. 6:24
8 [a]1 Tim. 6:3 [b]Neh. 5:9
9 [a]Eph. 6:5 [b]Eph. 5:24 [1]Or, *gainsaying*
10 [a]Mat. 5:16
11 [a]Rom. 5:15 [b]Luke 3:6 [1]Or, *that bringeth salvation to all men, hath appeared*
12 [a]Luke 1:75 [b]1 Pet. 4:2

C 13 [a]Looking for that blessed [b]hope, and the glorious [c]appearing of the great God and our Saviour Jesus Christ;

D 14 [a]Who gave himself for us, that he might redeem us from all iniquity, [b]and purify unto himself [c]a peculiar people, [d]zealous of good works.

15 These things speak, and [a]exhort, and rebuke with all authority. Let no man despise thee.

Faith and works

3 PUT THEM in mind [a]to be subject to principalities and powers, to obey magistrates, [b]to be ready to every good work,

2 [a]To speak evil of no man, [b]to be no brawlers, *but* [c]gentle, showing all [d]meekness unto all men.

C L 3 For [a]we ourselves also were sometimes foolish, disobedient, deceived, serving divers lusts and pleasures, living in malice and envy, hateful, *and* hating one another.

4 But after that [a]the kindness and [/]love of [b]God our Saviour toward man appeared,

B E R G 5 [a]Not by works of righteousness which we have done, but according to his mercy he saved us, by [b]the washing of regeneration, and renewing of the Holy Ghost;

C *2Ti 4:8* ◀ ▶ *Heb 9:26*
D *1Ti 2:5–6* ◀ ▶ *Heb 1:3*
C *Tit 1:16* ◀ ▶ *Heb 2:15*
L *Tit 2:11* ◀ ▶ *Heb 1:3*
B *Eph 5:18* ◀ ▶ *Heb 1:9*
E *2Ti 1:14* ◀ ▶ *Heb 2:4* **R** *Eph 2:18* ◀
G *2Ti 1:9* ◀ ▶ *Heb 11:6*

13 [a]1 Cor. 1:7 [b]Acts 24:15 [c]Col. 3:4
14 [a]Gal. 1:4 [b]Heb. 9:14 [c]Ex. 15:16 [d]Eph. 2:10
15 [a]2 Tim. 4:2
3:1 [a]1 Pet. 2:13 [b]Col. 1:10; Heb. 13:21
2 [a]Eph. 4:31 [b]2 Tim. 2:24 [c]Phil. 4:5 [d]Eph. 4:2; Col. 3:12
3 [a]1 Cor. 6:11; 1 Pet. 4:3
4 [a]ch. 2:11 [b]1 Tim. 2:3 [/]Or, *pity*
5 [a]Rom. 3:20; 2 Tim. 1:9 [b]John 3:3; 1 Pet. 3:21
6 [a]Ezek. 36:25; Joel 2:28 [/]Gk. *richly*
7 [a]Rom. 3:24 [b]Rom. 8:23 [c]ch. 1:2
8 [a]1 Tim. 1:15 [b]ch. 2:14
9 [a]1 Tim. 1:4 [b]2 Tim. 2:14
10 [a]2 Cor. 13:2 [b]Mat. 18:17
11 [a]Acts 13:46
12 [a]Acts 20:4
13 [a]Acts 18:24
14 [a]ver. 8 [b]Rom. 15:28; Phil. 1:11 [/]Or, *profess honest trades*

6 [a]Which he shed on us [/]abundantly through Jesus Christ our Saviour;

7 [a]That being justified by his grace, [b]we should be made heirs [c]according to the hope of eternal life.

8 [a]*This is* a faithful saying, and these things I will that thou affirm constantly, that they which have believed in God might be careful [b]to maintain good works. These things are good and profitable unto men. S

9 But [a]avoid foolish questions, and genealogies, and contentions, and strivings about the law; [b]for they are unprofitable and vain.

10 A man that is an heretic [a]after the first and second admonition [b]reject;

11 Knowing that he that is such is subverted, and sinneth, [a]being condemned of himself.

Closing instruction, benediction

12 When I shall send Artemas unto thee, or [a]Tychicus, be diligent to come unto me to Nicopolis: for I have determined there to winter.

13 Bring Zenas the lawyer and [a]Apollos on their journey diligently, that nothing be wanting unto them.

14 And let ours also learn [a]to [/]maintain good works for necessary uses, that they be [b]not unfruitful.

15 All that are with me salute thee. Greet them that love us in the faith. Grace *be* with you all. Amen.

S *Tit 2:11–14* ◀ ▶ *Heb 2:1–3*

2:13–14 Paul urges believers to be looking for the hope of the rapture and Christ's glorious second coming (see 1Th 4:16–17). Note also the mention of Jesus Christ as "the great God" (2:13), a clear affirmation of Christ's divinity.

Philemon

Author: Paul

Theme: Showing Christian love and forgiveness

Date of Writing: c. A.D. 60–62

Outline of Philemon

I. Greetings (1–3)
II. Paul's Concern and Love (4–7)
III. Paul's Intercession for Onesimus (8–21)
IV. Farewell (22–25)

During Paul's first imprisonment in Rome, Paul became associated with a runaway slave from Colosse named Onesimus. Under Paul's instruction Onesimus became a believer. Yet as a slave, Onesimus was the legal property of his owner, Philemon. Paul wrote this short letter from his prison cell, addressing it to Philemon, Apphia (who may have been Philemon's wife), Archippus (who may have been their son) and to the church which held meetings in Philemon's household, encouraging them to show Christian love and charity to Onesimus.

Slavery was a common practice in the Roman empire. Up to 50 percent of the population of some cities lived as slaves. Many slaves were respected stewards of their households. Yet this epistle does not endorse slavery as some critics have charged. With clear words and strong feelings Paul simply deals with the spiritual and moral issues involved in this incident between two believers. Onesimus had been a trusted slave who stole some of Philemon's goods when he ran away. Paul sent Onesimus back to his master with this letter, emphasizing that Christian conduct should permeate their relationship. Pleading with Philemon for forgiveness for Onesimus's sins, Paul calls upon Onesimus and Philemon to reconcile as brothers in the Lord.

1 PAUL, [a]A prisoner of Jesus Christ,
and Timothy *our* brother, unto Philemon
our dearly beloved, [b]and fellowlabourer,
2 And to *our* beloved Apphia, and [a]Ar-
chippus [b]our fellowsoldier, and to [c]the
church in thy house:
3 [a]Grace to you, and peace, from God
our Father and the Lord Jesus Christ.

Thanksgiving and prayer

4 [a]I thank my God, making mention of
thee always in my prayers,
5 [a]Hearing of thy love and faith, which
thou hast toward the Lord Jesus, and toward all saints;
T 6 That the communication of thy faith
may become effectual [a]by the acknowledging of every good thing which is in
you in Christ Jesus.
7 For we have great joy and consolation in thy love, because the bowels of
the saints [a]are refreshed by thee,
brother.

Appeal for Onesimus

8 Wherefore, [a]though I might be much
bold in Christ to enjoin thee that which is
convenient,
9 Yet for love's sake I rather beseech
thee, being such an one as Paul the aged,
[a]and now also a prisoner of Jesus Christ.
10 I beseech thee for my son [a]Onesi-
mus, [b]whom I have begotten in my
bonds:
11 Which in time past was to thee unprofitable, but now profitable to thee and
to me:
12 Whom I have sent again: thou
therefore receive him, that is, mine own
bowels:
13 Whom I would have retained with
me, [a]that in thy stead he might have
ministered unto me in the bonds of the
gospel:
14 But without thy mind would I do
nothing; [a]that thy benefit should not be
as it were of necessity, but willingly.
15 [a]For perhaps he therefore departed
for a season, that thou shouldest receive
him for ever;
16 Not now as a servant, but above a
servant, [a]a brother beloved, specially to
me, but how much more unto thee,
[b]both in the flesh, and in the Lord?
17 If thou count me therefore [a]a partner, receive him as myself.
18 If he hath wronged thee, or oweth
thee aught, put that on mine account;
19 I Paul have written *it* with mine
own hand, I will repay *it:* albeit I do not
say to thee how thou owest unto me even
thine own self besides.
20 Yea, brother, let me have joy of
thee in the Lord: [a]refresh my bowels in
the Lord.
21 [a]Having confidence in thy obedience I wrote unto thee, knowing that
thou wilt also do more than I say.
22 But withal prepare me also a lodging: for [a]I trust that [b]through your
prayers I shall be given unto you.
23 There salute thee [a]Epaphras, my
fellowprisoner in Christ Jesus;
24 [a]Marcus, [b]Aristarchus, [c]Demas,
[d]Lucas, my fellowlabourers.
25 [a]The grace of our Lord Jesus Christ
be with your spirit. Amen.

1:1 [a]ver. 9; Eph. 3:1 & 4:1; 2 Tim. 1:8 [b]Phil. 2:25
2 [a]Col. 4:17 [b]Phil. 2:25 [c]Rom. 16:5; 1 Cor. 16:19
3 [a]Eph. 1:2
4 [a]Eph. 1:16; 1 Thes. 1:2; 2 Thes. 1:3
5 [a]Eph. 1:15; Col. 1:4
6 [a]Phil. 1:9
7 [a]ver. 20; 2 Cor. 7:13; 2 Tim. 1:16
8 [a]1 Thes. 2:6
9 [a]ver. 1
10 [a]Col. 4:9 [b]1 Cor. 4:15; Gal. 4:19
13 [a]1 Cor. 16:17; Phil. 2:30
14 [a]2 Cor. 9:7
15 [a]Gen. 45:5,8
16 [a]Mat. 23:8; 1 Tim. 6:2 [b]Col. 3:22
17 [a]2 Cor. 8:23
20 [a]ver. 7
21 [a]2 Cor. 7:16
22 [a]Phil. 1:25 & 2:24 [b]2 Cor. 1:11
23 [a]Col. 1:7 & 4:12
24 [a]Acts 12:12,25 [b]Acts 19:29 & 27:2; Col. 4:10 [c]Col. 4:14 [d]2 Tim. 4:11
25 [a]2 Tim. 4:22

T *2Ti 2:12* ◀▶ *Heb 3:13*

Hebrews

Author: Uncertain; possibly Paul, Barnabas, Luke or Apollos

Theme: The priesthood of Jesus is superior to all others

Date of Writing: c. A.D. 60–70

Outline of Hebrews

I. A Superior Spokesman for God (1:1—4:13)
II. A Superior Intercessor and Priest (4:14—7:28)
III. A Superior Covenant and Offering (8:1—10:39)
IV. A Practical Appeal (11:1—13:25)

THOUGH THE BOOK of Hebrews does not name its author, early church scholars attributed this book to Paul. Later scholars suggested that Barnabas or Apollos wrote Hebrews. Still other scholars have suggested that this book came from the pen of Luke. Though its authorship is uncertain, the language in the book of Hebrews identifies the author as a mature, Jewish Christian who was well versed in the OT, a friend of Timothy and well known to the original recipients of this letter. The author possessed keen literary abilities and followed a style of writing that is closer to classical Greek than to the common Greek of the other NT books. The external and internal textual evidence suggests that this book was composed just prior to the destruction of Jerusalem in A.D. 70.

During the years surrounding the writing of the book of Hebrews, fear of persecution was a grim reality for the church in Rome. Directing his words to the Jewish Christians in both Palestine and throughout the Roman empire, the author of Hebrews encourages his readers to "hold fast" (3:6) despite the opposition and to press on "unto perfection" (6:1). In addition, Hebrews warns new believers against reverting to the legalism of the Law and stresses the utter preeminence of Jesus Christ as the only hope of salvation. Frequent warnings are given to believers against rejecting the great offer of salvation provided by Christ's completed work of atonement on the cross.

Jewish believers were also reminded that their OT religious system of sacrifices and regulations was no longer necessary. Hebrews presents Jesus as the culmination of God's revelation through the OT prophets, stating that Jesus Christ is superior in every respect to the Law. Forgiveness and salvation has been granted through the sacrificial death and resurrection of Jesus the Messiah. Hebrews also stresses the priesthood of Jesus Christ. In fact, more than twenty names and titles appear in reference to Christ in the book of Hebrews, with the office of Christ as our Priest-king receiving special consideration.

The Son is God's revelation

1 GOD, WHO at sundry times and [a]in divers manners spake in time past unto the fathers by the prophets,

V 2 Hath [a]in these last days [b]spoken unto us by *his* Son, [c]whom he hath appointed heir of all things, [d]by whom also he made the worlds;

D
L 3 [a]Who being the brightness of *his* glory, and the express image of his person, and [b]upholding all things by the word of his power, [c]when he had by himself purged our sins, [d]sat down on the right hand of the Majesty on high;

4 Being made so much better than the angels, as [a]he hath by inheritance obtained a more excellent name than they.

5 For unto which of the angels said he at any time, [a]Thou art my Son, this day have I begotten thee? And again, [b]I will be to him a Father, and he shall be to me a Son?

6 [/]And again, when he bringeth in [a]the first begotten into the world, he saith, [b]And let all the angels of God worship him.

7 And [/]of the angels he saith, [a]Who maketh his angels spirits, and his ministers a flame of fire.

M 8 But unto the Son *he saith,* [a]Thy throne, O God, *is* for ever and ever: a sceptre of [/]righteousness *is* the sceptre of thy kingdom.

B 9 Thou hast loved righteousness, and
F hated iniquity; therefore God, *even* thy
J God, [a]hath anointed thee with the oil of gladness above thy fellows.

N 10 And, [a]Thou, Lord, in the beginning hast laid the foundation of the earth; and the heavens are the works of thine hands:

11 [a]They shall perish; but thou remainest; and they all shall wax old as doth a garment;

12 And as a vesture shalt thou fold them up, and they shall be changed: but thou art the same, and thy years shall not fail.

13 But to which of the angels said he M
at any time, [a]Sit on my right hand, until I V
make thine enemies thy footstool?

14 [a]Are they not all ministering spir- L
its, sent forth to minister for them who shall be [b]heirs of salvation?

The role of Christ in salvation

2 THEREFORE WE ought to give the S
more earnest heed to the things which we have heard, lest at any time we should [/]let *them* slip.

2 For if the word [a]spoken by angels H
was stedfast, and [b]every transgression N
and disobedience received a just recompence of reward;

3 [a]How shall we escape, if we neglect so great salvation; [b]which at the first began to be spoken by the Lord, and was [c]confirmed unto us by them that heard *him;*

4 [a]God also bearing *them* witness, B
[b]both with signs and wonders, and with E
divers miracles, and [c]gifts[/] of the Holy G
Ghost, [d]according to his own will? H

5 For unto the angels hath he not put M
M

V *1Ti 6:15* ◀ ▶ *Heb 1:13*
D *Tit 2:14* ◀ ▶ *Heb 2:9*
L *Tit 3:3–5* ◀ ▶ *Heb 5:2*
M *2Ti 4:18* ◀ ▶ *Heb 1:13*
B *Tit 3:5–6* ◀ ▶ *Heb 2:4*
F *2Ti 1:7* ◀ ▶ *1Pe 1:22* **J** *1Th 1:6* ◀
N *Mt 5:5* ◀ ▶ *Heb 12:26–28*

M *Heb 1:8* ◀ ▶ *Heb 2:5–8*
V *Heb 1:2* ◀ ▶ *Rev 11:15*
L *1Ti 6:17* ◀ ▶ *Heb 13:5–6*
S *Tit 3:8* ◀ ▶ *Heb 3:6*
H *1Ti 6:9* ◀ ▶ *Heb 6:2*
N *2Ti 4:3–4* ◀ ▶ *Heb 3:7–9*
B *Heb 1:9* ◀ ▶ *Heb 10:14–15*
E *Tit 3:5–6* ◀ ▶ *Heb 3:7*
G *2Ti 3:16* ◀ ▶ *1Pe 4:10–11*
H *2Co 3:6* ◀ ▶ *1Pe 3:18*
M *2Ti 1:7* ◀ ▶ *2Pe 1:21*
M *Heb 1:13* ◀ ▶ *Heb 7:2*

1:1 [a]Num. 12:6
2 [a]Eph. 1:10 [b]John 1:17 [c]Ps. 2:8 [d]John 1:3
3 [a]John 1:14 [b]John 1:4; Rev. 4:11 [c]ch. 7:27 [d]Ps. 110:1
4 [a]Phil. 2:9,10
5 [a]Ps. 2:7; Acts 13:33 [b]2 Sam. 7:14
6 [a]Rom. 8:29 [b]Deut. 32:43; LXX [/]Or, *When he bringeth again*
7 [a]Ps. 104:4 [/]Gk. *unto*
8 [a]Ps. 45:6,7 [/]Gk. *rightness,* or, *straightness*
9 [a]Is. 61:1
10 [a]Ps. 102:25
11 [a]Is. 34:4
13 [a]Ps. 110:1; Luke 20:42
14 [a]Ps. 103:20; Mat. 18:10 [b]Rom. 8:17
2:1 [/]Gk. *run out as leaking vessels*
2 [a]Deut. 33:2; Acts 7:53 [b]Num. 15:30
3 [a]ch. 10:28 [b]Mat. 4:17 [c]Luke 1:2
4 [a]Mark 16:20 [b]Acts 2:22 [c]1 Cor. 12:4,7,11 [d]Eph. 1:5,9 [/]Or, *distributions*

1:2 This verse affirms that Jesus Christ made the world (see Jn 1:3; Col 1:16), and that, having performed the work of redemption, he was exalted to the position of the firstborn heir of God.

1:8 This reference to the ancient prophecy of Jacob (see Ge 49:10) confirms that Jesus of Nazareth is the Messiah, the King from the tribe of Judah. This prophetic fulfillment is verified in the genealogical records of both Matthew and Luke.

1:10–13 This passage is a restatement of Ps 102:25–27 and confirms Christ's hand as God in creation. Yet while the earth and heavens will ultimately change and perish, God remains unchangeable.

2:5–8 This passage clearly declares that Jesus Christ is the Son of God and that he is the fulfillment of King David's prophecy in Ps 8:4–6 (see 1Co 15:27; Eph 1:22).

in subjection [a]the world to come, whereof we speak.

6 But one in a certain place testified, saying, [a]What is man, that thou art mindful of him? or the son of man, that thou visitest him?

7 Thou madest him [/]a little lower than the angels; thou crownedst him with glory and honour, and didst set him over the works of thy hands:

8 [a]Thou hast put all things in subjection under his feet. For in that he put all in subjection under him, he left nothing *that is* not put under him. But now [b]we see not yet all things put under him.

D W 9 But we see Jesus, [a]who was made a little lower than the angels [/]for the suffering of death, [b]crowned with glory and honour; that he by the grace of God should taste death [c]for every man.

Christ the high priest

10 [a]For it became him, [b]for whom *are* all things, and by whom *are* all things, in bringing many sons unto glory, to make [c]the captain of their salvation [d]perfect through sufferings.

11 For [a]both he that sanctifieth and they who are sanctified [b]*are* all of one: for which cause [c]he is not ashamed to call them brethren,

12 Saying, [a]I will declare thy name unto my brethren, in the midst of the church will I sing praise unto thee.

13 And again, [a]I will put my trust in him. And again, [b]Behold I and the children [c]which God hath given me.

D 14 Forasmuch then as the children are partakers of flesh and blood, he [a]also himself likewise took part of the same; [b]that through death he might destroy him that had the power of death, that is, the devil;

C 15 And deliver them who [a]through fear of death were all their lifetime subject to bondage.

16 For verily [/]he took not on *him the nature of* angels; but he took on *him* the seed of Abraham.

17 Wherefore in all things it behooved him [a]to be made like unto *his* brethren, that he might be [b]a merciful and faithful high priest in things *pertaining* to God, to make reconciliation for the sins of the people.

18 [a]For in that he himself hath suffered being tempted, he is able to succour them that are tempted. K

Christ superior to Moses

3 WHEREFORE, HOLY brethren, partakers of [a]the heavenly calling, consider [b]the Apostle and High Priest of our profession, Christ Jesus;

2 Who was faithful to him that [/]appointed him, as also [a]Moses *was faithful* in all his house.

3 For this *man* was counted worthy of more glory than Moses, inasmuch as [a]he who hath builded the house hath more honour than the house.

4 For every house is builded by some *man;* but [a]he that built all things *is* God.

5 [a]And Moses verily *was* faithful in all his house, as [b]a servant, [c]for a testimony of those things which were to be spoken after;

6 But Christ as [a]a son over his own house; [b]whose house are we, [c]if we hold fast the confidence and the rejoicing of the hope firm unto the end. S

The disobedient generation

7 Wherefore (as [a]the Holy Ghost saith, E
[b]Today if ye will hear his voice, T
8 Harden not your hearts, as in the N
provocation, in the day of temptation in the wilderness:

9 When your fathers tempted me, proved me, and saw my works forty years.

10 Wherefore I was grieved with that C
generation, and said, They do always err in *their* heart; and they have not known my ways.

11 So I sware in my wrath, [/]They shall not enter into my rest.)

12 Take heed, brethren, lest there be S
in any of you an evil heart of unbelief, in departing from the living God.

13 But exhort one another daily, while T

5 [a]2 Pet. 3:13
6 [a]Job 7:17
7 [/]*Or, a little while inferior to*
8 [a]Mat. 28:18; Eph. 1:22 [b]1 Cor. 15:25
9 [a]Phil. 2:7-9 [b]Acts 2:33 [c]John 3:16; 2 Cor. 5:15; 1 John 2:2; Rev. 5:9 [/]*Or, by*
10 [a]Luke 24:46 [b]Rom. 11:36 [c]Acts 5:31 [d]Luke 13:32
11 [a]ch. 10:10 [b]Acts 17:26 [c]Mat. 28:10; John 20:17
12 [a]Ps. 22:22
13 [a]Ps. 18:2; Is. 12:2 [b]Is. 8:18 [c]John 10:29
14 [a]John 1:14; Phil. 2:7 [b]1 Cor. 15:54; Col. 2:15
15 [a]Luke 1:74; 2 Tim. 1:7
16 [/]Gk. *he taketh not hold of angels, but of the seed of Abraham he taketh hold*
17 [a]Phil. 2:7 [b]ch. 4:15
18 [a]ch. 4:15,16
3:1 [a]Rom. 1:7; 1 Cor. 1:2; Phil. 3:14; 2 Pet. 1:10 [b]Rom. 15:8
2 [a]Num. 12:7 [/]Gk. *made*
3 [a]Zech. 6:12; Mat. 16:18
4 [a]Eph. 2:10; ch. 1:2
5 [a]ver. 2 [b]Ex. 14:31; Deut. 3:24 [c]Deut. 18:19
6 [a]ch. 1:2 [b]1 Cor. 3:16 [c]Mat. 10:22; Rom. 5:2; Col. 1:23
7 [a]Acts 1:16 [b]Ps. 95:7
11 [/]Gk. *If they shall enter*

D *Heb 1:3* ◀▶ *Heb 2:14–17*
W *Tit 2:11* ◀▶ *Heb 5:9*
D *Heb 2:9* ◀▶ *Heb 7:27*
C *Tit 3:3* ◀▶ *Heb 3:10*

K *Tit 2:11* ◀▶ *Heb 5:9*
S *Heb 2:1–3* ◀▶ *Heb 3:12–14*
E *Heb 2:4* ◀▶ *Heb 9:8*
T *2Ti 3:16* ◀▶ *Heb 6:4*
N *Heb 2:2–3* ◀▶ *Heb 3:15*
C *Heb 2:15* ◀▶ *Jas 1:14–15*
S *Heb 3:6* ◀▶ *Heb 4:11*
T *Phm 6* ◀▶ *Heb 13:15–16*

it is called Today; lest any of you be hardened through the deceitfulness of sin.

14 For we are made partakers of Christ, [a]if we hold the beginning of our confidence stedfast unto the end;

N 15 While it is said, [a]Today if ye will hear his voice, harden not your hearts, as in the provocation.

16 [a]For some, when they had heard, did provoke: howbeit not all that came out of Egypt by Moses.

17 But with whom was he grieved forty years? *was it* not with them that had sinned, [a]whose carcases fell in the wilderness?

F N 18 And [a]to whom sware he that they should not enter into his rest, but to them that believed not?

19 So we see that they could not enter in because of unbelief.

The promise of rest

4 LET [a]US therefore fear, lest, a promise being left *us* of entering into his rest, any of you should seem to come short of it.

2 For unto us was the gospel preached, as well as unto them: but [1]the word preached did not profit them, [2]not being mixed with faith in them that heard *it.*

3 [a]For we which have believed do enter into rest, as he said, [b]As I have sworn in my wrath, if they shall enter into my rest: although the works were finished from the foundation of the world.

4 For he spake in a certain place of the seventh *day* on this wise, [a]And God did rest the seventh day from all his works.

5 And in this *place* again, If they shall enter into my rest.

6 Seeing therefore it remaineth that some must enter therein, [a]and they to whom [1]it was first preached entered not in because of unbelief:

7 Again, he limiteth a certain day, saying in David, Today, after so long a time; as it is said, [a]Today if ye will hear his voice, harden not your hearts.

8 For if [1]Jesus had given them rest, then would he not afterward have spoken of another day.

9 There remaineth therefore a [1]rest to the people of God.

10 For he that is entered into his rest, he also hath ceased from his own works, as God *did* from his.

11 Let us labour therefore to enter into that rest, lest any man fall after the same example of [1]unbelief. S

12 For the word of God *is* [a]quick, and powerful, and [b]sharper than any [c]twoedged sword, piercing even to the dividing asunder of soul and spirit, and of the joints and marrow, and *is* [d]a discerner of the thoughts and intents of the heart. E

13 [a]Neither is there any creature that is not manifest in his sight: but all things *are* naked [b]and opened unto the eyes of him with whom we have to do.

Christ the way to God

14 Seeing then that we have a great high priest, [a]that is passed into the heavens, Jesus the Son of God, [b]let us hold fast *our* profession.

15 For [a]we have not an high priest which cannot be touched with the feeling of our infirmities; but [b]was in all points tempted like as *we are,* [c]*yet* without sin.

16 [a]Let us therefore come boldly unto the throne of grace, that we may obtain mercy, and find grace to help in time of need.

5 FOR EVERY high priest taken from among men [a]is ordained for men in things *pertaining* to God, that he may offer both gifts and sacrifices for sins:

2 Who [1]can have compassion on the ignorant, and on them that are out of the way; for that he himself also is compassed with infirmity. L

3 And [a]by reason hereof he ought, as for the people, so also for himself, to offer for sins.

4 [a]And no man taketh this honour unto himself, but he that is called of God, as [b]*was* Aaron.

5 [a]So also Christ glorified not himself to be made an high priest; but he that said unto him, [b]Thou art my Son, today have I begotten thee.

6 As he saith also in another *place,* [a]Thou *art* a priest for ever after the order of Melchisedec.

7 Who in the days of his flesh, when he had [a]offered up prayers and supplica-

---

14 [a]ver. 6
15 [a]ver. 7
16 [a]Num. 14:2
17 [a]Num. 14:22; Ps. 106:26
18 [a]Num. 14:30
4:1 [a]ch. 12:15
2 [1]Gk. *the word of hearing* [2]Or, *because they were not united by faith to*
3 [a]ch. 3:14 [b]Ps. 95:11
4 [a]Ex. 20:11
6 [a]ch. 3:19 [1]Or, *the gospel was first preached*
7 [a]Ps. 95:7
8 [1]i.e. *Joshua*
9 [1]Or, *keeping of a sabbath*
11 [1]Or, *disobedience*
12 [a]Ps. 147:15; Jer. 23:29 [b]Is. 49:2 [c]Eph. 6:17; Rev. 1:16 [d]1 Cor. 14:25
13 [a]Ps. 90:8 [b]Job 26:6
14 [a]ch. 7:26 [b]ch. 10:23
15 [a]Is. 53:3 [b]Luke 22:28 [c]2 Cor. 5:21; 1 Pet. 2:22
16 [a]Eph. 2:18
5:1 [a]ch. 8:3
2 [1]Or, *can reasonably bear with*
3 [a]Lev. 4:3
4 [a]2 Chr. 26:18; John 3:27 [b]Ex. 28:1
5 [a]John 8:54 [b]Ps. 2:7
6 [a]Ps. 110:4
7 [a]Mat. 26:39; Mark 14:36; John 17:1

N *Heb 3:7–9* ◀ ▶ *Heb 3:18*
F *Php 3:9* ◀ ▶ *Heb 10:38–39*
N *Heb 3:15* ◀ ▶ *Heb 12:25*
S *Heb 3:12–14* ◀ ▶ *Heb 5:9*
E *1Th 2:4* ◀ ▶ *1Jn 3:20*
L *Heb 1:3* ◀ ▶ *Heb 7:25*

tions [b]with strong crying and tears unto
him [c]that was able to save him from
death, and was heard [d]in[1] that he feared;
T 8 [a]Though he were a Son, yet learned
he [b]obedience by the things which he
suffered;
K 9 And being made perfect, he became
S the author of eternal salvation unto all
W them that obey him;
10 Called of God an high priest after
the order of Melchisedec.
11 Of whom [a]we have many things to
say, and hard to be uttered, seeing ye are
[b]dull of hearing.
12 For when for the time ye ought to
be teachers, ye have need that one teach
you again which *be* the first principles of
the oracles of God; and are become such
as have need of [a]milk, and not of strong
meat.
13 For every one that useth milk [1]*is*
unskilful in the word of righteousness: for
he is [a]a babe.
14 But strong meat belongeth to them
that are [1]of full age, *even* those who by
reason [2]of use have their senses exercised [a]to discern both good and evil.

Warning against apostasy

S 6 THEREFORE [a]LEAVING [1]the principles of the doctrine of Christ, let us
go on unto perfection; not laying again
the foundation of repentance [b]from dead
works, and of faith toward God,
F 2 [a]Of the doctrine of baptisms, [b]and of
H laying on of hands, [c]and of resurrection
of the dead, [d]and of eternal judgment.
3 And this will we do, [a]if God permit.
T 4 For [a]*it is* impossible for those [b]who
were once enlightened, and have tasted
of [c]the heavenly gift, and [d]were made
partakers of the Holy Ghost,
5 And have tasted the good word of
God, and the powers of [a]the world to
come,

T *2Co 12:7–10* ◀▶ *Heb 12:5–13*
K *Heb 2:18* ◀▶ *Heb 6:18–19*
S *Heb 4:11* ◀▶ *Heb 6:1*
W *Heb 2:9* ◀▶ *Heb 7:25*
S *Heb 5:9* ◀▶ *Heb 6:8*
F *2Ti 2:17–18* ◀▶ *Heb 11:35*
H *Heb 2:2–3* ◀▶ *Heb 6:7–8*
T *Heb 3:7* ◀▶ *1Pe 1:11*

7 [b]Ps. 22:1; Mat. 27:46 [c]Mat. 26:53; Mark 14:36 [d]Mat. 26:37; Mark 14:33; Luke 22:43; John 12:27 [1]Or, *for his piety*
8 [a]ch. 3:6 [b]Phil. 2:8
11 [a]John 16:12; 2 Pet. 3:16 [b]Mat. 13:15
12 [a]1 Cor. 3:1
13 [a]1 Cor. 13:11; Eph. 4:14; 1 Pet. 2:2 [1]Gk. *hath no experience*
14 [a]Is. 7:15; 1 Cor. 2:14 [1]Or, *perfect;* see 1 Cor. 2:6 [2]Or, *of an habit,* or, *perfection*
6:1 [a]Phil. 3:12-14; ch. 5:12 [b]ch. 9:14 [1]Or, *the word of the beginning of Christ*
2 [a]Acts 19:4,5 [b]Acts 8:14 & 19:6 [c]Acts 17:31 [d]Acts 24:25; Rom. 2:16
3 [a]Acts 18:21
4 [a]Mat. 12:31; ch. 10:26; 2 Pet. 2:20; 1 John 5:16 [b]ch. 10:32 [c]John 4:10 & 6:32; Eph. 2:8 [d]Gal. 3:2,5; ch. 2:4
5 [a]ch. 2:5
6 [a]ch. 10:29
7 [a]Ps. 65:10 [1]Or, *for*
8 [a]Is. 5:6
10 [a]Prov. 14:31; Mat. 10:42 & 25:40; John 13:20 [b]Rom. 3:4; 2 Thes. 1:6,7 [c]1 Thes. 1:3 [d]Rom. 15:25; 2 Cor. 8:4; 2 Tim. 1:18
11 [a]ch. 3:6,14 [b]Col. 2:2
12 [a]ch. 10:36
13 [a]Gen. 22:16,17; Ps. 105:9; Luke 1:73
16 [a]Ex. 22:11
17 [a]ch. 11:9 [b]Rom. 11:29 [1]Gk. *interposed himself by an oath*
18 [a]ch. 12:1
19 [a]Lev. 16:15; ch. 9:7

6 If they shall fall away, to renew them
again unto repentance; [a]seeing they crucify to themselves the Son of God afresh,
and put *him* to an open shame.
7 For the earth which drinketh in the H
rain that cometh oft upon it, and bringeth
forth herbs meet for them [1]by whom it is
dressed, [a]receiveth blessing from God:
8 [a]But that which beareth thorns and S
briers *is* rejected, and *is* nigh unto cursing; whose end *is* to be burned.
9 But, beloved, we are persuaded better things of you, and things that accompany salvation, though we thus speak.
10 [a]For [b]God *is* not unrighteous to for- P
get [c]your work and labour of love, which
ye have shown toward his name, in that
ye have [d]ministered to the saints, and do
minister.
11 And we desire that [a]every one of S
you do show the same diligence [b]to the
full assurance of hope unto the end:
12 That ye be not slothful, but followers of them who through faith and patience [a]inherit the promises.

God's oath unchanging

13 For when God made promise to
Abraham, because he could swear by no
greater, [a]he sware by himself,
14 Saying, Surely blessing I will bless
thee, and multiplying I will multiply thee.
15 And so, after he had patiently endured, he obtained the promise.
16 For men verily swear by the
greater: and [a]an oath for confirmation *is*
to them an end of all strife.
17 Wherein God, willing more abundantly to show unto [a]the heirs of promise
[b]the immutability of his counsel, [1]con-
firmed *it* by an oath:
18 That by two immutable things, in K
which *it was* impossible for God to lie,
we might have a strong consolation, who
have fled for refuge to lay hold upon the
hope [a]set before us:
19 Which *hope* we have as an anchor
of the soul, both sure and stedfast, [a]and
which entereth into that within the veil;

H *Heb 6:2* ◀▶ *Heb 10:12–13*
S *Heb 6:1* ◀▶ *Heb 6:11–12*
P *1Ti 4:8* ◀ **S** *Heb 6:8* ◀▶ *Heb 9:14*
K *Heb 5:9* ◀▶ *Heb 7:25*

6:2 This verse indicates that one of the basic doctrines of the church is the "resurrection of the dead" (see 1Co 15:16–17).

20 [a]Whither the forerunner is for us
entered, *even* Jesus, [b]made an high priest
for ever after the order of Melchisedec.

The priesthood of Melchisedec

7 FOR THIS [a]Melchisedec, king of Salem, priest of the most high God,
who met Abraham returning from the
slaughter of the kings, and blessed him;
M 2 To whom also Abraham gave a tenth
part of all; first being by interpretation
King of righteousness, and after that also
King of Salem, which is, King of peace;
3 Without father, without mother,
[l]without descent, having neither beginning of days, nor end of life; but made
like unto the Son of God; abideth a priest
continually.
4 Now consider how great this man
was, [a]unto whom even the patriarch
Abraham gave the tenth of the spoils.
5 And verily [a]they that are of the sons
of Levi, who receive the office of the
priesthood, have a commandment to take
tithes of the people according to the law,
that is, of their brethren, though they
come out of the loins of Abraham:
6 But he whose [l]descent is not
counted from them received tithes of
Abraham, [a]and blessed [b]him that had the
promises.
7 And without all contradiction the
less is blessed of the better.
8 And here men that die receive
tithes; but there he *receiveth them,* [a]of
whom it is witnessed that he liveth.
9 And as I may so say, Levi also, who
receiveth tithes, paid tithes in Abraham.
10 For he was yet in the loins of his
father, when Melchisedec met him.
M 11 [a]If therefore perfection were by the
Levitical priesthood, (for under it the people received the law,) what further need
was there that another priest should rise
after the order of Melchisedec, and not
be called after the order of Aaron?
12 For the priesthood being changed,
there is made of necessity a change also
of the law.
13 For he of whom these things are
spoken pertaineth to another tribe, of
which no man gave attendance at the
altar.
14 For *it is* evident that [a]our Lord
sprang out of Judah; of which tribe Moses
spake nothing concerning priesthood.

Christ's priesthood superior

15 And it is yet far more evident: for M
that after the similitude of Melchisedec
there ariseth another priest,
16 Who is made, not after the law of a
carnal commandment, but after the
power of an endless life.
17 For he testifieth, [a]Thou *art* a priest
for ever after the order of Melchisedec.
18 For there is verily a disannulling of
the commandment going before for [a]the
weakness and unprofitableness thereof.
19 For [a]the law made nothing perfect,
[l]but the bringing in of [b]a better hope *did;*
by the which [c]we draw nigh unto God.
20 And inasmuch as not without an M
oath *he was made priest:*
21 (For those priests were made [l]with-
out an oath; but this with an oath by him
that said unto him, [a]The Lord sware and
will not repent, Thou *art* a priest for ever
after the order of Melchisedec:)
22 By so much [a]was Jesus made a
surety of a better testament.
23 And they truly were many priests,
because they were not suffered to continue by reason of death:
24 But this *man,* because he contin-

20 [a]ch. 4:14 & 8:1 & 9:24 [b]ch. 3:1 & 5:6,10 & 7:17
7:1 [a]Gen. 14:18
3 [l]Gk. *without pedigree*
4 [a]Gen. 14:20
5 [a]Num. 18:21,26
6 [a]Gen. 14:19 [b]Rom. 4:13 [l]Or, *pedigree*
8 [a]ch. 5:6 & 6:20
11 [a]ver. 18,19; Gal. 2:21; ch. 8:7
14 [a]Is. 11:1; Mat. 1:3; Luke 3:33; Rom. 1:3; Rev. 5:5
17 [a]Ps. 110:4; ch. 6:20
18 [a]Rom. 8:3; Gal. 4:9
19 [a]Acts 13:39; Rom. 3:20,21,28 [b]ch. 6:18 [c]Rom. 5:2; Eph. 2:18; ch. 4:16 [l]Or, *but it was the bringing in;* see Gal. 3:24
21 [a]Ps. 110:4 [l]Or, *without swearing of an oath*
22 [a]ch. 8:6

M *Heb 2:5–8* ◀▶ *Heb 7:11*
M *Heb 7:2* ◀▶ *Heb 7:15–17*
M *Heb 7:11* ◀▶ *Heb 7:20–21*
M *Heb 7:15–17* ◀▶ *Heb 10:13*

7:2 This prophetic reference describes Abram's honoring of Melchizedek (see Ge 14:17–20). Melchizedek was a "King of Salem" (Ge 14:18) and stands prophetically as a type of Christ is his role in the last days as "King of righteousness," the "King of peace" and "a priest for ever after the order of Melchizedek" (Ps 110:4).

7:11 The OT law, subject to the rule of the Levitical priesthood under Aaron, would be replaced with a better priesthood when "another priest should rise after the order of Melchisedec." This priest is clearly Jesus Christ the Messiah, who would bring salvation to all those who would follow him.

7:14–17 This passage clearly indicates that Jesus Christ, "our Lord" (7:14) fulfills the prophecy of King David that indicated the Messiah would be "a priest for ever after the order of Melchizedek" (Ps 110:4).

7:20–21 This passage is a reaffirmation that Jesus Christ is truly the fulfillment of King David's prophecy (see Ps 110:4).

ueth ever, hath [1]an unchangeable priesthood.

K 25 Wherefore he is able also to save
L them [1]to the uttermost that come unto
W God by him, seeing he ever liveth [a]to
make intercession for them.

26 For such an high priest became us, [a]*who is* holy, harmless, undefiled, separate from sinners, [b]and made higher than the heavens;

D 27 Who needeth not daily, as those
high priests, to offer up sacrifice, [a]first for
his own sins, [b]and then for the people's:
for [c]this he did once, when he offered up
himself.

28 For the law maketh [a]men high priests which have infirmity; but the word of the oath, which was since the law, *maketh* the Son, [b]who is [1]consecrated for evermore.

Superiority of the new covenant

8 NOW OF the things which we have spoken *this is* the sum: We have such an high priest, [a]who is set on the right hand of the throne of the Majesty in the heavens;

2 A minister [1]of [a]the sanctuary, and of [b]the true tabernacle, which the Lord pitched, and not man.

3 For [a]every high priest is ordained to offer gifts and sacrifices: wherefore [b]*it is* of necessity that this man have somewhat also to offer.

4 For if he were on earth, he should not be a priest, seeing that [1]there are priests that offer gifts according to the law:

5 Who serve unto the example and [a]shadow of heavenly things, as Moses

K *Heb 6:18–19* ◀▶ *Heb 8:10–12*
L *Heb 5:2* ◀▶ *Heb 8:12*
W *Heb 5:9* ◀▶ *2Pe 3:9*
D *Heb 2:14–17* ◀▶ *Heb 9:7*

24 [1]Or, *which passeth not from one to another*
25 [a]Rom. 8:34; 1 Tim. 2:5; 1 John 2:1 [1]Or, *evermore*
26 [a]ch. 4:15 [b]Eph. 1:20 & 4:10
27 [a]Lev. 9:7 [b]Lev. 16:15 [c]Rom. 6:10
28 [a]ch. 5:1,2 [b]ch. 2:10 & 5:9 [1]Gk. *perfected*
8:1 [a]Eph. 1:20; Col. 3:1; ch. 10:12
2 [a]ch. 9:8,12 [b]ch. 9:11 [1]Or, *of holy things*
3 [a]ch. 5:1 [b]Eph. 5:2; ch. 9:14
4 [1]Or, *they are priests*
5 [a]Col. 2:17; ch. 9:23 [b]Ex. 25:40; Num. 8:4; Acts 7:44
6 [a]2 Cor. 3:6,8; ch. 7:22 [1]Or, *testament*
7 [a]ch. 7:11,18
8 [a]Jer. 31:31
10 [a]ch. 10:16 [b]Zech. 8:8 [1]Gk. *give* [2]Or, *upon*
11 [a]Is. 54:13; John 6:45; 1 John 2:27
12 [a]Rom. 11:27
13 [a]2 Cor. 5:17

was admonished of God when he was about to make the tabernacle: [b]for, See, saith he, *that* thou make all things according to the pattern shown to thee in the mount.

6 But now [a]hath he obtained a more excellent ministry, by how much also he is the mediator of a better [1]covenant, which was established upon better promises.

7 [a]For if that first *covenant* had been faultless, then should no place have been sought for the second.

8 For finding fault with them, he saith, [a]Behold, the days come, saith the Lord, when I will make a new covenant with the house of Israel and with the house of Judah:

9 Not according to the covenant that I made with their fathers in the day when I took them by the hand to lead them out of the land of Egypt; because they continued not in my covenant, and I regarded them not, saith the Lord.

10 For [a]this *is* the covenant that I will K
make with the house of Israel after those
days, saith the Lord; I will [1]put my laws
into their mind, and write them [2]in their
hearts: and [b]I will be to them a God, and
they shall be to me a people:

11 And [a]they shall not teach every man his neighbour, and every man his brother, saying, Know the Lord: for all shall know me, from the least to the greatest.

12 For I will be merciful to their un- L
righteousness, [a]and their sins and their
iniquities will I remember no more.

13 [a]In that he saith, A new *covenant,* he hath made the first old. Now that which decayeth and waxeth old *is* ready to vanish away.

K *Heb 7:25* ◀▶ *Heb 9:13–14*
L *Heb 7:25* ◀▶ *Heb 9:13–14*

8:8 *New Covenant.* The new covenant is the last of the eight, major Biblical covenants. Established on God's unconditional promises to transform the hearts of his people, the new covenant grants the personal divine manifestation of the Lord to every believer and asserts that all sin has been effectively forgiven forever through Christ's atoning work on the cross. This final covenant will also be ratified with Israel, assuring their status as God's chosen people, their complete and ultimate redemption and conversion so that they will love and obey God forever and Israel's eternal relationship with God in the promised land.

NOTE: The seven additional covenants include the Edenic (Ge 2:15–17), Adamic (Ge 3:15–19), Noahic (Ge 9:8ff), Abrahamic (Ge 15:4ff; 17:1–22), Mosaic (Ex 19:5), Palestinian (Dt 30:1–10) and Davidic (2Sa 7:16). For further information, see the article on "The Biblical Covenants" on p. 8.

Temporary sacrifices by Levites

9 THEN VERILY the first *covenant* had
also 'ordinances of divine service,
and [a]a worldly sanctuary.
2 [a]For there was a tabernacle made;
the first, [b]wherein *was* [c]the candlestick,
and [d]the table, and the showbread;
which is called 'the sanctuary.
3 [a]And after the second veil, the tabernacle which is called the Holiest of all;
4 Which had the golden censer, and
[a]the ark of the covenant overlaid round
about with gold, wherein *was* [b]the
golden pot that had manna, and [c]Aaron's
rod that budded, and [d]the tables of the
covenant;
5 And [a]over it the cherubims of glory
shadowing the mercyseat; of which we
cannot now speak particularly.
6 Now when these things were thus
ordained, [a]the priests went always into
the first tabernacle, accomplishing the
service *of God.*
D 7 But into the second *went* the high
priest alone [a]once every year, not without blood, [b]which he offered for himself,
and *for* the errors of the people:
E 8 [a]The Holy Ghost this signifying, that
[b]the way into the holiest of all was not
yet made manifest, while as the first tabernacle was yet standing:
9 Which *was* a figure for the time then
present, in which were offered both gifts
and sacrifices, [a]that could not make him
that did the service perfect, as pertaining
to the conscience;
10 *Which stood* only in [a]meats and
drinks, and [b]divers washings, [c]and carnal
'ordinances, imposed *on them* until the
time of reformation.

The eternal sacrifice of Christ

D 11 But Christ being come [a]an high
priest [b]of good things to come, [c]by a
greater and more perfect tabernacle, not
made with hands, that is to say, not of
this building;
12 Neither [a]by the blood of goats and
calves, but [b]by his own blood he entered
in [c]once into the holy place, [d]having obtained eternal redemption *for us.*
13 For if [a]the blood of bulls and of K
goats, and [b]the ashes of an heifer sprin- L
kling the unclean, sanctifieth to the purifying of the flesh:
14 How much more [a]shall the blood of D
Christ, [b]who through the eternal Spirit E
offered himself without 'spot to God, L
[c]purge your conscience from [d]dead N
works [e]to serve the living God? S
15 [a]And for this cause [b]he is the mediator of the new testament, [c]that by
means of death, for the redemption of the
transgressions *that were* under the first
testament, [d]they which are called might
receive the promise of eternal inheritance.
16 For where a testament *is,* there
must also of necessity 'be the death of
the testator.
17 For [a]a testament *is* of force after
men are dead: otherwise it is of no
strength at all while the testator liveth.
18 [a]Whereupon neither the first *testament* was 'dedicated without blood.
19 For when Moses had spoken every
precept to all the people according to the
law, [a]he took the blood of calves and of
goats, [b]with water, and 'scarlet wool,
and hyssop, and sprinkled both the book,
and all the people,
20 Saying, [a]This *is* the blood of the testament which God hath enjoined unto
you.
21 Moreover [a]he sprinkled with blood
both the tabernacle, and all the vessels of
the ministry.
22 And almost all things are by the law O
purged with blood; and [a]without shed-
ding of blood is no remission.

Christ's once-for-all sacrifice

23 *It was* therefore necessary that [a]the
patterns of things in the heavens should
be purified with these; but the heavenly
things themselves with better sacrifices
than these.
24 For [a]Christ is not entered into the
holy places made with hands, *which are*
the figures of [b]the true; but into heaven

9:1 [a]Ex. 25:8 'Or, *ceremonies*
2 [a]Ex. 26:1 [b]Ex. 26:35 [c]Ex. 25:31 [d]Ex. 25:23 'Or, *holy*
3 [a]Ex. 26:31
4 [a]Ex. 25:10 [b]Ex. 16:33 [c]Num. 17:10 [d]Ex. 25:16; Deut. 10:2
5 [a]Lev. 16:2
6 [a]Num. 28:3
7 [a]Ex. 30:10 [b]ch. 7:27
8 [a]ch. 10:19 [b]John 14:6
9 [a]Gal. 3:21
10 [a]Col. 2:16 [b]Num. 19:7 [c]Eph. 2:15 'Or, *rites,* or, *ceremonies*
11 [a]ch. 3:1 [b]ch. 10:1 [c]ch. 8:2
12 [a]ch. 10:4 [b]Eph. 1:7; Col. 1:14 [c]Zech. 3:9 [d]Dan. 9:24
13 [a]Lev. 16:14 [b]Num. 19:2
14 [a]1 John 1:7 [b]Rom. 1:4 [c]ch. 10:22 [d]ch. 6:1 [e]Luke 1:74 'Or, *fault*
15 [a]1 Tim. 2:5 [b]ch. 7:22 [c]Rom. 3:25 [d]ch. 3:1
16 'Or, *be brought in*
17 [a]Gal. 3:15
18 [a]Ex. 24:6 'Or, *purified*
19 [a]Ex. 24:5,6 [b]Lev. 14:4 'Or, *purple*
20 [a]Ex. 24:8; Mat. 26:28
21 [a]Ex. 29:12; Lev. 8:15
22 [a]Lev. 17:11
23 [a]ch. 8:5
24 [a]ch. 6:20 [b]ch. 8:2

D *Heb 7:27* ◀▶ *Heb 9:11–28*
E *Heb 3:7* ◀▶ *Heb 9:14*
D *Heb 9:7* ◀▶ *Heb 10:12*

K *Heb 8:10–12* ◀▶ *Heb 10:16–17*
L *Heb 8:12* ◀▶ *Heb 9:28*
D *Eph 4:4* ◀▶ *1Jn 5:7*
E *Heb 9:8* ◀▶ *Heb 10:15*
L *1Th 5:19* ◀▶ *1Pe 1:12*
N *Eph 5:18* ◀▶ *Heb 10:29*
S *Heb 6:11–12* ◀▶ *Heb 10:26–31*
O *2Ti 2:11–12* ◀▶ *Jas 4:12*

itself, now [c]to appear in the presence of God for us:

25 Nor yet that he should offer himself often, as [a]the high priest entereth into the holy place every year with blood of others;

C 26 For then must he often have suffered since the foundation of the world:
but now [a]once [b]in the end of the world
hath he appeared to put away sin by the
sacrifice of himself.
J 27 [a]And as it is appointed unto men
J once to die, [b]but after this the judgment:
C 28 So [a]Christ was once [b]offered to
L bear the sins [c]of many; and unto them
that [d]look for him shall he appear the second time without sin unto salvation.

10

FOR THE law having [a]a shadow [b]of good things to come, *and* not the very image of the things, [c]can never with those sacrifices which they offered year by year continually make the comers thereunto [d]perfect.

2 For then [1]would they not have ceased to be offered? because that the worshippers once purged should have had no more conscience of sins.

3 [a]But in those *sacrifices there is* a remembrance again *made* of sins every year.

4 For [a]*it is* not possible that the blood of bulls and of goats should take away sins.

5 Wherefore when he cometh into the world, he saith, [a]Sacrifice and offering thou wouldest not, but a body [1]hast thou prepared me:

6 In burnt offerings and *sacrifices* for sin thou hast had no pleasure.

7 Then said I, Lo, I come (in the volume of the book it is written of me,) to do thy will, O God.

8 Above when he said, Sacrifice and offering and burnt offerings and *offering* for sin thou wouldest not, neither hadst pleasure *therein;* which are offered by the law;

9 Then said he, Lo, I come to do thy will, O God. He taketh away the first, that he may establish the second.

10 [a]By the which will we are sanctified [b]through the offering of the body of Jesus Christ once *for all.*

11 And every priest standeth [a]daily ministering and offering oftentimes the same sacrifices, [b]which can never take away sins:

12 [a]But this man, after he had offered D
one sacrifice for sins for ever, sat down H
on the right hand of God;
13 From henceforth expecting [a]till his M
enemies be made his footstool.
14 For by one offering [a]he hath per- B
fected for ever them that are sanctified. S
15 *Whereof* the Holy Ghost also is a E
witness to us: for after that he had said
before,
16 [a]This *is* the covenant that I will K
make with them after those days, saith
the Lord, I will put my laws into their
hearts, and in their minds will I write
them;
17 [1]And their sins and iniquities will I L
remember no more.

18 Now where remission of these *is, there is* no more offering for sin.

The appeal to hold fast

19 Having therefore, brethren, [a]boldness[1] to enter [b]into the holiest by the blood of Jesus,

20 By [a]a new and living way, which he hath [1]consecrated for us, [b]through the veil, that is to say, his flesh;

24 [c]Rom. 8:34; 1 John 2:1
25 [a]ver. 7
26 [a]ch. 7:27 [b]1 Cor. 10:11
27 [a]Gen. 3:19; Eccl. 3:20 [b]2 Cor. 5:10
28 [a]Rom. 6:10; 1 Pet. 3:18 [b]1 Pet. 2:24; 1 John 3:5 [c]Mat. 26:28; Rom. 5:15 [d]Tit. 2:13
10:1 [a]Col. 2:17 [b]ch. 9:11 [c]ch. 9:9 [d]ver. 14
2 [1]Or, *they would have ceased to be offered, because*
3 [a]ch. 9:7
4 [a]Mic. 6:6,7
5 [a]Ps. 40:6 [1]Or, *thou hast fitted me*
10 [a]John 17:19 [b]ch. 9:12
11 [a]Num. 28:3 [b]ver. 4
12 [a]Col. 3:1
13 [a]Ps. 110:1; Acts 2:35
14 [a]ver. 1
16 [a]ch. 8:10,12
17 [1]Some copies have, *Then he said, And their*
19 [a]Eph. 2:18 [b]ch. 9:8,12 [1]Or, *liberty*
20 [a]John 10:9 [b]ch. 9:3 [1]Or, *new made*

C *Tit 2:13* ◀▶ *Heb 9:28*
J *2Co 5:9–11* ◀▶ *Heb 10:30*
J *2Ti 4:1* ◀▶ *Heb 12:23*
C *Heb 9:26* ◀▶ *Heb 10:25*
L *Heb 9:13–14* ◀▶ *Heb 10:17*

D *Heb 9:11–28* ◀▶ *Heb 12:24*
H *Heb 6:7–8* ◀▶ *Heb 10:26–31*
M *Heb 7:20–21* ◀▶ *1Pe 5:1*
B *Heb 2:4* ◀▶ *1Pe 1:11*
S *2Th 2:13* ◀▶ *1Pe 1:2*
E *Heb 9:14* ◀▶ *Heb 11:11*
K *Heb 9:13–14* ◀▶ *Heb 12:24*
L *Heb 9:28* ◀▶ *Heb 13:8*

9:26–28 The ancient Israelites would put away the sin of the camp by sending a scapegoat loose into the wilderness (see Lev 16:21–22). Jesus Christ becomes the fulfillment of that symbolic scapegoat as he takes away the sins of the world through his own sacrifice on the cross. Every person who rejects Christ's sacrifice and offer of salvation will ultimately appear before God at life's end to account for their refusal to believe. Yet God's offer of salvation is still available for those who will repent and believe.

10:25 Hebrews urges us to gather together as believers, encouraging each other as we await the return of Jesus Christ in glory.

21 And *having* [a]an high priest over
[b]the house of God;
22 [a]Let us draw near with a true heart
[b]in full assurance of faith, having our
hearts sprinkled [c]from an evil conscience, and [d]our bodies washed with
pure water.
23 [a]Let us hold fast the profession of
our faith without wavering; (for [b]he *is*
faithful that promised;)
24 And let us consider one another to
provoke unto love and to good works:
C 25 [a]Not forsaking the assembling of
ourselves together, as the manner of
some *is;* but exhorting *one another:* and
[b]so much the more, as ye see [c]the day
approaching.
H 26 For [a]if we sin wilfully [b]after that
S we have received the knowledge of the
truth, there remaineth no more sacrifice
for sins,
27 But a certain fearful looking for of
judgment and [a]fiery indignation, which
shall devour the adversaries.
28 [a]He that despised Moses' law died
without mercy [b]under two or three witnesses:
N 29 [a]Of how much sorer punishment,
Q suppose ye, shall he be thought worthy,
who hath trodden under foot the Son of
God, and [b]hath counted the blood of the
covenant, wherewith he was sanctified,
an unholy thing, [c]and hath done despite
unto the Spirit of grace?
J 30 For we know him that hath said,
[a]Vengeance *belongeth* unto me, I will
recompense, saith the Lord. And again,
[b]The Lord shall judge his people.
31 [a]*It is* a fearful thing to fall into the
hands of the living God.
32 But [a]call to remembrance the former days, in which, [b]after ye were illumi-
nated, ye endured [c]a great fight of afflictions;
33 Partly, whilst ye were made [a]a gazingstock both by reproaches and afflictions; and partly, whilst [b]ye became companions of them that were so used.
34 For ye had compassion of me [a]in
my bonds, and [b]took joyfully the spoiling
of your goods, knowing [1]in yourselves
that [c]ye have in heaven a better and an
enduring substance.
35 Cast not away therefore your confi- S
dence, [a]which hath great recompence of
reward.
36 [a]For ye have need of patience, that,
after ye have done the will of God, [b]ye
might receive the promise.
37 For [a]yet a little while, and [b]he that C
shall come will come, and will not tarry.
38 Now [a]the just shall live by faith: but F
if *any man* draw back, my soul shall have S
no pleasure in him.
39 But we are not of them [a]who draw H
back unto perdition; but of them that [b]be-
lieve to the saving of the soul.

Faith defined

11 NOW FAITH is the [1]substance of
things hoped for, the evidence
[a]of things not seen.
2 For [a]by it the elders obtained a good
report.
3 Through faith we understand that
[a]the worlds were framed by the word of
God, so that things which are seen were
not made of things which do appear.

Examples of faith

4 By faith [a]Abel offered unto God a
more excellent sacrifice than Cain, by
which he obtained witness that he was
righteous, God testifying of his gifts: and
by it he being dead yet [1]speaketh.
5 By faith [a]Enoch was translated that
he should not see death; and was not
found, because God had translated him:
for before his translation he had this testimony, that he pleased God.

21 [a]ch. 4:14 [b]1 Tim. 3:15
22 [a]ch. 4:16 [b]Eph. 3:12 [c]ch. 9:14 [d]Ezek. 36:25
23 [a]ch. 4:14 [b]1 Cor. 1:9; 2 Thes. 3:3
25 [a]Acts 2:42 [b]Rom. 13:11 [c]Phil. 4:5; 2 Pet. 3:9
26 [a]Num. 15:30 [b]2 Pet. 2:20
27 [a]Zeph. 1:18; 2 Thes. 1:8
28 [a]ch. 2:2 [b]Mat. 18:16
29 [a]ch. 2:3 [b]1 Cor. 11:29 [c]Mat. 12:31; Eph. 4:30
30 [a]Deut. 32:35 [b]Deut. 32:36
31 [a]Luke 12:5
32 [a]Gal. 3:4 [b]ch. 6:4 [c]Phil. 1:29; Col. 2:1
33 [a]1 Cor. 4:9 [b]Phil. 1:7
34 [a]2 Tim. 1:16 [b]Mat. 5:12 [c]Mat. 6:20 [1]Or, *that ye have in yourselves,* or, *for yourselves*
35 [a]Mat. 5:12
36 [a]Luke 21:19 [b]Col. 3:24
37 [a]Luke 18:8 [b]Hab. 2:3,4
38 [a]Rom. 1:17; Gal. 3:11
39 [a]2 Pet. 2:20 [b]Acts 16:31; 1 Thes. 5:9; 2 Thes. 2:14
11:1 [a]Rom. 8:24; 2 Cor. 4:18 [1]Or, *ground,* or, *confidence*
2 [a]ver. 39
3 [a]Gen. 1:1; Ps. 33:6; John 1:3; 2 Pet. 3:5
4 [a]Gen. 4:4; 1 John 3:12 [1]Or, *is yet spoken of*
5 [a]Gen. 5:22

C *Heb 9:28* ◀ ▶ *Heb 10:37*
H *Heb 10:12–13* ◀ ▶ *Heb 10:39*
S *Heb 9:14* ◀ ▶ *Heb 10:35–36*
N *Heb 9:14* ◀ ▶ *1Pe 4:14*
Q *1Th 5:19* ◀ ▶ *1Jn 5:16*
J *Heb 9:27* ◀ ▶ *1Pe 4:5*
S *Heb 10:26–31* ◀ ▶ *Heb 10:38–39*
C *Heb 10:25* ◀ ▶ *Jas 5:7–9*
F *Heb 3:18–19* ◀ ▶ *Heb 11:6*
S *Heb 10:35–36* ◀ ▶ *Heb 12:1*
H *Heb 10:26–31* ◀ ▶ *Heb 11:28*

10:30 Despite the universal violence and evil during the last days, God will be the one to bring recompense, judgment and vengeance.
10:37 While the second coming of Christ seems delayed indefinitely, it will occur (see 2Pe 3:9). Once the conditions are right, the Lord will return in glory to defeat the antichrist and Satan.

F 6 But without faith *it is* impossible to
G please *him:* for he that cometh to God must believe that he is, and *that* he is a rewarder of them that diligently seek him.

7 By faith [a]Noah, being warned of God of things not seen as yet, [l]moved with fear, [b]prepared an ark to the saving of his house; by the which he condemned the world, and became heir of [c]the righteousness which is by faith.

8 By faith [a]Abraham, when he was called to go out into a place which he should after receive for an inheritance, obeyed; and he went out, not knowing whither he went.

9 By faith he sojourned in the land of promise, as *in* a strange country, [a]dwelling in tabernacles with Isaac and Jacob, [b]the heirs with him of the same promise:

10 For he looked for [a]a city which hath foundations, [b]whose builder and maker *is* God.

E 11 Through faith also [a]Sarah herself
E received strength to conceive seed, and [b]was delivered of a child when she was past age, because she judged him [c]faithful who had promised.

12 Therefore sprang there even of one, and [a]him as good as dead, [b]*so many* as the stars of the sky in multitude, and as the sand which is by the sea shore innumerable.

13 These all died [l]in faith, [a]not having received the promises, but [b]having seen them afar off, and were persuaded of *them,* and embraced *them,* and [c]confessed that they were strangers and pilgrims on the earth.

14 For they that say such things [a]declare plainly that they seek a country.

15 And truly, if they had been mindful of that *country* from whence they came out, they might have had opportunity to have returned.

16 But now they desire a better *country,* that is, an heavenly: wherefore God is not ashamed [a]to be called their God: for [b]he hath prepared for them a city.

17 By faith [a]Abraham, when he was tried, offered up Isaac: and he that had received the promises [b]offered up his only begotten *son,*

18 [l]Of whom it was said, [a]That in Isaac shall thy seed be called:

19 Accounting that God [a]*was* able to raise *him* up, even from the dead; from whence also he received him in a figure.

20 By faith [a]Isaac blessed Jacob and Esau concerning things to come.

21 By faith Jacob, when he was a-dying, [a]blessed both the sons of Joseph; and [b]worshipped, *leaning* upon the top of his staff.

22 By faith [a]Joseph, when he died, [l]made mention of the departing of the children of Israel; and gave commandment concerning his bones.

23 By faith [a]Moses, when he was born, was hid three months of his parents, because they saw *he was* a proper child; and they were not afraid of the king's [b]commandment.

24 By faith [a]Moses, when he was come to years, refused to be called the son of Pharaoh's daughter;

25 [a]Choosing rather to suffer affliction with the people of God, than to enjoy the pleasures of sin for a season;

26 Esteeming [a]the reproach [l]of Christ greater riches than the treasures in Egypt: for he had respect unto [b]the recompence of the reward.

27 By faith [a]he forsook Egypt, not fearing the wrath of the king: for he endured, as [b]seeing him who is invisible.

28 Through faith [a]he kept the pass- H
over, and the sprinkling of blood, lest he that destroyed the firstborn should touch them.

29 By faith [a]they passed through the Red sea as by dry *land:* which the Egyptians assaying to do were drowned.

30 By faith [a]the walls of Jericho fell down, after they were compassed about seven days.

31 By faith [a]the harlot Rahab perished not with them [l]that believed not, when [b]she had received the spies with peace.

32 And what shall I more say? for the V
time would fail me to tell of [a]Gedeon, and *of* Barak, and *of* [b]Samson, and *of* [c]Jephthae; *of* [d]David also, and [e]Samuel, and *of* the prophets:

33 Who through faith subdued king- S

7 [a]Gen. 6:13 [b]1 Pet. 3:20 [c]Rom. 3:22; Phil. 3:9 [l]Or, *being wary*
8 [a]Gen. 12:1; Acts 7:2-4
9 [a]Gen. 12:8 [b]ch. 6:17
10 [a]ch. 12:22 [b]Rev. 21:10
11 [a]Gen. 17:19 & 18:11,14 [b]Luke 1:36 [c]Rom. 4:21
12 [a]Rom. 4:19 [b]Rom. 4:18
13 [a]ver. 39 [b]John 8:56 [c]Gen. 23:4; 1 Chr. 29:15; Ps. 39:12; 1 Pet. 1:17 [l]Gk. *according to faith*
14 [a]ch. 13:14
16 [a]Ex. 3:6,15; Mat. 22:32; Acts 7:32 [b]ch. 13:14
17 [a]Gen. 22:1 [b]Jas 2:21
18 [a]Gen. 21:12; Rom. 9:7 [l]Or, *To*
19 [a]Rom. 4:17
20 [a]Gen. 27:27
21 [a]Gen. 48:5 [b]Gen. 47:31
22 [a]Gen. 50:24 [l]Or, *remembered*
23 [a]Ex. 2:2 [b]Ex. 1:16
24 [a]Ex. 2:10
25 [a]Ps. 84:10
26 [a]ch. 13:13 [b]ch. 10:35 [l]Or, *for Christ*
27 [a]Ex. 10:28 [b]ver. 13
28 [a]Ex. 12:21
29 [a]Ex. 14:22
30 [a]Josh. 6:20
31 [a]Josh. 6:23 [b]Josh. 2:1 [l]Or, *that were disobedient*
32 [a]Judg. 6:11 [b]Judg. 13:24 [c]Judg. 12:7 [d]1 Sam. 16:1 [e]1 Sam. 1:20

F *Heb 10:38–39* ◀ ▶ *Jas 2:23*
G *Tit 3:5* ◀ ▶ *1Pe 1:18–19*
E *Heb 10:15* ◀ ▶ *1Pe 1:2*
E *Php 2:27* ◀ ▶ *Heb 11:34–35*
H *Heb 10:39* ◀ ▶ *Heb 12:25*
V *2Ti 4:18* ◀ ▶ *1Jn 5:4–5*
S *Ro 8:31* ◀

doms, wrought righteousness, [a]obtained promises, [b]stopped the mouths of lions,

34 [a]Quenched the violence of fire, [b]escaped the edge of the sword, [c]out of weakness were made strong, waxed valiant in fight, [d]turned to flight the armies of the aliens.

35 [a]Women received their dead raised to life again: and others were [b]tortured, not accepting deliverance; that they might obtain a better resurrection:

36 And others had trial of *cruel* mockings and scourgings, yea, moreover [a]of bonds and imprisonment:

37 [a]They were stoned, they were sawn asunder, were tempted, were slain with the sword: [b]they wandered about [c]in sheepskins and goatskins; being destitute, afflicted, tormented;

38 (Of whom the world was not worthy:) they wandered in deserts, and *in* mountains, and [a]*in* dens and caves of the earth.

39 And these all, [a]having obtained a good report through faith, received not the promise:

40 God having [l]provided some better thing for us, that they without us should not be [a]made perfect.

Christ our example

12 WHEREFORE SEEING we also are compassed about with so great a cloud of witnesses, [a]let us lay aside every weight, and the sin which doth so easily beset *us,* and [b]let us run [c]with patience the race that is set before us,

2 Looking unto Jesus the [l]author and finisher of *our* faith; [a]who for the joy that was set before him endured the cross, despising the shame, and [b]is set down at the right hand of the throne of God.

3 [a]For consider him that endured such contradiction of sinners against himself, [b]lest ye be wearied and faint in your minds.

4 [a]Ye have not yet resisted unto blood, striving against sin.

5 And ye have forgotten the exhortation which speaketh unto you as unto children, [a]My son, despise not thou the chastening of the Lord, nor faint when thou art rebuked of him:

6 For [a]whom the Lord loveth he chasteneth, and scourgeth every son whom he receiveth.

7 [a]If ye endure chastening, God dealeth with you as with sons; for what son is he whom the father chasteneth not?

8 But if ye be without chastisement, [a]whereof all are partakers, then are ye bastards, and not sons.

9 Furthermore we have had fathers of our flesh which corrected *us,* and we gave *them* reverence: shall we not much rather be in subjection unto [a]the Father of spirits, and live?

10 For they verily for a few days chastened *us* [l]after their own pleasure; but he for *our* profit, [a]that *we* might be partakers of his holiness.

11 Now no chastening for the present seemeth to be joyous, but grievous: nevertheless afterward it yieldeth [a]the peaceable fruit of righteousness unto them which are exercised thereby.

An appeal for endurance

12 Wherefore [a]lift up the hands which hang down, and the feeble knees;

13 [a]And make [l]straight paths for your feet, lest that which is lame be turned out of the way; [b]but let it rather be healed.

14 [a]Follow peace with all *men,* and holiness, [b]without which no man shall see the Lord:

15 Looking diligently [a]lest any man [l]fail of the grace of God; [b]lest any root of bitterness springing up trouble *you,* and thereby many be defiled;

16 [a]Lest there *be* any fornicator, or profane person, as Esau, [b]who for one morsel of meat sold his birthright.

17 For ye know how that afterward, [a]when he would have inherited the blessing, he was rejected: for he found no [l]place of repentance, though he sought it carefully with tears.

33 [a]2 Sam. 7:11 [b]Judg. 14:5; 1 Sam. 17:34
34 [a]Dan. 3:25 [b]1 Sam. 20:1 [c]2 Ki. 20:7 [d]Judg. 15:8
35 [a]1 Ki. 17:22 [b]Acts 22:25
36 [a]Gen. 39:20; Jer. 20:2
37 [a]1 Ki. 21:13; Acts 7:58 [b]2 Ki. 1:8; Mat. 3:4 [c]Zech. 13:4
38 [a]1 Ki. 18:4
39 [a]ver. 2,13
40 [a]ch. 5:9 [l]Or, *foreseen*
12:1 [a]Col. 3:8 [b]1 Cor. 9:24 [c]Rom. 12:12
2 [a]Luke 24:26; Phil. 2:8 [b]Ps. 110:1; 1 Pet. 3:22 [l]Or, *beginner*
3 [a]Mat. 10:24; John 15:20 [b]Gal. 6:9
4 [a]1 Cor. 10:13
5 [a]Job 5:17
6 [a]Ps. 94:12; Jas. 1:12
7 [a]Deut. 8:5
8 [a]1 Pet. 5:9
9 [a]Job 12:10
10 [a]Lev. 11:44 [l]Or, *as seemed good,* or, *meet to them*
11 [a]Jas. 3:18
12 [a]Job 4:3,4
13 [a]Prov. 4:26 [b]Gal. 6:1 [l]Or, *even*
14 [a]Ps. 34:14; 2 Tim. 2:22 [b]Mat. 5:8; 2 Cor. 7:1
15 [a]Gal. 5:4 [b]ch. 3:12 [l]Or, *fall from*
16 [a]Eph. 5:3 [b]Gen. 25:33
17 [a]Gen. 27:34 [l]Or, *way to change his mind*

E *Heb 11:11–12* ◀
F *Heb 6:2* ◀ ▶ *Rev 20:5–6*
S *Heb 10:38–39* ◀ ▶ *Heb 12:14*
D *Php 2:30* ◀ **T** *Heb 5:8* ◀ ▶ *Jas 1:2–4*
S *Heb 12:1* ◀ ▶ *Heb 12:25*

11:35 The martyrs of the church gave their lives for their faith in Jesus Christ so that "they might obtain a better resurrection." This refers to the first resurrection to life (see Jn 5:29) that includes all those who participate in salvation and receive a complete transformation as they are raised to eternal life.

18 For ye are not come unto [a]the mount that might be touched, and that burned with fire, nor unto blackness, and darkness, and tempest,

19 And the sound of a trumpet, and the voice of words; which *voice* they that heard [a]entreated that the word should not be spoken to them any more:

20 (For they could not endure that which was commanded, [a]And if so much as a beast touch the mountain, it shall be stoned, or thrust through with a dart:

21 [a]And so terrible was the sight, *that* Moses said, I exceedingly fear and quake:)

22 But ye are come [a]unto mount Zion, [b]and unto the city of the living God, the heavenly Jerusalem, [c]and to an innumerable company of angels,

J 23 To the general assembly and church of [a]the firstborn, [b]which are [l]written in heaven, and to God [c]the Judge of all, and to the spirits of just men [d]made perfect,

D K 24 And to Jesus [a]the mediator of the new [l]covenant, and to [b]the blood of sprinkling, that speaketh better things [c]than *that of* Abel.

H N S 25 See that ye refuse not him that speaketh. For [a]if they escaped not who refused him that spake on earth, much more *shall not* we *escape,* if we turn away from him that *speaketh* from heaven:

N 26 [a]Whose voice then shook the earth: but now he hath promised, saying, [b]Yet once more I shake not the earth only, but also heaven.

27 And this *word,* Yet once more, signifieth [a]the removing of those things that [l]are shaken, as of things that are made, that those things which cannot be shaken may remain.

28 Wherefore we receiving a kingdom which cannot be moved, [l]let us have grace, whereby we may serve God acceptably with reverence and godly fear:

29 For [a]our God *is* a consuming fire. H

Warnings and requests

13 LET [a]BROTHERLY love continue.

2 [a]Be not forgetful to entertain strangers: for thereby [b]some have entertained angels unawares.

3 [a]Remember them that are in bonds, as bound with them; *and* them which suffer adversity, as being yourselves also in the body.

4 Marriage *is* honourable in all, and the bed undefiled: [a]but whoremongers and adulterers God will judge.

5 *Let your* conversation *be* without covetousness; *and* [a]*be* content with such things as ye have: for he hath said, [b]I will never leave thee, nor forsake thee. L W

6 So that we may boldly say, [a]The Lord *is* my helper, and I will not fear what man shall do unto me. J

7 [a]Remember them which [l]have the rule over you, who have spoken unto you the word of God: [b]whose faith follow, considering the end of *their* conversation.

8 Jesus Christ [a]the same yesterday, and today, and for ever. K L

9 [a]Be not carried about with divers and strange doctrines. For *it is* a good thing that the heart be established with grace; [b]not with meats, which have not profited them that have been occupied therein.

10 [a]We have an altar, whereof they have no right to eat which serve the tabernacle.

11 For [a]the bodies of those beasts, whose blood is brought into the sanctuary by the high priest for sin, are burned without the camp. D

18 [a]Deut. 4:11
19 [a]Ex. 20:19; Deut. 5:5
20 [a]Ex. 19:13
21 [a]Ex. 19:16
22 [a]Gal. 4:26; Rev. 3:12 [b]Phil. 3:20 [c]Deut. 33:2; Ps. 68:17
23 [a]Jas. 1:18 [b]Luke 10:20 [c]Ps. 94:2 [d]Phil. 3:12 [l]Or, *enrolled*
24 [a]ch. 9:15 [b]Ex. 24:8 [c]Gen. 4:10 [l]Or, *testament*
25 [a]ch. 2:2,3
26 [a]Ex. 19:18 [b]Hag. 2:6
27 [a]2 Pet. 3:10 [l]Or, *may be shaken*
28 [l]Or, *let us hold fast*
29 [a]Ex. 24:17; Deut. 4:24
13:1 [a]Rom. 12:10; 1 Pet. 1:22
2 [a]Mat. 25:35; 1 Tim. 3:2 [b]Gen. 18:3
3 [a]Mat. 25:26
4 [a]1 Cor. 6:9
5 [a]Phil. 4:11 [b]Gen. 28:15
6 [a]Ps. 27:1
7 [a]ver. 17 [b]ch. 6:12 [l]Or, *are the guides*
8 [a]John 8:58
9 [a]Eph. 4:14; Col. 2:4,8 [b]Rom. 14:17; 1 Tim. 4:3
10 [a]1 Cor. 9:13
11 [a]Ex. 29:14

J *Heb 9:27* ◀▶ *Jas 2:12–13*
D *Heb 10:12* ◀▶ *Heb 13:11–12*
K *Heb 10:16–17* ◀▶ *Heb 13:8*
H *Heb 11:28* ◀▶ *Heb 12:29*
N *Heb 3:18* ◀▶ *Jas 4:13–14*
S *Heb 12:14* ◀▶ *Heb 13:20–21*
N *Heb 1:10–12* ◀▶ *2Pe 3:13–14*
H *Heb 12:25* ◀▶ *1Pe 3:12*
L *Heb 1:14* ◀▶ *Jas 5:10–11*
W *1Ti 6:8* ◀▶ *1Pe 3:14*
J *Php 3:8* ◀▶ *Jas 1:2–4*
K *Heb 12:24* ◀▶ *Jas 1:21*
L *Heb 10:17* ◀▶ *Jas 4:10*
D *Heb 12:24* ◀▶ *1Pe 1:18–19*

12:26–28 This passage corresponds to several of the OT prophecies concerning the last days (see Isa 2:9; 13:13; Joel 3:16; Hag 2:6–7). At the coming judgment of Christ, he shall destroy the works of Satan and his antichrist at the Battle of Armageddon and establish his righteous rule in his millennial kingdom forever. Though the antichrist's kingdom will be shaken, Christ's kingdom is unshakable and will remain forever (12:28).

12 Wherefore Jesus also, that he might sanctify the people with his own blood, [a]suffered without the gate.

13 Let us go forth therefore unto him without the camp, bearing [a]his reproach.

14 [a]For here have we no continuing city, but we seek one to come.

T 15 [a]By him therefore let us offer [b]the sacrifice of praise to God continually, that is, [c]the fruit of *our* lips [1]giving thanks to his name.

16 [a]But to do good and to communicate forget not: for [b]with such sacrifices God is well pleased.

17 [a]Obey them that [1]have the rule over you, and submit yourselves: for [b]they watch for your souls, as they that must give account, that they may do it with joy, and not with grief: for that *is* unprofitable for you.

18 [a]Pray for us: for we trust we have [b]a good conscience, in all things willing to live honestly.

19 But I beseech *you* the rather to do this, that I may be restored to you the sooner.

S 20 Now [a]the God of peace, [b]that brought again from the dead our Lord Jesus, [c]that great shepherd of the sheep, [d]through the blood of the everlasting [1]covenant,

21 [a]Make you perfect in every good work to do his will, [b]working[1] in you that which is wellpleasing in his sight, through Jesus Christ; [c]to whom *be* glory for ever and ever. Amen.

22 And I beseech you, brethren, suffer the word of exhortation: for [a]I have written a letter unto you in few words.

23 Know ye that [a]*our* brother Timothy [b]is set at liberty; with whom, if he come shortly, I will see you.

24 Salute all them [a]that have the rule over you, and all the saints. They of Italy salute you.

25 [a]Grace *be* with you all. Amen.

12 [a]Acts 7:58
13 [a]1 Pet. 4:14
14 [a]Mic. 2:10; Phil. 3:20
15 [a]Eph. 5:20 [b]Lev. 7:12 [c]Hos. 14:2 [1]Gk. *confessing to*
16 [a]Rom. 12:13 [b]2 Cor. 9:12; Phil. 4:18
17 [a]Phil. 2:29; 1 Tim. 5:17 [b]Ezek. 3:17 [1]Or, *guide*
18 [a]Eph. 6:19 [b]Acts 23:1
20 [a]Rom. 15:33 [b]Rom. 4:24; Gal. 1:1 [c]1 Pet. 2:25 [d]Zech. 9:11 [1]Or, *testament*
21 [a]1 Pet. 5:10 [b]Phil. 2:13 [c]Gal. 1:5 [1]Or, *doing*
22 [a]1 Pet. 5:12
23 [a]1 Thes. 3:2 [b]1 Tim. 6:12
24 [a]ver. 7,17
25 [a]Tit. 3:15

James

Author: Uncertain; possibly the half-brother of Jesus

Theme: The need for a practical Christian faith

Date of Writing: c. A.D. 40–50

Outline of James

I. The Essence of True Religion (1:1–27)
II. True Faith in Practice (2:1—3:12)
III. True Wisdom in Practice (3:13—5:20)

THIS EPISTLE WAS written by James, who was probably the half-brother of Jesus (see Mk 6:3). James also was among the group gathered on Pentecost (see Ac 1:14) and became a leader in the Jerusalem church (see Ac 12:17), serving on the Jerusalem council where church leaders reached an agreement for the basis of Christian fellowship. The book of James may be the earliest of the NT epistles, probably written about the same time as Paul's letter to the Galatians.

Since the book of James is not directed to one particular church, it is referred to as a general epistle. Though its message reflects Jewish-Christian interests, this book is directed to all believers. James recognizes the need for a practical Christian faith that shows itself through belief and lifestyle. Using illustrations drawn from the OT, James relies on his Jewish background as he urges his readers to follow an ethical life of righteousness. Briefly mentioning the return of Christ, James emphasizes that genuine faith must produce results in good works and righteous deeds. James contends that genuine faith will be reflected in a changed life-style.

1 JAMES,[a] [b]A servant of God and of the Lord Jesus Christ, [c]to the twelve tribes [d]which are scattered abroad, greeting.

Patience in temptation

J T 2 My brethren, [a]count it all joy [b]when ye fall into divers temptations;

3 [a]Knowing *this,* that the trying of your faith worketh patience.

4 But let patience have *her* perfect work, that ye may be perfect and entire, wanting nothing.

5 [a]If any of you lack wisdom, [b]let him ask of God, that giveth to all *men* liberally, and upbraideth not; and [c]it shall be given him.

6 [a]But let him ask in faith, nothing wavering. For he that wavereth is like a wave of the sea driven with the wind and tossed.

7 For let not that man think that he shall receive any thing of the Lord.

8 [a]A double minded man *is* unstable in all his ways.

9 Let the brother of low degree [1]rejoice in that he is exalted:

10 But the rich, in that he is made low: because [a]as the flower of the grass he shall pass away.

11 For the sun is no sooner risen with a burning heat, but it withereth the grass, and the flower thereof falleth, and the grace of the fashion of it perisheth: so also shall the rich man fade away in his ways.

T 12 [a]Blessed *is* the man that endureth temptation: for when he is tried, he shall receive [b]the crown of life, [c]which the Lord hath promised to them that love him.

13 Let no man say when he is tempted, I am tempted of God: for God cannot be tempted with [1]evil, neither tempteth he any man:

C 14 But every man is tempted, when he is drawn away of his own lust, and enticed.

15 Then [a]when lust hath conceived, it bringeth forth sin: and sin, when it is finished, [b]bringeth forth death.

16 Do not err, my beloved brethren.

17 [a]Every good gift and every perfect gift is from above, and cometh down from the Father of lights, [b]with whom is no variableness, neither shadow of turning.

18 [a]Of his own will begat he us with the word of truth, [b]that we should be a kind of [c]firstfruits of his creatures.

The conduct of true religion

19 Wherefore, my beloved brethren, [a]let every man be swift to hear, [b]slow to speak, [c]slow to wrath:

20 For the wrath of man worketh not the righteousness of God.

21 Wherefore [a]lay apart all filthiness and superfluity of naughtiness, and receive with meekness the engrafted word, [b]which is able to save your souls. K S

22 But [a]be ye doers of the word, and not hearers only, deceiving your own selves.

23 For [a]if any be a hearer of the word, and not a doer, he is like unto a man beholding his natural face in a glass:

24 For he beholdeth himself, and goeth his way, and straightway forgetteth what manner of man he was.

25 But [a]whoso looketh into the perfect [b]law of liberty, and continueth *therein,* he being not a forgetful hearer, but a doer of the work, [c]this man shall be blessed in his [1]deed.

26 If any man among you seem to be religious, and [a]bridleth not his tongue, but deceiveth his own heart, this man's religion *is* vain.

27 Pure religion and undefiled before God and the Father is this, [a]To visit the fatherless and widows in their affliction, [b]*and* to keep himself unspotted from the world.

True faith impartial

2 MY BRETHREN, have not the faith of our Lord Jesus Christ, [a]*the Lord* of glory, with [b]respect of persons.

2 For if there come unto your [1]assembly a man with a gold ring, in goodly apparel, and there come in also a poor man in vile raiment;

3 And ye have respect to him that weareth the gay clothing, and say unto him, Sit thou here [1]in a good place; and

1:1 [a] Acts 12:17 [b] Tit. 1:1 [c] Acts 26:7 [d] Deut. 32:26; John 7:35; Acts 2:5; 1 Pet. 1:1
2 [a] Acts 5:41 [b] 1 Pet. 1:6
3 [a] Rom. 5:3
5 [a] 1 Ki. 3:9; Prov. 2:3 [b] Mat. 7:7; Luke 11:9; John 14:13 [c] Jer. 29:12; 1 John 5:14
6 [a] Mark 11:24; 1 Tim. 2:8
8 [a] ch. 4:8
9 [1] Or, *glory*
10 [a] Job 14:2; Ps. 37:2; 1 Cor. 7:31
12 [a] Job 5:17; Prov. 3:11 [b] 1 Cor. 9:25; 2 Tim. 4:8 [c] Mat. 10:22
13 [1] Or, *evils*
15 [a] Job 15:35; Ps. 7:14 [b] Rom. 6:21
17 [a] John 3:27 [b] Num. 23:19
18 [a] John 1:13; 1 Cor. 4:15 [b] Eph. 1:12 [c] Rev. 14:4
19 [a] Eccl. 5:1 [b] Prov. 10:19; Eccl. 5:2 [c] Prov. 14:17
21 [a] Col. 3:8; 1 Pet. 2:1 [b] Acts 13:26; Rom. 1:16; Eph. 1:13; Tit. 2:11
22 [a] Mat. 7:21; Rom. 2:13; 1 John 3:7
23 [a] Luke 6:47
25 [a] 2 Cor. 3:18 [b] ch. 2:12 [c] John 13:17 [1] Or, *doing*
26 [a] Ps. 34:13; 1 Pet. 3:10
27 [a] Is. 1:16; Mat. 25:36 [b] Rom. 12:2; 1 John 5:18
2:1 [a] 1 Cor. 2:8 [b] Lev. 19:15; Deut. 1:17; Mat. 22:16; Jude 16
2 [1] Gk. *synagogue*
3 [1] Or, *well,* or, *seemly*

J *Heb 13:6* ◀ ▶ *Jas 5:10*
T *Heb 12:5–13* ◀ ▶ *Jas 1:12*
T *Jas 1:2–4* ◀ ▶ *1Pe 1:6–7*
C *Heb 3:10* ◀ ▶ *Jas 2:14–15*
K *Heb 13:8* ◀ ▶ *Jas 4:12*
S *Heb 13:20–21* ◀ ▶ *Jas 2:8–26*

say to the poor, Stand thou there, or sit
here under my footstool:
4 Are ye not then partial in yourselves,
and are become judges of evil thoughts?
5 Hearken, my beloved brethren,
[a]Hath not God chosen the poor of this
world [b]rich in faith, and heirs of [1]the
kingdom [c]which he hath promised to
them that love him?
6 But [a]ye have despised the poor. Do
not rich men oppress you, [b]and draw you
before the judgment seats?
7 Do not they blaspheme that worthy
name by the which ye are called?
S 8 If ye fulfil the royal law according to
the scripture, [a]Thou shalt love thy neighbour as thyself, ye do well:
9 But [a]if ye have respect to persons, ye
commit sin, and are convinced of the law
as transgressors.
A 10 For whosoever shall keep the
whole law, and yet offend in one *point,*
[a]he is guilty of all.
11 For [1]he that said, [a]Do not commit
adultery, said also, Do not kill. Now if
thou commit no adultery, yet if thou kill,
thou art become a transgressor of the
law.
J 12 So speak ye, and so do, as they that
shall be judged by [a]the law of liberty.
13 For [a]he shall have judgment without mercy, that hath shown no mercy;
and [b]mercy [1]rejoiceth against judgment.

True faith evidenced by works

C 14 [a]What *doth it* profit, my brethren,
though a man say he hath faith, and have
not works? can faith save him?
15 [a]If a brother or sister be naked, and
destitute of daily food,
16 And [a]one of you say unto them, Depart in peace, be *ye* warmed and filled;
notwithstanding ye give them not those
things which are needful to the body;
what *doth it* profit?
17 Even so faith, if it hath not works,
is dead, being [1]alone.
18 Yea, a man may say, Thou hast
faith, and I have works: show me thy
faith [1]without thy works, [a]and I will
show thee my faith by my works.
19 Thou believest that there is one
God; thou doest well: the devils also believe, and tremble.
20 But wilt thou know, O vain man,
that faith without works is dead?
21 Was not Abraham our father justified by works, [a]when he had offered
Isaac his son upon the altar?
22 [1]Seest thou [a]how faith wrought
with his works, and by works was faith
made perfect?
23 And the scripture was fulfilled F
which saith, [a]Abraham believed God,
and it was imputed unto him for righteousness: and he was called [b]the Friend
of God.
24 Ye see then how that by works a
man is justified, and not by faith only.
25 Likewise also [a]was not Rahab the
harlot justified by works, when she had
received the messengers, and had sent
them out another way?
26 For as the body without the [1]spirit
is dead, so faith without works is dead
also.

True faith evidenced by words

3 MY BRETHREN, [a]be not many masters, [b]knowing that we shall receive
the greater [1]condemnation.
2 For [a]in many things we offend all. [b]If
any man offend not in word, [c]the same *is*
a perfect man, *and* able also to bridle the
whole body.
3 Behold, [a]we put bits in the horses'
mouths, that they may obey us; and we
turn about their whole body.
4 Behold also the ships, which though
they be so great, and *are* driven of fierce
winds, yet are they turned about with a
very small helm, whithersoever the governor listeth.
5 Even so [a]the tongue is a little member, and [b]boasteth great things. Behold,
how great [1]a matter a little fire kindleth!
6 And [a]the tongue *is* a fire, a world of
iniquity: so is the tongue among our
members, that [b]it defileth the whole
body, and setteth on fire the [1]course of
nature; and it is set on fire of hell.
7 For every [1]kind of beasts, and of
birds, and of serpents, and of things in
the sea, is tamed, and hath been tamed of
[2]mankind:
8 But the tongue can no man tame; *it*
is an unruly evil, [a]full of deadly poison.

5 [a]John 7:48 [b]Luke 12:21 [c]Ex. 20:6; Prov. 8:17 [1]Or, *that*
6 [a]1 Cor. 11:22 [b]Acts 13:50
8 [a]Lev. 19:18; Mat. 22:39
9 [a]ver. 1
10 [a]Deut. 27:26; Mat. 5:19; Gal. 3:10
11 [a]Ex. 20:13 [1]Or, *that* law *which said*
12 [a]ch. 1:25
13 [a]Job 22:6 [b]1 John 4:17 [1]Or, *glorieth*
14 [a]Mat. 7:26; Mat. 15:11
15 [a]Luke 3:11
16 [a]1 John 3:18
17 [1]Gk. *by itself*
18 [a]ch. 3:13 [1]Some copies read, *by thy works*
21 [a]Gen. 22:9
22 [a]Heb. 11:17 [1]Or, *Thou seest*
23 [a]Gen. 15:6; Rom. 4:3; Gal. 3:6 [b]2 Chr. 20:7; Is. 41:8
25 [a]Heb. 11:31
26 [1]Or, *breath*
3:1 [a]Mat. 23:8 [b]Luke 6:37 [1]Or, *Judgment*
2 [a]1 Ki. 8:46; 2 Chr. 6:36; Prov. 20:9 [b]Ps. 34:13; 1 Pet. 3:10 [c]Mat. 12:37
3 [a]Ps. 32:9
5 [a]Prov. 12:18 [b]Ps. 12:3 [1]Or, *wood*
6 [a]Prov. 16:27 [b]Mat. 15:11 [1]Gk. *wheel*
7 [1]Gk. *nature* [2]Gk. *nature of man*
8 [a]Ps. 140:3

S *Jas 1:21–27* ◀▶ *Jas 3:11–13*
A *Eph 2:1–3* ◀▶ *1Jn 8*
J *Heb 12:23* ◀▶ *1Pe 4:5*
C *Jas 1:14–15* ◀▶ *Jas 4:5*
F *Heb 11:6* ◀▶ *1Pe 1:8–9*

9 Therewith bless we God, even the Father; and therewith curse we men, [a]which are made after the similitude of God.

10 Out of the same mouth proceedeth blessing and cursing. My brethren, these things ought not so to be.

S 11 Doth a fountain send forth at the same [1]place sweet *water* and bitter?

12 Can the fig tree, my brethren, bear olive berries? either a vine, figs? so *can* no fountain both yield salt water and fresh.

True and false wisdom

13 [a]Who *is* a wise man and endued with knowledge among you? let him show out of a good conversation [b]his works [c]with meekness of wisdom.

14 But if ye have [a]bitter envying and strife in your hearts, [b]glory not, and lie not against the truth.

15 [a]This wisdom descendeth not from above, but *is* earthly, [1]sensual, devilish.

16 For [a]where envying and strife *is,* there *is* [1]confusion and every evil work.

17 But [a]the wisdom that is from above is first pure, then peaceable, gentle, *and* easy to be entreated, full of mercy and good fruits, [1]without partiality, [b]and without hypocrisy.

18 [a]And the fruit of righteousness is sown in peace of them that make peace.

Friendship and humility

4 FROM WHENCE *come* wars and [1]fightings among you? *come they* not hence, *even* of your [2]lusts [a]that war in your members?

2 Ye lust, and have not: ye [1]kill, and desire to have, and cannot obtain: ye fight and war, yet ye have not, because ye ask not.

3 [a]Ye ask, and receive not, [b]because ye ask amiss, that ye may consume *it* upon your [1]lusts.

4 [a]Ye adulterers and adulteresses, know ye not that [b]the friendship of the world is enmity with God? [c]whosoever therefore will be a friend of the world is the enemy of God.

S *Jas 2:8–26* ◀▶ *Jas 4:8*

C 5 Do ye think that the scripture saith in vain, [a]The spirit that dwelleth in us lusteth [1]to envy?

M 6 But he giveth more grace. Wherefore he saith, [a]God resisteth the proud, but giveth grace unto the humble.

7 Submit yourselves therefore to God. [a]Resist the devil, and he will flee from you.

R S 8 [a]Draw nigh to God, and he will draw nigh to you. [b]Cleanse *your* hands, *ye* sinners; and [c]purify *your* hearts, *ye* [d]double minded.

9 [a]Be afflicted, and mourn, and weep: let your laughter be turned to mourning, and *your* joy to heaviness.

L 10 [a]Humble yourselves in the sight of the Lord, and he shall lift you up.

Slander and false confidence

11 [a]Speak not evil one of another, brethren. He that speaketh evil of *his* brother, [b]and judgeth his brother, speaketh evil of the law, and judgeth the law: but if thou judge the law, thou art not a doer of the law, but a judge.

K O 12 There is one lawgiver, [a]who is able to save and to destroy: [b]who art thou that judgest another?

N 13 [a]Go to now, ye that say, Today or tomorrow we will go into such a city, and continue there a year, and buy and sell, and get gain:

14 Whereas ye know not what *shall be* on the morrow. For what *is* your life? [a]It[1] is even a vapour, that appeareth for a little time, and then vanisheth away.

15 For that ye *ought* to say, [a]If the Lord will, we shall live, and do this, or that.

16 But now ye rejoice in your boastings: [a]all such rejoicing is evil.

S 17 Therefore [a]to him that knoweth to do good, and doeth *it* not, to him it is sin.

C *Jas 2:14–15* ◀▶ *1Pe 2:25*
M *1Ti 6:3–4* ◀▶ *1Pe 5:5–6*
R *2Co 7:9–10* ◀▶ *2Pe 3:9*
S *Jas 3:11–13* ◀▶ *Jas 4:17*
L *Heb 13:8* ◀▶ *Jas 5:11*
K *Jas 1:21* ◀▶ *1Pe 1:4–5*
O *Heb 9:22* ◀▶ *1Jn 5:12*
N *Heb 12:25* ◀▶ *1Jn 5:10*
S *Jas 4:8* ◀▶ *Jas 5:9*

9 [a]Gen. 1:26
11 [1]Or, *hole*
13 [a]Gal. 6:4 [b]ch. 2:18 [c]ch. 1:21
14 [a]Rom. 13:13 [b]Rom. 2:17
15 [a]Phil. 3:19 [1]Or, *natural*
16 [a]1 Cor. 3:3; Gal. 5:20 [1]Gk. *tumult,* or, *unquietness*
17 [a]1 Cor. 2:6 [b]Rom. 12:9; 1 Pet. 1:22 [1]Or, *without wrangling*
18 [a]Prov. 11:18
4:1 [a]Rom. 7:23; Gal. 5:17 [1]Or, *brawlings* [2]Or, *pleasures*
2 [1]Or, *envy*
3 [a]Job 27:9; Ps. 18:41 [b]Ps. 66:18 [1]Or, *pleasures*
4 [a]Ps. 73:27 [b]1 John 2:15 [c]John 15:19; Gal. 1:10
5 [a]Gen. 6:5; Num. 11:29 [1]Or, *enviously?*
6 [a]Job 22:29; Ps. 138:6; Prov. 3:34; Mat. 23:12
7 [a]Eph. 4:27; 1 Pet. 5:9
8 [a]2 Chr. 15:2 [b]Is. 1:16 [c]1 Pet. 1:22; 1 John 3:3 [d]ch. 1:8
9 [a]Mat. 5:4
10 [a]Job 22:29
11 [a]1 Pet. 2:1 [b]Mat. 7:1
12 [a]Mat. 10:28 [b]Rom. 14:4
13 [a]Prov. 27:1
14 [a]Job 7:7 [1]Or, *For it is*
15 [a]Acts 18:21
16 [a]1 Cor. 5:6
17 [a]Luke 12:47; John 9:41

The miseries of the rich

E 5 GO [a]TO now, *ye* rich men, weep
and howl for your miseries that shall
come upon *you*.
2 Your riches are corrupted, and [a]your
garments are motheaten.
E 3 Your gold and silver is cankered; and
the rust of them shall be a witness against
you, and shall eat your flesh as it were
fire. [a]Ye have heaped treasure together
for the last days.
4 Behold, [a]the hire of the labourers
who have reaped down your fields,
which is of you kept back by fraud,
crieth: and [b]the cries of them which have
reaped are entered into the ears of the
Lord of sabaoth.
5 [a]Ye have lived in pleasure on the
earth, and been wanton; ye have nourished your hearts, as in a day of slaughter.
6 [a]Ye have condemned *and* killed the
just; *and* he doth not resist you.

The patience of the saints

C 7 ʹBe patient therefore, brethren, unto
E the coming of the Lord. Behold, the husbandman waiteth for the precious fruit
of the earth, and hath long patience for
it, until he receive [a]the early and latter
rain.
8 Be ye also patient; stablish your
hearts: [a]for the coming of the Lord draweth nigh.

9 [a]Grudgeʹ not one against another, S
brethren, lest ye be condemned: behold,
the judge [b]standeth before the door.
10 [a]Take, my brethren, the prophets, J
who have spoken in the name of the L
Lord, for an example of suffering affliction, and of patience.
11 Behold, [a]we count them happy L
which endure. Ye have heard of [b]the patience of Job, and have seen [c]the end of
the Lord; that [d]the Lord is very pitiful,
and of tender mercy.
12 But above all things, my brethren,
[a]swear not, neither by heaven, neither
by the earth, neither by any other oath:
but let your yea be yea; and *your* nay,
nay; lest ye fall into condemnation.

Prayer and confession

13 Is any among you afflicted? let H
him pray. Is any merry? [a]let him sing
psalms.
14 Is any sick among you? let him call
for the elders of the church; and let them
pray over him, [a]anointing him with oil in
the name of the Lord:
15 And the prayer of faith shall save
the sick, and the Lord shall raise him up;
[a]and if he have committed sins, they
shall be forgiven him.
16 Confess *your* faults one to another,
and pray one for another, that ye may be

5:1 [a]Prov. 11:28; Luke 6:24
2 [a]Job 13:28; Mat. 6:20
3 [a]Rom. 2:5
4 [a]Lev. 19:13 [b]Deut. 24:15
5 [a]Job 21:13; Amos 6:1
6 [a]ch. 2:6
7 [a]Deut. 11:14; Hos. 6:3 ʹOr, *Be long patient*, or, *Suffer with long patience*
8 [a]Phil. 4:5; 1 Pet. 4:7
9 [a]ch. 4:11 [b]Mat. 24:33 ʹOr, *Groan*, or, *Grieve not*
10 [a]Mat. 5:12
11 [a]Ps. 94:12 [b]Job 2:10 [c]Job 42:10 [d]Num. 14:18
12 [a]Mat. 5:34
13 [a]Eph. 5:19
14 [a]Mark 6:13
15 [a]Is. 33:24

E *2Ti 4:3–4* ◀▶ *Jas 5:3*
E *Jas 5:1* ◀▶ *Jas 5:7*
C *Heb 10:37* ◀▶ *1Pe 1:5*
E *Jas 5:3* ◀▶ *2Pe 3:3–10*

S *Jas 4:17* ◀▶ *Jas 5:19–20*
J *Jas 1:2–4* ◀▶ *1Pe 2:19–20*
L *Heb 13:5–6* ◀▶ *1Pe 3:12*
L *Jas 4:10* ◀▶ *1Pe 1:18–19*
H *Eph 6:2–3* ◀▶ *1Pe 3:10*

5:1–3 James warns that in the last days the rich will weep because their wealth will be worthless to help them during the famine and economic devastation that will unfold during the tribulation (see Rev 6:5–6). The rich will be left with nothing, for even gold and silver, the historic standard of value in troubled times, will be of no value. Though they have amassed great wealth for the last days, their gold and silver will tarnish because no one will want to buy.

5:7–9 James commands Christians to wait patiently for the Lord's coming and likens our waiting to a farmer who waits for the harvest. The farmer can tell by the rain when the final harvest is approaching. So also believers can tell by the fulfillment of the prophecies in our generation that Christ's return is near.

Yet James advises believers to be patient in light of the imminent reality of the second coming. Expectantly hoping that Christ might return at any moment, we must always remember that God looks at time very differently then we do (see 2Pe 3:8). Therefore we must not murmur and complain against each other for "the judge standeth before the door" (5:9). Such grudges violate Paul's command to "do all things without murmurings and disputings: That ye may be blameless and harmless, the sons of God, without rebuke, in the midst of a crooked and perverse nation" (Php 2:14–15).

healed. [a]The effectual fervent prayer of a
righteous man availeth much.
17 Elias was a man [a]subject to like passions as we are, and [b]he prayed [1]ear-
nestly that it might not rain: [c]and it
rained not on the earth by the space of
three years and six months.
18 And [a]he prayed again, and the
heaven gave rain, and the earth brought
forth her fruit.

16 [a]Num. 11:2; John 9:31
17 [a]Acts 14:15 [b]1 Ki. 17:1 [c]Luke 4:25 [1]Or, *in his prayer*
18 [a]1 Ki. 18:42,45
19 [a]Mat. 18:15
20 [a]Rom. 11:14 [b]Prov. 10:12; 1 Pet. 4:8

19 Brethren, [a]if any of you do err from **P**
the truth, and one convert him; **S**
20 Let him know, that he which con-
verteth the sinner from the error of his
way [a]shall save a soul from death, and
[b]shall hide a multitude of sins.

P *Ro 11:23–24* ◀ ▶ *1Jn 2:1–2*
S *Jas 5:9* ◀ ▶ *1Pe 1:2*

1 Peter

Author: Peter

Theme: Hope in the midst of suffering

Date of Writing: C. A.D. 60–64

Outline of 1 Peter

I. Salutation (1:1–2)
II. A Great Salvation (1:3—2:10)
III. Conduct of the Believer (2:11—4:11)
IV. Ministry Through Suffering (4:12—5:11)
V. Conclusion (5:12–14)

THIS LETTER WAS written by the apostle Peter shortly before his martyrdom under Emperor Nero of Rome. Peter wrote this letter from Babylon (see 5:13) and directed his words to the churches in the northern portion of the Roman province of Asia. Scholars disagree on the location of this "Babylon," suggesting that it could be a figurative reference to Rome or Jerusalem. There is little evidence to support these contentions since the context of 5:13 is not figurative in style, nor is there historical evidence from the first two centuries to indicate that Peter was ever in Rome or ever served as the leader of the Roman church. Other scholars suggest that Peter wrote this letter from a small, Egyptian military outpost called Babylon, though evidence to support this claim is also limited. Still other scholars contend that Peter penned these words from the small, first-century town of Babylon that was located on the Euphrates River in what is modern-day Iraq. Wherever the exact location of its composition, 1 Peter can be satisfactorily dated in the early A.D. 60s.

The recurring theme of this letter is the suffering of Christ and his saints and the glory of God that will ultimately be revealed through believers' lives. First-century Christians faced desperate times. During the rule of Emperor Nero, government policy shifted from tolerance to open persecution of Christians in Rome. Under the later rule of Emperor Domitian this persecution would spread throughout the empire. Yet sporadic waves of oppression had already begun in certain provinces and cities when Peter wrote this letter to struggling believers. Peter's message of hope, pilgrimage, courage and glory exhorts the believers to stand firm in their faith. Setting the readers' sights on their heavenly rewards, Peter's encouraging words testify to the true grace of God and fulfill Christ's command to Peter to "strengthen thy brethren" (Lk 22:32).

1

PETER, AN apostle of Jesus Christ, to the strangers [a]scattered throughout Pontus, Galatia, Cappadocia, Asia, and Bithynia,

E 2 [a]Elect [b]according to the foreknowl-
S edge of God the Father, [c]through sanctifi-
W cation of the Spirit, unto obedience and
S [d]sprinkling of the blood of Jesus Christ: [e]Grace unto you, and peace, be multiplied.

The risen Christ

3 [a]Blessed *be* the God and Father of our Lord Jesus Christ, which [b]according to his [/]abundant mercy [c]hath begotten us again unto a lively hope [d]by the resurrection of Jesus Christ from the dead,

K 4 To an inheritance incorruptible, and undefiled, and that fadeth not away, [a]reserved in heaven [/]for you,

C 5 [a]Who are kept by the power of God through faith unto salvation ready to be revealed in the last time.

T 6 [a]Wherein ye greatly rejoice, though now [b]for a season, if need be, [c]ye are in heaviness through manifold temptations:

C 7 That [a]the trial of your faith, being much more precious than of gold that perisheth, though [b]it be tried with fire, [c]might be found unto praise and honour and glory at the appearing of Jesus Christ:

F 8 [a]Whom having not seen, ye love; [b]in whom, though now ye see *him* not, yet believing, ye rejoice with joy unspeakable and full of glory:

E *Heb 11:11 ◀▶ 1Pe 1:11–12*
S *Heb 10:14–15 ◀▶ 1Pe 1:22*
W *1Ti 4:12 ◀▶ 1Pe 2:5*
S *Jas 5:19–20 ◀▶ 1Pe 1:15–17*
K *Jas 4:12 ◀▶ 1Pe 1:9*
C *Jas 5:7–9 ◀▶ 1Pe 1:7*
T *Jas 1:12 ◀▶ 1Pe 5:10*
C *1Pe 1:5 ◀▶ 1Pe 1:13*
F *Jas 2:23 ◀▶ 1Pe 2:6*

1:1 [a]John 7:35; Acts 2:5,9; Jas. 1:1
2 [a]Eph. 1:4 [b]Rom. 8:29 [c]2 Thes. 2:13 [d]Heb. 12:24 [e]Rom. 1:7
3 [a]Eph. 1:3 [b]Tit. 3:5 [c]John 3:3,5; Jas. 1:18 [d]1 Cor. 15:20 [/]Gk. *much*
4 [a]Col. 1:5 [/]Or, *for us*
5 [a]John 10:28
6 [a]Mat. 5:12 [b]2 Cor. 4:17 [c]Jas. 1:2
7 [a]Jas. 1:3 [b]Job 23:10; Prov. 17:3 [c]Rom. 2:7
8 [a]1 John 4:20 [b]John 20:29
9 [a]Rom. 6:22
10 [a]Gen. 49:10
11 [a]2 Pet. 1:21
12 [a]Dan. 9:24 [b]Heb. 11:13 [c]Acts 2:4 [d]Dan. 8:13
13 [a]Eph. 6:14 [b]Luke 21:34; Rom. 13:13 [c]1 Cor. 1:7 [/]Gk. *perfectly*
14 [a]Rom. 12:2 [b]Acts 17:30
15 [a]2 Cor. 7:1
16 [a]Lev. 11:44
17 [a]Deut. 10:17 [b]Heb. 12:28 [c]Heb. 11:13

9 Receiving [a]the end of your faith, *even* the salvation of *your* souls. K

10 [a]Of which salvation the prophets have inquired and searched diligently, who prophesied of the grace *that should come* unto you:

11 Searching what, or what manner of B
time [a]the Spirit of Christ which was in E
them did signify, when it testified before- T
hand the sufferings of Christ, and the glory that should follow.

12 [a]Unto whom it was revealed, that L
[b]not unto themselves, but unto us they did minister the things, which are now reported unto you by them that have preached the gospel unto you with [c]the Holy Ghost sent down from heaven; [d]which things the angels desire to look into.

An appeal for a holy life

13 Wherefore [a]gird up the loins of C
your mind, [b]be sober, and hope [/]to the end for the grace that is to be brought unto you [c]at the revelation of Jesus Christ;

14 As obedient children, [a]not fashioning yourselves according to the former lusts [b]in your ignorance:

15 [a]But as he which hath called you is S
holy, so be ye holy in all manner of conversation;

16 Because it is written, [a]Be ye holy; for I am holy.

17 And if ye call on the Father, [a]who without respect of persons judgeth according to every man's work, [b]pass the time of your [c]sojourning *here* in fear:

K *1Pe 1:4–5 ◀▶ 1Pe 2:6*
B *Heb 10:14–15 ◀▶ 1Pe 4:10–11*
E *1Pe 1:2 ◀▶ 1Pe 1:22*
T *Heb 6:4 ◀▶ 1Pe 4:10–11*
L *Heb 9:14 ◀▶ 1Pe 1:22*
C *1Pe 1:7 ◀▶ 1Pe 1:20*
S *1Pe 1:2 ◀▶ 1Pe 2:21–22*

1:5 Peter tells us that our spiritual preservation depends on "the power of God through faith" (1:5). The apostle also indicates that Jesus Christ will appear in the last days to establish his eternal kingdom of God on earth forever. No one can know how long Christ will delay until he returns, but the fulfillment of many specific prophecies in our generation strongly suggest that some of us may still be alive to witness the final coming of Jesus Christ to set up his kingdom on earth.

1:7 Faith will be rewarded amply when all Christians witness the glorious "appearing of Jesus Christ" (1:7).

1:13 Peter encourages Christians to be prepared and disciplined in light of Christ's unshakable prophecies that he will return in glory. When he comes he will bring the blessedness and deliverance from sin that is the hope of every believer and the mark of the grace of God.

D G L 18 Forasmuch as ye know [a]that ye were not redeemed with corruptible things, *as* silver and gold, from your vain conversation [b]*received* by tradition from your fathers;

19 But [a]with the precious blood of Christ, [b]as of a lamb without blemish and without spot:

C 20 [a]Who verily was foreordained before the foundation of the world, but was manifest [b]in these last times for you,

21 Who by him do believe in God, [a]that raised him up from the dead, and [b]gave him glory; that your faith and hope might be in God.

E F L S 22 Seeing ye [a]have purified your souls in obeying the truth through the Spirit unto unfeigned [b]love of the brethren, *see that ye* love one another with a pure heart fervently:

23 [a]Being born again, not of corruptible seed, but of incorruptible, [b]by the word of God, which liveth and abideth for ever.

24 [1]For [a]all flesh *is* as grass, and all the glory of man as the flower of grass. The grass withereth, and the flower thereof falleth away:

25 [a]But the word of the Lord endureth for ever. [b]And this is the word which by the gospel is preached unto you.

2 WHEREFORE [a]LAYING aside all malice, and all guile, and hypocrisies, and envies, and all evil speakings,

2 [a]As newborn babes, desire the sincere [b]milk of the word, that ye may grow thereby:

3 If so be ye have [a]tasted that the Lord *is* gracious.

Christ our corner stone

4 To whom coming, *as unto* a living stone, [a]disallowed indeed of men, but chosen of God, *and* precious,

5 [a]Ye also, as lively stones, [1]are built up [b]a spiritual house, [c]an holy priesthood, to offer up [d]spiritual sacrifices, [e]acceptable to God by Jesus Christ. E L W

6 Wherefore also it is contained in the scripture, [a]Behold, I lay in Zion a chief corner stone, elect, precious: and he that believeth on him shall not be confounded. F K L

7 Unto you therefore which believe *he is* [1]precious: but unto them which be disobedient, [a]the stone which the builders disallowed, the same is made the head of the corner,

8 [a]And a stone of stumbling, and a rock of offence, [b]*even to them* which stumble at the word, being disobedient: [c]whereunto also they were appointed.

9 But ye *are* [a]a chosen generation, [b]a royal priesthood, [c]an holy nation, [d]a [1] peculiar people; that ye should show forth the [2]praises of him who hath called you out of [e]darkness into his marvellous light: T

10 [a]Which in time past *were* not a people, but *are* now the people of God: which had not obtained mercy, but now have obtained mercy.

11 Dearly beloved, I beseech *you* [a]as strangers and pilgrims, [b]abstain from fleshly lusts, [c]which war against the soul;

12 [a]Having your conversation honest among the Gentiles: that, [1]whereas they speak against you as evildoers, [b]they may by *your* good works, which they shall behold, glorify God in the day of visitation.

Christian submission

13 [a]Submit yourselves to every ordinance of man for the Lord's sake: whether it be to the king, as supreme;

14 Or unto governors, as unto them that are sent by him [a]for the punishment of evildoers, and [b]for the praise of them that do well.

15 For so is the will of God, that [a]with

18 [a]1 Cor. 6:20 [b]Ezek. 20:18
19 [a]Acts 20:28 [b]Ex. 12:5
20 [a]Rom. 3:25 [b]Gal. 4:4
21 [a]Acts 2:24 [b]Acts 2:33
22 [a]Acts 15:9 [b]Heb. 13:1
23 [a]John 1:13 [b]Jas. 1:18
24 [a]Is. 40:6 [1]Or, *For that*
25 [a]Is. 40:8 [b]John 1:1
2:1 [a]Heb. 12:1
2 [a]Mat. 18:3 [b]1 Cor. 3:2
3 [a]Heb. 6:5
4 [a]Ps. 118:22; Acts 4:11
5 [a]Eph. 2:21 [b]Heb. 3:6 [c]Is. 61:6 [d]Hos. 14:2; Mal. 1:11 [e]Phil. 4:18 [1]Or, *be ye built*
6 [a]Is. 28:16
7 [a]Ps. 118:22 [1]Or, *an honour*
8 [a]Is. 8:14 [b]1 Cor. 1:23 [c]Rom. 9:22
9 [a]Deut. 10:15 [b]Rev. 5:10 [c]Is. 62:12 [d]Deut. 4:20 [e]Acts 26:18 [1]Or, *a purchased people* [2]Or, *virtues*
10 [a]Hos. 1:9
11 [a]Ps. 39:12 [b]Gal. 5:16 [c]Jas. 4:1
12 [a]Phil. 2:15 [b]Mat. 5:16 [1]Or, *wherein*
13 [a]Rom. 13:1
14 [a]Rom. 13:4 [b]Rom. 13:3
15 [a]Tit. 2:8

D *Heb 13:11–12* ◀▶ *1Pe 2:24*
G *Heb 11:6* ◀▶ *Rev 3:17–18*
L *Jas 5:11* ◀▶ *1Pe 2:6*
C *1Pe 1:13* ◀▶ *1Pe 4:7*
E *1Pe 1:11–12* ◀▶ *1Pe 2:5*
F *Heb 1:9* ◀ **L** *1Pe 1:12* ◀▶ *1Pe 2:5*
S *1Pe 1:2* ◀▶ *Jude 19–20*

E *1Pe 1:22* ◀▶ *1Pe 3:18–19*
L *1Pe 1:22* ◀▶ *1Pe 3:18–19*
W *1Pe 1:2* ◀▶ *1Pe 4:10–11*
F *1Pe 1:8–9* ◀▶ *1Jn 3:23*
K *1Pe 1:9* ◀▶ *1Pe 2:24*
L *1Pe 1:18–19* ◀▶ *1Pe 2:24–25*
T *Heb 13:15–16* ◀▶ *Rev 12:11*

1:20 This verse affirms Christ's preeminence (see Jn 17:24) and reveals that none of the events of Christ's earthly ministry, trial, death or resurrection was unexpected by God. God unfolded these things in his time and his plan to win salvation for humanity and deliver us from the curse of sin.

well doing ye may put to silence the ignorance of foolish men:

16 [a]As free, and not [l]using *your* liberty for a cloak of maliciousness, but as [b]the servants of God.

17 [a]Honour[l] all *men.* [b]Love the brotherhood. [c]Fear God. Honour the king.

18 [a]Servants, *be* subject to *your* masters with all fear; not only to the good and gentle, but also to the froward.

J 19 For this *is* [a]thankworthy,[l] if a man for conscience toward God endure grief, suffering wrongfully.

20 For what glory *is it,* if, when ye be buffeted for your faults, ye shall take it patiently? but if, when ye do well, and suffer *for it,* ye take it patiently, this *is* [l]acceptable with God.

Christ our great example

S 21 For [a]even hereunto were ye called: because Christ also suffered [l]for us, [b]leaving us an example, that ye should follow his steps:

22 [a]Who did no sin, neither was guile found in his mouth:

23 [a]Who, when he was reviled, reviled not again; when he suffered, he threatened not; but [b]committed[l] *himself* to him that judgeth righteously:

D K L S 24 [a]Who his own self bare our sins in his own body [l]on the tree, [b]that we, being dead to sins, should live unto righteousness: [c]by whose stripes ye were healed.

C 25 For [a]ye were as sheep going astray; but are now returned [b]unto the Shepherd and Bishop of your souls.

The husband and the wife

3 LIKEWISE, [a]YE wives, *be* in subjection to your own husbands; that, if any obey not the word, [b]they also may without the word [c]be won by the conversation of the wives;

2 [a]While they behold your chaste conversation *coupled* with fear.

3 [a]Whose adorning let it not be that outward *adorning* of plaiting the hair, and of wearing of gold, or of putting on of apparel;

4 But *let it be* [a]the hidden man of the heart, in that which is not corruptible, *even the ornament* of a meek and quiet spirit, which is in the sight of God of great price.

5 For after this manner in the old time the holy women also, who trusted in God, adorned themselves, being in subjection unto their own husbands:

6 Even as Sarah obeyed Abraham, [a]calling him lord: whose [l]daughters ye are, as long as ye do well, and are not afraid with any amazement.

7 [a]Likewise, ye husbands, dwell with *them* according to knowledge, giving honour unto the wife, [b]as unto the weaker vessel, and as being heirs together of the grace of life; [c]that your prayers be not hindered.

Christian conduct

8 Finally, [a]*be ye* all of one mind, having compassion one of another, [b]love[l] as brethren, [c]*be* pitiful, *be* courteous:

9 [a]Not rendering evil for evil, or railing for railing: but contrariwise blessing; knowing that ye are thereunto called, [b]that ye should inherit a blessing.

10 For [a]he that will love life, and see good days, [b]let him refrain his tongue from evil, and his lips that they speak no guile: S H

11 Let him [a]eschew evil, and do good; [b]let him seek peace, and ensue it.

12 For the eyes of the Lord *are* over the righteous, [a]and his ears *are open* unto their prayers: but the face of the Lord *is* [l]against them that do evil. H L U

13 [a]And who *is* he that will harm you, if ye be followers of that which is good?

14 [a]But and if ye suffer for righteousness' sake, happy *are ye:* and [b]be not afraid of their terror, neither be troubled; J W

15 But sanctify the Lord God in your hearts: and [a]*be* ready always to *give* an answer to every man that asketh you a reason of the hope that is in you with meekness and [l]fear:

16 [a]Gal. 5:1 [b]1 Cor. 7:22 [l]Gk. *having*
17 [a]Rom. 12:10 [b]Heb. 13:1 [c]Rom. 13:7 [l]Or, *Esteem*
18 [a]Eph. 6:5
19 [a]Mat. 5:10 [l]Or, *thank*
20 [l]Or, *thank*
21 [a]Mat. 16:24 [b]1 John 2:6 [l]Some read, *for you*
22 [a]Is. 53:9
23 [a]Is. 53:7 [b]Luke 23:46 [l]Or, *committed* his cause
24 [a]Heb. 9:28 [b]Rom. 7:6 [c]Is. 53:5 [l]Or, *to*
25 [a]Is. 53:6 [b]Ezek. 34:23; Heb. 13:20
3:1 [a]1 Cor. 14:34 [b]1 Cor. 7:16 [c]Mat. 18:15
2 [a]ch. 2:12
3 [a]1 Tim. 2:9
4 [a]Rom. 2:29
6 [a]Gen. 18:12 [l]Gk. *children*
7 [a]1 Cor. 7:3 [b]1 Cor. 12:23 [c]Job 42:8; Mat. 18:19
8 [a]Rom. 12:16 [b]Rom. 12:10; Heb. 13:1 [c]Eph. 4:32 [l]Or, *loving to the brethren*
9 [a]Prov. 17:13 [b]Mat. 25:34
10 [a]Ps. 34:12 [b]Jas. 1:26; Rev. 14:5
11 [a]Ps. 37:27; 3 John 11 [b]Rom. 12:18; Heb. 12:14
12 [a]John 9:31; Jas. 5:16 [l]Gk. *upon*
13 [a]Prov. 16:7
14 [a]Jas. 1:12; ch. 2:19 [b]Is. 8:12,13
15 [a]Ps. 119:46; Col. 4:6; 2 Tim. 2:25 [l]Or, *reverence*

J *Jas 5:10* ◀▶ *1Pe 3:14*
S *1Pe 1:15–17* ◀▶ *1Pe 2:24*
D *1Pe 1:18–19* ◀▶ *1Pe 3:18*
K *1Pe 2:6* ◀▶ *2Pe 2:9*
L *1Pe 2:6* ◀▶ *1Pe 3:18*
S *1Pe 2:21–22* ◀▶ *1Pe 3:10–12*
C *Jas 4:5* ◀▶ *2Pe 2:17*

S *1Pe 2:24* ◀▶ *1Pe 4:17–18*
H *Jas 5:13–18* ◀▶ *3Jn 2*
H *Heb 12:29* ◀▶ *1Pe 4:17–18*
L *Jas 5:10–11* ◀▶ *1Pe 5:7*
U *1Ti 4:8* ◀▶ *1Jn 4*
J *1Pe 2:19–20* ◀▶ *1Pe 4:12–14*
W *Heb 13:5–6* ◀▶ *1Pe 5:7*

16 [a]Having a good conscience; [b]that, whereas they speak evil of you, as of evildoers, they may be ashamed that falsely accuse your good conversation in Christ.

17 For *it is* better, if the will of God be so, that ye suffer for well doing, than for evil doing.

18 For Christ also hath [a]once suffered for sins, the just for the unjust, that he might bring us to God, [b]being put to death [c]in the flesh, but [d]quickened by the Spirit:

19 By which also he went and [a]preached unto the spirits [b]in prison;

20 Which sometime were disobedient, [a]when once the longsuffering of God waited in the days of Noah, while [b]the ark was a-preparing, [c]wherein few, that is, eight souls were saved by water.

21 [a]The like figure whereunto *even* baptism doth also now save us (not the putting away of [b]the filth of the flesh, [c]but the answer of a good conscience toward God,) [d]by the resurrection of Jesus Christ:

22 Who is gone into heaven, and [a]is on the right hand of God; [b]angels and authorities and powers being made subject unto him.

4 FORASMUCH THEN [a]as Christ hath suffered for us in the flesh, arm yourselves likewise with the same mind: for [b]he that hath suffered in the flesh hath ceased from sin;

2 [a]That he no longer [b]should live the rest of *his* time in the flesh to the lusts of men, [c]but to the will of God.

3 [a]For the time past of *our* life may suffice us [b]to have wrought the will of the Gentiles, when we walked in lasciviousness, lusts, excess of wine, revellings, banquetings, and abominable idolatries:

4 Wherein they think it strange that ye run not with *them* to the same excess of riot, [a]speaking evil of *you:*

5 Who shall give account to him that is ready [a]to judge the quick and the dead.

6 For for this cause [a]was the gospel preached also to them that are dead, that they might be judged according to men in the flesh, but live according to God in the spirit.

7 But [a]the end of all things is at hand: [b]be ye therefore sober, and watch unto prayer.

8 [a]And above all things have fervent charity among yourselves: for [b]charity [1]shall cover the multitude of sins.

9 [a]Use hospitality one to another [b]without grudging.

10 [a]As every man hath received the gift, *even so* minister the same one to another, [b]as good stewards of [c]the manifold grace of God.

11 [a]If any man speak, *let him speak* as the oracles of God; [b]if any man minister, *let him do it* as of the ability which God giveth: that [c]God in all things may be glorified through Jesus Christ, [d]to whom be praise and dominion for ever and ever. Amen.

The Christian and suffering

12 Beloved, think it not strange concerning [a]the fiery trial which is to try you, as though some strange thing happened unto you:

16 [a]Heb. 13:18 [b]Tit. 2:8
18 [a]Rom. 5:6 [b]2 Cor. 13:4 [c]Col. 1:21 [d]Rom. 1:4
19 [a]ch. 1:12 [b]Is. 42:7
20 [a]Gen. 6:3,5 [b]Heb. 11:7 [c]Gen. 7:7
21 [a]Eph. 5:26 [b]Tit. 3:5 [c]Rom. 10:10 [d]ch. 1:3
22 [a]Ps. 110:1; Rom. 8:34 [b]Rom. 8:38; 1 Cor. 15:24
4:1 [a]ch. 3:18 [b]Gal. 5:24
2 [a]Rom. 14:7 [b]Gal. 2:20 [c]John 1:13
3 [a]Ezek. 44:6 [b]Eph. 2:2; 1 Thes. 4:5; Tit. 3:3
4 [a]Acts 13:45
5 [a]Acts 10:42; Rom. 14:10; 2 Tim. 4:1
6 [a]ch. 3:19
7 [a]Rom. 13:12 [b]Mat. 26:41; Luke 21:34
8 [a]Col. 3:14; Heb. 13:1 [b]Prov. 10:12; 1 Cor. 13:7 [1]Or, *will*
9 [a]Heb. 13:2 [b]2 Cor. 9:7
10 [a]Rom. 12:6 [b]Mat. 24:45; Tit. 1:7 [c]1 Cor. 12:4; Eph. 4:11
11 [a]Jer. 23:22 [b]1 Cor. 3:10 [c]Eph. 5:20 [d]1 Tim. 6:16
12 [a]1 Cor. 3:13

E *1Pe 2:5 ◀▶ 1Pe 4:10–11*
H *Heb 2:4 ◀▶ Rev 11:11*
L *1Pe 2:5 ◀▶ 1Pe 4:10–11*
D *1Pe 2:24 ◀▶ 1Jn 7*
L *1Pe 2:24–25 ◀▶ 2Pe 3:9*
J *Heb 10:30 ◀▶ 2Pe 2:9*
J *Jas 2:12–13 ◀▶ 2Pe 2:4*
C *1Pe 1:20 ◀▶ 1Pe 4:13*
B *1Pe 1:11 ◀▶ 1Jn 2:20*
E *1Pe 3:18–19 ◀▶ 2Pe 1:21*
G *Heb 2:4 ◀▶ 2Pe 1:21*
L *1Pe 3:18–19 ◀▶ Jude 19–20*
T *1Pe 1:11 ◀▶ 2Pe 1:21*
W *1Pe 2:5 ◀▶ Jude 19–20*
J *1Pe 3:14 ◀▶ 1Pe 4:16*

4:5 Everyone, both the Christian saints and the wicked dead, will be judged by Jesus Christ. Whether they are living at the time of judgment or dead and buried, every human being that has ever lived will face Jesus Christ (see Ps 1:6; Mt 25:31–46; Jn 5:22–23, 28–29; Ro 14:10; 2Ti 4:1). For those who have truly repented of their sins, the completed atonement of Christ's death on the cross will grant them justification and eternal life in heaven. But those who have continued to be unrepentant will face his wrath and eternal punishment.

4:7 Peter did not mean that Jesus' return to resurrect the saints would occur immediately. Yet the NT repeatedly promises that Christ may return without warning at any moment. Timing is not the issue; readiness is.

C 13 [a]But rejoice, inasmuch as [b]ye are partakers of Christ's sufferings; that, when his glory shall be revealed, ye may be glad also with exceeding joy.

N 14 [a]If ye be reproached for the name of Christ, happy *are ye;* for the spirit of glory and of God resteth upon you: on their part he is evil spoken of, but on your part he is glorified.

15 But [a]let none of you suffer as a murderer, or *as* a thief, or *as* an evildoer, [b]or as a busybody in other men's matters.

J 16 Yet if *any man suffer* as a Christian, let him not be ashamed; [a]but let him glorify God on this behalf.

H S 17 For the time *is come* [a]that judgment must begin at the house of God: and [b]if *it* first *begin* at us, [c]what shall the end *be* of them that obey not the gospel of God?

18 [a]And if the righteous scarcely be saved, where shall the ungodly and the sinner appear?

19 Wherefore let them that suffer according to the will of God [a]commit the keeping of their souls *to him* in well doing, as unto a faithful Creator.

Christian life in God's care

M 5 THE ELDERS which are among you I exhort, who am also [a]an elder, and [b]a witness of the sufferings of Christ, and also [c]a partaker of the glory that shall be revealed:

2 [a]Feed the flock of God /which is among you, taking the oversight *thereof,* [b]not by constraint, but willingly; [c]not for filthy lucre, but of a ready mind;

3 Neither as [a]being/ lords over [b]*God's* heritage, but [c]being examples to the flock.

C *1Pe 4:7 ◀▶ 2Pe 1:16–19*
N *Heb 10:29 ◀▶ 1Jn 2:20*
J *1Pe 4:12–14 ◀▶ 1Jn 4:18*
H *1Pe 3:12 ◀▶ 2Pe 2:1*
S *1Pe 3:10–12 ◀▶ 2Pe 1:9–10*
M *Heb 10:13 ◀▶ 1Pe 5:4*

13 [a]Acts 5:41 [b]Rom. 8:17
14 [a]2 Cor. 12:10; Jas. 1:12
15 [a]ch. 2:20 [b]1 Thes. 4:11
16 [a]Acts 5:41
17 [a]Is. 10:12 [b]Luke 23:31 [c]Luke 10:12
18 [a]Luke 23:31
19 [a]2 Tim. 1:12
5:1 [a]Philem. 9 [b]Luke 24:48; Acts 1:8 [c]Rev. 1:9
2 [a]Acts 20:28 [b]1 Cor. 9:17 [c]1 Tim. 3:3 /Or, *as much as in you is*
3 [a]Ezek. 34:4 [b]Ps. 33:12 [c]Phil. 3:17 /Or, *overruling*
4 [a]Heb. 13:20 [b]2 Tim. 4:8
5 [a]Rom. 12:10 [b]Jas. 4:6 [c]Is. 57:15
6 [a]Jas. 4:10
7 [a]Ps. 37:5; Heb. 13:5
8 [a]Luke 21:34 [b]Job 1:7
9 [a]Eph. 6:11 [b]Acts 14:22
10 [a]1 Cor. 1:9 [b]2 Cor. 4:17 [c]Heb. 13:21 [d]2 Thes. 2:17
11 [a]Rev. 1:6
12 [a]2 Cor. 1:19 [b]Heb. 13:22 [c]Acts 20:24
13 [a]Acts 12:12
14 [a]Rom. 16:16 [b]Eph. 6:23

4 And when [a]the chief Shepherd shall appear, ye shall receive [b]a crown of glory that fadeth not away. M

5 Likewise, ye younger, submit yourselves unto the elder. Yea, [a]all *of you* be subject one to another, and be clothed with humility: for [b]God resisteth the proud, and [c]giveth grace to the humble. M

6 [a]Humble yourselves therefore under the mighty hand of God, that he may exalt you in due time:

7 [a]Casting all your care upon him; for he careth for you. L W

8 [a]Be sober, be vigilant; because [b]your adversary the devil, as a roaring lion, walketh about, seeking whom he may devour:

9 [a]Whom resist stedfast in the faith, [b]knowing that the same afflictions are accomplished in your brethren that are in the world.

10 But the God of all grace, [a]who hath called us unto his eternal glory by Christ Jesus, after that ye have suffered [b]a while, [c]make you perfect, [d]stablish, strengthen, settle *you.* T

11 [a]To him *be* glory and dominion for ever and ever. Amen.

Conclusion and benediction

12 [a]By Silvanus, a faithful brother unto you, as I suppose, I have [b]written briefly, exhorting, and testifying [c]that this is the true grace of God wherein ye stand.

13 The *church that is* at Babylon, elected together with *you,* saluteth you; and *so doth* [a]Marcus my son.

14 [a]Greet ye one another with a kiss of charity. [b]Peace *be* with you all that are in Christ Jesus. Amen.

M *1Pe 5:1 ◀▶ Rev 2:26–27*
M *Jas 4:6–10 ◀▶ Rev 3:17–18*
L *1Pe 3:12 ◀▶ 2Pe 2:9*
W *1Pe 3:14 ◀▶ 1Jn 4:18*
T *1Pe 1:6–7 ◀▶ Rev 3:19*

4:13 Peter promises that those who endure suffering for Christ's sake will be rewarded for their faithful service to him "when his glory shall be revealed" (4:13).

5:1 Peter concludes this epistle with a promise that those faithful believers in the church who experience persecution and stand firm will be glorified and blessed at the rapture when Christ "shall be revealed" (5:1) in glory at the second coming.

2 Peter

Author: Peter

Theme: Be on your guard against false teaching

Date of Writing: c. A.D. 64–68

Outline of 2 Peter

I. True Knowledge for the Believer (1:1–21)
II. False Teachers and Their Doom (2:1–22)
III. Warnings, Judgment and Exhortation (3:1–18)

THE AUTHOR IDENTIFIES himself in the first verse of this letter as "Simon Peter, a servant and an apostle of Jesus Christ" (1:1). This letter was written a short time after 1 Peter and was directed to the same readers in the northern portion of the Roman province of Asia to whom Peter had addressed his first letter. The style of writing, personal illustrations, vocabulary and thoughts in this letter are also similar to Peter's first epistle, though this second letter focuses on the pressing danger of false teachers.

Traveling philosophers and teachers were perverting the message of the gospel with false doctrines and erroneous teaching about Christ's second coming. Peter's second letter urges his readers to combine Christian faith and practice while awaiting the Lord's return. Peter calls attention to the importance of knowledge in discerning between false and true teaching. He also warns that those who pervert the Word of God will face God's judgment. The Lord is certain to return, so Peter urges the believers to be ready.

1 SIMON[1] PETER, a servant and an apostle of Jesus Christ, to them that have obtained [a]like precious faith with us through the righteousness [2]of God and our Saviour Jesus Christ:

2 [a]Grace and peace be multiplied unto you through the knowledge of God, and of Jesus our Lord,

The growth of true knowledge

3 According as his divine power hath given unto us all things that *pertain* unto life and godliness, through the knowledge of him [a]that hath called us [1]to glory and virtue:

4 [a]Whereby are given unto us exceeding great and precious promises: that by these ye might be [b]partakers of the divine nature, having escaped the corruption that is in the world through lust.

5 And beside this, [a]giving all diligence, add to your faith virtue; and to virtue [b]knowledge;

6 And to knowledge temperance; and to temperance patience; and to patience godliness;

7 And to godliness brotherly kindness; and [a]to brotherly kindness charity.

8 For if these things be in you, and abound, they make *you that ye shall* neither *be* [1]barren [a]nor unfruitful in the knowledge of our Lord Jesus Christ.

S 9 But he that lacketh these things [a]is blind, and cannot see afar off, and hath forgotten that he was [b]purged from his old sins.

10 Wherefore the rather, brethren, give diligence [a]to make your calling and election sure: for if ye do these things, ye shall never fall:

11 For so an entrance shall be ministered unto you abundantly into the everlasting kingdom of our Lord and Saviour Jesus Christ.

S *1Pe 4:17–18* ◀▶ *2Pe 2:19–21*

The basis of true knowledge

12 Wherefore [a]I will not be negligent to put you always in remembrance of these things, [b]though ye know *them,* and be established in the present truth.

13 Yea, I think it meet, [a]as long as I am in this tabernacle, to stir you up by putting *you* in remembrance;

14 [a]Knowing that shortly I must put off *this* my tabernacle, even as [b]our Lord Jesus Christ hath shown me.

15 Moreover I will endeavour that ye may be able after my decease to have these things always in remembrance.

16 For we have not followed [a]cunningly devised fables, when we made known unto you the power and coming of our Lord Jesus Christ, but [b]were eyewitnesses of his majesty. C

17 For he received from God the Father honour and glory, when there came such a voice to him from the excellent glory, [a]This is my beloved Son, in whom I am well pleased.

18 And this voice which came from heaven we heard, when we were with him in [a]the holy mount.

19 We have also a more sure word of prophecy; whereunto ye do well that ye take heed, as unto [a]a light that shineth in a dark place, until the day dawn, and [b]the day star arise in your hearts:

20 Knowing this first, that [a]no prophecy of the scripture is of any private interpretation.

21 For [a]the prophecy came not [1]in old time by the will of man: [b]but holy men of God spake *as they were* moved by the Holy Ghost. E G M T

C *1Pe 4:13* ◀▶ *2Pe 3:3–14*
E *1Pe 4:10–11* ◀▶ *1Jn 2:20*
G *1Pe 4:10–11* ◀▶ *1Jn 2:20*
M *Heb 2:4* ◀▶ *1Jn 2:20*
T *1Pe 4:10–11* ◀▶ *1Jn 2:20*

1:1 [a]Eph. 4:5 [1]Or, *Simeon,* as in Acts 15:14 [2]Gk. *of our God and Saviour*
2 [a]Dan. 4:1
3 [a]1 Thes. 2:12 [1]Or, *by*
4 [a]2 Cor. 7:1 [b]2 Cor. 3:18; Heb. 12:10
5 [a]ch. 3:18 [b]1 Pet. 3:7
7 [a]Gal. 6:10; 1 Thes. 3:12
8 [a]John 15:2; Tit. 3:14 [1]Gk. *idle*
9 [a]1 John 2:9 [b]Eph. 5:26; Heb. 9:14
10 [a]1 John 3:19
12 [a]Phil. 3:1; 1 John 2:21 [b]1 Pet. 5:12
13 [a]2 Cor. 5:1
14 [a]2 Tim. 4:6 [b]John 21:18,19
16 [a]1 Cor. 1:17 [b]Mark 9:2; 1 John 1:1
17 [a]Mat. 3:17; Luke 9:35
18 [a]Mat. 17:6
19 [a]Ps. 119:105; John 5:35 [b]Rev. 22:16
20 [a]Rom. 12:6
21 [a]2 Tim. 3:16; 1 Pet. 1:11 [b]2 Sam. 23:2; Acts 1:16 [1]Or, *at any time*

1:16–18 Peter confirms that he and the other NT writers were eyewitnesses of the life and resurrection of Christ, a life that fulfilled the OT prophecies of the Messiah. Peter declares personally hearing God the Father confirm Jesus' divinity (1:17; see Mt 3:17; 17:5).

1:19–21 Peter shares some very important principles by which we should evaluate the prophecies of the Bible. First, he validates the message of prophecy (1:19), explaining that prophecy is intended to be a spiritual light to enlighten the dark times in which believers live. Peter also urges vigilance and paying close attention to prophecy because it motivates us to holy living. He also notes that prophecy is an inspired message from the Holy Spirit, not from mere humans, given so that the church will live expectantly "until the day dawn, and the day star arise in your hearts" (1:19; see Rev 22:16).

False prophets and teachers

2 BUT [a]THERE were false prophets also among the people, even as [b]there shall be false teachers among you, who privily shall bring in damnable heresies, even [c]denying the Lord [d]that bought them, [e]and bring upon themselves swift destruction.

2 And many shall follow their [l]pernicious ways; by reason of whom the way of truth shall be evil spoken of.

3 And [a]through covetousness shall they with feigned words [b]make merchandise of you: [c]whose judgment now of a long time lingereth not, and their damnation slumbereth not.

4 For if God spared not [a]the angels [b]that sinned, but [c]cast *them* down to hell, and delivered *them* into chains of darkness, to be reserved unto judgment;

5 And spared not the old world, but saved [a]Noah the eighth *person,* [b]a preacher of righteousness, [c]bringing in the flood upon the world of the ungodly;

6 And [a]turning the cities of Sodom and Gomorrha into ashes condemned *them* with an overthrow, [b]making *them* an example unto those that after should live ungodly;

7 And [a]delivered just Lot, vexed with the filthy conversation of the wicked:

8 (For that righteous man dwelling among them, [a]in seeing and hearing, vexed *his* righteous soul from day to day with *their* unlawful deeds;)

9 [a]The Lord knoweth how to deliver the godly out of temptations, and to reserve the unjust unto the day of judgment to be punished:

10 But chiefly [a]them that walk after the flesh in the lust of uncleanness, and despise [l]government. [b]Presumptuous *are they,* self-willed, they are not afraid to speak evil of dignities.

11 Whereas [a]angels, which are greater in power and might, bring not railing accusation [l]against them before the Lord.

12 But these, [a]as natural brute beasts, made to be taken and destroyed, speak evil of the things that they understand not; and shall utterly perish in their own corruption;

13 [a]And shall receive the reward of unrighteousness, *as* they that count it pleasure [b]to riot in the day time. [c]Spots *they are* and blemishes, sporting themselves with their own deceivings while [d]they feast with you;

14 Having eyes full of [l]adultery, and that cannot cease from sin; beguiling unstable souls: [a]an heart they have exercised with covetous practices; cursed children:

15 Which have forsaken the right way, and are gone astray, following the way of [a]Balaam *the son* of Bosor, who loved the wages of unrighteousness;

16 But was rebuked for his iniquity: the dumb ass speaking with man's voice forbad the madness of the prophet.

17 [a]These are wells without water, clouds that are carried with a tempest; to whom the mist of darkness is reserved for ever.

18 For when [a]they speak great swelling *words* of vanity, they allure through the lusts of the flesh, *through much* wantonness, those that [b]were [l]clean escaped from them who live in error.

19 While they promise them [a]liberty, they themselves are [b]the servants of corruption: for of whom a man is overcome, of the same is he brought in bondage.

20 For [a]if after they [b]have escaped the pollutions of the world [c]through the

2:1 [a]Deut. 13:1 [b]Mat. 24:11; 1 John 4:1 [c]Jude 4 [d]1 Cor. 6:20; Heb. 10:29; Rev. 5:9 [e]Phil. 3:19
2 [l]Or, *lascivious ways,* as some copies read
3 [a]Rom. 16:18; Tit. 1:11 [b]2 Cor. 2:17 [c]Deut. 32:35; Jude 4,15
4 [a]Job 4:18; Jude 6 [b]John 8:44 [c]Luke 8:31; Rev. 20:2
5 [a]Gen. 7:1; Heb. 11:7; 1 Pet. 3:20 [b]1 Pet. 3:19 [c]ch. 3:6
6 [a]Gen. 19:24; Deut. 29:23 [b]Num. 26:10
7 [a]Gen. 19:16
8 [a]Ps. 119:139; Ezek. 9:4
9 [a]Ps. 34:17; 1 Cor. 10:13
10 [a]Jude 4,7,8 [b]Jude 8 [l]Or, *dominion*
11 [a]Jude 9 [l]Some read, *against themselves*
12 [a]Jude 10
13 [a]Phil. 3:19 [b]Rom. 13:13 [c]Jude 12 [d]1 Cor. 11:20
14 [a]Jude 11 [l]Gk. *an adulteress*
15 [a]Num. 22:5; Jude 11
17 [a]Jude 12,13
18 [a]Jude 16 [b]Acts 2:40 [l]Or, *for a little,* or, *a while,* as some read
19 [a]Gal. 5:13 [b]John 8:34; Rom. 6:16
20 [a]Mat. 12:45; Luke 11:26; Heb. 6:4 [b]ver. 18 [c]ch. 1:2

H *1Pe 4:17–18* ◀▶ *2Pe 2:3–9*
H *2Pe 2:1* ◀▶ *2Pe 2:12–13*
J *1Pe 4:5* ◀▶ *2Pe 2:9*
J *1Pe 4:5* ◀▶ *2Pe 3:7*
J *2Pe 2:4* ◀▶ *2Pe 3:7*
K *1Pe 2:24* ◀▶ *1Jn 7*
L *1Pe 5:7* ◀▶ *1Jn 3:1*

H *2Pe 2:3–9* ◀▶ *2Pe 2:17*
C *1Pe 2:25* ◀▶ *2Pe 2:22*
H *2Pe 2:12–13* ◀▶ *2Pe 3:6–7*
S *2Pe 1:9–10* ◀▶ *2Pe 3:11*

2:9 God can easily deliver believers from temptation if we follow his commands and resist the devil (see Ps 34:17; 1Co 10:13; 2Ti 2:22; Jas 4:7). Yet the Lord has promised to punish the wicked. Unrepentant souls who die will wait in Hades (hell) until they are resurrected to appear in heaven before God at the great white throne judgment (see Rev 20:11–15). All who appear at this judgment have chosen the punishment of hell since they have rejected the salvation of Jesus Christ. The issue to be settled at this judgment is exactly what form their punishment in hell will take (see Jer 17:10; Ro 2:5–6; Rev 2:23; 20:13).

knowledge of the Lord and Saviour Jesus
Christ, they are again entangled therein,
and overcome, the latter end is worse
with them than the beginning.
21 For [a]it had been better for them not
to have known the way of righteousness,
than, after they have known *it,* to turn
from the holy commandment delivered
unto them.
C 22 But it is happened unto them according to the true proverb, [a]The dog *is*
turned to his own vomit again; and the
sow that was washed to her wallowing in
the mire.

Christ's coming

3 THIS SECOND epistle, beloved, I
now write unto you; in *both* which
[a]I stir up your pure minds by way of remembrance:
2 That ye may be mindful of the words
which were spoken before by the holy
prophets, [a]and of the commandment of
us the apostles of the Lord and Saviour:
C 3 Knowing this first, that there shall
E come in the last days scoffers, [a]walking
C after their own lusts,

C *2Pe 2:17* ◀▶ *2Pe 3:3*
C *2Pe 1:16–19* ◀▶ *1Jn 2:28*
E *Jas 5:7* ◀▶ *1Jn 2:18*
C *2Pe 2:22* ◀▶ *1Jn 2:11*

21 [a]Luke 12:47
22 [a]Prov. 26:11
3:1 [a]ch. 1:13
2 [a]Jude 17
3 [a]ch. 2:10
4 [a]Is. 5:19; Jer. 17:15; Ezek. 12:22; Mat. 24:48; Luke 12:45
5 [a]Gen. 1:6,9; Ps. 33:6; Heb. 11:3 [b]Ps. 24:2; Col. 1:17 [1]Gk. *consisting*
6 [a]Gen. 7:11
7 [a]ver. 10 [b]Mat. 25:41; 2 Thes. 1:8
8 [a]Ps. 90:4
9 [a]Hab. 2:3; Heb. 10:37 [b]Is. 30:18; 1 Pet. 3:20 [c]Ezek. 33:11 [d]Rom. 2:4; 1 Tim. 2:4
10 [a]Mat. 24:43; Luke 12:39; 1 Thes. 5:2

4 And saying, [a]Where is the promise
of his coming? for since the fathers fell
asleep, all things continue as *they were*
from the beginning of the creation.
5 For this they willingly are ignorant
of, that [a]by the word of God the heavens
were of old, and the earth [b]standing[1] out
of the water and in the water:
6 [a]Whereby the world that then was, H
being overflowed with water, perished:
7 But [a]the heavens and the earth, J
which are now, by the same word are J
kept in store, reserved unto [b]fire against
the day of judgment and perdition of ungodly men.
8 But, beloved, be not ignorant of this
one thing, that one day *is* with the Lord
as a thousand years, and [a]a thousand
years as one day.
9 [a]The Lord is not slack concerning his L
promise, as some men count slackness; R
but [b]is longsuffering to us-ward, [c]not W
willing that any should perish, but [d]that
all should come to repentance.
10 But [a]the day of the Lord will come P

H *2Pe 2:17* ◀▶ *Jude 5–7*
J *2Pe 2:9* ◀▶ *1Jn 4:17*
J *2Pe 2:9* ◀▶ *1Jn 4:17*
L *1Pe 3:18* ◀▶ *1Jn 7* R *Jas 4:8* ◀▶ *1Jn 9*
W *Heb 7:25* ◀▶ *1Jn 7–9*
P *2Th 2:8–9* ◀▶ *2Jn 7*

3:3–7 The apostasy of the last days will be characterized by widespread scoffing and contempt for the doctrine of the second coming because of its long delay. Peter suggests that the scoffers will also deny the supernatural authority and truthfulness of the Scriptures, the creation by the Creator, the story of the flood and ignore the Bible's prophecies of a coming judgment. Many of these heretical tenets are taught in our modern-day seminaries. Can the "perdition of ungodly men" (3:7) be too far in the future?
3:8–9 Peter reminds us that God's view of time is different from ours (3:8; see Ps 90:4). Some suggest that these passages indicate that the six days of creation recorded in Ge 1—2 are a microcosm of six thousand years of God's dealings with humanity. These scholars suggest that just as creation took six days, with God resting on the seventh day, there would be six thousand years before the return of Christ and then the great Sabbath rest of one thousand years (the Millennium) as described in Heb 4:4, 7–9; Rev 20.

Others scholars contend that Peter's words are more direct, viewing time in its relation to eternity. Compared to eternity, an age seems no longer than a day, and a day seems no longer than a moment. These scholars suggest that Peter's words merely indicate God's patience and long-suffering versus humanity's impatience and haste. God's patience and mercy has even delayed the return of the Lord so that "all should come to repentance" (3:9).
3:10–14 Peter then warns that when the Lord appears, he will appear unexpectedly "as a thief in the night" (3:10) to the unbelievers who have not heeded the prophecies of Scripture. (The believer is to be alert and watching for the fulfillment of these signs, so Christ's coming in the air should not be a surprise to Christians.) Peter says that Christ's coming in these days will be marked with God's wrath poured out on the earth through the judgments of the tribulation. His description of the elements melting "with fervent heat" (3:10) may indicate multiple nuclear bombardments during the terrible judgments of the last days.

Because of such devastation, Peter urges people to consider the manner of their life (3:11). He calls upon believers to reflect their faith in Jesus in their words and actions, allowing the hope of the second coming to become a powerful motivator as they witness with urgency and walk in holiness. Note that Peter indicates that believers can speed up or hasten Christ's return by their faithful Christian walk. Since God is waiting for all who will come to salvation, the

as a thief in the night; in the which [b]the
heavens shall pass away with a great
noise, and the elements shall melt with
fervent heat, the earth also and the works
that are therein shall be burned up.
S 11 *Seeing* then *that* all these things
shall be dissolved, what manner *of persons*
ought ye to be [a]in *all* holy conversation and godliness,
12 [a]Looking for and [l]hasting unto the
coming of the day of God, wherein the
heavens being on fire shall [b]be dissolved,
and the elements shall [c]melt with fervent
heat?
N 13 Nevertheless we, according to his
S promise, look for [a]new heavens and a
new earth, wherein dwelleth righteousness.

The concluding appeal

14 Wherefore, beloved, seeing that ye
look for such things, be diligent [a]that ye
may be found of him in peace, without
spot, and blameless.
15 And account *that* [a]the longsuffering
of our Lord *is* salvation; even as our beloved brother Paul also according to the
wisdom given unto him hath written
unto you;
16 As also in all *his* epistles, [a]speaking
in them of these things; in which are
some things hard to be understood,
which they that are unlearned and unstable wrest, as *they do* also the other scriptures, unto their own destruction.
17 Ye therefore, beloved, [a]seeing ye
know *these things* before, [b]beware lest
ye also, being led away with the error of
the wicked, fall from your own stedfastness.
18 [a]But grow in grace, and *in* the
knowledge of our Lord and Saviour Jesus
Christ. [b]To him *be* glory both now and
for ever. Amen.

10 [b]Ps. 102:26; Is. 51:6; Mat. 24:35; Rom. 8:12
11 [a]1 Pet. 1:15
12 [a]1 Cor. 1:7; Tit. 2:13 [b]Ps. 50:3; Is. 34:4 [c]Mic. 1:4 [l]*Or, hasting the coming*
13 [a]Is. 65:17 & 66:22; Rev. 21:1
14 [a]1 Cor. 1:8 & 15:58; Phil. 1:10; 1 Thes. 3:13
15 [a]Rom. 2:4; 1 Pet. 3:20
16 [a]Rom. 8:19; 1 Cor. 15:24; 1 Thes. 4:15
17 [a]Mark 13:23 [b]Eph. 4:14
18 [a]Eph. 4:15; 1 Pet. 2:2 [b]2 Tim. 4:18; Rev. 1:6

S *2Pe 2:19–21* ◀▶ *2Pe 3:13–14*
N *Heb 12:26–28* ◀▶ *1Jn 2:17*
S *2Pe 3:11* ◀▶ *1Jn 5–7*

sooner we bring others to the Savior, the sooner he can return.

Finally, Peter reminds us that the final goal of our human journey is the "new heavens and a new earth" (3:13) where we will live under the righteous and just rule of Jesus Christ, the Messiah. When Jesus Christ establishes his kingdom on earth, humanity will finally experience the righteousness and justice it has desired for nearly two thousand years (see Isa 9:6–7). As we look for the fulfillment of these things, Paul urges us to live peaceful, blameless lives (3:14) just like Christ (see 1Pe 1:19).

1 John

Author: John

Theme: Walking in the light of Christian fellowship

Date of Writing: c. A.D. 85–95

Outline of 1 John

I. Introduction (1:1–4)
II. Light Is Essential for Fellowship (1:5—2:28)
III. Love Must Permeate Life (2:29—4:21)
IV. Faith and Certainty (5:1–21)

THIS SHORT LETTER is attributed to the apostle John, the son of Zebedee and one of Jesus' closest disciples. John also authored the Gospel of John, the book of Revelation and the other short epistles that bear his name. Though this letter does not denote its intended audience, content, style and vocabulary indicate that this epistle was probably directed to the same readers as the Gospel of John—most probably, the church in Asia for which John had some responsibilities. Though precise dating of this letter is difficult, internal and external evidence suggests that John composed this epistle shortly before his death.

False teachers had attempted to mislead first-century believers to follow their Gnostic ideas that matter is entirely evil and that the spirit is entirely good. The Gnostic solution to the tension between good and evil was to increase knowledge and thereby allow humanity to rise from the mundane to the spiritual. Gnostic teachings also perverted the gospel message by denying the true humanity of Christ, suggesting that Jesus was nothing more than a mere ghost who could manifest a dual personality, appearing at times human and at times divine. John's letter to the believers confronts this serious heresy by assuring the believers of the true message of the gospel and confirming his eyewitness testimony to the incarnation of Christ. With intimacy and warmth John also conveys the theme of Christian fellowship as he offers these first-century believers certainty for their faith in Christ.

The Word of life

1 THAT [a]WHICH was from the beginning, which we have heard, which we have seen with our eyes, [b]which we have looked upon, and [c]our hands have handled, of the Word of life;

2 (For [a]the life [b]was manifested, and we have seen *it,* [c]and bear witness, [d]and show unto you that eternal life, [e]which was with the Father, and was manifested unto us;)

3 That which we have seen and heard declare we unto you, that ye also may have fellowship with us: and truly [a]our fellowship *is* with the Father, and with his Son Jesus Christ.

U 4 And these things write we unto you, [a]that your joy may be full.

The test of righteousness

S 5 [a]This then is the message which we have heard of him, and declare unto you, that [b]God is light, and in him is no darkness at all.

6 [a]If we say that we have fellowship with him, and walk in darkness, we lie, and do not the truth:

D K L W 7 But if we walk in the light, as he is in the light, we have fellowship one with another, and [a]the blood of Jesus Christ his Son cleanseth us from all sin.

A 8 [a]If we say that we have no sin, we deceive ourselves, [b]and the truth is not in us.

L R 9 [a]If we confess our sins, he is faithful and just to forgive us *our* sins, and to [b]cleanse us from all unrighteousness.

A 10 If we say that we have not sinned, we make him a liar, and his word is not in us.

L P S W 2 MY LITTLE children, these things write I unto you, that ye sin not. And if any man sin, [a]we have an advocate with the Father, Jesus Christ the righteous:

2 And [a]he is the propitiation for our sins: and not for ours only, but [b]also for *the sins of* the whole world. D K

3 And hereby we do know that we know him, if we keep his commandments. S

4 [a]He that saith, I know him, and keepeth not his commandments, [b]is a liar, and the truth is not in him.

5 But [a]whoso keepeth his word, [b]in him verily is the love of God perfected: [c]hereby know we that we are in him.

6 [a]He that saith he abideth in him [b]ought himself also so to walk, even as he walked.

7 Brethren, [a]I write no new commandment unto you, but an old commandment [a]which ye had from the beginning. The old commandment is the word which ye have heard from the beginning.

8 Again, [a]a new commandment I write unto you, which thing is true in him and in you: [b]because the darkness is past, and [c]the true light now shineth.

9 [a]He that saith he is in the light, and hateth his brother, is in darkness even until now.

10 [a]He that loveth his brother abideth in the light, and [b]there is none [f]occasion of stumbling in him.

11 But he that hateth his brother is in darkness, and walketh in darkness, and knoweth not whither he goeth, because that darkness hath blinded his eyes. C

12 I write unto you, little children, because [a]your sins are forgiven you for his name's sake. L

13 I write unto you, fathers, because ye have known him [a]*that is* from the beginning. I write unto you, young men, because ye have overcome the wicked one. I write unto you, little children, because ye have known the Father.

14 I have written unto you, fathers, because ye have known him *that is* from the beginning. I have written unto you, young men, because [a]ye are strong, and the word of God abideth in you, and ye have overcome the wicked one.

15 [a]Love not the world, neither the C S

1:1 [a]John 1:1 [b]John 1:14; 2 Pet. 1:16 [c]Luke 24:39; John 20:27
2 [a]John 1:4 & 14:6 [b]Rom. 16:26; 1 Tim. 3:16 [c]John 21:24 [d]ch. 5:20 [e]John 1:1
3 [a]John 17:21; 1 Cor. 1:9
4 [a]John 16:24
5 [a]ch. 3:11 [b]John 1:9
6 [a]2 Cor. 6:14
7 [a]1 Cor. 6:11; Eph. 1:7; Heb. 9:14; 1 Pet. 1:19; Rev. 1:5
8 [a]Job 9:2; Eccl. 7:20; Jas. 3:2 [b]ch. 2:4
9 [a]Ps. 32:5 [b]Ps. 51:2
2:1 [a]Heb. 7:25
2 [a]Rom. 3:25; 2 Cor. 5:18 [b]John 1:29
4 [a]ch. 1:6 [b]ch. 1:8
5 [a]John 14:21,23 [b]ch. 4:12 [c]ch. 4:13
6 [a]John 15:4 [b]Mat. 11:29; 1 Pet. 2:21
7 [a]2 John 5
8 [a]John 13:34 [b]Rom. 13:12 [c]John 1:9
9 [a]1 Cor. 13:2; 2 Pet. 1:9
10 [a]ch. 3:14 [b]2 Pet. 1:10 [f]Gk. *scandal*
12 [a]Luke 24:47
13 [a]ch. 1:1
14 [a]Eph. 6:10
15 [a]Rom. 12:2

U *1Pe 3:12* ◀▶ *1Jn 3:22*
S *2Pe 3:13–14* ◀▶ *1Jn 2:1*
D *1Pe 3:18* ◀▶ *1Jn 2:2*
K *2Pe 2:9* ◀▶ *1Jn 2:2* **L** *2Pe 3:9* ◀▶ *1Jn 9*
W *2Pe 3:9* ◀▶ *1Jn 2:1–2*
A *Jas 2:10* ◀▶ *1Jn 10*
L *1Jn 7* ◀▶ *1Jn 2:1–2*
R *2Pe 3:9* ◀▶ *Rev 2:5* **A** *1Jn 8* ◀
L *1Jn 9* ◀▶ *1Jn 2:12*
P *Jas 5:19–20* ◀▶ *1Jn 5:16*
S *1Jn 5–7* ◀▶ *1Jn 2:3–6*
W *1Jn 7–9* ◀▶ *1Jn 4:14–15*

D *1Jn 7* ◀▶ *1Jn 3:5* **K** *1Jn 7* ◀▶ *1Jn 3:5*
S *1Jn 2:1* ◀▶ *1Jn 2:15*
C *2Pe 3:3* ◀▶ *1Jn 2:15–17*
L *1Jn 2:1–2* ◀▶ *1Jn 3:5*
C *1Jn 2:11* ◀▶ *1Jn 3:8*
S *1Jn 2:3–6* ◀▶ *1Jn 3:3–10*

things *that are* in the world. [b]If any man
love the world, the love of the Father is
not in him.
16 For all that *is* in the world, the lust
of the flesh, [a]and the lust of the eyes, and
the pride of life, is not of the Father, but
is of the world.
N 17 And [a]the world passeth away, and
the lust thereof: but he that doeth the
will of God abideth for ever.
E 18 [a]Little children, [b]it is the last time:
and as ye have heard that [c]antichrist shall
come, [d]even now are there many anti-
christs; whereby we know [e]that it is the
last time.
19 [a]They went out from us, but they
were not of us; for [b]if they had been of
us, they would *no doubt* have continued
with us: but *they went out,* [c]that they
might be made manifest that they were
not all of us.
B 20 But [a]ye have an unction [b]from the
E Holy One, and [c]ye know all things.
G 21 I have not written unto you be-
M cause ye know not the truth, but because
N ye know it, and that no lie is of the truth.
T 22 [a]Who is a liar but he that denieth
that Jesus is the Christ? He is antichrist,
that denieth the Father and the Son.
23 [a]Whosoever denieth the Son, the
same hath not the Father: *[but]* [b]*he that*
acknowledgeth the Son hath the Father
also.

N *2Pe 3:13–14* ◀▶ *Rev 21:1–5*
E *2Pe 3:3–10* ◀▶ *Jude 17–18*
B *1Pe 4:10–11* ◀
E *2Pe 1:21* ◀▶ *1Jn 2:27*
G *2Pe 1:21* ◀▶ *1Jn 2:27*
M *2Pe 1:21* ◀▶ *1Jn 2:27*
N *1Pe 4:14* ◀▶ *1Jn 2:27*
T *2Pe 1:21* ◀▶ *1Jn 2:27*

15 [b]Mat. 6:24
16 [a]Eccl. 5:11
17 [a]1 Cor. 7:31; 1 Pet. 1:24
18 [a]John 21:5 [b]Heb. 1:2 [c]2 Thes. 2:3 [d]Mat. 24:5; 2 John 7 [e]1 Tim. 4:1; 2 Tim. 3:1
19 [a]Deut. 13:13 [b]Mat. 24:24; John 6:37 [c]1 Cor. 11:19
20 [a]2 Cor. 1:21; Heb. 1:9 [b]Acts 3:14 [c]John 16:13
22 [a]2 John 7
23 [a]John 15:23; 2 John 9 [b]ch. 4:15
24 [a]2 John 6 [b]John 14:23
25 [a]John 17:3
26 [a]2 John 7
27 [a]ver. 20 [b]ver. 21 [c]John 14:26 [1]Or, *it*
28 [a]ch. 3:2 [b]ch. 4:17
29 [a]Acts 22:14 [b]ch. 3:7,10 [1]Or, *know ye*
3:1 [a]John 1:12 [b]John 16:3
2 [a]Is. 56:5; Rom. 8:15 [b]Rom 8:18; 2 Cor. 4:17

24 Let that therefore abide in you,
[a]which ye have heard from the beginning. If that which ye have heard from
the beginning shall remain in you, [b]ye
also shall continue in the Son, and in the
Father.
25 [a]And this is the promise that he
hath promised us, *even* eternal life.
26 These *things* have I written unto
you [a]concerning them that seduce you.
27 But [a]the anointing which ye have E
received of him abideth in you, and [b]ye G
need not that any man teach you: but as M
the same anointing [c]teacheth you of all N
things, and is truth, and is no lie, and T
even as it hath taught you, ye shall abide
in [1]him.
28 And now, little children, abide in C
him; that, [a]when he shall appear, we may
have confidence, [b]and not be ashamed
before him at his coming.
29 [a]If ye know that he is righteous, [1]ye
know that [b]every one that doeth righteousness is born of him.

Obedience and love

3 BEHOLD, WHAT manner of love the L
Father hath bestowed upon us, that
[a]we should be called the sons of God:
therefore the world knoweth us not, [b]be-
cause it knew him not.
2 Beloved, [a]now are we the sons of C
God, and [b]it doth not yet appear what we
shall be: but we know that, when he shall

E *1Jn 2:20* ◀▶ *1Jn 3:24*
G *1Jn 2:20* ◀▶ *Rev 1:4* **M** *1Jn 2:20* ◀
N *1Jn 2:20* ◀▶ *1Jn 4:1–2*
T *1Jn 2:20* ◀▶ *Rev 1:10*
C *2Pe 3:3–14* ◀▶ *1Jn 3:2–3*
L *2Pe 2:9* ◀▶ *1Jn 5:14–15*
C *1Jn 2:28* ◀▶ *Rev 1:7*

2:17 John prophesied that this age, which has been dominated by Satan and corruption, will pass away. However, the apostle promises that eternal life is the reward of those who are obedient to God's will, which "abideth for ever."

2:18 The apostle prophetically warned that the clock has started to tick in a countdown to the appearance of the antichrist and the return of Christ in victory (see Rev 13:1–10). John reminded his readers that there would be a proliferation of false Christs in the last days. This increase would signal the approach of the final antichrist who will take over the ten nations of the revived Roman empire in Europe in his bid to dominate the nations of the whole earth (see Da 2:40–45; 7:7–8; Rev 13:1–10).

2:22–23 The nature of the antichrist spirit is the denial of Jesus' incarnate divinity. John confirms that this antichrist spirit produces a person who has neither the spirit nor the presence of the Son or the Father.

2:28 John commands his readers to stand firm in their faith because of the promise of the second coming of Jesus Christ. When he returns, he will appear in the air to take his saints home to heaven.

3:2 This declaration of adoption refers to the supernatural relationship of the believers to God based on their faith in Christ's atonement on the cross. The passage affirms a wonderful revelation that our resurrection at the rapture will transform our natural bodies to become like Jesus' resurrection

appear, [c]we shall be like him; for [d]we shall see him as he is.

S 3 [a]And every man that hath this hope in him purifieth himself, even as he is pure.

4 Whosoever committeth sin transgresseth also the law: for [a]sin is the transgression of the law.

D K L 5 And ye know [a]that he was manifested [b]to take away our sins; and [c]in him is no sin.

6 Whosoever abideth in him sinneth not: [a]whosoever sinneth hath not seen him, neither known him.

7 Little children, [a]let no man deceive you: [b]he that doeth righteousness is righteous, even as he is righteous.

C K 8 [a]He that committeth sin is of the devil; for the devil sinneth from the beginning. For this purpose the Son of God was manifested, [b]that he might destroy the works of the devil.

9 [a]Whosoever is born of God doth not commit sin; for [b]his seed remaineth in him: and he cannot sin, because he is born of God.

10 In this the children of God are manifest, and the children of the devil: [a]whosoever doeth not righteousness is not of God, [b]neither he that loveth not his brother.

Love in action

11 For [a]this is the [/]message that ye heard from the beginning, [b]that we should love one another.

12 Not as [a]Cain, *who* was of that wicked one, and slew his brother. And wherefore slew he him? Because his own works were evil, and his brother's righteous.

13 Marvel not, my brethren, if [a]the world hate you.

14 [a]We know that we have passed from death unto life, because we love the brethren. [b]He that loveth not *his* brother abideth in death.

15 [a]Whosoever hateth his brother is a murderer: and ye know that [b]no murderer hath eternal life abiding in him. S

16 [a]Hereby perceive we the love *of God,* because he laid down his life for us: and we ought to lay down *our* lives for the brethren. D L

17 But [a]whoso hath this world's good, and seeth his brother have need, and shutteth up his bowels *of compassion* from him, [b]how dwelleth the love of God in him?

The test of belief

18 My little children, [a]let us not love in word, neither in tongue; but in deed and in truth.

19 And hereby we know [a]that we are of the truth, and shall [/]assure our hearts before him.

20 [a]For if our heart condemn us, God is greater than our heart, and knoweth all things. E

21 [a]Beloved, if our heart condemn us not, [b]*then* have we confidence toward God.

22 And [a]whatsoever we ask, we receive of him, because we keep his commandments, [b]and do those things that are pleasing in his sight. U

23 [a]And this is his commandment, That we should believe on the name of his Son Jesus Christ, [b]and love one another, [c]as he gave us commandment. F

24 And [a]he that keepeth his commandments [b]dwelleth in him, and he in him. And [c]hereby we know that he abideth in us, by the Spirit which he hath given us. E S

2 [c]Rom. 8:29; 2 Pet. 1:4 [d]Ps. 16:11; Mat. 5:8
3 [a]ch. 4:17
4 [a]Rom. 4:15
5 [a]ch. 1:2 [b]Is. 53:5,6 [c]2 Cor. 5:21; Heb. 4:15; 1 Pet. 2:22
6 [a]ch. 2:4
7 [a]ch. 2:26 [b]Rom. 2:13
8 [a]Mat. 13:38; John 8:44 [b]Luke 10:18; John 16:11
9 [a]ch. 5:18 [b]1 Pet. 1:23
10 [a]ch. 2:29 [b]ch. 4:8
11 [a]ch. 1:5 [b]John 13:34; 2 John 5 [/]Or, *commandment*
12 [a]Gen. 4:4,8; Heb. 11:4
13 [a]John 17:14
14 [a]ch. 2:10 [b]ch. 2:9,11
15 [a]Mat. 5:21 [b]Gal. 5:21
16 [a]John 3:16
17 [a]Deut. 15:7; Luke 3:11 [b]ch. 4:20
18 [a]Ezek. 33:31; Rom. 12:9; Eph. 4:15
19 [a]John 18:37 [/]Gk. *persuade*
20 [a]1 Cor. 4:4
21 [a]Job 22:26 [b]Heb. 10:22
22 [a]Ps. 34:15; Prov. 15:29; Jer. 29:12; Mat. 7:8 [b]John 8:29
23 [a]John 6:29 [b]Mat. 22:39; John 13:34; Eph. 5:2 [c]ch. 2:8,10
24 [a]John 14:23 [b]John 17:21 [c]Rom. 8:9

S *1Jn 2:15* ◀▶ *1Jn 3:15*
D *1Jn 2:2* ◀▶ *1Jn 3:16*
K *1Jn 2:2* ◀▶ *1Jn 3:8*
L *1Jn 2:12* ◀▶ *1Jn 3:16*
C *1Jn 2:15–17* ◀▶ *1Jn 5:12*
K *1Jn 3:5* ◀▶ *1Jn 4:4*

S *1Jn 3:3–10* ◀▶ *1Jn 3:24*
D *1Jn 3:5* ◀▶ *1Jn 4:9*
L *1Jn 3:5* ◀▶ *1Jn 4:8–10*
E *Heb 4:12–13* ◀▶ *Rev 2:23*
U *1Jn 4* ◀
F *1Pe 2:6* ◀▶ *1Jn 5:1*
E *1Jn 2:27* ◀▶ *1Jn 4:13*
S *1Jn 3:15* ◀▶ *1Jn 4:8*

body (see Php 3:21). For further information, see the article on "The Resurrection of the Body" on p. 1206.
3:3 John's prediction reminds believers of Paul's prophecy of the judgment of Christians (see Ro 14:10; 2Co 5:10), and motivates them to live in the constant expectation of the appearance of Jesus at the second coming.

N 4 BELOVED, [a]BELIEVE not every spirit, but [b]try the spirits whether they are of God: because [c]many false prophets are gone out into the world.

2 Hereby know ye the Spirit of God: [a]Every spirit that confesseth that Jesus Christ is come in the flesh is of God:

3 And [a]every spirit that confesseth not that Jesus Christ is come in the flesh is not of God: and this is that *spirit* of antichrist, whereof ye have heard that it should come; and [b]even now already is it in the world.

K 4 [a]Ye are of God, little children, and have overcome them: because greater is he that is in you, than [b]he that is in the world.

5 [a]They are of the world: therefore speak they of the world, and [b]the world heareth them.

N 6 We are of God: [a]he that knoweth God heareth us; he that is not of God heareth not us. Hereby know we [b]the spirit of truth, and the spirit of error.

The source of love

7 [a]Beloved, let us love one another: for love is of God; and every one that loveth is born of God, and knoweth God.

L S 8 He that loveth not [a]knoweth not God; for [b]God is love.

D 9 [a]In this was manifested the love of God toward us, because that God sent his only begotten Son into the world, [b]that we might live through him.

10 Herein is love, [a]not that we loved God, but that he loved us, and sent his Son [b]*to be* the propitiation for our sins.

11 Beloved, [a]if God so loved us, we ought also to love one another.

12 [a]No man hath seen God at any time. If we love one another, God dwelleth in us, and [b]his love is perfected in us.

13 [a]Hereby know we that we dwell in him, and he in us, because he hath given us of his Spirit. E

14 And [a]we have seen and do testify that [b]the Father sent the Son *to be* the Saviour of the world. K L W

15 [a]Whosoever shall confess that Jesus is the Son of God, God dwelleth in him, and he in God.

16 And we have known and believed the love that God hath to us. [a]God is love; and [b]he that dwelleth in love dwelleth in God, and God in him.

17 Herein is [1]our love made perfect, that [a]we may have boldness in the day of judgment: [b]because as he is, so are we in this world. J J

18 There is no fear in love; but perfect love casteth out fear: because fear hath torment. He that feareth [a]is not made perfect in love. J W

19 We love him, because he first loved us.

20 [a]If a man say, I love God, and hateth his brother, he is a liar: for he that loveth not his brother whom he hath seen, how can he love God [b]whom he hath not seen? S

21 And [a]this commandment have we from him, That he who loveth God love his brother also.

Faith through the Son

5 WHOSOEVER [a]BELIEVETH that [b]Jesus is the Christ is [c]born of God: [d]and every one that loveth him that begat loveth him also that is begotten of him. F L W

4:1 [a]Jer. 29:8; Mat. 24:4 [b]1 Cor. 14:29; 1 Thes. 5:21; Rev. 2:2 [c]Mat. 24:5; Acts 20:30; 1 Tim. 4:1; 2 Pet. 2:1
2 [a]1 Cor. 12:3
3 [a]2 John 7 [b]2 Thes. 2:7
4 [a]ch. 5:4 [b]John 12:31; Eph. 2:2
5 [a]John 3:31 [b]John 15:19
6 [a]John 8:47 [b]Is. 8:20
7 [a]ch. 3:10,11
8 [a]ch. 2:4 [b]ver. 16
9 [a]John 3:16 [b]ch. 5:11
10 [a]John 15:16; Rom. 5:8; Tit. 3:4 [b]ch. 2:2
11 [a]Mat. 18:33; ch. 3:16
12 [a]John 1:18; 1 Tim. 6:16 [b]ch. 2:5
13 [a]John 14:20
14 [a]John 1:14 [b]John 3:17
15 [a]Rom. 10:9
16 [a]ver. 8 [b]ch. 3:24
17 [a]Jas. 2:13 [b]ch. 3:3 [1]Gk. *love with us*
18 [a]ver. 12
20 [a]ch. 2:4 [b]ver. 12
21 [a]Mat. 22:37; John 13:34
5:1 [a]John 1:12 [b]ch. 2:22,23 [c]John 1:13 [d]John 15:23

N *1Jn 2:27* ◀▶ *1Jn 4:6*
K *1Jn 3:8* ◀▶ *1Jn 4:14*
N *1Jn 4:1–2* ◀▶ *1Jn 5:6*
L *1Jn 3:16* ◀▶ *1Jn 4:14*
S *1Jn 3:24* ◀▶ *1Jn 4:20–21*
D *1Jn 3:16* ◀▶ *Rev 1:5*
E *1Jn 3:24* ◀▶ *1Jn 5:6–8*
K *1Jn 4:4* ◀▶ *1Jn 5:4–5*
L *1Jn 4:8–10* ◀▶ *1Jn 5:1*
W *1Jn 2:1–2* ◀▶ *1Jn 5:1*
J *2Pe 3:7* ◀▶ *Jude 6* **J** *2Pe 3:7* ◀▶ *Jude 6*
J *1Pe 4:16* ◀ **W** *1Pe 5:7* ◀
S *1Jn 4:8* ◀▶ *1Jn 5:2–3*
F *1Jn 3:23* ◀▶ *1Jn 5:4–5*
L *1Jn 4:14* ◀▶ *1Jn 5:9–10*
W *1Jn 4:14–15* ◀▶ *1Jn 5:9–10*

4:3 The belief that Jesus, the Son of God, was incarnated in human flesh is essential to salvation. The spirit of antichrist denies this incarnation of Christ. In addition, the denial that Jesus of Nazareth is truly the Son of God is an essential component of almost every major cult and false religion that opposes Christianity.

4:17 Since we as believers have accepted Christ's atonement on the cross for our sins, we can "have boldness in the day of judgment." We will not be subject to God's wrath at the end of the Millennium when all of the wicked souls from Cain to the last rebel soul will be judged at the great white throne judgment.

S 2 By this we know that we love the
children of God, when we love God, and
keep his commandments.
3 [a]For this is the love of God, that we
keep his commandments: and [b]his commandments are not grievous.
F 4 For [a]whatsoever is born of God over-
K cometh the world: and this is the victory
V that overcometh the world, *even* our
faith.
5 Who is he that overcometh the
world, but [a]he that believeth that Jesus is
the Son of God?
E 6 This is he that came [a]by water and
N blood, *even* Jesus Christ; not by water
only, but by water and blood. [b]And it is
the Spirit that beareth witness, because
the Spirit is truth.
D 7 For there are three that bear record
in heaven, the Father, [a]the Word, and
the Holy Ghost: [b]and these three are one.
8 And there are three that bear witness in earth, the spirit, and the water,
and the blood: and these three agree in
one.
F 9 If we receive [a]the witness of men,
L the witness of God is greater: [b]for this is
W the witness of God which he hath testified of his Son.
N 10 He that believeth on the Son of God
[a]hath the witness in himself: he that believeth not God [b]hath made him a liar;
because he believeth not the record that
God gave of his Son.
11 [a]And this is the record, that God
hath given to us eternal life, and [b]this life
is in his Son.

S *1Jn 4:20–21 ◀▶ 1Jn 5:18*
F *1Jn 5:1 ◀▶ 1Jn 5:9–10*
K *1Jn 4:14 ◀▶ Jude 24*
V *Heb 11:32–35 ◀*
E *1Jn 4:13 ◀▶ Jude 19–20*
N *1Jn 4:6 ◀* **D** *Heb 9:14 ◀*
F *1Jn 5:4–5 ◀▶ 1Jn 5:13*
L *1Jn 5:1 ◀▶ 1Jn 5:16*
W *1Jn 5:1 ◀▶ Rev 3:20*
N *Jas 4:13–14 ◀▶ 1Jn 5:12*

3 [a]John 14:15; 2 John 6 [b]Mic. 6:8
4 [a]John 16:33
5 [a]1 Cor. 15:57
6 [a]John 19:34 [b]John 14:17; 1 Tim. 3:16
7 [a]John 1:1; Rev. 19:13 [b]John 10:30
9 [a]John 8:17 [b]Mat. 3:16
10 [a]Rom. 8:16 [b]John 3:33
11 [a]ch. 2:25 [b]ch. 4:9
12 [a]John 3:36
13 [a]John 20:31 [b]ch. 1:1,2
14 [a]ch. 3:22 [1]Or, *concerning him*
16 [a]Job 42:8; Jas. 5:14 [b]Mat. 12:31; Mark 3:29; Heb. 6:4,6 [c]Jer. 7:16; John 17:9
17 [a]ch. 3:4
18 [a]1 Pet. 1:23 [b]Jas. 1:27
19 [a]Gal. 1:4
20 [a]Luke 24:45 [b]John 17:3 [c]Is. 9:6; Acts 20:28; Tit. 2:13 [d]ver. 11,12
21 [a]1 Cor. 10:14

12 [a]He that hath the Son hath life; *and* C
he that hath not the Son of God hath not N
life. O

The certainties of faith

13 [a]These things have I written unto F
you that believe on the name of the Son
of God; [b]that ye may know that ye have
eternal life, and that ye may believe on
the name of the Son of God.
14 And this is the confidence that we L
have [1]in him, that, [a]if we ask any thing
according to his will, he heareth us:
15 And if we know that he hear us,
whatsoever we ask, we know that we
have the petitions that we desired of him.
16 If any man see his brother sin a sin Q
which is not unto death, he shall ask, and L
[a]he shall give him life for them that sin P
not unto death. [b]There is a sin unto
death: [c]I do not say that he shall pray
for it.
17 [a]All unrighteousness is sin: and
there is a sin not unto death.
18 We know that [a]whosoever is born S
of God sinneth not; but he that is begotten of God [b]keepeth himself, and that
wicked one toucheth him not.
19 *And* we know that we are of God, C
and [a]the whole world lieth in wickedness.
20 And we know that the Son of God
is come, and [a]hath given us an understanding, [b]that we may know him that is
true, and we are in him that is true, *even*
in his Son Jesus Christ. [c]This is the true
God, [d]and eternal life.
21 Little children, [a]keep yourselves
from idols. Amen.

C *1Jn 3:8 ◀▶ 1Jn 5:19*
N *1Jn 5:10 ◀▶ Jude 15*
O *Jas 4:12 ◀▶ Rev 7:9–12*
F *1Jn 5:9–10 ◀* **L** *1Jn 3:1 ◀*
Q *Heb 10:29 ◀*
L *1Jn 5:9–10 ◀▶ Rev 1:5*
P *1Jn 2:1–2 ◀▶ Rev 2:5*
S *1Jn 5:2–3 ◀▶ 2Jn 8–9*
C *1Jn 5:12 ◀▶ Jude 12*

5:7 This passage is one of the clearest Biblical declarations regarding the mystery of the triune nature of God. While the Scriptures clearly state that God is one (see Dt 6:4; Mk 12:29), this passage reveals the mystery of God presented to humanity in three persons: the Father, the Son and the Holy Spirit (see Mt 28:19; Jn 10:30).

2 John

Author: John

Theme: The search for Biblical truth in light of hospitality to strangers

Date of Writing: C. A.D. 85–95

Outline of 2 John

I. Introduction (1–3)
II. The Path of Love and Truth (4–6)
III. Warnings About the Deceiver (7–11)
IV. Conclusion (12–13)

THE APOSTLE JOHN wrote this short epistle as well as the other short letters that bear his name (see introduction to 1 John). This second letter of John was addressed to "the elect lady and her children" (v. 1). While some scholars feel that this greeting is used metaphorically to mean a church and its members, others feel John refers here to a specific individual and her family who allowed a church to be formed in their home. Because John's emphasis in this letter is similar to that of 1 John, scholars believe that these letters were composed at about the same time.

During the early development of the church, the gospel was taken from place to place by traveling evangelists. Believers opened their homes to these teachers and gave them provisions for their journey when they left. False teachers and philosophers also relied on this practice of hospitality, so John's letter to this "lady" urges discernment in offering hospitality to itinerant preachers. John emphasizes the importance of the knowledge of Biblical truth expressed through the life, teaching and person of Christ. With warm, personal words, John reminds this lady and her children that Jesus was truly God's Son and urges them to continue in God's love and reject false doctrine.

1 THE ELDER unto the elect lady and her children, [a]whom I love in the truth; and not I only, but also all they that have known [b]the truth;

2 For the truth's sake, which dwelleth in us, and shall be with us for ever.

3 [a]Grace [1]be with you, mercy, *and* peace, from God the Father, and from the Lord Jesus Christ, the Son of the Father, in truth and love.

Counsel and warnings

4 I rejoiced greatly that I found of thy children [a]walking in truth, as we have received a commandment from the Father.

5 And now I beseech thee, lady, [a]not as though I wrote a new commandment unto thee, but that which we had from the beginning, [b]that we love one another.

6 And [a]this is love, that we walk after his commandments. This is the commandment, That, as [b]ye have heard from the beginning, ye should walk in it.

P 7 For [a]many deceivers are entered into the world, [b]who confess not that Jesus Christ is come in the flesh. [c]This is a deceiver and an antichrist.

8 [a]Look to yourselves, [b]that we lose not those things which we have [1]wrought, but that we receive a full reward. S

9 [a]Whosoever transgresseth, and abideth not in the doctrine of Christ, hath not God. He that abideth in the doctrine of Christ, he hath both the Father and the Son.

10 If there come any unto you, and bring not this doctrine, receive him not into *your* house, [a]neither bid him God speed:

11 For he that biddeth him God speed is partaker of his evil deeds.

12 [a]Having many things to write unto you, I would not *write* with paper and ink: but I trust to come unto you, and speak [1]face to face, [b]that [2]our joy may be full.

13 [a]The children of thy elect sister greet thee. Amen.

1:1 [a]3 John 1 [b]Col. 1:5
3 [a]1 Tim. 1:2 [1]Gk. *shall be*
4 [a]3 John 3
5 [a]1 John 3:11 [b]John 13:34
6 [a]1 John 2:5 [b]1 John 2:24
7 [a]1 John 4:1 [b]1 John 4:2 [c]1 John 2:22
8 [a]Mark 13:9 [b]Gal. 3:4 [1]Or, *gained:* Some copies read, *which ye have gained, but that ye receive*
9 [a]1 John 2:23
10 [a]Rom. 16:17
12 [a]3 John 13 [b]John 17:13 [1]Gk. *mouth to mouth* [2]Or, *your*
13 [a]1 Pet. 5:13

P *2Pe 3:10–12* ◄► *Jude 14–15*

S *1Jn 5:18* ◄► *3Jn 11*

7 John said that there were many atheists even in his time who denied that Jesus was God incarnate. These "deceivers" possess the spirit of the antichrist and are fundamentally opposed to Jesus Christ. An antichrist spirit denies, at every opportunity, the gospel record that Jesus is real and that he came "in the flesh." Today, centuries later, the antichrist spirit of atheism still expresses itself in its total opposition to the historical reality that Jesus was born to the virgin Mary, lived among men, died on the cross and rose from the dead as the glorified Son of God.

3 John

Author: John

Theme: Daily life lived in the light of Biblical truth

Date of Writing: C. A.D. 85–95

Outline of 3 John

I. Introduction (1–4)
II. Gaius Is Commended (5–8)
III. Diotrephes Is Condemned (9–11)
IV. The Good Example of Demetrius (12)
V. Conclusion (13–14)

THIS LETTER WAS written by the apostle John, the son of Zebedee and beloved disciple of Jesus (see introduction to 1 John). Composed at about the same time as his other epistles, this letter is addressed by John to his friend Gaius, who may have been a first-century church leader.

This epistle reflects the difficult experience of the church during the closing decade of the first century. A domineering leader named Diotrephes had rejected itinerant preachers that had been sent out by John to one of the churches in the province of Asia. Diotrephes also had slandered John and repudiated John's authority to teach true doctrine by removing those believers from the church who disagreed with his teaching against John. In this brief letter, John rebukes Diotrephes for his actions and instructs Gaius to support and entertain those who come as God's true messengers. John reminds Gaius that the church should be walking daily in light of Biblical truth and commends Demetrius as a strong Christian leader for basing his life upon the fundamental truths of Christianity.

1 THE ELDER unto the wellbeloved Gaius, [a]whom I love [l]in the truth.

2 Beloved, I [l]wish above all things that thou mayest prosper and be in health, even as thy soul prospereth.

3 For I rejoiced greatly, when the brethren came and testified of the truth that is in thee, even as [a]thou walkest in the truth.

4 I have no greater joy than to hear that [a]my children walk in truth.

Encouragement and reproof

5 Beloved, thou doest faithfully whatsoever thou doest to the brethren, and to strangers;

6 Which have borne witness of thy charity before the church: whom if thou bring forward on their journey [l]after a godly sort, thou shalt do well:

7 Because that for his name's sake they went forth, [a]taking nothing of the Gentiles.

8 We therefore ought to receive such, that we might be fellowhelpers to the truth.

H *1Pe 3:10* ◀▶ *Rev 22:2*

1 [a]2 John 1 [l]Or, *truly*

2 [l]Or, *pray*

3 [a]2 John 4

4 [a]1 Cor. 4:15; Philem. 10

6 [l]Gk. *worthy of God*

7 [a]1 Cor. 9:12,15

11 [a]Ps. 37:27; Is. 1:16,17; 1 Pet. 3:11 [b]1 John 2:29 & 3:6,9

12 [a]1 Tim. 3:7 [b]John 21:24

13 [a]2 John 12

14 [l]Gk. *mouth to mouth*

9 I wrote unto the church: but Diotrephes, who loveth to have the preeminence among them, receiveth us not.

10 Wherefore, if I come, I will remember his deeds which he doeth, prating against us with malicious words: and not content therewith, neither doth he himself receive the brethren, and forbiddeth them that would, and casteth *them* out of the church.

11 Beloved, [a]follow not that which is evil, but that which is good. [b]He that doeth good is of God: but he that doeth evil hath not seen God.

12 Demetrius [a]hath good report of all *men,* and of the truth itself: yea, and we *also* bear record; [b]and ye know that our record is true.

13 [a]I had many things to write, but I will not with ink and pen write unto thee:

14 But I trust I shall shortly see thee, and we shall speak [l]face to face. Peace *be* to thee. *Our* friends salute thee. Greet the friends by name.

S *2Jn 8–9* ◀▶ *Jude 5–6*

Jude

Author: Jude

Theme: Believers must contend for the faith

Date of Writing: c. A.D. 65

Outline of Jude

I. Introduction (1–2)
II. The Reason for the Epistle (3–4)
III. Examples of Unbelief and Rebellion (5–16)
IV. Exhortations to Faithful Believers (17–23)
V. Conclusion (24–25)

THE AUTHOR OF this letter was Jude, the half-brother of Jesus and brother of the apostle James (see Mk 6:3). Directed to one or more of the churches dispersed throughout the Roman empire, this letter was probably composed during the mid to late A.D. 60s.

Though the first-century Christians faced open opposition, this letter addresses the problem of heresy and false teaching. Jude had intended to write about salvation (v. 3), but he changes his appeal to a defense of faith in Christ. The similarity of the content of Jude's letter to Peter's second letter may indicate the extent to which false teachers had led believers away from the true gospel. Jude contends that the errors raised by false teachers and critics must be refuted and urges his readers to contend for their faith in Jesus Christ. Citing three examples of judgment from the OT, Jude warns that God's judgment will fall upon those who turn away from the faith even as it fell upon Cain, Korah and Balaam.

1 JUDE, THE servant of Jesus Christ,
and [a]brother of James, to them that are
sanctified by God the Father, and [b]pre-
served in Jesus Christ, *and* [c]called:
2 Mercy unto you, and [a]peace, and
love, be multiplied.
3 Beloved, when I gave all diligence to
write unto you [a]of the common salvation,
it was needful for me to write unto you,
and exhort *you* that [b]ye should earnestly
contend for the faith which was once delivered unto the saints.
4 [a]For there are certain men crept in
unawares, [b]who were before of old ordained to this condemnation, ungodly
men, [c]turning [d]the grace of our God into
lasciviousness, and [e]denying the only
Lord God, and our Lord Jesus Christ.

The doom of false teachers

H 5 I will therefore put you in remem-
S brance, though ye once knew this, how
that [a]the Lord, having saved the people
out of the land of Egypt, afterward [b]de-
stroyed them that believed not.
J 6 And [a]the angels which kept not their
J [1]first estate, but left their own habitation,
[b]he hath reserved in everlasting chains
under darkness [c]unto the judgment of
the great day.
7 Even as [a]Sodom and Gomorrha, and
the cities about them in like manner, giving themselves over to fornication, and
going after [1]strange flesh, are set forth for
an example, suffering the vengeance of
eternal fire.
8 [a]Likewise also these *filthy* dreamers
defile the flesh, despise dominion, and
[b]speak evil of dignities.
9 Yet [a]Michael the archangel, when
contending with the devil he disputed
about the body of Moses, [b]durst not bring
against him a railing accusation, but said,
[c]The Lord rebuke thee.
10 [a]But these speak evil of those
things which they know not: but what
they know naturally, as brute beasts, in
those things they corrupt themselves.
11 Woe unto them! for they have gone
in the way [a]of Cain, and [b]ran greedily
after the error of Balaam for reward, and
perished [c]in the gainsaying of Core.
12 [a]These are spots in your [b]feasts of C
charity, when they feast with you, feeding themselves without fear: [c]clouds *they*
are without water, [d]carried about of
winds; trees whose fruit withereth, without fruit, twice dead, [e]plucked up by the
roots;
13 [a]Raging waves of the sea, [b]foaming H
out their own shame; wandering stars,
[c]to whom is reserved the blackness of
darkness for ever.
14 And Enoch also, [a]the seventh from P
Adam, prophesied of these, saying, Be- J
hold, [b]the Lord cometh with ten thousands of his saints,
15 To execute judgment upon all, and N
to convince all that are ungodly among
them of all their ungodly deeds which
they have ungodly committed, and of all
their [a]hard *speeches* which ungodly sinners have spoken against him.
16 These are murmurers, complainers, C
walking after their own lusts; and [a]their
mouth speaketh great swelling *words,*
[b]having men's persons in admiration because of advantage.

1 [a]Acts 1:13 [b]John 17:11; 1 Pet. 1:5 [c]Rom. 1:7
2 [a]1 Pet. 1:2; 2 Pet. 1:2
3 [a]Tit. 1:4 [b]Phil. 1:27; 2 Tim. 1:13
4 [a]Gal. 2:4; 2 Pet. 2:1 [b]Rom. 9:22 [c]2 Pet. 2:10 [d]Tit. 2:11 [e]Tit. 1:16
5 [a]1 Cor. 10:9 [b]Num. 14:29; Ps. 106:26
6 [a]John 8:44 [b]2 Pet. 2:4 [c]Rev. 20:10 [1]*Or, principality*
7 [a]Gen. 19:24; 2 Pet. 2:6 [1]*Gk. other*
8 [a]2 Pet. 2:10 [b]Ex. 22:28
9 [a]Dan. 10:13 [b]2 Pet. 2:11 [c]Zech. 3:2
10 [a]2 Pet. 2:12
11 [a]1 John 3:12 [b]2 Pet. 2:15 [c]Num. 16:1
12 [a]2 Pet. 2:13 [b]1 Cor. 11:21 [c]Prov. 25:14; 2 Pet. 2:17 [d]Eph. 4:14 [e]Mat. 15:13
13 [a]Is. 57:20 [b]Phil. 3:19 [c]2 Pet. 2:17
14 [a]Gen. 5:18 [b]Deut. 33:2
15 [a]1 Sam. 2:3; Ps. 31:18
16 [a]2 Pet. 2:18 [b]Prov. 28:21

H *2Pe 3:6–7* ◀ ▶ *Jude 13–15*
S *3Jn 11* ◀ ▶ *Rev 2:4–5*
J *1Jn 4:17* ◀ ▶ *Rev 20:11–15*
J *1Jn 4:17* ◀ ▶ *Jude 14–15*

C *1Jn 5:19* ◀ ▶ *Jude 16*
H *Jude 5–7* ◀ ▶ *Rev 1:7*
P *2Jn 7* ◀ ▶ *Rev 1:7*
J *Jude 6* ◀ ▶ *Rev 11:18*
N *1Jn 5:12* ◀ ▶ *Rev 3:17–18*
C *Jude 12* ◀ ▶ *Rev 3:17*

6–7 This prophecy refers to the evil angels who joined Satan in his wicked rebellion against God in the dateless past. Jude's prophecy reveals that these angels will be dealt with at the last judgment because of their rebellion and attempts to destroy humanity. Some scholars believe that these angels will also be judged for sexual sins because of Jude's comparison between their sin and the sin of Sodom and Gomorrah (see Ge 19). For further information, see the article on "Satan and the Fallen Angels" on p. 914.

14–15 Jude refers to an ancient prophecy of Enoch that has not survived the centuries. Yet Enoch's words echo Moses and Daniel as he prophesied that Jesus Christ will return from heaven with an enormous number of his resurrected saints (see Dt 33:2; Dan 7:9–10). Millions of resurrected saints will participate in Christ's glorious return to the earth, following his victory over the antichrist in the coming Battle of Armageddon. At that time Jesus Christ will judge everyone, convicting the ungodly of their wicked deeds.

Hold to the true faith

E 17 [a]But, beloved, remember ye the
words which were spoken before of the
apostles of our Lord Jesus Christ;
18 How that they told you [a]there
should be mockers in the last time, who
should walk after their own ungodly
lusts.
E 19 These be they [a]who separate them-
L selves, [b]sensual, having not the Spirit.
S 20 But ye, beloved, [a]building up your-
W selves on your most holy faith, [b]praying
in the Holy Ghost,
21 Keep yourselves in the love of God,
[a]looking for the mercy of our Lord Jesus
Christ unto eternal life.
22 And of some have compassion,
making a difference:
23 And others [a]save with fear, [b]pulling
them out of the fire; hating even [c]the garment spotted by the flesh.

Benediction

24 [a]Now unto him that is able to keep K
you from falling, and [b]to present *you*
faultless before the presence of his glory
with exceeding joy,
25 [a]To the only wise God our Saviour,
be glory and majesty, dominion and
power, both now and ever. Amen.

E *1Jn 2:18* ◀ ▶ *Rev 1:19*
E *1Jn 5:6–8* ◀ ▶ *Rev 1:4*
L *1Pe 4:10–11* ◀ ▶ *Rev 1:10*
S *1Pe 1:22* ◀ **W** *1Pe 4:10–11* ◀
K *1Jn 5:4–5* ◀ ▶ *Rev 1:18*

17 [a]2 Pet. 3:2
18 [a]1 Tim. 4:1; 2 Pet. 2:1
19 [a]Prov. 18:1 [b]Jas. 3:15
20 [a]Col. 2:7 [b]Rom. 8:26
21 [a]Tit. 2:13; 2 Pet. 3:12
23 [a]Rom. 11:14 [b]Amos 4:11; Zech. 3:2 [c]Zech. 3:4,5
24 [a]Eph. 3:20 [b]Col. 1:22
25 [a]Rom. 16:27

17–18 Jude's words sound a lot like Peter's words as he reminds his readers that in the last days mockers of the gospel would follow their own lusts and ignore the signs of Christ's return (see 2Pe 3:3). Despite the growing evidence that the prophetic signs are being fulfilled in our lifetime, there are still many "mockers" who reject the prophecies and Christ's promises that he would return.

Revelation

Author: John

Theme: Christ will overcome evil when he returns

Date of Writing: c. A.D. 90–96

Outline of Revelation

I. Jesus and the Seven Churches (1:1–20)
II. Letters to the Seven Churches (2:1—3:22)
III. The Throne, the Elders and the Lamb (4:1—5:14)
IV. The Seven Seals of Judgment (6:1—8:1)
V. The Seven Trumpets and Two Witnesses (8:2—11:19)
VI. Different Personifications and Events (12:1—14:20)
VII. The Seven Bowls and Armageddon (15:1—16:21)
VIII. The Great Prostitute: Babylon (17:1—19:5)
IX The Marriage Supper and Return of Christ (19:6–21)
X. The Millennium (20:1–6)
XI. Satan's Doom (20:7–10)
XII. The Great White Throne Judgment (20:11–15)
XIII. A New Heaven, New Earth and New Jerusalem (21:1—22:21)

THE AUTHOR OF this book clearly identifies himself as John (see 1:1, 4, 9; 22:8) and uses the word "I" repeatedly to verify this book's authenticity. During Emperor Domitian's tyranny (A.D. 81–96), opposition to Christianity increased throughout the Roman empire. Domitian commanded that everyone worship him as a god. Anyone who refused this order was severely punished; many were imprisoned, like John. During his imprisonment on the small island of Patmos in the Aegean Sea, John received this vision and wrote the book of Revelation. Though the book is directed primarily to the seven churches of Asia, John offers a divine perspective of human history for all believers as he proclaims the hope of God's judgment on apostasy and the vindication of his children.

Often referred to as the "Apocalypse," the book of Revelation reveals the hidden happenings of the future using metaphors, symbolic language, dreams, visions and displays of supernatural power. The interpretation of the symbols and figurative language in this divine prophecy has resulted in differing viewpoints among NT scholars. Some scholars suggest that the prophecies in Revelation deal only with the struggle between the Roman empire and the first-century church. Those who adopt this preterist view believe that the prophecies of Revelation and Mt 24 were totally fulfilled in A.D. 70 when Rome destroyed Jerusalem. This view also suggests an earlier date for the writing of Revelation.

Other scholars interpret Revelation from the historical view, suggesting that John's visions reveal the major, historical developments from the day of Pentecost up until Christ's second coming. Still other scholars hold to the allegorical view, interpreting John's prophecies as a reflection of the struggle between God and the forces of evil with no particular reference to actual future events. For further information on the historical and allegorical theories of prophetic interpretation, see the article "Introduction to Prophecy" on p. vi.

The majority of scholars in this century favor a futurist interpretation for this book, suggesting that John's prophecies will be fulfilled through actual events that will occur during a future world crisis. This crisis will culminate in Christ's second coming to earth to defeat evil and establish the Messianic kingdom. For further information about the futurist theory of prophetic interpretation, see the article "Introduction to Prophecy" on p. vi.

Despite the difficulties in interpretation, the book of Revelation has drawn the interest of Christians for centuries because of its focus on Jesus Christ as our glorified Lord and coming King. Throughout his vision, John presents Jesus Christ as the divine Judge who will destroy all satanic opposition and establish his everlasting kingdom of peace and justice. John also proclaims a blessing for those "that readeth, and they that hear the words of this prophecy, and keep those things which are written therein: for the time is at hand" (1:3).

The source of the revelation

1 THE REVELATION of Jesus Christ,
[a]which God gave unto him, to show
unto his servants things which must
shortly come to pass; and [b]he sent and
signified *it* by his angel unto his servant
John:
2 [a]Who bare record of the word of
God, and of the testimony of Jesus Christ,
and of all things [b]that he saw.
3 [a]Blessed *is* he that readeth, and they
that hear the words of this prophecy, and
keep those things which are written
therein: for [b]the time *is* at hand.

The salutation

4 John to the seven churches which
are in Asia: Grace *be* unto you, and

1:1 [a]John 3:32 [b]ch. 22:16
2 [a]1 Cor. 1:6 [b]1 John 1:1
3 [a]Luke 11:28 [b]Jas. 5:8

E Jude 19–20 ◄► Rev 1:10
G 1Jn 2:27 ◄► Rev 3:1

1:1–3 John declares that this vision was sent to him by God through his angel. Note that John issues a unique blessing of God on anyone who reads or listens to "the words of this prophecy" (1:3).

1:4–6 John begins the first portion of his book with messages to the Asiatic churches. Though John had been a leader in many churches in the Roman province of Asia (Turkey), these particular churches were singled out because each one represented a particular situation or problem. Each letter contained Jesus Christ's divine commands for correcting that particular problem in the church; and his words are still applicable to believers two thousand years later.

Note that the number seven, which relates to divine perfection, appears repeatedly throughout this prophecy. John's declaration that Jesus is "the first begotten of the dead" (1:5) reveals Christ's majesty in anticipation of his future rule as the King of kings. God's promise to make his faithful disciples "kings and priests unto God" (1:6) reveals that believers will rule and reign with him over the Jews and Gentiles that survive the tribulation and Armageddon and populate the earth during the

peace, from him [a]which is, and [b]which
was, and which is to come; [c]and from the
seven Spirits which are before his throne;
D 5 And from Jesus Christ, [a]*who is* the
L faithful witness, *and* the [b]first begotten of
the dead, and [c]the prince of the kings of
the earth. Unto him [d]that loved us, [e]and
washed us from our sins in his own
blood,

6 And hath [a]made us kings and priests
unto God and his Father; [b]to him *be* glory
and dominion for ever and ever. Amen.

C 7 [a]Behold, he cometh with clouds; and
P every eye shall see him, and [b]they *also*
H which pierced him: and all kindreds of
the earth shall wail because of him. Even
so, Amen.

8 [a]I am Alpha and Omega, the beginning and the ending, saith the Lord,
[b]which is, and which was, and which is
to come, the Almighty.

The voice and the vision

9 I John, who also am your brother,
and [a]companion in tribulation, and [b]in
the kingdom and patience of Jesus Christ,
was in the isle that is called Patmos, [c]for
the word of God, and for the testimony of
Jesus Christ.

D *1Jn 4:9* ◀ ▶ *Rev 5:9*
L *1Jn 5:16* ◀ ▶ *Rev 3:20*
C *1Jn 3:2–3* ◀ ▶ *Rev 3:11*
P *Jude 14–15* ◀ ▶ *Rev 2:27*
H *Jude 13–15* ◀ ▶ *Rev 3:16*

4 [a]Ex. 3:14 [b]John 1:1 [c]Zech. 3:9
5 [a]John 8:14; 1 Tim. 6:13 [b]Col. 1:18 [c]ch. 17:14 [d]John 13:34; Gal. 2:20 [e]Heb. 9:14; 1 John 1:7
6 [a]1 Pet. 2:5 [b]1 Tim. 6:16
7 [a]Dan. 7:13 [b]Zech. 12:10
8 [a]Is. 41:4 [b]ch. 4:8
9 [a]Phil. 1:7 [b]Rom. 8:17; 2 Tim. 2:12 [c]ch. 6:9
10 [a]Acts 10:10; 2 Cor. 12:2 [b]John 20:26 [c]ch. 4:1
11 [a]ver. 8 [b]ver. 17
12 [a]Ex. 25:37; Zech. 4:2
13 [a]ch. 2:1 [b]Ezek. 1:26; Dan. 7:13 & 10:16 [c]Dan. 10:5 [d]ch. 15:6
14 [a]Dan. 7:9 [b]Dan. 10:6
15 [a]Ezek. 1:7; Dan. 10:6 [b]Ezek. 43:2; Dan. 10:6; ch. 14:2
16 [a]ch. 2:1 [b]Is. 49:2; Eph. 6:17; Heb. 4:12 [c]Acts 26:13

10 [a]I was in the Spirit on [b]the Lord's E
day, and heard behind me [c]a great voice, L
as of a trumpet, T

11 Saying, [a]I am Alpha and Omega,
[b]the first and the last: and, What thou
seest, write in a book, and send *it* unto
the seven churches which are in Asia;
unto Ephesus, and unto Smyrna, and
unto Pergamos, and unto Thyatira,
and unto Sardis, and unto Philadelphia, and unto Laodicea.

12 And I turned to see the voice that
spake with me. And being turned, [a]I saw
seven golden candlesticks;

13 [a]And in the midst of the seven
candlesticks [b]*one* like unto the Son of
man, [c]clothed with a garment down to
the foot, and [d]girt about the paps with a
golden girdle.

14 His head and [a]*his* hairs *were* white
like wool, as white as snow; and [b]his eyes
were as a flame of fire;

15 [a]And his feet like unto fine brass,
as if they burned in a furnace; and [b]his
voice as the sound of many waters.

16 [a]And he had in his right hand
seven stars: and [b]out of his mouth went a
sharp twoedged sword: [c]and his countenance *was* as the sun shineth in his
strength.

E *Rev 1:4* ◀ ▶ *Rev 2:7*
L *Jude 19–20* ◀ ▶ *Rev 4:2*
T *1Jn 2:27* ◀ ▶ *Rev 2:7*

Millennium (see 5:10).

1:7–9 Though imprisoned on Patmos, John declared these words were written "for the testimony of Jesus Christ" (1:9) and to tell of Christ's glorious second coming in majesty and power, returning in judgment as the conquering King of kings. When he returns, there will be mourning as God's people recognize the Messiah they have rejected (see Mt 24:30).

Note that the Lord refers to himself with the first and last letters of the Greek alphabet (1:8) and declares that he alone is eternal, before everything and after everything (see Ex 3:14). This is an important declaration because some people think that Jesus only came into existence two thousand years ago when he was born in the flesh as a baby. The Scriptures clearly reveal that Jesus, the second person of the triune God, has always existed. The apostle Paul declared that Jesus created the universe (see Col 1:15–16).

1:10 This is the only place in Scripture that we find the expression "the Lord's day." This quite possibly refers to Sunday, the first day of the week when the Lord rose from the grave. Though Sunday was designated "the first day of the week" (Mt 28:1) throughout the NT (see Lk 24:1; 1Co 16:2), the phrase "the Lord's day" became a synonym for Sunday in the second century.

However, in this passage, "the Lord's day" may also be a simple rearrangement of the common expression, "the day of the Lord." Because the focus of John's vision of the last days is the future "day of the Lord" some scholars believe the burden of evidence suggests this interpretation. Whether or not John received his tremendous vision on Sunday, the focus of his prophetic vision manifests the glory of Jesus Christ in the last days.

1:12–18 In his vision John saw Jesus Christ standing "in the midst of the seven candlesticks" (1:13). The number seven appears repeatedly throughout Revelation. Seven candlesticks or lampstands represent the seven letters to the seven churches. The seven stars represent seven angelic messengers and point to the seven spirits or characteristics of God (see Zec 4:10). See study notes at Rev 4:5.

17 And [a]when I saw him, I fell at his feet as dead. And [b]he laid his right hand upon me, saying unto me, Fear not; [c]I am the first and the last:

K 18 [a]*I am* he that liveth, and was dead; and, behold, [b]I am alive for evermore, Amen; and [c]have the keys of hell and of death.

E 19 Write the things which thou hast seen, [a]and the things which are, [b]and the things which shall be hereafter;

20 The mystery of the seven stars which thou sawest in my right hand, and the seven golden candlesticks. The seven stars are [a]the angels of the seven churches: and [b]the seven candlesticks which thou sawest are the seven churches.

The message to Ephesus

2 UNTO THE angel of the church of Ephesus write; These things saith [a]he that holdeth the seven stars in his right hand, [b]who walketh in the midst of the seven golden candlesticks;

2 [a]I know thy works, and thy labour, and thy patience, and how thou canst not bear them which are evil: and [b]thou hast tried them [c]which say they are apostles, and are not, and hast found them liars:

3 And hast borne, and hast patience, and for my name's sake hast laboured, and hast [a]not fainted.

S 4 Nevertheless I have *somewhat* against thee, because thou hast left thy first love.

K *Jude 24* ◀ ▶ *Rev 7:14*
E *Jude 17–18* ◀ ▶ *Rev 4:1*
S *Jude 5–6* ◀ ▶ *Rev 2:10*

17 [a]Ezek. 1:28 [b]Dan. 8:18 & 10:10 [c]Is. 41:4 & 44:6 & 48:12; ch. 22:13
18 [a]Rom. 6:9 [b]ch. 4:9 [c]Ps. 68:20; ch. 20:1
19 [a]ch. 2:1 [b]ch. 4:1
20 [a]Mal. 2:7; ch. 2:1 [b]Zech. 4:2; Mat. 5:15; Phil. 2:15
2:1 [a]ch. 1:16 [b]ch. 1:13
2 [a]Ps. 1:6; ch. 3:1, 8 [b]1 John 4:1 [c]2 Cor. 11:13; 2 Pet. 2:1
3 [a]Gal. 6:9; Heb. 12:3,5
5 [a]Mat. 21:41
7 [a]Mat. 11:15 & 13:9,43; ch. 3:6,13 [b]ch. 22:2,14 [c]Gen. 2:9
8 [a]ch. 1:8,17
9 [a]Luke 12:21; 1 Tim. 6:18; Jas. 2:5 [b]Rom. 2:17 [c]ch. 3:9
10 [a]Mat. 10:22 [b]Mat. 24:13 [c]Jas. 1:12; ch. 3:11
11 [a]ch. 13:9

5 Remember therefore from whence thou art fallen, and repent, and do the first works; [a]or else I will come unto thee quickly, and will remove thy candlestick out of his place, except thou repent. P R

6 But this thou hast, that thou hatest the deeds of the Nicolaitans, which I also hate.

7 [a]He that hath an ear, let him hear what the Spirit saith unto the churches; To him that overcometh will I give [b]to eat of [c]the tree of life, which is in the midst of the paradise of God. E T

The message to Smyrna

8 And unto the angel of the church in Smyrna write; These things saith [a]the first and the last, which was dead, and is alive;

9 I know thy works, and tribulation, and poverty, (but thou art [a]rich) and *I know* the blasphemy of [b]them which say they are Jews, and are not, [c]but *are* the synagogue of Satan.

10 [a]Fear none of those things which thou shalt suffer: behold, the devil shall cast *some* of you into prison, that ye may be tried; and ye shall have tribulation ten days: [b]be thou faithful unto death, and I will give thee [c]a crown of life. S

11 [a]He that hath an ear, let him hear what the Spirit saith unto the churches; E T

P *1Jn 5:16* ◀ **R** *1Jn 9* ◀ ▶ *Rev 2:16*
E *Rev 1:10* ◀ ▶ *Rev 2:11*
T *Rev 1:10* ◀ ▶ *Rev 2:11*
S *Rev 2:4–5* ◀ ▶ *Rev 3:1–5*
E *Rev 2:7* ◀ ▶ *Rev 2:17*
T *Rev 2:7* ◀ ▶ *Rev 2:17*

1:19 John was told to divide his prophecy into three parts: the past, the present and the future. The past events were contained in the introductory vision of ch. 1. The present things were the seven messages to the seven churches. The bulk of this book concerns events that will occur in the end times. Understanding this structural analysis of the book will help us better interpret the prophetic vision of Revelation.

1:20 Christ emphasized his control over the spiritual and angelic realm by holding the seven stars in his hand. So that there would be no question about the meaning of John's vision, Christ interpreted the meaning of these symbols for him. Note that these candlesticks or lampstands might either refer to tall candelabra or to golden stands that held oil lamps at an appropriate height.

2:1 The letters to the seven churches are the last direct words we have from Jesus Christ. These seven messages are similar to the parables because they are composed of Christ's own words and use symbols to paint the spiritual conditions of the churches.

Located in the region of modern-day Turkey, these seven churches flourished during the first century, but were singled out because their specific problems were characteristic of the spiritual situations faced by believers throughout all generations. Addressed to the angels, or messengers, of these seven churches, these messages form the second portion of the threefold division of Revelation referred to in 1:19. For further information on Christ's messages to these seven churches, see the article "The Seven Letters to the Churches" on p. 1448.

He that overcometh shall not be hurt of [b]the second death.

The message to Pergamos

12 And to the angel of the church in Pergamos write; These things saith [a]he which hath the sharp sword with two edges;

13 I know thy works, and where thou dwellest, *even* where Satan's seat *is:* and thou holdest fast my name, and hast not denied my faith, even in those days wherein Antipas *was* my faithful martyr, who was slain among you, where Satan dwelleth.

14 But I have a few things against thee, because thou hast there them that hold the doctrine of [a]Balaam, who taught Balac to cast a stumblingblock before the children of Israel, [b]to eat things sacrificed unto idols, [c]and to commit fornication.

15 So hast thou also them that hold the doctrine of the Nicolaitans, which thing I hate.

R 16 Repent; or else I will come unto thee quickly, and [a]will fight against them with the sword of my mouth.

E T 17 He that hath an ear, let him hear what the Spirit saith unto the churches; To him that overcometh will I give to eat of the hidden manna, and will give him a white stone, and in the stone [a]a new name written, which no man knoweth saving he that receiveth *it.*

The message to Thyatira

18 And unto the angel of the church in Thyatira write; These things saith the Son of God, [a]who hath his eyes like unto a flame of fire, and his feet *are* like fine brass;

19 [a]I know thy works, and charity, and service, and faith, and thy patience, and thy works; and the last *to be* more than the first.

20 Notwithstanding I have a few things against thee, because thou sufferest that woman [a]Jezebel, which calleth herself a prophetess, to teach and to seduce my servants [b]to commit fornication, and to eat things sacrificed unto idols.

21 And I gave her space [a]to repent of her fornication; and she repented not.

22 Behold, I will cast her into a bed, and them that commit adultery with her into great tribulation, except they repent of their deeds.

23 And I will kill her children with death; and all the churches shall know that [a]I am he which searcheth the reins and hearts: and [b]I will give unto every one of you according to your works. **E**

24 But unto you I say, and unto the rest in Thyatira, as many as have not this doctrine, and which have not known the depths of Satan, as they speak; [a]I will put upon you none other burden.

25 But [a]that which ye have *already* hold fast till I come.

26 And he that overcometh, and keepeth [a]my works unto the end, [b]to him will I give power over the nations: **M**

27 [a]And he shall rule them with a rod of iron; as the vessels of a potter shall they be broken to shivers: even as I received of my Father. **P**

28 And I will give him [a]the morning star.

29 [a]He that hath an ear, let him hear what the Spirit saith unto the churches. **E T**

The message to Sardis

3 AND UNTO the angel of the church in Sardis write; These things saith he [a]that hath the seven Spirits of God, and the seven stars; [b]I know thy works, that thou hast a name that thou livest, [c]and art dead. **E G E S**

2 Be watchful, and strengthen the things which remain, that are ready to die: for I have not found thy works perfect before God.

3 [a]Remember therefore how thou hast received and heard, and hold fast, and [b]repent. [c]If therefore thou shalt not watch, I will come on thee as a thief, and thou shalt not know what hour I will come upon thee.

4 Thou hast [a]a few names even in Sardis which have not [b]defiled their garments; and they shall walk with me [c]in white: for they are worthy.

5 He that overcometh, [a]the same shall

---

11 [b]ch. 20:1 & 21:8
12 [a]ch. 1:16
14 [a]Num. 24:14 & 25:1 & 31:16; 2 Pet. 2:15; Jude 11 [b]Acts 15:29; 1 Cor. 8:9 & 10:19,20 [c]1 Cor. 6:13
16 [a]Is. 11:4; 2 Thes. 2:8; ch. 1:16
17 [a]ch. 3:12 & 19:12
18 [a]ch. 1:14,15
19 [a]ver. 2
20 [a]1 Ki. 16:31 & 21:25; 2 Ki. 9:7 [b]Ex. 34:15; Acts 15:20
21 [a]ch. 9:20
23 [a]1 Sam. 16:7; Jer. 11:20; John 2:24; Acts 1:24; Rom. 8:27 [b]Ps. 62:12; 2 Cor. 5:10
24 [a]Acts 15:28
25 [a]ch. 3:11
26 [a]John 6:29; 1 John 3:23 [b]Mat. 19:28; Luke 22:29; 1 Cor. 6:3
27 [a]Ps. 2:8,9; Dan. 7:22
28 [a]2 Pet. 1:19
29 [a]ver. 7
3:1 [a]ch. 1:4,16 [b]ch. 2:2 [c]Eph. 2:1, 5
3 [a]1 Tim. 6:20; 2 Tim. 1:13 [b]ver. 19 [c]Mat. 24:42; Mark 13:33; Luke 12:39; 1 Thes. 5:2, 6; 2 Pet. 3:10
4 [a]Acts 1:15 [b]Jude 23 [c]ch. 4:4 & 6:11
5 [a]ch. 19:8

R *Rev 2:5* ◀ **E** *Rev 2:11* ◀ ▶ *Rev 2:29*
T *Rev 2:11* ◀ ▶ *Rev 2:29*

E *1Jn 3:20* ◀ ▶ *Rev 3:1*
M *1Pe 5:4* ◀ ▶ *Rev 3:7*
P *Rev 1:7* ◀ ▶ *Rev 6:12*
E *Rev 2:17* ◀ ▶ *Rev 3:1*
T *Rev 2:17* ◀ ▶ *Rev 3:6*
E *Rev 2:29* ◀ ▶ *Rev 3:6*
G *Rev 1:4* ◀ ▶ *Rev 4:5* **E** *Rev 2:23* ◀
S *Rev 2:10* ◀ ▶ *Rev 3:14–16*

be clothed in white raiment; and I will
not [b]blot out his name out of the [c]book of
life, but [d]I will confess his name before
my Father, and before his angels.
E 6 [a]He that hath an ear, let him hear
T what the Spirit saith unto the churches.

The message to Philadelphia

M 7 And to the angel of the church in
Philadelphia write; These things saith
[a]he that is holy, [b]he that is true, he that
hath [c]the key of David, [d]he that openeth,
and no man shutteth; and [e]shutteth, and
no man openeth;
8 [a]I know thy works: behold, I have
set before thee [b]an open door, and no
man can shut it: for thou hast a little
strength, and hast kept my word, and
hast not denied my name.
9 Behold, I will make [a]them of the synagogue of Satan, which say they are Jews,
and are not, but do lie; behold, [b]I will
make them to come and worship before
thy feet, and to know that I have loved
thee.
10 Because thou hast kept the word of
my patience, [a]I also will keep thee from
the hour of temptation, which shall come
upon [b]all the world, to try them that
dwell [c]upon the earth.
C 11 Behold, [a]I come quickly: [b]hold that
fast which thou hast, that no man take
[c]thy crown.
D 12 Him that overcometh will I make [a]a
pillar in the temple of my God, and he
shall go no more out: and [b]I will write
upon him the name of my God, and the
name of the city of my God, *which is*
[c]new Jerusalem, which cometh down out
of heaven from my God: [d]and *I will write*
upon him my new name.
E 13 [a]He that hath an ear, let him hear
T what the Spirit saith unto the churches.

The message to Laodicea

S 14 And unto the angel of the church
[1]of the Laodiceans write; [a]These things
saith the Amen, [b]the faithful and true
witness, [c]the beginning of the creation of
God;
15 [a]I know thy works, that thou art
neither cold nor hot: I would thou wert
cold or hot.
16 So then because thou art lukewarm, H
and neither cold nor hot, I will spew thee
out of my mouth.
17 Because thou sayest, [a]I am rich, C
and increased with goods, and have need G
of nothing; and knowest not that thou art M
wretched, and miserable, and poor, and N
blind, and naked:
18 I counsel thee [a]to buy of me gold
tried in the fire, that thou mayest be rich;
and [b]white raiment, that thou mayest be
clothed, and *that* the shame of thy nakedness do not appear; and anoint thine eyes
with eyesalve, that thou mayest see.
19 [a]As many as I love, I rebuke and T
chasten: be zealous therefore, and
repent.
20 Behold, [a]I stand at the door, and L
knock: [b]if any man hear my voice, and W
open the door, [c]I will come in to him,
and will sup with him, and he with me.
21 To him that overcometh [a]will I M
grant to sit with me in my throne, even
as I also overcame, and am set down with
my Father in his throne.
22 [a]He that hath an ear, let him hear E
what the Spirit saith unto the churches. T

The heavenly worship

4 AFTER THIS I looked, and, behold, a E
door *was* opened in heaven: and [a]the
first voice which I heard *was* as it were of
a trumpet talking with me; which said,
[b]Come up hither, [c]and I will show thee
things which must be hereafter.

5 [b]Ex. 32:32 [c]Phil. 4:3 [d]Luke 12:8
6 [a]ch. 2:7
7 [a]Acts 3:14 [b]1 John 5:20 [c]Is. 22:22; Luke 1:32 [d]Mat. 16:19 [e]Job 12:14
8 [a]ver. 1 [b]1 Cor. 16:9
9 [a]ch. 2:9 [b]Is. 49:23
10 [a]2 Pet. 2:9 [b]Luke 2:1 [c]Is. 24:17
11 [a]Phil. 4:5 [b]ch. 2:25 [c]ch. 2:10
12 [a]1 Ki. 7:21; Gal. 2:9 [b]ch. 14:1 [c]Heb. 12:22 [d]ch. 22:4
13 [a]ch. 2:7
14 [a]Is. 65:16 [b]ch. 19:11 [c]Col. 1:15 [1]Or, *in Laodicea*
15 [a]ver. 1
17 [a]Hos. 12:8; 1 Cor. 4:8
18 [a]Is. 55:1; Mat. 13:44 [b]2 Cor. 5:3; ch. 7:13
19 [a]Job 5:17; Prov. 3:11; Heb. 12:5,6
20 [a]Sol. 5:2 [b]Luke 12:37 [c]John 14:23
21 [a]Mat. 19:28; Luke 22:30; 2 Tim. 2:12
22 [a]ch. 2:7
4:1 [a]ch. 1:10 [b]ch. 11:12 [c]ch. 1:19

E *Rev 3:1* ◄► *Rev 3:13*
T *Rev 2:29* ◄► *Rev 3:13*
M *Rev 2:26–27* ◄► *Rev 3:21*
C *Rev 1:7* ◄► *Rev 22:7* **D** *1Th 3:13* ◄
E *Rev 3:6* ◄► *Rev 3:22*
T *Rev 3:6* ◄► *Rev 3:22*
S *Rev 3:1–5* ◄► *Rev 20:12–13*
H *Rev 1:7* ◄► *Rev 6:15–17*
C *Jude 16* ◄ **G** *1Pe 1:18–19* ◄
M *1Pe 5:5–6* ◄
N *Jude 15* ◄► *Rev 6:15–16*
T *1Pe 5:10* ◄ **L** *Rev 1:5* ◄► *Rev 21:6*
W *1Jn 5:9–10* ◄► *Rev 21:6*
M *Rev 3:7* ◄► *Rev 5:10*
E *Rev 3:13* ◄► *Rev 4:2*
T *Rev 3:13* ◄► *Rev 4:2*
E *Rev 1:19* ◄► *Rev 5:1*

4:1 This chapter begins the third portion of John's revelation concerning "the things which shall be hereafter" (1:19). These events will be fulfilled during the seven-year tribulation and the Millennium.

The Seven Letters to the Churches

THE LETTERS TO the seven churches in Revelation are the last direct words we have from Jesus Christ. These seven short epistles are similar to Jesus' parables and his prophecy on the Mt. of Olives.

Ephesus (2:1–7)—The Need for Revival

Ephesus was the wealthy capital of the Roman province of Asia and an important commercial and political center. Though Ephesus was famous for its temple to Diana, one of the seven wonders of the ancient world, many of Ephesus' citizens came to faith in Christ under Paul's ministry. Paul founded the church at Ephesus and later asked Timothy to be its pastor (see Ac 19—20). The Ephesian church was also John's home church.

In the first of these brief letters the Lord commends the church at Ephesus for its genuine good works and its patient endurance. Yet Christ also criticized this church for abandoning their "first love" (Rev 2:4). Though their doctrine was uncompromised, their passion for Christ was growing dim. Jesus urged this church to "remember therefore from whence thou art fallen, and repent, and do the first works" (2:5), or else he would remove the light of God's truth from them. Tragically the church at Ephesus did not seek revival, and its spiritual light faded away, transferred to the growing, vibrant churches of the western Roman empire.

Smyrna (2:8–11)—Stand Firm in Persecution

Smyrna was a wealthy port city known for its devotion to Rome and its pagan gods. The apostle Paul probably founded the church at Smyrna on his missionary journey to Ephesus (see Ac 19:10). Christ's message to Smyrna is one of praise and commendation. Though the church was severely persecuted by both the Jews and the Romans and kept in a state of perpetual poverty, the church at Smyrna was rich in spiritual gifts, perseverance and steadfast faith.

Christ warned the believers in Smyrna that they would have to undergo more persecution, but he promised them a "crown of life" (2:10) if they would remain faithful. Christ also promised that whoever "overcometh shall not be hurt of the second death" (2:11), referring to the spiritual death of the soul who rejects salvation.

Surely it is no accident that Smyrna and Philadelphia—the only two churches of these seven to escape Christ's condemnation—have both survived over the centuries. Today Smyrna boasts a population of over 300,000, a large percentage of which claim to be Christians.

Pergamos (2:12–17)—The Seduction of Idolatry

Pergamos, located north of Smyrna in modern-day Turkey, was noted for its temples and sensual worship of pagan gods. After the fall of Babylon, Pergamos became the center of the Babylonian mystery religions. It also housed three huge temples that were used to worship the Roman emperor. One of the chief gods of Pergamos was Aesculapius, the god of healing, represented by a serpent. This serpent image was struck into many of the city's coins. Public festivals and ceremonies often centered on licentious parties and temple prostitution.

Christ commended the church at Pergamos for its faithfulness to his name and for its good works in the midst of idolatry and satanic spiritual assaults. Yet the church was in danger of losing its holy walk with God by tolerating those who committed sexual immorality and ate foods sacrificed to idols. Jesus warned that anyone who followed these practices should have no part in the church. Christ said he would give the believers in Pergamos spiritual food from heaven if they turned from food offered to idols, and he promised to also give them "a new name written, which no man knoweth saving he that receiveth it" (2:17).

Thyatira (2:18–29)—The Lack of Self-discipline

Thyatira was a wealthy city known for its manufacture of purple cloth (see Ac 16:14). Located in modern-day Turkey, Thyatira is now called Ak-hissar. The church at Thyatira was commended for its love in practical service to the Lord and to others. However, it also tolerated sin within its community and lacked a zeal for true doctrine and Christian discipline.

Certain antinomian philosophers in the days of the early church taught the false doctrine that Christians could indulge in immorality as much as they desired because their sins were automatically forgiven. Though this was a direct contradiction to Scripture (see Ro 6:15), a false prophetess pressed this belief on the church at Thyatira and led the church into immorality just as Jezebel in the OT had led Israel away from the true worship of God. These sinners forgot that without holiness no one can stand before the Lord (see Heb 12:14). Though she had been given time to repent, this prophetess refused, and Christ declared that he would punish her and her followers. Those who had rejected her sinful suggestions were promised a reward—"power over the nations" (Rev 2:26) and "the morning star" (2:28).

Sardis (3:1–7)—The Lure of Materialism

Sardis was the capital city of the wealthy King Croesus. The residents of this city carried sardis stones as amulets to ward off evil spirits. They also were consumed with securing material success and wealth. The church at Sardis had fallen prey to this lure of materialism and carnal concerns. Though they boasted in their accomplishments, this church had lost its spiritual vitality. Christ's only words of commendation were directed to a remnant who truly followed him. Christ's word to the church at Sardis was a command to "be watchful, and strengthen the things which remain, that are ready to die" (3:2).

The church at Sardis stands as a warning to churches today. While we tend to look at buildings, finances and the number of worshipers, God examines the heart of his church and its members as he evaluates the true spiritual health of the church. No matter how dead a church may seem, God may still have a faithful few "which have not defiled their garments" (3:4). Unless we, too, watch carefully for our Lord's return, our eyes will turn to this world and its cares. The prayer of every believer should be that we join that faithful remnant and walk closely with God.

Philadelphia (3:7–13)—Faithful Love and Service

Thirty miles inland from Sardis was the city of Philadelphia. The church at Philadelphia was composed of a small group of poor Christians, rich only in the eyes of God. Of the seven churches, Philadelphia and Smyrna were the only ones to escape the Lord's criticism.

Christ commends the church at Philadelphia for its strength, faithfulness and evangelical witness. They believed the promise of Christ's second coming as they patiently watched for his appearance. Christ knew about their service for him and others and responded by giving them "an open door" (3:8) of witness that no one could shut.

Because of their faithfulness to him, Christ issued an incredible promise to spare the church at Philadelphia "from the hour of temptation, which shall come upon all the world, to try them that dwell upon the earth" (3:10). Though some suggest that this verse meant that Christ would deliver the believers at Philadelphia from the horrible persecutions of the first century, some scholars contend that this verse may also indicate a deliverance from the horrors of the tribulation.

Christ also admonishes the believers at Philadelphia to "hold that fast which thou hast, that no man take thy crown" (3:11). Those who remained steadfast would become pillars in God's temple in heaven. This unusual statement refers to the custom in Philadelphia that rewarded noble citizens with the honor of having their name inscribed on a temple pillar.

Laodicea (3:14–22)—Lukewarm and Self-satisfied

Built along the Meander River, Laodicea was a profitable trade center that manufactured a special eye ointment that was valued throughout the Roman empire. It also produced a unique, rich, black wool as part of a flourishing garment industry. Laodicea suffered a devastating earthquake during the reign of Rome but refused all outside help to rebuild the city. This self-sufficient attitude spilled over into the church and propelled it toward spiritual disaster.

Though some of the churches exhibited serious spiritual faults, the Lord commended something in every one of the churches with the exception of the church of Laodicea. Many of the believers in Laodicea followed a "prosperity gospel" that focused on their worldly wealth, spiritual pride and personal needs and desires. The Laodiceans believed that their success was evidence that they were pleasing God. Utterly blinded to their true spiritual condition, these believers felt that they were almost perfect even though they tolerated a hybrid worship of materialism and Christ.

The only good thing that can be said about this church is that there were still a few souls remaining within it who loved the Lord, but even their love was growing cold. The

Lord's rebuke is clear: "Because thou art lukewarm, and neither cold nor hot, I will spew thee out of my mouth" (3:16). God hates lukewarm religiosity, and his judgment will fall on any church that compromises with evil.

Christ then urged the Laodiceans to turn back to true worship. To a city dependent on the garment industry and medicinal eye salve, the Lord advised the Laodicean believers to put on garments of righteousness and "anoint thine eyes with eyesalve" (3:18) to heal their spiritual vision. Although the letter to the Laodiceans is filled with warnings, the Lord's chastening indicates that he still loves them even though they have gone astray.

E 2 And immediately [a]I was in the spirit:
L and, behold, [b]a throne was set in heaven,
T and *one* sat on the throne.
3 And he that sat was to look upon like
a jasper and a sardine stone: [a]and *there*
was a rainbow round about the throne, in
sight like unto an emerald.
4 [a]And round about the throne *were*
four and twenty seats: and upon the seats
I saw four and twenty elders sitting,
[b]clothed in white raiment; and they had
on their heads crowns of gold.
G 5 And out of the throne proceeded
[a]lightnings and thunderings and voices:
[b]and *there were* seven lamps of fire burning before the throne, which are [c]the
seven Spirits of God.
6 And before the throne *there was* [a]a

E Rev 3:22 ◀▶ Rev 5:6 L Rev 1:10 ◀
T Rev 3:22 ◀▶ Rev 14:13
G Rev 3:1 ◀▶ Rev 5:6

2 [a]ch. 1:10 [b]Is. 6:1; Ezek. 1:26; Dan. 7:9
3 [a]Ezek. 1:28
4 [a]ch. 11:16 [b]ch. 3:4,5
5 [a]ch. 8:5 [b]Ex. 37:23; 2 Chr. 4:20; Ezek. 1:13; Zech. 4:2 [c]ch. 1:4
6 [a]Ex. 38:8; ch. 15:2 [b]Ezek. 1:5
7 [a]Num. 2:2; Ezek. 1:10
8 [a]Is. 6:2 [b]Is. 6:3 [c]ch. 1:8 [d]ch. 1:4 [l]Gk. *they have no rest*
9 [a]ch. 1:18
10 [a]ch. 5:8,14

sea of glass like unto crystal: [b]and in the
midst of the throne, and round about the
throne, *were* four beasts full of eyes before and behind.
7 [a]And the first beast *was* like a lion,
and the second beast like a calf, and the
third beast had a face as a man, and the
fourth beast *was* like a flying eagle.
8 And the four beasts had each of them
[a]six wings about *him;* and *they were* full
of eyes within: and [l]they rest not day and
night, saying, [b]Holy, holy, holy, [c]Lord
God Almighty, [d]which was, and is, and is
to come.
9 And when those beasts give glory
and honour and thanks to him that sat
on the throne, [a]who liveth for ever and
ever,
10 [a]The four and twenty elders fall
down before him that sat on the throne,
and worship him that liveth for ever and

4:1–3 John begins this section on the end time events by saying "After this..." (4:1), indicating that something important had transpired. Some scholars feel that this phrase refers to the rapture. Others believe that this phrase is merely a transition phrase between the two visions, indicating that John had acted on the instructions of the first vision and was thereby prepared for another word from God.

In this vision, John described a voice from heaven that called him to look at the things that would happen in the future. John saw a throne in heaven and Jesus Christ sitting on it in all his glory and majesty, surrounded by a rainbow. Note the similarity between this vision of Christ and Ezekiel's vision in Eze 1:26–28. Whenever God allows humans to see him, they see Christ, "for in him dwelleth all the fulness of the Godhead bodily" (Col 2:9; see Jn 1:18; Col 1:15).

4:4 John saw twenty-four elders seated on twenty-four seats. These elders were "clothed in white raiment." While some scholars believe these elders to be exalted angels, others believe that this court of heaven represents the resurrected saints of both the OT and NT. The fact that they are seated, wearing white raiment and golden crowns, repudiates the view that these are angelic beings but rather provides powerful evidence that these beings are raptured believers. Since we do not receive our resurrection bodies when we die (see 1Th 4:13–17), this event must take place after the rapture.

Note that the word translated "elder" almost always refers to the leading representative of a family, tribe or nation and is never applied to angels since they cannot grow old or mature. Since Jesus Christ, the twenty four elders, and the saints are the only ones seen in heaven with crowns, these twenty-four elders may represent the NT and OT saints who rose with Christ at his resurrection (Mt 27:52–53). Others contend that these twenty-four are the twelve OT patriarchs and the twelve NT disciples. Since the number twelve often relates to human government, the number twenty-four possibly suggests the perfection of the government of God's kingdom.

4:5 John's reference to "seven lamps" as the "seven Spirits of God," relates to seven aspects or characteristics of God. Compare this verse to Zec 4:10 and the prophet's vision of the seven eyes of the Lord, referring to seven distinct characteristics of the one triune God. Isaiah also describes the coming Messiah, the Son of God, as possessing these seven spirits or divine characteristics of God (see Isa 11:2).

4:6–9 John saw the crystal sea that stretches before the throne of God. In symbolic language, John described the "four beasts" which surround the throne of God. Some suggest that these beings, or "living creatures," are manifestations of the characteristics of God since Scripture records that they are "in the midst of the throne" (4:6). Other scholars believe that these "living ones" are angelic beings described as seraphim (see Isa 6:1–8) and cherubim (see Eze 1:4–28), seen in this vision surrounding God's throne, worshiping him, giving him glory and praising the Lamb with harps. Later they call forth the four horsemen (see 6:1–8) and provide the seven judgment bowls to the angels (see 15:7).

4:10–11 The twenty-four elders cast their crowns at the feet of Christ to give him glory. They announce that the purpose of all of his creation is to exist for his pleasure. Humanity's purpose is to love Christ and glorify him by their life, words and actions.

ever, and cast their crowns before the
throne, saying,
11 [a]Thou art worthy, O Lord, to receive glory and honour and power: [b]for
thou hast created all things, and for thy
pleasure they are and were created.

The book and the Lamb

E **5** AND I saw in the right hand of him
that sat on the throne [a]a book written within and on the backside, [b]sealed
with seven seals.
2 And I saw a strong angel proclaiming
with a loud voice, Who is worthy to open
the book, and to loose the seals thereof?
3 And no man in heaven, nor in earth,
neither under the earth, was able to open
the book, neither to look thereon.
4 And I wept much, because no man
was found worthy to open and to read the
book, neither to look thereon.
5 And one of the elders saith unto me,
Weep not: behold, [a]the Lion of the tribe
of Judah, [b]the Root of David, hath prevailed to open the book, [c]and to loose the
seven seals thereof.
E 6 And I beheld, and, lo, in the midst of
G the throne and of the four beasts, and in
the midst of the elders, stood [a]a Lamb as
it had been slain, having seven horns and
[b]seven eyes, which are [c]the seven Spirits
of God sent forth into all the earth.
7 And he came and took the book out
of the right hand [a]of him that sat upon
the throne.
8 And when he had taken the book,
[a]the four beasts and four *and* twenty elders fell down before the Lamb, having
every one of them [b]harps, and golden vi-

E *Rev 4:1* ◀▶ *Rev 22:6–7*
E *Rev 4:2* ◀▶ *Rev 11:11*
G *Rev 4:5* ◀▶ *Rev 19:10*

11 [a]ch. 5:12 [b]Gen. 1:1; Acts 17:24; Eph. 3:9
5:1 [a]Ezek. 2:9 [b]Is. 29:11; Dan. 12:4
5 [a]Gen. 49:9; Heb. 7:14 [b]Is. 11:1,10; ch. 22:16 [c]ch. 6:1
6 [a]Is. 53:7; John 1:29; 1 Pet. 1:19 [b]Zech. 3:9 [c]ch. 4:5
7 [a]ch. 4:2
8 [a]ch. 4:8,10 [b]ch. 14:2 [c]Ps. 141:2 [l]Or, *incense*
9 [a]Ps. 40:3 [b]ch. 4:11 [c]Acts 20:28; Rom. 3:24; 1 Cor. 6:20; Eph. 1:7; Col. 1:14; Heb. 9:12; 1 Pet. 1:18; 2 Pet. 2:1; 1 John 1:7 [d]Dan. 4:1
10 [a]Ex. 19:6; 1 Pet. 2:5
11 [a]Ps. 68:17; Dan. 7:10; Heb. 12:22
12 [a]ch. 4:11
13 [a]Phil. 2:10 [b]1 Chr. 29:11; Rom. 9:5 & 16:27; 1 Tim. 6:16; 1 Pet. 4:11 & 5:11 [c]ch. 6:16
14 [a]ch. 19:4 [b]ch. 4:9,10
6:1 [a]ch. 5:5-7 [b]ch. 4:7

als full of [l]odours, [c]which are the prayers
of saints.
9 And [a]they sung a new song, saying, D
[b]Thou art worthy to take the book, and
to open the seals thereof: for thou wast
slain, and [c]hast redeemed us to God by
thy blood [d]out of every kindred, and
tongue, and people, and nation;
10 [a]And hast made us unto our God M
kings and priests: and we shall reign on
the earth.
11 And I beheld, and I heard the voice
of many angels round about the throne
and the beasts and the elders: and the
number of them was [a]ten thousand times
ten thousand, and thousands of thousands;
12 Saying with a loud voice, [a]Worthy
is the Lamb that was slain to receive
power, and riches, and wisdom, and
strength, and honour, and glory, and
blessing.
13 And [a]every creature which is in
heaven, and on the earth, and under the
earth, and such as are in the sea, and all
that are in them, heard I saying, [b]Bless-
ing, and honour, and glory, and power,
be unto him [c]that sitteth upon the
throne, and unto the Lamb for ever and
ever.
14 [a]And the four beasts said, Amen.
And the four *and* twenty elders fell down
and worshipped him [b]that liveth for ever
and ever.

Six of the seals opened

6 AND [a]I saw when the Lamb opened
one of the seals, and I heard, as it
were the noise of thunder, [b]one of the
four beasts saying, Come and see.

D *Rev 1:5* ◀▶ *Rev 7:14*
M *Rev 3:21* ◀▶ *Rev 11:15–19*

5:1–4 John saw God, seated on his throne, holding a scroll that was "sealed with seven seals" (5:1). In ancient times a scroll addressed to a king often had a secret message written on the bottom of the page. When the scroll was rolled up and sealed, this message was effectively hidden from the courier who could only read the outer portion of the scroll.

5:5–7 Only Jesus, "the Lion of the tribe of Judah" (5:5), was able to break the seals and open the scroll.

5:8–10 John described the twenty-four elders worshiping Jesus with harps and a new song. These elders held golden bowls that were full of incense and described as "the prayers of saints" (5:8). That this incense represented the faithful prayers of believers reminds us of the incense offered in the Holy of Holies of the temple. Note also the use of harps in the worship of God. The twenty-four elders prophesied with their harps as they declared that God would make them "kings and priests; and we shall reign on the earth" (5:10).

5:11–14 The prophet described a glorious scene when the millions of inhabitants of heaven join to offer praise to Jesus Christ and worship "him that liveth for ever and ever" (5:14).

6:1 John watched Jesus open one of the seals on the scroll, indicating that the end-time judgment of the unrepentant sinners on earth had finally come.

2 And I saw, and behold [a]a white horse: [b]and he that sat on him had a bow; [c]and a crown was given unto him: and he went forth conquering, and to conquer.

3 And when he had opened the second seal, [a]I heard the second beast say, Come and see.

4 [a]And there went out another horse *that was* red: and *power* was given to him that sat thereon to take peace from the earth, and that they should kill one another: and there was given unto him a great sword.

5 And when he had opened the third seal, [a]I heard the third beast say, Come and see. And I beheld, and lo [b]a black horse; and he that sat on him had a pair of balances in his hand.

6 And I heard a voice in the midst of the four beasts say, [†]A measure of wheat for a penny, and three measures of barley for a penny; and [a]*see* thou hurt not the oil and the wine.

7 And when he had opened the fourth seal, [a]I heard the voice of the fourth beast say, Come and see.

8 [a]And I looked, and behold a pale horse: and his name that sat on him was Death, and Hell followed with him. And power was given [†]unto them over the fourth part of the earth, [b]to kill with sword, and with hunger, and with death, [c]and with the beasts of the earth.

9 And when he had opened the fifth seal, I saw under [a]the altar [b]the souls of them that were slain [c]for the word of

2 [a]Zech. 6:3; ch. 19:11 [b]Ps. 45:4,5; LXX [c]Zech. 6:11; ch. 14:14
3 [a]ch. 4:7
4 [a]Zech. 6:2
5 [a]ch. 4:7 [b]Zech. 6:2
6 [a]ch. 9:4 [†]The word *choenix* signifies a measure containing one wine quart, and the twelfth part of a quart
7 [a]ch. 4:7
8 [a]Zech. 6:3 [b]Ezek. 14:21 [c]Lev. 26:22 [†]Or, *to him*
9 [a]ch. 8:3 & 14:18 [b]ch. 20:4 [c]ch. 1:9

The opening of this first seal ushers in the tribulation, a seven-year period that also begins with the antichrist signing a seven-year covenant with Israel. This tribulation concludes with Christ's glorious return at the end of the Battle of Armageddon. From this moment until Christ destroys Satan's antichrist, "the great day of his wrath is come" (6:17).

6:2–8 *The Four Horsemen.* The first four seals of the seven seal judgments are commonly referred to as the four horsemen of the apocalypse because riders on horses carry out these judgments. These seven seal judgments begin the seven years of the tribulation and are part of "the great day of his wrath" (6:17). The apostle Paul clearly promised that the church would escape this coming wrath (see 1Th 1:10). Since the tribulation period begins with the wrath of God poured out in the seven seal judgments, the church will be in heaven at this time.

The first seal that begins the day of God's wrath is the white horseman of false peace. John saw a white horse and a rider with a bow. Though the color white usually represents peace, in this case this is a false peace because the rider rides out "conquering, and to conquer" (6:2). Note the absence of any arrows or a quiver. This may symbolize a disarmament and false peace before his attack on his enemies. Some scholars believe that this white horseman refers to a spirit of conquest as one of the natural calamities of these judgments. Others contend that this horseman represents the antichrist who will falsely present himself to the world as a peacemaker before conquering the world. Daniel's prophecy foreshadowed the coming of this antichrist who "by peace shall destroy many" (Da 8:25).

The second seal opens to reveal the red horseman of war. This horseman was given a "great sword" (6:4) to create cataclysmic wars. During the tribulation, bloody warfare will devastate the world by killing millions of people. Some scholars suggest that as many as two-thirds of the world's population may die during the tribulation.

The third seal opens to reveal the third horseman holding a set of weights and balances in his hand and riding on the black horse of famine. The angel revealed that the famine would be so severe that a daily wage will only buy enough food for one person, leaving no food for other family members. Strangely, despite worldwide famine, the angel prohibited the horseman from harming the oil and wine. Some scholars feel that since olive trees and grapevines have deep roots, this famine would not immediately affect these crops. Other suggest that since oil and wine were associated with ancient wealth and comfort, this may suggest that some people will still possess great wealth and not feel the immediate effects of this worldwide famine (see Jas 5:1–3).

The fourth seal is opened to reveal a pale horse with a rider that symbolizes death and who is given the authority to destroy a fourth of the earth. The four-part judgment delivered by this horseman echoes the four judgments that are often found together in the OT as symbols of God's wrath. These four instruments are described in Eze 14:21 as "the sword, and the famine, and the noisome beast, and the pestilence." Note that after the flood God instilled a fear of humanity in animals (see Ge 9:2). During the horrible judgments of the tribulation God will remove this fear, allowing the wild beasts to attack humans until the Messiah returns. The Messiah will then reinstitute a covenant of peace between humans and animals (see Isa 11:6–9; Hos 2:18).

6:9–11 When Jesus opened the fifth seal, John saw the souls of those who had died for their faith. The twenty-four crowned elders in Rev 4:1–10 represent the raptured church, so this new group of believers is made up of those Jewish and Gentile disciples who became believers during the early days of the tribulation.

John then described the response of the martyrs to their oppressors, crying out to God for vengeance.

God, and for [d]the testimony which they
held:
10 And they cried with a loud voice,
saying, [a]How long, O Lord, [b]holy and
true, [c]dost thou not judge and avenge our
blood on them that dwell on the earth?
11 And [a]white robes were given unto
every one of them; and it was said unto
them, [b]that they should rest yet for a little season, until their fellowservants also
and their brethren, that should be killed
as they *were,* should be fulfilled.
P 12 And I beheld when he had opened
the sixth seal, [a]and, lo, there was a great
earthquake; and [b]the sun became black
as sackcloth of hair, and the moon became as blood;
13 [a]And the stars of heaven fell unto
the earth, even as a fig tree casteth her
[l]untimely figs, when she is shaken of a
mighty wind.
14 [a]And the heaven departed as a
scroll when it is rolled together; and [b]ev-
ery mountain and island were moved out
of their places.
H 15 And the kings of the earth, and the
N great men, and the rich men, and the
chief captains, and the mighty men, and

P *Rev 2:27 ◀ ▶ Rev 9:12–15*
H *Rev 3:16 ◀ ▶ Rev 11:18*
N *Rev 3:17–18 ◀ ▶ Rev 13:9*

9 [d]2 Tim. 1:8; ch. 19:10
10 [a]See Zech. 1:12 [b]ch. 3:7 [c]ch. 11:18
11 [a]ch. 3:4,5 [b]Heb. 11:40
12 [a]ch. 16:18 [b]Joel 2:10 & 3:15; Mat. 24:29; Acts 2:20
13 [a]ch. 8:10 & 9:1 [l]Or, *green figs*
14 [a]Ps. 102:26; Is. 34:4; Heb. 1:12 [b]Jer. 3:23 & 4:24; ch. 16:20
15 [a]Is. 2:19
16 [a]Hos. 10:8; Luke 23:30
17 [a]Is. 13:6; Zeph. 1:14; ch. 16:14 [b]Ps. 76:7
7:1 [a]Dan. 7:2 [b]ch. 9:4
3 [a]ch. 6:6 [b]ch. 22:4
4 [a]ch. 9:16 [b]ch. 14:1

every bondman, and every free man, [a]hid
themselves in the dens and in the rocks
of the mountains;
16 [a]And said to the mountains and
rocks, Fall on us, and hide us from the
face of him that sitteth on the throne, and
from the wrath of the Lamb:
17 [a]For the great day of his wrath is
come; [b]and who shall be able to stand?

The sealing of God's servants

7 AND AFTER these things I saw four
angels standing on the four corners
of the earth, [a]holding the four winds of
the earth, [b]that the wind should not blow
on the earth, nor on the sea, nor on any
tree.
2 And I saw another angel ascending
from the east, having the seal of the living God: and he cried with a loud voice to
the four angels, to whom it was given to
hurt the earth and the sea,
3 Saying, [a]Hurt not the earth, neither
the sea, nor the trees, till we have sealed
the servants of our God [b]in their foreheads.
4 [a]And I heard the number of them
which were sealed: *and there were*
sealed [b]an hundred *and* forty *and* four
thousand of all the tribes of the children
of Israel.

This fifth seal provides additional confirmation that during the seven-year tribulation most believers will be martyred for their faith because these souls are told to wait until the other martyrs join them.

6:12–17 When Christ opens the sixth seal, he unleashes a devastating array of natural catastrophes. A massive earthquake will be the first in a series of major disturbances that mark God's wrath during the tribulation. Note that Jesus warned that the increase of earthquakes would signify his return (see Mt 24:7). In the last half-century, scientists have tracked the dramatic increase of killer earthquakes (6.5 or above on the Richter scale) from only 9 killer quakes during the 1950s to over 125 killer quakes in the first half of the 1990s alone. Jesus reminded his disciples to be alert for the signs of his coming for "when these things begin to come to pass, then look up, and lift up your heads; for your redemption draweth nigh" (Lk 21:28).

The heavens will also signal the wrath of the Lamb with celestial phenomena that will terrify the inhabitants of earth (see Isa 2:19). John prophesies a devastating meteor shower (6:13) and a tumultuous shaking of the heavens (see Isa 34:4) that will announce "the great day of his wrath" (6:17). (Though there are many similarities between the events of the sixth seal judgment and those at Armageddon, there will be an interval of at least three and a half-years between the sixth seal judgment and this final battle. The events of Rev 7:1—19:10 will occur during this interval.)

7:1–8 There is a pause after the sixth seal during which John describes two groups of redeemed souls. The first group is identified as twelve thousand persons from each of the twelve tribes of Israel—144,000 Jews. (Though today many Jews are unsure of their tribal lineage, this sealing of the Jews by tribe indicates that God will miraculously reveal the tribal identity of his people in the last days.)

God will choose these Jews to be his witnesses to share the gospel message with the world. Revelation does not reveal how or when these Jews become followers of the Messiah. After the rapture of the church, God would not leave the earth without a witness, so these 144,000 Jews will be divinely protected from the terrible persecution of the antichrist and the false prophet to share God's good news during the tribulation. After completing their special mission, the 144,000, identified as those who "were redeemed from among men, being the firstfruits unto God and to the Lamb" (14:4), will be transferred from earth to heaven.

5 Of the tribe of Judah *were* sealed
twelve thousand. Of the tribe of Reuben
were sealed twelve thousand. Of the tribe
of Gad *were* sealed twelve thousand.
6 Of the tribe of Aser *were* sealed
twelve thousand. Of the tribe of Neptha-
lim *were* sealed twelve thousand. Of the
tribe of Manasses *were* sealed twelve
thousand.
7 Of the tribe of Simeon *were* sealed
twelve thousand. Of the tribe of Levi
were sealed twelve thousand. Of the tribe
of Issachar *were* sealed twelve thousand.
8 Of the tribe of Zabulon *were* sealed
twelve thousand. Of the tribe of Joseph
were sealed twelve thousand. Of the tribe
of Benjamin *were* sealed twelve
thousand.

The saints in white robes

H 9 After this I beheld, and, lo, [a]a great
O multitude, which no man could number,
[b]of all nations, and kindreds, and people,
and tongues, stood before the throne, and
before the Lamb, [c]clothed with white
robes, and palms in their hands;
10 And cried with a loud voice, saying,
[a]Salvation to our God [b]which sitteth
upon the throne, and unto the Lamb.
11 [a]And all the angels stood round
about the throne, and *about* the elders
and the four beasts, and fell before the
throne on their faces, and worshipped
God,
12 [a]Saying, Amen: Blessing, and glory,
and wisdom, and thanksgiving, and honour, and power, and might, *be* unto our
God for ever and ever. Amen.
13 And one of the elders answered,
saying unto me, What are these which
are arrayed in [a]white robes? and whence
came they?
14 And I said unto him, Sir, thou D
knowest. And he said to me, [a]These are K
they which came out of great tribulation,
and have [b]washed their robes, and made
them white in the blood of the Lamb.
15 Therefore are they before the
throne of God, and serve him day and
night in his temple: and he that sitteth on
the throne shall [a]dwell among them.
16 [a]They shall hunger no more, neither thirst any more; [b]neither shall the
sun light on them, nor any heat.
17 For the Lamb which is in the midst S
of the throne [a]shall feed them, and shall
lead them unto living fountains of waters:
[b]and God shall wipe away all tears from
their eyes.

The seventh seal

8 AND [a]WHEN he had opened the
seventh seal, there was silence in
heaven about the space of half an hour.
2 [a]And I saw the seven angels which
stood before God; [b]and to them were
given seven trumpets.
3 And another angel came and stood at
the altar, having a golden censer; and
there was given unto him much incense,
that he should [1]offer *it* with [a]the prayers
of all saints upon [b]the golden altar which
was before the throne.
4 And [a]the smoke of the incense,
which came with the prayers of the
saints, ascended up before God out of the
angel's hand.
5 And the angel took the censer, and
filled it with fire of the altar, and cast *it*
[1]into the earth: and [a]there were voices,

9 [a]Rom. 11:25 [b]ch. 5:9 [c]ver. 14; ch. 3:5,18 & 4:4 & 6:11
10 [a]Ps. 3:8; Is. 43:11; Jer. 3:23; Hos. 13:4; ch. 19:1 [b]ch. 5:13
11 [a]ch. 4:6
12 [a]ch. 5:13,14
13 [a]ver. 9
14 [a]ch. 6:9 & 17:6 [b]Is. 1:18; See Zech. 3:3-5
15 [a]Is. 4:5,6; ch. 21:3
16 [a]Is. 49:10 [b]Ps. 121:6; ch. 21:4
17 [a]Ps. 23:1 & 36:8; John 10:11,14 [b]Is. 25:8; ch. 21:4
8:1 [a]ch. 6:1
2 [a]Mat. 18:10; Luke 1:19 [b]2 Chr. 29:25-28
3 [a]ch. 5:8 [b]Ex. 30:1; ch. 6:9 [1]Or, *add it to the prayers*
4 [a]Ps. 141:2; Luke 1:10
5 [a]ch. 16:18 [1]Or, *upon*

H *Eph 5:27* ◀▶ *Rev 14:1–5*
O *1Jn 5:12* ◀▶ *Rev 19:1*
D *Rev 5:9* ◀▶ *Rev 12:11*
K *Rev 1:18* ◀▶ *Rev 12:11*
S *Isa 61:3* ◀▶ *Rev 21:4*

7:9–17 John then describes "a great multitude" (7:9) from every nation and tribe who "came out of great tribulation" (7:14), the greatest harvest of souls in history. Though millions will accept Christ during the tribulation, the persecution of that period will be so severe that most of these tribulation saints will be martyred for their faith. This "great multitude" (7:9) will rejoice in the blessings of heaven and receive special rewards and honors as they minister "before the throne of God, and serve him day and night in his temple" (7:15).

8:1 The seventh seal judgment begins with an ominous "silence in heaven about the space of half an hour" (8:1). After the horrors of the first six seal judgments, God pauses for a little while to allow men to reconsider their choices and repent of their sins. Though the seventh seal does not contain any special instrument of judgment itself, it does introduce the seven trumpet judgments.

8:2–5 John then receives a vision of seven angels with seven trumpets, symbolizing the coming wrath of God that will be poured out on the earth as never before. Another angel appeared and offered the prayers of the saints to God like incense. These prayers likely cry, "Even so, come, Lord Jesus" (22:20).

and thunderings, and lightnings, [b]and an
earthquake.
6 And the seven angels which had the
seven trumpets prepared themselves to
sound.
7 The first angel sounded, [a]and there
followed hail and fire mingled with
blood, and they were cast [b]upon the
earth: and the third part [c]of trees was
burnt up, and all green grass was
burnt up.
8 And the second angel sounded, [a]and
as it were a great mountain burning with
fire was cast into the sea: [b]and the third
part of the sea [c]became blood;
9 [a]And the third part of the creatures
which were in the sea, and had life, died;
and the third part of the ships were destroyed.
10 And the third angel sounded, [a]and
there fell a great star from heaven, burning as it were a lamp, [b]and it fell upon the
third part of the rivers, and upon the
fountains of waters;
11 [a]And the name of the star is called
Wormwood: [b]and the third part of the
waters became wormwood; and many
men died of the waters, because they
were made bitter.
12 [a]And the fourth angel sounded, and
the third part of the sun was smitten, and
the third part of the moon, and the third
part of the stars; so as the third part of
them was darkened, and the day shone
not for a third part of it, and the night
likewise.
13 And I beheld, [a]and heard an angel
flying through the midst of heaven, saying with a loud voice, [b]Woe, woe, woe,
to the inhabiters of the earth by reason of
the other voices of the trumpet of the
three angels, which are yet to sound!

The plague of locusts

9 AND THE fifth angel sounded, [a]and I
saw a star fall from heaven unto the
earth: and to him was given the key of
[b]the bottomless pit.
2 And he opened the bottomless pit;
and there arose a smoke out of the pit, as
the smoke of a great furnace; and the sun
and the air were darkened by reason of
the smoke of the pit.
3 And there came out of the smoke [a]lo-
custs upon the earth: and unto them was
given power, [b]as the scorpions of the
earth have power.
4 And it was commanded them [a]that
they should not hurt [b]the grass of the
earth, neither any green thing, neither
any tree; but only those men which have
not [c]the seal of God in their foreheads.
5 And to them it was given that they
should not kill them, [a]but that they
should be tormented five months: and
their torment *was* as the torment of a
scorpion, when he striketh a man.
6 And in those days [a]shall men seek

5 [b]2 Sam. 22:8; 1 Ki. 19:11; Acts 4:31
7 [a]Ezek. 38:22 [b]ch. 16:2 [c]Is. 2:13; ch. 9:4
8 [a]Jer. 51:25; Amos 7:4 [b]ch. 16:3 [c]Ezek. 14:19
9 [a]ch. 16:3
10 [a]Is. 14:12; ch. 9:1 [b]ch. 16:4
11 [a]Ruth 1:20 [b]Ex. 15:23
12 [a]Is. 13:10; Amos 8:9
13 [a]ch. 14:6 & 19:17 [b]ch. 9:12 & 11:14
9:1 [a]Luke 10:18; ch. 8:10 [b]ver. 2,11; Luke 8:31; ch. 17:8 & 20:1
3 [a]Ex. 10:4; Judg. 7:12 [b]ver. 10
4 [a]ch. 6:6 & 7:3 [b]ch. 8:7 [c]See Ex. 12:23; Ezek. 9:4; ch. 7:3
5 [a]ver. 10; ch. 11:7
6 [a]Job 3:21; Is. 2:19; Jer. 8:3; ch. 6:16

8:7 The first trumpet triggers an outpouring of "hail and fire mingled with blood" (8:7). This cataclysmic judgment will burn one third of the trees and grass. Since humanity has abused the planet, the day of reckoning is at hand.

8:8–9 The second trumpet unleashes a huge chunk of a volcano or a large, burning meteor that impacts the ocean. Such an impact would create an astonishing tidal wave, sinking ships and devastating coastlands. John says this impact causes widespread death of one third of the marine life and the destruction of one third of the ships, affecting not only the food chain, but the economy as well.

8:10–11 The third trumpet judgment releases a huge meteor "called Wormwood" (8:11). Wormwood is a plant with a strong, bitter taste and is used in this passage to symbolize calamity. John warns that many will die because one third of the water will be poisoned.

8:12 The fourth trumpet will affect the heavens. One third of the sun, moon and stars will be darkened. Whether this means that daylight will be shortened or that the power of these light sources will be reduced by one-third is unclear.

8:13 The next three trumpet judgments are often called "the three woes," in recognition of the horrible judgments about to be unleashed upon the earth.

9:1–12 The fifth trumpet is also the first woe. When sounded, this trumpet releases demonic locusts from the bottomless pit that torment those "which have not the seal of God in their foreheads" (9:4) for five months, the same length of time as the flood (see Ge 7:24). The only humans on earth immune to this terrible plague are the 144,000 (see 7:3). This is not a normal plague of locusts, because these creatures serve "the angel of the bottomless pit" (9:11). The locusts' stings are not deadly, but so painful that people will want to die. Note that John indicates only two groups of persons on the earth during this time—the reprobate ones afflicted by the demonic locusts and the 144,000 sealed Jews—intimating that the church must be in heaven when this terrible judgment falls on the earth.

death, and shall not find it; and shall desire to die, and death shall flee from them.

7 And [a]the shapes of the locusts *were* like unto horses prepared unto battle; [b]and on their heads *were* as it were crowns like gold, [c]and their faces *were* as the faces of men.

8 And they had hair as the hair of women, and [a]their teeth were as *the teeth* of lions.

9 And they had breastplates, as it were breastplates of iron; and the sound of their wings *was* [a]as the sound of chariots of many horses running to battle.

10 And they had tails like unto scorpions, and there were stings in their tails: [a]and their power *was* to hurt men five months.

11 [a]And they had a king over them, *which is* [b]the angel of the bottomless pit, whose name in the Hebrew tongue *is* Abaddon, but in the Greek tongue hath *his* name [l]Apollyon.

P 12 [a]One woe is past; *and,* behold, there come two woes more hereafter.

13 And the sixth angel sounded, and I heard a voice from the four horns of the golden altar which is before God,

14 Saying to the sixth angel which had the trumpet, Loose the four angels which are bound [a]in the great river Euphrates.

15 And the four angels were loosed, which were prepared [l]for an hour, and a day, and a month, and a year, for to slay the third part of men.

16 And [a]the number of the army [b]of the horsemen *were* two hundred thousand thousand: [c]and I heard the number of them.

17 And thus I saw the horses in the vision, and them that sat on them, having breastplates of fire, and of jacinth, and brimstone: [a]and the heads of the horses *were* as the heads of lions; and out of their mouths issued fire and smoke and brimstone.

18 By these three was the third part of men killed, by the fire, and by the smoke, and by the brimstone, which issued out of their mouths. P

19 For their power is in their mouth, and in their tails: [a]for their tails *were* like unto serpents, and had heads, and with them they do hurt.

20 And the rest of the men which were not killed by these plagues [a]yet repented not of the works of their hands, that they should not worship [b]devils, [c]and idols of gold, and silver, and brass, and stone, and of wood: which neither can see, nor hear, nor walk: P

21 Neither repented they of their murders, [a]nor of their sorceries, nor of their fornication, nor of their thefts.

John eats the book

10 AND I saw another mighty angel come down from heaven, clothed with a cloud: [a]and a rainbow *was* upon his head, and [b]his face *was* as it were the sun, and [c]his feet as pillars of fire:

2 And he had in his hand a little book open: [a]and he set his right foot upon the sea, and *his* left *foot* on the earth,

3 And cried with a loud voice, as *when*

P *Rev 6:12* ◄► *Rev 9:18*

P *Rev 9:12–15* ◄► *Rev 9:20*
P *Rev 9:18* ◄► *Rev 10:5–7*

7 [a]Joel 2:4 [b]Nah. 3:17 [c]Dan. 7:8
8 [a]Joel 1:6
9 [a]Joel 2:5-7
10 [a]ver. 5
11 [a]Eph. 2:2 [b]ver. 1 [l]That is to say, *A destroyer*
12 [a]ch. 8:13
14 [a]ch. 16:12
15 [l]Or, *at*
16 [a]Ps. 68:17; Dan. 7:10 [b]Ezek. 38:4 [c]ch. 7:4
17 [a]1 Chr. 12:8; Is. 5:28,29
19 [a]Is. 9:15
20 [a]Deut. 31:29 [b]Lev. 17:7; Deut. 32:17; Ps. 106:37; 1 Cor. 10:20 [c]Ps. 115:4 & 135:15; Dan. 5:23
21 [a]ch. 22:15
10:1 [a]Ezek. 1:28 [b]Mat. 17:2; ch. 1:16 [c]ch. 1:15
2 [a]Mat. 28:18

9:13–21 The sixth trumpet (the second woe) will kill one third of humanity. God releases 200 million soldiers to wreak havoc throughout the earth (9:16). The enormous army of the kings of the east will cross into Israel from Asia to fight for world supremacy against the armies of the antichrist and his false prophet. This judgment will set the stage for the Battle of Armageddon, ending the seven-year tribulation (see Da 9:27).

For thousands of years the Euphrates River has served as a great military barrier to armies attacking from the East. However, in the late 1980s Turkey finished construction of the huge Ataturk Dam, designed to control these vast waters. For the first time in history, the flow of this great river can now be stopped at the push of a button. The prophecy of Rev 9:14 can be fulfilled in our lifetime.

Note that when God makes an appointment with destiny for a person or an empire, that appointment will not be postponed. Amazingly, despite every opportunity to repent, the sinners in the tribulation will refuse to turn from their wickedness (9:20).

10:1–4 John sees a mighty angel (see 5:2) come from heaven to announce the next series of judgments. A "little book" (10:2) is opened, containing information about the coming wrath of God, expressed by the "seven thunders" (10:3). Yet John is prevented from writing down these things because God seals them until their proper time (see 22:10).

a lion roareth: and when he had cried,
[a]seven thunders uttered their voices.
4 And when the seven thunders had
uttered their voices, I was about to write:
and I heard a voice from heaven saying
unto me, [a]Seal up those things which the
seven thunders uttered, and write them
not.
P 5 And the angel which I saw stand
upon the sea and upon the earth [a]lifted
up his hand to heaven,
6 And sware by him that liveth for
ever and ever, [a]who created heaven, and
the things that therein are, and the earth,
and the things that therein are, and the
sea, and the things which are therein,
[b]that there should be time no longer:
7 But [a]in the days of the voice of the
seventh angel, when he shall begin to
sound, the mystery of God should be finished, as he hath declared to his servants
the prophets.
8 And [a]the voice which I heard from
heaven spake unto me again, and said,
Go *and* take the little book which is open
in the hand of the angel which standeth
upon the sea and upon the earth.
9 And I went unto the angel, and said
unto him, Give me the little book. And
he said unto me, [a]Take *it,* and eat it up;
and it shall make thy belly bitter, but it
shall be in thy mouth sweet as honey.

P *Rev 9:20* ◀▶ *Rev 11:14*

3 [a]ch. 8:5
4 [a]Dan. 8:26 & 12:4,9
5 [a]Ex. 6:8; Dan. 12:7
6 [a]Neh. 9:6; ch. 4:11 & 14:7 [b]Dan. 12:7; ch. 16:17
7 [a]ch. 11:15
8 [a]ver. 4
9 [a]Jer. 15:16; Ezek. 2:8
10 [a]Ezek. 3:3 [b]Ezek. 2:10
11:1 [a]Ezek. 40:3; ch. 21:15 [b]Num. 23:18
2 [a]Ezek. 40:17 [b]Ps. 79:1; Luke 21:24 [c]Dan. 8:10 [d]ch. 13:5 [1]Gk. *cast out*
3 [a]ch. 20:4 [b]ch. 19:10 [c]ch. 12:6 [1]Or, *I will give unto my two witnesses that they may prophesy*
4 [a]Ps. 52:8; Jer. 11:16; Zech. 4:3
5 [a]2 Ki. 1:10; Jer. 1:10; Ezek. 43:3; Hos. 6:5 [b]Num. 16:29
6 [a]1 Ki. 17:1; Jas. 5:16

10 And I took the little book out of the
angel's hand, and ate it up; [a]and it was in
my mouth sweet as honey: and as soon as
I had eaten it, [b]my belly was bitter.
11 And he said unto me, Thou must
prophesy again before many peoples, and
nations, and tongues, and kings.

The two witnesses

11 AND THERE was given me [a]a
reed like unto a rod: and the angel stood, saying, [b]Rise, and measure the
temple of God, and the altar, and them
that worship therein.
2 But [a]the court which is without the G
temple [1]leave out, and measure it not;
[b]for it is given unto the Gentiles: and the
holy city shall they [c]tread under foot
[d]forty *and* two months.
3 And [1]I will give *power* unto my two
[a]witnesses, [b]and they shall prophesy [c]a
thousand two hundred *and* threescore
days, clothed in sackcloth.
4 These are the [a]two olive trees, and
the two candlesticks standing before the
God of the earth.
5 And if any man will hurt them, [a]fire
proceedeth out of their mouth, and devoureth their enemies: [b]and if any man
will hurt them, he must in this manner
be killed.
6 These [a]have power to shut heaven,

G *Ro 15:27* ◀▶ *Rev 12:3–6*

10:5–6 The mighty angel then declares that there would be no more delay. The next judgment was about to begin. Some have used this passage to mean that in heaven there would be no time. Yet Rev 22:2 indicates the passage of months in the new Jerusalem, intimating that eternity is not the absence of time; it is time without end.

10:7 The seventh trumpet (the third woe), though mentioned here, is not sounded until Rev 11:15.

11:1–2 The angel commands John to use a measuring rod and "measure the temple of God" (11:1). This seems to indicate the temple will be rebuilt during the tribulation and include the restoration of the great altar. Jerusalem will still be under the control of the Gentiles for another forty-two months (11:2) so the outer court cannot be measured. This 3 1/2 years corresponds to the great tribulation and will end at Armageddon (see Mt 24:21).

Some scholars believe that this outer court of the Gentiles encompasses the modern day Dome of the Rock. These scholars contend that the Moslem presence will still be strong in this area of Jerusalem and the court will not be completely rebuilt, so John did not need to measure it.

11:3–14 John then describes the supernatural ministry of God's two witnesses who will prophesy for 1260 days. Their supernatural power will authenticate their message. After 1260 days, they will finish their ministry and be killed by the antichrist. Unrepentant sinners will rejoice in their death, and the two will remain unburied on the streets of Jerusalem for three and a half days. The whole world will see their bodies. Yet, miraculously and fearfully, God will resurrect them and take them to heaven in the sight of their enemies. This prophecy clearly foreshadows modern-day, worldwide, television coverage. Only in this generation have people been able to see events as they occur from all over the world in live television broadcasts.

The resurrection of the two witnesses is closely followed by "a great earthquake" (11:13) which destroys one-tenth of Jerusalem and seven thousand people. Only then will the remnant be so frightened that they will give "glory to the God of heaven" (11:13).

that it rain not in the days of their prophecy: and have power over waters to turn
them to blood, and to smite the earth
with all plagues, as often as they will.
7 And when they [a]shall have finished
their testimony, [b]the beast that ascendeth [c]out of the bottomless pit [d]shall make
war against them, and shall overcome
them, and kill them.
8 And their dead bodies *shall lie* in the
street of [a]the great city, which spiritually
is called Sodom and Egypt, [b]where also
our Lord was crucified.
9 [a]And they of the people and kindreds and tongues and nations shall see
their dead bodies three days and an half,
[b]and shall not suffer their dead bodies to
be put in graves.
10 [a]And they that dwell upon the
earth shall rejoice over them, and make
merry, [b]and shall send gifts one to another; [c]because these two prophets tormented them that dwelt on the earth.
E 11 [a]And after three days and an half
H [b]the Spirit of life from God entered into
them, and they stood upon their feet;
and great fear fell upon them which saw
them.
12 And they heard a great voice from
heaven saying unto them, Come up
hither. [a]And they ascended up to heaven
[b]in a cloud; [c]and their enemies beheld
them.
13 And the same hour [a]was there a
great earthquake, [b]and the tenth part of
the city fell, and in the earthquake were
slain [/]of men seven thousand: and the
remnant were affrighted, [c]and gave glory
to the God of heaven.
P 14 [a]The second woe is past; *and*, behold, the third woe cometh quickly.

E *Rev 5:6* ◀ ▶ *Rev 14:13* H *1Pe 3:18* ◀
P *Rev 10:5–7* ◀ ▶ *Rev 11:18–19*

7 [a]Luke 13:32 [b]ch. 13:1,11 [c]ch. 9:2 [d]Dan. 7:21; Zech. 14:2
8 [a]ch. 14:8 [b]Heb. 13:12
9 [a]ch. 17:15 [b]Ps. 79:2,3
10 [a]ch. 12:12 [b]Esth. 9:19 [c]ch. 16:10
11 [a]ver. 9 [b]Ezek. 37:5
12 [a]Is. 14:13 [b]Is. 60:8; Acts 1:9 [c]2 Ki. 2:1
13 [a]ch. 6:12 [b]ch. 16:19 [c]Josh. 7:19 [/]Gk. *names of men*
14 [a]ch. 8:13
15 [a]ch. 10:7 [b]Is. 27:13 [c]ch. 12:10 [d]Dan. 2:44
16 [a]ch. 4:4
17 [a]ch. 16:5 [b]ch. 19:6
18 [a]ver. 2,9 [b]Dan. 7:9 [c]ch. 19:5 [d]ch. 13:10 [/]Or, *corrupt*
19 [a]ch. 15:5,8 [b]ch. 8:5 [c]ch. 16:21
12:1 [/]Or, *sign*
2 [a]Is. 66:7; Gal. 4:19

The seventh trumpet

15 And [a]the seventh angel sounded; K
[b]and there were great voices in heaven, M
saying, [c]The kingdoms of this world are V
become *the kingdoms* of our Lord, and of
his Christ; [d]and he shall reign for ever
and ever.
16 And [a]the four and twenty elders,
which sat before God on their seats, fell
upon their faces, and worshipped God,
17 Saying, We give thee thanks,
O Lord God Almighty, [a]which art, and
wast, and art to come; because thou hast
taken to thee thy great power, [b]and hast
reigned.
18 [a]And the nations were angry, and P
thy wrath is come, [b]and the time of the H
dead, that they should be judged, and J
that thou shouldest give reward unto thy
servants the prophets, and to the saints,
and them that fear thy name, [c]small and
great; [d]and shouldest destroy them which
[/]destroy the earth.
19 And [a]the temple of God was
opened in heaven, and there was seen
in his temple the ark of his testament:
and [b]there were lightnings, and voices,
and thunderings, and an earthquake, [c]and
great hail.

The woman and the dragon

12 AND THERE appeared a great R
[/]wonder in heaven; a woman
clothed with the sun, and the moon under her feet, and upon her head a crown
of twelve stars:
2 And she being with child cried, [a]tra-

K *1Co 15:24–28* ◀
M *Rev 5:10* ◀ ▶ *Rev 12:5*
V *Heb 1:13* ◀ ▶ *Rev 12:5*
P *Rev 11:14* ◀ ▶ *Rev 12:9–17*
H *Rev 6:15–17* ◀ ▶ *Rev 14:10–11*
J *Jude 14–15* ◀ ▶ *Rev 14:7*
R *1Th 2:16* ◀ ▶ *Rev 12:10–13*

11:15–18 The seventh trumpet sounds, ushering in the third woe. Though other significant events must still unfold, John records that the angels rejoice because the countdown to Christ's absolute victory over Satan has begun. The twenty-four elders fall upon their faces in worship of God, acknowledging that his glorious, majestic reign is about to be fulfilled at the second coming of Christ. Though the nations were angry as they endured God's judgments, when Christ returns the time for resurrection and final judgment approaches as well. Note also that God will hold people accountable for their stewardship of the earth, destroying those who destroy the earth.

11:19 John records his vision of God's temple in heaven and its "ark of his testament" as well as various phenomena that reflect God's coming judgments upon the earth. John's vision of the ark was an unspeakable privilege. While in the tabernacle, the ark resided in the Holy of Holies, hidden by curtains and accessible only to the high priest. John's vision of the ark symbolizes God's presence with his people and indicates that God has revealed his glory to them through Jesus Christ.

12:1 The book of Revelation follows a pattern

vailing in birth, and pained to be delivered.
G 3 And there appeared another [l]won-
der in heaven; and behold [a]a great red
dragon, [b]having seven heads and ten
horns, [c]and seven crowns upon his
heads.
4 And [a]his tail drew the third part [b]of
the stars of heaven, [c]and did cast them
to the earth: and the dragon stood [d]before
the woman which was ready to be delivered, [e]for to devour her child as soon as it
was born.
M 5 And she brought forth a man child,
V [a]who was to rule all nations with a rod of
iron: and her child was caught up unto
God, and *to* his throne.
6 And [a]the woman fled into the wilderness, where she hath a place prepared
of God, that they should feed her there [b]a
thousand two hundred *and* threescore
days.
7 And there was war in heaven: [a]Mi-
chael and his angels fought [b]against the
dragon; and the dragon fought and his
angels,
8 And prevailed not; neither was their
place found any more in heaven.
P 9 And [a]the great dragon was cast out,
[b]that old serpent, called the Devil, and

G *Rev 11:2* ◀ ▶ *Rev 13:1–18*
M *Rev 11:15–19* ◀ ▶ *Rev 20:1–6*
V *Rev 11:15* ◀ ▶ *Rev 17:14*
P *Rev 11:18–19* ◀ ▶ *Rev 14:6–11*

3 [a]ch. 17:3 [b]ch. 17:9,10 [c]ch. 13:1 [l]Or, *sign*
4 [a]ch. 9:10,19 [b]ch. 17:18 [c]Dan. 8:10 [d]ver. 2 [e]Ex. 1:16
5 [a]Ps. 2:9; ch. 19:15
6 [a]ver. 4 [b]ch. 11:3
7 [a]Dan. 10:13 [b]ch. 20:2
9 [a]Luke 10:18; John 12:31 [b]Gen. 3:1,4; ch. 20:2 [c]ch. 20:3 [d]ch. 9:1
10 [a]ch. 11:15 [b]Job 1:9; Zech. 3:1
11 [a]Rom. 16:20 [b]Luke 14:26
12 [a]Ps. 96:11; Is. 49:13; ch. 18:20 [b]ch. 8:13 [c]ch. 10:6
13 [a]ver. 5
14 [a]Ex. 19:4 [b]ver. 6 [c]ch. 17:3 [d]Dan. 7:25
15 [a]Is. 59:19

Satan, [c]which deceiveth the whole
world: [d]he was cast out into the earth,
and his angels were cast out with him.
10 And I heard a loud voice saying in R
heaven, [a]Now is come salvation, and
strength, and the kingdom of our God,
and the power of his Christ: for the ac-
cuser of our brethren is cast down,
[b]which accused them before our God day
and night.
11 And [a]they overcame him by the D
blood of the Lamb, and by the word of K
their testimony; [b]and they loved not their T
lives unto the death.
12 Therefore [a]rejoice, *ye* heavens, and
ye that dwell in them. [b]Woe to the inhabiters of the earth and of the sea! for the
devil is come down unto you, having
great wrath, [c]because he knoweth that
he hath but a short time.
13 And when the dragon saw that he
was cast unto the earth, he persecuted
[a]the woman which brought forth the
man *child.*
14 [a]And to the woman were given two
wings of a great eagle, [b]that she might fly
[c]into the wilderness, into her place,
where she is nourished [d]for a time, and
times, and half a time, from the face of
the serpent.
15 And the serpent [a]cast out of his

R *Rev 12:1–6* ◀ **D** *Rev 7:14* ◀
K *Rev 7:14* ◀ **T** *1Pe 2:9* ◀ ▶ *Rev 19:5*

---

that is consistent with Jewish apocalyptic literature as it retells the future events of the tribulation recorded in chs. 6—11 from a different vantage point in chs. 12—19.

12:1–6 This remarkable vision of a woman has spurred different interpretations and is critical to understanding Revelation. Some have suggested that this woman is Mary, but this view seems untenable since Mary never "fled into the wilderness" (12:6) for 1260 days. Other scholars suggest that the "woman" is the church. This view also does not hold up under scrutiny because the woman gives birth to one child, not many believers or multiple churches.

The only tenable interpretation is to identify this "woman" with the nation of Israel. In other passages of Scripture Israel is referred to as a woman, especially in regard to her relationship with God (see Hos 2:2–13). That the woman is clothed with the sun may refer to those of Israel who believed in their Messiah. Note that the twelve stars correspond to the twelve tribes (see Ge 37:9).

The woman gives birth to a male child. This child is Jesus Christ, the Messiah. John's vision then describes a spiritual war extending over thousands of years as Satan tries to destroy the Messiah who will someday annihilate him. Though Christ returned to heaven, God will protect the "woman" for the length of the great tribulation until Christ returns at Armageddon to destroy the antichrist.

12:7–14 When Christ declares war against Satan, the archangel Michael will marshal the awesome military forces of heaven to defeat Satan and his army of fallen angels. This war at the midpoint of the seven-year tribulation will result in Satan's final expulsion from heaven to the earth. This expulsion will so enrage him that his anger will burn against God's people. Satan will realize that his wicked rule is about to end in a short time and he will terrorize Israel. God will supernaturally intervene and protect Israel from the persecution of Satan "for a time, and times, and half a time" (12:14) or 3 1/2 years.

12:15–17 Satan will attempt to destroy the remnant of the righteous Jews with a flood. However, God will supernaturally open the earth and swallow

The Two Witnesses

GOD ESTABLISHED THE principle that two witnesses were required to settle the most important matters in judgment (see Dt 19:15). The Bible tells us that during the tribulation God will send two witnesses who will prophesy for 1,260 days, "standing before the God of the earth" (Rev 11:4), giving testimony and tormenting evil men. Because the deception of the antichrist will have confused many, these two witnesses will be empowered to destroy God's enemies with fire from heaven. Many will respond to their message of repentance but will face martyrdom at the hands of the antichrist (see 7:9, 14). Ultimately God's two witnesses will be killed by the antichrist and left unburied on the streets of Jerusalem.

The Identity of the Two Witnesses

Though the Bible does not name the two witnesses, scholars have attempted to determine their identity. Some scholars have suggested that the two witnesses are only symbols, possibly of the OT and NT, the Bible and the Holy Spirit, or the martyrs of the faith from both the OT and NT. Yet the Bible describes these two witnesses as human beings, making this symbolic interpretation untenable. Others contend that Elijah and Enoch will be the two witnesses because they are the only two human beings who never died but were instead translated to heaven. Still others believe that Elijah and Moses will be God's two witnesses during the tribulation. While Scripture does not name the exact identity of the two witnesses, several facts are given that may help in their identification.

Elijah the Prophet

Malachi intimates that one of the two witnesses will be the prophet Elijah (see Mal 4:5). For centuries the Jews have longed for Elijah's return, recognizing that Elijah's mission would precede the Messiah's appearance. Every Passover, Jews set a place at their seder meal in anticipation of the prophet's return, leaving a door or window slightly ajar in hopes that this will be the year for Elijah's entrance to usher in the Messianic kingdom. This longing prompted the priests and Sadducees to question whether John the Baptist or even Jesus was Elijah (see Mk 8:27–28; Jn 1:21).

Elijah was a vital leader of Israel during a critical time in the life of the nation. During his ministry Elijah prayed that God would stop the rain for three and one-half years (see 1Ki 17:1; Lk 4:25; Jas 5:17). This power over the rain corresponds to one of the supernatural signs of the two witnesses and their "power to shut heaven, that it rain not in the days of their prophecy" (Rev 11:6)—a total of 1,260 days or three and one-half years (see 11:3). Because Elijah did not experience physical death (see 2Ki 2:9–11), he could possibly be one of the two witnesses who will return and be martyred during the tribulation.

Enoch

Many commentators suggest that Enoch is the second of the two witnesses because he is the only other person in the Bible besides Elijah who was raptured to heaven without dying (see Ge 5:24). These scholars suggest that since "it is appointed unto men once to die, but after this the judgment" (Heb 9:27), both Enoch and Elijah must come back to earth and die since they escaped death the first time. To base the identification of one of God's witnesses on this interpretation of one verse of Scripture is a tenuous position at best. This interpretation overlooks the fact that those believers who are alive when Christ comes at the rapture will never experience death (see 1Th 4:17), yet these raptured believers are never suggested as being God's witnesses during the tribulation. Note too that the Bible indicates that several humans have actually died twice: Lazarus, Jairus's daughter and the widow of Nain's son. Complicating the identification of Enoch as one of the two witnesses is the fact that Enoch lived prior to the establishment of Israel as a nation and never figured prominently in its history or prophecy.

Moses

Because the prophet Malachi mentions both Elijah and Moses in his passage about the Messiah, some scholars conclude that Moses is the second of the two witnesses (see Mal 4:4–6). Moses was Israel's great leader and lawgiver who exercised God's miraculous power to authenticate his message and destroy Israel's spiritual enemies. Note that there are many similarities between the plagues and judgments against Egypt (see Ex 7—11) and the future plagues and judgments of the two witnesses during the tribulation.

Another indicator that suggests Moses' role as one of the two witnesses is his appearance with Elijah on the Mount of Transfiguration (see Mt 17:2–3). Moses, representing the Law, and Elijah, representing the prophets, appeared together to affirm Jesus' claim as God's Messiah. It is appropriate that these two great leaders should appear together again to witness to humanity at the end of this age.

mouth water as a flood after the woman,
that he might cause her to be carried
away of the flood.
16 And the earth helped the woman,
and the earth opened her mouth, and
swallowed up the flood which the dragon
cast out of his mouth.
17 And the dragon was wroth with the
woman, [a]and went to make war with
the remnant of her seed, [b]which keep the
commandments of God, and have [c]the
testimony of Jesus Christ.

The beast from the sea

G 13 AND I stood upon the sand of the
sea, and saw [a]a beast rise up out
of the sea, [b]having seven heads and ten
horns, and upon his horns ten crowns,
and upon his heads the [1]name of blasphemy.
2 [a]And the beast which I saw was like
unto a leopard, [b]and his feet were as *the*
feet of a bear, [c]and his mouth as the
mouth of a lion: and [d]the dragon gave
him his power, and his seat, [e]and great
authority.
3 And I saw one of his heads [a]as it
were [1]wounded to death; and his deadly
wound was healed: and [b]all the world
wondered after the beast.
4 And they worshipped the dragon
which gave power unto the beast: and
they worshipped the beast, saying, [a]Who
is like unto the beast? who is able to
make war with him?
5 And there was given unto him [a]a
mouth speaking great things and blasphemies; and power was given unto him [1]to
continue [b]forty *and* two months.
6 And he opened his mouth in blasphemy against God, to blaspheme his
name, [a]and his tabernacle, and them that
dwell in heaven.
7 And it was given unto him [a]to make
war with the saints, and to overcome
them: [b]and power was given him over all
kindreds, and tongues, and nations.
8 And all that dwell upon the earth
shall worship him, [a]whose names are
not written in the book of life of the
Lamb slain [b]from the foundation of the
world.
9 [a]If any man have an ear, let him N
hear.
10 [a]He that leadeth into captivity shall
go into captivity: [b]he that killeth with the
sword must be killed with the sword.

17 [a]Gen. 3:15; ch. 11:7 [b]ch. 14:12 [c]1 Cor. 2:1; 1 John 5:10
13:1 [a]Dan. 7:2,7 [b]ch. 12:3 [1]Or, *names;* see ch. 17:3
2 [a]Dan. 7:6 [b]Dan. 7:5 [c]Dan. 7:4 [d]ch. 12:9 [e]ch. 12:4
3 [a]ver. 12,14 [b]ch. 17:8 [1]Gk. *slain*
4 [a]ch. 18:18
5 [a]Dan. 7:8 [b]ch. 11:2 [1]Or, *to make war*
6 [a]John 1:14; Col. 2:9
7 [a]Dan. 7:21; ch. 11:7 [b]ch. 11:18
8 [a]Ex. 32:32; Dan. 12:1; Phil. 4:3; ch. 3:5 [b]ch. 17:8
9 [a]ch. 2:7
10 [a]Is. 33:1 [b]Gen. 9:6; Mat. 26:52

G *Rev 12:3–6* ◀ ▶ *Rev 14:8*

N *Rev 6:15–16* ◀ ▶ *Rev 22:11–12*

---

the water. John then describes Satan's anger and war against all who keep God's commands and believe in Jesus Christ. In fulfillment of this prophecy, modern-day armies can cause tidal waves to swamp low-lying enemy territory with a strategically placed nuclear bomb. Whether this prophecy of a flood will be fulfilled in this military manner or in a more supernatural way, God promises to deliver his people.

13:1–2 John describes his terrible vision of this beast (the antichrist) that rises to political prominence in the world. This antichrist has "ten horns," which represent the revived Roman empire—the ten nations of Europe that will unite together under his rule (see Da 7:23–24). The "ten crowns" indicate that he has usurped all political power over these ten nations. In gaining his authority over these nations, three of the leaders of the ten kingdoms are completely overthrown or killed leaving only "seven heads" (13:1) to help bring about "blasphemy" (13:1) against God. Whatever his status at birth, the antichrist will receive his power, throne and authority from Satan.

13:3–9 The antichrist miraculously survives an assassination attempt. Though "wounded to death" (13:3), the antichrist will be healed in a satanic imitation of Christ's resurrection, and receive the worship and wonderment of the world. For 3 1/2 years the antichrist will powerfully persecute the Jewish and Gentile tribulation saints. Everyone on earth who is not a follower of Christ will join the satanic worship of the antichrist.

13:11–18 Some say that because this second beast comes "out of the earth" (13:11) this beast is a symbol of the religious power that is now invested in the hands of secular authorities. Others propose that this beast is an individual, the antichrist's false prophet, his right-hand man, who enforces the worship of the antichrist with satanic miracles and oppression. Although countless writers have attempted to identify the future antichrist and this false prophet, it is probable that we will not know who these people are until the antichrist is revealed during the seven-year tribulation and after the rapture of the church.

Yet John give us a clear picture of the false prophet. This false prophet looks "like a lamb" (13:11) but behaves like a demon, attempting to bring down fire from heaven. Though he relies on Satan's limited power, this false prophet creates an automated image of the antichrist that people are forced to worship on penalty of death. He also

[c]Here is the patience and the faith of the
saints.

The beast from the earth

11 And I beheld another beast [a]com-
ing up out of the earth; and he had two
horns like a lamb, and he spake as a
dragon.
12 And he exerciseth all the power of
the first beast before him, and causeth
the earth and them which dwell therein
to worship the first beast, [a]whose deadly
wound was healed.
13 And [a]he doeth great wonders, [b]so
that he maketh fire come down from
heaven on the earth in the sight of men,
14 [a]And deceiveth them that dwell on
the earth [b]by *the means of* those miracles
which he had power to do in the sight of
the beast; saying to them that dwell on
the earth, that they should make an image to the beast, which had the wound by
a sword, [c]and did live.
15 And he had power to give [/]life
unto the image of the beast, that the
image of the beast should both speak,
[a]and cause that as many as would not
worship the image of the beast should
be killed.
16 And he causeth all, both small and
great, rich and poor, free and bond, [a]to[/]
receive a mark in their right hand, or in
their foreheads:
17 And that no man might buy or sell,
save he that had the mark, or [a]the name
of the beast, [b]or the number of his
name.
18 [a]Here is wisdom. Let him that hath
understanding count [b]the number of the
beast: [c]for it is the number of a man; and
his number *is* Six hundred threescore
and six.

10 [c]ch. 14:12
11 [a]ch. 11:7
12 [a]ver. 3
13 [a]Deut. 13:1; Mat. 24:24; 2 Thes. 2:9; ch. 16:14 [b]1 Ki. 18:38; 2 Ki. 1:10
14 [a]ch. 12:9 [b]2 Thes. 2:9 [c]2 Ki. 20:7
15 [a]ch. 16:2 [/]Gk. *breath*
16 [a]ch. 14:9 [/]Gk. *to give them*
17 [a]ch. 14:11 [b]ch. 15:2
18 [a]ch. 17:9 [b]ch. 15:2 [c]ch. 21:17
14:1 [a]ch. 5:6 [b]ch. 7:4 [c]ch. 13:16
2 [a]ch. 1:15 [b]ch. 5:8
3 [a]ch. 5:9 [b]ver. 1
4 [a]2 Cor. 11:2 [b]ch. 3:4 [c]ch. 5:9 [d]Jas. 1:18 [/]Gk. *were bought*
5 [a]Ps. 32:2; Zeph. 3:13 [b]Eph. 5:27; Jude 24
6 [a]ch. 8:13 [b]Eph. 3:9; Tit. 1:2 [c]ch. 13:7
7 [a]ch. 11:18 [b]Neh. 9:6; Ps. 33:6 & 124:8 & 146:5,6; Acts 14:15 & 17:24

The Lamb on mount Zion

14 AND I looked, and, lo, [a]a Lamb H
stood on the mount Zion, and
with him [b]an hundred forty *and* four
thousand, [c]having his Father's name
written in their foreheads.
2 And I heard a voice from heaven, [a]as
the voice of many waters, and as the
voice of a great thunder: and I heard the
voice of [b]harpers harping with their
harps:
3 And [a]they sung as it were a new
song before the throne, and before the
four beasts, and the elders: and no man
could learn that song [b]but the hundred
and forty *and* four thousand, which were
redeemed from the earth.
4 These are they which were not defiled with women; [a]for they are virgins.
These are they [b]which follow the Lamb
whithersoever he goeth. These [c]were[/]
redeemed from among men, [d]*being* the
firstfruits unto God and to the Lamb.
5 And [a]in their mouth was found no
guile: for [b]they are without fault before
the throne of God.

The angelic messages

6 And I saw another angel [a]fly in the P
midst of heaven, [b]having the everlasting
gospel to preach unto them that dwell on
the earth, [c]and to every nation, and kindred, and tongue, and people,
7 Saying with a loud voice, [a]Fear God, J
and give glory to him; for the hour of his
judgment is come: [b]and worship him that
made heaven, and earth, and the sea, and
the fountains of waters.

H *Rev 7:9–17* ◀▶ *Rev 15:2–4*
P *Rev 12:9–17* ◀▶ *Rev 14:14*
J *Rev 11:18* ◀▶ *Rev 20:1–15*

---

devises a marking system that will be needed in order to buy or sell in society. For the first time in history this prophecy can now be easily fulfilled. Scientists have recently developed tiny computer chips that can be inserted beneath the skin to hold complete financial, health and identification records. Such implants would remove the necessity for money and would easily prepare the way for the implementation of a society as described in John's prophecy in this chapter.

14:1–5 John sees the 144,000 Jewish witnesses in heaven, after they "were redeemed from the earth" (14:3). This is the same group seen earlier on earth in Rev 7. As faithful witnesses to Christ, this group is honored and called "the firstfruits unto God and to the Lamb" (14:4).

14:6–11 The first of a group of three angels appears and warns humanity of the coming final judgment of God. The first angel announces the gospel and calls for the worship of God. The second angel announces the fall of Babylon because of its unfaithfulness to God. This angelic announcement anticipates the final judgment of the apostate church (see ch. 17). The third angel warns humanity against worshiping the beast or receiving his mark. Anyone that gives in to the beast would be sent to the lake of fire for eternity.

G 8 And there followed another angel,
saying, [a]Babylon is fallen, is fallen, [b]that
great city, because she made all nations
drink of the wine of the wrath of her fornication.
9 And the third angel followed them,
saying with a loud voice, [a]If any man
worship the beast and his image, and receive *his* mark in his forehead, or in his
hand,
H 10 The same [a]shall drink of the wine
of the wrath of God, which is [b]poured out
without mixture into [c]the cup of his indignation; and [d]he shall be tormented
with [e]fire and brimstone in the presence
of the holy angels, and in the presence of
the Lamb:
11 And [a]the smoke of their torment ascendeth up for ever and ever: and they
have no rest day nor night, who worship
the beast and his image, and whosoever
receiveth the mark of his name.
12 [a]Here is the patience of the saints:
[b]here *are* they that keep the commandments of God, and the faith of Jesus.
E 13 And I heard a voice from heaven
T saying unto me, Write, [a]Blessed *are* the
dead [b]which die in the Lord [1]from henceforth: Yea, saith the Spirit, [c]that they may
rest from their labours; and their works
do follow them.
P 14 And I looked, and behold a white
H cloud, and upon the cloud *one* sat [a]like
unto the Son of man, [b]having on his head
a golden crown, and in his hand a sharp
sickle.
15 And another angel [a]came out of the
temple, crying with a loud voice to him

G *Rev 13:1–18* ◀▶ *Rev 17:1*
H *Rev 11:18* ◀▶ *Rev 14:14–20*
E *Rev 11:11* ◀▶ *Rev 17:3*
T *Rev 4:2* ◀▶ *Rev 17:3*
P *Rev 14:6–11* ◀▶ *Rev 15:5*
H *Rev 14:10–11* ◀▶ *Rev 15:1*

8 [a]Is. 21:9; ch. 18:2 [b]Jer. 51:7; ch. 16:19 & 17:2,5 & 18:3,10
9 [a]ch. 13:14
10 [a]Ps. 75:8; Is. 51:17; Jer. 25:15 [b]ch. 18:6 [c]ch. 16:19 [d]ch. 20:10 [e]ch. 19:20
11 [a]Is. 34:10
12 [a]ch. 13:10 [b]ch. 12:17
13 [a]Eccl. 4:1,2 [b]1 Cor. 15:18; 1 Thes. 4:16 [c]2 Thes. 1:7; Heb. 4:9,10 [1]Or, *from henceforth saith the Spirit, Yea*
14 [a]Ezek. 1:26; Dan. 7:13 [b]ch. 6:2
15 [a]ch. 16:17 [b]Joel 3:13; Mat. 13:39 [c]Jer. 51:33; ch. 13:12 [1]Or, *dried*
18 [a]ch. 16:8 [b]Joel 3:13
19 [a]ch. 19:15
20 [a]Is. 63:3; Lam. 1:15 [b]Heb. 13:12 [c]ch. 19:14
15:1 [a]ch. 12:1,3 [b]ch. 21:9 [c]ch. 14:10
2 [a]ch. 4:6 [b]Mat. 3:11 [c]ch. 13:15 [d]ch. 5:8
3 [a]Ex. 15:1

that sat on the cloud, [b]Thrust in thy
sickle, and reap: for the time is come for
thee to reap; for the harvest [c]of the earth
is [1]ripe.
16 And he that sat on the cloud thrust
in his sickle on the earth; and the earth
was reaped.
17 And another angel came out of the
temple which is in heaven, he also having a sharp sickle.
18 And another angel came out from
the altar, [a]which had power over fire;
and cried with a loud cry to him that had
the sharp sickle, saying, [b]Thrust in thy
sharp sickle, and gather the clusters of
the vine of the earth; for her grapes are
fully ripe.
19 And the angel thrust in his sickle
into the earth, and gathered the vine of
the earth, and cast *it* into [a]the great winepress of the wrath of God.
20 And [a]the winepress was trodden
[b]without the city, and blood came out of
the winepress, [c]even unto the horse bridles, by the space of a thousand *and* six
hundred furlongs.

The seven plagues

15 AND [a]I saw another sign in H
heaven, great and marvellous,
[b]seven angels having the seven last
plagues; [c]for in them is filled up the
wrath of God.
2 And I saw as it were [a]a sea of glass H
[b]mingled with fire: and them that had
gotten the victory over the beast, [c]and
over his image, and over his mark, *and*
over the number of his name, stand on
the sea of glass, [d]having the harps of God.
3 And they sing [a]the song of Moses the

H *Rev 14:14–20* ◀▶ *Rev 19:3*
H *Rev 14:1–5* ◀▶ *Rev 19:7–9*

14:14–20 Jesus Christ appears in John's vision wearing "a golden crown," (14:14) representing his identity as King of kings. He also carries a "sharp sickle" (14:14) that he uses to harvest grain (the Gentiles) and grapes (the unbelieving Jews)—the unrepentant sinners of the tribulation. Christ pours out his final wrath upon the godless enemies who have gathered against the city of Jerusalem in their attempt to destroy his chosen people. The place of the final battle becomes a river of blood outside of the city, running for over 180 miles and as deep as the bridle of a horse.

15:1–8 This chapter describes an interval before the last seven plagues that will complete the "wrath of God." (15:1). Once again John sees the "sea of glass like unto crystal" (4:6), but now he sees the martyrs of the tribulation who have been resurrected to heaven to receive their reward. They have their harps and sing "the song of Moses . . . and the song of the Lamb" (15:3) in glorious worship of Jesus Christ, their King. Then John sees the temple of God and seven angels coming out of the temple, preparing to pour out the final judgment of God.

servant of God, and the song of the Lamb,
saying, [b]Great and marvellous *are* thy
works, Lord God Almighty; [c]just and true
are thy ways, thou King of [l]saints.
4 [a]Who shall not fear thee, O Lord,
and glorify thy name? for *thou* only *art*
holy: for [b]all nations shall come and worship before thee; for thy judgments are
made manifest.
P 5 And after that I looked, and, behold,
[a]the temple of the tabernacle of the testimony in heaven was opened:
6 [a]And the seven angels came out of
the temple, having the seven plagues,
[b]clothed in pure and white linen, and
having their breasts girded with golden
girdles.
7 [a]And one of the four beasts gave
unto the seven angels seven golden vials
full of the wrath of God, [b]who liveth for
ever and ever.
8 And [a]the temple was filled with
smoke [b]from the glory of God, and from
his power; and no man was able to enter
into the temple, till the seven plagues of
the seven angels were fulfilled.

The vials of God's wrath

16 AND I heard a great voice out of
the temple saying [a]to the seven
angels, Go your ways, and pour out the
vials [b]of the wrath of God upon the earth.

P *Rev 14:14* ◀ ▶ *Rev 18:19*

3 [b]Deut. 32:4; Ps. 111:2 [c]Ps. 145:17; Hos. 14:9 [l]Or, *nations*, or, *ages*
4 [a]Ex. 15:14; Jer. 10:7 [b]Is. 66:23
5 [a]Num. 1:50
6 [a]ver. 1 [b]Ex. 28:6; Ezek. 44:17
7 [a]ch. 4:6 [b]1 Thes. 1:9
8 [a]Ex. 40:34; 2 Chr. 5:14 [b]2 Thes. 1:9
16:1 [a]ch. 15:1 [b]ch. 14:10

16:1–12 In this passage, John describes the last seven vial judgments. God commands the seven angels to carry out this final judgment against the earth and its wicked inhabitants. The first vial results in horrible boils and sores upon the skin of everyone who takes the mark of the beast and worships his image. The second vial will be poured out on the oceans, turning the waters to blood and killing every marine animal and fish.

The third vial will be poured out on all sources of fresh water, turning them to blood as God avenges the deaths of the saints and prophets who tried to

Stages of the Battle of Armageddon

Da 11:35–45; Rev 16:16

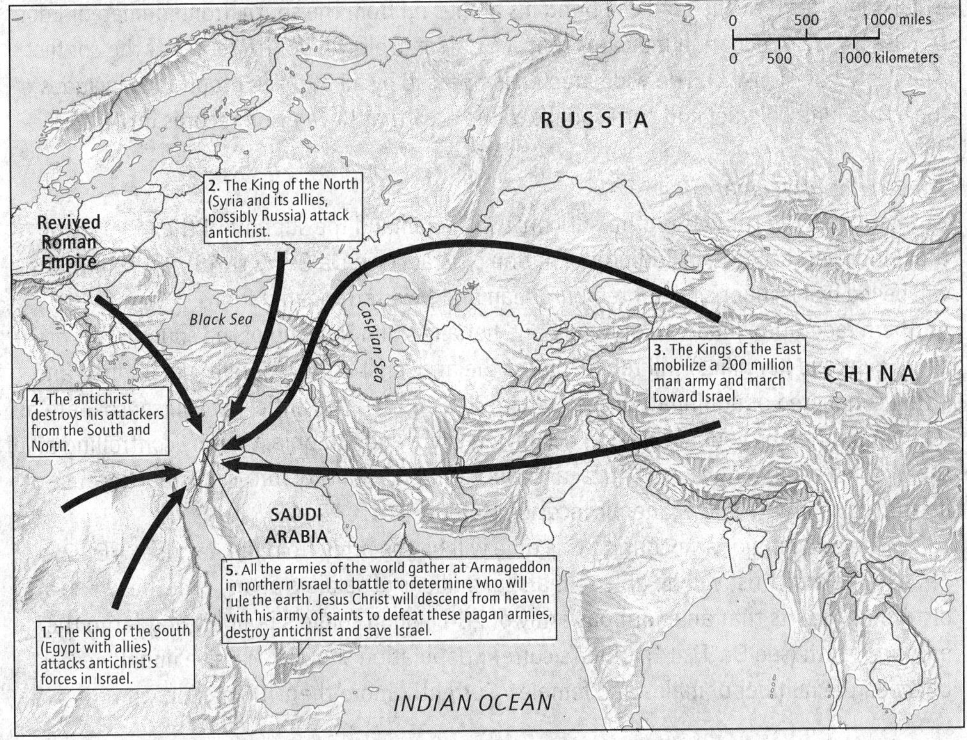

The Battle of Armageddon

THE LAST THREE years of the tribulation will be marked by a series of wars as many nations of the world rebel against the antichrist. God will allow "three unclean spirits" (Rev 16:13) to summon the "kings of the earth" (16:14) and their great armies to a valley in Israel. A fierce battle, the final conflict of the age, will then be enjoined at Armageddon.

The Location of Armageddon

Armageddon is the Greek term for the area of Palestine located along the southern rim of the plain of Esdraelon. Known alternately as the Valley of Jezreel, this great battlefield was the crossroads of two ancient trade routes and the site of major victories as well as disasters for the Israelites (see Jdg 4:15; 7; 1Sa 31:8; 2Ki 23:29–30; 2Ch 35:22). Thus Armageddon became synonymous to the Jews with terrible and final destruction.

The wars that will take place at the end of the tribulation will occur in various locations but will be centered in this area of Palestine. The prophet Joel foretold that God will "gather all nations, and will bring them down into the valley of Jehoshaphat" (Joel 3:2). Isaiah indicates that the Lord will bring his armies up from the south, from Idumea or Edom (see Isa 34; 63). Zechariah indicates that Jerusalem itself will be the center of the conflict (see Zec 12:2–11; 14:2). The wide area encompassed by all of these prophecies includes the entire land of Israel and corresponds to the area that Revelation records in 14:20.

The Armies of Armageddon

At the time of the tribulation the antichrist will command the support of the majority of the nations of the west, including the nation of Israel (see Da 9:27; 11:45). These nations will be led by his inner circle of ten European and Mediterranean nations. A weakened, northern federation made up of Russia and her allies and the king of the south (most probably Egypt and her allies) will rebel against the antichrist but eventually be subdued and either conquered or annihilated (see Da 11:40; Zec 12:4). The antichrist will consolidate his military position by conquering and occupying Libya and Ethiopia, thereby controlling all of the Middle East and northern Africa, and will center his military forces in Israel because of its strategic military and economic location (see Da 11:41–42, 45; Rev 13:7).

The other major army during this time will be the army from the east (see 16:12). Though the antichrist will be able to marshal millions of soldiers at any time, he will hear disturbing reports that an enormous army of 200 million soldiers is mobilizing far to the east and north (see Da 11:44). China's current population shows a massive imbalance between the number of males and females. Currently, more than 100 million young

Chinese men are of military age, and other countless millions are in its military reserve army. Should an alliance be forged between China and Japan, these eastern nations could effortlessly fill the ranks of Armageddon's prophesied 200 million soldiers (see Rev 9:14–16) and easily produce the armaments required for such an army. When the industrial might and engineering expertise of Japan is joined to the huge manpower and natural resources of China, the western world will face its greatest and final threat.

The final army to stand at the Battle of Armageddon will be the army of the Lord. Prophets in both the OT and NT foretold that the Lord would bring millions of his saints with him on the great day of the Lord (see Jude 14). Moses also described the army of heaven and the Lord coming in vengeance against Satan's forces (see Dt 33:2). The believers in Christ will return from heaven with their Messiah to join in the battle at Armageddon and win an incredible victory over the armies who attempt to destroy the Jews and each other (see Rev 19:14, 19).

The Battle Plan

At the midpoint of the seven-year tribulation, the antichrist and his ten nations will combine their forces to destroy the false church, the great whore of Babylon (see Rev 17:1–16). Obviously, this false church will have grown into a formidable power if the antichrist requires the military forces of ten nations to subdue her. Since the followers of the false church will not abandon her when she is attacked, she and her followers will be destroyed by the antichrist.

Though the nations of the world initially embrace the new world order of the antichrist, Israel and some Gentile nations will try to rebel during the tribulation (see 12:9–17). The king of the south (Egypt and her allies) will attack the antichrist's forces in Israel. The northern kingdoms will join the invasion by bringing in their forces in a lightning attack. The antichrist will swiftly retaliate and annihilate his enemies (see Da 11:9–12). Thus the forces of Satan will win the first round of the war.

The antichrist will then hear disturbing reports about an approaching army from the east. While for thousands of years the Euphrates River has stood as a great barrier between the nations of the east and west, John prophesied that this great river would somehow dry up to allow the passage of the armies of the east to invade Israel (see Rev 16:12).

Only recently has a large dam been completed in Turkey that can control the waters of the Euphrates River. At the dam's completion the president of Turkey pressed a button that closed some of the spillways, effectively reducing 75 percent of the river's flow. As a fulfillment of John's prophecy, the Euphrates River can now be dried up because of this massive dam.

The incredible army of the east will cross Asia, slaughtering one-third of humanity in its path as it moves toward the great Valley of Jezreel in northern Israel to meet the massed armies of the antichrist. After years of warfare this final battle between the forces of the east and the west will determine who will rule the world for the next millennium.

Although the final stages of the battle will center in Armageddon, skirmishes will engulf Asia, Africa, Europe and the Middle East. Untold millions will die in bloody warfare as nations pour their destructive nuclear, biological and chemical weapons on each other (see 19:17–18, 21).

Yet as the armies of the antichrist and the armies of the east join battle with each other, the Lord will return with his army to deliver the nation of Israel from annihilation. There will be nothing secret about his coming to destroy Satan's armies. Jesus promised that his return would be as brilliantly visible as lightning (see Mt 24:27). Yet to the consternation of the leaders of this titanic battle the armies of heaven will supernaturally intervene against both evil forces. Putting aside their own agenda, the armies of the antichrist and the armies of the east will join together to attack Christ and his heavenly army (see Rev 19:19). Despite their fearful array of military weapons, the armies of the world will be destroyed.

We are not told how long the Battle of Armageddon will rage. It may end quite quickly once the armies of heaven intervene, or it may continue for a period of time. Regardless of its duration, Christ will be the ultimate victor (see 2Th 2:8). His power and might will transcend the power of the antichrist's weapons of war (see Da 8:25; Mt 26:53). The enemies of Christ will be destroyed and the antichrist and the false prophet will be captured and thrown into the "lake of fire burning with brimstone" (Rev 19:20). Their final destruction will end the terrible persecution of God's people.

Though no one knows with certainty when this final conflict will occur, signs in the sky will announce to the nations that the Messiah's return is at hand. When Jesus returns he will not come as a meek Lamb or suffering servant. When the final day of reckoning arrives, Christ will call on the angels of heaven as well as the saints of the church to join in his triumphant return to establish his millennial kingdom. When Christ returns he will come in all the glory of Almighty God as "the King of kings, and Lord of lords" (1Ti 6:15).

2 And the first went, and poured out
his vial [a]upon the earth; and [b]there fell a
noisome and grievous sore upon the men
[c]which had the mark of the beast, and
upon them [d]which worshipped his
image.
3 And the second angel poured out his
vial [a]upon the sea; and [b]it became as the
blood of a dead *man:* [c]and every living
soul died in the sea.
4 And the third angel poured out his
vial [a]upon the rivers and fountains of waters; [b]and they became blood.
5 And I heard the angel of the waters
say, [a]Thou art righteous, O Lord, [b]which
art, and wast, and shalt be, because thou
hast judged thus.
6 For [a]they have shed the blood [b]of
saints and prophets, [c]and thou hast given
them blood to drink; for they are worthy.
7 And I heard another out of the altar
say, Even so, [a]Lord God Almighty, [b]true
and righteous *are* thy judgments.
8 And the fourth angel poured out his
vial [a]upon the sun; [b]and power was given
unto him to scorch men with fire.
9 And men were [1]scorched with great
heat, and [a]blasphemed the name of God,
which hath power over these plagues:
[b]and they repented not [c]to give him
glory.
10 And the fifth angel poured out his
vial [a]upon the seat of the beast; [b]and his
kingdom was full of darkness; [c]and they
gnawed their tongues for pain,
11 And [a]blasphemed the God of
heaven because of their pains and [b]their
sores, [c]and repented not of their deeds.
12 And the sixth angel poured out his
vial [a]upon the great river Euphrates; [b]and
the water thereof was dried up, [c]that the
way of the kings of the east might be prepared.
13 And I saw three unclean [a]spirits
like frogs *come* out of the mouth of [b]the
dragon, and out of the mouth of the
beast, and out of the mouth of [c]the false
prophet.
14 [a]For they are the spirits of devils,
[b]working miracles, *which* go forth unto
the kings of the earth [c]and of the whole
world, to gather them to [d]the battle of
that great day of God Almighty.
15 [a]Behold, I come as a thief. Blessed
is he that watcheth, and keepeth his garments, [b]lest he walk naked, and they see
his shame.
16 [a]And he gathered them together
into a place called in the Hebrew tongue
Armageddon.
17 And the seventh angel poured out
his vial into the air; and there came a
great voice out of the temple of heaven,
from the throne, saying, [a]It is done.
18 And [a]there were voices, and thunders, and lightnings; [b]and there was a
great earthquake, [c]such as was not since
men were upon the earth, so mighty an
earthquake, *and* so great.
19 And [a]the great city was divided into
three parts, and the cities of the nations
fell: and great Babylon [b]came in remembrance before God, [c]to give unto her the

2 [a]ch. 8:7 [b]Ex. 9:9-11 [c]ch. 13:16 [d]ch. 13:14
3 [a]ch. 8:8 [b]Ex. 7:17 [c]ch. 8:9
4 [a]ch. 8:10 [b]Ex. 7:20
5 [a]ch. 15:3 [b]ch. 1:4,8
6 [a]Mat. 23:34; ch. 13:15 [b]ch. 11:18 [c]Is. 49:26
7 [a]ch. 15:3 [b]ch. 13:10
8 [a]ch. 8:12 [b]ch. 9:17,18
9 [a]ver. 11,21 [b]Dan. 5:22 [c]ch. 11:13 [1]Or, *burned*
10 [a]ch. 13:2 [b]ch. 9:2 [c]ch. 11:10
11 [a]ver. 9,21 [b]ver. 2 [c]ver. 9
12 [a]ch. 9:14 [b]Jer. 50:38 [c]Is. 41:2,25
13 [a]1 John 4:1 [b]ch. 12:3,9 [c]ch. 19:20
14 [a]1 Tim. 4:1; Jas. 3:15 [b]2 Thes. 2:9 [c]Luke 2:1 [d]ch. 17:14
15 [a]Mat. 24:43 [b]2 Cor. 5:3
16 [a]ch. 19:19
17 [a]ch. 21:6
18 [a]ch. 4:5 [b]ch. 11:13 [c]Dan. 12:1
19 [a]ch. 14:8 & 17:18 [b]ch. 18:5 [c]Is. 51:17; ch. 14:10

---

warn the wicked. The fourth vial will be poured out on the sun, so that people will be burned "with great heat" (16:9). Yet the people will continue to blaspheme God and refuse "to give him glory" (16:9).

The fifth vial produces supernatural darkness throughout the antichrist's kingdom, similar to the plague in Egypt (see Ex 10:21–23). The sixth vial affects the "great river Euphrates"(16:12) and dries up its riverbed in preparation for the invasion of Israel by the armies of the kings of the east.

16:13–21 John describes three evil spirits that are sent from Satan, the antichrist and the false prophet to gather the wicked kings of the whole world together for a major battle. God will allow this battle to take place at Armageddon, a huge valley in northern Israel and the site of many major historical battles.

The seventh vial will be poured into the air and a great earthquake will devastate the earth and divide Jerusalem into three parts as cities around the world fall in ruins. John warns that Babylon's day of judgment is approaching (see Rev 18). Islands will be swamped and mountains will collapse as a terrible hailstorm falls from the skies. Yet despite these judgments, the wicked will continue to curse God rather than repent of their sins.

In the middle of this passage, almost as a parenthetical thought, Christ's followers are urged to watch for his coming and be alert. The unusual phrases of 16:15 referred to the custom in John's day of the treatment of a temple guard that fell asleep while on guard duty. His clothes were taken from him, and he was forced to go home naked and in disgrace. What a warning for Christ's followers to stand firm and alert, to heed the signs and be watchful for his coming.

cup of the wine of the fierceness of his
wrath.
20 And [a]every island fled away, and
the mountains were not found.
21 [a]And there fell upon men a great
hail out of heaven, *every stone* about the
weight of a talent: and [b]men blasphemed
God because of [c]the plague of the hail;
for the plague thereof was exceeding
great.

The woman on the beast

G 17 AND THERE came [a]one of the
seven angels which had the
seven vials, and talked with me, saying
unto me, Come hither; [b]I will show unto
thee the judgment of [c]the great whore
[d]that sitteth upon many waters:
2 [a]With whom the kings of the earth
have committed fornication, and [b]the inhabitants of the earth have been made
drunk with the wine of her fornication.
E 3 So he carried me away in the spirit
T

G *Rev 14:8* ◀
E *Rev 14:13* ◀ ▶ *Rev 21:10*
T *Rev 14:13* ◀

[a]into the wilderness: and I saw a woman
sit [b]upon a scarlet coloured beast, full of
[c]names of blasphemy, [d]having seven
heads and [e]ten horns.
4 And the woman [a]was arrayed in purple and scarlet colour, [b]and [1]decked with
gold and precious stones and pearls,
[c]having a golden cup in her hand [d]full of
abominations and filthiness of her fornication:
5 And upon her forehead *was* a name
written, [a]MYSTERY, BABYLON THE
GREAT, THE MOTHER OF [1]HARLOTS
AND ABOMINATIONS OF THE EARTH.
6 And I saw [a]the woman drunken
[b]with the blood of the saints, and with
the blood of [c]the martyrs of Jesus: and
when I saw her, I wondered with great
admiration.
7 And the angel said unto me, Wherefore didst thou marvel? I will tell thee the
mystery of the woman, and of the beast
that carrieth her, which hath the seven
heads and ten horns.
8 The beast that thou sawest was, and
is not; and [a]shall ascend out of the bottomless pit, and [b]go into perdition: and

20 [a]ch. 6:14
21 [a]ch. 11:19 [b]ver. 9,11 [c]Ex. 9:23
17:1 [a]ch. 21:9 [b]ch. 16:19 [c]Nah. 3:4; ch. 19:2 [d]Jer. 51:13
2 [a]ch. 18:3 [b]Jer. 51:7; ch. 18:3
3 [a]ch. 12:6,14 [b]ch. 12:3 [c]ch. 13:1 [d]ver. 9 [e]ver. 12
4 [a]ch. 18:12 [b]Dan. 11:38 [c]Jer. 51:7; ch. 18:6 [d]ch. 14:8 [1]Gk. *gilded*
5 [a]2 Thes. 2:7 [1]Or, *fornications*
6 [a]ch. 18:24 [b]ch. 13:15 [c]ch. 6:9,10
8 [a]ch. 11:7 [b]ch. 13:10

17:1–7 (Note that it is important to differentiate between the judgments of ecclesiastical Babylon, described in Rev 17 and the wrath of God poured out on the empire of Babylon, described in Rev 18.)

This passage is one of the most unusual prophecies in the Bible. One of the seven angels shows John "the judgment of the great whore" (17:1), referring to the worldwide, ecumenical apostate religion of the last days. The spiritual imagery of fornication is repeatedly used by John to emphasize the corruption of the religious system of the last days. A pagan revival of the ancient mystery religions of Babylon will cloak themselves in the outward symbols of Christianity. This false church will be allied with the antichrist and his ten allies (17:3) and will be characterized by blasphemy and drunkenness (17:5). This false church will claim to be the true church while persecuting the tribulation saints who worship God (17:6).

17:8–18 The events of this fascinating vision occur prior to the rise of the antichrist at the middle of the tribulation and refer to the satanic nature of the antichrist and his wicked kingdom. Some say that the opening phrase of 17:8 refers to the beast; though the beast appeared once, he is not presently evident, but will in the future make his presence known. Others suggest that this phrase is an imitation of the description of Christ (see 1:18; 2:8) and an indication of the antichrist's counterfeit of God's sovereignty. Still others contend that this passage deals with the final form of the Gentile world government.

There is also an allusion here to the rise and fall of Rome. Once a powerful empire that has ceased to rule, Rome will rise again to rule the world at the end of this age (17:12). The city of Rome was commonly known in ancient times as the city on seven hills (17:9). The seven kings in this prophecy might refer to Rome's emperors or to seven secular empires that have oppressed Israel throughout her history. The five fallen empires could be Egypt, Assyria, Babylon, Medo-Persia and Greece. When John wrote Revelation, Rome was still in power. The other empire that "is not yet come" (17:10) may refer to the revived Roman empire that will be established under the antichrist as a ten-nation confederacy.

The final ruler, the antichrist, will ultimately take over the seventh kingdom, the revived Roman empire, during the first half of the seven-year treaty period. He is the eighth ruler and his kingdom will differ markedly in character from the other kingdoms because of Satan's power over him. Yet the ten separate kings will bring their kingdoms under his authority (17:12) and will build this eighth kingdom by mutual consent (17:13). This kingdom will be the most oppressive and demonic reign in history, ushering in the last 3 1/2 years of the great tribulation. Together, in the power of Satan, "these shall make war with the Lamb" (17:14). Yet John prophesies that the Lamb of God will triumph.

John also sees in his vision that God will cause the

they that dwell on the earth [c]shall wonder, [d]whose names were not written in
the book of life from the foundation of
the world, when they behold the beast
that was, and is not, and yet is.
9 And [a]here *is* the mind which hath
wisdom. [b]The seven heads are seven
mountains, on which the woman sitteth.
10 And there are seven kings: five are
fallen, and one is, *and* the other is not
yet come; and when he cometh, he must
continue a short space.
11 And the beast that was, and is not,
even he is the eighth, and is of the seven,
[a]and goeth into perdition.
12 And [a]the ten horns which thou
sawest are ten kings, which have received no kingdom as yet; but receive
power as kings one hour with the beast.
13 These have one mind, and shall
give their power and strength unto the
beast.
V 14 [a]These shall make war with the
Lamb, and the Lamb shall overcome
them: [b]for he is Lord of lords, and King of
kings: [c]and they that are with him *are*
called, and chosen, and faithful.
15 And he saith unto me, [a]The waters
which thou sawest, where the whore sitteth, [b]are peoples, and multitudes, and
nations, and tongues.
16 And the ten horns which thou sawest upon the beast, [a]these shall hate the
whore, and shall make her desolate [b]and
naked, and shall eat her flesh, and [c]burn
her with fire.
17 [a]For God hath put in their hearts to
fulfil his will, and to agree, and give their
kingdom unto the beast, [b]until the words
of God shall be fulfilled.

V Rev 12:5 ◀▶ Rev 19:15–16

8 [c]ch. 13:3 [d]ch. 13:8
9 [a]ch. 13:18 [b]ch. 13:1
11 [a]ver. 8
12 [a]Dan. 7:20; Zech. 1:18
14 [a]ch. 16:14 [b]Deut. 10:17; 1 Tim. 6:15; ch. 19:16 [c]Jer. 50:44; ch. 14:4
15 [a]Is. 8:7 [b]ch. 13:7
16 [a]Jer. 50:41; ch. 16:12 [b]Ezek. 16:37; ch. 18:16 [c]ch. 18:8
17 [a]2 Thes. 2:11 [b]ch. 10:7
18 [a]ch. 16:19 [b]ch. 12:4
18:1 [a]ch. 17:1 [b]Ezek. 43:2
2 [a]Is. 13:19; Jer. 51:8 [b]Is. 13:21; Jer. 50:39 [c]Is. 14:23; Mark 5:2
3 [a]ch. 14:8 [b]Is. 47:15 [1]*Or, power*
4 [a]Is. 48:20; Jer. 50:8; 2 Cor. 6:17
5 [a]Gen. 18:20; Jer. 51:9; Jonah 1:2 [b]ch. 16:19
6 [a]Ps. 137:8; Jer. 50:15 [b]ch. 14:10 [c]ch. 16:19
7 [a]Ezek. 28:2 [b]Is. 47:7,8; Zeph. 2:15
8 [a]ver. 10; Is. 47:9 [b]ch. 17:16

18 And the woman which thou sawest
[a]is that great city, [b]which reigneth over
the kings of the earth.

The desolation of Babylon

18 AND [a]AFTER these things I saw
another angel come down from
heaven, having great power; [b]and the
earth was lightened with his glory.
2 And he cried mightily with a strong
voice, saying, [a]Babylon the great is fallen,
is fallen, and [b]is become the habitation of
devils, and the hold of every foul spirit,
and [c]a cage of every unclean and hateful
bird.
3 For all nations [a]have drunk of the
wine of the wrath of her fornication, and
the kings of the earth have committed
fornication with her, [b]and the merchants
of the earth are waxed rich through the
[1]abundance of her delicacies.
4 And I heard another voice from
heaven, saying, [a]Come out of her, my
people, that ye be not partakers of her
sins, and that ye receive not of her
plagues.
5 [a]For her sins have reached unto
heaven, and [b]God hath remembered her
iniquities.
6 [a]Reward her even as she rewarded
you, and double unto her double according to her works: [b]in the cup which she
hath filled [c]fill to her double.
7 [a]How much she hath glorified herself, and lived deliciously, so much torment and sorrow give her: for she saith
in her heart, I sit a [b]queen, and am no
widow, and shall see no sorrow.
8 Therefore shall her plagues come [a]in
one day, death, and mourning, and famine; and [b]she shall be utterly burned with

---

ten nations to join with the antichrist and destroy the false church (17:16) as a fulfillment of God's will (17:17). Though he used the worldwide, ecumenical church to consolidate his evil rule, the antichrist will turn on her and utterly destroy her, and will instead accept the worship and deification of the people.

18:1–19 This new vision describes the judgment of God upon the empire of Babylon, in all its commercial and political power. An angel announces the fall of this empire and focuses his words against the riches of this ungodly empire. The saints are urged to leave Babylon before God's judgment falls on this wicked nation (18:4). The antichrist will take the title "king of Babylon" (Isa 14:4) indicating his close connection with the wicked Babylonian empire during the tribulation.

In her wicked pride Babylon will show contempt for God, but John prophesies that her judgment will come and she will be destroyed by fire (18:8). Kings and merchants will mourn the loss of Babylon because they will lose their riches and wicked pleasures (18:11–13). As they watch her burning from afar, merchants and ship captains will cry out in dismay. Modern-day Iraq occupies the location of ancient Babylon. With great military power and large oil reserves, Iraq is ideally suited to become a vast commercial power that may figure prominently in the fulfillment of this prophecy in the future.

fire: [c]for strong *is* the Lord God who judgeth her.

9 And [a]the kings of the earth, who have committed fornication and lived deliciously with her, [b]shall bewail her, and lament for her, [c]when they shall see the smoke of her burning,

10 Standing afar off for the fear of her torment, saying, [a]Alas, alas, that great city Babylon, that mighty city! [b]for in one hour is thy judgment come.

11 And [a]the merchants of the earth shall weep and mourn over her; for no man buyeth their merchandise any more:

12 [a]The merchandise of gold, and silver, and precious stones, and of pearls, and fine linen, and purple, and silk, and scarlet, and all [l]thyine wood, and all manner vessels of ivory, and all manner vessels of most precious wood, and of brass, and iron, and marble,

13 And cinnamon, and odours, and ointments, and frankincense, and wine, and oil, and fine flour, and wheat, and beasts, and sheep, and horses, and chariots, and [l]slaves, and [a]souls of men.

14 And the fruits that thy soul lusted after are departed from thee, and all things which were dainty and goodly are departed from thee, and thou shalt find them no more at all.

15 [a]The merchants of these things, which were made rich by her, shall stand afar off for the fear of her torment, weeping and wailing,

16 And saying, Alas, alas, that great city, [a]that was clothed in fine linen, and purple, and scarlet, and decked with gold, and precious stones, and pearls!

17 [a]For in one hour so great riches is come to nought. And [b]every shipmaster, and all the company in ships, and sailors, and as many as trade by sea, stood afar off,

18 [a]And cried when they saw the smoke of her burning, saying, [b]What *city is* like unto this great city!

P 19 And [a]they cast dust on their heads, and cried, weeping and wailing, saying, Alas, alas, that great city, wherein were made rich all that had ships in the sea by reason of her costliness! [b]for in one hour is she made desolate.

20 [a]Rejoice over her, *thou* heaven, and *ye* holy apostles and prophets; for [b]God hath avenged you on her.

21 And a mighty angel took up a stone like a great millstone, and cast *it* into the sea, saying, [a]Thus with violence shall that great city Babylon be thrown down, and [b]shall be found no more at all.

22 [a]And the voice of harpers, and musicians, and of pipers, and trumpeters, shall be heard no more at all in thee; and no craftsman, of whatsoever craft *he be*, shall be found any more in thee; and the sound of a millstone shall be heard no more at all in thee;

23 [a]And the light of a candle shall shine no more at all in thee; [b]and the voice of the bridegroom and of the bride shall be heard no more at all in thee: for [c]thy merchants were the great men of the earth; [d]for by thy sorceries were all nations deceived.

24 And [a]in her was found the blood of prophets, and of saints, and of all that [b]were slain upon the earth.

The marriage supper of the Lamb

19 AND AFTER these things [a]I heard a great voice of much people in heaven, saying, Alleluia; [b]Salvation, and glory, and honour, and power, unto the Lord our God: O

2 For [a]true and righteous *are* his judgments: for he hath judged the great whore, which did corrupt the earth with her fornication, and [b]hath avenged the blood of his servants at her hand.

3 And again they said, Alleluia. And [a]her smoke rose up for ever and ever. H

4 And [a]the four and twenty elders and the four beasts fell down and worshipped God that sat on the throne, saying, [b]Amen; Alleluia.

8 [c]Jer. 50:34; ch. 11:17
9 [a]Ezek. 26:16 [b]Jer. 50:46 [c]ch. 19:3
10 [a]Is. 21:9; ch. 14:8 [b]ver. 17,19
11 [a]Ezek. 27:27
12 [a]ch. 17:4 [l]Or, *sweet*
13 [a]Ezek. 27:13 [l]Or, *bodies*
15 [a]ver. 3,11
16 [a]ch. 17:4
17 [a]ver. 10 [b]Is. 23:14; Ezek. 27:29
18 [a]Ezek. 27:30 [b]ch. 13:4
19 [a]Josh. 7:6; 1 Sam. 4:12; Job 2:12; Ezek. 27:30 [b]ver. 8
20 [a]Is. 44:23 & 49:13; Jer. 51:48 [b]Luke 11:49; ch. 19:2
21 [a]Jer. 51:64 [b]ch. 12:8 & 16:20
22 [a]Jer. 7:34 & 16:9 & 25:10; Ezek. 26:13
23 [a]Jer. 25:10 [b]Jer. 7:34 & 16:9 & 25:10 & 33:11 [c]Is. 23:8 [d]2 Ki. 9:22; ch. 17:2,5
24 [a]ch. 17:6 [b]Jer. 51:49
19:1 [a]ch. 11:15 [b]ch. 4:11 & 7:10, 12
2 [a]ch. 15:3 [b]Deut. 32:43
3 [a]Is. 34:10; ch. 14:11
4 [a]ch. 4:4,6 [b]1 Chr. 16:36; Neh. 5:13 & 8:6; ch. 5:14

P *Rev 15:5* ◀ ▶ *Rev 19:11*

O *Rev 7:9–12* ◀
H *Rev 15:1* ◀ ▶ *Rev 19:20*

18:20–24 John hears a voice commanding the apostles and prophets to rejoice over the destruction of their deadly enemy. The angel announces that Babylon will be utterly destroyed because of her deceptive sorceries (18:23) and because of the role she played in killing the prophets and saints.

19:1–6 Following the judgment upon Babylon, John hears the voices of heaven rejoicing that God has forever destroyed the enemies of Christ.

T 5 And a voice came out of the throne, saying, [a]Praise our God, all ye his servants, and ye that fear him, [b]both small and great.

6 [a]And I heard as it were the voice of a great multitude, and as the voice of many waters, and as the voice of mighty thunderings, saying, Alleluia: for [b]the Lord God omnipotent reigneth.

H 7 Let us be glad and rejoice, and give honour to him: for [a]the marriage of the Lamb is come, and his wife hath made herself ready.

8 And [a]to her was granted that she should be arrayed in fine linen, clean and [1]white: [b]for the fine linen is the righteousness of saints.

9 And he saith unto me, Write, [a]Blessed *are* they which are called unto the marriage supper of the Lamb. And he saith unto me, [b]These are the true sayings of God.

G 10 And [a]I fell at his feet to worship him. And he said unto me, [b]See *thou do it* not: I am thy fellowservant, and of thy brethren [c]that have the testimony of Jesus: worship God: for the testimony of Jesus is the spirit of prophecy.

T *Rev 12:11* ◄ **H** *Rev 15:2–4* ◄
G *Rev 5:6* ◄

5 [a]Ps. 134:1 [b]ch. 11:18 & 20:12
6 [a]Ezek. 1:24; ch. 14:2 [b]ch. 11:15
7 [a]Mat. 22:2 & 25:10; 2 Cor. 11:2; Eph. 5:32; ch. 21:2,9
8 [a]Ps. 45:13; Ezek. 16:10; ch. 3:18 [b]Ps. 132:9 [1]Or, *bright*
9 [a]Mat. 22:2; Luke 14:15 [b]ch. 22:6
10 [a]ch. 22:8 [b]Acts 10:26; ch. 22:9 [c]1 John 5:10; ch. 12:17
11 [a]ch. 15:5 [b]ch. 6:2 [c]ch. 3:14 [d]Is. 11:4
12 [a]ch. 1:14 [b]ch. 6:2 [c]ch. 2:17
13 [a]Is. 63:2,3 [b]John 1:1; 1 John 5:7
14 [a]ch. 14:20 [b]Mat. 28:3; ch. 4:4
15 [a]Is. 11:4; 2 Thes. 2:8; ch. 1:16 [b]Ps. 2:9; ch. 2:27 [c]Is. 63:3; ch. 14:19
16 [a]ver. 12 [b]Dan. 2:47; 1 Tim. 6:15; ch. 17:14
17 [a]ver. 21

The beast and false prophet

11 [a]And I saw heaven opened, and behold [b]a white horse; and he that sat upon him *was* called [c]Faithful and True, and [d]in righteousness he doth judge and make war. P

12 [a]His eyes *were* as a flame of fire, [b]and on his head *were* many crowns; [c]and he had a name written, that no man knew, but he himself.

13 [a]And he *was* clothed with a vesture dipped in blood: and his name is called [b]The Word of God.

14 [a]And the armies *which were* in heaven followed him upon white horses, [b]clothed in fine linen, white and clean.

15 And [a]out of his mouth goeth a sharp sword, that with it he should smite the nations: and [b]he shall rule them with a rod of iron: and [c]he treadeth the winepress of the fierceness and wrath of Almighty God. V

16 And [a]he hath on *his* vesture and on his thigh a name written, [b]KING OF KINGS, AND LORD OF LORDS.

17 And I saw an angel standing in the sun; and he cried with a loud voice, saying [a]to all the fowls that fly in the midst

P *Rev 18:19* ◄ ► *Rev 21:9*
V *Rev 17:14* ◄ ► *Rev 20:7–15*

19:7–9 John describes the glorious "marriage of the Lamb" (19:7) which will occur in heaven when the believers are spiritually united to Jesus Christ. The resurrected saints receive garments of "fine linen" (19:8) that signify their righteousness through the atonement of Christ's blood and God's sovereign grace. Note that this passage in ch. 19 contains the first reference to the church since the end of ch. 3 and the seven messages to the churches. This omission of the mention of the church during the seven-year tribulation reaffirms the rapture of the church before the tribulation. For further information, see the article "The Marriage Supper of the Lamb" on p. 1476.

19:11–13 John announces the second coming of Christ as heaven opens and Jesus appears in all of his glory, riding a white horse, ready to judge and make war with unrepentant sinners. Christ's garments are "dipped in blood" (19:13), reminding us of his terrible wrath and destruction of his enemies (see Isa 34:5–8).

Twice in this passage John makes reference to Jesus' name (19:12–13). Names carry a tremendous importance in the Bible because they are closely related to the character and destiny of the person so named. When the saints arrive in heaven they will even be given a "new name" (3:12). Though we do not know the name Jesus uses to refer to himself in 19:12, John reminds us that Jesus' name is "The Word of God" (19:13; see Jn 1:1).

19:14–18 Now John sees the armies of heaven which will follow Jesus out to battle. These resurrected saints are clothed in white linen and riding white horses, symbolic of their righteousness through the shed blood of Christ. These saints are probably the same ones seen at the marriage supper of the Lamb (19:7–8). Since this battle follows the marriage supper, the rapture and the judgment seat of Christ (see Ro 14:10; 2Co 5:10) must have taken place at an earlier time.

Jesus then treads the winepress in his judgment against those who have martyred his saints (see Isa 63:1–6). Jesus will rule the nations in righteousness and justice, destroying all evil during the Millennium. His glorious name is emblazoned on his garments: "KING OF KINGS, AND LORD OF LORDS" (19:16). At the end of the battle of Armageddon, an angel calls the birds of the air to come and scavenge the bodies of the wicked, to cleanse the land. This gruesome "supper of the great God" (19:17) is a grim contrast to the earlier wedding supper of the Lamb.

The Marriage Supper of the Lamb

THE USE OF marriage as a symbol of God's eternal spiritual union with people appears repeatedly in Scripture. In the OT, unrepentant Israel was likened to an adulterous wife (see Hos 2:1–8). In the NT, Jesus Christ referred to the faithful church as his virgin bride (see Jn 3:29).

In ancient Israel there were three phases to a legal marriage. The first stage was a betrothal, a legally binding agreement entered into by both parties. The second phase involved the coming of the bridegroom to meet his bride. The last part of a marriage celebration was the marriage supper hosted at the home of the groom.

Our spiritual life echoes this marriage ritual. Our spiritual betrothal as Christ's bride began when we accepted him as our Savior. Christ's appearance in the air to rapture the church is the equivalent of the bridegroom coming to meet the bride. John's vision in Revelation details the final phase of the church's marriage to Christ with his description of a glorious marriage supper in heaven between the complete bride of Christ and their Savior in the presence of the assembled angelic host.

Some posttribulation scholars suggest that the marriage supper of the Lamb will take place in the air while the church is being raptured. They contend that this will allow the church to rise in the air with Christ and immediately return to earth to participate in the Battle of Armageddon. This view presents some difficulties because of the clear words of Jesus' promise to bring believers to be with him in heaven (see Jn 14:3).

Other scholars suggest that the marriage supper of the Lamb must take place between Christ's coming for his church and his return with the saints at Armageddon. These scholars contend that after the rapture and the *bema* judgment, when all Christians have received their rewards for their righteous works, the believers will participate in the glorious marriage supper between Christ and his faithful bride. This supper will occur in heaven at the same time that the judgments of the tribulation are being felt on earth.

Specific grammar in John's prophecy affirms this sequence of events. Note that John says, "the marriage of the Lamb is come, and his wife hath made herself ready" (Rev 19:7). The Greek word translated "is come" is written in the Greek aorist tense, signifying an act that was completed in the past and needs no other action or limitation. This indicates that the marriage will be consummated by this point and will precede the second coming of Christ. Only after describing the marriage supper does John then record his vision of Christ's return to earth at Armageddon.

There will also be guests at this wedding, those "which are called unto the marriage supper of the Lamb" (19:9). Guests are "called" or invited to a wedding, whereas the bride and bridegroom are the honored hosts. The guests of the marriage supper of the Lamb are the tribulation martyrs, OT saints and the hosts of heaven. While the saints of Israel will live with the Christian saints in the new Jerusalem, the OT saints are not the bride of Christ. Even John the Baptist referred to himself only as a wedding guest when he likened himself to a friend of the Bridegroom (see Jn 3:29).

John's detailed vision of the marriage supper includes a description of the bride's garments. Dressed in "fine linen, clean and white" (Rev 19:8), the church is shown as completely cleansed through the atonement of Christ's completed work on the cross. Though some suggest that the church must suffer through the tribulation to cleanse and purify her in preparation for the marriage supper, these scholars have forgotten that we are not purified by tribulation. We are purified solely by Christ's righteousness applied to our hearts through faith in him as our Lord and Savior.

Because the bride is clothed with fine linen this also affirms that the church has already participated in the *bema* judgment where rewards are given for faithful works. Note also that John later describes the believers "clothed in fine linen, white and clean" (19:14) as they leave heaven to join in the Battle of Armageddon. This passage then confirms this order of events: the rapture, the *bema* judgment, the marriage supper and the return to earth at Armageddon.

of heaven, [b]Come and gather yourselves together unto the supper of the great God;

18 [a]That ye may eat the flesh of kings, and the flesh of captains, and the flesh of mighty men, and the flesh of horses, and of them that sit on them, and the flesh of all *men, both* free and bond, both small and great.

19 [a]And I saw the beast, and the kings of the earth, and their armies, gathered together to make war against him that sat on the horse, and against his army.

H 20 [a]And the beast was taken, and with him the false prophet that wrought miracles before him, with which he deceived them that had received the mark of the beast, and [b]them that worshipped his image. [c]These both were cast alive into a lake of fire [d]burning with brimstone.

21 And the remnant [a]were slain with the sword of him that sat upon the horse, which *sword* proceeded out of his mouth: [b]and all the fowls [c]were filled with their flesh.

H *Rev 19:3* ◄► *Rev 20:9–15*

17 [b]Ezek. 39:17
18 [a]Ezek. 39:18
19 [a]ch. 16:16
20 [a]ch. 16:13 [b]ch. 13:12 [c]Dan. 7:11; ch. 20:10 [d]ch. 14:10
21 [a]ver. 15 [b]ver. 17,18 [c]ch. 17:16
20:1 [a]ch. 1:18
2 [a]2 Pet. 2:4; Jude 6; ch. 12:9
3 [a]Dan. 6:17 [b]ch. 12:9
4 [a]Dan. 7:9; Mat. 19:28; Luke 22:30 [b]1 Cor. 6:2,3

The millennial reign

20 AND I saw an angel come down from heaven, [a]having the key of the bottomless pit and a great chain in his hand. M J

2 And he laid hold on [a]the dragon, that old serpent, which is the Devil, and Satan, and bound him a thousand years,

3 And cast him into the bottomless pit, and shut him up, and [a]set a seal upon him, [b]that he should deceive the nations no more, till the thousand years should be fulfilled: and after that he must be loosed a little season.

4 And I saw [a]thrones, and they sat upon them, and [b]judgment was given

M *Rev 12:5* ◄ J *Rev 14:7* ◄

19:19–21 The conclusion of Armageddon and the battle around Jerusalem (see Zec 12:2–9) will complete the total defeat of the antichrist and his allies by the supernatural power of Jesus Christ. The armies of the antichrist initially gathered to destroy Israel and oppose the 200 million soldiers of the kings of the east (see 9:13–21). When these armies see Jesus Christ and his armies descending from heaven, all of the wicked armies of the earth will join in battle against Jesus and his saints. However, Jesus Christ will be the ultimate victor and will annihilate the wicked, defeat the antichrist and his false prophet and cast them alive into the lake of fire in hell forever (19:20; see Da 7:11; 2Th 2:8). The remnant of the armies of the antichrist and the kings of the east will be slain with the sword of Christ (19:21).

20:1–3 John reveals the defeat of Satan as the angel of the Lord chains the Devil for a thousand years in "the bottomless pit" (20:3). This pit is not hell, the lake of fire, but is a real place where Satan will be imprisoned for the Millennium. However, John warns that after the thousand years are complete, "he must be loosed for a little season" (20:3).

Many have questioned why God would release Satan for a time after imprisoning him for a thousand years. Since the Bible does not tell us, we cannot be certain. It is interesting to note, however, that even after a Millennium of peace, prosperity, and justice under the rule of the Messiah, many humans will still rebel against God because their hearts are wicked apart from the grace of God (see 20:8–9; Jer 17:9).

20:4 *Dispensation of the Kingdom.* This last dispensation concludes God's plan of redemption for humanity and reflects the establishment of God's eternal kingdom on earth. The first one thousand years (the Millennium) will see the fulfillment of God's unshakable promises to Israel, the Gentile nations and the church. For the first time since Adam, humanity will be free of the temptation of Satan. The Messiah, Jesus Christ, will rule the earth from the throne of David, and the resurrected saints will govern with him. Humanity will be subject to Christ and the laws of God's kingdom. Righteousness and justice will replace oppression and misrule; Israel will be restored and converted. Creation will be delivered from its bondage to the effects of sin (see 1Co 15:24–28; Rev 22:3).

Yet despite the blessings of the initial years of this kingdom, some will choose to rebel when the Devil is loosed from the bottomless pit (see 20:7–10). God will destroy these rebels with fire from heaven and bring to an end the rebellion of Satan, his fallen angels and unrepentant sinners. These wicked ones will be resurrected to face the great white throne judgment and be condemned to hell (see Mt 25:41, 46; Rev 14:9–11; 19:20; 20:10). Those who remain true to God during this last rebellion will enjoy the full benefits of redemption through Christ for eternity.

The seven dispensations revealed in Scripture are the dispensations of innocence (Ge 1:28), conscience (Ge 3:7), human government (Ge 8:15), promise (Ge 12:1), law (Ex 19:1), the church (Ac 2:1) and the kingdom (Rev 20:4). For further information, see the article "The Seven Dispensations" on p. 4.

20:4–6 John then describes the saints, including those saints who resisted the antichrist (20:4), reigning from thrones and governing the kingdom of God

The Millennium

THE PREMILLENNIAL VIEW

THE POSTMILLENNIAL VIEW

THE AMILLENNIAL VIEW

The Millennium

THE SCRIPTURES PROMISE that Jesus Christ will rule over this earth for one thousand years. Yet the millennial kingdom of the coming Messiah is one of the most misunderstood subjects in the whole field of prophecy. Interpreters view this millennial period in three different ways.

Postmillennialism

This view suggests that Christ's spirit will work through established systems of preaching and teaching to root out evil and bring improvement to the world. Only when humanity has defeated evil will Christ return to initiate judgment and establish his kingdom for 1000 years. While this theory was popular in the late 1600s, most scholars today reject this viewpoint because of the progress of history and continued fulfillment of prophecy.

Amillennialism

Those who subscribe to a symbolic interpretation of prophecy usually advocate this view of the Millennium. This position maintains that the Millennium is currently in progress during this church age and that the 1000 years mentioned in Revelation is merely a symbol of God's kingdom promises throughout the OT. Amillennialists do not make a clear distinction between God's dealings with OT Israel and the church, but rather spiritualize one with the other. Those who hold to this viewpoint also contend that Satan is already bound because of Christ's promise in Mt 18:18 that his followers would have the power to do so. However, this view minimizes the evil conditions of this present age and overlooks the apostle Paul's clear distinctions between Israel and the church (see Ro 11; 1Co 10:32).

Premillennialism

This interpretation of the Millennium bases its belief on a literal interpretation of Biblical prophecy and stresses that the 1000 years in Revelation are actual years, not symbols. The majority of conservative Bible scholars subscribe to this view. Premillennialists also recognize the power of Christ's present rule in heaven and the importance of an earthly fulfillment of God's promises to Israel. Some critics suggest that an earthly kingdom that elevates Israel to prominence would negate the spiritual blessings of Christianity. Premillennialists counter this criticism with a rejoinder that God must keep his promises to Israel so that Christians can enjoy their eternal blessings too (see Isa 65:17; 66:22; 2Pe 3:13; Rev 21:1).

Those who hold to the premillennial view believe that Christ will return from heaven to defeat the antichrist at Armageddon and then will establish his peaceful kingdom on